VOLUME LIBRARY

A Modern, Authoritative Reference for Home and School Use

Clear and Complete • Colorfully Illustrated • Totally Indexed

SOUTHWESTERN

Nashville, Tennessee

Copyright © 2004
MapQuest.com, Inc.

Satellite images copyright © 2004
WorldSat International, Inc.

Photograph Credits

Photographs on pages 24–25, 54, 63, 78, 79 (Copenhagen), 84, 86, 89, 93, 96, 97, 98, 100, 102, 104, 105, 108 (China, Hong Kong), 114, 115, 116, 117 (Hong Kong), 118, 119, 122, 123, 124, 125, 126, 128, 130, 133, 134, 135, 137, 138 (Kenya), 144, 147, 150, 151 (Togo, Ghana), 152, 153, 157, 158, 159, 164 (New Zealand, Ayers Rock), 171, 174, 176 (Brazil, Peru), 188, 189, 193, 194 (Eastern Canada, Guadeloupe), 200, 201, 202, 203 (Costa Rica), 207 (Bahamas), 307, 356, 359, 368, 382 (Portland), 494–495, 496–497, 498, 499, 520, 644–645
Copyright © 2004 Corel Corp. and their suppliers.

Photographs on pages 50–51, 81, 83, 94, 95, 108 (Nepal), 117 (Taiwan), 138 (Egypt), 164 (Sydney), 172, 176 (Ecuador), 183, 185, 194 (Manitoba, Golden Gate), 203 (Panama), 207 (St. Kitts), 369, 380, 382 (Hawaii), 500, 501
Copyright © 2004 PhotoDisc, Inc.

Photograph on page 726
Copyright © 2004 Corbis

Photograph on page 496
Courtesy of the Pierre Auger Observatory

Additional photographs by:
Michael A. Heerschap . pages 145, 156, 160, 161, 175
Justin Louis . . . . pages 79, 120, 121, 148, 151
J. Scott Tharp . . . . pages 91, 146, 162
Matt Tharp . . . . pages 65, 67, 72, 79, 92, 190, 191, 192, 208, 209

ISBN 0-87197-454-1

Printed and manufactured in the
United States of America

THE
VOLUME
LIBRARY

**Maps and indexes by
MapQuest.com, Inc.**

MAPQUEST.COM

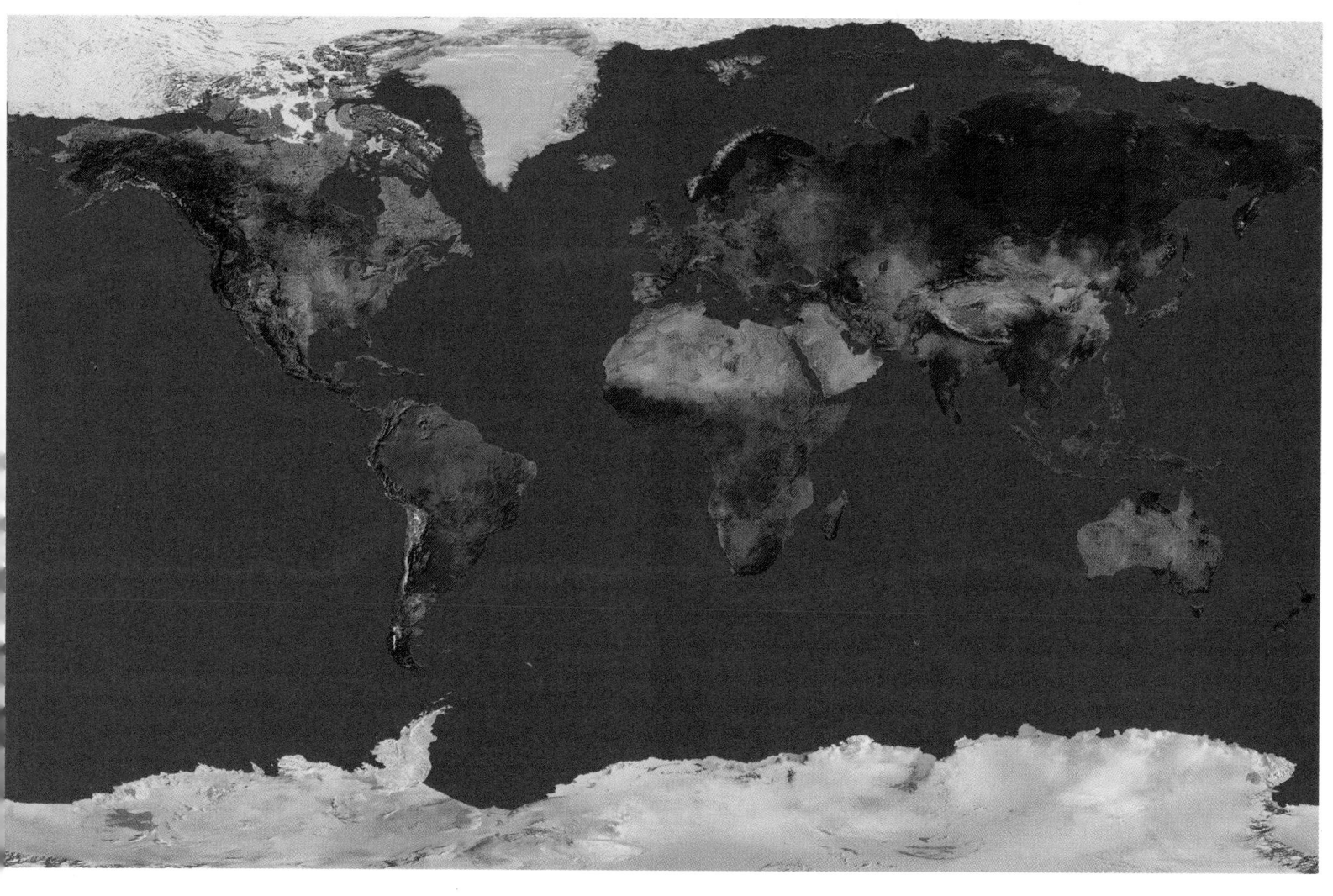

CONTRIBUTORS

Cartographic Staff, MapQuest.com, Inc.

Project Coordinator
Ian Turner

Layout
Ian Turner, Paul Yatabe

Research Librarian
Craig Haggit

Research & Compilation
Marley Amstutz, Candace Roper, Bill Truninger,
Paul Yatabe

Cartographers
Brian Goudreau, Erin Heithoff, Kendall Marten,
Jeff Martz, Chris Pfeiffer, Kathleen Resser,
Ian Turner, Martha Tyzenhouse

Database and Indexing
Mark Leitzell

Editors
Robert Harding, Dana Wolf

Text Editor
Candace Roper

Support Staff
Shawna Roberts

Project Manager
Keith Winters

Account Managers
Rita Hamlet, Bennett Moe

Consultants

British Cartography
Roger W. Anson
    Principal Lecturer and Field Chair for
    Cartography,
    Oxford Brookes University

Canadian Cartography
Deryck W. Holdsworth
    Professor, Department of Geography,
    The Pennsylvania State University

Glossary of Abbreviations 8

Map Skills 9

Solar System 22

Terrain Maps 24

Contents 25
Index 47

World Maps 50

WORLD 52
EUROPE 54
United Kingdom 60
    Scotland 62
    Wales 64
    Northern Ireland .65
    England – The North 66
    Midlands 68
    England – The Southeast 70
    England – The Southwest 72
    British Cities 74
    British Motorways 77
Ireland 78
Denmark and Iceland 79
Norway and Sweden 80
Estonia and Finland .81
Belarus, Latvia and Lithuania 82
Poland 83
Netherlands 84
Belgium and Luxembourg 85
Germany 86
France 88
Liechtenstein and Switzerland 90
Austria and Hungary 91
Czech Republic and Slovakia 92
Andorra and Portugal 93
Spain 94
Italy 95
Vatican City 96
Malta, Monaco and San Marino 97
Bosnia & Herzegovina, Croatia
    and Slovenia 98
Albania and Serbia & Montenegro 99
Greece and Macedonia 100
Bulgaria and Romania 101
Moldova and Ukraine 102
Armenia, Azerbaijan and Georgia 103
Russia 104
Europe Highway System 106

ASIA 108
Japan 114
Korea (North and South) 116
Hong Kong and Taiwan 117
Mongolia 118
China 119
Philippines 120
Brunei and Malaysia 121
East Timor and Indonesia 122
Singapore and Vietnam 123
Cambodia and Laos 124
Myanmar and Thailand 125
Bhutan, Nepal and Sri Lanka 126
Bangladesh and Maldives 127
India 128
Afghanistan and Pakistan 129
Iran and Iraq 130
Kazakhstan and Kyrgyzstan 131
Tajikistan, Turkmenistan
    and Uzbekistan .132
Cyprus and Turkey 133
Jordan, Lebanon and Syria 134
Israel 135
Kuwait, Saudi Arabia and United Arab Emirates . .136
Bahrain, Oman, Qatar, and Yemen 137

AFRICA 138
Egypt 144

Libya and Sudan .145
Algeria and Tunisia 146
Mauritania, Morocco
    and Western Sahara 147
Cape Verde, Gambia and Senegal 148
Guinea, Guinea-Bissau, Liberia
    and Sierra Leone 149
Côte d'Ivoire, Ghana and Mali 150
Benin, Burkina Faso and Togo 151
Niger and Nigeria .152
Cameroon and Chad 153
Central African Republic, Equatorial
    Guinea and São Tomé and Príncipe 154
Democratic Republic of the Congo, Gabon
    and Republic of the Congo 155
Djibouti, Eritrea and Ethiopia 156
Kenya, Somalia and Uganda 157
Burundi, Rwanda and Tanzania 158
Angola, Malawi and Zambia 159
Botswana, Namibia and Zimbabwe 160
Lesotho, Mozambique and Swaziland 161
South Africa 162
Comoros, Madagascar, Mauritius
    and Seychelles .163

AUSTRALIA AND OCEANIA 164
Australia 170
New Zealand 171
Micronesia, Palau
    and Papua New Guinea 172
Marshall Islands, Solomon Islands
    and Vanuatu 173
Fiji, Nauru and Tuvalu 174
Kiribati, Samoa and Tonga 175

SOUTH AMERICA 176
Venezuela 182
French Guiana, Guyana and Suriname 183
Colombia 184
Ecuador and Peru .185
Bolivia 186
Paraguay and Uruguay 187
Brazil 188
Chile 190
Argentina 191

POLAR REGIONS .192
Antarctica 192
North Pole and Greenland 193

NORTH AMERICA 194
Mexico 200
Belize and Guatemala 201
Honduras and Nicaragua 202
Costa Rica, El Salvador and Panama 203
Cuba and the West Indies 204
Dominican Republic and Haiti 205
Jamaica and Puerto Rico 206
Antigua & Barbuda, Bahamas
    and St. Kitts & Nevis 207
Dominica, St. Lucia
    and St. Vincent & the Grenadines 208
Barbados, Grenada
    and Trinidad & Tobago 209
Canada (Maps and Indexes) 210
    Alberta 212
    British Columbia 214
    Manitoba 215
    New Brunswick .217
    Newfoundland and Labrador 218
    Northwest Territories and Nunavut 220
    Nova Scotia 221
    Ontario 222
    Prince Edward Island 224
    Quebec 225
    Saskatchewan 227
    Yukon Territory .228
    Canadian Cities .229
United States of America (Maps and Indexes) . .232
    Alabama 238
    Alaska 240
    Arizona 242
    Arkansas 244
    California 246

    Colorado 250
    Connecticut 253
    Delaware 255
    Florida 256
    Georgia 260
    Hawaii 262
    Idaho 264
    Illinois 266
    Indiana 270
    Iowa 274
    Kansas 276
    Kentucky 280
    Louisiana 282
    Maine 285
    Maryland and the District of Columbia 288
    Massachusetts 292
    Michigan 294
    Minnesota 298
    Mississippi 300
    Missouri 302
    Montana 306
    Nebraska 308
    Nevada 310
    New Hampshire .312
    New Jersey 314
    New Mexico 317
    New York 320
    North Carolina .322
    North Dakota 326
    Ohio 328
    Oklahoma 330
    Oregon 334
    Pennsylvania 336
    Rhode Island 339
    South Carolina .340
    South Dakota 342
    Tennessee 344
    Texas 346
    Utah 350
    Vermont 352
    Virginia 354
    Washington 358
    West Virginia 360
    Wisconsin 364
    Wyoming 366
    American Cities .368
    United States Road Map 384
National Parks 386

Homework Maps 388

Contents 388

World Themes and Flags 494

World Theme Contents 495

FLAGS 520
Contents 520
Flags of the World 521
Flags of Canada 525
Flags of the United States 526

Index 528

World History 644

Contents 644

Current World Issues 726

Contents 726

How to Study 737

It is useful to know something of the manners of different nations, so that we may be enabled to form a more correct judgement regarding our own, and be prevented from thinking that everything contrary to our customs is ridiculous and irrational – a conclusion usually come to by those whose experience has been limited to their own country.

—René Descartes

The eye and the brain seem to be particularly felicitous partners in the act of map reading.

—Steven S. Hall

*Humility alone designs
Those short but admirable lines,
By which, ungirt and unconstrain'd,
Things greater are in less contain'd.*

—Andrew Marvell

*So geographers in Afric-Maps
With savage-pictures fill their gaps;
And o'er uninhabitable downs
Place elephants for want of towns.*

—Jonathan Swift

Maps break down our inhibitions, stimulate our glands, stir our imagination, loosen our tongues. The map speaks across the barriers of language; it is sometimes claimed as the language of geography.

—Carl Ortwin Sauer

Mathematical equations and literary phrases are useful, but they are no substitute for the spatial eloquence of the map.

—Arthur Robinson

Where in this small-talking world can I find a longitude with no platitude?

—Christopher Fry

I even know of an island...shown to be located between Prince of Wales Island and Bathurst Island, which does not exist, as found out recently by Panarctic Oil Company, which was given a lease to drill from it.

—Jean-Paul Drolet

Geographer: A chap who can tell you offhand the difference between the outside of the world and the inside.

—Ambrose Bierce

When I'm playful I use the meridians of longitude and parallels of latitude for a seine, and drag the Atlantic Ocean for whales.

—Mark Twain

Journey over all the universe in a map, without the expense and fatigue of traveling, without suffering the inconveniences of heat, cold, hunger, and thirst.

—Cervantes

Southwestern's *Volume Library* features an entirely new world atlas produced by MapQuest.com, Inc., one of the world's leading map suppliers. This atlas has been designed and created using completely digital production methods supported by extensive world and United States databases.

Here are some of the features which make this atlas one of the most informative and comprehensive references of its kind:

• All world maps are fully indexed and are thoroughly updated for each year's edition.

• All pages of the book have been designed specifically for this publication. The result is a clean, legible, consistent look from cover to cover.

• Color photographs of interesting landscapes enhance the student's appreciation of the geography of the world.

• The CD-ROM, GeoHelp™, is available as a complement to Southwestern's other products. The CD-ROM allows an interactive approach to the homework maps found in the book.

Volume 3 has been organized into color-coded sections according to map type. The following notes describe some of the features of each section of the atlas.

Key to Atlas Maps

The world map found on the inside cover of the book provides the student with a handy visual reference to the contents of the World Map section.

MapSkills

The MapSkills section has been assembled by the cartographers of MapQuest.com as a concise, stand-alone course on the use of maps. Students can use this section to learn more about the language of maps, and can test their knowledge by answering the exercise questions found throughout the MapSkills section.

Solar System

A graphic depiction of the Solar System has been specially prepared for this publication. Tables containing numerical statistics have been included to make this a quick reference for planetary data.

Terrain Maps

Terrain maps (also called physical maps) show the three-dimensional character of the earth's surface. Topographic features such as rivers, mountains, and glaciers are clearly labeled on each map, and indexed on pages 47-49. A legend on page 25 shows how color and symbols are used in this section of the book to indicate vegetation and elevation.

World Maps

The World Atlas section is the heart of the book. A master legend is provided on page 50. The World Atlas section is color-coded by continent along the outer margins of the page. The colors correspond to the continent colors found on the reference map on the inside cover.

Europe	Australia and Oceania
Asia	South America and Poles
Africa	North America

This section has been conceived as a one-stop reference for data pertaining to individual nations of the world. The entry for each nation contains the following features:

• A fully-indexed map showing as many cities and towns as scale permits, plus internal states or provinces where appropriate

• A table of basic cultural and economic facts

• A written description of the geography, economy and/or history of the country, which is meant to provide the student with a contemporary description of the nation, and will serve to remind the reader of each country's unique place in the world

• A full-color flag

Wherever possible, the following features have been added:

• Large-scale maps of major cities

• Special-interest maps for a few key nations, including Ireland and Israel

The entries for the United Kingdom and Canada include the following features:

• Detailed maps of British regions (showing new county/division boundaries) and Canadian provinces

• Large-scale maps of major cities

• On-page indexes with population figures from the latest British and Canadian census

• Flags and facts for individual regions and provinces

• A road map for the United Kingdom

• Verification by the academic consultants who are listed on page 4

Here are some of the features of the U.S. state maps and indexes:

• 2000 U.S. Census figures are given for counties and towns wherever possible.

• For over 12,000 unincorporated towns and villages, MapQuest.com has generated population estimates based on a one-mile circle around the town center. Estimates are necessary for these towns because they have no defined boundaries. Estimated figures are shown in an italic type style.

• For the states of Maine, New Hampshire, Vermont, Massachusetts, Connecticut, Rhode Island, and New Jersey, indexes have been expanded to accommodate the system of cities and towns which is unique to those states.

• Special-interest maps have been included where space permits.

Homework Maps

The maps in this section are designed to be traced for homework assignments. Boundaries of nations, provinces, regions and states are shown in heavy black ink, and can be seen clearly through another sheet of paper. Other basic information such as capital cities, rivers and non-subject country names are included to provide additional information for school projects, if necessary. This information is printed in a lighter color which is still traceable, but will not be easily confused with the boundaries of the subject area.

World Themes and Flags

The thematic map section is the place to turn to for information about the current state of the world. Cultural, environmental and economic themes are presented on the same base map of the world, in order to allow easy comparison among the various maps. Graphics and text enhance many of the maps.

Following the thematic maps are several pages depicting the flags of the world, with expanded coverage for the United Kingdom, Canada, and the United States.

Index

The master index contains entries for every label found on the maps in Volume 3. The entries are arranged alphabetically by feature name, which means that it is not necessary to know the country, state or province in order to find the feature. Each entry lists the page number and the map grid coordinate that can be used to find the label on the map. The grid coordinate refers to the small letters and numbers found around the edge of the map frame.

Population figures for world cities have been included wherever possible. These figures are the latest available from official census or U.N. sources.

World History

Current World Issues

These history sections have been designed to be as informative as possible without the need for additional reference to other texts. A text caption has been written to accompany each map. The text helps to summarize the story of the map in a way that is interesting and educational.

Maps have been grouped together by date or theme, and are arranged from prehistory to the present. All maps have been compiled from authoritative historical sources by the staff of MapQuest.com. Maps which have British or Canadian themes have been checked by the academic consultants listed on page 4.

How to Study

This section has been included by Southwestern to provide the student with information on how to improve study skills for all academic subjects and prepare for major standardized exams.

Glossary of Abbreviations

A. ... Arroyo
A.C.T. ... Australian Capital Territory
A.F.B. ... Air Force Base
Acad. ... Academy
Acc. ... Access
Admin. ... Administration, Administrative
Afg. ... Afghanistan
Afld. ... Airfield
Agcy. ... Agency
Ala., AL ... Alabama
Alaska, AK ... Alaska
Alb. ... Albania
Alg. ... Algeria
Alk. ... Alkali
Alt. ... Alternate
Alta., AB ... Alberta
Aly. ... Alley
Am. Sam., AS ... American Samoa
Amm. Dep. ... Ammunition Depot
Anch. ... Anchorage
And. ... Andorra
Ang. ... Angola
Angu. ... Anguilla
Ant. ... Antenna
Ant.-Bar. ... Antigua and Barbuda
Aprt. ... Airport
Aquar. ... Aquarium
Aqued. ... Aqueduct
Arch. ... Archipelago
Arg. ... Argentina
Ariz., AZ ... Arizona
Ark., AR ... Arkansas
Arm. ... Armenia
Art. Well ... Artesian Well
Aud. ... Auditorium
Aus. ... Austria
Aut. ... Autonomous
Austl. ... Australia
Aux. ... Auxiliary
Aux. Ldg. Fld., A.L.F. ... Auxiliary Landing Field
Av. ... Avenue
Azer. ... Azerbaijan
Azor. ... Azores
B. ... Bay, Bayou
B.C., BC, Br. Col. ... British Columbia
B.I.O.T. ... British Indian Ocean Territory
B.R. ... Business Route
B.V.I. ... British Virgin Islands
Bah. ... Bahamas The
Bahr. ... Bahrain
Bangl. ... Bangladesh
Barb. ... Barbados
Battleground Hist. Mon., Bgnd. Hist. Mon. ... Battleground Historical Monument
Battleground S.H.P., Bgnd. S.H.P. ... Battleground State Historic Park
Bch. ... Beach
Bdy. ... Boundary
Bel. ... Belize
Bela. ... Belarus
Belg. ... Belgium
Ben. ... Benin
Berm. ... Bermuda
Bfld. ... Battlefield
Bhu. ... Bhutan
Bk. ... Brook
Bkwr. ... Breakwater
Bl. ... Boulevard
Bldg. ... Building
Bol. ... Bolivia
Bos.-Her. ... Bosnia and Herzegovina
Bot. ... Bottom
Bots. ... Botswana
Br. ... Branch
Br. ... Bridge
Braz. ... Brazil
Bru. ... Brunei
Bs. ... Basin
Btwy. ... Beltway
Bul. ... Bulgaria
Bur. ... Bureau
Bur. ... Burundi
Burkina ... Burkina Faso
Bus. Dist. ... Business District
Bus. Pk. ... Business Park
Byp. ... Bypass
C. ... Cape
C. d'Iv. ... Côte D'Ivoire
C. Hall ... City Hall
C. of C. ... Chamber of Commerce
C.A.R. ... Central African Republic
C.C. ... Country Club
C.G.S. ... Coast Guard Station
C.H. ... Court House
C.R. ... Costa Rica
C.V. ... Cape Verde
Calif., CA ... California
Camb. ... Cambodia
Came. ... Cameroon
Can. ... Canada, Canal
Can. Is. ... Canary Islands
Cant. ... Canton
Cap. ... Capitol
Cas. ... Castle
Cat. ... Cataract
Cath. ... Cathedral
Cay. Is. ... Cayman Islands
Cem. ... Cemetery
Cen. ... Central
Ch. ... Church
Chan. ... Channel
Chan. Is. ... Channel Islands
Chp. ... Chapel
Christ. I. ... Christmas Island
Cir. ... Circle
Co. ... County
Co. Park, Co. Pk. ... County Park
Cocos Is. ... Cocos Islands (Keeling Islands)
Col. ... Colombia, Colony
Coll. ... College
Colo., CO ... Colorado
Com. ... Comoros
Comm. ... Community
Conn., CT ... Connecticut
Cont. ... Continent
Conv. Ctr. ... Convention Center
Cook Is. ... Cook Islands
Cor. ... Corner
Coral Sea Is. ... Coral Sea Islands Territory
Cord. ... Cordillera
Cr. ... Creek
Cres. ... Crescent
Cro. ... Croatia
Ct. ... Court
Cthse. ... Courthouse
Ctr. ... Center
Cwy. ... Causeway
Cyp. ... Cyprus
Czh. Rep. ... Czech Republic
D.C., DC, Dist. of Col. ... District of Columbia
Del., DE ... Delaware
Dem. Rep. ... Democratic Republic
Den. ... Denmark
Dep. ... Depot
Depr. ... Depression
Dept. ... Department
Des. ... Desert
Dist. ... District
Div. ... Divide, Division
Dji. ... Djibouti
Dkyd. ... Dockyard
Dom. ... Dominica
Dom. Rep. ... Dominican Republic
Dorm. ... Dormitory
Dr. ... Drive
Dtwn. ... Downtown
E. ... East
Ecua. ... Ecuador
Egy. ... Egypt
El. Salv. ... El Salvador
Elev. ... Elevation
Emb. ... Embankment
Emir. ... Emirates
Eng. ... England
Ent. ... Entrance
Eq. Gui. ... Equatorial Guinea
Erit. ... Eritrea
Escarp. ... Escarpment
Est. ... Estonia
Esty. ... Estuary
Eth. ... Ethiopia
Expwy. ... Expressway
Ext. ... Extension
F.A.C. ... Full Access Control
F.S.M. ... Federated States of Micronesia
Fact. ... Factory
Falk. Is. ... Falkland Islands
Far. Is. ... Faroe Islands
Fd. ... Fjord
Fd. ... Ford
Fed. ... Federal
Fin. ... Finland
Fk. ... Fork
Fla., FL ... Florida
Fld. ... Field
For. ... Forest
Fr. ... France
Fr. Gui. ... French Guiana
Fr. Poly. ... French Polynesia
Frgnd. ... Fairground
Frwy. ... Freeway
Ft. ... Feet, Foot, Fort
Fy. ... Ferry
G. ... Gulf
G.C. ... Golf Course
Ga., GA ... Georgia
Gal. Is. ... Galapagos Islands
Gam. ... The Gambia
Gaza ... Gaza Strip
Gdn. ... Garden
Gdns. ... Gardens
Gen. ... General
Geo. ... Georgia
Ger. ... Germany
Gha. ... Ghana
Gib. ... Gibraltar
Gl. ... Glacier
Govt. ... Government
Govt. Ctr. ... Government Center
Gr. ... Greece
Gren. ... Grenada
Grld. ... Greenland
Grnwy. ... Greenway
Grt. ... Great
Gtwy. ... Gateway
Guad. ... Guadeloupe
Guam, GU ... Guam
Guat. ... Guatemala
Guern. ... Guernsey
Gui.-B. ... Guinea-Bissau
Guin. ... Guinea
Guy. ... Guyana
H.K. ... Hong Kong
H.S. ... High School
Hawaii, HI ... Hawaii
Hbr. ... Harbor Harbour
Hd. ... Head
Hdqrs. ... Headquarters
Hol. ... Hollow
Hond. ... Honduras
Hosp. ... Hosptial
Hse. ... House
Hstd. ... Homestead
Hts. ... Heights
Hun. ... Hungary
Hwy. ... Highway
I. ... Island
I. of Man ... Isle of Man
Ice. ... Iceland
Ida., ID ... Idaho
Ill., IL ... Illinois
In. ... Inch, Inches
Ind. ... Industrial
Ind. Pk. ... Industrial Park
Ind. Res., I.R. ... Indian Reservation
Ind., IN ... Indiana
Indon. ... Indonesia
Inst. ... Institute, Institution
Interch. ... Interchange
Intl. ... International
Intl. Aprt. ... International Airport
Iowa, IA ... Iowa
Ire. ... Ireland
Is. ... Islands
Isr. ... Israel
Isth. ... Isthmus
It. ... Italy
Iv. C. ... Ivory Coast
Jam. ... Jamaica
Jap. ... Japan
Jct. ... Junction
Jers. ... Jersey
John. At. ... Johnston Atoll
Jor. ... Jordan
Kal. Nun. ... Kalaallit Nunaat
Kans., KS ... Kansas
Kaz. ... Kazakhstan
Kiri. ... Kiribati
Km. ... Kilometer, Kilometers
Kuw. ... Kuwait
Ky., KY ... Kentucky
Kyrg. ... Kyrgyzstan
L. ... Lake
L.H. ... Lighthouse
La., LA ... Louisiana
Lab. ... Laboratory
Lag. ... Lagoon
Lat. ... Latitude, Latvia
Ldg. ... Landing
Ldg. Fld. ... Landing Field
Ldg. Str. ... Landing Strip
Ldmk. ... Landmark
Leb. ... Lebanon
Leso. ... Lesotho
Lib. ... Libya
Liber. ... Liberia
Libr. ... Library
Liech. ... Liechtenstein
Lit. ... Little
Lith. ... Lithuania
Ln. ... Lane
Long. ... Longitude
Lp. ... Loop
Ltd. ... Limited
Ltd. Acc. ... Limited Access
Lux. ... Luxembourg
M. ... Meter, Meters
M.C.A.S. ... Marine Corps Air Station
Madag. ... Madagascar
Mal. ... Malawi
Malay. ... Malaysia
Mald. ... Maldives
Man., MB ... Manitoba
Mar. ... Marina
Marsh. Is. ... Marshall Islands
Mart. ... Martinique
Mass., MA ... Massachusetts
Maur. ... Mauritania
May. ... Mayotte
Md., MD ... Maryland
Mdw. ... Meadow
ME ... Maine
Mem. Pkwy. ... Memorial Parkway
Mem. S.P. ... Memorial State Park
Met. ... Meteor, Meteoric
Metro. ... Metropolitan
Mex. ... Mexico
Mgne. ... Montagne
Mi. ... Mile, Miles
Mich., MI ... Michigan
Micr. ... Micronesia
Mid. Is. ... Midway Islands
Mil. Res. ... Military Reservation
Minn., MN ... Minnesota
Miss., MS ... Mississippi
Mo., MO ... Missouri
Mol. ... Moldova
Mon. ... Monaco, Monument
Mon. S.P. ... Monument State Park
Mong. ... Mongolia
Mont., MT ... Montana
Monts. ... Montserrat
Mor. ... Morocco
Moz. ... Mozambique
Mt. ... Mount, Mont
Mte. ... Monte
Mtes. ... Montes
Mth. ... Mouth
Mths. ... Mouths
Mtn. ... Mountain
Mts. ... Mountains Monts
Mun. ... Municipal, Municipality
Mus. ... Museum
Mya. ... Myanmar
N. ... North
N. Ire. ... Northern Ireland
N. Kor. ... North Korea
N. Mar. Is. ... Northern Mariana Islands
N. Mex., NM ... New Mexico
N.B., NB ... New Brunswick
N.C., NC ... North Carolina
N. Dak., ND ... North Dakota
N.E. ... Northeast
N.H., NH ... New Hampshire
N.J., NJ ... New Jersey
N.S., NS ... Nova Scotia
N.S.W. ... New South Wales
N. Terr. ... Northern Territory
N.W. ... Northwest
N.W.R. ... National Wildlife Refuge
N.W.T., NT, N.W. Terr. ... Northwest Territories
N.Y., NY ... New York
N.Z. ... New Zealand
Nam. ... Namibia
Natl. ... National
Natl. Bfld. Park, N.B.P. ... National Battlefield Park
Natl. Bfld. Site, N.B.S. ... National Battlefield Site
Natl. Bfld., N.B. ... National Battlefield
Natl. Cap. Pk., N.C.P. ... National Capital Park
Natl. For., N.F. ... National Forest
Natl. Grassland, N.G. ... National Grassland
Natl. Hist. Park, N.H.P. ... National Historical Park
Natl. Hist. Res., N.H.R. ... Natl. Historical Reserve
Natl. Hist. Site, N.H.S. ... National Historic Site
Natl. Lakeshore, N.L. ... National Lakeshore
Natl. Mem., N. Mem. ... National Memorial
Natl. Mil. Park, N.M.P. ... National Military Park
Natl. Mon., N.M. ... National Monument
Natl. Park, N.P. ... National Park
Natl. Pkwy., N. Pkwy. ... National Parkway
Natl. Pres., N. Pres. ... National Preserve
Natl. Rec. Area, N.R.A. ... National Recreation Area
Natl. River ... National River
Natl. Scenic River, N.S.R. ... National Scenic River
Natl. Scenic Trail, N.S.T. ... National Scenic Trail
Natl. Seashore, N.S. ... National Seashore
Natl. Wilderness Area, N.W.A. ... National Wilderness Area
Naut. Mi. ... Nautical Mile
Naval Air Sta., N.A.S. ... Naval Air Station
Nbrhd. ... Neighborhood
Nebr., NE ... Nebraska
Neth. ... Netherlands
Neth. Ant. ... Netherlands Antilles
Nev., NV ... Nevada
New Cal. ... New Caledonia
Nfld., NF ... Newfoundland and Labrador
Nicar. ... Nicaragua
Nig. ... Nigeria
Nor. ... Norway
Norf. I. ... Norfolk Island
Nun. ... Nunavut
O. ... Ocean
Obl. ... Oblast
Obsv. ... Observatory
Ohio, OH ... Ohio
Okla., OK ... Oklahoma
Ont., ON ... Ontario
Oreg., OR ... Oregon
P.A.C. ... Partial Access Control
P.E.I., PE ... Prince Edward Island
P.N.G. ... Papua New Guinea
P.O. ... Post Office
P.R., PR ... Puerto Rico
Pa., PA, Penn., Penna. ... Pennsylvania
Pak. ... Pakistan
Pal. ... Palace
Pan. ... Panama
Par. ... Parish
Para. ... Paraguay
Pass. ... Passage
Pav. ... Pavilion
Pd. ... Pond
Pen. ... Peninsula
Phil. ... Philippines
Pitc. Is. ... Pitcairn Islands
Pk. ... Park, Peak, Pike
Pkg. ... Parking
Pks. ... Peaks
Pkwy. ... Parkway
Pl. ... Place
Plat. ... Plateau
Pln. ... Plain
Plns. ... Plains
Plz ... Plaza
Pol. ... Poland
Port. ... Portugal
Poss. ... Possession
Pref. ... Prefecture
Prom. ... Promontory
Prot. ... Protectorate
Prov. ... Province, Provincial
Pt. ... Point
Pta. ... Punta
Pte. ... Pointe
Pto. ... Puerto
Qnsld. ... Queensland
Qry. ... Quarry
Que., PQ ... Quebec
R. ... River
R.I., RI ... Rhode Island
R.R. ... Railroad
Ra. ... Range
Rap. ... Rapids
Ras. ... Ranges
Rav. ... Ravine
Rd ... Road
Rec. Area, R.A. ... Recreation Area
Ref. ... Refuge
Reg. ... Region
Rep. ... Republic
Res. ... Reservations, Reservoir
Resort S.P., R.S.P. ... Resort State Park
Reu. ... Reunion
Rom. ... Romania
Rte. ... Route
Russ. ... Russia
Rwa. ... Rwanda
Rwy ... Railway
Rwy. Sta. ... Railway Station
S. ... South
S. Afr. ... South Africa
S. Austl. ... South Australia
S. Dak., SD ... South Dakota
S. Kor. ... South Korea
S. Mar. ... San Marino
S.C., SC ... South Carolina
S.E. ... Southeast
S.L. ... Sierra Leone
S.P. ... State Park
S.W. ... Southwest
Sa. ... Sierra
Sa. Arab. ... Saudi Arabia
Sam. ... Samoa
Sanc. ... Sanctuary
São T. Prín. ... São Tome and Príncipe
Sas. ... Sierras
Sask., SK ... Saskatchewan
Sch. ... School
Scot. ... Scotland
Sd. ... Sound
Sem. ... Seminary
Sen. ... Senegal
Serb.-Mont. ... Serbia and Montenegro
Sey. ... Seychelles
Shop. Ctr. ... Shopping Center
Sing. ... Singapore
Slove. ... Slovenia
Slvk. ... Slovakia
Smt. ... Seamount
Snwfld. ... Snowfield
Sol. Is. ... Solomon Islands
Som. ... Somalia
Sp. ... Spain, Spur
Spr. ... Spring
Sprs. ... Springs
Sq. ... Square
Sri Lan. ... Sri Lanka
St. ... Saint, Street
St. Arch. Park, S.A.P. ... State Archaeological Park
St. Arch. Site, S.A.S. ... State Archaelogical Site
St. Beach, S.B. ... State Beach
St. Com. Area, S.C.A. ... State Commemorative Area
St. Fishing Lake, S.F.L. ... State Fishing Lake
St. For., S.F. ... State Forest
St. Hel. ... St. Helena
St. Hist. Area,S.H.A. ... State Historic Area State Historical Area
St. Hist. Mem., S.H. Mem. ... State Historical Memorial
St. Hist. Mon., S.H.M. ... State Historical Monument
St. Hist. Park, S.H.P. ... State Historical Park
St. Hist. Site, S.H.S. ... State Historical Site
St. Hist. Structure, S.H.S. ... State Historical Structure
St. K.-Nevis ... St. Kitts and Nevis
St. Luc. ... St. Lucia
St. Mem. ... State Memorial
St. Nat. Area, S.N.A. ... State Natural Area
St. P.-Miq. ... St. Pierre and Miquelon
St. Rec. Area, S.R.A. ... State Recreation Area
St. Rec. Site, S.R.S. ... State Recreation Site
St. Reserve, S.R. ... State Reserve
St. Resort Park, S.R.P. ... State Resort Park
St. Unique Area, S.U.A. ... State Unique Area
St. Veh. Rec. Area, S.V.R.A. ... State Vehicular Recreation Area
St. Vin.-Gren. ... St. Vincent and the Grenadines
St. Wayside Park, S.W.P. ... State Wayside Park
Sta. ... Station
Stad. ... Stadium
Ste. ... Sainte
Str. ... Strait
Str. ... Stream
Strs. ... Straits
Sur. ... Suriname
Sval. ... Svalbard
Swaz. ... Swaziland
Swe. ... Sweden
Switz. ... Switzerland
T.-C. Is. ... Turks and Caicos Islands
T.H. ... Town Hall
T.R. ... Truck Route
T.Z. ... Time Zone
Tai. ... Taiwan
Taj. ... Tajikistan
Tan. ... Tanzania
Tas. ... Tasmania
Tblnd. ... Tableland
Tech. ... Technical
Tenn., TN ... Tennessee
Ter. ... Terrace
Term. ... Terminal
Terr. ... Territory
Tex., TX ... Texas
Tfc. Cir. ... Traffic Circle
Thai. ... Thailand
Thoro. ... Thorofare
Thtr. ... Theater
Thwy. ... Throughway, Thruway
Tlwy. ... Tollway
Tmt. ... Tablemount
Tok. ... Tokelau
Toll ... Toll Bridge, Tollgate
Tpk. ... Turnpike
Tr. ... Trail
Trib. ... Tributary
Trin.-To. ... Trinidad and Tobago
Tun. ... Tunisia, Tunnel
Tur. ... Turkey
Turkm. ... Turkmenistan
Tuv. ... Tuvalu
Twp. ... Township
U.A.E. ... United Arab Emirates
U.C. ... Under Construction
U.K. ... United Kingdom
U.S. Vir. I., VI ... Virgin Islands
U.S., U.S.A. ... United States
Ug. ... Uganda
Ukr. ... Ukraine
Univ. ... University
Uru. ... Uruguay
Utah, UT ... Utah
Uzb. ... Uzbekistan
Va., VA ... Virginia
Val. ... Valley
Van. ... Vanuatu
Vat. ... Vatican City
Ven. ... Venezuela
Vet. ... Veteran
Viad. ... Viaduct
Vic. ... Vicinity
Vic. ... Victoria
Viet. ... Vietnam
Vil. ... Village
Vir. Is. ... Virgin Islands
Vol. ... Volcano
Vt., VT ... Vermont
W. ... West
W. Austl. ... West Australia
W. Bank ... West Bank
W. Sah. ... Western Sahara
W.H. ... Water Hole
W. Va., WV ... West Virginia
Wake I. ... Wake Island
Wal.-Fut. ... Wallis and Futuna
Wash., WA ... Washington
Wd. ... Ward
Whf. ... Wharf
Whvs. ... Wharves
Wisc., Wis., WI ... Wisconsin
Wtrwy. ... Waterway
Wyo., WY ... Wyoming
Y.C. ... Yacht Club
Yd. ... Yard
Yukon, YT ... Yukon Territory
Zam. ... Zambia
Zimb. ... Zimbabwe
Zn. ... Zone
Zoo. Gdn. ... Zoological Garden
Zoo. Pk. ... Zoological Park

MAPSKILLS™

The hundreds of informative, colorful maps found throughout Southwestern's *Volume 3* are the creation of MapQuest.com, Inc., one of the world's leading cartographic firms. To increase readers' enjoyment of maps, Mapquest.com created this *MAPSKILLS* section, designed as both an instructional aid and a visually exciting medium for learning.

Within *MAPSKILLS*, key topics such as map projections, latitude and longitude, map scale, symbols, and a glossary are discussed and illustrated. See the Bibliography on page 21 for a list of sources for further study on maps and their use.

Contents

Map Activities 10–11
Understanding Maps.........................12–13
Understanding Map Scale..................14–15
Understanding Latitude
    and Longitude.............................16–17
Understanding Map Projections.........18–19
Symbols and Glossary............................20
Further Study/Bibliography....................21

You can sharpen your map skills by completing the following questions. Use the following pages of the MapSkills section to help you answer the questions. The words that are in bold type refer to key words in the MapSkills section that will help you answer the questions. Also refer to maps that are included in volumes 1 and 2 of Southwestern's *Volume Library*.

Understanding Maps   see pages 12–13

1. Maps have three general uses. What are they?

2. Map types can be broken down into two broad categories. What are they?

3. Give an example of a **General Reference Map.**

4. Give an example of a **Thematic Map.**

Understanding Map Scale   see pages 14–15

1. Define "**map scale.**"

2. What are the **types** of map scales?

3. Define "**representative fraction.**"

4. Go to the map of your country or state and with a ruler and the scale bar, figure out approximately how many miles one inch represents.

Understanding Latitude and Longitude   see pages 16–17

1. Give a definition for "**latitude**" and "**longitude.**"

2. **Graticule** is another word for what?

3. Name a famous line of latitude.

4. Can you name other well known **parallel** lines?

5. Name a famous line of longitude.

6. Can you name other well known lines of longitude?

7. What degree of longitude is the **prime meridian**?

8. What degree of latitude is the **equator**?

9. How many **degrees** of latitude would you cross if you traveled north from the equator to the north pole?

10. How many **minutes** and **seconds** are in a degree of latitude and longitude?

11. What is another name for **90 degrees south**?

12. Find the map of your country or state and after finding the location of your town, figure out what line of latitude and longitude you are closest to.

Understanding Map Projections
see pages 18–19

1. Define a **projection**.

2. Name a **cylindrical** projection.

3. Name a kind of **azimuthal** projection.

4. Name a **conic** projection.

5. Go to the map of your country or state and look for the label that identifies the projection of that map. Look near the scale bar.

6. Go to the World Map on pages 52–53 and identify what projection it is.

Symbols and Glossary   see page 20

1. What kind of **symbol** is used to identify a **state** or **national capital**?

2. What kind of **symbol** is used to show where a **mountain peak** is located?

3. Using the map of your country or state, can you find and name the capital city?

4. Define **fjord**. Go to the map of Norway; it is a country that has many **fjords**.

5. How is a **hill** different than a **mountain**?

6. How can you tell the difference between a **perennial river** and an **intermittent river**?

7. Find the symbol for "continental divide". Define **continental divide**.

8. Think about which of the terms in the **glossary** identify any geographic features you live near or are familiar with. For example, you might live near or have visited the Grand **Canyon** or the English **Channel**.

9. Use the map of your country or state to see how many of the geographic features found in the **glossary** are located near to where you live. Do you have a **volcano** located near you?

MAP USE

Maps are tools that provide us with information about the world in which we live. As with all tools, we need to learn how to use them and for what purposes. Maps have three principal uses:

To **locate** places on the surface of the earth

To show **patterns of distribution** of natural and man-made phenomena

To **compare** and **contrast** map information and thereby discover **relationships** between different phenomena

MAP DEFINITION

We use the term map to refer to many things, including sketches, air photographs, radar images, and so forth. A stricter definition would limit the term map to images with an **orthogonal** viewpoint, where every point on the map is viewed as if looking straight down from above.

As a representation of reality, a map is made up of a selection of features. Whereas a photograph shows all objects in its view, a map is an abstraction of reality. The cartographer portrays only the information that is necessary to fulfill the purpose of the map, and that is suitable for its scale. Maps use symbols to convey information, such as points, lines, area patterns and colors, along with type.

Oblique **air photo** of Washington, D.C. Note how single focal point of camera lens skews buildings and street network from center of photo.

Portion of **topographic map** of Washington, D.C., showing the Mall from the Washington Monument to the U.S. Capitol. Note how only specific features have been selected and portrayed by use of conventional symbols.

Portion of **orthophotomap** of Washington's mall area. This map is a mosaic of many air photos. They have been rectified so that all points on the map are shown as if viewed directly from above.

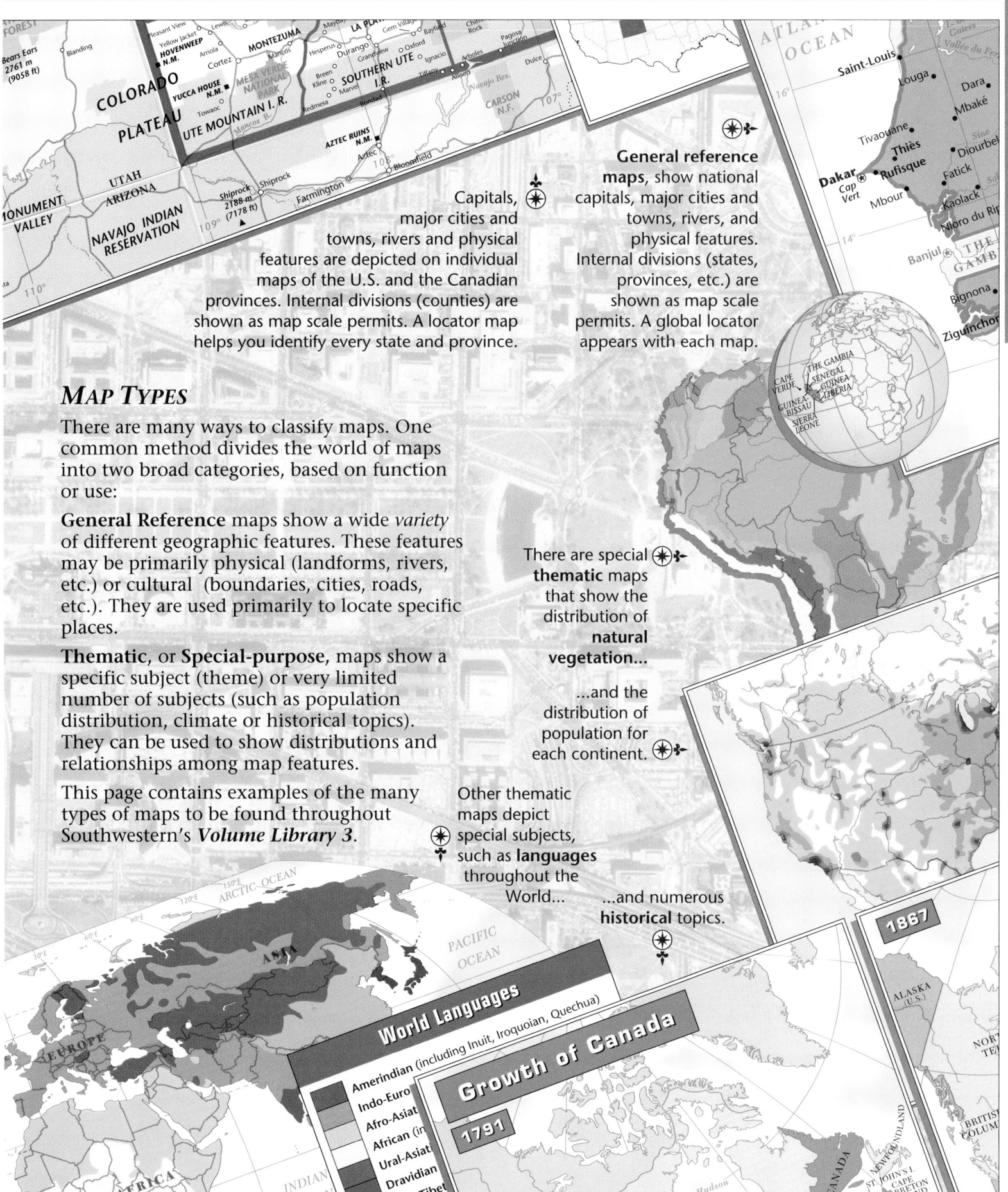

Capitals, major cities and towns, rivers and physical features are depicted on individual maps of the U.S. and the Canadian provinces. Internal divisions (counties) are shown as map scale permits. A locator map helps you identify every state and province.

General reference maps, show national capitals, major cities and towns, rivers, and physical features. Internal divisions (states, provinces, etc.) are shown as map scale permits. A global locator appears with each map.

MAP TYPES

There are many ways to classify maps. One common method divides the world of maps into two broad categories, based on function or use:

General Reference maps show a wide *variety* of different geographic features. These features may be primarily physical (landforms, rivers, etc.) or cultural (boundaries, cities, roads, etc.). They are used primarily to locate specific places.

Thematic, or **Special-purpose**, maps show a specific subject (theme) or very limited number of subjects (such as population distribution, climate or historical topics). They can be used to show distributions and relationships among map features.

This page contains examples of the many types of maps to be found throughout Southwestern's *Volume Library 3*.

There are special **thematic** maps that show the distribution of **natural vegetation**...

...and the distribution of population for each continent.

Other thematic maps depict special subjects, such as **languages** throughout the World...

...and numerous **historical** topics.

World Languages

Amerindian (including Inuit, Iroquoian, Quechua)
Indo-Euro
Afro-Asiat
African (in
Ural-Asiat
Dravidian
Sino-Tibet

Growth of Canada

1791

1867

The scale to which a map is drawn represents the **ratio** of the distance between two points on the earth and the distance between the two corresponding points on the map.

$$\text{Map Scale} = \frac{\text{Map Distance}}{\text{Ground Distance}}$$

TYPES OF SCALE

VERBAL SCALE

When a scale is expressed in words, for example *one inch represents one mile,* it is referred to as a **Verbal Scale.**

VISUAL SCALE

Almost every map has a bar scale, or a **Visual Scale,** that can be used for measuring. It shows graphically the relationship between map distance and ground distance.

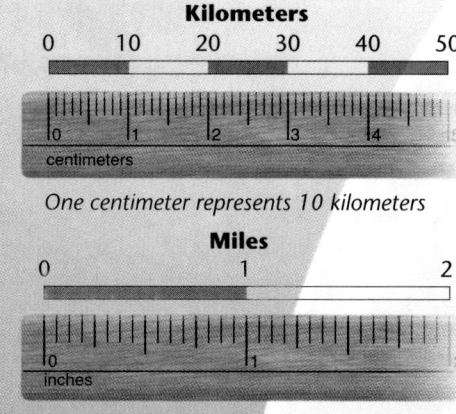

One centimeter represents 10 kilometers

One inch represents 1 mile

REPRESENTATIVE FRACTION

The scale of a map, expressed as a *numerical ratio* of map distance to ground distance, is called a **Representative Fraction** (or RF).
It is usually written as 1/50,000 or 1:50,000, meaning that one unit of measurement on the map represents 50,000 of the same units on the ground.

EXERCISES

Use the general reference map of WYOMING on page 366 to answer the following questions:

1. What is the map scale, expressed as a representative fraction ?

_____

2. Using a ruler to measure the bar scale, complete the following statement of verbal scale:
One inch represents approximately

_____ *miles.*

3. If you reduced the size of this map by half (50%) how long would 50 miles on the bar scale be?

_____

What would the representative fraction be?

1: _____

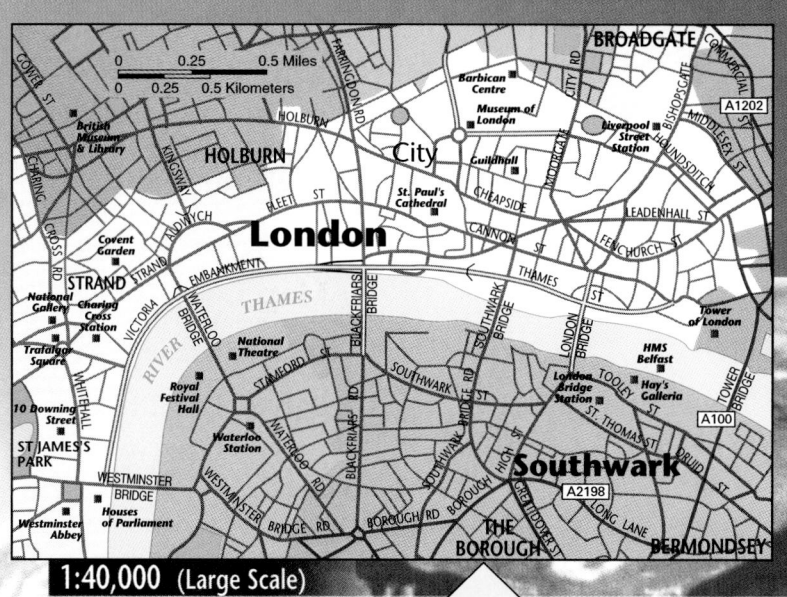

1:40,000 (Large Scale)

CHANGING SCALES

The maps on this page show how scale changes moving "closer" to or "farther" from the earth. A **large scale** map shows a small area with a large amount of detail. A **small scale** map shows a large area with small detail.

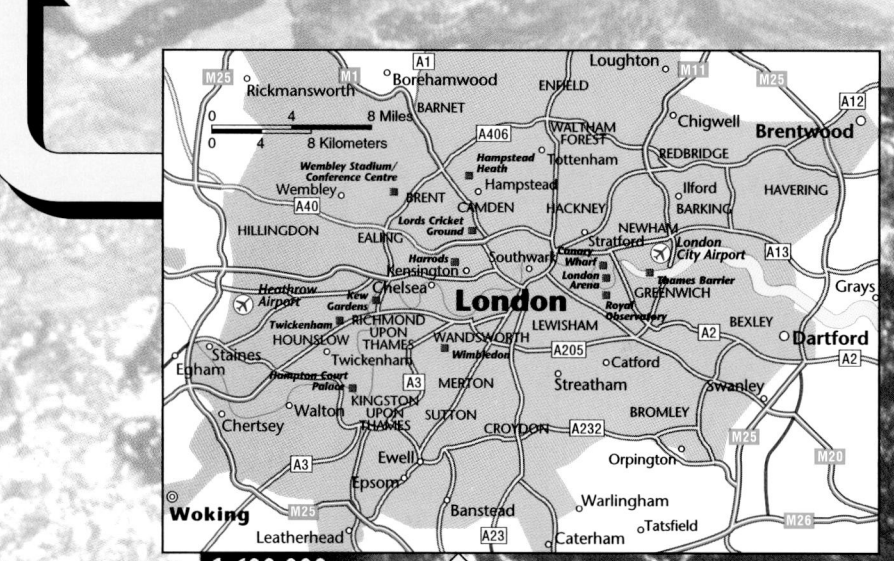

1:600,000

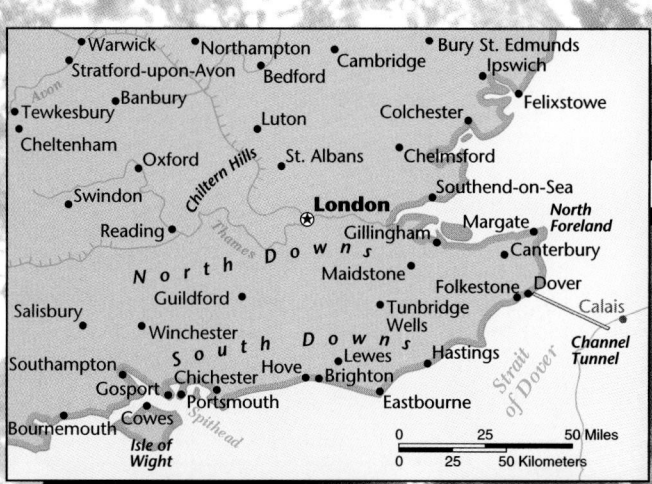

1:4,000,000 (Small Scale)

EXERCISES

Use the general reference map of the World on pages 52–53 to answer the following questions:

1. Trace the 80°W meridian. Does South America lie mainly to the east or west of this meridian? Is North America mainly to the east or west of it? What can you say about the location of South America in relation to the United States?

2. Find the 40°N parallel. Follow it from the left side of the map to the right. Through what countries does it pass? What countries are directly east of the United States? Describe the location of Ireland and the United Kingdom in relation to the United States.

3. Antipodes are two places that are directly opposite each other on the surface of the earth. They are therefore separated from each other by 180° of latitude and 180° of longitude.
   The antipode of the point where the prime meridian crosses the equator (0°, 0°) is the intersection of the equator and the International Date Line (0°, 180°). The antipode of 45°N, 90°W (in Wisconsin) is at 45°S, 90°E (in the Indian Ocean).

   Using a globe and atlas, answer the following questions:

   a. The antipode of Beijing, China (40°N, 116°E) lies in the country of:

   _____

   b. The antipode of Punta Arenas, Chile (53°S, 71°W) falls near:

   Lake _____

   c. The antipode of the capital of Brunei (5°N, 115°E) lies near the:

   _____ River

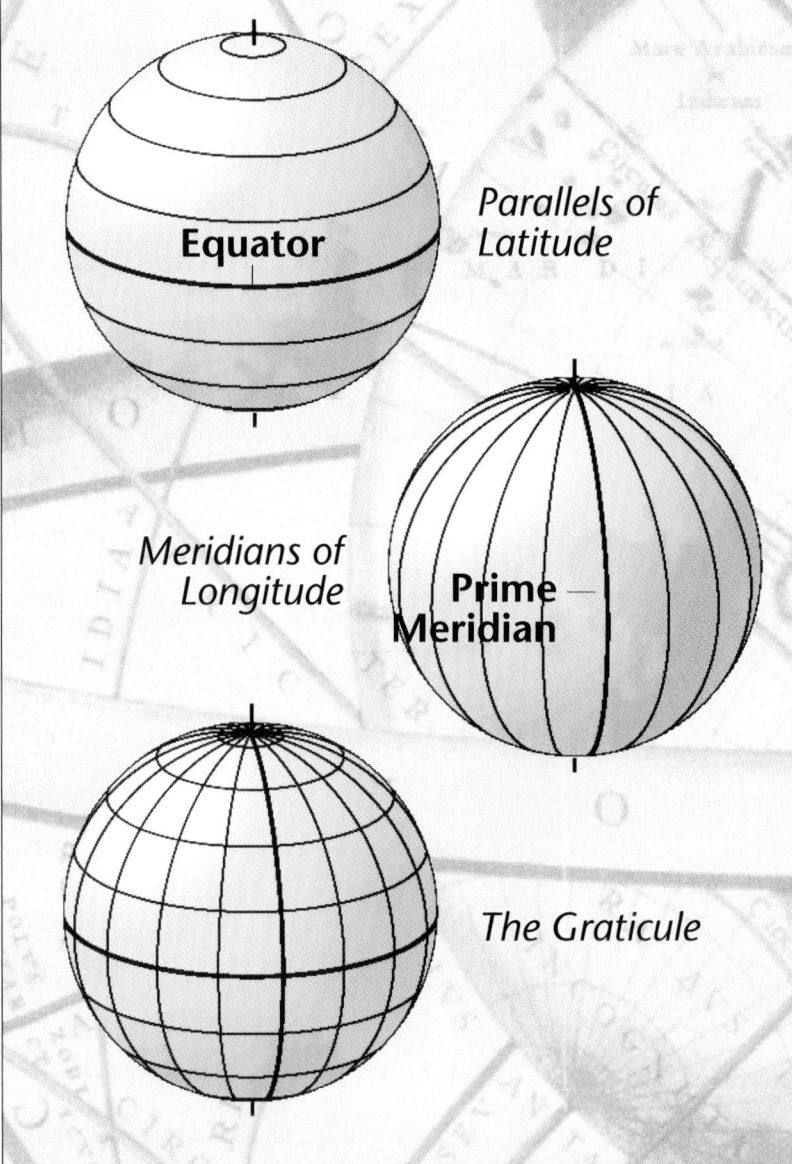

Latitude and longitude form a geographical coordinate system used for locating places on the surface of the earth. They are angular measurements, expressed as degrees of a circle measured from the center of the earth.

The earth spins on its axis, which intersects the surface at the north and south poles. The poles are the natural starting place for the graticule, a spherical grid of latitude and longitude lines.

Equator

Parallels of Latitude

Meridians of Longitude

Prime Meridian

The Graticule

LONGITUDE

Lines of longitude, called **meridians**, run in a north-south direction from pole to pole. Longitude is the angular measurement of a place east or west of the **prime meridian**. This meridian is also known as the Greenwich Meridian, because it runs through the original site of the Royal Observatory, which was located at Greenwich, just outside London, England.

Longitude runs from 0° at the prime meridian to 180° east or west, halfway around the globe. The International Date Line follows the 180° meridian, making a few jogs to avoid cutting through land areas.

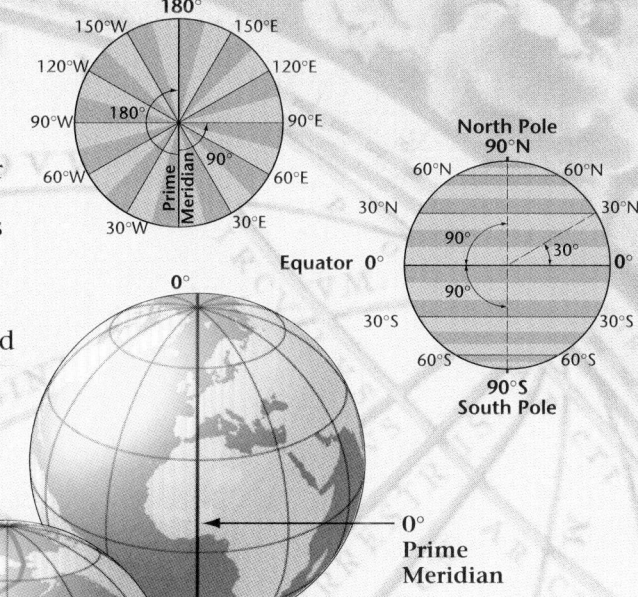

LATITUDE

Halfway between the poles lies the **equator**. Latitude is the angular measurement of a place expressed in degrees north or south of the equator. Latitude runs from 0° at the equator to 90°N or 90°S at the poles.

Lines of latitude run in an east-west direction. They are called **parallels** because they are equally distant from, or parallel to, one another.

Which way up . . .

The north and south poles are the earth's geographic poles, located at each end of its axis of rotation. All meridians meet at these poles.

The earth's magnetic fields cause the needle of a compass to align itself with magnetic north, not geographic north. The north **magnetic pole** is located in the Queen Elizabeth Islands group, in the Canadian Northwest Territories. The south magnetic pole lies near the edge of the continent of Antarctica, off the Adélie Coast.

The magnetic poles are constantly moving.

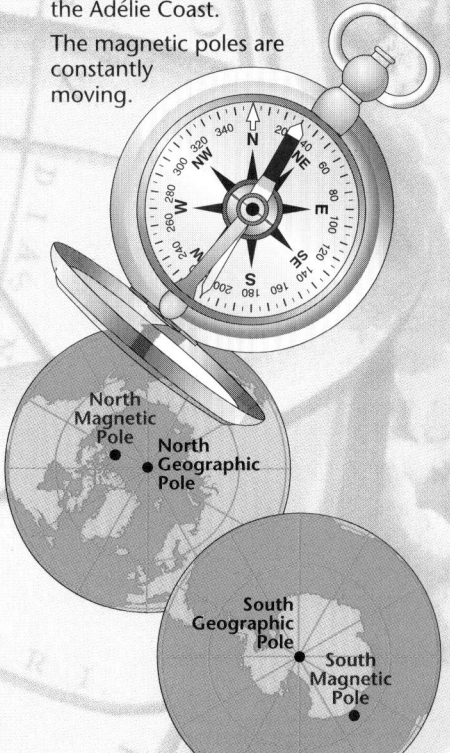

DEGREES, MINUTES, SECONDS

A **degree** (°) of latitude or longitude can be subdivided into 60 parts called minutes ('). Each minute can be further subdivided into 60 **seconds** ("). One degree of latitude equals approximately 69 miles (111 km). One minute is just over a mile (1.6 km), and one second is around 100 feet (30.5 m), which is a pretty precise location on a globe with a circumference of 25,000 miles (40,250 km). Because meridians converge at the poles, the length of a degree of longitude varies, from 69 miles (111 km) at the equator to 0 at the poles (longitude becomes a point at the poles).

The diagram at left is an example of a place located to the nearest second.

It is written as:

42° 21' 30" N   71° 03' 37" W

- This place is city center, Boston, Massachusetts.

MAP PROJECTIONS

The grid system of the globe is the only true representation of the earth. Note that on a globe the meridians are all of equal length; that each meridian is equal to one-half the length of the equator; that meridians come closer and closer together and meet at the poles; that the north and south poles are points; that the parallels between the equator and poles become shorter and shorter in length; that all lines of latitude are parallel to the equator and to one another; and that the distance between any two parallels a given number of degrees apart is the same as the distance between any other two parallels the same number of degrees apart. Each degree of latitude represents approximately 69 miles (111 km); each degree of longitude at the equator likewise represents about 69 miles (111 km), however at 60° latitude a degree of longitude is half that distance – approximately 35 miles (56 km); at the poles, where longitude meets at a point, the distance is zero.

Navigators use the **Gnomonic** and **Mercator** projections to plot and follow routes between two places. The shortest distance between two points is a **great circle route.** These appear as straight lines on the Gnomonic projection. Note that the bearing (compass direction) of this line constantly changes. On the Mercator projection routes of constant bearing, or rhumb lines, appear as straight lines. To plan a route, navigators first plot a great circle route on a Gnomonic projection. The next step is to transfer this route onto a Mercator projection. The route is then approximated by a number of short, straight-line segments. Each segment has a constant bearing, simplifying the task of navigating between points. Plot these routes for yourself:

Gnomonic Projection

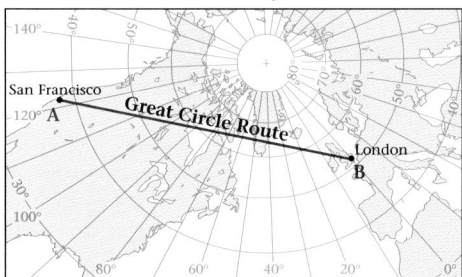

On the map above straight line A–B is a great circle route. Plot this on the Mercator projection below, then approximate the route with short straight-line segments.

Mercator Projection

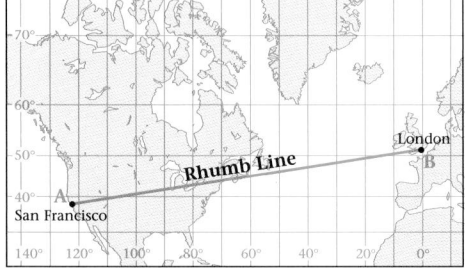

On the map above straight line A–B is a rhumb line. Plot this on the Gnomonic projection above. Note how following a rhumb line greatly increases the distance to be traveled.

The only true representation of the earth, free of distortion, is a globe. Maps are flat, and the process by which geographic locations (latitude and longitude) are transformed from a three-dimensional sphere to a two-dimensional flat map is called a **projection.**

PROPERTIES

Every map projection distorts at least three, and sometimes all four, of the following properties: *Shape, Area, Distance,* and *Direction.*

Conformal: *No map can preserve the* **shape** *of large areas, but a conformal projection maintains shape in small, localized areas.*

Equal Area: *These projections show the* **areas** *of all regions on the map in the same proportion to their true areas on the globe.*

Equidistant: *No map can show* **distance** *correctly between all points on the map, but only from one, or at most two, points to any other point.*

Azimuthal: *This projection correctly shows* **directions** *(azimuths) from a single point to all other points on the map.*

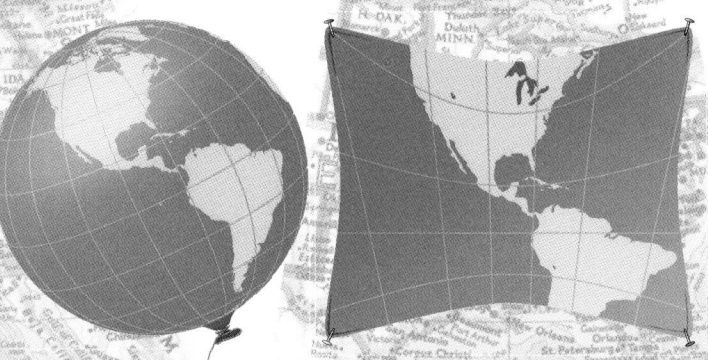

To better understand what happens during the projection process, imagine the earth as a large inflated balloon. Cut it apart, and flatten it to make a map. It will be stretched in some places, shrunk in others. Think of where and how the original balloon has been distorted.

This diagram illustrates how a Mercator (cylindrical) projection distorts the relative sizes of areas on the earth. Note how areas are increasingly enlarged towards higher latitudes.

VISUAL COMPARISONS

Visualize the properties of a map projection by comparing the arrangement of its meridians and parallels with the characteristics of the graticule on the globe:

- Lines of latitude are parallel.
- Parallels are spaced equal distances apart.
- The equator is the longest parallel.
  Length of parallels decreases moving toward the poles (which are points).
- All meridians are of equal length.
- Meridians converge at the poles.
- At a given latitude, meridians are equally spaced.
- Latitude and longitude meet at right angles.

CLASSIFICATION OF PROJECTIONS

One method of classifying map projections is to group them by the type of surface onto which the graticule is theoretically being projected: **Cylindrical**, **Conic**, and **Azimuthal**. Map projections that do not fit within these three classes are described as **Pseudo** or **Miscellaneous** projections. Though few maps are truly the result of such projection (most are derived from mathematical formulas), it is a useful way to visualize and understand the transformation process.

Where the projection surface touches (is tangent to) the globe, scale is true. This can be at a point, or along one or two lines (called standard lines, or, if along a line of latitude, standard parallels). Distortion increases with increasing distance from the standard point or lines.

CYLINDRICAL

Imagine a light bulb in the center of a globe, with a sheet of paper wrapped around it in the form of a cylinder. Meridians and parallels would be "projected" onto the cylinder as straight, parallel lines. Because meridians on these projections do not meet at the poles, as they do on the globe, these maps are increasingly stretched and distorted toward the poles.

Tangent
at Equator

Mercator Cylindrical Projection

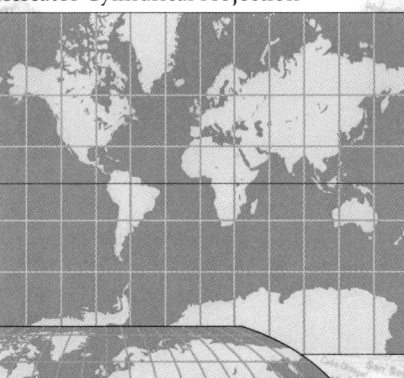

***Pseudocylindrical** projections normally have straight parallels and curved meridians (usually equally spaced). The Robinson Projection is a popular example. It was created to make the world "look" right by keeping angular and areal distortions to a minimum.*

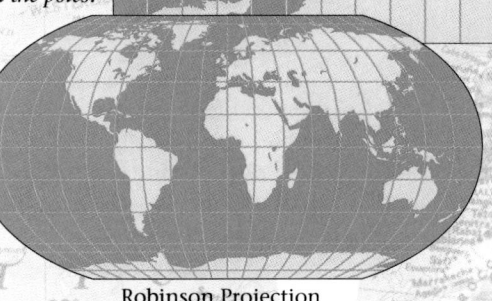

Robinson Projection

AZIMUTHAL

*A perfectly flat piece of paper (a plane) would touch the globe at a point. This projection is a good choice for maps with circular or square shapes. When the point of tangency is one of the poles, meridians are shown as straight lines radiating from the pole. If parallels are then drawn as equally spaced concentric circles, this projection would be **equidistant** (scale is true along any line radiating from the center point, in this case the pole).*

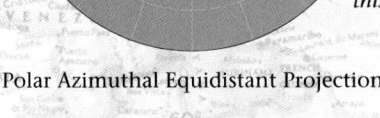

Polar Azimuthal Equidistant Projection

Gnomonic Projection.
Great circle routes (the shortest distance between two points on the globe) appear as straight lines on this Azimuthal *projection.*

Tangent Point

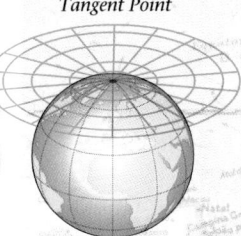

Albers Equal Area Conic Projection

CONIC

A cone of paper placed over a globe would touch its surface along one standard line (usually a parallel). A cone that sliced through the globe would intersect it twice, creating two standard parallels. Such a projection is well-suited for showing areas in the middle-latitudes with a mostly east-west extent (like the United States).

*Two
Standard
Parallels*

Background Notes . . .

The background image shows portions of map gores, which are used in the making of globes. The gores are printed on flat paper, cut into strips, and pasted onto the globe form – fitting a two-dimensional surface onto a three-dimensional sphere.

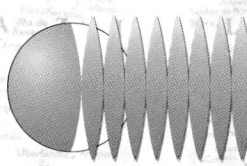

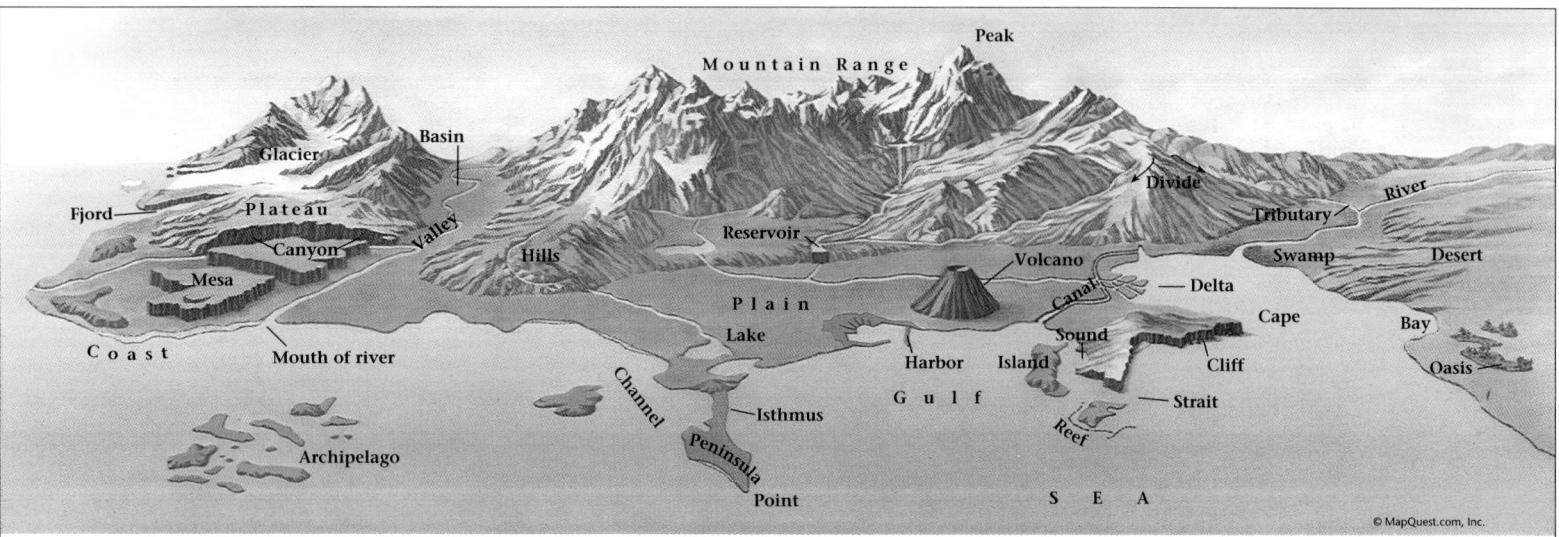

SYMBOLS

*The following symbols are used on **general reference maps** of the individual countries and states. Thematic (special subject) maps are accompanied by their own legends.*

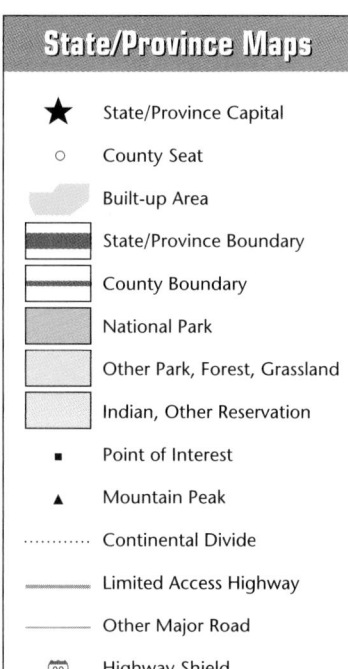

General Reference Maps

- ⊛ National Capital
- • Other City
- International Boundary (subject area)
- International Boundary (non-subject)
- Internal Boundary (state, province, etc.)
- Perennial River
- Intermittent River

State/Province Maps

- ★ State/Province Capital
- ○ County Seat
- Built-up Area
- State/Province Boundary
- County Boundary
- National Park
- Other Park, Forest, Grassland
- Indian, Other Reservation
- ■ Point of Interest
- ▲ Mountain Peak
- ·········· Continental Divide
- ———— Limited Access Highway
- ———— Other Major Road
- ⬡ Highway Shield

GLOSSARY

Archipelago a group of islands

Basin an area surrounded by higher land; an area drained by a river and its tributaries

Bay a coastal indentation of the sea or a lake into the land

Canal a man-made waterway, for irrigation or transportation

Canyon a deep valley with steep sides, usually with a river flowing through it

Cape a point of land extending out into a body of water

Channel a narrow stretch of water connecting two larger bodies of water

Cliff a high, steep rock-face

Coast a strip of land bordering the sea

Continental Divide a ridge of land (divide) that separates the great drainage basins of a continent, each basin emptying into a separate body of water

Delta an area of land formed by deposits at the mouth of a river

Desert an area of land with little rainfall or vegetation

Fjord a narrow inlet of the sea, with steep slopes, formed by a glacier

Glacier a large mass of ice that moves slowly, from higher to lower ground

Gulf an extension of the sea partly surrounded by land, larger than a bay

Harbor a sheltered area along a coast where ships can safely anchor

Hills an upland area, smaller than mountains, with gentle slopes

Island a body of land completely surrounded by water

Isthmus a narrow strip of land that connects two larger bodies of land

Lake a body of water completely surrounded by land

Mesa a flat upland area with steep sides, smaller than a plateau

Mountain an area of land rising much higher than the land around it, with steep slopes and pointed or rounded tops

Mouth, of river the point where a river empties into another body of water

Oasis a place in the desert with enough water to support vegetation

Peak the pointed top of a mountain

Peninsula a long piece of land surrounded on three sides by water

Plain a large area of flat or gently rolling land

Plateau a large elevated area of flat land

Point a narrow piece of land jutting out into a body of water, usually low-lying

Range a chain of mountains

Reef an underwater ridge, lying near the surface of the water

Reservoir a man-made lake, sometimes formed by a river dam

River any stream of fresh water flowing by gravity from an upland source into a body of water or another river. Perennial rivers flow all year; intermittent are dry part of the year

Sea a large body of salt water, smaller than an ocean

Sound a stretch of water between an island and the mainland

Strait a stretch of water joining two larger bodies of water, narrower than a channel

Swamp low-lying land permanently waterlogged

Tributary a river that flows into a larger river

Valley a long, low area, usually with a river flowing through it, and often lying between mountains or hills

Volcano a cone-shaped hill or mountain formed by lava and ash; may be active or extinct

FOR FURTHER STUDY/BIBLIOGRAPHY

For a general overview, see in particular articles in the following section: *Earth Sciences and Physical Geography, Southwestern Volume Library 1.*

This bibliography, listed alphabetically by author, identifies sources for further study:

Greenhood, David. *Mapping.* The University of Chicago Press, 1964. General interest, introductory level discussion of maps and mapmaking.

Maling, D.H. *Coordinate Systems and Map Projections.* Pergamon Press, Ltd., 1991. Advanced text on map projections.

Monmonier, Mark and George A. Schnell. *Map Appreciation.* Prentice-Hall, 1988. General survey of maps as tools, and types of maps.

Muehrcke, Phillip C. *Map Use: Reading, Analysis, Interpretation.* JP Publications, 3d ed., 1992. Introduction to maps and map usage.

Robinson, Morrison, Muehrcke, Kimerling and Guptill. *Elements of Cartography.* John Wiley & Sons, Inc., 6th ed., 1995. In depth review of entire subject of cartography, including history, research, production, and digital methods.

CREDITS

Text: Jeannine Schonta
Photo Research: Luis Freile
Design: Jeannine Schonta, Andy Skinner
Illustrations and Production: Andy Skinner, Andy Green

Title Page: Background World, Ortelio, *Planet Art*
Map Activities: Background USGS, *Concord, NH 7.5 Minute Digital Topographic Quadrangle*
Understanding Maps: Background and Orthophoto sample *USGS, Washington West 7.5 Minute Digital Orthophotoquad*; Oblique air photo, Washington, D.C. *Air Photographics, Inc.*; Map *USGS, Washington West 7.5 Minute Digital Topographic Quadrangle*
Understanding Map Scale: Background courtesy *NASA*
Understanding Latitude and Longitude: Background Atlas, Coelestis, *Planet Art*
Understanding Map Projections: Globe gores courtesy *National Geographic Society*

OUR SOLAR SYSTEM

	Sun	Mercury	Venus	Earth	Mars	Jupiter	Saturn	Uranus	Neptune	Pluto
Diameter (km)	1,390,000	4,878	12,102	12,800	6,800	143,000	120,500	51,100	49,528	2,300
Mean distance from Sun (millions of kilometers)	-----	58	108	150	228	778	1,427	2,871	4,504	5,900

Pluto

Neptune

	Time to orbit the Sun (years)	Average Temp. (°C)
Sun	---	5,500
Mercury	0.2	480
Venus	0.6	330
Earth	1.0	22
Mars	1.9	-23
Jupiter	11.9	-151
Saturn	29.5	-184
Uranus	84.0	-206
Neptune	164.8	-223
Pluto	247.7	?

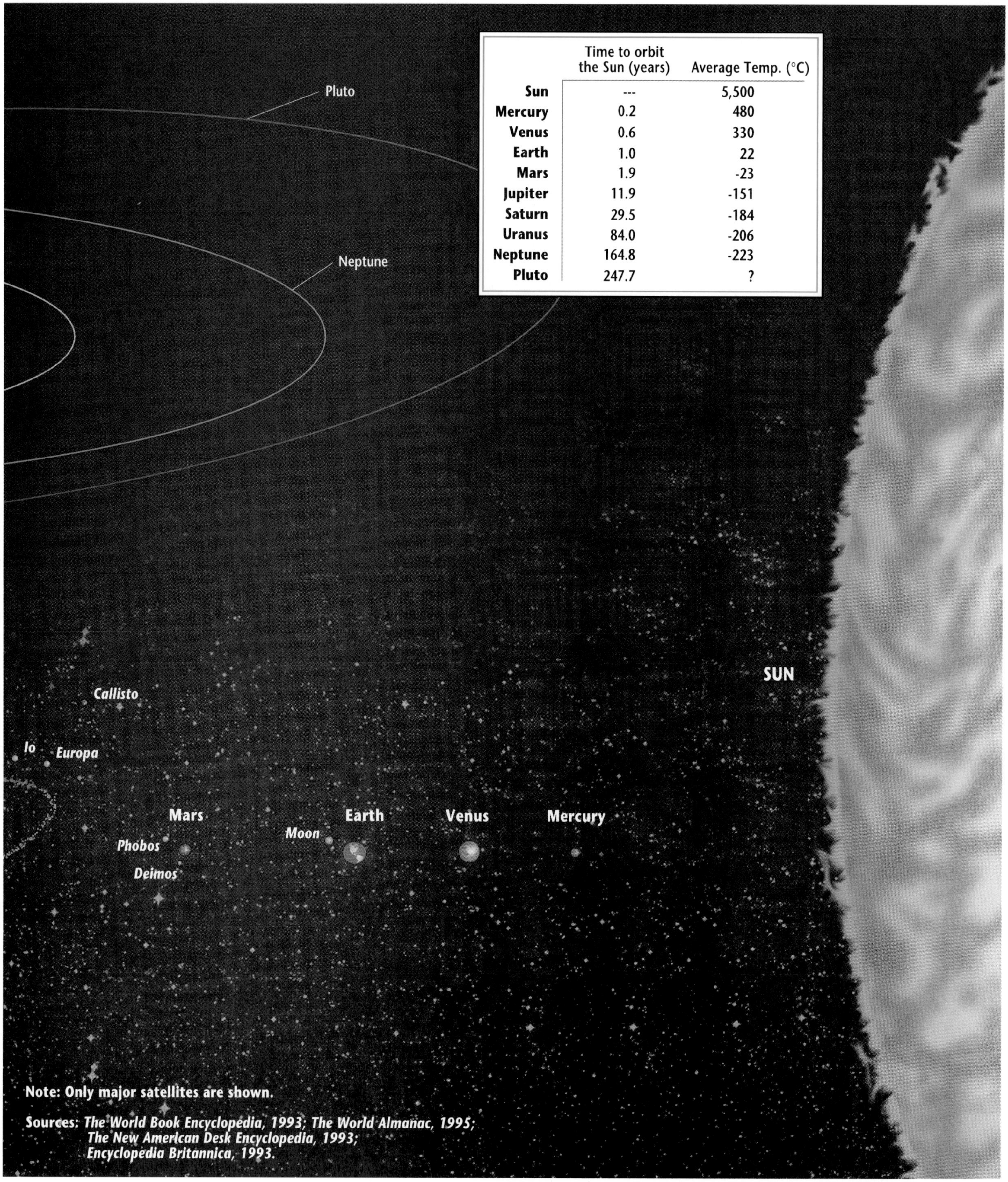

Callisto

Io Europa

SUN

Mars Moon Earth Venus Mercury

Phobos

Deimos

Note: Only major satellites are shown.

Sources: *The World Book Encyclopedia, 1993; The World Almanac, 1995; The New American Desk Encyclopedia, 1993; Encyclopedia Britannica, 1993.*

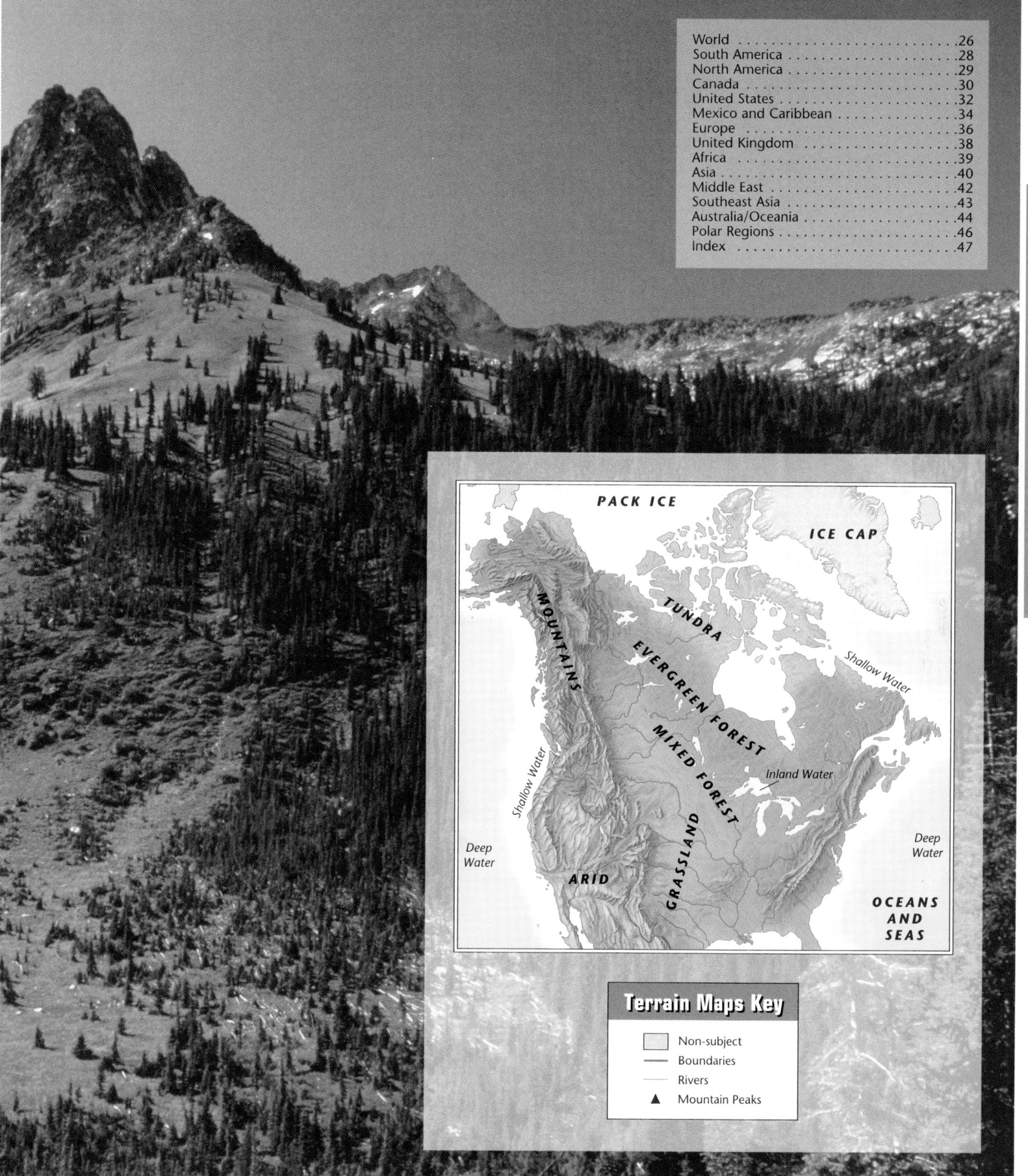

PACK ICE

ICE CAP

MOUNTAINS

TUNDRA

EVERGREEN FOREST

MIXED FOREST

Shallow Water

Shallow Water

Inland Water

Deep
Water

Deep
Water

ARID

GRASSLAND

OCEANS
AND
SEAS

Terrain Maps Key

- Non-subject
- Boundaries
- Rivers
- ▲ Mountain Peaks

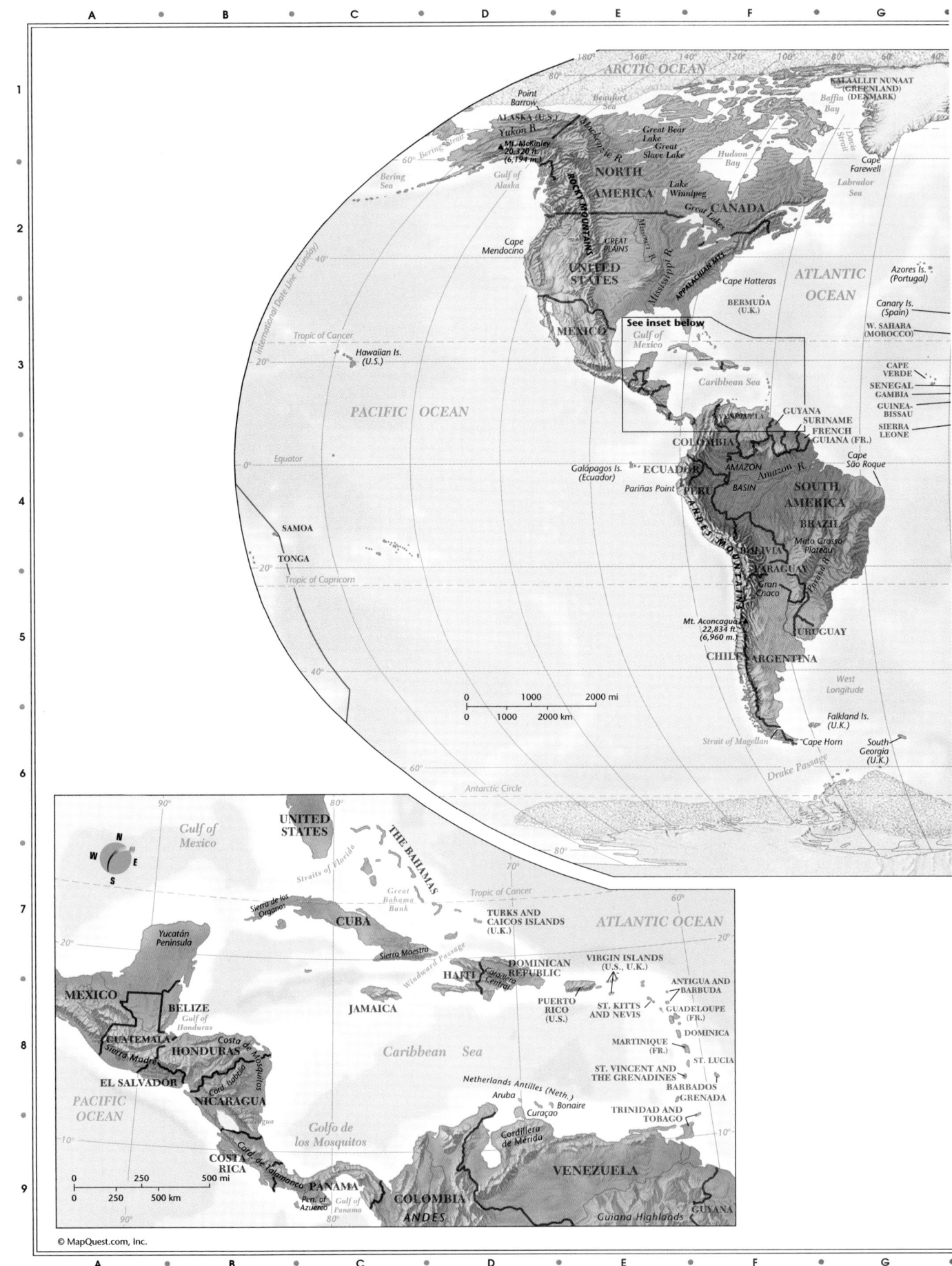

© MapQuest.com, Inc.

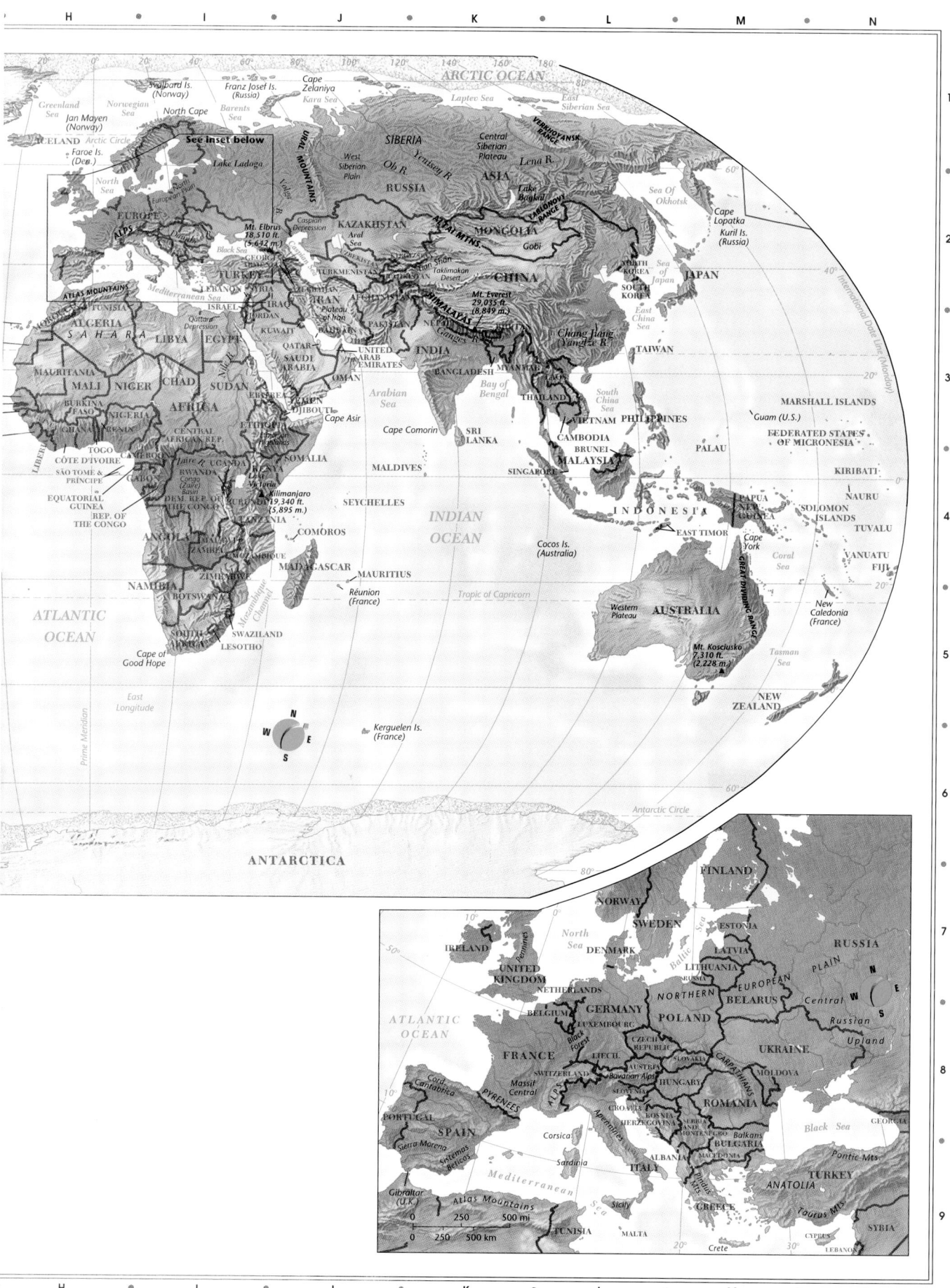

ARCTIC OCEAN

Svalbard Is. (Norway)
Franz Josef Is. (Russia)
Cape Zelaniya
North Cape
Laptev Sea
East Siberian Sea

Greenland Sea
Jan Mayen (Norway)
Norwegian Sea
Kara Sea

ICELAND
Arctic Circle
Faroe Is. (Den.)
Barents Sea

See inset below
SIBERIA
Central Siberian Plateau
Lena R.

URAL MOUNTAINS
Lake Ladoga
West Siberian Plain
Ob R.
Yenisey R.
ASIA
Lake Baikal
60°

North Sea
EUROPE
ALPS
RUSSIA
KAZAKHSTAN
ALTAI MTNS.
MONGOLIA
YABLONOVY RANGE
Sea Of Okhotsk

VERKHOYANSK RANGE

Mt. Elbrus 18,510 ft. (5,642 m.)
Aral Sea
Gobi
Cape Lopatka
Kuril Is. (Russia)

Caspian Depression
TURKEY
GEORGIA
Black Sea
Caspian Sea
TURKMENISTAN
Tian Shan
Taklimakon Desert
CHINA
SOUTH KOREA
NORTH KOREA
JAPAN

ATLAS MOUNTAINS
Mediterranean Sea
LEBANON
SYRIA
ISRAEL
AFGHANISTAN
HIMALAYAS
Mt. Everest 29,035 ft. (8,849 m.)
Sea of Japan
East China Sea
40°

TUNISIA
MOROCCO
ALGERIA
IRAQ
IRAN
Plateau of Iran
PAKISTAN
NEPAL
BHUTAN
Chang Jiang (Yangtze R.)
TAIWAN

LIBYA
EGYPT
JORDAN
KUWAIT
BAHRAIN
QATAR
SAUDI ARABIA
UNITED ARAB EMIRATES
OMAN
INDIA
BANGLADESH
MYANMAR
LAOS

Qattara Depression
SAHARA
20°

MAURITANIA
MALI
NIGER
CHAD
SUDAN
ERITREA
YEMEN
DJIBOUTI
Cape Asir
Arabian Sea
Cape Comorin
Bay of Bengal
THAILAND
VIETNAM
PHILIPPINES
South China Sea
MARSHALL ISLANDS

BURKINA FASO
NIGERIA
AFRICA
CENTRAL AFRICAN REP.
ETHIOPIA
Ethiopian Highlands
SRI LANKA
CAMBODIA
BRUNEI
PALAU
Guam (U.S.)
FEDERATED STATES OF MICRONESIA

GHANA
TOGO
CÔTE D'IVOIRE
LIBERIA
SÃO TOMÉ & PRÍNCIPE
CAMEROON
UGANDA
KENYA
SOMALIA
MALDIVES
MALAYSIA
SINGAPORE
KIRIBATI

EQUATORIAL GUINEA
GABON
REP. OF THE CONGO
DEM. REP. OF THE CONGO
Congo (Zaire) Basin
RWANDA
BURUNDI
Lake Victoria
Kilimanjaro 19,340 ft. (5,895 m.)
TANZANIA
SEYCHELLES
INDIAN OCEAN
INDONESIA
PAPUA NEW GUINEA
SOLOMON ISLANDS
NAURU
TUVALU

ANGOLA
ZAMBIA
MALAWI
MOZAMBIQUE
COMOROS
MADAGASCAR
EAST TIMOR
Cape York
Coral Sea
VANUATU
FIJI

Prime Meridian
NAMIBIA
ZIMBABWE
BOTSWANA
MAURITIUS
Réunion (France)
Tropic of Capricorn
Western Plateau
GREAT DIVIDING RANGE
AUSTRALIA
New Caledonia (France)
20°

ATLANTIC OCEAN
SOUTH AFRICA
SWAZILAND
LESOTHO
Mozambique Channel
Mt. Kosciusko 7,310 ft. (2,228 m.)
Tasman Sea

Cape of Good Hope
East Longitude
Kerguelen Is. (France)
NEW ZEALAND

N
W E
S

Antarctic Circle
80°
60°

ANTARCTICA

FINLAND
NORWAY
SWEDEN
RUSSIA

IRELAND
North Sea
DENMARK
Baltic Sea
ESTONIA
LATVIA
LITHUANIA
EUROPEAN PLAIN
Central Russian Upland

ATLANTIC OCEAN
UNITED KINGDOM
NETHERLANDS
BELGIUM
GERMANY
LUXEMBOURG
Black Forest
POLAND
BELARUS
NORTHERN
UKRAINE

FRANCE
Massif Central
SWITZERLAND
LIECH.
AUSTRIA
CZECH REPUBLIC
SLOVAKIA
HUNGARY
Bavarian Alps
SLOVENIA
CROATIA
CARPATHIANS
MOLDOVA
ROMANIA
GEORGIA

PORTUGAL
SPAIN
PYRENEES
Cordillera Cantabrica
Sierra Morena
Sistemas Béticos
ALPS
Apennines
Corsica
Sardinia
ITALY
BOSNIA AND HERZEGOVINA
SERBIA AND MONTENEGRO
Balkan Mts.
BULGARIA
Black Sea
Pontic Mts.
TURKEY
ANATOLIA
Taurus Mts.

Gibraltar (U.K.)
Atlas Mountains
Mediterranean Sea
Sicily
ALBANIA
MACEDONIA
GREECE
Crete
CYPRUS
LEBANON
SYRIA

TUNISIA
MALTA

0   250   500 mi
0   250   500 km

Caribbean Sea

Guajira
Peninsula

PANAMA

Gulf
of
Panama

Lake
Maracaibo

Pico Bolivar
16,427 ft. (5,007 m) ▲

VENEZUELA

Arauca River

Llanos

Orinoco   River

GUYANA

Angel
Falls

Mt. Roraima
9,094 ft.
(2,772 m) ▲

SURINAME

FRENCH GUIANA (FR.)

Meta River

COLOMBIA

Guainia R.

Orinoco R.

Guiana   Highlands

Vaupés R.

Pico da Neblina
9,889 ft. (3,014 m) ▲

Negro   River

Mt. Chimborazo
20,561 ft.
(6,267 m) ▲

Equator

ECUADOR

Gulf of
Guayaquil

Postaza   R.

Putumayo River

Içá R.

Japurá   River

AMAZON
BASIN

Amazon   R.

Amazon   River

Cape
São
Roque

Aguja Point

Marañón   River

Juruá River

Ucayali   River

Huallaga River

Napo

Purus

Madeira   River

Tapajóz   River

Xingu   River

Araguaia   River

BRAZIL

Mt. Huascarán
22,205 ft.
(6,768 m) ▲

PERU

Apurimac R.

Lake
Titicaca

Beni River

Mamoré

Grande R.

Guaporé River

Juruena   River

Aripuanã River

Tapajóz River

Teles Pires River

Tocantins River

Parnaíba

Mato Grosso
Plateau

Brazilian

Highlands

São Francisco River

Jequitinhonha R.

Paraguaçu R.

Mt. Ancohuma
21,489 ft. ▲
(6,550 m)

Lake
Poopó

BOLIVIA

ATACAMA DESERT

ANDES   MOUNTAINS

Chaco

Grande R.

Pilcomayo R.

Grande

Tietê River

Pico da Bandiera
9,482 ft. (2,890 m) ▲

PACIFIC

OCEAN

Tropic of Capricorn

Vol. Llullaillaco
22,057 ft.
(6,723 m) ▲

Mt. Ojos del Salado
22,572 ft.
(6,880 m) ▲

Gran

Bermejo
River

Paraguay

PARAGUAY

Salado

Paraná

Iguaçu
Falls

Paraná   River

Iguaçu River

Paraiba River

Mt. Aconcagua
22,834 ft.
(6,960 m) ▲

Salado River

Uruguay River

Negro River

URUGUAY

Río de la Plata

Lagoa dos Patos

Lagoa Mirin

ATLANTIC

OCEAN

Juan Fernandez
Islands
(Chile)

CHILE

ARGENTINA

Pampas

Colorado   River

Negro R.

Blanca Bay

Limay R.

San Matias
Gulf

Chiloé
Island

Chubut   River

Patagonia

Chico   River

Gulf of
San Jorge

Chonos
Archipelago

Deseado R.

Gulf of Penas

Falkland
Islands
(U.K.)

Santa
Cruz R.

Grande Bay

Queen Adelaide
Archipelago

Strait of Magellan

Tierra del Fuego

Cape Horn

South
Georgia
(U.K.)

N
W   E
S

| 0 | 250 | 500 mi |
| 0 | 250 | 500 km |

North America

RUSSIA
Chukchi Sea
Bering Sea
ARCTIC OCEAN
UNITED KINGDOM
ICELAND
Ellesmere Island
KALAALLIT NUNAAT (GREENLAND) (DENMARK)
Beaufort Sea
Banks Island
Parry Islands
Baffin Bay
BROOKS RANGE
Mt. McKinley 20,320 ft. (6,194 m)
Yukon River
ALASKA RANGE
Victoria Island
Baffin Island
Davis Strait
Gulf of Alaska
COAST MOUNTAINS
ROCKY
Great Bear Lake
Mackenzie River
Great Slave Lake
Labrador Sea
PACIFIC OCEAN
Peace River
River
Athabasca River
Lake Athabasca
Fraser River
Hudson Bay
CANADA
Newfoundland
Gulf of St. Lawrence
Mt. Rainier 14,410 ft. (4,391 m)
CASCADE RANGE
Columbia River
MOUNTAINS
Saskatchewan River
Canadian Shield
Lake Winnipeg
Lake Superior
St. Lawrence River
Great Plains
Snake River
Lake Huron
Lake Ontario
Lake Michigan
Allegheny Plateau
ATLANTIC OCEAN
COAST RANGES
Great Basin
Great Salt Lake
Lake Erie
APPALACHIAN MOUNTAINS
Mt. Whitney 14,491 ft. (4,418 m)
Mt. Elbert 14,431 ft. (4,400 m)
Missouri River
River
Central Plains
Mt. Mitchell 6,684 ft. (2,037 m)
Platte River
Colorado River
Arkansas River
Ozark Plateau
Ohio River
BERMUDA (U.K.)
Colorado Plateau
UNITED STATES
Red River
Mississippi River
Tennessee River
Atlantic Coastal Plain
Baja California
SIERRA MADRE OCCIDENTAL
Colorado River
Brazos River
Alabama River
Gulf Coastal Plain
Tropic of Cancer
Rio Grande
THE BAHAMAS
Gulf of California
SIERRA MADRE ORIENTAL
Gulf of Mexico
DOMINICAN REPUBLIC
Leeward Islands
MEXICO
Mt. Orizaba 18,855 ft. (5,747 m)
Bay of Campeche
Yucatán Peninsula
CUBA
HAITI
Hispaniola
PUERTO RICO (U.S.)
Greater Antilles
JAMAICA
Caribbean Sea
Lesser Antilles
BELIZE
GUATEMALA
HONDURAS
EL SALVADOR
NICARAGUA
Lake Nicaragua
Isthmus of Panama
VENEZUELA
COSTA RICA
PANAMA
COLOMBIA

0   500   1000 mi
0   500   1000 km

© MapQuest.com, Inc.

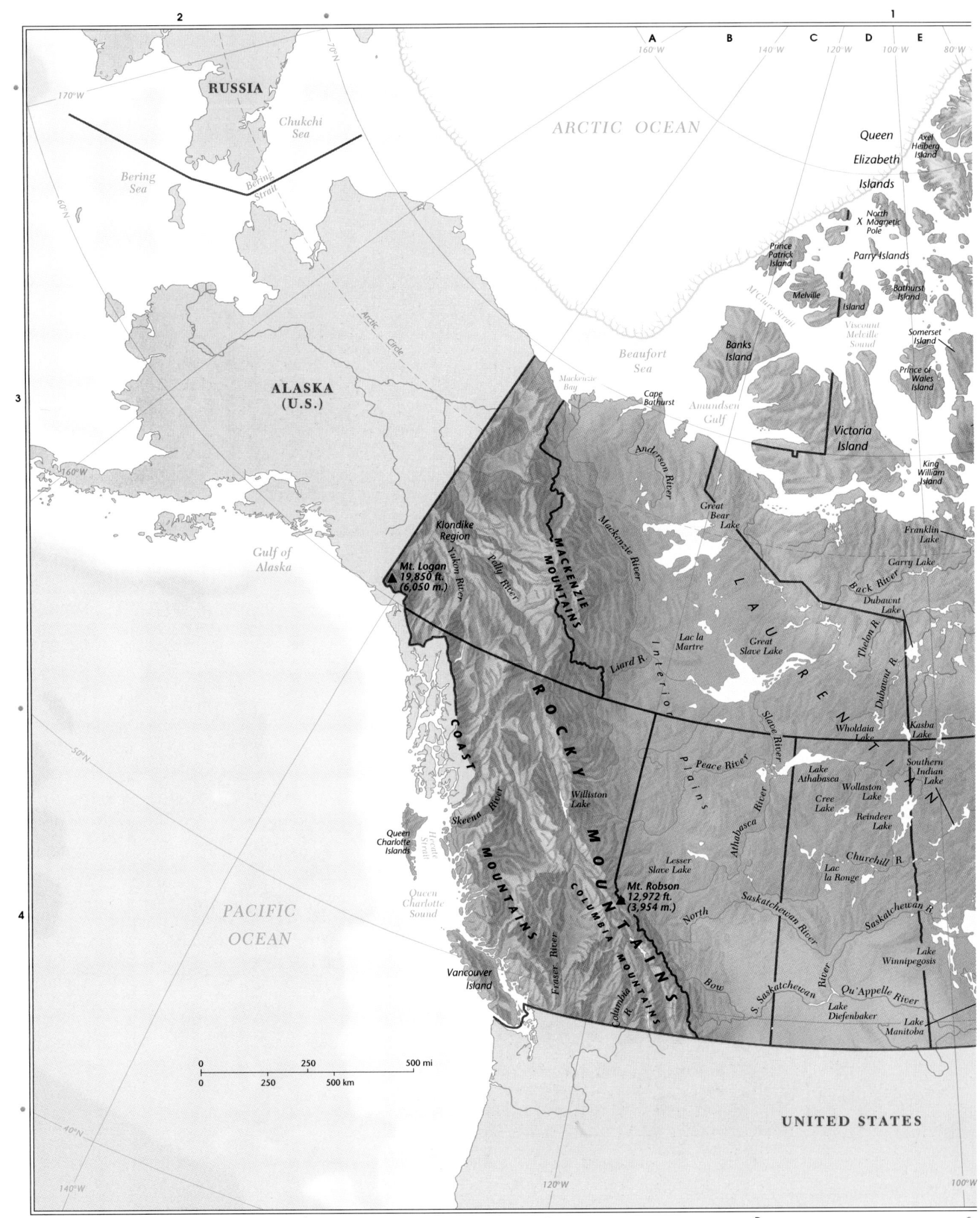

RUSSIA

Chukchi Sea

Bering Sea

Bering Strait

ARCTIC OCEAN

Queen
Elizabeth
Islands

Axel Heiberg Island

X North Magnetic Pole

Prince Patrick Island

Parry Islands

Melville Island

Bathurst Island

M'Clure Strait

Viscount Melville Sound

Somerset Island

Prince of Wales Island

Beaufort Sea

Banks Island

Amundsen Gulf

Victoria Island

King William Island

Mackenzie Bay

Cape Bathurst

Anderson River

ALASKA (U.S.)

Arctic Circle

Great Bear Lake

Franklin Lake

Garry Lake

MACKENZIE MOUNTAINS

Mackenzie River

Back River

Klondike Region

Mt. Logan
19,850 ft.
(6,050 m.)

Yukon River

Pelly River

Liard R.

Lac la Martre

Great Slave Lake

Dubawnt Lake

Thelon R.

Dubawnt R.

L A U R E N T I

Gulf of Alaska

ROCKY MOUNTAINS

Interior

Slave River

Wholdaia Lake

Kasba Lake

COAST MOUNTAINS

Peace River

Athabasca River

Lake Athabasca

Cree Lake

Wollaston Lake

Southern Indian Lake

Williston Lake

Plains

Reindeer Lake

Skeena River

Queen Charlotte Islands

Hecate Strait

Lesser Slave Lake

COLUMBIA MOUNTAINS

Mt. Robson
12,972 ft.
(3,954 m.)

Lac la Ronge

Churchill R.

Queen Charlotte Sound

PACIFIC OCEAN

Fraser River

Columbia R.

North

Saskatchewan River

Saskatchewan R.

Vancouver Island

Bow

S. Saskatchewan

Saskatchewan River

Lake Winnipegosis

Qu'Appelle River

Lake Diefenbaker

Lake Manitoba

| 0 | 250 | 500 mi |
| 0 | 250 | 500 km |

UNITED STATES

170°W 160°W 60°N 50°N 40°N 140°W 120°W 100°W

70°N 160°W 140°W 120°W 100°W 80°W

KALAALLIT NUNAAT (GREENLAND)
(DENMARK)

Cape Columbia

Ellesmere Island

Devon Island

Baffin Bay

Lancaster Sound

Brodeur Pen.

Baffin

Boothia Pen.

Island

Gulf of Boothia

Melville Pen.

Nettilling Lake

Prince Charles Island

Cumberland Sound

Amadjuak Lake

Foxe Basin

Frobisher Bay

Davis Strait

Arctic Circle

Denmark Strait

Southampton Island

Hudson Strait

Cape Chidley

Labrador Sea

Baker Lake

Ungava Peninsula

Ungava Bay

George River

Hudson

Bay

Kokosoak River

Caniapiscau R.

Labrador

Churchill R.

Cape Tatnam

Belcher Islands

Bienville Lake

Smallwood Reservoir

Newfoundland

Cape Race

Nelson River

Seven River

James Bay

Winisk River

Akimiski Islands

Attawapiskat R.

La Grande Reservoirs

Lake Sakami

Manicouagan Reservoir

Anticosti Island

St. PIERRE AND MIQUELON (FR.)

Lake Winnipeg

P L A T E A U

Albany River

Mistassini Reservoir

Gaspé Peninsula

Gulf of St. Lawrence

Cabot Strait

Cape Breton I.

Sable Island

Red R.

Canadian Shield

Lake Nipigon

Lac St.-Jean

Saguenay R.

Laurentian Highlands

Saint John R.

Lake of the Woods

Lawrence River

Bay of Fundy

Cape Sable

Lake Superior

Ottawa River

St.

Lake Michigan

Lake Huron

Lake Ontario

ATLANTIC OCEAN

Lake Erie

© MapQuest.com, Inc.

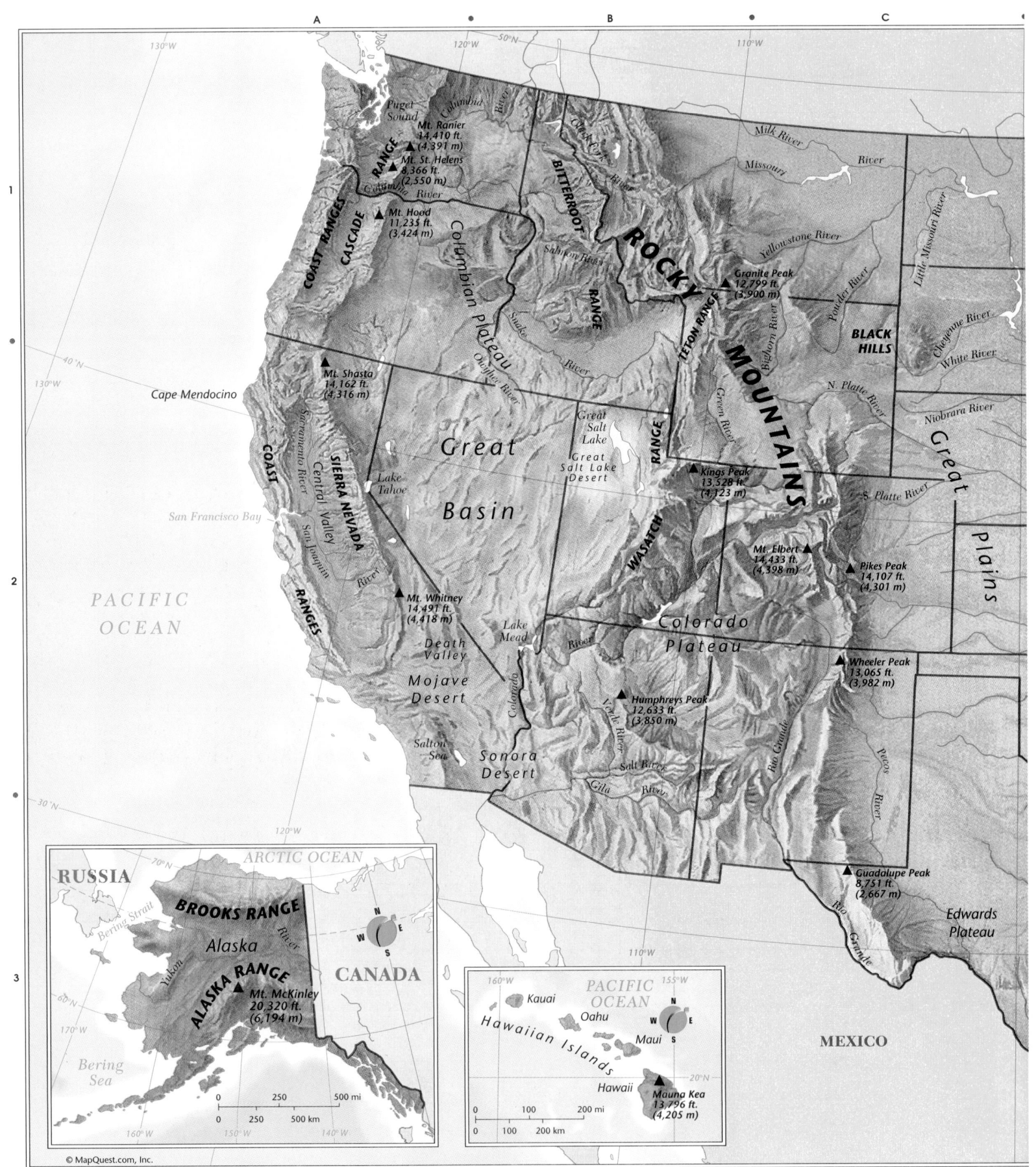

© MapQuest.com, Inc.

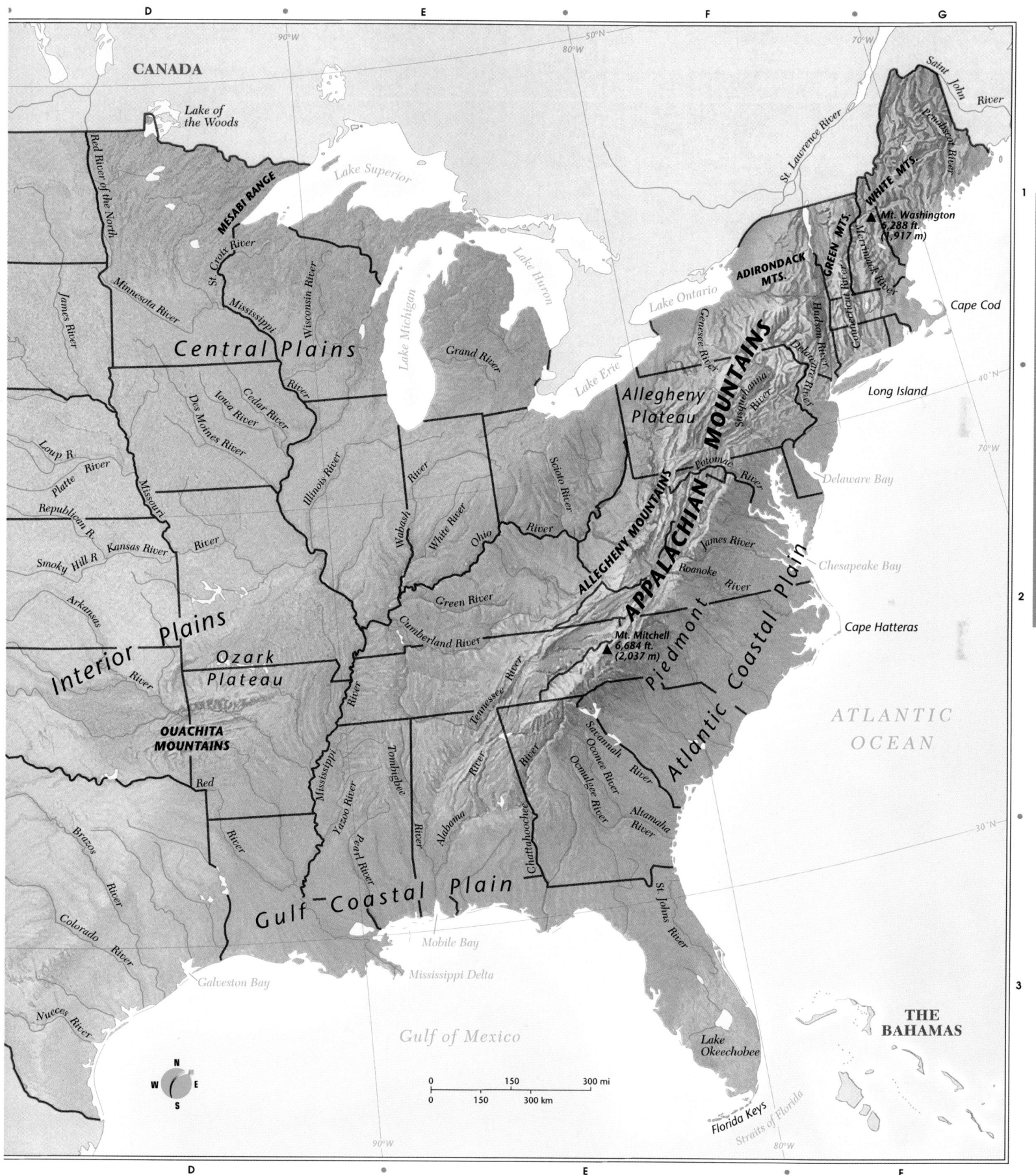

CANADA

Lake of
the Woods

Red River of the North

MESABI RANGE

Lake Superior

St. Croix River

Minnesota River

Mississippi

Wisconsin River

James River

Central Plains

Lake Michigan

Lake Huron

Grand River

Cedar River

Iowa River

Des Moines River

River

Loup R.

Platte River

Republican R.

Missouri

Smoky Hill R.

Kansas River

River

Illinois River

Wabash

White River

Ohio

River

Scioto River

Lake Ontario

Genesee River

Lake Erie

Allegheny
Plateau

Susquehanna River

ADIRONDACK
MTS.

St. Lawrence River

Saint John River

Penobscot River

WHITE MTS.

Mt. Washington
6,288 ft.
(1,917 m)

GREEN MTS.

Merrimack River

Connecticut River

Hudson River

Delaware River

APPALACHIAN MOUNTAINS

Cape Cod

Long Island

Delaware Bay

Chesapeake Bay

70°W

Arkansas

River

Interior

Plains

Ozark
Plateau

Green River

Cumberland River

ALLEGHENY MOUNTAINS

Potomac River

James River

Roanoke River

OUACHITA
MOUNTAINS

Red

Mississippi

River

Tennessee River

Mt. Mitchell
6,684 ft.
(2,037 m)

Piedmont

Atlantic Coastal Plain

Cape Hatteras

ATLANTIC
OCEAN

Brazos

River

Colorado

River

Nueces River

Yazoo River

Tombigbee River

Pearl River

River

Alabama

River

Chattahoochee

Savannah River

Ocmulgee River

Oconee River

River

Altamaha
River

Gulf Coastal Plain

St. Johns River

Mobile Bay

Mississippi Delta

Galveston Bay

Gulf of Mexico

Lake
Okeechobee

THE
BAHAMAS

N
W E
S

0   150   300 mi
0   150   300 km

Florida Keys

Straits of Florida

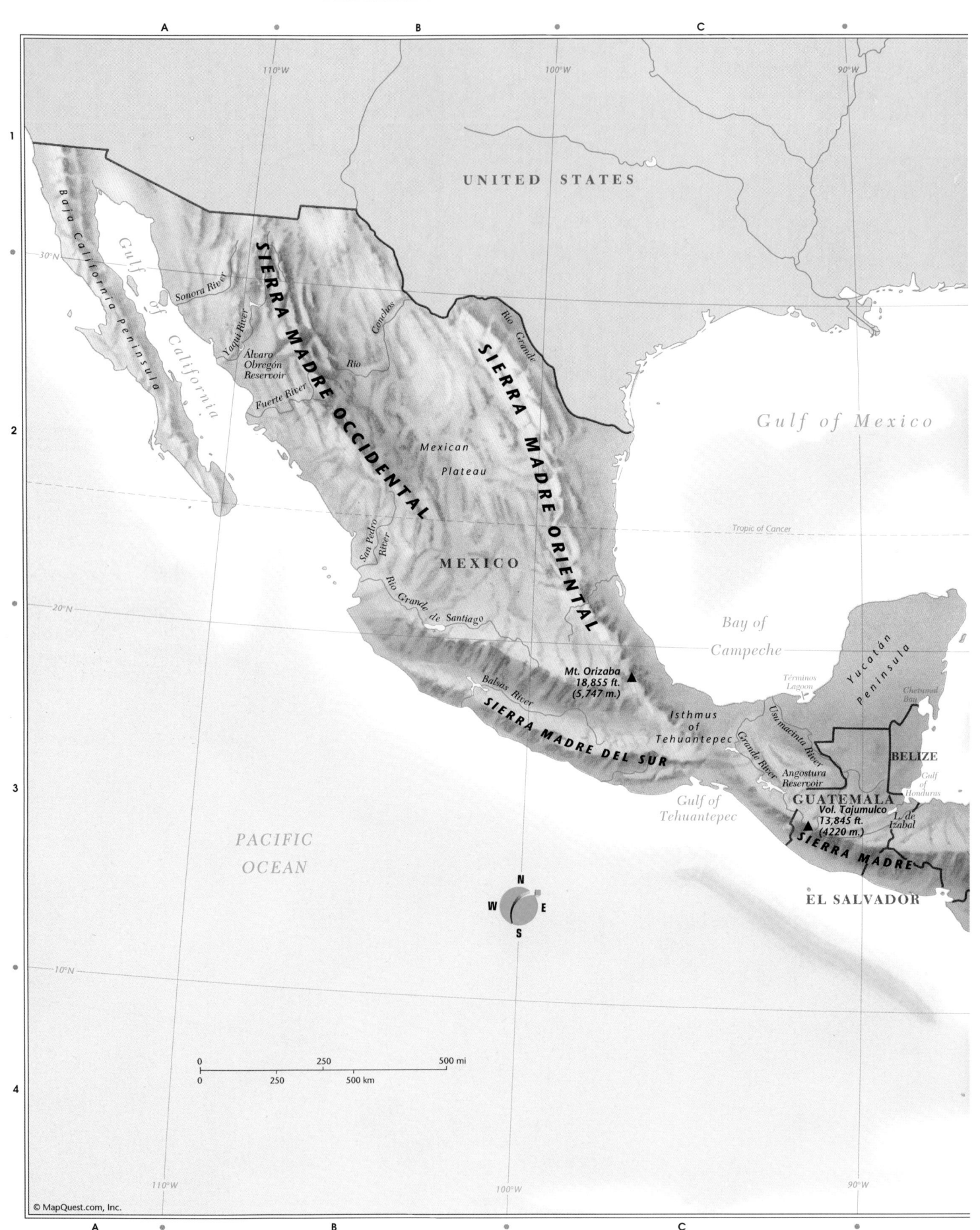

UNITED STATES

Baja California peninsula

Gulf of California

SIERRA MADRE OCCIDENTAL

Sonora River

Yaqui River

Álvaro Obregón Reservoir

Fuerte River

San Pedro River

Conchos

Rio

Rio Grande

SIERRA MADRE ORIENTAL

Mexican Plateau

MEXICO

Rio Grande de Santiago

Balsas River

SIERRA MADRE DEL SUR

Mt. Orizaba
18,855 ft.
(5,747 m.)

Isthmus of Tehuantepec

Grande River

Usumacinta River

Gulf of Mexico

Bay of Campeche

Términos Lagoon

Yucatán Peninsula

Chetumal Bay

BELIZE

Gulf of Honduras

Angostura Reservoir

GUATEMALA

Vol. Tajumulco
13,845 ft.
(4220 m.)

L. de Izabal

SIERRA MADRE

Gulf of Tehuantepec

EL SALVADOR

PACIFIC OCEAN

Tropic of Cancer

30°N

20°N

10°N

110°W

100°W

90°W

N
W   E
S

0   250   500 mi
0   250   500 km

© MapQuest.com, Inc.

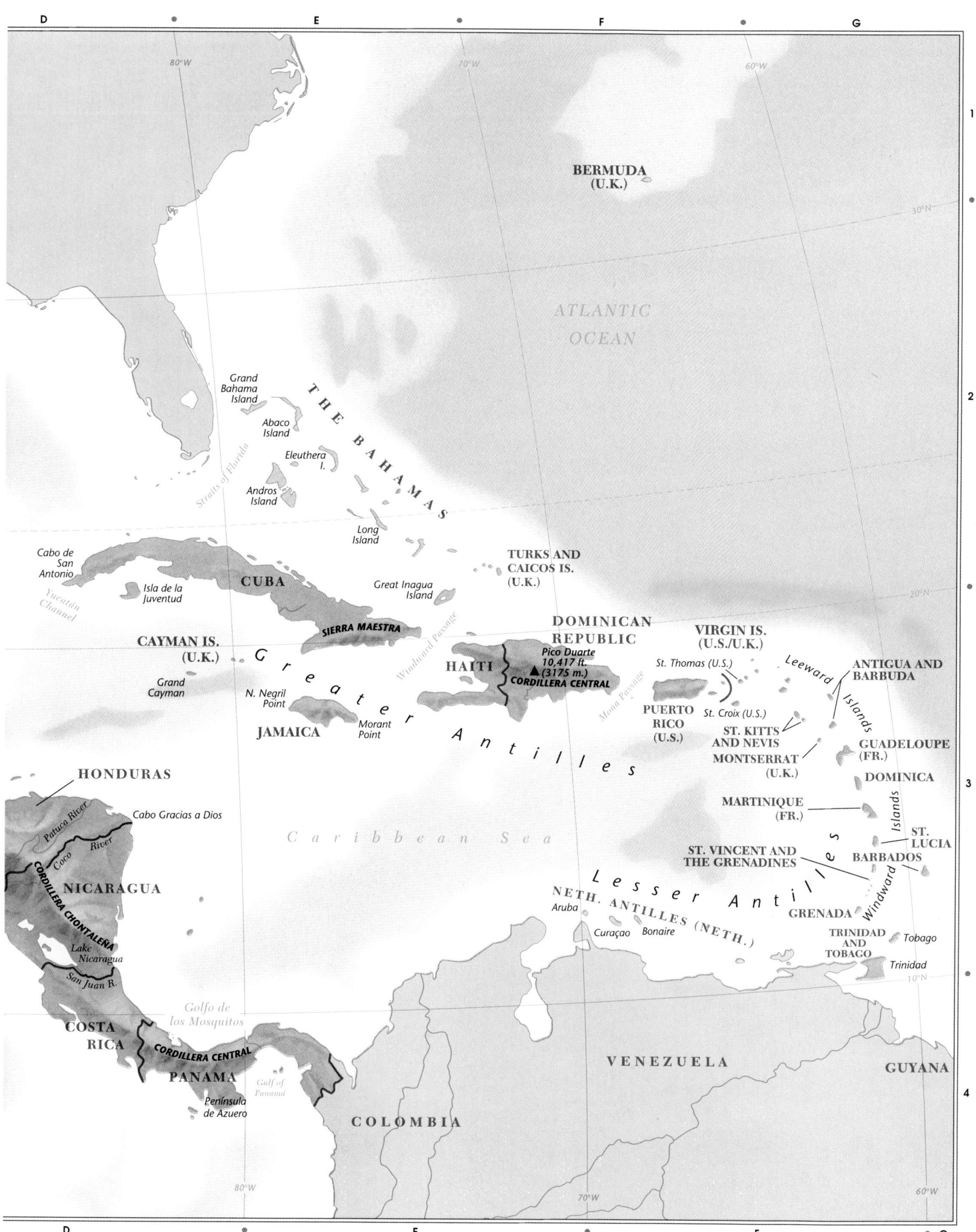

D · E · F · G

80°W · 70°W · 60°W

1

BERMUDA
(U.K.)

· 30°N

*ATLANTIC
OCEAN*

2

*Grand
Bahama
Island*

*Abaco
Island*

Straits of Florida

*Eleuthera
I.*

T H E   B A H A M A S

*Andros
Island*

*Long
Island*

TURKS AND
CAICOS IS.
(U.K.)

· 20°N

*Cabo de
San
Antonio*

*Isla de la
Juventud*

CUBA

*Great Inagua
Island*

DOMINICAN
REPUBLIC

VIRGIN IS.
(U.S./U.K.)

ANTIGUA AND
BARBUDA

*Yucatán
Channel*

SIERRA MAESTRA

Pico Duarte
10,417 ft.
▲ (3175 m.)

St. Thomas (U.S.)

Leeward

CAYMAN IS.
(U.K.)

G r e a t e r

Windward Passage

HAITI

CORDILLERA CENTRAL

PUERTO
RICO
(U.S.)

St. Croix (U.S.)

ST. KITTS
AND NEVIS

Islands

*Grand
Cayman*

*N. Negril
Point*

Mona Passage

MONTSERRAT
(U.K.)

GUADELOUPE
(FR.)

JAMAICA

*Morant
Point*

A n t i l l e s

DOMINICA

3

HONDURAS

MARTINIQUE
(FR.)

Islands

Cabo Gracias a Dios

C a r i b b e a n   S e a

A n t i l l e s

ST.
LUCIA

Patuca River

River

ST. VINCENT AND
THE GRENADINES

BARBADOS

Coco

CORDILLERA CHONTALEÑA

NICARAGUA

L e s s e r

Windward

GRENADA

NETH. ANTILLES (NETH.)

*Lake
Nicaragua*

Aruba

GRENADA

TRINIDAD
AND
TOBAGO

Tobago

San Juan R.

Curaçao

Bonaire

· 10°N

Trinidad

*Golfo de
los Mosquitos*

COSTA
RICA

CORDILLERA CENTRAL

VENEZUELA

GUYANA

4

PANAMA

*Península
de Azuero*

*Gulf of
Panamá*

COLOMBIA

80°W · 70°W · 60°W

D · E · F · G

ICELAND

Arctic Circle

Norwegian Sea

Faroe Is.
(Den.)

Shetland Is.
(U.K.)

NORWAY

Galdhøppiggen
8,097 ft.
(2,468 m.)

SWEDEN

Åland I.

Scandinavian Highlands

Dal River

Gulf of Bothnia

Muonio R.

Lake Vänern

Lake Vättern

Hiiumaa I.
Saaremaa I.
Gotland I.

Öland I.

Bornholm I.

Baltic Sea

RUSSIA

North

Vistula R.

Cape Wrath

Outer Hebrides Is.

Orkney Islands

SCOTLAND

Northern Ireland
(U.K.)

Isle of Man

IRELAND

Cape Clear

St. George's Channel

WALES

ENGLAND

UNITED KINGDOM

PENNINE RANGE

Irish Sea

North Sea

Skagerrak

Kattegat

Jutland

DENMARK

Kiel Canal

Elbe River

NETHERLANDS

Mittelland Canal

Weser River

GERMANY

POLAND

English Channel

Strait of Dover

Guernsey I. (U.K.)
Jersey I. (U.K.)

Breton Pen.

ATLANTIC OCEAN

Seine River

BELGIUM

LUXEMBOURG

Marne R.

Marne-Rhine Canal

Rhine R.

CZECH REPUBLIC

SLOVAKIA

Loire River

FRANCE

Danube River

LIECHTENSTEIN

AUSTRIA

HUNGARY

Cape Finisterre

Bay of Biscay

CANTABRIAN MTNS.

Ebro River

PYRENEES

Garonne River

Central Massif

Midi Canal

Bodensee

SWITZERLAND

L. Geneva

Mt. Blanc
15,771 ft.
(4,807 m.)

A L P S

Mt. Rosa
12,203 ft.
(4,634 m.)

Rhône River

Po Valley

Po R.

SLOVENIA

CROATIA

Lake Balaton

Tisza R.

Sava R.

DINARIC ALPS

BOSNIA-HERZEGOVINA

PORTUGAL

Duero River

Tagus River

Iberian Peninsula

SPAIN

Guadiana River

Aneto Peak
11,168 ft.
(3,404 m.)

ANDORRA

Gulf of Lions

MONACO

SAN MARINO

VATICAN CITY

ITALY

APENNINES

Corsica
(FR.)

Adriatic Sea

ALBANIA

Cape St. Vincent

SIERRA MORENA

Balearic Is.
(SP.)

Sardinia
(IT.)

Tyrrhenian Sea

Gulf of Taranto

Strait of Gibraltar

Gibraltar
(U.K.)

Mediterranean

SICILY

Pantelleria
(IT.)

Strait of Sicily

Ionian Sea

Kefallinia I.

MOROCCO

ALGERIA

TUNISIA

MALTA

Sea

North Cape

D 40°E 70°N E F 60°N 80°E 2

Barents Sea

Pechora River

Timan Ridge

Kola Peninsula

Torne R.

Kemi R.

White Sea

White Sea-Baltic Waterway

FINLAND

Lake Onega

N. Dvina River

Sukhona River

Vychegda River

Mt. Konzhakovskiy 5,147 ft. (1,569 m.)

URAL MOUNTAINS

Kama R.

Lake Saimaa

Lake Ladoga

Volga-Baltic Waterway

Rybinsk Reservoir

RUSSIA

Kama River

Gulf of Finland

ESTONIA

Chudskoye Lake

Volga River

Volga-Baltic Waterway

Kuybyshev Reservoir

Ural River

50°N

Gulf of Riga

LATVIA

W. Dvina Plain

Baltic Plain

Oka River

Volga River

LITHUANIA

European Plain

BELARUS

Central Russian Upland

Don R.

Volga Upland

Volgograd Reservoir

Ural River

3

KAZAKHSTAN

ARAL SEA

Pripet River

Desna R.

Don River

UKRAINE

Kremenchug Reservoir

Donets River

Tsimlyansk Reservoir

Volga River

Depression

Caspian

Delta of the Volga

40°N

Dnepr Upland

Dnestr River

Prut River

MOLDOVA

Dnepr Lowland

Kakhovka Reservoir

Dnepr River

Sea of Azov

Don River

Caspian Sea

60°E

CARPATHIAN MTNS

ROMANIA

Crimea

Mt. Elbrus 18,510 ft. (5,642 m.)

CAUCASUS

GEORGIA

AZERBAIJAN

4

Wallachia Plain

Danube River

SERBIA & MONTENEGRO

BULGARIA

Musala Peak 9,536 ft. (2,926 m.)

Bosporus

Peninsula

Black Sea

TURKEY

MACEDONIA

Balkan

Dardanelles

Sea of Marmara

0 150 300 mi

0 150 300 km

Aegean Sea

GREECE

30°N

Peloponese Pen.

Crete (GR.)

© MapQuest.com, Inc.

D E

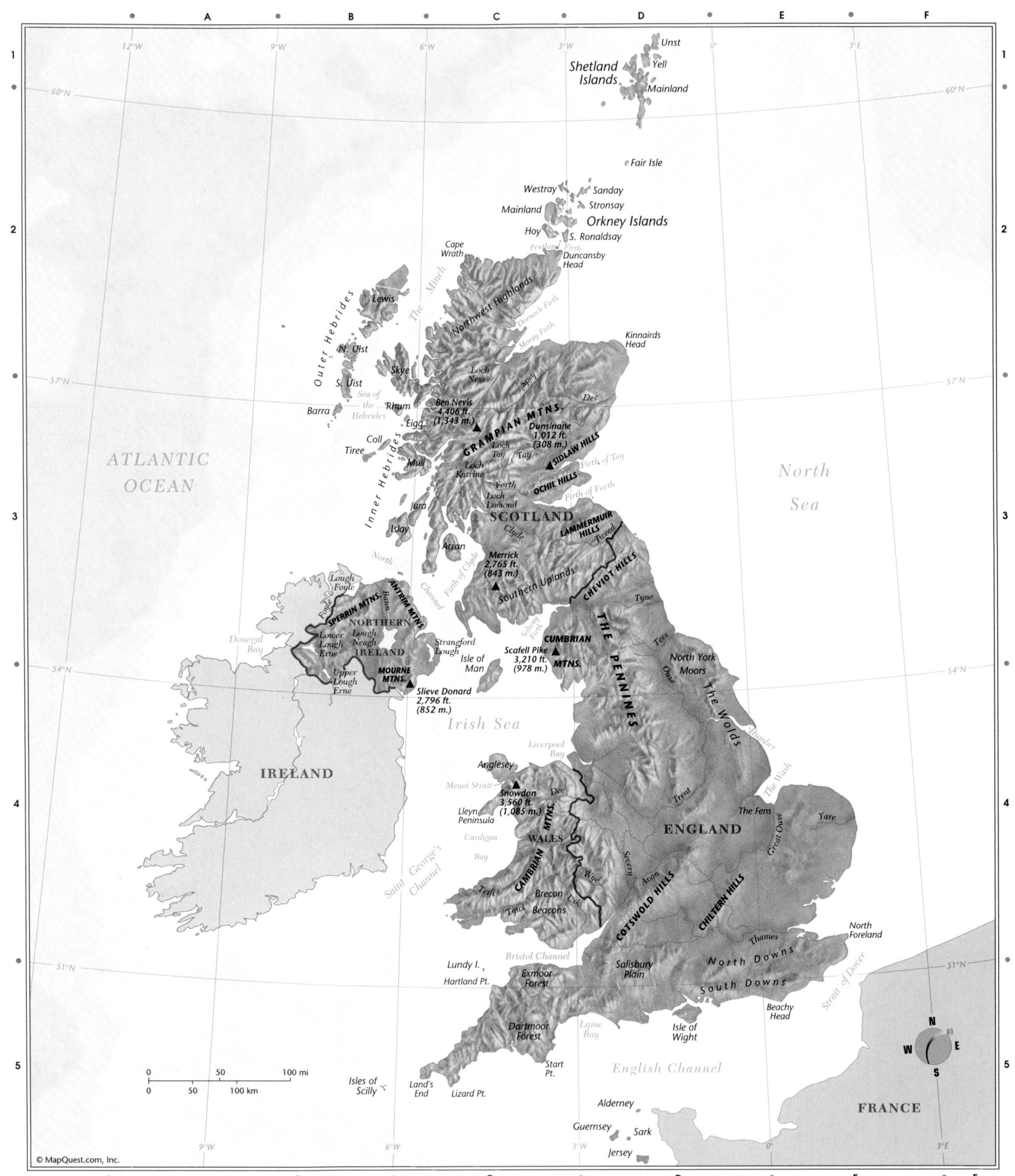

ATLANTIC
OCEAN

North
Sea

Shetland
Islands

Unst
Yell
Mainland

Fair Isle

Westray
Sanday
Mainland
Stronsay
Hoy
S. Ronaldsay
Orkney Islands

Cape
Wrath
Pentland Firth
Duncansby
Head

The Minch

Lewis

Northwest Highlands

Kinnairds
Head

Outer Hebrides

N. Uist
Skye

Loch
Ness

Dornoch Firth

Moray Firth

S. Uist
Sea of
the
Hebrides

Rhum

Spey

Dee

Barra

Eigg

Ben Nevis
4,406 ft.
(1,343 m.)

GRAMPIAN MTNS.

Dunsinane
1,012 ft.
(308 m.)

Coll
Tiree

Mull

Loch
Tay
Tay

SIDLAW HILLS

Firth of Tay

Inner Hebrides

Loch
Katrine

OCHIL HILLS

Firth of Forth

Jura

Forth
Loch
Lomond

SCOTLAND

LAMMERMUIR
HILLS

Islay

Clyde

Arran

North

Firth of Clyde

Merrick
2,765 ft.
(843 m.)

Southern Uplands

Tweed

CHEVIOT HILLS

Lough
Foyle

ANTRIM MTNS.

Channel

SPERRIN MTNS.

Foyle

NORTHERN
IRELAND

Bann

Lower
Lough
Erne

Lough
Neagh

Solway Firth

CUMBRIAN
MTNS.

Tyne

Donegal
Bay

Upper
Lough
Erne

MOURNE
MTNS.

Strangford
Lough

Isle of
Man

Scafell Pike
3,210 ft.
(978 m.)

THE PENNINES

Tees

North York
Moors

Ouse

The Wolds

Slieve Donard
2,796 ft.
(852 m.)

IRELAND

Irish Sea

Liverpool
Bay

Humber

The Wash

Anglesey

Dee

North

Menai Strait

Snowdon
3,560 ft.
(1,085 m.)

ENGLAND

The Fens

Great Ouse

Yare

Lleyn
Peninsula

CAMBRIAN
MTNS.

Trent

Cardigan
Bay

WALES

Severn

Teifi

Brecon
Beacons

Wye

Avon

COTSWOLD HILLS

CHILTERN HILLS

Saint George's Channel

Tywi

Usk

Thames

North
Foreland

Bristol Channel

Lundy I.

Salisbury
Plain

North Downs

South Downs

Beachy
Head

Hartland Pt.

Exmoor
Forest

Lyme
Bay

Isle of
Wight

Strait of Dover

51°N

English Channel

51°N

Dartmoor
Forest

FRANCE

Isles of
Scilly

Land's
End

Start
Pt.

Lizard Pt.

Alderney

Guernsey

Sark

Jersey

60°N

57°N

54°N

12°W

9°W

6°W

3°W

0°

3°E

N
W   E
S

0   50   100 mi
0   50   100 km

© MapQuest.com, Inc.

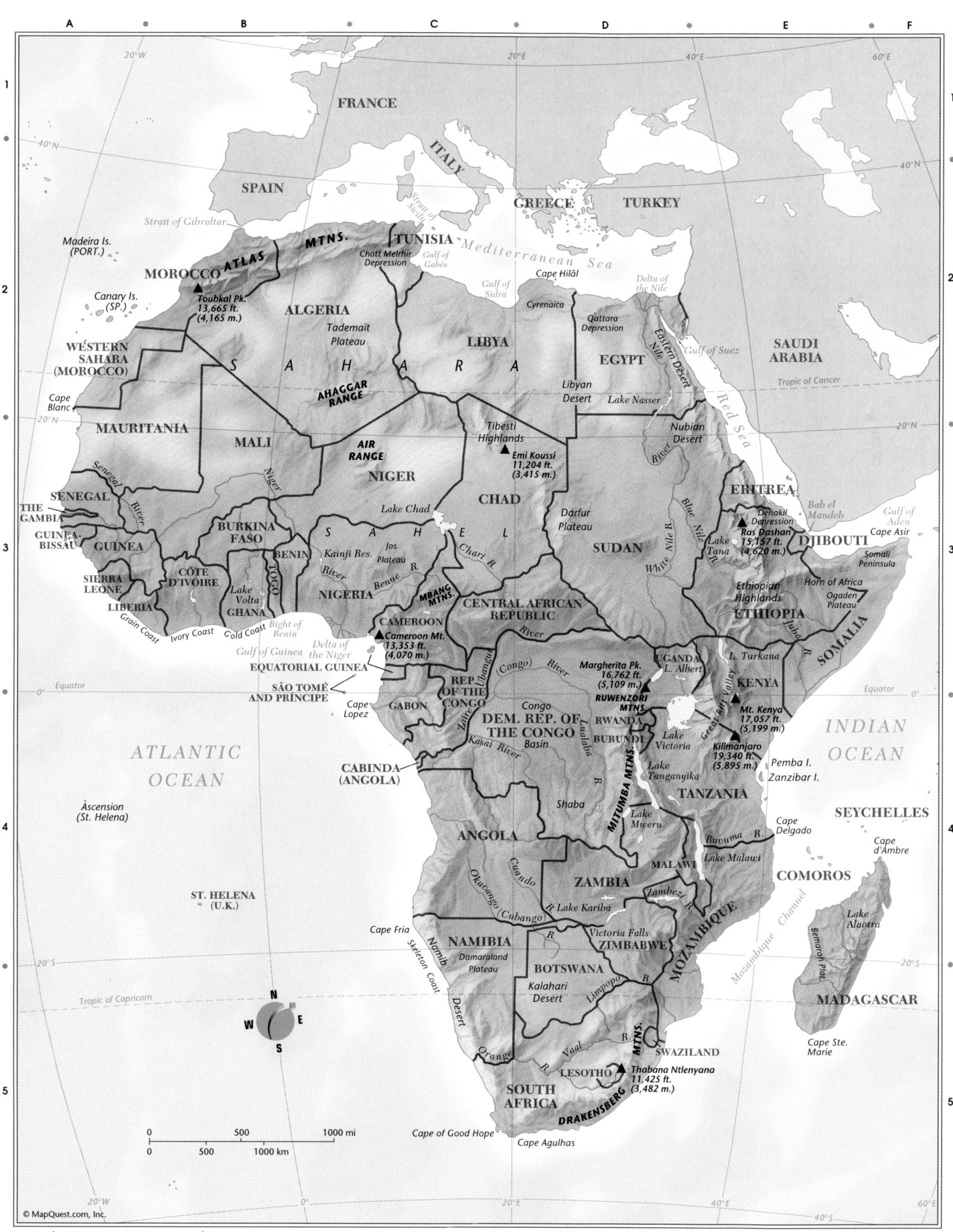

FRANCE

SPAIN

ITALY

GREECE

TURKEY

Mediterranean Sea

Madeira Is.
(PORT.)

Strait of Gibraltar

ATLAS **MTNS.**

MOROCCO

▲ Toubkal Pk.
13,665 ft.
(4,165 m.)

Canary Is.
(SP.)

TUNISIA

*Strait of
Sicily*

Chott Melrhir
Depression

*Gulf of
Gabès*

Cape Hilãl

*Gulf of
Sidra*

Cyrenaica

Delta of
the Nile

WESTERN
SAHARA
(MOROCCO)

ALGERIA

*Tademaït
Plateau*

LIBYA

EGYPT

*Qattara
Depression*

SAUDI
ARABIA

S   A   H   A   R   A

*Libyan
Desert*

Eastern Desert

Gulf of Suez

Red Sea

Tropic of Cancer

Cape
Blanc

AHAGGAR
RANGE

Lake Nasser

*Nubian
Desert*

20°N

MAURITANIA

MALI

AIR
RANGE

NIGER

Tibesti
Highlands

▲ Emi Koussi
11,204 ft.
(3,415 m.)

CHAD

*Darfur
Plateau*

SUDAN

ERITREA

*Bab el
Mandeb*

*Gulf of
Aden*

Cape Asir

*Senegal
River*

*Niger
River*

Lake Chad

Blue Nile

▲ Ras Dashan
15,157 ft.
(4,620 m.)

*Dahkil
Depression*

DJIBOUTI

SENEGAL

THE
GAMBIA

GUINEA-
BISSAU

GUINEA

BURKINA
FASO

BENIN

S   A   H   E   L

Kainji Res.

*Jos
Plateau*

Chari R.

Nile River

White Nile

Lake
Tana

*Ethiopian
Highlands*

*Ogaden
Plateau*

Horn of Africa

*Somali
Peninsula*

SIERRA
LEONE

CÔTE
D'IVOIRE

TOGO

GHANA

NIGERIA

Benue
River

MBANG
MTNS.

CENTRAL AFRICAN
REPUBLIC

ETHIOPIA

SOMALIA

Juba R.

LIBERIA

Grain Coast

Ivory Coast

Gold Coast

Lake
Volta

*Bight of
Benin*

CAMEROON

▲ Cameroon Mt.
13,353 ft.
(4,070 m.)

River

Margherita Pk.
16,762 ft.
(5,109 m.) ▲

UGANDA
L. Albert

L. Turkana

KENYA

Gulf of Guinea

*Delta of
the Niger*

EQUATORIAL GUINEA

SÃO TOMÉ
AND PRÍNCIPE

Cape
Lopez

REP.
OF THE
CONGO

GABON

*(Congo)
River*

*Congo
Basin*

RUWENZORI
MTNS.

RWANDA

BURUNDI

▲ Mt. Kenya
17,057 ft.
(5,199 m.)

Great Rift Valley

INDIAN
OCEAN

Equator

ATLANTIC
OCEAN

Ascension
(St. Helena)

CABINDA
(ANGOLA)

DEM. REP. OF
THE CONGO

Kasai River

Lualaba

Ubangi

Zambezi R.

Lake
Victoria

Lake
Tanganyika

MITUMBA MTNS.

Kilimanjaro
19,340 ft.
(5,895 m.) ▲

Pemba I.

Zanzibar I.

TANZANIA

Cape
Delgado

SEYCHELLES

Cape
d'Ambre

ST. HELENA
(U.K.)

Shaba

Lake
Mweru

Ruvuma R.

Lake Malawi

COMOROS

*Lake
Alaotra*

ANGOLA

Cuando

*Okavango
(Cubango)*

ZAMBIA

MALAWI

MOZAMBIQUE

Mozambique Channel

Bemaraha Plat.

Cape Fria

NAMIBIA

*Damaraland
Plateau*

R. Lake Kariba

Victoria Falls

ZIMBABWE

MADAGASCAR

Tropic of Capricorn

Skeleton Coast

*Namib
Desert*

BOTSWANA

*Kalahari
Desert*

Limpopo R.

Cape Ste.
Marie

N
W   E
S

Orange

Vaal

MTNS.

SWAZILAND

LESOTHO ▲ Thabana Ntlenyana
11,425 ft.
(3,482 m.)

SOUTH
AFRICA

DRAKENSBERG

Cape of Good Hope

Cape Agulhas

0	500	1000 mi
0	500	1000 km

KALAALLIT NUNAAT
(GREENLAND)
(DEN.)

ARCTIC OCEAN

Franz Josef Is.
(Russia)

Cape
Zelaniya

Novaya Zemlya

Kara Sea

Svalbard
(Nor.)

Barents Sea

North Cape

Yamal
Pen.

Jan Mayen
(Nor.)

Norwegian
Sea

Kola Pen.

West

Arctic Circle

ICELAND

SWEDEN

FINLAND

SCANDINAVIA

L. Saimaa

Lake Onega

Mt. Konzhakovskiy
5,147 ft.
(1,569 m.)

Siberian

NORWAY

Lake
Ladoga

North Dvina River

Faroe Is.
(Den.)

Lake
Ladoga

Rybinsk
Reservoir

Irtysh

Plain

ATLANTIC
OCEAN

North
Sea

L.
Vanern

ESTONIA

Kuybyshev
Reservoir

UNITED
KINGDOM

DENMARK

LATVIA

Baltic Sea

LITH.
RUSSIA

Volga Upland

Ural R.

Tobol R.

KAZAKHSTAN

IRELAND

NETHERLANDS

North European Plain

BELARUS

Kyrgyz Steppe

Aral
Sea

Lake
Balkhash

BELGIUM

Elbe R.

GERMANY

POLAND

Syr Darya

LUX.

Danube R.

CZECH REP.

Dnepr
Lowland

UKRAINE

Caspian
Depression

Bay of
Biscay

FRANCE

SWITZ.

AUSTRIA

SLOV.

HUNGARY

CARPATHIAN
MTNS.

MOLDOVA

Sea of
Azov

Volga R.

Mt. Elbrus
18,510 ft.
(5,642 m.)

UZBEKISTAN

Plains of
Turan

KYRGYZSTAN

Loire
R.

Mt. Blanc
18,771 ft.
(4,807 m.)

CR.

Kongur Pk.
25,324 ft.
(7,719 m.)

Cape
Finisterre

ANDORRA

MON.

S.M.

B.H.

ROMANIA

SERB.
MONT.

CAUCASUS

Black Sea

GEORGIA

Caspian
Sea

TURKMENISTAN

Amu
Darya

TAJIKISTAN

Communism Pk.
24,590 ft.
(7,495 m.)

Pamir

SPAIN

PYRENEES

Aneto Pk.
11,168 ft.
(3,404 m.)

Corsica

ITALY

ALBANIA

BULGARIA

MACE.

ARMENIA

AZERBAIJAN

AFGHANISTAN

Godwin Austen
Pk. (K-2)
28,251 ft.
(8,611 m.)

PORTUGAL

Tagus R.

VATICAN
CITY

Sardinia

GREECE

TURKEY

L. Van

ELBURZ MTNS.

KARAKORAM
RANGE

Iberian
Peninsula

Balearic Is.

Anatolia

L. Urmia

ZAGROS
MTNS.

Great Salt
Desert

IRAN

Plateau
of
Iran

PAKISTAN

Thar
Desert

Sicily

MALTA

Crete

CYPRUS

SYRIA

Euphrates R.

Tigris R.

Baluchistan

Helmand R.

INDIA

ALGERIA

TUNISIA

Mediterranean Sea

LEBANON

ISR.

JORDAN

IRAQ

KUW.

Sutlej R.

Narmada R.

MOROCCO

Dead Sea
Depression

Syrian
Desert

Persian Gulf

Deccan

Godavari R.

Tropic of Cancer

An Nafud
Desert

SAUDI
ARABIA

BAH.

QATAR

U.A.E.

OMAN

Gulf of
Oman

Arabian
Sea

Plateau

WESTERN

Hindu-
stan

Red Sea

Najd
Plateau

Arabian Peninsula
Rub Al
Khali

OMAN

GHATS

BAH. —Bahrain
B.H. —Bosnia and Herzegovina
CR. —Croatia
ISR. —Israel
KUW. —Kuwait
LIECH. —Liechtenstein
LITH. —Lithuania
LUX. —Luxembourg
MACE. —Macedonia
MON. —Monaco
S.M. —San Marino
SERB.- —Serbia and Montenegro
MONT.
SL. —Slovenia
SLOV. —Slovakia
SWITZ. —Switzerland
U.A.E. —United Arab Emirates

Cape Comorin

SRI LANKA

Ceylon

Shu'ayb
Mt. Nabi
12,336 ft.
(3,760 m.)

YEMEN

Gulf of
Aden

Socotra
(Yemen)

Cape Dondra

MALDIVES

Equator

0   500   1000 mi

0   500   1000 km

INDIAN OCEAN

N
W   E
S

© MapQuest.com, Inc.

F • G • H • J • K • L

75°E   90°E   105°E   120°E   135°E   150°E   165°E   180°   165°W   150°W   135°W

1

Severnaya Zemlya

Taymyr Peninsula

Laptev Sea   *New Siberian Islands*   *East Siberian Sea*   75°N

Wrangel Island

Central Siberian   *Kolyma Plain*   UNITED   2
Plateau   STATES

VERKHOYANSK RANGE   *Chukotsk Pen.*

Bering Strait

Lena Plateau   *Kolyma River*   KOLYMA RANGE   *Anadyr R.*   60°N

RUSSIA   *Cape Navarin*

Lower   *Tunguska*   *River*   *Lena*   *River*   S i b e r i a   *Bering Sea*

Angara   *River*   STANOVOY RANGE   *Mt. Klyuchevsk 15,584 ft.*   *Komandorskiy Is.*
▲*(4,750 m.)*
Bratsk Reservoir   *Lake Baikal*   *Sea of*   *Kamchatka Pen.*   3

Novosibirsk Reservoir   SAYAN MTNS.   YABLONOVY RANGE   *Amur River*   *Okhotsk*

ALTAI MTNS.   *Cape Lopatka*

L. Zaysan   **MONGOLIA**   DA HINGGAN LING   *Jiang*   *La Perouse Strait*   *Kuril Islands*   45°N

Dzungarian Basin   *Mongolian*   G o b i   *Northeast Songhua (Manchurian)*

TIEN SHAN   *Plateau*   *Plain*   *L. Khanka*   *Sea of*   4
Turfan Depression   *Huang*   N   *Japan*   **JAPAN**
Tarim He   *CHINA*   KOREA
Taklimakan Desert   *North*   S.
KUNLUN SHAN   *Wei He*   *He*   *China*   KOREA   *Yellow Sea*

HIMALAYAS
Annapurna Pk 26,502 ft.   *Plateau of*   *Jiang*   *Lake Tai*   *East China*   PACIFIC
▲*(8,078 m.)*   *Xizang*   *Sea*   30°N
Mt. Everest 29,035 ft.   *Chang*   *Lake Poyang*   OCEAN
▲*(8,849 m.) Mt. Kangchenjunga*
28,208 ft. (8,598 m.)   *Yungui Plateau*   *Ryukyu Is.*
NEPAL   *(Jap.)*
Ganges R.   BHUTAN   *Xi Jiang*   **TAIWAN**   *Tropic of Cancer*
Brahmaputra R.
BANGLADESH   *Formosa Strait*   5
Ganges Plain   MYANMAR   ANNAMESE CORD.
(BURMA)   *Luzon Strait*
Bay of   *Irrawaddy R.*   *Mekong R.*   LAOS   *Cape Engaño*   *Philippine*   15°N
Bengal   *Khorat*   *Sea*
Plateau   *Luzon*
THAILAND   *South*   **PHILIPPINES**
Preparis Channel   *China*
Andaman Is. (Ind.)   CAMBODIA   VIETNAM   *Mindoro*
Tonle Sap   *Sea*
Andaman   *Palawan*
Sea   *Mindanao*   6
Nicobar Is. (Ind.)
Malay   BRUNEI   *Sulu Arch. (Phil.)*
Peninsula
Strait of Malacca   M A L A Y S I A
Sumatra   SINGAPORE   *Borneo*   *Halmahera*   *Equator*   0°
BARISAN MTNS.   BORNEO HIGHLANDS
Celebes   *Cape d'Urville*
Java Sea   ▲*Jaya Pk. 16,499 ft. (5,029 m.)*   PAPUA
Banda Sea   NEW
Sunda Str.   *New Guinea*   GUINEA   7
Java   I N D O N E S I A

EAST TIMOR

90°E   105°E   120°E   135°E   150°E   165°E   15°S

AUSTRALIA

G • H • J

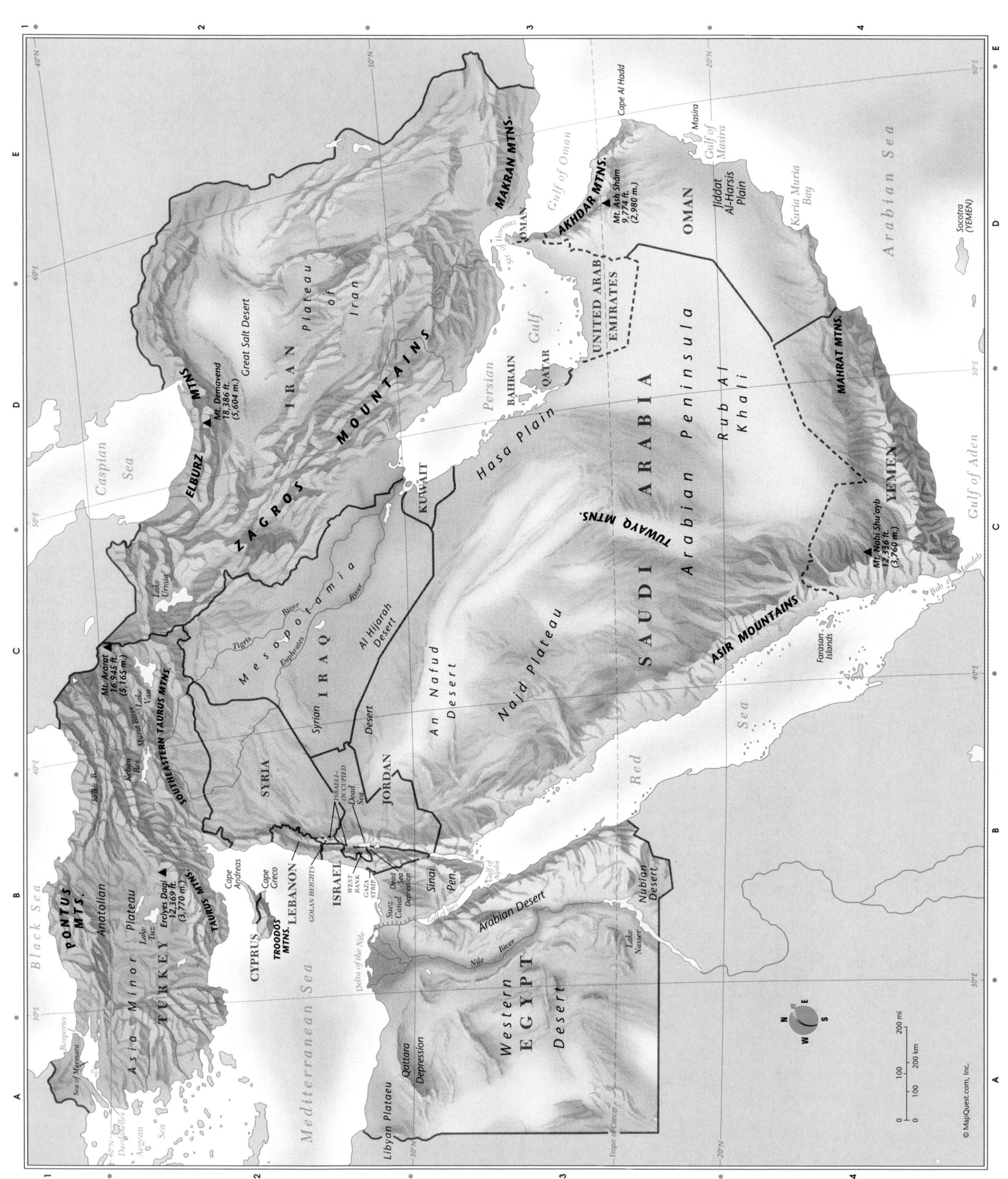

Black Sea

Caspian Sea

Sea of Marmara

Dardanelles

Bosporus

Aegean Sea

PONTUS MTS.

Anatolian Plateau

Asia Minor

TURKEY

Lake Tuz

Erciyes Dagi
12,369 ft.
(3,770 m.)

TAURUS MTNS.

Mt. Ararat
16,945 ft.
(5,165 m.)

Lake Van

Murat R.

Kizil R.

Keban Res.

Lake Urmia

SOUTHEASTERN TAURUS MTNS.

Mt. Demavend
18,386 ft.
(5,604 m.)

ELBURZ MTNS.

Great Salt Desert

Plateau of Iran

IRAN

ZAGROS MOUNTAINS

Tigris River

Euphrates River

Mesopotamia

Al Hijarah Desert

Syrian Desert

IRAQ

KUWAIT

SYRIA

LEBANON

CYPRUS

Cape Andreas

Cape Greco

TROODOS MTNS.

Mediterranean Sea

GOLAN HEIGHTS

ISRAEL

WEST BANK

GAZA STRIP

ISRAELI-OCCUPIED

Dead Sea

Dead Sea Depression

JORDAN

An Nafud Desert

Najd Plateau

TUWAYQ MTNS.

SAUDI ARABIA

Arabian Peninsula

Rub Al Khali

Hasa Plain

Persian Gulf

BAHRAIN

QATAR

UNITED ARAB EMIRATES

OMAN

AKHDAR MTNS.

Mt. Ash Sham
9,774 ft.
(2,980 m.)

Str. of Hormuz

Gulf of Oman

Cape Al Hadd

Masira

Gulf of Masira

Jiddat Al-Harsis Plain

Kuria Muria Bay

Socotra (YEMEN)

Arabian Sea

MAKRAN MTNS.

MAHRAT MTNS.

YEMEN

Mt. Nabi Shu'ayb
12,336 ft.
(3,760 m.)

ASIR MOUNTAINS

Farasan Islands

Bab el Mandeb

Gulf of Aden

Red Sea

Sinai Pen.

Gulf of Aqaba

Suez Canal

Gulf of Suez

Arabian Desert

Nile River

Delta of the Nile

EGYPT

Western Desert

Qattara Depression

Libyan Plateau

Lake Nasser

Nubian Desert

Tropic of Cancer

200 mi
200 km
0 100 200
0 100 200

© MapQuest.com, Inc.

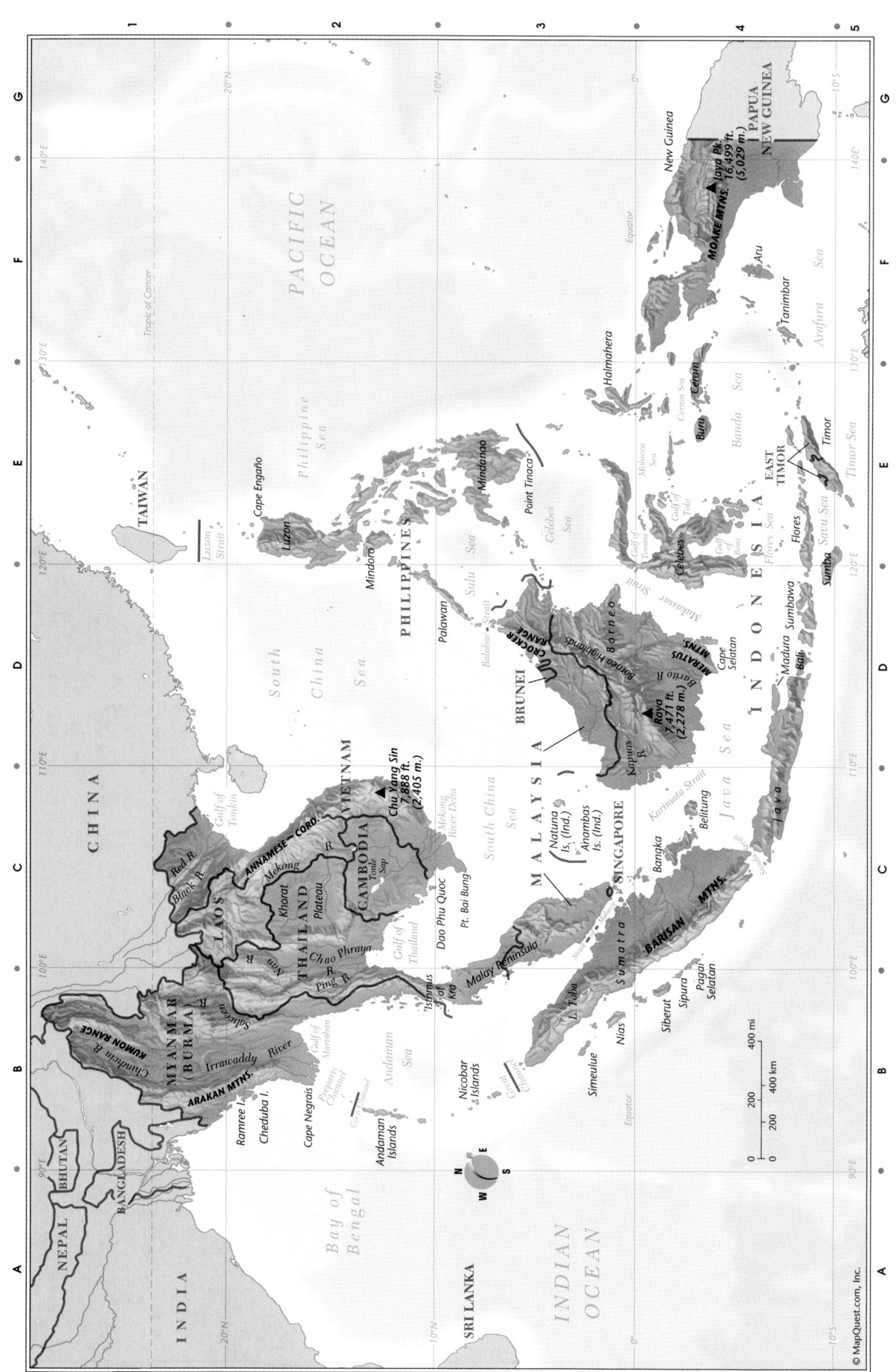

PACIFIC OCEAN

INDIAN OCEAN

Bay of Bengal

South China Sea

Java Sea

Banda Sea

Philippine Sea

Arafura Sea

Timor Sea

Celebes Sea

Sulu Sea

Andaman Sea

Flores Sea

Savu Sea

Ceram Sea

Molucca Sea

CHINA

INDIA

NEPAL

BHUTAN

BANGLADESH

SRI LANKA

TAIWAN

MYANMAR (BURMA)

LAOS

THAILAND

VIETNAM

CAMBODIA

MALAYSIA

SINGAPORE

BRUNEI

INDONESIA

PHILIPPINES

PAPUA NEW GUINEA

EAST TIMOR

New Guinea

MOAKE MTNS.

Jaya Pk. 16,499 ft. (5,029 m.)

Aru

Tanimbar

Halmahera

Buru

Ceram

Timor

Sumba

Bali

Sumbawa

Madura

Flores

Celebes

Gulf of Boni

Gulf of Tomini

Gulf of Tolo

Cape Selatan

Borneo

Borneo Highlands

MERATUS MTNS.

Barito R.

Kapuas R.

Raya 7,471 ft. (2,278 m.)

CROCKER RANGE

Natuna Is. (Ind.)

Anambas Is. (Ind.)

Karimata Strait

Makassar Strait

Belitung

Bangka

Sumatra

BARISAN MTNS.

L. Toba

Nias

Siberut

Sipura

Pagai Selatan

Simeulue

Java

Malay Peninsula

Isthmus of Kra

Gulf of Thailand

Dao Phu Quoc

Pt. Bai Bung

Mekong River Delta

Chu Yang Sin 7,888 ft. (2,405 m.)

ARNAMESE–CORD.

Tonie Sap

Khorat Plateau

Chao Phraya

Ping R.

Nan R.

Mekong

Red R.

Black R.

Salween R.

Chindwin R.

Irrawaddy River

ARAKAN MTNS.

KUMON RANGE

Gulf of Tonkin

Gulf of Martaban

Cape Negrais

Ramree I.

Cheduba I.

Pegu Mts.

Preparis Channel

Coco Channel

Andaman Islands

Nicobar Islands

Great Channel

Cape Engaño

Luzon

Mindoro

Palawan

Mindanao

Point Tinaca

Balabac Strait

Luzon Strait

Tropic of Cancer

Equator

20°N

10°N

10°S

90°E

100°E

110°E

120°E

130°E

140°E

400 mi

400 km

200

200

0

0

N S E W

© MapQuest.com, Inc.

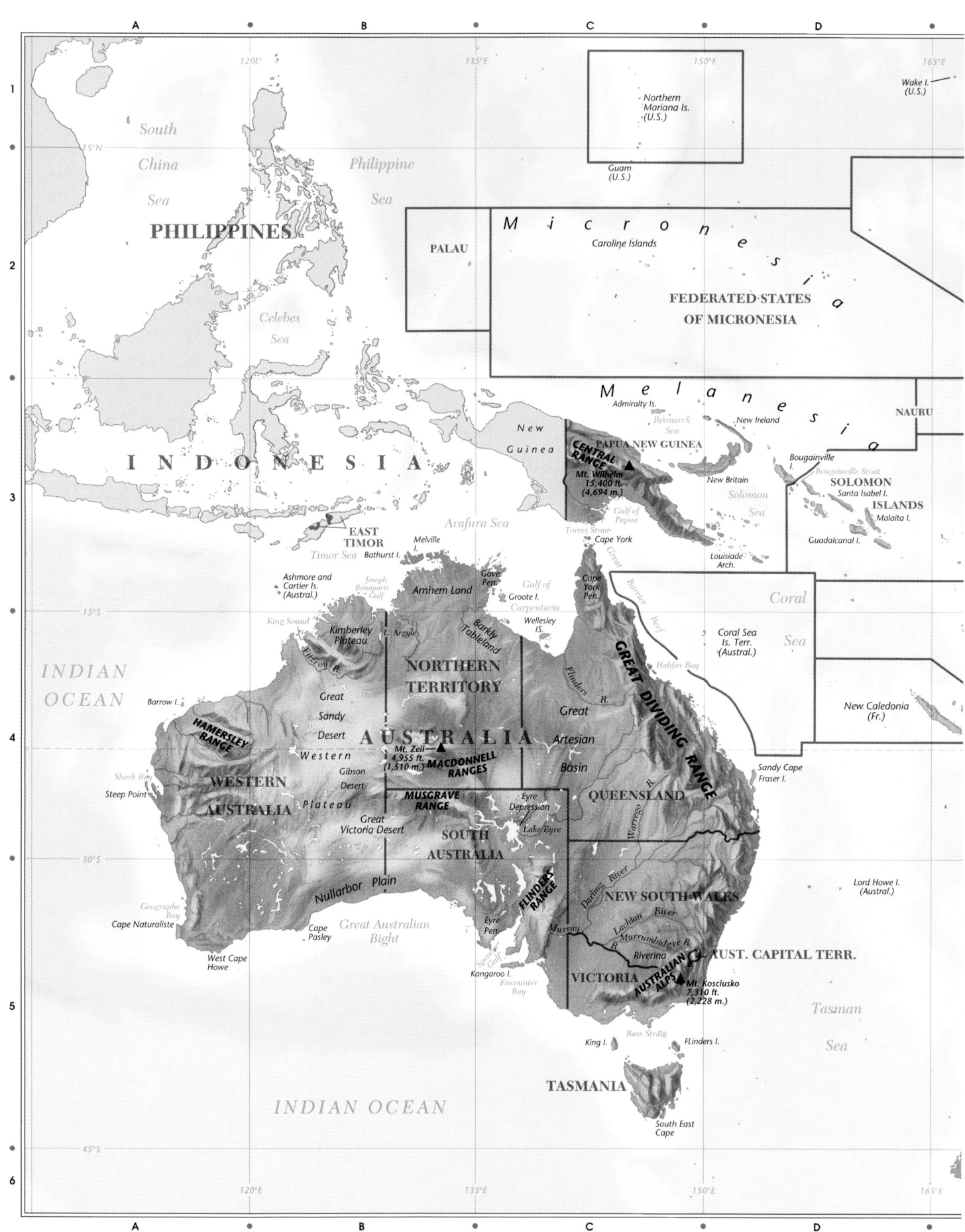

South
China
Sea

Philippine
Sea

PHILIPPINES

Celebes
Sea

I N D O N E S I A

Micronesia

Northern
Mariana Is.
(U.S.)

Guam
(U.S.)

PALAU

Caroline Islands

**FEDERATED STATES
OF MICRONESIA**

Melanesia

Admiralty Is.

*Bismarck
Sea*

New Ireland

NAURU

New
Guinea

PAPUA NEW GUINEA

**CENTRAL
RANGE**

Mt. Wilhelm
15,400 ft.
(4,694 m.)

Bougainville
I.

Bougainville Strait

SOLOMON

New Britain

*Solomon
Sea*

Santa Isabel I.

ISLANDS

Malaita I.

Arafura Sea

Torres Strait

Cape York

Guadalcanal I.

Louisiade
Arch.

**EAST
TIMOR**

Melville
I.

Timor Sea

Bathurst I.

Ashmore and
Cartier Is.
(Austral.)

*Joseph
Bonaparte
Gulf*

Arnhem Land

Gove
Pen.

*Gulf of
Carpentaria*

Groote I.

Wellesley
Is.

Cape
York
Pen.

Barrier Reef

Halifax Bay

*Coral
Sea*

**INDIAN
OCEAN**

King Sound

Kimberley
Plateau

L. Argyle

Barkly
Tableland

Coral Sea
Is. Terr.
(Austral.)

Barrow I.

Fitzroy R.

**HAMERSLEY
RANGE**

Great
Sandy
Desert

**NORTHERN
TERRITORY**

*Flinders
R.*

Great

GREAT DIVIDING RANGE

New Caledonia
(Fr.)

Shark Bay

Steep Point

WESTERN

Western

Mt. Zeil
4,955 ft.
(1,510 m.)

AUSTRALIA

Artesian

**MACDONNELL
RANGES**

Sandy Cape
Fraser I.

AUSTRALIA

Gibson
Desert

Plateau

**MUSGRAVE
RANGE**

Great
Victoria Desert

Eyre
Depression

Basin

QUEENSLAND

*Geographe
Bay*

Cape Naturaliste

Nullarbor Plain

**SOUTH
AUSTRALIA**

Lake Eyre

Lord Howe I.
(Austral.)

Cape
Pasley

*Great Australian
Bight*

Eyre
Pen.

**FLINDERS
RANGE**

NEW SOUTH WALES

Darling River

*Lachlan
River*

Murrumbidgee R.

Murray

Riverina

AUST. CAPITAL TERR.

West Cape
Howe

*Spencer
Gulf*

Kangaroo I.

*Encounter
Bay*

VICTORIA

**AUSTRALIAN
ALPS**

Mt. Kosciusko
7,310 ft.
(2,228 m.)

*Tasman
Sea*

King I.

Bass Strait

Flinders I.

INDIAN OCEAN

TASMANIA

South East
Cape

15°N

120°E

135°E

150°E

165°E

15°S

30°S

45°S

120°E

135°E

150°E

165°E

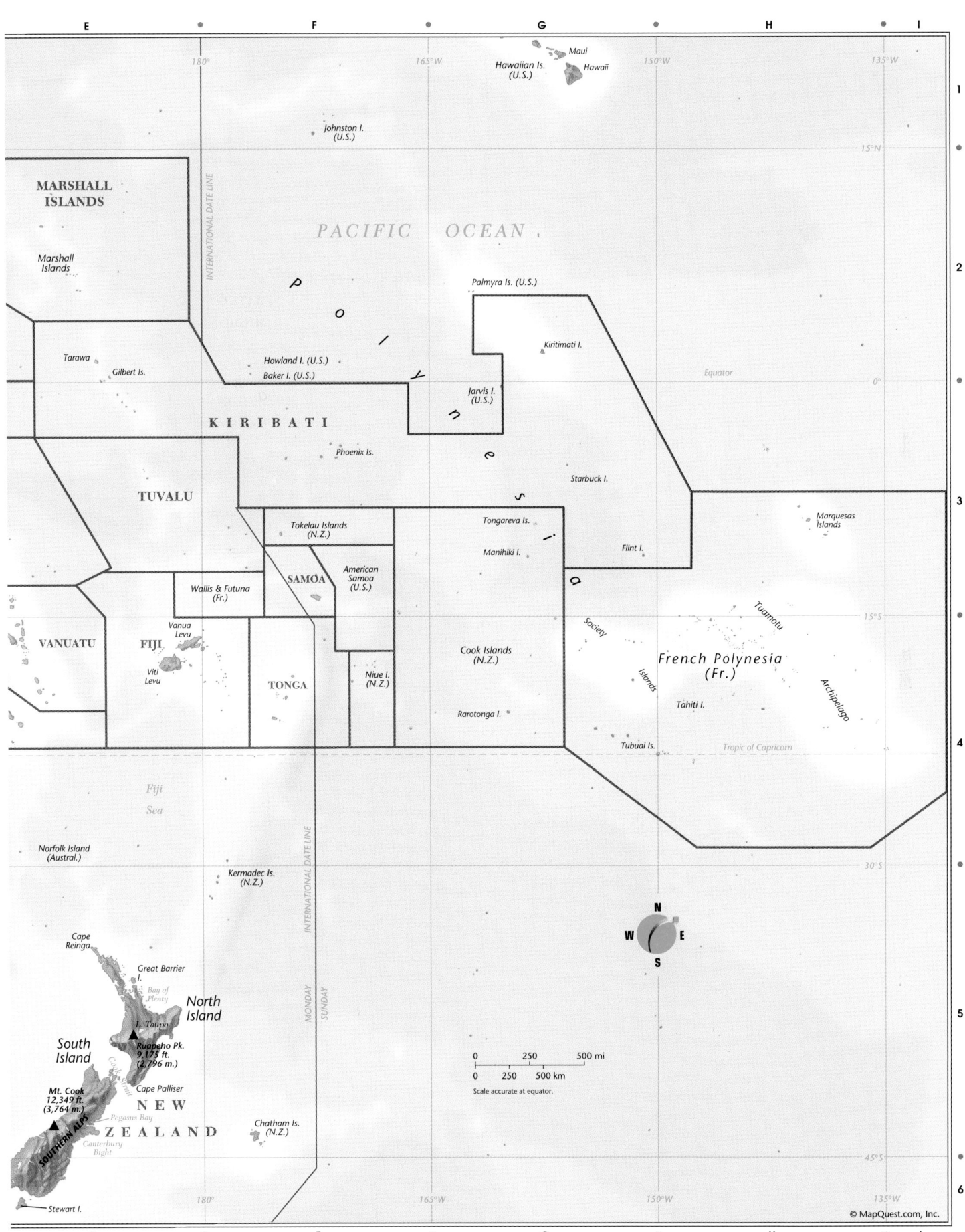

MARSHALL
ISLANDS

*Marshall
Islands*

PACIFIC OCEAN

INTERNATIONAL DATE LINE

*Johnston I.
(U.S.)*

*Hawaiian Is.
(U.S.)*

Maui

Hawaii

Palmyra Is. (U.S.)

Tarawa

Gilbert Is.

Howland I. (U.S.)

Baker I. (U.S.)

Kiritimati I.

Equator

K I R I B A T I

*Jarvis I.
(U.S.)*

Phoenix Is.

Starbuck I.

TUVALU

P o l y n e s i a

*Tokelau Islands
(N.Z.)*

Tongareva Is.

*Marquesas
Islands*

Manihiki I.

Flint I.

SAMOA

*Wallis & Futuna
(Fr.)*

*American
Samoa
(U.S.)*

VANUATU

FIJI

*Vanua
Levu*

*Viti
Levu*

TONGA

*Niue I.
(N.Z.)*

*Cook Islands
(N.Z.)*

Society

Islands

Tuamotu

French Polynesia
(Fr.)

Archipelago

Tahiti I.

Rarotonga I.

Tubuai Is.

Tropic of Capricorn

*Fiji
Sea*

INTERNATIONAL DATE LINE

*Norfolk Island
(Austral.)*

*Kermadec Is.
(N.Z.)*

*Cape
Reinga*

*Great Barrier
I.*

*Bay of
Plenty*

North
Island

MONDAY

SUNDAY

L. Taupo

▲*Ruapeho Pk.
9,175 ft.
(2,796 m.)*

South
Island

*Mt. Cook
12,349 ft.
(3,764 m.)*▲

Cook Strait

Cape Palliser

NEW

Pegasus Bay

*Chatham Is.
(N.Z.)*

ZEALAND

SOUTHERN ALPS

*Canterbury
Bight*

Stewart I.

0   250   500 mi

0   250   500 km

Scale accurate at equator.

N
W   E
S

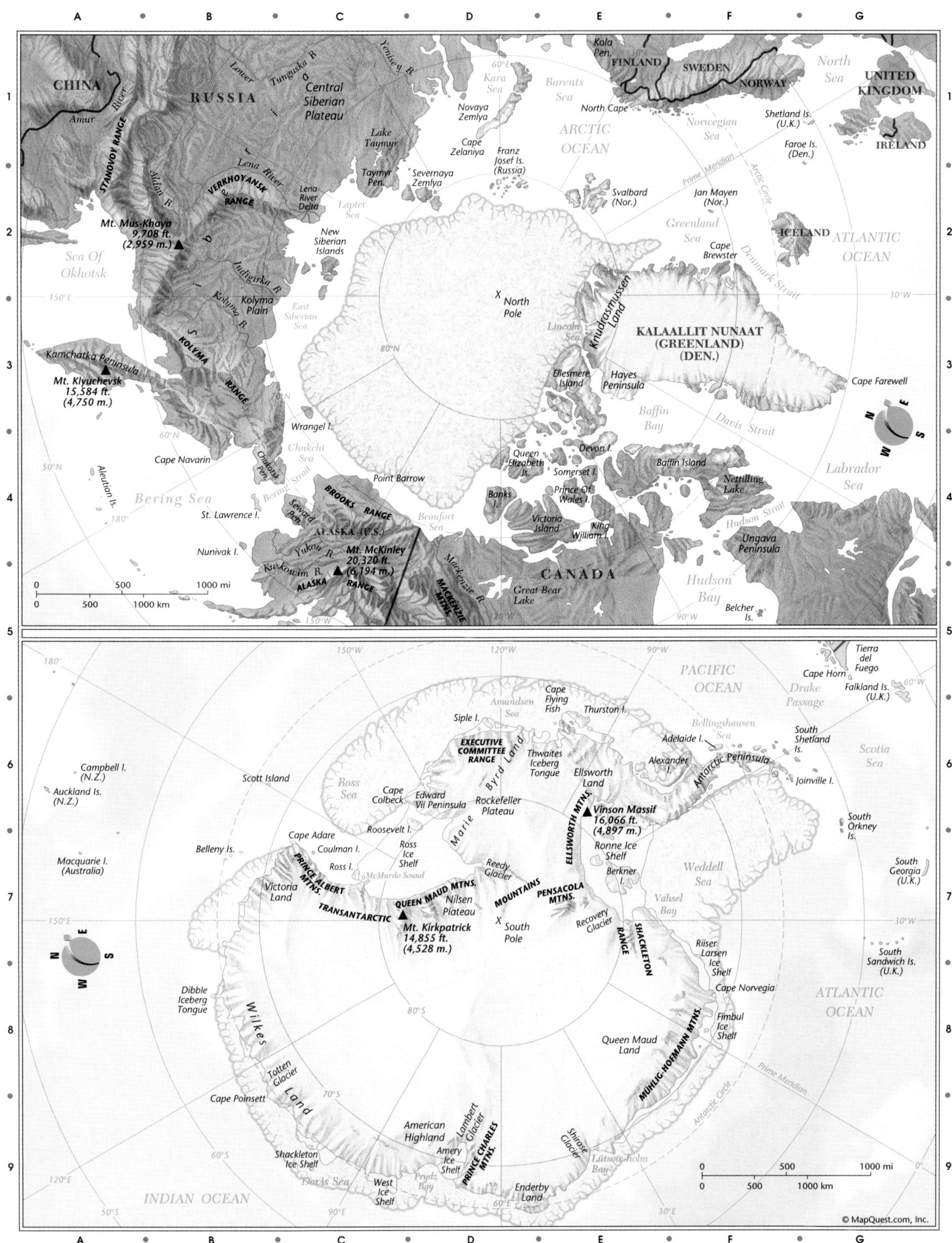

Arctic Region (top map):

A–G / 1–5 grid

CHINA
RUSSIA
Central Siberian Plateau
STANOVOY RANGE
VERKHOYANSK RANGE
Amur
Lower Tunguska R.
Tunguska R.
Yenisey R.
Lena River
Aldan R.
Indigirka R.
Kolyma R.
Kolyma Plain
KOLYMA RANGE
Mt. Mus-Khaya 9,708 ft. (2,959 m.)
Lena River Delta
Lake Taymyr
Taymyr Pen.
New Siberian Islands
Laptev Sea
East Siberian Sea
Sea Of Okhotsk
Kamchatka Peninsula
Mt. Klyuchevsk 15,584 ft. (4,750 m.)
Cape Navarin
Chukchi Pen.
Chukchi Sea
Wrangel I.
Aleutian Is.
Cape Zelaniya
Severnaya Zemlya
Novaya Zemlya
Kara Sea
Franz Josef Is. (Russia)
Barents Sea
Kola Pen.
FINLAND
SWEDEN
NORWAY
North Cape
North Sea
UNITED KINGDOM
IRELAND
Shetland Is. (U.K.)
Faroe Is. (Den.)
Norwegian Sea
Svalbard (Nor.)
Jan Mayen (Nor.)
Prime Meridian
Arctic Circle
ARCTIC OCEAN
North Pole
80°N
70°N
60°N
50°N
ICELAND
ATLANTIC OCEAN
Greenland Sea
Cape Brewster
Knudrasmussen Land
Denmark Strait
KALAALLIT NUNAAT (GREENLAND) (DEN.)
Lincoln Sea
Ellesmere Island
Hayes Peninsula
Cape Farewell
Davis Strait
Baffin Bay
Labrador Sea
Queen Elizabeth Is.
Devon I.
Somerset I.
Prince Of Wales I.
Banks I.
Victoria Island
King William I.
Baffin Island
Nettilling Lake
Hudson Strait
Ungava Peninsula
Great Bear Lake
CANADA
Hudson Bay
Belcher Is.
Point Barrow
Beaufort Sea
BROOKS RANGE
ALASKA (U.S.)
Mt. McKinley 20,320 ft. (6,194 m.)
ALASKA RANGE
MACKENZIE MTNS.
Mackenzie R.
Yukon R.
Kuskokwim R.
Seward Pen.
Nunivak I.
St. Lawrence I.
Bering Sea
Bering Strait
60°E
30°W
150°E
180°
150°W
90°W
60°N

0 500 1000 mi
0 500 1000 km

Antarctic Region (bottom map):

A–G / 5–9 grid

180°
150°W
120°W
90°W
150°E
120°E
90°E
60°E
30°E
Prime Meridian
Antarctic Circle
50°S
60°S
70°S
80°S
PACIFIC OCEAN
INDIAN OCEAN
ATLANTIC OCEAN
Campbell I. (N.Z.)
Auckland Is. (N.Z.)
Macquarie I. (Australia)
Scott Island
Ross Sea
Siple I.
Amundsen Sea
Cape Flying Fish
Thurston I.
Cape Colbeck
Edward VII Peninsula
EXECUTIVE COMMITTEE RANGE
Byrd Land
Thwaites Iceberg Tongue
Rockefeller Plateau
Marie Byrd Land
Ellsworth Land
Bellingshausen Sea
Adelaide I.
Alexander I.
Antarctic Peninsula
Cape Adare
Coulman I.
Roosevelt I.
Ross Ice Shelf
Ross I.
McMurdo Sound
Belleny Is.
PRINCE ALBERT MTNS.
Victoria Land
TRANSANTARCTIC
QUEEN MAUD MTNS.
Mt. Kirkpatrick 14,855 ft. (4,528 m.)
Nilsen Plateau
Reedy Glacier
MOUNTAINS
ELLSWORTH MTNS.
Vinson Massif 16,066 ft. (4,897 m.)
PENSACOLA MTNS.
South Pole
Ronne Ice Shelf
Berkner I.
Recovery Glacier
Weddell Sea
Vahsel Bay
SHACKLETON RANGE
Riiser Larsen Ice Shelf
Cape Norvegia
Fimbul Ice Shelf
MÜHLIG-HOFMANN MTNS.
Queen Maud Land
Lützow-holm Bay
Shirase Glacier
Enderby Land
Prydz Bay
West Ice Shelf
Amery Ice Shelf
Lambert Glacier
American Highland
PRINCE CHARLES MTNS.
Davis Sea
Shackleton Ice Shelf
Cape Poinsett
Totten Glacier
Wilkes Land
Dibble Iceberg Tongue
Tierra del Fuego
Cape Horn
Drake Passage
Falkland Is. (U.K.)
South Shetland Is.
Joinville I.
Scotia Sea
South Orkney Is.
South Georgia (U.K.)
South Sandwich Is. (U.K.)

0 500 1000 mi
0 500 1000 km

© MapQuest.com, Inc.

Terrain Map Index

Feature ....grid location/page number

Abaco, island E2/35
Aconcagua, mountain C6/28
Adare, cape C7/46
Adelaide, island E6/46
Aden, gulf E3/39
.... E6/40
.... C4/42
Adirondack, mountains F1/33
Admiralty, island C3/44
Adriatic, sea C3/36
Aegean, sea D4/37
.... A2/42
Africa, continent J3/27
Africa, Horn of, region E3/39
Aguja, point A3/28
Agulhas, cape D5/39
Ahaggar, range C2/39
Air, range C3/39
Akimiski, islands E3/31
Alabama, river L5/29
.... E2/33
Aland, island C1/36
Alaoira, lake E4/39
Alaska, gulf D2/26
.... E3/29
.... B3/30
Alaska, range D2/29
.... A3/32
.... C5/46
Albany, river E3/31
Albert, lake D3/39
Aldan, river B2/46
Alderney, island D5/38
Aleutian, islands A4/46
Alexander, island E6/46
Al Hijarah, desert C2/42
Allegheny, plateau L4/29
.... E1/33
Allegheny, mountains E2/33
Alps, mountains H2/27
.... C3/36
.... D3/40
Altai, mountains L2/27
.... F3/41
Altamaha, river E2/33
Atlantic Coastal, plain L5/29
Alvaro Obregon, reservoir B2/34
Amadjuak, lake F2/31
Amazon, basin F4/26
.... C3/28
Amazon, river F4/26
.... C3, D3/28
American, highland D9/46
American Samoa, islands F3/45
Amery, ice shelf D9/46
Amu Darya, river F4/40
Amundsen, gulf C1/30
Amundsen, island D6/46
Amur, river H3/41
.... A1/46
Anadyr, river J2/41
Anambas, islands C3/43
Anatolia, region N9/27
Anatolian, plateau B1/42
Ancoluma, mountain C4/28
Andaman, islands G6/41
.... B2/43
Andaman, sea G6/41
.... B2/43
Anderson, river C2/30
Andes, mountains C9, F4/26
.... B4/28
Andreas, cape B2/42
Andros, island E2/35
Aneto, peak C3/36
.... D4/40
Angara, river G3/41
Angel, falls C2/28
Anglesey, island C4/38
Angostura, reservoir C3/34
An Nafud, desert E5/40
.... B3/42
Annamese Cordillera, range G5/41
.... C2/43
Annapurns, range F5/41
Antarctic, peninsula F6/46
Antarctica, continent J6/27
Anticosti, island F4/31
Antigua and Barbuda, islands F3/35
Antrim, mountains B3/38
Apennines, mountains M8/27
.... C3/36
Appalachian, mountains E3/26
.... L5/29
.... E2/33
Apurímac, river B4/28
Aqaba, gulf B3/42
Arabian, desert B3/42
Arabian, peninsula E5/40
.... C3/42
Arabian, sea K3/27
.... F5/40
.... D4/42
Arafura, sea F4/43
.... B3/44
Araguaia, river D3/28
Arakan, mountains B1/43
Aral, sea K2/27
.... E3/37
.... E3/40
Ararat, mountain C2/42
Arauca, river B2/28
Arctic, ocean E1/26
.... L1/27
.... B1/30
.... A3/32
.... E1/40

.... E1/46
Argyle, lake B4/44
Aripuanã, river C3/28
Arkansas, river J5/29
.... D2/33
Arnhem Land, region B3/44
Arran, Island of, island C3/38
Aru, island F4/43
Aruba, island D8/26
.... E3/35
Ascension, island B4/39
Ashmore and Cartier, islands B3/44
Asia, continent L2/27
Asia Minor, region A2/42
Asir, cape K3/27
.... E3/39
Asir, mountains C3/42
Atacama, desert C4/28
Athabasca, lake J2/29
.... D3/30
Athabasca, river H3/29
.... D3/30
Atlantic, ocean E7, F2/26
.... H5, K8/27
.... F5/28
.... N5/29
.... F4/31
.... F2/33
.... B3/36
.... A3/38
.... B4/39
.... C3/40
.... G2, G8/46
Atlantic Coastal, plain E2/33
Atlas, mountains H2, L9/27
.... B2/39
Attawapiskat, river E3/31
Auckland, islands A6/46
Australian Alps, range C5/44
Avon, river D4/38
Axel Heiberg, island E1/30
Azores, islands G2/26
Azov, sea D3/37
.... E3/40
Azucro, peninsula C9/26
Azuero, Península de, peninsula D4/35
Bab el Mandeb, strait E3/39
.... C4/42
Baffin, bay G1/26
.... N1/29
.... F1/31
.... E3/46
Baffin, island L1/29
.... F1/31
.... E4/46
Bahamas, islands E2/35
Bai Bung, point C3/43
Baikal, lake H6/29
.... G3/41
Baja California, peninsula A1/34
.... H6/29
Baker, island F2/45
Baker, island E2/31
Balabac, strait D3/43
Balaton, lake C3/36
Balearic, islands C4/36
.... D4/40
Bali, island D4/43
Balkan, peninsula D3/37
Balkhash, lake F3/40
Balsas, river B3/34
Baltic, plain D2/37
Baltic, sea M7/27
.... C2/36
.... D3/40
Baluchistan, region E5/40
Banda, sea H7/41
.... E4/43
Bandiera, Pico da, mountain E5/28
Bangka, island C4/43
Banks, island G1/29
.... C1/30
.... D4/46
Bann, river B3/38
Barbados, island F3/35
Barents, sea D1/37
.... E2/40
.... E1/46
Barisan, mountains G7/41
.... C4/43
Barito, river D4/43
Barkly Tableland, plateau B4/44
Barra, island B3/38
Barrow, island A4/44
Barrow, point D1/26
.... C4/46
Bass, strait C5/44
Bathurst, cape C1/30
Bathurst, island D1/30
.... B3/44
Beachy Head, cape E5/38
Beaufort, sea E1/26
.... F2/29
.... C1/30
.... D4/46
Belcher, islands E3/31
Belcher, islands F5/46
Belitung, island C4/43
Belleny, islands B7/46
Bellingshausen, sea E4/39
Bemarah, plateau F6/46
Bengal, bay L3/27
.... F5/41
.... A2/43
Beni, river C4/28
Benin, Bight of, bay C3/39
Benue, river C3/39
Benue, river G5/41
Berents, sea J1/27
Bering, sea B2/29
.... A2/30
.... A3/32
.... J3/41
.... B4/46
Bering, strait A2/30

.... A3/32
.... K2/41
.... B4/46
Berkner, island E7/46
Bermejo, river C5/28
Bermuda, island F3/26
.... F1/35
Bienville, lake F3/31
Bighorn, river C1/32
Biscay, bay B3/36
.... C3/40
Bismarck, sea C3/44
Bitterroot, range B1/32
Black, hills C1/32
Black, river D2/30
Black, sea J2, P8/27
.... D3/37
.... E4/40
.... B1/42
Blanc, cape B2/39
Blanc, mountain C3/36
.... D3/40
Blanco, bay C6/28
Bodensee, lake C3/36
Boliviar, Pico, mountain B2/28
Bonaire, island E8/26
Bone, gulf E4/43
Boothia, gulf E2/31
Boothia, peninsula E1/31
Borneo, highlands G7/41
.... D3/43
Borneo, island G6/41
.... D3/43
Bornholm, island C2/36
Bosporus, strait D3/37
.... A1/42
Bothnia, gulf C1/36
Bougainville, island D3/44
Bougainville, strait D3/44
Brahmaputra, river G5/41
Branco, river C3/28
Bratsk, reservoir G3/41
Brazilian, highlands E4/28
Brazos, river K5/29
.... D2/33
Brecon Beacons, hills C4/38
Breton, peninsula B3/36
Brewster, cape F2/46
Bristol, channel B2/34
Brodeur, peninsula E1/31
Brooks, range D2/29
.... A3/32
Cabat, strait F4/31
California, gulf H6/29
.... A1/34
Cambrian, mountains C4/38
Cameroon, mountains C3/39
Campbell, island A6/46
Campeche, bay C8/26
.... K6/29
Canadian, shield C2/34
.... L3/29
.... E3/31
Canary, islands G2/26
.... B2/39
Caniapiscau, river F3/31
Cantabrian, mountains B2/36
Canterbury Bight, bay E5/45
Cape York, peninsula C3/44
Cardigan, bay C4/38
Caribbean, sea C8, F3/26
.... A1/28
.... M7/29
.... E3/35
Caroline, islands C2/44
Caroni, river C2/28
Carpathian, mountains N8/27
.... D3/37
.... D3/40
Carpentaria, gulf C3/44
Cascade, range G4/29
.... A1/32
Caspian, depression E3/37
.... E3/40
Caspian, sea K2/27
.... E3/37
.... E4/40
Cauca, river D2/42
.... B2/28
Caucasus, mountains E3/37
.... E4/40
Cayman, islands D2/35
.... D4/46
Cedar, river D1/33
Celebes, island H7/41
.... D4/43
Celebes, sea E3/43
.... B2/44
Central, plains L4/29
.... D1/33
Central, range C3/44
Central, valley A2/32
Central Massif, mountains C3/36
Central Russian, upland P8/27
.... D2/37
Central Siberian, plateau L1/27
.... G2/41
.... C1/46
Ceram, sea E4/43
Ceylon, island F6/40
Cgibis, archipelago B7/28
Chad, lake C3/39
Chang Jiang (Yangtze), river M3/27
Chao Phraya, river C2/43
Chari, river C3/39
Chatham, islands F5/45
Chattahoochee, river E2/33
Cheduba, island B2/43
Chesapeake, bay F2/33
Chetumal, bay D3/34

Cheviot, hills D3/38
Cheyenne, river C1/32
Chico, river C7/28
Chiloé, island B7/28
Chiltern, hills D4/38
Chimborazo, mountain B3/28
Chindwin, river B1/43
Chokotsk, peninsula K2/41
Chott Melrhir, depression C2/39
Chubut, river B7/28
Chuckchi, sea A2/30
Chudley, river F2/31
Chudskoye, lake D2/37
Chukchi, sea B2/29
.... C4/46
Chukotsk, peninsula B4/46
Churchill, river D3/30
.... F3/31
Chu Yang Sin, mountain C2/43
Clark Fork, river B1/32
Clear, cape B2/36
Clee, hills C3/38
Clyde, river C3/38
Clyde, Firth of, estuary C2/38
Coast, mountains F3/29
.... C3/30
Coast, ranges G4/29
.... A1, A2/32
Coco, channel B2/43
Coco, river D3/35
Cocos, islands M4/27
Cod, cape G1/33
Colbeck, cape C6/46
Coll, island B3/38
Colorado, plateau B2/32
Colorado, river H5, J5/29
.... B2/32
.... D2/33
Columbia, cape F1/31
Columbia, mountains C3/30
Columbia, river H4/29
.... D3/30
Columbian, plateau B1/32
Communism, peak F4/40
Comorin, cape K3/27
Comoros, islands E4/39
Conchos, Rio, river B2/34
Congo (Zaire), basin J4/27
.... D4/39
Connecticut, river F1/33
Cook, islands G4/45
Cook, mountain E5/45
Cook, strait E5/45
Coral, sea N4/27
.... D3/44
Coral Sea Island, territory D4/44
Cordillera Camabrica, mountains L8/27
Cordillera Central, mountains D7/26
.... D4, E3/35
Cordillera Chontaleña, range D3/35
Cordillera del Talamanca, mountains B9/26
Cordillera de Mérida, mountains C2/28
Cordillera Isabelia, mountains B8/26
Corsica, island M8/27
.... C3/36
.... D4/40
Cotswold, hills D4/38
Coulman, island C7/46
Courantyne, river D2/28
Cree, lake D3/30
Crete, island N9/27
.... D4/40
.... D4/40
Crimea, peninsula D3/37
Crocker, range D3/43
Cuando, river D4/39
Cuba, island E2/35
Cumberland, river C3/38
Cumberland, sound F2/31
Cumbrian, mountains C3/38
Curaçao, island D8/26
Cyrenaica, region C2/39
Da Hinggan Ling, range G4/41
Dal, river C1/36
Damaraland, plateau C5/39
d'Ambre, cape E4/39
Danube, river J2/27
.... D3/37
.... D3/37
.... D4/40
Dao Phu Quoc, island C3/43
Dardanelles, strait D4/37
.... A2/42
Darfur, plateau D2/39
Darling, river C5/44
Dartmoor, hills C5/38
Davis, sea C9/46
Davis, strait G1/26
.... P2/29
Dead, sea B2/42
Dead Sea, depression E5/40
Death, valley B2/32
Deccan, plateau F5/40
Dee, river C2, C4/38
Delaware, bay F2/33
Delaware, river F1/33
Delgado, cape E4/39
Demavend, mountain D2/42
Denakil, depression E3/39
Denmark, strait F2/46
Deseado, river B7/28
Des Moines, river D1/33
Desna, river D2/37
Devon, island E1/31

.... E4/46
Dibble, iceberg tongue B8/46
Dinaric Alps, mountains C3/36
Dnepr, lowland D3/37
.... D3/40
Dnepr, river D3/37
Dnepr, upland D3/37
Dnestr, river D3/37
Dominica, island F3/35
Don, river D2, D3/37
.... C3/38
Donard, Slieve, mountain F6/40
Dondra, cape B3/38
Donegal, bay B3/38
Donets, river D2/39
Dornoch Firth, estuary C2/38
Dover, strait B2/36
.... E5/38
Drake, passage F6/26
Drakensberg, mountains D5/39
Duarte, Pico, mountain E3/35
Dubawnt, lake D2/30
Dubawnt, river D2/30
Duero, river B3/36
Duncansby Head, cape C2/38
Dunsinane, hill C3/38
d'Urville, cape H7/41
Dvina, North, river E2/40
Dzungarian, basin F3/41
East China, sea M3/27
.... H5/41
Eastern, desert D2/39
East Siberian, sea M1/27
.... J2/41
.... C3/46
Ebro, river B3/36
Edward VII, peninsula D6/46
Edwards, plateau C2/32
Eigg, island B3/38
Elbe, river C2/36
Elbert, mountain J5/29
.... C2/32
Elbrus, mountain J2/27
.... E3/37
.... E3/40
Elburz, mountains E4/40
.... C2/42
Eleuthera, island E2/35
Ellesmere, island L1/29
.... F1/31
Ellsworth, mountains E6/46
Ellsworth Land, region E6/46
Emi Koussi, mountain C3/39
Encounter, bay C5/44
Enderby Land, region D9/46
Engaño, cape H5/41
.... E2/43
English, channel B3/36
.... D5/38
Erclyes Dagi, mountain B2/42
Erie, lake L4/29
.... E1/33
Erne, Lough, lake B3/38
Essequibo, river D2/28
Ethiopian, highlands J3/27
.... D3/39
Euphrates, river C2/42
Europe, continent H2/27
Everest, mountain L3/27
.... F4/41
Executive Committee, range D6/46
Exmoor, hills C4/38
Eyre, depression C4/44
Eyre, lake C4/44
Eyre, peninsula C5/44
Fair Isle, island D2/38
Falkland, islands G6/26
.... D8/28
.... G5/46
Farasan, islands C4/42
Farewell, cape G2/26
.... G3/46
Faroe, islands H1/27
.... B1/36
.... C2/40
.... F1/46
Fens, The, region D4/38
Fiji, sea E4/45
Fimbul, ice shelf F8/46
Finisterre, cape B3/36
.... C4/40
Finland, Gulf of, gulf D2/37
Fitzroy, river B4/44
Flinders, island C5/44
Flinders, range C5/44
Flinders, river C4/44
Flint, island G3/45
Flores, island E4/43
Flores, sea E4/43
Florida, key E3/33
Florida, straits B7/26
.... E3/33
.... D2/35
Flying Fish, cape E6/46
Formosa, strait G5/41
Forth, river C3/38
Forth, Firth of, estuary C3/38
Foxe, basin E2/31
Foyang, lake G5/41
Foyle, river B3/38
Foyle, Lough, estuary B3/38
Franklin, river D2/30
Franz Josef, islands J1/27
.... E1/40
.... D1/46
Fraser, island D4/44
Fraser, river G3/29
.... C3/30
French Polynesia, islands H4/45

Fria, cape C4/39
Frobisher, bay F2/31
Fuerte, river B2/34
Fundy, bay F4/31
Gabès, strait C2/39
Galápagos, islands E4/26
Galdhøppiggen, mountain C1/36
Galveston, bay D3/33
Ganges, plain F5/41
Ganges, river L3/27
.... F5/41
Garonne, river B3/36
Garry, lake D2/30
Gaspé, peninsula F4/31
Gaza Strip, region B2/42
Genesee, river F1/33
Geneva, lake C3/36
Geographe, bay A5/44
George, river F3/31
Ghats, Western, range F5/40
Gibraltar, strait B4/36
.... B2/39
Gibson, desert B4/44
Gila, river B2/32
Gilbert, island E2/45
Gobi, desert L2/27
.... G4/41
Godavari, river F5/40
Godwin Austen (K-2), peak F4/40
Golan Heights, region B2/42
Gold, coast B3/39
Good Hope, cape J5/27
.... C5/39
Gotland, island C2/36
Gracias a Dias, Cabo, cape D3/35
Grain, coast B3/39
Grampian, mountains C3/38
Gran Chaco, region F5/26
.... C5/28
Grand, river E1/33
Grand Bahama, island E2/35
Grand Cayman, island D2/35
Grande, bay C8/28
Grande, river E4/28
.... C3/34
Grande, Rio, river J5/29
.... C2/32
Granite, peak C1/32
Great, basin H4/29
.... B1/32
Great, channel B3/43
Great, plains E2/26
.... J4/29
.... C1/32
Great, lakes F2/26
Great Artesian, basin C4/44
Great Australian Bight, bay B5/44
Great Bahama, bank C7/26
Great Barrier, island E5/45
Great Barrier, reef C3/44
Great Bear, lake E1/26
.... G2/29
.... C2/30
.... D5/46
Great Dividing, range N4/27
.... C4/44
Greater Antilles, islands M7/29
.... E3/35
Great Inagua, island E2/35
Great Rift, valley D4/39
Great Salt, desert E4/40
.... D2/42
Great Salt, lake H4/29
.... B1/32
Great Salt Lake, desert B1/32
Great Sandy, desert B4/44
Great Slave, lake E1/26
.... H2/29
.... D2/30
Great Victoria, desert B4/44
Greco, cape B2/42
Green, mountains F1/33
Green, river C1/32
.... E2/33
Greenland, sea H1/27
.... F2/46
Grenada, island F3/35
Groote, island C3/44
Guadalcanal, island D3/44
Guadeloupe, island F3/35
Guadiana, river B4/36
Guadulupe, peak C2/32
Guainia, river B2/28
Guajira, peninsula B1/28
Guam, island N3/27
.... C2/44
Guaporé, river C4/28
Guayaquil, gulf A3/28
Guernsey, island B3/36
.... D5/38
Guiana, highlands E9/26
.... C2/28
Guinea, gulf K5/29
.... D2/33
Halifax, bay C4/44
Halmahera, island H6/41
.... E3/43
Hamersley, range A4/44
Hartland, point C4/38
Hasa, plain C3/42
Hatteras, cape F2/26
.... F2/33
Hawaii, island B3/32
.... G1/45
Hawaiian, islands C3/26
.... B3/32
.... G1/45
Hayes, peninsula E3/46
Hebrides, Sea of the, sea B2/38
Hecate, strait C3/30
Helmand, river F4/40
Hiiumaa, island C2/36

Hilal, cape D2/39
Himalayas, mountains L2/27
.... F4/41
Hindustan, region F5/40
Hispaniola, island M7/29
Honduras, gulf B8/26
.... D3/34
Hood, mountain A1/32
Hormuz, strait D3/42
Horn, cape F6/26
.... C8/28
.... G5/46
Howland, island F2/45
Hoy, island C2/38
Huallaga, river B3/28
Huang He, river G4/41
Huascarón, mountain B3/28
Hudson, bay F1/26
.... L2/29
.... E3/31
.... F5/46
Hudson, river F1/33
Hudson, strait F2/31
.... F4/46
Humber, river E4/38
Humphreys, peak B2/32
Huron, lake L4/29
.... E4/31
.... E1/33
Iberian, peninsula B3/36
.... C4/40
Içá, river C3/28
Iceland, island C2/40
Iguaçu, falls DE/28
Iguaçu, river D5/28
Illinois, river D1/33
Indian, ocean L4/27
.... E4/39
.... E7/40
.... A3/43
.... A4, B5/44
.... B9/46
Indigirka, river B2/46
Indus, river F5/40
Inner Hebrides, islands B3/38
Interior, plains C2/30
.... D2/33
Ionian, sea C4/36
Iowa, river D1/33
Iran, plateau K3/27
.... E4/40
.... D2/42
Irish, sea B2/36
.... C4/38
Irrawaddy, river G5/41
Irtysh, river F3/40
Islay, island B3/38
Ivory, coast B3/39
Izabel, lake D3/34
Jamaica, island E3/35
James, bay E3/31
James, river D1, F2/33
Jan Mayen, island H1/27
.... C2/40
.... F2/46
Japan, sea M2/27
.... H4/43
Japura, river B3/28
Jari, river D2/28
Jarvis, island G3/45
Java, island G7/41
.... C4/43
Java, sea G7/41
.... C4/43
Javari, river B3/28
Jaya, peak H7/41
.... F4/43
Jequitinhonha, river E4/28
Jersey, island B3/36
Jiddat al-Harsis, plain D4/42
Johnston, island F1/45
Joinville, island F6/46
Jos, plateau C3/39
Joseph Bonaparte, gulf B3/44
Juan Fernandez, islands A6/28
Juba, river E3/39
Juruá, river B3/28
Juruena, river D4/28
Jutland, peninsula C2/36
Juventud, Isla de la, island D2/35
Kainji, reservoir C3/39
Kakhovka, reservoir D3/37
Kalaallit Nunaat (Greenland), island G1/26
.... N1/29
.... G1/31
.... B1/40
Kalahari, desert D5/39
Kama, river E1, E2/37
Kamchatka, peninsula J3/41
.... A3/46
Kangaroo, island C5/44
Kangohenjunga, mountain G5/41
Kansas, river D2/33
Kapuas, river C3/43
Kara, sea K1/27
.... F2/40
.... D1/46
Karakoram, range F4/40
Kariba, lake D4/39
Karimata, strait C4/43
Kasai, river C4/39
Kasba, lake D2/30
Katrine, Loch, lake C3/38
Kattegat, strait C2/36
Kauai, island C2/30
.... B3/32
Keban, reservoir B2/42
Kefallinia, island C4/36
Kelkit, river B1/42
Kemi, river D1/37
Kenya, mountain D4/39

Kerguelen, island K6/27
Kermadec, islands F5/45
Khanka, lake H4/41
Khorat, plateau G5/41
.... C2/43
Kiel, canal C2/36
Kilimanjaro, mountain J4/27
.... D4/39
Kimberley, plateau B4/44
King, island C5/44
King, sound B4/44
King William, island E2/30
.... E4/46
Kings, peak B1/32
Kinnairds Head, cape D2/38
Kiritimati, island G2/45
Kirkpatrick, mountain C7/46
Klondike, region C2/30
Klyuchevsk, mountain J3/41
.... A3/46
Knudrasmussen Land, region E3/46
Kokosoak, river F3/31
Kola, peninsula D1/37
.... E2/40
.... E1/46
Kolyma, plain J2/41
.... B3/46
Kolyma, range J2/41
.... B3/46
Kolyma, river H2/41
.... B2/46
Komandorskiy, islands J3/41
Kongur, peak F4/40
Konzhakovskiy, mountain E1/37
.... F2/40
Kosciusko, mountain C5/44
Kra, isthmus B3/43
Kremenchug, reservoir D3/37
Kumon, range B1/43
Kunlun Shan, range F4/41
Kuria Muria, bay D4/42
Kuril, islands N2/27
.... H4/41
Kuskowim, river B5/46
Kuybyshev, reservoir E2/37
Kyrgyz, steppe E3/40
Labrador, region F3/31
Labrador, sea G2/26
.... P3/29
.... G3/31
.... G4/46
Lachian, river C5/44
Ladoga, lake D1/37
.... E2/40
La Grande, reservoirs F3/31
Laird, river C2/30
.... A2/42
Lake of the Woods, lake E4/31
.... D1/33
Lambert, glacier D9/46
Lammermuir, hills D3/38
Lancaster, sound E1/31
Land's End, cape C5/38
La Pérouse, strait H3/41
Lapland, region D2/40
Laptev, sea L1/27
.... H1/41
.... C2/46
Laurentian, highlands F4/31
Laurentian, plateau D2/30
Leeward, islands N7/29
.... F3/35
Lena, plateau G2/41
Lena, river L1/27
.... G2/41
.... B1/46
Lena River, delta C2/46
Lesser Antilles, islands N7/29
.... F3/35
Lesser Slave, lake D3/30
Lewis, Isle of, island B2/38
Libyan, desert D2/39
Libyan, plateau A2/42
Limay, river B7/28
Limpopo, river D5/39
Lincoln, sea E3/46
Lions, Gulf of, gulf C3/36
Little Missouri, river C1/32
Liullaillaco, volcano C5/28
Liverpool, bay C4/38
Lleyn, peninsula C4/38
Llsnos, plains C2/28
Logan, mountain C2/30
Loire, river C3/36
.... C3/40
Lomond, Loch, lake C3/38
Long, island F1/33
.... E2/35
Lopatka, cape N2/27
.... J3/41
Lopez, river C4/39
Lord Howe, island D5/44
Louisiade, archipelago D3/44
Loup, river D1/33
Lualaba, river D4/39
Lundy, island C4/38
Lütsow-holm, bay E9/46
Luzon, island H5/41
.... E2/43
Luzon, strait G5/41
.... E1/43
Lyme, bay D5/38
MacDonnell, ranges B4/44
Mackenzie, bay C2/30
Mackenzie, range D5/46
Mackenzie, river E1/26
.... G2/29
.... C2/30
.... D4/46
Mackenzie, mountains C2/30
Macquarie, island A7/46
Macquarie, river C5/44
Madagascar, island E5/39
Madeira, islands B2/39

Madeira, river C3/28
Madura, island D4/43
Magellan, strait F6/26
.... C8/28
Mahrat, mountains D3/42
Mainland, island C2, D1/38
Makassar, strait D4/43
Makran, region D3/42
Malacca, strait G6/41
.... C3/43
Malaita, island D3/44
Malawi, lake D4/39
Malay, peninsula G6/41
.... B3/43
Maldives, islands F6/40
Man, Isle of, island B2/36
.... C3/38
Manicouagan, reservoir F3/31
Manihiki, island G4/45
Manitoba, lake D3/30
Maracaibo, lake B1/28
Marañón, river B3/28
Margherita, peak D3/39
Marie Byrd Land, region D7/46
Marmara, sea D4/37
.... A1/42
Marne, river C3/36
Marne-Rhine, canal C3/36
Maroni, river D2/28
Marquesas, islands H3/45
Marshall, islands E2/45
Martaban, gulf B2/43
Martinique, island F3/35
Martre, Lac la, lake D2/30
Masira, gulf D4/42
Masira, island D4/42
Massif Central, mountains L8/27
Matinique, island E8/26
Mato Grosso, plateau F4/26
.... D4/28
.... C3/32
.... G1/45
Maui, island C3/32
Mauna Kea, mountain C3/32
Mbang, mountains C3/39
McKinley, mountain D1/26
.... D2/29
.... A3/32
.... C4/46
M'Clure, strait C1/30
McMurdo, sound C7/46
Mead, lake B2/32
Mediterranean, sea J2, L9/27
.... C4/36
.... C2/39
.... D4/40
Mekong, river G5/41
.... C2/43
Mekong River, delta C3/43
Melanesia, island group C3/44
Melville, island D1/30
.... B3/44
Melville, peninsula E2/31
Menai, strait C4/38
Mendocino, cape D2/26
.... A1/32
Meratus, mountains D4/43
Merrick, hill C3/38
Merrimack, river F1/33
Mesabi, range D1/33
Mesopotamia, region C2/42
Meta, river B2/28
Mexican, plateau B2/34
Mexico, gulf B6, E3/26
.... K6/29
.... E3/33
.... C2/34
Michigan, lake L4/29
.... E4/31
.... E1/33
Micronesia, island group C2/44
Midi, canal C3/36
Midlands, region D4/38
Milk, river C1/32
Minch, The, strait C2/38
Mindanao, island H6/41
.... E3/43
Mindoro, island G6/41
.... D2/43
Minnesota, river D1/33
Mirin, Lagoa, lagoon D6/28
Mississippi, delta E3/33
Mississippi, river E3/26
.... K5/29
.... D1, D2/33
Missouri, river E2/26
.... K4/29
.... C1/32
.... D1/33
Mistassini, reservoir F3/31
Mitchell, mountain L5/29
Mitchell, mountain E2/33
Mittelland, canal C2/36
Mitumba, mountains D4/39
Moake, mountains F4/43
Mobile, bay E3/33
Mojave, desert B2/32
Molucca, sea E4/43
Moluccas, island F3/35
Mona Passage, strait E1/43
Mongolian, plateau G3/41
Montserrat, island F3/35
Morant, point E3/35
Moray Firth, estuary C2/38
Mosquitos, Golfo de los, gulf D3/35
Mourne, mountains B3/38
.... G2/29
Mozambique, channel J5/27
.... D5/39
Mühlig-Hofmann, mountains E8/46
Mull, Island of, island B3/38
Muonio, river C1/36
Murat, river C2/42
Murray, river C5/44

Murrumbidgee, river C5/44
Musala, peak D3/37
Musgrave, range B4/44
Mus-Khaya, mountain B2/46
Mweru, lake D4/39
Nabi Shu'ayb, mountain C4/42
Najd, plateau E5/40
.... B3/42
Namib, desert C4/39
Nan, river B2/43
Narmada, river F5/40
Nasser, lake D2/39
.... B3/42
Natuna, islands C3/43
Naturaliste, cape A5/44
Nauru, island D3/44
Navarin, cape J2/41
.... B4/46
Neagh, Lough, lake B3/38
Neblina, Pico de, peak C2/28
Negrais, cape B2/43
Negro, river C3, C6, D6/28
.... E3/31
Nelson, river D2/30
Ness, Loch, lake C2/38
Netherlands Antilles, islands D8/26
.... E3/35
Nettilling, lake F2/31
.... F4/46
Nevis, Ben, mountain C3/38
New Britain, island D3/44
New Caledonia, island P5/27
.... D4/44
Newfoundland, island P4/29
.... G4/31
New Guinea, island H7/41
.... F4/43
.... C3/44
New Ireland, island D3/44
New Siberian, islands H1/41
.... C2/46
Nias, island B3/43
Nicaragua, lake B9/26
.... K7/29
.... D3/35
Nicobar, islands G6/41
.... B3/43
Niger, delta C3/39
Niger, river C3/39
Nile, delta D2/39
.... B2/42
Nile, river J3/27
.... D2/39
.... B3/42
Nile, Blue, river D3/39
Nile, White, river D3/39
Nilsen, plateau D7/46
Niobrara, river C1/32
Nipigon, lake E4/31
Niue, island F4/45
Norfolk, island E4/45
North, cape J1/27
.... D1/37
.... D2/40
.... E1/46
North, channel B3/38
North, island E5/45
North, sea H2, M7/27
.... C2/36
.... E3/38
.... D3/40
.... G1/46
North America, continent E2/26
North China, plain G4/41
North Downs, hills D4/38
North Dvina, river E1/37
Northeast (Manchurian), plain H3/41
Northern Mariana, islands C1/44
North European, plain J2/27
.... C2/36
.... D3/40
North Foreland, cape E4/38
North Magnetic, pole D1/30
North Negril, point E3/35
North Platte, river C1/32
North Pole, location D3/46
North Saskatchewan, river D3/30
North Uist, island B2/38
Northwest Highlands, range C2/38
Norvegia, cape F8/46
Norwegian, sea H1/27
.... C1/36
.... D2/40
.... F1/46
Novaya Zemlya, island E2/40
.... D1/46
Novosibirsk, reservoir F3/41
Nubian, desert D2/39
.... B3/42
Nueces, river D3/33
Nullarbor, plain B5/44
Nunivak, island B4/46
Oahu, island B3/32
Ob, river K1/27
.... F2/40
Ochil, hills C3/38
Ocmulgee, river E2/33
Oconee, river E2/33
Ogaden, plateau E3/39
Ohio, river L5/29
.... E2/33
Ojos del Salado, mountain C5/28
Oka, river D2/37
Okavango (Cubango), river C4/39
Okeechobee, lake E3/33
Okhotsk, sea M2/27
.... H3/41
.... A2/46
Öland, island C2/36
Oman, gulf E5/42
.... D3/42
Onega, lake D1/37
.... E2/40
Ontario, lake M4/29

. . . . . F4/31
. . . . . F1/33
Orange, *river* C5/39
Orinoco, *river* C2/28
Orizaba, *mountain* K7/29
. . . . . C3/34
Orkney, *islands* B2/36
. . . . . D2/38
Ottawa, *river* F4/31
Ouachita, *mountains* D2/33
Ouse, *river* D3/38
. . . . . E4/38
Outer Hebrides, *islands* B2/36
. . . . . B2/38
Owyhee, *river* B1/32
Ozark, *plateau* K5/29
. . . . . D2/33
Pacific, *ocean* A8, C3/29
. . . . . A4/28
. . . . . F4/29
. . . . . C4/30
. . . . . A2, B3/32
. . . . . J5/41
. . . . . F2/45
. . . . . F2/45
. . . . . F5/46
Pagai, *island* B4/43
Palau, *islands* B2/44
Palawan, *island* G6/41
. . . . . D3/43
Palliser, *cape* E5/45
Palmyra, *islands* G2/45
Pamir, *mountains* F4/40
Pampas, *plain* C6/28
Panama, *gulf* C9/26
. . . . . B2/28
. . . . . E4/35
Panama, *isthmus* L7/29
Pantelleria, *island* C4/36
Papua, *gulf* C3/44
Paraguaçu, *river* E4/28
Paraguay, *river* D5/28
Paraíba, *river* E5/28
Paraná, *river* F5/26
. . . . . D5/28
Pariñas, *point* E4/26
Parnaíba, *river* E3/28
Parry, *islands* J1/29
. . . . . D1/30
Pasley, *cape* B5/44
Pastaza, *river* C2/28
Patagonia, *region* C7/28
Patos, Lagoa dos, *lagoon* D6/28
Patuca, *river* D3/35
Peace, *river* H3/29
. . . . . D3/30
Pearl, *river* E2/33
Pechora, *river* E1/37
Pecos, *river* C2/32
Pegasus, *bay* E5/45
Pelly, *river* C2/30
Peloponese, *peninsula* D4/37
Pemba, *island* E4/39
Penas, *gulf* B7/28
Pennes, *range* L7/27
Pennines, *range* B2/36
. . . . . D3/38
Penobscot, *river* G1/33
Pensacola, *mountains* E7/46
Persian, *gulf* E5/40
. . . . . D3/42
Philippine, *sea* H5/41
. . . . . E2/43
. . . . . B2/44
Philippines, *islands* H6/41
. . . . . D2/43
. . . . . A2/44
Phoenix, *islands* F3/45
Piedmont, *hills* F2/33
Pikes, *peak* C2/32
Pilcomayo, *river* C5/28
Pindus, *mountains* N9/27
Ping, *river* B2/43
Plata, Rio de la, *river* D6/28
Platte, *river* J4/29
. . . . . D1/33
Plenty, *bay* E5/45
Po, *river* C3/36
Po, *valley* C3/36
Poinsett, *cape* B9/46
Polynesia, *island group* F2/45
Pontic, *mountains* P9/27
Pontus, *mountains* B1/42
Poopó, *river* C4/28
Potomac, *river* F2/33
Powder, *river* C1/32
Preparis, *channel* G5/41
. . . . . B2/43
Prince Albert, *mountains* C7/46
Prince Charles, *island* F2/31
Prince Charles, *mountains* D9/46
Prince of Wales, *island* E1/30
. . . . . E4/46
Prince Patrick, *island* C1/30
Pripet, *river* D2/37
Prut, *river* D3/37
Prydz, *bay* D9/46
Puerto Rico, *island* D8/26
. . . . . N7/29
. . . . . F3/35
Puget, *sound* A1/32
Purus, *river* C3/28
Putumayo, *river* B3/28
Pyrenees, *range* L8/27
. . . . . B3/36
. . . . . C4/40
Qattara, *depression* J3/27
. . . . . D2/39
. . . . . A2/42
Queen Adelaide, *archipelago* A8/28
Queen Charlotte, *islands* C3/30
Queen Charlotte, *sound* C3/30
Queen Elizabeth, *islands* D1/30

. . . . . D4/46
Queen Maud, *mountains* C7/46
Queen Maud Land, *region* E8/46
Race, *cape* G4/31
Rainier, *mountain* G4/29
. . . . . A1/32
Ramree, *island* B2/43
Rarotonga, *island* G4/45
Ras Dashan, *mountain* D3/39
Raya, *mountain* D4/43
Recovery, *glacier* E7/46
Red, *river* J5/29
. . . . . D2/33
. . . . . C1/43
Red, *sea* D2/39
. . . . . E5/40
. . . . . B3/42
Red, *river* E4/31
Red River of the North, *river* D1/33
Reedy, *glacier* D7/46
Reindeer, *lake* D3/30
Reinga, *cape* E5/45
Republican, *river* D1/33
Réunion, *island* K5/27
Rhine, *river* C3/36
Rhône, *river* C3/36
Rhum, *island* B2/38
Riga, Gulf of, *gulf* D2/37
Riiser Larsen, *ice shelf* F7/46
Riverina, *region* C5/44
Roanoke, *river* F2/33
Robinson, *mountain* D3/30
Rockefeller, *plateau* D6/46
Rocky, *mountains* E2/26
. . . . . G2/29
. . . . . C3/30
. . . . . B1/32
Ronge, Lac la, *lake* D3/30
Ronne, *ice shelf* E7/46
Roosevelt, *island* C6/46
Roraima, *mountain* C2/28
Rosa, *mountain* C3/36
Ross, *ice shelf* C7/46
Ross, *island* C7/46
Ross, *sea* C6/46
Ruapeho, *peak* E5/45
Rub al Khali, *desert* E5/40
. . . . . C4/42
Ruvuma, *river* D4/39
Ruwenzori, *mountains* D4/39
Rybinsk, *reservoir* D2/37
. . . . . E3/40
Ryukyu, *islands* H5/41
Saaremaa, *island* C2/36
Sable, *cape* F4/31
Sacramento, *river* A1/32
Saguenay, *river* F4/31
Sahara, *desert* H3/27
. . . . . B2/39
Sahel, *region* C3/39
Saimaa, *lake* D1/37
. . . . . D2/40
Saint Croix, *island* F3/35
Saint Croix, *river* D1/33
Sainte Marie, *cape* E5/39
Saint George's, *channel* B2/36
. . . . . B4/38
Saint Helena, *island* B4/39
Saint Helens, *mountain* A1/32
Saint-Jean, Lac, *lake* F4/31
Saint John, *river* G1/33
Saint Johns, *river* E2/33
Saint Kitts and Nevis, *islands* F3/35
Saint Lawrence, *gulf* N4/29
. . . . . F4/31
Saint Lawrence, *island* B4/46
Saint Lawrence, *river* M4/29
. . . . . F4/31
. . . . . F1/33
Saint Lucia, *island* G3/35
Saint Pierre and Miquelon, *islands* G4/31
Saint Thomas, *island* F3/35
Saint Vincent, *cape* B4/36
Saint Vincent and the Grenadines, *islands*
. . . . . F3/35
Sakami, Lake F3/31
Salado, *river* C5, C6/28
Salisbury, *plain* D4/38
Salmon, *river* B1/32
Salt, *river* B2/32
Salton, *sea* B2/32
Salween, *river* B2/43
San Antonia, Cabo de, *cape* D2/35
Sanday, *island* D2/38
Sandy, *cape* D4/44
San Francisco, *bay* A2/32
San Joaquin, *river* A2/32
San Jorge, *gulf* C7/28
San Juan, *river* D3/35
San Matías, *gulf* C7/28
San Pedro, *river* B2/34
Santa Cruz, *river* B7/28
Santa Isabel, *river* B2/34
Santiago, Rio Grande de, *river* B2/34
São Francisco, *river* E4/28
São Roque, *cape* G4/26
São Roque, *river* F3/28
Sardinia, *island* M9/27
. . . . . C3/36
. . . . . D4/40
Sark, *island* D5/38
Saskatchewan, *river* J3/29
. . . . . D3/30
Sava, *river* C3/36
Savannah, *river* E2/33
Savu, *sea* E4/43
Sayan, *mountains* G3/41
Scafell Pike, *mountain* C3/38
Scandinavia, *region* D2/40
Scandinavian, *highlands* C1/36
Scilly Isles, *islands* B5/38
Scioto, *river* E1/33
Scotia, *sea* G6/46

Scott, *island* B6/46
Seine, *river* C3/36
Selatan, *cape* D4/43
Selatan, *island* B4/43
Senegal, *river* B3/39
Severn, *river* E3/31
. . . . . D4/38
Severnaya Zemlya, *islands* G1/41
. . . . . D2/46
Seward, *peninsula* C4/46
Seychelles, *islands* E4/39
Shaba, *region* D4/39
Shackleton, *ice shelf* C9/46
Shackleton, *range* E7/46
Shark, *bay* A4/44
Shasta, *mountain* A1/32
Sherwood, *forest* D4/38
Shetland, *islands* B1/36
. . . . . D1/38
. . . . . F1/46
Shirase, *glacier* E9/46
Shu'ayb Mt. Nabul, *mountain* E6/40
Siberia, *region* K1/27
. . . . . G3/41
. . . . . B3/46
Siberut, *island* B4/43
Sicily, *island* M9/27
. . . . . D4/40
Sicily, *strait* C4/36
. . . . . C2/39
Sidlaw, *hills* C3/38
Sidra, *gulf* C2/39
Sierra Madre, *range* A8/26
. . . . . C3/34
Sierra Madre del Sur, *range* B3/34
Sierra Madre Occidental, *range* J6/29
. . . . . B1/34
Sierra Madre Oriental, *range* J6/29
. . . . . B2/34
Sierra Maestra, *range* C7/26
. . . . . E2/35
Sierra Morena, *range* L9/27
. . . . . B4/36
Sierra Nevada, *range* A2/32
Sierro de los Organos, *range* B7/26
Simeulue, *island* B3/43
Sinai, *peninsula* B3/42
Siple, *island* D6/46
Sipura, *island* B4/43
Sistemas Béticos, *mountains* L9/27
Skagerrak, *strait* C2/36
Skeena, *river* C3/30
Skeleton, *coast* C3/39
Skye, Island of, *island* B2/38
Slave, *river* D2/30
Smallwood, *reservoir* F3/31
Smoky Hill, *river* D2/33
Snake, *river* H4/29
. . . . . B1/32
Snowdon, *mountain* C4/38
Society, *islands* G4/45
Socotra, *island* E6/40
. . . . . D4/42
Solomon, *islands* D3/44
Solomon, *sea* D3/44
Solway Firth, *estuary* C3/38
Somali, *peninsula* E3/39
Somerset, *island* E1/30
. . . . . E4/46
Songhua Jiang, *river* H3/41
Sonora, *desert* B2/32
Sonora, *river* A2/34
South, *island* E5/45
South America, *continent* F4/26
Southampton, *island* E2/31
South China, *sea* M3/27
. . . . . G5/41
. . . . . C3, D2/43
. . . . . A1/44
South Downs, *hills* D5/38
South East, *cape* C5/44
Southern Alps, *range* E6/45
Southern Indian, *lake* D3/30
Southern Uplands, *hills* C3/38
South Georgia, *island* G6/26
. . . . . F8/28
South Orkney, *islands* G6/46
South Platte, *river* C1/32
South Pole, *location* D7/46
South Ronaldsay, *island* D2/38
South Sandwich, *islands* G7/46
South Saskatchewan, *river* D3/30
South Shetland, *islands* F6/46
South Uist, *island* B2/38
Spencer, *gulf* C5/44
Sperrin, *mountains* B3/38
Spey, *river* C2/38
Stanovoy, *range* H3/41
. . . . . A2/46
Starbuck, *island* G5/45
Start, *point* C5/38
Steep, *point* A4/44
Stewart, *island* E6/45
Stronsay, *island* D2/38
Suez, *canal* B2/42
Suez, *gulf* D2/39
. . . . . B3/42
Sukhona, *river* E2/37
Sulu, *archipelago* H6/41
Sulu, *sea* D3/43
Sumatra, *island* G6/41
. . . . . B3/43
Sumba, *island* D4/43
Sumbawa, *island* D4/43
Sunda, *strait* G7/41
. . . . . C4/43
Superior, *lake* L4/29
. . . . . E4/31
. . . . . E1/33
Susquehanna, *river* F1/33
Sutlej, *river* F5/40
Svalbard, *islands* J1/27

. . . . . D1/40
. . . . . E2/46
Syr Darya, *river* F3/40
Syrian, *desert* E4/40
. . . . . B2/42
Tademaït, *plateau* C2/39
Tagus, *river* B4/36
Tagus, *river* C4/40
Tahiti, *island* H4/45
Tahoe, *lake* B2/32
Tai, *lake* G4/41
Taiwan, *island* H5/41
. . . . . E1/43
Tajumulco, *volcano* C3/34
Taklimakan, *desert* L2/27
Taklimakan, *region* F4/41
Tana, *lake* D3/39
Tanganyika, *lake* D4/39
Tanimbar, *island* F4/43
Tapajóz, *river* D3/28
Taranto, Gulf of, *gulf* C3/36
Tarawa, *island* E2/45
Tarim He, *river* F4/41
Tasman, *sea* N5/27
. . . . . D5/44
Taurus, *mountains* N9/27
. . . . . B2/42
Taurus, Southeastern, *mountains* B2/42
Tay, *river* C3/38
Tay, Firth of, *estuary* D3/38
Tay, Loch, *lake* C3/38
Taymyr, *lake* C1/46
Taymyr, *peninsula* G1/41
. . . . . C2/46
Tees, *river* D3/38
Tehuantepec, *gulf* C3/34
Tehuantepec, *isthmus* C3/34
Teifi, *river* C4/38
Teles Pieres, *river* D3/28
Tennessee, *river* L5/29
. . . . . E2/33
Términos, *lagoon* C3/34
Teton, *range* B1/32
Thabana Ntlenyana, *mountain* D5/39
Thailand, *gulf* C2/43
Thames, *river* D4/38
Thar, *desert* F5/40
Thelon, *river* D2/30
Thurston, *island* E6/46
Thwaites, *iceberg tongue* D6/46
Tibesti, *highlands* C2/39
Tien Shan, *range* L2/27
. . . . . F4/41
Tierra del Fuego, *island* C8/28
. . . . . G5/46
Tietê, *river* E5/28
Tigris, *river* E4/40
. . . . . C2/42
Timan, *ridge* E1/37
Timor, *island* E4/43
Timor, *sea* E5/43
. . . . . B3/44
Tinaca, *point* E3/43
Tiree, *island* B3/38
Tisza, *river* C3/36
Titicaca, *lake* B4/28
Tobago, *island* F3/35
Tobol, *river* E4/40
Tocantins, *river* E4/28
Tokelau, *islands* F3/45
Tolo, *gulf* E4/43
Tombigbee, *river* E2/33
Tomini, *gulf* E4/43
Tongareva, *islands* G3/45
Tonkin, *gulf* C2/43
Tonle Sap, *lake* G6/41
. . . . . C2/43
Torne, *river* D1/37
Torres, *strait* C3/44
Totnam, *cape* E3/31
Totten, *glacier* B8/46
Toubkal, *peak* B2/39
Transantarctic, *mountains* C7/46
Trent, *river* D4/38
Trinidad, *island* F3/35
Troodos, *mountains* B2/42
Tsimlyansk, *reservoir* E3/37
Tuamotu, *archipelago* H3/45
Tubuai, *islands* G4/45
Tunguska, Lower, *river* G2/41
Turan, *plains* F4/40
Turfan, *depression* F4/41
Turkana, *lake* D3/39
Turks and Caicos, *islands* C3/42
Tuwayq, *mountains* C3/42
Tuz, *lake* B2/42
Tweed, *river* D3/38
Tyne, *river* D3/38
Tyrrhenian, *sea* C3/36
Tywi, *river* C4/38
Ubangui, *river* C3/39
Ucayali, *river* B3/28
Ungava, *bay* F3/31
Ungava, *peninsula* F2/31
Unst, *island* D1/38
Ural, *mountains* E1/37
. . . . . E2/37
Ural, *river* E3/40
. . . . . K1/27
Urmia, *lake* E4/40
Uruguay, *river* D6/28
Usk, *river* C4/38
Usumacinta, *river* C3/34
Vaal, *river* D5/39
Vahsel, *bay* E7/46
Van, *lake* C2/42
Vancouver, *island* C4/30
Vänern, *lake* C2/36

. . . . . D3/40
Vanua Levu, *island* E4/45
Vättern, *lake* C2/36
Vaupés, *river* B2/28
Verde, *cape* G3/26
Verde, *river* B2/32
Verkhoyansk, *range* L1/27
. . . . . H2/41
. . . . . B2/46
Victoria, *falls* D4/39
Victoria, *island* H1/29
. . . . . D1/30
. . . . . E4/46
Victoria, *lake* D4/39
Victoria Land, *region* B7/46
Vinson Massif, *mountain* E6/46
Virgin, *islands* E7/26
Virgin, *islands* F3/35
Viscount Melville, *sound* D1/30
Vistula, *river* C2/36
Viti Levu, *island* E4/45
Volga, *river* K2/27
. . . . . D2, E2, E3/37
. . . . . E3/40
. . . . . E3/40
Volga, *upland* E3/40
Volga-Baltic, *waterway* D2/37
Volga River, *delta* E3/37
Volgograd, *reservoir* E2/37
Volta, *lake* B3/39
Vychegda, *river* E1/37
Wabash, *river* E2/33
Wake, *island* D1/44
Wallachia, *plain* D3/37
Wallis & Futuna, *islands* F3/45
Warrego, *river* C4/44
Wasatch, *range* B2/32
Wash, The, *bay* E4/38
Washington, *mountain* F1/33
Weddell, *sea* F7/46
Wei He, *river* G4/41
Wellesley, *island* C2/36
Weser, *river* C2/36
West, *ice shelf* C9/46
West Bank, *region* B2/42
West Cape Howe, *cape* A5/44
West Dvina, *river* D2/37
Western, *desert* A3/42
Western, *plateau* M5/27
. . . . . B4/44
Westray, *island* D2/38
West Siberian, *plain* K1/27
. . . . . F2/40
Wheeler, *peak* C1/32
White, *mountains* F1/33
White, *river* E1/32
. . . . . E2/33
White, *sea* D1/37
White Sea-Baltic, *waterway* D1/37
Whitney, *mountain* H5/29
. . . . . B2/32
Wholdaia, *lake* D2/30
Wight, Isle of, *island* D5/38
Wilhelm, *mountain* C3/44
Wilkes Land, *region* B8/46
Williston, *lake* C3/30
Windward, *islands* F3/35
Windward Passage, *strait* C8/26
. . . . . E3/35
Winisk, *river* E3/31
Winnipeg, *lake* E2/26
. . . . . K3/29
. . . . . E3/31
Winnipegosis, *lake* D3/30
Wisconsin, *river* D1/33
Wolds, The, *hills* D4/38
Wollaston, *lake* D3/30
Wrangel, *island* K2/41
. . . . . C3/46
Wrath, *cape* B2/36
Wye, *river* D4/38
Xi Jiang, *river* G5/41
Xingu, *river* D3/28
Xizang, *plateau* G4/41
Yablonovy, *range* L2/27
Yamal, *peninsula* F2/40
Yaqui, *river* A2/34
Yare, *river* E4/38
Yazoo, *river* D3/33
Yell, *island* D1/38
Yellow, *sea* H4/41
Yellowstone, *river* C1/32
Yenisey, *river* L1/27
. . . . . F2/41
. . . . . C1/46
York, *cape* N4/27
. . . . . C3/44
Yucatán, *channel* D2/35
Yucatán, *peninsula* A7/26
. . . . . K6/29
. . . . . C3/34
Yukon, *river* D1/26
. . . . . D2/29
. . . . . A3/32
. . . . . C4/46
Yungui, *plateau* G5/41
Zagros, *mountains* E4/40
. . . . . C2/42
Zaire (Congo), *river* J4/27
. . . . . C4/39
Zambezi, *river* D4/39
Zanzibar, *island* E4/39
Zaysan, *lake* F3/41
Zelaniya, *cape* K1/27
. . . . . F1/40
. . . . . D1/46
Zell, *mountain* B4/44

LEGEND

General

⊛ National Capital	▭ International Boundary (subject area)	⎯⎯ Perennial River
★ Territorial Capital	▭ International Boundary (non-subject)	.... Intermittent River
• Other City	▭ Internal Boundary (state, province, etc.)	⊥⊥⊥⊥ Canal
▲ Mountain Peak	▭ Disputed Boundary	╱ Dam
		Compass Rose

U.S. States, Canadian Provinces & Territories, British Regions
(additions and changes to general legend)

★ State Capital	▭ National Park	■ Point of Interest
○ County Seat	▭ Other Park, Forest, Grassland	.... Continental Divide
⬚ Built Up Area	▭ Indian, Other Reservation	.... Time Zone Boundary
▭ State Boundary	▭ Military Area	⎯⎯⎯ Limited Access Highway
▭ County Boundary		⎯⎯⎯ Other Major Road
		〔90〕 Highway Shield

U.S., Canadian and British Cities
Type and symbol size indicate population, and color indicates administrative status, as follows:

American/Canadian cities and towns

County seat	Other city	Population
Jacksonville ⊙	⊙	500,000+
Tallahassee ⊙	⊙	100,000-499,999
Valdosta ⊚	⊚	25,000-99,999
St. Augustine ○	○	5,000-24,999
Macclenny ○	○	0-4,999

British cities and towns

Administrative center	Other city	Population
London ⊙	⊙	1,000,000+
Coventry ⊙	⊙	250,000-1,000,000
Nottingham ⊙	⊙	100,000-249,999
Dunstable ⊚	⊚	25,000-99,999
Buckingham ○	○	10,000-24,999
Compton ○	○	0-9,999

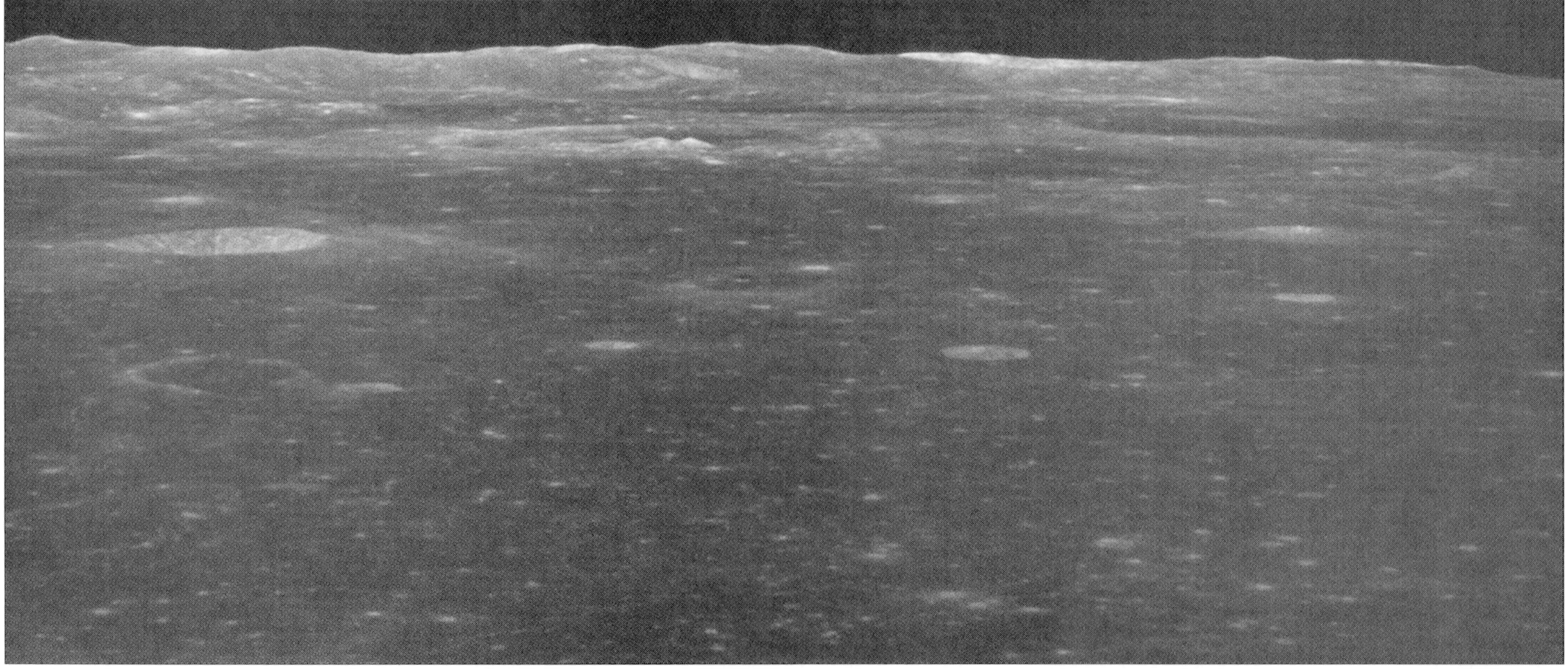

TABLE OF CONTENTS

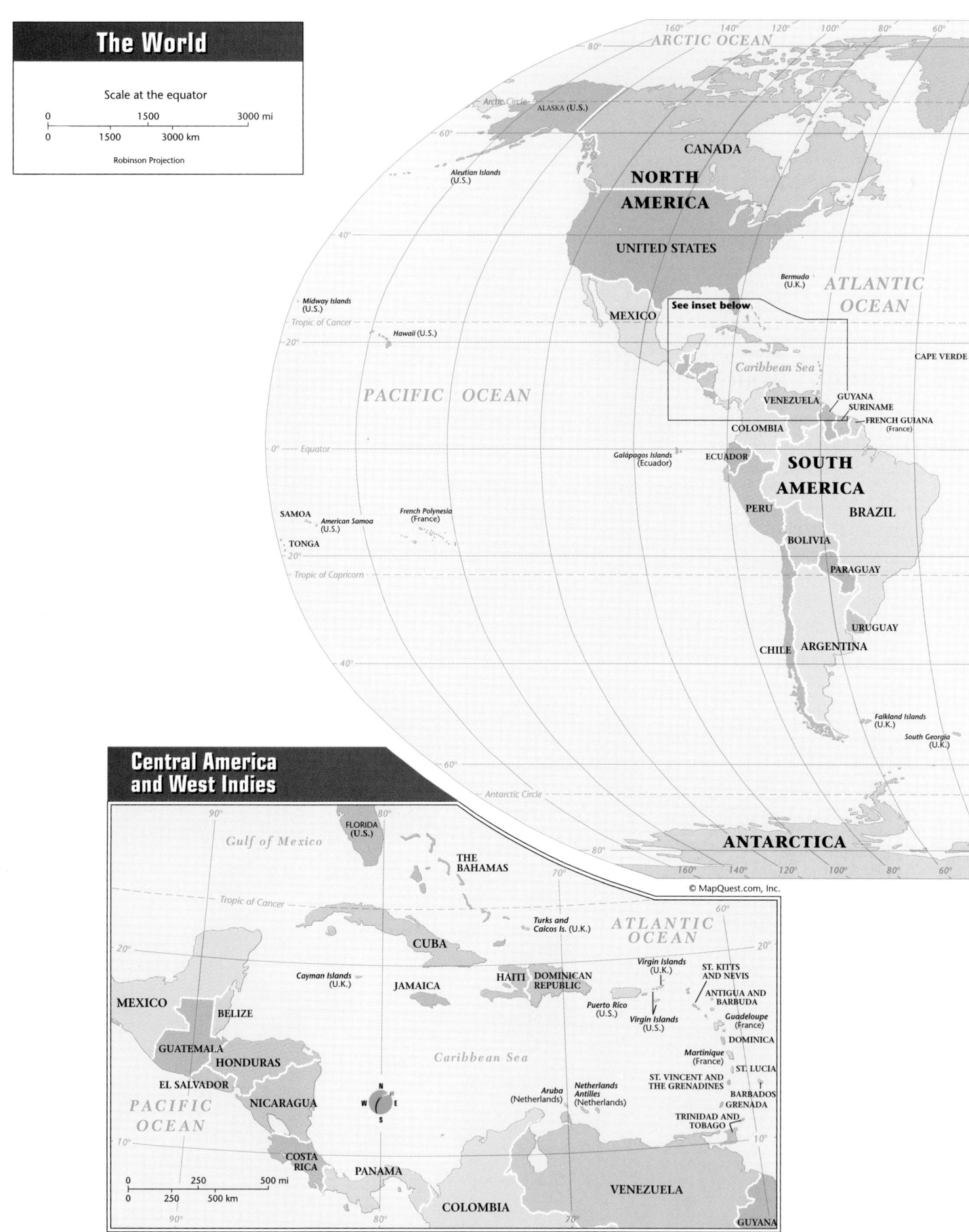

The World

Scale at the equator

| 0 | 1500 | 3000 mi |
| 0 | 1500 | 3000 km |

Robinson Projection

ARCTIC OCEAN

ALASKA (U.S.)

Arctic Circle

Aleutian Islands
(U.S.)

CANADA

**NORTH
AMERICA**

UNITED STATES

Bermuda
(U.K.)

*ATLANTIC
OCEAN*

Midway Islands
(U.S.)

Tropic of Cancer

MEXICO

See inset below

CAPE VERDE

Hawaii (U.S.)

Caribbean Sea

PACIFIC OCEAN

VENEZUELA   GUYANA
SURINAME
FRENCH GUIANA
(France)

COLOMBIA

Galápagos Islands
(Ecuador)

ECUADOR

**SOUTH
AMERICA**

Equator

PERU

BRAZIL

SAMOA

American Samoa
(U.S.)

French Polynesia
(France)

BOLIVIA

TONGA

PARAGUAY

Tropic of Capricorn

URUGUAY

CHILE   ARGENTINA

Falkland Islands
(U.K.)

South Georgia
(U.K.)

Antarctic Circle

ANTARCTICA

© MapQuest.com, Inc.

Central America and West Indies

Gulf of Mexico

FLORIDA
(U.S.)

THE
BAHAMAS

Tropic of Cancer

Turks and
Caicos Is. (U.K.)

*ATLANTIC
OCEAN*

CUBA

Cayman Islands
(U.K.)

JAMAICA

HAITI   DOMINICAN
REPUBLIC

Virgin Islands
(U.K.)

ST. KITTS
AND NEVIS

ANTIGUA AND
BARBUDA

MEXICO

BELIZE

Puerto Rico
(U.S.)

Virgin Islands
(U.S.)

Guadeloupe
(France)

DOMINICA

GUATEMALA

HONDURAS

Caribbean Sea

Martinique
(France)

ST. LUCIA

EL SALVADOR

N
W   E
S

ST. VINCENT AND
THE GRENADINES

BARBADOS

*PACIFIC
OCEAN*

NICARAGUA

Aruba
(Netherlands)

Netherlands
Antilles
(Netherlands)

GRENADA

TRINIDAD AND
TOBAGO

COSTA
RICA

PANAMA

| 0 | 250 | 500 mi |
| 0 | 250 | 500 km |

VENEZUELA

COLOMBIA

GUYANA

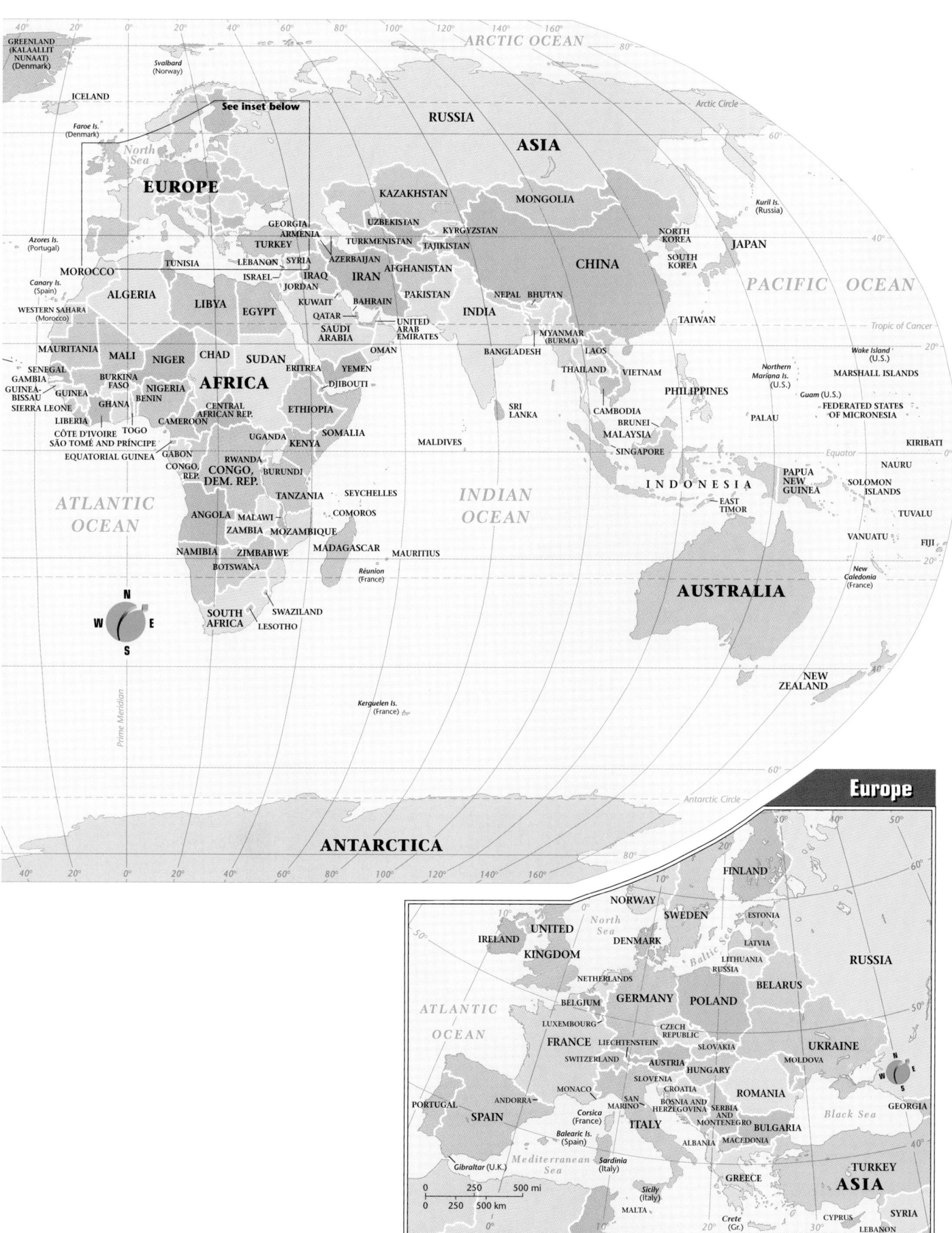

ARCTIC OCEAN

Arctic Circle

RUSSIA

ASIA

GREENLAND
(KALAALLIT
NUNAAT)
(Denmark)

Svalbard
(Norway)

ICELAND

See inset below

Faroe Is.
(Denmark)

North
Sea

EUROPE

KAZAKHSTAN

MONGOLIA

Kuril Is.
(Russia)

GEORGIA
ARMENIA
TURKEY

UZBEKISTAN

KYRGYZSTAN

NORTH
KOREA

JAPAN

Azores Is.
(Portugal)

TURKMENISTAN

TAJIKISTAN

SOUTH
KOREA

MOROCCO

TUNISIA

LEBANON SYRIA

AZERBAIJAN

AFGHANISTAN

CHINA

PACIFIC OCEAN

Canary Is.
(Spain)

ISRAEL

IRAQ

JORDAN

IRAN

ALGERIA

LIBYA

EGYPT

KUWAIT
QATAR
SAUDI
ARABIA

BAHRAIN

UNITED
ARAB
EMIRATES

PAKISTAN

NEPAL BHUTAN

INDIA

TAIWAN

Tropic of Cancer

WESTERN SAHARA
(Morocco)

MAURITANIA

MALI

NIGER

CHAD

SUDAN

OMAN

ERITREA YEMEN

BANGLADESH

MYANMAR
(BURMA)

LAOS

Wake Island
(U.S.)

SENEGAL
GAMBIA
GUINEA-
BISSAU
SIERRA LEONE

BURKINA
FASO

GUINEA

NIGERIA
BENIN

GHANA

AFRICA

CENTRAL
AFRICAN REP.

ETHIOPIA

DJIBOUTI

THAILAND

VIETNAM

Northern
Mariana Is.
(U.S.)

MARSHALL ISLANDS

PHILIPPINES

Guam (U.S.)

FEDERATED STATES
OF MICRONESIA

LIBERIA

CÔTE D'IVOIRE TOGO
SÃO TOMÉ AND PRÍNCIPE

CAMEROON

UGANDA

SOMALIA

SRI
LANKA

CAMBODIA
BRUNEI
MALAYSIA

PALAU

KIRIBATI

EQUATORIAL GUINEA

GABON
CONGO,
REP.

KENYA

MALDIVES

SINGAPORE

Equator

NAURU

RWANDA
CONGO,
DEM. REP.

BURUNDI

**ATLANTIC
OCEAN**

TANZANIA

SEYCHELLES

INDONESIA

PAPUA
NEW
GUINEA

SOLOMON
ISLANDS

ANGOLA
MALAWI
ZAMBIA MOZAMBIQUE

COMOROS

INDIAN
OCEAN

EAST
TIMOR

TUVALU

NAMIBIA ZIMBABWE

MADAGASCAR

MAURITIUS

VANUATU

FIJI

BOTSWANA

Réunion
(France)

New
Caledonia
(France)

N
W E
S

SOUTH
AFRICA

SWAZILAND

LESOTHO

AUSTRALIA

Kerguelen Is.
(France)

NEW
ZEALAND

Antarctic Circle

ANTARCTICA

See inset below

Europe

FINLAND

NORWAY

SWEDEN

ESTONIA

IRELAND

UNITED
KINGDOM

North
Sea

DENMARK

Baltic Sea

LATVIA

RUSSIA

LITHUANIA
RUSSIA

BELARUS

NETHERLANDS

ATLANTIC
OCEAN

BELGIUM

GERMANY

POLAND

LUXEMBOURG

CZECH
REPUBLIC

SLOVAKIA

UKRAINE

FRANCE LIECHTENSTEIN

MOLDOVA

SWITZERLAND

AUSTRIA HUNGARY

N
W E
S

SLOVENIA

MONACO

CROATIA

ROMANIA

PORTUGAL

ANDORRA

SAN
MARINO

BOSNIA AND
HERZEGOVINA

SERBIA
AND
MONTENEGRO

Black Sea

GEORGIA

SPAIN

Corsica
(France)

ITALY

BULGARIA

Balearic Is.
(Spain)

ALBANIA MACEDONIA

Gibraltar (U.K.)

Sardinia
(Italy)

GREECE

TURKEY

Mediterranean
Sea

Sicily
(Italy)

ASIA

0   250   500 mi
0   250   500 km

MALTA

Crete
(Gr.)

CYPRUS

SYRIA

LEBANON

Population: 749,792,000 (2002)
Area: 4,032,000 sq. mi.
      10,443,000 sq. km.
Highest Point: Mt. Elbrus
      18,510 ft. (5,642 m.)
Lowest Point: Caspian Sea
      92 ft. (28 m.)
      below sea level
Largest Urban Areas:
      Istanbul, Turkey
      Paris, France
      Moscow, Russia
      London, U.K.
      Essen, Germany
      St. Petersburg, Russia
      Milan, Italy
Countries: 46

Above: The Parthenon, Athens, Greece; **Right:** St. Basil's
Cathedral, Moscow, Russia; **Below:** Stonehenge, Wiltshire, England

Major Metropolitan Areas

Albania
Tirana 244,000

Andorra
Andorra la Vella 21,000

Armenia
Yerevan 1,247,000

Austria
Vienna 1,562,000

Azerbaijan
Baku 1,792,000

Belarus
Minsk 1,681,000

Belgium
Brussels 978,000
Antwerp 449,000

Bosnia & Herzegovina
Sarajevo 529,000

Bulgaria
Sofia 1,191,000

Croatia
Zagreb 692,000

Czech Republic
Prague 1,179,000

Denmark
Copenhagen 1,085,000

Estonia
Tallinn 398,000

Finland
Helsinki 965,000

France
Paris 9,645,000
Marseille 1,350,000
Lyon 1,349,000
Lille 1,001,000

Georgia
Tbilisi 1,399,000

Germany (core city only)
Berlin 3,382,000
Hamburg 1,715,000
Munich 1,210,000
Cologne 963,000
Frankfurt 647,000
Essen 595,000
Dortmund 589,000
Stuttgart 584,000
Düsseldorf 569,000

Greece
Athens 3,073,000

Hungary
Budapest 1,825,000

Iceland
Reykjavik 175,000

Ireland
Dublin 1,123,000

Italy
Rome 2,460,000
Milan 1,183,000
Naples 993,000
Turin 857,000
Palermo 653,000
Genoa 604,000

Latvia
Riga 793,000

Liechtenstein
Vaduz 5,000

Lithuania
Vilnius 578,000

Luxembourg
Luxembourg 77,000

F.Y.R. Macedonia
Skopje 545,000

Malta
Valletta 8,000

Moldova
Chişinău 658,000

Monaco
Monaco 27,000

Netherlands
Amsterdam 1,207,000
Rotterdam 1,161,000

Norway
Oslo 513,000

Poland
Warsaw 1,610,000
Łódź 787,000
Kraków 741,000
Wrocław 634,000

Portugal
Lisbon 1,947,000

Romania
Bucharest 2,009,000

Russia (European)
Moscow 8,538,000
St. Petersburg 4,678,000
Niżnij Novgorod 1,366,000
Samara 1,183,000
Kazan' 1,092,000
Ufa 1,094,000
Volgograd 1,025,000
Perm' 1,024,000
Rostov-na-Donu 1,004,000

San Marino
San Marino 5,000

Serbia & Montenegro
Belgrade 1,619,000

Slovakia
Bratislava 429,000

Slovenia
Ljubljana 264,000

Spain
Madrid 2,939,000
Barcelona 1,504,000
Valencia 738,000
Seville 685,000

Sweden
Stockholm 1,665,000

Switzerland
Zürich 933,000
Geneva 451,000

Turkey (European)
Istanbul 8,803,000

Ukraine
Kiev 2,590,000
Kharkiv 1,494,000
Dnipropetrovs'k 1,109,000
Donets'k 1,050,000
Odesa 1,002,000

United Kingdom
London 7,652,000
Birmingham 2,296,000
Manchester 2,277,000
Leeds-Bradford 1,446,000
Newcastle 886,000
Glasgow 867,000
Liverpool 838,000
Sheffield 633,000

International comparability of population data is limited by varying census methods. Where metropolitan population is unavailable, core city population is shown.

Population

Persons per sq. mile	Persons per sq. km
Over 520	Over 200
260 to 519	100 to 199
130 to 259	50 to 99
25 to 129	10 to 49
1 to 24	1 to 9
0	0

Major metropolitan areas
● Over 2 million
● 1 million to 2 million
● Under 1 million

Europe

⊛ National Capital

• Other City

0 — 250 — 500 mi
0 — 250 — 500 km
Azimuthal Equal Area Projection

© MapQuest.com, Inc.

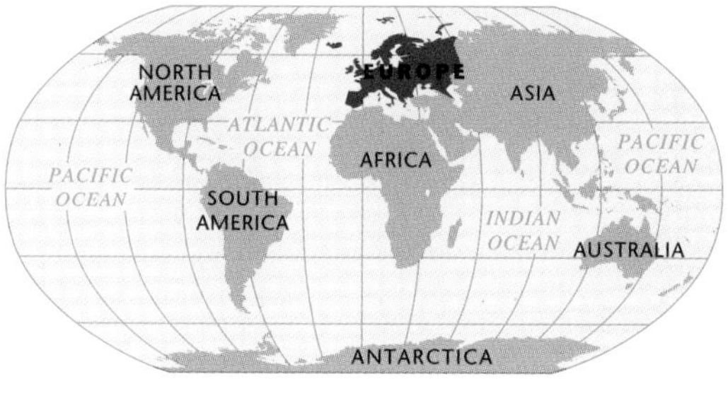

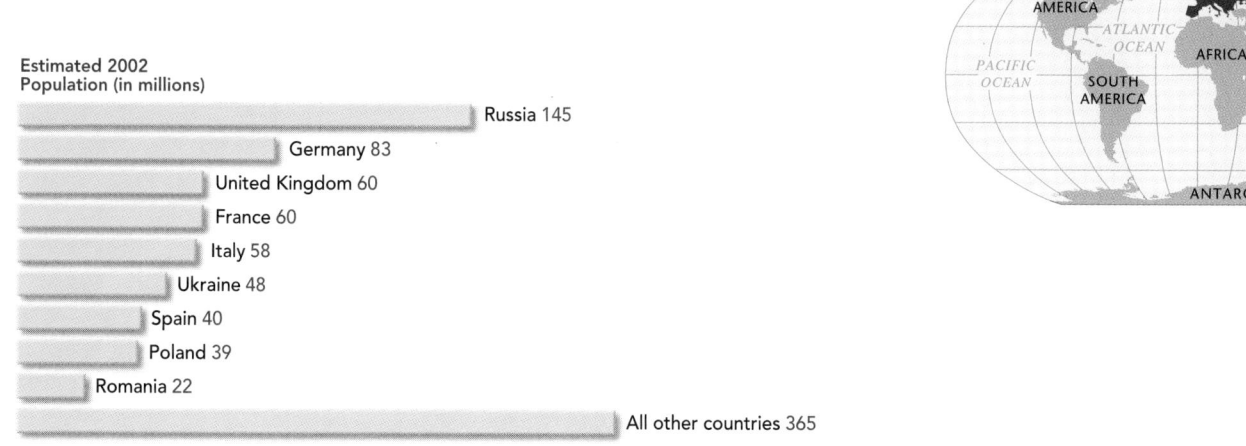

Estimated 2002
Population (in millions)

Country	Population
Russia	145
Germany	83
United Kingdom	60
France	60
Italy	58
Ukraine	48
Spain	40
Poland	39
Romania	22
All other countries	365

Source: U.S. Census Bureau

Vegetation

- Unclassified highlands or ice cap
- Tundra and alpine tundra
- Coniferous forest
- Midlatitude deciduous forest
- Mixed forest
- Midlatitude scrubland
- Midlatitude grassland

Forests, nourished by plentiful precipitation, dominate in Europe, but grassland and scrubland thrive where rainfall becomes sparse or is seasonal. Deciduous trees disappear as the winters grow harsh, replaced by vast and hardy stands of coniferous forest that are merely the western end of an immense belt stretching across Russia to the Pacific Ocean.

Europe, particularly Western Europe, is a consolidation of high-tech, market-driven, globally connected economies, where manufacturing and commercial agriculture predominate. Crucial to continental economic integration is the European Union, a partnership of member nations whose combined economic clout rivals the U.S. Russia and former Soviet-satellite nations are, in large part, reaching harmony with the rest of Europe after an initial and unsettling period of adjustment.

Despite centuries of exploration and exploitation, commercially-valuable mineral resources continue to be mined, notably in Russia, Ukraine, and Scandinavia. The bountiful oil and gas fields of the North Sea are one of the most important and most recent discoveries.

Land Use and Resources

Predominant land use

- Commercial agriculture
- Dairying
- Livestock ranching
- Nomadic herding
- Subsistence agriculture
- Primarily forestland
- Limited agricultural activity

Major resources

- Coal
- Natural gas
- Oil
- Au Gold
- Fe Iron ore
- Ag Silver
- U Uranium
- Al Bauxite
- Other minerals
- Fishing
- ● Major manufacturing and trade centers

Climate Graphs

Average daily temperature range (in °F)
100° High
65° Low
32°
0°

Average monthly precipitation (in inches)
20"
10"
0"

ARKHANGELSK, Russia

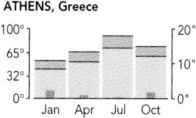
ATHENS, Greece

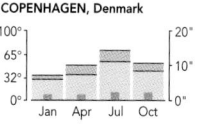
COPENHAGEN, Denmark

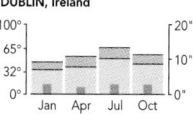
DUBLIN, Ireland

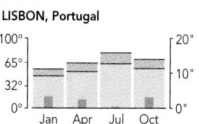
LISBON, Portugal

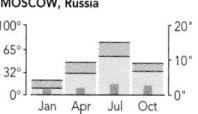
MOSCOW, Russia

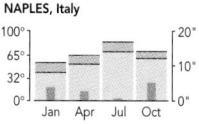
NAPLES, Italy

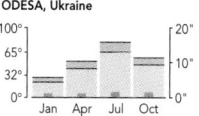
ODESA, Ukraine

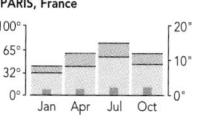
PARIS, France

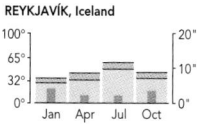
REYKJAVÍK, Iceland

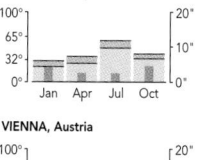
TROMSØ, Norway

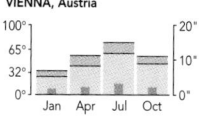
VIENNA, Austria

Climate

- Semiarid
- Mediterranean
- Humid subtropical
- Marine
- Humid continental
- Subarctic
- Tundra
- Ice cap
- Highland

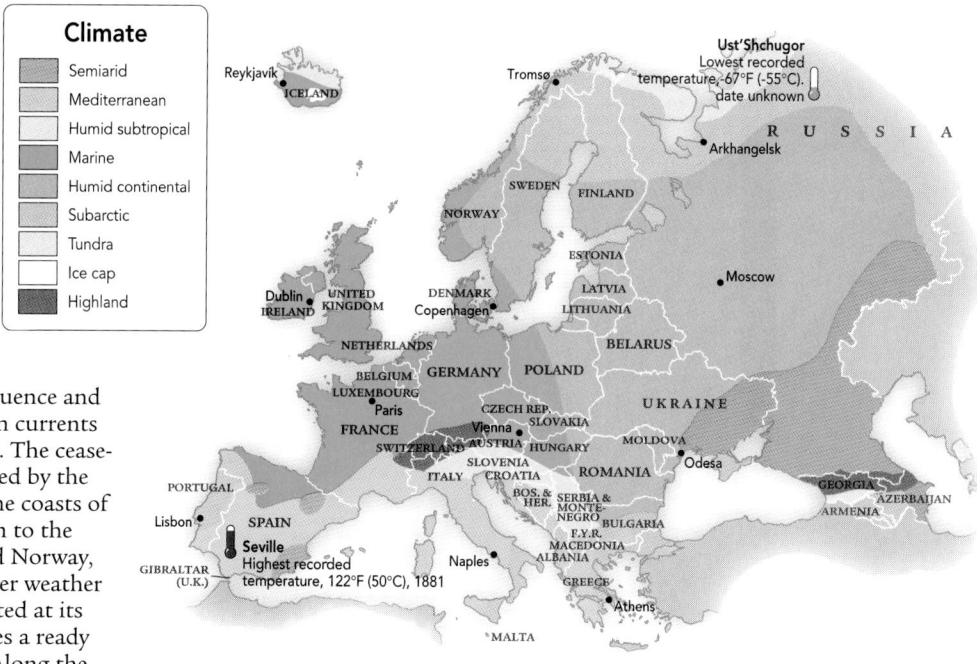

The far-reaching influence and effects of warm ocean currents cannot be overstated. The ceaseless torrent distributed by the Gulf Stream along the coasts of Western Europe, even to the shores of Iceland and Norway, produces much milder weather than would be expected at its latitudes and provides a ready source of moisture. Along the Mediterranean margin of Europe the typical weather—mild, wet winters and hot, dry summers—has been defined as a climate category that is now used worldwide.

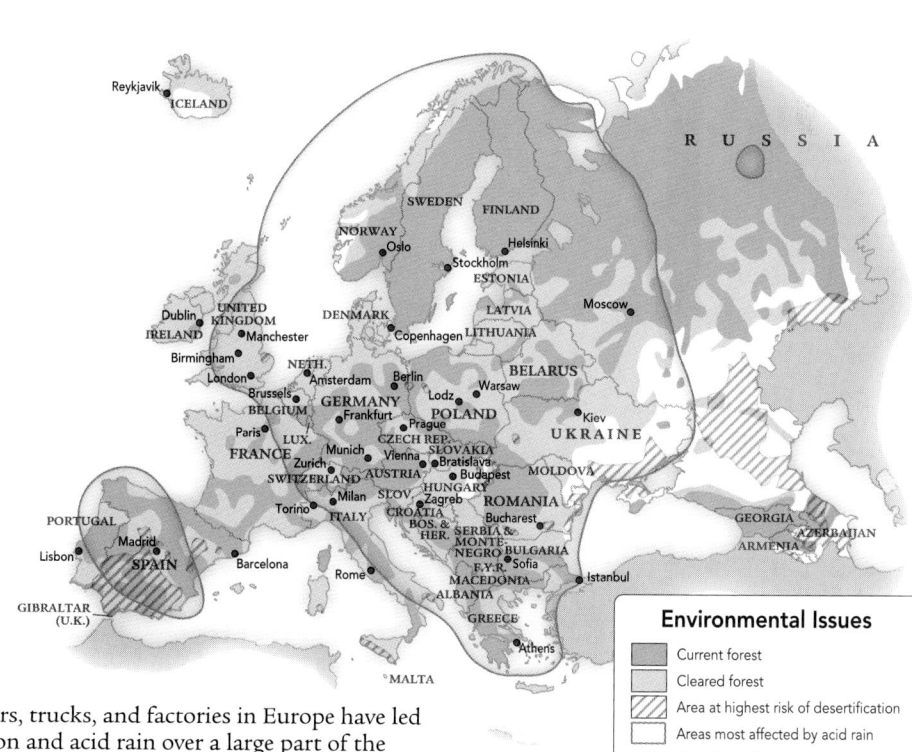

Environmental Issues

- Current forest
- Cleared forest
- Area at highest risk of desertification
- Areas most affected by acid rain
- Poor air quality*

*Cities exceeding at least one of the World Health Organization's (WHO) annual mean guidelines for air quality

Sources: Global Distribution of Original and Remaining Forests, UNEP-WCMC, 2002
World Soil Resources Map Index, USDA/NRCS, 2002
World Development Indicators, World Bank, 1999

Emissions from the many cars, trucks, and factories in Europe have led to problems with air pollution and acid rain over a large part of the continent. Land and water pollution (from fertilizers, pesticides, and industrial waste) is also widespread. Since the 1960's, the amount of forest area in Western and Central Europe has actually increased, but many forests (nearly 60%) are damaged due to acidification, pollution, drought, or fires. Overfishing—especially in the North Sea—is a serious problem for marine ecosystems.

United Kingdom

- ⊛ National Capital
- ★ Administrative Capital
- • Other Towns

0   25   50   75   100 mi
0   25   50   75   100   125   150 km

Lambert Conformal Conic Projection

Scotland

Cape Wrath, Thurso, Duncansby Head, Wick, Lewis, Stornoway, Lairg, Ullapool, Dornoch, Dornoch Firth, Fraserburgh, Kinnairds Head, Elgin, Inverness, Peterhead, Skye, Kyle of Lochalsh, Loch Ness, Aviemore, Aberdeen, Rhum, Mallaig, Ben Nevis 1343 m (4406 ft), Fort William, Pitlochry, Montrose, Eigg, Coll, Tiree, Mull, Oban, Dunsinane 308 m (1012 ft), Perth, Sidlaw Hills, Dundee, Bell Rock (Inchcape), Colonsay, Loch Katrine, Ochil Hills, Cupar, St. Andrews, Jura, Stirling, Kirkcaldy, Firth of Forth, Bass Rock, Islay, Loch Lomond, Dunfermline, Greenock, Clydebank, ★ Edinburgh, Lammermuir Hills, Paisley, Glasgow, Motherwell, Newtown St. Boswells, Berwick-upon-Tweed, Hamilton, Kilmarnock, Arran, Campbeltown, Ayr, SCOTLAND, Hawick, Merrick 843 m (2765 ft), Southern Uplands, Dumfries, Cheviot Hills, Stranraer, Carlisle

Northern Ireland / Ireland

Malin Head, Coleraine, Rathlin I., Antrim Mts., Londonderry, Sperrin Mts., Larne, Lough Foyle, Ballymena, Bangor, Donegal, Omagh, Lough Neagh, Belfast, Holywood, Sligo, Armagh, Portadown, Downpatrick, NORTHERN IRELAND, Newry, Mourne Mts., Slieve Donard 852 m (2796 ft), IRELAND, Carlingford, Douglas, ISLE OF MAN (U.K.)

England / Wales

Whitehaven, The Lake District, Scafell Pike 978 m (3210 ft), Cumbrian Mts., Penrith, Newcastle upon Tyne, North Shields, South Shields, Gateshead, Sunderland, Durham, Darlington, Middlesbrough, Kendal, THE PENNINES, Northallerton, Scarborough, Barrow-in-Furness, Lancaster, Harrogate, York, Kingston upon Hull, Fleetwood, Bradford, Grimsby, Blackpool, Preston, Bury, Burnley, Leeds, Wakefield, Scunthorpe, Southport, Blackburn, Bolton, Halifax, Huddersfield, Doncaster, Wigan, Rochdale, Oldham, Barnsley, Liverpool Bay, St. Helens, Salford, Manchester, Sheffield, Lincoln, Holyhead, Birkenhead, Liverpool, Warrington, Buxton, Chesterfield, Anglesey, Conwy, Chester, Stoke-on-Trent, Matlock, Boston, Caernarfon, Bangor, Mold, Crewe, Grantham, King's Lynn, Snowdon 1085 m (3560 ft), Lake Bala, Newcastle-under-Lyme, Derby, Nottingham, Norwich, Great Yarmouth, Lleyn Pen., Shrewsbury, Stafford, Telford, Lichfield, ENGLAND, Leicester, The Fens, Peterborough, Lowestoft, Cardigan Bay, WALES, Welshpool, Wolverhampton, Walsall, Ely, Thetford, Bury St. Edmunds, Aberystwyth, Black Country, Birmingham, Dudley, Coventry, Newmarket, Cambridge, Ipswich, Felixstowe, Llandrindod Wells, Kidderminster, Solihull, Kenilworth, Northampton, Lampeter, Worcester, Warwick, Stratford-upon-Avon, Bedford, Colchester, Fishguard, Hereford, Banbury, Luton, St. Albans, Chelmsford, St. David's, Carmarthen, Brecon Beacons, Merthyr Tydfil, Cheltenham, Tewkesbury, Gloucester, Oxford, Chiltern Hills, Southend-on-Sea, Milford Haven, Rhondda, Cotswold Hills, Swindon, Reading, London, Gillingham, Margate, North Foreland, Pembroke, Swansea, Caerleon, Newport, Bristol, Bath, North Downs, Canterbury, Port Talbot, Cardiff, Trowbridge, Maidstone, Folkestone, Dover, Calais, Bristol Channel, Glastonbury, Salisbury, Guildford, Tunbridge Wells, Channel Tunnel, Barnstaple, Exmoor Forest, Taunton, Winchester, South Downs, Lewes, Hastings, Tiverton, Yeovil, Southampton, Chichester, Hove, Brighton, Eastbourne, Dartmoor Forest, Dorchester, Bournemouth, Poole, Gosport, Portsmouth, Cowes, Isle of Wight, Spithead, Exeter, Launceston, Torbay, Lyme Bay, Newquay, Truro, St. Austell, Plymouth, Start Pt., Penzance, Land's End, Isles of Scilly, English Channel, Dieppe, FRANCE

Inset I (Shetland / Orkney):

Unst, Yell, Shetland Is., Mainland, Lerwick, Fair Isle, Westray, Sanday, Stronsay, Orkney Is., Kirkwall, Hoy, S. Ronaldsay — same scale as main map

Inset II (Channel Is.):

Alderney, Cherbourg, GUERNSEY (U.K.), FRANCE, Guernsey, St. Peter Port, Sark, JERSEY (U.K.), Channel Is., Jersey, St. Helier, Gulf of St. Malo — same scale as main map

Inset III (London area):

Dunstable, Stevenage, Braintree, Aylesbury, Hertford, Harlow, St. Albans, Chelmsford, Watford, High Wycombe, Brentwood, Slough, Basildon, London, Westminster, Thames, Gravesend, Windsor, Kingston upon Thames, Chatham, Camberley, Ewell, Epsom, Farnham, Reigate, Dorking, Tonbridge, Haslemere, Crawley

Atlantic Ocean, Outer Hebrides, The Minch, Inner Hebrides, Sea of the Hebrides, Barra, N. Uist, S. Uist, Portree, North Channel, Solway Firth, Firth of Clyde, Irish Sea, North Sea, Strait of Dover, Channel Tunnel

© MapQuest.com, Inc.

UNITED KINGDOM

United Kingdom

Capital: London
Area: 94,251 sq. mi.
244,174 sq. km.
Population: 59,912,000 (2002 est.)
Largest City: London, 7,172,036 (metro.)
Languages: English, Welsh, Scottish Gaelic
Major Religions: Anglican, Roman Catholic, Muslim, Presbyterian, Methodist, Sikh, Hindu, Jewish
Life Expectancy: 74 male, 80 female
Government: constitutional monarchy
Monetary Unit: pound
Industry: production machinery including machine tools, electric power equipment, automation equipment, railroad equipment, shipbuilding, aircraft, motor vehicles and parts, electronics and communications equipment, metals, chemicals, coal, petroleum, paper and paper products, food processing, textiles, clothing, and other consumer goods
Agriculture: wide variety of crops and livestock products
Minerals and Resources: coal, petroleum, natural gas, tin, limestone, iron ore, salt, clay, chalk, gypsum, lead, silica

The United Kingdom of Great Britain and Northern Ireland was originally established in 1801 as a constitutional monarchy and now comprises England, Wales, Scotland, and Northern Ireland. The British monarch serves as chief of state in the various countries which make up the British Commonwealth of Nations.

Britain was incorporated into the Roman empire after it was invaded by the Romans in 55 B.C. As Rome's power declined, the country was subject to many more invasions and migrations, mainly from Scandinavia and the continent. The territorial foundation of the 20th-century British Empire was laid during the 17th and 18th centuries with the expansion of its sea power and trade routes. The Commonwealth was created as an informal association of former colonies, most of them independent, which succeeded the empire.

The United Kingdom is one of the world's great trading powers and financial centers and it ranks fifth-largest in population of the European countries.

United Kingdom: Map Index

CHANNEL ISLANDS

Cities and Towns

St. Helier, *terr. capital* ....Inset II
St. Peter Port, *terr. capital* ....Inset II

Features

Alderney, *island* ....Inset II
Guernsey, *island* ....Inset II
Jersey, *island* ....Inset II
St. Malo, *gulf* ....Inset II
Sark, *island* ....Inset II

ENGLAND

Cities and Towns

Aylesbury ....Inset III
Banbury C3
Barnsley C3
Barnstaple B3
Barrow-in-Furness B2
Basildon ....Inset III
Bath C3
Bedford C3
Berwick-upon-Tweed C2
Birkenhead B3
Birmingham C3
Blackburn C3
Blackpool C3
Bolton C3
Boston C3
Bournemouth C4
Bradford C3
Braintree ....Inset III
Brentwood ....Inset III
Brighton C4
Bristol C3
Burnley C3
Bury C3
Bury St. Edmunds D3
Buxton C3
Camberley ....Inset III
Cambridge D3
Canterbury D3
Carlisle C2
Chatham ....Inset III
Chelmsford ....D3, Inset III
Cheltenham C3
Chester C3
Chesterfield C3
Chichester C4
Colchester D3
Coventry C3
Cowes C4
Crawley ....Inset III
Crewe C3
Darlington C2
Derby C3
Doncaster C3
Dorchester C4
Dorking ....Inset III
Dover D3
Dudley C3
Dunstable ....Inset III
Durham C2

Eastbourne D4
Ely D3
Epsom ....Inset III
Ewell ....Inset III
Exeter B4
Farnham ....Inset III
Felixstowe D3
Fleetwood C3
Folkestone D3
Gateshead C2
Gillingham D3
Glastonbury C3
Gloucester C3
Gosport C4
Grantham C3
Gravesend ....Inset III
Great Yarmouth D3
Grimsby C3
Guildford C3
Halifax C3
Harlow ....Inset III
Harrogate C3
Haslemere ....Inset III
Hastings D4
Hereford C3
Hertford ....Inset III
High Wycombe ....Inset III
Hove C4
Huddersfield C3
Ipswich D3
Kendal C2
Kenilworth C3
Kidderminster C3
King's Lynn D3
Kingston upon Hull C3
Kingston upon
Thames ....Inset III
Lancaster C2
Launceston B4
Leeds C3
Leicester C3
Lewes D4
Lichfield C3
Lincoln C3
Liverpool C3
London,
national capital ..C3, Inset III
Lowestoft D3
Luton C3
Maidstone D3
Manchester C3
Margate D3
Matlock C3
Middlesbrough C2
Newcastle-under-Lyme C3
Newcastle upon Tyne C2
Newmarket D3
Newquay B4
Northallerton C2
Northampton C3
North Shields C2
Norwich D3
Nottingham C3
Oldham C3
Oxford C3
Penrith C2
Penzance B4
Peterborough C3
Plymouth B4
Poole C4
Portsmouth C4
Preston C3
Reading C3
Reigate ....Inset III
Rochdale C3
Rotherham C3

St. Albans ....C3, Inset III
St. Austell B4
St. Helens C3
Salford C3
Salisbury C3
Scarborough C2
Scunthorpe C3
Sheffield C3
Shrewsbury C3
Slough ....Inset III
Solihull C3
Southampton C4
Southend-on-Sea D3
Southport C3
South Shields C2
Stafford C3
Stevenage ....Inset III
Stoke-on-Trent C3
Stratford-upon-Avon C3
Sunderland C2
Swindon C3
Taunton B3
Telford C3
Tewkesbury C3
Thetford D3
Tiverton B4
Tonbridge ....Inset III
Torbay B4
Trowbridge C3
Truro B4
Tunbridge Wells D3
Wakefield C3
Walsall C3
Warrington C3
Warwick C3
Watford ....Inset III
Westminster ....Inset III
Whitehaven B2
Wigan C3
Winchester C3
Windsor ....Inset III
Wolverhampton C3
Worcester C3
Yeovil C4
York C3

Other Features

Avon, *river* C3
Black Country, *region* C3
Bristol, *channel* B3
Channel, *tunnel* D3
Cheviot, *hills* C2
Chiltern, *hills* C3
Cotswold, *hills* C3
Cumbrian, *mts.* B2
Dartmoor Forest, *plateau* ...B4
Dee, *river* B3
Dover, *strait* D4
English, *channel* C4
Exmoor Forest, *plateau* B3
Fens, *region* D3
Great Ouse, *river* D3
Humber, *estuary* D3
Irish, *sea* B3
Lake, *district* B2
Land's End,
promontory B4
Liverpool, *bay* B3
Lyme, *bay* C4
Mersey, *river* C3
North, *sea* D2
North Downs, *hills* C3
North Foreland,
promontory D3
Ouse, *river* C2

Pennines, *mts.* C2
Scafell Pike, *mt.* B2
Scilly, *islands* A4
Severn, *river* C3
South Downs, *hills* C3
Spithead, *channel* C4
Start, *point* B4
Tees, *river* C2
Thames, *river* ....C3, Inset III
Trent, *river* C3
Tweed, *river* C2
Tyne, *river* C2
Wash, *bay* D3
Wight, *island* C4
Wye, *river* C3
Yare, *river* D3

ISLE OF MAN

City

Douglas, *terr. capital* B2

NORTHERN IRELAND

Cities and Towns

Armagh A2
Ballymena A2
Bangor B2
Belfast, *admin. capital* B2
Coleraine A2
Downpatrick B2
Holywood B2
Larne B2
Londonderry A2
Newry A2
Omagh A2
Portadown A2

Other Features

Antrim, *mts.* A2
Bann, *river* A2
Erne, *river* A2
Foyle, *lake* A2
Foyle, *river* A2
Irish, *sea* B3
Lough Erne, *lake* A2
Mourne, *mts.* A2
Neagh, *lake* A2
North, *channel* A2
Rathlin, *island* A2
Slieve Donard, *mt.* B2
Sperrin, *mts.* A2
Upper Lough Erne, *lake* A2

SCOTLAND

Cities and Towns

Aberdeen C1
Aviemore B1
Ayr B2
Campbeltown B2
Clydebank B2
Cupar B2
Dornoch B1
Dumfries B2
Dundee C2
Dunfermline B2

Edinburgh, *admin. capital* B2
Elgin B1
Fort William B2
Fraserburgh C1
Glasgow B2
Greenock B2
Hamilton B2
Hawick C2
Inverness B1
Kilmarnock B2
Kirkcaldy B2
Kirkwall ....Inset I
Kyle of Lochalsh B1
Lairg B1
Lerwick ....Inset I
Mallaig B1
Montrose C2
Motherwell B2
Newtown St. Boswells.........C2
Oban B2
Paisley B2
Perth B2
Peterhead C1
Pitlochry B2
Portree A1
St. Andrews C2
Stirling B2
Stornoway A1
Stranraer B2
Thurso B1
Ullapool B1
Wick B1

Other Features

Arran, *island* B2
Barra, *island* A2
Bass Rock, *islet* C2
Bell Rock (Inchcape),
reef C2
Ben Nevis, *mt.* B2
Bute, *island* B2
Cheviot, *hills* C2
Clyde, *estuary* B2
Clyde, *river* B2
Coll, *island* A2
Colonsay, *island* A2
Dee, *river* C1
Dornoch, *estuary* B1
Duncansby, *cape* B1
Dunsinane, *mt.* B2
Eigg, *island* A2
Fair, *island* ....Inset I
Forth, *estuary* C2
Forth, *river* B2
Grampian, *mts.* B2
Hebrides, *sea* A2
Hoy, *island* ....Inset I
Inner Hebrides, *islands* A2
Islay, *island* A2
Jura, *island* A2
Katrine, *lake* B2
Kinnairds, *cape* C1
Lammermuir, *hills* C2
Lewis, *island* A1
Linnhe, *lake* B2
Lomond, *lake* B2
Lorne, *estuary* A2
Mainland, *island*............Inset I
Merrick, *mt.* B2
Minch, *strait* B1
Moray, *estuary*...................B1
Mull, *island* A2
Ness, *lake* B1
North Uist, *island* A1
Ochil, *hills* B2

Orkney, *islands*...............Inset I
Outer Hebrides, *islands* A1
Rhum, *island* A1
Sanday, *island* ....Inset I
Shetland, *islands* ....Inset I
Sidlaw, *hills* B2
Skye, *island* A1
Solway, *estuary* B2
Southern Uplands, *mts.* B2
South Ronaldsay,
island ....Inset I
South Uist, *island* A1
Spey, *river* B1
Stronsay, *island* ....Inset I
Tay, *estuary* C2
Tay, *lake* B2
Tay, *river* B2
Tiree, *island* A2
Tweed, *river* C2
Unst, *island* ....Inset I
Westray, *island* ....Inset I
Wrath, *cape*......................B1
Yell, *island* ....Inset I

WALES

Cities and Towns

Aberystwyn B3
Bangor B3
Caerleon C3
Caernarfon B3
Cardiff, *admin. capital* B3
Carmarthen B3
Conwy B3
Fishguard B3
Holyhead B3
Lampeter B3
Llandrindod Wells B3
Merthyr Tydfil B3
Milford Haven B3
Mold B3
Newport C3
Pembroke B3
Port Talbot B3
Rhondda B3
St. David's B3
Swansea B3
Welshpool B3

Other Features

Anglesey, *island* B3
Bala, *lake* B3
Brecon Beacons, *mts.* B3
Bristol, *channel* B3
Cambrian, *mts.* B3
Cardigan, *bay* B3
Dee, *river* B3
Lleyn, *peninsula* B3
Menai, *strait* B3
Snowdon, *mt.* B3
Teifi, *river* B3
Tywi, *river* B3
Usk, *river* C3
Wye, *river* C3

Scotland

Administrative Capital (★)
Administrative Centre (○)
Motorways
Major Roads

0 25 50 mi
0 25 50 75 km

© MapQuest.com, Inc.

NUMBERED DISTRICTS
1 INVERCLYDE
2 WEST DUNBARTONSHIRE
3 RENFREWSHIRE
4 EAST RENFREWSHIRE
5 GLASGOW CITY
6 EAST DUNBARTONSHIRE
7 NORTH LANARKSHIRE
8 FALKIRK
9 CLACKMANNANSHIRE
10 WEST LOTHIAN
11 CITY OF EDINBURGH
12 MIDLOTHIAN
13 DUNDEE CITY

Scotland

Capital:	Edinburgh
Area:	30,420 sq. mi.
	78,789 sq. km.
Population:	5,062,011 (2001 Census)
Largest City:	Glasgow, 629,501
Highest Point:	Ben Nevis,
	4,409 ft.
	1,344 m.

Scotland:
Map Index

Unitary Authorities
(2001 census pop.)

Aberdeen City,
212,125 . . . . N4
Aberdeenshire,
226,871 . . . . L3
Angus, 108,400 . . . . K5
Argyll and Bute, 91,306 . . F6
Clackmannanshire,
48,077 . . . . J6

Dumfries and
Galloway, 147,765 . . . H9
Dundee City,
145,663 . . . . L5
East Ayrshire, 120,235 . . H8
East Dunbartonshire,
108,243 . . . . H7
East Lothian, 90,088 . . . M6
East Renfrewshire,
89,311 . . . . H7
Edinburgh, City of,
448,624 . . . . K7
Eilean Siar, 26,502 . . . . . C2
Falkirk, 145,191 . . . . J7

Fife, 349,429 . . . . L6
Glasgow City,
577,869 . . . . H7
Highland, 208,914 . . . . . G2
Inverclyde, 84,203 . . . . . G7
Midlothian, 80,941 . . . . . K7
Moray, 86,940 . . . . K4
North Ayrshire, 135,817 . . F7
North Lanarkshire,
321,067 . . . . J7
Orkney Islands,
19,245 . . . . J1, L2
Perth and Kinross,
134,949 . . . . H5

Renfrewshire, 172,867 . . G7
Scottish Borders,
106,764 . . . . K8
Shetland Islands,
21,988 . . . . P3
South Ayrshire,
112,097 . . . . F8
South Lanarkshire,
302,216 . . . . J7
Stirling, 86,212 . . . . H6
West Dunbartonshire,
93,378 . . . . G7
West Lothian, 158,714 . . J7

Cities and Towns

Aberchirder, 1,149 . . . . . L3
Aberdeen, 184,788 . . . . M4
Aberfeldy, 1,895 . . . . J5
Aberfoyle, 576 . . . . H6
Abington J8
Aboyne, 2,202 . . . . L4
Achallader G5
Acharn E5
Achavanich K2
Achfary G2
Achiltibuie F2
Achmore C2

Achnacroish E5
Achnasheen F3
Aikers L1, M2
Airdrie, 36,326 . . . . . .J7
Aith (Orkney Islands) . .L2
Aith (Shetland Islands) . .P2
Aitnoch J4
Alford, 1,925 . . . . . .L4
Allanton, 1,251 . . . . .M7
Alloa, 18,989 . . . . . .J6
Alness, 5,186 . . . . . .H3
Altnaharra H2
Alva, 5,181 . . . . . . .J6
Alves K3
Alvie J4
Alyth, 2,301 . . . . . .K5
Annan, 8,326 . . . . . .K9
Annbank, 854 . . . . . .H8
Anstruther, 3,442 . . . .L6
Arbroath, 22,785 . . . .L5
Ardbeg D7
Ardeonaig H6
Ardgay H3
Ardlussa E6
Arminish E7
Ardno G6
Ardrishaig, 1,283 . . . .F7
Ardrossan, 10,952 . . . .G7
Ardvourlie C2
Arileod C5
Arnisdale E4
Arnprior H6
Arrochar G6
Ashkirk L8
Auchallater K5
Auchencairn J9
Auchmull L5
Auchnagatt M4
Auchterarder, 3,945 . . .J6
Auchtermuchty, 2,010 . .K6
Auchtertyre J4
Aviemore, 2,397 . . . . .J4
Ayr, 46,431 . . . . . . .G8
Badenscoth M4
Badenyon K4
Balallan C2
Balfour M2
Balintore, 1,087 . . . .J3
Balivanich B4
Ballachulish, 615 . . . .F5
Ballantrae F8
Ballater, 1,446 . . . . .K4
Ballinluig J5
Ballyhaugh C5
Balmaha J6
Balmedie, 1,653 . . . . .M4
Balnacra F4
Balnaguard J5
Baltasound Q1
Balvicar E6
Banchory, 6,034 . . . . .M4
Banff, 3,991 . . . . . .M3
Bankend K9
Bankfoot, 1,136 . . . . .K6
Barcaldine F5
Bargrennan G8
Barr G8
Barrapoll C6
Barrhead, 17,244 . . . .H7
Barrhill G8
Barvas C2
Bayble D2
Bayhead B3
Beattock K8
Beauly, 1,164 . . . . . .H4
Beeswing J9
Bellheiglash K4
Belmont Q1
Benmore G6
Bentpath K2
Berriedale K2
Bettyhill H1
Big Carlae H8
Biggar, 2,098 . . . . . .J7
Bixter P2
Blackacre K8
Blackburn M4
Blackford, 556 . . . . .J6
Blackwaterfoot F8
Blaich F5
Blair Atholl J5
Blairgowrie, 7,965 . . .K5
Blairnamarrow K4
Boarhills L6
Bogend G7
Bogniebrae L4
Bolton L7
Bonar Bridge H3
Bo'ness, 13,961 . . . . .J6
Boreland K8
Bow M2
Bowmore, 862 . . . . . .D7
Brae, 660 . . . . .Q2
Braedownie K5
Braemar K5
Braeswick N1
Breascelete C2
Brechin, 7,199 . . . . .L5
Brenish B2
Bridgend, 765 . . . . . .D7
Bridge of Balgie H5
Bridge of Cally K5
Bridge of Don M4
Bridge of Dye L5
Bridge of Forss J1
Bridge of Orchy G6
Brig O'Turk H6
Brinyan M1
Broadford E4
Brora, 1,140 . . . . . .J2
Broughtown N1
Brove B3
Bualintur D4
Buchanty J6
Buckhaven, 16,391 . . . .L6
Buckie, 8,059 . . . . . .L3
Bunessan D6
Burg D5
Burghead, 1,640 . . . . .K3
Burnmouth M7
Burravoe Q2
Burwick L1, M2
Cabrach L4
Cairnbaan F6
Cairnryan F9
Calfsound N1
Callander, 2,754 . . . .H6

Calvine J5
Campbeltown, 5,144 . . .E8
Campmachmore M4
Caoles C5
Carlops K7
Carloway C2
Carnoustie, 10,561 . . .L5
Carrbridge J4
Carsphairn H8
Cashlie H5
Castle Douglas, 3,671 . .J9
Castle Lachlan F6
Castletown, 798 . . . . .K1
Catterline M5
Caulkerbush J9
Chapelhill J6
Chapelknowe K8
Charlestown of Aberlour K4
Clachan F6
Cladich F6
Claigan C4
Claonaig F7
Clarencefield K8
Clashmore H3
Cleadale D5
Cleat L1, M2
Cluanie F4
Clydebank, 29,858 . . . .H7
Coatbridge, 41,170 . . .J7
Cockburnspath M7
Col (Coll), 1,087 . . . .D2
Coldstream, 1,813 . . . .M7
Coldwells M4
Collafirth P2
Colliston N4
Colpy L4
Colvend J9
Connel F6
Contin G3
Corgarff K4
Cornhill L3
Corran F5
Corsock J8
Cortachy L5
Coulter J7
Coupar Angus, 2,190 . . .K5
Cove E3
Cowie, 2,387 . . . . . .J6
Coylton, 2,409 . . . . .H8
Coylumbridge J4
Craigellachie K4
Crail, 1,695 . . . . . .L6
Cranshaws M7
Crawford J8
Crawfordjohn J8
Creagorry B4
Creetown, 685 . . . . . .H9
Crianlarich G6
Crieff, 6,579 . . . . . .J6
Croggan E6
Cromarty, 719 . . . . . .H3
Cromdale J4
Cromra H5
Crosslee C2
Crulivig C2
Culkein F2
Cullivoe Q1
Culloch J6
Culnacraig F3
Culswick P2
Cumbernauld, 49,664 . . .J7
Cumnock, 9,358 . . . . .H8
Cunningsburgh Q3
Cupar, 8,506 . . . . . .L6
Currie K7
Dailly, 908 . . . . . . .G8
Dairsie L6
Dalbeattie, 4,289 . . . .J9
Dalblair H8
Daliburgh B4
Dalkeith, 11,566 . . . .K7
Dalmally G6
Dalmellington
  (Dalmellington and
  Burnton), 1,407 . . . .H8
Dalnaspidal Lodge H5
Dalnavie H3
Dalry, 5,398 . . . . . .G7
Dalrymple, 1,281 . . . .G8
Dalswinton J8
Dalwhinnie H5
Daviot H4
Denholm, 608 . . . . . .L8
Denmore M4
Denny, 9,797 . . . . . .J6
Dervaig D5
Dingwall, 5,026 . . . . .H3
Dinnet L4
Dodburn L8
Dollar, 2,877 . . . . . .J6
Dolphinton K7
Dornoch, 1,206 . . . . .H3
Dounby M2
Doune, 1,635 . . . . . .H6
Dowally J5
Drimsallie F5
Drumbeg F2
Drummore F9
Drumnadrochit, 813 . . .H4
Drumphail G8
Drymen, 681 . . . . . . .H6
Duchally G2
Dufftown, 1,454 . . . . .K4
Dulnain Bridge J4
Dumbarton, 20,527 . . . .G7
Dumfries, 31,146 . . . .J8
Dunbar, 6,354 . . . . . .M7
Dunbeath K2
Dunblane, 7,911 . . . . .J6
Dundee, 154,674 . . . . .L6
Dunderggan G4
Dundonnell F3
Dunecht M4
Dunfermline, 39,229 . . .K6
Dunoon, 8,251 . . . . . .G7
Dunragit G9
Duns, 2,594 . . . . . . .M7
Dunscore J8
Dunure G8
Durham J8
Durisdeer J8
Durness G1
Dyce, 5,661 . . . . . . .M4
Dykends K5
Eaglesfield, 616 . . . .K8

Eaglesham, 3,127 . . . .H7
Earlsferry L6
East Crachy H4
Easter Balmoral K4
East Kilbride, 73,796 . .H7
East Linton, 1,744 . . .L7
Ecclaw M7
Eccles M7
Eckford M7
Edinbane D4
Edinburgh, 430,082 . . .K7
Edzell, 783 . . . . . . .L5
Elgin, 20,829 . . . . . .K3
Elgol D4
Ellemford M7
Ellon, 8,754 . . . . . .M4
Elphin F2
Elsrickle K8
Eskdalemuir K8
Etteridge H5
Eyemouth, 3,383 . . . . .M7
Fairlie, 1,510 . . . . .G7
Fearnmore E3
Feolin Ferry D7
Ferryden, 929 . . . . . .M5
Fiag Lodge G2
Findhorn, 885 . . . . . .J3
Finstown M2
Fintry H6
Fladdabister Q2
Fochabers, 1,499 . . . .K3
Ford F6
Forfar, 13,206 . . . . .L5
Forres, 8,967 . . . . . .J3
Forsinard J2
Fort Augustus, 508 . . .G4
Forteviot K6
Fort George H3
Fortingall H5
Fortrose (Fortrose and
  Rosemarkie), 1,174 . .H3
Fort William, 9,908 . . .F5
Fountainhall L7
Fowlis Wester J6
Fraserburgh, 12,454 . . .N3
Freswick K1
Friockheim, 820 . . . . .L5
Funzie R1
Furnace F6
Fyvie M4
Gaick Lodge H5
Gairloch E3
Gairlochy F5
Galashiels, 14,361 . . .L7
Garderhouse P2
Garelochhead, 1,265 . . .G6
Garlogie M4
Garrow J5
Gartmore H6
Garve G3
Gatehouse of Fleet, 892 H9
Girlsta Q2
Girvan, 6,992 . . . . . .G8
Glamis L5
Glasgow, 629,501 . . . .H7
Glencoe F5
Glengolly J1
Glenkerry K8
Glenrothes, 38,679 . . .K6
Golspie, 1,404 . . . . .J3
Gordon L7
Grantown-on-Spey,
  2,166 . . . . .J4
Greenlaw, 579 . . . . . .M7
Greenock, 45,467 . . . .G7
Gualachulain F5
Gullane, 2,172 . . . . .L6
Gutcher Q1
Hackland M2
Haddington, 8,851 . . . .L7
Hamilton, 48,546 . . . .J7
Hamnavoe P2
Haroldswick Q1
Harris D5
Hawick, 14,573 . . . . .L8
Helensburgh, 14,626 . . .G7
Helmsdale J2
Heriot L7
Hermitage L8
Hillswick P2
Hobkirk L8
Holland N2
Hopeman, 1,624 . . . . .K3
Houbie Q1
Humbie L7
Huntly, 4,412 . . . . . .L4
Hurliness K1, M2
Hushinish B3
Hynish C6
Inchgrundle L5
Inchnadamph G2
Inchture, 735 . . . . . .K6
Innellan, 1,188 . . . . .F7
Innerleithen, 2,586 . . .K7
Insch, 1,523 . . . . . .L4
Insh J4
Inverallochy N3
Inveran H3
Inveraray F6
Inverarnan G6
Inverbervie, 2,094 . . .M5
Invergarry G4
Invergeldie H6
Invergordon, 3,890 . . .H3
Inverkeilor L5
Inverkeithing, 5,412 . .K6
Inverkip, 1,598 . . . . .G7
Inverlochlarig G6
Invermoriston G4
Inverness, 40,949 . . . .H4
Inveruglas G6
Inverurie, 10,882 . . . .M4
Irvine, 33,090 . . . . .G7
Isle of Whithorn H9
Isleornsay E4
Jedburgh, 4,090 . . . . .L8
John O'Groats K1, M2
Kames F7
Keillmore E7
Keiss K1
Keith, 4,491 . . . . . .L3
Kellas (Grampian) K3
Kellas (Tayside) L5
Kelso, 5,116 . . . . . .M7
Kenknock H6
Kennacraig F7
Kensaleyre D4

Kilbride B4
Kilchattan F7
Kilchenzie E8
Kilchrenan F6
Kildary (Milton and
  Kildary), 604 . . . . .H3
Kildavanan F7
Kildonan F8
Kilfinan F7
Killean E7
Killearn, 1,781 . . . . .H6
Killichonan G5
Killiecrankie J5
Killin, 666 . . . . . . .H6
Kilmaluag D3
Kilmarnock, 43,588 . . .H7
Kilmory (Highland) . . .D4
Kilmory (North Ayrshire) F8
Kilninver E6
Kilrenny L6
Kilsyth, 9,816 . . . . .H7
Kilwinning, 15,908 . . .G7
Kinbrace J2
Kinbuck J6
Kingarth F7
Kingsbarns L6
Kingshouse H6
Kingussie, 1,410 . . . .H4
Kinloch D4
Kinloch Hourn F4
Kinloch Rannoch H5
Kinlochbervie F2
Kinlochewe F3
Kinlochleven, 897 . . . .G5
Kinross, 4,681 . . . . .K6
Kintocher L4
Kintore, 1,696 . . . . .M4
Kirbister M2
Kirkabister Q2
Kirkcaldy, 46,912 . . . .K6
Kirkcolm F9
Kirkconnel, 2,074 . . . .J8
Kirkcudbright, 3,447 . .H9
Kirkinner H9
Kirkintilloch, 20,281 . .H7
Kirkoswald G8
Kirkton L8
Kirkwall, 6,206 . . . . .M2
Kirriemuir, 5,963 . . . .L5
Kyleakin E4
Kyle of Lochalsh, 739 . .E4
Kylerhea E4
Kylestrome F2
Ladybank, 1,487 . . . . .K6
Laggan H4
Laide E3
Lairg H2
Lamington J7
Lamlash, 1,010 . . . . .F7
Lanark, 8,253 . . . . . .J7
Langholm, 2,311 . . . . .L8
Langskaill M1
Largs, 11,241 . . . . . .G7
Latheron K2
Lauder, 1,081 . . . . . .L7
Laurencekirk, 1,808 . . .M5
Lawers H5
Laxford Bridge F2
Leadhills J8
Ledmore Junction G2
Leitholm M7
Lemreway D2
Lendalfoot G8
Lerwick, 8,685 . . . . .Q2
Lesmahagow, 3,685 . . . .J7
Leuchars, 2,518 . . . . .L6
Leven, 8,051 . . . . . .L6
Levenwick Q3
Lhanbryde, 1,845 . . . .K3
Linlithgow, 13,370 . . .J7
Lionel D2
Livingston, 50,826 . . .J7
Loanhead, 6,384 . . . . .K7
Lochans G9
Lochawe F6
Lochbuie E6
Lochcarron F4
Lochearnhead H6
Lochgelly, 6,749 . . . .K6
Lochgilphead, 2,326 . . .F6
Lochgoilhead G6
Lochinver F2
Lochside M5
Lochton M4
Lockerbie, 4,009 . . . .K8
Logie Coldstone L4
Longyester L7
Lossiemouth, 6,803 . . .K3
Lumsden L4
Lunan M5
Luncarty, 1,265 . . . . .K6
Luss G6
Lusta C3
Lybster K2
Lyness M2
Macduff, 3,767 . . . . .M3
Machrihanish E8
Mallaig, 797 . . . . . .D5
Manish C3
Marwick L1
Marykirk L5
Mauchline, 4,105 . . . .H7
Maud, 630 . . . . .M3
Maybole, 4,552 . . . . .G8
Melrose, 1,656 . . . . .L7
Melvaig E3
Melvich J1
Memus L5
Methlick M4
Mid Yell Q1
Middleyard H7
Millport, 1,253 . . . . .G7
Milovaig C4
Milton (Highland) G3
Milton (Tayside) J5
Minard F6
Mintlaw, 2,647 . . . . .N3
Mochrum G9
Monachylemore H6
Moniaive J8
Monifieth L6
Montrose, 10,845 . . . .M5
Morebattle M8
Morenish H6
Mossat L4
Mossbank Q2

Motherwell, 30,311 . . .J7
Mountbenger K7
Muir J5
Muirdrum L5
Muirkirk, 1,630 . . . . .H7
Muir of Ord, 1,812 . . .H3
Muthill, 675 . . . . . .J6
Nairn, 8,418 . . . . . .J3
Nethy Bridge J4
Newburgh K6
Newcastleton, 772 . . . .L8
New Cumnock, 3,165 . . .H8
New Deer, 519 . . . . . .M3
New Galloway H6
Newport-on-Tay, 4,214 . .L6
Newton K8
Newtonferry B3
Newtonhill, 2,940 . . . .M4
Newtonmore, 982 . . . . .H4
Newton Stewart, 3,573 . .H9
Newtown St. Boswells,
  1,199 . . . . .M7
Nigg J3
North Berwick, 6,223 . .L6
North Roe Q1
North Tolsta D2
Northton B3
Northwall N1
Norwick Q1
Oakley, 4,123 . . . . . .J6
Oban, 8,120 . . . . . . .F6
Oldmeldrum, 2,003 . . . .M4
Orphir M2
Oskamull D6
Otter Ferry F7
Paisley, 74,170 . . . . .H7
Park F6
Parton H9
Patna, 2,179 . . . . . .H8
Paxton M7
Peebles, 8,065 . . . . .K7
Penicuik, 14,759 . . . .K7
Pennan M3
Perth, 43,450 . . . . . .K6
Peterculter M4
Peterhead, 17,947 . . . .N3
Pierowall M1
Pinwherry G8
Pirnmill F7
Pitlochry, 2,564 . . . .J5
Pitmedden, 1,137 . . . .M4
Poolewe E3
Portavadie F7
Port Ellen, 819 . . . . .D7
Port Glasgow, 16,617 . .G7
Portknockie, 1,217 . . .L3
Port Logan G9
Portmahomack J3
Portnaguran D2
Portnahaven C7
Portnalong D4
Port of Ness D1
Portpatrick, 585 . . . .F9
Portree, 1,917 . . . . .D4
Portsoy, 1,734 . . . . .L3
Portuairk D5
Port William G9
Preston M7
Prestonpans, 7,153 . . .L7
Prestwick, 13,705 . . . .G8
Quarff Q2
Rackwick L2
Ranish D2
Rapness M1
Rathen N3
Rattray K5
Reawick P2
Redpoint E3
Reiff F2
Reiss K1
Rhynie L4
Rigg K9
Rigside, 741 . . . . . .J7
Rodel C3
Rodono K8
Rogart H3
Rosehall G3
Rosehearty, 1,194 . . . .M3
Rothes, 1,156 . . . . . .K3
Rothesay, 5,017 . . . . .F7
Rothiesholm N1
St. Abb's M7
St. Andrews, 14,209 . . .L6
St. Fergus N3
St. Margaret's Hope . . .M2
St. Mary's M2
Salen (Highland) E5
Salen (Strathclyde) . . .E6
Saltcoats, 11,260 . . . .G7
Sanaigmore D7
Sandgarth M2
Sandness P2
Sandwick Q3
Sanquhar, 2,028 . . . . .J8
Scalasaig D6
Scalloway, 812 . . . . .Q2
Scar N1
Scardroy G3
Scoraig F2
Scourie F2
Scousburgh P3
Scrabster J1
Seilebost C3
Selkirk, 5,742 . . . . .K7
Shandon G6
Sheigra F1
Shenval K4
Shiel Bridge F4
Shieldaig E3
Shinness H2
Shulishader D2
Sinclairston H8
Skaill N2
Skelmorlie, 1,828 . . . .G7
Skelwick M1
Skerray H1
Skigersta D2
Sligachan D4
Sollas B3
Sorisdale D5
Southend E8
Soutra Mains L7
Spean Bridge G5
Spittal of Glenshee . . .K5
Sprouston M7
Staffin D3

Stenness P2
Stewarton, 6,582 . . . .H7
Stilligarry B4
Stirling, 32,673 . . . .J6
Stonehaven, 9,577 . . . .M5
Stornoway D2
Stow, 548 . . . . .L7
Straad F7
Strachan L4
Straiton G8
Straloch J5
Stranraer, 10,851 . . . .F9
Strathan H1
Strathcarron F4
Strathcoil E6
Strathdon K4
Strath Kanaird F3
Strathy J1
Strathyre H6
Strichen, 879 . . . . . .M3
Stromeferry E4
Stromness, 1,609 . . . .L2
Strontian E5
Sumburgh Q3
Symbister Q2
Syre H2
Tain, 3,511 . . . . . . .H3
Talladale E3
Tarbert (Western Isles) .C3
Tarbert (Strathclyde) . .E7
Tarbert (Strathclyde) . .F7
Tarbet G6
Tarland, 520 . . . . . .L4
Tarskavaig E4
Tayinloan E7
Tayport, 3,847 . . . . .L6
The Braes D4
Thornhill J8
Thrumster K2
Thurso, 7,737 . . . . . .K1
Tigharry A3
Timsgarry B2
Tobermory, 980 . . . . .D5
Toft Q2
Toll of Birness N4
Tomatin J4
Tomintoul K4
Tongland H9
Tongue H2
Tore H3
Torphins, 1,094 . . . . .L4
Torrin E4
Toscaig E4
Toward F7
Town Yetholm M7
Tranent, 8,892 . . . . .L7
Troon, 14,766 . . . . . .G7
Trumpan C3
Turnberry G8
Turriff, 4,454 . . . . .M3
Twatt M1
Tweedsmuir K8
Ullapool, 1,308 . . . . .F3
Ulsta Q1
Veness N1
Vidlin Q2
Voe Q2
Walls P2
Wasbister M1
Watten K2
West Calder, 2,818 . . .J7
Westerdale K2
Westhill, 9,498 . . . . .M4
West Kilbride, 4,393 . .G7
West Linton, 1,459 . . .K7
Westruther L7
Whaness M1
Whitburn, 10,391 . . . .J7
Whitebridge H4
Whitehall N1
Whitehouse F7
Whitekirk L6
Whiterashes M4
Whithorn, 867 . . . . . .H9
Whiting Bay F8
Wick, 7,333 . . . . . . .K2
Wigtown, 987 . . . . . .H9
Wilkhaven J3

Other Features

Affric, river F4
Ailsa Craig, island . . .F8
An Daimh, lake G5
An Ruathair, lake J2
An Teallach, hill F3
Arkaig, lake F4
Arran, island F7
Assynt, lake F2
Assynt-Coigach N.P. . . .F2
Atholl, forest H5
Atlantic, ocean B6
Auskerry, island N2
Awe, lake F6
Barra, island A5
Beinn Alligin, hill . . .E3

Beinn Dearg, hill G3
Beinn Dearg, hill J5
Beinn Dhorain, hill . . .J2
Beinn Eighe, hill F3
Beinn Mhor, hill B4
Beinn Mhor, hill C3
Ben Aden, hill F4
Ben Alder, hill H5
Ben Hope, hill G2
Ben Klibreck, hill H2
Ben Macdhui, hill J4
Ben Nevis, hill F5
Ben Nevis and
  Glen Coe N.P. G5
Benbecula, island B4
Berneray, island B3
Bö, lake E6
Bora, lake H2
Boreray, island B3
Braeriach, hill J4
Bressay, island Q2
Broad, bay D2
Broom, lake G3
Bruichladic, lake G4
Burray, island M2
Bute, island F7
Cairn Toul, hill J4
Calder, lake J2
Canna, island C4
Carn Ban, hill H4
Carron, river J7
Cluanie, lake F4
Coll, island C5
Colonsay, island D6
Creag Meagaidh, hill . .G5
Cuillin, hills D4
Doon, lake H8
Dornoch, estuary J3
Duich, lake F4
Duntelchaig, lake H4
Eday, island N1
Eigg, island D5
Eil, lake F5
Ericht, lake H5
Eriskay, island B4
Etive, lake F6
Fannich, lake F3
Fetlar, island R1
Findhorn, river J4
Fionn, lake E3
Forth, estuary L6
Flannan, islands A2
Flotta, island M2
Foinaven, hill G2
Foula, island N2
Frisa, lake D5
Fyne, lake F6
Galloway Forest Park . .G8
Garry, lake G4
Gigha, island E7
Glascarnoch, lake G3
Glas Maol, hill K5
Glass, lake G3
Glen Affric N.P. F4
Glen Strathfarrar N.P. .G4
Glentrool, forest G8
Harris, island B3
Heisker or Monarch,
  islands A4
Holy, lake F7
Hope, lake G2
Hourn, lake E4
Hoy, island L2
Inner Hebrides,
  islands C7
Iona, island D6
Islay, island D7
Jura N.P. D7
Jura, island E6
Kintail N.P. F4
Knapdale N.P. E7
Knoydart N.P. E4
Kyle of Tongue N.P. . . .G1
Laggan, lake H5
Leven, lake C2
Lee, lake L4
Linnhe, lake F5
Lismore, island E5
Lewis, island B2
Lochan Fada, lake F3
Lochindorb, lake J4
Loch na Keal
  Isle of Mull N.P. . . .D6
Lochy, lake G5
Lomond, lake G6
Loyal, lake H2
Loyn, lake G4
Luing, island E6
Lynn of Lorn N.P. F5
Lyon, lake H5
Mainland, island M2
Mainland, island Q2
Maree, lake E3
May, lake M6
Meadie, lake H2
Merkland, lake G2
Mhor, lake H4

Mingulay, island A5
Monar, lake F4
Morar, lake E5
Morar Moidart and
  Ardnamurchan N.P. . . .D5
More, lake J2
Morlich, lake H3
Morven, hill J2
Mousa, island Q3
Muck, island D5
Muckle Roe, island . . .P2
Muick, lake K5
Mull, island D6
Mullardoch, lake F4
Nan Clar, lake H2
Na Shealling, lake . . .F3
Naver, lake H2
Ness, lake G4
Nevis, lake E5
North, sea P5, R2
North Arran N.P. F7
North Minch, strait . . .C2
North Ronaldsay, island N1
North Uist, island . . .B3
North-west Sutherland
  N.P. G2
Orkney, islands L2
Oronsay, island D7
Orrin, reservoir G3
Outer Hebrides,
  islands A4
Out Skerries, island . .Q2
Pabbay, island B3
Papa Stour, island . . .N2
Papa Westray, island . .M1
Pentland, hills K7
Quinag, hill F2
Quoich, lake F4
Raasay, island D4
Rannoch, lake H5
Rona, island D3
Ronay, island B4
Rosinish, island A5
Ross N.P. F3
Rousay, island M1
Sanday, island N1
Sandray, island B5
Scalpay, island C3
Scalpay, island E4
Scaraben, hill J2
Scarba, island E6
Scarba Lunga and the
  Garvellachs N.P. E6
Scarp, island B2
Seil, island E6
Sgurr na Lapaich, hill . .F4
Shapinsay, island N2
Shetland, islands P3
Shiant, islands D3
Shiel, lake E5
Shiel, lake E5
Shin, lake G2
Sinclairs, bay K1
Skye, island D4
Soay, island D4
Solway Firth J9
Sound of Eigg D5
Sound of Rhum D5
South Lewis Harris and
  North Uist N.P. B3
South Ronaldsay, island .M2
South Uist, island . . .B4
South Uist Machair N.P. .B4
Spean, river G5
Spey, river J4
Spey, river K3
Spey Bay K3
Strathconon Forest . . .F4
Stroma, island K1
Stronsay, island N1
Summer, islands E2
Taransay, island B3
Tay, lake H5
Teviotdale K8
The Small Isles, islands .C5
Tiree, island C5
Treig, lake G5
Trotternish N.P. D3
Tulla, lake G5
Tummel, lake J5
Tweed, river J4
Ulva, island D6
Unst, island R1
Upper Tweeddale N.P. . .K7
Vaich, lake G3
Vatersay, island A5
Watten, lake K1
West & East, island . . .P2
Westray, island M1
Whalsay, island Q2
Wiay, island B4
Yell, island Q2
Zetland, island P2

Edinburgh Castle

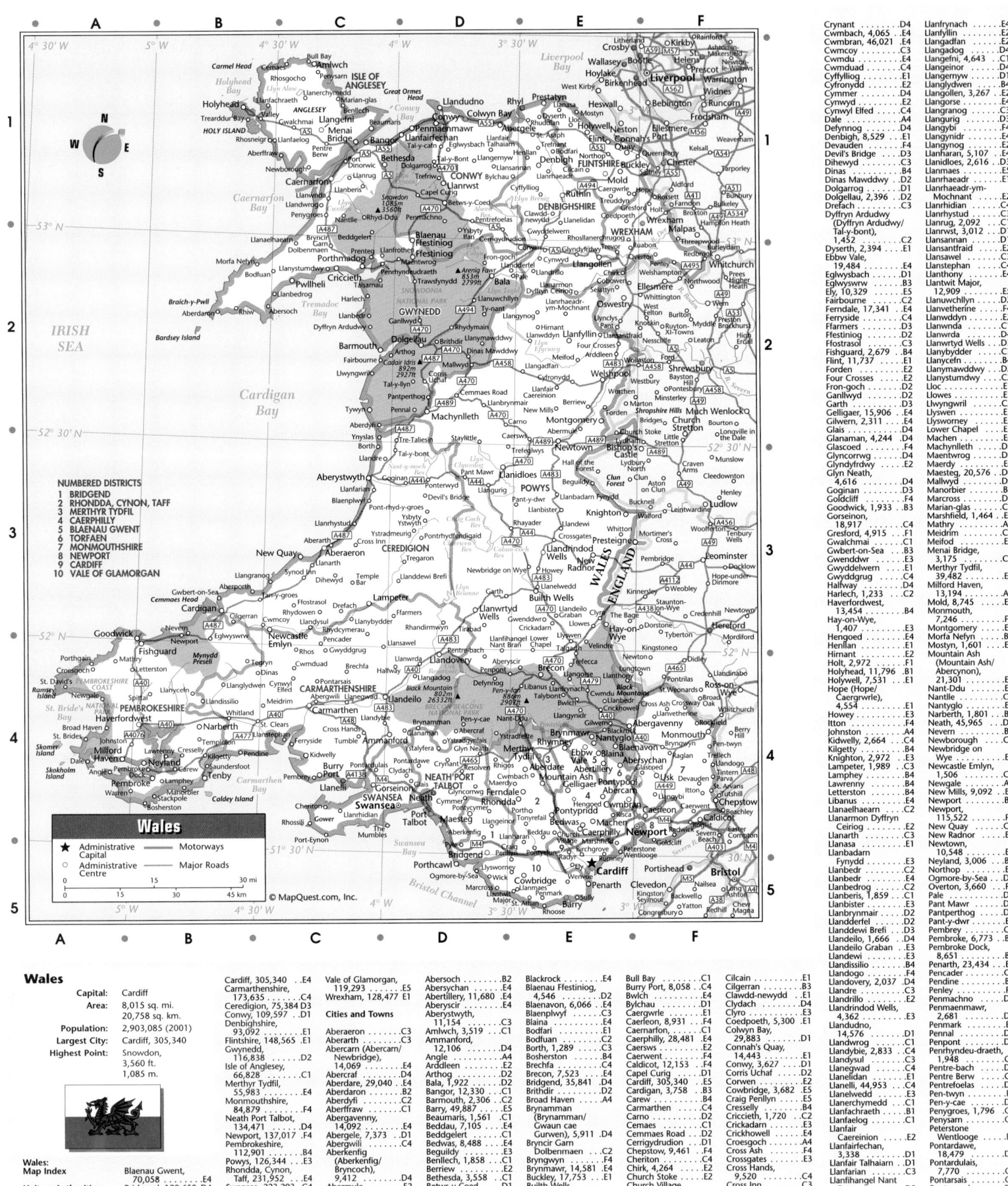

Wales

NUMBERED DISTRICTS
1 BRIDGEND
2 RHONDDA, CYNON, TAFF
3 MERTHYR TYDFIL
4 CAERPHILLY
5 BLAENAU GWENT
6 TORFAEN
7 MONMOUTHSHIRE
8 NEWPORT
9 CARDIFF
10 VALE OF GLAMORGAN

Wales — Legend:
★ Administrative Capital
○ Administrative Centre
— Motorways
— Major Roads
0 15 30 mi / 0 15 30 45 km

© MapQuest.com, Inc.

Wales

Capital:	Cardiff
Area:	8,015 sq. mi. / 20,758 sq. km.
Population:	2,903,085 (2001)
Largest City:	Cardiff, 305,340
Highest Point:	Snowdon, 3,560 ft. / 1,085 m.

Wales
Map Index
Unitary Authorities
(2001 census pop.)

Blaenau Gwent, 70,058 ......E4
Bridgend, 128,650 D4
Caerphilly, 169,521 E4
Cardiff, 305,340 ..E4
Carmarthenshire, 173,635 ....C4
Ceredigion, 75,384 D3
Conwy, 109,597 ..D1
Denbighshire, 93,092 ....E1
Flintshire, 148,565 .E1
Gwynedd, 116,838 ....D2
Isle of Anglesey, 66,828 ....C1
Merthyr Tydfil, 55,983 ....E4
Monmouthshire, 84,879 ....F4
Neath Port Talbot, 134,471 ....D4
Newport, 137,017 ..F4
Pembrokeshire, 112,901 ....B4
Powys, 126,344 ..E3
Rhondda, Cynon, Taff, 231,952 ....D4
Swansea, 223,293 ..C4
Torfaen, 90,967 ....E4
Vale of Glamorgan, 119,293 ....E5
Wrexham, 128,477 E1

Cities and Towns
Aberaeron C3
Aberarth C3
Abercarn (Abercarn/ Newbridge), 14,069 ....E4
Abercraf D4
Aberdare, 29,040 ..E4
Aberdaron B2
Aberdyfi C2
Aberffraw C1
Abergavenny, 14,092 ....E4
Abergele, 7,373 ..D1
Abergwili C4
Aberkenfig (Aberkenfig/ Bryncoch), 9,412 ....D4
Abermule, 1,431 ..E2
Aberporth B3

Abersoch B2
Aberychan E4
Abertillery, 11,680 ..E4
Aberyscir E4
Aberystwyth, 11,154 ....C3
Amlwch, 3,519 ..C1
Ammanford, 12,106 ....D4
Angle A4
Arddelen E2
Arthog D2
Bala, 1,922 ....D2
Bangor, 12,330 ..C1
Barmouth, 2,306 ..C2
Barry, 49,887 ....E5
Beaumaris, 1,561 ..C1
Beddau, 7,105 ....E4
Bedwas, 8,488 ....E4
Beguildy E3
Benllech, 1,858 ..C1
Berriew E2
Bethesda, 3,558 ..C1
Betws-y-Coed ..D1
Birchgrove E4

Blackrock E4
Blaenau Ffestiniog, 4,546 ....D2
Blaenavon, 6,066 ..E4
Blaenplwyf C3
Blaina E4
Bodfari E1
Borth, 1,289 ....C3
Bosherston B4
Brechfa C4
Brecon, 7,523 ....E4
Bridgend, 35,841 .D4
Brithdir D2
Broad Haven B4
Brynamman (Brynaman/ Gwaun cae Gurwen), 5,911 ..D4
Bryncir Garn B3
Bryngwyn E3
Brynmawr, 14,581 .E4
Buckley, 17,753 ..E1
Builth Wells, 2,474 ....E3

Bull Bay C1
Burry Port, 8,058 ..C4
Bwlch E4
Bylchau D1
Caergwrle E1
Caerleon, 8,931 ..F4
Caernarfon, ...C1
Caerphilly, 28,481 E4
Caersws E2
Caerwent F4
Caldicot, 12,153 .F4
Capel Curig D1
Cardiff, 305,340 .E5
Cardigan, 3,758 ..B3
Carew B4
Carmarthen C4
Carno D2
Cemaes C1
Cemmaes Road ..D2
Cerrigydrudion ..D1
Chepstow, 9,461 .F4
Cheriton C4
Chirk, 4,264 ....E2
Church Stoke E2
Church Village, 7,894 ....E4

Cilcain E1
Cilgerran B3
Clawdd-newydd ..E1
Clydach D4
Clyro E3
Coedpoeth, 5,300 .E1
Colwyn Bay, 29,883 ....D1
Connah's Quay, 14,443 ....E1
Conwy, 3,627 ..D1
Corris Uchaf D2
Corwen E2
Cowbridge, 3,682 E5
Craig Penllyn E5
Cressely B4
Criccieth, 1,720 ..C2
Crickadarn E3
Crickhowell E4
Croesgoch A4
Cross Ash F4
Cross Hands, 9,520 ....C4
Cross Inn C3
Crossway F4

Crynant D4
Cwmbach, 4,065 ..E4
Cwmbran, 46,021 .E4
Cwmcoy C3
Cwmdu E4
Cwmduad C4
Cyffylliog E1
Cyfronydd E2
Cymmer D4
Cynwyd E2
Cynwyl Elfed C4
Dale A4
Defynnog D4
Denbigh, 8,529 ..E1
Devauden F4
Devil's Bridge D3
Dihewyd C3
Dinas B4
Dinas Mawddwy ..D2
Dolgarrog D1
Dolgellau, 2,396 ..D2
Drefach C3
Dyffryn Ardudwy (Dyffryn Ardudwy/ Tal-y-bont), 1,452 ....C2
Dyserth, 2,394 ..E1
Ebbw Vale, 19,484 ....E4
Eglwysbach D1
Eglwyswrw B3
Ely, 10,329 ....E5
Fairbourne C2
Ferndale, 17,341 ..D4
Ferryside C4
Ffarmers D3
Ffestiniog D2
Ffostrasol C3
Fishguard, 2,679 ..B4
Flint, 11,737 ....E1
Forden E2
Four Crosses E2
Fron-goch D2
Ganllwyd D2
Garth D3
Gelligaer, 15,906 .E4
Gilwern, 2,311 ..E4
Glais D4
Glanamman, 4,244 D4
Glascoed F4
Glyncorrwg D4
Glyndyfrdwy E2
Glyn Neath, 4,616 ....D4
Goginan C3
Goldcliff F4
Goodwick, 1,933 .B3
Gorseinon, 18,917 ....C4
Gresford, 4,915 ..F1
Gwalchmai C1
Gwbert-on-Sea ..B3
Gwendraw E3
Gwyddelwern E1
Gwyddgrug C4
Halfway D3
Harlech, 1,233 ..C2
Haverfordwest, 13,454 ....B4
Hay-on-Wye, 1,407 ....E3
Hengoed E4
Henllan E1
Hirnant E2
Holt, 2,972 ....F1
Holyhead, 11,796 B1
Holywell, 7,531 ..E1
Hope (Hope/ Caergwrle), 4,554 ....E1
Howey E3
Itton F4
Johnston A4
Kidwelly, 2,664 ..C4
Kilgetty B4
Knighton, 2,972 ..E3
Lampeter, 1,989 ..C3
Lamphey B4
Lawrenny B4
Letterston B4
Libanus E4
Llanaelhaearn C2
Llanarmon Dyffryn Ceiriog E2
Llanarth C3
Llanasa E1
Llanbadarn Fynydd E3
Llanbedr C2
Llanbedr E4
Llanbedrog C2
Llanberis, 1,859 ..C1
Llanbister E3
Llanbrynmair D2
Llandderfel D2
Llanddewi Brefi ..D3
Llandeilo, 1,666 .D4
Llandeilo Graban ..E3
Llandewi E3
Llandissilio B4
Llandogo F4
Llandovery, 2,037 D4
Llandre C3
Llandrillo E2
Llandrindod Wells, 4,362 ....E3
Llandudno, 14,576 ....D1
Llandwrog C1
Llandybie, 2,833 .C4
Llandysul C3
Llanegwad C4
Llanelian E1
Llanelli, 44,953 ..C4
Llanerchymedd ..C1
Llanfachraeth B1
Llanfaelog C1
Llanfair Caereinion E2
Llanfairfechan, 3,338 ....D1
Llanfair Talhaiarn .D1
Llanfarian C3
Llanfihangel Nant Bran D3
Llanfrothen C2

Llanfrynach E4
Llanfyllin E2
Llangadfan E2
Llangadog D4
Llangefni, 4,643 ..C1
Llangeinor D4
Llangernyw D1
Llanglydwen B4
Llangollen, 3,267 .E2
Llangorse E4
Llangranog C3
Llangurig D3
Llangybi C2
Llangynidr E4
Llangynog E2
Llanharan, 5,107 .E4
Llanidloes, 2,616 .D3
Llanmaes E5
Llanrhaeadr E1
Llanrhaeadr-ym- Mochnant E2
Llanrhidian C4
Llanrhystud C3
Llanrug, 2,092 ..C1
Llanrwst, 3,012 ..D1
Llansannan D1
Llansantffraid E2
Llansawel C4
Llanstephan C4
Llanthony E4
Llantwit Major, 12,909 ....E5
Llanuwchllyn D2
Llanvetherine F4
Llanwddyn D2
Llanwnda C1
Llanwrda D4
Llanwrtyd Wells ..D3
Llanybydder C4
Llanycefn B4
Llanymawddwy ..D2
Llanystumdwy ..C2
Lloc E1
Llowes E3
Llwyngwril C2
Llysworney E5
Lower Chapel E3
Machen E4
Machynlleth D2
Maentwrog D2
Maerdy D4
Maesteg, 20,576 .D4
Mallwyd D2
Manorbier B4
Marcross D5
Marian-glas C1
Marshfield, 1,464 .E4
Mathry A4
Meidrim C4
Meifod E2
Menai Bridge, 3,175 ....C1
Merthyr Tydfil, 39,482 ....E4
Milford Haven, 13,194 ....A4
Mold, 8,745 ....E1
Monmouth, 7,246 ....F4
Montgomery E2
Morfa Nefyn B2
Mostyn, 1,601 ..E1
Mountain Ash (Mountain Ash/ Abercynon), 21,301 ....E4
Nant-Ddu E4
Nantle C1
Nantyglo E4
Narberth, 1,801 ..B4
Neath, 45,965 ..D4
Nevern B3
Newborough C1
Newbridge on Wye E3
Newcastle Emlyn, 1,506 ....C3
Newgale A4
New Mills, 9,092 .E2
Newport B3
Newport, 115,522 ..F4
New Quay C3
New Radnor E3
Newtown, 10,548 ....E2
Neyland, 3,006 ..B4
Northop E1
Ogmore-by-Sea ..D5
Overton, 3,660 ..F2
Pale D2
Pant Mawr D3
Pantperthog D2
Pant-y-dwr E3
Pembrey C4
Pembroke, 6,773 .B4
Pembroke Dock, 8,651 ....B4
Penarth, 23,434 ..E5
Pencader C3
Pendine B4
Penley F2
Penmachno D1
Penmaenmawr, 2,681 ....D1
Penmark E5
Pennal D2
Penpont D4
Penrhyndeu-draeth, 1,948 ....C2
Pentre-bach D4
Pentre Berw C1
Pentrefoelas D1
Pen-twyn F4
Pen-y-cae D4
Penygroes, 1,796 .C1
Penysarn C1
Peterstone Wentlooge E4
Pontardawe, 18,479 ....D4
Pontardulais, 7,770 ....C4
Pontarsais C4
Ponterwyd D3

Pontrhyd-fendigaid
................D3
Pont-rhyd-y-groes .D3
Pontyclun........E4
Pontycymer, 4,439 D4
Pontypool, 35,564 .E4
Pontypridd, 28,487 E4
Port Dinorwic, 1,664C1
Port-Eynon.......C4
Porth...........E4
Porthcawl, 15,922 .D5
Porthgain........A4
Porthmadog, 3,048 C2
Port Talbot, 37,647 D4
Prenteg..........C2
Prestatyn, 15,020 .E1
Presteigne, 1,815 .E3
Pwllheli, 3,974 ...C2
Pyle, 12,331......D4
Queensferry......F1
Radyr, 4,335 .....E4
Raglan...........E4
Redbrook........F2
Redwick.........E4
Resolven, 2,274 ..D4
Rhandirmwyn.....D3
Rhayader, 1,793 ..E3
Rhigos...........D4
Rhiw............B2
Rhondda, 59,947 ..E4
Rhoose, 3,574 ....E5
Rhos............C4
Rhosgoch........C1
Rhoslanerch-rugog,
  12,879.........E3
Rhosneigr........B1
Rhossili.........C4
Rhuddlan, 3,182 ..E1
Rhydcymerau.....D3
Rhyd-Ddu........C1
Rhydowen.........C3
Rhydymain.......D2
Rhyl, 24,909 .....E1
Rhymney, 7,991 ..E4
Risca, 15,124 ....E4
Rockfield........F4
Rogiet...........F4
Rossett, 1,986 ...F1
Ruabon, 2,828 ...E1
Rumney..........E4
Ruthin, 5,029 ....E1
St. Arvans.......E4
St. Asaph........E1
St. Athan........E5
St. Brides........A4
St. Clears........E4
St. David's, 1,627 ..E4
Saltney, 4,144 ...F1
Saundersfoot, 3,221B4
Spittal..........B4
Stackpole........B4
Staylittle........D2
Sully...........E5
Swansea, 171,038 .D4
Synod Inn........C3
Talgarth, 1,818 ..E3
Talsarnau........C2
Talybont........E4
Tal-y-Bont.......D1
Tal-y-bont.......D3
Tal-y-cafn.......D1
Tal-y-llyn........D2
Tan-y-groes......B3
Tegryn..........B4
Temple Bar......C3
Templeton........B4
Tenby, 5,619 ....B4
The Mumbles.....D4
Tintern Parva.....F4
Tirabad..........D3
Tonyrefail, 8,815 .E4
Trawsfynydd.....D2
Trearddur Bay....B1
Trefecca.........E4
Trefeglwys.......D3
Trefnant.........E1
Trefriw..........D1
Tregaron........D3

Trellech F4
Tre-Taliesin D2
Treuddyn E1
Trevor E2
Tumble C4
Ty-nant D2
Tywyn, 2,864 ....C2
Usk, 2,187 ....F4
Valley B1
Velindre E3
Warren A4
Welshpool, 5,725 ..E2
Wenvoe E5
Whitland, 1,518 ...B4
Whitton E3
Wick, 1,940 .....D5
Wrexham, 40,614 .F1
Ynyslas C2
Ysbyty Ifan D1
Ysbyty Ystwyth ..D3
Ystalyfera D4
Ystradfellte D4

Other Features

Alaw, lake B1
Alwen, reservoir . .D1
Anglesey, island . .C1
Arenig Fawr, hill ..D2
Bardsey, island ...B2
Black, mountain ..D4
Black, mountains ..E4
Braich-y-Pwll, point B2
Brecon Beacons N.P.D4
Brenig, lake D1
Brianne, lake D3
Bristol, channel ..D5
Caban-coch,
  reservoir D3
Cadair Idris, hill . .D2
Caernarfon, bay ..B1
Caldey, island ...B4
Cardigan, bay ...B3
Carmarthen, bay ..C4
Carmel Head, cape B1
Celyn, lake D2
Cemmaes Head,
  cape A4
Claerwen, reservoir D3
Clywedog, lake ..D3
Conwy, bay D1
Craig Goch, reservoirD3
Cwellyn, lake ...C1
Dee, river F1
Efyrnwy, lake E2
Gower, peninsula .C4
Great Ormes
  Head, cape D1
Holy, island B1
Holyhead, bay ...B1
Liverpool, bay ...E1
Mynydd Preseli, hill B4
Nant-y-moch,
  reservoir D3
Ogwen, lake D1
Pembrokeshire
  Coast N.P. A4
Pen-y-fan, hill ...E4
Pontsticill, reservoir E4
Ramsey, island ..A4
St. Bride's, bay ..A4
Severn, river F4
Skokholm, island .A4
Skomer, island ..A4
Snowdon, hill ...C1
Snowdonia
  National Park ...D2
Swansea, bay D4
Tegid, lake D2
Tremadoc, bay ...C2
Usk, reservoir ...D4

Dunluce Castle, near Portrush,
Northern Ireland

Northern Ireland

Capital:	Belfast
Area:	5,461 sq. mi.
	14,144 sq. km.
Population:	1,685,267 (2001 Census)
Largest City:	Belfast, 279,237
Highest Point:	Slieve Donard
	2,796 ft.
	852 m.

There has not been a
flag for Northern Ireland
since 1974. The Union
Flag is the official flag of
Northern Ireland.

Northern Ireland:
Map Index

Districts
(2001 census pop.)

Antrim, 48,366 ....E2
Ards, 73,244 .....F2
Armagh, 54,263 ..D3
Ballymena, 58,610 .E2
Ballymoney, 26,894.E1
Banbridge, 41,392 .E3
Belfast, 277,391 ..F2
Carrickfergus,
  37,659 ....F2
Castlereagh, 66,488 F2
Coleraine, 56,315 . .D2
Cookstown, 32,581 D2
Craigavon, 80,671 .E3
Derry, 105,066 ....C2
Down, 63,828 ....F3
Dungannon,
  47,735 ....D3
Fermanagh, 57,527 B3
Larne, 30,832 ....F2
Limavady, 32,422 ..D2
Lisburn, 108,694 . .E2
Magherafelt,
  39,780 ....D2
Moyle, 15,933 ....E1
Newry and Mourne,
  87,058 ....E3
Newtownabbey,
  79,995 ....F2
North Down,
  76,323 ....F2
Omagh, 47,952 ...C2
Strabane, 38,248 ..C2

Cities and Towns

Aghalee, 480 ....E2
Ahoghill, 2,260 ...E2
Annalong, 1,937 ..F3
Antrim, 20,878 ...E2
Arboe...........D2
Ardean E2

Ardglass, 1,651 ...F3
Armagh, 14,640 ..D3
Armoy, 560 .....E1
Augher, 430 .....C3
Aughnacloy, 597 ..D3
Ballinamallard,
  1,068 ....B3
Ballintoy, 184 ....E1
Ballycarry, 1,010 ..F2
Ballycarton D1
Ballycastle, 4,005 .E1
Ballyclare, 7,761 ..E2
Ballygalley, 496 ..F2
Ballygawley, 655 ..C3
Ballygowan, 2,384 .F2
Ballyhornan F3
Ballykelly, 2,277 ..C1
Ballymagorry, 493 .C2
Ballymartin, 472 ..F3
Ballymena, 28,717 .E2
Ballymoney, 8,242 .E1
Ballynahinch, 5,196.F3
Ballynure, 368 ...F2
Ballyronan E2
Ballyroney E3
Ballyvoy E1
Ballywalter, 1,162 .G2
Ballyward E3
Banbridge, 12,529 .E3
Bangor, 52,437 ...F2
Belcoo, 327 .....B3
Belfast, 279,237 ..F2
Bellaghy, 1,041 ..D2
Belleek, 550 .....A3
Belleek, 188 .....E3
Benburb, 287 ....D3
Beragh, 564 .....C2
Black Fort D2
Blaney...........B3
Brookeborough,
  541 ....B3
Broughshane, 1,873 E2
Bushmills, 1,348 ..E1
Caledon, 389 ....D3
Carnlough, 1,493 .E2
Carrickfergus,
  22,885 ....F2

Carrickmore, 524 .C2
Carrowreagh E1
Carryduff, 4,270 ..F2
Castledawson,
  1,770 ....D2
Castlederg, 2,579 .B2
Castlewellan, 2,230 F3
Clanabogan C2
Claudy, 970 .....C2
Clogher, 578 ....C3
Cloghy, 647 .....G3
Clonelly B2
Clough, 236 .....F3
Clough, 205 .....F3
Coalisland, 3,802 .D2
Coleraine, 20,721 .D1
Comber, 8,516 ...F2
Conor, 114 ......E2
Cookstown, 10,472 D2
Craigavon, 9,201 ..D3
Cranagh C2
Creggan C2
Crew............B2
Crossgar, 1,406 ..F3
Crossgare D1
Crossmaglen,
  1,586 ....D3
Crumlin, 2,697 ...E2
Cullion C2
Cullyhanna, 199 ..D3
Cushendall, 1,399 .E1
Cushendun, 347 ..E1
Derrylin, 321 ....B3
Derrytrasna, 209 ..E2
Doagh, 961 .....E2
Donagh, 230 ....C3
Donaghadee, 4,799 F2
Donaghmore, 768 .D2
Dooish D1
Downhill D1
Downpatrick,
  10,257 ....F3
Dromara, 511 ....F2
Dromore, 3,708 ..C2

Dromore, 655 ....E3
Drumaness, 1,026 .F3
Drumbadmeen ...B3
Drumdallagh E1
Drumquin, 558 ..C2
Dundrod F2
Dundrum, 1,131 ..F3
Dungannon, 9,420 .D3
Dungiven, 2,812 ..D2
Dunloy, 1,119 ...E2
Dunnamanagh,
  675 ....C2
Ederney, 626 ....B2
Enniskillen, 11,436 B3
Feeny, 583 ......C2
Fintona, 1,523 ...C3
Fivemiletown,
  1,107 ....C3
Forkhill, 343 ....E3
Garrison, 325 ....A3
Garvagh, 1,091 ..D2
Gilford, 1,639 ...E3
Glenanne D3
Glenarm, 603 ...F2
Glenavy, 497 ....E2
Gortin, 226 .....C2
Greenisland, 4,967 F2
Greyabbey, 697 ..F2
Hillsborough, 2,407 E3
Hilltown, 982 ....E3
Holywood, 9,252 .F2
Irvinestown, 1,906 .B3
Islandstown E2
Jonesborough, 460 .E3
Katesbridge, 174 ..E3
Keady, 2,467 ....D3
Kells, 1,130 .....E2
Killagan Fork E2
Killaloo C1
Killaloo C1
Killead E2
Killinchy, 779 ...F2
Killylea, 293 ....D3
Killyleagh, 2,221 .F3
Kilrea, 1,405 ....D2
Kilwaughter F2

Kircubbin, 1,098 ..F3
Larne, 17,575 ...F2
Letterbreen B3
Limavady, 10,764 .D1
Lisbellaw, 632 ...B3
Lisburn, 42,110 ..E2
Lislea E3
Lisnaskea, 2,457 ..C3
Londonderry,
  72,334 ....C1
Loughbrickland,
  674 ....E3
Lurgan, 21,905 ..E3
Mackan B3
Maggy's Leap ...F3
Maghera, 129 ...D2
Magherafelt, 7,143 .D2
Maghery, 723 ...D2
Maguiresbridge,
  645 ....C3
Markethill, 343 ..D3
Mayobridge, 933 ..E3
Middletown, 274 ..D3
Milford, 458 ....D3
Millisle, 1,531 ...F2
Milltown D1
Milltown F2
Moira, 2,772 ....E2
Moneymore, 1,231 D2
Moorfields F2
Mossley, 1,420 ...F2
Mountfield C2
Mountjoy C2
Moy, 875 ....D3
Muckleramer E2
Newcastle, 7,214 .F3
Newry, 22,975 ...E3
Newtownabbey,
  57,103 ....F2
Newtownards,
  11,644 ....F2
Newtownbutler,
  953 ....C3
Newtown
  Crommelin E2

Newtownhamilton,
  761 ....D3
Newtownstewart,
  1,520 ....C2
Nutt's Corner ...E2
Omagh, 17,280 ..C2
Park, 435 ....C2
Plumbridge, 257 ..C2
Pomeroy, 730 ...D2
Portadown, 21,299 .E3
Portaferry, 2,324 ..F3
Portavogie, 1,482 .G3
Portballintrae, 756 .D1
Portglenone, 1,243 .E2
Portmuck F2
Portrush, 5,703 ..D1
Portstewart, 6,459 .D1
Poyntz Pass, 380 ..E3
Randalstown, 4,290 E2
Rasharkin, 923 ...E2
Rathfriland, 2,126 .E3
Richill, 2,709 ....D3
Ringsend D1
Rosslea, 529 ....C3
Rostrevor, 2,269 ..E3
Rousky..........C2
Saintfield, 2,168 ..F3
Scraghy B2
Seskinore C2
Sion Mills, 1,998 .C2
Sixmilecross, 264 ..C2
Springfield B3
Stewartstown, 649 .D2
Strabane, 11,981 ..C2
Strangford, 548 ..F3
Templepatrick,
  1,414 ....E2
Tempo, 292 .....C3
The Sheddings ..E2
Tobermore, 621 ..D2
Toome..........D2
Trillick, 345 .....C3
Warrenpoint, 5,637 E3
Waterside C2
Whitehead, 3,761 .F2

Other Features

Atlantic, ocean ...B1
Bann, river E2
Beg, lake E2
Belfast Lough, lake .F2
Bush, river E1
Carntogher,
  mountain D2
Copeland, island ..F2
Cuileagh,
  mountain B3
Dundrum, bay ...F3
Fair Head, cape ..E1
Foyle, lake C1
Garron, point F1
Giant's Causeway .D1
Irish, sea F3
Knocklayd, hill ..C1
Loughermore, hill .C2
Lower Lough Erne,
  lake B3
Mourne, mountains .E3
Mourne, river ...C2
Mullaghcarn, hill ..C2
Neagh, lake E2
North, channel ..F1
Rathlin, island ...E1
Rathlin, sound ...E1
Red, bay E1
St. Johns, point ..F3
Sawel, mountain .C2
Sl. Donard,
  mountain F3
Sl. Gallion,
  mountain D2
Sl. Gullion,
  mountain E3
Sperrin, mountains .C2
Strangford, lake ..F3
Torr Head, cape ..E1
Trostan, hill E1
Upper Lough Erne,
  lake B3

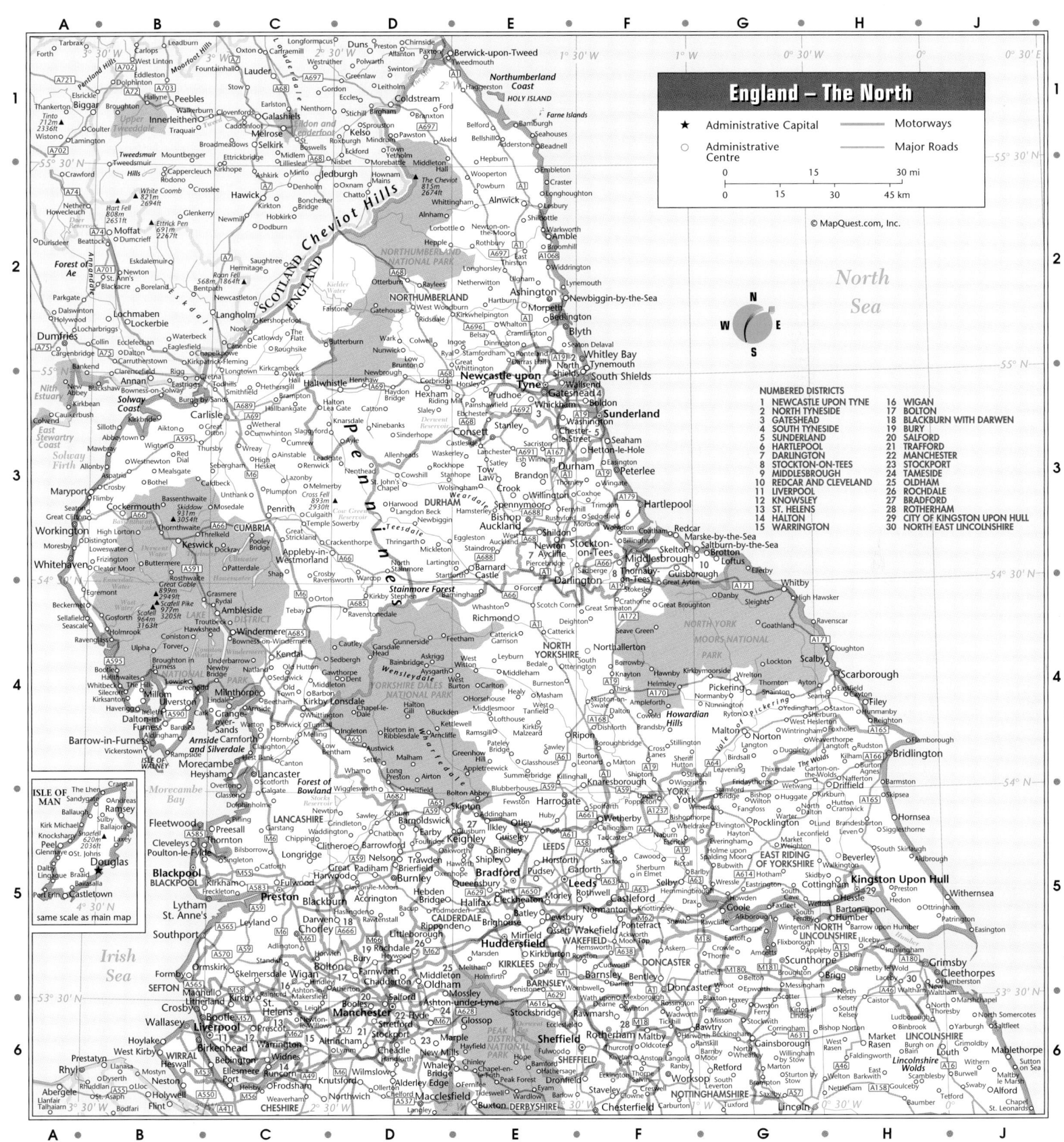

England – The North

★ Administrative Capital

○ Administrative Centre

Motorways

Major Roads

0   15   30 mi

0   15   30   45 km

© MapQuest.com, Inc.

NUMBERED DISTRICTS

1 NEWCASTLE UPON TYNE	16 WIGAN
2 NORTH TYNESIDE	17 BOLTON
3 GATESHEAD	18 BLACKBURN WITH DARWEN
4 SOUTH TYNESIDE	19 BURY
5 SUNDERLAND	20 SALFORD
6 HARTLEPOOL	21 TRAFFORD
7 DARLINGTON	22 MANCHESTER
8 STOCKTON-ON-TEES	23 STOCKPORT
9 MIDDLESBROUGH	24 TAMESIDE
10 REDCAR AND CLEVELAND	25 OLDHAM
11 LIVERPOOL	26 ROCHDALE
12 KNOWSLEY	27 BRADFORD
13 ST. HELENS	28 ROTHERHAM
14 HALTON	29 CITY OF KINGSTON UPON HULL
15 WARRINGTON	30 NORTH EAST LINCOLNSHIRE

ISLE OF MAN

same scale as main map

England

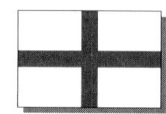

Capital: London
Area: 50,351 sq. mi.
130,410 sq. km.
Population: 49,138,831 (2001)
Largest City: London, 7,172,036 (metro.)
Highest Point: Scafell Pike, 3,210 ft. 979 m.

England – The North: Map Index

Unitary Authorities
(2001 census pop.)

Barnsley, 218,062 . . . . E5
Blackburn with Darwen, 137,471 . . . . D5
Blackpool, 142,284 . . B5
Bolton, 261,035 . . . . D5
Bradford, 467,668 . . E5
Bury, 180,612 . . . . . . D5
Calderdale, 192,396 D5
Cheshire, 673,777 . . C6
Cumbria, 487,607 . . C3
Darlington, 97,822 . . E3
Derbyshire, 734,581 E6
Doncaster, 286,865 . F5
Durham, 493,470 . . D3
East Riding of Yorkshire, 314,076 G5
Gateshead, 191,151 . E3
Halton, 118,215 . . . C6
Hartlepool, 88,629 . . F3
Kingston upon Hull, City of, 243,595 . . H5
Kirklees, 388,576 . . E5
Knowsley, 150,468 . C6
Lancashire, 1,134,976 . . . . . D5
Leeds, 715,404 . . . . E5
Lincolnshire, 646,646 . . . . H6
Liverpool, 439,476 . C6
Manchester, 392,819 . . . . . . D6
Middlesbrough, 134,847 . . . . F3
Newcastle upon Tyne, 259,573 . . E2
North East Lincolnshire, 157,983 . . H5
North Lincolnshire, 152,839 . . . . G5
North Tyneside, 191,663 . . . . E2
North Yorkshire, 569,660 . . . . E4
Northumberland, 307,186 . . . . D2
Nottinghamshire, 748,903 . . . . F6
Oldham, 217,393 . . D5
Redcar and Cleveland, 139,141 . . . . G3
Rochdale, 205,233 . D5
Rotherham, 248,176 F6
St. Helens, 176,845 . C6
Salford, 216,119 . . . D5
Sefton, 282,956 . . . B5
Sheffield, 513,234 . . E6
South Tyneside, 152,785 . . . . F3
Stockport, 284,544 . D6
Stockton-on-Tees, 178,405 . . . . F3
Sunderland, 280,807 F3
Tameside, 213,045 . D6
Trafford, 210,135 . . D6
Wakefield, 315,173 . E5
Warrington, 191,084 C6
Wigan, 301,417 . . . D5
Wirral, 312,289 . . . B6
York, 181,131 . . . . F4

Cities and Towns

Abbeytown B3
Aberford F5
Accrington, 36,466 . D5
Ackworth Moor Top, 5,851 . . . . F5
Adderstone E1
Addingham, 2,769 . E5
Adlington, 8,556 . . . D5
Aikton B3
Ainstable C3
Airton D4
Akeld D1
Aldbrough H5
Alderley Edge, 5,280 . . . . D6
Aldingham B4
Alford, 2,989 . . . . . J6
Alkborough G5
Allenheads D3
Allonby B3
Alnham D2
Alnwick, 7,419 . . . . D2
Altrincham, 40,042 . D6
Amble, 5,639 . . . . . E2
Ambleside, 2,905 . . C4
Amcotts G5
Ampleforth F4
Andreas B5
Anston (Anston/ Dinnington), 17,691 . . . . F6
Appleby, 2,570 . . . . G5
Appleby-in-Westmorland . . . C3
Appletreewick E4

Arncliffe D4
Arnside, 1,627 . . . . C4
Ashington, 27,962 . . E2
Ashton-in-Makersfield, 28,105 . . . . C5
Ashton-under-Lyne, 43,906 . . . . D6
Askern, 5,862 . . . . F5
Askrigg D4
Aspatria, 2,219 . . . B3
Atherton, 21,696 . . D5
Austwick D4
Ayle D3
Aysgarth D4
Ayton H4
Bacup, 13,682 . . . . D5
Bainbridge D4
Ballajora B5
Ballasalla A5
Ballaugh B5
Bamburgh E1
Bamford E6
Barbon D4
Bardsea B4
Barlby, 2,432 . . . . F5
Barlow E6
Barmston H4
Barnard Castle, 6,084 . . . . E3
Barnby Moor G6
Barnetby le Wold . . H5
Barningham E4
Barnoldswick, 10,038 . . . . D5
Barnsley, 75,120 . . F5
Barrowford, 5,212 . D5
Barrow-in-Furness, 48,947 . . . . B4
Barrow upon Humber, 2,161 . . . . H5
Barton-upon-Humber, 9,422 . . . . H5
Bassenthwaite B3
Batley, 48,030 . . . . E5
Baumber H6
Bawtry, 2,696 . . . . F6
Beadnell E1
Bebington, 60,148 . C6
Beckermet A4
Beckingham G6
Bedale, 2,828 . . . . E4
Bedlington, 15,430 . E2
Beetham C4
Belford E1
Bellshill E1
Belsay E2
Belton, 2,300 . . . . G5
Bentley, 32,675 . . . F5
Berwick-upon-Tweed, 13,544 . . . . E1
Billingham, 36,869 . F3
Bilsborrow C5
Binbrook H6
Bingley, 19,585 . . . E5
Birdsall G4
Birkenhead, 93,087 . B6
Bishop Auckland, 23,154 . . . . E3
Bishop Norton G6
Bishopthorpe, 3,148 F5
Bishop Wilton G5
Blackburn, 105,994 . D5
Blackpool, 146,262 . B5
Blaxton F6
Blubberhouses E4
Blyth, 35,327 . . . . E2
Boldon, 12,420 . . . F3
Bolton, 139,020 . . . D5
Bolton Abbey E5
Booles D6
Bootle, 65,454 . . . . B4
Bootle C6
Boroughbridge, 1,903 . . . . F4
Borrowby F4
Borwick C4
Bothel B3
Bowness-on-Solway . B3
Bowness-on-Windermere . . . C4
Braaid A5
Bradford, 289,376 . E5
Brampton (Cumbria), 3,957 . . . . C3
Brampton (Lincolnshire) G6
Brandesburton H5
Brandon, 9,162 . . . E3
Brandsby F4
Branston D1
Bridlington, 31,334 . H4
Brierfield, 9,567 . . D5
Brigg, 5,768 . . . . . H5
Brighouse, 32,198 . E5
Brotton, 4,735 . . . . G3
Broughton, 4,448 . . H5
Broughton in Furness B4
Broughton in Bubwith G5
Buckden, 2,534 . . . D4
Burgh by Sands . . . B3

Burgh on Bain H6
Burneston E4
Burnley, 74,661 . . . D5
Burton Agnes H4
Burton Leonard . . . E4
Burwell, 4,628 . . . . J6
Bury, 62,633 . . . . . D5
Butterburn C2
Buttermere B3
Buxton, 19,854 . . . E6
Caistor, 2,502 . . . . H6
Caldbeck B3
Canton C4
Carburton F6
Cark C4
Carlisle, 72,439 . . . C3
Carlton, 1,640 . . . . C4
Carnforth, 7,442 . . C4
Castleford, 38,536 . F5
Castleside, 4,555 . . E3
Castletown A5
Catforth C5
Catlowdy C2
Catterick, 2,629 . . . E4
Catterick Garrison, 8,694 . . . . E4
Catton D3
Cautley D4
Cawood F5
Cayton H4
Chadderton, 34,026 . . . . D5
Chapel-en-le-Frith, 8,715 . . . . E6
Chapel-le-Dale D4
Chapel St. Leonards, 2,884 . . . . J6
Chatburn D5
Cheadle, 10,833 . . . D6
Chelford D6
Chesterfield, 71,945 F6
Chester-le-Street, 35,123 . . . . E3
Chinley E6
Chipping C5
Chorley, 33,536 . . . C5
Claughton C4
Clayton-le-Moors, 6,961 . . . . D5
Cleator Moor, 6,410 B3
Cleckheaton (Cleck-heaton and Liver-sedge), 27,151 . . E5
Cleethorpes, 32,719 H5
Cleveleys B5
Clitheroe, 13,548 . . D5
Cloughton H4
Clowne, 7,234 . . . . F6
Coatham G3
Cockermouth, 7,702 B3
Collingham, 2,714 . E5
Colwell E2
Coniston B4
Consett, 20,148 . . . E3
Corbridge, 2,719 . . D3
Corringham G6
Cottingham H5
Cowold F4
Cowshill D3
Coxhoe, 2,395 . . . . E3
Crackenthorpe C3
Cramlington, 26,238 E2
Cranstal B4
Craster E2
Crathorne F4
Creswell, 4,655 . . . F6
Crook, 8,246 . . . . . E3
Crosby (Cumbria), 52,869 . . . . B3
Crosby (Merseyside) .B6
Crosby Ravensworth .C3
Cross Lanes F4
Crowle, 2,916 . . . . G5
Cudworth, 11,715 . . F5
Culgaith C3
Cumrew C3
Cumwhinton C3
Dalby A5
Dalton F4
Dalton-in-Furness, 7,550 . . . . B4
Danby G4
Darfield, 7,723 . . . F5
Darlington, 86,767 . E3
Darras Hall E2
Darwen, 29,864 . . . D5
Deighton F4
Denby Dale, 2,282 . E5
Dent D4
Dewsbury, 50,169 . E5
Dinnington, 1,722 . E2
Dishforth F4
Distington, 2,318 . . A3
Dockray C3
Dolphinholme C5
Doncaster, 71,595 . F5
Douglas B5
Drax G5
Driffield H4
Dronfield, 22,985 . . F6
Duggleby G4
Durham, 36,937 . . . E3
Earby, 4,957 . . . . . D5
Easington, 7,593 . . F3
Easington J5
East Barkwith H6
Eastfield, 9,708 . . . H4
Eastoft G5
Eastrington G5
East Thirston E2
Ebchester E3
Ecclesfield F6
Eckington, 7,167 . . F6
Eggleston D3
Egremont, 6,581 . . A4
Ellerby G3
Ellesmere Port, 64,504 . . . . C6
Elsham H5
Elvington G5
Embleton E2
Epworth, 3,359 . . . G5
Escrick F5
Esh Winning, 3,643 E3
Everingham G5
Eyam E6
Faldingworth H6

Falstone D2
Fangfoss G5
Farnworth, 25,053 . . D5
Faxfleet G5
Feetham D4
Fernilee E6
Ferryhill, 11,610 . . E3
Fewston E5
Filey, 6,044 . . . . . . H4
Finningley, 3,624 . . G6
Flamborough, 1,741 H4
Fleetwood, 27,227 . B5
Flimby, 1,775 . . . . B3
Flixborough G5
Forcett E4
Ford D1
Formby, 25,356 . . . B5
Foulridge D5
Foxholes H4
Freckleton (Freckleton/Warton), 8,273 . . C5
Fridaythorpe G4
Frizington, 2,472 . . A3
Frodsham, 8,903 . . C6
Fulwood C5
Fulwood E6
Gainsborough, 19,704 . . . . G6
Galgate C5
Garforth, 15,250 . . F5
Garsdale Head D4
Garstang, 5,697 . . . C5
Garthorpe G5
Garton-on-the-Wolds G4
Gatehouse D2
Gateshead, 83,159 . E3
Gawthorpe D4
Gisburn D5
Glasshouses E4
Glasson C5
Glenmaye A5
Glossop (Glossop/Hollingworth), 30,771 . . . . E6
Glusburn, 6,859 . . . E5
Goathland G4
Goole, 19,410 . . . . G5
Gosforth, 23,315 . . B4
Goulceby H6
Grange-over-Sands, 4,473 . . . . C4
Grasmere C4
Great Ayton, 3,592 . F3
Great Broughton . . E4
Great Clifton A3
Great Harwood, 10,562 . . . . D5
Great Orton B3
Great Smeaton F4
Great Strickland . . . C3
Great Whittington . E2
Greenhow Hill E4
Greenodd B4
Grimoldby J6
Grimsby, 90,703 . . H5
Grindleton D5
Guisborough, 18,156 . . . . F3
Guiseley (Guiseley/Yeadon), 31,104 . E5
Gunnerside D4
Haggerston E1
Halifax, 91,069 . . . E5
Hallbankgate C3
Hallthwaites B4
Halton Gill D4
Halton Lea Gate . . . C3
Haltwhistle, 3,773 . D3
Hamsterley E3
Handforth D6
Harrogate, 66,178 . E5
Hartburn E2
Hartlepool, 87,310 . F3
Harwood D3
Harworth (Harworth/Bircotes), 7,813 . . F6
Haslingden, 15,024 D5
Hatfield, 14,067 . . F5
Hathersage E6
Haverigg B4
Hawkshead C4
Hawnby F4
Haworth, 4,956 . . . E5
Haxey G6
Haydon Bridge, 1,784 . . . . D3
Hayfield, 2,293 . . . E6
Hayton G5
Healy E4
Hebden Bridge, 3,681 . . . . D5
Hedon, 6,646 . . . . H5
Hellifield D4
Helmsley F4
Helsby, 4,538 . . . . C6
Hemmingbrough . . G5
Hemsworth, 9,401 . F5
Henshaw D3
Hepburn E1
Hepple D2
Hessle H5
Hest Bank C4
Heswall, 31,093 . . . B6
Hethersgill C3
Hetton-le-Hole, 13,538 . . . . F3
Hexham, 11,008 . . D3
Heysham C4
Heywood, 29,286 . . D5
High Hawsker G4
High Hesket C3
High Lorton B3
Hindley, 22,581 . . . C5
Holme upon Spalding Moor, 2,629 . . . . G5
Holmfirth (Holmfirth/Honley), 21,979 . . E5
Holmrook B4
Hope E6
Hornby C4
Hornsea, 7,573 . . . H5
Horsehouse E4
Horsforth, 18,593 . . E5
Horsley E3
Horton in Ribblesdale D4

Horwich, 18,017 . . C5
Hotham G5
Howden, 3,673 . . . G5
Hoylake (Hoylake/West Kirby), 25,554 . . B6
Huby E5
Huddersfield, 143,726 . . . . . . E5
Huggate G5
Humberston, 6,877 . H5
Hunmanby, 3,068 . . H4
Hutton Cranswick . . H5
Hyde, 30,666 . . . . D6
Ilkley, 13,530 . . . . E5
Immingham, 12,278 H5
Ingleton, 1,979 . . . D4
Ingoe E2
Ireleth B4
Keighley, 49,567 . . E5
Kendal, 25,461 . . . C4
Kershopefoot C2
Keswick, 4,836 . . . B3
Kettlewell D4
Kilham H4
Killinghall E4
Kingston Upon Hull, 310,636 . . . . . . H5
Kirkbride B3
Kirkburn H5
Kirkburton, 4,121 . . E5
Kirkby, 43,017 . . . . C6
Kirkby Lonsdale . . . C4
Kirkby Malzeard . . . E4
Kirkbymoorside, 2,650 . . . . G4
Kirkby Stephen, 1,619 . . . . D4
Kirkcambeck C3
Kirkham, 9,038 . . . C5
Kirk Michael B5
Kirksanton B4
Kirkwhelpington . . E2
Kirton in Lindsey, 2,773 . . . . G6
Kiveton Park F6
Knaresborough, 13,380 . . . . F4
Knarsdale C3
Knayton F4
Knockharry A5
Knottingley, 14,690 F5
Knutsford, 13,352 . D6
Laceby, 2,666 . . . . H5
Lancaster, 44,497 . . C4
Lanchester, 3,599 . . E3
Langdon Beck D3
Langley D4
Langold, 2,802 . . . . F6
Langtoft H4
Langton G4
Lartington E3
Laxey B5
Lazonby C3
Leadgate, 4,736 . . . D3
Leavening G4
Leconfield, 1,436 . . H5
Leeds, 424,194 . . . E5
Leigh, 43,150 . . . . C6
Lesbury E2
Leven, 2,036 . . . . . H5
Leyburn, 1,716 . . . E4
Leyland, 37,331 . . . C5
Lincoln, 80,281 . . . G6
Lindale C4
Lingague A5
Litherland, 20,905 . B6
Littleborough, 13,638 . . . . D5
Liverpool, 481,786 . C6
Lockton G4
Lofthouse E4
Loftus, 5,931 . . . . . G3
Longhorsley E2
Longhoughton E2
Long Preston D4
Longridge, 7,351 . . C5
Longtown, 2,548 . . C2
Lorbottle E2
Louth, 14,248 . . . . H6
Low Bentham C4
Low Brunton D2
Loweswater B3
Lowick B4
Ludborough H6
Lund H5
Lymm, 9,721 . . . . . D6
Lynemouth, 2,024 . E2
Lytham St. Anne's, 40,866 . . . . C5
Mablethorpe (Mablethorpe/Sutton on Sea), 9,719 . . J6
Macclesfield, 50,270 D6
Maghull (Maghull/Lydiate), 29,206 . C5
Malham D4
Maltby, 18,158 . . . F6
Maltby le Marsh . . . J6
Malton, 4,294 . . . . G4
Manchester, 402,889 . . . . . . D6
Market Rasen, 2,948 H6
Market Weighton, 4,371 . . . . G5
Marple, 19,829 . . . D6
Marsden, 3,873 . . . E5
Marshchapel J6
Marske-by-the-Sea, 8,936 . . . . F3
Marton (North Yorkshire) F4
Marton (Lincolnshire) G6
Maryport, 9,797 . . A3
Masham E4
Mawbray B3
Mealsgate B3
Melling C4
Melmerby C3
Meltham, 7,514 . . . E5
Messingham, 2,952 . G5
Mexborough, 15,282 . . . . F6
Mickleton, 1,551 . . D3
Middleham E4
Middlesbrough, 147,430 . . . . . . F3

Middlesmoor E4
Middleton, 45,621 . . C4
Middleton D5
Middleton Hall D1
Millom, 6,455 . . . . B4
Milnthorpe, 1,934 . . C4
Mindrum D1
Mirfield, 18,459 . . . E5
Misson G6
Mordon E3
Morecambe, 46,657 C4
Moresby A3
Morley, 47,579 . . . . E5
Morpeth, 14,393 . . E2
Mosedale C3
Mossley, 10,569 . . . D5
Naburn F5
Nafferton, 1,979 . . H4
Natland C4
Nelson, 29,120 . . . D5
Nenthead D3
Neston, 15,585 . . . B6
Netherwitton E2
Nettleham, 3,152 . . H6
Newbiggin D3
Newbiggin-by-the-Sea, 7,100 . . . . E2
Newbrough D2
Newby Bridge C4
Newcastle upon Tyne, 189,150 . . . . . . E3
New Mills, 9,092 . . D6
Newton D5
Newton Aycliffe, 25,085 . . . . E3
Newton-le-Willows, 19,416 . . . . C6
Newton-on-the-Moor E2
New Waltham, 4,263 . . . . H5
Ninebanks D3
Nook C2
Normanby G5
Normanton, 13,774 F5
Northallerton, 13,774 . . . . F4
North Dalton G5
North Kelsey H5
North Shields, 38,119 . . . . F2
North Somercotes . J6
North Stainmore . . D3
North Thoresby . . . H6
Northwich, 34,520 . C6
Norton, 6,342 . . . . G4
Nunnington G4
Nunwick D2
Oakworth E5
Oldcotes F6
Oldham, 103,931 . . D5
Old Hutton C4
Old Town C4
Ollerton D6
Ormskirk, 23,425 . . C5
Orton C4
Ossett, 20,405 . . . . E5
Otley, 13,596 . . . . E5
Otterburn D2
Ottringham H5
Overton, 3,660 . . . C4
Owston Ferry G6
Oxenhope E5
Padiham, 12,570 . . D5
Painshawfield, 3,033 E3
Pateley Bridge, 1,943 . . . . E4
Patrington, 1,943 . . H5
Patterdale C3
Pawston D1
Peak Forest E6
Peel A5
Penistone, 8,627 . . E5
Penrith, 12,049 . . . C3
Peterlee, 31,139 . . . F3
Pickering, 5,914 . . G4
Piercebridge E3
Pilling C5
Plumpton C3
Pocklington, 5,908 . G5
Pontefract, 28,358 . F5
Ponteland, 9,933 . . E2
Pool E5
Pooley Bridge C3
Port Erin A5
Poulton-le-Fylde, 18,939 . . . . B5
Powburn E2
Preesall, 5,168 . . . C5
Prescot, 37,486 . . . C6
Preston (Lancashire), 177,660 . . . . . . C5
Preston (Humberside), 2,040 . . . . H5
Prudhoe, 11,204 . . E3
Pudsey, 31,636 . . . E5
Queensbury, 7,424 . E5
Rainford, 6,362 . . . C5
Rampside B4
Ramsey, 7,577 . . . . B5
Ramsgill E4
Ranby F6
Ranskill F6
Ravenglass B4
Ravenscar H4
Ravenstonedale . . . D4
Rawcliffe G5
Rawmarsh, 18,085 . F6
Rawtenstall, 21,933 D5
Raylees D2
Redcar, 35,877 . . . F3
Red Dial B3
Reighton H4
Renwick C3
Retford G6
Riccall, 1,949 . . . . F5
Ridsdale D2
Riding Mill E3
Ripon, 13,806 . . . . E4
Ripponden, 2,855 . E5
Rochdale, 94,313 . . D5
Rockhope D3
Rossington F6
Rosthwaite B3
Rothbury, 1,805 . . . E2
Rotherham, 121,380 F6

Rothwell, 18,336 . . F5
Roughsike C2
Royston, 9,638 . . . F5
Rudston H4
Runcorn, 64,154 . . C6
Rushyford E3
Ryal E2
Rydal C4
Ryton, 15,952 . . . . G4
Sacriston, 4,726 . . . E3
Sadberge E3
St. Helens, 106,293 C6
St. Johns A5
St. John's Chapel . . D3
Salford, 79,755 . . . D5
Saltburn-by-the-Sea, 6,145 . . . . G3
Saltfleet J6
Sandygate B5
Satley E3
Sawley D5
Sawley E4
Saxilby, 3,086 . . . . G6
Saxton F5
Scalby, 9,019 . . . . H4
Scambesby H6
Scarborough, 38,809 . . . . H4
Scotch Corner E4
Scotforth C5
Scotter, 2,415 . . . . G6
Scunthorpe, 75,982 G5
Seaham, 22,130 . . . F3
Seahouses E1
Seamer, 2,178 . . . . G4
Seascale, 1,766 . . . B4
Seaton, 4,380 . . . . A3
Seaton Delaval, 7,333 . . . . E2
Seave Green F4
Sebergham C3
Sedbergh, 1,670 . . C4
Sedgefield, 4,424 . . E3
Sedgwick C4
Selby, 15,292 . . . . F5
Sellafield A4
Settle, 3,082 . . . . . D4
Sheffield, 431,607 . E6
Shelf, 4,237 . . . . . E5
Sherburn, 2,832 . . . G4
Sherburn in Elmet, 5,396 . . . . F5
Sheriff Hutton F4
Shilbottle E2
Shildon, 11,136 . . . E3
Shipley, 28,165 . . . E5
Shipton F4
Sigglesthorne H5
Silecroft B4
Silloth, 2,942 . . . . B3
Sinderhope D3
Singleton C5
Skelmersdale, 42,104 . . . . C5
Skelton, 5,353 . . . . F3
Skidby H5
Skipsea H5
Skipton, 13,583 . . . D5
Skipton-on-Swale . . F4
Slaggyford C3
Slaley D3
Sleights, 2,061 . . . G4
Smithfield C3
Snainton G4
Snaith, 2,748 . . . . F5
South Cave, 2,669 . G5
South Ferriby G5
South Kelsey H6
South Leverton . . . G6
South Otterington . F4
Southport, 90,959 . B5
South Shields, 83,704 . . . . F3
South Skirlaugh . . . H5
Spennymoor, 17,381 E3
Spofforth F5
Staindrop E3
Stamford Bridge, 3,099 . . . . G5
Stamfordham E2
Standish, 12,196 . . C5
Stanhope, 1,342 . . D3
Stanley, 18,905 . . . E3
Startforth E3
Staveley, 27,665 . . F6
Staxton H4
Stillington F4
Stockport, 132,813 . D6
Stocksbridge, 13,182 . . . . E6
Stockton-on-Tees, 83,576 . . . . F3
Stockwith G6
Stokesley, 4,008 . . F4
Strensall, 4,432 . . . F4
Stretford, 43,953 . . D6
Sturton by Stow . . . G6

Sulby B5
Summerbridge E4
Sunderland, 183,310 . . . . . . F3
Sutton on Sea J6
Swaby J6
Swinton, 15,936 . . F6
Tadcaster, 6,915 . . F5
Tebay C4
Temple Sowerby . . C3
Tetford H6
The Flatt C2
The Hill B4
The Lhen B5
Thirsk, 6,860 . . . . F4
Thixendale G4
Thornaby-on-Tees, 24,189 . . . . F3
Thorne (Thorne/Moorends), 16,751 . . . . G5
Thornley, 2,970 . . . F3
Thornthwaite B3
Thornton B5
Thornton G4
Thorpe Salvin F6
Threlkeld B3
Thringarth D3
Thurcroft, 5,115 . . F6
Thursby B3
Tickhill, 5,572 . . . . F6
Tideswell, 1,717 . . E6
Todhills C3
Todmorden, 11,969 D5
Torver B4
Tow Law, 2,204 . . . E3
Trawden D5
Trimdon, 3,049 . . . F3
Troutbeck C4
Tunstall C4
Tuxford, 2,577 . . . . G6
Tweedmouth D1
Tynemouth, 17,422 F2
Ulceby H5
Ulgham E2
Ulpha B4
Ulverston, 11,866 . B4
Underbarrow C4
Unthank C3
Upper Poppleton . . F5
Vickerstown B4
Waddington, 4,781 . D5
Wadworth F6
Wakefield, 73,955 . E5
Walkington, 1,934 . G5
Wallasey, 60,895 . . B6
Wallsend, 45,280 . . E3
Waltham, 6,157 . . . H5
Warcop D3
Wardlow E6
Wark D2
Warkworth, 1,642 . E2
Warrington, 82,812 C6
Warter G4
Warton C4
Washington, 56,848 E3
Waskerley E3
Wath upon Dearne, 16,070 . . . . F5
Weaverham, 6,604 . C6
Weaverthorpe G4
Welton G5
Welton (Welton/Dunholme), 3,695 H6
West Auckland E3
West Burton E4
West Hall C3
West Heslerton . . . G4
West Kirby B6
Westnewton B3
West Rasen H6
West Tanfield E4
West Woodburn . . . D2
Wetheral C3
Wetherby, 8,154 . . F5
Wetwang G4
Whaley Bridge, 4,530 . . . . E6
Whalton E2
Wham D4
Whashton E4
Wheldrake G5
Whickham, 17,428 . E3
Whitbeck B4
Whitby, 13,640 . . . G4
Whitehaven, 26,542 A3
Whitley Bay, 33,335 F2
Whittingham D2
Whittington, 2,350 . C4
Widdington E2
Widnes, 57,162 . . . C6
Wigan, 85,819 . . . . C5
Wigginton F4
Wigglesworth D4
Wigton, 5,306 . . . . B3
Wilberfoss G5
Willingham by Stow G6
Willington, 4,913 . . E3

Wilmslow, 28,604 . . D6
Windermere, 6,847 . C4
Wingate, 4,541 . . . F3
Winterton, 4,895 . . G5
Wintringham G4
Witham D4
Withernsea, 6,433 . J5
Wolsingham, 1,286 . E3
Wolviston F3
Wombwell, 15,462 . E5
Wooperton E2
Workington, 25,579 A3
Worksop, 37,247 . . F6
Wreay C3
Wrelton G4
Wressle G5
Wroot G5
Yarburgh J6
Yedingham G4
York, 124,609 . . . . F5

Other Features

Ae, forest A2
Annandale, valley . . A2
Arnside and Silverdale . . . .
Bassenthwaite, lake .B3
Bowland, forest . . . C4
Cheviot, hills C2
Coniston Water, lake B4
Cow Green, reservoir D3
Cross Fell, hill C3
Daer, reservoir A2
Derwent, reservoir . E6
Derwent, reservoir . D3
Derwent Water, lake B3
East Stewartry Coast N.P. A3
Eildon and Leaderfoot N.P. . . . C1
Ennerdale Water, lake B4
Eskdale, valley B2
Ettrick Pen, hill . . . B2
Farne, islands E1
Great Gable, hill . . . B4
Hart Fell, hill B2
Haweswater, lake . . C3
Holy, island E1
Howardian, hills . . . F4
Humber, river H5
Irish, sea B5
Kielder Water, lake . C2
Lake District National Park B4
Lauderdale, valley . C1
Lincolnshire Wolds, hills H6
Man, island A5
Moorfoot, hills B1
Morecambe, bay . . B5
Nith, estuary A3
North, sea H2
Northumberland, coast E1
Northumberland National Park . . . D2
North York Moors National Park . . . F4
Peak District National Park . . . E6
Pennines, hills D3
Pentland, hills A1
Pickering, valley . . . G4
Roan Fell, hill C2
Scafell, hill B4
Scafell Pike, hill . . . B4
Skiddaw, hill B3
Snaefell, hill B5
Solway, coast A3
Solway, estuary . . . A3
Stainmore, forest . . D3
Stocks, reservoir . . D4
Teesdale, valley . . . D2
The Cheviot, hill . . . D2
The Merse, hill D1
The Wolds, hills . . . G4
Thirlmere, lake B3
Tinto, hill A1
Tweed, river B1
Tweedsmuir, hills . . B1
Ullswater, lake C3
Upper Tweeddale N.P. . . B1
Walney, island B4
Wast Water, lake . . B4
Weardale, valley . . D3
Wensleydale, valley . D4
Wharfedale, valley . E4
White Coomb, hill . B2
Windermere, lake . . C4
Yorkshire Dales National Park . . . D4

Richmond, North Yorkshire

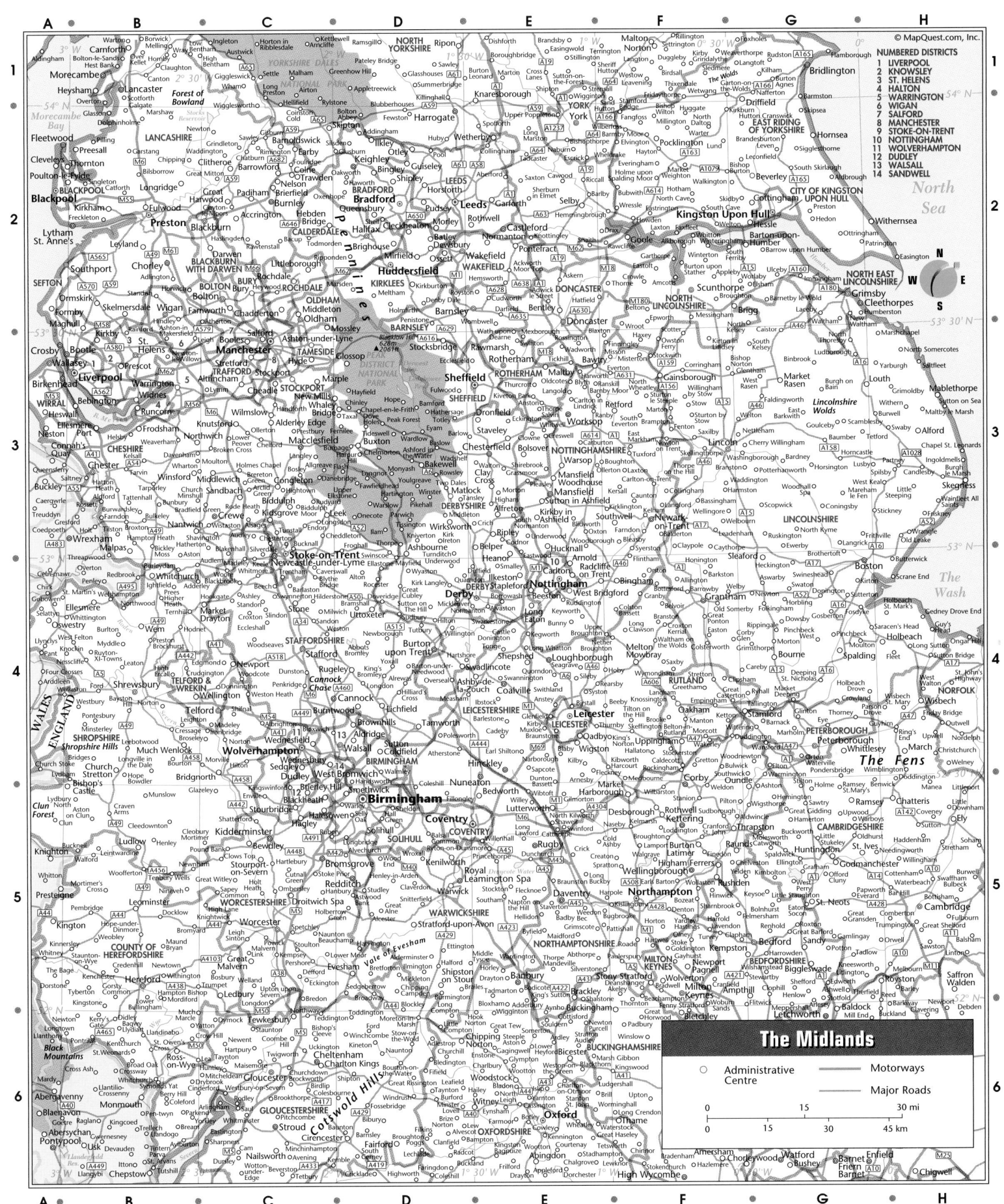

NUMBERED DISTRICTS
1. LIVERPOOL
2. KNOWSLEY
3. ST. HELENS
4. HALTON
5. WARRINGTON
6. WIGAN
7. SALFORD
8. MANCHESTER
9. STOKE-ON-TRENT
10. NOTTINGHAM
11. WOLVERHAMPTON
12. DUDLEY
13. WALSALL
14. SANDWELL

The Midlands

○ Administrative Centre

Motorways

Major Roads

0 ——— 15 ——— 30 mi

0 —— 15 —— 30 —— 45 km

Midlands:
Map Index

Unitary Authorities
(2001 census population)

Barnsley, 218,062 ...C2
Bedfordshire, 381,571 ...G5
Birmingham, 977,091 ...D4
Blackburn with Darwen, 137,471 ...C2
Blackpool, 142,284 ...A2
Bolton, 261,035 ...B2
Bradford, 467,668 ...C2
Buckinghamshire, 479,028 ...E6
Bury, 180,612 ...C2
Calderdale, 300,844 ...C2
Cambridgeshire, 552,655 ...G5
Cheshire, 673,777 ...B3
County of Herefordshire, 174,844 ...B5
Coventry, 300,844 ...D5
Derby, 221,716 ...D4
Derbyshire, 734,581 ...D3
Doncaster, 286,865 ...E2
Dudley, 305,164 ...C4
East Riding of Yorkshire, 314,076 ...G2
Gloucestershire, 564,559 ...C6
Halton, 118,215 ...B3
Hertfordshire, 1,033,977 ...G6
Kingston upon Hull, City of, 243,595 ...G2
Kirklees, 388,576 ...D2
Knowsley, 150,468 ...B3
Lancashire, 1,134,976 ...B2
Leeds, 715,404 ...D2
Leicester, 279,923 ...E4
Leicestershire, 609,579 ...E4
Lincolnshire, 646,646 ...G3
Liverpool, 439,476 ...B3
Manchester, 392,819 ...C3
Milton Keynes, 207,063 ...F5
Norfolk, 796,733 ...H4
Northamptonshire, 629,676 ...E5
North East Lincolnshire, 157,983 ...G2
North Lincolnshire, 152,839 ...F2
North Yorkshire, 569,660 ...D1
Nottingham, 266,995 ...E4
Nottinghamshire, 748,503 ...E3
Oldham, 217,393 ...C2
Oxfordshire, 605,492 ...E6
Peterborough, 156,060 ...G4
Rochdale, 205,233 ...C2
Rotherham, 248,176 ...E3
Rutland, 34,560 ...F4
St. Helens, 176,845 ...B3
Sandwell, 282,901 ...C4
Salford, 216,119 ...C2
Sefton, 282,956 ...A2
Sheffield, 513,234 ...D3
Shropshire, 283,240 ...B4
Solihull, 199,521 ...D5
Staffordshire, 806,737 ...C4
Stockport, 284,544 ...C3
Stoke-on-Trent, 240,643 ...C3
Tameside, 213,045 ...C3
Telford and Wrekin, 158,285 ...B4
Trafford, 210,135 ...C3
Wakefield, 315,173 ...E2
Walsall, 253,502 ...C4
Warrington, 191,084 ...B3
Warwickshire, 505,885 ...D5
Wigan, 301,417 ...B3
Wolverhampton, 236,573 ...C4
Worcestershire, 542,107 ...C5
York, 181,131 ...E1

Cities and Towns

Abbots Bromley, 1,356 ...D4
Abersychan ...A6
Abingdon, 35,234 ...E6
Accrington, 36,466 ...C2
Ackworth Moor Top, 5,851 ...E2
Adderbury, 2,348 ...E5
Adderley ...B4
Addingham, 2,769 ...C2
Adlington, 8,556 ...B2
Adwick le Street, 10,288 ...E2
Akeley ...F5
Albrighton, 6,135 ...C4
Alcester, 6,282 ...D5
Alderley Edge, 5,280 ...C3
Aldford ...B3
Aldridge, 16,862 ...D4
Alford, 2,989 ...H3
Alfreton, 22,822 ...E3
Allgreave ...C3
Alrewas, 2,907 ...D4
Alsager, 13,435 ...C3
Alton, 16,005 ...D4
Altrincham, 40,042 ...C3
Alvechurch, 3,317 ...D5
Amersham, 21,711 ...F6
Ampthill, 6,230 ...G5
Anstey, 6,192 ...E4
Anston (Anston/Dinnington), 17,691 ...E3
Appleby, 2,570 ...F2
Arclid Green ...C3
Arddleen ...A4
Ardley ...E6
Arlesey, 4,374 ...G5
Artingham ...C4
Arnold, 37,646 ...E4
Ashbourne, 6,300 ...D3
Ashby-de-la-Zouch, 10,595 ...D4
Ashford in the Water ...D3
Ashton ...C6
Ashton-in-Makersfield, 28,105 ...B3
Ashton-under-Lyne, 43,906 ...C3
Ashwell, 1,629 ...G5
Astern, 5,862 ...C2
Aston ...B5
Aston on Clun ...B5
Astwood Bank ...C5
Atherton, 21,696 ...C2
Audlem ...B4
Audley, 6,180 ...C3
Avening ...C6
Aylburton ...B6
Bacup, 13,682 ...C2
Bagwy Llydiart ...B6
Bakewell, 3,818 ...D3
Baldock, 9,232 ...G5
Ball Common ...D5
Bampton, 2,459 ...D6
Banbury, 39,906 ...E5
Bardney ...G3
Bar Hill, 4,397 ...H4
Barkway ...H5
Barlaston, 2,119 ...C4
Barlby, 2,432 ...E2
Barlestone, 2,547 ...E4
Barmby Moor ...F2
Barnet Friern Barnet ...G6
Barnoldswick, 10,038 ...C2
Barnsley, 75,120 ...D2
Barnsley ...C2
Barnwell, 2,084 ...F4
Barrowford, 5,212 ...C2
Barrow upon Humber, 2,161 ...G2
Barton-under-Needwood, 4,327 ...D4
Barton-upon-Humber, 9,422 ...G2
Baslow, 1,184 ...D3
Bassingham ...F3
Batley, 48,030 ...D2
Baunton ...C6
Bawtry, 2,696 ...E3
Bayston Hill, 5,462 ...B4

Bebington, 60,148 ...B3
Bedford, 73,917 ...G5
Bedworth, 31,932 ...D4
Beeston (Beeston and Stapleford), 66,626 ...E4
Belper, 18,213 ...D4
Belton, 2,300 ...G2
Bentley, 32,675 ...E2
Berry Hill ...B6
Beverley, 23,632 ...G2
Bewdley, 9,009 ...C5
Bibury ...D6
Bicester, 22,128 ...E6
Bickley Moss ...B4
Biddulph, 16,725 ...C3
Biddulph Moor ...C3
Bingham, 7,057 ...F4
Bingley, 19,585 ...D2
Birdlip ...C6
Birkenhead, 93,087 ...A3
Birmingham, 965,928 ...D5
Birstall, 11,770 ...E4
Bishop Burton ...G2
Bishop's Castle ...B4
Bishop's Cleeve, 10,098 ...C6
Bishopthorpe, 3,148 ...E2
Blaby, 6,358 ...E4
Blackbrook ...B3
Blackburn, 105,994 ...C2
Blackheath ...C4
Blackpool, 146,262 ...A2
Blackthorn ...E6
Bladon ...E6
Blaenavon, 6,066 ...A6
Blakenhall ...C3
Bleasby ...F3
Bletchley, 41,435 ...F5
Blidworth, 4,215 ...E3
Blockley ...D5
Bloxham, 2,356 ...E5
Bloxwich ...C4
Blyth, 35,327 ...E3
Blythe Bridge ...C4
Bodicote ...E5
Bolsover, 11,743 ...E3
Bolton, 139,020 ...C2
Bolton-le-Sands, 6,772 ...B1
Bootle, 65,454 ...B3
Boroughbridge, 1,903 ...E1
Borrowash, 7,092 ...E4
Bosley ...C3
Boston, 34,606 ...G4
Botley, 2,297 ...E6
Bottesford, 2,619 ...F4
Bottisham, 1,784 ...H5
Boughton (Boughton/Ollerton), 10,441 ...F3
Bourne, 8,777 ...G4
Bourton ...B4
Bourton-on-the-Water, 2,239 ...D6
Bozeat, 1,864 ...F5
Brackley, 9,113 ...E5
Bradfield Green ...C3
Bradford, 289,376 ...D2
Bramshall ...D4
Branston, 3,350 ...F4
Branston ...C4
Braunston, 1,669 ...E5
Bream, 2,704 ...B6
Bredon, 2,008 ...C5
Brereton Green ...C3
Bretforton ...D5
Bridges ...B4
Bridgnorth, 11,229 ...C4
Bridlington, 31,334 ...G1
Brierfield, 9,567 ...C2
Brierley Hill, 5,768 ...C4
Brigg, 5,768 ...G2
Brighouse, 32,198 ...D2
Brize Norton ...D6
Broad Oak, 1,764 ...B6
Broadway, 2,328 ...D5
Brockworth ...C6
Broken Cross ...C3
Bromsgrove, 26,366 ...C5
Bromyard, 3,117 ...B5
Brookthorpe ...C6
Broseley, 5,089 ...C4
Broughton (Humberside), 4,448 ...F2
Broughton (Northamptonshire), 2,005 ...F5
Broughton Poggs ...D6
Brownhills, 18,159 ...D4
Broxton ...B3
Buckingham, 10,168 ...F5
Buckland ...D6
Buckley, 17,753 ...A3
Bucknall ...C4
Bucknell ...B5
Budbrooke, 2,711 ...D5
Bulkeley ...B3
Bunbury ...B3
Burbage, 1,246 ...D3
Burford, 1,171 ...D6
Burgh le Marsh, 1,701 ...H3
Burleydam ...B4
Burlton ...B4
Burnley, 74,661 ...C2
Burntwood, 28,801 ...D4
Burton Latimer, 5,449 ...F5
Burton upon Stather ...F2
Burton upon Trent, 60,525 ...D4
Burwardsley ...B3
Burwell, 4,628 ...H5
Burwell ...H3
Bury, 62,633 ...C2
Bushey, 16,488 ...G6
Buxton, 19,854 ...D3
Caergwrle ...A3
Caistor, 2,502 ...G3
Cam ...C6
Cambridge, 95,682 ...H5
Candlesby ...H3
Cannock, 60,106 ...D4
Carlton (Nottinghamshire), 47,302 ...E4
Carlton in Lindrick, 6,376 ...E3
Carlton-on-Trent ...F3
Carnforth, 7,442 ...B1
Cassington ...E6
Castle Donington, 6,007 ...E4
Castleford, 38,536 ...E2
Catthorpe ...E5
Catworth ...G5
Caunton ...F3
Caversham ...A4
Cefn-mawr, 8,538 ...A4
Chadderton, 34,026 ...C2
Chalgrove, 2,832 ...E6
Chapel-en-le-Frith, 8,715 ...D3
Chapel St. Leonards, 2,884 ...H3
Charlbury, 2,694 ...E6
Charlton Kings, 11,332 ...C6
Charlton-on-Otmoor ...E6
Chatteris, 7,261 ...H4
Cheadle (Cheadle and Gatley), 58,457 ...C3
Cheddleton, 3,534 ...C3
Chelmorton ...D3
Cheltenham, 91,301 ...C6
Chelveston ...F5
Chepstow, 9,461 ...B6
Cherry Willingham (Cherry Willingham/Reepham), 3,670 ...G3
Chester, 80,110 ...B3
Chesterfield, 71,945 ...D3

Chesterton ...C3
Chigwell, 10,332 ...H6
Chinnor, 5,599 ...F6
Chipping Campden, 1,741 ...D5
Chipping Norton, 5,386 ...E6
Chirk, 4,264 ...A4
Chorley, 33,536 ...B2
Chorleywood, 9,025 ...F6
Christchurch, 36,379 ...H4
Churchdown ...C6
Church Minshull ...B3
Church Stoke ...A4
Church Stretton, 3,435 ...B4
Cinderford, 9,546 ...B6
Cirencester, 15,221 ...D6
Clapham, 3,501 ...F5
Claverdon ...D5
Clay Cross (Clay Cross/North Wingfield), 24,271 ...E3
Clayton-le-Moors, 6,961 ...C2
Cleckheaton (Cleckheaton and Liversedge), 27,151 ...D2
Cleedownton ...B5
Cleethorpes, 31,853 ...G2
Cleobury Mortimer, 2,164 ...C5
Clitheroe, 13,548 ...C2
Clophill, 2,372 ...G5
Clowne, 7,234 ...E3
Clows Top ...C5
Clun ...A5
Coalville, 30,408 ...E4
Coedpoeth, 5,300 ...A3
Colston Cold ...C2
Coleford (Gloucestershire), 9,567 ...B6
Colesbourne ...C6
Coleshill, 6,324 ...D5
Coleshill ...D6
Collingham (Nottinghamshire), 2,801 ...F3
Collingham (West Yorkshire), 2,714 ...
Colne, 18,776 ...C2
Comberton, 2,311 ...H5
Congleton, 24,569 ...C3
Coningsby, 5,126 ...G3
Connah's Quay, 14,443 ...A3
Coombe Hill ...C6
Corby, 49,053 ...F5
Cottenham, 4,486 ...H5
Courtenay ...E6
Coventry, 299,316 ...D5
Cowley ...E6
Cranfield, 4,142 ...F5
Cranford St. John ...F5
Craven Arms ...B5
Credenhill, 2,013 ...B5
Cressage ...B4
Creswell, 4,655 ...E3
Crewe, 63,351 ...C3
Crich ...E3
Crick, 1,314 ...E5
Cricklade, 3,808 ...D6
Crosby, 52,869 ...A3
Cross Ash ...B6
Crossway ...A5
Crow Hill ...B6
Crowland, 3,172 ...G4
Crowle, 2,916 ...F2
Crudgington ...B4
Cudworth, 11,715 ...E2
Cutnall Green ...C5
Danebridge ...C3
Darfield, 7,723 ...E2
Darwen, 29,864 ...C2
Davenham ...B3
Daventry, 18,099 ...E5
Deanshanger, 2,724 ...F5
Defford ...C5
Denby Dale, 2,282 ...D2
Denton, 37,785 ...C3
Desborough, 7,351 ...F5
Devauden ...B6
Dewsbury, 50,168 ...D2
Didley ...B6
Docklow ...B5
Doddington (Doddington/Wimblington), 2,810 ...H5
Doncaster, 71,595 ...E2
Donington, 2,569 ...G4
Donnington ...C4
Dorchester, 15,037 ...E6
Dorstone ...A5
Dove Holes ...D3
Doveridge ...D4
Drayton, 2,240 ...E5
Drayton ...C4
Droitwich Spa, 20,966 ...C5
Dronfield, 22,985 ...E3
Drybrook ...B6
Dudley (West Dudley), 192,171 ...C4
Duffield, 4,514 ...E4
Dunchurch, 2,251 ...E5
Dunston ...C4
Dunton Bassett ...E4
Dursley, 13,331 ...C6
Dymock ...C6
Earby, 4,957 ...C2
Earls Barton, 4,917 ...F5
Earl Shilton, 18,083 ...E4
Easington ...H2
Easingwold, 2,816 ...E1
Eastington ...C6
East Markham ...F3
Easton (Easton/Weston), 7,631 ...E5
Eastwood, 19,363 ...E4
Eaton Socon, 12,370 ...G5
Eccleshall, 2,748 ...C4
Eckington, 7,167 ...E3
Eckington ...C5
Edgmond, 1,376 ...C4
Edworth ...G5
Elastone ...D4
Ellesmere, 2,964 ...B4
Ellesmere Port, 64,504 ...B3
Ellington, 2,253 ...G5
Ely, 10,329 ...H5
Endon ...C3
Enfield, 256,664 ...G6
Enville ...C5
Epworth, 3,359 ...F2
Everton ...B3
Evesham, 17,823 ...D5
Eynsham, 4,764 ...E6
Eye (Cambridgeshire), 3,010 ...G4
Fairford, 2,633 ...D6
Faringdon, 5,235 ...D6
Farmoor ...E6
Farndon (Cheshire) ...B3
Farndon (Nottinghamshire) ...F3
Farnworth, 25,053 ...C2
Fawfieldhead ...C3
Felmersham ...F5
Fenny Stratford ...F5
Fenton ...F3
Finedon, 4,051 ...F5
Finningley, 3,624 ...F3
Flamborough, 1,741 ...G1
Flash ...C3
Fleckney, 4,295 ...E4
Fleet, 30,391 ...H4
Fleetwood, 27,227 ...A2
Flitwick, 11,063 ...F5
Fossebridge ...D6
Four Crosses ...A4
Freckleton (Freckleton/Warton), 8,273 ...B2
Friskney ...H3

Frithville ...G3
Frodsham, 8,903 ...B3
Froghall ...D3
Fulbourn, 3,896 ...H5
Fulwood ...B2
Gagingwell ...E5
Gainsborough, 19,704 ...F3
Gamlingay, 3,391 ...G5
Garforth, 15,250 ...E2
Garstang, 5,697 ...B2
Gayhurst ...F5
Giggleswick ...C1
Gilmorton ...E5
Glazeley ...C5
Glentham ...G3
Glinton, 1,663 ...G4
Glossop (Glossop/Hollingworth), 30,771 ...D3
Gloucester, 114,003 ...C6
Glusburn, 6,859 ...C2
Gobowen, 2,823 ...A4
Godmanchester, 5,243 ...G5
Goetre ...B6
Goole, 19,410 ...F2
Gorsty Common ...B5
Gosberton, 1,785 ...G4
Grassmoor ...E3
Great Alne ...D5
Great Barford, 1,754 ...G5
Great Cubley ...D4
Great Harwood, 10,562 ...C2
Great Malvern, 31,537 ...C5
Great Mitton ...C2
Great Rissington ...D6
Great Shelford, 6,522 ...H5
Great Witley ...C5
Gresford, 4,915 ...B3
Grimsby, 90,703 ...G2
Guiseley (Guiseley/Yeadon), 31,104 ...D2
Gwennesney ...B6
Haddenham (Cambridgeshire), 2,556 ...H5
Hagley, 5,417 ...C5
Halesowen, 57,918 ...C5
Halifax, 91,069 ...D2
Hallaton ...F4
Hall Green ...D5
Hampton Bishop ...B5
Hampton Heath ...B4
Hanbury ...C5
Handsworth ...D3
Harmston ...F3
Harpole ...E5
Harpur Hill ...D3
Harrogate, 66,178 ...D2
Hartington ...D3
Hartlebury ...C5
Hartpury ...C6
Hartwell (Northamptonshire), 1,780 ...F5
Harvington ...D5
Harworth (Harworth/Bircotes), 7,813 ...E3
Haslingden, 15,024 ...C2
Hatfield (South Yorkshire), 14,067 ...E2
Hatherton ...C3
Hatton Heath ...B3
Haworth, 4,956 ...D2
Hayfield, 2,293 ...D3
Hazlemere (Hazlemere/Tylers Green), 20,843 ...F6
Heanor, 22,180 ...E3
Hebden Bridge, 3,681 ...C2
Heckington, 2,723 ...G4
Hedon, 6,646 ...G2
Helsby, 4,538 ...B3
Hemington ...G5
Hemsworth, 9,401 ...E2
Henley ...B5
Henley-in-Arden, 2,803 ...D5
Henlow (Henlow/Shefford), 11,391 ...G5
Hereford, 54,326 ...B5
Heswall, 31,093 ...A3
Heywood, 29,286 ...C2
Higham, 2,670 ...C3
Higham Ferrers, 5,345 ...F5
High Bentham, 2,538 ...C1
High Ercall ...B4
High Lane, 4,861 ...C3
Hightown, 2,141 ...A3
Highworth, 8,259 ...D6
High Wycombe, 71,718 ...F6
Hilderstone ...C4
Hillard's Cross ...D4
Hilton, 1,755 ...D4
Hilton ...D4
Hinckley, 40,608 ...E4
Hindley, 22,581 ...C2
Hodnet ...B4
Holbeach, 6,088 ...H4
Holberrow Green ...D5
Holmes Chapel, 5,463 ...C3
Holme upon Spalding Moor, 2,629 ...F2
Holmfirth (Holmfirth/Honley), 21,979 ...D2
Holt, 2,922 ...B3
Holt Heath ...C5
Hookgate ...C4
Hook Norton, 1,913 ...E5
Hope Bowdler ...B4
Hope-under-Dinmore ...B5
Horley, 19,267 ...C5
Horncastle, 4,994 ...G3
Hornsea, 7,573 ...G2
Horsforth, 18,593 ...D2
Horsington ...G3
Horwich, 18,017 ...C2
Howden, 3,673 ...F2
Hucknall, 29,160 ...E3
Huddersfield, 143,726 ...D2
Humberston, 6,877 ...G2
Huntingdon, 15,575 ...G5
Hyde, 30,666 ...C3
Ibstock, 5,243 ...E4
Ightfield ...B4
Ilam ...D3
Ilkeston, 35,134 ...E4
Ilkley, 13,530 ...D2
Ilmington ...D5
Immingham, 12,278 ...G2
Ingleton, 1,979 ...C1
Ingoldmells, 2,874 ...H3
Ironbridge, 2,184 ...C4
Itton ...B6
Kegworth, 3,405 ...E4
Keighley, 49,567 ...D2
Kelham ...F3
Kelsall, 2,394 ...B3
Kelvedon Hatch, 2,738 ...H6
Kemble ...C6
Kempsey, 3,147 ...C5
Kempston, 18,233 ...F5
Kenchester ...B5
Kenilworth, 21,623 ...D5
Kennington, 4,290 ...E6
Kentchurch ...B6
Kerry's Gate ...B5
Kersall ...F3
Kettering, 47,186 ...F5
Ketton, 1,708 ...F4
Kibworth Harcourt, 3,973 ...E4
Kidderminster, 54,644 ...C5
Kidsgrove, 27,702 ...C3
Kimbolton ...G5
Kineton, 2,079 ...D5
Kingcoed ...B6
King's Bromley ...D4

King's Sutton, 2,073 ...E5
Kingston Bagpuize, 2,098 ...E6
Kingstone ...B5
Kingston Upon Hull, 310,636 ...G2
Kingswinford ...C5
Kingswood, 60,192 ...C6
Kington, 2,197 ...A5
Kinnersley ...A5
Kirby Grindalythe ...F1
Kirby Muxloe, 7,780 ...E4
Kirkburton, 4,121 ...D2
Kirkby, 43,017 ...B3
Kirkby in Ashfield, 27,014 ...E3
Kirkham, 9,038 ...B2
Kirk Ireton ...E3
Kirton, 2,328 ...G4
Kirton in Lindsey, 2,773 ...F3
Knaresborough, 13,380 ...E1
Knighton, 2,972 ...A5
Knightwick ...C5
Knockin ...B4
Knottingley, 14,690 ...E2
Knutsford, 13,352 ...C3
Laceby, 2,666 ...G2
Lancaster, 44,447 ...B1
Langford, 2,760 ...E5
Langold, 2,802 ...E3
Langton ...F1
Laxton ...C6
Laxton ...F3
Lea ...C6
Leadenham ...F3
Leaton ...B4
Lechlade, 1,638 ...D6
Leconfield, 1,436 ...G2
Ledbury, 6,216 ...C5
Leebotwood ...B4
Leeds, 424,194 ...D2
Leek, 18,167 ...C3
Leicester, 318,518 ...E4
Leigh, 43,150 ...B3
Leigh Sinton ...C5
Leighton ...B4
Leintwardine ...B5
Leominster, 9,543 ...B5
Letchworth, 31,418 ...G6
Leven, 2,036 ...G2
Lichfield, 28,666 ...D4
Lincoln, 80,281 ...F3
Linton, 3,959 ...H5
Litherland ...B3
Little ...C6
Littleborough, 13,638 ...C2
Little Compton ...D6
Little Downham, 1,728 ...H5
Littleport, 5,780 ...H5
Little Steeping ...H3
Liverpool, 481,786 ...B3
Llandinabo ...B6
Llandogo ...B6
Llangybi ...A6
Llanthony ...A6
Llantilio-Crossenny ...A6
Llynclys ...A4
Long Bennington ...F3
Long Buckby, 3,428 ...E5
Long Compton ...D6
Long Crendon, 2,505 ...F6
Longdon ...C5
Longsdon ...C3
Long Eaton, 44,826 ...E4
Long Lawford, 2,501 ...E5
Long Marston ...E2
Longnor ...D3
Longton ...B2
Longville in the Dale ...B4
Loughborough, 46,867 ...E4
Louth, 14,248 ...G3
Lower Bullingham ...B5
Lower Moor ...C5
Lower Peover ...C5
Ludgershall, 3,664 ...E5
Ludlow, 9,040 ...B5
Lusby ...H3
Lutterworth, 7,380 ...E5
Lydbury North ...B5
Lydham ...A4
Lymm, 9,721 ...B3
Lytham St. Anne's, 40,866 ...B2
Mablethorpe (Mablethorpe/Sutton on Sea), 9,839 ...H3
Macclesfield, 50,270 ...C3
Madeley (Shropshire), 17,909 ...C4
Madeley (Staffordshire), 2,254 ...C4
Maghull (Maghull/Lydiate), 29,206 ...B2
Maisemore ...C6
Malpas ...B3
Maltby, 18,158 ...E3
Malton, 4,294 ...F1
Malvern Link ...C5
Manchester, 402,889 ...C3
Manea, 1,786 ...H5
Mansfield, 71,858 ...E3
Mansfield Woodhouse, 18,204 ...E3
March, 16,221 ...H4
Marehay ...E4
Mareham le Fen ...G3
Market Deeping, 12,068 ...G4
Market Drayton, 9,482 ...C4
Market Harborough, 16,563 ...F5
Market Rasen, 2,948 ...G3
Market Weighton, 4,371 ...F2
Marple, 19,829 ...C3
Marsden, 3,873 ...D2
Marshaw ...C1
Marsh Gibbon ...E5
Marston (Lincolnshire) ...F3
Marton (North Yorkshire) ...E1
Matlock, 14,680 ...D3
Maund Bryan ...B5
Mayfield, 1,954 ...D4
Measham, 3,656 ...D4
Medbourne ...F4
Medmenham ...F6
Melbourn, 4,006 ...H5
Meltham, 7,514 ...D2
Melton Mowbray, 24,348 ...F4
Messingham, 2,952 ...F2
Mexborough, 15,282 ...E3
Mickleton, 1,551 ...D5
Middleton (Derbyshire) ...D3
Middleton (Manchester), 45,621 ...C2
Middlewich, 10,100 ...C3
Millington ...E2
Milton Keynes, 43,964 ...F5
Milwich ...C4
Minchinhampton, 3,201 ...C5
Minsterley ...B4
Mirfield, 18,459 ...D2
Misterton, 1,953 ...F3
Mitcheldean, 2,243 ...C6
Monmouth, 7,246 ...B6
Monyash ...D3
Mordiford ...B5
Morecambe, 46,657 ...B1
Moreton-in-Marsh, 3,895 ...D6
Morley, 47,529 ...D2
Mortimer's Cross ...B5
Morton ...G4
Morville ...C4
Mossley, 10,569 ...C2
Moulton (Cheshire), 5,060 ...B3
Moulton (Lincolnshire) ...G4
Much Marcle ...B6
Much Wenlock, 1,921 ...B4
Munslow ...B5
Myddle ...B4

Nafferton, 1,979 ...G1
Nailsworth, 5,242 ...C6
Nantwich, 11,695 ...B3
Narborough, 6,360 ...E4
Naunton ...D6
Naunton Beauchamp ...C5
Needingworth, 1,808 ...G5
Nelson, 29,120 ...C2
Nesscliffe ...B4
Neston, 15,585 ...A3
Nettleham, 3,152 ...G3
Newark-on-Trent, 35,129 ...F3
Newborough ...D4
Newcastle-under-Lyme, 73,731 ...C3
Newent, 4,111 ...C6
New Mills, 9,092 ...C3
Newnham ...B5
Newport (Essex), 2,178 ...H6
Newport (Shropshire), 10,964 ...C4
Newport Pagnell, 12,285 ...F5
Newton (Hereford & Worcester) ...B6
Newton (Lancashire) ...C2
Newton (Lincolnshire) ...G4
Newton-le-Willows, 19,416 ...B3
Newton on Trent ...F3
Newton, 10,548 ...B5
New Waltham, 4,263 ...G2
Nineveh ...B5
Normanton (Derbyshire) ...E4
Normanton (West Yorkshire), 18,775 ...E2
Northampton, 179,596 ...F5
North Cave ...F2
Northway ...C6
Northwich, 34,520 ...B3
Northwood, 1,961 ...B4
Norton (East Shropshire) ...C4
Norton (North Yorkshire), 6,342 ...F1
Norton (Derbyshire) ...B4
Nottingham, 270,222 ...E4
Nuneaton, 66,715 ...E4
Oadby, 18,538 ...E4
Ockbrook ...E4
Offord Cluny ...G5
Oldham, 103,931 ...C2
Ollerton ...C3
Olney, 4,484 ...F5
Ombersley ...C5
Onecote ...C3
Ormskirk, 23,425 ...B2
Ossett, 20,405 ...D2
Oswestry, 15,612 ...A4
Otley, 13,596 ...D2
Oundle, 3,996 ...G5
Outwell, 1,683 ...H4
Over Kellet ...B1
Overton, 3,660 ...A3
Overton ...B2
Oxford, 118,795 ...E6
Oxton ...E3
Padiham, 12,570 ...C2
Pant ...A4
Parbold ...B2
Partney ...H3
Parwich ...D3
Patrington, 1,943 ...H2
Pattishall ...E5
Pembridge ...B5
Penistone, 8,627 ...D2
Penkridge, 7,212 ...C4
Pen-twyn ...B6
Pershore, 7,087 ...C5
Peterborough, 134,788 ...G4
Pikehall ...D3
Pinchbeck, 3,655 ...G4
Pitchcombe ...C6
Pleasley ...E3
Pocklington, 5,908 ...F2
Pontefract, 28,358 ...E2
Ponterwyd ...A6
Pontllanfraith, 1,956 ...A6
Pontrilas ...B6
Pontypool, 35,564 ...A6
Potterhanworth ...F3
Potton, 4,230 ...G5
Poulton-le-Fylde, 18,939 ...A2
Pound Bank ...C5
Powick ...C5
Preesall, 5,168 ...A2
Prees Higher Heath ...B4
Prescot, 37,486 ...B3
Prestbury, 3,346 ...C3
Presteigne, 1,815 ...A5
Preston (Humberside), 2,040 ...G2
Preston (Lancashire), 177,660 ...B2
Preston Brockhurst ...B4
Pudsey, 31,636 ...D2
Queensbury, 7,424 ...D2
Queensferry ...A3
Quorndon, 4,614 ...E4
Radcliffe on Trent, 7,387 ...E4
Raglan ...B6
Rainford, 6,362 ...B2
Ramsey, 7,577 ...G5
Ramsey St. Mary's ...G5
Raunds, 7,493 ...F5
Rawmarsh, 18,085 ...E3
Rawtenstall, 21,933 ...C2
Redbrook ...B6
Redditch, 73,372 ...D5
Riccall, 1,949 ...E2
Rimington ...C2
Ripley, 18,310 ...E3
Ripon, 13,806 ...D1
Rippenden, 2,855 ...D2
Rishton, 6,380 ...C2
Roade, 2,239 ...F5
Rocester, 1,432 ...D4
Rochdale, 94,313 ...C2
Rode Heath, 2,078 ...C3
Rossett, 1,986 ...B3
Ross-on-Wye, 9,606 ...B6
Rotherham, 121,380 ...E3
Rothwell (Northamptonshire), 7,070 ...F5
Rothwell (West Yorkshire), 18,336 ...E2
Rowsley ...D3
Royston (Cambridgeshire/Hertfordshire), 14,087 ...G5
Royston (South/West Yorkshire), 9,638 ...E2
Rubery ...C5
Ruddington, 6,486 ...E4
Rudyard ...C3
Rugby, 61,106 ...E5
Rugeley, 22,975 ...D4
Runcorn, 64,154 ...B3
Rushden, 23,854 ...F5
Ruskington, 3,530 ...G3
Ruyton-Xi-Towns ...B4
Rylstone ...C2
Ryton-on-Dunsmore ...D5
St. Arvans ...B6
St. Helens, 106,293 ...B3
St. Ives, 16,510 ...G5
St. Martin's, 2,513 ...A4
St. Neots, 13,471 ...G5
St. Owen's Cross ...B6
St. Weonards ...B6
Salford, 79,755 ...C3
Saltney, 4,769 ...A3
Sandbach, 15,839 ...C3
Sand Hutton ...F1
Sandon ...C4
Sapcote, 2,628 ...E4
Sapey Common ...C5

Saul ...C6
Sawley (Lancashire) ...C2
Sawley (North Yorkshire) ...D1
Sawston, 7,172 ...H5
Sawtry, 4,766 ...G5
Saxilby, 3,086 ...F3
Scopwick ...G3
Scotter, 2,415 ...F3
Scunthorpe, 75,982 ...F2
Sedgeberrow ...D5
Sedgley ...C4
Selattyn ...A4
Selby, 15,292 ...E2
Selly Oak ...D5
Settle, 3,082 ...C1
Settrington ...F1
Sharnbrook, 1,984 ...F5
Sharpness ...C6
Shatterford ...C5
Shavington, 4,780 ...C3
Sheffield, 431,607 ...D3
Sheldon ...D5
Shelf, 4,237 ...D2
Shepshed, 12,361 ...E4
Sherburn in Elmet, 5,396 ...E2
Shifnal, 5,893 ...C4
Shipley, 28,165 ...D2
Shipston on Stour, 3,882 ...D5
Shipton ...D6
Shirebrook, 10,413 ...E3
Shrewsbury, 64,219 ...B4
Sileby, 7,190 ...E4
Silkstone ...D2
Silverdale, 1,551 ...C3
Skegness, 15,149 ...H3
Skellingthorpe, 2,776 ...F3
Skelmersdale, 42,104 ...B2
Skipton, 13,583 ...C2
Sleaford, 10,388 ...G4
Sledmere ...F1
Slindon ...C4
Smalley ...E4
Smeeth, 2,748 ...D2
Soham, 8,639 ...H5
Solihull, 94,531 ...D5
Southam, 5,304 ...D5
South Cave, 2,669 ...F2
South Cerney, 2,145 ...D6
South Normanton (South Normanton/Pinxton), 13,044 ...E3
Southport, 90,959 ...B2
Southwell, 6,498 ...F3
Southwick, 11,067 ...F4
Spalding, 18,731 ...G4
Spetchley ...C5
Spilsby, 2,324 ...H3
Spratton ...E5
Stafford, 61,885 ...C4
Stamford, 17,492 ...G4
Stamford Bridge, 3,099 ...F2
Standish, 12,196 ...B2
Standon, 2,731 ...C4
Stanton St. John ...E5
Stanton ...C6
Staunton-on-Wye ...B5
Staveley (Derbyshire), 27,665 ...E3
Stickney ...H3
Stilton, 2,219 ...G5
Stockport, 132,813 ...C3
Stocksbridge, 13,182 ...D3
Stokenchurch, 3,775 ...F6
Stoke-on-Trent, 266,543 ...C3
Stoke Prior ...C5
Stone (Staffordshire), 12,305 ...C4
Stotfold, 6,524 ...G5
Stoulton ...C5
Stourbridge, 55,624 ...C5
Stourport-on-Severn, 18,283 ...C5
Stow ...F3
Stow-on-the-Wold, 1,999 ...D6
Stratford-upon-Avon, 22,231 ...D5
Strensall, 4,835 ...E1
Stretford, 43,953 ...C3
Stretham, 1,471 ...H5
Stretton ...C4
Stroud, 38,835 ...C6
Studley, 5,883 ...D5
Sturton le Steeple ...F3
Sudbury, 19,512 ...D4
Sutton (Cambridgeshire) ...H5
Sutton, 5,168 ...C2
Sutton Bridge, 3,457 ...H4
Sutton Coldfield, 105,452 ...D4
Sutton in Ashfield, 37,890 ...E3
Sutton-on-the-Hill ...D4
Sutton on the Forest ...E1
Swadlincote, 36,859 ...D4
Swineshead, 1,576 ...G4
Swinscoe ...D3
Swinton, 15,936 ...C2
Swynnerton ...C4
Symonds Yat ...B6
Tadcaster, 6,915 ...E2
Tamworth, 68,440 ...D4
Tansley ...D3
Tarporley, 2,308 ...B3
Tarvin, 2,843 ...B3
Tattenhall, 1,854 ...B3
Taxal ...D3
Taynton ...C6
Teddington ...C6
Telford, 35,790 ...C4
Tenbury Wells, 2,219 ...B5
Ternhill ...B4
Terrington ...F1
Tetbury, 4,618 ...C6
Tetsworth ...F6
Tewkesbury, 9,488 ...C6
Thame, 10,806 ...F6
The Bage ...A5
Thorne (Thorne/Moorends), 16,751 ...F2
Thornton (Buckinghamshire) ...F5
Thornton (Lancashire-Thornton/Cleveleys), 28,061 ...B2
Thorpe ...D3
Thorpe on the Hill ...F3
Thrapston, 3,912 ...F5
Threapwood ...B3
Thurcroft, 5,115 ...E3
Tickhill, 5,228 ...E3
Tideswell, 1,717 ...D3
Tilton ...D3
Tintern Parva ...B6
Tissington ...D3
Tiverton ...B3
Todmorden, 11,999 ...C2
Totley ...D3
Trellech ...B6
Trentham ...C4
Tutbury (Tutbury/Hatton), 5,646 ...D4
Tuxford, 2,577 ...F3
Twigworth ...C6
Two Dales ...D3
Tyberton ...B5
Uckington ...C6
Underwood, 2,177 ...E3
Underwood ...C6
Upper Elkstone ...C3
Uppingham, 3,140 ...F4
Upton, 5,623 ...A2
Upton upon Severn, 1,756 ...C5
Utkinton ...B3
Uttoxeter, 10,329 ...D4
Waddington, 4,781 ...C2

Waddington ...F3
Wadshelf ...D3
Wainfleet All Saints ...H3
Wakefield, 73,955 ...D2
Wakerley ...F4
Walcott ...B5
Walkington, 1,934 ...G2
Wallasey, 60,895 ...A3
Walmley ...D4
Walsall, 174,739 ...D1
Walton, 4,157 ...G2
Walton, 3,323 ...G5
Warboys, 2,945 ...G5
Warley ...D4
Warrington, 82,812 ...B3
Warslow ...C3
Warsop, 10,083 ...E3
Warwick, 22,476 ...D5
Washingborough ...G3
Waterbeach, 4,148 ...H5
Watford, 113,080 ...G6
Wath upon Dearne, 16,070 ...E3
Weaverham, 6,604 ...B3
Wednesbury ...C4
Wednesfield ...C4
Weedon Bec, 2,363 ...E5
Welbourn ...F3
Welland ...C5
Wellingborough, 41,602 ...F5
Wellington (Shropshire), 18,494 ...B4
Welshampton ...B4
Welton (Humberside) ...G2
Welton (Lincolnshire-Welton/Dunholme), 3,695 ...G3
Wem, 4,882 ...B4
Weobley ...B5
West Bridgford, 33,883 ...E4
West Bromwich, 146,386 ...C4
Westbury, 11,863 ...B4
Westbury-on-Severn ...C6
West Felton ...B4
West Keal ...H3
Weston ...C4
Weston Heath ...C4
Westoning ...G5
West Perry ...G5
Wetherby, 8,154 ...E2
Whaley Bridge, 4,530 ...D3
Wharton ...B3
Wheatley, 3,661 ...E6
Whitchurch (Hereford & Worcester) ...B6
Whitchurch (Shropshire), 7,868 ...B4
Whitminster ...C6
Whitmore ...C4
Whitney ...A5
Whittington, 2,350 ...B4
Whittlesey, 10,275 ...G4
Whitton ...A5
Whitton ...G2
Whitwell, 4,016 ...E3
Widnes, 57,162 ...B3
Wigan, 85,819 ...B2
Wigston, 32,864 ...E4
Wilbarston ...F5
Willenhall ...C4
Willingham, 3,317 ...H5
Willington ...E4
Wilmslow, 28,604 ...C3
Wilshamstead, 2,188 ...F5
Winchcombe, 4,243 ...D6
Winsford, 26,839 ...B3
Winslow, 4,005 ...F6
Winster ...D3
Winteringham ...F2
Winterton, 4,895 ...F2
Wirksworth, 4,235 ...D3
Wisbech, 24,981 ...H4
Wistanstow ...B5
Withernsea, 6,433 ...H2
Withington ...C6
Witney, 20,377 ...E6
Wittering, 2,379 ...G4
Woburn Sands, 4,961 ...F5
Wollaston, 2,982 ...A4
Wollaton ...E4
Wolverhampton, 257,943 ...C4
Wolverton, 55,733 ...F5
Wombwell, 15,640 ...D2
Woodborough, 1,691 ...E3
Woodcote, 2,608 ...C4
Wood End ...D5
Woodhall Spa, 3,337 ...G3
Woodstock, 2,898 ...E6
Woofferton ...B5
Woore ...B4
Wootton (North Oxford) ...E6
Wootton (South Oxford) ...E6
Worcester, 82,661 ...C5
Worksop, 37,247 ...E3
Worlaby ...G2
Wotton-under-Edge, 5,316 ...C6
Wray ...B1
Wrexham, 40,614 ...A3
Wroxall, 1,656 ...D5
Wyaston ...D4
Wymondham, 10,159 ...F4
Yarnton, 2,431 ...E6
Yatton, 6,826 ...B6
Yelden ...F5
Yorkley ...B6
Youlgrave ...D3
Yoxall, 1,421 ...D4

Other Features

Black, mountains ...A6
Bleaklow, hill ...D3
Bowland, forest ...B1
Cannock Chase, region ...C4
Clun, forest ...A5
Cotswold, hills ...C6
Derwent, reservoir ...D3
Draycote Water, lake ...E5
Evesham, vale ...C5
Fens, The, region ...G4
Humber, river ...G2
Ladybower, reservoir ...D3
Lincolnshire Wolds, hills ...G3
Llandegfedd, reservoir ...A6
Mersey, river ...B3
Morecambe, bay ...A2
Nene, river ...H2
Peak District National Park ...D3
Pennines, range ...D2
Roden, river ...C4
Severn, river ...B4, B6
Shropshire, hills ...A4
Stocks, reservoir ...C1
Trent, river ...F3
Wash, The, bay ...H4
Wharfedale, valley ...C1
Wolds, The, hills ...F1
Yorkshire Dales National Park ...C1

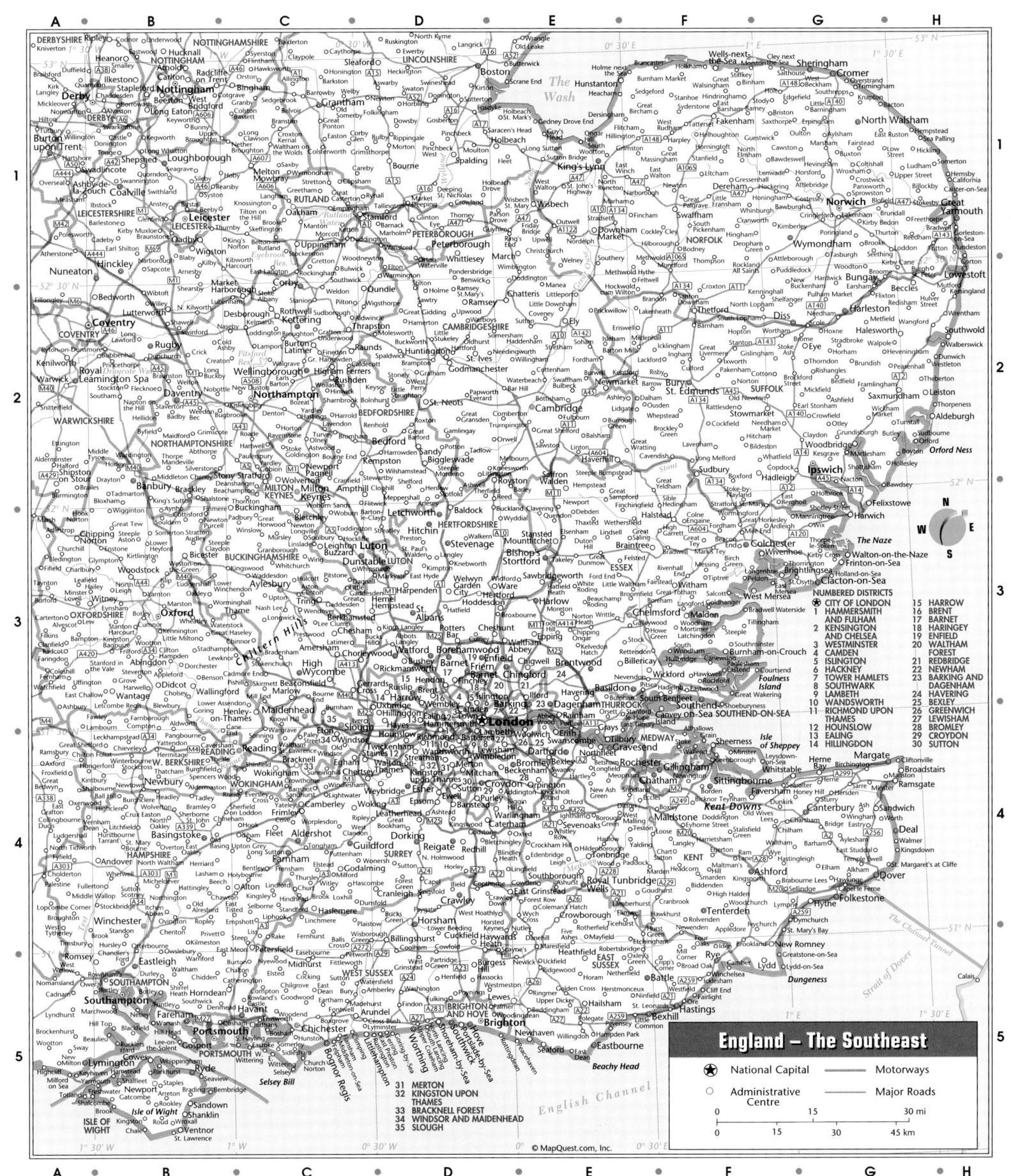

England – The Southeast

★ National Capital
○ Administrative Centre

— Motorways
— Major Roads

0   15   30 mi
0   15   30   45 km

NUMBERED DISTRICTS

① CITY OF LONDON
1 HAMMERSMITH AND FULHAM
2 KENSINGTON AND CHELSEA
3 WESTMINSTER
4 CAMDEN
5 ISLINGTON
6 HACKNEY
7 TOWER HAMLETS
8 SOUTHWARK
9 LAMBETH
10 WANDSWORTH
11 RICHMOND UPON THAMES
12 HOUNSLOW
13 EALING
14 HILLINGDON
15 HARROW
16 BRENT
17 BARNET
18 HARINGEY
19 ENFIELD
20 WALTHAM FOREST
21 REDBRIDGE
22 NEWHAM
23 BARKING AND DAGENHAM
24 HAVERING
25 BEXLEY
26 GREENWICH
27 LEWISHAM
28 BROMLEY
29 CROYDON
30 SUTTON
31 MERTON
32 KINGSTON UPON THAMES
33 BRACKNELL FOREST
34 WINDSOR AND MAIDENHEAD
35 SLOUGH

© MapQuest.com, Inc.

England – The Southeast: Map Index

Unitary Authorities
(2001 census pop.)

Barking and Dagenham, 163,944 E3
Barnet, 314,561 D3
Bedfordshire, 381,571 D2
Bexley, 218,307 E4
Bracknell Forest, 109,606 C4
Brent, 263,463 D3
Brighton and Hove, 247,820 D5
Bromley, 295,530 E4
Buckinghamshire, 479,028 C3
Cambridgeshire, 552,655 D2
Camden, 198,027 D3
Coventry, 300,844 A2
Croydon, 330,688 D4
Derby, 221,716 B1
Derbyshire, 734,581 A1
Ealing, 300,947 D3
East Sussex, 492,324 E5
Enfield, 273,563 D3
Essex, 1,310,922 E3
Greenwich, 214,540 E4
Hackney, 202,819 D3
Hammersmith and Fulham, 165,243 D4
Hampshire, 1,240,032 B4
Haringey, 216,510 D4
Harrow, 207,389 D3
Havering, 224,248 E3
Hertfordshire, 1,033,977 D3
Hillingdon, 242,435 D3
Hounslow, 212,344 D4
Isle of Wight, 132,719 B5
Islington, 175,787 D3
Kensington and Chelsea, 158,922 D3
Kent, 1,329,653 F4
Kingston Upon Thames, 147,295 D4
Lambeth, 266,170 D4
Leicester, 279,923 B1
Leicestershire, 609,579 C1
Lewisham, 248,924 D4
Lincolnshire, 646,646 D1
London, City of, 7,186 D3
Luton, 184,390 D3
Medway, 249,502 F4
Merton, 187,908 D4
Milton Keynes, 207,063 C2
Newham, 243,737 E3
Norfolk, 796,733 F1
Northamptonshire, 629,676 B2
Nottingham, 266,995 B1
Nottinghamshire, 748,503 C1
Oxfordshire, 605,492 B3
Peterborough, 156,060 D1
Portsmouth, 186,704 B5
Reading, 143,124 B4
Redbridge, 238,628 E3
Richmond Upon Thames, 172,327 D4
Rutland, 34,560 C1
Slough, 119,070 C3
Southampton, 217,478 B5
Southend-on-Sea, 160,256 F3
Southwark, 244,867 D4
Suffolk, 668,548 G2
Surrey, 1,059,015 D4
Sutton, 179,667 D4
Thurrock, 143,042 E3
Tower Hamlets, 196,121 D3
Waltham Forest, 218,277 D3
Wandsworth, 260,383 D4
Warwickshire, 505,885 A2
West Berkshire, 144,445 B4
Westminster, 181,279 D3
West Sussex, 753,612 C5
Windsor and Maidenhead, 133,606 C4
Wokingham, 150,257 C4

Cities and Towns

Abbey Wood E4
Abbots Langley D3
Abingdon, 35,234 B3
Abthorpe B2
Addington D4
Adlestrop A3
Aldeburgh, 2,654 H2
Aldermaston B4
Alderminster A2
Aldershot, 51,356 C4
Aldwincle C2
Aldworth B3
Alkham G4
Allhallows F4
Allington C1
Alton, 16,005 C4
Alvaston B1
Alvescot A3
Amberley C5
Amersham, 21,711 C3
Ampthill, 6,230 D2
Andover, 34,647 B4
Anstey, 6,192 B1
Appledore, 2,187 F4
Appleford B3
Ardleigh F3
Arlesey, 4,374 D3
Arnesby B1
Arnold, 37,646 B1
Arreton B5
Arundel, 3,033 C5
Ash, 2,024 G4
Ashbury A3
Ashby-de-la-Zouch, 10,595 B1
Ashfield G2
Ashford, 52,002 F4
Ashley E2
Ashtead D4
Ashurst (Ashurst/Netley Marsh), 2,541 E4
Ashwell D2
Aston Clinton, 3,467 C3
Astwood C2
Aswarby D1
Atherstone, 10,677 A1
Attleborough, 6,530 G1
Attlebridge G1
Axford A4
Aylesbury, 58,058 C3
Aylesham, 4,044 G4
Aylsham, 4,910 G1
Aynho B3
Bacton (Bacton/Walcott), 1,435 G1
Badby B2
Bagshot, 5,190 C4
Balderton C1
Baldock, 9,232 D3
Ball Hill B4
Balls Cross C4
Balsham E2
Bampton, 2,459 A3
Banbury, 39,906 B2
Banstead (Banstead/Tadworth), 37,245 D4
Barham G4
Bar Hill, 4,397 E2
Barking (Barking and Dagenham), 143,180 E3
Barkston C1
Barlestone, 2,547 B1
Barley E2
Barnack D1
Barnet, 292,783 D3
Barney F1
Barnham F2
Barrow F2
Barrowby, 2,084 C1
Bartley B5
Barton-le-Clay D3
Barton Mills F2
Basildon, 100,924 E3
Basingstoke, 77,837 B4
Battersea D4
Battle, 5,235 E5
Bawburgh G1
Bawdeswell G1
Bawdsey G2
Beachampton C2
Beacon End F3
Beaconsfield, 12,292 C3
Beauchamp Roding E3
Beaulieu B5
Beccles, 10,337 H2
Beckenham D4
Beddingham E5
Bedfield G2
Bedford, 73,917 D2
Bedworth, 31,932 B2
Beeby B1
Beech B4
Beeston (Beeston and Stapleford), 66,626 B1
Belton-in-Rutland C1
Belvoir C1
Bembridge, 3,397 B5
Benson, 4,796 B3
Bentley, 32,675 C4
Benwick D2
Berkhamsted, 18,044 C3
Betsham E4
Bexhill, 38,905 E5
Bexley, 210,257 E4
Bicester, 22,128 B3
Bicknor F4
Biddenden F4
Biggin Hill, 14,107 E4
Biggleswade, 12,350 D2
Bildeston F2
Billericay, 33,377 E3
Billingshurst, 4,980 D4
Billockby H1
Bingham, 7,057 C1
Binham F1
Birch Green F3
Birchington G4
Birstall, 11,770 B1
Bishop's Stortford, 28,403 E3
Blaby, 6,538 B1
Blackfield B5
Bledington A3
Bletchingley, 2,558 D4
Bletchley, 41,435 C3
Blewbury, 1,479 B3
Blindley Heath D4
Blofield G1
Bloxham, 2,356 B2
Blundeston H1
Bodney F1
Bognor Regis, 56,744 C5
Bolnhurst D2
Borden F4
Boreham, 3,170 F3
Borehamwood, 29,837 D3
Borough Green, 4,373 E4
Borrowash, 7,092 B1
Bosham, 2,270 C5
Boston, 34,606 D1
Botley, 2,297 B3
Botley B5
Bottisham, 1,784 E2
Bourne, 8,777 D1
Bourne End (Bourne End/Flackwell Heath), 13,562 C3
Boxford F2
Boxgrove C5
Boxley F4
Boyton G2
Bozeat, 1,864 C2
Brabourne Lees, 1,925 F4
Brackley, 9,113 B2
Bracknell, 60,895 C4
Bradenham C3
Brading, 2,077 B5
Bradwell (Essex) F3
Bradwell (Norfolk) H1
Bradwell Waterside F3
Brailes A2
Brailsford A1
Braintree, 33,229 F3
Bramley, 2,278 B4
Brampton, 4,673 D2
Brancaster F1
Brandon, 7,804 F2
Branston, 3,350 C1
Braunston, 1,669 B2
Braunstone B1
Brent, 243,025 D3
Brentwood, 49,463 E3
Bridge G4
Brightlingsea, 7,441 G3
Brighton, 124,851 D5
Briston, 2,184 G1
Broad Oak, 1,764 F5
Broadstairs, 22,116 G4
Brockenhurst, 3,048 A5
Brockford Street G2
Brockley Green F2
Brome G2
Bromham, 3,909 C2
Bromley, 275,841 E4
Brook (Hampshire) A4
Brook (Isle of Wight) B5
Brook (Surrey) C4
Brooke (Leicestershire) C1
Brooke (Norfolk) G1
Brookland F5
Broome G2
Broomfield E3
Broughton (Hampshire) A4
Broughton (Northamptonshire), 2,005 C2
Broxbourne D3
Brundall, 6,076 G1
Brundish G2
Bubbenhall B2
Buckingham, 10,168 C3
Buckland D3
Bucklers Hard B5
Bucks Green D4
Bucks Hill D3
Buckworth D2
Bugbrooke, 2,711 B2
Bulby D1
Bulphan E3
Bulwick C1
Bungay, 3,393 G2
Bunny B1
Burford, 1,171 A3
Burgess Hill, 26,077 D5
Burghclere B4
Burghfield B4
Burmington A2
Burnham C3
Burnham Market F1
Burnham-on-Crouch, 7,067 F3
Burrough Green E2
Burton, 3,651 C5
Burton Latimer, 5,549 C2
Burton upon Trent, 60,525 A1
Burwell, 4,628 E2
Bury, 62,633 C5
Bury St. Edmunds, 31,237 F2
Bushey, 16,488 D3
Butley G2
Butterwick E1
Buxton, 19,854 G1
Byfield B2
Cadeby B1
Cadmore End C3
Cadnam, 1,866 A5
Caister-on-Sea, 8,070 H1
Caldecott C2
California H1
Camber F5
Camberley (Camberley/Frimley), 46,120 C4
Cambridge, 95,682 E2
Camden Town (Camden), 170,444 D3
Cane End B4
Canewdon F3
Canterbury, 36,464 G4
Canvey Island, 36,406 F3
Capel D4
Capel le Ferne G4
Careby D1
Carlton, 47,302 B1
Carterton, 12,421 A3
Castle Donington, 6,007 B1
Caterham (Caterham and Warlingham), 30,177 D4
Catherington B5
Cavendish F2
Caversham B4
Cawston G1
Caythorpe C1
Chaddesden B1
Chale B5
Chalton C5
Chandler's Ford B5
Charlbury, 2,694 B3
Chartham, 2,464 G4
Chart Sutton F4
Chatham, 71,691 F4
Chatteris, 7,261 E2
Chawton B4
Chelmsford, 97,451 E3
Cheriton B4
Chertsey, 10,016 C4
Chesham, 20,290 C3
Cheshunt, 51,998 D3
Chichester, 26,572 C5
Chidden B5
Chidham C5
Chieveley B4
Chigwell, 10,332 E3
Chilgrove C5
Chilham F4
Chilton Foliat A4
Chineham B4
Chingford E3
Chinnor, 5,599 C3
Chipping Norton, 5,386 A3
Chipping Ongar, 5,974 E3
Cholderton A4
Cholsey, 3,262 B3
Chorleywood, 9,025 C3
Christchurch, 36,379 E1
Churchill A3
Church Norton C5
Churt C4
Clacton-on-Sea, 45,065 G3
Clanfield A3
Clavering E3
Claydon, 3,285 G2
Claypole C1
Cley next the Sea G1
Cliff End F5
Clifton Hampden B3
Cliftonville G4
Climping C5
Clipsham C1
Clophill, 2,372 D2
Coalville, 30,408 B1
Cockfield, 1,537 F2
Cocking C5
Cockley Cley F1
Codnor B1
Colchester, 96,063 F3
Cold Ashby B2
Coleman's Hatch E4
Coleshill, 6,324 A3
Collingbourne Ducis A4
Colne Engaine F3
Colsterworth C1
Colston Bassett C1
Coltishall, 1,992 G1
Comberton, 2,311 E2
Compton (Compton/Otterbourne), 1,609 B3
Compton C5
Coolham D5
Copdock G2
Copthorne, 3,930 D4
Corby, 49,053 C2
Corby Glen C1
Corton H1
Cosham B5
Costessey, 2,203 G1
Cotgrave, 7,364 B1
Cottenham, 4,486 E2
Cottisford B3
Cotton G2
Courtsend F3
Cove C4
Coveney E2
Coventry, 299,316 B2
Cowden E4
Cowes, 16,335 B5
Cowfold, 1,564 D5
Cranbrook, 3,522 F4
Cranfield, 4,142 C2
Cranleigh, 9,574 D4
Cranworth F1
Crawley, 88,203 D4
Crawley Down, 4,993 D4
Creaton C2
Crick, 1,314 B2
Cringleford, 2,190 G1
Cripp's Corner F5
Crockham Hill E4
Cromer, 7,267 G1
Cross Bush C5
Crostwick G1
Crowborough, 19,563 E4
Crowfield G2
Crowland, 3,172 D1
Crowthorne, 21,500 C4
Croxton F2
Croxton Kerrial C1
Croydon, 298,486 D4
Crux Easton B4
Cuckfield, 2,879 D4
Cuffley, 4,887 D3
Culford F2
Cumnor B3
Dagenham E3
Dagnall C3
Dalham F2
Danehill E4
Dartford, 59,411 E4
Daventry, 18,099 B2
Deal, 28,504 G4
Deanshanger, 2,724 C2
Debden E3
Deeping St. Nicholas D1
Denmead, 5,626 B5
Denton, 37,785 C2
Deopham Green G1
Derby, 223,836 B1
Dereham F1
Dersingham, 3,761 F1
Desborough, 7,351 C2
Didcot, 17,691 B3
Diss, 6,538 G2
Ditton E4
Doddington (Doddington/Wimblington), 2,810 E2
Doddington F4
Donington, 2,569 D1
Dorchester, 15,037 B3
Dorking, 15,658 D4
Dover, 34,179 G4
Downham Market, 5,841 E1
Dowsby D1
Drayton, 2,240 B2
Duddington C1
Duffield, 4,514 B1
Dunchurch, 2,251 B2
Dunkirk, 2,705 F4
Dunsfold C4
Dunstable, 49,666 C3
Dunwich H2
Durley B5
Dutton Hill E3
Dymchurch, 2,951 G4
Ealing, 275,257 D3
Earls Barton, 4,917 C2
Earl Shilton, 18,083 B1
Earl Stonham G2
Earsham G2
Eartham C5
Easebourne C5
East Barsham F1
East Bergholt G3
Eastbourne, 94,793 E5
East Challow B3
East Dean, 1,487 C5
East Dean E5
East Grafton A4
East Grinstead, 27,058 E4
East Hyde D3
East Langton C1
Eastleigh, 49,934 B5
East Meon B5
East Mersea F3
East Oakley B4
Eastoke C5
Easton C1
East Preston D5
East Ruston G1
Eastry, 2,273 G4
East Studdal G4
East Tilbury E4
East Tisted C4
East Walton F1
East Winch E1
East Wittering, 4,630 C5
Eastwood, 19,363 B1
Eastwood F3
Eccles, 36,000 E4
Edenbridge, 7,196 E4
Edgefield G1
Egerton F4
Egham, 23,816 C4
Elham, 1,429 G4
Elsenham E3
Elstead, 2,436 C4
Elsted C5
Elton D1
Ely, 10,329 E2
Empingham C1
Empshott C4
Emsworth (Emsworth/Southbourne), 18,310 C5
Enfield, 256,664 D3
Enstone B3
Epping, 9,922 E3
Epsom (Epsom and Ewell), 64,405 D4
Eriswell F2
Erith E4
Erpingham G1
Esher (Esher/Molesey), 46,599 D4
Etchingham E4
Eton C4
Ettington A2
Eversley Cross C4
Ewell D4
Ewerby D1
Eye (Cambridgeshire), 3,010 D1
Eye (Suffolk), 1,741 G2
Eyhorne Street F4
Eynsham, 4,764 B3
Fairlight, 1,605 F5
Fairstead (Essex) F3
Fairstead (Norfolk) G1
Fakenham, 6,471 F1
Falmer D5
Fareham (Fareham/Portchester), 54,866 B5
Faringdon, 5,235 A3
Farnborough, 52,535 B3
Farnham, 36,178 C4
Faversham, 17,070 F4
Fawley, 13,034 B3
Faygate D4
Felixstowe, 28,606 G3
Felpham C5
Felsted E3
Feltwell, 2,931 F2
Fernham A3
Fernhurst C4
Ferring D5
Fifield A3
Filkins A3
Fillongley A2
Fincham F1
Finchingfield E3
Finchley D3
Findon, 1,776 D5
Finedon, 4,051 C2
Finmere B3
Fittleworth C5
Five Ashes E4
Flansham C5
Flecknoe B2
Fleet (Hampshire), 30,391 C4
Fleet (Lincolnshire) E1
Flimwell E4
Flintham C1
Flitcham F1
Flitwick, 11,063 D3
Flixton G2
Folkestone G4
Folkingham D1
Fontwell C5
Ford End E3
Fordham (Cambridgeshire), 2,206 E2
Fordham (Essex) F3
Forest Green D4
Forest Row, 3,508 E4
Fosdyke D1
Four Oaks F5
Framlingham, 2,697 G2
Freethorpe H1
Frensham C4
Freshwater (Freshwater/Totland), 7,317 A5
Friday Bridge E1
Friern Barnet D3
Frilford B3
Frimley C4
Frinton-on-Sea (Frinton and Walton), 15,043 G3
Fritton H1
Froxfield A4
Fulbourn, 3,896 E2
Fulking D5
Fullerton B4
Funtley B5
Fyfield A4
Galleywood E3
Gamlingay, 3,391 D2
Gatcombe B5
Gedney Drove End E1
Gerrards Cross C3
Gillingham, 94,923 F4
Gislingham G2
Glenfield B1
Glinton, 1,663 D1
Glympton B3
Godalming, 20,630 C4
Godmanchester, 5,243 D2
Godstone, 2,399 D4
Golden Cross E5
Goldhanger F3
Goodwood C5
Goring B3
Goring-by-Sea D5
Gorleston-on-Sea H1
Gosberton, 1,785 D1
Gosport, 67,802 B5
Goudhurst E4
Grafham D2
Grafton Underwood C2
Grain F4
Granborough C3
Granby C1
Grantham, 33,243 C1
Gravesend, 51,435 E4
Grays, 50,145 E4
Great Barford, 1,754 D2
Great Bedwyn A4
Great Bircham F1
Great Bookham D4
Great Casterton C1
Great Dunmow, 4,907 E3
Great Gaddesden C3
Great Gidding D2
Great Gransden D2
Great Haseley B3
Great Horkesley F3
Great Horwood C3
Great Livermere F2
Great Massingham F1
Great Palgrave F1
Great Ponton C1
Great Saling E3
Great Sampford E3
Great Shefford B4
Great Shelford, 6,522 E2
Greatstone-on-Sea F5
Great Tew B3
Great Tey F3
Great Totham F3
Great Wakering F3
Great Walsingham F1
Great Wratting E2
Great Yarmouth, 56,190 H1
Great Yeldham, 1,513 F2
Greetham C1
Gressenhall F1
Gretton C1
Grimscote B2
Grimsthorpe D1
Grimston F1
Grove, 7,504 B3
Grundisburgh G2
Guestwick G1
Guildford, 65,998 C4
Guyhirn E1
Guy's Head E1
Haddenham (Cambridgeshire), 2,556 E2
Hadleigh, 6,595 F2
Hadleigh F3
Hadlow, 3,137 E4
Hailey A3
Hailsham, 18,426 E5
Halesworth, 4,575 G2
Halford A2
Halstead, 9,775 F3
Hamerton D2
Hammersmith (Hammersmith and Fulham), 148,502 D4
Hampden Park E5
Hamstead B5
Hardwick, 2,461 G2
Harleston, 3,717 G2
Harlow, 74,629 E3
Harpenden, 28,097 D3
Harpley F1
Harrietsham F4
Harrold C2
Harrow, 198,562 D3
Harrowden D2
Hartford D2
Hartley E4
Hartshore A1
Hartwell (Northamptonshire), 1,780 C2
Harwell, 2,236 B3
Harwich, 18,436 G3
Hascombe C4
Haslemere, 12,218 C4
Hassocks D5
Hastingleigh F4
Hastings, 81,139 F5
Hatfield (Hertfordshire), 31,104 D3
Hatfield Heath E3
Hattingley B4
Havant, 46,510 C5
Haverhill, 19,086 E2
Havering, 228,879 E3
Hawkhurst, 3,463 F4
Hawkinge, 2,224 G4
Hawksworth C1
Hawkwell F3
Hayes D3
Haywards Heath, 28,923 D4
Heacham, 4,064 E1
Headcorn, 2,295 F4
Headley, 5,176 B4
Heanor, 22,180 B1
Heathfield, 6,629 E5
Heckington, 2,723 D1
Helhoughton F1
Hellidon B2
Hemel Hempstead, 79,235 D3
Hempstead (Essex) E2
Hempstead (Norfolk) H1
Hemsby, 5,109 H1
Hendon D3
Henfield, 4,111 D5
Henley-on-Thames, 10,558 C3
Henlow (Henlow/Shefford), 11,391 D2
Hermitage, 1,557 B4
Herne G4
Herne Bay, 31,861 G4
Herriard B4
Hersden G4
Herstmonceux E5
Hertford, 21,665 D3
Heveningham G2
Hevingham G1
Hickling H1
Higham Ferrers, 5,345 C2
Highclere, 2,905 B4
Highcliff A5
High Garrett F3
High Halden F4
High Wycombe, 71,718 C3
Hilborough F1
Hildenborough E4
Hill Head B5
Hillingdon, 231,288 D3
Hillington F1
Hill Top B5
Hilton, 1,755 A1
Hinckley, 40,608 B1
Hindhead, 7,473 C4
Hindringham F1
Hingham, 1,995 F1
Hinwick C2
Hitcham F2
Hitchin, 32,221 D3
Hoby C1
Hockering G1
Hockliffe C3
Hockwold cum Wilton F2
Hoddesdon, 36,883 D3
Holbeach, 6,088 E1
Holbeach Drove D1
Holbeach St. Mark's E1
Holbrook G3
Holkham F1
Holland-on-Sea G3
Hollesley G2
Holme D2
Holme next the Sea F1
Holybourne C4
Honey Hill G4
Honingham G1
Honington C1
Hook, 6,471 C4
Hook Norton, 1,913 B3
Hopton F2
Horam, 1,962 E5
Horbling D1
Horham G2
Horley (Oxfordshire), 19,267 B2
Horley (Surrey) D4
Horndean B5
Horningtoft F1
Horsford, 2,255 G1
Horsham, 42,552 D4
Horsted Keynes D4
Horton C2
Hounslow, 204,397 D4
Hove, 67,602 D5
Howe Green F3
Hoxne G2
Hucknall, 29,160 B1
Hulcott C3
Hullbridge, 6,630 F3
Hulver Street H2
Hungerford, 5,046 A4
Hunstanton, 4,634 E1
Hunston C5
Huntingdon, 15,575 D2
Hursley B4
Hurstbourne Tarrant B4
Hurst Green E4
Hythe, 14,569 G4
Ibstock, 5,243 B1
Icklesham F5
Icklingham F2
Iden F5
Ifield D4
Ilford E3
Ilkeston, 35,134 B1
Ingham F2
Ipswich, 130,157 G2
Isleham, 1,953 E2
Islington, 164,686 D3
Islip B3
Itchen Abbas B4
Iver (Iver/Iver Heath), 7,134 C3
Ivychurch F4
Ixworth, 2,011 F2
Kegworth, 3,405 B1
Kelmarsh C2
Kelvedon Hatch, 2,738 E3
Kempston, 18,233 D2
Kenilworth, 21,623 A2
Kenninghall F2
Kennington, 4,290 B3
Kentford F2
Kesgrave G2
Kessingland, 3,167 H2
Kettering, 47,186 C2
Ketton, 1,708 C1
Keyhaven A5
Keysoe D2
Keyworth, 7,467 B1
Kibworth Harcourt, 3,973 C1
Kilby B1
Kilmeston B4
Kimberley, 10,488 G1
Kimpton, 2,247 D3
Kingsdown G4
Kingsfold D4
Kings Langley, 8,144 D3
Kingsley C4
King's Lynn, 41,281 E1
Kingsnorth F4
King's Norton C1
King's Sutton, 2,073 B2
Kingston B5
Kingston Bagpuize, 2,098 B3
Kingston upon Thames, 132,206 D4
Kingswood (Buckinghamshire), 60,192 C3
Kingswood (Surrey) D4
Kintbury, 2,072 B4
Kirby Bedon G1
Kirby Cane H2
Kirby Cross G3
Kirk Langley A1
Kirtlington B3
Kirton, 2,588 D1
Kislingbury C2
Knapton G1
Knebworth, 4,025 D3
Kneesworth D2
Kniveton A1
Knockholt Pound E4
Knossington C1
Knowl Hill C3
Lackford F2
Lakenham G1
Lakenheath, 9,226 F2
Lamberhurst E4
Lambeth, 244,834 D4
Lambourn, 2,850 A3
Lamport C2
Langenhoe F3
Langford, 2,760 F3
Langham C1
Langley (Hertfordshire) D3
Langley (Kent) F4
Langrick D1
Lasham B4
Latchingdon F3
Latimer C3
Lavendon C2
Lavenham, 1,231 F2
Leafield A3
Leatherhead, 42,903 D4
Leckhampstead B4
Lee Clump C3
Lee-on-the-Solent, 7,259 B5
Leicester, 318,518 B1
Leigh, 43,150 E4
Leighton Buzzard, 32,610 C3
Leiston, 5,950 H2
Lenwade G1
Letchworth, 31,418 D3
Letcombe Regis B3
Lew A3
Lewes, 15,376 D5
Lewisham, 231,175 D4
Lewknor B3
Leysdown-on-Sea, 2,483 F4
Lidgate F2
Lightwater, 6,432 C4
Linchmere C4
Lindford C4
Lindsell E3
Lingfield, 2,691 E4
Linslade C3
Linton, 3,959 E2
Liphook, 5,374 C4
Liss, 6,148 C4
Litcham F1
Litchfield B4
Litlington D2
Little Barningham G1
Little Common E5
Little Downham, 1,728 E2
Little Fransham F1
Little Gaddesden C3
Littlehampton, 50,408 C5
Little Milton B3
Littleport, 5,780 E2
Little Staughton D2
Little Stukeley D2
Little Waltham E3
Loddington C2
Loddon, 2,901 G1
London, 4,142 (city only) D4
Long Buckby, 3,428 B2
Long Clawson C1
Long Eaton, 44,826 B1
Longfield (Longfield/New Ash Green), 17,234 E4
Long Lawford, 2,501 B2
Long Melford, 2,808 F2
Long Sutton, 4,185 C4
Long Sutton E1
Long Whatton B1
Longwick C3
Loose F4
Lopcombe Corner A4
Loughborough, 46,867 B1
Lower Assendon C3
Lower Beeding D4
Lower Heyford B3
Lower Winchendon C3
Lowestoft, 62,907 H2
Low Street G1
Loxhill C4
Lubenham C2
Ludgershall, 3,664 A4
Ludgershall B3
Ludham H1
Luton, 171,671 D3
Lutterworth, 7,380 B2
Lydd, 3,173 F5
Lydd-on-Sea F5
Lymington, 13,508 A5
Lyminster C5
Lympne F4
Lyndhurst, 2,381 A5
Madehurst C5
Maidenhead, 59,605 C3
Maidford B2
Maidstone, 90,878 F4
Maldon, 15,841 F3
Maltman's Hill F4
Manea, 1,186 E2
Manningtree, 5,043 G3
Manston G4
Manton C1
March, 16,221 E1
Marchwood, 4,908 B5
Marden, 1,635 F4
Maresfield E5
Margate, 56,734 G4
Marham F1
Marholm D1
Market Deeping, 12,068 D1
Market Harborough, 16,563 C2
Mark's Tey F3
Markyate, 2,866 D3
Marlow, 17,771 C3
Marsh A3
Marsham G1
Marston B3
Martlesham G2
Mayfield, 1,954 E4
Measham, 3,656 A1
Melbourn, 4,006 E2
Melton Mowbray, 24,348 C1
Meopham, 4,956 E4
Meppershall D2
Merton, 168,470 D4
Messing F3
Metfield G2
Methwold F1
Methwold Hythe F1
Micheldever B4
Mickfield G2
Mickleover A1
Middleton Cheney, 3,306 B2
Middleton-on-Sea C5
Middle Tysoe A2
Middle Wallop A4
Midhurst, 6,451 C5
Mildenhall, 10,468 F2
Mile End F3
Milford (Milford/Witley), 6,476 C4
Milford on Sea, 4,434 A5
Mill Corner F5
Mill End C3
Milton Keynes, 43,964 C2
Minster, 15,448 F4
Minster (Minster/Manston), 4,591 G4
Minster Lovell A3
Mitcham D4
Molesworth D2
Morcott C1
Moreton E3
Morston F1
Morton D1
Moulton, 5,060 D1
Mundford F1
Mursley C3
Mutford H2
Nacton G2
Napton on the Hill B2

Cambridge University

Princethorpe B2
Privett B4
Puddledock G2
Pulham Market G2
Purfleet E4
Purley D4
Puttenham C3
Quarndon A1
Queenborough, 3,689 ..F4
Quendon E3
Quorndon, 4,614 .....B1
Radcliffe on Trent, 7,387 ..B1
Radcot A3
Rainham E3
Rake C4
Ram Lane F4
Ramsbury A4
Ramsey, 7,577 ......D2
Ramsgate, 37,895 ...G4
Rattlesden F2
Raunds, 7,493 ......C2
Ravenstone C2
Reading, 213,474 ...D4
Rearsby B1
Redhill D4
Redisham H2
Reed D2
Reedham H1
Reigate (Reigate/
  Redhill), 47,602 ..D4
Renhold D2
Rettendon F3
Richmond (Richmond upon
  Thames), 160,732 ..D4
Rickmansworth, 10,767 ..D3
Ridgewood E5
Ringmer, 3,119 .....E5
Ring's End E1
Ripley (Derbyshire),
  18,310 ....B1
Ripley (Surrey) D4
Rippingale D1
Risby F2
Riseley D3
Rishangles G2
Rivenhall End F3
Roade, 2,239 ......C2
Robertsbridge, 1,923 ..E5
Rochester, 23,971 ..E4
Rochford, 15,081 ...F3
Rockingham C1
Rockland All Saints ..F1
Rolvenden F4
Romsey, 17,032 ....B5
Rookley B5
Ropley B4
Rotherfield E4
Rothwell, 7,070 ...C2
Rottingdean (Rottingdean/
  Saltdean), 21,487 ..D5
Roud B5
Rowland's Castle ..C5
Rownham's B5
Roxton D2
Royal Leamington Spa ..A2
Royal Tunbridge Wells,
  60,272 ....E4
Royston, 14,087 ...D2
Rugby, 61,106 .....B2
Ruislip D3
Rushden, 23,854 ...C2
Ruskington, 3,530 ..D1
Rustington D5
Rye, 3,708 ....F5
Ryhall D1
Ryton-on-Dunsmore
  (Ryton), 15,952 ..A2
Saffron Walden, 13,201 ..E2
St. Albans, 80,376 ..D3
St. Ives, 16,510 ....D2
St. John's Highway ..E1
St. Lawrence B5
St. Leonards, 6,136 ..F5
St. Margaret's at Cliffe,
  2,415 ....G4
St. Mary Bourne ...B4
St. Mary's Bay, 3,163 ..F4
St. Neots, 13,471 ...D2
St. Paul's Walden ...D3
St. Osyth, 2,073 ....G3
Salcott F3
Salthouse G1
Sandhurst, 19,153 ..C4
Sandown (Sandown/
  Shanklin), 17,305 ..B5
Sandwich, 4,164 ....G4
Sandy, 8,554 ......D2
Santon Downham ...F2
Sapcote, 2,628 ....B1
Saracen's Head D1
Sarre G4
Sawbridgeworth, 9,432 ..E3
Sawston, 7,172 ....E2
Sawtry, 4,766 .....D2
Saxby C1
Saxmundham, 2,529 ..G2
Saxthorpe G1
Scayne's Hill D5
Scole G2

Scrane End E1
Seaford, 19,622 ....E5
Seagrave B1
Sea Palling H1
Seasalter G4
Seaview, 2,181 .....B5
Sedgebrook C1
Sedgeford, 4,424 ..F1
Seething G1
Selborne C4
Sellindge G4
Selsey, 8,754 ......C5
Sevenoaks, 24,489 ..E4
Shalbourne A4
Shalcombe B5
Shalfleet B5
Shalstone B2
Shanklin B5
Sharnbrook, 1,984 ..C2
Shawell B2
Shearsby B2
Sheerness, 11,653 ..F4
Shefford D2
Shelfanger G2
Shepshed, 12,961 ..B1
Sherborne St. John ..B4
Sherfield on Loddon,
  1,233 ....B4
Sheringham, 7,620 ..G1
Shinfield D4
Shipston on Stour,
  3,882 ....A2
Shirrel Heath B5
Shoeburyness F3
Shoreham-by-Sea
  (Shoreham), 17,332 ..D5
Shotley Street G3
Shottisham G2
Sible Hedingham, 3,947 ..E3
Sidlesham C5
Sileby, 7,190 .....B1
Silverstone B2
Sittingbourne, 38,771 ..F4
Skeffington C1
Skirmett C3
Sleaford, 10,388 ...D1
Slough, 110,708 ...C3
Smalley B1
Smarden F4
Snitterfield A2
Snodland, 8,814 ...E4
Soham, 6,639 .....E2
Somerley C5
Somersham, 3,257 ..E2
Somerton, 4,489 ...B3
Somerton H1
Sonning C3
Soulbury C3
Souldern B2
Southam, 5,304 ...B2
Southborough E4
Southend-on-Sea,
  158,517 ....F3
Southery E1
South Hayling C5
South Lancing D5
South Lopham F2
Southminster, 3,374 ..F3
South Pickenham ..F1
Southrepps G1
Southwick, 11,067 ..B5
Southwick D1
Southwick D5
Southwold, 3,905 ..H2
South Woodham ...F3
South Wootton ...E1
Spalding, 18,731 ..D1
Spaldwick D2
Sprowston G1
Stadhampton B3
Staines, 51,167 ...C4
Stalisfield Green ..F4
Stamford, 17,492 ..D1
Standford C4
Standon, 2,731 ...D3
Stanfield F1
Stanford in the Vale,
  1,708 ....A3
Stanford-le-Hope (Stanford
  le Hope/Corringham),
  30,747 ....E3
Stanhoe F1
Stanion C2
Stansted Mountfitchet,
  4,943 ....E3
Stanton, 2,131 ....F2
Stanton Harcourt ..B3
Stapleford B1
Staples B5
Staverton B2
Steep C4
Steeple F3
Steeple Aston B3
Steeple Bumpstead ..E2
Steeple Claydon, 2,269 ..C3
Steeple Morden ...D2
Stevenage, 76,064 ..D3
Steventon B3

Stewartby D2
Stiffkey F1
Stilton, 2,219 .....D2
Stock, 2,097 ......E3
Stockbridge B4
Stockcross B4
Stockerston C1
Stockton B2
Stody G1
Stoke F4
Stoke Albany C2
Stoke Ash G2
Stoke-by-Nayland ..F3
Stoke Goldington ..C2
Stokenchurch, 3,775 ..C3
Stokesby H1
Stonely D2
Stony Stratford ...C2
Stotfold, 6,524 ...D2
Stowmarket, 13,229 ..F2
Stradbroke G2
Stradsett E1
Stratford St. Mary ..F3
Stratton Audley ...B3
Streatham D4
Streatley D3
Stretham, 1,471 ...E2
Stretton C1
Sturry, 4,847 .....G4
Sudborough C2
Sudbourne H2
Sudbury, 19,512 ...F2
Sunninghill C4
Sutterton D1
Sutton (Cambridgeshire),
  3,076 ....E2
Sutton (London),
  166,041 ....D4
Sutton (Surrey) ...D4
Sutton (West Sussex) ..C5
Sutton Bridge, 3,457 ..E1
Sutton Scotney ...B4
Swadlincote, 36,859 ..A1
Swaffham, 5,332 ..F1
Swaffham Bulbeck ..E2
Swannington B1
Swanscombe, 5,973 ..E4
Swarkestone A1
Swaton D1
Sway, 2,072 ......A5
Swineshead, 1,576 ..D1
Swinford B2
Swithland B1
Syderstone F1
Syerston C1
Syston B1
Tadley, 15,520 ....B4
Tadlow D2
Tadmarton B2
Takeley, 1,703 ....E3
Tallington D1
Tasburgh G2
Tasset F1
Tatterset F1
Teigh C1
Temple Ewell G4
Tenterden, 6,803 ..F4
Teston E4
Teynham, 3,038 ..F4
Thame, 10,806 ...C3
Thatcham, 20,726 ..B4
Thaxted, 1,899 ...E3
Theale, 2,640 ....B4
Theberton H2
Therfield D2
Thetford, 20,058 ..F2
Thompson F1
Thorndon G2
Thorney D1
Thornton G2
Thorpe-le-Soken, 1,509 ..G3
Thorpe Mandeville ..B2
Thorpeness H2
Thorrington G3
Thrapston, 3,912 ..C2
Thurnby B1
Thursley C4
Thurton G1
Ticehurst E4
Tilbury, 11,658 ...E4
Tillingham F3
Tilton on the Hill ..C1
Timsbury, 2,396 ..A4
Tiptree, 7,679 ....F3
Toddington, 3,999 ..C3
Tonbridge, 34,260 ..E4
Tonge B1
Tongham C4
Toot Hill E3
Totland A5
Trimingham G1
Tring, 11,455 .....C3
Trumpington E2
Tunstall C4
Turvey C2
Tutbury (Tutbury/Hatton),
  5,646 ....A1
Twickenham D4
Uckfield, 13,531 ...E5
Uffington A3
Underwood, 2,177 ..B1

Upper Broughton ...B1
Upper Cokeham ...D5
Upper Dicker E5
Upper Street H1
Uppingham, 3,140 ..C1
Upton, 5,422 .....C3
Upton Grey C4
Upwell E1
Upwood D2
Uxbridge D3
Ventnor, 5,710 ....B5
Vernham Dean A4
Waddesdon C3
Walberswick H2
Walgrave C2
Walkern D3
Wallend F4
Wallingford, 9,315 ..B3
Walmer G4
Walpole G2
Waltham, 6,157 ...B5
Waltham F4
Waltham Abbey, 15,629 ..E3
Waltham on the Wolds ..C1
Waltham St. Lawrence ..C4
Walton-on-Thames
  (Walton and Weybridge),
  52,802 ....D4
Walton-on-the-Naze ..G3
Wandsworth, 252,425 ..D4
Wangford H2
Wansford D1
Wantage, 9,452 ...B3
Warboys, 2,945 ...D2
Wardington B2
Ware, 17,000 .....D3
Wargrave, 3,221 ..C4
Warlingham D4
Warmington D1
Warnford B4
Warsash B5
Warwick, 22,476 ..A2
Washington, 56,848 ..D5
Watchfield A3
Waterbeach, 4,148 ..E2
Watersfield C5
Waterstock B3
Watford, 113,080 ..D3
Weedon Bec, 2,363 ..B2
Welby C1
Weldon C2
Wellingborough, 41,602 ..C2
Wells-next-the-Sea,
  2,400 ....F1
Welney E1
Welton B2
Welwyn Garden City,
  42,087 ....D3
Wembley D3
Wendover, 6,985 ..C3
West Beckham G1
West Bridgford, 33,843 ..A1
West Clandon C4
Westfield F5
West Grinstead ...D4
West Hoathly D4
Westleton H2
West Malling, 2,056 ..E4
West Mersea, 6,602 ..F3
Westmeston D5
Weston-on-the-Green ..B3
West Rudham F1
West Tytherley ...A4
West Walton E1
West Wellow, 2,151 ..A5
West Wittering, 1,551 ..C5
Wethersfield E3
Weybridge D4
Whatfield F2
Wheatley, 3,661 ..B3
Whepstead F2
Wherwell B4

Whinburgh F1
Whippingham B5
Whipsnade C3
Whitchurch B4
White Roding E3
Whitley Row E4
Whittlesey, 10,275 ..D1
Wibtoft B2
Wickford, 26,294 ..F3
Wickham Market, 2,243 ..G2
Widford E3
Wigginton B3
Wigsthorpe C2
Wigston, 32,864 ..B1
Willey B2
Willingdon E5
Willingham, 3,317 ..E2
Willington, 2,292 ..A1
Wilshamstead, 2,188 ..D2
Wimbledon D4
Wimblington E1
Winchelsea F5
Winchester, 36,121 ..B4
Windlesham, 4,109 ..C4
Windsor (Windsor/Eton),
  30,136 ....C4
Wing, 2,805 .....C3
Wingham, 1,553 ..G4
Winslow, 4,005 ...C3
Winterbourne, 2,241 ..B4
Wisbech, 24,981 ..E1
Wisbech St. Mary ..E1
Wisborough Green ..C4
Witham, 22,684 ...F3
Witley C4
Witney, 20,377 ...B3
Wivenhoe, 7,073 ..F3
Wix G3
Woburn C3
Woburn Sands, 4,961 ..C2
Woking (Woking/Byfleet),
  98,138 ....C4
Wokingham, 38,063 ..C4
Wollaston, 2,982 ..C2
Wolverton (Hampshire) ..B4
Wolverton
  (Buckinghamshire-
  Wolverton/Stony
  Stratford), 55,733 ..C2
Wonersh C4
Wood E4
Woodbridge, 10,950 ..G2
Woodchurch, 1,419 ..F4
Woodend C5
Woodham Mortimer ..F3
Woodingdean D5
Woodnewton D1
Woodstock, 2,898 ..B3
Woodton G2
Woolwich E4
Wootton (Hampshire),
  4,353 ....A5
Wootton (Oxfordshire) ..B3
Wormingford F3
Worminghall B3
Worplesdon C4
Worth G4
Wortham G2
Worthing, 95,732 ..D5
Wrangle E1
Wrentham H2
Writtle, 5,128 ....E3
Wrotham, 1,656 ..E4
Wroxham
  (Wroxham/Hoveton),
  3,247 ....G1
Wych Cross E5
Wyddial E3
Wye, 1,608 ......F4
Wymondham (Leicester-
  shire), 10,159 ...C1

Wymondham (Norfolk) ..G1
Yalding E4
Yardley Gobion ...C2
Yardley Hastings ..C2
Yarmouth B5
Yarnton, 2,431 ...B3
Yateley, 15,663 ...C4
Yattendon B4

Other Features

Beachy Head, cape ..E5
Chiltern, hills C3
Dover, strait G5
Draycote Water, lake ..B2
Dungeness, cape ..F5
English, channel ..E5
Eyebrook, reservoir ..C1
Foulness, island ..F3
Great Ouse, river ..E2
Isle of Sheppey, island ..F4
Isle of Wight, island ..B5
Kennet, river B4
Kent, downs F4
Medway, river E4
Nene, river E1
Orford Ness, cape ..H2
Pitsford, reservoir ..C2
Rutland Water, lake ..C1
Selsey Bill, cape ..C5
Stout, river F2
Test, river A4
Thames, river B3
The Channel Tunnel ..G4
The Naze, cape ...G3
The Wash, bay ...E1
Welland, river D1

Narborough
  (Leicestershire), 6,360 ..B1
Narborough (Norfolk) ..F1
Naseby C2
Nash Lee C3
Needham G2
Needham Market, 4,312 ..G2
Needingworth, 1,808 ..D2
Nether Broughton ..C1
Netherfield E5
Netley, 6,327 ....B5
Nevendon E3
New Ash Green ...E4
New Buckenham ..G2
Newbury, 33,273 ..B4
New Duston C2
Newenden F4
Newhaven, 11,208 ..E5
Newick, 2,445 ...E5
Newington, 2,454 ..F4
Newmarket, 16,498 ..E2
New Milton (New Milton/
  Barton-on-Sea),
  24,324 ....A5
Newport (Isle of Wight),
  20,574 ....B5
Newport (Essex), 2,178 ..E3
Newport Pagnell,
  12,285 ....C2
New Romney F5
Newton (Lincolnshire) ..D1
Newton (Norfolk) ..F1
Newton Longville, 1,979 ..C3
Newton Purcell ...B3
Newtown, 10,548 ..B4
Ninfield E5
Nobottle B2
Nomansland A5
Nordelph E1
Normanton B1
Northampton, 179,596 ..C2
North Elmham F1
Northfleet, 21,397 ..E4
North Holmwood ..D4
Northington B4
North Kilworth ...B2
North Kyme D1
North Lancing ...D5
North Leigh B3
North Lopham F2
North Oakley B4
North Runcton ...E1
North Tidworth ..A4
North Walsham, 9,534 ..G1
North Waltham ..B4
Norton F2
Norton Heath ...E3
Norwich, 171,304 ..G1
Nottingham, 270,222 ..B1
Nuneaton, 66,715 ..B1
Nutley E4
Nyewood C5
Oadby, 18,538 ...B1
Oakham, 8,691 ...C1
Oakley B3
Odiham, 3,531 ...C4
Old Alresford B4
Old Basing B4
Oldhurst D2
Old Leake E1
Old Newton F2

Old Somerby C1
Old Windsor, 7,497 ..C4
Old Wives Lees F4
Olney, 4,484 ......C2
Ongar Hill E1
Ore F5
Orford H2
Orpington E3
Orsett E3
Orston C1
Orton Waterville ..D1
Orwell D2
Otford (Otford/
  Kemsing), 6,840 ..E4
Otley, 13,596 .....G2
Otterbourne B4
Oulton G1
Oundle, 3,996 ....D2
Ousden F2
Outwell, 1,683 ...E1
Overseal A1
Overstrand G1
Overton, 3,660 ...B4
Ovington B4
Ower A5
Owslebury B5
Oxenwood A4
Oxford, 118,795 ..B3
Oxley's Green E5
Oxted, 11,117 ...E4
Padbury C3
Paddock E4
Paglesham Eastend ..F3
Pakenham F2
Palestine A4
Paley Street C4
Pangbourne (Pangbourne/
  Whitchurch), 3,362 ..B4
Panxworth G1
Papworth Everard ..D2
Parkhurst B5
Parson Drove E1
Partridge Green ...D5
Paulerspury C2
Peacehaven, 16,517 ..E5
Peasenhall G2
Peldon F3
Peterborough, 134,788 ..D1
Petersfield, 12,177 ..C5
Petworth, 2,156 ..C5
Pevensey E5
Pilton C2
Pinchbeck, 3,655 ..D1
Pinchbeck West ...D1
Pishill C3
Pitsea F3
Pitstone C3
Plaistow C4
Polegate E5
Polesworth A1
Pondersbridge ...D1
Poringland, 4,684 ..G1
Portslade-by-Sea
  (Portslade), 17,762 ..D5
Portsmouth, 174,690 ..B5
Potters Bar, 22,414 ..D3
Potton, 4,230 ....D2
Poynings D5
Preston D3
Prestwood C3
Prickwillow E2

Devon countryside

England – The Southwest: Map Index

Unitary Authorities
(2001 census population)

Bath and North East
  Somerset, 169,045 ..H2
Bournemouth, 163,441 ..J3
Bristol, City of, 380,615 ..G2
Cornwall, 501,267 ...B4
Devon, 704,499 .....E3
Dorset, 390,986 .....H3
Gloucestershire, 564,559 ..H1
Hampshire, 1,240,032 ..J3
Isles of Scilly (see Cornwall) ..A3
North Somerset, 188,556 ..G2
Plymouth, 240,718 ....D4
Poole, 138,299 ......J3
Somerset, 498,093 ...F2
South Gloucestershire,
  245,644 ....H1
Swindon, 180,061 ...J1
Torbay, 129,702 .....E4

Wiltshire, 432,973 ....J2

Cities and Towns

Abbotsbury G3
Alternun C3
Alveston, 2,525 ....G1
Amesbury, 6,333 ...J2
Ashburton, 3,660 ..E3
Ashcott G2
Ashton H2
Ashwater D3
Avebury J2
Avonmouth G1
Axbridge G2
Axminster, 3,472 ..F3
Babbacombe E4
Bamwell, 1,850 ...G2
Barnstaple, 27,691 ..D2
Bath, 85,202 ......H2
Batheaston H2
Beaworthy D3
Beer F3
Bere Alston, 2,362 ..D4

Bere Regis, 1,767 ..H3
Bickington E3
Bickleigh E3
Bideford, 14,326 ..D2
Bigbury-on-Sea ...E4
Binegar G2
Bishop's Lydeard ..F2
Bishop's Tawton ..D2
Bishopstone J1
Bishop Sutton H2
Bishopswood F3
Black Dog E3
Blagdon G2
Blandford Forum, 8,880 ..H3
Bleadon G2
Bodmin, 12,553 ...C4
Boscastle C3
Bournemouth, 155,488 ..J3
Bovey Tracey, 3,492 ..E3
Bow E3
Box H2
Boyton D3
Bradford-on-Avon, 8,815 ..H2
Bradworthy D3

Bransgore, 3,843 ..J3
Bratton H2
Bratton Clovelly ..D3
Braunton, 9,227 ..D2
Brendon E2
Bridestowe D3
Bridgwater, 34,610 ..F2
Bridport, 11,667 ..G3
Brighton, 124,851 ..C4
Bristol, 407,992 ...G2
Brixham, 15,865 ...E4
Broadclyst E3
Broadmayne H3
Broadstone H3
Broadway, 2,328 ..J3
Broadwey G3
Broadwindsor G3
Bruton, 2,111 .....H2
Buckfastleigh, 2,786 ..E4
Buck's Cross D3
Bude, 3,681 ......C3
Budleigh Salterton, 4,801 ..F3
Bugle (Bugle/Stenalees),
  2,695 ....C4

Burnham-on-Sea (Burnham-on-
  Sea/Highbridge), 19,588 ..F2
Burtle G2
Callington, 3,511 ..D3
Calne, 11,516 .....H2
Cam H1
Camborne (Camborne/
  Redruth), 35,915 ..B4
Camelford C3
Cannington, 1,951 ..F2
Canworthy Water ..D3
Castle Cary, 2,904 ..G2
Cawsand D4
Cerne Abbas G3
Chaldon Herring ..H3
Chalford, 5,331 ...H1
Chalke J2
Challacombe E2
Chapmanslade ...H2
Chard, 10,770 ....F3
Charmonth G3
Chawleigh E3
Cheddar, 4,484 ...G2
Cheriton Bishop ..E3

Chetnole G3
Chicklade H2
Chideock G3
Chilsworthy D3
Chippenham, 25,961 ..H2
Christchurch, 36,379 ..J3
Churchill G2
Clevedon, 21,670 ..G2
Clovelly C2
Coldeast E3
Collingbourne Ducis ..J2
Colyton, 1,684 ....F3
Combe Martin, 2,453 ..D2
Compton H3
Congresbury, 3,435 ..G2
Copplestone E3
Corfe H2
Corfe Castle H3
Corston J1
Cove F2
Coverack B5
Crackington Haven ..C3
Crediton, 6,542 ...E3
Crewkerne, 7,142 ..G3
Crockerton H2

Crowcombe F2
Crownhill D4
Croyde D2
Cullompton, 5,676 ..F3
Culmstock F3
Damerham J3
Dartmouth, 5,676 ..E4
Dauntsey H1
Dawlish, 9,648 ....F3
Delabole C3
Devizes, 13,205 ...J2
Dobwalls C4
Dorchester, 15,037 ..H3
Dunster G2
Easter Compton ...G1
Eastertown G2
Easton H3
East Prawle E4
East Quantoxhead ..F2
Edington G2
Eggesford E3
Evercreech, 1,821 ..H2
Evershot G3
Exebridge E2

Exeter, 94,717 . . . . .E3
Exford E2
Exmouth, 28,414 . . . . .F3
Exton E2
Fairford, 2,633 . . . . .J1
Falmouth, 20,297 . . . . .B4
Faringdon, 5,235 . . . . .J1
Fillegh E2
Fittleton J2
Fontmell Magna H3
Fordingbridge, 4,301 . . . . . .J3
Fortuneswell, 4,584 . . . . . . .H3
Fovant H2
Fowey, 1,939 . . . . .C4
Frampton G3
Fremington, 3,727 . . . . .D2
Frome, 23,159 . . . . .G2
Fyfett F3
Gillingham, 6,404 . . . . .H2
Glastonbury, 7,747 . . . . . . .G2
Goonhavern B4
Gorra Haven C4
Great Bedwyn J2
Great Torrington, 4,073 . . . .D3
Hallworthy C3
Halwell D4
Hartland D3
Hatherleigh D3
Hayle, 7,034 . . . . .B4
Heathfield, 6,629 . . . . .E3
Helford B4
Helston, 8,505 . . . . .B4
Hemyock F3
Henley G2
Henstridge H3
Highampton D3
Highbridge G2
Highcliff J3
Highworth, 8,259 . . . . .J1
Hindon H2
Holford F2
Holsworthy, 1,892 . . . . .D3
Homington H2
Honiton, 7,859 . . . . .F3
Hugh Town A3
Hurn J3
Ilchester, 1,733 . . . . .G3
Ilfracombe, 10,429 . . . . .D2
Ilminster, 4,162 . . . . .G3
Ivybridge, 9,179 . . . . .E4
Kenton F3
Keynsham, 15,193 . . . . .G2
Kilkhampton D3
Kilmington F3

Kimmeridge H3
Kingsbridge, 5,258 . . . . .E4
Kingskerswell, 3,672 . . . . . . .E3
King's Nympton E3
Kingston H3
Kingston Seymour G2
Kingswear E4
Kingswood, 60,192 . . . . .G2
Knook H2
Lamerton D3
Lanreath C4
Larkhill, 2,108 . . . . .J2
Launceston, 6,466 . . . . .D3
Lechlade, 1,638 . . . . .J1
Lewdown D3
Lifton D3
Liskeard, 7,044 . . . . .D4
Lizard B5
Long Ashton, 4,080 . . . . . . .G2
Longburton H3
Longdown E3
Long Sutton, 4,185 . . . . .G2
Looe, 5,022 . . . . .D4
Lopcombe Corner J2
Lostwithiel, 2,452 . . . . .C4
Lyme Regis, 3,851 . . . . .G3
Lympstone, 1,855 . . . . .F3
Lyneham, 4,747 . . . . .J1
Lyng G2
Lynmouth E2
Lynton E2
Maiden Newton G3
Malmesbury, 4,439 . . . . .H1
Mangotsfield, 27,860 . . . . . .H2
Marazion, 1,381 . . . . .B4
Mark G2
Marksbury H2
Marlborough, 6,429 . . . . .J2
Marshfield, 1,464 . . . . .H2
Marston Magna G3
Martin J3
Martock, 4,051 . . . . .G3
Meddon D3
Meeth D3
Melcombe Bingham H3
Melksham, 13,074 . . . . .H2
Melplash G3
Mere, 2,257 . . . . .H2
Merriott, 1,956 . . . . .G3
Merton, 168,470 . . . . .D3
Meshaw E3
Mevagissey, 2,272 . . . . .C4
Midsomer Norton H2
Milborne St. Andrew H3

Milton Abbot D3
Milverton F2
Minehead, 9,158 . . . . .F2
Modbury E4
Monkleigh D3
Monksilver F2
Monkton F3
Monkton Deverill H2
Monkton Up J3
Morden H3
Morebath E2
Moreleigh E4
Mortehoe D2
Motcombe H2
Mullion, 2,040 . . . . .B4
Nailsea, 17,919 . . . . .G2
Nailsworth, 5,242 . . . . .H1
Newlyn A4
Newquay, 17,390 . . . . .B4
Newton Abbot, 23,801 . . . . . .E3
Newton Ferrers, 1,479 . . . . . .D4
Nomansland J3
Northam, 6,167 . . . . .D2
North Curry G3
Northleigh F3
North Molton E2
North Tawton E3
North Tidworth J2
Norton Fitzwarren F2
Oakford E2
Okehampton, 4,841 . . . . . . .D3
Othery G2
Ottery St. Mary, 3,253 . . . . . .F3
Padstow, 2,460 . . . . .C3
Paignton, 42,989 . . . . .E4
Parracombe E2
Patchole E2
Peasedown St.John, 3,398 . . .H2
Penryn, 7,027 . . . . .B4
Pensford G2
Pensilva, 1,528 . . . . .D4
Penzance, 19,709 . . . . .A4
Perranporth, 2,611 . . . . .B4
Pewsey, 2,452 . . . . .J2
Pillaton D4
Pilton D4
Plymouth, 245,295 . . . . .D4
Plympton D4
Plymstock D4
Polperro C4
Polyphant D3
Poole, 138,479 . . . . .J3
Porlock Weir E2
Porthleven, 3,123 . . . . .B4

Porthmeor A4
Port Isaac C3
Portishead, 14,721 . . . . .G2
Portloe D4
Portreath B4
Preston H3
Princetown D4
Puckington G3
Puddletown H3
Puncknowle G3
Puriton, 1,986 . . . . .G2
Purton, 3,879 . . . . .J1
Rackenford E2
Radstock H2
Ramsbury J2
Rawridge F3
Redhill G2
Redruth B4
Rewe E3
Ringwood, 11,959 . . . . .J3
Roachill E3
Rumford C3
St. Agnes, 2,899 . . . . .B4
St. Anne J4
St. Austell, 21,622 . . . . .C4
St. Blazey (St Blazey/Par),
  8,837 . . . . .C4
St. Columb Major, 2,119 . . . .C4
St. Dennis, 1,974 . . . . .C4
St. Heller H4
St. Ives, 10,092 . . . . .A4
St. John H4
St. Just, 2,092 . . . . .A4
St. Keverne B4
St. Mawes B4
St. Mawgan C4
St. Mellion D4
St. Peter Port G4
St. Quintin H1
St. Teath C3
Salcombe, 1,921 . . . . .E4
Salisbury, 39,268 . . . . .J2
Saltash, 14,139 . . . . .D4
Salwayash G3
Sandbanks J3
Sand Lane H2
Saunton D2
Seaton, 7,579 . . . . .F3
Sennen A4
Severn Beach, 1,468 . . . . . .G1
Shaftesbury, 6,203 . . . . .H3
Shaldon, 1,581 . . . . .E3
Shebbear D3
Shepton Mallet, 7,581 . . . . . .H2

Sherborne, 7,606 . . . . .G3
Sidmouth, 10,767 . . . . .F3
Silverton, 1,222 . . . . .E2
Simonsbath E2
Slapton E4
Somerton, 4,489 . . . . .G2
South Brent, 2,087 . . . . .E4
South Cerney, 2,145 . . . . .J1
South Molton, 4,066 . . . . . . .E2
South Perrott G3
South Zeal E3
Sparkford G3
Spreyton E3
Stalbridge, 2,344 . . . . .H3
Stanton, 2,131 . . . . .H1
Stapleford J2
Starcross F3
Stibb Cross D3
Stoke D3
Stourpaine H3
Stratton, 2,209 . . . . .D3
Street, 10,539 . . . . .G2
Strete E4
Studland J3
Swallowcliffe H2
Swanage, 9,947 . . . . .J3
Swindon, 145,236 . . . . .J1
Talaton F3
Tamerton Foliot D4
Taunton, 55,855 . . . . .F2
Tavistock, 10,222 . . . . .D3
Tedburn St. Mary E3
Teffont Magna H2
Teignmouth, 13,528 . . . . . . .F3
Thornbury, 12,108 . . . . .G1
Thurlestone E4
Tideford D4
Tilshead J2
Tintagel C3
Tiverton, 14,805 . . . . .F3
Torbay, 59,587 . . . . .E4
Torcross E4
Tormarton H1
Torpoint, 8,238 . . . . .D4
Totnes, 6,929 . . . . .E4
Treen A4
Tregony C4
Trowbridge, 29,334 . . . . . . .H2
Truro, 18,966 . . . . .B4
Two Bridges E3
Tytherleigh G3
Uplowman F3
Upton F2
Upton, 5,422 . . . . .H3

Upton Cross D3
Verwood, 8,926 . . . . .J3
Veryan C4
Wadebridge, 5,291 . . . . .C3
Wanstrow H2
Wareham, 2,454 . . . . .H3
Warminster, 16,379 . . . . .H2
Warmwell H3
Watchet, 3,147 . . . . .F2
Watchfield J1
Wedhampton J2
Wedmore, 2,222 . . . . .G2
Week St. Mary C3
Wellington, 9,621 . . . . .F3
Wells, 9,763 . . . . .G2
Westbury, 11,863 . . . . .H2
West Down D2
West Hill F3
West Knoyle H2
West Lulworth H3
West Moors J3
Weston-Super-Mare, 69,372 . .G2
Westonzoyland, 1,769 . . . . . .G2
Westward Ho! D2
Weymouth, 46,065 . . . . .H3
Whiddon Down E3
Whitstone D3
Wickwar H1
Widecombe in the Moor E3
Willand, 2,025 . . . . .F3
Williton F2
Wilton, 3,717 . . . . .J2
Wimbome Minster, 15,274 . . .H3
Wincanton, 3,973 . . . . .H2
Winkleigh E3
Winsford, 26,839 . . . . .E2
Winterbourne (Co. Avon) G1
Winterbourne (Co. Wiltshire) . .H2
Witchampton H3
Witcombe D3
Wiveliscombe, 1,753 . . . . . . .F2
Woodbury F3
Woodyates J3
Wookey G2
Wool, 2,097 . . . . .H3
Woolacombe D2
Wootton J3
Wotton-under-Edge H1
Wrantage G3
Wraxall G2
Wroughton, 7,111 . . . . .J1
Wylye H2
Yate H1
Yatton, 6,826 . . . . .G2
Yatton Keynell H2

Yelverton D4
Yeovil, 38,805 . . . . .G3
Yetminster G3

Other Features

Alderney, island J4
Bodmin, moor C3
Bristol, channel E2
Brown Willy, hill C3
Bryher, island A3
Channel, islands H4
Colliford Lake, reservoir C3
Dartmoor N.P. E3
Exmoor National Park E2
Fernworthy, reservoir D3
Guernsey, island G4
Hartland, point C2
Herm, island G4
Irish, sea B3
Jersey, island G4
Land's End, point A4
Lizard, point B5
Lundy, island C2
Lyme, bay F3
Mendip, hills G2
Mount's, bay B4
Portland, Isle of, island G3
Prawle, point E4
Roadford, reservoir D3
St. Agnes, island A3
St. Martin's, island J2
St. Mary's, island B3
Sark, island G4
Scilly, Isles of, islands A3
Severn, river G1
Stithian's, reservoir B4
Tresco, island A3
Trevose, point B3
Wimbeball, lake E2

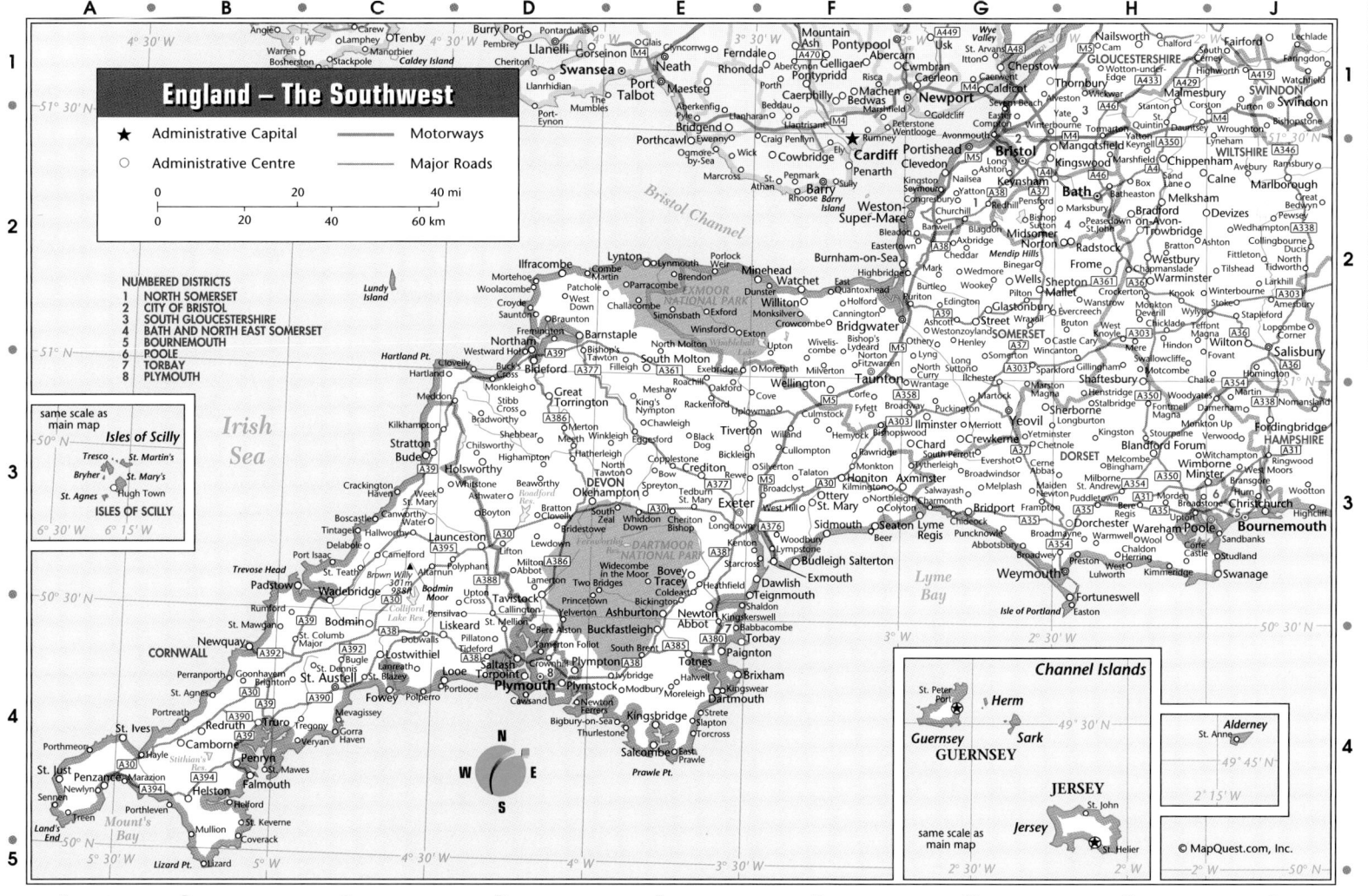

England – The Southwest

Administrative Capital ★
Administrative Centre ○
Motorways
Major Roads

0   20   40 mi
0   20   40   60 km

NUMBERED DISTRICTS
1   NORTH SOMERSET
2   CITY OF BRISTOL
3   SOUTH GLOUCESTERSHIRE
4   BATH AND NORTH EAST SOMERSET
5   BOURNEMOUTH
6   POOLE
7   TORBAY
8   PLYMOUTH

same scale as main map
Isles of Scilly
ISLES OF SCILLY

Channel Islands
GUERNSEY
JERSEY
Alderney
same scale as main map

© MapQuest.com, Inc.

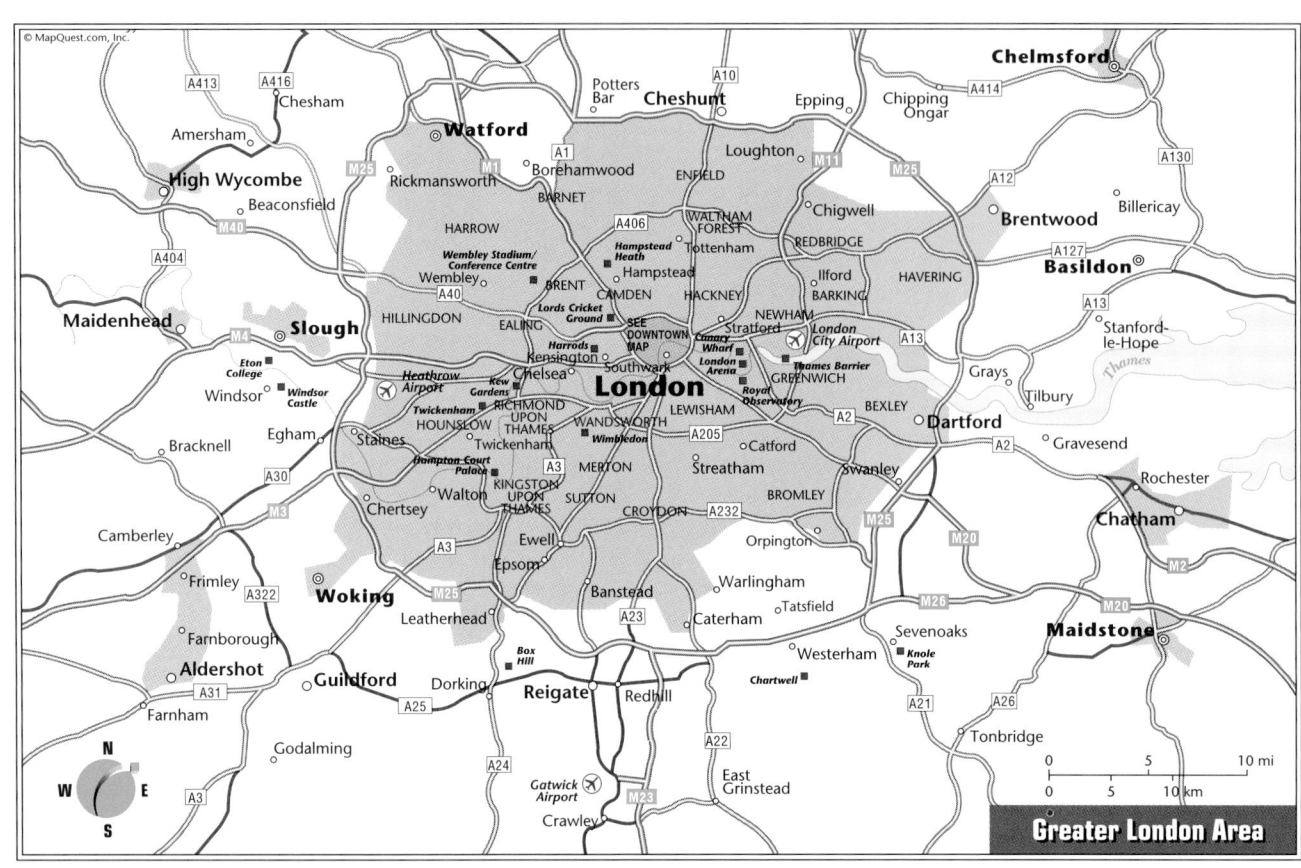

© MapQuest.com, Inc.
A413
A416
Chesham
Amersham
Potters Bar
Cheshunt
A10
Epping
Chipping Ongar
Chelmsford
A414
Watford
A1
Loughton
M11
M25
A12
A130
High Wycombe
M25
Rickmansworth
M1
Borehamwood
ENFIELD
Beaconsfield
BARNET
Chigwell
Brentwood
Billericay
M40
HARROW
A406
WALTHAM FOREST
A404
Wembley Stadium/ Conference Centre
Hampstead Heath
Tottenham
REDBRIDGE
A127
Hampstead
Basildon
Wembley
BRENT
Ilford
HAVERING
A40
CAMDEN
HACKNEY
BARKING
A13
Maidenhead
Slough
HILLINGDON
Lords Cricket Ground
NEWHAM
EALING
SEE DOWNTOWN MAP
Stratford
London City Airport
A13
Stanford-le-Hope
M4
Harrods
Canary Wharf
Kensington
London Arena
Eton College
Heathrow Airport
Chelsea
Southwark
Thames Barrier
Grays
Thames
Windsor
Windsor Castle
Kew Gardens
London
Royal Observatory
GREENWICH
Tilbury
Twickenham
RICHMOND UPON THAMES
LEWISHAM
BEXLEY
HOUNSLOW
WANDSWORTH
A2
Dartford
Egham
Staines
Twickenham
Wimbledon
A205
Catford
A2
Gravesend
Bracknell
Hampton Court Palace
A3
MERTON
Streatham
Swanley
Rochester
A30
KINGSTON UPON THAMES
Walton
SUTTON
BROMLEY
M3
Chertsey
CROYDON
A232
M25
M20
Chatham
Camberley
Ewell
Orpington
A3
Epsom
M2
Frimley
Woking
M25
Banstead
Warlingham
A322
Leatherhead
A23
Caterham
Tatsfield
M26
M20
Farnborough
Box Hill
Sevenoaks
Maidstone
Aldershot
Westerham
Knole Park
Guildford
Dorking
Reigate
Redhill
Chartwell
A31
Farnham
A25
A21
A26
Tonbridge
Godalming
A22
N
W
E
S
A24
Gatwick Airport
East Grinstead
0
5
10 mi
0
5
10 km
A3
M23
Crawley
Greater London Area

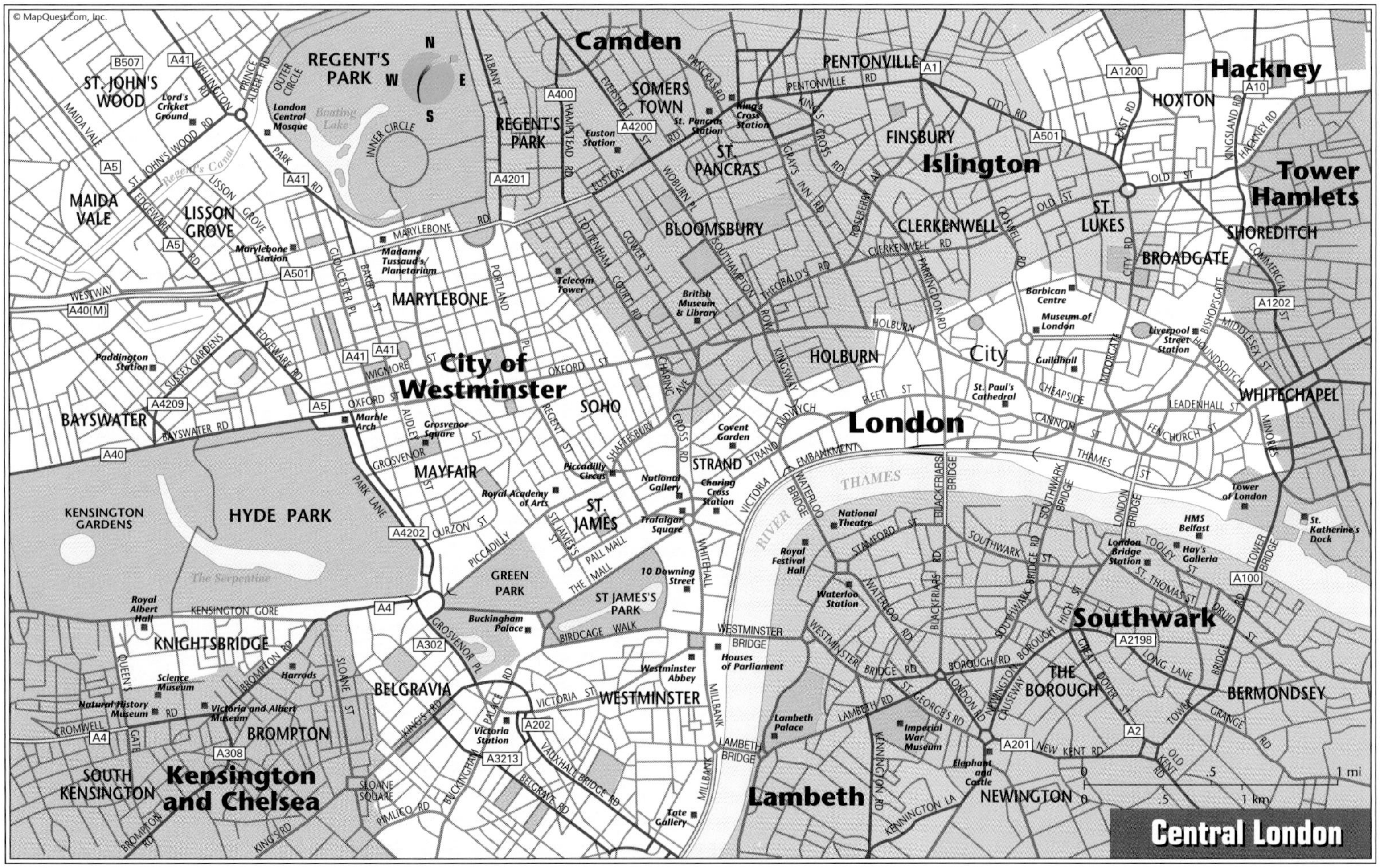
© MapQuest.com, Inc.
Camden
PENTONVILLE
A1
B507
A41
REGENT'S PARK
N
W
E
S
PENTONVILLE RD
A1200
Hackney
ST. JOHN'S WOOD
Lord's Cricket Ground
London Central Mosque
Boating Lake
INNER CIRCLE
A400
SOMERS TOWN
King's Cross Station
CITY RD
HOXTON
A10
REGENT'S PARK
Euston Station
A4200
St. Pancras Station
FINSBURY
A501
MAIDA VALE
A5
Regent's Canal
A41
A4201
ST. PANCRAS
Islington
OLD ST
Tower Hamlets
MAIDA VALE
LISSON GROVE
EUSTON RD
ST. LUKES
A5
MARYLEBONE RD
BLOOMSBURY
CLERKENWELL
SHOREDITCH
Marylebone Station
Madame Tussaud's Planetarium
CLERKENWELL RD
BROADGATE
A501
Telecom Tower
WESTWAY
A40(M)
MARYLEBONE
British Museum & Library
Barbican Centre
A1202
Museum of London
HOLBURN
Liverpool Street Station
Paddington Station
A41
A41
City of Westminster
OXFORD ST
HOLBURN
City
Guildhall
SOHO
St. Paul's Cathedral
WHITECHAPEL
A4209
A5
Marble Arch
Grosvenor Square
London
BAYSWATER
BAYSWATER RD
Covent Garden
A40
MAYFAIR
Piccadilly Circus
National Gallery
STRAND
Charing Cross Station
THAMES
Tower of London
Royal Academy of Arts
RIVER
National Theatre
KENSINGTON GARDENS
HYDE PARK
ST. JAMES
Trafalgar Square
HMS Belfast
St. Katherine's Dock
A4202
Royal Festival Hall
London Bridge Station
Hay's Galleria
The Serpentine
GREEN PARK
10 Downing Street
A100
Royal Albert Hall
KENSINGTON GORE
A4
ST JAMES'S PARK
Waterloo Station
Southwark
Buckingham Palace
KNIGHTSBRIDGE
WESTMINSTER BRIDGE
A2198
A302
Houses of Parliament
Harrods
Science Museum
Westminster Abbey
THE BOROUGH
BELGRAVIA
BERMONDSEY
Natural History Museum
Victoria and Albert Museum
WESTMINSTER
A202
Lambeth Palace
Imperial War Museum
A4
Victoria Station
LAMBETH BRIDGE
A2
A308
BROMPTON
A201
A3213
Elephant and Castle
SOUTH KENSINGTON
Kensington and Chelsea
0
.5
1 mi
Lambeth
NEWINGTON
0
.5
1 km
SLOANE SQUARE
Tate Gallery
Central London

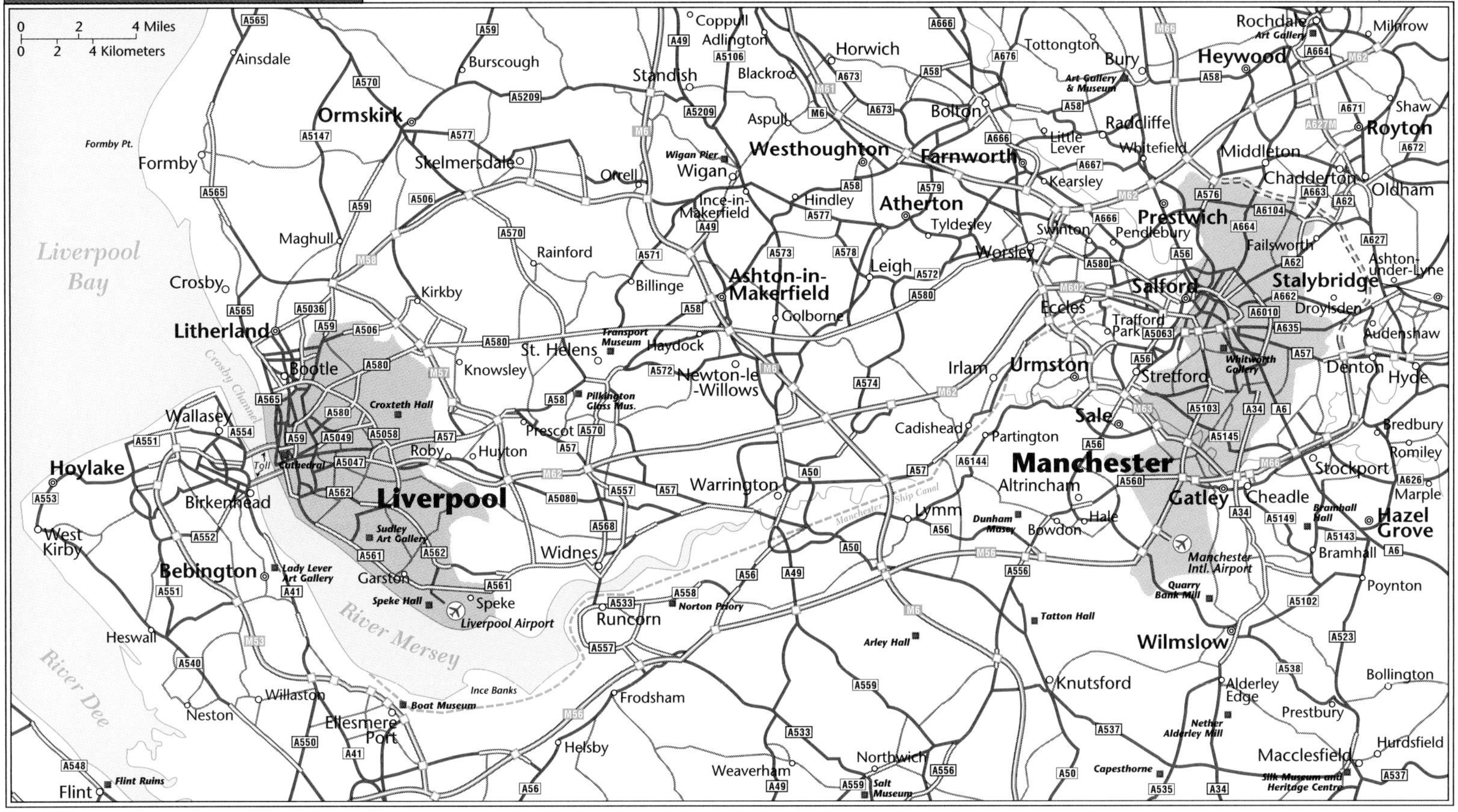

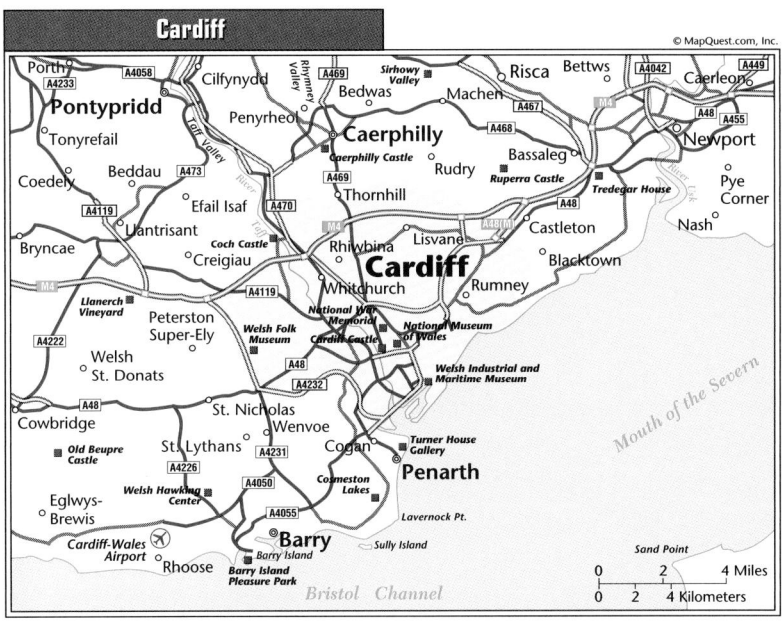

Glasgow

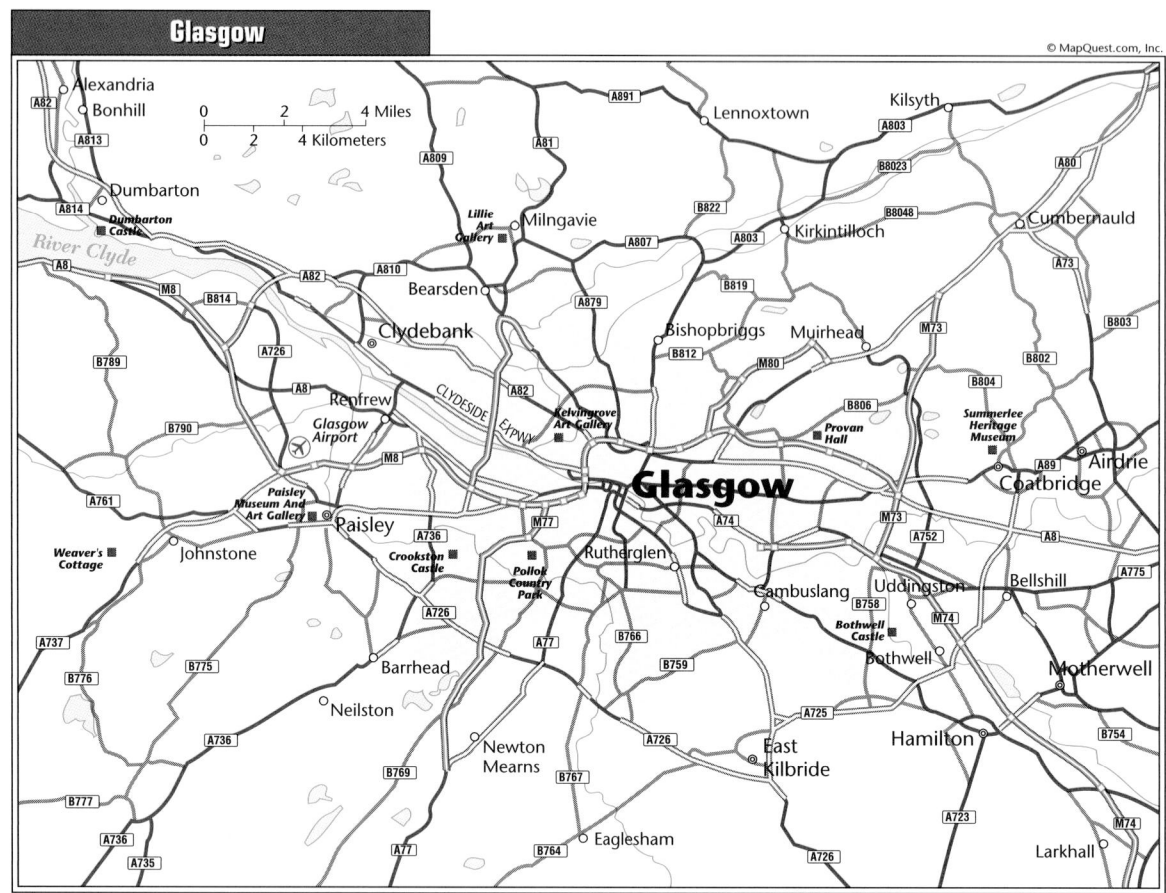

© MapQuest.com, Inc.

Glasgow • Edinburgh

Edinburgh

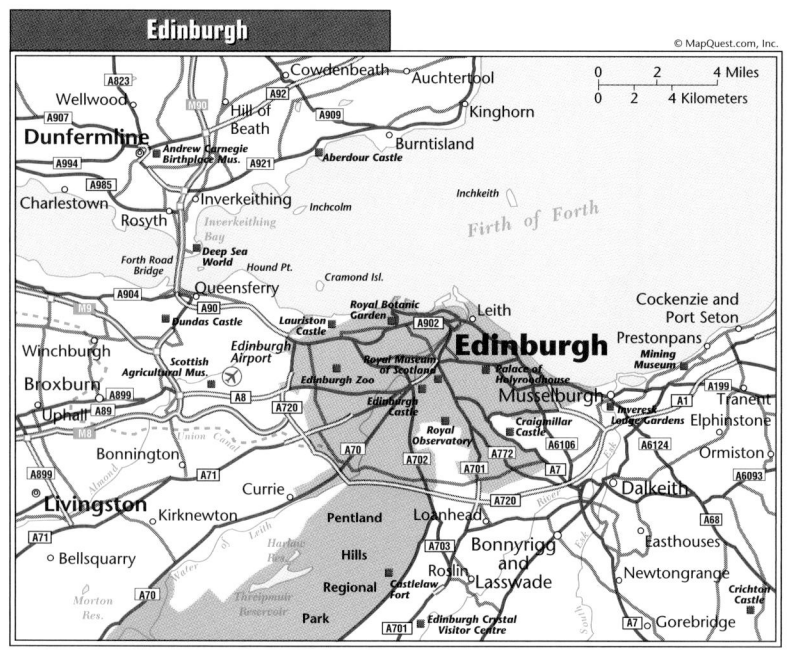

© MapQuest.com, Inc.

Central Edinburgh

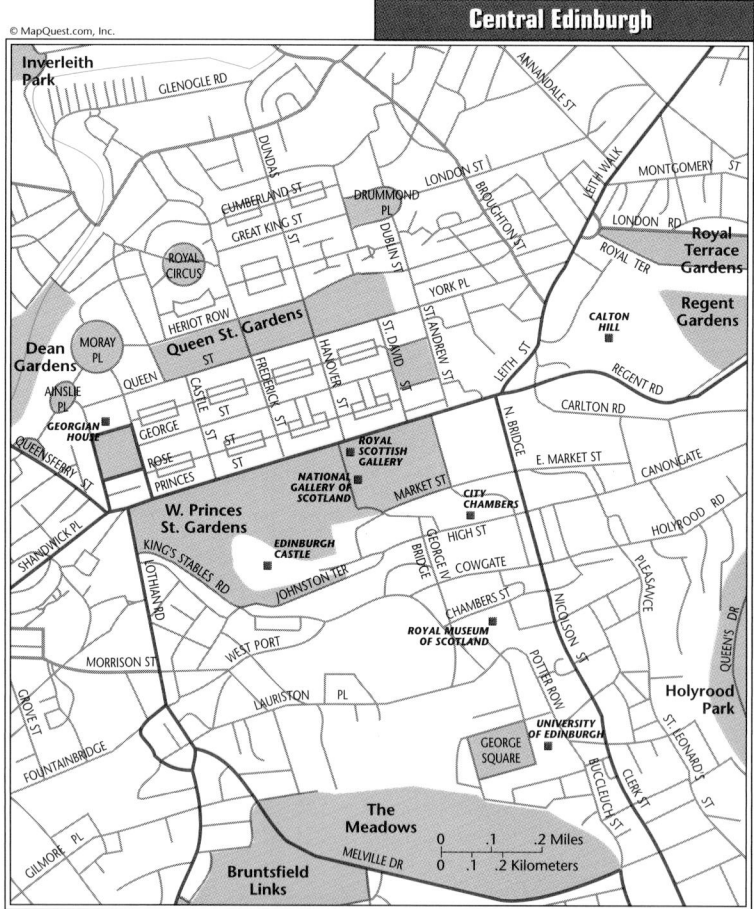

© MapQuest.com, Inc.

Ireland is an independent, democratic state with a parliamentary system of government. From 1800 to 1921, Ireland was part of the United Kingdom. In 1921 the Anglo-Irish Treaty established the Irish Free State, which after World War II left the British Commonwealth and became a republic. Six northern counties – Northern Ireland – remained part of the United Kingdom.

Resolving the Northern Ireland problem remains the leading political issue in Ireland. Nationalists in Northern Ireland want unification with Ireland, while unionists and loyalists want continued union with Great Britain.

The Irish people are predominantly Celtic, with an English minority. Almost two-thirds of Ireland's land area is meadows and pastures, giving it a pastoral beauty which is legendary. While agriculture was once the most important sector of the Irish economy, industry is now the largest by far.

Traditional Provinces and Counties

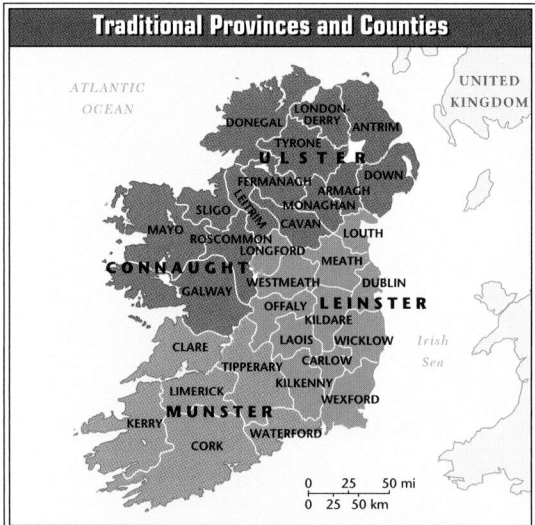

Landscape near Dingle, County Kerry

© MapQuest.com, Inc.

Ireland

Capital: Dublin
Area: 27,128 sq. mi.
    70,280 sq. km.
Population: 3,883,000 (2002 est.)
Largest City: Dublin, 495,000
Languages: English, Irish (Gaelic)
Major Religions: Roman Catholic, Anglican
Life Expectancy: 73 male, 79 female

Government: republic
Monetary Unit: euro
Industry: food products, brewing, textiles, clothing, chemicals, pharmaceuticals, machinery, transportation equipment, glass and crystal
Agriculture: turnips, barley, potatoes, sugar beets, wheat, meat and dairy products
Minerals and Resources: zinc, lead, natural gas, petroleum, barite, copper, gypsum, limestone, dolomite, peat, silver

Gullfoss, east of Thingvellir, Iceland

Capital: Reykjavik
Area: 39,758 sq. mi.
103,000 sq. km.
Population: 279,000 (2002 est.)
Largest City: Reykjavik, 111,000
Language: Icelandic
Major Religions: Evangelical Lutheran, other Protestant, Roman Catholic
Life Expectancy: 77 years male, 81 years female
Government: republic
Monetary Unit: Icelandic krona
Industry: fishing, fish processing, aluminum smelting, ferro-silicon production, hydropower, geothermal power
Agriculture: potatoes, turnips, cattle, sheep
Minerals and Resources: diatomite

After long being under the Danish crown in one capacity or another, Iceland was formally established as an independent republic in 1944.

Most Icelanders are descendants of Norwegian settlers and Celts from the British Isles, and the population is quite homogeneous.

Most of Iceland's land area, which is of recent volcanic origin, consists of glaciers, lakes, a mountainous lava desert and other wasteland. The remaining 20% is used for cultivation and grazing. The inhabited areas are along the coast, particularly the southwest coast.

Iceland's economy is one similar to those in the Scandinavian countries, basically capitalistic but with an extensive welfare system, relatively low unemployment, and comparatively even distribution of income. It is heavily dependent on the fishing industry, providing nearly 75% of export earnings and employing 12% of the work force.

Reykjavík, Iceland

Iceland

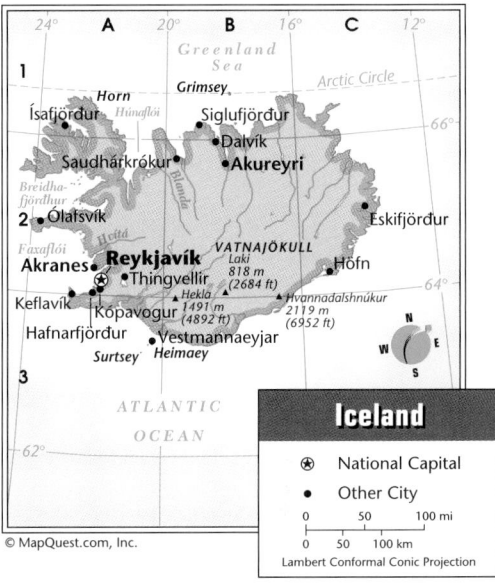

Iceland

⊛ National Capital
● Other City

0   50   100 mi
0   50   100 km
Lambert Conformal Conic Projection

© MapQuest.com, Inc.

© MapQuest.com, Inc.

Denmark

⊛ National Capital
★ Territorial Capital
● Other City

0   25   50 mi
0   25   50 km
Lambert Conformal Conic Projection

Denmark is a constitutional monarchy. The Queen has largely ceremonial functions, although she does appoint the prime minister and cabinet ministers. Denmark is divided into 14 counties (Amter) and 275 municipalities (Kommuner). The Faroe Islands and Greenland enjoy home rule, with the Danish government represented locally by high commissioners, and are responsible for most domestic affairs.

Denmark has been very active in international efforts to integrate the Central and Eastern European countries into the West. It has taken a leading role in assisting the Baltic states and is a strong supporter of international peacekeeping.

The Danish economy is a modern one, featuring high-tech agriculture, up-to-date small-scale and corporate industry, extensive government welfare measures, comfortable living standards and high dependence on foreign trade. It is self-sufficient in food production.

The Danes are a homogeneous Gothic-Germanic people and have inhabited Denmark since prehistoric times. Denmark's rich intellectual and cultural heritage are noted throughout the world.

Denmark

Capital: Copenhagen
Area: 16,625 sq. mi.
43,070 sq. km.
Population: 5,369,000 (2002 est.)
Largest City: Copenhagen, 501,000
Languages: Danish, Faroese, Greenlandic (an Eskimo dialect), German (small minority)

Major Religions: Evangelical Lutheran, other Protestant, Roman Catholic
Life Expectancy: 73 male, 79 female
Government: constitutional monarchy
Monetary Unit: Danish krone
Industry: fishing, food processing, machinery and equipment, textiles and clothing, chemical products, electronics, construction, furniture, and other wood products, shipbuilding
Agriculture: meat, dairy, grain, potatoes, rape, sugar beets
Minerals and Resources: petroleum, natural gas, salt, limestone

Boats along Nyhavn, Copenhagen

Capital: Oslo
Area: 125,182 sq. mi.
324,220 sq. km.
Population: 4,525,000 (2002 est.)
Largest City: Oslo, 513,000
Language: Norwegian
Major Religions: Evangelical Lutheran, Protestant, Roman Catholic
Life Expectancy: 74 male, 81 female
Government: constitutional monarchy

Monetary Unit: Norwegian krone
Industry: petroleum and gas, food processing, shipbuilding, pulp and paper products, metals, chemicals, timber, mining, textiles, fishing
Agriculture: fishing
Minerals and Resources: copper, pyrites, nickel, iron-ore, zinc, lead

Norway

Historically Norway has been in unions with both Denmark and Sweden. In 1905, Sweden recognized Norway's independence and a parliamentary monarchy was established with Danish Prince Carl (who took the name of Haakon VII) as monarch. The functions of the monarch are mainly ceremonial, but he has influence as the symbol of national unity.

Norwegians are a predominantly Germanic people, although there are communities of Sami (Lapps) in the far north, and there is a sizable immigrant population.

Norway is one of the world's richest countries and is well endowed with natural resources. Its large shipping fleet is one of the most modern among the maritime nations and it has become a major oil and gas producer.

Capital: Stockholm
Area: 173,732 sq. mi.
449,964 sq. km.
Population: 8,877,000 (2002 est.)
Largest City: Stockholm, 755,000
Language: Swedish
Major Religions: Evangelical Lutheran, Catholic, Pentecostal
Life Expectancy: 76 male, 81 female
Government: constitutional monarchy

Monetary Unit: Swedish krona
Industry: iron and steel, precision equipment, paper products, processed foods, motor vehicles
Agriculture: dairy products, grains, sugar beets, potatoes
Minerals and Resources: zinc, iron-ore, lead, copper, silver, uranium

Sweden

Sweden has a constitutional monarchy with a parliamentary system; the monarch's authority is formal, symbolic and representational. Sweden has long been a neutral country and has not fought a war for more than 175 years. This policy of neutrality has been backed by a strong national defense system which includes universal conscription.

Sweden is an industrial country and has become a leading producing and exporting nation, thanks to its extensive forests, rich iron ore deposits and hydroelectric power.

There is an extensive social welfare program in Sweden which accounts in part for the country's high standard of living. The Swedes are a very socially conscious people, devoting particular attention to issues of peacekeeping, humanitarian aid, arms control and nuclear proliferation.

Finland

Capital: Helsinki
Area: 130,128 sq. mi.
    337,030 sq. km.
Population: 5,184,000 (2002 est.)
Largest City: Helsinki, 560,000
Languages: Finnish, Swedish
Major Religions: Evangelical Lutheran, Greek Orthodox
Life Expectancy: 73 male, 80 female
Government: republic
Monetary Unit: euro
Industry: metal products, ship building, forestry and wood processing, copper refining, foodstuffs, chemicals, textiles, clothing
Agriculture: cereals, sugar beets, potatoes
Minerals and Resources: copper, zinc, iron-ore, silver

Although there is still some debate as to the origins of the Finnish people, most scholars agree that their original home was in what is now west-central Siberia. They arrived in their present territory thousands of years ago, pushing the indigenous Lapps into the more remote northern regions.

Finland was associated with the kingdom of Sweden for nearly 700 years, beginning in 1154. In 1809 Finland was conquered by the armies of Czar Alexander I and thereafter remained an autonomous grand duchy connected to the Russian Empire until the end of 1917. Finland declared its independence in 1918 and simultaneously experienced a brief but bitter civil war.

Finland has a dynamic industrial economy based on its abundant forest resources, capital investments and technology. Timber and steel are the main industries, and such export products as textiles, porcelain and glassware are world famous.

Helsinki Harbor Market

Estonia

Capital: Tallinn
Area: 17,413 sq. mi.
    45,100 sq. km.
Population: 1,416,000 (2002 est.)
Largest City: Tallinn, 398,000
Languages: Estonian, Latvian, Lithuanian, Russian
Major Religions: Lutheran
Life Expectancy: 65 male, 75 female
Government: republic
Monetary Unit: Estonian kroon
Industry: oil shale, ship building, phosphates, electric motors, excavators, cement, furniture, clothing, textiles, paper, shoes, apparel
Agriculture: dairy products, potatoes
Minerals and Resources: shale oil, phosphorite

Estonians are one of the longest-settled European peoples. Their history is one of foreign rule and struggles for independence. Estonia enjoyed 22 years of independence from the Russian empire between World Wars I and II, but in 1939, the Molotov-Ribbentrop pact provided for Soviet occupation of Estonia, Latvia, part of Finland and later, Lithuania. The Estonians then endured two years of Nazi occupation and many fled when in 1944, Soviet forces once again took over.

Free and fair parliamentary and presidential elections were held on September 20, 1992 and for the first time in more than 50 years, Estonians elected their leaders. The new Estonian government has pursued an ambitious program of market reforms and stabilization measures which is rapidly transforming the economy. Estonia's foreign trade has shifted quickly from East to West with the Western industrialized countries now accounting for two-thirds of foreign trade.

© MapQuest.com, Inc.

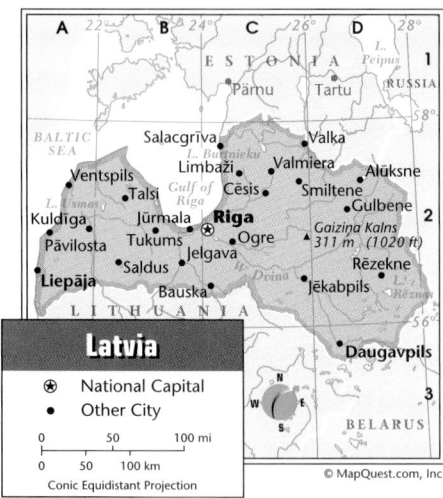

Latvia

- ✪ National Capital
- • Other City

0 — 50 — 100 mi
0 — 50 — 100 km
Conic Equidistant Projection

© MapQuest.com, Inc.

Capital: Riga
Area: 24,749 sq. mi.
64,100 sq. km.
Population: 2,367,000 (2002 est.)
Largest City: Riga, 793,000
Languages: Littish, Lithuanian, Russian
Major Religions: Lutheran, Roman Catholic, Russian Orthodox
Life Expectancy: 65 male, 75 female

Government: republic
Monetary Unit: lat
Industry: intermediate products, synthetic fibers, agricultural machinery, fertilizers, washing machines, electronics, pharmaceuticals, processed foods, textiles
Agriculture: dairy farming, eggs, grain, sugar beets, potatoes, vegetables, fishing
Minerals and Resources: limestone, dolomite

Latvia

The Latvian people consider themselves to be Nordics, after centuries of Germanic and Scandinavian colonization and settlement. Eastern Latvia, however, retains strong Polish and Russian cultural and linguistic influences and is predominantly Roman Catholic. Most Latvians belong to the Evangelical Lutheran Church, and there is also a sizeable Russian Orthodox minority.

Latvia is rapidly becoming a dynamic market economy, although the transition has been a painful one. Due to its strategic location on the Baltic Sea, its diverse (though inefficient and outdated) industrial structure and a well-educated population, it is gradually becoming more independent, although its economy still remains heavily dependent upon the markets of the states of the former Soviet Union.

Lithuania

- ✪ National Capital
- • Other City

0 — 30 — 60 mi
0 — 30 — 60 km
Conic Equidistant Projection

© MapQuest.com, Inc.

Capital: Vilnius
Area: 25,174 sq. mi.
65,200 sq. km.
Population: 3,601,000 (2002 est.)
Largest City: Vilnius, 578,000
Languages: Lithuanian, Polish, Russian
Major Religions: Roman Catholic, Lutheran
Life Expectancy: 67 male, 76

female
Government: republic
Monetary Unit: lita
Industry: electrical appliances, petroleum refining, shipbuilding, furniture making, food processing
Agriculture: sugar, grain, potatoes, sugar beets, vegetables, dairy products, eggs

Lithuania

Lithuania became independent in September 1991 after nearly fifty years of Soviet rule and a period of Nazi occupation. Until mid-1988, all political, economical and cultural life was controlled by the Soviet-dominated Lithuanian Communist Party. The Lithuanian reform movement Sajudis was formed by intellectuals in mid-1988 and quickly won national popularity.

Lithuania has endured a number of border changes, deportations by the Soviets, the massacre of its Jewish population and postwar German and Polish repatriations, but it has maintained a fairly stable percentage of ethnic Lithuanians (about 80%) and its constitution guarantees universal human and civil rights.

Capital: Minsk
Area: 80,155 sq. mi.
207,600 sq. km.
Population: 10,335,000 (2002 est.)
Largest City: Minsk, 1,677,000
Languages: Byelorussian, Russian
Major Religion: Eastern Orthodox
Life Expectancy: 66 male, 76

female
Government: republic
Monetary Unit: Belarusian ruble
Industry: heavy machinery, electronics, consumer goods
Agriculture: grain, potatoes, vegetables, dairy products
Minerals and Resources: oil

Belarus

Belarus declared its independence from the Soviet Union in August, 1991.

Among the former republics of the Soviet Union, Belarus has one of the highest standards of living, due to its relatively well-developed industrial base and a high education level. Belarusians face the difficult challenge of changing from a state-run economy with a high priority on military production to a civilian free-market system.

In fact the Belarusian government has lagged behind most of the other former Soviet state governments in economic reform, shying away from privatization and remaining almost solely dependent on trade with Russia. There are privatization plans but progress is quite slow and economic activity in Belarus has stagnated as businesses have had to wait for the results of negotiations over exchange rates and a monetary union with Russia.

Belarus

- ✪ National Capital
- • Other City

0 — 75 — 150 mi
0 — 75 — 150 km
Lambert Conformal Conic Projection

© MapQuest.com, Inc.

Poland

Capital: Warsaw
Area: 120,726 sq. mi.
  312,680 sq. km.
Population: 38,625,000 (2002 est.)
Largest City: Warsaw, 1,610,000
Language: Polish
Major Religions: Roman Catholic, Eastern Orthodox, Protestant
Life Expectancy: 69 male, 77 female
Government: democratic
Monetary Unit: zloty
Industry: machine building, iron and steel, extractive industries, chemicals, shipbuilding, food processing, glass, beverages, textiles
Agriculture: rye, rapeseed, potatoes
Minerals and Resources: coal, sulfur, copper, silver, lead, salt

Gdansk, Poland

The Solidarity movement in Poland, born in 1980 at the Lenin Shipyard in Gdansk, was the first step towards Poland's current fully democratic government and market economy. The election of former electrician Lech Walesa as president in 1990 marked the institution of freedom of speech, religion, assembly and the press in a country long plagued by totalitarian oppression.

Poland has undergone a profound and difficult transformation from a centrally planned, state-run Soviet economy to an independent free market system. It was the first of the Soviet-controlled countries to end its recession and return to growth, after the new independent government decontrolled prices, slashed subsidies and drastically reduced import barriers.

Before World War II Poland's industrial base was concentrated in the coal, textile, chemical, machinery, iron and steel sectors. Today it extends to fertilizers, petrochemicals, machine tools, electric machinery, electronics and shipbuilding. While agriculture employs one-third of the work force, it contributes only 8% to the GDP. State farms are currently being privatized. Poland is the leading producer in Eastern Europe of potatoes, rapeseed, sugar beets, grains, hogs and cattle.

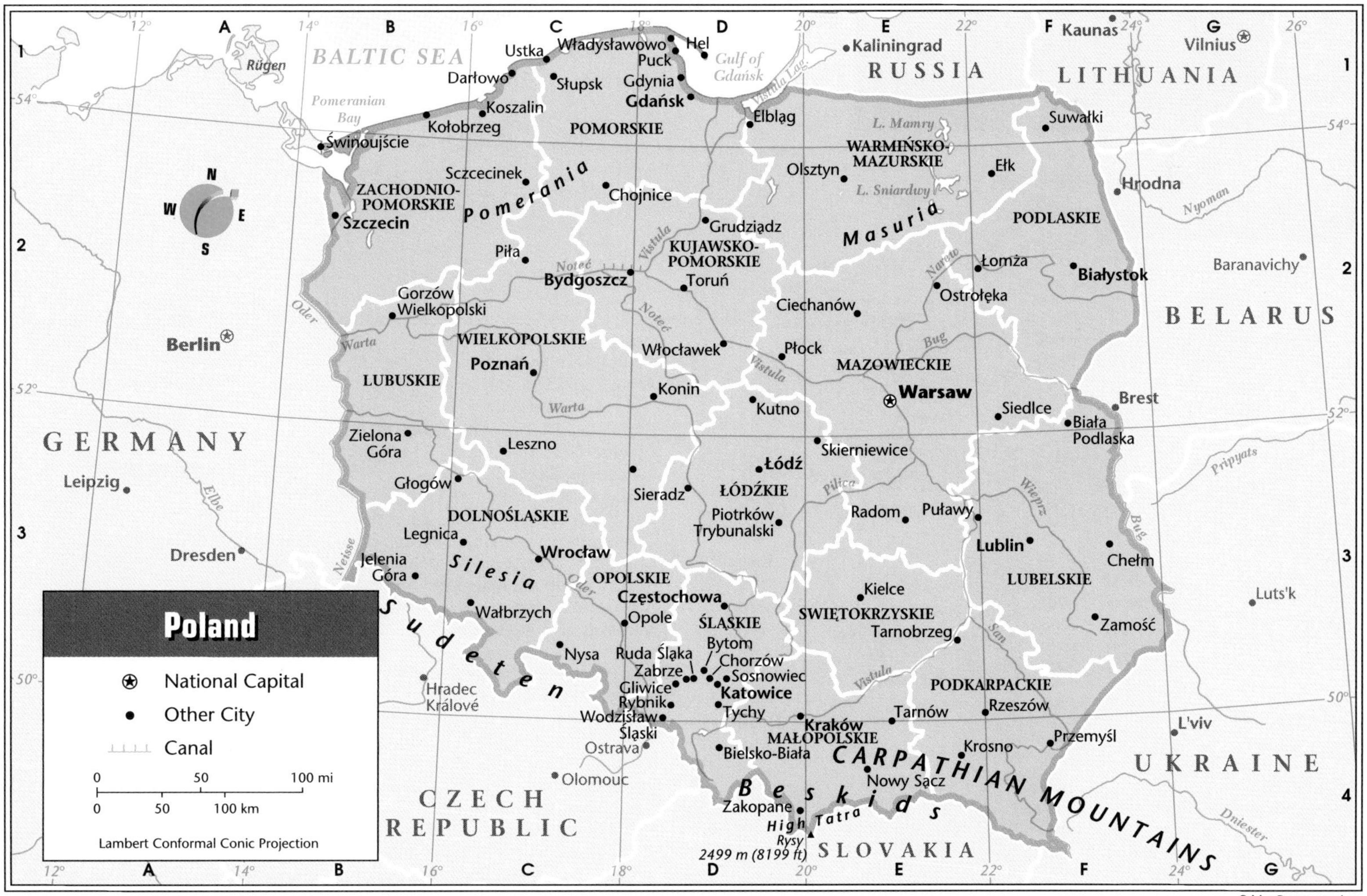

Poland

- ⊛ National Capital
- • Other City
- ⊥⊥⊥ Canal

0   50   100 mi
0   50   100 km

Lambert Conformal Conic Projection

Dutch windmills

© MapQuest.com, Inc.

Amsterdam - The Hague - Rotterdam

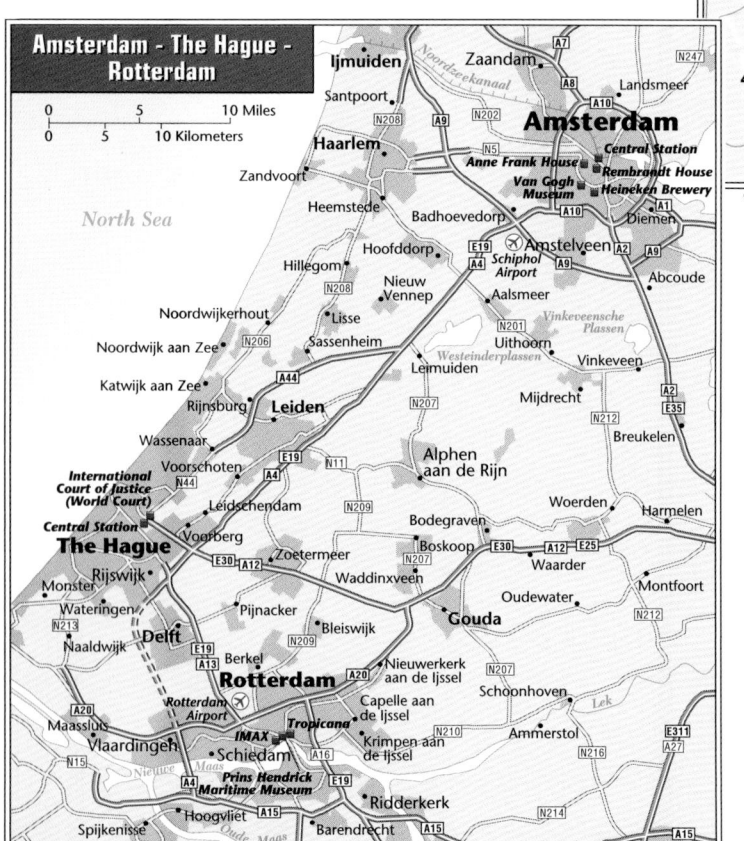

Capital: Amsterdam
Area: 16,033 sq. mi.
　　　41,536 sq. km.
Population: 16,068,000 (2002 est.)
Largest City: Amsterdam, 734,000
Language: Dutch
Major Religions: Roman Catholic, Protestant
Life Expectancy: 75 male, 81 female
Government: Parliamentary democracy under constitutional monarch
Monetary Unit: euro
Industry: metals, machinery, chemicals
Agriculture: grains, potatoes, sugar beets, vegetables, flowers
Minerals and Resources: natural gas, oil

Netherlands

The Netherlands is the most densely populated country in Europe. The Dutch people are primarily of Germanic stock with some Gallo-Celtic mixture.

The Netherlands was a founding member of the European Union and has long based its security upon membership in NATO, which it joined after World War II, abandoning its policy of neutrality.

The Dutch economy is based on private enterprise. Services, which account for more than half of the national income, are primarily in transport and financial areas, such as banking and insurance.

Environmental awareness plays a major role in Dutch life. Most of the land area is actually below sea level, having been "reclaimed" by the construction of numerous dikes withholding the sea.

Belgium

Map key:
- ★ National Capital
- ● Other City
- Canal

Scale: 0 — 15 — 30 mi / 0 — 15 — 30 km

Lambert Conformal Conic Projection

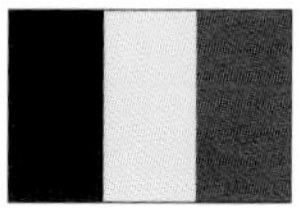

Capital: Brussels
Area: 11,787 sq. mi.
30,536 sq. km.
Population: 10,275,000 (2002 est.)
Largest City: Antwerp, 449,000
Languages: Flemish, French, German
Major Religion: Roman Catholic
Life Expectancy: 74 male, 80 female
Government: Parliamentary democracy under constitutional monarch
Monetary Unit: euro
Industry: steel, glassware, diamond cutting, textiles, chemicals
Agriculture: wheat, potatoes, sugar beets
Minerals and Resources: coal

Belgium has existed essentially in its present form since 1830, when an uprising led to independence from the Netherlands. The most significant factor in Belgian politics and every day life is the division of the Belgian people into two major language groups - French speakers and Flemish (which is closely related to Dutch) speakers.

Belgium is comprised of three regions and has three cultural communities: Flemish, Francophone and German. All major institutions are divided by language, and regional and linguistic concerns affect all important decisions. It is the second most densely populated country in Europe and has a highly developed market economy.

Belgium's climate is cool, temperate and rainy. Its terrain varies from coastal plains in the northwest, central rolling hills and the Ardennes mountains in the southeast.

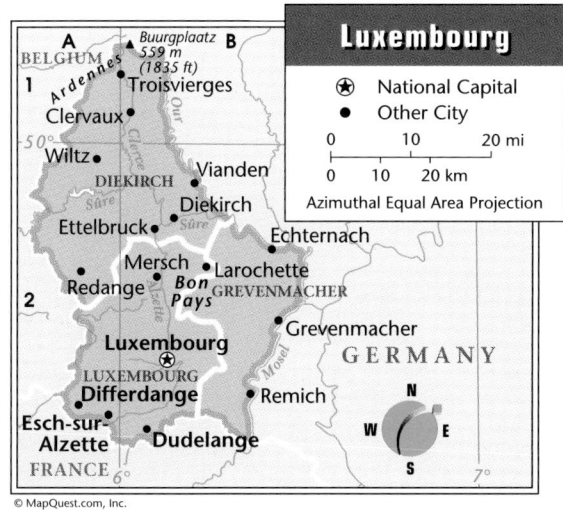

Luxembourg

Map key:
- ★ National Capital
- ● Other City

Scale: 0 — 10 — 20 mi / 0 — 10 — 20 km

Azimuthal Equal Area Projection

Capital: Luxembourg
Area: 999 sq. mi.
2,588 sq. km.
Population: 449,000 (2002 est.)
Largest City: Luxembourg, 77,000
Languages: French, German, Luxembourgish
Major Religion: Roman Catholic
Life Expectancy: 73 male, 81 female
Government: Constitutional monarchy
Monetary Unit: euro
Industry: steel, chemicals, beer, tires, electronics
Agriculture: corn, wine
Minerals and Resources: iron

Luxembourg enjoys a degree of economic prosperity almost unique among industrialized democracies. It has emerged as a world financial center, an audiovisual and communications center in Europe and offers favorable conditions for foreign investment. It is referred to as the "green heart of Europe" in tourist literature.

Luxembourgers are a blend of French and German with a Celtic base. The official languages are Luxembourgish, French and German. Luxembourg has long been a proponent of greater European political and economic integration.

© MapQuest.com, Inc.

Rhine River castles, cathedrals and vineyards, near Bingen

Germany has one of the world's highest levels of education, technological development and economic productivity. With the unification of East and West Germany in 1990, the new nation faced the challenge of bringing the standard of living in the former GDR up to that of West Germany. This is a complicated and ongoing task and such social problems as rising extremist violence have come along with the economic uncertainty in the former eastern state.

While progress towards economic integration between eastern and western Germany is visible, the eastern region will almost certainly remain dependent on subsidies funded by the western region for years to come. Assistance to the east is running at roughly 65 billion euros ($70 billion, £43 billion) annually.

The 165-kilometer wall surrounding western Berlin has been torn down and the city has been reunited. Russian withdrawal from the city was completed in August, 1994, followed by the departure of the Western Allied troops soon after. On May 23rd, 1999, the 50th anniversary of the German constitution, the Federal President was elected in the new Reichstag building. This event marked the official relocation of the German parliament and government to Berlin, but many federal government offices remain active in the former West German capital city of Bonn.

Germany, along with France, has played a leading role in creating the European Union and is a major force in providing for its security and prosperity.

Germany

Capital: Berlin
Area: 137,804 sq. mi.
356,910 sq. km.
Population: 82,351,000 (2002 est.)
Largest City: Berlin, 3,382,000
Language: German
Major Religions: Protestant, Roman Catholic
Life Expectancy: 74 male, 80 female
Government: federal republic
Monetary Unit: euro
Industry: iron, steel, coal, cement, chemicals, machinery, vehicles, machine tools electronics, food and beverages, metal fabrication, shipbuilding, textiles, petroleum refining
Agriculture: potatoes, wheat, barley, sugar beets, fruit, cabbage, wheat, rye
Minerals and Resources: iron ore, coal, potash, lignite, uranium, copper, salt, nickel

Berlin Metro Area

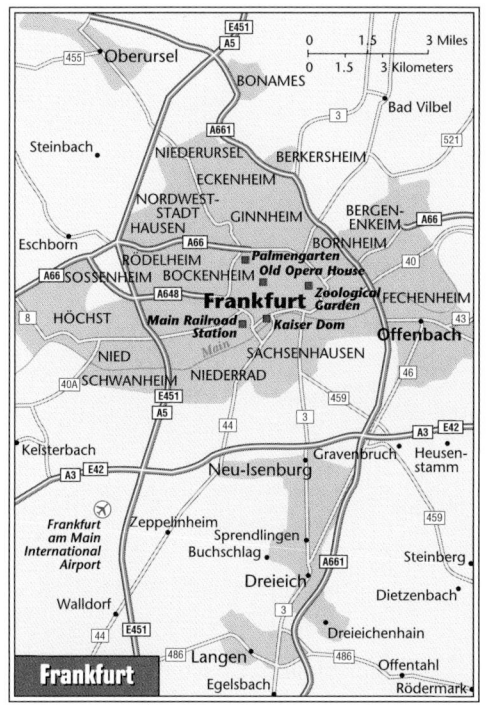

Frankfurt

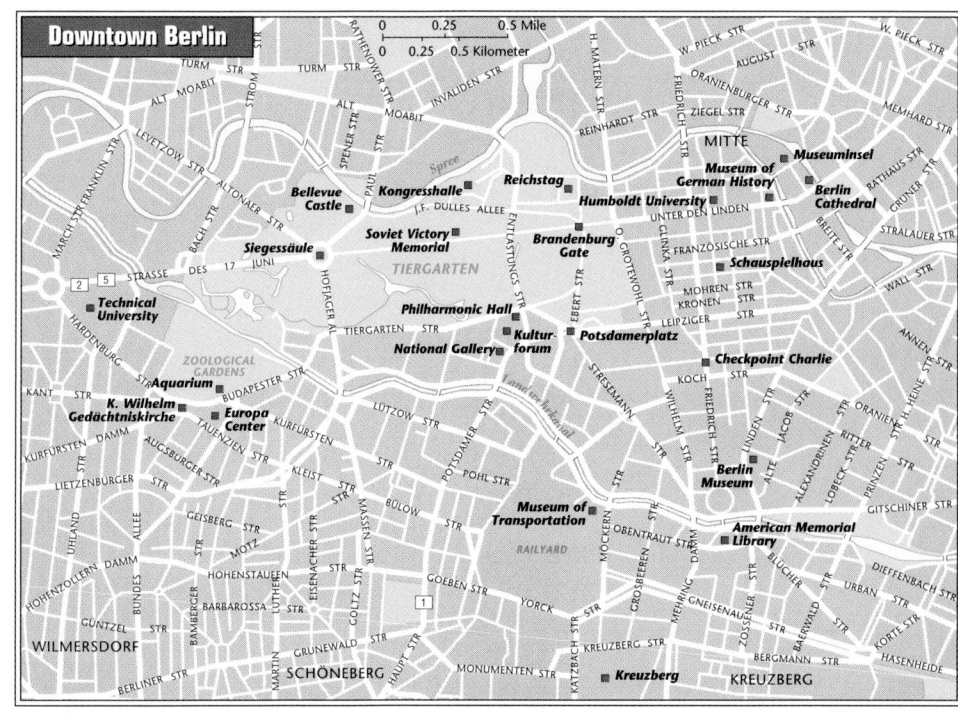

Downtown Berlin

France

⊛ National Capital
• Other City

0 — 50 — 100 mi
0 — 50 — 100 km

Lambert Conformal Conic Projection

Same scale as main map

© MapQuest.com, Inc.

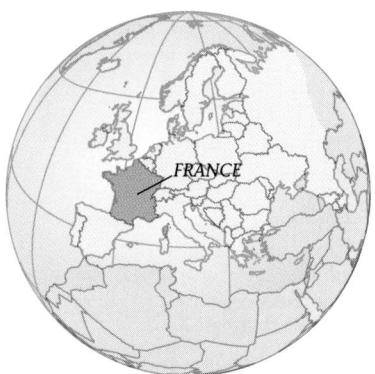

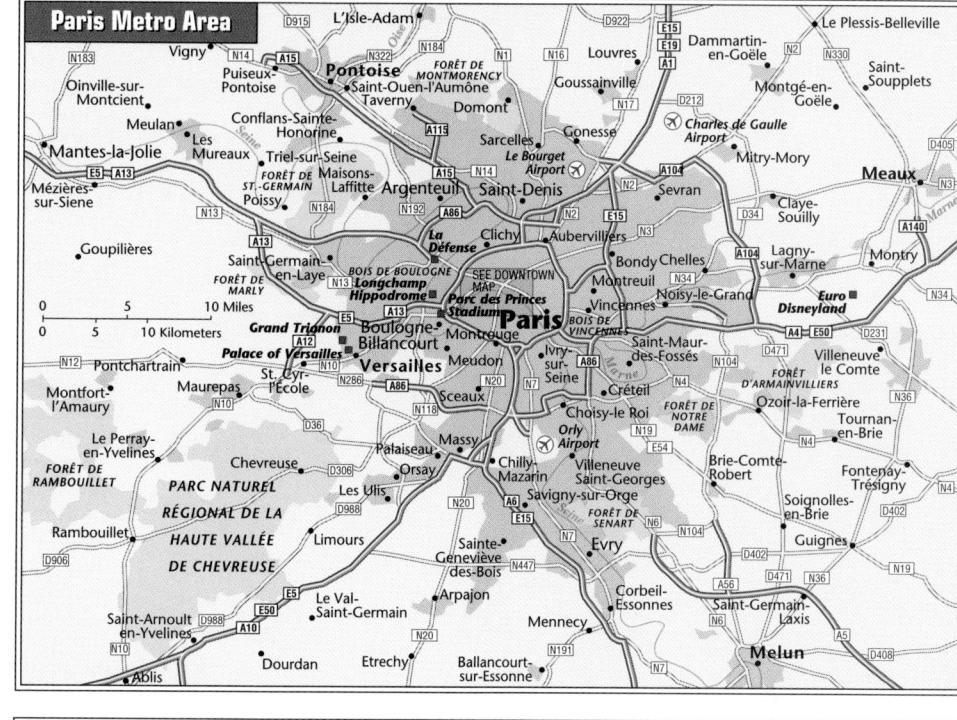

Paris Metro Area

Sunflower farm in Provence, near Avignon

France

Capital: Paris
Area: 211,209 sq. mi.
547,030 sq. km.
Population: 59,925,000 (2002 est.)
Largest City: Paris, 2,148,000
Language: French
Major Religions: Roman Catholic, Protestant, Jewish, Muslim
Life Expectancy: 75 male, 82 female
Government: republic
Monetary Unit: euro
Industry: steel, machinery, chemicals, automobiles, metallurgy, aircraft, electronics, mining, textiles, food processing, tourism
Agriculture: dairy products, cereals, sugar beets, potatoes, wine grapes
Minerals and Resources: coal, iron ore, bauxite, zinc, potash

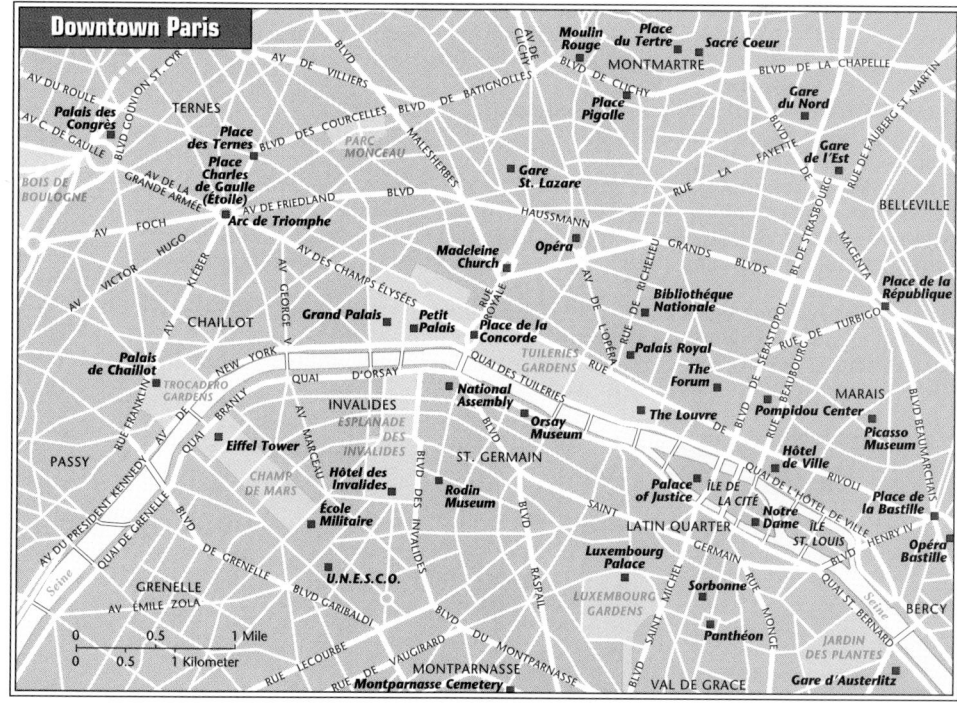

Downtown Paris

France has been a crossroads of travel, trade and invasion since prehistoric times. The population is a blend of Latin, Celtic and Teutonic (Frankish) ethnic stocks. French has been an international language for centuries and is a common second language throughout the world; in fact it has been a unifying factor in Africa, Asia, the Pacific and the West Indies where it often serves as the only common language.

France was one of the earliest countries to progress from feudalism into the era of the nation-state. It has one of the world's most highly developed economies with important agricultural resources and a diversified modern industrial sector.

France has been a leader in the formation of the European Union. It views Franco-German cooperation as the foundation of efforts to enhance European security as well as prosperity. French humanitarian organizations have long played a major role in providing assistance to the victims of war and disease. French troops represent the largest contingent of the UN Protection Force stationed in the former Yugoslavia and France has played a leading role in trying to resolve that conflict.

French culture is renowned the world over, as are its food, wine and many of its other export products, such as clothing.

The Orangérie at the Palace of Versailles

Liechtenstein

⊛ National Capital
• Other City

Oblique Mercator Projection

© MapQuest.com, Inc.

Liechtenstein

Capital: Vaduz
Area: 62 sq. mi.
160 sq. km.
Population: 33,000 (2002 est.)
Largest City: Vaduz, 5,000
Language: German
Major Religions: Roman Catholic, Protestant
Life Expectancy: 74 male, 81 female
Government: hereditary constitutional monarchy
Monetary Unit: Swiss franc
Industry: electronics, metal manufacturing, textiles, ceramics, pharmaceuticals, food products, precision instruments, tourism
Agriculture: vegetables, corn, wheat, potatoes, grapes
Minerals and Resources: negligible

Because of its strategic location on a north-south and east-west crossroads in central Europe, Liechtenstein has been permanently inhabited since the Neolithic Age.

The imperial Principality of Liechtenstein was established in 1719 when the territory was purchased by the princely House of Liechtenstein in order to maintain a seat in the Imperial Diet of the Holy Roman Empire. Liechtenstein has been politically independent since 1815, but has had customs agreements with Austria-Hungary and, since 1923, with Switzerland.

Despite its small size and limited natural resources, Liechtenstein has developed from a mainly agricultural into a highly industrialized, prosperous, free-enterprise economy. Although its domestic labor force is highly skilled, its size (about 9,000) has proven inadequate for its industry and about 13,800 foreign workers are employed to meet labor needs (about 8,200 of those commute from Austria and Switzerland to work each day).

Switzerland

So many cultures have influenced Switzerland that it is impossible to define its ethnic groups. Switzerland has three official languages – German, French and Italian – but Romansch is spoken by a small minority in Canton Graubünden and English is widely spoken.

About 70% of Switzerland's area is mountainous, the remaining 30% comprises the "Mittelland" which is the plateau that is home to the larger cities and industrial sections.

Switzerland's economy is one of the most prosperous and stable in the world. The decision not to become part of the EU's single market structure has not harmed Switzerland, which is renowned for it high labor value exports such as watches, precision instruments and items that do not lend themselves to mass production methods.

Switzerland has long maintained a policy of neutrality and avoids alliances that might entail military, political or direct economic action against another state or group of states. The Swiss do play an active role in international conflict resolution as well as humanitarian assistance in the world.

Capital: Bern
Area: 15,942 sq. mi.
41,290 sq. km.
Population: 7,302,000 (2002 est.)
Largest City: Zürich, 341,000
Languages: German, French, Italian, Romansch
Major Religions: Roman Catholic, Protestant

Life Expectancy: 75 male, 82 female
Government: federal republic
Monetary Unit: Swiss franc
Industry: machinery, chemicals, watches, textiles, precision instruments
Agriculture: dairy products
Minerals and Resources: salt

Switzerland

⊛ National Capital
• Other City

Lambert Conformal Conic Projection

© MapQuest.com, Inc.

Zürich

Austria

Capital: Vienna
Area: 32,375 sq. mi.
83,850 sq. km.
Population: 8,170,000 (2002 est.)
Largest City: Vienna, 1,562,000
Language: German
Major Religions: Roman Catholic, Protestant
Life Expectancy: 74 male, 80 female
Government: federal republic
Monetary Unit: euro
Industry: foods, iron and steel, machines, textiles, chemicals, electrical, paper and pulp, tourism, mining, motor vehicles
Agriculture: grains, fruit, potatoes, sugar beets
Minerals and Resources: iron ore, petroleum, magnesite, aluminum, lead, coal, lignite, copper

The present boundaries of Austria – once the center of the empire which was the second largest state in Europe – were established according to the Treaty of St. Germain in 1919. Austrians are a homogenous people, 98% being native German speakers. Many Austrians, particularly near Vienna, still have relatives in Hungary and the Czech Republic.

Austria is made up of nine Laender (provinces) which embody strong provincial and local loyalties based on tradition and history. It has traditionally been active in what Austrians call "bridge building to the East," involving contacts at all levels with Eastern Europe and the former Soviet Union. In this way, Austria has served in many ways as a gateway to eastern Europe through its transition in recent years.

Austria has a social market economy in which the government plays an important role. Thanks to its raw material endowment, a technically skilled labor force, and strong links to German industrial firms, Austria occupies specialized niches in European industry and services (tourism and banking).

Parliament, Budapest

Hungary

Capital: Budapest
Area: 35,919 sq. mi.
93,030 sq. km.
Population: 10,075,000 (2002 est.)
Largest City: Budapest, 1,825,000
Language: Hungarian
Major Religions: Roman Catholic, Calvinist, Lutheran
Life Expectancy: 68 male, 76 female
Government: republic
Monetary Unit: forint
Industry: mining, metallurgy, construction materials, processed foods, textiles, chemicals, pharmaceuticals, buses, automobiles
Agriculture: wheat, corn, sunflowers, potatoes, sugar beets, dairy products
Minerals and Resources: bauxite, coal, natural gas

Due to its geographic location, Hungary is considered to be one of the gateways to Eastern Europe. Historically it has enjoyed its role in the Austro-Hungarian Dual Monarchy (1867-1918) and endured both German and Soviet rule.

In 1990 Hungary had its first free, multiparty elections in more than 40 years.

Hungary's transition to a Western-style parliamentary democracy was the first and the smoothest among the former Soviet bloc. Hungary's current foreign policy has three equal priorities: integrating rapidly with the West and its institutions, improving relations with neighboring countries and supporting the rights of Hungarian minorities abroad.

Budapest is the country's leading tourist attraction, especially for its museums, historic houses and buildings of the Var (Royal Castle) area.

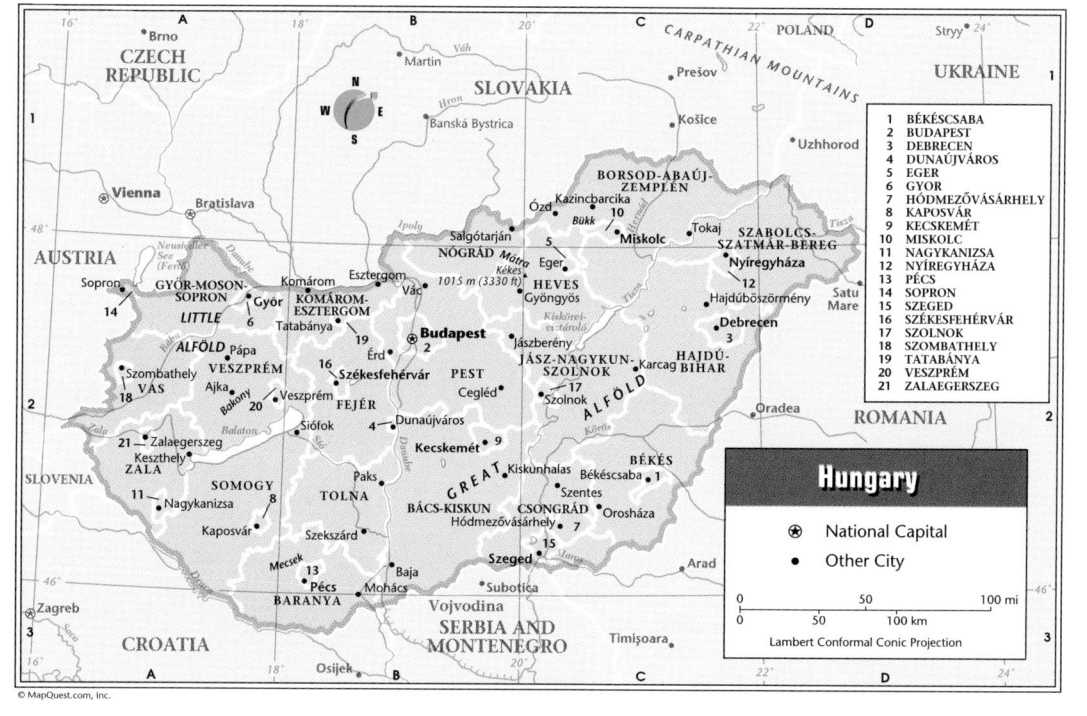

© MapQuest.com, Inc.

Czech Republic

The Czech Republic is made up of two main regions: Bohemia in the west, consisting of rolling plains, hills and plateaus surrounded by low mountains; and Moravia in the east, consisting of very hilly country. The majority of the inhabitants are ethnically and linguistically Czech, with only about 3% of the current population being Slovak.

The Czech and Slovak Federal Republic, or Czechoslovakia, was formed as a common state after World War I and remained one until 1993, when the two republics split to form two separate states. Since independence, the Czechs have made integration into Western institutions their chief foreign policy objective.

Of the emerging democracies in Central and Eastern Europe the Czech Republic has one of the most developed industrialized economies. The government has undertaken the ambitious task of privatizing state industries in all sectors of the economy.

Capital: Prague
Area: 30,387 sq. mi.
  78,703 sq. km.
Population: 10,257,000 (2002 est.)
Largest City: Prague, 1,179,000
Languages: Czech, Slovak
Major Religions: Roman Catholic, Protestant, Orthodox
Life Expectancy: 70 male, 77 female

Government: parliamentary democracy
Monetary Unit: koruna
Industry: fuels, ferrous metallurgy, machinery and equipment, coal, motor vehicles, glass, armaments
Agriculture: grains, potatoes, sugar beets, hops, fruit
Minerals and Resources: coal, kaolin, clay, graphite

Church of St. Nicholas, Old Town Square, Prague, Czech Republic

Slovakia

Capital: Bratislava
Area: 18,859 sq. mi.
  48,845 sq. km.
Population: 5,422,000 (2002 est.)
Largest City: Bratislava, 429,000
Languages: Slovak, Hungarian
Major Religions: Roman Catholic, Protestant, Orthodox
Life Expectancy: 69 male, 78 female
Government: parliamentary democracy
Monetary Unit: koruna
Industry: metal products, food and beverage, electricity, gas and water, coking, oil production, nuclear fuel production, chemicals and man-made fibers, machinery, paper and printing, earthenware and ceramics, transport vehicles, textiles, electrical and optical apparatus, rubber products
Agriculture: grains, potatoes, sugar beets, hops, fruit
Minerals and Resources: brown coal and lignite, iron ore, copper, manganese ore, salt

Slovakia became independent from Czechoslovakia in 1993. Most of Slovakia is mountainous, with lowlands in the south. Slovakia is a parliamentary democracy with a constitution.

Slovakia became part of Hungary in the 11th century and remained under Hungarian rule almost continuously through World War I. In 1918, the Slovaks joined the Czechs of Bohemia to form Czechoslovakia. There remains a sizable Hungarian minority (about 10%) in present-day Slovakia and Hungarian is widely spoken.

Slovakia has been striving to build its economy, privatize and attract foreign investment since its independence. Progress has been fairly slow but recovery in western Europe is boosting Slovak exports and production.

Andorra is the last independent survivor of the March states, a number of buffer states created by Charlemagne to keep the Muslim Moors from advancing into Christian France.

Andorrans are a minority in Andorra today, making up only about 30% of the population; Spanish, French and Portuguese residents make up the remainder. The national language is Catalan, but French and Spanish are spoken as well.

There are seven urbanized valleys, called parishes, that form Andorra's political districts. Until recently, Andorra's political system had no clear division of powers into executive, legislative and judicial branches. Upon the recommendation by the Council of Europe, Andorra ratified and approved a constitution in 1993 that established it as a sovereign parliamentary democracy that retains as its head of state a co-principality. The President of France and the Bishop of Seo de Urgel share limited powers and are represented by delegates in Andorra.

The 1993 constitution, in creating a modern legal framework for the country, has allowed Andorra to begin a shift from an economy based largely on duty free shopping to one based on international banking and finance.

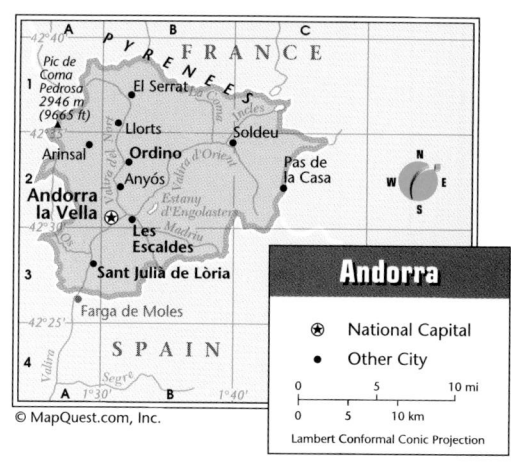

Capital: Andorra la Vella
Area: 174 sq. mi.
              450 sq. km.
Population: 68,000 (2002 est.)
Largest City: Andorra la Vella, 21,000
Languages: Catalan, French, Castilian
Major Religion: Roman Catholic
Life Expectancy: 76 male, 82 female
Government: parliamentary democracy
Monetary Unit: euro
Industry: tourism, sheep, timber, tobacco, banking
Agriculture: tobacco, wheat, barley, oats, vegetables
Minerals and Resources: mineral water, iron ore, lead

Andorra

Fortress town of Valença, along the Minho River, Portugal

Portugal

Capital: Lisbon
Area: 35,552 sq. mi.
              92,080 sq. km.
Population: 10,084,000 (2002 est.)
Largest City: Lisbon, 565,000
Language: Portuguese
Major Religions: Roman Catholic, Protestant
Life Expectancy: 72 male, 79 female
Government: republic
Monetary Unit: euro
Industry: textiles and footware, wood pulp, paper and cork, metal working, oil refining, chemicals, fish canning, wine, tourism
Agriculture: grains, potatoes, olives, grapes, dairy products
Minerals and Resources: tungsten, uranium ore, iron ore, marble

Portugal is a parliamentary democracy with a constitution that was adopted in 1976 and revised twice since, in 1982 and 1989. Each revision edited out more of the Marxist rhetoric and laid the groundwork for further privatization of public sector enterprise and the government-owned media.

Portugal's economy is based on traditional industries such as textiles, clothing, footwear, cork and wood products, wine and porcelain. Portugal is also a major European tourist destination and has recently strengthened its position in the automobile industry.

Portugal gave up many of its overseas possessions in the 1970s but still has two "autonomous regions," the Azores and Madeira Islands.

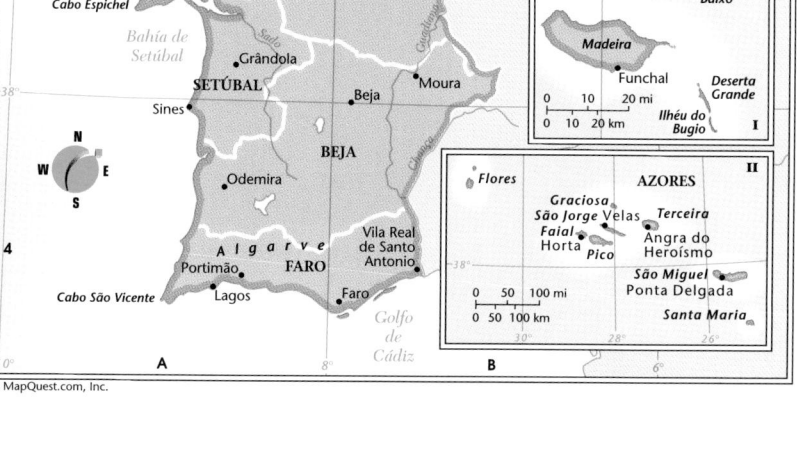

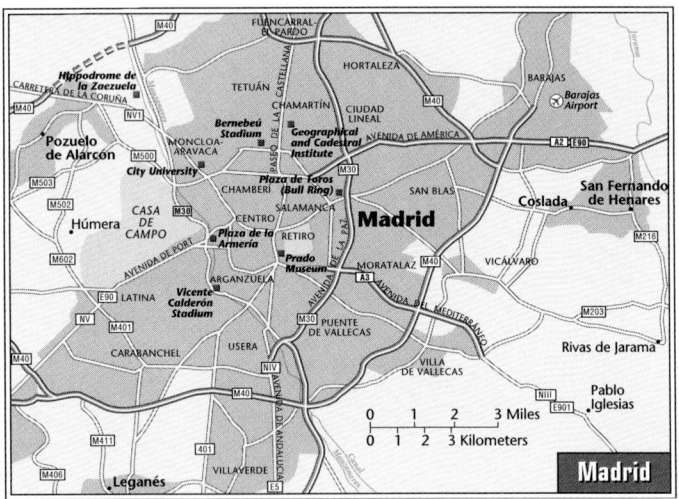

Madrid

Las Ramblas and Columbus Statue,
Barcelona, Spain

Spain

Capital: Madrid
Area: 194,834 sq. mi.
504,750 sq. km.
Population: 40,153,000 (2002 est.)
Largest City: Madrid, 2,939,000
Languages: Castilian Spanish, Catalan, Galician, Basque
Major Religion: Roman Catholic
Life Expectancy: 75 male, 81 female
Government: parliamentary monarchy
Monetary Unit: euro
Industry: textiles and apparel, food and beverages, metals and metal manufacturing, chemicals, shipbuilding, automobiles, machine tools, tourism
Agriculture: fishing, grain, vegetables, olives, wine grapes, sugar beets, citrus fruit, beef, pork, poultry, dairy
Minerals and Resources: coal, lignite, iron ore, uranium, mercury, pyrites, fluorspar, gypsum, zinc, lead, tungsten, copper, kaolin, potash, hydropower

Spain is comprised of seventeen autonomous communities covering all of peninsular Spain, the Canaries and the Balearic Islands. It is governed by a parliamentary monarchy that was established officially by the 1978 constitution.

Spain is still breaking out of the diplomatic and economic isolation of the thirty-six year reign of General Franco. Spain became a member of the European Community - now European Union - in 1986, which required it to open its economy, modernize its industrial base, improve infrastructure and revise economic legislation. It has been a good example of transition from authoritarianism to democracy, particularly for the Spanish-speaking nations of Latin America, with whom it maintains special economic and cultural cooperation.

Spain is rich in culture and history, as well as in beautiful beaches, and its tourism industry has blossomed since the 1970's, constituting a very important sector of the Spanish economy.

Italy

Capital: Rome
Area: 116,275 sq. mi.
301,230 sq. km.
Population: 57,927,000 (2002 est.)
Largest City: Rome, 2,460,000
Languages: Italian, German, French, Slovene
Major Religion: Roman Catholic
Life Expectancy: 75 male, 81 female
Government: republic
Monetary Unit: euro
Industry: machinery, iron and steel, chemicals, food processing, textiles, motor vehicles, clothings, footwear, ceramics
Agriculture: fruits, vegetables, grapes, potatoes, sugar beets, soybeans, grain, olives, fishing
Minerals and Resources: mercury, potash, marble, sulfur, dwindling natural gas and crude oil reserves, fish, coal

Italy

⊛ National Capital
• Other City

0   50   100 mi
0   50   100 km
Lambert Conformal Conic Projection

© MapQuest.com, Inc.

Leaning Tower of Pisa

Italy has been a democratic republic since 1946, when the monarchy was abolished by popular referendum. It is a largely homogeneous country linguistically and religiously, but is diverse culturally, economically and politically.

Italian culture has had a tremendous influence on Western civilization. Italy has been home to countless giants in literature, music, painting, sculpture, architecture, filmmaking, and design for centuries.

The Italian economy has changed dramatically since the end of World War II. It has developed from an agriculturally based economy into an industrial state that ranks as the word's fifth-largest industrial economy.

Despite frequent government turnovers and widespread political corruption since 1945, Italy has entered a period of political self-renewal. In recent years, Italian voters have demanded political, economic and and ethical reforms in their government and ambitious reform programs have been undertaken by its new leaders.

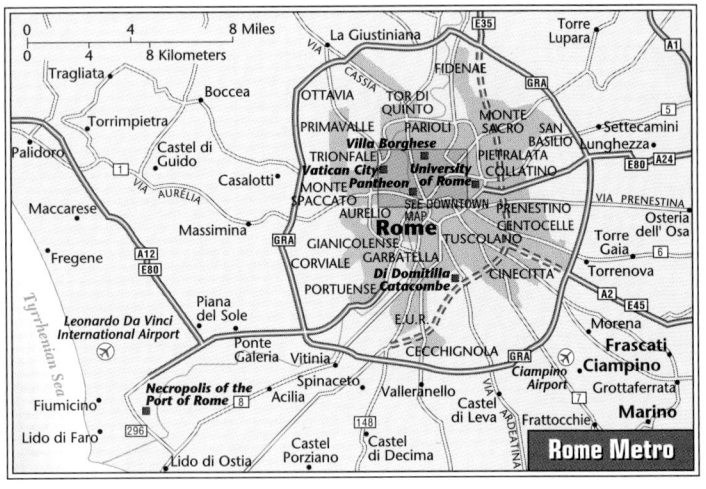

Rome Metro

Arched bridge with St. Peter's
in background

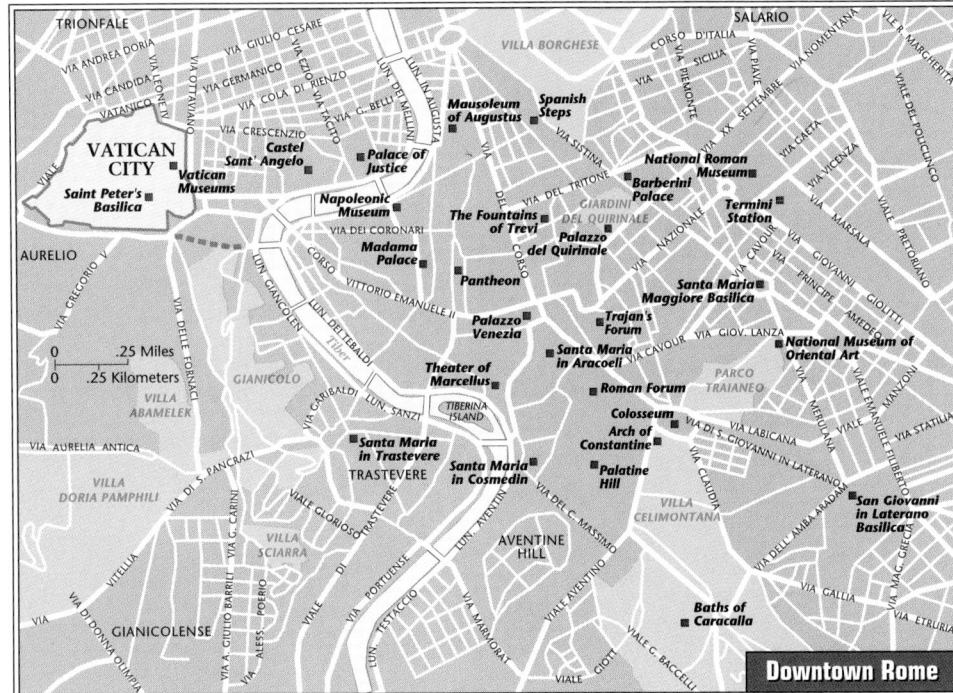

Downtown Rome

Roman Colosseum

View of St. Peter's Square, Vatican City

Vatican City

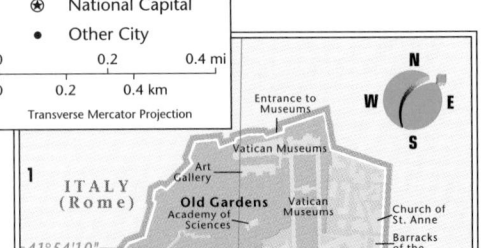

Vatican City

⊛ National Capital
• Other City

Transverse Mercator Projection

Capital: Vatican City
Area: 0.17 sq. mi.
0.44 sq. km.
Population: 840 (1996 est.)
Languages: Italian, Latin, various other languages
Life Expectancy: NA
Major Religions: Roman Catholic
Government: monarchical-sacerdotal state
Monetary Unit: euro
Industry: printing and production of a small amount of mosaics and staff uniforms; worldwide banking and financial activities
Minerals and Resources: none

Vatican City is the world's smallest state. It is home to the Holy See which directs the world-wide Catholic Church and was created in 1929 as an enclave of Rome to administer properties belonging to the Holy See. Vatican City is recognized under international law and enters into international agreements, but, unlike the Holy See, it does not receive or send diplomatic representatives.

The Pope is elected by the College of Cardinals for life and exercises supreme legislative, executive and judicial power over the Holy See and the state of Vatican City.

The unique, noncommercial economy of Vatican City is supported financially by contributions from Roman Catholics throughout the world, fees for admissions to its museums, the sale of postage stamps and tourist mementos, and the sale of publications.

© MapQuest.com, Inc.

Monaco is the second smallest state in the world, after Vatican City, with an area of just under two square kilometers. Monaco is a constitutional monarchy and has been independent and ruled by the House of Grimaldi since 1419. Since 1911, there has been a prince as chief of state.

The principality is noted for its beautiful natural scenery and mild sunny climate and has long been a resort for the wealthy. It is also known for its activity in the field of marine sciences.

Customs, postal services, telecommunications and banking in Monaco are governed by an economic and customs union with France. While France has agreed to defend the independence and sovereignty of Monaco, the Monegasque Government has agreed to exercise its sovereign rights in conformity with French intersts.

There is no unemployment in Monaco; in fact, thousands of French citizens commute there daily from nearby towns to work.

Capital: Monaco
Area: .73 sq. mi.
　　　 1.9 sq. km.
Population: 32,000 (2002 est.)
Largest City: Monaco, 27,000
Languages: French, English, Italian, Monegasque
Major Religions: Roman Catholic
Life Expectancy: 74 male, 82 female
Government: constitutional monarchy
Monetary Unit: euro
Industry: tourism
Agriculture: none
Minerals and Resources: none

The Casino of Monte Carlo, Monaco

Monaco

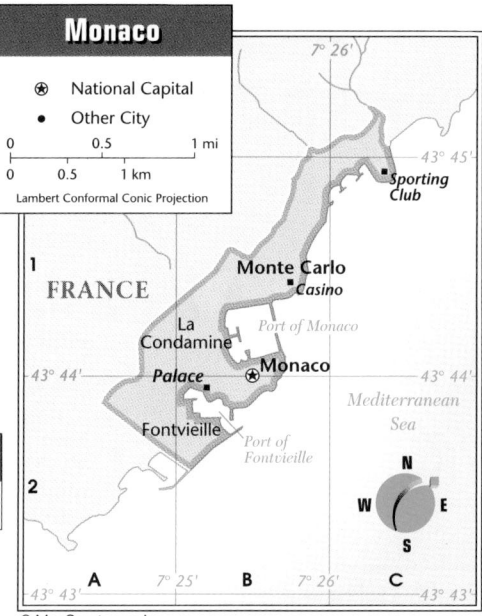

San Marino

Capital: San Marino
Area: 23 sq. mi.
　　　 60 sq. km.
Population: 28,000 (2002 est.)
Largest City: San Marino, 3,000
Language: Italian
Major Religions: Roman Catholic
Life Expectancy: 77 male, 85 female
Government: republic
Monetary Unit: euro
Industry: tourism, textiles, electronics, ceramics, cement, wine
Agriculture: wheat, grapes, maize, olives, meat, cheese, hides, cattle, pigs, horses
Minerals and Resources: building stone

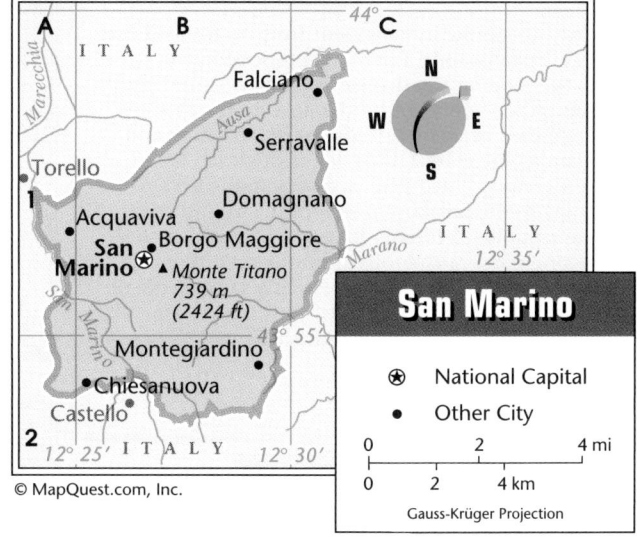

© MapQuest.com, Inc.

San Marino, located in north central Italy, is the world's smallest republic. Its terrain is ruggedly mountainous and it only has three towns of any size. Its population density is about one-fifth greater than that of Italy (358 per square kilometer). Its recorded history indicates that a monastery existed there in the ninth century and that a community grew around it and eventually formed a small state.

San Marino has had its own statutes and governmental institutions since the 11th century. Various assaults on its independence by the papacy, the Malatesta lords of Rimini, Cesare Borgia, Napoleon and Mussolini all failed.

San Marino's policies are inextricably tied to Italy's and thus political organizations and labor unions that are active in Italy are also active in San Marino. The key industries in San Marino are tourism, banking, wearing apparel, electronics and ceramics.

Malta

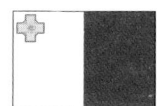

Malta comprises an archipelago, with only the three largest islands (Malta, Gozo and Comino) being inhabited. It is one of the most densely populated countries in the world, with about 1,160 inhabitants per square kilometer. Ethnically, the Maltese are a mixture of Arab, English, Sicilian, Norman, Italian and Spanish stock. Maltese and English are the official languages.

Malta has been ruled by the Romans, the Spanish, the French and the British. In 1964, Malta obtained independence from Britain, established itself as a parliamentary democracy and became a republic within the Commonwealth, with its own constitution and president.

Malta's economy is highly dependent on foreign trade and services and is tightly regulated by the government. Manufacturing and tourism are the most important industries in the Maltese economy.

Capital: Valletta
Area: 124 sq. mi.
　　　 320 sq. km.
Population: 397,000 (2002 est.)
Largest City: Valletta, 8,000
Languages: Maltese, English
Major Religions: Roman Catholic
Life Expectancy: 75 male, 80 female
Government: parliamentary democracy
Monetary Unit: Maltese lira
Industry: tourism, electronics, ship repairyard, construction, food manufacturing, textiles, footwear, clothing, beverages, tobacco
Agriculture: potatoes, cauliflower, grapes, wheat, barley, tomatoes, citrus, cut flowers, green peppers, hogs,poultry, eggs; generally adequate supplies of vegetables, poultry, milk, pork products;
Minerals and Resources: limestone, salt

© MapQuest.com, Inc.

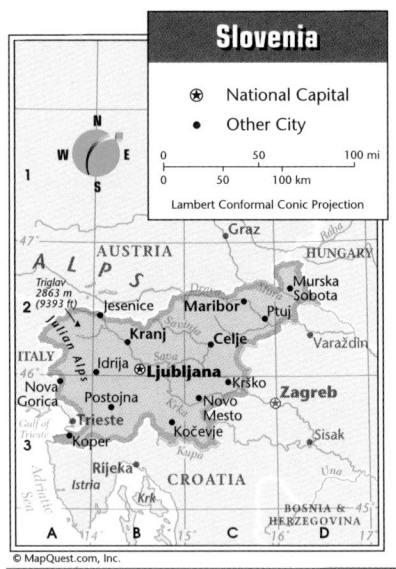

Slovenia is situated on the Adriatic Sea between Italy and Croatia, a gateway between east and west. It is a mountainous country with almost half its land area comprised of forests, yet it also enjoys a beautiful coastline.

Slovenia gained its independence from Yugoslavia in 1991 and is a progressive, young democracy headed by a prime minister.

Of the former Yugoslav republics, Slovenia was by far the most prosperous, having strong ties with western Europe and suffering relatively small physical damage in the break-up. Privatization is under way and there is already a majority of small companies.

Slovenia

Capital: Ljubljana
Area: 7,836 sq. mi.
20,296 sq. km.
Population: 1,933,000 (2002 est.)
Largest City: Ljubljana, 264,000
Languages: Slovenian, Serbo-Croatian
Major Religions: Roman Catholic, Muslim
Life Expectancy: 71 male, 79 female
Government: emerging democracy
Monetary Unit: tolar
Industry: ferrous metallurgy and rolling mill products, aluminum reduction and rolled products, lead and zinc smelting, electronics, trucks, electric power equipment, wood products, textiles, chemicals, machine tools
Agriculture: potatoes, hops, hemp, flax
Minerals: lignite coal, lead, zinc, mercury, uranium, silver

Gornji Grad (old town), Zagreb, Croatia

Capital: Zagreb
Area: 21,829 sq. mi.
56,538 sq. km.
Population: 4,391,000 (2002 est.)
Largest City: Zagreb, 692,000
Language: Serbo-Croatian
Major Religions: Catholic, Orthodox, Slavic Muslim, Protestant
Life Expectancy: 71 male, 78 female
Government: parliamentary democracy
Monetary Unit: Croatian kuna
Industry: chemicals and plastics, machine tools, fabricated metal, electronics, pig iron and rolled steel products, aluminum reduction, paper, wood products, building materials, textiles, shipbuilding, petroleum refining, food processing and beverages
Agriculture: wheat, corn, sugar beets, sunflowers, alfalfa, clover
Minerals and Resources: oil, coal, bauxite, low grade iron ore, calcium, natural asphalt, silica, mica, clays, salt

Croatia

Croatia became independent from Yugoslavia in 1991, establishing a parliamentary democracy. It is a geographically diverse country with flat plains along the Hungarian border, low mountains and highlands near the Adriatic coast, coastline and islands. There are 1,185 islands of which 66 are densely populated (the largest island is Krk).

Before the breakup of the former Yugoslavia, the republic of Croatia followed Slovenia as the second most prosperous and industrialized area. Four years of war followed Croatia's independence from Yugoslavia, but the last Serb troops left Croatian territory in 1998 under United Nations supervision.

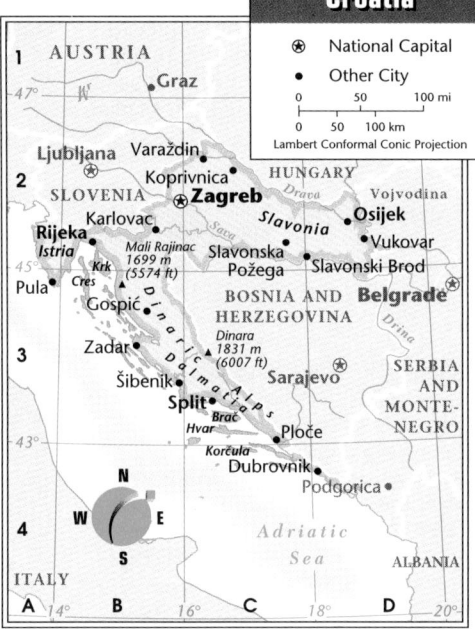

Before the breakup of the former Yugoslavia, Bosnia and Herzegovina ranked next to Macedonia as the poorest republic in the federation. Independence was declared by referendum on March 3, 1992, but the referendum was boycotted by Bosnian Serbs. A bitter ethnic war ravaged this small nation for the next three years, as Bosnian Serbs tried unsuccessfully to attach themselves to Yugoslavia to form a "Greater Serbia."

A peace agreement between warring factions was signed in Dayton, Ohio, in November 1995. Bosnia's boundaries remained intact, and internal government was restructured to create two separate entities: the Bosniak/Croat Federation of Bosnia and Herzegovina, and the Bosnian Serb-led Republika Srpska (RS). A NATO-led peacekeeping force remains active in Bosnia, but its troop levels are gradually being reduced.

Bosnia and Herzegovina

Capital: Sarajevo
Area: 19,781 sq. mi.
51,233 sq. km.
Population: 3,964,000 (2002 est.)
Largest City: Sarajevo, 529,000
Language: Serbo-Croatian
Major Religions: Muslim, Orthodox, Catholic, Protestant
Life Expectancy: 73 male, 78 female
Government: emerging democracy
Monetary Unit: dinar
Industry: steel production, mining, manufacturing
Agriculture: wine, wheat, corn
Minerals and Resources: coal, iron, bauxite, manganese, copper, chromium, lead, zinc

Serbia and Montenegro

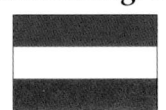

Following a European Union-sponsored deal in 2002 to prevent a final break-up of the last two Yugoslav republics, the Federal Republic of Yugoslavia formally dissolved itself on Feb. 4, 2003. The last two republics will form a loose federation to be called Serbia and Montenegro.

The new state still has many obstacles to overcome. The bloody ethnic warfare that led to the breakup of the former Yugoslavia still lingers and the status of NATO-controlled Kosovo still has to be resolved.

The terrain in Serbia and Montenegro is extremely varied, with rich, fertile plains in the north, limestone ranges and bases in the east, ancient mountains and hills in the southeast and a very high shoreline in the southwest with no islands off the coast.

Capital: Belgrade
Area: 39,518 sq. mi.
             102,350 sq. km.
Population: 10,658,000 (2002 est.)
Largest City: Belgrade, 1,619,000
Languages: Serbo-Croatian, Albanian
Major Religions: Orthodox, Muslim, Roman Catholic, Protestant
Life Expectancy: 71 male, 77 female
Government: republic
Monetary Unit: dinar (Serbia); euro (Montenegro, Kosovo)
Industry: machine building, metallurgy, mining, consumer goods, electronics, petroleum products, chemicals, pharmaceuticals
Agriculture: cereal, cotton, oil seeds, chicory, fruit, grapes, cereals, olives, citrus, rice
Minerals and Resources: oil, gas, coal, antimony, copper, lead, zinc, nickel, gold, pyrite, chrome

Albania

Capital: Tirana
Area: 11,100 sq. mi.
             28,750 sq, km.
Population: 3,545,000 (2002 est.)
Largest City: Tirana, 244,000
Languages: Albanian, Greek
Major Religions: Muslim, Albanian Orthodox, Roman Catholic
Life Expectancy: 71 male, 77 female
Government: emerging democracy
Monetary Unit: lek
Industry: food processing, textiles and clothing, lumber, oil, cement, chemicals, mining, basic metals, hydropower
Agriculture: temperate zone crops
Minerals and Resources: petroleum, natural gas, coal, chromium, copper, nickel

Albania, historically, has been a nation subjected to foreign domination, including 500 years of rule by the Ottoman Turks, followed by alliances with the Soviet Union, China and the former Yugoslavia. It became an independent state in 1912, although it lost some of its territories in the process, including the region of Kosovo in Serbia, which still has an Albanian majority that is fighting for independence.

Albania has long been the poorest nation in Europe and its strict communist government has kept the country cut off from the rest of the world for nearly fifty years. The late 1980s and 1990s have seen the Albanian government turn more and more from a communist system to a capitalist system and with that have come all the complexities which face an emerging democracy.

Albanians are divided into two ethnic groups: the Gegs in the north and the Tosks in the south. There have long been feuds between these two groups and the tensions have not been resolved.

© MapQuest.com, Inc.

Macedonia

Capital: Skopje
Area: 9,778 sq. mi.
    25,333 sq. km.
Population: 2,055,000
(2002 est.)
Largest City: Skopje, 545,000
Languages: Macedonian,
Albanian, Turkish, Serbo-Croatian
Major Religions: Eastern
Orthodox, Muslim
Life Expectancy: 72 male, 76
female
Government: emerging

democracy
Monetary Unit: denar
Industry: basic liquid fuels, coal,
metals, textiles, wood products,
tobacco
Agriculture: rice, tobacco, wheat,
corn, millet, cotton, sesame, mulberry leaves, citrus fruit, vegetables
Minerals and Resources: chromium, lead, zinc, manganese, tungsten, nickel, low-grade iron ore,
asbestos, sulphur, timber

The former Yugoslav republic of Macedonia gained its independence in 1991. Geographically, it is an isolated mountainous area covered with deep basins and valleys and bisected by the Vardar River.

Historically the poorest of the former Yugoslav republics, Macedonia faces a very difficult transition
period as it moves towards democracy and a free market economy. Economically, the country can meet
its own basic food and energy needs through agricultural and coal resources; however its economy
depends on outside sources for all of its oil and modern machinery and parts.

Politically, Macedonia is still very unstable and subject to the effects of the ongoing conflicts in the former Yugoslavia, as well as its own disputes with Greece and the presence of a large minority of ethnic
Albanians (22% of the population).

© MapQuest.com, Inc.

Greece

Capital: Athens
Area: 50,929 sq. mi.
    131,940 sq. km.
Population: 10,645,000 (2002 est.)
Largest City: Athens, 746,000
Languages: Greek, English, French
Major Religions: Greek Orthodox, Muslim
Life Expectancy: 75 male, 81 female
Government: presidential parliamentary
government
Monetary Unit: euro
Industry: tourism, food and tobacco pro-
cessing, textiles, chemicals, metal products,
mining, petroleum
Agriculture: fishing, forestry, wheat, corn,
barley, sugar beets, olives, tomatoes, wine,
tobacco, potatoes
Minerals and Resources: bauxite, lignite,
magnesite, petroleum, marble

Greece was inhabited as early as the Paleolithic period, and by 3000 BC had become home to a culture whose
art remains evocative today. Today's Greek governmental structure is similar to that of most Western
European countries and has been described as a compromise between the French and German models.

Greece is a mostly mountainous country, with ranges extending into into the sea as peninsulas or chains of
islands. It has gradually become a very urbanized society, with about one-third its population living in the
greater Athens area alone. Due to its rich cultural history as well as its countless beaches, Greece has a highly
developed and successful tourist industry.

Greece is a member of NATO and the EC. Because of its geographic location, it also has a special interest in
the Middle East.

Harbor at Oia, Thíra (Santorini)

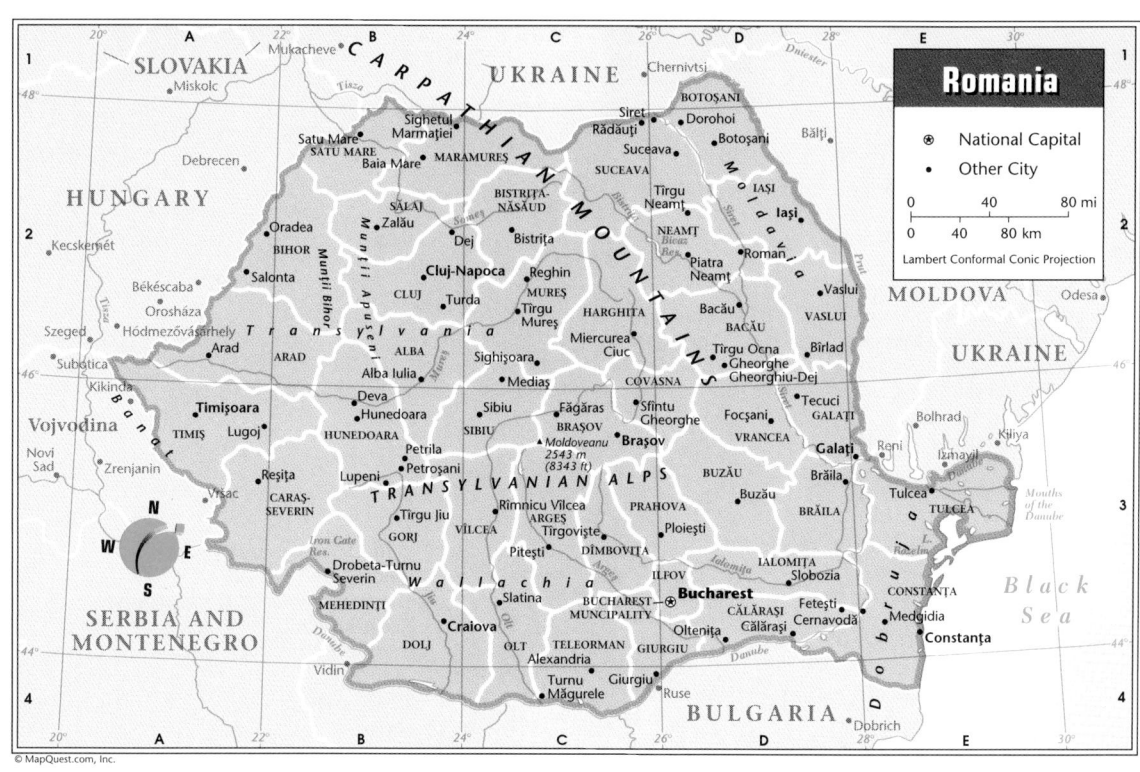

Romania

Capital: Bucharest
Area: 91,675 sq. mi.
237,500 sq. km.
Population: 22,318,000 (2002 est.)
Largest City: Bucharest, 2,009,000
Languages: Romanian, Hungarian, German
Major Religions: Romanian Orthodox, Roman Catholic, Protestant
Life Expectancy: 69 male, 75 female
Government: republic
Monetary Unit: leu
Industry: mining, timber, construction materials, metallurgy, chemicals, machine building, food processing, petroleum production and refining
Agriculture: wheat, corn, sugar beets, sunflower seed, potatoes, milk, eggs, meat, grapes
Minerals and Resources: petroleum (reserves declining), timber, natural gas, coal, iron ore, salt

Capital: Sofia
Area: 42,811 sq. mi.
110,910 sq. km.
Population: 7,621,000 (2002 est.)
Largest City: Sofia, 1,191,000
Life Expectancy: 70 male, 77 female
Major Religions: Bulgarian Orthodox, Muslim
Language: Bulgarian
Government: emerging democracy

Monetary Unit: lev
Industry: machine building and metal working, food processing, chemicals, textiles, building materials, ferrous and nonferrous metals
Agriculture: livestock, grain crops, oilseeds, vegetables, fruits, tobacco
Minerals and Resources: bauxite, copper, lead, zinc, coal, timber, arable land

Romania's history has been violent and dramatic for more than 22 centuries. It was an independent kingdom from 1881 to 1947 when the communist government forced the abdication of King Michael. The downfall of President Ceausescu and his brutal regime in 1989 started Romania on a path away from communism and towards democracy. A new constitution, based on France's Fifth Republic, was adopted in December 1991.

Economically, there is a growing private sector in Romania and many market-oriented reforms have been introduced. The process of conversion to a more open economy is slow and painful, however, and Romanians must continue to endure high inflation, frequent disruptions of basic services, high food prices and high unemployment, among other things.

Bulgaria

Bulgaria is a mostly mountainous country and has one of the lowest population densities in Eastern Europe. It is strategically located near the Turkish Straits and thus controls key land routes from Europe to the Middle East and Asia.

The removal of long-time Bulgarian leader Todor Zhivkov from government and party positions in November, 1989 began a period of significant change in Bulgarian political life. From 1944, when the communists seized power, up to this time, the Bulgarian Communist Party controlled all aspects of life in Bulgaria.

Present day Bulgaria is a young democracy, in transition from a centralized communist state to a free market economy. One of the keys to its economic recovery will be the re-establishment of market links lost with the other Soviet bloc economies.

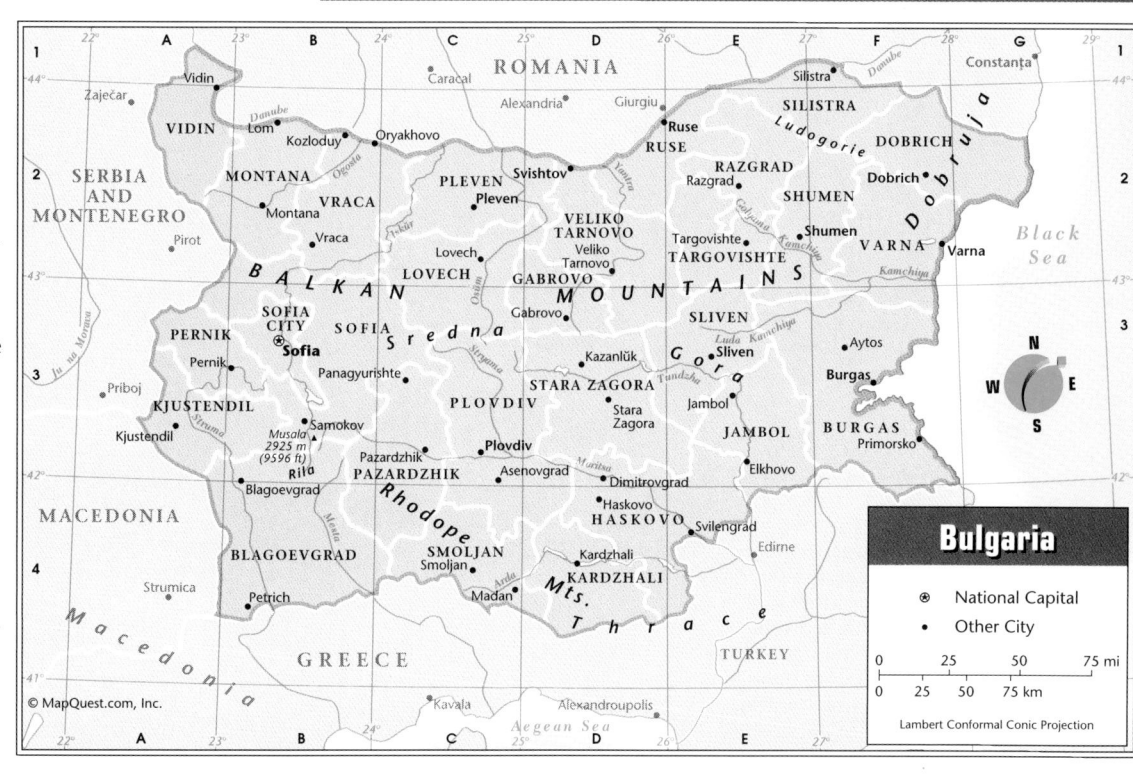

Moldova

Capital: Chişinău
Area: 13,008 sq. mi.
33,700 sq. km.
Population: 4,435,000
(2002 est.)
Largest City: Chişinău, 658,000
Languages: Moldovan
(Romanian), Russian, Gagauz (a
Turkish dialect)
Major Religions: Eastern
Orthodox, Jewish
Life Expectancy: 65 male, 72
female

Government: republic
Monetary Unit: leu
Industry: canned food, agricultural machinery, foundry equipment,
refrigerators and freezers, washing
machines, hosiery, refined sugar,
vegetable oil, shoes, textiles
Agriculture: vegetables, fruits,
wine, grain, sugar beets, sunflower seed, meat, milk, tobacco
Minerals and Resources: lignite,
phosphorites, gypsum

Moldova is the second-smallest of the former Soviet republics and is the most densely populated. It is landlocked, bounded by Ukraine on the east and Romania to the west. Its proximity to the Black Sea gives it a mild and sunny climate which provides it with good farmland.

Moldova declared its independence from the Soviet Union in 1991. In 1994 a new constitution and parliament were created and both have helped greatly in Moldova's transition to democracy and a privatized free-market economy. It is in fact considered to be a model of reform for the region.

Street sweeper, T'bilisi, Georgia

Capital: Kiev
Area: 233,028 sq. mi.
603,700 sq. km.
Population: 48,396,000 (2002 est.)
Largest City: Kiev, 2,590,000
Languages: Ukrainian, Russian, Romanian, Polish,
Hungarian
Major Religions: Ukrainian Orthodox, Ukrainian
Catholic, Protestant, Jewish
Life Expectancy: 66 male, 75 female

Government: republic
Monetary Unit: karbovanets (hryvnya in 1995)
Industry: coal, electric power, ferrous and nonferrous metals, machinery and transport equipment,
chemicals, food-processing
Agriculture: grain, vegetables, meat, milk, sugar
beets
Minerals and Resources: iron ore, coal, manganese, natural gas, oil, salt, sulphur, graphite, titanium, magnesium, kaolin, nickel, mercury, timber

Ukraine

Ukraine became independent from the Soviet Union in December, 1991 and soon after became a member of the Commonwealth of Independent States. Ukraine is larger than any other European state outside the former Soviet Union. Its terrain is mostly fertile plains.

Ethnically, Ukraine is 73% Ukrainian, 22% Russian and 5% other. The languages spoken in Ukraine are numerous: Ukrainian, Russian, Romanian, Polish and Hungarian.

After Russia, the Ukrainian republic was far and away the most important economic component of the former Soviet Union. Agriculture accounts for about 25% of its GDP and it has diversified heavy industries. Since President Kumcha's election in 1994 he has developed a comprehensive economic reform program which will be beneficial but difficult to implement.

Georgia

Capital: T'bilisi
Area: 26,904 sq. mi.
69,700 sq. km.
Population: 4,961,000 (2002 est.)
Largest City: T'bilisi, 1,399,000
Languages: Georgian, Armenian, Azeri, Russian
Major Religions: Georgian Orthodox, Russian Orthodox, Muslim
Life Expectancy: 69 male, 77 female
Government: republic
Monetary Unit: lari
Industry: steel, airplanes, locomotives, machinery, electric motors, cloth, hosiery, shoes, chemicals, wood-working industries
Agriculture: citrus fruits, grapes, vegetables, potatoes, livestock
Minerals and Resources: forest lands, hydropower, manganese deposits, iron ores, copper, minor coal and oil deposits

Since its independence from the Soviet Union in 1991, Georgia has been plagued by ethnic and civil strife. It has a largely mountainous terrain and a warm and pleasant climate. Georgia's economy has traditionally revolved around Black Sea tourism, cultivation of citrus fruits, tea and grapes, and several small industries. Due to the various conflicts in the country, much of industry in the past couple of years has been functioning at only a small fraction of its capacity, heavy disruptions in agricultural cultivation have been reported and the tourism industry has been shut down. Georgia continues to struggle with recovery and is precariously dependent on US and EU humanitarian grain shipments.

Capital: Yerevan
Area: 11,503 sq. mi.
29,800 sq. km.
Population: 3,330,000 (2002 est.)
Largest City: Yerevan, 1,247,000
Languages: Armenian, Russian
Major Religion: Armenian Orthodox
Life Expectancy: 69 male, 76 female
Government: republic
Monetary Unit: dram
Industry: machine tools, forging-pressing machines, electric motors, tires, knitted wear, hosiery, shoes, silk fabric, washing machines
Agriculture: fruits, vegetables, livestock, vineyards
Minerals and Resources: small deposits of gold, copper, molybdenum, zinc, alumina

Armenia

Armenia became independent from the Soviet Union in September, 1991. It is a member of the Commonwealth of Independent States.

Under the old Soviet central planning system, Armenia had developed a modern industrial sector, supplying machine building equipment, textiles and other manufactured goods to sister republics in exchange for raw materials and energy resources.

Armenia's economic decline in recent years has been severe due to the ongoing conflict over the ethnic Armenian-dominated region of Nagorno-Karabakh in Azerbaijan. The Armenian minority there has seized about 20% of the country's land and has declared independence. A full recovery for Armenia can only come after this conflict and its resulting blockades have been settled.

Azerbaijan

Capital: Baku (Baki)
Area: 33,428 sq. mi.
86,600 sq. km.
Population: 7,798,000 (2002 est.)
Largest City: Baku, 1,792,000
Languages: Azeri, Russian, Armenian
Major Religions: Muslim, Russian Orthodox, Armenian Orthodox
Life Expectancy: 67 male, 75 female
Government: republic
Monetary Unit: manat
Industry: petroleum, natural gas, oilfield equipment, steel, iron ore, cement, chemicals, textiles
Agriculture: cotton, grain, rice, grapes, fruit, vegetables, tea, tobacco, cattle, pigs, sheep and goats
Minerals and Resources: petroleum, natural gas, iron ore, nonferrous metals, alumina

Azerbaijan became an independent republic from the Soviet Union in August, 1991. It consists mainly of lowlands with the Great Caucasus Mountains in the north.

Azerbaijan is less developed industrially than either of the other two Transcaucasian states, Armenia and Georgia. Most Azerbaijanis are Muslim, at least nominally. The standard of living is low and unemployment is high, making Azerbaijan's transition from a planned to a market economy slow and painful.

A violent and longstanding dispute with ethnic Armenians in the Nagorno-Karabakh region continues to plague Azerbaijan. The Karabakh Armenians have seized almost 20% of the country's territory and declared independence. There have been Russian-mediated ceasefire agreements, but no long-term settlement has been negotiated yet.

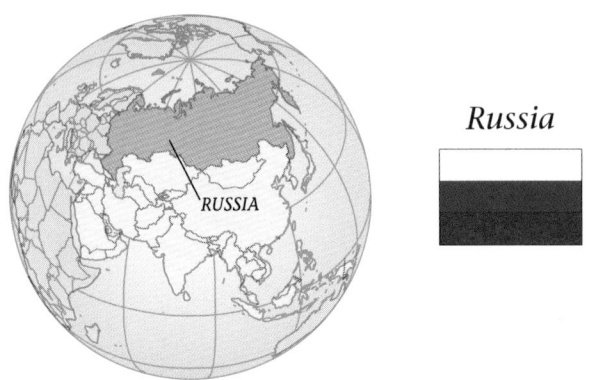

Russia

RUSSIA

Capital: Moscow
Area: 6,591,027 sq. mi.
  17,075,200 sq. km.
Population: 144,979,000 (2002 est.)
Largest City: Moscow, 8,297,000
Language: Russian
Major Religions: Russian Orthodox, Muslim
Life Expectancy: 64 male, 74 female
Government: federation
Monetary Unit: ruble
Industry: coal, oil, gas, chemicals, metals, machine building, rolling mills, aircraft, space vehicles, ship-building, road and rail transportation equipment, communications equipment, agricultural machinery, tractors construction equipment, electric power generating and transmitting equipment, medical and scientific instruments, consumer durables
Agriculture: grain, sugar beets, sunflower seeds, meat, milk, vegetables, fruits
Minerals and Resources: wide natural resource base including major deposits of oil, natural gas, coal, many strategic minerals, timber

Moscow Metro

Gold Towers of Kremlin Churches, Moscow

Russia is the largest country in the world by more than 2.5 million square miles. It has a predominantly urban society and one of the lowest population densities in the world.

After the December 1991 dissolution of the Soviet Union, the Russian Federation became its largest successor, inheriting its permanent seat on the UN Security Council as well as the bulk of its foreign assets and debt. While nominally Russia is a federation, the precise distribution of powers between the central government and the regional and local authorities is still evolving.

Making democracy a reality in Russia is hampered by the limited public trust of virtually all public institutions. Russia has a wealth of natural resources, a well-educated population and a diverse industrial base, all of which should facilitate its transition to a free market economy; however, Russia continues to face formidable difficulties in all aspects of its recovery.

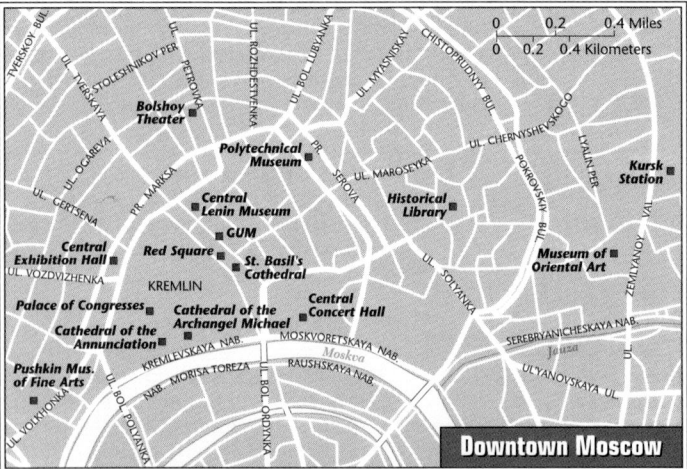

Downtown Moscow

St. Basil's Cathedral , Red Square, Moscow

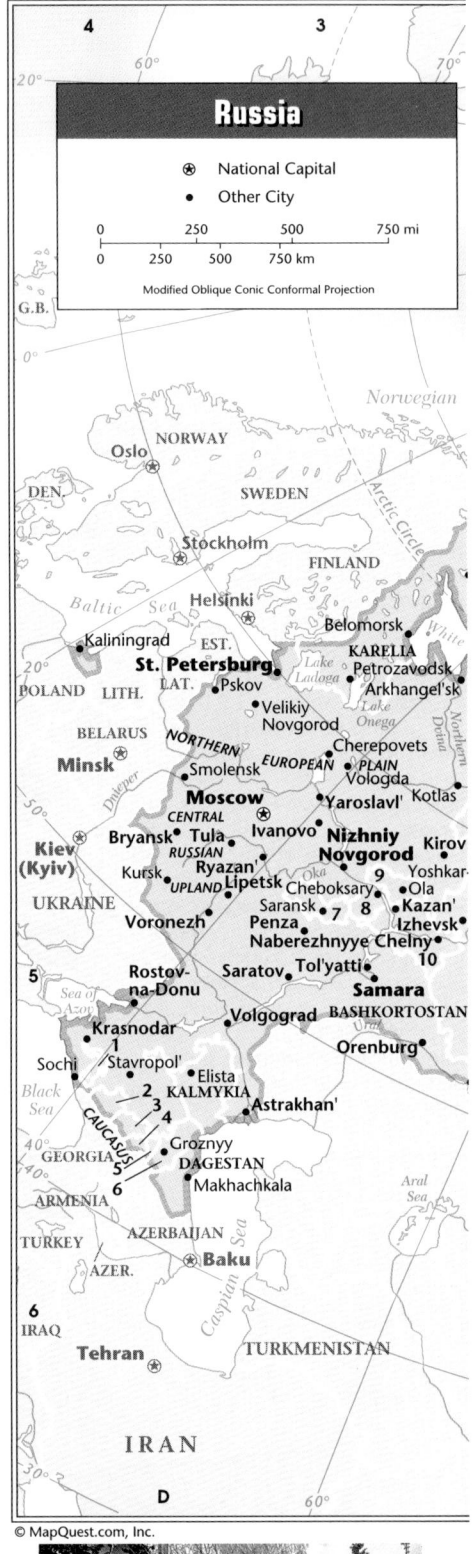

© MapQuest.com, Inc.

Tsar Cannon, the Kremlin, Moscow

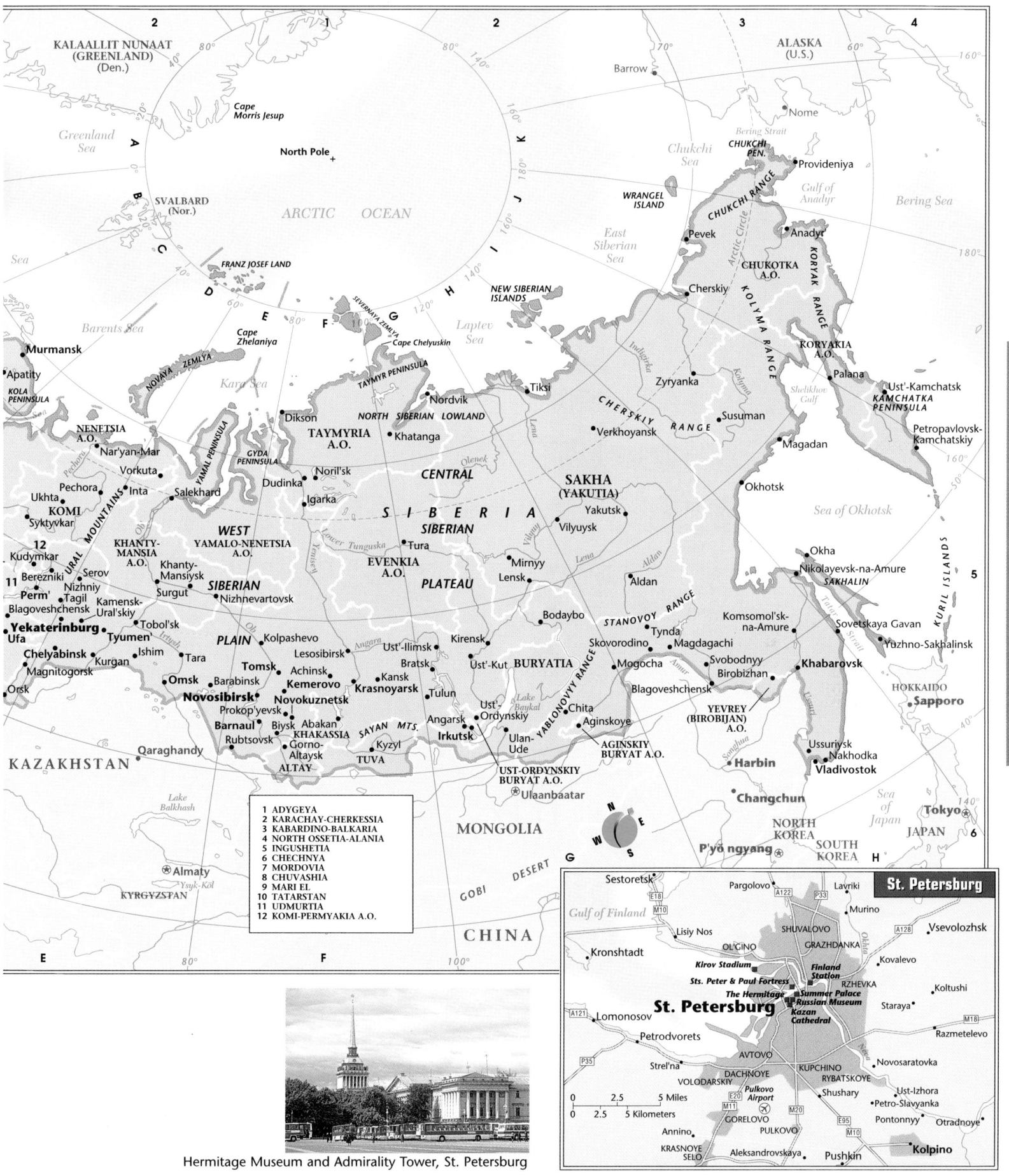

2

KALAALLIT NUNAAT
(GREENLAND)
(Den.)

1

2

3

ALASKA
(U.S.)

4

Cape
Morris Jesup

*Barrow

*Nome

*Greenland
Sea*

North Pole
+

Bering Strait

*Chukchi
Sea*

CHUKCHI
PEN.

ARCTIC OCEAN

SVALBARD
(Nor.)

Provideniya

WRANGEL
ISLAND

Pevek

Anadyr

CHUKOTKA
A.O.

FRANZ JOSEF LAND

Sea

Bering Sea

*East
Siberian
Sea*

Cherskiy

KORYAKIA
A.O.

Barents Sea

Murmansk

*Cape
Zhelaniya*

Kara Sea

Cape Chelyuskin

SEVERNAYA ZEMLYA

NEW SIBERIAN
ISLANDS

*Laptev
Sea*

CHERSKIY RANGE

Palana

Ust'-Kamchatsk

KAMCHATKA
PENINSULA

Apatity

KOLA
PENINSULA

NENETSIA
A.O.

Nar'yan-Mar

NOVAYA ZEMLYA

YAMAL PENINSULA

GYDA
PENINSULA

Dikson

TAYMYR PENINSULA

NORTH SIBERIAN LOWLAND

Nordvik

Tiksi

Zyryanka

Susuman

Magadan

Petropavlovsk-
Kamchatskiy

Vorkuta

Pechora

Inta

Salekhard

Dudinka

Khatanga

TAYMYRIA
A.O.

Verkhoyansk

Okhotsk

Sea of Okhotsk

Ukhta

KOMI

Syktyvkar

URAL MOUNTAINS

Noril'sk

Igarka

CENTRAL

SIBERIA

SAKHA
(YAKUTIA)

Yakutsk

12

Kudymkar

KHANTY-
MANSIA
A.O.

WEST
YAMALO-NENETSIA
A.O.

*Khanty-
Mansiysk*

SIBERIAN

Tura

EVENKIA
A.O.

Vilyuysk

Mirnyy

Lensk

Okha

Nikolayevsk-na-Amure

SAKHALIN

11

Berezniki

Serov

*Nizhniy
Tagil*

Surgut

Nizhnevartovsk

PLATEAU

Aldan

STANOVOY RANGE

Komsomol'sk-
na-Amure

Sovetskaya Gavan

Perm'

Blagoveshchensk

*Kamensk-
Ural'skiy*

PLAIN

Kolpashevo

Bodaybo

Skovorodino

Tynda

Magdagachi

Svobodnyy

Yuzhno-Sakhalinsk

Yekaterinburg

Ufa

Tyumen'

Tobol'sk

Kirensk

Mogocha

Birobizhan

Khabarovsk

Chelyabinsk

Kurgan

Ishim

Tara

Lesosibirsk

Ust'-Ilimsk

Ust'-Kut

BURYATIA

Blagoveshchensk

HOKKAIDO

Magnitogorsk

Tomsk

Achinsk

Bratsk

Chita

Sapporo

Orsk

Omsk

Barabinsk

Kemerovo

Kansk

Krasnoyarsk

Tulun

Angarsk

*Ust'-
Ordynskiy*

Aginskoye

YEVREY
(BIROBIJAN)
A.O.

Novosibirsk

Novokuznetsk

*Lake
Baykal*

Ussuriysk

Nakhodka

Prokop'yevsk

Abakan

Barnaul

Biysk

KHAKASSIA

SAYAN MTS.

*Ulan-
Ude*

Irkutsk

Kyzyl

YABLONOVYY RANGE

AGINSKIY
BURYAT A.O.

Harbin

Vladivostok

Rubtsovsk

*Gorno-
Altaysk*

TUVA

UST-ORDYNSKIY
BURYAT A.O.

Changchun

Tokyo

KAZAKHSTAN

Qaraghandy

ALTAY

Ulaanbaatar

MONGOLIA

NORTH
KOREA

SOUTH
KOREA

*Sea
of
Japan*

JAPAN

*Lake
Balkhash*

1 ADYGEYA
2 KARACHAY-CHERKESSIA
3 KABARDINO-BALKARIA
4 NORTH OSSETIA-ALANIA
5 INGUSHETIA
6 CHECHNYA
7 MORDOVIA
8 CHUVASHIA
9 MARI EL
10 TATARSTAN
11 UDMURTIA
12 KOMI-PERMYAKIA A.O.

N
E
W
S

P'yŏngyang

Almaty

Ysyk-Köl

KYRGYZSTAN

GOBI DESERT

CHINA

Hermitage Museum and Admirality Tower, St. Petersburg

St. Petersburg

Sestoretsk

Pargolovo

Lavriki

Gulf of Finland

Murino

Vsevolozhsk

Lisiy Nos

SHUVALOVO

GRAZHDANKA

Kovalevo

Kronshtadt

OL'GINO

Koltushi

Kirov Stadium

*Finland
Station*

RZHEVKA

Staraya

Sts. Peter & Paul Fortress

Summer Palace

The Hermitage

Russian Museum

St. Petersburg

Kazan
Cathedral

Razmetelevo

Lomonosov

Petrodvorets

AVTOVO

KUPCHINO

Novosaratovka

Strel'na

DACHNOYE

VOLODARSKIY

RYBATSKOYE

Shushary

Ust-Izhora

0   2.5   5 Miles

*Pulkovo
Airport*

Petro-Slavyanka

0   2.5   5 Kilometers

GORELOVO

PULKOVO

Pontonnyy

Otradnoye

Annino

KRASNOYE
SELO

Aleksandrovskaya

Pushkin

Kolpino

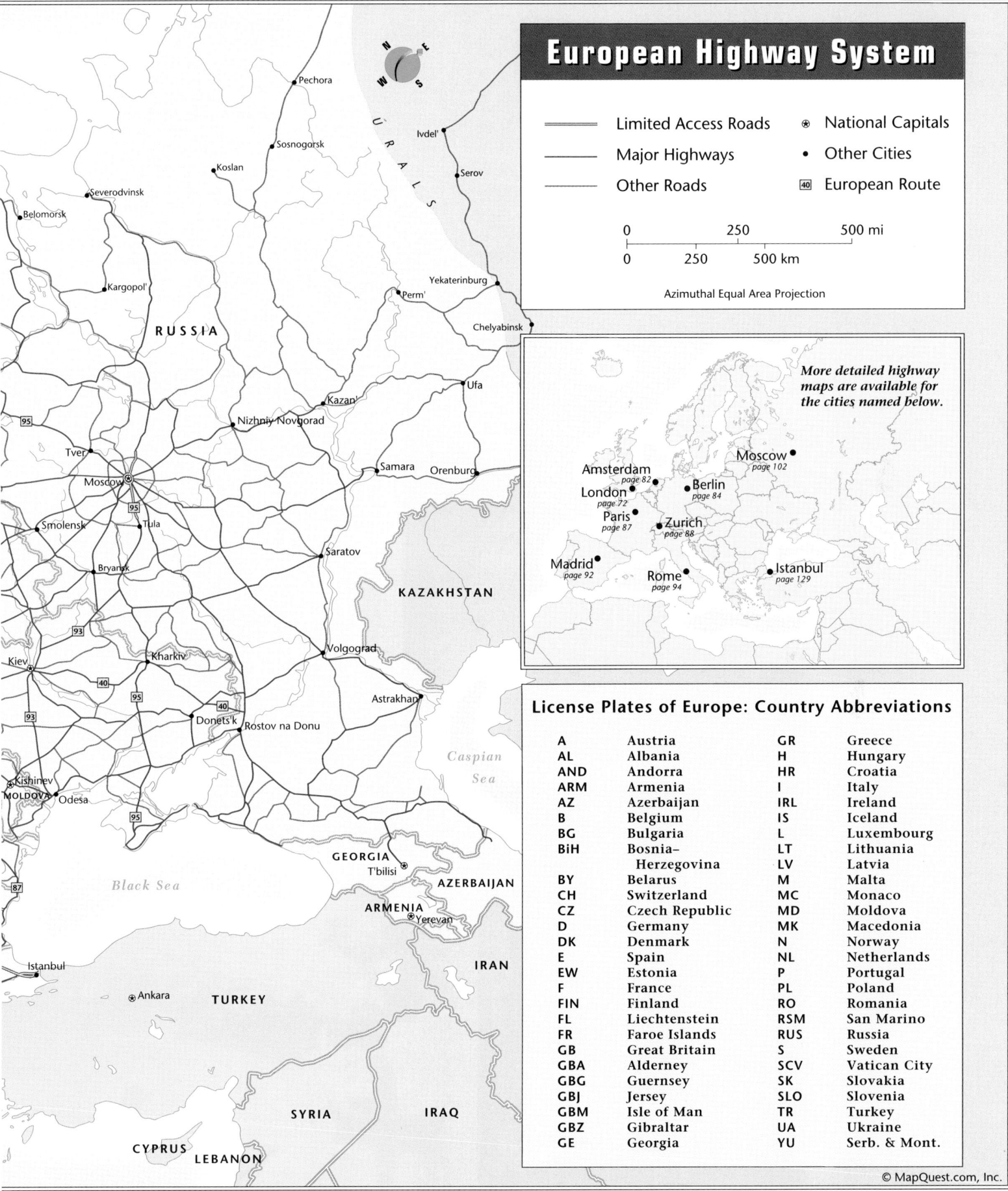

European Highway System

———	Limited Access Roads	⊛	National Capitals
———	Major Highways	•	Other Cities
----	Other Roads	⊡40	European Route

```
0          250          500 mi
0     250     500 km
```

Azimuthal Equal Area Projection

More detailed highway maps are available for the cities named below.

Amsterdam *page 82*
London *page 72*
Paris *page 87*
Berlin *page 84*
Zurich *page 88*
Moscow *page 102*
Madrid *page 92*
Rome *page 94*
Istanbul *page 129*

License Plates of Europe: Country Abbreviations

A	Austria	GR	Greece
AL	Albania	H	Hungary
AND	Andorra	HR	Croatia
ARM	Armenia	I	Italy
AZ	Azerbaijan	IRL	Ireland
B	Belgium	IS	Iceland
BG	Bulgaria	L	Luxembourg
BiH	Bosnia–	LT	Lithuania
	Herzegovina	LV	Latvia
BY	Belarus	M	Malta
CH	Switzerland	MC	Monaco
CZ	Czech Republic	MD	Moldova
D	Germany	MK	Macedonia
DK	Denmark	N	Norway
E	Spain	NL	Netherlands
EW	Estonia	P	Portugal
F	France	PL	Poland
FIN	Finland	RO	Romania
FL	Liechtenstein	RSM	San Marino
FR	Faroe Islands	RUS	Russia
GB	Great Britain	S	Sweden
GBA	Alderney	SCV	Vatican City
GBG	Guernsey	SK	Slovakia
GBJ	Jersey	SLO	Slovenia
GBM	Isle of Man	TR	Turkey
GBZ	Gibraltar	UA	Ukraine
GE	Georgia	YU	Serb. & Mont.

© MapQuest.com, Inc.

Population: 3,754,204,000 (2002)
Area: 17,139,000 sq. mi.
44,390,000 sq. km.
Highest Point: Mt. Everest
29,035 ft. (8,849 m.)
Lowest Point: Dead Sea
1302 ft. (397 m.)
below sea level
Largest Urban Areas:
Tokyo, Japan
Mumbai, India
Dhaka, Bangladesh
Kolkata (Calcutta), India
Karachi, Pakistan
Delhi, India
Jakarta, Indonesia
Countries: 46

Above Left: Buddhist Pagoda, Lijiang, Yunnan, China; **Above:** Millet fields in the Himalayas of Nepal; **Below Left:** The city and harbor of Hong Kong; **Below:** Fishermen near the village of Cheung Chau in Hong Kong.

Major Metropolitan Areas

Afghanistan
Kabul 2,029,000

Bahrain
Manama 151,000

Bangladesh
Dhaka 6,487,000

Bhutan
Thimphu 8,900

Brunei
Bandar Seri
Begawan 50,000

Cambodia
Phnom Penh 1,000,000

China
Shanghai 12,910,000
Beijing 10,820,000
Tianjin 8,970,000
Hong Kong 6,708,000
Shenyang 4,740,000
Wuhan 4,450,000
Chongqing 4,070,000
Guangzhou 3,910,000
Chengdu 3,120,000
Xi'an 2,990,000
Harbin 2,960,000
Nanjing 2,670,000

Cyprus
Nicosia 273,000

East Timor
Dili 140,000

India
Mumbai
(Bombay) 16,368,000
Kolkata
(Calcutta) 13,217,000
Delhi 12,791,000
Chennai
(Madras) 6,425,000
Bangalore 5,687,000
Hyderabad 5,534,000

Indonesia
Jakarta 9,374,000
Bandung 5,919,000
Bogor 5,000,000
Malang 3,174,000

Iran
Tehran 6,759,000
Mashhad 1,887,000

Iraq
Baghdad 4,336,000

Israel
Tel Aviv-Jaffa 2,595,000
Jerusalem 628,000

Japan
Tokyo 12,059,000
Yokohama 3,427,000
Osaka 2,599,000
Nagoya 2,171,000
Sapporo 1,822,000
Kobe 1,494,000
Kyoto 1,468,000
Fukuoka 1,341,000
Kawasaki 1,250,000
Hiroshima 1,126,000

Jordan
Amman 1,147,000

Kazakhstan
Almaty 1,129,000

North Korea
P'yŏngyang 2,741,000

South Korea (core city only)
Seoul 9,854,000
Busan 3,655,000
Daegu 2,474,000

Kuwait
Kuwait 193,000

Kyrgyzstan
Bishkek 753,000

Laos
Vientiane 331,000

Lebanon
Beirut 1,500,000

Malaysia
Kuala Lumpur 1,379,000

Maldives
Male 74,000

Mongolia
Ulaanbaatar 760,000

Myanmar (Burma)
Yangon
(Rangoon) 4,101,000

Nepal
Kathmandu 421,000

Oman
Muscat 477,000

Pakistan
Karachi 9,339,000
Lahore 5,143,000
Faisalabad 2,009,000
Islamabad 529,000

Philippines
Manila 9,933,000

Qatar
Doha 264,000

Russia (Asian)
Novosibirsk 1,400,000
Yekaterinburg 1,314,000
Omsk 1,177,000
Chelyabinsk 1,111,000

Saudi Arabia
Riyadh 2,776,000
Jeddah 2,046,000

Singapore
Singapore 4,131,000

Sri Lanka
Colombo 642,000

Syria
Halab (Aleppo) 1,813,000
Damascus 1,394,000

Taiwan
Taipei 2,720,000

Tajikistan
Dushanbe 529,000

Thailand
Bangkok 6,320,000

Turkey (Asian)
Ankara 3,203,000
Izmir 2,232,000

Turkmenistan
Ashgabat 407,000

United Arab Emirates
Abu Dhabi 904,000

Uzbekistan
Tashkent 2,142,000

Vietnam
Ho Chi Minh
City 4,990,000
Hanoi 2,464,000

Yemen
Sanaa 927,000

International comparability of population data is limited by varying census methods. Where metropolitan population is unavailable, core city population is shown.

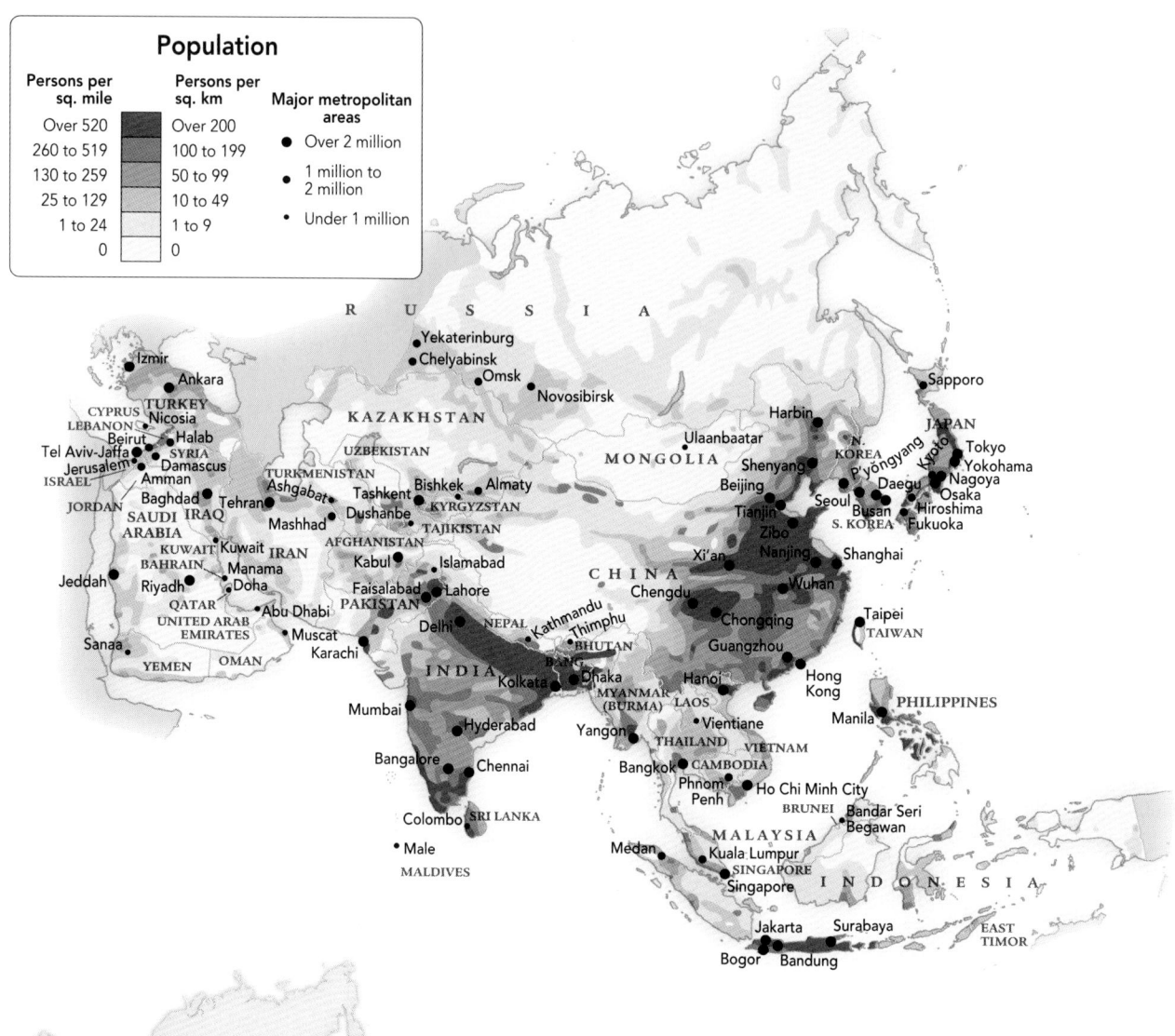

Population

Persons per sq. mile
Over 520
260 to 519
130 to 259
25 to 129
1 to 24
0

Persons per sq. km
Over 200
100 to 199
50 to 99
10 to 49
1 to 9
0

Major metropolitan areas
● Over 2 million
• 1 million to 2 million
· Under 1 million

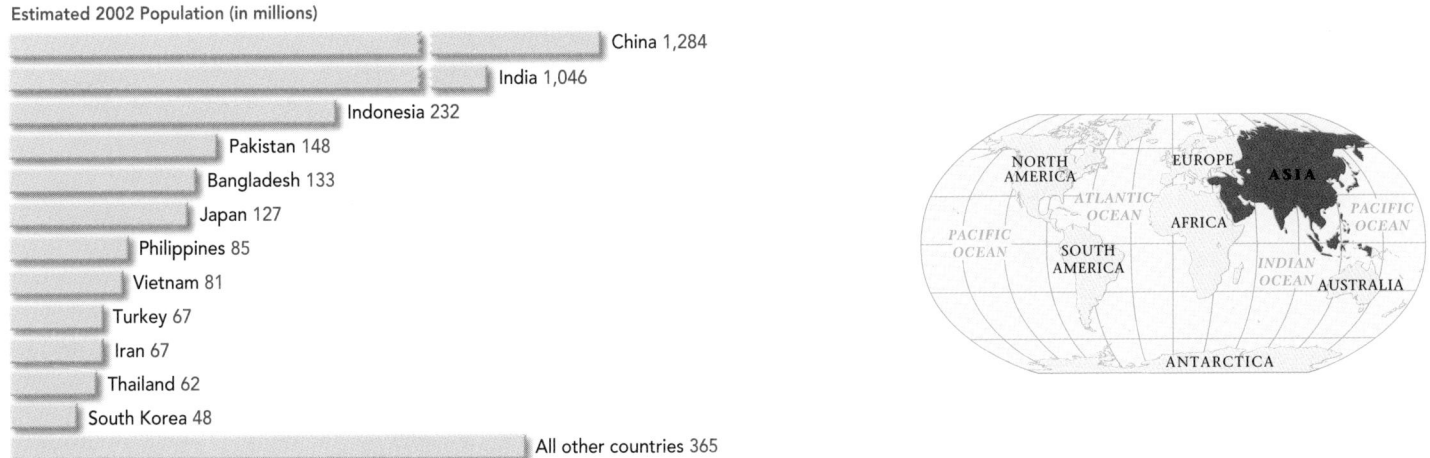

Asia

Legend:
- ⊛ National Capital
- ★ Territorial Capital
- • Other City

0 600 1200 mi
0 600 1200 km

Two-Point Equidistant Projection

© MapQuest.com, Inc.

Estimated 2002 Population (in millions)

- China 1,284
- India 1,046
- Indonesia 232
- Pakistan 148
- Bangladesh 133
- Japan 127
- Philippines 85
- Vietnam 81
- Turkey 67
- Iran 67
- Thailand 62
- South Korea 48
- All other countries 365

Source: U.S. Census Bueau

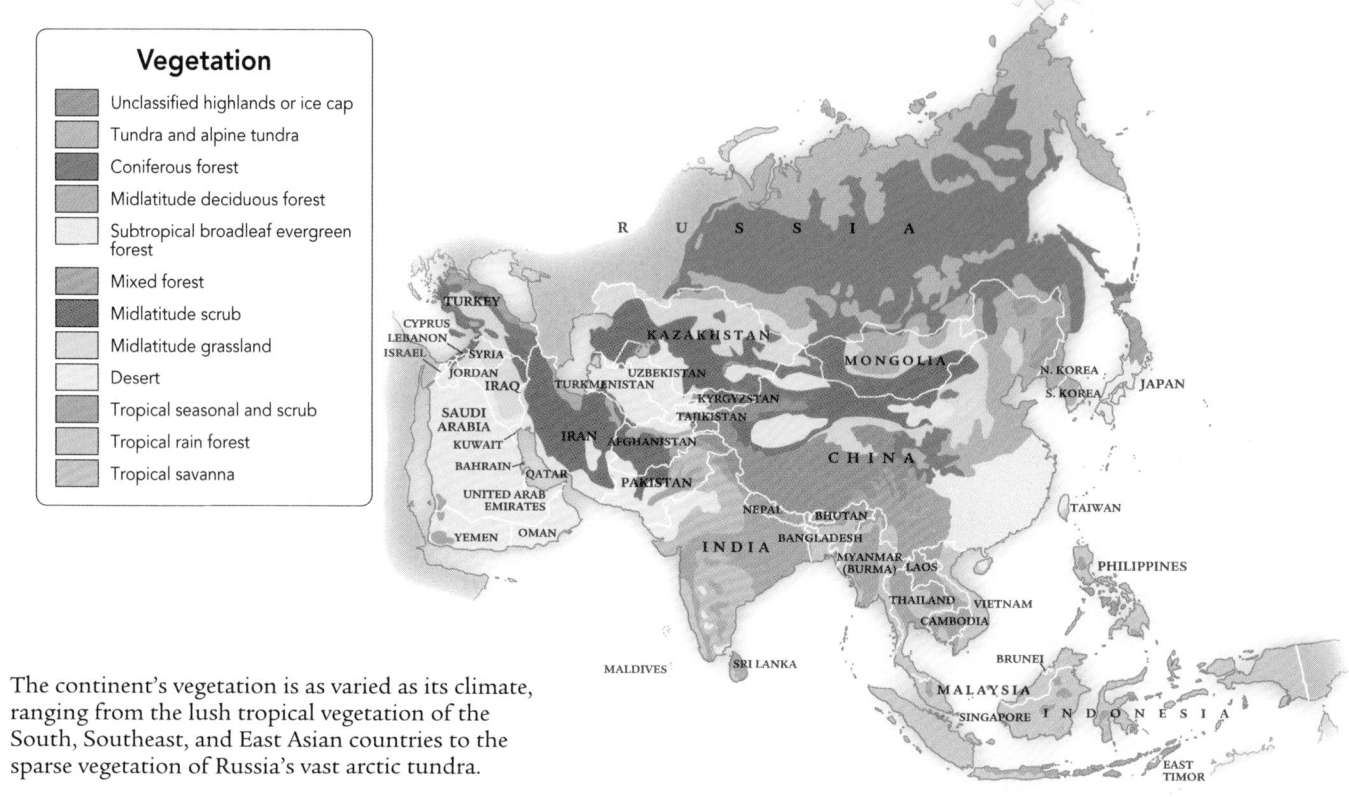

Vegetation

- Unclassified highlands or ice cap
- Tundra and alpine tundra
- Coniferous forest
- Midlatitude deciduous forest
- Subtropical broadleaf evergreen forest
- Mixed forest
- Midlatitude scrub
- Midlatitude grassland
- Desert
- Tropical seasonal and scrub
- Tropical rain forest
- Tropical savanna

The continent's vegetation is as varied as its climate, ranging from the lush tropical vegetation of the South, Southeast, and East Asian countries to the sparse vegetation of Russia's vast arctic tundra.

Agriculture is the predominant land use in Asia. Wet grains, such as rice, are the principal crops of China and Southeast Asian countries. Dry grains, such as wheat, are grown in limited areas of Russia and China. A lack of modern farming methods, except in Japan, Russia, and Israel has historically limited food production. However, production is increasing in some countries as governments supply the needed techonolgy. The rugged land and climate in Northern, Central and Southwest Asia limits land use to nomadic herding. Here, animals supply food, shelter, clothing, and transportation.

Most Asian countries have an insignificant number of manufacturing jobs relative to other occupations. Japan, South Korea, Taiwan, China, and Singapore are exceptions.

Natural resources are Asia's most important export. The oil fields of Southwest Asia supply much of the World's energy needs. Southeast Asia supplies the World with its tin, and coal is plentiful in areas of Russia, China and India. The lack of processing facilities limits many Asian countries in the use of their resources.

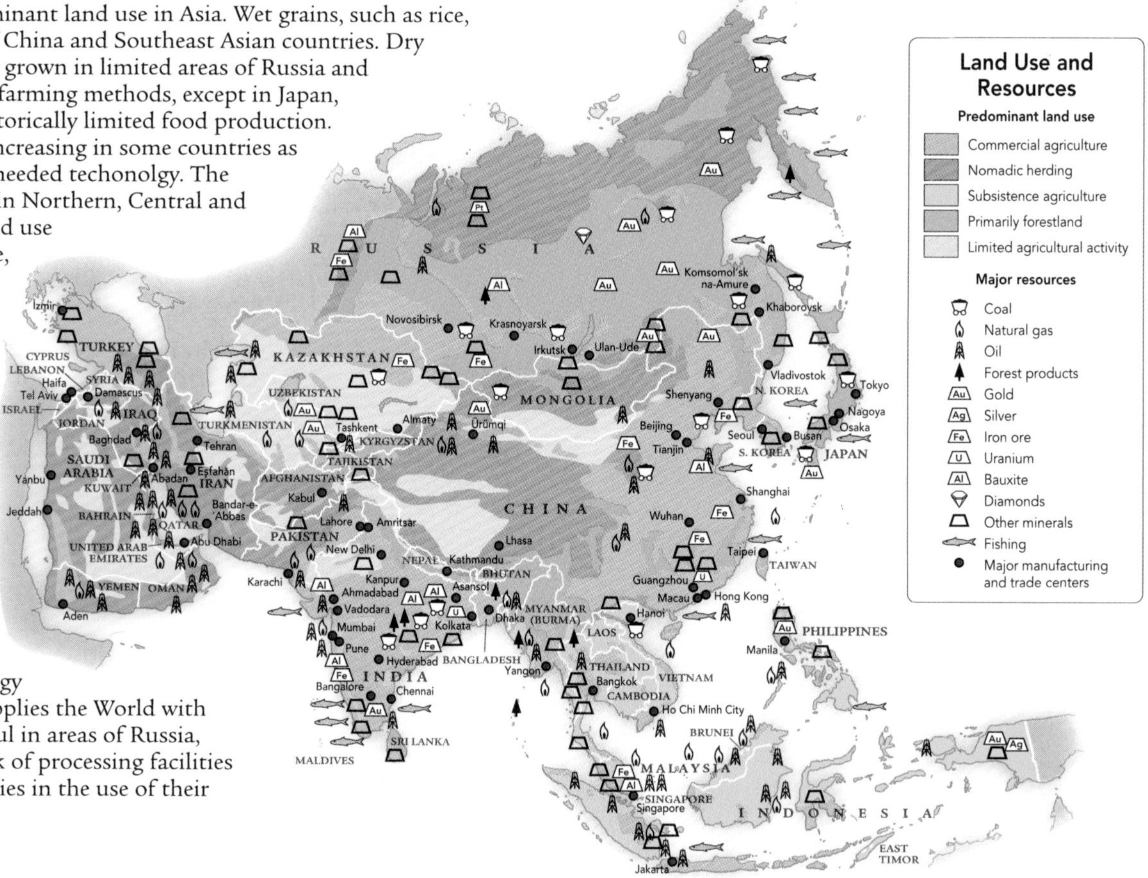

Land Use and Resources

Predominant land use

- Commercial agriculture
- Nomadic herding
- Subsistence agriculture
- Primarily forestland
- Limited agricultural activity

Major resources

- Coal
- Natural gas
- Oil
- Forest products
- Au Gold
- Ag Silver
- Fe Iron ore
- U Uranium
- Al Bauxite
- Diamonds
- Other minerals
- Fishing
- Major manufacturing and trade centers

Climate Graphs

Average daily temperature range (in °F)
High
Low
100°
65°
32°
0°

Average monthly precipitation (in inches)
20°
10°
0°

ALMATY, Kazakhstan

BEIRUT, Lebanon

COLOMBO, Sri Lanka

DHAKA, Bangladesh

HONG KONG, China

JAKARTA, Indonesia

NEW DELHI, India

RIYADH, Saudi Arabia

TEHRAN, Iran

TIANJIN, China

TOKYO, Japan

YAKUTSK, Russia
Temp. Range -53 to -45

Asia has many climates. This can be expected on a landmass that covers an area from below the Equator to the Arctic Ocean and from the Mediterranean Sea to the Pacific Ocean. Weather conditions fluctuate from the sub-freezing temperatures and snow of the tundra climate in northern Russia, through the more temperate humid continental climate, past the arid conditions of Southwest and Central Asia, and finally to the warm and wet zones of South and Southeast Asia.

Verkhoyansk
Lowest recorded temperature, -90°F (-68°C), 1892

Tirat Tsvi
Highest recorded temperature, 129°F (54°C)

Climate

- Tropical wet
- Tropical wet and dry
- Arid
- Semiarid
- Mediterranean
- Humid subtropical
- Humid continental
- Subarctic
- Tundra
- Highland

Environmental Issues

- Current forest
- Cleared forest
- Area at highest risk of desertification
- Areas most affected by acid rain
- ● Poor air quality*

*Cities exceeding at least one of the World Health Organization's (WHO) annual mean guidelines for air quality

Sources: Global Distribution of Original and Remaining Forests, UNEP-WCMC, 2002
World Soil Resources Map Index, USDA/NRCS, 2002
World Development Indicators, World Bank, 1999

Asia's high population densities have led to a multitude of environmental problems, including pollution, deforestation, overfishing, and water shortages. With rapid population growth, pressures on land and water resources will only continue to increase. In western Asia, desertification and groundwater issues are the most pressing concerns. Most land in the region is either currently desert or is vulnerable to becoming desert in the future, and water is being withdrawn more quickly than it can be replaced.

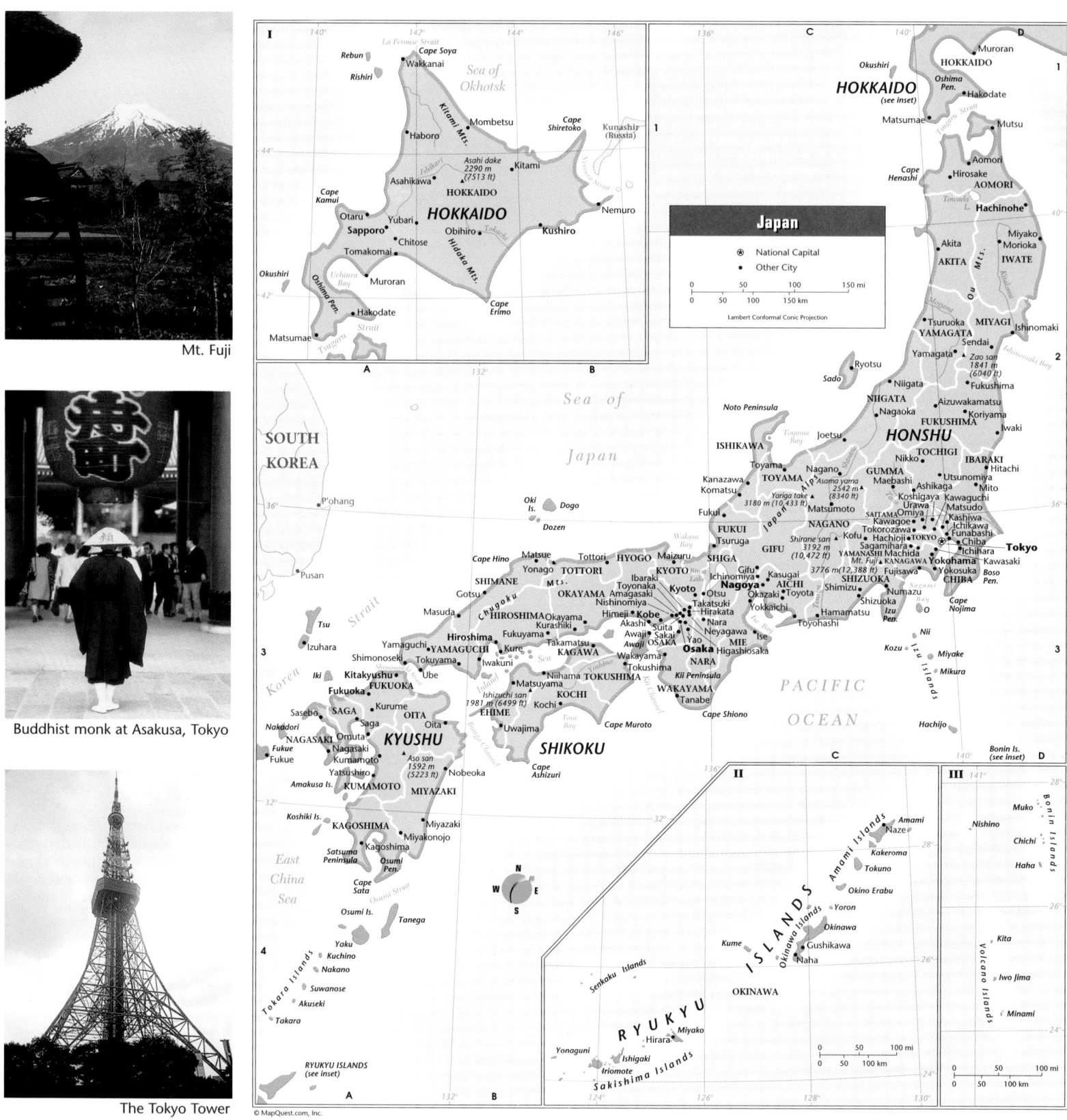

Mt. Fuji

Buddhist monk at Asakusa, Tokyo

The Tokyo Tower

© MapQuest.com, Inc.

Japan is one of the most densely populated nations in the world. It is mostly mountainous, with more than half of its area forested. Japan's economy ranks as the second most powerful in the world, thanks to good government-industry cooperation, a strong work ethic, mastery of high technology and a comparatively small defense allocation. Unemployment and inflation are quite low compared with other industrialized nations.

The government in Japan is a constitutional monarchy with a parliament. The cultural prestige of the imperial institution remains great for the Japanese and the emperor is defined as the symbol of the state. Buddhism, Shintoism and Confucianism all have strong influences in Japanese life.

Capital: Tokyo
Area: 145,844 sq. mi.
  377,835 sq. km.
Population: 127,066,000
(2002 est.)
Largest City: Tokyo,
8,130,000
Language: Japanese
Major Religions: Shinto, Buddhism
Life Expectancy: 77 male, 82
female
Government: constitutional
monarchy
Monetary Unit: yen
Industry: steel and non-ferrous
metallurgy, heavy electrical equip-

Japan

ment, construction and mining equipment, motor vehicles and parts, electronic and
telecommunication equip-
ment and components,
machine tools and automated
production systems, locomotives and railroad rolling
stock, shipbuilding, chemicals, textiles, food processing
Agriculture: rice, sugar beets, vegetables, fruit, pork, poultry, dairy,
eggs, fishing
Minerals and Resources: negligible
mineral resources, fish

The Torii-heian Jingu Shrine, Kyoto

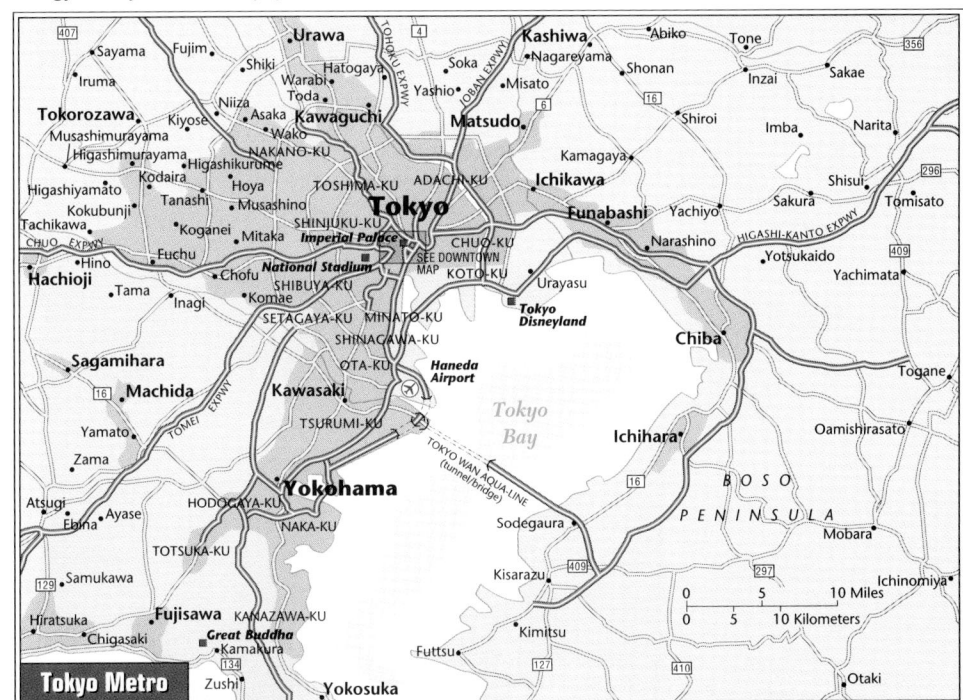
Tokyo Metro

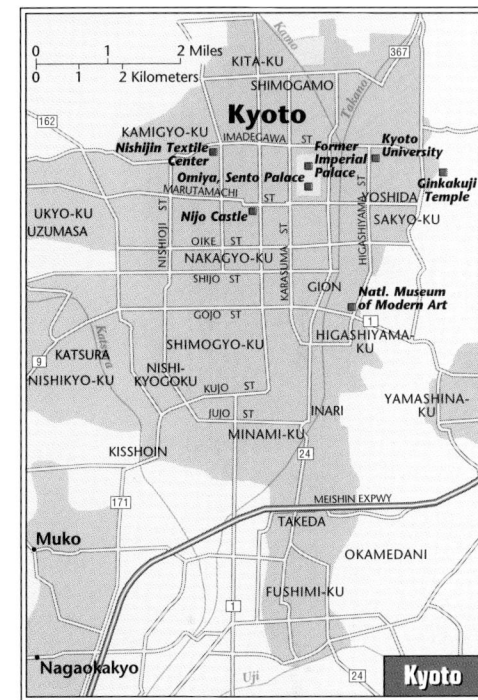
Kyoto

Tokyo's Commercial Center

Banrukun Rock Gardens

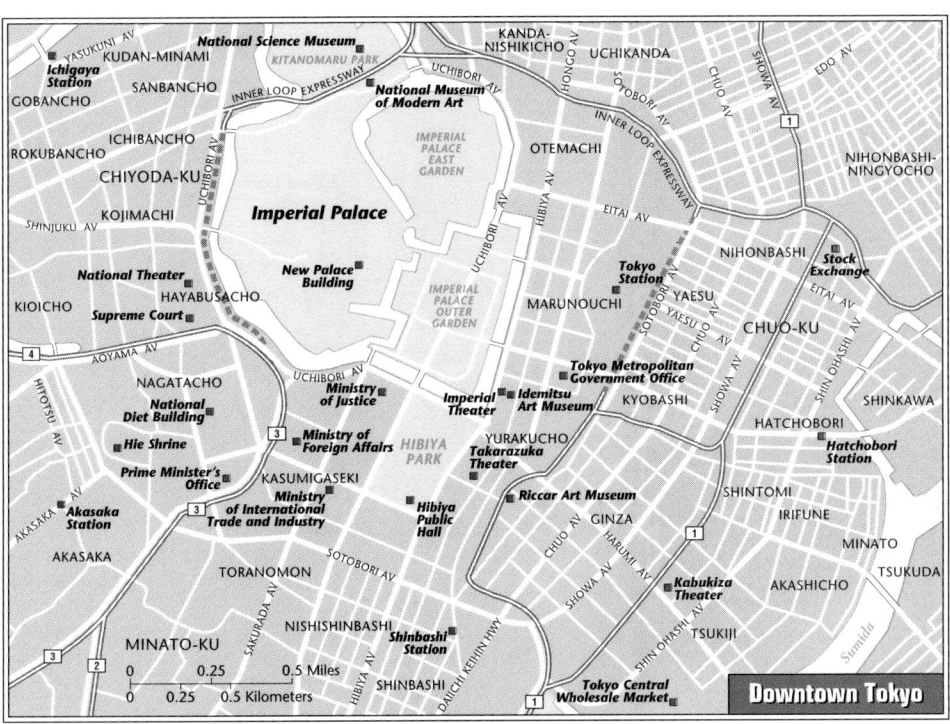
Downtown Tokyo

Capital: P'yongyang
Area: 46,528 sq. mi.
   120,540 sq. km
Population: 22,215,000 (2002 est.)
Largest City: P'yongyang, 2,741,000
Language: Korean
Major Religions: Buddhism, Confucianism, Christianity, Chondogyo
Life Expectancy: 67 male, 73 female
Government: Communist state;

North Korea

Stalinist dictatorship
Monetary Unit: North Korean won
Industry: machine building, military products, electric power, chemicals, mining, metallurgy, textiles, food processing
Agriculture: rice, corn, potatoes, soybeans, cattle, hogs, pork, eggs
Minerals and Resources: coal, lead, tungsten, zinc, graphite, magnesite, iron ore, copper, gold, pyrites, salt, fluorspar, hydropower

The Democratic People's Republic of Korea was formed in 1948 when the Soviet Union, which had a joint trusteeship over Korea with the US, did not honor the agreement to allow free elections to take place in order to establish a new Korean government. It instead created the DPRK which has become increasingly well-armed and belligerent. It now in fact has the fifth largest army in the world.

More than 90% of the DPRK's economy is socialized and state-owned industries produce 95% of manufactured goods. Abundant mineral resources and and hydropower have formed the basis of industrial development since WWII. North Korea remains far behind South Korea in economic development and living standards.

View of Downtown Seoul

Capital: Seoul
Area: 38,013 sq. mi.
   98,480 sq. km.
Population: 47,963,000 (2002 est.)
Largest City: Seoul, 9,854,000
Languages: Korean, English
Major Religions: Christianity, Buddhism, Confucianism, Shamanism, Chondogyo
Life Expectancy: 68 male, 74 female

South Korea

Government: republic
Monetary Unit: South Korean won
Industry: electronics, automobile production, chemicals, shipbuilding, steel, textiles, clothing, footwear, food processing
Agriculture: fishing, forestry, rice, root crops, barley, vegetables, fruit, cattle, hogs, chickens, milk, eggs
Minerals and Resources: coal, tungsten, graphite, molybdenum, lead, hydropower

South Korea has been an independent republic since 1948 when the Soviet Union ignored the provisions of its joint trusteeship with the US providing for UN-supervised elections throughout Korea. The 1945 Yalta Conference established that the Japanese, who had annexed Korea, would surrender to Soviet forces in the north of Korea and to US forces in the south.

Elections were held in the south and the Republic of Korea was established. The US withdrew its occupation forces in 1949 and one year later North Korea invaded, leading to the three year Korean War. The two Koreas have struggled with each other ever since and there is hope for reunification, but there is much progress to be made before that can be achieved.

The South Korean economy has grown dynamically due to the planned development of an export-oriented economy in a vigorously entrepreneurial society.

Taiwan comprises a group of islands off the southeastern coast of China. It has a multiparty democratic regime, although until 1986, it was a one-party system.

Over the past three decades, Taiwan has changed from an agricultural to an industrialized economy. It now has a dynamic capitalist economy with considerable government guidance of investment and foreign trade and partial government ownership of some large banks and industrial firms.

Taiwan's culture is a blend of its Chinese heritage and Western influences. A mixture of Buddhism, Taoism and Confucianism dominates religious identification.

Taiwan

Capital: Taipei
Area: 13,888 sq. mi.
    35,980 sq. km.
Population: 22,454,000 (2002 est.)
Largest City: Taipei, 2,720,000
Languages: Mandarin Chinese, Taiwanese, Hakka dialects
Major Religions: Buddhism, Confucian, Taoism, Christianity
Life Expectancy: 72 male, 79 female
Government: multiparty democratic regime
Monetary Unit: New Taiwan dollar
Industry: electronics, textiles, chemicals, clothing, food processing, plywood, sugar milling, cement, shipbuilding, petroleum refining
Agriculture: vegetables, rice, fruit, tea, hogs, poultry, beef, milk, fishing
Minerals and Resources: coal, natural gas, limestone, marble, asbestos

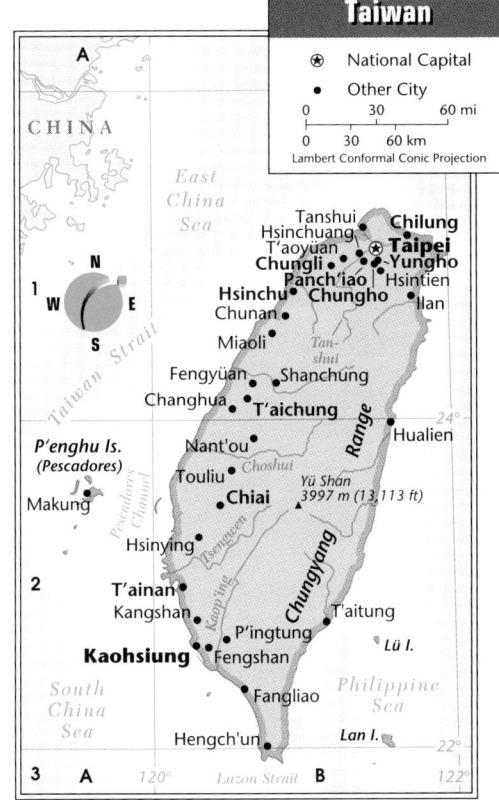

Lungshan Temple, Taiwan

Area: 401 sq. mi.
    1,040 sq. km.
Population: 7,303,000 (2002 est.)
Largest City: New Kowloon, 1,500,000
Languages: Chinese (Cantonese), English
Religions: eclectic mixture of local religions, Christianity
Life Expectancy: 77 male, 84 female
Government: special administrative region (S.A.R.) of China
Monetary Unit: Hong Kong dollar
Industry: textiles, clothing, tourism, electronics, plastics, toys, watches, clocks
Agriculture: vegetables, poultry
Minerals and Resources: outstanding deepwater harbor, feldspar

On July 1, 1997, Hong Kong was peacefully returned to Chinese control, in accordance with an agreement signed by the United Kingdom and China in December, 1984. Before 1997, Hong Kong was a dependent territory of the UK, ruled by a Governor appointed by the Queen.

Hong Kong is now a special administrative region of China, retaining its political, economic and judicial systems and participating in international agreements and organizations for at least 50 years after the reversion.

Hong Kong has a bustling free market economy. Its natural resources are limited and it imports food and raw materials, but, thanks to an ideal harbor, it has developed a very successful foreign trade economy.

Traditional junk in Hong Kong Harbor

Hong Kong

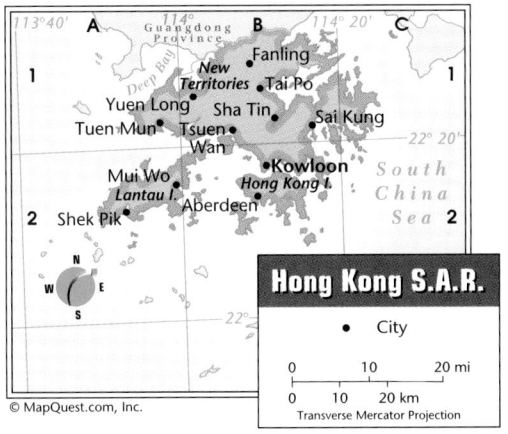

© MapQuest.com, Inc.

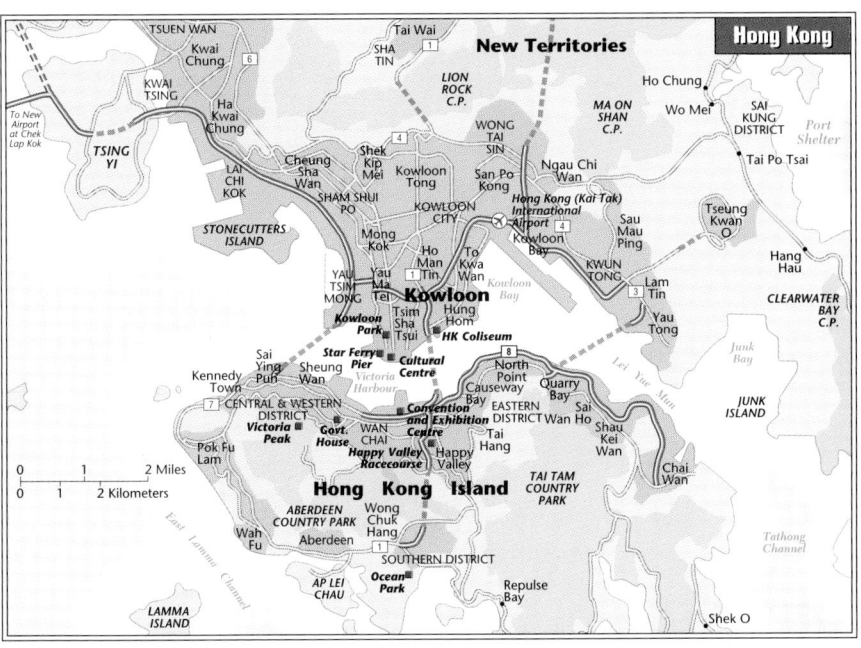

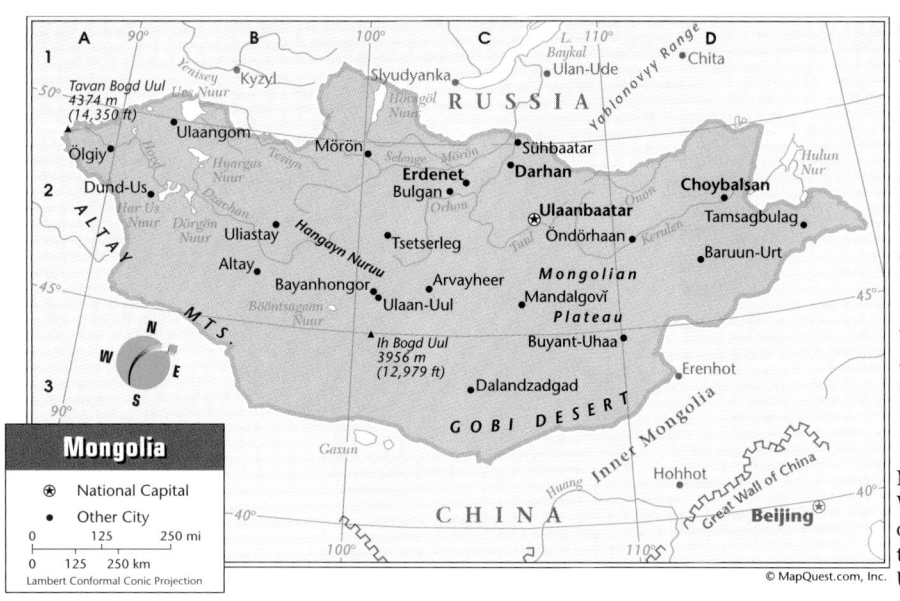

Capital: Ulaanbaatar
Area: 604,090 sq. mi.
1,565,000 sq. km.
Population: 2,674,000 (2002 est.)
Largest City: Ulaanbaatar, 760,000
Languages: Khalkha Mongol, Turkic, Russian, Chinese
Major Religions: Tibetan Buddhist, Muslim
Life Expectancy: 64 male, 69 female
Government: republic
Monetary Unit: tughrik
Industry: copper, processing of animal products, building materials, food and beverages, coal
Agriculture: livestock raising (primarily sheep, goats, cattle, camels, horses), wheat, barley, potatoes, forage
Minerals and Resources: oil, coal, copper, molybdenum, tungsten, phosphates, tin, nickel, zinc, wolfram, fluorspar, gold

Mongolia

Mongolia gained its independence from China in 1921. After WWII and until 1990, the Mongolian government was modeled on the Soviet system and only the Communist Party was allowed to function. However, the birth of perestroika in the former Soviet Union and the democracy movement in Eastern Europe were mirrored in Mongolia and brought swift and peaceful changes.

Nomadic life still predominates in the countryside in sparsely-populated Mongolia, although settled agricultural communities are becoming more common.

Traditionally, economic activity in Mongolia has been based on agriculture and the breeding of livestock. The Mongolian government has gradually been making the transition from Soviet-style central planning to a market economy through privatization and price reform, and by soliciting support from international financial agencies and foreign investors.

The Great Wall

Capital: Beijing
Area: 3,704,427 sq. mi.
9,596,960 sq. km.
Population: 1,279,161,000 (2002 est.)
Largest City: Shanghai, 8,214,000
Languages: Standard Chinese or Mandarin (Putonghua, based on the Beijing dialect), Yue (Cantonese), Wu (Shanghainese), Minbei (Fuzhou), Minnan (Hokkien-Taiwanese), Xiang, Gan, Hakka dialects
Major Religions: Daoism (Taoism), Buddhism, Muslim, Christianity
note: officially atheist, but traditionally pragmatic and eclectic
Life Expectancy: 67 male, 69 female
Government: Communist state

Monetary Unit: yuan
Industry: iron, steel, coal, machine building, armaments, textiles, apparel, petroleum, cement, chemical fertilizers, consumer durables, food processing, autos, consumer electronics, telecommunications
Agriculture: rice, potatoes, sorghum, peanuts, tea, millet, barley, pork, cotton, other fibers, oilseeds, fish
Minerals and Resources: coal, iron ore, petroleum, mercury, tin, tungsten, antimony, manganese, molybdenum, vanadium, magnetite, aluminum, lead, zinc, uranium, hydropower potential

China

China is the oldest continuous major world civilization, with records dating back about 3,500 years. China has gone from monolithic dynastic rule to monolithic communist rule. Since its establishment in 1949, the People's Republic has worked vigorously to win international support for its position that it is the sole legitimate government of all China, including Macau (which will revert to China in 1999) and Taiwan.

China is the world's third-largest country (after Russia and Canada) and has the largest population in the world. Despite the government's attempts to implement a strict population control policy, popular resistance, changes in central policy and loss of authority by rural officials have weakened the population control program. Population growth continues to be a major concern of the Chinese government.

Economically, the Chinese have developed a sort of hybrid socialist-capitalist system, trying to move towards a more productive and flexible economy while still in the communist framework. The results have been mixed, often yielding the worst of both systems.

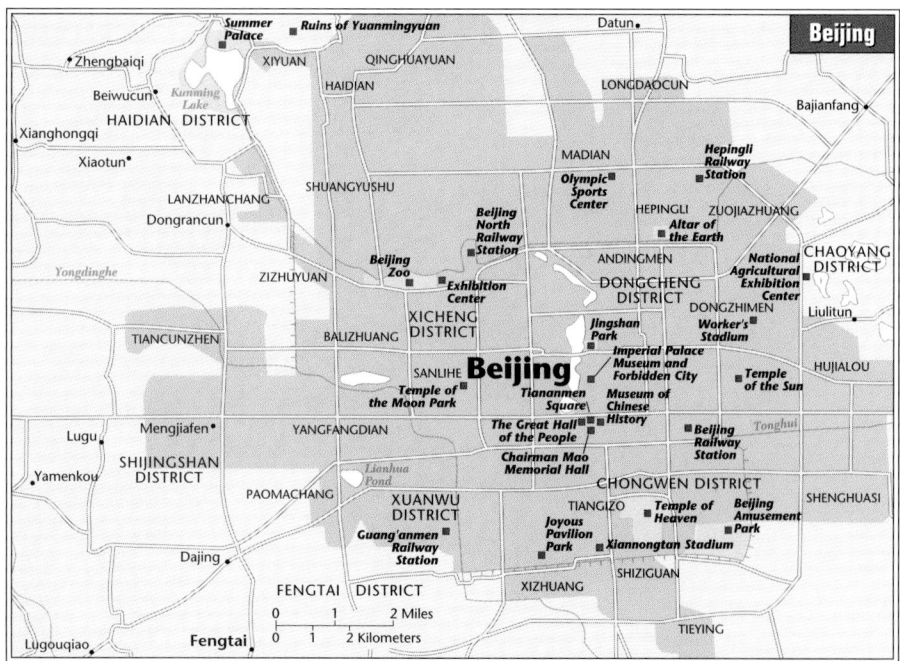

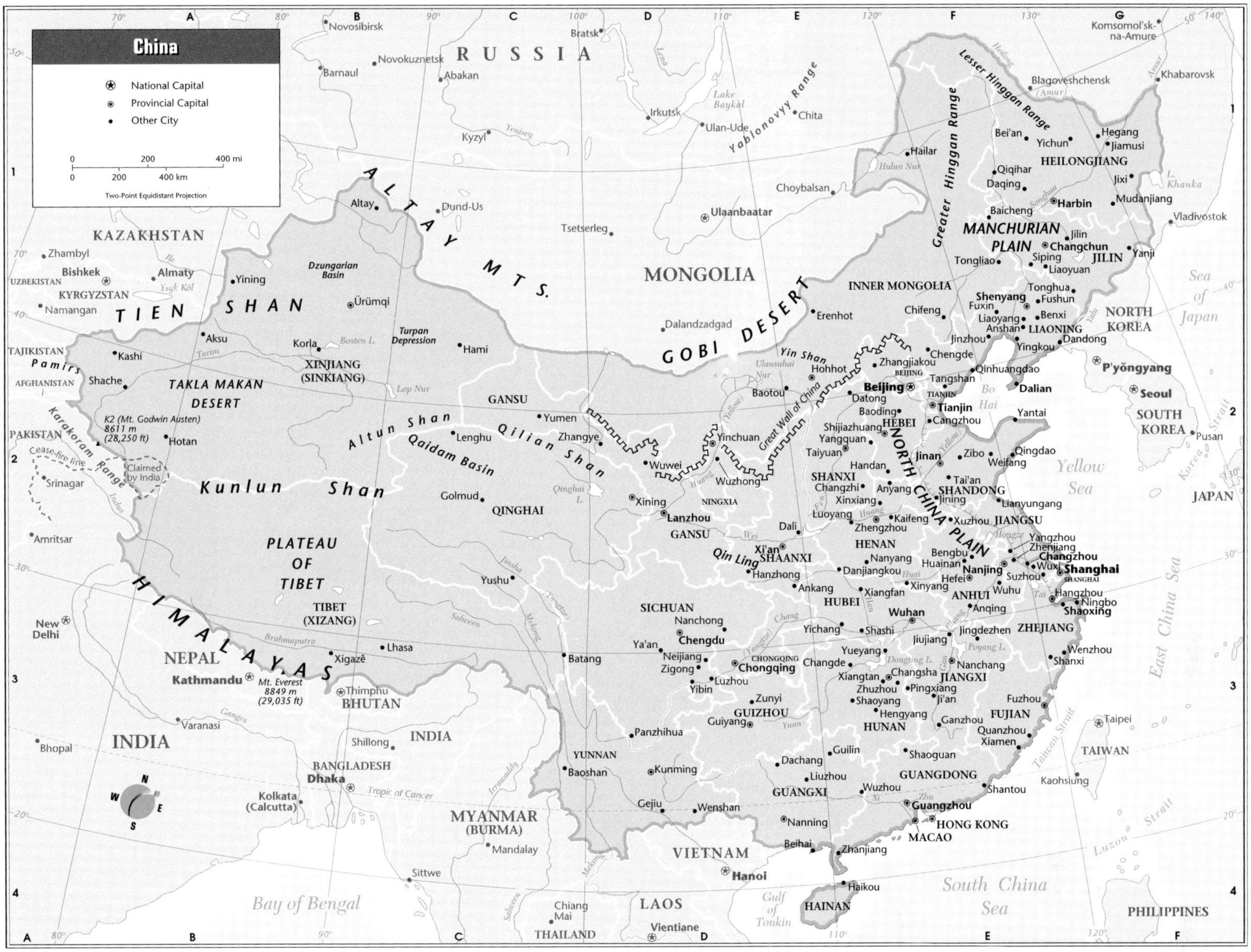

Pao-ho Tien, the Forbidden City, Beijing, China

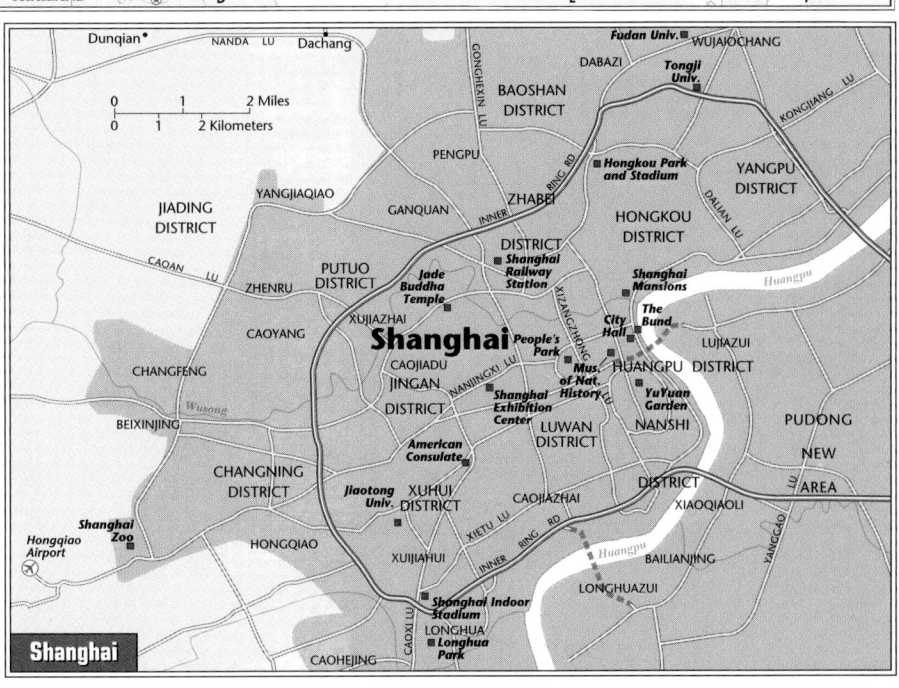

Map of the Philippines

Philippines

- ⊗ National Capital
- • Other City

0 — 100 — 200 mi
0 — 100 — 200 km

Lambert Conformal Conic Projection

Bashi Channel
Batan Is.
Luzon Strait
Babuyan Is.
Babuyan Channel

CORDILLERA ADMINISTRATIVE REGION
Laoag
Vigan
Tuguegarao
ILOCOS
San Fernando
CAGAYAN VALLEY
Baguio
Dagupan
LUZON
Cordillera Central
Sierra Madre
Cabanatuan
CENTRAL LUZON
Angeles
Quezon City
Olongapo
NATIONAL CAPITAL REGION
Bataan Pen.
Manila
Corregidor
Lamon Bay
Zambales Mts.
Lingayen Gulf
Manila Bay
Lipa
San Pablo
Lucena
BICOL
Batangas
Naga
Caramoan Pen.
Calapan
SOUTHERN
Marinduque
Catanduanes
Mamburao
TAGALOG
Mayon Vol.
2421 m
(7943 ft)
Legaspi
Mindoro
Tablas
Sibuyan
Laoang
Calamian Group
Sibuyan Sea
Masbate
Calbayog
Masbate
Samar
EASTERN VISAYAS
Roxas
Cuyo Is.
Panay
VISAYAN
Tacloban
Silay
Cadiz
Ormoc
Iloilo
Bacolod
Leyte
San Carlos
Cebu
Mandaue
Cebu
Dinagat
Panay Gulf
ISLANDS
Bohol
Siargao
WESTERN VISAYAS
Negros
CENTRAL VISAYAS
Surigao
Cagayan Is.
Dumaguete
Bohol Sea
Diuata Mts.
NORTHERN MINDANAO
Butuan
CARAGA
Dipolog
Iligan
Cagayan de Oro
Bislig
Sulu Sea
Pagadian
MINDANAO
WESTERN MINDANAO
Zamboanga Pen.
CENTRAL MINDANAO
Cotabato
Mt. Apo
2954 m
(9692 ft)
Davao
SOUTHERN MINDANAO
Zamboanga
Moro Gulf
Davao Gulf
Isabela
AUTONOMOUS REGION OF MUSLIM MINDANAO
Basilan
AUTONOMOUS REGION OF MUSLIM MINDANAO
General Santos
Cagayan Sulu
Jolo
Jolo
Balabac
Balabac Strait
Sandakan
Tawi Tawi
Sulu Archipelago
Celebes Sea
MALAYSIA
Borneo
INDONESIA
Karakelong

South China Sea
Philippine Sea
Mindoro Strait
Puerto Princesa
Palawan

© MapQuest.com, Inc.

Philippines

Capital: Manila
Area: 115,800 sq. mi.
300,000 sq. km.
Population: 82,995,000
(2002 est.)
Largest City: Manila, 1,581,000
Languages: Filipino, English
Major Religions: Roman Catholic, Protestant, Muslim, Buddhist
Life Expectancy: 63 male, 68 female
Government: republic
Monetary Unit: Philippine peso
Industry: textiles, pharmaceuticals, chemicals, wood products, food processing, electronics assembly, petroleum refining, fishing
Agriculture: rice, coconuts, corn, sugarcane, bananas, pineapples, mangos, pork, eggs, beef, fishing
Minerals and Resources: timber, petroleum, nickel, cobalt, silver, gold, salt, copper

JUSTIN LOUIS

Philippine sunset

The Philippines comprise an archipelago between the Philippine Sea and the South China Sea, east of Vietnam.

The Philippines has a representative democracy modeled on the U.S. system. The U.S.-Philippine relationship dates from Admiral Dewey's defeat of the Spanish fleet in Manila Bay and the subsequent cession of the Philippine Islands by Spain to the U.S. in 1898. The Philippines remained under the direct control of the U.S., until 1935, when it became a self-governing commonwealth. After being occupied by the Japanese from 1942–45, the Philippines became an independent republic.

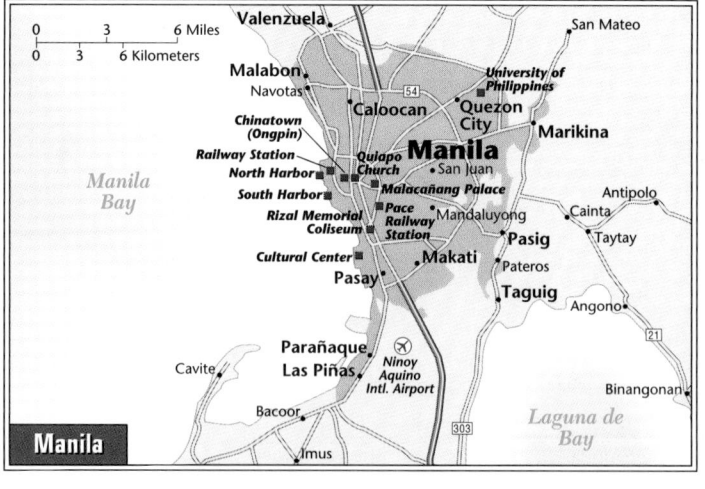

Manila

0 — 3 — 6 Miles
0 — 3 — 6 Kilometers

Valenzuela
San Mateo
Malabon
Navotas
Chinatown (Ongpin)
Caloocan
University of the Philippines
Quezon City
Marikina
Railway Station
Quiapo Church
Manila
Antipolo
North Harbor
San Juan
Cainta
Malacañang Palace
Taytay
South Harbor
Pace Railway Station
Mandaluyong
Pasig
Rizal Memorial Coliseum
Makati
Pateros
Cultural Center
Pasay
Angono
Manila Bay
Taguig
Parañaque
Las Piñas
Cavite
Ninoy Aquino Intl. Airport
Bacoor
Binangonan
Imus
Laguna de Bay

Market, Bandar Seri Begawan

Brunei has a constitutional sultanate; the sultan is both head of state and prime minister. Brunei's legal system is based on Islamic law and about 60% of its population is Muslim.

In 1888 Brunei became a British Protected State and remained so until 1984 when it received its independence. Since then it has undergone steady development, thanks mainly to its vast oil wealth. The economy is a mixture of foreign and domestic entrepreneurship, government regulation and welfare measures, and village tradition. Per capita GDP is among the highest in the developing countries.

Brunei

Capital: Bandar Seri Begawan
Area: 2,227 sq. mi.
   5,770 sq. km.
Population: 351,000 (2002 est.)
Largest City: Bandar Seri Begawan, 50,000
Languages: Malay, English, Chinese
Major Religions: Muslim, Buddhism, Christian
Life Expectancy: 70 male, 73 female
Government: constitutional sultanate
Monetary Unit: Bruneian dollar
Industry: petroleum, petroleum refining, liquefied natural gas, construction
Agriculture: rice, cassava, bananas, buffaloes, pigs
Minerals and Resources: petroleum, natural gas, timber

Palace, Bandar Seri Begawan

Brunei

National Capital
Other City
0   10   20 mi
0   10 20 km
Lambert Conformal Conic Projection

© MapQuest.com, Inc.

Water village, Sarawak, Malaysia

Malaysia

Capital: Kuala Lumpur
Area: 127,284 sq. mi.
   329,750 sq. km.
Population: 22,662,000 (2002 est.)
Largest City: Kuala Lumpur, 1,379,000
Languages: Malay, English, Chinese (Mandarin and Hakka dialects predominate), Tamil, numerous tribal dialects
Major Religions: Muslim, Buddhist, Hindu, Christian, Confucianist
Life Expectancy: 67 male, 73 female
Government: constitutional monarchy
Monetary Unit: ringgit
Industry: rubber and oil palm processing and manufacturing, light manufacturing industry, electronics, tin mining and smelting, logging, processing timber, petroleum production and refining, agriculture processing
Agriculture: natural rubber, palm oil, rice, timber, coconut, pepper
Minerals and Resources: tin, petroleum, timber, copper, iron ore, natural gas, bauxite

In 1946, the eleven separate states of Peninsular Malaysia were united as British Protectorates in the Malayan Union, and then became the Federation of Malaya in 1948. Malaya became independent in 1957 and in 1963 it merged with Singapore and the former British colonies of Sarawak and Sabah to form Malaysia (Singapore seceded two years later).

Malaysia today is a constitutional monarchy whose king is also the leader of the Islamic faith in the country. The king is elected for a five-year term from among the nine sultans of the peninsular Malaysian states.

Malaysia possesses abundant resources and land, a well-educated work force, adequate infrastructure and a stable political environment.

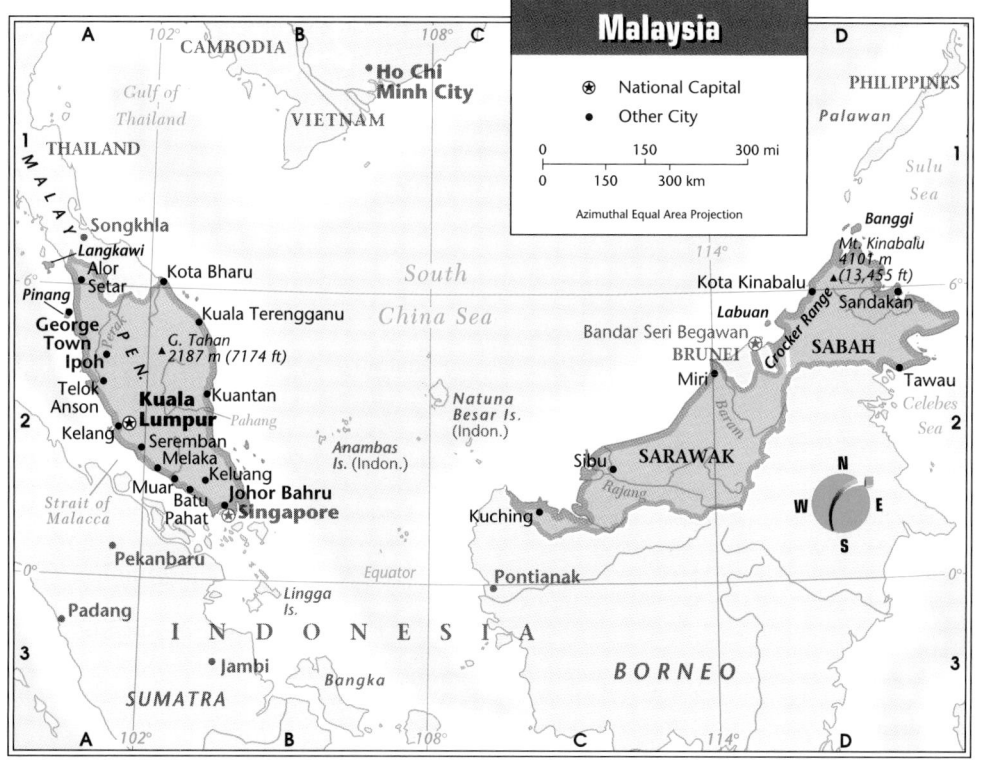

Malaysia

National Capital
Other City
0   150   300 mi
0   150   300 km
Azimuthal Equal Area Projection

© MapQuest.com, Inc.

Kuala Lumpur, Malaysia

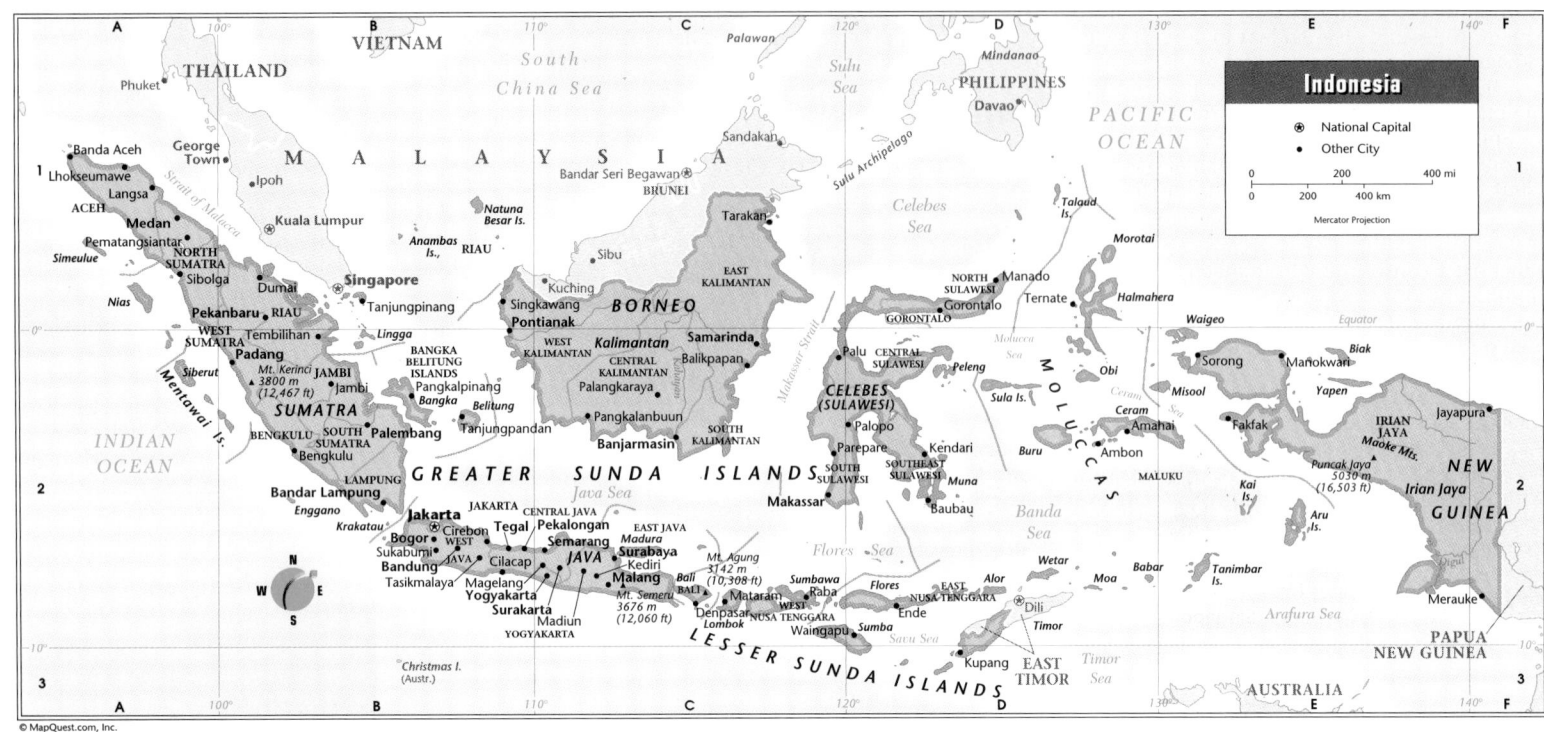

Indonesia comprises more than 17,000 islands and a multitude of ethnic groups. It became an independent republic in 1945 after three decades of Dutch rule. It is the world's largest Muslim nation.

Indonesia has a mixed economy with some socialist institutions and central planning but with a recent emphasis on deregulation and private enterprise. Agriculture, including forestry and fishing, is an important sector of the economy.

The Indonesian government has been fortunate that its poor human rights record has scarcely detracted from its international standing.

Capital: Jakarta
Area: 740,904 sq. mi.
1,919,440 sq. km.
Population: 231,326,000 (2002 est.)
Largest City: Jakarta, 9,374,000
Languages: Bahasa Indonesia, English, Dutch, Javanese
Major Religions: Muslim, Protestant, Roman Catholic, Hindu, Buddhist
Life Expectancy: 59 male, 63 female
Government: republic
Monetary Unit: Indonesian rupiah
Industry: petroleum and natural gas, textiles, mining, cement, chemical fertilizers, plywood, food, rubber
Agriculture: rice, cassava, peanuts, rubber, cocoa, coffee, palm oil, copra, other tropical products, poultry, beef, pork, eggs
Minerals and Resources: petroleum, tin, natural gas, nickel, timber, bauxite, copper, fertile soils, coal, gold, silver

Indonesia

Bali, Indonesia

East Timor

On October 20, 1999, Indonesia officially repealed the 1978 annexation of East Timor, ending its status as Indonesia's 27th province. Indonesia has turned over the administration of East Timor to the United Nations. The new nation will be administered for two to three years by a UN-controlled interim government until its formal independence.

Capital: Dili
Area: 7,297 sq. mi.
18,900 sq. km.
Population: 953,000 (2002 est.)
Largest City: Dili, 140,000
Languages: Portuguese, Tetum, Indonesian
Major Religions: Roman Catholic, Protestant, Muslim
Life Expectancy: 59 male, 63 female (1995)
Government: republic
Monetary Unit: US dollar
Industry: forestry, fishing
Agriculture: rice, spices, tea, coffee
Minerals and Resources: forests

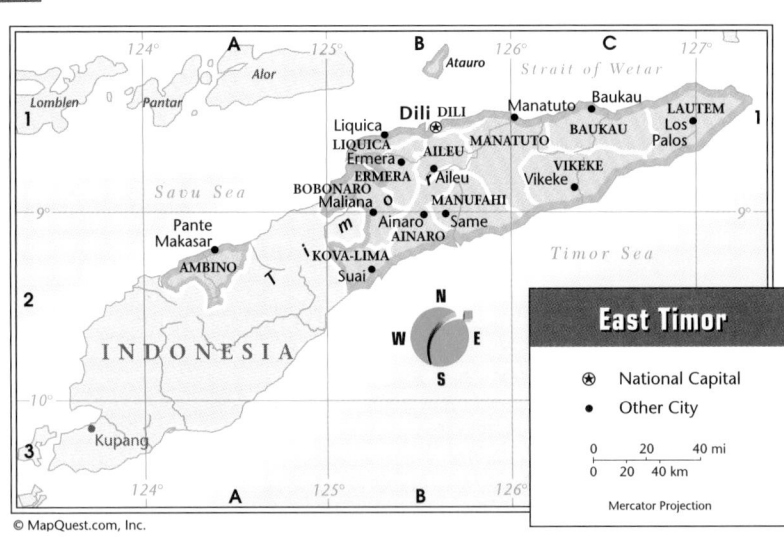

Singapore was a British Crown Colony from 1867–1959, when it achieved internal self-government. It became independent in 1965 after a two-year alliance in the Federation of Malaysia. Today, Singapore is a parliamentary republic.

The population in Singapore is predominantly Chinese. Its climate is tropical and it is a focal point for Southeast Asian trade routes due to its position along the Strait of Malacca.

Singapore's per capita income is second only in the region to that of Japan. The Singaporean economy is an open, entrepreneurial one with strong service and manufacturing sectors and excellent trading links derived from its entrepot history.

Singapore

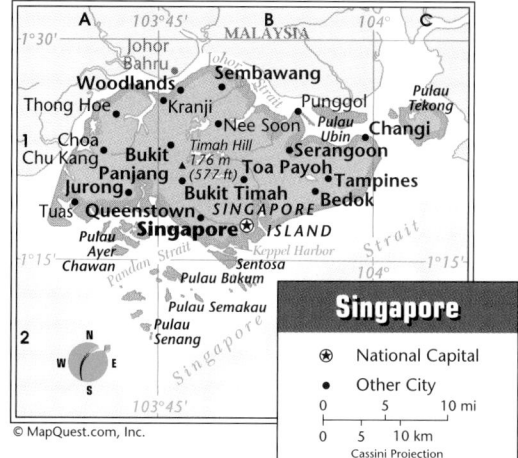

Paper mache dragon for Dragon Dance, Chinese New Year in Singapore

Capital: Singapore
Area: 244 sq. mi.
 633 sq. km.
Population: 4,453,000 (2002 est.)
Largest City: Singapore, 4,131,000
Languages: Chinese, Malay, Tamil, English
Major Religions: Buddhist, Muslim, Christian, Hindu, Sikh, Taoist, Confucianist
Life Expectancy: 73 male, 79 female
Government: republic within Commonwealth
Monetary Unit: Singapore dollar
Industry: petroleum refining, electronics, oil drilling equipment, rubber processing, rubber products, processed food and beverages, ship repair, entrepot trade, financial services, biotechnology
Agriculture: poultry, eggs, rubber, copra, fruit, vegetables
Minerals and Resources: fish, deepwater ports

Capital: Hanoi
Area: 127,210 sq. mi.
 329,560 sq. km.
Population: 80,577,000 (2002 est.)
Largest City: Ho Chi Minh City, 4,990,000
Languages: Vietnamese, French, Chinese, English, Khmer
Major Religions: Buddhist, Taoist, Roman Catholic, Islam, Protestant
Life Expectancy: 64 male, 68 female
Government: Communist state
Monetary Unit: new dong
Industry: food processing, textiles, machine building, mining, cement, chemical fertilizer, glass, tires, oil
Agriculture: paddy rice, corn, potatoes, rubber, soybeans, coffee, tea, bananas, fish
Minerals and Resources: phosphates, coal, manganese, bauxite, chromate, offshore oil deposits, forests

Vietnam

Seaside village on Vietnam coast

In 1884, France officially incorporated Vietnam into its empire. The Vietnamese, fiercely nationalistic, never truly accepted French rule. The Vietnamese communist movement began with Ho Chi Minh in 1920 but did not gain control of the country until 1945 when it proclaimed Vietnam's independence.

After an eight-year war, France ended its colonial rule in Indochina and a cease-fire agreement provided for the temporary division of Vietnam into two "zones." This partition proved to be more than temporary, leading to the U.S.-Vietnam war, and it was not until 1976 that the north and south reunified under Hanoi's communist rule.

Vietnam has made significant progress in recent years moving away from a planned economic system toward a more effective, market-based economy.

© MapQuest.com, Inc.

Laos

Capital: Vientiane
Area: 91,405 sq. mi.
236,800 sq. km.
Population: 5,778,000 (2002 est.)
Largest City: Vientiane, 331,000
Languages: Lao, French, English
Major Religions: Buddhist
Life Expectancy: 51 male, 54 female
Government: Communist state
Monetary Unit: new kip
Industry: tin and gypsum mining, timber, electric power, agricultural processing, construction
Agriculture: rice, sweet potatoes, vegetables, corn, coffee, sugarcane, cotton, buffaloes, hogs, cattle, poultry
Minerals and Resources: timber, hydropower, gypsum, tin, gold, gemstones

Laos is a small, landlocked country northeast of Thailand. It is made up mostly of rugged mountains and the climate is hot and tropical.

Laos obtained full independence from France in 1953 under the rule of King Sisavang Vong. Nationalist guerrillas opposed the monarchy as well as the French and later the Americans, and in 1975 the communist faction of this guerrilla force took over control of Laos. A repressive military campaign was undertaken by the new government causing about 10% of the Lao population to seek refugee status in foreign countries.

Since 1986 the government of Laos has been decentralizing control and encouraging private enterprise. Subsistence agriculture still accounts for about half of the GDP and provides 80% of total employment.

Orange robed monks at Angkor Wat, Cambodia

Giant stone sculpture, Cambodia

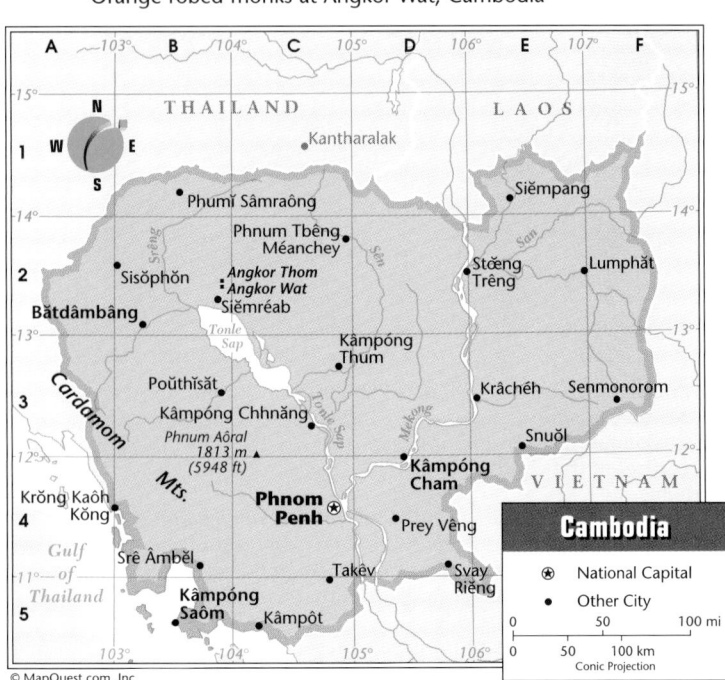

© MapQuest.com, Inc.

Cambodia

Capital: Phnom Penh
Area: 69,881 sq. mi.
181,040 sq. km.
Population: 12,890,000 (2002 est.)
Largest City: Phnom Penh, 1,000,000
Languages: Khmer, French
Major Religion: Theravada Buddhism
Life Expectancy: 48 male, 51 female
Government: multiparty liberal democracy under a constitutional monarchy
Monetary Unit: new riel
Industry: rice milling, fishing, wood and wood products, rubber, cement, gem mining
Agriculture: rice, rubber, corn, meat, vegetables, dairy products, sugar, flour
Minerals and Resources: timber, gemstones, some iron ore, manganese, phosphates, hydropower potential

Cambodia is a very poor, rural country. It is a land of paddies and forests dominated by the Mekong River. After decades of brutal war and repression, Cambodia has been recovering slowly.

In 1993 the Kingdom of Cambodia established itself as a multiparty liberal democracy under a constitutional monarchy. The government is working towards restoring fiscal and monetary discipline and establishing good working relations with international financial institutions.

Progress, however, is slow due to the persistence of internal political divisions, the total lack of basic infrastructure and widespread poverty.

Thailand is a constitutional monarchy that established its independence in the year 1238. The king has little direct power under the constitution but is a symbol of national identity and unity and commands enormous popular respect and moral authority.

Thailand is one of the more advanced developing countries in Asia. Tourism is Thailand's largest source of foreign exchange and agriculture accounts for more than half the GDP and employment in the country. The Thai economy recovered rapidly from the political unrest of 1992, but the government still has a lot of progress to make building infrastructure, protecting workers' rights and promoting business investment.

Capital: Bangkok
Area: 198,404 sq. mi.
    514,000 sq. km.
Population: 63,645,000 (2002 est.)
Largest City: Bangkok, 6,355,000
Languages: Thai, English
Major Religions: Buddhism, Muslim, Christianity, Hinduism
Life Expectancy: 65 male, 72 female
Government: constitutional monarchy
Monetary Unit: baht

Industry: tourism, textiles and garments, agricultural processing, beverages, tobacco, cement, light manufacturing, electric appliances and components, integrated circuits, furniture, plastics, tungsten and tin production
Agriculture: rice and cassava (tapioca), rubber, corn, sugarcane, coconuts, soybeans
Minerals and Resources: tin, rubber, natural gas, tungsten, tantalum, timber, lead, fish, gypsum, lignite, fluorite

Thailand

Grand Palace, Bangkok, Thailand

Myanmar (Burma)

Capital: Rangoon (Yangon)
Area: 261,901 sq. mi.
    678,500 sq. km.
Population: 42,282,000 (2002 est.)
Largest City: Rangoon (Yangon), 2,513,000
Languages: Burmese
Major Religions: Buddhist, Baptist, Roman Catholic, Muslim
Life Expectancy: 58 male, 63 female
Government: military regime
Monetary Unit: kyat
Industry: agricultural processing, textiles and footwear, wood and wood products, petroleum refining, copper, tin, tungsten, iron, construction materials, pharmaceuticals, fertilizer
Agriculture: fishing, animal husbandry, forestry, paddy rice, corn, oilseed, sugarcane, pulses
Minerals and Resources: petroleum, timber, tin, antimony, zinc, copper, tungsten, lead, coal, marble, limestone, precious stones, natural gas

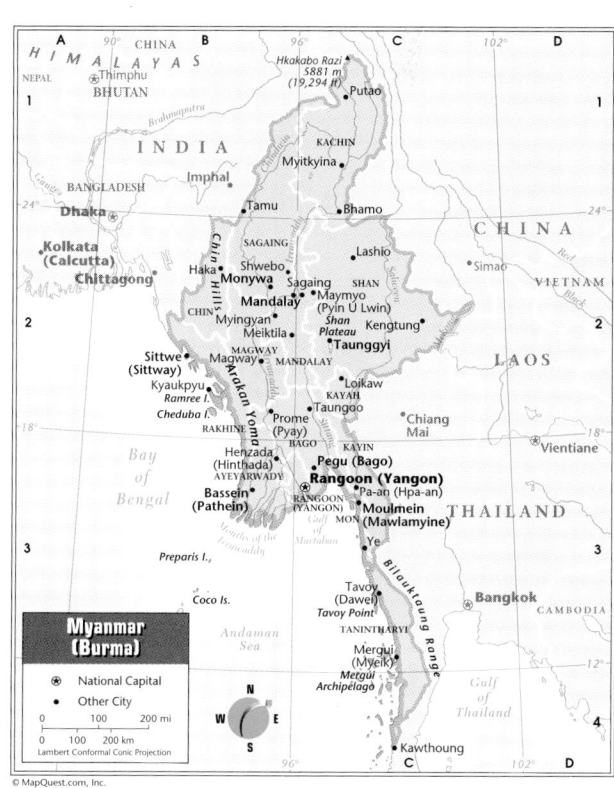

Myanmar, formerly Burma, gained its independence from the U.K. in 1948. The past decade has seen great political unrest in Myanmar and the current government is a military regime.

Although Myanmar is a poor country, it has rich resources which furnish the potential for substantial long-term increases in income, exports and living standards. Government policy in recent years has aimed at revitalizing the economy after four decades of tight central planning.

Myanmar's predominantly rural population is concentrated in the several lower river valleys in the country. Theravada Buddhism — an older form of Buddhism prevalent in most of mainland Southeast Asia — is practiced by about 85% of the Burmese.

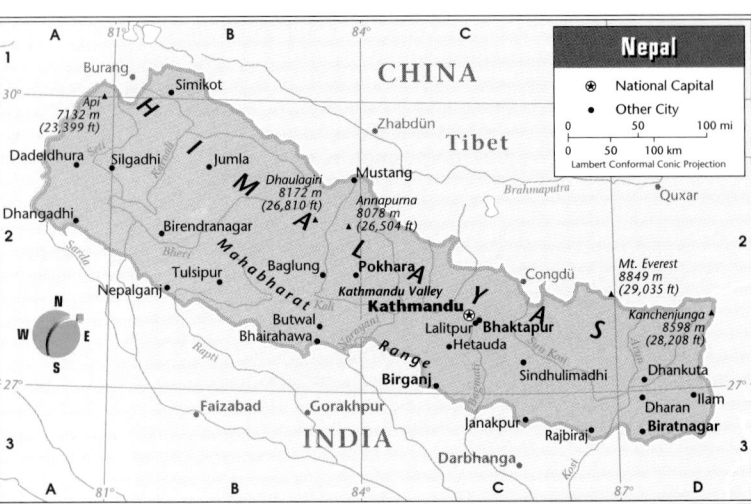

Nepal

Capital: Kathmandu
Area: 54,349 sq. mi.
140,800 sq. km.
Population: 25,874,000
(2002 est.)
Largest City: Kathmandu, 421,000
Language: Nepali
Major Religions: Hindu, Buddhist, Muslim
Life Expectancy: 53 male, 53 female
Government: parliamentary democracy
Monetary Unit: Nepalese rupee
Industry: small rice, jute, sugar, and oilseed mills; cigarettes, textile, carpet, cement, and brick production; tourism
Agriculture: rice, corn, wheat, sugarcane, root crops, milk, buffalo meat
Minerals and Resources: quartz, water, timber, hydroelectric potential, scenic beauty, small deposits of lignite, copper, cobalt, iron ore

The 1994 election defeat of the Nepali Congress Party by the UML (United Marxist and Leninist Party) has made Nepal the world's first communist monarchy. The UML has supported the country's recent free-market reforms and is a champion of multiparty democracy.

Nepal is 90% Hindu and religion is very important to its people. The Nepalese are descendants of three major migrations from India, Tibet and Central Asia.

Nepal ranks among the world's poorest countries; however, it has made progress and is committed to a program of economic liberalization. Agriculture remains Nepal's principal economic activity, employing 80% of the population and providing almost half of the country's income.

Traditionally a decentralized theocracy, and since 1907 a monarchy, Bhutan is moving gradually toward representative government. The country's political history is intimately tied to its religious history and relations among the various monastic schools and monasteries.

The spiritual head of Bhutan, the Je Khempo, is nominated by monastic leaders and appointed by the king. The monastic order is involved in government at many levels.

Bhutan's economy is largely rural-based. More than 90% of the work force is employed in subsistence farming and animal husbandry. Although the United Nations identifies Bhutan as "least developed", economic welfare levels and nutrition are probably above average for Asia.

Bhutan

Capital: Thimphu
Area: 18,142 sq. mi.
47,000 sq. km.
Population: 2,094,000 (2002 est.)
Largest City: Thimphu, 8,900
Languages: Dzongkha, various Tibetan and Nepalese dialects
Major Religions: Lamaistic Buddhism, Hinduism
Life Expectancy: 52 male, 50 female
Government: monarchy
Monetary Unit: ngultrum
Industry: cement, wood products, processed fruits, alcoholic beverages, calcium carbide
Agriculture: rice, corn, root crops, citrus fruit, dairy products, foodgrains, eggs
Minerals and Resources: timber, hydropower, gypsum, calcium carbide

---

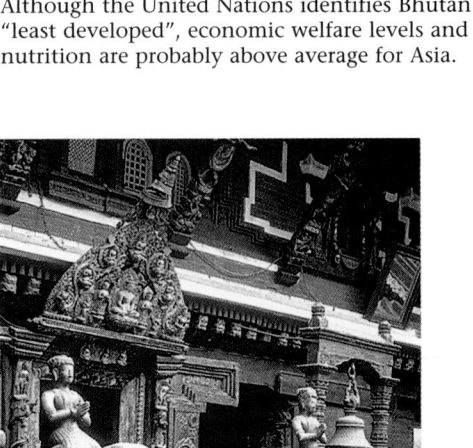

Capital: Colombo
Area: 25,326 sq. mi.
65,610 sq. km.
Population: 19,577,000
(2002 est.)
Largest City: Colombo, 642,000
Languages: Sinhala, Tamil, English
Major Religions: Buddhist, Hindu, Christian, Muslim
Life Expectancy: 70 male, 75 female
Government: republic
Monetary Unit: Sri Lankan rupee

Sri Lanka

Industry: processing of rubber, tea, coconuts, and other agricultural commodities; clothing, cement, petroleum refining, textiles, tobacco
Agriculture: rice, sugarcane, grains, pulses, oilseeds, roots, spices, tea, rubber, coconuts, milk, eggs, hides, meat
Minerals and Resources: limestone, graphite, mineral sands, gems, phosphates, clay

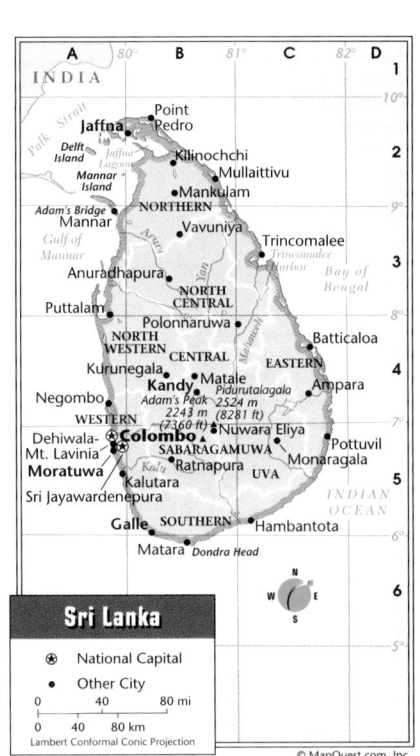

Sri Lanka is an island in the Indian Ocean, south of India. Formerly known as Ceylon, Sri Lanka was part of the British Empire from 1796 to 1948, when it became independent. It became a republic in 1972.

Sri Lanka is ethnically, linguistically, and religiously diverse. Sri Lankan politics since independence have been strongly democratic, and the government follows a moderate, non-aligned foreign policy.

The Tamil separatist movement has plagued Sri Lanka since 1956 and both the Tamils and the government forces have been accused of serious human rights violations in the past decade. The government is striving to to end hostilities and enter into peace negotiations to end the violence.

Hiranya Varna Mahabihar in Lalitpur, Nepal

Capital: Male
Area: 116 sq. mi.
300 sq. km.
Population: 320,000 (2002 est.)
Largest City: Male, 74,000
Languages: Divehi, English
Major Religions: Sunni Muslim
Life Expectancy: 64 male, 67 female
Government: republic
Monetary Unit: rufiyaa
Industry: fishing and fish processing, tourism, shipping, boat building, coconut processing, garments, woven mats, coir (rope), handicrafts
Agriculture: fishing, coconuts, corn, sweet potatoes
Minerals and Resources: fish

Maldives

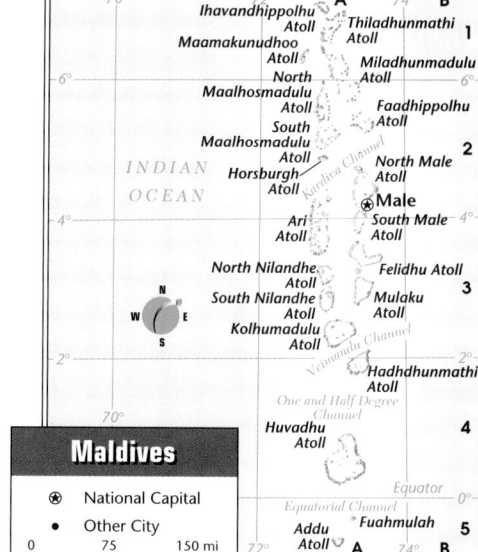

The Maldives are a chain of 19 atolls that form an archipelago in the northern Indian Ocean. Of the 1,200 coral islands that comprise the archipelago only about 200 are inhabited. Only four islands have a population of more than 3,000.

The Maldives were a British protectorate from 1887 until 1965. A sultanate was then established but lasted only three years and was replaced by a republic with a president and a constitution, which is the current system of government. The legal system is based on Islamic law.

The Maldivian economy is based on tourism and fishing.

Capital: Dhaka
Area: 55,584 sq. mi.
144,000 sq. km.
Population: 135,657,000 (2002 est.)
Largest City: Dhaka, 4,232,000
Languages: Bangla, English
Major Religions: Muslim, Hindu, Buddhist, Christian
Life Expectancy: 56 male, 55 female
Government: republic
Monetary Unit: taka
Industry: jute manufacturing, cotton textiles, food processing, steel, fertilizer
Agriculture: jute, rice, wheat, tea, sugarcane, potatoes, beef, milk, poultry
Minerals and Resources: natural gas, arable land, timber

Bangladesh

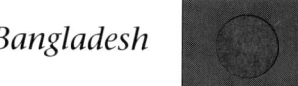

Bangladesh is the most densely populated agricultural nation in the world and one of the poorest. While a large majority of the population is Muslim, Hindus constitute a sizable minority (16%).

Present day Bangladesh was formerly East Pakistan. In 1971 Bangladesh seceded from Pakistan and a civil war ensued. At the end of that same year, Pakistan surrendered and Bangladesh achieved full independence. During the 1980s Bangladesh gradually improved relations with Pakistan, India and Burma, and started to make tentative economic progress.

Bangladesh's economy is predominantly agricultural, with the cultivation of rice the single most important activity in the economy. One of the major impediments to economic growth in Bangladesh are the frequent cyclones and floods it experiences as most of the country is flat alluvial plain.

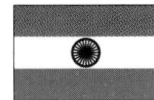

India

Capital: New Delhi
Area: 1,269,010 sq. mi.
3,287,590 sq. km.
Population: 1,034,173,000
(2002 est.)
Largest City: Mumbai
(Bombay), 11,914,000
Languages: English, Hindi,
Bengali, Telugu, Marathi, Tamil,
Urdu, Gujarati, Malayalam,
Kannada, Oriya, Punjabi,
Assamese, Kashmiri, Sindhi,
Sanskrit, Hindustani
Major Religions: Hindu, Muslim,
Christian, Sikh, Buddhist, Jains
Life Expectancy: 59 male, 60
female
Government: federal republic
Monetary Unit: Indian rupee
Industry: textiles, chemicals,
food processing, steel, trans-
portation equipment, cement,
mining, petroleum, machinery
Agriculture: rice, wheat,
oilseeds, cotton, jute, tea, sugar-
cane, potatoes, cattle, buffaloes,
sheep, goats, poultry, fish
Minerals and Resources: coal,
iron ore, manganese, mica,
bauxite, titanium ore, chromite,
natural gas, diamonds, petroleum, limestone

Raiphut Palace, Rajasthan, India

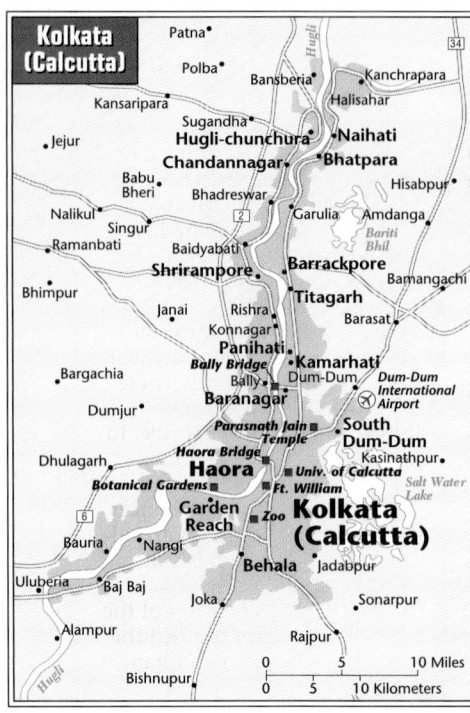

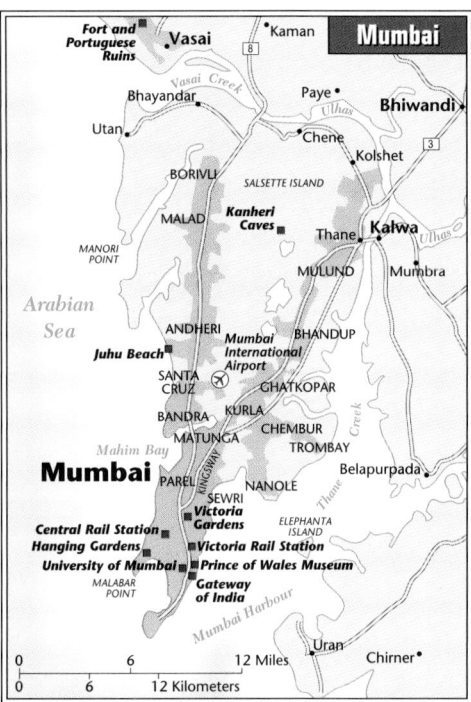

The people of India have had a continuous civilization since 2500 B.C. India was controlled by
Great Britain in varying degrees from 1639 until
1947, when it became independent.

While about 70% of India's population depend
on agriculture, India has an increasingly modern
industrial base with sophisticated industries in
electronics, avionics, and aluminum. India's size,
large population and strategic location give it a
prominent voice in international affairs, and its
growing industrial base, military strength and scientific and technical capacity give it added
weight.

Despite India's economic progress, it remains a
very impoverished country with a serious overpopulation problem.

© MapQuest.com, Inc.

Afghanistan

Afghanistan's population is ethnically and linguistically mixed, reflecting its geographic location at the crossroads of Central Asia along historic trade and invasion routes. Afghanistan is an Islamic country and Islamic practices pervade all aspects of life.

Most Afghans are divided into clans and tribal groups which follow ancient customs and religious practices. These allegiances have remained strong despite British and then Soviet rule. In fact, during the ten-year Soviet invasion and occupation of Afghanistan from 1978–88, these ethnic differences, combined with Soviet domination, culminated in a civil war which is still going on.

Over the past decade one-third of the population of Afghanistan has fled the country, mainly to Pakistan and Iran.

Capital: Kabul
Area: 249,936 sq. mi.
    647,500 sq. km.
Population: 27,756,000 (2002 est.)
Largest City: Kabul, 1,527,000
Languages: Pashtu, Afghan Persian (Dari), Uzbek, Turkmen, Balochi, Pashai
Major Religions: Sunni Muslim, Shi'a Muslim
Life Expectancy: 46 male, 45 female
Government: transitional government
Monetary Unit: afghani
Industry: textiles, soap, furniture, shoes, fertilizer, cement, handwoven carpets, natural gas, oil, coal, copper
Agriculture: wheat, fruits, nuts, karakul pelts, wool, mutton
Minerals and Resources: natural gas, petroleum, coal, copper, talc, barites, sulphur, lead, zinc, iron ore, salt, precious and semiprecious stones

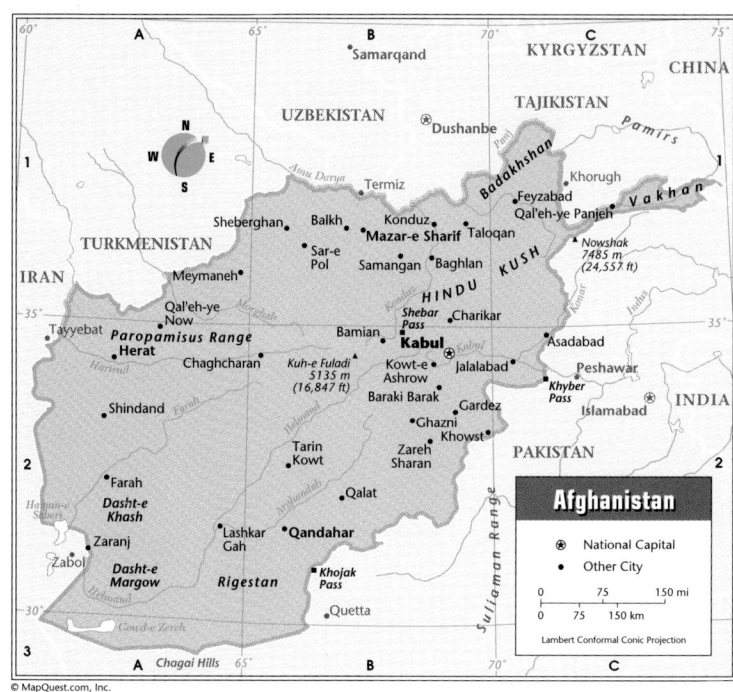

© MapQuest.com, Inc.

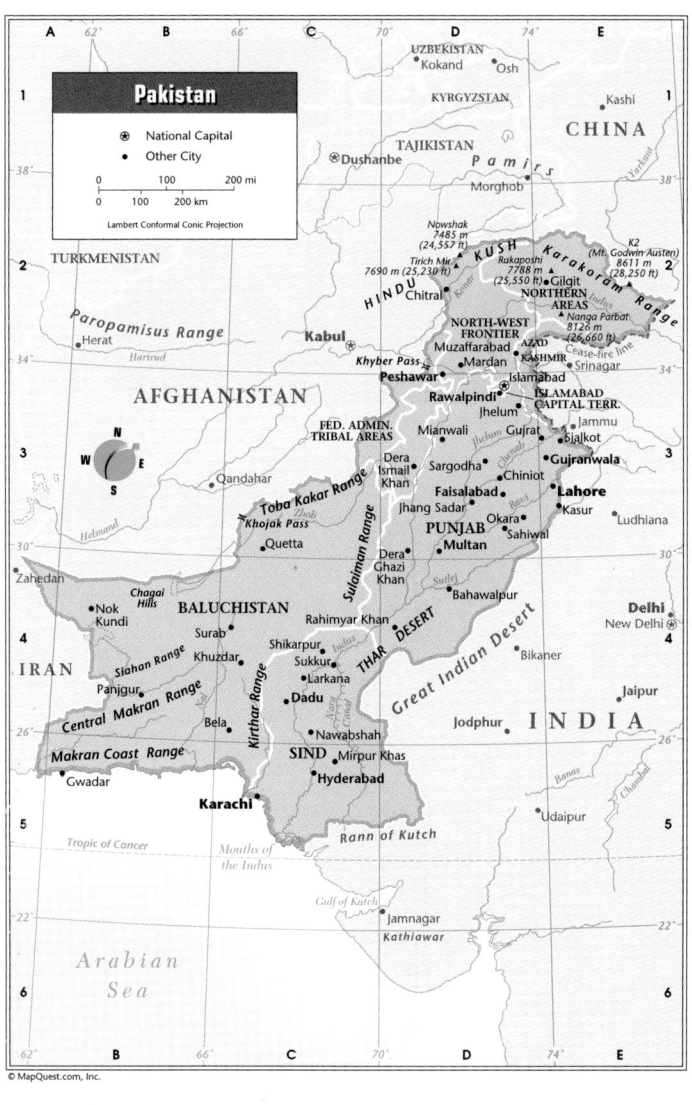

© MapQuest.com, Inc.

Pakistan

Capital: Islamabad
Area: 310,321 sq. mi.
    803,940 sq. km.
Population: 147,663,000 (2002 est.)
Largest City: Karachi, 9,339,000
Languages: Urdu, English, Punjabi, Sindhi, Pashtu, Urdu, Balochi
Major Religions: Muslim, Christian, Hindu
Life Expectancy: 57 male, 59 female
Government: republic
Monetary Unit: Pakistani rupee

Industry: textiles, food processing, beverages, construction materials, clothing, paper products, shrimp
Agriculture: cotton, wheat, rice, sugarcane, fruits, vegetables, milk, beef, mutton, eggs
Minerals and Resources: land, extensive natural gas reserves, limited petroleum, poor quality coal, iron ore, copper, salt, limestone

Pakistan was created in 1947 in response to Muslim demands for an Islamic state when India gained independence from Great Britain. Pakistan experienced political instability and economic difficulties for the next 26 years, due in part to the fact that it consisted of two areas, East and West Pakistan, separated by 1,600 kilometers of Indian territory. In 1970, East Pakistan gained independence as Bangladesh.

Pakistan is a relatively poor country with a large population; however, it has the resources and entrepreneurial skill to support rapid economic growth. Many challenges face the current government as it must deal with an inadequate and deteriorating infrastructure, a low literacy level and increasing sectarian, ethnic and tribal violence.

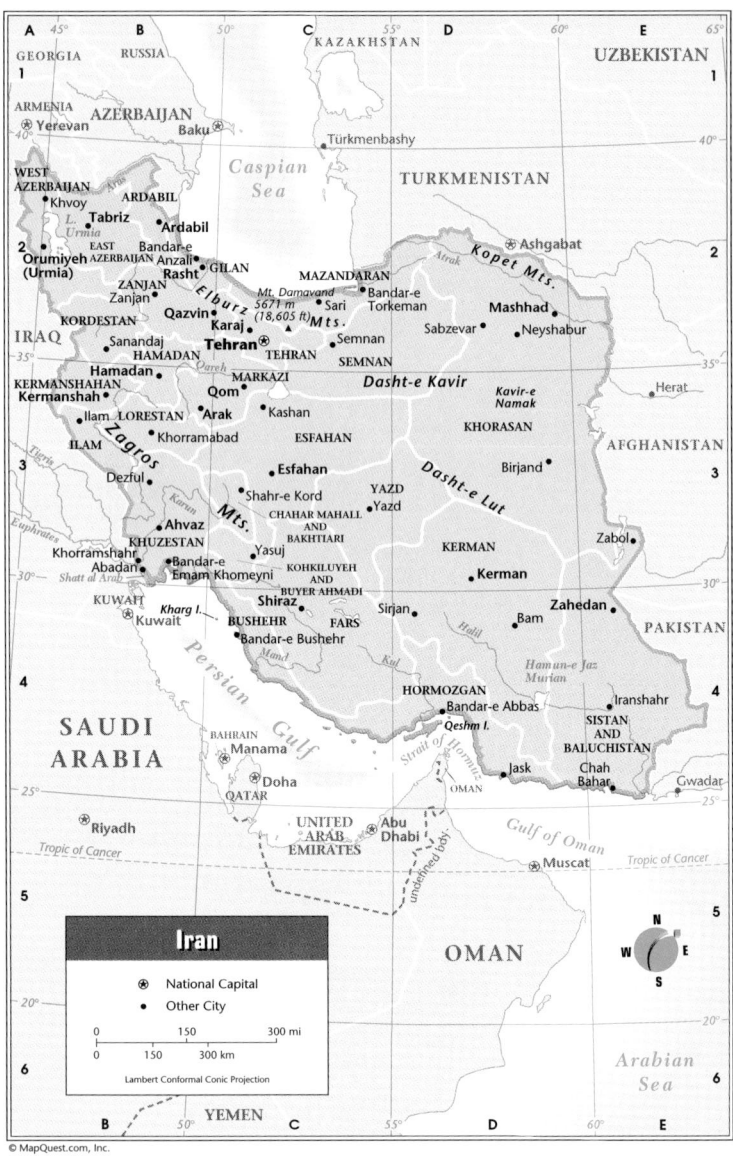

Iran

Capital: Tehran
Area: 636,128 sq. mi.
  1,648,000 sq. km.
Population: 67,538,000 (2002 est.)
Largest City: Tehran, 6,759,000
Languages: Persian, Turkic, Kurdish, Luri, Baloch, Arabic, Turkish
Major Religions: Shi'a Muslim, Sunni Muslim, Zoroastrian, Jewish, Christian, Baha'i
Life Expectancy: 66 male, 68 female
Government: theocratic republic
Monetary Unit: Iranian rial
Industry: petroleum, petrochemicals, textiles, cement and other building materials, food processing (particularly sugar refining and vegetable oil production), metal fabricating, armaments and military equipment
Agriculture: wheat, rice, other grains, sugar beets, fruits, nuts, cotton, dairy products, wool, caviar
Minerals and Resources: petroleum, natural gas, coal, chromium, copper, ironore, lead, manganese, zinc, sulfur

The ancient nation of Iran, formerly known as Persia and once a major empire in its own right, has been invaded frequently and had its territory altered through the centuries. Modern Iranian history began with a nationalist uprising against the Shah (who remained in power) in 1905, followed a year later by the granting of a limited constitution and, in 1908 with the discovery of oil.

In 1925 Reza Khan, a military officer, pronounced himself Shah and ruled Iran until 1941, when his son took over. Religious and political opposition to the Shah's rule culminated in his fleeing Iran in 1979, whereupon the Ayatollah Khomeini, an exiled religious leader, directed an Islamic revolution that resulted in a new republic.

Khomeini's regime brought about strong changes in Iran's foreign policy, particularly in reversing the country's orientation toward the West. Iran's only significant ally in the Middle East has been Syria.

Shrine of Hazrat Fatimeh, Sister of Shia 8th Iman, Iran

Iraq

Capital: Baghdad
Area: 168,710 sq. mi.
  437,072 sq. km.
Population: 24,002,000 (2002 est.)
Largest City: Baghdad, 3,841,000
Languages: Arabic, Kurdish, Assyrian, Armenian
Major Religions: Shi'a Muslim, Sunni Muslim, Christian
Life Expectancy: 66 male, 68 female
Government: republic
Monetary Unit: Iraqi dinar
Industry: petroleum production and refining, chemicals, textiles, construction materials, food processing
Agriculture: wheat, barley, rice, vegetables, dates, other fruit, cotton, wool, cattle, sheep
Minerals and Resources: petroleum, natural gas, phosphates, sulfur

Once known as Mesopotamia, Iraq historically was the site of flourishing ancient civilizations, including the Sumerian, Babylonian and Parthian cultures. At the end of World War I Iraq became a British-mandated territory and in 1932 it was declared independent and was ruled as a monarchy by the Hashemite family of Jordan. In 1945, Iraq joined the United Nations and became a founding member of the Arab League.

A series of coups started in 1958 and lasted a decade until Saddam Hussein's predecessor re-emerged as President of Iraq. In 1979, Saddam Hussein was chosen to take over as President and Chairman of the Revolutionary Command.

Iraq has been engaged in war (with Iran 1980–88, the 1990 seizure of Kuwait and 1991 Gulf War, and the 2003 U.S.-led war to remove Saddam Hussein's regime) for the better part of the past two-and-one-half decades and its economy and its people have suffered greatly.

Kyrgyzstan

Capital: Bishkek
Area: 76,621 sq. mi.
    198,500 sq. km.
Population: 4,822,000
(2002 est.)
Largest City: Bishkek, 753,000
Languages: Kirghiz, Russian
Major Religions: Muslim, Russian Orthodox
Life Expectancy: 64 male, 73 female
Government: republic
Monetary Unit: som
Industry: small machinery, textiles, food-processing, shoes, cement, sawn logs, refrigerators, furniture, electric motors, gold, and rare earth metals
Agriculture: wool, tobacco, cotton, livestock (sheep, goats, cattle), vegetables, meat, grapes, fruits and berries, eggs, milk, potatoes
Minerals and Resources: hydroelectric potential, gold and rare earth metal, coal, oil, natural gas, nepheline, mercury, bismuth, lead, zinc

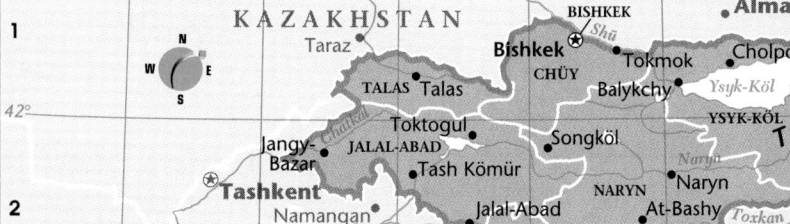

Kyrgyzstan is about the size of Great Britain. It is a member of the Commonwealth of Independent States, having become independent from the Soviet Union in 1991. It adopted a constitution in 1993. Kyrgyzstan is one of the smallest and poorest states in the former Soviet Union, but has been the most successful in reducing state controls over the economy and privatizing state industries. Its economy is heavily agricultural with an emphasis on livestock. Its people are Kyrgyz, Russian, Uzbek, Ukrainian and German and are predominantly Muslim.

Kazakhstan

Capital: Astana
Area: 1,048,878 sq. mi.
    2,717,300 sq. km.
Population: 16,742,000 (2002 est.)
Largest City: Almaty, 1,129,000
Languages: Kazakh, Russian
Major Religions: Muslim, Russian Orthodox, Protestant
Life Expectancy: 64 male, 73 female
Government: republic
Monetary Unit: tenge
Industry: extractive industries (oil, coal, iron ore, manganese, chromite, lead, zinc, copper, titanium, bauxite, gold, silver, phosphates, sulfur), iron and steel, nonferrous metal, tractors and other agricultural machinery, electric motors, construction materials
Agriculture: grain, mostly spring wheat; meat, cotton, wool
Minerals and Resources: coal, iron ore, manganese, chrome ore, nickel, cobalt, copper, molybdenum, lead, zinc, bauxite, gold, uranium

Kazakhstan is the second-largest republic in the former USSR, comprising a land area greater than that of Western Europe. The country's terrain is primarily an extensive flatland.

Kazakhstan is unique among the former Soviet republics in that it is the only one where the titular nationality accounted for a minority of the population; in recent years, however, the Kazakhstanis have come to outnumber the Russians slightly and there continue to be shifts in the population due to Kazakh resettlement from other states as well as the departure of many ethnic Europeans.

The government of Kazakhstan has committed itself to creating a market economy and has undertaken an ambitious program to privatize 60 to 70 percent of state property by the year 2000. The country possesses enormous untapped fossil-fuel reserves as well as abundant supplies of other minerals and metals.

Capital: Dushanbe
Area: 55,237 sq. mi.
143,100 sq. km.
Population: 6,720,000 (2002 est.)
Largest City: Dushanbe, 529,000
Languages: Tajik, Russian
Major Religions: Sunni Muslim, Shi'a Muslim
Life Expectancy: 66 male, 72 female
Government: republic
Monetary Unit: ruble
Industry: aluminum, zinc, lead, chemicals and fertilizers, cement, vegetable oil, metal-cutting machine tools, refrigerators and freezers
Agriculture: cotton, grain, fruits, grapes, vegetables, cattle, sheep, goats
Minerals and Resources: significant hydropower potential, some petroleum, uranium, mercury, brown coal, lead, zinc, antimony, tungsten

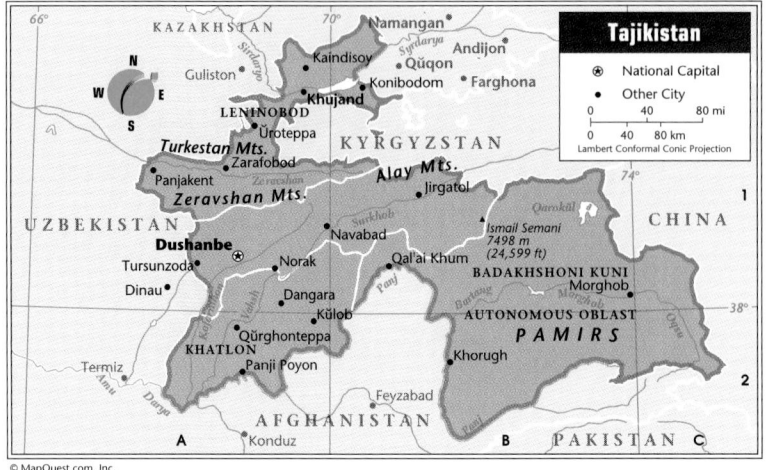

© MapQuest.com, Inc.

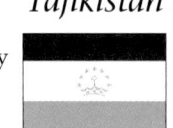

Tajikistan

Tajikistan gained independence from the Soviet Union in 1991 and adopted a new constitution in 1994. Since gaining its independence, Tajikistan has endured a civil war which is a deeply-rooted regional and clan-based conflict.

The population of Tajikistan is predominantly Sunni Muslim and is employed mainly in agriculture and forestry. Tajikistan had the next-to-lowest per capita GDP in the former USSR, the highest rate of population growth and an extremely low standard of living. The Tajik economy has further been weakened by the ongoing civil war which has caused it to lose subsidies and markets for its products, and by the lingering dominance of former Communist officials.

© MapQuest.com, Inc.

Turkmenistan is comprised mostly of sandy desert with dunes rising to mountains in the south and low mountains along the border with Iran. It became independent from the Soviet Union in 1991 but still has an authoritarian, ex-Communist regime.

The Turkmenistan government has taken a very cautious approach to economic restructuring. The Turkmen economy relies on nomadic cattle raising, intensive agriculture in irrigated oases and huge gas and oil resources. With half of Turkmenistan's irrigated land planted in cotton, it is the world's tenth largest cotton producer. It also has the world's fifth largest reserves of natural gas and significant oil reserves.

The Turkmen people are predominantly Muslim and have a tribal-based social structure.

Turkmenistan

Capital: Ashgabat
Area: 188,407 sq. mi.
488,100 sq. km.
Population: 4,689,000 (2002 est.)
Largest City: Ashgabat, 407,000
Languages: Turkmen, Russian, Uzbek
Major Religions: Muslim, Eastern Orthodox
Life Expectancy: 62 male, 69 female
Government: republic
Monetary Unit: manat
Industry: natural gas, oil, petroleum products, textiles, food processing
Agriculture: cotton, grain, animal husbandry
Minerals and Resources: petroleum, natural gas, coal, sulphur, salt

Uzbekistan

Uzbekistan is made up mostly of desert, interspersed with fertile oases. It became an independent republic in 1991 when the former Soviet Union broke up. It is one of the poorer former Soviet republics with 60% of its population living in overpopulated rural communities.

Since independence, the Uzbek government has sought to bolster the Soviet-style economy with subsidies and tight controls on prices and production. Economic reform in Uzbekistan is very slow to come and faces many obstacles; however, the country continues to be the world's third largest exporter of cotton and a major producer of gold and natural gas.

Capital: Tashkent
Area: 172,696 sq. mi.
447,400 sq. km.
Population: 25,563,000 (2002 est.)
Largest City: Tashkent, 2,143,000
Languages: Uzbek, Russian, Tajik
Major Religions: Muslim, Eastern Orthodox
Life Expectancy: 66 male, 72 female
Government: republic
Monetary Uint: som
Industry: textiles, food processing, machine building, metallurgy, natural gas
Agriculture: cotton, vegetables, fruits, grain, livestock
Minerals and Resources: natural gas, petroleum, coal, gold, uranium, silver, copper, lead and zinc, tungsten, molybdenum

© MapQuest.com, Inc.

Capital: Ankara
Area: 301,304 sq. mi.
 780,580 sq. km.
Population: 67,309,000 (2002 est.)
Largest City: İstanbul, 8,803,000
Languages: Turkish, Kurdish, Arabic
Major Religions: Muslim, Christian, Jewish
Life Expectancy: 69 male, 74 female
Government: republican parliamentary democracy
Monetary Unit: Turkish lira
Industry: textiles, food processing, mining (coal, chromite, copper, boron), steel, petroleum, construction, lumber, paper
Agriculture: tobacco, cotton, grain, olives, sugar beets, pulses, citrus fruit, variety of animal products
Minerals and Resources: antimony, coal, chromium, mercury, copper, borate, sulphur, iron ore

Turkey

The Republic of Turkey was founded in 1923 by a Turkish World War I hero, Mustafa Kemal (later known as "Ataturk") after the collapse of the 600-year-old Ottoman Empire. Social, political, linguistic and economic reforms and attitudes introduced by Ataturk before his death in 1938 continue to form the ideological base of modern Turkey.

Turkey is an eclectic blend of eastern and western cultures. Early efforts to Westernize Turkish society in the 1920s resulted in the arts, literature, drama and music flourishing under state support. Although 98% of the Turkish population is Sunni Muslim, the country has been officially secular since it became a republic. Turkey's primary political, economic and security ties are with the West and its free market orientation is dynamic.

Blue Mosque, Istanbul

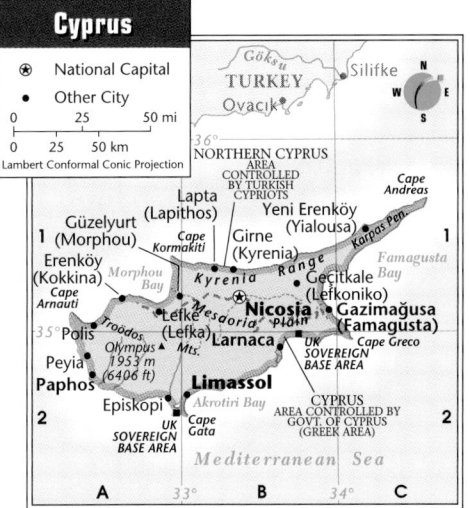

Cyprus

Capital: Nicosia
Area: 3,571 sq. mi.
 9,250 sq. km.
Population: 767,000 (2002 est.)
Largest City: Nicosia, 273,000
Languages: Greek, Turkish, English
Major Religions: Greek Orthodox, Muslim, Maronite, Armenian Apostolic
Life Expectancy: 74 male, 79 female
Government: republic
Monetary Unit: Cypriot pound
Industry: food, beverages, textiles, chemicals, metal products, tourism, wood products
Agriculture: potatoes, vegetables, barley, grapes, olives, citrus fruits
Minerals and Resources: copper, pyrites, asbestos, gypsum, timber, salt, marble, clay earth pigment

Cyprus, an island nation, is one of the oldest continuously inhabited countries. Although occupied and ruled by a succession of foreign powers for centuries, Cyprus' population was almost exclusively Greek Orthodox until the island was invaded and occupied by Ottoman Turks from 1571 to 1878, then by the British. During this period, a Turkish-speaking, Muslim minority grew alongside the Greek majority, setting the stage for an ongoing conflict between Greek Cypriots and Turkish Cypriots.

Four years of guerrilla war led by Greek Cypriots resulted in Cyprus' independence in 1959. An invasion by Turkey in 1974 established the self-proclaimed Turkish Republic of Northern Cyprus, which governs the Turkish Cypriots, a fifth of the island's population. However, the Republic of Cyprus is the officially recognized government. A UN peacekeeping force separates the two sides, and the process of establishing a unified country containing two states continues.

© MapQuest.com, Inc.

Syria

Capital: Damascus
Area: 71,480 sq. mi.
185,180 sq. km.
Population: 17,156,000 (2002 est.)
Largest City: Halab, 1,583,000
Languages: Arabic, Kurdish, Armenian, Aramaic, Circassian
Major Religions: Sunni Muslim, Alawite, Druze, Christian, Jewish
Life Expectancy: 66 male, 68 female
Government: republic under leftwing military regime
Monetary Unit: Syrian pound
Industry: textiles, food processing, beverages, tobacco, phosphate rock mining, petroleum
Agriculture: wheat, barley, cotton, lentils, chickpeas, beef, lamb, eggs, poultry, milk
Minerals and Resources: petroleum, phosphates, chrome and manganese ores, asphalt, iron ore, rock salt, marble, gypsum

Archaeology has shown that Syria was the center of one of the most ancient civilizations on earth. Damascus, settled about 2500 B.C., is one of the oldest continuously inhabited cities in the world and the excavated city of Ebla, discovered in 1975, was the home to a great Semitic empire that stretched from the Red Sea north to Turkey and east to Mesopotamia (now Iraq).

Since its independence in 1946, Syria has undergone a series of coups and political turmoil which culminated in 1970 with the bloodless military coup that established Syria's current leader, President Hafiz al-Asad. Asad's Ba'ath party emphasizes socialism and secular Arabism and his regime is a military one.

Syria's relations with Western nations were particularly strained in the past decade because of Syrian support for groups involved in international terrorism.

Lebanon

Capital: Beirut
Area: 4,014 sq. mi.
10,400 sq. km.
Population: 3,678,000 (2002 est.)
Largest City: Beirut, 475,000
Languages: Arabic, French, Armenian, English
Major Religions: Muslim, Christian
Life Expectancy: 67 male, 72 female
Government: republic
Monetary Unit: Lebanese pound
Industry: banking, food processing, textiles, cement, oil refining, chemicals, jewelry, some metal fabricating
Agriculture: citrus fruits, vegetables, potatoes, olives, tobacco, hemp (hashish), sheep, goats
Minerals and Resources: limestone, iron ore, salt, water-surplus state in a water-deficit region

The civil war that devastated Lebanon from 1975–1990 has given way to tentative peace and efforts to rebuild a battered economy. Although Lebanon is a parliamentary democracy and the people have a constitutional right to change their government, this right could not be exercised during the civil war. Balancing Christian and Muslim influences in the government has been at the heart of Lebanese politics since independence in 1943.

Lebanon has a higher proportion of skilled labor than any other Arab country and its urban population in Beirut and Tripoli is noted for its commercial enterprise. Many

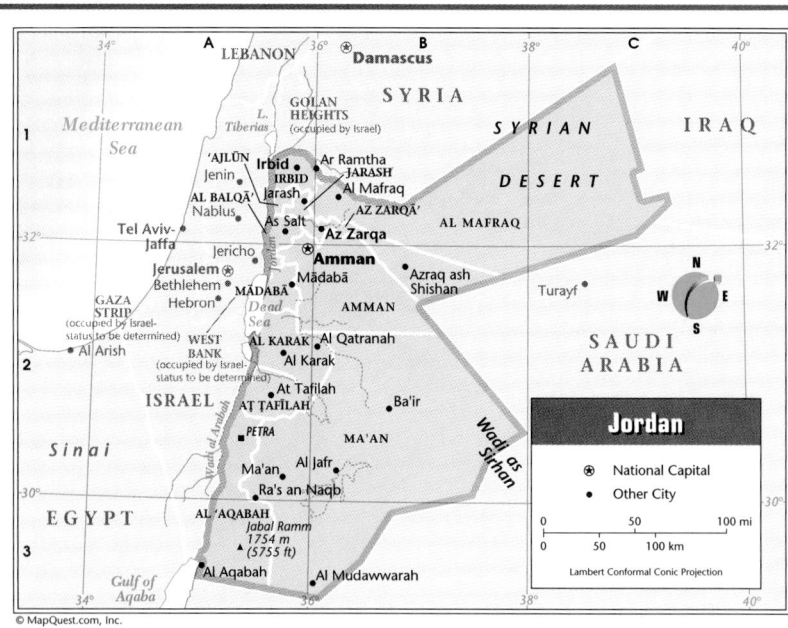

Dead Sea Marker, the Lowest Spot on Earth

Lebanese still derive their living from agriculture. Lebanon served historically as a haven for Arab capital and as a Middle East transit point.

Jordan

Jordan is a constitutional monarchy that gained its independence from Great Britain in 1946 through a League of Nations mandate. King Hussein has ruled Jordan since 1953 and is a strong symbol of unity and stability, as well as a proponent of democratization.

Jordan has consistently followed a pro-Western foreign policy and has traditionally had close relations with the United Kingdom and the United States. Jordan's Palestinian community's support for Iraq during the Gulf War only temporarily damaged its standing with the Western countries. In 1994 Jordan signed a non-belligerency agreement with Israel and participates in multilateral peace talks.

Capital: Amman
Area: 34,436 sq. mi.
89,213 sq. km.
Population: 5,307,000 (2002 est.)
Largest City: Amman, 1,147,000
Languages: Arabic, English
Major Religions: Sunni Muslim, Christian
Life Expectancy: 70 male, 74 female
Government: constitutional monarchy
Monetary Unit: Jordanian dinar
Industry: phosphate mining, petroleum refining, cement, potash, light manufacturing
Agriculture: wheat, barley, citrus fruit, tomatoes, melons, olives, sheep, goats, poultry
Minerals and Resources: phosphates, potash, shale oil

Israel was created in 1948 after more than 50 years of efforts by Zionist leaders to establish a sovereign nation as a homeland for the Jews. Since then, Israel's population has come from more than 100 countries on five continents and thus it is rich in cultural diversity and artistic creativity.

In its almost 50-year history, Israel has fought five wars against Arab forces and is seeking to end these hostilities via cease-fires and peace settlements. The Israeli government has also made it a priority to gain wide acceptance as a sovereign state with an important international role. Currently about 70% of all UN member countries have diplomatic relations with Israel.

An influx of Jewish immigrants from the former Soviet Union after 1990 increased unemployment, intensified housing problems and strained the government budget; however, with this large influx of immigrants came valuable scientific and professional expertise to be tapped.

Massive Gathering at the Western Wall, Jerusalem

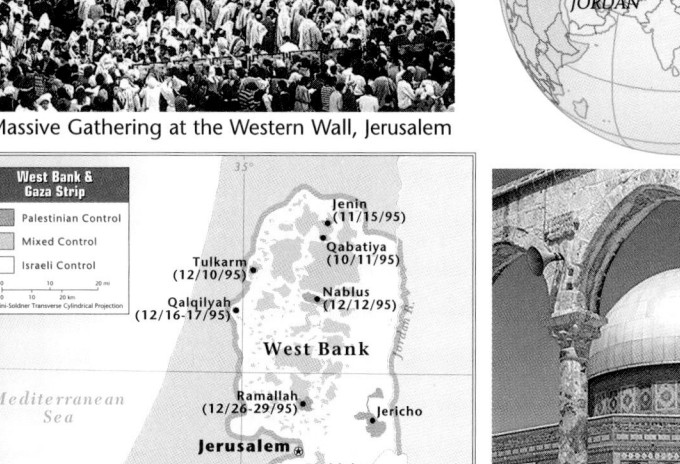

Dome of the Rock atop Temple Mount, Old Jerusalem

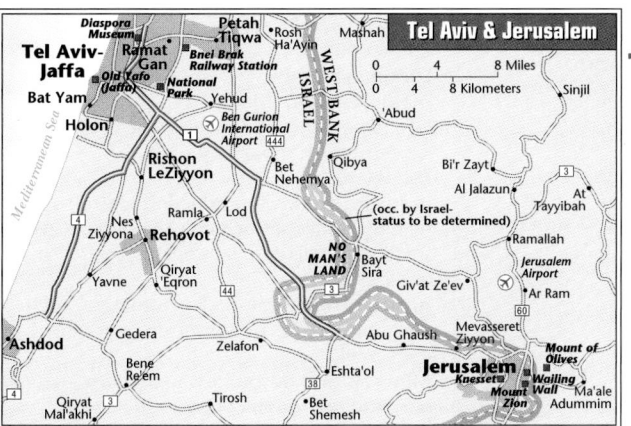

West Bank
Area: 2,262 sq. mi.
5,860 sq. km.
Languages: Arabic, Hebrew, English
Population: 2,164,000 (2002 est.)
Major Religions: Muslim, Jewish, Christian
Life Expectancy: 70 male, 73 female
Government: Under the Israeli-PLO Declaration of Principles on Interim Self-Government Arrangements. Final status is to be determined through direct negotiations within five years.
Monetary Unit: new Israeli shekel; Jordanian dinar
Industry: generally small family businesses that produce cement, textiles, soap, olive-wood carvings, and mother-of-pearl souvenirs; the Israelis have established some small-scale modern industries in the settlements and industrial centers
Agriculture: olives, citrus and other fruits; vegetables, beef, and dairy products
Minerals and Resources: negligible

Gaza Strip
Area: 139 sq. mi.
360 sq. km.
Population: 1,226,000 (2002 est.)
Languages: Arabic, Hebrew, English
Major Religions: Muslim, Christian, Jewish
Life Expectancy: 70 male, 73 female
Government: Under the Israeli-PLO Declaration of Principles on Interim Self-Government Arrangements. Final status is to be determined through direct negotiations within five years.
Monetary Unit: new Israeli shekel
Industry: generally small family businesses that produce textiles, soap, olive-wood carvings, and mother-of-pearl souvenirs; the Israelis have established some small-scale modern industries in an industrial center
Agriculture: olives, citrus and other fruits; vegetables, beef and dairy products
Minerals and Resources: negligible

Israel

Capital: Jerusalem
Area: 8,017 sq. mi.
20,770 sq. km.
Population: 6,030,000 (2002 est.)
Largest City: Jerusalem, 628,000
Languages: Hebrew, Arabic, English
Major Religions: Judaism, Islam, Christian, Druze
Life Expectancy: 76 male, 80 female
Government: republic
International disputes: West Bank and Gaza Strip are Israeli occupied with interim status subject to Israeli/Palestinian negotiations - final status to be determined
Monetary Unit: new Israeli shekel
Industry: food processing, diamond cutting and polishing, textiles and apparel, chemicals, metal products, military equipment, transport equipment, electrical equipment, miscellaneous machinery, potash mining, high-technology electronics, tourism
Agriculture: citrus and other fruits, vegetables, cotton, beef, poultry, dairy products
Minerals and Resources: copper, phosphates, bromide, potash, clay, sand, sulfur, asphalt, manganese, small amounts of natural gas and crude oil

Kuwait

- ⊛ National Capital
- • Other City

0   25   50 mi

0   25   50 km

Lambert Conformal Conic Projection

© MapQuest.com, Inc.

Kuwait

Capital: Kuwait
Area: 6,932 sq. mi.
   17,820 sq. km.
Population: 2,112,000
(2002 est.)
Largest City: Kuwait, 193,000
Languages: Arabic, English
Major Religions: Muslim, Christian, Hindu, Parsi
Life Expectancy: 73 male, 78 female
Government: nominal constitutional monarchy
Monetary Unit: Kuwaiti dinar
Industry: petroleum, petrochemicals, desalination, food processing, building materials, salt, construction
Agriculture: practically none, fishing
Minerals and Resources: petroleum, fish, shrimp, natural gas

The state of Kuwait is a constitutional monarchy and has been ruled by the Sabah family since 1751. The people residing in Kuwait are primarily Arab in origin, but fewer than half of them are from the Arabian Peninsula. Many Arabs from nearby states have taken up residence in Kuwait because of the prosperity that oil production after the 1940s brought.

Kuwait is a small country with huge oil reserves and whose economy has traditionally been dominated by the state and its oil industry. Thanks in large part to its oil wealth, Kuwait was transformed during the 1960s and 1970s into a highly developed welfare state with a free market economy. Social benefits for Kuwaiti citizens are substantial. The Iraqi invasion and occupation of Kuwait in 1990 ravaged the petroleum industry, but the Kuwaiti government has worked hard to restore it.

Capital: Abu Dhabi
Area: 29,401 sq. mi.
   75,581 sq. km.
Population: 2,446,000 (2002 est.)
Largest City: Dubai, 669,000
Languages: Arabic, Persian, English, Hindi, Urdu
Major Religions: Muslim, Christian, Hindu
Life Expectancy: 70 male, 75 female
Government: federation
Monetary Unit: Emirian dirham
Industry: petroleum, fishing, petrochemicals, construction materials, some boat building, handicrafts, pearling
Agriculture: dates, vegetables, watermelons, poultry, eggs, dairy, fish
Minerals and Resources: petroleum, natural gas

United Arab Emirates

- ⊛ National Capital
- • Other City

0   75   150 mi

0   75   150 km

Lambert Conformal Conic Projection

© MapQuest.com, Inc.

U.A.E.

The United Arab Emirates was formed from the group of tribally-organized Arabian Peninsula sheikhdoms along the southern coast of the Persian Gulf and the northwestern coast of the Gulf of Oman. After years of treaty agreements with Great Britain, it became independent in 1971. It is a loose federation of seven emirates, each with its own ruler who has substantial autonomy.

Since 1973, petroleum has dominated the UAE economy, giving it one of the highest living standards in the world.

Saudi Arabia is known as the birthplace of Islam. All aspects of life in Saudi Arabia adhere to a strict interpretation of Islamic religious law and its government, a monarchy, rules according to Islamic law.

Until the 1960s, most of Saudi Arabia's populace was nomadic or semi-nomadic, but due to rapid economic and urban growth, today more than 95% of the population is settled. Oil was discovered by American geologists in Saudi Arabia in the 1930s and large-scale oil production began after World War II. This transformed Saudi Arabia into one of the fastest-growing nations in the world during the 1970s. A worldwide oil glut that developed in the mid 1980s slowed Saudi Arabia's economy and forced the government to restrain public spending and encourage non-oil exports.

The Saudis often help mediate regional crises and actively support the Israeli-Palestinian peace negotiations.

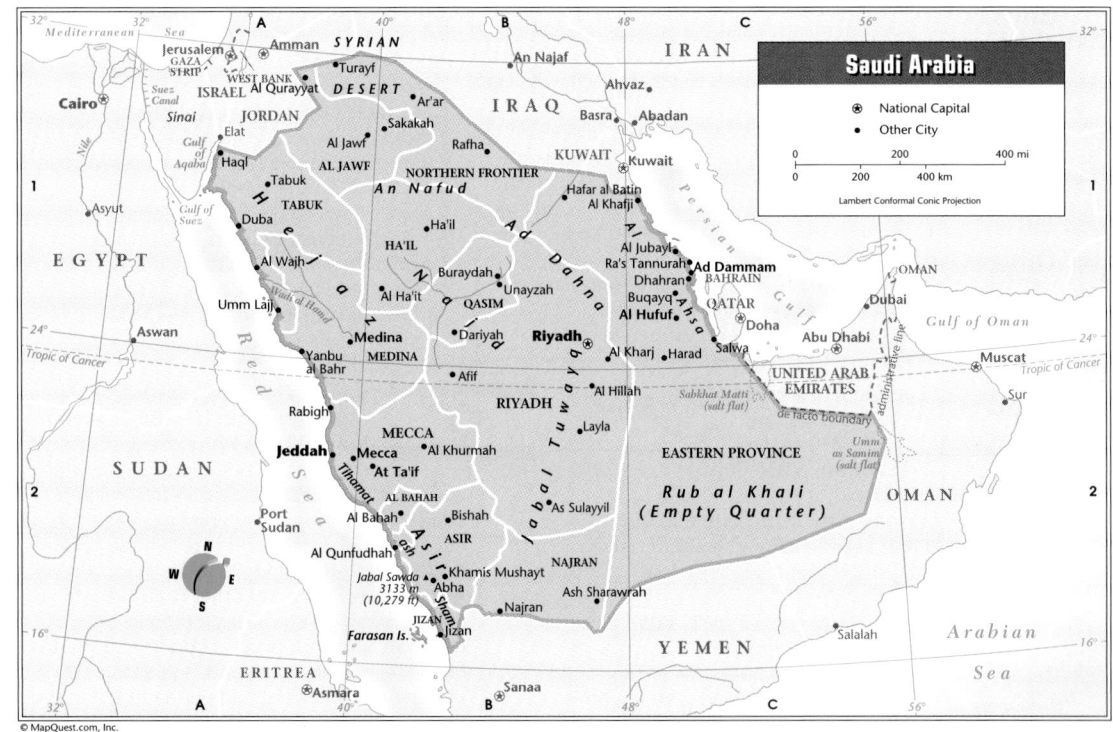

Saudi Arabia

- ⊛ National Capital
- • Other City

0   200   400 mi

0   200   400 km

Lambert Conformal Conic Projection

© MapQuest.com, Inc.

Saudi Arabia

Capital: Riyadh
Area: 762,666 sq. mi.
   1,960,582 sq. km.
Population: 23,513,000
(2002 est.)
Largest City: Riyadh, 2,776,000
Language: Arabic
Major Religion: Muslim
Life Expectancy: 67 male, 70 female
Government: monarchy
Monetary Unit: Saudi riyal
Industry: crude oil production, petroleum refining, basic petrochemicals, cement, two small steel-rolling mills, construction, fertilizer, plastics
Agriculture: wheat, barley, tomatoes, melons, dates, citrus fruit, mutton, chickens, eggs, milk
Minerals and Resources: petroleum, natural gas, iron ore, gold, copper

Bahrain

Capital: Manama
Area: 241 sq. mi.
  620 sq. km.
Population: 656,000 (2002 est.)
Largest City: Manama, 140,000
Languages: Arabic, English, Farsi, Urdu
Major Religion: Muslim
Life Expectancy: 71 male, 76 female
Government: traditional monarchy
Monetary Unit: Bahraini dinar
Industry: petroleum processing and refining, aluminum smelting, offshore banking, ship repairing
Agriculture: fishing, fruit, vegetables, poultry, dairy products, shrimp, fish
Minerals and Resources: oil, natural gas, fish

Bahrain consists of a group of islands in the Persian Gulf, the largest of which is Bahrain. It is a Muslim country with a constitutional emirate. After being involved in treaty agreements with Great Britain from 1905–1971, Bahrain became an independent state.

Most of Bahrain's population is concentrated in its two principal cities, Manama and Al Muharraq. In addition to its important oil industry, Bahrain is home to many multinational firms, thanks to its highly developed transport and communication facilities.

Bahrain and Qatar
- ⊛ National Capital
- • Other City
- 0   10   20 mi
- 0   10   20 km
Transverse Mercator Projection
© MapQuest.com, Inc.

Qatar

Capital: Doha
Area: 4,279 sq. mi.
  11,000 sq. km.
Population: 793,000 (2002 est.)
Largest City: Doha, 264,000
Languages: Arabic, English
Major Religion: Muslim
Life Expectancy: 70 male, 76 female
Government: traditional monarchy
Monetary Unit: Qatari riyal
Industry: crude oil production and refining, fertilizers, petrochemicals, steel (rolls reinforcing bars for concrete construction), cement
Agriculture: farming and grazing on small scale, commercial fishing
Minerals and Resources: petroleum, natural gas, fish

Qatar is a small Muslim country on the Arabian Peninsula. For centuries, pearling, fishing and trade were the main sources of income but when oil was discovered and oil production began just after World War II, the Qatari economy was transformed.

During the 1950s and 1960s, oil revenues brought prosperity, rapid immigration, and substantial social progress to Qatar. Foreign workers with temporary residence status make up about 75% of the Qatari population.

Oman

Capital: Muscat
Area: 82,647 sq. mi.
  212,460 sq. km.
Population: 2,713,000 (2002 est.)
Largest City: Muscat, 41,000
Languages: Arabic, English, Baluchi, Urdu, Indian dialects
Major Religions: Muslim, Hindu
Life Expectancy: 68 male, 72 female
Government: monarchy
Monetary Unit: Omani rial
Industry: crude oil production and refining, natural gas production, construction, cement, copper
Agriculture: fishing, dates, limes, bananas, alfalfa, vegetables, camels, cattle
Minerals and Resources: petroleum, copper, asbestos, some marble, limestone, chromium, gypsum, natural gas

Except for a brief period of Persian rule, the Omanis have remained independent since 1650. Oman is a monarchy with a sultan who rules according to a mixture of Islamic and English law.

Under its previous ruler, Oman had limited contacts with the outside world, but since Sultan Qaboos assumed power in 1970, the country has pursued a moderate foreign policy and has established close ties to its neighbors and encouraged foreign investment and diplomacy. It established a special treaty relationship with the United Kingdom which permits the UK close involvement in Oman's civil and military affairs.

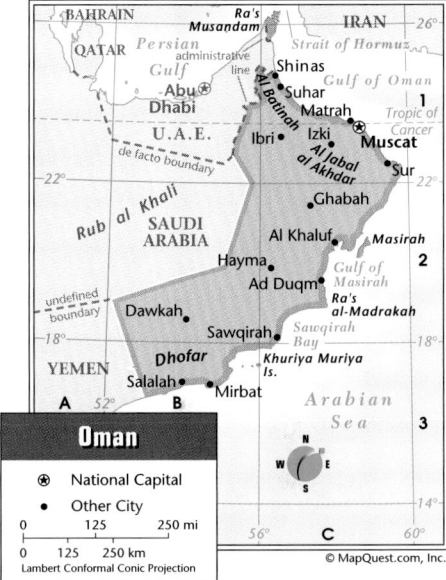

Oman
- ⊛ National Capital
- • Other City
- 0   125   250 mi
- 0   125   250 km
Lambert Conformal Conic Projection
© MapQuest.com, Inc.

Mosque in Yemen

Yemen

Capital: Sanaa
Area: 205,380 sq. mi.
  527,970 sq. km.
Population: 18,701,000 (2002 est.)
Largest City: Sanaa, 927,000
Language: Arabic
Major Religions: Muslim, Jewish, Christian, Hindu
Life Expectancy: 62 male, 64 female
Government: republic
Monetary Unit: Yemeni rial
Industry: crude oil production and petroleum refining, cotton textiles and leather goods, food processing, handicrafts, aluminum, cement
Agriculture: grain, fruits, vegetables, qat, coffee, cotton, dairy, poultry, meat, fish
Minerals and Resources: petroleum, fish, rock salt, marble, coal, gold, lead, nickel, and copper, fertile soil in west

In 1990 the Republic of Yemen was established with the unification of former North and South Yemen. After years of civil war and political instability, the two Yemens sought to resolve their differences and fuse their governments and economies. Whereas the northern city of Sanaa is the political capital, the southern city of Aden, with its refinery and port facilities, is the economic and commercial capital.

Prior to unification, the two Yemens pursued very different external relations: the North was isolated and aided by the USSR and China, and the South was closely allied with and heavily dependent on Egypt.

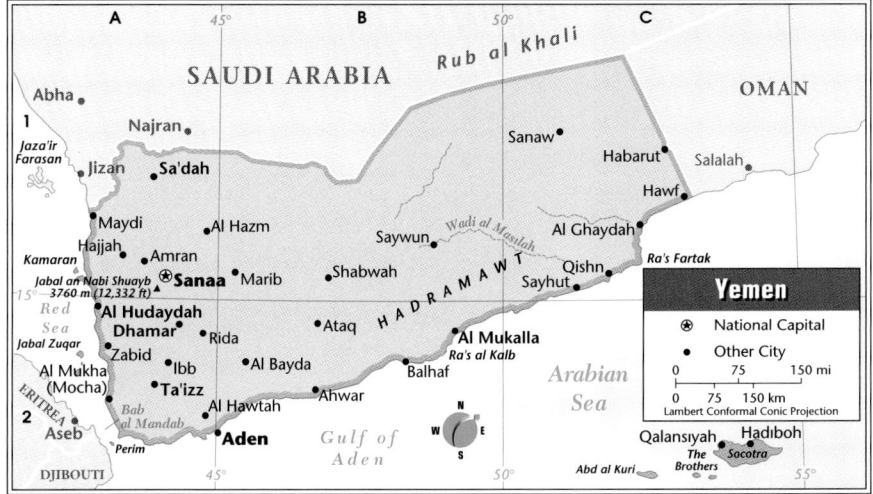

Yemen
- ⊛ National Capital
- • Other City
- 0   75   150 mi
- 0   75   150 km
Lambert Conformal Conic Projection
© MapQuest.com, Inc.

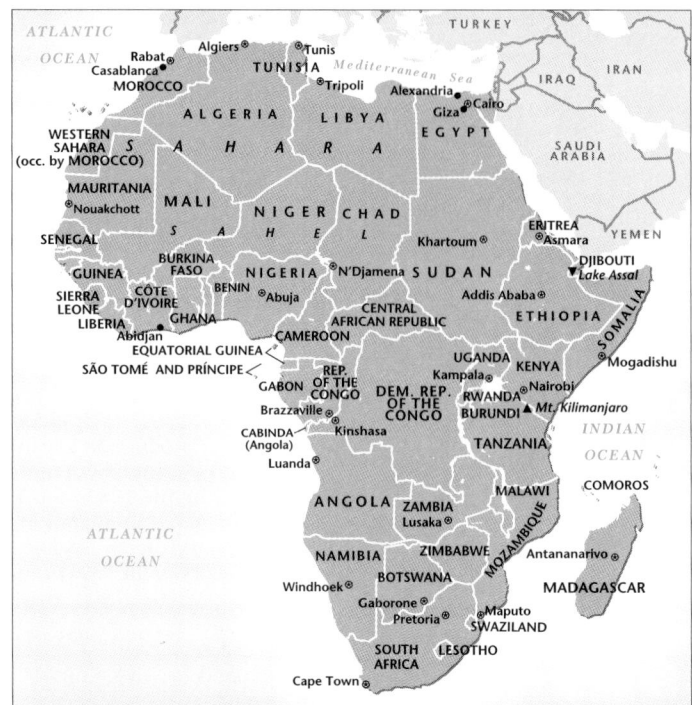

Population: 834,415,000 (2002)
Area: 11,677,239 sq. mi.
30,244,049 sq. km.
Highest Point: Mt. Kilimanjaro
19,340 ft. (5,899 m.)
Lowest Point: Lake Assal, Djibouti
512 ft. (156 m.)
below sea level
Largest Urban Areas:
Lagos, Nigeria
Cairo, Egypt
Kinshasa, Dem. Rep. Congo
Alexandria, Egypt
Casablanca, Morocco
Abidjan, Côte d'Ivoire
Maputo, Mozambique
Countries: 54

Above: Baobab Trees in Kenya; **Right:** Landscape near Lake Turkana, Kenya; **Below:** Ancient Pyramids near Cairo, Egypt.

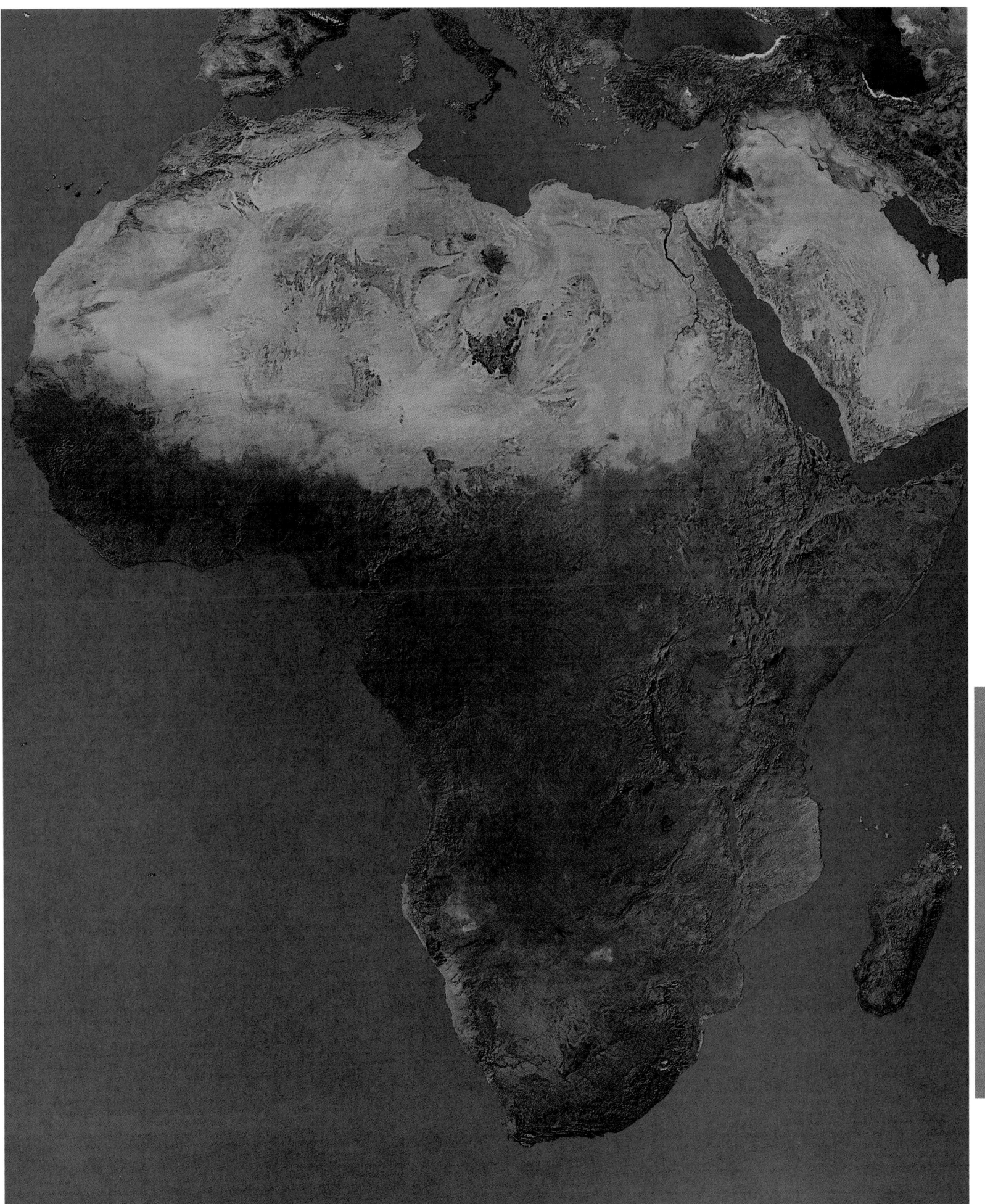

Major Metropolitan Areas

Algeria
Algiers	1,904,000 (metro)
Oran	745,000
Constantine	564,000

Angola
Luanda	1,822,000

Benin
Cotonou	537,000
Porto-Novo	179,000

Botswana
Gaborone	186,000

Burkina Faso
Ouagadougou	634,000

Burundi
Bujumbura	234,000

Cameroon
Douala	810,000
Yaoundé	649,000

Cape Verde
Praia	103,000

Central African Republic
Bangui	452,000

Chad
N'Djamena	547,000

Comoros
Moroni	30,000

Congo, Democratic Republic of the
Kinshasa	4,657,000
Lubumbashi	565,000

Congo, Republic of the
Brazzaville	596,000

Côte d'Ivoire
Abidjan	1,929,000
Yamoussoukro	107,000

Djibouti
Djibouti	62,000

Egypt
Cairo	6,801,000
Alexandria	3,339,000
Giza	2,222,000

Equatorial Guinea
Malabo	30,000

Eritrea
Asmara	358,000

Ethiopia
Addis Ababa	2,424,000

Gabon
Libreville	420,000

The Gambia
Banjul	271,000

Ghana
Accra	1,155,000

Guinea
Conakry	705,000

Guinea-Bissau
Bissau	109,000

Kenya
Nairobi	2,143,000
Mombasa	465,000

Lesotho
Maseru	138,000

Liberia
Monrovia	421,000

Libya
Tripoli	1,500,000

Madagascar
Antananarivo	1,103,000

Malawi
Blantyre	502,000
Lilongwe	440,000

Mali
Bamako	1,179,000

Mauritania
Nouakchott	612,000

Mauritius
Port Louis	128,000

Morocco
Casablanca	2,943,000
Rabat	1,220,000
Marrakesh	602,000

Mozambique
Maputo	989,000

Namibia
Windhoek	147,000

Niger
Niamey	397,000

Nigeria
Lagos	5,195,000
Kano	2,167,000
Ibadan	1,835,000

Rwanda
Kigali	234,000

São Tomé & Príncipe
São Tomé	6,000

Senegal
Dakar	1,977,000

Seychelles
Victoria	25,000

Sierra Leone
Freetown	470,000

Somalia
Mogadishu	230,000

South Africa
Durban	2,992,000
Cape Town	2,898,000
Johannesburg	2,885,000
Pretoria	2,086,000
Port Elizabeth	1,312,000

Sudan
Omdurman	1,271,000
Khartoum	947,000

Swaziland
Mbabane	38,000

Tanzania
Dar es Salaam	1,361,000

Togo
Lomé	450,000

Tunisia
Tunis	674,000

Uganda
Kampala	1,209,000

Western Sahara
el-Aaiún	90,000

Zambia
Lusaka	1,270,000

Zimbabwe
Harare	1,189,000

International comparability of population data is limited by varying census methods. Where metropolitan population is unavailable, core city population is shown.

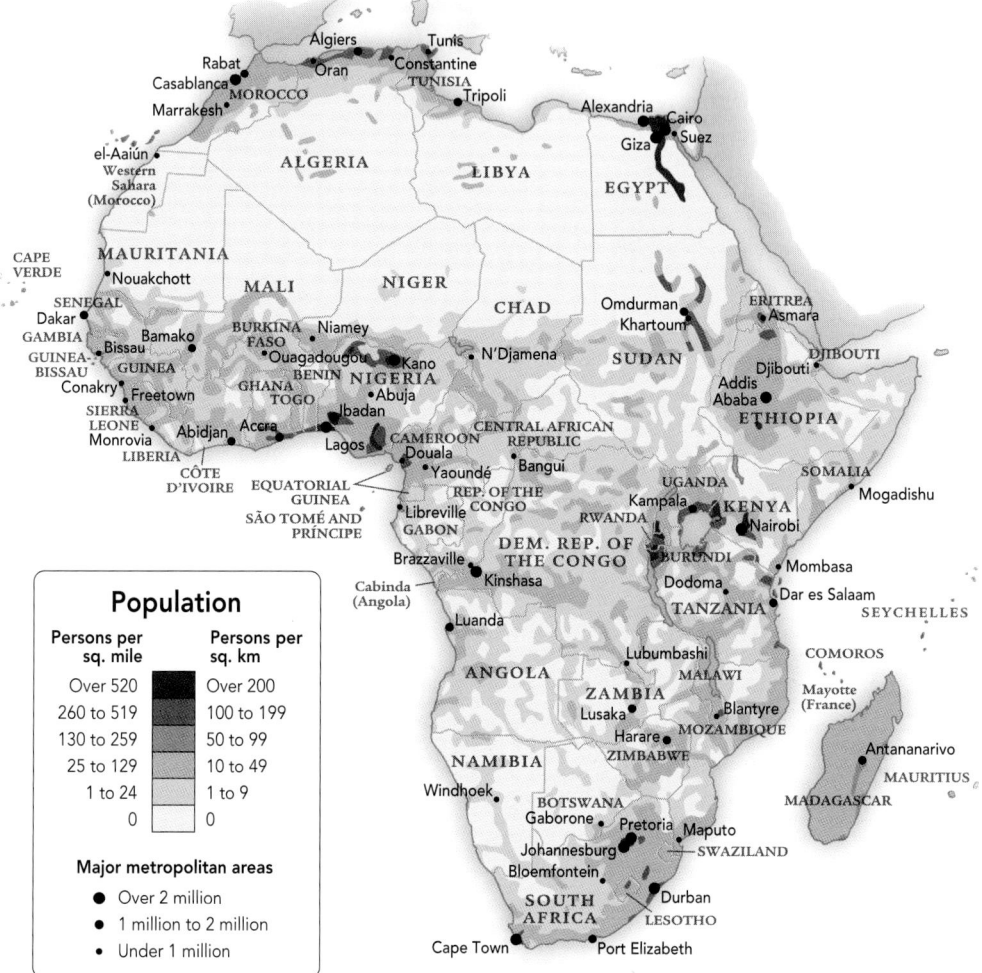

Population

Persons per sq. mile	Persons per sq. km
Over 520	Over 200
260 to 519	100 to 199
130 to 259	50 to 99
25 to 129	10 to 49
1 to 24	1 to 9
0	0

Major metropolitan areas
- Over 2 million
- 1 million to 2 million
- Under 1 million

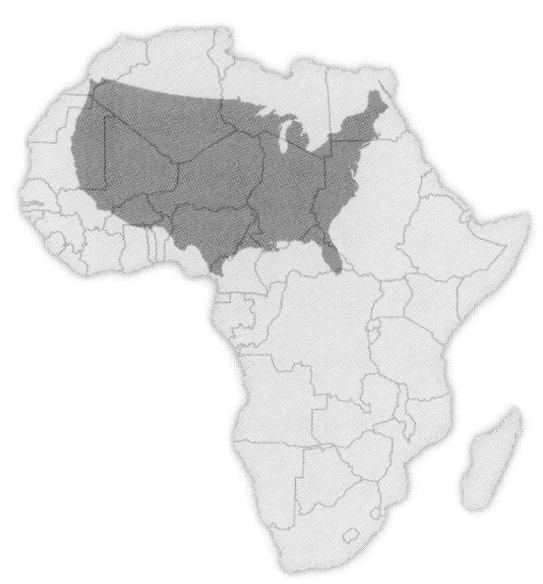

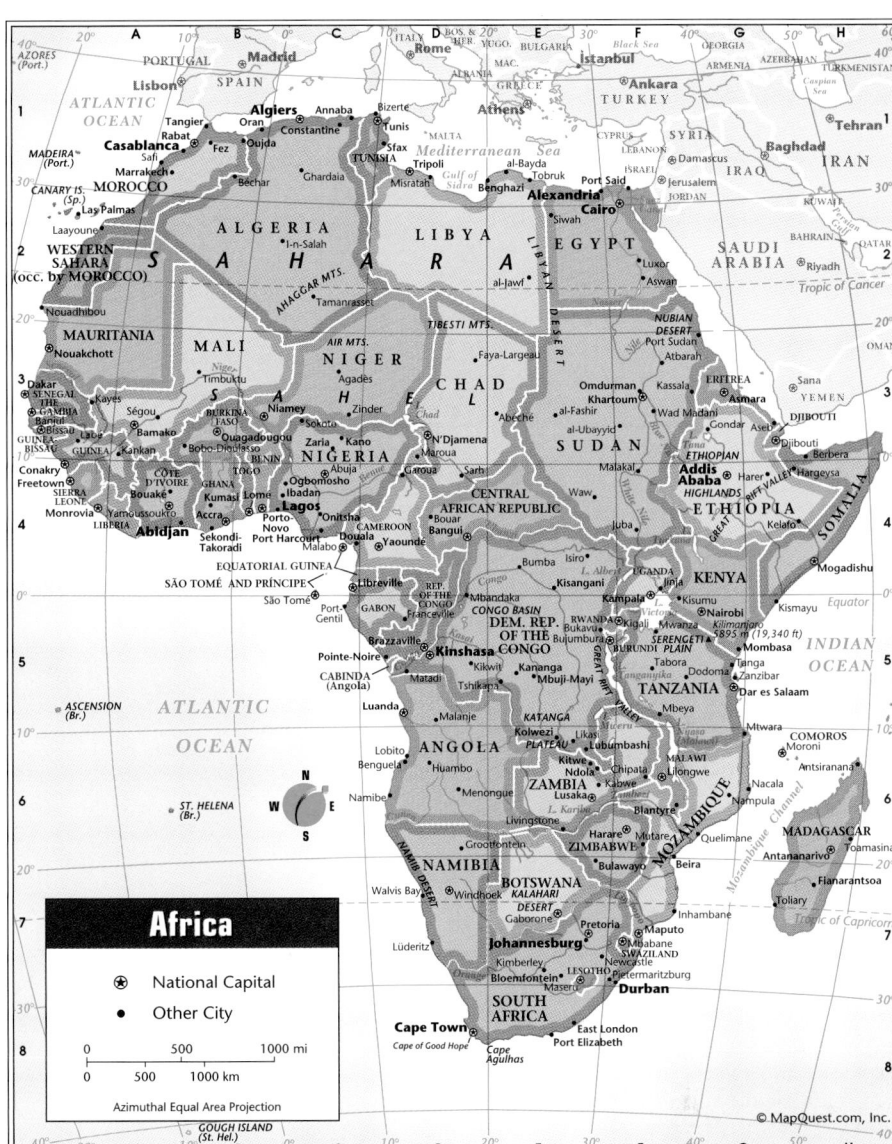

Africa

⊛ National Capital

• Other City

0 — 500 — 1000 mi

0 — 500 — 1000 km

Azimuthal Equal Area Projection

© MapQuest.com, Inc.

Estimated 2002 Population (in millions)

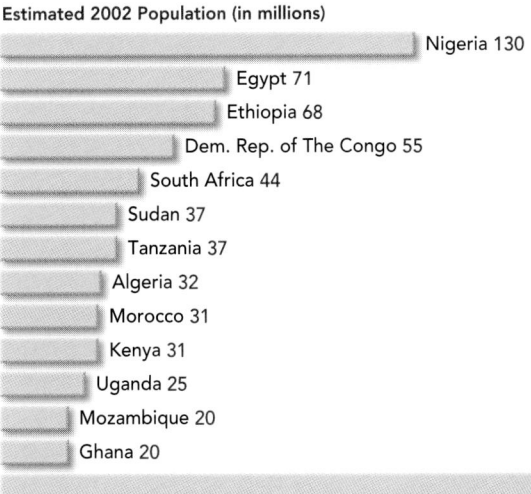

Nigeria 130
Egypt 71
Ethiopia 68
Dem. Rep. of The Congo 55
South Africa 44
Sudan 37
Tanzania 37
Algeria 32
Morocco 31
Kenya 31
Uganda 25
Mozambique 20
Ghana 20
All other countries 230

Source: U.S. Census Bureau

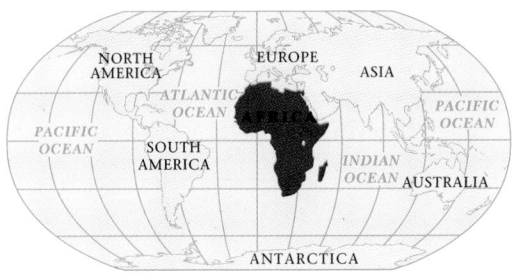

The dense, tropical rain forest surrounding the Equator is offset by the contrastingly sparse vegetation on the rest of the continent. Vast areas consist of grassland and scrub vegetation with trees only occasionally dotting the landscape. Evergreen and mixed forests of more temperate climates are limited to the Mediterranean areas of Morocco and Algeria, the Ethiopian Highlands, and Kenya.

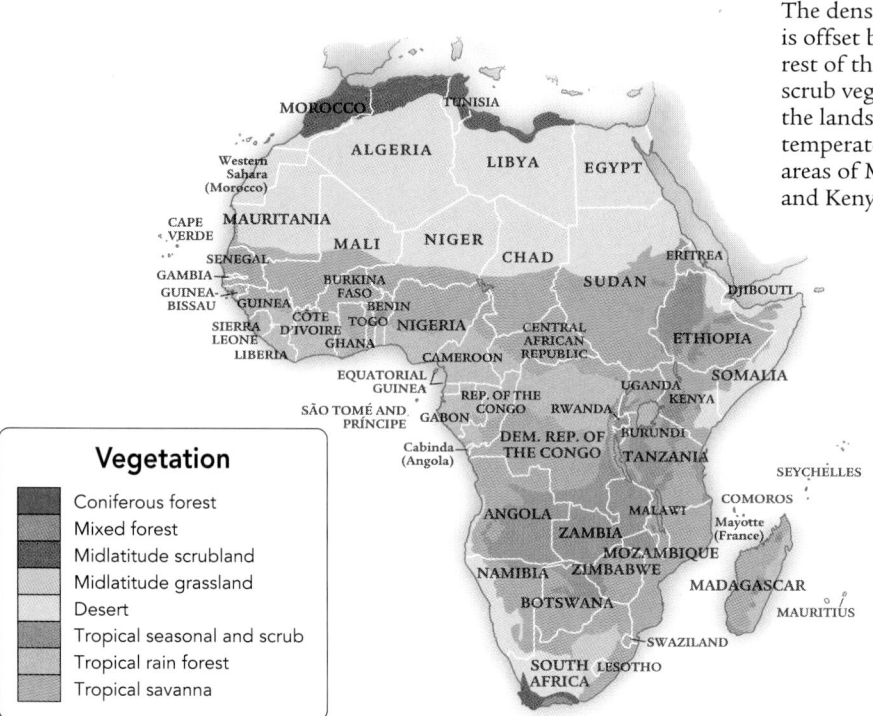

Vegetation

- Coniferous forest
- Mixed forest
- Midlatitude scrubland
- Midlatitude grassland
- Desert
- Tropical seasonal and scrub
- Tropical rain forest
- Tropical savanna

Agriculture supplies the livelihood for the vast majority of Africans. Agricultural exports include coffee, cocoa beans, peanuts, palm oil, and spices. These important export crops are mainly cultivated on plantations and large farms. Areas of subsistence farming supply the needs of local communities.

Unfortunately, poor soils and unfavorable climate conditions, as well as political unrest and unstable economies, all have an adverse impact on agricultural activity and therefore the standard of living.

Minerals account for more then one half of Africa's exports. Oil, diamonds, gold, cobalt, and several other minerals are leading exports. However, important mineral deposits are limited to a handful of countries.

Manufacturing has been slow to develop on the continent. Lack of money and skilled labor are the main deterrents.

Land Use and Resources

Predominant land use

- Commercial agriculture
- Livestock ranching
- Subsistence agriculture
- Nomadic herding
- Primarily forestland
- Limited agricultural activity

Major resources

- Coal
- Natural gas
- Oil
- Au Gold
- Fe Iron ore
- Pt Platinum
- U Uranium
- Al Bauxite
- Diamonds
- Other minerals
- Fishing
- ● Major manufacturing and trade centers

Climate Graphs

Average daily temperature range (in °F)
Average monthly precipitation (in inches)

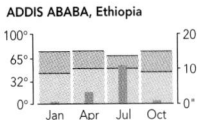
ADDIS ABABA, Ethiopia

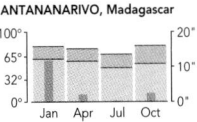
ANTANANARIVO, Madagascar

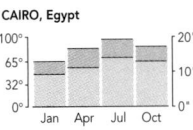
CAIRO, Egypt

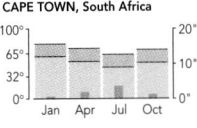
CAPE TOWN, South Africa

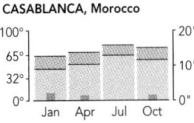
CASABLANCA, Morocco

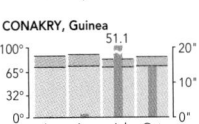
CONAKRY, Guinea

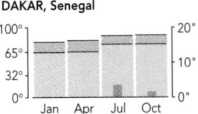
DAKAR, Senegal

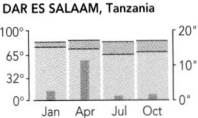
DAR ES SALAAM, Tanzania

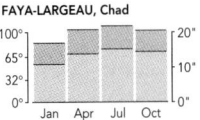
FAYA-LARGEAU, Chad

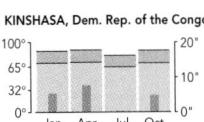
KINSHASA, Dem. Rep. of the Congo

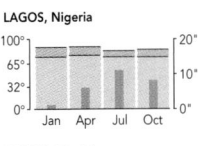
LAGOS, Nigeria

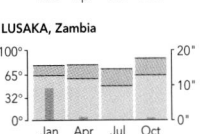
LUSAKA, Zambia

The climate of Africa is clearly a study in geographic contrasts. Perpetually wet and tropical areas surrounding the Equator quickly acquire seasonal variety as you move north and south. Roaming even farther leads to the vast, hot and arid zones of northern and southern Africa. The influence of neighboring water bodies is limited to small regions of northern Africa, namely Morocco, Algeria, and Libya, where the mild currents of the Mediterranean Sea temper the climate, and eastern South Africa, where the mixture of warm currents flowing close to shore and the seasonal onshore winds striking the Drakensberg uplands provide for a moist and temperate marine coast climate.

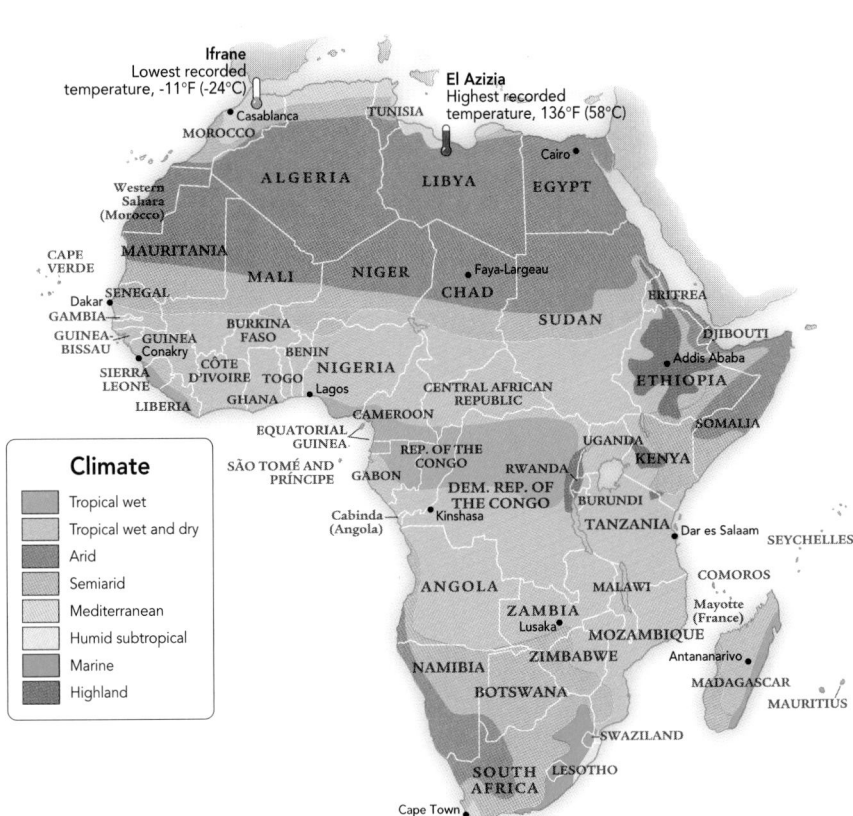

Climate

- Tropical wet
- Tropical wet and dry
- Arid
- Semiarid
- Mediterranean
- Humid subtropical
- Marine
- Highland

Ifrane — Lowest recorded temperature, -11°F (-24°C)

El Azizia — Highest recorded temperature, 136°F (58°C)

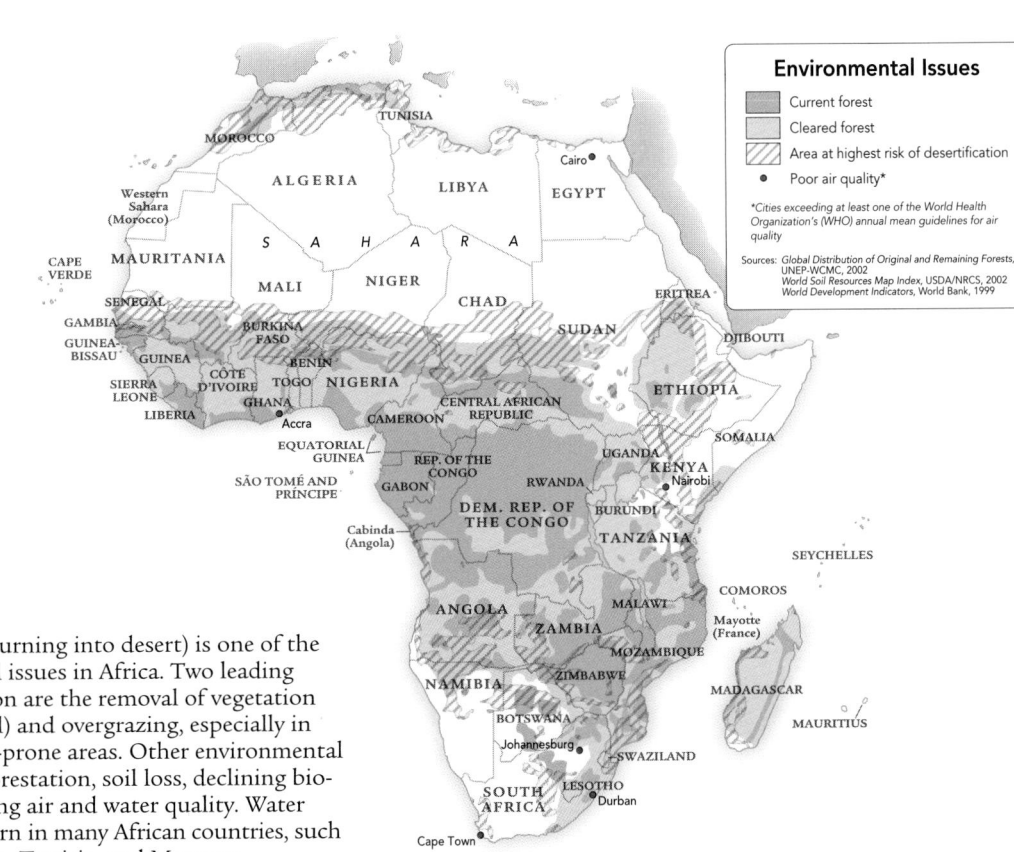

Environmental Issues

- Current forest
- Cleared forest
- Area at highest risk of desertification
- Poor air quality*

*Cities exceeding at least one of the World Health Organization's (WHO) annual mean guidelines for air quality

Sources: Global Distribution of Original and Remaining Forests, UNEP-WCMC, 2002
World Soil Resources Map Index, USDA/NRCS, 2002
World Development Indicators, World Bank, 1999

Desertification (land turning into desert) is one of the leading environmental issues in Africa. Two leading causes of desertification are the removal of vegetation (often for cooking fuel) and overgrazing, especially in semiarid and drought-prone areas. Other environmental problems include deforestation, soil loss, declining bio-diversity, and decreasing air and water quality. Water scarcity is also a concern in many African countries, such as Egypt, Libya, Algeria, Tunisia, and Morocco.

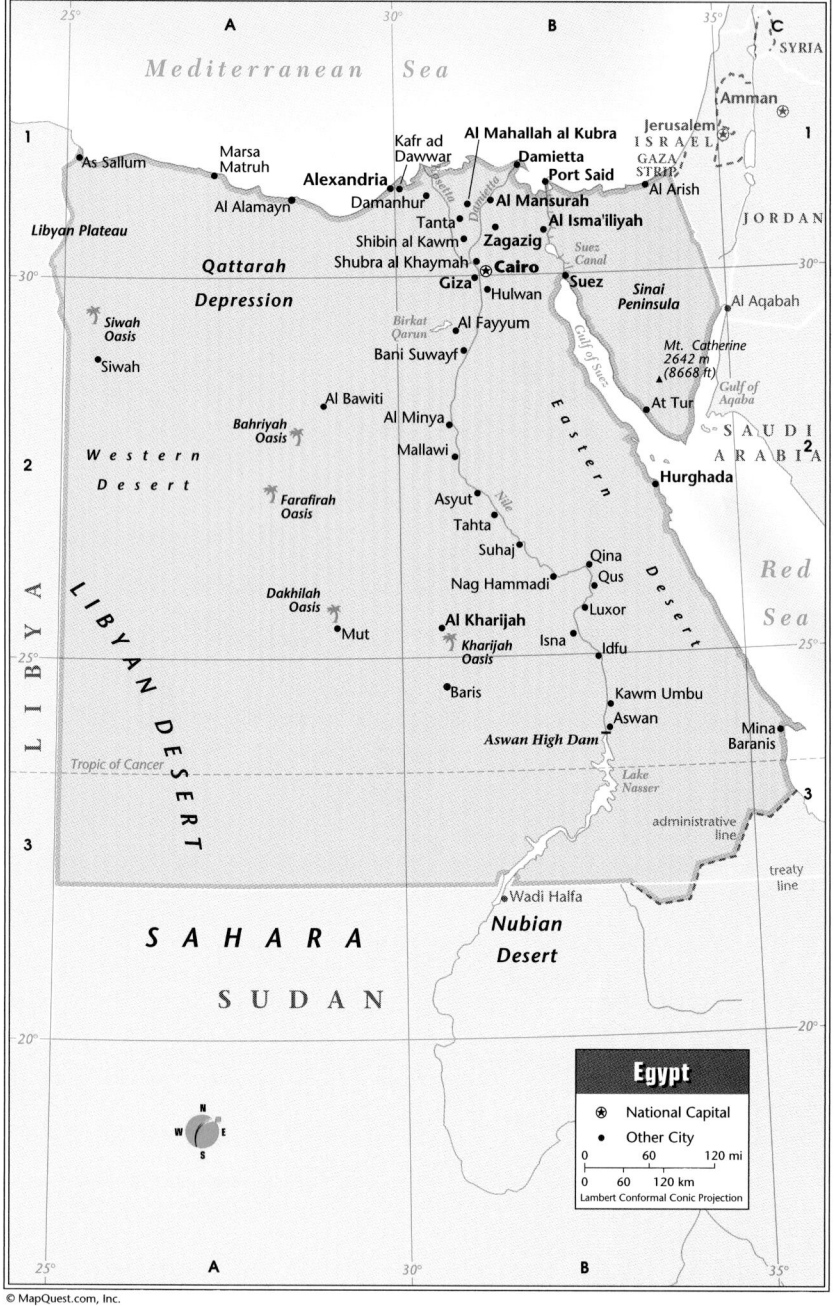

© MapQuest.com, Inc.

Capital: Cairo
Area: 389,564 sq. mi.
1,001,450 sq. km.
Population: 73,313,000
(2002 est.)
Largest City: Cairo, 6,801,000
Languages: Arabic, English, French
Major Religions: Muslim, Coptic Christian
Life Expectancy: 59 male, 63 female
Government: republic
Monetary Unit: Egyptian pound
Industry: textiles, food processing, tourism, chemicals, petroleum, construction, cement, metals
Agriculture: cotton, rice, corn, wheat, beans, fruit, vegetables, cattle, water buffalo, sheep, goats, fish
Minerals and Resources: petroleum, natural gas, iron ore, phosphates, manganese, limestone, gypsum, talc, asbestos, lead, zinc

Egypt

Egypt is the most populous country in the Arab world and the second-most populous on the continent of Africa. Egypt has endured as a unified state for more than 5,000 years, and archaeological evidence suggests that a developed Egyptian society has existed for much longer.

Life in Egypt is centered around the Nile River. Nearly all of Egypt's population lives in Cairo and Alexandria and elsewhere along the Nile and its delta. Practically all Egyptian agriculture takes place in some 2.5 million hectares of fertile soil in the Nile Valley and Delta, and more than one-third of the Egyptian labor force is engaged directly in farming.

Politically, Egypt has become more and more democratized since 1970 when President Nasser died. President Mubarak, first elected in 1981, has reestablished Egypt's position as an Arab leader and has maintained its commitment to the peace process in the Middle East.

The West Bank of the Nile River at Luxor

The Sphinx at Giza

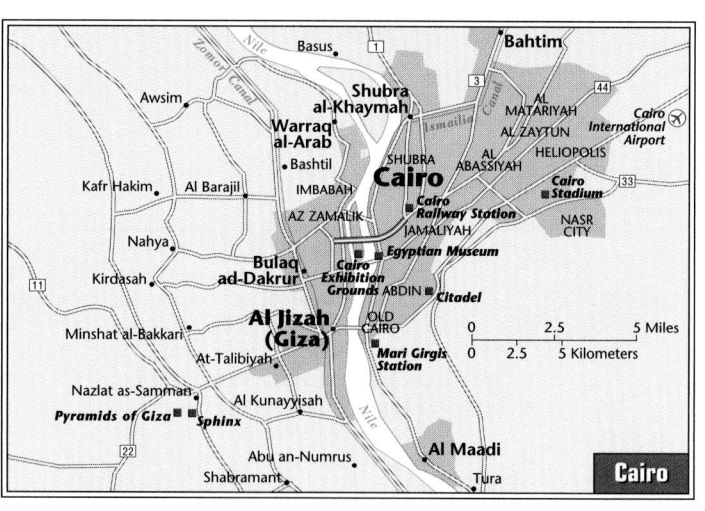

Ninety percent of the population of Libya lives in less than 10% of the land area, mainly along the coast. The Libyan people are primarily a mixture of Arabs and Berbers and have been subject to varying degrees of foreign control throughout their history.

Libya declared its independence from Italy in 1951 and in 1959 significant oil reserves were discovered, which transformed the Libyan economy from one of the poorest in the world to one of the very wealthy.

In 1969 a military-led coup overthrew the king of Libya and proclaimed the new Libyan Arab Republic. Mu'ammar al-Qadhafi emerged as leader of the new regime and eventually as de facto chief of state (a position he currently holds). While Qadhafi has no official position in Libya, he continues to control the government with absolute power. His primary foreign policy has been Arab unity, advancement of Islam and elimination of Western influence in the Middle East and Africa.

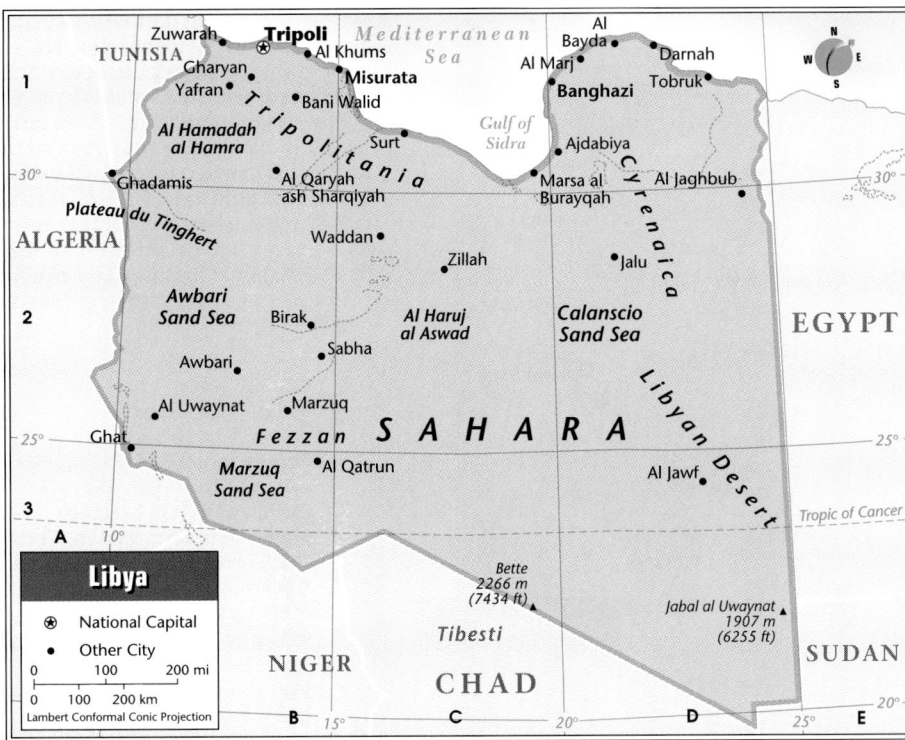

© MapQuest.com, Inc.

Libya

Capital: Tripoli
Area: 684,461 sq. mi.
1,759,540 sq. km.
Population: 5,369,000 (2002 est.)
Largest City: Tripoli, 1,500,000
Languages: Arabic, Italian, English,
Major Religion: Muslim
Life Expectancy: 62 male, 67 female
Government: military dictatorship

Monetary Unit: Libyan dinar
Industry: petroleum, food processing, textiles, handicrafts, cement
Agriculture: wheat, barley, olives, dates, citrus fruits, peanuts
Minerals and Resources: petroleum, natural gas, gypsum

Sudan

Sudan is the largest country in Africa. Historically, Sudan was a collection of small, independent states from the beginning of the Christian era until 1821 when Egypt conquered and unified the northern portion of the country. Although Egypt claimed all of present Sudan during most of the 19th century, it was not able to establish effective control of southern Sudan, which remained an area of fragmented tribes.

In 1953 Egypt and the United Kingdom concluded an agreement that provided for Sudanese self-government and self-determination, and in 1956 Sudan became independent. A series of provisional governments, coups, Islamicization measures and civil war has plagued Sudan since its independence.

MICHAEL A. HEERSCHAP

Sudan's Nile River Valley

© MapQuest.com, Inc.

Capital: Khartoum
Area: 947,760 sq. mi.
2,505,810 sq. km.
Population: 37,090,000 (2002 est.)
Largest City: Khartoum, 1,271,000
Languages: Arabic, Nubian, Ta Bedawie, Nilotic, Nilo-Hamitic, Sudanic languages, English
Major Religions: Muslim, indigenous beliefs, Christian
Life Expectancy: 54 male, 56 female

Government: military junta
Monetary Unit: Sudanese pound
Industry: cotton ginning, textiles, cement, edible oils, sugar, soap distilling, shoes, petroleum refining
Agriculture: cotton, oilseeds, sorghum, millet, wheat, gum arabic, sheep
Minerals and Resources: small reserves of petroleum, iron ore, copper, chromium ore, zinc, tungsten, mica, silver, gold

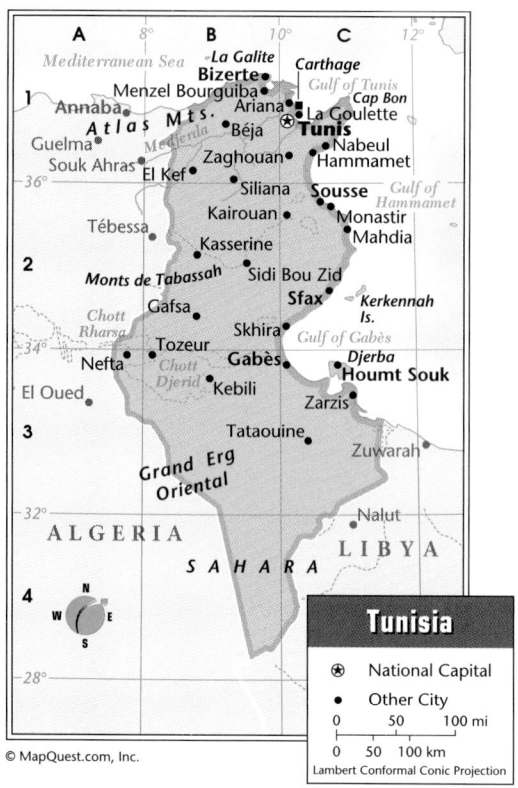

© MapQuest.com, Inc.

Tunisia was a French protectorate from 1881-1956, when it became an independent republic.

The Tunisian people are descendants of indigenous Berber and Arab tribes and are predominantly Muslim.

Tunisia's economic growth historically has depended on oil, phosphates, agriculture and tourism. In 1986, after a foreign exchange crisis, the Tunisian government launched a structural adjustment program to liberalize prices, reduce tariffs, and reorient the country toward a market economy. Its economic reform program has been lauded as a model by international financial institutions.

Tunisia has consistently played a moderating role in the negotiations for a comprehensive Middle East peace.

Tunisia

Capital: Tunis
Area: 63,153 sq. mi.
163,610 sq. km.
Population: 9,816,000 (2002 est.)
Largest City: Tunis, 702,000
Languages: Arabic, French
Major Religions: Muslim, Christian, Jewish
Life Expectancy: 71 male, 75 female
Government: republic
Monetary Unit: Tunisian dinar
Industry: petroleum, mining, tourism, textiles, footwear, food, beverages
Agriculture: olives, dates, oranges, almonds, grain, sugar beets, wine grapes, poultry, beef, dairy
Minerals & Resources: petroleum, phosphates, iron ore, lead, zinc, salt

Rabat Monastic, Sousse, Tunisia

Carthage, Tunisia

Algeria

Capital: Algiers
Area: 919,352 sq. mi.
2,381,740 sq. km.
Population: 32,278,000 (2002 est.)
Largest City: Algiers, 1,904,000
Languages: Arabic, French, Berber dialects
Major Religions: Sunni Muslim, Christian, Jewish
Life Expectancy: 67 male, 69 female
Government: republic
Monetary Unit: Algerian dinar
Industry: petroleum, light industries, natural gas, mining, electrical, petrochemical, food processing
Agriculture: wheat, barley, oats, grapes, olives, citrus, fruits, sheep, cattle, grain, vegetable oil, sugar
Minerals & Resources: petroleum, natural gas, iron ore, phosphates, uranium, lead, zinc

Algeria is the second-largest nation in Africa. About 90 percent of its population lives along the Mediterranean coast on 12 percent of the land and most of the remainder of the country is desert, steppes, wasteland, and mountains.

The borders of modern Algeria were created by the French, who colonized Algeria in 1830. In 1962, after almost ten years of revolution that resulted in a brutal two-way guerrilla war, France declared Algeria independent. Since then, Algeria has enjoyed relative political stability.

Algeria has the fifth largest natural gas reserve in the world and the fourteenth largest oil reserve.

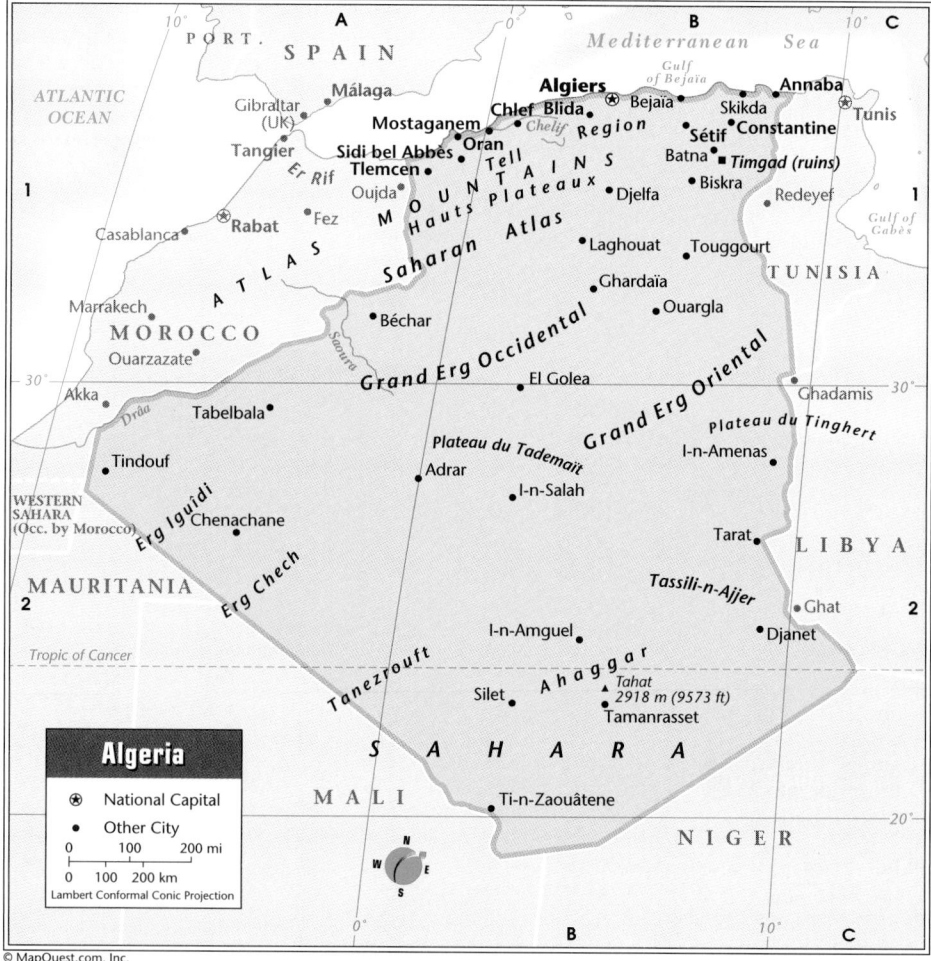

© MapQuest.com, Inc.

Morocco

Morocco is a constitutional monarchy whose king is of the Alaouite dynasty which has ruled Morocco since 1649 and which claims descent from the prophet Mohammed. From 1904–1956, Morocco was a French protectorate and was also subject to Spain's rule in the northern and southern (Sahara) zones.

Most Moroccans are Sunni Muslims of Arab, Berber or mixed Arab-Berber stock. Most people live west of the Atlas Mountains, a range which insulates the country from the Sahara Desert.

Morocco maintains close relations with Europe and the United States, but is also very active in regional and pan-Arab affairs. Morocco claims and administers Western Sahara, but the issue of sovereignty is unresolved.

Capital: Rabat
Area: 172,368 sq. mi.
446,550 sq. km.
Population: 31,168,000 (2002 est.)
Largest City: Casablanca, 2,943,000
Languages: Arabic, Berber dialects, French
Major Religions: Muslim, Christian, Jewish
Life Expectancy: 67 male, 71 female
Government: constitutional monarchy
Monetary Unit: Moroccan dirham
Industry: phosphate mining and processing, food processing, leather goods, textiles, construction, tourism
Agriculture: livestock, barley, wheat, citrus fruit, wine, vegetables, olives
Minerals & Resources: phosphates, iron ore, manganese, lead, zinc, fish, salt

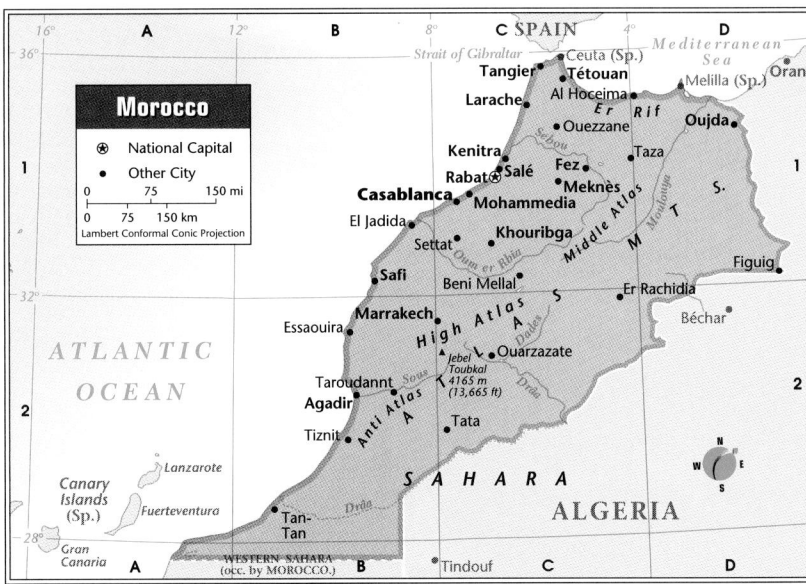

Western Sahara

Western Sahara, largely desert and wasteland, lies between Morocco and Mauritania. From 1904–1975, it was occupied by Spain. Pressure from surrounding countries and the United Nations for decolonization began in the 1960s and finally resulted in Spain's withdrawal in 1975. Morocco and Mauritania then occupied and claimed the territory and thereby entered into conflict with the Polisario, an independence movement based in the region of Tindouf, Algeria. Mauritania withdrew from the territory in 1978 and renounced all claims to the territory.

Morocco continues to administer and claim Western Sahara, basing its claim to sovereignty on the historical argument of the Saharan tribal leaders' loyalty to the Moroccan sultan as spiritual leader and ruler. A referendum to determine the area's sovereignty has been delayed repeatedly since 1992.

Open air market outside Fez city gate, Morocco

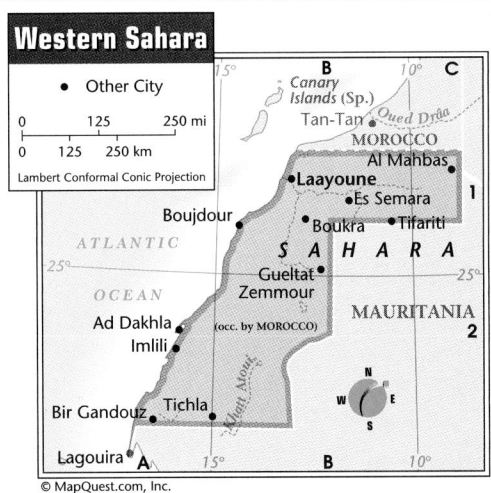

Capital: none
Area: 102,676 sq. mi.
266,000 sq. km.
Population: 256,000 (2002 est.)
Largest City: Laayoune, 90,000
Languages: Hassaniya Arabic, Moroccan Arabic
Major Religion: Muslim
Life Expectancy: 45 male, 48 female
Government: sovereignty disputed, administered by Morocco
Monetary Unit: Moroccan dirham
Industry: phosphate mining, handicrafts
Agriculture: subsistence agriculture and fishing, barley, limited fruit and vegetable production
Minerals & Resources: phosphates, iron ore

Mauritania

Capital: Nouakchott
Area: 397,850 sq.mi.
1,030,700 sq. km.
Population: 2,829,000 (2002 est.)
Largest City: Nouakchott, 612,000
Languages: Hassaniya Arabic, Pular, Soninke, Wolof
Major Religion: Muslim
Life Expectancy: 46 male, 52 female
Government: republic
Monetary Unit: ouguiya
Industry: fish processing, mining of iron ore and gypsum
Agriculture: subsistence farming and nomadic cattle and sheep herding, dates, millet, sorghum, root crops
Minerals & Resources: iron ore, gypsum, fish, copper, phosphate

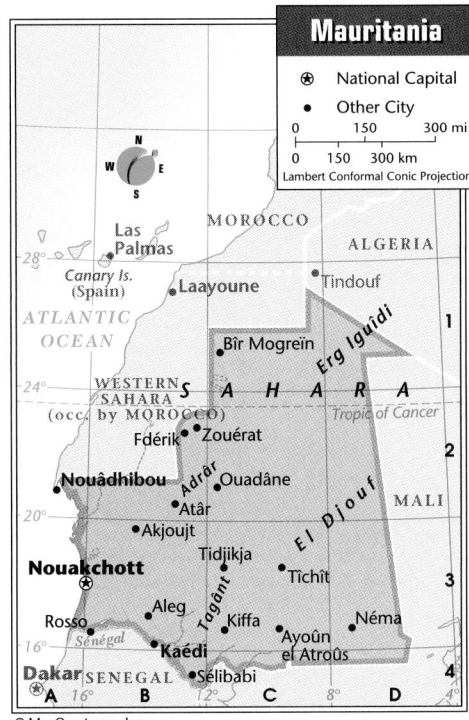

The Islamic Republic of Mauritania has been independent from France since 1960. From 1978 to 1992, Mauritania was governed by a military junta which alienated it from many nations due to its human rights abuses. Conflict between Moor and non-Moor ethnic groups continues to be a major challenge to national unity in Mauritania, even under the still relatively new civilian government. Democratic reform and decentralization since the military regime has somewhat eased ethnic tensions.

A majority of the population of Mauritania still depends on agriculture and livestock for its livelihood, even though most of the nomads and many subsistence farmers have been forced into the cities due to massive droughts.

Cape Verde

Cape Verde map

National Capital
Other City

0   40   80 mi
0   40   80 km
Lambert Conformal Conic Projection

Santo Antão, Ribeira Grande, Mindelo, São Vicente, Santa Luzia, Ribeira Brava, São Nicolau, Sal, Pedra Lume, Santa Maria, Sal-Rei, Boa Vista, Curral Velho, WINDWARD GROUP, ATLANTIC OCEAN, LEEWARD GROUP, Tarrafal, São Tiago, Maio, Pôrto Inglês, Pico 2829 m (9281 ft), Brava, Fogo, São Filipe, Praia

© MapQuest.com, Inc.

The Cape Verde Islands is an archipelago consisting of ten islands and five islets off the coast of western Africa. Cape Verde gained its independence from Portugal in 1975, after nearly five hundred years of colonization by the Portuguese.

The Cape Verde archipelago was uninhabited until the Portuguese discovered it in 1456. African slaves were brought to the islands to work on Portuguese plantations and, as a result, the population has mixed African and Portuguese origins. Survival in this country with few natural resources historically has induced Cape Verdeans to emigrate, and about two-thirds of the people of Cape Verdean ancestry live abroad.

Capital: Praia
Area: 1,568 sq. mi.
4,030 sq. km.
Population: 409,000 (2002 est.)
Largest City: Praia, 103,000
Languages: Portuguese, Crioulo
Major Religions: Roman Catholicism fused with indigenous beliefs
Life Expectancy: 61 male, 65 female
Government: republic

Monetary Unit: Cape Verdean escudo
Industry: fish processing, salt mining, garment industry, ship repair, construction materials, food and beverage production
Agriculture: bananas, corn, beans, sweet potatoes, coffee
Minerals and Resources: salt, basalt rock, pozzolana, limestone, kaolin, fish

CAPE VERDE, THE GAMBIA, SENEGAL, GUINEA-BISSAU, GUINEA, LIBERIA, SIERRA LEONE

JUSTIN LOUIS

Pico do Cano, Cape Verde

Senegal was under French control from 1895–1960, when it became independent. After a brief union with then French Soudan to form the Mali Federation, Senegal and Soudan (renamed Mali) each declared independence.

Senegal is a republic with a strong presidency, legislature, independent judiciary and multiple political parties. Its population is about 94% Muslim. The Senegalese economy is overwhelmingly agricultural, with more than 70% of the labor force engaged in farming. Peanut production accounts for half of the country's agricultural output. Despite migration to cities and towns, about 70% of the population is still rural.

Capital: Dakar
Area: 76,318 sq. mi.
196,190 sq. km.
Population: 10,311,000 (2002 est.)
Largest City: Dakar, 880,000
Languages: French, Wolof, Pulaar, Diola, Mandingo
Major Religions: Muslim, indigenous beliefs, Christian
Life Expectancy: 56 male, 59 female
Government: republic under multiparty democratic rule
Monetary Unit: CFA franc
Industry: agricultural and fish processing, phosphate mining, petroleum refining, building materials

Senegal

Agriculture: peanuts, millet, corn, sorghum, rice, cotton, tomatoes, green vegetables
Minerals and Resources: fish, phosphates, iron ore

JUSTIN LOUIS

Gambia River, The Gambia

Senegal map

Senegal

National Capital
Other City

0   40   80 mi
0   40   80 km
Lambert Conformal Conic Projection

MAURITANIA, L. Rkiz, Sénégal, Richard Toll, Haïré Lao, Saint-Louis, Kaédi, Louga, Ferlo, Matam, Tivaouane, Dara, Linguère, Sélibabi, Dakar, Thiès, Mbaké, Mamâri, Cap Vert, Rufisque, Diourbel, Vélingara, Bakel, Mbour, Fatick, Sine, Payar, Kaolack, Kaffrine, Kounghéul, SAHEL, Goudiri, Nioro du Rip, Saloum, Tambacounda, MALI, Banjul, THE GAMBIA, Dialakoto, Bignona, Casamance, Vélingara, Kolda, Saraya, Ziguinchor, Sédhiou, Koundara, Kédougou, GUINEA-BISSAU, Bissau, Bafatá, ATLANTIC OCEAN, Fouta Djalon, GUINEA, Labé

© MapQuest.com, Inc.

The Gambia

The Gambia map

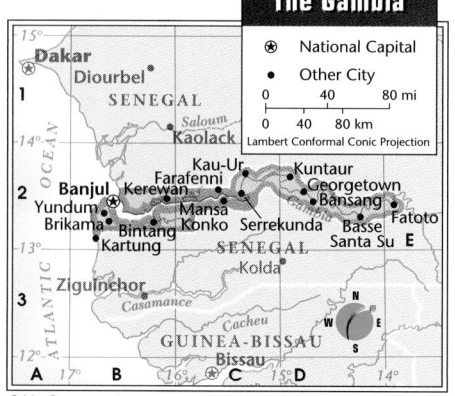

National Capital
Other City

0   40   80 mi
0   40   80 km
Lambert Conformal Conic Projection

Dakar, Diourbel, SENEGAL, Saloum, Kaolack, Kau-Ur, Farafenni, Kuntaur, Kerewan, Georgetown, Banjul, Mansa Konko, Bansang, Yundum, Serrekunda, Fatoto, Brikama, Bintang, Basse Santa Su, Kartung, SENEGAL, Kolda, Ziguinchor, Casamance, Cacheu, GUINEA-BISSAU, Bissau

© MapQuest.com, Inc.

Until 1994, when a military coup overthrew the government, the Gambia was one of the oldest existing multi-party democracies in Africa. From its independence from the United Kingdom in 1965, it conducted freely-contested elections every five years and its human rights record was often put forward as an example for other nations. The military regime that took over in 1994 has announced a transition back to democratic, civilian government.

The Gambia is home to a wide variety of ethnic groups, each with its own language and traditions, who live side by side with a minimum of inter-tribal friction. More than 80% of Gambians live in rural villages. Over 95% of the population is Muslim.

Capital: Banjul
Area: 4,396 sq. mi.
11,300 sq. km.

The Gambia

Population: 1,456,000 (2002 est.)
Largest City: Banjul, 42,000
Languages: English, Mandinka, Wolof, Fula,
Major Religions: Muslim, Christian, indigenous beliefs
Life Expectancy: 48 male, 53 female
Government: republic
Monetary Unit: dalasi
Industry: peanut processing, tourism, beverages, agricultural machinery assembly, woodworking, metalworking, clothing
Agriculture: peanuts, millet, sorghum, rice, corn, cassava, palm kernels, cattle, sheep, goats
Minerals and Resources: fish

Capital: Bissau
Area: 14,051 sq. mi.
36,120 sq. km.
Population: 1,333,000 (2002 est.)
Largest City: Bissau, 109,000
Languages: Portuguese, Criolo, African languages
Major Religions: indigenous beliefs, Muslim, Christian
Life Expectancy: 46 male, 50 female

Government: republic
Monetary Unit: Guinea-Bissauan peso
Industry: agricultural processing, beer, soft drinks
Agriculture: rice, corn, beans, cassava, cashew nuts, peanuts, palm kernels, cotton
Minerals and Resources: unexploited deposits of petroleum, bauxite, phosphates, fish, timber

Guinea-Bissau

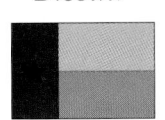

The rivers of Guinea were among the first areas to be explored by the Portuguese in the 15th century.

Like other Portuguese colonies, Guinea-Bissau suffered a protracted war of independence, and from 1963–1973 the country was ravaged by conflict. In 1974 the Portuguese withdrew and Guinea-Bissau achieved independence.

Guinea-Bissau is among the world's poorest nations. It's principal economic activities are agriculture and fishing. The government is committed to an economic reform program which emphasizes monetary stability and private sector growth. There are plans to develop its timber resources and rich offshore fish production.

Guinea was separated from Senegal in 1891 and administered as a separate colony by France until 1958, when it became an independent republic. The population of Guinea is predominantly Muslim and is made up of three main tribes, each of which has its own language.

Despite its great agricultural potential and major mineral and hydropower resources, Guinea is one of the poorest countries in the world. Agriculture employs about 80% of the work force and only contributes 40% to the GDP. Guinea has received a large number of refugees from the civil wars in Liberia and Sierra Leone, which has further strained its economy.

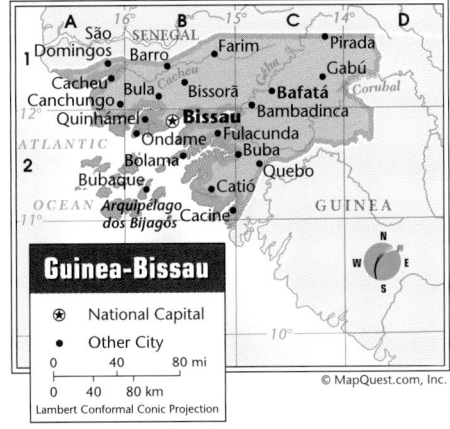

Capital: Conakry
Area: 95,640 sq. mi.
245,860 sq. km.
Population: 8,816,000 (2002 est.)
Largest City: Conakry, 705,000
Language: French
Major Religions: Muslim, Christian, indigenous beliefs
Life Expectancy: 42 male, 47 female

Guinea

Government: republic
Monetary Unit: Guinean franc
Industry: mining—bauxite, gold, diamonds; alumina refining; light manufacturing and agricultural processing industries
Agriculture: fishing, forestry, rice, coffee, pineapples, palm kernels, cassava, bananas, sweet potatoes, timber, cattle, sheep, goats
Minerals and Resources: bauxite, iron ore, diamonds, gold, uranium, hydropower, fish

Sierra Leone

Sierra Leone was one of the first West African British colonies, although it was not settled until 1787 when Britain began using it as a refuge for freed slaves who were later called Creoles. Despite revolts against British rule and Creole domination, Sierra Leone's colonial history was basically peaceful and independence was achieved in 1961 without violence.

Sierra Leone has substantial mineral, agricultural and fishery resources. Diamond mining alone accounts for more than half of the country's export earnings. Due to war-related disruptions in the mining and agricultural export sectors in recent years, the economic infrastructure in Sierra Leone has nearly collapsed.

Capital: Freetown
Area: 27,907 sq. mi.
71,740 sq. km.
Population: 5,565,000 (2002 est.)
Largest City: Freetown, 470,000
Languages: English, Mende, Temne, Krio
Major Religions: Muslim, indigenous beliefs, Christian
Life Expectancy: 44 male, 50 female
Government: military government
Monetary Unit: leone
Industry: mining (diamonds, bauxite, rutile), small-scale manufacturing (beverages, textiles, cigarettes, footwear), petroleum refinery
Agriculture: coffee, cocoa, palm kernels, rice, fish
Minerals and Resources: diamonds, titanium ore, bauxite, iron ore, gold, chromite

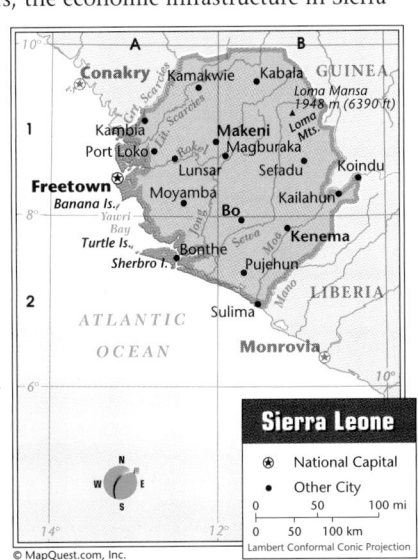

Liberia

Liberia was settled by freed American slaves beginning in 1822. In 1838 they united to form the Commonwealth of Liberia with a governor appointed by the American Colonization Society. In 1847, Liberia became Africa's first independent republic, and struggled for the next century to avoid French and British colonial encroachment.

A series of coups and military regimes have made Liberia a very unstable nation in recent years. Since 1990 Liberia has been ravaged by civil war and some 750,000 refugees have fled to neighboring countries.

Capital: Monrovia
Area: 43,323 sq. mi.
111,370 sq. km
Population: 3,262,000 (2002 est.)
Largest City: Monrovia, 421,000
Languages: English, Niger-Congo
Major Religions: indigenous beliefs, Muslim, Christian
Life Expectancy: 56 male, 61 female
Government: republic

Monetary Unit: Liberian dollar
Industry: rubber processing, food processing, construction materials, furniture, palm oil processing, mining (iron ore, diamonds)
Agriculture: fishing, forestry, rubber, timber, coffee, cocoa, rice, cassava, palm oil, sugarcane, bananas, sheep, goats
Minerals and Resources: iron ore, timber, diamonds, gold

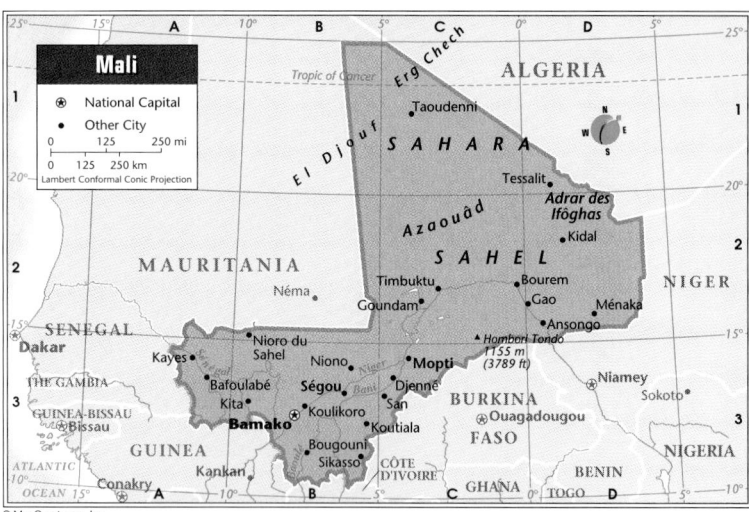

Shepherd with goats, Mali

The Gold Coast was renamed Ghana in 1957, when it became independent from the United Kingdom, due to the belief that its inhabitants descended from migrants who moved south from the ancient kingdom of Ghana.

Ethnically, Ghanians are divided into small groups speaking more than 50 languages and dialects.

Ghana is relatively well-off by West African standards. It is well endowed with natural resources and has a substantial physical and social infrastructure.

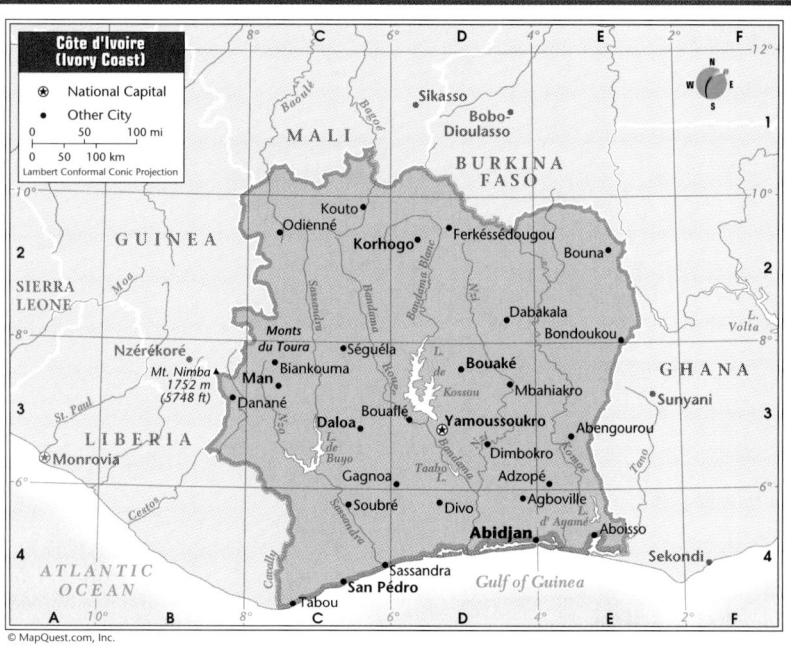

Mali

Mali is a multi-party democracy that gained its independence from France in 1960. As part of the colony that the French called Soudan, Mali was administered with other French colonial territories as the Federation of French West Africa.

Mali's population consists of diverse ethnic groups that share similar historic, cultural and religious traditions, with the exception of two desert nomad groups in the north who have been given a degree of autonomy by the government. Malians enjoy a harmony rare in African states.

Mali is one of the poorest countries in the world, with 65 percent of its land area desert or semi-desert. About 80 percent of the labor force is engaged in agriculture and fishing.

Capital: Bamako
Area: 478,714 sq. mi.
1,240,192 sq. km.
Population: 11,300,000 (2002 est.)
Largest City: Bamako, 1,179,000
Languages: French, Bambara, African languages
Major Religions: Muslim, indigenous beliefs, Christian
Life Expectancy: 45 male, 48 female
Government: republic
Monetary Unit: CFA franc
Industry: minor local consumer goods production and food processing, construction, phosphate and gold mining
Agriculture: cotton, millet, rice, corn, vegetables, peanuts, cattle, sheep, goats
Minerals & Resources: gold, phosphates, kaolin, salt, limestone, uranium, bauxite, iron ore, manganese, tin, and copper deposits

Ghana

Capital: Accra
Area: 92,076 sq. mi.
238,540 sq. km.
Population: 20,163,000 (2002 est.)
Largest City: Accra, 860,000
Languages: English, African languages
Major Religions: indigenous beliefs, Muslim, Christian
Life Expectancy: 54 male, 58 female
Government: constitutional democracy
Monetary Unit: new cedi
Industry: mining, lumbering, light manufacturing, aluminum, food processing
Agriculture: cocoa, rice, coffee, cassava, peanuts, corn, shea nuts, timber;
Minerals & Resources: gold, timber, industrial diamonds, bauxite, manganese, fish, rubber

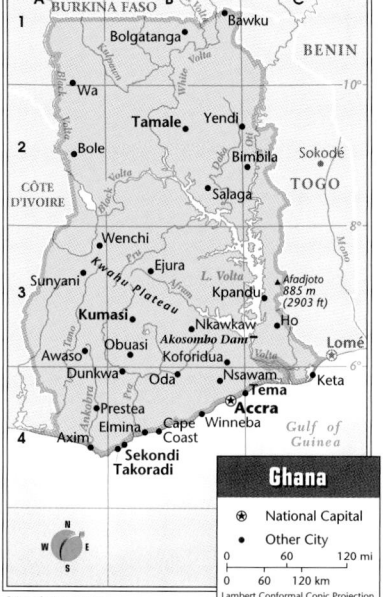

Côte d'Ivoire

Côte d'Ivoire is a stable, multi-party democracy which achieved independence from France in 1960 after being under French rule since 1893. Since its independence, it has developed into one of Africa's most prosperous countries, largely due to its coffee, cocoa bean and cotton exports.

There are more than 60 ethnic groups in Côte d'Ivoire, each with its own dialect. French is the unifying and official language.

Capital: Yamoussoukro
Area: 124,470 sq. mi.
322,460 sq. km.
Population: 16,598,000 (2002 est.)
Largest City: Abidjan, 1,929,000
Languages: French, native dialects
Major Religions: indigenous, Muslim, Christian
Life Expectancy: 47 male, 51 female
Government: republic
Monetary Unit: CFA franc
Industry: foodstuffs, wood processing, oil refining, automobile assembly, textiles, fertilizer, beverages
Agriculture: coffee, cocoa beans, timber, bananas, palm kernels, rubber, corn, rice, manioc, sweet potatoes
Minerals & Resources: petroleum, diamonds, manganese, iron ore, cobalt, bauxite, copper

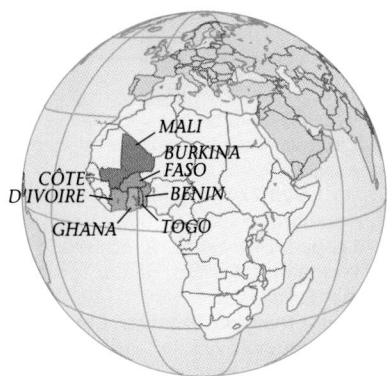

Burkina Faso is a landlocked Sahel country that shares borders with six nations. From 1896–1960, Burkina Faso was under French rule of varying degrees. Its more recent history has seen a series of military coups and economic instability.

With a high population density and growth rate, few natural resources and poor soil, Burkina Faso is one of the poorest nations in the world. Subsistence agriculture provides about 40% of the GDP and employs about 80% of the work force.

Burkina Faso

Capital: Ouagadougou
Area: 105,841 sq. mi.
274,200 sq. km.
Population: 12,887,000
(2002 est.)
Largest City: Ouagadougou, 634,000
Languages: tribal languages belonging to Sudanic family, French
Major Religions: indigenous beliefs, Muslim, Christian (Roman Catholic)
Life Expectancy: 46 male, 48 female
Government: parliamentary
Monetary Unit: CFA franc
Industry: cotton lint, beverages, agricultural processing, soap, cigarettes, textiles, gold mining and extraction
Agriculture: peanuts, shea nuts, sesame, cotton, sorghum, millet, corn, rice
Minerals & Resources: manganese, limestone, marble, small deposits of gold, antimony, copper, nickel, bauxite, lead, phosphates, zinc, silver

© MapQuest.com, Inc.

JUSTIN LOUIS

Traditional 'pito' beer brewing, Tamale, Ghana

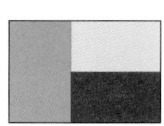

Marketplace in Benin

Benin

Benin, formerly known as Dahomey, was under French administration from 1892–1960. After becoming independent, the country experienced a string of coups and political upheavals. From 1972–1989, the government was a strict Marxist-Leninist regime, but mounting protest and unrest caused it to be abandoned and in 1990 a new pluralistic constitution was adopted.

Benin's economy is dependent on subsistence agriculture, cotton production and regional trade. About 80 percent of the population is rural and there are some 42 ethnic groups represented.

Capital: Porto-Novo
Area: 43,471 sq. mi.
112,620 sq. km.
Population: 6,835,000
(2002 est.)
Largest City: Cotonou, 651,000
Languages: French, Fon and Yoruba, tribal languages
Major Religions: indigenous beliefs, Muslim, Christian
Life Expectancy: 50 male, 54 female

Government: multiparty democratic rule
Monetary Unit: CFA franc
Industry: textiles, cigarettes, construction materials, beverages, food, petroleum
Agriculture: corn, sorghum, cassava, yams, beans, rice, cotton, palm oil, peanuts, livestock
Minerals & Resources: small offshore oil deposits, limestone, marble, timber

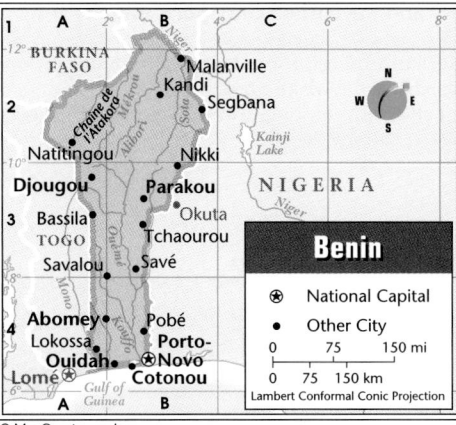

© MapQuest.com, Inc.

Togo's population is composed of about 37 ethnic groups, the three major of which are the Ewe and the Mina in the south, and the Kabye in the north. Historically, Togo was first a German protectorate, then a French/British United Nations trust territory, then an autonomous republic in the French Union and, finally in 1960, it became a fully independent republic.

The Togolese government is currently in transition from a republic to a multiparty democracy. Political unrest in recent years has stalled economic reform and disrupted vital economic activity. The country is heavily dependent on subsistence agriculture.

Togo

Capital: Lomé
Area: 21,921 sq. mi.
56,790 sq. km.
Population: 5,299,000
(2002 est.)
Largest City: Lomé, 450,000
Languages: French, Ewe, Mina, Dagomba, Kabye
Major Religions: indigenous beliefs, Christian, Muslim
Life Expectancy: 55 male, 60 female
Government: republic under transition to multiparty democratic rule
Monetary Unit: CFA franc
Industry: phosphate mining, agricultural processing, cement, handicrafts, textiles, beverages
Agriculture: coffee, cocoa, cotton, yams, cassava, corn, beans, rice, millet, sorghum, fish
Minerals & Resources: phosphates, limestone, marble

Perfectly balanced, Togo

© MapQuest.com, Inc.

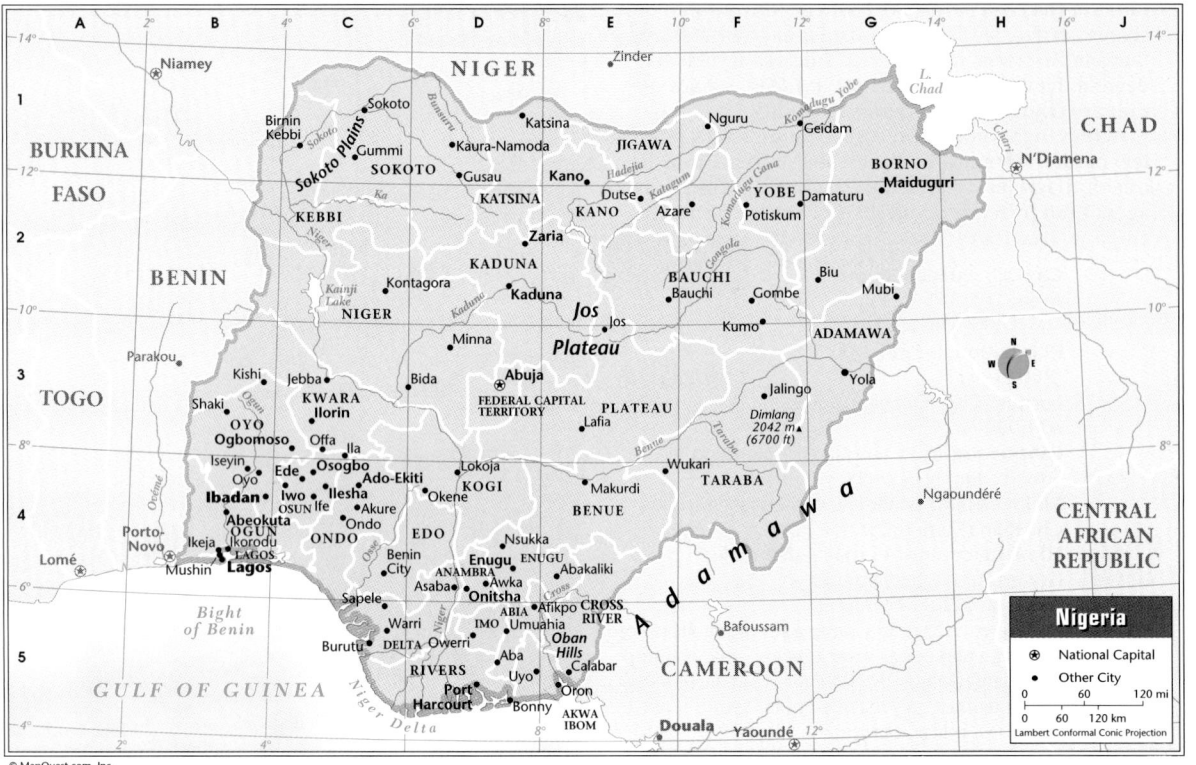

© MapQuest.com, Inc.

Nigeria

Capital: Abuja
Area: 359,346 sq. mi.
   923,770 sq. km.
Population: 130,500,000 (2002 est.)
Largest City: Lagos, 5,195,000
Languages: English, Hausa, Yoruba, Ibo, Fulani
Major Religions: Muslim, Christian, indigenous beliefs
Life Expectancy: 55 male, 57 female
Government: military government
Monetary Unit: naira
Industry: crude oil, mining (coal, tin, columbite), hides and skins, textiles, cement, building materials, food products, footwear, chemical, printing, ceramics, steel
Agriculture: cocoa, peanuts, palm oil, rubber, corn, rice, sorghum, millet, cassava, yams, cattle, sheep, goats, pigs, fishing, forestry
Minerals and Resources: petroleum, tin, columbite, iron ore, coal, limestone, lead, zinc, natural gas

Since its independence from the United Kingdom in 1960, Nigeria has experienced substantial political unrest. Regional, ethnic and religious tensions long present were magnified by the significant disparities in economic and educational development between the north and the south. A series of military coups, pro-democracy strikes and political upheavals have defined Nigeria's recent history and the current unpopular military leaders show no signs of wanting to restore democratic civilian rule.

The oil boom of the 1970s transformed Nigeria from a chiefly agricultural economy to one that relies on oil for more than 95% of its export earnings. Agriculture still employs about half of the labor force.

There are four main ethnic groups which make up about 65% of the entire population in Nigeria: the Hasua and Fulani in the north; the Yoruba in the southwest; and the Ibos in the southeast.

An inselberg rock formation, central Nigeria

Niger

Niger became independent from France in 1960 and adopted a new constitution in 1993 which established the Third Republic. The country is still in a transition stage of post-military rule.

Nigerians are about 80% Muslim and are comprised of two main ethnic groups, the Hausa and the Djerma-Songhai. Both groups are sedentary farmers.

Niger is one of the poorest countries in the world. It has a high population growth rate, a high infant and child mortality rate, poor nutrition, and drought and desertification conditions. Agricultural and livestock sectors are the mainstay of about 85% of the population, but generate only about 40% of the GDP. Uranium was once a major export commodity but the demand for it in recent years has decreased dramatically.

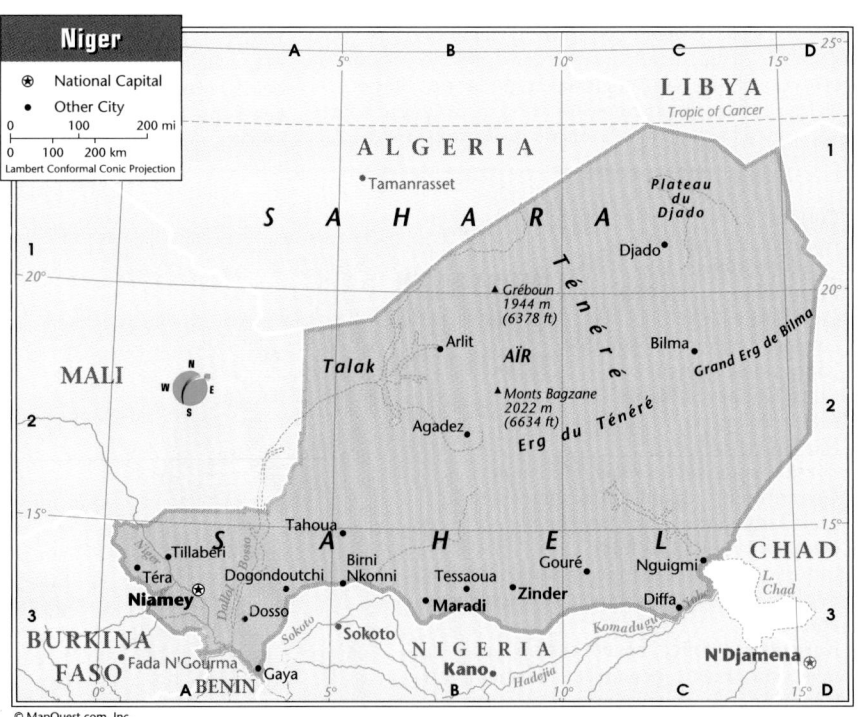

© MapQuest.com, Inc.

Water canal in Kano State, Nigeria

Capital: Niamey
Area: 492,863 sq. mi.
   1,267,000 sq. km,
Population: 10,760,000 (2002 est.)
Largest City: Niamey, 397,000
Languages: French, Hausa, Djerma
Major Religions: Muslim, indigenous beliefs, Christians
Life Expectancy: 43 male, 47 female
Government: republic
Monetary Unit: CFA franc
Industry: cement, brick, textiles, food processing, chemicals, slaughterhouses, uranium mining
Agriculture: cowpeas, cotton, peanuts, millet, sorghum, cassava, rice, cattle, sheep, goats
Minerals and Resources: uranium, coal, iron ore, tin, phosphates

The region that is now Chad was known to traders and geographers from the late Middle Ages. Since then, Chad has served as a crossroads for the Muslim peoples of the desert and savanna regions. Since its independence from France in 1960, Chad has experienced civil war, military coups, occupation of the northern part of the country by Libya, and economic instability.

More than 80% of Chadians are involved in subsistence farming and fishing. Due to chronic food shortages, Chad is heavily dependent on foreign aid, especially food credits. Geographic remoteness, drought, few natural resources and a lack of infrastructure make Chad one of the least developed countries in the world.

Chad is officially non-aligned, but has close relations with France and other Western countries.

Chad

Capital: N'Djamena
Area: 499,476 sq. mi.
1,284,000 sq. km.
Population: 8,971,000
(2002 est.)
Largest City: N'Djamena, 547,000
Languages: French, Arabic, Sara, Sango
Major Religions: Muslim, Christian, indigenous beliefs, animism
Life Expectancy: 40 male, 42 female
Government: republic
Monetary Unit: CFA franc
Industry: cotton textile mills, slaughterhouses, brewery, natron (sodium carbonate), soap, cigarettes
Agriculture: cotton, sorghum, millet, peanuts, rice, potatoes, manioc, cattle, sheep, goats, camels
Minerals and Resources: petroleum, uranium, natron, kaolin, fish

End of the Road, Sahara Desert, Chad

© MapQuest.com, Inc.

Cameroon

Capital: Yaoundé
Area: 184,946 sq. mi.
475,440 sq. km.
Population: 15,428,000
(2002 est.)
Largest City: Douala, 810,000
Languages: English, French
Major Religions: indigenous beliefs, Christian, Muslim
Life Expectancy: 55 male, 60 female
Government: unitary republic; multiparty presidential regime
Monetary Unit: CFA franc
Industry: petroleum production and refining, food processing, light consumer goods, textiles, lumber
Agriculture: coffee, cocoa, timber, cotton, rubber, bananas, oilseed, grains, livestock, root starches
Minerals and Resources: petroleum, bauxite, iron ore, timber, hydropower potential

Pulp logging of the 'Gmelin Arborea' tree near the Cameroon and Nigeria border

The area that is present-day Cameroon was once a German colony and, after World War I, was divided between the French and the British. French Cameroon gained independence in 1960 and the southern half of British Cameroon joined the French part to form the Republic of Cameroon.

Cameroon's economy is one of the largest in Africa, due to its offshore oil resources and favorable agricultural conditions. Abundant energy resources, lots of unused arable land and a well-educated population give Cameroon great development potential. However, political instability, slow economic liberalization and a generally unfavorable environment for business enterprise continue to hinder economic recovery. Cameroon's foreign relations are also clouded by concerns about human rights abuses.

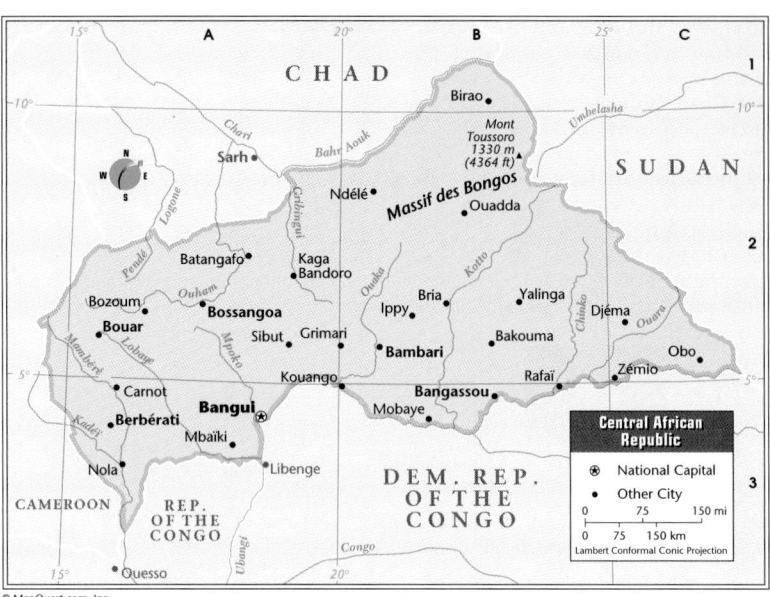

© MapQuest.com, Inc.

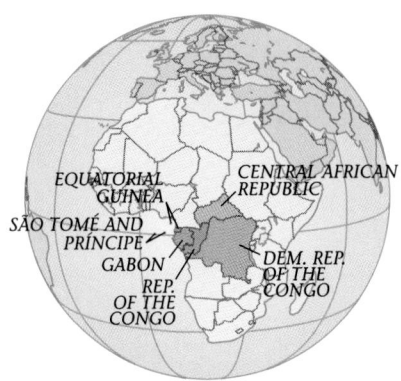

Capital: Bangui
Area: 240,470 sq. mi.
622,980 sq. km.
Population: 3,623,000 (2002 est.)
Largest City: Bangui, 452,000
Languages: French, Sangho, Arabic, Hunsa, Swahili
Major Religions: indigenous beliefs, Protestant, Roman Catholic, Muslim
Life Expectancy: 41 male, 44 female
Government: republic
Monetary Unit: CFA franc
Industry: diamond mining, sawmills, breweries, textiles, footwear, assembly of bicycles and motorcycles
Agriculture: cotton, coffee, tobacco, timber, manioc, yams, millet, corn, bananas
Minerals & Resources: diamonds, uranium, timber, gold, oil

In 1958 the French colony of Ubanghi Shari elected to remain within the French Community and adopted the title of the Central African Republic. In 1960 it became fully independent. Since then it has been through a number of coups and governments.

There are more than 80 ethnic groups in the country and more than 70% of Central Africans live in rural areas, relying mainly on subsistence farming.

Due to its poor infrastructure and resource base, the Central African Republic depends greatly on multilateral donors to supplement its agricultural and forestry revenues.

Central African Republic

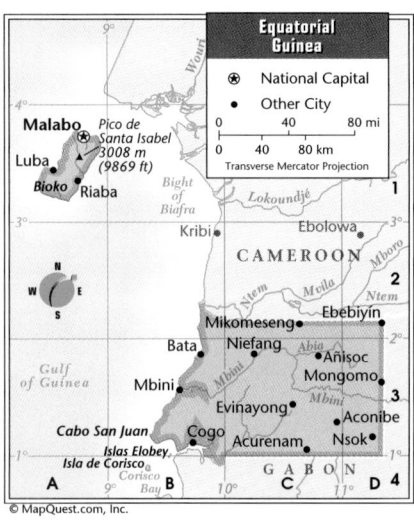

© MapQuest.com, Inc.

Present-day Equatorial Guinea was formerly two Spanish colonies that became provinces of metropolitan Spain in 1959 and then merged to form an independent Equatorial Guinea in 1968.

The country is still recovering from the brutal military regime which was in power from 1968–1979, but is in transition to a multiparty democracy.

Agriculture, forestry and fishing are the backbone of the Equatorial Guinean economy, accounting for about half of the GDP.

The majority of Equatoguinean people are of Bantu origin, the largest tribe of which is the Fang, who constitute 80% of the population and are divided into about 67 clans.

Capital: São Tomé
Area: 371 sq. mi.
960 sq. km.
Population: 170,000 (2002 est.)
Largest City: São Tomé, 6,000
Language: Portuguese
Major Religions: Roman Catholic, Evangelical Protestant, Seventh-Day Adventist
Life Expectancy: 62 male, 66 female
Government: republic
Monetary Unit: dobra
Industry: light construction, shirts, soap, beer, fisheries, shrimp processing
Agriculture: cocoa, coconuts, palm kernels, coffee, bananas, papaya, beans, poultry, fish
Minerals & Resources: fish

Capital: Malabo
Area: 10,827 sq. mi.
28,050 sq. km.
Population: 498,000 (2002 est.)
Largest City: Malabo, 30,000
Languages: Spanish, pidgin, English, Fang, Bubi
Major Religions: nominally Christian and predominantly Roman Catholic, pagan practices
Life Expectancy: 50 male, 55 female
Government: republic in transition to multiparty democracy
Monetary Unit: CFA franc
Industry: fishing, sawmilling
Agriculture: timber, coffee, cocoa, rice, yams, cassava, bananas, oil palm nuts, manioc, livestock
Minerals & Resources: timber, petroleum, small unexploited deposits of gold, manganese, uranium

Equatorial Guinea

São Tomé and Príncipe

The islands of São Tomé and Príncipe became independent from Portugal in 1975 after nearly 500 years of Portuguese influence and rule.

Ethnically, São Tomeans are a mix of descendants of African slaves, descendants of temporary contract workers on the islands, and Europeans, mainly Portuguese.

Plantation agriculture, primarily cocoa and coffee, has long been the base of the São Tomean economy. Production of such crops has been declining, however, due to drought and mismanagement. The islands have a great potential for development of the tourism industry and the government has been taking steps to expand this sector.

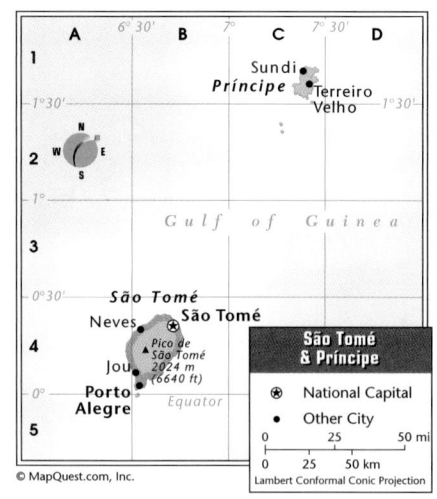

© MapQuest.com, Inc.

Republic of the Congo

Capital: Brazzaville
Area: 132,012 sq. mi.
342,000 sq. km.
Population: 2,908,000
(2002 est.)
Largest City: Brazzaville, 596,000
Languages: French (official), African languages (Lingala and Kikongo)
Major Religions: Christian, animist, Muslim
Life Expectancy: 45 male, 49 female
Government: republic
Monetary Unit: CFA franc
Industry: petroleum, cement, lumbering, brewing, sugar milling, palm oil, soap, cigarettes
Agriculture: cassava, rice, corn, peanuts, vegetables, coffee and cocoa, forest products
Minerals & Resources: petroleum, timber, potash, lead, zinc, uranium, copper, phosphates, natural gas

From 1883–1960, the Republic of the Congo was administered by France. Since independence, the Republic of the Congo has had a series of Marxist-Leninist governments which culminated in 1990 in the major party's renunciation of Marxism and the formation of a transitional, democratic, multiparty government.

A four-month civil war in 1997 brought former leader Denis Sassou-Nguesso back into power, ousting elected president Pascal Lissouba in the process. The capital city of Brazzaville was devastated during the conflict.

Despite years of political turmoil, the Republic of the Congo enjoys one of the highest per capita incomes in sub-Saharan Africa. Oil has supplanted forestry as the mainstay of the economy. The Republic of the Congo's location at the crossroads of transit trade to and from the Democratic Republic of the Congo, the Central African Republic, Chad, and Gabon, as well as the lingering importance of Brazzaville as the former administrative capital of French Equatorial Africa, have a positive effect on the country's economy.

Capital: Libreville
Area: 103,321 sq. mi.
267,670 sq. km.
Population: 1,288,000
(2002 est.)
Largest City: Libreville, 420,000
Languages: French, Fang, Myene, Bateke, Bapounou/Eschira, Bandjabi
Major Religions: Christian, Muslim, animist
Life Expectancy: 52 male, 58 female
Government: republic, multi-party presidential regime
Monetary Unit: CFA franc
Industry: food and beverages, lumbering and plywood, textiles, cement, petroleum refining, manganese, uranium, and gold mining
Agriculture: cocoa, coffee, palm oil, limited fishing and forest products
Minerals & Resources: petroleum, manganese, uranium, gold, timber, iron ore

Gabon lies along the Equator on the west coast of Africa and is covered with dense rain forest. Gabon was occupied by the French in 1885 and administered by France from 1903–1960, when it became an independent republic.

While Gabon is not without economic problems, it enjoys a per capita income more than twice that of most of its sub-Saharan neighbors, thanks to its bountiful natural resources.

Almost all Gabonese are of Bantu origin and there are at least 40 tribal groups with separate languages and cultures. French, the official language, is a unifying force.

Gabon

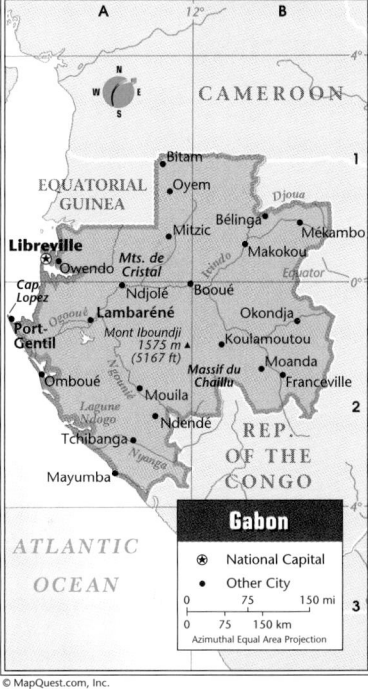

Democratic Republic of the Congo

Capital: Kinshasa
Area: 905,328 sq. mi.
2,345,410 sq. km.
Population: 55,042,000 (2002 est.)
Largest City: Kinshasa, 4,657,000
Languages: French, Lingala, Swahili, Kingwana, Kikongo, Tshiluba
Major Religions: Roman Catholic, Protestant, Kimbanguist, Muslim, other syncretic sects and traditional beliefs
Life Expectancy: 46 male, 49 female
Government: republic with a strong presidential system
Monetary Unit: new zaire is still in use until introduction of the DROC franc
Industry: mining, mineral processing, consumer products (including textiles, footwear, cigarettes, processed foods and beverages), cement, diamonds
Agriculture: coffee, palm oil, rubber, quinine, cassava, bananas, root crops, corn
Minerals & Resources: cobalt, copper, cadmium, petroleum, industrial and gem diamonds, gold, silver, zinc, manganese, tin, germanium, uranium, radium, bauxite, iron ore, coal, hydropower potential

The Belgian Congo was established in what is now the Democratic Republic of the Congo in 1895 and was administered by Belgium until it gained independence in 1960. In 1971 the country changed its name to Zaire and changed many place names to more African names.

From 1965 to 1997, Zaire had an extremely strong president, Mobutu Sese Seko, who was backed by a military regime. In 1994, however, under mounting domestic and foreign pressure, President Mobutu created a more democratic government. Rebel forces under Laurent Kabila defeated Mobutu's government in May 1997, and Kabila became president of the newly renamed nation.

The Congo is the third largest country in Africa and is potentially one of its richest as well. Sadly, widespread poverty and chaos remain the legacy of Mobutu's corrupt rule.

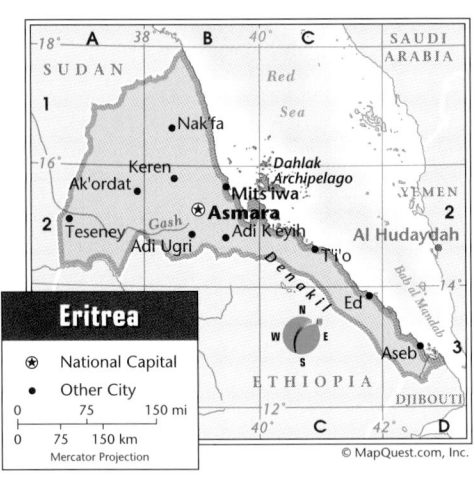

Capital: Asmara
Area: 47,194 sq. mi.
   121,320 sq. km.
Population: 4,306,000 (2002 est.)
Largest City: Asmara, 358,000
Languages: Tigre, Kunama, Cushitic dialects, Nora Bana, Arabic
Major Religions: Muslim, Coptic Christian, Roman Catholic, Protestant
Life Expectancy: 48 male, 52 female

Government: transitional government
Monetary Unit: Ethiopian birr
Industry: food processing, beverages, clothing and textiles
Agriculture: sorghum, livestock (including goats), fish, lentils, vegetables, maize, cotton, tobacco, coffee, sisal (for making rope)
Minerals and Resources: gold, potash, zinc, copper, salt, oil, fish

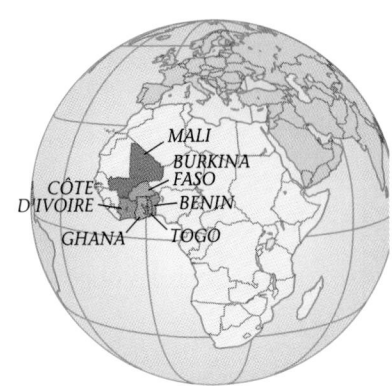

Eritrea

Eritrea officially celebrated its independence from Ethiopia in 1993, becoming the world's newest nation. Eritrea's people are comprised of nine ethnic groups which speak different but somewhat mutually intelligible languages. They are a mixture of Muslims and Christians.

The new government is dedicated to creating a democratic form of government and a free market economy. The challenges Eritrea faces are many. With no constitution or judicial system and an education system in shambles, the Eritrean government is having to build itself from scratch. It is an extremely poor country in which most people depend on subsistence farming.

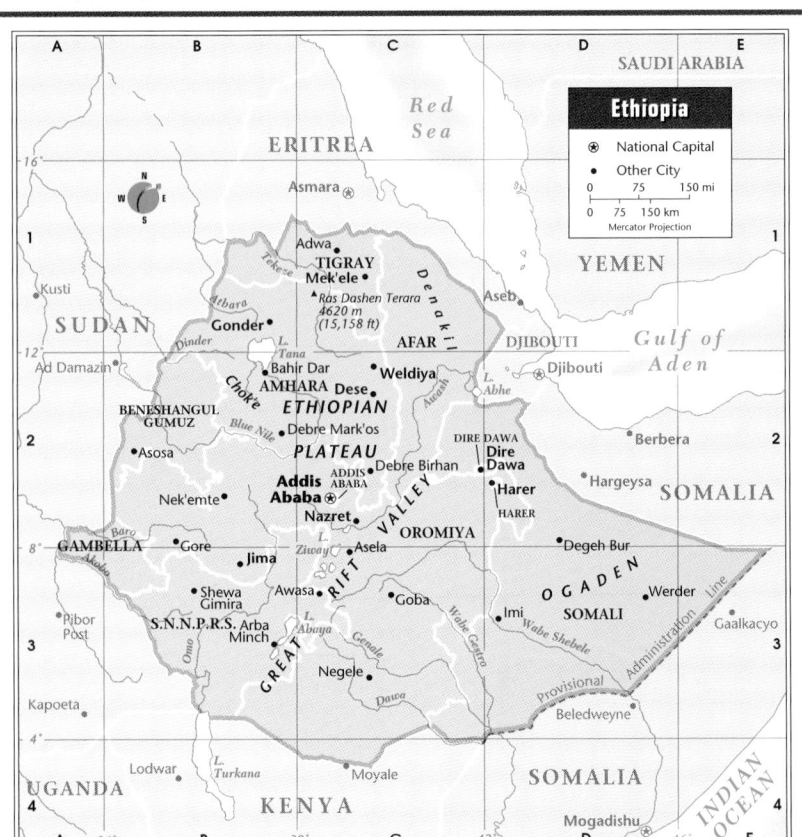

Capital: Djibouti
Area: 8,558 sq. mi.
   22,000 sq. km.
Population: 447,000 (2002 est.)
Largest City: Djibouti, 62,000
Languages: French, Arabic, Somali, Afar
Major Religions: Muslim, Christian
Life Expectancy: 48 male, 52 female
Government: republic
Monetary Unit: Djiboutian franc
Industry: dairy products, mineral-water bottling
Agriculture: fruit, vegetables, goats, sheep, camels
Minerals and Resources: geothermal areas

Djibouti

Formerly French Somaliland and the the French Territory of the Afars and the Issas, the Republic of Djibouti became independent from France in 1977.

More than half of the population of Djibouti live in the capital city, and the rest are mainly nomadic herders. Djibouti is a predominantly Muslim country, but there is freedom of religion.

Djibouti's economy is based on service activities connected with its strategic location and status as a free trade zone in northeast Africa.

Nile River Gorge, Ethiopia

Capital: Addis Ababa
Area: 438,452 sq. mi.
   1,127,127 sq. km.
Population: 65,254,000 (2002 est.)
Largest City: Addis Ababa, 2,424,000
Languages: Amharic, Tigrinya, Orominga, Guaraginga, Somali, Arabic, English
Major Religions: Muslim, Ethiopian Orthodox, animist
Life Expectancy: 48 male, 52 female

Government: federal republic
Monetary Unit: birr
Agriculture: coffee, oilseeds, cereals, pulses, coffee, oilseeds, sugarcane, potatoes, hides and skins, cattle, sheep, goats
Industry: food processing, beverages, textiles, chemicals, metals processing, cement
Natural resources: small reserves of gold, platinum, copper, potash

Ethiopia

Ethiopia is the oldest independent country in Africa, and one of the oldest in the world. In recent decades, Ethiopia has been plagued by drought, famine, civil war and brutal government regimes. In 1991, the Marxist-Leninist dictatorial government of Lt.-Col. Mengistu was overthrown by an opposition group seeking a more democratic government. Ethiopia has since been in transition to a multi-party democracy.

Years of civil strife and deadly droughts, plus the loss of Eritrea which became independent from Ethiopia in 1993, have left the Ethiopian economy gravely troubled. 80% of the population is employed in agriculture, which only accounts for a little less than half the GDP.

Somalia

Capital: Mogadishu
Area: 248,050 sq. mi.
636,660 sq. km.
637,660 sq. km.
Population: 7,753,000
(2002 est.)
Largest City: Mogadishu,
230,000
Languages: Somali, Arabic,
Italian, English
Major Religion: Muslim
Life Expectancy: 55 male, 56
female
Government: none
Monetary Unit: Somali
shilling
Industry: sugar refining, textiles, petroleum refining
Agriculture: cattle, sheep,
goats, bananas, sorghum,
corn, mangoes, sugarcane
Minerals and Resources: uranium, iron ore, tin, gypsum

Somalia was formed from two colonial territories, the British and Italian Somalilands, in 1960.

It is strategically located on the Horn of Africa along the route through the Red Sea and the Suez Canal.

The civil war which began in 1991 in Somalia has continued to devastate the country. The United Nation's intervention in 1992 to prevent massive starvation and, subsequently, to try to promote political reconciliation between the various waring factions was only minimally successful. When the final UN troops withdrew in March, 1995, clan fighting and starvation continued and there was no national government.

Rainbow at Lake Boragoi, Kenya

Capital: Kampala
Area: 91,820 sq. mi.
236,040 sq. km.
Population: 24,889,000
(2002 est.)
Largest City: Kampala, 1,209,000
Languages: English, Luganda,
Swahili, Bantu, Nilotic
Major Religions: Roman Catholic,
Protestant, Muslim, indigenous
beliefs
Life Expectancy: 36 male, 37
female
Government: republic
Monetary Unit: Ugandan shilling
Industry: sugar, brewing, tobacco,
cotton textiles, cement
Agriculture: coffee, tea, cotton, tobacco, cassava, potatoes, corn, millet, pulses, beef,
goat, meat, milk, poultry
Minerals and Resources: copper, cobalt, limestone, salt

Uganda

Uganda gained its independence from the United Kingdom in 1962. After independence, the country was plagued by chronic political instability and massive human rights violations. In 1986 the National Resistance Army, led by Yoweri Museveni, seized power in Kampala and set out to democratize the nation, putting an end to the brutality of former regimes.

Uganda has substantial natural resources, fertile soil and regular rainfall. Agriculture is the most important sector of the economy, employing over 80% of the population. Since 1986 the government has been working to rehabilitate and stabilize the economy.

Kenya

Capital: Nairobi
Area: 226,651 sq. mi.
582,650 sq. km.
Population: 31,223,000 (2002 est.)
Largest City: Nairobi, 2,143,000
Languages: English, Swahili
Major Religions: Protestant, Roman Catholic, indigenous beliefs
Life Expectancy: 51 male, 54 female
Government: republic
Monetary Unit: Kenyan shilling
Industry: plastic, furniture, batteries, textiles, soap, cigarettes,
flour, processing agricultural products, oil refining, cement,
tourism
Agriculture: coffee, tea, corn, wheat, sugarcane, fruit, vegetables, dairy products, beef, pork, poultry, eggs
Minerals and Resources: gold, limestone, soda ash, salt barytes,
rubies, fluorspar, garnets, wildlife

Since its independence from the United Kingdom in 1963, Kenya has maintained remarkable stability despite changes in its political system and crises in neighboring countries.

About 75% of the work force is engaged in agriculture, predominantly as subsistence farmers. In 1993, the government began a major economic reform and liberalization program which has been making substantial progress.

The national motto of Kenya is "harambee," meaning "pull together," and it is that belief which motivates volunteers in hundreds of communities in Kenya to build schools, clinics and other needed facilities.

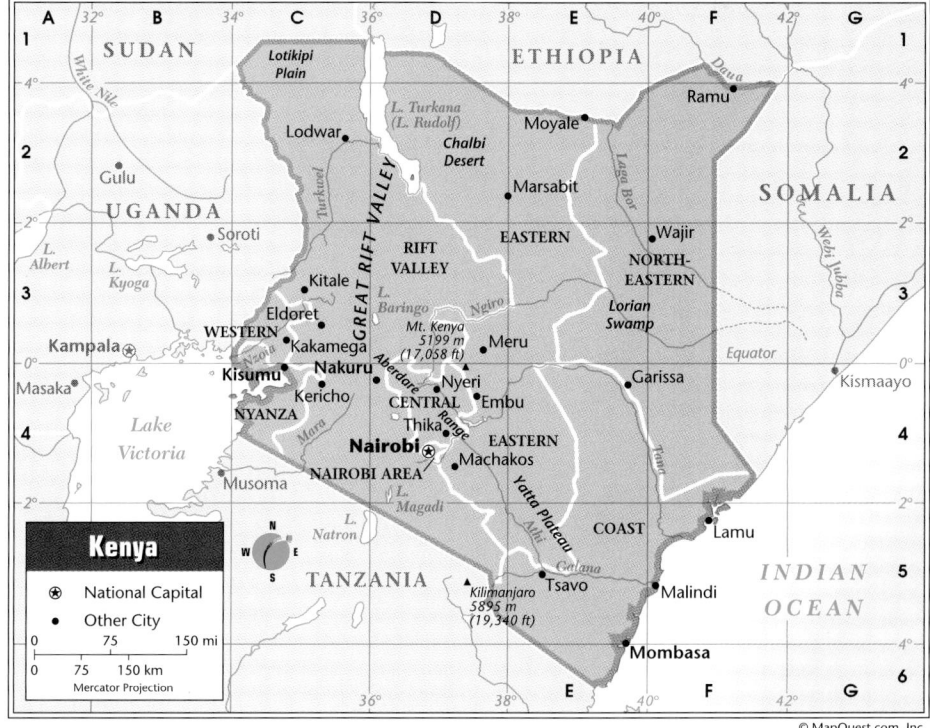

© MapQuest.com, Inc.

Capital: Bujumbura
Area: 10,742 sq. mi.
27,830 sq. km.
Population: 5,965,000 (2002 est.)
Largest City: Bujumbura, 235,000
Languages: Kirundi, French, Swahili
Major Religions: Roman Catholic, Protestant, indigenous beliefs, Muslim
Life Expectancy: 38 male, 42 female
Government: republic
Monetary Unit: Burundi franc
Industry: light consumer goods such as blankets, shoes, soap; assembly of imported components; public works construction; food processing
Agriculture: coffee, cotton, tea, corn, sorghum, sweet potatoes, bananas, manioc, livestock
Minerals & Resources: nickel, uranium, rare earth oxide, peat, cobalt, copper, platinum, vanadium

Formerly a Belgian trusteeship under the United Nations, Burundi became independent as a constitutional monarchy in 1962. In 1966 the monarchy was overthrown and the country became a republic.

Like Rwanda, Burundi has a long history of violence between the Tutsi minority and the Hutu majority. Recent efforts by the government to create a coalition government composed of equal numbers from each faction have not been very successful at solving the tensions, but they have achieved a plural political system and brought some measure of stability to this war-weary nation.

Burundi is landlocked and resource-poor. Its people depend primarily on subsistence agriculture.

Burundi

After World War II Rwanda and its southern neighbor Burundi were made UN trust territories with Belgium as the administrative authority. In 1962, Rwanda became an independent republic.

There have long been tensions between Rwanda's two largest ethnic groups, the Hutus, who comprise about 90% of the population, and the Tutsis, who comprise 9%. These tensions turned into civil war and genocide in 1994. This war left millions of Rwandans, mostly Tutsis, dead, displaced, or fleeing the country. The international community responded with one of the largest humanitarian relief efforts ever undertaken.

Rwanda's countryside is covered by grasslands and small farms extending over rolling hills. There are few villages and most Rwandan families live in self-contained compounds.

Capital: Kigali
Area: 10,167 sq. mi.
26,340 sq. km.
Population: 7,668,000 (2002 est.)
Largest City: Kigali, 234,000
Languages: Kinyarwanda, French, Kiswahili
Major Religions: Roman Catholic, Protestant, Muslim, indigenous beliefs
Life Expectancy: 39 male, 40 female
Government: republic, presidential system
Monetary Unit: Rwandan franc
Industry: mining of tin ore and tungsten ore, tin, cement, agricultural processing, soap, furniture, shoes, textiles
Agriculture: coffee, tea, pyrethrum, bananas, beans, sorghum, potatoes
Minerals & Resources: gold, tin ore, tungsten ore, natural gas, hydropower

Rwanda

Zebras, Ngorongoro Crater, Tanzania

Tanzania

Capital: Dar es Salaam
Area: 364,805 sq. mi.
945,090 sq. km.
Population: 35,302,000 (2002 est.)
Largest City: Dar es Salaam, 1,361,000
Languages: Swahili, English
Major Religions: Christian, Muslim, indigenous beliefs
Life Expectancy: 41 male, 44 female
Government: republic
Monetary Unit: Tanzanian shilling
Industry: agricultural processing of sugar, beer, cigarettes, sisal twine, diamond and gold mining, oil refining, shoes, cement, textiles, wood products, fertilizer
Agriculture: coffee, sisal, tea, cotton, pyrethrum (insecticide), cashews, tobacco, cloves, corn, wheat, cassava, bananas, fruits, vegetables, nominal livestock
Minerals & Resources: hydropower potential, tin, phosphates, iron ore, coal, diamonds, gemstones, gold, natural gas, nickel

Prior to the end of World War I, what is present-day Tanzania was under German colonial control. After World War II, it became a United Nations trust territory under British control.

Tanganyika became independent in 1961, united with Zanzibar in 1964, and then formed the United Republic of Tanzania later that year.

Tanzania depends heavily on agriculture, which provides almost 60% of its GDP and employs 90% of its people. Due to topography and climatic conditions, however, only about 5% of its land area can be used to cultivate crops.

In recent years, Tanzania has been making the transition from an autocratic, single-party state system to a more democratic, multi-party system.

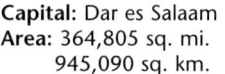

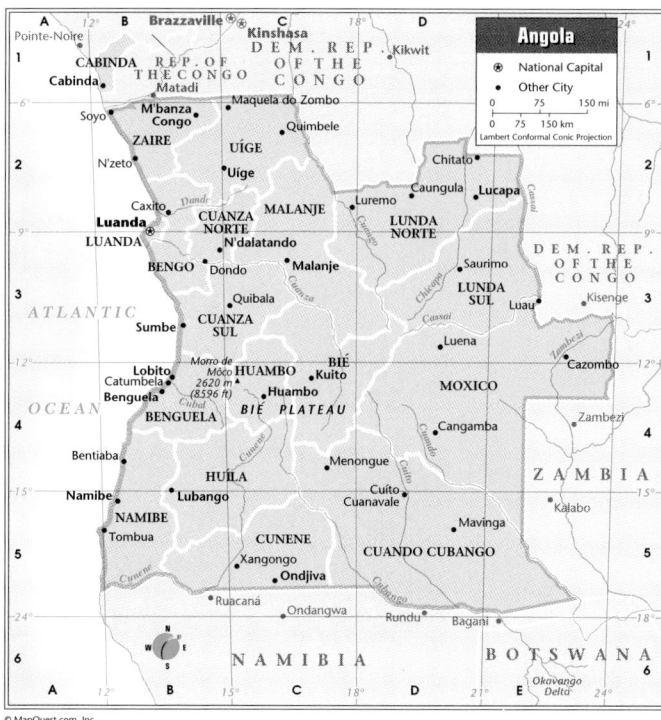

Angola was settled by the Portuguese in the 15th century and remained a Portuguese colony until 1975, when it gained independence. Since independence, Angola has been consumed with civil war. A peace accord signed between the government and the insurgent UNITA forces in 1994 implemented a cease-fire; however, sporadic fighting continues.

Long dependent on the Soviet Union and Cuba and a single Marxist-Leninist party system, Angola adopted a multi-party, democratic system in 1991. Since 1995, there have been UN peacekeeping forces in the country to oversee the peace process.

The vast majority of Angolans depend on subsistence agriculture for their livelihood, although it accounts for less than 15% of the GDP. While it has rich natural resources, Angola needs a more stable political system and successful cease-fire in order to begin rebuilding its devastated economy.

Capital: Luanda
Area: 481,226 sq. mi.
1,246,700 sq. km.
Population: 10,554,000 (2002 est.)
Largest City: Luanda, 1,822,000

Angola

Languages: Portuguese, Bantu, and other African languages
Major Religions: indigenous beliefs, Roman Catholic, Protestant
Life Expectancy: 44 male, 48 female
Government: transitional government nominally a multiparty democracy with a strong presidential system
Monetary Unit: new kwanza
Industry: petroleum, fish processing, brewing, tobacco, sugar, textiles, cement, basic metal products, diamond, iron ore, phosphate, feldspar, bauxite, uranium, and gold mining
Agriculture: bananas, sugarcane, coffee, sisal, corn, cotton, manioc, tobacco, cassava, vegetables, plantains, livestock, fishing, forestry
Minerals & Resources: petroleum, diamonds, iron ore, phosphates, copper, feldspar, gold, bauxite, uranium

Atlantic coast at Beguela, Angola

Capital: Lusaka
Area: 290,507 sq. mi.
752,610 sq. km.
Population: 10,149,000 (2002 est.)
Largest City: Lusaka, 1,270,000
Languages: English, numerous indigenous languages
Major Religions: Christian, Muslim and Hindu, indigenous beliefs
Life Expectancy: 43 male, 43 female
Government: republic
Monetary Unit: Zambian kwacha
Industry: copper mining and processing, construction, foodstuffs, beverages, chemicals, textiles, and fertilizer
Agriculture: corn, sorghum, rice, peanuts, sunflower, tobacco, cotton, sugarcane, cassava, cattle, goats, beef, eggs
Minerals & Resources: copper, cobalt, zinc, lead, coal, emeralds, gold, silver, uranium, hydropower potential

Zambia

Zambia became a republic immediately upon attaining independence from the United Kingdom in 1964.

Zambians are made up of more than 70 Bantu-speaking tribes, each of which constitutes a small percentage of the population. About half of the people are subsistence farmers; the other half are concentrated in a few urban zones, making Zambia one of sub-Saharan Africa's most highly urbanized nations.

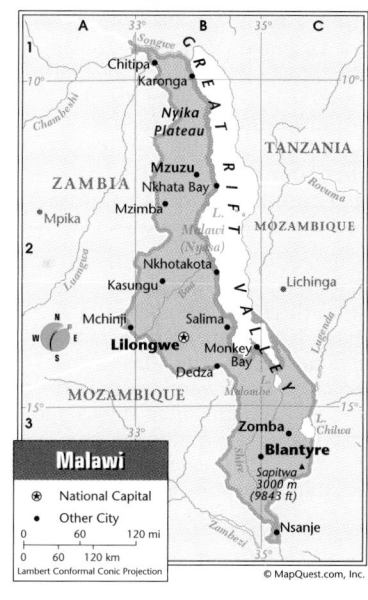

Malawi

Malawi, formerly Nyasaland, became independent from the United Kingdom in 1964. Malawi's transition to a multi-party democracy in 1993 has improved its human rights record and thus strengthened its standing in the international community and helped the economy restructure and grow.

About 90% of Malawians live in rural areas. The population is comprised of nine main tribal groups who, for the most part, have little friction between them.

Capital: Lilongwe
Area: 45,733 sq. mi.
118,480 sq. km.
Population: 11,393,000 (2002 est.)
Largest City: Blantyre, 502,000
Languages: English, Chichewa
Major Religions: Protestant, Roman Catholic, Muslim, indigenous beliefs
Life Expectancy: 38 male, 40 female
Government: multiparty democracy
Monetary Unit: Malawian kwacha
Industry: agricultural processing of tea, sugar, tobacco; sawmilling, cement, consumer goods
Agriculture: tobacco, sugarcane, cotton, tea, corn, potatoes, cassava, sorghum, pulses, cattle, goats
Minerals & Resources: limestone, unexploited deposits of uranium, coal, and bauxite

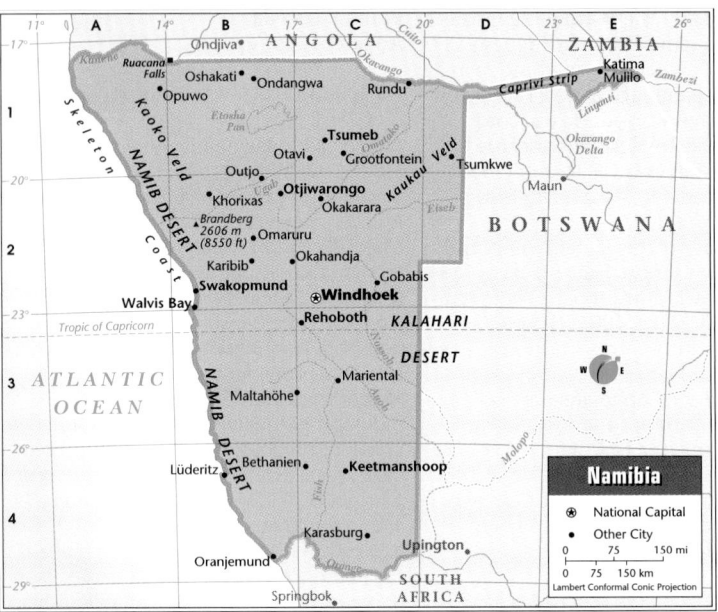

© MapQuest.com, Inc.

Namibia

Capital: Windhoek
Area: 318,611 sq. mi.
825,418 sq. km.
Population: 1,897,000 (2002 est.)
Largest City: Windhoek, 147,000
Languages: English, Afrikaans, German, indigenous languages: Oshivambo, Herero, Nama
Major Religions: Christian (Lutheran and other denominations)
Life Expectancy: 59 male, 65 female
Government: republic
Monetary Unit: South African rand
Industry: meat packing, fish processing, dairy products, mining of copper, lead, zinc, diamond, uranium
Agriculture: livestock, millet, peanuts, sorghum, fishing potential
Minerals & Resources: diamonds, copper, uranium, gold, lead, tin, lithium, cadmium, zinc, salt, vanadium, natural gas, fish, deposits of oil, natural gas, coal, iron ore

MICHAEL A. HEERSCHAP

Church in Windhoek, Namibia

From 1880 to 1915, Namibia was a German protectorate, named South West Africa. It was then administered by the Union of South Africa under the terms of the Treaty of Versailles, but when the League of Nations dissolved, the terms of South Africa's administrative position were nebulous.

South Africa continued to administer Namibia but in 1971, the International Court of Justice determined that this administration was illegal and that South Africa should immediately withdraw from Namibia. Implementation of this withdrawal was very slow and finally in 1990, Namibia became independent.

More than half of Namibians rely on agriculture for their livelihood, and the economy is also very dependent on the mining sector.

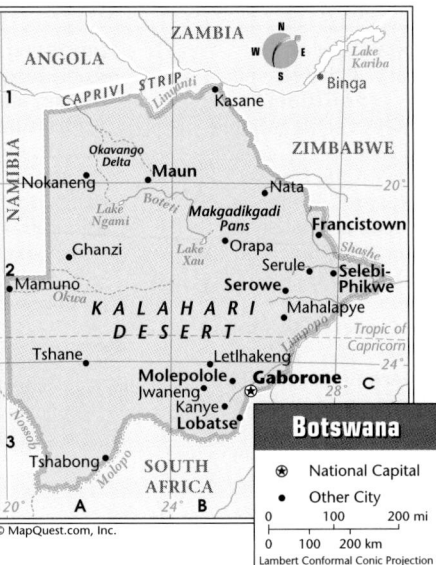

© MapQuest.com, Inc.

Botswana became independent from the United Kingdom in 1966. This parliamentary republic has a flourishing, multiparty constitutional democracy and its record for free and fair elections is very good.

Since independence, Botswana's economic growth rate has been impressive. Since the 1980s, the country has become the world's largest producer of quality diamonds. Agriculture employs about 80% of the population, but contributes only 2% of the GDP. Many of Botswana's citizens work in mines in South Africa.

Zimbabwe, formerly Southern Rhodesia, became independent from the United Kingdom in 1980. For the first ten years of independence, Zimbabwe's government was a very centralized socialist system. Since 1990 some free market economic reforms have been implemented to encourage exports and foreign investment.

Three quarters of Zimbabweans depend on agriculture for their livelihood and Zimbabwe is self-sufficient in food production. Tobacco is the most important export crop, Zimbabwe being its largest exporter in the world. Tourism is becoming an important sector of the economy.

© MapQuest.com, Inc.

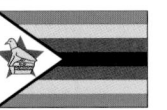

Zimbabwe

Capital: Harare
Area: 150,764 sq. mi.
390,580 sq. km.
Population: 12,463,000 (2002 est.)
Largest City: Harare, 1,189,000
Languages: English, Shona, Sindebele
Major Religions: syncretic (part Christian, part indigenous beliefs), Christian, indigenous beliefs, Muslim
Life Expectancy: 40 male, 43 female
Government: parliamentary democracy
Monetary Unit: Zimbabwean dollar
Industry: mining, steel, clothing and footwear, chemicals, foodstuffs, fertilizer, beverages, transportation equipment, wood products
Agriculture: corn, cotton, tobacco, wheat, coffee, sugarcane, peanuts, cattle, sheep, goats, pigs
Minerals & Resources: coal, chromium ore, asbestos, gold, nickel, copper, iron ore, vanadium, lithium, tin, platinum

Botswana

Capital: Gaborone
Area: 231,804 sq. mi.
600,370 sq. km.
Population: 1,579,000 (2002 est.)
Largest City: Gaborone, 186,000
Languages: English, Setswana
Major Religions: indigenous beliefs, Christian
Life Expectancy: 61 male, 67 female
Government: parliamentary republic
Monetary Unit: pula
Industry: mining of diamonds, copper, nickel, coal, salt, soda ash, potash, livestock processing
Agriculture: sorghum, maize, millet, pulses, groundnuts, beans, cowpeas, sunflower seeds, livestock
Minerals & Resources: diamonds, copper, nickel, salt, potash, coal, iron ore, silver

Mozambique gained its independence from Portugal in 1975, after ten years of sporadic warfare and some major political changes in Portugal. The new Mozambique government soon established itself as a one-party Marxist state, but one year later a civil war broke out between the ruling party and a national resistance movement which was born in Southern Rhodesia to discourage supporting the Zimbabwean and South African liberation movements.

In 1990 the two sides began peace negotiations and a new constitution was enacted that called for a multiparty system. The first multiparty democratic elections were held in 1994 and were pronounced free and fair by the UN and other international organizations.

Mozambique is one of Africa's poorest countries, yet it does have sizable agricultural, hydropower and transportation resources that have not been exploited.

MICHAEL A. HEERSCHAP

Maputo, Mozambique

Mozambique

Capital: Maputo
Area: 309,413 sq. mi.
  801,590 sq. km.
Population: 17,324,000 (2002 est.)
Largest City: Maputo, 967,000
Languages: Portuguese, indigenous dialects
Major Religions: indigenous beliefs, Christian, Muslim
Life Expectancy: 47 male, 51 female
Government: republic
Monetary Unit: metical
Industry: food, beverages, chemicals (fertilizer, soap, paints), petroleum products, textiles, nonmetallic mineral products (cement, glass, asbestos), tobacco
Agriculture: cotton, cashew nuts, sugarcane, tea, shrimp, cassava, corn, rice, tropical fruits
Minerals & Resources: coal, titanium

Formerly Basutoland, Lesotho is a small enclave surrounded by South Africa. It is a constitutional monarchy that gained its independence from the United Kingdom in 1966. Lesotho has been in a transition stage in the 1990s from a military regime to a multiparty democratic system.

Lesotho's only important natural resource is water, which it supplies to South Africa under a 1986 agreement, the Highlands Water Project. Its economy is based on agriculture, which employs the vast majority of Bathsoto. A large percentage of adult males are employed in South African mines.

Lesotho

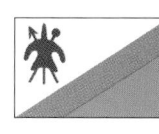

MICHAEL A. HEERSCHAP

Lesotho highlands

Capital: Maseru
Area: 11,715 sq. mi.
  30,350 sq. km.
Population: 1,858,000 (2002 est.)
Largest City: Maseru, 138,000
Languages: Sesotho, English, Zulu, Xhosa
Major Religions: Christian, indigenous beliefs
Life Expectancy: 61 male, 64 female
Government: constitutional monarchy
Monetary Unit: loti
Industry: food, beverages, textiles, handicrafts, tourism
Agriculture: subsistence farming, livestock, corn, wheat, pulses, sorghum, barley
Minerals & Resources: water, agricultural and grazing land, diamonds

---

Swaziland became independent from the United Kingdom in 1968, and established itself as a constitutional monarchy. The constitution was repealed and the parliament dissolved by the king in 1973, and though a new parliament was formed in 1979, political parties and trade unions remained banned. Swaziland has always been heavily dependent on South Africa, which all but surrounds it geographically.

Over half of the Swazi labor force relies on subsistence agriculture for a living, and about 70% of the population live in rural areas. Despite a relatively high population growth rate of 3.4%, Swaziland ranks among the more prosperous African countries.

Swaziland

Capital: Mbabane (administrative); Lobamba (legislative)
Area: 6,701 sq. mi.
  17,360 sq. km.
Population: 1,150,000 (2002 est.)
Largest City: Mbabane, 38,000
Languages: English, siSwati
Major Religions: Christian, indigenous beliefs
Life Expectancy: 53 male, 61 female
Government: monarchy
Monetary Unit: lilangeni
Industry: mining (coal and asbestos), wood pulp, sugar
Agriculture: mostly subsistence agriculture, sugarcane, cotton, maize, tobacco, rice, citrus, fruit, pineapples, corn, sorghum, peanuts, cattle, goats, sheep
Minerals & Resources: asbestos, coal, clay, cassiterite, hydropower, forests, small gold and diamond deposits, quarry stone, and talc

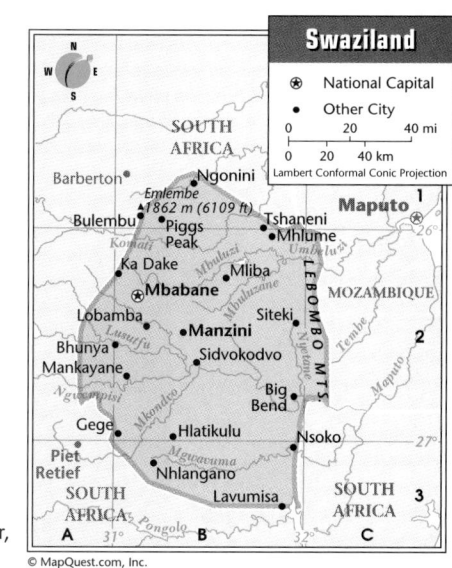

© MapQuest.com, Inc.

Pretoria skyline

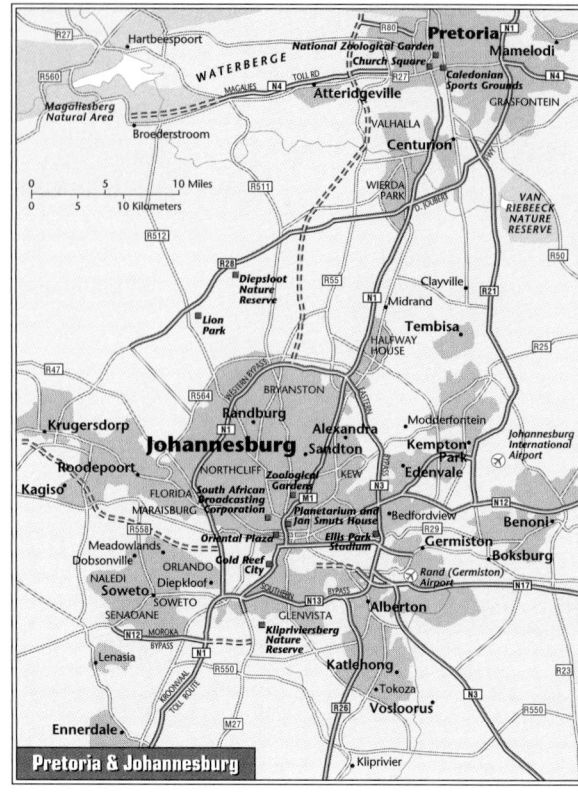

Pretoria & Johannesburg

The Cape of Good Hope

Capital: Pretoria (administrative); Cape Town (legislative); Bloemfontein (judicial)
Area: 470,886 sq. mi.
1,219,912 sq. km.
Population: 42,716,000 (2002 est.)
Largest City: Cape Town, 2,898,000
Languages: Afrikaans, English, Ndebele, Pedi, Sotho, Swazi, Tsonga, Tswana, Venda, Xhosa, Zulu
Major Religions: Christian, Hindu, Muslim
Life Expectancy: 63 male, 68 female
Government: republic
Monetary Unit: rand
Industry: mining of platinum, gold, and chromium; automobile assembly, metalworking, machinery, textile, iron and steel, chemical, fertilizer, foodstuffs
Agriculture: cattle, poultry, sheep, wool, milk, beef, corn, wheat, sugarcane, fruits, vegetables
Minerals & Resources: gold, chromium, antimony, coal, iron ore, manganese, nickel, phosphates, tin, uranium, gem diamonds, platinum, copper, vanadium, salt, natural gas

South Africa

South Africa became independent from the United Kingdom in 1910, but remained a self-governing dominion of the British Empire until 1961 when it became a republic.

Until 1991, South African law divided the population of the country into four major racial categories: Africans (black), whites, coloreds, and Asians. The white minority, which makes up about one-seventh of the population, has had complete political power since the early 1900s. South Africa held its first non-racial elections in 1994, electing Nelson Mandela as president, and is under a transitional constitution until 1999.

The new constitution grants more than 25 inalienable and fundamental rights to all South Africans. The Reconstruction and Development Program which the government embarked on in May 1994 addresses the broad range of inequities of the long-standing apartheid system.

South Africa has an industrialized economy which, despite a strong private sector, has substantial government intervention. Mining is one of its most important industries, and South Africa is the world's largest producer of platinum, gold, and chromium. Agriculture employs about 30% of the labor force but only accounts for 5% of the GDP.

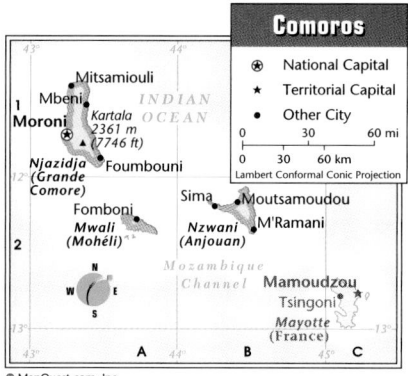

© MapQuest.com, Inc.

Comoros

Capital: Moroni
Area: 838 sq. mi.
2,170 sq. km.
Population: 614,000 (2002 est.)
Largest City: Moroni, 30,000
Languages: Arabic, French, Comoran
Major Religions: Sunni Muslim, Roman Catholic
Life Expectancy: 56 male, 61 female
Government: independent republic
Monetary Unit: Comoran franc
Industry: perfume distillation, textiles, furniture, jewelry, construction materials, soft drinks
Agriculture: vanilla, cloves, perfume essences, copra, coconuts, bananas, cassava, essence of ylang-ylang

Comoros is a group of islands off the coast of southeastern Africa. The islands became a French overseas territory after World War II and were granted political autonomy in 1961. In 1975, three years before it was to become officially independent, the Comorian parliament declared unilateral independence. The island of Mayotte abstained from this decision and is still under French administration, despite Comoros' claim to it.

Most Comorians share African-Arab origins and are Muslim, with the exception of the predominantly Catholic Mahorais of Mayotte.

Capital: Antananarivo
Area: 226,597 sq. mi.
587,040 sq. km.
Population: 16,473,000 (2002 est.)
Largest City: Antananarivo, 1,103,000
Languages: French, Malagasy
Major Religions: indigenous beliefs, Christian, Muslim
Life Expectancy: 52 male, 56 female
Government: republic
Monetary Unit: Malagasy franc
Industry: meat canneries, soap factories, breweries, tanneries, sugar refining plants, textiles, glassware, cement, automobile assembly plant, paper, petroleum
Agriculture: coffee, vanilla, sugarcane, cloves, cocoa, rice, cassava, beans, bananas, peanuts, cattle, rice
Minerals & Resources: graphite, chromite, coal, bauxite, salt, quartz, tar sands, semiprecious stones, mica

Madagascar

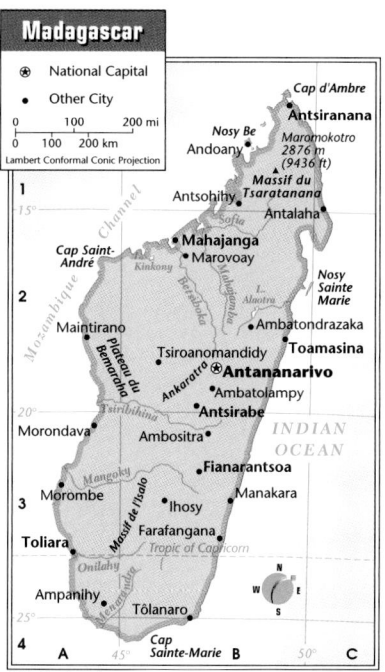

© MapQuest.com, Inc.

Madagascar lies off the southeast coast of Africa and is the fourth largest island in the world. Its people are of mixed Malayo-Polynesian, Arab and African origin. The French established control over the island by military force in 1895 and made it a colony. Madagascar gained independence from France in 1960.

Madagascar is a poor country that has considerable potential to grow but faces obstacles such as chronic malnutrition, a fast growth rate, a severe loss of forest cover and underfunded health and education facilities. Agriculture provides the livelihood for more than two-thirds of the population. The island has great tourism potential due to its unique and diverse flora and fauna, and its coastal waters are rich in shrimp and fish.

Capital: Victoria
Area: 176 sq. mi.
455 sq. km.
Population: 80,000 (2002 est.)
Largest City: Victoria, 25,000
Languages: English, French, Creole
Major Religions: Roman Catholic, Anglican
Life Expectancy: 67 male, 74 female
Government: republic
Monetary Unit: Seychelles rupee
Industry: tourism, processing of coconut and vanilla, fishing, coir rope factory, boat building, printing, furniture, beverages
Agriculture: coconuts, cinnamon, vanilla, sweet potatoes, cassava, bananas, chicken
Minerals & Resources: fish, copra, cinnamon trees

The Seychelles is an archipelago of 115 islands in the Indian Ocean. The islands were first colonized by the French in 1756 to establish spice plantations, but they were captured by the English in 1794 and later made a dependency of Mauritius in 1814. In 1903, the islands were formed into a separate colony and in 1976, they became an independent republic.

About 90% of the Seychellois people live on Mahé, the largest island. Seychelle culture is a mixture of French and African influences.

The tourist industry employs about 30% of the labor force in Seychelles and provides more than 70% of hard currency earnings. The government has worked to develop farming, fishing, and small-scale manufacturing.

© MapQuest.com, Inc.

Seychelles

In 1638, the Dutch colonized Mauritius, but abandoned their colony in 1710. Mauritius was claimed by France in 1715, and then taken by the British in 1810. Mauritius became independent and a member of the Commonwealth in 1968, and became a republic in 1992.

Mauritius is a parliamentary democracy whose politics since independence have been turbulent and characterized by coalition and alliance building. Despite this, Mauritius has developed from a low income, agriculturally based economy to a middle income, diversified economy with growing industrial and tourist sectors.

Mauritius

Capital: Port Louis
Area: 718 sq. mi.
1,860 sq. km.
Population: 1,200,000 (2002 est.)
Largest City: Port Louis, 128,000
Languages: English, Creole, French, Hindi, Urdu, Hakka, Bojpoori
Major Religions: Hindu, Roman Catholic, Protestant, Muslim
Life Expectancy: 67 male, 75 female
Government: parliamentary democracy
Monetary Unit: Mauritian rupee
Industry: food processing (largely sugar milling), textiles, wearing apparel, chemicals, metal products, transport equipment, non-electrical machinery, tourism
Agriculture: sugarcane, tea, corn, potatoes, bananas, pulses, cattle, goats, fish
Minerals & Resources: arable land, fish

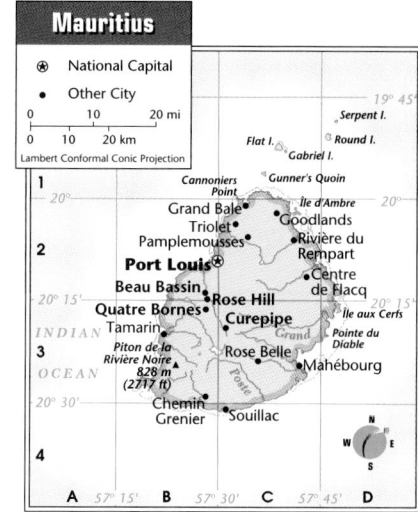

© MapQuest.com, Inc.

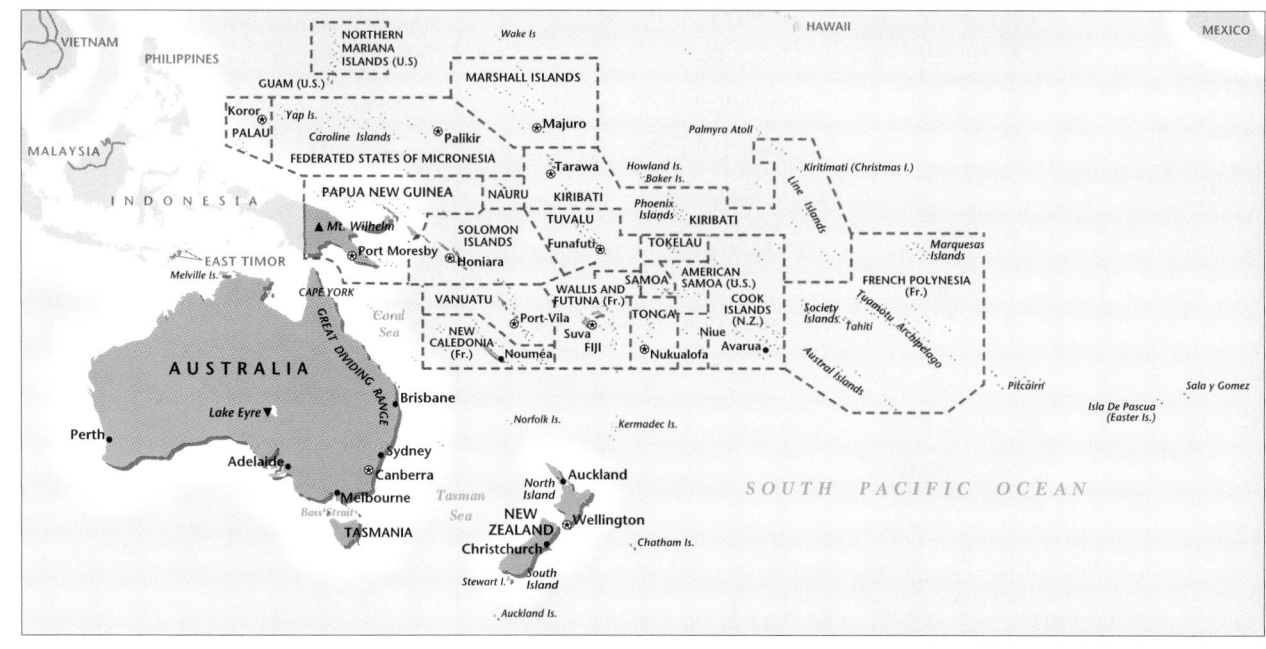

Population: 31,598,000 (2002)
Area: 3,300,000 sq. mi.
8,547,000 sq. km.
Highest Point: Mt. Wilhelm
14,790 ft. (4,509 m.)
Lowest Point: Lake Eyre
52 ft. (16 m.)
below sea level
Largest Urban Areas:
Sydney, Australia
Melbourne, Australia
Brisbane, Australia
Perth, Australia
Auckland, New Zealand
Adelaide, Australia
Christchurch, New Zealand
Countries: 14

Above Right: Bay of Islands, New Zealand; **Below Right:** Sydney Tower by moonlight, Australia; **Below:** Ayers Rock, Australia

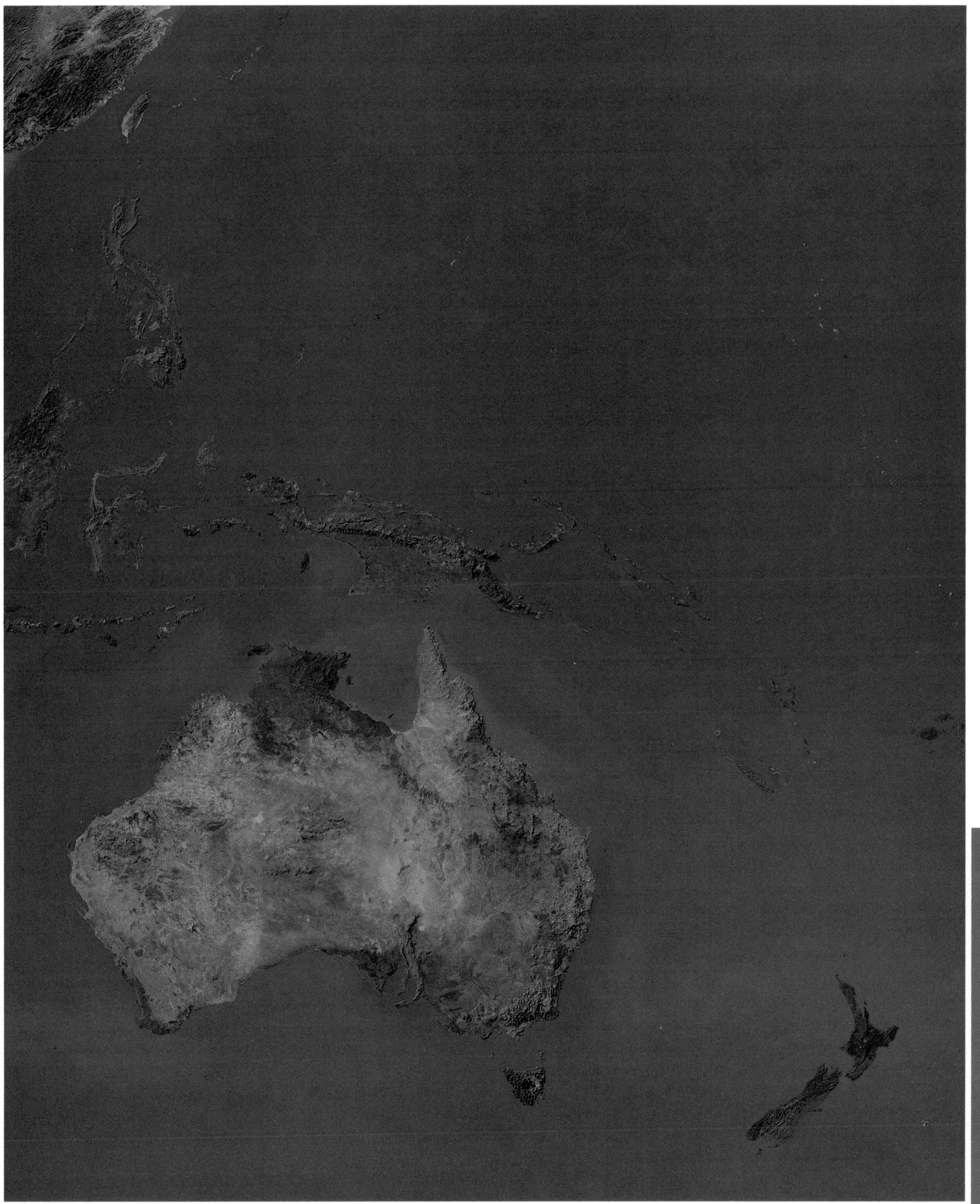

Major Metropolitan Areas

Australia

Sydney	3,997,000
Melbourne	3,367,000
Brisbane	1,628,000
Perth	1,340,000
Adelaide	1,073,000
Newcastle	471,000
Gold Coast (Southport)	397,000
Canberra	312,000

Fiji

Suva	167,000
Lautoka	29,000

Kiribati

Tarawa (Bairiki)	25,000

Marshall Islands

Majuro	18,000

Micronesia

Weno	15,000
Colonia	3,000

Nauru

Yaren	4,000

New Zealand

Auckland	1,075,000
Wellington	340,000
Christchurch	334,000

Palau

Koror	13,000

Papua New Guinea

Port Moresby	332,000
Lae	81,000
Madang	27,000
Wewak	23,000

Samoa

Apia	34,000

Solomon Islands

Honiara	61,000

Tonga

Nuku'alofa	30,000

Tuvalu

Funafuti	4,000

Vanuatu

Port-Vila	30,000

International comparability of population data is limited by varying census methods. Where metropolitan population is unavailable, core city population is shown.

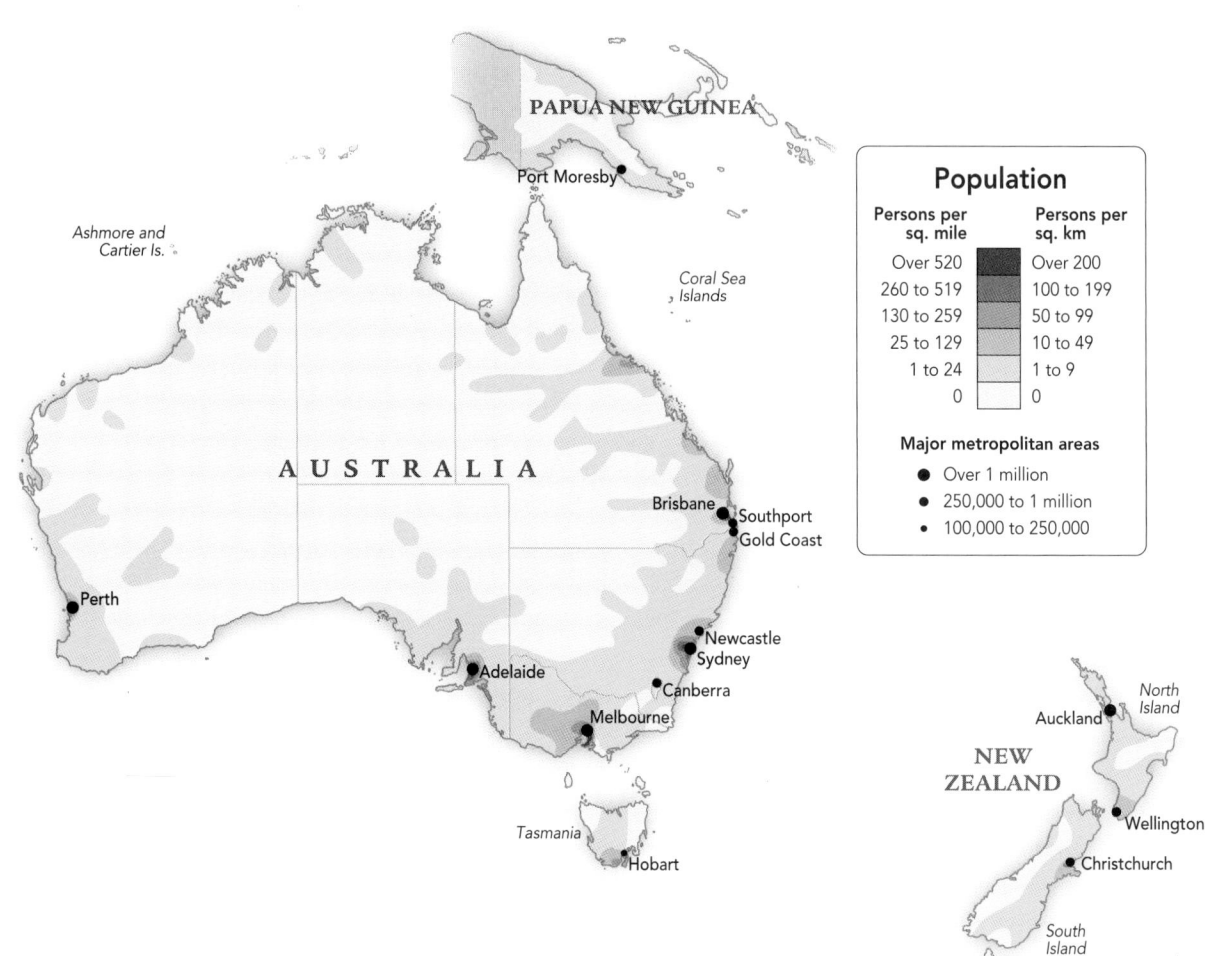

Population

Persons per sq. mile	Persons per sq. km
Over 520	Over 200
260 to 519	100 to 199
130 to 259	50 to 99
25 to 129	10 to 49
1 to 24	1 to 9
0	0

Major metropolitan areas

- ● Over 1 million
- ● 250,000 to 1 million
- • 100,000 to 250,000

Estimated
2002 Population (in millions)

Australia 20
Papua New Guinea 5
New Zealand 4
All other countries 2

Source: U.S. Census Bureau

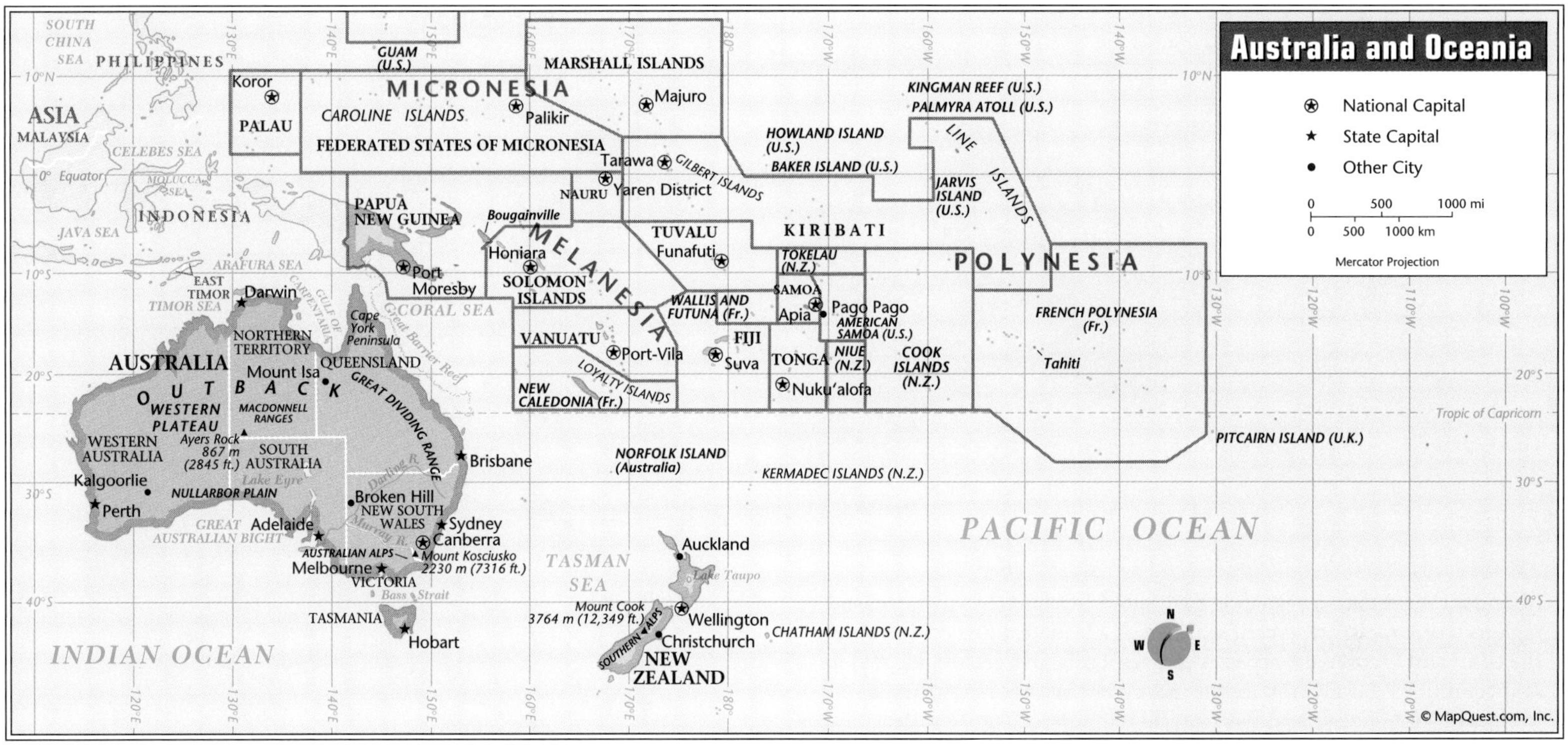

Australia and Oceania

- ⊛ National Capital
- ★ State Capital
- • Other City

| 0 | 500 | 1000 mi |
| 0 | 500 | 1000 km |

Mercator Projection

SOUTH CHINA SEA
PHILIPPINES
10°N
ASIA
MALAYSIA
CELEBES SEA
0° Equator
MOLUCCA SEA
INDONESIA
JAVA SEA
ARAFURA SEA
10°S
EAST TIMOR
TIMOR SEA

GUAM (U.S.)
MICRONESIA
CAROLINE ISLANDS
Koror
PALAU
⊛ Palikir
FEDERATED STATES OF MICRONESIA
Tarawa
NAURU Yaren District
PAPUA NEW GUINEA
Bougainville
⊛ Port Moresby
Honiara
SOLOMON ISLANDS
MELANESIA

MARSHALL ISLANDS
⊛ Majuro

KINGMAN REEF (U.S.)
PALMYRA ATOLL (U.S.)
HOWLAND ISLAND (U.S.)
BAKER ISLAND (U.S.)
⊛ GILBERT ISLANDS
JARVIS ISLAND (U.S.)
LINE ISLANDS

TUVALU
Funafuti
WALLIS AND FUTUNA (Fr.)
VANUATU
Port-Vila
NEW CALEDONIA (Fr.)
LOYALTY ISLANDS

KIRIBATI
TOKELAU (N.Z.)
SAMOA
Apia ⊛
Pago Pago
AMERICAN SAMOA (U.S.)
FIJI
Suva
TONGA
⊛ Nuku'alofa
NIUE (N.Z.)
COOK ISLANDS (N.Z.)

POLYNESIA
FRENCH POLYNESIA (Fr.)
Tahiti •

PITCAIRN ISLAND (U.K.)

Cape York Peninsula
GULF OF CARPENTARIA
CORAL SEA
Great Barrier Reef
GREAT DIVIDING RANGE

AUSTRALIA
Darwin
NORTHERN TERRITORY
Mount Isa •
QUEENSLAND
OUTBACK
WESTERN PLATEAU
MACDONNELL RANGES
Ayers Rock 867 m (2845 ft.) ▲
SOUTH AUSTRALIA
WESTERN AUSTRALIA
Kalgoorlie •
NULLARBOR PLAIN
Perth ★
GREAT AUSTRALIAN BIGHT
Adelaide ★
Lake Eyre
Darling R.
Murray R.
Broken Hill •
NEW SOUTH WALES
AUSTRALIAN ALPS
Melbourne ★
VICTORIA
Bass Strait
TASMANIA
Hobart ★
Brisbane ★
Sydney ★
Canberra ⊛
Mount Kosciusko 2230 m (7316 ft.)

INDIAN OCEAN

NORFOLK ISLAND (Australia)
KERMADEC ISLANDS (N.Z.)

PACIFIC OCEAN

Tropic of Capricorn

TASMAN SEA
Auckland •
Lake Taupo
Mount Cook 3764 m (12,349 ft.)
SOUTHERN ALPS
Wellington ⊛
Christchurch •
NEW ZEALAND
CHATHAM ISLANDS (N.Z.)

© MapQuest.com, Inc.

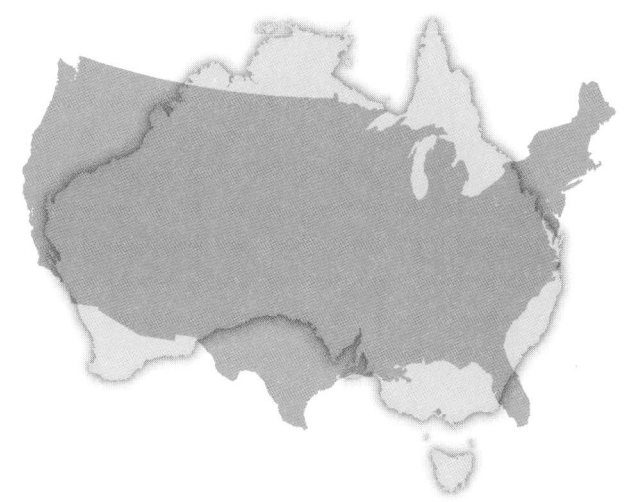

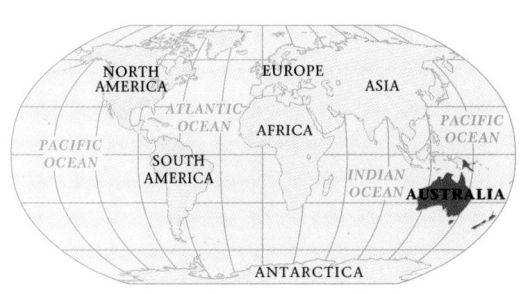

NORTH AMERICA
EUROPE
ASIA
ATLANTIC OCEAN
AFRICA
PACIFIC OCEAN
SOUTH AMERICA
INDIAN OCEAN
PACIFIC OCEAN
AUSTRALIA
ANTARCTICA

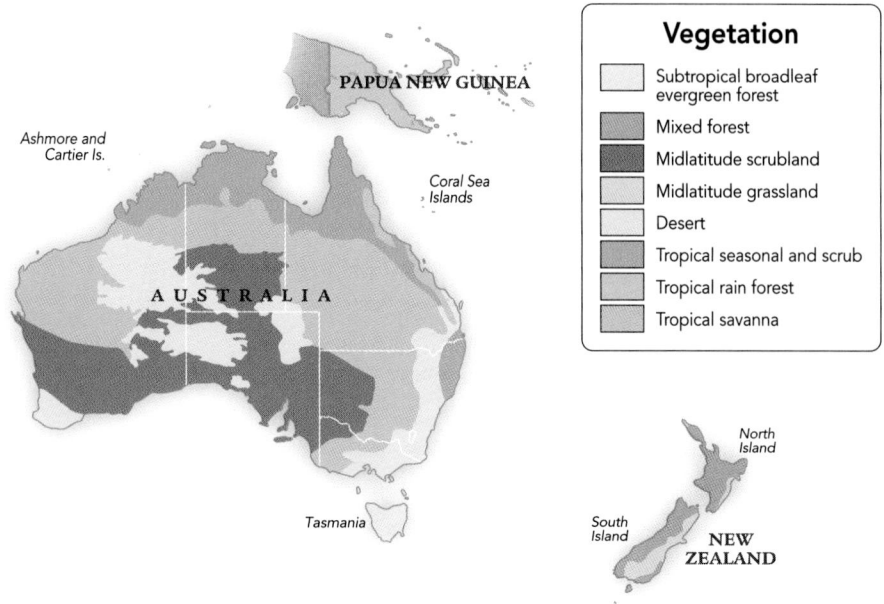

Vegetation

- Subtropical broadleaf evergreen forest
- Mixed forest
- Midlatitude scrubland
- Midlatitude grassland
- Desert
- Tropical seasonal and scrub
- Tropical rain forest
- Tropical savanna

Abundant Australian forestlands are limited to relatively narrow coastal regions where moisture, even if seasonal, is adequate. Most of the rest of the continent is covered by species of trees, bush, and grasses adapted to arid conditions. Eucalyptus are the most common trees in Australia.

Papua New Guinea has dense tropical rain forests, and New Zealand has mixed forests and grasslands arising from its temperate climate.

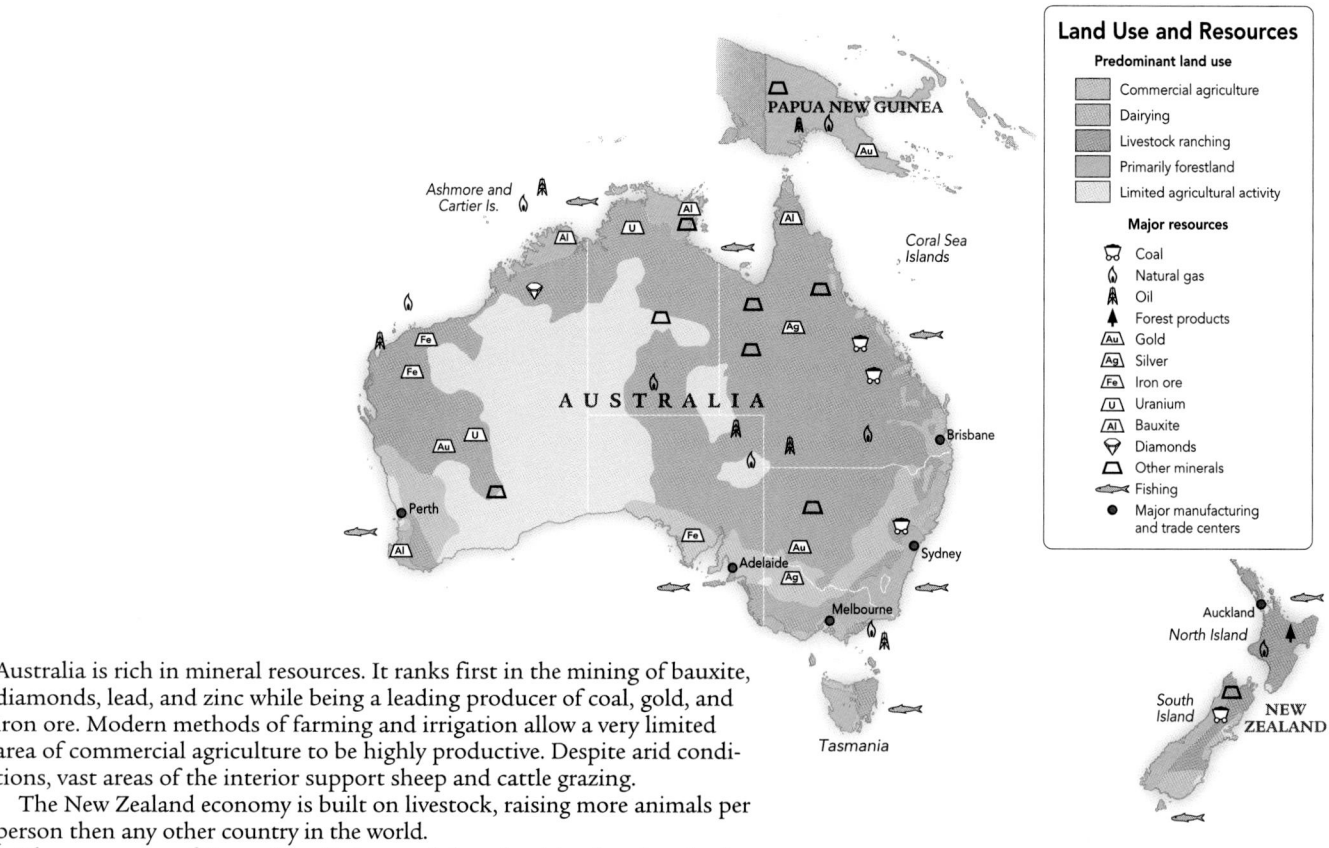

Land Use and Resources

Predominant land use

- Commercial agriculture
- Dairying
- Livestock ranching
- Primarily forestland
- Limited agricultural activity

Major resources

- Coal
- Natural gas
- Oil
- Forest products
- Au Gold
- Ag Silver
- Fe Iron ore
- U Uranium
- Al Bauxite
- Diamonds
- Other minerals
- Fishing
- ● Major manufacturing and trade centers

Australia is rich in mineral resources. It ranks first in the mining of bauxite, diamonds, lead, and zinc while being a leading producer of coal, gold, and iron ore. Modern methods of farming and irrigation allow a very limited area of commercial agriculture to be highly productive. Despite arid conditions, vast areas of the interior support sheep and cattle grazing.

The New Zealand economy is built on livestock, raising more animals per person then any other country in the world.

The economies of Papua New Guinea and the other island nations in the region rely primarily on subsistence agriculture and tourism.

Climate Graphs

Average daily temperature range (in °F)

100°
65°
32°
0°

High
Low

Average monthly precipitation (in inches)

20"
10"
0"

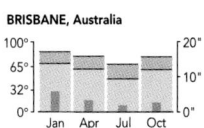

BRISBANE, Australia

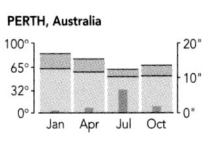

PERTH, Australia

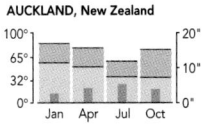

AUCKLAND, New Zealand

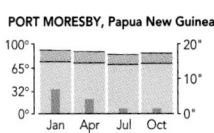

PORT MORESBY, Papua New Guinea

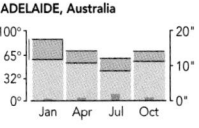

ADELAIDE, Australia

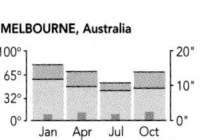

MELBOURNE, Australia

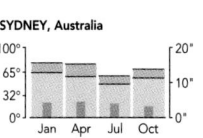

SYDNEY, Australia

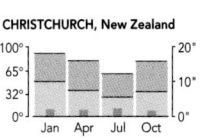

CHRISTCHURCH, New Zealand

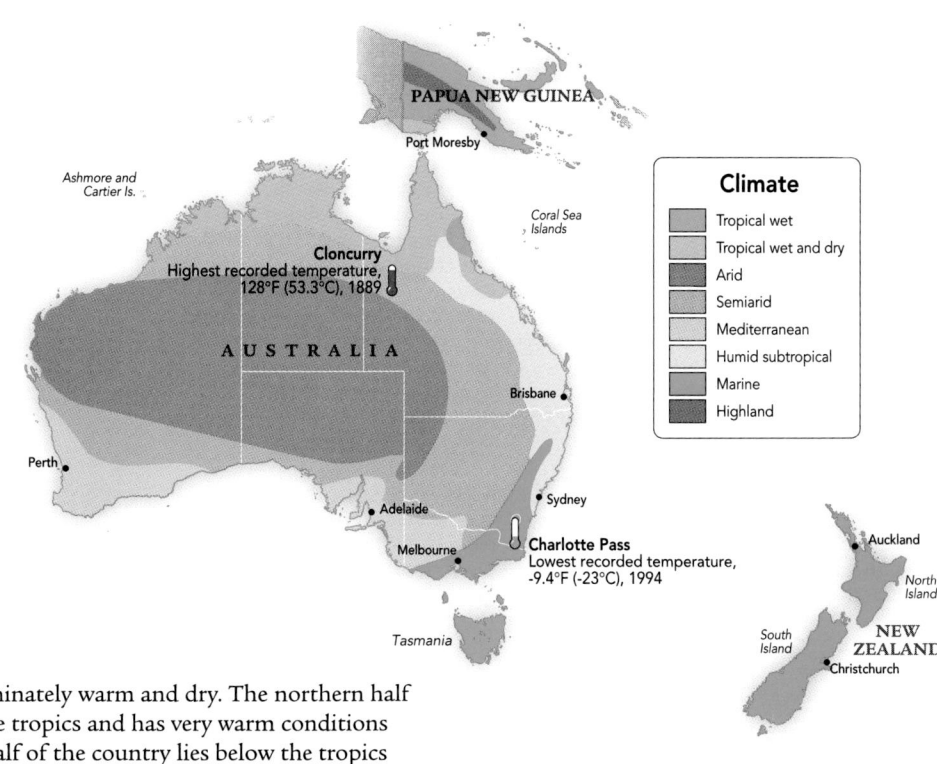

Climate

- Tropical wet
- Tropical wet and dry
- Arid
- Semiarid
- Mediterranean
- Humid subtropical
- Marine
- Highland

Cloncurry
Highest recorded temperature, 128°F (53.3°C), 1889

Charlotte Pass
Lowest recorded temperature, -9.4°F (-23°C), 1994

Australia's climate is predominately warm and dry. The northern half of the country lies within the tropics and has very warm conditions year round. The southern half of the country lies below the tropics and experiences a warm summer and a cool winter.

New Zealand's climate is like that of the U.S. Pacific Northwest—mild and moist. Papua New Guinea and other island nations surrounding the equator have climates that are mainly very warm and moist year round.

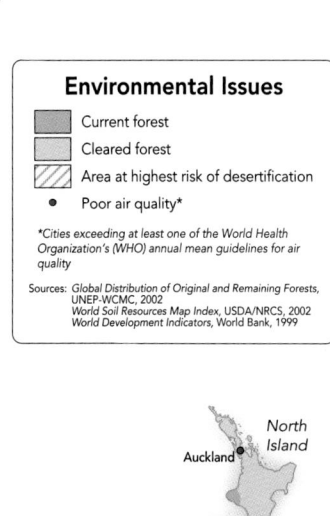

Environmental Issues

- Current forest
- Cleared forest
- Area at highest risk of desertification
- • Poor air quality*

*Cities exceeding at least one of the World Health Organization's (WHO) annual mean guidelines for air quality

Sources: *Global Distribution of Original and Remaining Forests,* UNEP-WCMC, 2002
World Soil Resources Map Index, USDA/NRCS, 2002
World Development Indicators, World Bank, 1999

Biodiversity loss is a leading environmental problem in both Australia and New Zealand. Over the past two hundred years, vast areas have been cleared for settlements and farmland. This land clearing, along with the introduction of non-native plant and animal species, has permanently altered the ecological balance. In New Zealand, it is estimated that eighty-five percent of the original lowland forests and wetlands have been lost due to human influences. Desertification, often brought on by overgrazing, is another serious environmental threat in many parts of Australia.

In 1901 the Commonwealth of Australia was established when the former British colonies of New South Wales, Victoria, Queensland, South Australia, Western Australia, and Tasmania joined in federation and changed their designation to states. In 1911 the territory for the federal capital at Canberra was acquired from New South Wales.

Australia comprises the continent and Tasmania, which is a group of islands. Australia's aboriginal inhabitants, a hunting-gathering people, have lived on the continent for some 40,000 years. The Aboriginal population currently makes up only slightly more than 1% of the population. Immigration, mainly from the United Kingdom, has been essential to Australia's development since the beginning of European settlement in 1788. Today, one of every five Australians is foreign-born.

Australia has a prosperous Western-style, capitalist economy. It is rich in natural resources and is a major exporter of agricultural products, minerals, metals, and fossil fuels.

Capital: Canberra
Area: 2,967,124 sq. mi.
7,686,850 sq. km.
Population: 19,547,000 (2002 est.)
Largest City: Sydney, 3,948,000
Languages: English, native languages
Major Religions: Anglican, Roman Catholic, other Christian
Life Expectancy: 75 male, 81 female
Government: federal parliamentary state
Monetary Unit: Australian dollar
Industry: mining, industrial and transportation equipment, food processing, chemicals, steel
Agriculture: beef, wool, mutton, wheat, barley, sugarcane, fruit, cattle, sheep, poultry
Minerals & Resources: bauxite, coal, iron ore, copper, tin, silver, uranium, nickel, tungsten, mineral sands, lead, zinc, diamonds, natural gas, petroleum

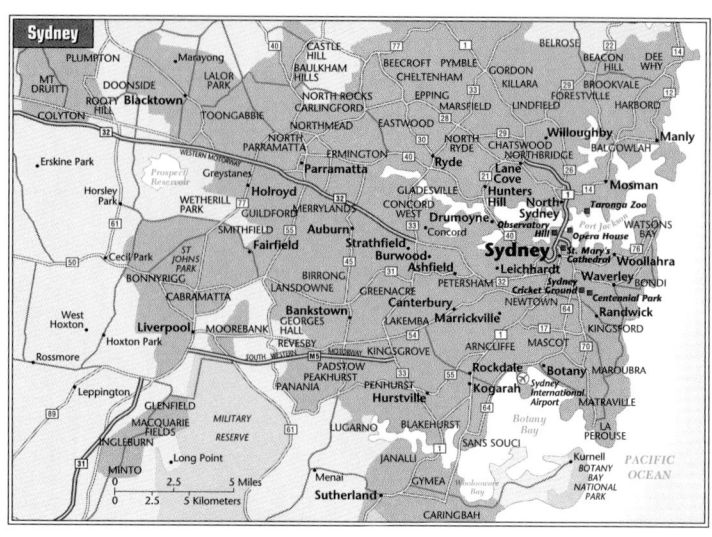

Australia

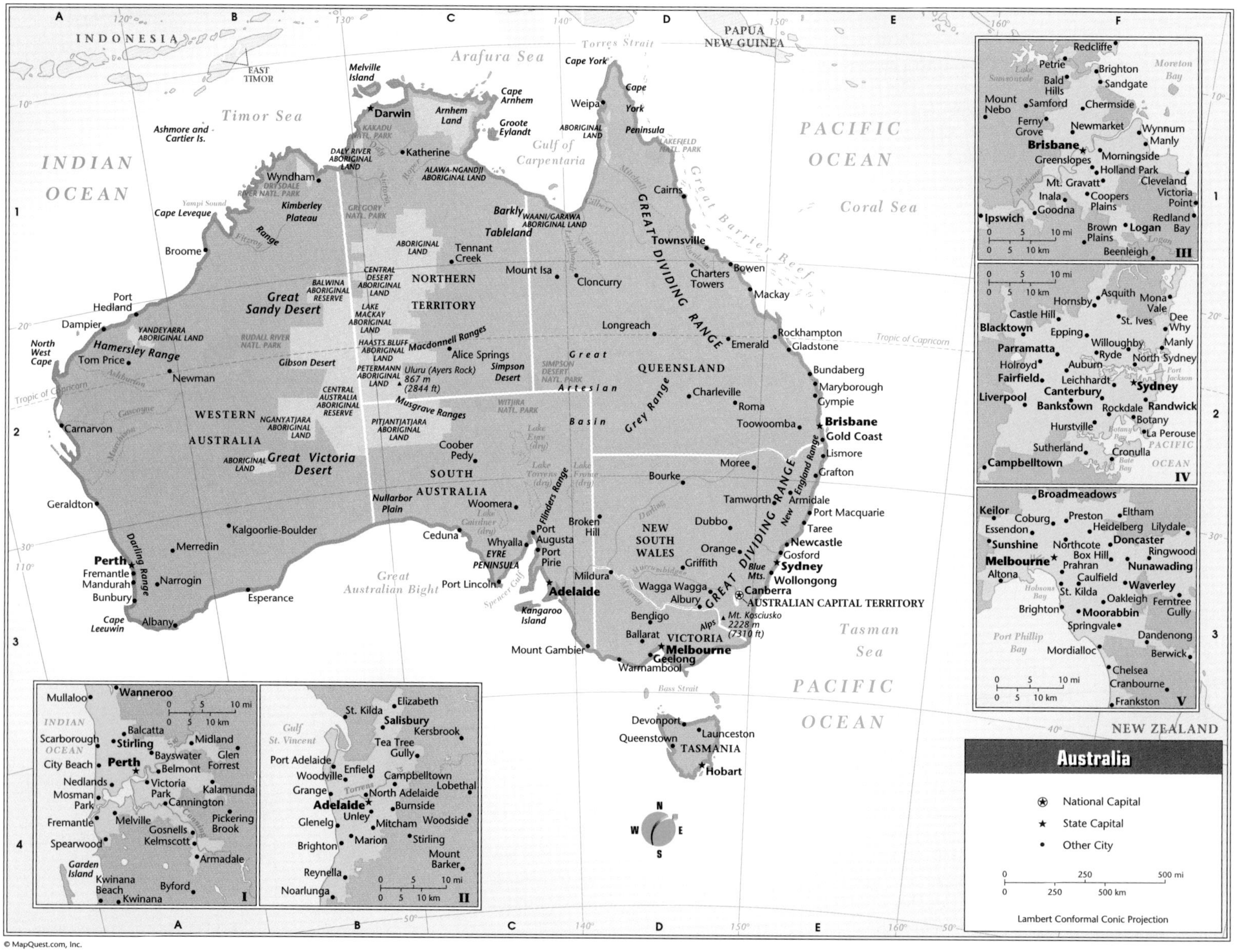

Melbourne

New Zealand consists of a number of islands in the Pacific Ocean, the larger two of which are North Island and South Island. It became a British colony in 1840 and gained independence from the United Kingdom as a dominion in 1907.

Polynesians, ancestors of New Zealand's Maori people, first discovered and settled New Zealand in the ninth century. The Maori currently represent about 9% of New Zealand's population, the remainder being mostly of European origin. The government is working to settle outstanding Maori land claims.

Since 1984, the New Zealand government has been reorienting an agrarian economy to a more industrialized, open, free market economy that can compete globally.

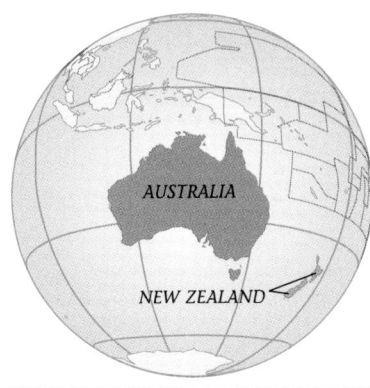

New Zealand

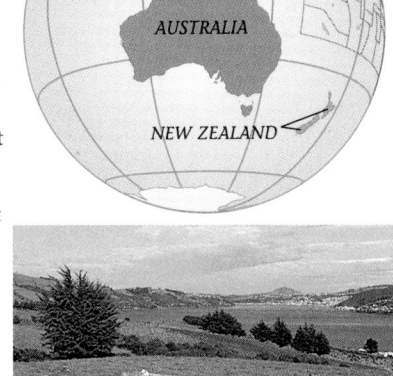
South Island Vista

Koala

Sydney Opera House

Lake Wanaka, New Zealand

Wallabies, Kakadu National Park, Northern Territory, Australia

Capital: Wellington
Area: 103,710 sq. mi.
268,680 sq. km.
Population: 3,908,000 (2002 est.)
Largest City: Auckland, 368,000
Languages: English, Maori
Major Religions: Anglican, Presbyterian, Roman Catholic, Methodist, Baptist, other Protestant
Life Expectancy: 73 male, 80 female
Government Type: parliamentary democracy
Monetary Unit: New Zealand dollar
Industry: food processing, wood and paper products, textiles, machinery, transportation equipment, banking and insurance, tourism, mining
Agriculture: wool, meat, dairy products, wheat, barley, potatoes, pulses, fruits, vegetables, fish
Minerals & Resources: natural gas, iron ore, sand, coal, timber, hydropower, gold, limestone

Parliament Building, Wellington, N.Z.

New Zealand

⊛ National Capital
• Other City

| 0 | 100 | 200 mi |
| 0 | 100 | 200 km |

Lambert Conformal Conic Projection

© MapQuest.com, Inc.

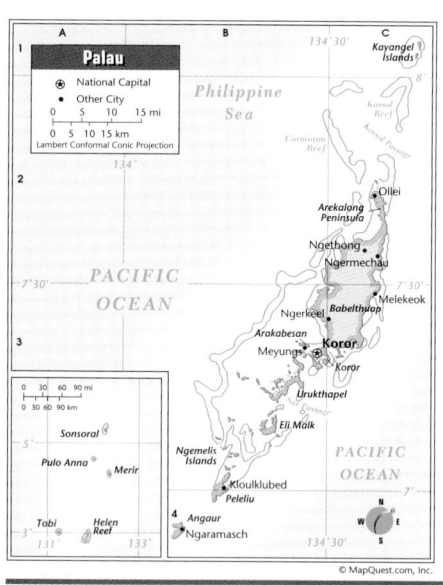

Capital: Koror (note: a new capital is under development)
Area: 177 sq. mi.
458 sq. km.
Population: 19,000 (2002 est.)
Largest City: Koror, 13,000
Languages: English, Sonsorolese, Angaur, Japanese, Tobi, Palauan
Major Religions: Christian beliefs, Modekngei religion (indigenous to Palau)
Life Expectancy: 69 male, 73 female
Government: self-governing

territory in free association with the US
Monetary Unit: United States dollar
Industry: tourism, craft items (shell, wood, pearl), some commercial fishing and agriculture
Agriculture: subsistence-level production of coconut, copra, cassava, sweet potatoes
Minerals & Resources: forests, minerals (especially gold), marine products, deep-seabed minerals

The Republic of Palau is comprised of more than two hundred islands in the Pacific Ocean, but only eight are permanently inhabited. Palau was administered by Germany from 1899-1914. It was then invaded by Japan and used as an administrative center for all Japanese possessions in Micronesia, until the United States occupied it in 1947 as part of the UN-created Trust Territory of the Pacific Islands. In 1994 Palau became a self-governing U.S. territory.

The Palauans are a mixture of Polynesian, Malayan, and Melanesian lineage and they adhere to very traditional customs. The backbone of the economy is subsistence farming and fishing, in addition to U.S. aid. Tourism promises to grow significantly in the near future.

Palau

Micronesia

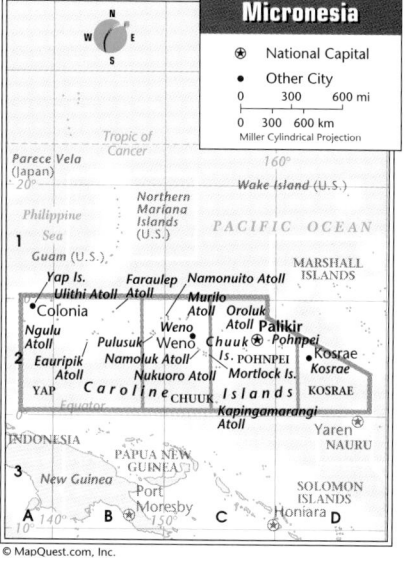

The Federated States of Micronesia (FSM) consist of about 600 islands extending across the archipelago of the Caroline Islands. The Carolines were claimed by the Spanish until 1899 when they were sold to Germany. The German administration of the Carolines encouraged development of trade and production of copra.

In 1914, the Japanese took possession of the islands, followed by the United States in World War II. In 1947, the islands became the Trust Territory of the Pacific Islands with the U.S. as administering authority. The FSM became fully independent in 1986.

The FSM comprises nine ethnic Micronesian and Polynesian groups. About two-thirds of the labor force are government employees and most of the remainder depend on subsistence farming and fishing.

Capital: Palikir
Area: 271 sq. mi.
702 sq. km.
Population: 136,000 (2002 est.)
Largest City: Palikir, 7,000
Languages: English, Trukese, Pohnpeian, Yapese, Kosrean
Major Religions: Roman Catholic, Protestant
Life Expectancy: 66 male, 70 female
Government: constitutional government in free association with the US
Monetary Unit: United States dollar
Industry: tourism, construction, fish processing, craft items from shell, wood, and pearls
Agriculture: mainly a subsistence economy; black pepper; tropical fruits and vegetables, coconuts, cassava, sweet potatoes, pigs, chickens
Mineral & Resources: forests, marine products, deep-seabed minerals

Papua New Guinea Tribal Costume

Papua New Guinea achieved full independence from an Australian-administered UN trusteeship in 1975. Papua New Guinea is a constitutional monarchy, recognizing the Queen of England as head of state and representing her by a governor-general who performs mostly ceremonial duties.

Papua New Guineans comprise five main ethnic groups which speak more than 700 indigenous languages. Agriculture provides a subsistence livelihood for 85% of the population and mining is important as the country is richly endowed with natural resources.

Papua New Guinea

Capital: Port Moresby
Area: 178,212 sq. mi.
461,690 sq. km.
Population: 5,172,000 (2002 est.)
Largest City: Port Moresby, 174,000
Languages: English, pidgin English, Motu, 715 indigenous languages
Major Religions: Roman Catholic, Lutheran, Protestant, indigenous beliefs
Life Expectancy: 56 male, 58 female
Government: parliamentary democracy
Monetary Unit: kina
Industry: copra crushing, palm oil processing, plywood production, wood chip production, mining of gold, silver, and copper, construction, tourism
Agriculture: coffee, cocoa, coconuts, palm kernels, tea, rubber, sweet potatoes, fruit, vegetables, poultry, pork
Minerals & Resources: gold, copper, silver, natural gas, timber, oil potential

Marshall Islands

Marshall Islands

- ⊛ National Capital
- • Other City

0   150   300 mi
0   150   300 km
Mercator Projection

© MapQuest.com, Inc.

The Marshall Islands is a group of atolls and reefs which form two parallel groups, the "Ratak" (sunrise) chain and the "Ralik" (sunset) chain, in the North Pacific Ocean. The islands achieved independence from a U.S.-administered trusteeship in 1986 after having been administered consecutively by the Spanish, the Germans, and the Japanese.

Government in the Marshall Islands is a relatively new democratic political system combined with a hierarchical traditional culture. The government is the largest employer, employing about one-third of the work force.

Capital: Majuro
Area: 70 sq. mi.
           181 sq. km.
Population: 55,000 (2002 est.)
Largest City: Majuro, 18,000
Languages: English, Marshallese dialects, Japanese
Major Religion: Christian
Life Expectancy: 62 male, 65 female
Government: constitutional government in free association with the US
Monetary Unit: United States dollar
Industry: copra, fish, tourism, crafts from shell, wood, and pearls, offshore banking
Agriculture: coconuts, cacao, taro, breadfruit, fruits, pigs, chickens
Minerals & Resources: phosphate deposits, marine products, deep seabed minerals

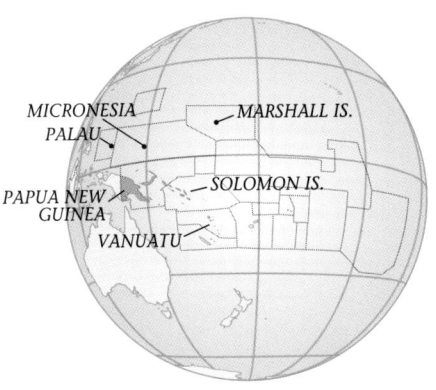

Solomon Islands

The Solomon Islands form an archipelago in the Southwest Pacific Ocean. They became independent from the United Kingdom in 1978, and formed a parliamentary democracy which recognizes the British Sovereign as Head of State.

The vast majority of Solomon Islanders are Melanesian. Most people live in small, widely dispersed rural settlements along the coasts. About one-third of the work force relies on subsistence agriculture, forestry and fishing for their livelihood. The islands are rich in undeveloped mineral resources such as lead, zinc, nickel, and gold.

Solomon Islands

- ⊛ National Capital
- • Other City

0   150   300 mi
0   150   300 km
Mercator Projection

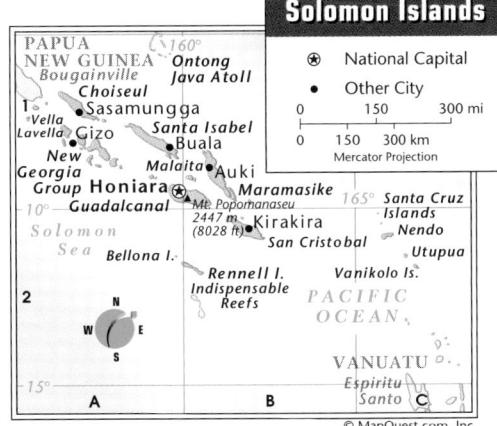

© MapQuest.com, Inc.

Capital: Honiara
Area: 10,982 sq. mi.
           28,450 sq. km.
Population: 495,000 (2002 est.)
Largest City: Honiara, 49,000
Languages: Melanesian pidgin, English, 120 indigenous languages
Major Religions: Anglican, Roman Catholic, Baptist, Protestant, traditional beliefs
Life Expectancy: 68 male, 73 female
Government: parliamentary democracy
Monetary Unit: Solomon Islands dollar
Industry: copra, fish (tuna)
Agriculture: cocoa, beans, coconuts, palm kernels, timber, rice, potatoes, vegetables, fruit, cattle, pigs, fish
Minerals & Resources: fish, forests, gold, bauxite, phosphates, lead, zinc, nickel

---

Vanuatu

Capital: Port-Vila
Area: 5,697 sq. mi.
           14,760 sq. km.
Population: 196,000 (2002 est.)
Largest City: Port-Vila, 30,000
Languages: English, French, pidgin (known as Bislama or Bichelama)
Major Religions: Presbyterian, Anglican, Catholic, indigenous beliefs, Seventh-Day Adventist
Life Expectancy: 58 male, 62 female
Government: republic
Monetary Unit: vatu
Industry: food and fish freezing, wood processing, meat canning
Agriculture: coconuts, cocoa, coffee, fish, taro, yams, coconuts, fruits, vegetables
Minerals & Resources: manganese, hardwood forests, fish

Formerly New Hebrides, Vanuatu is a "Y"-shaped archipelago that comprises 80 islands. It gained its independence from France and the United Kingdom in 1980 after 74 years of a unique joint administration by the two.

The Ni-Vanuatu people are predominantly indigenous Melanesian. Both society and government in Vanuatu tend to divide along linguistic lines — French and English. About 80% of the population is engaged in agricultural activities ranging from subsistence farming to smallholder farming of coconuts and other cash crops. Fishing and tourism are also important sectors of the economy.

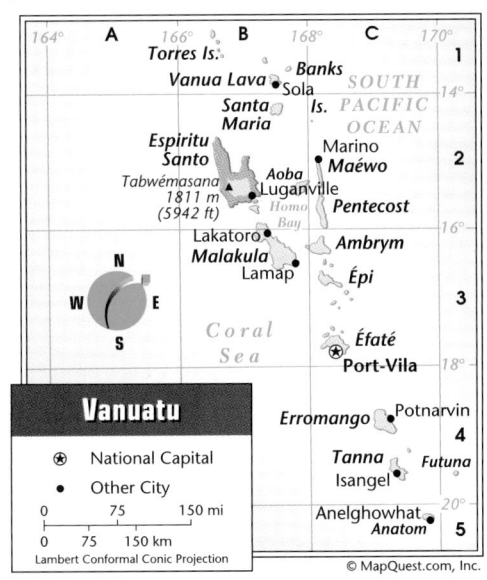

Vanuatu

- ⊛ National Capital
- • Other City

0   75   150 mi
0   75   150 km
Lambert Conformal Conic Projection

© MapQuest.com, Inc.

Nauru

National Capital
Other City

Lambert Conformal Conic Projection

Anna Point
Anetan
Ewa
Baiti
Anabar
Uaboe
Nibok
Ijuw
Central Plateau
Denigomodu
Buada
Buada Lagoon
Anibare Bay
Aiwo
Anibare
Meneng Point
Yaren
Moqua Well
Meneng

PACIFIC OCEAN

© MapQuest.com, Inc.

Capital: no official capital; government offices in Yaren District
Area: 8 sq. mi.
 21 sq. km.
Population: 12,000 (2002 est.)
Largest City: Yaren, 4,000
Languages: Nauruan, English
Major Religion: Christian
Life Expectancy: 64 male, 69 female
Government: republic
Monetary Unit: Australian dollar
Industry: phosphate mining, financial services, coconut products
Agriculture: coconuts; other agricultural activity negligible; almost completely dependent on imports for food and water
Minerals & Resources: phosphates

Formerly Pleasant Island, the Republic of Nauru gained its independence from a UN trusteeship jointly administered by Australia, New Zealand and the United Kingdom. This isolated island remained free of European contact for much longer than other Pacific islands, coming under German control in 1881. Following World War I, the island was administered through a League of Nations mandate by Australia, New Zealand and Britain.

Nauru's main source of income has been the mining of phosphates, which are one of the nation's only resources. Phosphate reserves are expected to be depleted by about the year 2000, which will leave the economy badly in need of replacement activity. Most necessities, including water, must be imported.

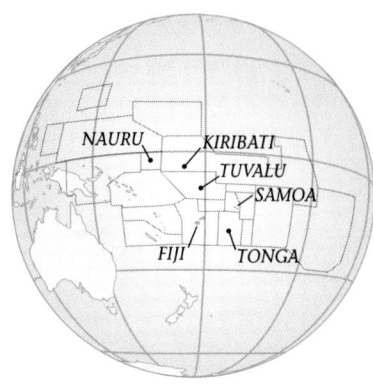

Nauru

Tuvalu

Tuvalu is a group of islands consisting of nine coral atolls in the South Pacific Ocean. Formerly the Ellice Islands in the Gilbert and Ellice Islands, they were a British Protectorate from 1892 until 1978, when they became an independent nation. Tuvalu recognizes the British Monarch as Head of State.

Ethnically, Tuvaluans are 96% Polynesian. Most people rely on subsistence farming and fishing for a living. The country has no known mineral resources, few exports, and is too small and remote for tourism to develop. It receives substantial income from a trust fund established in 1987 by Australia, New Zealand, and the United Kingdom.

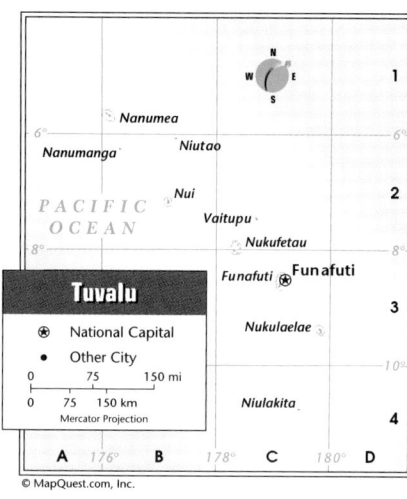

Nanumea
Nanumanga
Niutao
Nui
Vaitupu
Nukufetau
Funafuti
Funafuti

Tuvalu

National Capital
Other City

Mercator Projection

Nukulaelae
Niulakita

© MapQuest.com, Inc.

Capital: Funafuti
Area: 10 sq. mi.
 26 sq. km.
Population: 11,000 (2002 est.)
Largest City: Funafuti, 4,000
Languages: Tuvaluan, English
Major Religions: Church of Tuvalu, Seventh-Day Adventist, Baha'i
Life Expectancy: 62 male, 64 female
Government: democracy
Monetary Unit: Tuvaluan dollar
Industry: fishing, tourism, copra
Agriculture: coconuts and fish
Minerals & Resources: fish

 *Fiji*

Fiji is an island group in the South Pacific Ocean. It gained its independence from the United Kingdom in 1970, remaining part of the Commonwealth until 1987, when two military coups established it as a republic.

More than half of Fiji's population lives on the island coasts, either in Suva, the capital, or in smaller urban centers. Ethnically, Fijians are about half indigenous Fijian and half Indian.

Nearly two-thirds of the work force is employed in subsistence agriculture, and tourism has been growing in importance. Fiji is a well-endowed country with a well-educated labor force and a per capita income that is double that of many other countries in the region.

Fiji

National Capital
Other City

Azimuthal Equal Area Projection

Cikobia
Great Sea Reef
Vetauua
Udu Point
Qelelevu
Vanua Levu
Labasa
Rabi
Yasawa Group
Naduri
Kioa
Laucala
High Water
Nabouwalu
Qamea
Taveuni
Lautoka
Viti Levu
Koro
Vanua Balavu
Nadi
Tomanivi (4340 ft)
Nakodu
Lau Group
Ovalau
Cicia
Lomawai
Navua
Lami
Gau
Koro Sea
Lakeba
Galoa
Suva
Beqa
Vatulele
Kadavu
Ono
Moala Group
Vunisea
Kadavu Passage
Cape Washington
PACIFIC OCEAN

© MapQuest.com, Inc.

Capital: Suva
Area: 7,052 sq. mi.
 18,270 sq. km.
Population: 856,000 (2002 est.)
Largest City: Suva, 92,000
Languages: English, Fijian, Hindustani
Major Religions: Methodist, Roman Catholic, Hindu, Muslim
Life Expectancy: 63 male, 68 female
Government: republic
Monetary Unit: Fijian dollar
Industry: sugar, tourism, copra, gold, silver, clothing, lumber, small cottage industries
Agriculture: sugarcane, coconuts, cassava, rice, sweet potatoes, bananas, cattle, pigs, horses, goats, fish
Minerals & Resources: timber, fish, gold, copper, offshore oil potential

Carvings from Balabala Tree, Fiji

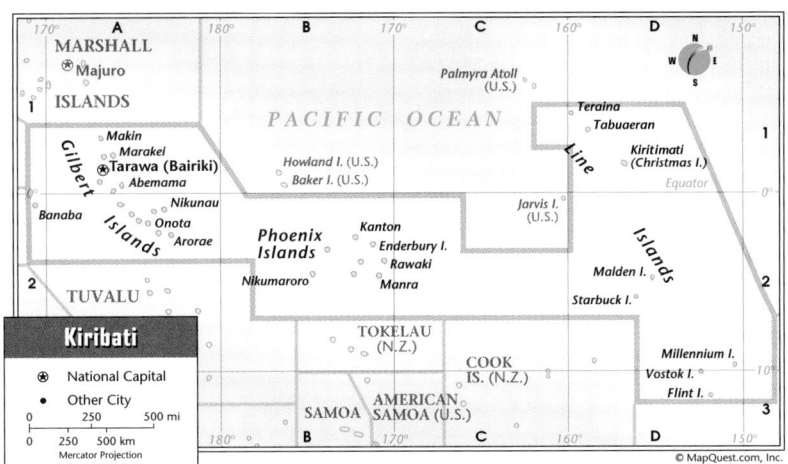

Kiribati

Capital: Tarawa
Area: 277 sq. mi.
          717 sq. km.
Population: 96,000 (2002 est.)
Largest City: Tarawa, 25,000
Languages: English, Gilbertese
Major Religions: Roman Catholic, Protestant, Seventh-Day Adventist, Baha'i, Church of God, Mormon
Life Expectancy: 53 male, 56 female
Government: republic
Monetary Unit: Australian dollar
Industry: fishing, handicrafts
Agriculture: copra, fish, taro, breadfruit, sweet potatoes, vegetables
Minerals & Resources: phosphate (production, discontinued in 1979)

Formerly the Gilbert Islands, Kiribati became independent from the United Kingdom in 1979, becoming a republic within the Commonwealth. There are three island groups that make up Kiribati: Gilbert Islands, Line Islands and Phoenix Islands. Their terrain is mostly low-lying coral atolls surrounded by extensive reefs.

The I'Kiribati people are Micronesians. Most people live in small villages and rely on fishing, subsistence farming, and/or copra production for a living. At independence, Kiribati's important phosphate reserves were depleted, and since then the government has been trying to diversify the stagnant economy through fisheries projects and tourism.

Samoa gained its independence from a UN trusteeship administered by New Zealand in 1962. The nation was known as Western Samoa until July 1997. It is a group of islands which are mainly formed from ranges of extinct volcanos.

Samoans are the second largest Polynesian group after the Maoris of New Zealand. Most Samoans live within a traditional social system based on the "aiga," or extended family group, headed by a "matai" or chief. A majority of the population lives in coastal villages and relies on agriculture for a living. Tourism has become the most important growth industry in the country.

Samoa

Capital: Apia
Area: 1,104 sq. mi.
          2,860 sq. km.
Population: 179,000 (2002 est.)
Largest City: Apia, 34,000
Languages: Samoan, English
Major Religions: Roman Catholic, Methodist, Latter Day Saints, Seventh-Day Adventist
Life Expectancy: 66 male, 71 female
Government: constitutional monarchy under native chief
Monetary Unit: tala
Industry: timber, tourism, food processing, fishing
Agriculture: coconuts, bananas, taro, yams, other fruits
Minerals & Resources: hardwood forests, fish

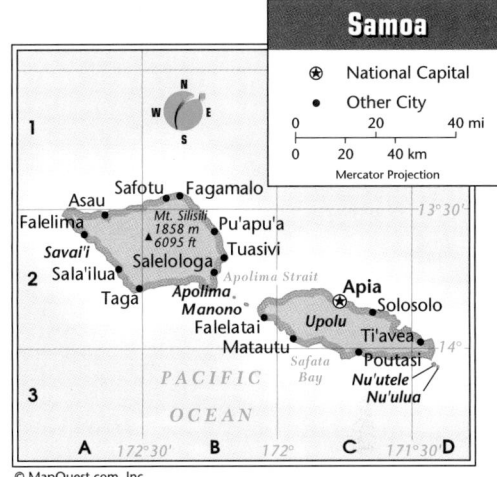

Tongatapu Island, Tonga

Tonga

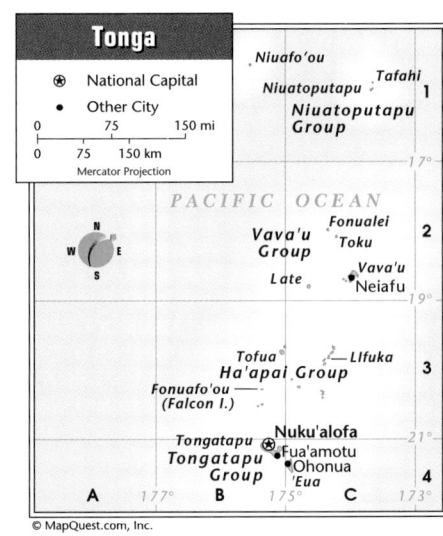

Tonga is an archipelago of 170 islands in the South Pacific Ocean. The islands are made up of three main groups, the Vava'u, Ha'api and Tongatapu; only thirty-six are inhabited. Tonga became independent in 1970, after being a protectorate of the United Kingdom.

Tongans are a Polynesian people and everyday life is heavily influenced by the Christian faith and Polynesian traditions. Tonga has a hereditary constitutional monarchy and no political parties. Agriculture employs about 70% of the labor force and is the backbone of the economy, followed by tourism and fishing.

Capital: Nuku'alofa
Area: 289 sq. mi.
          748 sq. km.
Population: 106,000 (2002 est.)
Largest City: Nuku'alofa, 22,000
Languages: Tongan, English
Major Religions: Christian (Free Wesleyan Church claims over 30,000 adherents)
Life Expectancy: 66 male, 71 female
Government: hereditary constitutional monarchy
Monetary Unit: pa'anga
Industry: tourism, fishing
Agriculture: coconut, copra, bananas, vanilla beans, cocoa, coffee, ginger, black pepper
Minerals & Resources: fish, fertile soil

Population: 359,469,000 (2002)
Area: 6,900,300 sq. mi.
17,871,777 sq. km.
Highest Point: Mt. Aconcagua
22,834 ft. (6,964 m.)
Lowest Point: Valdes Peninsula
131 ft. (40 m.)
below sea level
Largest Urban Areas:
São Paulo, Brazil
Buenos Aires, Argentina
Rio de Janeiro, Brazil
Lima, Peru
Bogotá, Colombia
Santiago, Chile
Belo Horizonte, Brazil
Countries: 13

Above: Local market in Ecuador; **Above Right:** Machu Picchu, Peru;
Below Right: Tropical fruits and vegetables at a market in Brazil;
Below: Cove along the Brazilian coast near Rio de Janeiro.

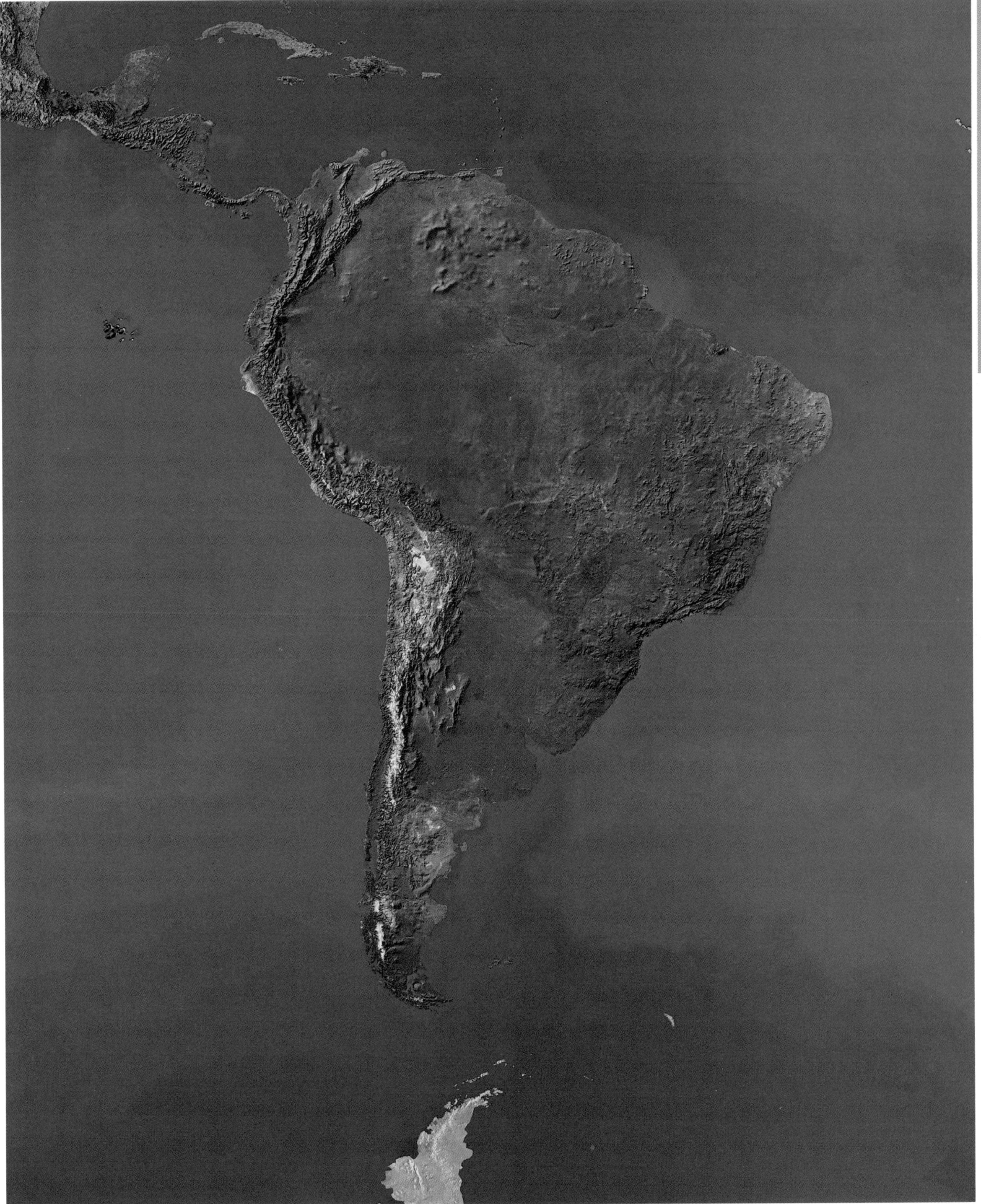

Major Metropolitan Areas

Argentina
Buenos Aires	11,298,000
Córdoba	1,209,000
Rosario	1,119,000

Bolivia
La Paz	1,484,000
Santa Cruz	1,136,000
Cochabamba	517,000

Brazil
São Paulo	17,834,000
Rio de Janeiro	10,612,000
Belo Horizonte	4,800,000
Pôrto Alegre	3,655,000
Recife	3,332,000
Salvador	3,018,000
Fortaleza	2,975,000
Brasília	2,942,000
Curitiba	2,726,000
Belém	1,816,000
Manaus	1,011,000

Chile
Santiago	4,647,000
Viña del Mar	299,000

Colombia
Bogotá	6,422,000
Cali	2,129,000
Medellín	1,885,000
Barranquilla	1,549,000

Ecuador
Guayaquil	2,118,000
Quito	1,616,000

French Guiana
Cayenne	50,000

Guyana
Georgetown	187,000

Paraguay
Asunción	513,000

Peru
Lima	6,988,000
Arequipa	830,000
Chiclayo	766,000

Suriname
Paramaribo	291,000

Uruguay
Montevideo	1,303,000

Venezuela
Caracas	3,061,000
Maracaibo	1,220,000
Barquisimeto	896,000
Valencia	742,000

International comparability of population data is limited by varying census methods. Where metropolitan population is unavailable, core city population is shown.

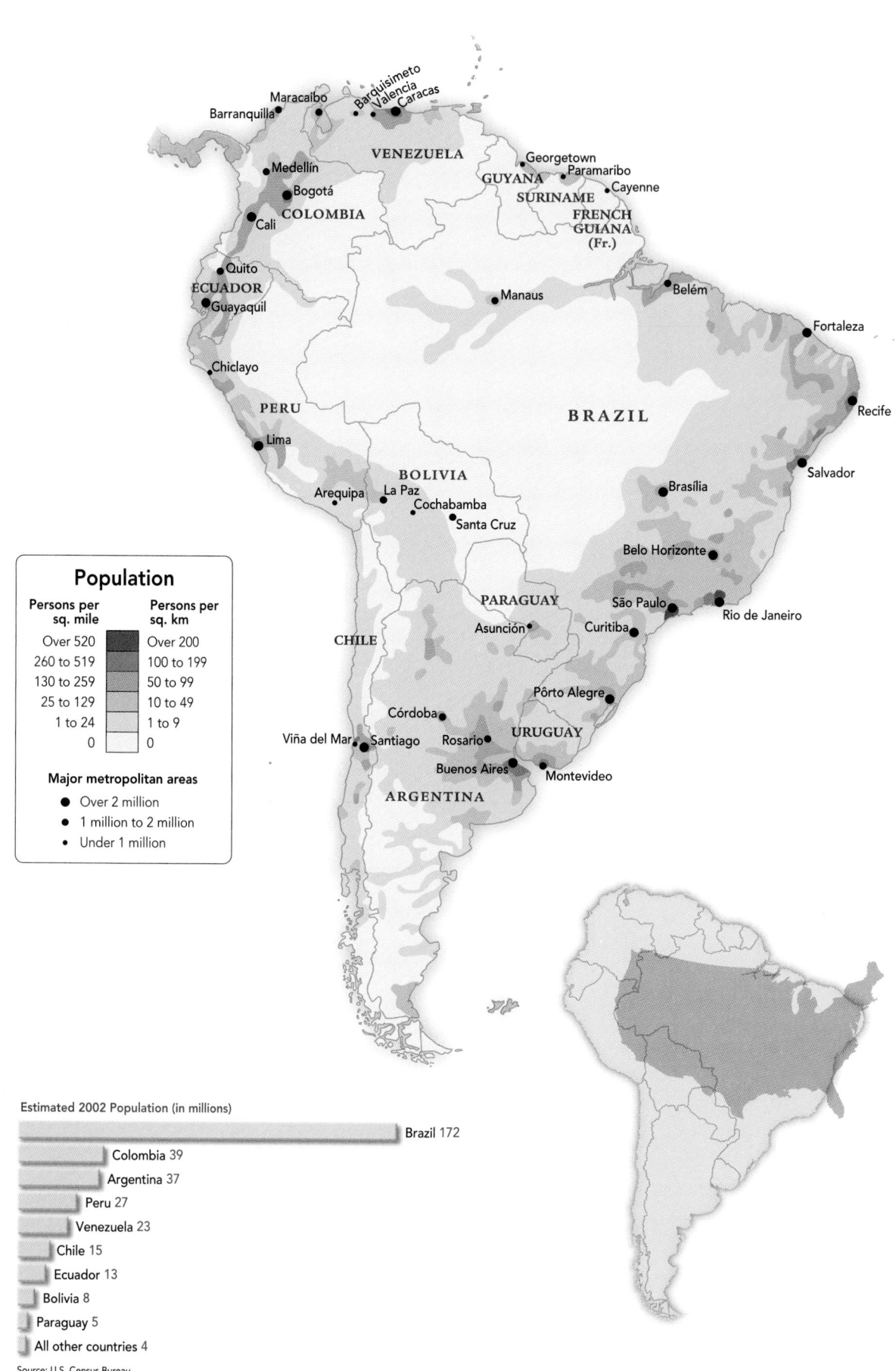

Population

Persons per sq. mile	Persons per sq. km
Over 520	Over 200
260 to 519	100 to 199
130 to 259	50 to 99
25 to 129	10 to 49
1 to 24	1 to 9
0	0

Major metropolitan areas
- Over 2 million
- 1 million to 2 million
- Under 1 million

Estimated 2002 Population (in millions)

Brazil 172
Colombia 39
Argentina 37
Peru 27
Venezuela 23
Chile 15
Ecuador 13
Bolivia 8
Paraguay 5
All other countries 4

Source: U.S. Census Bureau

Caribbean Sea

ATLANTIC OCEAN

PACIFIC OCEAN

TRINIDAD AND TOBAGO

VENEZUELA
COLOMBIA
ECUADOR
PERU
BRAZIL
GUYANA
SURINAME
FRENCH GUIANA (Fr.)

AMAZON BASIN
SELVAS
GUIANA HIGHLANDS
BRAZILIAN HIGHLANDS
MATO GROSSO PLATEAU
LLANOS
ANDES

BOLIVIA
PARAGUAY
CHILE
ARGENTINA
URUGUAY

GRAN CHACO
ATACAMA DESERT
ALTIPLANO
PAMPAS
PATAGONIA

Tropic of Capricorn
Equator

South America
⊛ National Capital
★ Territorial Capital
• Other City

0   400   800 mi
0   400   800 km
Azimuthal Equal Area Projection

© MapQuest.com, Inc.

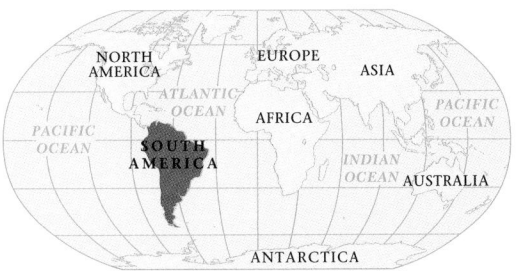

NORTH AMERICA
EUROPE
ASIA
AFRICA
AUSTRALIA
ANTARCTICA
SOUTH AMERICA
ATLANTIC OCEAN
PACIFIC OCEAN
INDIAN OCEAN

South America is dominated by tropical vegetation, including Earth's most extensive rain forest. Farther south, a vast grassland, the Pampa, fades gradually into the dry and meager vegetation of Patagonia.

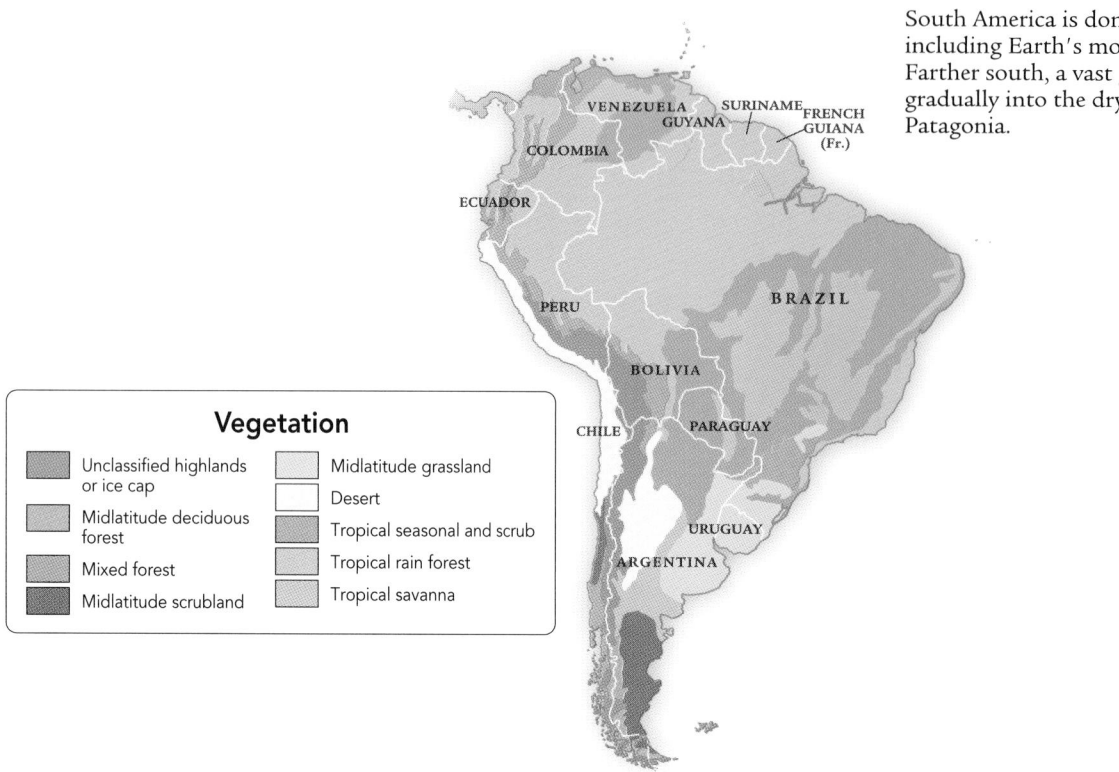

Vegetation

- Unclassified highlands or ice cap
- Midlatitude deciduous forest
- Mixed forest
- Midlatitude scrubland
- Midlatitude grassland
- Desert
- Tropical seasonal and scrub
- Tropical rain forest
- Tropical savanna

Non-manufacturing economic activity is generated primarily by commercial plantation agriculture, livestock raising, and the harvest of forest products, plus the extraction of oil and minerals. Manufacturing, like population, is concentrated in the continent's coastal areas.

Land Use and Resources

Predominant land use

- Commercial agriculture
- Livestock ranching
- Subsistence agriculture
- Primarily forestland
- Limited agricultural activity

Major resources

- Coal
- Natural gas
- Oil
- Forest products
- Au Gold
- Ag Silver
- Fe Iron ore
- U Uranium
- Al Bauxite
- Diamonds
- Other minerals
- Fishing
- ● Major manufacturing and trade centers

Climate Graphs

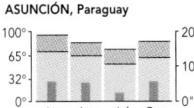

Average daily temperature range (in °F)	Average monthly precipitation (in inches)
High / Low	

ASUNCIÓN, Paraguay

BOGOTÁ, Colombia
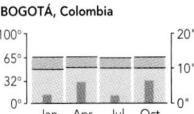

BUENOS AIRES, Argentina
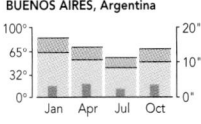

CARACAS, Venezuela
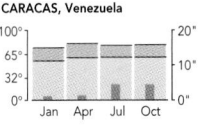

CAYENNE, French Guiana
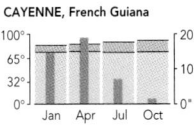

LA PAZ, Bolivia
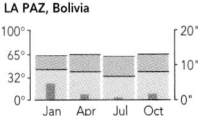

LIMA, Peru
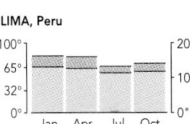

MANAUS, Brazil
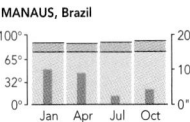

PUNTA ARENAS, Chile
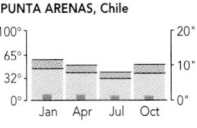

RECIFE, Brazil
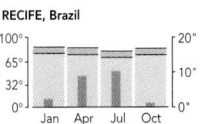

RIO DE JANEIRO, Brazil
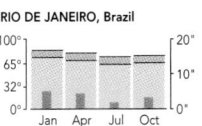

SANTIAGO, Chile
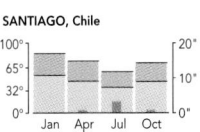

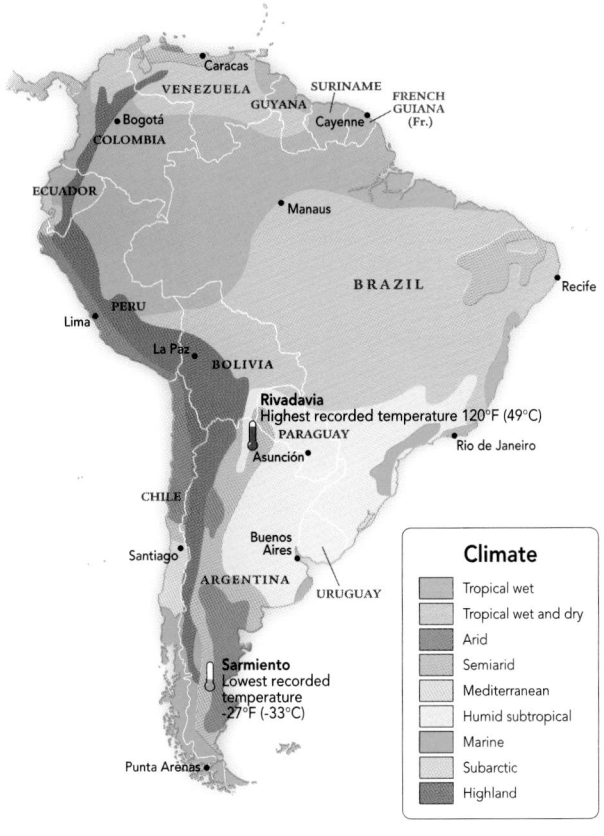

Rivadavia
Highest recorded temperature 120°F (49°C)

Sarmiento
Lowest recorded temperature -27°F (-33°C)

Climate

- Tropical wet
- Tropical wet and dry
- Arid
- Semiarid
- Mediterranean
- Humid subtropical
- Marine
- Subarctic
- Highland

Most of the continent is under the influence of wet and tropical air. Warm currents in the Atlantic Ocean as well as wet lowland elevations lying within the confines of the tropical latitudes directly affect the climate of the majority of the land area. The Andes Mountains and cold currents that hug the Pacific coast keep the Western and Southern regions of the continent temperate but dry.

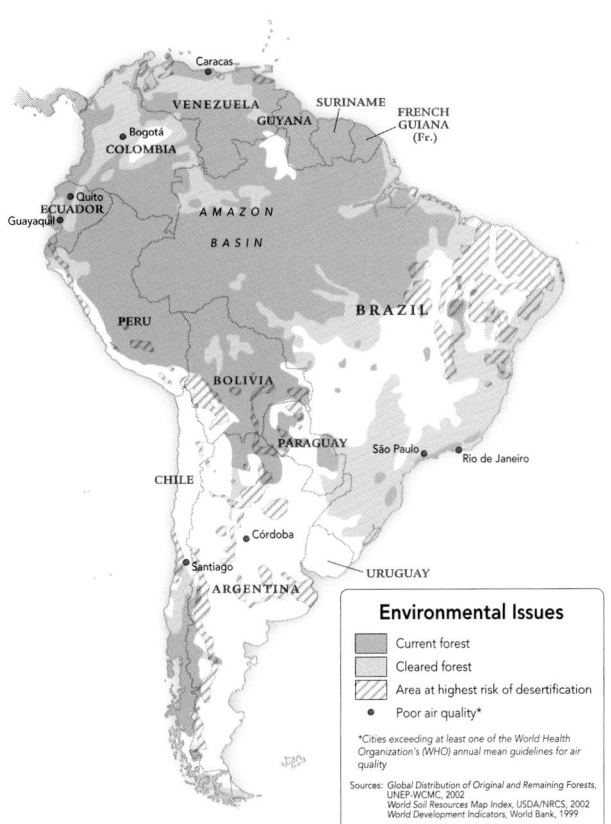

Environmental Issues

- Current forest
- Cleared forest
- Area at highest risk of desertification
- Poor air quality*

*Cities exceeding at least one of the World Health Organization's (WHO) annual mean guidelines for air quality

Sources: Global Distribution of Original and Remaining Forests, UNEP-WCMC, 2002
World Soil Resources Map Index, USDA/NRCS, 2002
World Development Indicators, World Bank, 1999

The destruction of forest areas—especially in the Amazon Basin—is one of the leading environmental issues in South America. In Brazil, it is estimated that an average of 15,000 acres of forest are lost each day as people clear land for timber and to grow crops. Human activities have impacted other types of vegetation, as well. For example, over-grazing has caused damage to grasslands in many areas, putting them at risk of becoming infertile deserts. Poor urban air quality is another serious concern in the region, with nearly 80 percent of the population living in cities.

Venezuela achieved independence from Spain in 1821 and much of its history since has been characterized by political instability, dictatorial rule, and revolutionary turbulence. From 1958–1992, however, Venezuela had regular, free and open elections and a lack of military dominance which earned it a reputation as one of the more stable democracies in Latin America. In 1992, two military coups again put the nation into a politically and economically unstable situation, with which it has since struggled.

Most Venezuelans are of European, Indian, and/or African descent. About 85% of the population live in urban areas, most of which are along the coast or in the Andes.

Petroleum plays a dominant role in the Venezuelan economy and there is an abundance of other natural resources which are in various stages of development.

Capital: Caracas
Area: 352,051 sq. mi.
          912,050 sq. km.
Population: 24,288,000 (2002 est.)
Largest City: Caracas, 1,836,000
Languages: Spanish, native dialects (Amerindians)
Major Religions: Roman Catholic, Protestant
Life Expectancy: 70 male, 76 female
Government: republic
Monetary Unit: bolivar
Industry: petroleum, iron-ore mining, construction materials, food processing, textiles, steel, aluminum, motor vehicle assembly
Agriculture: corn, sorghum, sugarcane, rice, bananas, vegetables, coffee, beef, pork, milk, eggs, fish
Minerals & Resources: petroleum, natural gas, iron ore, gold, bauxite, other minerals, hydropower, diamonds

Venezuela

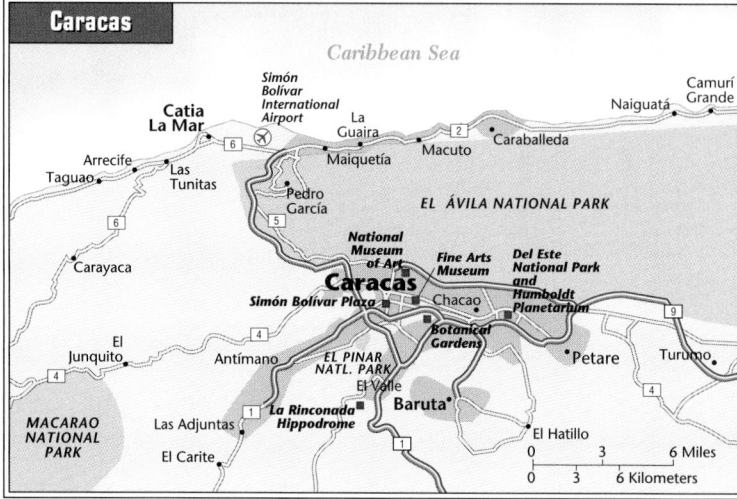

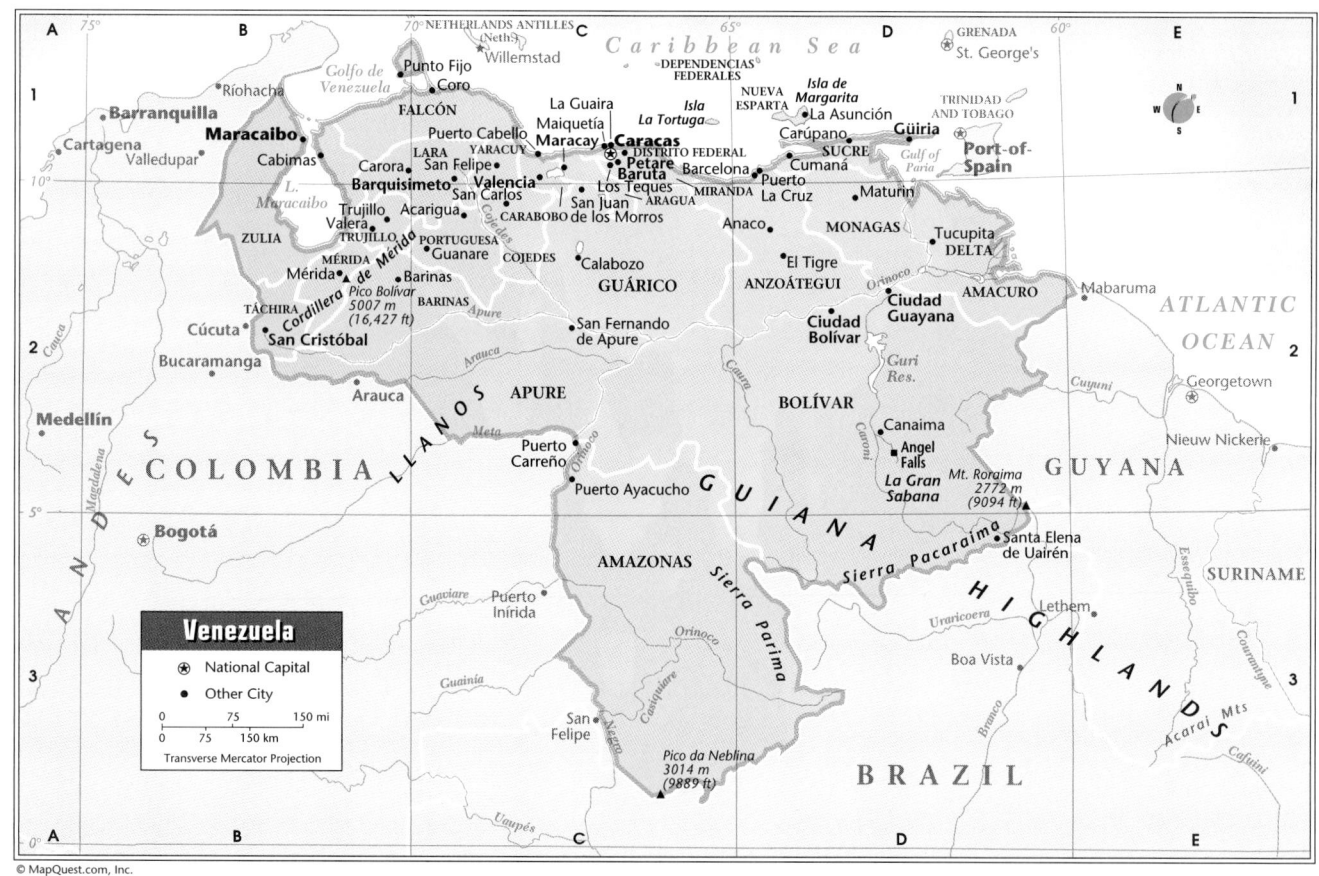

© MapQuest.com, Inc.

© MapQuest.com, Inc.

Guyana

Capital: Georgetown
Area: 82,978 sq. mi.
214,970 sq. km.
Population: 700,000 (2002 est.)
Largest City: Georgetown,
72,000
Languages: English, Amerindian dialects
Major Religions: Christian, Hindu, Muslim
Life Expectancy: 62 male, 69 female
Government: republic
Monetary Unit: Guyanese dollar
Industry: bauxite mining, sugar, rice milling,
timber, fishing, shrimping, textiles, gold mining
Agriculture: sugar, rice, greater potential for
fishing and forestry
Minerals & Resources: bauxite, gold, dia-
monds, hardwood timber, shrimp, fish

Aerial view of Guyana rainforest

Guyana gained its independence from the United Kingdom
in 1966 after being under British rule for nearly two centuries. More than three quarters of Guyana's land area is rainforest and woodland.

Guyana is one of the poorest countries in the Western
Hemisphere but in recent years it has made good economic
progress. The government's role in the economy has been
significantly reduced since 1989, allowing for privatization
and foreign investment. Agriculture and mining are Guyana's
most important economic activities.

Ethnically, the Guyanese are about half East Indian, slightly less than half African and mixed, and a small percentage
of Amerindian, European and Chinese. The vast majority of
the population lives on the narrow coastal plain.

Suriname gained its independence from the Netherlands
in 1975 after nearly a century
of Dutch administration.
Since independence, the
country has experienced considerable political instability
characterized by military
coups and ethnic politics.

Surinamers are one of the

most ethnically varied populations in the world, comprising more than seven ethnic
groups and four major religions. Most people live in the
narrow, northern coastal
plain. Suriname is known for
its diverse flora and fauna
which thrives due to lack of
development.

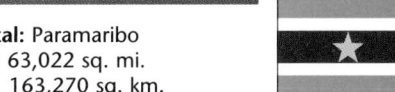

Suriname

Capital: Paramaribo
Area: 63,022 sq. mi.
163,270 sq. km.
Population: 434,000 (2002 est.)
Largest City: Paramaribo,
219,000
Languages: Dutch, English, Sranang Tongo,
Hindustani, Javanese
Major Religions: Hindu, Muslim, Roman
Catholic, Protestant, indigenous beliefs
Life Expectancy: 67 male, 72 female
Government: republic
Monetary Unit: Surinamese guilder, gulden, or
florin
Industry: bauxite mining, alumina and aluminum
production, lumbering, food processing, fishing
Agriculture: rice, bananas, palm kernels,
coconuts, plantains, peanuts, beef, chicken,
shrimp, forest products
Minerals & Resources: timber, hydropower
potential, fish, shrimp, bauxite, iron ore, and
small amounts of nickel, copper, platinum, gold

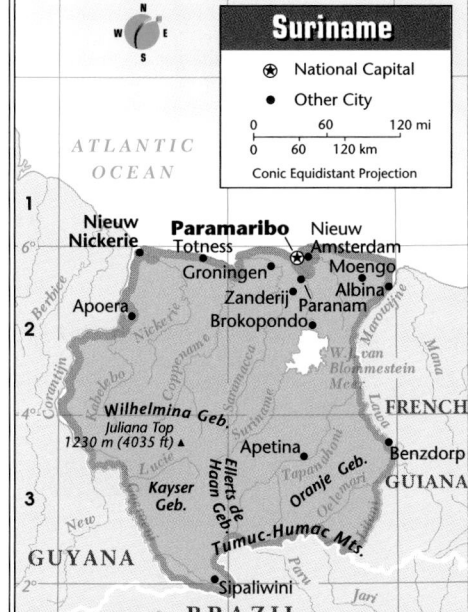

© MapQuest.com, Inc.

French Guiana has been an overseas department of France since 1946. Most of the
country is unsettled and covered by a dense
tropical rain forest. The first known indigenous inhabitants of French Guiana were
Arawak and Carib Indians. The first permanent French settlement was established in
1634 and part of what is French Guiana
today became a French possession in 1817.

As an integral part of France, French
Guiana has a political system that is basically an extension of that in France. Similarly,
the country's economy is tied closely with
the French economy through subsidies and
imports. Fishing and forestry are the most
important economic activities and since the
mid-1960s there has been a French space
center in Kourou.

© MapQuest.com, Inc.

French Guiana

Capital: Cayenne
Area: 35,126 sq. mi.
91,000 sq. km.
Population: 182,000
(2002 est.)
Largest City: Cayenne,
50,000
Language: French
Major Religion: Roman
Catholic
Life Expectancy: 72 male,
79 female

Government: overseas
department of France
Monetary Unit: French franc
Industry: construction,
shrimp processing, forestry
products, rum, gold mining
Agriculture: rice, corn, manioc, cocoa, bananas, sugar,
cattle, pigs, poultry
Minerals & Resources:
bauxite, timber, gold,
cinnabar, kaolin, fish

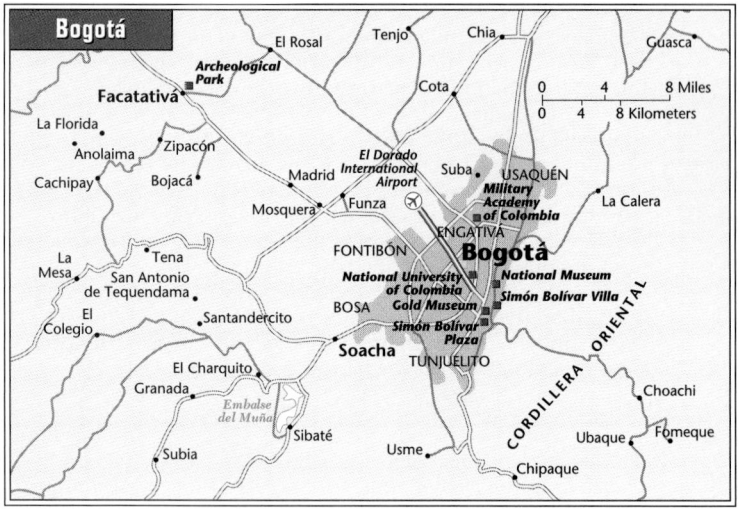

Bogotá

Colombia gained independence from Spain in 1810 after almost three hundred years of Spanish rule, and became the Republic of Greater Colombia nine years later. Today it is the third most populous country in Latin America.

The population of Colombia is ethnically diverse as a result of the intermingling of indigenous Indians, Spanish colonists and African slaves. Colombians have become increasingly urbanized, with three quarters of the population now residing in urban areas.

Economically, Colombia enjoys very diverse industrial and agricultural sectors. It is well-endowed with minerals and energy resources, including coal, oil and gas, gold, silver and emeralds.

Colombia has been plagued by left-wing insurgency movements and the drug cartels which dominate Cali.

Colombia

Capital: Bogotá
Area: 439,619 sq. mi.
  1,138,910 sq. km.
Population: 41,008,000 (2002 est.)
Largest City: Bogotá, 6,422,000
Language: Spanish
Major Religion: Roman Catholic
Life Expectancy: 70 male, 75 female
Government Type: republic
Monetary Unit: Colombian peso
Industry: textiles, food processing, oil, clothing and footwear, beverages, chemicals, metal products, cement; mining - gold, coal, emeralds, iron, nickel, silver, salt
Agriculture: coffee, rice, tobacco, corn, sugarcane, cocoa beans, oilseeds, vegetables, forest products and shrimp farming are becoming more important
Minerals & Resources: petroleum, natural gas, coal, iron ore, nickel, gold, copper, emeralds

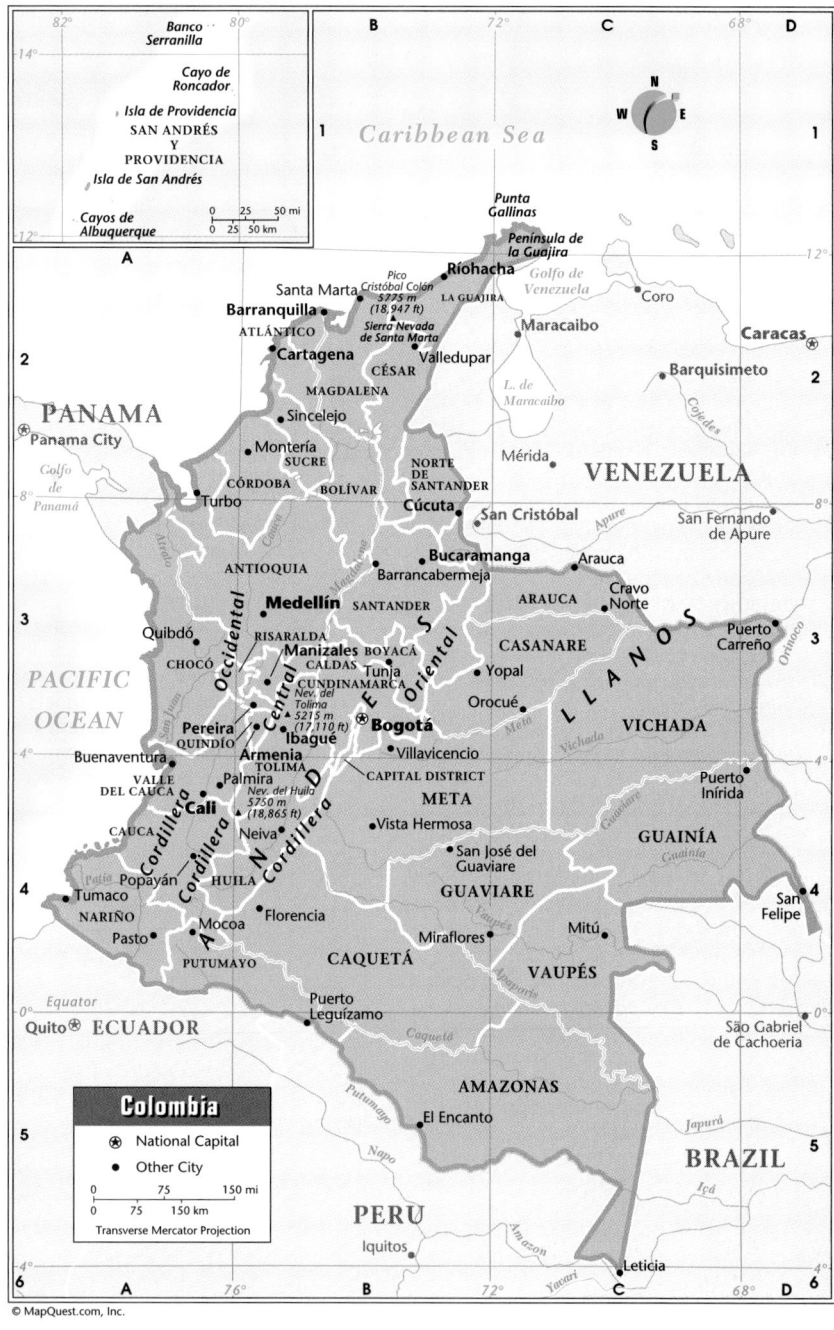

© MapQuest.com, Inc.

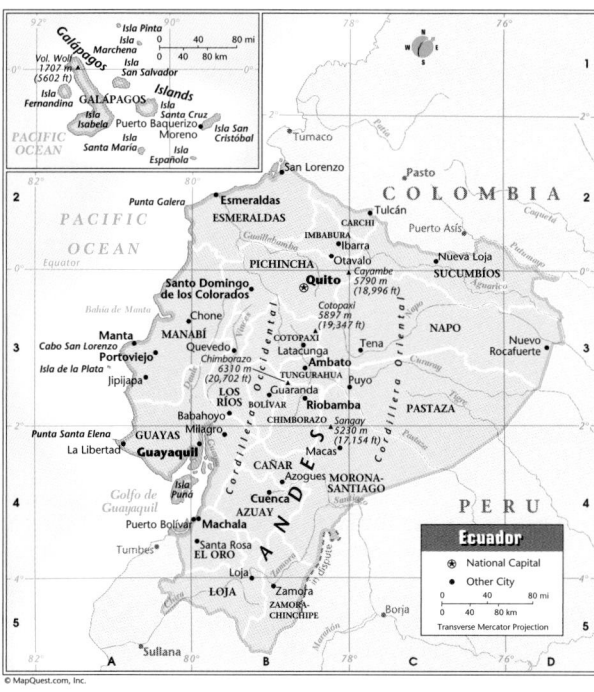

Ecuador gained independence from Spain in 1822 as part of the federation of Gran Colombia from which it withdrew in 1830. Ecuador is an equatorial country which extends across the Western Andes and includes the Galapagos Islands.

Ecuadorians are ethnically mixed with a majority mestizo population. Although people were concentrated in the mountainous central highland region several decades ago, the current population is divided between that area and the coastal lowlands.

Agriculture is the most important sector of the economy, supporting about half the population. There are also important oil reserves. The current government has been working to make economic reforms and encourage foreign investment.

Ecuador

Capital: Quito
Area: 109,454 sq. mi.
283,560 sq. km.
Population: 13,447,000 (2002 est.)
Largest City: Guayaquil, 2,118,000
Languages: Spanish, Indian languages
Major Religion: Roman Catholic
Life Expectancy: 68 male, 73 female
Government: republic
Monetary Unit: sucre
Industry: petroleum, food processing, textiles, metal work, paper products, wood products, chemicals, plastics, fishing, lumber
Agriculture: bananas, balsawood, coffee, cocoa, fish, shrimp, rice, potatoes, manioc, plantains, sugarcane, cattle, sheep, hogs, beef, pork
Minerals & Resources: petroleum, fish, timber

Ecuador Indian market

Machu Picchu ruins in Peru

In 1531 when the Spanish landed, Peru's territory was the nucleus of the highly developed Inca civilization. By 1542 the Spanish had established control and Peru became the main source of Spanish wealth and power in South America. In 1821 Peru declared its independence from Spain. Since then, Peru has had a dominant military and coups have repeatedly interrupted civilian constitutional government.

Ethnically, Peru's population is made up primarily of Indians, mestizos, and Caucasians and there are also some people of African, Chinese, and Japanese descent. The Hispanic and Indian cultures in the country influence many aspects of life in Peru.

The Peruvian economy has become increasingly market-oriented and privatization has recently become common.

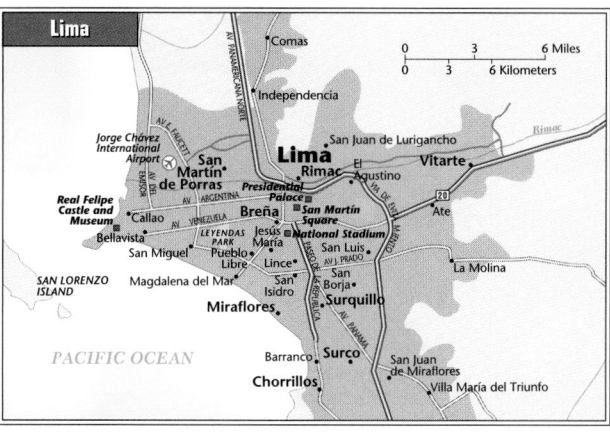

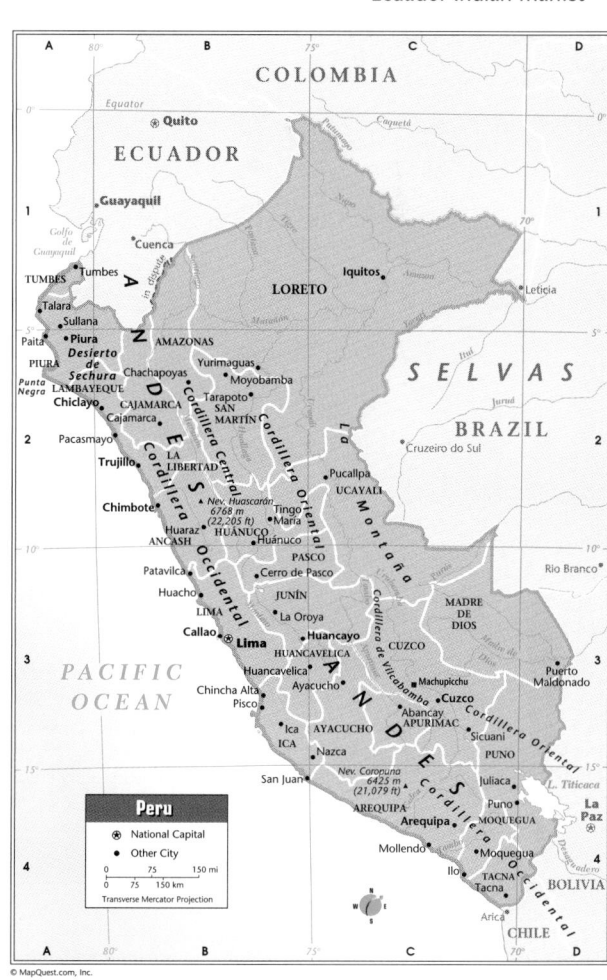

Peru

Capital: Lima
Area: 496,094 sq. mi.
1,285,220 sq. km.
Population: 27,950,000 (2002 est.)
Largest City: Lima, 6,988,000
Languages: Spanish, Quechua, Aymara
Major Religion: Roman Catholic
Life Expectancy: 64 male, 68 female
Government Type: republic
Monetary Unit: nuevo sol

Industry: mining of metals, petroleum, fishing, textiles, clothing, food processing, cement, auto assembly, steel, shipbuilding, metal fabrication
Agriculture: coffee, cotton, sugarcane, rice, wheat, potatoes, plantains, coca, poultry, red meats, dairy, wool, fish
Minerals & Resources: copper, silver, gold, petroleum, timber, fish, iron ore, coal, phosphate, potash

Bolivia

- ⊛ National Capital
- • Other City

| 0 | 100 | 200 mi |
| 0 | 100 | 200 km |

Transverse Mercator Projection

A 65° **B** 60° **C**

1

Rio Branco

Iñapari
Cobija
PANDO
Riberalta
Guajará-Mirim

BRAZIL

Puerto
Maldonado

Chapada dos Parecis

Vilhena

2

LA PAZ
Santa Ana
Magdalena
Mojos
San
Borja
BENI
San Cristóbal
Trinidad

PERU

Cordillera
Titicaca
Illampu
6485 m (21,276 ft)
YUNGAS
Cordillera
Tarvo

Mato Grosso Plateau

15°

Guaqui
⊛ La Paz
Illimani
6462 m
(21,201 ft)
Real
COCHABAMBA
Cochabamba
Cordillera
Oriental
SANTA CRUZ
San
Ignacio
Santa Rosa
del Palmar
San
Matías

3

Nevado
Sajama
6542 m
(21,463 ft)
Oruro
Llallagua
ALTIPLANO
ORURO
L.
Poopó
Aiquile
Montero
Santa Cruz
San José
de Chiquitos
Roboré

Sucre ⊛
Salar
de
Uyuni
Potosí
Camiri
CENTRAL
CHACO
Puerto Suárez
Fortín Ravelo

20°

A
N
D
E
S
Occidental
Uyuni
CHUQUISACA
POTOSÍ
Vol.
Ollagüe
5869 m
(19,255 ft)
Tupiza
Tarija
TARIJA
Yacuiba
PARAGUAY

4

Calama
Villazón
La Quiaca
Tartagal
Mariscal
Estigarribia

CHILE
ARGENTINA
GRAN
San Salvador
de Jujuy
Concepción

© MapQuest.com, Inc.

Bolivia gained its independence from Spain and became a republic in 1825 after three centuries of Spanish influence and rule. The struggle for independence was led by Simón Bolívar, for whom the country is named. Its history since independence has been marked by coups, political instability and poverty for many of its people. Bolivia is in fact the least-developed country in South America, although recent government policies are having a positive effect.

The Bolivians are of indigenous Indian, European and mixed descent. Many people depend on subsistence farming or mining for a living. Education and literacy are poor and a majority of people live in poverty.

Bolivia

Capital: La Paz (seat of government); Sucre (legal capital and seat of judiciary)
Area: 424,052 sq. mi.
1,098,580 sq. km.
Population: 8,445,000 (2002 est.)
Largest City: La Paz, 1,484,000
Languages: Spanish, Quechua, Aymara
Major Religions: Roman Catholic, Protestant
Life expectancy: 61 male, 66 female
Government: republic
Monetary Unit: boliviano
Industry: mining, smelting, petroleum, food and beverage, tobacco, handicrafts, clothing; illicit drug industry reportedly produces 15% of its revenues
Agriculture: coffee, coca, cotton, corn, sugarcane,
rice, potatoes, timber; self-sufficient in food
Minerals and Resources: tin, natural gas, petroleum, zinc, tungsten, antimony, silver, iron, lead, gold, timber

Paraguay

National Capital
Other City

0   75   150 mi
0   75   150 km

Conic Equidistant Projection

© MapQuest.com, Inc.

Capital: Asunción
Area: 157,006 sq. mi.
406,750 sq. km.
Population: 5,884,000 (2002 est.)
Largest City: Asunción, 513,000
Languages: Spanish, Guaraní
Major Religions: Roman Catholic, Mennonite, and other Protestant denominations
Life Expectancy: 72 male, 75 female
Government: republic
Monetary Unit: guaraní
Industry: meat packing, oilseed crushing, milling, brewing, textiles, other light consumer goods, cement, construction
Agriculture: cotton, sugarcane, soybeans, corn, wheat, tobacco, cassava
Minerals and Resources: iron ore, manganese

 *Paraguay*

Paraguay declared its independence from Spain in 1811 when it overthrew the local Spanish authorities. Since independence, Paraguay has seen civil war, dictatorships, and periods of extreme political instability. The highly centralized government was fundamentally changed by the 1992 constitution, which provides for a division of powers.

The vast majority of Paraguayans live in the east, most within about 150 kilometers of Asunción. Ethnically, culturally and socially, Paraguay has one of the most homogeneous populations in South America. About 95% of the people are of mixed Spanish and Guarani Indian descent.

Agriculture, including forestry, employs nearly half the labor force and accounts for a quarter of the GDP. Paraguay lacks substantial mineral or petroleum resources but possesses a large hydrocarbon potential.

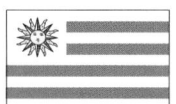 *Uruguay*

Capital: Montevideo
Area: 68,038 sq. mi.
176,220 sq. km.
Population: 3,387,000 (2002 est.)
Largest City: Montevideo, 1,303,000
Language: Spanish
Major Religions: Roman Catholic, Protestant, Jewish
Life Expectancy: 71 male, 78 female
Government: republic
Monetary Unit: Uruguayan peso
Industry: meat processing, wool and hides, sugar, textiles, footwear, leather apparel, tires, cement, petroleum refining, wine
Agriculture: wheat, rice, corn, sorghum
Minerals and Resources: soil, hydropower potential

Uruguay's early 19th century history was shaped by ongoing fights between the British, Spanish, and Portuguese for dominance in the Argentina-Brazil-Uruguay region. In 1821 Uruguay was annexed to Brazil by Portugal, but Uruguayan patriots declared independence from Brazil in 1825 and three years later Uruguay officially became independent.

Although Uruguayans share a Spanish linguistic and cultural background, one quarter of the population is of Italian origin and most are Roman Catholic. Uruguay is distinguished by its high literacy rate and large urban middle class. The average standard of living compares favorably with that of most other Latin American countries.

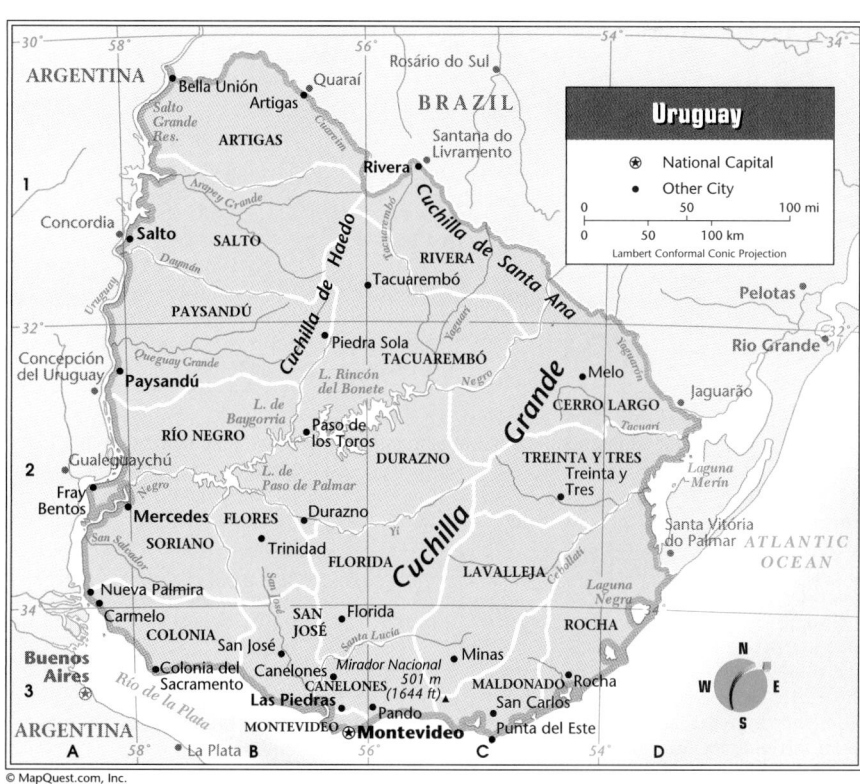

Uruguay

National Capital
Other City

0   50   100 mi
0   50   100 km

Lambert Conformal Conic Projection

© MapQuest.com, Inc.

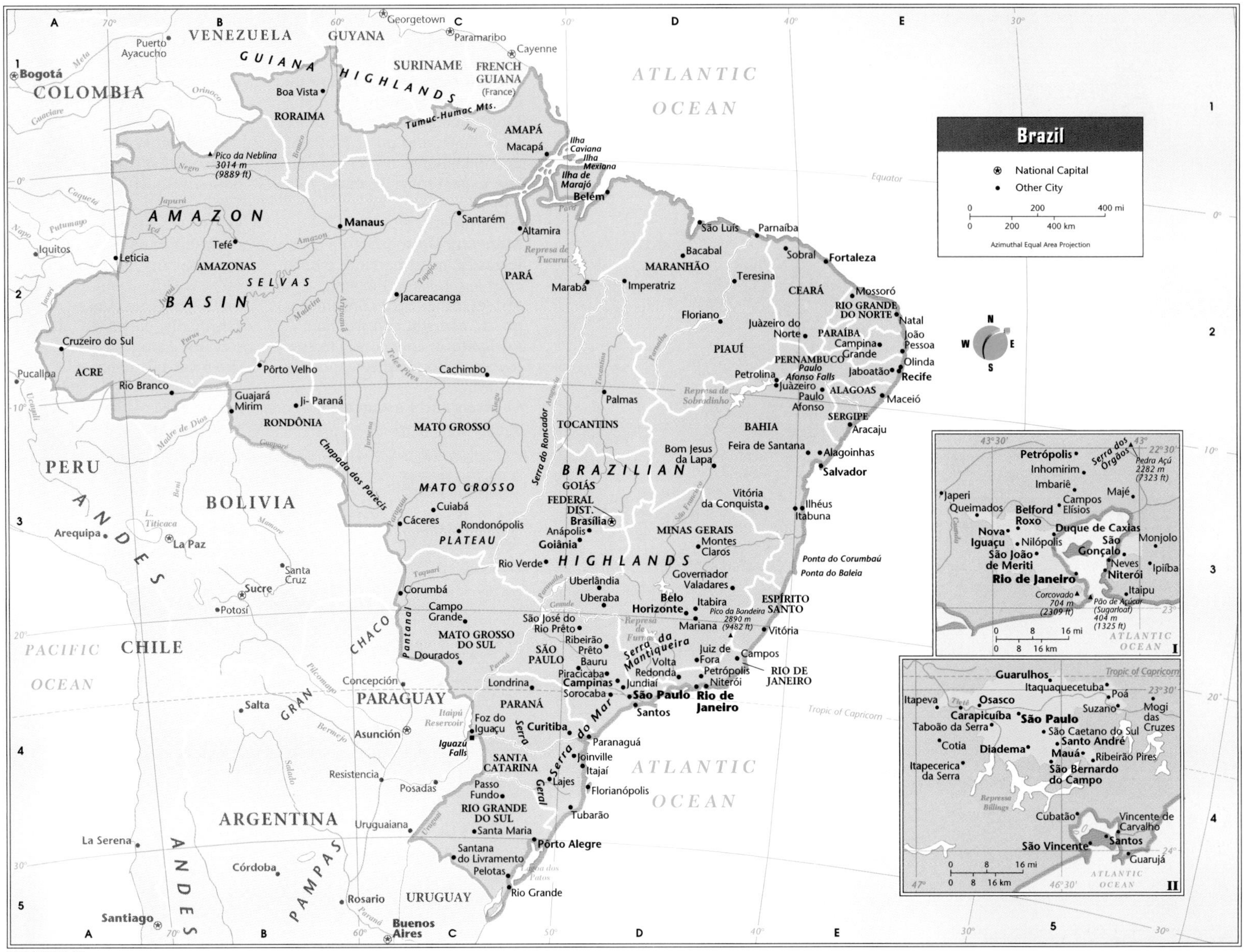

Brazil Map

VENEZUELA • GUYANA • Georgetown • Paramaribo • **SURINAME** • **FRENCH GUIANA (France)** • Cayenne

COLOMBIA • Bogotá • Puerto Ayacucho

GUIANA HIGHLANDS • Boa Vista • **RORAIMA** • Tumuc-Humac Mts.

AMAPÁ • Macapá • Ilha Caviana • Ilha Mexiana • Ilha de Marajó • Belém

Pico da Neblina 3014 m (9889 ft)

AMAZON • Manaus • Santarém • Altamira

AMAZONAS • Tefé • SELVAS • BASIN

Iquitos • Leticia • Cruzeiro do Sul

São Luís • Parnaíba • Bacabal • Sobral • **Fortaleza**

MARANHÃO • Teresina • **CEARÁ** • Mossoró

PARÁ • Marabá • Imperatriz • Floriano

PIAUÍ • Juàzeiro do Norte • **RIO GRANDE DO NORTE** • Natal • **PARAÍBA** • Campina Grande • João Pessoa

PERNAMBUCO • Paulo Afonso Falls • Olinda • Recife • Jaboatão • Petrolina • Juàzeiro • Paulo Afonso • **ALAGOAS** • Maceió

ACRE • Rio Branco • Pôrto Velho • Cachimbo

Cruzeiro do Sul • Pucallpa • Guajará Mirim • Ji-Paraná

RONDÔNIA • **MATO GROSSO** • **TOCANTINS** • Palmas

PERU • ANDES • **BOLIVIA** • Arequipa • La Paz • Santa Cruz • Sucre • Potosí

MATO GROSSO • PLATEAU • Cuiabá • Cáceres • Rondonópolis

GOIÁS • **FEDERAL DIST.** • **Brasília** • Anápolis • Goiânia • Rio Verde

BRAZILIAN • HIGHLANDS

Bom Jesus da Lapa • Feira de Santana • **BAHIA** • Alagoinhas • **Salvador**

SERGIPE • Aracaju

Vitória da Conquista • Ilhéus • Itabuna

MINAS GERAIS • Montes Claros

Ponta do Corumbaú • Ponta do Baleia

Uberlândia • Uberaba • Governador Valadares • Itabira • **Belo Horizonte** • Pico da Bandeira 2890 m (9482 ft) • **ESPÍRITO SANTO**

Corumbá • Campo Grande • São José do Rio Prêto • Ribeirão Prêto • Bauru • Mariana • Vitória

MATO GROSSO DO SUL • Dourados • **SÃO PAULO** • Piracicaba • **Campinas** • Jundiaí • Juiz de Fora • Volta Redonda • Petrópolis • Campos • **RIO DE JANEIRO**

Concepción • Londrina • Sorocaba • **São Paulo** • Niterói • **Rio de Janeiro**

PARAGUAY • Asunción • Salta • Itaipú Reservoir • **PARANÁ** • Santos

Iguazu Falls • Foz do Iguaçu • **Curitiba** • Paranaguá

Resistencia • **SANTA CATARINA** • Joinville • Itajaí • Lajes • Florianópolis

ARGENTINA • Posadas • Passo Fundo • **RIO GRANDE DO SUL** • Santa Maria • Tubarão

Córdoba • Uruguaiana • Santana do Livramento • Pelotas • **Pôrto Alegre** • Rio Grande

Santiago • Rosario • **URUGUAY** • Buenos Aires

PACIFIC OCEAN • CHILE • ANDES • GRAN CHACO • PAMPAS

ATLANTIC OCEAN • Equator • Tropic of Capricorn

Map Legend: Brazil
⊛ National Capital
• Other City
0 200 400 mi
0 200 400 km
Azimuthal Equal Area Projection

Inset I (Rio de Janeiro region)
Petrópolis • Inhomirim • Imbariê • Majé • Campos Elísios • Japeri • Queimados • Belford Roxo • Nova Iguaçu • Nilópolis • Duque de Caxias • São João de Meriti • São Gonçalo • Monjolo • **Rio de Janeiro** • Niterói • Ipiíba • Corcovado 704 m (2309 ft) • Pão de Açúcar (Sugarloaf) 404 m (1325 ft) • Pedra Açú 2282 m (7323 ft) • Serra dos Órgãos
0 8 16 mi / 0 8 16 km
ATLANTIC OCEAN

Inset II (São Paulo region)
Guarulhos • Itaquaquecetuba • Poá • Suzano • Mogi das Cruzes • Itapeva • Osasco • Carapicuíba • **São Paulo** • Taboão da Serra • Cotia • São Caetano do Sul • Santo André • Ribeirão Pires • Itapecerica da Serra • Diadema • Mauá • São Bernardo do Campo • Cubatão • Vincente de Carvalho • São Vicente • **Santos** • Guarujá
0 8 16 mi / 0 8 16 km
ATLANTIC OCEAN
Tropic of Capricorn

© MapQuest.com, Inc.

Brazil was claimed in 1500 by the Portuguese navigator Pedro Cabral and was ruled as a colony until 1808, when the Portuguese royal family fled to Brazil to escape Napoleon's army and established Salvador and later Rio de Janeiro as the seat of government. In 1822, Brazil declared its independence from Portugal and established itself as an empire. The monarchy was overthrown in 1889 and a republic was declared.

Brazil is the largest and most populous country in South America. Most Brazilians live in the south-central area and urban growth has been rapid in recent years. The Brazilian population comprises four major groups: indigenous Indians, Portuguese, Africans and various European and Asian immigrant groups. National identity is strong and racial friction is a relatively new phenomenon.

Brazil's economy has large agricultural, mining and manufacturing sectors. Since the return to civilian rule in 1985, successive Brazilian governments have introduced various plans to reduce high inflation and large budget deficits. These measures have been fairly successful and economic reform is progressing.

Capital: Brasilia
Area: 3,311,154 sq. mi.
8,511,965 sq. km.
Population: 179,914,000 (2002 est.)
Largest City: São Paulo, 10,406,000
Languages: Portuguese, Spanish, English, French
Major Religion: Roman Catholic
Life Expectancy: 57 male, 67 female
Government: federal republic
Monetary Unit: real
Industry: textiles, shoes, chemicals, cement, lumber, mining (iron ore, tin), steel making, machine building - including aircraft, motor vehicles, motor vehicle parts and assemblies, and other machinery and equipment
Agriculture: coffee, orange juice concentrate, soybeans, rice, corn, sugarcane, cocoa, beef
Minerals and Resources: bauxite, gold, iron ore, manganese, nickel, phosphates, platinum, tin, uranium, petroleum, hydropower, timber

Brazil

Bird of Paradise flower blooming in the Amazon

Macaw in Belém courtyard

Rio de Janeiro

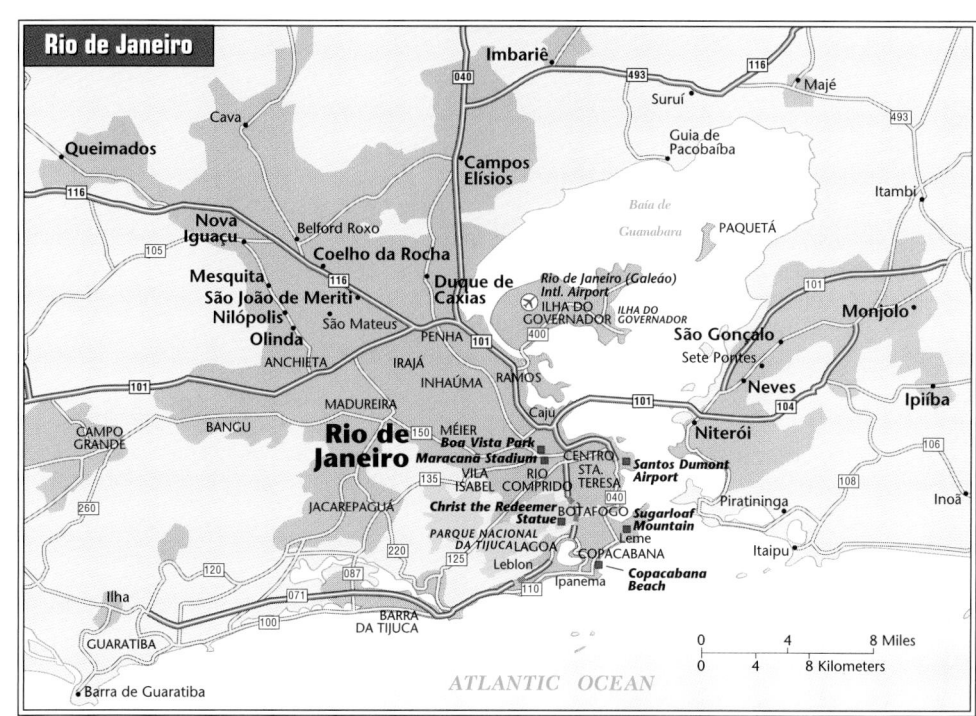

Queimados
Cava
Imbariê
Suruí
Majé
Guia de Pacobaíba
Itambi
Campos Elísios
Belford Roxo
Nova Iguaçu
Coelho da Rocha
Mesquita
São João de Meriti
Nilópolis
Olinda
São Mateus
Duque de Caxias
Rio de Janeiro (Galeão) Intl. Airport
ILHA DO GOVERNADOR
ILHA DO GOVERNADOR
Baía de Guanabara
PAQUETÁ
Monjolo
São Gonçalo
Sete Pontes
Neves
Ipiíba
Inoã
ANCHIETA
IRAJÁ
INHAÚMA
PENHA
RAMOS
Caju
Rio de Janeiro
MÉIER
Boa Vista Park
Maracanã Stadium
VILA ISABEL
RIO COMPRIDO
CENTRO
STA. TERESA
Santos Dumont Airport
Niterói
Piratininga
CAMPO GRANDE
BANGU
MADUREIRA
JACAREPAGUÁ
Christ the Redeemer Statue
BOTAFOGO
Sugarloaf Mountain
Leme
COPACABANA
PARQUE NACIONAL DA TIJUCA
LAGOA
Leblon
Ipanema
Copacabana Beach
Itaipu
Ilha
GUARATIBA
BARRA DA TIJUCA
Barra de Guaratiba
ATLANTIC OCEAN

0   4   8 Miles
0   4   8 Kilometers

BRAZIL

Pão de Açúcar (Sugarloaf Mt.) in Rio de Janeiro

São Paulo Metro

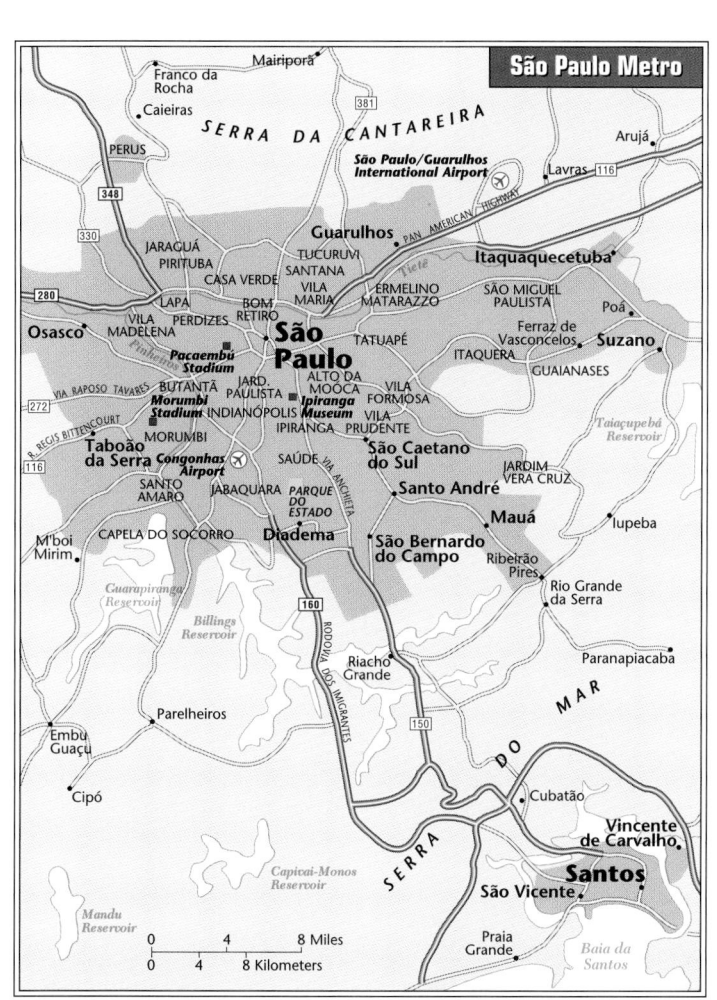

Mairiporã
Franco da Rocha
Caieiras
SERRA DA CANTAREIRA
Arujá
PERUS
São Paulo/Guarulhos International Airport
Lavras
PAN AMERICAN HIGHWAY
JARAGUÁ
PIRITUBA
Guarulhos
TUCURUVI
SANTANA
CASA VERDE
VILA MARIA
ERMELINO MATARAZZO
Itaquaquecetuba
SÃO MIGUEL PAULISTA
Poá
LAPA
PERDIZES
BOM RETIRO
Osasco
VILA MADELENA
Pacaembú Stadium
São Paulo
TATUAPÉ
Ferraz de Vasconcelos
Suzano
BUTANTÃ
JARD. PAULISTA
ALTO DA MOÓCA
ITAQUÉRA
GUAIANASES
Morumbi Stadium
INDIANÓPOLIS
Ipiranga Museum
IPIRANGA
VILA FORMOSA
VILA PRUDENTE
Taiaçupebá Reservoir
MORUMBI
Taboão da Serra
Congonhas Airport
SAÚDE
VIA ANCHIETA
São Caetano do Sul
JARDIM VERA CRUZ
SANTO AMARO
JABAQUARA
PARQUE DO ESTADO
Santo André
CAPELA DO SOCÓRRO
Maúa
Iupeba
M'boi Mirim
Diadema
São Bernardo do Campo
Ribeirão Pires
Rio Grande da Serra
Guarapiranga Reservoir
Billings Reservoir
Riacho Grande
Paranapiacaba
Parelheiros
Embú Guaçu
SERRA DO MAR
Cipó
Capivai-Monos Reservoir
Cubatão
Vincente de Carvalho
Mandu Reservoir
Santos
São Vicente
Praia Grande
Baía da Santos

0   4   8 Miles
0   4   8 Kilometers

Downtown São Paulo

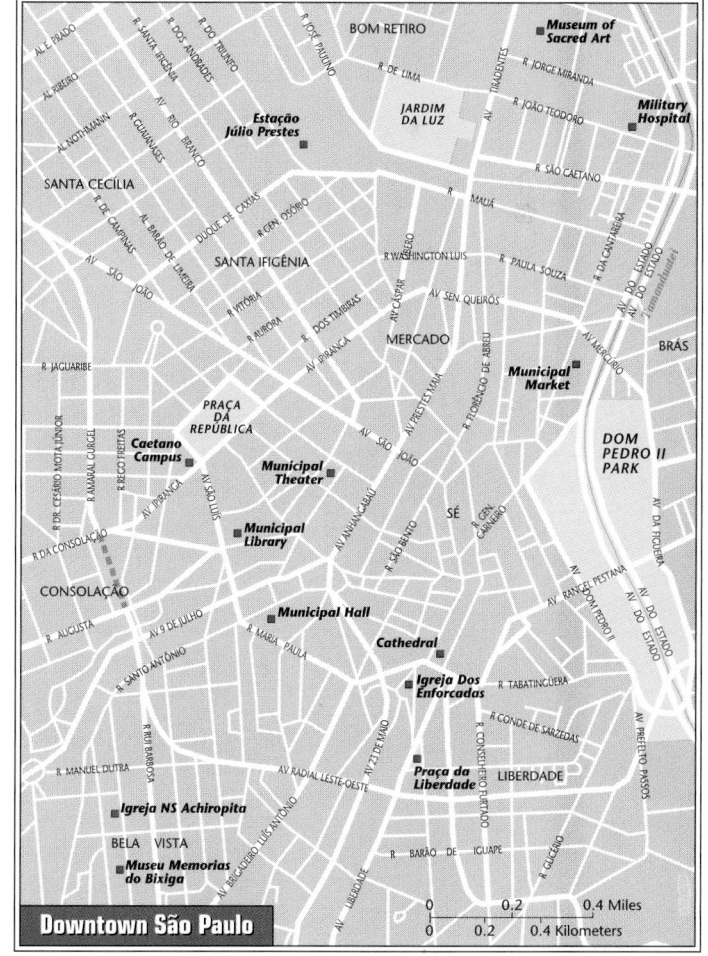

BOM RETIRO
Museum of Sacred Art
JARDIM DA LUZ
Military Hospital
SANTA CECÍLIA
Estação Júlio Prestes
SANTA IFIGÉNIA
MERCADO
Municipal Market
BRÁS
PRAÇA DA REPÚBLICA
Caetano Campus
Municipal Theater
DOM PEDRO II PARK
Municipal Library
SÉ
CONSOLAÇÃO
Municipal Hall
Cathedral
Igreja Dos Enforcadas
Praça da Liberdade
LIBERDADE
Igreja NS Achiropita
BELA VISTA
Museu Memorias do Bixiga

0   0.2   0.4 Miles
0   0.2   0.4 Kilometers

What is present-day Chile was first settled some 10,000 years ago by migrating Indians who followed the line of the Andes Mountains and settled in fertile valleys and along the coast. Chile became part of the Spanish Viceroyalty of Peru in the 16th century and remained so until 1818 when Chilean independence was formally proclaimed.

About 85% of Chileans live in urban centers, 40% in greater Santiago. The majority are of Spanish or Spanish-Indian descent. Chileans make up one of the most educated work forces in Latin America. Chile has a prosperous, essentially free market economy. It depends heavily on copper, of which it is the world's largest producer and exporter.

Chile

Capital: Santiago
Area: 292,183 sq. mi.
756,950 sq. km.
Population: 15,499,000 (2002 est.)
Largest City: Santiago, 4,647,000
Language: Spanish
Major Religions: Roman Catholic, Protestant, Jewish
Life Expectancy: 72 male, 78 female
Government: republic
Monetary Unit: Chilean peso

Industry: copper, other minerals, foodstuffs, fish processing, iron and steel, wood and wood products, transport equipment, cement, textiles
Agriculture: wheat, corn, grapes, beans, sugar beets, potatoes, deciduous fruit
Minerals and Resources: copper, iron ore, nitrates, precious metals, molybdenum

Tierra del Fuego National Park, Argentina-Chile border

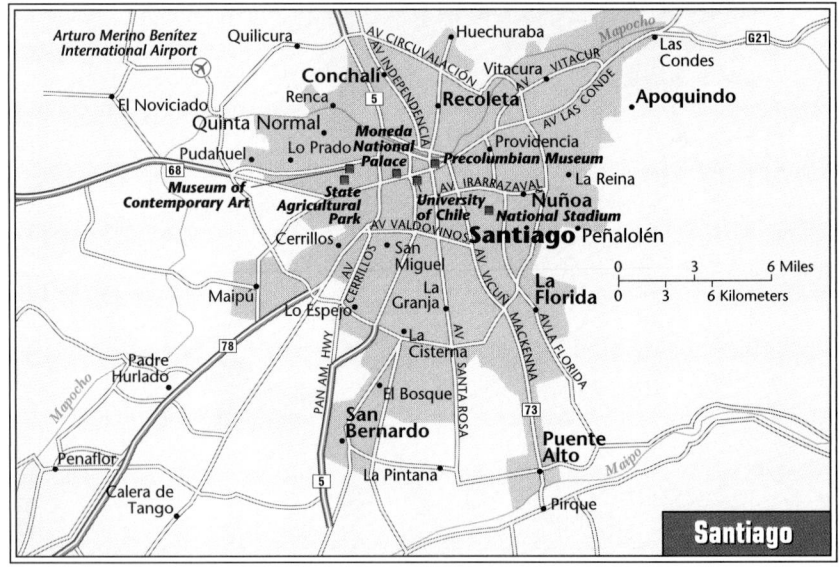

Santiago

Argentina

In 1580 Spain established a permanent colony on the site of Buenos Aires. Argentina was further integrated into the Spanish empire following the establishment of the Viceroyalty of Rio de la Plata in 1776. Buenos Aires declared its independence from Spain in 1816.

Argentines are a fusion of diverse national and ethnic groups, predominantly Italian and Spanish. Eighty percent of the population resides in urban areas, more than one-third in the greater Buenos Aires area. The Argentines enjoy a relatively high standard of living and have one of Latin America's lowest growth rates.

Argentina has a well-educated work force and substantial natural resources, making it one of Latin America's richest countries.

However, political conflict and uneven economic performance over the past decades have impeded full realization of its potential. Recently, a comprehensive economic restructuring program was implemented and, to date, it has proven successful.

Capital: Buenos Aires
Area: 1,068,020 sq. mi.
　　　 2,766,890 sq. km.
Population: 38,331,000 (2002 est.)
Largest City: Buenos Aires, 2,965,000
Languages: Spanish, English, Italian, German, French
Major Religions: Roman Catholic, Protestant, Jewish
Life Expectancy: 68 male, 75 female
Government: republic
Monetary Unit: nuevo peso argentino
Industry: food processing, motor vehicles, consumer durables, textiles, chemicals and petrochemicals, printing, metallurgy, steel
Agriculture: wheat, corn, sorghum, soybeans, sugar beets
Minerals and Resources: lead, zinc, tin, copper, iron ore, manganese, petroleum, uranium

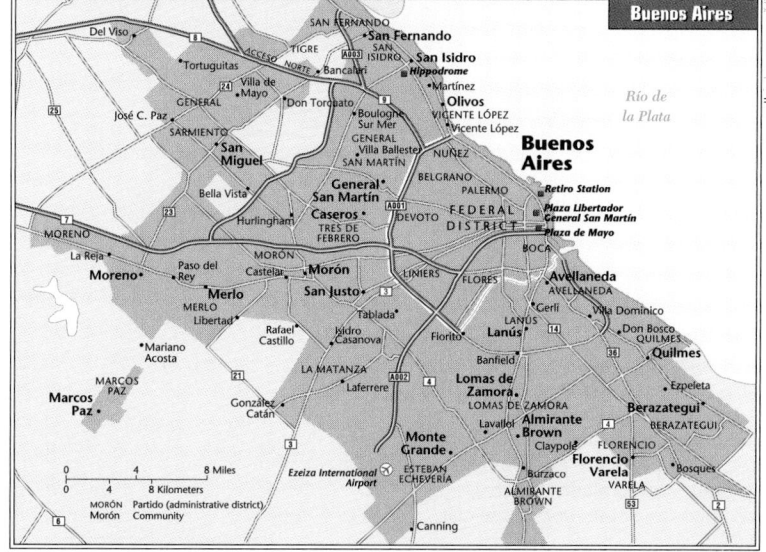

MATT THARP

National Congress, Buenos Aires

Antarctica is a continent south of the Antarctic Circle that contains the South Pole. Several nations have claimed sections of Antarctica, including Argentina, Australia, Chile, France, New Zealand, Norway, and the United Kingdom; however the Antarctic Treaty of 1959 defers these claims and most other countries do not recognize them.

The Antarctic Treaty establishes the legal framework for the management of Antarctica. There are currently 42 treaty member nations, including the seven which claim portions of Antarctica.

Antarctica is the coldest, windiest, highest, and driest continent. There are no indigenous inhabitants, but there are 42 permanent and about 40 summer research stations which are staffed and operated by various countries. Military activity is prohibited except for scientific research.

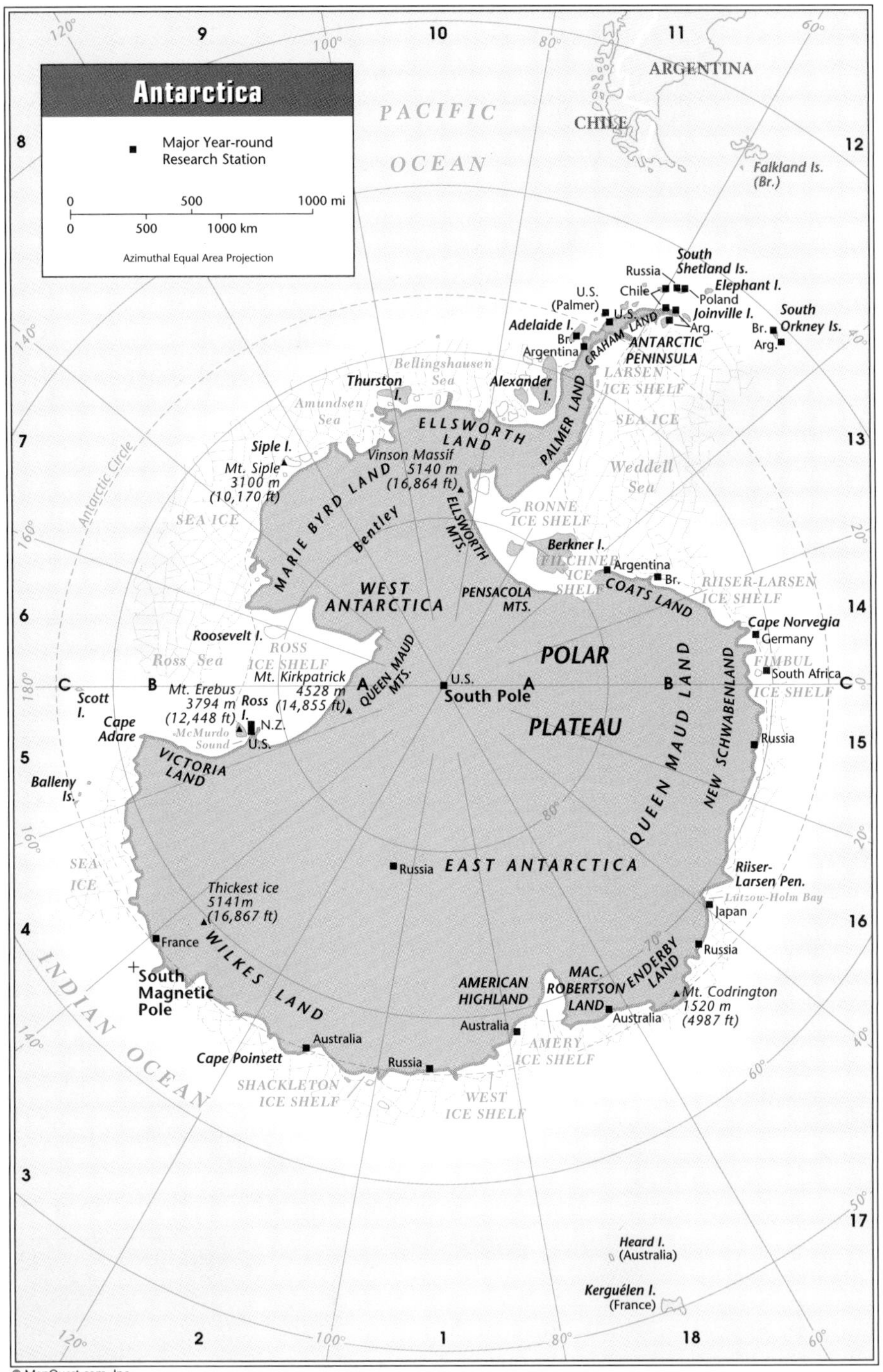

Gentoo Penguins among whale vertebrae

Iceberg off coast of Antarctica

Abandoned Norwegian whaling station, Antarctica

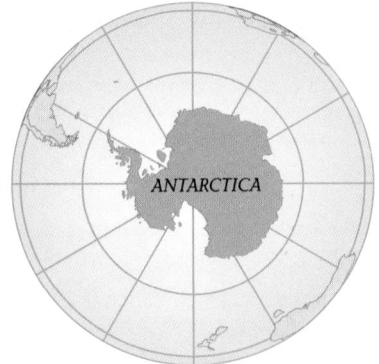

ANTARCTICA

Area: 5.4 million sq. mi. (est.)
14 million sq. km. (est.)
Population: no indigenous inhabitants; note: summer population of research stations is 4,115
Government: Antarctic Treaty Summary: The Antarctic Treaty, signed on December 1, 1959, and entered into force on June 23, 1961, establishes the legal framework for the management of Antarctica. Administration is carried out through consultative meetings of the 42 treaty member nations. Of these, 26 are consultative and 16 acceding.

Consultative (voting) members include the seven nations that claim portions of Antarctica as national territory (some claims overlap) and 19 nonclaimant nations. Certain nations that have made no claims have reserved the right to do so. The United States does not recognize the claims of others.
Industry: fishing, small-scale tourism (both based abroad)
Minerals and Resources: none presently exploited; iron ore, chromium, copper, gold, nickel, platinum, coal, and hydrocarbons have been found in small, uncommercial quantities

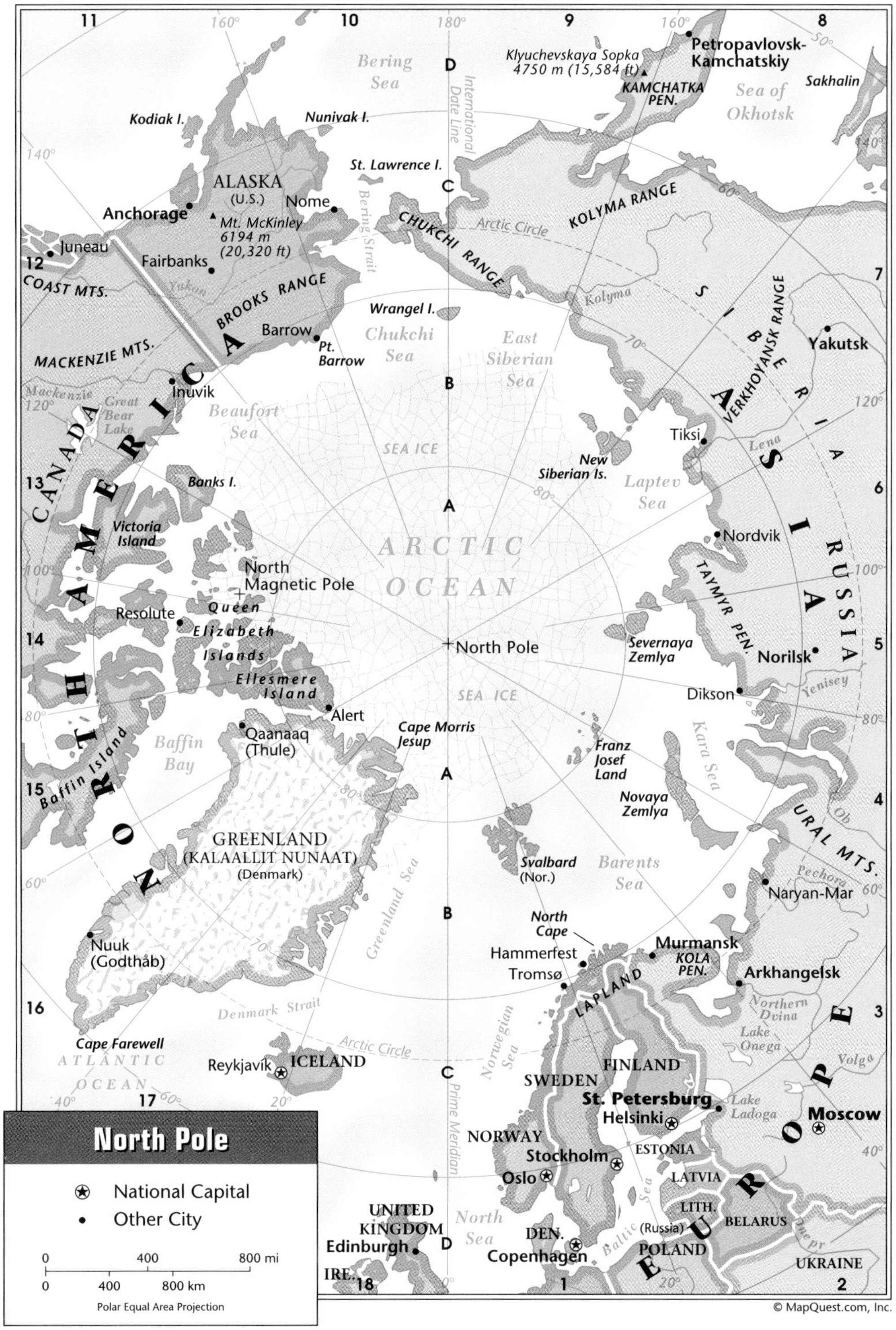

North Pole

11 10 180° 9 160° 8

Bering Sea

D

Klyuchevskaya Sopka 4750 m (15,584 ft) Petropavlovsk-Kamchatskiy

KAMCHATKA PEN.

Sakhalin

Kodiak I. Nunivak I.

St. Lawrence I.

Sea of Okhotsk

C

ALASKA (U.S.) Nome

KOLYMA RANGE

Anchorage Mt. McKinley 6194 m (20,320 ft)

Arctic Circle

Juneau Fairbanks

Kolyma

7

COAST MTS. Yukon

CHUKCHI RANGE

BROOKS RANGE

S I B E R I A R U S S I A

VERKHOYANSK RANGE

MACKENZIE MTS.

Barrow Pt. Barrow

Chukchi Sea

Yakutsk

B

Mackenzie

Inuvik

Beaufort Sea

Tiksi

Lena

120°

Great Bear Lake

SEA ICE

East Siberian Sea

New Siberian Is.

Laptev Sea

CANADA

Banks I.

A

Nordvik

100°

Victoria Island

ARCTIC OCEAN

North Magnetic Pole

TAYMYR PEN.

Severnaya Zemlya

Norilsk

Resolute Queen Elizabeth Islands

North Pole

Dikson

Yenisey

Kara Sea

Ellesmere Island

SEA ICE

80°

Alert

Cape Morris Jesup

Baffin Bay

Qaanaaq (Thule)

A

Franz Josef Land

Novaya Zemlya

Ob

NORTH AMERICA

Baffin Island

GREENLAND (KALAALLIT NUNAAT) (Denmark)

Svalbard (Nor.)

Barents Sea

URAL MTS.

Pechora

Naryan-Mar

Greenland Sea

60°

Nuuk (Godthåb)

B

North Cape

Murmansk

Hammerfest KOLA PEN.

Tromsø

Arkhangelsk

Cape Farewell

Denmark Strait

Northern Dvina

ATLANTIC OCEAN 40°

Arctic Circle

LAPLAND

Lake Onega

EUROPE

Reykjavík ICELAND

Norwegian Sea

FINLAND

Volga

SWEDEN

St. Petersburg

Lake Ladoga

North Pole

⊛ National Capital
• Other City

0   400   800 mi
0   400   800 km

Polar Equal Area Projection

NORWAY

Stockholm

Helsinki

ESTONIA

Oslo

LATVIA

UNITED KINGDOM

North Sea

LITH. (Russia)

BELARUS

Edinburgh

DEN.

POLAND

IRE. 18 Copenhagen

UKRAINE

1 2

© MapQuest.com, Inc.

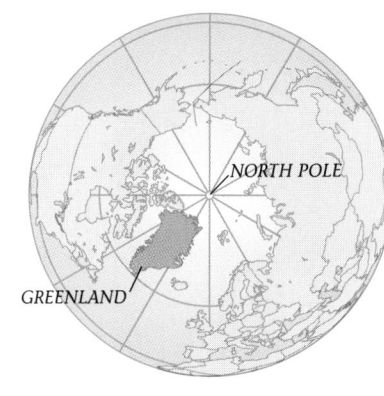

Ellesmere Island National Park, Canada

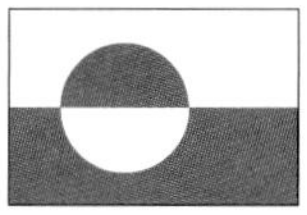

Capital: Nuuk (Godthåb)
Area: 839,782 sq. mi.
2,175,600 sq. km.
Population: 56,000 (2002 est.)
Languages: Eskimo dialects, Danish
Major Religions: Evangelical Lutheran
Life Expectancy: 63 male, 72 female
Government: part of the Danish realm; self-governing overseas administrative division
Monetary Unit: Danish krone
Industry: fish processing (mainly shrimp), lead and zinc mining, handicrafts, some small shipyards, potential for platinum and gold mining
Agriculture: fish, sheep, crops limited to forage and small garden vegetables
Minerals and Resources: zinc, lead, iron ore, coal, molybdenum, cryolite, uranium, fish

Greenland

Polar Bear and Cub

Greenland is an island between the Arctic Ocean and the North Atlantic Ocean. It is part of the Danish realm and is a self-governing overseas administrative division.

Greenlanders constitute a sparse population confined to small settlements along the coast. Two-thirds of the work force are employed by the central government, its commercial entities, and the municipalities. The remainder are primarily engaged in fishing, hunting, and sheep breeding.

Greenland relies on grants from the Danish government for about half of its revenues. Fishing and fish processing account for 95% of Greenland's exports, but prospects for fisheries in the future are not bright. Tourism is the only sector with potential for growth in the near future.

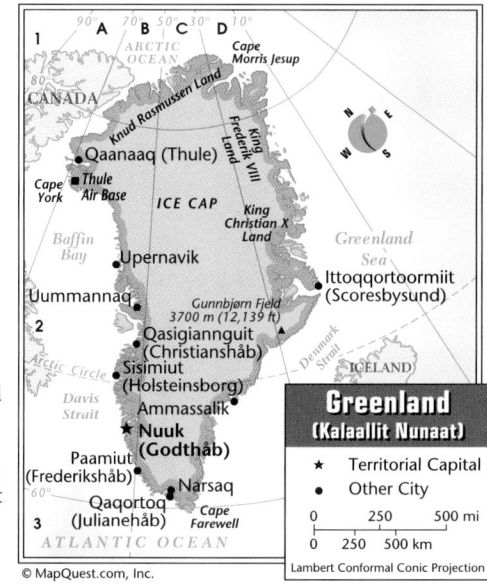

A B C D

1

ARCTIC OCEAN

Cape Morris Jesup

CANADA

Knud Rasmussen Land

King Frederik VIII Land

Qaanaaq (Thule)

Cape York Thule Air Base

ICE CAP

King Christian X Land

Greenland Sea

Baffin Bay

Upernavik

Gunnbjørn Fjeld 3700 m (12,139 ft)

Ittoqqortoormiit (Scoresbysund)

Uummannaq

2

Qasigiannguit (Christianshåb)

Denmark Strait

Sisimiut (Holsteinsborg)

ICELAND

Ammassalik

Davis Strait

★ Nuuk (Godthåb)

Paamiut (Frederikshåb)

Narsaq

Qaqortoq (Julianehåb)

Cape Farewell

3

ATLANTIC OCEAN

Greenland (Kalaallit Nunaat)

★ Territorial Capital
• Other City

0   250   500 mi
0   250   500 km

Lambert Conformal Conic Projection

© MapQuest.com, Inc.

Population: 498,916,000 (2002)
Area: 9,361,791 sq. mi.
24,247,038 sq. km.
Highest Point: Mt. McKinley
20,320 ft. (6,198 m.)
Lowest Point: Death Valley
282 ft. (86 m.)
below sea level
Largest Urban Areas:
Mexico City, Mexico
New York City, U.S.
Los Angeles, U.S.
Chicago, U.S.
Toronto, Canada
Philadelphia, U.S.
San Francisco, U.S.
Countries: 25

Above: Golden Gate Bridge, United States; **Above Right:** Banana plantation in Guadeloupe; **Below Right:** Ropes, traps, and buoys in eastern Canada; **Below:** Farmland in Manitoba, Canada.

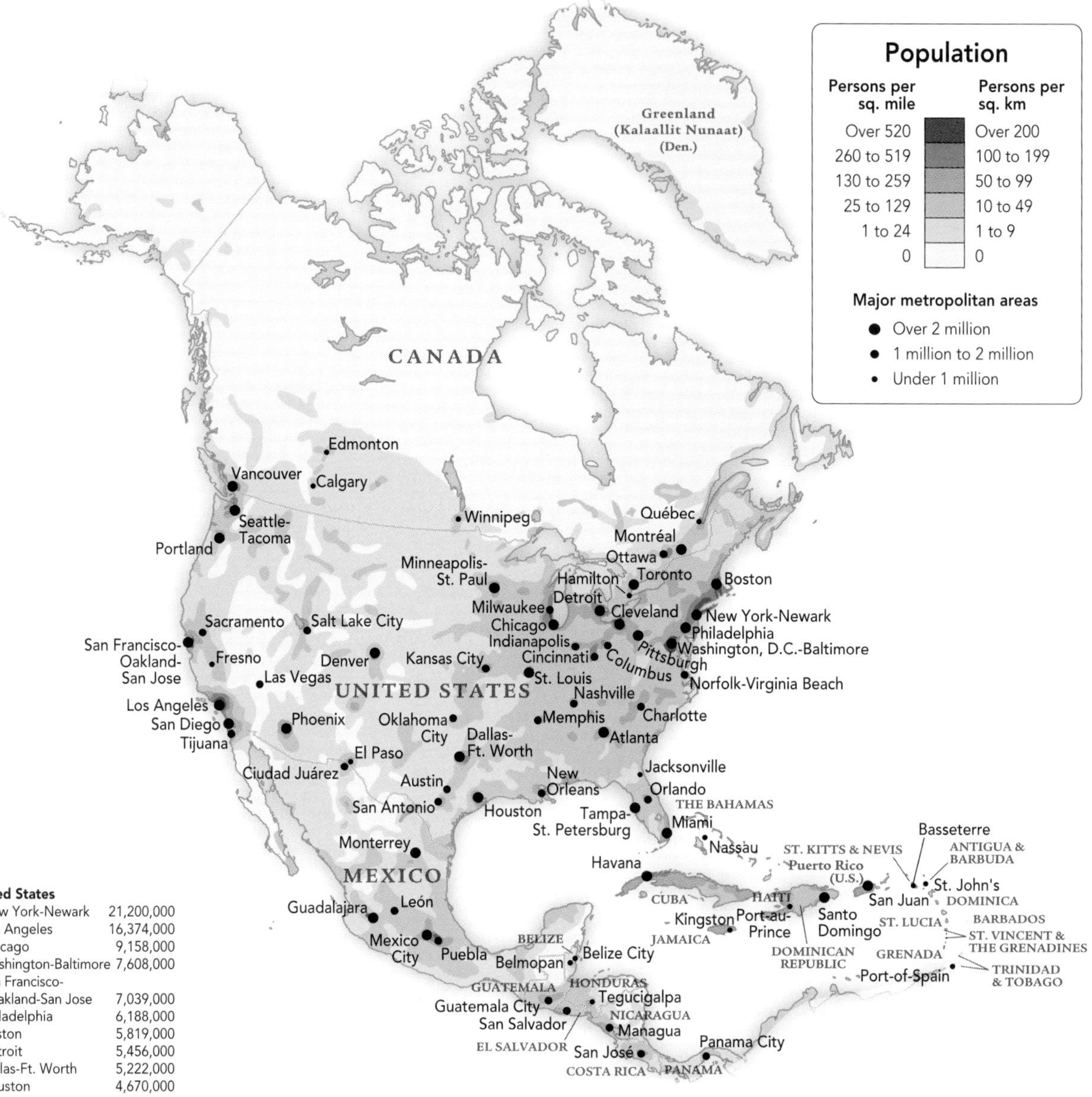

Major Metropolitan Areas

Antigua & Barbuda
St. John's — 22,000

Bahamas
Nassau — 211,000

Barbados
Bridgetown — 6,000

Belize
Belize City — 49,000
Belmopan — 8,000

Canada
Toronto — 5,030,000
Montréal — 3,549,000
Vancouver — 2,123,000
Ottawa — 1,129,000
Calgary — 993,000
Edmonton — 967,000
Québec — 698,000
Hamilton — 687,000
Winnipeg — 686,000

Costa Rica
San José — 1,305,000

Cuba
Havana — 2,192,000

Dominica
Roseau — 16,000

Dominican Republic
Santo Domingo — 2,677,000

El Salvador
San Salvador — 1,909,000

Grenada
St. George's — 5,000

Guatemala
Guatemala City — 1,007,000

Haiti
Port-au-Prince — 991,000

Honduras
Tegucigalpa — 835,000

Jamaica
Kingston — 578,000

Mexico
Mexico City — 16,203,000
Guadalajara — 3,349,000
Monterrey — 3,131,000
Puebla — 1,272,000
Ciudad Juárez — 1,187,000
Tijuana — 1,149,000
León — 1,021,000

Nicaragua
Managua — 1,148,000

Panama
Panama City — 1,002,000

Puerto Rico
San Juan — 2,450,000

St. Kitts & Nevis
Basseterre — 13,000

St. Lucia
Castries — 11,000

St. Vincent & Grenadines
Kingstown — 15,000

Trinidad & Tobago
Port of Spain — 48,000

United States
New York-Newark — 21,200,000
Los Angeles — 16,374,000
Chicago — 9,158,000
Washington-Baltimore — 7,608,000
San Francisco-
Oakland-San Jose — 7,039,000
Philadelphia — 6,188,000
Boston — 5,819,000
Detroit — 5,456,000
Dallas-Ft. Worth — 5,222,000
Houston — 4,670,000
Atlanta — 4,112,000
Miami — 3,876,000
Seattle-Tacoma — 3,555,000
Phoenix — 3,252,000
Minneapolis-St. Paul — 2,969,000
Cleveland-Akron — 2,946,000
San Diego — 2,814,000
St. Louis — 2,604,000
Denver — 2,582,000
Tampa-St. Petersburg — 2,396,000
Pittsburgh — 2,359,000
Portland — 2,265,000
Cincinnati — 1,979,000
Sacramento — 1,797,000
Kansas City — 1,776,000
Milwaukee — 1,690,000

International comparability of population data is limited by varying census methods. Where metropolitan population is unavailable, core city population is shown.

Population

Persons per sq. mile	Persons per sq. km
Over 520	Over 200
260 to 519	100 to 199
130 to 259	50 to 99
25 to 129	10 to 49
1 to 24	1 to 9
0	0

Major metropolitan areas
- Over 2 million
- 1 million to 2 million
- Under 1 million

Greenland
(Kalaallit Nunaat)
(Den.)

CANADA

Edmonton
Vancouver • Calgary
Seattle-Tacoma
Portland
Winnipeg
Québec
Montréal
Ottawa
Minneapolis-St. Paul
Hamilton • Toronto
Milwaukee • Detroit • Boston
Sacramento • Salt Lake City • Chicago • Cleveland
San Francisco-Oakland-San Jose • Fresno • Denver • Kansas City • Indianapolis • Cincinnati • New York-Newark
Las Vegas • Columbus • Pittsburgh • Philadelphia • Washington, D.C.-Baltimore
St. Louis • Norfolk-Virginia Beach
UNITED STATES • Nashville
Los Angeles • Phoenix • Oklahoma City • Memphis • Charlotte
San Diego • Dallas-Ft. Worth • Atlanta
Tijuana • El Paso • Jacksonville
Ciudad Juárez • Austin • New Orleans • Orlando
San Antonio • Houston • Tampa-St. Petersburg • THE BAHAMAS • Miami
Monterrey • Nassau
Havana
MEXICO • CUBA
Guadalajara • León • ST. KITTS & NEVIS • Basseterre
Mexico City • Puebla • BELIZE • Kingston • Port-au-Prince • Puerto Rico (U.S.) • San Juan • ANTIGUA & BARBUDA
Belmopan • Belize City • JAMAICA • Santo Domingo • DOMINICA • St. John's
GUATEMALA • HONDURAS • DOMINICAN REPUBLIC • ST. LUCIA • BARBADOS
Guatemala City • Tegucigalpa • NICARAGUA • GRENADA • ST. VINCENT & THE GRENADINES
San Salvador • Managua • Panama City • TRINIDAD & TOBAGO
EL SALVADOR • San José • Port-of-Spain
COSTA RICA • PANAMA

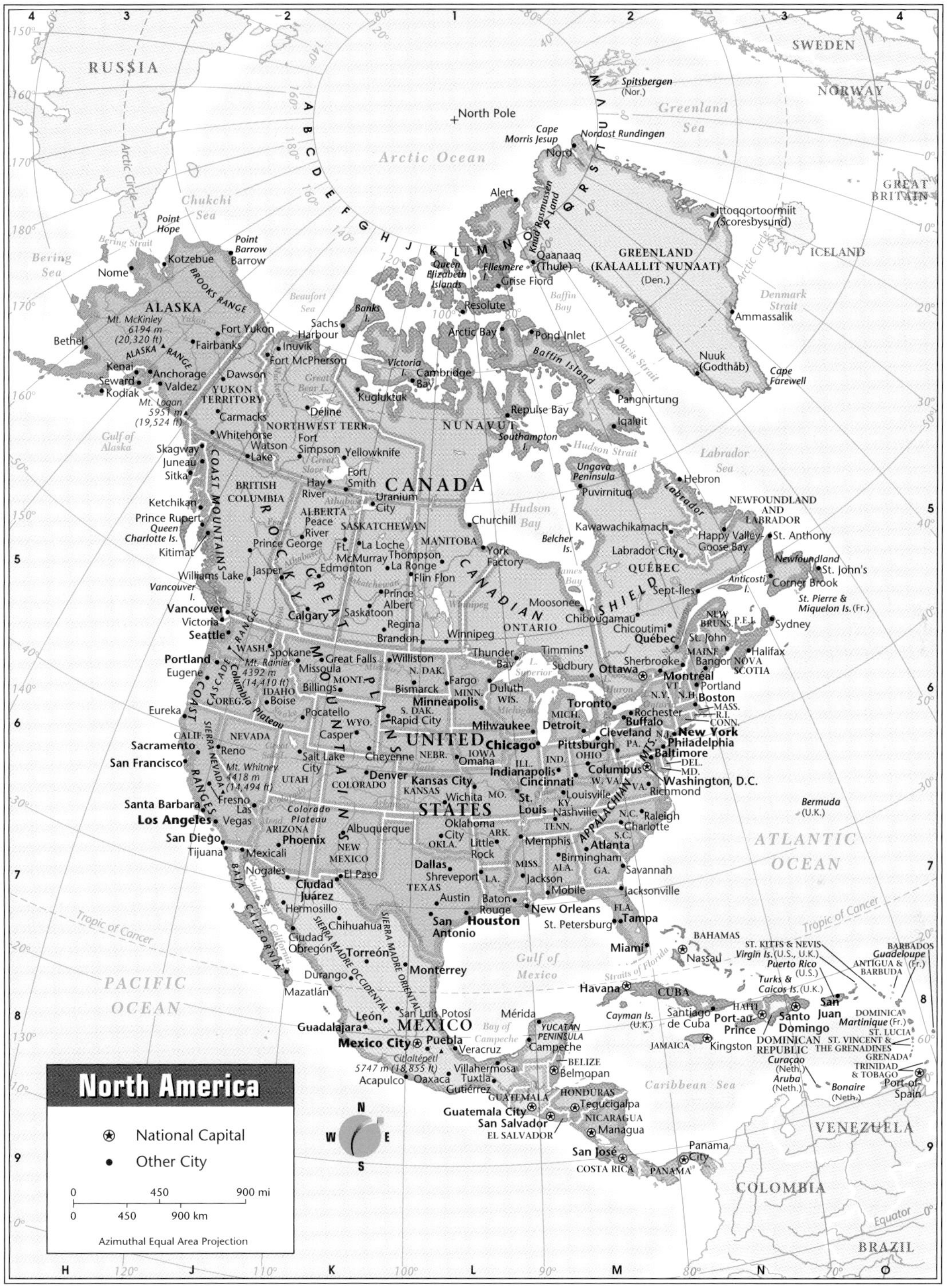

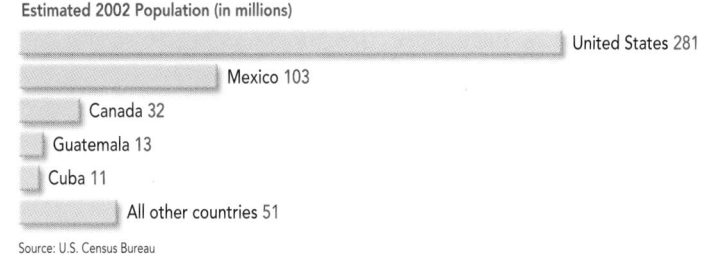

Estimated 2002 Population (in millions)

- United States 281
- Mexico 103
- Canada 32
- Guatemala 13
- Cuba 11
- All other countries 51

Source: U.S. Census Bureau

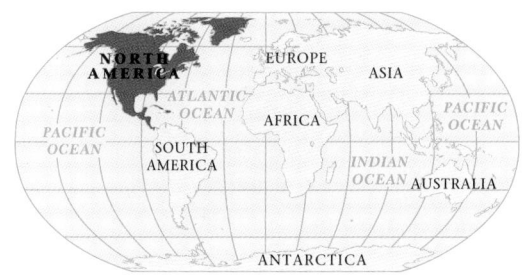

North America

- ⊛ National Capital
- • Other City

Azimuthal Equal Area Projection

© MapQuest.com, Inc.

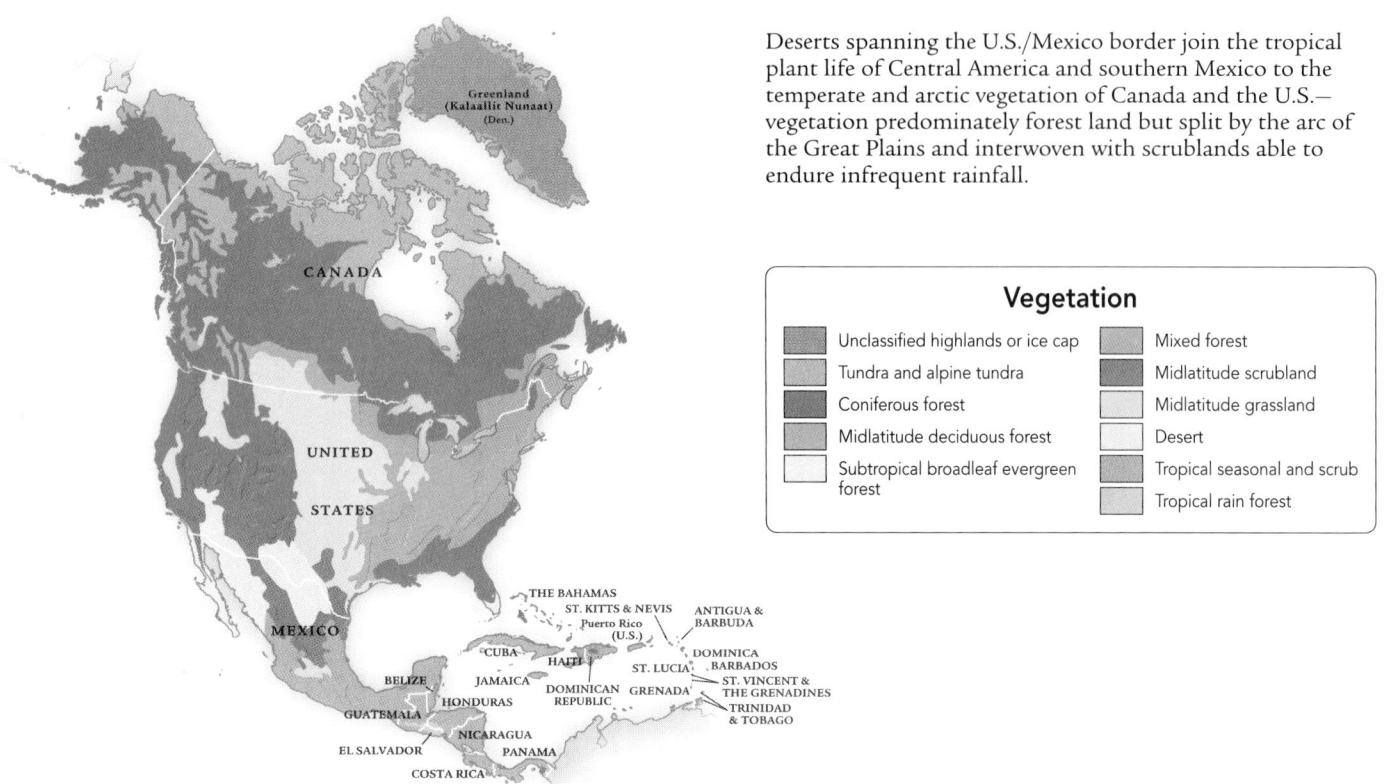

Deserts spanning the U.S./Mexico border join the tropical plant life of Central America and southern Mexico to the temperate and arctic vegetation of Canada and the U.S.— vegetation predominately forest land but split by the arc of the Great Plains and interwoven with scrublands able to endure infrequent rainfall.

Vegetation

- Unclassified highlands or ice cap
- Tundra and alpine tundra
- Coniferous forest
- Midlatitude deciduous forest
- Subtropical broadleaf evergreen forest
- Mixed forest
- Midlatitude scrubland
- Midlatitude grassland
- Desert
- Tropical seasonal and scrub
- Tropical rain forest

There is a profound north-south difference in North America. Canada and the U.S. are models of high-tech, globally connected economies—where a relative handfull of farmers produces a surplus of foodstuffs.

Although Mexico has substantial oil and mineral resources, much of its growing prosperity is linked to increased trade with the U.S. Central America and the Caribbean continue to wrestle with the legacy of commercial plantation agriculture.

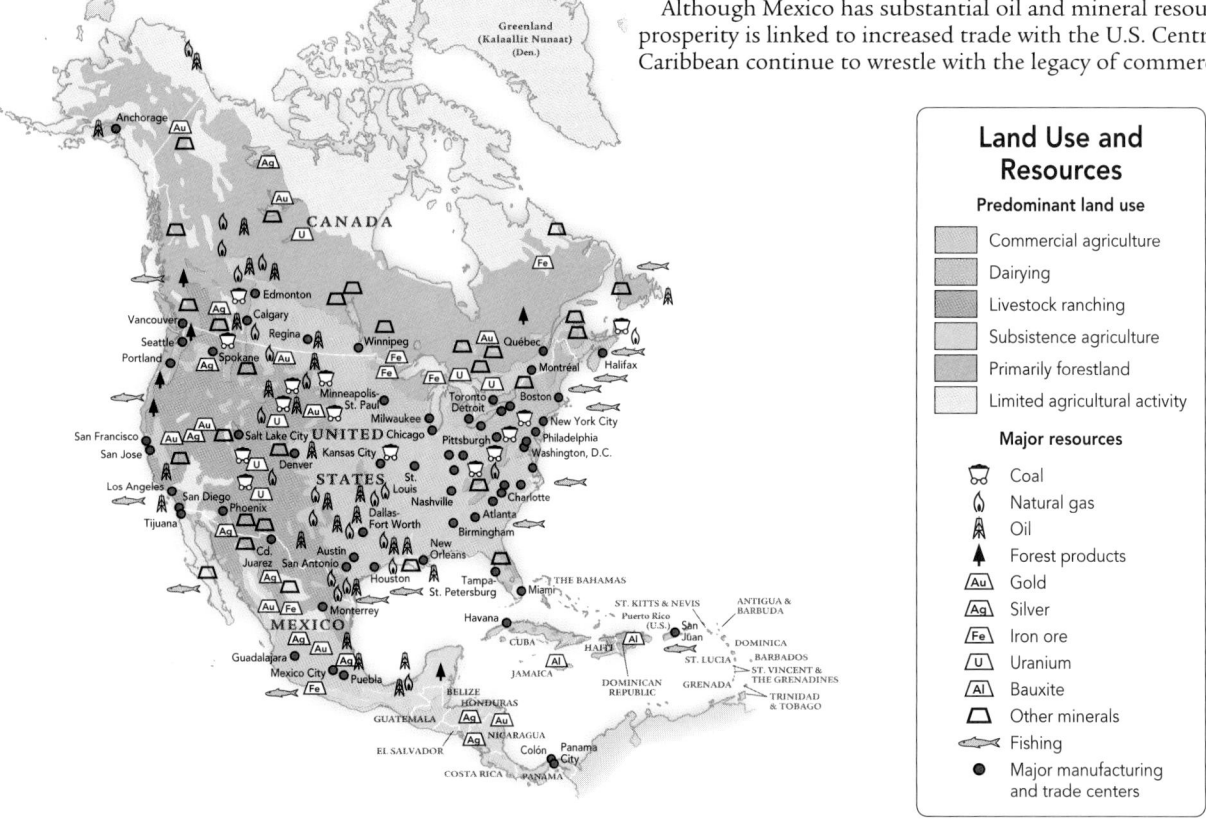

Land Use and Resources

Predominant land use

- Commercial agriculture
- Dairying
- Livestock ranching
- Subsistence agriculture
- Primarily forestland
- Limited agricultural activity

Major resources

- Coal
- Natural gas
- Oil
- Forest products
- Au Gold
- Ag Silver
- Fe Iron ore
- U Uranium
- Al Bauxite
- Other minerals
- Fishing
- Major manufacturing and trade centers

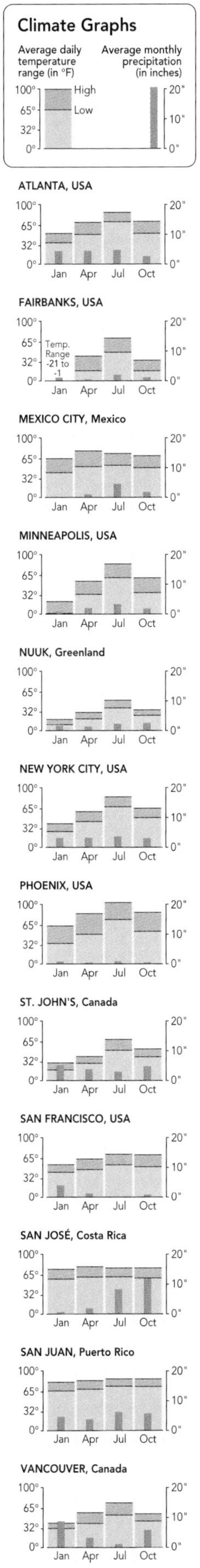

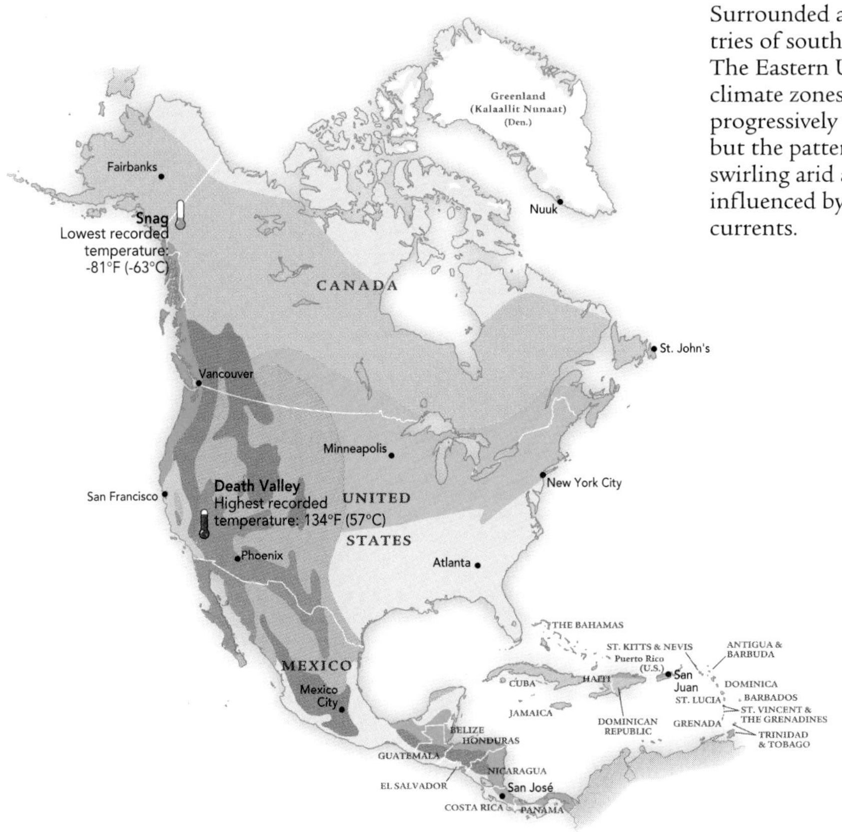

Surrounded and enveloped by warm water, the countries of southern North America are warm and wet. The Eastern U.S. and most of Canada are striped by climate zones offering adequate precipitation and progressively lower temperatures as one travels north, but the pattern goes topsy-turvy in the West, where swirling arid and semiarid zones abut coastal regions influenced by both rain-bearing winds and cool ocean currents.

Climate Graphs

Average daily temperature range (in °F) — High / Low

Average monthly precipitation (in inches)

ATLANTA, USA

FAIRBANKS, USA — Temp. Range -21 to -1

MEXICO CITY, Mexico

MINNEAPOLIS, USA

NUUK, Greenland

NEW YORK CITY, USA

PHOENIX, USA

ST. JOHN'S, Canada

SAN FRANCISCO, USA

SAN JOSÉ, Costa Rica

SAN JUAN, Puerto Rico

VANCOUVER, Canada

Snag — Lowest recorded temperature: -81°F (-63°C)

Death Valley — Highest recorded temperature: 134°F (57°C)

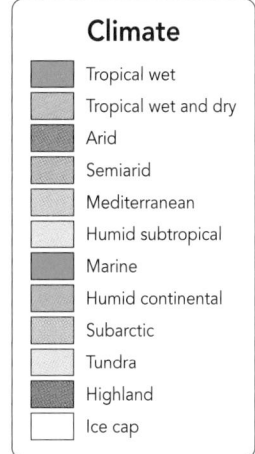

Climate

- Tropical wet
- Tropical wet and dry
- Arid
- Semiarid
- Mediterranean
- Humid subtropical
- Marine
- Humid continental
- Subarctic
- Tundra
- Highland
- Ice cap

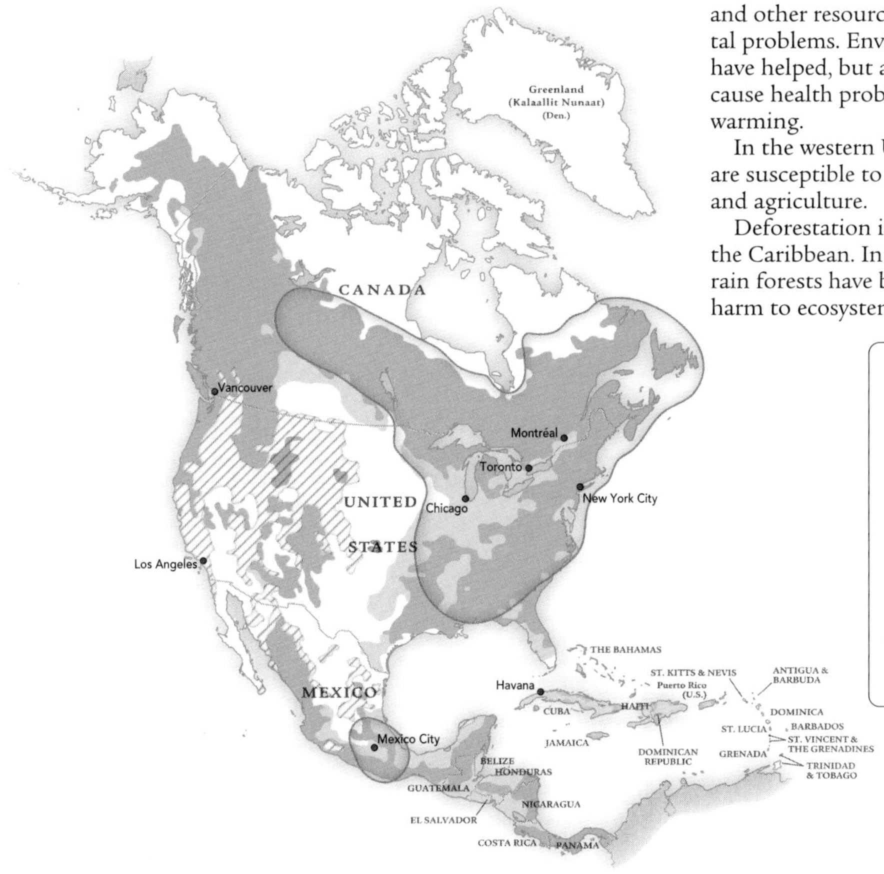

In the U.S. and Canada, heavy consumption of energy and other resources is a source of many environmental problems. Environmental laws and regulations have helped, but air pollutants and gases continue to cause health problems and may contribute to global warming.

In the western U.S. and parts of Mexico, large areas are susceptible to desertification from overgrazing and agriculture.

Deforestation is a major issue in Latin America and the Caribbean. In Haiti, for example, all the native rain forests have been destroyed, causing irreversible harm to ecosystems.

Environmental Issues

- Current forest
- Cleared forest
- Area at highest risk of desertification
- Areas most affected by acid rain
- Poor air quality*

*Cities exceeding at least one of the World Health Organization's (WHO) annual mean guidelines for air quality

Sources: *Global Distribution of Original and Remaining Forests*, UNEP-WCMC, 2002
World Soil Resources Map Index, USDA/NRCS, 2002
World Development Indicators, World Bank, 1999

Capital: Mexico City
Area: 761,404 sq. mi.
   1,972,550 sq. km.
Population: 103,400,000 (2002 est.)
Largest City: Mexico City, 8,605,000
Languages: Spanish, various Mayan dialects
Major Religions: Roman Catholic, Protestant
Life Expectancy: 70 male, 77 female
Government: federal republic operating under a centralized government
Monetary Unit: New Mexican peso
Industry: food and beverages, tobacco, chemicals, iron and steel, petroleum, mining, textiles, clothing, motor vehicles, consumer durables, tourism
Agriculture: corn, wheat, rice, beans, cotton, coffee, fruit, tomatoes
Minerals and Resources: petroleum, silver, copper, gold, lead, zinc, natural gas, timber

The National Cathedral, Mexico City

Mexico

© MapQuest.com, Inc.

Mexico was colonized by the Spanish in the early 16th century and became independent from Spain in 1821. At the end of the Mexican-American war in 1848, Mexico was forced to cede its northern provinces of California and New Mexico.

Mexico today is a federal republic which comprises 31 states and one federal district.

It is the most populous Spanish-speaking country in the world, and is the second-most populous country in Latin America, after Brazil. About 70% of Mexicans live in urban areas; many of them emigrate there from rural regions seeking employment opportunities. According to some estimates, the population of the area around Mexico City is about 20 million, which would make it the largest concentration of people in the world.

Mexico is in a transition stage to becoming a more competitive democracy, implementing liberalized trade regimes and tough economic stabilization measures. These measures have begun to show promising signs of recovery.

Teotihuacán Complex, Pyramids of the Moon and Sun

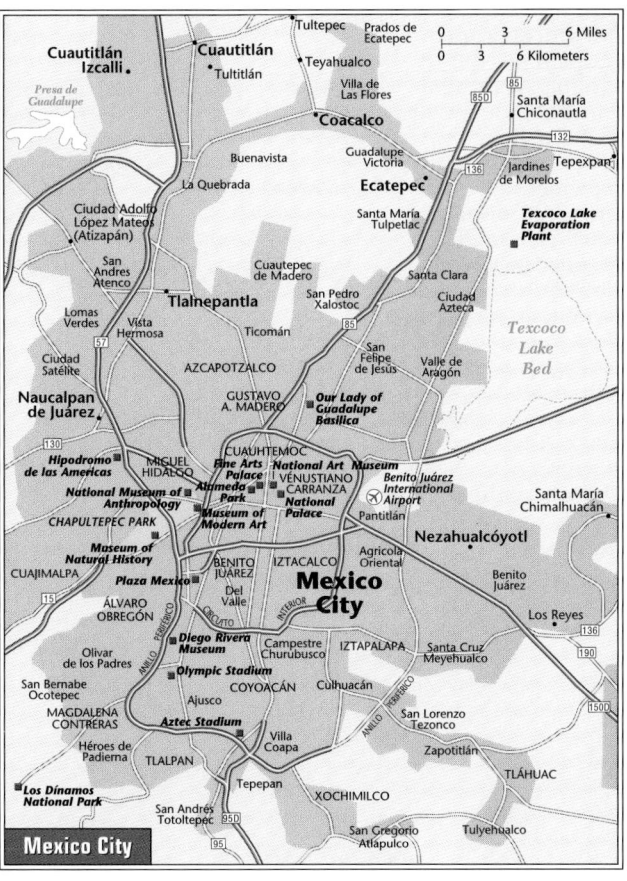

Mexico City

The Fine Arts Palace, Mexico City

Capital: Belmopan
Area: 8,863 sq. mi.
    22,960 sq. km.
Population: 260,000 (2002 est.)
Largest City: Belize City, 49,000
Languages: English, Spanish, Maya, Garifuna
Major Religions: Roman Catholic, Protestant
Life Expectancy: 66 male, 70 female
Government: parliamentary democracy
Monetary Unit: Belizean dollar
Industry: garment production, food processing, tourism, construction
Agriculture: commercial crops: bananas, cocoa, citrus fruits, fish, cultured shrimp, lumber
Minerals and Resources: arable land potential, timber, fish

Formerly British Honduras, Belize gained its independence from the United Kingdom in 1981. Belize is a parliamentary democracy and a member of the Commonwealth.

Belize is the most sparsely populated nation in Central America. About a quarter of its population lives in Belize City and another quarter inhabits other urban areas, primarily along the coast. In recent years there has been a steady inflow of Central American refugees and other immigrants. Most Belizeans are of multiracial descent.

While Belize's once important forestry sector has dwindled, its tourism industry is booming. Due to a combination of natural factors—climate, the longest barrier reef in the Western Hemisphere, numerous islands, excellent fishing, safe boating waters, jungle wildlife and Mayan ruins—Belize has a thriving tourist business.

Belize

Belize

⊛ National Capital
● Other City

© MapQuest.com, Inc.

Guatemala

The Mayan civilization which had flourished throughout Guatemala and the surrounding region was already in decline when the Spaniards established colonial rule in the area in 1524. Guatemala gained independence from Spain in 1821, and briefly became part of the Mexican Empire. It later belonged to a federation called the United Provinces of Central America before encountering a long line of dictatorships, coups, and military rulers.

More than half of Guatemala's population are descendants of Mayan Indians, and most of the population is rural, although it is beginning to become more urbanized. Agriculture employs about 60% of the work force and the economy is based on family and corporate agriculture. Since 1986, when Guatemala returned to civilian democratic rule, tourism and exports of textiles, apparel, and non-traditional agricultural products such as cut flowers and winter vegetables have boomed.

Guatemala

⊛ National Capital
● Other City

© MapQuest.com, Inc.

Capital: Guatemala City
Area: 42,032 sq. mi.
    108,890 sq. km.
Population: 13,542,000 (2002 est.)
Largest City: Guatemala City, 1,007,000
Languages: Spanish, Indian dialects
Major Religions: Roman Catholic, Protestant, traditional Mayan
Life Expectancy: 62 male, 68 female
Government: republic
Monetary Unit: quetzal
Industry: sugar, textiles and clothing, furniture, chemicals, petroleum, metals, rubber, tourism
Agriculture: sugarcane, corn, bananas, coffee, beans, cardamom, cattle, sheep, pigs, chickens
Minerals and Resources: petroleum, nickel, rare woods, fish, chicle

Temple I and Plaza Major in Tikal, Guatemala

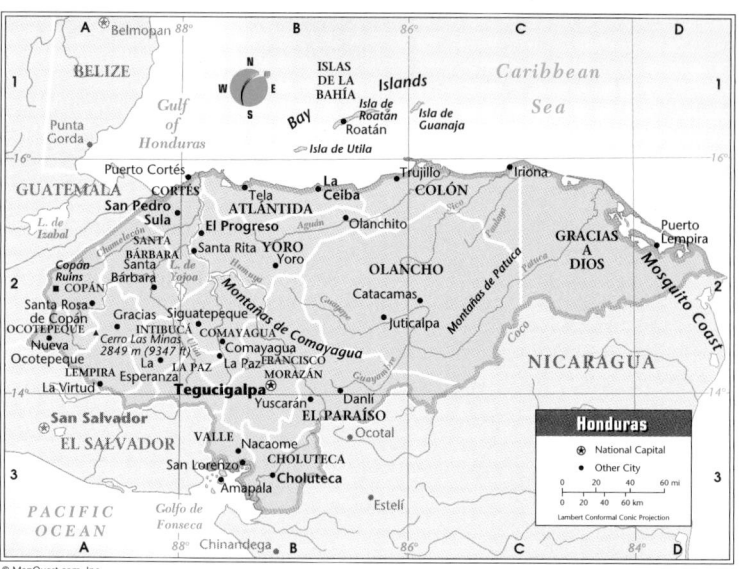

Honduras, along with the other Central American provinces, gained independence from Spain in 1821. It was then annexed to the Mexican Empire briefly and in 1823 joined the newly formed United Provinces of Central America until it collapsed in 1838. Since its independence, Honduras has experienced continual internal rebellion, civil wars, and changes of government. The government returned to civilian rule in 1981.

About 90% of Hondurans are mestizo (mixed Indian and European) and more than half of the labor force is employed in agriculture. Honduras is one of the poorest and least developed countries in Latin America. About three quarters of the country is covered by pine forest, but slash-and-burn agricultural practices have destroyed much of the forest. Environmental issues such as this have recently become more of a public and governmental concern.

Honduras

Capital: Tegucigalpa
Area: 43,267 sq. mi.
　　　112,090 sq. km.
Population: 6,514,000 (2002 est.)
Largest City: Tegucigalpa, 835,000
Languages: Spanish, Indian dialects
Major Religions: Roman Catholic, Protestant
Life Expectancy: 66 male, 71 female
Government: republic
Monetary Unit: lempira
Industry: agricultural processing (sugar and coffee), textiles, clothing, wood products
Agriculture: bananas, coffee, timber, beef, citrus fruit, shrimp
Minerals and Resources: timber, gold, silver, copper, lead, zinc, iron ore, antimony, coal, fish

Sugarcane and cattle, Nicaragua

Nicaragua

Capital: Managua
Area: 49,985 sq mi.
　　　129,494 sq. km.
Population: 5,024,000 (2002 est.)
Largest City: Managua, 903,000
Languages: Spanish, English
Major Religions: Roman Catholic, Protestant
Life Expectancy: 62 male, 68 female
Government: republic
Monetary Unit: gold cordoba
Industry: food processing, chemicals, metal products, textiles, clothing, petroleum refining and distribution, beverages, footwear
Agriculture: coffee, bananas, sugarcane, cotton, rice, corn, cassava, citrus fruit, beans, beef, veal, pork, poultry, dairy products
Minerals and Resources: gold, silver, copper, tungsten, lead, zinc, timber, fish

The Spanish colonial period in Nicaragua began in 1522 and virtually wiped out the native population. In 1821, Nicaragua gained independence from Spain, briefly joining the Mexican Empire and later becoming a member of the United Provinces of Central America federation. In 1838, it became an independent republic.

Most Nicaraguans have both European and Indian ancestry.

Indians on the Caribbean coast and a large black minority of Jamaican origin, also on the coast, remain ethnically distinct. More than half of Nicaraguans live in urban areas.

Nicaragua is the second poorest nation after Haiti in the Western Hemisphere. However, since 1991 an ambitious economic stabilization program has been very successful in bringing inflation down and obtaining vital aid from abroad.

Barbados

When the British first landed on Barbados in 1625, they found it uninhabited. Barbados was under British control from that time until its independence in 1966. It remains a member of the Commonwealth.

Most Barbadians trace their descent to African slaves brought to the island to work on sugar plantations.

Barbados has one of the highest standards of living in the eastern Caribbean. Manufacturing and tourism have joined sugar production as the most important industries.

Capital: Bridgetown
Area: 166 sq. mi.
  430 sq. km.
Population: 276,000 (2002 est.)
Largest City: Bridgetown, 6,000
Language: English
Major Religions: Protestant, Roman Catholic
Life Expectancy: 71 male, 77 female
Government: parliamentary democracy
Monetary Unit: Barbadian dollar
Industry: tourism, sugar, light manufacturing, component assembly for export
Agriculture: sugarcane, vegetables, cotton
Minerals and Resources: petroleum, fishing, natural gas

Grenada

Inhabited by the Carib Indians, Grenada remained uncolonized for more than 100 years after Columbus landed there in 1498. In 1650, the French bought the island from the British. After several skirmishes with the Caribs, the French slaughtered the entire Indian population and controlled Grenada until 1763 when it was ceded to the British. Grenada became independent from the United Kingdom in 1974, but remains a part of the Commonwealth.

Historically, Grenada has depended on the production of spices such as nutmeg and mace for its livelihood. Today tourism and agriculture are the two main components of the Grenadian economy. The fishing industry is underdevelopment.

Capital: St. George's
Area: 131 sq. mi.
  340 sq. km.
Population: 89,000 (2002 est.)
Largest City: St. George's, 5,000
Languages: English, French patois
Major Religions: Roman Catholic, Anglican, other Protestant sects
Life Expectancy: 68 male, 73 female

Government Type: parliamentary democracy
Monetary Unit: EC dollar
Industry: food and beverage, textile, light assembly operations, tourism, construction
Agriculture: bananas, cocoa, nutmeg, mace, citrus fruits, avocados, root crops, sugarcane, corn, and vegetables
Minerals and Resources: timber, tropical fruit, deepwater harbors

Trinidad & Tobago

Christopher Columbus landed on Trinidad in 1498, and one century later the Spanish settled the island and virtually wiped out the native Arawak and Carib Indians. Trinidad remained under Spanish rule until the British captured it in 1797. The island of Tobago changed hands 22 times during its colonial period and finally went to Britain in 1814. Trinidad and Tobago were merged into a single colony in 1888 and gained independence from the United Kingdom in 1962.

Trinidad and Tobago's petroleum and natural gas-based economy provides it with a high per capita income by Latin American standards, even though the country suffers from widespread unemployment and large foreign debt payments. The economy has shifted from a centrally planned to a free market system which has affected all sectors of the economy.

Capital: Port of Spain
Area: 1,980 sq. mi.
  5,130 sq. km.
Population: 1,112,000 (2002 est.)
Largest City: Port of Spain, 48,000
Languages: English, Hindi, French, Spanish
Major Religions: Roman Catholic, Hindu, Anglican, Protestant, Muslim
Life Expectancy: 68 male, 73 female

Government: parliamentary democracy
Monetary Unit: Trinidad and Tobago dollar
Industry: petroleum, chemicals, tourism, food processing, cement, beverage, cotton textiles
Agriculture: cocoa, sugarcane, rice, citrus, coffee, vegetables, poultry
Minerals and Resources: petroleum, natural gas, asphalt

MATT THARP

St. George's, Grenada

Trinidad & Tobago

Canada

Canada's early history was dominated by rivalry between the French and the British over territorial claims. The Native American population was decimated following the arrival of Europeans in the late 15th century. For more than a century, Canada was a French colony, "New France." Although New France came under British control in 1759 it was permitted to retain its religious and civil code. Today, Canada is still trying to find a solution to the dilemma of French-speaking Quebec's desire for autonomy.

Industry has transformed Canada from a rural, agri-cultural society into a primarily urban, industrial one. Canada ranks seventh in the world in both gross domestic product and total volume of trade. It is one of the world's largest producers of a variety of minerals.

Canada's lakes have more than 50% of the world's fresh surface water and the country supplies more than 75% of its own power needs with hydroelectric energy.

Eighty percent of Canadians live within 160 kilometers (100 miles) of the U.S. border and half live near the Great Lakes and St. Lawrence River. The vast majority of Canadians are of European heritage.

Capital: Ottawa
Area: 3,851,792 sq. mi.
9,976,140 sq. km.
Population: 31,902,000 (2002 est.)
Largest City: Toronto, 2,481,494
Languages: English, French
Major Religions: Roman Catholic, United Church, Anglican
Life Expectancy: 75 male, 82 female
Government: confederation with parliamentary democracy
Monetary Unit: Canadian dollar

Industry: processed and unprocessed minerals, food products, wood and paper products, transportation equipment, chemicals, fish products, petroleum and natural gas
Agriculture: grain (wheat and barley), forest resources, commercial fisheries
Minerals and Resources: nickel, zinc, copper, gold, lead, molybdenum, potash, silver, fish, timber, wildlife, coal, petroleum, natural gas

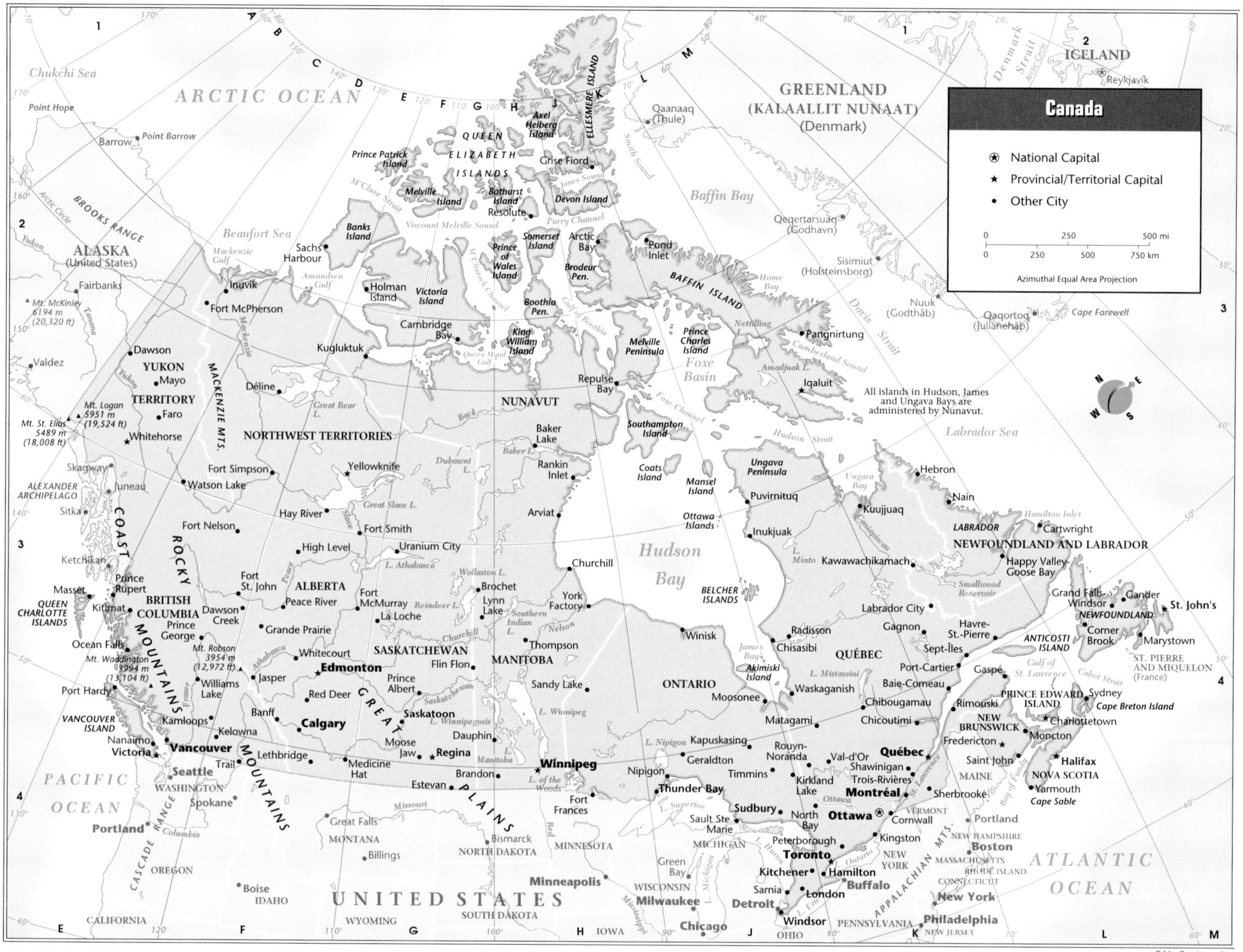

Canada

⊛ National Capital
★ Provincial/Territorial Capital
• Other City

0 ___ 250 ___ 500 mi
0 ___ 250 ___ 500 ___ 750 km

Azimuthal Equal Area Projection

© MapQuest.com, Inc.

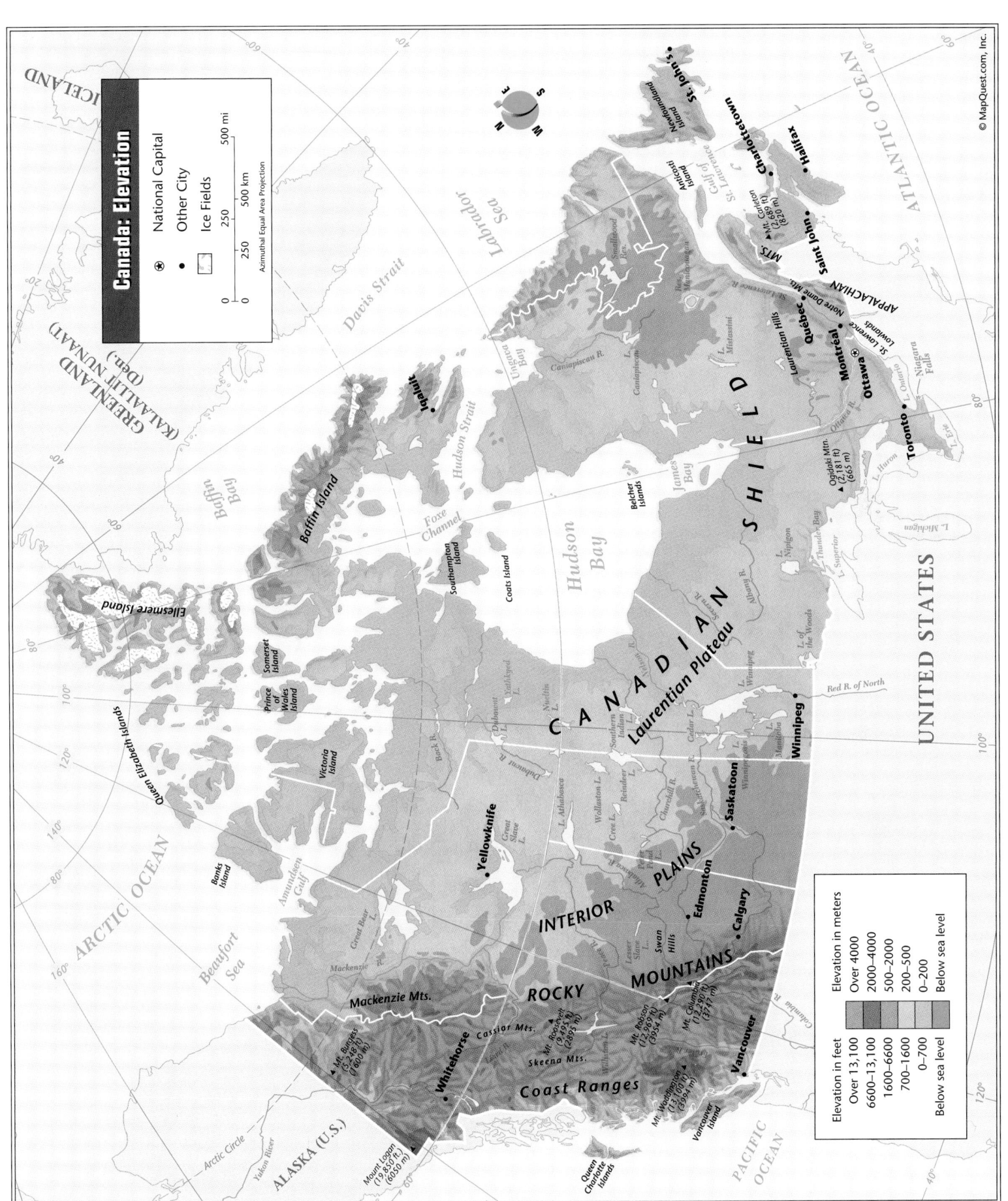

© MapQuest.com, Inc.

Canada: Elevation

- ⊛ National Capital
- • Other City
- ☐ Ice Fields

500 mi

500 km
250
250
0

Azimuthal Equal Area Projection

ICELAND

GREENLAND (KALAALLIT NUNAAT) (Den.)

ATLANTIC OCEAN

St. John's
Newfoundland Island
Charlottetown
Anticosti Island
Gulf of St. Lawrence
Halifax
Mt. Carleton (2,690 ft) (820 m)
Saint John
APPALACHIAN MTS
Notre Dame Mts
Laurentian Hills
Québec
Montréal
St. Lawrence Lowland
Ottawa ⊛
Niagara Falls
Toronto
L. Ontario
L. Erie
L. Huron

Davis Strait

Labrador Sea

Ungava Bay

Caniapiscau R.

L. Mistassini

Baffin Bay

Iqaluit

Baffin Island

Hudson Strait

Foxe Channel

Belcher Islands

James Bay

C A N A D I A N   S H I E L D

Ogidaki Mtn. (2,181 ft) (665 m)

L. Michigan

Ellesmere Island

Somerset Island

Prince of Wales Island

Southampton Island

Coats Island

Hudson Bay

Laurentian Plateau

L. Nipigon
Thunder Bay
L. Superior

Albany R.
Severn R.

UNITED STATES

Queen Elizabeth Islands

Victoria Island

Back R.

Dubawnt L.

Thelon R.

Nueltin L.

Southern Indian L.

Cedar L.
L. Winnipeg
Lake of the Woods

Red R. of North

ARCTIC OCEAN

Banks Island

Amundsen Gulf

Great Bear L.

Mackenzie R.

Yellowknife

Great Slave L.

L. Athabasca

Wollaston L.

Reindeer L.

Cree L.

Churchill R.

Saskatoon

Saskatchewan R.

L. Manitoba

Winnipeg

Beaufort Sea

Mackenzie Mts.

Liard R.

Whitehorse

Cassiar Mts.

Skeena Mts.

I N T E R I O R

Lesser Slave L.

Swan Hills

Edmonton

Calgary

P L A I N S

R O C K Y   M O U N T A I N S

Mt. Burgess (5,148 ft) (1,600 m)

Mt. Roosevelt (9,495 ft) (2,895 m)

Mt. Robson (12,969 ft) (3,954 m)

Mt. Columbia (12,290 ft) (3,747 m)

Coast Ranges

Mt. Waddington (13,100 ft) (3,994 m)

Vancouver Island

Vancouver

Columbia R.

PACIFIC OCEAN

Queen Charlotte Islands

Mount Logan (19,850 ft) (6,050 m)

ALASKA (U.S.)

Yukon River

Arctic Circle

Elevation in feet	Elevation in meters
Over 13,100	Over 4000
6600–13,100	2000–4000
1600–6600	500–2000
700–1600	200–500
0–700	0–200
Below sea level	Below sea level

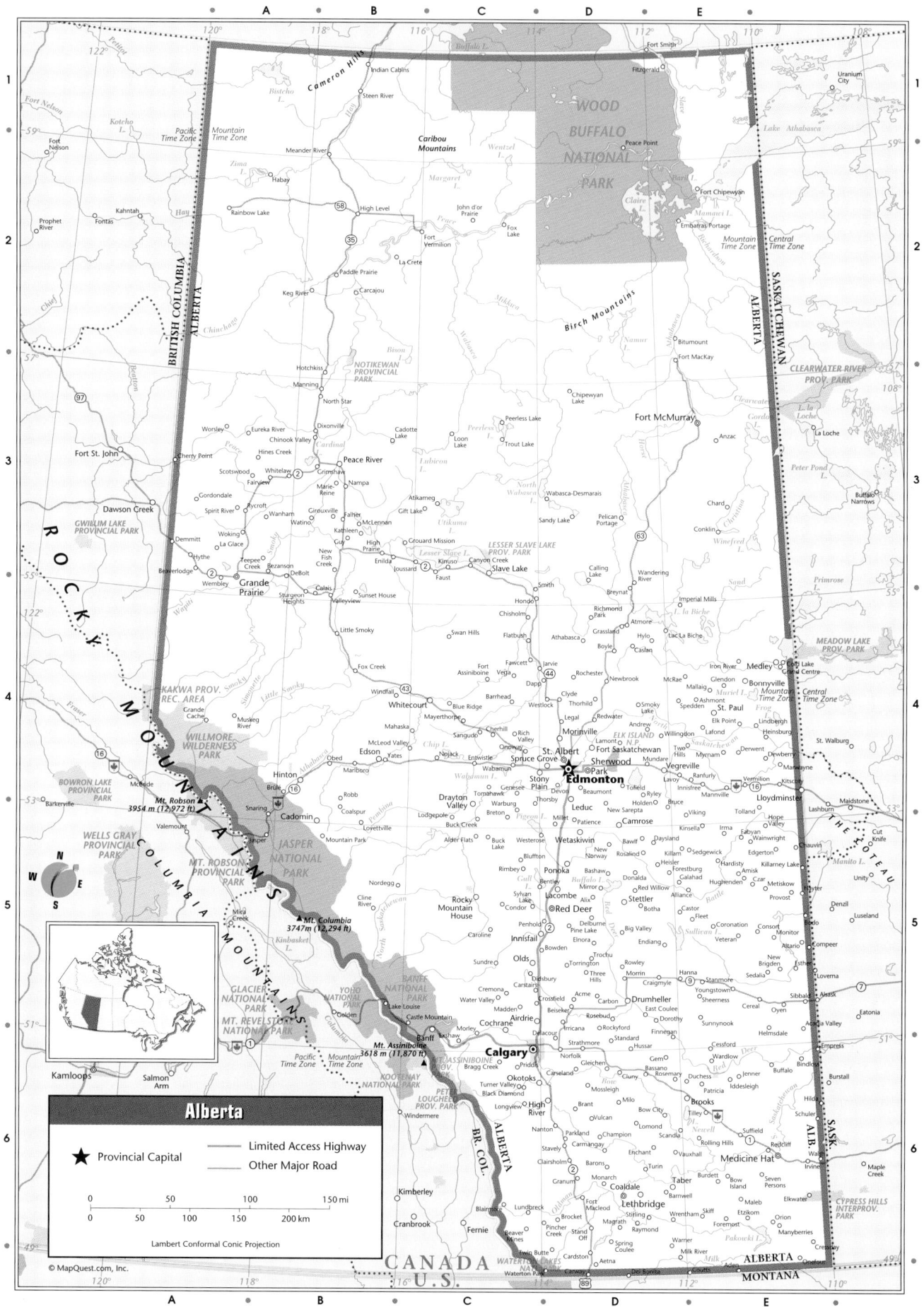

Alberta

★ Provincial Capital
Limited Access Highway
Other Major Road

0   50   100   150 mi
0   50   100   150   200 km

Lambert Conformal Conic Projection

© MapQuest.com, Inc.

Alberta

Capital: Edmonton
Area: 255,219 sq. mi. / 661,190 sq. km.
Population: 2,974,807 (2001 Census)
Largest City: Calgary, 878,866
Highest Point: Mt. Columbia / 12,294 ft. / 3,747 m.
Entered the Dominion: September 1, 1905
Floral Emblem: Wild Rose

Alberta: Map Index

Cities and Towns

Acadia Valley, 122 .... E5
Acme, 648 .... D5
Aden E6
Aetna D6
Airdrie, 20,382 .... C5
Alder Flats, 133 .... C5
Alix, 825 .... D5
Alliance, 171 .... E5
Altario E5
Amisk, 181 .... E5
Andrew, 485 .... D4
Anzac, 460 .... E3
Ashmont, 160 .... E4
Athabasca, 2,415 .... D4
Atikameg C3
Atmore, 37 .... D4
Banff, 7,135 .... C5
Barnwell, 548 .... D6
Barons, 284 .... D6
Barrhead, 4,213 .... C4
Bashaw, 825 .... D5
Bassano, 1,320 .... D6
Bawlf, 362 .... D5
Beaumont, 7,006 .... D4
Beaverlodge, 2,110 .... A3
Beaver Mines, 65 .... C6
Beiseker, 838 .... D5
Bentley, 1,035 .... D5
Bezanson, 81 .... A3
Big Valley, 340 .... D5
Bindloss E6
Bitumount E2
Black Diamond, 1,866 .... C6
Blairmore, 1,993 .... C6
Blue Ridge, 230 .... C4
Bluffton, 127 .... C5
Bodo E5
Bonnyville, 5,709 .... E4
Botha, 186 .... D5
Bow City D6
Bowden, 1,174 .... D5
Bow Island, 1,704 .... E6
Boyle, 836 .... D4
Bragg Creek, 678 .... C6
Brant D6
Breton, 573 .... C4
Breynat D3
Brocket D6
Brooks, 11,604 .... E6
Bruce D4
Brûlé, 162 .... B4
Buck Creek C4
Buck Lake, 79 .... C5
Buffalo E6
Burdett, 264 .... E6
Cadomin, 64 .... B4
Cadotte Lake, 151 .... B3
Calais B3
Calgary, 878,866 .... C5
Calling Lake D3
Camrose, 14,854 .... D4
Canyon Creek, 251 .... C3
Carbon, 530 .... D5
Carcajou B2
Cardston, 3,475 .... D6
Carmangay, 255 .... D6
Caroline, 556 .... C5
Carseland, 662 .... D6
Carstairs, 2,254 .... C5
Carway D6
Caslan D4
Castle Mountain C5
Castor, 935 .... E5
Cereal, 187 .... E5
Cessford E6
Champion, 355 .... D6
Chard E3
Chauvin, 366 .... E5
Cherhill C4
Cherry Point A3
Chinook Valley B3
Chipewyan Lake D3
Chisholm, 20 .... C4
Claresholm, 3,622 .... D6
Cline River B5
Cluny D6
Clyde, 491 .... D4
Coaldale, 6,008 .... D6
Coalspur B4
Cochrane, 11,798 .... C5
Cold Lake, 11,520 .... E4
Compeer E5
Condor C5
Conklin, 166 .... E3
Consort, 634 .... E5
Coronation, 902 .... E5
Coutts, 364 .... E6
Craigmyle D5
Cremona, 415 .... C5
Cressday E6
Crossfield, 2,389 .... C5
Czar, 205 .... E5
Dapp, 27 .... D4
Daysland, 779 .... D5
DeBolt, 124 .... A3
Delacour D5
Del Bonita D6
Delburne, 719 .... D5
Demmitt A3
Derwent, 111 .... E4
Devon, 4,969 .... D4
Dewberry, 200 .... E4
Didsbury, 3,932 .... C5
Dixonville, 97 .... B3
Donalda, 230 .... D5
Dorothy D5
Drayton Valley, 5,801 .... C4
Drumheller, 7,785 .... D5
Duchess, 836 .... E6
East Coulee, 156 .... D5
Edgerton, 403 .... E5
Edmonton, 666,104 .... D4
Edson, 7,585 .... B4
Elk Point, 1,440 .... E4
Elkwater, 50 .... E6
Elnora, 290 .... D5
Embarras Portage E2
Empress, 171 .... E6
Enchant D6
Endiang, 35 .... D5
Enilda, 154 .... B3
Entwistle C4
Esther E5
Etzikom E6
Eureka River A3
Exshaw, 231 .... C5
Fabyan E5
Fairview, 3,150 .... A3
Falher, 1,109 .... B3
Faust, 365 .... C3
Fawcett, 102 .... C4
Finnegan D5
Fitzgerald E1
Flatbush, 30 .... C4
Fleet E5
Foremost, 531 .... E6
Forestburg, 870 .... D5
Fort Assiniboine C4
Fort Chipewyan, 902 .... E2
Fort MacKay, 437 .... E2
Fort Macleod, 2,990 .... D6
Fort McMurray, 38,667 .... E3
Fort Saskatchewan, 13,121 .... D4
Fort Vermilion, 818 .... C2
Fox Creek, 2,337 .... B4
Fox Lake C2
Galahad, 161 .... E5
Gem D6
Genesee C4
Gift Lake, 809 .... C3
Girouxville, 306 .... B3
Gleichen, 408 .... D6
Glendon, 459 .... E4
Gordondale A3
Grand Centre, 11,780 .... E4
Grande Cache, 3,828 .... A4
Grande Prairie, 36,983 .... A3
Granum, 392 .... D6
Grassland, 101 .... D4
Grimshaw, 2,435 .... B3
Grouard Mission, 436 .... B3
Guy B3
Habay A2
Hanna, 2,986 .... E5
Hardisty, 743 .... E5
Hayter E5
Heinsburg E4
Heisler, 183 .... D5
Helmsdale E5
High Level, 3,444 .... B2
High Prairie, 2,737 .... B3
High River, 9,345 .... D6
Hilda, 55 .... E6
Hines Creek, 437 .... A3
Hinton, 9,405 .... B4
Holden, 374 .... D4
Hondo C3
Hope Valley E5
Hotchkiss B2
Hughenden, 235 .... E5
Hussar, 181 .... D5
Hylo D4
Hythe, 582 .... A3
Iddesleigh E6
Imperial Mills E4
Indian Cabins B1
Innisfail, 6,928 .... D5
Innisfree, 219 .... E4
Irma, 435 .... E4
Iron River E4
Irricana, 1,038 .... D5
Irvine E6
Jarvie, 112 .... D4
Jasper, 3,716 .... A5
Jenner E6
John d'or Prairie C2
Joussard, 219 .... C3
Kathleen B3
Keg River B2
Killam, 1,004 .... E5
Killarney Lake E5
Kinsella E5
Kinuso, 231 .... C3
Kitscoty, 671 .... E4
Lac La Biche, 2,776 .... E4
Lacombe, 9,384 .... D5
La Crete, 1,783 .... B2
Lafond E4
La Glace, 213 .... A3
Lake Louise, 1,041 .... B5
Lamont, 1,692 .... D4
Lavoy E4
Leduc, 15,032 .... D4
Legal, 1,058 .... D4
Lethbridge, 67,374 .... D6
Lindbergh E4
Little Smoky B4
Lloydminster, 13,148 .... E4
Lodgepole, 165 .... C4
Lomond, 171 .... D6
Longview, 300 .... C6
Loon Lake, 399 .... C3
Lovettville B4
Lundbreck, 263 .... C6
Madden C5
Magrath, 1,993 .... D6
Mahaska C4
Maleb E6
Mallaig, 162 .... E4
Manning, 1,293 .... B3
Mannville, 722 .... E4
Manyberries E6
Marie-Reine B3
Marlboro, 160 .... B4
Marwayne, 495 .... E4
Mayerthorpe, 1,570 .... C4
McLennan, 804 .... B3
McLeod Valley C4
McRae E4
Meander River B1
Medicine Hat, 51,249 .... E6
Medley E4
Metiskow E5
Milk River, 879 .... D6
Millet, 2,037 .... D4
Milo, 115 .... D6
Mirror, 492 .... D5
Monarch, 195 .... D6
Monitor E5
Morinville, 6,540 .... D4
Morley C5
Morrin, 252 .... D5
Mossleigh D6
Mountain Park B5
Mundare, 653 .... D4
Muskeg River A4
Myrnam, 322 .... E4
Nampa, 372 .... B3
Nanton, 1,841 .... D6
New Brigden E5
Newbrook, 85 .... D4
New Fish Creek B3
New Norway, 292 .... D5
New Sarepta, 382 .... D4
Nojack C4
Nordegg B5
Norfolk D5
North Star B3
Obed B4
Okotoks, 11,664 .... C6
Olds, 6,607 .... C5
Onefour E6
Onoway, 847 .... C4
Orion E6
Oyen, 1,020 .... E5
Paddle Prairie, 581 .... B2
Parkland D6
Patience D4
Patricia, 116 .... E6
Peace Point D1
Peace River, 6,240 .... B3
Peerless Lake, 402 .... C3
Pelican Portage D3
Penhold, 1,729 .... D5
Pincher Creek, 3,666 .... D6
Pine Lake D5
Ponoka, 6,330 .... D5
Priddis C6
Provost, 1,980 .... E5
Rainbow Lake, 976 .... A2
Ranfurly, 60 .... E4
Raymond, 3,200 .... D6
Redcliff, 4,372 .... E6
Red Deer, 67,707 .... D5
Redwater, 2,172 .... D4
Red Willow, 40 .... D5
Richmond Park D4
Rich Valley C4
Rimbey, 2,118 .... C5
Robb, 183 .... B4
Rochester, 116 .... D4
Rockyford, 375 .... D5
Rocky Mountain House, 6,208 .... C5
Rolling Hills, 234 .... E6
Rosalind, 190 .... D5
Rosebud, 87 .... D5
Rosemary, 366 .... D6
Rowley D5
Rycroft, 609 .... A3
Ryley, 437 .... D4
St. Albert, 53,081 .... D4
St. Paul, 5,061 .... E4
Sandy Lake D3
Sangudo, 377 .... C4
Scandia, 114 .... D6
Schuler, 89 .... E6
Scotswood A3
Sedalia E5
Sedgewick, 865 .... E5
Seven Persons, 245 .... E6
Sheerness E5
Sherwood Park, 47,645 .... D4
Sibbald E5
Skiff E6
Slave Lake, 6,600 .... C3
Smith, 262 .... C3
Smoky Lake, 1,011 .... D4
Snaring A4
Spedden E4
Spirit River, 1,100 .... A3
Spring Coulee D6
Spruce Grove, 15,983 .... D4
Standard, 389 .... D5
Stand Off D6
Stanmore E5
Stavely, 442 .... D6
Steen River B1
Stettler, 5,215 .... D5
Stirling, 877 .... D6
Stony Plain, 9,589 .... D4
Strathmore, 7,621 .... D5
Sturgeon Heights B3
Suffield, 205 .... E6
Sundre, 2,267 .... C5
Sunnynook E5
Sunset House B3
Swan Hills, 1,807 .... C4
Sylvan Lake, 7,493 .... C5
Taber, 7,671 .... D6
Teepee Creek A3
Thorhild, 462 .... D4
Thorsby, 799 .... C4
Three Hills, 2,902 .... D5
Tilley, 422 .... E6
Tofield, 1,818 .... D4
Tolland E4
Tomahawk, 61 .... C4
Torrington D5
Trochu, 1,033 .... D5
Trout Lake, 315 .... C3
Turin, 123 .... D6
Turner Valley, 1,608 .... C6
Twin Butte, 10 .... D6
Two Hills, 1,091 .... E4
Valleyview, 1,856 .... B3
Vauxhall, 1,112 .... D6
Vega C4
Vegreville, 5,376 .... D4
Vermilion, 3,948 .... E4
Veteran, 292 .... E5
Viking, 1,052 .... E4
Vulcan, 1,762 .... D6
Wabamun, 601 .... C4
Wabasca-Desmarais, 1,114 .... D3
Wainwright, 5,117 .... E5
Walsh, 70 .... E6
Wandering River D3
Wanham A3
Warburg, 560 .... C4
Wardlow E6
Warner, 379 .... D6
Waterton Park, 155 .... D6
Water Valley C5
Watino B3
Wembley, 1,497 .... A3
Westerose D5
Westlock, 4,819 .... D4
Wetaskiwin, 11,154 .... D5
Whitecourt, 8,334 .... C4
Whitelaw, 124 .... A3
Willingdon, 287 .... D4
Windfall B4
Woking, 87 .... A3
Worsley A3
Wrentham D6
Yates B4
Youngstown, 184 .... E5

Other Features

Athabasca, *lake* E1
Athabasca, *river* B4, D3, E2
Banff Natl. Park B5
Baril, *lake* E2
Battle, *river* E5
Biche, *lake* E4
Birch, *mts.* D2
Bison, *lake* B2
Bistcho, *lake* A1
Bow, *river* D6
Buffalo, *lake* D5
Cameron, *hills* B1
Cardinal, *lake* B3
Chinchaga, *river* A2
Chip, *lake* C4
Christina, *river* E3
Claire, *lake* D2
Clearwater, *river* E3
Cypress Hills Interprov. Park E6
Elk Island Natl. Park D4
Frog, *lake* E4
Gordon, *lake* E3
Gull, *lake* C5
Hay, *river* A2, B1
Horse, *river* D3
Jasper Natl. Park B5
Kakwa Prov. Rec. Area A4
Kinbasket, *lake* B5
Lesser Slave, *lake* C3
Lesser Slave Lake Prov. Park C3
Little Smoky, *river* A4
Lubicon, *lake* C3
Mamawi, *lake* E2
Margaret, *lake* C2
Mikkwa, *river* C2
Milk, *river* E6
Muriel, *lake* E4
Namur, *lake* D2
Newell, *lake* E6
North Saskatchewan, *river* B5, D4
North Wabasca, *lake* D3
Notikewan Prov. Park B2
Oldman, *river* D6
Pakowki, *lake* E6
Peace, *river* A3, C2
Peerless, *lake* C3
Pembina, *river* B4
Peter Lougheed Prov. Park C6
Pigeon, *lake* C4
Red Deer, *river* D5, E6
Richardson, *river* E2
Rocky, *mts.* A4
Sand, *river* E3
Simonette, *river* A4
Slave, *river* E1
Smoky, *river* A3, A4
South Saskatchewan, *river* E6
Sullivan, *lake* E5
Utikuma, *lake* C3
Wabamun, *lake* C4
Wabasca, *river* C2
Wapiti, *river* A4
Waterton Lakes Natl. Park D6
Wentzel, *lake* C1
Willmore Wilderness Park A4
Winefred, *lake* E3
Wood Buffalo Natl. Park D1
Zima, *lake* A2

British Columbia

Capital: Victoria
Area: 365,851 sq. mi. / 947,800 sq. km.
Population: 3,907,738 (2001 Census)
Largest City: Vancouver, 545,671
Highest Point: Mt. Fairweather / 15,300 ft. / 4,663 m.
Entered the Dominion: July 20, 1871
Floral Emblem: Pacific Dogwood

British Columbia: Map Index

Cities and Towns

100 Mile House, 1,739 .... M5
150 Mile House, 1,142 .... M5
70 Mile House M5
Abbotsford, 115,463 .... L6
Alexis Creek, 162 .... L5
Alice Arm H3
Anahim Lake, 163 .... K5
Armstrong, 4,256 .... N6
Ashcroft, 1,788 .... M6
Atlin F1
Barkerville M4
Barrière M5
Bear Lake, 227 .... L4
Beaton O6
Bella Coola, 167 .... J5
Bellingham L7
Big Creek L5
Blind Bay, 2,464 .... N6
Blue River N5
Boston Bar, 233 .... M6
Boswell O6
Bralorne L6
Bridge Lake M5
Burns Lake, 1,942 .... K4
Cache Creek, 1,056 .... M6
Campbell River, 28,456 .... K6
Canal Flats, 709 .... P6
Cassiar H1
Castlegar, 7,002 .... O6
Charlie Lake, 1,727 .... M3
Chase, 2,460 .... N6
Cherryville, 619 .... N6
Chetwynd, 2,591 .... M3
Chilliwack, 62,927 .... M6
Clearwater M5
Clinton, 621 .... M5
Coal River J1
Comox, 11,172 .... K6
Courtenay, 18,304 .... K6
Cranbrook, 18,476 .... P6
Crawford Bay, 328 .... O6
Creston, 4,795 .... O6
Cumberland, 2,618 .... K6
Dawson Creek, 10,754 .... M3
Dease Lake, 318 .... G2
Donald Station O5
Duncan, 4,699 .... L7
Dunster N4
Elkford, 2,589 .... P6
Elko P6
Enderby, 2,818 .... N6
Fairmont Hot Springs, 429 .... P6
Farmington M3
Fauquier, 219 .... N6
Fernie, 4,611 .... P6
Field O5
Fireside J1
Fontas M2
Fort Fraser, 308 .... K4
Fort Nelson, 4,188 .... L2
Fort St. James, 1,927 .... K4
Fort St. John, 16,034 .... M3
Fort Steele P6
Fraser E1
Fraser Lake, 1,268 .... K4
Galena Bay O6
Glenora G2
Golden, 4,020 .... O5
Gold River, 1,359 .... J6
Grand Forks, 4,054 .... N6
Granisle, 353 .... J4
Greenwood, 666 .... N6
Groundbirch M3
Halfmoon Bay, 358 .... L6
Hartley Bay H4
Hazelton, 345 .... J3
Hedley, 272 .... M6
Heriot Bay, 625 .... K6
Hixon, 264 .... L4
Hope, 6,184 .... M6
Houston, 3,577 .... J4
Hudson's Hope, 1,039 .... M3
Hyland Post H2
Kahntah M2
Kamloops, 77,281 .... M6
Kaslo, 1,032 .... O6
Kelowna, 96,288 .... N6
Kemano J4
Keremeos, 1,197 .... N6
Kimberley, 6,484 .... O6
Kingcome Inlet J6
Kitimat, 10,285 .... H4
Kitwanga H3
Klemtu H5
Lac La Hache, 396 .... M5
Lakelse Lake H4
Langley, 23,643 .... L6
Liard River J1
Lillooet, 2,741 .... M6
Little Fort M5
Lone Butte, 266 .... M5
Lower Post, 28 .... H1
Lund, 265 .... K6
Lytton, 319 .... M6
Mackenzie, 5,206 .... L3
Manson Creek K3
Masset, 926 .... F4
McBride, 711 .... M4
McDame H1
McLeese Lake, 261 .... L5
McLeod Lake L4
McLure M5
Merritt, 7,088 .... M6
Mica Creek N5
Mill Bay, 1,974 .... L7
Moricetown J3
Moyie P6
Muncho Lake K2
Nakusp, 1,698 .... O6
Nanaimo, 73,000 .... L6
Nazko L5
Needles N6
Nelson, 9,298 .... O6
Nelson Forks L1
New Denver, 538 .... O6
Nicola M6
Ocean Falls J5
Okanagan Falls, 1,971 .... N6
Oliver, 4,224 .... N6
Osoyoos, 4,295 .... N6
Parksville, 10,323 .... K6
Peachland, 4,654 .... N6
Pemberton, 1,637 .... L6
Penticton, 30,985 .... N6
Pink Mountain L3
Port Alberni, 17,743 .... K6
Port Clements, 516 .... F4
Port Coquitlam, 51,257 .... L6
Port Hardy, 4,574 .... J6
Port McNeill, 2,821 .... J6
Port Moody, 23,816 .... L6
Port Renfrew K7
Powell River, 12,983 .... K6
Prince George, 72,406 .... L4
Prince Rupert, 14,643 .... G4
Princeton, 2,610 .... M6
Prophet River L2
Queen Charlotte F4
Quesnel, 10,044 .... L5
Quilchena M6
Radium Hot Springs, 583 .... O6
Redstone L5
Revelstoke, 7,500 .... N6
Richmond, 164,345 .... L6
Riske Creek L5
Rivers Inlet J5
Rossland, 3,646 .... O6
Rutland N6
Salmon Arm, 15,210 .... N6
Saltery Bay K6
Sandspit, 435 .... G4
Savona M6
Sayward, 379 .... K6
Shelter Bay N6
Sicamous, 2,720 .... N6
Sidney, 10,929 .... L7
Sikanni Chief L2
Sinclair Mills M4
Skookumchuck P6
Smithers, 5,414 .... J4
Smithers Landing J3
Smith River J1
Sooke, 8,735 .... L7
Sparwood, 3,812 .... P6
Spences Bridge M6
Squamish, 14,247 .... L6
Stewart, 661 .... H3
Stikine G3
Strathnaver L4
Stuie J5
Summerland, 10,713 .... N6
Summit Lake K2
Summit Lake L4
Surprise F1
Tatla Lake K5
Tatlayoko Lake K5
Telegraph Creek G2
Telkwa, 1,371 .... J4
Terrace, 12,109 .... H4
Tête Jaune Cache N5
Toad River K2
Tofino, 1,466 .... K6
Topley Landing J4
Trail, 7,575 .... O6
Trutch L2
Tulsequah F2
Tumbler Ridge, 1,851 .... M3
Ucluelet, 1,559 .... K7
Valemount, 1,195 .... N5
Vancouver, 545,671 .... L6
Vanderhoof, 4,390 .... K4
Vavenby N5
Vernon, 33,494 .... N6
Victoria, 74,125 .... L7
Ware K2
Wasa, 259 .... P6
Westbank, 15,700 .... N6
Whaletown K6
Whistler, 8,896 .... L6
White Rock, 18,250 .... L6
Williams Lake, 11,153 .... L5
Windermere, 1,060 .... O6
Winfield N6
Winter Harbour H6
Wonowon M3
Yahk, 168 .... O6
Yale, 171 .... M6

Other Features

Adams, *lake* N5
Assiniboine, *mt.* P6
Atlin, *lake* F1
Atlin Prov. Park F1
Babine, *lake* J4
Babine, *river* J3
Banks, *island* G4
Bowron Lake Prov. Park M4
Bowser, *lake* H3
Burke, *channel* J5
Cassiar, *mts.* G1
Cathedral Prov. Park M6
Chatham, *sound* G4
Chief, *river* L2
Chilcotin, *river* K5
Chilko, *lake* K5
Coast, *mts.* F2, J5
Columbia, *mts.* M4
Columbia, *river* N5
Continental Divide, *mt. ridge* H2
Crooked, *river* L4
Dean, *channel* J5
Dean, *river* K5
Dixon Entrance, *channel* F4
Douglas, *channel* H4
Eutsuk, *lake* J4
Fairweather, *mt.* D1
Finlay, *river* J2
Fiordland Prov. Rec. Area H5
Fort Nelson, *river* L1
François, *lake* K4
Fraser, *river* L5, M4
Gardner, *canal* H4
Garibaldi Prov. Park L6
Glacier Natl. Park O5
Golden Ears Prov. Park L6
Graham, *island* F4
Gwillim Lake Prov. Park M3
Hamber Prov. Park O5
Hay, *river* M2
Hart, *ranges* L3
Hazelton, *mts.* H3
Hecate, *strait* G4
Homathko, *river* K5
Juan de Fuca, *strait* L7
Kate's Needle, *mt.* F2
Kechika, *river* J2
Kinbasket, *lake* O5
Knight, *inlet* K6
Kokanee Glacier Prov. Park O6
Kootenay, *lake* O6
Kootenay, *river* P6
Kootenay Natl. Park O5
Kotcho, *lake* M1
Kwadacha Wilderness Prov. Park K2
Liard, *river* K1
Lillooet, *river* L6
Lower Arrow, *lake* N6
Manning Prov. Park M6
Monashee Prov. Park N6
Moresby, *island* F5
Morice, *lake* J4
Mt. Assiniboine Prov. Park P6
Mount Edziza Prov. Park G2
Mt. Revelstoke Natl. Park N5
Mt. Robson Prov. Park N5
Muncho Lake Prov. Park K1
Muskwa, *ranges* J2
Nass, *river* H3
Natalkuz, *lake* K4
Nechako, *river* K4
Nesselrode, *mt.* E1
Nootka, *island* J6
North Cascades Natl. Park M7
N. Thompson, *river* N5
Okanagan, *lake* N6
Omineca, *mts.* J2
Omineca, *river* K3
Ootsa, *lake* J4
Osilinka, *river* K3
Pacific Rim Natl. Park Res. K7
Parsnip, *river* L4
Peace, *river* L3
Pitt, *island* H4
Portland, *inlet* G4
Princess Royal, *island* H4
Queen Charlotte, *islands* G4
Queen Charlotte, *sound* H5
Queen Charlotte, *strait* H5
Quesnel, *lake* M5
Robson, *mt.* N4
Rocky, *mts.* K2
St. Elias, *mts.* D1
Salmon, *river* L4
Silver Star Prov. Park N6
Skeena, *mts.* H3
Skeena, *river* H4
South Moresby Natl. Park Reserve G5
Spatsizi Plateau Wilderness Prov. Park H2
Stikine, *river* G2
Stone Mountain Prov. Park K2
Strathcona Prov. Park K6
Stuart, *lake* K4
Tagish, *lake* E1
Takla, *lake* K3
Taseko, *lake* L5
Tchentlo, *lake* K3
Teslin, *lake* F1
Teslin, *river* G1
Tezzeron, *lake* K4
Thompson, *river* M6
Trembleur, *lake* K4
Tuya, *lake* G1
Tweedsmuir Prov. Park J4
Upper Arrow, *lake* O6
Vancouver, *island* J6
Waddington, *mt.* K5
Wells Gray Prov. Park M5
West Road, *river* K4
Williston, *lake* K3
Yoho Natl. Park O5

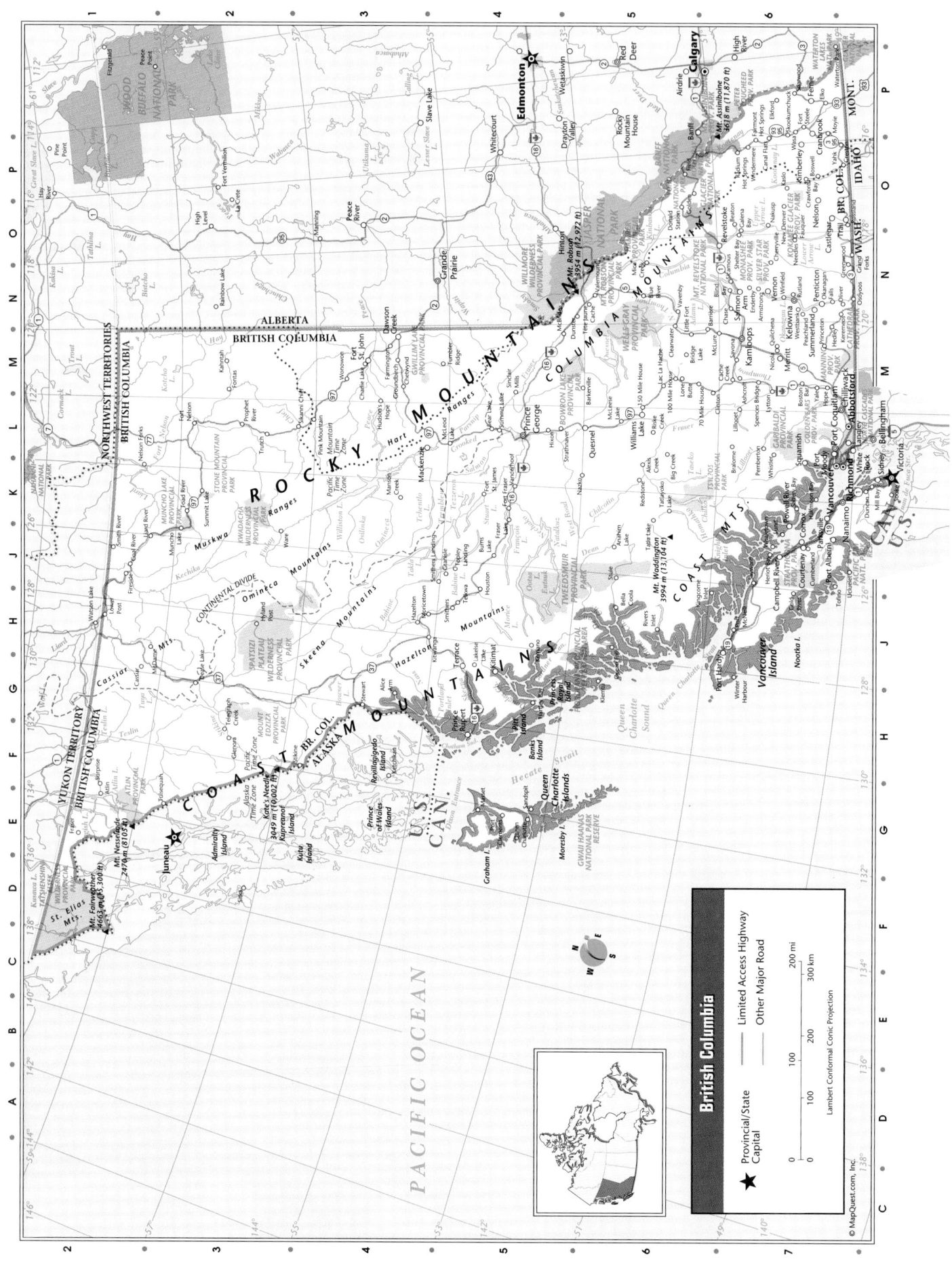

PACIFIC OCEAN

British Columbia

★ Provincial/State Capital
— Limited Access Highway
— Other Major Road

200 mi
300 km

Lambert Conformal Conic Projection

© MapQuest.com, Inc.

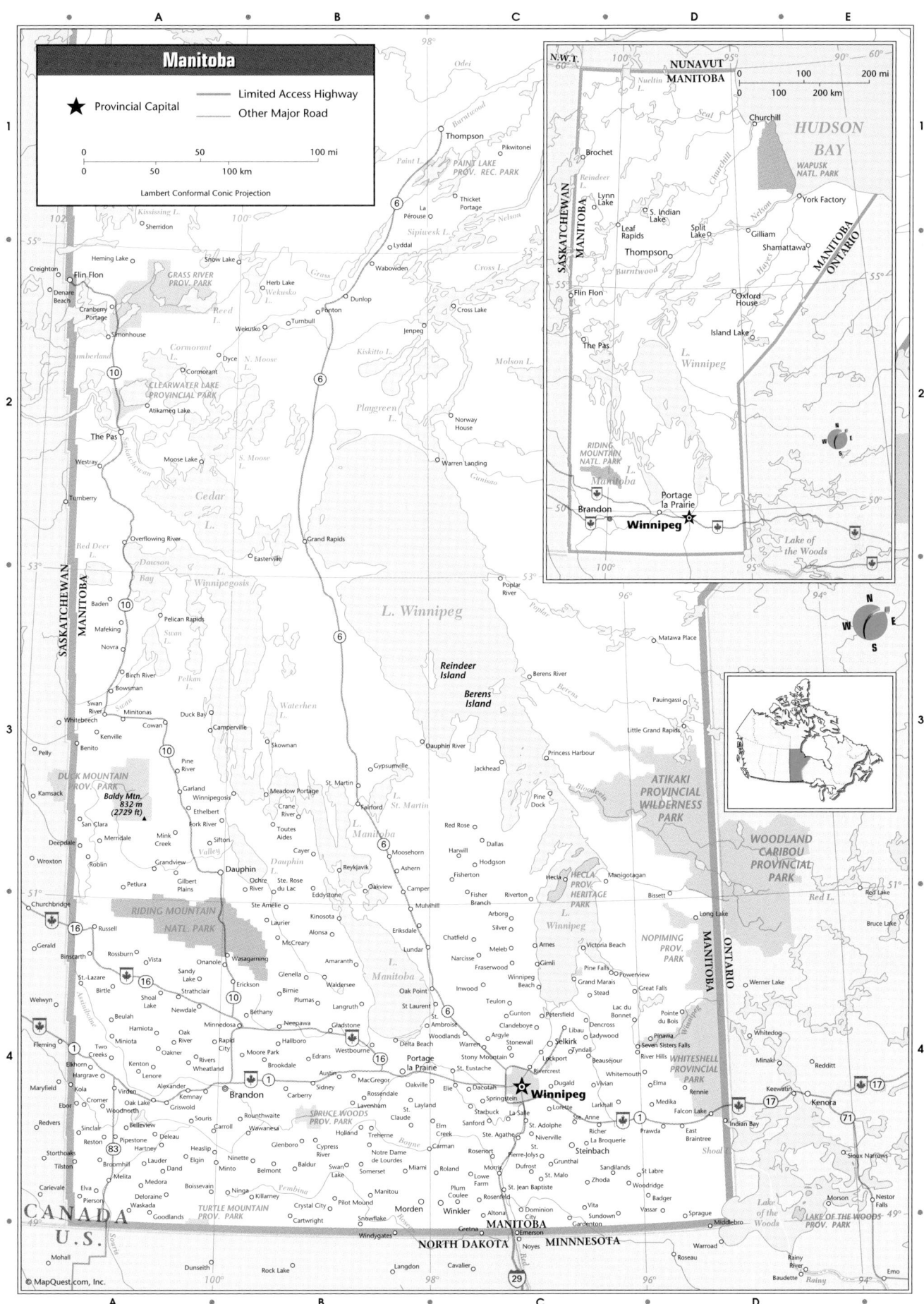

Manitoba

★ Provincial Capital

━━ Limited Access Highway
── Other Major Road

0   50   100 mi
0   50   100 km

Lambert Conformal Conic Projection

Manitoba

Capital: Winnipeg
Area: 250,881 sq. mi. 649,950 sq. km.
Population: 1,119,583 (2001 Census)
Largest City: Winnipeg, 619,544
Highest Point: Mt. Baldy 2,730 ft. 832 m.
Entered the Dominion: July 15, 1870
Floral Emblem: Prarie Crocus

Manitoba: Map Index

Cities and Towns

Alexander ... A4
Alonsa ... B4
Altona, 3,434 ... C4
Amaranth ... B4
Arborg, 959 ... C4
Argyle ... C4
Arnes ... C4
Ashern ... B3
Atikameg Lake ... A2
Austin ... B4
Baden, 38 ... A3
Badger ... D4
Baldur ... B4
Beauséjour, 2,772 ... C4
Belleview ... A4
Belmont ... B4
Benito, 415 ... A3
Berens River, 42 ... C3
Bethany ... B4
Beulah ... A4
Binscarth, 445 ... A4
Birch River ... A3
Birnie ... B4
Birtle, 715 ... A4
Bissett, 243 ... D3
Boissevain, 1,495 ... A4
Bowsman, 320 ... A3
Brandon, 39,716 ... B4, C2
Brochet, 226 ... C1
Brookdale ... B4
Broomhill ... A4
Camper ... B3
Camperville, 524 ... A3
Carberry, 1,513 ... B4
Carievale ... A4
Carman, 2,831 ... B4
Carroll ... A4
Cartwright, 304 ... B4
Cayer ... B3
Charles ... A1
Chatfield ... C4
Churchbridge ... A4
Churchill, 963 ... D1
Clandeboye ... C4
Cormorant, 400 ... A2
Cowan ... A3
Cranberry Portage ... A2
Crane River, 161 ... B3
Cromer ... A4
Cross Lake, 294 ... C2
Crystal City, 414 ... B4
Cypress River ... B4
Dacotah ... C4
Dallas, 65 ... C3
Dand ... A4
Dauphin, 8,085 ... A3
Dauphin River, 10 ... B3
Deepdale ... A3
Deleau ... A4
Deloraine, 1,026 ... A4
Delta Beach ... B4
Dencross ... C4
Dominion City ... C4
Duck Bay, 454 ... A3
Dufrost ... C4
Dugald ... C4
Dunlop ... B2
Dyce ... A2
East Braintree ... D4
Easterville, 80 ... B2
Ebor ... A4
Eddystone ... B3
Edrans ... B4
Elgin ... A4
Elie ... C4
Elkhorn, 470 ... A4
Elma ... D4
Elm Creek ... C4
Elva ... A4
Emerson, 655 ... C4
Erickson, 448 ... B4
Eriksdale ... B4
Ethelbert, 335 ... A3
Fairford ... B3
Falcon Lake ... D4
Fisher Branch ... C3
Fisherton ... C3
Fleming ... A4
Flin Flon, 6,000 ... A2, C2
Fork River ... A3
Fraserwood ... C4
Garden Hill ... D2
Gardenton ... C4
Garland ... A3
Gerald ... A4
Gilbert Plains, 757 ... A3
Gillam, 1,178 ... D1
Gimli, 1,657 ... C4
Gladstone, 848 ... B4
Glenboro, 656 ... B4
Glenella ... B4
Goodlands ... A4
Grand Marais ... C4
Grand Rapids, 355 ... B2
Grandview, 814 ... A3
Granville Lake, 69 ... A1
Great Falls ... C4
Gretna, 563 ... C4
Griswold ... A4
Grunthal ... C4
Gunton ... C4
Gypsumville ... B3
Hallboro ... B4
Hamiota, 858 ... A4
Hargrave ... A4
Hartney, 446 ... A4
Harwill, 19 ... C3
Heaslip ... A4
Hecla ... C3
Heming Lake ... A2
Herb Lake ... B2
Highrock ... A1
Hodgson ... C3
Holland ... B4
Ilford, 143 ... D1
Indian Bay ... D4
Inwood ... C4
Island Lake, 59 ... D2
Jackhead ... C3
Jenpeg ... B2
Jetait ... A1
Kelsey ... C1
Kemnay ... A4
Kenton ... A4
Kenville ... A3
Killarney, 2,221 ... B4
Kinosota ... B4
Kola ... A4
La Broquerie ... C4
Lac du Bonnet, 1,089 ... C4
Ladywood ... C4
Langruth ... B4
La Pérouse ... B1
Larkhall ... C4
La Salle ... C4
Lauder ... A4
Laurier ... B4
Laurie River ... A1
Lavenham ... B4
Layland ... B4
Leaf Rapids, 1,309 ... D1
Lenore ... A4
Libau ... C4
Little Grand Rapids, 10 ... D3
Lockport ... C4
Long Lake ... D4
Lorette ... C4
Lowe Farm ... C4
Lundar ... B4
Lyddal ... B1
Lynn Lake, 699 ... C1
Macgregor, 882 ... B4
Mafeking ... A3
Manigotagan, 192 ... C3
Manitou, 775 ... B4
Maryfield ... A4
Matawa Place ... D3
McCreary, 522 ... B4
Meadow Portage, 80 ... B3
Medika ... D4
Medora ... A4
Meleb ... C4
Melita, 1,111 ... A4
Merridale ... A3
Miami ... B4
Middlebro ... D4
Miniota ... A4
Minitonas, 538 ... A3
Mink Creek ... A3
Minnedosa, 2,426 ... B4
Minto ... B4
Moore Park ... B4
Moosehorn ... B3
Moose Lake, 740 ... A2
Morden, 6,142 ... B4
Morris, 1,673 ... C4
Mulvihill ... B4
Narcisse ... C4
Neepawa, 3,325 ... B4
Nelson House, 54 ... B1
Newdale ... A4
Ninette ... B4
Ninga ... B4
Niverville, 1,921 ... C4
Norway House, 456 ... C2
Notre Dame de Lourdes, 619 ... B4
Novra ... A3
Oak Lake, 359 ... A4
Oakner ... A4
Oak Point ... C4
Oak River ... A4
Oakview ... B3
Oakville ... C4
Ochre River ... B3
Onanole ... B4
Overflowing River ... A2
Oxford House ... D1, D2
Pauingassi ... D3
Pelican Rapids, 123 ... A3
Petersfield ... C4
Petlura ... A3
Pierson ... A4
Pikwitonei, 117 ... C1
Pilot Mound, 676 ... B4
Pinawa, 1,500 ... D4
Pine Dock, 108 ... C3
Pine Falls ... C4
Pine River ... A3
Pipestone ... A4
Plumas ... B4
Plum Coulee, 725 ... C4
Pointe du Bois ... D4
Ponton ... B2
Poplar River ... C3
Portage la Prairie, 12,976 ... B4, D2
Powerview, 750 ... C4
Prawda ... D4
Princess Harbour, 10 ... C3
Pukatawagan ... A1
Rafter ... A1
Rapid City, 424 ... A4
Red Rose ... C3
Redvers ... A4
Rennie ... D4
Reston ... A4
Reykjavik ... B3
Richer ... C4
Rivercrest ... C4
River Hills ... C4
Rivers, 1,119 ... A4
Riverton, 594 ... C3
Roblin, 1,818 ... A3
Roland ... C4
Rosenfeld ... C4
Rosenort ... C4
Rossburn, 568 ... A4
Rossendale ... B4
Rounthwaite ... B4
Russell, 1,587 ... A4
St. Adolphe, 1,140 ... C4
St. Ambroise ... B4
St. Claude, 558 ... B4
Ste. Agathe ... C4
Ste-Amélie ... B4
Ste. Anne, 1,513 ... C4
Ste. Rose du Lac, 1,047 ... B3
St. Eustache ... C4
St. Jean Baptiste ... C4
St. Labre ... C4
St. Laurent ... C4
St.-Lazare, 265 ... A4
St. Malo ... C4
St. Martin ... B3
St. Pierre-Jolys, 893 ... C4
San Clara ... A3
Sandilands ... C4
Sandy Lake ... A4
Sanford ... C4
Selkirk, 9,752 ... C4
Seven Sisters Falls ... C4
Shamattawa ... E2
Sherridon, 113 ... A1
Shoal Lake, 801 ... A4
Sidney ... B4
Sifton ... A3
Silver ... C4
Simonhouse ... A2
Sinclair ... A4
Skownan ... B3
Snowflake ... B4
Snow Lake, 1,207 ... A2
Somerset, 459 ... B4
Souris, 1,683 ... A4
S. Indian Lake, 808 ... D1
Split Lake ... D1
Sprague ... D4
Springstein ... C4
Starbuck ... C4
Stead ... C4
Steinbach, 9,227 ... C4
Stonewall, 4,012 ... C4
Stony Mountain, 1,700 ... C4
Storthoaks ... A4
Strathclair ... A4
Sundown ... C4
Swan Lake ... B4
Swan River, 4,032 ... A3
Takipy ... A1
Teulon, 1,058 ... C4
The Pas, 5,795 ... A2, C2
Thicket Portage, 137 ... C1
Thompson, 13,256 ... C1, D2
Tilston ... A4
Toutes Aides ... B3
Treherne, 644 ... B4
Turnberry ... A2
Turnbull ... B2
Two Creeks ... A4
Tyndall ... C4
Vassar ... D4
Victoria Beach ... C4
Virden, 3,109 ... A4
Vista ... A4
Vita ... C4
Vivian ... C4
Wabowden, 497 ... B2
Waldersee ... B4
Wapawsik ... B1
Warren ... C4
Warren Landing ... C2
Wasagaming ... B4
Waskada, 208 ... A4
Wawanesa, 516 ... B4
Wekusko ... B2
Welwyn ... A4
Westbourne ... B4
Westray ... A2
Wheatland ... A4
Whitemouth ... D4
Winkler, 7,943 ... C4
Winnipeg, 619,544 ... C4, D2
Winnipeg Beach, 801 ... C4
Winnipegosis, 621 ... B3
Woodlands ... C4
Woodnorth ... A4
Woodridge ... C4
York Factory ... E1
Zhoda ... C4

Other Features

Assiniboine, *river* ... A4
Atikaki Prov. Wilderness Park ... D3
Baldy, *mt.* ... A3
Beaver Hill, *lake* ... D2
Berens, *island* ... C3
Berens, *river* ... C3
Bigstone, *river* ... D1
Bloodvein, *river* ... C3
Boyne, *river* ... B4
Burntwood, *lake* ... A1
Burntwood, *river* ... B1, C1, D2
Cedar, *lake* ... A2
Churchill, *river* ... D1
Clearwater Lake Prov. Park ... A2
Cobham, *river* ... D2
Cormorant, *lake* ... A2
Cross, *lake* ... C2
Cumberland, *lake* ... A2
Dauphin, *lake* ... B3
Dawson, *bay* ... A2
Duck Mountain Prov. Park ... A3
Gods, *lake* ... D2
Grass, *river* ... A3, B2
Grass River Prov. Park ... A2
Gunisao, *river* ... C2
Hayes, *river* ... D1, D2
Hecla Prov. Park ... C3
Highrock, *lake* ... A1
Island, *lake* ... D2
Kiskitto, *lake* ... B2
Kississing, *lake* ... A1
Knee, *lake* ... D1
Manitoba, *lake* ... B3, B4, D2
Molson, *lake* ... C2
Nelson, *river* ... C1, D1
Nopiming Prov. Park ... D4
N. Moose, *lake* ... B2
Nueltin, *lake* ... D1
Odei, *river* ... C1
Oxford, *lake* ... D2
Paint, *lake* ... B1
Paint Lake Prov. Rec. Park ... C1
Pelkan, *lake* ... A3
Pembina, *river* ... B4
Playgreen, *lake* ... B2
Poplar, *river* ... C3
Red, *river* ... C4
Red Deer, *lake* ... A2
Red Sucker, *lake* ... E2
Reed, *lake* ... A2
Reindeer, *island* ... C3
Reindeer, *lake* ... C1
Riding Mountain Natl. Park ... A4, C2
Roseau, *river* ... B4
St. Martin, *lake* ... B3
Saskatchewan, *river* ... A2
Seal, *river* ... D1
Sipiwesk, *lake* ... C1
Souris, *river* ... A4
S. Moose, *lake* ... B2
Spruce Woods Prov. Park ... B4
Stevenson, *lake* ... C2
Swan, *lake* ... A3
Swan, *river* ... A3
Turtle Mountain Prov. Park ... A4
Valley, *river* ... A3
Wapusk National Park ... D1
Waterhen, *lake* ... B3
Wekusko, *lake* ... B2
Whiteshell Prov. Park ... D4
Winnipeg, *lake* ... B3, C4, D2
Winnipeg, *river* ... D4
Winnipegosis, *lake* ... A3

New Brunswick

Capital: Fredericton
Area: 28,348 sq. mi. 73,440 sq. km.
Population: 729,498 (2001 Census)
Largest City: Saint John, 69,661
Highest Point: Mt. Carleton 2,690 ft. 820 m.
Entered the Dominion: July 1, 1867
Floral Emblem: Purple Violet

New Brunswick: Map Index

Counties

Albert ... E3
Carleton ... B2
Charlotte ... B3
Gloucester ... D1
Kent ... D2
Kings ... D3
Madawaska ... A1
Northumberland ... C1
Queens ... D2
Restigouche ... C1
St. John ... D3
Sunbury ... C3
Victoria ... B1
Westmorland ... D2
York ... C2

Cities and Towns

Acadieville ... D2
Acton ... C3
Allardville, 463 ... D1
Alma, 290 ... E3
Anagance ... D3
Anse-Bleue, 409 ... D1
Apohaqui ... D3
Aroostook, 380 ... B2
Arthurette ... B2
Astle ... C2
Atholville, 1,381 ... C1
Aulac ... E3
Back Bay ... C3
Baie-Ste.-Anne, 1,600 ... E1
Baie Verte, 413 ... E2
Baker Brook, 599 ... A1
Balmoral, 1,836 ... C1
Barachois ... E2
Barnaby River ... D2
Bartibog Bridge, 255 ... D1
Bas-Caraquet, 1,689 ... E1
Bass River ... D2
Bath, 592 ... B2
Bathurst, 12,924 ... D1
Bathurst Mines ... D1
Bay du Vin ... D1
Bayfield, 56 ... E2
Beechwood ... B2
Belledune, 1,923 ... D1
Ben Lomond ... D3
Benton, 109 ... B3
Beresford, 4,414 ... D1
Bertrand, 1,269 ... D1
Berwick ... D3
Black River ... D3
Blacks Harbour, 1,082 ... C3
Blackville, 1,015 ... D2
Blissfield ... C2
Blissville ... C3
Bloomfield ... D3
Boiestown ... C2
Bon Accord ... B2
Bonny River, 415 ... C3
Bouctouche, 2,426 ... E2
Bristol, 719 ... B2
Brockway ... B3
Burnsville ... D1
Burnt Church ... D1
Burtts Corner ... C2
Calais ... B3
Cambridge-Narrows, 654 ... D3
Campbellton, 7,798 ... C1
Canaan ... D2
Canaan Forks ... D2
Canterbury, 399 ... B3
Cap-des-Caissie ... E2
Cape Enrage ... E3
Cape Tormentine, 157 ... E2
Cap-Pelé, 2,266 ... E2
Caraquet, 4,442 ... E1
Central Blissville ... C3
Centreville, 535 ... B2
Chance Harbour ... C3
Charlo, 1,449 ... C1
Chatham ... D1
Chipman, 1,432 ... D2
Clair, 863 ... A1
Cloverdale ... B2
Coal Branch ... D2
Cocagne, 2,659 ... E2
Codys ... D3
Coldstream, 134 ... B2
Coles Island ... D3
Collette, 522 ... D2
Connors ... A1
Cormierville ... E2
Cornhill ... D3
Cross Creek ... C2
Cumberland Bay ... D2
Currie ... B2
Dalhousie, 3,975 ... C1
Dawsonville ... C1
Debec, 135 ... B2
Dieppe, 14,951 ... E2
Doaktown, 955 ... C2
Dorchester, 954 ... E3
Douglastown ... D1
Drummond, 932 ... B2
Edmundston, 17,373 ... A1
Eel River Crossing, 1,335 ... C1
Elgin, 220 ... D3
Escuminac, 252 ... E1
Evandale ... C3
Everett ... B1
Fairvale ... C3
Florenceville, 762 ... B2
Fosterville ... B3
Four Falls ... B2
Fredericton, 47,560 ... C3
Fredericton Jct., 692 ... C3
Gagetown, 682 ... C3
Gaspereau Forks ... D2
Geary ... C3
Glassville, 108 ... B2
Gondola Pt. ... C3
Grafton ... B2
Grand-Aldouane ... E2
Grand Bay, 4,949 ... C3
Grande-Anse, 853 ... D1
Grand Falls, 5,858 ... B1
Grand Manan, 2,610 ... C4
Hammondvale ... D3
Hampstead, 312 ... C3
Hampton, 3,997 ... D3
Hanford Brook ... D3
Harcourt ... D2
Hardwood Ridge ... C2
Hartland, 902 ... B2
Harvey, 349 ... C3
Hatfield Point ... D3
Havelock, 380 ... D2
Heath Steele ... C1
Hillsborough, 1,288 ... E3
Hopewell Cape ... E3
Howard ... D2
Hoyt ... C3
Indian Island ... E2
Inkerman, 936 ... E1
Irishtown ... E2
Jacquet River ... C1
Janeville ... D1
Jemseg ... C3
Juniper ... B2
Kedgwick, 1,184 ... B1
Kedgwick River ... B1
Kent Junction ... D2
Keswick Ridge, 1,331 ... C2
Kilburn ... B2
King's Landing ... B3
Kingston ... D3
Kouchibouguac ... D2
Lac-Baker, 226 ... A1
Lake Edward ... B2
Lakeville, 381 ... B2
Lamèque, 1,580 ... E1
Lavillette ... D1
Lawrence Station ... B3
Lepreau ... C3
Letete ... C3
Lindsay ... B2
Little Ridge ... B3
Loggieville ... D1
Lords Cove ... C4
Lorne ... C1
Losier Settlement ... E1
Lower Hainesville ... B2
Ludlow ... C2
Lutes Mountain ... E2
Maces Bay ... C3
Maisonnette, 605 ... D1
Maltais ... C1
McAdam, 1,513 ... B3
McGraw Brook ... C2
McLean Settlement ... E2
Meadow Brook ... E2
Mechanic Settlement ... D3
Meductic, 189 ... B3
Melrose ... E2
Menneval, 83 ... B1
Millerton ... D2
Millville, 319 ... B2
Minto, 2,776 ... C2
Moncton, 61,046 ... E2
Moores Mills ... B3
Nackawic, 1,042 ... B3
Napadogan ... C2
Nash Creek, 279 ... C1
Nashwaak Bridge ... C2
Nashwaak Village, 255 ... C2
Nauwigewauk, 1,508 ... D3
Neguac, 1,697 ... D1
Nelson-Miramichi ... D2
New Bandon, 968 ... D1
New Canaan ... D2
Newcastle ... D2
New Denmark ... B2
New Maryland, 4,284 ... C3
New Mills ... C1
Newtown ... D3
Nictau ... B1
Nigadoo, 983 ... D1
North Esk Boom ... D2
Norton, 1,370 ... D3
Notre-Dame ... E2
Oak Point ... C3
Oromocto, 8,843 ... C3
Paquetville, 667 ... D1
Parker Ridge ... C2
Parkindale ... E3
Penobsquis ... D3
Perth-Andover, 1,908 ... B2
Petitcodiac, 1,444 ... D3
Petite-Cap ... E2
Petit-Rocher, 1,966 ... D1
Petit-Shippegan ... E1
Pigeon Hill, 537 ... E1
Pine Ridge ... D2
Plaster Rock, 1,219 ... B2
Pointe Sapin, 627 ... E2
Pointe-Verte, 1,041 ... D1
Pokemouche, 558 ... E1
Pokeshaw ... D1
Pokiok ... B3
Pomeroy ... C3
Pont-Lafrance, 754 ... E1
Port Elgin, 436 ... E3
Price Settlement ... D1
Prince of Wales ... C3
Quarryville ... D2
Quispamsis, 13,757 ... D3
Red Bank ... D2
Renous, 1,183 ... D2
Rexton, 810 ... E2
Richibucto, 1,341 ... E2
Riley Brook, 78 ... B1
River de Chute ... B2
Riverside-Albert, 393 ... E3
Riverview, 17,010 ... E2
Rivière-du-Portage ... E1
Rivière-Verte, 856 ... A1
Robertville, 954 ... D1
Robinsonville ... C1
Rogersville, 1,248 ... D2
Rosaireville ... D2
Rothesay, 11,505 ... D3
Rothwell ... C2
Rowena ... B2
Sackville, 5,361 ... E3
St.-André, 415 ... B1
St. Andrews, 1,869 ... B3
St-Antoine, 1,472 ... E2
St.-Arthur, 832 ... C1
St.-Basile ... A1
St-Charles, 806 ... E2
St. Croix ... B3
Ste-Anne de Kent, 1,150 ... E2
Ste.-Anne-de-Madawaska, 1,168 ... A1
Ste-Marie-de-Kent ... E2
St.-François-de-Madawaska, 572 ... A1
St. George, 1,509 ... C3
St.-Hilaire, 237 ... A1
St-Ignace, 651 ... D2
St.-Isidore, 877 ... D1
St.-Jacques ... A1
St-Jean-Baptiste-de-Restigouche, 214 ... B1
Saint John, 69,661 ... C3
St. Joseph ... E2
St.-Léonard, 1,385 ... B1
St-Léonard-Parent ... B1
St.-Louis-de-Kent, 991 ... E2
St. Margarets, 386 ... D2
St-Martin-de-Restigouche, 146 ... B1
St. Martins, 374 ... D3
St-Paul ... E2
St.-Quentin, 2,280 ... B1
St-Sauveur, 817 ... D1
St. Stephen, 4,667 ... B3
Salisbury, 1,954 ... D2
Scotch Ridge ... B3
Sevogle ... D1
Shediac, 4,892 ... E2
Shediac Ridge ... D2
Shemogue ... E2
Shippagan, 2,872 ... E1
Siegas, 272 ... B1
Smiths Corner ... D2
Somerville, 368 ... B2
South Tetagouche ... D1
Springfield ... D3
Stanley, 460 ... C2
Stickney ... B2
Sunny Corner, 910 ... D2
Sussex, 4,182 ... D3
Sussex Corner, 1,321 ... D3
Tabusintac, 893 ... D1
Tay Creek ... C2
Taymouth ... C2
Thomaston Corner ... B3
Three Brooks ... B2
Tide Head, 1,149 ... C1
Tidnish ... E3
Tracadie-Sheila, 4,724 ... E1
Tracy, 601 ... C3
Turtle Creek ... E3
Tweedside ... B3
Upper Blackville ... D2
Upper Brockway ... B3
Upper Gagetown, 314 ... C3
Upper Hainesville ... B2
Upper Kent, 167 ... B2
Upper Woodstock ... B2
Val Comeau, 823 ... E1
Waterborough ... C3
Waterside ... E3
Welsford ... C3
Westfield ... C3
West Quaco ... D3
Whites Brook, 158 ... B1
Williamsburg ... C2
Wilsons Beach ... C4
Windsor ... B2
Wishart Point ... E1
Woodstock, 5,198 ... B2
York Mills ... B3
Youngs Cove ... D2
Zealand ... C2

Other Features

Campobello, *island* ... C4
Chaleur, *bay* ... D1
Chignecto, *bay* ... E3
Fundy, *bay* ... D3
Fundy Natl. Park ... D3
Grand, *lake* ... D2
Grand Manan, *island* ... C4
Kouchibouguac Natl. Park ... E2
Lamèque, *island* ... E1
Minas, *channel* ... E3
Miramichi, *bay* ... E1
Miscou, *island* ... E1
Mt. Carleton Prov. Park ... C1
Nepisiguit, *river* ... C1
Northumberland, *strait* ... E2
Restigouche, *river* ... B1
Roosevelt Campobello Intl. Hist. Park ... C4
Saint John, *river* ... B2
SW Miramichi, *river* ... C2

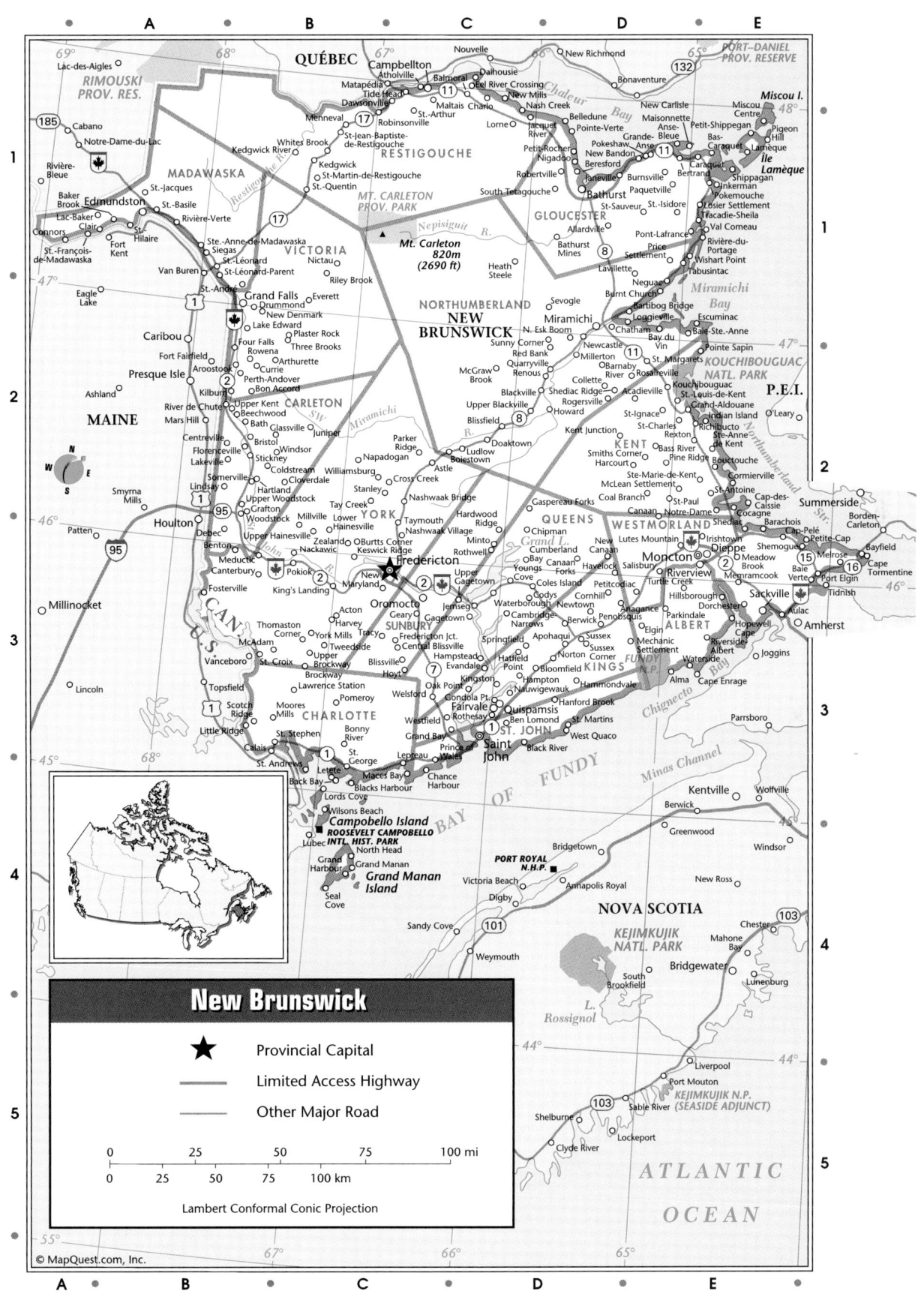

New Brunswick

★ Provincial Capital
— Limited Access Highway
— Other Major Road

| 0 | 25 | 50 | 75 | 100 mi |

| 0 | 25 | 50 | 75 | 100 km |

Lambert Conformal Conic Projection

© MapQuest.com, Inc.

Newfoundland and Labrador

★ Provincial Capital — Major Road

0   50   100 mi
0   50   100   150 km

Lambert Conformal Conic Projection

MAIN MAP

LABRADOR SEA

LABRADOR

NFLD. & LAB.
QUÉ.

© MapQuest.com, Inc.

Newfoundland and Labrador

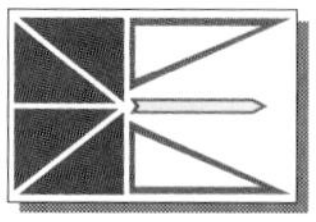

Capital: St. John's
Area: 156,608 sq. mi. 405,720 sq. km.
Population: 512,930 (2001 Census)
Largest City: St. John's, 99,182
Highest Point: Torngat Mts. (highest peak) 5,420 ft. 1,652 m.
Entered the Dominion: March 31, 1949
Floral Emblem: Pitcher Plant

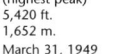

Newfoundland and Labrador: Map Index

Cities and Towns

Aillik B1
Argentia D5
Arnold's Cove, 1,024 . . . . . .D5
Badger, 906 . . . . .C5
Baie Verte, 1,492 . . . . .C4
Batteau D2
Bay Bulls, 1,014 . . . . .E5
Bay de Verde, 534 . . . . .E5
Bay Roberts, 5,237 . . . . . . .E5
Beachside, 174 . . . . .D4
Bellburns, 80 . . . . .C4
Benoit's Cove B5
Birchy Bay, 612 . . . . .D4
Bishop's Falls, 3,688 . . . . . .D4
Black Tickle, 249 . . . . .D2
Bonavista, 4,021 . . . . .E5
Botwood, 3,221 . . . . .D4
Boyd's Cove, 258 . . . . .D4
Branch, 318 . . . . .E5
Britannia E5
Buchans, 877 . . . . .C5
Burgeo, 1,782 . . . . .C5
Burin, 2,470 . . . . .D5
Cape Charles D3
Cape Race E5
Cape Ray, 399 . . . . .B5
Cape St. George, 926 . . . . .B5
Carbonear, 4,759 . . . . .E5
Carmanville, 798 . . . . .D4
Cartwright, 629 . . . . .C2
Catalina, 995 . . . . .E5
Centreville, 1,146 . . . . .E4
Channel-Port aux Basques, 4,637 . . . . .B5
Charlottetown, 346 . . . . . . .C3
Churchill Falls D3
Clarenville, 5,104 . . . . .D5
Conche, 263 . . . . .D4
Cook's Harbour, 226 . . . . . .D3
Cormack, 675 . . . . .C4
Corner Brook, 20,103 . . . . .C5
Cow Head, 511 . . . . .C4
Cox's Cove, 719 . . . . .B4
Daniel's Harbour, 350 . . . . .C4
Davis Inlet E3
Deer Lake, 4,769 . . . . .C4
Eastport, 509 . . . . .E5
Eddies Cove C3
Englee, 694 . . . . .C4
Esker D3
Ferryland, 607 . . . . .E5
Fleur de Lys, 348 . . . . .C4
Fogo, 803 . . . . .D4
Forteau, 477 . . . . .C3
Fortune, 1,615 . . . . .D5
Francois, 162 . . . . .C5
Gambo, 2,084 . . . . .D5
Gander, 9,651 . . . . .D5
Gander Bay, 315 . . . . .D4
Garnish, 665 . . . . .D5
Gaultois, 321 . . . . .D5
Glenwood, 845 . . . . .D5
Glovertown, 2,163 . . . . . . .D5
Goobies, 108 . . . . .E5
Grand Bank, 2,841 . . . . . . .D5
Grand Bruit, 44 . . . . .B5
Grand Falls-Windsor, 13,340 D5
Grey River, 169 . . . . .C5
Hampden, 544 . . . . .C4
Happy Valley-Goose Bay, 7,969 . . . . .A2, E4
Harbour Breton, 2,079 . . . .D5
Harbour Deep C4
Hare Bay, 1,065 . . . . .D5
Hawke Harbour D2
Hawke's Bay, 445 . . . . .C4
Heart's Content, 495 . . . . . .E5
Hebron E3
Henley Harbour D3
Hermitage-Sandyville, 602 . .D5
Holton C2
Holyrood, 1,906 . . . . .E5
Hopedale, 559 . . . . .A1, E3
Howley, 271 . . . . .C4
Isle aux Morts, 813 . . . . . . .B5
Jackson's Arm, 420 . . . . . . .C4
Joe Batt's Arm, 889 . . . . . .D4
King's Cove, 159 . . . . .E5
King's Point, 771 . . . . .C4
Labrador City, 7,744 . . . . . .D3
Lamaline, 346 . . . . .D5
L'Anse-au-Loup, 635 . . . . . .C3
Lark Harbour, 613 . . . . .B4
La Scie, 1,063 . . . . .D4
Lawn, 779 . . . . .D5
Leading Tickles, 453 . . . . . .D4
Lethbridge E5
Lewisporte, 3,312 . . . . .D4
Little Bay B5
Little Seldom (Seldom-Little Seldom) D4
Lumsden, 622 . . . . .E4
Main Brook, 357 . . . . .C3
Makkovik, 384 . . . . .B1
Mary's Harbour, 450 . . . . . .D3
Marystown, 5,908 . . . . . . .D5
McCallum, 134 . . . . .C5
Menihek D3
Middle Arm, 546 . . . . .C4
Milltown, 884 . . . . .D5
Musgrave Harbour, 1,294 . .E4
Musgravetown, 640 . . . . . . .E5
Nain, 1,159 . . . . .E3
New Ferolle, 345 . . . . .C4
Norris Arm, 843 . . . . .D4
Norris Point, 786 . . . . .C4
North West River, 551 . . . . .A2
Notre Dame Junction D4
Nutak E3
Old Perlican, 714 . . . . .E5
Paradise River C2
Parson's Pond, 427 . . . . . . .C4
Pasadena, 3,133 . . . . .C5
Placentia, 4,426 . . . . .D5
Point Leamington, 685 . . . .D4
Pond Cove C3
Port au Choix, 1,010 . . . . . .C4
Port au Port B5
Port Blandford, 580 . . . . . .D5
Port Burwell D3
Port Hope Simpson, 509 . . .C3
Portland Creek, 98 . . . . . . .C4
Port Saunders, 812 . . . . . . .C4
Postville B2
Pouch Cove, 1,669 . . . . .E5
Purbeck's Cove C4
Ramea, 754 . . . . .C5
Red Bay, 264 . . . . .C3
Rencontre East, 202 . . . . . .D5
Rigolet, 317 . . . . .B2
Rocky Harbour, 1,002 . . . . .C4
Roddickton, 1,003 . . . . . . .C4
Rose Blanche, 668 . . . . . . .B5
St. Alban's, 1,372 . . . . .D5
St. Anthony, 2,730 . . . . . . .D3
St. Barbe, 158 . . . . .C3
St. Bernard's, 657 . . . . .D5
St. Brendan's, 251 . . . . .E5
St. Bride's, 473 . . . . .D5
St. Catherine's E5
St. George's, 1,354 . . . . . . .B5
St. John's, 99,182 . . . . .E5
St. Lawrence, 1,558 . . . . . .D5
St. Lewis, 290 . . . . .D3
St. Mary's, 505 . . . . .E5
St. Shotts, 144 . . . . .E5
Sally's Cove, 37 . . . . .C4
Salvage, 203 . . . . .E5
Seal Cove, 417 . . . . .C4
Ship Cove, 133 . . . . .D3
Snug Harbour D3
South Branch B5
South Brook, 578 . . . . .C4
Springdale, 3,045 . . . . .C4
Square Islands D3
Stephenville, 7,109 . . . . . . .B5
Summerford, 1,010 . . . . . .D4
Summerville, 541 . . . . .E5
Swift Current, 255 . . . . . . .D5
Terrenceville, 630 . . . . .D5
Torbay, 5,474 . . . . .E5
Trepassey, 889 . . . . .E5
Trinity East E5
Triton, 1,102 . . . . .D4
Trout River, 616 . . . . .B4
Twillingate, 2,611 . . . . .D4
Wabana, 2,679 . . . . .E5
Wabush, 1,894 . . . . .D4
Wesleyville E4
West St. Modeste, 175 . . . .C3
Whitbourne, 930 . . . . .E5
Williams Harbour, 61 . . . . . .D3
Williamsport C4
Wiltondale C4
Witless Bay, 1,056 . . . . .E5
Woody Point, 366 . . . . .C4
Wreck Cove D5

Other Features

Alexis, *river* C3
Avalon, *peninsula* E5
Belle, *island* C3
Belle Isle, *strait* C3
Big, *river* B2
Bonavista, *bay* E5
Burin, *peninsula* D5
Deep, *inlet* B1
Deer, *lake* C4
Eagle, *river* B2
Fortune, *bay* D5
George, *river* D3
Grand, *lake* C4
Grey, *river* C5
Gros Morne Natl. Park C4
Hamilton, *inlet* B2
Jeddore, *lake* D5
Jubilee, *lake* D5
Kikkertavak, *island* B2
L'Anse Aux Meadows Natl. Hist. Site D3
Lloyds, *river* C5
Long Range, *mts.* B5
Long Range, *mts.* C4
Mealy, *mts.* A3
Meelpaeg, *reservoir* C5
Melville, *lake* B2
North, *river* B2
Northwest Gander, *river* . . .D5
Notre Dame, *bay* D4
Paradise, *river* C3
Placentia, *bay* D5
Red Indian, *lake* C5
Round, *pond* C5
St. George's, *bay* B5
St. Lewis, *river* C3
St. Paul, *river* C3
Sandwich, *bay* C2
Sandy, *lake* C4
Smallwood, *reservoir* D3
S. Aulatsivik, *island* E3
Terra Nova Natl. Park D5
Torngat, *mts.* D3
Trinity, *bay* E5
Ungava, *bay* D3
White, *bay* C4

Northwest Territories

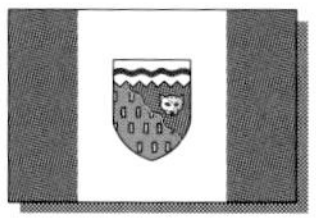

Capital: Yellowknife
Area: 501,574 sq. mi. 1,299,070 sq. km.
Population: 37,360 (2001 Census)
Largest City: Yellowknife, 16,541
Highest Point: Unnamed peak in Mackenzie Mts. 9,098 ft. 2,773 m.
Entered the Dominion: July 15, 1870
Floral Emblem: Mountain Avens

Northwest Territories: Map Index

Cities and Towns

Aklavik, 632 . . . . A3
Déline, 536 . . . . D3
Echo Bay. E3
Fort Good Hope, 549 . . . . . C3
Fort Liard, 530 . . . . D4
Fort McPherson, 761 . . . . . . B3
Fort Providence, 753 . . . . . . E4
Fort Resolution, 525. . . . . . . F4
Fort Simpson, 1,163 . . . . . . D4
Fort Smith, 2,185 . . . . F4
Hay River, 3,510 . . . . E4
Holman, 398. . . . . E2
Inuvik, 2,894. . . . . B3
Łutselkė, 248 . . . . F4
Mould Bay E1
Norman Wells, 666 . . . . C3
Parry D2
Paulatuk, 286 . . . . D3
Pine Point F4
Rae-Edzo, 1,552 . . . . E4
Reliance G4
Sachs Harbour, 114. . . . . . . C2
Tsiigehtchic, 195 . . . . B3
Tuktoyaktuk, 930. . . . . B3
Tulita, 473 . . . . C4
Tungsten C4
Wekweti, 131 . . . . F4
Wha Ti, 453 . . . . E4
Wrigley, 165. . . . . D4
Yellowknife, 16,541 . . . . F4

Other Features

Amundsen, *gulf*. C2
Anderson, *river* C3
Aulavik Natl. Park E2
Aylmer, *lake* G4
Banks, *island*. D2
Borden, *island* F1
Brock, *island* F1
Buffalo, *lake*. E4
Clinton Colden, *lake* G4
Contwoyto, *lake* G3
Coppermine, *river* F3
Dubawnt, *river* H4
Eglinton, *island* E1
Emerald, *island* F1
Gras, *lake* F4
Great Bear, *lake* D3
Great Slave, *lake* F4
Hay, *river*. E4
Hecla and Griper, *bay* F1
Highest Point in Northwest Territories C4
Horton, *river*. D3
Hottah, *lake*. E3
Kasba, *lake* H4
Keele, *river* C4
La Martre, *lake* E4
Liard, *river* D4
Lougheed, *island*. G1
MacKay, *lake* F4
Mackenzie King, *island*. F1
Mackenzie, *mts.* C4
Mackenzie, *river* B3, D4
M'Clure, *strait*. D2
Melville, *island*. F1
Nahanni, *river*. C4
Nahanni Natl. Park D4
Nonacho, *lake* G4
Point, *lake*. F3
Prince Albert, *peninsula* E2
Prince Patrick, *island* E1
Queen Elizabeth, *islands* H1
Slave, *river*. F4
Taltson, *river* F4
Tathlina, *lake*. E4
Thekulthili, *lake*. G4
Thelon, *river*. H4
Trout, *lake* D4
Tuktut Nogait Natl. Park . . . D3
Victoria, *island*. F2
Viscount Melville, *sound*. . . . F2
Wholdaia, *lake* H4
Wollaston, *peninsula*. E3
Wood Buffalo Natl. Park. . . . F4

Nunavut

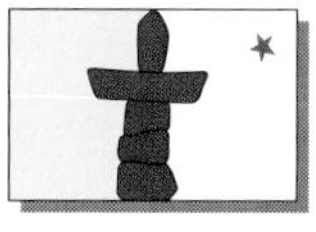

Capital: Iqaluit
Area: 769,888 sq. mi. 1,994,000 sq. km
Population: 26,745 (2001 Census)
Largest City: Iqaluit, 5,236
Highest Point: Barbeau Peak 8,583 ft. 2,616 m.
Entered the Dominion: April 1, 1999
Floral Emblem: Arctic Poppy

Nunavut: Map Index

Cities and Towns

Alert Q1
Arctic Bay, 646 . . . . L2
Arviat, 1,899. . . . . K4
Baker Lake, 1,507. . . . . J4
Cambridge Bay, 1,309 . . . . G3
Cape Dorset, 1,148 . . . . . . N4
Chesterfield Inlet, 345 . . . . K4
Clyde River, 785 . . . . P2
Coral Harbour, 712. . . . . . . N4
Gjoa Haven, 960 . . . . J3
Grise Fiord M1
Hall Beach, 609 . . . . M3
Igloolik, 1,286 . . . . M3
Iqaluit, 5,236 . . . . P4
Kimmirut O4
Kugluktuk, 1,212. . . . . E3
Nanisivik M2
Pangnirtung, 1,276 . . . . P3
Pelly Bay L3
Pond Inlet, 1,220 . . . . N2
Qikiqtarjuag Q3
Rankin Inlet, 2,177 . . . . K4
Repulse Bay, 612. . . . . L3
Resolute, 215. . . . . J2
Taloyoak, 720 . . . . K3
Whale Cove K4

Other Features

Aberdeen, *lake* H4
Air Force, *island* O3
Akpatok, *island* P4
Amadjuak, *lake*. O4
Amund Ringnes, *island* J1
Angikuni, *lake*. H4
Auyuittuq Natl. Park P3
Axel Heiberg, *island*. K1
Back, *river*. H3
Baffin, *bay*. P2
Baffin, *island* M2
Baffin, *region* N2
Baker, *lake* J4
Barbeau Peak, *mountain* . . . N1
Barnes, *ice cap* O3
Bathurst, *island*. J1
Big, *island* O4
Bjorne, *peninsula* L1
Bluenose, *lake* E3
Boothia, *gulf* K2
Boothia, *peninsula* K2
Borden, *peninsula*. M2
Brodfur, *peninsula* L2
Byam Martin, *channel* G1
Byam Martin, *island* H1
Bylot, *island* N2
Cameron, *island* H1
Coats, *island* M4
Coburg, *island* N1
Committee, *bay*. L3
Contwoyto, *lake* G3
Coppermine, *river* F3
Cornwall, *island*. K1
Cornwallis, *island* J1
Coronation, *gulf* F3
Cumberland, *peninsula* P3
Cumberland, *sound* P3
Davis, *strait*. R3
Devon, *island*. L1
Dubawnt, *lake* H4
Ellef Ringnes, *island*. H1
Ellesmere, *island*. M1
Ellesmere Island Natl. Park Reserve O1
Ellice, *river* G3
Ennadai, *lake* H4
Foxe, *basin*. N3
Foxe, *channel*. M3
Foxe, *peninsula* N4
Franklin, *strait* J2
Garry, *lake* H3
Gifford, *river*. M2
Graham, *island* K1
Greely, *fjord*. L1
Grinnell, *peninsula* J1
Hall, *peninsula*. P4
Hantzsch, *river* O3
Hudson, *bay* L4
Hudson, *strait*. O4
Jones, *sound* L1
Kaminak, *lake*. J4
Kane, *basin* P1
Kasba, *lake* H4
King William, *island* J3
Kitikmeot, *region*. G3
La Martre, *lake* E4
Liard, *river* D4
Lougheed, *island*. G1
MacAlpine, *lake* H3
Maclean, *strait* G1
Mansel, *island* M4
M'Clintock, *channel*. H2
Meighen, *island* J1
Melville, *island*. F1
Melville, *peninsula* M3
Meta Incognita, *peninsula*. P4
Napaktulik, *lake*. F3
Nares, *strait* O1
Nettilling, *lake* O3
Norwegian, *bay* K1
Nottingham, *island*. N4
Nueltin, *lake*. J4
Parry, *channel*. J2
Prince Albert, *hills* L3
Prince Charles, *island* N3
Prince of Wales, *island* J2
Prince Regent, *inlet* K2
Queen Elizabeth, *islands* H1
Queen Maude, *gulf*. H3
Raanes, *peninsula*. L1
Resolution, *island*. P4
Salisbury, *island* N4
Somerset, *island* K2
Southampton, *island* L4
South Henik, *lake*. J4
Stefanson, *island*. G2
Storkerson, *peninsula*. G2
Tehek, *lake*. J4
Thelon, *river*. H4, J4
Thlewiaza, *river*. J4
Ungava, *bay*. P5
Vansittart, *island*. M3
Victoria, *island*. F2
Viscount Melville, *sound* F2
White, *island* L3
Wollaston, *peninsula*. E3
Yathkyed, *lake* J4

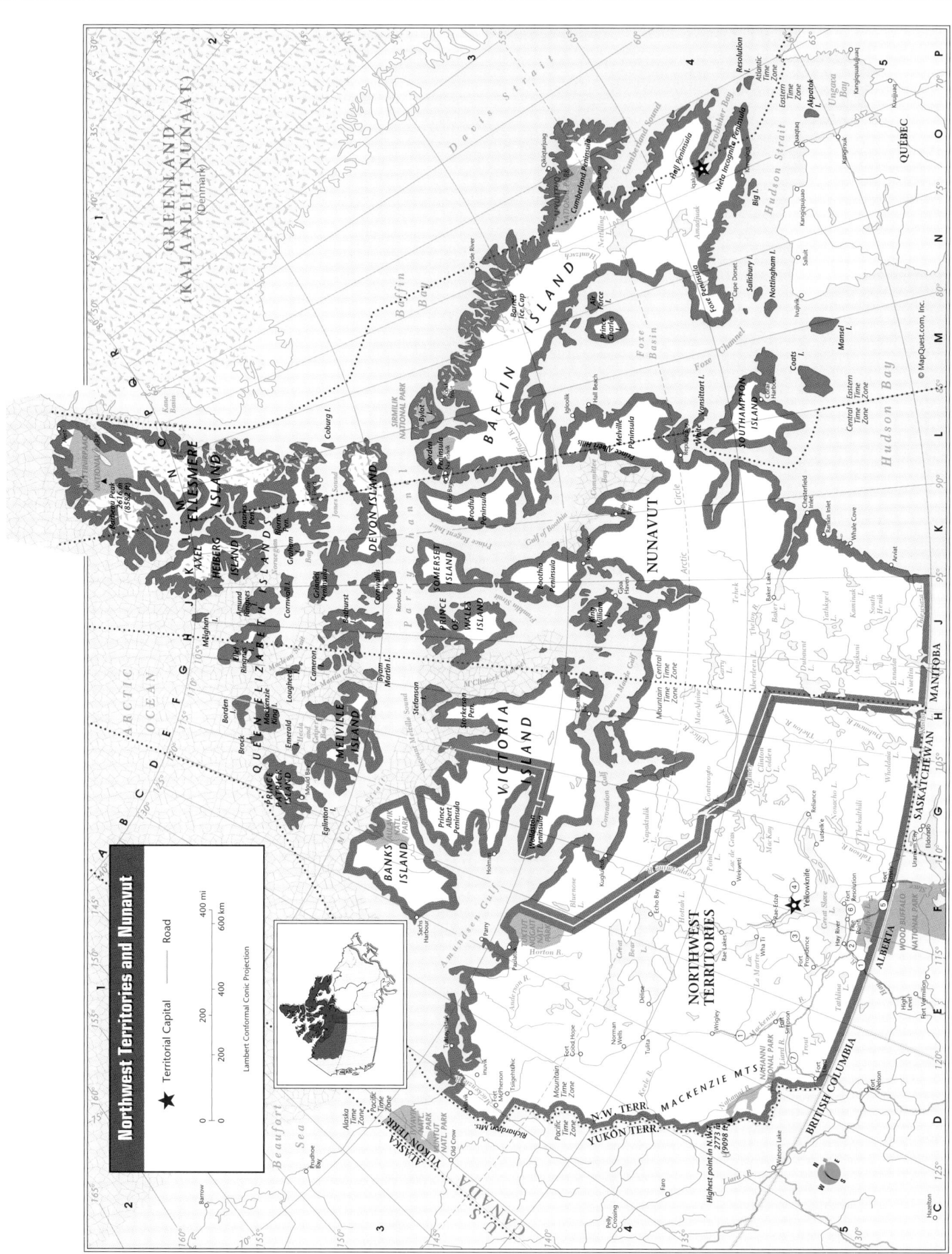

Northwest Territories and Nunavut

★ Territorial Capital
— Road

0   200   400   600 km
0   200   400 mi

Lambert Conformal Conic Projection

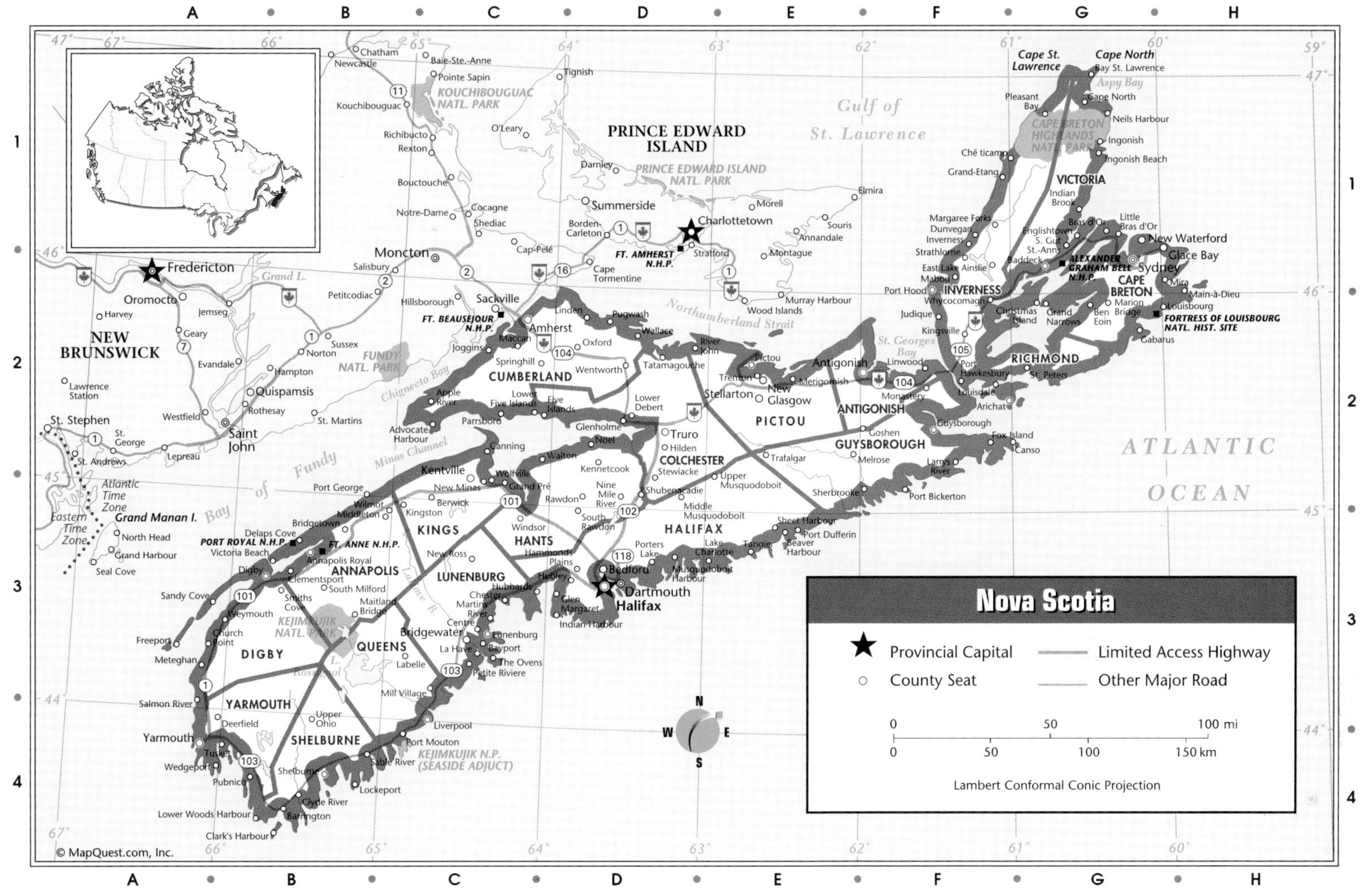

Nova Scotia

Capital:	Halifax
Area:	21,419 sq. mi.
	55,490 sq. km.
Population:	908,007 (2001 Census)
Largest City:	Halifax, 359,111
Highest Point:	Cape Breton Highlands
	1,745 ft.
	532 m.
Entered the Dominion:	July 1, 1867
Floral Emblem:	Mayflower

Nova Scotia: Map Index

Counties

Annapolis	B3
Antigonish	E1
Cape Breton	G1
Colchester	D2
Cumberland	C2
Digby	B3
Guysborough	E2
Halifax	D3
Hants	C3
Inverness	F1
Kings	C3
Lunenburg	C3
Pictou	E2
Queens	B3
Richmond	G2
Shelburne	B4
Victoria	G1
Yarmouth	B3

Cities and Towns

Advocate Harbour	C2
Amherst, 9,470	C2
Annapolis Royal, 550	B3
Antigonish, 4,754	F2
Apple River	C2
Arichat	F2
Baddeck, 907	G1
Barrington	B4
Bayport	C3
Bay St. Lawrence	G1
Beaver Harbour	E3
Bedford	D3
Ben Eoin	G2
Berwick, 2,282	C2
Bras d'Or	G1
Bridgetown, 1,035	B3
Bridgewater, 7,621	C3
Canning, 811	C2
Canso, 992	G2
Cape North	G1
Centre	C3
Chester, 1,590	C3
Chéticamp	G1
Christmas Island	G2
Church Point	A3
Clark's Harbour, 944	B4
Clementsport	B3
Clyde River	B4
Dartmouth	D3
Deerfield	A4
Delaps Cove	B3
Digby, 2,111	B3
Dunvegan	F1
East Lake Ainslie	F1
Englishtown	G1
Five Islands	C2
Fox Island	F2
Freeport, 345	A3
Gabarus	G2
Glace Bay, 21,187	H1
Glenholme	D2
Glen Margaret	D3
Goshen	F2
Grand-Etang	F1
Grand Narrows	G2
Grand Pré	C2
Guysborough, 462	F2
Halifax, 359,111	D3
Hammonds Plains	D3
Hilden	D2
Hubbards	C3
Hubley	D3
Indian Brook	G1
Indian Harbour	D3
Ingonish	G1
Ingonish Beach	G1
Inverness, 1,702	F1
Joggins	C2
Judique	F2
Kennetcook	D2
Kentville, 5,610	C2
Kingston, 3,009	C3
Kingsville	F2
Labelle	C3
La Have (La Have Islands)	C3
Lake Charlotte	E3
Larrys River	F2
Linden	D2
Linwood	F2
Little Bras d'Or	G1
Liverpool, 2,888	C3
Lockeport, 701	B4
Louisbourg, 1,071	H2
Louisdale	G2
Lower Debert	D2
Lower Five Islands	C2
Lower Woods Harbour	B4
Lunenburg, 2,568	C3
Mabou	F1
Maccan	C2
Main-à-Dieu	H1
Maitland Bridge	B3
Margaree Forks	F1
Marion Bridge	G2
Martins River	C3
Melrose	E2
Merigomish	E2
Meteghan	A3
Middle Musquodoboit	D2
Middleton, 1,744	B3
Mill Village	C3
Mira	H1
Monastery	F2
Musquodoboit Harbour	D3
Neils Harbour	G1
New Glasgow, 9,432	E2
New Minas	C2
New Ross	C3
New Waterford, 10,185	G1
Nine Mile River	D2
Noel	D2
Oxford, 1,332	D2
Parrsboro, 1,529	C2
Petite Riviere	C3
Pictou, 3,875	E2
Pleasant Bay	G1
Port Bickerton	F2
Port Dufferin	E3
Porters Lake	D3
Port George	B2
Port Hawkesbury, 3,701	F2
Port Hood	F1
Port Mouton	C4
Pubnico	B4
Pugwash, 810	D2
Rawdon	D2
River John	D2
Sable River	B4
St. Peters	G2
Salmon River, 2,259	A3
Sandy Cove	A3
Sheet Harbour	E3
Shelburne, 2,013	B4
Sherbrooke	E2
Shubenacadie, 906	D2
Smiths Cove (Smiths Cove Station)	B3
So. Gut St.-Anns	G1
South Milford	B3
South Rawdon	C2
Springhill, 4,091	C2
Stellarton, 4,809	E2
Stewiacke, 1,388	D2
Strathlorne	F1
Sydney, 33,913	G1
Tangier	E2
Tatamagouche, 738	D2
The Ovens	C3
Trafalgar	D2
Trenton, 2,798	E2
Truro, 11,457	D2
Tusket	B4
Upper Musquodoboit	E2
Upper Ohio	B4
Victoria Beach	B3
Wallace	D2
Walton	C2
Wedgeport, 1,217	A4
Wentworth	D2
Weymouth	A3
Whycocomagh	F2
Wilmot	B3
Windsor, 3,778	C3
Wolfville, 3,658	C2
Yarmouth, 7,561	A4

Other Features

Alexander Graham Bell Natl. Hist. Park	G1
Aspy, bay	G1
Cape Breton Highlands Natl. Park	G1
Chignecto, bay	C2
Ft. Anne Natl. Hist. Park	B3
Fortress of Louisbourg Natl. Hist. Park	H2
Fundy, bay	A3
Kejimkujik Natl. Park	B3
Kejimkujik Natl. Park (Seaside Adjunct)	C4
Lahave, river	C3
Minas, channel	C2
North, cape	G1
Northumberland, strait	D2
Port Royal Natl. Hist. Park	B3
Rossignol, lake	B3
St. Georges, bay	F2
St. Lawrence, cape	G1

© MapQuest.com, Inc.

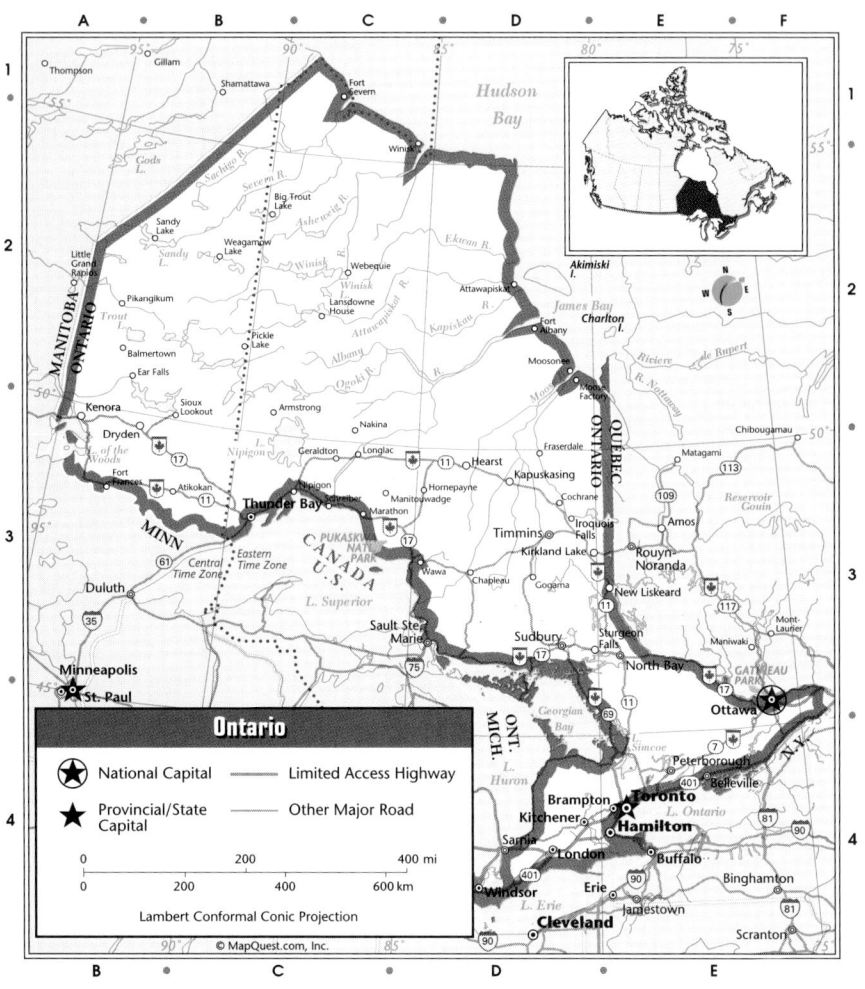

Ontario

Capital: Toronto
Area: 412,472 sq. mi.
1,068,580 sq. km.
Population: 11,410,046 (2001 Census)
Largest City: Toronto, 2,481,494
Highest Point: Timiskaming District 2,274 ft. 693 m.
Entered the Dominion: July 1, 1867
Floral Emblem: White Trillium

Ontario:
Map Index

Cities and Towns

Armstrong, 250 . . . . .C2
Atikokan, 3,560 . . . . .B3
Attawapiskat, 1,293 . .D2
Balmertown B2
Belleville, 45,986 . . . .E4
Big Trout Lake C2
Brampton, 325,428 . . .E4
Chapleau, 2,832 . . . . .D3
Cochrane, 5,690 . . . . .D3
Dryden, 8,198 . . . . . .B3
Ear Falls B2
Fort Albany D2
Fort Frances, 8,315 . . .B3
Fort Severn C1
Fraserdale D2
Geraldton, 2,224 . . . .C3
Gogama, 467 . . . . . . .D3
Hamilton, 490,268 . . .E4
Hearst, 5,825 . . . . . . .D3
Hornepayne, 1,312 . .C3
Iroquois Falls, 5,217 . .D3
Kapuskasing, 9,238 . .D3
Kenora, 15,838 . . . . .B3
Kirkland Lake, 8,616 . .D3
Kitchener, 190,399 . .D4
Lansdowne House,
270 . . . . .C2
London, 336,539 . . . .D4
Longlac, 1,748 . . . . . .C3
Manitouwadge, 2,949 C3
Marathon, 4,416 . . . .C3
Moose Factory, 1,950 D2
Moosonee, 936 . . . . .D2
Nakina C3
New Liskeard, 4,906 . .E3
Nipigon, 1,964 . . . . . .C3
North Bay, 52,771 . . .E3
Ottawa, 774,072 . . . .E3
Peterborough, 71,446 E4
Pickle Lake B2

Pikangikum B2
Sandy Lake B2
Sarnia, 70,876 . . . . . .D4
Sault Ste. Marie,
74,566 . . . . .D3
Schreiber C3
Sioux Lookout, 5,336 .B2
Sturgeon Falls, 5,978 .D3
Sudbury, 103,879 . . .D3
Thunder Bay, 109,016 C3
Timmins, 43,686 . . . .D3
Toronto, 2,481,494 . .E4
Wawa, 3,279 . . . . . . .D3
Weagamow Lake B2
Webequie, 600 . . . . .C2
Windsor, 208,402 . . .D4
Winisk C1

Other Features

Albany, river C2
Asheweig, river C2
Attawapiskat, river . . .C2
Ekwan, river D2
Erie, lake D4
Georgian, bay D3
Hudson, bay D1
Huron, lake D4
James, bay D2
Kapiskau, river D2
Moose, river D2
Nipigon, lake C3
Ogoki, river C2
Ontario, lake E4
Pukaskwa Natl. Park . .C3
Sachigo, river B2
Sandy, lake B2
Severn, river B2
Simcoe, lake E4
Superior, lake C3
Trout, lake B2
Winisk, lake C2
Winisk, river C2
Woods, lake B3

Southern Ontario:
Map Index

Counties

Algoma B1
Brant E4
Bruce D3
Dufferin E3
Durham G3
Elgin D5
Essex C5
Frontenac J3
Grenville and
Leeds K3
Grey E3
Haldimand-Norfolk E5
Haliburton G2
Halton F4
Hamilton-
Wentworth F4
Hastings H3
Huron D4
Kent C5
Lambton C5
Lanark J2
Lennox and
Addington H2
Manitoulin C2
Middlesex D4
Muskoka F2
Niagara F4
Nipissing G2
Northumberland . . .G3
Ottawa-
Carleton G5, K2
Oxford E4
Parry Sound E2
Peel F4, J5
Perth D4
Peterborough G3
Prescott and
Russel K2
Prince Edward H3
Regional Municipality
of Sudbury D1
Renfrew H2
Simcoe F3
Stormont, Dundas,
and Glengarry L2
Sudbury D1
Victoria G3
Waterloo E4

Wellington E4
York F4, J5

Cities and Towns

Acton, 7,767 . . . . . . .E4
Adolphustown . . .H3
Ahmic Harbour . . .F2
Ajax, 73,753 . . . . . .G4
Alban, 1,084 . . . . . . .E1
Alexandria, 3,369 . .L2
Alfred, 1,348 . . . . . . .L2
Allenford D3
Alliston (Alliston,
Beeton, Tecumseth,
and Tottenham),
9,679 . . . . .F3
Almonte, 4,659 . . . .J2
Alvinston D5
Amberley D3
Amherstburg,
20,339 . . . . . . .B5
Angus, 9,722 . . . . .F3
Apsley G3
Ardbeg E2
Argyle F3
Arkona, 598 . . . . . . .D4
Arnprior, 7,192 . . . .J2
Arthur, 2,284 . . . . . .E4
Aurora, 40,167 . . . .F3
Aylmer, 7,126 . . . . .E5
Bailieboro G3
Bainsville L2
Bala F2
Bancroft, 4,089 . . . .H2
Bannockburn H3
Barrie, 103,710 . . . .F3
Barry's Bay, 1,259 . .H2
Bayfield, 909 . . . . . .D4
Beaverton, 3,065 . . .F3
Belleville, 45,986 . . .H3
Birch Cliff K5
Blenheim, 4,795 . . .D5
Blind River, 3,969 . .C1
Bloomfield, 643 . . . .H4
Blossom Park H6
Blyth, 987 . . . . .D4
Bobcaygeon,
2,854 . . . . .G3
Bolton, 20,553 . . . . .F4
Bracebridge,
13,751 . . . . . . .F2
Bramalea H5

Brampton,
325,428 . . . . . . .F4
Brantford, 86,417 . .E4
Brighton, 9,449 . .H3
Britt, 367 . . . . .E2
Brockville, 21,375 . .K3
Bruce Mines, 627 . .B1
Brussels, 1,143 . . . .D4
Burk's Falls, 940 . . .F2
Burlington,
150,836 . . . . . . .F4
Buttonville K5
Calabogie J2
Caledon E4
Caledonia, 8,582 . .F4
Cambridge,
110,372 . . . . . .E4
Capreol, 3,471 . . . .D1
Cardinal, 1,739 . . . .K3
Carleton Place,
9,083 . . . . .J2
Carnarvon G2
Cartier, 332 . . . . . . .D1
Casselman, 2,910 . .K2
Chatham, 44,156 . .C5
Chatsworth, 517 . .E3
Chesley, 1,880 . . .D3
City View G6
Clear Creek E5
Clifford, 792 . . . . . . .E4
Clinton, 3,117 . . . . .D4
Cloyne H3
Cobden H2
Cobourg, 17,172 . . .G4
Coe Hill H3
Collingwood,
16,039 . . . . . . .E3
Combermere H2
Consecon, 1,449 . . .H3
Cookstown, 1,449 . .F3
Cornwall, 45,640 . . .L2
Deep River, 4,135 . .H1
Delhi, 4,002 . . . . . . .E5
Denbigh H2
Desberats B1
Deseronto, 1,796 . . .H3
Deux Rivieres G1
Dresden, 2,582 . . .C5
Dunnville, 5,686 . . .F4
Durham, 2,709 . . . .E3
East York K5
Echo Bay A1
Eganville, 1,230 . . . .H2
Elliot Lake, 11,956 .C1
Elmira, 8,155 . . . . . .E4
Elmvale, 2,176 . . . . .F3
Espanola, 5,449 . . .D1
Essex, 20,085 . . . . .C5
Estaire E1
Etobicoke J5
Evansville C2
Exeter, 4,452 . . . . . .D4
Fenelon Falls,
1,874 . . . . .G3
Fergus, 16,732 . . . .E4
Field E1
Flesherton, 617 . . . .E3
Forest, 2,857 . . . . . .D4
Fort Erie, 28,143 . . .F5
Frankford, 2,487 . . .H3
French River E1
Gananoque, 5,167 . .J3
Glencoe, 2,152 . . . .D5
Gloucester K2
Goderich, 7,604 . . .D4
Godfrey J3
Golden Lake H2
Gore Bay, 898 . . . . .C2
Grand Bend, 1,949 D4
Grand Valley,
1,757 . . . . .E4
Gravenhurst,
10,899 . . . . . . .F3
Guelph, 106,170 . .E4
Haldimand F5
Haliburton G2
Halton Hills F4
Hamilton, 490,268 . .F4
Hanover, 6,869 . . . .D3
Hardwood Lake H2
Hastings, 1,208 . . . .H3
Havelock, 1,328 . . . .H3
Hawkesbury,
10,314 . . . . . . .L2

Hensall, 1,194 . . .D4
Hilton Beach, 174 . .B1
Huntsville, 17,338 . .F2
Ingleside K3
Innisfil F3
Iron Bridge, 686 . .B1
Islington J6
Jarvis, 2,180 . . . . . .E5
Kagawong C2
Kaladar H3
Kanata, 70,320 . . .K2
Kearney, 773 . . . .F2
Kemptville, 4,004 . .K2
Killaloe, 661 . . . . . .H2
Killarney, 428 . . . . .D1
Kimberley E3
Kincardine, 6,410 . .D3
Kingston, 114,195 . .J3
Kingsville, 19,619 . .C5
Kinloss D3
Kinmount G3
Kiosk G1
Kirkfield G3
Kitchener, 190,399 E4
Kleinburg J5
Lakefield, 2,734 . . .G3
Lake St. Peter G2
Lanark, 869 . . . . . . .J2
Lancaster, 797 . . . .L2
Langstaff K5
Langton E5
Lansdowne J3
Leamington,
27,138 . . . . . . .C5
Leitrim H6
Levack D1
Lindsay, 17,757 . . . .G3
Lions Head, 500 . .D3
Listowel, 5,905 . . . .E4
Little Current,
1,564 . . . . .D2
Lombardy J3
London, 336,539 . .D5
L'Orignal, 2,033 . . .L2
Lucknow, 1,207 . .D4
Maberly J3
Mackey H1
Mac Tier F2
Madawaska, 407 . .G2
Madoc, 1,730 . . . . .H3
Magnetawan, 244 . .F2
Malton J5
Manitowaning D2
Manor Park H5
Maple J5
Markham,
208,615 . . . .F4, K5
Markstay E1
Marmora, 1,589 . . .H3
Marten River F1
Massey C1
Mattawa, 2,270 . . .G1
Maynooth H2
McKerrow D1
Meaford, 4,559 . . .E3
Meldrum Bay B2
Metcalfe, 1,610 . . .K2
Midland, 16,214 . .F3
Miller Lake D2
Milliken K5
Milton, 31,471 . . . .F4
Milverton, 1,707 . . .E4
Mimico J6
Mindemoya D2
Minden G3
Miner's Bay G3
Mississauga,
612,925 . . . .F4, J6
Mitchell, 4,181 . . . .D4
Morpeth D5
Morrisburg, 2,583 . .K3
Mt. Forest, 4,584 . .E4
Nanticoke E5
Napanee, 7,760 . . .J3
Nepean, G6, K2
Newboro, 309 . . . .J3
New Hamburg,
7,003 . . . . .E4
Newmarket,
65,788 . . . . . . .F3
Niagara Falls,
78,815 . . . . . . .F4
Niagara-on-the-Lake,
13,839 . . . . . . .F4

Nipissing F1
Norland G3
North Bay, 52,771 .F1
North York K5
Norwich, 2,510 . . . .E4
Oakville, 144,738 . .F4
Omemee, 1,319 . .G3
Orangeville,
25,248 . . . . . . .E4
Orillia, 29,121 . . . .F3
Oshawa, 139,051 .G4
Ottawa,
774,072 . . .H5, K2
Owen Sound,
21,431 . . . . . . .E3
Palmerston, 2,518 . .E4
Paris, 9,881 . . . . . . .E4
Parkhill, 1,752 . . . . .D4
Parry Sound, 6,124 E2
Pembroke, 13,490 . .H2
Penetanguishene,
8,316 . . . . .F3
Perth, 6,003 . . . . . .J3
Petawawa, 14,398 H2
Peterborough,
71,446 . . . . . . .G3
Petrolia, 4,849 . . . .C5
Pickering, 87,139 . .F4
Picton, 4,563 . . . .H3
Plantagenet, 1,103 K2
Plevna J3
Pointe au Baril E2
Port Bruce E5
Port Burwell E5
Port Colborne,
18,450 . . . . . . .F5
Port Elgin, 6,766 . . .D3
Port Franks D4
Port Hope, 11,718 G4
Port Loring E2
Port Perry, 7,244 . .G3
Port Rowan E5
Port Stanley, 2,521 D5
Powassan, 3,252 . .F1
Prescott, 4,228 . . . .K3
Providence Bay . . .C2
Ranger Lake B1
Rayside-Balfour . . .D1
Redbridge F1
Renfrew, 7,942 . . . .J2
Restoule, 415 . . . . .F1
Rexdale J5
Richards Landing . .A1
Richmond Hill,
132,030 . . . .F4, K5
Rockcliffe Park H5
Rockland, 8,542 . . .K2
Rodney, 1,102 . . . .D5
Rolphton H1
Round Lake Centre H2
Rutherglen F1
St. Catharines,
129,170 . . . . . .F4
St. Marys, 6,293 . . .D4
St. Thomas,
33,236 . . . . . . .D5
Sarnia (Sarnia-
Clearwater),
70,876 . . . . . . .C5
Sauble Beach D3
Sault Ste. Marie . . .A1
Scarborough . .F4, L5
Seaforth, 2,692 . . . .D4
Searchmont, 365 . .A1
Sebright F3
Seeley's Bay J3
Sharbot Lake J3
Sheguianda D2
Shelburne, 4,122 . .E3
Simcoe, 14,175 . . .E5
Skead E1
Smiths Falls, 9,140 .J3
Smithville, 3,317 . . .F4
Sombra C5
Southampton,
3,360 . . . . .D3
South Baymouth . .C2
South River, 1,040 .F1
Spanish C1
Spragge C1
Spring Bay C2
Stayner, 3,885 . . . .E3
Stirling, 2,149 . . . . .H3
Stonecliffe H1
Stoney Creek F4
Stoney Point,
1,316 . . . . .C5
Stratford, 29,676 . .D4
Strathroy, 12,805 . .D5
Sturgeon Falls,
5,978 . . . . .E1
Sudbury, 103,879 . .E1
Sunderland F3
Sundridge, 983 . . . .F2
Sutton West F3
Teeswater, 1,109 . .D3
Tehkummah D2
Thamesville, 928 . .D5
Thedford, 755 . . . .D4
Thessalon, 1,386 . .A1
Thornhill K5
Thorold, 18,048 . . .F4
Tilbury, 4,599 . . . . .C5
Tillsonburg,
14,052 . . . . . . .E5
Tiverton, 743 . . . . .D3

Toronto,
2,481,494 . .F4, K5
Tory Hill G3
Trenton H3
Trout Creek, 591 . .F1
Tweed, 1,539 . . . . .H3
Vanier H5
Vaughan, 182,022 .J5
Verner E1
Verona J3
Walden D1
Walkerton, 4,970 . .D3
Wallaceburg,
11,114 . . . . . . .C5
Walton D4
Warren E1
Wasaga Beach,
12,419 . . . . . . .F3
Washago F3
Waterloo, 86,543 . .E4
Watford, 1,625 . . . .D5
Webbwood, 507 . . .D1
Welland, 48,402 . . .F4
Weston J5
Westport J3
Wheatley, 1,920 . . .C5
Whitby, 87,413 . . . .G4
Whitefish Falls,
273 . . . . .D1
White Lake J2
Whitney G2
Wiarton, 2,349 . . . .D3
Wilberforce G2
Winchester, 2,427 .K2
Windermere F2
Windsor, 208,402 . .C5
Wingham, 2,885 . . .D4
Woodbridge J5
Woodstock, 33,061 E4
York K5

Other Features

Algonquin Prov.
Park G2
Allumette, lake H2
Bark, lake H2
Bays, lake F2
Big Gull, lake J3
Bon Echo
Prov. Park H3
Bruce Peninsula
Natl. Park D2
Cockburn, island . .B2
Erie, lake E5
Fathom Five Natl.
Marine Park C2
French, river E1
Frontenac Prov.
Park J3
Garden, river A1
Georgian, bay E2
Georgian Bay Islands
Natl. Park F3
Grundy Lake Prov.
Park E2
Huron, lake C4
Killarney Prov. Park D1
Loughborough,
lake J3
Manitoulin, island . .C2
Mattawa River Prov.
Park F1
Mississippi, lake . . .J2
Muskoka, lake F2
Nipissing, lake F1
North, channel C1
Ontario, lake . .H4, K6
Opeongo, lake G2
Ottawa, river
. . . . . . .G1, G5 H5, K2
Pelee, island C6
Pigeon, lake G3
Point Pelee Natl.
Park C6
Ranger, lake B1
Rice, lake G3
Rideau, lake J3
Rideau, river H6
Rocky Island, lake . .C1
Rondeau Prov. Park D5
Rosseau, lake F2
St. Clair, lake C5
St. Clair, river C5
St. Joseph, island . .B1
St. Lawrence, river . K3
St. Lawrence Islands
Natl. Park J3
Scugog, lake F3
Simcoe, lake F3
Temagami, lake . . .E1
Thames, river D5
Tomiko, lake F1
Toronto Islands
Park K6
Wakomata, lake . . .B1
Wanapitei, lake . . .E1
Whitefish, bay A1

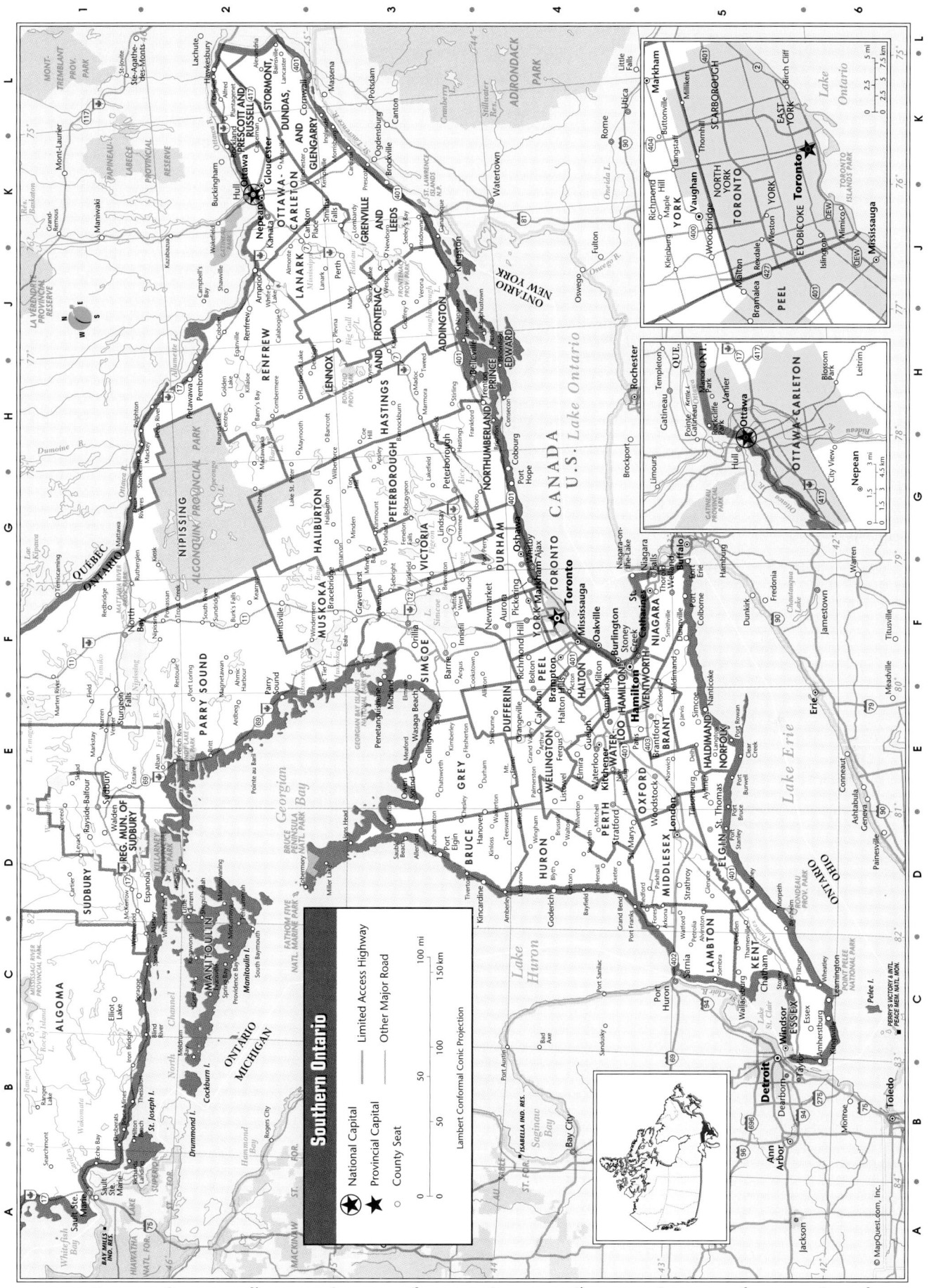

Southern Ontario

National Capital ⊛
Provincial Capital ★
County Seat ○

Limited Access Highway
Other Major Road

100 mi
150 km

Lambert Conformal Conic Projection

© MapQuest.com, Inc.

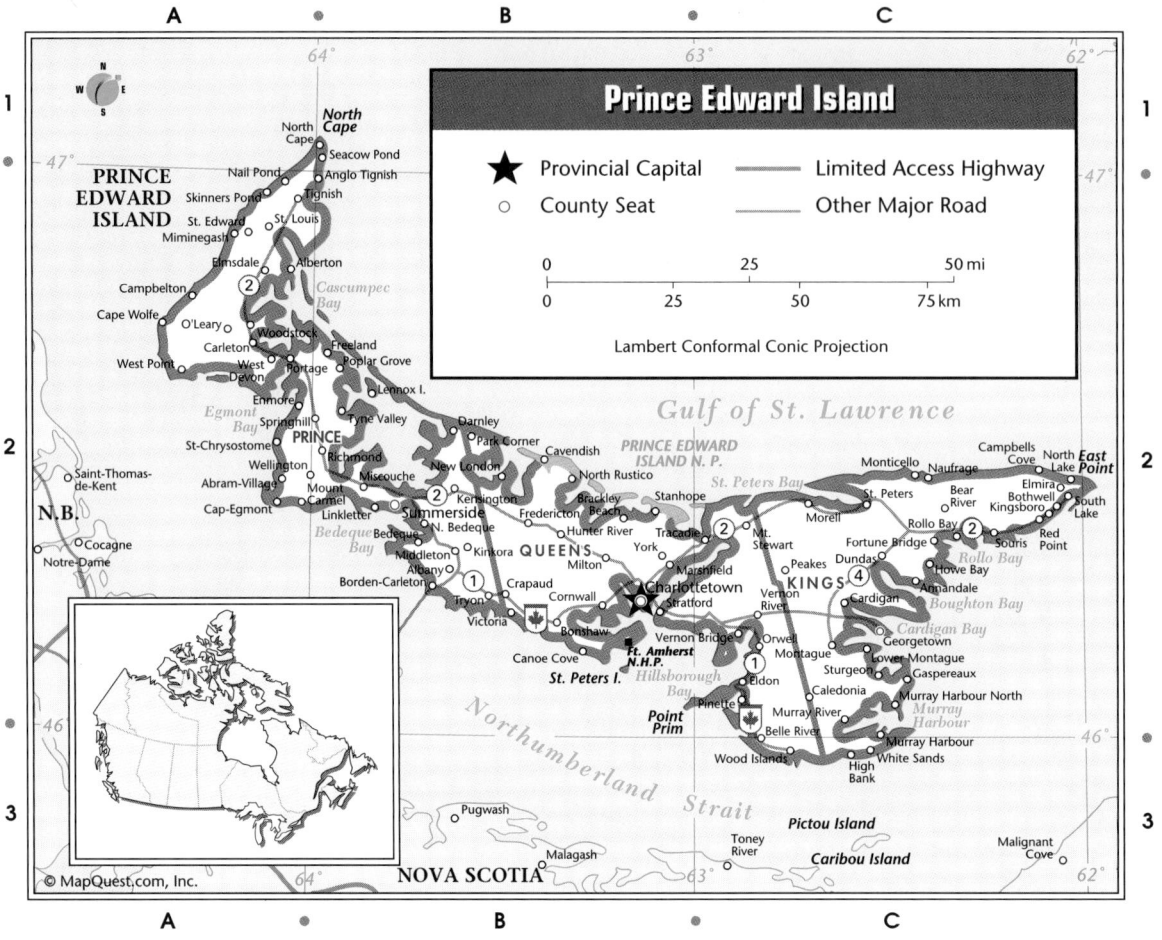

Prince Edward Island

Capital:	Charlottetown
Area:	2,185 sq. mi.
	5,660 sq. km.
Population:	135,294 (2001 Census)
Largest City:	Charlottetown, 32,245
Highest Point:	Queens County
	466 ft.
	142 m.
Entered the Dominion:	July 1, 1873
Floral Emblem:	Lady's Slipper

Prince Edward Island:
Map Index

Counties

Kings C2
Prince A2
Queens B2

Cities and Towns

Abram-Village, 342 . . . . . . A2
Albany B2
Alberton, 1,115 . . . . A2
Anglo Tignish A2
Annandale C2
Bear River C2

Bedeque, 154 . . . . B2
Belle River C3
Bonshaw B2
Borden, 798 . . . . B2
Bothwell C2
Brackley Beach B2
Caledonia C2
Campbells Cove C2
Campbelton A2
Canoe Cove B2
Cap-Egmont A2
Cape Wolfe A2
Cardigan, 382 . . . . C2
Carleton A2
Cavendish, 267 . . . . B2
Charlottetown, 32,245 . . . . B2
Cornwall, 4,412 . . . . B2

Crapaud, 382 . . . . B2
Darnley B2
Dundas C2
Eldon C2
Elmira C2
Elmsdale A2
Enmore A2
Fortune Bridge C2
Fredericton B2
Freeland B2
Gaspereaux C2
Georgetown, 721 . . . . C2
High Bank C3
Howe Bay C2
Hunter River, 354 . . . . B2
Kensington, 1,385 . . . . B2
Kingsboro C2
Kinkora, 315 . . . . B2
Lennox Island B2
Linkletter, 332 . . . . B2
Lower Montague C2
Marshfield B2
Middleton B2
Milton B2
Miminegash, 188 . . . . A2
Miscouche, 766 . . . . B2
Montague, 1,945 . . . . C2
Monticello C2
Morell, 332 . . . . C2
Mount Carmel A2
Mt. Stewart, 312 . . . . C2
Murray Harbour, 357 . . . . . C3
Murray Harbour North C2
Murray River, 435 . . . . C2

Nail Pond A2
Naufrage C2
New London B2
North Bedeque B2
North Cape B1
North Lake C2
North Rustico, 637 . . . . B2
O'Leary, 860 . . . . A2
Orwell C2
Park Corner B2
Peakes C2
Pinette C2
Poplar Grove B2
Portage A2
Red Point C2
Richmond B2
Rollo Bay C2
St.-Chrysostome A2
St. Edward A2
St. Louis, 98 . . . . A2
St. Peters C2
Seacow Pond B1
Skinners Pond A2
Souris, 1,248 . . . . C2
South Lake C2
Southport B2
Springhill B2
Stanhope B2
Sturgeon C2
Summerside, 14,654 . . . . . B2
Tignish, 831 . . . . A2
Tracadie B2
Tryon B2
Tyne Valley, 223 . . . . B2

Vernon Bridge C2
Vernon River C2
Victoria, 119 . . . . B2
Wellington, 382 . . . . A2
West Devon A2
West Point A2
White Sands C3
Wood Islands C3
Woodstock A2
York B2

Other Features

Bedeque, *bay* B2
Boughton, *bay* C2
Cardigan, *bay* C2
Cascumpec, *bay* B2
East, *point* C2
Egmont, *bay* A2
Ft. Amherst N.H.P. B2
Hillsborough, *bay* B2
Murray, *harbour* C2
North, *cape* B1
Northumberland,
   strait B3
Prim, *point* B2
Prince Edward Island
   Natl. Park B2
Rollo, *bay* C2
St. Lawrence, *gulf* C2
St. Peters, *bay* C2
St. Peters, *island* B2

Québec

Capital: Québec City
Area: 594,702 sq. mi.
1,540,680 sq. km.
Population: 7,237,479 (2001 Census)
Largest City: Montréal, 1,039,534
Highest Point: Mt. d'Iberville
5,420 ft.
1,652 m.
Entered the Dominion: July 1, 1867
Floral Emblem: Iris

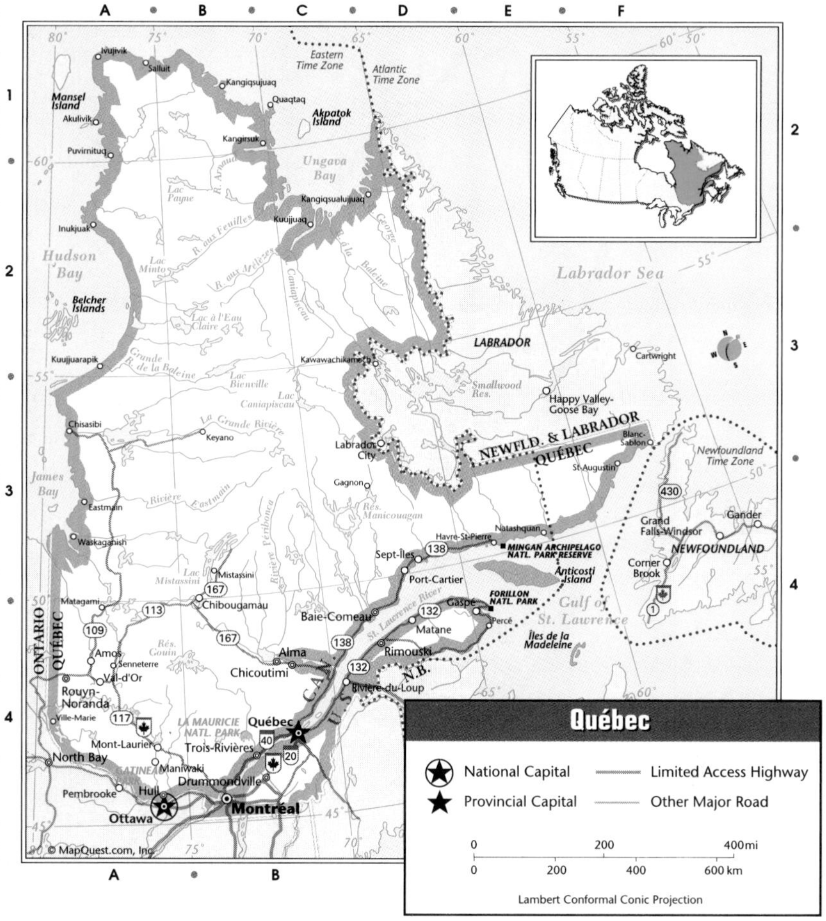

Eastern Time Zone
Atlantic Time Zone
Hudson Bay
James Bay
Ungava Bay
Labrador Sea
Gulf of St. Lawrence
LABRADOR
NEWFOUNDLAND
NEWFLD. & LABRADOR
QUÉBEC
ONTARIO
Newfoundland Time Zone
Ivujivik
Salluit
Kangiqsujuaq
Quaqtaq
Akpatok Island
Mansel Island
Akulivik
Kangirsuk
Puvirnituq
Kangiqsualujjuaq
Kuujjuaq
Inukjuak
Belcher Islands
Kuujjuarapik
Kawawachikamach
Cartwright
Happy Valley-Goose Bay
Smallwood Res.
Chisasibi
Keyano
Labrador City
Blanc-Sablon
St-Augustin
Gagnon
Eastmain
Waskaganish
Rés. Manicouagan
Natashquan
Havre-St-Pierre
MINGAN ARCHIPELAGO NATL. PARK RESERVE
Sept-Îles
Port-Cartier
Anticosti Island
Grand Falls-Windsor
Gander
Corner Brook
Mistassini
Lac Mistassini
Chibougamau
Matagami
Baie-Comeau
Gaspé
FORILLON NATL. PARK
Percé
Matane
Îles de la Madeleine
Rimouski
Amos
Senneterre
Val-d'Or
Chicoutimi
Alma
Rouyn-Noranda
Rivière-du-Loup
Ville-Marie
LA MAURICIE NATL. PARK
Québec
Mont-Laurier
Trois-Rivières
North Bay
Maniwaki
Drummondville
Pembrooke
Hull
Ottawa
Montréal
U.S.A.
N.B.
© MapQuest.com, Inc.
Québec
National Capital
Provincial Capital
Limited Access Highway
Other Major Road
0 200 400mi
0 200 400 600 km
Lambert Conformal Conic Projection

Québec: Map Index

Cities and Towns

Akulivik A1
Alma, 25,918 ..... B4
Amos, 13,044 ..... A4
Baie-Comeau, 23,079 ..... C4
Blanc-Sablon, 1,201 ..... E3
Chibougamau, 7,922 ..... B3
Chicoutimi, 60,008 ..... B4
Chisasibi, 3,467 ..... A3
Drummondville, 46,599 ..... B4
Eastmain A3
Gagnon C3
Gaspé, 14,932 ..... D4
Havre-St-Pierre, 3,291 ..... D3
Hull, 66,246 ..... A4
Inukjuak A2
Ivujivik, 298 ..... A1
Kangiqsualujjuaq C2
Kangiqsujuaq B1
Kangirsuk B1
Kawawachikamach C2
Keyano B3
Kuujjuaq, 1,932 ..... C2
Kuujjuarapik, 555 ..... A2
Maniwaki, 3,571 ..... A4
Matagami, 1,939 ..... A4
Matane, 11,635 ..... C4
Mistassini, 1,814 ..... B3
Mont-Laurier, 7,365 ..... A4
Montréal, 1,039,534 ..... B4
Natashquan D3
Percé, 3,614 ..... D4
Port-Cartier, 6,412 ..... C3
Povungnituk A1
Quantaq C1
Québec, 169,076 ..... B4
Rimouski, 31,305 ..... C4
Rivière du Loup, 17,772 ..... C4
Rouyn-Noranda, 28,270 ..... A4
St-Augustin, 626 ..... E3
Salluit, 1,072 ..... A1
Senneterre, 3,275 ..... A4
Sept-Iles, 23,791 ..... C3
Trois-Rivières, 46,264 ..... B4
Val-d'Or, 22,748 ..... A4
Ville-Marie, 2,770 ..... A4
Waskaganish, 1,699 ..... A3

Other Features

Anticosti, *island* D4
Arnaud, *river* B2
Baleine, *river* C2
Bienville, *lake* B2
Caniapiscau, *lake* C3
Caniapiscau, *river* C2
Eastmain, *river* B3
Feuilles, *river* B2
Forillon Natl. Park D4
Gatineau, *park* A4
George, *river* C2
Gouin, *reservoir* A4
Grande Baleine, *river* A2
Hudson, *bay* A2
James, *bay* A3
La Grande, *river* B3
La Mauricie Natl. Park B4
l'Eau Claire, *lake* B2
Manicouagan, *reservoir* C3
Mélèzes, *river* B2
Mingan Archipelago Natl. Park Reserve D3
Minto, *lake* B2
Mistassini, *lake* B3
Payne, *lake* B2
Péribonca, *river* B3
Saint Lawrence, *gulf* D4
Saint Lawrence, *river* C4
Ungava, *bay* C2

Southern Québec: Map Index

Cities and Towns

Acton Vale, 7,299 ..... D6
Alma, 25,918 ..... E3
Amqui, 6,473 ..... J3
Anjou, 38,015 ..... J5
Asbestos, 6,580 ..... E6
Ayer's Cliff, 1,102 ..... D6
Aylmer, 36,085 ..... A6
Baie-Comeau, 23,079 ..... H2
Baie-des-Sables, 654 ..... J3
Baie-Ste-Catherine, 273 ..... G3
Baie-St-Paul, 7,290 ..... F4
Barachois M3
Beauceville, 6,261 ..... F5
Beaulac E6
Beauport, 72,813 ..... L5
Beaupré, 2,761 ..... F4
Bécancour, 11,051 ..... D5
Bedford, 2,667 ..... D6
Beloeil C6
Bernières K6
Berthierville, 3,939 ..... C5
Betsiamites, 1,625 ..... H3
Blainville, 36,029 ..... H5
Boilleau F3
Bois-des-Filion H5
Bonaventure, 2,756 ..... L3
Boucherville J5
Bromptonville, 5,571 ..... E6
Brossard, 65,026 ..... J6
Buckingham, 11,668 ..... A6
Cabano, 3,213 ..... H4
Cacouna G4
Candiac J6
Cap-aux-Os M3
Cap-Chat, 2,913 ..... K2
Cap-de-la-Madeleine, 32,534 ..... D5
Caplan, 2,010 ..... L3
Cap-Rouge, 13,700 ..... K6
Cap-St-Ignace, 3,204 ..... F4
Carleton, 4,010 ..... K3
Caspascal, 2,634 ..... J3
Chambord, 1,693 ..... D3
Champlain, 1,623 ..... D5
Chandler, 2,817 ..... M3
Charlesbourg, 70,310 ..... E5, L5
Charny, 10,507 ..... E5, K6
Châteauguay, 41,003 ..... C6, H6
Chénéville, 738 ..... A6
Chibougamau, 7,922 ..... B2
Chicoutimi, 60,008 ..... E3
Chute-aux-Outardes, 1,968 ..... H2
Clermont, 3,078 ..... F4
Cloridorme M2
Coaticook, 8,988 ..... E6
Colombier, 890 ..... H3
Compton E6
Contrecoeur, 5,222 ..... C6
Cookshire, 1,543 ..... E6
Cowansville, 12,032 ..... D6
Danville, 4,301 ..... D6
Dégelis, 3,317 ..... H4
Delson J6
Deschaillons (Deschaillons-Sur-St-Laurent), 1,061 ..... D5
Deux-Montagnes H5
Dolbeau, 14,879 ..... D3
Donnacona, 5,479 ..... E5
Dorval, 17,706 ..... H6
Dosquet, 889 ..... E5
Douglastown M3
Drummondville, 46,599 ..... D6
East Angus, 3,570 ..... E6
Escuminac, 604 ..... K3
Farrellton A6
Ferme-Neuve, 2,947 ..... A5
Forestville, 3,748 ..... G3
Franquelin J2
Gaspé, 14,932 ..... M3
Gatineau, 102,898 ..... A6
Godbout, 327 ..... J2
Granby, 44,121 ..... D6
Grande-Rivière, 3,556 ..... M3
Grande-Vallée M2
Grand-Mère, 13,179 ..... D5
Grand-Remous, 1,216 ..... A5
Gros-Morne L2
Hampstead, 6,974 ..... J5
Hull, 66,246 ..... A6
Joliette, 17,837 ..... C5
Jonquière, 54,842 ..... E3
Kahnawake H6
La Baie, 19,940 ..... F3
Labrieville G2
Lac-aux-Sables, 1,313 ..... D5
Lac-Bouchette, 1,370 ..... D3
Lac-des-Aigles, 657 ..... H4
Lac-des-Îles A5
Lac-Édouard, 137 ..... D4
Lac-Etchemin, 2,276 ..... F5
Lachenaie J5
Lachine, 40,222 ..... H6
Lachute, 11,628 ..... B6
Lac-Mégantic, 5,897 ..... F6
Lac-Nominingue, 2,064 ..... A5
La Conception, 1,050 ..... B5
Lac-Saguay, 382 ..... A5
La Doré D3
La Guadeloupe, 1,716 ..... F6
La Malbaie, 9,143 ..... F4
La Martre, 266 ..... K2
Lambton, 1,525 ..... E6
L'Ancienne-Lorette, 15,929 ..... K5
L'Annonciation, 1,984 ..... B5
L'Anse-aux-Gascons M3
L'Anse-à-Valleau M2
L'Anse-St-Jean, 1,155 ..... F3
La Pocatière, 4,518 ..... F4
La Prairie, 18,896 ..... J6
LaSalle, 73,983 ..... J6
L'Ascension (L'Ascension-De-Patapedia), 783 ..... B5
La Tuque, 11,298 ..... D4
Laval, 343,005 ..... C6, J5
Le Bic, 2,872 ..... H3
Les Éboulements, 1,027 ..... F4
Les Escoumins, 2,009 ..... G3
Les Islets-Caribou J2
Les Méchins, 1,220 ..... K3
Lévis (Lévis-Lauzon), 40,926 ..... E5, L6
L'Isle-Verte, 1,519 ..... G3
Longueuil, 128,016 ..... J5
Loretteville, 13,737 ..... K5
Lorraine H5
Louiseville, 7,622 ..... D5
Magog, 14,283 ..... D6
Maniwaki, 3,571 ..... A5
Manouane B4
Maria, 2,458 ..... L3
Marsoui, 373 ..... L2
Mascouche, 29,556 ..... C6
Matane, 11,635 ..... J3
Matapédia, 707 ..... K4
Métabetchouan, 4,198 ..... E3
Métis-sur-Mer J3
Mirabel, 27,330 ..... B6
Mistassini, 1,814 ..... D3
Mont-Carmel, 1,244 ..... G4
Montebello, 1,039 ..... B6
Mont-Joli, 5,886 ..... H3
Mont-Laurier, 7,365 ..... A5
Montmagny, 11,654 ..... F5
Montréal, 1,039,534 ..... C6, J5
Montréal-Nord, 83,600 ..... J5
Mont-Royal, 18,682 ..... J5
Mont-St-Pierre, 239 ..... L2
Mont-Tremblant-Village B5
Murdochville, 1,171 ..... L3
New Carlisle, 1,431 ..... L4
New Richmond, 3,760 ..... L3
Nicolet, 7,928 ..... D5
Normandin, 3,524 ..... D3
Notre-Dame-de-la-Merci, 811 ..... B5
Notre-Dame-de-la-Salette, 706 ..... A6
Notre-Dame-de-Lorette D2
Notre-Dame-du-Bon-Conseil D5
Notre-Dame-du-Lac, 2,152 ..... H4
Notre-Dame-du-Laus, 1,382 ..... A5
Nouvelle, 1,960 ..... K3
Parent, 326 ..... B4
Percé, 3,614 ..... M3
Péribonka, 538 ..... D3
Pierrefonds, 54,963 ..... G5
Plessisville, 6,756 ..... E5
Pointe-à-la-Croix, 1,513 ..... K3
Pointe-Claire H6
Pointe-des-Monts J2
Pointe-Lebel, 1,931 ..... H2
Poltimore A6
Pont-Rouge, 7,146 ..... E5
Princeville, 5,703 ..... E5
Québec, 169,076 ..... E5, L6
Ragueneau H2
Repentigny, 54,550 ..... K5
Richmond, 3,424 ..... D6
Rimouski, 31,305 ..... H3
Rivière-à-Pierre, 689 ..... D4
Rivière-au-Renard, 2,524 ..... M3
Rivière-aux-Rats D4
Rivière-Bleue G4
Rivière-du-Loup, 17,772 ..... G4
Rivière-Matawin D5
Rivière-Ste-Marguerite G3
Roberval, 10,906 ..... D3
Rock Island, 1,025 ..... D6
Routhierville J3
St-Alexis-des-Monts (St-Alexis) C5
St-Ambroise, 3,463 ..... E3
St-André, 634 ..... G4
St-Antoine C6
St-Apollinaire, 3,930 ..... E5
St-Bruno, 2,384 ..... E3
St-Camille-de-Lellis, 907 ..... F5
St-Côme, 1,923 ..... C5
St-Constant J6
St-Cyprien, 1,231 ..... H4
St-David-de-Falardeau, 2,347 ..... E3
St-Donat, 847 ..... B5
Ste-Agathe-des-Monts, 7,116 ..... B5
Ste-Angèle-de-Mérici, 1,066 ..... J3
Ste-Anne-des-Monts, 6,835 ..... K2
Ste-Anne-du-Lac, 570 ..... A5
Ste-Apolline F5
Ste-Claire, 3,135 ..... F5
Ste-Croix, 1,533 ..... E5
Ste-Eulalie D5
Ste-Foy, 72,547 ..... E5, K6
Ste-Luce, 1,478 ..... H3
Ste-Marie, 11,320 ..... E5
St-Émile, 10,940 ..... K5
Ste-Monique, 930 ..... E3
Ste-Rose-du-Nord, 409 ..... F3
Ste-Thérèse, 24,269 ..... H5
St-Eustache, 40,378 ..... H5
Ste-Véronique, 1,050 ..... A5
St-Fabien, 1,848 ..... H3
St-Fabien-de-Panet, 1,021 ..... F5
St-Félicien, 10,622 ..... D3
St-Félix-d'Otis, 790 ..... F3
St-Gédéon, 1,923 ..... E3
St-Georges, 20,787 ..... F5
St-Germain (St-Germain-De-Grantham), 3,661 ..... G4
St-Henri-de-Taillon, 776 ..... E3
St-Hubert, 75,912 ..... G4
St-Hyacinthe, 38,739 ..... D6
St-Ignace-du-Lac C5
St-Jacques-de-Leeds, 771 ..... E5
St-Jean-Chrysostome, 17,089 ..... L6
St-Jean-de-Matha, 3,602 ..... C5
St-Jean-Port-Joli, 1,898 ..... F4
St-Jean-sur-Richelieu, 37,386 ..... C6
St-Jérôme, 24,583 ..... B6
St-Joseph-de-Beauce, 4,487 ..... F5
St-Lambert, 21,051 ..... J5
St-Laurent, 77,391 ..... J5
St-Leonard, 69,604 ..... J5
St-Ludger, 1,203 ..... F6
St-Ludger-de-Milot, 764 ..... E3
St-Malo, 518 ..... E6
St-Marc-du-Lac-Long, 469 ..... H4
St-Marcel, 531 ..... F5
St-Marcellin H3
St-Michel, 1,633 ..... F5
St-Michel-des-Saints, 1,805 ..... C5
St-Nicolas, 16,645 ..... E5
St-Pacôme, 1,706 ..... G4
St-Pamphile, 2,847 ..... G5
St-Pascal, 3,643 ..... G4
St-Philémon, 855 ..... F5
St-Raphaël, 2,231 ..... F5
St-Rédempteur, 6,349 ..... K6
St-Rémi-d'Amherst B5
St-Romuald, 10,825 ..... L6
St-Siméon, 984 ..... G4
St-Tite-des-Caps, 1,426 ..... F4
St-Vallier F5
St-Zacharie, 2,100 ..... F5
Salaberry-de-Valleyfield, 26,170 ..... B6
Sault-au-Mouton, 1,352 ..... G3
Sayabec, 1,999 ..... J3
Scotstown, 600 ..... E6
Shawinigan, 17,535 ..... D5
Sherbrooke, 75,916 ..... E6
Sillery, 11,909 ..... K6
Sorel, 34,194 ..... C5
Stoneham E4
Stornoway, 606 ..... E6
Stratford (Stratford-Centre), 873 ..... E6
Tadoussac, 870 ..... G3
Terrebonne, 43,149 ..... J5
Thetford Mines, 16,628 ..... E5
Tracy C5
Trois-Pistoles, 3,635 ..... G3
Trois-Rivières, 46,264 ..... D5
Valcourt, 2,411 ..... D6
Val-des-Bois, 732 ..... A6
Vanier, 11,054 ..... L5
Vaudreuil, 19,920 ..... C6
Verdun, 60,564 ..... J6
Victoriaville, 38,841 ..... E5
Villeroy, 519 ..... E5
Waterloo, 3,993 ..... D6
Windsor, 5,321 ..... D6
Woburn F6

Other Features

Ashuapmushuan, *river* C2
Ashuapmushuan Prov. Reserve C2
Assinica Prov. Reserve A1
Aylmer, *lake* E6
Baskatong, *reservoir* A5
Bazin, *river* A4
Betsiamites, *river* G2
Bizard, *island* H5
Blanc, *reservoir* C4
Bonaventure, *river* L3
Cascapedia, *river* K3
Chibougamau, *lake* B2
Chic-Chocs Prov. Reserve L3
Duchénier Prov. Reserve H3
Édouard, *lake* D4
Etchemin, *river* L6
Forillon Natl. Park M3
Frontenac Prov. Park E6
Gaspé, *peninsula* L3
Gaspésie Prov. Park K3
Gatineau, *river* A4, A5
Gatineau Park A6
Gouin, *reservoir* B3
Grands Jardins Prov. Park F4
Îles-de-Boucherville Prov. Park J5
Jacques-Cartier, *river* E4
Jacques Cartier Prov. Park E4
Jésus, *island* J5
Kempt, *lake* B4
Lac Albanel, Mistassini & Waconichi Prov. Reserve B1
La Mauricie Natl. Park C5
Laurentides Prov. Reserve E4
Lièvre, *river* A5
Malbaie, *river* F4
Manicougan Deux, *reservoir* H2
Mastigouche Prov. Reserve C5
Matane Prov. Reserve K3
Mattawin, *river* C5
Mékinac, *lake* D4
Memphrémagog, *lake* D6
Mistassibi, *river* D1
Mistassini, *river* D2
Mitchinamécus, *lake* A4
Montréal, *island* J5
Mont-Tremblant Prov. Park B5
Nestaocano, *river* C2
Orléans, *island* F5, L5
Ottawa, *river* A6
Outarde, *river* H2
Papineau-Labelle Prov. Reserve A5
Parke Prov. Reserve G4
Péribonca, *river* E2
Perrot, *island* G6
Pipmuacan, *reservoir* F2
Pointe-Taillon Prov. Park D3
Poisson Blanc, *reservoir* A6
Port-Daniel Prov. Reserve M3
Portneuf, *river* G3
Portneuf Prov. Reserve D4
Restigouche, *river* J4
Richelieu, *river* C6
Rimouski Prov. Reserve H3
Rouge-Matawin Prov. Reserve B5
Saguenay, *river* F3
Saguenay Prov. Park F3
St-Charles, *lake* K5
St-François, *lake* E6
St-François, *river* D5
St-Jean, *lake* D3
St. Lawrence, *river* B6, G3, J6, L6
St-Louis, *lake* H6
St-Maurice, *river* C4
St-Maurice Prov. Reserve C4
Simon, *lake* A6
Taureau, *reservoir* C5
Trenche, *river* C3
Vermillion, *river* C4

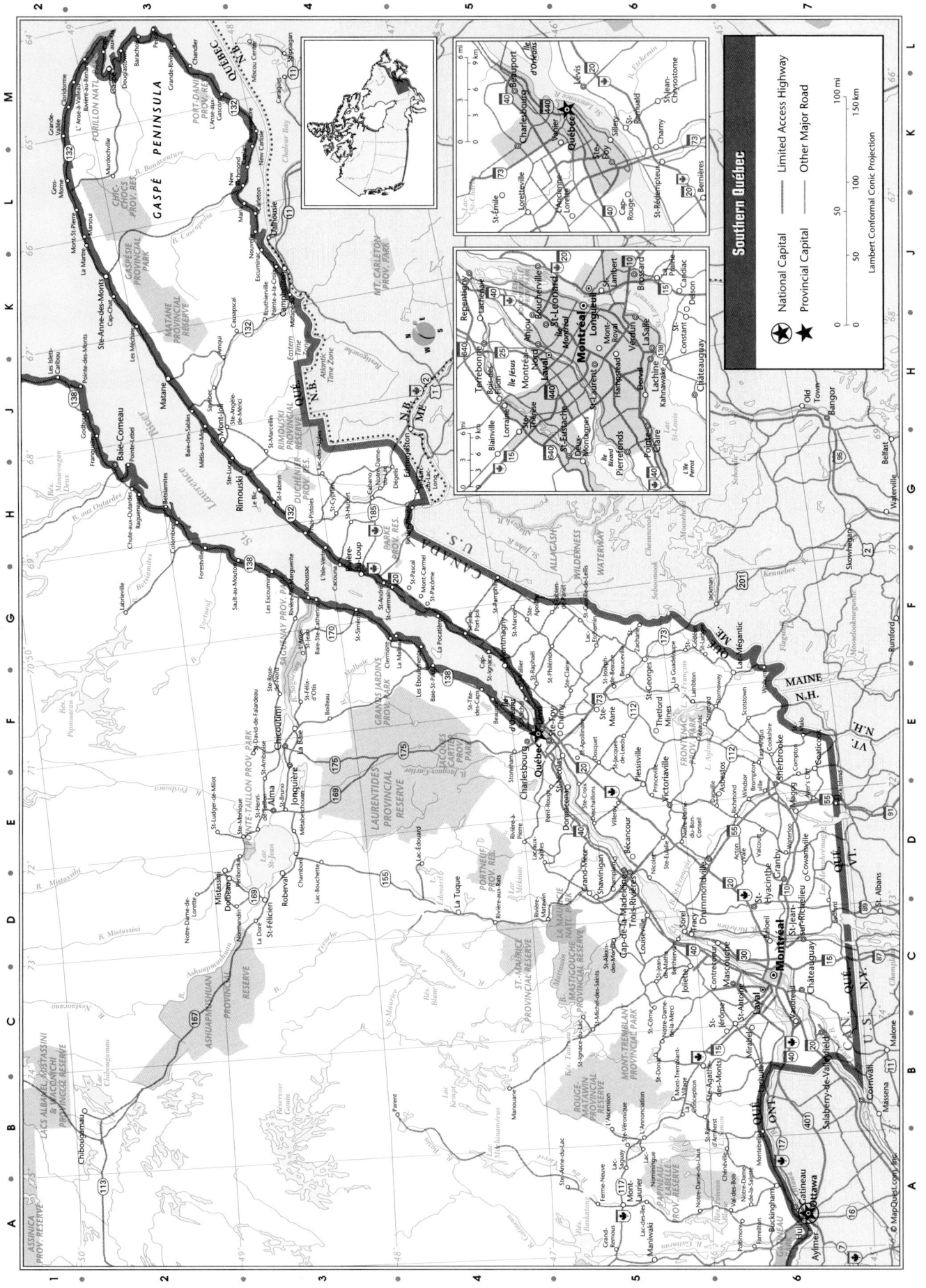

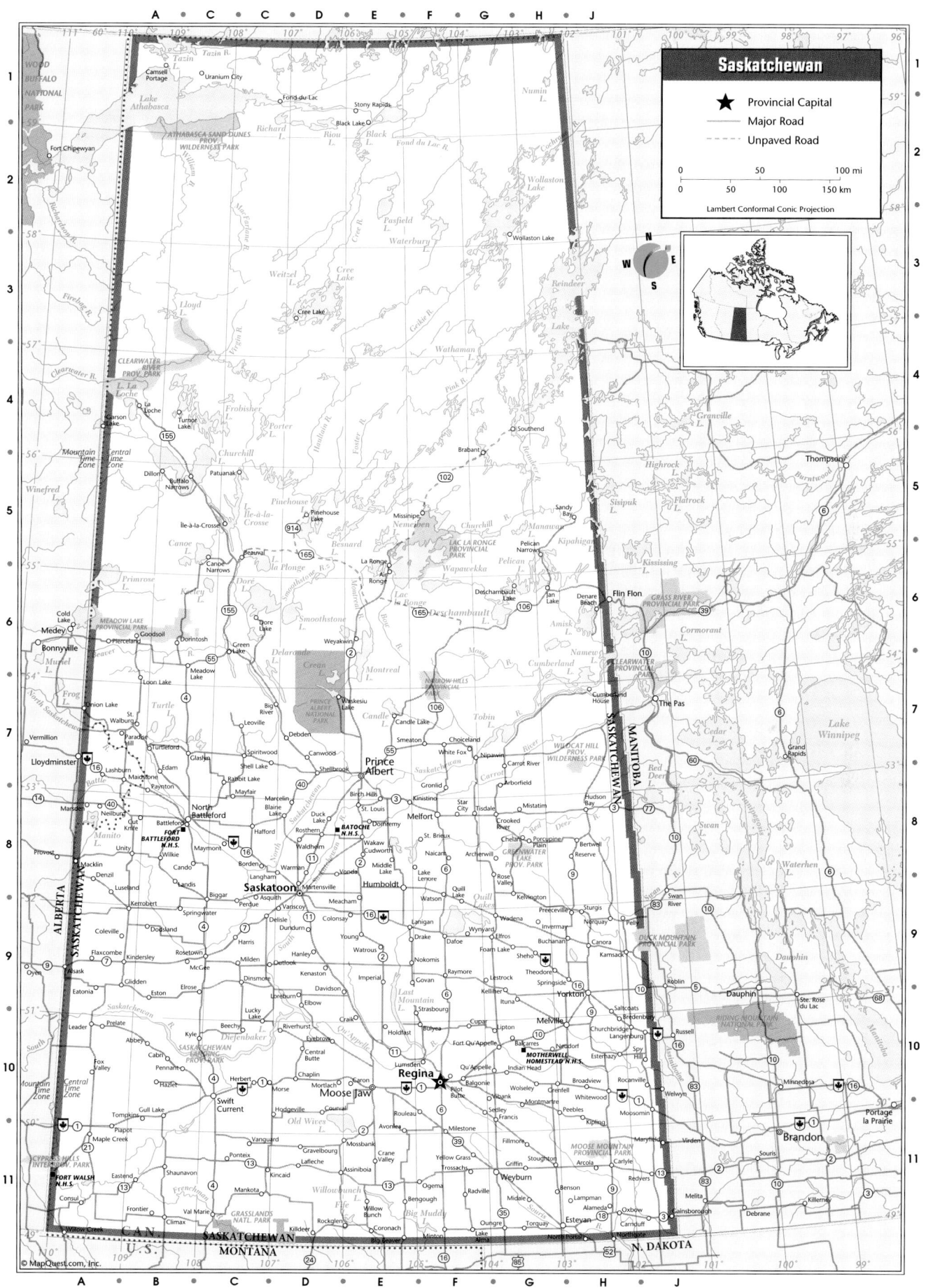

Saskatchewan

Capital: Regina
Area: 251,793 sq. mi.
652,330 sq. km.
Population: 978,933 (2001 Census)
Largest City: Saskatoon, 196,811
Highest Point: Cypress Hills
4,567 ft.
1,392 m.
Entered the Dominion: September 1, 1905
Floral Emblem: Western Red Lily

Saskatchewan: Map Index

Cities and Towns

Abbey, 137 . . . . B10
Air Ronge, 955. . . . . . E5
Alameda, 311 . . . . . H11
Alsask, 178 . . . . A9
Arborfield, 411 . . . . . G7
Archerwill, 215 . . . . . G8
Arcola, 532 . . . . H11
Asquith, 574 . . . . C8
Assiniboia, 2,483 . . . D11
Avonlea, 412 . . . . . . E10
Balcarres, 622 . . . . . G10
Balgonie, 1,239 . . . . F10
Battleford, 3,820 . . . . B8
Beauval, 843 . . . . C5
Beechy, 295 . . . . . . C10
Bengough, 401 . . . . E11
Benson, 95 . . . . G11
Bertwell H8
Big Beaver, 20 . . . . . E11
Biggar, 2,243 . . . . . . C8
Big River, 741 . . . . . . C7
Birch Hills, 957. . . . . . E7
Black Lake E1
Blaine Lake, 508 . . . . D8
Borden, 225 . . . . C8
Brabant. G4
Bredenbury, 354 . . . H10
Broadview, 669 . . . . H10
Buchanan, 233 . . . . . H9
Buffalo Narrows, 1,137. . . . . B5
Bulyea, 107 . . . . F10
Cabri, 483 . . . . B10
Camsell Portage. A1
Candle Lake, 503 . . . . E7
Cando, 102. . . . . B8
Canoe Narrows B5
Canora, 2,200. . . . . . . H9
Canwood, 374 . . . . . . D7
Carlyle, 1,260 . . . . . H11
Carnduff, 1,017 . . . . J11
Caron, 120 . . . . E10
Carrot River, 1,017 . . G7
Central Butte, 439 . . D10
Chaplin, 292. . . . . . D10
Chelan, 52 . . . . G8
Choiceland, 370. . . . . F7
Churchbridge, 796 . . J10
Climax, 206. . . . . . . B11
Coleville, 313 . . . . . . A9
Colonsay, 426 . . . . . . E9
Consul, 91. . . . . A11
Coronach, 822. . . . . . E11
Courval, 10. . . . . . . D10
Craik, 418 . . . . E9
Crane Valley, 40 . . . . E11
Cree Lake D3
Crooked River, 64 . . . G8
Cudworth, 766 . . . . . E8
Cumberland House, 632. . . . . H7
Cupar, 602 . . . . F10
Cut Knife, 556. . . . . . A8
Dafoe, 15 . . . . F9
Davidson, 1,035 . . . . D9
Debden, 355. . . . . . . D7
Delisle, 884. . . . . C9
Denare Beach, 784 . . H6
Denzil, 161 . . . . A8
Deschambault Lake, 896. . . . . G6
Dillon B5
Dinsmore, 337 . . . . . C9
Dodsland, 211. . . . . . . B9
Domremy, 135. . . . . . E8
Dore Lake, 27 . . . . . . C6
Dorintosh, 125 . . . . . B6
Drake, 248. . . . . E9
Duck Lake, 624 . . . . . D8
Dundurn, 596. . . . . . . D9
Eastend, 576 . . . . . . B11
Eatonia, 474 . . . . A9
Edam, 429. . . . . B7
Elbow, 298 . . . . D9
Elfros, 161. . . . . G9
Elrose, 517 . . . . B9
Esterhazy, 2,348 . . . H10
Estevan, 10,242. . . . G11
Eston, 1,048 . . . . B9
Eyebrow, 136 . . . . . D10
Fillmore, 246. . . . . . G11
Flaxcombe, 128. . . . . A9
Foam Lake, 1,218 . . . G9
Fond-du-Lac C1
Fort Qu'Appelle, 1,940 . . . . G10
Fox Valley, 326 . . . . A10
Francis, 172 . . . . . . G10
Frontier, 302 . . . . . . B11
Gainsborough, 286 . . J11
Garson Lake. A4
Glaslyn, 375 . . . . B7
Glidden. A9
Goodsoil, 284 . . . . . . A6
Govan, 274 . . . . E9
Gravelbourg, 1,187 . D11
Green Lake, 498 . . . . C6
Grenfell, 1,067 . . . . H10
Griffin, 70 . . . . G11
Gronlid, 70 . . . . F7
Gull Lake, 1,016. . . . B10
Hafford, 401 . . . . C8
Hanley, 495. . . . . D9
Harris, 232 . . . . C9
Hazlet, 126 . . . . B10
Herbert, 812 . . . . . . C10
Hodgeville, 175. . . . D10
Holdfast, 190. . . . . . E10
Hudson Bay, 1,783 . . H8
Humboldt, 5,161 . . . . E8
Île-à-la-Crosse, 1,268 . C5
Imperial, 339 . . . . E9
Indian Head, 1,758 . G10
Invermay, 284. . . . . . G9
Ituna, 709. . . . . G9
Jan Lake H6
Kamsack, 2,009 . . . . . J9
Kelliher, 317 . . . . G9
Kelvington, 1,007 . . . G8
Kenaston, 282. . . . . . D9
Kerrobert, 1,111 . . . . A9
Key Lake Mine E3
Killdeer D11
Kincaid, 161 . . . . . . C11
Kindersley, 4,548 . . . . A9
Kinistino, 702. . . . . . . E8
Kipling, 1,037 . . . . . H10
Kyle, 478. . . . . B10
Lafleche, 446. . . . . . D11
Lake Alma, 35 . . . . . F11
Lake Lenore, 314 . . . . F8
La Loche, 2,136. . . . . A4
Lampman, 650 . . . . H11
Landis, 161 . . . . B8
Langenburg, 1,107 . . J10
Langham, 1,145 . . . . D8
Lanigan, 1,289. . . . . . E9
La Ronge, 2,727. . . . . E5
Lashburn, 783 . . . . . . A7
Leader, 914 . . . . A10
Leoville, 343 . . . . C7
Lestrock, 226 . . . . . . G9
Lipton, 331. . . . . . . G10
Lloydminster, 7,840 . . A7
Loon Lake, 318 . . . . . A6
Loreburn, 143. . . . . . D9
Lucky Lake, 354. . . . . C9
Lumsden, 1,581 . . . . F10
Luseland, 602 . . . . . . A8
Macklin, 1,330 . . . . . A8
Maidstone, 995 . . . . . A7
Mankota, 248 . . . . . . C11
Maple Creek, 2,270 . A11
Marcelin, 167 . . . . . . D8
Marsden, 276 . . . . . . A8
Martensville, 4,365 . . D8
Maryfield, 359 . . . . . J11
Mayfair, 48 . . . . C7
Maymont, 164 . . . . . C8
McGee B9
Meacham, 90 . . . . E8
Meadow Lake, 4,582 . B6
Melfort, 5,559 . . . . . . F8
Melville, 4,453 . . . . H10
Midale, 496 . . . . . . G11
Middle Lake, 300 . . . . E8
Milden, 196 . . . . C9
Milestone, 542. . . . . F10
Minton, 95 . . . . F11
Missinipe, 38 . . . . F5
Mistatim, 104 . . . . . . G8
Montmartre, 465. . . G10
Moose Jaw, 32,131. . E10
Moosomin, 2,361 . . . J10
Morse, 248 . . . . C10
Mortlach, 241 . . . . . D10
Mossbank, 379. . . . . E11
Naicam, 761 . . . . F8
Neilburg, 366 . . . . . . A8
Neudorf, 304 . . . . . G10
Nipawin, 4,275 . . . . . F7
Nokomis, 436 . . . . . . E9
Norquay, 485 . . . . . . H9
North Battleford, 13,692. . . . . B8
Northgate H11
North Portal, 136 . . H11
Ogema, 292 . . . . F11
Onion Lake A7
Oungre, 15 . . . . G11
Outlook, 2,129 . . . . . C9
Oxbow, 1,132. . . . . . H11
Paradise Hill, 486. . . . A7
Patuanak, 72. . . . . . . C5
Paynton, 172. . . . . . . B7
Peebles, 20 . . . . H10
Pelican Narrows, 690. H5
Pelly, 303 . . . . J9
Pennant, 150. . . . . . B10
Perdue, 372 . . . . C8
Piapot, 55 . . . . A10
Pierceland, 449 . . . . . A6
Pilot Butte, 1,850 . . . F10
Pinehouse Lake D5
Ponteix, 550 . . . . C11
Porcupine Plain, 820 . G8
Preeceville, 1,074 . . . H9
Prelate, 164. . . . . . . A10
Prince Albert, 34,291 . E7
Qu'Appelle, 648 . . . G10
Quill Lake, 439. . . . . . F8
Rabbit Lake, 87 . . . . . C7
Radville, 735 . . . . . . F11
Raymore, 625 . . . . . . F9
Redvers, 917. . . . . . . J11
Regina, 178,225. . . . F10
Reserve H8
Riverhurst, 143 . . . . D10
Rocanville, 887 . . . . . J10
Rockglen, 450 . . . . . E11
Rosetown, 2,471 . . . . B9
Rose Valley, 395 . . . . G8
Rosthern, 1,504. . . . . D8
Rouleau, 434 . . . . . . F10
St. Brieux, 505 . . . . . . F8
St. Louis, 474. . . . . . . E8
St. Walburg, 672 . . . . A7
Saltcoats, 494 . . . . . . H9
Sandy Bay, 1,092. . . . H5
Saskatoon, 196,811. . D8
Sedley, 322 . . . . F10
Shaunavon, 1,775 . . B11
Sheho, 148. . . . . G9
Shellbrook, 1,276 . . . D7
Shell Lake, 185 . . . . . C7
Smeaton, 178 . . . . . . F7
Southend, 696 . . . . . G4
Spiritwood, 907. . . . . C7
Springside, 525. . . . . H9
Springwater, 20. . . . . B9
Spy Hill, 213. . . . . . . J10
Star City, 482. . . . . . . F8
Stony Rapids, 189 . . . E1
Stoughton, 720. . . . G11
Strasbourg, 760 . . . . . F9
Sturgis, 627 . . . . H9
Swift Current, 14,821. . . . . C10
Theodore, 381 . . . . . H9
Tisdale, 3,063 . . . . . . F8
Tompkins, 191. . . . . B10
Torquay, 231. . . . . . G11
Trossachs, 30 . . . . . . F11
Turnor Lake, 155 . . . . B4
Turtleford, 465. . . . . . B7
Unity, 2,243 . . . . A8
Uranium City. B1
Val Marie, 134. . . . . C11
Vanguard, 187. . . . . . C11
Vanscoy, 345. . . . . . . D8
Vibank, 381. . . . . . . G10
Vonda, 322. . . . . D8
Wadena, 1,412 . . . . . G9
Wakaw, 884 . . . . E8
Waldheim, 889 . . . . . D8
Warman, 3,481 . . . . . D8
Waskesiu Lake D7
Watrous, 1,808 . . . . . E9
Watson, 794 . . . . F8
Weyakwin, 183 . . . . . E6
Weyburn, 9,534 . . . G11
White Fox, 436 . . . . . F7
Whitewood, 947 . . . . H10
Wilkie, 1,282 . . . . B8
Willow Bunch, 395. . E11
Willow Creek A11
Wollaston Lake G2
Wolseley, 766 . . . . . G10
Wynyard, 1,919. . . . . . F9
Yellow Grass, 422. . . F11
Yorkton, 15,107 . . . . H9
Young, 299 . . . . E9

Other Features

Amisk, *lake* H6
Athabasca, *lake* A1
Batoche N.H.S. D8
Battle, *river* A7
Beaver, *river*. A6
Besnard, *lake*. D5
Big Muddy, *lake* F11
Black, *lake* E1
Bow, *river*. E6
Candle, *lake*. E7
Canoe, *lake* B5
Carrot, *river*. G7
Churchill, *lake* B4
Churchill, *river*. G5
Clearwater River Prov. Park. A4
Cochrane, *river* H2
Crean, *lake* D6
Cree, *lake* D3
Cree, *river* E2
Cumberland, *lake* . . . H6
Cypress Hills Interprov. Park. A11
Delaronde, *lake* C6
Deschambault, *lake* . . G6
Diefenbaker, *lake* . . . C10
Dor, *lake* C6
Duck Mountain Prov. Park J9
Fife, *lake* E11
Fond du Lac, *river*. . . . F2
Fort Battleford N.H.S. . B8
Fort Walsh N.H.S. . . . A11
Foster, *river* E4
Frenchman, *river* . . . B11
Frobisher, *lake* C4
Geikie, *river* F3
Grasslands Natl. Park C11
Greenwater Lake Prov. Park G8
Haultain, *river* D4
Île-à-la-Crosse, *lake* . . C5
Keeley, *lake* B6
Lac La Ronge Prov. Park. F5
La Plonge, *lake* C5
La Ronge, *lake* E6
Last Mountain, *lake* . . E9
Lloyd, *lake*. B3
Macfarlane, *river* C2
Manawan, *lake* G5
Manito, *lake* A8
Meadow Lake Prov. Park A6
Montreal, *lake* E6
Montreal, *river*. E6
Moose Mountain Prov. Park H11
Mossy, *river* F6
Motherwell Homestead N.H.S.. . . . . G10
Namew, *lake*. H6
Narrow Hills Prov. Park F6
Nemeiben, *lake* E5
North Saskatchewan, *river*. D8
Numin, *lake* H1
Old Wives, *lake* D10
Pasfield, *lake* E2
Pelican, *lake* G5
Pinehouse, *lake* D5
Pink, *river*. F4
Porter, *lake* C4
Primrose, *lake* A6
Qu'Appelle, *river* . . . D10
Quill, *lakes*. F8
Red Deer, *river*. G8
Reindeer, *lake* H3
Reindeer, *river* G4
Richard, *lake* C1
Riou, *lake* D1
Saskatchewan, *river* . . E7
Saskatchewan Landing Prov. Park. C10
Smoothstone, *lake*. . . D6
Smoothstone, *river* . . D6
Souris, *river*. G11
South Saskatchewan, *river*. D8
Tazin, *lake*. A1
Tazin, *river*. B1
Tobin, *lake* G7
Turtle, *lake*. B7
Virgin, *river* C3
Wapawekka, *lake* F5
Waterbury, *lake* F2
Wathaman, *lake*. G3
Weitzel, *lake* D3
William, *river* B2
Willowbunch, *lake* . . E11
Wollaston, *lake* H2

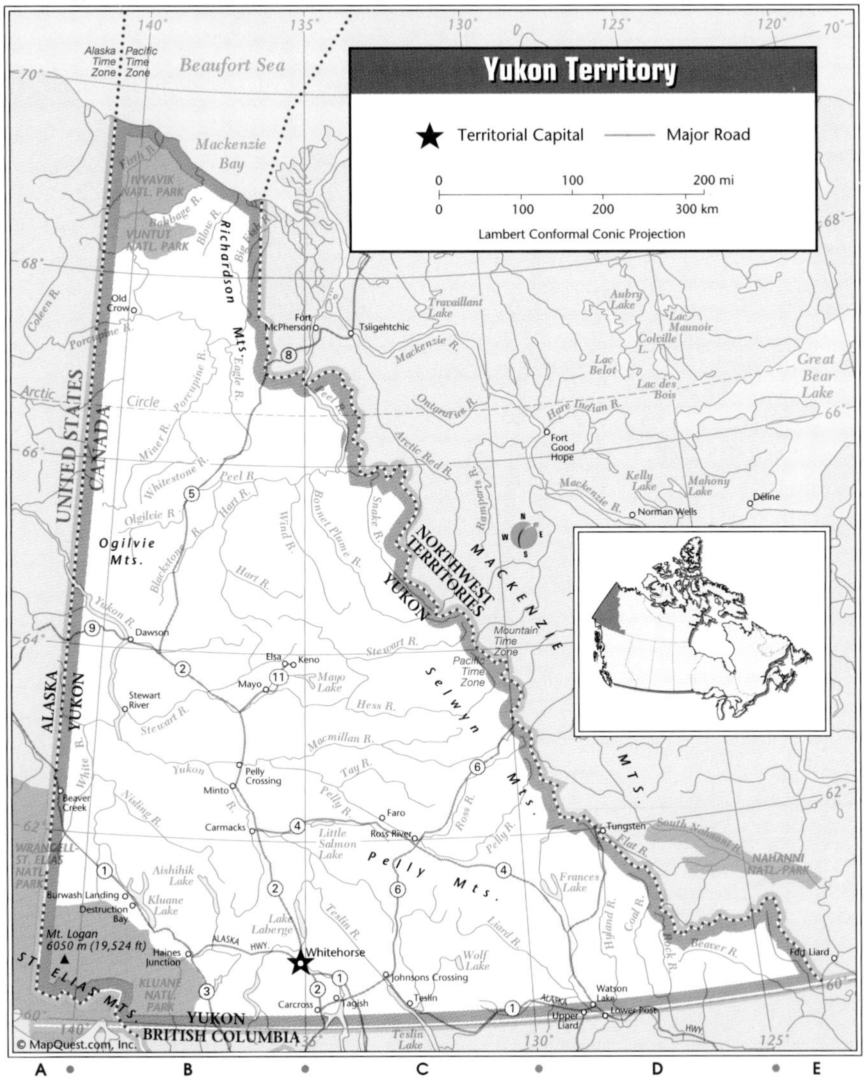
Yukon Territory
Territorial Capital
Major Road
0 100 200 mi
0 100 200 300 km
Lambert Conformal Conic Projection
Beaufort Sea
Mackenzie Bay
UNITED STATES
CANADA
ALASKA
YUKON
BRITISH COLUMBIA
NORTHWEST TERRITORIES
Richardson Mts.
Ogilvie Mts.
Selwyn Mts.
Pelly Mts.
Mackenzie Mts.
St. Elias Mts.
Whitehorse
Dawson
Mt. Logan 6050 m (19,524 ft)
© MapQuest.com, Inc.

Yukon Territory

Capital: Whitehorse
Area: 186,607 sq. mi.
483,450 sq. km.
Population: 28,674 (2001 Census)
Largest City: Whitehorse, 19,058
Highest Point: Mt. Logan
19,524 ft.
6,050 m.
Entered the Dominion: June 13,1898
Floral Emblem: Fireweed

Yukon Territory: Map Index

Cities and Towns

Beaver Creek, 88 . . . . A4
Burwash Landing, 68 . B5
Carcross, 152 . . . . . . C5
Carmacks, 431 . . . . . B4
Dawson, 1,251 . . . . . B3
Destruction Bay, 43 . . B5
Elsa. B4
Faro, 313 . . . . C4
Haines Junction, 531 . B5
Johnsons Crossing, 20 C5
Keno. B4
Mayo, 366 . . . . B4
Minto B4
Old Crow, 299 . . . . . B2
Pelly Crossing, 328 . . B4
Ross River, 337 . . . . . C4
Stewart River. B4
Tagish, 206. . . . . C5
Teslin, 123 . . . . C5
Upper Liard, 159. . . . D5
Watson Lake, 912 . . . D5
Whitehorse, 19,058. . C5

Other Features

Aishihik, *lake* B5
Babbage, *river* B1
Beaufort, *sea* B1
Beaver, *river* D5
Big Fish, *river*. B1
Blackstone, *river*. B3
Blow, *river*. B1
Bonnet Plume, *river*. . C3
Coal, *river*. D5
Eagle, *river* B2
Firth, *river* A1
Frances, *lake* D5
Hart, *river* B3
Hess, *river* C4
Hyland, *river* D5
Ivvavik Natl. Park B1
Kluane, *lake*. B5
Kluane Natl. Park. B5
Laberge, *lake*. B5
Liard, *river*. C5
Little Salmon, *lake*. . . C4
Logan, *mt* A5
Mackenzie, *bay* B1
Macmillan, *river*. C4
Mayo, *lake* C4
Miner, *river* B3
Nisling, *river* B4
Ogilvie, *mts.* B3
Olgilvie, *river*. B3
Peel, *river* B3, C2
Pelly, *mts* C5
Pelly, *river* C4, C5
Porcupine, *river* B2
Richardson, *mts.* B1
Rock, *river*. D5
Ross, *river* C4
St. Elias, *mts.* A5
Selwyn, *mts.* C4
Snake, *river*. C3
Stewart, *river*. . . . B4, C3
Tay, *river*. C4
Teslin, *lake* C5
Teslin, *river* C5
Vuntut Natl. Park. . . . A1
White, *river* A4
Whitestone, *river* B3
Wind, *river* B3
Wolf, *lake* C5
Yukon, *river*. B4

Québec City

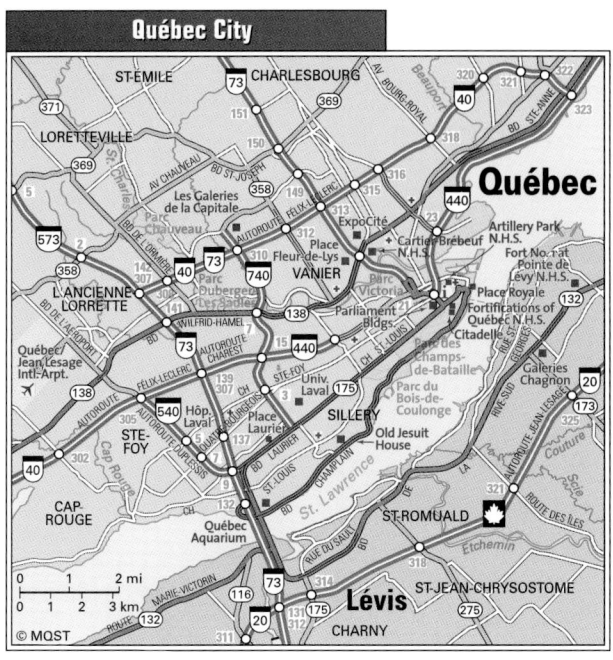

Montréal

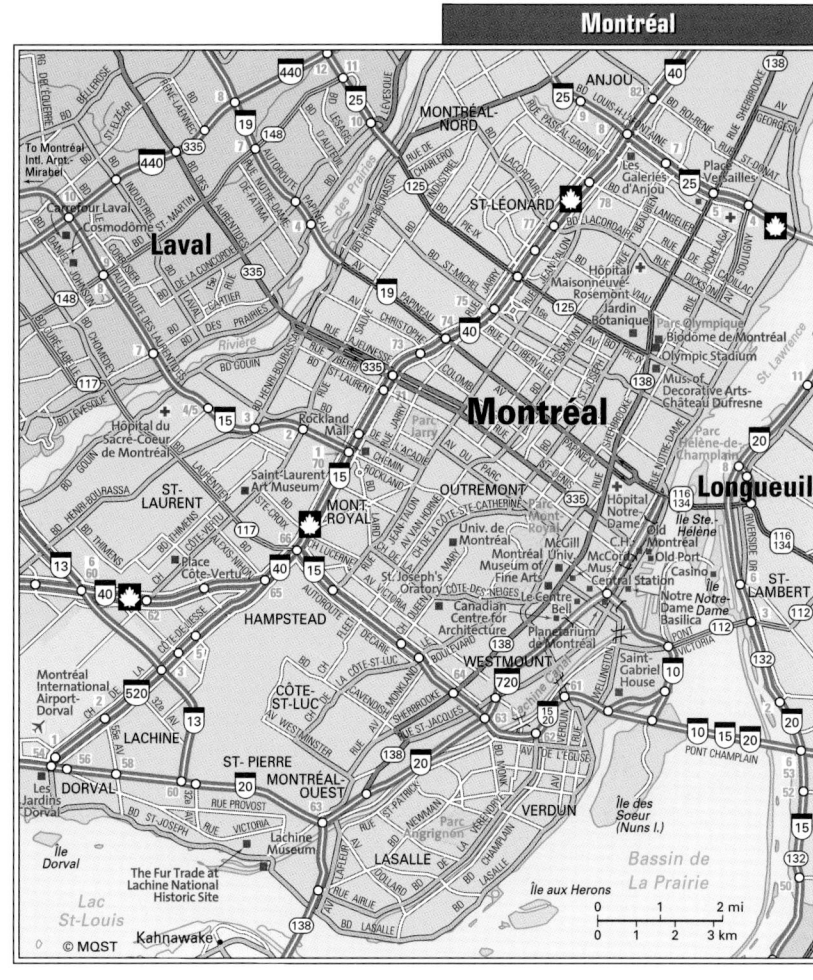

Ottawa

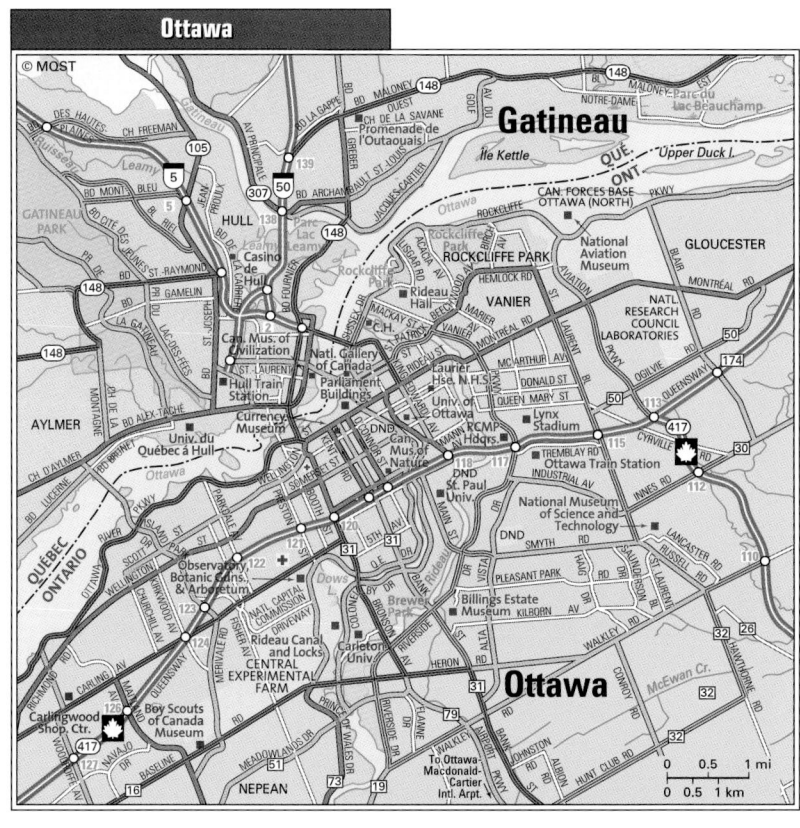

Halifax

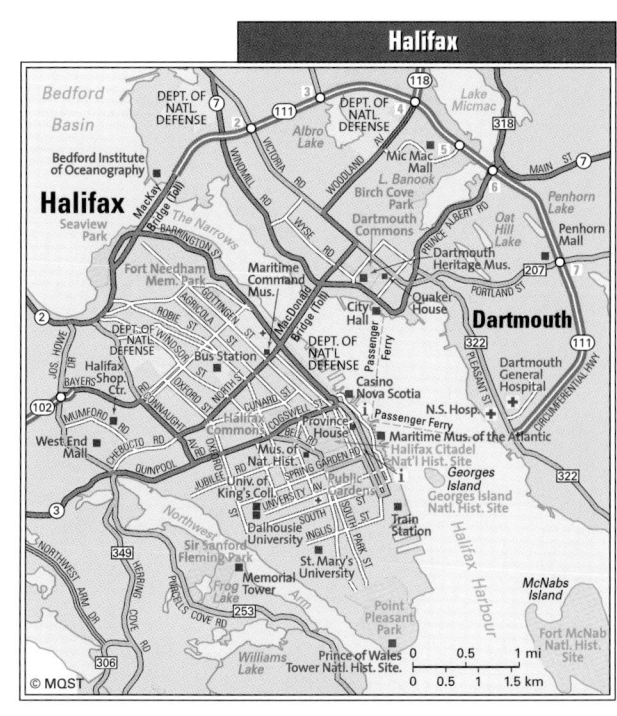

Toronto

Downtown Toronto

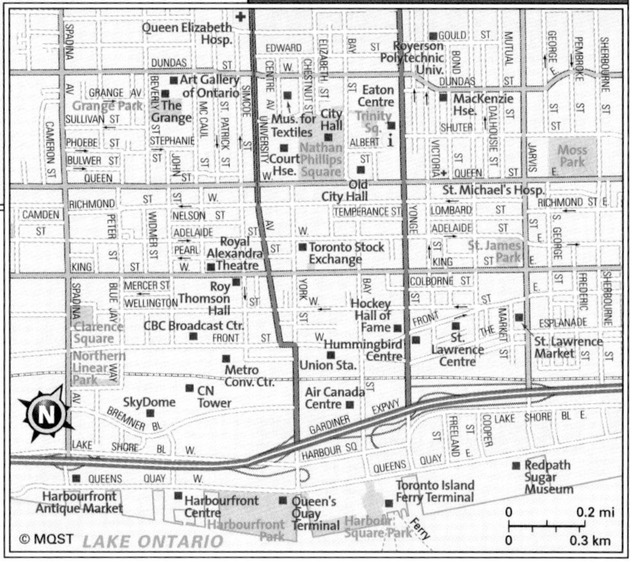

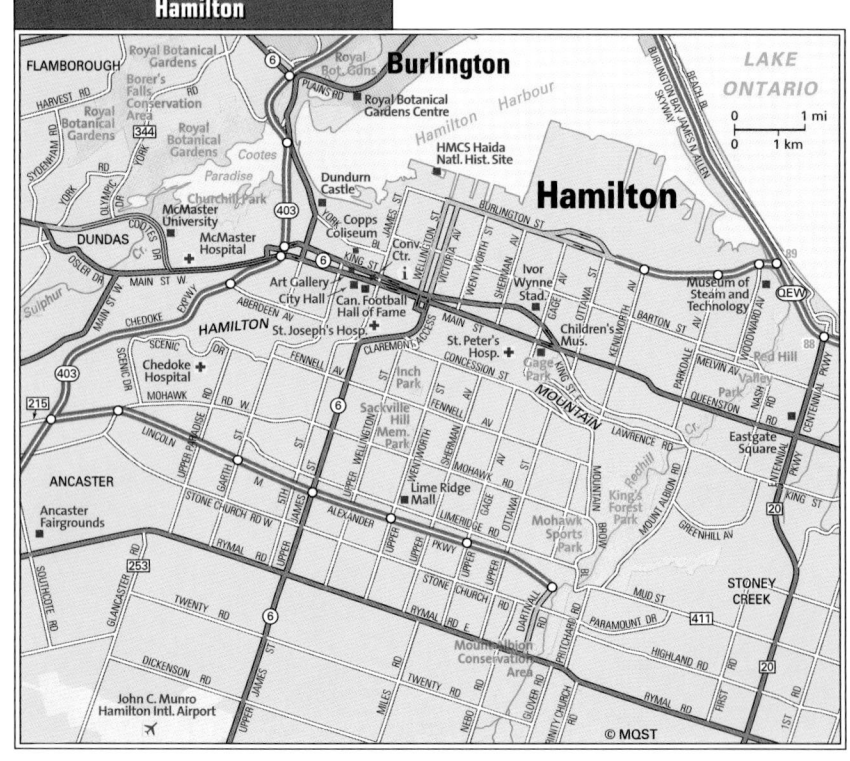

Hamilton

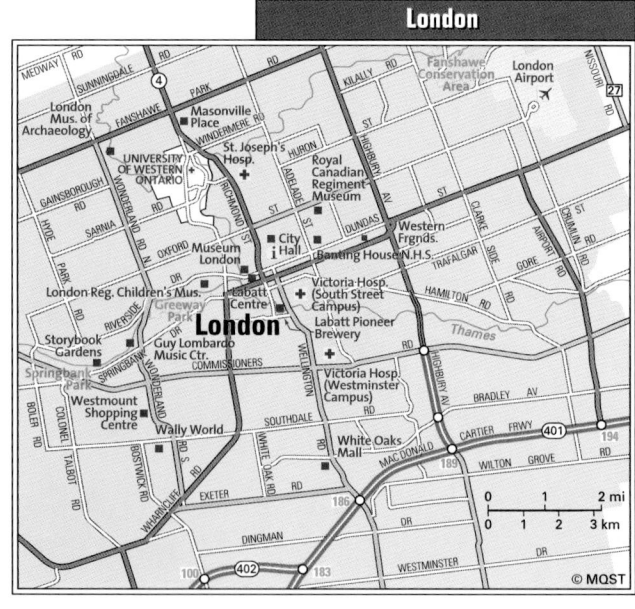

London

Winnipeg

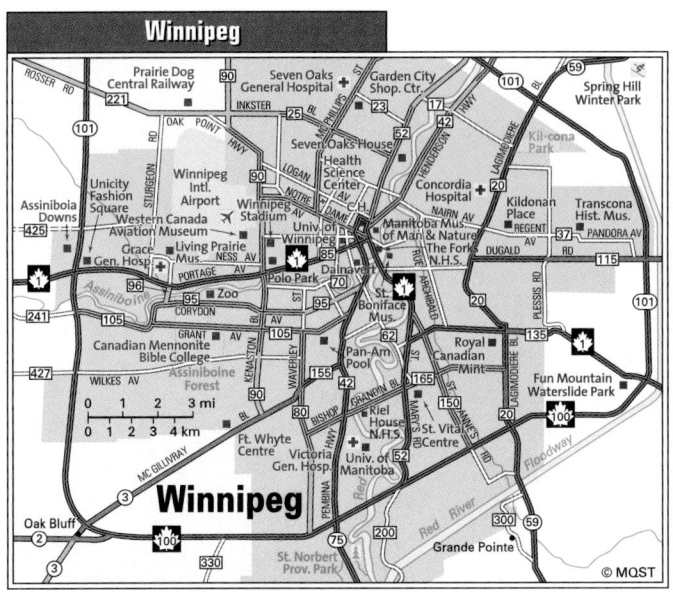

Edmonton

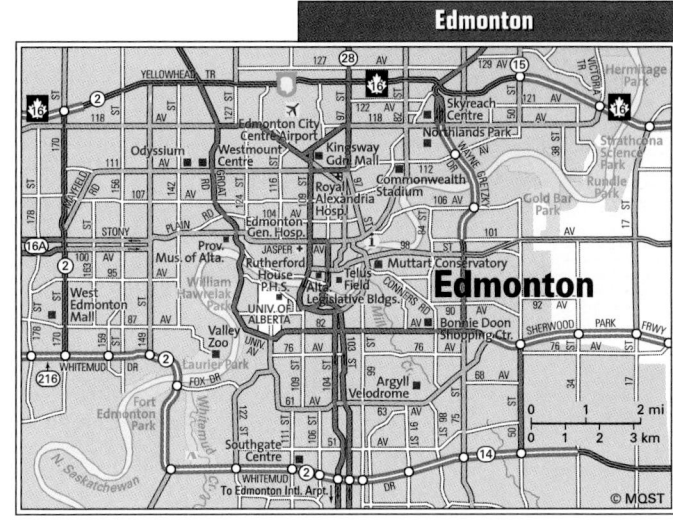

Victoria

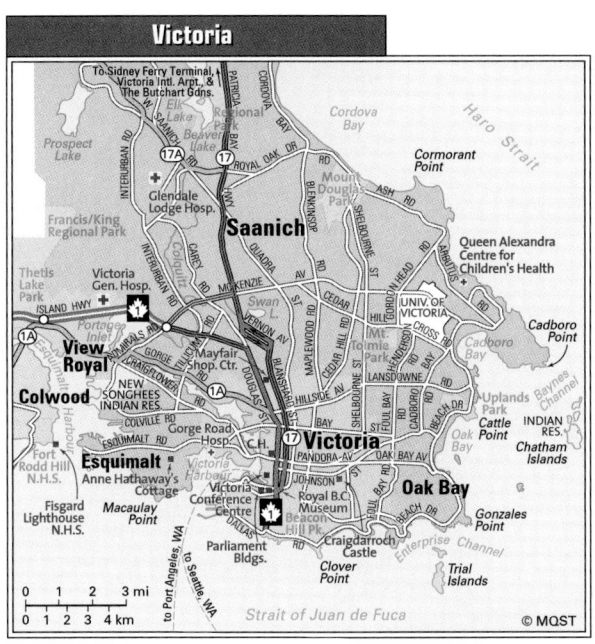

Calgary

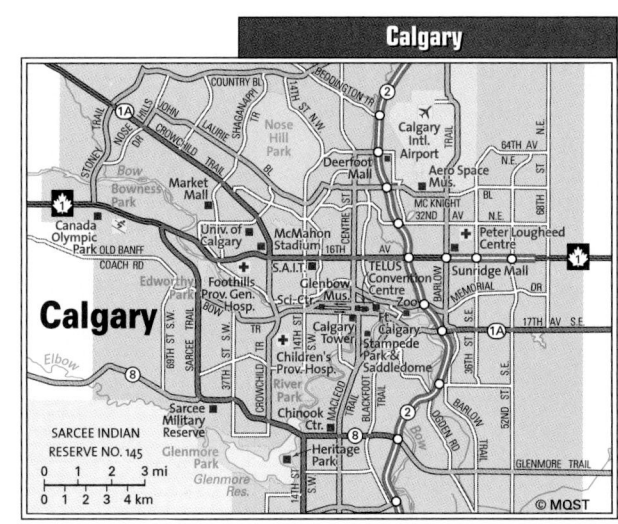

Vancouver

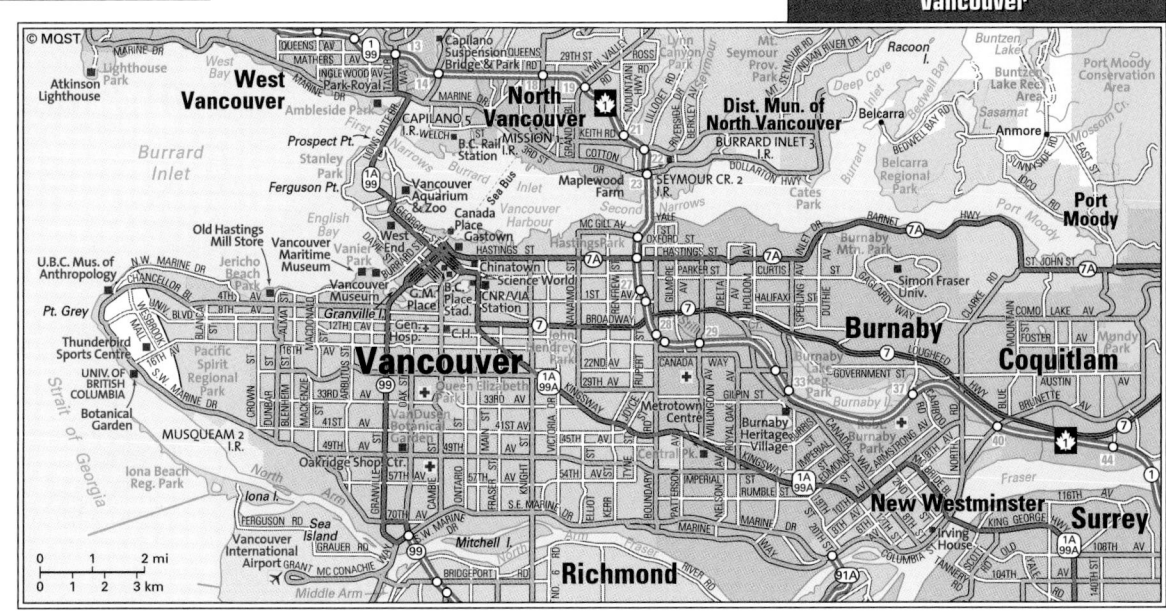

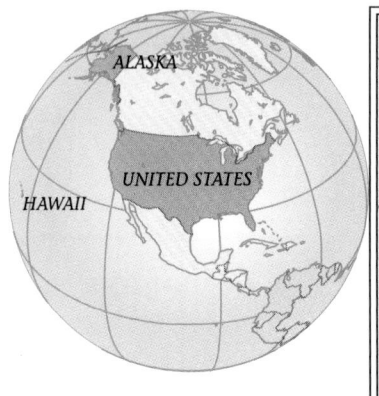

ALASKA

UNITED STATES

HAWAII

★ Edmonton

Vancouver

Calgary

Saskatoon

Winnipegosis L.

Victoria ★ Bellingham
Mt. Olympus 2424 m (7954 ft) ▲ Everett
Tacoma ★ Seattle
Olympia ★
Mt. Rainier 4392 m (14,410 ft) ▲ WASHINGTON
Portland Yakima
Salem ★
Corvallis
Eugene
Coos Bay

Spokane
Coeur d'Alene
Lewiston
Pendleton

Missoula ● Great Falls
Helena ★
Butte ●

Havre
Glasgow

Lethbridge

★ Regina

Missouri

Minot ●

Winnipeg

Grand Forks ●

MONTANA

Bozeman Miles City

Billings

NORTH DAKOTA

Bismarck ★

Aberdeen ●

Medford ● Klamath Falls
OREGON
Bend
Columbia Plateau
Cascade Range
Columbia R.
Snake R.

Eureka
Redding ●

SIERRA

Coast Ranges

IDAHO
★ Boise
Idaho Falls
Twin Falls
Pocatello

Salmon

Cody ●
Sheridan ●

Jackson ●
WYOMING
Lander ●
Casper ●

Rapid City ●
Pierre ★
SOUTH DAKOTA
Black Hills

Sioux Falls

Missouri R.

Winnemucca ●
Elko ●
Logan ●
Great Salt L.
Ogden ●
Salt Lake City ★
Provo ●
UTAH
Vernal ●

Laramie ●
Cheyenne ★
Fort Collins
Boulder ● Greeley ●
Denver ★
North Platte
Kearney ●
NEBRASKA
Grand Island ●

San Francisco ★ Sacramento
Oakland
San Jose
NEVADA
Reno ●
Carson City ●
Great Basin
Ely ●
NEVADA
Mt. Whitney 4418 m (14,494 ft) ▲
Death Valley

Grand Junction ●
Mt. Elbert 4399 m (14,433 ft) ▲
COLORADO
Pikes Peak 4301 m (14,110 ft) ▲
Colorado Springs ●
Pueblo ●
Durango ●
Colorado R.
Moab ●
Farmington ●

Salina ●
KANSAS
Hutchinson ●
Dodge City ●
Wichita ●

Arkansas R.

Monterey
Fresno ●
CALIFORNIA
Bakersfield ●
Santa Barbara
Channel Is.
Los Angeles
Long Beach
San Bernardino
Riverside
San Diego
Tijuana
Mexicali

Coast Ranges

Las Vegas ●
MOJAVE DESERT
Kingman ●
Flagstaff ●
Prescott ●
ARIZONA
Phoenix ★
Yuma ●
Casa Grande ●
Tucson ●
Nogales ●

Cedar City ●
St. George ●
GRAND CANYON
Colorado Plateau
Winslow ●
Santa Fe ★
Albuquerque ●
Socorro ●
NEW MEXICO
Silver City ●
Las Cruces ●
El Paso ●
Ciudad Juárez

Las Vegas ●
Tucumcari ●
Clovis ●
Roswell ●
Carlsbad ●

Amarillo ●
OKLAHOMA
Oklahoma City ★
Lawton ●
Wichita Falls ●
Lubbock ●
Abilene ●
Midland ●
San Angelo ●
Odessa ●
TEXAS
Fort Stockton ●

Enid ●

Dallas ●
Fort Worth
Waco ●

Edwards Plateau
Killeen ●
Austin ★

PACIFIC OCEAN

Del Rio ●
San Antonio ●
Laredo ●
Corpus Christi ●
McAllen ●
Brownsville ●

MEXICO
Torreón ●
Monterrey ●
Rio Grande
GULF
Victoria ●

Kauai
Niihau ● Oahu
Honolulu ★
Molokai
Lanai Maui
Kahoolawe
PACIFIC OCEAN
Mauna Loa 4169 m (13,677 ft) ▲ Hilo
Hawaii

ARCTIC OCEAN
Barrow ●
Arctic Circle
Inuvik ●
RUSSIA
Brooks Range
ALASKA
Nome ●
Fairbanks ●
CANADA
Dawson ●
Mt. McKinley 6194 m (20,320 ft) ▲
Yukon R.
Alaska Range
Mackenzie R.
Whitehorse ●
Bethel ●
Anchorage ●
Homer ● Seward ●
Juneau ●
Sitka ●
Ketchikan ●
Kodiak ●
Bering Sea
Gulf of Alaska
Aleutian Is.

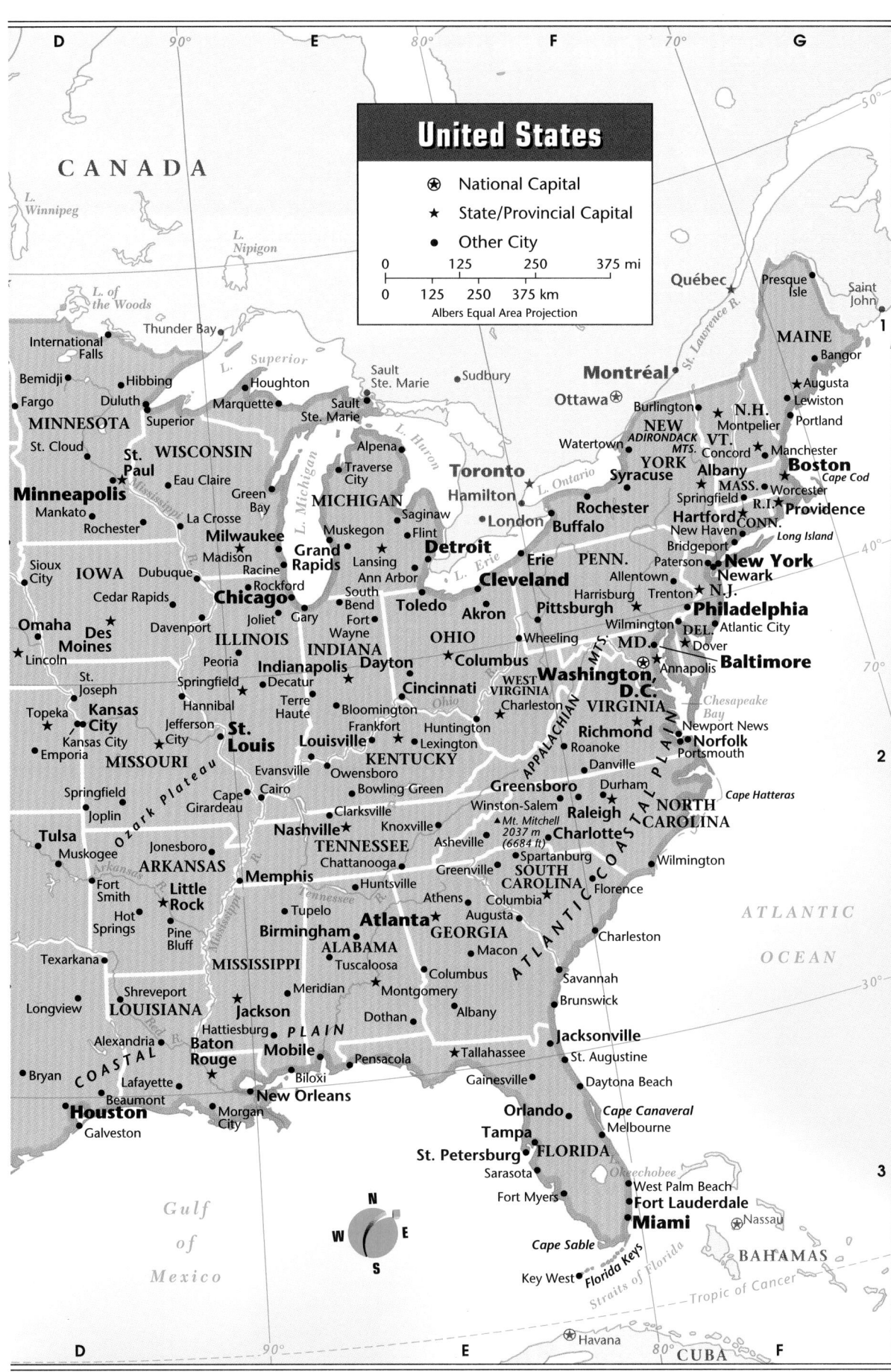

United States

⊛ National Capital

★ State/Provincial Capital

● Other City

0   125   250   375 mi

0   125   250   375 km

Albers Equal Area Projection

CANADA

L. Winnipeg

L. Nipigon

L. of the Woods

L. Superior

Thunder Bay

International Falls

Bemidji   Hibbing

Fargo   Duluth   Houghton   Marquette

MINNESOTA   Superior

St. Cloud   WISCONSIN   Sault Ste. Marie   Sault Ste. Marie

Minneapolis   Eau Claire   Green Bay   Alpena

St. Paul   Traverse City

Mankato   La Crosse   MICHIGAN   Saginaw

Rochester   Madison   Muskegon   Flint

Sioux City   IOWA   Dubuque   Milwaukee   Grand Rapids   Lansing   Detroit

Racine   Rockford   Ann Arbor

Cedar Rapids   Chicago   South Bend   Toledo   Cleveland

Omaha   Des Moines   Davenport   Joliet   Gary   Fort Wayne   OHIO   Akron   Pittsburgh

Lincoln   ILLINOIS   INDIANA   Columbus

St. Joseph   Peoria   Dayton

Topeka   Springfield   Decatur   Indianapolis   Cincinnati

Kansas City   Hannibal   Terre Haute   WEST VIRGINIA

Jefferson City   St. Louis   Bloomington   Frankfort   Huntington   Charleston

Emporia   Kansas City   Louisville   Lexington

MISSOURI   Evansville   Owensboro   KENTUCKY

Springfield   Cairo   Bowling Green

Joplin   Cape Girardeau   Clarksville   Knoxville   Asheville

Tulsa   Jonesboro   Nashville   TENNESSEE   Greenville

Muskogee   ARKANSAS   Chattanooga   Huntsville   Athens

Fort Smith   Memphis   SOUTH CAROLINA   Columbia

Little Rock   Tupelo   Birmingham   Atlanta   GEORGIA   Augusta

Hot Springs   Pine Bluff   ALABAMA   Macon

Texarkana   MISSISSIPPI   Tuscaloosa   Columbus

Shreveport   Meridian   Montgomery   Savannah

Longview   LOUISIANA   Jackson   Dothan   Albany   Brunswick

Alexandria   Hattiesburg   PLAIN   Jacksonville

Bryan   Lafayette   Baton Rouge   Mobile   Pensacola   Tallahassee   St. Augustine

Beaumont   Biloxi   New Orleans   Gainesville   Daytona Beach

Houston   Morgan City   Galveston   Orlando   Cape Canaveral

Tampa   Melbourne

St. Petersburg   FLORIDA

Sarasota   West Palm Beach

Fort Myers   Fort Lauderdale   Nassau

Cape Sable   Miami   BAHAMAS

Gulf of Mexico   Key West   Florida Keys   Straits of Florida   Tropic of Cancer

Québec   Presque Isle   Saint John

MAINE   Bangor

Montréal   Augusta   Lewiston

Ottawa   Burlington   N.H.   Portland

Watertown   ADIRONDACK MTS.   VT.   Montpelier   Manchester

NEW   Concord   Boston

Toronto   YORK   Albany   MASS.   Cape Cod

Hamilton   Syracuse   Springfield   R.I.   Worcester   Providence

London   Rochester   Buffalo   Hartford   CONN.

New Haven   Long Island

Erie   PENN.   Bridgeport   New York

Allentown   Newark

Harrisburg   Paterson   N.J.

Wheeling   Trenton   Philadelphia

Wilmington   DEL.   Atlantic City

MD.   Dover

Washington, D.C.   Annapolis   Baltimore

VIRGINIA   Chesapeake Bay

Richmond   Newport News

Roanoke   Norfolk   Portsmouth

Danville   Cape Hatteras

Greensboro   Durham

Winston-Salem   Raleigh   NORTH CAROLINA

Mt. Mitchell 2037 m (6684 ft)   Charlotte   Wilmington

Spartanburg

Florence

Charleston

ATLANTIC   OCEAN

APPALACHIAN   ATLANTIC   COASTAL   PLAIN

OZARK PLATEAU   COASTAL PLAIN

St. Lawrence R.

L. Huron   L. Ontario   L. Erie   L. Michigan

Sudbury   Sault Ste. Marie

Ohio R.   Tennessee R.   Arkansas R.   Red R.   Mississippi R.

Okeechobee

Havana   CUBA

N E S W

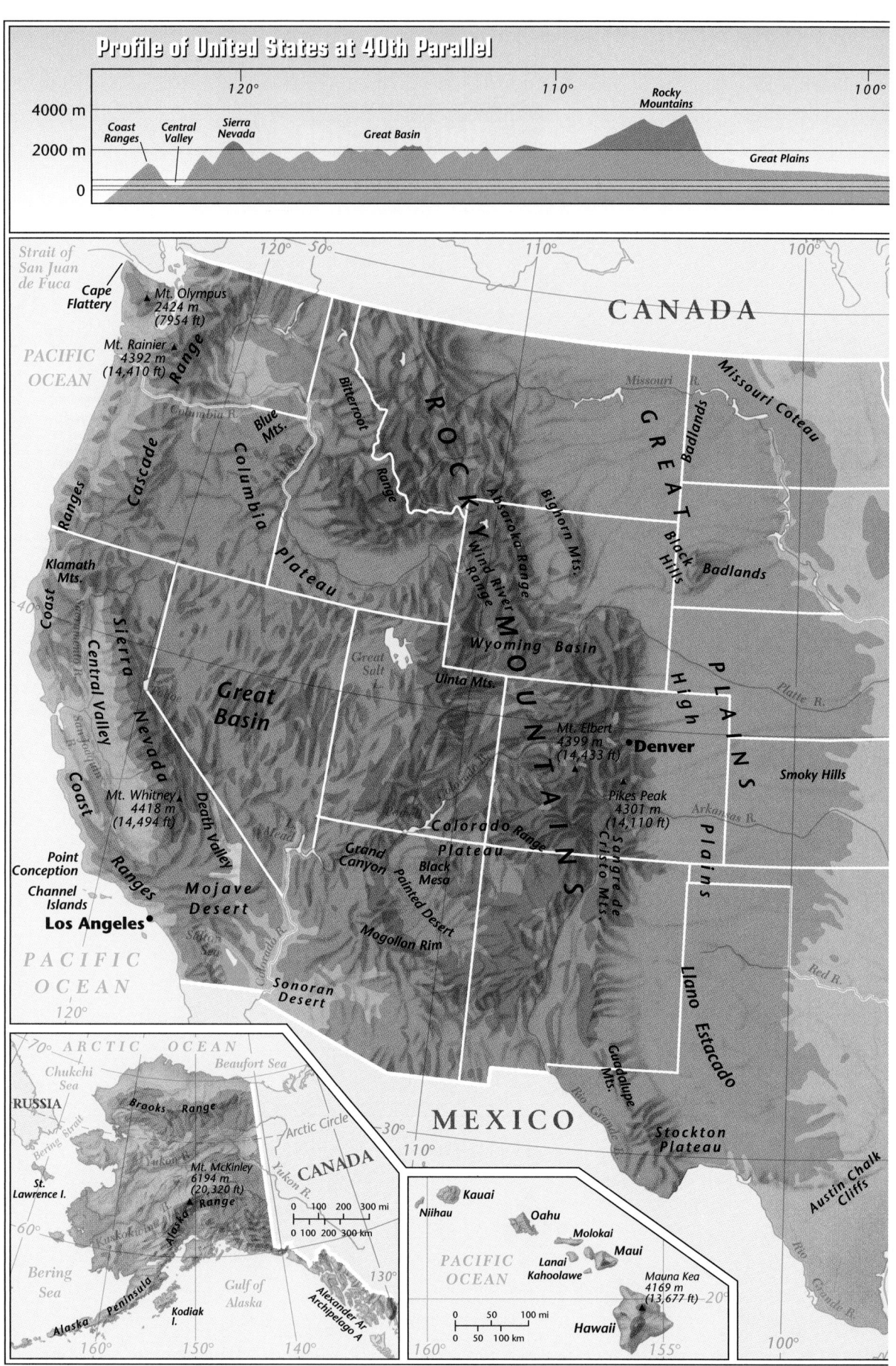

Profile of United States at 40th Parallel

120°   110°   Rocky Mountains   100°

4000 m
2000 m
0

Coast Ranges   Central Valley   Sierra Nevada   Great Basin   Great Plains

Strait of San Juan de Fuca
Cape Flattery
▲ Mt. Olympus 2424 m (7954 ft)
Mt. Rainier ▲ 4392 m (14,410 ft)
PACIFIC OCEAN
120°   50°   110°   100°
CANADA
Columbia R.
Blue Mts.
Bitterroot Range
R O C K Y
Missouri R.
Missouri Coteau
Cascade Range
Columbia Plateau
Absaroka Range
Bighorn Mts.
G R E A T
Badlands
Black Hills
Badlands
Klamath Mts.
Wind River Range
M O U N T A I N S
Wyoming Basin
P L A I N S
Coast Ranges
Great Salt L.
Uinta Mts.
40°
Sierra Nevada
Central Valley
Great Basin
Mt. Elbert 4399 m (14,433 ft)
•Denver
High Plains
Smoky Hills
Platte R.
Mt. Whitney ▲ 4418 m (14,494 ft)
Death Valley
Pikes Peak 4301 m (14,110 ft)
Arkansas R.
Point Conception
Coast Ranges
Mead
Colorado Range
Plateau
Sangre de Cristo Mts.
Channel Islands
Los Angeles•
Mojave Desert
Grand Canyon
Black Mesa
Painted Desert
Colorado Plateau
Mogollon Rim
Llano Estacado
PACIFIC OCEAN
120°
Sonoran Desert
Colorado R.
Red R.
Guadalupe Mts.
ARCTIC OCEAN
Chukchi Sea
Beaufort Sea
70°
Stockton Plateau
Austin Chalk Cliffs
RUSSIA
Brooks Range
Arctic Circle
MEXICO
30°
110°
Rio Grande
Bering Strait
Yukon R.
CANADA
St. Lawrence I.
Mt. McKinley 6194 m (20,320 ft)
Alaska Range
0 100 200 300 mi
0 100 200 300 km
60°
Kauai
Niihau
Oahu
Molokai
Maui
Lanai
Kahoolawe
Bering Sea
Gulf of Alaska
130°
PACIFIC OCEAN
Mauna Kea 4169 m (13,677 ft)
Alaska Peninsula
Kodiak I.
Alexander Archipelago
Alaska
160°   150°   140°
160°   155°
Hawaii
0 50 100 mi
0 50 100 km
–20°
100°

© MapQuest.com, Inc.

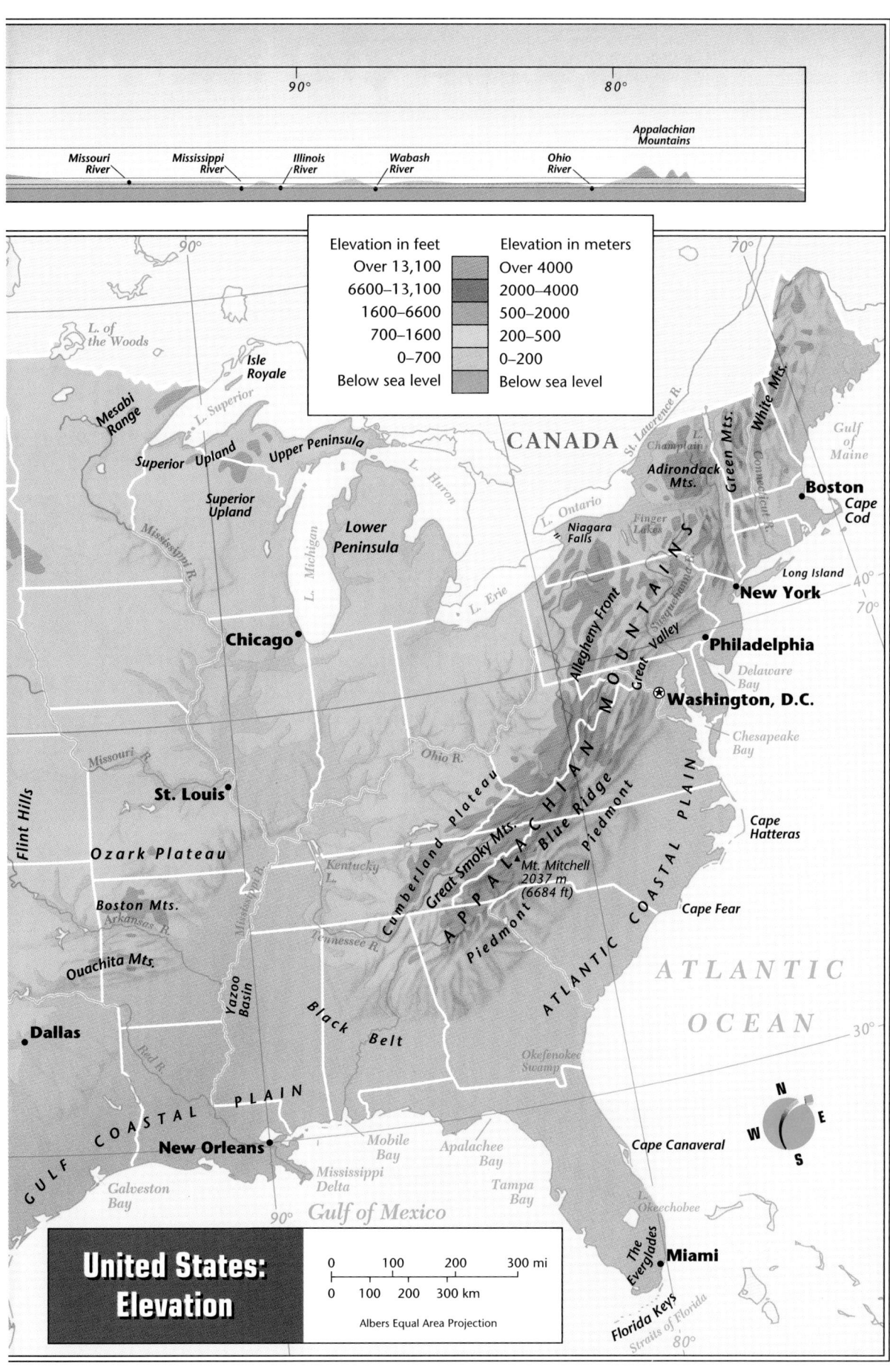

90° 80°

Appalachian Mountains

Missouri River · Mississippi River · Illinois River · Wabash River · Ohio River

Elevation in feet
Over 13,100
6600–13,100
1600–6600
700–1600
0–700
Below sea level

Elevation in meters
Over 4000
2000–4000
500–2000
200–500
0–200
Below sea level

CANADA

L. of the Woods

Mesabi Range

Isle Royale

Superior Upland

L. Superior

Upper Peninsula

Superior Upland

Lower Peninsula

L. Michigan

L. Huron

L. Ontario

St. Lawrence R.

Niagara Falls

L. Erie

Finger Lakes

Adirondack Mts.

L. Champlain

Green Mts.

White Mts.

Connecticut R.

Gulf of Maine

Boston
Cape Cod

Long Island

New York

Mississippi R.

Chicago

Allegheny Front

Susquehanna R.

Philadelphia

Great Valley

⊗ **Washington, D.C.**

Delaware Bay

Missouri

Ohio R.

A P P A L A C H I A N   M O U N T A I N S

Chesapeake Bay

Flint Hills

St. Louis

Cumberland Plateau

Blue Ridge

Piedmont

Cape Hatteras

Ozark Plateau

Kentucky L.

Great Smoky Mts.

Mt. Mitchell 2037 m (6684 ft)

Piedmont

A T L A N T I C   C O A S T A L   P L A I N

Boston Mts.

Arkansas R.

Tennessee R.

Mississippi R.

Piedmont

Cape Fear

Ouachita Mts.

Yazoo Basin

A T L A N T I C

Dallas

Red R.

Black Belt

O C E A N

30°

Okefenokee Swamp

G U L F   C O A S T A L   P L A I N

Mobile Bay

Apalachee Bay

Cape Canaveral

New Orleans

Mississippi Delta

Tampa Bay

Galveston Bay

90°

Gulf of Mexico

L. Okeechobee

The Everglades

Miami

Florida Keys

Straits of Florida

80°

N E S W

United States: Elevation

0   100   200   300 mi
0   100   200   300 km

Albers Equal Area Projection

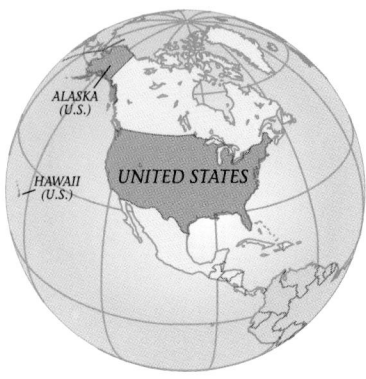

United States of America

The United States is a federal republic that consists of 50 states, the federal District of Columbia, and more than a dozen dependent territories. It is the world's fourth-largest country, after Russia, Canada and China. The United States declared its independence from England in 1776 and its thirteen colonies became the thirteen original states. The American Constitution became effective in 1789.

The United States has the most powerful, diverse and technically advanced economy in the world, with the highest per capita GDP among major industrial nations. Despite this fact, the country faces some major economic problems, including rapidly rising medical costs for an aging population, inadequate economic infrastructure, and large budget and trade deficits.

Historically, the U.S. has been a "melting pot" for immigrants from countries around the world, and the population reflects a wide mix of ethnic backgrounds.

Capital: Washington, D.C.
Area: 3,655,318 sq. mi.
9,372,610 sq. km.
Population: 281,421,906 (2000 Census)
Largest City: New York, 8,008,278
Languages: English, Spanish (spoken by a sizable minority)
Major Religions: Protestant, Roman Catholic, Jewish
Life Expectancy: 73 male, 80 female
Government: federal republic; strong democratic tradition
Monetary Unit: dollar
Industry: leading industrial power in the world, highly diversified and technologically advanced; petroleum, steel, motor vehicles, aerospace, telecommunications, chemicals, electronics, food processing, consumer goods, lumber, mining
Agriculture: wide variety of crops and livestock production; world's second largest producer and number one exporter of grain; surplus food producer; fishing
Minerals and Resources: coal, copper, lead, molybdenum, phosphates, uranium, bauxite, gold, iron, mercury, nickel, potash, silver, tungsten, zinc, petroleum, natural gas, timber

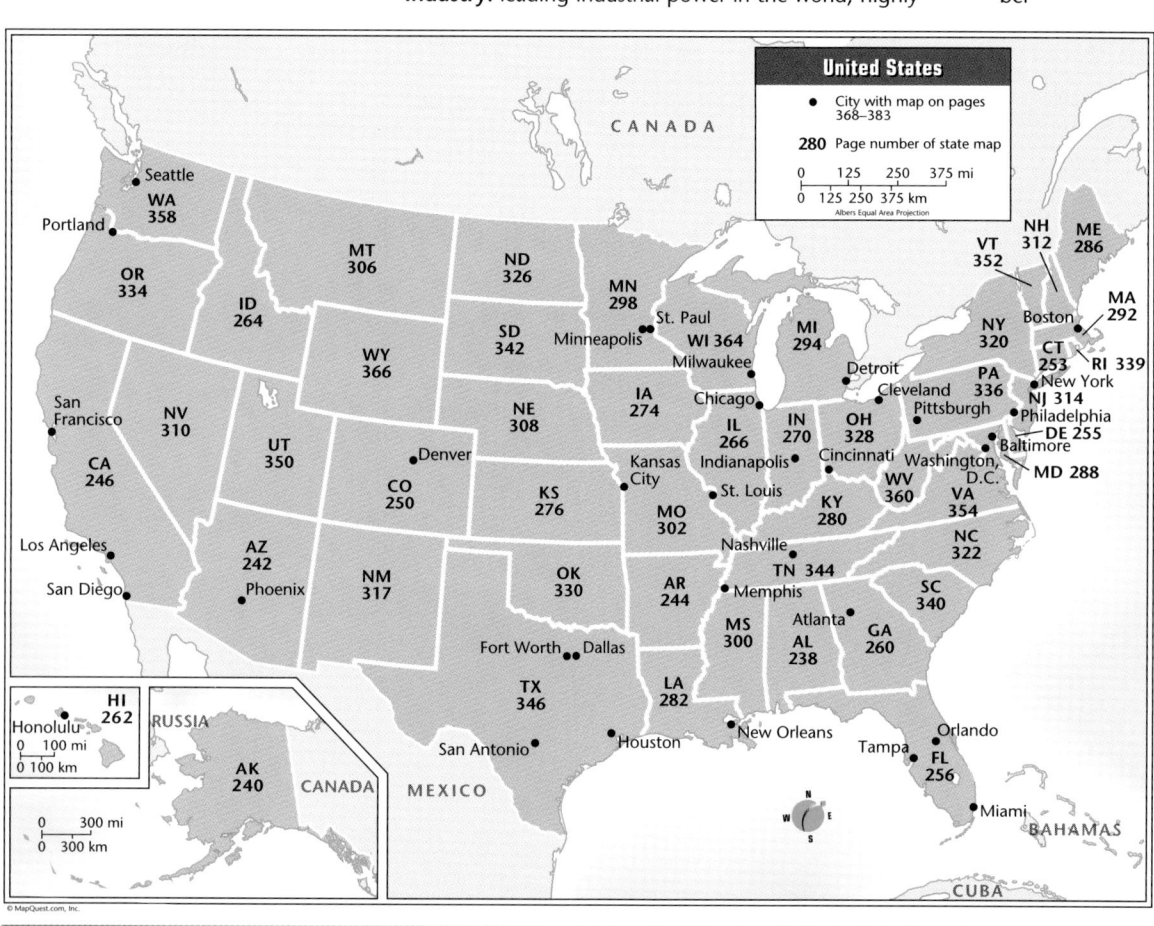

UNITED STATES POSTAL CODE ABBREVIATIONS

code	state name	page
AL	Alabama	238
AK	Alaska	240
AZ	Arizona	242
AR	Arkansas	244
CA	California	246
CO	Colorado	250
CT	Connecticut	253
DE	Delaware	255
DC	District of Columbia	288
FL	Florida	256
GA	Georgia	260
HI	Hawaii	262
ID	Idaho	264
IL	Illinois	266
IN	Indiana	270
IA	Iowa	274
KS	Kansas	276
KY	Kentucky	280
LA	Louisiana	282
ME	Maine	285
MD	Maryland	288
MA	Massachusetts	292
MI	Michigan	294
MN	Minnesota	298
MS	Mississippi	300
MO	Missouri	302
MT	Montana	306
NE	Nebraska	308
NV	Nevada	310
NH	New Hampshire	312
NJ	New Jersey	314
NM	New Mexico	317
NY	New York	320
NC	North Carolina	322
ND	North Dakota	326
OH	Ohio	328
OK	Oklahoma	330
OR	Oregon	334
PA	Pennsylvania	336
RI	Rhode Island	339
SC	South Carolina	340
SD	South Dakota	342
TN	Tennessee	344
TX	Texas	346
UT	Utah	350
VT	Vermont	352
VA	Virginia	354
WA	Washington	358
WV	West Virginia	360
WI	Wisconsin	364
WY	Wyoming	366

EXPLANATION OF UNITED STATES INDEXES

Populations in **bold** type are from the 2000 U.S. Census.

Populations in *italics* are *estimated* from 2000 census data.

Crystal Beach is a community within Palm Harbor. See the listing for Palm Harbor for the total population.

Florida:
Map Index

Counties

Brevard, **476,230** H4
...

Cities and Towns

Allentown, **40** A1
Altamonte Springs,
41,200 . . . . .C4, G3
Altha, **506** C1
Alton, *80* E1
...
Cross City, **1,775** E2
Crystal Beach
(see Palm Harbor) **4,000** . .C6
Crystal Lake C1

...
Fort Myers, **48,208** G5
Fort Myers Beach, **6,561** G5
Fort Myers Villas (Villas), **11,346** .G5
...
Hillsboro Beach, **2,163** B5
Hines E2
Hinson, *750* D1

Palm Harbor, **59,248** C6, F3

Other Features

Aucilla, *river* E1
Avon Park A.F.B. G4
Bald, *point* D2
Big Cypress I.R. H5
Big Cypress
National Preserve G5
Big Cypress *swamp* G5

Alternate place name.

For places without a population figure, the population is estimated to be less than 40.

This category lists all physical features and points of interest labeled in the subject state.

See the abbreviations list on page 8.

Italics indicate the type of feature listed.

Alabama

Capital: Montgomery
Land Area: 50,750 sq. mi.
131,443 sq. km.
Population: 4,447,100 (2000 Census)
Largest City: Birmingham, 242,820
Highest Point: Cheaha Mtn.
2,405 ft.
733 m.
Admitted to Union: December 14, 1819
Nickname: Heart of Dixie
Cotton State
Yellowhammer State
State Flower: Camellia
State Bird: Yellowhammer

Alabama:
Map Index

Counties

Autauga, **43,671** C3
Baldwin, **140,415** B5
Barbour, **29,038** D4
Bibb, **20,826** B2
Blount, **51,024** C2
Bullock, **11,714** D3
Butler, **21,399** C4
Calhoun, **112,249** D2
Chambers, **36,583** D3
Cherokee, **23,988** D1
Chilton, **39,593** C3
Choctaw, **15,922** A3
Clarke, **27,867** B4
Clay, **14,254** D2
Cleburne, **14,123** D2
Coffee, **43,615** C4
Colbert, **54,984** B1
Conecuh, **14,089** C4
Coosa, **12,202** C3
Covington, **37,631** C4
Crenshaw, **13,665** C4
Cullman, **77,483** C1
Dale, **49,129** D4
Dallas, **46,365** B3
De Kalb, **64,452** D1
Elmore, **65,874** C3
Escambia, **38,440** B4
Etowah, **103,459** D1
Fayette, **18,495** B2
Franklin, **31,223** B1
Geneva, **25,764** D4
Greene, **9,974** A3
Hale, **17,185** B3
Henry, **16,310** D4
Houston, **88,787** D4
Jackson, **53,926** C1
Jefferson, **662,047** C2, E1
Lamar, **15,904** A2
Lauderdale, **87,966** B1
Lawrence, **34,803** B1
Lee, **115,092** D3
Limestone, **65,676** C1
Lowndes, **13,473** C3
Macon, **24,105** D3
Madison, **276,700** C1
Marengo, **22,539** B3
Marion, **31,214** B1
Marshall, **82,231** C1
Mobile, **399,843** A5
Monroe, **24,324** B4
Montgomery, **223,510** C3
Morgan, **111,064** C1
Perry, **11,861** B3
Pickens, **20,949** A2
Pike, **29,605** D4
Randolph, **22,380** D2
Russell, **49,756** D3
St. Clair, **64,742** C2
Shelby, **143,293** C2, E1
Sumter, **14,798** A3
Talladega, **80,321** C2
Tallapoosa, **41,475** D3
Tuscaloosa, **164,875** B2
Walker, **70,713** B2
Washington, **18,097** A4
Wilcox, **13,183** B4
Winston, **24,843** B1

Cities and Towns

Abbeville, **2,987** D4
Aberfoil, *125* D3
Abernant, *175* B2
Adamsville, **4,965** C2, D1
Addison, **723** B1
Akron, **521** B3
Alabaster, **22,619** C2
Alberta, *175* B3
Albertville, **17,247** C1
Alexander City, **15,008** D3
Aliceville, **2,567** A2
Allgood, **629** C2
Alma, *250* B4
Altoona, **984** C1
Andalusia, **8,794** C4
Anderson, **354** B1
Anniston, **24,276** D2
Ansley, *70* C4
Arab, **7,174** C1
Ardmore, **1,034** C1
Argo, **1,780** C2
Ariton, **772** D4
Arkadelphia, *100* C2
Arley, **290** B1
Ashby, *125* C2
Ashford, **1,853** D4
Ashland, **1,965** D2
Ashville, **2,260** C2
Athens, **18,967** B1
Atmore, **7,676** B4
Attalla, **6,592** C1
Auburn, **42,987** D3
Autaugaville, **820** C3
Avon, **466** D4
Axis, *400* A5
Babbie, **627** C4
Baileyton, **684** C1
Baker Hill, *90* D4
Banks, **224** D4
Bankston, *80* B2
Bashi B4
Batesville D3
Bay Minette, **7,820** B5
Bayou La Batre, **2,313** A5
Bear Creek, **1,053** B1
Beatrice, **412** B4
Beaverton, **226** A2
Belgreen, *150* B1
Belk, **214** B2
Bellamy, *600* A3
Benton, **47** C3
Berry, **1,238** B2
Bessemer, **29,672** C2, D1
Bexar, *60* A1
Billingsley, **116** C3
Birmingham, **242,820** C2, E1
Black, **202** D4
Blacksher B4
Blanche D1
Bleecker, *150* D3
Blountsville, **1,768** C1
Blue Mountain, **233** D2
Blue Ridge, **1,331** C3
Blue Springs, **121** D4
Boaz, **7,411** C1
Boligee, **369** A3
Bolling, *80* C4
Bon Air, **96** C2
Booth, *80* C3
Borden Springs D2
Boyd, *125* A3
Bradley, *40* C4
Braggs, *80* C3
Branchville, **825** C2
Brantley, **920** C4
Bremen, *250* C2
Brent, **4,024** B3
Brewton, **5,498** B4
Bridgeport, **2,728** D1
Brilliant, **762** B1
Brooklyn C4
Brookside, **1,393** D1
Brooksville, *100* C1
Brookwood, **1,483** B2
Browns B3
Brownville B2
Brundidge, **2,341** D4
Bucks, *40* A4
Burkville C3
Burnsville, *175* C3
Burnt Corn, *90* B4
Butler, **1,952** A3
Bynum, **1,863** D2
Cahaba Heights, **5,203** E1
Calera, **3,158** C2
Calhoun, *100* C3
Camden, **2,257** B4
Campbell B4
Camp Hill, **1,273** D3
Carbon Hill, **2,071** B2
Cardiff, **82** D1
Carlowville, *40* B3
Carlton B4
Carolina, **248** C4
Carrollton, **987** A2
Castleberry, **590** B4
Catherine, *50* B3
Cedar Bluff, **1,467** D1
Center Point, **22,784** C2, E1
Central, *125* C3
Centre, **3,216** D1
Centreville, **2,466** B3
Chalkville (see Pinson), **3,829** E1
Chancellor, *200* D4
Chapman, *100* C4
Chatom, **1,193** A4
Chelsea, **2,949** C2
Cherokee, **1,237** B1
Chickasaw, **6,364** A5
Childersburg, **4,927** C2
Chrysler, *40* B4
Chunchula, *275* A5
Citronelle, **3,659** A4
Claiborne, *40* B4
Clanton, **7,800** C3
Clay (see Pinson), **4,947** E1
Clayhatchee, **501** D4
Clayton, **1,475** D4
Cleveland, **1,241** C2
Clinton, *175* B3
Clio, **2,206** D4
Clopton D4
Cloverdale, *150* B1
Coaling, **1,115** B2
Coatopa A3
Cochrane A2
Coffee Springs, **251** D4
Coffeeville, **360** A4
Coker, **808** B2
Collbran, *50* D1
Collinsville, **1,644** D1
Colony, **385** C2
Columbia, **804** D4
Columbiana, **3,316** C2
Comer, *40* D3
Cooper, *250* C3
Coosada, **1,382** C3
Cordova, **2,423** B2
Cottondale, *2,000* B2
Cottonton D3
Cottonwood, **1,170** D4
County Line (Blount Co.), **257** C2
County Line (Covington Co.), **125** C4
Courtland, **769** B1
Cowarts, **1,546** D4
Cragford, *90* D2
Crawford, *275* D3
Creola, **2,002** A5
Cromwell A3
Crossville (De Kalb Co.), **1,431** D1
Crossville (Lamar Co.), *150* B2
Cuba, **363** A3
Cullman, **13,995** C1
Cullomburg, *175* A4
Curry, *125* C2
Cusseta, *125* D3
Cypress, *60* B3
Dadeville, **3,212** D3
Daleville, **4,653** D4
Dancy, *100* A2
Daphne, **16,581** B5
Dauphin Island, **1,371** A5
Daviston, **267** D2
Dayton, *60* B3
Deatsville, **340** C3
Decatur, **53,929** C1
Deer Park, **30** A4
Delta, *90* D2
Demopolis, **7,540** B3
Detroit, **247** A1
Dickinson, *250* B4
Dixons Mills, *400* B3
Dixonville B4
Dodge City, **612** C1
Dolomite, *120* D1
Dora, **2,413** B2
Dothan, **57,737** D4
Double Springs, **1,003** B1
Douglas, **530** C1
Dozier, **391** C4
Duncanville, *175* B2
Dutton, **310** D1
East Brewton, **2,496** B4
Echo, *50* D4
Eclectic, **1,037** C3
Edwardsville, **186** D2
Elba, **4,185** C4
Elberta, **552** B5
Eldridge, **184** B2
Elkmont, **470** C1
Elmore, **199** C3
Elrod, *150* B2
Emelle, **31** A3
Enterprise, **21,178** D4
Eoline, *70* B2
Epes, **206** A3
Equality, *60* C3
Ethelsville, **81** A2
Eufaula, **13,908** D4
Eunola, **182** D4
Eutaw, **1,878** B3
Eva, **491** C1
Evergreen, **3,630** C4
Excel, **582** B4
Fackler, *175* D1
Fairfield (Covington Co.), *60* C4
Fairfield (Jefferson Co.), **12,381** C2, E1
Fairhope, **12,480** B5
Fairview, **522** C1
Falkville, **1,202** C1
Faunsdale, **87** B3
Fayette, **4,922** B2
Fayetteville, *200* C2
Five Points, **146** D2
Flat Rock, *175* D1
Flatwood B3
Flomaton, **1,588** B4
Florala, **1,964** C4
Florence, **36,264** B1
Foley, **7,590** B5
Forestdale, **10,509** E1
Forest Home C4
Forkland, **629** B3
Forney, *50* D1
Fort Davis, *80* D3
Fort Deposit, **1,270** C4
Fort Mitchell, *200* D3
Fort Morgan, *350* A5
Fort Payne, **12,938** D1
Fosters, *200* B2
Fountain, *50* B4
Franklin (Macon Co.), **149** D3
Franklin (Monroe Co.) B4
Frankville, *125* A4
Freemanville, *450* B4
Frisco City, **1,460** B4
Fruitdale, *125* A4
Fruithurst, **270** D2
Fulton, **308** B4
Fultondale, **6,595** C2, E1
Furman C3
Fyffe, **971** D1
Gadsden, **38,978** C1
Gainesville, **220** A3
Gallion, *100* B3
Gantt, **241** C4
Garden City, **564** C1
Gardendale, **11,626** C2, E1
Garland, *40* C4
Gasque, *350* B5
Gaylesville, **140** D1
Geiger, **161** A3
Geneva, **4,388** D4
Georgetown, *300* A5
Georgiana, **1,737** C4
Geraldine, **786** C1
Gilbertown, **187** A4
Glen Allen, **442** B2
Glencoe, **5,152** D2
Glenville D3
Glenwood, **191** C4
Goldville, **37** D2
Good Hope, **1,966** C1
Goodwater, **1,633** C2
Gordo, **1,677** B2
Gordon, **408** D4
Gordonsville, **318** C3
Gorgas, *40* B2
Goshen, **300** C4
Grady, *100* C4
Graham, *125* D2
Grand Bay, **3,918** A5
Grangeburg, **10** D4
Grant, **665** C1
Grayson, *100* B1
Graysville, **2,344** D1
Greensboro, **2,731** B3
Greenville, **7,228** C4
Grimes, **459** D4
Grove Hill, **1,438** B4
Guin, **2,389** B2
Gulf Crest, *90* A4
Gulf Shores, **5,044** B5
Guntersville, **7,395** C1
Gurley, **876** C1
Gu-Win, **204** B2
Hackleburg, **1,527** B1
Hacoda, *50* C4
Haleburg, **108** D4
Haleyville, **4,182** B1
Halsell A3
Hamilton, **6,786** B1
Hammondville, **486** D1
Hanceville, **2,951** C1
Hardaway, *40* D3
Harpersville, **1,620** C2
Hartford, **2,369** D4
Hartselle, **12,019** C1
Harvest, **3,054** C1
Hatchechubbee, *40* D3
Hatton, *400* B1
Hayden, **470** C2
Hayneville, **1,177** C3
Hazel Green, **3,805** C1
Hazen, *60* B3
Headland, **3,523** D4
Heath, **249** C4
Heflin, **3,002** D2
Heiberger B3
Helena, **10,296** C2
Henagar, **2,400** D1
Hendrix, *175* C1
Heron Bay, *550* A5
Highland Home, *125* C4
Highland Lake, **408** C2
Hillsboro, **608** B1
Hodges, **261** B1
Hokes Bluff, **4,149** D2
Hollis Crossroads, *225* D2
Holly Pond, **645** C1
Hollywood, **950** D1
Holt, **4,103** B2
Homewood, **25,043** C2, E1
Honoraville, *90* C4
Hoover, **62,742** C2, E1
Horn Hill, **235** C4
Hueytown, **15,364** B2, D1
Huguley, **2,953** D3
Hulaco, *400* C1
Huntsville, **158,216** C1
Hurtsboro, **592** D3
Huxford, *80* B4
Hybart B4
Hytop, **315** C1
Ider, **664** D1
Indian Springs Village, **2,225** C2, E1
Inverness E1
Irondale, **9,813** C2, E1
Isbell, *200* B1
Jack, *90* C4
Jackson, **5,419** B4
Jacksons Gap, **761** D3
Jacksonville, **8,404** D2
Jasper, **14,052** B2
Jemison, **2,248** C3
Jenifer, *550* D2
Jones, *70* C3
Jones Chapel, *50* B1
Keener, *150* D1
Kennedy, **541** B2
Kent, *175* D3
Killen, **1,119** B1
Kimberly, **1,801** C2
Kimbrough, *70* B3
Kinsey, **1,796** D4
Kinston, **602** C4
Knoxville B3
Laceys Spring, *750* C1
Ladonia, **3,229** D3
Lafayette, **3,234** D3
Lake Purdy, **5,799** E1
Lakeview, **163** D1
Lamison, *50* B3
Landersville, *150* B1
Lanett, **7,897** D3
Langston, **254** C1
Lavaca, *100* A3
Lawley, *125* C3
Leeds, **10,455** C2
Leesburg, **799** D1
Leighton, **849** B1
Lester, **107** B1
Letohatchee, *175* C3
Level Plains, **1,544** D4
Lexington, **840** B1
Libertyville, **106** C4
Lillian, *350* B5
Lincoln, **4,577** C2
Linden, **2,424** B3
Lineville, **2,401** D2
Lipscomb, **2,458** D1
Lisman, **653** A3
Littleville, **978** B1
Livingston, **3,297** A3
Loachapoka, **165** D3
Lockhart, **548** C4
Locust Fork, **1,016** C2
Lomax, *150* C3
Louisville, **612** D4
Lower Peach Tree, *100* B4
Lowndesboro, **140** C3
Loxley, **1,348** B5
Luverne, **2,635** C4
Lynn, **597** B1
Madison, **29,329** C1
Madrid, **303** D4
Malone D2
Malvern, **1,215** D4
Maplesville, **672** C3
Margaret, **1,169** C2
Marion, **3,511** B3
Marion Junction, *50* B3
Maytown, **435** D1
McCullough, *200* B4
McIntosh, **244** A4
McKenzie, **644** C4
McMullen, **66** A2
McWilliams, *125* B4
Meadowbrook, **4,697** E1
Megargel, *90* B4
Melvin, *60* A4
Memphis, **33** A2
Mentone, **451** D1
Meridianville, **4,117** C1
Midfield, **5,626** C2, D1
Midland City, **1,703** D4
Midway (Bullock Co.), **457** D3
Midway (Monroe Co.) B4
Mignon, **1,348** C2
Millbrook, **10,386** C3
Miller, *40* B3
Millers Ferry B3
Millerville, *200* D2
Millport, **1,160** A2
Millry, **615** A4
Milstead D3
Minter, *80* C3
Mitchell D3
Mobile, **198,915** A5
Monroeville, **6,862** B4
Montevallo, **4,825** C2
Montgomery, **201,568** C3
Moody, **8,053** C2
Moores Bridge B2
Moores Mill, **5,178** C1
Mooresville, **59** C1
Morgan City, *550* C1
Morris, **1,827** C2
Mosses, **1,101** C3
Moulton, **3,260** B1
Moundville, **1,809** B3
Mountainboro, **338** C1
Mountain Brook, **20,604** C2, E1
Mountain Creek, *300* C3
Mount Andrew, *40* D4
Mount Vernon, **844** A4
Mulga, **973** D1
Muscle Shoals, **11,924** B1
Myrtlewood, **139** B3
Napier Field, **404** D4
Natural Bridge, **28** B1
Nauvoo, **284** B2
Nectar, **372** C2
Needham, **97** A4
Newbern, **231** B3
New Brockton, **1,250** D4
New Hope, **2,539** C1
New Market, **1,864** C1
New Site, **848** D2
Newton, **1,708** D4
Newtonville, *40* B2
Newville, **553** D4
North Courtland, **799** B1
North Johns, **142** B2
Northport, **19,435** B2
Notasulga, **916** D3
Oak Grove, **457** C2
Oak Hill, **37** B4
Oakman, **944** B2
Odenville, **1,131** C2
Ohatchee, **1,215** C2
Oneonta, **5,576** C2
Onycha, **208** C4
Opelika, **23,498** D3
Opp, **6,607** C4
Orange Beach, **3,784** B5
Orion D4
Orrville, **230** B3
Overbrook, *400* C2
Owens Crossroads, **1,124** C1
Oxford, **14,592** D2
Ozark, **15,119** D4
Paint Rock, **185** C1
Panola, *90* A3
Parrish, **1,268** B2
Pea Ridge, *175* C2
Pelham, **14,369** C2
Pell City, **9,565** C2
Pennington, **353** A3
Penton, *80* D2
Perdido, *375* B4
Perote D4
Peterson, *475* B2
Petersville (Underwood-Petersville), **3,137** B1
Petrey, **63** C4
Phenix City, **28,265** D3
Phil Campbell, **1,091** B1
Pickensville, **662** A2
Piedmont, **5,120** D2
Pike Road, **310** C3
Pinckard, **667** D4
Pine Apple, **145** C4
Pine Hill, **966** B4
Pine Level, *100* C3
Pine Ridge, **243** D1
Pinson (Pinson-Clay-Chalkville), **5,033** C2, E1
Pisgah, **706** D1
Pittsview, *70* D3
Plantersville, *325* C3
Pleasant Grove, **9,983** D1
Pleasant Groves, **447** D1
Pleasant Site, *50* A1
Pletcher, *90* C3
Plevna, *50* C1
Point Clear, **1,876** B5
Pollard, **120** B4
Pondville, *60* B3
Portersville D1
Powell, **926** D1
Prattville, **24,303** C3
Priceville, **1,631** C1
Prichard, **28,633** A5
Providence, **311** B3
Putnam A3
Pyriton, *70* D2
Rabun, *100* B4
Ragland, **1,918** C2
Rainbow City, **8,428** C2
Rainsville, **4,499** D1
Ralph, *40* B2
Ramer, *100* C3
Ranburne, **459** D2
Randolph C3
Range, *80* B4
Red Bay, **3,374** A1
Red Hill, *350* D3
Red Level, **556** C4
Reece City, **634** C1
Reform, **1,978** A2
Repton, **280** B4
Riderwood, *40* A3
Ridgeville, **158** C1
River Falls, **616** C4
Riverside, **1,564** C2
Riverview, **99** B4
Roanoke, **6,563** D2
Robertsdale, **3,782** B5
Rockford, **428** C3
Rockledge, *600* C1
Rogersville, **1,199** B1
Rosa, **313** C2

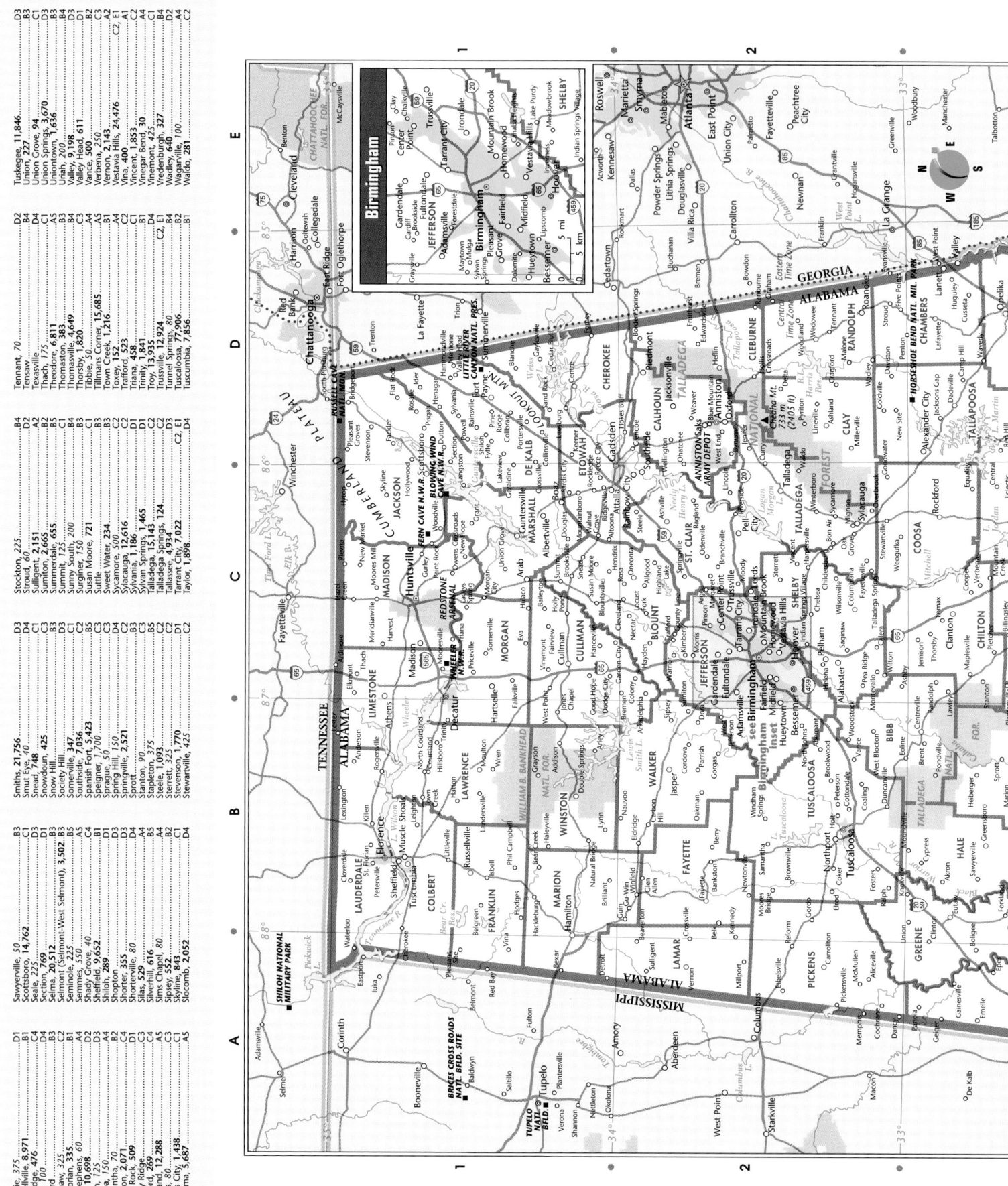

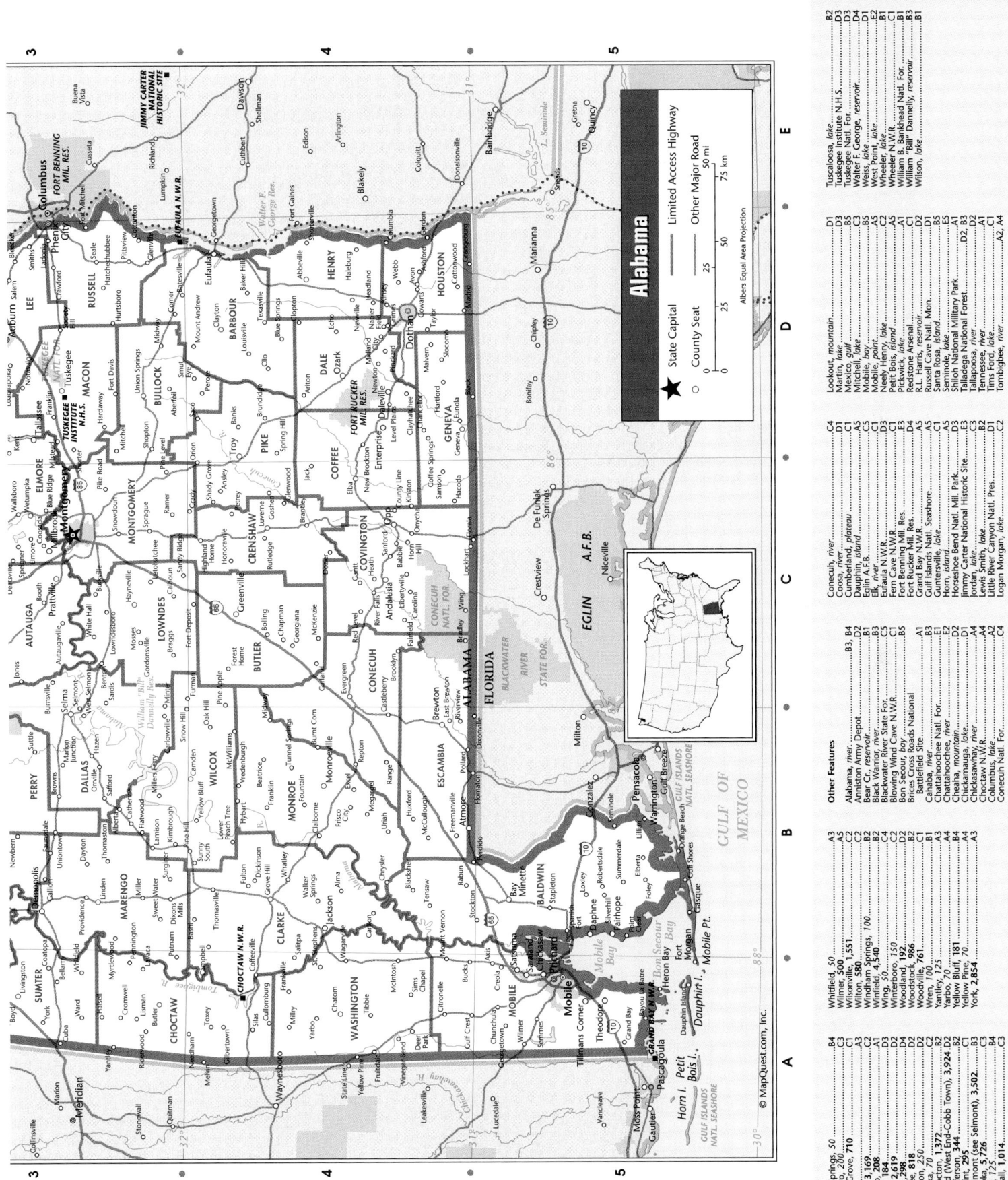

Alabama

Map Legend:
- ★ State Capital
- ○ County Seat
- Limited Access Highway
- Other Major Road

Albers Equal Area Projection

0   25   50   50 mi
0   25   50   75 km

Walker Springs, 50 .... B4
Walsboro, 200 .... C1
Walnut Grove, 710 .... A3
Warrior, 3,169 .... A1
Waterloo, 208 .... D3
Waverly, 184 .... D2
Weaver, 2,619 .... D2
Webb, 1,298 .... C2
Wedowee, 818 .... C2
Wellington, 250 .... B2
Weogufka, 70 .... B2
West Blocton, 1,372 .... D2
West End (West End-Cobb Town), 3,924 .. D2
West Jefferson, 344 .... B2
West Point, 295 .... C1
West Selmont (see Selmont), 3,502 ..... B3
Wetumpka, 5,726 .... C3
Whatley, 125 .... B4
White Hall, 1,014 .... C3

Whitfield, 50 .... A3
Wilmer, 500 .... C1
Wilsonville, 1,551 .... C2
Wiltonville, 580 .... B2
Windham Springs, 100 .... B1
Winfield, 4,540 .... A1
Wing, 50 .... C4
Winterboro, 150 .... C1
Woodland, 192 .... D2
Woodstock, 986 .... B2
Woodville, 761 .... B1
Wren, 100 .... A3
Yantley, 125 .... A4
Yarbo, 70 .... B4
Yellow Bluff, 181 .... B3
Yellow Pine, 70 .... A4
York, 2,854 .... A3

Other Features

Alabama, river B3, B4
Anniston Army Depot D2
Bear Cr., reservoir B1
Blackwater River State For. C5
Black Warrior, river B2
Blowing Wind Cave N.W.R. C1
Bon Secour, bay D2
Brices Cross Roads National
  Battlefield Site A1
Cahaba, river B3
Chattahoochee Natl. For. E1
Chattahoochee, river E2
Cheaha, mountain D1
Chickamauga, lake D1
Chickasawhay, river A4
Choctaw N.W.R. A4
Columbus, lake A2
Conecuh Natl. For. C4

Conecuh, river C4
Coosa, river D1
Cumberland, plateau A5
Dauphin, island C3
Eglin A.F.B. C5
Elk, river C1
Eufaula N.W.R. E3
Fern Cave N.W.R. C1
Fort Benning Mil. Res. D2
Fort Rucker Mil. Res. D4
Grand Bay N.W.R. A5
Gulf Islands Natl. Seashore B5
Guntersville, lake C1
Horn, island B5
Jimmy Carter National Historic Site ... E3
Jordan, lake D1
Lewis Smith, lake A4
Little River Canyon Natl. Pres. A2
Logan Martin, lake C4

Lookout, mountain B2
Martin, lake D3
Mexico, gulf D4
Mitchell, lake D1
Mobile, bay E2
Mobile, point B1
Neely Henry, lake A5
Petit Bois, island C1
Pickwick, lake A5
R.L. Harris, reservoir C1
Redstone Arsenal D2
Russell Cave Natl. Mon. D1
Santa Rosa, island B5
Seminole, lake E5
Shiloh National Military Park A1
Talladega National Forest D2, B3
Tallapoosa, river B2
Tennessee, river A1
Tims Ford, lake A2
Tombigbee, river C2

Tuscaloosa, lake B2
Tuskegee Institute N.H.S. D3
Tuskegee Natl. For. D4
Walter F. George, reservoir E2
Weiss, lake A5
West Point, lake C1
Wheeler, lake A5
Wheeler N.W.R. C1
William B. Bankhead Natl. For. B3
William "Bill" Dannelly, reservoir B1
Wilson, lake B1

© MapQuest.com, Inc.

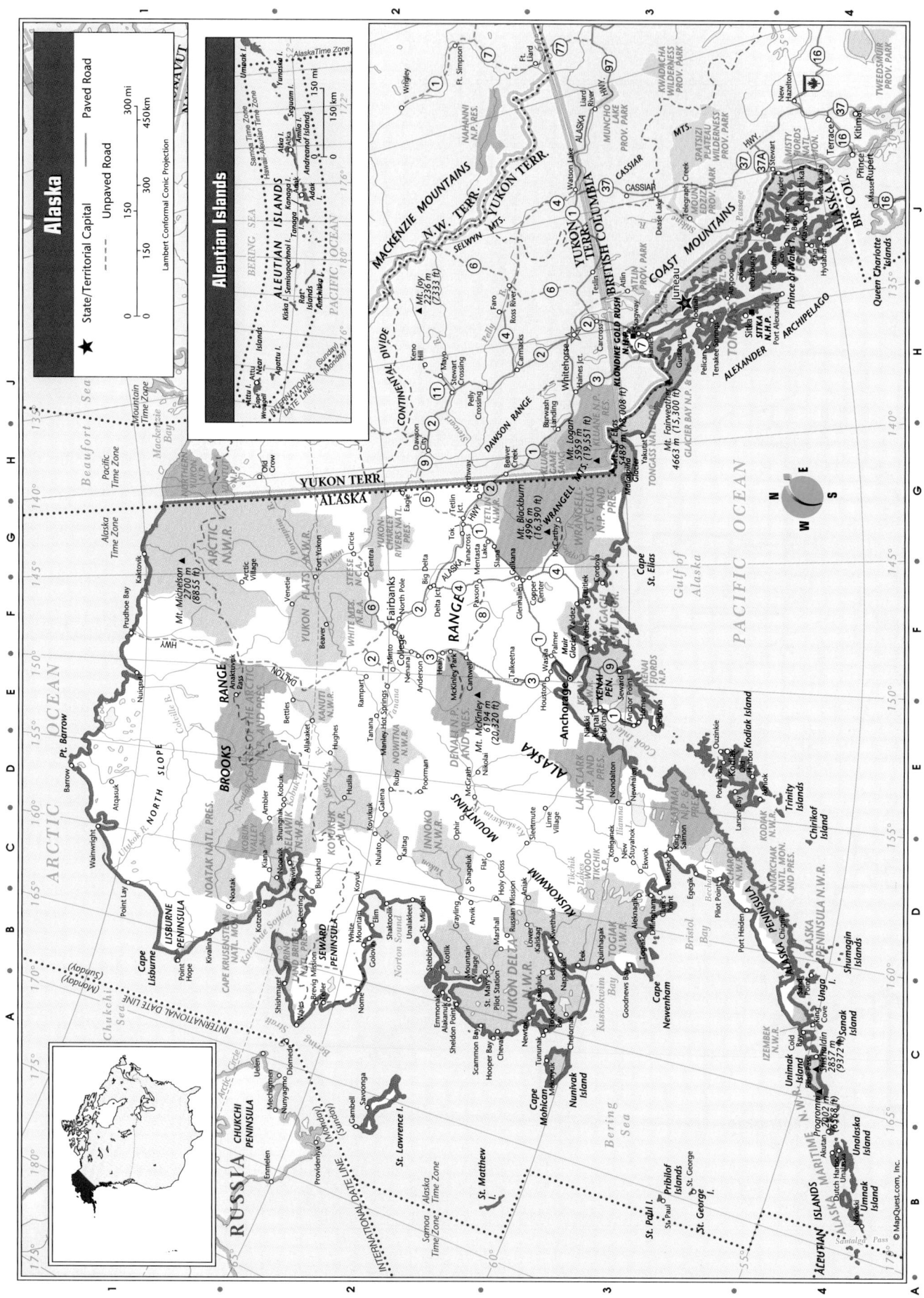

Alaska

State/Territorial Capital
★

Unpaved Road
Paved Road

0   150   300   450km
0   150   300 mi

Lambert Conformal Conic Projection

Aleutian Islands

0   150   300 km
0   150 mi

© MapQuest.com, Inc.

Alaska

Capital:	Juneau
Land Area:	570,374 sq. mi.
	1,477,268 sq. km.
Population:	626,932 (2000 Census)
Largest City:	Anchorage, 260,283
Highest Point:	Mt. McKinley
	20,320 ft.
	6,194 m.
Admitted to Union:	January 3, 1959
Nickname:	The Last Frontier
State Flower:	Forget-Me-Not
State Bird:	Willow Ptarmigan

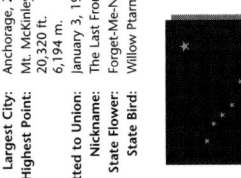

Alaska: Map Index

Cities and Towns

Adak (Adak Station), 316 .... Inset
Akhiok, 80 .... E3
Akutan, 713 .... B4
Alakanuk, 652 .... C2
Aleknagik, 221 .... D3
Allakaket, 97 .... E1
Ambler, 309 .... D1
Anaktuvuk Pass, 282 .... E1
Anchorage, 260,283 .... F2
Anchor Point, 1,845 .... E3
Anderson, 367 .... F2
Angoon, 572 .... J3
Aniak, 572 .... D2
Anvik, 104 .... C2
Arctic Village, 152 .... F1
Atka, 92 .... Inset
Atqasuk, 228 .... D1
Attu .... Inset
Barrow, 4,581 .... D1
Beaver, 84 .... F1
Bethel, 5,471 .... C2
Bettles, 43 .... E1
Big Delta, 749 .... F2
Brevig Mission, 276 .... B1
Buckland, 406 .... C1
Cantwell, 222 .... F2
Central, 134 .... F1
Chefornak, 394 .... C2
Chevak, 765 .... B2
Chignik, 79 .... D3
Circle, 100 .... F1
Clark's Point, 75 .... D3
Coffman Cove, 199 .... K3
Cold Bay, 88 .... C3
College, 11,402 .... F2
Copper Center, 362 .... G2
Cordova, 2,454 .... F2
Craig, 1,397 .... J3
Deering, 136 .... C1
Delta Jct., 840 .... F2
Dillingham, 2,466 .... D3
Diomede, 146 .... B1
Dutch Harbor B4
Eagle, 129 .... G2
Eek, 280 .... C2
Egegik, 116 .... D3

Ekwok, 130 .... D3
Elim, 313 .... C2
Emmonak, 767 .... C2
Fairbanks, 30,224 .... F2
False Pass, 64 .... C4
Flat, 4 .... D2
Fort Yukon, 595 .... F1
Galena, 675 .... D2
Gambell, 649 .... A2
Glennallen, 554 .... F2
Golovin, 144 .... C2
Goodnews Bay, 230 .... C3
Grayling, 194 .... C2
Gulkana, 88 .... F2
Gustavus, 429 .... H3
Haines, 1,811 .... H3
Healy, 1,000 .... F2
Holy Cross, 227 .... D2
Homer, 3,946 .... F3
Hoonah, 860 .... H3
Hooper Bay, 1,014 .... B2
Houston, 1,202 .... F2
Hughes, 78 .... E1
Huslia, 293 .... D1
Hydaburg, 382 .... J3
Hyder, 97 .... J3
Kake, 710 .... J3
Kaktovik, 293 .... G1
Kaltag, 230 .... D2
Kasigluk, 543 .... C2
Kenai, 6,942 .... E2
Ketchikan, 7,922 .... J3
Kiana, 388 .... C1
King Cove, 792 .... C3
King Salmon, 442 .... D3
Kivalina, 377 .... C1
Klawock, 854 .... J3
Kobuk, 109 .... D1
Kodiak, 6,334 .... E3
Koliganek, 182 .... D3
Kotlik, 591 .... C2
Kotzebue, 3,082 .... C1
Koyuk, 297 .... C2
Koyukuk, 101 .... D2
Kwethluk, 713 .... C2
Larsen Bay, 115 .... E3
Lime Village, 6 .... E2
Lower Kalskag, 267 .... C2
Manley Hot Springs, 72 .... E1
Marshall, 349 .... C2
McCarthy, 42 .... G2
McGrath, 401 .... D2
McKinley Park F2
Mekoryuk, 210 .... B2
Mentasta Lake, 142 .... G2
Metlakatla, 1,375 .... J3
Minto, 258 .... F2
Mountain Village, 755 .... C2
Naknek, 678 .... D3
Napaskiak, 390 .... C2
Nenana, 402 .... F2
Newhalen, 160 .... E3
New Stuyahok, 471 .... D3
Newtok, 321 .... C2
Nikiski, 4,327 .... E2
Nikolai, 100 .... E2
Nikolski, 39 .... B4
Noatak, 428 .... C1
Nome, 3,505 .... B2

Nondalton, 221 .... E2
Noorvik, 634 .... C1
North Pole, 1,570 .... F2
Northway Jct. (Northway), 95 .... G2
Nuiqsut, 433 .... E1
Nulato, 336 .... D2
Old Harbor, 237 .... E3
Ophir D2
Ouzinkie, 225 .... E3
Palmer, 4,533 .... F2
Paxson, 43 .... F2
Pelican, 163 .... H3
Petersburg, 3,224 .... J3
Pilot Point, 100 .... D3
Pilot Station, 550 .... C2
Point Hope, 757 .... B1
Point Lay, 247 .... C1
Poorman D2
Port Alexander, 81 .... J3
Port Heiden, 119 .... D3
Port Lions, 256 .... E3
Prudhoe Bay, 5 .... F1
Quinhagak, 555 .... C3
Rampart, 45 .... E1
Ruby, 188 .... D1
Russian Mission, 296 .... C2
St. George, 152 .... B3
St. Mary's, 500 .... C2
St. Michael, 368 .... C2
St. Paul, 532 .... A3
Sand Point, 952 .... C3
Savoonga, 643 .... A2
Scammon Bay, 465 .... B2
Selawik, 772 .... C1
Seldovia, 286 .... E3
Seward, 2,830 .... F2
Shageluk, 129 .... D2
Shaktoolik, 230 .... C2
Sheldon Point
 (Sheldon Point Nunam Iqua), 164 .... C2
Shishmaref, 562 .... B1
Shungnak, 256 .... D1
Sitka, 8,835 .... H3
Skagway, 862 .... H3
Slana, 124 .... G2
Sleetmute, 100 .... D2
Soldotna, 3,759 .... E2
Stebbins, 547 .... C2
Talkeetna, 772 .... F2
Tanacross, 140 .... G2
Tanana, 308 .... E1
Tatitlek, 107 .... F2
Teller, 268 .... B1
Tenakee Springs, 104 .... H3
Tetlin Jct. (Tetlin), 117 .... G2
Thorne Bay, 557 .... J3
Togiak, 809 .... C3
Tok, 1,393 .... G2
Toksook Bay, 532 .... B2
Tununak, 325 .... B2
Unalakleet, 747 .... C2
Unalaska, 4,283 .... B4
Valdez, 4,036 .... F2
Venetie, 202 .... F1
Wainwright, 546 .... C1
Wales, 152 .... B1
Wasilla, 5,469 .... F2
White Mountain, 203 .... C2
Whittier, 182 .... F2
Wrangell, 2,308 .... J3
Yakutat, 680 .... H3

Other Features

Adak, island .... Inset
Admiralty Island Natl. Monument .... Inset
Agattu, island .... Inset
Alaska, gulf F3
Alaska, peninsula C3
Alaska, range E2
Alaska Maritime Natl.
 Wildlife Refuge B4
Alaska Peninsula Natl.
 Wildlife Refuge D3
Aleutian, islands .... A4, Inset
Alexander, archipelago H3
Amchitka, island .... Inset
Amlia, island .... Inset
Andreanof, islands .... Inset
Aniakchak Natl.
 Monument and Preserve D3
Arctic Natl. Wildlife Refuge G1
Atka, island .... Inset
Attu, island .... Inset
Barrow, point D1
Beaufort, sea H1
Becharof, lake D3
Becharof Natl. Wildlife Refuge D3
Bering, sea B3
Bering, strait B2
Bering Land Bridge Natl. Preserve C1
Blackburn, mt. G2
Bristol, bay D1
Brooks, range C1
Cape Krusenstern Natl. Monument C1
Chirikof, island D3
Chugach Natl. Forest F2
Chukchi, sea A1
Colville, river E1
Cook, inlet E3
Copper, river G2
Denali Natl. Park and Preserve E2
Fairweather, mt. H3
Gates of the Arctic
 Natl. Park and Preserve E1
Glacier Bay Natl. Park and Preserve H3
Iliamna, lake D3
Innoko Natl. Wildlife Refuge D2
Inside Passage, waterway J3
Izembek Natl. Wildlife Refuge C3
Kanaga, island .... Inset
Kanuti Natl. Wildlife Refuge E1
Katmai Natl. Park and Preserve D3
Kenai, peninsula F2
Kenai Fjords Natl. Park F3
Kenai Natl. Wildlife Refuge E2
Kiska, island .... Inset
Klondike Gold Rush N.H.P. H3
Kobuk, river D1
Kobuk Valley Natl. Park D1
Kodiak, island E3
Kodiak Natl. Wildlife Refuge E3
Kotzebue, sound C1
Koyukuk, river D1
Koyukuk Natl. Wildlife Refuge E1
Kuskokwim, bay C3
Kuskokwim, mts. D2
Kuskokwim, river D2
Lake Clark Natl. Park and Preserve E2
Lisburne, cape B1

Lisburne, peninsula C1
Logan, mt. G2
Lynn, canal J3
Mackenzie, bay H1
McKinley, mt. E2
Malaspina, glacier G3
Michelson, mt. G1
Mohican, cape B2
Muir, glacier F2
Near, islands .... Inset
Newenham, cape C3
Noatak, river D1
Noatak Natl. Preserve C1
North Slope, plain D1
Norton, sound C2
Nowitna Natl. Wildlife Refuge E2
Nunivak, island B3
Porcupine, river G1
Pribilof, islands B3
Prince of Wales, island J3
Progromni, volcano C4
Rat, islands .... Inset
St. Elias, cape G3
St. Elias, mt. G2
St. George, island B3
St. Lawrence, island A2
St. Matthew, island A2
St. Paul, island A3
Samalga, pass B4
Sanak, island C4
Seguam, island .... Inset
Selawik Natl. Wildlife Refuge D1
Semisopochnoi, island .... Inset
Seward, peninsula C1
Shishaldin, volcano C4
Shumagin, islands D4
Sitka N.H.P. H3
Steese Natl. Cons. Area F1
Stikine, river J3
Tanaga, island F3
Tanana, river E2
Tetlin Natl. Wildlife Refuge G2
Tikchik, lakes D2
Togiak Natl. Wildlife Refuge C3
Tongass Natl. Forest H3
Trinity, islands E3
Umnak, island .... Inset
Unalaska, island B4
Unga, island C3
Unimak, island C4
Utukok, river C1
White Mts. Natl. Rec. Area F1
Wood-Tikchik State Park D2
Wrangell, cape .... Inset
Wrangell, mts. G2
Wrangell-St. Elias
 Natl. Park and Preserve G2
Yukon, river D2
Yukon-Charley Rivers Natl. Preserve G2
Yukon Delta Natl. Wildlife Refuge C2
Yukon Flats Natl. Wildlife Refuge F1
Yunaska, island .... Inset

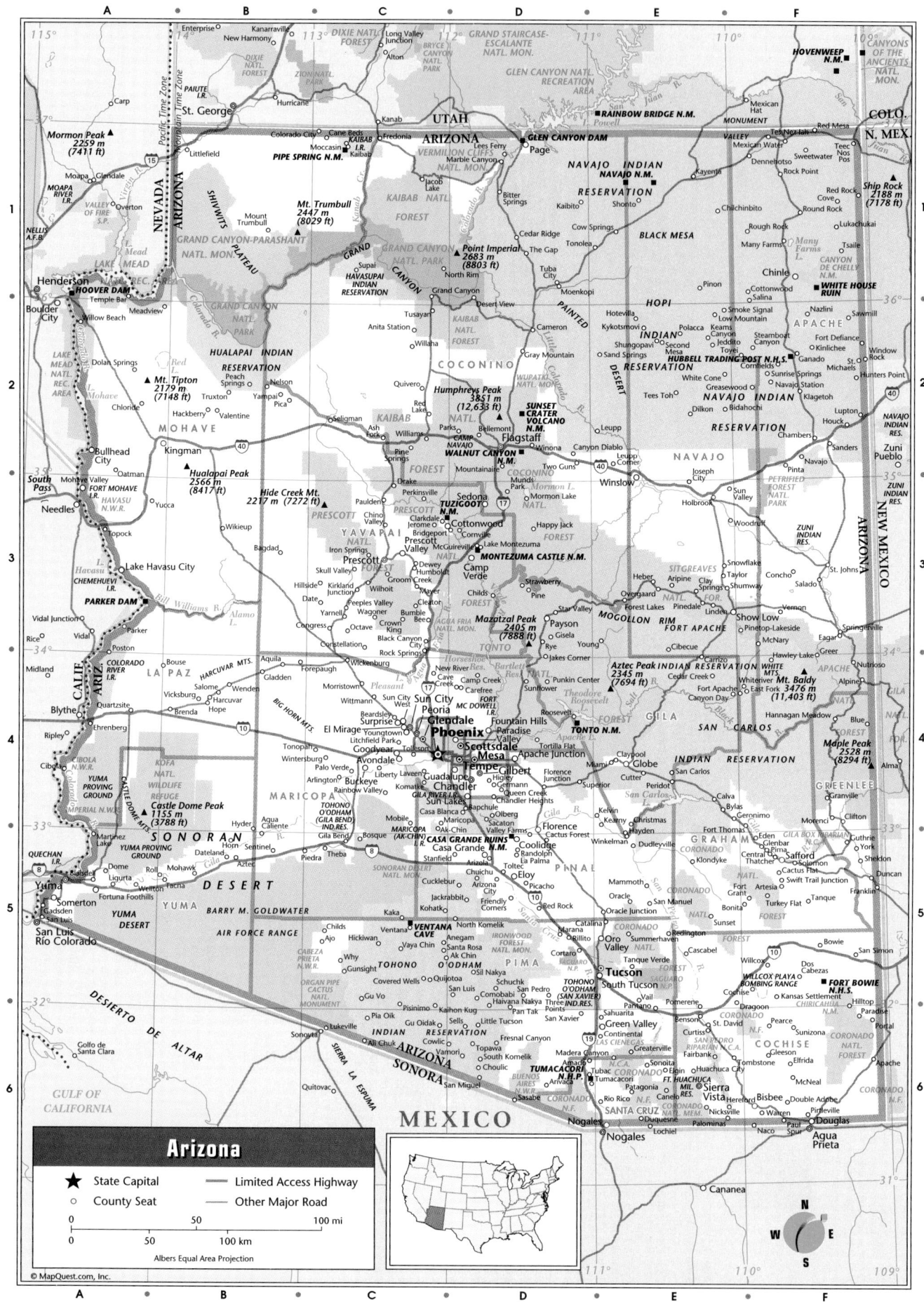

Arizona

★ State Capital
○ County Seat
— Limited Access Highway
— Other Major Road

0   50   100 mi
0   50   100 km
Albers Equal Area Projection

© MapQuest.com, Inc.

Arizona

Capital: Phoenix
Land Area: 113,642 sq. mi.
294,334 sq. km.
Population: 5,130,632 (2000 Census)
Largest City: Phoenix, 1,321,045
Highest Point: Humphreys Peak
12,633 ft.
3,851 m.
Admitted to Union: February 14, 1912
Nickname: Grand Canyon State
State Flower: Saguaro Cactus Blossom
State Bird: Cactus Wren

Arizona:
Map Index

Counties

Apache, 69,423 ....F2
Cochise, 117,755 ....F6
Coconino, 116,320 ....D2
Gila, 51,335 ....E4
Graham, 33,489 ....E5
Greenlee, 8,547 ....F4
La Paz, 19,715 ....A4
Maricopa, 3,072,149 ....B4
Mohave, 155,032 ....B2
Navajo, 97,470 ....E2
Pima, 843,746 ....D5
Pinal, 179,727 ....D5
Santa Cruz, 38,381 ....E6
Yavapai, 167,517 ....C3
Yuma, 160,026 ....B5

Cities and Towns

Agua Caliente, 50 ....B4
Ajo, 3,705 ....C5
Ak Chin, 150 ....D5
Ak-Chuk, 669 ....C6
Ali Chuk, 450 ....C6
Alpine, 60 ....F4
Amado, 275 ....D6
Anegam, 175 ....C5
Anita Station, 110 ....C2
Apache F6
Apache Junction, 31,814 ....D4
Aquila, 90 ....B4
Aripine, 100 ....E3
Arivaca, 100 ....D6
Arizola, 550 ....D5
Arizona City, 4,385 ....D5
Arlington, 90 ....C4
Artesia, 200 ....F5
Ash Fork, 457 ....C2
Avondale, 35,883 ....C4
Aztec B5
Bagdad, 1,578 ....B3
Bapchule, 70 ....C4
Beardsley D2
Bellemont D2
Benson, 4,711 ....E6
Bidahochi E2
Bisbee, 6,090 ....F6
Bitter Springs, 547 ....D1
Black Canyon City, 2,697 ....C3
Blaisdell A5
Blue F4
Bonita F5
Bosque, 100 ....C5
Bouse, 615 ....B4
Bowie, 550 ....F5
Brenda, 50 ....B4
Bridgeport C3
Buckeye, 6,537 ....C4
Bullhead City, 33,769 ....A2
Bumble Bee C3
Bylas, 1,200 ....E4
Cactus Flat, 550 ....D5
Cactus Forest D5
Calva, 50 ....E4
Cameron, 978 ....D2
Camp Creek, 80 ....D4
Camp Verde, 9,451 ....D3
Cane Beds C1
Canelo, 60 ....E6
Canyon Day, 1,092 ....E4
Canyon Diablo D2
Carefree, 2,927 ....D4
Carrizo, 150 ....E4
Casa Blanca, 300 ....D4
Casa Grande, 25,224 ....D5
Cascabel, 50 ....E5
Catalina, 7,025 ....E5
Cave Creek, 3,728 ....D4
Cedar Creek, 70 ....E4
Cedar Ridge, 225 ....D1
Central, 425 ....F5
Chambers, 250 ....F2
Chandler, 176,581 ....D4
Chandler Heights, 950 ....D4
Chilchinbito, 462 ....E1
Childs (Pima Co.) C5
Childs (Yavapai Co.) D3
Chinie, 5,366 ....F1
Chino Valley, 7,835 ....C3
Chloride, 175 ....A2
Choulic, 40 ....D6
Christmas, 70 ....E4
Chuichu, 339 ....D5
Cibecue, 1,331 ....E3
Cibola, 172 ....A4
Clarkdale, 3,422 ....C3
Claypool, 1,794 ....E4
Clay Springs, 250 ....E3
Cleator C3

Clifton, 2,596 ....F4
Cochise, 40 ....F5
Colorado City, 3,334 ....C1
Comobabi, 50 ....D5
Concho F3
Congress, 1,717 ....C3
Constellation, 100 ....C3
Continental E6
Coolidge, 7,786 ....D5
Cornfields, 300 ....F2
Cornville, 3,335 ....D3
Cortaro, 1,700 ....D5
Cottonwood (Apache Co.) F1
Cottonwood (Yavapai Co.), 9,179 ...D3
Cove, 125 ....F1
Covered Wells, 60 ....C5
Cowlic, 100 ....C6
Cow Springs, 225 ....E1
Crown King, 60 ....C3
Cucklebur, 150 ....D5
Curtiss, 40 ....E6
Cutter E4
Date C3
Dateland, 70 ....B5
Dennehotso, 734 ....F1
Desert View D1
Dewey (Dewey-Humboldt), 6,295 ...C3
Dilkon, 1,265 ....E2
Dolan Springs, 1,867 ....A2
Dome A5
Dos Cabezas, 40 ....F5
Double Adobe, 125 ....F6
Douglas, 14,312 ....F6
Dragoon, 70 ....E5
Drake, 50 ....C2
Dudleyville, 1,323 ....E5
Duncan, 812 ....F5
Duquesne E6
East Fork, 880 ....F4
Eden, 70 ....F5
Ehrenberg, 1,357 ....A4
Elfrida, 475 ....F6
Elgin, 309 ....E6
El Mirage, 7,609 ....C4
Eloy, 10,375 ....D5
Fairbank E6
Flagstaff, 52,894 ....D2
Florence, 17,054 ....D4
Florence Junction, 275 ......D4
Forepaugh, 60 ....B4
Forest Lakes, 90 ....E3
Fort Apache, 100 ....F4
Fort Defiance, 4,061 ....F2
Fort Grant, 800 ....F5
Fort Thomas, 125 ....F5
Fortuna Foothills, 20,478 ....A5
Fountain Hills, 20,235 ....D4
Franklin, 100 ....F5
Fredonia, 1,036 ....C1
Fresnal Canyon D6
Friendly Corners D5
Gadsden, 953 ....A5
Ganado, 1,505 ....F2
Germann, 45 ....D4
Geronimo E4
Gila Bend, 1,980 ....C5
Gilbert, 109,697 ....D4
Gisela, 532 ....D3
Gladden, 400 ....B4
Gleeson F6
Glenbar F5
Glendale, 218,812 ....C4
Globe, 7,486 ....E4
Goodyear, 18,911 ....C4
Grand Canyon, 1,460 ....C1
Granville F4
Gray Mountain D2
Greasewood, 581 ....F2
Greaterville, 60 ....E6
Green Valley, 17,283 ....E6
Greer F3
Groom Creek, 250 ....C3
Guadalupe, 5,228 ....D4
Gunsight, 200 ....C5
Gu Oidak, 150 ....C6
Guthrie F5
Gu Vo, 175 ....C5
Hackberry B2
Haivana Nakya, 200 ....D5
Hannagan Meadow F4
Happy Jack D3
Harcuvar, 40 ....B4
Hawley Lake F4
Hayden, 892 ....E4
Heber, 2,722 ....E3
Hereford (part of Sierra Vista Southeast, pop. 14,348) ...E6
Hickiwan C5
Higley, 425 ....D4
Hillside, 100 ....C3
Hilltop F5
Holbrook, 4,917 ....E3
Hope B4
Horn, 150 ....B5
Hotevilla, 767 ....E2
Houck, 1,087 ....F2
Huachuca City, 1,751 ....E6
Humboldt (see Dewey), 6,295 ...C3
Hunters Point, 400 ....F2
Hyder, 40 ....B4
Iron Springs C3
Jackrabbit D5
Jacob Lake C1
Jakes Corner D3
Jeddito, 390 ....E2
Jerome, 329 ....C3
Joseph City, 1,000 ....E2
Kaibab, 275 ....C1
Kaibito, 1,607 ....D1
Kaihon Kug C5
Kaka, 175 ....C5
Kansas Settlement F5
Kayenta, 4,922 ....E1
Keams Canyon, 260 ....E2
Kearny, 2,249 ....E4
Kelvin, 150 ....E4
Kingman, 20,069 ....A2
Kinlichee F2
Kirkland Junction C3
Klagetoh, 50 ....F2
Klondyke, 50 ....E5
Kohatk, 50 ....C5
Komatke, 1,100 ....C4

Kykotsmovi, 776 ....E2
Lake Havasu City, 41,938 ....A3
Lake Montezuma, 3,344 ......D3
La Palma, 100 ....D5
Laveen, 850 ....C4
Lees Ferry, 100 ....D1
Leupp, 970 ....E2
Leupp Corner, 100 ....E2
Liberty, 250 ....C4
Ligurta, 40 ....A5
Linden, 60 ....E3
Litchfield Park, 3,810 ....C4
Littlefield B1
Little Tucson D6
Lochiel E6
Low Mountain, 175 ....E2
Lukachukai, 1,565 ....F1
Lukeville, 125 ....C6
Lupton, 375 ....F2
Madera Canyon, 70 ....E6
Mammoth, 1,762 ....E5
Many Farms, 1,548 ....F1
Marana, 13,556 ....D5
Marble Canyon, 100 ....D1
Maricopa, 1,040 ....C4
Martinez Lake, 50 ....A5
Mayer, 1,408 ....C3
McGuireville D3
McNary, 349 ....F3
McNeal, 100 ....F6
Meadview A2
Mesa, 396,375 ....D4
Mexican Water, 60 ....F1
Miami, 1,936 ....E4
Mobile, 40 ....C4
Mocassin, 80 ....C1
Moenkopi, 901 ....D1
Mohave Valley, 13,694 ......A3
Mohawk B5
Morenci, 1,879 ....F4
Mormon Lake, 50 ....D3
Morristown, 80 ....C4
Mountainaire, 1,014 ....D2
Mount Trumbull B1
Munds Park, 1,250 ....D3
Naco, 833 ....F6
Navajo F2
Navajo Station, 80 ....F2
Nazlini, 397 ....F2
Nelson B2
New River, 10,740 ....C4
Nicksville (part of Sierra Vista Southeast, pop. 14,348), 425 ...E6
Nogales, 20,878 ....E6
North Komelik, 100 ....D5
North Rim C1
Nutrioso, 40 ....F4
Oatman, 150 ....A2
Octave, 50 ....C3
Olberg, 40 ....D4
Oracle, 3,563 ....E5
Oracle Junction, 550 ....E5
Oro Valley, 29,700 ....E5
Overgaard, 2,722 ....E3
Page, 6,809 ....D1
Palominas (part of Sierra Vista Southeast, pop. 14,348) ...E6
Palo Verde, 100 ....C4
Pan Tak, 40 ....D5
Pantano, 350 ....E5
Paradise F6
Paradise Valley, 13,664 ......D4
Parker, 3,140 ....A3
Parks, 1,137 ....D2
Patagonia, 881 ....E6
Paulden, 3,420 ....C3
Paul Spur F6
Payson, 13,620 ....D3
Peach Springs, 600 ....B2
Pearce F6
Peeples Valley, 374 ....C3
Peoria, 108,364 ....C4
Peridot, 1,266 ....E4
Perkinsville C3
Phoenix, 1,321,045 ....C4
Pia Oik, 450 ....C6
Pica B2
Picacho, 475 ....D5
Piedra C5
Pima, 1,989 ....F5
Pine, 1,931 ....D3
Pinedale, 100 ....E3
Pine Springs C2
Pinetop-Lakeside, 3,582 .....F3
Pinon, 1,190 ....E1
Pinta F2
Pirtleville, 1,550 ....F6
Pisinimo, 237 ....C6
Polacca, 1,100 ....E2
Pomerene, 40 ....E5
Portal F6
Poston, 389 ....A3
Prescott, 33,938 ....C3
Prescott Valley, 23,535 ......C3
Punkin Center D4
Quartzsite, 3,354 ....A4
Queen Creek, 4,316 ....D4
Quijotoa, 150 ....C5
Quivero C2
Rainbow Valley C4
Randolph, 275 ....D5
Redington E5
Red Lake, 225 ....C2
Red Mesa, 50 ....F1
Red Rock (Apache Co.) F1
Red Rock (Pinal Co.), 70 .....D5
Rillito, 275 ....D5
Rio Rico, 3,164 ....E6
Rock Point, 724 ....F1
Rock Springs C3
Roll, 70 ....A5
Roosevelt D4
Rough Rock, 469 ....F1
Round Rock, 601 ....F1
Rye, 40 ....D3
Sacaton, 1,584 ....D4
Safford, 9,232 ....F5
Sahuarita, 3,242 ....E6
St. David, 1,744 ....E6
St. Johns, 3,269 ....F3
St. Michaels, 1,295 ....F2
Salado, 125 ....F3
Salina, 150 ....F1
Salome, 1,690 ....B4

San Carlos, 3,716 ....E4
Sanders, 200 ....F2
Sand Springs E2
San Luis (Pima Co.), 60 ......D5
San Luis (Yuma Co.), 15,322 ...A5
San Manuel, 4,375 ....E5
San Miguel, 90 ....D6
San Pedro D5
San Simon, 125 ....F5
Santa Rosa, 438 ....C5
San Xavier, 50 ....D6
Sasabe D6
Sawmill, 612 ....F2
Schuchk, 50 ....D5
Scottsdale, 202,705 ....D4
Second Mesa, 814 ....E2
Sedona, 10,192 ....D3
Seligman, 456 ....C2
Sells, 2,799 ....D6
Sentinel B5
Sheldon F5
Shonto, 568 ....E1
Show Low, 7,695 ....E3
Shumway, 125 ....E3
Shungopavi, 632 ....E2
Sierra Vista, 37,775 ....E6
Sil Nakya, 125 ....D5
Skull Valley, 60 ....C3
Smoke Signal E2
Snowflake, 4,460 ....E3
Solomon, 475 ....F5
Somerton, 7,266 ....A5
Sonoita, 826 ....E6
South Komelik, 90 ....D6
South Tucson, 5,490 ....E5
Springerville, 1,972 ....F3
Stanfield, 651 ....D5
Star Valley, 550 ....D3
Steamboat Canyon, 1,100 ...F2
Strawberry, 1,028 ....D3
Summerhaven E5
Sun City, 38,309 ....C4
Sun City West, 26,344 ....C4
Sunflower D4
Sunizona, 200 ....F6
Sun Lakes, 11,936 ....D4
Sunrise Springs, 40 ....F2
Sunset, 80 ....E5
Sun Valley E3
Supai C1
Superior, 3,254 ....D4
Surprise, 30,848 ....C4
Sweetwater, 225 ....F1
Swift Trail Junction, 2,195 ...F5
Tacna, 555 ....B5
Tanque, 40 ....F5
Tanque Verde, 16,195 ....E5
Taylor, 3,176 ....E3
Teec Nos Pos, 799 ....F1
Tees Toh E2
Tempe, 158,625 ....D4
Temple Bar A1
Tes Nez Iah F1
Thatcher, 4,022 ....F5
Theba C5
The Gap, 175 ....D1
Three Points, 5,273 ....D5
Tolleson, 4,974 ....C4
Toltec D5
Tombstone, 1,504 ....E6
Tonolea, 562 ....E1
Tonopah C4
Topawa, 150 ....D6
Topock A3
Tortilla Flat, 40 ....D4
Toyei, 70 ....F2
Truxton B2
Tsaile, 1,078 ....F1
Tubac, 569 ....D6
Tuba City, 8,225 ....D1
Tucson, 486,699 ....E5
Tumacacori, 569 ....D6
Turkey Flat F5
Tusayan, 562 ....C2
Two Guns D2
Vail, 2,484 ....E5
Valentine B2
Valley Farms, 300 ....D4
Vamori, 60 ....D6
Vaya Chin, 70 ....C5
Ventana, 70 ....C5
Vernon F3
Vicksburg B4
Wagoner C3
Warren F6
Wellton, 1,829 ....A5
Wenden, 556 ....B4
White Cone E2
Whiteriver, 5,220 ....F4
Why, 225 ....C5
Wickenburg, 5,082 ....C4
Wikieup B3
Wilhoit, 664 ....C3
Willaha C2
Willcox, 3,733 ....F5
Williams, 2,842 ....C2
Willow Beach A2
Window Rock, 3,059 ....F2
Winkelman, 443 ....E5
Winona D2
Winslow, 9,520 ....E2
Wintersburg, 125 ....C4
Wittmann, 350 ....C4
Woodruff, 150 ....E3
Yampai B2
Yarnell, 645 ....C3
York, 50 ....F5
Young, 561 ....D3
Youngtown, 3,010 ....C4
Yucca, 100 ....A3
Yuma, 77,515 ....A5

Other Features

Agua Fria, river C4
Agua Fria Natl. Mon. D3
Alamo, lake B3
Apache, lake D4
Apache Natl. Forest F4
Aztec, peak E4
Baldy, mountain F4
Barry M. Goldwater Air Force Range B5
Bartlett, reservoir D4

Big Horn, mountains B4
Bill Williams, river A3
Black, mesa E1
Black, river E4
Buenos Aires N.W.R. D6
Cabeza Prieta N.W.R. B5
California, gulf A6
Canyon De Chelly N.M. F1
Casa Grande Ruins N.M. D5
Castle Dome, mountains A4
Castle Dome, peak A4
Chemehuevi I.R. A3
Chiricahua N.M. F6
Cibola N.W.R. A4
Coconino Natl. Forest D2
Colorado, river A2, A4, B1, D1
Colorado River I.R. A4
Coronado Natl. Mem. E6
Coronado N.F. D6, E5, E6, F6
Desierto De Altar, desert A5
Dixie Natl. Forest B1
Fort Apache Indian Reservation ...E3
Fort Bowie N.H.S. F5
Ft. Huachuca Mil. Res. E6
Fort Mc Dowell I.R. D4
Fort Mohave I.R. A3
Gila, river B5, D4, F4
Gila Box Riparian Natl. Cons. Area ...F5
Gila Natl. For. F4
Gila River I.R. C4
Glen Canyon, dam D1
Glen Canyon Natl. Recreation Area ...E1
Grand, canyon C1
Grand Canyon Natl. Park ...B2, C1
Grand Canyon-Parashant Natl. Mon. ...B1
Harcuvar, mountains B4
Havasu, lake A3
Havasu N.W.R. A3
Havasupai Indian Reservation ...C1
Hide Creek, mountain C3
Hoover, dam A1
Hopi Indian Reservation E2
Horseshoe, reservoir D4
Hualapai Indian Reservation ...B2
Hualapai, peak B2
Hubbell Trading Post N.H.S. ...F2
Humphreys, peak D2
Imperial N.W.R. A4
Ironwood Forest Natl. Mon. ...D5
Kaibab I.R. C1
Kaibab Natl. Forest ...C1, C2, D2
Kanab, creek C1
Kofa Natl. Wildlife Refuge ...B4
La Cienegas Natl. Cons. Area ...E6
Lake Mead Natl. Rec. Area ...A1, A2, B1
Little Colorado, river D2
Many Farms, lake F1
Maple, peak F4
Maricopa (Ak-Chin) I.R. C5
Mazatzal, peak D3
Mead, lake A1
Moapa River I.R. A1
Mogollon Rim, cliffs D3
Mohave, lake A2
Montezuma Castle N.M. D3
Monument, valley E1
Mormon, lake D3
Mormon, peak A1
Navajo Army Depot E2
Navajo Indian Reservation ...E1, F2
Navajo N.M. E1
Nellis A.F.B. A1
Organ Pipe Cactus Natl. Monument ...C5
Painted, desert D1
Paiute I.R. B1
Parker, dam A3
Petrified Forest Natl. Park ...F3
Pipe Spring N.M. C1
Pleasant, lake C4
Point Imperial, peak D1
Powell, lake D1
Prescott Natl. Forest C3
Quechan I.R. A5
Rainbow Bridge N.M. E1
Red, lake B2
Saguaro N.P. D5, E5
Salt, river E4
San Carlos, lake E4
San Carlos Indian Reservation ...E4
San Juan, river E1, F1
San Pedro, river E5
San Pedro Riparian N.C.A. ...E6
Santa Cruz, river D5
Ship Rock, mountain F1
Shivwits, plateau B1
Sierra La Espuma, range C6
Sitgreaves Natl. Forest E3
Sonoran, desert B5
Sonoran Desert Natl. Mon. ...C5
South, pass A3
Sunset Crater Volcano N.M. ...D2
Theodore Roosevelt, lake ...D4
Tipton, mountain A2
Tohono O'Odham (Gila Bend) I.R. ...C4
Tohono O'Odham Indian Reservation ...C5
Tohono O'Odham (San Xavier) I.R. ...D5
Tonto Natl. Forest D3
Tonto N.M. D4
Trumbull, mountain B1
Tumacacori N.H.P. D6
Tuzigoot N.M. C3
Valley Of Fire S.P. A1
Ventana, cave C5
Verde, river D3
Vermilion Cliffs Natl. Mon. ...D1
Virgin, river A1
Walnut Canyon N.M. D2
White, mountains F4
White House Ruin F1
Willcox Playa Bombing Range ...F5
Wupatki Natl. Mon. D2
Yuma, desert A5
Yuma Proving Ground ...A4, A5
Zion Natl. Park C1
Zuni Indian Res. F3

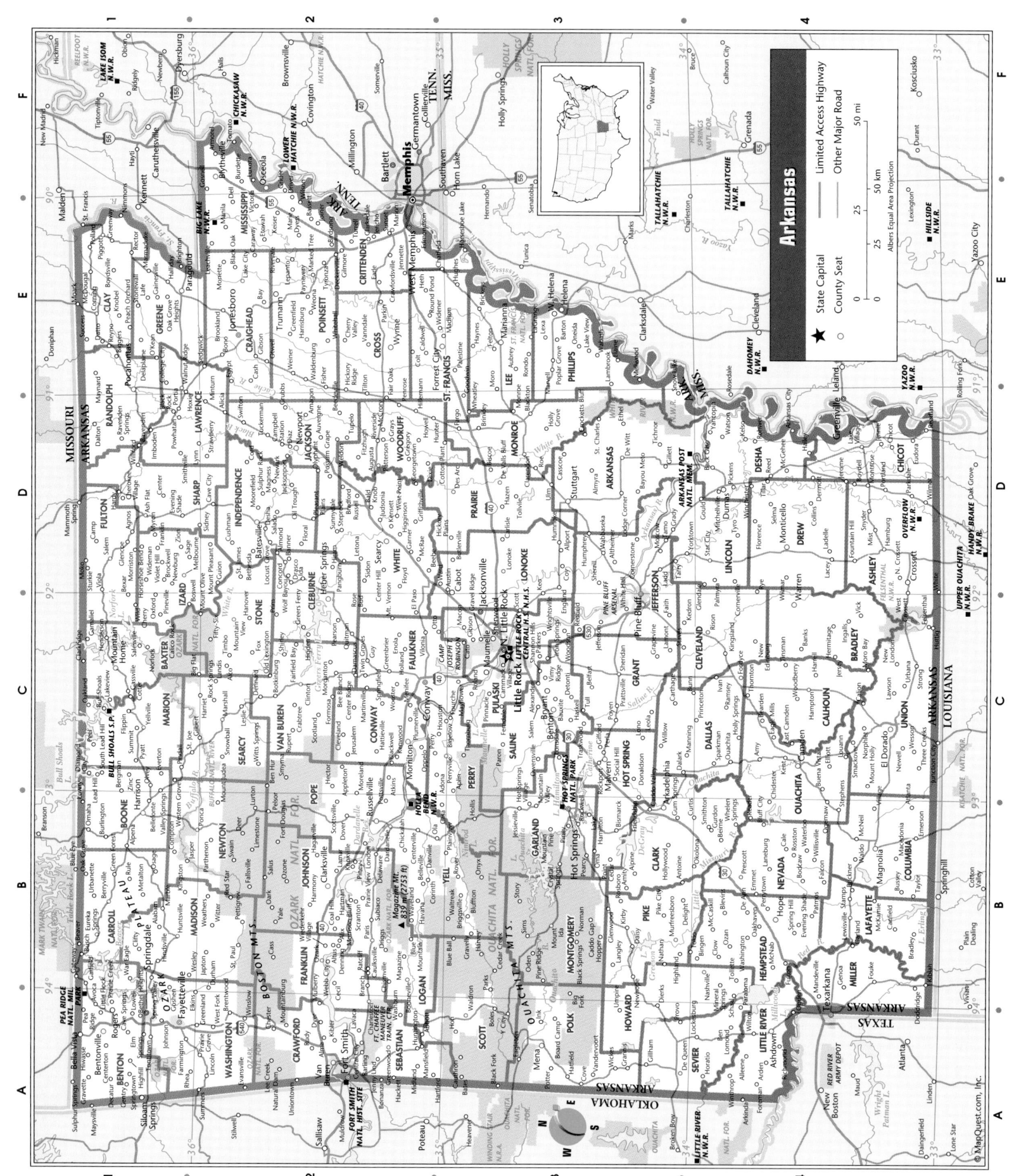

Arkansas

Capital: Little Rock
Land Area: 52,075 sq. mi.
134,875 sq. km.
Population: 2,673,400 (2000 Census)
Largest City: Little Rock, 183,133
Highest Point: Magazine Mtn.
2,753 ft.
839 m.
Admitted to Union: June 15, 1836
Nickname: Land of Opportunity
State Flower: Apple Blossom
State Bird: Mockingbird

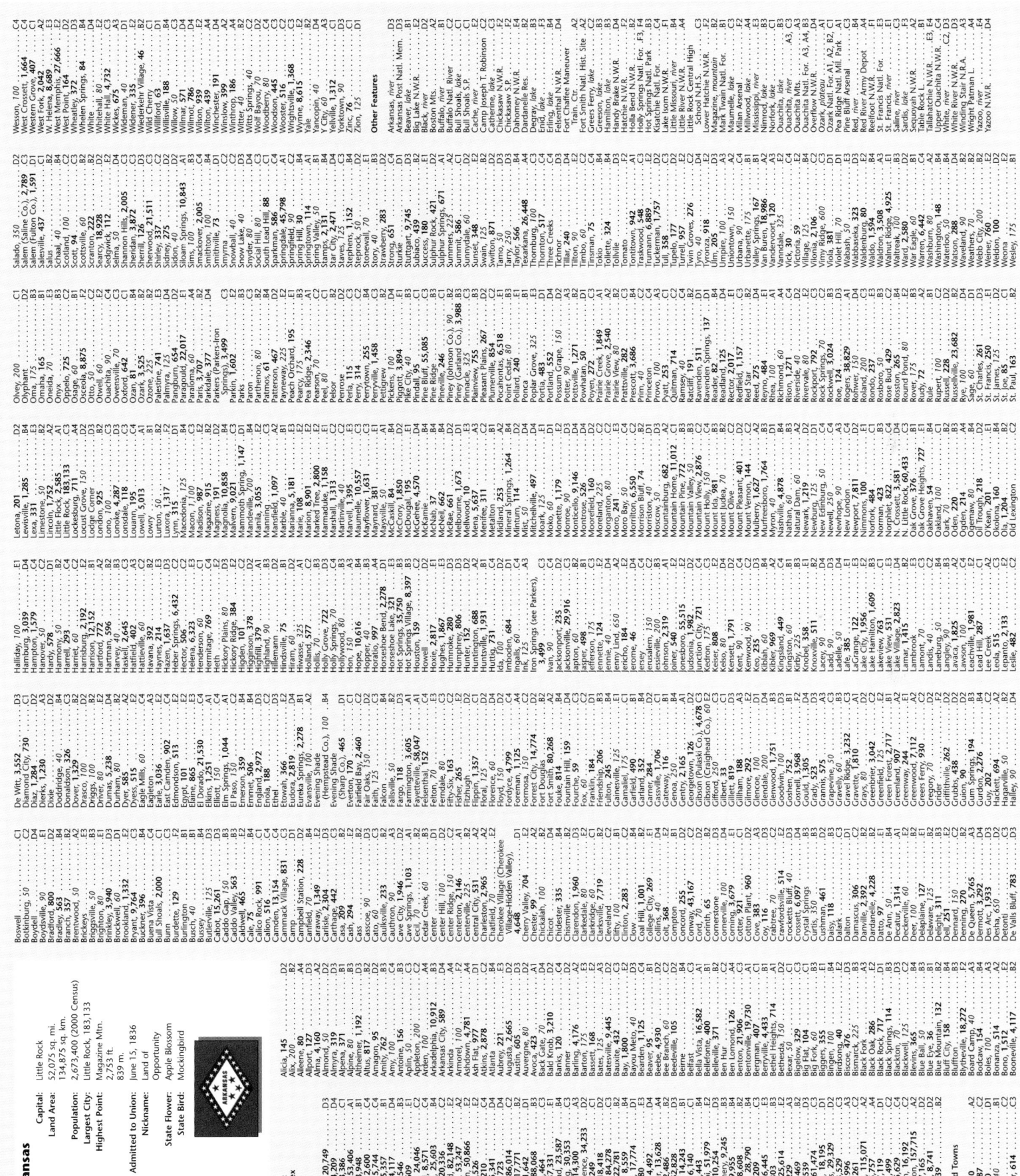

Arkansas: Map Index

Counties

Arkansas, **20,749** D3
Ashley, **24,209** D4
Baxter, **38,386** C1
Benton, **153,406** A1
Boone, **33,948** B1
Bradley, **12,600** C4
Calhoun, **5,744** C4
Carroll, **25,357** B1
Chicot, **14,117** D4
Clark, **23,546** B3
Clay, **17,609** E1
Cleburne, **24,046** C2
Cleveland, **8,571** C4
Columbia, **25,603** B4
Conway, **20,336** C2
Craighead, **82,148** E2
Crawford, **53,247** A2
Crittenden, **50,866** E2
Cross, **19,526** E2
Dallas, **9,210** C4
Desha, **15,341** D4
Drew, **18,723** D4
Faulkner, **86,014** C2
Franklin, **17,771** B2
Fulton, **11,642** D1
Garland, **88,068** B3
Grant, **16,464** C3
Greene, **37,331** E1
Hempstead, **23,587** B4
Hot Spring, **30,353** C3
Howard, **14,300** A3
Independence, **34,233** D2
Izard, **13,249** C1
Jackson, **18,418** D2
Jefferson, **84,278** C3
Johnson, **22,781** B2
Lafayette, **8,559** B4
Lawrence, **17,774** D1
Lee, **12,580** E3
Lincoln, **14,492** D4
Little River, **13,628** A4
Logan, **22,486** B2
Lonoke, **52,828** D3
Madison, **14,243** B1
Marion, **16,140** C1
Miller, **40,443** B4
Mississippi, **51,979** E2
Monroe, **10,254** D3
Montgomery, **9,245** B3
Nevada, **9,955** B4
Newton, **8,608** B2
Ouachita, **28,790** B4
Perry, **10,209** C3
Phillips, **26,445** E3
Pike, **11,303** B3
Poinsett, **25,614** E2
Polk, **20,229** A3
Pope, **54,469** B2
Prairie, **9,539** D3
Pulaski, **361,474** C3
Randolph, **18,195** D1
St. Francis, **29,329** D2
Saline, **83,529** C3
Scott, **10,996** A3
Searcy, **8,261** C2
Sebastian, **115,071** A2
Sevier, **15,757** A4
Sharp, **17,119** D1
Stone, **11,499** C2
Union, **45,629** C4
Van Buren, **16,192** C2
Washington, **157,715** A2
White, **67,165** D2
Woodruff, **8,741** D2
Yell, **21,139** B2

Cities and Towns

Abbott, **50** A2
Adona, **187** C2
Agnos, **50** D1
Alabam, *40* B1
Alco, *50* C2
Alexander, **614** C3
Alicia, **145** D2
Alix, *200* B2
Alleene, **80** A4
Allport, **127** D3
Alma, **4,160** A2
Almond, *50* D2
Almyra, **319** D3
Alpena, **371** B1
Alpine, *80* B3
Altheimer, **1,192** D3
Altus, **817** B2
Amagon, **95** D2
Amity, **762** B3
Amy, *100* C4
Antoine, **156** B3
Aplin, *50* C3
Appleton, *200* C2
Arden, *100* A4
Arkadelphia, **10,912** B3
Arkansas City, **589** D4
Arkinda A4
Armorel, *100* F2
Ashdown, **4,781** A4
Ash Flat, **977** D1
Atkins, **2,878** C2
Atlanta B4
Aubrey, **221** E3
Augusta, **2,665** D2
Austin, **605** D3
Auvergne, *80* D2
Avoca, **423** A1
Back Gate, *70* D4
Bald Knob, **3,210** D2
Banks, **120** C4
Banner D2
Barling, **4,176** A2
Barton, *175* E3
Bassett, **168** E2
Bates, *125* A3
Batesville, **9,445** D2
Bauxite, **432** C3
Bay, **1,800** E2
Bayou Meto, *40* D3
Bearden, **1,125** C4
Beaver, **95** B1
Beebe, **4,930** D2
Bee Branch, *60* C2
Beedeville, **105** D2
Beirne B4
Belfast C3
Bella Vista, **16,582** A1
Bellefonte, **400** B1
Belleville, **371** B2
Ben Hur C2
Ben Lomond, **126** A4
Benton, **21,906** C3
Bentonville, **19,730** A1
Bergman, **407** C1
Berryville, **4,433** B1
Bethel Heights, **714** A1
Bethesda, *150* D2
Bexar, *50* C1
Bigelow, **329** C3
Big Flat, **104** C1
Big Fork, *60* B3
Biggers, **355** E1
Bingen, *100* B4
Birdsong, **40** E2
Biscoe, **476** D3
Bismarck, *225* B3
Black Fork A3
Black Oak, **286** E2
Black Rock, **717** D1
Black Springs, **114** B3
Blackton, *70* D3
Blackwell, *125* C2
Blevins, **365** B4
Blue Ball, *50* B3
Blue Eye, **36** B1
Blue Mountain, **132** B2
Bluff City, **158** B4
Bluffton B3
Blytheville, **18,272** F2
Board Camp, *40* A3
Bodcaw, **154** B4
Boles, *100* A3
Bonanza, **514** A2
Bono, **1,512** E2
Booneville, **4,117** B2
Boswell C1
Botkinburg, *50* C2
Boydell D4
Boydsville, *90* E1
Bradford, **800** D2
Bradley, **563** B4
Branch, **357** B2
Brentwood, *50* A2
Brickeys E3
Briggsville, *50* B3
Brighton, *80* E1
Brinkley, **3,940** D3
Brockwell, *60* D1
Brookland, **1,332** E2
Bryant, **9,764** C3
Buckner, **396** B4
Buena Vista C4
Bull Shoals, **2,000** C1
Bunn C3
Burdette, **129** F2
Burlington B1
Busch, *40* B1
Bussey B4
Butlerville, *125* D3
Cabot, **15,261** D3
Caddo Gap, *150* B3
Caddo Valley, **563** B3
Caldwell, **465** E2
Cale, **75** B4
Calico Rock, **991** C1
Calion, **516** C4
Camden, **13,154** C4
Cammack Village, **831** C3
Camp D1
Campbell Station, **228** D2
Canfield, *70* B4
Caraway, **1,349** E2
Carlisle, **2,304** D3
Carthage, **442** C3
Casa, **209** B2
Cash, **294** E2
Cass B2
Casscoe, *90* D3
Cato, *60* C3
Caulksville, **233** B2
Cauthron, *90* A3
Cave City, **1,946** D2
Cave Springs, **1,103** A1
Cecil, *70* B2
Cedar Creek, *60* B3
Center D1
Center Hill, *100* D2
Center Ridge, *150* C2
Centerton, **2,146** A1
Centerville, *225* B2
Central City, **531** A2
Charleston, **2,965** A2
Chatfield, *70* E2
Cherokee Village (Cherokee Village-Hidden Valley), **4,648** D1
Cherry Valley, **704** E2
Chester, **99** A2
Chickalah, *100* B2
Chicot D4
Chidester, **335** B4
Chismville B2
Clarendon, **1,960** D3
Clarkedale, *80* E2
Clarkridge, *60* C1
Clarksville, **7,719** B2
Cleveland C2
Clifty, *100* B1
Clinton, **2,283** C2
Clow B4
Coal Hill, **1,001** B2
College City, **269** E1
Collins, *40* D4
Colt, **368** E2
Compton B1
Concord, **255** D2
Conway, **43,167** C2
Cord, *70* D2
Corinth, **65** B2
Cornerstone D3
Cornerville, *100* D4
Corning, **3,679** E1
Cotter, **921** C1
Cotton Plant, **960** D2
Cove, **383** A3
Coy, **116** D3
Crabtree, *70* C2
Crawfordsville, **514** E2
Crocketts Bluff, *40* D3
Crossett, **6,097** D4
Crystal Springs B3
Curtis, *350* B3
Cushman, **461** D2
Daisy, **118** B3
Dalark C3
Dalton D1
Damascus, **306** C2
Danville, **2,392** B2
Dardanelle, **4,228** B2
Datto, **97** E1
De Ann, *50* B4
Decatur, **1,314** A1
Deckerville, *60* E2
Deer, *100* B2
Delaplaine, **127** E1
Delaware, *125* B2
Delight, **311** B3
Dell, **251** E2
Dennard, *150* C2
Denning, **270** B2
De Queen, **5,765** A3
Dermott, **3,292** D4
Des Arc, **1,933** D3
Desha, *650* D2
Detonti C3
De Valls Bluff, **783** D3
De Witt, **3,552** D3
Diamond City, **730** C1
Diaz, **1,284** D2
Dierks, **1,230** A3
Dixie D2
Doddridge, *40* B4
Donaldson, **326** C3
Dover, **1,329** B2
Drasco, *100* D2
Driggs, *100* B2
Driver, *80* E2
Dumas, **5,238** D4
Durham, *80* B2
Dyer, **585** A2
Dyess, **515** E2
Eagle Mills, *60* C4
Eagleton A3
Earle, **3,036** E2
East Camden, **902** C4
Edmondson, **513** E2
Egypt, **101** E2
Elaine, **865** E3
El Dorado, **21,530** C4
Elkins, **1,251** A1
Elliott, *150* C4
Elm Springs, **1,044** A1
El Paso, *150* C2
Emerson, **359** B4
Emmet, **506** B4
England, **2,972** D3
Enola, **188** C2
Ethel D3
Etowah, **366** E2
Eudora, **2,819** D4
Eureka Springs, **2,278** B1
Evansville, *100* A2
Evening Shade (Hempstead Co.), *100* B4
Evening Shade (Sharp Co.), **465** D1
Everton, **170** C1
Fairfield Bay, **2,460** C2
Fair Oaks, *150* D2
Faith, *125* C3
Falcon B4
Fallsville, *50* B2
Fargo, **118** D3
Farmington, **3,605** A1
Fayetteville, **58,047** A1
Felsenthal, **152** C4
Felton, *70* E3
Ferndale, *80* C3
Fifty-Six, **163** C2
Fisher, **265** E2
Fitzhugh D2
Flippin, **1,357** C1
Floral, *125* D2
Florence, *60* D4
Floyd, *150* D2
Fordyce, **4,799** C4
Foreman, **1,125** A4
Formosa, *150* C2
Forrest City, **14,774** D2
Fort Douglas B2
Fort Smith, **80,268** A2
Fouke, **814** B4
Fountain Hill, **159** D4
Fourche, **59** C3
Fox, *60* C2
Franklin, **184** D1
Friendship, **206** B3
Fulton, **245** B4
Gainesville, *125* E1
Gamaliel, *175* C1
Garfield, **490** B1
Garland, **352** B4
Garner, **284** D2
Gassville, **1,706** C1
Gateway, **116** B1
Genoa, *250* B4
Gentry, **2,165** A1
Georgetown, **126** D2
Gibson (Pulaski Co.), **4,678** C3
Gibson (Craighead Co.), *60* E2
Gifford, *250* C3
Gilbert, **33** C1
Gillett, **819** D3
Gillham, **188** A3
Gilmore, **292** E2
Glencoe, *100* D1
Glendale, *200* D4
Glenwood, **1,751** B3
Goodwin, *100* D3
Goshen, **752** B1
Gosnell, **3,968** F2
Gould, **1,305** D4
Grady, **523** D3
Grannis, **575** A3
Grapevine, *50* C3
Gravelly, *60* B3
Gravel Ridge, **3,232** C3
Gravette, **1,810** A1
Grays, *80* D2
Greenbrier, **3,042** C2
Greenfield, *125* E2
Green Forest, **2,717** B1
Greenland, **907** A2
Greenway, **244** E1
Greenwood, **7,112** A2
Greers Ferry, **930** C2
Gregory, *70* D2
Grider F2
Griffithville, **262** D2
Grubbs, **438** D2
Guion, **90** D2
Gum Springs, **194** B3
Gurdon, **2,276** B4
Guy, **202** C2
Hackett, **694** A2
Hagarville, *50* B2
Halley, *90* D4
Halliday, *100* E1
Hamburg, **3,039** D4
Hampton, **1,579** C4
Hanover, *50* C2
Hardy, **578** D1
Harmony, *50* B2
Harrell, **293** C4
Harriet, *60* C2
Harrisburg, **2,192** E2
Harrison, **12,152** B1
Hartford, **772** A2
Hartman, **596** B2
Harvey, *40* B3
Haskell, **2,645** C3
Hatfield, **402** A3
Hattieville, *60* C2
Havana, **392** B2
Haynes, **214** E3
Hazen, **1,637** D3
Heber Springs, **6,432** C2
Hector, **506** C2
Helena, **6,323** E3
Henderson, *60* C1
Hermitage, **769** C4
Heth E2
Hickory Plains, *80* D3
Hickory Ridge, **384** E2
Higden, **101** C2
Higginson, **378** D2
Highfill, **379** A1
Highland, *90* B3
Hillemann D2
Hindsville, **75** B1
Hiram, *60* D2
Hiwasse, *325* A1
Holland, **577** C2
Hollis, *70* B3
Holly Grove, **722** D3
Holly Springs, *70* C4
Hollywood, *80* B3
Hon, *150* A3
Hope, **10,616** B4
Hopper, *40* B3
Horatio, **997** A4
Horseshoe Bend, **2,278** D1
Horseshoe Lake, **321** E3
Hot Springs, **35,750** B3
Hot Springs Village, **8,397** B3
Houston, **159** C2
Howell D2
Hoxie, **2,817** E1
Hughes, **1,867** E3
Humnoke, **280** D3
Humphrey, **806** D3
Hunter, **152** D2
Huntington, **688** A2
Huntsville, **1,931** B1
Huttig, **731** C4
Ida, *100* D2
Imboden, **684** D1
Ingalls, *60* C4
Ink, *125* A3
Iron Springs (see Parkers), **3,499** C3
Ivan, *90* C4
Jacksonport, **235** D2
Jacksonville, **29,916** C3
Japton, *60* B2
Jasper, **498** B1
Jefferson, *175* C3
Jennette, **124** E2
Jennie, *40* D4
Jenny Lind, *650* A2
Jericho, **184** E2
Jerome, **46** D4
Jersey C4
Jerusalem, *150* C2
Jessieville, *200* B3
Johnson, **2,319** A1
Joiner, **540** E2
Jonesboro, **55,515** E2
Judsonia, **1,982** D2
Junction City, **721** C4
Kedron, *175* C3
Keiser, **808** E2
Kelso, *80* D4
Kensett, **1,791** D2
Kent, *90* C4
Kenwood, *90* C2
Keo, **235** D3
Kiblah, *60* B4
Kibler, **969** A2
Kingsland, **449** C4
Kingston, *60* B1
Kirby, *225* B3
Knobel, **358** E1
Knoxville, **511** B2
Lacey, *90* D4
Ladd, *90* D3
Ladelle, *50* D4
Lafe, **385** E1
LaGrange, **122** E3
Lake City, **1,956** E2
Lake Hamilton, **1,609** B3
Lakeview, **763** C1
Lake View, **531** E3
Lake Village, **2,823** D4
Lamar, **1,415** B2
Lambrook E3
Lamont, *70* C3
Landis, *40* C2
Laneburg, *50* B4
Langley, *90* B3
Lavaca, **1,825** A2
Lawson, *100* C4
Leachville, **1,981** E2
Lead Hill, **287** C1
Lee Creek A2
Leola, **515** C3
Lepanto, **2,133** E2
Leslie, **482** C2
Letona, **201** D2
Lewisville, **1,285** B4
Lexa, **331** E3
Limestone, *50* B2
Lincoln, **1,752** A2
Little Flock, **2,585** A1
Little Rock, **183,133** C3
Lockesburg, **711** A4
Locust Grove, *150* D2
Lodge Corner D3
London, **925** B2
Lono, *100* C3
Lonoke, **4,287** D3
Lonsdale, **118** C3
Louann, **195** C4
Lowell, **5,013** A1
Lowry B1
Lurton, *50* B2
Luxora, **1,317** F2
Lynn, **315** D1
Macedonia, *125* B4
Macon, *1,100* C3
Madison, **987** E2
Magazine, **915** B2
Magness, **191** D2
Magnolia, **10,858** B4
Malvern, **9,021** C3
Mammoth Spring, **1,147** D1
Mandeville, *700* B4
Manila, **3,055** E2
Manning C3
Mansfield, **1,097** A2
Marble, *40* B1
Marianna, **5,181** E3
Marie, **108** E2
Marion, **8,901** E2
Marked Tree, **2,800** E2
Marmaduke, **1,158** E1
Marshall, **1,313** C2
Martinville, *40* C2
Marvell, **1,395** E3
Maumelle, **10,557** C3
Mayflower, **1,631** C3
Maynard, **381** E1
Maysville, *50* A1
McCaskill, **84** B4
McCrory, **1,850** D2
McDougal, **195** E1
McGehee, **4,570** D4
McKamie B4
McNab, **37** B4
McNeil, **662** B4
McRae, **661** D2
Melbourne, **1,673** D1
Mellwood, **10** E3
Mena, **5,637** A3
Menifee, **311** C2
Metalton B1
Midland, **253** A2
Mineral Springs, **1,264** B4
Minturn, **114** D2
Mist, *50* D4
Mitchellville, **497** D4
Moark, *125* E1
Moko, *60* D1
Monette, **1,179** E2
Monroe, *90* D3
Monticello, **9,146** D4
Montrose, **526** D4
Moorefield, **160** D2
Moreland, *225* C2
Morganton, *80* C2
Moro, **241** E3
Moro Bay, *50* C4
Morrilton, **6,550** C2
Morrison Bluff, **74** B2
Morriston, *40* D1
Moscow, *50* D3
Mountainburg, **682** A2
Mountain Home, **11,012** C1
Mountain Pine, **772** B3
Mountain Valley, *50* B3
Mountain View, **2,876** C2
Mount Holly, *150* C4
Mount Ida, **981** B3
Mount Judea, *70* B2
Mount Olive C2
Mount Pleasant, **401** D2
Mount Vernon, **144** C2
Mulberry, **1,627** A2
Murfreesboro, **1,764** B3
Myron, *40* D1
Nashville, **4,878** B4
Nathan, *60* B3
Natural Dam, *60* A2
Newark, **1,219** D2
Newburg, *125* D1
New Edinburg, *50* C4
Newell, *250* C4
Newhope, *90* A3
New London C4
Newport, **7,811** D2
Nimmons, **100** E1
Norfork, **484** C1
Norman, **423** B3
Norphlet, **822** C4
N. Crossett, **3,581** D4
N. Little Rock, **60,433** C3
Oak Grove, **376** B1
Oak Grove Heights, **727** E1
Oakhaven, **54** B4
Oakland, *100* C1
Oark, *70* B2
Oden, **220** B3
Ogden, **214** A4
Ogemaw, *80* B4
Oil Trough, **218** D2
O'Kean, **201** E1
Okolona, **160** B4
Ola, **1,204** B2
Old Lexington C2
Olvey, *200* C1
Olyphant D2
Oma, *175* B3
Omaha, **165** B1
Oneida, *70* E3
Onyx B3
Oppelo, **725** C2
Osage, *60* B1
Osceola, **8,875** F2
Otto, *50* C2
Otwell, *60* E2
Ouachita, *90* C4
Owensville, *70* C3
Oxford, **642** C1
Ozan, **81** B4
Ozark, **3,525** B2
Ozone, *225* B2
Palestine, **741** E3
Palmyra, *125* D4
Pangburn, **654** D2
Paragould, **22,017** E1
Paraloma, *60* A4
Paris, **3,707** B2
Parkdale, **377** D4
Parkers (Parkers-Iron Springs), **3,499** C3
Parkin, **1,602** E2
Parks B3
Paron C3
Parthenon, *80* B2
Patmos, **61** B4
Patterson, **467** D2
Payneway, *225* E2
Peach Orchard, **195** E1
Pearcy, *175* B3
Pea Ridge, **2,346** A1
Pearson, *70* C2
Peel, *80* C1
Pelsor B2
Penrose D2
Perla, **115** C3
Perry, **314** C2
Perrytown, **255** B4
Perryville, **1,458** C3
Pettigrew B2
Pickens, *100* D4
Piggott, **3,894** E1
Pike City, *40* B3
Pindall, **95** C1
Pine Bluff, **55,085** C3
Pine Ridge B3
Pineville, **246** C1
Piney (Johnson Co.), *90* B2
Piney (Garland Co.), **3,988** B3
Pinnacle, *325* C3
Plainview, **755** B3
Pleasant Plains, **267** D2
Plumerville, **854** C2
Pocahontas, **6,518** E1
Point Cedar, *80* B3
Pollard, **240** E1
Ponca B1
Poplar Grove, *325* E3
Portia, **483** D1
Portland, **552** D4
Possum Grape, *150* D2
Potter, *90* A3
Pottsville, **1,271** B2
Powhatan, **50** D1
Poyen, **272** C3
Prairie Creek, **1,849** A1
Prairie Grove, **2,540** A2
Prairie View, *80* B2
Prattsville, **282** C3
Prescott, **3,686** B4
Prim, *40* C2
Princeton C4
Provo, *100* A3
Pyatt, **253** C1
Quitman, **714** C2
Ramsey, *40* C4
Ratcliff, **191** B2
Ravenden, **511** D1
Ravenden Springs, **137** D1
Reader, **82** B4
Readland, **125** D4
Rector, **2,017** E1
Redfield, **1,157** C3
Red Star B2
Reed, **275** D4
Reyno, **484** E1
Rhea, *100* A1
Richmond, *60* A4
Rison, **1,271** C4
Riverside, *40* D2
Rivervale, *80* E2
Rockport, **792** C3
Rock Springs, *70* C2
Rockwell, **3,024** B3
Roe, **124** D3
Rogers, **38,829** A1
Rohwer, *150* D4
Roland, *200* C3
Rondo, **237** E3
Rosboro, *50* B3
Rose Bud, **429** C2
Rosston, **265** B4
Round Pond, *80* E2
Rover, *175* B3
Rudy, **72** A2
Rule B1
Rupert, *100* C2
Russell, **228** D2
Russellville, **23,682** B2
Rye, *100* D4
Sage, *60* D1
St. Charles, **261** D3
St. Francis, **250** E1
St. James, *125* D2
St. Joe, **85** C1
St. Paul, **163** B2
Salado, *350* D2
Salem (Saline Co.), **2,789** C3
Salem (Fulton Co.), **1,591** D1
Salesville, **437** C1
Salus B2
Schaal, *40* B4
Scotland, *100* C2
Scott, **94** C3
Scottsville, *60* B2
Scranton, **222** B2
Searcy, **18,928** D2
Sedgwick, **112** E2
Selma, *50* D4
Shannon Hills, **2,005** C3
Sheridan, **3,872** C3
Sherrill, **126** D3
Sherwood, **21,511** C3
Shirley, **337** C2
Sidney, **275** D2
Sidon, *40* D2
Siloam Springs, **10,843** A1
Sims, *100* B3
Smackover, **2,005** C4
Smithton, *100* B4
Smithville, **73** D1
Smyrna C2
Snowball, *40* C2
Snow Lake, *40* D3
Snyder, *80* D4
Social Hill, *80* C3
South Lead Hill, **88** C1
Sparkman, **586** C4
Springdale, **45,798** A1
Springfield, *90* C2
Spring Hill, **30** B4
Springtown, **114** A1
Spring Valley, *50* B1
Stamps, **2,131** B4
Star City, **2,471** D4
Staves, *125* C3
Stephens, **1,152** B4
Steprock, *50* D2
Stonewall, *70* E1
Story, *40* B3
Strawberry, **283** D2
Strong, **651** C4
Sturkie D1
Stuttgart, **9,745** D3
Subiaco, **439** B2
Success, **180** E1
Sulphur Rock, **421** D2
Sulphur Springs, **671** A1
Summers, *225* A2
Summit, **586** C1
Sunnydale, *60* D2
Sunset, **348** E2
Swain, *125* B2
Swifton, **871** D2
Tamo, *50* D3
Tarry, *250* D3
Taylor, **566** B4
Texarkana, **26,448** A4
Thornburg, *100* C3
Thornton, **517** C4
Three Creeks C4
Tichnor D3
Tillar, **240** D4
Tilton, *90* E2
Timbo, *60* C2
Tinsman, **75** C4
Tokio B4
Tollette, **324** B4
Tollvile D3
Tomato F2
Tontitown, **942** A1
Traskwood, **548** C3
Trumann, **6,889** E2
Tuckerman, **1,757** D2
Tull, **358** C3
Tupelo, **177** D2
Turrell, **957** E2
Twin Groves, **276** C2
Tyro, *40* D4
Tyronza, **918** E2
Ulm, **205** D3
Umpire, *100* A3
Uniontown, *150* A2
Urbana, *90* C4
Urbanette, *175* B1
Valley Springs, **167** B1
Van Buren, **18,986** A2
Vandervoort, **120** A3
Vanndale, *325* E2
Vick, **30** C4
Victoria, **59** E2
Village, *125* B4
Vilonia, **2,106** C2
Vimy Ridge, *600* C3
Viola, **381** D1
Violet Hill, *70* D1
Wabash, *50* E3
Wabbaseka, **323** D3
Waldenburg, **80** E2
Waldo, **1,594** B4
Waldron, **3,508** A3
Walnut Ridge, **4,925** E1
Waltreak, *100* B3
Ward, **2,580** D2
War Eagle, *60* B1
Warren, **6,442** C4
Washburn, *80* A2
Washington, **148** B4
Waterloo, *50* B4
Watson, **288** D4
Waveland, *90* B2
Weathers, *70* B2
Webb City, *200* B2
Weiner, **760** E2
Weldon, **100** D2
Weona E2
Wesley, *175* B1
Wesson, *100* C4
West Crossett, **1,664** C4
Western Grove, **407** C1
West Fork, **2,042** A2
W. Helena, **8,689** E3
West Memphis, **27,666** E2
West Point, **164** D2
Wheatley, **372** D3
Whelen Springs, **84** B4
White D4
Whitehall, *80* E2
White Hall, **4,732** C3
Wickes, **675** A3
Wideman, *40* D1
Widener, **335** E2
Wiederkehr Village, **46** B2
Wild Cherry C1
Williford, **63** D1
Willisville, **188** B4
Willow, *50* C3
Wilmar, **571** D4
Wilmot, **786** D4
Wilson, **939** E2
Wilton, **439** A4
Winchester, **191** D4
Winslow, **399** A2
Winthrop, **186** A4
Witter, *40* B2
Witts Springs, *40* C2
Wolf Bayou, *70* D2
Woodberry, *80* C4
Woodson, **445** C3
Wooster, **516** C2
Wrightsville, **1,368** C3
Wynne, **8,615** E2
Yale B2
Yancopin, *40* D4
Y City, *60* A3
Yellville, **1,312** C1
Yorktown, *90* D3
Zinc, **76** C1
Zion, *125* D1

Other Features

Arkansas, *river* D3
Arkansas Post Natl. Mem. D3
Beaver, *lake* B1
Big Lake N.W.R. E2
Black, *river* D2
Boston Mts. A2
Buffalo, *river* B1
Buffalo Natl. River C2
Bull Shoals, *lake* C1
Bull Shoals S.P. C1
Cache, *river* E2
Camp Joseph T. Robinson C2
Catherine, *lake* C3
Chickasaw N.W.R. F2
Chickasaw S.P. F2
Dahomey N.W.R. E4
Dardanelle Res. B2
Degray, *lake* B3
Enid, *lake* F3
Erling, *lake* B4
Felsenthal N.W.R. D4
Fort Chaffee Maneuver Train. Ctr. A2
Fort Smith Natl. Hist. Site A2
Greers Ferry, *lake* C2
Greeson, *lake* B3
Hamilton, *lake* B3
Handy Brake N.W.R. D4
Hatchie N.W.R. F2
Holla Bend N.W.R. B2
Holly Springs Natl. For. F3, F4
Hot Springs Natl. Park B3
Kisatchie Natl. For. C4
Lake Isom N.W.R. F1
Little Missouri, *river* B4
Little River N.W.R. A4
Little Rock Central High School N.H.S. C3
Lower Hatchie N.W.R. F2
Magazine, *mountain* B2
Mark Twain Natl. For. B1
Maumelle, *lake* C3
Milan Arsenal F2
Millwood, *lake* A4
Mississippi, *river* E3
Nimrod, *lake* B3
Norfork, *lake* C1
Ouachita, *lake* B3
Ouachita, *river* A3, C3
Ouachita Mts. A3
Ouachita Natl. For. A3, A4, B3
Overflow N.W.R. D4
Ozark, *plateau* A1
Ozark Natl. For. A1, A2, B2, C1
Pea Ridge Natl. Mil. Park A1
Pine Bluff Arsenal C3
Red, *river* B4
Red River Army Depot A4
Reelfoot N.W.R. F1
St. Francis Natl. For. E3
St. Francis, *river* E1
Saline, *river* C3
Sardis, *lake* F3
Sequoyah N.W.R. A2
Table Rock L. B1
Tallahatchie N.W.R. E3, E4
Upper Ouachita N.W.R. C4
White, *river* C2, D3
White River N.W.R. D3
Winding Stair N.R.A. A3
Wright Patman L. A4
Yazoo, *river* E4
Yazoo N.W.R. D4

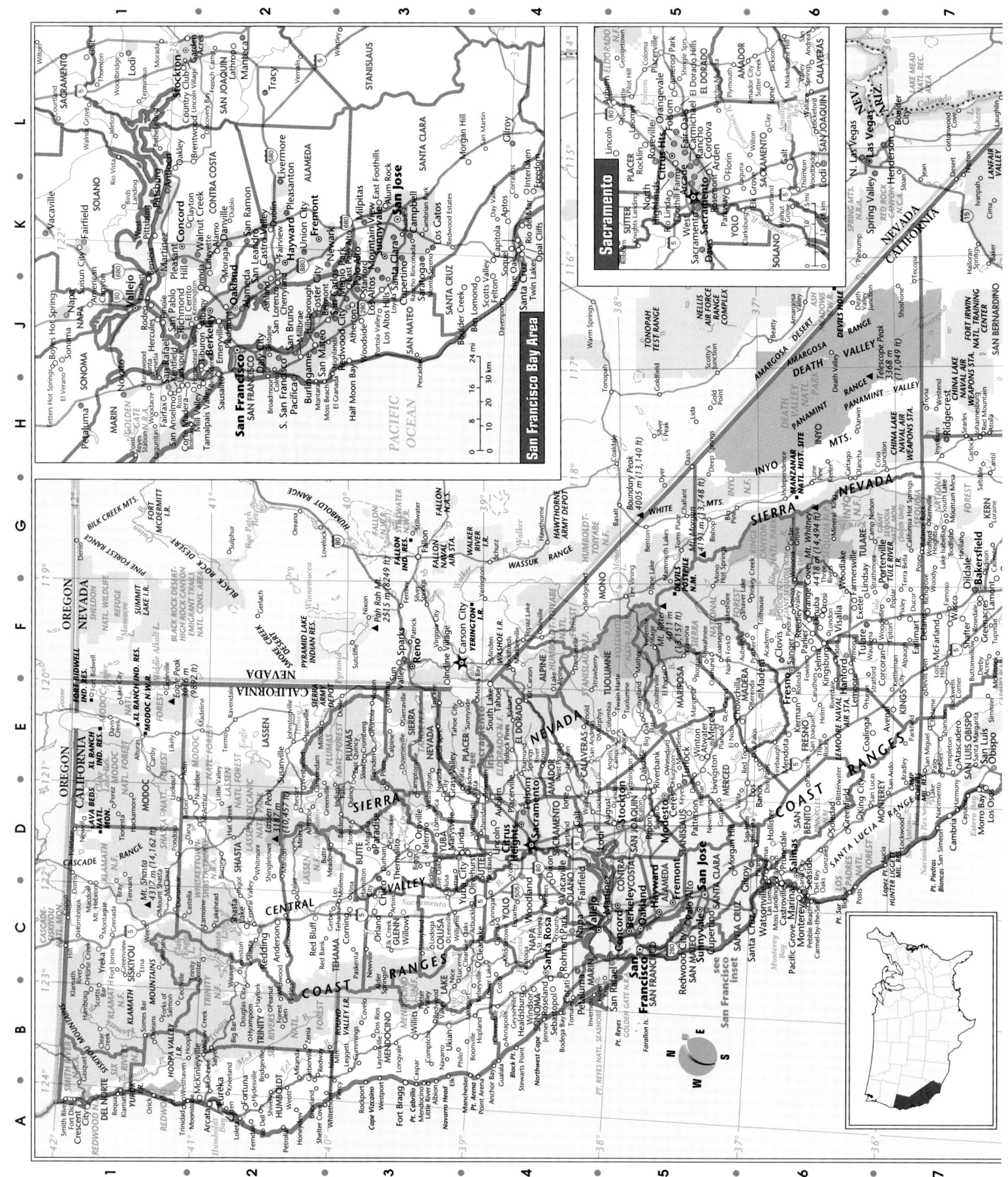

Sacramento

San Francisco Bay Area

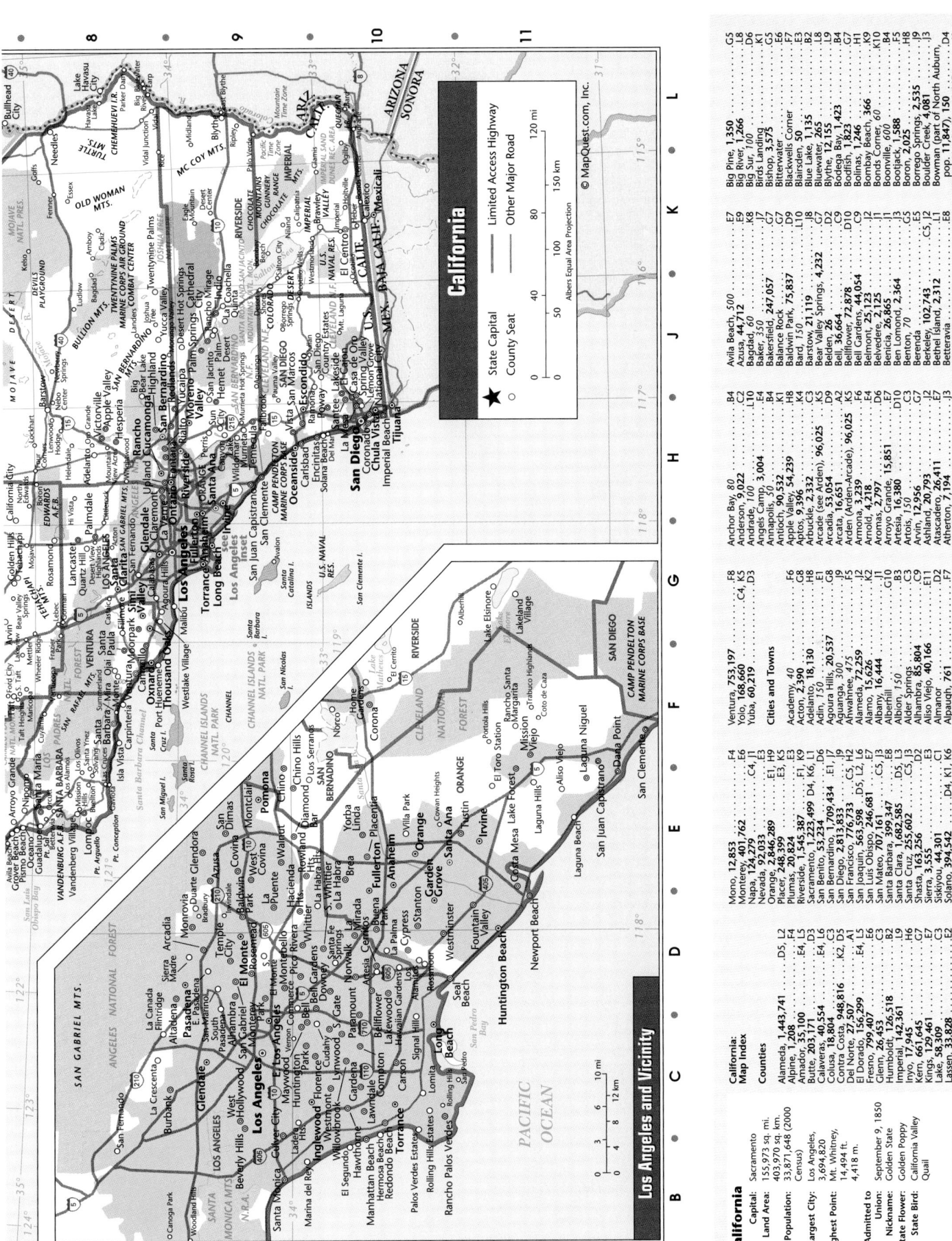

California

Capital:	Sacramento
Land Area:	155,973 sq. mi.
	403,970 sq. km.
Population:	33,871,648 (2000 Census)
Largest City:	Los Angeles, 3,694,820
Highest Point:	Mt. Whitney, 14,494 ft.
	4,418 m.
Admitted to Union:	September 9, 1850
Nickname:	Golden State
State Flower:	Golden Poppy
State Bird:	California Valley Quail

California: Map Index

Counties

Alameda, 1,443,741	D5, L2
Alpine, 208	F4
Amador, 35,100	E4, L5
Butte, 203,171	D3
Calaveras, 40,554	E4, L6
Colusa, 18,804	C3
Contra Costa, 948,816	K2, D5
Del Norte, 27,507	A1
El Dorado, 156,299	E4, L5
Fresno, 799,407	E6
Glenn, 26,453	C3
Humboldt, 126,518	B2
Imperial, 142,361	L9
Inyo, 17,945	G7
Kern, 661,645	E7
Kings, 129,461	E6
Lake, 58,309	C3
Lassen, 33,828	E2
Los Angeles, 9,519,338	B9, G8
Madera, 123,109	F5
Marin, 247,289	C4, H1
Mariposa, 17,130	F5
Mendocino, 86,265	B3
Merced, 210,554	D5
Modoc, 9,449	D1
Mono, 12,853	F4
Monterey, 401,762	E6
Napa, 124,279	C4, J1
Nevada, 92,033	E3, E3
Orange, 2,846,289	E8
Placer, 248,399	E3
Plumas, 20,824	E2
Riverside, 1,545,387	F8, F1, K9
Sacramento, 1,223,499	D4, K6, L1
San Benito, 53,234	D6
San Bernardino, 1,709,434	E1, I7
San Diego, 2,813,833	F9
San Francisco, 776,733	C5, H2
San Joaquin, 563,598	D5, L2, L6
San Luis Obispo, 246,681	D7
San Mateo, 707,161	C5, J3
Santa Barbara, 399,347	D7
Santa Clara, 1,682,585	D5, L3
Santa Cruz, 255,602	D5
Shasta, 163,256	D2
Sierra, 3,555	E3
Siskiyou, 44,301	C1
Solano, 394,542	D4, K1, K6
Sonoma, 458,614	B4, J1
Stanislaus, 446,997	D5, L5
Sutter, 78,930	D4, K5
Tehama, 56,039	C3
Trinity, 13,022	B2
Tulare, 368,021	G6
Tuolumne, 54,501	F4

Ventura, 753,197	F8
Yolo, 168,660	C4, K5
Yuba, 60,219	D3

Cities and Towns

Academy, 40	F6
Acton, 2,390	G8
Adelanto, 18,130	H8
Adin, 150	E1
Agoura Hills, 20,537	G8
Aguanga, 300	J9
Ahwahnee, 475	F5
Alameda, 15,626	K2
Alamo, 16,444	J2
Albany, 16,380	J2
Albion, 150	B3
Alder Springs, 150	C3
Alhambra, 85,804	C9
Aliso Viejo, 40,166	E11
Almanor, 761	D2
Alpaugh, 761	F7
Altadena, 42,610	C9
Alturas, 2,892	E1
Alum Rock, 13,479	K3
Amador City, 196	L6
Amboy, 300	K8
American Canyon, 9,774	G9, H9
Anaheim, 328,014	F4

Anchor Bay, 80	B4
Anderson, 9,022	C2
Andrade, 100	L10
Angels Camp, 3,004	L6
Annapolis, 90,532	K1
Antioch, 90,532	K1
Apple Valley, 54,239	H8
Aptos, 9,396	C3
Arbuckle, 2,332	C3
Arcade (see Arden), 96,025	K5
Arcadia, 53,054	C3
Arcata, 16,651	A2
Arden (Arden-Arcade), 96,025	K5
Armona, 3,239	F6
Arnold, 4,218	K2
Aromas, 2,125	D6
Arroyo Grande, 15,851	D7
Artesia, 16,380	D10
Artois, 150	C3
Arvin, 12,956	G7
Ashland, 20,793	J2
Atascadero, 26,411	D7
Atherton, 7,194	J3
Atolia, 150	H7
Atwater, 23,113	E5
Auberry, 2,053	F5
Auburn, 12,462	L6
August, 7,808	K8
Avalon, 3,127	G9
Avenal, 14,674	E6

Avila Beach, 500	B4
Azusa, 44,712	C9
Bagdad, 60	K8
Baker, 350	G7
Bakersfield, 247,057	B4
Balance Rock	K1
Baldwin Park, 75,837	D9
Bard, 150	L10
Barstow, 21,119	J8
Bear Valley Springs, 4,232	G7
Belden, 26	D2
Bell, 36,664	C9
Bell Gardens, 44,054	C9
Bellflower, 72,878	D10
Belmont, 25,123	J3
Belvedere, 2,125	J2
Benicia, 26,865	J1
Ben Lomond, 2,364	J3
Benton, 70	G5
Berenda, 150	E5
Berkeley, 102,743	J2
Bethel Island, 2,312	L1
Betteravia	J7
Beverly Hills, 33,784	B9
Bieber, 225	D1
Big Bar, 40	B2
Big Bear Lake, 5,438	J8
Biggs, 1,793	D3
Big Oak Flat (see Groveland), 3,388	E5

Big Pine, 1,350	G5
Big River, 1,266	L8
Birds Landing	K1
Bishop, 3,575	G5
Bitterwater	E6
Blackwells Corner	F7
Blairsden, 80	E3
Blue Lake, 1,135	B2
Bluewater, 265	L9
Blythe, 12,155	L9
Bodfish, 1,823	G7
Bodega Bay, 1,423	B4
Bolinas, 1,246	H1
Bombay Beach, 366	K9
Bonds Corner, 60	K10
Boonville, 600	B4
Bootjack, 1,588	F5
Boron, 2,025	H8
Borrego Springs, 2,535	J9
Boulder Creek, 4,081	J3
Bowman (part of North Auburn), pop. 11,847), 150	D4
Boyes Hot Springs, 6,665	J1
Bradbury, 855	E7
Bradley, 120	E7
Brawley, 22,052	K10
Bray, 35,410	D1
Brentwood, 23,302	E10, L1

Los Angeles and Vicinity

Briceland, 80 .... B2
Bridgeport, 200 .... F4
Bridgeville B2
Brisbane, 3,597 .... J2
Broadmoor, 4,026 .... H2
Buellton, 3,828 .... E8
Buena Park, 78,282 .... D10
Burbank (Los Angeles Co.), 100,316 .... C9
Burbank (Santa Clara Co.), 5,239 .... K3
Burlingame, 28,158 .... J2
Burney, 3,217 .... D2
Butte Meadows, 40 .... D2
Buttonwillow, 1,266 .... F7
Cadiz K8
Calabasas, 20,033 .... G8
Calexico, 27,109 .... K10
Caliente G7
California City, 8,385 .... H7
California Hot Springs, 125 .... G7
Calipatria, 7,289 .... K9
Calistoga, 5,190 .... C4
Callahan C1
Calpine, 150 .... E3
Camarillo, 57,077 .... F8
Cambria, 6,232 .... D7
Cambrian Park, 3,258 .... K3
Cameron Park, 14,549 .... L5
Campbell, 38,138 .... K3
Camp Nelson, 100 .... G6
Camptonville, 175 .... D3
Canby, 300 .... E1
Canoga Park, 70 .... A9
Cantil H7
Canyondam, 37 .... D2
Canyon Lake, 9,952 .... H9
Capitola, 10,033 .... K4
Carlsbad, 78,247 .... H9
Carmel-by-the-Sea, 4,081 .... D6
Carmichael, 49,742 .... L5
Carpinteria, 14,194 .... F8
Carson, 89,730 .... C10
Cartago, 109 .... G6
Caruthers, 2,103 .... F6
Casa de Oro (Casa de Oro-Mount Helix), 18,874 .... J10
Caspar, 375 .... B3
Castaic, 1,700 .... G8
Castella, 150 .... C1
Castro Valley, 57,292 .... K2
Castroville, 6,724 .... D6
Cathedral City, 42,647 .... J9
Cayucos, 2,943 .... E7
Cecilville B1
Cedar Grove G6
Central Valley C2
Ceres, 34,609 .... E5
Cerritos, 51,488 .... D10
Chalfant, 70 .... G5
Cherokee, 90 .... D3
Cherryland, 13,837 .... J2
Chester, 2,316 .... D2
Chico, 59,954 .... D3
Chino, 67,168 .... E9
Chino Hills, 66,787 .... E9
Cholame E7
Chowchilla, 11,127 .... E5
Chula Vista, 173,556 .... H10
Cima K7
Citrus Heights, 85,071 .... D4, K5
Claremont, 33,998 .... H8
Clarksburg, 475 .... K5
Clay, 225 .... L6
Clayton, 10,762 .... K1
Clear Creek, 100 .... B1
Clearlake, 13,142 .... C4
Clearlake Oaks, 2,402 .... C3
Cloverdale, 6,831 .... B4
Clovis, 68,468 .... F6
Coachella, 22,724 .... J9
Coalinga, 11,668 .... E6
Coarsegold, 275 .... F5
Cobb, 1,638 .... C4
Coleville F4
Colfax, 1,496 .... E3
Colma, 1,191 .... H2
Coloma, 325 .... L5
Columbia, 2,405 .... F4
Colusa, 5,402 .... D3
Commerce, 12,568 .... C9
Comptche, 90 .... B3
Compton, 93,493 .... C10
Concord, 121,780 .... C5, K1
Copco C1
Corcoran, 14,458 .... F6
Corning, 6,741 .... C3
Corona, 124,966 .... F10
Coronado, 24,100 .... H10
Corralitos, 2,431 .... K4
Corte Madera, 9,100 .... H1
Coso Junction H6
Costa Mesa, 108,724 .... E11
Cotati, 6,471 .... C4
Coto de Caza, 13,057 .... F11
Cottonwood, 2,960 .... C2
Coulterville, 100 .... E5
Country Club, 9,462 .... L1
Courtland, 375 .... D4, K6, L1
Covelo, 1,175 .... C3
Covina, 46,837 .... E9
Cowan Heights (part of Tustin Foothills, pop. 24,044), 4,700 .... E10
Crescent City, 4,006 .... A1
Crockett, 3,194 .... K1
Cromberg, 290 .... E3
Cudahy, 24,208 .... C10
Culver City, 38,816 .... B9
Cummings B2
Cupertino, 50,546 .... C5, K3
Cutten, 2,933 .... A2
Cuyama, 40 .... F8
Cypress, 46,229 .... D10
Dales C2

Daly City, 103,621 .... J2
Dana, 50 .... D1
Dana Point, 35,110 .... E11
Danville, 41,715 .... K2
Dardanelle F4
Darwin, 54 .... H6
Davenport, 175 .... J4
Davis, 60,308 .... K5
Davis Creek, 70 .... E1
Day Valley, 3,587 .... K4
Death Valley, 386 .... J6
Death Valley Junction J6
Deep Springs H5
Delano, 38,824 .... F7
Del Mar, 4,389 .... H10
Del Rey Oaks, 1,650 .... D6
Derby Acres, 376 .... F7
Desert, 70 .... K7
Desert Center, 60 .... K9
Desert Hot Springs, 16,582 .... J9
Desert Shores, 792 .... J9
Desert View Highlands, 2,337 .... G8
Devils Den F7
Diablo, 988 .... K2
Diamond Bar, 56,287 .... E9
Diamond Springs, 4,888 .... E4
Dinkey Creek F5
Dinuba, 16,844 .... F6
Discovery Bay, 8,981 .... L2
Dixon, 16,103 .... D4
Dorris, 886 .... D1
Dos Palos, 4,581 .... E6
Dos Rios, 40 .... B3
Douglas City, 200 .... C2
Downey, 107,323 .... D10
Downieville, 80 .... E3
Doyle, 225 .... E2
Ducor, 504 .... F7
Dunnigan, 150 .... D4
Dunsmuir, 1,923 .... C1
Durham, 5,220 .... D3
Eagle Mountain, 125 .... K9
Eagleville E1
Earlimart, 6,583 .... F7
Earp L8
East Blythe, 3 .... L9
East Foothills, 8,133 .... K3
East Los Angeles, 124,283 .... C9
East Palo Alto, 29,506 .... J3
East Pasadena, 6,045 .... D9
E. Quincy (see Quincy), 2,398 .... E3
Edison, 375 .... G7
El Cajon, 94,869 .... J10
El Centro, 37,835 .... K10
El Cerrito (Contra Costa Co.), 23,171 .... J1
El Cerrito (Riverside Co.), 4,590 .... F10
El Dorado Hills, 18,016 .... L5
El Granada, 5,724 .... H2
Elk, 60 .... B3
Elk Creek C3
Elk Grove, 59,984 .... K5
Elkhorn, 1,591 .... D6
El Monte, 115,965 .... D9
El Nido, 325 .... E5
El Portal, 200 .... F5
El Segundo, 16,033 .... B10
El Toro Station E11
El Verano, 3,954 .... J1
Emeryville, 6,882 .... J2
Encinitas, 58,014 .... H9
Escalon, 5,963 .... D5
Escondido, 133,559 .... H9
Esparto, 1,858 .... C4
Essex K8
Etna, 781 .... C1
Eureka, 26,128 .... A2
Exeter, 9,168 .... F6
Fairfax, 7,319 .... H1
Fairfield, 96,178 .... D4, K1
Fair Oaks, 28,008 .... L5
Fairview, 9,470 .... K2
Fallbrook, 29,100 .... H9
Famoso F7
Farmersville, 8,737 .... F6
Farmington, 262 .... E5
Felton, 1,051 .... J4
Fenner K8
Ferndale, 1,382 .... A2
Fetters Hot Springs (Fetters Hot Springs-Agua Caliente), 2,505 .... J1
Fillmore, 13,643 .... G8
Firebaugh, 5,743 .... E6
Florence (Florence-Graham), 60,197 .... C10
Florin, 27,653 .... D4, L5
Folsom, 51,884 .... D4, L5
Fontana, 128,929 .... H8
Foothill Farms, 17,426 .... L5
Ford City, 3,512 .... F7
Forest Glen B2
Forest Knoll (see Lagunitas), 1,835 .... C4
Forks of Salmon B1
Fort Bidwell, 80 .... E1
Fort Bragg, 7,026 .... B3
Fort Dick, 300 .... A1
Fort Jones, 660 .... C1
Fortuna, 10,497 .... A2
Foster City, 28,803 .... J2
Fountain Valley, 54,978 .... D11
Four Corners H8
Fowler, 3,979 .... F6
Frazier Park, 2,348 .... G8
Freedom, 6,000 .... K4
Fremont, 203,413 .... D5, K2
French Camp, 4,109 .... L2
Fresno, 427,652 .... F6
Fullerton, 126,003 .... D10, H9
Galt, 19,472 .... D4, K6, L1
Garberville, 300 .... B2

Gardena, 57,746 .... C10
Garden Acres, 9,747 .... L1
Garden Grove, 165,196 .... D10
Garlock H7
Gasquet, 300 .... B1
Gaviota E8
Georgetown, 962 .... L5
Gerber (Gerber-Las Flores), 1,389 .... C2
Geyserville, 700 .... C4
Gilroy, 41,464 .... D5, L4
Glamis K10
Glendale, 194,973 .... C9, G8
Glendora, 49,415 .... E9
Goffs K8
Golden Hills, 7,434 .... G7
Gonzales, 7,525 .... D6
Gorman G8
Grass Valley, 10,922 .... E3
Greenacres, 7,400 .... F7
Greenfield, 12,583 .... D6
Greenview, 200 .... C1
Greenville, 1,160 .... E2
Grenada, 351 .... C1
Gridley, 5,382 .... D3
Grover Beach, 13,067 .... E7
Guadalupe, 5,659 .... E8
Gualala, 275 .... B4
Guinda, 100 .... C4
Gustine, 4,698 .... D5
Hacienda Heights, 53,122 .... D9
Hackamore D1
Half Moon Bay, 11,842 .... J3
Halloran Springs, 350 .... K7
Hamburg, 50 .... B1
Hamilton City, 1,903 .... C3
Hanford, 41,686 .... F6
Harmony E7
Hat Creek, 40 .... D2
Havasu Lake, 125 .... L8
Havilah G7
Hawaiian Gardens, 14,779 .... D10
Hawthorne, 84,112 .... C10
Hayfork, 2,315 .... B2
Hayward, 140,030 .... C5, K2
Healdsburg, 10,722 .... C4
Heber, 2,988 .... K10
Helendale, 250 .... H8
Helm, 60 .... E6
Hemet, 58,812 .... J9
Hercules, 19,488 .... J1
Hermosa Beach, 18,566 .... B10
Hesperia, 62,582 .... H8
Highland, 44,605 .... H8
Highlands J2
Hillsborough, 10,825 .... J2
Hilmar, 4,807 .... E5
Hilt C1
Hi Vista, 40 .... H8
Hodge, 100 .... H8
Hollister, 34,413 .... D6
Holtville, 5,612 .... K10
Home Gardens, 9,461 .... F10
Homestead Valley (Tamalpais-Homestead Valley), 10,691 .... H1
Honeydew, 60 .... A2
Hoopa, 300 .... B1
Hopland, 300 .... B4
Hornbrook, 286 .... C1
Horse Creek C1
Hughson, 3,980 .... E5
Huntington Beach, 189,594 .... D11
Huntington Park, 61,348 .... C9
Huron, 6,306 .... E6
Hyampom, 60 .... B2
Hydesville, 1,209 .... A2
Imperial, 7,560 .... K10
Imperial Beach, 26,992 .... H10
Independence, 574 .... G6
Indian Falls, 37 .... E2
Indio, 49,116 .... J9
Ingot C2
Inglewood, 112,580 .... C10
Interlaken, 7,328 .... K4
Inverness, 1,421 .... C4
Inyokern, 984 .... H7
Ione, 7,129 .... E4, L6
Irvine, 143,072 .... E11, H9
Irwindale, 1,446 .... D9
Island Mountain B2
Isla Vista, 18,344 .... F8
Isleton, 828 .... L1
Ivanpah K7
Jackson, 3,989 .... E4, L6
Janesville, 550 .... E2
Jenner, 50 .... B4
Johannesburg, 176 .... H7
Johnstonville, 450 .... E2
Joshua Tree, 4,207 .... J8
Julian, 1,621 .... J9
June Lake, 300 .... F5
Keeler, 66 .... H6
Kelseyville, 2,928 .... C4
Kelso K7
Kensington, 4,936 .... J1
Kentfield, 6,351 .... H1
Kerman, 8,551 .... E6
Kernville, 1,736 .... G7
Kettleman City, 1,499 .... F6
Keyes, 4,575 .... E5
King City, 11,094 .... D6
Kings Beach, 9,199 .... F6
Kit Carson E4
Klamath, 651 .... A1
Klamath River C1
Kneeland, 70 .... B2
Knights Landing, 1,000 .... K5
Kyburz, 80 .... E4
La Canada Flintridge, 20,318 .... C8
La Crescenta (La Crescenta-Montrose), 18,532 .... C8
Ladera Heights, 6,568 .... B9
Lafayette, 23,908 .... K2

Laguna, 34,309 .... K5
Laguna Beach, 23,727 .... E11
Laguna Hills, 31,178 .... E11
Laguna Niguel, 61,891 .... E11
Lagunitas (Lagunitas-Forest Knolls), 1,835 .... H1
La Habra, 58,974 .... D10
La Habra Heights, 5,712 .... D9
Lake Alpine F4
Lake City, 50 .... E1
Lake Elsinore, 28,928 .... G11
Lake Forest, 58,707 .... E11
Lakehead (Lakehead-Lakeshore), 549 .... C2
Lake Isabella, 3,315 .... G7
Lakeland Village, 5,626 .... G11
Lake Nacimiento, 2,176 .... E7
Lakeport, 4,820 .... C3
Lakeshore F5
Lakeside, 19,560 .... J10
Lakeview (Kern Co.), 80 .... F7
Lakewood, 79,345 .... D10
La Mesa, 54,749 .... H10
La Mirada, 46,783 .... D10
Lamoine, 80 .... C2
Lamont, 13,296 .... G7
La Palma, 15,408 .... D10
La Porte, 43 .... E3
La Puente, 41,063 .... D9
La Quinta, 23,694 .... J9
Larkspur, 12,014 .... H1
Las Cruces E8
Las Lomas, 3,078 .... D6
Lathrop, 10,445 .... L2
Laton, 1,236 .... F6
La Verne, 31,638 .... H8
Lawndale, 31,711 .... C10
Laytonville, 1,301 .... B3
Lebec, 1,285 .... G8
Leesville C3
Lee Vining, 175 .... F5
Leggett B3
Le Grand, 1,760 .... E5
Lemon Grove, 24,918 .... H10
Lemoore, 19,712 .... F6
Lenwood, 3,222 .... H8
Lewiston, 1,305 .... C2
Likely, 100 .... E1
Lincoln, 11,205 .... D4, L4
Lincoln Village, 4,216 .... L1
Linda, 13,474 .... D3
Linden, 1,103 .... D4
Lindsay, 10,297 .... F6
Little River, 70 .... B3
Littlerock, 1,402 .... H8
Little Valley D2
Live Oak (Santa Cruz Co.), 16,628 .... K4
Live Oak (Sutter Co.), 6,229 .... D3
Livermore, 73,345 .... K2
Livingston, 10,473 .... E5
Lockeford, 3,179 .... D4, L6
Lockhart, 50 .... H7
Lockwood, 150 .... D7
Lodi, 56,999 .... D4, K6, L1
Lodoga C3
Loleta, 600 .... A2
Loma Rica, 2,075 .... D3
Lomita, 20,046 .... C10
Lompoc, 41,103 .... E8
London, 1,848 .... F6
Lone Pine, 1,655 .... G6
Long Beach, 461,522 .... C10, G9
Longvale, 50 .... B3
Lookout D1
Loomis, 6,260 .... L5
Loraine, 125 .... G7
Los Alamitos, 11,536 .... D10
Los Alamos, 1,372 .... E8
Los Altos, 27,693 .... J3
Los Altos Hills, 7,902 .... J3
Los Angeles, 3,694,820 .... C9, G9
Los Banos, 25,869 .... E5
Los Gatos, 28,592 .... K3
Los Molinos, 1,952 .... C2
Los Olivos, 950 .... E8
Los Osos (Baywood-Los Osos), 14,351 .... E7
Los Serranos E9
Lost Hills, 1,938 .... F7
Lower Lake, 1,755 .... C4
Loyalton, 862 .... E3
Loyola, 3,478 .... J3
Lucerne, 2,870 .... C3
Lucia, 90 .... D6
Ludlow J8
Lynwood, 69,845 .... C10
Macdoel, 140 .... C1
Madeline E1
Madera, 43,207 .... E6
Magalia, 10,569 .... D3
Malibu, 12,575 .... G8
Mammoth Lakes, 7,093 .... G5
Manchester, 125 .... B4
Manhattan Beach, 33,852 .... B10
Manteca, 49,258 .... L2
Manton, 372 .... D2
Maricopa, 1,111 .... F7
Marina, 25,101 .... D6
Marina del Rey, 8,176 .... B9
Marinwood, 6,357 .... H1
Mariposa, 1,373 .... F5
Markleeville, 197 .... F4
Martinez, 35,866 .... C4, K1
Marysville, 12,268 .... D3
Mather E4
Maywood, 28,083 .... C9
McArthur, 365 .... D1
McCloud, 1,343 .... C1
McFarland, 9,618 .... F7
McKinleyville, 13,599 .... A2
McKittrick, 160 .... F7
Meadow Vista, 3,096 .... D3

Meeks Bay, 50 .... E3
Mendocino, 824 .... B3
Mendota, 7,890 .... E6
Menlo Park, 30,785 .... J2
Merced, 63,893 .... E5
Mettler, 157 .... G7
Middletown, 1,020 .... C4
Midland K9
Milford, 90 .... E2
Millbrae, 20,718 .... J2
Mill Valley, 13,600 .... H1
Milpitas, 62,698 .... K3
Mineral, 143 .... D2
Mineral King G6
Mira Monte F8
Miranda, 225 .... B2
Mission Hills, 3,142 .... E8
Mission Viejo, 93,102 .... F11
Modesto, 188,856 .... E5
Mojave, 3,836 .... G7
Mokelumne Hill, 774 .... L6
Mono Hot Springs, 40 .... G5
Monrovia, 36,929 .... D9
Montague, 1,456 .... C1
Montara, 2,950 .... H2
Montclair, 33,049 .... E9
Montebello, 62,150 .... D9
Monterey, 29,674 .... D6
Monterey Park, 60,051 .... D9
Monte Sereno, 3,483 .... K3
Montpelier, 50 .... E5
Moonstone (see Westhaven), 1,044 .... A1
Moorpark, 31,415 .... G8
Morada, 3,726 .... L1
Moraga, 16,290 .... J2
Moreno Valley, 142,381 .... H9
Morgan Hill, 33,556 .... D5, L3
Morongo Valley, 1,929 .... J8
Morro Bay, 10,350 .... E7
Moss Beach, 1,953 .... H2
Moss Landing, 300 .... D6
Mountain Mesa, 716 .... G7
Mountain View, 70,708 .... K3
Mountain View Acres, 2,521 .... H8
Mount Hebron, 92 .... C1
Mount Laguna J10
Mount Shasta, 3,621 .... C1
Murphys, 2,061 .... L6
Murrieta, 44,282 .... H9
Murrieta Hot Springs, 2,948 .... H9
Napa, 72,585 .... C4, J1
National City, 54,260 .... H10
Navarro, 40 .... B3
Nebo Center, 1,174 .... J8
Needles, 4,830 .... L8
Nevada City, 3,001 .... D3
Newark, 42,471 .... K2
Newberry Springs, 40 .... J8
Newcastle, 1,000 .... L5
Newell, 400 .... D1
Newman, 7,093 .... D5
Newport Beach, 70,032 .... D11
Newville C3
Nice, 2,509 .... C3
Nicolaus, 100 .... D4
Niland, 1,143 .... K9
Nipomo, 12,626 .... E7
Nipton K7
Norco, 24,157 .... F10
North Edwards, 1,227 .... H7
North Fork, 500 .... F5
North Highlands, 44,187 .... K5
Norwalk, 103,298 .... D10
Novato, 47,630 .... H1
Nubieber, 50 .... D1
Oakdale, 15,503 .... E5
Oakhurst, 2,868 .... F5
Oakland, 399,484 .... C5, J2
Oakley, 25,619 .... L1
Oasis H5
Oceano, 7,260 .... E7
Oceanside, 161,029 .... H9
Ocotillo, 296 .... K10
Ocotillo Wells, 100 .... J9
Ogilby, 70 .... L10
Oildale, 27,885 .... F7
Ojai, 7,862 .... F8
Olancha, 134 .... H6
Olivehurst, 11,061 .... D3
Ontario, 158,007 .... H8
Opal Cliffs, 6,458 .... K4
Orange, 128,821 .... E10
Orange Cove, 7,722 .... F6
Orangevale, 26,705 .... L5
Orcutt, 28,830 .... E8
Orick, 350 .... A1
Orinda, 17,599 .... J1
Orland, 6,281 .... C3
Orleans, 80 .... B1
Orosi, 7,318 .... F6
Oroville, 13,004 .... D3
Oxnard, 170,358 .... F8
Pacifica, 38,390 .... H2
Pacific Grove, 15,522 .... D6
Pajaro, 3,384 .... D6
Palermo, 5,720 .... D3
Palmdale, 116,670 .... G8
Palm Desert, 41,155 .... J9
Palm Springs, 42,807 .... J9
Palo Alto, 58,598 .... C5, J3
Palo Verde, 236 .... L9
Palos Verdes Estates, 13,340 .... B10
Panoche E6
Paradise, 26,408 .... D3
Paramount, 55,266 .... C10
Parker Dam, 100 .... L9
Parkfield E7
Parkway (Parkway-South Sacramento), 36,468 .... K5
Parlier, 11,145 .... F6
Pasadena, 133,936 .... D9
Paskenta C3
Paso Robles, 24,297 .... E7

Patterson, 11,606 .... D5
Pauma Valley, 325 .... J9
Peanut C2
Pebble Beach, 100 .... D6
Perez D1
Perris, 36,189 .... H9
Pescadero, 475 .... J3
Petaluma, 54,548 .... C4, H1
Petrolia, 50 .... A2
Philo, 325 .... B3
Pico Rivera, 63,428 .... D9
Piedmont, 10,952 .... J2
Piedra, 80 .... F6
Piercy, 50 .... B3
Pilot Hill, 200 .... L5
Pinole, 19,039 .... J1
Pismo Beach, 8,551 .... E7
Pittsburg, 56,769 .... K1
Pixley, 2,586 .... F7
Placentia, 46,488 .... D10
Placerville, 9,610 .... D4, L5
Planada, 4,369 .... E5
Platina C2
Pleasant Hill, 32,837 .... K1
Pleasanton, 63,654 .... K2
Plymouth, 980 .... L5
Point Arena, 474 .... B4
Point Reyes Station, 818 .... H1
Pollock Pines, 4,728 .... E4
Pomona, 149,473 .... E9
Pondosa D2
Poplar, 1,496 .... F6
Porterville, 39,615 .... G6
Port Hueneme, 21,845 .... F8
Portola, 2,227 .... E3
Portola Hills, 6,391 .... F11
Portola Valley, 4,462 .... J3
Posey G7
Posts, 250 .... D6
Potter Valley, 650 .... B3
Poway, 48,044 .... H10
Prather, 150 .... F5
Prunedale, 16,432 .... D6
Quartz Hill, 9,890 .... G8
Quincy (Quincy-East Quincy), 1,879 .... E3
Ramona, 15,691 .... J9
Rancho Cordova, 55,060 .... K5
Rancho Cucamonga, 127,743 .... H8
Rancho Mirage, 13,249 .... J9
Rancho Murieta, 4,193 .... L5
Rancho Palos Verdes, 41,145 .... C10
Rancho Rinconada, 4,200 .... K3
Rancho Santa Margarita, 47,214 .... F11
Ravendale E2
Red Bank, 40 .... C2
Red Bluff, 13,147 .... C2
Redding, 80,865 .... C2
Redlands, 63,591 .... H8
Red Mountain, 150 .... H7
Redondo Beach, 63,261 .... B10
Red Top, 40 .... E5
Redway, 1,188 .... B2
Redwood City, 75,402 .... C5, J2
Redwood Estates (part of Lexington Hills, pop. 2,454), 1,600 .... K3
Redwood Valley, 1,200 .... B3
Reedley, 20,756 .... F6
Requa, 100 .... A1
Rialto, 91,873 .... H8
Rice L8
Richgrove, 2,723 .... F7
Richmond, 99,216 .... J1
Ridgecrest, 24,927 .... H7
Rio Dell, 3,174 .... A2
Rio del Mar, 9,198 .... K4
Rio Linda, 10,466 .... K5
Rio Vista, 4,571 .... L1
Ripley, 650 .... L9
Ripon, 10,146 .... E5
Riverbank, 15,826 .... E5
Riverdale, 2,416 .... F6
River Pines, 400 .... E4
Riverside, 255,166 .... H9
Robbins, 325 .... K5
Rocklin, 36,330 .... L5
Rockport B3
Rodeo, 8,717 .... J1
Rohnert Park, 42,236 .... C4
Rolinda, 200 .... F6
Rolling Hills, 1,871 .... C10
Rolling Hills Estates, 7,676 .... C10
Rosamond, 14,349 .... G8
Rosedale, 8,445 .... F7
Roseland, 6,369 .... C4
Rosemead, 53,505 .... D9
Rosemont, 22,904 .... K5
Roseville, 79,921 .... K5
Ross, 2,329 .... H1
Rossmoor, 10,298 .... D10
Rowland Hts., 48,553 .... E9
Sacramento, 407,018 .... D4, K5
St. Helena, 5,950 .... C4
Salida, 12,560 .... D5
Salinas, 151,060 .... D6
Saltdale H7
Salton City, 978 .... K9
Salyer, 50 .... B2
San Andreas, 2,615 .... E4, L6
San Anselmo, 12,378 .... H1
San Ardo, 501 .... D6
San Bernardino, 185,401 .... H8
San Bruno, 40,165 .... J2
San Carlos, 27,718 .... J3
San Clemente, 49,936 .... F11, H9
Sand City, 261 .... D6
San Diego, 1,223,400 .... H10
San Diego Country Estates, 9,262 .... J9
San Dimas, 34,980 .... E9
San Fernando, 23,564 .... B8, G8
San Francisco, 776,733 .... C5, J2
San Gabriel, 39,804 .... D9

Sanger, 18,931 . . . . .F6
San Jacinto, 23,779 . . . . .J9
San Joaquin, 3,270 . . . . .J2
San Jose, 894,943 . . . . .D5, K3
San Juan Bautista, 1,549 . . . .D6
San Juan Capistrano,
 33,826 . . . . .F11, H9
San Leandro, 79,452 . . . . . . .J2
San Lorenzo, 21,898 . . . . . . .J2
San Lucas, 419 . . . . .E6
San Luis Obispo, 44,174 . . . .E7
San Marcos, 54,977 . . . . . . .H9
San Marino, 12,945 . . . . .D9
San Martin, 4,230 . . . . .L4
San Mateo, 92,482 . . . . .J2
San Miguel, 1,427 . . . . .E7
San Pablo, 30,215 . . . . .J1
San Pedro, 1,900 . . . . .C11
San Rafael, 56,063 . . . . .C5, H1
San Ramon, 44,722 . . . . .K2
San Simeon D7
Santa Ana, 337,977 . . . . .E10, H9
Santa Barbara, 92,325 . . . . . .F8
Santa Clara, 102,361 . . . . . . .K3
Santa Clarita, 151,088 . . . . . .G8
Santa Cruz, 54,593 . . . . .C6, K4
Santa Fe Springs, 17,438 . . . .D10
Santa Margarita, 950 . . . . . . .E7
Santa Maria, 77,423 . . . . .E8
Santa Monica, 84,084 . . . . . .B9
Santa Paula, 28,598 . . . . .F8
Santa Rosa, 147,595 . . . . . . .C4
Santa Venetia, 4,298 . . . . . . .H1
Santa Ynez, 4,584 . . . . .E8
Santee, 52,975 . . . . .J10
Saratoga, 29,843 . . . . .K3
Sausalito, 7,330 . . . . .H2
Scotts Bar, 40 . . . . .B1
Scotts Valley, 11,385 . . . . . . .K4
Seal Beach, 24,157 . . . . .D10
Searles H7
Seaside, 31,696 . . . . .D6
Sebastopol, 7,774 . . . . .C4
Selma, 19,444 . . . . .F6
Shafter, 12,736 . . . . .F7
Shandon, 986 . . . . .E7
Shasta, 375 . . . . .C2
Shasta Lake, 9,008 . . . . .C2

Shaver Lake, 705 . . . . .F5
Shelter Cove, 125 . . . . .A2
Sheridan, 750 . . . . .D4
Shingle Springs, 2,643 . . . . . .L5
Shingletown, 2,222 . . . . .D2
Shively B2
Shoshone, 52 . . . . .J7
Sierra Madre, 10,578 . . . . . . .D8
Sierraville, 80 . . . . .E3
Signal Hill, 9,333 . . . . .C10
Simi Valley, 111,351 . . . . . . .G8
Simmler F7
Sloat, 50 . . . . .E3
Smith River, 750 . . . . .A1
Soda Springs, 100 . . . . .E3
Solana Beach, 12,979 . . . . . .H10
Soledad, 11,263 . . . . .D6
Solvang, 5,332 . . . . .E8
Somes Bar B1
Sonoma, 9,128 . . . . .J1
Sonora, 4,423 . . . . .E5
Soquel, 5,081 . . . . .K4
South Dos Palos, 1,385 . . . . .E6
South El Monte, 21,144 . . . . .D9
South Gate, 96,375 . . . . .C10
South Lake G7
South Lake Tahoe, 23,609 . . .F4
South Pasadena, 24,292 . . . . .C9
South San Francisco, 60,552 . .J2
South Taft, 1,898 . . . . .F7
South Whittier, 55,193 . . . . . .D10
Spring Valley, 26,663 . . . . . . .J10
Squaw Valley, 2,691 . . . . .F6
Stanford, 13,315 . . . . .J3
Stanton, 37,403 . . . . .D10
Stewarts Point B3
Stockton, 243,771 . . . . . .D5, L1
Stonyford, 40 . . . . .C3
Storrie, 5 . . . . .D3
Stratford, 1,264 . . . . .F6
Strathmore, 2,584 . . . . .F6
Strawberry, 125 . . . . .F4
Suisun City, 26,118 . . . . .K1
Summerland, 1,545 . . . . .F8
Sun City, 17,773 . . . . .H9
Sunnyside (Sunnyside-Tahoe City),
 1,761 . . . . .E3
Sunnyvale, 131,760 . . . . .C5, K3

Susanville, 13,541 . . . . .E2
Sutter, 2,885 . . . . .D3
Sutter Creek, 2,303 . . . . .L6
Taft, 6,400 . . . . .F7
Taft Heights, 1,865 . . . . .F7
Tahoe City (see Sunnyside),
 1,761 . . . . .E3
Tamalpais Valley (Tamalpais-
 Homestead Valley), 10,691 . .H1
Tecopa, 99 . . . . .J7
Tehachapi, 10,957 . . . . .G7
Tehama, 432 . . . . .C2
Temecula, 57,716 . . . . .H9
Temple City, 33,377 . . . . .D9
Templeton, 4,687 . . . . .E7
Tennant, 63 . . . . .D1
Terminous, 475 . . . . .L1
Termo E2
Terra Bella, 3,466 . . . . .F7
Thermalito, 6,045 . . . . .D3
Thornton, 850 . . . . .K6, L1
Thousand Oaks, 117,005 . . . .G8
Three Rivers, 2,248 . . . . .G6
Three Rocks E6
Tiburon, 8,666 . . . . .J1
Tionesta D1
Tipton, 1,790 . . . . .F6
Tollhouse, 275 . . . . .F5
Tomales, 210 . . . . .C4
Toms Place, 125 . . . . .G5
Torrance, 137,946 . . . . .C10, G9
Trabuco Highlands F11
Tracy, 56,929 . . . . .L2
Trinidad, 311 . . . . .A1
Trinity Center, 50 . . . . .C2
Trona (part of Searles Valley,
 pop. 1,885), 650 . . . . .H7
Truckee, 13,864 . . . . .F3
Tulare, 43,994 . . . . .F6
Tulelake, 1,020 . . . . .D1
Tuolumne, 1,865 . . . . .E5
Tupman, 227 . . . . .F7
Turlock, 55,810 . . . . .E5
Tustin, 67,504 . . . . .E10
Twain Harte, 2,586 . . . . .E4
Twentynine Palms, 14,764 . . .J8
Twin Lakes, 5,533 . . . . .K4
Ukiah, 15,497 . . . . .B3

Union City, 66,869 . . . . .K2
Upland, 68,393 . . . . .H8
Vacaville, 88,625 . . . . . .D4, K1
Vallejo, 116,760 . . . . . . .C4, J1
Valley Springs, 2,560 . . . . . . .L6
Vandenberg Village, 5,802 . . .E8
Ventucopa F8
Ventura, 100,916 . . . . .F8
Vernalis, 70 . . . . .L2
Vernon, 91 . . . . .C9
Victorville, 64,029 . . . . .H8
Vidal L8
Vidal Junction L8
Villa Park, 5,999 . . . . .E10
Vina, 175 . . . . .C3
Vinton, 387 . . . . .E3
Visalia, 91,565 . . . . .F6
Vista, 89,857 . . . . .H9
Volta, 125 . . . . .E5
Wallace, 220 . . . . .E4, L6
Walnut, 30,004 . . . . .E9
Walnut Creek, 64,296 . . . . . . .K1
Walnut Grove, 669 . . . . . .L1, K6
Wasco, 21,263 . . . . .F7
Washington, 125 . . . . .E3
Waterford, 6,924 . . . . .E5
Watsonville, 44,265 . . . . .D6
Waukena, 225 . . . . .F6
Wawona F5
Weaverville, 3,554 . . . . .C2
Weed, 2,978 . . . . .C1
Weott, 125 . . . . .B2
West Covina, 105,080 . . . . . .E9
Westend, 175 . . . . .H7
Westhaven (Humboldt Co.),
 1,044 . . . . .A1
West Hollywood, 35,716 . . . .C9
Westlake Village, 8,368 . . . . .G8
Westley, 747 . . . . .L3
Westminster, 88,207 . . . . . . .D10
Westmont, 31,623 . . . . .C10
Westmorland, 2,131 . . . . .K9
West Pittsburg K1
West Point, 746 . . . . .E4
West Sacramento, 31,615 . . . .K5
Westport, 70 . . . . .B3
Westwood, 1,998 . . . . .E2
Wheatland, 2,275 . . . . .D3

Wheeler Ridge G8
Whitethorn B2
Whitmore, 100 . . . . .D2
Whittier, 83,680 . . . . .D9
Wildomar, 14,064 . . . . .H9
Wildwood B2
Williams, 3,670 . . . . .C3
Willits, 5,073 . . . . .B3
Willowbrook, 34,138 . . . . . . .C10
Willow Creek, 1,743 . . . . .B2
Willows, 6,220 . . . . .C3
Wilsonia, 50 . . . . .G6
Wilton, 4,551 . . . . .K5, L1
Windsor, 22,744 . . . . .C4
Winters, 6,125 . . . . .D4
Winton, 8,832 . . . . .E5
Wofford Heights, 2,276 . . . . .G7
Woodacre, 1,393 . . . . .H1
Woodbridge K6, L1
Woodfords, 50 . . . . .F4
Woodlake, 6,651 . . . . .F6
Woodland, 49,151 . . . . .D4
Woodside, 5,352 . . . . .J3
Woodville, 1,678 . . . . .F6
Woody G7
Wrightwood, 3,837 . . . . .H8
Yolo, 550 . . . . .D4
Yorba Linda, 58,918 . . . . . . .E10
Yosemite Village, 265 . . . . . . .F5
Yountville, 2,916 . . . . .C4
Yreka, 7,290 . . . . .C1
Yuba City, 36,758 . . . . .D3
Yucaipa, 41,207 . . . . .H8
Yucca Valley, 16,865 . . . . . . .J8
Zenia B2

Other Features

Almanor, lake D2
Amador Camanche, reservoir . .L6
Amargosa, desert H6
Amargosa, river J7
Amargosa, range J6
Angeles National Forest . . .C8, H8
Arena, point B4
Arguello, point E8
Ash Meadows N.W.R. J6
Berryessa, lake C4
Bilk Creek, mountains G1
Black, point B4
Black Rock, desert F2
Boundary, peak G5
Bullion, mountains J8
Cabrillo, point B3
Camp Pendelton Marine
 Corps Base F11, H9
Camp Roberts Mil. Res. E7
Carrizo Plain Natl. Mon. F7
Cascade, range D1
Central, valley C2
Channel, islands F9
Channel Islands Natl. Park F9
Chemehuevi I.R. L8
China Lake Naval Air
 Weapons Center H7
Chocolate Mountains
 Gunnery Range K9
Chocolate, mountains K9
Clair Engle, lake C1
Clear, lake C3
Clear Lake, reservoir D1
Cleveland N.F. F10, J10, J9
Coast, ranges B2, D6
Colorado, desert J9
Colorado, river L7, L9
Conception, point E8
Cosumnes, river L5
Death, valley H6
Death Valley Natl. Park H6
Devils Hole J6
Devils Playground K8
Devils Postpile N.M. F5
Dry, lake F2
Eagle, lake E2
Eagle, peak E1
Edwards A.F.B. H8
Eel, river B2
Eldorado N.F. E4, L5
Elsinore, lake G11
Estero, bay E7
Fallon Ind. Res. G3
Fallon N.W.R. G3
Fallon Naval Air Sta. G3
Farallon, islands B5
Folsom, lake L5
Fort Bidwell Ind. Res. E1
Fort Irwin Natl. Training Ctr. . .J7
Fort McDermitt I.R. G1
Giant Sequoia Natl. Mon.
 (North Unit) G6
Giant Sequoia Natl. Mon.
 (South Unit) G6
Golden Gate N.R.A. C5, H1
Goose, lake E1
Hawthorne Ammunition Depot G4
Honey, lake E2
Hoopa Valley I.R. B1
Humboldt, bay A2
Humboldt, range G2
Hunter Liggett Mil. Res. D7
Imperial, valley K9
Imperial Sand Dunes Rec. Area K10
Inyo, mountains H6
Inyo N.F. G5, G6
Joshua Tree Natl. Park K8
Kern, river G6
Kings, river F6
Kings Canyon Natl. Park G5
Klamath, mountains B1
Klamath, river B1
Klamath N.F. B1, D1
Lanfair, valley K7
Lassen, peak D2
Lassen N.F. D2, E2

Lassen Volcanic Natl. Park D2
Lava Beds Natl. Mon. D1
Lemoore Naval Air Sta. E6
Lopez, point D6
Los Padres Natl. Forest . . .D6, E8
Mad, river B2
Manzanar Natl. Hist. Site G6
Massacre, lake F1
Mathews, lake F10
McCoy, mountains K9
Mendocino N.F. C3
Merced, river E5
Middle Alkali, lake F1
Modoc Natl. Forest E1
Modoc N.W.R. E1
Mohave, lake L7
Mojave, river J8
Mojave Desert J7
Mojave Natl. Preserve K7
Mono, lake G4
Monterey, bay C6
Morgan, mountain G5
Nacimiento, reservoir D7
Navarro, head B3
Nellis Air Force Range J5
Nevada Test Site J5
Northwest, cape B4
Old Woman, mountains K8
Oroville, reservoir D3
Pacific, ocean B6, C11, H3
Pah Rah, mountain F3
Panamint, range H6
Panamint, valley H6
Piedras Blancas, point D7
Pine Forest, range G1
Pinnacles N.M. E6
Plumas Natl. Forest E2
Point Reyes Natl. Seashore . . .C4
Pyramid, lake F2
Pyramid Lake Indian Res. F2
Quechan I.R. L10
Quinn, river G1
Red Rock N.C.A. K6
Redwood N.P. A1
Reyes, point B5
Ritter, mountain F5
Round Valley I.R. B3
Rye Patch, reservoir G2
Sacramento, river C3, K6
Sal, point E8
Salton, sea K9
San Antonio, reservoir D7
San Bernardino, mountains . . .J8
San Bernardino N.F. J9
San Clemente, island G10
San Gabriel, mountains . . .C8, G8
San Joaquin, river E5
San Luis Obispo Bay D7
San Miguel, island E8
San Nicolas, island F9
San Pedro Bay C11
San Rafael Mts. F8
Santa Ana, river E10
Santa Barbara Channel E8
Santa Barbara, island G9
Santa Catalina, island G9
Santa Cruz, island F8
Santa Lucia Range D6
Santa Monica Mountains
 N.R.A. B9
Santa Rosa, island G9
Santa Rosa and San Jacinto
 Mountains Natl. Mon. J9
Sequoia Natl. Park G6
Sequoia N.F. G6, G8
Shasta, lake C2
Shasta, mountain C1
Shasta Natl. Forest D1
Sheldon N.W.R. F1
Sierra Army Depot E2
Sierra National Forest F5
Sierra Nevada, range D3, G5
Siskiyou, mountains B1
Six Rivers N.F. B1, B2
Smith River N.R.A. B1
Smoke Creek, desert F2
Stanislaus N.F. E4
Stillwater N.W.R. G3
Summit Lake I.R. F1
Sur, point D6
Tahoe, lake F3
Tahoe N.F. E3
Tehachapi, mountains G8
Telescope, peak H6
Toiyabe N.F. F3, F4, G4, K6
Trinity, river B2
Trinity N.F. B2
Tule, river F6
Tule River I.R. G6
Turtle, mountains L8
Twentynine Palms Marine Corps
 Air Ground Combat Center . .J8
U.S. Naval Res. G10, K10
Upper, lake E1
Vandenburg A.F.B. E8
Vizcaino, cape B3
Walker, lake G4
Walker, river F3
Walker River I.R. G3
Washoe I.R. F4
Wassuk, range G4
Whiskeytown-Shasta-Trinity
 N.R.A. D1
White, mountains G5
Whitney, mountain G6
Winnemucca, lake F2
XL Ranch Ind. Res. E1
Yerington I.R. F3
Yosemite Natl. Park F5
Yurok I.R. B1

California Landforms

Elevation in feet	Elevation in meters	
Over 6,000	Over 1,800	▲ Highest point
3,000–6,000	900–1,800	▼ Lowest point
1,500–3,000	450–900	— Landform boundary
600–1,500	180–450	
300–600	90–180	
0–300	0–90	
Below sea level	Below sea level	

0 50 100 150 mi
0 50 100 150 200 km

Map labels: Goose L., MODOC PLATEAU, WARNER MTS., SISKIYOU MTS., Klamath Mts., SALMON MTS., Trinity, Shasta L., Cascade Range, Basin and Range, Honey L., Mad R., Eel R., Russian R., Clear L., NAPA VALLEY, SACRAMENTO VALLEY, Pit R., Feather R., Yuba R., American R., L. Tahoe, Coast Ranges, Sierra Nevada, PACIFIC OCEAN, San Francisco Bay, DIABLO RANGE, Mokelumne R., Stanislaus R., Tuolumne R., Merced R., Mono L., CENTRAL VALLEY, SAN JOAQUIN VALLEY, SANTA CLARA VALLEY, SANTA CRUZ MTS., Monterey Bay, SALINAS VALLEY, Salinas R., SANTA LUCIA RANGE, San Joaquin R., Kings R., Kern R., TEMBLOR RANGE, Owens R., INYO MTS., WHITE MTS., Mt. Whitney 14,494 ft (4,418 m), 282 ft (86 m) Below Sea Level, DEATH VALLEY, Basin and Range, San Luis Obispo Bay, MOJAVE DESERT, Santa Barbara Channel, LOS ANGELES RANGES, SAN GABRIEL MTS., SAN BERNARDINO MTS., PENINSULAR RANGES, CHOCOLATE MTS., Colorado R., COACHELLA VALLEY, COLORADO DESERT, LAGUNA MTS., Salton Sea, IMPERIAL VALLEY, San Miguel I., Santa Rosa I., Santa Cruz I., Santa Barbara I., San Nicolas I., Channel Islands, Santa Catalina I., San Clemente I., Gulf of Santa Catalina

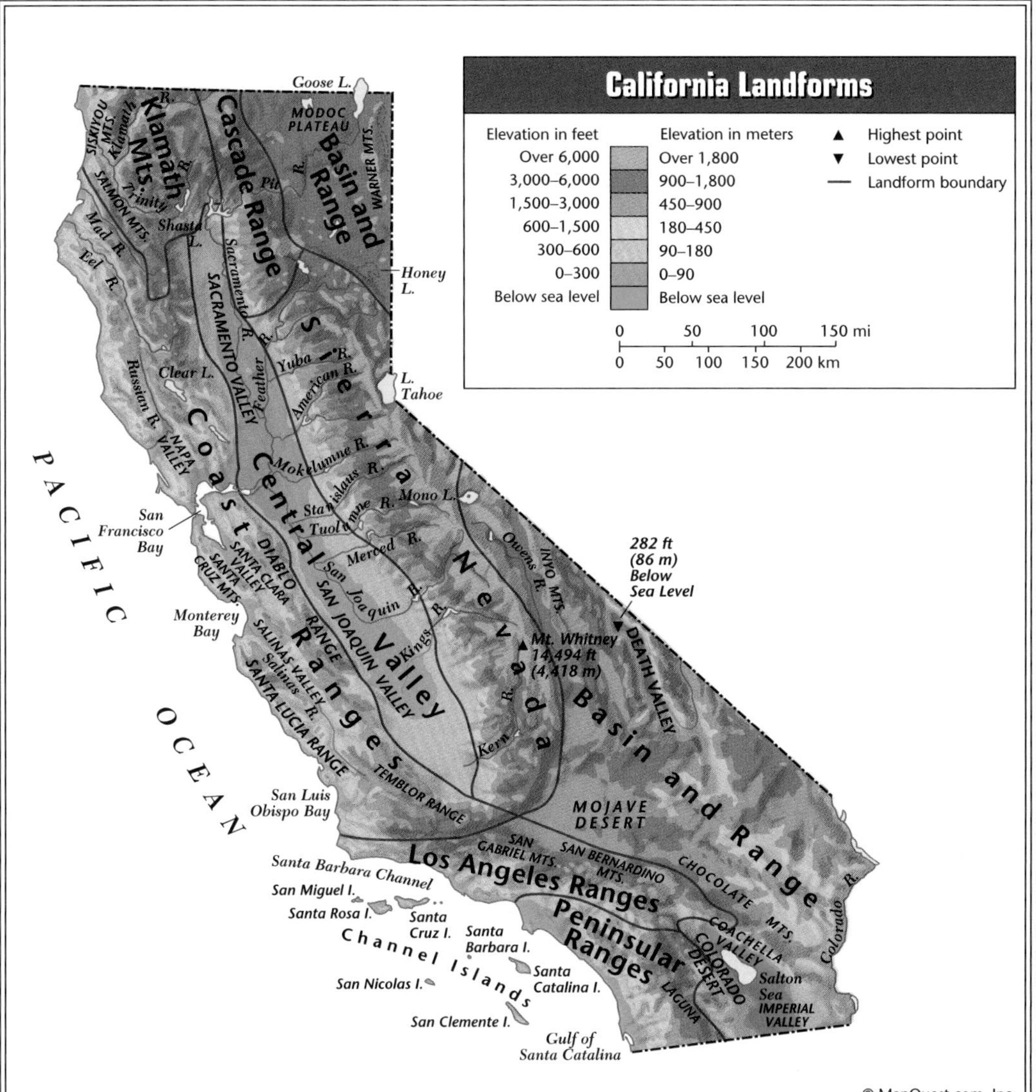

© MapQuest.com, Inc.

Colorado

Capital: Denver
Land Area: 103,730 sq. mi.
268,660 sq. km.
Population: 4,301,261 (2000 Census)
Largest City: Denver, 554,636
Highest Point: Mt. Elbert
14,433 ft.
4,399 m.
Admitted to Union: August 1, 1876
Nickname: Centennial State
State Flower: Rocky Mountain Columbine
State Bird: Lark Bunting

Colorado: Map Index

Counties

Colorado

State Capital
County Seat
Limited Access Highway
Other Major Road

0   25   50 mi
0   25   50   75 km
Albers Equal Area Projection

Denver

© MapQuest.com, Inc.

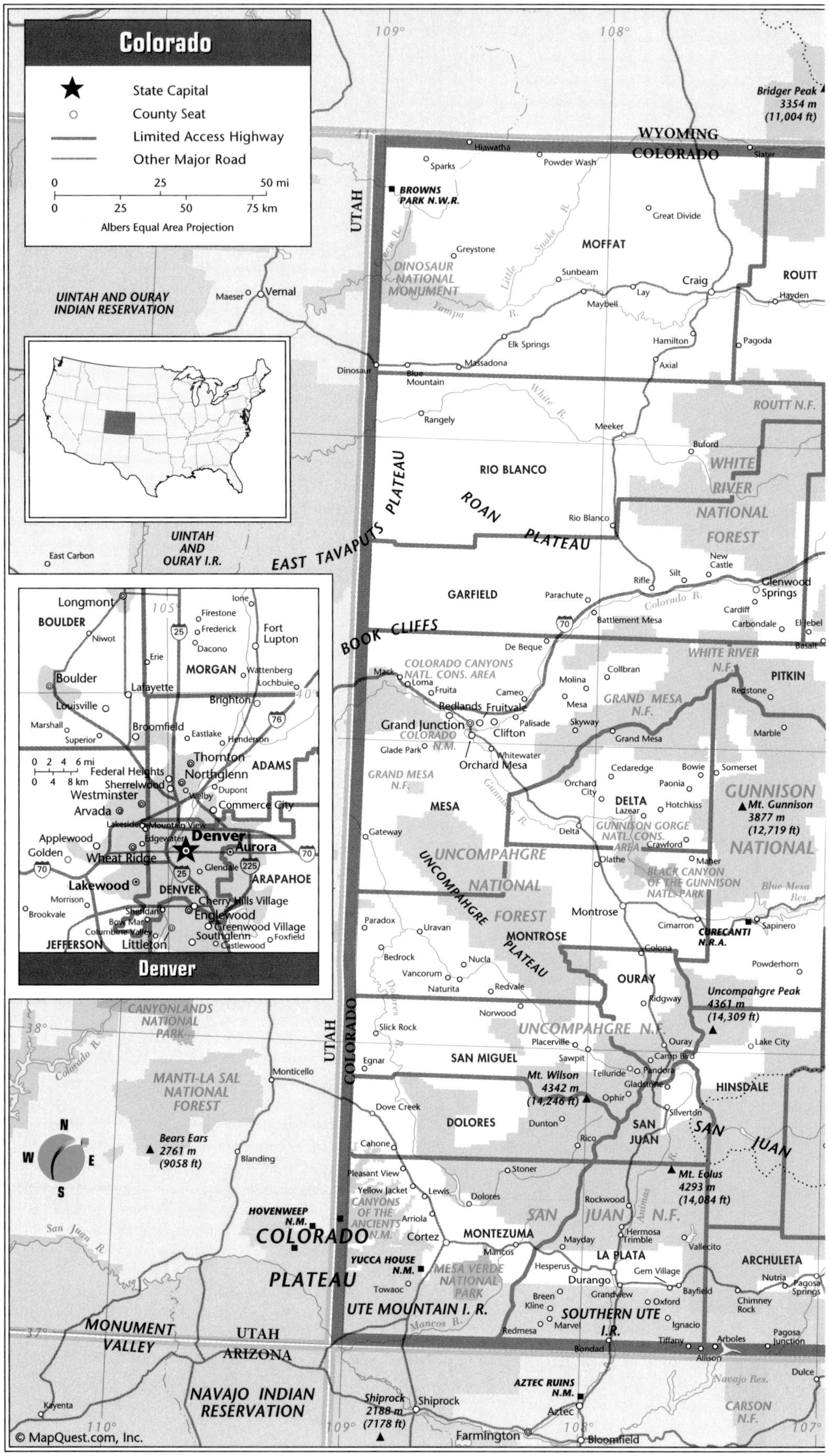

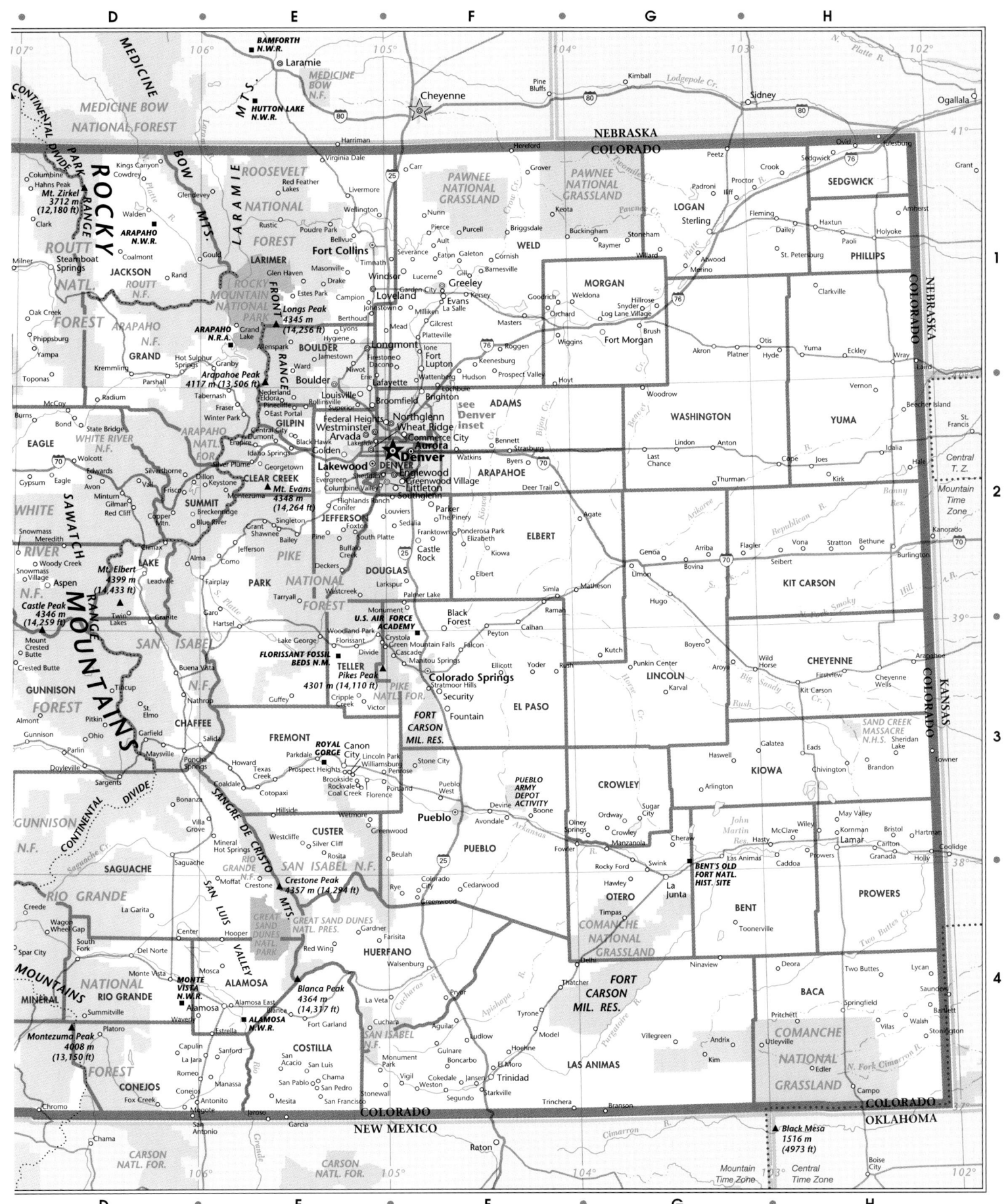

Beecher Island ...H2
Bellvue, 500 ...E1
Bennett, 2,021 ...F2
Berthoud, 4,839 ...E1
Bethune, 225 ...H2
Beulah, 1,164 ...F3
Black Forest, 13,247 ...E3
Black Hawk, 118 ...E2
Blanca, 391 ...E4
Blue Mountain, 50 ...B1
Blue River, 685 ...D2
Bonanza, 14 ...D3
Boncarbo ...F4
Bond, 80 ...D2
Bondad ...C4
Boone, 323 ...F3
Boulder, 94,673 ...A2, E1
Bovina ...G2
Bowie ...C3
Bow Mar, 847 ...A3
Boyero ...G3
Brandon ...H3
Branson, 77 ...F4
Breckenridge, 2,408 ...D2
Breen ...B4
Briggsdale, 80 ...F1
Brighton, 20,905 ...A2, F2
Bristol, 70 ...H3
Brookside, 219 ...E3
Brookvale, 350 ...A3
Broomfield, 38,272 ...A3, E2
Brush, 5,117 ...G1
Buckingham ...G1
Buena Vista, 2,195 ...D3
Buffalo Creek, 50 ...E2
Buford ...C2
Burlington, 3,678 ...H2
Burns, 50 ...D2
Byers, 1,233 ...F2
Caddoa ...H3
Cahone, 50 ...B4
Calhan, 896 ...F2
Cameo ...B2
Camp Bird ...C4
Campion, 1,832 ...E1
Campo, 150 ...H4
Canon City, 15,431 ...E3
Capulin, 275 ...D4
Carbondale, 5,196 ...C2
Cardiff, 175 ...C2
Carlton, 175 ...H3
Carr ...F1
Cascade (Cascade-Chipita Park), 1,709 ...F3
Castle Rock, 20,224 ...F2
Castlewood, 25,567 ...A3
Cedaredge, 1,854 ...C3
Cedarwood ...F3
Center, 2,392 ...D4
Central City, 515 ...E2
Chama, 275 ...E4
Cheraw, 211 ...G3
Cherry Hills Village, 5,958 ...A3
Cheyenne Wells, 1,010 ...H3
Chimney Rock ...H3
Chivington ...H3
Chromo ...D4
Cimarron ...C3
Clark, 40 ...D1
Clarkville ...H1
Clifton, 17,345 ...B2
Climax, 40 ...D2
Coal Creek, 303 ...E3
Coaldale, 40 ...E3
Coalmont ...D1
Cokedale, 139 ...F4
Collbran, 388 ...C2
Colona, 50 ...C3
Colorado City, 2,018 ...F3
Colorado Springs, 360,890 ...F3
Columbine ...D1
Columbine Valley, 1,132 ...A3, E2
Commerce City, 20,991 ...A3, F2
Como ...E2
Conejos, 125 ...D4
Conifer, 325 ...E2
Cope, 50 ...H2
Copper Mtn., 150 ...D2
Cornish ...F1
Cortez, 7,977 ...B4
Cotopaxi ...E3
Cowdrey ...D1
Craig, 9,189 ...C1
Crawford, 366 ...C3
Creede, 377 ...D4
Crested Butte, 1,529 ...D3
Crestone, 73 ...E4
Cripple Creek, 1,115 ...E3
Crook, 128 ...H1
Crowley, 187 ...G3
Crystola ...E3
Cuchara, 40 ...F4
Dacono, 3,015 ...A2, F1
Dailey ...H1
De Beque, 451 ...B2
Deckers ...E2
Deer Trail, 598 ...F2
Delhi ...F4
Del Norte, 1,705 ...D4
Delta, 6,400 ...B3
Denver, 554,636 ...A3, F2
Deora ...H4
Devine, 500 ...F3
Dillon, 802 ...D2
Dinosaur, 319 ...A1
Divide, 40 ...E3
Dolores, 857 ...B4
Dove Creek, 698 ...A4
Doyleville ...D3
Drake ...E1
Dumont, 364 ...E2
Dunton ...B4
Dupont (Derby), 4,500 ...A3
Durango, 13,922 ...C4
Eads, 747 ...H3
Eagle, 3,032 ...D2
Eastlake, 100 ...A3
East Portal, 70 ...E2
Eaton, 2,690 ...F1
Eckley, 278 ...H1
Edgewater, 5,445 ...A3
Edler ...H4
Edwards, 8,257 ...D2
Egnar ...B4
Elbert, 100 ...F2
Eldora, 170 ...E2
Elizabeth, 1,434 ...F2
El Jebel, 4,488 ...C2
Elk Springs ...B1
Ellicott, 80 ...F3
El Moro, 70 ...F4

Empire, 355 ...E2
Englewood, 31,727 ...A3, F2
Erie, 6,291 ...E1
Estes Park, 5,413 ...E1
Estrella ...G2
Evans, 9,514 ...F1
Evergreen, 9,216 ...E2
Fairplay, 610 ...E2
Falcon, 225 ...F3
Farisita ...E4
Federal Heights, 12,065 ...A3, F2
Firestone, 1,908 ...A2, F1
Firstview ...H3
Flagler, 612 ...G2
Fleming, 426 ...H1
Florence, 3,653 ...E3
Florissant, 60 ...E3
Fort Collins, 118,652 ...E1
Fort Garland, 432 ...E4
Fort Lupton, 6,787 ...A2, F1
Fort Morgan, 11,034 ...G1
Fountain, 15,197 ...F3
Fowler, 1,206 ...F3
Fox Creek ...D4
Foxfield, 746 ...A3
Foxton, 70 ...E2
Franktown, 99 ...F2
Fraser, 910 ...D2
Frederick, 2,467 ...A2
Frisco, 2,443 ...D2
Fruita, 6,478 ...B2
Fruitvale, 6,936 ...B2
Galatea ...G3
Galeton, 150 ...F1
Garcia ...E4
Garden City, 357 ...F1
Gardner, 70 ...E4
Garfield ...D3
Garo ...E2
Gateway ...B3
Gem Village, 175 ...C4
Genoa, 211 ...G2
Georgetown, 1,088 ...E2
Gilcrest, 1,162 ...F1
Gill, 250 ...F1
Gilman ...D2
Glade Park, 125 ...B3
Gladstone ...C4
Glendale, 4,547 ...A3
Glendevey ...E1
Glen Haven ...E1
Glenwood Springs, 7,736 ...C2
Golden, 17,159 ...A3, E2
Goodrich ...F1
Gould ...D1
Granada, 640 ...H3
Granby, 1,525 ...E1
Grand Junction, 41,986 ...B2
Grand Lake, 447 ...E1
Grand Mesa ...C2
Grandview, 600 ...C4
Granite ...D2
Grant, 60 ...E2
Great Divide ...C1
Greeley, 76,930 ...F1
Green Mountain Falls, 773 ...F3
Greenwood (Custer Co.) ...E3
Greenwood (Pueblo Co.) ...F4
Greenwood Village, 11,035 ...A3, F2
Greystone ...B1
Grover, 153 ...F1
Guffey ...E3
Gulnare ...F4
Gunnison, 5,409 ...D3
Gypsum, 3,654 ...D2
Hahns Peak, 40 ...D1
Hale ...H2
Hamilton ...C1
Hartman, 111 ...H3
Hartsel, 40 ...E2
Haswell, 84 ...G3
Hawley, 80 ...G4
Haxtun, 982 ...H1
Hayden, 1,634 ...C1
Henderson, 250 ...A3
Hereford, 50 ...F1
Hermosa, 700 ...C4
Hesperus ...B4
Hiawatha ...B1
Highlands Ranch, 70,931 ...F2
Hillrose, 254 ...G1
Hillside ...E3
Hoehne, 90 ...F4
Holly, 1,048 ...H3
Holyoke, 2,261 ...H1
Hooper, 123 ...E4
Hotchkiss, 968 ...C3
Hot Sulphur Springs, 521 ...D1
Howard, 80 ...E3
Hoyt ...F1
Hudson, 1,565 ...F1
Hugo, 885 ...G2
Hyde ...H1
Hygiene, 450 ...E1
Idaho Springs, 1,889 ...E2
Idalia, 90 ...H2
Ignacio, 669 ...C4
Iliff, 213 ...G1
Ione, 40 ...A2, F1
Jamestown, 205 ...E1
Jansen, 125 ...F4
Jefferson ...E2
Jaroso ...E4
Joes, 100 ...H2
Johnstown, 3,827 ...F1
Julesburg, 1,467 ...H1
Karval ...G3
Keenesburg, 855 ...F1
Keota, 10 ...F1
Kersey, 1,389 ...F1
Keystone, 825 ...D2
Kim, 65 ...G4
Kings Canyon ...D1
Kiowa, 581 ...F2
Kirk, 100 ...H2
Kit Carson, 253 ...H3
Kline, 100 ...B4
Kornman, 100 ...H3
Kremmling, 1,578 ...D1
Kutch ...G3
Lafayette, 23,197 ...A2, E1
La Garita, 40 ...D4
Laird, 60 ...H1
La Jara, 877 ...E4
La Junta, 7,568 ...G3
Lake City, 375 ...C3
Lake George, 50 ...E3
Lakeside, 20 ...A3
Lakewood, 144,126 ...A3, E2

Lamar, 8,869 ...H3
Larkspur, 234 ...F2
La Salle, 1,849 ...F1
Las Animas, 2,758 ...G3
Last Chance ...G2
La Veta, 924 ...F4
Lay, 40 ...C1
Lazear, 200 ...C3
Leadville, 2,821 ...D2
Lewis, 125 ...B4
Limon, 2,071 ...G2
Lincoln Park, 3,904 ...E3
Lindon ...G2
Littleton, 40,340 ...A3, F2
Livermore ...E1
Lochbuie, 2,049 ...A2, F1
Log Lane Village, 1,006 ...G1
Loma, 175 ...B2
Longmont, 71,093 ...A2, E1
Louisville, 18,937 ...A2, E2
Louviers, 237 ...E2
Loveland, 50,608 ...E1
Lucerne, 175 ...F1
Ludlow ...F4
Lycan ...H4
Lyons, 1,585 ...E1
Mack, 150 ...B2
Maher, 70 ...C3
Manassa, 1,042 ...E4
Mancos, 1,119 ...B4
Manitou Springs, 4,980 ...F3
Manzanola, 525 ...G3
Marble, 105 ...C2
Marshall, 300 ...A3
Marvel, 80 ...B4
Masonville, 150 ...E1
Massadona ...B1
Masters ...F1
Matheson, 50 ...G2
Maybell, 60 ...B1
Mayday, 40 ...B4
Maysville, 40 ...D3
May Valley, 60 ...H3
McClave, 90 ...H3
McCoy, 50 ...D2
Mead, 2,017 ...F1
Meeker, 2,242 ...C1
Meredith ...C2
Merino, 246 ...G1
Mesa, 100 ...B2
Mesita ...E4
Milliken, 2,888 ...F1
Milner, 150 ...C1
Mineral Hot Springs ...E3
Minturn, 1,068 ...D2
Model ...F4
Moffat, 114 ...E4
Mogote, 50 ...D4
Molina, 50 ...C2
Monte Vista, 4,529 ...D4
Montezuma, 42 ...E2
Montrose, 12,344 ...C3
Monument, 1,971 ...F2
Monument Park ...A3
Morrison, 430 ...A3
Mosca, 150 ...E4
Mountain View, 569 ...A3
Mount Crested Butte, 707 ...D3
Nathrop, 100 ...D3
Naturita, 635 ...B3
Nederland, 1,394 ...E2
New Castle, 1,984 ...C2
Ninaview ...G4
Niwot, 4,160 ...A2, E1
Northglenn, 31,575 ...A3, F2
Norwood, 438 ...B3
Nucla, 734 ...B3
Nunn, 471 ...F1
Nutria, 100 ...C4
Oak Creek, 849 ...D1
Ohio, 40 ...D3
Olathe, 1,573 ...C3
Olney Springs, 389 ...G3
Ophir, 113 ...C4
Orchard, 100 ...F1
Orchard City, 2,880 ...C3
Orchard Mesa, 6,456 ...B2
Ordway, 1,248 ...G3
Otis, 534 ...H1
Ouray, 813 ...C3
Ovid, 330 ...H1
Oxford, 70 ...G1
Padroni, 97 ...G1
Pagoda ...H3
Pagosa Junction ...C4
Pagosa Springs, 1,591 ...C4
Palisade, 2,579 ...B2
Palmer Lake, 2,179 ...F2
Pandora, 125 ...C4
Paoli, 42 ...H1
Paonia, 1,497 ...C3
Parachute, 1,006 ...B2
Paradox, 60 ...B3
Parkdale ...E3
Parker, 23,558 ...F2
Parlin ...D3
Parshall, 50 ...D1
Peetz, 192 ...G1
Penrose, 4,070 ...E3
Peyton, 70 ...F3
Phippsburg, 150 ...D1
Pierce, 884 ...F1
Pine, 100 ...E2
Pinecliffe, 50 ...E2
Pitkin, 124 ...D3
Placerville, 40 ...C3
Platner, 40 ...G1
Platoro ...D4
Platteville, 2,370 ...F1
Pleasant View, 60 ...B4
Poncha Springs, 466 ...D3
Ponderosa Park, 3,112 ...F2
Portland ...E3
Poudre Park, 70 ...E1
Powderhorn ...C3
Powder Wash, 50 ...B1
Pritchett, 137 ...H4
Proctor ...H1
Prospect Heights ...E3
Prospect Valley, 125 ...F1
Prowers ...H3
Pryor ...F4
Pueblo, 102,121 ...F3
Pueblo West, 16,899 ...F3
Punkin Center ...G3
Purcell ...F2
Radium ...D2
Ramah, 117 ...F2
Rand ...D1
Rangely, 2,096 ...B1

Raymer, 91 ...G1
Red Cliff, 289 ...D2
Red Feather Lakes, 525 ...E1
Redlands, 8,043 ...B2
Redmesa, 40 ...B4
Redstone ...C2
Redvale, 60 ...B3
Red Wing ...E4
Rico, 205 ...B4
Ridgway, 713 ...C3
Rifle, 6,784 ...C2
Rio Blanco ...C2
Rockvale, 426 ...E3
Rockwood ...C4
Rocky Ford, 4,286 ...G3
Roggen, 90 ...F1
Rollinsville, 40 ...E2
Romeo, 375 ...E4
Rosita, 40 ...E3
Rush ...F3
Rustic ...E1
Rye, 202 ...F4
Saguache, 578 ...D3
St. Elmo ...D3
St. Petersburg ...H1
Salida, 5,504 ...E3
San Acacio, 60 ...E4
San Antonio, 150 ...D4
Sanford, 817 ...E4
San Francisco, 30 ...D4
San Luis, 739 ...E4
San Pablo, 125 ...E4
San Pedro, 100 ...E4
Sapinero ...C3
Sargents ...D3
Sawpit, 25 ...B4
Security (Security-Widefield), 29,845 ...F3
Sedalia, 211 ...F2
Sedgwick, 191 ...H1
Segundo, 40 ...F4
Seibert, 180 ...H2
Severance, 597 ...F1
Shawnee, 80 ...E2
Sheridan, 5,600 ...A3, F2
Sheridan Lake, 66 ...H3
Sherrelwood, 17,657 ...A3
Silt, 1,740 ...C2
Silver Cliff, 512 ...E3
Silver Plume, 203 ...E2
Silverthorne, 3,196 ...D2
Silverton, 531 ...C4
Simla, 663 ...F2
Singleton ...E2
Skyway ...B2
Slater ...C1
Slick Rock ...B3
Snowmass, 250 ...D2
Snowmass Village, 1,822 ...D2
Snyder, 125 ...G1
Somerset, 90 ...C3
South Fork, 604 ...D4
Southglenn, 43,520 ...A3, F2
South Platte ...E2
Spar City ...D4
Sparks ...B1
Springfield, 1,562 ...H4
Starkville, 128 ...F4
State Bridge, 60 ...D2
Steamboat Springs, 9,815 ...D1
Sterling, 11,360 ...G1
Stone City ...F3
Stoneham ...G1
Stoner ...B4
Stonewall, 40 ...E4
Stonington ...H4
Strasburg, 1,402 ...F2
Stratmoor Hills (Stratmoor), 6,650 ...F3
Stratton, 669 ...H2
Sugar City, 279 ...G3
Summitville ...D4
Sunbeam, 40 ...B1
Superior, 9,011 ...A3, E2
Swink, 696 ...G3
Tabernash, 165 ...D2
Tarryall ...E2
Telluride, 2,221 ...C4
Texas Creek ...E3
Thatcher, 40 ...F4
The Pinery, 7,253 ...F2
Thornton, 82,384 ...A3
Thurman ...G2
Tiffany ...C4
Timnath, 223 ...F1
Timpas ...G3
Tincup ...D3
Toonerville ...G4
Toponas ...D1
Towaoc, 1,097 ...B4
Towner, 40 ...H3
Trimble, 650 ...C4
Trinchera ...G4
Trinidad, 9,078 ...F4
Twin Lakes ...D2
Two Buttes, 67 ...H4
Tyrone ...F4
Utavan ...B3
Utleyville ...G4
Vail, 4,531 ...D2
Vallecito ...C4
Vancorum, 40 ...B3
Vernon, 40 ...H2
Victor, 445 ...E3
Vigil ...F4
Vilas, 110 ...H4
Villa Grove ...E3
Villegreen ...G4
Virginia Dale ...E1
Vona, 95 ...H2
Wagon Wheel Gap ...D4
Walden, 734 ...D1
Walsenburg, 4,182 ...F4
Walsh, 723 ...H4
Ward, 169 ...E1
Watkins, 80 ...F2
Wattenberg, 450 ...A2, F1
Waverly, 60 ...E1
Welby, 12,973 ...A3
Weldona, 175 ...G1
Wellington, 2,672 ...E1
Westcliffe, 417 ...E3
Westcreek, 105 ...E2
Westminster, 100,940 ...A3, E2
Weston, 50 ...F4
Wetmore, 100 ...F3
Wheat Ridge, 32,913 ...A3, E2
Whitewater, 50 ...B3
Wiggins, 838 ...F1
Wild Horse ...G3
Wiley, 483 ...H3
Willard ...G1

Williamsburg, 714 ...E3
Windsor, 9,896 ...F1
Winter Park, 662 ...E2
Wolcott, 50 ...D2
Woodland Park, 6,515 ...E3
Woodrow ...G2
Woody Creek, 275 ...D2
Wray, 2,187 ...H1
Yampa, 443 ...D1
Yellow Jacket ...B4
Yoder ...F3
Yuma, 3,285 ...H1

Other Features

Alamosa N.W.R. ...E4
Animas, river ...C4
Apishapa, river ...F4
Arapaho National Forest ...D1, E2
Arapaho N.R.A. ...E1
Arapaho N.W.R. ...D1
Arapahoe, peak ...E1
Arikaree, river ...G2
Arkansas, river ...F3
Aztec Ruins N.M. ...B4
Barnforth N.W.R. ...E1
Bears Ears, mountain ...A4
Beaver, creek ...G2
Bent's Old Fort Natl. Hist. Site ...G3
Big Sandy, creek ...G3
Bijou, creek ...F2
Black, mesa ...H4
Black Canyon of the Gunnison N.P. ...C3
Blanca, peak ...E4
Blue Mesa, reservoir ...C3
Bonny, reservoir ...H2
Book, cliffs ...A2
Bridger, peak ...C1
Browns Park N.W.R. ...B1
Canyonlands National Park ...A3
Canyons of the Ancients Natl. Mon. ...B4
Carson Natl. For. ...C4, D4, E4
Castle, peak ...D2
Cimarron, river ...G4
Colorado, plateau ...A4
Colorado, river ...A4, C2
Colorado Canyons Natl. Cons. Area ...B2
Colorado N.M. ...B2
Comanche National Grassland ...G4, H4
Continental Divide ...C1, D3
Crestone, peak ...E4
Crow, creek ...F1
Cucharas, river ...F4
Curecanti N.R.A. ...C3
Dinosaur National Monument ...B1
Dolores, river ...B3
East Tavaputs Plateau ...A2
Elbert, mountain ...D2
Eolus, mountain ...C4
Evans, mountain ...E2
Florissant Fossil Beds N.M. ...E3
Fort Carson Mil. Res. ...F3, G3
Front, range ...E1
Grand Mesa N.F. ...B3, C2
Great Sand Dunes N.P. ...E4
Great Sand Dunes Natl. Pres. ...E4
Green, river ...A1
Gunnison, river ...B3
Gunnison, mountain ...C3
Gunnison Gorge Natl. Cons. Area ...C3
Gunnison National Forest ...C3, D3
Horse, creek ...G3
Hovenweep N.M. ...B4
Hutton Lake N.W.R. ...E1
John Martin, reservoir ...G3
Kiowa, creek ...F2
Laramie, mountains ...E1
Laramie, river ...E1
Little Snake, river ...B1
Lodgepole, creek ...G1
Longs, peak ...E1
Mancos, river ...B4
Manti-La Sal National Forest ...A3
Medicine Bow, mountains ...D1
Medicine Bow National Forest ...D1, E1
Mesa Verde National Park ...B4
Monte Vista N.W.R. ...D4
Montezuma, peak ...D4
Monument, valley ...A4
Navajo, reservoir ...C4
Navajo Indian Reservation ...A4
N. Fork Cimarron, river ...H4
N. Fork Smoky Hill, river ...H2
N. Platte, river ...D1
Park, range ...D1
Pawnee, creek ...G1
Pawnee National Grassland ...F1, G1
Peale, mountain ...A3
Pike National Forest ...E2, E3
Pikes, peak ...E3
Platte, river ...H1
Pueblo Ordnance Depot ...F3
Purgatoire, river ...G4
Rio Grande, river ...E4
Rio Grande National Forest ...D4, E4
Roan, plateau ...B2
Rocky, mountains ...D1
Rocky Mountain National Park ...E1
Roosevelt National Forest ...E1
Routt Natl. Forest ...C1, D1
Royal, gorge ...E3
Rush, creek ...G3
Sand Creek Massacre N.H.S. ...H3
Sangre De Cristo Mts. ...E3
San Isabel N.F. ...D3, E3, E4
San Juan, mountains ...A4
San Juan, river ...A4
San Juan N.F. ...C4
San Luis, valley ...E4
Sawatch, range ...D3
Shiprock, mountain ...B4
S. Fk. Republican, river ...H2
S. Platte, river ...E2, G1
Southern Ute I.R. ...C4
Two Buttes, creek ...H4
Twomile, creek ...G1
Uintah And Ouray I.R. ...A1, A2
Uncompahgre National Forest ...B3
Uncompahgre, peak ...C3
Uncompahgre, plateau ...B3
U.S. Air Force Academy ...F3
Ute Mountain
  Indian Reservation ...B4
White, river ...C2, B2
White River National Forest ...C2, D2
Wilson, mountain ...B4
Yampa, river ...B1
Yucca House N.M. ...B4
Zirkel, mountain ...D1

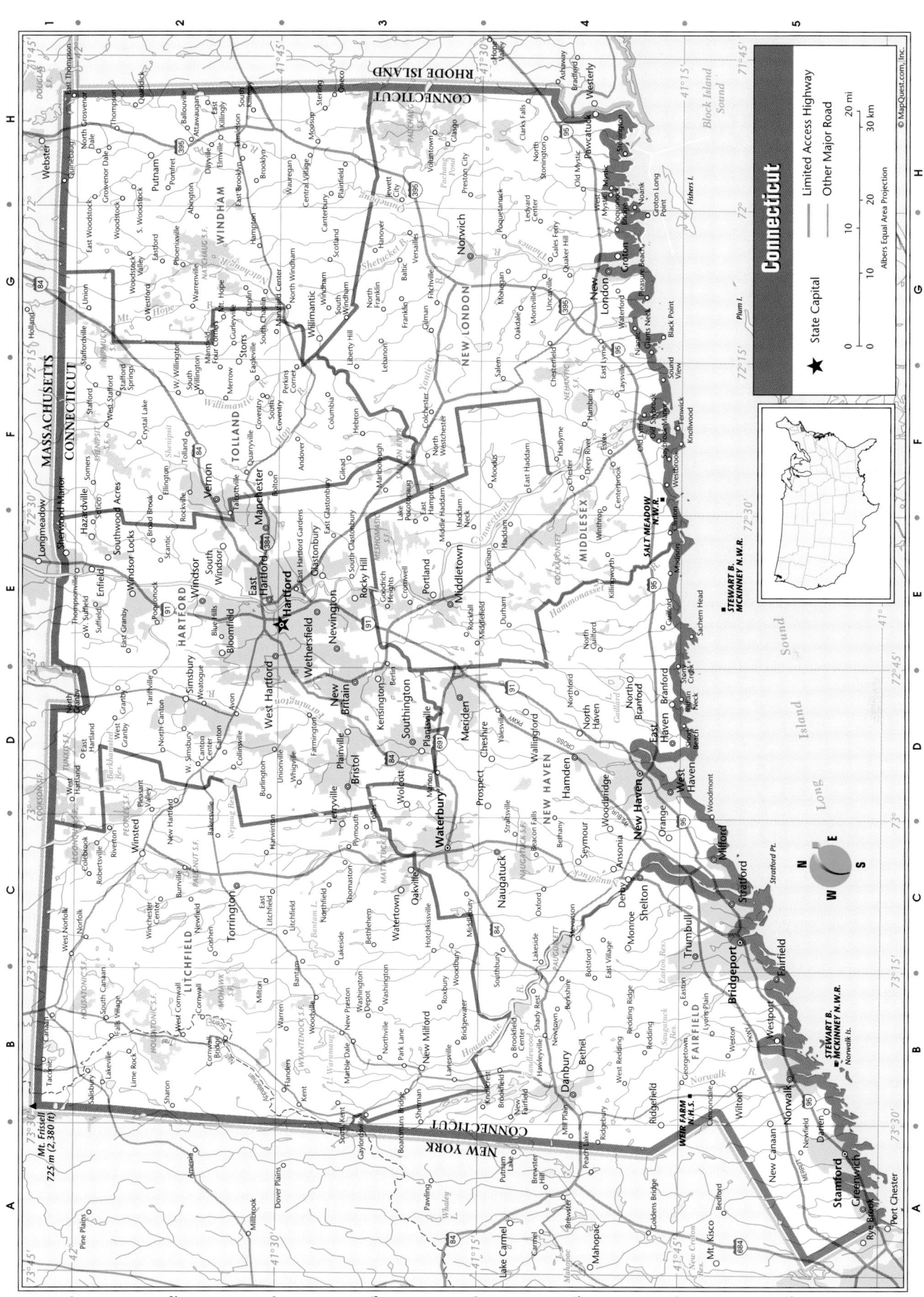

Connecticut

Limited Access Highway
Other Major Road

★ State Capital

© MapQuest.com, Inc.

20 mi
30 km

Albers Equal Area Projection

Connecticut

Capital: Hartford
Land Area: 4,845 sq. mi. 12,550 sq. km.
Population: 3,405,565 (2000 Census)
Largest City: Bridgeport, 139,529
Highest Point: Mt. Frissell 2,380 ft. 725 m.
Admitted to Union: January 9, 1788
Nickname: Constitution State, Nutmeg State
State Flower: Mountain Laurel
State Bird: Robin

Connecticut: Map Index

Counties

Fairfield, **882,567** B5
Hartford, **857,183** E2
Litchfield, **182,193** C2
Middlesex, **155,071** E4
New Haven, **824,008** D4
New London, **259,088** G3
Tolland, **136,364** F2
Windham, **109,091** G2

Cities and Towns

Cities and towns that are not labeled on the map are shown with an asterisk. They are included here only for population reference.

Andover, **3,036** F3
Ansonia, **18,554** C4
Ashford, **4,098** . . . . *
Avon, **15,832** D2
Barkhamsted, **3,494** . . . . *
Beacon Falls, **5,246** C4
Berlin, **18,215** E3
Bethany, **5,040** C4
Bethel, **18,067** B4
Bethlehem, **3,422** C3
Bloomfield, **19,587** E2
Bolton, **5,017** F2
Bozrah, **2,357** . . . . *
Branford, **28,683** D4
Bridgeport, **139,529** C5
Bridgewater, **1,824** B3
Bristol, **60,062** D3
Brookfield, **15,664** B4
Brooklyn, **7,173** H2
Burlington, **8,190** D2
Canaan, **1,081** B1
Canterbury, **4,692** H3
Canton, **8,840** D2
Chaplin, **2,250** G2
Cheshire, **28,543** D4
Chester, **3,743** F4
Clinton, **13,094** E4
Colchester, **14,551** F3
Colebrook, **1,471** C2
Columbia, **4,971** F3
Cornwall, **1,434** B2
Coventry, **11,504** F2
Cromwell, **12,871** E3
Danbury, **74,848** B4
Darien, **19,607** B5
Deep River, **4,610** F4
Derby, **12,391** C4
Durham, **6,627** E4
Eastford, **1,618** G2
East Granby, **4,745** E2
East Haddam, **8,333** F4
East Hampton, **13,352** E3
East Hartford, **49,575** E2
East Haven, **28,189** D4
East Lyme, **18,118** G4
Easton, **7,272** B5
East Windsor, **9,818** . . . . *
Ellington, **12,921** F2
Enfield, **45,212** E2
Essex, **6,505** F4
Fairfield, **57,340** B5
Farmington, **23,641** D3
Franklin, **1,835** G3
Glastonbury, **31,876** E3
Goshen, **2,697** C2
Granby, **10,347** D2
Greenwich, **61,101** A5
Griswold, **10,807** . . . . *
Groton, **39,907** G4
Guilford, **21,398** E4
Haddam, **7,157** E4
Hamden, **56,913** D4
Hampton, **1,758** G2
Hartford, **121,578** E3
Hartland, **2,012** . . . . *
Harwinton, **5,283** C2
Hebron, **8,610** F3
Kent, **2,858** B3
Killingly, **16,472** . . . . *
Killingworth, **6,018** E4
Lebanon, **6,907** G3
Ledyard, **14,687** . . . . *
Lisbon, **4,069** . . . . *
Litchfield, **8,316** C3
Lyme, **2,016** . . . . *
Madison, **17,858** E4
Manchester, **54,740** E2
Mansfield, **20,720** . . . . *
Marlborough, **5,709** F3
Meriden, **58,244** D3
Middlebury, **6,451** C3
Middlefield, **4,203** E3
Middletown, **43,167** E3
Milford, **52,305** C5
Monroe, **19,247** C4
Montville, **18,546** G4
Morris, **2,301** . . . . *
Naugatuck, **30,989** C4
New Britain, **71,538** D3
New Canaan, **19,395** A5
New Fairfield, **13,953** B4
New Hartford, **6,088** D2
New Haven, **123,626** D4
Newington, **29,306** E3
New London, **25,671** G4
New Milford, **27,121** B3
Newtown, **25,031** B4
Norfolk, **1,660** C2
North Branford, **13,906** D4
North Canaan, **3,350** . . . . *
North Haven, **23,035** D4
North Stonington, **4,991** H4
Norwalk, **82,951** B5
Norwich, **36,117** G3
Old Lyme, **7,406** F4
Old Saybrook, **10,367** F4
Orange, **13,233** C4
Oxford, **9,821** C4
Plainfield, **14,619** H3
Plainville, **17,328** D3
Plymouth, **11,634** C3
Pomfret, **3,798** H2
Portland, **8,732** E3
Preston, **4,688** . . . . *
Prospect, **8,707** D4
Putnam, **9,002** H2
Redding, **8,270** B4
Ridgefield, **23,643** B4
Rocky Hill, **17,966** E3
Roxbury, **2,136** B3
Salem, **3,858** F4
Salisbury, **3,977** B2
Scotland, **1,556** G3
Seymour, **15,454** C4
Sharon, **2,968** B2
Shelton, **38,101** C4
Sherman, **3,827** B3
Simsbury, **23,234** D2
Somers, **10,417** F2
Southbury, **18,567** C4
Southington, **39,728** D3
South Windsor, **24,412** E2
Sprague, **2,971** . . . . *
Stafford, **11,307** F2
Stamford, **117,083** A5
Sterling, **3,099** H3
Stonington, **17,906** H4
Stratford, **49,976** C5
Suffield, **13,552** E2
Thomaston, **7,503** C3
Thompson, **8,878** H2
Tolland, **13,146** F2
Torrington, **35,202** C2
Trumbull, **34,243** C5
Union, **693** G2
Vernon, **28,063** F2
Voluntown, **2,528** H3
Wallingford, **43,026** D4
Warren, **1,254** B3
Washington, **3,596** B3
Waterbury, **107,271** C3
Waterford, **19,152** G4
Watertown, **21,661** C3
Westbrook, **6,292** F4
West Hartford, **63,589** E2
West Haven, **52,360** D4
Weston, **10,037** B5
Westport, **25,749** B5
Wethersfield, **26,271** E3
Willington, **5,959** . . . . *
Wilton, **17,633** B5
Winchester, **10,664** . . . . *
Windham, **22,857** G3
Windsor, **28,237** E2
Windsor Locks, **12,043** E2
Wolcott, **15,215** D3
Woodbridge, **8,983** C4
Woodbury, **9,198** C3
Woodstock, **7,221** H2

Other Places

The city or town containing each entry is shown in italics. See the "Cities and Towns" listing for total city/town population.

Attawaugan *(Killingly)*, **950** H2
Bakersville *(New Hartford)*, **475** C2
Ballouville *(Killingly)*, **950** H2
Baltic *(Sprague)*, **1,500** G3
Bantam *(Litchfield)*, **802** C3
Berkshire *(Newtown)*, **950** B4
Black Point *(East Lyme)*, **300** G4
Blue Hills *(Bloomfield)*, **3,020** E2
Boardman Bridge *(New Milford)*, **600** B3
Botsford *(Newtown)*, **1,000** B4
Broad Brook *(East Windsor)*, **3,469** E2
Brookfield Center *(Brookfield)*, **1,800** B4
Burrville *(Torrington)*, **70** C2
Canaan *(North Canaan)*, **1,288** B1
Cannondale *(Wilton)*, **1,400** B5
Canton Center *(Canton)*, **750** D2
Centerbrook *(Essex)*, **950** F4
Central Village *(Plainfield)*, **1,400** H3
Chesterfield *(Montville)*, **425** G4
Clarks Falls *(North Stonington)*, **275** H4
Collinsville *(Canton)*, **2,686** D2
Cornwall Bridge *(Cornwall)*, **125** B2
Crystal Lake *(Ellington)*, **1,459** F2
Danielson *(Killingly)*, **4,265** H2
Dayville *(Killingly)*, **1,600** H2
Eagleville *(Mansfield)*, **500** F2
E. Brooklyn *(Brooklyn)*, **1,473** H2
East Glastonbury *(Glastonbury)*, **1,400** E3
East Hartford Gardens *(East Hartford)* E3
E. Hartland *(Hartland)*, **500** D2
East Killingly *(Killingly)*, **350** H2
E. Litchfield *(Litchfield)*, **250** C2
East Thompson *(Thompson)*, **275** H1
East Village *(Monroe)*, **1,500** C4
East Woodstock *(Woodstock)*, **450** H2
Elmville *(Killingly)*, **1,300** H2
Falls Village *(Canaan)*, **500** B2
Fenwick *(Old Saybrook)*, **52** F4
Fitchville *(Bozrah)*, **750** G3
Flanders *(Kent)*, **200** B3
Gales Ferry *(Ledyard)*, **2,400** G4
Gaylordsville *(New Milford)*, **750** B3
Georgetown *(Redding, Weston and Wilton)*, **1,650** B5
Giants Neck *(East Lyme)*, **1,000** G4
Gilead *(Hebron)*, **325** F3
Gilman *(Bozrah)*, **275** G3
Glasgo *(Griswold)*, **500** H3
Goodrich Heights *(Cromwell)* E3
Grosvenor Dale *(Thompson)*, **700** H2
Groton Long Point *(Groton)*, **667** G4
Gurleyville *(Mansfield)*, **100** G2
Haddam Neck *(Haddam)*, **300** E3
Hadlyme *(Lyme)*, **300** F4
Hamburg *(Lyme)*, **125** F4
Hanover *(Sprague)*, **700** G3
Hawleyville *(Newtown)*, **800** B4
Hazardville *(Enfield)*, **4,900** E2
Higganum *(Haddam)*, **1,671** E4
Hotchkissville *(Woodbury)*, **1,200** C3
Indian Neck *(Branford)*, **3,400** D5
Jewett City *(Griswold)*, **3,053** H3
Kensington *(Berlin)*, **8,541** D3
Knollcrest *(New Fairfield)*, **1,300** B4
Knollwood *(Old Saybrook)*, **2,500** F4
Lake Pocotopaug *(East Hampton)*, **3,169** E3
Lakeside *(Morris)*, **275** C3
Lakeside *(Southbury)*, **1,300** C4
Lakeville *(Salisbury)*, **900** B2
Lanesville *(New Milford)*, **3,100** B3
Laysville *(Old Lyme)*, **1,100** F4
Ledyard Center *(Ledyard)*, **800** G4
Liberty Hill *(Lebanon)*, **300** F3
Lime Rock *(Salisbury)*, **250** B2
Lyons Plain *(Weston)*, **2,100** B5
Mansfield Center *(Mansfield)*, **973** G2
Mansfield Four Corners *(Mansfield)*, **700** F2
Marble Dale *(Washington)*, **475** B3
Marion *(Southington)*, **1,900** D3
Merrow *(Mansfield)*, **1,000** F2
Middle Haddam *(East Hampton)*, **900** E3
Mill Plain *(Danbury)*, **20** A4
Milton *(Litchfield)*, **275** B2
Mohegan *(Montville)*, **3,500** G4
Moodus *(East Haddam)*, **1,263** F4
Moosup *(Plainfield)*, **3,237** H3
Mt. Hope *(Mansfield)*, **275** G2
Mystic *(Stonington and Groton)*, **4,001** H4
Newfield *(Stamford)*, **20** A5
Newfield *(Torrington)*, **20** C2
New Preston *(Washington)*, **1,110** B3
Niantic *(East Lyme)*, **3,085** G4
Noank *(Groton)*, **1,830** H4
North Canton *(Canton)*, **325** D2
Northfield *(Litchfield)*, **800** C3
Northford *(North Branford)*, **1,600** D4
N. Franklin *(Franklin)*, **150** G3
N. Granby *(Granby)*, **1,720** D2
North Grosvenor Dale *(Thompson)*, **1,424** H2
North Guilford (Guilford) E4
Northville *(New Milford)*, **175** B3
North Westchester *(Colchester)*, **800** F3
North Windham *(Windham)*, **550** G3
Oakdale *(Montville)*, **1,100** G4
Oakville *(Watertown)*, **8,618** C3
Old Mystic *(Groton and Stonington)*, **3,205** H4
Oneco *(Sterling)*, **475** H3
Park Lane *(New Milford)*, **650** B3
Pawcatuck *(Stonington)*, **5,474** H4
Perkins Corner *(Mansfield)*, **1,000** F3
Phoenixville *(Eastford)*, **150** G2
Plantsville *(Southington)*, **6,400** D3
Pleasant Valley *(Barkhamsted)*, **550** D2
Pleasure Beach *(Waterford)*, **1,600** G4
Poquetanuck *(Preston)*, **1,100** G4
Poquonock *(Windsor)*, **2,200** E2
Poquonock Bridge *(Groton)*, **1,592** G4
Preston City *(Preston)*, **425** H3
Quaddick *(Thompson)*, **425** H2
Quaker Hill *(Waterford)*, **4,200** G4
Quarryville *(Bolton)*, **2,500** F2
Quinebaug *(Thompson)*, **1,122** H1
Redding Ridge *(Redding)*, **900** B4
Ridgebury *(Ridgefield)*, **1,200** A4
Riverton *(Barkhamsted)*, **225** C2
Robertsville *(Colebrook)*, **225** C2
Rockfall *(Middlefield)*, **1,500** E3
Rockville *(Vernon)*, **7,708** F2
Sachem Head *(Guilford)*, **600** E5
Saybrook Manor *(Old Saybrook)*, **1,133** F4
Scantic *(East Windsor)*, **200** E2
Scitico *(Enfield)*, **550** E2
Shady Rest *(Newtown)*, **550** B4
Sherwood Manor *(Enfield)*, **5,689** E1
Short Beach *(Branford)*, **5,100** D5
Sound View *(Old Lyme)*, **1,200** F4
S. Canaan *(Canaan)*, **125** B2
S. Chaplin *(Chaplin)*, **550** G2
S. Coventry *(Coventry)*, **1,381** F2
South Glastonbury *(Glastonbury)*, **1,900** E3
South Kent *(Kent)*, **225** B3
S. Killingly *(Killingly)*, **750** H2
South Willington *(Willington)*, **1,700** F2
South Windham *(Windham)*, **1,278** G3
Southwood Acres *(Enfield)*, **8,067** E2
South Woodstock *(Woodstock)*, **1,211** H2
Stafford Springs *(Stafford)*, **4,100** F2
Staffordville *(Stafford)*, **550** F2
Stevenson *(Monroe)*, **800** C4
Stony Creek *(Branford)*, **900** E4
Storrs *(Mansfield)*, **10,996** F2
Straitsville *(Naugatuck)*, **1,000** C4
Taconic *(Salisbury)*, **200** B1
Talcottville *(Vernon)*, **4,500** F2
Tariffville *(Simsbury)*, **1,371** D2
Terryville *(Plymouth)*, **5,360** C3
Thompsonville *(Enfield)*, **1,600** E2
Tolles *(Plymouth)*, **650** C3
Uncasville *(Montville)*, **1,500** G4
Unionville *(Farmington)*, **5,100** D3
Versailles *(Lisbon and Sprague)*, **750** G3
Warrenville *(Ashford)*, **350** G2
Washington Depot *(Washington)*, **550** B3
Wauregan *(Plainfield)*, **1,085** H3
Weatogue *(Simsbury)*, **2,805** D2
W. Cornwall *(Cornwall)*, **40** B2
Westford *(Ashford)*, **175** G2
West Granby *(Granby)*, **450** D2
W. Hartland *(Hartland)*, **175** D1
West Mystic *(Groton)*, **3,600** H4
West Norfolk *(Norfolk)*, **275** C1
W. Redding *(Redding)*, **500** B4
West Simsbury *(Simsbury)*, **2,395** D2
West Stafford *(Stafford)*, **375** F2
West Suffield *(Suffield)*, **600** E2
West Willington *(Willington)*, **450** F2
Whigville *(Burlington)*, **850** D3
Willimantic *(Windham)*, **15,823** G3
Winchester Center *(Winchester)*, **275** C2
Winsted *(Winchester)*, **7,321** C2
Winthrop *(Deep River)*, **400** F4
Woodmont *(Milford)*, **1,711** D5
Woodstock Valley *(Woodstock)*, **750** G2
Woodville *(Washington)*, **225** B3
Yalesville *(Wallingford)*, **3,600** D4

Other Features

Algonquin State Forest C2
Appalachian National Scenic Trail B2
Bantam, *lake* C3
Barkhamsted, *reservoir* D2
Block Island, *sound* H5
Brimfield State Forest G1
Candlewood, *lake* B4
Cockaponset State Forest E4
Connecticut, *river* E3
Cookson State Forest D1
Crane Neck, *point* C5
Douglas State Forest H1
Easton, *reservoir* B4
Eatons Neck, *point* B5
Farmington, *river* D3
Fishers, *island* H5
Gaillard, *lake* D4
Hammonasset, *river* E4
Hop, *river* F3
Housatonic, *river* B3
Housatonic State Forest B2
Little Wappinger, *creek* A2
Lloyd, *point* B5
Long, *island* D5
Long Island, *sound* C5
Mahopac, *lake* A4
Mattatuck State Forest C3
Merritt Parkway A5
Meshomasic State Forest E3
Mohawk State Forest B2
Mt. Frissell, *hill* B1
Mt. Hope, *river* G2
Mt. Misery, *point* C5
Mt. Washington State Forest B1
Natchaug, *river* G2
Natchaug State Forest G2
Naugatuck, *river* C4
Naugatuck State Forest C4
Nehantic State Forest F4
Nepaug, *reservoir* D2
New Croton, *reservoir* A5
Nipmuck State Forest G2
Norwalk, *island* B5
Norwalk, *river* B5
Orient, *point* G5
Pachaug, *pond* H3
Pachaug State Forest H3
Paugnut State Forest C2
Paugussett State Forest C4
Peoples State Forest C2
Plum, *island* G5
Quinebaug, *river* H3
Rocky, *point* F5
Salmon River State Forest F3
Salt Meadow National Wildlife Refuge F4
Sandisfield State Forest C1
Saugatuck, *reservoir* B4
Shenipsit, *lake* F2
Shenipsit State Forest F2
Shetucket, *river* G3
Smithtown, *bay* B5
Stewart B. McKinney National Wildlife Refuge B5, E5
Stratford, *point* C5
Taconic S.P. A1
Thames, *river* G4
Tunxis State Forest D1
Waramaug, *lake* B3
Weir Farm N.H.S. B5
Whaley, *lake* A3
Wilbur Cross Parkway C4
Willimantic, *river* F2
Wyantenock State Forest B3
Yantic, *river* F3

Delaware

Capital: Dover
Land Area: 1,955 sq. mi. 5,063 sq. km.
Population: 783,600 (2000 Census)
Largest City: Wilmington, 72,664
Highest Point: Ebright Road 442 ft. 135 m.
Admitted to Union: December 7, 1787
Nickname: First State Diamond State
State Flower: Peach Blossom
State Bird: Blue Hen Chicken

Delaware: Map Index

Counties

Kent, **126,697** B4
New Castle, **500,265** B2
Sussex, **156,638** C6

Cities and Towns

Adamsville, **90** B5
Andrewville, **150** B5
Arden, **474** C1
Ardencroft, **267** C1
Ardentown, **300** C1
Argos Corner, **550** C5
Bellefonte, **1,249** C1
Belltown D5
Bethany Beach, **903** D6
Bethel, **184** B6
Blackbird, **700** B3
Blades, **956** B6
Bowers Beach, **305** C4
Bridgeville, **1,436** B6
Broadkill Beach, **70** D5
Brookside, **14,806** B2
Burrsville B5
Camden, **2,100** B4
Cannon, **175** B6
Canterbury, **1,200** B4
Capitol Park, **700** B4
Cheswold, **313** B4
Clarksville, **900** D6
Claymont, **9,220** C1
Clayton, **1,273** B3
Collins Park, **8,300** B2
Dagsboro, **519** C6
Delaware City, **1,453** B2
Delmar, **1,407** B7
Dewey Beach, **301** D6
Dover, **32,135** B4
Dunleith, **9,100** B2
Edgemoor, **5,992** B1
Ellendale, **327** C5
Elsmere, **5,800** B1
Fairfax, **2,300** B1
Farmington, **75** B5
Felton, **784** B4
Fenwick Island, **342** D7
Frankford, **714** D6
Frederica, **648** C4
Georgetown, **4,643** C6
Glasgow, **12,840** B2
Greenwood, **837** B5
Gumboro, **275** C7
Harbeson, **375** C6
Harrington, **3,174** B5
Hartly, **78** B4
Hazlettville, **450** B4
Henlopen Acres, **139** D6
Hickman B5
Hockessin, **12,902** B1
Houston, **430** B5
Indian Beach D6
Jimtown, **175** D6
Kent Acres, **1,637** B4
Kenton, **237** B4
Kirkwood, **1,800** B2
Kitts Hummock, **250** C4
Laurel, **3,668** B6
Lebanon, **2,458** B4
Leipsic, **203** B4
Lewes, **2,932** D5
Lincoln, **950** C5
Little Creek, **195** C4
Little Heaven, **1,400** C4
Llangollen Estates, **5,600** B2
Lynch Heights, **550** C5
Magnolia, **226** C4
Marshallton, **1,700** B2
Marydel B4
Mastens Corner, **175** B5
McClellandville, **2,400** A2

Meadowbrook Acres B4
Middletown, 6,161 . . . . . .B3
Midway, 1,500 . . . . .D6
Milford, 6,732 . . . . .C5
Millsboro, 2,360 . . . . . . .C6
Millville, 259 . . . . .D6
Milton, 1,657 . . . . .C5
Nanticoke Acres B6
Nassau, 1,600 . . . . .D5
Newark, 28,547 . . . . . . .A2
New Castle, 4,862 . . . . . .B2
Newport, 1,122 . . . . . . .B2
Oak Grove C4
Oak Orchard, 750 . . . . . .D6
Ocean View, 1,006 . . . . .D6
Odessa, 286 . . . . .B3
Owens, 125 . . . . .B5
Petersburg, 225 . . . . . . .B4
Pinetown, 1,100 . . . . . . .D5
Plymouth, 350 . . . . .B4
Primehook Beach, 30 . . . .C5
Reeves Crossing, 450 . . . .B5
Rehoboth Beach, 1,495 . .D6
Reliance B6
Rising Sun, 2,458 . . . . . .B4
Rodney Village, 1,602 . . .B4
Rosedale Beach, 750 . . . .D6
Roseville Park, 6,200 . . . .B2
Roxana, 375 . . . . .D7
Sandtown, 325 . . . . .B4
Seaford, 6,699 . . . . .B6
Selbyville, 1,645 . . . . . . .D7
Slaughter Beach, 198 . . . .C5
Smyrna, 5,679 . . . . .B3
South Bethany, 492 . . . . .D6
Stanton, 5,000 . . . . .B2
Star Hill, 600 . . . . .B4
Swann Keys, 700 . . . . . . .D7
Talleyville, 6,300 . . . . . . .B1
Taylors Bridge, 20 . . . . . .B3
Townsend, 346 . . . . .B3
Viola, 156 . . . . .B4
Whitesville, 125 . . . . .D7
Williamsville (Kent Co.),
    300 . . . . .B5
Williamsville (Sussex Co.),
    350 . . . . .D7
Wilmington, 72,664 . . . . .B1
Wilmington Manor, 8,262 .B2
Woodenhawk, 200 . . . . . .B5
Woodland Beach, 100 . . . .C3
Woodside, 184 . . . . .B4
Workmans Corners, 400 . . .C6
Wyoming, 1,141 . . . . . . .B4

Other Features

Assawoman, bay D7
Atlantic, ocean E6
Belleplain State Forest E4
Bellevue State Park C1
Ben Davis, point C3
Blackbird State Forest B3
Bombay Hook National
    Wildlife Refuge C3
Broad, creek B6
Broadkill, river C5
Cape Henlopen State Park .D5
Cape May, point E5
Chesapeake &
    Delaware, canal B2
Cohansey, river C3
Delaware, bay D4
Delaware, river B2
Delaware Seashore
    State Park D6
Dover A.F.B. C4
Egg Island, point D4
Elk Neck State Forest A2
Fort Delaware State Park . .B2
Henlopen, cape D5
Indian R., bay D6
Kelly, island C4
Kent, island C4
Marshyhope, creek A6
Maurice, river D4
Maurice River, cove D4
Mispillion, river C5
Murderkill, river B5
Nanticoke, river B6
Prime Hook National
    Wildlife Refuge C5
Redden State Forest C6
Rehoboth, bay D6
Smyrna, river B3
Supawna Meadows National
    Wildlife Refuge B2
Tuckahoe State Park A5

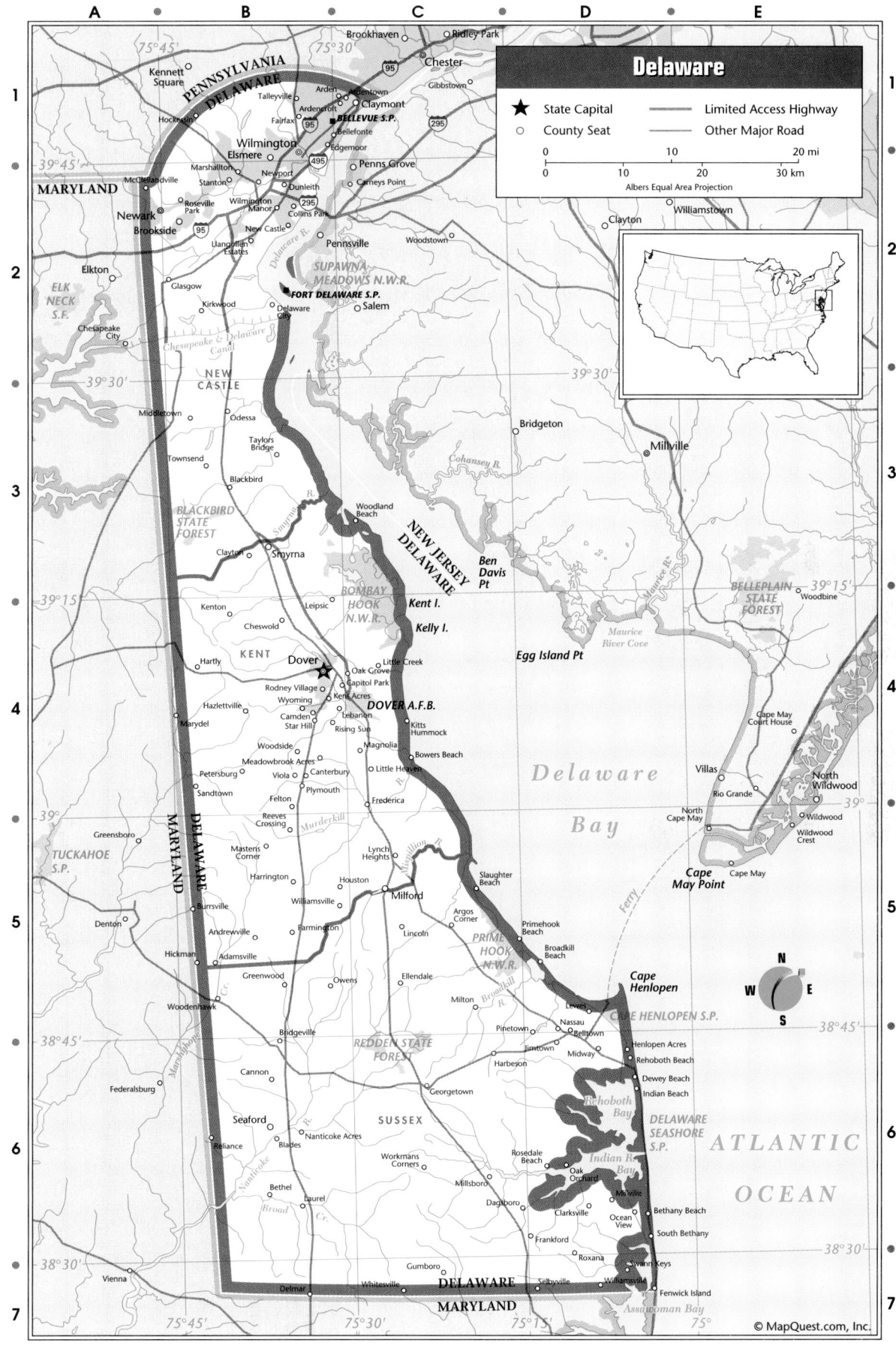

Florida

Capital:	Tallahassee
Land Area:	53,997 sq. mi. 139,852 sq. km.
Population:	15,982,378 (2000 Census)
Largest City:	Jacksonville, 735,617
Highest Point:	Walton County 345 ft. 105 m.
Admitted to Union:	March 3, 1845
Nickname:	Sunshine State Peninsula State
State Flower:	Orange Blossom
State Bird:	Mockingbird

Florida: Map Index

Counties

Alachua, 217,955 F2
Baker, 22,259 F1
Bay, 148,217 C1
Bradford, 26,088 F2
Brevard, 476,230 H4
Broward, 1,623,018 A6, H5
Calhoun, 13,017 C1
Charlotte, 141,627 G5
Citrus, 118,085 F3
Clay, 140,814 G2
Collier, 251,377 G5
Columbia, 56,513 F1
De Soto, 32,209 G4
Dixie, 13,827 E2
Duval, 778,879 G1
Escambia, 294,410 A1
Flagler, 49,832 G2
Franklin, 11,057 D2
Gadsden, 45,087 D1
Gilchrist, 14,437 F2
Glades, 10,576 G5
Gulf, 13,332 C2
Hamilton, 13,327 F1
Hardee, 26,938 G4
Hendry, 36,210 G5
Hernando, 130,802 F3
Highlands, 87,366 G4
Hillsborough, 998,948 D6, F4
Holmes, 18,564 C1
Indian River, 112,947 H4
Jackson, 46,755 C1
Jefferson, 12,902 E1
Lafayette, 7,022 E2
Lake, 210,528 C4, G3
Lee, 440,888 F5
Leon, 239,452 D1
Levy, 34,450 F2
Liberty, 7,021 D1
Madison, 18,733 E1
Manatee, 264,002 D7, F4
Marion, 258,916 G2
Martin, 126,731 A4, H4
Miami-Dade, 2,253,362 A6, H6
Monroe, 79,589 G6, G7
Nassau, 57,663 G1
Okaloosa, 170,498 B1
Okeechobee, 35,910 H4
Orange, 896,344 D4, G3
Osceola, 172,493 D4, G3
Palm Beach, 1,131,184 A4, H5
Pasco, 344,765 F3
Pinellas, 921,482 C6, F4
Polk, 483,924 C4, G3
Putnam, 70,423 G2
St. Johns, 123,135 G1
St. Lucie, 192,695 A3, H4
Santa Rosa, 117,743 A1
Sarasota, 325,957 F4
Seminole, 365,196 D3, G3
Sumter, 53,345 F3
Suwannee, 34,844 E1
Taylor, 19,256 E1
Union, 13,442 F1
Volusia, 443,343 G2
Wakulla, 22,863 D1
Walton, 40,601 B1
Washington, 20,973 C1

Cities and Towns

Alachua, 6,098 F2
Alford, 466 C1
Allentown, 40 A1
Altamonte Springs, 41,200 C4, G3
Altha, 506 C1
Alton, 80 E1
Altoona, 88 G3
Alva, 2,182 G5
Amelia City, 1,300 G1
Anna Maria, 1,814 F4
Anthony, 1,600 F2
Apalachicola, 2,334 D2
Apollo Beach, 7,444 D7, F4
Apopka, 26,642 C4, G3
Arcadia, 6,604 G4
Archer, 1,289 F2
Aripeka, 650 F3
Ashville, 90 E1
Astatula, 1,298 C3, G3
Astor, 1,487 G2
Athena E2
Atlantic Beach, 13,368 G1
Atlantis, 2,005 B5
Auburndale, 11,032 G3
Avon Park, 8,542 G4
Babcock, 50 G5
Babson Park, 1,182 G4
Bagdad, 1,490 A1
Baker, 300 B1
Baldwin, 1,634 G1
Bal Harbour, 3,305 B6
Barberville, 200 G2
Barrineau Park, 60 A1
Bartow, 15,340 G4
Basinger, 50 G4
Bay Hill, 5,177 C4
Bay Lake (Lake Co.), 100 G3
Bay Lake (Orange Co.), 23 C4
Bayonet Point, 23,577 F3
Bayport, 36 F3
Bay Springs, 50 A1
Beacon Hill, 100 C2
Becker, 40 G1
Bee Ridge, 8,744 F4
Bell, 349 F2
Belleair, 4,067 C6
Belleair Beach, 1,751 C6
Belleair Bluffs, 2,243 C6
Belleair Shore C6
Belle Glade, 14,906 H5
Belle Isle, 5,531 C4
Belleview, 3,478 F2
Bellwood, 450 H3
Berrydale, 50 A1
Beverly Beach, 547 G2
Beverly Hills, 8,317 F3
Big Pine Key, 5,032 G7
Biscayne Park, 3,269 B6
Bithlo, 4,626 D4, G3
Blackman B1
Blanton, 200 F3
Bloomingdale, 19,839 D6
Blountstown, 2,444 C1
Bloxham, 425 D1
Boca Grande, 700 F5
Boca Raton, 74,764 B5, H5
Bogia, 50 A1
Bokeelia, 1,997 F5
Bonifay, 4,078 C1
Bonita Springs, 32,797 G5
Bostwick, 350 G2
Boulogne, 150 G1
Bowling Green, 2,892 G4
Boyd, 175 E1
Boyette, 5,895 D6
Boynton Beach, 60,389 B5, H5
Bradenton, 49,504 F4
Bradenton Beach, 1,482 F4
Bradfordville, 1,100 D1
Brandon, 77,895 D6, F4
Branford, 695 F2
Bratt, 225 A1
Brighton G4
Briny Breezes, 411 B5
Bristol, 845 D1
Bronson, 964 F2
Brooker, 352 F2
Brooksville, 7,264 F3
Buckhead Ridge, 1,390 H4
Buena Ventura Lakes, 14,100 C4
Bunnell, 2,122 G2
Bushnell, 2,050 F3
Callahan, 962 G1
Callaway, 14,233 C1
Campbellton, 212 C1
Campton, 150 B1
Canal Point, 525 H5
Cantonment, 2,300 A1
Cape Canaveral, 8,829 H3
Cape Coral, 102,286 G5
Capps, 40 E1
Captiva, 379 F5
Carol City, 59,443 A6, H6
Carrabelle, 1,303 D2
Carrollwood, 33,519 D6
Caryville, 218 C1
Casselberry, 22,629 D4
Cedar Key, 790 E2
Center Hill, 910 G3
Century, 1,714 A1
Century Village, 7,616 B4
Chaires, 300 D1
Charlotte Beach, 1,600 F5
Chassahowitzka, 700 F3
Chattahoochee, 3,287 D1
Cherry Lake, 80 E1
Chiefland, 1,993 F2
Chipley, 3,592 C1
Chokoloskee, 404 G6
Citra, 800 F2
Citrus Springs, 4,157 F2
Clearwater, 108,787 C6, F4
Clearwater Beach, 175 C6
Clermont, 9,333 C4, G3
Cleveland, 3,268 G5
Clewiston, 6,460 H5
Cloud Lake, 167 B4
Cocoa, 16,412 H3
Cocoa Beach, 12,482 H3
Coconut Creek, 43,566 B5
Coleman, 647 F3
Columbia, 550 F1
Compass Lake, 200 C1
Cooks Hammock E2
Cooper City, 27,939 A6
Copeland, 80 G6
Coral Gables, 42,249 A6, H6
Coral Springs, 117,549 A5, H5
Cornwell, 70 G4
Cottage Hill, 1,300 A1
Cottondale, 869 C1
Crawfordville, 750 D1
Crescent Beach, 985 G2
Crescent City, 1,776 G2
Crestview, 14,766 B1
Cross City, 1,775 E2
Crystal Beach (see Palm Harbor), 4,000 C6
Crystal Lake C1
Crystal River, 3,485 F3
Crystal Springs, 1,175 D6, F3
Curlew (see Palm Harbor), 5,900 C6
Cutler, 17,390 A7
Cutler Ridge, 24,781 A7
Dade City, 6,188 F3
Dania, 20,061 B6
Darlington, 175 B1
Davenport, 1,924 G3
Davie, 75,720 B6, H5
Day, 90 E1
Daytona Beach, 64,112 G2
Daytona Beach Shores, 4,299 H2
De Bary, 15,559 G3
Deerfield Beach, 64,583 B5, H5
Deer Park, 60 H3
De Funiak Springs, 5,089 B1
Dekle Beach E2
De Land, 20,904 G2
De Leon Springs, 2,358 G2
Dellwood, 125 C1
Delray Beach, 60,020 B5, H5
Del Rio D6
Deltona, 69,543 G3
De Soto City, 550 G4
Destin, 11,119 B1
Doctor Phillips, 9,548 C4
Dover, 2,798 D6
Dowling Park, 650 E1
Drifton, 200 E1
Duette F4
Dukes, 70 F2
Dunedin, 35,691 C6, F3
Dunnellon, 1,898 F2
Durbin G1
Eagle Lake, 2,496 G4
East Naples, 23,000 G5
Eastpoint, 2,158 D2
Eatonville, 2,432 C4
Ebro, 250 C1
Edgewater, 18,668 H3
Edgewood, 1,901 C4
Egypt Lake D6
Effers, 13,161 F3
Ellaville E1
Ellzey, 60 F2
El Portal, 2,505 B6
Englewood, 16,196 F5
Eridu, 40 E1
Espanola, 40 G2
Estero, 9,503 G5
Eustis, 15,106 C3, G3
Everglades City, 479 G6
Fairbanks, 750 F2
Falmouth E1
Fanning Springs, 737 F2
Favoretta, 650 G2
Feather Sound, 3,597 C6
Felda, 300 G5
Fellsmere, 3,813 H4
Fenholloway E1
Fernandina Beach, 10,549 G1
Ferndale, 233 C4
Flagler Beach, 4,954 G2
Flamingo, 200 H6
Florida City, 7,843 A7, H6
Forest City, 12,612 C4
Fort Basinger G4
Fort Drum, 150 H4
Fort Green, 40 G4
Fort Lauderdale, 152,397 B6, H5
Fort Meade, 5,691 G4
Fort Myers, 48,208 G5
Fort Myers Beach, 6,561 G5
Fort Myers Villas (Villas), 11,346 G5
Fort Ogden, 225 G4
Fort Pierce, 37,516 H4
Fort Walton Beach, 19,973 B1
Fort White, 409 F2
Fountain, 225 C1
Freeport, 1,190 B1
Frink C1
Frostproof, 2,975 G4
Gainesville, 95,447 F2
Gardner G4
Gaskin, 80 B1
Geneva, 2,601 D3
Genoa, 50 F1
Georgetown, 450 G2
Gibsonton, 8,752 D6, F4
Gifford, 7,599 H4
Glendale, 80 B1
Glen Ridge, 276 B4
Glen St. Mary, 473 G1
Golden Beach, 919 B6
Golden Gate, 20,951 G5
Goldenrod, 12,871 D4
Golf, 230 B5
Golfview, 150 B4
Gonzalez, 11,365 A1
Goulds, 7,453 A7, H6
Graceville, 2,402 C1
Grand Ridge, 792 C1
Grant, 275 H4
Greenacres, 27,569 B5, H5
Green Cove Springs, 5,378 G2
Greensboro, 619 D1
Greenville, 837 E1
Greenwood, 735 C1
Gretna, 1,709 D1
Grove City, 2,092 F5
Groveland, 2,360 B4
Gulf Breeze, 5,665 A1
Gulf Hammock, 40 F2
Gulfport, 12,527 C7
Gulf Stream, 716 B5
Haines City, 13,174 G3
Hallandale, 34,282 B6, H6
Hampton, 431 F2
Hampton Springs, 40 E1
Hanson, 175 E1
Harlem, 2,730 H5
Hastings, 521 G2
Hatchbend, 50 F2
Havana, 1,713 D1
Haverhill, 1,454 B4
Hawthorne, 1,415 F2
Hernando, 8,253 F3
Hialeah, 226,419 B6, H6
Hialeah Gardens, 19,297 A6
Highland, 80 F1
Highland Beach, 3,775 B5
Highland View, 450 C2
High Springs, 3,863 F2
Hillcrest Heights, 266 G4
Hilliard, 2,702 G1
Hillsboro Beach, 2,163 B5
Hines E2
Hinson, 750 D1
Hobe Sound, 11,376 B4, H4
Holden Heights, 3,856 C4
Holder, 225 F3
Holiday, 21,904 C6, F3
Holley, 650 B1
Holly Hill, 12,119 G2
Hollywood, 139,357 B6, H5
Holmes Beach, 4,966 F4
Holopaw, 425 G3
Holt, 125 B1
Homeland, 325 G4
Homestead, 31,909 A7, H6
Homosassa Springs, 12,458 F3
Honeyville, 400 C1
Horseshoe Beach, 206 E2
Hosford, 450 D1
Houston, 125 F1
Howey-in-the-Hills, 956 C3
Hudson, 12,765 F3
Hypoluxo, 2,015 B5
Immokalee, 19,763 G5
Indian Harbour Beach, 8,152 H3
Indian Lake Estates, 250 G4
Indian River Shores, 3,448 H4
Indian Rocks Beach, 5,072 C6, F4
Indian Shores, 1,705 C6
Indiantown, 5,588 A4, H4
Indrio, 550 H4
Inglis, 1,491 F2
Interlachen, 1,475 G2
Inverness, 6,789 F3
Islamorada, 6,846 H7
Islandia, 6 H6
Istachatta, 65 F3
Italia, 50 G1
Izagora, 80 C1
Jacksonville, 735,617 G1
Jacksonville Beach, 20,990 G1
Jacobs, 281 C1
Jasper, 1,780 F1
Jay, 579 A1
Jena, 400 E2
Jennings, 833 E1
Jensen Beach, 11,100 A3, H4
Jerome, 40 G6
Juno Beach, 3,262 B4, H5
Jupiter, 39,328 B4, H5
Jupiter Inlet Colony, 368 B4
Jupiter Island, 620 B4
Kathleen, 3,280 F3
Keaton Beach, 80 E2
Kenansville H4
Kendall, 75,226 A7, H6
Kenneth City, 4,400 C6
Key Biscayne, 10,507 B6
Key Colony Beach, 788 G7
Key Largo, 11,886 H6
Keystone Heights, 1,349 F2
Key West, 25,478 G7
Kinard C1
Kingsley, 425 G2
Kissimmee, 47,814 C4, G3
Korona, 40 G2
La Belle, 4,210 G5
La Crosse, 143 F2
Lady Lake, 11,828 G3
Laguna Beach, 2,909 C1
Lake Bird, 50 E1
Lake Buena Vista, 16 C4, G3
Lake Butler, 1,927 F1
Lake City, 9,980 F1
Lake Clarke Shores, 3,451 B5
Lake Harbor, 195 H5
Lake Helen, 2,743 G3
Lakeland, 78,452 G3
Lake Magdalene, 28,755 D6
Lake Mary, 11,458 D3, G3
Lake Monroe, 700 D3
Lake Panasoffkee, 3,413 F3
Lake Park, 8,721 B4
Lake Placid, 1,668 G4
Lake Wales, 10,194 G4
Lake Worth, 35,133 B5, H5
Lamont, 125 E1
Lanark Village, 550 D2
Land O' Lakes, 20,971 F3
Lantana, 9,437 B5, H5
Largo, 69,371 C6, F4
Lauderdale-by-the-Sea, 2,563 B5
Lauderdale Lakes, 31,705 B5
Lauderhill, 57,585 B6
Laurel, 8,393 F4
Laurel Hill, 549 B1
Lawtey, 656 F1
Layton, 186 H7
Lazy Lake, 38 B5
Lebanon, 50 F2
Lecanto, 5,161 F3
Lee, 352 E1
Leesburg, 15,956 F3
Leisure City, 22,152 A7
Leonia, 40 B1
Liberty, 50 B1
Lighthouse Point, 10,767 B5
Limestone G4
Live Oak, 6,480 F1
Lloyd, 200 D1
Longboat Key, 7,603 F4
Longwood, 13,745 D3
Lorida, 375 G4
Loughman, 1,385 G3
Lulu, 90 F1
Luraville E1
Lutz, 17,081 D6, F3
Lynne, 300 G2
Lynn Haven, 12,451 C1
Macclenny, 4,459 F1
Madeira Beach, 4,511 C6
Madison, 3,061 E1
Maitland, 12,019 C4
Malabar, 2,622 H3
Malone, 2,007 C1
Manalapan, 321 B5
Mango, 8,842 D6
Mangonia Park, 1,283 B4
Marathon, 10,255 G7
Marco, 14,879 G6
Margate, 53,909 B5, H5
Marianna, 6,230 C1
Marineland, 6 G2
Marion Oaks, 100 F2
Martel, 375 F2
Mary Esther, 4,055 B1
Masaryktown, 920 F3
Mascotte, 2,687 G3
Matlacha, 735 F5
Mayo, 988 E1
McAlpin, 80 E1
McDavid, 175 A1
McIntosh, 453 F2
Medart, 175 D1
Medley, 1,098 A6
Melbourne, 71,382 H3
Melbourne Beach, 3,335 H3
Merritt Island, 36,090 H3
Mexico Beach, 1,017 C2
Miami, 362,470 B6, H6
Miami Beach, 87,933 B6, H6
Miami Shores, 10,380 B6
Miami Springs, 13,712 A6
Micanopy, 653 F2
Micco, 9,498 H4
Miccosukee, 150 D1
Middleburg, 10,338 G1

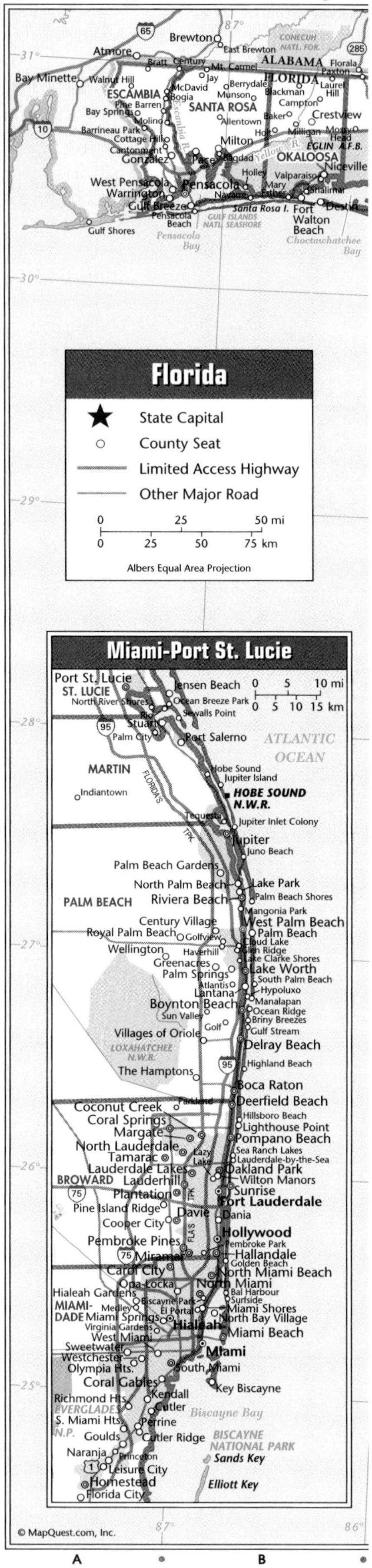

Midway, 1,446 ....D1
Milligan, 425 ....B1
Milton, 7,045 ....A1
Mims, 9,147 ....H3
Minneola, 5,435 ....C4
Miramar, 72,739 ....B6, H6
Molino, 1,312 ....A1
Monticello, 2,533 ....E1
Montverde, 882 ....C4
Moore Haven, 1,635 ....G5
Morriston, 125 ....F2
Mossy Head, 100 ....B1
Mount Carmel, 100 ....A1
Mount Dora, 9,418 ....C3, G3
Mount Pleasant, 150 ....D1
Mount Plymouth, 2,814 ....C3
Mulberry, 3,230 ....G4
Munson, 60 ....B1
Myakka City, 200 ....F4
Naples, 20,976 ....G5
Naples Manor, 5,186 ....G5
Naples Park, 6,741 ....G5
Naranja, 4,034 ....A7, H6
Narcoossee, 475 ....D4
Navarre, 450 ....B1
Newberry, 3,316 ....F2
Newburn, 60 ....E1
New Port Richey, 16,117 ....F3
New Smyrna Beach, 20,048 ....H2
Niceville, 11,684 ....B1
Nocatee, 700 ....G4
Noma, 213 ....C1
North Bay Village, 6,733 ....B6
Northdale (Greater Northdale), 20,461 ....D6
North Fort Myers, 40,214 ....G5
North Lauderdale, 32,264 ....B5
North Miami, 59,880 ....B6, H6
North Miami Beach, 40,786 ....B6
North Naples, 13,400 ....G5
North Palm Beach, 12,064 ....B4
North Port, 22,797 ....F4
North Redington Beach, 1,474 ....C6
North River Shores, 3,101 ....A3
Oakdale, 125 ....C1
Oak Hill, 1,378 ....H3
Oakland, 936 ....C4
Oakland Park, 30,966 ....B5, H5
O'Brien, 80 ....F1
Ocala, 45,943 ....F2
Ocean Breeze Park, 463 ....A3, H4
Ocean Ridge, 1,636 ....B5
Ochopee H6
Ocoee, 24,391 ....C4, G3
Odessa, 3,173 ....D6, F3
Okeechobee, 5,376 ....H4
Okeelanta, 90 ....H5
Old Myakka, 225 ....F4
Oldsmar, 11,910 ....C6, F3
Old Town, 100 ....F2
Olympia Hts., 13,452 ....A6
Ona, 700 ....G4
Oneco, 7,500 ....F4
Opa-Locka, 14,951 ....B6
Orange C1
Orange City, 6,604 ....G3
Orange Heights, 150 ....F2
Orange Park, 9,081 ....G1
Orchid, 140 ....H4
Orient Park (East Lake-Orient Park), 5,703 ....D6
Orlando, 185,951 ....C4, G3

Ormond Beach, 36,301 ....G2
Ormond-by-the-Sea, 8,430 ....G2
Oslo, 1,900 ....H4
Osprey, 4,143 ....F4
Osteen, 450 ....D3
Otter Creek, 121 ....F2
Oviedo, 26,316 ....D4, G3
Oxford, 350 ....F3
Pace, 7,393 ....A1
Pahokee, 5,985 ....H5
Palatka, 10,033 ....G2
Palm Bay, 79,413 ....H3
Palm Beach, 10,468 ....B4, H5
Palm Beach Gardens, 35,058 ....B4, H5
Palm Beach Shores, 1,269 ....B4
Palm City, 20,097 ....A4
Palm Coast, 32,732 ....G2
Palmdale, 175 ....G5
Palmetto, 12,571 ....F4
Palm Harbor, 59,248 ....C6, F3
Palm River (Palm River-Clair Mel), 17,589 ....D6
Palm Shores, 794 ....H3
Palm Springs, 11,699 ....B5
Panacea, 865 ....D1
Panama City, 36,417 ....C1
Panama City Beach, 7,671 ....C1
Parkland, 13,835 ....A5
Parrish, 1,252 ....D7, F4
Pasco, 100 ....F3
Paxton, 656 ....B1
Pembroke Park, 6,299 ....B6
Pembroke Pines, 137,427 ....B6
Penney Farms, 580 ....G2
Pensacola, 56,255 ....A1
Pensacola Beach, 750 ....A1
Perrine, 15,600 ....A7, H6
Perry, 6,847 ....E1
Pierson, 2,596 ....G2
Pine Barren, 150 ....A1
Pine Castle, 8,803 ....C4, G3
Pinecrest, 600 ....F4
Pineda, 1,700 ....H3
Pine Island Ridge, 5,199 ....A6
Pinellas Park, 45,658 ....C6
Pinetta, 275 ....E1
Piney Point, 175 ....D7
Pinland, 80 ....E1
Pirate Harbor, 200 ....F5
Placida, 325 ....F5
Plantation, 82,934 ....A6, H5
Plant City, 29,915 ....F3
Polk City, 1,516 ....G3
Pomona Park, 789 ....G2
Pompano Beach, 78,191 ....B5, H5
Ponce de Leon, 457 ....C1
Ponce Inlet, 2,513 ....H2
Port Charlotte, 46,451 ....F5
Portland, 275 ....B1
Port Mayaca H5
Port Orange, 45,823 ....H2
Port Richey, 3,021 ....F3
Port St. Joe, 3,644 ....C2
Port St. Lucie, 88,769 ....A3, H4
Port Salerno, 10,141 ....A4, H4
Princeton, 10,090 ....A7
Prosperity, 150 ....F2
Providence, 1,100 ....F3
Punta Gorda, 14,344 ....F5
Quincy, 6,982 ....D1
Raiford, 187 ....F1
Raleigh, 300 ....F2

Reddick, 571 ....F2
Red Head, 60 ....C1
Redington Beach, 1,539 ....C6, F4
Redington Shores, 2,338 ....C6
Richmond Heights, 8,479 ....A7
Ridge Manor, 4,108 ....F3
Rio, 1,028 ....A3
Riverview, 12,035 ....D6, F4
Riviera Beach, 29,884 ....B4, H5
Rock Hill B1
Rockledge, 20,170 ....H3
Roseland, 1,775 ....H4
Round Lake, 200 ....C1
Royal Palm Beach, 21,523 ....A4, H5
Rubonia, 1,700 ....D7
Ruskin, 8,321 ....D7
Russell, 100 ....G1
Safety Harbor, 17,203 ....C6
St. Augustine, 11,592 ....G2
St. Augustine Beach, 4,683 ....G2
St. Augustine Shores, 4,922 ....G2
St. Cloud, 20,074 ....G3
St. Leo, 595 ....F3
St. Lucie, 604 ....H4
St. Marks, 272 ....D1
St. Pete Beach, 9,929 ....C7, F4
St. Petersburg, 248,232 ....C7, F4
St. Teresa D2
Salem, 80 ....E2
Salt Springs, 600 ....G2
San Carlos Park, 16,317 ....F5
Sanderson, 500 ....F1
Sanford, 38,291 ....D3, G3
Sanibel, 6,064 ....F5
San Mateo, 1,000 ....G2
Santa Rosa Beach, 300 ....B1
Santos, 550 ....G2
Sarasota, 52,715 ....F4
Satellite Beach, 9,577 ....H3
Scottsmoor, 600 ....H3
Seagrove Beach, 150 ....B1
Sea Ranch Lakes, 1,392 ....B5
Sebastian, 16,181 ....H4
Sebring, 9,667 ....G4
Seffner, 5,467 ....D6
Seminole, 10,890 ....C6
Seville, 475 ....G2
Sewalls Point, 1,946 ....A3
Shady Grove, 90 ....E1
Shalimar, 718 ....B1
Shamrock, 200 ....E2
Silver Springs, 6,400 ....F2
Sink Creek, 50 ....E1
Sirmans E1
Sneads, 1,919 ....C1
Sopchoppy, 426 ....D1
South Bay, 3,859 ....H5
South Daytona, 13,177 ....G2
South Miami, 10,741 ....H6
South Miami Heights, 33,522 ....A7
South Palm Beach, 699 ....B5
South Pasadena, 5,778 ....C7
South Ponte Vedra Beach, 150 ....G1
Southport, 1,500 ....C1
South Venice, 13,539 ....F4
Sparr, 400 ....F2
Springfield, 8,810 ....C1
Spring Hill, 69,078 ....F3
Starke, 5,593 ....F2
Steinhatchee, 700 ....E2
Stuart, 14,633 ....A3, H4

Sumatra, 60 ....D1
Summerfield, 550 ....F2
Summerville, 250 ....C1
Sun City, 175 ....D7, F4
Sun City Center, 16,321 ....D7
Sunnyside C3
Sunrise, 85,779 ....B5
Sun Valley B5
Surfside, 4,909 ....B6
Suwannee, 425 ....E2
Suwannee Springs, 70 ....F1
Sweetwater, 14,226 ....A6, H6
Taft, 1,938 ....C4, G3
Tallahassee, 150,624 ....D1
Tamarac, 55,588 ....A5, H5
Tampa, 303,447 ....D6, F4
Tangelo Park, 2,430 ....C4
Tarpon Springs, 21,003 ....F3
Tavares, 9,700 ....C3, G3
Tavernier, 2,173 ....H6
Taylor, 150 ....F1
Telogia, 200 ....D1
Temple Terrace, 20,918 ....D6, F3
Tenille D1
Tequesta, 5,273 ....H5
The Hamptons (Hamptons at Boca Raton), 11,306 ....B5
Theressa, 175 ....F2
Titusville, 40,670 ....H3
Treasure Island, 7,450 ....C7, F4
Trenton, 1,617 ....F2
Umatilla, 2,214 ....G3
University West D6
Valkaria, 200 ....H4
Valparaiso, 6,408 ....B1
Venice, 17,764 ....F4
Venus G5
Verna F4
Vernon, 743 ....C1
Vero Beach, 17,705 ....H4
Vilano Beach, 2,533 ....G2
Vilas D1
Villages of Oriole, 4,758 ....B5
Virginia Gardens, 2,348 ....A6
Wabasso, 918 ....H4
Wacissa, 350 ....E1
Wakulla, 175 ....D1
Waldo, 821 ....F2
Walnut Hill, 375 ....A1
Walton, 100 ....C1
Ward Ridge, 60 ....C2
Warrington, 15,207 ....A1
Watertown, 2,837 ....F1
Wauchula, 4,368 ....G4
Wausau, 398 ....C1
Webster, 805 ....F3
Weeki Wachee, 12 ....F3
Weirsdale, 750 ....G3
Welaka, 586 ....G2
Wellborn, 350 ....F1
Wellington, 38,216 ....A5
West Bay, 225 ....C1
West Frostproof, 125 ....G4
Westchester, 30,271 ....A6
West Melbourne, 9,824 ....H3
West Miami, 5,863 ....A6
West Palm Beach, 82,103 ....B4, H5
West Pensacola, 21,939 ....A1
Westwood Acres, 125 ....F2
Wewahitchka, 1,722 ....C1
White City, 275 ....C2
White Springs, 819 ....F1

Wildwood, 3,924 ....F3
Williston, 2,297 ....F2
Wilma D1
Wilton Manors, 12,697 ....B6
Wimauma, 4,246 ....D7
Windermere, 1,897 ....C4
Winfield, 225 ....B1
Winter Beach, 965 ....H4
Winter Garden, 14,351 ....C4, G3
Winter Haven, 26,487 ....G3
Winter Park, 24,090 ....D4, G3
Winter Springs, 31,666 ....D4
Woodville, 3,006 ....D1
Worthington Springs, 193 ....F2
Yalaha, 1,175 ....C3
Yankeetown, 629 ....F2
Yeehaw Junction, 21,778 ....H4
Youngstown, 40 ....C1
Yulee, 8,392 ....G1
Zellwood, 2,540 ....C3
Zephyrhills, 10,833 ....F3
Zolfo Springs, 1,641 ....G4

Other Features

Amelia, island G1
Andrews, bay C1
Apalachee, bay D2
Apalachicola, bay C2
Apalachicola, river C1
Apalachicola National Forest D1
Atlantic, ocean B4, H3
Aucilla, river E1
Avon Park A.F. Range G4
Bald, point D2
Big Cypress, swamp G5
Big Cypress I.R. H5
Big Cypress National Preserve H5
Biscayne, bay B7, H6
Biscayne National Park B7, H6
Boca Chica, key G7
Brighton I.R. G4
Caloosahatchee, river G5
Canaveral, cape H3
Canaveral Natl. Seashore H3
Cape Canaveral Air Station H3
Castillo de San Marcos N.M. G2
Cecil Field N.A.S. G1
Cedar, keys E2
Cedar Keys N.W.R. E2
Charlotte, harbor F5
Chassahowitzka N.W.R. F3
Chattahoochee, river C1
Choctawhatchee, bay B1
Crocodile Lake N.W.R. H6
Crooked, lake G4
Deadman, bay E2
De Soto Natl. Mem. F4
Dog, island D2
Dry Tortugas Natl. Park F7
Eglin A.F.B. B1
Egmont Key N.W.R. C7
Elliott, key B7, H6
Escanbia, bay A1
Everglades, swamp A7, H6
Everglades National Park A7, H6
Florida, bay H6
Florida, keys G7
Florida, straits H7
Florida Panther N.W.R. G5
Florida's Turnpike G3

Ft. Jefferson F7
Fort Matanzas N.M. G2
Gasparilla, island F5
George, lake G2
Great White Heron N.W.R. G7
Gulf Islands Natl. Seashore B1
Highest Point in Florida B1
Hobe Sound N.W.R. B4, H4
Homosassa, bay F3
Indian, river B1
Iron, mountain G4
Island Bay N.W.R. F5
Istokpoga, lake G4
John F. Kennedy Space Center H3
Key West N.W.R. F7
Kissimmee, lake G4
Largo, key H6
Lochloosa, lake F2
Lower Suwannee N.W.R. E2
Loxahatchee N.W.R. A5, H5
Marquesas, keys F7
Matlacha Pass N.W.R. F5
Mexico, gulf C6, E5
Miccosukee Indian Res. H5
Myakka River S.P. F4
National Key Deer Refuge G7
Ocala National Forest G2
Ochlockonee, river D1
Okeechobee, lake H5
Okefenokee, swamp F1
Osceola Natl. Forest F1
Peace, river G4
Pensacola, bay A1
Piney, point E2
Ponce de Leon, bay G6
Romano, cape G6
Sable, cape G6
St. George, island D2
St. Johns N.W.R. H3
St. Johns, river G3
St. Joseph, bay C2
St. Marks N.W.R. D1
St. Marys, river G1
St. Vincent, island C2
St. Vincent N.W.R. C2
San Blas, cape C2
Sands, key B7, H6
Sanibel, island F5
Santa Rosa, island B1
Sugarloaf Key G7
Suwannee, river F1, F2
Talquin, lake D1
Tampa, bay D7, F4
Timucuan Ecological And Hist. Pres. G1
Tyndall A.F.B. C2
Waccasassa, bay F2
Walt Disney World, resort C4
Withlacoochee, river E1
Yellow, river B1

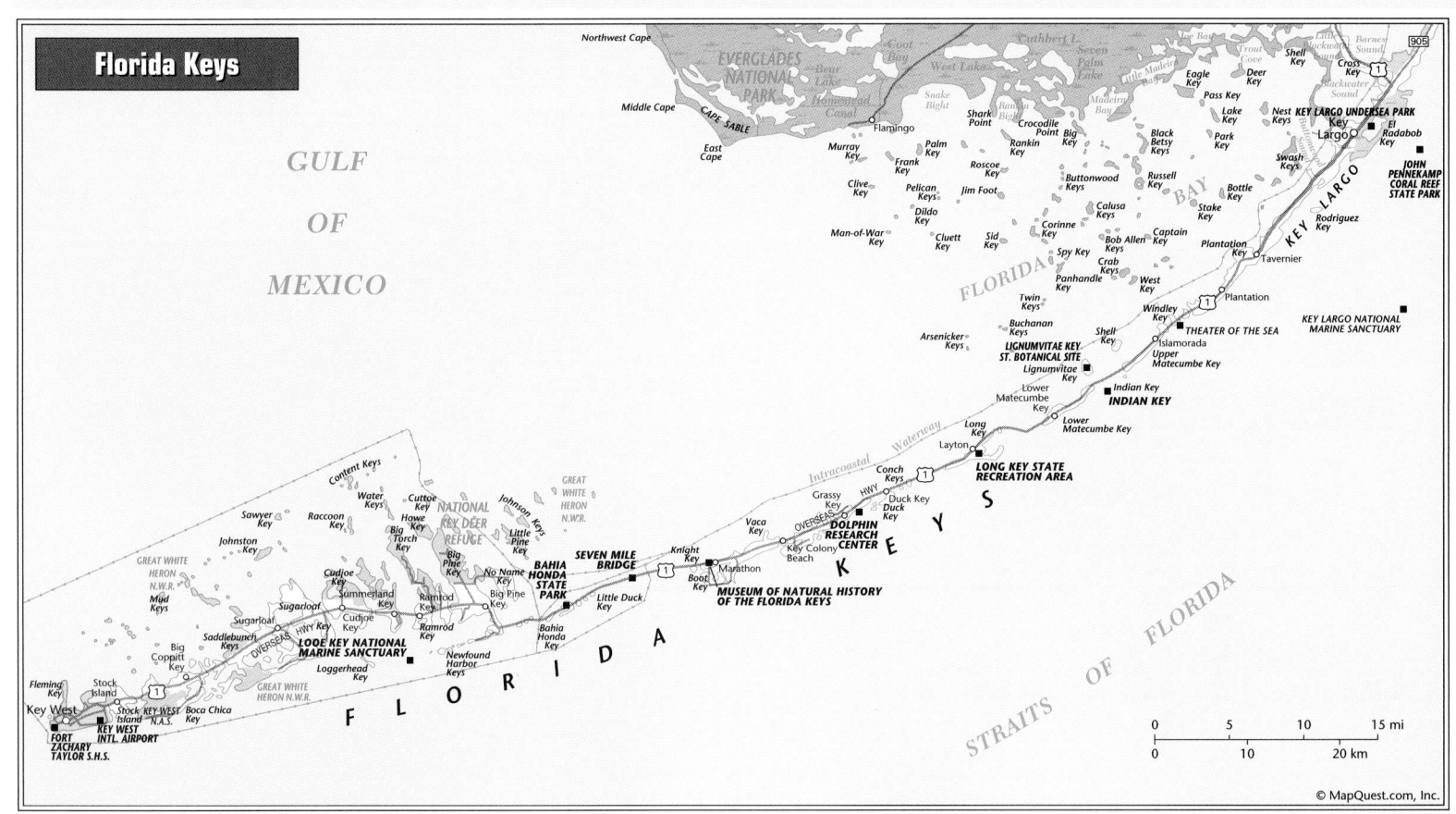

Florida Keys

Georgia

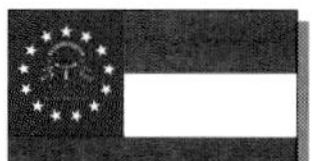

Capital: Atlanta
Land Area: 57,919 sq. mi.
150,010 sq. km.
Population: 8,186,453 (2000 Census)
Largest City: Atlanta,
416,474
Highest Point: Brasstown Bald
4,784 ft.
1,458 m.
Admitted to Union: January 2, 1788
Nickname: Empire State of the South
Peach State
State Flower: Cherokee Rose
State Bird: Brown Thrasher

Georgia: Map Index

Counties

Appling, **17,419** ... G8
Atkinson, **7,609** ... F9
Bacon, **10,103** ... F8
Baker, **4,074** ... C9
Baldwin, **44,700** ... E5
Banks, **14,422** ... D3
Barrow, **46,144** ... D3
Bartow, **76,019** ... B3
Ben Hill, **17,484** ... E8
Berrien, **16,235** ... E9
Bibb, **153,887** ... D6
Bleckley, **11,666** ... E7
Brantley, **14,629** ... H9
Brooks, **16,450** ... D1
Bryan, **23,417** ... H7
Bulloch, **55,983** ... H7
Burke, **22,243** ... G5
Butts, **19,522** ... C5
Calhoun, **6,320** ... B8
Camden, **43,664** ... H1
Candler, **9,577** ... G7
Carroll, **87,268** ... A4
Catoosa, **53,282** ... A2
Charlton, **10,282** ... G1
Chatham, **232,048** ... J7
Chattahoochee, **14,882** ... B7
Chattooga, **25,470** ... A2
Cherokee, **141,903** ... B3, G1
Clarke, **101,489** ... E4
Clay, **3,357** ... B8
Clayton, **236,517** ... C4, H3
Clinch, **6,878** ... F1
Cobb, **607,751** ... B4, G2
Coffee, **37,413** ... F9
Colquitt, **42,053** ... D9
Columbia, **89,288** ... G4
Cook, **15,771** ... E9
Coweta, **89,215** ... B5
Crawford, **12,495** ... C6
Crisp, **21,996** ... D8
Dade, **15,154** ... A2
Dawson, **15,999** ... C3
Decatur, **28,240** ... B9
De Kalb, **665,865** ... C4, J3
Dodge, **19,171** ... E7
Dooly, **11,525** ... D7
Dougherty, **96,065** ... C9
Douglas, **92,174** ... B4, G3
Early, **12,354** ... B9
Echols, **3,754** ... E1
Effingham, **37,535** ... J7
Elbert, **20,511** ... F3
Emanuel, **21,837** ... G6
Evans, **10,495** ... H7
Fannin, **19,798** ... C2
Fayette, **91,263** ... B5, H4
Floyd, **90,565** ... A3
Forsyth, **98,407** ... C3, J1
Franklin, **20,285** ... E3
Fulton, **816,006** ... B4, G3
Gilmer, **23,456** ... C2
Glascock, **2,556** ... F5
Glynn, **67,568** ... H9
Gordon, **44,104** ... A3
Grady, **23,659** ... C9
Greene, **14,406** ... E4
Gwinnett, **588,448** ... C3, J2
Habersham, **35,902** ... D2
Hall, **139,277** ... D3
Hancock, **10,076** ... E5
Haralson, **25,690** ... A4
Harris, **23,695** ... A6
Hart, **22,997** ... E3
Heard, **11,012** ... A5
Henry, **119,341** ... C5, J4
Houston, **110,765** ... D7
Irwin, **9,931** ... E8
Jackson, **41,589** ... D3
Jasper, **11,426** ... D5
Jeff Davis, **12,684** ... F8
Jefferson, **17,266** ... F5
Jenkins, **8,575** ... G6
Johnson, **8,560** ... F6
Jones, **23,639** ... D6
Lamar, **15,912** ... C5
Lanier, **7,241** ... E9
Laurens, **44,874** ... E7
Lee, **24,757** ... C8
Liberty, **61,610** ... H8
Lincoln, **8,348** ... F4
Long, **10,304** ... H8
Lowndes, **92,115** ... E1
Lumpkin, **21,016** ... C2
Macon, **14,074** ... C7
Madison, **25,730** ... E3
Marion, **7,144** ... B7
McDuffie, **21,231** ... F5
McIntosh, **10,847** ... H9
Meriwether, **22,534** ... B5
Miller, **6,383** ... B9
Mitchell, **23,932** ... C9
Monroe, **21,757** ... C6
Montgomery, **8,270** ... F7
Morgan, **15,457** ... D4
Murray, **36,506** ... B2
Muscogee, **186,291** ... B6
Newton, **62,001** ... D5, K4
Oconee, **26,225** ... D4
Oglethorpe, **12,635** ... E4
Paulding, **81,678** ... B4
Peach, **23,668** ... D6
Pickens, **22,983** ... B3
Pierce, **15,636** ... G9
Pike, **13,688** ... C5
Polk, **38,127** ... A3
Pulaski, **9,588** ... D7
Putnam, **18,812** ... E5
Quitman, **2,598** ... A8
Rabun, **15,050** ... D2
Randolph, **7,791** ... B8
Richmond, **199,775** ... G5
Rockdale, **70,111** ... C4, K3
Schley, **3,766** ... C7
Screven, **15,374** ... H6
Seminole, **9,369** ... B1
Spalding, **58,417** ... C5
Stephens, **25,435** ... E3
Stewart, **5,252** ... B7
Sumter, **33,200** ... C7
Talbot, **6,498** ... B6
Taliaferro, **2,077** ... F4
Tattnall, **22,305** ... G8
Taylor, **8,815** ... C6
Telfair, **11,794** ... E8
Terrell, **10,970** ... B8
Thomas, **42,737** ... C1
Tift, **38,407** ... D8
Toombs, **26,067** ... G7
Towns, **9,319** ... D2
Treutlen, **6,854** ... F7
Troup, **58,779** ... A6
Turner, **9,504** ... D8
Twiggs, **10,590** ... D6
Union, **17,289** ... C2
Upson, **27,597** ... C6
Walker, **61,053** ... A2
Walton, **60,687** ... D4
Ware, **35,483** ... F9
Warren, **6,336** ... F5
Washington, **21,176** ... F6
Wayne, **26,565** ... G8
Webster, **2,390** ... B7
Wheeler, **6,179** ... F7
White, **19,944** ... D2
Whitfield, **83,525** ... A2
Wilcox, **8,577** ... D7
Wilkes, **10,687** ... F4
Wilkinson, **10,220** ... E6
Worth, **21,967** ... D8

Cities and Towns

Abbeville, **2,298** ... E8
Acree, *200* ... C8
Acworth, **13,422** ... B3, G1
Adairsville, **2,542** ... B3
Adel, **5,307** ... E9
Adgateville ... D5
Adrian, **579** ... F6
Ailey, **394** ... F7
Alamo, **1,943** ... F7
Alapaha, **682** ... E9
Albany, **76,939** ... C8
Aldora, **98** ... C5
Alexander, *125* ... H5
Allenhurst, **788** ... D7
Allentown, **287** ... E6
Alma, **3,236** ... G8
Almon, *1,000* ... D4
Alpharetta, **34,854** ... C3, J1
Alston, **159** ... G7
Alto, **876** ... D3
Alvaton, *125* ... B5
Ambrose, **320** ... F8
Americus, **17,013** ... C7
Andersonville, **331** ... C7
Apalachee, *100* ... E4
Appling, *225* ... G4
Arabi, **456** ... D8
Aragon, **1,039** ... A3
Arcade, **1,643** ... D3
Argyle, **151** ... F9
Arlington, **1,602** ... B9
Arnoldsville, **312** ... E4
Ashburn, **4,419** ... D8
Athens, **101,489** ... E4
Atkinson, *100* ... H9
Atlanta, **416,474** ... C4, H3
Attapulgus, **492** ... C1
Auburn, **6,904** ... D3
Augusta, **199,775** ... H5
Austell, **5,359** ... B4, G2
Avalon, **278** ... E2
Avera, **217** ... F5
Avondale Estates, **2,609** ... J3
Axson, *90* ... F9
Baconton, **804** ... C9
Bainbridge, **11,722** ... B1
Baldwin, **2,425** ... D3
Ball Ground, **730** ... C3
Barnesville, **5,972** ... C5
Barney, *300* ... D9
Barretts, *550* ... E9
Bartow, **223** ... G6
Barwick, **444** ... D1
Baxley, **4,150** ... G8
Bellville, **130** ... H7
Belvedere (part of Belvedere Park pop. **18,945**), **11,100** ... C4, J3
Bemiss, *1,500* ... E1
Benevolence, *40* ... B8
Berkeley Lake, **1,695** ... C4, J2
Berlin, **595** ... D9
Bethlehem, **716** ... D4
Between, **148** ... D4
Bibb City, **510** ... B6
Bishop, **146** ... E4
Blackshear, **3,283** ... G9
Blacksville, **4** ... C5
Blackwells, *2,200* ... B3, H1
Blairsville, **659** ... D2
Blakely, **5,696** ... B9
Blitchton, *200* ... J7
Bloomingdale, **2,665** ... J7
Blue Ridge, **1,210** ... C2
Bluffton, **118** ... B8
Blythe, **718** ... G5
Bogart, **1,049** ... D4
Bolingbroke, *250* ... D6
Bonaire, *800* ... D6
Bonanza, **2,904** ... C5
Boston, **1,417** ... D1
Bostwick, **322** ... D4
Bowdon, **1,959** ... A4
Bowdon Junction, *600* ... A4
Bowersville, **334** ... E3
Bowman, **898** ... E3
Boykin, *125* ... B9
Braselton, **1,206** ... D3
Braswell, **80** ... B4
Bremen, **4,579** ... A4
Brewton, *150* ... F6
Bridgeboro, *200* ... D9
Brinson, **225** ... B1
Broadhurst ... H9
Bronwood, **513** ... C8
Brookfield, *375* ... E9
Brooklet, **1,113** ... H7
Brooklyn ... B7
Brooks, **553** ... C5
Broxton, **1,428** ... F8
Brunswick, **15,600** ... J9
Brynwood ... G5
Buchanan, **941** ... A4
Buckhead, **205** ... E4
Buena Vista, **1,664** ... B7
Buford, **10,668** ... C3, K1
Bullard, *80* ... E6
Butler, **1,907** ... C6
Byromville, **415** ... D7
Byron, **2,887** ... D6
Cadley ... F4
Cadwell, **329** ... E7
Cairo, **9,239** ... C1
Calhoun, **10,667** ... B2
Calvary, *300* ... C1
Camak, **165** ... F5
Camilla, **5,669** ... C9
Campton, *400* ... D4
Canon, **755** ... E3
Canton, **7,709** ... B3
Carl, **205** ... D3
Carlton, **233** ... E3
Carnegie, *60* ... B8
Carnesville, **541** ... E3
Carrollton, **19,843** ... A4
Cartersville, **15,925** ... B3
Cary, *125* ... E6
Cass, *1,625* ... B3
Cataula, *300* ... B6
Cave Spring, **975** ... A3
Cecil, **265** ... E9
Cedar Creek Park ... E4
Cedartown, **9,470** ... A3
Center, *325* ... E3
Centerpost, *250* ... A2
Centerville, **4,278** ... D6
Centralhatchee, **383** ... A5
Chamblee, **9,552** ... C4, J2
Charing ... C7
Chatsworth, **3,531** ... B2
Chauncey, **295** ... E7
Cherrylog, *80* ... C2
Chester, **305** ... E7
Chestnut Mountain, *650* ... D3
Chickamauga, **2,245** ... A2
China Hill ... E8
Chula, *175* ... D8
Cisco, *450* ... B2
Clarkesville, **1,248** ... D2
Clarkston, **7,231** ... C4, J2
Claxton, **2,276** ... H7
Clayton, **2,019** ... E2
Clem, *275* ... A4
Clermont, **419** ... D3
Cleveland, **1,907** ... D2
Climax, **297** ... C1
Clyattville, *450* ... E1
Clyo, *300* ... J7
Coal Mountain, *700* ... C3
Cobbtown, **311** ... G7
Cochran, **4,455** ... E7
Cogdell, *40* ... F9
Cohutta, **582** ... B2
Colbert, **488** ... E3
Coleman, **149** ... B8
College Park, **20,382** ... C4, H3
Collins, **528** ... G7
Colquitt, **1,939** ... B9
Columbus, **186,291** ... B7
Comer, **1,052** ... E3
Commerce, **5,292** ... E3
Concord, **336** ... B5
Conley, **6,188** ... J3
Conyers, **10,689** ... C4, K3
Coolidge, **552** ... D9
Cooper Heights, *175* ... A2
Coosa ... A3
Cordele, **11,608** ... D8
Corinth, **213** ... B5
Cornelia, **3,674** ... D2
Cotton, *80* ... C9
Council ... F1
Country Club Estates, **7,594** J9
Coverdale, *50* ... D8
Covington, **11,547** ... D4
Cox, *60* ... H9
Crawford, **807** ... A3
Crawfordville, **572** ... F4
Culloden, **223** ... C6
Culverton, *80* ... F5
Cumming, **4,220** ... C3
Cusseta, **1,196** ... B7
Cuthbert, **3,731** ... B8
Dacula, **3,848** ... D4
Dahlonega, **3,638** ... D2
Daisy, **126** ... H7
Dakota, *80* ... D8
Dallas, **5,056** ... B4
Dalton, **27,912** ... B2
Damascus, **277** ... B9
Dames Ferry, *70* ... D5
Danielsville, **457** ... E3
Danville, **373** ... E6
Darien, **1,719** ... J9
Dasher, **834** ... E1
Davisboro, **1,544** ... F6
Dawson, **5,058** ... C8
Dawsonville, **619** ... C3
Dearing, **441** ... G5
Decatur, **18,147** ... C4, J3
Deenwood, **1,836** ... G9
Deepstep, **132** ... F5
Demorest, **1,465** ... D2
Denmark, *150* ... H7
Denton, **269** ... F8
De Soto, **214** ... C8
Devereux, *100* ... E5
Dewy Rose, *225* ... F3
Dexter, **509** ... E7
Dillard, **198** ... E2
Dixie, *125* ... D1
Dixie Union, *125* ... G9
Dock Junction, **6,951** ... H9
Doctortown ... H8
Doerun, **828** ... D9
Doles, *100* ... D8
Donalsonville, **2,796** ... B9
Donovan, *50* ... F6
Dooling, **163** ... D7
Doraville, **9,862** ... C4, J2
Douglas, **10,639** ... F8
Douglasville, **20,065** ... B4
Doyle, *40* ... C7
Draketown, *300* ... A4
Druid Hills, **12,741** ... J3
Dublin, **15,857** ... F6
Dudley, **447** ... E6
Duluth, **22,122** ... C3, J2
Dunwoody, **32,808** ... C4, J2
Dupont, **139** ... F1
Durand, *175* ... B6
East Dublin, **2,484** ... F6
East Ellijay, **707** ... C2
East Griffin, **1,635** ... C5
Eastman, **5,440** ... E7
East Newnan, **1,305** ... B5
East Point, **39,595** ... C4, H3
Eatonton, **6,764** ... E5
Edge Hill, **30** ... F5
Edison, **1,340** ... B8
Egypt, *70* ... J7
Elberton, **4,743** ... F3
Eldorendo, *100* ... B9
Elko, *175* ... D7
Ellabell, *425* ... J7
Ellaville, **1,609** ... C7
Ellenton, **336** ... D9
Ellijay, **1,584** ... C2
Elliotts Bluff, *475* ... H1
Elmodel ... C9
Emerson, **1,092** ... B3
Emmalane, *125* ... G6
Empire, *450* ... E7
Enigma, **869** ... E9
Ephesus, **388** ... A5
Esom Hill, *125* ... A4
Eton, **319** ... B2
Euharlee, **3,208** ... B3
Eulonia, *70* ... J8
Evans, **17,727** ... G4
Evansville, *50* ... A5
Everett, *70* ... H9
Experiment, **3,233** ... C5
Faceville, *70* ... B1
Fairburn, **5,464** ... B4, H3
Fairmount, **745** ... B3
Fair Oaks, **8,443** ... B4, H2
Fairview, **6,601** ... A2
Fargo, **380** ... F1
Farmington, *250* ... E4
Fayetteville, **11,148** ... C5
Felton, *275* ... A4
Fitzgerald, **8,758** ... E8
Flemington, **369** ... J8
Flippen, *900* ... C5, J4
Flovilla, **652** ... D5
Flowery Branch, **1,806** ... D3
Folkston, **2,178** ... G1
Forest Park, **21,447** ... C4, H3
Forsyth, **3,776** ... D5
Fort Gaines, **1,110** ... A8
Fort Oglethorpe, **6,940** ... A2
Fortsonia, *125* ... F3
Fort Valley, **8,005** ... D6
Fowlstown, *275* ... B1
Franklin, **902** ... A5
Franklin Springs, **762** ... E3
Free Home, *550* ... C3
Friendship ... C7
Funston, **426** ... D9
Gainesville, **25,578** ... D3
Gainesville Mills ... D3
Garden City, **11,289** ... J7
Gardi, *150* ... H8
Garfield, **152** ... G6
Gay, **149** ... B5
Geneva, **114** ... B6
Georgetown, **973** ... A8
Gibson, **694** ... F5
Gillsville, **195** ... D3
Girard, **227** ... H5
Glennville, **3,641** ... H8
Glenwood, **884** ... F7
Godfrey, *100* ... D5
Good Hope, **210** ... D4
Gordon, **2,152** ... E6
Gordy, *125* ... D9
Gough, *225* ... G5
Gracewood, *550* ... G5
Graham, **312** ... G8
Grange ... F5
Grantville, **1,309** ... B5
Gray, **1,811** ... D5
Grayson, **765** ... D4
Greensboro, **3,238** ... E4
Greenville, **946** ... B5
Gresham Park, **9,215** ... C4, J3
Gresston, *275* ... E7
Griffin, **23,451** ... C5
Grovania ... D7
Groveland, *100* ... H7
Grovetown, **6,089** ... G5
Gum Branch, **273** ... H8
Gumlog, **2,025** ... E3
Guyton, **917** ... J7
Haddock, *475* ... E5
Hagan, **898** ... H7
Hahira, **1,626** ... E1
Hamilton, **307** ... B6
Hampton, **3,857** ... C5
Hapeville, **6,180** ... C4, H3
Haralson, **144** ... B5
Hardwick, **5,135** ... E5
Harlem, **1,814** ... G5
Harrison, **509** ... F6
Hartwell, **4,188** ... F3
Hatley, *60* ... D8
Hawkinsville, **3,280** ... E7
Hayneville, *400* ... D7
Hazlehurst, **3,787** ... F8
Helen, **430** ... D2
Helena, **2,307** ... F7
Henderson, *125* ... D7
Hephzibah, **3,880** ... G5
Herod, *40* ... C8
Hiawassee, **808** ... D2
Hickox, *200* ... H9
Higgston, **316** ... G7
Hillsboro, *50* ... D5
Hilltonia, **421** ... H6
Hinesville, **30,392** ... H8
Hiram, **1,361** ... B4
Hoboken, **463** ... G9
Hogansville, **2,774** ... B5
Holland, *90* ... A3
Holly Springs, **3,195** ... C3
Hollywood, *400* ... E2
Homeland, **765** ... C1
Homer, **950** ... D3
Homerville, **2,803** ... F9
Hopeful, *40* ... C9
Horns, *200* ... C6
Hortense, *225* ... H9
Hoschton, **1,070** ... D3
Howard, *60* ... C6
Howell, *60* ... E1
Huber, *275* ... D6
Hull, **160** ... E3
Ideal, **518** ... C7
Ila, **328** ... E3
Indian Springs, **1,982** ... A2
Inman, *650* ... C5
Iron City, **321** ... B9
Irondale, **7,727** ... C5, H4
Irwinton, **587** ... E6
Irwinville, *125* ... E8
Isle of Hope, **2,605** ... J8
Ivey, **1,100** ... E6
Jackson, **3,934** ... D5
Jacksonville, **118** ... F8
Jakin, **157** ... B9
James, *150* ... E6
Jasper, **2,167** ... C3
Jefferson, **3,825** ... E3
Jeffersonville, **1,209** ... E6
Jenkinsburg, **203** ... C5
Jersey, **163** ... D4
Jesup, **9,279** ... H8
Jonesboro, **3,829** ... C4, J4
Juliette, *200* ... D5
Junction City, **179** ... C6
Juniper ... B6
Juno, *100* ... C3
Kathleen, *650* ... D7
Keithsburg, *300* ... C3
Keller, *80* ... J8
Kennesaw, **21,675** ... B3, G2
Keysville, **180** ... G5
Kingsland, **10,506** ... H1
Kingston, **659** ... B3
Kirkland ... F9
Kite, **241** ... F6
Knoxville, *60* ... D6
La Fayette, **6,702** ... A2
LaGrange, **25,998** ... A5
Lake City, **2,886** ... C4, J3
Lakeland, **2,730** ... E9
Lakemont, *325* ... E2
Lake Park, **549** ... E1
Lakeview, **4,820** ... A2
Lakeview Estates, **2,637** ... K3
Lavonia, **1,827** ... E3
Lawrenceville, **22,397** ... D4, K2
Leary, **666** ... C9
Leesburg, **2,633** ... C8
Lenox, **889** ... E9
Leslie, **455** ... C8
Lexington, **239** ... E4
Lilburn, **11,307** ... C4, J2
Lilly, **221** ... D7
Lincolnton, **1,595** ... G4
Lindale, **4,088** ... A3
Linton, *150* ... E5
Lithia Springs, **2,072** ... B4, G2
Lithonia, **2,187** ... C4, K3
Lizella, *600* ... D6
Locust Grove, **2,322** ... C5
Loganville, **5,435** ... D4
Lone Oak, **104** ... B5
Lookout Mountain, **1,617** ... A2
Louisville, **2,712** ... G5
Lovejoy, **2,495** ... C5
Lovett, *70* ... F6
Lucile ... B9
Ludowici, **1,440** ... H8
Ludville, *200* ... B3
Luella, *125* ... C5
Lula, **1,438** ... D3
Lumber City, **1,247** ... F8
Lumpkin, **1,369** ... B7
Luthersville, **783** ... B5
Lyerly, **488** ... A3
Lyons, **4,169** ... G7
Mableton, **29,733** ... B4, H2
Macon, **97,255** ... D6
Madison, **3,636** ... E4
Madras, *350* ... B5
Manassas, **100** ... G7
Manchester, **3,988** ... B6
Manor, *200* ... F9
Mansfield, **392** ... D4
Marietta, **58,748** ... B4, H2
Marshallville, **1,335** ... D7
Martin, **311** ... E3
Martinez, **27,749** ... G4
Mauk, *60* ... C6
Maxeys, **210** ... E4
Mayday ... F1
Mayfield, *150* ... F5
Maysville, **1,247** ... D3
McBean, *125* ... H5
McCaysville, **1,071** ... C2
McDonough, **8,493** ... C5, J4
McIntyre, **718** ... E6
McKinnon, *70* ... H9
McRae, **2,682** ... F7
Meansville, **192** ... C5
Meigs, **1,090** ... C9
Mendes, *125* ... H8
Menlo, **485** ... A3
Meridian, *300* ... J9
Merrillville, *175* ... D1
Mershon, *90* ... G9
Metcalf, *150* ... D1
Metter, **3,879** ... G7
Midville, **457** ... G6
Midway, **1,100** ... J8
Milan, **1,012** ... E8
Milford, *50* ... B9
Milledgeville, **18,757** ... E5
Millen, **3,492** ... H6
Millhaven, *40* ... H6
Millwood, *90* ... F9
Milner, **522** ... C5
Mineral Bluff, **150** ... C2
Minter, *80* ... F7
Mitchell, **173** ... F5
Modoc ... G6
Molena, **475** ... C6
Moniac, *40* ... G1
Monroe, **11,407** ... D4
Montezuma, **3,999** ... C7
Montgomery, **4,134** ... J8
Monticello, **2,428** ... D5
Montrose, **154** ... E6
Moreland, **393** ... B5
Morgan, **1,464** ... B8
Morganton, **299** ... C2
Morris ... B8
Morrow, **4,882** ... C4, J3
Morven, **634** ... D1
Moultrie, **14,387** ... D9
Mountain City, **829** ... E2
Mountain Park (Fulton Co.), **506** ... C3, H1
Mountain Park (Gwinnett Co.), **11,753** ... J2
Mountain View (part of Chattanooga Valley, **4,065**) ... A2
Mount Airy, **604** ... E2
Mount Berry, *225* ... A3
Mount Vernon, **2,082** ... F7
Mountville ... B5
Mount Zion, **1,275** ... A4
Munnerlyn ... H6
Murphy, *70* ... D9
Musella, *125* ... C6
Nahunta, **930** ... H9
Nashville, **4,697** ... E9
Naylor, **125** ... E1
Needmore ... F1
Nelson, **626** ... C3
Newborn, **520** ... D4
New Branch, *50* ... G7
New Hope, *750* ... B4
Newington, **322** ... H6
Newnan, **16,242** ... B5
Newton, **851** ... C9
Nicholls, **1,008** ... F8
Nicholson, **1,247** ... E3
Nicklesville ... E6
Norcross, **8,410** ... C4, J2
Norman Park, **849** ... D9
Normantown, *225* ... G7
Norristown, *100* ... F7
North Atlanta, **38,579** ... J2
North Decatur, **15,270** ... J2
North Druid Hills, **18,852** ... C4, J2
North High Shoals, **439** ... E4
Norwood, **299** ... F5
Nunez, **131** ... G7
Oakfield, *125* ... D8
Oakman ... B2
Oak Park, **366** ... G7
Oakwood, **2,689** ... D3
Ochlocknee, **605** ... C1
Ocilla, **3,270** ... E8
Oconee, **280** ... F6
Odum, **414** ... G8
Offerman, **403** ... G9
Oglethorpe, **1,200** ... C7
Oliver, **253** ... H6
Omaha, **125** ... A7
Omega, **1,340** ... D9
Orchard Hill, **230** ... C5
Osierfield ... E8
Oxford, **1,892** ... D4
Palmetto, **3,400** ... B4, G4
Panthersville, **11,791** ... J3
Parrott, **156** ... B8
Patterson, **627** ... G9
Pavo, **711** ... D1
Payne, **178** ... D6
Peach Orchard ... G5
Peachtree City, **31,580** ... B5
Pearson, **1,805** ... F9
Pelham, **4,126** ... C9
Pembroke, **2,379** ... H7
Pendergrass, **431** ... D3
Perkins, *80* ... H6
Perry, **9,602** ... D7
Phillipsburg, **887** ... D9
Philomath, *50* ... E4
Piedmont ... C5
Pinehurst, **307** ... D7
Pine Lake, **621** ... J3
Pine Log, *250* ... B3
Pine Mountain, **1,141** ... B6
Pine Mountain Valley, *475* ... B6
Pineview, **532** ... E7
Pitts, **308** ... D8
Plains, **637** ... C7
Plainville, **257** ... A3
Pooler, **6,239** ... J7
Portal, **597** ... H6
Porterdale, **1,281** ... D4
Port Wentworth, **3,276** ... J7
Potterville, *175* ... C6
Poulan, **946** ... D8
Powder Springs, **12,481** ... B4, G2
Powelton, **20** ... F5
Preston, **453** ... B7
Pretoria ... C8
Pridgen, *125* ... F8
Primrose, *175* ... B5
Pulaski, **261** ... H7
Putney, **2,998** ... C9
Queensland, *200* ... E8
Quitman, **4,638** ... D1
Race Pond ... G1
Raines, *50* ... D8
Raleigh, *125* ... B6
Ramhurst, *400* ... B2
Ranger, **85** ... B3
Raoul, **1,816** ... D3
Ray City, **746** ... E9
Rayle, **139** ... F4
Raymond, *300* ... B5
Rebecca, **246** ... E8
Redan, **33,841** ... J3
Reed Creek, **2,148** ... F3
Register, **164** ... H7
Reidsville, **2,235** ... G7
Remerton, **847** ... E1
Renfroe ... B7
Rentz, **304** ... F7
Resaca, **815** ... B2
Rest Haven, **151** ... D3
Reynolds, **1,036** ... C6
Reynoldsville, *175* ... B1
Rhine, **422** ... E8
Riceboro, **736** ... J8
Richland, **1,794** ... B7
Richmond Hill, **6,959** ... J8
Riddleville, **124** ... F6
Rincon, **4,376** ... J7
Ringgold, **2,422** ... A2
Rising Fawn, *200* ... A2
Riverdale, **12,478** ... C4, H3
Riverside, **57** ... D9
Roberta, **808** ... C6
Rochelle, **1,415** ... E8
Rockmart, **3,870** ... A3
Rock Spring, *550* ... A2
Rocky Ford, **186** ... H6
Rome, **34,980** ... A3
Roopville, **177** ... A5
Rosier ... G6
Rossville, **3,511** ... A2
Roswell, **79,334** ... C3, J2
Round Oak ... D5
Royston, **2,493** ... E3
Rupert ... C7
Russell ... D4
Rutledge, **707** ... D4
St. Clair ... G5
St. George, *275* ... G1
St. Marys, **13,761** ... H1

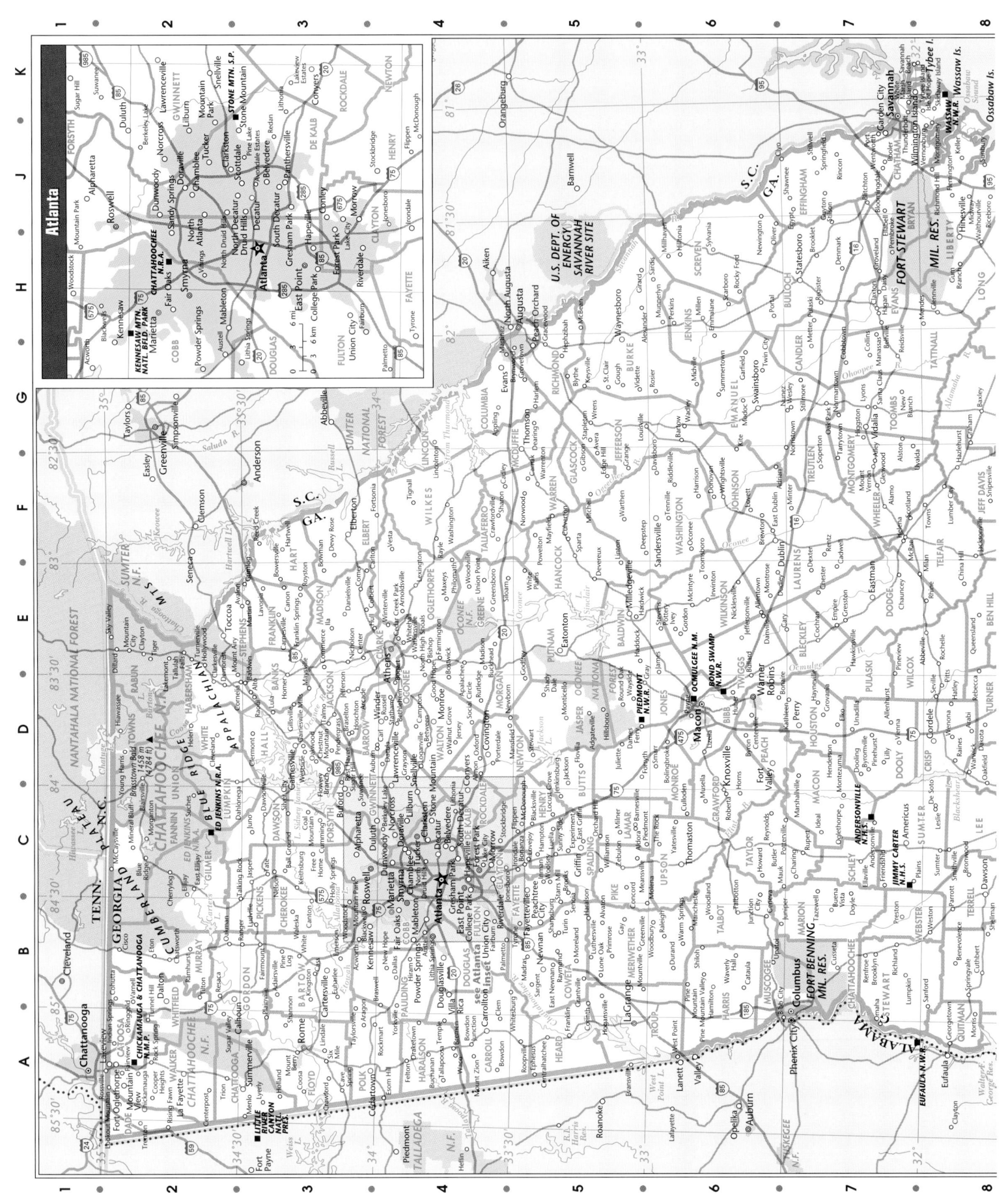

Atlanta

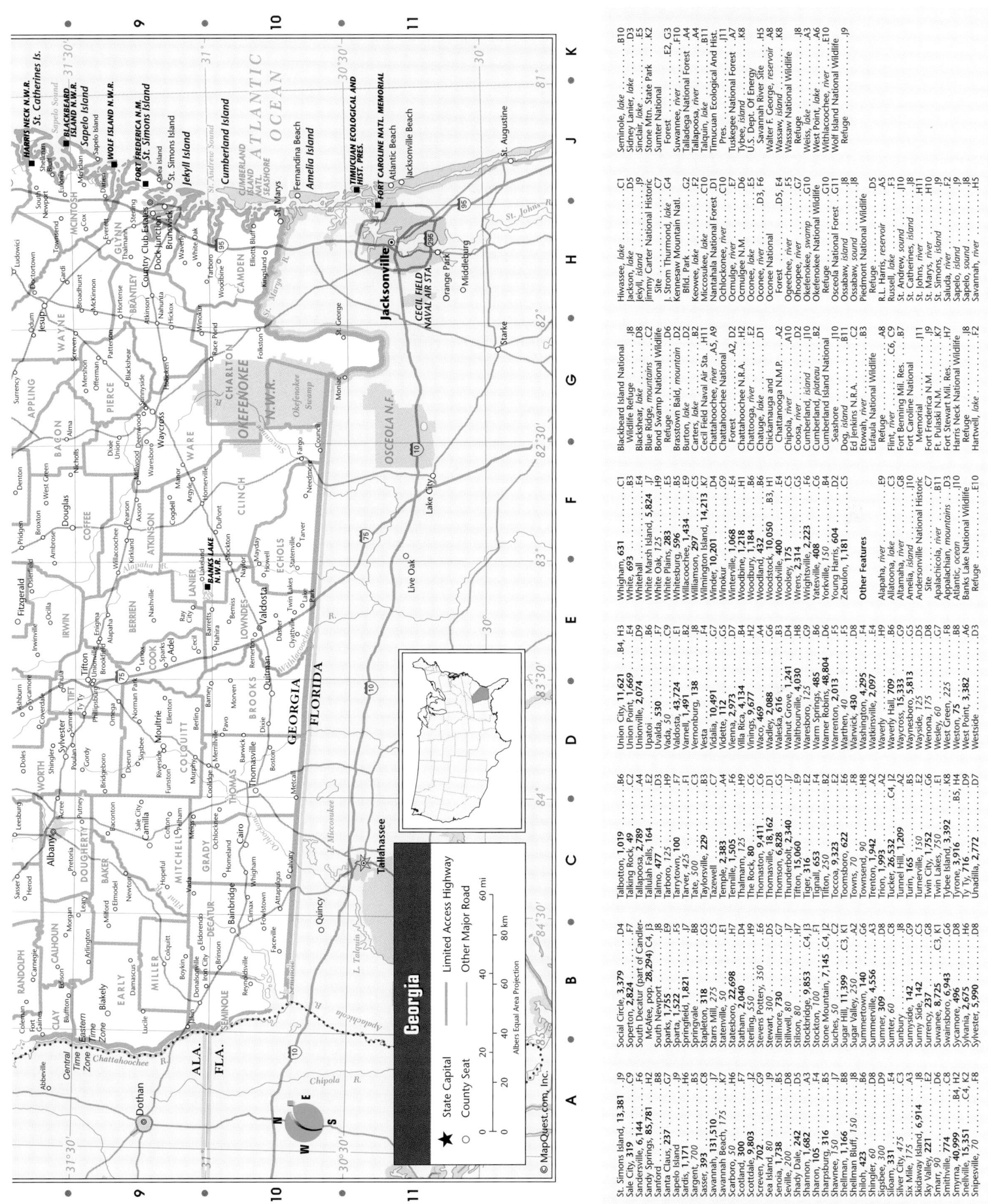

St. Simons Island, 13,381 .....J9
Sale City, 319 .....C9
Sandersville, 6,144 .....F6
Sandy Springs, 85,781 .....H2
Sanford B8
Santa Claus, 237 .....G7
Sapelo Island J9
Sardis, 1,171 .....H6
Sargent, 700 .....C8
Sasser, 393 .....C8
Savannah, 131,510 .....J7
Savannah Beach, 175 .....K7
Scarboro, 50 .....H6
Scotland, 300 .....F7
Scottdale, 9,803 .....G9
Screven, 702 .....G7
Sea Island, 80 .....B5
Seville, 1,738 .....D8
Seville, 200 .....D8
Shady Dale, 242 .....A3
Shannon, 1,682 .....A3
Sharon, 105 .....F4
Sharpsburg, 316 .....B5
Shawnee, 150 .....J7
Shellman, 1,166 .....B8
Shellman Bluff, 150 .....J8
Shiloh, 423 .....D8
Shingler, 60 .....D8
Sigsbee, 300 .....D9
Siloam, 331 .....E4
Silver City, 475 .....A3
Six Mile, 175 .....J8
Skidaway Island, 6,914 .....J8
Sky Valley, 221 .....E2
Smarr, 90 .....D6
Smithville, 774 .....C8
Smyrna, 40,999 .....B4, H2
Snellville, 15,351 .....C4, K2
Snipesville, 70 .....F8

Social Circle, 3,379 .....D4
Soperton, 2,824 .....F6
South Decatur (part of Candler-McAfee, pop. 28,294) C4, J3
South Newport J8
Sparks, 1,755 .....E9
Springfield, 1,821 .....H6
Springvale B8
Stapleton, 318 .....G5
Starrs Mill, 275 .....C3
Statenville, 50 .....E10
Statesboro, 22,698 .....H6
Statham, 2,040 .....D4
Sterling, 550 .....J8
Stevens Pottery, 350 .....E6
Stewart, 300 .....B5
Stillmore, 730 .....G7
Stillwell, 80 .....D8
Stilson, 80 .....C4, J3
Stockbridge, 9,853 .....C4, J3
Stockton, 100 .....E9
Stone Mountain, 7,145 .....C4, J2
Suches, 50 .....C2
Sugar Hill, 11,399 .....C3, K1
Sugar Valley, 250 .....A2
Summertown, 140 .....H6
Summerville, 4,556 .....A2
Sumner, 309 .....D8
Sumter, 60 .....C8
Sunbury C8
Sunnyside, 142 .....C9
Sunny Side, 142 .....G5
Surrency, 237 .....G8
Suwanee, 8,725 .....C3, K1
Swainsboro, 6,943 .....G6
Sycamore, 496 .....D8
Sylvania, 2,675 .....H6
Sylvester, 5,990 .....D8

Talbotton, 1,019 .....D4
Talking Rock, 49 .....C2
Tallapoosa, 2,789 .....A4
Tallulah Falls, 164 .....D2
Talmo, 477 .....D3
Tarboro, 125 .....H9
Tarrytown, 100 .....F7
Tarver, 425 .....E10
Tate, 500 .....C2
Taylorsville, 229 .....B3
Tazewell C7
Temple, 2,383 .....A4
Tennille, 1,505 .....F6
Thalmann, 125 .....H9
The Rock, 80 .....D4
Thomaston, 9,411 .....C6
Thomasville, 18,162 .....D1
Thomson, 6,828 .....F5
Thunderbolt, 2,340 .....J7
Tiger, 316 .....E2
Tignall, 653 .....F4
Tifton, 250 .....E9
Toccoa, 9,323 .....E2
Toomsboro, 622 .....F6
Towns, 70 .....F8
Townsend, 90 .....H8
Trenton, 1,942 .....A2
Trion, 1,993 .....A3
Tucker, 26,532 .....C4, J2
Tunnel Hill, 1,209 .....A2
Turin, 165 .....B5
Turnerville, 150 .....D2
Twin City, 1,752 .....G6
Twin Lakes, 150 .....E1
Tybee Island, 3,392 .....C3, K1
Tyrone, 3,916 .....G6
Ty Ty, 716 .....D8
Unadilla, 2,772 .....D8

Union City, 11,621 .....B6
Union Point, 1,669 .....E4
Unionville, 2,074 .....D9
Upatoi B6
Uvalda, 530 .....F7
Vada, 50 .....C9
Valdosta, 43,724 .....E1
Varnell, 1,491 .....B2
Vernonburg, 138 .....J8
Vesta F4
Vidalia, 10,491 .....G7
Vidette, 112 .....G5
Vienna, 2,973 .....D7
Villa Rica, 9,177 .....B4
Vinings, 9,677 .....H2
Waco, 469 .....A4
Wadley, 2,088 .....G6
Walnut Grove, 1,241 .....C4
Walthourville, 4,030 .....H8
Waresboro, 125 .....G9
Warm Springs, 485 .....C6
Warner Robins, 48,804 .....D6
Warrenton, 2,013 .....F5
Warthen, 40 .....F5
Warwick, 430 .....D8
Washington, 4,295 .....F4
Watkinsville, 2,097 .....A2
Waverly H9
Waverly Hall, 709 .....B6
Waycross, 15,333 .....G9
Waynesboro, 5,813 .....G5
Wayside, 125 .....D5
Wenona, 175 .....D8
Wesley, 60 .....G6
West Green, 225 .....F8
Weston, 75 .....B8
West Point, 3,382 .....A6
Westside D3

Whigham, 631 .....C1
White, 693 .....B3
Whitehall E4
White Marsh Island, 5,824 .....J7
White Oak, 125 .....H9
White Plains, 283 .....E5
Whitesburg, 596 .....B5
Willacoochee, 1,434 .....E9
Williamson, 297 .....C5
Wilmington Island, 14,213 .....K7
Winder, 10,201 .....C4
Winokur G9
Winterville, 1,068 .....E4
Woodbine, 1,218 .....H9
Woodbury, 1,184 .....C6
Woodland, 432 .....C6
Woodstock, 10,050 .....B3, H1
Woodville, 400 .....E4
Woolsey, 175 .....C5
Wrens, 2,314 .....F5
Wrightsville, 2,223 .....F6
Yatesville, 408 .....D6
Yorkville, 150 .....B4
Young Harris, 604 .....D2
Zebulon, 1,181 .....C5

Seminole, lake B10
Sidney Lanier, lake D3
Sinclair, lake E5
Stone Mtn. State Park K2
Sumter National
Forest E2, G3
Suwannee, river A4
Talladega National Forest A4
Tallapoosa, river A4
Talquin, lake B11
Timucuan Ecological And Hist.
Pres. J11
Tuskegee National Forest A7
Tybee, island K8
U.S. Dept. Of Energy
Savannah River Site H5
Walter F. George, reservoir A8
Wassaw, island K8
Wassaw National Wildlife
Refuge J8
Weiss, lake A3
West Point, lake A6
Withlacoochee, river E10
Wolf Island National Wildlife
Refuge J9

Hiwassee, lake C1
Jackson, lake D5
Jekyll, island J9
Jimmy Carter National Historic
Site G4
J. Strom Thurmond, lake G2
Kennesaw Mountain Natl.
Bfld. Park G2
Keowee, lake F2
Miccosukee, lake C10
Nantahala National Forest D1
Ochlockonee, river C10
Ocmulgee, river D6
Ocmulgee N.M. E5
Oconee, lake D1
Oconee, river D5, E4
Oconee National
Forest D5, E4
Ogeechee, river G7
Ohoopee, river A10
Okefenokee, swamp G10
Okefenokee National Wildlife
Refuge G10
Osceola National Forest G11
Ossabaw, island J8
Ossabaw, sound J8

Blackbeard Island National
Wildlife Refuge C1
Blackshear, lake B3
Blue Ridge, mountains C2
Bond Swamp National Wildlife
Refuge D6
Brasstown Bald, mountain D2
Burton, lake D2
Carters, lake B2
Cecil Field Naval Air Sta. K7
Chattahoochee N.M. G9
Chattahoochee National
Forest A2, D2
Chattahoochee N.R.A. H2
Chattooga, river E2
Chatuge, lake D1
Chickamauga and
Chattanooga N.M.P. A2
Chipola, river D2
Cumberland, island J10
Cumberland Island National
Seashore J10
Dog, island B11
Ed Jenkins N.R.A. C2
Etowah, river B3

Eufaula National Wildlife
Refuge E9
Flint, river C3
Fort Benning Mil. Res. C6, C9
Fort Caroline National
Memorial J10
Andersonville National Historic
Site C7
Appalachicola, river B11
Appalachin, mountains D3
Atlantic, ocean K8
Banks Lake National Wildlife
Refuge E10

Alapaha, river E9
Allatoona, lake C3
Amelia, island J10
Ft. Pulaski N.M. K7
Fort Stewart Mil. Res. H7
Harris Neck National Wildlife
Refuge J8
Hartwell, lake F2

Other Features

St. Andrew, sound J11
St. Catherines, island J8
St. Johns, river H10
St. Marys, river H11
St. Simons, island J9
Saluda, river F2
Sapelo, island J9
Sapelo, sound J8
Savannah, river H5

Blackbeard Island National
R.L. Harris, reservoir A5
Russell, lake F3

Georgia

★ State Capital
○ County Seat

Limited Access Highway
Other Major Road

0   20   40   60 mi
0   20   40   60   80 km

Albers Equal Area Projection

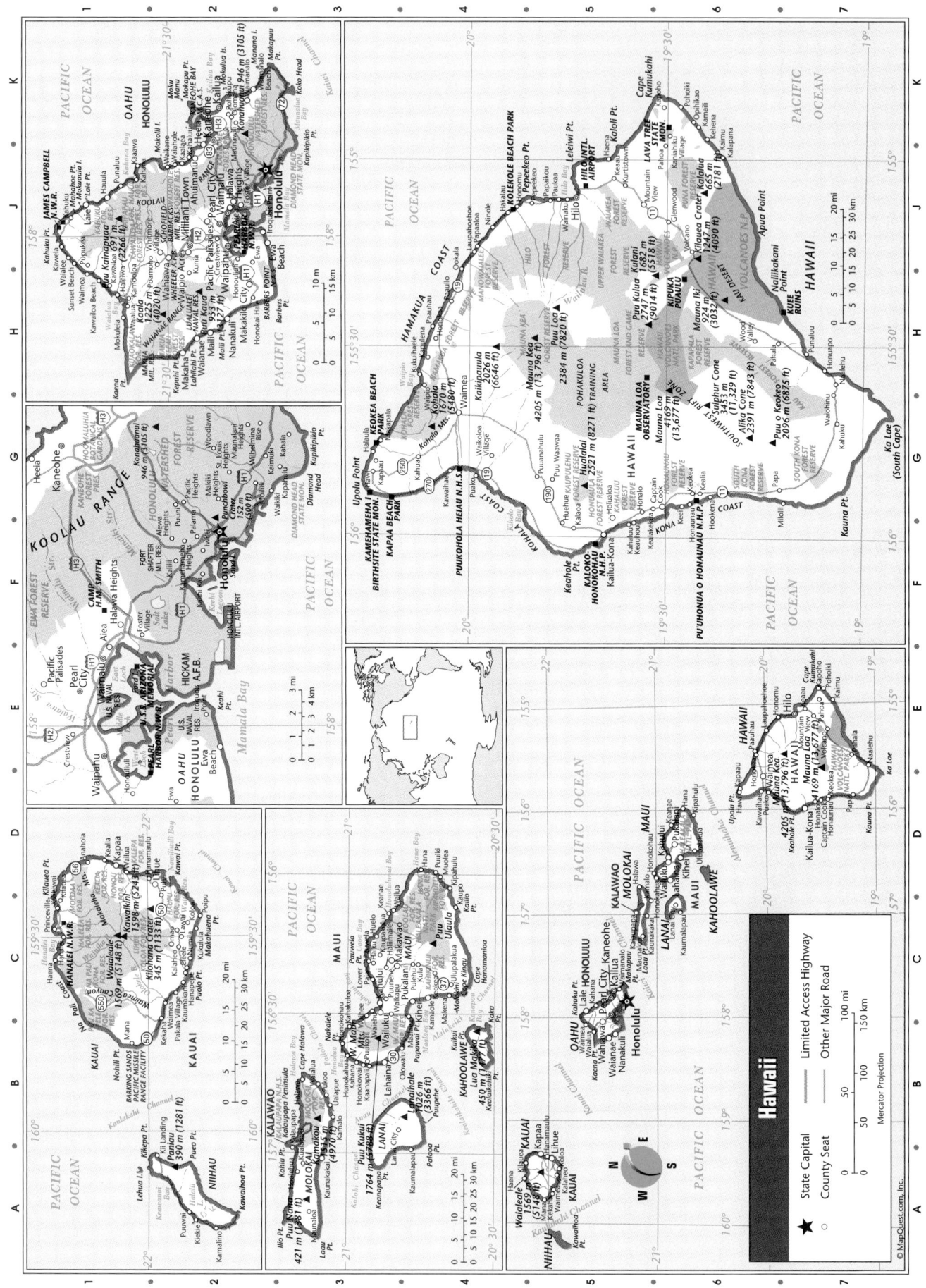

Hawaii

State Capital
County Seat
Limited Access Highway
Other Major Road

Mercator Projection

© MapQuest.com, Inc.

Hawaii

Capital: Honolulu
Land Area: 6,423 sq. mi.
16,637 sq. km.
Population: 1,211,537 (2000 Census)
Largest City: Honolulu, 371,657
Highest Point: Mauna Kea
13,796 ft.
4,205 m.
Admitted to Union: August 21, 1959
Nickname: Aloha State
State Flower: Yellow Hibiscus
State Bird: Hawaiian Goose

Hawaii Map Index

Counties

Hawaii, 148,677.....E7, G5
Honolulu, 876,156 ..C5, D2, K1
Kalawao, 147.....A5, B2
Kauai, 58,463.....C3, D6
Maui, 128,094.....

Cities and Towns

Note: There are no incorporated cities or towns in Hawaii. Populations are shown only for places designated by the U.S. Census Bureau for the 2000 census.

Ahuimanu, 8,506.....J2
Aiea, 9,019.....F1, J2
Alewa Heights.....A3
Anahola, 1,932.....D1
Captain Cook, 3,206.....F2
Crestview.....E1, J2
Eleele, 2,040.....D2, J3
Ewa.....E2, J3
Ewa Beach, 14,650.....F1, J2
Foster Village.....J2
Glenwood.....J5
Haena (Hawaii Co.).....J5
Haena (Kauai Co.).....C3
Haiku (Haiku-Pauwela).....
Hakalau, 495.....J4
Halaula, 13,891.....G3
Halawa Heights.....F1, J2
Haleiwa, 2,225.....C3
Halimaile, 895.....D4
Hana, 709.....J5
Hanamaulu, 3,272.....D1
Hanapepe, 2,153.....C2
Hauula, 3,651.....J1
Hawi, 938.....G3
Heeia.....G1, K2
Hilo, 40,759.....E7, J5
Holualoa, 6,107.....G5
Honalo, 1,987.....
Honaunau (Honaunau-Napoopoo), 2,414.....G6
Honokaa, 2,233.....H4
Honokahua.....B3
Honokohau Hale.....B3
Honokowai (Napili-Honokowai), 6,788.....B3
Honomu, 541.....J4
Honouliuli.....D1, J2
Honuapo.....H7
Hookena.....G6
Hoolehua.....A3
Huehue.....F2
Huelo.....D1
Iroquois Point, 2,462.....E2, J2
Iwilei.....J2
Kaaawa, 1,324.....J1
Kaalaea.....J2
Kaanapali, 1,375.....B3
Kahakuloa.....B3
Kahala.....K2
Kahaluu (Hawaii Co.).....G4
Kahaluu (Honolulu Co.), 2,935.....J2
Kahana (Maui Co.).....B3
Kahana (Honolulu Co.), J1.....
Kahuku (Hawaii Co.).....G7
Kahuku (Honolulu Co.), 2,097.....C3
Kahului, 20,146.....C3, D6
Kailua (Hawaii Co.).....
Kailua (Honolulu Co.), 36,513.....C5, K2
Kailua-Kona (Hawaii Co., Kailua).....D7, F5
Kaimu.....J6
Kaimuki.....K2
Kalaheo, 3,913.....C2
Kalaoa, 6,794.....F5
Kalapana.....J6
Kalaupapa.....A3
Kalihi Kai, 717.....F2
Kalihiwai, 717.....C1
Kalilii.....F2
Kamalino.....K6
Kamalino.....A2
Kamalo.....B3
Kamaole.....C4
Kamehameha Heights.....F2
Kamooloa.....J1
Kaneohe, 34,970.....C5, G1, K2
Kaniahiku Village.....J5
Kapaa, 9,472.....D1
Kapaau, 1,159.....G3
Kapahulu.....K2
Kapoho.....K6
Kapulena.....H4
Kaumakani, 607.....C2
Kaumalapau.....A4
Kaunakakai, 2,726.....A3
Kaupakulua.....C3
Kaupo.....G4
Kawaihae.....H1
Kawailoa.....H1
Kawailoa Beach (Kawela Bay), 410.....J1
Keaau, 2,010.....J5
Kealakekua, 1,645.....G5
Kealia (Hawaii Co.).....G6
Kealia (Kauai Co.).....D1
Keanae.....J4
Keauhou (Kahaluu-Keauhou), 2,414.....F5
Kei.....G6
Kekaha, 3,175.....B2
Kehena.....A3
Keokea (Hawaii Co.).....F5
Keokea (Maui Co.).....C4
Kiekie.....E2, J2
Kii Landing.....J1
Kilauea, 2,092.....C1
Koloa, 1,942.....D4
Kualapuu, 1,936.....A3
Kukuihaele, 317.....H4
Kukuiula.....C2
Kula.....H2
Kunia.....H2
Kurtistown, 1,157.....J5
Lahaina, 9,118.....B3, D6
Lanai City, 3,164.....C5, J1
Laupahoehoe, 473.....J4
Lawai, 1,984.....C2
Lihue, 5,674.....A5, D2
Lower Paia.....C4
Maalaea, 454.....C4
Maili, 5,943.....H2
Wahiawa, 16,151.....H2
Waiahole.....F2
Waialua (Hawaii Co.), 3,761.....H1
Waialua (Maui Co.).....B5, H1
Waianae, 10,506.....B5, H2
Waiehu (Wailee-Waiehu), 7,310.....
Waikane, 726.....J2
Waikiki, 1,115.....J2
Waikoloa Village, 4,806.....G3
Wailua (Kauai Co.), 2,083.....D1
Makaha, 7,753.....H2
Makakilo City, 13,156.....J2
Makapala.....H1
Makawao, 6,327.....C3
Makena (Wailea-Makena), 5,671.....C4
Makiki Heights.....B1
Mana.....B1
Maunalani Heights.....C3
Maunaloa, 230.....A3
Maunawili, 4,869.....K2
Mililani Town, 28,608.....G7
Milolii.....G7
Moiliili.....K2
Mokuleia, 1,839.....H1
Mountain View, 2,799.....J5
Muolea.....D4
Naalehu, 919.....H7
Nanakuli, 10,814.....B5, H2
Ninole.....J4
Numila.....C2
Olomana.....K2
Olowalu.....B4
Omao, 1,221.....D1
Ookala.....H4
Opihikao.....G3
Paauhau.....K6
Paauilo, 571.....H4
Pacific Heights.....B4
Pacific Palisades.....A3
Pahala, 1,378.....C3
Pahoa, 962.....C4
Pakala Village, 478.....G4
Palama.....H1
Papa.....J2
Papaaloa, 1,414.....G4
Papaikou, 1,414.....J4
Paukaa, 495.....J5
Pauwela (Haiku-Pauwela), 6,578.....J4
Pearl City, 30,976.....C5, E1, J2
Pepeekeo, 1,697.....J5
Poamoho.....K2
Pohakupu.....K6
Poholoi.....K6
Poipu, 1,075.....C2
Princeville, 1,698.....C1
Puako, 429.....G4
Puhi, 1,186.....D2
Pukalani, 7,380.....C3, D6
Pukoo.....B3
Pulehu.....C4
Punaluu (Hawaii Co.).....H7
Punaluu (Honolulu Co.), 881.....J1
Pupukea, 4,250.....G5
Puuanahulu.....D4
Puuiki.....B3
Puukolii.....H2
Puunene.....A2
Puu Waawaa.....A5
Puuwai.....A2
St. Louis Heights.....C1, J1
Sunset Beach.....B3
Ualapue.....J4
Ulupalakua.....B3
Volcano, 2,231.....C2
Waiahole.....G6

Other Features

Alalakeik, channel.....B4
Alenuihaha, channel.....D6
Alika Cone, mt.....G6
Apua, channel.....B3
Auau, channel.....B3
Barbers, point.....E1, J2
Barbers Point Naval Air Station.....F2
Barking Sands Pacific Missile Range Facility.....B1
Camp H. M. Smith.....F1
Diamond Head, point.....D7, F5
Diamond Head State Mon.....G3, J3
East Loch, harbor.....E1
Ewa Forest Reserve.....F1
Ford, island.....E1
Fort Shafter Mil. Res.....F2
Halalii, lake.....A2
Halawa, bay.....B3
Halawa, cape.....B3
Haleakala Natl. Park.....C4, D6
Halelea Forest Reserve.....C1
Hamakua, coast.....E7, H6
Hamakua Forest Reserve.....H4
Hana, bay.....A2
Hanalei Natl. Wildlife Refuge.....C1
Hanamanioa, cape.....C4
Haupu Forest Reserve.....C2
Hauula Forest Reserve.....J1
Hawaii, island.....E6, G5
Hawaii Volcanoes Natl. Park.....E7, H6
Hickam Air Force Base.....J2
Hilo, bay.....A5
Hilo Forest Reserve.....J5
Hilo Intl. Airport.....J5
Honaunau Forest Reserve.....G6
Honolua, bay.....B3
Honolulu, bay.....F2
Honolulu Intl. Airport.....C3
Honolulunui, bay.....B3
Honouliuli Watershed Forest Reserve.....J2
Hoomaluhia Botanical Gardens.....G1
Hualalai, mt.....A3
Ilio, point.....
James Campbell Natl. Wildlife Refuge.....J1
Kaala, mt.....
Kaena, point.....B5, H1
Kahaluu Forest Reserve.....G5
Kahana, bay.....
Kahikinui Forest Reserve.....C4
Kahoolawe, island.....B4, D6
Kahiu, point.....
Kahuku, point.....C1, J1
Kahului, bay.....C3
Kaikipauula, mt.....H4
Kailio, point.....C4
Kailua, bay.....K2
Kaiwi, channel.....B4
Ka Lae (South Cape), cape.....D7, G7
Kalalua, mt.....J6
Kalaupapa, peninsula.....B3
Kalaupapa Natl. Hist. Park.....B3
Kalepa Forest Reserve.....D1
Kalohi, channel.....A3
Kaloko-Honokohau Natl. Hist. Park.....F5
Kaloli, point.....K5
Kamakou, mt.....B3
Kamehameha I Birthsite State Monument.....G3
Kanapou, bay.....B4
Kaneohe Bay Marine Corps Air Station.....
Kaneohe Forest Reserve.....
Kapaa Beach Park.....G1, J2
Kapapala Forest Reserve.....H6
Kau, desert.....H6
Kau Forest Reserve.....G7
Kauai, island.....B5, D2
Kaulakahi, channel.....A5, B1
Kauna, point.....D7, G7
Kaupulehu Forest Reserve.....D1
Kawai, point.....D2
Kawaihoa, point.....A2, A5
Kawaikini, mt.....B1
Kawailoa Forest Reserve.....J1
Keahi, point.....E2
Keahole, point.....F5
Kealaikahiki, channel.....B4
Kealaikahiki, point.....B1
Kealia Forest Reserve.....D1
Keanapapa, point.....A3
Keehi, lagoon.....F2
Keokea Beach Park.....G3
Kepuhi, point.....H2
Kiholo, bay.....G4
Kikepa, point.....A1
Kilauea, point.....C1
Kilauea, crater.....J6
Kilohana, mt.....C2
Kinau, cape.....C4
Kipahulu Forest Reserve.....C4
Kipuka Puaulu, mt.....H6
Kohala, coast.....F5
Kohala, mt.....G4
Kohala, mts.....G3
Kohala Forest Reserve.....G4
Koko Head, point.....K3
Kokole Beach Park.....J4
Kona, coast.....C4
Konahuanui, mt.....G2, K2
Koolau Forest Reserve.....C4
Koolau Range, mts.....F1, J1
Kuaokala Forest Reserve.....H1
Kuee Ruins.....H7
Kuhio, point.....G6
Kukui, mt.....B3
Kulani, point.....F2
Kumukahi, cape.....E7, K5
Kupikipikio, point.....G3, K3
Laau, point.....A3, Q5
Lahilahi, point.....
Lanai, island.....B3, C6
Lanai City, mt.....B4
Lanaihale, mt.....
Lava Tree State Monument.....K5
Lehua, island.....A1
Leleiwi, point.....J5
Lihue Koloa Forest Reserve.....C1
Lualualei Naval Res.....B4
Lua Makika, mt.....C4
Maalaea, bay.....C4
Mahaoe, point.....J1
Mahukona, point.....H2
Maili, point.....H2
Makaeha, island.....C1
Makaleha, mts.....C3
Makapuu, point.....H4
Makapuu, point.....C4
Makua Mil. Res.....H1
Makua Keeau Forest Reserve.....H2
Mamala, bay.....E2, J3
Mamala, point.....F1
Manana, point.....K2
Manowaialee Forest Reserve.....J5
Maui, island.....C3, D6
Mauna Iki, mt.....H6
Mauna Kea, mt.....E6, H5
Mauna Kea Forest Reserve.....H4
Mauna Loa, mt.....D7, H6
Mauna Loa Forest and Game Reserve.....H5
Mauna Loa Observatory.....H5
Maunalua, bay.....K3
Middle Loch, harbor.....E1
Mokapu, point.....K2
Mokolii, island.....J1
Mokuaia, island.....K2
Moku Manu, island.....K2
Moloaa Forest Reserve.....C1
Molokai, island.....A3, C5
Molokini, island.....C4
Na Pali, coast.....B1
Na Pali Kona Forest Reserve.....C1
Nakalele, point.....B3
Nalilikani, point.....H6
Niihau, island.....A2, A5
Nohili, point.....B1
Nonou Forest Reserve.....D1
Oahu, island.....B5, D2, K1
Pailolo, channel.....B3
Palaoa, point.....B4
Paniau, mt.....A4
Papawai, point.....B4
Pauwela, point.....C3
Pearl, harbor.....E2
Pearl Harbor Natl. Wildlife Refuge.....D2, J2
Pepeekeo, point.....F2
Pohakuloa Training Area.....H5
Pueo, point.....J6
Puna Forest Reserve.....G4
Punchbowl, crater.....C2
Puolo, point.....C1
Pu'uhonua O Honaunau Natl. Hist. Park.....G6
Puu Kainapuaa, mt.....J1
Puu Kainapuaa, mt.....
Puu Ka Pele Forest Reserve.....C1
Puu Kaua, mt.....H2
Puu Kukui, mt.....G4
Puu Kulua, mt.....B3
Puu Loa, mt.....H5
Puu Nana, mt.....H6
Puu O Keokeo, mt.....G6
Puupehe, point.....C4
Puu Ulaula, mt.....F2
Salt, lake.....
Sand, island.....F2
Schofield Barracks.....
Mil. Res.....J2
South Kona Forest Reserve.....G4
Southwest Rift Zone, mt.....G6
Sulphur Cone, mt.....G6
Uaoa, bay.....C3
Upolu, point.....D6, G3
Upper Waiakea Forest Reserve.....J5
U.S. Naval Reservation.....E1, E2
U.S.S. Arizona Memorial.....E1
Waiahole Forest Reserve.....J2
Waiakea Forest Reserve.....J5
Waialeale, mt.....A5, C1
Waialae, bay.....H1
Waianae Range, mts.....B4
Waiawa, stream.....C4
Wailuku, river.....J1
Waimea, stream.....H2
Waimea, canyon.....C2
Waipio, bay.....H4
West Loch, harbor.....
West Maui, mts.....B3
West Maui Forest.....
Wheeler Air Force Base.....J2

Wailua (Maui Co.).....C3
Wailuku, 12,296.....E1, J2
Waimalu, 29,371.....K2
Waimanalo, 3,664.....G7
Waimanalo Beach, 4,271.....H1
Waimea (Honolulu Co.)...B5, H1
Waimea (Kauai Co.), 1,787.....C2
Wainaku, 1,227.....J5
Waiohinu.....
Waipahu, 33,108.....E1, J2
Waipio.....B5, D2, K1
Waipio Acres, 5,298.....
Whitmore Village, 4,057.....
Wilhelmina Rise.....
Woodlawn.....
Wood Valley.....

Hawaiian Island Chain

PACIFIC OCEAN

Midway Island
Kure Atoll
Lisianski Island
Laysan Island
Gardner Pinnacles
La Perouse Pinnacle
Necker Island
Nihoa
Niihau
Kaula
Kauai
Oahu
Honolulu
Molokai
Lanai
Kahoolawe
Maui
Hawaii

Tropic of Cancer

0 100 200 mi
0 100 200 300 km

© MapQuest.com, Inc.

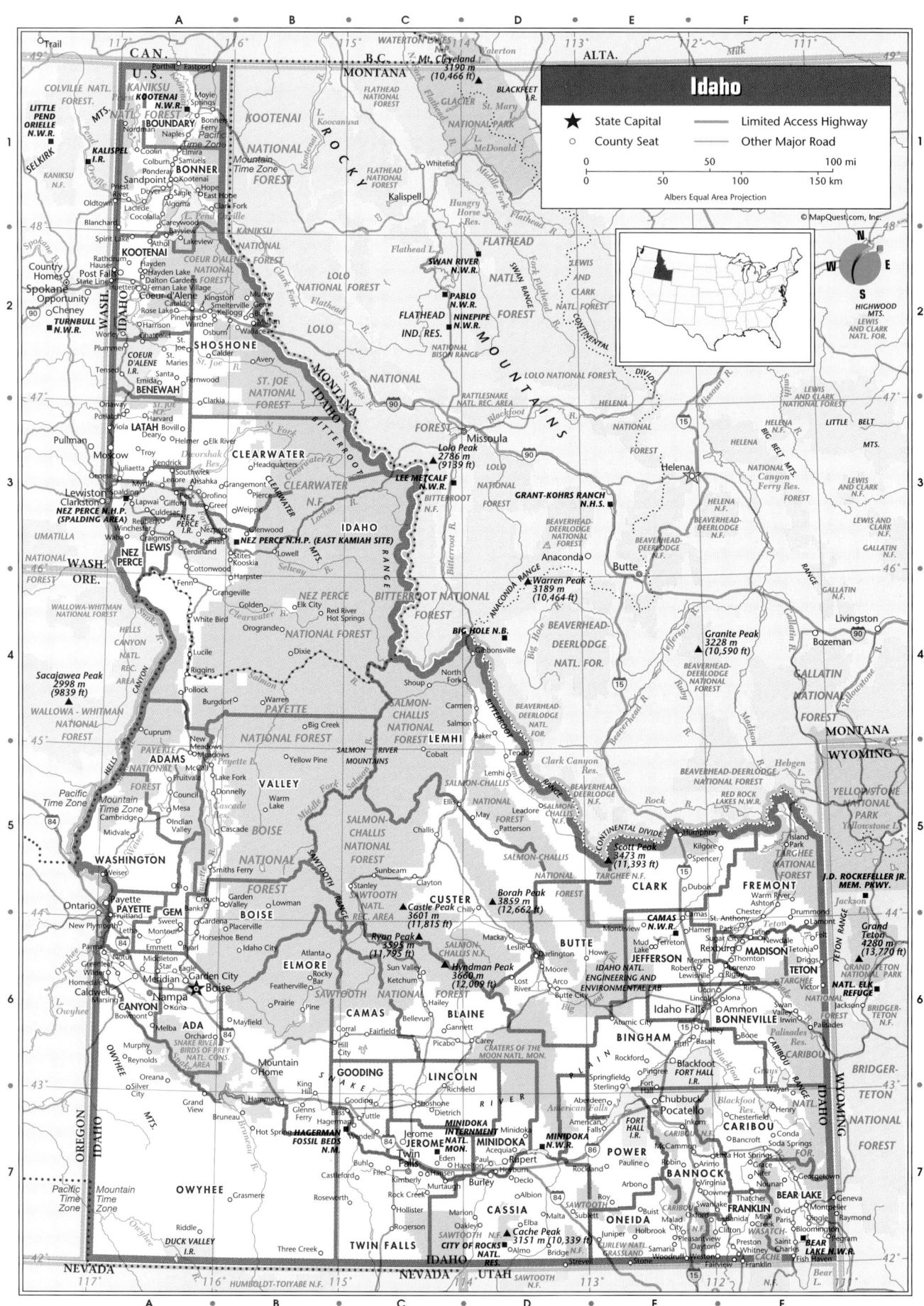

Idaho

★ State Capital
○ County Seat

─── Limited Access Highway
─── Other Major Road

0   50   100 mi
0   50   100   150 km
Albers Equal Area Projection

© MapQuest.com, Inc.

Idaho

Capital:	Boise
Land Area:	82,751 sq. mi.
	214,325 sq. km.
Population:	1,293,953 (2000 Census)
Largest City:	Boise, 185,787
Highest Point:	Borah Peak
	12,662 ft.
	3,859 m.
Admitted to Union:	July 3, 1890
Nickname:	Gem State
State Flower:	Syringa
State Bird:	Mountain Bluebird

Idaho: Map Index

Counties

Ada, 300,904 . . . . .A6
Adams, 3,476 . . . . .A5
Bannock, 75,565 . . . . .E7
Bear Lake, 6,411 . . . . .F7
Benewah, 9,171 . . . . .A2
Bingham, 41,735 . . . . .E6
Blaine, 18,991 . . . . .C6
Boise, 6,670 . . . . .B5
Bonner, 36,835 . . . . .A1
Bonneville, 82,522 . . . . . . .F6
Boundary, 9,871 . . . . .A1
Butte, 2,899 . . . . .D6
Camas, 991 . . . . .C6
Canyon, 131,441 . . . . .A6
Caribou, 7,304 . . . . .F7
Cassia, 21,416 . . . . .D7
Clark, 1,022 . . . . .E5
Clearwater, 8,930 . . . . . . .B3
Custer, 4,342 . . . . .C5
Elmore, 29,130 . . . . .B6
Franklin, 11,329 . . . . .F7
Fremont, 11,819 . . . . .F5
Gem, 15,181 . . . . .A5
Gooding, 14,155 . . . . .B6
Idaho, 15,511 . . . . .B3
Jerome, 18,342 . . . . .C7
Jefferson, 19,155 . . . . . . .E6
Kootenai, 108,685 . . . . . . .A2
Latah, 34,935 . . . . .A3
Lemhi, 7,806 . . . . .C4
Lewis, 3,747 . . . . .A3
Lincoln, 4,044 . . . . .C6
Madison, 27,467 . . . . .F6
Minidoka, 20,174 . . . . .D7
Nez Perce, 37,410 . . . . . . .A3
Oneida, 4,125 . . . . .E7
Owyhee, 10,644 . . . . .A7
Payette, 20,578 . . . . .A5
Power, 7,538 . . . . .E7
Shoshone, 13,771 . . . . .A2
Teton, 5,999 . . . . .F6
Twin Falls, 64,284 . . . . . . .C7
Valley, 7,651 . . . . .B5
Washington, 9,977 . . . . . . .A5

Cities and Towns

Aberdeen, 1,840 . . . . .E7
Acequia, 144 . . . . .D7
Ahsahka, 600 . . . . .A3
Albion, 262 . . . . .D7
Algoma, 575 . . . . .A1
Almo, 40 . . . . .D7
American Falls, 4,111 . . . . .E7
Ammon, 6,187 . . . . .F6
Arbon E7
Arco, 1,026 . . . . .D6
Arimo, 348 . . . . .E7
Ashton, 1,129 . . . . .F5
Athol, 676 . . . . .A2
Atlanta B6
Atomic City, 25 . . . . .E6
Avery B2
Baker, 70 . . . . .D4
Bancroft, 382 . . . . .F7
Banida, 100 . . . . .F7
Banks, 40 . . . . .A5
Basalt, 419 . . . . .E6
Bayview, 350 . . . . .A2
Bellevue, 1,876 . . . . .C6
Big Creek B4
Blackfoot, 10,419 . . . . . . .E6
Blanchard, 90 . . . . .A1
Bliss, 275 . . . . .C7
Bloomington, 251 . . . . .F7
Boise, 185,787 . . . . .A6
Bone F6
Bonners Ferry, 2,515 . . . . . .A1
Bovill, 305 . . . . .A3
Bowmont, 125 . . . . .A6
Bridge D7
Bruneau B7
Buhl, 3,985 . . . . .C7
Buist, 40 . . . . .E7
Burgdorf B4
Burke, 90 . . . . .B2
Burley, 9,316 . . . . .D7
Butte City, 76 . . . . .D6
Calder A2

Caldwell, 25,967 . . . . .A6
Camas, 80 . . . . .E5
Cambridge, 360 . . . . .A5
Carey, 513 . . . . .D6
Careywood A1
Carmen, 40 . . . . .D4
Cascade, 997 . . . . .A5
Castleford, 277 . . . . .C7
Cataldo, 80 . . . . .A2
Challis, 909 . . . . .C5
Chatcolet A2
Chester, 175 . . . . .F5
Chesterfield, 40 . . . . .F7
Chilly D5
Chubbuck, 9,700 . . . . .E7
Clark Fork, 530 . . . . .A1
Clarkia A2
Clayton, 27 . . . . .C5
Clifton, 213 . . . . .F7
Cobalt C5
Cocolalla, 90 . . . . .A1
Coeur d'Alene, 34,514 . . . . .A2
Colburn, 175 . . . . .A1
Conda F7
Coolin, 100 . . . . .A1
Corral C6
Cottonwood, 944 . . . . .A3
Council, 816 . . . . .A5
Craigmont, 556 . . . . .A3
Crouch, 154 . . . . .B5
Culdesac, 378 . . . . .A3
Cuprum A4
Dalton Gardens, 2,278 . . . . .A2
Darlington, 60 . . . . .D6
Dayton, 444 . . . . .E7
Deary, 552 . . . . .A3
Declo, 338 . . . . .D7
Dietrich, 150 . . . . .C7
Dingle, 100 . . . . .F7
Dixie B4
Donnelly, 138 . . . . .A5
Dover, 342 . . . . .A1
Downey, 613 . . . . .E7
Driggs, 1,100 . . . . .F6
Drummond, 15 . . . . .F5
Dubois, 647 . . . . .E5
Eagle, 11,085 . . . . .A6
East Hope, 200 . . . . .A1
Eastport A1
Eden, 411 . . . . .C7
Elba D7
Elk City, 150 . . . . .B4
Elk River, 156 . . . . .A3
Ellis C5
Elmira, 60 . . . . .A1
Emida, 70 . . . . .A2
Emmett, 5,490 . . . . .A6
Fairfield, 395 . . . . .C6
Fairview, 145 . . . . .F7
Featherville B6
Felt, 40 . . . . .F6
Fenn A4
Ferdinand, 145 . . . . .A3
Fernan Lake Village, 186 . . . .A2
Fernwood, 200 . . . . .A2
Filer, 1,620 . . . . .C7
Firth, 408 . . . . .E6
Fish Haven F7
Fort Hall, 3,193 . . . . .E6
Franklin, 641 . . . . .F7
Fruitland, 3,805 . . . . .A5
Fruitvale, 175 . . . . .A5
Gannett C6
Gardena, 40 . . . . .A6
Garden City, 10,624 . . . . . .A6
Garden Valley, 100 . . . . . . .B5
Gem, 125 . . . . .B2
Genesee, 946 . . . . .A3
Geneva F7
Georgetown, 538 . . . . .F7
Gibbonsville C4
Gifford A3
Glenns Ferry, 1,611 . . . . . .B7
Glenwood, 60 . . . . .B3
Golden B4
Gooding, 3,384 . . . . .C7
Grace, 990 . . . . .F7
Grand View, 470 . . . . .A7
Grangemont A3
Grangeville, 3,228 . . . . . . .A4
Grasmere B7
Greenleaf, 862 . . . . .A6
Greer A3
Hagerman, 656 . . . . .C7
Hailey, 6,200 . . . . .C6

Hamer, 12 . . . . .E6
Hammett, 300 . . . . .B7
Hansen, 970 . . . . .C7
Harpster, 40 . . . . .B4
Harrison, 267 . . . . .A2
Harvard, 125 . . . . .A3
Hauser, 668 . . . . .A2
Hayden, 9,159 . . . . .A2
Hayden Lake, 494 . . . . .A2
Hazelton, 687 . . . . .C7
Headquarters B3
Helmer A3
Henry F7
Heyburn, 2,899 . . . . .D7
Hill City B6
Holbrook, 60 . . . . .E7
Hollister, 237 . . . . .C7
Homedale, 2,528 . . . . .A6
Hope, 79 . . . . .A1
Horseshoe Bend, 770 . . . . . .A5
Hot Spring, 60 . . . . .B7
Howe, 70 . . . . .E6
Huetter, 96 . . . . .A2
Humphrey E5
Idaho City, 458 . . . . .B6
Idaho Falls, 50,730 . . . . . .E6
Indian Valley, 60 . . . . . . .A5
Inkom, 738 . . . . .E7
Iona, 1,201 . . . . .F6
Irwin, 157 . . . . .F6
Island Park, 215 . . . . .F5
Jerome, 7,780 . . . . .C7
Juliaetta, 609 . . . . .A3
Juniper E7
Kamiah, 1,160 . . . . .A3
Kellogg, 2,395 . . . . .B2
Kendrick, 369 . . . . .A3
Ketchum, 3,003 . . . . .C6
Kilgore E5
Kimberly, 2,614 . . . . .C7
King Hill, 150 . . . . .B6
Kingston, 650 . . . . .B2
Kooskia, 675 . . . . .B3
Kootenai, 441 . . . . .A1
Kuna, 5,382 . . . . .A6
Laclede, 150 . . . . .A1
Lake Fork, 50 . . . . .A5
Lakeview A1
Lamont F6
Lapwai, 1,134 . . . . .A3
Lava Hot Springs, 521 . . . . .E7
Leadore, 90 . . . . .D5
Lemhi D4
Lenore, 70 . . . . .A3
Leslie, 50 . . . . .D6
Letha, 70 . . . . .A6
Lewiston, 30,904 . . . . .A3
Lewisville, 467 . . . . .E6
Lincoln, 2,800 . . . . .F6
Lorenzo, 275 . . . . .F6
Lost River, 26 . . . . .D6
Lowell B3
Lowman B5
Lucile A4
Mackay, 566 . . . . .D6
Malad City, 2,158 . . . . . . .E7
Malta, 177 . . . . .D7
Marion, 50 . . . . .D7
Marsing, 890 . . . . .A6
May D5
Mayfield A6
McCall, 2,084 . . . . .A5
McCammon, 805 . . . . .E7
Meadows A5
Melba, 439 . . . . .A6
Menan, 707 . . . . .E6
Meridian, 34,919 . . . . .A6
Mesa A5
Middleton, 2,978 . . . . .A6
Midvale, 176 . . . . .A5
Minidoka, 129 . . . . .D7
Mink Creek, 40 . . . . .F7
Monteview, 40 . . . . .E6
Montour A6
Montpelier, 2,785 . . . . . . .F7
Moore, 196 . . . . .D6
Moscow, 21,291 . . . . .A3
Mountain Home, 11,143 . . . . .B6
Moyie Springs, 656 . . . . . . .A1
Mud Lake, 270 . . . . .E6
Mullan, 840 . . . . .B2
Murphy, 40 . . . . .A6
Murray, 60 . . . . .B2
Murtaugh, 139 . . . . .C7
Myrtle, 200 . . . . .A6
Nampa, 51,867 . . . . .A6
Naples, 175 . . . . .A1
Newdale, 358 . . . . .F6
New Meadows, 533 . . . . .A4
New Plymouth, 1,400 . . . . . .A6
Nezperce, 523 . . . . .A3
Niter F7
Nordman A1
North Fork C4
Notus, 458 . . . . .A6
Nounan F7
Oakley, 668 . . . . .D7
Ola A5
Oldtown, 190 . . . . .A1
Onaway, 230 . . . . .A3
Orchard A6
Oreana, 60 . . . . .A6

Orofino, 3,247 . . . . .A3
Orogrande B4
Osburn, 1,545 . . . . .A2
Ovid, 50 . . . . .F7
Oxford, 53 . . . . .E7
Palisades F6
Paris, 576 . . . . .F7
Parker, 319 . . . . .F6
Parma, 1,771 . . . . .A6
Patterson D5
Paul, 998 . . . . .D7
Pauline E7
Payette, 7,054 . . . . .A5
Pearl, 70 . . . . .A6
Peck, 186 . . . . .A3
Pegram F7
Picabo, 60 . . . . .C6
Pierce, 617 . . . . .B3
Pine B6
Pinehurst, 1,661 . . . . .A2
Pingree, 90 . . . . .E6
Placerville, 60 . . . . .B6
Pleasantview, 60 . . . . .E7
Plummer, 990 . . . . .A2
Pocatello, 51,466 . . . . . . .E7
Pollock, 50 . . . . .A4
Ponderay, 638 . . . . .A1
Porthill A1
Post Falls, 17,247 . . . . . . .A2
Potlatch, 791 . . . . .A3
Prairie B6
Preston, 4,682 . . . . .F7
Priest River, 1,754 . . . . . .A1
Rathdrum, 4,816 . . . . .A2
Raymond F7
Red River Hot Springs B4
Reubens, 72 . . . . .A3
Rexburg, 17,257 . . . . .F6
Reynolds, 100 . . . . .A6
Richfield, 412 . . . . .C6
Riddle A7
Rigby, 2,998 . . . . .F6
Riggins, 410 . . . . .A4
Ririe, 545 . . . . .F6
Roberts, 647 . . . . .E6
Robin, 60 . . . . .E7
Rock Creek C7
Rockford, 350 . . . . .E6
Rockland, 316 . . . . .E7
Rocky Bar B6
Rogerson, 60 . . . . .C7
Rose Lake, 40 . . . . .A2
Roseworth C7
Roy E7
Rupert, 5,645 . . . . .D7
Sagle, 425 . . . . .A1
St. Anthony, 3,342 . . . . . . .F6
St. Charles, 156 . . . . .F7
St. Joe A2
St. Maries, 2,652 . . . . . . .A2
Salmon, 3,122 . . . . .D4
Samaria E7
Samuels, 80 . . . . .A1
Sandpoint, 6,835 . . . . .A1
Santa, 100 . . . . .A2
Shelley, 3,813 . . . . .E6
Shoshone, 1,398 . . . . .C7
Shoup C4
Silver City A6
Smelterville, 651 . . . . . . .A2
Smiths Ferry A5
Soda Springs, 3,381 . . . . . .F7
Southwick A3
Spalding, 50 . . . . .A3
Spencer, 38 . . . . .E5
Spirit Lake, 1,376 . . . . . . .A2
Springfield, 60 . . . . .E6
Stanley, 100 . . . . .C5
Star, 1,795 . . . . .A6
State Line, 28 . . . . .A2
Sterling E6
Stites, 226 . . . . .B3
Stone E7
Strevell D7
Sublett D7
Sugar City, 1,242 . . . . . . .F6
Sunbeam C5
Sun Valley, 1,427 . . . . . . .C6
Swanlake, 40 . . . . .E7
Swan Valley, 213 . . . . .F6
Sweet, 125 . . . . .A6
Tendoy D5
Tensed, 126 . . . . .A2
Terreton, 125 . . . . .E6
Teton, 569 . . . . .F6
Tetonia, 247 . . . . .F6
Thatcher F7
Thornton, 300 . . . . .F6
Three Creek, 50 . . . . .B7
Troy, 798 . . . . .A3
Tuttle, 50 . . . . .C7
Twin Falls, 34,469 . . . . . . .C7
Ucon, 943 . . . . .F6
Victor, 840 . . . . .F6
Viola, 80 . . . . .A3
Virginia, 80 . . . . .E7
Waha, 100 . . . . .A3
Wallace, 960 . . . . .B2
Wardner, 215 . . . . .B2
Warm Lake B5
Warm River, 10 . . . . .F5
Warren B4

Wayan F7
Weippe, 416 . . . . .B3
Weiser, 5,343 . . . . .A5
Wendell, 2,338 . . . . .C7
Weston, 425 . . . . .E7
White Bird, 106 . . . . .A4
Whitney, 225 . . . . .F7
Wilder, 1,462 . . . . .A6
Winchester, 308 . . . . .A3
Woodruff, 50 . . . . .E7
Worley, 223 . . . . .A2
Yellow Pine, 60 . . . . .B5

Other Features

American Falls, reservoir . . .E7
Anaconda, range D4
Bear, lake F7
Bear, river F7
Bear Lake National Wildlife
    Refuge F7
Beaverhead, river E4
Beaverhead-Deerlodge National
    Forest D3-4, E3-5, F3-5
Big Belt, mountains F3
Big Hole N.B. D4
Big Hole, river D4
Big Lost, river D6
Bitterroot, range B3, D4
Bitterroot, river C3, C4
Bitterroot National Forest . .C4
Blackfeet Indian
    Reservation D1
Blackfoot, river (Montana) . .D3
Blackfoot, river (Idaho) . . .F6
Blackfoot, reservation F7
Boise National Forest B5
Borah, peak D5
Bridger, peak F3
Bridger-Teton National
    Forest F6
Bruneau, river B7
Cache, peak D7
Camas National
    Wildlife Refuge E6
Canyon Ferry, reservoir F3
Caribou, range F6
Caribou National Forest .E7, F6
Cascade, reservoir A5
Castle, peak C5
City Of Rocks Natl. Res. . . .D7
Clark Canyon, reservoir E5
Clearwater, mountains B3
Clearwater, river B3, B4
Clearwater, S. Fork, river . .A3
Clearwater National Forest . .B3
Coeur D'Alene Indian
    Reservation A2
Coeur D'Alene
    National Forest A2
Colville National Forest . . .A1
Continental Divide . . .D2, E5
Craters Of The Moon
    National Monument D6
Curlew Natl. Grassland E7
Deer Flat National Wildlife
    Refuge A6
Duck Valley
    Indian Reservation A7
Dworshak, reservoir A3
Flathead, lake C2
Flathead, Clark Fork, river . .B2
Flathead, Middle Fork, river .D1
Flathead, North Fork,
    river B2, C1
Flathead, South Fork, river . .D1
Flathead Indian Reservation .C2
Flathead
    National Forest C1, D2
Fort Hall
    Indian Reservation . . .E6, E7
Gallatin, river F4
Gallatin National Forest .F3, F4
Glacier National Park C1
Grand Teton, mountain F6
Grand Teton National Park . . .F6
Granite, peak F4
Grant-Kohrs Ranch National
    Historic Site E3
Grays, lake F6
Hagerman Fossil Beds National
    Monument C7
Hebgen, lake F5
Helena National Forest .E3, F3
Hells, canyon A5
Hells Canyon National
    Recreation Area A4
Highwood, mountains F2
Humboldt National Forest . . .B7
Hungry Horse, reservoir D1
Hyndman, peak C6
Idaho National Engineering
    and Environmental Lab . . .E6
J.D. Rockefeller Jr.
    Memorial Parkway F5
Jackson, lake F5
Jefferson, river E4
Kalispel Indian Reservation . .A1
Kaniksu National Forest .A1, B2
Kootenai, river A1, B1
Kootenai National Forest . . .B1

Kootenai National Wildlife
    Refuge A1
Koocanusa, lake B1
Lee Metcalf National
    Wildlife Refuge C3
Lemhi, river D5
Lewis And Clark
    National Forest . . .E2, F2, F3
Little Belt Mts. F3
Little Pend Orielle National
    Wildlife Refuge A1
Lochsa, river B3
Lolo, peak C3
Lolo National
    Forest B2, D2, D3
McDonald, lake D1
Madison, river F4
Milk, river F1
Minidoka Internment Natl.
    Mon. C7
Minidoka National Wildlife
    Refuge D7
Missouri, river F3
National Bison Range C2
National Elk Refuge F6
Nez Perce Indian
    Reservation A3
Nez Perce National Forest . .B4
Nez Perce N.H.P.
    (East Kamiah Site) B3
Nez Perce N.H.P.
    (Spalding Area) A3
Ninepipe National Wildlife
    Refuge C2
Owyhee, lake A6
Owyhee, mountains A6
Owyhee, river A6, A7
Pablo National
    Wildlife Refuge C2
Palisades, reservoir F6
Payette, lake A5
Payette, river A5
Payette National Forest .A5, B4
Pend Oreille, lake A1
Pend Oreille, river A1
Priest, lake A1
Rattlesnake National
    Recreation Area D2
Red Rock Lakes
    National Wildlife Refuge . .F5
Red Rock, river E5
Rocky, mountains B1
Ruby, river E4
Ryan, peak C6
Sacajawea, peak A4
St. Joe National Forest .A3, B2
St. Joe, river A2
St. Mary, lake D1
St. Regis, river B2
Salmon, river B4
Salmon, Middle Fork, river . .B5
Salmon-Challis National
    Forest C4, C5, C6, D5
Salmon River, mountains C5
Sawtooth, range B5
Sawtooth National
    Forest C6, D7
Sawtooth National
    Recreation Area C5
Scott, peak E5
Selkirk, mountains A1
Selway, river B3
Smith, river F2
Snake, river . . .A4, A5, A6, F6
Snake River, plain B6
Snake River Birds of Prey
    Natl. Cons. Area A6
Spokane, river A2
Swan, range D2
Swan River National
    Wildlife Refuge D2
Targhee National
    Forest E5, F5, F6
Teton, river F6
Teton, range F6
Turnbull National Wildlife
    Refuge A2
Umatilla National Forest . . .A3
Wallowa-Whitman National
    Forest D4
Warren, peak D4
Wasatch-Cache National
    Forest F7
Waterton, lake D1
Waterton Lakes N.P. C1
Weiser, river A5
Yellowstone, lake F5
Yellowstone, river F4
Yellowstone National Park . . .F5

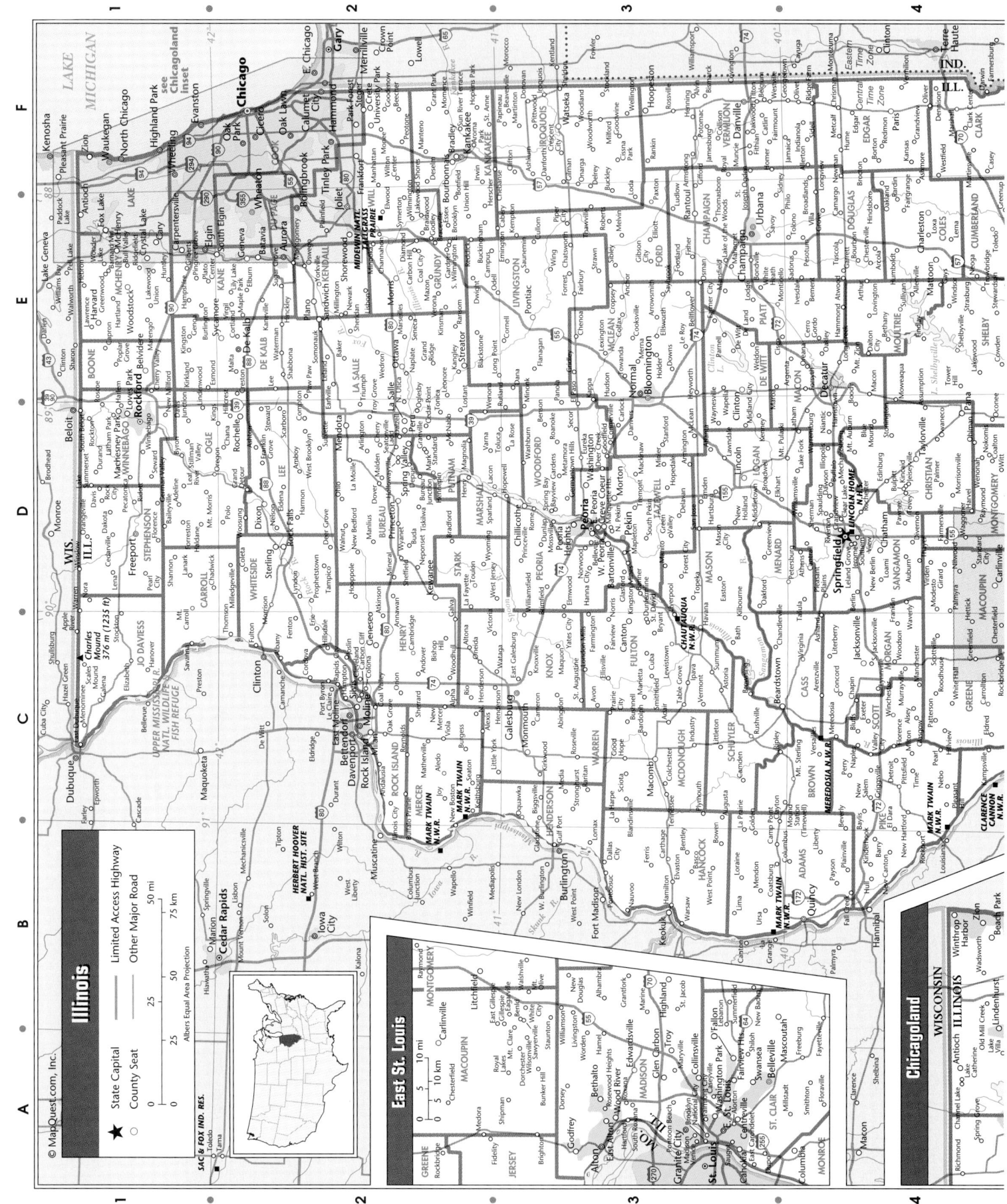

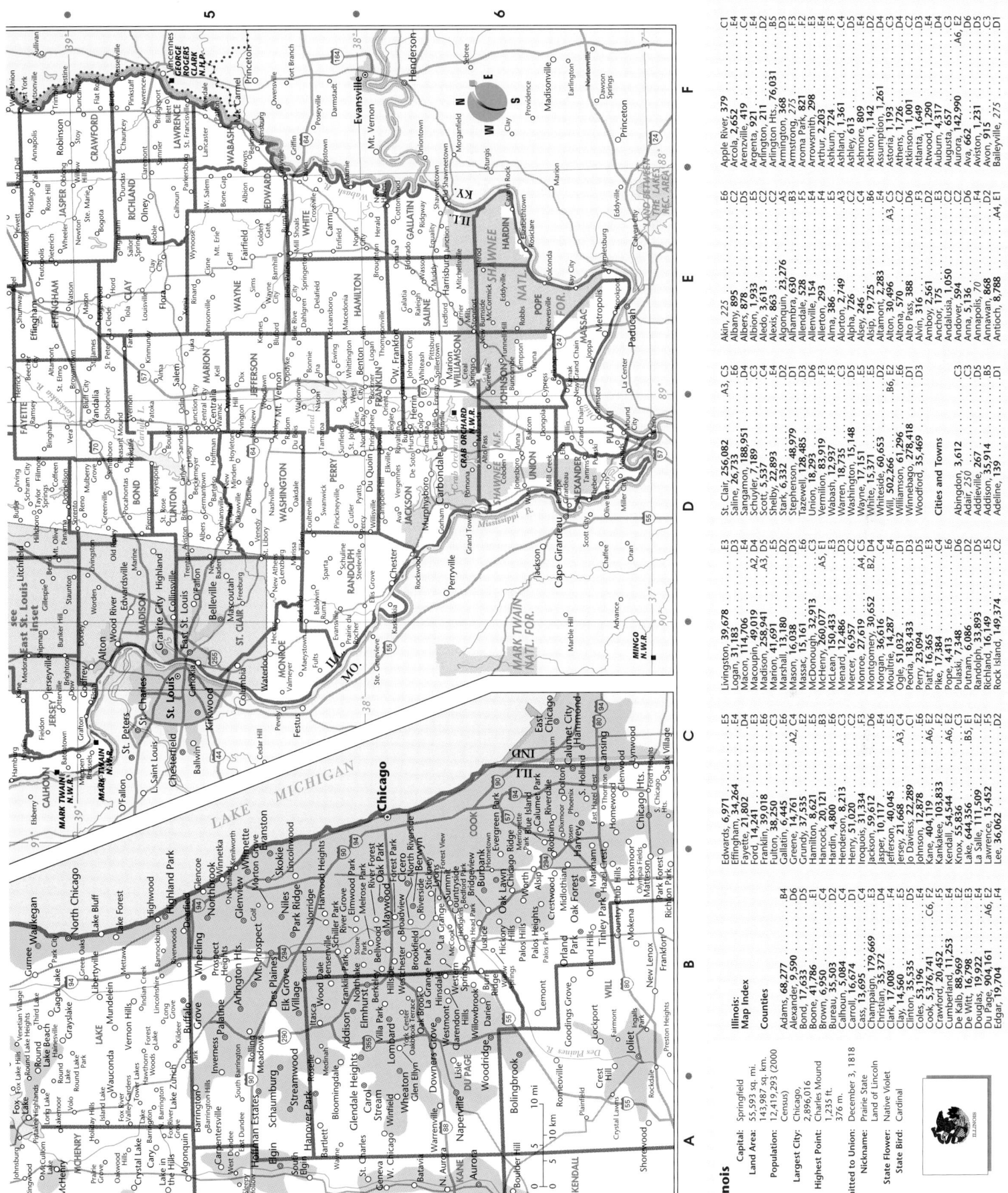

Illinois

Capital:	Springfield
Land Area:	55,593 sq. mi.
	143,987 sq. km.
Population:	12,419,293 (2000 Census)
Largest City:	Chicago, 2,896,016
Highest Point:	Charles Mound 1,235 ft. 376 m.
Admitted to Union:	December 3, 1818
Nickname:	Prairie State, Land of Lincoln
State Flower:	Native Violet
State Bird:	Cardinal

Illinois:
Map Index

Counties

Adams, 68,277 ... B4
Alexander, 9,590 ... D6
Bond, 17,633 ... E1
Boone, 41,786 ... C4
Brown, 6,950 ... D2
Bureau, 35,503 ... C4
Calhoun, 5,084 ... D1
Carroll, 16,674 ... C3
Cass, 13,695 ... E3
Champaign, 179,669 ... D4
Christian, 35,372 ... F4
Clark, 17,008 ... E5
Clay, 14,560 ... D5
Clinton, 35,535 ... E4
Coles, 53,196 ... C6, F2
Cook, 5,376,741 ... F4
Crawford, 20,452 ... E4
Cumberland, 11,253 ... E2
De Kalb, 88,969 ... D3
De Witt, 16,798 ... E4
Douglas, 19,922 ... A6, F2
Du Page, 904,161 ... F4
Edgar, 19,704 ... D2

Edwards, 6,971 ... E5
Effingham, 34,264 ... E4
Fayette, 21,802 ... D4
Ford, 14,241 ... E3
Franklin, 39,018 ... D5
Fulton, 38,250 ... C3
Gallatin, 6,445 ... E6
Greene, 14,761 ... C4
Grundy, 37,535 ... D1
Hamilton, 8,621 ... E5
Hancock, 20,121 ... B3
Hardin, 4,800 ... E6
Henderson, 8,213 ... B3
Henry, 51,020 ... C2
Iroquois, 31,334 ... F3
Jackson, 59,612 ... D6
Jasper, 10,117 ... E4
Jefferson, 40,045 ... D5
Jersey, 21,668 ... C4
Jo Daviess, 22,289 ... D1
Johnson, 12,878 ... E6
Kane, 404,119 ... A6, F2
Kankakee, 103,833 ... F2
Kendall, 54,544 ... A6, E2
Knox, 55,836 ... C2
Lake, 644,356 ... B5, F1
La Salle, 111,509 ... E2
Lawrence, 15,452 ... F5
Lee, 36,062 ... D2

Livingston, 39,678 ... E3
Logan, 31,183 ... D3
Macon, 114,706 ... D4
Macoupin, 188,951 ... D4
Madison, 258,941 ... D5
Marion, 41,691 ... D5
Marshall, 13,180 ... D2
Mason, 16,038 ... D3
Massac, 15,161 ... D6
McDonough, 32,913 ... C3
McHenry, 260,077 ... F1
McLean, 150,433 ... D3
Menard, 12,486 ... D3
Mercer, 16,957 ... C2
Monroe, 27,619 ... C5
Montgomery, 30,652 ... D4
Morgan, 36,616 ... C4
Moultrie, 14,287 ... E4
Ogle, 51,032 ... D1
Peoria, 183,433 ... D3
Perry, 23,094 ... D5
Piatt, 16,365 ... E3
Pike, 17,384 ... C4
Pope, 4,413 ... E6
Pulaski, 7,348 ... D6
Putnam, 6,086 ... D2
Randolph, 33,893 ... D5
Richland, 16,149 ... E5
Rock Island, 149,374 ... C2

St. Clair, 256,082 ... A3, C5
Saline, 26,733 ... E6
Sangamon, 188,951 ... D4
Schuyler, 7,189 ... C3
Scott, 5,537 ... C4
Shelby, 22,893 ... D4
Stark, 6,332 ... D2
Stephenson, 48,979 ... D1
Tazewell, 128,485 ... D3
Union, 18,293 ... D6
Vermilion, 83,919 ... F3
Wabash, 12,486 ... F5
Warren, 18,735 ... C2
Washington, 15,148 ... D5
Wayne, 17,151 ... E5
White, 15,371 ... E5
Whiteside, 60,653 ... C1
Will, 502,266 ... B6, F2
Williamson, 61,296 ... D6
Winnebago, 278,418 ... E1
Woodford, 35,469 ... D3

Cities and Towns

Abingdon, 3,612 ... C3
Adair, 250 ... C3
Addieville, 267 ... D5
Addison, 35,914 ... B5
Adeline, 139 ... D1

Apple River, 379 ... E6
Arcola, 2,652 ... C2
Arenzville, 419 ... D5
Argenta, 921 ... E5
Arlington, 211 ... E5
Arlington Hts., 76,031 ... B5
Armington, 368 ... A5
Armstrong, 275 ... F3
Aroma Park, 821 ... F2
Arrowsmith, 298 ... E3
Arthur, 2,203 ... E4
Ashkum, 724 ... F3
Ashland, 1,361 ... C4
Ashley, 613 ... A3
Ashmore, 809 ... C4
Ashton, 1,142 ... E4
Assumption, 1,261 ... D4
Astoria, 1,193 ... A3, C3
Athens, 1,726 ... D3
Atkinson, 1,001 ... C2
Atlanta, 1,649 ... F3
Atwood, 1,290 ... E4
Auburn, 4,317 ... D4
Augusta, 657 ... C2
Aurora, 142,990 ... A6, E2
Ava, 662 ... D6
Aviston, 1,231 ... D5
Avon, 915 ... C3
Baileyville, 275 ... D1

Baker, 80 ....E2
Balcom, 150 ....D6
Baldwin, 3,627 ....D5
Banner, 149 ....D3
Bannockburn, 1,429 ....B5
Bardolph, 253 ....C3
Barnard Mill E1
Barnhill, 90 ....E5
Barrington, 10,168 ....A5
Barrington Hills, 3,915 ....A5
Barry, 1,368 ....B4
Bartelso, 593 ....D5
Bartlett, 36,706 ....A5
Bartonville, 6,310 ....D3
Basco, 107 ....B3
Batavia, 23,866 ....A6, E2
Batchtown, 218 ....C4
Bath, 310 ....C4
Bay City E6
Baylis, 265 ....B4
Bayview Gardens, 366 ....D3
Beach Park, 10,072 ....B4
Beardstown, 5,766 ....C3
Beaverville, 391 ....F3
Beckemeyer, 1,043 ....D5
Bedford Park, 574 ....B6
Beecher, 2,033 ....F2
Beecher City, 493 ....E4
Belgium, 466 ....F3
Belknap, 133 ....E6
Belle Prairie City, 60 ....E5
Belle Rive, 371 ....E5
Belleville, 41,410 ....A3, D5
Bellevue, 1,887 ....D3
Bellflower, 408 ....E3
Bellmont, 297 ....E5
Bellwood, 20,535 ....B6
Belvidere, 20,820 ....E1
Bement, 1,784 ....E4
Benld, 1,541 ....B3, D4
Bensenville, 20,703 ....B5
Benson, 408 ....D3
Bentley, 43 ....B3
Benton, 6,880 ....E5
Berkeley, 5,245 ....B6
Berlin, 140 ....D4
Berwyn, 54,016 ....B6
Bethalto, 9,454 ....A3
Bethany, 1,287 ....E4
Beverly, 40 ....C4
Biggsville, 343 ....C3
Billett, 150 ....F5
Bingham, 117 ....D4
Birds, 51 ....F5
Bishop Hill, 125 ....C2
Bismarck, 542 ....F3
Blackstone, 70 ....E2
Blandinsville, 777 ....C3
Bloomingdale, 21,675 ....B5
Bloomington, 64,808 ....E3
Blue Island, 23,463 ....C6
Blue Mound, 1,129 ....D4
Bluff City, 200 ....D5
Bluffs, 748 ....C4
Bluford, 785 ....E5
Bogota, 100 ....E5
Bolingbrook, 56,321 ....B6, E2
Bondville, 455 ....E3
Bone Gap, 272 ....F5
Bonfield, 364 ....E2
Bonnie, 424 ....E5
Boody, 300 ....D4
Borton, 80 ....E4
Boulder, 70 ....D5
Boulder Hill, 8,169 ....A6
Bourbon, 100 ....E4
Bourbonnais, 15,256 ....F2
Bowen, 535 ....B3
Braceville, 792 ....E2
Bradford, 787 ....D2
Bradley, 12,784 ....F2
Braidwood, 5,203 ....E2
Breese, 4,048 ....D5
Bridgeport, 2,168 ....F5
Bridgeview, 15,335 ....B6
Brighton, 2,196 ....A3, C4
Brimfield, 933 ....D3
Broadlands, 312 ....E4
Broadview, 8,264 ....B6
Broadwell, 169 ....D3
Brocton, 322 ....E4
Brookfield, 19,085 ....B6
Brooklyn, 676 ....C4
Brookport, 1,054 ....E6
Broughton, 193 ....E6
Browning, 130 ....C4
Browns, 175 ....F5
Brownstown, 705 ....E4
Brussels, 141 ....C5
Bryant, 255 ....D3
Buckingham, 237 ....E2
Buckley, 593 ....E3
Buckner, 479 ....D6
Buda, 592 ....D2
Buffalo, 491 ....D4
Buffalo Grove, 42,909 ....B5
Buffalo Prairie, 60 ....C2
Bull Valley, 726 ....E1
Bulpitt, 206 ....D4
Buncombe, 186 ....E6
Bunker Hill, 1,801 ....A3, D4
Burbank, 27,902 ....B6
Bureau Junction, 368 ....D2
Burgess, 80 ....C4
Burlington, 452 ....E1
Burnham, 4,170 ....C6
Burnt Prairie, 58 ....E5
Burr Ridge, 10,408 ....B6
Bush, 257 ....D6
Bushnell, 3,221 ....C3
Butler, 197 ....D4
Byron, 2,917 ....D1

Cabery, 263 ....E3
Cahokia, 16,391 ....A3, C5
Cairo, 3,632 ....D6
Calhoun, 222 ....E5
Calumet City, 39,071 .....C6, F2
Calumet Park, 8,516 ....C6
Calvin, 70 ....E5
Camargo, 469 ....E4
Cambria, 1,330 ....D6
Cambridge, 2,180 ....C2
Camden, 97 ....C3
Cameron, 300 ....C3
Campbell Hill, 333 ....D6
Camp Point, 1,244 ....B3
Campus, 145 ....E2
Canton, 15,288 ....C3
Cantrall, 139 ....D4
Capron, 961 ....E1
Carbon Cliff, 1,689 ....C2
Carbondale, 20,681 ....D6
Carbon Hill, 392 ....E2
Carlinville, 5,685 ....A2, D4
Carlock, 456 ....D3
Carlyle, 3,406 ....D5
Carmi, 5,422 ....E5
Carol Stream, 40,438 ....A5
Carpentersville, 30,586 ..A5, E1
Carrier Mills, 1,886 ....E6
Carrollton, 2,605 ....C4
Carterville, 4,616 ....D6
Carthage, 2,725 ....B3
Cary, 15,531 ....A5, E1
Casey, 2,942 ....F4
Caseyville, 4,310 ....A3
Catlin, 2,087 ....F3
Cave in Rock, 346 ....E6
Cedar Point, 262 ....D2
Cedarville, 719 ....D1
Central City, 1,371 ....D5
Centralia, 14,136 ....D5
Centreville, 5,951 ....A3
Cerro Gordo, 1,436 ....E4
Chadwick, 505 ....D1
Champaign, 67,518 ....E3
Chana, 225 ....D2
Chandlerville, 704 ....C3
Channahon, 7,344 ....E2
Channel Lake, 1,785 ....A4
Chapin, 592 ....C4
Charleston, 21,039 ....E4
Chatham, 8,583 ....D4
Chatsworth, 1,265 ....E3
Chauncey, 100 ....F5
Chebanse, 1,148 ....F2
Chenoa, 1,845 ....E3
Cherry, 509 ....D2
Cherry Valley, 2,191 ....E1
Chester, 5,185 ....D6
Chesterfield, 223 ....A2, C4
Chesterville, 225 ....E4
Chicago, 2,896,016 ....C6, F2
Chicago Hts., 32,776 ....C6
Chicago Ridge, 14,127 ....B6
Chillicothe, 5,996 ....D3
Chrisman, 1,318 ....F4
Christopher, 2,836 ....D6
Cicero, 85,616 ....B6, F2
Cisco, 264 ....E3
Cisne, 673 ....E5
Cissna Park, 811 ....F3
Claremont, 212 ....F5
Clarendon Hills, 7,610 ....B6
Clark Center, 100 ....F4
Clay City, 1,000 ....E5
Clayton, 904 ....C3
Clear Lake, 267 ....D4
Cleveland, 253 ....C2
Clifton, 1,317 ....F3
Clinton, 7,485 ....E3
Coal City, 4,797 ....E2
Coalton, 307 ....D4
Coal Valley, 3,606 ....C2
Coatsburg, 226 ....B3
Cobden, 1,116 ....D6
Coffeen, 709 ....D4
Colchester, 1,493 ....C3
Coleta, 155 ....D2
Colfax, 989 ....E3
Collinsville, 24,707 ......A3, D5
Collison, 100 ....F3
Colona, 5,173 ....C2
Colp, 224 ....D6
Columbia, 7,922 ....A4, C5
Columbus, 112 ....B4
Compton, 347 ....D2
Concord, 176 ....C4
Congerville, 466 ....D3
Cooksville, 213 ....E3
Cordova, 633 ....C2
Cornell, 511 ....E3
Cortland, 2,066 ....E2
Cottonwood, 60 ....E6
Coulterville, 1,230 ....D5
Country Club Hills, 16,169 ....B6
Countryside, 5,991 ....B6
Cowden, 612 ....E4
Crainville, 992 ....D6
Creal Springs, 702 ....E6
Crescent City, 631 ....F3
Crest Hill, 13,329 ....B6
Creston, 543 ....E2
Crestwood, 11,251 ....B6
Crete, 7,346 ....F2
Creve Coeur, 5,448 ....D3
Cropsey, 150 ....E3
Crossville, 782 ....E5
Crystal Lake, 38,000 .....A5, E1
Crystal Lawns, 2,933 ....A6
Cuba, 1,418 ....C3
Cullom, 563 ....E3
Cutler, 543 ....D5
Cypress, 271 ....D6

Dahlgren, 514 ....E5
Dakota, 499 ....D1
Dallas City, 1,055 ....B3
Dalton City, 581 ....E4
Dalzell, 717 ....D2
Damiansville, 368 ....D5
Dana, 171 ....E3
Danforth, 587 ....F3
Danvers, 1,183 ....D3
Danville, 33,904 ....F3
Darien, 22,860 ....B6
Darwin, 80 ....F4
Davis, 662 ....D1
Davis Junction, 491 ....D1
Dawson, 466 ....D4
Deer Creek, 605 ....D3
Deerfield, 18,420 ....B5
Deer Grove, 48 ....D2
Deer Park, 3,102 ....B5
De Kalb, 39,018 ....E2
Delafield, 40 ....E5
De Land, 475 ....E3
Delavan, 1,825 ....D3
Delrey E3
Dennison, 125 ....F4
Depue, 1,842 ....D2
Deselm, 80 ....F2
Des Plaines, 58,720 ....B5
De Soto, 1,653 ....D6
Detroit, 93 ....C4
De Witt, 188 ....E3
Diamond, 1,393 ....E2
Dieterich, 591 ....E4
Divernon, 1,201 ....D4
Dix, 494 ....E5
Dixmoor, 3,934 ....C6
Dixon, 15,941 ....D2
Dolton, 25,614 ....C6
Dongola, 806 ....D6
Donnellson, 243 ....D4
Donovan, 351 ....F3
Dorchester, 142 ....A3, C5
Dorsey, 150 ....A3, C5
Dover, 172 ....D2
Dow, 300 ....C4
Dowell, 441 ....D6
Downers Grove, 48,724 ....B6
Downs, 776 ....E3
Du Bois, 222 ....D5
Duncanville, 125 ....F5
Dundas, 225 ....E5
Dunfermline, 262 ....C3
Dunlap, 926 ....D3
Dupo, 3,933 ....A3
Du Quoin, 6,448 ....D6
Durand, 1,081 ....D1
Dwight, 4,363 ....E2

Eagarville, 128 ....B3
Earlville, 1,778 ....E2
East Alton, 6,830 ....A3
East Brooklyn, 123 ....C4
East Cape Girardeau, 437 ......D6
East Carondelet, 267 ....A3
East Dubuque, 1,995 ....C1
East Dundee, 2,955 ....A5
East Galesburg, 839 ....C3
East Gillespie, 234 ....B2
East Hazel Crest, 1,607 ....C6
East Moline, 20,333 ....C2
Easton, 373 ....D3
East Peoria, 22,638 ....D3
East St. Louis, 31,542 ...A3, C5
Eddyville, 153 ....E6
Edgar, 40 ....F4
Edgewood, 527 ....E5
Edinburg, 1,135 ....D4
Edwardsville, 21,491 ......A3, D5
Effingham, 12,384 ....E4
Elburn, 2,756 ....E2
Elco, 60 ....D6
El Dara, 89 ....C4
Eldena, 175 ....D2
Eldorado, 4,534 ....E6
Eldred, 211 ....C4
Elgin, 94,487 ....A5, E1
Elizabeth, 682 ....C1
Elizabethtown, 348 ....E6
Elk Grove Village, 34,727 .....B5
Elkhart, 443 ....D3
Elkville, 1,001 ....D6
Elliott, 341 ....E3
Ellis Grove, 381 ....D6
Ellisville, 87 ....C3
Ellsworth, 271 ....E3
Elmhurst, 42,762 ....B6
Elmwood, 1,945 ....D3
Elmwood Park, 25,405 ....B5
El Paso, 2,695 ....D3
Elsah, 635 ....C5
Elvaston, 152 ....B3
Elwood, 1,620 ....E2
Emden, 515 ....D3
Emington, 120 ....E2
Energy, 1,175 ....D6
Enfield, 625 ....E5
Equality, 721 ....E6
Erie, 1,589 ....C2
Esmond, 100 ....E1
Essex, 554 ....E2
Eureka, 4,871 ....D3
Evanston, 74,239 ....B5, F1
Evansville, 724 ....D5
Evergreen Park, 20,821 ....B6
Ewing, 310 ....E5
Exeter, 70 ....C4

Fairbury, 3,968 ....E3
Fairfield, 5,421 ....E5
Fairgrange, 491 ....E4
Fairmont, 2,563 ....B6
Fairmont City, 2,436 ....A3
Fairmount, 640 ....F3
Fairview, 493 ....C3
Fairview Hts., 15,034 ....A3
Fall Creek B4
Farina, 558 ....E5
Farmer City, 2,055 ....E3
Farmersville, 768 ....D4
Farmington, 2,601 ....C3
Fayetteville, 384 ....B4
Fenton, 150 ....C2
Ferris, 168 ....B3
Fidelity, 105 ....A2
Fieldon, 271 ....C4
Fillmore, 362 ....D4
Findlay, 723 ....E4
Fisher, 1,647 ....E3
Fithian, 506 ....F3
Flanagan, 1,083 ....E3
Flat Rock, 415 ....F5
Flora, 5,086 ....E5
Floraville, 200 ....A4
Florence (Pike Co.), 71 ....C4
Florence (Stephenson Co.),
   125 ....D1
Flossmoor, 9,301 ....C6
Foosland, 90 ....E3
Ford Heights, 3,456 ....C6
Forest City, 287 ....D3
Forest Lake, 1,530 ....B5
Forest Park, 15,688 ....B6
Forest View, 778 ....B6
Forrest, 1,225 ....E3
Forreston, 1,469 ....D1
Forsyth, 2,434 ....E4
Fox Lake, 9,178 ....A4, E1
Fox Lake Hills, 2,561 ....A4
Fox River Grove, 4,862 ....A5
Fox River Valley Gardens, 788 .A5
Frankfort, 10,391 ....B6, F2
Franklin, 586 ....C4
Franklin Grove, 1,052 ....D2
Franklin Park, 19,434 ....B5
Freeburg, 3,872 ....A4, D5
Freemanspur, 273 ....E6
Freeport, 26,443 ....D1
Fulton, 3,881 ....C2
Fults, 28 ....C5

Gages Lake, 10,415 ....B4
Galatia, 1,013 ....E6
Galena, 3,460 ....C1
Galesburg, 33,706 ....C3
Galva, 2,758 ....C2
Gardner, 1,406 ....E2
Garrett, 198 ....E4
Gays, 259 ....E4
Geff, 366 ....E5
Geneseo, 6,480 ....C2
Geneva, 19,515 ....A6, E2
Genoa, 4,169 ....E1
Georgetown, 3,628 ....F4
Germantown, 1,181 ....D5
Germantown Hills, 2,111 ....D3
German Valley, 481 ....D1
Gibson City, 3,373 ....E3
Gifford, 815 ....E3
Gilberts, 1,279 ....E1
Gillespie, 3,412 ....B3, D4
Gilman, 1,793 ....F3
Girard, 2,245 ....D4
Gladstone, 280 ....C3
Glasford, 1,076 ....D3
Glasgow, 90 ....C4
Glen Carbon, 10,425 ....A3
Glencoe, 8,762 ....B5
Glendale Heights, 31,765 ......B5
Glen Ellyn, 26,999 ....B6
Glenview, 41,847 ....B5
Glenwood, 9,000 ....C6
Godfrey, 16,286 ....A3, C5
Godley, 594 ....E2
Golconda, 726 ....E6
Golden, 629 ....B3
Golden Gate, 100 ....E5
Golf, 451 ....B5
Goodenow, 725 ....F2
Goodfield, 686 ....D3
Good Hope, 415 ....C3
Goodings Grove, 17,084 ....B6
Goodwine, 80 ....F3
Goreville, 938 ....E6
Gorham, 256 ....D6
Grafton, 609 ....C5
Grand Chain D6
Grand Detour, 550 ....D2
Grand Ridge, 546 ....E2
Grand Tower, 624 ....D6
Grandview (Edgar Co.), 80 .....F4
Grandview (Sangamon Co.),
   1,537 ....D4
Granite City, 31,301 .....A3, C5
Grantfork, 254 ....B3
Grant Park, 1,358 ....F2
Granville, 1,414 ....D2
Grayslake, 18,506 ....B4
Grayville, 1,725 ....E5
Greenfield, 1,179 ....C4
Green Oaks, 3,572 ....B5
Green Rock C2
Greenup, 1,532 ....E4
Green Valley, 728 ....D3
Greenview, 862 ....D3
Greenville, 6,955 ....D5
Greenwood, 244 ....E1
Gridley, 1,411 ....E3
Griggsville, 1,258 ....C4
Gulf Port, 207 ....B3
Gurnee, 28,834 ....B4

Hainesville, 2,129 ....B4
Haldane, 125 ....D1
Hamburg, 126 ....C4
Hamel, 570 ....B3
Hamilton, 3,029 ....B3
Hametsburg, 90 ....E6

Hammond, 518 ....E4
Hampshire, 2,900 ....E1
Hampton, 1,626 ....C2
Hanna City, 1,013 ....D3
Hanover, 836 ....C1
Hanover Park, 38,278 ....A5
Hardin, 959 ....C4
Harlem, 550 ....D1
Harmon, 149 ....D2
Harrisburg, 9,860 ....E6
Harristown, 1,338 ....E4
Hartford, 1,545 ....A3
Hartland, 325 ....E1
Hartsburg, 358 ....D3
Harvard, 7,996 ....E1
Harvel, 235 ....D4
Harvey, 30,000 ....C6
Harwood Heights, 8,297 ....B5
Havana, 3,577 ....C3
Hawthorn Woods, 6,002 ....B5
Hazel Crest, 14,816 ....C6
Hazel Dell, 125 ....E4
Hebron, 1,038 ....E1
Hecker, 475 ....C5
Henderson, 319 ....C2
Hennepin, 707 ....D2
Henning, 241 ....F3
Henry, 2,540 ....D2
Herald, 60 ....E6
Herod E6
Herrick, 524 ....E4
Herrin, 11,298 ....D6
Herscher, 1,523 ....E2
Hettick, 182 ....C4
Heyworth, 2,431 ....E3
Hickory Hills, 13,926 ....B6
Hidalgo, 123 ....E4
Highland, 8,438 ....B3, D5
Highland Park, 31,365 .....B5, F1
Highwood, 4,143 ....B5
Hillcrest, 1,158 ....D2
Hillsboro, 4,359 ....D4
Hillsdale, 588 ....C2
Hillside, 8,155 ....B6
Hillview, 179 ....C4
Hinckley, 1,994 ....E2
Hindsboro, 361 ....E4
Hinsdale, 17,349 ....B6
Hodgkins, 2,134 ....B6
Hoffman, 460 ....D5
Hoffman Estates, 49,495 ....A5
Holder, 60 ....E3
Holiday Hills, 831 ....A5
Hollowayville, 90 ....D2
Homer, 1,200 ....F3
Hometown, 4,467 ....B6
Homewood, 19,543 ....C6
Hookdale, 40 ....D5
Hoopeston, 5,965 ....F3
Hooppole, 162 ....D2
Hopedale, 929 ....D3
Hopewell, 396 ....D3
Hopkins Park, 711 ....F2
Hord, 90 ....E5
Hoyleton, 520 ....D5
Hudson, 1,510 ....E3
Huey, 196 ....D5
Hull, 474 ....B4
Humboldt, 481 ....E4
Hume, 382 ....F4
Huntley, 5,730 ....E1
Hurst, 805 ....D6
Hutsonville, 568 ....F4
Illinois City, 200 ....C2
Iliopolis, 916 ....D4
Ina, 2,455 ....E5
Indian Creek, 194 ....B5
Indian Head Park, 3,685 ....B6
Indianola, 207 ....F4
Industry, 540 ....C3
Ingalls Park, 3,082 ....B6
Ingraham, 150 ....E5
Inverness, 6,749 ....A5
Iola, 171 ....E5
Ipava, 506 ....C3
Iroquois, 207 ....F3
Irving, 2,484 ....D4
Irvington, 736 ....D5
Irwin, 92 ....F2
Island Lake, 8,153 ....A5
Itasca, 8,302 ....B5
Iuka, 598 ....E5
Ivesdale, 288 ....E4
Jacksonville, 18,940 ....C4
Jamaica, 80 ....F4
Jamesburg, 70 ....F3
Jeiseyville, 128 ....C4
Jerome, 1,414 ....D4
Jerseyville, 7,984 ....C4
Jewett, 232 ....E4
Johnsburg, 5,391 ....A4
Johnsonville, 89 ....E5
Johnston City, 3,557 ....E6
Joliet, 106,221 ....B6, E2
Jonesboro, 1,853 ....D6
Joppa, 409 ....E6
Joslin, 60 ....C2
Joy, 373 ....C2
Junction, 139 ....E6
Junction City, 559 ....D5
Justice, 12,193 ....B6
Kampsville, 302 ....C4
Kane, 459 ....C4
Kaneville, 375 ....E2
Kankakee, 27,491 ....F2
Kansas, 842 ....F4
Kappa, 170 ....D3
Karnak, 619 ....D6
Kaskaskia, 9 ....D6
Keenes, 99 ....E5
Keensburg, 252 ....F5

Keithsburg, 714 ....C2
Kell, 231 ....E5
Kempton, 235 ....E3
Kenilworth, 2,494 ....B5
Kenney, 374 ....D3
Kewanee, 12,944 ....D2
Keyesport, 481 ....D5
Kilbourne, 375 ....C3
Kildeer, 3,460 ....B5
Kincaid, 1,441 ....D4
Kinderhook, 249 ....B4
Kings, 150 ....D1
Kingston, 980 ....E1
Kingston Mines, 259 ....D3
Kinmundy, 892 ....E5
Kinsman, 109 ....E2
Kirkland, 1,166 ....E1
Kirkwood, 794 ....C3
Knoxville, 3,183 ....C3
La Clede, 100 ....E5
Lacon, 1,979 ....D2
Ladd, 1,313 ....D2
La Fayette, 227 ....D2
La Grange, 15,608 ....B6
La Grange Park, 13,295 ....B6
La Harpe, 1,385 ....C3
Lake Barrington, 4,757 ....A5
Lake Bluff, 6,056 ....B5
Lake Catherine, 1,490 ....A4
Lake Forest, 20,059 ....B5
Lake Fork, 100 ....D4
Lake in the Hills, 23,152 .....A5
Lakemoor, 2,788 ....A4
Lake of the Woods, 3,026 ......E3
Lake Summerset, 2,061 ....D1
Lake Villa, 5,864 ....A4
Lakewood (McHenry Co.),
   2,337 ....E1
Lakewood (Shelby Co.), 125 ....E4
Lakewood Shores, 1,487 ....E2
Lake Zurich, 18,104 ....A5
La Moille, 773 ....D2
Lanark, 1,584 ....D1
Lancaster, 100 ....F5
Lansing, 28,332 ....C6
La Prairie, 60 ....B3
La Rose, 159 ....D3
La Salle, 9,796 ....D2
Latham, 371 ....D4
Latham Park, 425 ....D1
Lawndale, 150 ....D4
Lawrence, 350 ....E1
Lawrenceville, 4,745 ....F5
Leaf River, 555 ....D1
Lebanon, 3,523 ....B3
Ledford, 475 ....E6
Lee, 313 ....E2
Leland, 970 ....E2
Leland Grove, 1,592 ....D4
Lemont, 13,098 ....B6
Lena, 2,887 ....D1
Lenzburg, 577 ....D5
Leonore, 110 ....E2
Lerna, 322 ....E4
Le Roy, 3,332 ....E3
Lewistown, 2,522 ....C3
Lexington, 1,912 ....E3
Liberty, 519 ....B4
Libertyville, 20,742 ....B5
Lily Lake, 825 ....E2
Lima, 159 ....B3
Lincoln, 15,369 ....D3
Lincolnshire, 6,108 ....B5
Lincolnwood, 12,359 ....C6
Lindenhurst, 12,539 ....B4
Lindenwood, 275 ....D1
Lisbon, 248 ....E2
Lisle, 21,182 ....B6
Litchfield, 6,815 ....B2, D4
Literberry, 125 ....C4
Littleton, 197 ....C3
Little York, 269 ....C2
Liverpool, 119 ....C3
Livingston, 825 ....B3, D5
Loami, 804 ....D4
Lockport, 15,191 ....B6
Loda, 419 ....E3
Lodge, 125 ....E3
Logan, 55 ....E6
Lomax, 477 ....B3
Lombard, 42,322 ....B6
London Mills, 447 ....C3
Long Creek, 1,364 ....E4
Long Grove, 6,735 ....B5
Long Lake, 3,356 ....A4
Long Point, 247 ....E2
Longview, 153 ....E4
Loraine, 363 ....B3
Lostant, 486 ....E2
Louisville, 1,242 ....E5
Loves Park, 20,044 ....D1
Lovington, 1,222 ....E4
Loxa, 50 ....E4
Ludlow, 324 ....E3
Lyndon, 566 ....D2
Lynnville, 137 ....C4
Lynwood, 7,377 ....C6
Lyons, 10,255 ....B6
Macedonia, 51 ....E5
Machesney Park, 20,759 ....D1
Mackinaw, 1,452 ....D3
Macomb, 18,558 ....C3
Macon, 1,213 ....D4
Madison, 4,545 ....A3
Maeystown, 148 ....C5
Magnolia, 279 ....D2
Mahomet, 4,877 ....E3
Makanda, 419 ....D6
Malden, 343 ....D2
Malta, 969 ....E2
Manchester, 354 ....C4
Manhattan, 3,330 ....F2

Manito, 1,733 ....D3
Manlius, 355 ....D2
Mansfield, 949 ....E3
Manteno, 6,414 ....F2
Maple Park, 765 ....E2
Mapleton, 227 ....D3
Maquon, 318 ....C3
Marengo, 6,355 ....E1
Marietta, 150 ....C3
Marine, 910 ....B3, D5
Marion, 16,035 ....E6
Marissa, 2,141 ....D5
Mark, 491 ....D2
Markham, 12,620 ....C6
Maroa, 1,654 ....E3
Marquette Hts., 2,794 ....D3
Marseilles, 4,655 ....E2
Marshall, 3,771 ....F4
Martinsville, 1,225 ....F4
Martinton, 375 ....F3
Maryville, 4,651 ....A3
Mascoutah, 5,659 ....B3, D5
Mason, 396 ....E5
Mason City, 2,558 ....D3
Matherville, 772 ....C2
Matteson, 12,928 ....B6
Mattoon, 18,291 ....E4
Maunie, 177 ....E5
Maywood, 26,987 ....B6
Mazon, 904 ....E2
McCook, 40 ....E6
McCormick, 40 ....E6
McCullom Lake, 1,038 ....A4
McHenry, 21,501 ....A4, E1
McLean, 808 ....D3
McLeansboro, 2,945 ....E5
McNabb, 310 ....D2
Mechanicsburg, 456 ....D4
Media, 130 ....C3
Medinah, 2,500 ....B5
Medora, 501 ....A2, C4
Melrose Park, 23,171 ....B6
Melvin, 465 ....E3
Mendon, 883 ....B3
Mendota, 7,272 ....D2
Menominee, 237 ....C1
Meppen, 60 ....C5
Meredosia, 1,041 ....C4
Merna, ...E3
Merrionette Park, 1,999 ....B6
Metamora, 2,700 ....D3
Metcalf, 213 ....F4
Metropolis, 6,482 ....E6
Mettawa, 367 ....B5
Middletown, 434 ....D3
Midland City, 100 ....D3
Midlothian, 14,315 ....B6
Milan, 5,348 ....C2
Milford, 1,369 ....F3
Mill Creek, 76 ....D6
Milledgeville, 1,016 ....D2
Miller City, ...D6
Millington, 458 ....E2
Mill Shoals, 235 ....E5
Millstadt, 2,794 ....A4
Milton, 274 ....C4
Mineral, 272 ....D2
Minier, 1,244 ....D3
Minonk, 2,168 ....D3
Minooka, 3,971 ....E2
Mitchellsville, 90 ....E6
Modesto, 252 ....D4
Mokena, 14,583 ....B6
Moline, 43,768 ....C2
Momence, 3,171 ....F2
Monee, 2,924 ....F2
Monmouth, 9,841 ....C3
Montgomery, 5,471 ....E2
Monticello, 5,138 ....E3
Montrose, 257 ....E4
Morris, 11,928 ....E2
Morrison, 4,447 ....D2
Morrisonville, 1,068 ....D4
Morton, 15,198 ....D3
Morton Grove, 22,451 ....B5
Mossville, 1,000 ....D3
Mound City, 692 ....D6
Mounds, 1,117 ....D6
Mound Station (Timewell), 127 ....C3
Mount Auburn, 515 ....D4
Mount Carmel, 7,982 ....F5
Mount Carroll, 1,832 ....D1
Mount Clare, 433 ....B3
Mount Erie, 105 ....E5
Mount Morris, 3,013 ....D1
Mount Olive, 2,150 ....B3, D4
Mount Prospect, 56,265 ....B5
Mount Pulaski, 1,701 ....D3
Mount Sterling, 2,070 ....C4
Mount Vernon, 16,269 ....E5
Mount Zion, 4,845 ....E4
Moweaqua, 1,923 ....D4
Muddy, 78 ....E6
Mulberry Grove, 671 ....D5
Muncie, 155 ....F3
Mundelein, 30,935 ....B5
Murphysboro, 13,295 ....D6
Murrayville, 644 ....C4
Naperville, 128,358 ....A6
Naplate, 523 ....E2
Naples, 134 ....C4
Nashville, 3,147 ....D5
Nason, 234 ....E5
National City, ...A3
Nauvoo, 1,063 ....B3
Nebo, 408 ....C4
Nelson, 163 ....D2
Neoga, 1,854 ....E4
Neponset, 519 ....D2
Newark, 887 ....E2
New Athens, 1,981 ....D5

New Baden, 3,001 ....B3, D5
New Bedford, 95 ....D2
New Berlin, 1,030 ....D4
New Boston, 632 ....C2
New Burnside, 242 ....E6
New Canton, 417 ....B4
New Douglas, 369 ....B3
New Grand Chain, 233 ....D6
New Hartford, 60 ....C4
New Haven, 477 ....E6
New Holland, 318 ....D3
New Lenox, 17,771 ....B6
Newman, 956 ....F4
New Memphis, 225 ....D5
New Mercer, ...C2
New Millford, 541 ....D1
New Minden, 204 ....D5
New Salem, 136 ....C4
Newton, 3,069 ....E5
Niantic, 738 ....D4
Niles, 30,068 ....B5
Nilwood, 284 ....D4
Noble, 746 ....E5
Nokomis, 2,389 ....D4
Nora, 118 ....D1
Normal, 45,386 ....E3
Norridge, 14,582 ....B5
Norris, 194 ....C3
Norris City, 1,057 ....E6
North Aurora, 10,585 ....A6
North Barrington, 2,918 ....A5
Northbrook, 33,435 ....B5
North Chicago, 35,918 ....B4, F1
North City, 630 ....D6
Northfield, 5,389 ....B5
North Henderson, 187 ....C2
Northlake, 11,878 ....B5
North Pekin, 1,574 ....D3
North Riverside, 6,688 ....B6
North Utica, 977 ....D2
Norwood, 473 ....D3
Oak Brook, 8,702 ....B6
Oakbrook Terrace, 2,300 ....B6
Oakdale, 213 ....D5
Oakford, 309 ....D3
Oak Forest, 28,051 ....B6
Oak Grove, 1,318 ....C2
Oakland, 996 ....E4
Oak Lawn, 55,245 ....B6, E6
Oakley, 125 ....E4
Oak Park, 52,524 ....B6, F2
Oakwood, 1,502 ....F3
Oakwood Hills, 2,194 ....A5
Oblong, 1,580 ....F4
Oconee, 202 ....D4
Odell, 1,014 ....E2
Odin, 1,122 ....D5
O'Fallon, 21,910 ....B3, D5
Ogden, 743 ....F3
Oglesby, 3,647 ....D2
Ohio, 540 ....D2
Ohlman, ...D4
Okawville, 1,355 ....D5
Old Mill Creek, 251 ....B4
Old Ripley, 127 ....D5
Old Shawneetown, 278 ....E6
Olive Branch, 500 ....D6
Oliver, 125 ....F4
Olivet, 400 ....F4
Olmsted, 299 ....D6
Olney, 8,631 ....E5
Olympia Fields, 4,732 ....C6
Omaha, 263 ....E6
Onarga, 1,438 ....F3
Oneida, 752 ....C2
Opdyke, 300 ....E5
Oquawka, 1,539 ....C3
Orangeville, 751 ....D1
Oreana, 892 ....E4
Oregon, 4,060 ....D1
Orient, 296 ....E6
Orion, 1,713 ....C2
Orland Hills, 6,779 ....B6
Orland Park, 51,077 ....B6
Osman, 612 ....E3
Oswego, 13,326 ....E2
Ottawa, 18,307 ....E2
Otterville, 120 ....C4
Owaneco, 256 ....D4
Palatine, 65,479 ....B5
Palestine, 1,366 ....F4
Palmer, 248 ....D4
Palmyra, 733 ....C4
Palos Heights, 11,260 ....B6
Palos Hills, 17,665 ....B6
Palos Park, 4,689 ....B6
Pana, 5,614 ....D4
Panama, 323 ....D4
Panola, 33 ....D3
Papineau, 196 ....F3
Paris, 9,077 ....F4
Park City, 6,637 ....B4
Parkersburg, 234 ....E5
Park Forest, 23,462 ....B6, F2
Park Ridge, 37,775 ....B5
Parnell, 40 ....E2
Patoka, 633 ....D5
Patterson, 120 ....C4
Patton, 125 ....F5
Pawnee, 2,647 ....D4
Paw Paw, 852 ....E2
Paxton, 4,525 ....F3
Payson, 1,066 ....B4
Pearl, 187 ....C4
Pearl City, 780 ....D1
Pecatonica, 1,997 ....D1
Pekin, 33,857 ....D3
Peoria, 112,936 ....D3
Peoria Heights, 6,635 ....D3
Peotone, 3,385 ....F2
Percy, 942 ....D5
Perry, 437 ....C4

Peru, 9,835 ....D2
Pesotum, 521 ....E4
Petersburg, 2,299 ....D4
Phillipstown, 28 ....E5
Philo, 1,314 ....E3
Phoenix, 2,157 ....C6
Pierron, 653 ....D5
Pinckneyville, 5,464 ....D5
Pingree Grove, 124 ....E1
Pinkstaff, 225 ....F5
Piper City, 781 ....F3
Pistakee Highlands, 3,812 ....A4
Pittsburg, 575 ....E6
Pittsfield, 4,211 ....C4
Pittwood, 50 ....F3
Plainfield, 13,038 ....A6, E2
Plainville, 248 ....B4
Plano, 5,633 ....E2
Plato Center, 225 ....E1
Pleasant Hill, 1,047 ....C4
Pleasant Mound, 100 ....D5
Pleasant Plains, 777 ....D4
Plymouth, 562 ....C3
Pocahontas, 727 ....D5
Polo, 2,477 ....D2
Pomona, 125 ....D6
Pontiac, 11,864 ....E3
Pontoon Beach, 5,620 ....A3
Pontoosuc, 171 ....B3
Poplar Grove, 1,368 ....E1
Port Byron, 1,535 ....C2
Posen, 4,730 ....C6
Potomac, 681 ....F3
Prairie City, 461 ....C3
Prairie du Rocher, 613 ....C5
Prairie Grove, 960 ....A5
Preston Heights, 2,527 ....B6
Princeton, 7,501 ....D2
Princeville, 1,621 ....D3
Prophetstown, 2,023 ....D2
Prospect Heights, 17,081 ....B5
Pulaski, 274 ....D6
Pyatts, ...D5
Quincy, 40,366 ....B4
Radom, 395 ....D5
Raleigh, 330 ....E6
Ramsey, 1,056 ....D4
Rankin, 617 ....F3
Ransom, 409 ....E2
Rantoul, 12,857 ....E3
Rapids City, 953 ....C2
Rardin, 100 ....E4
Raritan, 140 ....C3
Raymond, 927 ....B2, D4
Red Bud, 3,422 ....D5
Reddick, 219 ....E2
Redmon, 199 ....F4
Reevesville, 70 ....E6
Reno, 60 ....D5
Reynolds, 508 ....C2
Richmond, 1,091 ....A4
Richton Park, 12,533 ....B6
Richview, 308 ....D5
Ridge Farm, 912 ....F4
Ridgefield, 325 ....E1
Ridgway, 928 ....E6
Ridott, 159 ....D1
Rinard, 100 ....E5
Ringwood, 471 ....A4
Rio, 240 ....C2
Ripley, 103 ....C3
Riverdale, 15,055 ....C6
River Forest, 11,635 ....B6
River Grove, 10,668 ....B5
Riverside, 8,895 ....B6
Riverton, 3,048 ....D4
Riverwoods, 3,843 ....B5
Roanoke, 1,994 ....D3
Robbins, 6,635 ....B6
Robbs, 60 ....E6
Roberts, 387 ....E3
Robinson, 6,822 ....F4
Rochelle, 9,424 ....D2
Rochester, 2,893 ....D4
Rockbridge, 189 ....A2, C4
Rock City, 313 ....D1
Rockdale, 1,888 ....B6
Rock Falls, 9,580 ....D2
Rockford, 150,115 ....D1
Rock Island, 39,684 ....C2
Rockport, 80 ....B4
Rockton, 5,296 ....D1
Rockwood, 41 ....D6
Rolling Meadows, 24,604 ....B5
Rome, 1,776 ....D3
Romeoville, 21,153 ....B6
Roodhouse, 2,214 ....C4
Roscoe, 6,244 ....D1
Rose Hill, 79 ....E4
Roselle, 23,115 ....B5
Rosemont, 4,224 ....B5
Roseville, 1,083 ....C3
Rosewood Heights, 4,262 ....A3
Rosiclare, 1,213 ....E6
Rossville, 1,217 ....F3
Round Lake, 5,842 ....A4
Round Lake Beach, 25,859 ....A4
Round Lake Heights, 1,347 ....A4
Round Lake Park, 6,038 ....B4
Roxana, 1,547 ....A3
Royal, 279 ....F3
Royal Lakes, 190 ....A3
Royalton, 1,130 ....D6
Ruma, 260 ....D5
Rushville, 3,212 ....C3
Russellville, 119 ....F5
Rutland, 354 ....D3
Sadorus, 426 ....E4
Sailor Springs, 128 ....E5
St. Anne, 1,212 ....F2
St. Augustine, 152 ....C3

St. David, 587 ....C3
St. Elmo, 1,456 ....E4
Ste. Marie, 261 ....E5
St. Francisville, 759 ....F5
St. Jacob, 801 ....B3
St. James, 80 ....E5
St. Johns, 218 ....D5
St. Joseph, 2,912 ....E3
St. Libory, 583 ....D5
St. Peter, 386 ....D4
St. Rose, 350 ....D5
Salem, 7,909 ....E5
Sandoval, 1,434 ....D5
Sandwich, 6,509 ....E2
San Jose, 696 ....D3
Sauget, 249 ....A3
Sauk Village, 10,411 ....C6
Saunemin, 456 ....E3
Savanna, 3,542 ....C1
Savoy, 4,476 ....E3
Sawyerville, 295 ....B3
Saybrook, 764 ....E3
Scales Mound, 401 ....C1
Scarboro, 50 ....D2
Schaumburg, 75,386 ....A5
Schiller Park, 11,850 ....B5
Schram City, 653 ....D4
Sciota, 70 ....C3
Scioto, 58 ....C3
Scottville, 140 ....C4
Seaton, 242 ....C2
Seatonville, 303 ....D2
Secor, 379 ....D3
Seneca, 2,053 ....E2
Sesser, 2,128 ....D5
Seward, 225 ....D1
Shabbona, 929 ....E2
Shannon, 854 ....D1
Shawneetown, 1,410 ....E6
Sheffield, 946 ....D2
Sheldon, 1,232 ....F3
Shelbyville, 4,971 ....E4
Sheridan, 2,411 ....E2
Sherman, 2,871 ....D4
Sherrard, 694 ....C2
Shiloh, 7,643 ....A3
Shipman, 655 ....A3, C4
Shobonier, 125 ....D5
Shorewood, 7,686 ....A6, E2
Shumway, 217 ....E4
Sibley, 329 ....E3
Sidell, 626 ....F4
Sidney, 1,062 ....E3
Sigel, 386 ....E4
Silvis, 7,269 ....C2
Simpson, 54 ....E6
Sims, 273 ....E5
Skokie, 63,348 ....B5
Sleepy Hollow, 3,553 ....A5
Smithboro, 200 ....D5
Smithfield, 214 ....C3
Smithton, 2,248 ....A4
Somonauk, 1,295 ....E2
Sorento, 601 ....D4
South Barrington, 3,760 ....A5
South Beloit, 5,397 ....D1
South Chicago Hts., 3,970 ....C6
South Elgin, 16,100 ....A5, E2
Southern View, 1,695 ....D4
South Holland, 22,147 ....C6
South Jacksonville, 3,475 ....C4
South Pekin, 1,162 ....D3
South Roxana, 1,888 ....A3
South Wilmington, 621 ....E2
Sparland, 504 ....D2
Sparta, 4,486 ....D5
Spaulding, 559 ....D4
Spillertown, 220 ....E6
Spring Bay, 436 ....D3
Springerton, 134 ....E5
Springfield, 111,454 ....D4
Spring Grove, 3,880 ....A4
Spring Valley, 5,398 ....D2
Standard, 256 ....D2
Standard City, 138 ....D4
Stanford, 670 ....D3
Staunton, 5,030 ....B3, D4
Steeleville, 2,077 ....D5
Steger, 9,682 ....F2
Sterling, 15,451 ....D2
Steward, 271 ....D2
Stewardson, 747 ....E4
Stickney, 6,148 ....B6
Stillman Valley, 1,048 ....D1
Stockland, 100 ....F3
Stockton, 1,926 ....C1
Stonefort, 292 ....E6
Stone Park, 5,127 ....B6
Stonington, 960 ....D4
Stoy, 119 ....F5
Strasburg, 603 ....E4
Strawn, 104 ....E3
Streamwood, 36,407 ....A5
Streator, 14,190 ....E2
Stronghurst, 896 ....C3
Sublette, 456 ....D2
Sugar Grove, 3,909 ....E2
Sullivan, 4,326 ....E4
Summerfield, 472 ....B3
Summit, 10,637 ....B6
Summum, 175 ....C3
Sumner, 1,022 ....F5
Sunfield, 425 ....D5
Sun River Terrace, 383 ....F2
Swansea, 10,579 ....A3
Swanwick, 125 ....D5
Sycamore, 12,020 ....E2
Symerton, 106 ....F2
Table Grove, 396 ....C3
Tallula, 638 ....D4
Tamaroa, 740 ....D5
Tamms, 724 ....D6

Tampico, 772 ....D2
Taylor Springs, 583 ....D4
Taylorville, 11,427 ....D4
Tennessee, 144 ....C3
Teutopolis, 1,559 ....E4
Thawville, 258 ....E3
Thayer, 750 ....D4
Thebes, 478 ....D6
Third Lake, 1,355 ....B4
Thomasboro, 1,233 ....E3
Thompsonville, 571 ....E6
Thomson, 559 ....C2
Thornton, 2,582 ....C6
Tilden, 922 ....D5
Tilton, 2,976 ....F3
Time, 29 ....C4
Tinley Park, 48,401 ....B6, F2
Tiskilwa, 787 ....D2
Toledo, 1,166 ....E4
Tolono, 2,700 ....E4
Toluca, 1,339 ....D2
Tonica, 685 ....D2
Topeka, 90 ....D3
Toulon, 1,400 ....D2
Tovey, 516 ....D4
Towanda, 493 ....E3
Tower Hill, 609 ....E4
Tower Lakes, 1,310 ....A5
Tremont, 2,029 ....D3
Trenton, 2,610 ....D5
Trimble, 125 ....F4
Triumph, 225 ....D2
Trowbridge, 100 ....E4
Troy, 8,524 ....A3
Troy Grove, 305 ....D2
Tunnel Hill, 80 ....E6
Tuscola, 4,448 ....E4
Ullin, 779 ....D6
Union, 576 ....E1
Union Hill, 66 ....E2
University Park, 6,662 ....F2
Urbana, 36,395 ....E3
Ursa, 595 ....B3
Valier, 662 ....D5
Valley City, 14 ....C4
Valmeyer, 608 ....C5
Vandalia, 6,975 ....D5
Varna, 436 ....D2
Venedy, 137 ....D5
Venetian Village, 3,082 ....B4
Venice, 2,528 ....A3
Vera, 125 ....D4
Vergennes, 491 ....D6
Vermilion, 239 ....F4
Vermont, 792 ....C3
Vernon, 178 ....D5
Vernon Hills, 20,120 ....B5
Verona, 257 ....E2
Versailles, 567 ....C4
Victoria, 323 ....C2
Vienna, 1,234 ....E6
Villa Grove, 2,553 ....E4
Villa Park, 22,075 ....B6
Viola, 956 ....C2
Virden, 3,488 ....D4
Virgil, 266 ....E2
Virginia, 1,728 ....C4
Volo, 180 ....A4
Wadsworth, 3,083 ....B4
Waggoner, 245 ....D4
Walnut, 1,461 ....D2
Walnut Hill, 109 ....D5
Walshville, 89 ....B3
Waltonville, 422 ....D5
Wamac, 1,378 ....D5
Wapella, 651 ....E3
Ware, 125 ....D6
Warren, 1,496 ....D1
Warrensburg, 1,289 ....D4
Warrenville, 13,363 ....A6
Warsaw, 1,793 ....B3
Washburn, 1,147 ....D3
Washington, 10,841 ....D3
Washington Park, 5,345 ....A3
Wasson, 300 ....E6
Wataga, 857 ....C2
Waterloo, 7,614 ....C5
Waterman, 1,224 ....E2
Watseka, 5,670 ....F3
Watson, 729 ....E4
Wauconda, 9,448 ....A5
Waukegan, 87,901 ....B4, F1
Waverly, 1,346 ....D4
Wayne, 2,137 ....A5
Wayne City, 1,089 ....E5
Waynesville, 452 ....D3
Wedron, 300 ....E2
Weldon, 440 ....E3
Wellington, 265 ....F3
Wenona, 1,065 ....D2
Wenonah, 44 ....D4
West Brooklyn, 174 ....D2
Westchester, 16,824 ....B6
West Chicago, 23,469 ....A6
West City, 716 ....E5
West Dundee, 5,428 ....A5
Western Springs, 12,493 ....B6
Westfield, 678 ....F4
West Frankfort, 8,196 ....E6
West Jersey, 50 ....D2
Westmont, 24,554 ....B6
West Peoria, 4,762 ....D3
West Point, 195 ....B3
West Salem, 1,001 ....F5
West Union, 300 ....F4
Westville, 3,175 ....F3
West York, 225 ....F4
Wheaton, 55,416 ....A6, E2
Wheeler, 119 ....E4
Wheeling, 34,496 ....B5, F1
Whiteash, 268 ....E6
White City, 221 ....B3

White Hall, 2,629 ....C4
White Heath, 375 ....E3
Whittington, 250 ....E5
Williamsfield, 620 ....C3
Williamson, 251 ....B3
Williamsville, 1,439 ....D4
Willisville, 694 ....D6
Willowbrook, 8,967 ....B6
Willow Hill, 250 ....E5
Willow Springs, 5,027 ....B6
Wilmette, 27,651 ....B5
Wilmington, 5,134 ....E2
Wilsonville, 604 ....B3
Wilton Center, 125 ....F2
Winchester, 1,650 ....C4
Windsor, 1,125 ....E4
Winfield, 8,718 ....A6
Wing, 80 ....E3
Winnebago, 2,958 ....D1
Winnetka, 12,419 ....B5
Winslow, 345 ....D1
Winthrop Harbor, 6,670 ....B4
Witt, 991 ....D4
Wonder Lake, 1,345 ....E1
Wood Dale, 13,535 ....B5
Woodhull, 809 ....C2
Woodland, 319 ....F3
Woodlawn, 630 ....D5
Woodridge, 30,934 ....B6
Wood River, 11,296 ....A3, C5
Woodson, 559 ....C4
Woodstock, 20,151 ....E1
Woodworth, 150 ....F3
Woosung, 125 ....D2
Worden, 905 ....B3, D5
Worth, 11,047 ....B6
Wyanet, 1,028 ....D2
Wynoose, 40 ....E5
Wyoming, 1,424 ....D2
Xenia, 407 ....E5
Yale, 97 ....E4
Yates City, 725 ....C3
York Center, ...B6
Yorkville, 6,189 ....E2
Zeigler, 1,669 ....D6
Zion, 22,866 ....B4, F1

Other Features

Carlyle, lake D5
Charles Mound, hill C1
Chautauqua National Wildlife
  Refuge C3
Clarence Cannon National
  Wildlife Refuge C4
Clinton, lake E3
Crab Orchard, lake D6
Crab Orchard National Wildlife
  Refuge D6
Des Plaines, river B6
Fox, river A5, E2
Herbert Hoover National
  Historic Site B2
Illinois, river C3, C4, E2
Iowa, river A2, B2
Kankakee, river F2
Kaskaskia, river D4
Land Between The Lakes
  Recreation Area E6
Lincoln Home National
  Historic Site D4
Mark Twain National Wildlife
  Refuge B2, B3, B4, C2, C4, C5
Mark Twain National Forest C6
Meredosia National Wildlife
  Refuge C4
Michigan, lake C5, F1
Midewin Natl. Tallgrass Prairie E2
Mingo National Wildlife
  Refuge C6
Mississippi, river B3, D6
Ohio, river D6
Rend, lake D5
Rock, river D2
Sac & Fox Indian Reservation A2
Sangamon, river C3
Shawnee National Forest D6, E6
Shelbyville, lake E4
Skunk, river B3
Spoon, river C3
Upper Mississippi River National
  Wildlife & Fish Refuge C1
Wabash, river E6

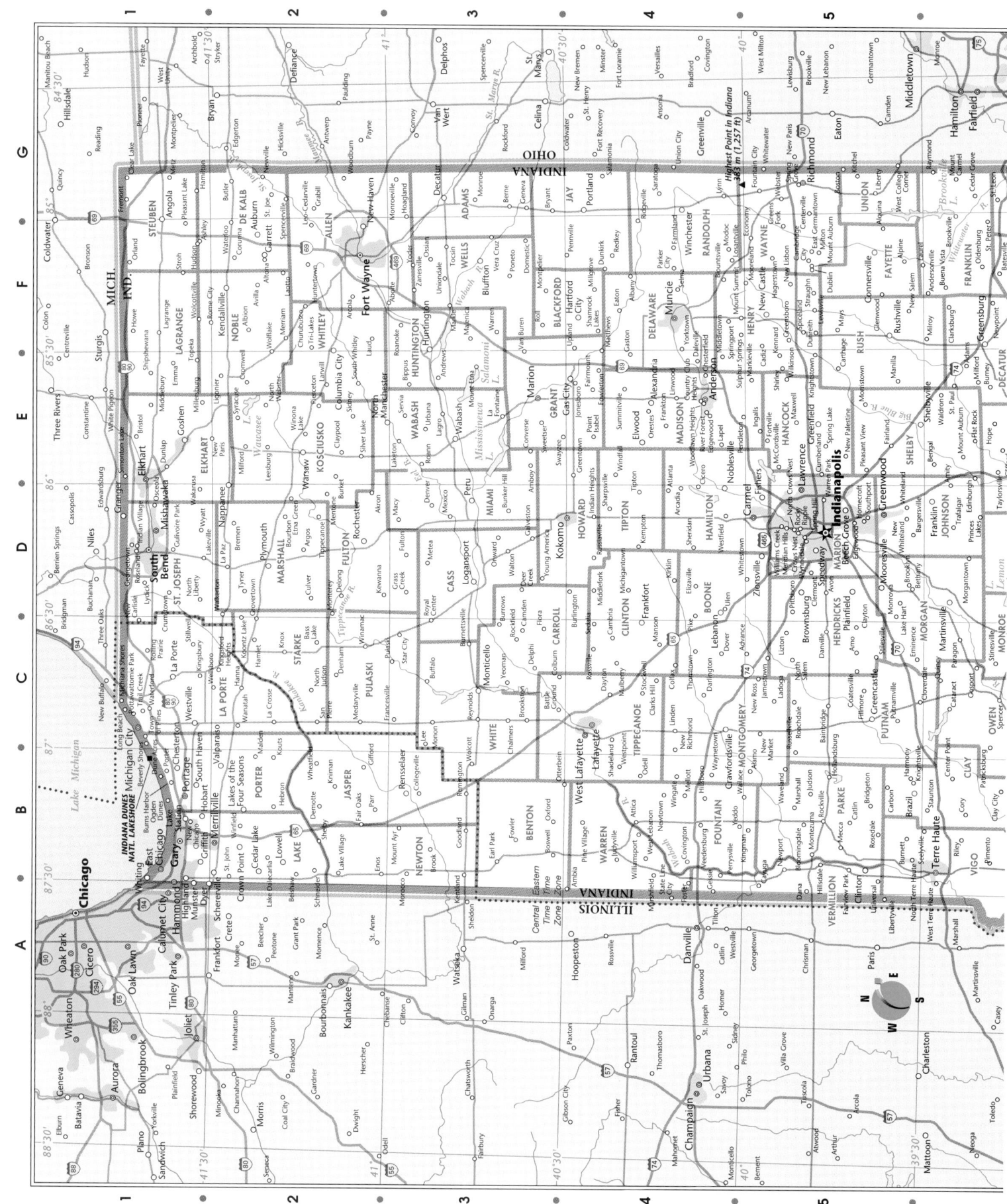

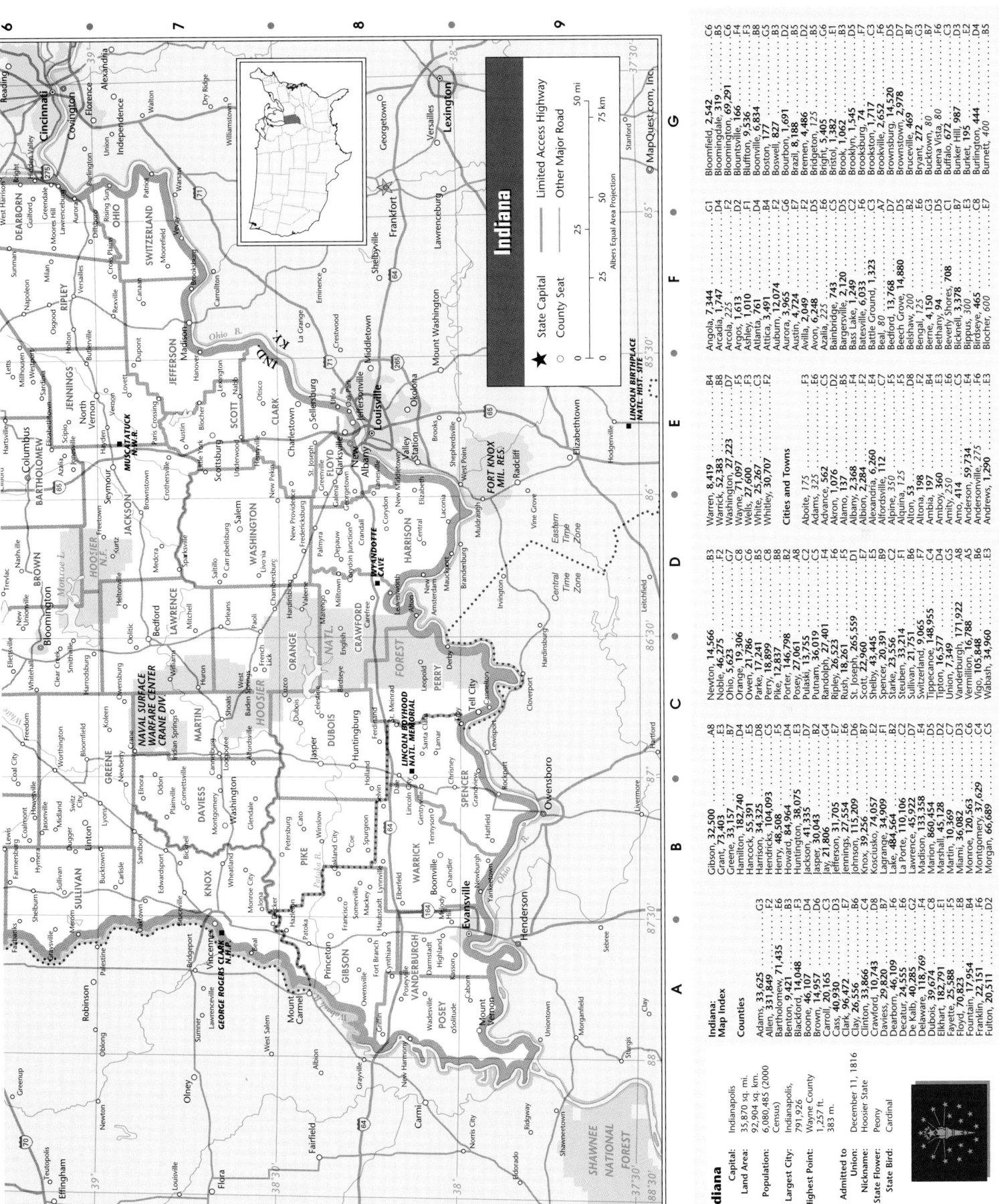

Indiana

Indiana

Capital:	Indianapolis
Land Area:	35,870 sq. mi. / 92,904 sq. km.
Population:	6,080,485 (2000 Census)
Largest City:	Indianapolis, 791,926
Highest Point:	Wayne County 1,257 ft. / 383 m.
Admitted to Union:	December 11, 1816
Nickname:	Hoosier State
State Flower:	Peony
State Bird:	Cardinal

Legend:
★ State Capital
○ County Seat
— Limited Access Highway
— Other Major Road
Albers Equal Area Projection
© MapQuest.com, Inc.

Map Index

Counties

Adams, 33,625	G3	Gibson, 32,500	A8	Newton, 14,566	A3
Allen, 331,849	F2	Grant, 73,403	E3	Noble, 46,275	F2
Bartholomew, 71,435	E6	Greene, 33,157	B7	Ohio, 5,623	G7
Benton, 9,421	B3	Hamilton, 182,740	D4	Orange, 19,306	C8
Blackford, 14,048	F3	Hancock, 55,391	E5	Owen, 21,786	C6
Boone, 46,107	D4	Harrison, 34,325	D8	Parke, 17,241	B5
Brown, 14,957	D6	Hendricks, 104,093	C5	Perry, 18,899	C8
Carroll, 20,165	C3	Henry, 48,508	F4	Pike, 12,837	B8
Cass, 40,930	D3	Howard, 84,964	D4	Porter, 146,798	B2
Clark, 96,472	E7	Huntington, 38,075	F3	Posey, 27,061	A8
Clay, 26,556	B6	Jackson, 41,335	D7	Pulaski, 13,755	C2
Clinton, 33,866	C4	Jasper, 30,043	B2	Putnam, 36,019	C5
Crawford, 10,743	D8	Jay, 21,806	G4	Randolph, 27,401	F4
Daviess, 29,820	B7	Jefferson, 31,705	F6	Ripley, 26,523	F6
Dearborn, 46,109	G6	Jennings, 27,554	E6	Rush, 18,261	E5
Decatur, 24,555	F6	Johnson, 115,209	D6	St. Joseph, 265,559	D1
De Kalb, 40,285	G2	Knox, 39,256	A7	Scott, 22,960	E7
Delaware, 118,769	F4	Kosciusko, 74,057	E2	Shelby, 43,445	E5
Dubois, 39,674	C8	Lagrange, 34,909	F1	Spencer, 20,391	B9
Elkhart, 182,791	E1	Lake, 484,564	B1	Starke, 23,556	C2
Fayette, 25,588	F5	La Porte, 110,106	C1	Steuben, 33,214	F1
Floyd, 70,823	E8	Lawrence, 45,922	C7	Switzerland, 9,065	F7
Fountain, 17,954	B4	Madison, 133,358	E4	Tippecanoe, 148,955	C4
Franklin, 22,151	F6	Marion, 860,454	D5	Tipton, 16,577	D4
Fulton, 20,511	D2	Marshall, 45,128	D2	Union, 7,349	G5
		Martin, 10,369	C7	Vanderburgh, 171,922	A8
		Miami, 36,082	D3	Vermillion, 16,788	A5
		Monroe, 120,563	C6	Vigo, 105,848	A6
		Montgomery, 37,629	C4	Wabash, 34,960	E3
		Morgan, 66,689	D5	Warren, 8,419	B4
				Warrick, 52,383	B8
				Washington, 27,223	D7
				Wayne, 71,097	G5
				Wells, 27,600	F3
				Whitley, 30,707	F2

Cities and Towns

Aboite, 175	F3	Angola, 7,344	G1	Bloomfield, 2,542	C6
Adams, 225	E6	Arcadia, 1,747	D4	Bloomingdale, 319	B5
Akron, 562	D2	Arcola, 225	F2	Bloomington, 69,291	C6
Alamo, 137	C5	Argos, 1,613	D2	Bluffton, 9,536	F3
Albany, 2,368	F4	Ashley, 1,010	F1	Boonville, 6,834	B8
Albion, 2,284	F2	Atlanta, 761	D4	Boston, 177	G5
Alexandria, 6,260	E4	Attica, 3,491	B4	Boswell, 827	B3
Alfordsville, 112	C7	Auburn, 12,074	F2	Bourbon, 1,691	D2
Alpine, 125	B9	Aurora, 3,965	G6	Brazil, 8,188	B5
Alquina, 125	F5	Austin, 4,724	E7	Bremen, 4,486	D2
Alton, 53	D8	Avilla, 2,049	F2	Bridgeton, 125	B5
Altona, 197	F2	Avon, 6,248	D5	Bright, 5,405	G6
Ambia, 197	B4	Azalia, 225	E6	Bristol, 1,382	E1
Amboy, 360	E3	Bainbridge, 743	C5	Brook, 1,062	B3
Amity, 250	D6	Bargersville, 2,120	D5	Brooklyn, 1,545	D5
Amo, 414	C5	Bass Lake, 1,249	C2	Brooksburg, 74	F7
Anderson, 59,734	E4	Batesville, 6,033	F6	Brookston, 1,717	C3
Andersonville, 275	F6	Battle Ground, 1,323	C3	Brookville, 2,652	F6
Andrews, 1,290	E3	Beal, 80	A7	Brownsburg, 14,520	D5
		Bedford, 13,768	C7	Brownstown, 2,978	D7
		Beech Grove, 14,880	D5	Bruceville, 469	B7
		Belshaw, 200	B2	Bryant, 272	G3
		Bengal, 125	C8	Bucktown, 80	G3
		Berne, 4,150	G3	Buena Vista, 80	F6
		Bethany, 94	D6	Buffalo, 672	C3
		Beverly Shores, 708	B1	Bunker Hill, 987	D3
		Bicknell, 3,378	B7	Burlington, 444	D4
		Bippus, 300	E3	Burnett, 400	B5
		Birdseye, 465	C8		
		Blocher, 600	E7		

Burnettsville, 373 . . . . .C3
Burney, 275 . . . . .E6
Burns Harbor, 766 . . . . . . .B1
Burrows, 250 . . . . .C3
Butler, 2,725 . . . . .G2
Butlerville, 450 . . . . .E6
Caborn, 200 . . . . .A9
Cadiz, 161 . . . . .F5
Cambria, 582 . . . . .C3
Cambridge City, 2,121 . . . . .F5
Camden, 582 . . . . .C3
Campbellsburg, 578 . . . . . .D7
Canaan, 90 . . . . .F7
Cannelburg, 140 . . . . .C7
Cannelton, 1,209 . . . . .C9
Carbon, 334 . . . . .B5
Carefree, 30 . . . . .D8
Carlisle, 2,660 . . . . .B7
Carmel, 37,733 . . . . .D5
Carthage, 928 . . . . .E5
Cataract, 150 . . . . .C6
Catlin, 150 . . . . .B5
Cato, 125 . . . . .B8
Cayuga, 1,109 . . . . .B5
Cedar Grove, 185 . . . . .G6
Cedar Lake, 9,279 . . . . . . .B2
Celestine, 275 . . . . .C8
Center Point, 292 . . . . .B6
Centerville, 2,427 . . . . .F5
Central, 200 . . . . .D8
Chalmers, 513 . . . . .C3
Chambersburg, 80 . . . . . . .D7
Chandler, 3,094 . . . . .B8
Charlestown, 5,993 . . . . . . .E8
Chesterfield, 2,969 . . . . . . .E4
Chesterton, 10,488 . . . . . . .B1
Chrisney, 544 . . . . .B8
Churubusco, 1,666 . . . . . . .F2
Cicero, 4,303 . . . . .D4
Clarksburg, 125 . . . . .F6
Clarks Hill, 680 . . . . .C4
Clarksville, 21,400 . . . . . . .E8
Clay City, 1,019 . . . . .B6
Claypool, 311 . . . . .E2
Clayton, 693 . . . . .C5
Clear Creek, 1,800 . . . . . . .C6
Clear Lake, 244 . . . . .G1
Clermont, 1,477 . . . . .D5
Clifford, 291 . . . . .E6
Clinton, 5,126 . . . . .B5
Cloverdale, 2,243 . . . . .C5
Coal City, 150 . . . . .B6
Coalmont, 425 . . . . .B6
Coatesville, 516 . . . . .C5
Coe, 80 . . . . .B8
Colburn, 325 . . . . .C3
Colfax, 768 . . . . .C4
Collegeville, 865 . . . . .B3
Columbia City, 7,077 . . . . . .E2
Columbus, 39,059 . . . . .E6
Connersville, 15,411 . . . . . .F5
Converse, 1,137 . . . . .E3
Cornettsville, 70 . . . . .B7
Corunna, 254 . . . . .F2
Cory, 175 . . . . .B6
Corydon, 2,715 . . . . .D8
Corydon Junction, 650 . . . . .D8
Country Club Heights, 91 . . .E4
Covington, 2,565 . . . . .B4
Crandall, 131 . . . . .D8
Crane, 203 . . . . .C7
Crawfordsville, 15,243 . . . . .C4
Cromwell, 452 . . . . .E2
Cross Plains, 150 . . . . .F7
Crothersville, 1,570 . . . . . . .E7
Crown Point, 19,806 . . . . . .B2
Crows Nest, 96 . . . . .D5
Crumstown, 350 . . . . .D1
Culver, 1,539 . . . . .D2
Cumberland, 5,500 . . . . . . .E5
Cuzco, 125 . . . . .C8
Cynthiana, 693 . . . . .A8
Dale, 1,568 . . . . .B8
Daleville, 1,658 . . . . .E4
Dana, 662 . . . . .B5
Danville, 6,418 . . . . .C5
Darlington, 854 . . . . .C4
Darmstadt, 1,313 . . . . .A8
Dayton, 1,120 . . . . .C4
Decatur, 9,528 . . . . .G3
Decker, 283 . . . . .A7
Deer Creek, 250 . . . . .D3
Delong, 450 . . . . .D2
Delphi, 3,015 . . . . .C3
Demotte, 3,234 . . . . .B2
Denham, 125 . . . . .C2
Denver, 541 . . . . .D3
Depauw, 250 . . . . .D8
Derby, ...C9
Dillsboro, 1,436 . . . . .F6
Domestic, 70 . . . . .C4
Dover, 100 . . . . .C4
Dublin, 697 . . . . .F5
Dubois, 425 . . . . .C8
Dugger, 955 . . . . .B6
Dune Acres, 213 . . . . .B1
Dunkirk, 2,646 . . . . .F4
Dunlap, 5,887 . . . . .E1
Dunreith, 184 . . . . .F5
Dupont, 392 . . . . .E7
Dyer, 13,895 . . . . .A1
Earl Park, 485 . . . . .B3
East Chicago, 32,414 . . . . .B1
East Germantown, 243 . . . . .F5
Eaton, 1,603 . . . . .F4
Economy, 199 . . . . .F5
Edgewood (Madison Co.),
  1,988 . . . . .E4
Edgewood (Marion Co.) D5
Edinburgh, 4,505 . . . . .D6
Edwardsport, 363 . . . . .B7
Elberfeld, 636 . . . . .B8
Elizabeth, 137 . . . . .D8
Elizabethtown, 391 . . . . . . .E6

Elizaville, 150 . . . . .D4
Elkhart, 51,874 . . . . .E1
Ellettsville, 5,078 . . . . .C6
Elnora, 721 . . . . .B7
Elwood, 9,737 . . . . .E4
Eminence, 275 . . . . .C5
Emma, 325 . . . . .E1
English, 673 . . . . .D8
Enos, 60 . . . . .B2
Etna Green, 663 . . . . .D2
Evansville, 121,582 . . . . . . .A9
Fairbanks, 175 . . . . .A6
Fairland, 1,276 . . . . .E5
Fairmount, 2,992 . . . . .E4
Fair Oaks, 175 . . . . .B2
Fairview Park, 1,496 . . . . . . .B5
Farmersburg, 1,180 . . . . . . .B6
Farmland, 1,456 . . . . .F4
Ferdinand, 2,277 . . . . .C8
Fillmore, 545 . . . . .C5
Fishers, 37,835 . . . . .D5
Flat Rock, 325 . . . . .E6
Flora, 2,227 . . . . .C3
Fortville, 3,444 . . . . .E5
Fort Branch, 2,320 . . . . . . .A8
Fort Wayne, 205,727 . . . . . .F2
Foster, 125 . . . . .B4
Fountain City, 735 . . . . .G5
Fowler, 2,415 . . . . .B3
Fowlerton, 298 . . . . .E4
Francesville, 905 . . . . .C3
Francisco, 543 . . . . .B8
Frankfort, 16,662 . . . . .C4
Franklin, 19,463 . . . . .D6
Frankton, 1,905 . . . . .E4
Fredericksburg, 92 . . . . .D8
Freedom, 150 . . . . .C6
Freetown, 600 . . . . .D7
Fremont, 1,696 . . . . .G1
French Lick, 1,941 . . . . .C7
Fulton, 326 . . . . .D3
Galena, 1,831 . . . . .E8
Galveston, 1,532 . . . . .D3
Garrett, 5,803 . . . . .F2
Gas City, 5,940 . . . . .E4
Gaston, 1,010 . . . . .E4
Geneva, 1,368 . . . . .G3
Gentryville, 262 . . . . .B8
Georgetown (Floyd Co.), 2,227 .E8
Georgetown (St. Joseph Co.),
  4,497 . . . . .D1
Gessie, 100 . . . . .B4
Gifford, 80 . . . . .B2
Glendale, 50 . . . . .B7
Glenwood, 318 . . . . .F5
Goodland, 1,096 . . . . .B3
Goshen, 29,383 . . . . .E1
Gosport, 715 . . . . .C6
Grabill, 1,113 . . . . .G2
Grandview, 696 . . . . .C9
Granger, 28,284 . . . . .D1
Grass Creek, 100 . . . . .D3
Graysville, 125 . . . . .A6
Greencastle, 9,880 . . . . . . .C5
Greendale, 4,296 . . . . .G6
Greenfield, 14,600 . . . . .E5
Greensboro, 174 . . . . .F5
Greensburg, 10,260 . . . . . . .F6
Greens Fork, 371 . . . . .F5
Greentown, 2,546 . . . . .E4
Greenville, 591 . . . . .E8
Greenwood, 36,037 . . . . . . .D5
Griffin, 160 . . . . .A8
Griffith, 17,334 . . . . .B1
Grovertown, 350 . . . . .C2
Guilford, 100 . . . . .G6
Gulivoire Park, 2,974 . . . . . .D1
Hagerstown, 1,768 . . . . .F5
Hamilton, 1,233 . . . . .G1
Hamlet, 820 . . . . .C2
Hammond, 83,048 . . . . .A1
Hanna, 500 . . . . .C2
Hanover, 2,834 . . . . .F7
Hardinsburg, 244 . . . . .D8
Harmony, 589 . . . . .B5
Harrodsburg, 375 . . . . .C6
Hartford City, 6,928 . . . . . . .F4
Hartsville, 376 . . . . .E6
Hatfield, 1,000 . . . . .B9
Haubstadt, 1,529 . . . . .A8
Hayden, 550 . . . . .E7
Hazleton, 288 . . . . .A8
Hebron, 3,596 . . . . .B2
Heltonville, 225 . . . . .D7
Henryville, 1,545 . . . . .E7
Hidden Valley, 4,417 . . . . . .G6
Highland (Lake Co.), 23,546 . .B1
Highland (Vanderburgh Co.),
  4,107 . . . . .A8
Hillsboro, 489 . . . . .B4
Hillsdale, 300 . . . . .B5
Hoagland, 550 . . . . .G3
Hobart, 25,363 . . . . .B1
Holland, 695 . . . . .B8
Hollandsburg, 125 . . . . .B5
Holton, 407 . . . . .F6
Homecroft, 751 . . . . .D5
Hope, 2,140 . . . . .E6
Howe, 850 . . . . .F1
Howesville, 80 . . . . .B6
Hudson, 396 . . . . .F1
Huntertown, 1,771 . . . . .F2
Huntingburg, 5,598 . . . . . . .C8
Huntington, 17,450 . . . . . . .F3
Huron, 200 . . . . .C7
Hymera, 833 . . . . .B6
Indianapolis, 791,926 . . . . . .D5
Indian Heights, 3,274 . . . . . .D4
Indian Springs, 100 . . . . . . .C7
Indian Village, 144 . . . . .D1
Ingalls, 1,168 . . . . .E5
Iona, 50 . . . . .B7
Jamestown, 886 . . . . .C5

Jasonville, 2,490 . . . . .B6
Jasper, 12,100 . . . . .C8
Jeffersonville, 27,362 . . . . . .E8
Jonesboro, 1,887 . . . . .E4
Jonesville, 220 . . . . .E6
Judson, 60 . . . . .B5
Judyville, 50 . . . . .B4
Kasson, 1,500 . . . . .A8
Kempton, 380 . . . . .D4
Kendallville, 9,616 . . . . .F2
Kennard, 455 . . . . .E5
Kentland, 1,822 . . . . .B3
Kewanna, 614 . . . . .D2
Kingman, 538 . . . . .B5
Kingsbury, 229 . . . . .C1
Kingsford Heights, 1,453 . . . .C2
Kirklin, 766 . . . . .D4
Kitchel, 70 . . . . .G5
Knightstown, 2,148 . . . . . . .E5
Knightsville, 624 . . . . .B5
Kniman, 175 . . . . .B2
Knox, 3,721 . . . . .C2
Kokomo, 46,113 . . . . .D3
Koleen, 70 . . . . .C7
Koontz Lake, 1,554 . . . . . . .C2
Kouts, 1,698 . . . . .B2
Kurtz, 200 . . . . .D7
Laconia, 29 . . . . .D8
La Crosse, 561 . . . . .C2
Ladoga, 1,047 . . . . .C5
Lafayette, 56,397 . . . . .C4
La Fontaine, 900 . . . . .E3
Lagrange, 2,919 . . . . .F1
Lagro, 454 . . . . .E3
Lake Dalecarlia, 1,285 . . . . .B2
Lake Hart, 250 . . . . .D5
Lakes of the Four Seasons,
  7,291 . . . . .B2
Lake Station, 13,948 . . . . . .B1
Laketon, 700 . . . . .E3
Lake Village, 855 . . . . .B2
Lakeville, 567 . . . . .D1
Lamar, 150 . . . . .C8
Lanesville, 614 . . . . .E8
Laotto, 425 . . . . .F2
La Paz, 489 . . . . .D2
Lapel, 1,855 . . . . .E4
La Porte, 21,621 . . . . .C1
Larwill, 282 . . . . .E2
Laud, 250 . . . . .F2
Laurel, 579 . . . . .F5
Lawrence, 38,915 . . . . .D5
Lawrenceburg, 4,685 . . . . . .G6
Leavenworth, 353 . . . . .D8
Lebanon, 14,222 . . . . .D4
Lee, 70 . . . . .C3
Leesburg, 625 . . . . .E2
Leo-Cedarville, 2,782 . . . . . .F2
Leopold, 90 . . . . .C8
Letts, 150 . . . . .E6
Lewis, 225 . . . . .B6
Lewisville, 395 . . . . .F5
Lexington, 325 . . . . .E7
Liberty, 2,061 . . . . .G5
Libertyville, 225 . . . . .A5
Ligonier, 4,357 . . . . .E2
Lincoln City, 150 . . . . .B8
Linden, 700 . . . . .C4
Linton, 5,774 . . . . .B6
Linwood, 700 . . . . .E4
Little York, 185 . . . . .E7
Livonia, 112 . . . . .D7
Lizton, 372 . . . . .C5
Logansport, 19,684 . . . . . . .D3
Long Beach, 1,559 . . . . . . .C1
Loogootee, 2,741 . . . . .C7
Losantville, 280 . . . . .F4
Lovett, 80 . . . . .E7
Lowell, 7,505 . . . . .B2
Lydick, 1,300 . . . . .D1
Lynn, 1,143 . . . . .G4
Lynnville, 781 . . . . .B8
Lyons, 748 . . . . .B7
Mackey, 142 . . . . .B8
Macy, 248 . . . . .D3
Madison, 12,004 . . . . .F7
Majenica, 175 . . . . .F3
Malden, 225 . . . . .B2
Manilla, 425 . . . . .E5
Manson, 125 . . . . .C4
Marengo, 829 . . . . .D8
Marion, 31,320 . . . . .E3
Markle, 1,102 . . . . .F3
Markleville, 383 . . . . .E5
Marshall, 360 . . . . .B5
Marshfield, 100 . . . . .B4
Martinsville, 11,698 . . . . . . .D6
Matthews, 595 . . . . .F4
Mauckport, 83 . . . . .D8
Maxwell, 550 . . . . .E5
Mays, 225 . . . . .F5
McCordsville, 1,134 . . . . . . .E5
Mecca, 355 . . . . .B5
Medaryville, 565 . . . . .C2
Medora, 565 . . . . .D7
Mellott, 207 . . . . .B4
Melody Hill A8
Mentone, 898 . . . . .D2
Meridian Hills, 1,713 . . . . . . .D5
Merom, 294 . . . . .A6
Merriam, 225 . . . . .F2
Merrillville, 30,560 . . . . .B2
Metea, 100 . . . . .D3
Metz, 250 . . . . .G1
Mexico, 984 . . . . .D3
Miami, ...D3
Michiana Shores, 330 . . . . . .C1
Michigan City, 32,900 . . . . . .C1
Michigantown, 406 . . . . .D4
Middlebury, 2,956 . . . . .E1
Middlefork, 150 . . . . .D4
Middletown, 2,488 . . . . .E4
Midland, 350 . . . . .B6
Milan, 1,816 . . . . .F6
Milford (Decatur Co.), 121 . . .E6

Milford (Kosciusko Co.), 1,550 .E2
Millersburg, 868 . . . . .E1
Millgrove, 200 . . . . .F4
Millhousen, 136 . . . . .F6
Milltown, 932 . . . . .D8
Milroy, 800 . . . . .F6
Milton, 611 . . . . .F5
Mishawaka, 46,557 . . . . . . .D1
Mitchell, 4,567 . . . . .D7
Modoc, 225 . . . . .F4
Monon, 1,733 . . . . .C3
Monroe, 734 . . . . .G3
Monroe City, 548 . . . . .B7
Monroeville, 1,236 . . . . .G3
Monrovia, 628 . . . . .D5
Monterey, 231 . . . . .D2
Montezuma, 1,179 . . . . .B5
Montgomery, 368 . . . . .B7
Monticello, 5,723 . . . . .C3
Montpelier, 1,929 . . . . .F3
Moorefield, 125 . . . . .F7
Mooreland, 393 . . . . .F5
Moores Hill, 635 . . . . .F6
Mooresville, 9,273 . . . . .D5
Morgantown, 964 . . . . .D6
Morocco, 1,127 . . . . .B3
Morristown, 1,133 . . . . .E5
Mount Auburn (Shelby Co.),
  125 . . . . .E6
Mount Auburn (Wayne Co.), 75 .F5
Mount Ayr, 147 . . . . .B3
Mount Carmel, 106 . . . . . . .G6
Mount Etna, 110 . . . . .E3
Mount Summit, 313 . . . . . . .F4
Mount Vernon, 7,478 . . . . . .A9
Mulberry, 1,387 . . . . .C4
Muncie, 67,430 . . . . .F4
Munster, 21,511 . . . . .A1
Nabb, 200 . . . . .E7
Napoleon, 238 . . . . .F6
Nappanee, 6,710 . . . . .D2
Nashville, 825 . . . . .D6
New Albany, 37,603 . . . . . . .E8
New Amsterdam, 1 . . . . . . .D8
Newberry, 206 . . . . .B7
Newburgh, 3,088 . . . . .B9
New Carlisle, 1,505 . . . . . . .C1
New Castle, 17,780 . . . . . . .F5
New Chicago, 2,063 . . . . . . .B1
New Harmony, 916 . . . . . . .A8
New Haven, 12,406 . . . . . . .F2
New Lisbon, 325 . . . . .F5
New Market, 659 . . . . .C5
New Middletown, 77 . . . . . . .D8
New Palestine, 1,264 . . . . . .E5
New Paris, 1,006 . . . . .E2
New Pekin, 1,334 . . . . .D7
Newpoint, 290 . . . . .F6
Newport, 578 . . . . .B5
New Richmond, 349 . . . . . . .C4
New Ross, 334 . . . . .C5
New Salem, 200 . . . . .F5
Newtown, 162 . . . . .B4
New Unionville, 500 . . . . . . .D6
Newville, 200 . . . . .G2
New Whiteland, 4,579 . . . . . .D5
Noblesville, 28,590 . . . . . . .D4
North Crows Nest, 42 . . . . . .D5
North Judson, 1,675 . . . . . . .C2
North Liberty, 1,402 . . . . . . .D1
North Manchester, 6,260 . . . .E2
North Salem, 591 . . . . .C5
North Terre Haute, 4,606 . . . .B5
North Vernon, 6,515 . . . . . . .E6
North Webster, 1,067 . . . . . .E2
Oakland City, 2,588 . . . . . . .B8
Oak Park, 5,379 . . . . .E8
Oaktown, 633 . . . . .B7
Odell, 80 . . . . .B4
Odon, 1,376 . . . . .C7
Ogden Dunes, 1,313 . . . . . .B1
Oldenburg, 647 . . . . .F6
Onward, 81 . . . . .D3
Oolitic, 1,152 . . . . .C7
Orestes, 334 . . . . .E4
Orland, 341 . . . . .F1
Orleans, 2,273 . . . . .D7
Osceola, 1,859 . . . . .D1
Osgood, 1,669 . . . . .F6
Ossian, 2,943 . . . . .F3
Otisco, 225 . . . . .E7
Otterbein, 1,312 . . . . .B3
Owensburg, 200 . . . . .C7
Owensville, 1,322 . . . . .A8
Oxford, 1,271 . . . . .B3
Palmyra, 633 . . . . .D8
Paoli, 3,844 . . . . .D7
Paragon, 663 . . . . .C6
Paris Crossing, 200 . . . . . . .E7
Parker City, 1,416 . . . . .F4
Parr, 150 . . . . .B2
Patoka, 749 . . . . .A8
Patricksburg, 250 . . . . .C6
Patriot, 202 . . . . .G7
Pendleton, 3,873 . . . . .E4
Pennville, 706 . . . . .F4
Perrysville, 502 . . . . .B4
Peru, 12,994 . . . . .D3
Petersburg, 2,570 . . . . .B8
Pierceton, 695 . . . . .E2
Pike, 150 . . . . .D4
Pimento, 275 . . . . .B6
Pine Village, 255 . . . . .B4
Pittsboro, 1,588 . . . . .D5
Plainfield, 18,396 . . . . .D5
Plainville, 513 . . . . .B7
Pleasant Lake, 750 . . . . .F1
Pleasant View, 850 . . . . . . .E5
Plymouth, 9,840 . . . . .D2
Point Isabel, 125 . . . . .E4
Poneto, 240 . . . . .F3
Portage, 33,496 . . . . .B1
Porter, 4,972 . . . . .B1

Portland, 6,437 . . . . .G4
Poseyville, 1,187 . . . . .A8
Pottawattomie Park, 300 . . . .C1
Princes Lakes, 1,506 . . . . . .D6
Princeton, 8,175 . . . . .A8
Pulaski, 175 . . . . .C3
Putnamville, 225 . . . . .C5
Quincy, 250 . . . . .C6
Raymond, 50 . . . . .G6
Redkey, 1,427 . . . . .F4
Remington, 1,323 . . . . .B3
Rensselaer, 5,294 . . . . .B3
Rexville, 175 . . . . .F7
Reynolds, 547 . . . . .C3
Richmond, 39,124 . . . . .G5
Ridgeville, 843 . . . . .F4
Riley, 160 . . . . .B6
Rising Sun, 2,470 . . . . .G7
River Forest, 28 . . . . .E3
Roachdale, 975 . . . . .C5
Roann, 400 . . . . .E3
Roanoke, 1,495 . . . . .F3
Rochester, 6,414 . . . . .D2
Rockfield, 225 . . . . .C3
Rockport, 2,160 . . . . .B9
Rockville, 2,765 . . . . .B5
Rocky Ripple, 712 . . . . .D5
Roll, 275 . . . . .F3
Rolling Prairie, 800 . . . . .C1
Rome City, 1,615 . . . . .F1
Rosedale, 750 . . . . .B5
Roseland, 800 . . . . .D1
Rossville, 1,513 . . . . .C4
Royal Center, 832 . . . . .C3
Rushville, 5,995 . . . . .F5
Russellville, 340 . . . . .C5
Russiaville, 1,092 . . . . .D4
St. Joe, 478 . . . . .G2
St. John, 8,382 . . . . .A1
St. Joseph, 375 . . . . .E8
St. Leon, 387 . . . . .G6
St. Meinrad, 700 . . . . .C8
St. Paul, 1,022 . . . . .E6
St. Peter, 175 . . . . .F6
Salamonia, 158 . . . . .G4
Salem, 6,172 . . . . .D7
Saltillo, 107 . . . . .D7
Sandborn, 451 . . . . .B7
San Pierre, 156 . . . . .C2
Santa Claus, 2,041 . . . . . . .C8
Saratoga, 288 . . . . .G4
Sardinia, 150 . . . . .E6
Schererville, 24,851 . . . . . . .B2
Schneider, 317 . . . . .B2
Scipio, 275 . . . . .E6
Scottsburg, 6,040 . . . . .E7
Sedalia, 175 . . . . .C4
Seelyville, 1,182 . . . . .B6
Sellersburg, 6,071 . . . . .E8
Selma, 880 . . . . .F4
Selvin, 200 . . . . .B8
Servia, 225 . . . . .E3
Seymour, 18,101 . . . . .E7
Shadeland, 1,682 . . . . .C4
Shamrock Lakes, 168 . . . . . .F4
Sharpsville, 618 . . . . .D4
Shelburn, 1,268 . . . . .B6
Shelby, 475 . . . . .B2
Shelbyville, 17,951 . . . . .E5
Sheridan, 2,520 . . . . .D4
Shipshewana, 536 . . . . .E1
Shirley, 806 . . . . .E5
Shoals, 807 . . . . .C7
Sidney, 168 . . . . .E2
Silver Lake, 546 . . . . .E2
Simonton Lake, 4,053 . . . . . .E1
Smithville, 750 . . . . .C6
Solitude, 125 . . . . .A8
Somerville, 312 . . . . .B8
South Bend, 107,789 . . . . . .D1
South Haven, 5,619 . . . . . . .B1
Southport, 1,852 . . . . .D5
South Whitley, 1,782 . . . . . . .E2
Sparksville, 100 . . . . .D7
Speedway, 12,881 . . . . .D5
Spencer, 2,508 . . . . .C6
Spencerville, 350 . . . . .G2
Spiceland, 807 . . . . .F5
Spring Grove, 386 . . . . .G5
Spring Hill, 97 . . . . .G4
Spring Lake, 262 . . . . .E5
Springport, 174 . . . . .F4
Spurgeon, 227 . . . . .B8
Star City, 377 . . . . .C3
State Line City, 141 . . . . . . .A4
Staunton, 550 . . . . .B6
Stilesville, 261 . . . . .C5
Stillwell, 375 . . . . .C1
Stinesville, 194 . . . . .C6
Stockwell, 425 . . . . .C4
Straughn, 263 . . . . .F5
Stroh, 700 . . . . .F1
Sullivan, 4,617 . . . . .B6
Sulphur Springs, 346 . . . . . .F4
Summitville, 1,090 . . . . .E4
Sunman, 805 . . . . .F6
Swayzee, 1,011 . . . . .E4
Sweetser, 906 . . . . .E3
Switz City, 311 . . . . .B6
Syracuse, 3,038 . . . . .E2
Taylorsville, 936 . . . . .E6
Tell City, 7,845 . . . . .C9
Tennyson, 290 . . . . .B8
Terre Haute, 59,614 . . . . . . .B6
Thorntown, 1,562 . . . . .C4
Tippecanoe D2
Tipton, 5,251 . . . . .D4
Tocsin, 275 . . . . .F3
Topeka, 1,159 . . . . .E1
Town of Pines, 798 . . . . . . .C1
Trafalgar, 798 . . . . .D6
Trail Creek, 2,296 . . . . .C1
Trevlac, 350 . . . . .D6
Tri-Lakes, 3,925 . . . . .F2

Troy, 392 . . . . .C8
Tyner, 300 . . . . .D2
Ulen, 123 . . . . .D4
Underwood, 425 . . . . .E7
Union City, 3,622 . . . . .G4
Uniondale, 277 . . . . .F3
Universal, 419 . . . . .B5
Upland, 3,803 . . . . .F4
Urbana, 325 . . . . .E3
Utica, 591 . . . . .E8
Valeene, 200 . . . . .D8
Valparaiso, 27,428 . . . . . . .B2
Van Buren, 935 . . . . .E3
Veedersburg, 2,299 . . . . . . .B4
Vera Cruz, 55 . . . . .F3
Vernon, 330 . . . . .E7
Versailles, 1,784 . . . . .F6
Vevay, 1,735 . . . . .F7
Vincennes, 18,701 . . . . . . .A7
Wabash, 11,743 . . . . .E3
Wadesville, 500 . . . . .A8
Wakarusa, 1,618 . . . . .D1
Waldron, 1,100 . . . . .E6
Walkerton, 2,274 . . . . .D2
Wallace, 100 . . . . .B4
Walton, 1,069 . . . . .D3
Wanatah, 1,013 . . . . .C2
Warren, 1,272 . . . . .F3
Warren Park, 1,656 . . . . . . .D5
Warsaw, 12,415 . . . . .E2
Washington, 11,380 . . . . . .B7
Waterford, 225 . . . . .C1
Waterloo, 2,200 . . . . .F2
Waveland, 416 . . . . .B5
Waynetown, 909 . . . . .B4
Webster, 550 . . . . .G5
Wellsboro, 600 . . . . .C2
West Baden Springs, 618 . . .C7
West College Corner, 634 . . .G5
Westfield, 9,293 . . . . .D4
West Harrison, 284 . . . . . . .G6
West Lafayette, 28,778 . . . . .C4
West Lebanon, 793 . . . . . . .B4
Westpoint, 425 . . . . .B4
Westport, 1,515 . . . . .E6
West Terre Haute, 2,330 . . . .B6
Westville, 2,116 . . . . .C1
Wheatfield, 772 . . . . .B2
Wheatland, 504 . . . . .B7
Whitehall, 175 . . . . .C6
Whiteland, 3,958 . . . . .D5
Whitestown, 471 . . . . .D5
Whitewater, 78 . . . . .G5
Whiting, 5,137 . . . . .B1
Wilkinson, 356 . . . . .E5
Williams, 275 . . . . .C7
Williams Creek, 413 . . . . . . .D5
Williamsport, 1,935 . . . . . . .B4
Winamac, 2,418 . . . . .C2
Winchester, 5,037 . . . . .G4
Windfall, 712 . . . . .E4
Winfield, 2,298 . . . . .B2
Wingate, 299 . . . . .B4
Winona Lake, 3,987 . . . . . . .E2
Winslow, 881 . . . . .B8
Wolcott, 989 . . . . .B3
Wolcottville, 933 . . . . .F1
Wolflake, 350 . . . . .F2
Woodburn, 1,579 . . . . .G2
Woodlawn Heights, 73 . . . . .E4
Worthington, 1,481 . . . . . . .C6
Wyatt, 225 . . . . .D1
Wynnedale, 275 . . . . .D5
Yankeetown, 375 . . . . .B9
Yeddo, 200 . . . . .B4
Yeoman, 96 . . . . .C3
Yoder, 300 . . . . .F3
Yorktown, 4,785 . . . . .F4
Young America, 300 . . . . . .D3
Zanesville, 602 . . . . .F3
Zionsville, 8,775 . . . . .D5

Other Features

Big Blue, river E5
Brookville, lake G6
Eel, river E3
Fort Knox Mil. Res. E9
George Rogers Clark N.H.P. . .A7
Highest Point in Indiana G4
Hoosier National Forest . .C7, D6
Indiana Dunes Natl.
  Lakeshore B1
Kankakee, river C2
Lemon, lake D6
Lincoln Birthplace National
  Historic Site E9
Lincoln Boyhood National
  Memorial C8
Maumee, river G2
Michigan, lake B1
Mississinewa, lake E3
Monroe, lake D6
Muscatatuck National Wildlife
  Refuge E7
Naval Surface Warfare Center
  Crane Division C7
Ohio, river A9, F7
Patoka, river B8
St. Joseph, river G2
St. Marys, river G3
Salamoni, lake E3
Shawnee National Forest . . .A9
Tippecanoe, river D2
Wabash, river A8, B4, F3
Wawasee, lake E2
White, river B7
Whitewater, river F6
Wyandotte, cave D8

Iowa

- **Capital:** Des Moines
- **Land Area:** 55,875 sq. mi. 144,716 sq. km.
- **Population:** 2,926,324 (2000 Census)
- **Largest City:** Des Moines, 198,682
- **Highest Point:** Osceola County, 1,670 ft. 509 m.
- **Admitted to Union:** December 28, 1846
- **Nickname:** Hawkeye State
- **State Flower:** Wild Rose
- **State Bird:** Eastern Goldfinch

Iowa:
Map Index

Counties

Adair, 8,243 ... F5
Adams, 4,482 ... E5
Allamakee, 14,675 ... M1
Appanoose, 13,721 ... J6
Audubon, 6,830 ... E4
Benton, 25,308 ... K3
Black Hawk, 128,012 ... K2
Boone, 26,224 ... G4
Bremer, 23,325 ... K2
Buchanan, 21,093 ... L2
Buena Vista, 20,411 ... D2
Butler, 15,305 ... J2
Calhoun, 11,115 ... E3
Carroll, 21,421 ... E3
Cass, 14,684 ... E5
Cedar, 18,187 ... M4
Cerro Gordo, 46,447 ... H1
Cherokee, 13,035 ... C2
Chickasaw, 13,095 ... K2
Clarke, 9,133 ... G6
Clay, 17,372 ... D2
Clayton, 18,678 ... M1
Clinton, 50,149 ... P4
Crawford, 16,942 ... D3
Dallas, 40,750 ... F4
Davis, 8,541 ... K6
Decatur, 8,689 ... G6
Delaware, 18,404 ... M3
Des Moines, 42,351 ... M6
Dickinson, 16,424 ... D1
Dubuque, 89,143 ... N3
Emmet, 11,027 ... E1
Fayette, 22,008 ... L2
Floyd, 16,900 ... J2
Franklin, 10,704 ... H2
Fremont, 8,010 ... C6
Greene, 10,366 ... F4
Grundy, 12,369 ... J3
Guthrie, 11,353 ... E4
Hamilton, 16,438 ... G3
Hancock, 12,100 ... G1
Hardin, 18,812 ... H3
Harrison, 15,666 ... C4
Henry, 20,336 ... L5
Howard, 9,932 ... K1
Humboldt, 10,381 ... F2
Ida, 7,837 ... D3
Iowa, 15,671 ... K4
Jackson, 20,296 ... N3
Jasper, 37,213 ... H4
Jefferson, 16,181 ... K5
Johnson, 111,006 ... L4
Jones, 20,221 ... M3
Keokuk, 11,400 ... K5
Kossuth, 17,163 ... F1
Lee, 38,052 ... M6
Linn, 191,701 ... L3
Louisa, 12,183 ... M5
Lucas, 9,422 ... H6
Lyon, 11,763 ... B1
Madison, 14,019 ... F5
Mahaska, 22,335 ... J5
Marion, 32,052 ... H5
Marshall, 39,311 ... J3
Mills, 14,547 ... C6
Mitchell, 10,874 ... J1
Monona, 10,020 ... C3
Monroe, 8,016 ... J5
Montgomery, 11,771 ... D5
Muscatine, 41,722 ... M5
O'Brien, 15,102 ... C1
Osceola, 7,003 ... C1
Page, 16,976 ... D6
Palo Alto, 10,147 ... E1
Plymouth, 24,849 ... B2
Pocahontas, 8,662 ... E2
Polk, 374,601 ... H4
Pottawattamie, 87,704 ... D5
Poweshiek, 18,815 ... J4
Ringgold, 5,469 ... F6
Sac, 11,529 ... D3
Scott, 158,668 ... N4
Shelby, 13,173 ... D4
Sioux, 31,589 ... B1
Story, 79,981 ... H4
Tama, 18,103 ... K3
Taylor, 6,958 ... E6
Union, 12,309 ... F6
Van Buren, 7,809 ... K6
Wapello, 36,051 ... K5
Warren, 40,671 ... G5
Washington, 20,670 ... L5
Wayne, 6,730 ... H6
Webster, 40,235 ... F3
Winnebago, 11,723 ... G1
Winneshiek, 21,310 ... L1
Woodbury, 103,877 ... B3
Worth, 7,909 ... H1
Wright, 14,334 ... G2

Cities and Towns

Abingdon, 50 ... K5
Ackley, 1,809 ... H2
Ackworth, 85 ... H5
Adair, 839 ... E4
Adel, 3,435 ... F4
Afton, 917 ... F5
Agency, 622 ... K6
Ainsworth, 524 ... L5
Akron, 1,489 ... A2
Albert City, 709 ... E2
Albia, 3,706 ... J5
Albion, 592 ... J3
Alburnett, 559 ... L3
Alden, 904 ... H2
Alexander, 165 ... H2
Algona, 5,741 ... F1
Alleman, 439 ... G4
Allerton, 559 ... H6
Allison, 1,006 ... J2
Alta, 1,865 ... D2
Alta Vista, 286 ... K1
Alton, 1,095 ... B2
Altoona, 10,345 ... H4
Alvord, 187 ... B1
Amana, 700 ... L4
Amber, 125 ... M3
Ames, 50,731 ... G3
Anamosa, 5,494 ... M3
Anderson, 80 ... C6
Andover, 87 ... P4
Andrew, 460 ... N3
Anita, 1,049 ... E5
Ankeny, 27,117 ... G4
Anthon, 649 ... C3
Aplington, 1,054 ... J2
Arbor Hill, ... F5
Arcadia, 443 ... D3
Archer, 126 ... C1
Aredale, 89 ... J2
Argyle, 200 ... L6
Arion, 136 ... D4
Arispe, 89 ... F6
Arlington, 490 ... L2
Armstrong, 979 ... F1
Arnolds Park, 1,162 ... D1
Arthur, 245 ... D3
Asbury, 2,450 ... N2
Ashton, 461 ... C1
Aspinwall, 58 ... D4
Athelstan, 18 ... E6
Atkins, 977 ... L3
Atlantic, 7,257 ... D5
Attica, 125 ... H5
Auburn, 296 ... E3
Audubon, 2,382 ... E4
Aurelia, 1,062 ... D2
Aurora, 194 ... L2
Avery, 125 ... J5
Avoca, 1,610 ... D5
Ayrshire, 202 ... E1
Badger, 610 ... F2
Bagley, 354 ... F4
Baldwin, 127 ... N3
Balltown, 73 ... N2
Bancroft, 808 ... F1
Bankston, 27 ... N2
Barnes City, 201 ... K4
Barnum, 195 ... F2
Bartlett, ... C6
Bassett, 74 ... J1
Batavia, 500 ... K5
Battle Creek, 743 ... C3
Baxter, 1,052 ... H4
Bayard, 536 ... E4
Beacon, 518 ... J5
Beaconsfield, 11 ... F6
Beaman, 210 ... J3
Beaver, 53 ... F3
Bedford, 1,620 ... E6
Belknap, 70 ...
Belle Plaine, 2,878 ... K4
Bellevue, 2,350 ... P3
Belmond, 2,560 ... G2
Bennett, 395 ... N4
Bentley, 90 ... C5
Benton, 40 ... F6
Bentonsport, ... L6
Berkley, 24 ... F4
Bernard, 97 ... N3
Bertram, 681 ... L4
Berwick, 450 ... G4
Bettendorf, 31,275 ... P4
Bevington, 58 ... G5
Bingham, 60 ... D6
Birmingham, 423 ... L6
Blairsburg, 235 ... G3
Blairstown, 682 ... K4
Blakesburg, 374 ... J6
Blanchard, 61 ... D6
Blencoe, 231 ... B4
Blockton, 192 ... F6
Bloomfield, 2,601 ... K6
Blue Grass, 1,169 ... N4
Bluffton, 80 ... L1
Bode, 327 ... F2
Bonaparte, 458 ... L6
Bondurant, 1,846 ... H4
Boone, 12,803 ... G3
Botna, ... D4
Bouton, 150 ... F4
Boxholm, 215 ... F3
Boyden, 672 ... B1
Boyer, ... D3
Braddyville, 176 ... D6
Bradford, 150 ... H2
Bradgate, 101 ... F2
Brandon, 311 ... K3
Brayton, 145 ... E4
Breda, 477 ... E3
Bremer, 90 ... K2
Bridgewater, 178 ... E5
Brighton, 687 ... L5
Bristow, 202 ... J2
Britt, 2,052 ... G1
Bronson, 269 ... B3
Brooklyn, 1,367 ... K4
Brooks, 100 ...
Brunsville, 146 ... B2
Buckeye, 110 ... H3
Buck Grove, 49 ... D4
Buckingham, 70 ... K3
Buffalo, 1,321 ... N5
Buffalo Center, 963 ... G1
Burchinal, 90 ... H1
Burlington, 26,839 ... M6
Burr Oak, 175 ... L1
Burt, 556 ... F1
Bussey, 450 ... J5
Calamus, 394 ... N4
Callender, 424 ... F3
Calmar, 1,058 ... L1
Calumet, 181 ... C2
Camanche, 4,215 ... P4
Cambridge, 819 ... G4
Canton, ... N3
Cantril, 257 ... K6
Carbon, 28 ... E5
Carl, ... E5
Carlisle, 3,497 ... H4
Carnarvon, 100 ... D3
Carmel, 150 ... B1
Carpenter, 130 ... H1
Carroll, 10,106 ... E3
Carson, 668 ... D5
Carter Lake, 3,248 ... C5
Cascade, 1,958 ... M3
Castalia, 175 ... L1
Castana, 178 ... C3
Casey, 478 ... E4
Cedar Falls, 36,145 ... K2
Cedar Rapids, 120,758 ... L4
Center Junction, 131 ... M3
Center Point, 2,007 ... L3
Centerville, 5,924 ... J6
Central City, 1,157 ... L3
Centralia, 101 ... N3
Chapin, 175 ... H2
Chariton, 4,573 ... H5
Charles City, 7,812 ... J1
Charleston, 50 ... L6
Charlotte, 421 ... P4
Charter Oak, 530 ... C3
Chatsworth, 89 ... A2
Chelsea, 287 ... K4
Cherokee, 5,369 ... C2
Chester, 151 ... K1
Chillicothe, 90 ... J5
Churdan, 418 ... F3
Cincinnati, 428 ... J6
Clare, 190 ... F2
Clarence, 1,008 ... M4
Clarinda, 5,690 ... D6
Clarion, 2,968 ... G2
Clarksville, 1,441 ... J2
Clayton, 55 ... M2
Clearfield, 371 ... F6
Clear Lake, 8,161 ... H1
Cleghorn, 250 ... C2
Clemons, 148 ... H3
Clermont, 716 ... L1
Cleves, ... J3
Climbing Hill, 100 ... B3
Clinton, 27,772 ... P4
Clio, 91 ... H6
Clive, 12,855 ... G4
Cloverdale, 40 ... C1
Clutier, 229 ... K3
Coburg, 31 ... D6
Coggon, 745 ... L3
Coin, 252 ... D6
Colesburg, 412 ... M2
Colfax, 2,151 ... H4
College Springs, 246 ... D6
Collins, 499 ... H4
Colo, 868 ... H3
Columbia, 135 ... H5
Columbus City, 376 ... M5
Columbus Junction, 1,900 ... M5
Colwell, 76 ... J1
Conesville, 424 ... M5
Conrad, 1,055 ... J3
Conroy, 175 ... L4
Conway, 63 ... E6
Coon Rapids, 1,305 ... E4
Cooper, 50 ... F4
Coppock, 57 ... L5
Coralville, 15,123 ... L4
Cornelia, 150 ... G2
Corning, 1,783 ... E6
Correctionville, 851 ... C3
Corwith, 350 ... G2
Corydon, 1,591 ... H6
Cotter, 48 ... M5
Coulter, 262 ... H2
Council Bluffs, 58,268 ... C5
Craig, 102 ... B2
Crawfordsville, 295 ... L5
Crescent, 537 ... C5
Cresco, 3,905 ... K1
Creston, 7,597 ... F5
Cromwell, 120 ... F5
Croton, ... L6
Crystal Lake, 285 ... G1
Cumberland, 281 ... E5
Cumming, 162 ... G5
Curlew, 62 ... E2
Cushing, 246 ... C3
Cylinder, 110 ... E1
Dakota City, 911 ... F2
Dallas Center, 1,595 ... G4
Dana, 84 ... F3
Danbury, 384 ... C3
Danville, 914 ... M6
Davenport, 98,359 ... N4
Davis City, 275 ... G6
Dawson, 155 ... F4
Dayton, 884 ... F3
Decatur City, 199 ... G6
Decorah, 8,172 ... L1
Dedham, 280 ... E4
Deep River, 288 ... K4
Defiance, 346 ... D4
Delaware, 188 ... M3
Delhi, 458 ... M3
Delmar, 514 ... N3
Deloit, 288 ... D3
Delphos, 25 ... F6
Delta, 410 ... K5
Denison, 7,339 ... D3
Denmark, 400 ... M6
Denver, 1,627 ... K2
Derby, 131 ... H6
Des Moines, 198,682 ... G4
De Soto, 1,009 ... F4
De Witt, 5,049 ... N4
Dexter, 689 ... F4
Diagonal, 312 ... F6
Dickens, 202 ... D1
Dike, 944 ... J3
Dixon, 276 ... N4
Dolliver, 77 ... E1
Donahue, 293 ... N4
Donnan, 10 ... L2
Donnellson, 963 ... L6
Doon, 533 ... B1
Dorchester, 80 ... M1
Douds, 165 ... K6
Dougherty, 80 ... H2
Dow City, 503 ... D4
Downey, 125 ... N4
Dows, 675 ... G2
Drakesville, 185 ... K6
Dubuque, 57,686 ... N2
Dumont, 676 ... J2
Dunbar, 100 ... J4
Duncombe, 474 ... F3
Dundee, 179 ... L2
Dunkerton, 749 ... K2
Dunlap, 1,139 ... C4
Durango, 24 ... N2
Durant, 1,677 ... N4
Dyersville, 4,035 ... M3
Dysart, 1,303 ... K3
Eagle Grove, 3,712 ... G2
Earlham, 1,298 ... F5
Earling, 471 ... D4
Earlville, 900 ... M3
Early, 605 ... D3
East Amana, 90 ... L4
East Peru, 153 ... G5
Eddyville, 1,064 ... J5
Edgewood, 923 ... M2
Edna, ... B1
Elberon, 245 ... K3
Eldon, 998 ... K6
Eldora, 3,035 ... H3
Eldridge, 4,159 ... N4
Elgin, 676 ... L2
Elk Horn, 649 ... D4
Elkader, 1,465 ... M2
Elkhart, 362 ... G4
Elkport, 88 ... M2
Elk Run Heights, 1,052 ... K3
Elliott, 402 ... D5
Ellston, 57 ... F6
Ellsworth, 531 ... H3
Elma, 598 ... K1
Ely, 1,149 ... L4
Emerson, 480 ... D5
Emmetsburg, 3,958 ... E1
Epworth, 1,428 ... N3
Essex, 884 ... D6
Estherville, 6,656 ... E1
Evans, 90 ... J5
Evansdale, 4,526 ... K3
Everly, 647 ... D1
Ewart, ... J4
Exira, 810 ... E4
Exline, 191 ... J6
Fairbank, 1,041 ... K2
Fairfax, 889 ... L4
Fairfield, 9,509 ... L5
Fairport, 175 ... N5
Farley, 1,334 ... M3
Farlin, 40 ... F3
Farmersburg, 300 ... M2
Farmington, 756 ... L6
Farnhamville, 430 ... F3
Farragut, 509 ... D6
Faulkner, 60 ... H2
Fayette, 1,300 ... L2
Fenton, 317 ... F1
Ferguson, 126 ... J4
Fertile, 360 ... H1
Finchford, 125 ... J2
Floris, 153 ... K6
Floyd, 361 ... J1
Folletts, 150 ... P4
Fonda, 648 ... E2
Fontanelle, 680 ... E5
Forest City, 4,362 ... G1
Fort Atkinson, 389 ... L1
Fort Dodge, 25,136 ... F2
Fort Madison, 10,715 ... M6
Fostoria, 230 ... D1
Franklin, 136 ... L6
Frankville, 125 ... L1
Fraser, 82 ... G3
Fredericksburg, 984 ... K2
Frederika, 199 ... K2
Fredonia, 251 ... M5
Fremont, 704 ... K5
Fruitland, 703 ... M5
Fulton, 100 ... N3
Galt, 30 ... G2
Galva, 368 ... D2
Gambrill, 175 ... N4
Garber, 103 ... M2
Garden City, 100 ... H3
Garden Grove, 250 ... G6
Garnavillo, 754 ... M2
Garner, 2,922 ... G1
Garrison, 413 ... K3
Garwin, 565 ... J3
Gaza, 70 ... C1
Geneva, 171 ... H2
George, 1,051 ... B1
Germantown, 100 ... H3
Gibson, 92 ... K5
Gifford, 70 ... H3
Gilbert, 987 ... G3
Gilbertville, 767 ... K3
Gillett Grove, 55 ... D1
Gilman, 600 ... H4
Gilmore City, 556 ... F2
Gladbrook, 1,015 ... J3
Glasgow, 40 ... L6
Glenwood, 5,358 ... C5
Glidden, 1,253 ... E3
Goldfield, 680 ... G2
Goodell, 174 ... G2
Goose Lake, 232 ... P4
Gowrie, 1,038 ... F3
Graettinger, 900 ... E1
Graf, 73 ... N2
Grafton, 290 ... H1
Grand Junction, 964 ... F3
Grand Mound, 676 ... N4
Grand River, 225 ... G6
Grandview, 600 ... M5
Granger, 583 ... G4
Grant, 102 ... E5
Grant Center, ... B3
Gravity, 218 ... E6
Gray, 82 ... E4
Greeley, 276 ... M2
Greene, 1,099 ... J2
Greenfield, 2,129 ... F5
Green Island, 30 ... P3
Greenville, 93 ... D1
Grimes, 5,098 ... G4
Grinnell, 9,105 ... J4
Griswold, 1,039 ... D5
Grundy Center, 2,596 ... J3
Gruver, 106 ... E1
Guernsey, 70 ... K4
Gunder, 50 ... L2
Guthrie Center, 1,668 ... E4
Guttenberg, 1,987 ... M2
Halbur, 202 ... E3
Hale, 60 ... M3
Halfa ... E1
Hamburg, 1,240 ... C6
Hamilton, 144 ... J5
Hamlin, 70 ... E4
Hancock, 207 ... D5
Hanlontown, 229 ... H1
Hansell, 96 ... H2
Harcourt, 340 ... F3
Hardy, 57 ... F2
Harlan, 5,282 ... D4
Harper, 134 ... K5
Harpers Ferry, 330 ... M1
Harris, 200 ... D1
Hartford, 759 ... H5
Hartley, 1,733 ... D1
Hartwick, 83 ... K4
Harvey, 277 ... J5
Hastings, 214 ... D5
Havelock, 177 ... E2
Haverhill, 170 ... J4
Hawarden, 2,478 ... B1
Hawkeye, 489 ... L2
Hawley, 64 ... K5
Hayfield, 60 ... G1
Hazleton, 950 ... L2
Hedrick, 837 ... K5
Henderson, 171 ... D5
Hepburn, 39 ... D6
Hiawatha, 6,480 ... L3
Highland Center, ... K5
Highlandville ... L1
Hills, 679 ... L4
Hillsboro, 205 ... L6
Hinton, 808 ... B2
Hiteman, 60 ... J5
Holland, 250 ... J3
Holstein, 1,470 ... C2
Holy Cross, 339 ... N2
Hopkinton, 681 ... M3
Hornick, 253 ... B3
Hospers, 672 ... C1
Houghton, 130 ... L6
Hubbard, 885 ... H3
Hudson, 2,117 ... K3
Hull, 1,960 ... B1
Humboldt, 4,452 ... F2
Humeston, 543 ... G6
Huntington, 50 ... E1
Hurstville, 100 ... N3
Huxley, 2,316 ... G4
Iconium ... J6
Ida Grove, 2,350 ... D3
Imogene, 60 ... D6
Independence, 6,014 ... L3
Indianola, 12,998 ... G5
Inwood, 875 ... B1
Ionia, 182 ... K1
Iowa City, 62,220 ... L4
Iowa Falls, 5,193 ... H2
Ira, 100 ... H4
Ireton, 585 ... B2
Irvington, 40 ... F1
Irwin, 357 ... D4
Jackson Junction, 60 ... K1
Jamaica, 237 ... F4
Jamison ... G5
Janesville, 829 ... K2
Jefferson, 4,626 ... F3
Jerico ... K1
Jesup, 2,212 ... K3
Jewell, 1,239 ... G3
Johnston, 8,649 ... G4
Joice, 231 ... G1
Jolley, 54 ... E3
Jordan, 60 ... G4
Kalona, 2,293 ... L5
Kamrar, 229 ... G3
Kanawha, 739 ... G2
Kellerton, 372 ... F6
Kelley, 300 ... G4
Kellogg, 606 ... J4
Kensett, 280 ... H1
Kent, 52 ... F6
Keokuk, 11,427 ... M7
Keomah Village, 97 ... J5
Keosauqua, 1,066 ... L6
Keota, 1,025 ... K5
Kesley, 150 ... J2
Keswick, 295 ... K5
Keystone, 687 ... K4
Kilduff, 150 ... J4
Kimballton, 342 ... D4
King, 450 ... N3
Kingsley, 1,245 ... C2
Kinross, 80 ... K5
Kirkman, 76 ... D4
Kirkville, 214 ... J5
Kiron, 273 ... D3
Klemme, 593 ... G2
Knierim, 70 ... F3
Knoke, 60 ... L2
Knoxville, 7,731 ... H5
Koszta, 70 ... K4
Lacey, 70 ... J5
Lacona, 360 ... H5
Ladora, 287 ... K4
Lake City, 1,787 ... E3
Lake Mills, 2,140 ... G1
Lake Park, 1,023 ... D1
Lakeside, 484 ... D2
Lake View, 1,278 ... D3
Lakota, 255 ... F1
Lambs Grove, 225 ... H4
Lamoni, 2,444 ... G6
Lamont, 503 ... L2
La Motte, 272 ... N3
Lanesboro, 152 ... E3
Langdon, 125 ... D1
Langworthy, 90 ... M3
Lansing, 1,012 ... M1
Lanyon, 100 ... F3
La Porte City, 2,275 ... K3
Larchwood, 788 ... B1
Larrabee, 149 ... C2
Latimer, 535 ... H2
Laurel, 266 ... J4
Laurens, 1,476 ... E2
Lawler, 461 ... K1
Lawton, 697 ... B3
Le Claire, 2,847 ... P4
Ledyard, 147 ... F1
Le Grand, 883 ... J3
Lehigh, 497 ... F3
Leighton, 153 ... J5
Leland, 258 ... G1
Lenox, 1,401 ... E6
Leon, 1,983 ... G6
Le Roy, 13 ... G6
Lester, 291 ... B1
Letts, 392 ... M5
Lewis, 438 ... D5
Libertyville, 325 ... K6
Lidderdale, 186 ... E3
Lime Springs, 496 ... K1
Linby, 60 ... K5
Lincoln, 182 ... J3
Linden, 226 ... F4
Lineville, 273 ... G6
Linn Grove, 211 ... D2
Lisbon, 1,898 ... M4
Liscomb, 272 ... H3
Littleport, 26 ... M2
Little Rock, 489 ... C1
Little Sioux, 217 ... B4
Livermore, 431 ... F2
Lockridge, 275 ... L6
Logan, 1,545 ... C4
Lohrville, 431 ... E3
Lone Rock, 157 ... F1
Lone Tree, 1,151 ... M5
Long Grove, 597 ... N4
Lorimor, 427 ... F5
Lost Nation, 497 ... N3
Lourdes ... K1
Lovilia, 583 ... J5
Lowden, 794 ... N4
Lowell, 100 ... M6
Low Moor, 240 ... P4
Luana, 249 ... M1
Lucas, 243 ... H5
Luther, 158 ... G4
Luton ... B3
Lu Verne, 299 ... F2
Luxemburg, 246 ... M2
Luzerne, 105 ... K4
Lyman, 125 ... E5
Lynnville, 366 ... J4
Lytton, 305 ... E3
Macedonia, 325 ... D5
Macksburg, 142 ... F5
Madrid, 2,264 ... G4
Magnolia, 200 ... C4
Malcom, 352 ... J4
Mallard, 298 ... E2
Maloy, 28 ... F6
Malvern, 1,256 ... C5
Manchester, 5,257 ... M3
Manilla, 839 ... D4
Manly, 1,342 ... H1
Manning, 1,490 ... D4
Manson, 1,893 ... E2
Mapleton, 1,416 ... C3
Maquoketa, 6,112 ... N3
Marathon, 302 ... E2
Marble Rock, 326 ... J2
Marcus, 1,139 ... C2
Marengo, 2,535 ... K4
Marion, 26,294 ... L3
Mark, 60 ... K6
Marne, 149 ... D5
Marquette, 421 ... M1
Marshalltown, 26,009 ... J3
Martelle, 280 ... M3
Martensdale, 467 ... G5
Martinsburg, 126 ... K5
Marysville, 96 ... H5
Mason City, 29,172 ... H1
Masonville, 104 ... L3
Massena, 414 ... E5
Massillon, 100 ... N4
Matlock, 83 ... C1
Maurice, 254 ... B2
Maxwell, 807 ... H4
May City, 100 ... D1
Maynard, 500 ... L2
Maysville, 163 ... N4
McCallsburg, 318 ... H3
McCausland, 299 ... P4
McClelland, 129 ... C5
McGregor, 871 ... M1
McIntire, 173 ... J1
Mechanicsville, 1,173 ... M4
Mediapolis, 1,644 ... M5
Melbourne, 794 ... H4
Melcher-Dallas, 1,298 ... H5
Melrose, 130 ... H6
Melvin, 243 ... C1
Menlo, 365 ... F4
Meriden, 184 ... C2
Merrill, 754 ... B2
Meservey, 252 ... H2
Middletown, 535 ... M6
Miles, 462 ... P3
Milford, 2,474 ... D1
Miller, 80 ... G1
Millersburg, 184 ... K4
Millerton, 48 ... H6
Millville, 23 ... M2
Milo, 839 ... H5
Milton, 550 ... K6
Minburn, 391 ... F4
Minden, 564 ... C5
Mineola, 150 ... C5
Mingo, 269 ... H4
Missouri Valley, 2,992 ... C4
Mitchell, 155 ... J1
Mitchellville, 1,715 ... H4
Modale, 303 ... B4
Moingona, 175 ... G3
Mondamin, 423 ... B4
Moneta, 30 ... D1
Monmouth, 180 ... N3
Monona, 1,550 ... M1
Monroe, 1,808 ... H4
Monteith, 70 ... F4
Montezuma, 1,440 ... J4
Monticello, 3,607 ... M3
Montour, 285 ... J4
Montrose, 957 ... M6
Moorhead, 232 ... C4
Moorland, 197 ... F3
Moravia, 713 ... J6
Morley, 88 ... M3
Morning Sun, 872 ... M5
Morrison, 97 ... J3
Morse, 125 ... M4
Morton Mills, 40 ... E5
Moulton, 658 ... J6
Mount Auburn, 160 ... K3
Mount Ayr, 1,822 ... F6
Mount Etna, 40 ... E5
Mount Hamill, 50 ... L6
Mount Pleasant, 8,751 ... L5
Mount Sterling, 40 ... L6
Mount Union, 132 ... M5
Mount Vernon, 3,390 ... M4
Mount Zion, 40 ... L6
Moville, 1,583 ... B3
Murray, 766 ... G5
Muscatine, 22,697 ... M5
Mystic, 588 ... J6
Nashua, 1,618 ... J2
Nemaha, 102 ... D2
Neola, 845 ... C5
Nevada, 6,658 ... H3
Nevinville ... E5
New Albin, 527 ... M1
Newburg, 100 ... J4
Newell, 887 ... D2
Newhall, 886 ... L4
New Hampton, 3,692 ... K1
New Hartford, 659 ... J2
New Haven, 100 ... J1
New London, 1,937 ... L6
New Market, 456 ... E6
New Providence, 227 ... H3
New Sharon, 1,301 ... J5
Newton, 15,579 ... H4
New Vienna, 400 ... M2
New Virginia, 469 ... G5
Nichols, 374 ... M5
Nodaway, 132 ... E6
Nora Springs, 1,532 ... J1
Northboro, 60 ... D6
North Buena Vista, 124 ... N2
North English, 991 ... K4
North Liberty, 5,367 ... L4
North Washington, 118 ... K1
Northwood, 2,050 ... H1
Norwalk, 6,884 ... G5
Norway, 601 ... L4
Norwood ... H5
Numa, 109 ... J6
Oakland, 1,487 ... D5
Oakland Acres, 166 ... J4
Oakville, 439 ... M5
Ocheyedan, 536 ... C1
Odebolt, 1,153 ... D3
Oelwein, 6,692 ... L2
Ogden, 2,023 ... F3
Okoboji, 820 ... D1
Olds, 249 ... L5
Olin, 716 ... M4
Ollie, 224 ... K5
Onawa, 3,091 ... B3
Oneida, 50 ... M2
Onslow, 225 ... M3
Orange City, 5,582 ... B1
Orchard, 83 ... J1
Orient, 402 ... F5
Orleans, 583 ... D1
Osage, 3,451 ... J1
Osceola, 4,659 ... G5
Oskaloosa, 10,938 ... J5
Ossian, 853 ... L1
Osterdock, 50 ... M2
Otho, 537 ... F3
Otley, 150 ... H5
Oto, 145 ... C3
Otranto ... J1
Otter Creek, 50 ... N3
Ottosen, 61 ... F2
Ottumwa, 24,998 ... K5
Owasa, 38 ... H3
Oxford, 705 ... L4
Oxford Junction, 573 ... N3
Oyens, 132 ... B2
Pacific Junction, 507 ... C5
Packard, 60 ... J2
Packwood, 223 ... K5
Palmer, 214 ... E2
Palo, 614 ... L3
Panama, 212 ... D4
Panora, 1,175 ... F4
Panorama Park, 111 ... P4
Paris, 80 ... L2
Parkersburg, 1,889 ... J2
Parnell, 220 ... L4
Paton, 265 ... F3
Patterson, 126 ... G5

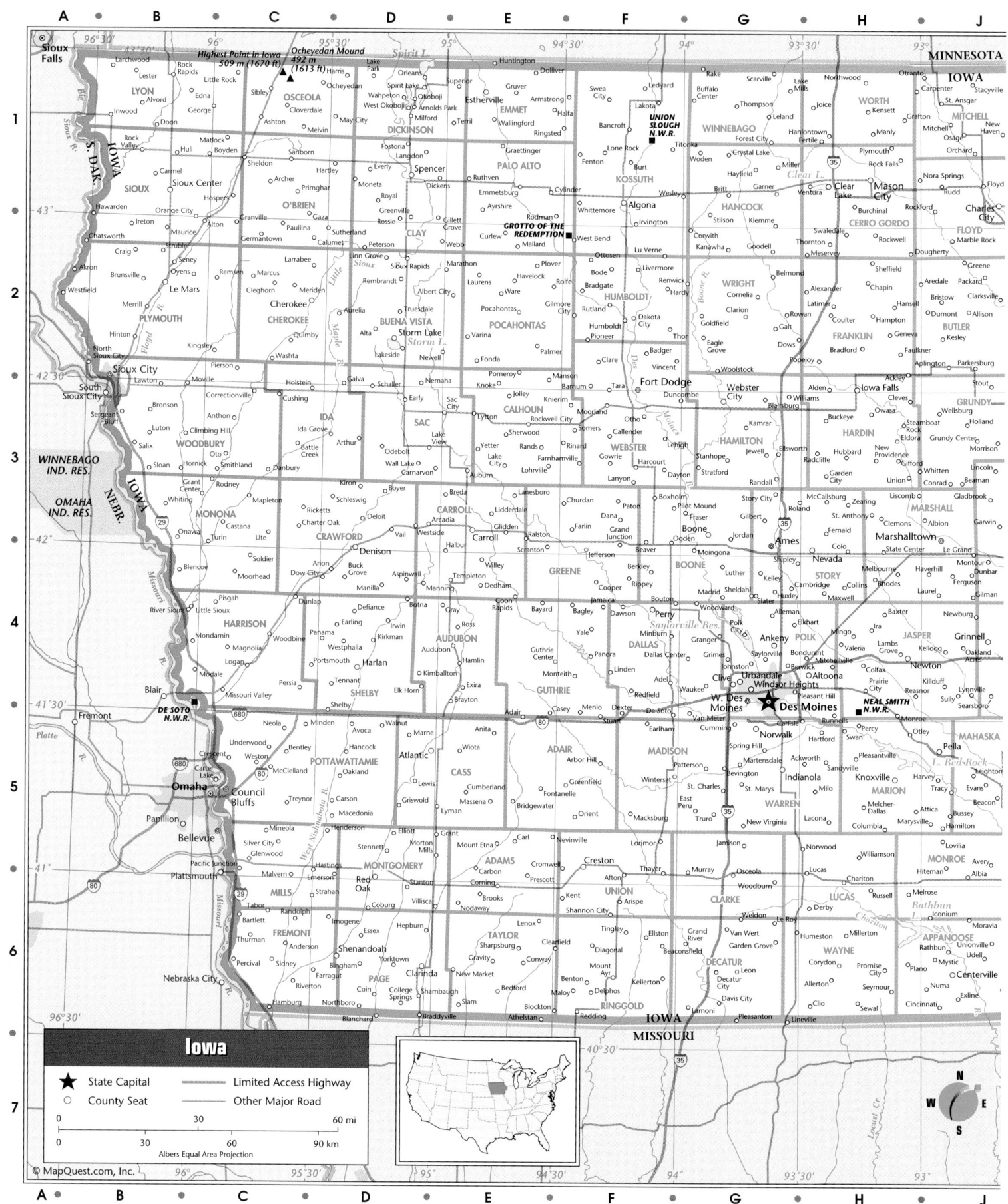

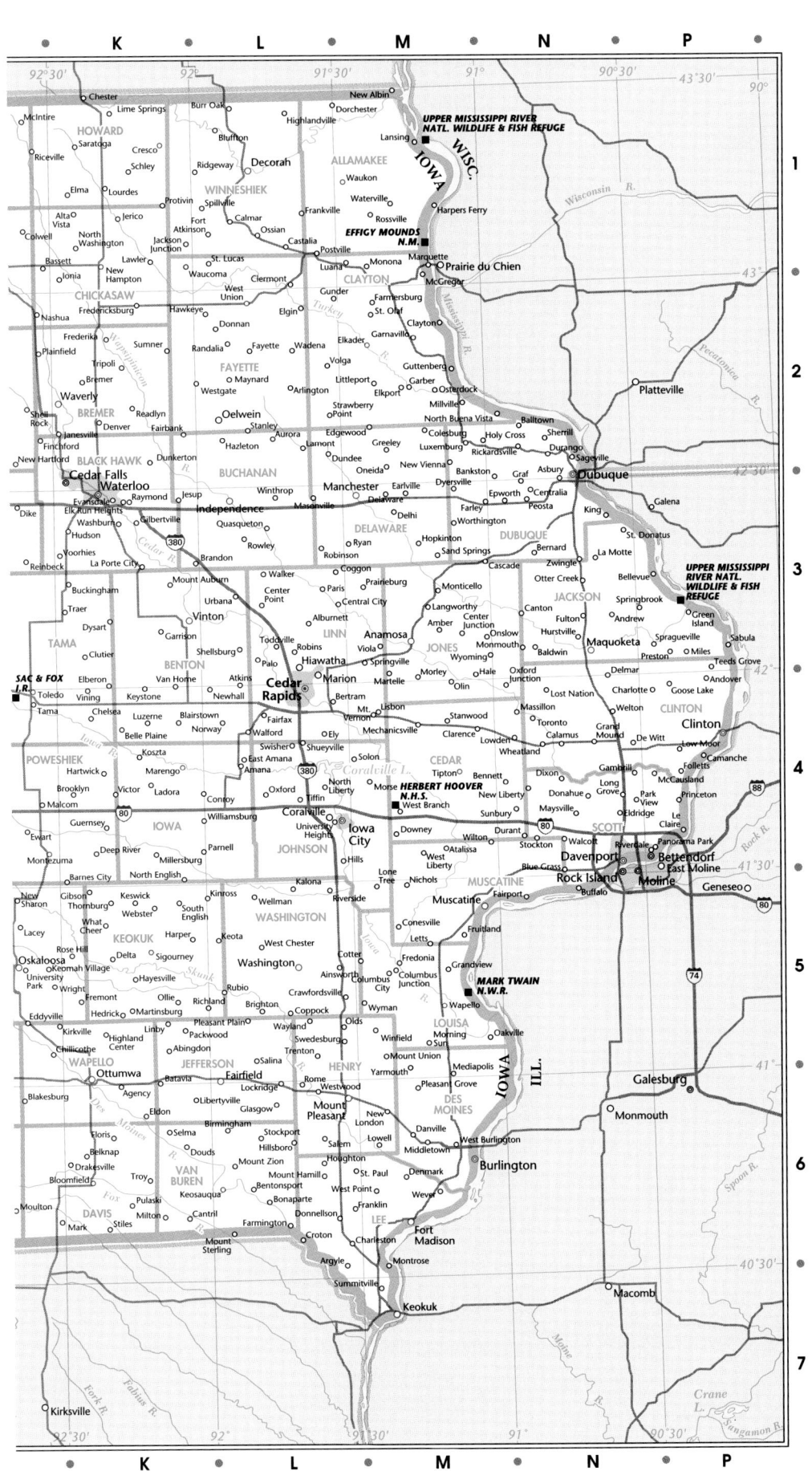

Paullina, 1,124 . . . . C2
Pella, 9,832 . . . . . J5
Peosta, 651 . . . . . N3
Percival, 125 . . . . C6
Percy, 100 . . . . . . H5
Perry, 7,633 . . . . F4
Persia, 363 . . . . . C4
Peterson, 372 . . . . D2
Pierson, 371 . . . . C2
Pilot Mound, 214 . . F3
Pioneer, 21 . . . . . F2
Pisgah, 316 . . . . . C4
Plainfield, 438 . . . J2
Plano, 58 . . . . H6
Pleasant Grove, 70 . . M6
Pleasant Hill, 5,070 . . G4
Pleasanton, 37 . . . . G6
Pleasant Plain, 131 . . L5
Pleasantville, 1,539 . . H5
Plover, 95 . . . . . . E2
Plymouth, 429 . . . . F1
Pocahontas, 1,970 . . E2
Polk City, 2,344 . . . G4
Pomeroy, 710 . . . . E2
Popejoy, 78 . . . . . . H2
Portsmouth, 225 . . . . C4
Postville, 2,273 . . . L1
Prairieburg, 175 . . . M3
Prairie City, 1,365 . . H4
Prescott, 266 . . . . . E5
Preston, 949 . . . . . P3
Primghar, 891 . . . . C1
Princeton, 946 . . . . P4
Promise City, 105 . . H6
Protivin, 317 . . . . K1
Pulaski, 249 . . . . . K6
Quasqueton, 574 . . L3
Quimby, 368 . . . . . C2
Radcliffe, 607 . . . . H3
Rake, 227 . . . . . . G1
Ralston, 98 . . . . . E3
Randall, 148 . . . . . G3
Randolph, 209 . . . . C6
Rands E3
Rathbun, 88 . . . . . J6
Raymond, 537 . . . . K3
Readlyn, 786 . . . . K2
Reasnor, 194 . . . . H4
Redding, 78 . . . . . F6
Redfield, 833 . . . . F4
Red Oak, 6,197 . . . D5
Reinbeck, 1,751 . . . J3
Rembrandt, 228 . . . D2
Remsen, 1,762 . . . C2
Renwick, 306 . . . . G2
Rhodes, 294 . . . . H4
Riceville, 840 . . . . J1
Richland, 587 . . . . K5
Rickardsville, 191 . . N2
Ricketts, 144 . . . . C3
Ridgeway, 293 . . . L1
Rinard, 72 . . . . . E3
Ringsted, 436 . . . . E1
Rippey, 319 . . . . . F3
Riverdale, 656 . . . . P4
Riverside, 928 . . . . L5
River Sioux, 90 . . . B4
Riverton, 304 . . . . C6
Robins, 1,806 . . . . L3
Robinson, 90 . . . . L3
Rock Falls, 170 . . . H1
Rockford, 907 . . . . J1
Rock Rapids, 2,573 . . B1
Rock Valley, 2,702 . . B1
Rockwell, 989 . . . . H2
Rockwell City, 2,264 . E3
Rodman, 56 . . . . . E1
Rodney, 74 . . . . . C3
Roland, 1,324 . . . . G3
Rolfe, 675 . . . . . . E2
Rome, 113 . . . . . . L6
Rose Hill, 205 . . . . K5
Ross, 80 . . . . E4
Rossie, 58 . . . . . . D1
Rossville, 125 . . . . M1
Rowan, 218 . . . . . G2
Rowley, 290 . . . . . L3
Royal, 479 . . . . . . D1
Rubio, 50 . . . . . . L5
Rudd, 431 . . . . . . J1
Runnells, 352 . . . . H4
Russell, 559 . . . . . H6
Ruthven, 711 . . . . E1
Rutland, 145 . . . . F2
Ryan, 410 . . . . . . M3
Sabula, 670 . . . . . P3
Sac City, 2,368 . . . E3
Sageville, 203 . . . . N2
St. Ansgar, 1,031 . . J1
St. Anthony, 109 . . H3
St. Charles, 619 . . . G5
St. Donatus, 140 . . N3
St. Lucas, 178 . . . . L1
St. Marys, 134 . . . . G5
St. Olaf, 136 . . . . M2
St. Paul, 118 . . . . L6
Salem, 464 . . . . . L6
Salina, 50 . . . . . . L5
Salix, 370 . . . . . . B3
Sanborn, 1,353 . . . C1
Sand Springs, 70 . . M3
Sandyville, 61 . . . H5
Saratoga, 100 . . . K1
Saylorville, 3,238 . . G4
Scarville, 97 . . . . G1
Schaller, 779 . . . . D2
Schleswig, 833 . . . D3
Schley, 40 . . . . . K1
Scranton, 604 . . . . E3
Searsboro, 155 . . . J4
Selma, 80 . . . . . . K6
Seney, 100 . . . . . B2
Sergeant Bluff, 3,321 . . . . B3
Sewal, 60 . . . . . . H6
Seymour, 810 . . . H6
Shambaugh, 188 . . D6
Shannon City, 70 . . F6
Sharpsburg, 98 . . . E6
Sheffield, 930 . . . H2
Shelby, 664 . . . . D4
Sheldahl, 336 . . . G4
Sheldon, 4,914 . . . C1
Shell Rock, 1,298 . . J2

Shellsburg, 938 . . . L3
Shenandoah, 5,546 . D6
Sherrill, 186 . . . . N2
Sherwood E3
Shipley, 80 . . . . . G4
Shueyville, 250 . . . L4
Siam, 40 . . . . . . E6
Sidney, 1,300 . . . . C6
Sigourney, 2,209 . . K5
Silver City, 259 . . . C5
Sioux Center, 6,002 . B1
Sioux City, 85,013 . . B2
Sioux Rapids, 720 . . D2
Slater, 1,306 . . . . G4
Sloan, 1,032 . . . . B3
Smithland, 221 . . . C3
Soldier, 207 . . . . C4
Solon, 1,177 . . . . M4
Somers, 165 . . . . F3
South English, 213 . K5
Spencer, 11,317 . . . D1
Spillville, 386 . . . L1
Spirit Lake, 4,261 . . D1
Spragueville, 89 . . . P3
Springbrook, 182 . . P3
Spring Hill, 92 . . . G5
Springville, 1,091 . . M3
Stacyville, 469 . . . J1
Stanhope, 488 . . . G3
Stanley, 128 . . . . L2
Stanton, 714 . . . . D6
Stanwood, 680 . . . M4
State Center, 1,349 . H3
Steamboat Rock, 336 . . . . H3
Stennett, 40 . . . . D5
Stiles K6
Stilson G1
Stockport, 284 . . . L6
Stockton, 182 . . . . N4
Storm Lake, 10,076 . D2
Story City, 3,228 . . G3
Stout, 217 . . . . . J2
Strahan, 40 . . . . . D6
Stratford, 746 . . . G3
Strawberry Point, 1,386 . . . . L2
Struble, 85 . . . . . B2
Stuart, 1,712 . . . . F4
Sully, 904 . . . . . J4
Summitville, 125 . . M7
Sumner, 2,106 . . . K2
Sunbury, 100 . . . . N4
Superior, 142 . . . . E1
Sutherland, 707 . . . D2
Swaledale, 174 . . . H2
Swan, 121 . . . . . H4
Swea City, 642 . . . F1
Swedesburg, 150 . . L5
Swisher, 813 . . . . L4
Tabor, 993 . . . . . C6
Tama, 2,731 . . . . J3
Tara J2
Teeds Grove, 100 . . P3
Templeton, 334 . . . E4
Tennant, 73 . . . . D4
Terril, 404 . . . . . E1
Thayer, 66 . . . . . F5
Thompson, 596 . . . G1
Thor, 174 . . . . . . F2
Thornburg, 84 . . . K5
Thornton, 422 . . . H2
Thurman, 236 . . . C6
Tiffin, 975 . . . . . L4
Tipton, 3,155 . . . . M4
Titonka, 584 . . . . F1
Toddville, 450 . . . L3
Toledo, 2,539 . . . . J4
Toronto, 134 . . . . N4
Tracy, 275 . . . . . J5
Traer, 1,594 . . . . K3
Trenton, 125 . . . . L5
Treynor, 950 . . . . C5
Tripoli, 1,310 . . . . K2
Troy, 60 . . . . . . K6
Truesdale, 91 . . . . D2
Truro, 471 . . . . . G5
Turin, 75 . . . . . . C3
Udell, 58 . . . . . . J6
Underwood, 688 . . C5
Union, 427 . . . . . H3
Unionville, 127 . . . J6
University Heights, 987 . . . . L4
University Park, 536 . J5
Urbana, 1,019 . . . L3
Urbandale, 29,072 . G4
Ute, 378 . . . . . . C3
Valeria, 62 . . . . . H4
Valley, 452 . . . . . D3
Van Horne, 716 . . . K3
Van Meter, 866 . . . G4
Van Wert, 231 . . . G6
Varina, 90 . . . . . E2
Ventura, 670 . . . . H1
Victor, 952 . . . . . K4
Villisca, 1,344 . . . E6
Vincent, 158 . . . . F2
Vining, 70 . . . . . K4
Vinton, 5,102 . . . . K3
Viola, 70 . . . . . . M3
Volga, 247 . . . . . L2
Voorhies, 90 . . . . K3
Wadena, 243 . . . . L2
Wahpeton, 462 . . . D1
Walcott, 1,528 . . . N4
Walford, 1,224 . . . L4
Walker, 750 . . . . L3
Wallingford, 210 . . E1
Wall Lake, 841 . . . D3
Walnut, 778 . . . . D5
Wapello, 2,124 . . . M5
Ware E2
Washburn, 1,000 . . K3
Washington, 7,047 . L5
Washta, 282 . . . . C2
Waterloo, 68,747 . . K3
Waterville, 145 . . . M1
Waucoma, 299 . . . K1
Waukee, 5,126 . . . G4
Waukon, 4,131 . . . M1
Waverly, 8,968 . . . K2
Wayland, 945 . . . . L5
Webb, 165 . . . . . . D2

Webster, 110 . . . . . K5
Webster City, 8,176 . G3
Weldon, 145 . . . . . G6
Wellman, 1,393 . . . L5
Wellsburg, 716 . . . J3
Welton, 159 . . . . N4
Wesley, 467 . . . . F1
West Bend, 834 . . . F2
West Branch, 2,188 M4
West Burlington,
   3,161 . . . . M6
West Chester, 159 . . L5
West Des Moines,
   46,403 . . . . G4
Westfield, 189 . . . . A2
Westgate, 234 . . . . L2
West Liberty, 3,332 M4
West Okoboji, 432 . D1
Weston, 175 . . . . . C5
Westphalia, 160 . . D4
West Point, 980 . . M6
Westside, 327 . . . . D3
West Union, 2,549 . . L2
Westwood, 127 . . . L6
Wever, 250 . . . . . M6
What Cheer, 678 . . . K5
Wheatland, 772 . . . N4
Whiting, 707 . . . . B3
Whittemore, 530 . . F1
Whitten, 160 . . . . H3
Willey, 103 . . . . . E4
Williams, 427 . . . . G3
Williamsburg, 2,622 . L4
Williamson, 163 . . . H5
Wilton, 2,829 . . . . M4
Windsor Heights,
   4,805 . . . . G4
Winfield, 1,131 . . . M5
Winterset, 4,768 . . . F5
Winthrop, 772 . . . . L3
Woden, 243 . . . . . G1
Woodbine, 1,564 . . C4
Woodburn, 244 . . . G5
Woodward, 1,200 . . G4
Woolstock, 204 . . . G2
Worthington, 381 . . M3
Wright, 80 . . . . . . J5
Wyman, 50 . . . . . M5
Wyoming, 626 . . . M3
Yale, 287 . . . . . . F4
Yarmouth, 100 . . . M5
Yetter, 36 . . . . . . E3
Yorktown, 82 . . . . D6
Zearing, 617 . . . . H3
Zwingle, 100 . . . . N3

Other Features

Big Sioux, river . . . A1
Boone, river G2
Cedar, river K3
Chariton, river H6
Clear, lake H1
Coralville, lake . . . L4
Crane, lake P7
Des Moines,
   river F2, K6
De Soto N.W.R. . . . B4
Effigy Mounds
   N.M. M1
Fabius, river K7
Floyd, river B2
Fork, river K7
Fox, river K6
Grotto Of The
   Redemption F2
Herbert Hoover
   N.H.S. M4
Highest Point
   in Iowa C1
Iowa, river K4, M5
Little Sioux, river . . D2
Locust Cr. H7
Maple, river D2
Mark Twain N.W.R. . M5
Mississippi, river . . M2
Missouri, river . . B4, C6
Moine, river M4
Neal Smith N.W.R. . H4
Ocheyedan Mound . C1
Omaha Ind. Res. . . B3
Pecatonica, river . . P2
Platte, river A5
Rathbun, lake J5
Red Rock, lake . . . H5
Rock, river P4
Sac & Fox I.R. . . . J3
Sangamon, river . . P7
Saylorville Res. . . . G4
Skunk, river D1
Spirit, lake D1
Spoon, river P6
Storm, lake D2
Turkey, river L2
Union Slough N.W.R. F1
Upper Mississippi River
   Natl. Wildlife & Fish
   Refuge M1, P3
Wapsipinicon, river . K2
West Nishnabota,
   river C5
Winnebago Ind. Res. A3
Wisconsin, river . . . N1

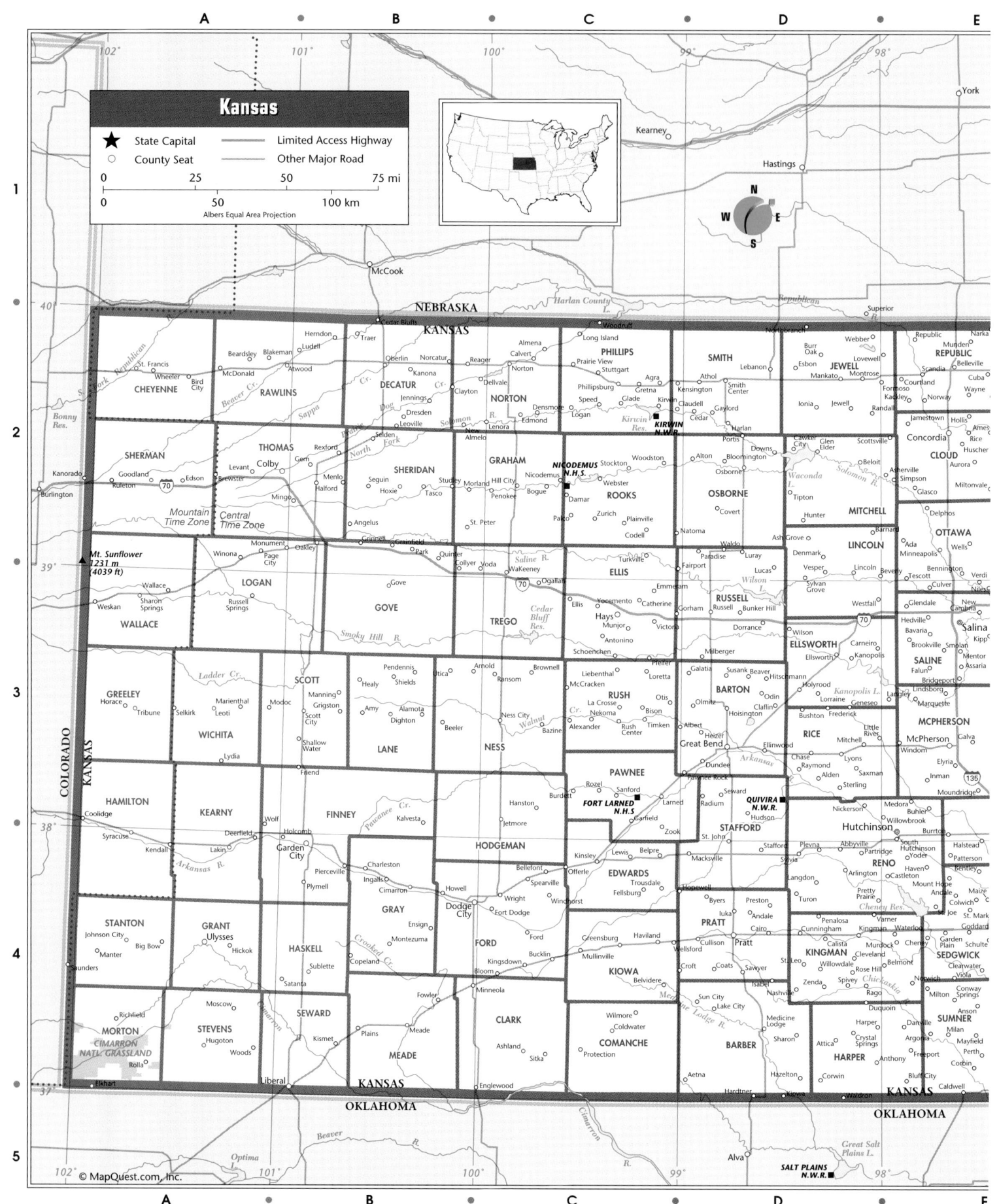

Kansas

★ State Capital
○ County Seat

Limited Access Highway
Other Major Road

0 — 25 — 50 — 75 mi
0 — 50 — 100 km

Albers Equal Area Projection

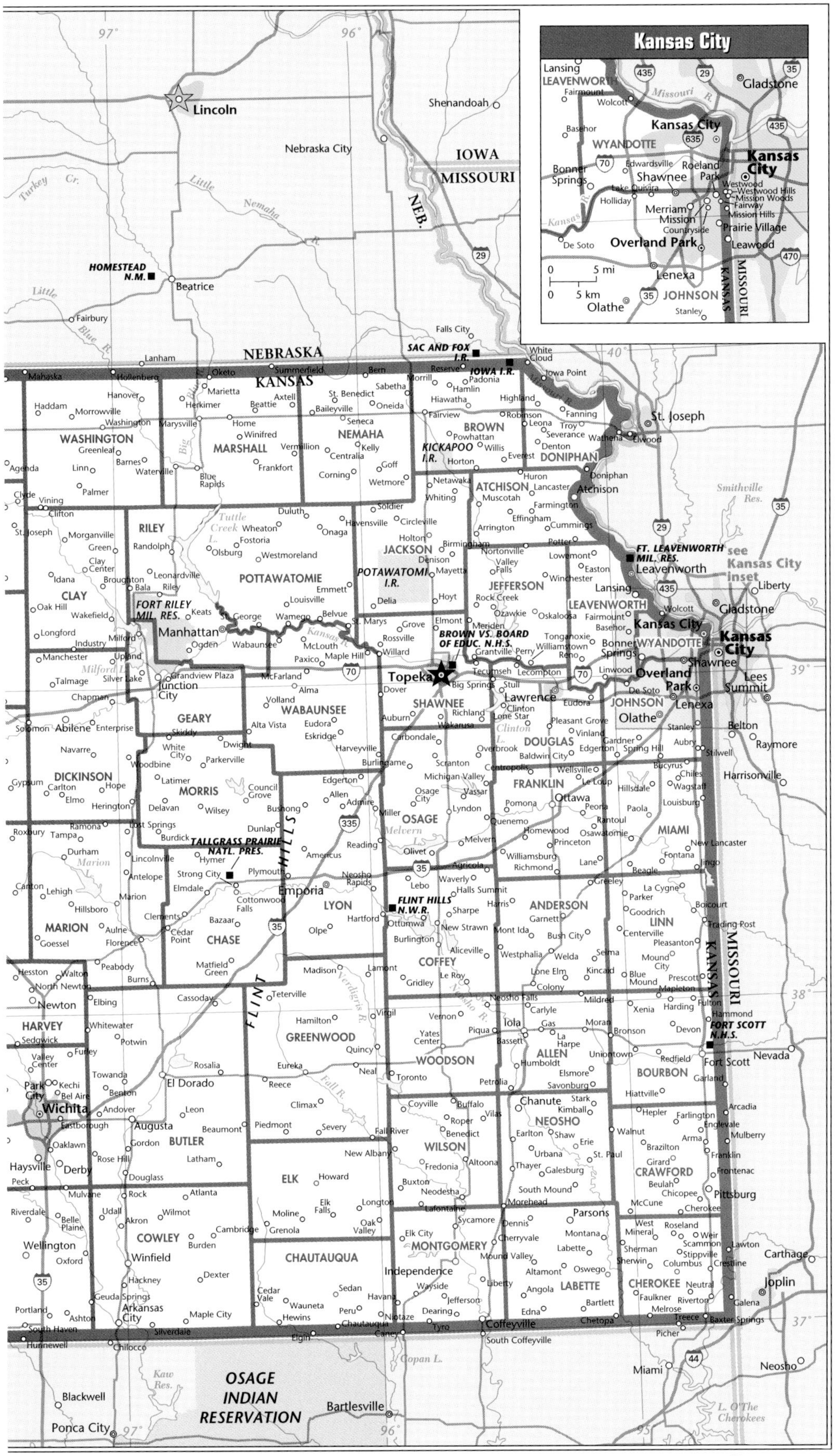

Kansas City

Lansing
LEAVENWORTH
Fairmount
Wolcott
Basehor
WYANDOTTE
Bonner Springs
Edwardsville
Roeland Park
Kansas City
Lake Quivira
Holliday
Merriam
Mission
Countryside
Prairie Village
Leawood
De Soto
Overland Park
Lenexa
Olathe
Stanley
JOHNSON
Westwood
Westwood Hills
Mission Woods
Mission Hills
Fairway
Shawnee
Gladstone
Kansas City
MISSOURI

0 5 mi
0 5 km

Kansas

Capital:	Topeka
Land Area:	81,823 sq. mi.
	211,922 sq. km.
Population:	2,688,418 (2000 Census)
Largest City:	Wichita, 344,284
Highest Point:	Mt. Sunflower
	4,039 ft.
	1,231 m.
Admitted to Union:	January 29, 1861
Nickname:	Sunflower State
State Flower:	Sunflower
State Bird:	Western Meadowlark

Kansas:
Map Index

Counties

Allen, 14,385 ....G4
Anderson, 8,110 ......G3
Atchison, 16,774 .....G2
Barber, 5,307 ....D4
Barton, 28,205 ....D3
Bourbon, 15,379 .....H4
Brown, 10,724 ....G2
Butler, 59,482 ....F4
Chase, 3,030 ....F3
Chautauqua, 4,359 ...F4
Cherokee, 22,605 ....H4
Cheyenne, 3,165 .....A2
Clark, 2,390 ....C4
Clay, 8,822 ....E2
Cloud, 10,268 ....E2
Coffey, 8,865 ....G3
Comanche, 1,967 ....C4
Cowley, 36,291 ......F4
Crawford, 38,242 ....H4
Decatur, 3,472 ....A2
Dickinson, 19,344 ....E3
Doniphan, 8,249 .....G2
Douglas, 99,962 .....G3
Edwards, 3,449 ......C4
Elk, 3,261 ....F4
Ellis, 27,507 ....C2
Ellsworth, 6,525 .....D3
Finney, 40,523 ......B3
Ford, 32,458 ....C4
Franklin, 24,784 .....G3
Geary, 27,947 ....F3
Gove, 3,068 ....B3
Graham, 2,946 ......C2
Grant, 7,909 ....A4
Gray, 5,904 ....B4
Greeley, 1,534 ......A3
Greenwood, 7,673 ...F3
Hamilton, 2,670 .....A3
Harper, 6,536 ....D4
Harvey, 32,869 .....E4
Haskell, 4,307 ......B4
Hodgeman, 2,085 ...C4
Jackson, 12,657 .....G2
Jefferson, 18,426 ...G2
Jewell, 3,791 ....D2
Johnson, 451,086 ...H1, H3
Kearny, 4,531 ......A4
Kingman, 8,673 .....D4
Kiowa, 3,278 ....C4
Labette, 22,835 .....G4
Lane, 2,155 ....B3
Leavenworth, 68,691 .G1, G2
Lincoln, 3,578 ......D2
Linn, 9,570 ....H3
Logan, 3,046 ....A3
Lyon, 35,935 ....F3
Marion, 13,361 .....E3
Marshall, 10,965 ...F2
McPherson, 29,554 ..E3
Meade, 4,631 ......B4
Miami, 28,351 .....H3
Mitchell, 6,932 .....D2
Montgomery, 36,252 .G4
Morris, 6,104 ......F3
Morton, 3,496 .....A4
Nemaha, 10,717 ...G2
Neosho, 16,997 ....G4
Ness, 3,454 ....C3
Norton, 5,953 ......C2
Osage, 16,712 .....G3
Osborne, 4,452 ....D2
Ottawa, 6,163 .....E2
Pawnee, 7,233 ....C3
Phillips, 6,001 .....C2
Pottawatomie, 18,209 .F2
Pratt, 9,647 ....D4
Rawlins, 2,966 .....A2
Reno, 64,790 ......D4
Republic, 5,835 ....E2
Rice, 10,761 ....D3
Riley, 62,843 ......F2
Rooks, 5,685 ......C2
Rush, 3,551 ....C3
Russell, 7,370 .....D3
Saline, 53,597 .....E3
Scott, 5,120 ....B3
Sedgwick, 452,869 ..E4
Seward, 22,510 ....B4
Shawnee, 169,871 ..F3
Sheridan, 2,813 ...B2
Sherman, 6,760 ...A2
Smith, 4,536 ....D2
Stafford, 4,789 ....D3
Stanton, 2,406 ....A4
Stevens, 5,463 ....A4
Sumner, 25,946 ....E4
Thomas, 8,180 .....B2
Trego, 3,319 ....C3
Wabaunsee, 6,885 ..G3
Wallace, 1,749 .....A3

Washington, 6,483 ....E2
Wichita, 2,531 ....A3
Wilson, 10,332 ....G4
Woodson, 3,788 .....G4
Wyandotte, 157,882 ..H1, H2

Cities and Towns

Abbyville, 128 ....D4
Abilene, 6,543 ......E3
Ada, 100 ....E2
Admire, 177 ....F3
Aetna D4
Agenda, 81 ....E2
Agra, 306 ....C2
Agricola G3
Akron E4
Alamota B3
Albert, 181 ....C3
Alden, 168 ....D3
Alexander, 75 ......C3
Aliceville, 60 ......G3
Allen, 211 ....F3
Almena, 469 ....C2
Altamont, 1,092 ....G4
Alta Vista, 442 ....F3
Alton, 117 ....D2
Altoona, 485 ......G4
Americus, 938 .....F3
Ames, 50 ....E2
Amy B3
Andale, 766 ....D4, E4
Andover, 6,698 ....E4
Angelus, 40 ....B2
Angola G4
Anson, 70 ....E4
Antelope F3
Anthony, 2,440 ....D4
Antonino C3
Arcadia, 391 ......H4
Argonia, 534 ......E4
Arkansas City, 11,963 .E4
Arlington, 459 ....D4
Arma, 1,529 ......H4
Arnold, 60 ....B3
Arrington G2
Asherville, 60 .....E2
Ash Grove D2
Ashland, 975 .....C4
Ashton, 50 ....C4
Assaria, 438 ......E3
Atchison, 10,232 ..G2
Athol, 51 ....D2
Atlanta, 255 ......F4
Attica, 636 ....D4
Atwood, 1,279 ....A2
Aubry, 1,200 ......H3
Auburn, 1,121 ....G3
Augusta, 8,423 ....F4
Aulne, 50 ....E3
Aurora, 79 ....E2
Axtell, 445 ....F2
Baileyville, 200 ...F2
Bala E2
Baldwin City, 3,400 ..G3
Barnard, 123 .....D2
Barnes, 152 ......E2
Bartlett, 124 .....G4
Basehor, 2,238 ...G1, H2
Bassett, 22 ....G4
Bavaria, 90 ......E3
Baxter Springs, 4,602 .H4
Bazaar F3
Bazine, 311 ......C3
Beagle, 125 ......H3
Beardsley A2
Beattie, 277 ......F2
Beaumont, 90 ....F4
Beaver, 50 ....D3
Beeler B3
Bel Aire, 5,836 ...E4
Bellefont C4
Belle Plaine, 1,708 ..E4
Belleville, 2,239 ..E2
Belmont E4
Beloit, 4,019 .....D2
Belpre, 104 ......C4
Belvidere C4
Belvue, 228 ......F2
Benedict, 103 ....G4
Bennington, 623 ..E2
Bentley, 368 ......E4
Benton, 827 ......E4
Bern, 204 ....G2
Beulah H4
Beverly, 199 .....D2
Big Bow, 50 ......A4
Big Springs, 150 ..G3
Bird City, 482 ....A2
Birmingham, 50 ...G2
Bison, 235 ....C3
Blakeman A2
Bloom, 60 ....C4
Bloomington D2
Blue Mound, 277 ..G3
Blue Rapids, 1,088 ..F2

Bluff City, 80 . . . . .E4
Bogue, 179 . . . . .C2
Boicourt H3
Bonner Springs, 6,768 . . . . .G1, H2
Brazilton, 60 . . . . .H4
Brewster, 285 . . . . .A2
Bridgeport, 100 . . . . .E3
Bronson, 346 . . . . .G4
Brookville, 259 . . . . .D3
Broughton E2
Brownell, 48 . . . . .C3
Bucklin, 725 . . . . .C4
Bucyrus, 250 . . . . .H3
Buffalo, 284 . . . . .G4
Buhler, 1,358 . . . . .E3
Bunker Hill, 101 . . . . .D3
Burden, 564 . . . . .E4
Burdett, 256 . . . . .C3
Burdick, 80 . . . . .F3
Burlingame, 1,017 . . . . .G3
Burlington, 2,790 . . . . .G3
Burns, 268 . . . . .F3
Burr Oak, 265 . . . . .D2
Burrton, 932 . . . . .E3
Bush City G4
Bushong, 55 . . . . .F3
Bushton, 314 . . . . .D3
Buxton D4
Byers, 50 . . . . .D4
Cairo, 80 . . . . .D4
Caldwell, 1,284 . . . . .E4
Calista E3
Calvert, 40 . . . . .C2
Cambridge, 103 . . . . .F4
Caney, 2,092 . . . . .G4
Canton, 829 . . . . .E3
Carbondale, 1,478 . . . . .G3
Carlton, 38 . . . . .E3
Carlyle, 90 . . . . .G4
Carneiro D3
Cassoday, 130 . . . . .F3
Castleton, 40 . . . . .E4
Catherine, 100 . . . . .C3
Cawker City, 521 . . . . .D2
Cedar, 26 . . . . .D2
Cedar Bluffs B2
Cedar Point, 53 . . . . .F3
Cedar Vale, 723 . . . . .F4
Centerville, 90 . . . . .G4
Centralia, 534 . . . . .F2
Centropolis, 90 . . . . .G3
Chanute, 9,411 . . . . .G4
Chapman, 1,241 . . . . .E2
Charleston B4
Chase, 490 . . . . .D3
Chautauqua, 113 . . . . .F4
Cheney, 1,783 . . . . .E4
Cherokee, 722 . . . . .H4
Cherryvale, 2,386 . . . . .G4
Chetopa, 1,281 . . . . .G4
Chicopee, 350 . . . . .H4
Chiles, 90 . . . . .G3
Cimarron, 1,934 . . . . .B4
Circleville, 185 . . . . .G2
Claflin, 705 . . . . .D3
Claudell C2
Clay Center, 4,564 . . . . .E2
Clayton, 66 . . . . .B2
Clearwater, 2,178 . . . . .E4
Clements F3
Cleveland D4
Clifton, 557 . . . . .E2
Climax, 64 . . . . .F4
Clinton, 80 . . . . .G3
Clyde, 740 . . . . .E2
Coats, 112 . . . . .D4
Codell, 90 . . . . .C3
Coffeyville, 11,021 . . . . .G4
Colby, 5,450 . . . . .A2
Collyer, 133 . . . . .B2
Colony, 397 . . . . .G3
Columbus, 3,396 . . . . .H4
Colwich, 1,229 . . . . .E4
Concordia, 5,714 . . . . .E2
Conway Springs, 1,322 . . . . .E4
Coolidge, 86 . . . . .A3
Copeland, 339 . . . . .B4
Corbin, 60 . . . . .E4
Corning, 170 . . . . .F2
Corwin . . . .
Council Grove, 2,321 . . . . .F3
Countryside, 295 . . . . .H1
Courtland, 334 . . . . .E2
Covert D2
Coyville, 71 . . . . .G4
Crestline, 150 . . . . .H4
Croft D4
Crystal Springs, 50 . . . . .D4
Cuba, 231 . . . . .E2
Cullison, 80 . . . . .D4
Culver, 64 . . . . .E3
Cummings, 80 . . . . .G2
Cunningham, 514 . . . . .D4
Damar, 155 . . . . .C2
Danville, 59 . . . . .E4
Dearing, 415 . . . . .G4
Deerfield, 884 . . . . .A4
Delavan, 40 . . . . .F3
Delia, 179 . . . . .F2
Dellvale B2
Delphos, 469 . . . . .E2
Denison, 231 . . . . .G2
Denmark D2
Dennis, 150 . . . . .G4
Densmore C2
Denton, 186 . . . . .G2
Derby, 17,807 . . . . .E4
De Soto, 4,561 . . . . .G1, H3
Devon, 80 . . . . .H4
Dexter, 364 . . . . .F4
Dighton, 1,261 . . . . .B3
Dodge City, 25,176 . . . . .B4
Doniphan, 50 . . . . .G2
Dorrance, 205 . . . . .D3
Douglass, 1,813 . . . . .F4
Dover, 125 . . . . .G3
Downs, 1,038 . . . . .D2
Dresden, 51 . . . . .B2
Duluth, 50 . . . . .F2
Dundee, 100 . . . . .D3
Dunlap, 81 . . . . .F3
Duquoin D4
Durham, 114 . . . . .E3
Dwight, 330 . . . . .F3
Earlton, 80 . . . . .G4
Eastborough, 826 . . . . .E4

Easton, 362 . . . . .G2
Edgerton, 1,440 . . . . . .F3, G3
Edmond, 47 . . . . .C2
Edna, 423 . . . . .G4
Edson, 50 . . . . .A2
Edwardsville, 4,146 . . . . .H1
Effingham, 588 . . . . .G2
Elbing, 218 . . . . .E3
El Dorado, 12,057 . . . . .F4
Elgin, 82 . . . . .F4
Elk City, 305 . . . . .G4
Elk Falls, 112 . . . . .F4
Elkhart, 2,233 . . . . .A4
Ellinwood, 2,164 . . . . .D3
Ellis, 1,873 . . . . .C3
Ellsworth, 2,965 . . . . .D3
Elmdale, 50 . . . . .F3
Elmo, 50 . . . . .E3
Elmont, 425 . . . . .G2
Elsmore, 73 . . . . .G4
Elwood, 1,145 . . . . .H2
Elyria, 90 . . . . .E3
Emmeram C3
Emmett, 277 . . . . .F2
Emporia, 26,760 . . . . .F3
Englevale, 50 . . . . .H4
Englewood, 109 . . . . .C4
Ensign, 203 . . . . .B4
Enterprise, 836 . . . . .E3
Erie, 1,211 . . . . .G4
Esbon, 148 . . . . .D2
Eskridge, 589 . . . . .F3
Eudora, 4,307 . . . . . .F3, G3
Eureka, 2,914 . . . . .F4
Everest, 314 . . . . .G2
Fairmount, 250 . . . . . .G1, H2
Fairport . . . .
Fairview, 271 . . . . .G2
Fairway, 3,952 . . . . .H1
Fall River, 156 . . . . .F4
Falun, 125 . . . . .E3
Fanning, 40 . . . . .G2
Farlington, 125 . . . . .H4
Farmington G4
Faulkner, 40 . . . . .G4
Fellsburg C3
Florence, 671 . . . . .F3
Fontana, 149 . . . . .H3
Ford, 314 . . . . .C4
Formoso, 129 . . . . .E2
Fort Dodge, 550 . . . . .C4
Fort Scott, 8,297 . . . . .H4
Fostoria, 80 . . . . .F2
Fowler, 567 . . . . .B4
Frankfort, 855 . . . . .F2
Franklin, 475 . . . . .H4
Frederick, 11 . . . . .D3
Fredonia, 2,600 . . . . .G4
Freeport, 6 . . . . .E4
Friend B3
Frontenac, 2,996 . . . . .H4
Fulton, 184 . . . . .H4
Furley, 80 . . . . .E4
Galatia, 61 . . . . .D3
Galena, 3,287 . . . . .H4
Galesburg, 150 . . . . .G4
Galva, 701 . . . . .E3
Garden City, 28,451 . . . . .B4
Garden Plain, 797 . . . . .E4
Gardner, 9,396 . . . . .H3
Garfield, 198 . . . . .C3
Garland, 100 . . . . .H4
Garnett, 3,368 . . . . .G3
Gas, 556 . . . . .G4
Gaylord, 145 . . . . .D2
Gem, 96 . . . . .B2
Geneseo, 272 . . . . .D3
Geuda Springs, 212 . . . . .E4
Girard, 2,773 . . . . .H4
Glade, 111 . . . . .C2
Glasco, 536 . . . . .E2
Glendale . . . .
Glen Elder, 439 . . . . .D2
Goddard, 2,037 . . . . .E4
Goessel, 565 . . . . .E3
Goff, 181 . . . . .G2
Goodland, 4,948 . . . . .A2
Goodrich, 90 . . . . .H3
Gordon, 60 . . . . .H4
Gorham, 360 . . . . .C3
Grainfield, 327 . . . . .B2
Grandview Plaza, 1,184 . . . . .F2
Grantville, 280 . . . . .G2
Great Bend, 15,345 . . . . .D3
Greeley, 327 . . . . .G3
Green, 147 . . . . .E2
Greenleaf, 357 . . . . .F2
Greensburg, 1,574 . . . . .C4
Grenola, 231 . . . . .F4
Gretna C2
Gridley, 372 . . . . .G3
Grigston B3
Grinnell, 329 . . . . .B2
Grove . . . .
Gypsum, 414 . . . . .E3
Hackney . . . .
Haddam, 169 . . . . .E2
Halford B2
Halls Summit G3
Halstead, 1,873 . . . . .E3
Hamilton, 334 . . . . .F4
Hamlin, 53 . . . . .G2
Hammond H4
Hanover, 653 . . . . .F2
Hanston, 259 . . . . .C3
Harding H4
Hardtner, 199 . . . . .D4
Harlan D2
Harper, 1,567 . . . . .D4
Harris, 53 . . . . .G3
Hartford, 500 . . . . .G3
Harveyville, 267 . . . . .G3
Havana, 86 . . . . .G4
Haven, 1,175 . . . . .E4
Havensville, 146 . . . . .F2
Haviland, 612 . . . . .C4
Hays, 20,013 . . . . .C3
Haysville, 8,502 . . . . .E4
Hazelton, 144 . . . . .D4
Healy, 250 . . . . .B3
Hedville, 80 . . . . .E3
Heizer, 80 . . . . .D3
Hepler, 154 . . . . .H4
Herington, 2,563 . . . . .F3
Herkimer, 100 . . . . .F2
Herndon, 149 . . . . .B2
Hesston, 3,509 . . . . .E3

Hewins F4
Hiattville, 60 . . . . .H4
Hiawatha, 3,417 . . . . .G2
Hickok, 50 . . . . .A4
Highland, 976 . . . . .G2
Hill City, 1,604 . . . . .C2
Hillsboro, 2,854 . . . . .E3
Hillsdale, 275 . . . . .H3
Hitschmann D3
Hoisington, 2,975 . . . . .D3
Holcomb, 2,026 . . . . .B4
Hollenberg, 31 . . . . .F2
Holliday H1
Hollis F2
Holton, 3,353 . . . . .G2
Holyrood, 464 . . . . .D3
Home, 175 . . . . .F2
Homewood, 100 . . . . .G3
Hope, 372 . . . . .E3
Hopewell D4
Horace, 143 . . . . .A3
Horton, 1,967 . . . . .G2
Howell, 40 . . . . .B4
Hoxie, 1,244 . . . . .B2
Hoyt, 571 . . . . .G2
Hudson, 133 . . . . .D3
Hugoton, 3,708 . . . . .A4
Humboldt, 1,999 . . . . .G4
Hunnewell, 83 . . . . .E4
Hunter, 77 . . . . .D2
Huron, 87 . . . . .G2
Huscher, 40 . . . . .E2
Hutchinson, 40,787 . . . . .E3
Hymer F3
Idana, 70 . . . . .E2
Independence, 9,846 . . . . .G4
Industry, 40 . . . . .E2
Ingalls, 328 . . . . .B4
Inman, 1,142 . . . . .E3
Iola, 6,302 . . . . .G4
Iowa Point G2
Isabel, 108 . . . . .D4
Iuka, 185 . . . . .D4
Jamestown, 399 . . . . .E2
Jefferson, 90 . . . . .G2
Jennings, 146 . . . . .B2
Jewell, 483 . . . . .D2
Jingo H3
Johnson City, 1,528 . . . . .A4
Junction City, 18,886 . . . . .F2
Kackley E2
Kalvesta B3
Kanona B2
Kanopolis, 543 . . . . .D3
Kanorado, 248 . . . . .A2
Kansas City, 146,866 . . . . .H1
Keats, 150 . . . . .F2
Kechi, 1,038 . . . . .E4
Kelly, 50 . . . . .F2
Kendall A4
Kensington, 529 . . . . .C2
Kimball, 60 . . . . .C2
Kincaid, 178 . . . . .G3
Kingman, 3,387 . . . . .D4
Kingsdown, 50 . . . . .C4
Kinsley, 1,658 . . . . .C4
Kiowa, 1,055 . . . . .D4
Kipp, 100 . . . . .E3
Kirwin, 229 . . . . .C2
Kismet, 484 . . . . .B4
Labette, 68 . . . . .G4
La Crosse, 1,376 . . . . .C3
La Cygne, 1,115 . . . . .H3
Lafontaine, 90 . . . . .G4
La Harpe, 706 . . . . .G4
Lake City D4
Lake Quivira, 932 . . . . .H1
Lakin, 2,316 . . . . .A4
Lamont, 60 . . . . .F3
Lancaster, 291 . . . . .G2
Lane, 256 . . . . .G3
Langdon, 72 . . . . .D4
Langley . . . .
Lansing, 9,199 . . . . . .G1, H2
Larned, 4,236 . . . . .C3
Latham, 164 . . . . .F4
Latimer, 47 . . . . .F3
Lawrence, 80,098 . . . . .G3
Lawton, 80 . . . . .H4
Leavenworth, 35,420 . . . . .H2
Leawood, 27,656 . . . . .H1
Lebanon, 303 . . . . .D2
Lebo, 961 . . . . .G3
Lecompton, 608 . . . . .G2
Lehigh, 215 . . . . .E3
Le Loup, 125 . . . . .G3
Lenexa, 40,238 . . . . . .H1, H3
Lenora, 306 . . . . .C2
Leon, 645 . . . . .F4
Leona, 88 . . . . .G2
Leonardville, 398 . . . . .F2
Leoti, 1,598 . . . . .A3
Leoville, 50 . . . . .B2
Le Roy, 593 . . . . .G3
Levant, 90 . . . . .A2
Lewis, 486 . . . . .C4
Liebenthal, 111 . . . . .C3
Lincoln, 1,349 . . . . .D2
Lincolnville, 225 . . . . .F3
Lindsborg, 3,321 . . . . .E3
Linn, 425 . . . . .E2
Linwood, 374 . . . . .G2
Little River, 536 . . . . .D3
Logan, 603 . . . . .C2
Lone Elm, 27 . . . . .G3
Lone Star, 50 . . . . .G3
Longford, 94 . . . . .E2
Long Island, 155 . . . . .C2
Longton, 394 . . . . .F4
Loretta C3
Lorraine, 136 . . . . .D3
Lost Springs, 71 . . . . .F3
Louisburg, 2,576 . . . . .H3
Louisville, 209 . . . . .F2
Lovewell E2
Lowemont, 125 . . . . .G2
Lucas, 436 . . . . .D2
Ludell, 80 . . . . .B2
Luray, 203 . . . . .D2
Lydia . . . .
Lyons, 3,732 . . . . .D3
Macksville, 514 . . . . .C4
Madison, 857 . . . . .F3
Mahaska, 107 . . . . .E2

Maize, 1,868 . . . . .E4
Manchester, 102 . . . . .E2
Manhattan, 44,831 . . . . .F2
Mankato, 976 . . . . .D2
Manning B3
Manter, 178 . . . . .A4
Maple City F4
Maple Hill, 469 . . . . .G2
Mapleton, 98 . . . . .H3
Marienthal, 90 . . . . .A3
Marietta . . . .
Marion, 2,110 . . . . .E3
Marquette, 542 . . . . .E3
Marysville, 3,271 . . . . .F2
Matfield Green, 60 . . . . .F3
Mayetta, 312 . . . . .G2
Mayfield, 113 . . . . .E4
McCracken, 211 . . . . .C3
McCune, 426 . . . . .G4
McDonald, 159 . . . . .A2
McFarland, 271 . . . . .F2
McLouth, 868 . . . . .G2
McPherson, 13,770 . . . . .E3
Meade, 1,672 . . . . .B4
Medicine Lodge, 2,193 . . . .D4
Medora, 350 . . . . .E3
Melrose, 60 . . . . .H4
Melvern, 429 . . . . .G3
Menlo, 57 . . . . .B2
Mentor, 100 . . . . .E3
Meriden, 706 . . . . .G2
Merriam, 11,008 . . . . .H1
Michigan Valley, 90 . . . . .G3
Milan, 137 . . . . .E4
Milberger D3
Mildred, 36 . . . . .G3
Milford, 502 . . . . .F2
Miller, 50 . . . . .G3
Milton, 100 . . . . .E4
Miltonvale, 523 . . . . .E2
Mingo B2
Minneapolis, 2,046 . . . . .E2
Minneola, 717 . . . . .B4
Mission, 9,727 . . . . .H1
Mission Hills, 3,593 . . . . .H1
Mission Woods, 165 . . . . .H1
Mitchell D3
Modoc A3
Moline, 457 . . . . .F4
Montana, 80 . . . . .G4
Montezuma, 966 . . . . .B4
Mont Ida, 60 . . . . .G3
Montrose D2
Monument, 80 . . . . .A2
Moran, 562 . . . . .G4
Morehead . . . .
Morganville, 198 . . . . .E2
Morland, 164 . . . . .C2
Morrill, 277 . . . . .G2
Morrowville, 168 . . . . .E2
Moscow, 247 . . . . .A4
Moundridge, 1,593 . . . . .E3
Mound Valley, 418 . . . . .G4
Mount Hope, 830 . . . . .E4
Mulberry, 577 . . . . .H4
Mullinville, 279 . . . . .C4
Mulvane, 5,155 . . . . .E4
Munden, 122 . . . . .E2
Munjor, 325 . . . . .C3
Murdock, 100 . . . . .E4
Muscotah, 200 . . . . .G2
Narka, 93 . . . . .E2
Nashville, 111 . . . . .D4
Natoma, 367 . . . . .C2
Navarre, 60 . . . . .E3
Neal, 70 . . . . .F4
Nekoma C3
Neodesha, 2,848 . . . . .G4
Neosho Falls, 179 . . . . .G3
Neosho Rapids, 274 . . . . .G3
Ness City, 1,534 . . . . .C3
Netawaka, 170 . . . . .G2
Neutral, 60 . . . . .H4
New Albany, 73 . . . . .G4
New Almelo, 40 . . . . .B2
New Cambria, 150 . . . . .E3
New Lancaster H3
New Strawn, 425 . . . . .G3
Newton, 17,190 . . . . .E3
Nickerson, 1,194 . . . . .D3
Nicodemus C2
Niles, 90 . . . . .E3
Niotaze, 122 . . . . .F4
Norcatur, 169 . . . . .B2
Northbranch D2
North Newton, 1,522 . . . . .E3
Norton, 3,012 . . . . .C2
Nortonville, 620 . . . . .G2
Norway, 40 . . . . .E2
Norwich, 551 . . . . .E4
Oak Hill, 35 . . . . .E2
Oaklawn (Oaklawn-Sunview), 3,135 . . . . .E4
Oakley, 2,173 . . . . .B2
Oak Valley F4
Oberlin, 1,994 . . . . .B2
Odin, 100 . . . . .D3
Offerle, 220 . . . . .C4
Ogallah, 40 . . . . .C3
Ogden, 1,762 . . . . .F2
Oketo, 87 . . . . .F2
Olathe, 92,962 . . . .H1, H3
Olivet, 64 . . . . .G3
Olmitz, 138 . . . . .D3
Olpe, 504 . . . . .F3
Olsburg, 192 . . . . .F2
Onaga, 704 . . . . .F2
Oneida, 70 . . . . .G2
Osage City, 3,034 . . . . .G3
Osawatomie, 4,645 . . . . .H3
Osborne, 1,607 . . . . .D2
Oskaloosa, 1,165 . . . . .G2
Oswego, 2,046 . . . . .G4
Otis, 325 . . . . .C3
Ottawa, 11,921 . . . . .G3
Ottumwa, 9 . . . . .G3
Overbrook, 947 . . . . .G3
Overland Park, 149,080 . . . . .H1
Oxford, 1,173 . . . . .E4
Ozawkie, 552 . . . . .G2
Padonia . . . .
Page City, 60 . . . . .A2
Palco, 248 . . . . .C2
Palmer, 108 . . . . .E2
Paola, 5,011 . . . . .H3
Paradise, 64 . . . . .D2
Park, 151 . . . . .B2

Park City, 5,814 . . . . .E4
Parker, 281 . . . . .H3
Parkerville, 73 . . . . .F3
Parsons, 11,514 . . . . .G4
Partridge, 259 . . . . .D4
Patterson E4
Pawnee Rock, 356 . . . . .D3
Paxico, 211 . . . . .F2
Peabody, 1,384 . . . . .E3
Peck, 175 . . . . .E4
Penalosa, 27 . . . . .D4
Pendennis B3
Penokee, 60 . . . . .C2
Peoria, 90 . . . . .G3
Perry, 901 . . . . .G2
Perth, 70 . . . . .E4
Peru, 183 . . . . .F4
Petrolia, 70 . . . . .G4
Pfeifer, 40 . . . . .C3
Phillipsburg, 2,668 . . . . .C2
Piedmont, 50 . . . . .F4
Pierceville, 90 . . . . .B4
Piqua, 125 . . . . .G4
Pittsburg, 19,243 . . . . .H4
Plains, 1,163 . . . . .B4
Plainville, 2,029 . . . . .C2
Pleasant Grove, 300 . . . . .G3
Pleasanton, 1,387 . . . . .H3
Plevna, 99 . . . . .D4
Plymell B4
Plymouth, 90 . . . . .F3
Pomona, 923 . . . . .G3
Portis, 123 . . . . .D2
Portland E4
Potter, 90 . . . . .G2
Potwin, 457 . . . . .E4
Powhattan, 91 . . . . .G2
Prairie View, 141 . . . . .C2
Prairie Village, 22,072 . . . .H1
Pratt, 6,570 . . . . .D4
Prescott, 280 . . . . .H3
Preston, 164 . . . . .D4
Pretty Prairie, 615 . . . . .D4
Princeton, 317 . . . . .G3
Protection, 558 . . . . .C4
Quenemo, 468 . . . . .G3
Quincy F4
Quinter, 961 . . . . .B2
Radium, 40 . . . . .D3
Rago D4
Ramona, 94 . . . . .E3
Randall, 90 . . . . .D2
Randolph, 175 . . . . .F2
Ransom, 338 . . . . .C3
Rantoul, 241 . . . . .G3
Raymond, 95 . . . . .D3
Reading, 247 . . . . .G3
Reager B2
Redfield, 140 . . . . .H4
Reece F4
Reno, 50 . . . . .G3
Republic, 161 . . . . .E2
Reserve, 100 . . . . .G2
Rexford, 157 . . . . .B2
Rice E2
Richfield, 48 . . . . .A4
Richland, 70 . . . . .G3
Richmond, 510 . . . . .G3
Riley, 886 . . . . .F2
Riverdale, 60 . . . . .E4
Riverton, 850 . . . . .H4
Robinson, 216 . . . . .G2
Rock E4
Rock Creek, 150 . . . . .A3
Roeland Park, 6,817 . . . .H1
Rolla, 482 . . . . .A4
Roper G4
Rosalia, 100 . . . . .F4
Rose Hill, 3,432 . . . .D4, E4
Roseland, 101 . . . . .H4
Rossville, 1,014 . . . . .G2
Roxbury, 100 . . . . .E3
Rozel, 182 . . . . .C3
Ruleton, 40 . . . . .A2
Rush Center, 176 . . . . .C3
Russell, 4,696 . . . . .D3
Russell Springs, 32 . . . . .A3
Sabetha, 2,589 . . . . .G2
St. Benedict, 80 . . . . .F2
St. Francis, 1,497 . . . . .A2
St. George, 434 . . . . .F2
St. Joe, 70 . . . . .E4
St. John, 1,318 . . . . .D3
St. Joseph E2
St. Leo, 70 . . . . .D4
St. Mark, 50 . . . . .E4
St. Marys, 2,198 . . . . .F2
St. Paul, 646 . . . . .G4
St. Peter B2
Salina, 45,679 . . . . .E3
Sanford C3
Satanta, 1,239 . . . . .B4
Saunders A4
Savonburg, 91 . . . . .G4
Sawyer, 124 . . . . .D4
Saxman D3
Scammon, 496 . . . . .H4
Scandia, 436 . . . . .E2
Schoenchen, 214 . . . . .C3
Schulte, 125 . . . . .E4
Scott City, 3,855 . . . . .B3
Scottsville, 21 . . . . .E2
Scranton, 724 . . . . .G3
Sedan, 1,342 . . . . .F4
Sedgwick, 1,537 . . . . .E4
Seguin B2
Selden, 201 . . . . .B2
Selkirk A3
Selma G3
Seneca, 2,122 . . . . .F2
Severance, 108 . . . . .G2
Severy, 359 . . . . .F4
Seward, 63 . . . . .D3
Shallow Water, 125 . . . . .B3
Sharon, 210 . . . . .D4
Sharpe G3
Shaw C3
Shawnee, 47,996 . . . .H1, H2
Sherman, 60 . . . . .G4
Sherwin, 60 . . . . .H4
Shields B3
Silverdale, 80 . . . . .F4
Silver Lake, 1,358 . . . . .F2
Simpson, 114 . . . . .D2
Sitka C4
Skiddy F3
Smith Center, 1,931 . . . .D2

Smolan, 218 . . . . .E3
Soldier, 122 . . . . .G2
Solomon, 1,072 . . . . .E3
South Haven, 390 . . . . .E4
South Hutchinson, 2,539 E3
South Mound, 80 . . . . .G4
Spearville, 813 . . . . .C4
Speed, 44 . . . . .C2
Spivey, 80 . . . . .D4
Spring Hill, 2,727 . . . . .H3
Stafford, 1,161 . . . . .D4
Stanley, 100 . . . . . .H1, H3
Stark, 106 . . . . .G4
Sterling, 2,642 . . . . .D3
Stilwell, 1,200 . . . . .H3
Stippville, 125 . . . . .H4
Stockton, 1,558 . . . . .C2
Strong City, 584 . . . . .F3
Studley B2
Stull, 60 . . . . .G3
Stuttgart, 80 . . . . .C2
Sublette, 1,592 . . . . .B4
Summerfield, 211 . . . . .F2
Sun City, 81 . . . . .D4
Susank, 57 . . . . .D3
Sycamore, 125 . . . . .G4
Sylvan Grove, 324 . . . . .D2
Sylvia, 297 . . . . .D4
Syracuse, 1,824 . . . . .A4
Talmage, 125 . . . . .E2
Tampa, 144 . . . . .E3
Tasco B2
Tecumseh, 600 . . . . .G2
Tescott, 339 . . . . .E2
Teterville F3
Thayer, 500 . . . . .G4
Timken, 83 . . . . .C3
Tipton, 243 . . . . .D2
Tonganoxie, 2,728 . . . . .G2
Topeka, 122,377 . . . . .G2
Toronto, 312 . . . . .G4
Towanda, 1,338 . . . . .E4
Trading Post, 60 . . . . .H3
Treece, 149 . . . . .H4
Trousdale C4
Troy, 1,054 . . . . .G2
Turkville C2
Turon, 436 . . . . .D4
Tyro, 226 . . . . .G4
Udall, 794 . . . . .E4
Ulysses, 5,960 . . . . .A4
Uniontown, 288 . . . . .H4
Upland, 40 . . . . .E2
Urbana, 50 . . . . .G4
Utica, 223 . . . . .B3
Valley Center, 4,883 . . . . .E4
Valley Falls, 1,254 . . . . .G2
Varner D4
Vassar, 125 . . . . .G3
Verdi F2
Vermillion, 107 . . . . .F2
Vernon G3
Vesper D2
Victoria, 1,208 . . . . .C3
Vilas G4
Vining, 58 . . . . .E2
Vinland, 100 . . . . .G3
Viola, 211 . . . . .E4
Virgil, 113 . . . . .F4
Voda B2
Volland F3
Wabaunsee, 60 . . . . .F2
Wagstaff, 70 . . . . .H3
Wakarusa, 150 . . . . .G3
WaKeeney, 1,924 . . . . .C2
Wakefield, 838 . . . . .E2
Waldo, 48 . . . . .D2
Waldron, 17 . . . . .D4
Wallace, 67 . . . . .A3
Walnut, 221 . . . . .G4
Walton, 284 . . . . .E3
Wamego, 4,246 . . . . .F2
Washington, 1,223 . . . . .E2
Waterloo, 30 . . . . .E4
Waterville, 681 . . . . .F2
Wathena, 1,348 . . . . .H2
Wauneta F4
Waverly, 589 . . . . .G3
Wayside G4
Webber, 37 . . . . .D2
Webster C2
Weir, 780 . . . . .H4
Welda, 60 . . . . .G3
Wellington, 8,647 . . . . .E4
Wells, 40 . . . . .E2
Wellsford C4
Wellsville, 1,606 . . . . .G3
Weskan, 150 . . . . .A3
Westfall, 40 . . . . .D3
West Mineral, 243 . . . . .H4
Westphalia, 165 . . . . .G3
Westwood, 1,533 . . . . .H1
Westwood Hills, 378 . . . .H1
Wetmore, 362 . . . . .G2
Wheaton, 92 . . . . .F2
Wheeler A2
White City, 518 . . . . .F3
White Cloud, 239 . . . . .G2
Whitewater, 653 . . . . .E4
Whiting, 206 . . . . .G2
Wichita, 344,284 . . . . .E4
Willard, 86 . . . . .G2
Williamsburg, 351 . . . . .G3
Williamstown, 100 . . . . .G2
Willis, 69 . . . . .G2
Willowbrook, 36 . . . . .E3
Willowdale, 50 . . . . .D4
Wilmore, 57 . . . . .C4
Wilsey, 191 . . . . .F3
Wilson, 799 . . . . .D3
Winchester, 579 . . . . .G2
Windhorst C4
Windom, 137 . . . . .E3
Winfield, 12,206 . . . . .F4
Winifred F2
Winona, 228 . . . . .A2
Wolcott H1, H2
Wolf A3
Woodbine, 207 . . . . .F3
Woodruff C2
Woods A4
Woodston, 116 . . . . .C2
Wright, 200 . . . . .C4
Xenia H4

Yates Center, 1,599 . . .G4
Yocemento, 70 . . . . .C3
Yoder, 200 . . . . .E4
Zenda, 123 . . . . .D4
Zook, 40 . . . . .C3
Zurich, 126 . . . . .C2

Other Features

Arkansas, river A4, D3
Beaver, creek A2
Beaver, river B5
Big Blue, river F2
Bonny, reservoir A2
Brown vs. Board of Education N.H.S. G2
Cedar Bluff, reservoir C3
Cheney, reservoir E4
Cherokees, Lake O' The, lake H5
Chickaskia, river D4
Cimarron, river A4, C5
Cimarron Natl. Grassland A4
Clinton, lake G3
Copan, lake G5
Crooked, creek B4
Fall, river F4
Flint Hills F4
Flint Hills N.W.R. F3
Fort Larned N.H.S. C3
Ft. Leavenworth Mil. Res. H2
Fort Riley Mil. Res. F2
Fort Scott N.H.S. H4
Great Salt Plains, lake D5
Harlan County, lake C1
Homestead N.M. F1
Iowa Indian Reservation G2
Kanopolis, lake D3
Kansas, river F2, G1
Kaw, reservoir F5
Kickapoo Indian Reservation G2
Kirwin, reservoir C2
Kirwin N.W.R. C2
Ladder, creek A3
Little Blue, river E1
Little Nemaha, river F1
Marion, lake E3
Medicine Lodge, river C4
Melvern, lake G3
Milford, lake F2
Missouri, river G2, H1
Mt. Sunflower A2
Neosho, river G4
Nicodemus N.H.S. C2
Optima, lake A5
Osage Indian Reservation F5
Pawnee, creek C3
Potawatomi I.R. G2
Prairie Dog, creek B2
Quivira N.W.R. D3
Republican, river D1
Republican, S. Fork, river A2
Sac And Fox I.R. G1
Saline, river C2
Salt Plains N.W.R. D5
Sappa, creek B2
Smith, reservoir H2
Smoky Hill, river B3
Solomon, river D2
Solomon, N. Fork, river B2
Squaw Creek N.W.R. G1
Tallgrass Prairie Natl. Preserve F3
Turkey, creek E1
Tuttle Creek, lake F2
Verdigris, river F2
Waconda, lake D2
Walnut, creek C3
Wilson, lake D3

Kentucky:
Map Index

Counties

Adair, 17,244 . . . . .E3
Allen, 17,800 . . . . .D4
Anderson, 19,111 . . . . .E3
Ballard, 8,286 . . . . .B3
Barren, 38,033 . . . . .E4
Bath, 11,085 . . . . .G2
Bell, 30,060 . . . . .G4
Boone, 85,991 . . . .F2, G1
Bourbon, 19,360 . . . . .F2
Boyd, 49,752 . . . . .H2
Boyle, 27,697 . . . . .F3
Bracken, 8,279 . . . . .G1
Breathitt, 16,100 . . . . .G3
Breckinridge, 18,648 . . . .D3
Bullitt, 61,236 . . . . .E3
Butler, 13,010 . . . . .D3
Caldwell, 13,060 . . . . .C3
Calloway, 34,177 . . . . .B4
Campbell, 88,616 . .F2, G1
Carlisle, 5,351 . . . . .B3
Carroll, 10,155 . . . . .E2
Carter, 26,889 . . . . .G2
Casey, 15,447 . . . . .F3
Christian, 72,265 . . . . .C4
Clark, 33,144 . . . . .F3
Clay, 24,556 . . . . .G3
Clinton, 9,634 . . . . .E4
Crittenden, 9,384 . . . . .B3
Cumberland, 7,147 . . . . .E4
Daviess, 91,545 . . . . .C3
Edmonson, 11,644 . . . . .D3
Elliott, 6,748 . . . . .G2
Estill, 15,307 . . . . .F3
Fayette, 260,512 . . . . .F3
Fleming, 13,792 . . . . .G2
Floyd, 42,441 . . . . .H3
Franklin, 47,687 . . . . .F2
Fulton, 7,752 . . . . .A4
Gallatin, 7,870 . . . . .F2
Garrard, 14,792 . . . . .F3
Grant, 22,384 . . . . .F2
Graves, 37,028 . . . . .B4
Grayson, 24,053 . . . . .D3
Green, 11,518 . . . . .E3
Greenup, 36,891 . . . . .G2
Hancock, 8,392 . . . . .D3
Hardin, 94,174 . . . . .D3
Harlan, 33,202 . . . . .G4
Harrison, 17,983 . . . . .F2
Hart, 17,445 . . . . .E3
Henderson, 44,829 . . . . .C3
Henry, 15,060 . . . . .E2
Hickman, 5,262 . . . . .A4
Hopkins, 46,519 . . . . .C3
Jackson, 13,495 . . . . .F3
Jefferson, 693,604 . .B2, D2
Jessamine, 39,041 . . . . .F3
Johnson, 23,445 . . . . .H3
Kenton, 151,464 . . .F2, G1
Knott, 17,649 . . . . .H3
Knox, 31,795 . . . . .G4
Larue, 13,373 . . . . .E3
Laurel, 52,715 . . . . .F3
Lawrence, 15,569 . . . . .H2
Lee, 7,916 . . . . .G3
Leslie, 12,401 . . . . .G3
Letcher, 25,277 . . . . .H3
Lewis, 14,092 . . . . .G2
Lincoln, 23,361 . . . . .F3
Livingston, 9,804 . . . . .B3
Logan, 26,573 . . . . .C4
Lyon, 8,080 . . . . .C3
Madison, 70,872 . . . . .F3
Magoffin, 13,332 . . . . .G3
Marion, 18,212 . . . . .E3
Marshall, 30,125 . . . . .B3
Martin, 12,578 . . . . .H3
Mason, 16,800 . . . . .G2
McCracken, 65,514 . . . . .B3
McCreary, 17,080 . . . . .F4
McLean, 9,938 . . . . .C3
Meade, 26,349 . . . . .D3
Menifee, 6,556 . . . . .G3
Mercer, 20,817 . . . . .F3
Metcalfe, 10,037 . . . . .E4
Monroe, 11,756 . . . . .E4
Montgomery, 22,554 . . . . .G2
Morgan, 13,948 . . . . .G3
Muhlenberg, 31,839 . . . . .C3
Nelson, 37,477 . . . . .E3
Nicholas, 6,813 . . . . .F2
Ohio, 22,916 . . . . .D3
Oldham, 46,178 . . .B1, E2
Owen, 10,547 . . . . .F2
Owsley, 4,858 . . . . .G3
Pendleton, 14,390 . . . . .F2
Perry, 29,390 . . . . .G3
Pike, 65,024 . . . . .H3
Powell, 13,237 . . . . .G3
Pulaski, 56,217 . . . . .F3
Robertson, 2,266 . . . . .F2
Rockcastle, 16,582 . . . . .F3
Rowan, 22,094 . . . . .G2
Russell, 16,315 . . . . .F4
Scott, 33,061 . . . . .F2
Shelby, 33,337 . . . . .E2
Simpson, 16,405 . . . . .D4
Spencer, 11,766 . . . . .E2
Taylor, 22,927 . . . . .E3
Todd, 11,971 . . . . .C4
Trigg, 12,597 . . . . .C4
Trimble, 8,125 . . . . .E2
Union, 15,637 . . . . .B3
Warren, 92,522 . . . . .D4
Washington, 10,916 . . . . .E3
Wayne, 19,923 . . . . .F4
Webster, 14,120 . . . . .C3
Whitley, 35,865 . . . . .F4
Wolfe, 7,065 . . . . .G3
Woodford, 23,208 . . . . .F2

Cities and Towns

Adairville, 920 . . . . .D4
Adams, 60 . . . . .H2
Adolphus, 175 . . . . .D4
Albany, 2,220 . . . . .E4
Alexandria, 8,286 . . . . .G1
Allegre, 100 . . . . .C4
Allen, 150 . . . . .G3
Allensville, 189 . . . . .C4
Almo, 225 . . . . .B4

Kentucky

Capital:	Frankfort
Land Area:	39,732 sq. mi. 102,906 sq. km.
Population:	4,041,769 (2000 Census)
Largest City:	Lexington, 260,512
Highest Point:	Black Mountain 4,139 ft. 1,262 m.
Admitted to Union:	June 1, 1792
Nickname:	Bluegrass State
State Flower:	Goldenrod
State Bird:	Cardinal

Alpine, *80* ... F4
Alton, *750* ... F2
Alva, *150* ... G4
Alvaton, *375* ... D4
Anchorage, **2,264** ... B2
Anneta, *175* ... D3
Annville, **589** ... G3
Anthoston, *350* ... C3
Anton, *300* ... C3
Argo ... H3
Arlington, **395** ... A4
Ashbyburg, *40* ... C3
Ashland, **21,981** ... H2
Athertonville, *60* ... E3
Auburn, **1,444** ... D4
Audubon Park, **1,545** ... A2
Augusta, **1,204** ... F2
Aurora, *150* ... B4
Austin, *200* ... D4
Avawam, *450* ... G3
Bagdad, *150* ... E2
Baileys Switch, *400* ... G4
Baizetown, *40* ... D3
Balltown, *250* ... E3
Bancroft, **536** ... B2
Bandana, *150* ... B3
Barbourmeade, **1,260** ... B1
Barbourville, **3,589** ... G4
Bardstown, **10,374** ... E3
Bardwell, **799** ... B4
Barlow, **715** ... A3
Barrier, *150* ... F4
Baskett, *550* ... C3
Battletown, *40* ... D2
Beattyville, **1,193** ... G3
Beaumont, *225* ... E4
Beaver Dam, **3,033** ... D3
Beaverlick, *200* ... F2
Beda, *250* ... D3
Bedford, **677** ... E2
Beechburg, *150* ... G2
Beech Grove, *250* ... C3
Beechwood, *125* ... F2
Beechwood Village,
1,173 ... B2
Bee Spring, *225* ... D3
Belcher, *175* ... H3
Bell City, *40* ... B4
Bellefonte, **837** ... H2
Bellemeade, **871** ... B2
Bellevue, **6,480** ... G1
Belmont, *425* ... E3
Belton, *500* ... C3
Benham, **599** ... H4
Benton, **4,197** ... B4
Berea, **9,851** ... F3
Bernstadt, *475* ... F3
Berry, **310** ... F2
Beulah, *200* ... C3
Bewleyville, *125* ... D3
Big Clifty, *250* ... D3
Big Spring, *70* ... D3
Birdsville, *40* ... B3
Blackey, **153** ... H3
Blackford, *125* ... C3
Blacks Ferry ... F4
Blaine, **245** ... H2
Blairs Mills ... G2
Blandville, **99** ... B4
Bloomfield, **855** ... E3
Blue Ridge Manor, **623** ... B2
Bohon, *60* ... F3
Bondurant ... A4
Bonnieville, **354** ... E3
Boone, *275* ... F3
Booneville, **111** ... G3
Boston, *375* ... E3
Botto, *550* ... G3
Bourne, *80* ... F3
Bradfordsville, **304** ... E3
Brandenburg, **2,049** ... D3
Breckinridge Center,
1,874 ... C3
Bremen, **365** ... C3
Briarwood, **554** ... B2
Briensburg, *400* ... B4
Broad Fields, **250** ... B2
Brodhead, **1,193** ... F3
Bromley, **838** ... G1
Brooklyn, *70* ... D3
Brooks, **2,678** ... E2
Brooksville, **589** ... F2
Brownsboro Farm, **676** ... B1
Browns Valley, *100* ... C3
Brownsville, **921** ... D3
Bruin, *175* ... G2
Bryants Store ... G4
Bryantsville, *300* ... F3
Buckhorn, **144** ... G3
Buckner, **4,000** ... E2
Buechel, **7,272** ... B2, E2
Buffalo, *475* ... E3
Burgin, **874** ... F3
Burkesville, **1,756** ... E4
Burlington, **10,779** ... F1
Burna, *225* ... B3
Burning Springs, *600* ... G3
Burnside, **637** ... F4
Bush, *375* ... G3
Butler, **613** ... F2
Cadiz, **2,373** ... C4
Cains Store, *90* ... F3
Cairo, *250* ... C3
Calhoun, **836** ... C3
California, **86** ... F2
Calvary, *175* ... E3
Calvert City, **2,701** ... B3
Camargo, **923** ... G3
Campbellsburg, **705** ... E2
Campbellsville, **10,498** ... E3
Camp Dix, *50* ... G2
Camp Nelson, *225* ... F3
Camp Springs, *350* ... G1
Campton, **424** ... G3
Cane Valley, *225* ... E3
Caneyville, **627** ... D3
Canmer, *100* ... E3
Cannel City, *375* ... G3
Cannonsburg, *1,300* ... H2
Canton, *150* ... C4
Cardwell, *80* ... E3
Carlisle, **1,917** ... F2
Carntown, *100* ... F2
Carrollton, **3,846** ... E2
Carrsville, **64** ... B3
Carter, *100* ... G2
Carver, *40* ... G3
Casky, *150* ... C4
Catlettsburg, **1,960** ... H2
Cave City, **1,880** ... E3
Cawood, *800* ... G4
Cayce, *150* ... A4
Cecilia, *600* ... E3
Cedarville, **52** ... H3
Centertown, **416** ... C3
Central City, **5,893** ... C3
Cerulean, *350* ... C4
Chapel Hill, *125* ... D4
Chaplin, *500* ... E3
Charters ... G2
Chavies, *60* ... G3
Cherokee ... H2
Chilton ... F3
Clarkson, **794** ... D3
Claryville, **2,588** ... F2
Clay, **1,179** ... C3
Clay City, **1,303** ... G3
Claysville, *70* ... F2
Clay Village, *90* ... E2
Cleaton, *500* ... C3
Clifty, *80* ... C4
Clinton, **1,415** ... B4
Closplint, *50* ... G4
Cloverport, **1,256** ... D3
Coal Run Village, **577** ... H3
Cobb, *50* ... C4
Cold Spring, **3,806** ... G1
Coldstream, **956** ... B1
Colesburg, *50* ... E3
Colfax ... G2
Colmar, *125* ... G4
Colson, *175* ... H3
Columbia, **4,014** ... E3
Columbus, **229** ... A4
Concord
(Lewis Co.), **28** ... G2
Concord
(McCracken Co.) ... B3
Concordia, *50* ... D2
Conway, *225* ... F3
Cool Springs ... D3
Cooper, *100* ... F4
Co-Operative, *125* ... F4
Corbin, **7,742** ... F4
Corinth (Grant Co.),
181 ... F2
Corinth (Logan Co.),
50 ... D4
Cornettsville, *125* ... G3
Corydon, **744** ... C3
Covington, **43,370** ... G1
Cowan, *200* ... G2
Crab Orchard, **842** ... F3
Cranston, *40* ... G2
Creelsboro, *40* ... E4
Crescent Park ... G1
Crescent Springs, **3,931** G1
Crestview, **471** ... G1
Crestview Hills, **2,889** ... G1
Crestwood, **1,999** ... B1, E2
Crider, *50* ... C3
Crittenden, **2,401** ... F2
Crockett ... G4
Crofton, **838** ... C3
Cromwell, *175* ... D3
Cropper, *100* ... E2
Crutchfield, *150* ... B4
Cumberland, **2,611** ... H4
Cumberland City, *125* ... E4
Cundiff, *175* ... E4
Custer, *70* ... D3
Cynthiana, **6,258** ... F2
Dalton, *100* ... C3
Dan, *50* ... G3
Danville, **15,477** ... F3
David, *300* ... H3
Dawson Springs, **2,980** ... C3
Daysville, *90* ... C4
Dayton, **5,966** ... F1, G1
Decoy ... G3
Dekoven, *225* ... B3
Dexter, *375* ... B4
Dimple, *100* ... D3
Dingus ... G3
Dixon, **632** ... C3
Dizney, *300* ... G4
Dorton, *250* ... H3
Douglass Hills, **5,718** ... B2
Dover, **316** ... G2
Drakesboro, **627** ... C3
Drip Rock, *100* ... G3
Dry Ridge, **1,995** ... F2
Dublin, *175* ... B4
Duncan, *100* ... F3
Dundee, *50* ... D3
Dunmor, *250* ... D3
Dunnville, *40* ... F3
Dwarf, *550* ... G3
Dycusburg, **39** ... B3
Dyer, *175* ... D3
Earles, *60* ... C3
Earlington, **1,649** ... C3
East Bernstadt, *774* ... F3
Eddyville, **2,350** ... B3
Edgewood, **9,400** ... F1, G1
Edmonton, **1,586** ... E4
Ekron, **170** ... D3
Elihu, *650* ... F3
Elizabethtown, **22,542** ... E3
Elkatawa, *40* ... G3
Elk Creek, *150* ... E2
Elk Horn, *60* ... E3
Elkhorn City, **1,060** ... H3
Elkton, **1,984** ... C4
Elrod ... F3
Elsmere, **8,139** ... G1
Emerson, *80* ... G2
Eminence, **2,231** ... E2
Ensor, *500* ... D3
Eolia, *50* ... H3
Epleys, *275* ... D4
Erlanger, **16,676** ... G1
Ermine, *300* ... H3
Erose, *100* ... G4
Eubank, **358** ... F3
Evarts, **1,101** ... G4
Ewing, **278** ... G2
Ezel, *225* ... G3
Fairdale, **7,658** ... A2
Fairfield, **72** ... E3
Fairview
(Christian Co.), *150* ... C4
Fairview
(Fleming Co.), *70* ... G2
Fairview
(Kenton Co.), **156** ... G1
Falcon, *225* ... H3
Fallsburg, *175* ... H2
Falmouth, **2,058** ... F2
Fancy Farm, *500* ... B4
Farmington, *225* ... B4
Farristown, *200* ... F3
Fearisville, *150* ... G2
Ferguson, **881** ... F3
Fern Creek, **17,870** ... B2
Fincastle, **825** ... B1
Finchville, *200* ... E2
Firebrick, *300* ... G2
Flaherty, *175* ... D3
Flatgap, *200* ... H3
Flat Lick, *700* ... G4
Flatwoods, **7,605** ... H2
Fleming-Neon, **840** ... H3
Flemingsburg, **3,010** ... G2
Fletcher, *80* ... G3
Florence, **23,551** ... F2, G1
Fonde, *80* ... G4
Fordsville, **531** ... D3
Forest Hills, **494** ... B2
Fort Mitchell,
8,089 ... F1, G1
Fort Thomas,
16,495 ... F1, G1
Fort Wright, **5,681** ... F1, G1
Foster, **70** ... F2
Fount ... G4
Fountain Run, **236** ... E4
Fox Chase, **476** ... E2
Fox Creek, *100* ... F3
Frances, *125* ... B3
Frankfort, **27,741** ... F2
Franklin, **7,996** ... D4
Fredonia, **420** ... B3
Fremont, *325* ... B4
Frenchburg, **551** ... G3
Fritz, *80* ... G3
Fullerton, *175* ... H2
Fulton, **2,775** ... B4
Furnace, *50* ... G3
Gallup, *75* ... H2
Galveston, *450* ... H3
Gamaliel, **439** ... E4
Garlin, *325* ... E3
Garner, *600* ... H3
Garrison, *950* ... G2
Gasper, *125* ... D4
Gatliff, *80* ... F4
Georgetown, **18,080** ... F2
Germantown, **190** ... G2
Ghent, **371** ... E2
Gilpin, *40* ... F3
Glasgow, **13,019** ... E3
Glencoe, **251** ... F2
Glendale, *350* ... D3
Glen Dean ... D3
Glensboro, *70* ... E2
Glenview, **558** ... B1
Glenville, *150* ... C3
Goshen, **907** ... E2
Gracey, *125* ... C4
Gradyville, *70* ... E3
Graham, *475* ... C3
Grand Rivers, **343** ... B3
Grassy Creek, *100* ... G3
Gratz, **89** ... F2
Gravel Switch, *125* ... E3
Gray, *650* ... F4
Gray Hawk, *250* ... G3
Graymoor-Devondale,
2,925 ... B2
Grays Branch, *225* ... H2
Grayson, **3,877** ... H2
Greensburg, **2,396** ... E3
Green Spring, **759** ... B1
Greenup, **1,198** ... H2
Greenville, **4,398** ... C3
Greenwood, *50* ... F4
Grove Center, *90* ... B3
Guage, *80* ... G3
Gulnare, *100* ... H3
Guston, *350* ... D3
Guthrie, **1,469** ... C4
Hagerhill, *900* ... H3
Haldeman, *350* ... G2
Halfway, *40* ... D4
Hall, *225* ... F3
Halls Gap, *450* ... F3
Hampton, *100* ... B3
Handshoe, *70* ... H3
Hanson, **625** ... C3
Hardin, **564** ... B4
Hardinsburg, **2,345** ... D3
Hargett, *40* ... F3
Hargis ... F4
Harlan, **2,081** ... G4
Harold, *1,400* ... H3
Harrodsburg, **8,014** ... F3
Hartford, **2,571** ... D3
Hawesville, **971** ... D3
Hazard, **4,806** ... G3
Hazel, **440** ... B4
Hazel Green, *275* ... G3
Head of Grassy, *40* ... G2
Hebbardsville, *175* ... C3
Hebron, *1,300* ... F1
Hebron Estates, **1,104** ... E2
Heidrick, *275* ... G4
Helena, *125* ... G2
Helton ... G4
Hendricks, *125* ... G3
Hendron, **4,239** ... B3
Henshaw, *125* ... B3
Herndon, *70* ... C4
Hesler, *60* ... F2
Hickman, **2,560** ... A4
Hickory, *250* ... B4
Highland Heights,
6,554 ... G1
Highview, **15,161** ... B2
Hills and Dales, **153** ... B1
Hillsboro, *250* ... G2
Hill Top, *100* ... G2
Hillview, **7,037** ... E2
Hindman, **787** ... H3
Hinton, *100* ... F2
Hiseville, **224** ... E3
Hitchins, *475* ... H2
Hobson, *100* ... E3
Hodgenville, **2,874** ... E3
Hollow Creek, **815** ... B2
Hollyhill, *80* ... F4
Hollyvilla, **481** ... E2
Horse Branch, *250* ... D3
Horse Cave, **2,252** ... E3
Hoskinston, *90* ... G3
Houston Acres, **491** ... B2
Howardstown ... E3
Huddy, *900* ... H3
Hudson, *100* ... D3
Hulen, *350* ... G4
Hunters Hollow, **372** ... E2
Huntsville, *150* ... D3
Hurstbourne, **3,884** ... B2
Hurstbourne Acres,
1,504 ... B2
Hustonville, **347** ... F3
Hyden, **204** ... G3
Idamay, *90* ... G3
Independence, **14,982** ... F2
Indian Fields, *90* ... G3
Indian Hills, **2,882** ... A2
Indian Hills Cherokee
Section ... B2
Inez, **466** ... H3
Iron Hill, *70* ... G2
Irvine, **2,843** ... G3
Irvington, **1,257** ... D3
Island, **435** ... C3
Island City, *70* ... G3
Jackson, **2,490** ... G3
Jackstown, *40* ... F2
Jamestown, **1,624** ... E4
Jeffersontown, **26,633** ... B2
Jeffersonville, **1,804** ... G3
Jenkins, **2,401** ... H3
Jessietown, *175* ... E3
Johnetta, *80* ... F3
Jonancy, *350* ... H3
Jonestown, *650* ... F3
Jonesville, *225* ... F2
Junction City, **2,184** ... F3
Keavy, *450* ... F3
Keene, *225* ... F3
Kelly, *225* ... C4
Kenton, *375* ... F2
Kenton Vale, **156** ... G1
Kevil, **574** ... B3
Kimper, *50* ... H3
Kingsley, **428** ... A2
Kingston, *600* ... F3
Kirkmansville, *50* ... C3
Kirksey, *175* ... B4
Kirkwood, *70* ... F3
Knifley, *225* ... E3
Knob Lick, *150* ... E3
Kuttawa, **596** ... B3
La Center, **1,038** ... A3
La Fayette, **193** ... C4
La Grange, **5,676** ... E2
Lair, *100* ... F2
Lakeside Park, **2,869** ... G1
Lakeview Heights, **251** ... G2
Lamasco, *40* ... C4
Lancaster, **3,734** ... F3
Langdon Place, **974** ... B2
Langley, *375* ... H3
Latonia Lakes, **325** ... F2
Laura, *600* ... H3
Lawrenceburg, **9,014** ... F2
Leatherwood, *125* ... G3
Lebanon, **5,718** ... E3
Lebanon Junction,
1,801 ... E3
Ledbetter, **1,700** ... B3
Lee City, *100* ... G3
Leesburg, *250* ... F2
Leitchfield, **6,139** ... D3
Lenoxburg, *125* ... F2
Letcher, *425* ... H3
Lewisburg
(Logan Co.), **903** ... D4
Lewisburg
(Mason Co.), *225* ... G2
Lewisport, **1,639** ... D3
Lexington, **260,512** ... F2
Liberty, **1,850** ... F3
Ligon, *150* ... H3
Lily, *1,200* ... F3
Limestone, *275* ... G2
Lincolnshire, **154** ... B2
Lindseyville, *175* ... D3
Linton ... C4
Linwood, *90* ... E3
Lisman, *100* ... C3
Little Rock, *100* ... F2
Livermore, **1,482** ... C3
Livia, *125* ... C3
Livingston, **228** ... F3
Lola, *150* ... B3
London, **5,692** ... F3
Lone Oak, **454** ... B3
Long Ridge, *90* ... F2
Loretto, **623** ... E3
Lost Creek, *425* ... G3
Louellen, *80* ... G4
Louisa, **2,018** ... H2
Louisville, **256,231** ... A2
Lowes, *175* ... B4
Loyall, **766** ... G4
Lucas, *200* ... D4
Ludlow, **4,409** ... G1
Lynch, **900** ... H4
Lyndon, **9,369** ... B2, E2
Lynn Grove, *225* ... B4
Lynnview, **965** ... A2
Lynnville, *100* ... B4
Maceo, *400* ... D3
Mackville, **206** ... E3
Madisonville, **19,307** ... C3
Magnolia, *425* ... E3
Majestic, *600* ... H3
Mammoth Cave ... D3
Manchester, **1,738** ... G3
Mannington, *80* ... C3
Mannsville, *200* ... E3
Mariba, *50* ... G3
Marion, **3,196** ... B3
Marrowbone, *100* ... E4
Martin, **633** ... H3
Maryhill Estates, **175** ... B2
Mason, *125* ... F2
Masonville, **1,075** ... C3
Massac, **3,888** ... B3
Mattoon, *100* ... B3
Mayfield, **10,349** ... B4
Mayo, *200* ... F3
Mays Lick, *325* ... G2
Maysville, **8,993** ... G2
Mazie, *300* ... H2
McDaniels, *90* ... D3
McHenry, **417** ... D3
McKee, **878** ... G3
McQuady, *100* ... D3
McRoberts, **921** ... H3
McVeigh, *550* ... H3
Meadow Vale, **765** ... B2
Meadowview Estates,
422 ... B2
Melbourne, **457** ... G1
Meldrum, *225* ... G4
Memphis Junction, *550* ... D4
Mentor, **181** ... F2
Merrimac, *40* ... E3
Middlesboro, **10,384** ... G4
Middleton, *50* ... D4
Middletown, **5,744** ... B2, E2
Midway, **1,620** ... F2
Milford, *80* ... F2
Millersburg, **842** ... F2
Millers Creek, *80* ... G3
Millstone, *650* ... H3
Milltown, *90* ... E3
Millville, *325* ... F2
Millwood, *125* ... D3
Milton, **525** ... E2
Minerva, *150* ... G2
Minor Lane Heights,
1,435 ... A2
Mitchellsburg, *175* ... F3
Monterey, **167** ... F2
Monticello, **5,981** ... F4
Mooleyville, *40* ... D2
Moon, *150* ... G3
Moorman, *225* ... C3
Morehead, **5,914** ... G2
Moreland, *550* ... F3
Morgan, *70* ... F2
Morganfield, **3,494** ... C3
Morgantown, **2,544** ... D3
Morrill ... F3
Mortons Gap, **952** ... C3
Mortonsville, *150* ... F3
Moscow, *60* ... A4
Mountain Valley, *40* ... G3
Mount Carmel, *125* ... G2
Mount Eden, *50* ... E2
Mount Hermon, *125* ... E4
Mount Olivet, **289** ... F2
Mount Sterling, **5,876** ... G2
Mount Vernon, **2,592** ... F3
Mount Washington,
8,485 ... E2
Mousie, *200* ... H3
Mozelle, *125* ... G4
Muldraugh, **1,298** ... D3
Munfordville, **1,563** ... E3
Murray, **14,950** ... B4
Murray Hill, **616** ... B2
Myers, *50* ... G2
Nancy, *200* ... F3
Narrows, *40* ... D3
Nazareth, *1,000* ... E3
Nebo, **220** ... C3
Nevada, *225* ... F3
Newburg, **20,636** ... A2
New Castle, **919** ... E2
New Concord, *150* ... B4
Newfoundland, *80* ... G2
New Haven, **849** ... E3
New Market ... E3
Newport, **17,048** ... G1
Newtown, *90* ... F2
Niagara, *275* ... C3
Nicholasville, **19,680** ... F3
Nina, *90* ... F3
Norbourne Estates, **461** ... B2
North Corbin, **1,662** ... F4
Northfield, **970** ... B2
North Middletown, **562** ... F2
Nortonville, **1,264** ... C3
Norwood, **395** ... B2
Oakbrook, **7,726** ... F2
Oakdale, **4,937** ... B3
Oak Grove, **7,064** ... C4
Oakland, **260** ... D3
Oak Level, *150* ... B4
Oakton, *150* ... A4
Okolona, **17,807** ... A2, E2
Olaton, *90* ... D3
Oldtown, *60* ... H2
Olive Hill, **1,813** ... G2
Olmstead, *70* ... C4
Olympia, *225* ... G2
Oneida, *325* ... G3
Orchard Grass Hills,
1,031 ... B1
Ottusville ... F2
Owensboro, **54,067** ... C3
Owenton, **1,387** ... F2
Owingsville, **1,488** ... G2
Oxford, *300* ... F2
Paint Lick, *200* ... F3
Paintsville, **4,132** ... H3
Panco, *80* ... G3
Panther, *175* ... C3
Paris, **9,183** ... F2
Park City, **517** ... D3
Parkers Lake ... F4
Park Hills, **2,977** ... G1
Park Lake, **537** ... E2
Parkway Village, **715** ... A2
Patesville, *50* ... D3
Pathfork, *350* ... G4
Paw Paw, *175* ... H3
Peaks Mill, *300* ... F2
Pellville, *175* ... D3
Pembroke, **797** ... C4
Pendleton, *225* ... E2
Perryville, **763** ... F3
Petersburg, *450* ... F1
Petersville, *80* ... G2
Pewee Valley, **1,436** ... B1
Phelps, **1,053** ... H3
Phillipsburg ... E3
Philpot, *850* ... D3
Pierce, *200* ... E3
Pike View, *125* ... E3
Pikeville, **6,295** ... H3
Pine Grove ... F2
Pine Knot, **1,680** ... F4
Pineville, **2,093** ... G4
Pioneer Village, **2,555** ... E2
Pippa Passes, **297** ... H3
Plantation, **902** ... B2
Pleasure Ridge Park,
25,776 ... E2
Pleasureville, **869** ... E2
Plum ... F2
Plum Springs, **447** ... D3
Poindexter, *60* ... F2
Poole, *275* ... C3
Poplar Hills, **396** ... A2
Poplar Plains, *100* ... G2
Port Royal, *175* ... E2
Powderly, **846** ... C3
Prestonsburg, **3,612** ... H3
Prestonville, **164** ... E2
Pride, *150* ... C3
Primrose ... G3
Princeton, **6,536** ... C3
Prospect, **4,657** ... E2
Providence, **3,611** ... C3
Pryorsburg, *275* ... B4
Pueblo, *60* ... F4
Pulaski, *425* ... F3
Putney, *600* ... G4
Raceland, **2,355** ... H2
Radcliff, **21,961** ... E3
Ravenna, **693** ... G3
Raywick, **144** ... E3
Ready, *70* ... D3
Rectorville, *375* ... G2
Reed, *175* ... C3
Reidland, **4,353** ... B3
Repton, *80* ... B3
Reynoldsville ... G2
Riceville, *150* ... H3
Richardsville, *425* ... D3
Richmond, **27,152** ... F3
Rich Pond, *425* ... D4
Riley, *175* ... E3
Rineyville, *550* ... E3
Ritchie, *825* ... G3
River Bluff, **402** ... E2
Riverwood, **469** ... A2
Robards, **564** ... C3
Robinson, *125* ... F2
Rochester, **186** ... D3
Rockholds, *325* ... F4
Rockport, **334** ... D3
Rolling Fields, **648** ... A2
Rolling Hills, **907** ... B2
Rome, *275* ... C3
Rosine, *175* ... D3
Roundhill, *125* ... D3
Rowdy, *150* ... G3
Royalton, *325* ... G3
Rush, *175* ... H2
Russell, **3,645** ... H2
Russell Springs, **2,399** ... E3
Russellville, **7,149** ... D4
Ryland Heights, **799** ... F2
Sacramento, **517** ... C3
Sadieville, **263** ... F2
St. Charles, **309** ... C3
St. Dennis, **9,177** ... E2
St. Francis, *125* ... E3
St. John, *275* ... E3
St. Matthews, **15,852** ... B2
St. Regis Park, **1,520** ... B2
Salem, **769** ... B3
Salt Lick, **342** ... G2
Salvisa, *325* ... F3
Salyersville, **1,604** ... G3
Samuels, *400* ... E3
Sanders, **246** ... F2
Sandgap, *350* ... F3
Sandy Hook, **678** ... G2
Sardis, **149** ... G2
Saxton, *350* ... F4
Science Hill, **634** ... F3
Scottsburg, *125* ... C3
Scottsville, **4,327** ... D4
Sebree, **1,558** ... C3
Seneca Gardens, **699** ... A2
Shady Grove ... C3
Sharpe, *300* ... B4
Sharpsburg, **295** ... G2
Shawhan, *125* ... F2
Shelbiana, *600* ... H3
Shelbyville, **10,085** ... E2
Shepherdsville, **8,334** ... E3
Sheridan, *60* ... B3
Sherman, *100* ... F2
Shipley, *225* ... E4
Shively, **15,157** ... E2
Shopville, *150* ... F3
Short Creek ... D3
Silver Grove, **1,215** ... G1
Silverhill, *100* ... G3
Simpsonville, **1,281** ... E2
Sitka ... H3
Slade ... G3
Slaughters, **238** ... C3
Slemp, *300* ... G3
Smith, *50* ... G4
Smithfield, **102** ... E2
Smithland, **401** ... B3
Smith Mills, *325* ... C3
Smiths Creek, *40* ... G2
Smiths Grove, **784** ... D3
Somerset, **11,352** ... F3
Sonora, **350** ... E3
South Carrollton, **184** ... C3
South Fork, *175* ... F3
Southgate, **3,472** ... G1
South Park View, **196** ... A2
South Shore, **1,226** ... H2
South Wallins, **996** ... G4
South Williamson, *600* ... H3
Sparta, **230** ... F2
Speight, *100* ... H3
Spottsville, *600* ... C3
Springfield, **2,634** ... E3
Springlee, **426** ... B2
Spring Mill, **380** ... B2
Sprout, *80* ... G2
Stamping Ground, **566** ... F2
Stanford, **3,430** ... F3
Stanley, *400* ... C3
Stanton, **3,029** ... G3
State Line, *60* ... A4
Stearns, **1,586** ... F4
Stella, *300* ... B4
Stephensburg, *325* ... D3
Stephensport, *80* ... D3
Steubenville, *550* ... F4
Stinnett, *250* ... G3
Strathmoor Manor, **333** ... A2
Strathmoor Village, **625** A2
Sturgis, **2,030** ... B3
Sublett, *325* ... G3
Sugar Grove, *125* ... D3
Sullivan, *125* ... C3
Summersville, *325* ... E3
Summit (Boyd Co.),
3,400 ... H2
Summit (Hardin Co.),
300 ... D3
Sunnybrook, *150* ... F4
Sunrise, *100* ... F2
Sutherland, *100* ... C3
Symsonia, *450* ... B4
Talbert, *225* ... G3
Taylor Mill, **6,913** ... G1
Taylorsville, **1,009** ... E2
Temple Hill, *175* ... E4
Thousandsticks, *70* ... G3
Threelinks ... F3
Tilden, *100* ... C3
Tiline, *40* ... B3
Tobacco, *275* ... B4
Tolu, *100* ... B3
Tompkinsville, **2,660** ... E4
Topmost, *250* ... H3
Totz, *325* ... G4
Tracy, *80* ... E4
Trent, *150* ... G3
Trenton, **419** ... C4
Turkey, *125* ... G3
Ulysses, *175* ... H3
Union, **2,893** ... F2
Union City, *175* ... F3
Uniontown, **1,064** ... C3
Upton, **654** ... E3
Valeria, *60* ... G3
Valley View, *70* ... F3
Van Buren ... E3
Vanceburg, **1,731** ... G2
Vancleve ... G3
Van Lear, **1,100** ... H3
Vaughns Mill, *275* ... G3
Vernon ... E4
Verona, *175* ... F2
Versailles, **7,511** ... F2
Vicco, **318** ... G3
Villa Hills, **7,948** ... G1
Vine Grove, **4,169** ... E3
Viper, *250* ... G3
Visalia, **111** ... F2
Vortex ... G3
Waddy, *275* ... E2
Wallins Creek, **257** ... G4
Walton, **2,450** ... F2
Warfield, **284** ... H3
Warsaw, **1,811** ... F2
Watergap, *150* ... H3
Water Valley, **316** ... B4
Watterson Park, **953** ... A2
Waverly, **297** ... C3
Wax, *70* ... D3
Wayland, **298** ... H3
Waynesburg, *400* ... F3
Webbville ... H2
Weir, *60* ... C3
Wellington, **561** ... A2
Westbend, *250* ... G3
West Buechel, **1,301** ... A2
West Liberty, **3,277** ... G3
West Louisville, *150* ... C3
West Point, **1,100** ... E2
Westport, *250* ... E2
Westwood
(Boyd Co.), **4,888** ... H2
Westwood
(Jefferson Co.), **4,888** B2
Wheatcroft, **173** ... C3
Wheatley, *80* ... F2
Wheeler, *90* ... G4
Wheelwright, **1,042** ... H3
White City ... E3
White Oak, *125* ... G3
White Plains, **800** ... C3
Whitesburg, **1,600** ... H3
Whitesville, **632** ... D3
Whitley City, **1,111** ... F4
Wickliffe, **794** ... A4
Wilder, **2,624** ... G1
Wildwood, **247** ... B2
Willard, *90* ... H2
Williamsburg, **5,143** ... F4
Williamstown, **3,227** ... F2
Willisburg, **304** ... E3
Wilmore, **5,905** ... F3
Winchester, **16,724** ... F3
Winding Falls ... B2
Windy Hills, **2,480** ... B2
Wingo, **581** ... B4
Wofford, *375* ... F4
Wolf Creek, *90* ... D2
Wonnie, *250* ... G3
Woodbine, *550* ... F4
Woodburn, **323** ... D4
Woodbury, **87** ... D3
Woodland Hills, **657** ... B2
Woodlawn
(Campbell Co.), **268** ... G1
Woodlawn
(McCracken Co.), **268** B3
Woodlawn Park, **1,033** ... B2
Worthington, **1,673** ... H2
Worthington Hills,
1,594 ... B1
Worthville, **215** ... E2
Wrigley ... G2
Wurtland, **1,049** ... H2
Yerkes, *500* ... G3
York ... G2
Yosemite, *175* ... F3
Zag ... G3
Zebulon, *700* ... H3
Zion, *550* ... C3

Other Features

Barkley, *lake* ... C4
Barren, *river* ... D3
Barren River, *lake* ... D4
Big Sandy, *river* ... H2
Big South Fork Natl.
River And Rec. Area ... F4
Black, *mountain* ... H4
Blue Grass Army Depot ... F3
Buckhorn, *lake* ... G3
Cave Run, *lake* ... G2
Clinch, *river* ... H4
Crab Orchard N.W.R. ... A3
Crane Naval Weapons
Support Center ... D2
Cumberland, *lake* ... F4
Cumberland, *mountains* G4
Cumberland, *river* ... F4
Cumberland Gap
N.H.P. ... G4
Dale Hollow, *lake* ... E4
Daniel Boone
National Forest ... G3
Fishtrap, *lake* ... H3
Fort Campbell Mil. Res. ... C4
Fort Donelson Natl.
Bfld. ... C4
Fort Knox Mil. Res. ... E3
Green, *river* ... C3, E3
Green River, *lake* ... E3
Guyandotte, *river* ... H2
Hocking, *river* ... H1
Hoosier N.F. ... D1, D2
Jefferson Natl. Forest ... H4
Jefferson Proving
Ground ... E2
Kentucky, *river* ... E2, F3
Land Between The Lakes
Rec. Area. ... B4
Licking, *river* ... G2
Lincoln Birthplace Natl.
Hist. Site ... E3
Lincoln Boyhood
Natl. Memorial ... D2
Lincoln Home Natl.
Hist. Site ... A1
Little Miami, *river* ... F1
Mammoth Cave
Natl. Park ... D3
Miami, *river* ... F1
Mississippi, *river* ... A3
Muscatatuck N.W.R. ... E2
Nolin River, *lake* ... D3
Ohio, *river* ... A2, B3, G1, G2
Patoka, *lake* ... D2
Pennyrile Forest St.
Resort Park ... C3
Powell, *river* ... G4
Rough, *river* ... D3
Rough River, *lake* ... D3
Scioto, *river* ... G2
Shawnee Natl. For. ... A3
Tug Fork, *river* ... H3
Wabash, *river* ... B3
Wayne National Forest ... H2

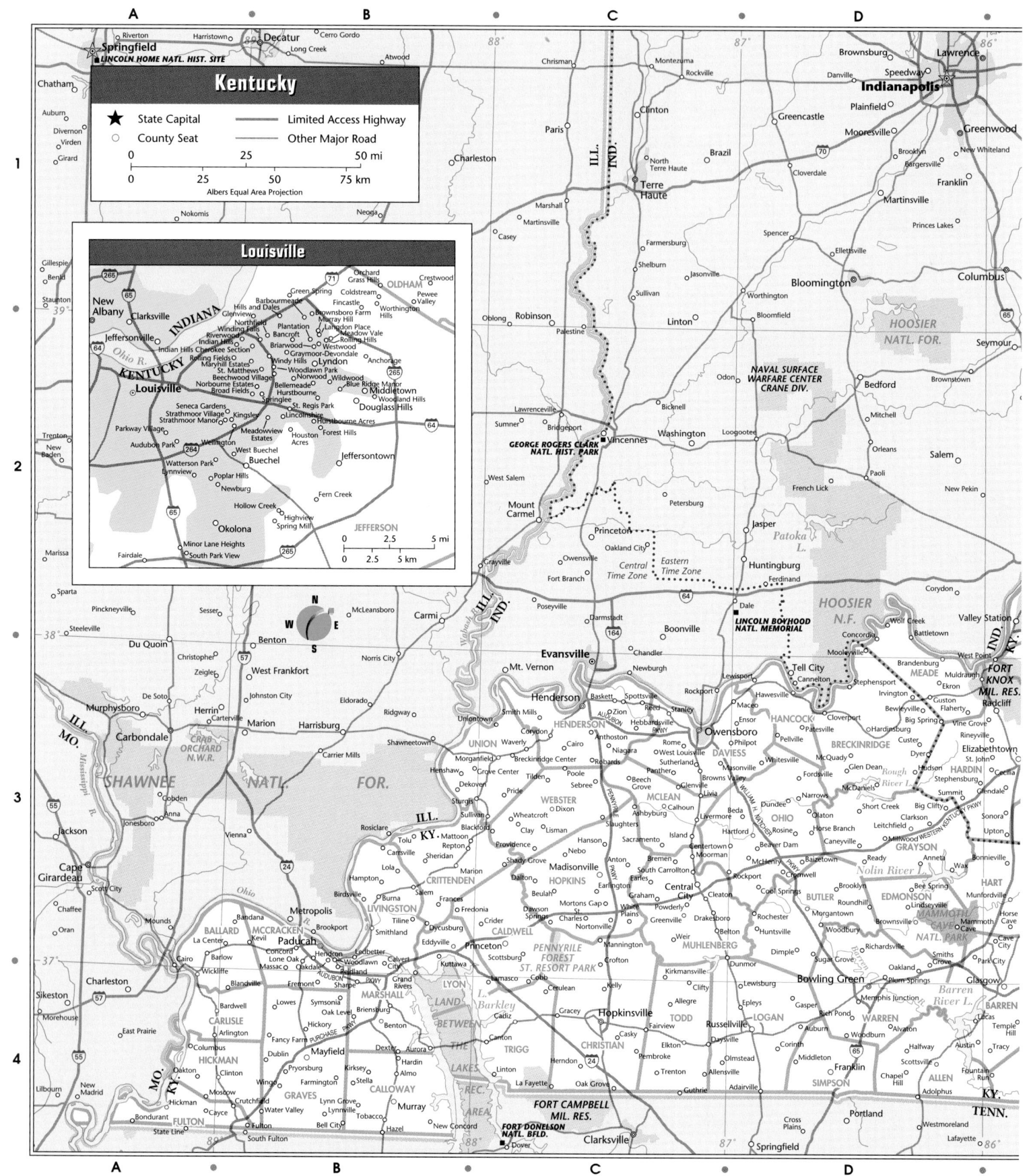

Kentucky

★ State Capital — Limited Access Highway
○ County Seat — Other Major Road

0 — 25 — 50 mi
0 — 25 — 50 — 75 km
Albers Equal Area Projection

Louisville

JEFFERSON

0 — 2.5 — 5 mi
0 — 2.5 — 5 km

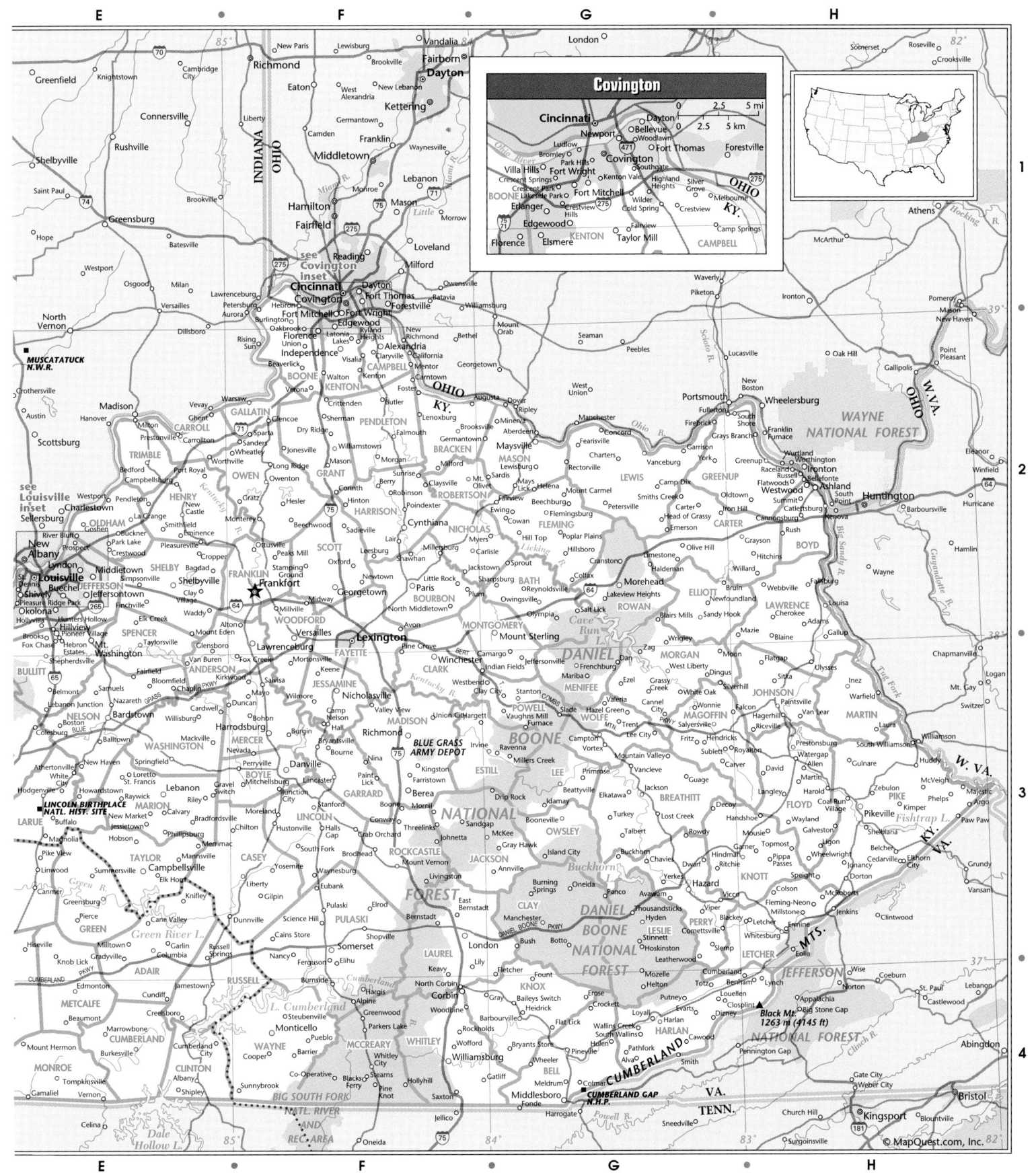

Covington

Cincinnati
Newport
Dayton
Bellevue
Woodlawn
Forestville
Bromley
Ludlow
Park Hills
Kenton Vale
Villa Hills
Fort Wright
Covington
Southgate
Fort Thomas
Crescent Springs
Highland
Heights
Silver
Grove
Crescent Park
Fort Mitchell
Melbourne
Erlanger
Lakeside Park
Crestview
Hills
Cold Spring
Crestview
Edgewood
Fairview
Camp Springs
Florence
Elsmere
Taylor Mill
KENTON
CAMPBELL

Louisiana

Capital:	Baton Rouge
Land Area:	43,566 sq. mi.
	112,836 sq. km.
Population:	4,468,976 (2000 Census)
Largest City:	New Orleans, 484,674
Highest Point:	Driskill Mtn.
	535 ft.
	163 m.
Admitted to Union:	April 30, 1812
Nickname:	Pelican State
State Flower:	Magnolia
State Bird:	Eastern Brown Pelican

Louisiana:
Map Index

Parishes

Acadia, 58,861 . . . . .D6
Allen, 25,440 . . . . .D5
Ascension, 76,627 . . . . .H6
Assumption, 23,388 . . . . .G7
Avoyelles, 41,481 . . . . .E4
Beauregard, 32,986 . . . . .C5
Bienville, 15,752 . . . . .C2
Bossier, 98,310 . . . . .B1
Caddo, 252,161 . . . . .B2
Calcasieu, 183,577 . . . . .C6
Caldwell, 10,560 . . . . .E2
Cameron, 9,991 . . . . .C7
Catahoula, 10,920 . . . . .F3
Claiborne, 16,851 . . . . .C1
Concordia, 20,247 . . . . .F4
De Soto, 25,494 . . . . .B2
East Baton Rouge, 412,852 . . . . . . .H5
East Carroll, 9,421 . . . . .G1
East Feliciana, 21,360 . . . . .H5
Evangeline, 35,434 . . . . .D5
Franklin, 21,263 . . . . .F2
Grant, 18,698 . . . . .D3
Iberia, 73,266 . . . . .F7
Iberville, 33,320 . . . . .G6
Jackson, 15,397 . . . . .D2
Jefferson, 455,466 . . . . .J7, K3
Jefferson Davis, 31,435 . . . . .D6
Lafayette, 190,503 . . . . .E6
Lafourche, 89,974 . . . . .J7
La Salle, 14,282 . . . . .E3
Lincoln, 42,509 . . . . .D1
Livingston, 91,814 . . . . .H5
Madison, 13,728 . . . . .G3
Morehouse, 31,021 . . . . .F1
Natchitoches, 39,080 . . . . .C3
Orleans, 484,674 . . . . .K6, L2
Ouachita, 147,250 . . . . .E2
Plaquemines, 26,757 . . . . .K7, L4
Pointe Coupee, 22,763 . . . . .F5
Rapides, 126,337 . . . . .D5
Red River, 9,622 . . . . .C2
Richland, 20,981 . . . . .F2
Sabine, 23,459 . . . . .B3
St. Bernard, 67,229 . . . . .K7, L3
St. Charles, 48,072 . . . . .J3, J7
St. Helena, 10,525 . . . . .H5
St. James, 21,216 . . . . .H7
St. John the Baptist, 43,044 . . . .H2, J7
St. Landry, 87,700 . . . . .F5
St. Martin, 48,583 . . . . .F6, G7
St. Mary, 53,500 . . . . .G7
St. Tammany, 191,268 . . . . .J5
Tangipahoa, 100,588 . . . . .J5
Tensas, 6,618 . . . . .G3
Terrebonne, 104,503 . . . . .G7
Union, 22,803 . . . . .E1
Vermilion, 53,807 . . . . .E7
Vernon, 52,531 . . . . .C4
Washington, 43,926 . . . . .J5
Webster, 41,831 . . . . .C1
West Baton Rouge, 21,601 . . . . .G6
West Carroll, 12,314 . . . . .F1
West Feliciana, 15,111 . . . . .G5
Winn, 16,894 . . . . .D3

Cities and Towns

Abbeville, 11,887 . . . . .E7
Abita Springs, 1,957 . . . . .J6
Acme, 100 .F4
Ada, 325 . . . . .C1
Addis, 2,238 . . . . .G6
Afton, 40 . . . . .G2
Akers, 70 . . . . .J6
Albany, 865 . . . . .H5
Alden Bridge, 40 . . . . .B1
Alexandria, 46,342 . . . . .E4
Allen C3
Alluvial City, 300 . . . . .K7
Alsatia, 70 .G1
Alsen, 950 .H5
Alto, 80 . . . . .F2
Amelia, 2,423 . . . . .J7
Amite, 4,110 . . . . .J5
Anacoco, 866 . . . . .C4
Anandale, 100 . . . . .E4
Andrew, 125 . . . . .E6
Angie, 240 .K5
Ansley D2
Arabi, 8,093 . . . . .K3
Arcadia, 3,041 . . . . .D1
Archibald, 325 . . . . .F2
Archie F3
Arlington F2
Arnaudville, 1,398 . . . . .F6
Ashland, 291 . . . . .C2
Athens, 262 . . . . .C1

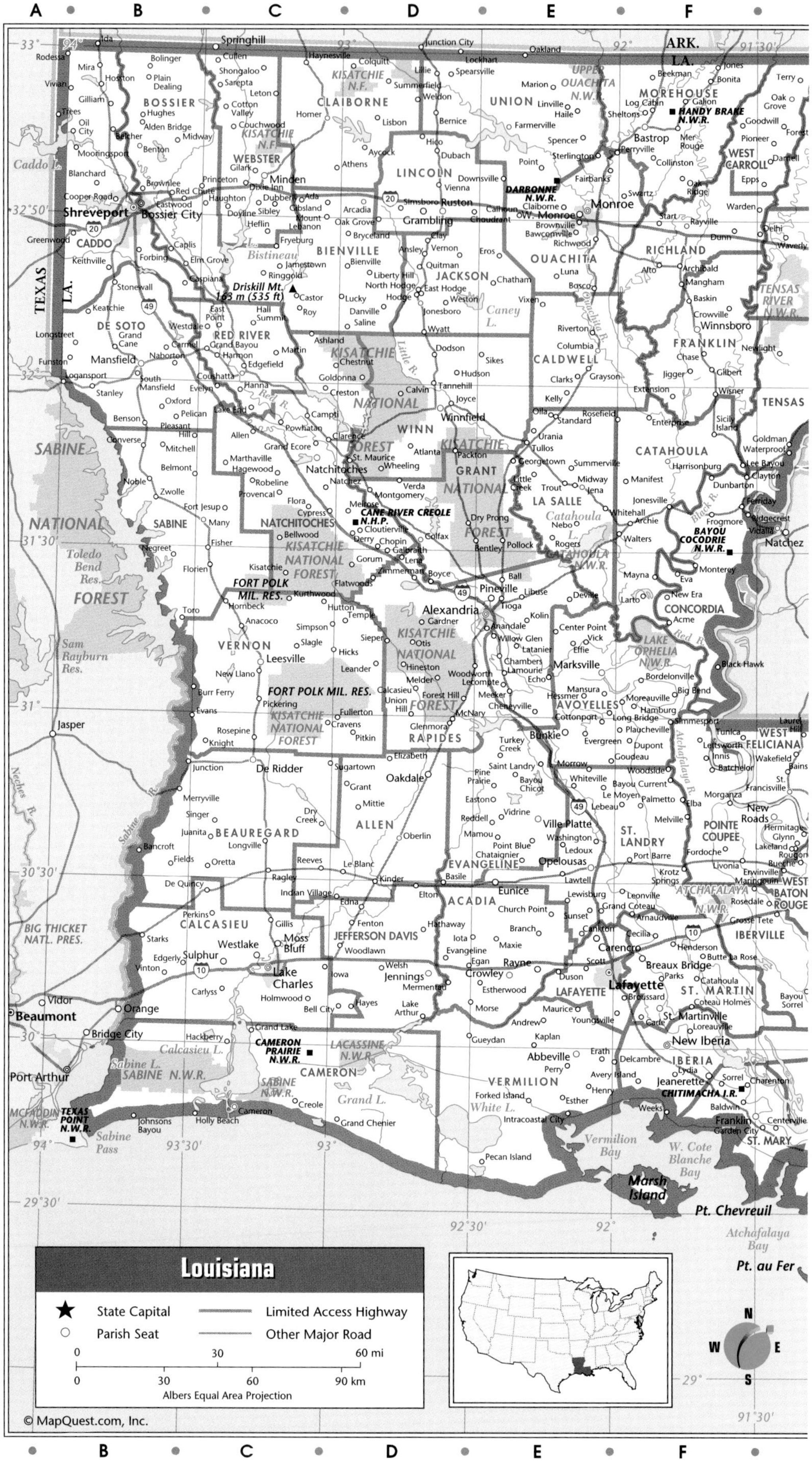

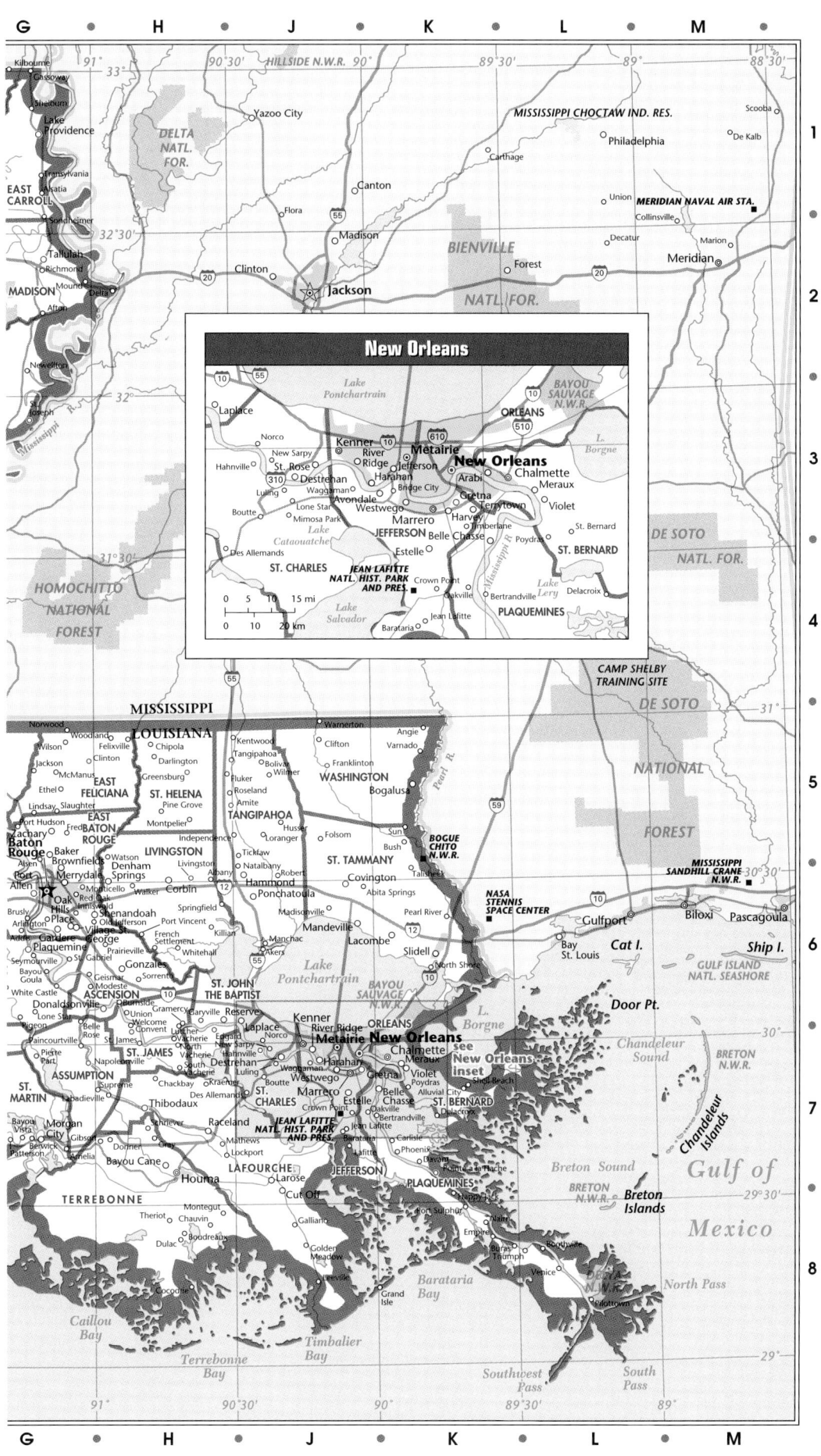

New Orleans

0 5 10 15 mi
0 10 20 km

Atlanta, 150 . . . . .D3
Avery Island, 225 . . . . .F7
Avondale, 5,441 . . . . .K3
Aycock D1
Bains, 150 . . . . .G5
Baker, 13,793 . . . . .G5
Baldwin, 2,497 .F7
Ball, 3,681 . . . . .E4
Bancroft, 60 . . . . .B5
Barataria, 1,333 . . . . .J7, K4
Basile, 1,660 . . . . .D5
Baskin, 188 . . . . .F2
Bastrop, 12,988 .F1
Batchelor, 200 . . . . .F5
Baton Rouge, 227,818 . . . . .G6
Bawcomville (Brownville-Bawcomville), 7,616 . . .E2
Bayou Cane, 17,046 . . . . .H7
Bayou Chicot, 200 . . . . .E5
Bayou Current, 60 . . . . .F5
Bayou Goula, 750 . . . . .G6
Bayou Sorrel, 350 . . . . .G6
Bayou Vista, 4,351 . . . . .G7
Beekman, 125 . . . . .F1
Belcher, 272 . . . . .B1
Bell City, 125 . . . . .D6
Belle Chasse, 9,848 . . . . .K3, K7
Belle Rose, 1,944 . . . . .G6
Bellwood, 40 . . . . .C3
Belmont, 125 . . . . .B3
Benson, 80 . . . . .B3
Bentley, 150 . . . . .E3
Benton, 2,035 . . . . .B1
Bernice, 1,809 . . . . .D1
Bertrandville, 200 . . . . .K4, K7
Berwick, 4,418 .G7
Bienville, 262 . . . . .D2
Big Bend F4
Black Hawk F4
Blanchard, 2,050 . . . . .B1
Bogalusa, 13,365 . . . . .K5
Bolinger, 200 . . . . .B1
Bolivar, 150 . . . . .J5
Bonita, 335 . . . . .F1
Boothville (Boothville-Venice), 2,220 . . . . . .L8
Bordelonville, 100 . . . . .F4
Bosco E2
Bossier City, 56,461 . . . . .B1
Boudreaux, 350 .H8
Boutte, 2,181 . . . . .J3, J7
Boyce, 1,190 . . . . .D4
Branch, 275 . . . . .E6
Breaux Bridge, 7,281 . . . . .F6
Bridge City, 8,323 . . . . .K3
Broussard, 5,874 . . . . .F6
Brownfields, 5,222 . . . . .G5
Brownlee B1
Brownville (see Bawcomville), 7,616 . . . . . .E2
Brusly, 2,020 . . . . .G6
Bryceland, 114 . . . . .D2
Bueche, 125 . . . . .G5
Bunkie, 4,662 . . . . .E5
Buras (Buras-Triumph), 3,358 . . . . .K8
Burnside, 450 . . . . .H6
Burr Ferry, 50 . . . . .C4
Bush, 200 . . . . .K5
Butte La Rose, 60 . . . . .F6
Cade, 700 . . . . .F6
Calcasieu, 225 . . . . .D4
Calhoun, 250 . . . . .E1
Calvin, 236 . . . . .D3
Cameron, 1,965 .C7
Campti, 1,057 . . . . .C3
Cankton, 362 . . . . .E6
Caplis, 90 . . . . .B2
Carencro, 6,120 .E6
Carlisle, 60 . . . . .K7
Carlyss, 4,049 . . . . .C6
Carmel, 175 . . . . .B2
Caspiana B2
Castor, 209 . . . . .C2
Catahoula, 450 . . . . .F6
Cecilia, 1,505 . . . . .F6
Center Point, 250 . . . . .E4
Centerville, 800 .G7
Chackbay, 4,018 . . . . .H6
Chalmette, 32,069 . . . . .K7, L3
Chambers E4
Charenton, 1,944 . . . . .F7
Chase, 150 . . . . .F2
Chataignier, 383 . . . . .E5
Chatham, 623 . . . . .E2
Chauvin, 3,229 .H8
Cheneyville, 901 . . . . .E4
Chestnut D2
Chipola H5
Chopin D3
Choudrant, 582 .D1
Church Point, 4,756 . . . . .E6
Claiborne, 9,830 .E1
Clarence, 516 . . . . .D3
Clarks, 1,071 . . . . .E2
Clay, 50 . . . . .D2
Clayton, 858 . . . . .F3
Clifton, 100 . . . . .J5
Clinton, 1,998 . . . . .G5
Cloutierville, 225 . . . . .D3
Cocodrie, 225 . . . . .H8
Colfax, 1,659 . . . . .D3
Collinston, 327 . . . . .F1
Colquitt D1
Columbia, 477 . . . . .E2
Convent, 250 . . . . .H6
Converse, 400 . . . . .B3
Cooper Road, 175 . . . . .B1
Corbin H6
Coteau Holmes, 175 . . . . .F6
Cottonport, 2,316 . . . . .E5
Cotton Valley, 1,189 . . . . .C1
Couchwood, 100 . . . . .C1
Coushatta, 2,299 . . . . .C2
Covington, 8,483 . . . . .J6
Cravens, 225 . . . . .C5
Creole, 175 . . . . .C7
Creston, 125 . . . . .C3
Crowley, 14,225 .E6
Crown Point, 650 . . . . .J7, K4
Crowville, 225 . . . . .F2
Cullen, 1,296 . . . . .C1
Cut Off, 5,635 . . . . .J7
Cypress, 40 . . . . .C3
Danville D2
Darlington, 150 .H5
Darnell, 80 . . . . .G1
Davant, 275 . . . . .K7

Delacroix K7, L4
Delcambre, 2,168 . . . . .F7
Delhi, 3,066 . . . . .G2
Delta, 239 . . . . .H2
Denham Springs, 8,757 . . . . .H5
De Quincy, 3,398 . . . . .C6
De Ridder, 9,808 . . . . .C5
Derry, 100 . . . . .D3
Des Allemands, 2,500 . . . . . . .H3, J7
Destrehan, 11,260 . . . . .J3, J7
Deville, 1,007 . . . . .E4
Dixie Inn, 352 . . . . .C1
Dodson, 357 . . . . .D2
Donaldsonville, 7,605 . . . . .H6
Donner, 275 . . . . .H7
Downsville, 118 . . . . .E1
Doyline, 841 . . . . .C1
Dry Creek C6
Dry Prong, 421 . . . . .D3
Dubach, 800 . . . . .D1
Dubberly, 290 . . . . .C1
Dulac, 2,458 . . . . .H8
Dunbarton, 50 . . . . .F3
Dunn, 125 . . . . .F2
Dupont, 50 . . . . .F5
Duson, 1,672 . . . . .E6
East Hodge, 366 . . . . .D2
Easton, 150 . . . . .C4
East Point C2
Eastwood, 3,374 . . . . .B1
Echo, 250 . . . . .E4
Edgard, 2,637 . . . . .H6
Edgefield, 190 . . . . .C2
Edgerly, 225 . . . . .B6
Edna, 90 .D6
Effie, 250 . . . . .E4
Egan, 325 . . . . .E6
Elba F5
Elizabeth, 574 . . . . .D5
Elm Grove B2
Elton, 1,261 . . . . .D6
Empire, 2,211 . . . . .K8
Enterprise, 125 . . . . .F3
Epps, 1,153 . . . . .G1
Erath, 2,187 . . . . .E7
Eros, 202 . . . . .E2
Erwinville, 700 . . . . .G5
Estelle, 15,880 . . . . .J7, K3
Esther E7
Estherwood, 807 . . . . .E6
Ethel, 125 . . . . .G5
Eunice, 11,499 . . . . .E6
Eva, 225 .F4
Evangeline, 150 . . . . .D6
Evans, 100 . . . . .C5
Evelyn, 50 . . . . .C3
Evergreen, 314 . . . . .E5
Extension, 150 . . . . .F3
Fairbanks, 150 . . . . .E1
Farmerville, 3,808 . . . . .E1
Felixville, 70 . . . . .H5
Fenton, 380 . . . . .D6
Ferriday, 3,723 . . . . .G3
Fields B5
Fisher, 268 . . . . .C3
Flatwoods, 125 . . . . .D3
Flora C3
Florien, 692 . . . . .C4
Fluker, 150 . . . . .H5
Folsom, 525 . . . . .J5
Forbing, 250 . . . . .B2
Fordoche, 933 . . . . .F5
Forest, 275 . . . . .G1
Forest Hill, 456 . . . . .D4
Forked Island, 325 . . . . .E7
Fort Jesup, 200 . . . . .C4
Franklin, 8,354 . . . . .F7
Franklinton, 3,657 . . . . .J5
Fred, 125 . . . . .G5
French Settlement, 945 . . . . .H6
Frogmore F3
Fryeburg, 80 . . . . .C2
Fullerton, 90 . . . . .D5
Funston, 50 . . . . .A2
Galbraith, 80 . . . . .D4
Galion F1
Galliano, 7,356 . . . . .J8
Garden City, 275 . . . . .G7
Gardere, 8,992 . . . . .G6
Gardner, 125 . . . . .D4
Garyville, 2,775 . . . . .H6
Gassoway G1
Geismar, 80 . . . . .G6
Georgetown, 301 . . . . .E3
Gibsland, 1,119 . . . . .C1
Gibson, 475 . . . . .H7
Gilark, 250 . . . . .C1
Gilbert, 561 . . . . .F2
Gilliam, 178 . . . . .B1
Gillis, 300 . . . . .C6
Glenmora, 1,558 . . . . .D5
Glynn, 275 . . . . .G5
Golden Meadow, 2,193 . . . . .J8
Goldman .G3
Goldonna, 457 . . . . .D2
Gonzales, 8,156 . . . . .H6
Goodwill, 150 . . . . .F1
Gorum, 60 . . . . .D4
Goudeau, 150 . . . . .E5
Grambling, 4,693 . . . . .D1
Gramercy, 3,066 . . . . .H6
Grand Bayou, 40 . . . . .C2
Grand Cane, 191 . . . . .B2
Grand Chenier, 125 . . . . .D7
Grand Coteau, 1,040 . . . . .E6
Grand Ecore C3
Grand Isle, 1,541 . . . . .K8
Grand Lake, 40 . . . . .C6
Grant, 50 . . . . .D5
Gray, 4,958 . . . . .H7
Grayson, 531 . . . . .E2
Greensburg, 631 . . . . .H5
Greenwood, 2,458 . . . . .A1
Gretna, 17,423 . . . . .J7, K3
Grosse Tete, 670 . . . . .G6
Gueydan, 1,598 . . . . .E6
Hackberry, 1,699 . . . . .C6
Hagewood, 225 . . . . .C3
Hahnville, 2,792 . . . . .J3, J7
Haile, 60 .E1
Hall Summit, 264 . . . . .C2
Hamburg, 60 . . . . .F4
Hammond, 17,639 . . . . .J5
Hanna C3

Happy Jack, 250 . . . . .K7
Harahan, 9,885 . . . . .J7, K3
Harmon, 80 . . . . .C1
Harrisonburg, 746 . . . . .F3
Harvey, 22,226 . . . . .K3
Hathaway, 275 . . . . .D6
Haughton, 2,792 . . . . .C1
Hayes, 750 . . . . .D6
Haynesville, 2,679 . . . . .C1
Heflin, 245 . . . . .C2
Henderson, 1,531 . . . . .F6
Henry, 275 . . . . .E7
Hermitage, 375 . . . . .G5
Hessmer, 642 . . . . .E4
Hicks, 225 . . . . .D4
Hico, 70 .D1
Hineston, 175 . . . . .D4
Hodge, 492 . . . . .D2
Holly Beach, 60 . . . . .C7
Holmwood, 90 . . . . .C6
Homer, 3,788 . . . . .C1
Hornbeck, 435 . . . . .C4
Hosston, 387 . . . . .B1
Houma, 32,393 . . . . .H7
Hudson, 50 . . . . .D2
Hughes, 70 . . . . .B1
Husser, 150 . . . . .J5
Hutton C4
Ida, 258 .B1
Independence, 1,724 . . . . .H5
Indian Village, 100 . . . . .D6
Innis, 175 . . . . .F5
Inniswold, 4,944 . . . . .G6
Intracoastal City E7
Iota, 1,376 . . . . .E6
Iowa, 2,663 . . . . .C6
Jackson, 4,130 . . . . .G5
Jamestown, 149 . . . . .C2
Jean Lafitte, 2,137 . . . . .J7, K4
Jeanerette, 5,997 . . . . .F7
Jefferson, 11,843 . . . . .K3
Jena, 2,971 . . . . .E3
Jennings, 10,986 . . . . .D6
Jigger, 90 . . . . .F2
Johnsons Bayou, 500 . . . . .B7
Jones F1
Jonesboro, 3,914 . . . . .D2
Jonesville, 2,469 . . . . .F3
Joyce, 200 . . . . .D3
Juanita, 150 . . . . .C5
Junction, 125 . . . . .C5
Junction City, 652 . . . . .D1
Kaplan, 5,177 . . . . .E6
Keatchie, 323 . . . . .B2
Keithville, 550 . . . . .B2
Kelly, 125 .E3
Kenner, 70,517 . . . . .J3, J6
Kentwood, 2,205 . . . . .J5
Kilbourne, 436 . . . . .G1
Killian, 1,053 . . . . .H6
Kinder, 2,148 . . . . .D5
Kisatchie .C4
Knight C5
Kolin, 600 . . . . .D4
Kraemer, 325 . . . . .H7
Krotz Springs, 1,219 . . . . .F5
Kurthwood, 60 . . . . .C4
Labadieville, 1,811 . . . . .H7
Lacombe, 7,518 . . . . .K6
Lafayette, 110,257 . . . . .E6
Lafitte, 1,576 . . . . .J7
Lake Arthur, 3,007 . . . . .D6
Lake Charles, 71,757 . . . . .C6
Lake End, 50 . . . . .C3
Lakeland, 375 . . . . .G5
Lake Providence, 5,104 . . . . .G1
Lamourie, 100 . . . . .E4
Laplace, 27,684 . . . . .H3, J6
Larose, 7,306 . . . . .J7
Larto, 225 . . . . .F4
Latanier, 90 . . . . .E4
Laurel Hill G5
Lawtell, 850 . . . . .E5
Leander, 100 . . . . .D4
Lebeau, 110 . . . . .E5
Lecompte, 1,366 . . . . .E4
Ledoux, 250 . . . . .E5
Lee Bayou, 60 . . . . .F3
Leesville, 6,753 . . . . .C4
Leeville, 80 . . . . .J8
Le Moyen, 80 . . . . .E5
Lena D4
Leonville, 1,007 . . . . .F6
Leton, 50 .C1
Lettsworth, 150 . . . . .F5
Lewisburg, 425 . . . . .E6
Liberty Hill D2
Libuse, 475 . . . . .E4
Lillie, 139 . . . . .D1
Lindsay G5
Linville, 80 . . . . .E1
Lisbon, 162 . . . . .D1
Little Creek, 40 . . . . .E3
Livingston, 1,342 . . . . .H5
Livonia, 1,339 . . . . .F5
Lockhart .D1
Lockport, 2,624 . . . . .H7
Logansport, 1,630 . . . . .B3
Log Cabin, 325 . . . . .F1
Lone Star (Iberville Par.), 80 . . . . . .G6
Lone Star (St. Charles Par.), 1,400 . . .J3
Long Bridge, 70 . . . . .E4
Longstreet, 163 . . . . .B2
Longville, 225 . . . . .C5
Loranger, 425 . . . . .J5
Loreauville, 938 . . . . .F6
Lucky, 355 . . . . .D2
Luling, 11,512 . . . . .J3, J7
Luna, 70 .E2
Lutcher, 3,735 . . . . .H6
Lydia, 1,079 . . . . .F7
Madisonville, 677 . . . . .J6
Mamou, 3,566 . . . . .E5
Manchac, 70 . . . . .J6
Mandeville, 10,489 . . . . .J6
Mangham, 595 . . . . .F2
Manifest, 70 . . . . .F3
Mansfield, 5,582 . . . . .B2
Mansura, 1,573 . . . . .E4
Many, 2,889 . . . . .C3
Maringouin, 1,262 . . . . .F6
Marion, 806 . . . . .E1
Marksville, 5,537 . . . . .E4

Marrero, 36,165 . . . . .J7, K3
Marthaville, 200 . . . . .C3
Martin, 625 . . . . .C3
Mathews, 2,003 . . . . .H7
Maurice, 642 . . . . .E6
Maxie, 125 . . . . .E6
Mayna, 70 . . . . .F4
McManus, 350 . . . . .G5
McNary, 211 . . . . .D5
Meeker, 40 . . . . .E4
Melder, 90 . . . . .D4
Melrose, 90 . . . . .D3
Melville, 1,376 . . . . .F5
Meraux, 10,192 . . . . .K7, L3
Mermentau, 721 . . . . .D6
Mer Rouge, 721 . . . . .F1
Merrydale, 10,427 . . . . .G5
Merryville, 1,126 . . . . .B5
Metairie, 146,136 . . . . .J7, K3
Midway (La Salle Parish), 1,505 . . . .E3
Midway (BossierParish) B1
Mimosa Park, 4,500 . . . . .J3
Minden, 13,027 . . . . .C1
Mira, 40 .B1
Mitchell, 100 . . . . .B3
Mittie, 90 .D5
Modeste, 125 . . . . .G6
Monroe, 53,107 . . . . .E1
Montegut, 1,803 . . . . .H8
Monterey, 80 . . . . .F4
Montgomery, 787 . . . . .D3
Monticello, 4,763 . . . . .G6
Montpelier, 214 . . . . .H5
Mooringsport, 833 . . . . .B1
Moreauville, 922 . . . . .F4
Morgan City, 12,703 . . . . .G7
Morganza, 659 . . . . .F5
Morrow, 200 . . . . .E5
Morse, 759 . . . . .E6
Moss Bluff, 10,535 . . . . .C6
Mound, 12 . . . . .G2
Mount Lebanon, 73 . . . . .C1
Naborton, 125 . . . . .B2
Nairn (part of Empire, pop. 2,211), 350 . .K8
Napoleonville, 686 . . . . .G7
Natalbany, 1,739 . . . . .J5
Natchez, 583 . . . . .C3, G3
Natchitoches, 17,865 . . . . .C3
Nebo, 125 . . . . .E3
Negreet, 90 . . . . .B4
Newellton, 1,482 . . . . .G2
New Era, 70 . . . . .F4
New Iberia, 32,623 . . . . .F6
Newlight .G2
New Llano, 2,415 . . . . .C4
New Orleans, 484,674 . . . . .J7, K3
New Roads, 4,966 . . . . .G5
New Sarpy, 1,568 . . . . .J3, J7
Noble, 259 . . . . .B3
Norco, 3,579 . . . . .J3, J6
North Hodge, 436 . . . . .D2
North Shore (part of Eden Isle,
  pop. 3,768), 1,800 . . . . .K6
North Vacherie, 2,411 . . . . .H7
Norwood, 337 . . . . .G5
Oakdale, 8,137 . . . . .D5
Oak Grove (Lincoln Parish) D2
Oak Grove (West Carroll Parish), 2,174 . . .G1
Oak Hills Place, 7,996 . . . . .G6
Oakland .E1
Oak Ridge, 142 . . . . .F1
Oakville, 3,007 . . . . .J7, K4
Oberlin, 1,853 . . . . .D5
Oil City, 1,219 . . . . .B1
Old Jefferson, 5,631 . . . . .H6
Olla, 1,417 . . . . .E3
Opelousas, 22,860 . . . . .E5
Oretta, 250 . . . . .C5
Otis, 50 . . . . .D4
Oxford, 90 . . . . .B3
Packton D3
Paincourtville, 884 . . . . .G6
Palmetto, 188 . . . . .F5
Parks, 533 . . . . .F6
Patterson, 5,130 . . . . .G7
Pearl River, 1,839 . . . . .K6
Pecan Island, 125 . . . . .E7
Pelican B3
Perkins, 40 . . . . .C6
Perry, 1,300 . . . . .E7
Perryville, 50 . . . . .F1
Phoenix, 475 . . . . .K7
Pickering, 400 . . . . .C4
Pierre Part, 3,239 . . . . .G7
Pigeon, 600 . . . . .G7
Pilottown, 100 . . . . .L8
Pine Grove, 150 . . . . .H5
Pine Prairie, 1,087 . . . . .E5
Pineville, 13,829 . . . . .E4
Pioneer, 171 . . . . .G1
Pitkin, 400 . . . . .D5
Plain Dealing, 1,071 . . . . .B1
Plaquemine, 7,064 . . . . .G6
Plaucheville, 281 . . . . .F5
Pleasant Hill, 786 . . . . .B3
Point, 175 . . . . .F5
Point Blue, 175 . . . . .E5
Pointe a la Hache, 475 . . . . .K7
Pollock, 376 . . . . .E3
Ponchatoula, 5,180 . . . . .J6
Port Allen, 5,278 . . . . .G6
Port Barre, 2,287 . . . . .F5
Port Hudson, 275 . . . . .G5
Port Sulphur, 3,115 . . . . .K8
Port Vincent, 463 . . . . .H6
Poydras, 3,886 . . . . .K7, L3
Prairieville, 950 . . . . .H6
Princeton, 225 . . . . .C1
Provencal, 708 . . . . .C3
Quitman, 168 . . . . .D2
Raceland, 10,224 . . . . .H7
Ragley, 125 . . . . .C5
Rayne, 8,552 . . . . .E6
Rayville, 4,234 . . . . .F2
Red Chute, 5,984 . . . . .B1
Reddell, 1,075 . . . . .E5
Red Oak, 375 . . . . .C2
Reeves, 209 . . . . .C5
Reserve, 9,111 . . . . .H6
Richmond, 499 . . . . .G2
Richwood, 2,115 . . . . .E2
Ridgecrest, 801 . . . . .F3
Ringgold, 1,660 . . . . .C2

River Ridge, 14,588 . . . . .J3, J6
Riverton, 40 . . . . .E2
Robeline, 183 . . . . .C3
Robert, 375 . . . . .J5
Rodessa, 307 . . . . .A1
Rogers E3
Rosedale, 753 . . . . .G6
Rosefield .E3
Roseland, 1,162 . . . . .J5
Rosepine, 1,390 . . . . .C5
Rougon, 250 . . . . .G5
Roy, 125 . . . . .C2
Ruston, 20,546 . . . . .D1
St. Bernard, 1,500 . . . . .L3
St. Francisville, 1,712 . . . . .G5
St. Gabriel, 5,514 . . . . .G6
St. James, 275 . . . . .H6
St. Joseph, 1,340 . . . . .G3
St. Landry, 300 . . . . .E5
St. Martinville, 6,989 . . . . .F6
St. Maurice, 100 . . . . .D3
St. Rose, 6,540 . . . . .J3
Saline, 296 . . . . .D2
Sarepta, 925 . . . . .C1
Schriever, 5,880 . . . . .H7
Scott, 7,870 . . . . .E6
Seymourville, 2,200 . . . . .G6
Shelburn, 50 . . . . .E1
Shell Beach, 300 . . . . .K7
Sheltons, 450 . . . . .F1
Shenandoah, 17,070 . . . . .H6
Shongaloo, 162 . . . . .C1
Shreveport, 200,145 . . . . .B1
Sibley, 1,098 . . . . .C1
Sicily Island, 453 . . . . .F3
Sieper, 70 . . . . .D4
Sikes, 120 . . . . .E2
Simmesport, 2,239 . . . . .F5
Simpson, 583 . . . . .C4
Simsboro, 684 . . . . .D1
Singer, 70 . . . . .C5
Slagle, 225 . . . . .C4
Slaughter, 1,011 . . . . .G5
Slidell, 25,695 . . . . .K6
Sondheimer, 80 . . . . .G1
Sorrel, 550 . . . . .F7
Sorrento, 1,227 . . . . .H6
South Mansfield, 352 . . . . .B2
South Vacherie, 3,543 . . . . .H7
Spearsville, 155 . . . . .D1
Spencer, 90 . . . . .E1
Springfield, 395 . . . . .H6
Springhill, 5,439 . . . . .C1
Standard, 250 . . . . .E3
Stanley, 145 . . . . .B3
Starks, 500 . . . . .B6
Start, 475 . . . . .F2
Sterlington, 1,276 . . . . .E1
Stonewall, 1,668 . . . . .B2
Sugartown, 60 . . . . .D5
Sulphur, 20,512 . . . . .C6
Summerfield D1
Summerville, 125 . . . . .E3
Sun, 471 .K5
Sunset, 2,352 . . . . .E6
Supreme, 1,119 . . . . .H7
Swartz, 4,247 . . . . .F1
Talisheek, 60 . . . . .K5
Tallulah, 9,189 . . . . .G2
Tangipahoa, 747 . . . . .J5
Tannehill, 100 . . . . .D2
Temple D4
Terry, 225 . . . . .G1
Terrytown, 25,430 . . . . .K3
Theriot, 225 . . . . .H8
Thibodaux, 14,431 . . . . .H7
Tickfaw, 617 . . . . .J5
Timberlane, 11,405 . . . . .K3
Tioga, 1,500 . . . . .E4
Toro B4
Transylvania, 90 . . . . .G1
Trees A1
Triumph (see Buras), 3,358 . . . . .L8
Trout, 350 . . . . .E3
Tullos, 419 . . . . .E3
Tunica, 90 . . . . .F5
Turkey Creek, 356 . . . . .E5
Union, 500 . . . . .H6
Union Hill, 60 . . . . .D4
Urania, 700 . . . . .E3
Vacherie, 250 . . . . .H6
Varnado, 342 . . . . .K5
Venice (see Boothville), 2,220 . . . . . .L8
Verda, 275 . . . . .D3
Vernon D2
Vick, 50 . . . . .E4
Vidalia, 4,543 . . . . .G3
Vidrine, 225 . . . . .E5
Vienna, 424 . . . . .D1
Village St. George, 6,993 . . . . .G6
Ville Platte, 8,145 . . . . .E5
Vinton, 3,338 . . . . .B6
Violet, 8,555 . . . . .K7, L3
Vivian, 4,031 . . . . .B1
Vixen E2
Waggaman, 9,435 . . . . .J3, J7
Wakefield, 150 . . . . .G5
Walker, 4,801 . . . . .H6
Walters F3
Warden, 150 . . . . .G1
Warnerton, 50 . . . . .J5
Washington, 1,082 . . . . .E5
Waterproof, 834 . . . . .G3
Watson, 1,400 . . . . .H5
Waverly, 40 . . . . .G2
Weeks F7
Welcome, 950 . . . . .H6
Weldon D3
Welsh, 3,380 . . . . .D6
Westlake, 70 . . . . .C6
Westlake, 4,668 . . . . .C6
West Monroe, 13,250 . . . . .E1
Weston, 150 . . . . .D2
Westwego, 10,763 . . . . .J7, K3
Wheeling .D3
White Castle, 1,946 . . . . .G6
Whitehall (La Salle Parish), 150 . . . . .E3
Whitehall (Livingston Parish), 275 . . .H6
Whiteville, 80 . . . . .E5
Willow Glen, 175 . . . . .E4
Wilmer, 60 . . . . .J5
Wilson, 668 . . . . .G5
Winnfield, 5,749 . . . . .D3
Winnsboro, 5,344 . . . . .F2

Wisner, 1,140 . . . . .F3
Woodland, 70 . . . . .H5
Woodlawn, 100 . . . . .B5
Woodside E4
Woodworth, 1,080 . . . . .E4
Wyatt, 70 .D2
Youngsville, 3,992 . . . . .F6
Zachary, 11,275 . . . . .G5
Zimmerman, 125 . . . . .D4
Zwolle, 1,783 . . . . .B3

Other Features

Atchafalaya, bay F8
Atchafalaya, river F5
Atchafalaya N.W.R. F6
Barataria, bay K8
Bayou Cocodrie N.W.R. F3
Bayou Sauvage N.W.R. K6, L2
Bienville Natl. For. K2
Bistineau, lake C2
Black, river F3
Bogue Chito N.W.R. K5
Borgne, lake K6, L3
Breton, islands L8
Breton, sound L7
Breton N.W.R. L7, M7
Caddo, lake A1
Caillou, bay G8
Calcasieu, lake C7
Cameron Prairie N.W.R. C7
Camp Shelby Mil. Res. L4
Cane River Creole N.H.P. D3
Caney, lake D1
Cat, island L6
Catahoula, lake E3
Catahoula N.W.R. E4
Cataouatche, lake J3
Chandeleur, islands M7
Chandeleur, sound L7
Chitimacha I.R. F7
Darbonne N.W.R. E1
Delta N.W.R. L8
Delta Natl. For. H1
De Soto National
  Forest M3, M4
Door, point L6
Driskill, mountain C2
Fort Polk Mil. Res. C4
Grand, lake D7
Gulf Island Natl. Seashore M6
Handy Brake N.W.R. F1
Hillside N.W.R. J1
Homochitto National Forest G4
Jean Lafitte Natl. Hist.
  Park And Pres. J7, K3
Kisatchie National
  Forest C1, C4, C5, D1-4
Lacassine N.W.R. D7
Lake Ophelia N.W.R. F4
Lery, lake .L3
Little, river D2
Marsh, island F7
McFaddin N.W.R. A7
Meridian Naval Air Sta. M1
Mexico, gulf G8
Mississippi, river G3, K3
Mississippi Choctaw
  Ind. Res. .L1
Mississippi Sandhill
  Crane N.W.R. M5
Nasa Test Site K6
Neches, river A5
North, pass M8
Ouachita, river E2
Pearl, river K5
Pt. au Fer, point G8
Pt. Chevreuil, point F7
Pontchartrain, lake J2, J6
Red, river C3, F4
Sabine, lake B7
Sabine, pass B7
Sabine, river B7
Sabine N.W.R. B7, C7
Sabine National Forest B3
Salvador, lake J4
Sam Rayburn Res. B4
Ship, island M6
South, pass L8
Southwest, pass L8
Tensas River N.W.R. G2
Terrebonne, bay H8
Texas Point N.W.R. B7
Timbalier, bay J8
Toledo Bend, reservoir B4
Upper Ouachita N.W.R. E1
Vermillion, bay E7
W. Cote Blanche, bay F7
White, lake E7

Maine

Capital:	Augusta
Land Area:	30,865 sq. mi. 79,940 sq. km.
Population:	1,274,923 (2000 Census)
Largest City:	Portland, 64,249
Highest Point:	Mt. Katahdin, 5,267 ft. 1,605 m.
Admitted to Union:	March 15, 1820
Nickname:	Pine Tree State
State Flower:	White Pine Cone & Tassel
State Bird:	Chickadee

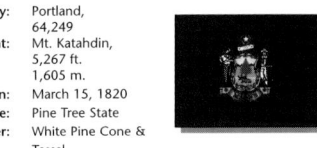

Maine:
Map Index

Counties

Androscoggin, **103,793** B4
Aroostook, **73,938** D2
Cumberland, **265,612** B5
Franklin, **29,467** B4
Hancock, **51,791** D4
Kennebec, **117,114** C4
Knox, **39,618** C4
Lincoln, **33,616** C4
Oxford, **54,755** B4
Penobscot, **144,919** D3
Piscataquis, **17,235** C3
Sagadahoc, **35,214** C5
Somerset, **50,888** B3
Waldo, **36,280** C4
Washington, **33,941** E4
York, **186,742** B5

Cities and Towns

Cities and towns that are not labeled on the map are shown with an asterisk. They are included here only for population reference. Italics indicate township groupings that are used only for census purposes.

Abbot, **630** .... *
Acton, **2,145** B5
Addison, **1,209** E4
Albion, **1,946** C4
Alexander, **514** E4
Alfred, **2,497** B5
Allagash, **277** C1
Alna, **675** C4
Alton, **816** .... *
Amherst, **230** D4
Amity, **199** .... *
Andover, **864** B4
Anson, **2,583** C4
Appleton, **1,271** C4
Argyle (unorg.), **253** D3
Arrowsic, **477** C5
Arundel, **3,571** B5
Ashland, **1,474** D2
Athens, **847** C4
Atkinson, **323** .... *
Auburn, **23,203** B4
Augusta, **18,560** C4
Aurora, **121** D4
Avon, **504** B4
Baileyville, **1,686** .... *
Baldwin, **1,290** .... *
Bancroft, **61** D3
Bangor, **31,473** D4
Bar Harbor, **4,820** D4
Baring, **273** E3
Bath, **9,266** C5
Beals, **618** E4
Beaver Cove, **91** C3
Beddington, **29** D4
Belfast, **6,381** C4
Belgrade, **2,978** C4
Belmont, **821** .... *
Benton, **2,557** C4
Berwick, **6,353** B5
Bethel, **2,411** B4
Biddeford, **20,942** B5
Bingham, **989** C3
Blaine, **806** E2
Blanchard (unorg.), **83** C3
Blue Hill, **2,390** D4
Boothbay, **2,960** C5
Boothbay Harbor, **2,334** C5
Bowdoin, **2,727** C4
Bowdoinham, **2,612** C4
Bowerbank, **123** C3
Bradford, **1,186** D3
Bradley, **1,242** D4
Bremen, **782** C4
Brewer, **8,987** D4
Bridgewater, **612** E2
Bridgton, **4,883** B4
Brighton, **86** C3
Bristol, **2,644** .... *
Brooklin, **841** D4
Brooks, **1,022** C4
Brooksville, **911** D4
Brownfield, **1,251** B5
Brownville, **1,259** C3
Brunswick, **21,172** C5
Buckfield, **1,723** B4
Bucksport, **4,908** D4
Burlington, **351** D3
Burnham, **1,142** C4
Buxton, **7,452** .... *
Byron, **121** B4
Calais, **3,447** E3
Cambridge, **492** C3
Camden, **5,254** C4
Canaan, **2,017** C4
Canton, **1,121** B4
Cape Elizabeth, **9,068** B5
Caratunk, **108** C3
Caribou, **8,312** D2
Carmel, **2,416** C4
Carrabassett Valley (Carrabassett), **399** B3
Carroll, **144** D3
Carthage, **520** .... *
Cary, **217** E3
Casco, **3,469** B4
Castine, **1,343** D4
Castle Hill, **454** D2
Caswell, **326** E2
Centerville, **26** E4
Central Aroostook (unorg.), 95 .... *
Central Hancock (unorg.), 138 .... *
Central Somerset (unorg.), 336 .... *
Chapman, **465** D2
Charleston, **1,397** C3
Charlotte, **324** E3
Chelsea, **2,559** C4
Cherryfield, **1,157** E4
Chester, **525** D3
Chesterville, **1,170** B4
China, **4,106** C4
Clifton, **743** D4
Clinton, **3,340** C4
Codyville, **19** E3
Columbia, **459** E4
Columbia Falls, **599** E4
Connor, **424** D2
Cooper, **145** E4
Coplin, **135** B3
Corinna, **2,145** C4
Corinth, **2,511** .... *
Cornish, **1,269** B5
Cornville, **1,208** C4
Cranberry Isles, **128** D4
Crawford, **108** E3
Crystal, **285** D2
Cumberland, **7,159** .... *
Cushing, **1,322** C4
Cutler, **623** E4
Cyr, **117** E1
Dallas, **250** B4
Damariscotta, **2,041** C4
Danforth, **629** E3
Dayton, **1,805** .... *
Deblois, **49** D4
Dedham, **1,422** .... *
Deer Isle, **1,876** D4
Denmark, **1,004** B5
Dennistown, **30** B3
Dennysville, **319** E4
Detroit, **816** C4
Dexter, **3,890** C3
Dixfield, **2,514** B4
Dixmont, **1,065** C4
Dover-Foxcroft, **4,211** C3
Dresden, **1,625** .... *
Drew, **57** .... *
Durham, **3,381** B5
Dyer Brook, **199** .... *
Eagle Lake, **815** D1
Eastbrook, **370** D4
East Central Franklin (unorg.), 526 .... *
East Central Penobscot (unorg.), 324 .... *
East Central Washington (unorg.), 768 .... *
East Hancock (unorg.), 73 .... *
East Machias, **1,298** E4
East Millinocket, **1,828** D3
Easton, **1,249** E2
Eastport, **1,640** F4
Eddington, **2,052** .... *
Edgecomb, **1,090** C5
Edinburg, **98** D3
Eliot, **5,954** .... *
Ellsworth, **6,456** D4
Embden, **881** C4
Enfield, **1,616** D3
Etna, **1,012** C4
Eustis, **685** B3
Exeter, **997** .... *
Fairfield, **6,573** C4
Falmouth, **10,310** B5
Farmingdale, **2,804** C4
Farmington, **7,410** B4
Fayette, **1,040** B4
Fort Fairfield, **3,579** E2
Fort Kent, **4,233** D1
Frankfort, **1,041** D4
Franklin, **1,370** D4
Freedom, **645** C4
Freeport, **7,800** B5
Frenchboro, **38** D4
Frenchville, **1,225** D1
Friendship, **1,204** C4
Fryeburg, **3,083** A4
Frye Island B5
Gardiner, **6,198** C4
Garfield, **86** D2
Garland, **990** C3
Georgetown, **1,020** .... *
Gilead, **156** A4
Glenburn, **3,964** .... *
Glenwood D3
Gorham, **14,141** B5
Gouldsboro, **1,941** D4
Grand Isle, **518** D1
Grand Lake Stream, **150** E3
Gray, **6,820** B5
Great Pond, **47** D4
Greenbush, **1,421** D3
Greene, **4,076** B4
Greenville, **1,623** C3
Greenwood, **802** B4
Guilford, **1,531** C3
Hallowell, **2,467** C4
Hamlin, **257** E1
Hammond, **98** .... *
Hampden, **6,327** D4
Hancock, **2,147** D4
Hanover, **251** B4
Harmony, **954** C4
Harpswell, **5,239** .... *
Harrington, **882** E4
Harrison, **2,315** B4
Hartford, **963** .... *
Hartland, **1,816** C4
Haynesville, **122** D3
Hebron, **1,053** B4
Hermon, **4,437** D4
Hersey, **63** D2
Hibberts, **1** .... *
Highland, **52** .... *
Hiram, **1,423** B5
Hodgdon, **1,240** E2
Holden, **2,827** .... *
Hollis, **4,114** .... *
Hope, **1,310** C4
Houlton, **6,476** E2
Howland, **1,362** D3
Hudson, **1,393** D4
Industry, **790** .... *
Island Falls, **793** D3
Isle au Haut, **79** D4
Islesboro, **603** D4
Jackman, **718** B3
Jackson, **506** C4
Jay, **4,985** .... *
Jefferson, **2,388** C4
Jonesboro, **594** E4
Jonesport, **1,408** E4
Kenduskeag, **1,171** D4
Kennebunk, **10,476** B5
Kennebunkport, **3,720** B5
Kingfield, **1,103** B4
Kingman, **213** D3
Kingsbury, **9** C3
Kittery, **9,543** B5
Knox, **747** .... *
Lagrange, **747** D3
Lake View, **43** .... *
Lakeville, **63** .... *
Lamoine, **1,495** .... *
Lebanon, **5,083** .... *
Lee, **845** D3
Leeds, **2,001** B4
Levant, **2,171** D4
Lewiston, **35,690** B4
Liberty, **927** C4
Limerick, **2,240** B5
Limestone, **2,361** E2
Limington, **3,403** B5
Lincoln (Oxford Co.), **46** .... *
Lincoln (Penobscot Co.), **5,221** D3
Lincolnville, **2,042** D4
Linneus, **892** E2
Lisbon, **9,077** B4
Litchfield, **3,110** C4
Littleton, **955** E2
Livermore, **2,106** B4
Livermore Falls, **3,227** B4
Long Island, **202** .... *
Lovell, **974** B4
Lowell, **291** D3
Lubec, **1,652** F4
Ludlow, **402** D2
Lyman, **3,795** B5
Machias, **2,353** E4
Machiasport, **1,160** E4
Macwahoc, **98** D3
Madawaska, **4,534** D1
Madison, **4,523** C4
Madrid, **173** B4
Magalloway, **37** A4
Manchester, **2,465** C4
Mapleton, **1,889** D2
Mariaville, **414** D4
Marshfield, **494** E4
Mars Hill, **1,480** .... *
Masardis, **255** D2
Matinicus Isle, **51** D5
Mattawamkeag, **825** D3
Maxfield, **87** D3
Mechanic Falls, **3,138** B4
Meddybemps, **150** E3
Medford, **231** .... *
Medway, **1,489** D3
Mercer, **647** C4
Merrill, **249** .... *
Mexico, **2,959** B4
Milbridge, **1,279** E4
Milford, **2,950** D4
Millinocket, **5,203** D3
Milo, **2,383** D3
Milton (unorg.), **123** B4
Minot, **2,248** B4
Monhegan, **75** C5
Monmouth, **3,785** B4
Monroe, **882** C4
Monson, **666** C3
Monticello, **790** E2
Montville, **1,002** .... *
Moose River, **219** B3
Moro, **63** D2
Morrill, **774** C4
Moscow, **577** C3
Mount Chase, **247** .... *
Mount Desert, **2,109** .... *
Mount Vernon, **1,524** C4
Naples, **3,274** B5
Nashville, **55** D2
Newburgh, **1,394** .... *
New Canada, **306** .... *
Newcastle, **1,748** C4
Newfield, **1,328** B5
New Gloucester, **4,803** B5
New Limerick, **523** E2
Newport, **3,017** C4
New Portland, **785** B4
Newry, **344** B4
New Sharon, **1,297** C4
New Sweden, **621** D2
New Vineyard, **725** B4
Nobleboro, **1,626** C4
Norridgewock, **3,294** C4
North Berwick, **4,293** B5
Northeast Piscataquis (unorg.), 347 .... *
Northeast Somerset (unorg.), 354 .... *
Northfield, **131** E4
North Franklin (unorg.), 41 .... *
North Haven, **381** D4
North Oxford (unorg.), 17 .... *
North Penobscot (unorg.), 443 .... *
Northport, **1,331** D4
North Washington (unorg.), 547 .... *
Northwest Aroostook (unorg.), 27 .... *
Northwest Hancock (unorg.), 4 .... *
Northwest Piscataquis (unorg.), 159 .... *
Northwest Somerset (unorg.), 46 .... *
North Yarmouth, **3,210** .... *
Norway, **4,611** B4
Oakfield, **732** D2
Oakland, **5,959** C4
Ogunquit, **1,226** B5
Old Orchard Beach, **8,856** B5
Old Town, **8,130** D4
Orient, **145** E3
Orland, **2,134** D4
Orono, **9,112** D4
Orrington, **3,526** D4
Osborn, **69** D4
Otis, **543** D4
Otisfield, **1,560** B4
Owls Head, **1,601** C4
Oxbow, **56** D2
Oxford, **3,960** B4
Palermo, **1,220** C4
Palmyra, **1,953** C4
Paris, **4,793** B4
Parkman, **811** C3
Parsonsfield, **1,584** B5
Passadumkeag, **441** D3
Passamaquoddy Indian Township Reservation, **676** .... *
Passamaquoddy Pleasant Point Reservation, **640** .... *
Patten, **1,111** D3
Pembroke, **879** E4
Penobscot, **1,344** D4
Penobscot Indian Island Reservation, **562** .... *
Perham, **434** D2
Perkins (unorg.) C4
Perry, **847** E4
Peru, **1,515** .... *
Phillips, **990** B4
Phippsburg, **2,106** .... *
Pittsfield, **4,214** C4
Pittston, **2,548** .... *
Pleasant Ridge, **83** C3
Plymouth, **1,257** C4
Poland, **4,866** B4
Portage Lake, **390** .... *
Porter, **1,438** .... *
Portland, **64,249** B5
Pownal, **1,491** .... *
Prentiss, **214** D3
Presque Isle, **9,511** E2
Princeton, **892** E3
Prospect, **642** D4
Randolph, **1,911** C4
Rangeley (plantation), **123** B4
Rangeley (town), **1,052** B4
Raymond, **4,299** B5
Readfield, **2,360** C4
Reed, **207** D3
Richmond, **3,298** C4
Ripley, **452** C3
Robbinston, **525** E3
Rockland, **7,609** C4
Rockport, **3,209** C4
Rome, **980** C4
Roque Bluffs, **264** E4
Roxbury, **384** B4
Rumford, **6,472** B4
Sabattus, **4,486** B4
Saco, **16,822** B5
St. Agatha, **802** D1
St. Albans, **1,836** C4
St. Francis, **577** D1
St. George, **2,580** C4
St. John, **282** D1
Sandy River, **93** B4
Sanford, **20,806** B5
Sangerville, **1,270** C3
Scarborough, **16,970** B5
Searsmont, **1,174** C4
Searsport, **2,641** D4
Sebago, **1,433** .... *
Sebec, **612** C3
Seboeis, **41** D3
Seboomook Lake (unorg.), **45** C3
Sedgwick, **1,102** D4
Shapleigh, **2,326** B5
Sherman, **937** D3
Shirley, **183** .... *
Sidney, **3,514** C4
Skowhegan, **8,824** C4
Smithfield, **930** C4
Smyrna, **415** .... *
Solon, **940** C4
Somerville, **509** C4
Sorrento, **290** D4
South Aroostook (unorg.), 486 .... *
South Berwick, **6,671** B5
South Bristol, **897** C5
Southeast Piscataquis (unorg.), 254 .... *
South Franklin (unorg.), 70 .... *
South Oxford (unorg.), 515 .... *
Southport, **684** C5
South Portland, **23,324** B5
South Thomaston, **1,416** .... *
Southwest Harbor, **1,966** D4
Springfield, **379** D3
Square Lake (unorg.), 615 .... *
Stacyville, **405** D3
Standish, **9,285** .... *
Starks, **578** C4
Stetson, **981** C4
Steuben, **1,126** E4
Stockholm, **271** D1
Stockton Springs, **1,481** D4
Stoneham, **255** .... *
Stonington, **1,152** D4
Stow, **288** A4
Strong, **1,259** B4
Sullivan, **1,185** .... *
Sumner, **854** B4
Surry, **1,361** D4
Swans Island, **327** D4
Swanville, **1,357** C4
Sweden, **324** B4
Talmadge, **70** E3
Temple, **572** B4
The Forks, **35** C3
Thomaston, **3,748** C4
Thorndike, **712** C4
Topsfield, **225** E3
Topsham, **9,100** C5
Tremont, **1,529** .... *
Trenton, **1,370** D4
Troy, **963** C4
Turner, **4,972** B4
Twombly (unorg.), **2** .... *
Union, **2,209** C4
Unity (Kennebec Co.), **31** C4
Unity (Waldo Co.), **1,889** C4
Upton, **62** A4
Van Buren, **2,631** E1
Vanceboro, **147** E3
Vassalboro, **4,047** .... *
Veazie, **1,744** D4
Verona, **533** D4
Vienna, **527** C4
Vinalhaven, **1,235** D4
Wade, **250** .... *
Waite, **105** E3
Waldo, **733** .... *
Waldoboro, **4,916** C4
Wales, **1,322** .... *
Wallagrass, **561** D1
Waltham, **306** D4
Warren, **3,794** C4
Washburn, **1,627** D2
Washington, **1,345** C4
Waterboro, **6,214** B5
Waterford, **1,455** B4
Waterville, **15,605** C4
Wayne, **1,112** B4
Webster, **82** D3
Weld, **402** B4
Wellington, **258** C3
Wells, **9,400** B5
Wesley, **114** E4
West Bath, **1,798** .... *
Westbrook, **16,142** B5
West Central Franklin (unorg.) .... *
Westfield, **559** E2
West Forks, **47** C3
West Gardiner, **2,902** C4
Westmanland, **71** D2
Weston, **203** E3
West Paris, **1,722** B4
Westport, **745** C5
Whitefield, **2,273** C4
Whiting, **430** E4
Whitney (unorg.) .... *
Whitneyville, **262** E4
Willimantic, **135** C3
Wilton, **4,123** B4
Windham, **14,904** .... *
Windsor, **2,204** .... *
Winn, **420** D3
Winslow, **7,743** C4
Winter Harbor, **988** D4
Winterport, **3,602** D4
Winterville, **196** D2
Winthrop, **6,232** C4
Wiscasset, **3,603** C5
Woodland, **1,403** E3
Woodstock, **1,307** .... *
Woodville, **286** .... *
Woolwich, **2,810** C5
Wyman (unorg.), **70** E4
Yarmouth, **8,360** B5
York, **12,854** B5

Other Places

The city, town or census subdivision containing each entry is shown in italics. See the "Cities and Towns" listing for total population.

Abbot Village *(Abbot)*, **60** C3
Allens Mills *(Industry)*, **275** B4
Atkinson Corner *(Atkinson)*, **70** C3
Atlantic *(Swans Island)*, **125** D4
Ayers *(Pembroke)*, **10** E4
Bailey Island *(Harpswell)*, **400** B5
Bass Harbor *(Tremont)*, **600** D4
Belgrade Lakes *(Belgrade and Rome)*, **350** C4
Belmont Corner *(Belmont)*, **375** C4
Belvedere *(Crystal)*, **70** D2
Benedicta *(South Aroostook)*, **50** D3
Bernard *(Tremont)*, **600** D4
Berry Mills *(Carthage)*, **225** B4
Biddeford Pool *(Biddeford)* B5
Bigelow *(Carrabassett Valley)*, **40** B3
Bingo *(Waite)* E3
Birch Harbor *(Gouldsboro)*, **175** D4
Blue Hill Falls *(Blue Hill)*, **40** D4
Bodfish *(Elliottsville)*, **20** C3
Bradbury *(St. Francis)*, **100** D1
Bradford Center *(Bradford)*, **175** D3
Brassua *(Northeast Somerset)* C3
Brookton *(North Washington)*, **50** E3
Brownville Junction *(Brownville)*, **750** C3
Bryant Pond *(Woodstock)*, **250** B4
Bucks Harbor *(Machiasport)*, **200** E4
Bucksport Center *(Bucksport)*, **650** D4
Buxton Center *(Buxton)* B5
Cape Neddick *(York)*, **2,997** B5
Cape Porpoise *(Kennebunkport)*, **650** B5
Cardville *(Greenbush)*, **200** D3
Carson *(Woodland)*, **125** D2
Carys Mills *(Houlton)*, **60** E2
Center Lovell *(Lovell)*, **60** B4
Center Montville *(Montville)*, **60** C4
Charles Chase Corner *(Wells)* B5
Chesuncook *(Greenville)* C2
Chisholm *(Jay)*, **1,399** B4
City Point *(Belfast)*, **30** C4
Clark Island *(St. George)*, **200** C5
Clarks Mills *(Dayton and Hollis)*, **450** B5
Clayton Lake *(Northwest Aroostook)*, **10** C2
Coburn Gore *(Eustis)* B3
Colby *(Woodland)*, **200** D2
Cooks Mills *(Casco)*, **325** B5
Coopers Mills *(Whitefield)*, **350** C4
Corea *(Gouldsboro)*, **450** E4
Costigan *(Milford)*, **100** D3
Crouseville *(Washburn)*, **275** D2
Cumberland Center *(Cumberland)*, **2,596** B5
Cumberland Foreside *(Cumberland)*, **500** B5
Daigle *(New Canada)*, **50** D1
Danville *(Auburn)*, **125** B4
Davidson *(North Penobscot)* D3
Dickey *(Allagash)*, **10** C1
Dunns *(North Yarmouth)*, **300** B5
Dyer Cove *(Harpswell)*, **600** C5
East Andover *(Andover)*, **150** B4
East Baldwin *(Baldwin)*, **225** B5
East Corinth *(Corinth)*, **125** C4
East Dixfield *(Dixfield and Wilton)*, **125** B4
East Dover *(Dover-Foxcroft)*, **40** C3
East Eddington *(Eddington)*, **300** D4
East Hampden *(Hampden)*, **800** D4
East Hiram *(Hiram)* B5
East Holden *(Holden)*, **475** D4
East Lebanon *(Lebanon)*, **650** B5
East Madison *(Madison)*, **125** C4
East Newport *(Newport)*, **175** C4
East New Portland *(New Portland)*, **70** B4
East Orland *(Orland)*, **250** D4
East Parsonsfield *(Parsonsfield)*, **200** B5
East Peru *(Peru)*, **225** B4
East Stoneham *(Stoneham)*, **150** B4
East Vassalboro *(Vassalboro)*, **300** C4
East Waterboro *(Waterboro)*, **275** B5
East Winn *(Winn)*, **100** D3
Eaton *(Danforth)*, **30** E3
Ellsworth Falls *(Ellsworth)* D4
Emery Mills *(Shapleigh)*, **350** B5
Exeter Corners *(Exeter)*, **100** C4
Fairfield Center *(Fairfield)*, **500** C4
Falmouth *(Falmouth)* B5
Falmouth Foreside *(Falmouth)*, **1,964** B5
Farmington Falls *(Chesterville and Farmington)*, **225** B4
Five Islands *(Georgetown)* C5
Forest *(Brookton)*, **80** E3
Forest City *(Brookton)*, **10** E3
Fort Kent Mills *(Fort Kent)*, **325** D1
Frenchville *(Ashland)*, **175** D2
Frye *(Roxbury)*, **90** B4
Gerard *(Northwest Somerset)* B3
Gerry *(Alton)*, **40** D3
Glenburn Center *(Glenburn)* D4
Glen Cove *(Rockport)*, **375** C4
Goodrich *(Fort Fairfield)*, **40** E2
Goose Rocks Beach *(Kennebunkport)*, **250** B5
Grants *(North Franklin)* B3
Great Works *(Old Town)* D4
Green Lake *(Dedham)*, **70** D4
Greenville Junction *(Greenville)*, **850** C3
Grimes Mill *(Caribou)* E2
Grindstone *(Medway)*, **30** D3
Grove *(Cooper)*, **70** E4
Groveville *(Buxton)* B5
Guerette *(Stockholm)*, **50** D1
Haines Landing *(Rangeley)*, **40** B4
Hall Quarry *(Mount Desert)*, **125** D4
Hampden Highlands *(Hampden)* D4
Hanford *(Perham)*, **30** D2
Harborside *(Brooksville)*, **20** D4
Harvey *(Monticello)* E2
Head Tide *(Alna)* C4
Higgins Beach *(Scarborough)*, **800** B5
Hinckley *(Fairfield)*, **125** C4
Hodgdon Corners *(Houlton)*, **300** E2
Holeb *(Northwest Somerset)* B3
Hollis Center *(Hollis)*, **450** B5
Houghton *(Byron)* B4
Howe Brook *(Central Aroostook)* D2
Indian River *(Addison)*, **50** E4
Jackman Station *(Jackman)*, **750** B3
Jacksonville *(East Machias)*, **350** E4
Jemtland *(New Sweden)*, **100** D1
Keegan *(Van Buren)*, **550** E1
Kelleyland *(Woodland)* E3
Kennebago Lake *(North Franklin)* B3
Kennebec *(Machias)*, **225** E4
Kennebunk Beach *(Kennebunk)*, **800** B5
Kents Hills *(Readfield)*, **375** C4
Kezar Falls *(Parsonsfield and Porter)*, **750** B5
Kineo *(Northwest Piscataquis)* C3
Kittery Point *(Kittery)*, **1,135** B5
Knights Landing *(Brownville)*, **20** D3
Knowles Corner *(Moro)*, **10** D2
Kokadjo *(Greenville)* C3
Lake Moxie *(The Forks)* C3
Lake Parlin *(Northeast Somerset)* B3
Lakewood *(Madison)*, **225** C4
Lambert Lake *(North Washington)*, **20** E3
Lamoine Beach *(Lamoine)* D4
Lille *(Grand Isle)*, **150** D1
Lily Bay *(Greenville)* C3
Lincoln Center *(Lincoln)*, **275** D3
Lincolnville Center *(Lincolnville)*, **325** C4
Lisbon Falls *(Lisbon)*, **4,420** B5
Locke Mills *(Greenwood)*, **150** B4
Long Beach *(Sebago)*, **300** B5
Long Pond *(Northeast Somerset)*, **30** B3
Loon Lake *(Dallas)*, **10** B3
Lowelltown *(North Franklin)* B3
Mackamp *(Northeast Somerset)* B3
Maple Grove *(Fort Fairfield)*, **80** E2
Maplewood *(Newfield and Parsonsfield)*, **90** B5
Marion *(Dennysville)*, **20** E4
Marlboro *(Lamoine)*, **70** D4
McNally *(Winterville)* D2
Medford Center *(Medford)*, **10** D3
Michaud *(Wallagrass)*, **150** D1
Millvale *(Bucksport)*, **125** D4
Minturn *(Swans Island)*, **175** D4
Molunkus *(Kingman)*, **20** D3
Monarda *(Sherman Mills)*, **20** D3
Montsweag *(Woolwich)* C5
Moody *(Wells)*, **1,000** B5
Moosehead *(Northwest Piscataquis)* C3
Mountainville *(Deer Isle)*, **150** D4
Myra *(Northwest Hancock)* D4
Naskeag *(Brooklin)*, **80** D4
Newburgh Village *(Newburgh)*, **250** C4
New Harbor *(Bristol)*, **225** C5
Norcross *(North Penobscot)* D3
North Amity *(Amity)*, **30** E3

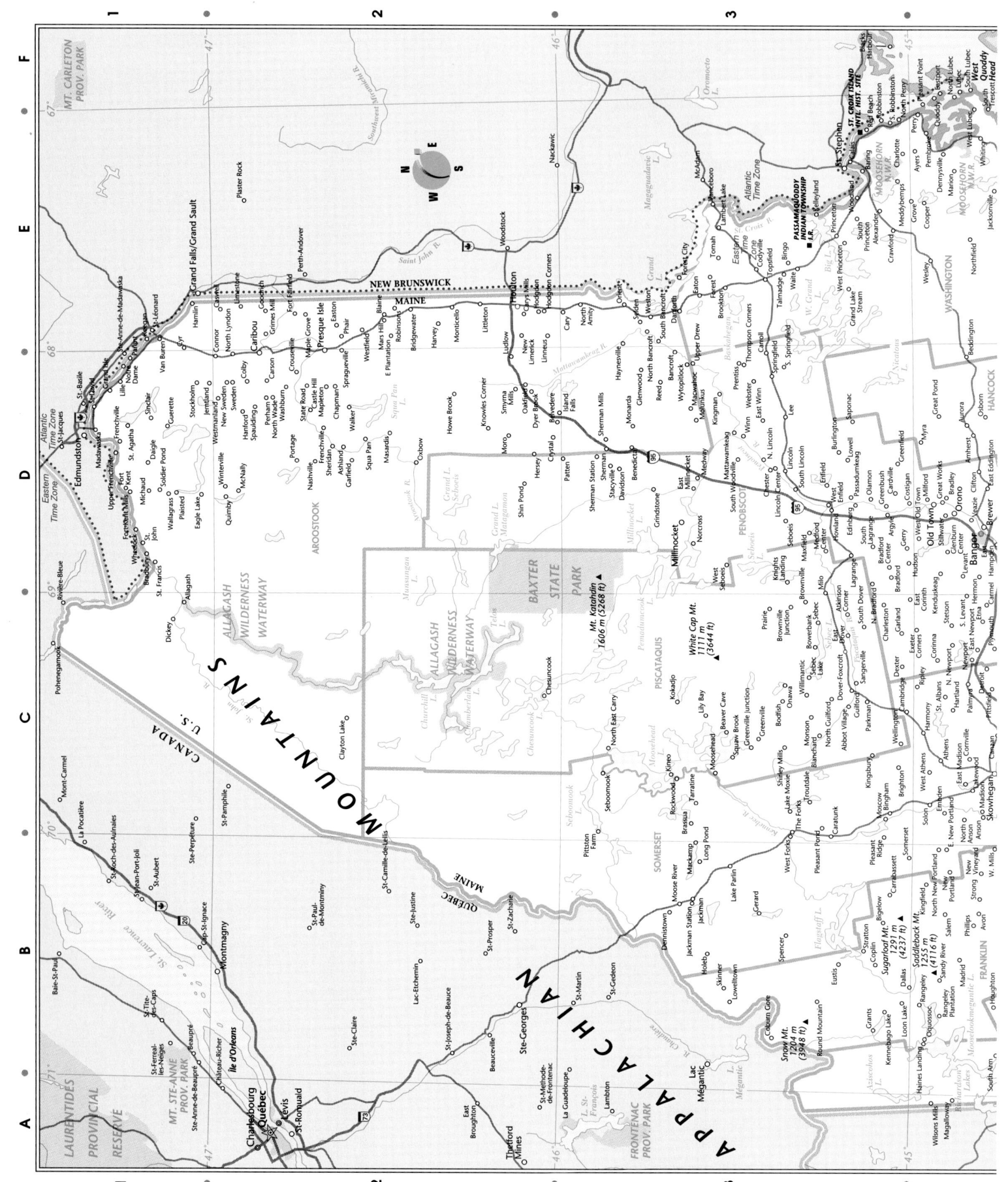

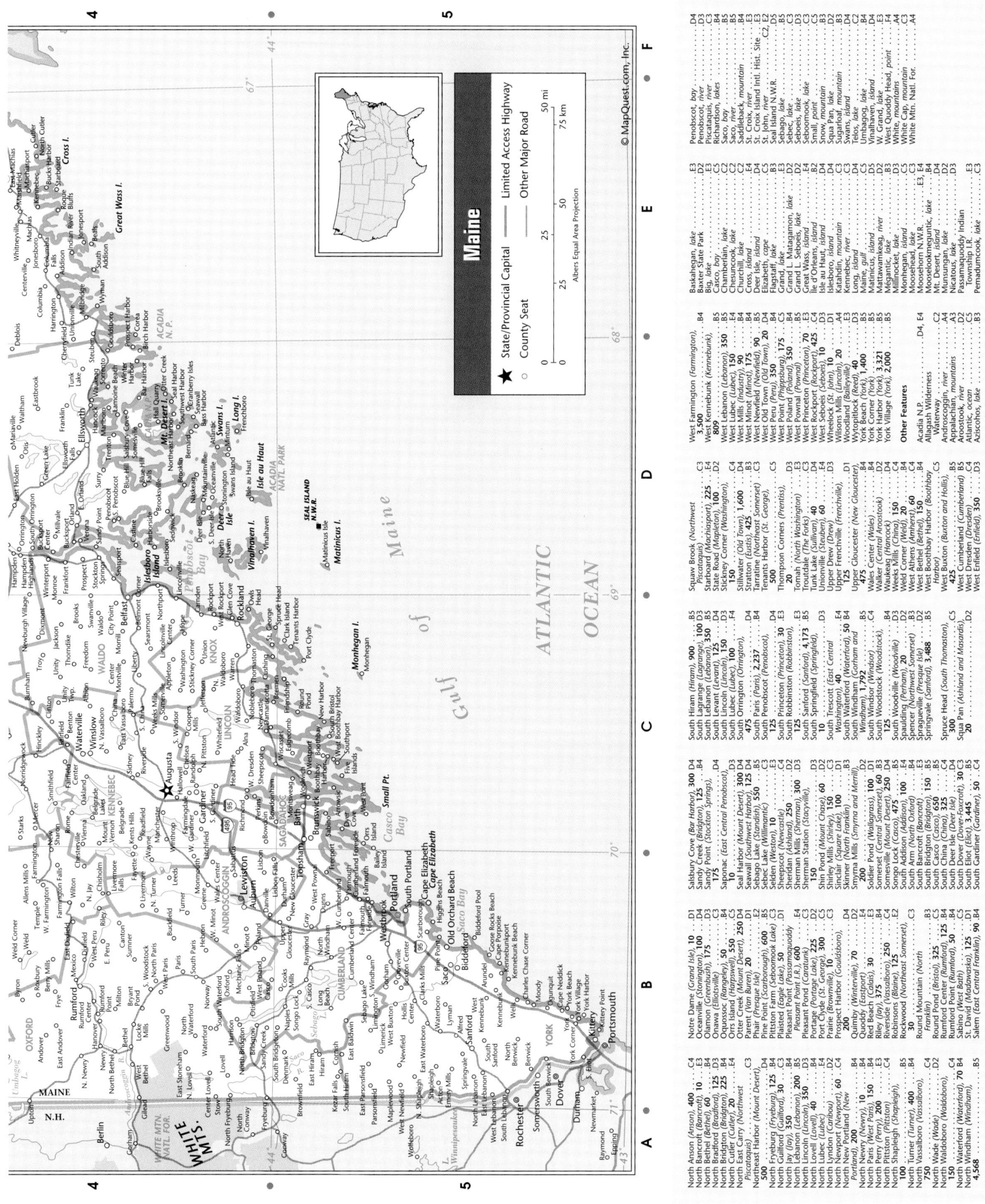

Maine

★ State/Provincial Capital
○ County Seat

— Limited Access Highway
— Other Major Road

© MapQuest.com, Inc.

Albers Equal Area Projection

0   25   50 mi
0   25   50   75 km

North Anson (Anson), 400 ....C4
North Bancroft (Bancroft), 10 ...D1
North Bethel (Bethel), 60 ....B4
North Bradford (Bradford), 225 ..B4
North Bridgton (Bridgton), 175 ..B4
North East Carry (Northwest
  Piscataquis) C3
North Fryeburg (Fryeburg), 125 ..B4
North Jay (Jay), 350 ....C3
North Lebanon (Lebanon), 200 ..B5
North Lincoln (Lincoln), 350 ...D3
North Lovell (Lovell), 40 ......B4
North Lyndon (Caribou), 60 ....C2
North Newport (New
  Portland), 200 ....B4
North Newry (Newry), 10 ......B4
North Paris (North Paris), 150 ..B4
North Perry (Perry), 200 ......D3
North Pittston (Pittston) C4
North Shapleigh (Shapleigh) ...B5
North Turner (Turner), 400 ....C4
North Wade (Wade), 150 ......D2
North Waldoboro (Waldoboro) ..C4
North Waterford (Waterford), 70 B4
North Windham (Windham),
  4,568 ....B5

Notre Dame (Grand Isle), 10 ...D1
Oceanville (Stonington), 100 ...D5
Olamon (Greenbush), 175 .....D3
Onawa (Elliottsville) C3
Oquossoc (Rangeley), 50 .....B4
Orrs Island (Harpswell), 550 ...C5
Otter Creek (Mount Desert), 250 D4
Parent (Van Buren), 20 ....D1
Phair (Presque Isle) D2
Phillips Lake (Dedham), 600 ...D4
Pittston Farm (Seboomook Lake) C3
Plaisted (Eagle Lake), 50 .....D1
Pleasant Point (Passamaquoddy
  Pleasant Point I.R.), 600 ...E4
Pleasant Pond (Caratunk) C3
Portage (Portage Lake), 225 ...D2
Port Clyde (St. George), 300 ...C5
Prairie (Brownville), 10 ......C3
Prospect Harbor (Gouldsboro),
  200 ....D4
Quimby (Winterville), 70 .....D1
Quoddy (Eastport) E4
Red Beach (Calais), 30 ......E3
Riley (Jay), 375 ....B4
Riverside (Vassalboro), 250 ...C4
Rockwood (Northeast Somerset),
  30 ....C3
Round Mountain (North
  Franklin) B3
Round Pond (Bristol), 325 ....C5
Rumford Center (Rumford), 125 B4
Rumford Point (Rumford), 50 ...B4
Sabino (West Bath) C5
St. David (Madawaska), 125 ...D1
Salem (East Central Franklin), 90 B4

Salsbury Cove (Bar Harbor), 300 D4
Sandy Creek (Bridgton), 125 ...B4
Sandy Point (Stockton Springs),
  175 ....D4
Saponac (East Central Penobscot) D3
Seal Harbor (Mount Desert), 300 D4
Seawall (Southwest Harbor), 125 D4
Sebago Lake (Standish), 550 ...B5
Selden (Weston), 10 ....E3
Sheepscot (Newcastle) C4
Sheridan (Ashland), 250 .....D2
Sherman Mills (Sherman), 300 ..D3
Sherman Station (Stacyville) ...D3
Shin Pond (Mount Chase), 60 ..D3
Shirley Mills (Shirley), 150 ....C3
Skinner (Square Central
  Washington), 40 ......D4
Smyrna Mills (Smyrna and Merrill) B3
Soldier Pond (Wallagrass), 100 ..D1
Somerset (Central Somerset), 60 .B3
Somesville (Mount Desert), 250 .D4
South Addison (Addison), 100 ..E4
South Arm (North Oxford) B4
South Berwick (Berwick), 150 ..B5
Springvale (Sanford), 3,488 ...B5
South Bridgton (Bridgton), 150 ..B5
South Casco (Casco), 650 ....B5
South China (China), 325 ....C4
South Deer Isle (Deer Isle),
  300 ....D4
South Dover (Dover-Foxcroft), 30 C3
South Eliot (Eliot), 3,445 ......B5
South Gardiner (Gardiner), 50 ...C4

South Hiram (Hiram), 900 ....B5
South Lagrange (Lagrange), 100 D3
South Lebanon (Lebanon), 350 ..B5
South Lincoln (Lincoln), 150 ...D3
South Lubec (Lubec), 125 ....E4
South Orrington (Orrington) ...D4
South Paris (Paris), 2,237 ....B4
South Penobscot (Penobscot) ...D4
South Princeton (Princeton), 30 .E3
South Robbinston (Robbinston) .E3
South Sanford (Sanford), 4,173 .B5
South Springfield (Springfield) ..D3
South Thomaston (South
  Thomaston) C4
South Trescott (East Central
  Washington) E4
Stillwater (Old Town), 1,600 ...D3
Stratton (Eustis), 425 ......B3
Tarratine (Northeast Somerset) ..C3
Tenants Harbor (St. George),
  500 ....C5
Thompson Corners (Prentiss),
  20 ....D3
Tomah (North Washington) E3
Troutdale (The Forks) C3
Tunk Lake (Sullivan), 40 .....D4
Unionville (Steuben), 60 .....D4
Upper Drew (Drew) D3
Upper Frenchville (Frenchville),
  40 ....D1
Waldoboro (Waldoboro), 50 ...C4
Wales Center (Wales) B4
Walker (Central Aroostook) D2
Waukeag (Hancock) D4
Weeks Mills (China), 150 .....C4
Weld Corner (Weld), 20 .....B4
Wesley (Central Washington) ...E3
West Athens (Amherst), 60 ....C4
West Bethel (Bethel), 150 ....B4
West Boothbay Harbor (Boothbay
  Harbor) C5
West Buxton (Buxton and Hollis),
  425 ....B5
West Cumberland (Cumberland) B5
West Dresden (Dresden), 350 ...C4
West Enfield (Enfield), 350 ....D3

West Farmington (Farmington),
  3,500 ....B4
West Kennebunk (Kennebunk),
  809 ....B5
West Lebanon (Lebanon), 350 ..B5
West Lubec (Lubec), 150 .....E4
West Mills (Industry), 90 .....B4
West Minot (Minot), 175 ....B4
West Newfield (Newfield), 90 ...B5
West Paris (Old Town), 20 ....D4
West Peru (Peru), 350 ......B4
West Point (Phippsburg), 175 ...C5
West Poland (Poland), 350 ....B4
West Pownal (Pownal) B5
West Princeton (Princeton), 70 ..E3
West Rockport (Rockport), 425 ..C4
West Seboeis (Seboeis), 10 ....D3
Wheelock (St. John), 10 .....D1
Wilsons Mills (Lincoln), 20 ....B3
Woodland (Baileyville), 50 ....E3
Wyotopitlock (Reed), 40 .....D3
York Beach (York), 1,400 .....B5
York Corner (York) B5
York Harbor (York), 3,321 ....B5
York Village (York), 2,000 ....B5

Penobscot, bay D4
Penobscot, river D3
Piscataquis, river C3
Richardson, lakes B4
Saco, bay B5
Saco, river B4
Saddleback, mountain B4
St. Croix, river E3
St. Croix Island Intl. Hist. Site ..E3
St. John, river C2, D5
Seal Island N.W.R. D5
Sebago, lake B5
Sebec, lake D3
Seboeis, lake D3
Seboomook, lake C3
Small, point B5
Snow, mountain B3
Squa Pan, lake D2
Sugarloaf, mountain B4
Telos, lake C2
Umbagog, lake B4
Vinalhaven, island D4
W. Grand, lake E3
West Quoddy Head, point E4
White, mountains A4
White Cap, mountain C3
White Mtn. Natl. For. A4

Other Features

Acadia N.P. D4, E4
Allagash Wilderness
  Waterway C2
Androscoggin, river A4
Appalachian, mountains A3
Aroostook, river D2
Atlantic, ocean C5
Azischohos, lake B3

Baskahegan, lake E3
Baxter State Park C2
Big, lake E3
Casco, bay C5
Chamberlain, lake C2
Chesuncook, lake C3
Churchill, lake C2
Cross, island E4
Deer Isle, island D4
Elizabeth, cape C5
Grand, lake E3
Grand L. Matagamon, lake ...C2
Grand L. Seboeis, lake D2
Great Wass, island D4
Isle d'Orleans, island B2
Isle au Haut, island D4
Islesboro, island D4
Katahdin, mountain C3
Kennebec, river C4
Long, island D4
Maine, gulf C5
Matinicus, island D5
Mattawamkeag, river D3
Megantic, lake B3
Millinocket, lake C3
Monhegan, island C5
Moosehead, lake C3
Mooselookmeguntic, lake B4
Moosehorn N.W.R. E3
Mt. Desert, island D4
Munsungan, lake C2
Nicatous, lake D3
Passamaquoddy Indian
  Township I.R. E3
Pemadumcook, lake C3

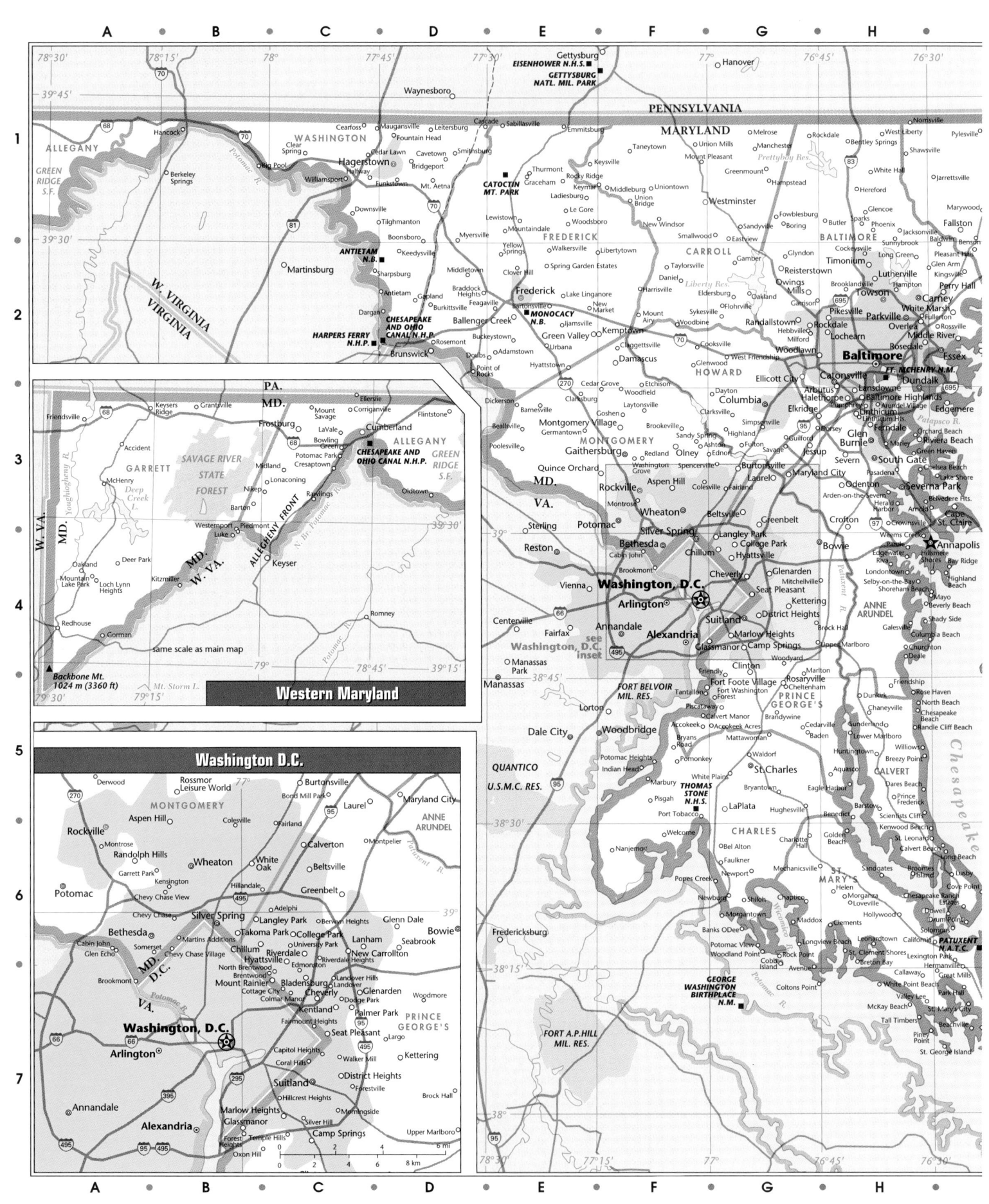

Western Maryland

Washington D.C.

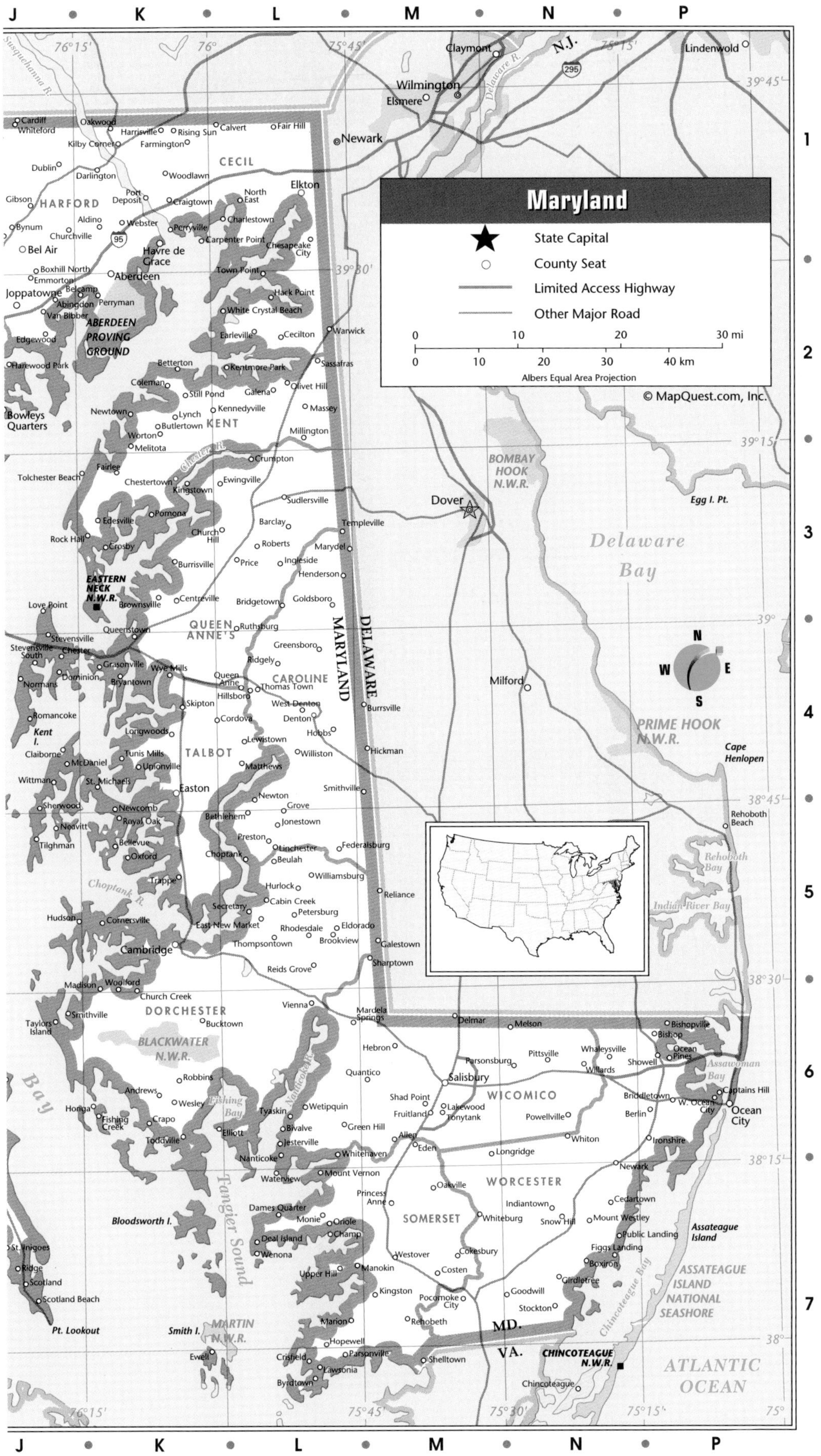

Map Labels (Maryland and the District of Columbia)

Grid columns: J K L M N P

Grid rows: 1 2 3 4 5 6 7

76°15' 76° 75°45' 75°15'

N.J.

Claymont
Lindenwold
Wilmington
Elsmere
Newark

39°45'

Cardiff
Whiteford
Oakwood
Kilby Corner
Harrisville
Rising Sun
Calvert
Fair Hill
CECIL
Dublin
Darlington
Woodlawn
North East
Elkton
Gibson
HARFORD
Port Deposit
Craigtown
Charlestown
Bynum
Aldino
Webster
Perryville
Carpenter Point
Chesapeake City
Churchville
Havre de Grace
Town Point
Bel Air
Boxhill North
Emmorton
Aberdeen
39°30'
Hack Point
Joppatowne
Belcamp
Perryman
White Crystal Beach
Warwick
Abingdon
Van Bibber
ABERDEEN PROVING GROUND
Earleville
Ceciliton
Edgewood
Betterton
Sassafras
Harewood Park
Coleman
Kentmore Park
Still Pond
Galena
Olivet Hill
Bowleys Quarters
Newtown
Lynch
Kennedyville
Massey
Worton
Butlertown
KENT
Millington
Melitota
Fairlee
Crumpton
Tolchester Beach
Chestertown
Ewingville
39°15'
BOMBAY HOOK N.W.R.
Kingstown
Sudlersville
Dover
Rock Hall
Edesville
Pomona
Church Hill
Templeville
Egg I. Pt.
Crosby
Burrisville
Price
Ingleside
Marydel
Roberts
EASTERN NECK N.W.R.
Brownsville
Centreville
Henderson
Delaware Bay
Love Point
Bridgetown
Goldsboro
Queenstown
Ruthsburg
39°
QUEEN ANNE'S
Stevensville
Chester
Greensboro
Stevensville South
Grasonville
Ridgely
Normans
Dominion
Wye Mills
Queen Anne
Bryantown
CAROLINE
Thomas Town
Romancoke
Longwoods
Skipton
Hillsboro
West Denton
Milford
Kent I.
Claiborne
Cordova
Denton
Burrsville
38°45'
McDaniel
Tunis Mills
Lewistown
Hobbs
Wittman
Unionville
Williston
Hickman
St. Michaels
TALBOT
Matthews
Newcomb
Easton
Newton
Smithville
PRIME HOOK N.W.R.
Sherwood
Royal Oak
Bethlehem
Grove
Neavitt
Bellevue
Preston
Jonestown
Cape Henlopen
Tilghman
Oxford
Choptank
Linchester
Federalsburg
Rehoboth Beach
Trappe
Beulah
Williamsburg
Hurlock
38°30'
Hudson
Cornersville
Secretary
Cabin Creek
Reliance
Rehoboth Bay
Madison
Wingate
Petersburg
Eldorado
Indian River Bay
East New Market
Rhodesdale
Brookview
Galestown
Thompsontown
Reids Grove
Sharptown
CAMBRIDGE
Church Creek
Vienna
Mardela Springs
Delmar
Melson
Bishopville
38°15'
Taylors Island
Bucktown
DORCHESTER
Hebron
Bishop
Smithville
BLACKWATER N.W.R.
Parsonsburg
Pittsville
Whaleysville
Ocean Pines
Showell
Robbins
Quantico
Salisbury
Willards
Assawoman Bay
Andrews
Wesley
Wetipquin
Shad Point
WICOMICO
Captains Hill
38°
Honga
Fishing Bay
Tyaskin
Lakewood
Briddletown
W. Ocean City
Fishing Creek
Crapo
Bivalve
Fruitland
Tonytank
Berlin
Ocean City
Toddville
Elliott
Jesterville
Green Hill
Powellville
Nanticoke
Whitehaven
Allen
Whiton
Ironshire
Mount Vernon
Eden
Longridge
Newark
Waterview
Oakville
Cedartown
WORCESTER
Dames Quarter
Princess Anne
Indiantown
Bloodsworth I.
Monie
Oriole
Whiteburg
Snow Hill
Mount Westley
Assateague Island
SOMERSET
Public Landing
Tangier Sound
Deal Island
Champ
Figgs Landing
Wenona
Westover
Cokesbury
Boxiron
ASSATEAGUE ISLAND NATIONAL SEASHORE
St. Inigoes
Upper Hill
Manokin
Goodwill
Girdletree
Ridge
Kingston
Costen
Scotland
Pocomoke City
Stockton
Scotland Beach
Marion
Rehobeth
MD.
Pt. Lookout
Smith I.
MARTIN N.W.R.
Hopewell
VA.
CHINCOTEAGUE N.W.R.
Ewell
Crisfield
Parsonville
Shelltown
ATLANTIC OCEAN
Byrdtown
Chincoteague
Lawsonia

Susquehanna R.
Delaware R.
Choptank R.
Chester R.
Nanticoke R.
Pocomoke R.
Tangier Sound

76°15' 75°45' 75°30' 75°15' 75°

Maryland (map legend box)

- ★ State Capital
- ○ County Seat
- ── Limited Access Highway
- ── Other Major Road

Scale:
0 10 20 30 mi
0 10 20 30 40 km
Albers Equal Area Projection

© MapQuest.com, Inc.

District of Columbia
Land Area: 61 sq. mi.
159 sq. km.
Population: 572,059 (2000 Census)
Largest City: Washington, 572,059
Highest Point: Tenleytown (NW), 410 ft. 125 m.

Maryland
Capital: Annapolis
Land Area: 9,775 sq. mi.
25,317 sq. km.
Population: 5,296,486 (2000 Census)
Largest City: Baltimore, 651,154
Highest Point: Backbone Mountain, 3,360 ft. 1,024 m.
Admitted to Union: April 28, 1788
Nickname: Old Line State, Free State
State Flower: Black-eyed Susan
State Bird: Baltimore Oriole

District of Columbia:
Map Index

Cities and Towns

Washington, 572,059 ....B7, F4

Maryland:
Map Index

Counties

Allegany, 74,930 ....A1, D3
Anne Arundel, 489,656 ....D5, H4
Baltimore, 754,292 ....H1
Baltimore City, 651,154 ....H2
Calvert, 74,563 ....H5
Caroline, 29,772 ....L4
Carroll, 150,897 ....G2
Cecil, 85,951 ....L1
Charles, 120,546 ....G6
Dorchester, 30,674 ....K6
Frederick, 195,277 ....E1
Garrett, 29,846 ....A3
Harford, 218,590 ....J1
Howard, 247,842 ....G2
Kent, 19,197 ....L2
Montgomery, 873,341 ....B5, F3
Prince Georges, 801,515 ....D7, G5
Queen Anne's, 40,563 ....K3
St. Mary's, 86,211 ....H6
Somerset, 24,747 ....M7
Talbot, 33,812 ....K4
Washington, 131,923 ....C1
Wicomico, 84,644 ....M6
Worcester, 46,543 ....N7

Cities and Towns

Aberdeen, 13,842 ....K2
Abingdon, 950 ....J2
Accident, 353 ....A3
Accokeek, 7,349 ....F5
Accokeek Acres, 1,500 ....G5
Adamstown, 650 ....E2
Adelphi, 14,998 ....C6
Aldino, 375 ....K1
Allen, 200 ....M6
Andrews, 70 ....K6
Annapolis, 35,838 ....J4
Antietam, 275 ....D2
Aquasco, 250 ....H5
Arbutus, 20,116 ....H3
Arden-on-the-Severn, 1,971 ....H3
Arnold, 23,422 ....H3
Arundel Village, 8,000 ....H3
Ashton (Ashton-Sandy Springs), 3,437 .....F3
Aspen Hill, 50,228 ....B5, F3
Avenue, 475 ....G6
Baden, 225 ....G5
Baldwin, 850 ....J2
Ballenger Creek, 13,518 ....E2
Baltimore, 651,154 ....H2
Baltimore Highlands (see Lansdowne), 15,724 ....H3
Banks Odee G6
Barclay, 143 ....L3
Barnesville, 161 ....E3
Barstow, 750 ....H5
Barton, 478 ....B3
Bartonsville (Linganore-Bartonsville), 12,529 ....E2
Bay Ridge, 2,300 ....J4
Beachville, 225 ....J7

Beallsville, 150 ....E3
Bel Air, 10,080 ....J1
Bel Alton, 425 ....G6
Belcamp, 1,900 ....K2
Bellevue, 175 ....K5
Beltsville, 15,690 ....C6, G3
Belvedere Hts., 7,900 ....H3
Benedict, 450 ....H5
Benson, 950 ....J1
Bentley Springs, 175 ....H1
Berlin, 3,491 ....P6
Berwyn Heights, 2,942 ....C6
Bethesda, 55,277 ....A6, F4
Bethlehem, 600 ....L5
Betterton, 376 ....K2
Beulah, 125 ....L5
Beverly Beach, 1,600 ....H4
Big Pool, 200 ....B1
Bishop, 200 ....P6
Bishopville, 300 ....P6
Bivalve, 450 ....L6
Bladensburg, 7,661 ....C7
Bond Mill Park (West Laurel),
3,400 ....C5
Boonsboro, 2,803 ....D1
Boring, 600 ....G1
Bowie, 50,269 ....D6, H4
Bowleys Quarters, 6,314 ....J2
Boxhill North (Bel Air South),
2,900 ....J1
Boxiron, 30 ....N7
Braddock Heights, 4,627 ....D2
Brandywine, 1,410 ....G5
Breezy Point, 800 ....H5
Brentwood, 2,844 ....C7
Breton Bay, 750 ....H6
Briddletown, 50 ....P6
Bridgeport, 2,700 ....D1
Bridgetown, 100 ....L3
Brock Hall (Greater Upper
Marlboro), 1,200 ....D7, G4
Brookeville, 120 ....F3
Brooklandville (Mays Chapel),
2,200 ....H2
Brookmont (see Cabin John),
3,202 ....A7, F4
Brookview, 65 ....L5
Broomes Island, 425 ....H6
Brownsville, 125 ....K3
Brunswick, 4,894 ....D2
Bryans Road, 4,912 ....F5
Bryantown (Charles Co.), 550 ....G5
Bryantown (Queen Anne's Co.),
550 ....K4
Buckeystown, 425 ....E2
Bucktown, 425 ....K6
Burkittsville, 171 ....D2
Burrisville, 175 ....K3
Burrsville, 150 ....M4
Burtonsville, 7,305 ....C5, G3
Butler, 225 ....H1
Butlertown, 350 ....K2
Bynum J1
Byrdtown, 475 ....L7
Cabin Creek, 100 ....L5
Cabin John (Cabin John-
Brookmont), 1,734 ....A6, F4
California, 9,307 ....H6
Callaway, 400 ....H7
Calvert, 450 ....L1
Calvert Beach (Calvert Beach-Long
Beach), 2,487 ....J6
Calvert Manor, 650 ....F5
Calverton, 12,610 ....C6
Cambridge, 10,911 ....K5
Camp Springs, 17,968 ....C7, G4
Cape St. Claire, 8,022 ....J3
Capitol Heights, 4,138 ....C7
Captains Hill (see West Ocean
City), 600 ....P6
Cardiff, 650 ....J1
Carney, 28,264 ....H2
Carpenter Point, 400 ....K1
Cascade, 1,141 ....D1
Catonsville, 39,820 ....H2
Cavetown, 1,486 ....D1
Cearfoss, 800 ....C1
Cecilton, 474 ....L2
Cedar Grove, 950 ....F2
Cedar Lawn, 900 ....C1
Cedartown N7
Cedarville, 275 ....G5
Centreville, 1,970 ....K3
Champ, 150 ....L7
Chaneyville, 475 ....H5
Chaptico, 175 ....G6
Charlestown, 1,019 ....L1
Charlotte Hall, 1,214 ....G6
Chelsea Beach, 4,400 ....H3
Cheltenham, 650 ....G5
Chesapeake Beach, 3,180 ....H5
Chesapeake City, 787 ....L1
Chesapeake Ranch Estates,
11,503 ....J6
Chester, 3,723 ....J4
Chestertown, 4,746 ....K3
Cheverly, 6,433 ....C7, G4
Chevy Chase, 2,726 ....B6
Chevy Chase View, 863 ....B6
Chevy Chase Village, 2,043 ....B6
Chillum, 34,252 ....B6, G4
Choptank, 250 ....L5
Church Creek, 450 ....K6
Church Hill, 530 ....L3
Churchton, 1,800 ....H4
Churchville, 1,200 ....J1
Claggettville, 250 ....F2
Claiborne, 225 ....J4
Clarksburg, 1,834 ....E3
Clarksville, 900 ....G3
Clear Spring, 455 ....C1
Clements, 150 ....H6
Clinton, 26,064 ....G4
Clover Hill, 3,260 ....E2

Cobb Island, 750 ....G6
Cockeysville, 19,388 ....H2
Cokesbury, 200 ....M7
Coleman, 250 ....K2
Colesville, 19,810 ....B6, F3
College Park, 24,657 ....C6, G4
Colmar Manor, 1,257 ....C7
Coltons Point, 375 ....G7
Columbia, 88,254 ....G3
Columbia Beach, 700 ....H4
Cooksville, 125 ....F2
Coral Hills, 10,720 ....C7
Cordova, 592 ....L4
Cornersville, 175 ....K5
Corriganville, 1,000 ....C3
Costen, 80 ....M7
Cottage City, 1,136 ....C7
Cove Point, 275 ....J6
Craigtown, 550 ....K1
Crapo, 70 ....K6
Cresaptown (Cresaptown-Bel Air),
5,884 ....C3
Crisfield, 2,723 ....L7
Crofton, 20,091 ....H3
Crosby, 300 ....K3
Crownsville, 1,670 ....H3
Crumpton, 500 ....L3
Cumberland, 21,518 ....C3
Damascus, 11,430 ....F2
Dames Quarter, 188 ....L7
Daniel, 650 ....F2
Dares Beach, 1,400 ....H5
Dargan, 350 ....D2
Darlington, 350 ....K1
Dayton, 600 ....G3
Deale, 4,796 ....H4
Deal Island, 578 ....L7
Deer Park, 405 ....A4
Delmar, 1,859 ....M6
Denton, 2,960 ....L4
Derwood, 2,000 ....A5
Dickerson, 250 ....E3
District Heights, 5,958 ....C7, G4
Dodge Park C7
Dominion, 600 ....J4
Dorsey, 1,000 ....G3
Doubs, 750 ....E2
Dowell, 750 ....J6
Downsville, 175 ....C1
Drum Point (see Chesapeake Ranch
Estates), 11,503 ....J6
Dublin, 650 ....J1
Dundalk, 62,306 ....H2
Dunkirk, 2,363 ....H5
Eagle Harbor, 55 ....H5
Earleville, 125 ....L2
East New Market, 167 ....L5
Easton, 11,708 ....K4
Eastview, 650 ....G1
Eden, 793 ....M6
Edesville, 275 ....K3
Edgemere, 9,248 ....J3
Edgewater, 2,900 ....H4
Edgewood, 23,378 ....J2
Edmonston, 959 ....C7
Ednor G3
Eldersburg, 27,741 ....G2
Eldorado, 60 ....L5
Elkridge, 22,042 ....G3
Elkton, 11,893 ....L1
Ellerslie, 600 ....C3
Ellicott City, 56,397 ....G2
Elliott, 10 ....K6
Emmitsburg, 2,290 ....E1
Emmorton, 4,000 ....J2
Essex, 39,078 ....J2
Etchison, 325 ....F2
Ewell, 364 ....K7
Ewingville, 150 ....L3
Fair Hill L1
Fairland, 21,738 ....C6, G3
Fairlee, 250 ....K3
Fairmount Heights, 1,508 ....C7
Fallston, 8,427 ....J1
Farmington, 375 ....K1
Faulkner, 250 ....G6
Feagaville, 600 ....E2
Federalsburg, 2,620 ....L5
Ferndale, 16,056 ....H3
Figgs Landing N7
Fishing Creek, 300 ....K6
Flintstone, 275 ....D3
Flohrville, 950 ....G2
Forest Heights, 2,585 ....B7
Forestville, 12,707 ....C7
Fort Foote Village (Fort
Washington) F5
Fort Washington Forest F5
Fountain Head (Long Meadow) D1
Fowblesburg, 600 ....G1
Frederick, 52,767 ....E2
Friendly, 10,938 ....G4
Friendship, 425 ....H5
Friendsville, 539 ....A3
Frostburg, 7,873 ....C3
Fruitland, 3,774 ....M6
Fullerton, 10,100 ....H2
Fulton, 850 ....G3
Funkstown, 983 ....D1
Gaithersburg, 52,613 ....F3
Galena, 428 ....L2
Galestown, 101 ....M5
Galesville, 600 ....H4
Gamber, 1,000 ....G2
Gapland, 325 ....D2
Garrett Park, 917 ....B6
Garrison, 7,969 ....G2
Germantown, 55,419 ....E3
Gibson, 850 ....J1
Girdletree, 117 ....N7
Glassmanor (See Oxon Hill),
35,355 ....B7, F4
Glenarden, 6,318 ....C7, G4
Glen Arm, 500 ....J2

Glen Burnie, 38,922 ....H3
Glencoe, 450 ....H1
Glen Echo, 242 ....A6
Glenn Dale, 12,609 ....D6
Glenwood, 650 ....F2
Glyndon, 1,200 ....G2
Golden Beach, 2,665 ....H6
Goldsboro, 216 ....L3
Goodwill, 150 ....N7
Goshen, 1,300 ....F3
Graceham, 475 ....E1
Grantsville, 619 ....B3
Grasonville, 2,193 ....K4
Great Mills, 2,600 ....J7
Greenbelt, 21,456 ....C6, G3
Green Haven, 17,415 ....H3
Green Hill, 50 ....L6
Greenmount, 600 ....G1
Greensboro, 1,632 ....L4
Green Valley, 12,262 ....F2
Grove L4
Guilford (see Savage), 12,918 ....G3
Hack Point, 400 ....L2
Hagerstown, 36,687 ....D1
Halethorpe, 150 ....H3
Halfway, 10,065 ....C1
Hampstead, 5,060 ....G1
Hampton, 5,004 ....H2
Hancock, 1,725 ....B1
Harewood Park, 3,400 ....J2
Harrisville (Carroll Co.), 475 ....F2
Harrisville (Cecil Co.), 600 ....K1
Havre de Grace, 11,331 ....K1
Hebbville (Milford Mill), 10,900 ....G2
Hebron, 807 ....M6
Helen, 500 ....H6
Henderson, 118 ....L3
Herald Harbor, 2,313 ....H3
Hereford, 550 ....H1
Hermanville, 1,100 ....J6
Hickman M4
Highland, 800 ....G3
Highland Beach, 109 ....J4
Hillandale, 3,054 ....B6
Hillcrest Heights, 16,359 ....C7
Hillsboro, 163 ....L4
Hillsmere Shores, 2,977 ....J4
Hobbs, 150 ....L4
Hollywood, 650 ....H6
Honga, 225 ....K6
Hopewell, 550 ....L7
Hudson, 275 ....J5
Hughesville, 1,537 ....G5
Huntingtown, 2,436 ....H5
Hurlock, 1,874 ....L5
Hyattstown, 60 ....E2
Hyattsville, 14,733 ....C6, G4
Ijamsville, 225 ....E2
Indian Head, 3,422 ....F5
Indiantown N7
Ingleside, 125 ....L3
Ironshire, 225 ....P6
Jacksonville, 900 ....H1
Jarrettsville, 2,756 ....J1
Jessup, 7,865 ....G3
Jesterville, 225 ....L6
Jonestown, 475 ....L5
Joppatowne, 11,391 ....J2
Keedysville, 482 ....D2
Kemptown F2
Kennedyville, 175 ....L2
Kensington, 1,873 ....B6
Kentland C7
Kentmore Park, 20 ....L2
Kenwood Beach, 600 ....H6
Kettering, 11,008 ....D7, G4
Keymar, 350 ....E1
Keysers Ridge A3
Keysville, 80 ....E1
Kilby Corner K1
Kingston, 175 ....M7
Kingstown, 1,644 ....K3
Kingsville, 4,214 ....J2
Kitzmiller, 302 ....B4
Ladiesburg, 275 ....E1
Lake Linganore (Linganore-
Bartonsville) E2
Lake Shore, 13,065 ....J3
Lakewood M6
Landover, 22,900 ....C7
Landover Hills, 1,534 ....C7
Langley Park, 16,214 ....B6, G4
Lanham (Lanham-Seabrook),
18,190 ....D6
Lansdowne (Lansdowne-Baltimore
Heights), 15,724 ....H3
La Plata, 6,551 ....G5
Largo, 8,408 ....D7
Laurel, 19,960 ....C5, G3
La Vale, 4,613 ....C3
Lawsonia, 1,300 ....L7
Laytonsville, 277 ....F3
Le Gore, 375 ....E1
Leitersburg, 325 ....D1
Leonardtown, 1,896 ....H6
Lewistown (Frederick Co.), 600 ....E1
Lewistown (Talbot Co.), 175 ....L4
Lexington Park, 11,021 ....J6
Libertytown, 275 ....F2
Linchester L5
Linthicum, 7,539 ....H3
Linthicum Hts. H3
Lochearn, 25,269 ....G2
Loch Lynn Heights, 469 ....A4
Londontown (Londontowne),
7,595 ....H4
Long Beach (see Calvert Beach),
2,487 ....J6
Long Green, 1,000 ....J2
Longridge, 40 ....M6
Longview Beach, 275 ....G6
Longwoods, 250 ....K4
Love Point, 30 ....J3

Loveville, 650 ....H6
Lower Marlboro, 450 ....H5
Luke, 80 ....B4
Lusby, 1,666 ....J6
Lutherville (Lutherville-Timonium),
15,814 ....H2
Lynch, 200 ....K2
Maddox, 225 ....G6
Madison, 70 ....K5
Manchester, 3,329 ....G1
Manokin, 100 ....L7
Marbury, 1,200 ....F5
Mardela Springs, 364 ....L6
Marion, 600 ....L7
Marley, 11,200 ....H3
Marlow Heights, 6,059 ....C7, G4
Marlton, 7,798 ....H4
Martins Additions, 875 ....B6
Marydel, 147 ....L3
Maryland City, 6,814 ....D5, G3
Marywood (Bel Air North), 6,000 ....J1
Massey, 200 ....L2
Mattawoman, 3,100 ....G5
Matthews, 100 ....L4
Maugansville, 2,295 ....C1
Mayo, 3,153 ....J4
McDaniel, 425 ....J4
McHenry, 250 ....A3
McKay Beach, 600 ....H7
Mechanicsville, 750 ....H6
Melitota, 225 ....K2
Melrose, 750 ....G1
Melson, 225 ....N6
Middleburg, 300 ....F1
Middle River, 23,958 ....J2
Middletown, 2,668 ....D2
Midland, 473 ....C3
Milford, 26,527 ....C7
Millington, 416 ....L2
Mitchellville, 9,611 ....G4
Monie, 50 ....L7
Montgomery Village, 38,051 ....F3
Montpelier (South Laurel),
11,800 ....C6
Montrose, 4,800 ....A6, F3
Morganton, 275 ....G6
Morganza, 500 ....H6
Morningside, 1,295 ....C7
Mount Aetna, 838 ....D1
Mountaindale, 325 ....E1
Mountain Lake Park, 2,248 ....A4
Mount Airy, 6,425 ....F2
Mount Pleasant, 550 ....F1
Mount Rainier, 8,498 ....C7
Mount Savage, 1,200 ....C3
Mount Vernon, 761 ....M7
Mount Westley, 80 ....N7
Myersville, 1,382 ....D1
Nanjemoy, 300 ....F6
Nanticoke, 275 ....L6
Neavitt, 250 ....J5
Newark, 339 ....N7
Newburg, 300 ....G6
New Carrollton, 12,589 ....C7
Newcomb, 100 ....K4
New Market, 427 ....E2
Newport, 175 ....G6
Newton, 250 ....L4
Newtown, 80 ....K2
New Windsor, 1,303 ....F1
Nikep, 650 ....B3
Normans, 650 ....J4
Norrisville, 300 ....H1
North Beach, 1,880 ....H5
North Brentwood, 469 ....C7
North East, 2,733 ....L1
Oakland (Carroll Co.), 2,100 ....G2
Oakland (Garrett Co.), 1,930 ....A4
Oakville, 50 ....M7
Oakwood, 425 ....K1
Ocean City, 7,173 ....P6
Ocean Pines, 10,496 ....P6
Odenton, 20,534 ....H3
Oldtown, 200 ....D3
Olivet Hill, 250 ....L3
Olney, 31,438 ....F3
Orchard Beach, 4,400 ....H3
Oriole, 200 ....L7
Overlea, 12,148 ....H2
Owings Mills, 20,193 ....H2
Oxford, 771 ....K5
Oxon Hill (Oxon Hill-Glassmanor),
35,355 ....B7
Palmer Park, 7,000 ....C7
Park Hall, 800 ....J7
Parkville, 31,118 ....H2
Parole, 14,031 ....H4
Parsonsburg, 600 ....N6
Parsonville L7
Pasadena, 12,093 ....H3
Perry Hall, 28,705 ....J2
Perryman, 2,461 ....K2
Perryville, 3,672 ....K1
Petersburg, 175 ....L5
Phoenix, 500 ....H1
Pikesville, 29,123 ....H2
Piney Point, 700 ....H7
Pisgah, 175 ....F5
Pittsville, 1,182 ....N6
Pleasant Hills, 2,851 ....J2
Pocomoke City, 4,098 ....M7
Point of Rocks, 850 ....D2
Pomona, 150 ....K3
Pomonkey, 750 ....F5
Poolesville, 5,151 ....E3
Popes Creek, 125 ....G6
Port Deposit, 676 ....K1
Port Tobacco, 15 ....F5
Potomac, 44,822 ....A6, F3
Potomac Heights, 1,154 ....F5
Potomac Park, 1,900 ....C3
Potomac View, 200 ....G6
Powellville, 225 ....N6

Preston, 566 ....L5
Price, 100 ....L3
Prince Frederick, 1,432 ....H5
Princess Anne, 2,313 ....M7
Public Landing, 90 ....N7
Pumphrey, 5,317 ....H3
Pylesville, 350 ....J1
Quantico, 325 ....M6
Queen Anne, 617 ....K4
Queenstown, 616 ....K4
Quince Orchard (North Potomac),
23,044 ....F3
Randallstown, 30,870 ....G2
Randle Cliff Beach, 800 ....H5
Randolph Hills (North Bethesda),
14,300 ....A6
Rawlings, 750 ....C3
Redhouse A4
Redland, 16,998 ....F3
Rehobeth, 50 ....M7
Reids Grove, 80 ....L5
Reisterstown, 22,438 ....G2
Reliance, 20 ....M5
Rhodesdale, 70 ....L5
Ridge, 400 ....J7
Ridgely, 1,352 ....L4
Rising Sun, 1,702 ....K1
Riva, 3,966 ....H4
Riverdale C6
Riverdale Heights (East Riverdale),
750 ....C6
Riviera Beach, 12,695 ....H3
Robbins, 40 ....K6
Roberts, 350 ....L3
Rockdale (northern Baltimore Co.),
16,100 ....G1
Rockdale (southern Baltimore Co.,
Milford Mill), 16,100 ....G2
Rock Hall, 1,396 ....K3
Rock Point, 750 ....G6
Rockville, 47,388 ....A6, F3
Rocky Ridge, 425 ....E1
Romancoke, 800 ....J4
Rosaryville, 12,322 ....G5
Rosedale, 19,199 ....H2
Rose Haven, 1,400 ....H5
Rosemont, 273 ....D2
Rossmoor Leisure World, 7,569 ....B5
Rossville, 11,515 ....J2
Royal Oak, 750 ....K5
Ruthsburg, 125 ....L3
Sabillasville, 350 ....E1
St. Charles, 33,379 ....G5
St. Clement Shores, 800 ....H6
St. George Island, 275 ....H7
St. Inigoes, 650 ....J7
St. Leonard, 536 ....H6
St. Mary's City, 900 ....J7
St. Michaels, 1,193 ....K4
Salisbury, 23,743 ....M6
Sandgates, 550 ....H6
Sandy Spring (see Ashton), 3,437 ....F3
Sandyville, 1,000 ....G1
Sassafras, 100 ....L2
Savage (Savage-Guilford),
12,918 ....G3
Scientists Cliffs, 500 ....H5
Scotland, 300 ....J7
Scotland Beach, 125 ....J7
Seabrook (see Lanham), 18,190 ....D6
Seat Pleasant, 4,885 ....C7, G4
Secretary, 503 ....L5
Selby-on-the-Bay, 3,674 ....H4
Severn, 35,076 ....H3
Severna Park, 28,507 ....H3
Shad Point M6
Shady Side, 5,559 ....H4
Sharpsburg, 691 ....C2
Sharptown, 649 ....M5
Shawsville, 275 ....H1
Shelltown, 40 ....M7
Sherwood, 100 ....J4
Shiloh, 250 ....E1
Shoreham Beach, 1,300 ....H4
Showell, 225 ....P6
Silver Hill (see Suitland), 33,515 ....C7
Silver Spring, 76,540 ....B6, F3
Simpsonville, 4,400 ....G3
Skipton, 200 ....K4
Smallwood, 950 ....G1
Smithsburg, 2,146 ....D1
Smithville (Caroline Co.), 150 ....M4
Smithville (Dorchester Co.), 30 ....J6
Snow Hill, 2,409 ....N7
Solomons, 1,536 ....J6
Somerset, 1,124 ....B6
South Gate, 28,672 ....H3
Sparks, 1,800 ....H1
Spencerville (Cloverly), 2,900 ....G3
Spring Garden Estates (Discovery-
Spring Garden), 2,400 ....E2
Stevensville, 5,880 ....J4
Stevensville South J4
Still Pond, 325 ....K2
Stockton, 143 ....N7
Sudlersville, 391 ....L3
Suitland (Suitland-Silver Hill),
33,515 ....C7, G4
Sunderland, 1,400 ....H5
Sunnybrook, 2,300 ....H1
Sykesville, 4,197 ....G2
Takoma Park, 17,299 ....B6
Tall Timbers, 275 ....H7
Taneytown, 5,128 ....F1
Tantallon, 7,900 ....F5
Taylors Island, 100 ....J6
Taylorsville, 900 ....F2
Temple Hills, 7,792 ....C7
Templeville, 80 ....L3
Thomas Town L4
Thompsontown, 90 ....J4
Thurmont, 5,588 ....E1
Tilghman, 854 ....J5
Tilghmanton, 475 ....D1
Timonium (see Lutherville) H2

Toddville, 150 ....K6
Tolchester Beach, 175 ....K3
Tonytank, 3,500 ....M6
Town Point, 550 ....L2
Towson, 51,793 ....H2
Trappe, 1,146 ....K5
Tunis Mills, 225 ....K4
Tyaskin, 250 ....L6
Union Bridge, 989 ....F1
Union Mills, 300 ....F1
Uniontown, 275 ....F1
Unionville, 175 ....K4
University Park, 2,318 ....C6
Upper Hill, 175 ....L7
Upper Marlboro, 648 ....D7, G4
Urbana, 400 ....E2
Valley Lee, 400 ....H7
Van Bibber J2
Vienna, 280 ....L6
Waldorf, 22,312 ....G5
Walker Mill, 11,104 ....C7
Walkersville, 5,192 ....E2
Warwick, 300 ....L2
Washington Grove, 515 ....F3
Waterview, 100 ....L7
Webster, 1,200 ....K1
Weems Creek H4
Welcome, 175 ....F6
Wenona, 475 ....L7
Wesley, 80 ....K6
West Denton, 325 ....L4
Westernport, 2,104 ....B3
West Friendship, 700 ....G2
West Liberty, 325 ....H1
Westminster, 16,731 ....G1
West Ocean City, 3,311 ....P6
Westover, 100 ....M7
Wetipquin, 100 ....L6
Whaleysville, 250 ....N6
Wheaton, 57,694 ....B6, F3
Whiteburg M7
White Crystal Beach L2
Whiteford, 700 ....J1
White Hall, 300 ....H1
Whitehaven, 70 ....L6
White Marsh, 8,485 ....J2
White Oak, 20,973 ....B6
White Plains, 3,600 ....G5
White Point Beach, 200 ....H7
Whiton, 30 ....N6
Willards, 938 ....N6
Williamsburg, 60 ....L5
Williamsport, 1,868 ....C1
Willows, 900 ....H5
Williston, 425 ....L4
Wittman, 325 ....J4
Woodbine, 425 ....F2
Woodfield, 2,500 ....F3
Woodland Point, 125 ....G6
Woodlawn (Baltimore Co.),
36,079 ....G2
Woodlawn (Cecil Co.), 1,600 ....K1
Woodmore, 6,077 ....D7
Woodsboro, 846 ....E1
Woodyard G4
Woolford, 150 ....K5
Worton, 225 ....K2
Wye Mills, 325 ....K4
Yellow Springs, 1,100 ....E2

Other Features

Aberdeen Proving Ground K2
Allegheny Front, ridge B4
Antietam N.B. C2
Appalachian N.S.T. D1
Assateague, island P7
Assateague Island
National Seashore P7
Assawoman, bay P6
Atlantic, ocean P7
Backbone, mountain A4
Blackwater N.W.R. K6
Bloodsworth, island K7
Catoctin Mt. Park E1
Chesapeake, bay J5
Chesapeake And Ohio Canal
N.H.P. C3, D2
Chester, river K3
Chincoteague, bay N7
Choptank, river K5
Deep Creek, lake A3
Eastern Neck N.W.R. K3
Fishing, bay L6
Fort McHenry N.M. H2
Green Ridge S.F. A1, D3
Kent, island J4
Liberty, reservoir G2
Lookout, point J7
Martin N.W.R. K7
Monocacy N.B. E2
Nanticoke, river L6
Patapsco, river H3
Patuxent N.A.T.C. J6
Patuxent, river D6, H4
Potomac, river B1, B7, G7
Potomac, North Branch, river C4
Prettyboy, reservoir G1
Savage River State Forest B3
Smith, island K7
Susquehanna, river J1
Tangier, sound K7
Thomas Stone N.H.S. F5
Wicomico, river G6
Youghiogheny, river A3

Massachusetts

Capital: Boston
Land Area: 7,838 sq. mi.
20,300 sq. km.
Population: 6,349,097 (2000 Census)
Largest City: Boston, 589,141
Highest Point: Mt. Greylock,
3,487 ft.
1,063 m.
Admitted to Union: February 6, 1788
Nickname: Bay State
State Flower: Mayflower
State Bird: Chickadee

Massachusetts: Map Index

Counties

Barnstable, 222,230 . . . N6
Berkshire, 134,953 . . . A3
Bristol, 534,678 . . . K5
Dukes, 14,987 . . . M7
Essex, 723,419 . . . D6, L2
Franklin, 71,535 . . . C2
Hampden, 456,228 . . . C4
Hampshire, 152,251 . . . C3
Middlesex, 1,465,396 . . . B7, H2
Nantucket, 9,520 . . . P7
Norfolk, 650,308 . . . B8, J4, L3
Plymouth, 472,822 . . . L4
Suffolk, 689,807 . . . C8, L3
Worcester, 750,963 . . . F3

Cities and Towns

Cities and towns that are not labeled on the map are shown with an asterisk. They are included here only for population reference.

Abington, 14,605 . . . L4
Acton, 20,331 . . . J3
Acushnet, 10,161 . . . L6
Adams, 8,809 . . . B2
Agawam, 28,144 . . . D4
Alford, 399 . . . A4
Amesbury, 16,450 . . . L1
Amherst, 34,874 . . . D3
Andover, 31,247 . . . K2
Aquinnah (Gay Head), 344 . . . L7
Arlington, 42,389 . . . C7, K3
Ashburnham, 5,546 . . . G2
Ashby, 2,845 . . . G2
Ashfield, 1,800 . . . C2
Ashland, 14,674 . . . J3
Athol, 11,299 . . . F2
Attleboro, 42,068 . . . J5
Auburn, 15,901 . . . G4
Avon, 4,443 . . . K4
Ayer, 7,287 . . . H2
Barnstable, 47,821 . . . N6
Barre, 5,113 . . . F3
Becket, 1,755 . . . B3
Bedford, 12,595 . . . B6, J3
Belchertown, 12,968 . . . E3
Bellingham, 15,314 . . . J4
Belmont, 24,194 . . . C7
Berkley, 5,749 . . . K5
Berlin, 2,380 . . . H3
Bernardston, 2,155 . . . D2
Beverly, 39,862 . . . L2
Billerica, 38,981 . . . B6, J2
Blackstone, 8,804 . . . H4
Blandford, 1,214 . . . C4
Bolton, 4,148 . . . H3
Boston, 589,141 . . . C7, L3
Bourne, 18,721 . . . M6
Boxborough, 4,868 . . . H2
Boxford, 7,921 . . . L2
Boylston, 4,008 . . . *
Braintree, 33,828 . . . K4
Brewster, 10,094 . . . P5
Bridgewater, 25,185 . . . L5
Brimfield, 3,339 . . . F4
Brockton, 94,304 . . . K4
Brookfield, 3,051 . . . F4
Brookline, 57,107 . . . C8, K3
Buckland, 1,991 . . . C2
Burlington, 22,876 . . . B6, K2
Cambridge, 101,355 . . . C7, K3
Canton, 20,775 . . . K4
Carlisle, 4,717 . . . J2
Carver, 11,163 . . . L5
Charlemont, 1,358 . . . C2
Charlton, 11,263 . . . G4
Chatham, 6,625 . . . Q6
Chelmsford, 33,858 . . . J2
Chelsea, 35,080 . . . D7
Cheshire, 3,401 . . . B2
Chester, 1,308 . . . C3
Chesterfield, 1,201 . . . C3
Chicopee, 54,653 . . . D4
Chilmark, 843 . . . M7
Clarksburg, 1,686 . . . B2
Clinton, 13,435 . . . H3
Cohasset, 7,261 . . . L4
Colrain, 1,813 . . . D2
Concord, 16,993 . . . J3
Conway, 1,809 . . . D2
Cummington, 978 . . . C3
Dalton, 6,892 . . . B3
Danvers, 25,212 . . . D6, L2
Dartmouth, 30,666 . . . K6
Dedham, 23,464 . . . K4
Deerfield, 4,750 . . . D2
Dennis, 15,973 . . . P6
Dighton, 6,175 . . . K5
Douglas, 7,045 . . . H4
Dover, 5,558 . . . J4
Dracut, 28,562 . . . J2
Dudley, 10,036 . . . G4
Dunstable, 2,829 . . . J2
Duxbury, 14,248 . . . M4
East Bridgewater, 12,974 . . . L4
East Brookfield, 2,097 . . . F4
Eastham, 5,453 . . . Q5
Easthampton, 15,994 . . . D3
East Longmeadow, 14,100 . . . D4
Easton, 22,299 . . . *
Edgartown, 3,779 . . . M7
Egremont, 1,345 . . . *
Erving, 1,467 . . . E2
Essex, 3,267 . . . L2
Everett, 38,037 . . . D7, K3
Fairhaven, 16,159 . . . L6
Fall River, 91,938 . . . K6
Falmouth, 32,660 . . . M6
Fitchburg, 39,102 . . . G2
Florida, 676 . . . B2
Foxboro, 16,246 . . . K4
Framingham, 66,910 . . . J3
Franklin, 29,560 . . . J4
Freetown, 8,472 . . . *
Gardner, 20,770 . . . G2
Georgetown, 7,377 . . . L2
Gill, 1,363 . . . E2
Gloucester, 30,273 . . . M2
Goshen, 921 . . . C3
Gosnold, 86 . . . *
Grafton, 14,894 . . . H4
Granby, 6,132 . . . D3
Granville, 1,521 . . . C4
Great Barrington, 7,527 . . . A4
Greenfield, 18,168 . . . D2
Groton, 9,547 . . . H2
Groveland, 6,038 . . . K1
Hadley, 4,793 . . . D3
Halifax, 7,500 . . . L5
Hamilton, 8,315 . . . L2
Hampden, 5,171 . . . E4
Hancock, 721 . . . A2
Hanover, 13,164 . . . L4
Hanson, 9,495 . . . L4
Hardwick, 2,622 . . . F3
Harvard, 5,981 . . . H2
Harwich, 12,386 . . . P6
Hatfield, 3,249 . . . D3
Haverhill, 58,969 . . . K1
Hawley, 336 . . . C2
Heath, 805 . . . C2
Hingham, 19,882 . . . L3
Hinsdale, 1,872 . . . B3
Holbrook, 10,785 . . . K4
Holden, 15,621 . . . G3
Holland, 2,407 . . . F4
Holliston, 13,801 . . . J4
Holyoke, 39,838 . . . D4
Hopedale, 5,907 . . . H4
Hopkinton, 13,346 . . . H4
Hubbardston, 3,909 . . . G3
Hudson, 18,113 . . . H3
Hull, 11,050 . . . L3
Huntington, 2,174 . . . C4
Ipswich, 12,987 . . . L2
Kingston, 11,780 . . . M5
Lakeville, 9,821 . . . L5
Lancaster, 7,380 . . . H3
Lanesboro, 2,990 . . . B2
Lawrence, 72,043 . . . K2
Lee, 5,985 . . . B3
Leicester, 10,471 . . . G3
Lenox, 5,077 . . . A3
Leominster, 41,303 . . . G2
Leverett, 1,663 . . . D3
Lexington, 30,355 . . . B7, K3
Leyden, 772 . . . D2
Lincoln, 8,056 . . . B7, J3
Littleton, 8,184 . . . H2
Longmeadow, 15,633 . . . D4
Lowell, 105,167 . . . J2
Ludlow, 21,209 . . . E4
Lunenburg, 9,401 . . . H2
Lynn, 89,050 . . . D7, L3
Lynnfield, 11,542 . . . D6, K2
Malden, 56,340 . . . C7, K3
Manchester-by-the-Sea (Manchester), 5,228 . . . L2
Mansfield, 22,414 . . . K4
Marblehead, 20,377 . . . L3
Marion, 5,123 . . . L6
Marlborough, 36,255 . . . H3
Marshfield, 24,324 . . . M4
Mashpee, 12,946 . . . N6
Mattapoisett, 6,268 . . . L6
Maynard, 10,433 . . . J3
Medfield, 12,273 . . . J4
Medford, 55,765 . . . C7, K3
Medway, 12,448 . . . J4
Melrose, 27,134 . . . C7, K3
Mendon, 5,286 . . . H4
Merrimac, 6,138 . . . K1
Methuen, 43,789 . . . K2
Middleboro, 19,941 . . . L5
Middlefield, 542 . . . B3
Middleton, 7,744 . . . D5, K2
Milford, 26,799 . . . H4
Millbury, 12,784 . . . G4
Millis, 7,902 . . . J4
Millville, 2,724 . . . H4
Milton, 26,062 . . . K3
Monroe, 93 . . . *
Monson, 8,359 . . . E4
Montague, 8,489 . . . D2
Monterey, 934 . . . B4
Montgomery, 654 . . . C4
Mount Washington, 130 . . . A4
Nahant, 3,632 . . . L3
Nantucket, 9,520 . . . P7
Natick, 32,170 . . . J3
Needham, 28,911 . . . K3
New Ashford, 247 . . . B2
New Bedford, 93,768 . . . L6
New Braintree, 927 . . . F3
Newbury, 6,717 . . . *
Newburyport, 17,189 . . . L1
New Marlborough, 1,494 . . . B4
New Salem, 929 . . . E2
Newton, 83,829 . . . B7, K3
Norfolk, 10,460 . . . J4
North Adams, 14,681 . . . B2
Northampton, 28,978 . . . D3
North Andover, 27,202 . . . K2
North Attleboro, 27,143 . . . J5
Northborough, 14,013 . . . H3
Northbridge, 13,182 . . . H4
North Brookfield, 4,683 . . . F3
Northfield, 2,951 . . . E2
North Reading, 13,837 . . . C6, K2
Norton, 18,036 . . . K5
Norwell, 9,765 . . . L4
Norwood, 28,587 . . . K4
Oak Bluffs, 3,713 . . . M7
Oakham, 1,673 . . . F3
Orange, 7,518 . . . E2
Orleans, 6,341 . . . Q5
Otis, 1,365 . . . B4
Oxford, 13,352 . . . G4
Palmer, 12,497 . . . E4
Paxton, 4,386 . . . G3
Peabody, 48,129 . . . E6, L2
Pelham, 1,403 . . . E3
Pembroke, 16,927 . . . L4
Pepperell, 11,142 . . . H2
Peru, 821 . . . B3
Petersham, 1,180 . . . F3
Phillipston, 1,621 . . . F2
Pittsfield, 45,793 . . . B3
Plainfield, 589 . . . C2
Plainville, 7,683 . . . J4
Plymouth, 51,701 . . . M5
Plympton, 2,637 . . . L5
Princeton, 3,353 . . . G3
Provincetown, 3,431 . . . P4
Quincy, 88,025 . . . K3
Randolph, 30,963 . . . K4
Raynham, 11,739 . . . K5
Reading, 23,708 . . . C6, K2
Rehoboth, 10,172 . . . K5
Revere, 47,283 . . . D7, K3
Richmond, 1,604 . . . A3
Rochester, 4,581 . . . L6
Rockland, 17,670 . . . L4
Rockport, 7,767 . . . M2
Rowe, 351 . . . C2
Rowley, 5,500 . . . L2
Royalston, 1,254 . . . F2
Russell, 1,657 . . . C4
Rutland, 6,353 . . . G3
Salem, 40,407 . . . L2
Salisbury, 7,827 . . . L1
Sandisfield, 824 . . . B4
Sandwich, 20,136 . . . N5
Saugus, 26,078 . . . D6, K3
Savoy, 705 . . . B2
Scituate, 17,863 . . . L4
Seekonk, 13,425 . . . J5
Sharon, 17,408 . . . K4
Sheffield, 3,335 . . . A4
Shelburne, 2,058 . . . D2
Sherborn, 4,200 . . . J3
Shirley, 6,373 . . . H2
Shrewsbury, 31,640 . . . H3
Shutesbury, 1,810 . . . E3
Somerset, 18,234 . . . K5
Somerville, 77,478 . . . C7, K3
Southampton, 5,387 . . . D4
Southborough, 8,781 . . . H3
Southbridge, 17,214 . . . F4
South Hadley, 17,196 . . . D3
Southwick, 8,835 . . . C4
Spencer, 11,691 . . . G3
Springfield, 152,082 . . . D4
Sterling, 7,257 . . . G3
Stockbridge, 2,276 . . . A3
Stoneham, 22,219 . . . C6, K3
Stoughton, 27,149 . . . K4
Stow, 5,902 . . . H3
Sturbridge, 7,837 . . . F4
Sudbury, 16,841 . . . J3
Sunderland, 3,777 . . . D3
Sutton, 8,250 . . . G4
Swampscott, 14,412 . . . L3
Swansea, 15,901 . . . K5
Taunton, 55,976 . . . K5
Templeton, 6,799 . . . F2
Tewksbury, 28,851 . . . B5, K2
Tisbury, 3,755 . . . *
Tolland, 426 . . . B4
Topsfield, 6,141 . . . L2
Townsend, 9,198 . . . H2
Truro, 2,087 . . . P5
Tyngsborough, 11,081 . . . J2
Tyringham, 350 . . . B4
Upton, 5,642 . . . H4
Uxbridge, 11,156 . . . H4
Wakefield, 24,804 . . . C6, K2
Wales, 1,737 . . . F4
Walpole, 22,824 . . . J4
Waltham, 59,226 . . . B7, J3
Ware, 9,707 . . . F3
Wareham, 20,335 . . . L5, M5
Warren, 4,776 . . . F4
Warwick, 750 . . . E2
Washington, 544 . . . B3
Watertown, 32,986 . . . C7, K3
Wayland, 13,100 . . . J3
Webster, 16,415 . . . G4
Wellesley, 26,613 . . . B8, J3
Wellfleet, 2,749 . . . P5
Wendell, 986 . . . E2
Wenham, 4,440 . . . L2
Westborough, 17,997 . . . H3
West Boylston, 7,481 . . . G3
West Bridgewater, 6,634 . . . K4
West Brookfield, 3,804 . . . F4
Westfield, 40,072 . . . D4
Westford, 20,754 . . . J2
Westhampton, 1,468 . . . C3
Westminster, 6,907 . . . G2
West Newbury, 4,149 . . . K1
Weston, 11,469 . . . B7, J3
Westport, 14,183 . . . K6
West Springfield, 27,899 . . . D4
West Stockbridge, 1,416 . . . A3
West Tisbury, 2,467 . . . M7
Westwood, 14,117 . . . K4
Weymouth, 53,988 . . . L4
Whately, 1,573 . . . D3
Whitman, 13,882 . . . L4
Wilbraham, 13,473 . . . E4
Williamsburg, 2,427 . . . D3
Williamstown, 8,424 . . . B2
Wilmington, 21,363 . . . C6, K2
Winchendon, 9,611 . . . F2
Winchester, 20,810 . . . C7, K3
Windsor, 875 . . . B2
Winthrop, 18,303 . . . D7, L3
Woburn, 37,258 . . . C6, K3
Worcester, 172,648 . . . G3
Worthington, 1,270 . . . *
Wrentham, 10,554 . . . J4
Yarmouth, 24,807 . . . P6

Other Places

The city or town containing each entry is shown in italics. See the "Cities and Towns" listing for total city/town population.

Accord (*Hingham*), 2,300 . . . L4
Acoaxet (*Westport*), 175 . . . K6
Adamsville (*Colrain*), 200 . . . D2
Ashdod (*Duxbury*) . . . L4
Ashley Falls (*Sheffield*), 450 . . . A4
Assinippi (*Hanover and Norwell*), 2,700 . . . L4
Assonet (*Freetown*), 1,200 . . . K5
Baldwinville (*Templeton*), 1,852 . . . F2
Ballardvale (*Andover*), 3,500 . . . K2
Bancroft (*Middlefield*), 125 . . . B3
Barre Plains (*Barre*), 1,200 . . . F3
Becket Center (*Becket*), 100 . . . B3
Berkshire (*Lanesborough*), 400 . . . B2
Bliss Corner (*Dartmouth*), 5,466 . . . L6
Bondsville (*Belchertown and Palmer*), 1,876 . . . E4
Brant Rock (*Marshfield*), 5,100 . . . M4
Briarwood Beach (*Wareham*) . . . M6
Briggsville (*Clarksburg*), 750 . . . B2
Bryantville (*Hanson and Pembroke*), 2,600 . . . L4
Buzzards Bay (*Bourne*), 3,549 . . . M5
Byfield (*Newbury*), 850 . . . L1
Cahoon Hollow (*Wellfleet*) . . . Q5
Cedarville (*Plymouth*) . . . M5
Centerville (*Barnstable*), 9,200 . . . N6
Central Village (*Westport*), 600 . . . K6
Chaffinville (*Holden*), 3,100 . . . G3
Charlton City (*Charlton*), 1,400 . . . G4
Charlton Depot (*Charlton*), 1,200 . . . G4
Chartley (*Norton*), 1,600 . . . K5
Chelmsford Center (*Chelmsford, Tyngsboro and Westford*) . . . J2
Cheshire Harbor (*Cheshire*), 450 . . . B2
Clayton (*New Marlboro*), 50 . . . A4
Clifford (*New Bedford*) . . . L6
Cochituate (*Natick and Wayland*), 6,768 . . . J3
Cold Spring (*Otis*), 30 . . . B4
Cordaville (*Southborough*), 2,515 . . . H3
Cotuit (*Barnstable*), 2,400 . . . N6
Dennis Port (*Dennis*), 3,612 . . . P6
Drury (*Florida*), 100 . . . C2
Dwight (*Belchertown*), 550 . . . E3
East Blackstone (*Blackstone*), 1,600 . . . H4
East Brewster (*Brewster*), 850 . . . P5
East Dennis (*Dennis*), 3,299 . . . P6
East Douglas (*Douglas*), 2,319 . . . H4
East Falmouth (*Falmouth*), 6,615 . . . M6
East Freetown (*Freetown*), 1,200 . . . L5
East Harwich (*Harwich*), 4,744 . . . P6
East Leverett (*Leverett*), 275 . . . E3
East Marion (*Marion*), 550 . . . L6
East Northfield (*Northfield*), 150 . . . E2
East Orleans (*Orleans*), 1,800 . . . Q5
East Otis (*Otis*), 200 . . . B4
East Pepperell (*Pepperell*), 2,034 . . . H2
East Princeton (*Princeton*), 300 . . . G3
East Sandwich (*Sandwich*), 3,720 . . . N6
East Templeton (*Templeton*), 1,200 . . . F2
East Wareham (*Wareham*), 1,700 . . . M5
East Windsor (*Windsor*), 80 . . . C3
Farley (*Erving*), 200 . . . E2
Feeding Hills (*Agawam*) . . . D4
Fiskdale (*Sturbridge*), 2,156 . . . F4
Five Corners (*Easton*), 2,100 . . . K4
Forestdale (*Sandwich*), 3,992 . . . N6
Forge Village (*Westford*), 2,300 . . . H2
Gilbertville (*Hardwick*), 1,000 . . . F3
Glendale (*Stockbridge*), 250 . . . A3
Glen Mills (*Rowley*), 750 . . . L1
Greenbush (*Scituate*), 550 . . . L4
Green Harbor (*Marshfield*), 2,397 . . . M4
Griswoldville (*Colrain*), 150 . . . D2
Hartsville (*New Marlborough*), 150 . . . B4
Harwich Port (*Harwich*), 1,809 . . . P6
Haydenville (*Williamsburg*), 700 . . . D3
Hixville (*Dartmouth*), 500 . . . K6
Hortonville (*Swansea*), 850 . . . K5
Housatonic (*Great Barrington*), 1,335 . . . A3
Humarock (*Scituate*), 2,000 . . . M4
Hyannis (*Barnstable*), 14,100 . . . N6
Hyannis Port (*Barnstable*), 3,100 . . . N6
Interlaken (*Stockbridge*), 225 . . . A3
Jefferson (*Holden*), 1,600 . . . G3
Katama (*Edgartown*), 125 . . . M7
Knights Corner (*Pelham*), 50 . . . E3
Lake Pleasant (*Montague*), 350 . . . D2
Lakeside (*Westport*), 300 . . . K6
Lenox Dale (*Lenox*), 1,100 . . . B3
Lithia (*Goshen*), 60 . . . C3
Littleton Common (*Littleton*), 2,816 . . . J2
Locks Village (*Shutesbury*), 225 . . . E2
Long Pond (*Plymouth*), 1,500 . . . M5
Ludlow City (*Ludlow*), 375 . . . E4
Madaket (*Nantucket*), 125 . . . P7
Manchaug (*Sutton*), 850 . . . H4
Manomet (*Plymouth*), 2,900 . . . M5
Marshfield Hills (*Marshfield*), 2,369 . . . M4
Marstons Mills (*Barnstable*), 8,000 . . . N6
Matfield (*West Bridgewater*) . . . L4
Menemsha (*Chilmark*), 100 . . . M7
Millers Falls (*Erving and Montague*), 1,072 . . . E2
Mill River (*New Marlborough*), 225 . . . A4
Minot (*Scituate*), 1,100 . . . L4
Monponsett (*Halifax and Hanson*), 1,700 . . . L4
Monroe Bridge (*Monroe*), 60 . . . C2
Montville (*Sandisfield*), 60 . . . B4
Monument Beach (*Bourne*), 2,438 . . . M6
Moody Corner (*Granby and South Hadley*) . . . D3
Morningdale (*Boylston*), 2,500 . . . G3
Myricks (*Berkley*), 600 . . . K5
Nameloc Heights (*Plymouth*), 1,500 . . . M5
Nashaquitsa (*Chilmark*), 30 . . . L7
New Boston (*Sandisfield*), 200 . . . B4
Newbury Old Town (*Newbury*), 475 . . . L1
Nonquitt (*Dartmouth*), 350 . . . L6
North Acton (*Acton*), 3,000 . . . J2
North Amherst (*Amherst*), 6,019 . . . D3
North Billerica (*Billerica*), 5,200 . . . B6, J2
North Carver (*Carver*), 700 . . . L5
North Chatham (*Chatham*), 750 . . . Q6
North Chelmsford (*Chelmsford*), 4,900 . . . J2
North Cohasset (*Cohasset*), 1,600 . . . L3
North Dartmouth (*Dartmouth*), 2,200 . . . L6
North Dighton (*Dighton*), 1,400 . . . K5
North Eastham (*Eastham*), 1,915 . . . Q5
North Easton (*Easton*), 3,700 . . . K4
North Egremont (*Egremont*), 200 . . . A4
North Falmouth (*Falmouth*), 3,355 . . . M6
North Grafton (*Grafton*), 3,600 . . . H4
North Harwich (*Harwich*) . . . P6
North Hatfield (*Hatfield*), 550 . . . D3
North Leverett (*Leverett*), 250 . . . E2
North Middleboro (*Middleboro*), 850 . . . L5
North New Salem (*New Salem*), 275 . . . E2
North Orange (*Orange*), 200 . . . E2
North Otis (*Otis*), 40 . . . B4
North Oxford (*Oxford*), 1,200 . . . G4
North Pembroke (*Pembroke*), 2,913 . . . L4
North Plymouth (*Plymouth*), 3,593 . . . M5
North Plympton (*Plympton*), 475 . . . L5
North Scituate (*Scituate*), 5,065 . . . L4
North Seekonk (*Seekonk*), 2,598 . . . J5
North Swansea (*Swansea*), 1,100 . . . J5
North Tisbury (*West Tisbury*), 200 . . . M7
North Truro (*Truro*), 550 . . . P4
North Uxbridge (*Uxbridge*), 4,200 . . . H4
Northville (*East Bridgewater*), 2,400 . . . L4
Norwich (*Huntington*), 350 . . . C3
Nutting Lake (*Billerica*), 5,700 . . . B6, J2
Oakdale (*West Boylston*), 1,100 . . . G3
Ocean Bluff (*Marshfield*), 5,100 . . . M4
Ocean Grove (*Swansea*), 3,012 . . . K6
Onset (*Wareham*), 1,292 . . . M6
Osterville (*Barnstable*), 2,900 . . . N6
Otter River (*Templeton*), 850 . . . F2
Pigeon Cove (*Rockport*), 1,700 . . . M2
Pinehurst (*Billerica*), 6,941 . . . B6, K2
Pleasant Lake (*Harwich*), 800 . . . P6
Pocasset (*Bourne*), 2,671 . . . M6
Polpis (*Nantucket*), 90 . . . P7
Popponesset Beach (*Mashpee*), 310 . . . N6
Princeton Sta. (*Princeton*), 225 . . . G3
Quidnet (*Nantucket*), 10 . . . Q7
Raynham Center (*Raynham*), 3,633 . . . K5
Ringville (*Worthington*), 100 . . . C3
Risingdale (*Great Barrington*), 225 . . . A4
Rochdale (*Leicester*), 1,400 . . . G4
Rock (*Middleboro*), 850 . . . L5
Sagamore (*Bourne*), 3,544 . . . M5
Sagamore Beach (*Bourne*), 1,200 . . . M5
Salisbury Beach (*Salisbury*), 1,300 . . . L1
Sand Hills (*Scituate*), 2,400 . . . M4
Santuit (*Cotuit*), 375 . . . N6
Scotland (*Bridgewater*), 1,900 . . . K5
Shattuckville (*Colrain*), 225 . . . D2
Shelburne Falls (*Buckland and Shelburne*), 1,951 . . . D2
Sheldonville (*Wrentham*), 500 . . . J4
Siasconset (*Nantucket*), 275 . . . Q7
Silver Beach (*Falmouth*), 500 . . . M6
Silver Lake (*Kingston and Plympton*), 1,000 . . . L4
Silver Lake (*Tewksbury and Wilmington*), 3,300 . . . B6
Sippewisset (*Falmouth*), 950 . . . M6
Smith Mills (*Dartmouth*), 4,432 . . . L6
South Acton (*Acton*), 2,700 . . . J3
South Amherst (*Amherst*), 5,039 . . . D3
South Ashburnham (*Ashburnham*), 1,013 . . . G2
South Berlin (*Berlin*), 800 . . . H3
South Bridgewater (*Bridgewater*), 2,600 . . . L5
South Carver (*Carver*), 375 . . . M5
South Chatham (*Chatham*), 800 . . . P6
South Dartmouth (*Dartmouth*), 1,900 . . . L6
South Deerfield (*Deerfield*), 1,868 . . . D3
South Dennis (*Dennis*), 3,679 . . . P6
South Duxbury (*Duxbury*), 3,062 . . . M4
South Easton (*Easton*), 3,600 . . . K4
South Egremont (*Egremont*), 450 . . . A4
Southfield (*New Marlborough*), 100 . . . B4
South Hadley Falls (*South Hadley*), 4,300 . . . D4
South Lancaster (*Lancaster*), 1,742 . . . H3
South Middleboro (*Middleboro*), 750 . . . L5
South Orleans (*Orleans*), 1,100 . . . Q5
South Royalston (*Royalston*), 300 . . . F2
South Sandisfield (*Sandisfield*), 20 . . . B4
South Truro (*Truro*) . . . P5
South Walpole (*Walpole*), 1,900 . . . J4
South Wareham (*Wareham*), 375 . . . L5
South Wellfleet (*Wellfleet*), 500 . . . P5
South Westport (*Westport*), 600 . . . K6
South Weymouth (*Weymouth*), 11,100 . . . L4
South Worthington (*Worthington*), 80 . . . C3
South Yarmouth (*Yarmouth*), 11,603 . . . P6
Standish (*Taunton*), 425 . . . L4
Stanley (*Bridgewater*) . . . L4
Still River (*Harvard*), 400 . . . H3
Surfside (*Nantucket*), 175 . . . P8
Swifts Beach (*Wareham*), 2,700 . . . M6
Teaticket (*Falmouth*), 1,907 . . . M6
Texas (*Oxford*), 1,300 . . . G4
Three Rivers (*Palmer*), 2,939 . . . E4
Townsend Harbor (*Townsend*), 1,700 . . . H2
Tully (*Orange*), 275 . . . E2
Turners Falls (*Montague*), 4,441 . . . D2
Vallersville (*Plymouth*), 2,000 . . . M5

Vineyard Haven (Tisbury), 2,048 . . . . .M7
Wades Corner (Taunton), 150 . . . . .K5
Wakeby (Sandwich), 1,600 . . . . .N6
Warrentown (Middleboro), 400 . . . . . . .L5
Waterville (Winchendon), 950 . . . . . . .F2
Watson (Ashfield), 80 . . . . .C2
Wauwinet (Nantucket), 10 . . . . .P7
West Barnstable (Barnstable), 1,500 . . . .N6
West Becket (Becket), 80 . . . . .B3
West Boxford (Boxford), 1,200 . . . . . .K2
West Brimfield (Brimfield), 125 . . . . . .E4
West Chatham (Chatham), 1,446 . . . . .Q6
West Chelmsford (Chelmsford), 1,400 . . .J2
West Chesterfield (Chesterfield), 100 . . .C3
West Concord (Concord), 5,632 . . . . .J3
West Cummington (Cummington), 125 . . .C3
West Dennis (Dennis), 2,570 . . . . . . .P6
West Falmouth (Falmouth), 1,867 . . . .M6
West Granville (Granville), 20 . . . . . .C4
West Groton (Groton), 750 . . . . .H2
West Harwich (Harwich), 750 . . . . . . .P6
West Hawley (Hawley), 50 . . . . .C2
West Medway (Medway), 3,500 . . . . . .J4
West Northfield (Northfield) E2
West Otis (Otis), 125 . . . . .B4
West Pelham (Pelham), 1,300 . . . . . . .E3
Westport Point (Westport), 350 . . . . . .K6
West Royalston (Royalston), 40 . . . . . .F2
West Sterling (Sterling), 450 . . . . . . .G3
West Sutton (Sutton), 350 . . . . .G4
West Townsend (Townsend), 1,300 . . . .H2
West Upton (Upton), 2,326 . . . . .H4
West Wareham (Wareham), 1,908 . . . .L5
West Warren (Warren), 1,100 . . . . . . .F4
West Yarmouth (Yarmouth), 6,460 . . . .P6
Wheelwright (Hardwick), 425 . . . . . . .F3
White Horse Beach (Plymouth), 2,300 . . .M5
White Island Shores (Wareham), 2,133 . .M5
Whitinsville (Northbridge), 6,340 . . . . .H4
Williamsville (Hubbardston), 225 . . . . .F3
Winnecunnet (Norton), 750 . . . . .K5
Woods Hole (Falmouth), 925 . . . . . . .M6
Woodville (Hopkinton), 500 . . . . .H4
Worthington Center (Worthington) C3
Worthington Corners (Worthington), 250 . .C3
Yarmouth Port (Yarmouth), 5,395 . . . . .P6
Zoar (Charlemont), 175 . . . . .C2

Other Features

Adams N.H.P. L4
Ann, cape M2
Appalachian N.S.T. A4, A6
Assawompset, pond L5
Atlantic, ocean J8, N2
Barkhamsted, reservoir C5
Berkshire, hills B4
Block, island H8
Block Island, sound G8
Block Island N.W.R. H8
Boston, harbor D7
Boston Harbor Islands N.R.A. D8
Boston Natl. Hist. Park D7
Broad, sound D7
Buzzards, bay M6
Cape Cod, bay N5
Cape Cod, canal M6
Cape Cod National Seashore P5
Chicopee, river D4
Cobble Mt. Res. C4
Cod, cape P4
Connecticut, river E2
Elizabeth, islands M7
Everett Tpk. H1
Fishers, island G7
Frissell, mountain A4
Gardiners, island F8
Great, point P7
Great Meadows N.W.R. J3
Great Quittacus, pond L5
Green, mountains B1
Greylock, mountain B2
Harriman, reservoir C1
Housatonic, river A4, A5
John F. Kennedy Natl. Hist. Site C8
Lake Candlewood, lake A6
Long, pond L5
Longfellow Natl. Hist. Site C7
Long Island, sound C8
Lowell N.H.P. J2
Maine, gulf M1
Martha's Vineyard M7
Mass. Tpk. C4
Merrimack, river L1
Minute Man N.H.P. J3
Monomoy, island P6
Monomoy, point P6
Monomoy N.W.R. Q6
Montauk, point G8
Muskeget, channel N7
Nantucket, island P7
Nantucket, sound N6
Nantucket N.W.R. P7
Narragansett, bay J6
New Bedford Whaling N.H.P. L6
Ninigret N.W.R. H7
Otis, reservoir B4
Parker River N.W.R. L1
Plum, island F8
Quabbin, reservoir F3
Quinebaug, river G6
Rhode Island, sound J7
Sachuest Point N.W.R. J7
Salem Maritime N.H.S. L2
Saugus Iron Works N.H.S D6
Scituate, reservoir H5
Springfield Armory N.H.S. D4
Swift, river E4
Taconic, mountains A3
Thacher Island N.W.R. M2
Thames, river F7
Trustom Pond N.W.R. H7
Vineyard, sound L7
Wachusett, mountain G3
Wachusett, reservoir H3
Watuppa, pond K6
Weir Farm N.H.S. A7

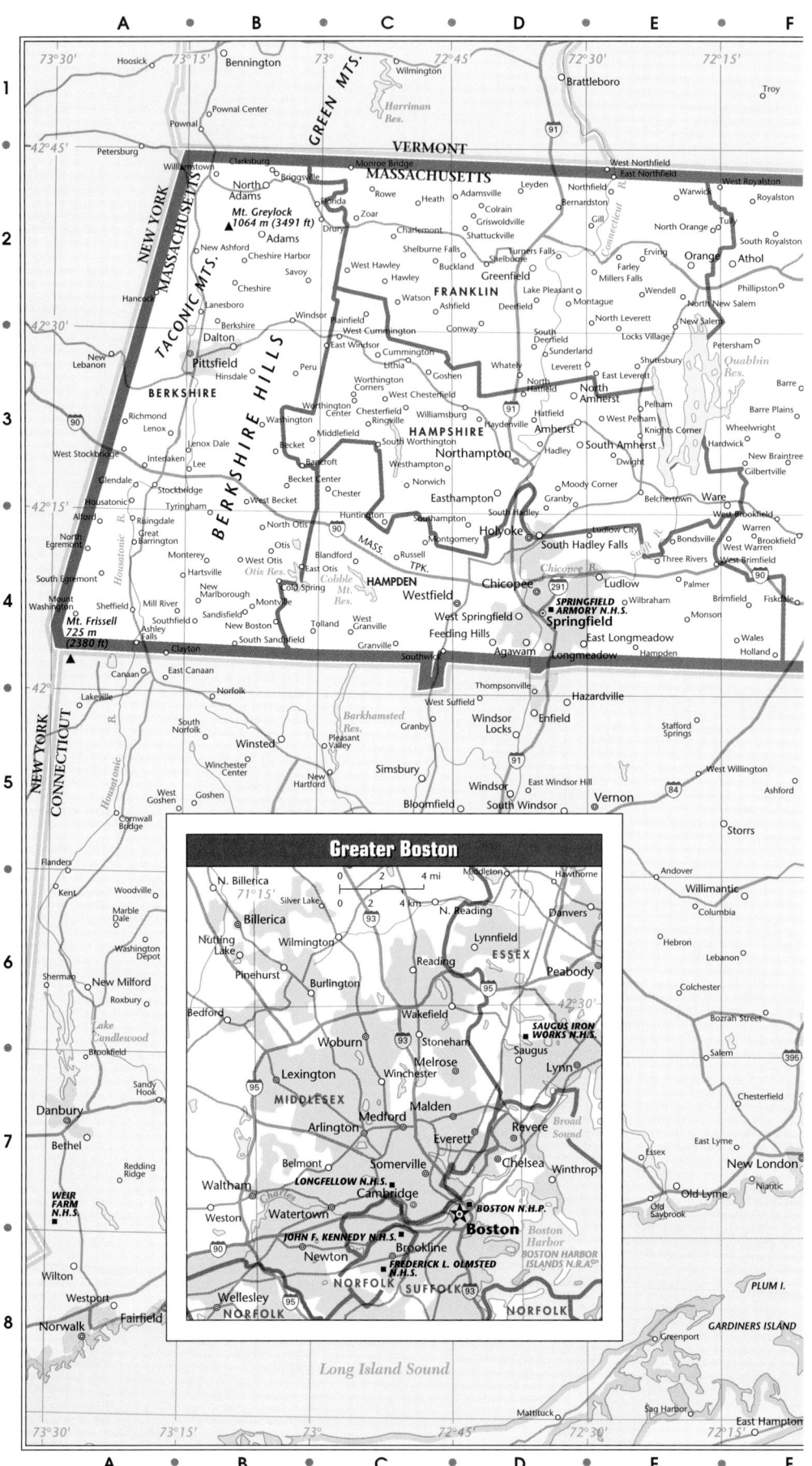

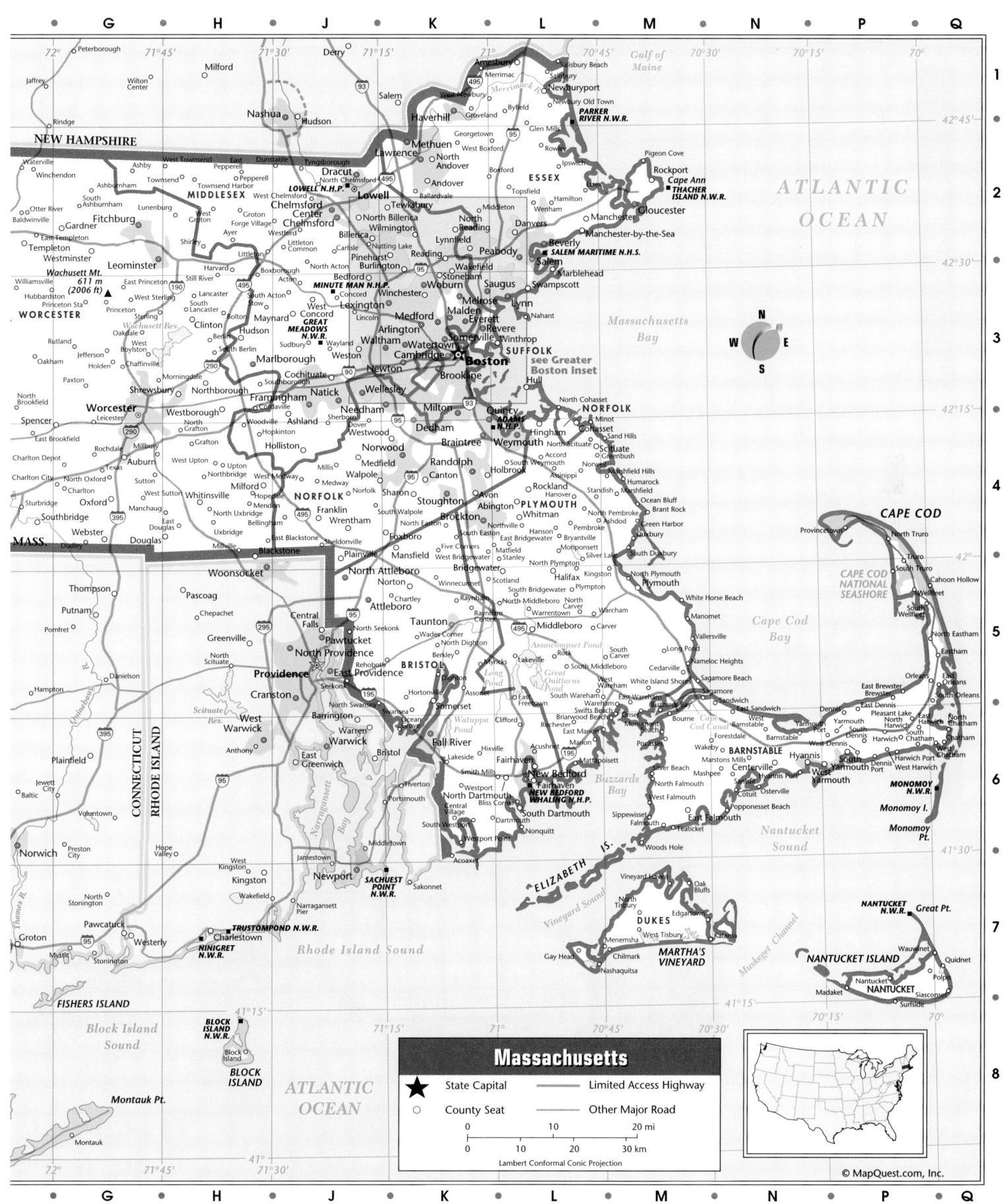

Massachusetts

★ State Capital
○ County Seat
━━ Limited Access Highway
── Other Major Road

0   10   20 mi
0   10   20   30 km
Lambert Conformal Conic Projection

© MapQuest.com, Inc.

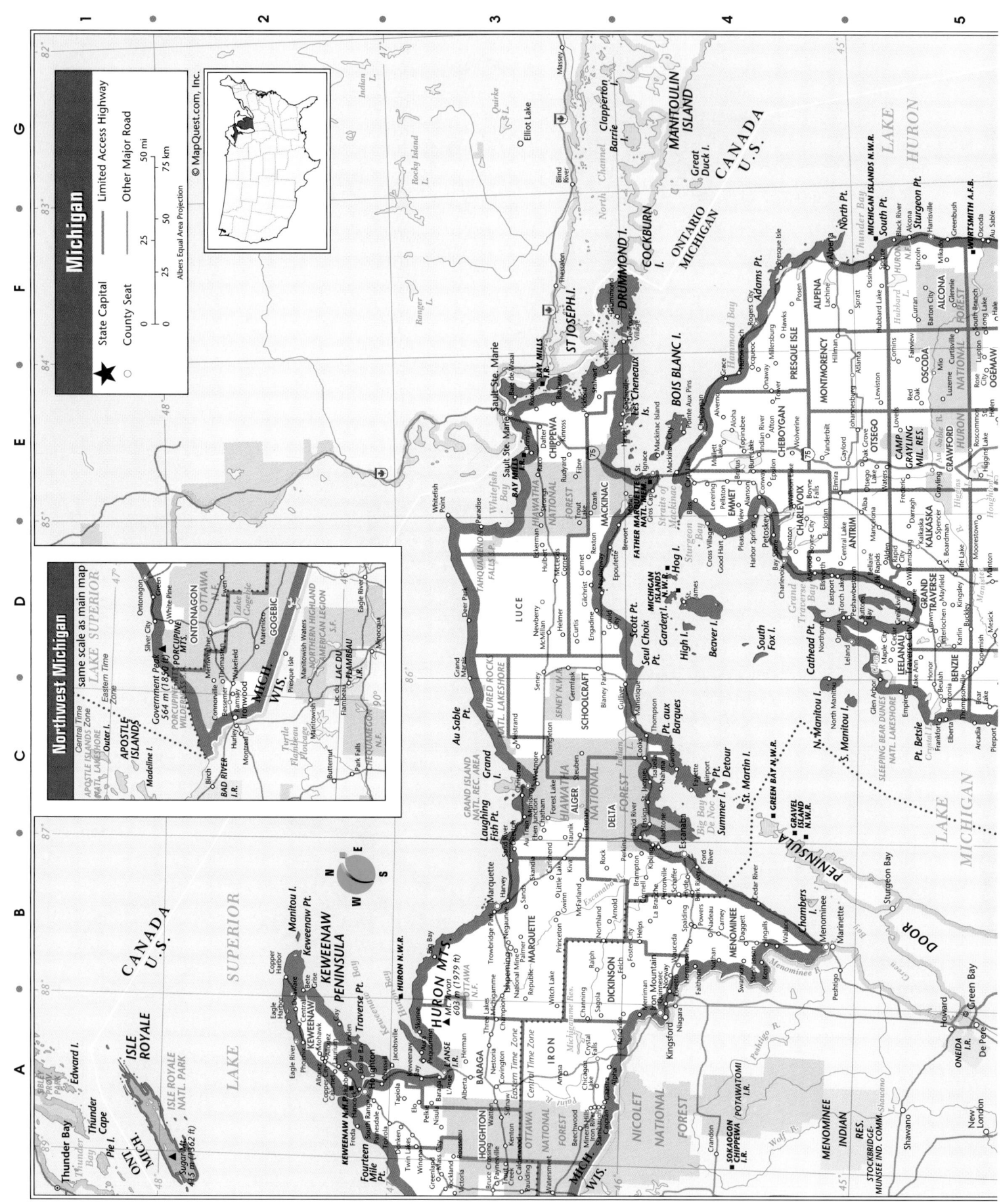

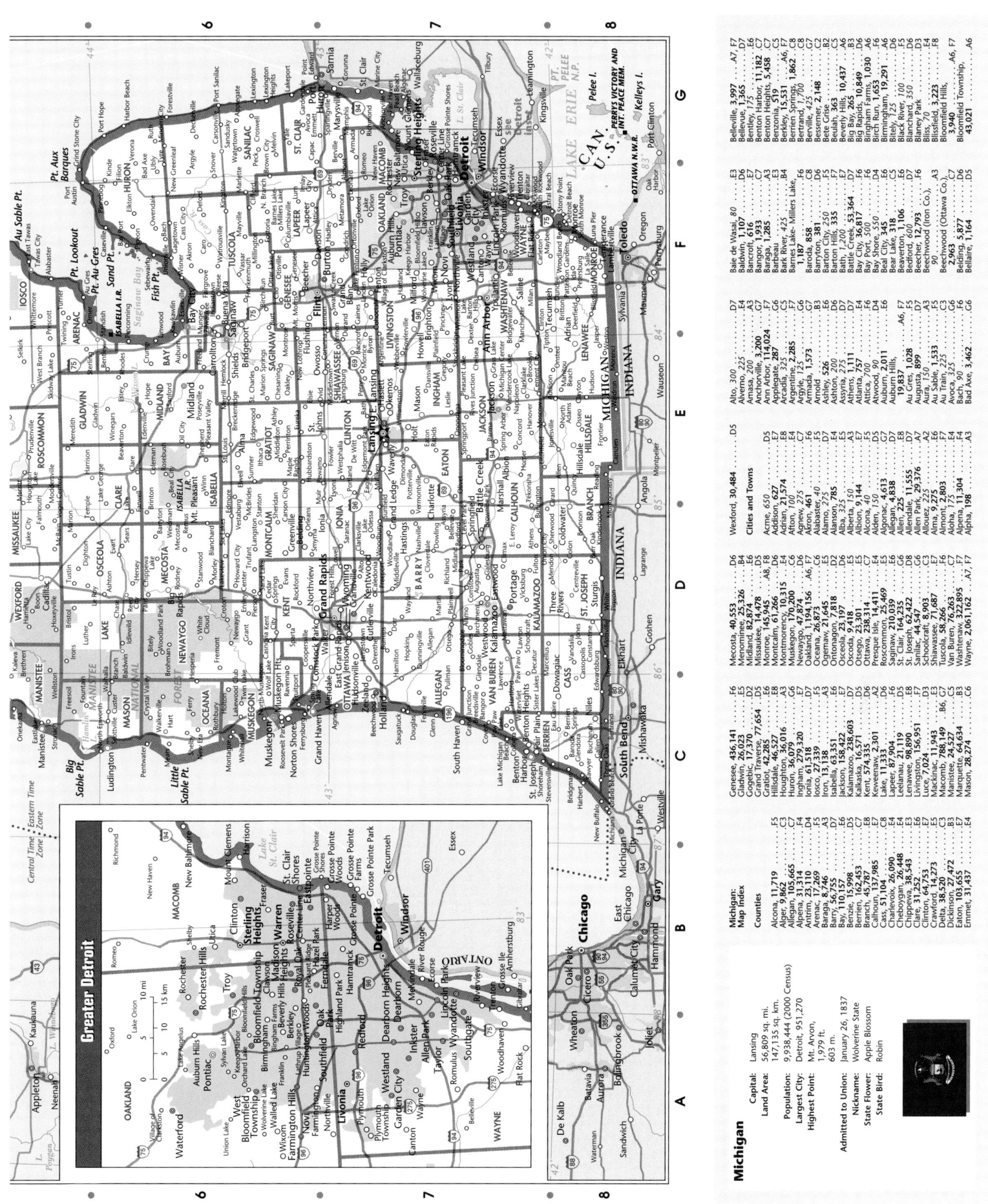

Greater Detroit

Michigan

Capital: Lansing
Land Area: 56,809 sq. mi. / 147,135 sq. km.
Population: 9,938,444 (2000 Census)
Largest City: Detroit, 951,270
Highest Point: Mt. Arvon, 1,979 ft. / 603 m.
Admitted to Union: January 26, 1837
Nickname: Wolverine State
State Flower: Apple Blossom
State Bird: Robin

Michigan: Map Index

Counties

Name	Ref
Alcona, 11,719	F5
Alger, 9,862	C3
Allegan, 105,665	C7
Alpena, 31,314	F4
Antrim, 23,110	D4
Arenac, 17,269	F5
Baraga, 8,746	A3
Barry, 56,755	D7
Bay, 110,157	E6
Benzie, 15,998	C5
Berrien, 162,453	B7
Branch, 45,787	D8
Calhoun, 137,985	D7
Cass, 51,104	C8
Charlevoix, 26,090	D4
Cheboygan, 26,448	E3
Chippewa, 38,543	E3
Clare, 31,252	E5
Clinton, 64,753	E7
Crawford, 14,273	E5
Delta, 38,520	C3
Dickinson, 27,472	B3
Eaton, 103,655	E7
Emmet, 31,437	E4
Genesee, 436,141	E6
Gladwin, 26,023	E5
Gogebic, 17,370	A3
Grand Traverse, 77,654	D5
Gratiot, 42,285	E6
Hillsdale, 46,527	E8
Houghton, 36,016	A3
Huron, 36,079	G5
Ingham, 279,320	E7
Ionia, 61,518	D6
Iosco, 27,339	F5
Iron, 13,138	A3
Isabella, 63,351	E6
Jackson, 158,422	E7
Kalamazoo, 238,603	D7
Kalkaska, 16,571	D5
Kent, 574,335	D6
Keweenaw, 2,301	A2
Lake, 11,333	D6
Lapeer, 87,904	F6
Leelanau, 21,119	D4
Lenawee, 98,890	E8
Livingston, 156,951	F7
Luce, 7,024	D3
Mackinac, 11,943	E3
Macomb, 788,149	B6, C7
Manistee, 24,527	C5
Marquette, 64,634	B3
Mason, 28,274	C6
Mecosta, 40,553	D6
Menominee, 25,326	B4
Midland, 82,874	E6
Missaukee, 14,478	D5
Monroe, 145,945	F7
Montcalm, 61,266	D6
Montmorency, 10,315	E4
Muskegon, 170,200	C6
Newaygo, 47,874	D6
Oakland, 1,194,156	A6, F6
Oceana, 26,873	C6
Ogemaw, 21,645	F5
Ontonagon, 7,818	A3
Osceola, 23,197	D5
Oscoda, 9,418	E5
Otsego, 23,301	E4
Ottawa, 238,314	C7
Presque Isle, 14,411	F4
Roscommon, 25,469	E5
Saginaw, 210,039	E6
St. Clair, 164,235	G6
St. Joseph, 62,422	D8
Sanilac, 44,547	G5
Schoolcraft, 8,903	C3
Shiawassee, 71,687	E6
Tuscola, 58,266	F6
Van Buren, 76,263	C7
Washtenaw, 322,895	E7
Wayne, 2,061,162	A7, F7
Wexford, 30,484	D5

Cities and Towns

Name	Ref
Acme, 650	D5
Addison, 627	E7
Adrian, 21,574	E8
Arcadia, 325	C5
Applegate, 287	G6
Agnew	C7
Akron, 461	F6
Alamo	D7
Alanson, 785	E4
Alba	E4
Alberta, 150	A3
Albion, 9,144	E7
Alcona, 40	F5
Alden, 150	D5
Algonac, 4,613	G6
Allegan, 4,838	D7
Allen, 225	E8
Allen Park, 29,376	A7, F7
Allouez, 225	A3
Alma, 9,275	E6
Almont, 2,803	F6
Aloha, 175	E4
Alpena, 11,304	F4
Alpha, 198	B3
Alto, 300	D5
Amasa, 200	A3
Anchorville, 87	G6
Ann Arbor, 114,024	E7
Applegate, 287	G6
Arcadia, 325	C5
Argentine, 2,285	F6
Armada, 1,573	G6
Ashley, 526	E6
Ashton, 200	D5
Assyria, 275	D7
Athens, 1,111	D7
Atlanta, 757	E4
Attica, 700	F6
Atwood, 90	D4
Auburn, 2,011	E6
Auburn Hills, 19,837	A6, F6
Augusta, 899	D7
Aura, 150	A3
Au Sable, 1,533	F5
Au Train, 225	C3
Avoca, 325	G6
Bach, 90	F6
Bad Axe, 3,462	G5
Baie de Wasai, 80	D7
Baldwin, 1,107	D6
Bancroft, 616	E6
Bangor, 1,933	C7
Baraga, 1,285	A3
Barbeau	E3
Bark River, 425	B4
Bark Lake - Millers Lake, 1,700	G6
Barryton, 381	D6
Barton City, 250	F5
Barton Hills, 335	E7
Battle Creek, 53,364	D7
Bay City, 36,817	F6
Bay Port, 500	F6
Bay Shore, 350	D4
Bear Lake, 318	C5
Beaverton, 1,106	E5
Bedford	D7
Beechwood (Iron Co.), 90	A3
Beechwood (Ottawa Co.)	C7
Belding, 5,877	D6
Bellaire, 1,164	D5
Belleville, 3,997	A7, F7
Bellevue, 1,365	D7
Bentley, 175	E6
Benton Harbor, 11,182	C7
Benton Heights, 5,458	C7
Benzonia, 519	C5
Berkley, 15,531	A6, F7
Berrien Springs, 1,862	C8
Berville, 425	G6
Bessemer, 2,148	A3
Bete Grise	B2
Beulah, 363	C5
Beverly Hills, 10,437	A6
Big Bay, 265	B3
Big Rapids, 10,849	D6
Bingham Farms, 1,030	A6
Birch Run, 1,653	F6
Birmingham, 19,291	A6, F6
Bitely, 125	D6
Black River, 100	F5
Blanchard, 350	D6
Bliss, 70	E4
Blissfield, 3,223	E8
Bloomfield Hills, 3,940	A6, F7
Bloomfield Township, 43,021	A6

Bloomingdale, 528 ...D7
Boon, 150 ...D5
Boyne City, 3,503 ...D4
Boyne Falls, 370 ...E4
Brampton, 80 ...B4
Branch, 150 ...C6
Breckenridge, 1,339 ...E6
Breedsville, 235 ...C7
Brethren, 275 ...C5
Brevort ...C3
Bridgeport, 7,849 ...F6
Bridgewater, 175 ...F7
Bridgman, 2,428 ...C8
Brighton, 6,701 ...F7
Brimley, 450 ...E3
Brinton, 100 ...D6
Bristol, 60 ...D5
Britton, 699 ...F8
Brohman, 175 ...D6
Bronson, 2,421 ...D8
Brooklyn, 1,176 ...E7
Brown City, 1,334 ...G6
Brownlee Park, 2,588 ...D7
Bruce Crossing, 225 ...A3
Brutus, 175 ...D4
Buchanan, 4,681 ...C8
Buckley, 550 ...D5
Buena Vista, 7,845 ...F6
Burlington, 405 ...D7
Burnips, 375 ...D7
Burr Oak, 797 ...D8
Burt, 1,122 ...F6
Burt Lake, 225 ...E4
Burton, 30,308 ...F6
Byron, 595 ...F7
Cadillac, 10,000 ...D5
Calderwood ...A3
Caledonia, 1,102 ...D7
Calumet, 879 ...A2
Camden, 550 ...E8
Canton, 76,366 ...A7, F7
Capac, 1,775 ...G6
Carleton, 2,562 ...F7
Carlshend, 90 ...B3
Carney, 225 ...B4
Caro, 4,145 ...F6
Carp Lake, 150 ...E4
Carrollton, 6,602 ...F6
Carson City, 1,190 ...E6
Carsonville, 502 ...G6
Caseville, 888 ...F5
Casnovia, 315 ...D6
Caspian, 997 ...A3
Cass City, 2,643 ...F6
Cassopolis, 1,740 ...C8
Cedar, 215 ...D4
Cedar River ...B4
Cedar Springs, 3,112 ...D6
Cedarville, 425 ...E4
Cement City, 452 ...E7
Center Line, 8,531 ...B6, F7
Central ...A2
Central Lake, 990 ...D4
Centreville, 1,579 ...D8
Champion, 250 ...B3
Channing, 250 ...A3
Charlevoix, 2,994 ...D4
Charlotte, 8,389 ...E7
Chase, 275 ...D6
Chassell, 800 ...A2
Cheboygan, 5,295 ...E4
Chelsea, 4,398 ...E7
Chesaning, 2,548 ...E6
Chicagon Lake ...A3
Chippewa Lake, 125 ...D6
Christmas, 250 ...C3
Clare, 3,173 ...E6
Clarklake, 250 ...E7
Clarksville, 317 ...D7
Clawson, 12,732 ...B6, F7
Clayton, 326 ...E8
Clifford, 324 ...F6
Climax, 791 ...D7
Clinton (Lenawee Co.), 2,293 ...F7
Clinton (Macomb Co.), 95,648 ...B6
Clio, 2,483 ...F6
Cloverdale, 400 ...D7
Cohoctah, 275 ...F7
Coldwater, 12,697 ...D8
Coleman, 1,296 ...E6
Coloma, 1,595 ...C7
Colon, 1,227 ...D8
Columbiaville, 815 ...F6
Comins, 150 ...E5
Comstock, 4,472 ...D7
Comstock Park, 10,674 ...D6
Concord, 1,101 ...E7
Connorville ...C2
Constantine, 2,095 ...D8
Conway, 275 ...E4
Cooks, 100 ...C3
Coopersville, 3,910 ...D6
Copemish, 232 ...D5
Copper City, 205 ...A2
Copper Harbor, 50 ...B2
Cornell, 90 ...B4
Corunna, 3,381 ...E6, G7
Covert, 650 ...C7
Covington, 40 ...A3
Cross Village, 70 ...D4
Croswell, 2,467 ...G6
Croton, 275 ...D6
Crump, 275 ...E6
Crystal Falls, 1,791 ...A3
Crystal Valley, 175 ...C6
Curran, 40 ...F5
Curtis, 250 ...D3
Curtisville, 50 ...F5
Custer, 318 ...C6
Cutlerville, 15,114 ...D7
Daggett, 270 ...B4
Dansville, 429 ...E7
Darragh, 200 ...D5
Davison, 5,536 ...F6
Dearborn, 97,775 ...A7
Dearborn Heights, 58,264 ...A7
Decatur, 1,838 ...C7
Deckerville, 944 ...G6
Deerfield, 1,005 ...F8
Deer Park ...D3
Deerton ...B3
Deford, 325 ...F6

Delaware ...A2
De Tour Village, 421 ...F4
Detroit, 951,270 ...B7, F7
Detroit Beach, 2,289 ...F8
De Witt, 4,702 ...E7
Dexter, 2,338 ...F7
Dighton, 100 ...D5
Dimondale, 1,342 ...E7
Dollar Bay, 950 ...A2
Donken ...A2
Dorr, 2,800 ...D7
Douglas, 1,214 ...C7
Dowagiac, 6,147 ...C7
Dowling, 150 ...D7
Drenthe, 325 ...D7
Drummond, 200 ...F3
Dryden, 815 ...F7
Dundee, 3,522 ...F8
Dunningville, 150 ...D7
Durand, 3,933 ...F7
Eagle, 130 ...E7
Eagle Harbor ...A2
Eagle River ...A2
East Grand Rapids, 10,764 ...D7
East Jordan, 2,507 ...D4
Eastlake, 441 ...C5
East Lansing, 46,525 ...E7
East Leroy, 275 ...D7
Eastpointe, 34,077 ...B6
Eastport, 200 ...D4
East Tawas, 2,951 ...F5
Eastwood, 6,265 ...D7
Eaton Rapids, 5,330 ...E7
Eau Claire, 656 ...C7
Eben Junction, 200 ...C3
Eckerman, 50 ...D3
Edenville, 250 ...E6
Edgemont Park, 2,442 ...E7
Edgewood ...A3
Edmore, 1,244 ...D6
Edwardsburg, 1,147 ...C8
Elberta, 457 ...C5
Elk Rapids, 1,700 ...D5
Elkton, 863 ...F6
Ellsworth, 483 ...D4
Elmira, 200 ...E4
Elo, 70 ...A3
Elsie, 1,055 ...E6
Elwell, 300 ...E6
Emmett, 251 ...G6
Empire, 378 ...C5
Engadine, 275 ...D3
Ensign, 40 ...C4
Ensley Center, 175 ...D6
Epoufette, 40 ...D3
Epsilon, 200 ...E4
Escanaba, 13,140 ...B4
Essexville, 3,766 ...F6
Estey, 150 ...E6
Estral Beach, 486 ...F7
Eureka, 300 ...E6
Evans, 225 ...D6
Evart, 1,738 ...D6
Ewen, 175 ...D2
Fairgrove, 627 ...F6
Fair Haven, 1,500 ...G7
Fair Plain, 7,828 ...C7
Fairport, 125 ...C4
Fairview, 600 ...E5
Faithorn, 20 ...B4
Falmouth, 275 ...D5
Farmington, 10,423 ...A6
Farmington Hills, 82,111 ...A6
Farwell, 855 ...E6
Fayette, 10 ...C4
Felch, 80 ...B4
Fennville, 1,459 ...C7
Fenton, 10,582 ...F7
Ferndale, 22,105 ...B6
Ferry, 250 ...C6
Ferrysburg, 3,040 ...C6
Fibre ...E3
Fife Lake, 466 ...D5
Filion, 225 ...F5
Flat Rock, 8,488 ...A7, F7
Flint, 124,943 ...F6
Flushing, 8,348 ...F6
Ford River, 150 ...B4
Forest Hills, 20,942 ...D7
Forest Lake ...C3
Forestville, 127 ...G6
Foster City, 60 ...B4
Fostoria, 600 ...F6
Fountain, 175 ...C5
Fowler, 1,136 ...E6
Fowlerville, 2,972 ...E7
Frankenmuth, 4,838 ...F6
Frankfort, 1,513 ...C5
Franklin, 2,937 ...A6, F7
Fraser, 15,297 ...B6, G7
Freda, 50 ...A2
Frederic, 425 ...E5
Freeland, 5,147 ...E6
Freeport, 444 ...D7
Freesoil, 177 ...C5
Fremont, 4,224 ...D6
Frontier, 250 ...E8
Fruitport, 1,124 ...C6
Fulton, 350 ...D7
Gaastra, 339 ...A3
Gagetown, 389 ...F6
Gaines, 366 ...F7
Galesburg, 1,988 ...D7
Galien, 593 ...C8
Garden, 240 ...C4
Garden City, 30,047 ...A7, F7
Gardendale, 800 ...G6
Garnet, 40 ...D3
Gay, 40 ...A2
Gaylord, 3,681 ...E5
Genesee, 1,800 ...F6
Germfask, 70 ...D3
Gibraltar, 4,264 ...B7, F7
Gilchrist ...D7
Girard, 275 ...D7
Gladstone, 5,032 ...B4
Gladwin, 3,001 ...E6
Glen Arbor, 200 ...C5
Glendale, 300 ...D7
Glendora, 325 ...C8
Glenn, 325 ...C7
Glennie, 90 ...F5
Gobles, 815 ...D7
Goetzville, 70 ...E3

Good Hart, 50 ...D4
Goodrich, 1,353 ...F7
Gould City, 80 ...D3
Grace, 40 ...E4
Grand Beach, 221 ...C8
Grand Blanc, 8,242 ...F7
Grand Haven, 11,168 ...C6
Grand Junction, 325 ...C7
Grand Ledge, 7,813 ...E7
Grand Marais, 300 ...D7
Grand Rapids, 197,800 ...D7
Grandville, 16,263 ...D7
Grant, 881 ...D6
Grass Lake, 1,082 ...E7
Grawn, 1,600 ...D5
Grayling, 1,952 ...E5
Green, 80 ...D1
Greenbush, 225 ...F5
Greenland, 325 ...A3
Greenville, 7,935 ...D6
Gregory, 500 ...E7
Greilickville, 1,415 ...D5
Grind Stone City, 100 ...G5
Gros Cap, 90 ...E4
Grosse Ile, 10,894 ...B7
Grosse Pointe, 5,670 ...B7
Grosse Pointe Farms, 9,764 ...B7
Grosse Pointe Park, 12,443 ...B7
Grosse Pointe Shores, 2,823 ...B6, G7
Grosse Pointe Woods, 17,080 ...B7
Gulliver, 90 ...C3
Gwinn, 1,965 ...B3
Hadley, 450 ...F7
Hale, 600 ...F5
Hamilton, 1,300 ...C7
Hamtramck, 22,976 ...B7, F7
Hancock, 4,323 ...A2
Hanover, 424 ...E7
Harbert, 1,619 ...C8
Harbor Beach, 1,837 ...G6
Harbor Springs, 1,567 ...D4
Harper Woods, 14,254 ...B7
Harrietta, 169 ...D5
Harrison (Clare Co.), 2,108 ...E5
Harrison (Macomb Co.), 24,461 ...B6
Harrisville, 514 ...F5
Hart, 1,950 ...C6
Hartford, 2,476 ...C7
Hartland, 375 ...F7
Harvey, 1,321 ...B3
Haslett, 11,283 ...E7
Hastings, 7,095 ...D7
Hawks, 80 ...E4
Hazel Park, 18,963 ...B6
Helmer, 50 ...D3
Helps ...B4
Hemlock, 1,585 ...E6
Herman, 60 ...A3
Hermansville, 325 ...B4
Hersey, 374 ...D6
Hesperia, 954 ...C6
Hessel, 200 ...E3
Higgins Lake, 400 ...E5
Highland Park, 16,746 ...B7
Hillman, 500 ...F4
Hillsdale, 8,233 ...E8
Holland, 35,048 ...C7
Holly, 6,135 ...F7
Holt, 11,315 ...E7
Holton, 600 ...C6
Homer, 1,851 ...E7
Honor, 299 ...C5
Hope, 200 ...E6
Hopkins, 592 ...D7
Houghton, 7,010 ...A2
Houghton Lake, 3,749 ...E5
Howard City, 1,585 ...D6
Howell, 9,232 ...F7
Hoxeyville, 40 ...D5
Hubbard Lake, 993 ...F5
Hubbardston, 394 ...E6
Hubbell, 1,051 ...A2
Hudson, 2,499 ...E8
Hudsonville, 7,160 ...D7
Hulbert, 80 ...D3
Huntington Woods, 6,151 ...B6
Huron Beach, 225 ...E4
Hyde, 275 ...B4
Ida, 1,100 ...F8
Idlewild, 350 ...D6
Imlay City, 3,869 ...F6
Indian River, 2,008 ...E4
Indiantown, 1,158 ...F6
Ingalls, 175 ...B4
Inkster, 30,115 ...A7, F7
Interlochen, 600 ...D5
Ionia, 10,569 ...D6
Iron Mountain, 8,154 ...A4
Iron River, 3,386 ...A3
Irons, 90 ...D5
Ironton, 200 ...D4
Ironwood, 6,293 ...C2
Isabella, 40 ...C4
Ishpeming, 6,686 ...B3
Ithaca, 3,098 ...E6
Jackson, 36,316 ...E7
Jacobsville ...A2
Jamestown, 750 ...D7
Jasper, 400 ...E8
Jenison, 17,211 ...D7
Johannesburg, 80 ...E5
Jones, 450 ...D7
Jonesville, 2,337 ...E7
Junction City, 242 ...G6
Kalamazoo, 77,145 ...D7
Kaleva, 509 ...D5
Kalkaska, 2,226 ...D5
Karlin, 100 ...D5
Kawkawlin, 1,500 ...F6
Keego Harbor, 2,769 ...A6, F7
Kent City, 1,061 ...D6
Kenton ...A3
Kentwood, 45,255 ...D7
Keweenaw Bay, 150 ...A3
Kinde, 534 ...G6
Kinderhook, 350 ...D8
Kingsford, 5,549 ...A4
Kingsley, 1,469 ...D5
Kingston, 450 ...F6
Kinross, 175 ...E3

Kiva, 50 ...B3
Koss, 80 ...B4
La Branche ...B4
Lachine, 225 ...F4
Laingsburg, 1,223 ...E7
Lake, 475 ...D6
Lake Angelus, 326 ...A6
Lake Ann, 276 ...D5
Lake City, 923 ...D5
Lake Fenton, 4,876 ...F7
Lake George, 400 ...E6
Lake Linden, 1,081 ...A2
Lake Michigan Beach, 1,509 ...C7
Lake Odessa, 2,272 ...D7
Lake Orion, 2,715 ...A6, F7
Lakeport, 700 ...G6
Lakeview, 1,112 ...D6
Lakewood Club, 1,006 ...C6
Lambertville, 9,299 ...F8
Langston, 300 ...D6
L'Anse, 2,107 ...A3
Lansing, 119,128 ...E7
Lapeer, 9,072 ...F6
La Salle, 350 ...F8
Lathrup Village, 4,236 ...A6, F7
Laurium, 2,126 ...A2
Lawrence, 1,059 ...C7
Lawton, 1,859 ...D7
Leland, 350 ...D4
Lennon, 517 ...F6
Leonard, 332 ...F7
Le Roy, 267 ...D5
Leslie, 2,044 ...E7
Level Park, 3,605 ...D7
Levering, 300 ...E4
Lewiston, 990 ...E5
Lexington, 1,104 ...G6
Lexington Heights, 1,000 ...G6
Lincoln, 364 ...F5
Lincoln Park, 40,008 ...B7, F7
Linden, 2,861 ...F7
Linwood, 1,200 ...F6
Litchfield, 1,458 ...E7
Little Lake, 225 ...B3
Livonia, 100,545 ...A7, F7
Long Lake, 200 ...F5
Loretto, 150 ...B4
Lovells, 80 ...E5
Lowell, 4,013 ...D7
Ludington, 8,357 ...C6
Lum, 500 ...F6
Luna Pier, 1,483 ...F8
Lupton, 350 ...E5
Luther, 339 ...D5
Luzerne, 275 ...E5
Lyons, 726 ...E6
Mackinac Island, 523 ...E4
Mackinaw City, 859 ...E4
Madison Heights, 31,101 ...B6
Mancelona, 1,408 ...D5
Manchester, 2,160 ...E7
Manistee, 6,586 ...C5
Manistique, 3,583 ...C4
Manitou Beach, 2,080 ...E8
Manton, 1,221 ...D5
Maple City, 225 ...D5
Maple Rapids, 643 ...E6
Marcellus, 1,162 ...D7
Marenisco, 300 ...D2
Marine City, 4,652 ...G7
Marion, 836 ...D5
Marion Springs, 200 ...E6
Marlette, 2,104 ...F6
Marquette, 19,661 ...B3
Marshall, 7,459 ...E7
Martin, 435 ...D7
Marysville, 9,684 ...G7
Mason, 6,714 ...E7
Mass City, 300 ...A3
Mattawan, 2,536 ...D7
Maybee, 505 ...F7
Mayfield, 225 ...D5
Mayville, 1,055 ...F6
McBain, 584 ...D5
McBrides, 232 ...D6
McFarland ...D3
McLeods Corner, 20 ...D3
McMillan, 100 ...D3
Mears, 425 ...C6
Mecosta, 450 ...D6
Melstrand, 10 ...C3
Melvin, 160 ...G6
Melvindale, 10,735 ...B7
Memphis, 1,129 ...G7
Mendon, 917 ...D7
Menominee, 9,131 ...B4
Meredith, 125 ...E5
Merrill, 782 ...E6
Merriman, 125 ...A4
Merritt, 90 ...D5
Merriweather, 125 ...D2
Mesick, 447 ...D5
Metamora, 507 ...F7
Michiana, 200 ...C8
Michigamme, 287 ...A3
Michigan Center, 4,641 ...E7
Middleton, 475 ...E6
Middletown, 966 ...E7
Middleville, 2,721 ...D7
Midland, 41,685 ...E6
Midland Park, 475 ...D7
Mikado, 175 ...F5
Milan, 4,775 ...F7
Milford, 6,272 ...F7
Millersburg, 263 ...E4
Millington, 1,137 ...F6
Minden City, 242 ...G6
Mineral Hills, 214 ...A3
Mio, 2,016 ...E5
Moddersville, 40 ...E5
Mohawk, 750 ...A2
Monroe, 22,076 ...F7
Montague, 2,407 ...C6
Montgomery, 386 ...E8
Montrose, 1,619 ...F6
Moorestown, 90 ...D5
Moran, 175 ...E4
Morenci, 2,398 ...E8
Morley, 495 ...D6
Morrice, 882 ...E7
Moscow, 250 ...E7
Mottville, 400 ...D8
Mount Clemens, 17,312 ...B6, G7

Mt. Morris, 3,194 ...F6
Mt. Pleasant, 25,946 ...E6
Muir, 634 ...E6
Mullett Lake, 325 ...E4
Mulliken, 557 ...E7
Munger, 350 ...F6
Munising, 2,539 ...C3
Muskegon, 40,105 ...C6
Muskegon Hts., 12,049 ...C6
Nadeau, 175 ...B4
Nahma ...C4
Napoleon, 1,254 ...E7
Nashville, 1,684 ...D7
Nathan ...B4
National Mine, 400 ...B3
Naubinway, 175 ...D3
Negaunee, 4,576 ...B3
Nestoria ...A3
Newaygo, 1,670 ...D6
New Baltimore, 7,405 ...C6, G7
Newberry, 2,686 ...D3
New Buffalo, 2,200 ...C8
New Era, 461 ...C6
New Greenleaf, 125 ...F6
New Haven, 3,071 ...B6, G7
New Lothrop, 603 ...F6
Niles, 12,204 ...C8
Nisula, 40 ...A3
North Adams, 514 ...E8
North Branch, 1,027 ...F6
North Epworth, 275 ...C6
Northland, 50 ...B3
North Manitou ...C4
North Muskegon, 4,031 ...C6
Northport, 648 ...D4
Northview, 6,459 ...D6
Norway, 2,959 ...B4
Norton Shores, 22,527 ...C6
Novi, 47,386 ...A6, F7
Oak Grove, 700 ...E5
Oakley, 339 ...E6
Oak Park, 29,793 ...A6, F7
Ocqueoc ...E4
Oil City, 190 ...E6
Okemos, 22,805 ...E7
Olivet, 1,758 ...E7
Omena, 150 ...D4
Omer, 337 ...F5
Onaway, 993 ...E4
Onekama, 647 ...C5
Onondaga, 425 ...E7
Onsted, 813 ...E7
Ontonagon, 1,769 ...D1
Orchard Lake, 2,215 ...A6
Orleans, 275 ...D6
Ortonville, 1,535 ...F7
Oscoda, 992 ...F5
Osseo, 550 ...E8
Ossineke, 1,059 ...F5
Otisville, 882 ...F6
Otsego, 3,933 ...D7
Otsego Lake, 325 ...E5
Otter Lake, 437 ...F6
Ovid, 1,514 ...E6
Owendale, 296 ...F6
Owosso, 15,713 ...E6
Oxford, 3,540 ...A6, F7
Ozark ...E3
Painesdale, 550 ...A2
Palmer, 449 ...B3
Paradise, 225 ...D3
Parchment, 1,936 ...D7
Paris, 450 ...D6
Parma, 907 ...E7
Patterson Gardens, 3,900 ...F8
Paulding, 70 ...A3
Paw Paw, 3,363 ...D7
Paw Paw Lake, 3,944 ...C7
Paynesville, 125 ...A3
Pearl Beach, 3,224 ...G7
Peck, 599 ...G6
Pelkie, 40 ...A3
Pellston, 771 ...E4
Pentwater, 958 ...C6
Pequaming ...A3
Perkins, 150 ...B4
Perrinton, 439 ...E6
Perronville, 100 ...B4
Perry, 2,065 ...E7
Peshawbestown, 200 ...D4
Petersburg, 1,157 ...F7
Petoskey, 6,080 ...E4
Pewamo, 560 ...E6
Phoenix ...A2
Pickford, 500 ...E3
Pierport, 70 ...C5
Pierson, 185 ...D6
Pigeon, 1,207 ...F6
Pinckney, 2,141 ...F7
Pinconning, 1,386 ...F6
Pinnebog, 40 ...F5
Plainfield, 250 ...E7
Plainwell, 3,933 ...D7
Pleasant Lake, 850 ...E7
Pleasant Ridge, 2,594 ...B6
Pleasant Valley, 80 ...A3
Pleasant View, 40 ...D4
Plymouth, 9,022 ...A7
Plymouth Township, 27,798 ...A7
Pointe Aux Pins, 40 ...E4
Pontiac, 66,337 ...A6, F7
Portage, 44,897 ...D7
Port Austin, 737 ...F5
Port Hope, 310 ...G6
Port Huron, 32,338 ...G7
Portland, 3,789 ...E7
Port Sanilac, 658 ...G6
Posen, 292 ...E4
Poseyville, 2,168 ...E7
Potterville, 2,168 ...E7
Powers, 430 ...B4
Prescott, 286 ...F5
Presque Isle, 125 ...F4
Princeton, 200 ...B3
Prudenville, 1,737 ...E5
Pullman, 700 ...C7
Quincy, 1,701 ...E8
Quinnesec, 1,187 ...B4
Raco, 40 ...E3
Ralph, 40 ...B3
Ramsay, 750 ...C2
Randville, 40 ...A3
Rapid City, 550 ...D5

Rapid River, 500 ...C4
Ravenna, 1,206 ...D6
Reading, 1,134 ...E8
Redford, 51,622 ...A7
Red Oak, 40 ...E5
Reed City, 2,430 ...D6
Reese, 1,375 ...F6
Remus, 250 ...D6
Republic, 614 ...B3
Rexton, 70 ...D3
Rhodes, 125 ...E6
Richland, 593 ...D7
Richmond, 4,897 ...C6, G7
River Rouge, 9,917 ...B7
Riverview, 13,272 ...B7, F7
Rives Junction, 650 ...E7
Rochester, 10,467 ...B6, F7
Rochester Hills, 68,825 ...A6
Rock, 150 ...B3
Rockford, 4,626 ...D6
Rockland, 250 ...A3
Rockwood, 3,442 ...F7
Rodney, 175 ...D6
Rogers City, 3,322 ...F4
Romeo, 3,721 ...B6, F7
Romulus, 22,979 ...A7, F7
Roosevelt Park, 3,890 ...C6
Roscommon, 1,133 ...E5
Rosebush, 379 ...E6
Rose City, 721 ...E5
Rosedale, 50 ...E3
Roseville, 48,129 ...B6, G7
Rothbury, 416 ...C6
Rousseau ...A3
Royal Oak, 60,062 ...B6
Rudyard, 500 ...E3
Ruth, 275 ...G6
Saginaw, 61,799 ...F6
Sagola, 50 ...A3
St. Charles, 2,215 ...E6
St. Clair, 5,802 ...G7
St. Clair Shores, 63,096 ...B6
St. Helen, 2,993 ...E5
St. Ignace, 2,678 ...E4
St. Jacques, 50 ...C4
St. James, 200 ...D4
St. Johns, 7,485 ...E6
St. Joseph, 8,789 ...C7
St. Louis, 4,494 ...E6
Saline, 8,034 ...F7
Sand Lake, 492 ...D6
Sand River, 80 ...B3
Sands, 100 ...B3
Sandusky, 2,745 ...G6
Sanford, 943 ...E6
Saranac, 1,326 ...D7
Saugatuck, 1,065 ...C7
Sault Ste. Marie, 16,542 ...E3
Sawyer, 200 ...C8
Schaffer, 325 ...B4
Schoolcraft, 1,587 ...D7
Scottville, 1,266 ...C6
Sears, 100 ...D6
Sebewaing, 1,974 ...F6
Selkirk, 90 ...E5
Seney, 70 ...D3
Shelby (Macomb Co.), 65,159 ...B6
Shelby (Oceana Co.), 1,914 ...C6
Shepherd, 1,536 ...E6
Sheridan, 705 ...D6
Sherwood, 324 ...D7
Shields, 6,590 ...F6
Shingleton, 475 ...C3
Shoreham, 860 ...C7
Sidnaw, 40 ...A3
Silver City ...D1
Sister Lakes, 1,000 ...C7
Six Lakes, 425 ...D6
Skandia, 325 ...B3
Skanee, 40 ...A3
Skidway Lake, 3,147 ...E5
Smyrna, 275 ...D6
Snover, 275 ...G6
South Boardman, 500 ...D5
South Branch, 125 ...F5
Southfield, 78,296 ...A6, F7
Southgate, 30,136 ...A7
South Haven, 5,021 ...C7
South Lyon, 10,036 ...F7
South Monroe, 6,370 ...F8
South Range, 727 ...A2
South Rockwood, 1,284 ...F7
Sparlingville ...G7
Sparta, 4,159 ...D6
Spencer, 100 ...D5
Spratt, 50 ...F5
Spring Arbor, 2,188 ...E7
Springfield, 5,189 ...D7
Spring Lake, 2,514 ...C6
Springport, 704 ...E7
Spruce, 125 ...E5
Stalwart, 60 ...E3
Stambaugh, 1,243 ...A3
Standish, 1,581 ...F6
Stanton, 1,504 ...D6
Stanwood, 204 ...D6
Stephenson, 875 ...B4
Sterling, 533 ...E5
Sterling Heights, 124,471 ...B6, F7
Steuben, 10 ...C3
Stevensville, 1,191 ...C7
Stockbridge, 1,260 ...E7
Stony Point, 1,775 ...F8
Stronach, 350 ...C5
Strongs ...D3
Sturgis, 11,285 ...D8
Sumner, 300 ...E6
Sunfield, 591 ...E7
Suttons Bay, 589 ...D5
Swanson ...B4
Swartz Creek, 5,102 ...F7
Sylvan Lake, 1,735 ...A6
Tapiola, 40 ...A3
Tawas City, 2,005 ...F5
Taylor, 65,868 ...A7
Tecumseh, 8,574 ...F7
Tekonsha, 712 ...E7
Temple, 200 ...E5
Thomaston, 90 ...C2
Thompson ...C4
Thompsonville, 457 ...D5

Three Oaks, 1,829 ...C8
Three Rivers, 7,328 ...D8
Tipton, 325 ...E7
Toivola ...A2
Topinabee, 250 ...E4
Torch Lake, 175 ...D4
Tower, 375 ...E4
Traunik ...C3
Traverse City, 14,532 ...D5
Trenary, 125 ...C3
Trenton, 19,584 ...B7, F7
Trout Creek, 225 ...A3
Trout Lake, 175 ...D3
Trowbridge Park, 2,012 ...B3
Troy, 80,959 ...B6, F7
Trufant, 600 ...D6
Turner, 139 ...F5
Tustin, 237 ...D5
Twining, 192 ...F5
Twin Lake, 1,613 ...C6
Twin Lakes ...A3
Tyre, 60 ...G6
Ubly, 873 ...G6
Union, 475 ...D8
Union City, 1,804 ...D7
Union Lake, 2,500 ...A6
Unionville, 605 ...F6
Utica, 4,577 ...B6, F7
Vandalia, 429 ...D8
Vanderbilt, 587 ...E4
Vandercook Lake, 4,809 ...E7
Vassar, 2,823 ...F6
Vermontville, 789 ...D7
Vernon, 847 ...E7
Vestaburg, 550 ...E6
Vicksburg, 2,320 ...D7
Victoria ...A3
Village of Clarkston, 175 ...A6, F7
Vogel Center, 175 ...D5
Wakefield, 2,085 ...C2
Waldron, 590 ...E8
Walhalla, 275 ...C6
Walkerville, 254 ...C6
Wallace, 200 ...B4
Walled Lake, 6,713 ...A6
Walloon Lake, 375 ...D4
Warren, 138,247 ...B6
Waterford, 73,150 ...A6
Waters, 60 ...E5
Watersmeet, 450 ...A3
Watertown, 225 ...G6
Watervliet, 1,843 ...C7
Watrousville, 200 ...F6
Watton, 40 ...A3
Wauceda, 175 ...B4
Waverly, 16,194 ...E7
Wayland, 3,939 ...D7
Wayne, 19,051 ...A7, F7
Webberville, 1,503 ...E7
Weidman, 879 ...E6
Wellston, 425 ...D5
West Bloomfield Township, 64,862 ...A6
West Branch, 1,926 ...E5
Westland, 86,602 ...A7, F7
Weston, 300 ...E8
Westphalia, 876 ...E7
Westwood, 9,122 ...D7
Wetmore, 300 ...C3
White Cloud, 1,420 ...D6
Whitefish Point ...E3
Whitehall, 2,884 ...C6
White Pigeon, 1,627 ...D8
White Pine, 700 ...D1
Whitmore Lake, 6,574 ...F7
Whittemore, 476 ...F5
Williamsburg, 350 ...D5
Williamston, 3,441 ...E7
Winegars, 50 ...E7
Winn, 275 ...E6
Winona ...A3
Wisner, 200 ...F6
Witch Lake, 60 ...A3
Wixom, 13,263 ...A6, F7
Wolf Lake, 4,455 ...C6
Wolverine, 359 ...E4
Wolverine Lake, 4,415 ...A6, F7
Woodbury, 175 ...D7
Woodhaven, 12,530 ...A7, F7
Woodland, 495 ...D7
Woodland Beach, 2,179 ...F8
Woodland Park, 150 ...D6
Wyandotte, 28,006 ...B7, F7
Wyoming, 69,368 ...D7
Yale, 2,063 ...G6
Ypsilanti, 22,362 ...F7
Zeeland, 5,805 ...D7
Zilwaukee, 1,799 ...F6

Other Features

Adams, point ...F4
Apostle, islands ...C1
Apostle Islands Natl. Lakeshore ...C1
Arvon, mountain ...A3
Au Gres, point ...F5
Au Sable, point ...C3, F5
Au Sable, river ...E5
Aux Barques, point ...G5, C4
Bad River I.R. ...C2
Barrie, island ...D4
Bay Mills I.R. ...E3
Beaver, island ...D4
Betsie, river ...C5
Big Bay De Noc, bay ...C4
Big Sable, point ...C5
Bois Blanc, island ...E4
Camp Grayling Mil. Res. ...E5
Cass, river ...F6
Cathead, point ...D4
Chambers, island ...B4
Chequamegon N.F. ...C2
Clapperton, island ...G3
Cockburn, island ...F3
Crystal, lake ...C5
Detour, point ...F4
Door, peninsula ...B5
Drummond, island ...F3
Edward, island ...A1
Erie, lake ...G8
Escanaba, river ...B3
Father Marquette Natl. Mem. ...E4

Fish, point ...F6
Fourteen Mile, point ...A2
Garden, island ...D4
Glen, lake ...C5
Gogebic, lake ...D2
Government, peak ...D1
Grand, island ...C3
Grand Island N.R.A. ...C3
Grand Traverse, bay ...D4
Gravel Island N.W.R. ...C4
Great Duck, island ...G4
Green, bay ...B5
Green Bay N.W.R. ...C5
Hamlin, lake ...C5
Hammond, bay ...E4
Hiawatha National Forest ...C3, E3
Higgins, lake ...E5
High, island ...D4
Hog, island ...D4
Houghton, lake ...E5
Hubbard, lake ...F5
Huron, bay ...A3
Huron, lake ...G5
Huron, mountains ...A3
Huron National Forest ...E5, F5
Huron N.W.R. ...A2
Indian, lake ...C3, G2
Isabella I.R. ...E6, F6
Isle Royale, island ...A2
Isle Royale Natl. Park ...A2
Kelleys, island ...G8
Keweenaw, bay ...A2
Keweenaw, peninsula ...A2
Keweenaw, point ...B2
Lac du Flambeau I.R. ...D2
L'Anse I.R. ...A3
Laughing Fish, point ...C3
Les Cheneaux, islands ...E4
Little Sable, point ...C6
Lookout, point ...F5
Mackinac, straits ...E4
Madeline, island ...C1
Manistee, river ...D5
Manistee National Forest ...C5
Manitou, island ...B2
Manitoulin, island ...G4
Menominee, river ...B4
Menominee Indian Res. ...A4
Michigamme, reservoir ...A3
Michigan, lake ...C4
Michigan Islands N.W.R. ...D4, F5
Nicolet National Forest ...A4
North, channel ...F3
North, point ...F4
Northern Highland American Legion S.F. ...D2
North Fox, island ...C4
North Manitou, island ...C4
Oneida I.R. ...A5
Ottawa National Forest ...A3, B3, D2
Ottawa N.W.R. ...F8
Outer, island ...C1
Paint, river ...A3
Pelee, island ...G8
Perrys Victory And Int. Peace Mem. ...G8
Peshtigo, river ...A4
Pictured Rocks Natl. Lakeshore ...C3
Pie, island ...A1
Pt. Pelee N.P. ...G8
Porcupine, mountains ...D1
Porcupine Mts. Wilderness S.P. ...D1
Potawatomi I.R. ...A4
Poygan, lake ...A5
Quirke, lake ...G3
Ranger, lake ...G3
Rocky Island, lake ...G3
Saginaw, bay ...F5
St. Clair, lake ...B6, C7, G7
St. Joseph, island ...F3
St. Martin, island ...C4
Sand, point ...F5
Scott, point ...D4
Seney N.W.R. ...D3
Shawano, lake ...A5
Sibley Prov. Park ...A1
Sleeping Bear Dunes Natl. Lakeshore ...C5
Sokaogon Chippewa I.R. ...A4
South, point ...F5
South Fox, island ...D4
South Manitou, island ...C4
Stockbridge I.R. ...A5
Sturgeon, bay ...D4
Sturgeon, point ...F5
Sugar, mountain ...A2
Summer, island ...C4
Superior, lake ...C1
Tahquamenon Falls S.P. ...D3
Thunder, bay ...A1, F5
Thunder, cape ...A1
Traverse, point ...A2
Turtle Flambeau Flowage ...C2
Whitefish, bay ...E3
Winnebago, lake ...A5
Wixom, lake ...E6
Wolf, river ...A4
Wurtsmith A.F.B. ...F5

Minnesota

Capital: St. Paul
Land Area: 79,617 sq. mi.
206,208 sq. km.
Population: 4,919,479 (2000 Census)
Largest City: Minneapolis, 382,618
Highest Point: Eagle Mountain,
2,301 ft.
701 m.
Admitted to Union: May 11, 1858
Nickname: North Star State,
Gopher State
State Flower: Lady's Slipper
State Bird: Common Loon

Minnesota: Map Index

Counties

Aitkin, 15,301 . . . . .D4
Anoka, 298,084 . . . .D5, F5
Becker, 30,000 . . . . . . .B3
Beltrami, 39,650 . . . . . .B2
Benton, 34,226 . . . . . .C5
Big Stone, 5,820 . . . . . .A5
Blue Earth, 55,941 . . . .C7
Brown, 26,911 . . . . . . .C6
Carlton, 31,671 . . . . . .D4
Carver, 70,205 . . . . . . .C6
Cass, 27,150 . . . . .C4
Chippewa, 13,088 . . . . .B5
Chisago, 41,101 . . . . . .E5
Clay, 51,229 . . . . .A3
Clearwater, 8,423 . . . . .B3
Cook, 5,168 . . . . . .F2, F3
Cottonwood, 12,167 . . .B6
Crow Wing, 55,099 . . . .C4
Dakota, 355,904 . . .D6, F6
Dodge, 17,731 . . . . . . .E7
Douglas, 32,821 . . . . . .B5
Faribault, 16,181 . . . . .D7
Fillmore, 21,122 . . . . . .E7
Freeborn, 32,584 . . . . .D7
Goodhue, 44,127 . . . . .E6
Grant, 6,289 . . . . .A4
Hennepin,
1,116,200 . . . . . .D5, E6
Houston, 19,718 . . . . . .F7
Hubbard, 18,376 . . . . .C3
Isanti, 31,287 . . . . .D5
Itasca, 43,992 . . . . . . .D3
Jackson, 11,268 . . . . . .B7
Kanabec, 14,996 . . . . .D5
Kandiyohi, 41,203 . . . . .B5
Kittson, 5,285 . . . . . . .A2
Koochiching, 14,355 . . .D2
Lac Qui Parle, 8,067 . . .A6
Lake, 11,058 . . . . .F3
Lake of the Woods,
4,522 . . . . .C2
Le Sueur, 25,426 . . . . .D6
Lincoln, 6,429 . . . . . . .A6
Lyon, 25,425 . . . . .B6
Mahnomen, 5,190 . . . . .B3
Marshall, 10,155 . . . . .A2
Martin, 21,802 . . . . . . .C7
McLeod, 34,898 . . . . . .C6
Meeker, 22,644 . . . . . .C5
Mille Lacs, 22,330 . . . .D5
Morrison, 31,712 . . . . .C4
Mower, 38,603 . . . . . . .E7
Murray, 9,165 . . . . . . .B6
Nicollet, 29,771 . . . . . .C6
Nobles, 20,832 . . . . . . .B7
Norman, 7,442 . . . . . . .A3
Olmsted, 124,277 . . . . .E7
Otter Tail, 57,159 . . . . .B4
Pennington, 13,584 . . .A2
Pine, 26,530 . . . . .E4
Pipestone, 9,895 . . . . .A6
Polk, 31,369 . . . . .A3
Pope, 11,236 . . . . .B5
Ramsey, 511,035 . . .D5, F6
Red Lake, 4,299 . . . . . .A3
Redwood, 16,815 . . . . .B6
Renville, 17,154 . . . . . .C6
Rice, 56,665 . . . . .D6
Rock, 9,721 . . . . .A7
Roseau, 16,338 . . . . . .B2
St. Louis, 200,528 . . . .E2
Scott, 89,498 . . . . .D6
Sherburne, 64,417 . . . .D5
Sibley, 15,356 . . . . . . .C6
Stearns, 133,166 . . . . .C5
Steele, 33,680 . . . . . . .D6
Stevens, 10,053 . . . . . .A5
Swift, 11,956 . . . . .B5
Todd, 24,426 . . . . .C4
Traverse, 4,134 . . . . . .A5
Wabasha, 21,610 . . . . .E6
Wadena, 13,713 . . . . . .C4
Waseca, 19,526 . . . . . .D6
Washington,
201,130 . . . . . . .E5, F5
Watonwan, 11,876 . . . .C6
Wilkin, 7,138 . . . . .A4
Winona, 49,985 . . . . . .F7
Wright, 89,986 . . . . . . .D5
Yellow Medicine,
11,080 . . . . .B6

Cities and Towns

Ada, 1,657 . . . . .A3
Adams, 800 . . . . .E7
Adrian, 1,234 . . . . .B7
Afton, 2,839 . . . . .E6
Aitkin, 1,984 . . . . .D4
Akeley, 412 . . . . .C3
Albany, 1,796 . . . . .C5
Alberta, 142 . . . . .A5
Albert Lea, 18,356 . . . .D7
Albertville, 3,621 . . . . . .D5
Alborn, 60 . . . . .E4
Alden, 652 . . . . .D7
Aldrich, 53 . . . . .C4
Alexandria, 8,820 . . . . .B5
Alida B3
Almora, 50 . . . . .B4
Alpha, 126 . . . . .C7
Altura, 417 . . . . .F6
Alvarado, 371 . . . . .A2
Alwwood C3
Amboy, 575 . . . . .C7
Amiret, 70 . . . . .B6
Andover, 26,588 . . . . . .D5
Angle Inlet B1
Angora E3
Angus, 40 . . . . .A2
Annandale, 2,684 . . . . .C5
Anoka, 18,076 . . . .D5, E5
Appleton, 2,871 . . . . . .A5
Apple Valley, 45,527 . . .D6
Arco, 100 . . . . .A6
Arden Hills, 9,652 . . . . .F5
Argyle, 656 . . . . .A2
Arlington, 2,048 . . . . . .C6
Arnold, 3,032 . . . . .E4
Ashby, 472 . . . . .B4
Askov, 368 . . . . .E4
Atkinson, 50 . . . . .E4
Atwater, 1,079 . . . . . . .C5
Audubon, 445 . . . . .B4
Aurora, 1,850 . . . . .E3
Austin, 23,314 . . . . . . .E7
Averill A4
Avoca, 146 . . . . .B7
Avon, 1,242 . . . . .C5
Babbitt, 1,670 . . . . . . .F3
Backus, 311 . . . . .C4
Badger, 470 . . . . .A2
Bagley, 1,235 . . . . .B3
Baker, 80 . . . . .A4
Balaton, 637 . . . . .B6
Ball Bluff D4
Ball Club, 80 . . . . .D3
Barnesville, 2,173 . . . . .A4
Barnum, 525 . . . . .E4
Barrett, 355 . . . . .B5
Barrows, 80 . . . . .C4
Barry, 25 . . . . .A5
Basswood, 80 . . . . .B4
Battle Lake, 686 . . . . . .B4
Baudette, 1,104 . . . . . .C2
Baxter, 5,555 . . . . .C4
Bay Lake, 50 . . . . .D4
Beardsley, 262 . . . . . . .A5
Bear River D3
Beaulieu B3
Beaver Bay, 175 . . . . . .F3
Beaver Creek, 250 . . . .A7
Bechyn, 40 . . . . .B6
Becida, 50 . . . . .B3
Becker, 2,673 . . . . .D5
Bejou, 94 . . . . .B3
Belgrade, 750 . . . . .B5
Bellaire, 1,400 . . . . . . .F5
Bellechester, 172 . . . . .E6
Belle Plaine, 3,789 . . . .D6
Bellingham, 205 . . . . . .A5
Beltrami, 101 . . . . .A3
Belview, 417 . . . . .B6
Bemidji, 11,917 . . . . . .C3
Bena, 110 . . . . .C3
Benedict, 150 . . . . .C3
Benson, 3,376 . . . . . . .B5
Bergen, 40 . . . . .C7
Bergville C3
Berner B3
Beroun, 125 . . . . .E5
Bertha, 470 . . . . .B4
Bethel, 443 . . . . .D5
Big Bend City, 100 . . . .B5
Bigelow, 231 . . . . .B7
Big Falls, 264 . . . . .D2
Bigfork, 469 . . . . .D3
Big Lake, 6,063 . . . . . . .D5
Bingham Lake, 167 . . . .B7
Birchdale, 50 . . . . .C2
Birchwood Village, 968 . .F5
Bird Island, 1,195 . . . . .C6
Biscay, 114 . . . . .C6
Biwabik, 954 . . . . .E3
Bixby, 60 . . . . .D7
Blackberry, 100 . . . . . . .D3
Blackduck, 696 . . . . . . .C3
Blaine, 44,942 . . . . . . .F5
Blakeley, 50 . . . . .D6
Blomkest, 186 . . . . .B6
Blooming Prairie, 1,933 .D7
Bloomington,
85,172 . . . . .D6, F6
Blue Earth, 3,621 . . . . .C7
Blue Grass, 50 . . . . . . .C4
Bluffton, 210 . . . . .B4
Bock, 106 . . . . .D5
Border, 40 . . . . .C2
Borup, 91 . . . . .A3
Bovey, 662 . . . . .D3

Bowlus, 260 . . . . .C5
Bowstring, 40 . . . . . . .D3
Boy River, 38 . . . . . . .C3
Bradford, 200 . . . . . . .D5
Braham, 1,276 . . . . . .D5
Brainerd, 13,178 . . . . .C4
Brandon, 450 . . . . . . .B5
Breckenridge, 3,559 . . .A4
Breezy Point, 979 . . . .C4
Brennyville, 100 . . . . . .C5
Brevik, 50 . . . . .D5
Brewster, 502 . . . . . . .B7
Bricelyn, 379 . . . . .D7
Brimson F3
Britt, 125 . . . . .E3
Brooklyn Center, 29,172 E5
Brooklyn Park,
67,388 . . . . .D5, E5
Brook Park, 156 . . . . . .D5
Brooks, 141 . . . . .A3
Brookston, 98 . . . . . . .E4
Brooten, 649 . . . . .B5
Browerville, 735 . . . . . .C4
Brownsdale, 718 . . . . .E7
Browns Valley, 690 . . . .A5
Brownsville, 517 . . . . . .F7
Brownton, 807 . . . . . . .C6
Bruno, 102 . . . . .E4
Brunswick, 225 . . . . . .A4
Brushvale A4
Buckman, 208 . . . . . . .C5
Buffalo, 10,097 . . . . . .D5
Buffalo Lake, 768 . . . . .C6
Buhl, 983 . . . . .E3
Burchard, 40 . . . . .B6
Burnett, 60 . . . . .E4
Burnsville, 60,220 . . . .F6
Burr, 40 . . . . .A6
Burtrum, 146 . . . . .C5
Butler B4
Butterfield, 564 . . . . . .C7
Buyck E2
Bygland, 50 . . . . .A3
Byron, 3,500 . . . . .E6
Caledonia, 2,965 . . . . .F7
Callaway, 200 . . . . . . .B4
Calumet, 383 . . . . .D3
Cambridge, 5,520 . . . .D5
Campbell, 241 . . . . . . .A4
Canby, 1,903 . . . . .A6
Cannon Falls, 3,795 . . .E6
Canton, 343 . . . . .F7
Canyon E3
Caribou A2
Carlisle, 60 . . . . .A4
Carlos, 329 . . . . .B5
Carlton, 810 . . . . .E4
Carp C2
Carver, 1,266 . . . . .D6
Cass Lake, 860 . . . . . . .C3
Castle Danger F3
Cedar Mills, 53 . . . . . .C6
Celina D3
Center City, 582 . . . . . .E5
Centerville, 3,202 . . . . .F5
Central C4
Ceylon, 413 . . . . .C7
Champlin, 22,193 . . . . .E5
Chandler, 276 . . . . . . .B7
Chanhassen, 20,321 . . .D6
Charlesville A5
Chaska, 17,449 . . . . . .D6
Chatfield, 2,394 . . . . . .E7
Chickamaw Beach, 148 .C4
Chisago City, 2,622 . . . .E5
Chisholm, 4,960 . . . . . .E3
Chokio, 443 . . . . .A5
Circle Pines, 4,663 . . . .F5
Clara City, 1,393 . . . . . .B6
Claremont, 620 . . . . . . .E6
Clarissa, 609 . . . . .C4
Clarkfield, 944 . . . . . . .B6
Clarks Grove, 734 . . . . .D7
Clearbrook, 551 . . . . . .B3
Clear Lake, 266 . . . . . .D5
Clearwater, 858 . . . . . .C5
Clements, 191 . . . . . . .B6
Clementson, 40 . . . . . .C2
Cleveland, 673 . . . . . . .D6
Climax, 243 . . . . .A3
Clinton, 453 . . . . .A5
Clitherall, 118 . . . . .B4
Clontarf, 173 . . . . .B5
Cloquet, 11,201 . . . . . .E4
Clotho C4
Cloverdale, 70 . . . . . . .E4
Cloverton E4
Coates, 163 . . . . .C6
Cobden, 61 . . . . .C6
Cohasset, 2,481 . . . . . .D3
Cokato, 2,727 . . . . . . .C5
Cold Spring, 2,975 . . . .C5
Coleraine, 1,110 . . . . . .D3
Collis A5
Cologne, 1,012 . . . . . . .D6
Columbia Heights,
18,520 . . . . .F5
Comfrey, 367 . . . . .C6
Comstock, 123 . . . . . . .A4
Conger, 133 . . . . .D7
Cook, 622 . . . . .E2
Coon Rapids,
61,607 . . . . .D5, E5
Corcoran, 5,630 . . . . . .D5
Cormorant, 70 . . . . . . .A4
Correll, 47 . . . . .A5
Cosmos, 582 . . . . .C6
Cottage Grove, 30,582 .F6
Cotton, 70 . . . . .E3
Cottonwood, 1,148 . . . .B6
Courtland, 538 . . . . . . .C6
Craigville D3
Crane Lake E2
Cromwell, 143 . . . . . . .E4
Crookston, 8,192 . . . . .A3
Crosby, 2,389 . . . . . . .D4
Cross Lake, 1,893 . . . . .C4
Crown, 80 . . . . .D5
Crow River, 40 . . . . . . .D5
Crystal, 22,698 . . . . . . .E5
Culver, 40 . . . . .E4
Currie, 225 . . . . .B6
Cushing, 40 . . . . .C4
Cusson E2
Cutler D4
Cuyuna, 231 . . . . .D4

Cyrus, 303 . . . . .B5
Dakota, 329 . . . . .F7
Dalbo, 80 . . . . .D5
Dale, 50 . . . . .A4
Dalton, 258 . . . . .B4
Danube, 529 . . . . .B6
Danvers, 108 . . . . .B5
Darfur, 137 . . . . .C6
Darwin, 276 . . . . .C5
Dassel, 1,233 . . . . . . .C5
Dawson, 1,539 . . . . . .A6
Day, 215 . . . . .D5
Dayton, 4,699 . . . . . . .D5
Debs B3
Deephaven, 3,853 . . . .E6
Deer Creek, 328 . . . . .B4
Deer River, 903 . . . . . .D3
Deerwood, 590 . . . . . .D4
De Graff, 133 . . . . .B5
Delano, 3,837 . . . . . . .D5
Delavan, 223 . . . . .C7
Delft, 90 . . . . .B7
Delhi, 69 . . . . .B6
Dellwood, 1,033 . . . . . .F5
Denham, 40 . . . . .E4
Dennison, 168 . . . . . . .D6
Dent, 192 . . . . .B4
Detroit Lakes, 7,348 . . .B4
Dexter, 333 . . . . .E7
Dilworth, 3,001 . . . . . .A4
Dodge Center, 2,226 . . .E7
Donaldson, 41 . . . . . . .A2
Donnelly, 254 . . . . .B5
Doran, 59 . . . . .A4
Dorothy A4
Dorset, 100 . . . . .B4
Douglas, 175 . . . . .E6
Dover, 438 . . . . .E7
Dovray, 67 . . . . .B6
Downer A4
Duelm, 100 . . . . .D5
Dumont, 122 . . . . .A5
Dundas, 547 . . . . .D6
Dundee, 102 . . . . .B7
Dunnell, 197 . . . . .C7
Dunvilla, 80 . . . . .A4
Duquette, 60 . . . . .E4
Eagan, 63,557 . . . . . . .F6
Eagle Bend, 595 . . . . .B4
Eagle Lake, 1,787 . . . . .D6
East Bethel, 10,941 . . .D5
East Grand Forks, 7,501 A3
East Gull Lake, 978 . . .C4
Easton, 214 . . . . .D7
Ebro, 60 . . . . .B3
Echo, 278 . . . . .B6
Eden Prairie, 54,901 . . .D6
Eden Valley, 866 . . . . .C5
Edgerton, 1,033 . . . . . .A7
Edina, 47,425 . . . .D6, E6
Effie, 91 . . . . .D3
Eitzen, 229 . . . . .F7
Elba, 214 . . . . .E6
Elbow Lake, 1,275 . . . .B5
Eldred, 50 . . . . .A3
Elgin, 826 . . . . .E6
Elizabeth, 172 . . . . . . .A4
Elko, 472 . . . . .D6
Elk River, 16,447 . . . . .D5
Elkton, 149 . . . . .E7
Ellendale, 590 . . . . . . .D7
Ellsworth, 540 . . . . . . .A7
Elmdale, 107 . . . . .C5
Elmer, 50 . . . . .D4
Elmore, 735 . . . . .C7
Elrosa, 166 . . . . .C5
Ely, 3,724 . . . . .F3
Elysian, 486 . . . . .D6
Embarrass, 70 . . . . . . .E3
Emily, 847 . . . . .D4
Emmons, 432 . . . . . . .D7
Erdahl B5
Erhard, 150 . . . . .A4
Ericsburg, 60 . . . . .D2
Erie B2
Erskine, 437 . . . . .A3
Esko, 1,300 . . . . .E4
Etna, 40 . . . . .E7
Euclid, 70 . . . . .A3
Evan, 91 . . . . .C6
Evansville, 566 . . . . . . .B4
Eveleth, 3,865 . . . . . . .E3
Everdell A4
Evergreen, 72 . . . . . . .D6
Excelsior, 2,393 . . . . . .D6
Eyota, 1,644 . . . . .E7
Fairbanks F3
Fairfax, 1,295 . . . . . . .C6
Fairmont, 10,889 . . . . .C7
Faith, 50 . . . . .A3
Falcon Heights, 5,572 . .F5
Faribault, 20,818 . . . . .D6
Farmington, 12,365 . . .D6
Farwell, 57 . . . . .B5
Federal Dam, 101 . . . . .C3
Felton, 216 . . . . .A3
Fergus Falls, 13,471 . . .A4
Fernando, 50 . . . . .C6
Fertile, 893 . . . . .A3
Fifty Lakes, 392 . . . . . .C4
Finland, 40 . . . . .F3
Finlayson, 314 . . . . . . .E4
Fisher, 435 . . . . .A3
Flensburg, 244 . . . . . . .C5
Flom, 60 . . . . .A3
Floodwood, 503 . . . . . .E4
Florence, 61 . . . . .A6
Florenton, 125 . . . . . . .E3
Foley, 2,154 . . . . .D5
Forada, 197 . . . . .B5
Forbes, 50 . . . . .E3
Forest Center F3
Forest City, 125 . . . . . .C5
Forest Lake, 6,798 . . . .E5
Foreston, 389 . . . . .D5
Fossum A3
Fountain, 343 . . . . .E7
Fourtown B2
Fox, 175 . . . . .B2
Foxhome, 143 . . . . . . .A4
Franklin (Renville Co.),
498 . . . . .C6
Frazee, 1,377 . . . . .B4
Freeborn, 305 . . . . . . .D7

Freedhem, 50 . . . . . . .C4
Freeport, 454 . . . . . . .C5
French River, 325 . . . . .E4
Fridley, 27,449 . . . . . . .F5
Frost, 251 . . . . .D7
Fulda, 1,283 . . . . .B7
Funkley, 15 . . . . .C3
Garden City, 275 . . . . .C6
Garfield, 281 . . . . .B5
Garrison, 213 . . . . .D4
Garvin, 159 . . . . .B6
Gary, 215 . . . . .A3
Gaylord, 2,279 . . . . . . .C6
Gemmell C3
Geneva, 449 . . . . .D7
Genola, 71 . . . . .C5
Gentilly, 100 . . . . .A3
Georgetown, 125 . . . . .A3
Gheen E3
Ghent, 315 . . . . .B6
Gibbon, 808 . . . . .C6
Gilbert, 1,847 . . . . . . .E3
Gilman, 215 . . . . .D5
Glen, 50 . . . . .D4
Glencoe, 5,453 . . . . . .C6
Glenville, 720 . . . . .D7
Glenwood, 2,594 . . . . .B5
Gluek, 40 . . . . .B6
Glyndon, 1,049 . . . . . .A4
Golden Valley, 20,281 . .E5
Gonvick, 294 . . . . .B3
Goodhue, 778 . . . . . . .E6
Goodland, 60 . . . . .D3
Goodridge, 98 . . . . . . .A2
Good Thunder, 592 . . . .C6
Goodview, 3,373 . . . . .F6
Gordonsville, 125 . . . . .D7
Gowan E4
Graceton C2
Graceville, 605 . . . . . . .A5
Granada, 317 . . . . .C7
Grand Falls D2
Grand Marais, 1,353 . . .F2
Grand Meadow, 945 . . .E7
Grand Portage, 100 . . . .F2
Grand Rapids, 7,764 . . .D3
Grandy, 175 . . . . .D5
Granger, 50 . . . . .E7
Granite Falls, 3,070 . . . .B6
Grasston, 105 . . . . . . .D5
Greaney D3
Greenbush, 784 . . . . . .A2
Greenfield, 2,544 . . . . .D5
Green Isle, 334 . . . . . .C6
Greenleaf, 40 . . . . .C5
Greenleafton, 125 . . . . .E7
Green Valley, 150 . . . . .B6
Greenview A3
Greenwald, 201 . . . . . .C5
Grey Eagle, 335 . . . . . .C5
Grove City, 608 . . . . . .C5
Grove Lake, 50 . . . . . .B5
Grygla, 228 . . . . .B2
Gully, 106 . . . . .B3
Guthrie, 50 . . . . .C3
Hackensack, 285 . . . . .C4
Hadley, 81 . . . . .B6
Hallock, 1,196 . . . . . . .A2
Halma, 78 . . . . .A2
Halstad, 622 . . . . .A3
Hamburg, 538 . . . . . . .D6
Ham Lake, 12,710 . . . .D5
Hammond, 198 . . . . . .E6
Hampton, 434 . . . . . . .D6
Hancock, 717 . . . . . . .B5
Hanley Falls, 323 . . . . .B6
Hanover, 1,355 . . . . . .D5
Hanska, 443 . . . . .C6
Harding, 105 . . . . .C4
Hardwick, 222 . . . . . . .A7
Harmony, 1,080 . . . . . .E7
Harris, 1,121 . . . . .E5
Hartland, 288 . . . . .D7
Hassman, 40 . . . . .D4
Hastings, 18,204 . . . . .E6
Hatfield, 47 . . . . .A7
Hawick, 125 . . . . .C5
Hawley, 1,882 . . . . . . .A4
Hay Creek, 90 . . . . . . .E6
Hayfield, 1,325 . . . . . . .E7
Hayward, 249 . . . . . . .D7
Hazel Run, 64 . . . . . . .B6
Hector, 1,166 . . . . .C6
Heidelberg, 72 . . . . . . .D6
Henderson, 910 . . . . . .D6
Hendricks, 725 . . . . . .A6
Hendrum, 315 . . . . . . .A3
Henning, 719 . . . . .B4
Henriette, 101 . . . . . . .D5
Herman, 452 . . . . .A5
Hermantown, 7,448 . . .E4
Heron Lake, 768 . . . . .B7
Hewitt, 267 . . . . .B4
Hibbing, 17,071 . . . . . .E3
Highland
(Fillmore Co.), 40 . . . .F7
Highland (Lake Co.) F3
High Landing A2
High Forest E7
Hill City, 479 . . . . .D4
Hillman, 29 . . . . .D4
Hills, 565 . . . . .A7
Hilltop, 766 . . . . .F5
Hillview B4
Hinckley, 1,291 . . . . . .E4
Hines, 50 . . . . .C3
Hitterdal, 201 . . . . .A4
Hoffman, 672 . . . . .B5
Hokah, 614 . . . . .F7
Holdingford, 736 . . . . . .C5
Holland, 215 . . . . .A6
Hollandale, 292 . . . . . .D7
Holloway, 112 . . . . . . .B5
Holmes City, 100 . . . . .B5
Holt, 80 . . . . .A2
Holyoke, 100 . . . . .F4
Hope, 125 . . . . .D7
Hopkins, 17,145 . . . . . .E6
Houston, 1,020 . . . . . .F7
Hovland F2
Howard Lake, 1,853 . . .C5
Hoyt Lakes, 2,082 . . . .E3
Hubbard, 200 . . . . . . .B4
Hugo, 6,363 . . . . .F5
Humboldt, 61 . . . . .A2
Huntersville C4
Huntley, 150 . . . . .C7

Hutchinson, 13,080 . . .C6
Idington, 50 . . . . .E3
Ihlen, 107 . . . . .A7
Illgen City F3
Independence, 40 . . . . .E5
Indus D2
Inger, 100 . . . . .D3
Inguadona C4
International Falls,
6,703 . . . . .D2
Inver Grove Heights,
29,751 . . . . .F6
Iona, 173 . . . . .B7
Iron Junction, 93 . . . . .E3
Ironton, 498 . . . . .D4
Isabella F3
Isanti, 2,324 . . . . .D5
Island Lake
(Beltrami Co.), 40 . . .B3
Island Lake
(St. Louis Co.), 50 . . .E3
Island View, 150 . . . . .D2
Isle, 707 . . . . .D4
Ivanhoe, 679 . . . . .A6
Jackson, 3,501 . . . . . .B7
Jacobson, 80 . . . . .D4
Janesville, 2,109 . . . . .D6
Jasper, 597 . . . . .A7
Jeffers, 396 . . . . .B6
Jenkins, 287 . . . . .C4
Johnson, 32 . . . . .A5
Jordan, 3,833 . . . . . . .D6
Judson, 70 . . . . .C6
Kabekona, 40 . . . . . . .C3
Kabetogama, 40 . . . . .D2
Kanaranzi, 80 . . . . . . .A7
Kandiyohi, 555 . . . . . .C5
Karlstad, 794 . . . . .A2
Kasota, 680 . . . . .C6
Kasson, 4,398 . . . . . . .E7
Keewatin, 1,164 . . . . . .D3
Kelliher, 294 . . . . .C3
Kellogg, 439 . . . . .F6
Kelsey, 40 . . . . .E3
Kennedy, 255 . . . . .A2
Kennel, 61 . . . . .A7
Kensington, 286 . . . . . .B5
Kent, 120 . . . . .A4
Kenyon, 1,661 . . . . . . .E6
Kerkhoven, 759 . . . . . .B5
Kerrick, 71 . . . . .E4
Kettle River, 168 . . . . . .E4
Kiester, 540 . . . . .D7
Kilkenny, 148 . . . . .D6
Kimball, 635 . . . . .C5
Kimberly D4
Kinbrae, 21 . . . . .B7
Kingsdale E4
Kingston, 120 . . . . .C5
Kinney, 199 . . . . .E3
Klossner, 100 . . . . . . .C6
Knife River, 300 . . . . . .F4
Kragnes, 41 . . . . .A4
Lac qui Parle, 50 . . . . .B6
La Crescent, 4,923 . . . .F7
Lafayette, 529 . . . . . . .C6
Lake Benton, 703 . . . . .A6
Lake Bronson, 246 . . . .A2
Lake City, 4,950 . . . . . .E6
Lake Crystal, 2,420 . . . .C6
Lake Elmo, 6,863 . . . . .F5
Lakefield, 1,721 . . . . . .B7
Lake George, 150 . . . . .C3
Lake Henry, 90 . . . . . . .C5
Lake Itasca B3
Lakeland, 1,917 . . . . . .F6
Lake Lillian, 257 . . . . . .C6
Lake Park, 782 . . . . . . .A4
Lake Shore, 966 . . . . . .C4
Lakeville, 43,128 . . . . .D6
Lake Wilson, 270 . . . . .B6
Lamberton, 859 . . . . . .B6
Lamoille, 60 . . . . .F7
Lancaster, 363 . . . . . . .A2
Landfall, 700 . . . . .F6
Lanesboro, 788 . . . . . .E7
Lansing, 225 . . . . .E7
Laporte, 145 . . . . .C3
La Prairie, 605 . . . . . . .D3
Larsmont, 100 . . . . . . .F4
La Salle, 90 . . . . .C6
Lastrup, 99 . . . . .C4
Lauderdale, 2,364 . . . . .F5
Lavinia, 100 . . . . .C3
Lawler D4
Lawndale A4
Leader C4
Leavenworth C6
Le Center, 2,240 . . . . .D6
Leetonia, 40 . . . . .E3
Lengby, 79 . . . . .B3
Leonard, 29 . . . . .B3
Leonidas, 60 . . . . .E3
Leota, 230 . . . . .A7
Le Roy, 925 . . . . .E7
Lester Prairie, 1,377 . . .C6
Le Sueur, 3,922 . . . . . .D6
Lewiston, 1,484 . . . . . .F7
Lewisville, 274 . . . . . . .C7
Lexington, 2,214 . . . . .F5
Libby D4
Lilydale, 552 . . . . .F6
Lime Creek, 50 . . . . . .B7
Lincoln, 40 . . . . .D4
Lindford D2
Lindstrom, 3,015 . . . . .E5
Lino Lakes, 16,791 . . . .F5
Lismore, 238 . . . . .B7
Litchfield, 6,562 . . . . . .C5
Little Canada, 9,771 . . .F5
Little Falls, 7,719 . . . . .C5
Littlefork, 680 . . . . .D2
Little Marais F3
Little Rock
(Beltrami Co.) B3
Little Rock
(Morrison Co.), 50 . . .C5
Little Sauk, 125 . . . . . .C5
Lockhart A3
Loman, 60 . . . . .D2
London, 90 . . . . .D7
Long Beach, 271 . . . . .B5
Long Lake, 1,842 . . . . .D5
Long Prairie, 3,040 . . . .C5
Longville, 180 . . . . .C4
Lonsdale, 1,491 . . . . . .D6
Louisburg, 26 . . . . .A5

Lowry, 271 . . . . .B5
Lucan, 226 . . . . .B6
Lude, 60 . . . . .C2
Lutsen, 100 . . . . .F2
Luverne, 4,617 . . . . . . .A7
Lyle, 566 . . . . .E7
Lynd, 346 . . . . .B6
Mabel, 766 . . . . .F7
Madelia, 2,340 . . . . . . .C6
Madison, 1,768 . . . . . .A5
Madison Lake, 837 . . . .D6
Magnolia, 221 . . . . . . .A7
Mahnomen, 1,202 . . . .B3
Mahtomedi, 7,563 . . . . .F5
Mahtowa, 80 . . . . .E4
Makinen, 60 . . . . .E3
Malmo, 60 . . . . .D4
Manannah, 100 . . . . . .C5
Manchester, 81 . . . . . .D7
Manhattan Beach, 50 . .C4
Mankato, 32,427 . . . . .C6
Mantorville, 1,054 . . . . .E6
Maple Bay, 80 . . . . . . .A3
Maple Grove,
50,365 . . . . . .D5, E5
Maple Lake, 1,633 . . . .C5
Maple Plain, 2,088 . . . .D5
Mapleton, 1,678 . . . . . .D7
Maplewood, 34,947 . . .F5
Marble, 695 . . . . .D3
Marcell, 60 . . . . .D3
Marcoux A3
Marietta, 174 . . . . .A5
Marine on St. Croix,
602 . . . . .E5
Markham, 60 . . . . .E3
Markville E4
Marshall, 12,735 . . . . .B6
Matawan, 40 . . . . .D7
Max, 40 . . . . .C3
Maynard, 388 . . . . . . .B6
Mazeppa, 778 . . . . . . .E6
McGrath, 65 . . . . .D4
McGregor, 404 . . . . . .D4
McIntosh, 638 . . . . . . .B3
Meadowlands, 111 . . . .E3
Medford, 845 . . . . .D6
Medina, 4,005 . . . . . . .D5
Meire Grove, 149 . . . . .C5
Melby, 80 . . . . .B4
Melrose, 3,091 . . . . . . .C5
Melrude E3
Menahga, 1,220 . . . . . .B4
Mendota, 197 . . . . . . .F6
Mendota Heights,
11,434 . . . . .F6
Mentor, 150 . . . . .A3
Merrifield, 275 . . . . . . .C4
Middle River, 319 . . . . .A2
Midway E4
Miesville, 135 . . . . .E6
Milaca, 2,580 . . . . . . .D5
Milan, 326 . . . . .B5
Millerville, 115 . . . . . . .B4
Millville, 186 . . . . .E6
Milroy, 317 . . . . .B6
Miltona, 279 . . . . .B4
Minneapolis,
382,618 . . . . . .D5, E6
Minneiska, 116 . . . . . .F6
Minneota, 1,449 . . . . .B6
Minnesota City, 235 . . .F6
Minnesota Lake, 681 . .D7
Minnetonka, 51,301 . . .E6
Minnetrista, 4,358 . . . .D6
Mizpah, 78 . . . . .C3
Money Creek, 70 . . . . .F7
Montevideo, 5,346 . . . .B6
Montgomery, 2,794 . . . .D6
Monticello, 7,868 . . . . .D5
Montrose, 1,143 . . . . . .D5
Moorhead, 32,177 . . . .A4
Moose Lake, 2,239 . . . .E4
Mora, 3,193 . . . . .D5
Morgan, 903 . . . . .C6
Morrill, 175 . . . . .C5
Morris, 5,068 . . . . .B5
Morristown, 981 . . . . . .D6
Morton, 442 . . . . .C6
Motley, 585 . . . . .C4
Mound, 9,435 . . . . . . .D6
Mounds View, 12,738 . .F5
Mountain Iron, 2,999 . .E3
Mountain Lake, 2,082 . .C7
Murdock, 303 . . . . . . .B5
Murphy City F3
Myrtle, 63 . . . . .D7
Nashua, 69 . . . . .A4
Nashwauk, 935 . . . . . .D3
Nassau, 83 . . . . .A5
Naytahwaush, 583 . . . .B3
Nebish, 90 . . . . .C3
Nelson, 172 . . . . .B5
Nerstrand, 233 . . . . . . .D6
Nett Lake, 50 . . . . .D2
Nevis, 364 . . . . .C4
New Auburn, 480 . . . . .C6
New Brighton, 22,206 . .F5
Newfolden, 362 . . . . . .A2
New Germany, 346 . . . .D6
New Hope, 20,873 . . . .E5
New London, 1,066 . . .C5
New Market, 332 . . . . .D6
New Munich, 352 . . . . .C5
Newport, 3,715 . . . . . .F6
New Prague, 4,559 . . . .D6
New Richland, 1,197 . . .D7
New Trier, 116 . . . . . . .D6
New Ulm, 13,594 . . . . .C6
New York Mills, 1,158 . .B4
Nickerson, 40 . . . . . . .E4
Nicollet, 889 . . . . .C6
Nielsville, 91 . . . . .A3
Nimrod, 75 . . . . .C4
Nisswa, 1,953 . . . . . . .C4
Norcross, 59 . . . . .A5
Noreland, 50 . . . . .E4
North Branch, 8,023 . . .E5
Northcote A2
Northfield, 17,147 . . . . .D6
North Mankato, 11,798 .C6
North Oaks, 3,883 . . . .F5
Northome, 230 . . . . . . .C3
North Redwood B6
Northrop, 262 . . . . .C7
North St. Paul, 11,929 . .F5

Norwood (Norwood-Young
America), 3,108 . . . . .C6
Noyes A2
Oakdale, 26,653 . . . . . .F5
Oak Grove, 6,903 . . . . .D5
Oakland, 60 . . . . .D7
Oak Park, 125 . . . . . . .D5
Oak Park Heights, 3,957 F5
Oakport, 1,334 . . . . . . .A4
Odessa, 113 . . . . .A5
Odin, 125 . . . . .C7
Ogema, 143 . . . . .B3
Ogilvie, 474 . . . . .D5
Okabena, 185 . . . . . . .B7
Oklee, 396 . . . . .B3
Olivia, 2,570 . . . . .C6
Onamia, 847 . . . . .D4
Orleans A2
Ormsby, 154 . . . . .C7
Orono, 7,538 . . . . .D6
Oronoco, 883 . . . . .E6
Orr, 249 . . . . .E2
Ortonville, 2,158 . . . . . .A5
Osage, 150 . . . . .B4
Osakis, 1,567 . . . . .B5
Oslo, 347 . . . . .A2
Osseo, 2,434 . . . . .E5
Ostrander, 212 . . . . . . .E7
Otisco, 60 . . . . .D7
Otsego, 6,389 . . . . . . .D5
Ottawa, 125 . . . . .D6
Ottertail, 451 . . . . .B4
Outing, 100 . . . . .C4
Owatonna, 22,434 . . . .D6
Oylen, 50 . . . . .C4
Palisade, 118 . . . . .D4
Palmers, 80 . . . . .F4
Parkers Prairie, 991 . . . .B4
Park Rapids, 3,276 . . . .B4
Payne E3
Paynesville, 2,267 . . . . .C5
Pease, 163 . . . . .D5
Pelican Rapids, 2,374 . .A4
Pelland, 90 . . . . .D2
Pemberton, 246 . . . . . .D6
Pencer B2
Pengilly, 350 . . . . .D3
Pennock, 500 . . . . . . .B5
Pequot Lakes, 947 . . . .C4
Perley, 121 . . . . .A3
Petersburg C7
Peterson, 269 . . . . . . .F7
Phelps, 40 . . . . .B4
Philbrook C4
Pierz, 1,277 . . . . .C5
Pigeon River F2
Pillager, 420 . . . . .C4
Pine Brook, 175 . . . . . .D5
Pine Center, 80 . . . . . .D4
Pine City, 3,043 . . . . . .E5
Pinecreek B2
Pine Island, 2,337 . . . .E6
Pine River, 928 . . . . . .C4
Pine Springs, 421 . . . . .F5
Pinewood, 50 . . . . .B3
Pipestone, 4,280 . . . . .A7
Pitt C2
Plainview, 3,190 . . . . . .E6
Plato, 336 . . . . .C6
Pleasant Lake, 504 . . . .C5
Plummer, 279 . . . . . . .A3
Plymouth, 65,894 . . . . .E5
Ponemah, 874 . . . . . . .C2
Ponsford, 200 . . . . . . .B4
Porter, 190 . . . . .A6
Preston, 1,426 . . . . . . .E7
Princeton, 3,933 . . . . . .D5
Prinsburg, 458 . . . . . . .B6
Prior Lake, 15,917 . . . .D6
Proctor, 2,852 . . . . . . .E4
Prosit, 40 . . . . .E4
Puposky, 40 . . . . .C3
Quamba, 98 . . . . .D5
Racine, 355 . . . . .E7
Radium A2
Ramsey, 18,510 . . . . . .D5
Randall, 535 . . . . .C4
Randolph, 318 . . . . . . .D6
Ranier, 188 . . . . .D2
Ray D2
Raymond, 803 . . . . . . .B5
Reading, 125 . . . . .B7
Redby, 957 . . . . .C3
Red Lake, 1,430 . . . . . .B3
Red Lake Falls, 1,590 . .A3
Red Wing, 16,116 . . . . .E6
Redwood Falls, 5,459 . .B6
Regal, 40 . . . . .C5
Remer, 372 . . . . .D3
Reno F7
Renville, 1,323 . . . . . . .C6
Revere, 100 . . . . .B6
Rice, 711 . . . . .C5
Richfield, 34,439 . . . . .E6
Richmond, 1,213 . . . . .C5
Richville, 124 . . . . .B4
Richwood, 100 . . . . . . .B4
Rindal, 40 . . . . .A3
Riverton, 115 . . . . .D4
Robbin, 40 . . . . .A2
Robbinsdale, 14,123 . . .E5
Robinson E3
Rochert, 350 . . . . .B4
Rochester, 85,806 . . . .E6
Rock Creek, 1,119 . . . .E5
Rockford, 3,484 . . . . . .D5
Rockville, 749 . . . . .C5
Rogers, 3,588 . . . . . . .D5
Rollag, 60 . . . . .A4
Rollins D5
Ronneby, 16 . . . . .D5
Roosevelt, 166 . . . . . . .B2
Roscoe, 116 . . . . .C5
Roseau, 2,756 . . . . . . .B2
Rose City, 90 . . . . .B4
Rose Creek, 354 . . . . .E7
Rosemount, 14,619 . . .D6
Rosen, 60 . . . . .A5
Rosendale, 40 . . . . . . .C5
Roseville, 33,690 . . . . .F5
Rosewood, 100 . . . . . .A3
Ross B2
Rossburg, 40 . . . . .B4
Rothsay, 497 . . . . .A4
Round Lake, 424 . . . . .B7
Round Prairie, 100 . . . .C5

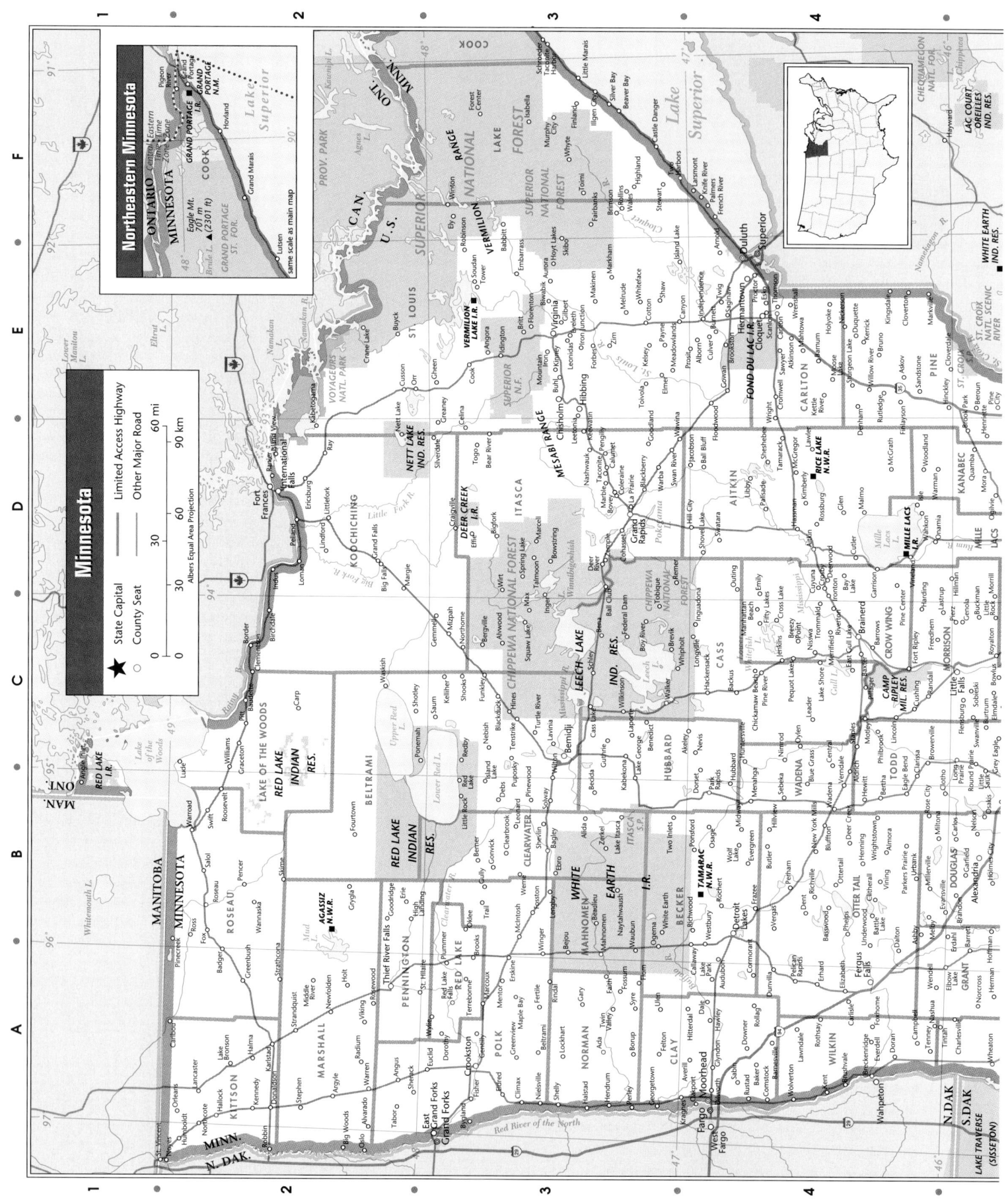

Minnesota

Legend:
★ State Capital
○ County Seat
— Limited Access Highway
— Other Major Road

0 30 60 90 km
0 30 60 mi

Albers Equal Area Projection

Northeastern Minnesota
Eagle Mt. 701 m (2301 ft)
same scale as main map

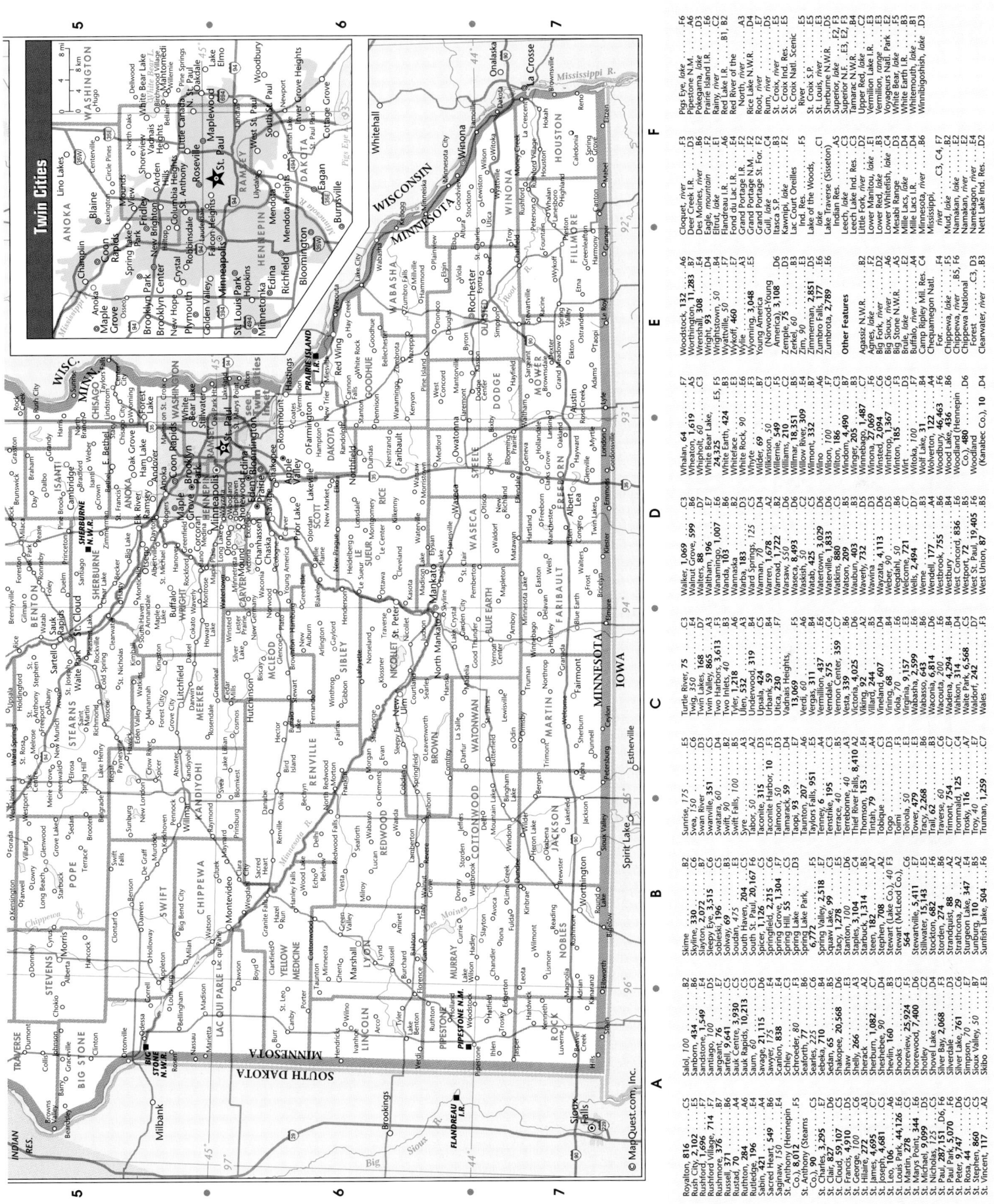

Royalton, 816 .... C5
Rush City, 2,102 .... E5
Rushford, 1,696 .... F7
Rushford Village, 714 ... F7
Rushmore, 376 .... B6
Russell, 70 .... B6
Rustad, 70 .... A4
Rutledge, 196 .... E4
Sabin, 421 .... A4
Sacred Heart, 549 ...... B5
Saginaw, 150 .... E4
St. Anthony (Stearns
  Co.), 90 .... C5
St. Charles, 3,295 ...... E7
St. Clair, 829 .... D6
St. Cloud, 59,107 ...... C5
St. Francis, 4,910 ...... D5
St. George A3
St. Hilaire, 272 .... A2
St. James, 4,695 .... C6
St. Joseph, 4,681 ...... C5
St. Leo, 106 .... B5
St. Louis Park, 44,126 .. D6
St. Martin, 278 .... C5
St. Marys Point, 344 ... E6
St. Michael, 9,099 ..... D5
St. Nicholas, 125 ...... C5
St. Paul, 287,151 ...... D6, F6
St. Paul Park, 5,070 ... F6
St. Peter, 9,747 .... D6
St. Rosa, 44 .... C5
St. Stephen, 860 .... C5
St. Vincent, 117 .... A2

Salol, 100 .... C5
Sanborn, 434 .... C6
Sandstone, 1,549 ...... E4
Santiago, 100 .... D5
Sartell, 9,641 .... C5
Sauk Centre, 3,930 .... C5
Sauk Rapids, 10,213 ... C5
Savage, 21,115 .... D6
Sawyer, 175 .... E4
Scanlon, 838 .... E4
Schley C5
Schroeder, 80 .... F3
Seaforth, 77 .... B6
Searles, 225 .... C6
Sebeka, 710 .... B4
Sedan, 65 .... B5
Shafer, 932 .... E5
Shakopee, 20,568 ..... D6
Shelly, 266 .... A3
Sherburn, 1,082 ...... C7
Sheshebee, 90 .... D4
Shevlin, 160 .... B3
Shooks C3
Shoreview, 25,924 .... D5
Shorewood, 7,400 .... D6
Shotley C3
Shovel Lake D4
Silver Bay, 2,068 ..... F3
Silver Lake, 761 ...... C6
Silverdale D3
Sioux Valley, 50 ...... B7
Skibo, 117 .... E3

Skime C2
Skyline, 330 .... C6
Slayton, 2,072 .... B7
Sleepy Eye, 3,515 .... C6
Sobieski, 196 .... C5
Solway, 69 .... B3
Soudan, 475 .... E3
South Haven, 204 .... C5
South St. Paul, 20,167 F6
Spicer, 1,126 .... C5
Springfield, 2,215 .... C6
Spring Grove, 1,304 .. F7
Spring Hill, 55 .... C5
Spring Lake Park,
  6,772 .... D6
Spring Valley, 2,518 . E7
Squaw Lake, 99 ...... C3
Stacy, 1,178 .... E5
Staples, 3,104 .... C4
Starbuck, 1,314 ..... B5
Steen, 182 .... A7
Stephen, 708 .... A2
Stewart (Lake Co.), 40 F3
Stewart (McLeod Co.),
  564 .... C6
Stewartville, 5,411 .. E7
Stillwater, 15,143 ... E6
Storden, 274 .... B6
Stockton, 682 .... F6
Strandquist, 88 ..... A2
Strathcona, 38 ...... A2
Sturgeon Lake, 347 .. E4
Sunburg, 110 .... B5
Sunfish Lake, 504 ... F6

Sunrise, 175 .... E5
Svea, 150 .... C6
Swan River, 351 .... D4
Swanville, 60 .... C5
Swatara, 60 .... D4
Swift, 90 .... A3
Swift Falls, 100 .... B5
Syre, 532 .... A3
Taconite, 319 ...... D4
Taconite Harbor, 10 . F3
Talmoon, 60 .... D3
Tamarack, 59 .... E4
Taopi, 93 .... D7
Taunton, 207 .... A6
Taylors Falls, 951 .. E5
Tenney, 6 .... A5
Tenstrike, 195 ..... C3
Terrebonne, 40 .... A2
Terrace, 40 .... B5
Thief River Falls,
  8,410 .... A2
Thomson, 153 ..... E4
Tintah, 79 .... A5
Togo D3
Toimi E3
Toivola, 50 .... E3
Tower, 479 .... E3
Tracy, 2,268 ...... B6
Trail, 62 .... B3
Trimont, 754 ...... C7
Trommald, 125 .... D4
Trosky, 116 .... A7
Troy, 40 .... E7
Truman, 1,259 .... C7

Turtle River, 75 ... C3
Twig, 350 .... E4
Twin Lakes, 168 ... D7
Twin Valley, 865 .. A3
Two Harbors, 3,613 F3
Two Inlets, 40 .... A6
Tyler, 1,218 ...... A6
Ulen, 532 .... A3
Underwood, 319 ... B4
Upsala, 424 .... C5
Urbank, 59 .... B4
Utica, 230 .... E7
Vadnais Heights,
  13,069 .... D6
Verdi, 60 .... A6
Vergas, 311 ...... B4
Vermillion, 437 ... C4
Vernon Center, 359 C7
Vesta, 339 .... B6
Victoria, 4,025 ... D6
Viking, 92 .... A2
Villard, 244 ...... B5
Vineland, 607 .... D4
Vining, 68 .... B4
Viola, 90 .... E7
Virginia, 9,157 ... E3
Wabasha, 2,599 .. E6
Wabasso, 643 .... B6
Waconia, 6,814 .. D6
Wadena, 4,294 ... B4
Wahkon, 306 ..... D4
Waite Park, 6,568 . C5
Waldorf, 242 ..... C7

Walker, 1,069 ...... C3
Walnut Grove, 599 .. B6
Waltham, 196 ...... D7
Wanamingo, 1,007 .. E6
Wanda, 103 .... B6
Wannaska C2
Warba, 183 .... D4
Ward Springs, 125 .. C5
Warren, 1,678 ..... A2
Warroad, 1,722 .... B2
Warsaw, 70 .... D6
Waseca, 8,493 ..... D6
Waskish, 50 .... C2
Watab, 425 .... C5
Waterville, 1,833 .. D6
Watkins, 880 ...... C5
Watson, 209 ...... B5
Waubun, 403 ..... A3
Waverly, 732 ..... D6
Wawina D4
Wayzata, 4,113 .. D6
Webster, 90 ...... D6
Wegdahl B5
Welcome, 721 .... C7
Wells, 2,494 ..... D7
Wendell, 177 .... B4
Westbrook, 755 .. B6
West Concord, 836 E6
Westport, 72 .... B5
West St. Paul, 19,405 F6
West Union, 87 .. B5

Whalan, 64 .... F7
Wheaton, 1,619 ... A5
White Bear Lake,
  24,325 .... E5, F6
White Earth, 424 .. A3
White Rock, 90 ... A5
Whiteface E4
Whyte A3
Wilder, 69 .... B7
Wilkinson, 50 .... D6
Willernie, 549 .... E5
Willmar, 18,351 .. B5
Willow River, 309 . E4
Wilmont, 332 .... A6
Wilson, 100 ...... E7
Windom, 186 .... B6
Winger, 205 ..... A3
Winnebago, 1,487 . C7
Winona, 27,069 .. F6
Winsted, 2,094 .. C6
Winthrop, 1,367 . C6
Winton, 185 ..... E3
Wirt D3
Witoka, 100 ..... F6
Wolf Lake, 31 ... B4
Wolverton, 177 .. A4
Woodland (Hennepin
  Co.), 480 ...... D6
Woodland (Kanabec
  Co.), 10 .... D4

Woodstock, 132 .. A6
Worthington, 11,283 B7
Wrenshall, 308 .. E4
Wright, 93 ...... D4
Wrightstown, 50 . F7
Wyattville, 50 .. F6
Wykoff, 460 .... E7
Wylie A3
Wyoming, 3,048 . D5
Young America;
  Young America),
  3,108 .... D6
Zerkel, 60 ...... C3
Zemple, 75 ..... D3
Zim, 90 .... E3
Zimmerman, 2,851 D5
Zumbro Falls, 177 E6
Zumbrota, 2,789 . E6

Other Features
Agassiz N.W.R. B2
Agnes, lake F2
Big Fork, river ... D3
Big Stone N.W.R. . A5
Brule, lake E2
Buffalo, river ... B4
Camp Ripley Mil. Res. C4
Cannon (Hennepin
  Co.), 480 ...... D6

Cloquet, river ... E4
Deer Creek I.R. .. D3
Eagle, mountain .. F2
Eltrut, lake E1
Flandreau I.R. ... A6
Fond du Lac I.R. . E4
Grand Portage I.R.
  North A3
Grand Portage N.M. F2
Grand Portage St. For. F2
Gull, lake C4
Itasca S.P. B3
Lac Court Oreilles .. B3
Indian Res. F5
Lake Traverse (Sisseton)
  Indian Res. A5
Leech, lake C3
Leech Lake Ind. Res. . C3
Little Fork, river . D2
Lower Manitou, lake E1
Lower Red, lake . C2
Lower Whitefish, lake C4
Mille Lacs, lake . D4
Mille Lacs Ind. Res. . D4
Minnesota, river . C4
Mississippi, river . F4
Mud, lake B2
Namakan, lake . E2
Namakan, river . E2
Nett Lake Ind. Res. . D2

Pigs Eye, lake ... F6
Pipestone N.M. .. A6
Pokegama, lake . D3
Prairie Island I.R. . E6
Rainy, river C2
Red River of the
  North A3
Red Lake I.R. ... C2
Rice Lake N.W.R. . D4
Root, river E7
Rum, river D5
St. Croix, river .. E5
St. Croix Natl. Scenic
  Riverway E5
St. Croix S.P. .. E5
St. Louis, river . E3
Sherburne N.W.R. . D5
Superior, lake . F2, F3
Superior N.F. ... E3
Tamarac N.W.R. . B4
Upper Red, lake . C2
Vermilion, lake . E3
Vermillion, range . E3
Voyageurs Natl. Park . E2
White Bear, lake . E5
White Earth I.R. . B3
Whitemouth, river . B1
Winnibigoshish, lake . D3

© MapQuest.com, Inc.

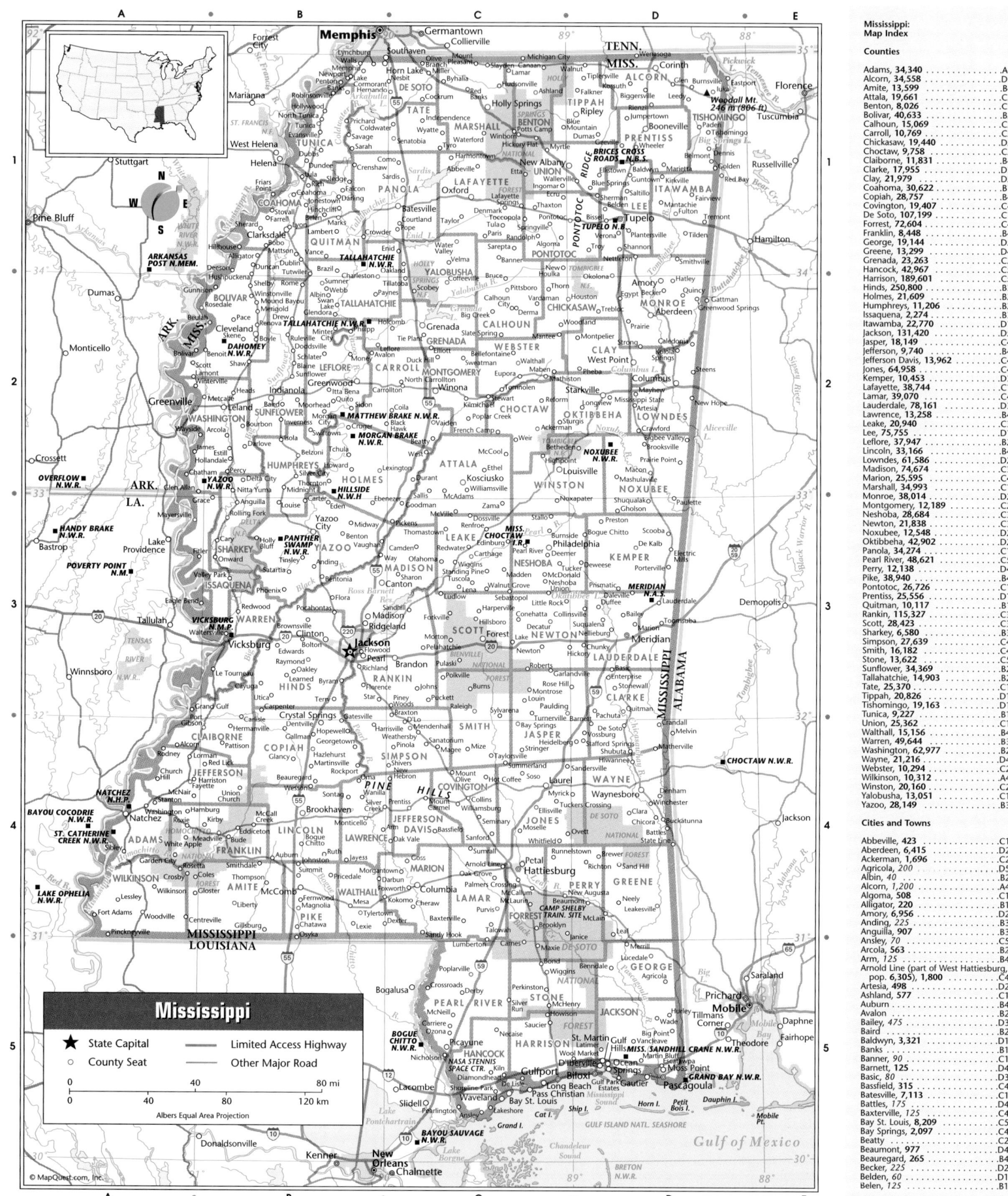

Mississippi:
Map Index

Counties

Adams, 34,340 ....A4
Alcorn, 34,558 ....D1
Amite, 13,599 ....B4
Attala, 19,661 ....C2
Benton, 8,026 ....C1
Bolivar, 40,633 ....B2
Calhoun, 15,069 ....C2
Carroll, 10,769 ....C2
Chickasaw, 19,440 ....D2
Choctaw, 9,758 ....C2
Claiborne, 11,831 ....B4
Clarke, 17,955 ....D3
Clay, 21,979 ....D2
Coahoma, 30,622 ....B1
Copiah, 28,757 ....B4
Covington, 19,407 ....C4
De Soto, 107,199 ....C1
Forrest, 72,604 ....C4
Franklin, 8,448 ....B4
George, 19,144 ....D5
Greene, 13,299 ....D4
Grenada, 23,263 ....C2
Hancock, 42,967 ....C5
Harrison, 189,601 ....C5
Hinds, 250,800 ....B3
Holmes, 21,609 ....B2
Humphreys, 11,206 ....B2
Issaquena, 2,274 ....B3
Itawamba, 22,770 ....D1
Jackson, 131,420 ....D5
Jasper, 18,149 ....C4
Jefferson, 9,740 ....B4
Jefferson Davis, 13,962 .....C4
Jones, 64,958 ....C4
Kemper, 10,453 ....D3
Lafayette, 38,744 ....C1
Lamar, 39,070 ....C4
Lauderdale, 78,161 ....D3
Lawrence, 13,258 ....B4
Leake, 20,940 ....C3
Lee, 75,755 ....D1
Leflore, 37,947 ....B2
Lincoln, 33,166 ....B4
Lowndes, 61,586 ....D2
Madison, 74,674 ....C3
Marion, 25,595 ....C4
Marshall, 34,993 ....C1
Monroe, 38,014 ....D2
Montgomery, 12,189 ....C2
Neshoba, 28,684 ....C3
Newton, 21,838 ....C3
Noxubee, 12,548 ....D2
Oktibbeha, 42,902 ....D2
Panola, 34,274 ....C1
Pearl River, 48,621 ....C5
Perry, 12,138 ....D4
Pike, 38,940 ....B4
Pontotoc, 26,726 ....C1
Prentiss, 25,556 ....D1
Quitman, 10,117 ....B1
Rankin, 115,327 ....C3
Scott, 28,423 ....C3
Sharkey, 6,580 ....B3
Simpson, 27,639 ....C4
Smith, 16,182 ....C4
Stone, 13,622 ....C5
Sunflower, 34,369 ....B2
Tallahatchie, 14,903 ....B2
Tate, 25,370 ....C1
Tippah, 20,826 ....D1
Tishomingo, 19,163 ....D1
Tunica, 9,227 ....B1
Union, 25,362 ....C1
Walthall, 15,156 ....B4
Warren, 49,644 ....B3
Washington, 62,977 ....B2
Wayne, 21,216 ....D4
Webster, 10,294 ....C2
Wilkinson, 10,312 ....A4
Winston, 20,160 ....C2
Yalobusha, 13,051 ....C1
Yazoo, 28,149 ....B3

Cities and Towns

Abbeville, 423 ....C1
Aberdeen, 6,415 ....D2
Ackerman, 1,696 ....C2
Agricola, 200 ....D5
Albin, 40 ....B2
Alcorn, 1,200 ....A4
Algoma, 508 ....C1
Alligator, 220 ....B1
Amory, 6,956 ....D2
Anding, 225 ....B3
Anguilla, 907 ....B3
Ansley, 70 ....C5
Arcola, 563 ....B2
Arm, 125 ....B4
Arnold Line (part of West Hattiesburg,
 pop. 6,305), 1,800 ....C4
Artesia, 498 ....D2
Ashland, 577 ....C1
Auburn, ...B4
Avalon, ...B2
Bailey, 475 ....D3
Baird, ...B2
Baldwyn, 3,321 ....D1
Banks, ...B1
Banner, 90 ....C1
Barnett, 125 ....D4
Basic, 80 ....D3
Bassfield, 315 ....C4
Batesville, 7,113 ....C1
Battles, 175 ....D4
Baxterville, 125 ....C4
Bay St. Louis, 8,209 ....C5
Bay Springs, 2,097 ....C4
Beatty, ...
Beaumont, 977 ....D4
Beauregard, 265 ....B4
Becker, 225 ....D2
Belden, 60 ....D1
Belen, 125 ....B1

Mississippi

Capital: Jackson
Land Area: 46,914 sq. mi.
121,507 sq. km.
Population: 2,844,658 (2000 Census)
Largest City: Jackson, 184,256
Highest Point: Woodall Mountain
806 ft.
246 m.
Admitted to Union: December 10, 1817
Nickname: Magnolia State
State Flower: Magnolia
State Bird: Mockingbird

Bellefontaine, *80* ... C2
Belmont, **1,961** ... D1
Belzoni, **2,663** ... B2
Benndale, *100* ... D5
Benoit, **611** ... B2
Benton, *275* ... B3
Bentonia, **500** ... B3
Betheden ... D2
Beulah, **473** ... B2
Bigbee Valley, *175* ... D2
Big Creek, **127** ... C2
Biggersville, *175* ... D1
Big Point, **115** ... D5
Biloxi, **50,644** ... D5
Bissell ... D1
Black Hawk, *70* ... C2
Blaine, *100* ... B2
Blue Mountain, **670** ... C1
Blue Springs, **144** ... D1
Bobo, *200* ... B1
Bogue Chitto (Lincoln Co.), *375* ... B4
Bogue Chitto (Neshoba Co.), **533** ... D3
Bolivar, *60* ... A2
Bolton, **629** ... B3
Bond, *375* ... C5
Booneville, **8,625** ... D1
Bourbon, *40* ... B2
Boyle, **720** ... B2
Brandon, **16,436** ... C3
Braxton, **181** ... C3
Brazil, *60* ... B1
Brewer, *225* ... D4
Brookhaven, **9,861** ... B4
Brooklyn, *350* ... C4
Brooksville, **1,182** ... D2
Brownsville, *70* ... B3
Bruce, **2,097** ... C2
Buckatunna, *300* ... D4
Bude, **1,037** ... B4
Burns, *70* ... C3
Burnside ... C3
Burnsville, **1,034** ... D1
Byhalia, **706** ... C1
Byram, **7,386** ... B3
Caledonia, **1,015** ... D2
Calhoun City, **1,872** ... C2
Camden ... C3
Canaan ... C1
Canton, **12,911** ... B3
Carlisle, *50* ... B3
Carnes, *250* ... C5
Carpenter ... B3
Carriere, *600* ... C5
Carrollton, **408** ... C2
Carter, *80* ... B3
Carthage, **4,637** ... C3
Cary, **427** ... B3
Cayuga, *60* ... B3
Centreville, **1,680** ... A4
Charleston, **2,198** ... B1
Chatawa, *150* ... B4
Chatham, *40* ... A2
Cheraw, *150* ... C4
Chicora, *90* ... D4
Chunky, **344** ... D3
Church Hill ... A4
Clara, *375* ... D4
Clarksdale, **20,645** ... B1
Cleveland, **13,841** ... B2
Clinton, **23,347** ... B3
Coahoma, **325** ... B1
Cockrum, *175* ... C1
Coffeeville, **930** ... C2
Coila ... C2
Coldwater, **1,674** ... C1
Coles, *125* ... A4
Collins, **2,683** ... C4
Collinsville, **1,823** ... D3
Columbia, **6,603** ... C4
Columbus, **25,944** ... D2
Como, **1,310** ... C1
Conehatta, **997** ... C3
Corinth, **14,054** ... D1
Courtland, **460** ... C1
Crandall ... D4
Crawford, **655** ... D2
Crenshaw, **916** ... B1
Crosby, **360** ... A4
Crossroads, *90* ... C5
Crowder, **766** ... B1
Cruger, **449** ... B2
Crystal Springs, **5,873** ... B3
Daleville, *175* ... D3
Darbun, *80* ... B4
Darling, *325* ... B1
Darlove ... B2
Decatur, **1,426** ... C3
Deemer, *350* ... C3
Deeson ... B1
De Kalb, **972** ... D3
De Lisle, *800* ... C5
Delta City, *100* ... B2
Denham ... D4
Denmark, *80* ... C1
Dennis, *250* ... D1
Dentville ... B4
Derby, *225* ... C5
Derma, **1,023** ... C2
De Soto, *250* ... D4
Deweese ... D3
Dexter, *90* ... C4
Diamondhead, **5,912** ... C5
D'Iberville, **7,608** ... D5
D'Lo, **394** ... C4
Doddsville, **108** ... B2
Dossville, *70* ... C3
Drew, **2,434** ... B2
Dubbs ... B1
Dublin, *70* ... B1
Duck Hill, **746** ... C2
Duffee, *60* ... D3
Dumas, **452** ... D1
Duncan, **578** ... B1
Dundee, *125* ... B1
Durant, **2,932** ... C2
Eagle Bend, *80* ... A3
Eastport ... D1
Ebenezer, *80* ... B3
Ecru, **947** ... C1
Eddiceton, *80* ... B4
Eden, **126** ... B3
Edinburg, *100* ... C3
Edwards, **1,347** ... B3
Egypt, *40* ... D2
Electric Mills, *40* ... D3
Elliott, *175* ... C2
Ellistown, *175* ... D1
Ellisville, **3,465** ... C4
Enid, *225* ... C1
Enterprise, **474** ... D3
Escatawpa, **3,566** ... D5
Estill, *70* ... B2
Ethel, **452** ... C2
Etta, *50* ... C1
Eupora, **2,326** ... C2
Evansville, *60* ... B1
Fairview, *150* ... D1
Falcon, **317** ... B1
Falkner, **212** ... D1
Farrell, *200* ... B1
Fayette, **2,242** ... A4
Fernwood, *325* ... B4
Fitler ... A3
Flora, **1,546** ... B3
Florence, **2,396** ... B3
Flowood, **4,750** ... B3
Forest, **5,987** ... C3
Forkville ... C3
Fort Adams ... A4
Foxworth, *500* ... C4
French Camp, **393** ... C2
Friars Point, **1,480** ... B1
Fulton, **3,882** ... D1
Gallman, *275* ... B4
Garden City, *80* ... A4
Garlandville, *50* ... C3
Gatesville, *70* ... B3
Gattman, **114** ... D2
Gautier, **11,681** ... D5
Geeville, *40* ... D1
Georgetown, **344** ... B4
Gholson ... D3
Gillsburg ... B4
Glancy ... B4
Glen, **286** ... D1
Glen Allan, *400* ... A2
Glendora, **285** ... B2
Gloster, **1,073** ... A4
Golden, **201** ... D1
Goodman, **1,252** ... C3
Goss, *125* ... C4
Grace, *125* ... B3
Grand Gulf ... A3
Greenville, **41,633** ... A2
Greenwood, **18,425** ... B2
Greenwood Springs, *50* ... D2
Grenada, **14,879** ... C2
Gulf Hills, **5,900** ... D5
Gulf Park Estates, **4,272** ... D5
Gulfport, **71,127** ... C5
Gunnison, **633** ... B2
Guntown, **1,183** ... D1
Hamburg, *90* ... A4
Harmontown, *60* ... C1
Harperville, *250* ... C3
Harriston, *60* ... A4
Harrisville, *175* ... B4
Hatley, **476** ... D2
Hattiesburg, **44,779** ... C4
Hazlehurst, **4,400** ... B4
Heads ... B2
Heidelberg, **840** ... D4
Hermanville, *125* ... B4
Hernando, **6,812** ... B1
Hickory, **499** ... C3
Hickory Flat, **565** ... C1
Highpoint, *150* ... C2
Hillhouse ... B1
Hillsboro, *300* ... C3
Hinchcliff, *40* ... B1
Hiwannee, *90* ... D4
Holcomb, *250* ... C2
Hollandale, **3,437** ... B2
Holly Bluff, *200* ... B3
Holly Springs, **7,957** ... C1
Hollywood, *150* ... B1
Hopewell, *150* ... B4
Horn Lake, **14,099** ... B1
Hot Coffee, *150* ... C4
Houston, **4,079** ... D2
Howard ... B2
Howison, *100* ... C5
Hudsonville, *70* ... C1
Hurley, **985** ... D5
Hushpuckena ... B1
Independence, *300* ... C1
Indianola, **12,066** ... B2
Ingomar, *400* ... C1
Inverness, **1,153** ... B2
Isola, **768** ... B2
Itta Bena, **2,208** ... B2
Iuka, **3,059** ... D1
Jackson, **184,256** ... B3
James, *90* ... A2
Janice ... C4
Jayess, *175* ... B4
Johns, *175* ... C3
Johnston, *125* ... B4
Jonestown, **1,701** ... B1
Jumpertown, **404** ... D1
Kilmichael, **830** ... C2
Kiln, **2,040** ... C5
Kirby ... B4
Kirkville, *40* ... D1
Kokomo, *125* ... C4
Kolola Springs, *150* ... D2
Kosciusko, **7,372** ... C2
Kossuth, **170** ... D1
Lafayette Springs, *100* ... C1
Lake, **408** ... C3
Lake Cormorant, *150* ... B1
Lakeshore, *225* ... C5
Lamar, *175* ... C1
Lambert, **1,967** ... B1
Lamont, *275* ... A2
Latimer, **4,288** ... D5
Lauderdale, *325* ... D3
Laurel, **18,393** ... C4
Leaf, *100* ... D4
Leakesville, **1,026** ... D4
Learned, **50** ... B3
Leedy, *175* ... D1
Leflore, *50* ... B2
Leland, **5,502** ... B2
Lena, **167** ... C3
Lessley ... A4
Le Tourneau, *200* ... B3
Lexie, *125* ... B4
Lexington, **2,025** ... B2
Liberty, **633** ... B4
Little Rock, *150* ... C3
Long Beach, **17,320** ... C5
Longview, *350* ... D2
Lorman, *50* ... A4
Louin, **339** ... C3
Louise, **315** ... B3
Louisville, **7,006** ... C2
Lucedale, **2,458** ... D5
Ludlow, *250* ... C3
Lula, **370** ... B1
Lumberton, **2,228** ... C5
Lynchburg, **2,959** ... B1
Lyon, **418** ... B1
Maben, **803** ... C2
Macon, **2,461** ... D2
Madden ... C3
Madison, **14,692** ... B3
Magee, **4,200** ... C4
Magnolia, **2,071** ... B4
Mantachie, **1,107** ... D1
Mantee, **169** ... C2
Marietta, **248** ... D1
Marion, **1,305** ... D3
Marks, **1,551** ... B1
Martin Bluff ... D5
Martinsville, *200* ... B4
Mashulaville, *50* ... D2
Matherville, *50* ... D4
Mathiston, **720** ... C2
Mattson, *125* ... B1
Maxie ... C5
Mayersville, **795** ... A3
Mayhew, *40* ... D2
McAdams, *200* ... C2
McCall Creek, *125* ... B4
McCallum, *40* ... C4
McComb, **13,337** ... B4
McCool, **182** ... C2
McDonald, *70* ... C3
McHenry, *225* ... C5
McLain, **603** ... D4
McLaurin, *250* ... C4
McNair, *50* ... A4
McNeill, *425* ... C5
McVille, *50* ... C3
Meadville, **519** ... B4
Memphis, **87** ... B1
Mendenhall, **2,555** ... C4
Meridian, **39,968** ... D3
Merigold, **664** ... B2
Merrill ... D5
Mesa, *90* ... B4
Metcalfe, **1,109** ... B2
Michigan City, *40* ... C1
Midnight, *225* ... B2
Midway, *80* ... B3
Miller, *125* ... C1
Minter City, *90* ... B2
Mississippi State, *3,500* ... D2
Mize, **285** ... C4
Money, *80* ... B2
Monticello, **1,726** ... B4
Montpelier ... D2
Montrose, **127** ... C3
Moorhead, **2,573** ... B2
Morgan City, **305** ... B2
Morgantown, *225* ... C4
Morton, **3,482** ... C3
Moselle, *325* ... C4
Moss Point, **15,851** ... D5
Mound Bayou, **2,102** ... B2
Mount Carmel, *125* ... C4
Mount Olive, **893** ... C4
Mount Pleasant, *300* ... C1
Myrick, *325* ... C4
Myrtle, **407** ... C1
Natchez, **18,464** ... A4
Necaise, *80* ... C5
Neely ... D4
Nellieburg, **1,354** ... D3
Nesbit, *700* ... C1
Neshoba, *60* ... C3
Nettleton, **1,932** ... D1
New Albany, **7,607** ... D1
New Augusta, **715** ... C4
New Hebron, **447** ... C4
New Hope, **1,964** ... D2
New Houlka, **710** ... C1
Newport, **40** ... B1
Newton, **3,699** ... C3
Nicholson, *1,400* ... C5
Nitta Yuma, *70* ... B2
North Carrollton, **499** ... C2
North Tunica, **1,450** ... B1
Noxapater, **419** ... C3
Oak Grove, *1,400* ... C4
Oakland, **586** ... C1
Oakley, *250* ... B3
Oak Vale, *150* ... C4
Ocean Springs, **17,225** ... D5
Ofahoma ... C3
Okolona, **3,056** ... D1
Olive Branch, **21,054** ... C1
Oma, *40* ... B4
Onward ... B3
Osyka, **481** ... B4
Ovett, *150* ... C4
Oxford, **11,756** ... C1
Ozona, *425* ... C5
Pace, **364** ... B2
Pachuta, **245** ... D3
Paden, **106** ... D1
Palmers Crossing, *1,700* ... C4
Paris, *175* ... C1
Pascagoula, **26,200** ... D5
Pass Christian, **6,579** ... C5
Pattison, *175* ... B4
Paulding, *200* ... C3
Paulette ... D3
Paynes, *150* ... B2
Pearl, **21,961** ... B3
Pearlington, **1,684** ... C5
Pearl River, **3,156** ... C3
Pelahatchie, **1,461** ... C3
Penton, *40* ... B1
Percy, *50* ... B2
Perkinston, *700* ... C5
Petal, **7,579** ... C4
Pheba, *175* ... D2
Philadelphia, **7,303** ... C3
Philipp, *250* ... B2
Phoenix, *60* ... B3
Picayune, **10,535** ... C5
Pickens, **1,325** ... C3
Pinckneyville, *40* ... A4
Piney Woods, *80* ... C3
Pinola, *150* ... C4
Pittsboro, **212** ... C2
Plantersville, **1,144** ... D1
Pocahontas, *40* ... B3
Polkville, **132** ... C3
Pontotoc, **5,253** ... D1
Pope, **241** ... C1
Poplar Creek, *60* ... C2
Poplarville, **2,601** ... C5
Porterville, *40* ... D3
Port Gibson, **1,840** ... B4
Potts Camp, **494** ... C1
Prairie ... D2
Prairie Point ... D2
Prentiss, **1,158** ... C4
Preston, *250* ... D3
Pricedale, *125* ... B4
Prichard ... B1
Prismatic, *60* ... D3
Puckett, **354** ... C3
Pulaski, *90* ... C3
Purvis, **2,164** ... C4
Quincy, *40* ... D2
Quitman, **2,463** ... D3
Quito, *100* ... B2
Raleigh, **1,255** ... C3
Randolph, *150* ... C1
Raymond, **1,664** ... B3
Red Banks, *125* ... C1
Red Lick, *100* ... B4
Redwater, **409** ... C3
Redwood, *125* ... B3
Reform, *125* ... C2
Renfroe, *90* ... C3
Renova, **623** ... B2
Rich, *60* ... B1
Richland, **6,027** ... B3
Richton, **1,038** ... D4
Ridgeland, **20,173** ... B3
Rienzi, **330** ... D1
Ripley, **5,478** ... D1
Roberts ... C3
Robinsonville, *100* ... B1
Rockport, *40* ... B4
Rodney ... A4
Rolling Fork, **2,486** ... B3
Rome, *90* ... B2
Rosedale, **2,414** ... A2
Rose Hill, *90* ... C3
Rosetta, *70* ... A4
Roxie, **569** ... A4
Ruleville, **3,234** ... B2
Runnelstown, *250* ... C4
Ruth, *100* ... B4
St. Martin, **6,676** ... D5
Sallis, **114** ... C2
Saltillo, **3,393** ... D1
Sanatorium, *900* ... C4
Sandersville, **789** ... C4
Sandhill, *125* ... C3
Sand Hill, *40* ... D4
Sandy Hook, *50* ... C4
Sanford, *300* ... C4
Sarah, *70* ... B1
Sardis, **2,038** ... C1
Sarepta, *60* ... C1
Satartia, **68** ... B3
Saucier, **1,303** ... C5
Savage, *100* ... B1
Schlater, **388** ... B2
Scobey ... C2
Scooba, **632** ... D3
Scott, *150* ... A2
Sebastopol, **233** ... C3
Seminary, **335** ... C4
Senatobia, **6,682** ... C1
Shannon, **1,657** ... D1
Sharon ... C3
Shaw, **2,312** ... B2
Shelby, **2,926** ... B2
Sherard, *40* ... B1
Sherman, **548** ... D1
Shivers, *70* ... C4
Shoreline Park, **4,058** ... C5
Shubuta, **651** ... D4
Shuqualak, **562** ... D3
Sibley, *300* ... A4
Sidon, **672** ... B2
Silver City, **337** ... B2
Silver Creek, **209** ... B4
Silver Run ... C5
Skene, *200* ... B2
Slate Spring, **121** ... C2
Slayden, *60* ... C1
Sledge, **529** ... B1
Smithdale, *100* ... B4
Smithville, **882** ... D1
Sontag, *125* ... B4
Soso, **379** ... C4
Southaven, **28,977** ... B1
Springville, *90* ... C1
Stafford Springs, *175* ... D4
Stallo, *125* ... C3
Standing Pine, **509** ... C3
Stanton, *275* ... A4
Star, *400* ... B3
Starkville, **21,869** ... D2
State Line, **555** ... D4
Steens, *70* ... D2
Stewart, *175* ... C2
Stonewall, **1,149** ... D3
Stovall ... B1
Stringer, *125* ... C4
Strong ... D2
Sturgis, **206** ... C2
Summerland ... C4
Summit, **1,428** ... B4
Sumner, **407** ... B2
Sumrall, **1,005** ... C4
Sunflower, **696** ... B2
Suqualena, *150* ... D3
Swan Lake, *60* ... B2
Sweatman ... C2
Swiftown, *80* ... B2
Sylvarena, **120** ... C3
Talowah, *100* ... C4
Taylor, **289** ... C1
Taylorsville, **1,341** ... C4
Tchula, **2,332** ... B2
Terry, **664** ... B3
Thaxton, **513** ... C1
Thomastown, *100* ... C3
Thompson ... B4
Thorn, *200* ... C2
Thornton, *70* ... B2
Tie Plant, *450* ... C2
Tilden, *100* ... D1
Tillatoba, **121** ... C2
Tinsley, *50* ... B3
Tiplersville, *100* ... D1
Tishomingo, **316** ... D1
Toccopola, **189** ... C1
Tomnolen, *90* ... C2
Toomsuba, *175* ... D3
Trebloc, *40* ... D2
Tremont, **390** ... D1
Troy, *60* ... D1
Tucker, **534** ... C3
Tuckers Crossing, *350* ... C4
Tula, *200* ... C1
Tunica, **1,132** ... B1
Tupelo, **34,211** ... D1
Turnerville, *50* ... C3
Tuscola, *125* ... C3
Tutwiler, **1,364** ... B1
Tylertown, **1,910** ... B4
Tyro ... C1
Union, **2,021** ... C3
Union Church, *50* ... B4
Utica, **966** ... B3
Vaiden, **840** ... C2
Valley Park, *60* ... B3
Vance, *80* ... B1
Vancleave, **4,910** ... D5
Vardaman, **1,065** ... C2
Vaughan, *60* ... B3
Velma, *90* ... C1
Verona, **3,334** ... D1
Vicksburg, **26,407** ... B3
Vossburg, *80* ... D4
Wade, **491** ... D5
Wallerville, *200* ... D1
Walls, *200* ... B1
Walnut, **754** ... D1
Walnut Grove, **488** ... C3
Waltersville, *1,000* ... B3
Walthall, **170** ... C2
Wanilla, *90* ... B4
Washington, *250* ... A4
Waterford, *90* ... C1
Water Valley, **3,677** ... C1
Waveland, **6,674** ... C5
Way, *125* ... B3
Waynesboro, **5,197** ... D4
Wayside, *70* ... A2
Weathersby, *100* ... C4
Webb, **587** ... B2
Weir, **553** ... C2
Wenasoga, *175* ... D1
Wesson, **1,693** ... B4
West, **220** ... C2
West Point, **12,145** ... D2
Wheeler, **300** ... D1
White Apple, *80* ... A4
Whitfield, *90* ... C4
Wiggins (Leake Co.), *100* ... C3
Wiggins (Stone Co.), **3,849** ... C5
Wilkinson, *125* ... A4
Williamsburg, *90* ... C4
Williamsville, *400* ... C2
Winborn, *125* ... C1
Winchester, *50* ... D4
Winona, **5,482** ... C2
Winstonville, **319** ... B2
Winterville, *175* ... A2
Woodland, **159** ... C2
Woodville, **1,192** ... A4
Wool Market ... C5
Wyatte ... C1
Yazoo City, **14,550** ... B3
Zama, *40* ... C3

Other Features

Alabama, *river* ... E4
Aliceville, *lake* ... D2
Arkabutla, *lake* ... B1
Arkansas, *river* ... A1
Arkansas Post N.Mem. ... A1
Bayou Cocodrie N.W.R. ... A4
Bayou Sauvage N.W.R. ... C5
Bear, *creek* ... E1
Bienville National Forest ... C3
Big, *lake* ... D5
Big Black, *river* ... B3
Big Springs, *lake* ... D1
Big Sunflower, *river* ... B2
Black, *creek* ... C4
Black Warrior, *river* ... E3
Bogue Chitto, *river* ... B4
Bogue Chitto N.W.R. ... C5
Borgne, *lake* ... C5
Breton N.W.R. ... D5
Brices Cross Roads N.B.S. ... D1
Buttahatchee, *river* ... D2
Camp Shelby Training Site ... C4
Cat, *island* ... C5
Chandeleur, *sound* ... C5
Chicasawhay, *river* ... D3
Choctaw N.W.R. ... D4
Coldwater, *river* ... B1
Columbus, *lake* ... D2
Dahomey N.W.R. ... B2
Dauphin, *island* ... D5
Delta N.F. ... B3
De Soto National Forest ... D4, D5
Enid, *lake* ... C1
Grand, *island* ... C5
Grand Bay N.W.R. ... D5
Grenada, *lake* ... C2
Gulf Island Natl. Seashore ... D5
Handy Brake N.W.R. ... A3
Hillside N.W.H ... B2
Holly Springs National Forest ... C1
Homochitto, *river* ... A4
Homochitto National Forest ... A4
Horn, *island* ... D5
Lake Ophelia N.W.R. ... A4
Leaf, *river* ... C4
Matthew Brake N.W.R. ... B2
Meridian N.A.S. ... D3
Mexico, *gulf* ... D5
Mississippi, *river* ... A4, B1
Mississippi, *sound* ... D5
Miss. Choctaw I.R. ... C3
Miss. Sandhill Crane N.W.R. ... D5
Mobile, *bay* ... D5
Mobile, *point* ... D5
Morgan Brake N.W.R. ... B2
NASA Stennis Space Ctr. ... C5
Natchez N.H.P. ... A4
Noxubee, *river* ... D2
Noxubee N.W.R. ... D2
Okatibbee, *lake* ... D3
Overflow N.W.R. ... A2
Panther Swamp N.W.R. ... B3
Pascagoula, *river* ... D5
Pearl, *river* ... B4, C3
Petit Bois, *island* ... D5
Pickwick, *lake* ... D1
Pine, *hills* ... B4
Pontchartrain, *lake* ... C5
Pontotoc, *ridge* ... D1
Poverty Point N.M. ... A3
Red, *river* ... A4
Ross Barnett, *reservoir* ... C3
St. Catherine Creek N.W.R. ... A4
St. Francis, *river* ... B1
St. Francis N.F. ... B1
Sardis, *lake* ... C1
Ship, *island* ... D5
Sipsey, *river* ... E2
Tallahatchie, *river* ... B1
Tallahatchie N.W.R. ... B2, C1
Tennessee, *river* ... D1
Tensas River N.W.R. ... A3
Tombigbee, *river* ... D1, D3
Tombigbee N.F. ... C2, D1
Tupelo N.B. ... D1
Vicksburg N.M.P. ... B3
White, *river* ... A1
White River N.W.R. ... A1
Woodall, *mountain* ... D1
Yalobusha, *river* ... C2
Yazoo, *river* ... B2
Yazoo N.W.R. ... B2

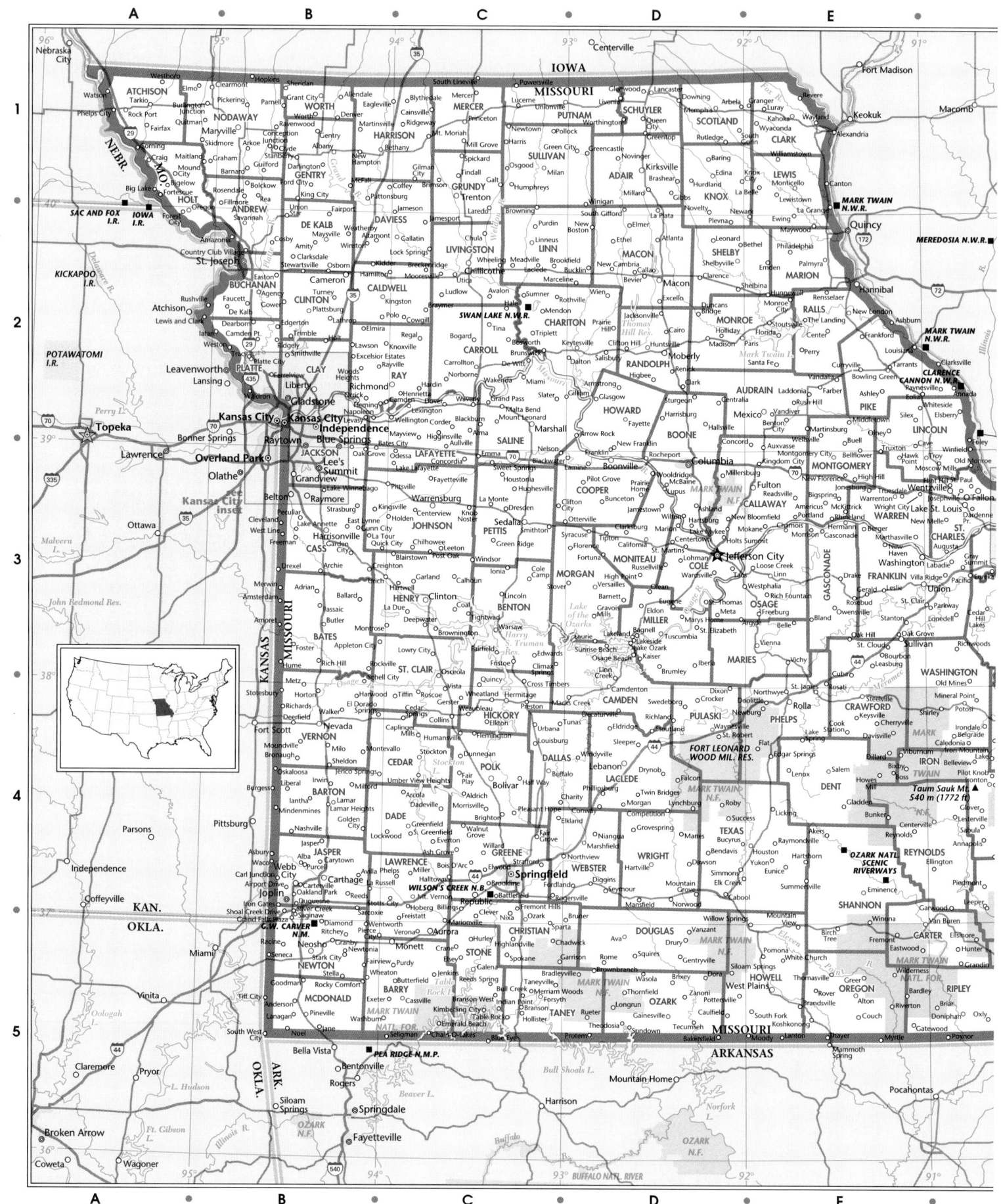

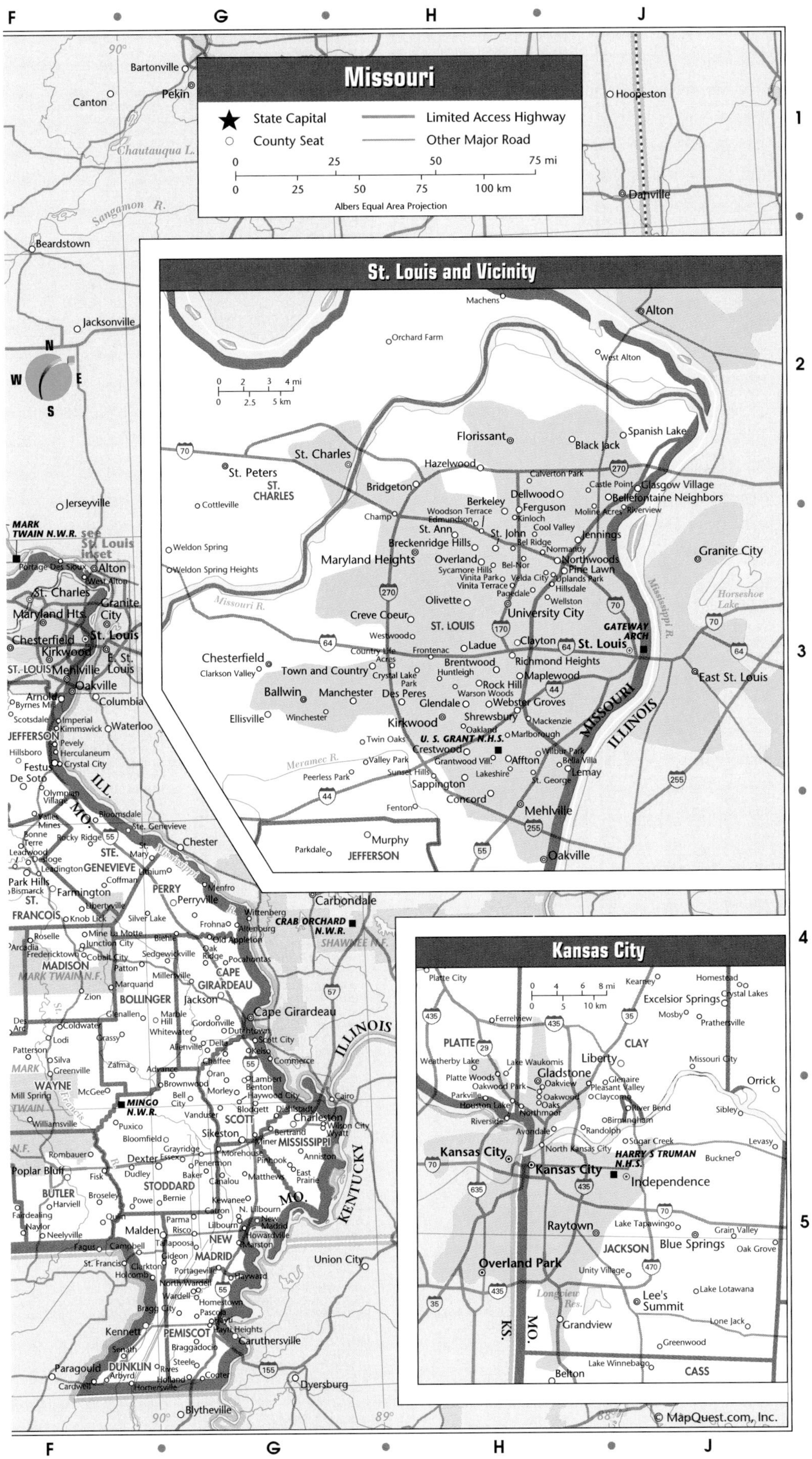

Missouri

Capital:	Jefferson City
Land Area:	68,898 sq. mi.
	178,446 sq. km.
Population:	5,595,211 (2000 Census)
Largest City:	Kansas City, 441,545
Highest Point:	Taum Sauk Mtn.
	1,772 ft.
	540 m.
Admitted to Union:	August 10, 1821
Nickname:	Show Me State
State Flower:	Hawthorn
State Bird:	Bluebird

Map labels (Missouri main map)

Missouri

★ State Capital   — Limited Access Highway
○ County Seat   — Other Major Road

0   25   50   75 mi
0   25   50   75   100 km
Albers Equal Area Projection

St. Louis and Vicinity

0 2 3 4 mi
0 2.5 5 km

Kansas City

0 4 6 8 mi
0 10 km

© MapQuest.com, Inc.

Missouri:
Map Index

Counties

Adair, 24,977 . . . . .D1
Andrew, 16,492 . . . . . . .B2
Atchison, 6,430 . . . . . . .A1
Audrain, 25,853 . . . . . . .D2
Barry, 34,010 . . . . .C5
Barton, 12,541 . . . . . . .B4
Bates, 16,653 . . . . .B3
Benton, 17,180 . . . . . . .C3
Bollinger, 12,029 . . . . . .F4
Boone, 135,454 . . . . . . .D2
Buchanan, 85,998 . . . . . .B2
Butler, 40,867 . . . . .F5
Caldwell, 8,969 . . . . . . .B2
Callaway, 40,766 . . . . . .E3
Camden, 37,051 . . . . . . .D4
Cape Girardeau, 68,693 . .G4
Carroll, 10,285 . . . . . . .C2
Carter, 5,941 . . . . .E5
Cass, 82,092 . . . . . .B3, J5
Cedar, 13,733 . . . . .C4
Chariton, 8,438 . . . . . . .C2
Christian, 54,285 . . . . . .C5
Clark, 7,416 . . . . .E1
Clay, 184,006 . . . . .B2, J4
Clinton, 18,979 . . . . . . .B2
Cole, 71,397 . . . . .D3
Cooper, 16,670 . . . . . . .D3
Crawford, 22,804 . . . . . .E4
Dade, 7,923 . . . . .C4
Dallas, 15,661 . . . . .C4
Daviess, 8,016 . . . . .B2
De Kalb, 11,597 . . . . . . .B2
Dent, 14,927 . . . . .E4
Douglas, 13,084 . . . . . . .D5
Dunklin, 33,155 . . . . . . .F5
Franklin, 93,807 . . . . . . .E3
Gasconade, 15,342 . . . . .E3
Gentry, 6,861 . . . . .B1
Greene, 240,391 . . . . . . .C4
Grundy, 10,432 . . . . . . .C1
Harrison, 8,850 . . . . . . .B1
Henry, 21,997 . . . . .C3
Hickory, 8,940 . . . . .C4
Holt, 5,351 . . . . .A1
Howard, 10,212 . . . . . . .D2
Howell, 37,238 . . . . .E5
Iron, 10,697 . . . . .E4
Jackson, 654,880 . . . .B3, J5
Jasper, 104,686 . . . . . . .B4
Jefferson, 198,099 . .F3, G4
Johnson, 48,258 . . . . . . .C3
Knox, 4,361 . . . . .D1
Laclede, 32,513 . . . . . . .D4
Lafayette, 32,960 . . . . . .C3
Lawrence, 35,204 . . . . . .C4
Lewis, 10,494 . . . . .E1
Lincoln, 38,944 . . . . . . .E2
Linn, 13,754 . . . . .C2
Livingston, 14,558 . . . . .C2
Macon, 15,762 . . . . .D2
Madison, 11,800 . . . . . . .F4
Maries, 8,903 . . . . .D3
Marion, 28,289 . . . . .E2
McDonald, 21,681 . . . . .B5
Mercer, 3,757 . . . . .C1
Miller, 23,564 . . . . .D3
Mississippi, 13,427 . . . . .G5
Moniteau, 14,827 . . . . . .D3
Monroe, 9,311 . . . . .D2
Montgomery, 12,136 . . . .E3
Morgan, 19,309 . . . . . . .C3
New Madrid, 19,760 . . . .G5
Newton, 52,636 . . . . . . .B5
Nodaway, 21,912 . . . . . .B1
Oregon, 10,344 . . . . . . .E5
Osage, 13,062 . . . . .E3
Ozark, 9,542 . . . . .D5
Pemiscot, 20,047 . . . . . .G5

Perry, 18,132 . . . . .G4
Pettis, 39,403 . . . . .C3
Phelps, 39,825 . . . . . . .E4
Pike, 18,351 . . . . .E2
Platte, 73,781 . . . . .B2, H4
Polk, 26,992 . . . . .C4
Pulaski, 41,165 . . . . . . .D4
Putnam, 5,223 . . . . .C1
Ralls, 9,626 . . . . .E2
Randolph, 24,663 . . . . .D2
Ray, 23,354 . . . . .C2
Reynolds, 6,689 . . . . . . .E4
Ripley, 13,509 . . . . .F5
St. Charles, 283,883 . .F3, G2
St. Clair, 9,652 . . . . . . .C3
Ste. Genevieve, 17,842 . .F4
St. Francois, 55,641 . . . .F4
St. Louis (city),
   348,189 . . . . . . .F3, H3
St. Louis (county),
   1,016,315 . . . . .F3, H3
Saline, 23,756 . . . . .C2
Schuyler, 4,170 . . . . . . .D1
Scotland, 4,983 . . . . . . .D1
Scott, 40,422 . . . . .G5
Shannon, 8,324 . . . . . . .E4
Shelby, 6,799 . . . . .D2
Stoddard, 29,705 . . . . . .F5
Stone, 28,658 . . . . .C5
Sullivan, 7,219 . . . . . . .C1
Taney, 39,703 . . . . .C5
Texas, 23,003 . . . . .D4
Vernon, 20,454 . . . . . . .B4
Warren, 24,525 . . . . . . .E3
Washington, 23,344 . . . .F3
Wayne, 13,259 . . . . .F4
Webster, 31,045 . . . . . . .D4
Worth, 2,382 . . . . .B1
Wright, 17,955 . . . . .D4

Cities and Towns

Adrian, 1,780 . . . . .B3
Advance, 1,244 . . . . . . .G4
Affton, 20,535 . . . . . . .H3
Agency, 599 . . . . .B2
Airport Drive, 622 . . . . .B4
Akers E4
Alba, 588 . . . . .B4
Albany, 1,937 . . . . .B1
Aldrich, 75 . . . . .C4
Alexandria, 166 . . . . . . .E1
Allendale, 54 . . . . .B1
Allenville, 104 . . . . .G4
Alma, 399 . . . . .C2
Altamont, 218 . . . . .B2
Altenburg, 309 . . . . . . .G4
Alton, 668 . . . . .E5
Amazonia, 277 . . . . . . .B2
Americus, 100 . . . . .E3
Amity, 70 . . . . .B2
Amoret, 211 . . . . .B3
Amsterdam, 281 . . . . . .B3
Anderson, 1,856 . . . . . .B5
Annada, 48 . . . . .F2
Annapolis, 310 . . . . . . .F4
Anniston, 285 . . . . .G5
Appleton City, 1,314 . . . .B3
Arbela, 40 . . . . .D1
Arbyrd, 528 . . . . .F5
Arcadia, 567 . . . . .F4
Archie, 890 . . . . .B3
Arcola, 45 . . . . .C4
Argyle, 164 . . . . .D3
Armstrong, 287 . . . . . . .D2
Arnold, 19,965 . . . . . . .F3
Arrow Rock, 79 . . . . . . .D2
Asbury, 218 . . . . .B4
Ashburn, 51 . . . . .E2
Ash Grove, 1,430 . . . . . .C4
Ashland, 1,869 . . . . . . .D3
Ashley, 80 . . . . .E2
Atlanta, 450 . . . . .D2

Augusta, 218 ...F3
Aullville, 86 ...C2
Aurora, 7,014 ...D5
Auxvasse, 901 ...E2
Ava, 3,021 ...D5
Avalon, 100 ...C2
Avilla, 137 ...B4
Avondale, 529 ...H5
Bagnell, 86 ...D3
Baker, 5 ...G5
Bakersfield, 285 ...D5
Ballard, 60 ...B3
Ballwin, 31,283 ...G3
Bardley, 40 ...E5
Baring, 159 ...D1
Barnard, 257 ...B1
Barnett, 207 ...D3
Bates City, 245 ...B2
Battlefield, 2,385 ...C4
Belgrade, 200 ...F4
Bella Villa, 687 ...H3
Bell City, 461 ...G4
Belle, 1,344 ...E3
Bellefontaine Neighbors, 11,271 ...J2
Belleview, 125 ...F4
Bellflower, 427 ...E3
Bel-Nor, 1,598 ...H3
Bel Ridge, 3,082 ...H3
Belton, 21,730 ...B3, H5
Bendavis, 80 ...D4
Benton, 732 ...G4
Benton City, 122 ...E2
Berger, 206 ...E3
Berkeley, 10,063 ...H2
Bernie, 1,777 ...G5
Bertrand, 740 ...G5
Bethany, 3,087 ...B1
Bethel, 121 ...D2
Bevier, 723 ...D2
Biehle, 11 ...G4
Bigelow, 38 ...A1
Big Lake, 127 ...A1
Bigspring, 200 ...E3
Billings, 1,091 ...C4
Birch Tree, 634 ...E5
Birmingham, 214 ...J5
Bismarck, 1,470 ...F4
Bixby, 125 ...E4
Blackburn, 284 ...C2
Black Jack, 6,792 ...J2
Blackwater, 199 ...D3
Blairstown, 141 ...C3
Bland, 565 ...E3
Blodgett, 265 ...G5
Bloomfield, 1,952 ...G5
Bloomsdale, 419 ...F3
Blue Eye, 129 ...C5
Blue Springs, 48,080 ...B2, J5
Blythedale, 233 ...C1
Bogard, 234 ...C2
Bois d'Arc, 300 ...C4
Bolckow, 234 ...B1
Bolivar, 9,143 ...C4
Bonne Terre, 4,039 ...F4
Boonville, 8,202 ...D3
Boss, 80 ...E4
Bosworth, 382 ...C2
Bourbon, 1,348 ...E3
Bowling Green, 3,260 ...E2
Bradleyville, 50 ...C5
Braggadocio, 200 ...G5
Bragg City, 189 ...G5
Brandsville, 174 ...D5
Branson, 6,050 ...C5
Branson West, 408 ...C5
Brashear, 280 ...D1
Braymer, 910 ...C2
Breckenridge, 454 ...C2
Breckenridge Hills, 4,817 ...H3
Brentwood, 7,693 ...H3
Briar ...F5
Bridgeton, 15,550 ...H2
Brighton, 225 ...C4
Brimson, 63 ...C1
Brixey ...D5
Bronaugh, 245 ...B4
Brookfield, 4,769 ...C2
Brookline, 326 ...C4
Broseley, 250 ...F5
Brownbranch ...D5
Browning, 317 ...C1
Brownington, 119 ...C3
Brownwood, 150 ...G4
Brumley, 102 ...D3
Bruner, 175 ...C5
Brunswick, 925 ...C2
Bucklin, 524 ...D2
Buckner, 2,725 ...J5
Bucyrus ...D4
Buell, 100 ...E2
Buffalo, 2,781 ...C4
Bull Creek, 225 ...C5
Bunceton, 348 ...D3
Bunker, 427 ...E4
Burgess, 70 ...
Burlington Junction, 632 ...A1
Butler, 4,209 ...B3

Butterfield, 397 ...C5
Byrnes Mill, 2,376 ...F3
Cabool, 2,168 ...D4
Cainsville, 370 ...C1
Cairo, 293 ...D2
Caledonia, 158 ...F4
Calhoun, 491 ...C3
California, 4,005 ...D3
Callao, 291 ...D2
Calverton Park, 1,322 ...H2
Camden, 209 ...B2
Camden Point, 484 ...B2
Camdenton, 2,779 ...D4
Cameron, 8,312 ...B2
Campbell, 1,883 ...F5
Canalou, 348 ...G5
Canton, 2,557 ...E1
Cape Girardeau, 35,349 ...G4
Caplinger Mills, 50 ...C4
Cardwell, 789 ...F5
Carl Junction, 5,294 ...B4
Carrollton, 4,122 ...C2
Carterville, 1,850 ...B4
Carthage, 12,668 ...B4
Caruthersville, 6,760 ...G5
Carytown, 217 ...B4
Cassville, 2,890 ...C5
Castle Point, 4,559 ...J2
Catron, 68 ...G5
Caulfield, 150 ...D5
Cave, 7 ...E2
Cedar Hill Lakes, 229 ...F3
Cedar Springs, 50 ...C4
Center, 644 ...E2
Centertown, 257 ...D3
Centerview, 249 ...C3
Centerville, 171 ...E4
Centralia, 3,774 ...D2
Chadwick ...C5
Chaffee, 3,044 ...G4
Chain-O-Lakes, 127 ...C5
Chamois, 456 ...E3
Champ, 12 ...H2
Charity, 70 ...C4
Charleston, 4,732 ...G5
Cherryville, 125 ...E4
Chesterfield, 46,802 ...F3, G3
Chilhowee, 329 ...C3
Chillicothe, 8,968 ...C2
Chula, 198 ...C2
Clarence, 915 ...D2
Clark, 275 ...D2
Clarksburg, 375 ...D3
Clarksdale, 351 ...B2
Clarkson Valley, 2,675 ...G3
Clarkton, 1,330 ...G5
Claycomo, 1,267 ...J5
Clayton, 12,825 ...H3
Clearmont, 191 ...A1
Cleveland, 592 ...B3
Clever, 1,010 ...C4
Clifton City ...C3
Clifton Hill, 124 ...D2
Climax Springs, 80 ...C3
Clinton, 9,311 ...C3
Clyde, 74 ...B1
Coal, 60 ...C3
Cobalt City, 189 ...F4
Coffey, 140 ...B1
Coffman, 50 ...F4
Coldwater ...F4
Cole Camp, 1,028 ...C3
Collins, 176 ...C4
Columbia, 84,531 ...D3
Commerce, 110 ...G4
Competition ...D4
Conception Junction, 202 ...B1
Concord (Callaway Co.), 70 ...E2
Concord (St. Louis Co.), 16,689 ...H3
Concordia, 2,360 ...C3
Conway, 743 ...D4
Cook Station ...E4
Cool Valley, 1,081 ...H3
Cooter, 440 ...G5
Corder, 427 ...C2
Corning, 21 ...A1
Cosby, 143 ...B2
Cottleville, 1,928 ...G2
Couch ...D5
Country Club Village, 1,846 ...A2
Country Life Acres, 81 ...H3
Cowgill, 247 ...C2
Craig, 309 ...A1
Crane, 1,390 ...C4
Creighton, 322 ...B3
Crestwood, 11,863 ...H3
Creve Coeur, 16,500 ...H3
Crocker, 1,033 ...D4
Cross Timbers, 185 ...C3
Crystal City, 4,247 ...F3
Crystal Lake Park, 457 ...H3
Crystal Lakes, 383 ...J4
Cuba, 3,230 ...E3
Curryville, 251 ...E2
Dadeville, 224 ...C4
Dalton, 27 ...D2

Dardenne Prairie, 4,384 ...F3
Darlington, 113 ...B1
Davisville ...E4
Dawson, 50 ...D4
Dearborn, 529 ...B2
Decaturville, 50 ...D4
Deepwater, 507 ...C3
Deerfield, 75 ...B4
De Kalb, 257 ...B2
Dellwood, 5,255 ...H2
Delta, 517 ...G4
Denver, 40 ...B1
Des Arc, 187 ...F4
Desloge, 4,802 ...F4
De Soto, 6,375 ...F3
Des Peres, 8,592 ...H3
De Witt, 120 ...C2
Dexter, 7,356 ...G5
Diamond, 807 ...B5
Diehlstadt, 163 ...G5
Diggins, 298 ...D4
Dillard ...E4
Dixon, 1,570 ...D4
Doniphan, 1,932 ...F5
Doolittle, 644 ...E4
Dora ...D5
Dover, 108 ...C2
Downing, 396 ...D1
Drake ...E3
Dresden, 175 ...C3
Drexel, 1,090 ...B3
Drury, 50 ...D5
Drynob ...D4
Dudley, 289 ...F5
Duncans Bridge, 50 ...D2
Dunnegan, 125 ...C4
Duquesne, 1,640 ...B4
Dutchtown, 99 ...G4
Eagleville, 321 ...B1
East Lynne, 300 ...B3
Easton, 258 ...B2
East Prairie, 3,227 ...G5
Eastwood ...E5
Edgar Springs, 190 ...E4
Edgerton, 533 ...B2
Edina, 1,233 ...D1
Edmundson, 840 ...H2
Edwards ...C3
Eldon, 4,895 ...D3
El Dorado Springs, 3,775 ...B4
Eldridge, 80 ...D4
Elkland, 225 ...C4
Elkton, 60 ...C4
Ellington, 1,045 ...F4
Ellisville, 9,104 ...G3
Ellsinore, 363 ...F5
Elmer, 98 ...D2
Elmira, 82 ...B2
Elmo, 166 ...A1
Elsberry, 2,047 ...F2
Elsey, 150 ...C5
Elwood, 350 ...C4
Emden, 70 ...E2
Emerald Beach, 250 ...C5
Eminence, 548 ...E4
Emma, 243 ...C3
Eolia, 435 ...E2
Essex, 524 ...G5
Ethel, 100 ...D2
Eugene, 175 ...D3
Eunice, 40 ...E4
Eureka, 7,676 ...F3
Everton, 322 ...C4
Ewing, 464 ...E2
Excello, 40 ...D2
Excelsior Estates, 263 ...B2
Excelsior Springs, 10,847 ...J4
Exeter, 707 ...C5
Fagus, 60 ...F5
Fairdealing, 225 ...F5
Fairfax, 645 ...A1
Fairfield ...C3
Fair Grove, 1,107 ...C4
Fair Play, 418 ...C4
Fairport, 80 ...B2
Fairview, 395 ...B5
Falcon, 50 ...D4
Farber, 411 ...E2
Farmington, 13,924 ...F4
Faucett, 300 ...B2
Fayette, 2,793 ...D2
Fayetteville, 90 ...C3
Fenton, 4,360 ...H3
Ferguson, 22,406 ...H2
Ferrelview, 593 ...B2, H4
Festus, 9,660 ...F3
Fillmore, 211 ...B1
Fisk, 363 ...F5
Flat, 90 ...E4
Fleming, 122 ...B2
Flemington, 124 ...C4
Flint Hill, 379 ...F3
Florence, 125 ...D3
Florida, 9 ...E2
Florissant, 50,497 ...H2
Foley, 178 ...F2
Ford City, 30 ...B1

Fordland, 684 ...D4
Forest City, 338 ...A2
Forsyth, 1,686 ...C5
Fortescue, 51 ...A1
Fortuna, 225 ...D3
Foster, 130 ...B3
Frankford, 351 ...E2
Franklin, 112 ...D2
Fredericktown, 3,928 ...F4
Freeburg, 423 ...E3
Freeman, 521 ...B3
Freistatt, 184 ...C4
Fremont, 125 ...E5
Fremont Hills, 597 ...C4
Frohna, 192 ...G4
Frontenac, 3,483 ...H3
Fulton, 12,128 ...E3
Gainesville, 632 ...D5
Galena, 451 ...C5
Gallatin, 1,789 ...C2
Galt, 275 ...C1
Garden City, 1,500 ...B3
Garland, 100 ...C3
Garrison, 40 ...C5
Garwood ...F4
Gasconade, 267 ...E3
Gatewood, 50 ...E5
Gentry, 101 ...B1
Gentryville ...D5
Gerald, 1,171 ...E3
Gerster, 35 ...C4
Gibbs, 300 ...D1
Gideon, 1,113 ...G5
Gilliam, 229 ...D2
Gilman City, 380 ...C1
Gladden ...E4
Gladstone, 26,365 ...B2, H4
Glasgow, 1,263 ...D2
Glasgow Village, 5,234 ...J2
Glenaire, 553 ...J4
Glenallen, 145 ...F4
Glendale, 5,767 ...H3
Glenwood, 203 ...D1
Glover ...F4
Golden City, 884 ...B4
Goodman, 1,183 ...B5
Gordonville, 425 ...G4
Gower, 1,399 ...B2
Graham, 191 ...A1
Grain Valley, 5,160 ...J5
Granby, 2,121 ...B5
Grand Falls Plaza, 104 ...B4
Grandin, 236 ...F5
Grand Pass, 53 ...C2
Grandview, 24,881 ...B3, H5
Granger, 44 ...E1
Grant City, 926 ...B1
Grantwood Village, 883 ...H3
Grassy, 50 ...F4
Gravois Mills, 208 ...D3
Grayridge, 150 ...G5
Gray Summit, 2,640 ...F3
Greencastle, 308 ...D1
Green City, 688 ...D1
Greenfield, 1,358 ...C4
Green Ridge, 445 ...C3
Greentop, 427 ...D1
Greenville, 451 ...F4
Greenwood, 3,952 ...J5
Greer, 50 ...E5
Grovespring, 125 ...D4
Guilford, 87 ...B1
Gunn City, 85 ...B3
Hale, 473 ...C2
Half Way, 176 ...C4
Hallsville, 978 ...D2
Halltown, 189 ...C4
Hamilton, 1,813 ...C2
Hannibal, 17,757 ...E2
Hardin, 614 ...C2
Harris, 105 ...C1
Harrisburg, 184 ...D2
Harrisonville, 8,946 ...B3
Hartsburg, 108 ...D3
Hartshorn, 70 ...E4
Hartville, 607 ...D4
Hartwell, 16 ...C3
Harviell, 125 ...F5
Harwood, 90 ...B4
Hawk Point, 459 ...E3
Hayti, 3,207 ...G5
Hayti Heights, 771 ...G5
Hayward, 123 ...G5
Haywood City, 239 ...G4
Hazelwood, 26,206 ...H2
Henrietta, 457 ...C2
Herculaneum, 2,805 ...F3
Hermann, 2,674 ...E3
Hermitage, 406 ...C4
Higbee, 623 ...D2
Higginsville, 4,682 ...C2
High Hill, 231 ...E3
Highlandville, 872 ...C5
High Point, 80 ...D3
Hillsboro, 1,675 ...F3
Hillsdale, 1,477 ...H3
Hoberg, 60 ...C4

Holcomb, 696 ...F5
Holden, 2,510 ...C3
Holland, 246 ...G5
Holliday, 129 ...D2
Hollister, 3,867 ...C5
Holt, 405 ...B2
Holts Summit, 2,935 ...D3
Homestead, 181 ...J4
Homestown, 181 ...G5
Hopkins, 579 ...B1
Hornersville, 686 ...F5
Horton, 40 ...B4
Houston, 1,992 ...E4
Houstonia, 275 ...C3
Houston Lake, 284 ...H5
Howardville, 342 ...G5
Howes Mill ...E4
Hughesville, 174 ...C3
Hume, 337 ...B3
Humansville, 946 ...C4
Humphreys, 164 ...C1
Hunnewell, 227 ...E2
Hunter ...F5
Huntleigh, 323 ...H3
Huntsville, 1,553 ...D2
Hurdland, 239 ...D1
Hurley, 157 ...C5
Iantha, 125 ...B4
Iatan, 54 ...B2
Iberia, 605 ...D3
Imperial, 4,373 ...F3
Independence, 113,288 ...B2, J5
Indian Point, 588 ...C5
Ionia, 108 ...C3
Irondale, 437 ...F4
Iron Gates ...B4
Iron Mountain Lake, 693 ...F4
Ironton, 1,471 ...F4
Irwin, 50 ...B4
Jackson, 11,947 ...G4
Jacksonville, 163 ...D2
Jameson, 120 ...C1
Jamesport, 505 ...C2
Jamestown, 382 ...D3
Jane, 200 ...B5
Jasper, 1,011 ...B4
Jefferson City, 39,636 ...D3
Jenkins, 50 ...C5
Jennings, 15,469 ...J3
Jerico Springs, 259 ...B4
Jonesburg, 695 ...E3
Joplin, 45,504 ...B4
Josephville, 270 ...F3
Junction City, 319 ...F4
Kahoka, 2,241 ...E1
Kaiser, 500 ...D3
Kansas City, 441,545 ...B2, J5
Kearney, 5,472 ...J4
Kelso, 527 ...G4
Kennett, 11,260 ...F5
Kewanee, 175 ...G5
Keysville ...B2
Keytesville, 533 ...D2
Kidder, 271 ...B2
Kimberling City, 2,253 ...C5
Kimmswick, 94 ...F3
King City, 1,012 ...B1
Kingdom City, 121 ...E3
Kingston, 287 ...C2
Kingsville, 257 ...B3
Kinloch, 449 ...H2
Kirksville, 16,988 ...D1
Kirkwood, 27,324 ...F3, H3
Knob Lick, 200 ...F4
Knob Noster, 2,462 ...C3
Knox City, 223 ...D1
Knoxville, 50 ...B2
Koshkonong, 205 ...E5
Labadie, 225 ...F3
La Belle, 669 ...E1
Laclede, 415 ...C2
Laddonia, 620 ...E2
Ladue, 8,645 ...H3
La Due, 39 ...
La Grange, 1,000 ...E1
Lake Annette, 163 ...B3
Lake Lafayette, 346 ...C3
Lakeland ...D3
Lake Lotawana, 1,872 ...J5
Lake Mykee, 326 ...D3
Lake Ozark, 1,489 ...D3
Lake St. Louis, 10,169 ...F3
Lakeshire, 1,375 ...H3
Lakeside, 37 ...D3
Lake Spring ...E4
Lake Tapawingo, 843 ...J5
Lake Waukomis, 917 ...H4
Lake Winnebago, 902 ...B3, J5
Lamar, 4,425 ...B4
Lamar Heights, 216 ...B4
Lambert, 49 ...G4
Lamine ...D3
La Monte, 1,064 ...C3
Lanagan, 411 ...B5
Lancaster, 737 ...D1
Lanton, 70 ...E5
La Plata, 1,486 ...D1
Laredo, 250 ...C1

La Russell, 138 ...B4
Lathrop, 2,092 ...B2
La Tour, 65 ...B3
Laurie, 663 ...D3
Lawson, 2,336 ...B2
Leadington, 206 ...F4
Leadwood, 1,160 ...F4
Leasburg, 323 ...E3
Lebanon, 12,155 ...D4
Leeper, 60 ...F4
Lee's Summit, 70,700 ...B3, J5
Leeton, 619 ...C3
Lemay, 17,215 ...H3
Lenox, 125 ...E4
Leonard, 66 ...D2
Leslie, 87 ...E3
Lesterville, 225 ...F4
Levasy, 108 ...B2, J5
Lewis and Clark (Lewis and Clark Village), 155 ...A2
Lewistown, 595 ...E1
Lexington, 4,453 ...C2
Liberal, 779 ...B4
Liberty, 26,232 ...B2, J4
Libertyville, 70 ...F4
Licking, 1,471 ...E4
Lilbourn, 1,303 ...G5
Lincoln, 1,026 ...C3
Linn, 1,354 ...E3
Linn Creek, 280 ...D3
Linneus, 369 ...C2
Lithium ...G4
Livonia, 114 ...D1
Lock Springs, 69 ...C2
Lockwood, 989 ...C4
Lodi ...F4
Lohman, 168 ...D3
Lonedell, 300 ...F3
Lone Jack, 528 ...J5
Longrun ...D5
Loose Creek, 80 ...E3
Louisburg, 147 ...C4
Louisiana, 3,863 ...E2
Lowry City, 728 ...C3
Lucerne, 92 ...C1
Ludlow, 204 ...C2
Lupus, 29 ...D3
Luray, 102 ...E1
Lynchburg ...D4
Machens, 60 ...H2
Mackenzie, 137 ...H3
Macks Creek, 267 ...D4
Macon, 5,538 ...D2
Madison, 586 ...D2
Maitland, 342 ...A1
Malden, 4,782 ...G5
Malta Bend, 249 ...C2
Manchester, 19,161 ...H3
Manes, 100 ...D4
Mansfield, 1,349 ...D4
Maplewood, 9,228 ...H3
Marble Hill, 1,502 ...G4
Marceline, 2,558 ...D2
Marion, 60 ...D3
Marionville, 2,113 ...C4
Marlborough, 2,235 ...H3
Marquand, 251 ...F4
Marshall, 12,433 ...C2
Marshfield, 5,720 ...D4
Marston, 610 ...G5
Marthasville, 837 ...E3
Martinsburg, 326 ...E2
Martinsville ...B1
Maryland Heights, 25,756 ...H3, F3
Marys Home, 80 ...D3
Maryville, 10,581 ...B1
Matthews, 605 ...G5
Maysville, 1,212 ...B2
Mayview, 294 ...C2
Maywood, 225 ...E2
McBaine, 17 ...D3
McFall, 135 ...B1
McGee ...F4
McKittrick, 72 ...E3
Meadville, 457 ...C2
Mehlville, 28,822 ...F3, H3
Memphis, 2,061 ...D1
Mendon, 208 ...C2
Menfro, 60 ...G4
Mercer, 342 ...C1
Merriam Woods, 1,142 ...C5
Merwin, 83 ...B3
Meta, 249 ...D3
Metz, 67 ...B3
Mexico, 11,320 ...E2
Miami, 160 ...C2
Middletown, 199 ...E2
Milan, 1,958 ...C1
Milford, 52 ...B4
Millard, 75 ...D1
Miller, 754 ...C4
Millersburg, 175 ...D3
Millersville, 250 ...G4
Mill Grove, 50 ...C1
Mill Spring, 219 ...F4
Milo, 84 ...B4
Mindenmines, 409 ...B4

Mine La Motte, 100 . . . . . .F4
Miner, 1,056 . . . . .G5
Mineral Point, 363 . . . . . .F4
Missouri City, 295 . . . . . .J4
Moberly, 11,945 . . . . . . .D2
Mokane, 188 . . . . .E3
Moline Acres, 2,662 . . . . .J2
Monett, 7,396 . . . . .C5
Monroe City, 2,588 . . . . .E2
Montevallo B4
Montgomery City, 2,442 . . .E3
Monticello, 126 . . . . . . .E1
Montrose, 417 . . . . .B3
Moody, 125 . . . . .E5
Mooresville, 89 . . . . .C2
Morehouse, 1,015 . . . . . .G5
Morgan, 90 . . . . .D4
Morley, 792 . . . . .G4
Morrison, 123 . . . . .E3
Morrisville, 344 . . . . . . .C4
Mosby, 242 . . . . .J4
Moscow Mills, 1,742 . . . . .F3
Mound City, 1,193 . . . . . .A1
Moundville, 103 . . . . . . .B4
Mountain Grove, 4,574 . . .D4
Mountain View, 2,430 . . . .E4
Mount Leonard, 123 . . . . .C2
Mount Moriah, 143 . . . . . .C1
Mount Vernon, 4,017 . . . .C4
Murphy, 9,048 . . . . .H4
Myrtle, 90 . . . . .E5
Napoleon, 208 . . . . .B2
Nashville, 60 . . . . .B4
Naylor, 610 . . . . .F5
Neelyville, 487 . . . . .F5
Nelson, 212 . . . . .C3
Neosho, 10,505 . . . . . . .B5
Nevada, 8,607 . . . . .B4
Newark, 100 . . . . .E1
New Bloomfield, 599 . . . . .D3
New Boston, 40 . . . . . . .D2
Newburg, 484 . . . . .E4
New Cambria, 222 . . . . . .D2
New Florence, 764 . . . . . .E3
New Franklin, 1,145 . . . . .D2
New Hampton, 349 . . . . . .B1
New Haven, 1,867 . . . . . .E3
New London, 1,001 . . . . .E2
New Madrid, 3,334 . . . . . .G5
New Melle, 124 . . . . .F3
Newtonia, 231 . . . . .B5
Newtown, 209 . . . . .C1
Niangua, 445 . . . . .D4
Nixa, 12,124 . . . . .C4
Noel, 1,480 . . . . .B5
Norborne, 805 . . . . .C2
Normandy, 5,153 . . . . . . .H3
North Kansas City, 4,714 . .H5
North Lilbourn, 95 . . . . . .G5
Northmoor, 399 . . . . .H5
Northview, 125 . . . . .D4
North Wardell, 170 . . . . . .G5
Northwoods, 4,643 . . . . . .H3
Northwye, 550 . . . . .E4
Norwood, 552 . . . . .D4
Novelty, 119 . . . . .D1
Novinger, 534 . . . . .D1
Oak Grove (Franklin Co.),
  382 . . . . .E3
Oak Grove (Jackson Co.),
  5,535 . . . . .B3, J5
Oak Hill, 60 . . . . .E3
Oakland, 1,540 . . . . .H3
Oakland Park B4
Oak Ridge, 202 . . . . .G4
Oaks, 136 . . . . .H5
Oakview, 386 . . . . .H4
Oakville, 35,309 . . . . . F3, H4
Oakwood, 197 . . . . .H4
Oakwood Park, 183 . . . . . .H4
Odessa, 4,818 . . . . .C3
O'Fallon, 46,169 . . . . . . .F3
Old Appleton, 82 . . . . . . .G4
Old Mines, 350 . . . . .F3
Old Monroe, 250 . . . . . . .F3
Olean, 157 . . . . .D3
Olivette, 7,438 . . . . .H3
Olney, 40 . . . . .E2
Olympian Village, 669 . . . .F3
Oran, 1,264 . . . . .G4
Orchard Farm, 275 . . . . . .H2
Oregon, 935 . . . . .A2
Orrick, 889 . . . . .B2, J5
Osage Beach, 3,662 . . . . .D3
Osborn, 455 . . . . .B2
Osceola, 835 . . . . .C3
Osgood, 51 . . . . .C1
Oskaloosa, 40 . . . . .B4
Otterville, 476 . . . . .D3
Overland, 16,838 . . . . . . .H3
Owensville, 2,500 . . . . . .E3
Oxly, 175 . . . . .F5
Ozark, 9,665 . . . . .C4
Pacific, 5,482 . . . . .F3
Pagedale, 3,616 . . . . . . .H3
Palmyra, 3,467 . . . . .E2
Paris, 1,529 . . . . .D2
Parkdale, 205 . . . . .G4

Park Hills, 7,861 . . . . . . .F4
Parkville, 4,059 . . . . .H5
Parkway, 280 . . . . .F3
Parma, 852 . . . . .G5
Parnell, 197 . . . . .B1
Pascola, 138 . . . . .G5
Passaic, 40 . . . . .B3
Patterson, 250 . . . . .F4
Patton, 125 . . . . .F4
Pattonsburg, 261 . . . . . . .B1
Paynesville, 91 . . . . .F2
Peculiar, 2,604 . . . . .B3
Peerless Park, 80 . . . . . . .G3
Penermon, 75 . . . . .G5
Perry, 666 . . . . .E2
Perryville, 7,667 . . . . .G4
Pevely, 3,768 . . . . .F3
Phelps, 90 . . . . .C4
Phelps City, 40 . . . . .A1
Philadelphia, 250 . . . . . . .E2
Phillipsburg, 201 . . . . . . .D4
Pickering, 154 . . . . .B1
Piedmont, 1,992 . . . . . . .F4
Pierce City, 1,385 . . . . . . .B5
Pilot Grove, 723 . . . . .D3
Pilot Knob, 697 . . . . .F4
Pine Lawn, 4,204 . . . . . . .J3
Pineville, 768 . . . . .B5
Pinhook, 48 . . . . .G5
Pittsville, 50 . . . . .E3
Platte City, 3,866 . . . .B2, H4
Platte Woods, 474 . . . . . .H4
Plattsburg, 2,354 . . . . . . .B2
Pleasant Hope, 548 . . . . . .C4
Pleasant Valley, 3,321 . . . .H4
Plevna, 40 . . . . .D2
Pocahontas, 127 . . . . . . .G4
Pollock, 131 . . . . .C1
Polo, 582 . . . . .B2
Pomona, 300 . . . . .E5
Poplar Bluff, 16,651 . . . . . .F5
Portage Des Sioux, 351 . . .F3
Portageville, 3,295 . . . . . .G5
Portland, 90 . . . . .E3
Post Oak, 60 . . . . .C3
Potosi, 2,662 . . . . .F4
Pottersville, 50 . . . . .D5
Powe, 100 . . . . .F5
Powersville, 86 . . . . .C1
Poynor, 90 . . . . .F5
Prairie Hill, 100 . . . . .D2
Prairie Home, 220 . . . . . . .D3
Prathersville, 111 . . . . . . .J4
Preston, 113 . . . . .C4
Princeton, 1,047 . . . . .C1
Protem D5
Purcell, 357 . . . . .B4
Purdin, 223 . . . . .C2
Purdy, 1,103 . . . . .C5
Puxico, 1,145 . . . . .F5
Queen City, 638 . . . . . . .D1
Quick City B3
Quincy C3
Quitman, 46 . . . . .A1
Qulin, 467 . . . . .F5
Racine, 200 . . . . .B5
Randolph, 47 . . . . .H5
Ravenwood, 448 . . . . . . .B1
Raymondville, 442 . . . . . .E4
Raymore, 11,146 . . . . . . .B3
Raytown, 30,388 . . . . .B2, H5
Rayville, 204 . . . . .B2
Rea, 56 . . . . .B1
Readsville E3
Reeds, 103 . . . . .B4
Reeds Spring, 465 . . . . . .C5
Regal, 50 . . . . .C2
Renick, 221 . . . . .D2
Rensselaer, 145 . . . . .E2
Republic, 8,438 . . . . .C4
Revere, 121 . . . . .E1
Reynolds, 125 . . . . .E4
Rhineland, 176 . . . . .E3
Richards, 95 . . . . .B4
Rich Fountain, 90 . . . . . . .E3
Rich Hill, 1,461 . . . . .B3
Richland, 1,805 . . . . .D4
Richmond, 6,116 . . . . . . .C2
Richmond Heights, 9,602 . .H3
Richwoods, 225 . . . . .F3
Ridgely, 64 . . . . .B2
Ridgeway, 530 . . . . .C1
Risco, 392 . . . . .G5
Ritchey, 76 . . . . .B5
River Bend, 10 . . . . .J5
Riverside, 2,979 . . . . .H5
Riverton E5
Riverview, 3,146 . . . . .J2
Rives, 88 . . . . .F5
Roby, 60 . . . . .D4
Rocheport, 208 . . . . .D3
Rock Hill, 4,765 . . . . .H3
Rock Port, 1,395 . . . . .A1
Rockville, 162 . . . . .B3
Rocky Comfort, 175 . . . . . .B5
Rocky Ridge, 350 . . . . . . .F4
Rogersville, 1,508 . . . . . .C4
Rolla, 16,367 . . . . .E4

Rombauer, 80 . . . . .F5
Rome D5
Rosati, 125 . . . . .E4
Roscoe, 112 . . . . .C4
Rosebud, 364 . . . . .E3
Roselle, 100 . . . . .F4
Rosendale, 180 . . . . .B1
Rothville, 93 . . . . .C2
Rover, 60 . . . . .E5
Rueter D5
Rush Hill, 130 . . . . .E2
Rushville, 280 . . . . .A2
Russellville, 758 . . . . .D3
Rutledge, 103 . . . . .D1
Sabula F4
Saginaw, 276 . . . . .B4
St. Ann, 13,607 . . . . .H3
St. Charles, 60,321 . . .F3, H2
St. Clair, 4,390 . . . . .E3
St. Cloud, 56 . . . . .F3
Ste. Genevieve, 4,476 . . . .F4
St. Elizabeth, 297 . . . . . . .D3
St. George, 1,288 . . . . . . .H3
St. James, 3,704 . . . . . . .E4
St. John, 6,871 . . . . .H3
St. Joseph, 73,990 . . . . . .B2
St. Louis, 348,189 . . . .F3, J3
St. Martins, 1,023 . . . . . . .D3
St. Mary, 377 . . . . .G4
St. Paul, 1,634 . . . . .H2
St. Peters, 51,381 . . . . . .G2
St. Robert, 2,760 . . . . . . .D4
St. Thomas, 287 . . . . .D3
Salem, 4,854 . . . . .E4
Salisbury, 1,726 . . . . .D2
Santa Fe, 70 . . . . .E2
Sappington, 7,287 . . . . . . .H3
Sarcoxie, 1,354 . . . . .B4
Savannah, 4,762 . . . . . . .B2
Schell City, 286 . . . . .B3
Scotsdale, 211 . . . . .F3
Scott City, 4,591 . . . . .G4
Sedalia, 20,339 . . . . .C3
Sedgewickville, 197 . . . . . .G4
Seligman, 877 . . . . .C5
Senath, 1,650 . . . . .F5
Seneca, 2,135 . . . . .B5
Seymour, 1,834 . . . . .D4
Shelbina, 1,943 . . . . .D2
Shelbyville, 682 . . . . .D2
Sheldon, 529 . . . . .B4
Sheridan, 185 . . . . .B1
Shirley, 125 . . . . .F4
Shoal Creek Drive, 346 . . .B4
Shrewsbury, 6,644 . . . . . .H3
Sibley, 347 . . . . .J5
Sikeston, 16,992 . . . . .G5
Silex, 206 . . . . .E2
Siloam Springs, 70 . . . . . .D5
Silva, 125 . . . . .F4
Silver Creek, 608 . . . . . . .B4
Silver Lake, 60 . . . . .G4
Simmons D4
Skidmore, 342 . . . . .A1
Slater, 2,083 . . . . .C2
Sleeper, 175 . . . . .D4
Smithton, 510 . . . . .C3
Smithville, 5,514 . . . . .B2
South Fork, 50 . . . . .E5
South Gifford, 72 . . . . . . .D1
South Gorin, 143 . . . . . . .D1
South Greenfield, 136 . . . . .C4
South Lineville, 37 . . . . . . .C1
South West City, 855 . . . . .B5
Spanish Lake, 21,337 . . . . .J2
Sparta, 1,144 . . . . .C5

Spickard, 315 . . . . .C1
Spokane, 133 . . . . .C5
Springfield, 151,580 . . . . . .C4
Squires D5
Stanberry, 1,243 . . . . .B1
Stanton, 225 . . . . .E3
Stark City, 156 . . . . .B5
Steele, 2,263 . . . . .G5
Steelville, 1,429 . . . . .E4
Stella, 178 . . . . .B5
Stewartsville, 759 . . . . . . .B2
Stockton, 1,960 . . . . .C4
Stotesbury, 43 . . . . .B4
Stotts City, 250 . . . . .C4
Stoutland, 177 . . . . .D4
Stoutsville, 44 . . . . .E2
Stover, 968 . . . . .D3
Strafford, 1,845 . . . . .C4
Strasburg, 136 . . . . .B3
Sturgeon, 944 . . . . .D2
Success, 100 . . . . .D4
Sugar Creek, 3,839 . . . . . .J5
Sullivan, 6,351 . . . . .E3
Summersville, 544 . . . . . . .E4
Sumner, 142 . . . . .C2
Sundown, 38 . . . . .D5
Sunrise Beach, 368 . . . . . .D3
Sunset Hills, 8,267 . . . . . .H3
Swedeborg, 250 . . . . .D4
Sweet Springs, 1,628 . . . . .C3
Sycamore Hills, 722 . . . . . .H3
Syracuse, 172 . . . . .D3
Table Rock, 229 . . . . .C5
Tallapoosa, 204 . . . . .G5
Taneyville, 359 . . . . .C5
Taos, 870 . . . . .D3
Tarkio, 1,935 . . . . .A1
Tarrants, 30 . . . . .E2
Tecumseh, 50 . . . . .D5
Thayer, 2,201 . . . . .E5
The Landing, 10 . . . . .E2
Theodosia, 240 . . . . .D5
Thomasville, 40 . . . . .E5
Thornfield, 60 . . . . .D5
Tiff City, 125 . . . . .B5
Tiffin, 40 . . . . .C4
Tightwad, 63 . . . . .C3
Tina, 193 . . . . .C2
Tindall, 65 . . . . .C1
Tipton, 3,261 . . . . .D3
Town and Country, 10,894 . .H3
Tracy, 213 . . . . .B2
Trenton, 6,216 . . . . .C1
Trimble, 451 . . . . .B2
Triplett, 64 . . . . .C2
Troy, 6,737 . . . . .F3
Truesdale, 397 . . . . .E3
Truxton, 96 . . . . .E2
Tunas, 50 . . . . .C4
Turney, 155 . . . . .B2
Tuscumbia, 218 . . . . .D3
Twin Bridges, 42 . . . . .D4
Twin Oaks, 362 . . . . .H3
Umber View Heights, 52 . . .C4
Union, 7,757 . . . . .F3
Union Star, 433 . . . . .B2
Unionville, 2,041 . . . . .C1
Unity Village, 140 . . . . . . .J5
University City, 37,428 . . . .H3
Uplands Park, 460 . . . . . . .H3
Urbana, 407 . . . . .C4
Urich, 495 . . . . .B3
Utica, 274 . . . . .C2
Valles Mines, 275 . . . . . . .F3
Valley Park, 6,518 . . . . . . .H3
Van Buren, 845 . . . . .E4

Vandalia, 2,529 . . . . .E2
Vandiver, 83 . . . . .E2
Vanduser, 217 . . . . .G5
Vanzant D5
Velda City, 1,616 . . . . .H3
Verona, 714 . . . . .C5
Versailles, 2,565 . . . . .D3
Viburnum, 825 . . . . .E4
Vichy, 70 . . . . .E3
Vienna, 628 . . . . .E3
Villa Ridge, 2,417 . . . . . . .F3
Vinita Park, 1,924 . . . . . . .H3
Vinita Terrace, 292 . . . . . . .H3
Vista, 55 . . . . .C4
Waco, 86 . . . . .B4
Wakenda, 90 . . . . .C2
Waldron, 175 . . . . .B2
Walker, 275 . . . . .B4
Walnut Grove, 630 . . . . . . .C4
Wardell, 278 . . . . .G5
Wardsville, 976 . . . . .D3
Warrensburg, 16,340 . . . . .C3
Warrenton, 5,281 . . . . .E3
Warsaw, 2,070 . . . . .C3
Warson Woods, 1,983 . . . . .H3
Washburn, 448 . . . . .C5
Washington, 13,243 . . . . . .E3
Wasola, 90 . . . . .D5
Watson, 121 . . . . .A1
Waverly, 806 . . . . .C2
Wayland, 425 . . . . .E1
Waynesville, 3,507 . . . . . . .D4
Weatherby, 123 . . . . .B2
Weatherby Lake, 1,873 . . . .H4
Weaubleau, 518 . . . . .C4
Webb City, 9,812 . . . . .B4
Webster Groves, 23,230 . . .H3
Weldon Spring, 5,270 . . . . .G3
Weldon Spring Heights, 79 . .G3
Wellington, 784 . . . . .C2
Wellston, 2,460 . . . . .H3
Wellsville, 1,423 . . . . .E2
Wentworth, 141 . . . . .B5
Wentzville, 6,896 . . . . .F3
Westboro, 163 . . . . .A1
West Line, 95 . . . . .B3
Weston, 1,631 . . . . .B2
Westphalia, 320 . . . . .E3
West Plains, 10,866 . . . . . .E5
Westwood, 284 . . . . .H3
Wheatland, 388 . . . . .C4
Wheaton, 721 . . . . .B5
Wheeling, 268 . . . . .C2
White Church, 50 . . . . .E5
Whiteside, 67 . . . . .E2
Whitewater, 113 . . . . .G4
Wien, 50 . . . . .D2
Wilbur Park, 475 . . . . .H3
Wilderness, 40 . . . . .E5
Willard, 3,193 . . . . .C4
Williamstown, 100 . . . . . . .E1
Williamsville, 379 . . . . .F5
Willow Springs, 2,147 . . . . .E4
Wilson City, 165 . . . . .G5
Wilton, 70 . . . . .D3
Winchester, 1,651 . . . . . . .H3
Windsor, 3,087 . . . . .C3
Windyville D4
Winfield, 723 . . . . .F2
Winigan D1
Winona, 1,290 . . . . .E4
Winston, 247 . . . . .B2
Wittenberg G4
Woods Heights, 742 . . . . . .B2
Woodson Terrace, 4,189 . . .H3

Wooldridge, 47 . . . . .D3
Worth, 94 . . . . .B1
Worthington, 89 . . . . .D1
Wright City, 1,532 . . . . . . .E3
Wyaconda, 310 . . . . .E1
Wyatt, 364 . . . . .G5
Yukon, 60 . . . . .E4
Zalma, 93 . . . . .F4
Zanoni, 50 . . . . .D5
Zion, 80 . . . . .F4

Other Features

Beaver, lake C5
Buffalo, river C5
Bull Shoals, lake D5
Chautauqua, lake F1
Clarence Cannon N.W.R. . .F2
Crab Orchard N.W.R. G4
Delaware, river A2
Eleven Point, river E5
Fort Gibson, lake A5
Fort Leonard Wood
  Mil. Res. D4
Fox, river E1
Grand, river B1
G.W. Carver N.M. B5
Harry S Truman, reservoir . .C3
Harry S Truman N.H.S. J5
Horseshoe, lake J3
Hudson, lake A5
Illinois, river B5, F2
Iowa I.R. A2
John Redmond, reservoir . . .A3
Kansas, river H5
Kickapoo I.R. A2
Lake of the Ozarks, lake . . .D3
Longview, reservoir H5
Malvern, lake A3
Mark Twain, lake E2
Mark Twain N.F. . .C5, D3, D4,
  D5, E4, E5, F4
Mark Twain N.W.R. E1, F2
Meramec, river E4, G3
Meredosia N.W.R. F2
Milan Arsenal H5
Mingo N.W.R. F5
Mississippi, river G4, J3
Missouri, river C2, G3, J5
Norfolk, lake D5
Oologah, lake A5
Osage, river B4, D3
Ozark Natl. Scenic
  Riverways E4
Ozark N.F. B5, D4
Perry, lake A2
Platte, river B2
Potawatomi I.R. A2
Sac And Fox I.R. A2
St. Francis, river F4
Sangamon, river F1
Shawnee N.F. G4
Stockton, lake C4
Swan Lake N.W.R. C2
Table Rock, lake C5
Taum Sauk, mountain F4
Thomas Hill, reservoir D2
Wilson's Creek Natl. Bfld. . .C4
Weldon, river C2

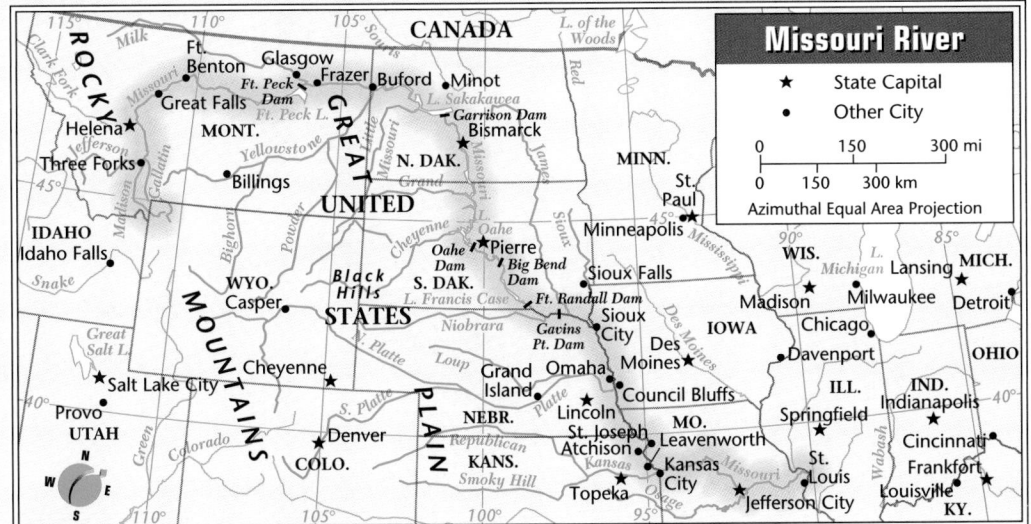

Missouri River

★ State Capital
• Other City

0   150   300 mi
0   150 300 km
Azimuthal Equal Area Projection

© MapQuest.com, Inc.

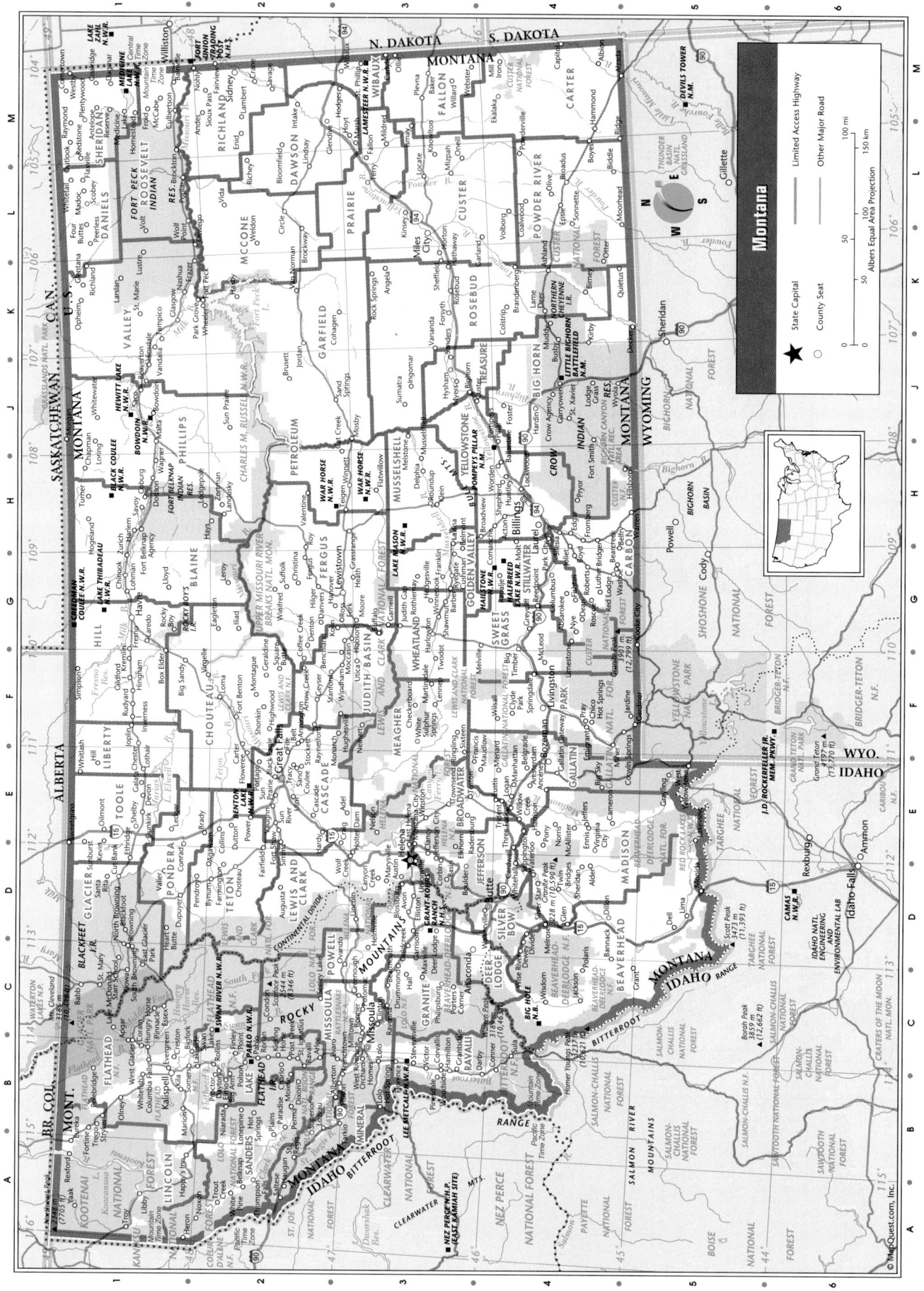

Montana

Montana

Capital: Helena
Land Area: 145,556 sq. mi.
376,990 sq. km.
Population: 902,195 (2000 Census)
Largest City: Billings, 89,847
Highest Point: Granite Peak
12,799 ft.
3,901 m.
Admitted to Union: November 8, 1889
Nickname: Treasure State
Big Sky Country
State Flower: Bitterroot
State Bird: Western Meadowlark

Montana: Map Index

Counties

Beaverhead, 9,202 . . . D4
Big Horn, 12,671 . . . J4
Blaine, 7,009 . . . G1
Broadwater, 4,385 . . . E3
Carbon, 9,552 . . . G4
Carter, 1,360 . . . M4
Cascade, 80,357 . . . E2
Chouteau, 5,970 . . . F2
Custer, 11,696 . . . L3
Daniels, 2,017 . . . L1
Dawson, 9,059 . . . L2
Deer Lodge, 9,417 . . . C3
Fallon, 2,837 . . . M3
Fergus, 11,893 . . . G2
Flathead, 74,471 . . . B1
Gallatin, 67,831 . . . E4
Garfield, 1,279 . . . K2
Glacier, 13,247 . . . D1
Golden Valley, 1,042 . . . G3
Granite, 2,830 . . . C3
Hill, 16,673 . . . G1
Jefferson, 10,049 . . . D3
Judith Basin, 2,329 . . . F3
Lake, 26,507 . . . B2
Lewis and Clark, 55,716 . . . D2
Liberty, 2,158 . . . E1
Lincoln, 18,837 . . . A1
Madison, 6,851 . . . E4
McCone, 1,977 . . . L2
Meagher, 1,932 . . . F3
Mineral, 3,884 . . . B3
Missoula, 95,802 . . . C2
Musselshell, 4,497 . . . H3
Park, 15,694 . . . F4
Petroleum, 493 . . . H2
Phillips, 4,601 . . . J1
Pondera, 6,424 . . . D1
Powder River, 1,858 . . . L4
Powell, 7,180 . . . C2
Prairie, 1,199 . . . L3
Ravalli, 36,070 . . . C3
Richland, 9,667 . . . M2
Roosevelt, 10,620 . . . L1
Rosebud, 9,383 . . . K3
Sanders, 10,227 . . . A2
Sheridan, 4,105 . . . M1
Silver Bow, 34,606 . . . D4
Stillwater, 8,195 . . . G4
Sweet Grass, 3,609 . . . G4
Teton, 6,445 . . . D2
Toole, 5,267 . . . E1
Treasure, 861 . . . J3
Valley, 7,675 . . . K1
Wheatland, 2,259 . . . G3
Wibaux, 1,068 . . . M3
Yellowstone, 129,352 . . . H3

Cities and Towns

Absarokee, 1,234 . . . G4
Acton, 50 . . . H4
Adel, 125 . . . E2
Agawam . . . D2
Alberton, 374 . . . B2
Albion . . . M4
Alder, 116 . . . D4
Alzada, 50 . . . M4
Amsterdam, 727 . . . E4
Anaconda, 9,417 . . . D3
Anceney . . . E4
Andes . . . M2
Angela . . . K3
Antelope, 43 . . . M1
Apgar . . . C1
Arlee, 602 . . . B2
Armington, 150 . . . F2
Arrow Creek . . . F2
Ashland, 464 . . . K4
Augusta, 284 . . . D2
Austin . . . D3
Avon, 124 . . . D3
Babb . . . C1
Bainville, 153 . . . M1
Baker, 1,695 . . . M3
Ballantine, 346 . . . H4
Bannack . . . D4
Barber . . . G3
Basin, 255 . . . D3
Bearcreek, 83 . . . G4
Bearmouth . . . C3
Beaverton . . . J1
Belfry, 219 . . . H4
Belgrade, 5,728 . . . E4
Belknap, 50 . . . A2
Belmont . . . H3
Belt, 633 . . . F2
Benchland . . . F2
Biddle . . . L4
Big Arm, 131 . . . B2
Bigfork, 1,421 . . . B1
Bighorn . . . J3
Big Sandy, 703 . . . F1
Big Sky, 1,221 . . . E4
Big Timber, 1,650 . . . G4
Billings, 89,847 . . . H4
Birney, 108 . . . K4
Black Eagle, 914 . . . E2
Blackfoot . . . D1
Bloomfield . . . M2
Blossburg . . . D3
Bonner (Bonner-West Riverside), 1,693 . . . C3
Boulder, 1,300 . . . D3
Bowdoin . . . J1
Box Elder, 794 . . . F1
Boyd . . . G4
Boyes . . . L4
Bozeman, 27,509 . . . E4
Brady, 150 . . . E1
Brandenberg . . . K4
Bridger, 745 . . . H4
Broadus, 451 . . . L4
Broadview, 150 . . . H3
Brockton, 245 . . . M1
Brockway . . . L2
Browning, 1,065 . . . C1
Brusett . . . J2
Buffalo . . . G3
Busby, 695 . . . K4
Butte, 34,606 . . . D3
Bynum . . . D2
Cameron . . . E4
Canyon Creek . . . D3
Capitol . . . M4
Cardwell, 40 . . . E4
Carlyle . . . M3
Carter, 62 . . . F2
Cascade, 819 . . . E2
Cat Creek . . . J2
Chapman . . . H1
Charlo, 439 . . . B2
Checkerboard . . . F3
Chester, 871 . . . F1
Chico Hot Springs, 50 . . . F4
Chinook, 1,386 . . . G1
Choteau, 1,781 . . . D2
Christina . . . G2
Circle, 644 . . . L2
Clancy, 1,406 . . . E3
Clinton, 549 . . . C3
Clyde Park, 310 . . . F4
Coalridge, 50 . . . M1
Coalwood . . . L4
Coburg . . . H1
Coffee Creek . . . F2
Cohagen . . . K2
Collins . . . E2
Colstrip, 2,346 . . . K4
Columbia Falls, 3,645 . . . B1
Columbus, 1,748 . . . G4
Comanche . . . H3
Comertown . . . M1
Condon, 60 . . . C2
Conner, 40 . . . B4
Conrad, 2,753 . . . D1
Cooke City, 140 . . . G4
Coram, 337 . . . B1
Corbin, 100 . . . D3
Corvallis, 443 . . . B3
Corwin Springs . . . F4
Craig, 60 . . . E2
Crane, 40 . . . M2
Creston, 125 . . . B1
Crow Agency, 1,552 . . . J4
Culbertson, 716 . . . M1
Cushman . . . G3
Custer, 145 . . . J3
Cut Bank, 3,105 . . . D1
Dagmar . . . M1
Danvers . . . G2
Darby, 710 . . . B3
Dayton, 95 . . . B2
Dean . . . G4
Decker . . . K4
Deer Lodge, 3,421 . . . D3
Dell . . . D5
Delphia . . . H3
Denton, 301 . . . G2
Devon . . . E1
Dewey, 40 . . . D4
Dillon, 3,752 . . . D4
Divide . . . D4
Dixon, 216 . . . B2
Dodson, 122 . . . H1
Drummond, 318 . . . C3
Dunkirk . . . E1
Dupuyer, 40 . . . D1
Dutton, 389 . . . E2
Eagleton . . . G2
East Glacier Park, 396 . . . C1
East Helena, 1,642 . . . E3
Edgar, 125 . . . H4
Ekalaka, 410 . . . M4
Elkhorn . . . E3
Elliston, 225 . . . D3
Elmo, 143 . . . B2
Emigrant . . . F4
Enid . . . M2
Ennis, 840 . . . E4
Epsie . . . L4
Essex . . . C1
Ethridge . . . D1
Eureka, 1,017 . . . A1
Eustis, 50 . . . E4
Evaro, 329 . . . B2
Evergreen, 6,215 . . . B1
Fairfield, 659 . . . D2
Fairview, 709 . . . M2
Fallon, 138 . . . L3
Farmington . . . D2
Fergus . . . G2
Fife . . . E2
Finley Point, 493 . . . B2
Fishtail, 60 . . . G4
Flatwillow . . . H3
Flaxville, 87 . . . L1
Florence, 901 . . . B3
Floweree . . . E2
Forsyth, 1,944 . . . K3
Fort Belknap Agency, 1,262 . . . H1
Fort Benton, 1,594 . . . F2
Fortine, 169 . . . B1
Fort Peck, 240 . . . K2
Fort Shaw, 274 . . . E2
Fort Smith, 122 . . . J4
Foster . . . J4
Four Buttes . . . L1
Francis . . . E3
Franklin . . . G3
Frazer, 452 . . . K1
Frenchtown, 883 . . . B3
Fresno . . . G1
Froid, 195 . . . M1
Fromberg, 486 . . . H4
Galata . . . E1
Gallatin Gateway, 350 . . . E4
Gardiner, 851 . . . F4
Garland . . . L3
Garneill . . . G3
Garrison, 112 . . . D3
Garryowen . . . J4
Geraldine, 284 . . . F2
Geyser, 40 . . . F2
Gildford, 185 . . . F1
Glasgow, 3,253 . . . K1
Glen . . . D4
Glendive, 4,729 . . . M2
Glentana . . . K1
Goldcreek, 40 . . . D3
Grant, 50 . . . C4
Grantsdale, 750 . . . B3
Grassrange, 149 . . . H2
Grayling . . . E5
Great Falls, 56,690 . . . E2
Greenough . . . C3
Greycliff, 56 . . . G4
Hall, 150 . . . C3
Hamilton, 3,705 . . . B3
Hammond . . . M4
Hanover . . . G2
Happy's Inn . . . A1
Hardin, 3,384 . . . J4
Hardy, 50 . . . E2
Harlem, 848 . . . H1
Harlowton, 1,062 . . . G3
Harrison, 162 . . . E4
Hathaway . . . K3
Haugan . . . A2
Havre, 9,621 . . . G1
Haxby . . . K2
Hays, 702 . . . H2
Heart Butte, 698 . . . D1
Heath . . . G3
Hedgesville . . . G3
Helena, 25,780 . . . D3
Helmville . . . D3
Heron, 149 . . . A1
Highwood, 189 . . . F2
Hilger, 70 . . . G2
Hill . . . E1
Hillsboro . . . H4
Hingham, 157 . . . F1
Hinsdale, 125 . . . J1
Hobson, 244 . . . G3
Hodges . . . M3
Hogeland . . . H1
Holter Dam . . . D3
Homestead . . . M1
Horton . . . K3
Hot Springs, 531 . . . B2
Hoyt . . . M3
Hughesville . . . F2
Hungry Horse, 934 . . . B1
Huntley, 411 . . . H4
Huson, 125 . . . B2
Hysham, 330 . . . J3
Iliad . . . G2
Ingomar . . . J3
Intake . . . M2
Inverness, 103 . . . F1
Ismay, 26 . . . M3
Jackson . . . C4
Jardine . . . F4
Jeffers, 70 . . . E4
Jefferson City, 295 . . . D3
Joliet, 575 . . . H4
Joplin, 210 . . . F1
Jordan, 364 . . . K2
Judith Gap, 164 . . . G3
Kalispell, 14,223 . . . B1
Kevin, 178 . . . E1
Kicking Horse, 80 . . . B2
Kila, 225 . . . B1
Kinsey . . . L3
Kiowa . . . C1
Kirby . . . K4
Klein, 188 . . . H3
Knowlton . . . L3
Kolin . . . G2
Kremlin, 126 . . . F1
Lake McDonald . . . C1
Lakeside, 1,679 . . . B1
Lakeview . . . E5
Lambert, 150 . . . M2
Lame Deer, 2,018 . . . K4
Landusky, 200 . . . H2
Laredo . . . G1
Larslan . . . K1
Laurel, 6,255 . . . H4
Lavina, 209 . . . H3
Ledger . . . E1
Lennep . . . F3
Leroy, 40 . . . G2
Lewistown, 5,813 . . . G2
Libby, 2,626 . . . A1
Lima, 242 . . . D5
Limestone . . . G4
Lincoln, 1,100 . . . D3
Lindsay . . . L2
Livingston, 6,851 . . . F4
Lloyd, 60 . . . G1
Locate . . . L3
Lockwood, 4,306 . . . H4
Lodge Grass, 510 . . . J4
Lodgepole, 214 . . . H1
Logan, 90 . . . E4
Lohman, 40 . . . G1
Lolo, 3,388 . . . B3
Lolo Hot Springs . . . B3
Loma, 92 . . . F2
Lonepine, 137 . . . B2
Loring . . . J1
Lothair . . . E1
Lozeau . . . B2
Lustre . . . L1
Luther, 50 . . . G4
Madoc . . . L1
Malta, 2,120 . . . J1
Manhattan, 1,396 . . . E4
Marion, 100 . . . B1
Marsh . . . M3
Martinsdale . . . F3
Marysville . . . D3
Maudlow . . . E3
Maxville, 40 . . . C3
McAllister, 150 . . . E4
McCabe . . . M1
McLeod . . . F4
Medicine Lake, 269 . . . M1
Melrose . . . D4
Melstone, 136 . . . J3
Melville . . . G3
Menard . . . E4
Mildred . . . M3
Miles City, 8,487 . . . L3
Mill Iron . . . M4
Milltown . . . C3
Miner . . . F4
Missoula, 57,053 . . . C3
Mizpah . . . L3
Moccasin, 40 . . . G2
Moiese . . . B2
Molt . . . H4
Monarch . . . F2
Monida . . . D5
Montague . . . F2
Montana City, 2,094 . . . E3
Moore, 186 . . . G3
Moorhead . . . L4
Morgan . . . J1
Mosby . . . J3
Muddy, 627 . . . K4
Musselshell, 60 . . . H3
Myers . . . J3
Nashua, 325 . . . K1
Neihart, 91 . . . F3
Nelson . . . E3
Niarada, 50 . . . B2
Nohly . . . M2
Norris . . . E4
North Browning, 2,200 . . . D1
Noxon, 230 . . . A2
Nye . . . G4
Oilmont . . . E1
Olive . . . L4
Ollie . . . M3
Olney, 60 . . . B1
Oneill . . . L3
Opheim, 111 . . . K1
Orchard Homes, 5,199 . . . B3
Oswego, 60 . . . L1
Otter . . . K4
Outlook, 82 . . . M1
Ovando, 71 . . . C2
Pablo, 1,814 . . . B2
Paradise, 184 . . . B2
Park City, 870 . . . H4
Park Grove . . . K1
Peerless, 60 . . . L1
Pendroy . . . D1
Perma . . . B2
Philipsburg, 914 . . . C3
Pinesdale, 742 . . . B3
Pinnacle . . . C1
Plains, 1,126 . . . B2
Plentywood, 2,061 . . . M1
Plevna, 138 . . . M3
Polaris, 60 . . . C4
Polebridge . . . B1
Polson, 4,041 . . . B2
Pompeys Pillar . . . J4
Pony, 40 . . . E4
Poplar, 911 . . . L1
Portage . . . E2
Porters Corner . . . C3
Post Creek, 70 . . . B2
Potomac, 125 . . . C3
Powderville . . . L4
Power, 171 . . . E2
Pray, 50 . . . F4
Proctor . . . B2
Pryor, 628 . . . H4
Quietus . . . K4
Radersburg, 70 . . . E3
Rapalje, 70 . . . G4
Ravalli, 119 . . . B2
Ravenna . . . C3
Raymond . . . M1
Raynesford . . . F2
Red Lodge, 2,177 . . . G4
Redstone, 40 . . . M1
Reedpoint, 185 . . . G4
Reserve, 37 . . . M1
Rexford, 151 . . . A1
Richey, 189 . . . L2
Richland . . . K1
Ridge . . . L4
Ringling . . . F3
Roberts, 200 . . . G4
Rock Springs . . . K3
Rocky Boy, 175 . . . G1
Rollins, 183 . . . B2
Ronan, 1,812 . . . B2
Roscoe . . . G4
Rosebud . . . K3
Ross Fork . . . G2
Rothiemay . . . G3
Roundup, 1,931 . . . H3
Roy, 100 . . . H2
Rudyard, 275 . . . F1
Ryegate, 268 . . . G3
Saco, 224 . . . J1
St. Ignatius, 788 . . . B2
St. Marie, 183 . . . K1
St. Mary . . . C1
St. Phillip . . . M3
St. Regis, 315 . . . A2
St. Xavier, 67 . . . J4
Saltese . . . A2
Sand Coulee, 200 . . . E2
Sanders, 40 . . . J3
Sand Springs, 40 . . . J2
Santa Rita, 100 . . . D1
Sappington . . . E4
Savage, 250 . . . M2
Savoy . . . H1
Scobey, 1,082 . . . L1
Seeley Lake, 1,436 . . . C2
Shawmut, 90 . . . G3
Sheffield . . . K3
Shelby, 3,216 . . . E1
Shepherd, 193 . . . H4
Sheridan, 659 . . . D4
Shonkin . . . F2
Sidney, 4,774 . . . M2
Silesia . . . H4
Silver Star . . . D4
Simms, 373 . . . E2
Simpson . . . F1
Sioux Pass . . . M2
Sixteen . . . F3
Somers, 556 . . . B1
Sonnette . . . L4
South Browning, 1,677 . . . C1
Springdale . . . F4
Square Butte . . . F2
Stanford, 454 . . . F2
Starr School, 248 . . . C1
Stevensville, 1,553 . . . B3
Stockett, 200 . . . E2
Stryker . . . B1
Suffolk . . . G2
Sula . . . C4
Sumatra . . . J3
Sunburst, 415 . . . E1
Sun Prairie (Cascade Co.), 1,772 . . . E2
Sun Prairie (Phillips Co.) . . . J2
Sun River, 131 . . . E2
Superior, 893 . . . B2
Swan Lake . . . C2
Sweetgrass, 175 . . . E1
Tampico, 60 . . . K1
Tarkio . . . B3
Teigen . . . H2
Terry, 611 . . . L3
Thompson Falls, 1,321 . . . A2
Three Forks, 1,728 . . . E4
Toston, 105 . . . E3
Townsend, 1,867 . . . E3
Tracy, 150 . . . E2
Trego . . . B1
Trident . . . E4
Trout Creek, 261 . . . A2
Troy, 957 . . . A1
Turner, 80 . . . H1
Twin Bridges, 400 . . . D4
Twodot . . . F3
Ulm, 750 . . . E2
Unionville, 175 . . . D3
Utica . . . F3
Valentine . . . H2
Valier, 498 . . . D1
Vananda . . . K3
Vandalia . . . K1
Van Norman . . . K2
Vaughn, 701 . . . E2
Victor, 859 . . . B3
Vida . . . L2
Virgelle . . . F1
Virginia City, 130 . . . E4
Volborg . . . L4
Volt . . . L1
Wagner . . . H1
Walkerville, 714 . . . D3
Warren . . . H4
Washoe . . . G4
Waterloo . . . D4
Webster . . . M3
Weldon . . . L2
Westby, 172 . . . M1
West Glacier, 125 . . . B1
West Riverside (Bonner-West Riverside), 1,693 . . . C3
West Yellowstone, 1,177 . . . E5
Wheeler . . . K2
Whitefish, 5,032 . . . B1
Whitehall, 1,044 . . . D4
White Pine, 70 . . . A2
White Sulphur Springs, 984 . . . F3
Whitetail . . . L1
Whitewater, 40 . . . J1
Whitlash . . . E1
Wibaux, 567 . . . M3
Willard, 50 . . . M3
Willow Creek, 209 . . . E4
Wilsall, 237 . . . F4
Windham, 50 . . . F2
Winifred, 156 . . . G2
Winnecook, 40 . . . G3
Winnett, 185 . . . H2
Winston, 73 . . . E3
Wisdom, 114 . . . C4
Wise River, 60 . . . D4
Wolf Creek . . . D2
Wolf Point, 2,663 . . . L1
Woodside, 175 . . . B3
Worden, 506 . . . H4
Wyola, 186 . . . J4
Yaak . . . A1
Zortman, 175 . . . H2
Zurich . . . G1

Other Features

Beaverhead-Deerlodge National Forest . . . C4, D3, D4, E5
Belle Fourche, *river* . . . L5
Benton Lake N.W.R. . . . E2
Big Hole N.B. . . . C4
Bighorn, *basin* . . . H5
Bighorn, *river* . . . H5, J4
Bighorn Canyon Natl. Rec. Area . . . H4
Bighorn National Forest . . . J5
Bitterroot, *range* . . . A3, C4
Bitterroot, *river* . . . B4
Bitterroot N.F. . . . B4
Black Coulee N.W.R. . . . H1
Blackfeet I.R. . . . C1
Boise National Forest . . . A5
Bowdoin N.W.R. . . . J1
Bridger-Teton N.F. . . . F5, F6
Bull, *mountains* . . . H3
Camas N.W.R. . . . D6
Canyon Ferry, *lake* . . . E3
Caribou N.F. . . . E6
Charles M. Russell N.W.R. . . . J2
Clark Fork, *river* . . . A2
Clearwater, *mountains* . . . A3
Clearwater National Forest . . . A3
Cleveland, *mountain* . . . C1
Coeur D'Alene N.F. . . . A2
Continental Divide . . . D2
Creedman Coulee N.W.R. . . . G1
Crow Indian Res. . . . H4
Custer National Forest . . . G4, H4, K4, M4
Devils Tower N.M. . . . M5
Dworshak, *reservoir* . . . A3
Elwell, *lake* . . . E1
Flathead I.R. . . . B2
Flathead, *lake* . . . B2
Flathead, *river* . . . B1
Flathead N.F. . . . B1, C2
Fort Belknap Indian Res. . . . H1
Fort Peck, *lake* . . . K2
Fort Peck Indian Res. . . . L1
Fort Union Trading Post N.H.S. . . . M2
Fresno, *reservoir* . . . F1
Gallatin National Forest . . . F4
Glacier Natl. Park . . . C1
Grand Teton, *peak* . . . F6
Grand Teton Natl. Park . . . F6
Granite, *peak* (highest point) . . . G4
Granite, *peak* . . . D4
Grant-Kohrs Ranch N.H.S. . . . D3
Grasslands Natl. Park . . . J1
Hailstone N.W.R. . . . G3
Halfbreed Lake N.W.R. . . . G4
Helena National Forest . . . D3, E3
Hewitt Lake N.W.R. . . . J1
Homer Youngs, *peak* . . . C4
Hungry Horse Res. . . . C1
Idaho Natl. Engineering Lab . . . D6
J.D. Rockefeller Jr. Mem. Pkwy. . . . F5
Kaniksu National Forest . . . A1
Koocanusa, *lake* . . . A1
Kootenai, *river* . . . A1
Kootenai National Forest . . . A1
Lake Mason N.W.R. . . . H3
Lake Thibadeau N.W.R. . . . G1
Lake Zahl N.W.R. . . . M1
Lamesteer N.W.R. . . . M3
Lee Metcalf N.W.R. . . . B3
Lewis And Clark National Forest . . . D2, F2, F3
Little Bighorn Battlefield N.M. . . . J4
Little Missouri, *river* . . . M5
Lolo National Forest . . . A2, B2, C2, C3
Madison, *river* . . . E4
Marias, *river* . . . E1
Medicine Lake N.W.R. . . . M1
Middle Fork, *river* . . . C1
Milk, *river* . . . D1, G1, K1
Missouri, *river* . . . F2, G2, M1
Musselshell, *river* . . . G3
Natl. Bison Range . . . B2
Nez Perce National Forest . . . A4
Nez Perce N.H.P. (East Kamiah Site) . . . A3
Northern Cheyenne I.R. . . . K4
Northwest, *peak* . . . A1
Pablo N.W.R. . . . B2
Payette National Forest . . . A4
Pompeys Pillar Natl. Mon. . . . H3
Powder, *river* . . . K5, L3, L4
Rattlesnake N.R.A. . . . C2
Red Rock Lakes N.W.R. . . . E5
Rocky, *mountains* . . . C2
Rocky Boy's I.R. . . . G1
St. Joe National Forest . . . A2
St. Mary, *river* . . . C1
St. Regis, *river* . . . A2
Salmon, *river* . . . A4
Salmon-Challis National Forest . . . B4, B5, C5, D5
Salmon River, *mountains* . . . B5
Scarface, *peak* . . . C2
Scott, *peak* . . . D5
Shoshone National Forest . . . G5
South Fork, *river* . . . C2
Swan, *river* . . . C2
Swan River N.W.R. . . . C2
Targhee National Forest . . . D5, E5
Teton, *river* . . . E2
Thunder Basin Natl. Grassland . . . L5
Tongue, *river* . . . K4
Upper Missouri River Breaks Natl. Mon. . . . G2
War Horse N.W.R. . . . H2, H3
Warren, *peak* . . . C4
Waterton Lakes N.P. . . . C1
Yellowstone, *lake* . . . F5
Yellowstone, *river* . . . H3, L3
Yellowstone Natl. Park . . . F5

Glacier National Park

Nebraska

Capital: Lincoln
Land Area: 76,878 sq. mi.
199,114 sq. km.
Population: 1,711,263 (2000 Census)
Largest City: Omaha, 390,007
Highest Point: Kimball County
5,426 ft.
1,654 m.
Admitted to Union: March 1, 1867
Nickname: Cornhusker State
State Flower: Goldenrod
State Bird: Western Meadowlark

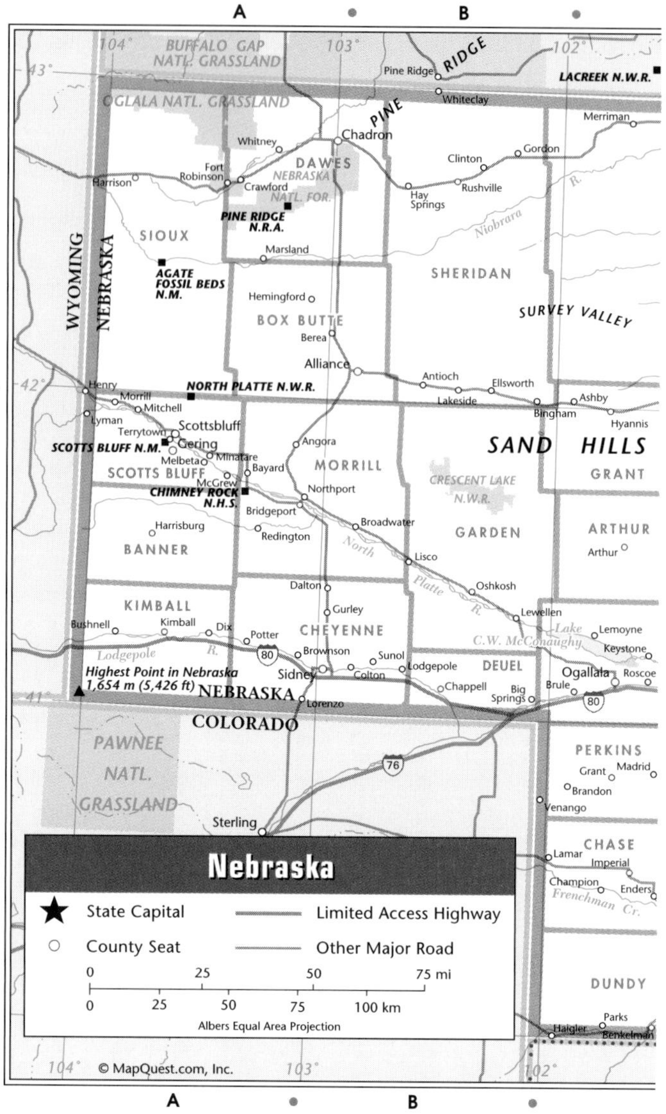
A
B
1
2
3
BUFFALO GAP NATL. GRASSLAND
OGLALA NATL. GRASSLAND
PINE RIDGE
LACREEK N.W.R.
Pine Ridge
Whiteclay
Merriman
Whitney
Chadron
Fort Robinson
Crawford
DAWES
NEBRASKA NATL. FOR.
Harrison
Hay Springs
Clinton
Rushville
Gordon
PINE RIDGE N.R.A.
SIOUX
Marsland
AGATE FOSSIL BEDS N.M.
SHERIDAN
Hemingford
BOX BUTTE
Berea
SURVEY VALLEY
WYOMING
NEBRASKA
Alliance
Antioch
Ellsworth
Lakeside
Bingham
Ashby
Hyannis
Henry
Morrill
Mitchell
NORTH PLATTE N.W.R.
Lyman
Terrytown
Scottsbluff
SCOTTS BLUFF N.M.
Gering
Melbeta
Minatare
McGrew
Angora
SCOTTS BLUFF
Bayard
MORRILL
SAND HILLS
GRANT
CHIMNEY ROCK N.H.S.
Northport
CRESCENT LAKE N.W.R.
Bridgeport
Harrisburg
Redington
Broadwater
BANNER
GARDEN
ARTHUR
Arthur
Lisco
Dalton
Oshkosh
KIMBALL
Gurley
Lewellen
Bushnell
Kimball
Dix
Potter
CHEYENNE
Lemoyne
Keystone
Brownson
Sunol
Lodgepole
DEUEL
Ogallala
Roscoe
Highest Point in Nebraska 1,654 m (5,426 ft)
Sidney
Colton
Chappell
Big Springs
Brule
NEBRASKA
Lorenzo
COLORADO
PAWNEE NATL. GRASSLAND
PERKINS
Grant
Madrid
Brandon
Venango
Sterling
CHASE
Lamar
Imperial
Champion
Enders
DUNDY
Haigler
Parks
Benkelman
Nebraska
State Capital
Limited Access Highway
County Seat
Other Major Road
0 25 50 75 mi
0 25 50 75 100 km
Albers Equal Area Projection
© MapQuest.com, Inc.

Nebraska: Map Index

Counties

Adams, 31,151 . . . . F3
Antelope, 7,452 . . . . F1
Arthur, 444 . . . . C2
Banner, 819 . . . . A2
Blaine, 583 . . . . D2
Boone, 6,259 . . . . F2
Box Butte, 12,158 . . . . A1
Boyd, 2,438 . . . . F1
Brown, 3,525 . . . . E1
Buffalo, 42,259 . . . . E3
Burt, 7,791 . . . . H2
Butler, 8,767 . . . . G2
Cass, 24,334 . . . . H3
Cedar, 9,615 . . . . G1
Chase, 4,068 . . . . C3
Cherry, 6,148 . . . . C1
Cheyenne, 9,830 . . . . B2
Clay, 7,039 . . . . G3
Colfax, 10,441 . . . . G2
Cuming, 10,203 . . . . H1
Custer, 11,793 . . . . D2
Dakota, 20,253 . . . . H1
Dawes, 9,060 . . . . A1
Dawson, 24,365 . . . . E3
Deuel, 2,098 . . . . B2
Dixon, 6,339 . . . . H1
Dodge, 36,160 . . . . H2
Douglas, 463,585 . . . . H2
Dundy, 2,292 . . . . C3
Fillmore, 6,634 . . . . G3
Franklin, 3,574 . . . . F3
Frontier, 3,099 . . . . D3
Furnas, 5,324 . . . . E3
Gage, 22,993 . . . . H3
Garden, 2,292 . . . . B2
Garfield, 1,902 . . . . E2
Gosper, 2,143 . . . . E3
Grant, 747 . . . . C2
Greeley, 2,714 . . . . F2
Hall, 53,534 . . . . F3
Hamilton, 9,403 . . . . F3
Harlan, 3,786 . . . . E3
Hayes, 1,068 . . . . C3
Hitchcock, 3,111 . . . . C3
Holt, 11,551 . . . . F1
Hooker, 783 . . . . C2
Howard, 6,567 . . . . F2
Jefferson, 8,333 . . . . G3
Johnson, 4,488 . . . . H3
Kearney, 6,882 . . . . E3
Keith, 8,875 . . . . C2
Keya Paha, 983 . . . . E1
Kimball, 4,089 . . . . A2
Knox, 9,374 . . . . G1
Lancaster, 250,291 . . . . H3
Lincoln, 34,632 . . . . D3
Logan, 774 . . . . D2
Loup, 712 . . . . E2
Madison, 35,226 . . . . G2
McPherson, 533 . . . . C2
Merrick, 8,204 . . . . G2
Morrill, 5,440 . . . . B2
Nance, 4,038 . . . . F2
Nemaha, 7,576 . . . . J3
Nuckolls, 5,057 . . . . F3
Otoe, 15,396 . . . . H3
Pawnee, 3,087 . . . . H3
Perkins, 3,200 . . . . C3
Phelps, 9,747 . . . . E3
Pierce, 7,857 . . . . G1
Platte, 31,662 . . . . G2
Polk, 5,639 . . . . G2
Red Willow, 11,448 . . . . D3
Richardson, 9,531 . . . . J3
Rock, 1,756 . . . . E1
Saline, 13,843 . . . . G3
Sarpy, 122,595 . . . . H2
Saunders, 19,830 . . . . H2
Scotts Bluff, 36,951 . . . . A2
Seward, 16,496 . . . . G3
Sheridan, 6,198 . . . . B1
Sherman, 3,318 . . . . E2
Sioux, 1,475 . . . . A1
Stanton, 6,455 . . . . G2
Thayer, 6,055 . . . . G3
Thomas, 729 . . . . D2
Thurston, 7,171 . . . . H1
Valley, 4,647 . . . . E2
Washington, 18,780 . . . . H2
Wayne, 9,851 . . . . G1
Webster, 4,061 . . . . F3
Wheeler, 886 . . . . F2
York, 14,598 . . . . G3

Cities and Towns

Abie, 108 . . . . H2
Adams, 489 . . . . H3
Agnew, *100* H2
Ainsworth, 1,862 . . . . E1
Albion, 1,797 . . . . G2
Alda, 652 . . . . E3
Alexandria, 216 . . . . G3
Allen, 411 . . . . H1
Alliance, 8,959 . . . . B1
Alma, 1,214 . . . . E3
Almeria E2
Aloys, *50* H2
Altona, *40* G1
Alvo, 142 . . . . H3
Amelia E1
Amherst, 277 . . . . E3
Angora A2
Angus G3
Anoka, 10 . . . . E1
Anselmo, 159 . . . . E2
Ansley, 520 . . . . E2
Antioch B1
Arapahoe, 1,028 . . . . E3
Arcadia, 359 . . . . E2
Archer, *90* E2
Arlington, 1,197 . . . . H2
Arnold, 630 . . . . D2
Arthur, 145 . . . . C2
Ashby C1
Ashland, 2,262 . . . . H2
Ashton, 237 . . . . E2
Assumption, *70* E3
Atkinson, 1,244 . . . . E1
Atlanta, 130 . . . . E3
Auburn, 3,350 . . . . J3
Aurora, 4,225 . . . . E3
Avoca, 270 . . . . H3
Axtell, 696 . . . . E3
Ayr, 98 . . . . E3
Bancroft, 520 . . . . H1
Barada, 28 . . . . J3
Barneston, 122 . . . . H3
Bartlett, 128 . . . . E2
Bartley, 355 . . . . D3
Bassett, 743 . . . . E1
Battle Creek, 1,158 . . . . G2
Bayard, 1,247 . . . . A2
Bazile Mills, 26 . . . . G1
Beatrice, 12,496 . . . . H3
Beaver City, 641 . . . . E3
Beaver Crossing, 457 . . . . G3
Bee, 223 . . . . G2
Beemer, 773 . . . . H2
Belden, 131 . . . . G1
Belgrade, 134 . . . . E2
Bellevue, 44,382 . . . . J2
Bellwood, 446 . . . . G2
Belvidere, 98 . . . . G3
Benedict, 278 . . . . G2
Benkelman, 1,006 . . . . C3
Bennet, 570 . . . . H3
Bennington, 937 . . . . H2
Berea, *70* A1
Bertrand, 786 . . . . E3
Berwyn, 134 . . . . E2
Big Springs, 418 . . . . B2
Bingham B1
Bladen, 291 . . . . E3
Blair, 7,512 . . . . H2
Bloomfield, 1,126 . . . . G1
Bloomington, 124 . . . . E3
Blue Hill, 867 . . . . E3
Blue Springs, 383 . . . . H3
Boelus, 221 . . . . E2
Boone, *50* G2
Bostwick E3
Bow Valley, *125* G1
Boys Town, 818 . . . . H2
Bradshaw, 336 . . . . G3
Brady, 366 . . . . D2
Brainard, 351 . . . . H2
Brandon C3
Brewster, 29 . . . . E2
Bridgeport, 1,594 . . . . A2
Bristow, 88 . . . . E1
Broadwater, 140 . . . . B2
Brock, 162 . . . . J3
Broken Bow, 3,491 . . . . E2
Brownlee D1
Brownson A2
Brownville, 146 . . . . J3
Brule, 372 . . . . C2
Bruning, 300 . . . . G3
Bruno, 112 . . . . H2
Brunswick, 179 . . . . G1
Bucktail C2
Burchard, 103 . . . . H3
Burr, 66 . . . . H3
Burton, 11 . . . . E1
Burwell, 1,130 . . . . E2
Bushnell, 162 . . . . A2
Butte, 366 . . . . E1
Byron, 144 . . . . G3
Cairo, 790 . . . . E3
Callaway, 637 . . . . E2
Cambridge, 1,041 . . . . D3
Campbell, 387 . . . . E3
Carleton, 136 . . . . G3
Carroll, 238 . . . . G1
Cedar Bluffs, 615 . . . . H2
Cedar Creek, 396 . . . . H2
Cedar Rapids, 407 . . . . E2
Center, 90 . . . . G1
Central City, 2,998 . . . . E2
Ceresco, 920 . . . . H2
Chadron, 5,634 . . . . B1
Chalco, 10,736 . . . . H2
Chambers, 333 . . . . E1
Champion, *150* C3
Chapman, 341 . . . . E2
Chappell, 983 . . . . B2
Chester, 294 . . . . G3
Clarks, 361 . . . . G2
Clarkson, 685 . . . . G2
Clatonia, 275 . . . . H3
Clay Center, 861 . . . . E3
Clearwater, 384 . . . . E1
Clinton, 30 . . . . B1
Cody, 149 . . . . C1
Coleridge, 541 . . . . G1
Colon, 138 . . . . H2
Colton B2
Columbus, 20,971 . . . . G2
Comstock, 110 . . . . E2
Concord, 160 . . . . H1
Cook, 322 . . . . H3
Cordova, 127 . . . . G3
Cornlea, 41 . . . . G2
Cortland, 488 . . . . H3
Cotesfield, 66 . . . . E2
Cowles, 48 . . . . E3
Cozad, 4,163 . . . . E3
Crab Orchard, 49 . . . . H3
Craig, 241 . . . . H2
Crawford, 1,107 . . . . A1
Creighton, 1,270 . . . . G1
Creston, 215 . . . . G2
Crete, 6,028 . . . . H3
Crofton, 754 . . . . G1
Crookston, 98 . . . . D1
Crowell, *40* H2
Culbertson, 594 . . . . D3
Curtis, 832 . . . . D3
Cushing, 31 . . . . E2
Dakota City, 1,821 . . . . H1
Dalton, 332 . . . . B2
Danbury, 127 . . . . D3
Dannebrog, 352 . . . . E2
Darr E3
Davenport, 339 . . . . G3
Davey, 153 . . . . H3
David City, 2,597 . . . . G2
Dawson, 209 . . . . J3
Daykin, 177 . . . . G3
Decatur, 618 . . . . H1
Denman E3
Denton, 189 . . . . H3
Deshler, 879 . . . . G3
Deweese, 80 . . . . E3
De Witt, 572 . . . . H3
Dickens, 20 . . . . D3
Diller, 287 . . . . H3
Dix, 267 . . . . A2
Dixon, 108 . . . . H1
Dodge, 700 . . . . H2
Doniphan, 763 . . . . E3
Dorchester, 615 . . . . G3
Douglas, 231 . . . . H3
Dubois, 166 . . . . H3
Dunbar, 237 . . . . H3
Duncan, 359 . . . . G2
Dunning, 109 . . . . D2
Dwight, 259 . . . . G2
Eagle, 1,105 . . . . H3
Eddyville, 96 . . . . E2
Edgar, 539 . . . . G3
Edison, 154 . . . . E3
Elba, 243 . . . . E2
Eldorado G3
Elgin, 735 . . . . E2
Eli C1
Elk City, *125* H2
Elk Creek, 112 . . . . H3
Elkhorn, 6,062 . . . . H2
Ellis H3
Ellsworth B1
Elm Creek, 894 . . . . E3
Elmwood, 668 . . . . H3
Elsie, 139 . . . . C3
Elsmere D1
Elwood, 761 . . . . E3
Elyria, 54 . . . . E2
Emerson, 817 . . . . H1
Emmet, 77 . . . . E1
Enders, *70* C3
Endicott, 139 . . . . G3
Ericson, 104 . . . . E2
Eustis, 464 . . . . D3
Ewing, 433 . . . . E1
Exeter, 712 . . . . G3
Fairbury, 4,262 . . . . G3
Fairfield, 467 . . . . E3
Fairmont, 691 . . . . G3
Falls City, 4,671 . . . . J3
Farnam, 223 . . . . D3
Farwell, 148 . . . . E2
Filley, 174 . . . . H3
Firth, 564 . . . . H3
Flats C2
Fordyce, 182 . . . . G1
Fort Calhoun, 856 . . . . H2
Fort Robinson A1
Foster, 63 . . . . G1
Franklin, 1,026 . . . . E3
Fremont, 25,174 . . . . H2
Friend, 1,174 . . . . G3
Fullerton, 1,378 . . . . G2
Funk, 204 . . . . E3
Gandy, 30 . . . . D2
Garland, 247 . . . . G3
Garrison, 67 . . . . G2
Geneva, 2,226 . . . . G3
Genoa, 981 . . . . G2
Gering, 7,751 . . . . A2
Gibbon, 1,759 . . . . E3
Gilead, 40 . . . . G3
Giltner, 389 . . . . E3
Glenvil, 332 . . . . E3
Glenwood Park, *550* E3
Goehner, 186 . . . . G3
Gordon, 1,756 . . . . B1
Gothenburg, 3,619 . . . . D3
Grafton, 152 . . . . G3
Grainton, 20 . . . . C3
Grand Island, 42,940 . . . . E3
Grant, 1,225 . . . . C3
Greeley, 531 . . . . E2
Greenwood, 544 . . . . H3
Gresham, 270 . . . . G2
Gretna, 2,355 . . . . H2
Gross, 5 . . . . E1
Guide Rock, 245 . . . . E3
Gurley, 228 . . . . B2
Hadar, 312 . . . . G1
Haigler, 211 . . . . C3
Hallam, 276 . . . . H3
Halsey, 59 . . . . D2
Hamlet, 54 . . . . C3
Hampton, 439 . . . . G3
Hansen, *90* E3
Harbine, 56 . . . . H3
Hardy, 179 . . . . G3
Harrisburg, 75 . . . . A2
Harrison, 279 . . . . A1
Hartington, 1,640 . . . . G1
Harvard, 998 . . . . E3
Hastings, 24,064 . . . . E3
Havens G2
Hayes Center, 240 . . . . C3
Hay Springs, 652 . . . . B1
Hazard, 66 . . . . E2
Heartwell, 80 . . . . E3
Hebron, 1,565 . . . . G3
Hemingford, 993 . . . . A1
Henderson, 986 . . . . G3
Hendley, 38 . . . . E3
Henry, 162 . . . . A2
Herman, 310 . . . . H2
Hershey, 572 . . . . D2
Hickman, 1,084 . . . . H3
Hildreth, 370 . . . . E3
Holbrook, 225 . . . . D3
Holdrege, 5,636 . . . . E3
Hollinger E3
Holmesville, *90* H3
Holstein, 229 . . . . E3
Homer, 590 . . . . H1
Hooper, 827 . . . . H2
Hordville, 150 . . . . G2
Hoskins, 283 . . . . G1
Howe, *50* J3
Howells, 632 . . . . G2
Hubbard, 234 . . . . H1
Hubbell, 73 . . . . G3
Humboldt, 941 . . . . J3
Humphrey, 786 . . . . G2
Huntley, 67 . . . . E3
Hyannis, 287 . . . . C2
Imperial, 1,982 . . . . C3
Inavale, *150* E3
Indianola, 642 . . . . D3
Inglewood, 382 . . . . H2
Inland, *70* E3
Inman, 148 . . . . E1
Irvington, *950* H2
Ithaca, 168 . . . . H2
Jackson, 205 . . . . H1
Jansen, 143 . . . . G3
Johnson, 280 . . . . H3
Johnstown, 53 . . . . D1
Julian, 63 . . . . J3
Juniata, 693 . . . . E3
Kearney, 27,431 . . . . E3
Keene E3
Kenesaw, 873 . . . . E3
Kennard, 371 . . . . H2
Keystone, *60* C2
Kilgore, 99 . . . . D1
Kimball, 2,559 . . . . A2
Kramer, *80* H3
Kronborg, *40* G2
Lakeside B1
Lamar, 19 . . . . C3
Lanham, *40* H3
LaPlatte, *350* J2
Laurel, 986 . . . . G1
La Vista, 11,699 . . . . H2
Lawrence, 312 . . . . E3
Lebanon, 70 . . . . D3
Leigh, 442 . . . . G2
Lemoyne, *60* C2
Leshara, 111 . . . . H2
Lewellen, 282 . . . . B2
Lewiston, 86 . . . . H3
Lexington, 10,011 . . . . E3
Liberty, 86 . . . . H3
Lincoln, 225,581 . . . . H3
Lindsay, 276 . . . . G2
Lindy G1
Linwood, 118 . . . . H2
Lisco B2
Litchfield, 280 . . . . E2
Lodgepole, 348 . . . . B2
Loma, *60* H2
Long Pine, 341 . . . . E1
Loomis, 397 . . . . E3
Lorenzo, *40* A2
Loretto E2
Lorton, 39 . . . . H3
Louisville, 1,046 . . . . H3
Loup City, 996 . . . . E2
Lowell E3
Lushton, 33 . . . . G3
Lyman, 421 . . . . A2
Lynch, 269 . . . . E1
Lyons, 963 . . . . H2
Macon, *40* E3
Macy, 956 . . . . H1
Madison, 2,367 . . . . G2
Madrid, 265 . . . . C3
Magnet, 79 . . . . G1
Malcolm, 413 . . . . H3
Malmo, 109 . . . . H2
Manley, 191 . . . . H3
Marion, *50* D3
Marquette, 282 . . . . E3
Marsland, 10 . . . . A1
Martinsburg, 103 . . . . G1
Maskell, 67 . . . . H1
Mason City, 178 . . . . E2
Max, *60* C3
Maxwell, 315 . . . . D2
Maywood, 331 . . . . D3
McCook, 7,994 . . . . D3
McCool Junction, 385 . . . . G3
McGrew, 103 . . . . A2
McLean, 38 . . . . G1
Mead, 564 . . . . H2
Meadow Grove, 311 . . . . G1
Melbeta, 138 . . . . A2
Memphis, 106 . . . . H2
Merna, 391 . . . . E2
Merriman, 118 . . . . C1
Milburn E2
Milford, 2,070 . . . . G3
Miller, 156 . . . . E3
Milligan, 315 . . . . G3
Mills E1
Minatare, 810 . . . . A2
Minden, 2,964 . . . . E3
Mitchell, 1,831 . . . . A2
Monowi, 2 . . . . E1
Monroe, 307 . . . . G2
Monterey H2
Moorefield, 52 . . . . D3
Morrill, 957 . . . . A2
Morse Bluff, 134 . . . . H2
Mullen, 491 . . . . C1
Murdock, 269 . . . . H3
Murray, 481 . . . . J3
Mynard, *100* J3
Naper, 105 . . . . E1
Naponee, 132 . . . . E3
Nebraska City, 7,228 . . . . J3
Nehawka, 232 . . . . J3
Neligh, 1,651 . . . . E1
Nelson, 587 . . . . E3
Nemaha, 178 . . . . J3

Nenzel, 13 . . . . .C1
Newcastle, 299 . . . . .H1
Newman Grove, 797 . . . . . . .G2
Newport, 98 . . . . .E1
Nickerson, 431 . . . . .H2
Niobrara, 379 . . . . .E1
Nora, 20 . . . . .G3
Norden D1
Norfolk, 23,516 . . . . .G1
Norman, 49 . . . . .F3
North Bend, 1,213 . . . . .H2
North Loup, 339 . . . . .E2
North Platte, 23,878 . . . . . . .D2
Northport, 50 . . . . .A2
Oak, 60 . . . . .G3
Oakdale, 345 . . . . .G1
Oakland, 1,367 . . . . .H2
Obert, 49 . . . . .G1
Oconto, 141 . . . . .D2
Octavia, 145 . . . . .G2
Odell, 345 . . . . .H3
Odessa, 175 . . . . .E3
Ogallala, 4,930 . . . . .C2
Ohiowa, 142 . . . . .G3
Omaha, 390,007 . . . . .J2
O'Neill, 3,733 . . . . .E1
Ong, 67 . . . . .G3
Orchard, 391 . . . . .E1
Ord, 2,269 . . . . .E2
Orleans, 425 . . . . .E3
Osceola, 921 . . . . .G2
Oshkosh, 887 . . . . .C1
Osmond, 796 . . . . .G1
Otoe, 217 . . . . .H3
Overton, 646 . . . . .E3
Oxford, 876 . . . . .E3
Page, 157 . . . . .E1
Palisade, 386 . . . . .C3
Palmer, 472 . . . . .E2
Palmyra, 546 . . . . .H3
Panama, 253 . . . . .H3
Papillion, 16,363 . . . . .H2
Parks C3
Paul J3
Pauline, 90 . . . . .E3
Pawnee City, 1,033 . . . . .H3
Paxton, 614 . . . . .C2
Pender, 1,148 . . . . .H1
Peru, 569 . . . . .J3

Petersburg, 374 . . . . .E2
Phillips, 336 . . . . .E3
Pickrell, 182 . . . . .H3
Pierce, 1,774 . . . . .G1
Pilger, 378 . . . . .G2
Plainview, 1,353 . . . . .G1
Platte Center, 359 . . . . .G2
Plattsmouth, 6,887 . . . . .J2
Pleasant Dale, 245 . . . . .H3
Pleasanton, 360 . . . . .E2
Plymouth, 477 . . . . .H3
Polk, 322 . . . . .G2
Ponca, 1,062 . . . . .H1
Poole E3
Potter, 390 . . . . .A2
Powell G3
Prague, 346 . . . . .H2
Precept E3
Preston, 50 . . . . .J3
Primrose, 69 . . . . .E2
Princeton, 100 . . . . .H3
Prosser, 94 . . . . .E3
Purdum D1
Raeville, 50 . . . . .E2
Ragan, 46 . . . . .E3
Ralston, 6,314 . . . . .H2
Randolph, 955 . . . . .G1
Ravenna, 1,341 . . . . .E2
Raymond, 186 . . . . .H3
Red Cloud, 1,131 . . . . .E3
Redington A2
Republican City, 209 . . . . . . .E3
Reynolds, 88 . . . . .G3
Richland, 89 . . . . .G2
Ringgold D2
Rising City, 386 . . . . .G2
Riverdale, 213 . . . . .E3
Riverton, 145 . . . . .E3
Roca, 220 . . . . .H3
Rockford, 30 . . . . .H3
Rockville, 111 . . . . .E2
Rogers, 95 . . . . .G2
Rosalie, 194 . . . . .H1
Roscoe, 70 . . . . .C2
Rose E1
Roseland, 242 . . . . .E3
Rosemont, 40 . . . . .E3
Royal, 75 . . . . .E1
Rulo, 226 . . . . .J3

Rushville, 999 . . . . .B1
Ruskin, 195 . . . . .G3
St. Edward, 796 . . . . .G2
St. Helena, 86 . . . . .G1
St. Libory, 275 . . . . .E2
St. Mary, 60 . . . . .H3
St. Paul, 2,218 . . . . .E2
St. Stephens E3
Salem, 138 . . . . .J3
Santee, 302 . . . . .G1
Sarben C2
Sargent, 649 . . . . .E2
Saronville, 61 . . . . .G3
Schuyler, 5,371 . . . . .G2
Scotia, 308 . . . . .E2
Scottsbluff, 14,732 . . . . .A2
Scribner, 971 . . . . .H2
Seneca, 51 . . . . .D1
Seward, 6,319 . . . . .G3
Shelby, 690 . . . . .G2
Shelton, 1,140 . . . . .E3
Shickley, 376 . . . . .G3
Sholes, 24 . . . . .G1
Shubert, 252 . . . . .J3
Sidney, 6,282 . . . . .B2
Silver Creek, 441 . . . . .G2
Skyline H2
Smithfield, 68 . . . . .E3
Snyder, 318 . . . . .H2
South Bend, 86 . . . . .H2
South Sioux City, 11,925 . . . . .H1
Spalding, 537 . . . . .E2
Sparks D1
Spencer, 541 . . . . .E1
Sprague, 146 . . . . .H3
Springfield, 1,450 . . . . .H2
Springview, 244 . . . . .E1
Stamford, 202 . . . . .E3
Stanton, 1,627 . . . . .G2
Staplehurst, 270 . . . . .G3
Stapleton, 301 . . . . .D2
Steele City, 84 . . . . .H3
Steinauer, 74 . . . . .H3
Stella, 220 . . . . .J3
Sterling, 507 . . . . .H3
Stockham, 60 . . . . .G3
Stockville, 36 . . . . .D3
Strang, 32 . . . . .G3
Stratton, 396 . . . . .C3

Stromsburg, 1,232 . . . . .G2
Stuart, 625 . . . . .E1
Sumner, 237 . . . . .E3
Sunol, 80 . . . . .B2
Superior, 2,055 . . . . .E3
Surprise, 44 . . . . .G2
Sutherland, 1,129 . . . . .C2
Sutton, 1,447 . . . . .G3
Swanton, 106 . . . . .G3
Sweetwater, 70 . . . . .H2
Sweetwater E2
Syracuse, 1,762 . . . . .H3
Table Rock, 345 . . . . .H3
Talmage, 268 . . . . .J3
Tamora, 50 . . . . .G3
Tarnov, 63 . . . . .G2
Taylor, 207 . . . . .E2
Tecumseh, 1,716 . . . . .H3
Tekamah, 1,892 . . . . .H2
Terrytown, 646 . . . . .A2
Thayer, 71 . . . . .G3
Thedford, 211 . . . . .D2
Thurston, 125 . . . . .H1
Tilden, 1,078 . . . . .G1
Tobias, 158 . . . . .G3
Touhy, 50 . . . . .H2
Trenton, 507 . . . . .C3
Trumbull, 212 . . . . .E3
Tryon, 100 . . . . .C2
Uehling, 275 . . . . .H2
Ulysses, 276 . . . . .G2
Unadilla, 342 . . . . .H3
Union, 260 . . . . .J3
Upland, 179 . . . . .E3
Utica, 844 . . . . .G3
Valentine, 2,820 . . . . .D1
Valley, 1,788 . . . . .H2
Valparaiso, 563 . . . . .H2
Venango, 175 . . . . .B3
Verdel, 58 . . . . .E1
Verdigre, 519 . . . . .E1
Verdon, 223 . . . . .J3
Vesta, 40 . . . . .H3
Virginia, 67 . . . . .H3
Waco, 256 . . . . .G3
Wahoo, 3,942 . . . . .H2
Wakefield, 1,411 . . . . .H1
Wallace, 329 . . . . .C3
Walthill, 909 . . . . .H1

Wann, 80 . . . . .H2
Washington, 126 . . . . .H2
Waterbury, 89 . . . . .H1
Waterloo, 459 . . . . .H2
Wauneta, 625 . . . . .C3
Wausa, 636 . . . . .G1
Waverly, 2,448 . . . . .H3
Wayne, 5,583 . . . . .G1
Weeping Water, 1,103 . . . . . .H3
Weissert E2
Wellfleet, 76 . . . . .D3
Western, 287 . . . . .G3
Westerville E2
Weston, 310 . . . . .H2
West Point, 3,660 . . . . .H2
Whiteclay, 40 . . . . .B1
Whitman C1
Whitney, 87 . . . . .A1
Wilber, 1,761 . . . . .H3
Wilcox, 360 . . . . .E3
Willow Island, 20 . . . . .D3
Wilsonville, 118 . . . . .D3
Winnebago, 768 . . . . .H1
Winnetoon, 70 . . . . .G1
Winside, 468 . . . . .G1
Winslow, 104 . . . . .H2
Wisner, 1,270 . . . . .G1
Wolbach, 287 . . . . .E2
Wood Lake, 72 . . . . .D1
Wood River, 1,204 . . . . .E3
Wymore, 1,656 . . . . .H3
Wynot, 191 . . . . .G1
York, 8,081 . . . . .G3
Yutan, 1,216 . . . . .H2

Other Features

Agate Fossil Beds N.M. A1
Big Blue, river G2, H3
Big Rock, river H1
Boyer, river J2
Buffalo Gap Natl. Grassland . . .A1
Calamus, river E1
Calamus, reservoir E1
Cedar, river F2
Chimney Rock N.H.S. A2
Crescent Lake N.W.R. B2
C.W. McConaughy, lake C2
Elkhorn, river E1, H2

Fort Niobrara N.W.R. D1
Francis Case, lake F1
Frenchman, creek C3
Harlan Co., lake E3
Highest Point in Nebraska A2
Homestead N.M. H3
Iowa I.R. J3
Karl E. Mundt N.W.R. F1
Lacreek N.W.R. C1
Lake Andes N.W.R. F1
Lewis and Clark, lake F1
Little Blue, river G3
Little Sioux, river H1
Lodgepole, river A2
Loup, river E2
Middle Loup, river E2
Missouri, river J3
Nebraska Natl. For. A1, D2
Niobrara, river B1, E1
Nishnabotna, river J3
North Loup, river C1, D2
North Platte, river B2
North Platte N.W.R. A1
Oglala Natl. Grassland A1
Omaha I.R. H1
Pawnee Natl. Grassland A1
Pine, ridge B1
Pine Ridge Natl. Rec. Area A1
Platte, river D3, D2
Red Willow Cr. C3
Republican, river D3, F3
Rosebud Indian Reservation . . .D1
Sac And Fox I.R. J3
Samuel R. McKelvie Natl. For. . .C1
Sand, hills B2
Santee I.R. G1
Scotts Bluff N.M. A2
South Loup, river E2
Survey, valley B1
Valentine N.W.R. D1
Vermillion, river G1
Winnebago I.R. H1
Yankton I.R. F1

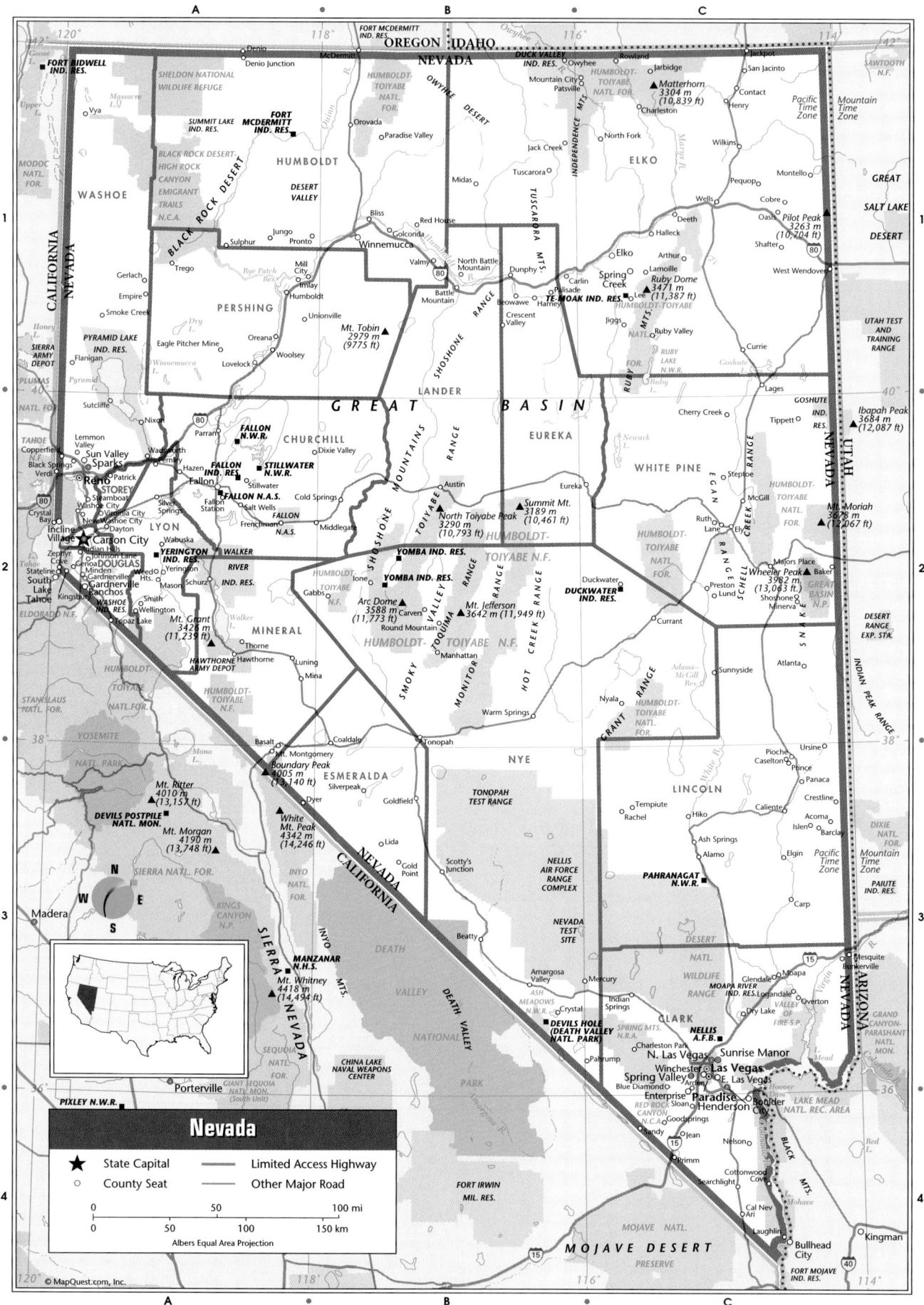

Nevada

★ State Capital
○ County Seat

Limited Access Highway
Other Major Road

0 — 50 — 100 mi
0 — 50 — 100 — 150 km
Albers Equal Area Projection

© MapQuest.com, Inc.

Nevada

Capital: Carson City
Land Area: 109,806 sq. mi.
284,398 sq. km.
Population: 1,998,257 (2000 Census)
Largest City: Las Vegas, 478,434
Highest Point: Boundary Peak,
13,140 ft.
4,005 m.
Admitted to Union: October 31, 1864
Nickname: Silver State
State Flower: Sagebrush
State Bird: Mountain Bluebird

Nevada:
Map Index

Counties

Carson City, 52,457 ....*
Churchill, 23,982 ....A2
Clark, 1,375,765 ....C3
Douglas, 41,259 ....A2
Elko, 45,291 ....C1
Esmeralda, 971 ....B3
Eureka, 1,651 ....B2
Humboldt, 16,106 ....A1
Lander, 5,794 ....B1
Lincoln, 4,165 ....C3
Lyon, 34,501 ....A2
Mineral, 5,071 ....A2
Nye, 32,485 ....B3
Pershing, 6,693 ....A1
Storey, 3,399 ....A2
Washoe, 339,486 ....A1
White Pine, 9,181 ....C2

Cities and Towns

Acoma C3
Alamo C3
Amargosa Valley B3
Arden, 125 ....C3
Arthur, 60 ....C1
Ash Springs C3
Atlanta, 50 ....C2
Austin, 600 ....B2
Baker, 50 ....C2
Barclay C3
Basalt A2
Battle Mountain, 2,871 ....B1
Beatty, 1,154 ....B3
Beowawe, 60 ....B1
Black Springs, 950 ....A2
Bliss, 100 ....B1
Blue Diamond, 282 ....C3
Boulder City, 14,966 ....C4
Bunkerville, 1,014 ....C3
Caliente, 1,123 ....C3
Cal Nev Ari, 278 ....C4
Carlin, 2,161 ....B1
Carp C3
Carson City, 52,457 ....A2
Carvers B2
Caselton C3
Charleston C1
Charleston Park, 125 ....C3
Cherry Creek C2
Coaldale B2
Cobre, 50 ....C1
Cold Springs B2
Contact C1
Copperfield A2
Cottonwood Cove, 100 ....C4
Crescent Valley, 50 ....B1
Crestline C3
Crystal B3
Crystal Bay, 9,952 ....A2
Currant C2
Currie C1
Dayton, 5,907 ....A2
Deeth C1
Denio, 40 ....A1
Denio Junction A1
Dixie Valley A2
Dry Lake, 300 ....C3
Duckwater C2
Dunphy B1
Dyer A3
Eagle Pitcher Mine A1
East Las Vegas C3
Elgin C3
Elko, 16,708 ....C1
Ely, 4,041 ....C2
Empire, 350 ....A1

Enterprise, 14,676 ....C3
Eureka, 550 ....C2
Fallon, 7,536 ....A2
Fallon Station, 1,265 ....A2
Fernley, 8,543 ....A2
Flanigan A1
Frenchman A2
Gabbs, 318 ....B2
Gardnerville, 3,357 ....A2
Gardnerville Ranchos, 11,054 ...A2
Genoa, 250 ....A2
Gerlach, 80 ....A1
Glendale C3
Golconda, 175 ....B1
Goldfield, 175 ....B3
Gold Point B3
Goodsprings, 232 ....C4
Halleck C1
Harney B1
Hawthorne, 3,311 ....A2
Hazen A2
Henderson, 175,381 ....C3
Henry C1
Hiko, 100 ....C3
Humboldt, 500 ....A1
Imlay, 300 ....A1
Incline Village, 9,952 ....A2
Indian Hills, 4,407 ....A2
Indian Springs, 1,302 ....C3
Ione, 50 ....B2
Islen C3
Jack Creek, 50 ....B1
Jackpot, 1,100 ....C1
Jarbidge C1
Jean C4
Jiggs C1
Johnson Lane, 4,837 ....A2
Jungo A1
Kingsbury, 2,624 ....A2
Lages C1
Lamoille, 100 ....C1
Lane C2
Las Vegas, 478,434 ....C3
Laughlin, 7,076 ....C4
Lee, 40 ....C1
Lemmon Valley, 6,855 ....A2
Lida B3
Logandale, 800 ....C3
Lovelock, 2,003 ....A1
Lund, 60 ....C2
Luning, 100 ....A2
Majors Place C2
Manhattan, 60 ....B2
Mason, 500 ....A2
McDermitt, 269 ....B1
McGill, 1,054 ....C2
Mercury C3
Mesquite, 9,389 ....C3
Midas B1
Middlegate B2
Mill City, 300 ....A1
Mina, 275 ....A2
Minden, 2,836 ....A2
Minerva C2
Moapa, 928 ....C3
Montello, 10 ....C1
Mountain City C1
Mount Montgomery A3
Nelson, 50 ....C4
New Washoe City, 2,900 ....A2
Nixon, 418 ....A2
North Battle Mountain B1
North Fork C1
North Las Vegas, 115,488 ....C3
Nyala C2
Oasis, 200 ....C1
Oreana A1
Orovada B1
Overton, 1,700 ....C3
Owyhee, 1,017 ....B1
Pahrump, 24,631 ....C3
Palisade B1
Panaca, 550 ....C3
Paradise, 186,070 ....C3
Paradise Valley, 60 ....B1
Parran A2
Patrick A2
Patsville C1
Pequop, 150 ....C1
Pioche, 475 ....C3
Preston C2
Primm C4
Prince C3
Pronto A1
Rachel, 90 ....C3
Red House B1
Reno, 180,480 ....A2
Round Mountain, 550 ....B2
Rowland C1
Ruby Valley, 50 ....C1
Ruth, 500 ....C2
Salt Wells A2
Sandy, 90 ....C4

San Jacinto C1
Schurz, 721 ....A2
Scotty's Junction B3
Searchlight, 576 ....C4
Shafter, 50 ....C1
Shoshone C2
Silverpeak B3
Silver Springs, 4,708 ....A2
Sloan C4
Smith, 1,425 ....A2
Smoke Creek, 175 ....A1
Sparks, 66,346 ....A2
Spring Creek, 10,548 ....C1
Spring Valley, 117,390 ....C3
Stateline, 1,215 ....A2
Steamboat, 1,100 ....A2
Steptoe, 40 ....C2
Stillwater, 50 ....A2
Sulphur A1
Sunnyside C2
Sunrise Manor, 156,120 ....C3
Sun Valley, 19,461 ....A2
Sutcliffe, 281 ....A2
Tempiute C3
Thorne, 40 ....A2
Tippett C2
Tonopah, 2,627 ....B2
Topaz Lake, 60 ....A2
Trego A1
Tuscarora B1
Unionville, 250 ....A1
Ursine, 90 ....C3
Valmy, 100 ....B1
Verdi, 2,949 ....A2
Virginia City, 800 ....A2
Vya A1
Wabuska A2
Wadsworth, 881 ....A2
Warm Springs B2
Washoe City, 225 ....A2
Weed Heights, 300 ....A2
Wellington A2
Wells, 1,346 ....C1
West Wendover, 4,721 ....C1
Wilkins C1
Winchester, 26,958 ....C3
Winnemucca, 7,174 ....B1
Woolsey A1
Yerington, 2,883 ....A2
Zephyr Cove, 1,649 ....A2

Other Features

Adams-McGill, reservoir C2
Amargosa, river B4
Arc Dome, peak B2
Ash Meadows N.W.R. B3
Black, mountains C4
Black Rock, desert A1
Black Rock Desert-High Rock Canyon Emigrant
   Trails Natl. Cons. Area. A1
Boundary, peak A3
China Lake Naval Weapons Center B3
Colorado, river C3, C4
Death, valley B3
Death Valley National Park B3
Deseret Test Center C1
Desert, valley A1
Desert Natl. Wildlife Range C3
Desert Range Exp. Sta. C2
Devils Hole (Death Valley Natl. Park) B3
Devils Postpile Natl. Mon. A3
Dixie Natl. For. C3
Dry, lake A1
Duck Valley Ind. Res. B1
Duckwater Ind. Res. C2
Egan, range C2
Eldorado N.F. A2
Fallon Ind. Res. A2
Fallon N.A.S. A2
Fallon N.W.R. A2
Fort Bidwell Ind. Res. A1
Fort Irwin Mil. Res. B4
Fort McDermitt Ind. Res. A1, B1
Fort Mojave Ind. Res. C4
Goose, lake A1
Goshute, lake C1
Goshute Ind. Res. C2
Grant, mountain A2
Grant, range C2
Great Basin B2
Great Basin N.P. C2
Great Salt Lake, desert C1
Hawthorne Army Depot A2
Honey, lake A1
Hoover, dam C3
Hot Creek, range B2
Humboldt, river B1
Humboldt-Toiyabe Natl. For. A2, B1-2, C1-3
Ibapah, peak C2
Independence, mountains C1
Indian Peak, range C2
Inyo, mountains B3

Inyo Natl. For. A3
Jefferson, mountain B2
Kern, river A3
Kings Canyon N.P. A3
Kings Canyon Natl. Park A3
Lake Mead Natl. Rec. Area C4
Marys, river C1
Massacre, lake A1
Matterhorn, peak C1
Mead, lake C3
Moapa River Ind. Res. C3
Modoc Natl. For. A1
Mohave, lake C4
Mojave, desert C4
Mojave Natl. Preserve C4
Monitor, range B2
Mono, lake A3
Morgan, mountain A3
Moriah, mountain C2
Nellis A.F.B. C3
Nellis Air Force Range Complex B3
Nevada Test Site B3
Newark, lake C2
North Toiyabe, peak B2
Owyhee, desert B1
Owyhee, river B1
Pahranagat N.W.R. C3
Paiute Ind. Res. C3
Pilot, peak C1
Pixley N.W.R. A4
Plumas Natl. For. A1
Pyramid, lake A1
Pyramid Lake Ind. Res. A1
Quinn, river B1
Red, lake A2
Red Rock Canyon N.C.A. C4
Ritter, mountain A3
Ruby, lake C1
Ruby, mountains C1
Ruby Dome, peak C1
Ruby Lake N.W.R. C1
Rye Patch, reservoir A1
Sawtooth N.F. C1
Schell Creek, range C2
Sequoia Natl. For. A3
Sheldon N.W.R. A1
Shoshone, mountains B2
Shoshone, range B1
Sierra Army Depot A1
Sierra Natl. For. A3
Sierra Nevada, range A3
Smoky, valley B2
Snake, range C2
Spring Mts. N.R.A. C3
Stanislaus Natl. For. A2
Stillwater N.W.R. A2
Summit, mountain B2
Summit Lake Ind. Res. A1
Tahoe, lake A2
Tahoe N.F. A2
Te-Moak Ind. Res. C1
Tobin, mountain B1
Toiyabe, range B2
Tonopah Test Range B3
Toquima, range B2
Tuscarora, mountains B1
Upper, lake A1
Valley Of Fire S.P. C3
Virgin, river C3
Walker, lake A2
Walker River Ind. Res. A2
Washoe Ind. Res. A2
Wendover, range C1
Wheeler, peak C2
White, river C3
White Mt., peak A3
Whitney, mountain A3
Winnemucca, lake A1
Yerington Ind. Res. A2
Yomba Ind. Res. B2
Yosemite Natl. Park A2

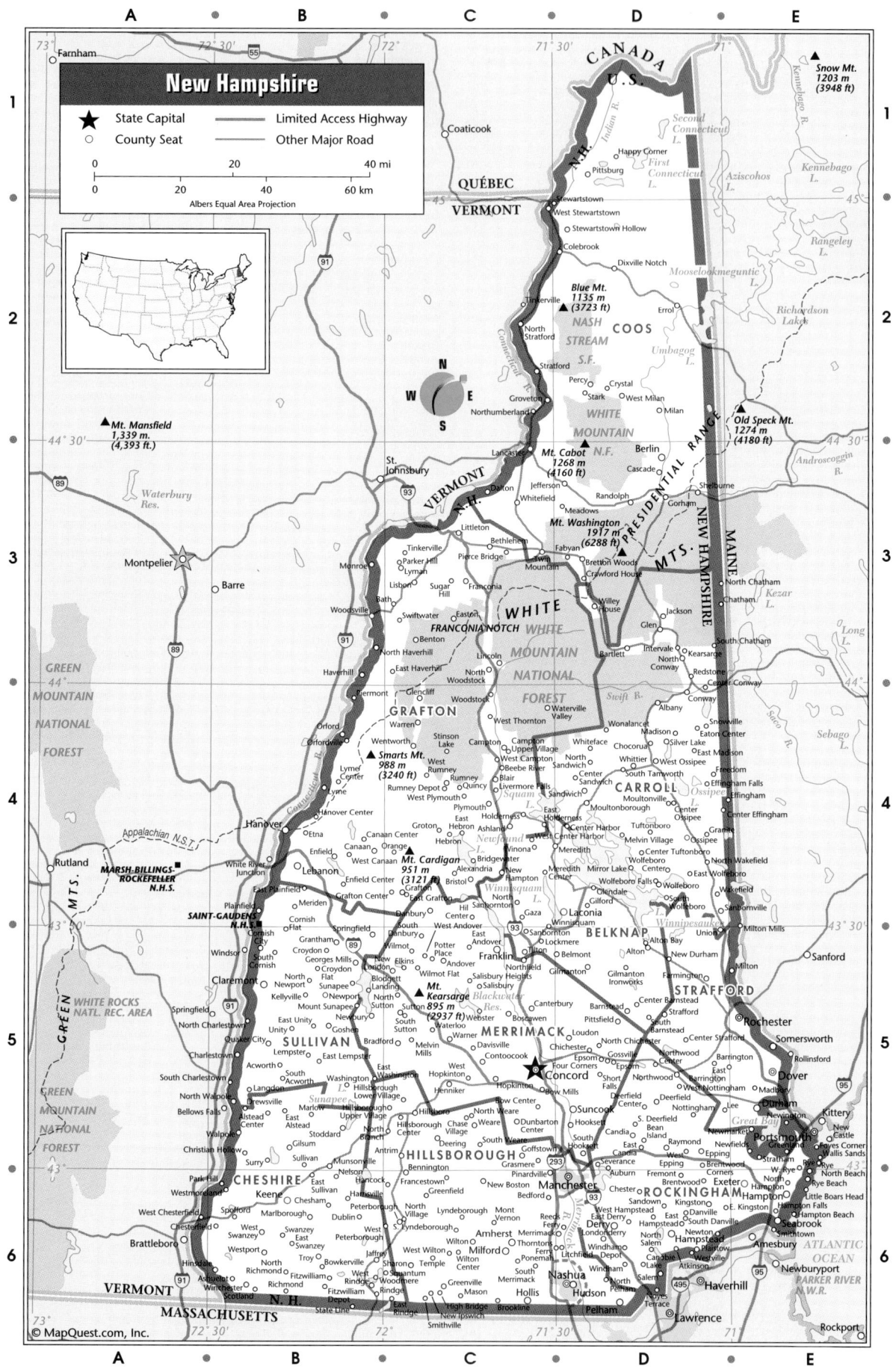

New Hampshire

- ★ State Capital
- ○ County Seat
- ═══ Limited Access Highway
- ─── Other Major Road

0   20   40 mi
0   20   40   60 km
Albers Equal Area Projection

© MapQuest.com, Inc.

New Hampshire

Capital: Concord
Land Area: 8,969 sq. mi.
23,230 sq. km.
Population: 1,235,786 (2000 Census)
Largest City: Manchester, 107,006
Highest Point: Mt. Washington, 6,288 ft. 1,917 m.
Admitted to Union: June 21, 1788
Nickname: Granite State
State Flower: Purple Lilac
State Bird: Purple Finch

New Hampshire: Map Index

Counties

Belknap, 56,325 ....D5
Carroll, 43,666 ....D4
Cheshire, 73,825 ....B6
Coos, 33,111 ....D2
Grafton, 81,743 ....C4
Hillsborough, 380,841 ....C5
Merrimack, 136,225 ....C5
Rockingham, 277,359 ....D6
Strafford, 112,233 ....D5
Sullivan, 40,458 ....B5

Cities and Towns

Cities and towns that are not labeled on the map are shown with an asterisk. They are included here only for population reference.

Acworth, 836 ....B5
Albany, 654 ....D4
Alexandria, 1,329 ....C4
Allenstown, 4,843 ....*
Alstead, 1,944 ....B5
Alton, 4,502 ....D5
Amherst, 10,769 ....C6
Andover, 2,109 ....C5
Antrim, 2,449 ....C5
Ashland, 1,955 ....C4
Atkinson, 6,178 ....D6
Auburn, 4,682 ....D6
Barnstead, 3,886 ....D5
Barrington, 7,475 ....D5
Bartlett, 2,705 ....D3
Bath, 893 ....C3
Bedford, 18,274 ....C6
Belmont, 6,716 ....D5
Bennington, 1,401 ....C5
Benton, 314 ....C3
Berlin, 10,331 ....D2
Bethlehem, 2,199 ....C3
Boscawen, 3,672 ....C5
Bow, 7,138 ....*
Bradford, 1,454 ....C5
Brentwood, 3,197 ....D6
Bridgewater, 974 ....C4
Bristol, 3,033 ....C4
Brookfield, 604 ....*
Brookline, 4,181 ....C6
Campton, 2,719 ....C4
Canaan, 3,319 ....B4
Candia, 3,911 ....D5
Canterbury, 1,979 ....C5
Carroll, 663 ....*
Center Harbor, 996 ....D4
Charlestown, 4,749 ....B5
Chatham, 260 ....D3
Chester, 3,792 ....D6
Chesterfield, 3,542 ....B6
Chichester, 2,236 ....D5
Claremont, 13,151 ....B5
Clarksville, 294 ....*
Colebrook, 2,321 ....D2
Columbia, 750 ....*
Concord, 40,687 ....C5
Conway, 8,604 ....D4
Cornish, 1,661 ....B5
Croydon, 661 ....B5
Dalton, 927 ....C3
Danbury, 1,071 ....C5
Danville, 4,023 ....D6
Deerfield, 3,678 ....D5
Deering, 1,875 ....C5
Derry, 34,021 ....D6
Dixville, 75 ....*
Dorchester, 353 ....*
Dover, 26,884 ....E5
Dublin, 1,476 ....B6
Dummer, 309 ....*
Dunbarton, 2,226 ....*
Durham, 12,664 ....E5
East Kingston, 1,784 ....D6
Easton, 256 ....C3
Eaton, 375 ....*
Effingham, 1,273 ....E4

Ellsworth, 87 ....*
Enfield, 4,618 ....B4
Epping, 5,476 ....D5
Epsom, 4,021 ....D5
Errol, 298 ....D2
Exeter, 14,058 ....E6
Farmington, 5,774 ....D5
Fitzwilliam, 2,141 ....B6
Francestown, 1,480 ....C6
Franconia, 924 ....C3
Franklin, 8,405 ....C5
Freedom, 1,303 ....D4
Fremont, 3,510 ....D6
Gilford, 6,803 ....D4
Gilmanton, 3,060 ....D5
Gilsum, 777 ....B5
Goffstown, 16,929 ....C6
Gorham, 2,895 ....D3
Goshen, 741 ....B5
Grafton, 1,138 ....C4
Grantham, 2,167 ....B5
Greenfield, 1,657 ....C6
Greenland, 3,208 ....E5
Greenville, 2,224 ....C6
Groton, 456 ....C4
Hampstead, 8,297 ....D6
Hampton, 14,937 ....E6
Hampton Falls, 1,880 ....E6
Hancock, 1,739 ....C6
Hanover, 10,850 ....B4
Harrisville, 1,075 ....B6
Hart's Location, 37 ....*
Haverhill, 4,416 ....B3
Hebron, 459 ....C4
Henniker, 4,433 ....C5
Hill, 992 ....*
Hillsboro, 4,928 ....C5
Hinsdale, 4,082 ....B6
Holderness, 1,930 ....C4
Hollis, 7,015 ....C6
Hooksett, 11,721 ....D5
Hopkinton, 5,399 ....C5
Hudson, 22,928 ....D6
Jackson, 835 ....D3
Jaffrey, 5,476 ....B6
Jefferson, 1,006 ....D3
Keene, 22,563 ....B6
Kensington, 1,893 ....*
Kingston, 5,862 ....D6
Laconia, 16,411 ....D4
Lancaster, 3,280 ....C3
Landaff, 378 ....*
Langdon, 586 ....B5
Lebanon, 12,568 ....B4
Lee, 4,145 ....D5
Lempster, 971 ....B5
Lincoln, 1,271 ....C3
Lisbon, 1,587 ....C3
Litchfield, 7,360 ....D6
Littleton, 5,845 ....C3
Livermore, 3 ....*
Londonderry, 23,236 ....D6
Loudon, 4,481 ....D5
Lyman, 487 ....C3
Lyme, 1,679 ....B4
Lyndeborough, 1,585 ....C6
Madbury, 1,509 ....E5
Madison, 1,984 ....D4
Manchester, 107,006 ....D6
Marlborough, 2,009 ....B6
Marlow, 747 ....B5
Mason, 1,147 ....C6
Meredith, 5,943 ....D4
Merrimack, 25,119 ....D6
Middleton, 1,440 ....*
Milan, 1,331 ....D2
Milford, 13,535 ....C6
Millsfield, 22 ....*
Milton, 3,910 ....E5
Monroe, 759 ....B3
Mont Vernon, 2,034 ....C6
Moultonborough, 4,484 ....D4
Nashua, 86,605 ....D6
Nelson, 634 ....B6
New Boston, 4,138 ....C6
Newbury, 1,702 ....B5
New Castle, 1,010 ....*
New Durham, 2,220 ....D5
Newfields, 1,551 ....E5
New Hampton, 1,950 ....C4
New Ipswich, 4,289 ....C6
New London, 4,116 ....C5
Newmarket, 8,027 ....E5
Newport, 6,269 ....B5
Newton, 4,289 ....D6
Northfield, 4,548 ....C5
North Hampton, 4,259 ......E6
Northumberland, 2,438 .....C2
Northwood, 3,640 ....D5
Nottingham, 3,701 ....D5
Orange, 299 ....C4
Orford, 1,091 ....B4
Ossipee, 4,211 ....D4
Pelham, 10,914 ....D6
Pembroke, 6,897 ....*
Peterborough, 5,883 ....C6
Piermont, 709 ....B4
Pinkhams ....*
Pittsburg, 867 ....D1
Pittsfield, 3,931 ....D5
Plainfield, 2,241 ....B4

Plaistow, 7,747 ....D6
Plymouth, 5,892 ....C4
Portsmouth, 20,784 ....E5
Randolph, 339 ....D3
Raymond, 9,674 ....D5
Richmond, 1,077 ....B6
Rindge, 5,451 ....B6
Rochester, 28,461 ....E5
Rollinsford, 2,648 ....E5
Roxbury, 237 ....*
Rumney, 1,480 ....C4
Rye, 5,182 ....E5
Salem, 28,112 ....D6
Salisbury, 1,137 ....C5
Sanbornton, 2,581 ....C5
Sandown, 5,143 ....D6
Sandwich, 1,286 ....D4
Seabrook, 7,934 ....E6
Sharon, 360 ....C6
Shelburne, 379 ....D3
Somersworth, 11,477 ....E5
South Hampton, 844 ....*
Springfield, 945 ....B5
Stark, 516 ....D2
Stewartstown, 1,012 ....D2
Stoddard, 928 ....B5
Strafford, 3,626 ....D5
Stratford, 942 ....C2
Stratham, 6,355 ....E5
Sugar Hill, 563 ....C3
Sullivan, 746 ....B5
Sunapee, 3,055 ....B5
Surry, 673 ....B5
Sutton, 1,544 ....C5
Swanzey, 6,800 ....B6
Tamworth, 2,510 ....*
Temple, 1,297 ....C6
Thornton, 1,843 ....C4
Tilton, 3,477 ....C5
Troy, 1,962 ....B6
Tuftonboro, 2,148 ....D4
Unity, 1,530 ....B5
Wakefield, 4,252 ....D4
Walpole, 3,594 ....B5
Warner, 2,760 ....C5
Warren, 873 ....C4
Washington, 895 ....B5
Waterville Valley, 257 ....C4
Weare, 7,776 ....C5
Webster, 1,579 ....C5
Wentworth Location (Coos Co.), 44 ...*
Wentworth (Grafton Co.), 798 ...C4
Westmoreland, 1,747 ....B6
Whitefield, 2,038 ....C3
Wilmot, 1,144 ....C5
Wilton, 3,743 ....C6
Winchester, 4,144 ....B6
Windham, 10,709 ....D6
Windsor, 201 ....C5
Wolfeboro, 6,083 ....D4
Woodstock, 1,139 ....C4

Other Places

The city or town containing each entry is shown in italics. See the "Cities and Towns" listing for total population.

Alstead Center (*Alstead*), 60 ....B5
Alton Bay (*Alton*), 400 ....D5
Ashuelot (*Winchester*), 375 ....B6
Bean Island (*Candia*) D5
Beebe River (*Campton*), 175 ...C4
Blair (*Campton*), 225 ....C4
Blodgett Landing (*Newbury*) B5
Bow Center (*Bow*), 600 ....C5
Bowkerville (*Fitzwilliam*), 450 ...B6
Bow Mills (*Bow*), 650 ....C5
Brentwood Corners (*Brentwood*) ...D5
Bretton Woods (*Carroll*) D3
Campton Upper Village (*Campton*)...C4
Canaan Center (*Canaan*), 500 ...B4
Canobie Lake (*Salem*), 2,500 ...D6
Cascade (*Gorham*), 350 ....D3
Center Barnstead (*Barnstead*), 500 ..D5
Center Conway (*Conway*), 275 ...D4
Center Effingham (*Effingham*), 100 ..D4
Center Ossipee (*Ossipee*), 650 ......D4
Center Sandwich (*Sandwich*), 300 ...D4
Center Strafford (*Strafford*), 175 ...D5
Center Tuftonboro (*Tuftonboro*), 300 ....D4
Chase Village (*Weare*) C5
Chesham (*Harrisville*), 200 .....B6
Chocorua (*Tamworth*), 125 ....D4
Christian Hollow (*Walpole*), 80 ...B5
Contoocook (*Hopkinton*), 1,444 ...C5
Cornish Flat (*Cornish*), 325 ....B5
Crawford House (*Carroll*) D3
Croydon Flat (*Croydon*), 250 ...B5
Crystal (*Stark*), 100 ....D2
Davisville (*Warner*), 225 ....C5
Deerfield Center (*Deerfield*), 275 ...D5
Dixville Notch (*Dixville*), 40 ....D2
Drewsville (*Walpole*), 175 ......B5
Dunbarton Center (*Dunbarton*), 200 C5
East Alstead (*Alstead*), 175 ....B5
East Andover (*Andover*), 300 ..C5
East Barrington (*Barrington*), 400 ...D5
East Candia (*Candia*) D5
East Derry (*Derry*), 350 ....D6
East Grafton (*Grafton*), 100 ....C4
East Hampstead (*Hampstead*), 1,400 D6

East Haverhill (*Haverhill*), 60 ....C3
East Hebron (*Hebron*), 90 ....C4
East Holderness (*Holderness*), 175 ...C4
East Lempster (*Lempster*), 175 ......B5
East Madison (*Madison*), 20 ...D4
East Plainfield (*Plainfield*), 125 ....B4
East Rindge (*Rindge*), 600 .....C6
East Sullivan (*Sullivan*), 225 ...B6
East Swanzey (*Swanzey*), 475 ...B6
East Unity (*Unity*), 60 ....B5
East Washington (*Washington*), 125 ..B5
East Wolfeboro (*Wolfeboro*), 80 ...D4
Eaton Center (*Eaton*), 80 ....D4
Effingham Falls (*Effingham*), 175 ...D4
Elkins (*New London*) C5
Enfield Center (*Enfield*), 600 ...B4
Epsom Four Corners (*Epsom*), 275 ..D5
Etna (*Hanover*), 275 ....B4
Fabyan (*Carroll*) D3
Fitzwilliam Depot (*Fitzwilliam*), 450 ..B6
Foyes Corner (*Rye*), 450 ....E5
Gaza (*Sanbornton*), 100 ....C4
Georges Mills (*Sunapee*), 300 ...B5
Gilmanton Ironworks (*Gilmanton*), 225 ....D5
Glen (*Bartlett*), 200 ....D3
Glencliff (*Warren*), 40 ....C4
Glendale (*Gilford*), 700 ....D4
Gossville (*Epsom*), 600 ....D5
Grafton Center (*Grafton*), 150 ...C4
Granite (*Ossipee*), 90 ....D4
Grasmere (*Goffstown*), 1,100 ...C5
Groveton (*Northumberland*), 1,197 ..C2
Hampton Beach (*Hampton*), 1,800 ..E6
Hanover Center (*Hanover*), 225 ...B4
Happy Corner (*Pittsburg*), 20 ...D1
High Bridge (*New Ipswich*), 300 ...C6
Hill Center (*Hill*), 70 ....C4
Hillsborough Center (*Hillsborough*) ...C5
Hillsborough Lower Village (*Hillsborough*), 400 .....C5
Hillsborough Upper Village (*Hillsborough*), 225 ....C5
Intervale (*Bartlett and Conway*), 200 ....D3
Kearsarge (*Bartlett and Conway*), 325 ....D3
Kellyville (*Newport*) B5
Little Boars Head (*North Hampton*) ...E6
Livermore Falls (*Campton and Plymouth*), 350 ......C4
Lockmere (*Belmont and Tilton*), 600 ..C5
Lyme Center (*Lyme*), 175 ....B4
Meadows (*Jefferson*), 100 ......D3
Melvin Mills (*Warner*), 125 .....C5
Melvin Village (*Tuftonboro*), 275 ...D4
Meredith Center (*Meredith*), 425 ....C4
Meriden (*Plainfield*), 250 ....B4
Milton Mills (*Milton*), 300 ......E5
Mirror Lake (*Tuftonboro*), 350 ...D4
Moultonville (*Ossipee*) D4
Mount Sunapee (*Newbury*), 150 ...B5
Munsonville (*Nelson*), 175 ......B5
North Branch (*Antrim*), 225 ....C5
North Charlestown (*Charlestown*), 425 ....B5
North Chatham (*Chatham*), 30 ...D3
North Chichester (*Chichester*), 700 ..D5
North Conway (*Conway*), 2,069 ...D3
North Haverhill (*Haverhill*), 450 ...B3
North Newport (*Newport*), 300 ...B5
North Pelham (*Pelham*), 750 ...D6
North Richmond (*Richmond*), 100 ..B6
North Salem (*Salem*), 1,600 ...D6
North Sanbornton (*Sanbornton*), 125 ....C4
North Sandwich (*Sandwich*), 60 ...D4
North Stratford (*Stratford*), 100 ...C2
North Sutton (*Sutton*), 225 .....C5
North Village (*Peterborough*), 125 ...C6
North Wakefield (*Wakefield*), 150 ...D4
North Walpole (*Walpole*), 750 ...B5
North Weare (*Weare*), 350 ......C5
Northwood Center (*Northwood*) ...D5
Noyes Terrace (*Salem*) D6
Orfordville (*Orford*), 200 ....B4
Park Hill (*Lyman*), 80 ....C3
Park Hill (*Westmoreland*) B6
Percy (*Stark*), 40 ....D2
Pierce Bridge (*Bethlehem*), 80 ...C3
Pinardville (*Goffstown*), 5,779 ...C6
Ponemah (*Amherst*), 1,000 ....C6
Potter Place (*Andover*), 150 ...C5
Quaker City (*Unity*) B5
Quincy (*Rumney*), 250 ....C4
Redstone (*Conway*), 350 ....D3
Reeds Ferry (*Merrimack*), 1,400 ...D6
Rumney Depot (*Rumney*), 300 ...C4
Rye Beach (*Rye*), 750 ....E6
Rye North Beach (*Rye*), 475 ...E5
Salisbury Heights (*Salisbury*), 150 ...C5
Sanbornville (*Wakefield*), 950 ...D4
Scotland (*Winchester*), 300 ....B6
Severance (*Auburn*), 500 ....D5
Short Falls (*Epsom*), 550 ....D5
Silver Lake (*Madison*), 200 .....D4
Smithtown (*Seabrook*) E6
Smithville (*New Ipswich*) C6
Snowville (*Eaton*), 60 ....D4
South Acworth (*Acworth*), 150 ...B5
South Barnstead (*Barnstead*), 150 ....D5

South Charlestown (*Charlestown*), 175 ....B5
South Chatham (*Chatham*), 40 ...D3
South Cornish (*Cornish*), 275 ...B5
South Danbury (*Danbury*), 50 ...C5
South Danville (*Danville*) D6
South Deerfield (*Deerfield*) D5
South Hooksett (*Hooksett*), 5,282 ...D5
S. Lyndeborough (*Lyndeborough*), 275 ....C6
South Merrimack (*Merrimack*), 1,900 ....C6
South Sutton (*Sutton*), 175 .....C5
South Tamworth (*Tamworth*), 150 ...D4
South Weare (*Weare*), 375 .....C5
South Wolfeboro (*Wolfeboro*), 350 ...D4
Spofford (*Chesterfield*), 500 ...B6
Squantum (*Jaffrey*), 400 ....C6
State Line (*Fitzwilliam*), 60 ....B6
Stewartstown Hollow (*Stewartstown*), 50 ....D2
Stinson Lake (*Rumney*), 30 ....C4
Suncook (*Allenstown and Pembroke*), 5,362 ....D5
Swiftwater (*Bath*), 175 ....C3
Thorntons Ferry (*Merrimack*) ...C6
Tinkerville (*Lyman*), 20 ....C3
Twin Mountain (*Carroll*), 100 ...C3
Union (*Wakefield*), 425 ....D5
Wallis Sands (*Rye*), 850 ....E5
Waterloo (*Warner*) C5
West Andover (*Andover*), 100 ...C5
West Campton (*Campton*), 225 ...C4
West Canaan (*Canaan*), 275 ...B4
West Center Harbor (*Center Harbor*), 175 ....C4
West Chesterfield (*Chesterfield*), 500 .A6
West Epping (*Epping*), 1,200 ...D5
West Hampstead (*Hampstead*), 700 .D6
West Hopkinton (*Hopkinton*), 175 ...C5
West Milan (*Milan*), 100 ....D2
West Nottingham (*Nottingham*), 300 ....D5
West Ossipee (*Ossipee*), 325 ...D4
West Peterborough (*Peterborough*), 650 ....C6
West Plymouth (*Plymouth*), 100 ...C4
Westport (*Swanzey*) B6
West Rindge (*Rindge*), 475 .....B6
West Rumney (*Rumney*), 175 ...C4
W. Rye (*Rye*), 1,400 ....E5
West Stewartstown (*Stewartstown*) ..C2
West Swanzey (*Swanzey*), 1,118 ...B6
West Thornton (*Thornton*), 225 ...C4
Westville (*Plaistow*), 2,100 .....D6
West Wilton (*Wilton*), 175 ......C6
Whiteface (*Sandwich*), 30 ......D4
Whittier (*Tamworth*), 275 ......D4
Willey House (*Hart's Location*) ...D3
Wilmot Flat (*Wilmot*) C5
Wilton Center (*Wilton*) C6
Windham Depot (*Windham*) D6
Winnisquam (*Belmont, Sanbornton, and Tilton*), 850 ....C4
Winona (*New Hampton*), 150 ...C4
Wolfeboro Center (*Wolfeboro*), 80 ...D4
Wolfeboro Falls (*Wolfeboro*), 1,000 ...D4
Wonalancet (*Tamworth*), 40 ...D4
Woodmere (*Rindge*) B6
Woodsville (*Haverhill*), 1,081 ...B3

Other Features

Androscoggin, *river* E3
Appalachian N.S.T. A4
Atlantic, *ocean* E6
Blackwater, *reservoir* C5
Blue, *mountain* D2
Cabot, *mountain* D3
Cardigan, *mountain* C4
Connecticut, *river* B4, C2
First Connecticut, *lake* D1
Franconia Notch, *pass* C3
Great, *bay* E5
Indian, *river* D1
Kearsarge, *mountain* C5
Merrimack, *river* D6
Nash Stream S.F. D2
Newfound, *lake* C4
Old Speck, *mountain* E2
Ossipee, *lake* D4
Parker River N.W.R. E6
Presidential, *range* D3
Saco, *river* E4
Saint-Gaudens N.H.S. B4
Second Connecticut, *lake* D1
Smarts, *mountain* B4
Snow, *mountain* E1
Squam, *lake* D4
Sunapee, *lake* B5
Swift, *river* D4
Umbagog, *lake* D2
Washington, *mountain* D3
White, *mountains* C3
White Mountain National Forest C3, D2
Winnipesaukee, *lake* D4
Winnisquam, *lake* D4

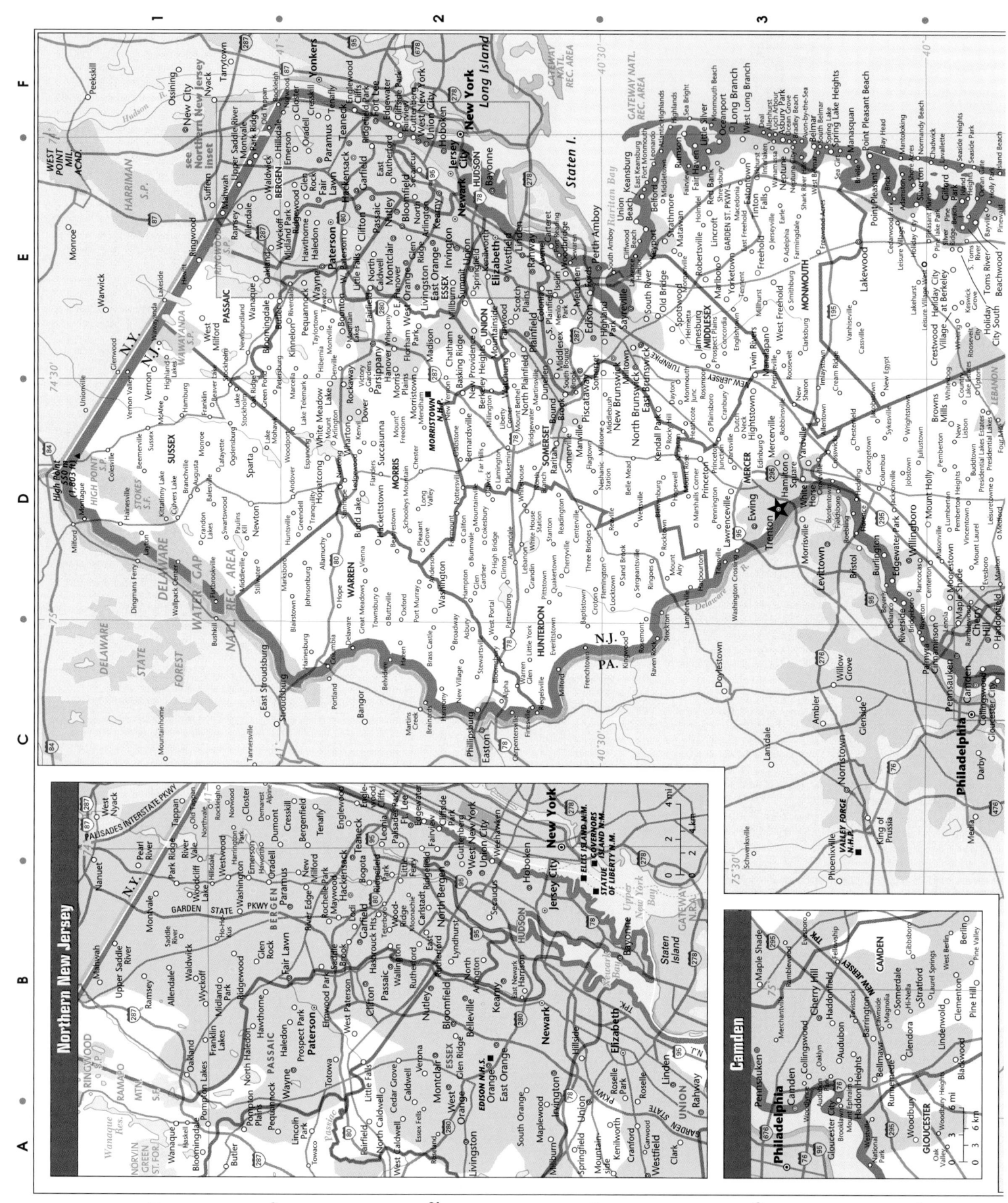

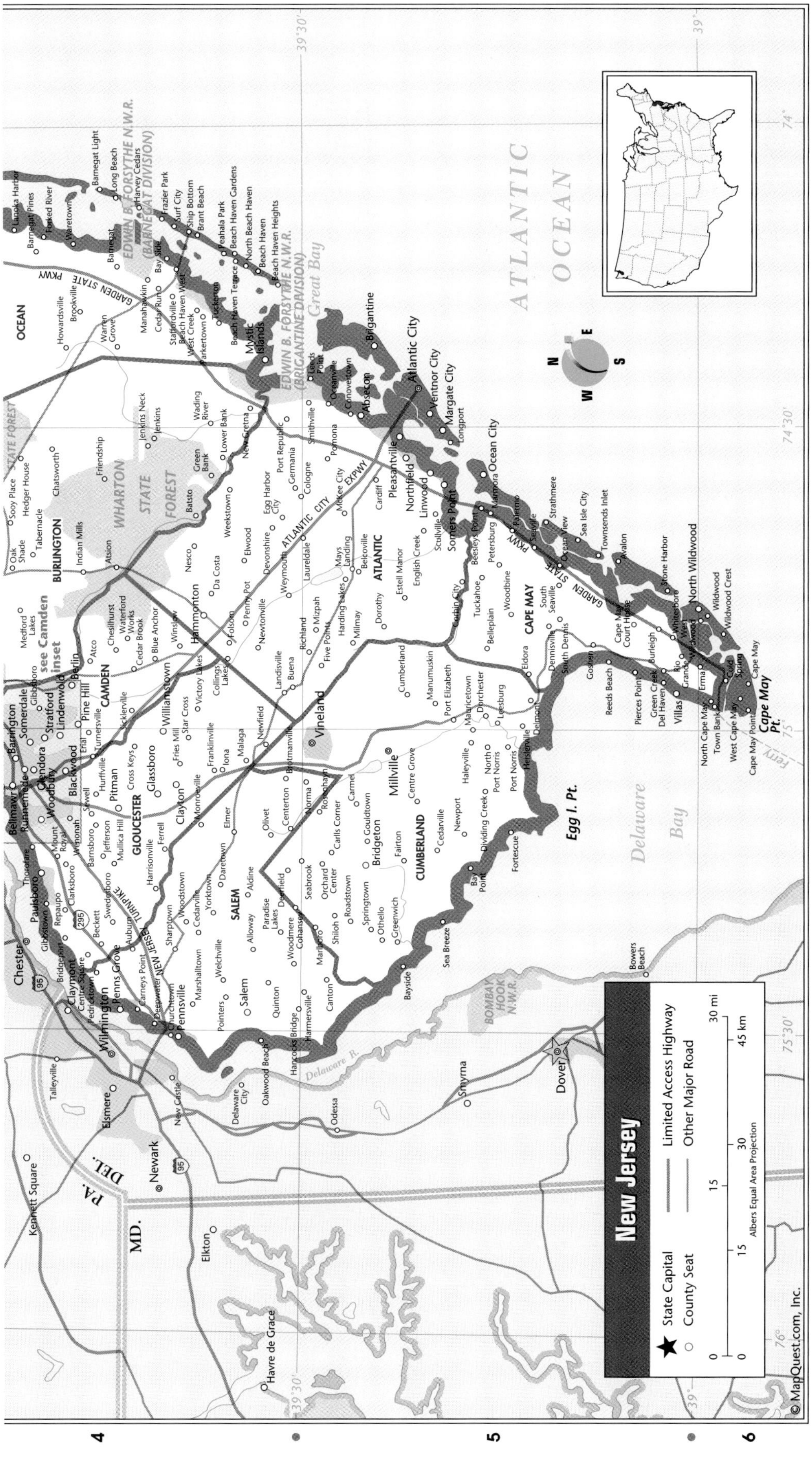

New Jersey

Capital:	Trenton
Land Area:	7,419 sq. mi.
	19,215 sq. km.
Population:	8,414,350 (2000 Census)
Largest City:	Newark, 273,546
Highest Point:	High Point,
	1,803 ft.
	550 m.
Admitted to Union:	December 18, 1787
Nickname:	Garden State
State Flower:	Purple Violet
State Bird:	Eastern Goldfinch

New Jersey: Map Index

Counties

Atlantic, 252,552	D5
Bergen, 884,118	B1, E2
Burlington, 423,394	D4
Camden, 508,932	B3, D4
Cape May, 102,326	D5
Cumberland, 146,438	C5
Essex, 793,633	B2, E2
Gloucester, 254,673	A4, C4
Hudson, 608,975	B2, E2
Hunterdon, 121,989	C2
Mercer, 350,761	D3
Middlesex, 750,162	E3
Monmouth, 615,301	E3
Morris, 470,212	D2
Ocean, 510,916	E4
Passaic, 489,049	A1, E1
Salem, 64,285	C4
Somerset, 297,490	D2
Sussex, 144,166	D1
Union, 522,541	E2
Warren, 102,437	D2

Boroughs, Cities, Towns and Townships

Boroughs, cities, towns and townships that are not labeled on the map are shown with an asterisk. They are included here only for population reference.

Aberdeen, 17,454	*
Absecon, 7,638	E5
Alexandria, 4,698	D2
Allamuchy, 3,877	D2
Allendale, 6,699	B1, E1
Allenhurst, 718	F3
Allentown, 1,882	D3
Alloway, 2,774	C4
Alpha, 2,482	C2
Alpine, 2,183	C1
Andover (borough), 658	D2
Andover (township), 6,033	D2
Asbury Park, 16,930	E3
Atlantic City, 40,517	E5
Atlantic Highlands, 4,705	E3
Audubon, 9,182	B3
Audubon Park, 1,102	B3
Avalon, 2,143	D5
Avon-by-the-Sea, 2,244	E3
Barnegat, 15,270	E4
Barnegat Light, 764	E4
Barrington, 7,084	B3, C4
Bass River, 1,510	*
Bay Head, 1,238	E4
Bayonne, 61,842	B3, E2
Beach Haven, 1,278	E4
Beachwood, 10,375	E4
Bedminster, 8,302	*
Belleville, 35,928	B2
Bellmawr, 11,262	B3, C4
Belmar, 6,045	E3
Belvidere, 2,771	C2
Bergenfield, 26,247	C2
Berkeley, 39,991	*
Berkeley Heights, 13,407	E2
Berlin (borough), 6,149	B4, D4
Berlin (township), 5,290	*
Bernards, 24,575	*
Bernardsville, 7,345	D2
Bethlehem, 3,820	*
Beverly, 2,661	D3
Blairstown, 5,747	D2
Bloomfield, 47,683	B2, E2
Bloomingdale, 7,610	A1, E1
Bloomsbury, 886	C2
Bogota, 8,249	B2
Boonton (town), 8,496	E2
Boonton (township), 4,287	*
Bordentown (city), 3,969	D3
Bordentown (township), 8,380	*
Bound Brook, 10,155	D2
Bradley Beach, 4,793	E3
Branchburg, 14,566	*
Branchville, 845	D1
Brick, 76,119	E3
Bridgeton, 22,771	C5
Bridgewater, 42,940	D2
Brielle, 4,893	E3
Brigantine, 12,594	E5
Brooklawn, 2,354	B3
Buena, 3,873	C4
Buena Vista, 7,436	*
Burlington (city), 9,736	D3
Burlington (township), 20,294	E1
Butler, 7,420	*
Byram, 8,254	*
Caldwell, 7,584	A2
Califon, 1,055	D2
Camden, 79,904	B3, C4
Cape May, 4,034	D6
Cape May Point, 241	D6
Carlstadt, 5,917	B2
Carneys Point, 7,684	C4
Carteret, 20,709	E2
Cedar Grove, 12,300	B2
Chatham (borough), 8,460	E2
Chatham (township), 10,086	*

Cherry Hill, 69,965	B3, C4
Chesilhurst, 1,520	D4
Chester (borough), 1,635	D2
Chester (township), 7,282	*
Chesterfield, 5,955	*
Cinnaminson, 14,595	D4
Clark, 14,597	A3
Clayton, 7,139	C4
Clementon, 4,986	B4
Cliffside Park, 23,007	C2, F2
Clifton, 78,672	B2, E2
Clinton (town), 2,632	D2
Clinton (township), 12,957	*
Closter, 8,383	C1, F2
Collingswood, 14,326	B3, C4
Colts Neck, 12,331	*
Commercial, 5,259	*
Corbin City, 468	D5
Cranbury, 3,227	*
Cranford, 22,578	A3
Cresskill, 7,746	C2, F2
Deal, 1,070	F3
Deerfield, 2,927	C4
Delanco, 3,237	D3
Delaware, 4,478	C2
Delran, 15,536	*
Demarest, 4,845	C1
Dennis, 6,492	*
Denville, 15,824	E2
Deptford, 26,763	*
Dover (town), 18,188	D2
Dover (township), 89,706	*
Downe, 1,631	*
Dumont, 17,503	C2
Dunellen, 6,823	E2
Eagleswood, 1,441	*
Eastampton, 6,202	*
East Amwell, 4,455	*
East Brunswick, 46,756	E3
East Greenwich, 5,430	*
East Hanover, 11,393	E2
East Newark, 2,377	B2
East Orange, 69,824	B2, E2
East Rutherford, 8,716	B2, E2
East Windsor, 24,919	*
Eatontown, 14,008	E3
Edgewater, 7,677	C2, F2
Edgewater Park, 7,864	D3
Edison, 97,687	E2
Egg Harbor (township), 30,726	*
Egg Harbor City, 4,545	D4
Elizabeth, 120,568	B3, E2
Elk, 3,514	*
Elmer, 1,384	C4
Elmwood Park, 18,925	B2
Elsinboro, 1,092	*
Emerson, 7,197	B1, E2
Englewood, 26,203	C2
Englewood Cliffs, 5,322	C2, F2
Englishtown, 1,764	*
Essex Fells, 2,162	A2
Estell Manor, 1,585	D5
Evesham, 42,275	*
Ewing, 35,707	*
Fairfield (Cumberland Co.), 6,283	*
Fairfield (Essex Co.), 7,063	A2, E2
Fair Haven, 5,937	E3
Fair Lawn, 31,637	B2, E2
Fairview (Bergen Co.), 13,255	C2, F2
Fanwood, 7,174	E2
Far Hills, 859	D2
Farmingdale, 1,587	E3
Fieldsboro, 522	D3
Flemington, 4,200	D3
Florence, 10,746	D3
Florham Park, 8,857	E2
Folsom, 1,972	D4
Fort Lee, 35,461	C2, F2
Frankford, 5,420	*
Franklin (Gloucester Co.), 15,466	*
Franklin (Hunterdon Co.), 2,990	*
Franklin (Somerset Co.), 50,903	*
Franklin (Sussex Co.), 5,160	D1
Franklin (Warren Co.), 2,768	*
Franklin Lakes, 10,422	B1
Fredon, 2,860	*
Freehold (borough), 10,976	E3
Freehold (township), 31,537	E3
Frelinghuysen, 2,083	*
Frenchtown, 1,488	C2
Galloway, 31,209	*
Garfield, 29,786	B2, E2
Garwood, 4,153	A3
Gibbsboro, 2,435	B3, D4
Glassboro, 19,068	C4
Glen Gardner, 1,902	D2
Glen Ridge, 7,271	B2, E2
Glen Rock, 11,546	B1, E2
Gloucester (township), 64,350	*
Gloucester City, 11,484	B3, C4
Green, 3,220	*
Green Brook, 5,654	*
Greenwich (Cumberland Co.), 847	C5
Greenwich (Gloucester Co.), 4,879	*
Greenwich (Warren Co.), 4,365	C2
Guttenberg, 10,807	C2, F2
Hackensack, 42,677	B2
Hackettstown, 10,403	D2
Haddon, 14,651	*
Haddonfield, 11,659	B3, C4
Haddon Heights, 7,547	B3

Map labels (water, parks, regions):

ATLANTIC OCEAN

OCEAN

Great Bay

EDWIN B. FORSYTHE N.W.R. (BARNEGAT DIVISION)

EDWIN B. FORSYTHE N.W.R. (BRIGANTINE DIVISION)

GARDEN STATE PKWY

Delaware Bay

WHARTON STATE FOREST

STATE FOREST

BURLINGTON

CAMDEN

GLOUCESTER

SALEM

CUMBERLAND

CAPE MAY

ATLANTIC

Egg I. Pt.

Cape May Pt.

BOMBAY HOOK N.W.R.

Delaware R.

MD.

DEL.

PA.

NEW JERSEY TURNPIKE

ATLANTIC CITY EXPWY

New Jersey

Legend:
- ★ State Capital
- ○ County Seat
- Limited Access Highway
- Other Major Road

Scale:
- 0 15 30 mi
- 0 15 30 45 km

Albers Equal Area Projection

© MapQuest.com, Inc.

Hainesport, 4,126 ... *
Haledon, 8,252 ... B2, E2
Hamburg, 3,105 ... D1
Hamilton (Atlantic Co.), 20,499 ... *
Hamilton (Mercer Co.), 87,109 ... *
Hammonton, 12,604 ... D4
Hampton (Hunterdon Co.), 1,546 ... D2
Hampton (Sussex Co.), 4,943 ... *
Hanover (Morris Co.), 12,898 ... E2
Harding, 3,180 ... *
Hardwick, 1,464 ... *
Hardyston, 6,171 ... *
Harmony, 2,729 ... C2
Harrington Park, 4,740 ... C1
Harrison (Gloucester Co.), 8,788 ... *
Harrison (Hudson Co.), 14,424 ... B2
Harvey Cedars, 359 ... E4
Hasbrouck Heights, 11,662 ... B2
Haworth, 3,390 ... C1
Hawthorne, 18,218 ... B1, E2
Hazlet, 21,378 ... *
Helmetta, 1,825 ... E3
High Bridge, 3,776 ... D2
Highland Park, 13,999 ... E3
Highlands, 5,097 ... F3
Hightstown, 5,216 ... D3
Hillsborough, 36,634 ... *
Hillsdale, 10,087 ... B1, E1
Hillside, 21,747 ... B3
Hi-Nella, 1,029 ... B3
Hoboken, 38,577 ... B2, E2
Ho-Ho-Kus, 4,060 ... B1
Holland, 5,124 ... *
Holmdel, 15,781 ... E3
Hopatcong, 15,888 ... D2
Hope, 1,891 ... D2
Hopewell (Cumberland Co.), 4,434 ... *
Hopewell (borough, Mercer Co.), 2,035 ... D3
Hopewell (township, Mercer Co.), 16,105 ... *
Howell, 48,903 ... *
Independence, 5,603 ... *
Interlaken, 900 ... E3
Irvington, 60,695 ... B2, E2
Island Heights, 1,751 ... E4
Jackson, 42,816 ... *
Jamesburg, 6,025 ... E3
Jefferson, 19,717 ... C4
Jersey City, 240,055 ... B2, E2
Keansburg, 10,732 ... E3
Kearny, 40,513 ... B2, E2
Kenilworth, 7,675 ... A3, E2
Keyport, 7,568 ... E3
Kingwood, 3,782 ... C3
Kinnelon, 9,365 ... E2
Knowlton, 2,977 ... *
Lacey, 25,346 ... *
Lafayette, 2,300 ... D1
Lakehurst, 2,522 ... E3
Lakewood, 60,352 ... E3
Lambertville, 3,868 ... D3
Laurel Springs, 1,970 ... B4
Lavallette, 2,665 ... E4
Lawnside, 2,692 ... B3
Lawrence (Cumberland Co.), 2,721 ... *
Lawrence (Mercer Co.), 29,159 ... *
Lebanon (borough, Hunterdon Co.), 1,065 ... D2
Lebanon (township, Hunterdon Co.), 5,816 ... *
Leonia, 8,914 ... C2
Liberty, 2,765 ... *
Lincoln Park, 10,930 ... A2
Linden, 39,394 ... B3, E2
Lindenwold, 17,414 ... B4, C4
Linwood, 7,172 ... D5
Little Egg Harbor, 15,945 ... *
Little Falls, 10,855 ... B2, E2
Little Ferry, 10,800 ... B2
Little Silver, 6,170 ... E3
Livingston, 27,391 ... A2, E2
Loch Arbour, 280 ... F3
Lodi, 23,971 ... B2
Logan, 6,032 ... *
Long Beach, 3,329 ... E4
Long Branch, 31,340 ... F3
Long Hill (formerly Passic Twp.), 8,777 ... *
Longport, 1,054 ... D5
Lopatcong, 5,765 ... *
Lower, 22,945 ... *
Lower Alloways Creek, 1,851 ... *
Lumberton, 10,461 ... D4
Lyndhurst, 19,383 ... B2
Madison, 16,530 ... E2
Magnolia, 4,409 ... B3
Mahwah, 24,062 ... B1, E1
Manalapan, 33,423 ... E3
Manasquan, 6,310 ... E3
Manchester, 38,928 ... *
Mannington, 1,559 ... *
Mansfield (Burlington Co.), 5,090 ... *
Mansfield (Warren Co.), 6,653 ... *
Mantoloking, 423 ... E3
Mantua, 14,217 ... *
Manville, 10,343 ... D2
Maple Shade, 19,079 ... B3, D4
Maplewood, 23,868 ... A2
Margate City, 8,193 ... E5
Marlboro, 36,398 ... C5, E3
Matawan, 8,910 ... E3
Maurice River, 6,928 ... *
Maywood, 9,523 ... B2
Medford, 22,253 ... D4
Medford Lakes, 4,173 ... D4
Mendham (borough), 5,097 ... D2
Mendham (township), 5,400 ... *
Merchantville, 3,801 ... B3
Metuchen, 12,840 ... E2
Middle, 16,405 ... *
Middlesex, 13,717 ... E2
Middletown, 66,327 ... E3
Midland Park, 6,947 ... B1, E2
Milford, 1,195 ... C2
Millburn, 19,765 ... A2, E2
Millstone (Monmouth Co. township), 8,970 ... *
Millstone (Somerset Co., borough), 410 ... D3
Milltown, 7,000 ... E3
Millville, 26,847 ... C5
Mine Hill, 3,679 ... *
Monmouth Beach, 3,595 ... F3
Monroe (Gloucester Co.), 28,967 ... *
Monroe (Middlesex Co.), 27,999 ... *
Montague, 3,412 ... D1
Montclair, 38,977 ... B2, E2
Montgomery, 17,481 ... *
Montvale, 7,034 ... B1, E1
Montville, 20,839 ... E2
Moonachie, 2,754 ... B2
Moorestown, 19,017 ... D4
Morris, 21,796 ... *
Morris Plains, 5,236 ... E2
Morristown, 18,544 ... E2
Mountain Lakes, 4,256 ... E2
Mountainside, 6,602 ... A3, E2
Mount Arlington, 4,663 ... D2
Mount Ephraim, 4,495 ... B3
Mount Holly, 10,728 ... D4
Mount Laurel, 40,221 ... D4
Mount Olive, 24,193 ... *
Mullica, 5,912 ... *
National Park, 3,205 ... A3
Neptune, 27,690 ... E3
Neptune City, 5,218 ... E3
Netcong, 2,580 ... D2
Newark, 273,546 ... B2, E2
New Brunswick, 48,573 ... E3
Newfield, 1,616 ... C4
New Hanover, 9,744 ... *
New Milford, 16,400 ... B2
New Providence, 11,907 ... E2
Newton, 8,244 ... D1
North Arlington, 15,181 ... B2, E2
North Bergen, 58,092 ... B2
North Brunswick, 36,287 ... E3
North Caldwell, 7,375 ... B2, E2
Northfield, 7,725 ... D5
North Haledon, 7,920 ... B1
North Hanover, 7,347 ... *
North Plainfield, 21,103 ... E2
Northvale, 4,460 ... C1
North Wildwood, 4,935 ... D5
Norwood, 5,751 ... C1, F2
Nutley, 27,362 ... B2, E2
Oakland, 12,466 ... B1, E1
Oaklyn, 4,188 ... B3
Ocean (Monmouth Co.), 26,959 ... *
Ocean (Ocean Co.), 6,450 ... *
Ocean City, 15,378 ... D5
Ocean Gate, 2,076 ... E4
Oceanport, 5,807 ... E3
Ogdensburg, 2,638 ... D1
Old Bridge, 60,456 ... E3
Oldmans, 1,798 ... *
Old Tappan, 5,482 ... C1, F1
Oradell, 8,047 ... B1, E2
Orange (City of Orange), 32,868 ... B2
Oxford, 2,307 ... D2
Palisades Park, 17,073 ... C2
Palmyra, 7,091 ... C3
Paramus, 25,737 ... B2, E2
Park Ridge, 8,708 ... B1, E1
Parsippany (Parsippany-Troy Hills), 50,649 ... E2
Passaic, 67,861 ... B2, E2
Paterson, 149,222 ... B2, E2
Paulsboro, 6,160 ... C4
Peapack and Gladstone, 2,433 ... *
Pemberton (borough), 1,210 ... D4
Pemberton (township), 28,691 ... *
Pennington, 2,696 ... D3
Pennsauken, 35,737 ... B3, C4
Penns Grove, 4,886 ... C4
Pennsville, 13,194 ... B4
Pequannock, 13,888 ... A1, E2
Perth Amboy, 47,303 ... E2
Phillipsburg, 15,166 ... C2
Pilesgrove, 3,923 ... *
Pine Beach, 1,950 ... E4
Pine Hill, 10,880 ... B4, D4
Pine Valley, 20 ... B4
Piscataway, 50,482 ... E2
Pitman, 9,331 ... C4
Pittsgrove, 8,893 ... *
Plainfield, 47,829 ... E2
Plainsboro, 20,215 ... D3
Pleasantville, 19,012 ... D5
Plumsted, 7,275 ... *
Pohatcong, 3,416 ... *
Point Pleasant, 19,306 ... E3
Point Pleasant Beach, 5,314 ... E3
Pompton Lakes, 10,640 ... A1
Port Republic, 1,037 ... E4
Princeton (borough), 14,203 ... D3
Princeton (township), 16,027 ... *
Prospect Park, 5,779 ... B2
Quinton, 2,786 ... C4
Rahway, 26,500 ... A3, E2
Ramsey, 14,351 ... B1, E1
Randolph, 24,847 ... *
Raritan (Hunterdon Co.), 19,809 ... *
Raritan (Somerset Co.), 6,338 ... D2
Readington, 15,803 ... D2
Red Bank, 11,844 ... E3
Ridgefield, 10,830 ... C2
Ridgefield Park, 12,873 ... B2, E2
Ridgewood, 24,936 ... B1, E2
Ringwood, 12,396 ... E1
Riverdale, 2,498 ... A1, E2
River Edge, 10,946 ... B2
Riverside, 7,911 ... D3
Riverton, 2,759 ... C3
River Vale, 9,449 ... B1
Rochelle Park, 5,528 ... B2
Rockaway (borough), 6,473 ... D2
Rockaway (township), 22,930 ... *
Rockleigh, 391 ... C1, F1
Rocky Hill, 662 ... D3
Roosevelt, 933 ... E3
Roseland, 5,298 ... A2
Roselle, 21,274 ... A3
Roselle Park, 13,281 ... B3
Roxbury, 23,883 ... *
Rumson, 7,137 ... E3
Runnemede, 8,533 ... B3, C4
Rutherford, 18,110 ... B2
Saddle Brook, 13,155 ... B2
Saddle River, 3,201 ... B1
Salem, 5,857 ... C4
Sandyston, 1,825 ... *
Sayreville, 40,377 ... E3
Scotch Plains, 22,732 ... E2
Sea Bright, 1,818 ... F3
Sea Girt, 2,148 ... E3
Sea Isle City, 2,835 ... D5
Seaside Heights, 3,155 ... E4
Seaside Park, 2,263 ... E4
Secaucus, 15,931 ... B2, E2
Shamong, 6,462 ... *
Shiloh, 534 ... C5
Ship Bottom, 1,384 ... E4
Shrewsbury (borough), 3,590 ... E3
Shrewsbury (township), 1,098 ... *
Somerdale, 5,192 ... B3, C4
Somers Point, 11,614 ... D5
Somerville, 12,423 ... D2
South Amboy, 7,913 ... E3
Southampton, 10,388 ... *
South Belmar, 1,806 ... E3
South Bound Brook, 4,492 ... D2
South Brunswick, 37,734 ... *
South Hackensack, 2,249 ... *
South Harrison, 2,417 ... *
South Orange (South Orange Village), 16,964 ... B2
South Plainfield, 21,810 ... E2
South River, 15,322 ... E3
South Toms River, 3,634 ... E4
Sparta, 18,080 ... D1
Spotswood, 7,880 ... E3
Springfield (Burlington Co.), 3,227 ... *
Springfield (Union Co.), 14,429 ... A2, E2
Spring Lake, 3,567 ... E3
Spring Lake Heights, 5,227 ... E3
Stafford, 22,532 ... *
Stanhope, 3,584 ... D2
Stillwater, 4,267 ... D1
Stockton, 560 ... D3
Stone Harbor, 1,128 ... D5
Stow Creek, 1,429 ... *
Stratford, 7,271 ... B3, C4
Summit, 21,131 ... E2
Surf City, 1,442 ... E4
Sussex, 2,145 ... D1
Swedesboro, 2,055 ... C4
Tabernacle, 7,170 ... D4
Tavistock, 24 ... B3
Teaneck, 39,260 ... C2, E2
Tenafly, 13,806 ... C2, F2
Teterboro, 18 ... B2
Tewksbury, 5,541 ... *
Tinton Falls, 15,053 ... E3
Totowa, 9,892 ... B2
Trenton, 85,403 ... D3
Tuckerton, 3,517 ... E4
Union (Hunterdon Co.), 6,160 ... *
Union (Union Co.), 54,405 ... B2, E2
Union Beach, 6,649 ... E3
Union City, 67,088 ... B2, E2
Upper, 12,115 ... *
Upper Deerfield, 7,556 ... *
Upper Freehold, 4,282 ... *
Upper Pittsgrove, 3,468 ... *
Upper Saddle River, 7,741 ... B1, E1
Ventnor City, 12,910 ... E5
Vernon, 24,686 ... E1
Verona, 13,533 ... B2
Victory Gardens, 1,546 ... D2
Vineland, 56,271 ... C5
Voorhees, 28,126 ... *
Waldwick, 9,622 ... B1, E1
Wall, 25,261 ... *
Wallington, 11,583 ... B2
Walpack, 41 ... *
Wanaque, 10,266 ... A1, E1
Wantage, 10,387 ... *
Warren, 14,259 ... *
Washington (Bergen Co.), 8,938 ... B1
Washington (Burlington Co.), 621 ... *
Washington (Gloucester Co.), 47,114 ... *
Washington (Mercer Co.), 10,275 ... *
Washington (Morris Co.), 17,592 ... *
Washington (borough, Warren Co.), 6,712 ... *
Washington (township, Warren Co.), 6,248 ... D2
Watchung, 5,613 ... E2
Waterford, 10,494 ... *
Wayne, 54,069 ... A2, E2
Weehawken, 13,501 ... B2
Wenonah, 2,317 ... C4
Westampton, 7,217 ... *
West Amwell, 2,383 ... *
West Caldwell, 11,233 ... A2
West Cape May, 1,095 ... D6
West Deptford, 19,368 ... *
Westfield, 29,644 ... A3, E2
West Long Branch, 8,258 ... E3
West Milford, 26,410 ... E1
West New York, 45,768 ... C2, E2
West Orange, 44,943 ... A2, E2
West Paterson, 10,987 ... B2, E2
Westville, 4,500 ... A3
West Wildwood, 448 ... D5
West Windsor, 21,907 ... *
Westwood, 10,999 ... B1
Weymouth, 2,257 ... D4
Wharton, 6,298 ... D2
White, 4,245 ... *
Wildwood, 5,436 ... D6
Wildwood Crest, 3,980 ... D6
Willingboro, 33,008 ... D3
Winfield, 1,514 ... *
Winslow, 34,611 ... D4
Woodbine, 2,716 ... D5
Woodbridge, 97,203 ... E2
Woodbury, 10,307 ... A3, C4
Woodbury Heights, 2,988 ... A4
Woodcliff Lake, 5,745 ... B1
Woodland, 1,170 ... *
Woodlynne, 2,796 ... B3
Wood-Ridge, 7,644 ... B2
Woodstown, 3,136 ... C4
Woolwich, 3,032 ... *
Wrightstown, 748 ... D3
Wyckoff, 16,508 ... B1, E1

Other Places

The borough, city, town or township containing each entry is shown in italics. See the "Boroughs, Cities, Towns and Townships" listing for total population.

Adamston _(Brick)_, 4,900 ... E3
Adelphia _(Howell)_, 700 ... E3
Aldine _(Alloway)_, 150 ... C4
Anderson _(Mansfield)_, 500 ... D2
Annandale _(Clinton)_, 1,276 ... D2
Asbury _(Bethlehem and Franklin)_, 550 ... C2
Atco _(Waterford)_, 4,500 ... D4
Atsion _(Shamong)_ ... D4
Auburn _(Oldmans)_, 550 ... C4
Augusta _(Frankford)_, 300 ... D1
Avenel _(Woodbridge)_, 17,552 ... E2
Balesville _(Hampton)_, 475 ... D1
Baptistown _(Kingwood)_, 275 ... C2
Barnegat Pines _(Lacey)_, 1,300 ... E4
Barnsboro _(Mantua)_, 2,500 ... C4
Basking Ridge _(Bernards)_, 3,600 ... D2
Batsto _(Washington, Burlington Co.)_, 175 ... D4
Bay Point _(Lawrence)_ ... C5
Bayside _(Greenwich)_, 1,800 ... C5
Bay Side _(Stafford)_, 1,800 ... E4
Bayville _(Berkeley)_, 4,700 ... E4
Beach Haven Gardens _(Long Beach)_, 1,200 ... E4
Beach Haven Heights _(Long Beach)_, 125 ... E4
Beach Haven Terrace _(Long Beach)_, 1,100 ... E4
Beach Haven West _(Stafford)_, 4,444 ... E4
Beatyestown _(Mansfield)_, 3,223 ... D2
Beaver Lake _(Hardyston)_, 30 ... D1
Beckett _(Logan)_, 4,726 ... C4
Beemerville _(Wantage)_, 600 ... D1
Beesleys Point _(Upper)_, 1,400 ... D5
Belcoville _(Weymouth)_, 425 ... D5
Belford _(Middletown)_, 1,340 ... E3
Belle Mead _(Hillsborough and Montgomery)_, 550 ... D3
Belleplain _(Dennis)_, 425 ... D5
Blackwood _(Gloucester)_, 4,692 ... B4, C4
Blawenburg _(Montgomery)_, 1,300 ... D3
Blue Anchor _(Winslow)_, 1,500 ... D4
Brainards _(Harmony)_, 225 ... C2
Brant Beach _(Long Beach)_, 800 ... E4
Brass Castle _(Washington, Warren Co.)_, 1,507 ... C2
Bridgeboro _(Delran)_, 250 ... D3
Bridgeport _(Logan)_, 600 ... C4
Broadway _(Franklin)_, 700 ... C2
Brookville _(Barnegat and Ocean)_, 90 ... E4
Brotmanville _(Pittsgrove)_, 500 ... C4
Browns Mills _(Pemberton)_, 11,257 ... D4
Budd Lake _(Mount Olive)_, 8,100 ... D2
Buddtown _(Southampton)_, 150 ... D4
Bunnvale _(Lebanon)_, 950 ... D2
Burleigh _(Middle)_, 1,836 ... D5
Buttzville _(White)_, 700 ... C2
Canton _(Lower Alloways Creek)_, 400 ... C5
Cape May Court House _(Middle)_, 4,704 ... D5
Cardiff _(Egg Harbor)_, 2,100 ... D5
Carlls Corner _(Upper Deerfield)_, 1,100 ... C5
Carmel _(Deerfield)_, 275 ... C5
Carpentersville _(Pohatcong)_, 175 ... C2
Cassville _(Jackson)_, 900 ... E3
Cedar Brook _(Winslow)_, 1,100 ... D4
Cedar Run _(Stafford)_, 450 ... E4
Cedarville _(Lawrence)_, 793 ... C5
Cedarville _(Pilesgrove)_, 325 ... C4
Cedarwood Park _(Brick)_ ... E3
Centerton _(Mount Laurel)_, 2,000 ... D4
Centerton _(Pittsgrove)_, 475 ... C4
Centerville _(Branchburg and Readington)_ ... D2
Centre Grove _(Lawrence)_, 250 ... C5
Centre Square _(Logan)_, 50 ... C4
Chadwick _(Dover)_, 200 ... E4
Chatsworth _(Woodland)_, 225 ... D4
Cherryville _(Franklin)_, 350 ... D2
Churchtown _(Pennsville)_, 3,300 ... B4
Clarksboro _(East Greenwich)_, 2,600 ... C4
Clarksburg _(Millstone)_, 450 ... E3
Clarksville ... D3
Cliffwood Beach _(Aberdeen)_, 3,538 ... E3
Cohansey _(Alloway, Hopewell and Stow Creek)_, 200 ... C4
Cokesbury _(Clinton and Tewksbury)_, 850 ... D2
Cold Spring _(Lower)_, 950 ... D6
Colesville _(Wantage)_, 400 ... D1
Collings Lakes _(Buena Vista)_, 1,726 ... D4
Cologne _(Galloway)_, 800 ... D4
Colonia _(Woodbridge)_, 17,811 ... E2
Columbia _(Knowlton)_, 375 ... C2
Columbus _(Mansfield)_, 750 ... D3
Concordia _(Monroe)_, 3,658 ... E3
Conovertown _(Galloway)_, 1,000 ... E5
Country Lake Estates _(Pemberton)_, 4,012 ... D4
Crandon Lakes _(Hampton and Stillwater)_, 1,180 ... D1
Cream Ridge _(Upper Freehold)_, 400 ... D3
Crestwood Village _(Manchester)_, 8,392 ... E4
Cross Keys _(Monroe and Washington)_, 3,600 ... C4
Crosswicks _(Chesterfield)_, 900 ... D3
Croton _(Delaware and Raritan)_, 400 ... D2
Culvers Lake _(Frankford)_ ... D1
Cumberland _(Maurice River)_, 225 ... D5
Da Costa _(Hammonton)_, 30 ... D4
Daretown _(Upper Pittsgrove)_, 225 ... C4
Dayton _(South Brunswick)_, 6,235 ... D3
Deepwater _(Pennsville)_, 1,700 ... C4
Del Haven _(Middle)_, 1,200 ... D5
Delmont _(Maurice River)_, 80 ... D5
Dennisville _(Dennis)_, 350 ... D5
Devonshire _(Mullica)_, 475 ... D4
Dividing Creek _(Downe)_, 475 ... C5
Dorchester _(Maurice River)_, 600 ... D5
Dorothy _(Weymouth)_, 600 ... D5
Dutch Neck _(West Windsor)_, 4,400 ... D3
Earle _(Colts Neck, Howell and Wall)_, 550 ... E3
East Freehold _(Freehold and Marlboro)_, 4,936 ... E3
East Keansburg _(Middletown)_ ... E3
Edinburg _(West Windsor)_, 900 ... D3
Eldora _(Dennis)_, 150 ... D5
Elwood _(Mullica)_, 1,392 ... D4
English Creek _(Egg Harbor)_, 550 ... D5
Erial _(Gloucester)_, 6,200 ... C4
Erma _(Lower)_, 2,088 ... D6
Espanong _(Jefferson)_, 2,700 ... D2
Everittstown _(Alexandria)_, 275 ... C2
Evesboro _(Evesham)_, 2,400 ... B3, D4
Fairmount _(Tewksbury and Washington)_, 300 ... D2
Fairton _(Fairfield)_, 2,253 ... C5
Fellowship _(Mount Laurel)_, 4,900 ... B3
Ferrell _(Elk)_, 1,100 ... C4
Finesville _(Pohatcong)_, 400 ... C2
Five Points ... D5
Flagtown _(Hillsborough)_, 3,000 ... D2
Flanders _(Mount Olive)_, 3,300 ... D2
Flatbrookville _(Walpack)_, 20 ... D1
Fords _(Woodbridge)_, 15,032 ... E2
Forked River _(Lacey)_, 4,914 ... E4
Fortescue _(Downe)_, 225 ... C5
Four Mile, 900 ... D4
Franklinville _(Franklin, Gloucester Co.)_, 1,500 ... C4
Frazier Park _(Long Beach)_, 225 ... E4
Freewood Acres _(Howell)_, 3,100 ... E3
Friendship ... D4
Fries Mill _(Franklin, Gloucester Co.)_, 600 ... C4
Georgetown _(Mansfield)_, 550 ... D3
Germania _(Galloway)_, 750 ... D4
Gibbstown _(Greenwich)_, 3,758 ... C4
Gilford Park _(Dover)_, 8,700 ... E4
Gladstone _(Peapack and Gladstone)_, 2,433 ... D2
Glendora _(Gloucester)_, 4,907 ... B3, C4
Goshen _(Middle)_, 350 ... D5
Gouldtown _(Fairfield)_, 2,300 ... C5
Grandin _(Franklin and Union)_, 1,800 ... D2
Great Meadows _(Independence)_, 1,264 ... D2
Green Bank _(Washington, Burlington Co.)_, 125 ... D4
Green Creek _(Middle)_, 1,300 ... D5
Greendell _(Green)_, 550 ... D2
Green Pond _(Rockaway)_, 1,400 ... E1
Groveville _(Hamilton)_, 9,208 ... D3
Hainesburg _(Knowlton)_, 400 ... C2
Hainesville _(Sandyston)_, 400 ... D1
Haleyville _(Commercial)_, 250 ... C5
Hamilton Square _(Hamilton)_, 26,419 ... D3
Hancocks Bridge _(Lower Alloways Creek)_, 350 ... C4
Harbourton _(Hopewell)_, 250 ... D3
Harding Lakes _(Hamilton)_, 1,900 ... D5
Harmersville _(Lower Alloways Creek)_, 125 ... C5
Harrisonville _(South Harrison)_, 325 ... C4
Haskell _(Wanaque)_ ... A1
Hazen _(White)_, 225 ... C2
Heathcote _(South Brunswick)_, 4,755 ... D3
Hedding _(Mansfield)_, 475 ... D3
Hedger House ... D4
Heislerville _(Maurice River)_, 275 ... D5
Hewitt _(West Milford)_, 50 ... E1
Hibernia _(Rockaway)_, 175 ... E2
Highland Lakes _(Vernon)_, 5,051 ... E1
Holiday City _(Dover)_ ... E3
Holiday City at Berkeley _(Berkeley)_, 13,884 ... E4
Holiday City South _(Berkeley)_, 4,047 ... E4
Holly Park _(Berkeley)_, 2,200 ... E4
Howardsville ... E4
Huntsville _(Green)_, 250 ... D2
Hurffville _(Washington, Gloucester Co.)_, 4,300 ... C4
Imlaystown _(Upper Freehold)_, 175 ... D3
Indian Mills _(Shamong)_, 300 ... D4
Iona _(Franklin)_ ... C4
Iselin _(Woodbridge)_, 16,698 ... E2
Island Beach, 60 ... E4
Jacksonville _(Springfield)_, 500 ... D3
Jacobstown _(North Hanover)_, 950 ... D3
Jenkins _(Washington, Burlington Co.)_, 20 ... D4
Jenkins Neck ... D4
Jerseyville _(Howell)_, 1,000 ... E3
Jobstown _(Springfield)_, 250 ... D3
Johnsonburg _(Frelinghuysen)_, 375 ... D2
Juliustown _(Springfield)_, 450 ... D3
Kendall Park _(South Brunswick)_, 9,006 ... D3
Kenvil _(Roxbury)_, 12,569 ... D2
Keswick Grove _(Manchester)_ ... E4
Kingston _(Franklin)_, 1,292 ... D3
Kittatinny Lake _(Sandyston)_ ... D1
Lake Mohawk _(Sparta)_, 1,500 ... D1
Lake Stockholm _(Holland)_ ... D1
Lake Telemark _(Rockaway)_, 1,202 ... D2
Lamington _(Bedminster)_, 80 ... D2
Landisville _(Buena)_, 500 ... D4
Lanoka Harbor _(Lacey)_, 3,800 ... E4
Laureldale _(Hamilton)_, 800 ... D5
Laurence Harbor _(Old Bridge)_, 6,227 ... E3
Lawrenceville _(Lawrence)_, 4,081 ... D3
Layton _(Sandyston)_, 225 ... D1
Ledgewood _(Roxbury)_, 1,100 ... D2
Leeds Point _(Galloway)_, 350 ... E5
Leesburg _(Maurice River)_, 850 ... D5
Leisuretowne _(Southampton)_, 2,535 ... D4
Leisure Village _(Lakewood)_, 4,443 ... E3
Leisure Village West _(Manchester)_, 11,085 ... E3
Lenola _(Moorestown)_, 13,860 ... D4
Leonardo _(Middletown)_, 2,823 ... E3
Liberty Corner _(Bernards)_, 1,700 ... D2
Lincroft _(Middletown)_, 6,255 ... E3
Little York _(Alexandria and Holland)_, 300 ... C2
Locktown _(Delaware)_, 400 ... D3
Long Valley _(Washington, Morris Co.)_, 1,818 ... D2
Lower Bank _(Washington, Burlington Co.)_, 70 ... D4
Macedonia _(Tinton Falls)_, 30 ... E3
Malaga _(Franklin, Gloucester Co.)_, 1,700 ... C4
Manahawkin _(Stafford)_, 2,004 ... E4
Manumuskin _(Maurice River)_ ... D5
Marcella _(Rockaway)_, 475 ... E2
Marksboro _(Frelinghuysen)_, 325 ... D2
Marlton _(Evesham)_, 10,260 ... D4
Marmora _(Upper)_, 1,600 ... D5
Marshalls Corner _(Hopewell)_, 400 ... D3
Marshalltown _(Mannington)_, 80 ... C4
Martinsville _(Bridgewater)_, 1,800 ... D2
Masonville _(Mount Laurel)_, 7,300 ... D4
Mauricetown _(Commercial)_, 250 ... D5
Mays Landing _(Hamilton)_, 2,321 ... D5
McAfee _(Vernon)_, 2,600 ... D1
McKee City _(Egg Harbor)_, 2,800 ... D5
Menlo Park _(Edison)_ ... E2
Mercerville _(Hamilton)_, 26,419 ... D3
Middlebush _(Franklin, Somerset Co.)_, 500 ... D3
Middleville _(Stillwater)_, 375 ... D1
Millhurst _(Manalapan)_, 300 ... E3
Millington _(Long Hill)_, 3,500 ... D2
Milmay _(Buena Vista)_, 275 ... D5
Mizpah _(Hamilton)_, 500 ... D5
Monmouth Junction _(South Brunswick)_, 2,721 ... D3
Monroeville _(Upper Pittsgrove)_, 300 ... C4
Morganville _(Marlboro)_, 11,255 ... E3
Mountainville _(Tewksbury)_, 475 ... D2
Mount Airy _(West Amwell)_, 250 ... D3
Mount Bethel _(Warren)_, 1,000 ... D2
Mount Freedom _(Randolph)_, 2,000 ... D2
Mount Rose _(Hopewell)_, 550 ... D3
Mount Royal _(East Greenwich)_, 1,800 ... C4
Mullica Hill _(Harrison)_, 1,658 ... C4
Mystic Islands _(Little Egg Harbor)_, 8,694 ... E4
Nesco _(Mullica)_, 375 ... D4
Neshanic Station _(Branchburg)_ ... D2
New Egypt _(Plumsted)_, 2,519 ... D3
Newfoundland _(Jefferson and West Milford)_, 250 ... E1
New Gretna _(Bass River)_, 600 ... E4
New Lisbon _(Pemberton)_, 450 ... D4
Newport _(Downe)_, 325 ... C5
New Sharon _(Upper Freehold and Washington)_, 300 ... D3
Newtonville _(Buena Vista)_, 800 ... D4
New Vernon _(Harding)_, 1,200 ... D2
New Village _(Franklin, Warren Co.)_, 350 ... C2
Norma _(Pittsgrove)_, 500 ... C5
Normandy Beach _(Brick)_ ... E3
North Beach Haven _(Long Beach)_, 2,427 ... E4
North Branch _(Branchburg)_, 1,500 ... D2
North Cape May _(Lower)_, 3,618 ... D6
North Port Norris _(Commercial)_, 80 ... C5
Oakhurst _(Ocean)_, 4,152 ... E3
Oak Ridge _(West Milford)_, 750 ... E1
Oak Shade _(Aberdeen)_, 1,500 ... D4
Oak Valley _(Deptford)_, 3,747 ... A4
Oakwood Beach _(Elsinboro)_, 700 ... B4
Ocean Grove _(Neptune)_, 4,256 ... E3
Ocean View _(Dennis)_, 450 ... D5
Oceanville _(Galloway)_, 475 ... E5
Oldwick _(Tewksbury)_, 250 ... D2
Olivet _(Pittsgrove)_, 1,420 ... C4
Orchard Center, 550 ... C5
Othello _(Greenwich)_ ... C5
Palermo _(Upper)_, 2,300 ... D5
Paradise Lakes _(Alloway and Quinton)_, 425 ... C4
Parkertown _(Little Egg Harbor)_, 1,700 ... E4
Pattenburg _(Union)_, 800 ... C2
Paulins Kill _(Stillwater)_, 1,400 ... D1
Peahala Park _(Long Beach)_, 850 ... E4
Pedricktown _(Oldmans)_, 550 ... C4
Pemberton Heights _(Pemberton)_, 2,512 ... D4
Penny Pot _(Hammonton)_, 90 ... D4
Perrineville _(Millstone)_, 550 ... E3
Petersburg _(Upper)_, 650 ... D5
Petersburg _(Jefferson)_, 2,900 ... D1
Pierces Point _(Middle)_, 125 ... D5
Pine Lake Park _(Manchester)_ ... E4
Pinewald _(Berkeley)_, 2,500 ... E4
Pittstown _(Alexandria and Franklin)_, 550 ... D2
Pleasant Grove _(Washington, Morris Co.)_, 1,100 ... D2
Pleasant Plains _(Dover)_, 2,600 ... E4
Pluckemin _(Bedminster)_, 6,000 ... D2
Pointers _(Mannington)_, 550 ... C4
Pomona _(Galloway)_, 4,019 ... D5
Pompton Plains _(Pequannock)_, 6,500 ... A1
Port Elizabeth _(Maurice River)_, 425 ... D5
Port Monmouth _(Middletown)_, 3,742 ... E3
Port Murray _(Mansfield)_, 425 ... D2
Port Norris _(Commercial)_, 1,507 ... C5
Port Reading _(Woodbridge)_, 3,829 ... E2
Pottersville _(Bedminster and Tewksbury)_ D2
Presidential Lakes _(Pemberton)_ ... D4
Presidential Lakes Estates _(Pemberton)_, 2,332 ... D4
Princeton Junction _(West Windsor)_, 2,382 ... D3
Prospect Plains _(Monroe)_, 550 ... E3
Quakertown _(Franklin)_, 400 ... D2
Ramblewood _(Mount Laurel)_, 6,003 ... B3, D4
Rancocas _(Westampton)_, 8,400 ... D3
Raven Rock _(Delaware)_, 150 ... C3
Reaville _(East Amwell and Raritan)_, 1,200 ... D3
Reeds Beach _(Middle)_, 100 ... D5
Repaupo _(Logan)_, 275 ... C4
Richland _(Buena Vista)_, 750 ... D5
Riegelsville _(Pohatcong)_ ... C2
Ringoes _(East Amwell and West Amwell)_, 1,100 ... D3
Rio Grande _(Middle)_, 2,444 ... D5
Roadstown _(Hopewell and Stow Creek)_, 175 ... C5
Robbinsville _(Washington, Mercer Co.)_, 1,900 ... D3
Robertsville _(Marlboro)_, 9,800 ... E3
Rocktown _(East Amwell and West Amwell)_ ... D3
Roebling _(Florence)_, 8,200 ... D3
Roosevelt City _(Manchester)_, 325 ... E4
Rosemont _(Delaware)_, 450 ... D3
Rosenhayn _(Deerfield)_, 1,099 ... C5
Rossmoor _(Monroe)_, 3,129 ... E3
Sand Brook _(Delaware)_, 400 ... D3
Schooleys Mountain _(Washington)_, 1,100 ... D2
Scullville _(Egg Harbor)_, 600 ... D5
Sea Breeze _(Fairfield)_, 40 ... C5
Seabrook _(Upper Deerfield)_, 1,719 ... C5
Seaville _(Upper)_, 1,700 ... D5
Sergeantsville _(Delaware)_, 650 ... D3
Sewaren _(Woodbridge)_, 2,780 ... E2
Sewell _(Mantua)_, 3,400 ... C4
Shark River Hills _(Neptune)_, 3,878 ... E3
Sharptown _(Pilesgrove)_, 350 ... C4
Shore Acres _(Brick)_, 4,500 ... E3
Sicklerville _(Winslow)_, 6,000 ... D4
Silver Ridge _(Berkeley)_, 1,211 ... E4
Silverton _(Dover)_, 9,200 ... E3
Smithburg _(Freehold and Millstone)_, 350 ... E3
Smithville _(Galloway)_, 3,100 ... E5
Somerset _(Franklin)_, 23,040 ... E2
Sooy Place, 550 ... D4
South Dennis _(Dennis)_, 600 ... D5
South Seaville _(Dennis)_, 600 ... D5
Springtown _(Greenwich)_, 250 ... C5
Staffordville _(Eagleswood)_, 425 ... E4
Stanton _(Readington)_, 500 ... D2
Star Cross _(Franklin)_, 1,400 ... C4
Stewartsville _(Greenwich)_, 650 ... C2
Stockholm _(Hardyston)_, 200 ... D1
Strathmere _(Upper)_, 175 ... D5
Strathmore _(Aberdeen)_, 6,740 ... E3
Succasunna _(Roxbury)_, 12,569 ... D2
Swartswood _(Stillwater)_, 500 ... D1
Sykesville _(Chesterfield)_, 375 ... D3
Taylortown _(Boonton and Montville)_, 1,200 ... E2
Tennent _(Manalapan)_, 1,100 ... E3
Thorofare _(West Deptford)_, 1,500 ... C4
Three Bridges _(Readington)_, 850 ... D2
Titusville _(Hopewell)_, 800 ... D3
Toms River _(Dover)_, 86,327 ... E4
Towaco _(Montville)_, 2,700 ... E2
Town Bank _(Lower)_, 2,700 ... D6
Townsbury _(Liberty)_, 550 ... D2
Townsends Inlet _(Sea Isle City)_ ... D5
Tranquility _(Green)_, 425 ... D2
Tuckahoe _(Upper)_, 600 ... D5
Turnersville _(Washington)_, 3,867 ... C4
Twin Rivers _(East Windsor)_, 7,422 ... E3
Upton _(Pemberton)_ ... D4
Vanhiseville _(Jackson)_, 700 ... E3
Vernon Valley _(Vernon)_, 1,737 ... E1
Victory Lakes _(Monroe)_, 2,118 ... D4
Vienna _(Independence)_, 1,264 ... D2
Villas _(Lower)_, 9,064 ... D5
Vincentown _(Southampton)_, 750 ... D4
Wading River _(Washington)_, 20 ... E4
Wallpack Center _(Walpack)_, 20 ... D1
Wanamassa _(Ocean)_, 4,551 ... E3
Waretown _(Ocean)_, 1,582 ... E4
Warren Glen _(Stafford)_, 650 ... C2
Warren Grove _(Stafford)_, 150 ... E4
Washington Crossing _(Hopewell)_, 950 ... D3
Waterford Works _(Waterford and Winslow)_, 1,000 ... D4
Wawayanda ... E1
Weekstown _(Mullica)_, 150 ... D4
Welchville ... C4
Wertsville, 550 ... D3
West Belmar _(Wall)_, 2,606 ... E3
West Berlin _(Berlin)_, 4,000 ... B4
West Creek _(Eagleswood)_, 1,500 ... E4
West Freehold _(Freehold)_, 12,498 ... E3
West Portal _(Bethlehem)_, 225 ... C2
Whippany _(Hanover)_, 3,800 ... E2
White Horse _(Hamilton)_, 9,373 ... D3
Whitehouse _(Readington)_ ... D2
White House Station _(Readington)_, 1,951 ... D2
White Meadow Lake _(Rockaway)_, 9,052 ... D2
Whitesbog _(Pemberton)_, 70 ... D4
Whitesboro _(Middle)_, 1,836 ... D5
Whiting _(Manchester)_, 1,800 ... E4
Williamstown _(Monroe)_, 11,812 ... D4
Woodmere _(Jackson)_, 150 ... C4
Woodport _(Jefferson)_, 2,000 ... D2
Yardville _(Hamilton)_, 9,208 ... D3
Yorketown _(Manalapan)_, 6,712 ... E3
Yorktown _(Pilesgrove)_, 250 ... C4

Other Features

A.C. Expwy. ... D4
Atlantic, _ocean_ ... E5
Bombay Hook N.W.R. ... C5
Cape May, _point_ ... D6
Delaware, _bay_ ... C5
Delaware, _river_ ... B5, D3
Delaware State Forest ... C1
Delaware Water Gap Natl. Rec. Area ... D1
Edison N.H.S. ... B2
Edwin B. Forsythe N.W.R. (Barnegat Division) ... E4
Edwin B. Forsythe N.W.R. (Brigantine Division) ... E4
Egg I., _point_ ... C5
Ellis Island N.M. ... B2
Garden St. Pkwy. ... D4, D5, E1
Gateway Natl. Rec. Area ... F2, F3
Great, _bay_ ... E5
Harriman S.P. ... E1
High Point, _hill_ ... D1
High Point S.P. ... D1
Hudson, _river_ ... F1
Lebanon State Forest ... D4
Long, _island_ ... C3, F2
Morristown N.H.P. ... D2
N.J. Tpk. ... C4, D4, E3
Norvin Green St. For. ... A1
Pa. Tpk. ... C3
Palisades Pkwy. ... E1
Pecos N.H.P. ... E2
Ramapo Mtn. S.F. ... B1
Raritan, _bay_ ... E3
Ringwood S.P. ... B1, E1
Staten, _island_ ... B3, E2
Statue of Liberty N.M. ... B2
Stokes S.F. ... D1
Wanaque, _reservoir_ ... A1
Wawayanda S.P. ... E1
West Point Mil. Acad. ... E1
Wharton State Forest ... D4

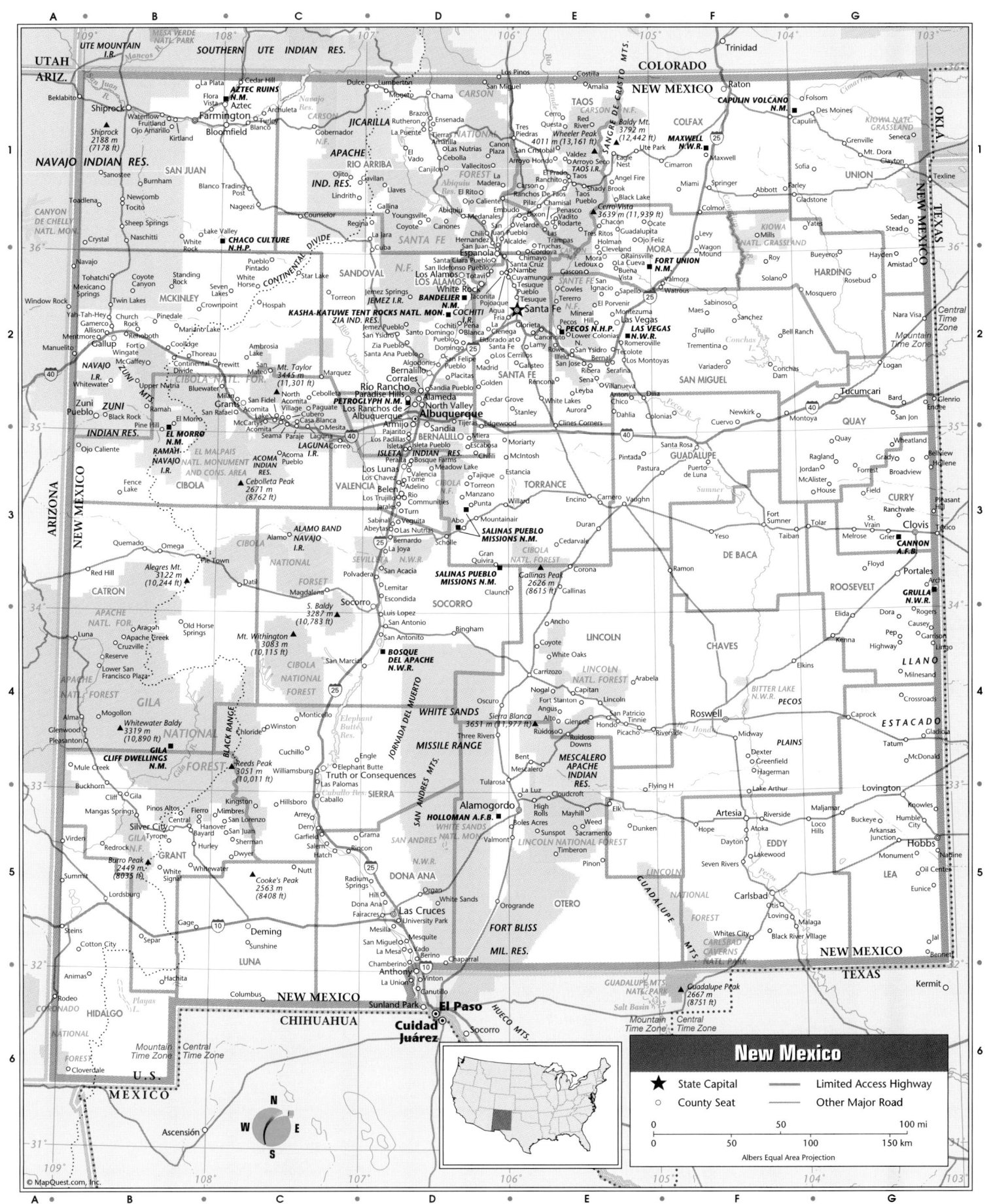

New Mexico

Capital: Santa Fe
Land Area: 121,364 sq. mi.
314,333 sq. km.
Population: 1,819,046 (2000 Census)
Largest City: Albuquerque, 448,607
Highest Point: Wheeler Peak
13,161 ft.
4,011 m.
Admitted to Union: January 6, 1912
Nickname: Land of Enchantment
State Flower: Yucca
State Bird: Roadrunner

New Mexico: Map Index

Counties

Bernalillo, **556,678** ... D3
Catron, **3,543** ... B3
Chaves, **61,382** ... F4
Cibola, **25,595** ... B3
Colfax, **14,189** ... F1
Curry, **45,044** ... G3
De Baca, **2,240** ... F3
Doña Ana, **174,682** ... D5
Eddy, **51,658** ... F5
Grant, **31,002** ... B5
Guadalupe, **4,680** ... F3
Harding, **810** ... G2
Hidalgo, **5,932** ... B6
Lea, **55,511** ... G5
Lincoln, **19,411** ... E4
Los Alamos, **18,343** ... D2
Luna, **25,016** ... C5
McKinley, **74,798** ... B2
Mora, **5,180** ... F1
Otero, **62,298** ... E5
Quay, **10,155** ... G2
Rio Arriba, **41,190** ... C1
Roosevelt, **18,018** ... G3
Sandoval, **89,908** ... C2
San Juan, **113,801** ... B1
San Miguel, **30,126** ... F2
Santa Fe, **129,292** ... E2
Sierra, **13,270** ... D5
Socorro, **18,078** ... D3
Taos, **29,979** ... E1
Torrance, **16,911** ... E3
Union, **4,174** ... G1
Valencia, **66,152** ... C3

Cities and Towns

Abbott ... F1
Abeytas, *60* ... D3
Abiquiu, *225* ... D1
Abo, *60* ... D3
Acoma Pueblo, *40* ... C3
Acomita, **288** ... C2
Acomita Lake, **312** ... C2
Adelino, **2,211** ... D3
Agua Fria, **2,051** ... D2
Alameda, **4,200** ... D2
Alamo, **1,183** ... C3
Alamogordo, **35,582** ... E5
Albuquerque, **448,607** ... D2
Alcalde, **377** ... D1
Algodones, **688** ... D2
Allison, *125* ... B2
Alma, *60* ... B4
Alto, *80* ... E4
Amalia, *100* ... E1
Ambrosia Lake ... C2
Amistad ... G2
Ancho ... E4
Angel Fire, **1,048** ... E1
Angus, *50* ... E4
Animas, *125* ... B6
Anthony, **7,904** ... D6
Anton Chico, *200* ... E2
Apache Creek ... B4
Arabela, *125* ... E4
Aragon, *150* ... B4
Arch ... G3
Archuleta, *50* ... C1
Arkansas Junction ... G5
Armijo, **9,500** ... D2
Arrey, *150* ... C5
Arroyo Hondo, *550* ... E1
Arroyo Seco, **1,149** ... E1
Artesia, **10,692** ... F5
Atoka, *150* ... F5
Aurora ... E2
Aztec, **6,378** ... C1
Bard, *50* ... G2
Bayard, **2,534** ... B5
Beklabito, *70* ... A1
Belen, **6,901** ... D3
Bell Ranch, *40* ... F2
Bellview ... G3
Bennett, *50* ... G5
Bent ... E4
Berino, *900* ... D5
Bernal, *50* ... E2
Bernalillo, **6,611** ... D2
Bernardo ... D3
Bingham, *50* ... D4
Black Lake ... E1
Black River Village ... F5
Black Rock, **1,252** ... B2
Blanco, *40* ... C1
Blanco Trading Post, *70* ... C1
Bloomfield, **6,417** ... C1
Bluewater, *90* ... C2
Boles Acres, **1,172** ... E5
Bosque Farms, **3,931** ... D3
Brazos, *150* ... D1
Broadview, *40* ... G3
Buckeye ... G5
Buckhorn ... B4
Buena Vista, *70* ... E2
Bueyeros ... G2
Burnham ... B1
Caballo, *80* ... C5
Canjilon, *175* ... D1
Canoncito, *225* ... E2
Canones, *50* ... D1
Canon Plaza, *80* ... D1
Capitan, **1,443** ... E4
Caprock ... G4
Capulin, *50* ... G1
Carlsbad, **25,625** ... F5
Carnero ... E3
Carrizozo, **1,036** ... E4
Carson ... E1
Casa Blanca, **669** ... C2
Causey, **52** ... G4
Cebolla, *50* ... D1
Cebolleta, *70* ... C2
Cedar Grove, **599** ... D2
Cedar Hill, *250* ... C1
Cedarvale ... E3
Central, **1,944** ... B5
Cerro, *150* ... E1
Chacon, *40* ... E1
Chama, **1,199** ... D1
Chamberino, *425* ... D5
Chamisal, **301** ... E1
Chaparral, **6,117** ... D5
Chili, *175* ... D1
Chilili, **113** ... D3
Chimayo, **2,924** ... E1
Chloride ... C4
Church Rock, **1,077** ... B2
Cimarron, **917** ... F1
Claunch ... E3
Clayton, **2,524** ... G1
Cleveland, *175* ... E1
Cliff, *175* ... B5
Clines Corners, *100* ... E2
Cloudcroft, **749** ... E5
Cloverdale, *50* ... B6
Clovis, **32,667** ... G3
Cochiti, **507** ... D2
Colmor ... F1
Colonias ... F2
Columbus, **1,765** ... C6
Conchas Dam ... F2
Continental Divide, *70* ... B2
Coolidge, *50* ... B2
Cordova, *225* ... E1
Corona, **165** ... E3
Corrales, **7,334** ... D2
Correo ... C3
Costilla, *100* ... E1
Cotton City, *100* ... B5
Counselor, *50* ... C1
Cowles ... E2
Coyote (Lincoln Co.) ... E4
Coyote (Rio Arriba Co.), *80* ... D1
Coyote Canyon, *40* ... B2
Crossroads ... G4
Crownpoint, **2,630** ... B2
Cruzville ... B4
Crystal, **347** ... B1
Cuba, **590** ... D1
Cubero, *150* ... C2
Cuchillo, *60* ... C4
Cuervo ... F2
Cuyamungue, **421** ... E2
Dahlia ... E2
Datil, *60* ... C3
Dayton ... F5
Deming, **14,116** ... C5
Derry, *200* ... C5
Des Moines, **177** ... G1
Dexter, **1,235** ... F4
Dilia ... E2
Dixon, *275* ... E1
Domingo, *70* ... D2
Doña Ana, **1,379** ... D5
Dora, **130** ... G4
Dulce, **2,623** ... C1
Dunken ... E5
Duran ... E3
Dwyer ... C5
Eagle Nest, **306** ... E1
Edgewood, **1,893** ... D2
Eldorado at Santa Fe, **5,799** ... E2
Elephant Butte, **1,390** ... C4
Elida, **183** ... G4
Elk ... E5
Elkins ... F4
El Morro, *60* ... B2
El Porvenir ... E2
El Prado, *400* ... E1
El Rito, *425* ... D1
El Vado ... D1
Embudo, *70* ... E1
Encino, **94** ... E3
Endee ... G2
Engle ... C4
Ensenada, *80* ... D1
Escabosa ... D3
Escondida, *150* ... D3
Espanola, **9,688** ... D1
Estancia, **1,584** ... D3
Eunice, **2,562** ... G5
Fairacres, *1,100* ... D5
Farley ... F1
Farmington, **37,844** ... B1
Fence Lake ... B3
Field ... G3
Fierro ... B5
Flora Vista, **1,383** ... B1
Floyd, **78** ... G3
Flying H ... E4
Folsom, **75** ... G1
Forrest ... G3
Fort Stanton, *150* ... E4
Fort Sumner, **1,249** ... F3
Fort Wingate, *550* ... B2
Fruitland, *650* ... B1
Gage ... B5
Galisteo, **265** ... E2
Gallina, *175* ... D1
Gallinas, *40* ... E3
Gallup, **20,209** ... B2
Gamerco, *300* ... B2
Garfield, *175* ... C5
Garrison ... G4
Gascon ... E2
Gavilan, *60* ... C1
Gila, *90* ... B5
Gladiola ... G4
Gladstone ... G1
Glencoe ... E4
Glenrio ... G2
Glenwood, *80* ... B4
Glorieta, **859** ... E2
Gobernador, *60* ... C1
Golden ... D2
Grady, **98** ... G3
Grama, *70* ... C5
Gran Quivira ... D3
Grants, **8,806** ... C2
Greenfield, *175* ... F4
Grenville, **25** ... G1
Grier ... G3
Guadalupita ... E1
Hachita ... B6
Hagerman, **1,168** ... F4
Hanover, *150* ... B5
Hatch, **1,673** ... C5
Hayden ... G2
Hernandez, *600* ... D1
High Rolls, *425* ... E5
Highway ... G4
Hill, *175* ... D5
Hillsboro, *50* ... C5
Hobbs, **28,657** ... G5
Hollene ... G3
Holman, *175* ... E1
Hondo ... E4
Hope, **107** ... F5
Hospah ... C2
House, **72** ... G3
Humble City, *90* ... G5
Hurley, **1,464** ... B5
Ilfeld, *100* ... E2
Isleta, **496** ... D3
Isleta Pueblo ... D3
Jaconita, **343** ... D2
Jal, **1,996** ... G5
Jarales, **1,434** ... D3
Jemez Pueblo, **1,953** ... D2
Jemez Springs, **375** ... D2
Jordan ... G3
Kenna ... G4
Kingston, *125* ... C5
Kirtland, **6,190** ... B1
Knowles ... G5
La Cienega, **3,007** ... D2
La Cueva, *40* ... E2
Laguna, **423** ... C2
La Jara, **209** ... D1
La Joya, *70* ... D3
Lake Arthur, **432** ... F5
Lake Valley, *60* ... B1
Lakewood, *70* ... F5
La Luz, **1,615** ... E5
La Madera, *40* ... D1
La Mesa, *800* ... D5
Lamy, **137** ... E2
La Plata, *60* ... B1
La Puente, *175* ... D1
Las Cruces, **74,267** ... D5
Las Nutrias (Rio Arriba Co.) ... D1
Las Nutrias (Socorro Co.), *70* ... D3
Las Palomas, *100* ... C4
Las Trampas, *100* ... E1
Las Vegas, **14,565** ... E2
La Union, *850* ... D6
Ledoux, *60* ... E2
Lemitar, *400* ... D3
Levy ... F1
Leyba, *70* ... E2
Lincoln, *150* ... E4
Lindrith, *125* ... C1
Lingo ... G4
Llaves, *175* ... D1
Loco Hills, *80* ... G5
Logan, **1,094** ... G2
Lordsburg, **3,379** ... B5
Los Alamos, **11,909** ... D2
Los Cerrillos, *229* ... D2
Los Chavez, **5,033** ... D3
Los Lunas, **10,034** ... D3
Los Montoyas, *275* ... E2
Los Padillas, **1,800** ... D3
Los Pinos ... D1
Los Ranchos de Albuquerque, **5,092** ... D2
Los Trujillo (Los Trujillos-Gabaldon), **2,166** ... D3
Loving, **1,326** ... F5
Lovington, **9,471** ... G5
Lower Colonias ... E2
Lower San Francisco Plaza, *275* ... B4
Luis Lopez, *125* ... D4
Lumberton, *80* ... D1
Luna ... B4
Madrid, **149** ... D2
Maes ... F2
Magdalena, **913** ... C3
Malaga, *100* ... F5
Maljamar ... G5
Mangas Springs ... B5
Manuelito, *125* ... A2
Manzano, **54** ... D3
Mariano Lake, *250* ... B2
Marquez, *250* ... C2
Maxwell, **274** ... F1
Mayhill ... E5
McAlister ... G3
McCartys, *325* ... C2
McDonald ... G4
McGaffey ... B2
McIntosh, *100* ... D3
Meadow Lake, **4,491** ... D3
Medanales, *450* ... D1
Melrose, **736** ... G3
Mentmore, *150* ... B2
Mescalero, **1,233** ... E4
Mesilla, **2,180** ... D5
Mesita, **776** ... C2
Mesquite, **948** ... D5
Mexican Springs, **250** ... B2
Miami ... F1
Midway, *700* ... F4
Miera, *100* ... D3
Milan, **1,891** ... C2
Mills ... F1
Milnesand ... G4
Mimbres, *50* ... C5
Mineral Hill ... E2
Mogollon ... B4
Monero ... D1
Montezuma, *325* ... E2
Monticello, *50* ... C4
Montoya ... F2
Monument, *125* ... G5
Mora, *450* ... E2
Moriarty, **1,765** ... D3
Mosquero, **120** ... G2
Mountainair, **1,116** ... D3
Mount Dora ... G1
Mule Creek, *40* ... B4
Nadine, *175* ... G5
Nageezi, **296** ... C1
Nambe, **1,200** ... E2
Nara Visa, *70* ... G2
Naschitti, **360** ... B1
Navajo, **2,097** ... A2
Newcomb, **387** ... B1
Newkirk ... F2
Nogal ... E4
North Acomita Village, **288** ... C2
North San Ysidro ... E2
North Valley, **11,923** ... D2
Nutt ... C5
Ocate, *100* ... F1
Oil Center ... G5
Ojito ... C1
Ojo Amarillo, **829** ... B1
Ojo Caliente (Cibola Co.) ... B3
Ojo Caliente (Taos Co.), *50* ... D1
Ojo Feliz, *90* ... E1
Old Horse Springs ... B4
Omega, *60* ... B3
Organ, *300* ... D5
Orogrande, *70* ... D5
Oscuro, *40* ... D4
Otis, *175* ... F5
Paguate, **474** ... C2
Pajarito, **2,700** ... D2
Paradise Hills, **5,500** ... D2
Paraje ... C2
Pastura ... F3
Pecos, **1,441** ... E2
Pena Blanca, **661** ... D2
Penasco, **572** ... E1
Pep ... G4
Peralta, **3,750** ... D3
Picacho ... E4
Pie Town ... B3
Pilar, *90* ... E1
Pinedale, *70* ... B2
Pine Hill, **116** ... B2
Pinon ... E5
Pinos Altos ... B5
Pintada, *40* ... E3
Placitas, **3,452** ... D2
Pleasant Hill, *40* ... G3
Pleasanton, *80* ... B4
Pojoaque, **1,261** ... D2
Polvadera, *250* ... D3
Portales, **11,131** ... G3
Prewitt ... B2
Pueblo Pintado, **247** ... C2
Puerto de Luna, *50* ... F3
Punta, *40* ... D3
Quay ... G3
Quemado, *125* ... B3
Questa, **1,864** ... E1
Radium Springs, **1,518** ... D5
Ragland ... G3
Rainsville, *100* ... E2
Ramah, **407** ... B2
Ramon, **20** ... F3
Ranchito, *800* ... E1
Ranchos de Taos, **2,390** ... E1
Ranchvale ... G3
Raton, **7,282** ... F1
Red Hill, *90* ... B3
Red River, **484** ... E1
Redrock ... B5
Regina, **99** ... D1
Rehoboth, *375* ... B2
Rencona ... E2
Reserve, **387** ... B4
Ribera, *125* ... E2
Rincon, **220** ... C5
Rio Communities, **4,213** ... D3
Rio Rancho, **51,765** ... D2
Riverside (Eddy Co.), *40* ... F5
Riverside (Lincoln Co.) ... E4
Rodarte, *350* ... E1
Rodeo, *100* ... A6
Rogers ... G4
Romeroville ... E2
Rosebud ... G2
Roswell, **45,293** ... F4
Rowe ... E2
Roy, **304** ... F2
Ruidoso, **7,698** ... E4
Ruidoso Downs, **1,824** ... E4
Rutheron, *90* ... D1
Sabinal, *100* ... D3
Sabinoso ... F2
Sacramento, *50* ... E5
St. Vrain ... G3
Salem, **795** ... C5
San Acacia, *100* ... D3
San Antonio, *125* ... D4
San Antonito ... D3
Sanchez ... F2
San Cristobal, *150* ... E1
Sandia ... D2
Sandia Pueblo ... D2
San Felipe Pueblo, **2,080** ... D2
San Fidel, *60* ... C2
San Ignacio ... E2
San Ildefonso Pueblo, **458** ... D2
San Jon, **306** ... G2
San Jose ... E2
San Juan (Grant Co.), *50* ... C5
San Juan (Rio Arriba Co.), **592** ... D1
San Juan Pueblo ... D1
San Lorenzo, *40* ... C5
San Marcial, *175* ... D4
San Mateo, *225* ... C2
San Miguel (Doña Ana Co.), *1,100* ... D5
San Miguel (Rio Arriba Co.) ... D1
Sanostee, **429** ... B1
San Patricio ... E4
San Rafael, *175* ... C2
Santa Ana Pueblo, **479** ... D2
Santa Clara Pueblo, **980** ... D2
Santa Cruz, **423** ... D2
Santa Fe, **62,203** ... E2
Santa Rosa, **2,744** ... F3
Santo Domingo Pueblo, **2,550** ... D2
San Ysidro, **238** ... D2
Sapello ... E2
Scholle ... D3
Seama, **333** ... C2
Sedan ... G1
Sena, *250* ... E2
Seneca ... G1
Separ ... B5
Serafina, *50* ... E2
Seven Lakes ... C2
Seven Rivers, *125* ... F5
Shady Brook, *200* ... E1
Sheep Springs, **237** ... B1
Sherman, *90* ... C5
Shiprock, **8,156** ... B1
Silver City, **10,545** ... B5
Socorro, **8,877** ... D3
Sofia ... G1
Solano ... F2
Springer, **1,285** ... F1
Standing Rock, *60* ... B2
Stanley ... E2
Star Lake, *150* ... C2
Stead ... G1
Steins, *60* ... B5
Summit, *150* ... B5
Sunland Park, **13,309** ... D6
Sunshine, *90* ... C5
Sunspot, *80* ... E5
Taiban ... F3
Tajique, **148** ... D3
Taos, **4,700** ... E1
Taos Pueblo, **1,264** ... E1
Tatum, **683** ... G4
Tecolote, *125* ... E2
Tererro ... E2
Tesuque, **909** ... E2
Tesuque Pueblo, *225* ... E2
Texico, **1,065** ... G3
Thoreau, **1,863** ... B2
Three Rivers ... D4
Tierra Amarilla, *90* ... D1
Tijeras, **474** ... D2
Timberon, **309** ... E5
Tinnie ... E4
Toadlena, *125* ... B1
Tocito, *60* ... B1
Tohatchi, **1,037** ... B2
Tolar ... G3
Tome, **2,211** ... D3
Torreon (Sandoval Co.), **297** ... C2
Torreon (Torrance Co.), **244** ... D3
Totavi ... D2
Trementina ... F2
Tres Piedras ... E1
Tres Ritos ... E1
Truchas, *125* ... E1
Trujillo ... F2
Truth or Consequences, **7,289** ... C4
Tucumcari, **5,989** ... G2
Tularosa, **2,864** ... D4
Turley, *425* ... C1
Turn, *125* ... D3
Twin Lakes, **1,069** ... B2
Tyrone, *500* ... B5
University Park, **2,732** ... D5
Upper Nutria ... B2
Ute Park ... E1
Vadito, **242** ... E1
Vado, **3,003** ... D5
Valdez, *250* ... E1
Valencia, **4,500** ... D3
Vallecitos, *200* ... D1
Valmont, *100* ... E5
Valmora, *125* ... F2
Variadero ... F2
Vaughn, **539** ... E3
Veguita, *100* ... D3
Velarde, *325* ... E1
Villanueva, *70* ... E2
Virden, **143** ... B5
Wagon Mound, **369** ... F1
Waterflow, *175* ... B1
Watrous ... F2
Weed, *60* ... E5
Wheatland ... G3
White Horse ... C2
White Lakes ... E2
White Oaks ... E4
White Rock (Los Alamos Co.), **6,045** ... D2
White Rock (San Juan Co.) ... B1
White Sands ... D5
Whites City, *40* ... F5
White Signal ... B5
Whitewater (Grant Co.) ... B5
Whitewater (McKinley Co.) ... B2
Willard, **240** ... D3
Williamsburg, **527** ... C4
Winston ... C4
Yah-Tah-Hey, **580** ... B2
Yates ... G1
Yeso ... F3
Youngsville ... D1
Zia Pueblo, **646** ... D2
Zuni Pueblo, **6,367** ... B2

Other Features

Abiquiu, *reservoir* ... D1
Acoma Indian Res. ... C3
Alamo Band Navajo I.R. ... C3
Alegres, *mountain* ... B3
Apache Natl. Forest ... A4, B4
Aztec Ruins N.M. ... C1
Baldy, *mountain* ... E1
Bandelier N.M. ... D2
Bitter Lake N.W.R. ... F4
Black, *range* ... C4
Bosque Del Apache N.W.R. ... D4
Burro, *peak* ... B5
Caballo, *reservoir* ... C5
Canadian, *river* ... F1
Cannon A.F.B. ... G3
Canyon De Chelly Natl. Mon. ... A1
Capulin Volcano N.M. ... F1
Carlsbad Caverns Natl. Park ... F5
Carson National Forest ... C1, D1, E1
Cebolleta, *peak* ... C3
Cerro Vista, *peak* ... E1
Chaco Culture N.H.P. ... C1
Cibola National Forest ... B2, C3, C4, D3, E3
Cimarron, *river* ... G1
Cochiti I.R. ... D2
Conchas, *lake* ... F2
Continental Divide ... C2
Cooke's, *peak* ... C5
Coronado National Forest ... A6
Elephant Butte, *reservoir* ... C4
El Malpais Natl. Monument and Conservation Area ... B3
El Morro N.M. ... B3
Fort Bliss Mil. Res. ... D5
Fort Union N.M. ... F2
Gallinas, *peak* ... E3
Gila, *river* ... B5
Gila Cliff Dwellings N.M. ... B4
Gila National Forest ... B4, B5
Grulla N.W.R. ... G3
Guadalupe, *mountains* ... E5
Guadalupe, *peak* ... F6
Guadalupe Mts. Natl. Park ... F6
Holloman A.F.B. ... D5
Hueco, *mountains* ... D6
Isleta Indian Res. ... D3
Jemez Ind. Res. ... D2
Jicarilla Apache Ind. Res. ... C1
Jornada Del Muerto ... D4
Kasha-Katuwe Tent Rocks Natl. Mon. ... D2
Kiowa Natl. Grassland ... F1, G1
Laguna I.R. ... C3
Las Vegas N.W.R. ... E2
Lincoln National Forest ... E4, E5
Llano Estacado, *plains* ... G4
Mancos, *river* ... B1
Maxwell N.W.R. ... F1
Mesa Verde Natl. Park ... B1
Mescalero Apache Indian Res. ... E4
Navajo, *reservoir* ... C1
Navajo Indian Res. ... A1, B2
Pecos, *plains* ... F4
Pecos, *river* ... F2, F5
Pecos N.H.P. ... E2
Petroglyph N.M. ... D2
Playas, *lake* ... B6
Ramah Navajo I.R. ... B3
Reeds, *peak* ... C4
Rio Grande, *river* ... E1
Rio Hondo, *river* ... F4
Rio Puerco, *river* ... C2
Salinas Pueblo Missions N.M. ... D3
Salt Basin, *dry lake* ... E6
San Andres, *mountains* ... D5
San Andres N.W.R. ... D5
Sangre De Cristo, *mountains* ... E1
San Juan, *river* ... B1
Santa Fe N.F. ... D1, E2
Sevilleta N.W.R. ... C3
Shiprock, *peak* ... B1
Sierra Blanca, *mountains* ... E4
South Baldy, *peak* ... C3
Southern Ute Indian Res. ... B1
Sumner, *lake* ... F3
Taos I.R. ... E1
Taylor, *mountain* ... C2
Ute Mountain I.R. ... B1
Wheeler, *peak* ... E1
White Sands Missile Range ... D4
White Sands Natl. Mon. ... D5
Whitewater Baldy, *peak* ... B4
Withington, *mountain* ... C4
Zia Ind. Res. ... D2
Zuni, *mountains* ... B2
Zuni Indian Res. ... B2

New York

Capital: Albany
Land Area: 47,224 sq. mi.
122,310 sq. km.
Population: 18,976,457 (2000 Census)
Largest City: New York, 8,008,278
Highest Point: Mt. Marcy, 5,344 ft. 1,629 m.
Admitted to Union: July 26, 1788
Nickname: Empire State
State Flower: Rose
State Bird: Bluebird

New York: Map Index

Counties

Albany, 294,565 ...N5
Allegany, 49,927 ...F6
Bronx, 1,332,650 ...B2
Broome, 200,536 ...K6
Cattaraugus, 83,955 ...D6
Cayuga, 81,963 ...J5
Chautauqua, 139,750 ...C6
Chemung, 91,070 ...H6
Chenango, 51,401 ...K6
Clinton, 79,894 ...P1
Columbia, 63,094 ...P6
Cortland, 48,599 ...J5
Delaware, 48,055 ...L6
Dutchess, 280,150 ...P7
Erie, 950,265 ...D5
Essex, 38,851 ...P2
Franklin, 51,134 ...N1
Fulton, 55,073 ...N4
Genesee, 60,370 ...E5
Greene, 48,195 ...N6
Hamilton, 5,379 ...M3
Herkimer, 64,427 ...M4
Jefferson, 111,738 ...K2
Kings, 2,465,326 ...B2
Lewis, 26,944 ...K3
Livingston, 64,328 ...F5
Madison, 69,441 ...K5
Monroe, 735,343 ...F4
Montgomery, 49,708 ...N5
Nassau, 1,334,544 ...C2
New York, 1,537,195 ...B2
Niagara, 219,846 ...D4
Oneida, 235,469 ...K4
Onondaga, 458,336 ...J5
Ontario, 100,224 ...G5
Orange, 341,367 ...A1, N8
Orleans, 44,171 ...E4
Oswego, 122,377 ...J4
Otsego, 61,676 ...M5
Putnam, 95,745 ...P8
Queens, 2,229,379 ...B2
Rensselaer, 152,538 ...Q5
Richmond, 443,728 ...A1
Rockland, 286,753 ...A1
St. Lawrence, 111,931 ...L2
Saratoga, 200,635 ...P4
Schenectady, 146,555 ...N5
Schoharie, 31,582 ...N5
Schuyler, 19,224 ...H6
Seneca, 33,342 ...H5
Steuben, 98,726 ...G6
Suffolk, 1,419,369 ...E2
Sullivan, 73,966 ...M7
Tioga, 51,784 ...J6
Tompkins, 96,501 ...J5
Ulster, 177,749 ...N7
Warren, 63,303 ...P3
Washington, 61,042 ...Q4
Wayne, 93,765 ...G4
Westchester, 923,459 ...C1
Wyoming, 43,424 ...E5
Yates, 24,621 ...G5

Cities and Towns

Acra, 550 ...N6
Adams, 1,624 ...K3
Adams Center, 1,500 ...K3
Addison, 1,797 ...G6
Afton, 836 ...K6
Airmont, 7,799 ...A1
Akron, 3,085 ...E4
Albany, 95,658 ...P5
Albion, 7,438 ...E4
Alden, 2,666 ...E5
Alder Creek, 200 ...L4
Alexander, 481 ...E5
Alexandria Bay, 1,088 ...K2
Alfred, 3,954 ...F6
Allegany, 1,883 ...D6
Almond, 461 ...F6
Alpine, 275 ...H6
Altamont, 1,737 ...N5
Altmar, 351 ...K3
Alton, 475 ...H4
Altona, 1,056 ...P1
Amagansett, 1,067 ...G1
Amenia, 1,115 ...P7
Ames, 173 ...M5
Amherst, 13,200 ...D5
Amityville, 9,441 ...C2
Amsterdam, 18,355 ...N5
Andes, 289 ...M6
Andover, 1,073 ...F6
Angelica, 903 ...F5
Angola, 2,266 ...C5
Angola on the Lake, 1,771 ...C5
Antwerp, 716 ...K2
Apalachin, 1,126 ...J6
Aquebogue, 2,254 ...F1
Arcade, 2,026 ...E5
Ardsley, 4,269 ...A1
Argyle, 289 ...Q4
Arkport, 832 ...G6
Arlington, 12,481 ...P7
Asharoken, 625 ...D2
Ashford Hollow, 100 ...D6
Athens, 1,695 ...P6
Atlanta, 650 ...G5
Atlantic Beach, 1,986 ...C3
Attica, 2,597 ...E5
Auburn, 28,574 ...H5
Aurora, 720 ...H5
Au Sable Forks, 670 ...P2
Averill Park, 1,517 ...P5
Avoca, 1,008 ...G6
Avon, 2,977 ...F5
Babylon, 12,615 ...D2
Bainbridge, 1,365 ...L6
Bakers Mills, 60 ...N3
Baldwinsville, 7,053 ...J4
Ballston Spa, 5,556 ...P5
Barker, 577 ...D4
Barnes Corners, 50 ...K3
Barneveld, 332 ...L4
Barryville, 125 ...M8
Batavia, 16,256 ...E4
Bayport, 8,662 ...E2
Bayville, 7,135 ...C2
Beacon, 13,808 ...P7
Bedford, 1,724 ...C1
Belfast, 800 ...F6
Belle Terre, 832 ...E1
Bellport, 2,363 ...E2
Belmont, 952 ...F6
Bemus Point, 340 ...C6
Bergen, 1,240 ...F4
Berkshire, 300 ...J6
Big Flats, 2,482 ...H6
Big Moose ...M3
Billington Heights, 1,691 ...D5
Binghamton, 47,380 ...K6
Black River, 1,285 ...J3
Blasdell, 2,718 ...D5
Bliss, 375 ...E5
Bloomfield, 1,267 ...G5
Bloomingburg, 353 ...N7
Bolivar, 1,173 ...E6
Bombay, 325 ...M1
Boonville, 2,138 ...L4
Branchport, 375 ...G5
Brandreth ...M3
Brasher Falls (Brasher Falls-Winthrop), 1,140 ...M1
Brentwood, 53,917 ...D2
Brewerton, 3,453 ...J4
Brewster, 2,162 ...P8
Brewster Hill, 2,226 ...P8
Briarcliff Manor, 7,696 ...B1
Bridgehampton, 1,381 ...G1
Bridgeport, 1,665 ...K4
Bridgewater, 579 ...L5
Brier Hill, 200 ...K1
Brighton, 35,584 ...F4
Brinckerhoff, 2,734 ...P7
Broadalbin, 1,411 ...N4
Brockport, 8,103 ...F4
Brocton, 1,547 ...C6
Bronx (see New York) ...B2
Bronxville, 6,543 ...B2
Brooklyn (see New York) ...B2
Brookville, 2,126 ...C2
Brownville, 1,022 ...K2
Brushton, 479 ...M1
Buchanan, 2,189 ...B1
Buffalo, 292,648 ...D5
Burdett, 357 ...H6
Burke, 213 ...N1
Cairo, 1,390 ...N6
Calcium, 3,346 ...K2
Caledonia, 2,327 ...F5
Callicoon, 216 ...L7
Calverton, 5,704 ...F2
Cambridge, 1,925 ...Q4
Camden, 2,330 ...K4
Camillus, 1,249 ...J4
Canajoharie, 2,257 ...M5
Canandaigua, 11,264 ...G5
Canaseraga, 594 ...F6
Canastota, 4,425 ...K4
Candor, 855 ...J6
Canisteo, 2,336 ...G6
Canton, 5,882 ...L1
Cape Vincent, 760 ...J2
Carlisle, 325 ...N5
Carmel, 5,650 ...P8
Caroga Lake, 500 ...N4
Carthage, 3,721 ...K3
Cassadaga, 676 ...C6
Cassville, 250 ...L5
Castile, 1,051 ...E5
Castleton-on-Hudson, 1,619 ...P5
Castorland, 306 ...L3
Cato, 601 ...J4
Cattaraugus, 1,075 ...D6
Cayuga, 509 ...H5
Cayuga Hts., 3,273 ...J6
Cazenovia, 2,614 ...K5
Cedarhurst, 6,164 ...C3
Cedarville, 325 ...L5
Celoron, 1,295 ...C6
Centereach, 27,285 ...E2
Center Moriches, 6,655 ...F2
Centerville, 150 ...E6
Central Bridge, 900 ...N5
Central Islip, 31,950 ...D2
Central Square, 1,646 ...J4
Central Valley, 1,857 ...A1
Champlain, 1,173 ...Q1
Champlain Park (part of Cumberland Head, pop. 1,532) ...Q1
Chateaugay, 798 ...N1
Chatham, 1,758 ...P6
Chaumont, 592 ...J2
Chazy, 600 ...Q1
Cheektowaga, 79,988 ...D5
Chenango Bridge, 4,100 ...K6
Cherry Creek, 551 ...C6
Cherryplain, 90 ...Q5
Cherry Valley, 592 ...M5
Chester, 3,445 ...A1
Chestnut Ridge, 7,829 ...B1
Childwold, 50 ...M2
Churchville, 1,887 ...F4
Cincinnatus, 600 ...K5
Clarence Center, 1,747 ...D4
Clark Mills, 1,424 ...L4
Clayton, 1,821 ...J2
Clayville, 445 ...L5
Cleveland, 758 ...K4
Clifton Park, 4,600 ...P5
Clifton Springs, 2,223 ...G5
Clinton, 1,952 ...L4
Clintondale, 1,424 ...N7
Clyde, 2,269 ...H4
Cobleskill, 4,533 ...N5
Cohocton, 854 ...F5
Cohoes, 15,521 ...P5
Cold Brook, 336 ...L4
Colden, 700 ...D5
Cold Spring, 1,983 ...P8
Colonie, 7,916 ...P5
Colton, 450 ...M1
Commack, 36,367 ...D2
Conklin, 850 ...K6
Constableville, 305 ...L3
Constantia, 1,107 ...J4
Cooperstown, 2,032 ...M5
Copenhagen, 865 ...K3
Coram, 34,923 ...E2
Corfu, 795 ...E5
Corinth, 2,474 ...P4
Corning, 10,842 ...G6
Cornwall on Hudson, 3,058 ...N8
Cortland, 18,740 ...J5
Country Knolls, 2,155 ...P5
Coxsackie, 2,895 ...P6
Croghan, 85 ...L3
Croton-on-Hudson, 7,606 ...B1
Crown Heights, 2,992 ...P7
Cuba, 1,633 ...E6
Cutchogue, 2,849 ...F1
Dannemora, 4,129 ...P1
Dansville, 4,832 ...F5
Davenport, 60 ...M6
Deer Park, 28,316 ...D2
Deferiet, 309 ...K2
De Kalb Junction, 450 ...L2
De Lancey, 150 ...M6
Delanson, 385 ...N5
Delevan, 1,089 ...E6
Delhi, 2,583 ...M6
Delmar, 8,292 ...P5
Depew, 16,629 ...D5
Deposit, 1,699 ...L6
Derby, 900 ...D5
Dering Harbor, 13 ...G1
DeRuyter, 531 ...K5
De Witt, 8,200 ...J4
Dexter, 1,120 ...J2
Dobbs Ferry, 10,622 ...B1
Dolgeville, 2,166 ...M4
Dover Plains, 1,996 ...P7
Downsville, 325 ...L6
Dresden, 307 ...H5
Dryden, 1,832 ...J6
Dundee, 1,690 ...H6
Dunkirk, 13,131 ...C6
Earlville, 791 ...K5
East Aurora, 6,673 ...D5
East Branch, 250 ...L7
East Cayuga Hts. ...J6
East Glenville, 6,064 ...P5
East Greenbush, 4,085 ...P5
East Hampton, 1,334 ...G1
East Hampton North, 3,587 ...G1
East Hills, 6,842 ...C2
East Ithaca, 2,192 ...J6
East Meredith, 150 ...M6
East Moriches, 4,550 ...F2
Eastport, 1,454 ...F2
East Quogue, 4,265 ...F2
East Randolph, 630 ...D6
East Rochester, 6,650 ...G5
East Rockaway, 10,414 ...C2
East Shoreham, 5,809 ...E1
East Syracuse, 3,178 ...J4
East Wilson, 175 ...D4
Eden, 3,579 ...D5
Edenville, 650 ...A1
Edgewater, 225 ...N6
Edmeston, 575 ...L5
Edwards, 465 ...L2
Elba, 696 ...E4
Elbridge, 1,103 ...J4
Eldred, 375 ...M7
Elizabethtown, 750 ...P2
Ellenburg Depot, 300 ...P1
Ellenville, 4,130 ...N7
Ellicott, 2,200 ...D5
Ellicottville, 472 ...D6
Ellington, 300 ...C6
Ellisburg, 269 ...J3
Elma, 2,491 ...D5
Elmira, 30,940 ...H6
Elmira Heights, 4,170 ...H6
Elmont, 32,657 ...C2
Elmsford, 4,676 ...B1
Endicott, 13,038 ...J6
Endwell, 11,706 ...J6
Esperance, 380 ...N5
Essex, 175 ...Q2
Evans Mills, 605 ...K2
Fabius, 355 ...J5
Fair Haven, 884 ...H4
Fairmount, 10,795 ...J4
Fairport, 5,740 ...F4
Fairview, 5,421 ...P7
Falconer, 2,540 ...C6
Farmington, 475 ...G5
Farnham, 322 ...C5
Fayette, 275 ...H5
Fayetteville, 4,190 ...K4
Fernwood, 2,600 ...P4
Fillmore, 450 ...E6
Fine, 200 ...L2
Fisherville (part of Big Flats Airport, pop. 2,184), 400 ...H6
Fishkill, 1,735 ...P7
Flanders, 3,646 ...F2
Fleischmanns, 351 ...M6
Floral Park, 15,967 ...C2
Florida, 2,571 ...A1
Fonda, 810 ...N5
Forest Home, 941 ...J6
Forestville, 770 ...C6
Fort Ann, 471 ...Q4
Fort Covington, 700 ...N1
Fort Edward, 3,141 ...P4
Fort Johnson, 491 ...N5
Fort Plain, 2,288 ...M5
Fowler, 300 ...L2
Frankfort, 2,537 ...L4
Franklin, 402 ...L6
Franklin Square, 29,342 ...B2
Franklinville, 1,855 ...E6
Fredonia, 10,706 ...C6
Freeport, 43,783 ...C2
Freeville, 505 ...J5
Frewsburg, 1,965 ...C6
Friendship, 1,176 ...E6
Fulton, 11,855 ...J4
Fultonville, 710 ...N5
Gainesville, 304 ...E5
Galway, 214 ...N4
Gang Mills, 3,304 ...G6
Gansevoort, 800 ...P4
Gasport, 1,248 ...D4
Gates, 15,138 ...F4
Geneseo, 7,509 ...F5
Geneva, 13,617 ...H5
Gilbertsville, 375 ...L6
Glasco, 1,692 ...P6
Glen Cove, 26,622 ...C2
Glenfield, 475 ...L3
Glen Park, 487 ...K2
Glens Falls, 14,354 ...P4
Gloversville, 15,413 ...N4
Golden Bridge, 1,578 ...C1
Gorham, 650 ...G5
Goshen, 5,676 ...N8
Gouverneur, 4,263 ...L2
Gowanda, 2,842 ...D6
Granville, 2,644 ...Q4
Great Neck, 9,538 ...C2
Great Neck Plaza, 6,433 ...C2
Greece, 14,614 ...F4
Greene, 1,701 ...K6
Green Island, 2,278 ...P5
Greenport, 2,048 ...G1
Greenville, 493 ...N6
Greenwich, 1,902 ...Q4
Greenwood, 325 ...F6
Greenwood Lake, 3,411 ...A1
Groton, 2,470 ...J5
Hadley (see Lake Luzerne), 2,240 ...P4
Hagaman, 1,357 ...N5
Hague, 150 ...P3
Hamburg, 10,116 ...D5
Hamilton, 3,509 ...K5
Hammond, 302 ...K2
Hammondsport, 731 ...G6
Hampton Bays, 12,236 ...F2
Hampton Manor, 2,525 ...P5
Hancock, 1,189 ...L7
Hannawa Falls, 550 ...M1
Hannibal, 542 ...H4
Harriman, 2,252 ...A1
Harris Hill, 4,881 ...D5
Harrison, 24,154 ...C1
Harrisville, 653 ...L2
Hartwick, 550 ...L5
Hastings-on-Hudson, 7,648 ...B1
Haverstraw, 10,117 ...B1
Head of the Harbor, 1,447 ...D2
Helena, 40 ...M1
Hempstead, 56,554 ...C2
Henrietta, 6,600 ...F4
Herkimer, 7,498 ...M4
Hermon, 402 ...L2
Herrings, 129 ...K2
Heuvelton, 804 ...L1
Hicksville, 41,260 ...C2
Higgins Bay ...M4
Highland, 5,060 ...P7
Highland Falls, 3,678 ...B1
Highland Mills, 3,468 ...A1
Hillburn, 881 ...A1
Hillsdale, 375 ...P6
Hillside Lake, 2,022 ...P7
Hilton, 5,856 ...F4
Hobart, 390 ...M6
Hoffmeister, 40 ...M4
Hogansburg, 450 ...M1
Holbrook, 27,512 ...E2
Holland, 1,261 ...D5
Holland Patent, 461 ...L4
Holley, 1,802 ...E4
Homer, 3,368 ...J5
Honeoye, 800 ...G5
Honeoye Falls, 2,595 ...F5
Hoosick Falls, 3,436 ...Q5
Hopewell Junction, 2,610 ...P7
Hornell, 9,019 ...F6
Horseheads, 6,452 ...H6
Houghton, 1,748 ...E5
Hudson, 7,524 ...P6
Hudson Falls, 6,927 ...P4
Hunter, 490 ...N6
Huntington Bay, 1,496 ...D2
Huntington Station, 29,910 ...D2
Hurley, 3,561 ...N7
Hyde Park, 2,900 ...P7
Ilion, 8,610 ...L4
Indian Lake, 325 ...N3
Inlet, 70 ...M3
Interlaken, 674 ...H5
Irondequoit, 52,354 ...F4
Irvington, 6,631 ...B1
Islandia, 3,057 ...D2
Island Park, 4,732 ...C3
Ithaca, 29,287 ...J6
Jamaica (see New York) ...B2
Jamesport, 1,526 ...F1
Jamestown, 31,730 ...C6
Jamesville, 550 ...J5
Jasper, 375 ...G6
Java Center, 225 ...E5
Jay, 350 ...P2
Jefferson Heights, 1,104 ...P6
Jefferson Valley, 14,891 ...B1
Jeffersonville, 420 ...M7
Johnsburg, 175 ...P3
Johnson City, 15,535 ...K6
Johnstown, 8,511 ...N4
Jordan, 1,314 ...J4
Keene, 100 ...P2
Keeseville, 1,850 ...Q1
Kendall, 750 ...E4
Kenmore, 16,426 ...D5
Kerhonkson, 1,732 ...N7
Keuka, 150 ...G6
Kinderhook, 1,275 ...P6
Kingston, 23,456 ...P7
Kiryas Joel, 13,138 ...A1
Lackawanna, 19,064 ...D5
Lacona, 590 ...J3
La Fargeville, 588 ...K2
Lake Carmel, 8,663 ...P8
Lake Clear Junction, 100 ...N2
Lake Erie Beach, 4,499 ...C5
Lake George, 985 ...P4
Lake Grove, 10,250 ...E2
Lake Katrine, 2,396 ...P7
Lake Luzerne (Lake Luzerne-Hadley), 2,240 ...P4
Lake Placid, 2,638 ...N2
Lake Pleasant, 100 ...N4
Lake Success, 2,797 ...C2
Lake View, 2,100 ...D5
Lakewood, 3,258 ...C6
Lancaster, 11,188 ...D5
Lansing, 3,417 ...J5
Larchmont, 6,485 ...C2
Lattingtown, 1,860 ...C2
Laurel, 1,188 ...F1
Laurens, 277 ...L5
Lawrence, 6,522 ...C3
Leicester, 469 ...F5
Leonardsville, 275 ...L5
Le Roy, 4,462 ...E5
Levittown, 53,067 ...C2
Lewiston, 2,781 ...C4
Liberty, 3,975 ...M7
Lima, 2,459 ...F5
Lime Lake (Lime Lake-Machias), 1,422 ...E6
Limestone, 411 ...D6
Lindenhurst, 27,819 ...D2
Lindley, 225 ...G6
Lisbon, 400 ...L1
Lisle, 302 ...J6
Little Falls, 5,188 ...M4
Little Valley, 1,130 ...D6
Liverpool, 2,505 ...J4
Livingston Manor, 1,355 ...M7
Livonia, 1,373 ...F5
Lloyd Harbor, 3,675 ...C2
Locke, 550 ...J5
Lockport, 22,279 ...D4
Lodi, 338 ...H5
Long Beach, 35,462 ...C3
Long Eddy, 100 ...L7
Long Lake, 325 ...N3
Loon Lake ...N1
Loudonville, 10,800 ...P5
Lowville, 3,476 ...K3
Ludlowville, 600 ...H5
Lynbrook, 19,911 ...C2
Lyncourt, 4,268 ...J4
Lyndonville, 862 ...E4
Lyon Mountain, 458 ...P1
Lyons, 3,695 ...H4
Lyons Falls, 591 ...L3
Macedon, 1,496 ...G4
Machias (see Lime Lake), 1,422 ...E6
Madison, 315 ...K5
Madrid, 657 ...L1
Mahopac, 8,478 ...C1, P8
Maine, 1,000 ...J6
Malone, 6,075 ...N1
Malverne, 8,934 ...C2
Mamaroneck, 18,752 ...C2
Manchester, 1,475 ...G5
Manhasset, 8,362 ...C2
Manlius, 4,819 ...K4
Mannsville, 400 ...J3
Manorhaven, 6,138 ...C2
Manorville, 11,131 ...F2
Marathon, 1,063 ...J6
Marcellus, 1,826 ...J5
Margaretville, 643 ...M6
Marion, 1,400 ...G4
Marlboro, 2,339 ...P7
Masonville, 225 ...L6
Massena, 11,209 ...M1
Mastic, 15,436 ...E2
Mastic Beach, 11,543 ...F2
Mattituck, 4,198 ...F1
Mattydale, 6,367 ...J4
Maybrook, 3,084 ...N8
Mayfield, 800 ...N4
Mayville, 1,756 ...B6
McGraw, 1,000 ...J5
Mechanicville, 5,019 ...P5
Medford, 21,985 ...E2
Medina, 6,415 ...E4
Melrose Park, 2,359 ...H5
Menands, 3,910 ...P5
Meridian, 350 ...H4
Merrill, 125 ...P1
Mexico, 1,572 ...J4
Middleburgh, 1,398 ...N5
Middleport, 1,917 ...D4
Middlesex, 275 ...G5
Middletown, 25,388 ...N8
Middleville, 550 ...M4
Milford, 511 ...M5
Millbrook, 1,429 ...P7
Miller Place, 10,580 ...E1
Millerton, 925 ...P7
Millport, 297 ...H6
Milton (Saratoga Co.), 1,251 ...P4
Milton (Ulster Co.), 1,251 ...N7
Mineola, 19,234 ...C2
Minerva, 125 ...P3
Minetto, 1,086 ...J4
Mineville (Mineville-Witherbee), 1,747 ...P2
Minoa, 3,348 ...J4
Mohawk, 2,660 ...M5
Monroe, 7,780 ...A1
Montebello, 3,688 ...A1
Montgomery, 3,636 ...N7
Monticello, 6,512 ...M7
Montour Falls, 1,797 ...H6
Mooers, 440 ...P1
Moravia, 1,363 ...J5
Morris, 591 ...L5
Morrisonville, 1,702 ...P1
Morristown, 456 ...K1
Morrisville, 2,148 ...K5
Mount Kisco, 9,983 ...B1
Mount Morris, 3,266 ...F5
Mount Sinai, 8,734 ...E1
Mount Upton, 175 ...L6
Mount Vernon (Erie Co.), 4,400 ...D5
Mount Vernon (Westchester Co.), 68,381 ...B2
Mumford, 600 ...F5
Munnsville, 437 ...K5
Munsons Corners, 2,426 ...J5
Muttontown, 3,412 ...C2
Napanoch, 1,168 ...N7
Naples, 1,072 ...G5
Narrowsburg, 414 ...L7
Nassau, 1,161 ...P5
Natural Bridge, 392 ...K2
Nelliston, 622 ...M5
Nelsonville, 565 ...P8
Newark, 9,682 ...G4
Newark Valley, 1,071 ...J6
New Berlin, 1,129 ...L5
Newburgh, 28,259 ...N7
New City, 34,038 ...B1
Newcomb, 40 ...N3
Newfane, 3,129 ...D4
Newfield, 647 ...H6
New Hartford, 1,886 ...L4
New Haven, 375 ...J4
New Hempstead, 4,767 ...B1
New Hyde Park, 9,523 ...C2
New Paltz, 6,034 ...N7
Newport, 640 ...L4
New Rochelle, 72,182 ...B2
New Square, 4,624 ...B1
Newton Falls, 225 ...M2
New Windsor, 9,077 ...N8
New York, 8,008,278 ...B2
New York Mills, 3,191 ...L4
Niagara Falls, 55,593 ...C4
Nichols, 574 ...J6
Nicholville, 150 ...M1
Niskayuna, 4,892 ...P5
Nissequogue, 1,543 ...D2
Niverville, 1,737 ...P6
Norfolk, 1,334 ...M1
North Boston, 2,680 ...D5
North Chili, 4,300 ...F4
North Collins, 1,079 ...D5
North Creek, 425 ...P3
North Haven, 743 ...G1
North Hornell, 851 ...F6
North Hudson ...P3
North Patchogue, 7,825 ...E2
North Rose, 700 ...H4
North Sea, 4,493 ...G1
North Syracuse, 6,862 ...J4
North Tonawanda, 33,262 ...D4
Northport, 7,606 ...D2
Northville, 1,133 ...N4
Northwest Harbor, 3,059 ...G1
Norwich, 7,355 ...K5
Norwood, 1,685 ...M1
Noyack, 2,696 ...G1
Nunda, 1,330 ...F5
Nyack, 6,737 ...B1
Oakfield, 1,805 ...E4
Ocean Beach, 138 ...D2
Oceanside, 32,733 ...C2
Odessa, 617 ...H6
Ogdensburg, 12,364 ...L1
Olcott, 1,156 ...D4
Old Field, 947 ...D1
Old Forge, 800 ...M3
Olean, 15,347 ...E6
Oneida, 10,987 ...K4
Oneida Castle, 627 ...K4
Oneonta, 13,292 ...L6
Orchard Park, 3,294 ...D5
Oriskany, 1,459 ...L4
Oriskany Falls, 698 ...L5
Osceola, 50 ...L3
Ossining, 24,010 ...B1
Oswego, 17,954 ...J4
Otego, 1,052 ...L6
Otisville, 989 ...M8
Otselic, 90 ...K5
Ovid, 612 ...H5
Owego, 3,911 ...J6
Oxford, 1,584 ...K6
Painted Post, 1,842 ...G6
Palatine Bridge, 706 ...M5
Palenville, 1,120 ...N6
Palmyra, 3,490 ...G4
Panama, 491 ...C6
Parish, 512 ...J4
Parishville, 600 ...M1
Parksville, 150 ...M7
Patchogue, 11,919 ...E2
Patterson, 950 ...P7
Paul Smiths, 50 ...N2
Pavilion, 550 ...E5
Pawling, 2,233 ...P7
Peach Lake, 1,671 ...C1, P8
Pearl River, 15,553 ...B1
Peconic, 1,081 ...F1
Peekskill, 22,441 ...B1
Pelham, 6,400 ...B2
Pelham Manor, 5,466 ...B2
Penn Yan, 5,219 ...G5
Perry, 3,945 ...F5
Perrysburg, 408 ...C5
Peru, 1,514 ...P1
Petersburg, 350 ...Q5
Phelps, 1,969 ...G5
Philadelphia, 1,519 ...K2
Philmont, 1,480 ...P6
Phoenicia, 381 ...N6
Phoenix, 2,251 ...J4
Piercefield, 150 ...M2
Piermont, 2,607 ...B1
Pike, 382 ...E5
Pine Bush, 1,539 ...N7
Pine Plains, 1,412 ...P7
Pine Valley (Chemung Co.), 950 ...H6
Pine Valley (Suffolk Co.) ...F2
Pittsford, 1,418 ...F4
Plainview, 25,637 ...C2
Plattsburgh, 18,816 ...P1
Plattsburgh West ...P1
Pleasant Valley, 1,839 ...P7
Pleasantville, 7,172 ...B1
Poland, 451 ...L4
Pomona, 2,726 ...B1
Pond Eddy, 225 ...M8
Poquott, 975 ...E1
Port Byron, 1,297 ...H4
Port Chester, 27,867 ...C1
Port Dickinson, 1,697 ...K6
Port Ewen, 3,650 ...P7
Port Henry, 1,152 ...Q2
Port Jefferson, 7,837 ...E1
Port Jefferson Station, 7,527 ...E2
Port Kent, 250 ...Q1
Port Leyden, 665 ...L3
Portville, 1,024 ...E6
Potsdam, 9,425 ...M1
Poughkeepsie, 29,871 ...P7
Prattsburgh, 650 ...G5
Prattsville, 400 ...N6
Preble, 325 ...J5
Prospect, 330 ...L4
Pulaski, 2,398 ...J3
Putnam Lake, 3,855 ...P8
Quogue, 1,018 ...F2
Randolph, 1,316 ...D6
Ransomville, 1,488 ...D4
Rapids, 1,356 ...D4
Raquette Lake, 80 ...M3
Ravena, 3,369 ...P6
Raymondville, 475 ...M1
Red Creek, 521 ...H4
Redfield, 60 ...K3
Red Hook, 1,805 ...P7
Red Mills (Claverack-Red Mills), 1,061 ...P6
Redwood, 584 ...K2
Remsen, 531 ...L4
Rensselaer, 7,761 ...P5
Rensselaer Falls, 337 ...L1
Rhinebeck, 3,077 ...P7
Richburg, 448 ...E6
Richfield Springs, 1,255 ...M5
Richford, 225 ...J6
Richmondville, 786 ...M5
Richville, 274 ...L2
Ripley, 930 ...B6
Riverhead, 10,513 ...F1
Riverside (Steuben Co.), 594 ...G6
Riverside (Suffolk Co.), 2,875 ...F2
Rochester, 219,773 ...F4
Rocky Point, 10,185 ...E1
Roessleville, 10,800 ...P5
Rome, 34,950 ...L4
Roscoe, 597 ...M7
Rosendale, 1,374 ...N7
Roslyn, 2,570 ...C2
Rotterdam, 20,536 ...P5
Round Lake, 604 ...P5
Rouses Point, 2,277 ...Q1
Roxbury, 375 ...M6
Rushford, 350 ...E6
Rushville, 621 ...G5
Russell, 125 ...L2
Rye, 14,955 ...C2
Rye Brook, 8,602 ...C1
Sabael, 40 ...N3
Sabattis ...M2
Sackets Harbor, 1,386 ...J3
Sag Harbor, 2,313 ...G1
St. Bonaventure, 2,127 ...E6
St. George (see New York) ...B2
St. Johnsville, 1,685 ...M4
St. Regis Falls, 750 ...M1
Salamanca, 6,097 ...D6
Salem, 964 ...Q4
Saltaire, 43 ...D2
Sand Ridge, 906 ...J4
Sandy Creek, 789 ...J3
Sangerfield, 200 ...L5
Santa Clara, 70 ...N1
Saranac, 275 ...P1
Saranac Lake, 5,041 ...N2
Saratoga Springs, 26,186 ...P4
Saugerties, 4,955 ...P6
Sauquoit, 1,000 ...L5
Savona, 822 ...G6
Scarsdale, 17,823 ...B1
Schaghticoke, 676 ...P5
Schenectady, 61,821 ...P5
Schenevus, 500 ...M5
Schoharie, 1,030 ...N5
Schroon Lake, 650 ...P3
Schuyler Lake, 275 ...L5
Schuylerville, 1,197 ...P4
Scotchtown, 8,954 ...N8
Scotia, 7,957 ...P5
Scottsville, 2,128 ...F4
Sea Cliff, 5,066 ...C2
Seneca Falls, 6,861 ...H5
Sharon Springs, 547 ...M5
Shelter Island, 1,234 ...G1
Shelter Island Heights, 981 ...G1
Sherburne, 1,455 ...L5
Sherman, 714 ...B6
Sherrill, 3,147 ...K4
Shinnecock Hills, 1,749 ...G2
Shoreham, 417 ...E1
Shortsville, 1,320 ...G5
Sidney, 4,068 ...L6
Sidney Center, 275 ...L6
Silver Creek, 2,896 ...C5
Silver Springs, 844 ...E5
Sinclairville, 665 ...C6
Skaneateles, 2,616 ...J5
Slaterville Springs, 275 ...J6
Sleepy Hollow (formerly N. Tarrytown), 9,212 ...B1
Sloan, 3,775 ...D5
Sloatsburg, 3,117 ...A1

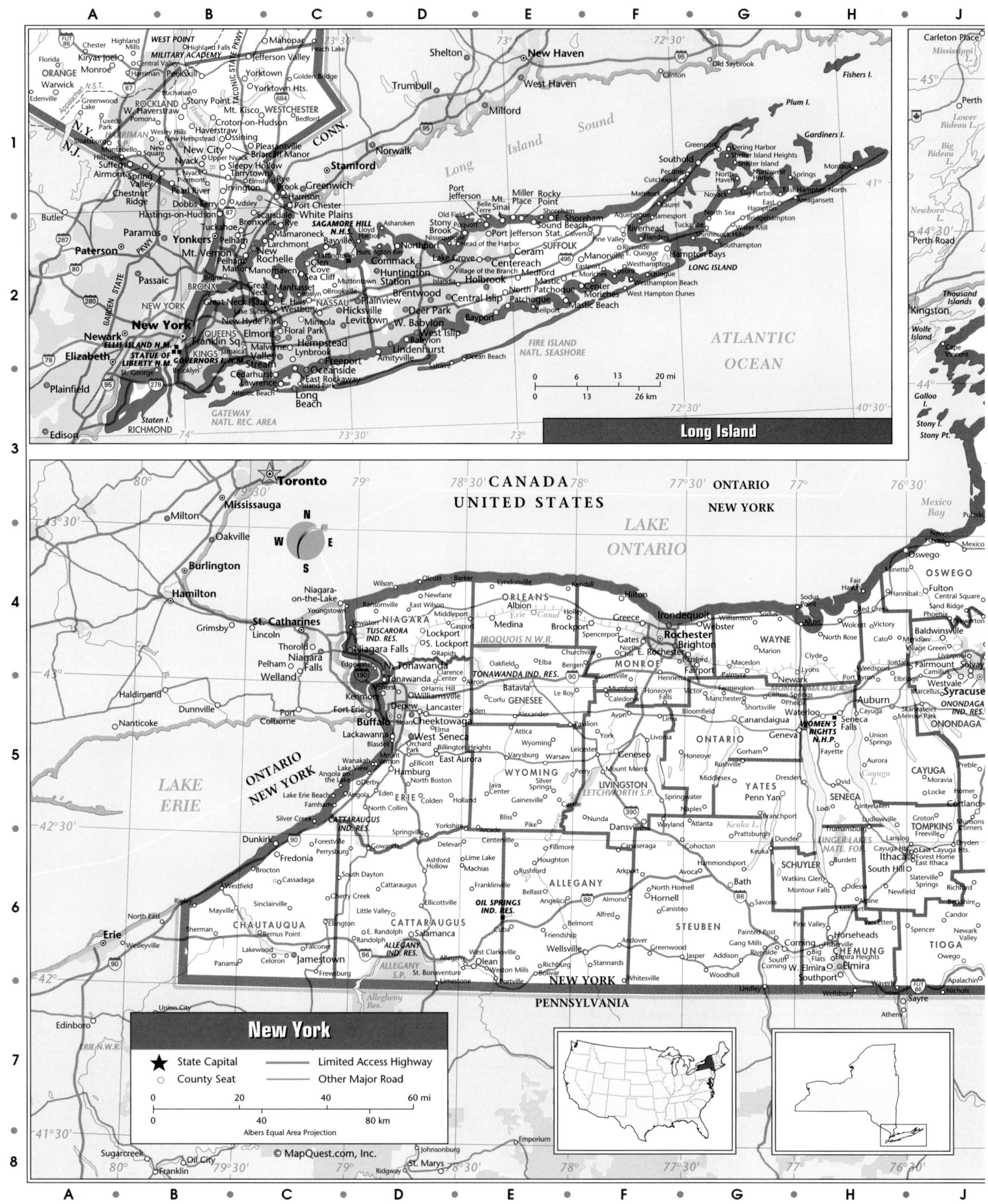

Long Island

New York

★ State Capital — Limited Access Highway
○ County Seat — Other Major Road

0 — 20 — 40 — 60 mi
0 — 40 — 80 km
Albers Equal Area Projection

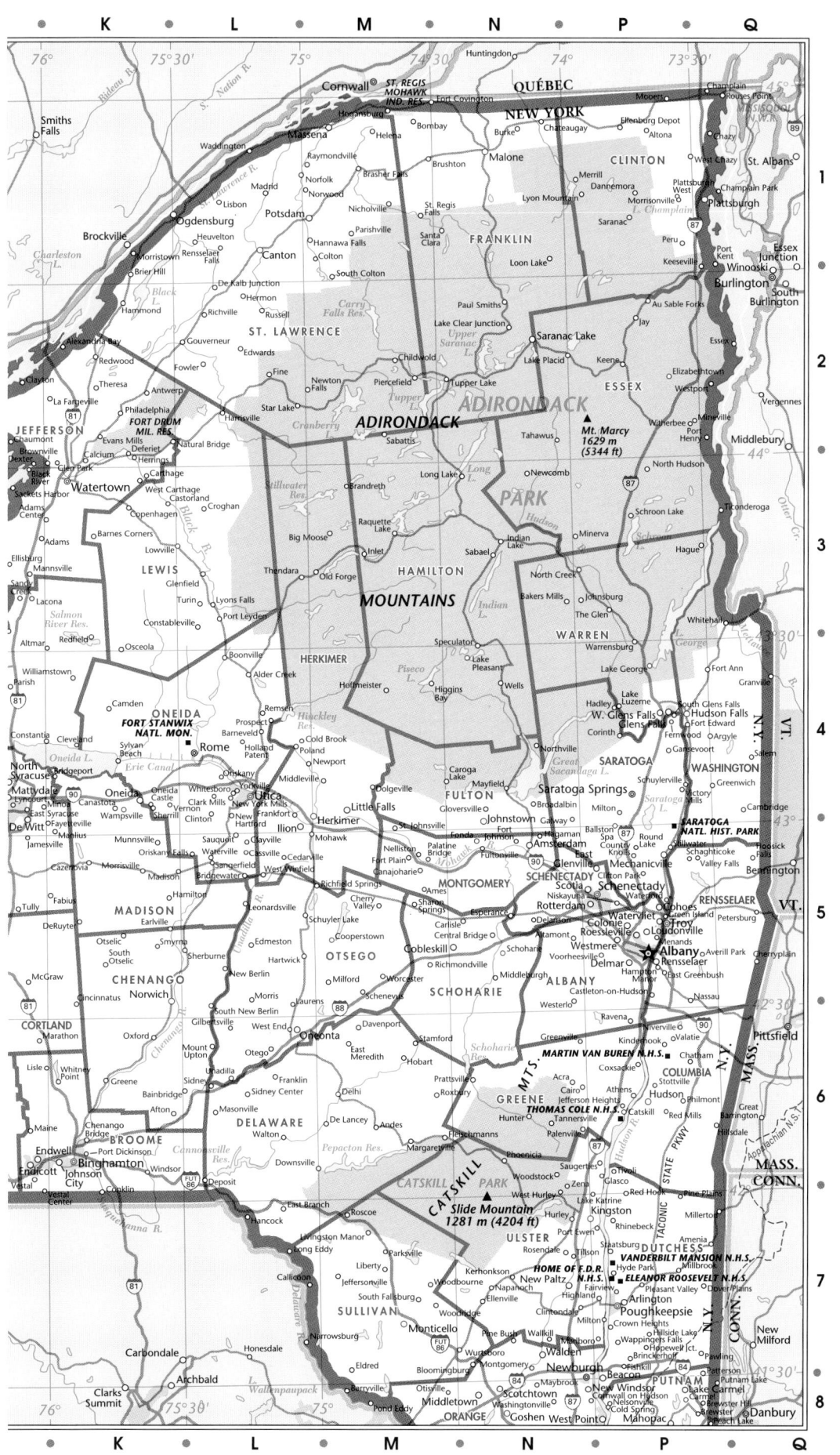

Smyrna, 241 . . . . .K5
Sodus, 1,735 . . . . .G4
Sodus Point, 1,160 . . . . . .H4
Solvay, 6,845 . . . . .J4
Sound Beach, 9,807 . . . . . .E1
Southampton, 3,965 . . . . . .G2
South Colton, 200 . . . . . . .M1
South Corning, 1,147 . . . . .G6
South Dayton, 662 . . . . . . .C6
South Fallsburg, 2,061 . . . .M7
South Glens Falls, 3,368 . . .P4
South Hill, 6,003 . . . . .H6
South Lockport, 8,552 . . . .D4
South New Berlin, 400 . . . .L5
South Nyack, 3,473 . . . . . .B1
Southold, 5,465 . . . . .G1
South Otselic, 300 . . . . . . .K5
Southport, 7,396 . . . . .H6
Speculator, 348 . . . . .N3
Spencer, 731 . . . . .J6
Spencerport, 3,559 . . . . . . .F4
Speonk (Remsenburg-Speonk),
  2,675 . . . . .F2
Springs, 4,950 . . . . .G1
Spring Valley, 25,464 . . . . .B1
Springville, 4,252 . . . . .D5
Springwater, 700 . . . . .F5
Staatsburg, 911 . . . . .P7
Stamford, 1,265 . . . . .M6
Stannards, 868 . . . . .F6
Star Lake, 860 . . . . .L2
Stillwater, 1,644 . . . . .P5
Stony Brook, 13,727 . . . . . .D2
Stony Point, 11,744 . . . . . .P6
Stottville, 1,355 . . . . .P6
Suffern, 11,006 . . . . .A1
Sylvan Beach, 1,071 . . . . . .K4
Syracuse, 147,306 . . . . . . .J4
Tahawus N2
Tannersville, 448 . . . . .N6
Tarrytown, 11,090 . . . . . . .B1
The Glen P3
Thendara, 300 . . . . .L3
Theresa, 812 . . . . .K2
Ticonderoga, 2,800 . . . . . . .Q3
Tillson, 1,709 . . . . .N7
Tivoli, 1,163 . . . . .P6
Tonawanda, 16,136 . . . . . . .D4
Troy, 49,170 . . . . .P5
Trumansburg, 1,581 . . . . . .H5
Tuckahoe (Suffolk Co., part of
  Southampton, pop. 3,965),
  1,741 . . . . .G1
Tuckahoe (Westchester Co.),
  6,211 . . . . .B2
Tully, 924 . . . . .J5
Tupper Lake, 3,935 . . . . . .N2
Turin, 263 . . . . .L3
Tuxedo Park, 731 . . . . .A1
Unadilla, 1,127 . . . . .L6
Union Springs, 1,074 . . . . .H5
Upper Nyack, 1,863 . . . . . .B1
Utica, 60,651 . . . . .L4
Valatie, 1,712 . . . . .P6
Valley Falls, 491 . . . . .P5
Valley Stream, 36,368 . . . . .C2
Van Etten, 581 . . . . .H6
Varysburg, 375 . . . . .D5
Vernon, 1,155 . . . . .K4
Vestal, 3,900 . . . . .J6
Vestal Center, 850 . . . . . . .J6
Victor, 2,433 . . . . .G5
Victory, 250 . . . . .H4
Victory Mills, 544 . . . . .P4
Village Green, 3,945 . . . . . .J4
Village of the Branch, 1,895 . D2
Voorheesville, 2,705 . . . . . .P5
Waddington, 923 . . . . .L1
Walden, 6,164 . . . . .N7
Wallkill, 2,143 . . . . .N7
Walton, 3,070 . . . . .L6
Wampsville, 561 . . . . .K4
Wanakah, 3,200 . . . . .D5
Wappingers Falls, 4,929 . . . .P7
Warrensburg, 3,208 . . . . . . .P4
Warsaw, 3,814 . . . . .E5
Warwick, 6,412 . . . . .A1
Washingtonville, 5,851 . . . .N8
Waterford, 2,204 . . . . .P5
Waterloo, 5,115 . . . . .H5
Watertown, 26,705 . . . . . . .K3
Waterville, 1,721 . . . . .L5
Watervliet, 10,207 . . . . . . .P5
Watkins Glen, 2,149 . . . . . .H5
Waverly, 4,607 . . . . .H6
Wayland, 1,893 . . . . .F5
Webster, 5,216 . . . . .G4
Weedsport, 2,017 . . . . .H4
Wells, 300 . . . . .N4
Wellsburg, 631 . . . . .H6
Wellsville, 5,171 . . . . .F6
Wesley Hills, 4,848 . . . . . . .B1
West Babylon, 43,452 . . . . .D2
West Carthage, 2,102 . . . . .K3
West Chazy, 600 . . . . .Q1
West Clarksville, 125 . . . . . .E6
West Elmira, 5,136 . . . . . . .H6
West End, 1,813 . . . . .L6
Westerlo, 275 . . . . .N5
Westfield, 3,481 . . . . .B6
West Glens Falls, 6,721 . . . .P4
Westhampton, 2,869 . . . . . .F2
Westhampton Beach, 1,902 . .F2
West Hampton Dunes, 11 . . .F2
West Haverstraw, 10,295 . . . .B1
West Hurley, 2,105 . . . . . . .N6
West Islip, 28,907 . . . . .D2
Westmere, 7,188 . . . . .P5
Weston Mills E6
West Point P8
Westport, 550 . . . . .Q2
West Seneca, 45,943 . . . . . .D5
Westvale, 5,166 . . . . .J4
West Winfield, 862 . . . . . . .L5
Whitehall, 2,667 . . . . .Q3
White Plains, 53,077 . . . . . .C1
Whitesboro, 3,943 . . . . .L4
Whitesville, 400 . . . . .F6
Whitney Point, 965 . . . . . . .K6
Williamson, 2,100 . . . . .G4
Williamstown, 475 . . . . .K4
Williamsville, 5,573 . . . . . . .D5
Wilson, 1,213 . . . . .D4

Windsor, 901 . . . . .K6
Witherbee (Mineville-
  Witherbee), 1,747 . . . . . .P2
Wolcott, 1,712 . . . . .H4
Woodbourne, 1,600 . . . . . .M7
Woodhull, 400 . . . . .G6
Woodridge, 902 . . . . .M7
Woodstock, 2,187 . . . . .N6
Worcester, 900 . . . . .M5
Wurtsboro, 1,234 . . . . .N7
Wyoming, 513 . . . . .E5
Yonkers, 196,086 . . . . .B2
York, 450 . . . . .F5
Yorkshire, 1,403 . . . . .E5
Yorktown (Jefferson Valley-
  Yorktown) 14,891 . . . . . .B1
Yorktown Heights, 7,972 . . .B1
Yorkville, 2,675 . . . . .L4
Youngstown, 1,957 . . . . . . .C4
Zena, 1,119 . . . . .N6

Other Features

Adirondack, mountains M2
Adirondack Park N2
Allegany Ind. Res. D6
Allegany S.P. D6
Allegheny, reservoir D7
Appalachian N.S.T. A1, Q6
Atlantic, ocean G2
Big Rideau, lake J1
Black, lake K2
Black, river L3
Cannonsville, reservoir L6
Carry Falls, reservoir M2
Catskill, mountains M7
Catskill Park M6
Cattaraugus Ind. Res. C5
Cayuga, lake H5
Champlain, lake P1
Charleston, lake K1
Chenango, river K6
Cranberry, lake M2
Delaware, river L7
Eleanor Roosevelt N.H.S. . . .P7
Ellis Island N.M. A2
Erie, canal E4, K4
Erie, lake B5
Erie N.W.R. A7
Finger Lakes Natl. For. H5
Fire Island Natl. Seashore . . .E2
Fishers, island H1
Fort Drum Mil. Res. K2
Fort Stanwix Natl. Mon. L4
Galloo, island J3
Gardiners, island H1
Gateway Natl. Rec. Area B3
Genesee, river E5
George, lake P3
Grand, river B4
Great Sacandaga, lake N4
Harriman S.P. A1
Hinckley, reservoir L4
Home of F.D.R. N.H.S. N7
Hudson, river B1, N3, P6
Indian, lake N3
Iroquois N.W.R. E4
Keuka, lake G5
Letchworth S.P. E5
Long, island G2
Long, lake N3
Long Island, sound D1
Lower Rideau, lake J1
Martin Van Buren N.H.S. P6
Mettawee, river Q3
Mexico, bay J3
Missisquoi N.W.R. Q1
Mississippi, lake J1
Mohawk, river M5
Montezuma N.W.R. H4
Marcy, mountain P2
Newboro, lake J1
Oil Springs Ind. Res. E6
Oneida, lake K4
Onondaga Ind. Res. J5
Ontario, lake F3
Otter, creek Q3
Pepacton, reservoir M6
Piseco, lake M4
Plum, island G1
Rideau, river K1
Sagamore Hill N.H.S. C2
St. Lawrence, river L1
St. Regis Mohawk Ind. Res. . .M1
Salmon River, reservoir K3
Saratoga, lake P4
Saratoga Natl. Hist. Park P5
Schoharie, reservoir N6
Schroon, lake P3
Slide, mountain N7
South Nation, river L1
Staten, island A3
Statue of Liberty N.M. A2
Stillwater, reservoir L3
Stony, island J3
Stony, point J3
Susquehanna, river K7
Susquehanna St. For. F7
Taconic State Pkwy P7
Thomas Cole N.H.S. P6
Tonawanda Ind. Res. E4
Tupper, lake M2
Tuscarora Ind. Res. D4
Unadilla, river L5
Upper Saranac, lake N2
Vanderbilt Mansion N.H.S. . .P7
Wallenpaupack, lake L7
West Point
  Military Academy A1
Wolfe, island J2
Women's Rights N.H.P. H5

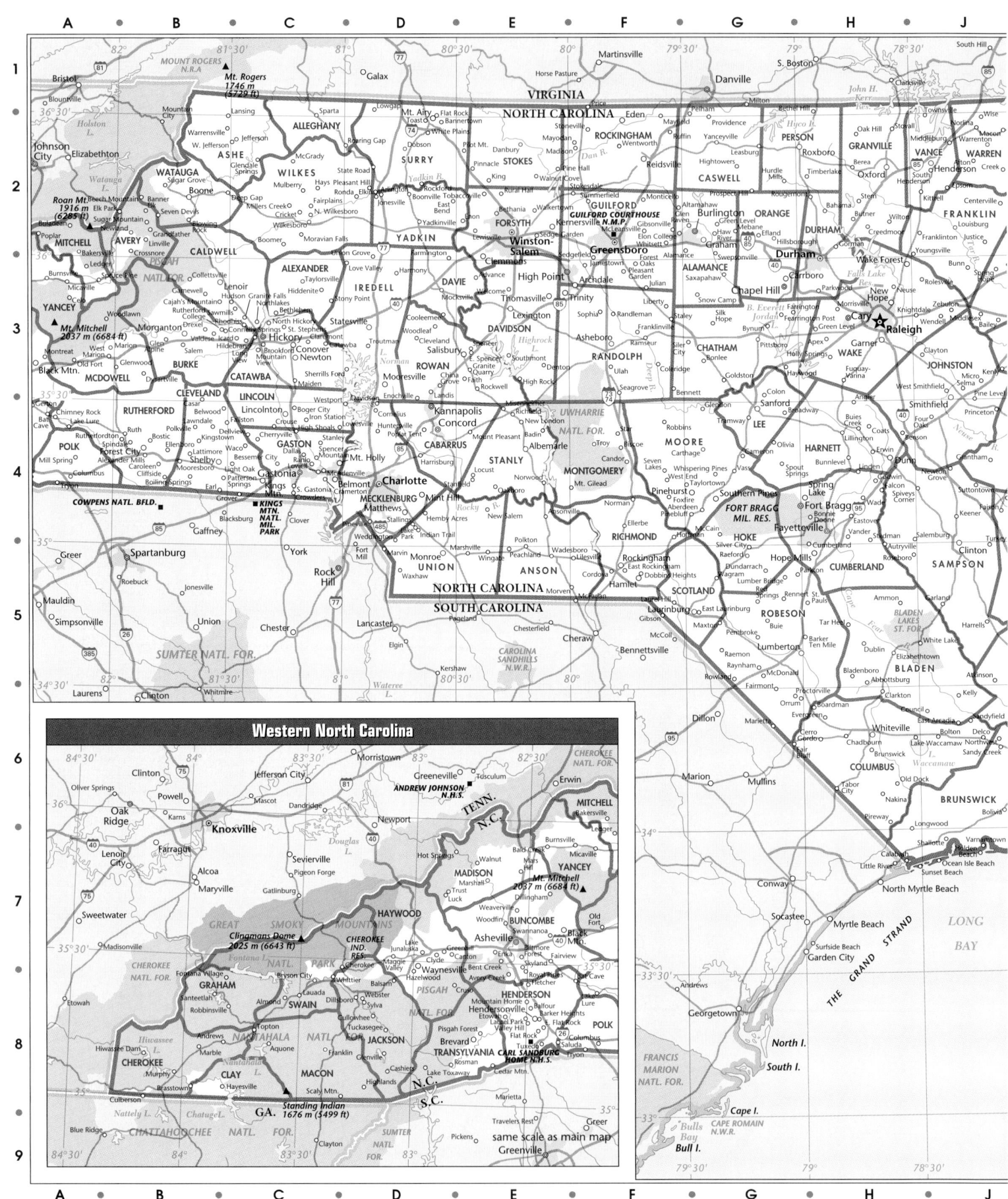

Western North Carolina

same scale as main map

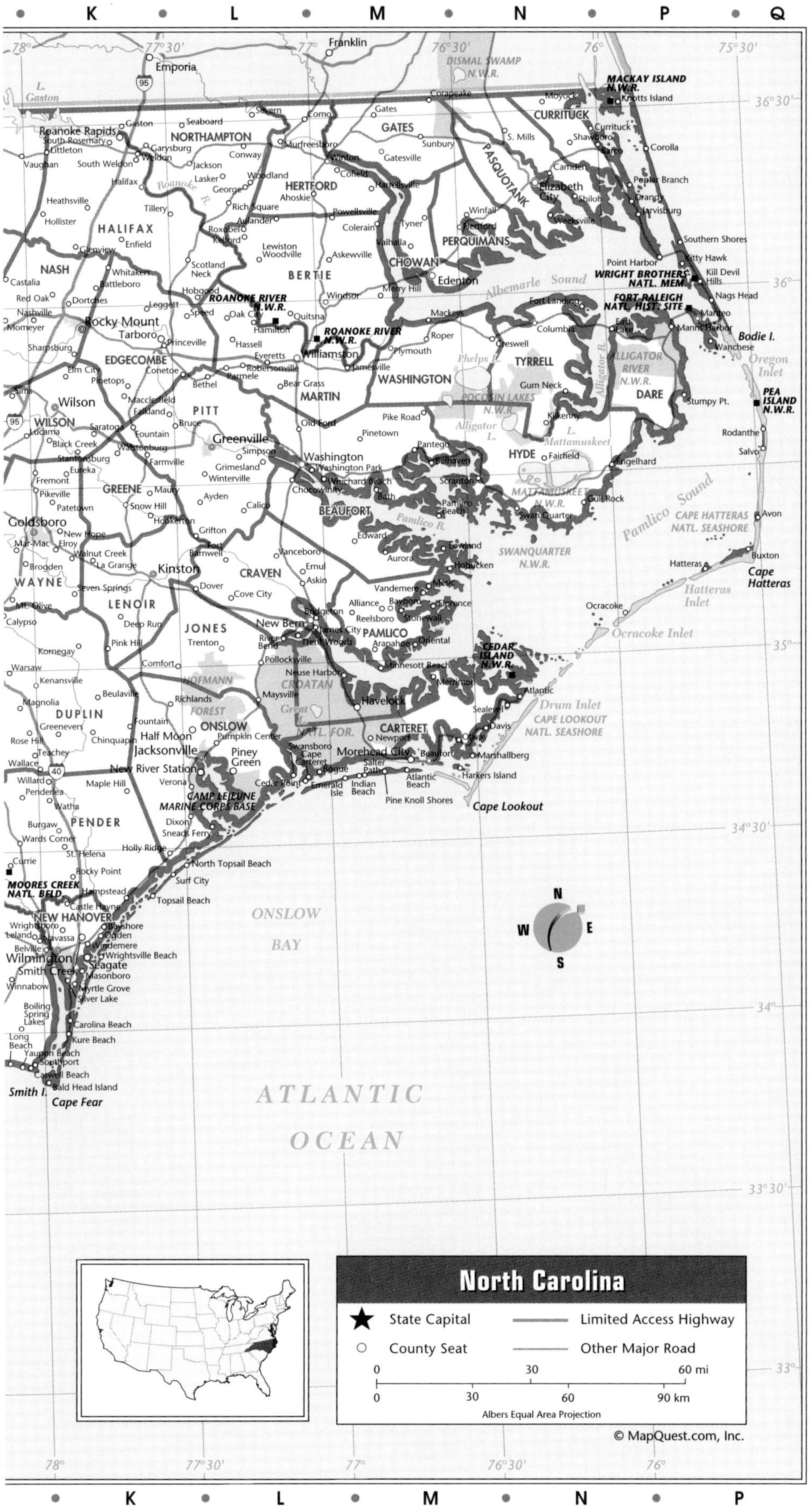

North Carolina

Capital: Raleigh
Land Area: 48,718 sq. mi.
126,180 sq. km.
Population: 8,049,313 (2000 Census)
Largest City: Charlotte, 540,828
Highest Point: Mt. Mitchell, 6,684 ft. 2,037 m.
Admitted to Union: November 21, 1789
Nickname: Tar Heel State
State Flower: Dogwood
State Bird: Cardinal

North Carolina: Map Index

Counties

Alamance, 130,800	G3
Alexander, 33,603	C3
Alleghany, 10,677	C2
Anson, 25,275	E5
Ashe, 24,384	C2
Avery, 17,167	B2
Beaufort, 44,958	M4
Bertie, 19,773	L2
Bladen, 32,278	H5
Brunswick, 73,143	J6
Buncombe, 206,330	E7
Burke, 89,148	B3
Cabarrus, 131,063	D4
Caldwell, 77,415	B2
Camden, 6,885	N2
Carteret, 59,383	M5
Caswell, 23,501	G2
Catawba, 141,685	C3
Chatham, 49,329	G3
Cherokee, 24,298	B8
Chowan, 14,526	M2
Clay, 8,775	C8
Cleveland, 96,287	B3
Columbus, 54,749	H6
Craven, 91,436	L4
Cumberland, 302,963	H5
Currituck, 18,190	N2
Dare, 29,967	P3
Davidson, 147,246	E3
Davie, 34,835	D3
Duplin, 49,063	K5
Durham, 223,314	H2
Edgecombe, 55,606	K3
Forsyth, 306,067	E2
Franklin, 47,260	J2
Gaston, 190,365	C4
Gates, 10,516	M2
Graham, 7,993	B8
Granville, 48,498	H2
Greene, 18,974	K4
Guilford, 421,048	F2
Halifax, 57,370	K2
Harnett, 91,025	H4
Haywood, 54,033	D7
Henderson, 89,173	E8
Hertford, 22,601	L2
Hoke, 33,646	G4
Hyde, 5,826	N3
Iredell, 122,660	D3
Jackson, 33,121	D8
Johnston, 121,965	J3
Jones, 10,381	L4
Lee, 49,040	G4
Lenoir, 59,648	K4
Lincoln, 63,780	C3
Macon, 29,811	C8
Madison, 19,635	E7
Martin, 25,593	L3
McDowell, 42,151	A3
Mecklenburg, 695,454	D4
Mitchell, 15,687	A2, F6
Montgomery, 26,822	F4
Moore, 74,769	F4
Nash, 87,420	K2
New Hanover, 160,307	K6
Northampton, 22,086	L2
Onslow, 150,355	L5
Orange, 118,227	G2
Pamlico, 12,934	M4
Pasquotank, 34,897	N2
Pender, 41,082	K5
Perquimans, 11,368	N2
Person, 35,623	G2
Pitt, 133,798	L3
Polk, 18,324	A4, F8
Randolph, 130,454	F3
Richmond, 46,564	F4
Robeson, 123,339	G5
Rockingham, 91,928	F2
Rowan, 130,340	D3
Rutherford, 62,899	B4
Sampson, 60,161	J5
Scotland, 35,998	F5
Stanly, 58,100	E4
Stokes, 44,711	E2
Surry, 71,219	D2
Swain, 12,968	C8
Transylvania, 29,334	D8
Tyrrell, 4,149	N3
Union, 123,677	D5
Vance, 42,954	J2
Wake, 627,846	H3
Warren, 19,972	J2
Washington, 13,723	M3
Watauga, 42,695	B2
Wayne, 113,329	J4
Wilkes, 65,632	C2
Wilson, 73,814	K3
Yadkin, 36,348	D2
Yancey, 17,774	A3, E7

Cities and Towns

Abbottsburg, 125	H5
Aberdeen, 3,400	G4
Advance, 250	E3
Afton, 200	J2
Ahoskie, 4,523	M2
Alamance, 310	G2
Albemarle, 15,680	E4
Alexander Mills	B4
Alliance, 781	M4
Almond	C8
Altamahaw (Altamahaw-Ossipee), 996	F2
Ammon, 40	H5
Andrews, 1,602	C8
Angier, 3,419	H3
Ansonville, 636	E4
Apex, 20,212	H3
Aquone, 125	C8
Arapahoe, 436	M4
Archdale, 9,014	F3
Arlington, 795	D2
Asheboro, 21,672	F3
Asheville, 68,889	E7
Askewville, 180	M2
Askin, 125	L4
Atkinson, 236	J5
Atlantic, 400	N5
Atlantic Beach, 1,781	M5
Aulander, 888	L2
Aurora, 583	M4
Autryville, 196	H5
Avery Creek, 1,405	E8
Avon, 550	Q4
Ayden, 4,622	L4
Badin, 1,154	E4
Bahama, 550	H2
Bailey, 670	J3
Bakersville, 357	A2, F6
Bald Creek, 125	E7
Bald Head Island, 173	K7
Balfour, 1,200	E8
Balsam, 450	D8
Banner Elk, 811	B2
Bannertown, 950	D2
Barco, 300	P2
Barker Heights, 1,237	E8
Barker Ten Mile, 976	H5
Bat Cave, 125	A4, F8
Bath, 275	M4
Battleboro	K2
Bayboro, 741	M4
Bayshore, 2,512	K6
Bear Grass, 53	L3
Beaufort, 3,771	M5
Beech Mountain, 310	B2
Belhaven, 1,968	M3
Belmont, 8,705	C4
Belville, 285	K6
Belwood, 962	B4
Bennett, 250	F3
Benson, 2,923	H4
Bent Creek, 1,389	E7
Berea, 225	H2
Bessemer City, 5,119	C4
Bethania, 354	E2
Bethel, 1,681	L3
Bethel Hill, 175	H1
Bethlehem, 3,713	C3
Beulaville, 1,067	K5
Biltmore Forest, 1,440	E7
Biscoe, 1,700	F4
Black Creek, 714	K3
Black Mtn., 7,511	A3, E7
Bladenboro, 1,718	H5
Blowing Rock, 1,418	B2
Boardman, 202	H6
Boger City, 554	C4
Bogue, 590	L5
Boiling Spring Lakes, 2,972	J6
Boiling Springs, 3,866	B4

© MapQuest.com, Inc.

North Carolina

★ State Capital — Limited Access Highway
○ County Seat — Other Major Road

0 ... 30 ... 60 mi
0 ... 30 ... 60 ... 90 km
Albers Equal Area Projection

Bolivia, 148 . . . . .J6
Bolton, 494 . . . . .J6
Bonlee, 325 . . . . .G3
Bonnie Doone, 3,900 .H4
Boomer, 425 . . . . .C2
Boone, 13,472 . . . . . . .B2
Boonville, 1,138 . . . . .D2
Bostic, 328 . . . . .B4
Brevard, 6,789 . . . . . . .E8
Bridgeton, 328 . . . . . .L4
Broadway, 1,015 . . . . .G4
Brogden, 2,907 . . . . . .J4
Brookford, 434 . . . . . .C3
Bruce, 80 . . . . .L3
Brunswick, 360 . . . . . .H6
Bryson City, 1,411 . . . .C8
Buie, 125 . . . . .G5
Buies Creek, 2,215 . . .H4
Buladean, 200 . . . . . . .A2
Bunn, 357 . . . . .J3
Bunnlevel, 300 . . . . . .H4
Burgaw, 3,337 . . . . . . .K5
Burlington, 44,917 . . .G2
Burnsville, 1,623 . .A3, F7
Butner, 5,792 . . . . . . .H2
Buxton, 550 . . . . .P4
Bynum, 425 . . . . .G3
Cajah's Mountain,
   2,683 . . . . .B3
Calabash, 711 . . . . . . .H7
Calico, 70 . . . . .L4
Calypso, 410 . . . . .J4
Camden, 350 . . . . . . .N2
Cameron, 151 . . . . . . .G4
Candor, 825 . . . . .F4
Canton, 4,029 . . . . . . .D7
Cape Carteret, 1,214 . .L5
Caroleen, 1,200 . . . . . .B4
Carolina Beach, 4,701 .K6
Carrboro, 16,782 . . . . .G3
Carthage, 1,871 . . . . . .G4
Cary, 94,536 . . . . .H3
Casar, 308 . . . . .B3
Cashiers, 196 . . . . . . .D8
Castalia, 340 . . . . .J2
Castle Hayne, 1,116 . . .K6
Caswell Beach, 370 . . .J7
Catawba, 698 . . . . . . .C3
Cedar Mtn., 100 . . . . . .E8
Cedar Point, 929 . . . . .L5
Celo, 425 . . . . .A3
Centerville, 99 . . . . . . .J2
Cerro Gordo, 244 . . . .H6
Chadbourn, 2,129 . . . .H6
Chapel Hill, 48,715 . . .G3
Charlotte, 540,828 . . . .D4
Cherokee, 250 . . . . . . .D7
Cherryville, 5,361 . . . .C4
Chimney Rock, 175 . . .A4
China Grove, 3,616 . . .D3
Chinquapin, 375 . . . . . .K5
Chocowinity, 733 . . . .L3
Claremont, 1,038 . . . .C3
Clarkton, 705 . . . . . . .H6
Clayton, 6,973 . . . . . . .J3
Clemmons, 13,827 . . . .E2
Cleveland, 808 . . . . . .D3
Cliffside, 600 . . . . .B4
Clinton, 8,600 . . . . . . .J5
Clyde, 1,324 . . . . .D7
Coats, 1,845 . . . . .H4
Cofield, 347 . . . . .M2
Colerain, 221 . . . . . . .M2
Coleridge, 200 . . . . . . .F3
Collettsville, 175 . . . . .B3
Colon, 300 . . . . .G3
Columbia, 819 . . . . . . .N3
Columbus, 992 . . .A4, F8
Comfort, 200 . . . . . . .K4
Como, 78 . . . . .L2
Concord, 55,977 . . . . .D4
Conetoe, 365 . . . . . . .L3
Connelly Springs, 1,814 B3
Conover, 6,604 . . . . . .C3
Conway, 734 . . . . .L2
Cooleemee, 905 . . . . .D3
Corapeake, 350 . . . . . .M1
Cordova, 1,100 . . . . . . .F5
Cornelius, 11,969 . . . .D4
Corolla P2
Council, 60 . . . . .J6
Cove City, 433 . . . . . . .L4
Cramerton, 2,976 . . . .C4
Creedmoor, 2,232 . . . .H2
Creek J2
Creswell, 278 . . . . . . .N3
Cricket, 2,053 . . . . . . .C2
Crossnore, 242 . . . . . .B2
Crouse, 475 . . . . .C4
Crowders, 200 . . . . . . .C4
Cruso, 100 . . . . .E8
Culberson, 70 . . . . . . .B8
Cullowhee, 3,579 . . . .D8
Cumberland, 4,400 . . .H4
Currie, 250 . . . . .J6
Currituck, 125 . . . . . . .N2
Dallas, 3,402 . . . . .C4
Danbury, 108 . . . . . . .E2
Davidson, 7,139 . . . . .D3
Davis, 275 . . . . .N5
Deep Gap, 200 . . . . . .C2
Deep Run, 300 . . . . . .K4

Delco, 275 . . . . .J6
Dellview C4
Denton, 1,450 . . . . . . .E3
Dillingham, 90 . . . . . . .C7
Dillsboro, 205 . . . . . . .D8
Dixon, 125 . . . . .L5
Dobbins Heights, 936 . .F5
Dobson, 1,457 . . . . . . .D2
Dortches, 809 . . . . . . .K2
Dover, 443 . . . . .L4
Drexel, 1,938 . . . . .B3
Dublin, 250 . . . . .H6
Dundarrach, 62 . . . . . .G5
Dunn, 9,196 . . . . .H4
Dysartville, 100 . . . . . .B3
Earl, 234 . . . . .B4
East Arcadia, 524 . . . . .J6
East Bend, 659 . . . . . .D2
East Flat Rock, 4,151 . .E8
East Lake, 100 . . . . . . .P3
East Laurinburg, 295 . .G5
Eastover, 1,376 . . . . . .H4
East Rockingham,
   3,885 . . . . .F5
East Spencer, 1,755 . . .E3
Eden, 15,908 . . . . . . .F2
Edenton, 5,394 . . . . . .M2
Edward, 250 . . . . .M4
Efland, 650 . . . . .G2
Elizabeth City, 17,188 .N2
Elizabethtown, 3,698 . .H5
Elkin, 4,109 . . . . .D2
Elk Park, 459 . . . . .B2
Ellenboro, 479 . . . . . . .B4
Ellerbe, 1,021 . . . . . . .F4
Elm City, 1,165 . . . . . .K3
Elon College F2
Elroy, 3,896 . . . . .K4
Emerald Isle, 3,488 . . .M5
Enfield, 2,347 . . . . . . .K2
Engelhard, 425 . . . . . .P3
Enka, 1,500 . . . . .E7
Enochville, 2,851 . . . . .D3
Enon, 275 . . . . .E2
Epsom, 275 . . . . .J2
Ernul, 425 . . . . .L4
Erwin, 4,537 . . . . .H4
Etowah, 2,766 . . . . . . .E8
Eureka, 244 . . . . .K3
Everetts, 179 . . . . .L3
Evergreen, 325 . . . . . .H6
Fair Bluff, 1,181 . . . . . .G6
Fairfield, 125 . . . . .N3
Fairmont, 2,604 . . . . . .G5
Fairplains, 2,051 . . . . .C2
Fairview, 2,495 . . . . . .E7
Faison, 744 . . . . .J4
Faith, 695 . . . . .E3
Falcon, 328 . . . . .H4
Falkland, 112 . . . . .K3
Fallston, 603 . . . . .C4
Farmington, 125 . . . . . .D2
Farmville, 4,302 . . . . . .K3
Farrington, 100 . . . . . .G3
Fayetteville, 121,015 . .H4
Fearrington Post
   (Fearrington), 903 . .G3
Flat Rock, 1,690 . . . . .D1
Fletcher, 4,185 . . . . . .E8
Florence, 175 . . . . . . .M4
Fontana Village, 175 . .C8
Forest City, 7,549 . . . .B4
Forest Oaks, 3,241 . . .F3
Fort Barnwell, 250 . . . .L4
Fort Bragg, 29,183 . . .H4
Fort Landing, 40 . . . . .N3
Fountain (Duplin Co.) .K5
Fountain (Pitt Co.), 533 K3
Four Oaks, 1,424 . . . . .J4
Foxfire, 474 . . . . .F4
Franklin, 3,490 . . . . . .C8
Franklinton, 1,745 . . . .J2
Franklinville, 1,258 . . .F3
Fremont, 1,463 . . . . . .K3
Fuquay-Varina, 7,898 . .H3
Gamewell, 3,644 . . . . .B3
Garland, 808 . . . . .J5
Garner, 17,757 . . . . . .H3
Garysburg, 1,254 . . . . .K2
Gaston, 973 . . . . .K2
Gastonia, 66,277 . . . . .C4
Gates, 300 . . . . .M1
Gatesville, 281 . . . . . .M2
George, 125 . . . . .L2
Gerton, 175 . . . . .A4
Gibson, 584 . . . . .F5
Gibsonville, 4,372 . . . .F2
Glen Alpine, 1,090 . . . .B3
Glendale Springs, 225 .C2
Glendon G4
Glen Raven, 2,750 . . . .G2
Glenview, 150 . . . . . . .K2
Glenville, 200 . . . . . . .D8
Glenwood, 475 . . . . . .B3
Godwin, 112 . . . . .H4
Goldsboro, 39,043 . . . .J4
Goldston, 319 . . . . . . .G3
Gorman, 1,200 . . . . . .H2
Graham, 12,833 . . . . .G2
Grandfather, 73 . . . . . .B2
Grandy, 1,000 . . . . . . .P2

Granite Falls, 4,612 . . .C3
Granite Quarry, 2,175 . .E3
Grantham, 100 . . . . . . .J4
Greenevers, 560 . . . . .K5
Greenhill
   (West Canton) D7
Green Level H3
Greensboro, 223,891 . .F2
Greenville, 60,476 . . . .L3
Grifton, 2,073 . . . . . . .L4
Grimesland, 440 . . . . .L3
Grover, 698 . . . . .C4
Gull Rock N4
Gum Neck, 150 . . . . . .N3
Half Moon, 6,645 . . . . .L5
Halifax, 344 . . . . .K2
Hamilton, 516 . . . . . . .L3
Hamlet, 6,018 . . . . . . .F5
Hampstead, 475 . . . . .K6
Harkers Island, 1,525 .M5
Harmony, 526 . . . . . . .D3
Harrells, 187 . . . . .J5
Harrellsville, 102 . . . . .M2
Harrisburg, 4,493 . . . . .D4
Hassell, 72 . . . . .L3
Hatteras, 650 . . . . . . .P4
Havelock, 22,442 . . . .M5
Haw River, 1,908 . . . . .G2
Hayesville, 297 . . . . . .C8
Hays, 1,731 . . . . .C2
Haywood, 475 . . . . . . .G3
Hazelwood D8
Heathsville, 100 . . . . . .K2
Hemby Acres (Hemby
   Bridge), 897 . . . . . .D4
Henderson, 16,095 . . . .J2
Hendersonville, 10,420 .E8
Hertford, 2,070 . . . . . .N2
Hickory, 37,222 . . . . . .C3
Hiddenite, 650 . . . . . . .C3
Highlands, 909 . . . . . .D8
High Point, 85,839 . . . .E3
High Rock, 90 . . . . . . .E3
High Shoals, 729 . . . . .C4
Hightowers, 225 . . . . .G2
Hildebran, 1,472 . . . . .C3
Hillsborough, 5,446 . . .G2
Hiwassee Dam, 60 . . . .B8
Hobgood, 404 . . . . . . .L2
Hobucken, 225 . . . . . .M4
Hoffman, 624 . . . . . . .F4
Holden Beach, 787 . . . .J7
Hollister, 600 . . . . .K2
Holly Ridge, 831 . . . . .K6
Holly Springs, 9,192 . .H3
Hookerton, 467 . . . . . .K4
Hope Mills, 11,237 . . . .H5
Hot Springs, 645 . . . . .D7
Hudson, 3,078 . . . . . . .C3
Huntersville, 24,960 . . .D4
Hurdle Mills, 225 . . . . .H2
Icard, 2,734 . . . . .C3
Indian Beach, 95 . . . . .M5
Indian Trail, 11,905 . . .D4
Iron Station, 450 . . . . .C4
Jackson, 695 . . . . .L2
Jacksonville, 66,715 . .L5
James City, 5,420 . . . .L4
Jamestown, 3,088 . . . .F3
Jamesville, 502 . . . . . .M3
Jarvisburg, 200 . . . . . .P2
Jefferson, 1,422 . . . . .C2
Jonesville, 1,464 . . . . .C2
Julian, 600 . . . . .F3
Justice, 150 . . . . .J2
Kannapolis, 36,910 . . .D4
Keener, 508 . . . . .J4
Kelford, 245 . . . . .L2
Kelly, 454 . . . . .J6
Kenansville, 1,149 . . . .K5
Kenly, 1,569 . . . . .J3
Kernersville, 17,126 . . .E2
Kilkenny, 50 . . . . .N3
Kill Devil Hills, 5,897 . .P2
King, 5,952 . . . . .E2
Kings Mtn., 9,693 . . . .C4
Kingstown, 845 . . . . . .B4
Kinston, 23,688 . . . . . .K4
Kittrell, 148 . . . . .J2
Kitty Hawk, 2,991 . . . .P2
Knightdale, 5,958 . . . .J3
Knotts Island, 175 . . . .P1
Kornegay K4
Kure Beach, 1,507 . . . .K7
La Grange, 2,844 . . . .K4
Lake Junaluska, 2,675 .D7
Lake Lure, 1,027 . .A4, F8
Lake Park, 2,093 . . . . .D4
Lake Waccamaw, 1,411 H6
Landis, 2,996 . . . . . . .D3
Lansing, 151 . . . . .C1
Lasker, 103 . . . . .L2
Lattimore, 419 . . . . . . .B4
Lauada, 125 . . . . .C8
Laurel Hill, 1,400 . . . . .F5
Laurel Park, 1,835 . . . .E8
Laurinburg, 15,874 . . .G5
Lawndale, 642 . . . . . . .B4
Leasburg, 300 . . . . . . .G2
Ledger, 500 . . . . . .A3, F6
Leggett, 77 . . . . .K3
Leland, 1,938 . . . . .J6

Lenoir, 16,793 . . . . . . .B3
Lewiston Woodville,
   613 . . . . .L2
Lewisville, 8,826 . . . . .E2
Lexington, 19,953 . . . .E3
Liberty, 2,661 . . . . . . .F3
Light Oak, 779 . . . . . . .C4
Lilesville, 459 . . . . .F5
Lillington, 2,915 . . . . . .H4
Lincolnton, 9,965 . . . . .C4
Linden, 127 . . . . .H4
Linville, 300 . . . . .B2
Littleton, 692 . . . . .K2
Locust, 2,416 . . . . .E4
Long Beach J7
Long View, 4,722 . . . . .C3
Longwood, 375 . . . . . .H6
Louisburg, 3,111 . . . . . .J2
Love Valley, 30 . . . . . .D3
Lowell, 2,662 . . . . .C4
Lowesville, 1,440 . . . . .C4
Lowgap, 475 . . . . .D1
Lowland, 200 . . . . .M4
Lucama, 847 . . . . .J3
Lumber Bridge, 118 . . .G5
Lumberton, 20,795 . . .G5
Macclesfield, 458 . . . .K3
Mackeys, 225 . . . . . . .M3
Macon, 115 . . . . .J2
Madison, 2,262 . . . . . .F2
Maggie Valley, 607 . . .D7
Magnolia, 932 . . . . . . .J5
Maiden, 3,282 . . . . . . .C3
Manns Harbor, 325 . . .P3
Manteo, 1,052 . . . . . . .P3
Maple Hill, 40 . . . . .K5
Marble, 350 . . . . .B8
Marietta, 164 . . . . .G6
Marion, 4,943 . . . . . . .A3
Mar-Mac, 3,004 . . . . . .J4
Marshall, 840 . . . . .E7
Marshallberg, 650 . . . .M5
Mars Hill, 1,764 . . . . . .E7
Marshville, 2,360 . . . . .E5
Marvin, 1,039 . . . . . . .D5
Masonboro, 11,812 . . .K6
Matthews, 22,127 . . . .D4
Maury, 400 . . . . .K4
Maxton, 2,551 . . . . . . .G5
Mayfield, 100 . . . . .F2
Mayodan, 2,417 . . . . . .F2
Maysville, 1,002 . . . . . .L5
McAdenville, 619 . . . . .C4
McCain, 400 . . . . .G4
McDonald, 119 . . . . . .G5
McFarlan, 89 . . . . .F5
McGrady, 250 . . . . . . .C2
McLeansville, 1,080 . . .F2
Mebane, 7,284 . . . . . .G2
Merrimon, 175 . . . . . . .M5
Merry Hill, 70 . . . . .M2
Mesic, 257 . . . . .M4
Micaville, 750 . . . .A3, F7
Micro, 454 . . . . .J3
Middleburg, 162 . . . . . .J2
Middlesex, 838 . . . . . . .J3
Millers Creek, 2,071 . . .C2
Mill Spring, 325 . . . . . .A4
Milton, 132 . . . . .G1
Minnesott Beach, 311 .M5
Mint Hill, 14,922 . . . . .D4
Misenheimer, 750 . . . .E4
Mocksville, 4,178 . . . . .D3
Momeyer, 291 . . . . . . .J3
Monroe, 26,228 . . . . . .D4
Monticello, 500 . . . . . .F2
Montreat, 630 . . . . . . .A4
Mooresboro, 314 . . . . .B4
Mooresville, 18,823 . . .D3
Moravian Falls, 1,440 . .C2
Morehead City, 7,691 .M5
Morganton, 17,310 . . .B3
Morrisville, 5,208 . . . . .H3
Morven, 579 . . . . .E5
Mountain Home, 2,169 E8
Mountain View, 3,768 . .C3
Mount Airy, 8,484 . . . .D1
Mount Gilead, 1,389 . .F4
Mount Holly, 9,618 . . . .C4
Mount Olive, 4,567 . . .J4
Mount Pleasant, 1,259 .E4
Moyock, 400 . . . . .N1
Mulberry, 2,269 . . . . . .C2
Murfreesboro, 2,045 . .L2
Murphy, 1,568 . . . . . . .B8
Myrtle Grove, 7,125 . . .K6
Nags Head, 2,700 . . . .P3
Nakina, 90 . . . . .H6
Nashville, 4,309 . . . . . .K3
Navassa, 479 . . . . .J6
Neuse, 250 . . . . .H3
Neuse Harbor, 150 . . .M5
New Bern, 23,128 . . . .L4
New Hope (Wake Co.) H3
New Hope (Wayne Co.),
   4,500 . . . . .K4
Newland, 704 . . . . . . .B2
New London, 326 . . . .E4
Newport, 3,349 . . . . . .L5
New River Station L5
New Salem, 70 . . . . . .E4
Newton, 12,560 . . . . . .C3

Newton Grove, 606 . . .J4
Norlina, 1,107 . . . . . . .J2
Norman, 72 . . . . .F4
North Hickory, 4,300 . .C3
Northlakes, 1,390 . . . .C3
North Topsail Beach,
   843 . . . . .L6
Northwest, 671 . . . . . .J6
N. Wilkesboro, 4,116 . .C2
Norwood, 2,216 . . . . . .E4
Oakboro, 1,198 . . . . . .E4
Oak City, 339 . . . . .L3
Oak Hill, 90 . . . . .J2
Ocean Isle Beach, 426 .J7
Ocracoke, 769 . . . . . . .P4
Ogden, 5,481 . . . . . . .K6
Old Dock, 150 . . . . . . .H6
Old Ford, 100 . . . . .L3
Old Fort, 963 . . . .A3, F7
Olivia, 475 . . . . .G4
Oriental, 875 . . . . .M4
Orrum, 79 . . . . .G6
Otway, 700 . . . . .M5
Oxford, 8,338 . . . . . . .H2
Pamlico Beach, 125 . . .M4
Pantego, 170 . . . . .M3
Parkton, 428 . . . . .G5
Parkwood H3
Parmele, 290 . . . . .L3
Patetown, 50 . . . . .K4
Patterson Springs, 620 .B4
Peachland, 554 . . . . . .E5
Pelham, 150 . . . . .G1
Pembroke, 2,399 . . . . .G5
Penderlea, 225 . . . . . . .J5
Pike Road, 275 . . . . . .M3
Pikeville, 719 . . . . .K4
Pilot Mt., 1,281 . . . . . .E2
Pinebluff, 1,109 . . . . . .G4
Pine Hall, 275 . . . . . . .E2
Pinehurst, 9,706 . . . . .G4
Pine Knoll Shores,
   1,524 . . . . .M5
Pine Level, 1,313 . . . . .J3
Pinetops, 1,419 . . . . . .K3
Pinetown, 225 . . . . . . .M3
Pineville, 3,449 . . . . . .D4
Piney Green, 11,658 . .L5
Pink Hill, 521 . . . . .K4
Pinnacle, 550 . . . . . . .E2
Pireway, 100 . . . . .H6
Pisgah Forest, 1,100 . .E8
Pittsboro, 2,226 . . . . . .G3
Pleasant Garden, 4,714 F3
Pleasant Hill, 1,109 . . .D2
Plymouth, 4,107 . . . . .M3
Point Harbor, 200 . . . .P2
Polkton, 1,195 . . . . . . .E4
Polkville, 535 . . . . .B4
Pollocksville, 269 . . . . .L4
Poplar A2
Poplar Branch, 225 . . .P2
Poplar Tent D4
Powellsville, 259 . . . . .M2
Price F1
Princeton, 1,066 . . . . .J4
Princeville, 940 . . . . . .K3
Proctorville, 133 . . . . . .G6
Prospect Hill, 125 . . . .G2
Providence, 325 . . . . .G2
Pumpkin Center, 2,228 .L5
Quitsna, 100 . . . . .L3
Raeford, 3,386 . . . . . . .G5
Raemon, 212 . . . . . . .G5
Raleigh, 276,093 . . . . .H3
Ramseur, 1,588 . . . . . .F3
Randleman, 3,557 . . . .F3
Ranlo, 2,198 . . . . .C4
Raynham, 67 . . . . .G5
Red Oak, 2,723 . . . . . .K2
Red Springs, 3,493 . . .G5
Reelsboro, 800 . . . . . .M4
Reidsville, 14,485 . . . .F2
Rennert, 283 . . . . .G5
Rhodhiss, 366 . . . . . . .C3
Richfield, 515 . . . . .E4
Richlands, 928 . . . . . . .K5
Rich Square, 931 . . . . .L2
River Bend, 2,923 . . . .L4
Roanoke Rapids,
   16,957 . . . . .K2
Roaring Gap, 20 . . . . .D2
Robbins, 1,195 . . . . . . .F4
Robbinsville, 747 . . . . .C8
Robersonville, 1,731 . .L3
Rockford, 125 . . . . . . .D2
Rockingham, 9,672 . . .F5
Rockwell, 1,971 . . . . . .E3
Rocky Mount, 55,893 . .K3
Rocky Point, 275 . . . . .K6
Rodanthe, 275 . . . . . .Q3
Roduco, 90 . . . . .M2
Ronda, 460 . . . . .D2
Roper, 613 . . . . .M3
Rosman, 490 . . . . .D8
Rougemont, 600 . . . . .H2
Rowland, 1,146 . . . . . .G6
Roxboro, 8,696 . . . . . .H2
Roxobel, 263 . . . . .L2
Royal Pines, 5,334 . . . .E7

Ruffin, 375 . . . . .F2
Rural Hall, 2,464 . . . . .E2
Ruth, 329 . . . . .B4
Rutherford College,
   1,293 . . . . .B3
Rutherfordton, 4,131 . .B4
St. Helena, 395 . . . . . .K5
St. Pauls, 2,137 . . . . . .H5
St. Stephens, 9,439 . . .C3
Salem, 2,923 . . . . .B3
Salemburg, 469 . . . . . .H4
Salisbury, 26,462 . . . . .E3
Salter Path, 450 . . . . .M5
Saluda, 575 . . . . .E8
Salvo, 250 . . . . .Q3
Sandy Creek, 246 . . . .J6
Sandyfield, 340 . . . . . .J6
Sanford, 23,220 . . . . .G4
Santeetlah B8
Saratoga, 379 . . . . . . .K3
Sawmills, 4,921 . . . . . .C3
Saxapahaw, 1,418 . . . .G3
Scaly Mtn., 125 . . . . . .D8
Scotland Neck, 2,362 . .L2
Scranton, 50 . . . . .N4
Seaboard, 695 . . . . . . .L2
Seagate, 4,590 . . . . . .K6
Seagrove, 246 . . . . . . .F3
Sealevel, 225 . . . . . . .N5
Sedgefield, 1,100 . . . .F2
Sedge Garden E2
Selma, 5,914 . . . . .J3
Seven Devils, 129 . . . .B2
Seven Lakes, 3,214 . . .F4
Seven Springs, 86 . . . .K4
Severn, 263 . . . . .L1
Shallotte, 1,381 . . . . . .J7
Sharpsburg, 2,421 . . . .K3
Shawboro, 90 . . . . . . .N2
Shelby, 19,477 . . . . . .B4
Sherrills Ford, 941 . . . .D3
Shiloh, 300 . . . . .N2
Siler City, 6,966 . . . . . .G3
Silk Hope, 125 . . . . . . .G3
Silver City, 1,146 . . . . .G5
Silver Lake, 5,788 . . . .K6
Simpson, 464 . . . . . . .L3
Sims, 128 . . . . .J3
Skyland, 50 . . . . .E7
Smith Creek K6
Smithfield, 11,510 . . . .J4
Sneads Ferry, 2,248 . . .L5
Snow Camp, 175 . . . .G3
Snow Hill, 1,514 . . . . .K4
Sophia, 325 . . . . .F3
Southern Pines, 10,918 G4
Southern Shores, 2,201 P2
South Gastonia, 5,433 .C4
South Henderson,
   1,220 . . . . .J2
South Mills, 700 . . . . .N2
Southmont, 850 . . . . .E3
Southport, 2,351 . . . . . .J7
South Rosemary, 2,843 K2
South Weldon, 1,414 . .K2
Sparta, 1,817 . . . . . . .C1
Speed, 70 . . . . .L3
Spencer, 3,355 . . . . . .E3
Spencer Mountain, 51 .C4
Spindale, 4,022 . . . . . .B4
Spiveys Corner, 448 . . .J4
Spout Springs, 550 . . .G4
Spring Hope, 1,261 . . .J3
Spring Lake, 8,098 . . . .H4
Spruce Pine, 2,030 . . .A3
Staley, 347 . . . . .F3
Stallings, 3,189 . . . . . .D4
Stanfield, 1,113 . . . . . .E4
Stanley, 3,053 . . . . . . .C4
Stantonsburg, 726 . . . .K3
Star, 807 . . . . .F4
State Road, 900 . . . . .D2
Statesville, 23,320 . . . .D3
Stedman, 664 . . . . . . .H4
Stem, 229 . . . . .H2
Stokesdale, 3,267 . . . .F2
Stoneville, 1,002 . . . . .F2
Stonewall, 285 . . . . . . .M4
Stony Point, 1,380 . . . .C3
Stovall, 376 . . . . .H2
Stumpy Pt., 200 . . . . . .P3
Sugar Grove, 325 . . . .B2
Sugar Mountain, 226 . .B2
Summerfield, 7,018 . . .F2
Sunbury, 175 . . . . . . .M2
Sunset Beach, 1,824 . .H7
Surf City, 1,393 . . . . . .K6
Suttontown, 80 . . . . . .J4
Swannanoa, 4,132 . . . .E7
Swan Quarter, 275 . . .N4
Swansboro, 1,426 . . . .L5
Swepsonville, 922 . . . .G2
Sylva, 2,435 . . . . .D8
Tabor City, 2,509 . . . . .H6
Tarboro, 11,138 . . . . . .L3
Tar Heel, 70 . . . . .H5
Taylorsville, 1,799 . . . .C3
Taylortown, 845 . . . . . .G4
Teachey, 245 . . . . .J5
Thomasville, 19,788 . . .E3
Tillery, 40 . . . . .L2
Timberlake, 225 . . . . . .H2

Toast, 1,922 . . . . .D2
Tobaccoville, 2,209 . . .E2
Topsail Beach, 471 . . . .K6
Topton, 30 . . . . .C8
Townsville, 175 . . . . . . .J1
Tramway, 750 . . . . . . .G4
Trenton, 206 . . . . .L4
Trent Woods, 4,192 . . .L4
Trinity, 6,690 . . . . .E3
Troutman, 1,592 . . . . .D3
Troy, 3,430 . . . . .F4
Trust D7
Tryon, 1,760 . . . .A4, F8
Tuckasegee, 50 . . . . . .D8
Turkey, 262 . . . . .J5
Tuxedo, 475 . . . . .E8
Tyner, 100 . . . . .M2
Ulah, 800 . . . . .F3
Union Grove, 350 . . . .D2
Valdese, 4,485 . . . . . .B3
Valhalla, 90 . . . . .M2
Valley Hill, 2,137 . . . . .E8
Vanceboro, 898 . . . . . .L4
Vandemere, 289 . . . . .M4
Vander, 1,204 . . . . . . .H4
Varnamtown, 481 . . . .J7
Vass, 750 . . . . .G4
Vaughan, 90 . . . . .J2
Verona, 700 . . . . .L5
Waco, 328 . . . . .B4
Wade, 480 . . . . .H4
Wadesboro, 3,552 . . . .E5
Wagram, 801 . . . . . . .G5
Wake Forest, 12,588 . .H3
Walkertown, 4,009 . . . .E2
Wallace, 3,344 . . . . . . .K5
Walnut, 450 . . . . .E7
Walnut Cove, 1,465 . . .E2
Walnut Creek, 859 . . . .K4
Walstonburg, 224 . . . .K3
Wanchese, 1,527 . . . . .P3
Wards Corner, 40 . . . . .J5
Warrensville, 275 . . . . .B2
Warrenton, 811 . . . . . .J2
Warsaw, 3,051 . . . . . .J5
Washington, 9,583 . . . .L3
Washington Park, 440 .L3
Watha, 151 . . . . .K5
Waxhaw, 2,625 . . . . . .D5
Waynesville, 9,232 . . . .D7
Weaverville, 2,416 . . . .E7
Webster, 486 . . . . .D8
Weddington, 6,696 . . .D4
Weeksville, 150 . . . . . .N2
Welcome, 3,538 . . . . .E3
Weldon, 1,374 . . . . . . .K2
Wendell, 4,247 . . . . . . .J3
Wentworth, 2,779 . . . .F2
West End, 450 . . . . . . .F4
West Jefferson, 1,081 .B2
West Marion, 1,556 . . .A3
Westport, 2,006 . . . . . .D4
West Smithfield J3
Whichard Beach (River
   Road), 30 . . . . .M3
Whispering Pines,
   2,090 . . . . .G4
Whitakers, 799 . . . . . .K2
White Lake, 529 . . . . . .J5
White Plains, 1,049 . . .D2
Whiteville, 5,148 . . . . .H6
Whitsett, 686 . . . . .F2
Wilkesboro, 3,159 . . . .C2
Willard, 300 . . . . .K5
Williamston, 5,843 . . . .L3
Wilmington, 75,838 . . .K6
Wilson, 44,405 . . . . . .K3
Wilton, 125 . . . . .H2
Windemere K6
Windsor, 2,283 . . . . . .M3
Winfall, 554 . . . . .N2
Wingate, 2,406 . . . . . .E5
Winnabow, 125 . . . . . .J6
Winston-Salem,
   185,776 . . . . .E2
Winterville, 4,791 . . . . .L3
Winton, 956 . . . . .M2
Wise, 250 . . . . .J2
Woodfin, 3,162 . . . . . .E7
Woodland, 833 . . . . . .L2
Woodlawn, 250 . . . . . .A3
Woodleaf, 350 . . . . . . .D3
Wrightsboro, 4,496 . . .K6
Wrightsville Beach,
   2,593 . . . . .K6
Yadkinville, 2,818 . . . .D2
Yanceyville, 2,091 . . . .G2
Yaupon Beach J7
Youngsville, 651 . . . . . .J2
Zebulon, 4,046 . . . . . .J3

Other Features

Albemarle, *sound* . . . N2
Alligator, *lake* . . . N3
Alligator, *river* . . . N3
Alligator River N.W.R. . . P3
Atlantic, *ocean* . . . L7
B. Everett Jordan, *lake* . G3
Bladen Lakes St. For. . . H5
Bodie, *island* . . . P3
Bull, *island* . . . F9
Bulls, *bay* . . . F9
Camp Lejeune Marine Corps Base . . . L5
Cape, *island* . . . G8
Cape Fear, *river* . . . H5
Cape Hatteras Natl. Seashore . . . P4
Cape Lookout Natl. Seashore . . . N5
Cape Romain N.W.R. . . G9
Carl Sandburg N.H.S. . E8
Carolina Sandhills N.W.R. . . . E5
Cedar Island N.W.R. . . N4
Chattahoochee Natl. For. . . . B9
Chatuge, *lake* . . . C9
Cherokee Ind. Res. . . . D7
Cherokee Natl. For. . . . B7, F6
Clingmans Dome, *peak* . . . C7
Croatan Natl. For. . . . L5
Dan, *river* . . . F2
Deep, *river* . . . F3
Dismal Swamp N.W.R. N1
Douglas, *lake* . . . D7
Drum, *inlet* . . . N5
Falls Lake, *reservoir* . . . H3
Fear, *cape* . . . K7
Fontana, *lake* . . . C7
Fort Bragg Mil. Res. . . G4
Fort Raleigh Natl. Hist. Site . . . P3
Francis Marion Natl. For. . . . F8
Gaston, *lake* . . . K1
Grand Strand, The, *beach* . . . H8
Great, *lake* . . . L5
Great Smoky Mountains Natl. Park . . . C7
Guilford Courthouse N.M.P. . . . F2
Hatteras, *cape* . . . P4
Hatteras, *inlet* . . . P4
Highrock, *lake* . . . E3
Hiwassee, *lake* . . . B8
Hofmann Forest . . . L5
Holston, *lake* . . . A2
Hyco, *lake* . . . G2
John H. Kerr, *reservoir* . H1
Long, *bay* . . . J7
Lookout, *cape* . . . M5
Mackay Island N.W.R. . P1
Mattamuskeet, *lake* . . . N3
Mattamuskeet N.W.R. . N4
Mitchell, *mountain* . A3, F7
Moores Creek Natl. Bfld. . . . J6
Mount Rogers N.R.A . . B1
Nantahala, *lake* . . . C8
Nantahala Natl. For. . C8
Natteley, *lake* . . . B9
Neuse, *river* . . . J4
Norman, *lake* . . . D3
North, *island* . . . G8
Ocracoke, *inlet* . . . N4
Onslow, *bay* . . . L6
Oregon, *inlet* . . . Q3
Pamlico, *river* . . . M4
Pamlico, *sound* . . . P4
Pea Island N.W.R. . . . Q3
Phelps, *lake* . . . N3
Pisgah Natl. For. . . B3, D8
Pocosin Lakes N.W.R. . N3
Roan, *mountain* . . . A2
Roanoke, *river* . . . K2
Roanoke River N.W.R. . . . L3, M3
Rocky, *river* . . . E4
Rogers, *mountain* . . . B1
Smith, *island* . . . J7
South, *island* . . . C8
Standing Indian . . . C8
Sumter Natl. For. . B5, D9
Swanquarter N.W.R. . . N4
Tar, *river* . . . J2
Uwharrie Natl. For. . . . F4
Waccamaw, *lake* . . . J6
Watauga, *lake* . . . A2
Wateree, *lake* . . . D5
Wright Brothers Natl. Mem. . . . P2
Yadkin, *river* . . . D2

North Dakota

Capital: Bismarck
Land Area: 68,994 sq. mi.
178,694 sq. km.
Population: 642,200 (2000 Census)
Largest City: Fargo, 90,599
Highest Point: White Butte
3,506 ft.
1,069 m.
Admitted to Union: November 2, 1889
Nickname: Peace Garden State
State Flower: Wild Prairie Rose
State Bird: Western Meadowlark

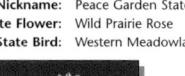

North Dakota: Map Index

Counties

Adams, **2,593** . . . C3
Barnes, **11,775** . . . G3
Benson, **6,964** . . . F2
Billings, **888** . . . B2
Bottineau, **7,149** . . . E1
Bowman, **3,242** . . . B3
Burke, **2,242** . . . C1
Burleigh, **69,416** . . . E3
Cass, **123,138** . . . H3
Cavalier, **4,831** . . . G1
Dickey, **5,757** . . . G3
Divide, **2,283** . . . B1
Dunn, **3,600** . . . C2
Eddy, **2,757** . . . F2
Emmons, **4,331** . . . E3
Foster, **3,759** . . . F2
Golden Valley, **1,924** . B3
Grand Forks, **66,109** . H2
Grant, **2,841** . . . D3
Griggs, **2,754** . . . G2
Hettinger, **2,715** . . . C3
Kidder, **2,753** . . . F3
La Moure, **4,701** . . . G3
Logan, **2,308** . . . F3
McHenry, **5,987** . . . E1
McIntosh, **3,390** . . . F3
McKenzie, **5,737** . . . B2
McLean, **9,311** . . . D2
Mercer, **8,644** . . . C2
Morton, **25,303** . . . D3
Mountrail, **6,631** . . . C1
Nelson, **3,715** . . . G2
Oliver, **2,065** . . . D2
Pembina, **8,585** . . . H1
Pierce, **4,675** . . . E1
Ramsey, **12,066** . . . G1
Ransom, **5,890** . . . H3
Renville, **2,610** . . . D1
Richland, **17,998** . . . J3
Rolette, **13,674** . . . F1
Sargent, **4,366** . . . H3
Sheridan, **1,710** . . . E2
Sioux, **4,044** . . . D3
Slope, **767** . . . B3
Stark, **22,636** . . . C3
Steele, **2,258** . . . H2
Stutsman, **21,908** . . . F3
Towner, **2,876** . . . F1
Traill, **8,477** . . . H2
Walsh, **12,389** . . . H1
Ward, **58,795** . . . D1
Wells, **5,102** . . . F2
Williams, **19,761** . . . B1

Cities and Towns

Abercrombie, **296** . . . J3
Adams, **203** . . . G1
Akra, *50* . . . H1
Alamo, **51** . . . B1
Alexander, **217** . . . B2
Alfred . . . F3
Alice, **56** . . . H3
Alkabo . . . B1
Almont, **89** . . . D3
Alsen, **68** . . . G1
Ambrose, **23** . . . B1
Amenia, **89** . . . H2
Amidon, **26** . . . B3
Anamoose, **282** . . . E2
Aneta, **284** . . . H2
Antler, **47** . . . D1
Appam . . . B1
Ardoch, **61** . . . H1
Argusville, **147** . . . J2
Armourdale . . . F1
Arnegard, **105** . . . B2
Arthur, **402** . . . H2
Ashley, **882** . . . F3
Aylmer . . . E2
Ayr, **23** . . . H2
Baker . . . F1
Baldwin, *50* . . . E2
Balfour, **20** . . . E2
Balta, **73** . . . E1
Bantry, **19** . . . E1
Barlow, *40* . . . F2
Barney, **69** . . . H3
Barton, **20** . . . E1
Bathgate, **66** . . . H1
Battleview . . . C1
Beach, **1,116** . . . A3
Belcourt, **2,440** . . . F1
Belden . . . C1
Belfield, **866** . . . B3
Benedict, **53** . . . D2
Bergen, **11** . . . E2
Berlin, **35** . . . G3
Berthold, **466** . . . D1
Berwick . . . E1
Beulah, **3,152** . . . D2
Binford, **201** . . . G2
Bisbee, **167** . . . F1
Bismarck, **55,532** . . . E3
Blaisdell . . . C1
Blanchard, *70* . . . H2
Bonetraill . . . B1
Bordulac . . . G2
Bottineau, **2,336** . . . E1
Bowbells, **406** . . . C1
Bowdon, **139** . . . F2
Bowesmont, *40* . . . H1
Bowman, **1,600** . . . B3
Braddock, **43** . . . E3
Brampton . . . H4
Brantford . . . G2
Breien . . . E3
Bremen, *40* . . . F2
Briarwood, **78** . . . J3
Brinsmade, **29** . . . F1
Brocket, **65** . . . G1
Buchanan, **77** . . . G2
Bucyrus, **26** . . . C3
Buffalo, **209** . . . H3
Buford . . . B1
Burlington, **1,096** . . . D1
Burnstad . . . F3
Burt . . . C3
Butte, **92** . . . E2
Buxton, **350** . . . H2
Caledonia, *40* . . . J2
Calio, **24** . . . G1
Calvin, **26** . . . G1
Cando, **1,342** . . . F1
Cannon Ball, **864** . . . E3
Carpio, **148** . . . D1
Carrington, **2,268** . . . F2
Carson, **319** . . . D3
Cartwright . . . B2
Cashel . . . H1
Casselton, **1,855** . . . H3
Cathay, **56** . . . F2
Cavalier, **1,537** . . . H1
Cayuga, **61** . . . H3
Center, **678** . . . D2
Chaffee, *90* . . . H3
Chaseley . . . F2
Christine, **153** . . . J3
Churchs Ferry, **77** . . . F1
Cleveland, **112** . . . F3
Clifford, **51** . . . H2
Clyde . . . G1
Cogswell, **165** . . . H3
Coleharbor, **106** . . . D2
Colfax, **91** . . . J3
Colgate, *40* . . . H2
Columbus, **151** . . . C1
Conway, **23** . . . H1
Cooperstown, **1,053** . . G2
Coteau . . . C1
Coulee . . . C1
Courtenay, **53** . . . G2
Crary, **149** . . . G1
Crete, *50* . . . H3
Crosby, **1,089** . . . B1
Crystal, **167** . . . H1
Crystal Springs . . . F3
Cummings, *60* . . . H2
Dahlen, *40* . . . H1
Davenport, **261** . . . H3
Dawson, **75** . . . F3
Dazey, **91** . . . G2
Deering, **118** . . . D1
Denbigh . . . E1
Denhoff . . . E2
De Sart . . . C3
Des Lacs, **209** . . . D1
Devils Lake, **7,222** . . . G1
Dickey, **57** . . . G3
Dickinson, **16,010** . . . C3
Dodge, **125** . . . C2
Donnybrook, **90** . . . D1
Dore, *40* . . . A2
Douglas, **64** . . . D2
Doyon, *40* . . . G1
Drake, **322** . . . E2
Drayton, **913** . . . H1
Driscoll, *100* . . . E3
Dunn Center, **122** . . . C2
Dunseith, **739** . . . E1
Dwight, **75** . . . J3
East Dunseith, **219** . . . E1
Eckman . . . D1
Edgeley, **637** . . . G3
Edinburg, **252** . . . H1
Edmore, **256** . . . G1
Egeland, **49** . . . F1
Eldridge, *40* . . . G3
Elgin, **659** . . . D3
Ellendale, **1,559** . . . G3
Elliott, **44** . . . H3
Embden, *70* . . . H3
Emerado, **510** . . . H2
Enderlin, **947** . . . H3
Epping, **79** . . . B1
Erie, **65** . . . H2
Esmond, **159** . . . F1
Fairdale, **51** . . . G1
Fairfield . . . B2
Fairmount, **406** . . . J3
Falkirk . . . D2
Fargo, **90,599** . . . J3
Fessenden, **625** . . . F2
Fillmore . . . F1
Fingal, **133** . . . H3
Finley, **515** . . . H2
Flasher, **285** . . . D3
Flaxton, **73** . . . C1
Forbes, **64** . . . G4
Fordville, **266** . . . H1
Forest River, **154** . . . H1
Forman, **506** . . . H3
Fort Clark . . . D2
Fort Ransom, **70** . . . H3
Fort Rice . . . E3
Fort Totten, **952** . . . F2
Fortuna, **31** . . . B1
Fort Yates, **228** . . . E3
Four Bears Village, **364** C2
Freda . . . D3
Fredonia, **51** . . . F3
Frontier, **273** . . . J3
Fryburg . . . B3
Fullerton, **85** . . . G3
Gackle, **335** . . . F3
Galchutt, *50* . . . J3
Galesburg, **157** . . . H2
Gardar, *50* . . . H1
Gardena, **38** . . . E1
Gardner, **80** . . . J2
Garrison, **1,318** . . . D2
Garske . . . G1
Gascoyne, **23** . . . B3
Gilby, **243** . . . H1
Gladstone, **248** . . . C3
Glenburn, **374** . . . D1
Glenfield, **134** . . . G2
Glen Ullin, **865** . . . D3
Golden Valley, **183** . . . C2
Golva, **106** . . . B3
Goodrich, **163** . . . E2
Grace City, **71** . . . G2
Grafton, **4,516** . . . H1
Grand Forks, **49,321** . . H2
Grandin, **181** . . . J2
Grand Rapids . . . G3
Grano, **9** . . . D1
Granville, **286** . . . E1
Grassy Butte . . . B2
Great Bend, **118** . . . J3
Grenora, **202** . . . B1
Guelph . . . G3
Guthrie . . . E2
Gwinner, **717** . . . H3
Hague, **91** . . . F3
Haley . . . B4
Halliday, **227** . . . C2
Hamberg, **28** . . . F2
Hamilton, **73** . . . H1
Hampden, **60** . . . G1
Hankinson, **1,058** . . . J3
Hanks, **10** . . . B1
Hannaford, **181** . . . G2
Hannah, **20** . . . G1
Hannover, *40* . . . D2
Hansboro, **8** . . . F1
Harlow, *50* . . . F1
Hartland . . . D1
Harvey, **1,989** . . . F2
Harwood, **607** . . . J3
Hatton, **707** . . . H2
Havana, **94** . . . H4
Havelock . . . C3
Haynes, **19** . . . C4
Hazelton, **237** . . . E3
Hazen, **2,457** . . . D2
Heaton . . . F2
Hebron, **803** . . . C3
Heil . . . D3
Heimdal, *40* . . . F2
Hensel, **42** . . . H1
Hensler, *60* . . . D2
Hettinger, **1,307** . . . C3
Hickson, *80* . . . J3
Hillsboro, **1,563** . . . H2
Hoople, **292** . . . H1
Hope, **303** . . . H2
Horace, **915** . . . J3
Hove Mobile Park, **2** . . G1
Hunter, **326** . . . H2
Hurdsfield, **91** . . . F2
Inkster, **102** . . . H1
Jamestown, **15,527** . . G3
Jessie, *50* . . . G2
Joliette . . . H1
Juanita . . . G2
Jud, **76** . . . G3
Judson . . . D3
Karlsruhe, **119** . . . E1
Kathryn, **63** . . . H3
Keene, *50* . . . C2
Kelvin . . . E1
Kempton . . . H2
Kenmare, **1,081** . . . C1
Kensal, **161** . . . G2
Kief, **13** . . . E2
Killdeer, **713** . . . C2
Kindred, **614** . . . H3
Kintyre . . . F3
Kloten, *40* . . . G2
Knox, **59** . . . F1
Kramer, **44** . . . E1
Kulm, **422** . . . G3
Lake Williams . . . F2
Lakewood Park, *425* . G1
Lakota, **781** . . . G1
La Moure, **944** . . . G3
Landa, **28** . . . E1
Langdon, **2,101** . . . G1
Lankin, **131** . . . H1
Lansford, **253** . . . D1
Larimore, **1,433** . . . H2
Lark . . . D3
Larson, **17** . . . C1
Lawton, **42** . . . G1
Leal, **36** . . . G2
Leeds, **464** . . . F1
Lefor, *40* . . . C3
Lehr, **114** . . . F3
Leith, **28** . . . D3
Leonard, **255** . . . H3
Leroy . . . H1
Lidgerwood, **738** . . . H3
Lignite, **174** . . . C1
Lincoln, **1,730** . . . E3
Linton, **1,321** . . . E3
Lisbon, **2,292** . . . H3
Litchville, **191** . . . G3
Livona . . . E3
Loma, **21** . . . G1
Loraine, **19** . . . D1
Lostwood . . . C1
Lucca . . . H3
Ludden, **29** . . . G3
Luverne, **44** . . . H2
Maddock, **498** . . . F2
Maida . . . G1
Makoti, **145** . . . D2
Mandan, **16,718** . . . E3
Mandaree, **558** . . . C2
Manfred . . . F2
Manning . . . C2
Mantador, **71** . . . J3
Manvel, **370** . . . H1
Mapleton, **606** . . . H3
Marion, **146** . . . G3
Marmarth, **140** . . . B3
Marshall . . . C2
Martin, **96** . . . E2
Max, **278** . . . D2
Maxbass, **91** . . . D1
Mayville, **1,953** . . . H2
Maza, **5** . . . F1
McCanna . . . H2
McClusky, **415** . . . E2
McGregor, *60* . . . C1
McHenry, **71** . . . G2
McKenzie . . . E3
McLeod . . . H3
McVille, **470** . . . G2
Medina, **335** . . . F3
Medora, **100** . . . B3
Mekinock, *125* . . . H1
Melville . . . F2
Menoken, *40* . . . E3
Mercer, **86** . . . E2
Merricourt, **10** . . . G3
Michigan, **345** . . . G1
Millarton . . . G3
Milnor, **711** . . . H3
Milton, **85** . . . G1
Minnewaukan, **318** . . F1
Minot, **36,567** . . . D1
Minto, **657** . . . H1
Moffit, *70* . . . E3
Mohall, **812** . . . D1
Monango, **28** . . . G3
Montpelier, **103** . . . G3
Mooreton, **204** . . . J3
Mott, **808** . . . C3
Mountain, **133** . . . H1
Munich, **268** . . . G1
Mylo, **19** . . . F1
Nanson . . . F1
Napoleon, **857** . . . F3
Nash, *40* . . . H1
Neche, **437** . . . H1
Nekoma, **51** . . . G1
Newburg, **88** . . . E1
New England, **555** . . C3
New Hradec, *90* . . . C2
New Leipzig, **274** . . . D3
New Rockford, **1,463** . . F2
New Salem, **938** . . . D3
New Town, **1,367** . . . C2
Niagara, **57** . . . H2
Niobe . . . C1
Nome, **70** . . . H3
Noonan, **154** . . . B1
Northgate . . . C1
North River, **65** . . . J3
Northwood, **959** . . . H2
Nortonville, *60* . . . G3
Norwich, *80* . . . E1
Oakes, **1,979** . . . G3
Oberon, **81** . . . F2
Olga . . . G1
Omemee . . . E1
Oriska, **128** . . . H3
Orrin . . . E1
Osnabrock, **174** . . . G1
Overly, **19** . . . E1
Oxbow, **248** . . . J3
Page, **225** . . . H2
Palermo, **77** . . . C1
Park River, **1,535** . . . H1
Parshall, **981** . . . C2
Pekin, **80** . . . G2
Pembina, **642** . . . H1
Penn, *90* . . . F1
Perth, **13** . . . F1
Petersburg, **195** . . . H2
Pettibone, **88** . . . F2
Pick City, **166** . . . D2
Pillsbury, **24** . . . H2
Pingree, **66** . . . G2
Pisek, **96** . . . H1
Plaza, **167** . . . D1
Portal, **131** . . . C1
Portland, **604** . . . H2
Powers Lake, **309** . . . C1
Prairie Rose, **68** . . . J3
Price, *40* . . . E2
Raleigh . . . D3
Raub . . . C2
Rawson, **6** . . . B2
Ray, **534** . . . B1
Reeder, **181** . . . C3
Regan, **43** . . . E2
Regent, **211** . . . C3
Reile's Acres, **254** . . . J3
Reynolds, **350** . . . H2
Rhame, **189** . . . B3
Richardton, **619** . . . C3
Riverdale, **273** . . . D2
Robinson, **71** . . . F2
Rocklake, **194** . . . F1
Rogers, **61** . . . G2
Rolette, **538** . . . F1
Rolla, **1,417** . . . F1
Roseglen . . . D2
Ross, **48** . . . C1
Rugby, **2,939** . . . F1
Ruso, **6** . . . E2
Russell, **10** . . . E1
Rutland, **220** . . . H3
Ryder, **92** . . . D2
St. Anthony, *40* . . . E3
St. John, **358** . . . F1
St. Thomas, **447** . . . H1
Sanborn, **194** . . . G3
Sarles, **25** . . . G1
Sawyer, **377** . . . D1
Scranton, **304** . . . B3
Selfridge, **223** . . . E3
Selz, *60* . . . F2
Sentinel Butte, **62** . . . B3
Sharon, **109** . . . H2
Sheldon, **135** . . . H3
Shell Valley, **395** . . . F1
Sherwood, **255** . . . D1
Sheyenne, **318** . . . F2
Shields . . . D3
Sibley, **46** . . . H2
Simcoe . . . E1
Solen, **86** . . . E3
Souris, **83** . . . E1
Southam . . . G1
South Heart, **307** . . . C3
Spiritwood, *50* . . . G3
Spiritwood Lake, **72** . . G2
Springbrook, **26** . . . B1
Stanley, **1,279** . . . C1
Stanton, **345** . . . D2
Starkweather, **157** . . . G1
Steele, **761** . . . F3
Sterling, *70* . . . E3
Strasburg, **549** . . . E3
Streeter, **172** . . . F3
Surrey, **917** . . . D1
Sutton, *50* . . . G2
Sykeston, **153** . . . F2
Tagus . . . D1
Tappen, **210** . . . F3
Taylor, **150** . . . C3
Temvik . . . E3
Thompson, **1,006** . . . H2
Tioga, **1,125** . . . C1
Tokio, *100* . . . G2
Tolley, **63** . . . D1
Tolna, **202** . . . G2
Tower City, **252** . . . H3
Towner, **574** . . . E1
Trenton, *350* . . . B1
Trotters . . . B2
Turtle Lake, **580** . . . E2
Tuttle, **106** . . . E2
Twin Buttes, *80* . . . C2
Underwood, **812** . . . D2
Upham, **155** . . . E1
Valley City, **6,826** . . . H3
Velva, **1,049** . . . E1
Venturia, **23** . . . F3
Verona, **108** . . . G3
Voltaire, **51** . . . E1
Voss, *70* . . . H1
Wahpeton, **8,586** . . . J3
Walcott, **189** . . . J3
Wales, **30** . . . G1
Walhalla, **1,057** . . . H1
Walum . . . G2
Warwick, **75** . . . G2
Washburn, **1,389** . . . D2
Watford City, **1,435** . . B2
Webster, *40* . . . G1
Wellsburg . . . F2
West Fargo, **14,940** . . . J3
Westfield, *40* . . . E3
Westhope, **533** . . . D1
Wheelock, **20** . . . B1
White Earth, **63** . . . C1
White Shield, **348** . . . D2
Whitman . . . G1
Wildrose, **129** . . . B1
Williston, **12,512** . . . B1
Willow City, **221** . . . E1
Wilton, **807** . . . E2
Wimbledon, **237** . . . G2
Wing, **124** . . . E2
Wishek, **1,122** . . . F3
Wolford, **50** . . . F1
Woodworth, **80** . . . F2
Wyndmere, **533** . . . H3
York, **26** . . . F1
Ypsilanti, *125* . . . G3
Zahl . . . B1
Zap, **231** . . . D2
Zeeland, **141** . . . F4

Other Features

Antler, *river* . . . D1
Ardoch N.W.R. . . . J1
Arrowwood N.W.R. . . G2
Audubon N.W.R. . . . D2
Bois de Sioux, *river* . . J4
Buffalo Lake N.W.R. . . F1
Canfield Lake N.W.R. . E2
Cannonball, *river* . . . D3
Cedar River Natl. Grassland . . . D3
Chase Lake N.W.R. . . . F2
Custer Natl. For. . . A4, B4
Des Lacs N.W.R. . . . C1
Devils, *lake* . . . G1
Florence Lake N.W.R. . E2
Fort Berthold Ind. Res. . C2
Fort Peck Ind. Res. . . . A1
Fort Union Trading Post Natl. Hist. Site . . . A2
Green, *river* . . . B2
Heart, *river* . . . D3
Hobart Lake N.W.R. . . G2
Intl. Peace Garden . . . E1
James, *river* . . F2, G3, G4
Jamestown Res. . . . G2
J. Clark Salyer N.W.R. . E1
Johnson Lake N.W.R. . G2
Kellys Slough N.W.R. . . H2
Knife, *river* . . . C2
Knife River Indian Villages Natl. Hist. Site . . . D2
Lake Alice N.W.R. . . . F1
Lake George N.W.R. . . F3
Lake Ilo N.W.R. . . . C2
Lake Nettie N.W.R. . . E2
Lake Traverse (Sisseton) Ind. Res. . . . H4
Lake Zahl N.W.R. . . . B1
Lamesteer N.W.R. . . . A3
Little Missouri, *river* . . B3
Little Missouri Natl. Grassland . . B1, B2, B3
Long, *lake* . . . E3
Long Lake N.W.R. . . . E3
Lostwood N.W.R. . . . C1
Maple, *river* . . . G3, H2
McLean N.W.R. . . . D2
Medicine, *lake* . . . A1

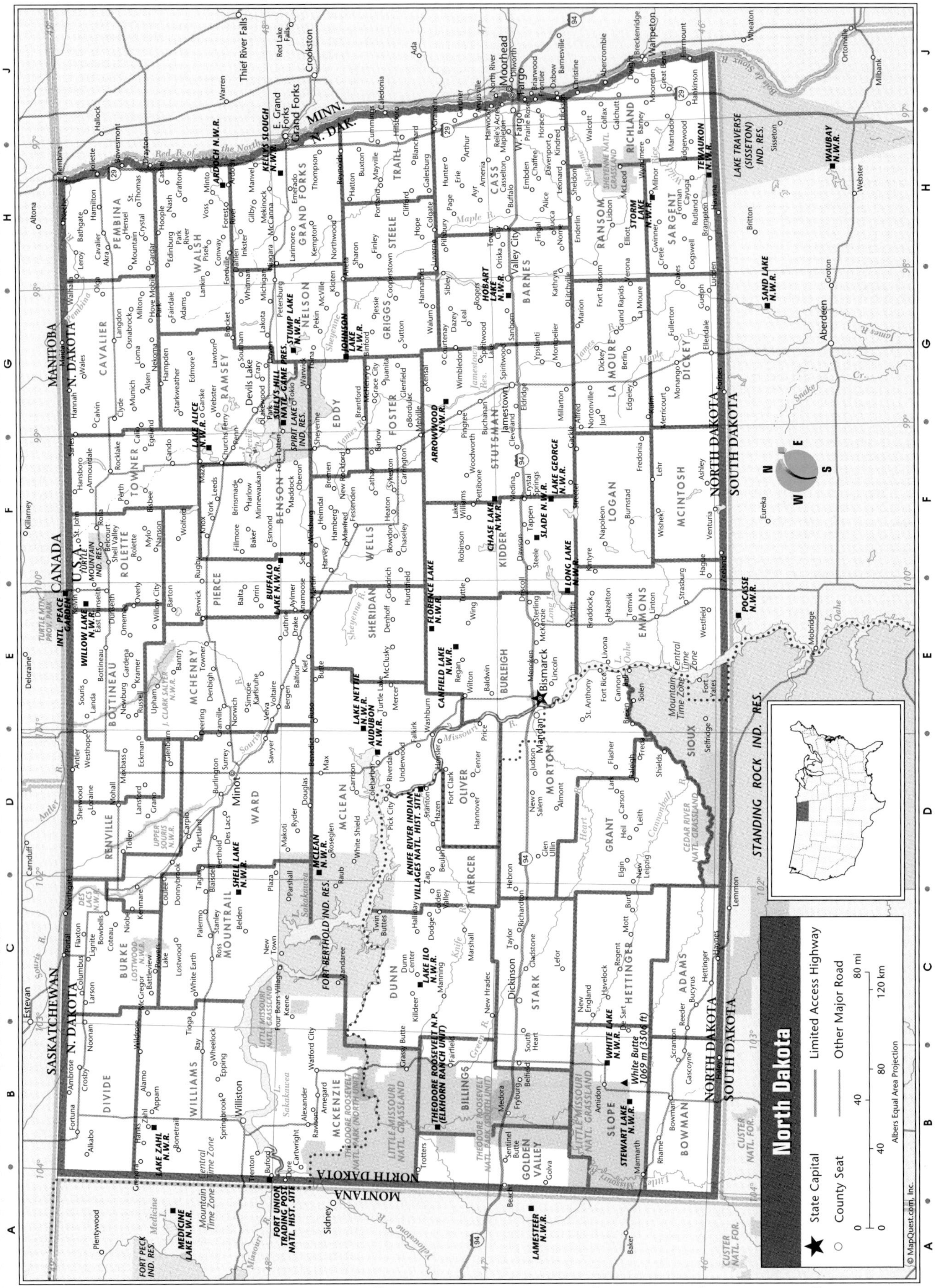

Ohio

Capital:	Columbus
Land Area:	40,953 sq. mi.
	106,067 sq. km.
Population:	11,353,140 (2000 Census)
Largest City:	Columbus, 711,470
Highest Point:	Campbell Hill, 1,549 ft.
	472 m.
Admitted to Union:	March 1, 1803
Nickname:	Buckeye State
State Flower:	Scarlet Carnation
State Bird:	Cardinal

Ohio:
Map Index

Counties

Adams, 27,330 . . . . . . C8
Allen, 108,473 . . . . . . B4
Ashland, 52,523 . . . . . F4
Ashtabula, 102,728 . . . J2
Athens, 62,223 . . . . . . G7
Auglaize, 46,611 . . . . . B4
Belmont, 70,226 . . . . . H6
Brown, 42,285 . . . . . . C8
Butler, 332,807 . . B7, B9
Carroll, 28,836 . . . . . . H4
Champaign, 38,890 . . . C5
Clark, 144,742 . . . . . . C6
Clermont, 177,977 B8, C1
Clinton, 40,543 . . . . . . C7
Columbiana, 112,075 . . J4
Coshocton, 36,655 . . . G5
Crawford, 46,966 . . . . E4
Cuyahoga, 1,393,978 . . . . . . G3, G9
Darke, 53,309 . . . . . . A5
Defiance, 39,500 . . . . . A3
Delaware, 109,989 D8, E5
Erie, 79,551 . . . . E3
Fairfield, 122,759 . E1, E6
Fayette, 28,433 . . . . . . D7
Franklin, 1,068,978 E5, E9
Fulton, 42,084 . . . . . . B2
Gallia, 31,069 . . . . . . F8
Geauga, 90,895 . H3, J9
Greene, 147,886 . C6, G2
Guernsey, 40,792 . . . . H5
Hamilton, 845,303 A1, A7
Hancock, 71,295 . . . . . C3
Hardin, 31,945 . . . . . . C4
Harrison, 15,856 . . . . . H5
Henry, 29,210 . . . . . . B3
Highland, 40,875 . . . . C7
Hocking, 28,241 . . . . . E7
Holmes, 38,943 . . . . . G4
Huron, 59,487 . . . . . . E3
Jackson, 32,641 . . . . . E8
Jefferson, 73,894 . . . . J5
Knox, 54,500 . . . . F5
Lake, 227,511 . . . H2, J8
Lawrence, 62,319 . . . . E8
Licking, 145,491 . . . . F5
Logan, 46,005 . . . . . . C5
Lorain, 284,664 . . F1, F3
Lucas, 455,054 . . . . . . C2
Madison, 40,213 . . . . . D6
Mahoning, 257,555 . . . J4
Marion, 66,217 . . . . . . D4
Medina, 151,095 . G1, G3
Meigs, 23,072 . . . . . . F7
Mercer, 40,924 . . . . . . A4
Miami, 98,868 . . . B5, G1
Monroe, 15,180 . . . . . H6
Montgomery, 559,062 . . . . . . B6, F2
Morgan, 14,897 . . . . . G6
Morrow, 31,628 . . . . . E4
Muskingum, 84,585 . . . G6
Noble, 14,058 . . . . . . H6
Ottawa, 40,985 . . . . . D2
Paulding, 20,293 . . . . A3
Perry, 34,078 . . . . . . F6
Pickaway, 52,727 . . . . D6
Pike, 27,695 . . . . D7
Portage, 152,061 . H3, J1
Preble, 42,337 . . . . . . A6
Putnam, 34,726 . . . . . B3
Richland, 128,852 . . . . E4
Ross, 73,345 . . . . D7
Sandusky, 61,792 . . . . D3
Scioto, 79,195 . . . . . . D8
Seneca, 58,683 . . . . . D3
Shelby, 47,910 . . . . . . B5
Stark, 378,098 . . . . . . H4
Summit, 542,899 . G3, H1
Trumbull, 225,116 . . . . J3
Tuscarawas, 90,914 . . . G5
Union, 40,909 . . . . . . D5
Van Wert, 29,659 . . . . A4
Vinton, 12,806 . . . . . . E7
Warren, 158,383 . . B7, C9
Washington, 63,251 . . . G7
Wayne, 111,564 . . . . . G4
Williams, 39,188 . . . . . A2
Wood, 121,065 . . . . . . C3
Wyandot, 22,908 . . . . D4

Cities and Towns

Aberdeen, 1,603 . . . . . C8
Ada, 5,582 . . . . C4
Adamsville, 127 . . . . . G5
Addison, 225 . . . . F8
Addyston, 1,010 . . . . . A9

Adelphi, 371 . . . . E7
Adena, 815 . . . . J5
Aid, 125 . . . . F8
Akron, 217,074 . . . . . G3
Albany, 808 . . . . F7
Alexandria, 85 . . . . . . E5
Alger, 888 . . . . C4
Allensville, 100 . . . . . . E7
Alliance, 23,253 . . . . . H4
Alvordton, 305 . . . . . . B2
Amanda, 707 . . . . E6
Amberley, 3,425 . . . . . B9
Amelia, 2,752 . . . . . . B7
Amesville, 184 . . . . . . G7
Amherst, 11,797 . . . . . F3
Amsden, 175 . . . . D3
Amsterdam, 568 . . . . . J5
Andersonville, 800 . . . D7
Andover, 1,269 . . . . . J2
Anna, 1,319 . . . . B5
Ansonia, 1,145 . . . . . A5
Antioch, 89 . . . . H6
Antrim, 175 . . . . H5
Antwerp, 1,740 . . . . . A3
Apple Creek, 999 . . . . G4
Aquilla, 372 . . . . . H2, J8
Arabia F8
Arcadia, 537 . . . . C3
Arcanum, 2,076 . . . . . A6
Archbold, 4,290 . . . . . B2
Arlington, 1,351 . . . . . C4
Armstrong Mills J6
Ashland, 21,249 . E9, F4
Ashley, 1,216 . . . . . . E5
Ashtabula, 20,962 . . . J2
Ashville, 3,174 . . . . . . E6
Athalia, 328 . . . . F8
Athens, 21,342 . . . . . F7
Attica, 955 . . . . E3
Atwater, 950 . . . . H3
Aurora, 13,556 . . . H3, J9
Austinburg, 450 . . . . . J2
Austintown, 31,627 . . J3
Ava, 250 . . . . G6
Avon, 11,446 . . . . . . F9
Avon Lake, 18,145 . . . F3
Bailey Lakes, 397 . . . . F4
Bainbridge (Geauga Co.), 3,417 . . . . J9
Bainbridge (Ross Co.), 1,012 . . . . D7
Bairdstown, 130 . . . . . C3
Ballville, 3,255 . . . . . . D3
Baltic, 743 . . . . G5
Baltimore, 2,881 . . . . E6
Barberton, 27,899 . . . G3
Barnesville, 4,225 . . . H6
Barnhill, 364 . . . . H5
Bartlett, 100 . . . . G7
Barton, 800 . . . . J5
Batavia, 1,617 . . . B7, C10
Batesville, 100 . . . . . . H6
Bay Bridge, 90 . . . . . E3
Bay View, 692 . . . . . . E3
Bay Village, 16,087 . . . F9
Beach City, 1,137 . . . . G4
Beachwood, 12,186 . . H9
Beallsville, 423 . . . . . H6
Beaver, 464 . . . . E7
Beavercreek, 37,984 . . . . B6, G2
Beaverdam, 356 . . . . . C4
Bedford, 14,214 . . . . . H9
Bedford Heights, 11,375 . . . . H9
Bellaire, 4,892 . . . . . . J5
Bellbrook, 7,009 . . . . . G2
Belle Center, 807 . . . . C4
Bellefontaine, 13,069 . C5
Belle Valley, 263 . . . . G6
Bellevue, 8,193 . . . . . E3
Bellville, 1,773 . . . . . . F4
Belmont, 532 . . . . . . H5
Belmore, 171 . . . . . . C3
Beloit, 1,024 . . . . H4
Belpre, 6,660 . . . . . . G7
Bentleyville, 947 . . . . . H9
Benton Ridge, 315 . . . C3
Bentonville, 250 . . . . . C8
Berea, 18,970 . . . . . . G9
Bergholz, 769 . . . . . . J4
Berkey, 265 . . . . C2
Berlin, 1,300 . . . . G4
Berlin Heights, 685 . . . F3
Bethel, 2,637 . . . . . . B8
Bethesda, 1,413 . . . . . H5
Bettsville, 784 . . . . . . D3
Beverly, 1,282 . . . . . . G6
Bevis (part of Northgate, pop. 8,016), 5,700 . . A9
Bexley, 13,203 . . . . . E9
Big Plain, 200 . . . . . . D6
Bladensburg, 250 . . . . F5

Blakeslee, 130 . . . . . . A2
Blanchester, 4,220 . . . C7
Blissfield, 150 . . . . . . G5
Bloomdale, 724 . . . . . C3
Bloomingburg, 874 . . . D6
Bloomingdale, 221 . . . J5
Bloomville, 1,045 . . . . D3
Blue Ash, 12,513 . . . . B9
Bluffton, 3,896 . . . . . C4
Boardman, 37,215 . . . J3
Bolivar, 894 . . . . H4
Boston Heights, 1,186 . . . . H10
Botkins, 1,205 . . . . . . B5
Bowerston, 414 . . . . . H5
Bowersville, 290 . . . . C6
Bowling Green, 29,636 . . . . C3
Bradford, 1,859 . . . . . B5
Bradner, 1,171 . . . . . D3
Brady Lake, 513 . . . . H3
Brandon, 200 . . . . . . F5
Bratenahl, 1,337 . . . . H8
Brecksville, 13,382 . . . H1
Bremen, 1,265 . . . . . F6
Brewster, 2,324 . . . . . G4
Briarwood Beach G3
Brice, 70 . . . . E9
Bridgeport, 2,186 . . . . J5
Bridgetown, 12,569 . . . . A7, A9
Brilliant, 1,600 . . . . . . J5
Brinkhaven, 143 . . . . . F5
Broadview Heights, 15,967 . . . . G9
Broadway, 250 . . . . . D5
Brooklyn, 11,586 . . . . G9
Brooklyn Heights, 1,558 . . . . G9
Brook Park, 21,218 . . . G9
Brookside, 644 . . . . . J5
Brookville, 5,289 . . . . B6
Broughton, 166 . . . . . A3
Brunersburg, 325 . . . . B3
Brunswick, 33,388 . . . . G3, G10
Bryan, 8,333 . . . . A3
Buchtel, 574 . . . . F7
Buckeye Lake, 3,049 . . E6
Buckland, 255 . . . . . . B4
Bucyrus, 13,224 . . . . E4
Buena Vista, 150 . . . . D7
Buford, 100 . . . . C7
Burbank, 279 . . . . . . F4
Burgoon, 199 . . . . . . D3
Burkettsville, 254 . . . . A5
Burlington, 2,794 . . . . E9
Burton, 1,450 . . . . . . H3
Butler, 921 . . . . F4
Butlerville, 231 . . . . . B7
Byer, 200 . . . . E7
Byesville, 2,574 . . . . . G6
Byhalia, 125 . . . . D5
Cadiz, 3,308 . . . . H5
Cadmus, 60 . . . . F8
Cairo, 499 . . . . B4
Calcutta, 3,491 . . . . . J4
Caldwell, 1,956 . . . . . G6
Caledonia, 578 . . . . . E4
Cambridge, 11,520 . . . G5
Camden, 2,302 . . . . . A6
Campbell, 9,460 . . . . . J3
Canal Fulton, 5,061 . . G4
Canal Winchester, 4,478 . . . . E10
Canfield, 7,374 . . . . . J3
Canton, 80,806 . . . . . H4
Carbondale, 175 . . . . F7
Cardington, 1,849 . . . E5
Carey, 3,901 . . . . D4
Carlisle, 5,121 . . . . . . B6
Carroll, 488 . . . . E6
Carrollton, 3,190 . . . . H4
Carrothers, 85 . . . . . . E3
Casstown, 322 . . . . . B5
Castalia, 935 . . . . . . E3
Castine, 129 . . . . A6
Catawba, 312 . . . . . . C5
Catawba Island, 850 . . E2
Cecil, 216 . . . . A3
Cedarville, 3,828 . . . . C6
Celina, 10,303 . . . . . . A4
Centerburg, 1,432 . . . E5
Centerville (Gallia Co.), 134 . . . . F8
Centerville (Montgomery Co.), 23,024 . . . . . . B6
Chagrin Falls, 4,024 . . H9
Champion, 4,727 . . . . J3
Chardon, 5,156 . . . H2, J8
Charm, 400 . . . . G4
Chatfield, 218 . . . . . . E4
Chattanooga, 175 . . . A4
Chauncey, 1,067 . . . . F7
Cherry Fork, 127 . . . . C8
Cherry Grove, 4,555 . . . . B7, C10
Chesapeake, 842 . . . . F9
Cheshire, 221 . . . . . . F8
Chester, 150 . . . . F7
Chesterhill, 305 . . . . . G7
Chesterville, 193 . . . . E5
Cheviot, 9,015 . . . A7, A9
Chickasaw, 364 . . . . . A5
Chillicothe, 21,796 . . . D7
Chilo, 97 . . . . B8
Chippewa-on-the-Lake, 823 . . . . G3
Christiansburg, 553 . . . B5
Cincinnati, 331,285 . . . . . . A7, B10
Circleville, 13,485 . . . E6
Clarington, 444 . . . . . J6
Clarksburg, 516 . . . . . D6
Clarksfield, 425 . . . . . F3
Clarksville, 497 . . . . . C7
Clay Center, 294 . . . . D2
Claysville, 125 . . . . . . H5
Clayton, 13,347 . . . . . B6
Cleveland, 478,403 . . . . . . G3, G9

Cleveland Heights, 49,958 . . . . . . G2, H9
Cleves, 2,790 . . . . . . A9
Clifton, 179 . . . . C6
Clinton, 1,337 . . . . . . G4
Cloverdale, 201 . . . . . B3
Clyde, 6,064 . . . . E3
Coal Grove, 2,027 . . . E8
Coal Run, 325 . . . . . . G6
Coalton, 545 . . . . . . E7
Coldwater, 4,482 . . . . A5
College Corner, 424 . . A6
Collins, 450 . . . . A5
Columbus, 711,470 . . . . . . D6, D9
Columbus Grove, 2,200 . . . . B4
Commercial Point, 776 D6
Condit, 325 . . . . E5
Conesville, 364 . . . . . G5
Congress, 192 . . . . . F4
Conneaut, 12,485 . . . J2
Conneautville, 1,188 . . B3
Convoy, 1,110 . . . . . . A4
Coolville, 528 . . . . . . G7
Cooperdale, 175 . . . . F5
Corning, 593 . . . . . . F6
Cortland, 6,830 . . . . . J3
Corwin, 256 . . . . B6
Coshocton, 11,682 . . . G5
Covington, 2,559 . . . . B5
Craig Beach, 1,254 . . . H3
Creola, 60 . . . . F7
Crestline, 5,088 . . . . . E4
Creston, 2,161 . . . . . G4
Cridersville, 1,817 . . . B4
Crooksville, 2,483 . . . F6
Crown City, 411 . . . . . F8
Cuba, 325 . . . . C7
Cumberland, 402 . . . . G6
Custar, 208 . . . . C3
Cutler, 125 . . . . G7
Cuyahoga Falls, 49,374 H3
Cuyahoga Heights, 599 G9
Cygnet, 564 . . . . C3
Dalton, 1,605 . . . . . . G4
Danville, 1,104 . . . . . F5
Darbyville, 293 . . . . . D6
Day Heights, 2,823 . . . C9
Dayton, 166,179 . . B6, F2
Decatur, 150 . . . . . . C8
Deerfield, 300 . . . . . . H3
Deer Park, 5,982 . . . . B9
Deersville, 82 . . . . . . H5
Defiance, 16,465 . . . . B3
DeForest (Bolindale), 2,800 . . . . J3
De Graff, 1,212 . . . . . C5
Delaware, 25,243 . . . . D5
Delhi, 1,450 . . . . H3
Delphos, 6,944 . . . . . B4
Delta, 2,930 . . . . B2
Dennison, 2,992 . . . . H5
Dent, 7,612 . . . . A9
Deshler, 1,831 . . . . . C3
Devola, 2,771 . . . . . . H7
Dexter, 70 . . . . F7
Dexter City, 166 . . . . . H6
Dillonvale, 781 . . . . . J5
Dodsonville, 275 . . . . C7
Donnelsville, 293 . . . . C6
Dorset, 225 . . . . J2
Dover, 12,210 . . . . . . H4
Doylestown, 2,799 . . . G4
Dresden, 1,423 . . . . . F5
Dublin, 31,392 . . . D5, D9
Duncan Falls, 950 . . . G6
Dunkinsville, 90 . . . . . D8
Dunkirk, 952 . . . . C4
Dupont, 268 . . . . B3
Eagle Mills, 50 . . . . . E7
Eagleport, 300 . . . . . G6
Eagleville, 175 . . . . . J2
East Canton, 1,629 . . . H4
East Claridon, 325 . . . H2
East Cleveland, 27,217 . . . . G2, H9
Eastlake, 20,255 . . . . H8
East Liverpool, 13,089 . J4
East Palestine, 4,917 . . J4
East Sparta, 806 . . . . H4
Eaton, 8,133 . . . . . . A6
Eaton Estates, 1,409 . . F9
Edgerton, 2,117 . . . . A3
Edgewood, 4,762 . . . . J2
Edison, 437 . . . . E4
Edon, 898 . . . . A2
Eldorado, 543 . . . . . . A6
Elgin, 50 . . . . B4
Elida, 1,917 . . . . B4
Elkton, 325 . . . . J4
Elm Grove, 200 . . . . . D7
Elmore, 1,426 . . . . . . D3
Elmwood Place, 2,681 . B9
Elyria, 55,953 . . . . . . F3
Empire, 300 . . . . J4
Englewood, 12,235 . . . F1
Enon, 2,638 . . . . C6
Epworth Heights, 3,300 C9
Euclid, 52,717 . . . G2, H8
Evendale, 3,090 . . . . B9
Fairborn, 32,052 . . B6, G1
Fairfax, 1,938 . . . . . . B9
Fairfield, 42,097 . . A7, B9
Fairfield Beach, 1,163 . F6
Fairlawn, 7,307 . . . . . G3
Fairport Harbor, 3,180 . H2
Fairview, 81 . . . . A3
Fairview Park, 17,572 . G9
Farmer, 150 . . . . A3
Farmersville, 980 . . . . B6
Fayette, 1,340 . . . . . . B2
Fayetteville, 372 . . . . C7
Felicity, 922 . . . . B8
Findlay, 38,967 . . . . . C3
Fitchville, 250 . . . . . . F3
Flat Rock, 400 . . . . . . E3
Fletcher, 510 . . . . . . B5
Florida, 246 . . . . B3
Flushing, 900 . . . . . . H5
Forest, 1,488 . . . . . . C4

Forest Park, 19,463 A7, B9
Forestville, 10,978 . . . B10
Fort Jennings, 432 . . . B4
Fort Loramie, 1,344 . . B5
Fort McKinley, 3,989 . . F1
Fort Recovery, 1,273 . . A5
Fort Shawnee, 3,855 . . B4
Foster, 425 . . . . C9
Fostoria, 13,931 . . . . . D3
Frankfort, 1,011 . . . . . D7
Franklin, 11,396 . . . . . B6
Franklin Furnace, 1,537 E8
Frazeysburg, 1,201 . . . F5
Fredericksburg, 487 . . G4
Fredericktown, 2,428 . . E5
Freeport, 398 . . . . . . H5
Fremont, 17,375 . . . . . D3
Fresno, 225 . . . . G5
Fruitdale, 80 . . . . D7
Fruit Hill, 3,945 . . . . . B10
Fulton, 264 . . . . E5
Fultonham, 151 . . . . . F6
Gahanna, 32,636 . . E5, E9
Galena, 305 . . . . E5
Galion, 11,341 . . . . . . E4
Gallipolis, 4,180 . . . . . F8
Gambier, 1,871 . . . . . F5
Garfield Heights, 30,734 . . . . G3, H9
Garrettsville, 2,262 . . . H3
Gates Mills, 2,493 . . . . H9
Geneva, 6,595 . . . . . . J2
Geneva-on-the-Lake, 1,545 . . . . J2
Genoa, 2,230 . . . . . . D2
Georgetown, 3,691 . . . C8
Gerald, 150 . . . . B3
Gettysburg, 558 . . . . . A5
Ghent (see Montrose), 5,261 . . . . G3
Gibsonburg, 2,506 . . . D3
Gilboa, 170 . . . . C3
Girard, 10,902 . . . . . . J3
Glandorf, 919 . . . . . . B3
Glendale, 2,188 . . . . . B9
Glenford, 198 . . . . . . F6
Glenmont, 283 . . . . . F4
Glenmoor, 2,192 . . . . J4
Glenwillow, 449 . . . . . H9
Gloria Glens Park, 538 . G3
Glouster, 1,972 . . . . . F6
Gnadenhutten, 1,280 . . H5
Golf Manor, 3,999 . . . B9
Good Hope, 275 . . . . . D7
Gordon, 190 . . . . A6
Grafton, 2,302 . . F3, F10
Grand River, 345 . . H2, J8
Grandview Heights, 6,695 . . . . D6, D9
Grant, 125 . . . . C4
Granville, 3,167 . . . . . E5
Gratiot, 187 . . . . F6
Gratis, 934 . . . . A6
Graysville, 113 . . . . . . H6
Green, 22,817 . . . . . . H4
Green Camp, 342 . . . . D4
Greenfield, 4,906 . . . . D7
Greenhills, 4,103 . . . . B9
Green Springs, 1,247 . . D3
Greenville, 13,294 . . . A5
Greenwich, 1,525 . . . . E3
Grove City, 27,075 . . . . . . D6, D10
Groveport, 3,865 . . . . E10
Grover Hill, 412 . . . . . B3
Gustavus, 275 . . . . . . J3
Hamden, 871 . . . . . . E7
Hamersville, 515 . . . . C8
Hamilton, 60,690 . . . . A7
Hamler, 650 . . . . B3
Hanging Rock, 279 . . . E8
Hannibal, 300 . . . . . . J6
Hanover, 885 . . . . . . F5
Hanoverton, 387 . . . . J4
Harbor View, 99 . . . . . D2
Harpster, 203 . . . . . . D4
Harrisburg, 332 . . . . . D6
Harrison, 7,487 . . . . . A7
Harrisonville, 150 . . . . F7
Harrisville, 259 . . . . . J5
Harrod, 491 . . . . C4
Hartford, 412 . . . . . . E5
Hartville, 2,174 . . . . . H4
Harveysburg, 563 . . . . B6
Haskins, 638 . . . . C3
Havana, 90 . . . . E3
Haviland, 180 . . . . . . A3
Haydenville, 475 . . . . F7
Hayesville, 348 . . . . . F4
Heath, 8,527 . . . . F5
Hebardville, 200 . . . . . F7
Hebron, 2,034 . . . . . . F6
Helena, 234 . . . . D3
Hemlock, 142 . . . . . . F6
Hepburn, 300 . . . . . . C4
Hicksville, 3,649 . . . . . A3
Higginsport, 291 . . . . C8
Highland, 283 . . . . . . C7
Highland Heights, 8,082 . . . . H8
Highland Hills, 1,618 . . H9
Hilliard, 24,230 . . . D5, D9
Hills and Dales, 260 . . H4
Hillsboro, 6,368 . . . . . C7
Hiram, 1,242 . . . . H3
Holgate, 1,194 . . . . . . B3
Holland, 1,306 . . . . . . C2
Hollansburg, 214 . . . . A5
Holloway, 345 . . . . . . H5
Holmesville, 386 . . . . G4
Hopedale, 984 . . . . . J5
Hoytville, 296 . . . . . . C3
Hubbard, 8,284 . . . . . J3
Huber Heights, 38,212 . . . . B6, G1
Huber Ridge, 4,883 E5, E9
Hudson Village, 22,439 . . . . . . H3, H10
Hunting Valley, 735 . . . H9
Huntsville, 454 . . . . . C5

Huron, 7,958 . . . . E3
Independence, 7,109 . . H9
Indian Hill B7, C9
Irondale, 418 . . . . . . J4
Ironton, 11,211 . . . . . E8
Ithaca, 102 . . . . A6
Jackson, 6,184 . . . . . E7
Jacksonburg, 67 . . . . . A6
Jackson Center, 1,369 . B5
Jacksonville, 544 . . . . F7
Jamestown, 1,917 . . . . C6
Jasper, 350 . . . . D7
Jefferson, 3,572 . . . . . J2
Jeffersonville, 1,288 . . C6
Jelloway, 175 . . . . . . F4
Jenera, 235 . . . . C4
Jeromesville, 478 . . . . F4
Jerry City, 453 . . . . . . C3
Jerusalem, 152 . . . . . H6
Jewell, 150 . . . . B3
Jewett, 784 . . . . H5
Johnstown, 3,440 . . . . E5
Junction City, 818 . . . . F6
Kalida, 1,031 . . . . B4
Keene, 200 . . . . G5
Kelleys Island, 367 . . . E2
Kent, 27,906 . . . . H3
Kenton, 8,336 . . . . . . C4
Kenwood, 7,423 . . . . . B9
Kettering, 57,502 . B6, G2
Kettlersville, 175 . . . . B5
Kilbourne, 275 . . . . . . E5
Killbuck, 839 . . . . G5
Kimball, 150 . . . . J2
Kimbolton, 190 . . . . . G5
Kingston, 1,032 . . . . . E7
Kinsman, 800 . . . . . . J3
Kipton, 265 . . . . F3
Kirby, 132 . . . . D4
Kirkersville, 520 . . . . . E6
Kirtland, 6,670 . . . H2, J8
Kirtland Hills, 597 . . . . J8
Kitts Hill, 650 . . . . E8
Kunkle, 400 . . . . B2
La Croft, 1,307 . . . . . . J4
Lafayette (Allen Co.), 304 . . . . C4
Lafayette (Madison Co.), 350 . . . . D6
Lagrange, 1,815 . . . . . F3
Lakeline, 165 . . . . . . H8
Lakemore, 2,561 . . . . H3
Lakeside, 1,000 . . . . . E2
Lakeview, 1,074 . . . . . C5
Lakewood, 56,646 G3, G9
Lancaster, 35,335 . . . . E6
Laporte, 1,600 . . . F3, F9
La Rue, 775 . . . . D4
Lattasburg, 275 . . . . . F4
Latty, 200 . . . . A3
Laura, 487 . . . . B5
Laurelville, 533 . . . . . E7
Lawrenceville, 302 . . . C5
Lebanon, 16,962 . . . . B7
Leesburg, 1,253 . . . . . C7
Leesville (Carroll Co.), 184 . . . . H5
Leesville (Crawford Co.), 350 . . . . E4
Leetonia, 2,043 . . . . . J4
Leipsic, 2,236 . . . . . . C3
Lewisburg, 1,798 . . . . A6
Lewis Center, 500 . . . . D5
Lewisville, 233 . . . . . . H6
Lexington, 4,165 . . . . F4
Liberty Center, 1,109 . . C3
Lima, 40,081 . . . . B4
Limaville, 193 . . . . . . H4
Lincoln Heights, 4,113 . B9
Lincoln Village, 9,482 . . D9
Lindsey, 504 . . . . D3
Linndale, 117 . . . . . . G9
Lisbon, 2,788 . . . . . . J4
Litchfield, 650 . . . . . . F3
Lithopolis, 600 . . . E6, E10
Lockbourne, 280 . E6, E10
Lockington, 208 . . . . . B5
Locust Grove, 225 . . . D8
Lodi, 3,061 . . . . F3
Logan, 6,704 . . . . F6
London, 8,771 . . . . . . D6
Londonderry, 200 . . . . E7
Lorain, 68,652 . . . . . . F3
Lordstown, 3,633 . . . . J3
Lore City, 305 . . . . . . H6
Loudonville, 2,906 . . . F4
Louisville, 8,904 . . . . . H4
Loveland, 11,677 . . . . C9
Loveland Park, 1,799 . . C9
Lowell, 628 . . . . G6
Lowellville, 1,281 . . . . J3
Lower Salem, 109 . . . . H6
Lucas, 620 . . . . F4
Lucasville, 1,588 . . . . D8
Luckey, 998 . . . . D3
Ludlow Falls, 210 . . . . B5
Lynchburg, 1,350 . . . . C7
Lyndhurst, 15,279 . . . . H9
Lynx, 350 . . . . D8
Lyons, 559 . . . . B2
Macedonia, 9,224 . G3, H9
Mack, 8,900 . . . . A9
Macksburg, 202 . . . . . H6
Macon, 250 . . . . C8
Madeira, 8,923 . . . B7, B9
Madison, 2,921 . . . . . H2
Madison Mills, 150 . . . D6
Madison-on-the-Lake (part of North Madison, pop. 8,451), 3,900 . . . . H2
Magnetic Springs, 323 D5
Magnolia, 931 . . . . . . H4
Maineville, 885 . . . B7, C9
Malinta, 285 . . . . B3
Malta, 696 . . . . G6
Malvern, 1,218 . . . . . H4
Manchester, 2,043 . . . C8
Mansfield, 49,346 . . . . E4
Mantua, 1,046 . . . . . . J10
Maple Heights, 26,156 . . . . G3, H9

Maple Ridge, 910 . . . . H4
Marble Cliff, 646 . . . . . D9
Marblehead, 762 . . . . E2
Marengo, 297 . . . . . . E5
Mariemont, 3,408 . . . . B9
Marietta, 14,515 . . . . . H7
Marion, 35,318 . . . . . D4
Marseilles, 124 . . . . . D4
Marshall, 150 . . . . . . D7
Marshallville, 826 . . . . G4
Martel, 200 . . . . E4
Martinsburg, 185 . . . . F5
Martins Ferry, 7,226 . . J5
Martinsville, 440 . . . . . C7
Marysville, 15,942 . . . . D5
Mason, 22,016 . . . . B7, C9
Massieville, 750 . . . . . E7
Massillon, 31,325 . . . . G4
Matamoras, 957 . . . . . H6
Maud, 4,800 . . . . B9
Maumee, 15,237 . . . . C2
Mayfield, 3,435 . . . . . H8
Mayfield Heights, 19,386 . . . . H9
McArthur, 1,888 . . . . . F7
McClure, 761 . . . . . . C3
McComb, 1,676 . . . . . C3
McConnelsville, 1,676 . G6
McCuneville, 100 . . . . F6
McDermott, 650 . . . . . D8
McDonald, 3,481 . . . . J3
McGuffey, 522 . . . . . . C4
Mecca, 300 . . . . J3
Mechanicsburg, 1,744 . C5
Medina, 25,139 . . . . . G3
Meeker, 250 . . . . D4
Melmore, 275 . . . . . . D3
Melrose, 322 . . . . B3
Mendon, 697 . . . . . . A4
Mentor, 50,278 . . . H2, J8
Mentor-on-the-Lake, 8,127 . . . . J8
Metamora, 563 . . . . . B2
Meyers Lake, 565 . . . . H4
Miamisburg, 19,489 . . . F2
Middleburg Heights, 15,542 . . . . G9
Middlefield, 2,233 . . . . H3
Middle Point, 593 . . . . B4
Middleport, 2,525 . . . . F7
Middletown, 51,605 . . . B6
Midland, 265 . . . . C7
Midvale, 547 . . . . H5
Midway, 274 . . . . D6
Mifflin, 144 . . . . F4
Milan, 1,445 . . . . E3
Milford, 6,284 . . . . B7, C9
Milford Center, 626 . . . D5
Millbury, 1,161 . . . . . . D2
Milledgeville, 122 . . . . C6
Miller City, 136 . . . . . . B3
Millersburg, 3,326 . . . . G4
Millersport, 963 . . . . . E6
Millville, 817 . . . . A7
Milton Center, 195 . . . C3
Miltonsburg, 29 . . . . . H6
Mineral City, 841 . . . . H4
Mineral Ridge, 3,900 . . J3
Minerva, 3,934 . . . . . H4
Minerva Park, 1,288 . . E9
Minford, 700 . . . . E8
Mingo Junction, 3,631 . J5
Minster, 2,794 . . . . . . B5
Mogadore, 3,893 . . . . H3
Monclova, 4,500 . . . . . C2
Monroe, 7,133 . . . . . . B7
Monroeville, 1,433 . . . E3
Montezuma, 191 . . . . A5
Montgomery, 10,163 . . . . B7, B9
Montpelier, 4,320 . . . . A2
Montrose (Montrose-Ghent), 5,261 . . . . . G3
Montville, 225 . . . . . . H2
Moraine, 6,897 . . . . B6, F2
Moreland Hills, 3,298 . . H9
Morgantown, 60 . . . . . D7
Morral, 388 . . . . D4
Morristown, 299 . . . . . H5
Morrow, 1,286 . . . . . . B7
Moscow, 244 . . . . B8
Mount Blanchard, 484 . C4
Mount Carmel, 4,308 . . C10
Mount Cory, 203 . . . . C4
Mount Eaton, 246 . . . . G4
Mount Gilead, 3,290 . . E4
Mount Healthy, 7,149 . . . . A7, B9
Mount Liberty, 300 . . . E5
Mount Orab, 2,307 . . . C7
Mount Pleasant, 535 . . J5
Mount Repose, 4,102 . . C9
Mount Sterling, 1,865 . . D6
Mount Vernon, 14,375 . F5
Mount Victory, 600 . . . C4
Mowrystown, 373 . . . . C7
Moxahala, 300 . . . . . . F6
Mulberry, 3,139 . . . . . C9
Munroe Falls, 5,314 . . . H3
Murray City, 452 . . . . F6
Mutual, 132 . . . . C5
Nankin, 550 . . . . F4
Napoleon, 9,318 . . . . . B3
Nashville, 172 . . . . . . F4
Navarre, 1,440 . . . . . . G4
Neapolis, 1,000 . . . . . C3
Neffs, 1,138 . . . . J5
Nellie, 134 . . . . F5
Nelsonville, 5,230 . . . . F7
Neptune, 250 . . . . . . A4
Nevada, 814 . . . . D4
Neville, 127 . . . . B8
New Alexandria, 222 . . J5
New Athens, 342 . . . . H5
New Bavaria, 78 . . . . . B3
New Bloomington, 548 . . . . D4
New Boston, 2,340 . . . D8
New Bremen, 2,909 . . . B5

Newburgh Heights, 2,389 . . . . G9
New Carlisle, 5,735 . . . B6
Newcomerstown, 4,008 . . . . G5
New Concord, 2,651 . . G5
New Holland, 785 . . . . D6
New Knoxville, 891 . . . B4
New Lebanon, 4,231 . . B6
New Lexington, 4,689 . . F6
New London, 2,696 . . . F3
New Madison, 817 . . . A6
New Matamoras, 957 . . H6
New Miami, 2,469 . . . . A7
New Middletown, 1,682 . . . . J4
New Paris, 1,623 . . . . . A6
New Petersburg, 70 . . . D7
New Philadelphia, 17,056 . . . . H5
Newport (Shelby Co.), 375 . . . . B5
Newport (Washington Co.), 1,100 . . . . . . H7
New Richmond, 2,219 . B8
New Riegel, 226 . . . . . D3
New Rome, 60 . . . . . . D9
New Straitsville, 774 . . F6
Newton Falls, 5,002 . . . J3
Newtonsville, 492 . . . . B7
Newtown, 2,420 . . . . . B10
New Vienna, 1,294 . . . C7
New Washington, 987 . E4
New Waterford, 1,391 . J4
New Weston, 135 . . . . A5
Ney, 364 . . . . A3
Niles, 20,932 . . . . J3
North Baltimore, 3,361 . C3
North Bend, 603 . . . . A9
North Bloomfield, 325 . J3
Northbrook, 11,076 . . . B9
North Canton, 16,369 . H4
North College Hill, 10,082 . . . . B9
North Fairfield, 573 . . . E3
Northfield, 3,827 . . . . . H9
North Hampton, 370 . . C5
North Industry, 1,800 . . H4
North Kingsville, 2,658 . J2
North Lewisburg, 1,588 . . . . C5
North Olmsted, 34,113 . . . . F9, G3
North Perry, 838 . . . . H2
North Randall, 906 . . . H9
Northridge (Clark Co.), 6,853 . . . . C6
Northridge (Montgomery Co.), 8,487 . . . . . . F1
North Ridgeville, 22,338 . . . . F9
North Robinson, 211 . . E4
North Royalton, 28,648 . . . . G9
North Star, 209 . . . . . A5
Northwood, 5,471 . . . . C2
North Zanesville, 3,013 F6
Norton, 11,523 . . . . . . G3
Norwalk, 16,238 . . . . . E3
Norwich, 113 . . . . G6
Norwood, 21,675 . B7, B9
Nova, 425 . . . . F3
Oak Harbor, 2,841 . . . D2
Oak Hill, 1,685 . . . . . . E8
Oakshade, 275 . . . . . B2
Oakwood (Cuyahoga Co.), 3,667 . . . . . . H9
Oakwood (Montgomery Co.), 9,215 . . . . . . F2
Oakwood (Paulding Co.), 607 . . . . B3
Oberlin, 8,195 . . . . . . F3
Obetz, 3,977 . . . . E10
Octa, 83 . . . . C6
Ohio City, 784 . . . . . . A4
Okolona, 200 . . . . B3
Old Washington, 265 . . H5
Olena, 250 . . . . E3
Olmsted Falls, 7,962 . . G9
Omega, 225 . . . . E7
Ontario, 5,303 . . . . . . E4
Orange, 3,236 . . . . . . H9
Orangeville, 189 . . . . . J3
Oregon, 19,355 . . . . . D2
Oregonia, 175 . . . . . . B7
Orient, 269 . . . . D6
Orrville, 8,551 . . . . . . G4
Orwell, 1,519 . . . . . . J2
Osgood, 255 . . . . A5
Ostrander, 405 . . . . . . D5
Otsego B3
Ottawa, 4,367 . . . . . . B3
Ottawa Hills, 4,564 . . . C2
Ottoville, 873 . . . . B4
Otway, 86 . . . . D8
Owensville, 816 . . . . . B7
Oxford, 21,943 . . . . . A6
Page Manor (Overlook-Page Manor) G2
Painesville, 17,503 . H2, J8
Palestine, 170 . . . . . . A5
Pandora, 1,188 . . . . . C4
Parkertown, 225 . . . . . E3
Parkman, 600 . . . . . . H3
Parma, 85,655 . . . G3, G9
Parma Heights, 21,659 G9
Parral, 241 . . . . G4
Pataskala, 10,249 . . . . E5
Patterson, 138 . . . . . . C4
Paulding, 3,595 . . . . . A3
Payne, 1,166 . . . . A3
Pedro, 325 . . . . E8
Peebles, 1,739 . . . . . . D8
Pemberville, 1,365 . . . D3
Peninsula, 602 . . . G3, H10
Peoria, 250 . . . . D5
Pepper Pike, 6,040 . . . H9
Perry, 1,195 . . . . H2
Perry Heights, 8,900 . . H4
Perrysburg, 16,945 . . . C2
Perrysville, 816 . . . . . F4

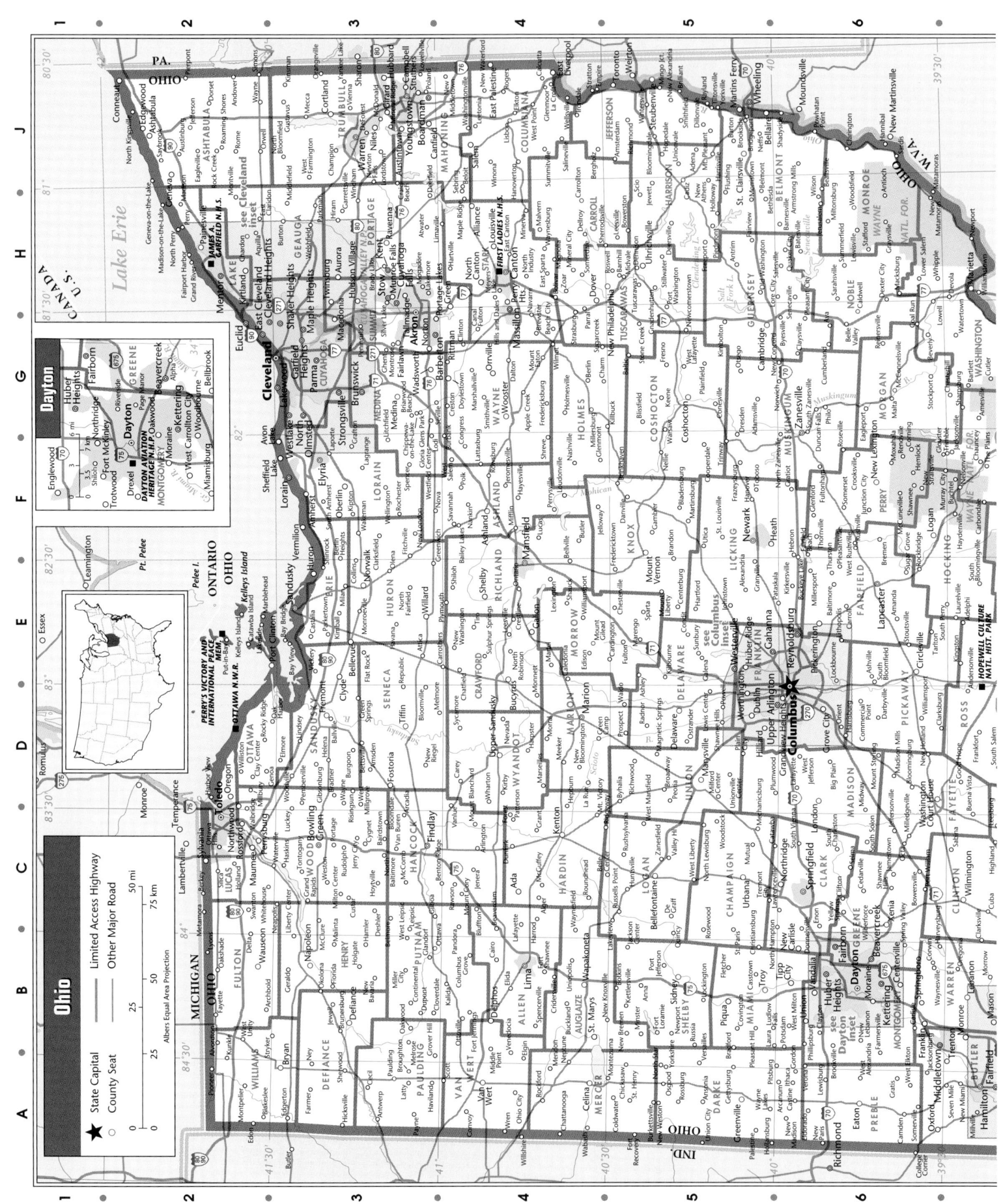

Maps: Cincinnati; Cleveland; Columbus

© MapQuest.com, Inc.

Index

Phillipsburg, 628 ... F6
Philo, 769 ... D3
Pickerington, 9,792 ... E6, E10
Piedmont, 225 ... F6
Pierpont, 300 ... J2
Piketon, 1,907 ... D7
Pioneer, 1,460 ... A2
Piqua, 20,738 ... B5
Pitsburg, 392 ... A6
Plain City, 2,832 ... D5
Plainfield, 158 ... F6
Pleasant City, 439 ... G6
Pleasant Hill, 1,134 ... B5
Pleasant Plain, 156 ... B7
Pleasant Run, 5,267 ... E6
Pleasantville, 877 ... E6
Plymouth, 1,852 ... E4
Poland, 2,866 ... C3
Polk, 357 ... F4
Pomeroy, 1,966 ... G3
Portage, 428 ... D2
Portage Lakes, 9,870 ... J4
Port Clinton, 6,391 ... E8
Port Jefferson, 321 ... J4
Portsmouth, 20,909 ... D8
Port Washington, 552 ... B6
Port William, 258 ... E6
Potsdam, 203 ... B6
Powell, 6,247 ... E4
Powhatan Point, 1,744 ... J4
Prospect, 1,191 ... D5
Put-in-Bay, 128 ... E2
Quaker City, 563 ... A5
Quincy, 734 ... H6
Racine, 746 ... G3
Radnor, 275 ... D7
Rarden, 11,771 ... D8
Rawson, 465 ... H4
Rayland, 434 ... B7, J9
Reading, 11,292 ... G7
Reedsville, 175 ... G6
Reinersville, 70 ... H9
Remindersville, 2,347 ... H9

Rendville, 46 ... B6
Republic, 614 ... G6
Reynoldsburg, 32,069 ... E6, E10
Richfield, 3,286 ... H5
Richmond, 471 ... B7
Richmond Dale, 500 ... E7
Richmond Heights, 10,944 ... H8
Richwood, 2,156 ... D5
Ridgeway, 354 ... C4
Rio Grande, 915 ... G3
Ripley, 1,745 ... C8
Risley, 11,620 ... B5
Rittman, 6,314 ... G5
Riverlea, 499 ... E6
Riverside, 23,545 ... E4
Roaming Shores, 1,239 ... J2
Rochester, 190 ... F4
Rockbridge, 550 ... F6
Rock Creek, 584 ... J2
Rockford, 1,126 ... A4
Rocky Hill, 70 ... D2
Rocky Ridge, 389 ... J4
Rogers, 266 ... B8
Rome (Adams Co.), 117 ... D8
Rome (Ashtabula Co.) ... J2
Rosemount, 2,043 ... E8
Roseville, 1,936 ... F6
Ross, 1,971 ... A9
Rossburg, 60 ... A5
Rossford, 6,406 ... C2
Roswell, 276 ... B6
Roundhead, 125 ... B4
Rudolph, 600 ... D2
Rushsylvania, 543 ... C4
Rushville, 268 ... E6
Russells Point, 1,619 ... C4
Russellville, 453 ... G4
Russia, 551 ... B5
Rutland, 401 ... F7

Sabina, 2,780 ... C7
St. Bernard, 4,924 ... B9
St. Clairsville, 5,057 ... A5
St. Henry, 2,271 ... F5
St. Louisville, 346 ... C7
St. Martin, 91 ... B4
St. Marys, 8,342 ... C5
St. Paris, 1,998 ... J4
Salem, 12,197 ... H6
Salesville, 154 ... D5
Sandusky, 27,844 ... G4
Saratoga, 198 ... F8
Sardinia, 862 ... G4
Sardis, 750 ... D4
Saybrook, 850 ... J6
Savannah, 372 ... H5
Scio, 799 ... E8
Sciotodale, 982 ... A4
Scott, 322 ... C8
Seaman, 1,039 ... H4
Sebring, 4,912 ... C6
Selma, 225 ... A7
Senecaville, 453 ... H6
Seven Hills, 12,080 ... C9
Seven Mile, 678 ... G3
Seville, 2,160 ... J6
Shade, 100 ... G3, H9
Shadyside, 3,675 ... D7
Shaker Heights, 29,405 ... E8
Shandon, 425 ... B9
Sharonville, 13,804 ... A9
Sharpsburg, 60 ... E4
Shauck, 400 ... A5
Shawnee, 608 ... F6
Shawnee Hills (Delaware Co.), 419 ... D5
Shawnee Hills (Greene Co.), 11,272 ... F1

Shiloh (Richland Co.), 721 ... H3
Shinrock, 200 ... G4
Shreve, 1,582 ... J10
Sidney, 20,211 ... J3
Silica, 1,100 ... J3
Silver Lake, 3,019 ... E6
Silverton, 5,178 ... E6
Simons, 225 ... D7
Sinking Spring, 158 ... H6
Smithfield, 867 ... D4
Smithville, 1,333 ... E4
Solon, 21,802 ... C10
Somerdale, 275 ... H4
Somerset, 1,549 ... F6
Somerville, 294 ... A6
South Amherst, 1,863 ... F3
South Bloomfield, 1,179 ... F6
South Bloomingville, 90 ... E6
South Charleston, 1,850 ... G3, D4
South Euclid, 23,537 ... C10
South Lebanon, 2,538 ... C9
South Perry, 150 ... E6
South Point, 3,742 ... F6
South Russell, 4,022 ... C9
South Salem, 213 ... D7
South Solon, 405 ... D7
South Vienna, 469 ... H8
South Webster, 764 ... C10
South Zanesville, 1,936 ... B6
Spargursville, 175 ... J3, H9
Sparta, 191 ... D7
Spencer, 747 ... G5
Spencerville, 2,235 ... B4
Springboro, 12,380 ... A9
Springdale, 10,563 ... B9
Spring Valley, 510 ... B7
Stafford, 86 ... H6
Steubenville, 19,015 ... A9
Stewart, 225 ... G7
Stillwater, 150 ... H5
Stockdale, 150 ... D8
Stockport, 540 ... G6
Stone Creek, 184 ... G5
Stoutsville, 581 ... E6

Stow, 32,139 ... C7
Strasburg, 2,310 ... B9
Stratton, 277 ... F4
Streetsboro, 12,311 ... B5
Strongsville, 43,858 ... G3, D5
Struthers, 11,756 ... B4
Stryker, 1,406 ... H9
Sugar Bush Knolls, 227 ... C7
Sugarcreek, 4,022 ... F10
Sulphur Springs, 400 ... D4
Summerfield, 296 ... H6
Summerside, 5,523 ... E4
Summit Station, 108 ...
Summitville, 108 ... J4
Sunbury, 2,630 ... D6
Swanton, 3,307 ... C2
Sycamore, 914 ... G5
Sylvania, 18,670 ... C2
Tallmadge, 16,390 ... F3
Tarlton, 298 ... E6
Terrace Park, 2,273 ... E6
The Plains, 2,931 ... F7
Thornville, 755 ... F6
Thurston, 555 ... E6
Tiffin, 18,135 ... G4
Tiltonsville, 1,329 ... B6
Timberlake, 775 ... H8
Tipp City, 9,221 ... B6
Tiro, 281 ... G4
Tobosco, 125 ...
Toledo, 313,619 ... B8
Tontogany, 446 ...
Toronto, 5,676 ... B7
Trenton, 8,746 ... A8
Trimble, 466 ... F7
Trinway, 450 ...
Trotwood, 27,420 ... H5
Troy, 21,999 ... B6
Turpin Hills, 4,960 ... B10
Tuscarawas, 934 ... H4
Twinsburg, 17,006 ... H3, B9
Tylersville, 3,484 ... B9
Uhrichsville, 5,662 ... H5

Union, 5,574 ... B6
Union City, 1,767 ... A5
Unionvale, 80 ... D5
Uniontown, 256 ... B4
Uniopolis, 256 ... H9
University Heights, 14,146 ...
Upper Arlington, 33,686 ... D5, D9
Upper Sandusky, 6,533 ... D4
Urbana, 11,613 ... C6
Urbancrest, 868 ... E7
Utica, 2,130 ... F5, F10
Valley Hi, 244 ... D9
Valley View, 2,179 ... C9
Valleyview, 601 ... H3
Vandalia, 14,603 ... B6
Van Buren, 313 ...
Vanlue, 371 ... A6
Van Wert, 10,690 ... A4
Venedocia, 160 ... B4
Vermilion, 10,927 ... F3
Verona, 430 ... B5
Versailles, 2,589 ... B5
Vickery, 300 ... D3
Vienna (Vienna Center), 650 ... J3
Vinton, 324 ... J3
Wadsworth, 18,437 ... G5
Wakeman, 951 ... F3
Waldo, 332 ... D5
Walton Hills, 2,400 ... B9
Wapakoneta, 9,474 ... B4
Warren, 46,832 ... B8
Warrensville Heights, 15,109 ... C9
Warsaw, 781 ... F5
Washington Court House, 13,524 ... D6
Washingtonville, 789 ... J4
Watertown, 225 ... G7

Waterville, 4,828 ... C2, B6
Wauseon, 7,091 ... A5
Waverly, 4,433 ... E7
Wayne (Ashtabula Co.), 725 ...
Wayne (Wood Co.), 842 ... D6
Wayne Lakes, 684 ... A5
Waynesburg, 1,003 ... H4
Waynesfield, 803 ... C4
Waynesville, 2,558 ... B6
Wellington, 4,511 ... F3
Wellston, 6,078 ... E7
Wellsville, 4,133 ... G4
Welshfield, 350 ... H3, J9
West Alexandria, 1,395 ... A6
West Carrollton City, 13,818 ...
West Elkton, 194 ... A6
Westerville, 35,318 ... E5, E9
West Farmington, 519 ... J3
West Jefferson, 1,054 ... G2
Westfield Center, 1,054 ... D4, G4
West Lafayette, 2,313 ... B9
Westlake, 31,719 ... F9, G9
West Leipsic, 271 ... B3
West Liberty, 1,813 ... C5
West Mansfield, 700 ... D3
West Milton, 4,645 ... B6
Weston, 1,659 ... B6
West Point, 375 ... A4
West Portsmouth, 3,458 ... G3
Westville, 99 ... J4
Wharton, 409 ... G4
Wheelersburg, 6,471 ... C8
Whipple, 225 ... E8
White Oak, 13,277 ... B9
Whitehall, 19,201 ... E10
Whitehouse, 2,733 ... H9
Wickliffe, 13,484 ... C5
Wilberforce, 1,579 ... D6
Willard, 6,806 ... H5

Williamsburg, 2,358 ... C2, B7
Williamsport (Morrow Co.) ... B2
Williamsport (Pickaway Co.), 725 ... E7
Willoughby, 22,621 ... D6, D2
Willoughby Hills, 8,595 ... H8
Willowick, 14,361 ... H8
Willshire, 463 ... A4
Wilmington, 11,921 ... C7
Wilmot, 335 ... G4
Wilson, 118 ... H6
Winchester, 1,025 ... C8
Windham, 2,806 ... H3
Winkle, 225 ...
Winona, 475 ... C7
Wintersville, 4,067 ... J4
Withamsville, 3,145 ... B10
Woodbourne (Woodbourne-Hyde Park), 7,910 ... D9
Woodlawn, 2,816 ... B9
Woodmere, 828 ... H9
Woodsfield, 2,598 ... F2
Woodstock, 317 ... C5
Woodville, 1,977 ... D3
Wooster, 24,811 ... G4
Worthington, 14,125 ... D5, D9
Wren, 195 ... A4
Wyoming, 8,261 ... B9
Xenia, 24,164 ... C6
Yankee Lake, 99 ... B8
Yellow Springs, 3,761 ... C6
Yorkshire, 110 ... B5
Yorkville, 1,230 ... J9
Youngstown, 82,026 ... B8
Zaleski, 375 ... F7
Zanesfield, 220 ... C5
Zanesville, 25,586 ... F6
Zoar, 193 ... H4

Other Features

Alum, river ... E10
Clendening, lake ... H5

Cuyahoga, river ... H9
Cuyahoga Valley N.P. ... G3, H10
Dayton Aviation Heritage ... F2
Erie, lake ... G8, H2
First Ladies N.H.S. ... G4
Gr. Miami, river ... A9, F2
Hocking, river ... F7
Hopewell Culture Natl. Hist. Park ... E7
James A. Garfield N.H.S. ... H2, J8
Kanawha, river ... G8
Kelleys, island ... E2
Little Kanawha, river ... C9, G8
Little Miami, river ... C9, F4
Mohican, river ... G6
Muskingum, river ... D9
Ohio, river ... A10, D8, J6
Ottawa N.W.R. ... F2
Pelee, island ... A9, F2
Pelee, point ... F2
Perry's Victory And International Peace Mem. ... E2
Raccoon, creek ... F7
Salt Fork, lake ... H5
Sandusky, river ... D3
Scioto, river ... C9, D8
Senecaville, lake ... D4, H6
Wayne Nat. For. ... E7, F8, F6
William H. Taft N.H.S. ... B10

Oklahoma

Capital:	Oklahoma City
Land Area:	68,679 sq. mi.
	177,879 sq. km.
Population:	3,450,654 (2000 Census)
Largest City:	Oklahoma City, 506,132
Highest Point:	Black Mesa, 4,973 ft. 1,516 m.
Admitted to Union:	November 16, 1907
Nickname:	Sooner State
State Flower:	Mistletoe
State Bird:	Scissor-tailed Flycatcher

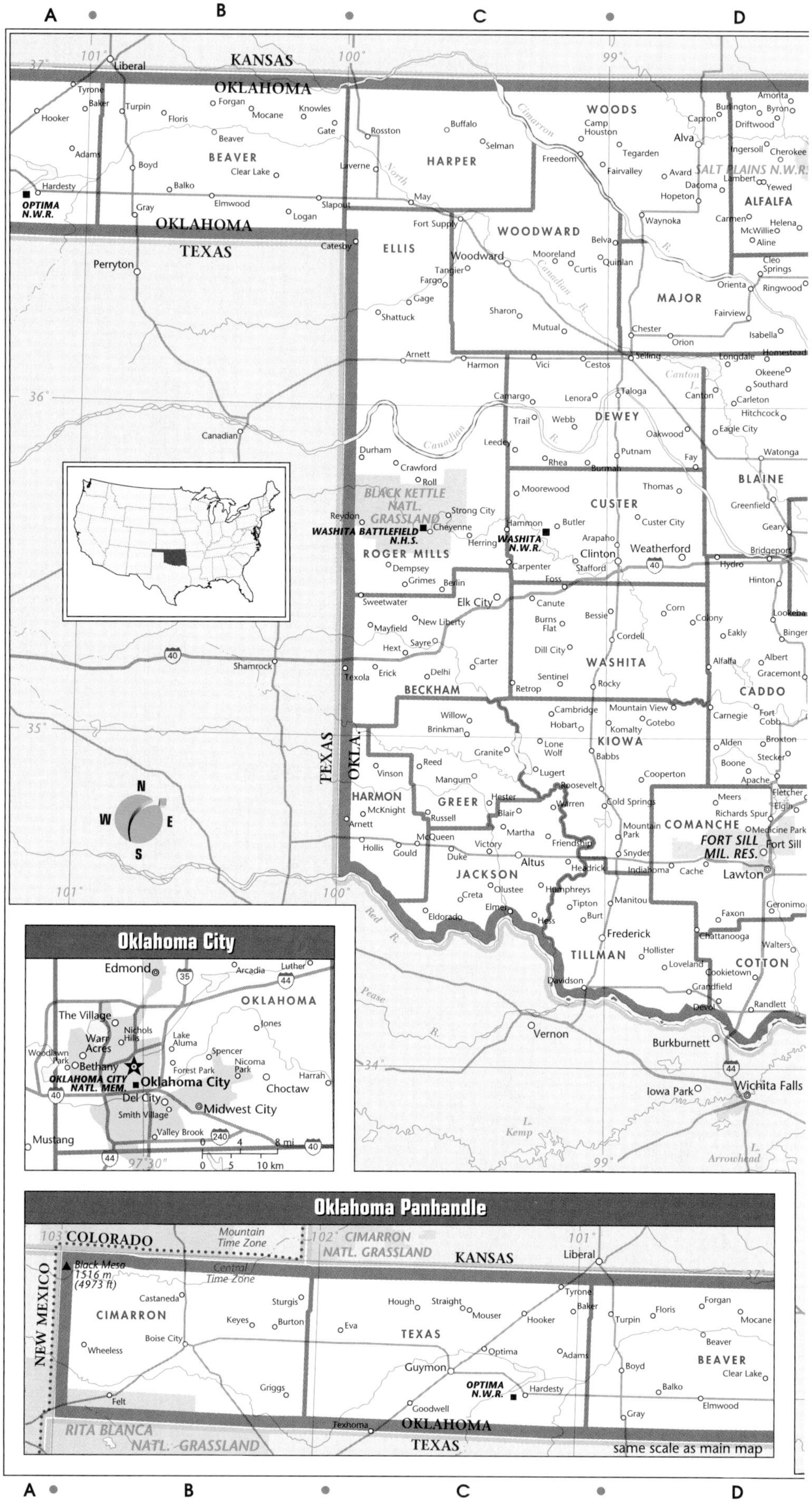

Oklahoma: Map Index

Counties

Adair, 21,038	H2
Alfalfa, 6,105	D1
Atoka, 13,879	G3
Beaver, 5,857	B1, D4
Beckham, 19,799	C2
Blaine, 11,976	D2
Bryan, 36,534	F3
Caddo, 30,150	D2
Canadian, 87,697	E2
Carter, 45,621	E3
Cherokee, 42,521	G2
Choctaw, 15,342	G3
Cimarron, 3,148	B4
Cleveland, 208,016	E2
Coal, 6,031	F3
Comanche, 114,996	D3
Cotton, 6,614	D3
Craig, 14,950	G1
Creek, 67,367	F2
Custer, 26,142	D2
Delaware, 37,077	H1
Dewey, 4,743	D2
Ellis, 4,075	C1
Garfield, 57,813	E1
Garvin, 27,210	E3
Grady, 45,516	E2
Grant, 5,144	E1
Greer, 6,061	C3
Harmon, 3,283	C3
Harper, 3,562	C1
Haskell, 11,792	G2
Hughes, 14,154	F2
Jackson, 28,439	C3
Jefferson, 6,818	E3
Johnston, 10,513	F3
Kay, 48,080	E1
Kingfisher, 13,926	E2
Kiowa, 10,227	D3
Latimer, 10,692	G3
Le Flore, 48,109	H3
Lincoln, 32,080	F2
Logan, 33,924	E2
Love, 8,831	E4
Major, 7,545	D1
Marshall, 13,184	F3
Mayes, 38,369	G1
McClain, 27,740	E3
McCurtain, 34,402	H3
McIntosh, 19,456	G2
Murray, 12,623	E3
Muskogee, 69,451	G2
Noble, 11,411	E1
Nowata, 10,569	G1
Okfuskee, 11,814	F2
Oklahoma, 660,448	B3, E2
Okmulgee, 39,685	G2
Osage, 44,437	F1
Ottawa, 33,194	H1
Pawnee, 16,612	F1
Payne, 68,190	E1
Pittsburg, 43,953	G3
Pontotoc, 35,143	F3
Pottawatomie, 65,521	F2
Pushmataha, 11,667	G3
Roger Mills, 3,436	C2
Rogers, 70,641	G1
Seminole, 24,894	F2
Sequoyah, 38,972	H2
Stephens, 43,182	E3
Texas, 20,107	C4
Tillman, 9,287	C3
Tulsa, 563,299	G1
Wagoner, 57,491	G2
Washington, 48,996	G1
Washita, 11,508	D2
Woods, 9,089	C1
Woodward, 18,486	C1

Cities and Towns

Achille, 506	F4
Ada, 15,691	F3
Adair, 704	G2
Adams, 175	A1, C4
Addington, 117	E3
Afton, 1,118	H1
Agawam, 70	E3
Agra, 356	F2
Ahloso, 175	F3
Albany, 80	F4
Albert, 100	D2
Albion, 143	G3
Alden	D3
Alderson, 261	G3
Alex, 635	E3
Alfalfa, 40	D2
Aline, 214	D1
Allen, 951	F3
Altus, 21,447	C3
Alva, 5,288	D1
Amber, 490	E2
Ames, 199	D1
Amorita, 44	D1
Anadarko, 6,645	D2
Antioch, 70	E3
Antlers, 2,552	G3
Apache, 1,616	D3
Arapaho, 748	C2
Arcadia, 279	B3, E2
Ardmore, 23,711	E3
Arkoma, 2,180	H2
Armstrong, 141	F3
Arnett (Ellis Co.), 520	C1
Arnett (Harmon Co.)	C3
Arpelar, 50	G3
Asher, 419	F3
Ashland, 53	F3
Atoka, 2,988	F3
Atwood, 113	F3
Avant, 372	F1
Avard, 26	D1
Avery, 60	F2
Babbs	C3
Baker, 60	A1, C4
Balko, 40	B1, D4
Barnsdall, 1,325	F1
Baron, 70	H2
Bartlesville, 34,748	F1
Bearden, 140	F2
Beaver, 1,570	B1, D4
Beckett	E3
Beggs, 1,364	F2
Belva	D1
Bennington, 289	F3
Berlin	C2
Bernice, 504	H1
Bessie, 190	D2
Bethany, 20,307	B4, E2
Bethel, 70	H3
Bethel Acres, 2,735	E2
Big Cabin, 293	G1
Big Cedar	H3
Billings, 436	E1
Binger, 708	D2
Bison, 100	E1
Bixby, 13,336	G2
Blackburn, 102	F1
Blackwell, 7,668	E1
Blair, 894	C3
Blanchard, 2,816	E2
Blanco, 90	G3
Blocker, 60	G2
Bluejacket, 274	G1
Boatman, 325	G1
Boise City, 1,483	B4
Bokchito, 564	F3
Bokhoma, 100	H4
Bokoshe, 450	H2
Boley, 1,126	F2
Boone, 100	D3
Boswell, 703	G3
Bowlegs, 371	F2
Bowring, 40	F1
Boyd	B1, D4
Boynton, 274	G2
Bradley, 182	E3
Braggs, 301	G2
Braman, 244	E1
Bray, 1,035	E3
Breckinridge, 239	E1
Briartown, 150	G2
Bridgeport, 109	D2
Brinkman	C2
Bristow, 4,325	F2
Broken Arrow, 74,859	G1
Broken Bow, 4,230	H3
Bromide, 163	F3

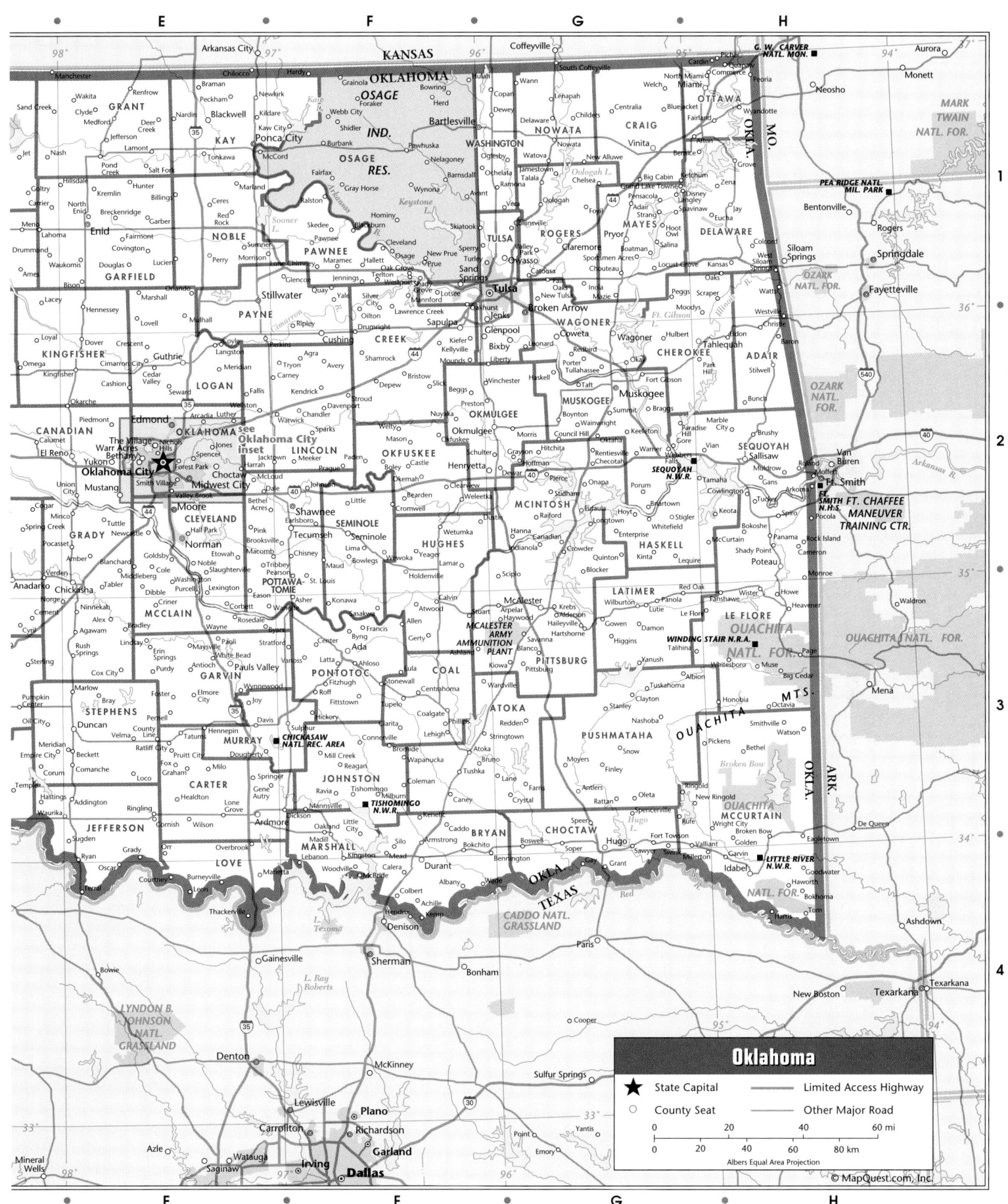

Oklahoma

★ State Capital ——— Limited Access Highway
○ County Seat ——— Other Major Road

0   20   40   60 mi
0   20   40   60   80 km
Albers Equal Area Projection

© MapQuest.com, Inc.

Brooksville, 90 ...F2
Broxton ...D3
Bruno, 80 ...F3
Brushy, 787 ...H2
Buffalo, 1,200 ...C1
Bunch, 40 ...H2
Burbank, 155 ...F1
Burlington, 156 ...D1
Burmah ...C2
Burneyville, 70 ...E4
Burns Flat, 1,782 ...C2
Burt ...C3
Burton ...B4
Butler, 345 ...C2
Byars, 280 ...E3
Byng, 1,090 ...F3
Byron, 45 ...D1
Cache, 2,371 ...D3
Caddo, 944 ...F3
Calera, 1,739 ...F4
Calumet, 535 ...D2
Calvin, 279 ...F3
Camargo, 115 ...C1
Cambridge ...C2
Cameron, 312 ...H2
Camp Houston ...C1
Canadian, 239 ...G2
Caney, 199 ...F3
Canton, 618 ...D1
Canute, 524 ...C2
Capron, 42 ...D1
Cardin, 150 ...H1
Carleton ...D1
Carmen, 411 ...D1
Carnegie, 1,637 ...D2
Carney, 649 ...E2
Carpenter ...C2
Carrier, 77 ...D1
Carter, 254 ...C2
Cashion, 635 ...E2
Castaneda ...B4
Castle, 122 ...F2
Catesby ...C1
Catoosa, 5,449 ...G1
Cedar Valley, 58 ...E2
Cement, 530 ...D3
Center, 175 ...F3
Centrahoma, 110 ...F3
Centralia ...G1
Ceres ...E1
Cestos ...C1
Chandler, 2,842 ...F2
Chattanooga, 432 ...D3
Checotah, 3,481 ...G2
Chelsea, 2,136 ...G1
Cherokee, 1,630 ...D1
Chester, 125 ...D1
Cheyenne, 778 ...C2
Chickasha, 15,850 ...E2
Childers ...G1
Chilocco ...E1
Chisney, 50 ...F2
Choctaw, 9,377 ...B4, E2
Chouteau, 1,931 ...G1
Christie, 166 ...H2
Cimarron City, 110 ...E2
Claremore, 15,873 ...G1
Clarita, 80 ...F3
Clayton, 719 ...G3
Clear Lake ...B1, D4
Clearview, 56 ...F2
Cleo Springs, 326 ...D1
Cleveland, 3,282 ...F1
Clinton, 8,833 ...D2
Clyde ...E1
Coalgate, 2,005 ...F3
Cogar, 40 ...D2
Colbert, 1,065 ...F4
Colcord, 819 ...H1
Cold Springs ...D3
Cole, 473 ...E2
Coleman, 150 ...F3
Collinsville, 4,077 ...G1
Colony, 147 ...D2
Comanche, 1,556 ...E3
Connerville, 80 ...F3
Cookietown ...D3
Cooperton, 20 ...D3
Copan, 796 ...G1
Corbett, 125 ...C2
Cordell, 2,867 ...D2
Corn, 591 ...D2
Cornish, 172 ...E3
Corum, 40 ...D3
Council Hill, 129 ...G2
County Line, 200 ...E3
Courtney ...E4
Covington, 553 ...E1
Coweta, 7,139 ...G2
Cowlington, 133 ...H2
Cox City ...E3
Coyle, 337 ...E2
Crawford ...C2
Crescent, 1,281 ...E2
Creta ...C3
Criner ...E3
Cromwell, 265 ...F2
Crowder, 436 ...G2
Crystal, 60 ...G3
Curtis, 50 ...C1
Cushing, 8,371 ...F2
Custer City, 393 ...D2
Cyril, 1,168 ...D3
Dacoma, 148 ...D1
Dale, 200 ...E2
Damon, 50 ...G3
Davenport, 881 ...F2

Davidson, 375 ...C3
Davis, 2,610 ...E3
Deer Creek, 147 ...E1
Delaware, 456 ...G1
Delhi ...C2
Dempsey ...C2
Depew, 564 ...F2
Devol, 150 ...D3
Dewar, 919 ...G2
Dewey, 3,179 ...G1
Dibble, 289 ...E2
Dickson, 1,139 ...F3
Dill City, 526 ...C2
Disney, 226 ...G1
Dougherty, 224 ...E3
Douglas, 32 ...E1
Dover, 367 ...E2
Driftwood ...D1
Drummond, 405 ...D1
Drumright, 2,905 ...F2
Duke, 445 ...C3
Duncan, 22,505 ...E3
Durant, 13,549 ...F4
Durham ...C2
Dustin, 452 ...F2
Eagle City, 60 ...D2
Eagletown, 475 ...H3
Eakly, 276 ...D2
Earlsboro, 633 ...F2
Eason, 50 ...E2
Edmond, 68,315 ...B3, E2
Eldon, 991 ...H2
Eldorado, 527 ...C3
Elgin, 1,210 ...D3
Elk City, 10,510 ...C2
Elmer, 96 ...C3
Elmore City, 756 ...E3
Elmwood ...B1, D4
El Reno, 16,212 ...E2
Empire City, 734 ...D3
Enid, 47,045 ...E1
Enterprise ...G2
Erick, 1,023 ...C2
Erin Springs, 114 ...E3
Etowah, 122 ...E2
Eucha, 300 ...H1
Eufaula, 2,639 ...G2
Eva ...C4
Fairfax, 1,555 ...F1
Fairland, 1,025 ...H1
Fairmont, 147 ...E1
Fair Oaks, 122 ...G1
Fairvalley ...C1
Fairview, 2,733 ...D1
Fallis, 28 ...E2
Fanshawe, 384 ...H3
Fargo, 326 ...C1
Farris, 80 ...G3
Faxon, 134 ...D3
Fay, 100 ...D2
Felt, 100 ...B4
Finley, 40 ...G3
Fittstown, 175 ...F3
Fitzhugh, 204 ...F3
Fletcher, 1,022 ...D3
Floris ...B1, D4
Foraker, 23 ...F1
Forest Park, 1,066 ...B3, E2
Forgan, 532 ...B1, D4
Fort Cobb, 667 ...D2
Fort Gibson, 4,054 ...G2
Fort Sill ...D3
Fort Supply, 328 ...C1
Fort Towson, 611 ...G3
Foss, 153 ...C2
Foster, 50 ...E3
Fox, 225 ...E3
Foyil, 234 ...G1
Francis, 332 ...F3
Frederick, 4,637 ...D3
Freedom, 271 ...C1
Friendship, 70 ...C3
Gage, 429 ...C1
Gans, 208 ...H2
Garber, 845 ...E1
Garvin, 143 ...H4
Gate, 112 ...B1
Gay, 100 ...G4
Geary, 1,258 ...D2
Gene Autry, 99 ...E3
Geronimo, 959 ...D3
Gerty, 101 ...F3
Glencoe, 583 ...F1
Glenpool, 8,123 ...G2
Golden, 125 ...H3
Goldsby, 1,204 ...E2
Goltry, 268 ...D1
Goodwater, 70 ...H4
Goodwell, 1,192 ...C4
Gore, 850 ...G2
Gotebo, 272 ...D2
Gould, 206 ...C3
Gowen, 175 ...G3
Gracemont, 336 ...D2
Grady ...E3
Graham, 50 ...E3
Grainola, 31 ...F1
Grandfield, 1,110 ...D3
Grand Lake Towne, 65 ...G1
Granite, 1,844 ...C3
Grant, 300 ...G4
Gray ...B1, D4
Gray Horse ...F1
Grayson, 134 ...G2
Greenfield, 123 ...D2
Griggs ...B4
Grimes ...C2

Grove, 5,131 ...H1
Guthrie, 9,925 ...E2
Guymon, 10,472 ...C4
Haileyville, 891 ...G3
Hallett, 168 ...F1
Hall Park, 1,088 ...E2
Hammon, 469 ...C2
Hanna, 133 ...G2
Hardesty, 277 ...A1, C4
Hardy ...F1
Harmon ...C1
Harrah, 4,719 ...B4, E2
Hartshorne, 2,102 ...G3
Haskell, 1,765 ...G2
Hastings, 155 ...D3
Haworth, 354 ...H4
Haywood, 80 ...G3
Headrick, 130 ...C3
Healdton, 2,786 ...E3
Heavener, 3,201 ...H3
Helena, 443 ...D1
Hendrix, 79 ...F4
Hennepin, 125 ...E3
Hennessey, 2,058 ...E1
Henryetta, 6,096 ...F2
Herd ...F1
Herring ...C2
Hess ...C3
Hester ...C3
Hext ...C2
Hickory, 87 ...F3
Higgins ...G3
Hillsdale, 101 ...E1
Hinton, 2,175 ...D2
Hitchcock, 141 ...D2
Hitchita, 113 ...G2
Hobart, 3,997 ...C2
Hoffman, 148 ...G2
Holdenville, 4,732 ...F2
Hollis, 2,264 ...C3
Hollister, 60 ...D3
Homestead, 80 ...D1
Hominy, 2,584 ...F1
Honobia, 50 ...H3
Hooker, 1,788 ...A1, C4
Hoot Owl ...G1
Hopeton, 40 ...D1
Hough ...C4
Howe, 697 ...H3
Hoyt, 70 ...G2
Hugo, 5,536 ...G3
Hulah ...F1
Hulbert, 543 ...G2
Humphreys, 70 ...C3
Hunter, 173 ...E1
Hydro, 1,060 ...D2
Idabel, 6,952 ...H4
Indiahoma, 374 ...D3
Indianola, 191 ...G2
Ingersoll ...D1
Inola, 1,589 ...G1
Isabella, 150 ...D1
Jacktown ...E2
Jamestown, 10 ...G1
Jay, 2,482 ...H1
Jefferson, 37 ...E1
Jenks, 9,557 ...G1
Jennings, 373 ...F1
Jet, 230 ...D1
Johnson, 223 ...E2
Jones, 2,517 ...B3, E2
Joy, 100 ...E3
Kansas, 685 ...H1
Kaw City, 372 ...F1
Keefeton, 225 ...G2
Kellyville, 906 ...F2
Kemp, 144 ...F4
Kendrick, 138 ...F2
Kenefic, 192 ...F3
Keota, 517 ...H2
Ketchum, 286 ...G1
Keyes, 410 ...B4
Kiefer, 1,026 ...F2
Kildare, 92 ...E1
Kingfisher, 4,380 ...E2
Kingston, 1,390 ...F3
Kinta, 243 ...G2
Kiowa, 693 ...G3
Knowles, 32 ...B1
Komalty ...D2
Konawa, 1,479 ...F3
Krebs, 2,051 ...G3
Kremlin, 240 ...E1
Lacey ...D1
Lahoma, 577 ...D1
Lake Aluma, 97 ...B3
Lamar, 172 ...F2
Lambert, 9 ...D1
Lamont, 465 ...E1
Lane, 300 ...G3
Langley, 669 ...G1
Langston, 1,670 ...E2
Latta, 800 ...F3
Laverne, 1,097 ...C1
Lawrence Creek, 119 ...F1
Lawton, 92,757 ...D3
Lebanon, 125 ...F4
Leedey, 345 ...C2
Le Flore, 168 ...H3
Lehigh, 315 ...F3
Lenapah, 298 ...G1
Lenora ...C1
Leon, 96 ...E4
Leonard, 325 ...G2
Lequire, 125 ...H2
Lexington, 2,086 ...E2
Liberty, 184 ...G2

Lima, 74 ...F2
Lindsay, 2,889 ...E3
Little, 125 ...F2
Little City, 100 ...F3
Loco, 150 ...E3
Locust Grove, 1,366 ...G1
Logan ...B1
Lone Chimney, 50 ...F1
Lone Grove, 4,631 ...E3
Lone Wolf, 500 ...C3
Longdale, 310 ...D1
Longtown, 2,397 ...G2
Lookeba, 131 ...D2
Lotsee, 11 ...F1
Loveland, 14 ...D3
Lovell, 50 ...E1
Loyal, 81 ...D2
Lucien, 100 ...E1
Lugert ...C3
Lula, 60 ...F3
Luther, 612 ...B3, E2
Lutie, 80 ...G3
Macomb, 61 ...E2
Madill, 3,410 ...F3
Manchester, 104 ...D1
Mangum, 2,924 ...C3
Manitou, 278 ...D3
Mannford, 2,095 ...F1
Mannsville, 587 ...F3
Maramec, 104 ...F1
Marble City, 242 ...H2
Marietta, 2,445 ...E4
Marland, 280 ...E1
Marlow, 4,592 ...E3
Marshall, 258 ...E1
Martha, 205 ...C3
Mason ...F2
Maud, 1,136 ...F2
May, 33 ...C1
Mayfield ...C2
Maysville, 1,313 ...E3
Mazie, 88 ...G1
McAlester, 17,783 ...G3
McBride, 80 ...F4
McCord, 1,711 ...E1
McCurtain, 466 ...H2
McKnight ...C3
McLoud, 3,548 ...E2
McQueen ...C3
McWillie ...D1
Mead, 123 ...F3
Medford, 1,172 ...E1
Medicine Park, 373 ...D3
Meeker, 978 ...F2
Meers, 40 ...D3
Meno, 195 ...D1
Meridian
(Logan Co.), 54 ...E2
Meridian
(Stephens Co.), 1,485 ...E3
Miami, 13,704 ...H1
Middleberg, 90 ...E2
Midwest City,
54,088 ...B4, E2
Milburn, 312 ...F3
Mill Creek, 340 ...F3
Millerton, 359 ...G4
Milo ...E3
Minco, 1,672 ...E2
Mocane ...B1, D4
Moffett, 179 ...H2
Monroe, 225 ...H2
Moodys, 125 ...H1
Moore, 41,138 ...E2
Mooreland, 1,226 ...C1
Moorewood ...C2
Morris, 1,294 ...G2
Morrison, 636 ...E1
Mounds, 1,153 ...F2
Mountain Park, 390 ...D3
Mountain View, 880 ...D2
Mouser ...C4
Moyers, 90 ...G3
Muldrow, 3,104 ...H2
Mulhall, 239 ...E1
Muse, 175 ...H3
Muskogee, 38,310 ...G2
Mustang, 13,156 ...A4, E2
Mutual, 76 ...C1
Nardin, 80 ...E1
Nash, 224 ...D1
Nashoba, 50 ...G3
Nelagoney, 40 ...F1
New Alluwe, 95 ...G1
Newcastle, 5,434 ...E2
Newkirk, 2,243 ...E1
New Liberty ...E3
New Prue, 40 ...F1
New Ringold, 50 ...G3
New Tulsa, 568 ...G2
Nichols Hills, 4,056 ...B3, E2
Nicoma Park, 2,415 ...B4
Ninnekah, 994 ...E3
Noble, 5,260 ...E2
Norge, 82 ...D3
Norman, 95,694 ...E2
North Enid, 796 ...E1
North Miami, 433 ...H1
Nowata, 3,971 ...G1
Nuyaka, 60 ...F2
Oak Grove, 18 ...F1
Oakhurst, 2,731 ...G1
Oakland, 674 ...F3
Oaks, 412 ...H1
Oakwood, 72 ...D2
Ochelata, 494 ...G1
Octavia, 60 ...H3
Oglesby, 175 ...G1

Oil City, 125 ...D3
Oilton, 1,099 ...F1
Okarche, 1,110 ...E2
Okay, 597 ...G2
Okeene, 1,240 ...D1
Okemah, 3,038 ...F2
Okfuskee ...F2
Oklahoma City,
506,132 ...B4, E2
Okmulgee, 13,022 ...G2
Oktaha, 327 ...G2
Oleta, 40 ...G3
Olustee, 680 ...C3
Omega, 40 ...D2
Onapa, 150 ...G2
Oologah, 883 ...G1
Optima, 266 ...C4
Orienta, 50 ...D1
Orion ...D1
Orlando, 201 ...E1
Orr ...E3
Osage, 188 ...F1
Oscar ...E4
Overbrook, 80 ...E3
Owasso, 18,502 ...G1
Paden, 446 ...F2
Page ...H3
Panama, 1,362 ...H2
Panola, 70 ...G3
Paoli, 649 ...E3
Paradise Hill, 100 ...H2
Park Hill, 3,936 ...H2
Pauls Valley, 6,256 ...E3
Pawhuska, 3,629 ...F1
Pawnee, 2,230 ...F1
Pearson, 50 ...F2
Peckham, 60 ...E1
Peggs, 175 ...G1
Pensacola, 71 ...G1
Peoria, 141 ...H1
Perkins, 2,272 ...E2
Pernell, 60 ...E3
Perry, 5,230 ...E1
Phillips, 150 ...F3
Picher, 1,640 ...H1
Pickens, 50 ...G3
Piedmont, 3,650 ...E2
Pierce, 60 ...G2
Pink, 1,165 ...E2
Pittsburg, 280 ...G3
Pocasset, 192 ...E2
Pocola, 3,994 ...H2
Ponca City, 25,919 ...E1
Pond Creek, 896 ...E1
Porter, 574 ...G2
Porum, 725 ...G2
Poteau, 7,939 ...H2
Prague, 2,138 ...F2
Preston, 125 ...F2
Prue, 433 ...F1
Pruitt City, 200 ...E3
Pryor, 8,659 ...G1
Pumpkin Center, 70 ...D3
Purcell, 5,571 ...E2
Purdy, 50 ...E3
Putnam, 46 ...D2
Quapaw, 984 ...H1
Quay, 47 ...F1
Quinlan ...C1
Quinton, 1,071 ...G2
Raiford, 40 ...G2
Ralston, 355 ...F1
Ramona, 564 ...G1
Randlett, 511 ...D3
Rattan, 247 ...G3
Ravia, 459 ...F3
Reagan, 70 ...F3
Redbird, 153 ...G2
Redden ...G3
Red Oak, 581 ...G3
Red Rock, 293 ...E1
Reed ...C3
Renfrow, 16 ...E1
Rentiesville, 102 ...G2
Retrop ...C2
Reydon, 177 ...C2
Rhea ...C2
Richards Spur, 200 ...D3
Ringling, 1,135 ...E3
Ringold ...G3
Ringwood, 424 ...D1
Ripley, 444 ...F1
Rock Island, 709 ...H2
Rocky, 174 ...C2
Roff, 734 ...F3
Roland, 2,842 ...H2
Roll, 40 ...C2
Roosevelt, 280 ...C3
Rosedale, 66 ...E3
Rosston, 66 ...C1
Rufe, 80 ...G3
Rush Springs, 1,278 ...E3
Russell ...C3
Ryan, 894 ...E3
St. Louis, 206 ...F2
Salina, 1,422 ...G1
Sallisaw, 7,989 ...H2
Salt Fork ...E1
Sand Creek ...D1
Sand Springs, 17,451 ...F1
Sapulpa, 19,166 ...F1
Sasakwa, 150 ...F3
Savanna, 730 ...G3
Sawyer, 274 ...G3
Sayre, 4,114 ...C2
Schulter, 600 ...G2
Scipio, 70 ...G2

Scraper, 475 ...H1
Seiling, 875 ...D1
Selman, 40 ...C1
Seminole, 6,899 ...F2
Sentinel, 859 ...C2
Seward, 70 ...E2
Shady Grove, 44 ...F1
Shady Point, 848 ...H2
Shamrock, 125 ...F2
Sharon, 122 ...C1
Shattuck, 1,274 ...C1
Shawnee, 28,692 ...F2
Shidler, 520 ...F1
Silo, 282 ...F3
Silver City, 100 ...F1
Skedee, 102 ...F1
Skiatook, 5,396 ...F1
Slapout ...B1
Slaughterville, 3,609 ...E2
Slick, 148 ...F2
Smith Village, 40 ...B4, E2
Smithville, 123 ...H3
Snow ...G3
Snyder, 1,509 ...D3
Soper, 300 ...G3
Southard, 70 ...D1
South Coffeyville, 790 ...G1
Sparks, 137 ...F2
Spavinaw, 563 ...G1
Speer, 50 ...G3
Spencer, 3,746 ...B3, E2
Spencerville, 40 ...G3
Sperry, 981 ...G1
Spiro, 2,227 ...H2
Sportsmen Acres, 204 ...G1
Spring Creek ...D2
Springer, 577 ...E3
Stafford, 40 ...C2
Stanley ...G3
Stecker, 100 ...D3
Sterling, 762 ...D3
Stidham, 23 ...G2
Stigler, 2,731 ...G2
Stillwater, 39,065 ...E1
Stilwell, 3,276 ...H2
Stonewall, 465 ...F3
Straight ...C4
Strang, 100 ...G1
Stratford, 1,474 ...F3
Stringtown, 396 ...F3
Strong City, 42 ...C2
Stroud, 2,758 ...F2
Stuart, 220 ...F3
Sturgis ...B4
Sugden, 59 ...E3
Sulphur, 4,794 ...F3
Summit, 226 ...G2
Sumner, 70 ...E1
Sweetwater ...C2
Swink, 83 ...G3
Tabler ...E2
Taft, 349 ...G2
Tahlequah, 14,458 ...H2
Talala, 270 ...G1
Talihina, 1,211 ...G3
Taloga, 372 ...D2
Tamaha, 198 ...H2
Tangier, 40 ...C2
Tatums, 172 ...E3
Tecumseh, 6,098 ...F2
Tegarden ...D1
Temple, 1,146 ...D3
Terlton, 85 ...F1
Terral, 386 ...E4
Texhoma, 935 ...C4
Texola, 47 ...C2
Thackerville, 404 ...E4
The Village, 10,157 ...B3, E2
Thomas, 1,238 ...D2
Tipton, 916 ...C3
Tishomingo, 3,162 ...F3
Tom, 225 ...H4
Tonkawa, 3,299 ...E1
Trail ...C2
Tribbey, 273 ...E2
Tryon, 448 ...F2
Tucker ...H2
Tullahassee, 106 ...G2
Tulsa, 393,049 ...G1
Tupelo, 377 ...F3
Turley, 3,231 ...G1
Turpin, 475 ...B1, D4
Tushka, 345 ...F3
Tuskahoma, 125 ...G3
Tuttle, 4,294 ...E2
Tyrone, 880 ...A1, C4
Union City, 1,375 ...E2
Valley Brook, 874 ...B4, E2
Valley Park, 24 ...E3
Valliant, 771 ...G4
Vanoss, 100 ...F3
Velma, 664 ...E3
Vera, 188 ...G1
Verden, 509 ...D2
Vian, 1,362 ...H2
Vici, 668 ...C1
Victory ...C3
Vinita, 6,472 ...G1
Vinson ...C3
Wade ...F4
Wagoner, 7,669 ...G2
Wainwright, 197 ...G2
Wakita, 420 ...E1
Walters, 2,657 ...D3
Wanette, 402 ...E2
Wann, 132 ...G1
Wapanucka, 445 ...F3
Wardville, 50 ...F3

Warner, 1,430 ...G2
Warr Acres, 9,735 ...B3, E2
Warren, 80 ...C3
Warwick, 235 ...F2
Washington, 520 ...E2
Watonga, 4,658 ...D2
Watova, 100 ...G1
Watson, 70 ...H3
Watts, 316 ...H1
Waukomis, 1,261 ...E1
Waurika, 1,988 ...D3
Wayne, 714 ...E3
Waynoka, 993 ...D1
Weatherford, 9,859 ...D2
Webb ...C2
Webb City, 95 ...F1
Webbers Falls, 726 ...G2
Welch, 597 ...G1
Weleetka, 1,014 ...F2
Wellston, 825 ...F2
Welty, 80 ...F2
Westport, 264 ...F1
West Siloam Springs,
877 ...H1
Westville, 1,596 ...H1
Wetumka, 1,451 ...F2
Wewoka, 3,562 ...F2
Wheeless ...B4
White Bead, 150 ...E3
Whitefield, 231 ...G2
Whitesboro, 70 ...H3
Wilburton, 2,972 ...G3
Willow, 114 ...C2
Wilson, 1,584 ...E3
Winchester, 424 ...G2
Wister, 1,002 ...H3
Woodlawn Park, 161 ...B4
Woodville, 69 ...F4
Woodward, 11,853 ...C1
Wright City, 848 ...H3
Wyandotte, 363 ...H1
Wynnewood, 2,367 ...E3
Wynona, 531 ...F1
Yale, 1,342 ...F1
Yanush, 50 ...G3
Yeager, 67 ...F2
Yewed ...D1
Yukon, 21,043 ...E2
Zena, 123 ...H1

Other Features

Arkansas, river ...F1, H2
Arrowhead, lake ...D4
Black, mesa ...B4
Black Kettle Natl.
Grassland ...C2
Broken Bow, lake ...H3
Caddo Natl.
Grassland ...G4
Canadian, river ...D1
Canton, lake ...D1
Chickasaw Natl.
Rec. Area ...F3
Cimarron, river ...C1, F1
Fort Chaffee Mil. Res. ...H2
Ft. Gibson, lake ...G1
Fort Sill Mil. Res. ...D3
G. W. Carver
Natl. Mon. ...H1
Hugo, lake ...G3
Illinois, river ...H1
Kaw, lake ...F1
Kemp, lake ...C4
Keystone, lake ...F1
Little River N.W.R. ...H4
Lyndon B. Johnson
Natl. Grassland ...E4
Mark Twain Natl. For. ...
McAlester Army
Ammunition Plant ...G3
North Canadian, river ...C1
Oklahoma City
Natl. Mem. ...B4
Oologah, lake ...G1
Optima N.W.R. ...A1, C4
Osage Ind. Res. ...F1
Ouachita, mountains ...G3
Ouachita Natl.
For. ...H3, H4
Ozark Natl. For. ...H1, H2
Pea Ridge Natl.
Mil. Park ...H1
Pease, river ...C4
Ray Roberts, lake ...F4
Red, river ...C3, G4
Rita Blanca Natl.
Grassland ...B4
Salt Plains N.W.R. ...D1
Sequoyah N.W.R. ...G2
Sooner, lake ...E1
Texoma, lake ...F4
Tishomingo N.W.R. ...F3
Washita Battlefield
N.H.S. ...C2
Washita N.W.R. ...C2
Winding Stair N.R.A. ...H3

Oregon

Capital: Salem
Land Area: 96,002 sq. mi. 248,645 sq. km.
Population: 3,421,399 (2000 Census)
Largest City: Portland, 529,121
Highest Point: Mt. Hood, 11,235 ft. 3,424 m.
Admitted to Union: February 14, 1859
Nickname: Beaver State
State Flower: Oregon Grape
State Bird: Western Meadowlark

Oregon: Map Index

Counties

Baker, **16,741** . . . J3
Benton, **78,153** . . . C3
Clackamas, **338,391** . . . B3, D2
Clatsop, **35,630** . . . C1
Columbia, **43,560** . . . C2
Coos, **62,779** . . . C4
Crook, **19,182** . . . F3
Curry, **21,137** . . . B5
Deschutes, **115,367** . . . E4
Douglas, **100,399** . . . D4
Gilliam, **1,915** . . . F2
Grant, **7,935** . . . H3
Harney, **7,609** . . . G4
Hood River, **20,411** . . . E2
Jackson, **181,269** . . . D5
Jefferson, **19,009** . . . E3
Josephine, **75,726** . . . C5
Klamath, **63,775** . . . E5
Lake, **7,422** . . . F4
Lane, **322,959** . . . D4
Lincoln, **44,479** . . . C3
Linn, **103,069** . . . D3
Malheur, **31,615** . . . J4
Marion, **284,834** . . . D3
Morrow, **10,995** . . . G2
Multnomah, **660,486** . . . A2, D2
Polk, **62,380** . . . C3
Sherman, **1,934** . . . F2
Tillamook, **24,262** . . . C2
Umatilla, **70,548** . . . H2
Union, **24,530** . . . H2
Wallowa, **7,226** . . . J2
Wasco, **23,791** . . . E2
Washington, **445,342** . . . A3, C2
Wheeler, **1,547** . . . F3
Yamhill, **84,992** . . . C2

Cities and Towns

Adair Village, **536** . . . C3
Adams, **297** . . . H2
Adel, *90* . . . G5
Adrian, **147** . . . J4
Agness . . . B5
Albany, **40,852** . . . C3
Alfalfa, *90* . . . E3
Algoma . . . E5
Alkali Lake . . . G5
Allegany, *200* . . . B4
Aloha, **41,741** . . . A2
Alsea, *125* . . . C3
Altamont, **19,603** . . . E5
Amity, **1,478** . . . C2
Andrews, *100* . . . H5
Antelope, **59** . . . F3
Arch Cape, *40* . . . C2
Arlington, **524** . . . F2
Arock . . . J5
Ash, *40* . . . C4
Ashland, **19,522** . . . D5
Ashwood, *40* . . . F3
Astoria, **9,813** . . . C1
Athena, **1,221** . . . H2
Aumsville, **3,003** . . . D3
Aurora, **655** . . . D2
Baker City, **9,860** . . . J3
Bandon, **2,833** . . . B4
Banks, **1,286** . . . C2
Basque . . . J5
Bates . . . H3
Bay City, **1,149** . . . C2
Beatty, *60* . . . E5
Beaver, **145** . . . C2
Beaver Marsh, *40* . . . E4
Beaverton, **76,129** . . . A2, D2
Belknap Springs . . . D3
Bend, **52,029** . . . E3
Beulah . . . H4
Biggs . . . F2
Blachly, *175* . . . C3
Blalock, *40* . . . F2
Blue River, *70* . . . D3
Bly, *250* . . . E5
Boardman, **2,855** . . . G2
Bonanza, **415** . . . E5
Boring, *1,000* . . . B2
Bourne . . . H3
Bridgeport . . . J3
Brightwood, *80* . . . D2
Broadbent, *100* . . . B4
Brogan . . . J3
Brookings, **5,447** . . . B5
Brothers . . . F4
Brownsville, **1,449** . . . D3
Buchanan . . . H4
Bunker Hill, **1,462** . . . B4
Burlington, *225* . . . A2, D2
Burns, **3,064** . . . G4
Burns Junction . . . J5
Butte Falls, **439** . . . D5
Camas Valley, *125* . . . C4
Canby, **12,790** . . . D2
Cannon Beach, **1,588** . . . C2
Canyon City, **669** . . . H3
Canyonville, **1,293** . . . C5
Carlton, **1,514** . . . C2
Carpenterville . . . B5
Carson, *80* . . . J3
Cascade Locks, **1,115** . . . E2
Cascadia, *125* . . . D3
Cave Junction, **1,363** . . . C5
Cayuse, **59** . . . H2
Cecil . . . G2
Cedar Hills, **8,949** . . . A2
Cedar Mill, **12,597** . . . A2
Central Point, **12,493** . . . D5
Charleston, *300* . . . B4
Chenoweth, **3,412** . . . E2
Chiloquin, **716** . . . E5
Christmas Valley . . . F4
Clackamas, **5,177** . . . A3
Clarno . . . F3
Clatskanie, **1,528** . . . C1
Cloverdale, **242** . . . C2
Coburg, **969** . . . C3
Columbia City, **1,571** . . . D2
Condon, **759** . . . F2
Coos Bay, **15,374** . . . B4
Coquille, **4,184** . . . B4
Corvallis, **49,322** . . . C3
Cottage Grove, **8,445** . . . C4
Cove, **594** . . . J2
Crabtree, *350* . . . D3
Crane, *70* . . . H4
Crawfordsville, *125* . . . D3
Crescent, *175* . . . E4
Crescent Lake . . . E4
Creswell, **3,579** . . . C4
Crowley . . . J4
Culp Creek, *375* . . . D4
Culver, **802** . . . E3
Cushman, *125* . . . B4
Dairy, *50* . . . E5
Dale, *50* . . . H3
Dallas, **12,459** . . . C3
Days Creek, *100* . . . C5
Dayton, **2,119** . . . C2
Dayville, **138** . . . G3
Dee, *200* . . . E2
Denmark, *70* . . . B5
Depoe Bay, **1,174** . . . B3
Deschutes River Woods, **4,631** . . . E4
Detroit, **262** . . . D3
Dexter, *750* . . . D4
Diamond . . . H4
Diamond Lake, *100* . . . D4
Dillard, *500* . . . C4
Disston, *200* . . . D4
Dora . . . C4
Dorena, *375* . . . D4
Drain, **1,021** . . . C4
Drew, *100* . . . D5
Drewsey . . . H4
Dufur, **588** . . . E2
Dundee, **2,598** . . . D2
Dunes City, **1,241** . . . B4
Durham, **1,382** . . . A3
Durkee . . . J3
Eagle Point, **4,797** . . . D5
Echo, **650** . . . G2
Elgin, **1,654** . . . J2
Elkhorn . . . D3
Elkton, **147** . . . C4
Elsie . . . C2
Enterprise, **1,895** . . . J2
Estacada, **2,371** . . . D2
Eugene, **137,893** . . . C3
Fairview (Coos Co.), *60* . . . B4
Fairview (Multnomah Co.), **7,561** . . . B2
Fields, *40* . . . H5
Flora . . . J2
Florence, **7,263** . . . B4
Fort Klamath, *80* . . . E5
Fort Rock . . . E4
Fossil, **469** . . . F3
Foster, *175* . . . D3
Four Corners, **13,922** . . . D3
Fox . . . G3
Frenchglen . . . H5
Fruitdale (Harbeck-Fruitdale), **3,780** . . . C5
Galena . . . H3
Galice . . . C5
Garden Home (Garden Home-Whitford), **6,931** . . . A2
Gardiner, *325* . . . B4
Garibaldi, **899** . . . C2
Gaston, **600** . . . C2
Gates, **471** . . . D3
Gaylord . . . B5
Gearhart, **995** . . . C1
Gervais, **2,009** . . . D2
Gibbon . . . H2
Gilchrist, *450* . . . E4
Gladstone, **11,438** . . . A3
Glendale, **855** . . . C5
Glenwood, *60* . . . C2
Glide, **1,690** . . . C4
Gold Beach, **1,897** . . . B5
Gold Hill, **1,073** . . . C5
Government Camp, *150* . . . E2
Grand Ronde, **271** . . . C2
Granite, **24** . . . H3
Grants Pass, **23,003** . . . C5
Grass Valley, **171** . . . F2
Gravelford . . . B4
Green, **6,174** . . . C4
Greenhorn . . . H3
Gresham, **90,205** . . . A2
Gunter . . . C4
Haines, **426** . . . J3
Halfway, **337** . . . J3
Halsey, **724** . . . C3
Hamilton . . . G3
Hampton . . . F4
Happy Valley, **4,519** . . . A2
Harbor, **2,622** . . . B5
Hardman . . . G2
Harlan, *40* . . . C3
Harney . . . H4
Harper, *70* . . . J4
Harrisburg, **2,795** . . . C3
Hauser, *475* . . . B4
Hayesville, **18,222** . . . D3
Hazelwood . . . A2
Hebo, **231** . . . C2
Helix, **183** . . . H2
Heppner, **1,395** . . . G2
Hereford . . . H3
Hermiston, **13,154** . . . G2
Hilgard . . . H2
Hillsboro, **70,186** . . . D2
Hines, **1,623** . . . G4
Homestead . . . K3
Hood River, **5,831** . . . E2
Hubbard, **2,483** . . . D2
Huntington, **515** . . . J3
Idanha, **232** . . . D3
Idleyld Park, *200* . . . C4
Imbler, **284** . . . J2
Imnaha, *50* . . . K2
Independence, **6,035** . . . C3
Ione, **321** . . . G2
Ironside . . . J3
Irrigon, **1,702** . . . G2
Island City, **916** . . . H2
Jacksonville, **2,235** . . . D5
Jamieson, *40* . . . J3
Jasper, *700* . . . D4
Jefferson, **2,487** . . . D3
Jennings Lodge, **7,036** . . . A3
John Day, **1,821** . . . H3
Johnson City, **634** . . . A3
Jordan Valley, **239** . . . J5
Joseph, **1,054** . . . J2
Junction City, **4,721** . . . C3
Juntura . . . H4
Kamela . . . H2
Keating . . . J3
Keizer, **32,203** . . . C3
Kellogg . . . C4
Keno, *650* . . . E5
Kent, *40* . . . F2
Kerby, *450* . . . C5
Kernville, *125* . . . C3
Kimberly, *50* . . . G3
King City, **1,949** . . . A3
Kings Valley . . . C3
Kinzua . . . F3
Kirk, *80* . . . E5
Klamath Falls, **19,462** . . . E5
Knappa, *275* . . . C1
Lacomb, *300* . . . D3
Lafayette, **2,586** . . . C2
La Grande, **12,327** . . . H2
Lakecreek . . . D5
Lake Oswego, **35,278** . . . A2, D2
Lakeside, **1,371** . . . B4
Lakeview, **2,474** . . . F5
Langell Valley . . . E5
Langlois, *50* . . . B5
La Pine, **5,799** . . . E4
Lawen . . . H4
Leaburg, *300* . . . D3
Lebanon, **12,950** . . . D3
Leland, *40* . . . C5
Lexington, **263** . . . G2
Lime . . . J3
Lincoln Beach, **2,078** . . . B3
Lincoln City, **7,437** . . . B3
Logsden, *125* . . . C3
London, *150* . . . C4
Lonerock, **24** . . . G2
Long Creek, **228** . . . G3
Lorane, *125* . . . C4
Lorella . . . E5
Lostine, **263** . . . J2
Lowell, **857** . . . D4
Lyons, **1,008** . . . D3
Madras, **5,078** . . . E3
Malin, **638** . . . E5
Manzanita, **564** . . . C2
Mapleton, *300* . . . C3
Marcola, *400* . . . D3
Marion Forks . . . E3
Maupin, **411** . . . E2
Mayville . . . F2
Maywood Park, **777** . . . A2
McCredie Springs, *90* . . . D4
McDermitt . . . J6
McKenzie Bridge, *150* . . . D3
McMinnville, **26,499** . . . C2
Meacham . . . H2
Medford, **63,154** . . . D5
Medical Springs . . . J3
Melrose, *350* . . . C4
Merrill, **897** . . . E5
Metolius, **635** . . . E3
Metzger, **3,354** . . . A2
Midland, *200* . . . E5
Mikkalo . . . F2
Mill City, **1,537** . . . D3
Millersburg, **651** . . . C3
Millican . . . F4
Milo, *40* . . . C5
Milton-Freewater, **6,470** . . . H2
Milwaukie, **20,490** . . . A2
Minam . . . J2
Mission, **1,019** . . . H2
Mist . . . C2
Mitchell, **170** . . . F3
Molalla, **5,647** . . . D2
Monmouth, **7,741** . . . C3
Monroe, **607** . . . C3
Monument, **151** . . . G3
Moro, **337** . . . F2
Mosier, **410** . . . E2
Mount Angel, **3,121** . . . D2
Mount Vernon, **595** . . . G3
Murphy, *325* . . . C5
Myrtle Creek, **3,419** . . . C4
Myrtle Point, **2,451** . . . B4
Narrows . . . H4
Nehalem, **203** . . . C2
Neotsu, *650* . . . C3
Nesika Beach, *200* . . . B5
Neskowin, **169** . . . C2
Netarts, **744** . . . C2
Newberg, **18,064** . . . D2
New Pine Creek, *80* . . . F6
Newport, **9,532** . . . B3
North Bend, **9,544** . . . B4
North Plains, **1,605** . . . D2
North Powder, **489** . . . J2
North Springfield . . . C3
Norway, *40* . . . B4
Nyssa, **3,163** . . . J4
Oak Grove, **12,808** . . . A3
Oak Hills, **9,050** . . . A2
Oakland, **954** . . . C4
Oakridge, **3,148** . . . D4
Oatfield, **15,750** . . . A2
O'Brien, *225* . . . C5
Oceanside, **326** . . . C2
Odell, **1,849** . . . E2
Olene, *100* . . . E5
Olex . . . F2
Ontario, **10,985** . . . K3
Ophir, *50* . . . B5
Oregon City, **25,754** . . . A3, D2
Otis, *80* . . . C3
Otter Rock, *175* . . . B3
Pacific City, **1,027** . . . C2
Paisley, **247** . . . F5
Parkdale, **266** . . . E2
Paulina, *40* . . . G3
Pendleton, **16,354** . . . H2
Philomath, **3,838** . . . C3
Phoenix, **4,060** . . . D5
Pilot Rock, **1,532** . . . H2
Pine . . . J3
Pine Grove, **162** . . . E2
Pinehurst . . . D5
Pistol River, *70* . . . B5
Pleasant Valley . . . J3
Plush . . . G5
Portland, **529,121** . . . A2, D2
Port Orford, **1,153** . . . B5
Post . . . F3
Powell Butte, *80* . . . E3
Powers, **734** . . . B5
Prairie City, **1,080** . . . H3
Prescott, **72** . . . D1
Princeton . . . H4
Prineville, **7,356** . . . F3
Prospect, *250* . . . D5
Quartz Mountain . . . F5
Quincy, *275* . . . C1
Rainier, **1,687** . . . D1
Raleigh Hills, **5,865** . . . A2
Redmond, **13,481** . . . E3
Redwood, **5,844** . . . C5
Reedsport, **4,378** . . . B4
Remote, *90* . . . C4
Rhododendron (part of Mount Hood Village, pop. **3,306**) . . . E2
Rice Hill, *150* . . . C4
Richland, **147** . . . J3
Riddle, **1,014** . . . C5
Rieth, *90* . . . H2
Riley, *50* . . . G4
Ritter . . . G3
Rivergrove, **324** . . . A3
River Road . . . C3
Riverside . . . H4
Riverton, *50* . . . B4
Rockaway Beach, **1,267** . . . C2
Rockcreek . . . A2
Rock Creek . . . F2
Rogue River, **1,847** . . . C5
Rome, *40* . . . J5
Roseburg, **20,017** . . . C4
Rose Lodge, **1,708** . . . C3
Ruch, *700* . . . C5
Rufus, **268** . . . F2
Ruggs . . . G2
St. Helens, **10,019** . . . D2
St. Paul, **354** . . . D2
Salem, **136,924** . . . C3
Sandy, **5,385** . . . D2
Santa Clara, **12,800** . . . C3
Scappoose, **4,976** . . . D2
Scio, **695** . . . D3
Scottsburg, *50* . . . C4
Scotts Mills, **312** . . . D2
Seal Rock, *275* . . . B3
Seaside, **5,900** . . . C2
Selma, *300* . . . C5
Seneca, **223** . . . H3
Shady Cove, **2,307** . . . D5
Shaniko, **26** . . . F3
Shedd, *90* . . . C3
Sheridan, **3,570** . . . C2
Sherwood, **11,791** . . . A3, D2
Siletz, **1,133** . . . C3
Siltcoos, *40* . . . B4
Silver Lake, *60* . . . E4
Silverton, **7,414** . . . D3
Silvies . . . H3
Simnasho, *70* . . . E3
Siskiyou . . . D5
Sisters, **959** . . . E3
Sitkum, *50* . . . C4
Sixes, *90* . . . B5
Sodaville, **290** . . . D3
South Beach, *150* . . . B3
South Junction . . . E3
Sprague River . . . E5
Spray, **140** . . . G3
Springfield, **52,864** . . . D3
Stanfield, **1,979** . . . G2
Starkey . . . H2
Stayton, **6,816** . . . D3
Steamboat . . . D4
Sublimity, **2,148** . . . D3
Summer Lake . . . F5
Summerville, **117** . . . J2
Summit . . . C3
Sumner, *40* . . . B4
Sumpter, **171** . . . H3
Sunnyside, **6,791** . . . A2
Sunny Valley, *150* . . . C5
Sunriver, *450* . . . E4
Suplee . . . G3
Sutherlin, **6,669** . . . C4
Sweet Home, **8,016** . . . D3
Swisshome, *40* . . . C3
Takilma, *125* . . . C5
Talent, **5,589** . . . D5
Tangent, **933** . . . C3
Telocaset, *70* . . . J2
Tenmile, *225* . . . C4
Terrebonne, **1,469** . . . E3
The Dalles, **12,156** . . . E2
Three Rivers, **2,445** . . . E4
Tidewater, *100* . . . C3
Tiernan, *40* . . . C3
Tigard, **41,223** . . . A3, D2
Tillamook, **4,352** . . . C2
Tiller, *150* . . . D5
Timber, *100* . . . C2
Toledo, **3,472** . . . C3
Trail, *100* . . . D5
Troutdale, **13,777** . . . B2, D2
Troy . . . J2
Tualatin, **22,791** . . . A3, D2
Tumalo, *375* . . . E3
Turner, **1,199** . . . D3
Tygh Valley, **224** . . . E2
Ukiah, **255** . . . H2
Umapine, *250* . . . H2
Umatilla, **4,978** . . . G2
Umpqua . . . C4
Union, **1,926** . . . J2
Union Creek . . . D5
Unity, **131** . . . H3
Upper Soda . . . D3
Vale, **1,976** . . . J4
Valley Falls . . . F5
Valsetz . . . C3
Veneta, **2,755** . . . C3
Vernonia, **2,228** . . . C2
Vida, *200* . . . D3
Wagontire . . . G4
Waldport, **2,050** . . . B3
Wallowa, **869** . . . J2
Walterville, *350* . . . D3
Walton, *60* . . . C3
Wamic, **36** . . . E2
Warm Springs, **2,431** . . . E3
Warrenton, **4,096** . . . C1
Wasco, **381** . . . F2
Waterloo, **239** . . . D3
Wedderburn, *300* . . . B5
Westfall . . . J3
Westfir, **276** . . . D4
West Haven-Sylvan, **7,147** . . . A2
West Linn, **22,261** . . . A3
Weston, **717** . . . H2
Westport, *500* . . . C1
West Slope, **6,442** . . . A2
Wheeler, **391** . . . C2
White City, **5,466** . . . D5
Wilbur, *125* . . . C4
Wilderville, *125* . . . C5
Willamina, **1,844** . . . C2
Williams, *200* . . . C5
Willow Creek, *125* . . . J3
Willowdale . . . F3
Wilsonville, **13,991** . . . D2
Winchester, *275* . . . C4
Winchester Bay, **488** . . . B4
Winston, **4,613** . . . C4
Wolf Creek, *175* . . . C5
Wonder . . . C5
Woodburn, **20,100** . . . D2
Wood Village, **2,860** . . . B2
Worden . . . E5
Yachats, **617** . . . B3
Yamhill, **794** . . . C2
Yoncalla, **1,052** . . . C4

Other Features

Abert, *lake* . . . F5
Adams, *mountain* . . . E1
Alvord, *lake* . . . H5
Ankeny N.W.R. . . . C3
Antelope, *reservoir* . . . J5
Baskett Slough N.W.R. . . . C3
Bear Valley N.W.R. . . . E5
Blanco, *cape* . . . B5
Blue, *mountains* . . . H3
Blue Mt., *pass* . . . J5
Boise Natl. For. . . . K3
Burns Ind. Res. . . . G4
Calapooya, *mountains* . . . D4
Cascade, *range* . . . D4
Cascade-Siskiyou Natl. Mon. . . . D5
Charles Sheldon Antelope Range . . . G6

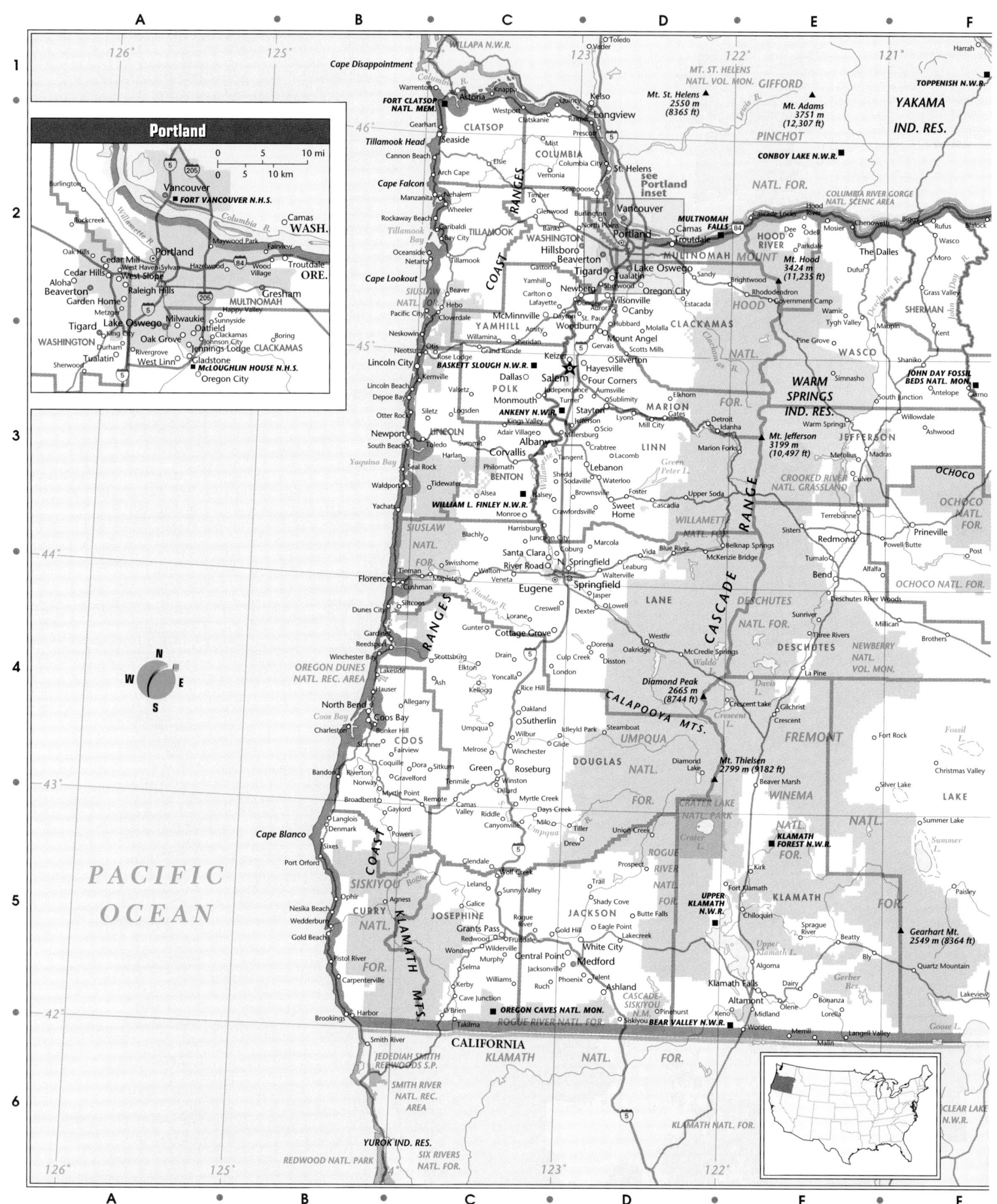

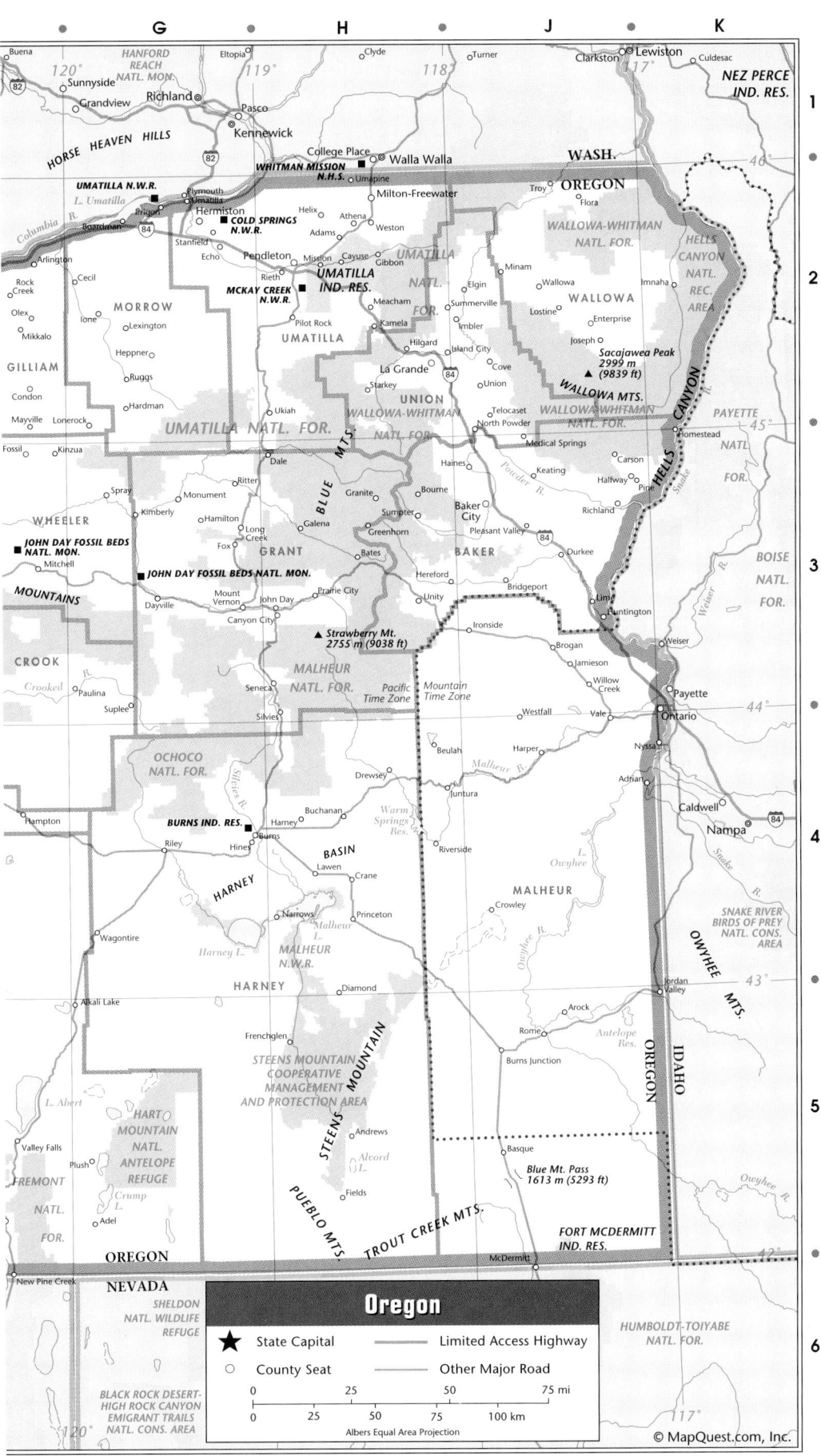

Clackamas, river D2
Clear Lake N.W.R. F6
Coast, ranges B5, C2
Cold Springs N.W.R. G2
Columbia, river A2, B1, F2
Columbia River Gorge Natl. Scenic
     Area E2
Conboy Lake N.W.R. E2
Coos, bay .B4
Crater, lake D5
Crater Lake Natl. Park D4
Crescent, lake E4
Crooked, river F3
Crooked River Natl. Grassland E3
Crump, lake G5
Davis, lake .E4
Deschutes, river E2
Deschutes Natl. For. E4
Diamond, peak D4
Disappointment, cape B1
Falcon, cape B2
Fort Clatsop Natl. Mem. C1
Fort McDermitt Ind. Res. H6, J5
Fort Vancouver N.H.S. A2
Fossil, lake .F4
Fremont Natl. For. E4, F5
Gearhart, mountain F5
Gerber, reservoir E5
Gifford Pinchot Natl. For. E1
Goose, lake F5
Green Peter, lake D3
Harney, basin G4
Harney, lake G4
Hart Mountain Natl.
     Antelope Refuge G5
Hells, canyon K3
Hells Canyon Natl. Rec. Area K2
Hood, mountain E2
Horse Heaven, hills F1
Humboldt Natl. For. J6
Jedediah Smith Redwoods S.P. B6
Jefferson, mountain E3
John Day, river F2
John Day Fossil Beds
     Natl. Mon. F3, G3
Klamath, mountains B5
Klamath Forest N.W.R. E5
Klamath Natl. For. D6
Lewis, river E1
Lookout, cape B2
Malheur, lake H4
Malheur, river H4
Malheur Natl. For. H3
Malheur N.W.R. H4
McKay Creek N.W.R. H2
McLoughlin House N.H.S. A3
Mount Hood Natl. For. E2
Mt. St. Helens Natl. Vol. Mon. D1
Multnomah, falls D2
Newberry Natl. Vol. Mon. E4
Nez Perce Ind. Res. K1
Ochoco, mountains F3
Ochoco Natl. For. F3, G4
Oregon Caves Natl. Mon. C5
Oregon Dunes Natl. Rec. Area B4
Owyhee, lake J4
Owyhee, mountains K4
Owyhee, river J4, K5
Pacific, ocean A5
Payette Natl. For. K2
Powder, river J3
Pueblo, mountains H5
Redwood Natl. Park B6
Rogue, river C5
Rogue River Natl. For. C5, D5
Sacajawea, peak J2
St. Helens, mountain D1
Silvies, river G4
Siskiyou Natl. For. B5
Siuslaw, river C4
Siuslaw Natl. For. C2, C3
Six Rivers Natl. For. C6
Snake, river K3, K4
South Umpqua, river C5
Steens, mountain H5
Steens Mountain Cooperative
     Management and Protection Area .H5
Strawberry, mountain H3
Summer, lake F5
Summit Lake Ind. Res. H6
Thielsen, mountain D4
Tillamook, bay C2
Tillamook, head B2
Toppenish N.W.R. F1
Trout Creek, mountains H5
Umatilla, lake G2
Umatilla Ind. Res. H2
Umatilla N.W.R. G2
Umatilla Natl. For. G2, H2
Umpqua Natl. For. D4
Upper Klamath, lake E5
Upper Klamath N.W.R. E5
Waldo, lake D4
Wallowa, mountains J2
Wallowa-Whitman Natl. For. H2, J2
Warm Springs, reservoir H4
Warm Springs Ind. Res. E3
Weiser, river K3
Whitman Mission N.H.S. H1
Willamette, river A2, C3
Willamette Natl. For. D3
Willapa N.W.R. C1
William L. Finley N.W.R. C3
Winema Natl. For. E4
Yakima Ind. Res. F1
Yaquina, bay B3
Yurok Ind. Res. B6

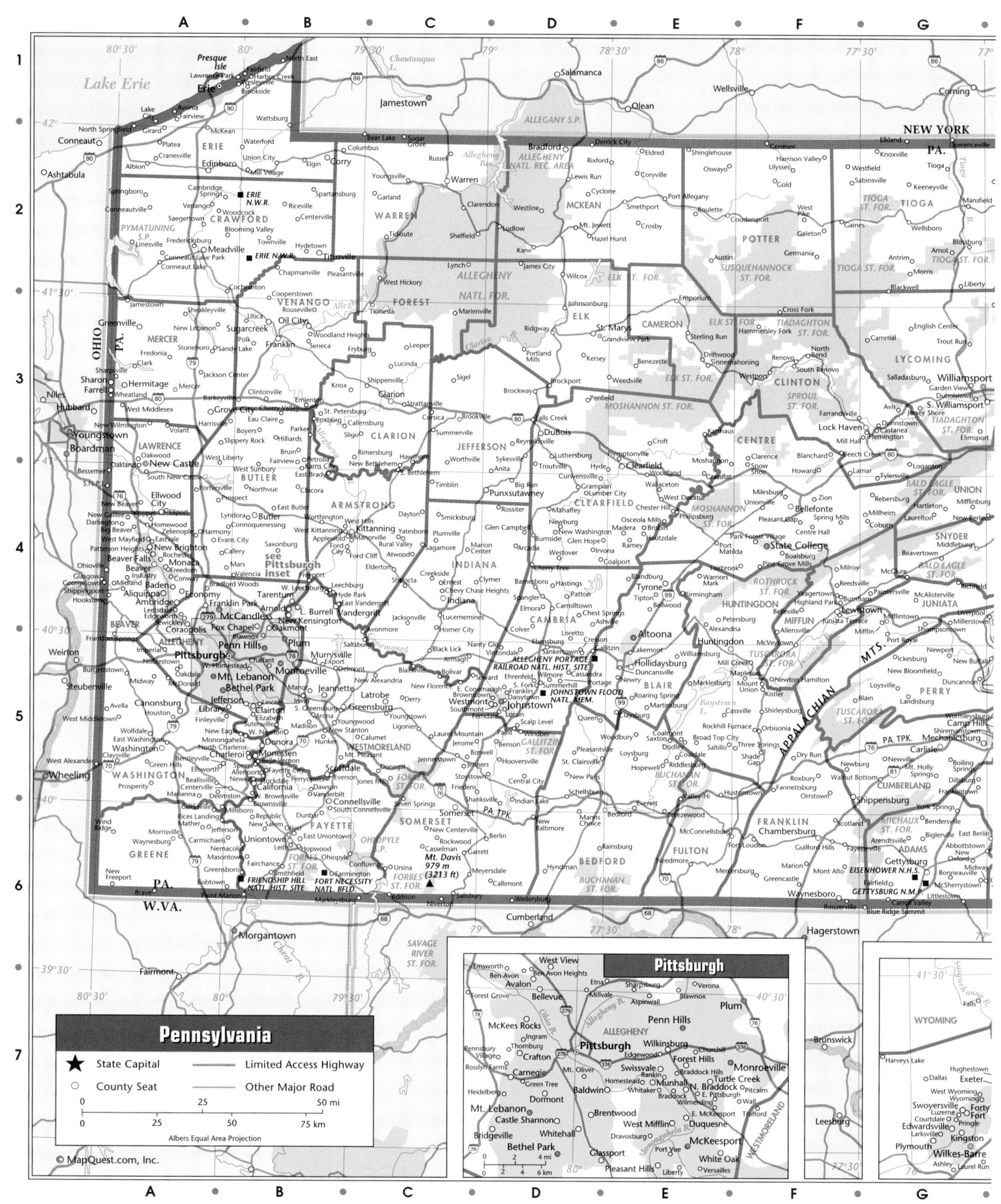

Pennsylvania

★ State Capital
○ County Seat

Limited Access Highway
Other Major Road

0   25   50 mi
0   25   50   75 km

Albers Equal Area Projection

© MapQuest.com, Inc.

Pittsburgh

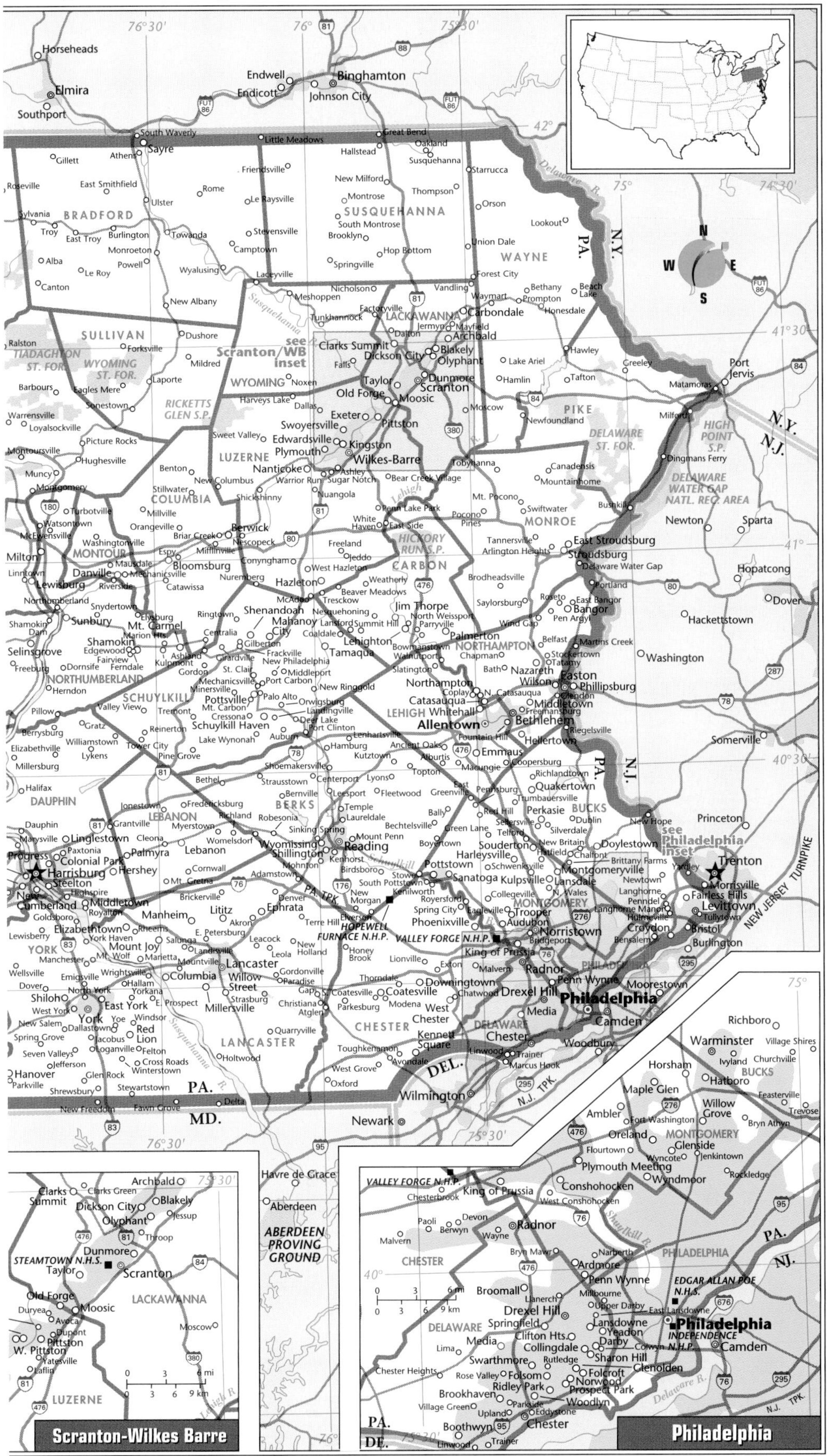

Pennsylvania

Capital:	Harrisburg
Land Area:	44,820 sq. mi.
	116,084 sq. km.
Population:	12,281,054 (2000 Census)
Largest City:	Philadelphia, 1,517,550
Highest Point:	Mt. Davis,
	3,213 ft.
	979 m.
Admitted to Union:	December 12, 1787
Nickname:	Keystone State
State Flower:	Mountain Laurel
State Bird:	Ruffed Grouse

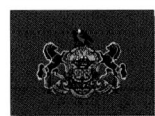

Pennsylvania: Map Index

Counties

Adams, 91,292 . . . . . .G6
Allegheny,
  1,281,666 . . . . . .A5, E7
Armstrong, 72,392 . . . .C4
Beaver, 181,412 . . . . . .A4
Bedford, 49,984 . . . . . .D6
Berks, 373,638 . . . . . . .J5
Blair, 129,144 . . . . . . .E5
Bradford, 62,761 . . . . .H2
Bucks, 597,635 . . .L5, M6
Butler, 174,083 . . . . . .B4
Cambria, 152,598 . . . . .D4
Cameron, 5,974 . . . . . .E3
Carbon, 58,802 . . . . . .K4
Centre, 135,758 . . . . . .F3
Chester, 433,501 . .K6, K7
Clarion, 41,765 . . . . . .C3
Clearfield, 83,382 . . . .D4
Clinton, 37,914 . . . . . .F3
Columbia, 64,151 . . . . .J3
Crawford, 90,366 . . . . .A2
Cumberland, 213,674 . .G5
Dauphin, 251,798 . . . . .H5
Delaware, 550,864 . .K6, K7
Elk, 35,112 . . . . .D3
Erie, 280,843 . . . . . . .A2
Fayette, 148,644 . . . . .B6
Forest, 4,946 . . . . . . .C3
Franklin, 129,313 . . . . .F6
Fulton, 14,261 . . . . . . .E6
Greene, 40,672 . . . . . .A6
Huntingdon, 45,586 . . .E4
Indiana, 89,605 . . . . . .C4
Jefferson, 45,932 . . . . .D3
Juniata, 22,821 . . . . . .G4
Lackawanna,
  213,295 . . . . . .H7, K2
Lancaster, 470,658 . . . .J6
Lawrence, 94,643 . . . . .A3
Lebanon, 120,327 . . . . .J5
Lehigh, 312,090 . . . . . .K4
Luzerne, 319,250 . . .H7, J3
Lycoming, 120,044 . . . .G3
McKean, 45,936 . . . . . .D2
Mercer, 120,293 . . . . . .A3
Mifflin, 46,486 . . . . . . .F4
Monroe, 138,687 . . . . .L3
Montgomery,
  750,097 . . . . . .L5, M6
Montour, 18,236 . . . . . .H3
Northampton, 267,066 . .K4
Northumberland,
  94,556 . . . . .H4
Perry, 43,602 . . . . . . .G5
Philadelphia,
  1,517,550 . . . . .L5, M7
Pike, 46,302 . . . . .L3
Potter, 18,080 . . . . . . .F2
Schuylkill, 150,336 . . . .H4
Snyder, 37,546 . . . . . .G4
Somerset, 80,023 . . . . .C6
Sullivan, 6,556 . . . . . . .H3
Susquehanna, 42,238 . .K2
Tioga, 41,373 . . . . . . .G2
Union, 41,624 . . . . . . .G4
Venango, 57,565 . . . . .B3
Warren, 43,863 . . . . . .C2
Washington, 202,897 . .A5
Wayne, 47,722 . . . . . . .L2
Westmoreland,
  369,993 . . . . .B5, F7
Wyoming, 28,080 . . .G7, J3
York, 381,751 . . . . . . .H5

Cities and Towns

Abbottstown, 905 . . . .G6
Adamstown, 1,203 . . . .J5
Addison, 214 . . . . . . .C6
Akron, 4,046 . . . . .J5
Alba, 186 . . . . .H2
Albion, 1,607 . . . . . . .A2
Alburtis, 2,117 . . . . . .K4
Alexandria, 401 . . . . . .E4
Aliquippa, 11,734 . . . . .A4
Allenport, 549 . . . . . . .B5
Allensville, 500 . . . . . .F4
Allentown, 106,632 . . .L4
Altoona, 49,523 . . . . . .E4
Ambler, 6,426 . . . . . . .L6
Ambridge, 7,769 . . . . .A4
Ancient Oaks, 3,161 . . .K4
Antrim, 175 . . . . .G2
Applewold, 356 . . . . . .C4
Arcadia, 250 . . . . .D4
Archbald, 6,220 . . .J6, K2
Ardmore, 12,616 . . . . .L7
Arendtsville, 848 . . . . .G6
Arlington Heights,
  5,132 . . . . .L3
Armagh, 131 . . . . . . .C5

Arnold, 5,667 . . . . . . .B4
Arnot, 300 . . . . .G2
Arona, 407 . . . . .B5
Ashland, 3,283 . . . . . .J4
Ashley, 2,866 . . . .G7, K3
Ashville, 279 . . . . .D4
Aspinwall, 2,960 . . . . .E7
Atglen, 1,217 . . . . . . .K6
Athens, 3,415 . . . . . . .H2
Atwood, 112 . . . . .C4
Auburn, 839 . . . . .J4
Audubon, 6,549 . . . . . .L5
Austin, 623 . . . . .E2
Avalon, 5,294 . . . . . . .D7
Avella, 750 . . . . .A5
Avis, 1,492 . . . . .G3
Avoca, 2,851 . . . . . . .H7
Avondale, 1,108 . . . . . .K6
Avonia, 1,331 . . . . . . .A1
Avonmore, 820 . . . . . .C4
Baden, 4,377 . . . . . . .A4
Baldwin, 19,999 . . . . . .E7
Bally, 1,062 . . . . .K5
Bangor, 5,319 . . . . . . .L4
Barbours, 225 . . . . . . .H3
Barkeyville, 237 . . . . . .B3
Barnesboro D4
Bath, 2,678 . . . . .L4
Beach Lake, 450 . . . . .L2
Beallsville, 511 . . . . . .A5
Bear Creek Village, 284 .K3
Bear Lake, 193 . . . . . .C2
Beaver, 4,775 . . . . . . .A4
Beaver Falls, 9,920 . . . .A4
Beaver Meadows, 968 . .K4
Beavertown, 870 . . . . .G4
Bechtelsville, 931 . . . . .K5
Bedford, 3,141 . . . . . . .E5
Beech Creek, 717 . . . . .F3
Belfast, 1,301 . . . . . . .L4
Bellefonte, 6,395 . . . . .F4
Belle Vernon, 1,211 . . . .B5
Belleville, 1,386 . . . . . .F4
Bellevue, 8,770 . . . . . .D7
Bellwood, 2,016 . . . . . .E4
Ben Avon, 1,917 . . . . . .D6
Ben Avon Heights, 392 .D6
Bendersville, 576 . . . . .G6
Benezette, 60 . . . . . . .E3
Bensalem (part of Cornwells
  Hts.-Eddington, pop.
  3,406) M5
Benson, 194 . . . . .D5
Bentleyville, 2,502 . . . .A5
Benton, 955 . . . . .J3
Berlin, 2,192 . . . . .D6
Bernville, 865 . . . . . . .J5
Berrysburg, 354 . . . . . .H4
Berwick, 10,774 . . . . . .J3
Berwyn (see Devon),
  5,067 . . . . .K7
Bessemer, 1,172 . . . . .A4
Bethany, 292 . . . . .L2
Bethel, 650 . . . . .J5
Bethel Park, 33,556 .A5, D7
Bethlehem, 71,329 . . . .L4
Big Beaver, 2,186 . . . . .A4
Biglerville, 1,101 . . . . .G6
Big Run, 686 . . . . .D4
Birdsboro, 5,064 . . . . . .K5
Birmingham, 91 . . . . . .E4
Black Lick, 1,438 . . . . .C5
Blackwell, 40 . . . . .G2
Blain, 252 . . . . .F5
Blairsville, 3,607 . . . . .C5
Blakely, 7,027 . . . .H6, K3
Blanchard, 621 . . . . . .F3
Blandburg, 425 . . . . . .E4
Blawnox, 1,550 . . .B5, E7
Blooming Valley, 378 . . .A2
Bloomsburg, 12,375 . . .J4
Blossburg, 1,480 . . . . .G2
Blue Ridge Summit,
  1,400 . . . . .G6
Boalsburg, 3,578 . . . . .F4
Bobtown, 1,000 . . . . . .B6
Boiling Springs, 2,769 . .G5
Bolivar, 501 . . . . .C5
Bonneauville, 1,378 . . .G6
Boothwyn, 5,206 . . . . .K7
Boswell, 1,364 . . . . . . .C5
Bowmanstown, 895 . . . .K4
Boyers, 400 . . . . .B3
Boyertown, 3,940 . . . . .K5
Braddock, 2,912 . . . . . .E7
Braddock Hills, 1,998 . .E7
Bradford, 9,175 . . . . . .D2
Bradford Woods, 1,149 .A4
Brave, 200 . . . . .A6
Breezewood, 200 . . . . .E5
Brentwood, 10,466 . . . .D7
Briar Creek, 651 . . . . . .J3
Brickerville, 1,287 . . . . .J5
Bridgeport, 4,371 . . . . .L5
Bridgeville, 5,341 . . . . .D7
Bristol, 413 . . . . .E4
Bristol, 9,923 . . . . . . .M5

Maps: Scranton-Wilkes Barre · Philadelphia

Brittany Farms (Brittany Farms-Highlands), 3,268 ... M5
Broad Top City, 384 ... E5
Brockport, 550 ... D3
Brockway, 2,182 ... D3
Brodheadsville, 1,637 ... L4
Brookhaven, 7,985 ... L7
Brookline, 325 ... K2
Brookside (part of Northwest Harborcreek, pop. 8,658) ... B1
Brookville, 4,230 ... C3
Broomall, 11,046 ... L7
Brownstown, 883 ... B5
Brownsville, 2,804 ... B5
Bruin, 534 ... B4
Bryn Athyn, 1,351 ... M6
Bryn Mawr, 4,382 ... L7
Burgettstown, 1,576 ... A5
Burlington, 182 ... H2
Burnham, 2,144 ... F4
Burnside, 283 ... C4
Bushkill, 225 ... L3
Butler, 15,121 ... B4
California, 5,274 ... B5
Callensburg, 224 ... B3
Callery, 444 ... A4
Callimont, 51 ... C6
Calumet (Calumet-Norvelt), 1,682 ... C5
Cambridge Springs, 2,363 ... A2
Cammal, 30 ... G3
Camp Hill, 7,636 ... H5
Camptown, 325 ... H2
Canadensis, 450 ... L3
Canonsburg, 8,607 ... A5
Canton, 1,807 ... H2
Carbondale, 9,804 ... K2
Carlisle, 17,970 ... G5
Carmichaels, 556 ... B6
Carnegie, 8,389 ... D7
Carrolltown, 1,049 ... D4
Carroll Valley, 3,291 ... G6
Cassandra, 136 ... D5
Casselman, 99 ... C6
Cassville, 152 ... E5
Castanea, 1,189 ... G3
Castle Shannon, 8,556 ... D7
Catasauqua, 6,588 ... L4
Catawissa, 1,589 ... J4
Centerport, 327 ... J5
Centerville, 3,390 ... A5
Centerville, 247 ... B2
Central City, 1,258 ... D5
Centralia, 21 ... J4
Centre Hall, 1,079 ... F4
Chalfant, 870 ... B5
Chalfont, 3,900 ... L5
Chambersburg, 17,862 ... F6
Chapman, 234 ... L4
Chapmanville, 225 ... B2
Charleroi, 4,871 ... B5
Chatwood (part of West Goshen, pop. 8,472), 3,600 ... K6
Cherry Tree, 443 ... D4
Cherry Valley, 72 ... B3
Chesterbrook, 4,623 ... K6
Chester Heights, 2,481 ... K7
Chester Hill, 918 ... E4
Chest Springs, 110 ... D4
Chevy Chase Heights, 1,511 ... C4
Chicora, 1,021 ... B4
Christiana, 1,124 ... J6
Churchill, 3,566 ... E7
Churchville, 4,469 ... M6
Clairton, 8,491 ... B5
Clarence, 577 ... F3
Clarendon, 564 ... C2
Clarion, 6,185 ... C3
Clark, 633 ... A3
Clarks Green, 1,630 ... H6
Clarks Summit, 5,126 ... H6, K3
Clarksville, 234 ... A6
Claysburg, 1,503 ... D5
Claysville, 724 ... A5
Clearfield, 6,631 ... E4
Cleona, 2,148 ... J5
Clifton Heights, 6,779 ... L7
Clintonville, 528 ... B3
Clymer, 1,547 ... C4
Coaldale (Bedford Co.), 146 ... E5
Coaldale (Schuylkill Co.), 2,295 ... K4
Coalmont, 128 ... E5
Coalport, 490 ... D4
Coatesville, 10,838 ... K6
Coburn, 145 ... G4
Cochranton, 1,148 ... A2
Collegeville, 8,032 ... L5
Collingdale, 8,664 ... L7
Colonial Park, 13,259 ... H5
Columbia, 10,311 ... J5
Columbus, 550 ... B2
Colver, 1,035 ... D4
Colwyn, 2,453 ... L7
Confluence, 834 ... C6
Conneaut Lake, 708 ... A2
Conneaut Lake Park, 2,502 ... A2
Conneautville, 848 ... A2
Connellsville, 9,146 ... B5
Connoquenessing, 564 ... A4
Conshohocken, 7,589 ... L6
Conway, 2,290 ... A4
Conyngham, 1,958 ... J4
Coopersburg, 2,582 ... L4
Cooperstown, 460 ... B2
Coplay, 3,387 ... K4
Coraopolis, 6,131 ... A4
Cornwall, 3,486 ... J5
Corry, 6,834 ... B2
Corsica, 354 ... C3
Coryville, 200 ... E2
Coudersport, 2,650 ... F2
Courtdale, 791 ... J3
Cranesville, 600 ... A2
Creekside, 323 ... C4
Cresson, 1,631 ... D5
Cressona, 1,635 ... J4

Croft, 175 ... E3
Crosby, 125 ... E2
Cross Fork ... F3
Cross Roads, 518 ... H6
Croydon, 9,993 ... M5
Curwensville, 2,650 ... D4
Cyclone, 225 ... D2
Daisytown, 356 ... C5
Dallas, 2,557 ... G7, K3
Dallastown, 4,087 ... H6
Dalton, 1,294 ... K2
Danville, 4,897 ... H4
Darby, 10,299 ... L7
Darlington, 299 ... A4
Dauphin, 773 ... H5
Dawson, 451 ... B5
Dayton, 543 ... C4
Deemston, 809 ... B5
Deer Lake, 528 ... J4
Delaware Water Gap, 744 ... L4
Delmont, 2,497 ... B5
Delta, 741 ... J6
Denver, 3,332 ... J5
Derrick City, 350 ... D2
Derry, 2,991 ... C5
Devon (Devon-Berwyn), 5,067 ... K7
Dickson City, 6,205 ... H7, K3
Dillsburg, 2,063 ... G5
Dingmans Ferry, 10 ... M3
Donegal, 165 ... C5
Donora, 5,653 ... B5
Dormont, 9,305 ... D7
Dornsife, 200 ... H4
Dover, 1,815 ... H5
Downingtown, 7,589 ... K6
Doylestown, 8,227 ... L5
Dravosburg, 2,015 ... E7
Drexel Hill, 29,364 ... L6, L7
Driftwood, 103 ... E3
Dry Run, 325 ... F5
Dublin, 2,083 ... L5
DuBois, 8,123 ... D3
Duboistown, 1,280 ... G3
Dudley, 192 ... E5
Dunbar, 1,219 ... B5
Duncannon, 1,508 ... G5
Duncansville, 1,238 ... D5
Dunmore, 14,018 ... H7, K3
Dunnstown, 1,365 ... G3
Dupont, 2,719 ... H7
Duquesne, 7,332 ... E7
Duryea, 4,593 ... H7
Dushore, 663 ... J2
Eagles Mere, 153 ... H3
Eagleville, 4,458 ... L5
East Bangor, 979 ... L4
East Berlin, 1,365 ... H6
East Brady, 1,038 ... B4
East Butler, 694 ... B4
East Conemaugh, 1,291 ... D5
East Greenville, 3,103 ... K5
East Lansdowne, 2,586 ... L7
East McKeesport, 2,343 ... E7
East Petersburg, 4,450 ... J5
East Pittsburgh, 2,017 ... E7
East Prospect, 678 ... H6
East Side, 290 ... K3
East Smithfield, 375 ... H2
East Stroudsburg, 9,888 ... L3
East Troy, 250 ... H2
East Uniontown, 2,760 ... B6
Eastvale, 293 ... A4
East Vandergrift, 742 ... B4
East Washington, 1,930 ... A5
East York, 8,782 ... H6
Eau Claire, 355 ... B3
Ebensburg, 3,091 ... D5
Economy, 9,363 ... A4
Eddystone, 2,442 ... L7
Edgewood (Allegheny Co.), 3,311 ... E7
Edgewood (Northumberland Co.), H4
Edgeworth, 1,730 ... A4
Edinboro, 6,950 ... A2
Edwardsville, 4,984 ... G7, K3
Ehrenfeld, 234 ... D5
Elderton, 358 ... C4
Eldred, 858 ... E2
Elgin, 236 ... B2
Elimsport, 275 ... G3
Elizabeth, 1,609 ... B5
Elizabethtown, 11,887 ... H5
Elizabethville, 1,344 ... H4
Elkland, 1,786 ... G2
Ellport, 1,148 ... A4
Ellsworth, 1,083 ... B5
Ellwood City, 8,688 ... A4
Elmora, 700 ... D5
Elverson, 959 ... K5
Elysburg, 2,067 ... H4
Emigsville, 2,467 ... H5
Emlenton, 784 ... B3
Emmaus, 11,313 ... L4
Emporium, 2,526 ... E2
Emsworth, 2,598 ... D7
English Center, 10 ... G3
Ephrata, 13,213 ... J5
Erie, 103,717 ... A1
Ernest, 501 ... C4
Espy, 1,428 ... J3
Etna, 3,924 ... D7
Evans City, 2,009 ... A4
Everett, 1,905 ... E5
Everson, 842 ... B5
Exeter, 5,955 ... H7, K3
Export, 895 ... B5
Exton, 4,267 ... K6
Factoryville, 1,144 ... K2
Fairbrook (part of Ramblewood, pop. 1,054), 600 ... F4
Fairchance, 2,174 ... B6
Fairfield (Adams Co.), 486 ... G6
Fairfield (Erie Co., part of Northwest Harborcreek, pop. 8,658), 486 ... B1
Fairless Hills, 8,365 ... M5
Fairview (Butler Co.), 220 ... B3
Fairview (Erie Co.), 1,900 ... A1

Fairview (Northumberland Co., Fairview-Ferndale), 2,411 ... H4
Falls, 550 ... G7, K3
Falls Creek, 983 ... D3
Fannettsburg, 375 ... F5
Farmington, 650 ... B6
Farrandsville, 40 ... F3
Fawn Grove, 463 ... J6
Fayette City, 714 ... B5
Fayetteville, 2,774 ... F6
Feasterville (Feasterville-Trevose), 6,525 ... M6
Felton, 449 ... H6
Ferndale (Cambria Co.), 1,834 ... D5
Ferndale (Northumberland Co., see Fairview), 900 ... H4
Finleyville, 459 ... A5
Fleetwood, 4,018 ... K5
Flemington, 1,319 ... G3
Flourtown, 4,669 ... L6
Folcroft, 6,978 ... L7
Folsom, 8,072 ... L7
Ford City, 3,451 ... B4
Ford Cliff, 412 ... B4
Forest City, 1,855 ... L2
Forest Grove (part of Robinson Township, pop. 12,289), 3,800 ... C7
Forest Hills, 6,831 ... E7
Forksville, 147 ... H2
Fort Loudon, 500 ... F6
Fort Washington, 3,680 ... L6
Forty Fort, 4,579 ... G7
Fountain Hill, 4,614 ... L4
Foxburg, 275 ... B3
Fox Chapel, 5,436 ... B4
Frackville, 4,361 ... J4
Frankfort Springs, 130 ... A5
Franklin (Cambria Co.), 442 ... D5
Franklin (Venango Co.), 7,212 ... B3
Franklin Park, 11,364 ... A4
Franklintown, 532 ... G5
Fredericksburg (Crawford Co.), 1,140 ... A2
Fredericksburg (Lebanon Co.), 987 ... J5
Fredonia, 652 ... A3
Freeburg, 584 ... H4
Freedom, 1,763 ... A4
Freeland, 3,643 ... K3
Freemansburg, 1,897 ... L4
Freeport, 1,962 ... B4
Friedens, 1,673 ... C5
Friendsville, 91 ... J2
Fryburg, 350 ... C3
Gaines, 125 ... F2
Galeton, 1,325 ... F2
Gallitzin, 1,756 ... D5
Gap, 1,611 ... J6
Garden View, 2,679 ... G3
Garland, 225 ... C2
Garrett, 449 ... C6
Genesee, 425 ... F2
Georgetown, 182 ... A4
Germania, 80 ... F2
Gilberton, 867 ... J4
Gillett, 375 ... H2
Girard, 3,164 ... A2
Girardville, 1,742 ... J4
Glasgow, 63 ... A4
Glassport, 4,993 ... D7
Glen Campbell, 306 ... D4
Glendon, 367 ... L4
Glen Hope, 149 ... D4
Glenolden, 7,476 ... L7
Glen Rock, 1,809 ... H6
Glenside, 7,914 ... M6
Gold, 125 ... F2
Goldsboro, 939 ... H5
Gordon, 781 ... J4
Gordonville, 800 ... J5
Grampian, 441 ... D4
Grandview Park, 3 ... C4
Grantville, 1,000 ... H5
Grassflat, 650 ... E3
Gratz, 676 ... H4
Great Bend, 700 ... K2
Greeley, 250 ... L3
Greencastle, 3,722 ... F6
Green Hills, 18 ... A5
Green Lane, 584 ... L5
Greensboro, 295 ... B6
Greensburg, 15,889 ... B5
Green Tree, 4,719 ... D7
Greenville, 6,380 ... A3
Grove City, 8,024 ... A3
Guilford Hills (Guilford), 2,100 ... F6
Halfax, 875 ... H4
Hallam, 1,532 ... H5
Hallstead, 1,216 ... K2
Hamburg, 4,114 ... K4
Hamlin, 300 ... L3
Hammersley Fork, 3 ... F3
Hanover, 14,535 ... H6
Harborcreek ... B1
Harleysville, 8,795 ... L5
Harmony, 937 ... A4
Harrisburg, 48,950 ... H5
Harrison Valley, 250 ... F2
Harrisville, 883 ... A3
Hartleton, 260 ... G4
Harveys Lake, 2,888 ... G7, J3
Hastings, 1,398 ... D4
Hatboro, 7,393 ... M6
Hatfield, 2,605 ... L5
Hawley, 1,303 ... L3
Hawthorn, 587 ... C3
Hazel Hurst, 200 ... D2
Hazleton, 23,329 ... K4
Heidelberg, 1,225 ... D7
Hellertown, 5,606 ... L4
Hermitage, 16,157 ... A3
Herndon, 383 ... H4
Hershey, 12,771 ... H5
Highland Park (part of Old Orchard, pop. 2,443), 1,446 ... L4
Highspire, 2,720 ... H5
Hilliards, 175 ... B3
Hollidaysburg, 5,368 ... E5

Holtwood, 325 ... J6
Homer City, 1,844 ... C4
Homestead, 3,569 ... E7
Homewood, 147 ... A4
Honesdale, 4,874 ... L2
Honey Brook, 1,287 ... K5
Hookstown, 152 ... A4
Hooversville, 779 ... D5
Hop Bottom, 333 ... K2
Hopewell, 222 ... E5
Hopwood, 2,006 ... B6
Horsham, 14,779 ... M6
Houston, 1,314 ... A5
Houtzdale, 941 ... E4
Howard, 699 ... F3
Hughestown, 1,541 ... G7
Hughesville, 2,220 ... H3
Hulmeville, 893 ... M5
Hunker, 329 ... B5
Huntingdon, 6,918 ... E5
Hustontown, 400 ... E5
Hyde, 1,491 ... D3
Hyde Park, 513 ... B4
Hydetown, 605 ... B2
Hyndman, 1,005 ... D6
Icksburg, 425 ... G5
Imperial (Imperial-Enlow), 3,514 ... A5
Indiana, 14,895 ... C4
Indian Lake, 450 ... D5
Industry, 1,921 ... A4
Ingram, 3,712 ... D7
Irvona, 680 ... D4
Irwin, 4,366 ... B5
Ivyland, 842 ... M5
Jackson Center, 221 ... A3
Jacksonville, 675 ... C4
Jacobus, 1,203 ... H6
James City, 200 ... D2
Jamestown, 636 ... A3
Jeannette, 10,654 ... B5
Jeddo, 98 ... K4
Jefferson (Allegheny Co.) B5
Jefferson (Greene Co.), 337 ... A6
Jefferson (York Co.), 631 ... H6
Jenkintown, 4,478 ... M6
Jenners, 850 ... D5
Jennerstown, 714 ... C5
Jermyn, 2,287 ... K2
Jerome, 1,068 ... C5
Jersey Shore, 4,482 ... G3
Jessup, 4,718 ... J7
Jim Thorpe, 4,804 ... K4
Johnsonburg, 3,003 ... D3
Johnstown, 23,906 ... C5
Jones Mills, 275 ... C5
Jonestown, 1,028 ... J5
Juniata Terrace, 502 ... F4
Kane, 4,126 ... D2
Karns City, 244 ... B3
Karthaus, 300 ... E3
Keeneyville, 80 ... G2
Kenhorst, 2,679 ... K5
Kenilworth, 1,576 ... K5
Kennett Square, 5,273 ... K6
Kersey, 750 ... D3
King of Prussia, 18,511 ... L5, L6
Kistler, 344 ... F5
Kittanning, 4,787 ... B4
Knox, 1,176 ... B3
Knoxville, 617 ... G2
Koppel, 856 ... A4
Kulpmont, 2,985 ... J4
Kulpsville, 8,005 ... L5
Kutztown, 5,067 ... K4
Laceyville, 396 ... J2
Laflin, 1,502 ... H7
Lake Ariel, 1,000 ... L3
Lake Burrell ... B4
Lake City, 2,811 ... A1
Lakemont, 1,600 ... E5
Lake Wynonah, 1,961 ... J4
Lamar, 600 ... F3
Lancaster, 56,348 ... J5
Landingville, 175 ... J4
Landisburg, 195 ... G5
Landisville (see Salunga), 4,771 ... J5
Langhorne, 1,981 ... M5
Langhorne Manor, 927 ... M5
Lansdale, 16,071 ... L5
Lansdowne, 11,044 ... L7
Lansford, 4,230 ... K4
Laporte, 290 ... H3
Larksville, 4,694 ... G7
Latrobe, 8,994 ... C5
Laureldale, 3,759 ... K5
Laurel Mountain, 185 ... C5
Laurel Run, 723 ... G7
Laureltown, 475 ... G4
Lawrence Park, 4,048 ... A1
Lawrenceville, 627 ... G2
Leacock (Leacock-Leola-Bareville), 6,625 ... J5
Lebanon, 24,461 ... J5
Leechburg, 2,386 ... B4
Leeper, 250 ... C3
Leesport, 1,805 ... K5
Leetsdale, 1,232 ... A4
Lehighton, 5,537 ... K4
Leith (Leith-Hatfield), 2,820 ... B6
Lenhartsville, 181 ... K4
Leola (see Leacock) ... J5
Le Raysville, 318 ... J2
Le Roy, 175 ... H2
Levittown, 53,966 ... M5
Lewisberry, 385 ... H5
Lewisburg, 5,620 ... H4
Lewis Run, 577 ... D2
Lewistown, 8,998 ... F4
Liberty (Allegheny Co.), 2,670 ... E7
Liberty (Tioga Co.), 230 ... G2
Library (part of South Park Township, pop. 14,340), 5,600 ... A5
Ligonier, 1,695 ... C5
Lima, 3,075 ... L7
Lincoln, 1,218 ... B5
Linesville, 1,155 ... A2
Linglestown, 6,414 ... H5
Linntown, 1,542 ... H4

Linwood, 3,374 ... K7, L6
Lionville (Lionville-Marchwood), 6,298 ... K5
Lititz, 9,029 ... J5
Little Meadows, 290 ... J2
Littlestown, 3,947 ... G6
Liverpool, 876 ... H4
Llanerch ... L7
Lock Haven, 9,149 ... G3
Loganton, 435 ... G3
Loganville, 908 ... H6
Lookout, 80 ... L2
Lorain, 747 ... D5
Loretto, 1,190 ... D4
Loyalsockville, 375 ... H3
Loysburg, 275 ... E5
Loysville, 450 ... G5
Lucernemines, 951 ... C4
Lucinda, 600 ... C3
Ludlow, 251 ... D2
Lumber City, 86 ... D4
Luthersburg, 375 ... D3
Luzerne, 2,952 ... G7
Lykens, 1,937 ... H4
Lynch ... C2
Lyndora (Homeacre-Lyndora), 6,685 ... B4
Lyons, 504 ... K5
Macungie, 3,039 ... K4
Madera, 425 ... E4
Madison, 510 ... B5
Mahaffey, 402 ... D4
Mahanoy City, 4,647 ... J4
Malvern, 3,059 ... K5, K7
Manchester, 2,350 ... H5
Manheim, 4,784 ... J5
Manns Choice, 291 ... D6
Manor, 2,796 ... B5
Manorville, 401 ... B4
Mansfield, 3,411 ... G2
Maple Glen, 7,042 ... M6
Mapleton, 473 ... F5
Marcus Hook, 2,314 ... L6
Marianna, 626 ... A5
Marienville, 350 ... C3
Marietta, 2,689 ... J5
Marion, 1,100 ... F6
Marion Center, 451 ... C4
Marion Heights, 735 ... J4
Marklesburg, 216 ... E5
Markleysburg, 282 ... C6
Mars, 1,746 ... A4
Martinsburg, 2,236 ... E5
Martins Creek, 950 ... L4
Marysville, 2,306 ... H5
Masontown, 3,611 ... B6
Matamoras, 2,312 ... M3
Mather, 1,200 ... A6
Mausdale, 500 ... H4
Mayfield, 1,756 ... K2
McAdoo, 2,274 ... J4
McAlisterville, 765 ... G4
McCandless, 29,022 ... A4
McClure, 975 ... G4
McConnellsburg, 1,073 ... E6
McDonald, 2,281 ... A5
McEwensville, 314 ... H3
McKean, 389 ... A2
McKeesport, 24,040 ... E7
McKees Rocks, 6,622 ... D7
McSherrystown, 2,691 ... G6
McVeytown, 405 ... F4
Meadville, 13,685 ... A2
Mechanicsburg, 9,042 ... G5
Mechanicsville (Montour Co.), 3,099 ... H4
Mechanicsville (Schuylkill Co.), 515 ... J4
Media, 5,533 ... L6, L7
Mercer, 2,391 ... A3
Mercersburg, 1,540 ... F6
Meshoppen, 459 ... J2
Meyersdale, 2,473 ... C6
Middleburg, 1,382 ... G4
Middleport, 458 ... J4
Middletown (Dauphin Co.), 9,242 ... H5
Middletown (Northampton Co.), 7,378 ... L4
Midland, 3,137 ... A4
Midway (Adams Co.), 2,323 ... G6
Midway (Washington Co.), 982 ... A5
Mifflin, 627 ... G4
Mifflinburg, 3,594 ... G4
Mifflintown, 861 ... G4
Mifflinville, 1,213 ... J3
Mildred, 425 ... J3
Milesburg, 1,187 ... F4
Milford, 1,104 ... M3
Millbourne, 943 ... L7
Mill Creek, 351 ... F5
Millersburg, 2,562 ... H4
Millerstown, 679 ... G4
Millersville, 7,774 ... J6
Mill Hall, 1,568 ... G3
Millheim, 749 ... G4
Millsboro (Fredericktown-Millsboro), 1,094 ... A6
Millvale, 4,028 ... D7
Mill Village, 412 ... B2
Millville, 991 ... H3
Milroy, 1,386 ... F4
Milton, 6,650 ... H3
Minersville, 4,552 ... J4
Modena, 610 ... K6
Mohnton, 2,963 ... K5
Monaca, 6,286 ... A4
Monessen, 8,669 ... B5
Monongahela, 4,761 ... B5
Monroeton, 514 ... J2
Monroeville, 29,349 ... B5, E7
Mont Alto, 1,357 ... F6
Montgomery, 1,695 ... H3
Montgomeryville, 12,031 ... L5
Montoursville, 4,777 ... H3
Montrose, 1,664 ... K2
Moosic, 5,575 ... H7, K3
Morris, 100 ... G2
Morrisville (Bucks Co.), 10,023 ... M5
Morrisville (Greene Co.), 1,443 ... A6
Moscow, 1,883 ... J7, K3
Moshannon, 450 ... E3
Mountainhome, 1,169 ... L3

Mount Carbon, 87 ... J4
Mount Carmel, 6,390 ... J4
Mount Gretna, 242 ... J5
Mount Holly Springs, 1,925 ... G5
Mount Jewett, 1,070 ... D2
Mount Joy, 6,765 ... J5
Mount Lebanon, 33,017 ... A5, C7
Mount Oliver, 3,970 ... D7
Mount Penn, 3,016 ... K5
Mount Pleasant, 4,728 ... B5
Mount Pocono, 2,742 ... L3
Mount Union, 2,504 ... F5
Mount Wolf, 1,373 ... H5
Muncy, 2,663 ... H3
Munhall, 12,264 ... E7
Murrysville, 18,872 ... B5
Myerstown, 3,171 ... J5
Nanticoke, 10,955 ... J3
Nanty Glo, 3,054 ... D5
Narberth, 4,233 ... L7
Nazareth, 6,023 ... L4
Needmore, 225 ... E6
Nemacolin, 1,034 ... B6
Nescopeck, 1,528 ... J3
Nesquehoning, 3,288 ... K4
New Albany, 306 ... J2
New Alexandria, 595 ... C5
New Baltimore, 168 ... D6
New Beaver, 1,677 ... A4
New Berlin, 838 ... H4
New Bethlehem, 1,057 ... C3
New Bloomfield, 1,077 ... G5
New Brighton, 6,641 ... A4
New Britain, 3,125 ... L5
New Buffalo, 123 ... H5
Newburg (Clearfield Co.), 81 ... D4
Newburg (Cumberland Co.), 372 ... F5
New Castle, 26,309 ... A4
New Centerville, 193 ... C6
New Columbus, 215 ... J3
New Cumberland, 7,349 ... H5
New Eagle, 2,262 ... B5
Newell, 551 ... B5
New Florence, 784 ... C5
New Freedom, 3,512 ... H6
New Freeport, 50 ... A6
New Galilee, 424 ... A4
New Holland, 5,092 ... J5
New Hope, 2,252 ... M5
New Kensington, 14,701 ... B4
New Lebanon, 205 ... A3
New Milford, 878 ... K2
New Morgan ... K5
New Oxford, 1,696 ... G6
New Paris, 224 ... D6
New Philadelphia, 1,149 ... J4
Newport, 1,506 ... G5
New Ringgold, 291 ... J4
Newry, 245 ... E5
New Salem (Fayette Co., New Salem-Buffington), 808 ... B6
New Salem (York Co.), 648 ... H6
New Stanton, 1,906 ... B5
Newton Hamilton, 272 ... F5
Newtown, 2,312 ... M5
Newville, 1,367 ... G5
New Washington, 89 ... D4
New Wilmington, 2,452 ... A3
Nicholson, 713 ... K2
Niverton, 225 ... C6
Noblestown (Sturgeon-Noblestown), 1,764 ... A5
Norristown, 31,282 ... L5
Northampton, 9,405 ... K4
North Bend, 425 ... F3
North Braddock, 6,410 ... E7
North Catasauqua, 2,814 ... L4
North Charleroi, 1,409 ... B5
North Apollo, 4,601 ... B4
North Springfield, 300 ... A2
Northumberland, 3,714 ... H4
Northvue, 4,825 ... B4
North Wales, 3,342 ... L5
North Weissport (part of Weissport East, 1,936) ... K4
North York, 1,689 ... H6
Norwood, 5,985 ... L7
Noxen, 500 ... J3
Nuangola, 671 ... K3
Nuremberg, 700 ... J4
Oakdale, 1,551 ... A5
Oakland (Lawrence Co.), 1,516 ... A4
Oakland (Susquehanna Co.), 622 ... K2
Oakmont, 6,911 ... B4
Oakwood, 2,249 ... A3
Ohiopyle, 77 ... B6
Ohioville, 3,759 ... A4
Oil City, 11,504 ... B3
Old Forge, 8,798 ... H7, K3
Oliver, 2,925 ... B6
Olyphant, 4,978 ... H7, K3
Orangeville, 500 ... J3
Orbisonia, 425 ... F5
Oreland, 5,509 ... L6
Orrstown, 231 ... F5
Orson, 60 ... L2
Orwigsburg, 3,106 ... J4
Osceola Mills, 1,249 ... E4
Oswayo, 159 ... E2
Oxford, 4,315 ... K6
Paint, 1,103 ... D5
Painterville, 550 ... G4
Palmerton, 5,248 ... K4
Palmyra, 7,096 ... H5
Palo Alto, 1,052 ... J4
Paoli, 5,425 ... K7
Paradise, 1,028 ... J5
Parker, 799 ... B3
Parkesburg, 3,373 ... K6
Park Forest Village, 8,830 ... F4
Parkside, 2,267 ... L7
Parkville, 6,593 ... H6
Parryville, 478 ... K4
Patterson Heights, 670 ... A4
Patton, 2,023 ... D4
Paxtang, 5,254 ... H5
Paxtonia ... H5
Pen Argyl, 3,615 ... L4

Penfield, 350 ... D3
Penndel, 2,420 ... M5
Penn Hills, 46,809 ... B5, E7
Pennsburg, 2,732 ... L5
Pennsbury Village, 738 ... D7
Penn Wynne, 5,382 ... L6, L7
Perkasie, 8,828 ... L5
Perryopolis, 1,764 ... B5
Petersburg, 455 ... E4
Petrolia, 218 ... B3
Philadelphia, 1,517,550 ... L6, M7
Philipsburg, 3,056 ... E4
Phoenixville, 14,788 ... K5
Picture Rocks, 693 ... H3
Pillow, 304 ... H4
Pine Grove, 2,154 ... J4
Pine Grove Mills, 1,141 ... F4
Pitcairn, 3,689 ... E7
Pittsburgh, 334,563 ... A5, D7
Pittston, 8,104 ... H7, K3
Platea, 474 ... A2
Pleasant Gap, 1,611 ... F4
Pleasant Hills, 8,397 ... E7
Pleasantville (Bedford Co.) ... D5
Pleasantville (Venango Co.), 850 ... B2
Plum, 26,940 ... B5, E7
Plumville, 342 ... C4
Plymouth, 6,507 ... G7, K3
Plymouth Meeting, 5,593 ... L6
Plymptonville, 1,040 ... E3
Pocono Pines, 1,013 ... L3
Point Marion, 1,333 ... B6
Polk, 1,031 ... B3
Portage, 2,837 ... D5
Port Allegany, 2,355 ... E2
Port Carbon, 2,019 ... J4
Port Clinton, 288 ... J4
Portersville, 268 ... A4
Portland, 579 ... L4
Portland Mills, 30 ... D3
Port Matilda, 638 ... E4
Port Royal, 977 ... G4
Port Vue, 4,228 ... E7
Pottsgrove, 21,859 ... K5
Pottsville, 15,549 ... J4
Powell, 300 ... H2
Pringle, 991 ... G7
Progress, 9,647 ... H5
Prompton, 243 ... L2
Prospect, 1,234 ... A4
Prospect Park, 6,594 ... L7
Prosperity, 200 ... A5
Punxsutawney, 6,271 ... D4
Quakertown, 8,931 ... L5
Quarryville, 1,994 ... J6
Queen, 180 ... D5
Radnor, 30,878 ... L5, L7
Rainsburg, 146 ... D6
Ralston, 200 ... H2
Ramey, 525 ... E4
Rankin, 2,315 ... E7
Reading, 81,207 ... K5
Rebersburg, 492 ... G4
Red Hill, 2,196 ... L5
Red Lion, 6,149 ... H6
Reedsville, 858 ... F4
Reinerton (Reinerton-Orwin-Muir), 1,037 ... H4
Renovo, 1,318 ... F3
Republic, 1,396 ... B6
Reynoldsville, 2,710 ... D3
Rheems, 1,557 ... H5
Rices Landing, 443 ... A6
Riceville, 82 ... B2
Richboro, 6,678 ... M6
Richfield, 459 ... G4
Richland, 1,508 ... J5
Richlandtown, 1,283 ... L5
Ridgway, 4,591 ... D3
Ridley Park, 7,196 ... L7
Riegelsville, 863 ... L4
Rimersburg, 1,051 ... B3
Riverside, 1,861 ... H4
Rixford, 250 ... D2
Roaring Spring, 2,418 ... E5
Robesonia, 2,036 ... J5
Rochester, 4,014 ... A4
Rockhill Furnace, 414 ... F5
Rockledge, 2,577 ... M6
Rockwood, 954 ... C6
Rome, 382 ... J2
Roseto, 1,653 ... L4
Rose Valley, 944 ... L7
Roseville, 207 ... G2
Rossiter, 790 ... D4
Rosslyn Farms, 464 ... D7
Roulette, 600 ... E2
Rouseville, 472 ... B3
Rouzerville, 862 ... F6
Roxbury, 350 ... F5
Royalton, 963 ... H5
Royersford, 4,246 ... K5
Rural Valley, 922 ... C4
Russell, 1,200 ... C2
Rutledge, 860 ... L7
Sabinsville, 225 ... F2
Saegertown, 1,071 ... A2
Sagamore, 400 ... C4
St. Clair, 3,254 ... J4
St. Clairsville, 86 ... D5
St. Marys, 14,502 ... D3
St. Petersburg, 405 ... B3
Salisbury, 878 ... C6
Salladasburg, 260 ... G3
Saltillo, 385 ... E5
Saltsburg, 955 ... C5
Salunga (Salunga-Landisville), 4,771 ... J5
Sanatoga, 7,734 ... K5
Sandy Lake, 743 ... A3
Sankertown, 680 ... D5
Saxonburg, 1,629 ... B4
Saxton, 803 ... E5
Saylorsburg, 1,100 ... L4
Sayre, 5,813 ... H2
Scalp Level, 851 ... D5
Schellsburg, 316 ... D6
Schuylkill Haven, 5,548 ... J4
Schwenksville, 1,693 ... L5
Scotland, 1,700 ... F6

Scottdale, 4,772 ... B5
Scranton, 76,415 ... H7, K3
Selinsgrove, 5,383 ... H4
Sellersville, 4,564 ... L5
Seneca, 966 ... B3
Seven Springs, 127 ... C5
Seven Valleys, 492 ... H6
Seward, 484 ... C5
Sewickley, 3,902 ... A4
Shade Gap, 97 ... F5
Shamokin, 8,009 ... H4
Shamokin Dam, 1,502 ... H4
Sharksville, 245 ... C5
Sharon, 16,328 ... A3
Sharon Hill, 5,468 ... L7
Sharpsburg, 3,594 ... E7
Sharpsville, 4,500 ... A3
Sheakleyville, 164 ... A3
Sheffield, 1,268 ... C2
Shelocta, 127 ... C4
Shenandoah, 5,624 ... J4
Shickshinny, 959 ... J3
Shillington, 5,059 ... K5
Shiloh, 10,192 ... H6
Shinglehouse, 1,250 ... E2
Shippensburg, 5,586 ... F5
Shippenville, 505 ... C3
Shippingport, 237 ... A4
Shiremanstown, 1,521 ... H5
Shirleysburg, 140 ... F5
Shoemakersville, 2,124 ... K4
Shrewsbury, 3,378 ... H6
Sigel, 100 ... C3
Silverdale, 1,001 ... L5
Sinking Spring, 2,639 ... J5
Sinnemahoning, 100 ... E3
Slatington, 4,434 ... K4
Sligo, 728 ... C3
Slippery Rock, 3,068 ... A3
Smethport, 1,684 ... E2
Smicksburg, 49 ... C4
Smithfield, 854 ... B6
Snow Shoe, 771 ... F3
S.N.P.J. ... A3
Snydertown, 357 ... H4
Somerset, 6,762 ... C5
Sonestown, 225 ... H3
Souderton, 6,730 ... L5
South Bethlehem, 444 ... C4
South Coatesville, 997 ... K6
South Connellsville, 2,281 ... B6
South Fork, 1,138 ... D5
South Greensburg, 2,280 ... B5
Southmont, 2,262 ... C5
South Monroe, 400 ... K2
South New Castle, 808 ... A4
South Pottstown, 2,135 ... K5
South Renovo, 557 ... F3
South Waverly, 987 ... H2
South Williamsport, 6,412 ... G3
Spangler ... D4
Spartansburg, 333 ... B2
Speers, 1,241 ... B5
Springboro, 491 ... A2
Spring City, 3,305 ... K5
Springdale, 23,677 ... L7
Spring Grove, 2,050 ... H6
Spring Mills, 289 ... F4
Springville, 325 ... K2
Starrucca, 216 ... L2
State College, 38,420 ... F4
Steelton, 5,858 ... H5
Sterling Run, 40 ... E3
Stevensville, 125 ... J2
Stewartstown, 1,752 ... H6
Stillwater, 194 ... J3
Stockdale, 555 ... B5
Stockertown, 687 ... L4
Stoneboro, 1,104 ... A3
Stowe, 3,585 ... K5
Stoystown, 428 ... D5
Strasburg, 2,800 ... J6
Strattanville, 542 ... C3
Strausstown, 339 ... J5
Stroudsburg, 5,756 ... L4
Sugarcreek, 5,331 ... B3
Sugar Grove, 613 ... C2
Sugar Notch, 1,023 ... G7
Summerhill, 521 ... D5
Summerville, 525 ... C3
Summit Hill, 2,974 ... K4
Sunbury, 10,610 ... H4
Susquehanna, 1,690 ... K2
Sutersville, 636 ... B5
Swarthmore, 6,170 ... L7
Sweet Valley, 600 ... J3
Swiftwater, 800 ... L3
Swissvale, 9,653 ... E7
Swoyersville, 5,157 ... G7, K3
Sykesville, 1,246 ... D3
Sylvania, 200 ... H2
Tafton, 200 ... L3
Tamaqua, 7,174 ... K4
Tannersville, 1,000 ... L3
Tarentum, 4,993 ... B4
Tatamy, 930 ... L4
Taylor, 6,475 ... H7, K3
Telford, 4,680 ... L5
Temple, 1,400 ... K5
Terre Hill, 1,237 ... J5
Thompson, 299 ... K2
Thompsontown, 711 ... G4
Thornburg, 468 ... D7
Thorndale, 3,561 ... K6
Three Springs, 445 ... F5
Throop, 4,010 ... H7
Tidioute, 792 ... C2
Timblin, 151 ... C4
Tioga, 622 ... G2
Tionesta, 615 ... C3
Tipton, 1,225 ... E5
Titusville, 6,146 ... B2
Tobyhanna, 325 ... L3
Topton, 1,948 ... K4
Toughkenamon, 1,375 ... K6
Towanda, 3,024 ... J2
Tower City, 1,396 ... H4
Townville, 306 ... B2
Trafford, 3,236 ... E7
Trainer, 1,901 ... K7, L6
Tremont, 1,784 ... J4
Tresckow, 964 ... K4
Trevose (see Feasterville), 6,525 ... M6
Trooper, 6,061 ... L5

Trout Run, *300* G3
Troutville, 224 . . . . .D3
Troy, 1,508 . . . . .H2
Trumbauersville, 1,059 . .L5
Tullytown, 2,031 . . . . . .M5
Tunkhannock, 1,911 . . . .K2
Turbotville, 691 . . . . . . .H3
Turtle Creek, 6,076 . . . .E7
Tylersville, *100* G4
Ulster, *325* H2
Ulysses, 684 . . . . .H2
Union City, 3,463 . . . . . .B2
Union Dale, 368 . . . . . . .K2
Uniontown, 12,422 . . . . .B6
Unionville, 313 . . . . .F4
Upland, 2,977 . . . . .L7
Upper Darby, *1,900* L7
Ursina, 254 . . . . .C6
Utica, 211 . . . . .B3
Valencia, 384 . . . . .B4
Valley-Hi, 20 . . . . .E5
Valley View, 1,677 . . . . .H4
Vanderbilt, 553 . . . . . . .B5
Vandergrift, 5,455 . . . . .B4
Vandling, 738 . . . . .L2
Venango, 288 . . . . .A2
Verona, 3,124 . . . . .E7
Versailles, 1,724 . . . . . .E7
Village Green (Village
  Green-Green Ridge),
  8,279 . . . . .K7
Village Shires, 4,137 . . .M6
Vintondale, 528 . . . . . . .D5
Volant, 113 . . . . .A3
Wall, 727 . . . . .F7
Wallaceton, 350 . . . . . .E4
Walnut Bottom, *650* . . .G5
Walnutport, 2,043 . . . . .K4
Warminster, *650* M6
Warren, 10,259 . . . . . . .C2
Warrensville, *1,100* . . .H3
Warrior Run, 624 . . . . . .K3
Warriors Mark, *375* . . .E4
Washington, 15,268 . . . .A5
Washingtonville, 201 . . .H3
Waterford, 1,449 . . . . . .B2
Watsontown, 2,255 . . . .H3
Wattsburg, 378 . . . . . . .B1
Waymart, 1,429 . . . . . . .L2
Wayne, *1,000* L7
Waynesboro, 9,614 . . . . .F6
Waynesburg, 4,184 . . . .A6
Weatherly, 2,612 . . . . . .K4
Weedville, *400* E3
Wellersburg, 176 . . . . . .D6
Wellsboro, 3,328 . . . . . .G2
Wellsville, 279 . . . . .H5
Wesleyville, 3,617 . . . . .A1
West Alexander, 320 . . .A5
West Brownsville, 1,075 .B5
West Chester, 17,861 . . .K6
West Conshohocken,
  1,446 . . . . .L7
West Decatur, *600* E4
Westfield, 1,190 . . . . . . .F2
West Grove, 2,652 . . . . .K6
West Hazleton, 3,542 . . .J4
West Hickory, *200* C2
West Hills, 1,229 . . . . . .B4
West Homestead, 2,197 .B5
West Kittanning, 1,199 . .B4
West Leechburg, 1,290 . .B4

West Liberty, 325 . . . . .A3
Westline D2
West Mayfield, 1,187 . . .A4
West Middlesex, 929 . . .A3
West Middletown, 144 . .A5
West Mifflin, 22,464 . . . .E7
Westmont, 5,523 . . . . . .D5
West Newton, 3,083 . . . .B5
Westover, 458 . . . . .D4
West Pike, *70* F2
West Pittston, 5,072 . . . .H7
Westport F3
West Sunbury, *104* B3
West View, 7,277 . . . . . .D6
West Wyoming, 2,833 . . .G7
West York, 4,321 . . . . . .H6
Wheatland, 748 . . . . . . .A3
Whitaker, 1,338 . . . . . . .E7
Whitehall (Allegheny Co.),
  14,444 . . . . .D7
Whitehall (Lehigh Co.),
  14,268 . . . . .L4
White Haven, 1,182 . . . .K3
White Oak, 8,437 . . . . . .E7
Wilcox, *500* D2
Wilkes-Barre, 43,123 G7, K3
Wilkinsburg, 19,196 . . . .E7
Williamsburg, 1,345 . . . .E5
Williamsport, 30,706 . . .G3
Williamstown, 1,433 . . . .H4
Willow Grove, 16,234 . . .M6
Willow Street, 7,258 . . . .J6
Wilmerding, 2,145 . . . . .E7
Wilmore, 252 . . . . .D5
Wilson, 7,682 . . . . .L4
Windber, 4,395 . . . . . . .D5
Wind Gap, 2,812 . . . . . .L4
Wind Ridge, *90* A6
Windsor, 1,331 . . . . . . .H6
Winterstown, 546 . . . . . .H6
Wolfdale, 2,873 . . . . . . .A5
Womelsdorf, 2,599 . . . . .J5
Woodbury, 269 . . . . . . .E5
Woodcock, 146 . . . . . . .A2
Woodland, *550* E3
Woodland Heights,
  1,402 . . . . .B3
Woodlyn, 10,036 . . . . . .L7
Wormleysburg, 2,607 . . .H5
Worthington, 778 . . . . . .B4
Worthville, 85 . . . . .C3
Wrightsville, 2,223 . . . . .H5
Wyalusing, 564 . . . . . . .J2
Wyncote, 3,046 . . . . . . .M6
Wyndmoor, 5,601 . . . . . .M6
Wyoming, 3,221 . . . . . . .G7
Wyomissing, 8,587 . . . . .J5
Yardley, 2,498 . . . . .M5
Yatesboro, *275* C4
Yatesville, 649 . . . . .H7
Yeadon, 11,762 . . . . . . .L7
Yeagertown, 1,035 . . . . .F4
Yoe, 1,022 . . . . .H6
York, 40,862 . . . . .H6
Yorkana, 239 . . . . .H6
York Haven, 809 . . . . . .H5
York Springs, 574 . . . . .G5
Youngstown, 400 . . . . . .C5
Youngsville, 1,834 . . . . .C2
Youngwood, 4,138 . . . . .B5
Zelienople, 4,123 . . . . . .A4
Zion, 2,054 . . . . .F4

Other Features

Aberdeen Proving
  Grounds J7
Allegany State Park D1
Allegheny, *river* B3, D7
Allegheny, *reservoir* . . .D2
Allegheny Natl. For. C2
Allegheny Natl.
  Rec. Area D2
Allegheny Portage Railroad
  Natl. Hist. Site D5
Appalachian, *mountains* .F5
Bald Eagle State Forest .G4
Buchanan State
  Forest D6, E5
Chautauqua, *lake* C1
Cheat, *river* B6
Clarion, *river* C3
Conemaugh, *river* C4
Delaware, *river* L2, L7
Delaware State Forest . . .L3
Delaware Water Gap
  Natl. Rec. Area M3
Eisenhower N.H.S. G6
Elk State Forest D2, E3
Erie, *lake* A1
Erie N.W.R. B2
Forbes State
  Forest B6, C5, C6
Fort Necessity Natl. Bfld. B6
Friendship Hill Natl.
  Hist. Site B6
Gallitzin State Forest . . .D5
Gettysburg Natl.
  Mil. Park G6
Hickory Run State Park . .K3
High Point State Park . . .M3
Hopewell Furnace N.H.S. K5
Independence N.H.P. . . .M7
Johnstown Flood
  Natl. Mem. D5
Juniata, *river* F5
Lehigh, *river* J7, K3
Michaux State Forest . . .G6
Monongahela, *river* E7
Moshannon State
  Forest D3, E4
Mt. Davis, *mountain* C6
Ohio, *river* D7
Ohiopyle State Park C6
Pa. Tpk. D6, G5, J5
Presque Isle, *peninsula* .A1
Pymatuning State Park . .A2
Raystown, *lake* E5
Ricketts Glen State Park . .J3
Rothrock State Forest . . .F4
Savage River State Forest C6
Schuylkill, *river* K5, L7
Sproul State Forest F3
Steamtown N.H.S. H7
Susquehanna,
  river G6, J2, J6
Susquehannock State
  Forest F2
Tiadaghton State
  Forest F3, G3, H3
Tioga, *river* G2
Tioga State Forest . .F2, G2
Tuscarora State Forest . .F5
Valley Forge N.H.P. . .K6, L5
Wyoming State Forest . .H3

Rhode Island

Capital:	Providence
Land Area:	1,045 sq. mi.
	2,707 sq. km.
Population:	1,048,319 (2000 Census)
Largest City:	Providence, 173,618
Highest Point:	Jerimoth Hill,
	812 ft.
	247 m.
Admitted to Union:	May 29, 1790
Nickname:	Little Rhody,
	Ocean State
State Flower:	Violet
State Bird:	Rhode Island Red

Rhode Island:
Map Index

Counties

Bristol, 50,648 . . . . .E3
Kent, 167,090 . . . . .C4
Newport, 85,433 . . . . .E4
Providence, 621,602 . . . . .C2
Washington, 123,546 . . . . .C4

Cities and Towns

*Cities and towns that are not labeled on the
map are shown with an asterisk. They are
included here only for population reference.*

Barrington, 16,819 . . . . .E3
Bristol, 22,469 . . . . .E3
Burrillville, 15,796 . . . .*
Central Falls, 18,928 . . . . .D2
Charlestown, 7,859 . . . . .C5
Coventry, 33,668 . . . .*
Cranston, 79,269 . . . . .D3
Cumberland, 31,840 . . . .*
East Greenwich, 12,948 . . . . . .D4
East Providence, 48,688 . . . . . .D3
Exeter, 6,045 . . . . .C4
Foster, 4,274 . . . .*
Glocester, 9,948 . . . .*
Hopkinton, 7,836 . . . . .B5
Jamestown, 5,622 . . . . .D5
Johnston, 28,195 . . . .*

Lincoln, 20,898 . . . .*
Little Compton, 3,593 . . . . .E5
Middletown, 17,334 . . . . .E4
Narragansett, 16,361 . . . .*
Newport, 26,475 . . . . .E5
New Shoreham, 1,010 . . . .*
North Kingstown, 26,326 . . . . . .D4
North Providence, 32,411 . . . . .D2
North Smithfield, 10,618 . . . .*
Pawtucket, 72,958 . . . . .D2
Portsmouth, 17,149 . . . . .E4
Providence, 173,618 . . . . .D3
Richmond, 7,222 . . . .*
Scituate, 10,324 . . . .*
Smithfield, 20,613 . . . .*
South Kingstown, 27,921 . . . .*
Tiverton, 15,260 . . . . .E4
Warren, 11,360 . . . . .E3
Warwick, 85,808 . . . . .D3
Westerly, 22,966 . . . . .B5
West Greenwich, 5,085 . . . .*
West Warwick, 29,581 . . . . .C3
Woonsocket, 43,224 . . . . .C1

Other Places

*The city or town containing each entry is
shown in italics. See the Cities and Towns listing for total population.*

Adamsville *(Little Compton)*, 550 . . . . . .F4
Allenton *(North Kingstown)*, 1,400 . . . . . .D4
Alton *(Richmond and Hopkinton)*, 350 . . . .B5

Anthony *(Coventry)* C3
Arcadia *(Exeter and Richmond)*, 150 . . . . .B4
Ashaway *(Hopkinton)*, 1,537 . . . . .B5
Ashton *(Cumberland)*, 2,600 . . . . .D2
Avondale *(Westerly)*, 425 . . . . .A6
Berkeley *(Cumberland)*, 2,800 . . . . .D2
Block Island *(New Shoreham)*, 150 . . . . . .C7
Bonnet Shores *(Narragansett)*, 2,200 . . .D5
Bradford *(Westerly)*, 1,497 . . . . .B5
Carolina *(Charlestown and Richmond)*, 850 C5
Chepachet *(Glocester)*, 900 . . . . .B2
Clayville *(Scituate and Foster)*, 250 . . . . .B3
Coventry Center *(Coventry)*, 850 . . . . . . .C3
Cumberland Hill *(Cumberland)*, 7,738 . . .D2
Diamond Hill *(Cumberland)*, 1,100 . . . . .D2
DunnsCorners *(Westerly)*, 500 . . . . .B5
Fiskeville *(Cranston)* C3
Foster Center *(Foster)*, 500 . . . . .B3
Galilee *(Narragansett)*, 700 . . . . .C5
Glendale *(Burrillville)*, 800 . . . . .C2
Green Hill *(South Kingstown)*, 275 . . . . . .C5
Greenville *(Smithfield)*, 8,626 . . . . .C2
Hamilton *(North Kingstown)*, 2,500 . . . . .D4
Harmony *(Glocester)*, 850 . . . . .C2
Harrisville *(Burrillville)*, 1,561 . . . . .B2
Hope *(Scituate)*, 1,900 . . . . .C3
Hope Valley *(Hopkinton)*, 1,649 . . . . .B5
Jerusalem *(Narragansett)*, 800 . . . . .C5
Kingston *(South Kingstown)*, 5,446 . . . . .C5
Lonsdale *(Lincoln)* D2
Manville *(Lincoln)*, 3,800 . . . . .D2
Matunuck *(South Kingstown)*, 750 . . . . . .C5

Moosup Valley *(Foster)*, 150 . . . . .B3
Mount View *(North Kingstown)*, 750 . . . .D4
Narragansett Pier *(Narragansett)*, 3,671 . .D5
Nooseneck *(West Greenwich)*, 200 . . . . .C4
North Foster *(Foster)*, 275 . . . . .B2
North Scituate *(Scituate)*, 950 . . . . .C3
Pascoag *(Burrillville)*, 4,742 . . . . .B2
Pawtuxet *(Warwick)* D3
Perryville *(South Kingstown)*, 300 . . . . . .C5
Plum Point *(North Kingstown)*, 850 . . . . .D4
Point Judith *(Narragansett)*, 900 . . . . . . .D5
Prudence *(Portsmouth)*, 40 . . . . .E4
Quidnessett *(North Kingstown)*, 3,600 . . .D4
Quidnick *(Coventry)*, 6,300 . . . . .C3
Quonochontaug *(Charlestown)*, 350 . . . .B6
Rice City *(Coventry)*, 425 . . . . .B3
Riverside *(East Providence)* D3
Rockville *(Hopkinton)*, 425 . . . . .B4
Rumford *(East Providence)* D2
Sakonnet *(Little Compton)*, 125 . . . . . . .E5
Saunderstown *(North Kingstown)*, 1,600 .D5
Saylesville *(Lincoln)* D2
Shannock *(Richmond and Charlestown)*,
  900 . . . . .C5
Slatersville *(North Smithfield)*, 2,600 . . . .C2
Slocum *(North Kingstown)*, 350 . . . . .C4
South Foster *(Foster)*, 225 . . . . .B3
Spragueville *(Smithfield)*, 300 . . . . .C2
Tarkiln *(Burrillville)*, 950 . . . . .C2
Usquepaug *(Richmond and South Kingstown)*,
  350 . . . . .C5
Valley Falls *(Cumberland)*, 11,599 . . . . . .D2

Wakefield *(South Kingstown)*, 8,468 . . . . .C5
Wallum Lake *(Burrillville)*, 300 . . . . .B2
Washington *(Coventry)* C3
Watch Hill *(Westerly)*, 325 . . . . .A6
Weekapaug *(Westerly)*, 350 . . . . .B6
West Barrington *(Barrington)*, 4,500 . . . .D3
West Glocester *(Glocester)*, 175 . . . . . . .B2
West Kingston *(South Kingstown)*, 500 . . .C5
Wickford *(North Kingstown)*, 1,900 . . . . .D4
Wyoming *(Richmond and Hopkinton)*, 475 B4

Other Features

Block, *island* C6
Block Island, *sound* B6
Block Island N.W.R. C6
Jerimoth, *hill* B2
Mt. Hope, *bay* .E4
Narragansett, *bay* D4
Ninigret N.W.R. C5
Rhode Island, *sound* E5
Roger Williams Natl. Mem. D3
Sachuest Point N.W.R. E5
Sakonnet, *river* E4
Sandy, *point* C6
Scituate, *reservoir* C3
Southeast, *point* C7
Touro Synagogue N.H.S. E5
Trustom Pond N.W.R. C5
Worden, *pond* .C5

Rhode Island

★ State Capital
— Limited Access Highway
— Other Major Road

0 . . . 5 . . . 10 . . . 15 mi

0 . . 5 . . 10 . . 15 . . 20 km

Albers Equal Area Projection

© MapQuest.com, Inc.

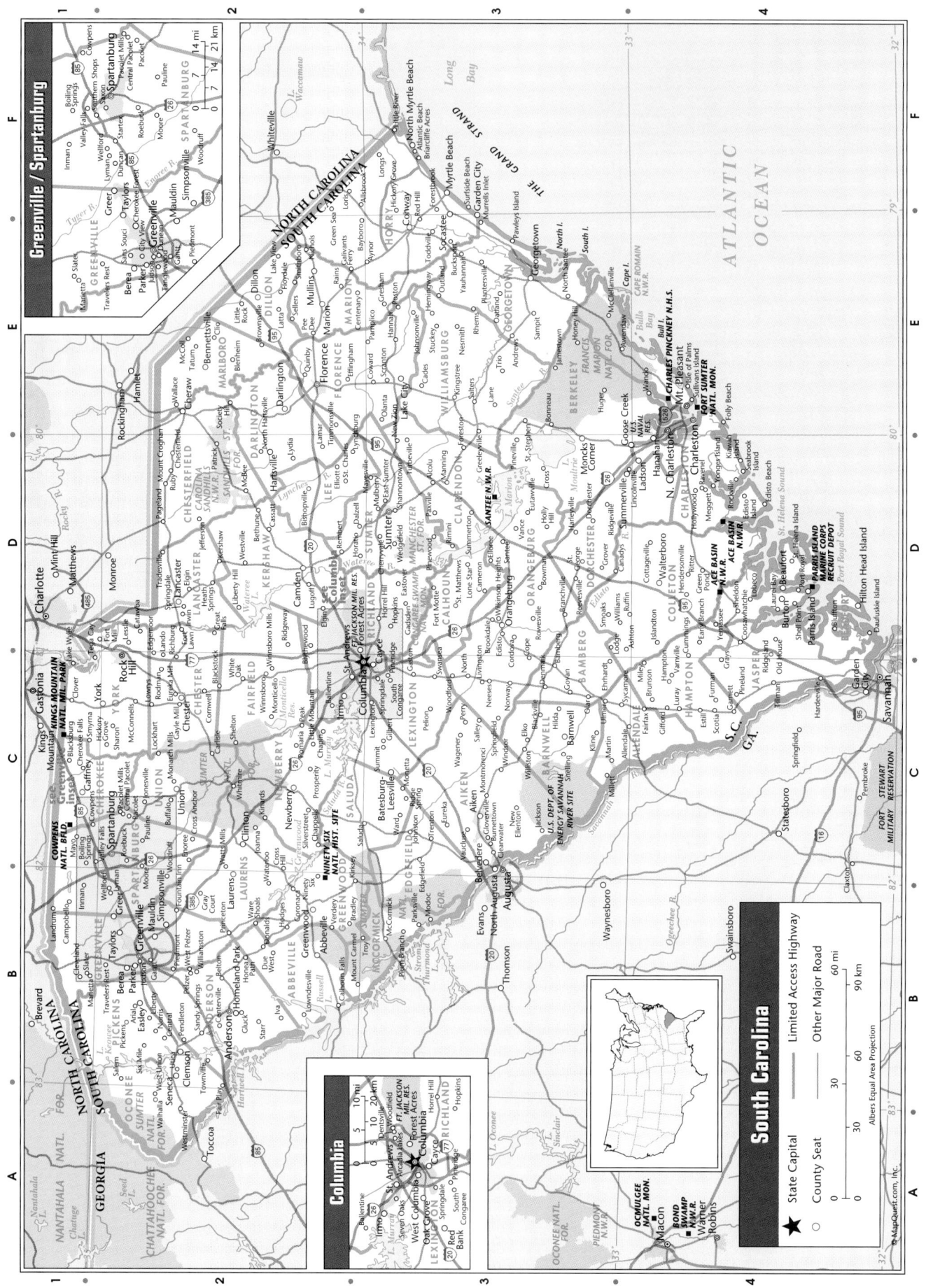

South Carolina

State Capital
County Seat
Limited Access Highway
Other Major Road

Greenville / Spartanburg

Columbia

ATLANTIC OCEAN

South Carolina

Capital: Columbia
Land Area: 30,111 sq. mi.
77,987 sq. km.
Population: 4,012,012 (2000 Census)
Largest City: Columbia, 116,278
Highest Point: Sassafras Mountain
3,560 ft.
1,085 m.
Admitted to Union: May 23, 1788
Nickname: Palmetto State
State Flower: Yellow Jessamine
State Bird: Carolina Wren

South Carolina: Map Index

Counties

Abbeville, 26,167 . . . B2
Aiken, 142,552 . . . C3
Allendale, 11,211 . . . C4
Anderson, 165,740 . . . B2
Bamberg, 16,658 . . . C3
Barnwell, 23,478 . . . C3
Beaufort, 120,937 . . . D4
Berkeley, 142,651 . . . E3
Calhoun, 15,185 . . . D3
Charleston, 309,969 . . . D4
Cherokee, 52,537 . . . C2
Chester, 34,068 . . . C2
Chesterfield, 42,768 . . . D2
Clarendon, 32,502 . . . D3
Colleton, 38,264 . . . D4
Darlington, 67,394 . . . E2
Dillon, 30,722 . . . E2
Dorchester, 96,413 . . . D3
Edgefield, 24,595 . . . C3
Fairfield, 23,454 . . . C2
Florence, 125,761 . . . E2
Georgetown, 55,797 . . . E3
Greenville, 379,616 . . . B2, E1
Greenwood, 66,271 . . . B2
Hampton, 21,386 . . . C4
Horry, 196,629 . . . E3
Jasper, 20,678 . . . C4
Kershaw, 52,647 . . . D2
Lancaster, 61,351 . . . D2
Laurens, 69,567 . . . B2
Lee, 20,119 . . . D2
Lexington, 216,014 . . . A3, C3
Marion, 35,466 . . . E2
Marlboro, 28,818 . . . E2
McCormick, 9,958 . . . B3
Newberry, 36,108 . . . C2
Oconee, 66,215 . . . A2
Orangeburg, 91,582 . . . D3
Pickens, 110,757 . . . B2
Richland, 320,677 . . . A3, D3
Saluda, 19,181 . . . C2
Spartanburg, 253,791 . . . C2, F2
Sumter, 104,646 . . . D3
Union, 29,881 . . . C2
Williamsburg, 37,217 . . . E3
York, 164,614 . . . C2

Cities and Towns

Abbeville, 5,840 . . . B2
Aiken, 25,337 . . . C3
Alcolu, *375* . . . D3
Allendale, 4,052 . . . C3
Allsbrook, *250* . . . F2
Anderson, 25,514 . . . B2
Andrews, 3,068 . . . E3
Arcadia Lakes, 882 . . . A3
Arial, 2,607 . . . B2
Ashton, *100* . . . D3
Atlantic Beach, 351 . . . F3
Awendaw, 1,195 . . . E3
Aynor, 587 . . . E3
Ballentine, *850* . . . A3, C2
Bamberg, 3,733 . . . C3
Barnwell, 5,035 . . . C3
Batesburg-Leesville, 5,517 . . . C3
Bayboro, *80* . . . E2
Beaufort, 12,950 . . . D4
Belton, 4,461 . . . B2
Belvedere, 5,631 . . . C3
Bennettsville, 9,425 . . . E2
Berea, 14,158 . . . B2, E2
Bethune, 352 . . . D2
Bishopville, 3,670 . . . D2
Blacksburg, 1,880 . . . C1
Blackstock, *125* . . . C2
Blackville, 2,973 . . . C3
Blenheim, 137 . . . E2
Bluffton, 1,275 . . . D4
Blythewood, 170 . . . D2
Boiling Springs, 4,544 . . . C1, F1
Bonneau, 354 . . . E3
Bowman, 1,198 . . . D3
Bradley, 171 . . . B2
Branchville, 1,083 . . . D3
Briarcliffe Acres, 470 . . . F3
Brookdale, 4,724 . . . D3
Brownsville, *90* . . . E2
Brunson, 589 . . . C4
Bucksport, 1,117 . . . E3
Buffalo, 1,426 . . . C2
Burnettown, 2,720 . . . C3
Burton, 7,180 . . . D4
Cades, *70* . . . E3
Calhoun Falls, 2,303 . . . B2
Camden, 6,682 . . . D2
Cameron, 449 . . . D3
Campobello, 449 . . . B1
Canadys, *150* . . . D3
Carlisle, 496 . . . C2
Cassatt, *100* . . . D2
Catawba, *700* . . . D2
Cayce, 12,150 . . . A3, C3
Centenary, *350* . . . E2
Centerville, 5,181 . . . B2
Central, 3,522 . . . B2
Central Pacolet, 267 . . . C2, F2
Chapin, 628 . . . C2
Chappells, 50 . . . C2
Charleston, 96,650 . . . E4
Cheraw, 5,524 . . . E2
Cherokee Falls, *225* . . . C1
Cherokee Forest, 8,000 . . . E2
Cherryvale, 2,461 . . . D3
Chester, 6,476 . . . C2
Chesterfield, 1,318 . . . D2
City View, 1,254 . . . E2
Clearwater, 4,199 . . . C3
Clemson, 11,939 . . . B2
Cleveland, *150* . . . B1
Clinton, 8,091 . . . C2
Clio, 774 . . . E2
Clover, 4,014 . . . C1
Columbia, 116,278 . . . A3, C2
Conway, 11,788 . . . E3
Coosawhatchie, *150* . . . D4
Cope, 107 . . . C3
Cordova, 157 . . . D3
Cornwell, *125* . . . C2
Coronaca, 170 . . . B2
Cottageville, 707 . . . D4
Coward, 650 . . . E3
Cowpens, 2,279 . . . C1, F1
Cross, *250* . . . D3
Cross Anchor, *325* . . . C2
Cross Hill, 601 . . . C2
Cummings, *250* . . . D4
Dalzell, 2,260 . . . D2
Darlington, 6,720 . . . E2
Daufuskie Island, *60* . . . D4
Denmark, 3,328 . . . C3
Dentsville, 13,009 . . . A3
Dillon, 6,316 . . . E2
Donalds, 354 . . . B2
Dorchester, *200* . . . D3
Due West, 1,209 . . . B2
Duncan, 2,870 . . . F2
Dunean, 4,158 . . . E2
Early Branch, *80* . . . D4
Easley, 17,754 . . . B2
Eastover, 830 . . . D3
East Sumter, 1,220 . . . D3
Edgefield, 4,449 . . . C3
Edgemoor, *450* . . . D2
Edisto, 2,632 . . . D3
Edisto Beach, 641 . . . D4
Edisto Island, *90* . . . D4
Effingham, *200* . . . E2
Ehrhardt, 614 . . . C3
Elgin (Kershaw Co.), 806 . . . D2
Elgin (Lancaster Co.), 2,426 . D2
Elko, 212 . . . C3
Elliott, *425* . . . D2
Elloree, 742 . . . D3
Enoree, *700* . . . C2
Estill, 2,425 . . . C4
Eureka, *200* . . . C3
Eureka Mill, 1,737 . . . C2
Eutawville, 344 . . . D3
Fairfax, 3,206 . . . C4
Fair Play, *375* . . . B2
Florence, 30,248 . . . E2
Floydale, *450* . . . E2
Folly Beach, 2,116 . . . E4
Forest Acres, 10,558 . . . A3, D2
Forestbrook, 3,391 . . . F3
Foreston, *100* . . . D3
Fort Lawn, 864 . . . D2
Fort Mill, 7,587 . . . D1
Fort Motte, *100* . . . D3
Fountain Inn, 6,017 . . . B2
Furman, 286 . . . C4
Gadsden, *550* . . . D3
Gaffney, 12,968 . . . C1
Galivants Ferry, *70* . . . E2
Gantt, 13,962 . . . B2, E2
Garden City, 9,357 . . . F3
Garnett, *80* . . . C4
Gaston, 1,304 . . . C3
Gayle Mill, 1,094 . . . C2
Georgetown, 8,950 . . . E3
Gifford, 370 . . . C4
Gilbert, 500 . . . C3
Gloverville, 2,805 . . . C3
Gluck, *300* . . . B2
Goose Creek, 29,208 . . . D3
Govan, 67 . . . C3
Gray Court, 1,021 . . . B2
Grays . . . C4
Great Falls, 2,194 . . . D2
Greeleyville, 452 . . . E3
Green Pond, *175* . . . D4
Green Sea, *150* . . . F2
Greenville, 56,002 . . . B2, E2
Greenwood, 22,071 . . . B2
Greer, 16,843 . . . B2, F2
Gresham, *125* . . . E3
Grover, *250* . . . D3
Hampton, 2,837 . . . C4
Hanahan, 12,937 . . . D4
Hannah, *100* . . . E3
Hardeeville, 1,793 . . . C4
Harleyville, 594 . . . D3
Hartsville, 7,556 . . . D2
Heath Springs, 864 . . . D2
Hemingway, 573 . . . E3
Hendersonville, *100* . . . D4
Hickory Grove (Horry Co.), *600* . . . C2
Hickory Grove (York Co.), 337 . . . F3
Hilda, 436 . . . C3
Hilton Head Island, 33,862 . D4
Hodges, 158 . . . B2
Holly Hill, 1,281 . . . D3
Hollywood, 3,946 . . . D4
Homeland Park, 6,337 . . . B2
Honea Path, 3,504 . . . B2
Honey Hill, *90* . . . E3
Hopkins, *600* . . . A3, D3
Horatio, *100* . . . D2
Horrel Hill, *600* . . . A3, D3
Huger . . . E3
Inman, 1,884 . . . B1, F1
Irmo, 11,039 . . . A3, C2
Irwin, 1,343 . . . D2
Islandton, *50* . . . D4
Isle of Palms, 4,583 . . . E4
Iva, 1,156 . . . B2
Jackson, 1,625 . . . C3
Jamestown, 97 . . . E3
Jefferson, 704 . . . D2
Joanna, 1,609 . . . C2
Johnsonville, 1,418 . . . E3
Johnston, 2,336 . . . C3
Jonesville, 982 . . . C2
Judson, 2,456 . . . B2, E2
Kershaw, 1,645 . . . D2
Kiawah Island, 1,163 . . . D4
Kinards, *125* . . . C2
Kingstree, 3,496 . . . E3
Kirksey, *40* . . . B2
Kline, 238 . . . C3
Ladson, 13,264 . . . D4
Lake City, 6,478 . . . E3
Lake View, 789 . . . E2
Lake Wylie, 3,061 . . . C1
Lamar, 1,015 . . . D2
Lancaster, 8,177 . . . D2
Lando, *250* . . . D2
Landrum, 2,472 . . . B1
Lane, 585 . . . E3
Latta, 1,410 . . . E2
Laurel Bay, 6,625 . . . D4
Laurens, 9,916 . . . B2
Lesslie, 2,268 . . . D2
Lexington, 9,793 . . . C3
Liberty, 3,009 . . . B2
Liberty Hill, 40 . . . D2
Lincolnville, 904 . . . D3
Little Mountain, 255 . . . C2
Little River, 7,027 . . . F3
Little Rock, *325* . . . E2
Livingston, 148 . . . C3
Lobeco, *125* . . . D4
Lockhart, 39 . . . C2
Lodge, 114 . . . D3
Lone Star, *90* . . . D3
Longs, *375* . . . F3
Loris, 2,079 . . . F2
Lowndesville, 166 . . . B2
Lowrys, 207 . . . C2
Lugoff, 6,278 . . . D2
Luray, 115 . . . C4
Lydia, *550* . . . D2
Lyman, 2,659 . . . B2, F2
Lynchburg, 588 . . . D3
Manning, 4,025 . . . D3
Marietta, 2,228 . . . B1, E1
Marion, 7,042 . . . E2
Martin . . . C3
Mauldin, 15,224 . . . B2, E2
Mayesville, 1,001 . . . D3
Mayo, 1,842 . . . C1
McBee, 714 . . . D2
McClellanville, 459 . . . E3
McColl, 2,498 . . . E2
McConnells, 287 . . . C2
McCormick, 1,489 . . . B3
Meggett, 1,230 . . . D4
Miley . . . C4
Millett, *80* . . . C3
Modoc, 256 . . . B3
Monarch Mills, 1,930 . . . C2
Moncks Corner, 5,952 . . . D3
Monetta, 220 . . . C3
Monticello . . . C2
Montmorenci, *300* . . . C3
Moore, *350* . . . C2, F2
Mount Carmel, 237 . . . B2
Mount Croghan, 155 . . . D2
Mount Pleasant, 47,609 . . . E4
Mulberry, 841 . . . D3
Mullins, 5,029 . . . E2
Murrells Inlet, 5,519 . . . E3
Myrtle Beach, 22,759 . . . F3
Neeses, 413 . . . C3
Nesmith, *100* . . . E3
Newberry, 10,580 . . . C2
New Ellenton, 2,250 . . . C3
New Zion, *200* . . . D3
Nichols, 408 . . . E2
Ninety Six, 1,936 . . . B2
Norris, 847 . . . B2
North, 813 . . . C3
North Augusta, 17,574 . . . C3
North Charleston, 79,641 . . . E4
North Hartsville, 3,136 . . . D2
North Myrtle Beach, 10,974 . F3
North Santee, *225* . . . E3
Norway, 389 . . . C3
Oak Grove, 8,183 . . . A3, E2
Oatland, *400* . . . E3
Olanta, 613 . . . E3
Olar, 237 . . . C3
Old House, *225* . . . D4
Orangeburg, 12,765 . . . D3
Outland, *100* . . . E3
Pacolet, 2,690 . . . C2, F2
Pacolet Mills . . . C2, F2
Pageland, 2,521 . . . D2
Pamplico, 1,139 . . . E3
Parker, 10,760 . . . B2, E2
Parksville, 120 . . . B3
Parris Island, 4,841 . . . D4
Patrick, 354 . . . D2
Pauline, *350* . . . C2, F2
Pawleys Island, 138 . . . E3
Paxville, 248 . . . D3
Peak, 61 . . . C2
Pee Dee, *175* . . . E2
Pelion, 553 . . . C3
Pelzer, 97 . . . B2
Pendleton, 2,966 . . . B2
Perry, 237 . . . C3
Pickens, 3,012 . . . B2
Piedmont, 4,684 . . . B2, E2
Pineland, *200* . . . C4
Pineridge, 1,593 . . . A3, C3
Pineville, *300* . . . D3
Pinewood, 459 . . . D3
Plantersville, *250* . . . E3
Plum Branch, 98 . . . B3
Pomaria, 177 . . . C2
Port Royal, 3,950 . . . D4
Poston, *175* . . . E3
Princeton, 65 . . . B2
Prosperity, 1,047 . . . C2
Quinby, 842 . . . E2
Rains, *650* . . . E2
Ravenel, 2,214 . . . D4
Red Bank, 8,811 . . . A3
Red Hill, 10,509 . . . E3
Reevesville, 207 . . . D3
Rembert, 406 . . . D2
Rhems . . . E3
Richburg, 332 . . . C2
Ridgeland, 2,518 . . . D4
Ridge Spring, 823 . . . C3
Ridgeville, 1,690 . . . D3
Ridgeway, 328 . . . D2
Rimini, *200* . . . D3
Ritter, *500* . . . D4
Rock Hill, 49,765 . . . C2
Rockville, 137 . . . D4
Rodman, *70* . . . C2
Roebuck, 1,725 . . . C2, F2
Rowesville, 378 . . . D3
Ruby, 348 . . . D2
Ruffin, *275* . . . D3
St. Andrews, 21,814 . . . A3, C2
St. Charles, *70* . . . D2
St. George, 2,092 . . . D3
St. Helena Island, *400* . . . D4
St. Matthews, 2,107 . . . D3
St. Stephen, 1,776 . . . E3
Salem, 126 . . . B2
Salley, 410 . . . C3
Salters, *200* . . . E3
Saluda, 3,066 . . . C3
Sampit, *700* . . . E3
Sandy Springs, *750* . . . B2
Sans Souci, 7,836 . . . E2
Santee, 740 . . . D3
Saxon, 3,707 . . . F2
Scotia, 227 . . . C4
Scranton, 942 . . . E3
Seabrook Island, 1,250 . . . D4
Sellers, 277 . . . E2
Seneca, 7,652 . . . B2
Seven Oaks, 15,755 . . . A3
Shannontown, 4,100 . . . D3
Sharon, 421 . . . C2
Sheldon, *225* . . . D4
Shell Point, 2,856 . . . D4
Shelton . . . C2
Silverstreet, 216 . . . C2
Simpsonville, 14,352 . . . B2, F2
Six Mile, 553 . . . B2
Slater, 2,228 . . . B1, E1
Smithboro, *350* . . . E2
Smoaks, 140 . . . D3
Smyrna, 59 . . . C1
Snelling, 246 . . . C3
Socastee, 14,295 . . . E3
Society Hill, 700 . . . E2
South Congaree, 2,266 . A3, C3
Southern Shops, 3,707 . . . F1
Spartanburg, 39,673 . . . C2, F2
Springdale (Lancaster Co.), 2,864 . . . D2
Springdale (Lexington Co.), 2,877 . . . A3, C3
Springfield, 504 . . . C3
Starr, 173 . . . B2
Startex, 988 . . . F2
Stuckey, 263 . . . E3
Sullivans Island, 1,911 . . . E4
Summerton, 1,061 . . . D3
Summerville, 27,752 . . . D3
Summit, 219 . . . C3
Sumter, 39,643 . . . D3
Surfside Beach, 4,425 . . . F3
Swansea, 533 . . . C3
Sycamore, 185 . . . C3
Tanglewood . . . E2
Tatum, 69 . . . E2
Taylors, 20,125 . . . B2, F2
Tega Cay, 4,044 . . . C1
Tillman, *150* . . . C4
Timmonsville, 2,315 . . . E2
Toddville, *200* . . . E3
Townville, *300* . . . B2
Tradesville, *200* . . . D2
Travelers Rest, 4,099 . . . B2, E2
Trenton, 226 . . . C3
Trio, *50* . . . E3
Troy, 105 . . . B3
Turbeville, 602 . . . D3
Ulmer, 102 . . . C3
Union, 8,793 . . . C2
Utica, 1,322 . . . B2
Valencia Heights . . . E2
Valley Falls, 3,990 . . . C1, F1
Vance, 208 . . . D3
Varnville, 2,074 . . . C4
Vaucluse, *125* . . . C3
Verdery, *175* . . . B2
Wagener, 863 . . . C3
Walhalla, 3,801 . . . A2
Wallace, *550* . . . E2
Walterboro, 5,153 . . . D4
Wando, *375* . . . E4
Ward, 110 . . . C3
Ware Shoals, 2,363 . . . B2
Waterloo, 203 . . . B2
Watts Mills, 1,479 . . . C2
Wedgefield, *275* . . . D3
Wellford, 2,030 . . . B2, F2
West Columbia, 13,064 . . . A3
Westminster, 2,743 . . . A2
West Pelzer, 879 . . . B2
West Union, 297 . . . A2
Westville, *275* . . . D2
White Oak, *40* . . . C2
Whitmire, 1,512 . . . C2
Wilkinson Heights, 3,068 . . . D3
Williams, 116 . . . D3
Williamston, 3,791 . . . B2
Williston, 3,307 . . . C3
Windsor, 127 . . . C3
Winnsboro, 3,599 . . . C2
Winnsboro Mills, 2,263 . . . C2
Woodfield, 9,238 . . . A3
Woodford, 196 . . . C3
Woodruff, 4,229 . . . B2, F2
Yauhannah, *50* . . . E3
Yemassee, 807 . . . D4
Yonges Island, *80* . . . D4
York, 6,985 . . . C2

Other Features

Ace Basin N.W.R. . . . D4
Atlantic, *ocean* . . . F4
Bladen Lakes St. For. . . . F2
Bond Swamp N.W.R. . . . A4
Bull, *island* . . . E4
Bulls, *bay* . . . E4
Cape, *island* . . . E3
Cape Fear, *river* . . . F2
Cape Romain N.W.R. . . . E4
Carolina Sandhills N.W.R. . . . D2
Charles Pinckney N.H.S. . . . E4
Chattahoochee Natl. For. . . . A2
Chatuge, *lake* . . . A1
Congaree Swamp Natl. Mon. D3
Cowpens Natl. Bfld. . . . C1
Edisto, *river* . . . D3
Enoree, *river* . . . F2
Fort Bragg Mil. Res. . . . E1
Ft. Jackson Mil. Res. . . . A3, D2
Fort Stewart Military Reservation . . . C4
Fort Sumter Natl. Mon. . . . E4
Francis Marion Natl. For. . . . E3
Greenwood, *lake* . . . C2
Hartwell, *lake* . . . A2
J. Strom Thurmond, *lake* . . . B3
Kings Mountain Natl. Mil. Park . . . C1
Keowee, *lake* . . . B2
Long, *bay* . . . F3
Lynches, *river* . . . D2
Manchester St. For. . . . D3
Marion, *lake* . . . D3
Monticello, *reservoir* . . . C2
Moultrie, *lake* . . . D3
Murray, *lake* . . . A3, C2
Nantahala, *lake* . . . A1
Nantahala Natl. For. . . . A1
Ninety Six Natl. Hist. Site . . . B2
North, *island* . . . E3
Oconee, *lake* . . . A3
Oconee, *river* . . . A2
Oconee Natl. For. . . . A3
Ogeechee, *river* . . . B4
Parris Island Marine Corps Recruit Depot . . . D4
Piedmont N.W.R. . . . A3
Port Royal, *sound* . . . D4
Rocky, *river* . . . D1
Russell, *lake* . . . B2
St. Helena, *sound* . . . D4
Saluda, *river* . . . C2
Sandhills St. For. . . . D2
Santee, *river* . . . E3
Santee N.W.R. . . . D3
Savannah, *river* . . . C3
Seed, *lake* . . . A2
Sinclair, *lake* . . . A3
South, *island* . . . E3
Sumter Natl. For. . . . A2, B3, C2
The Grand Strand, *beach* . . . F3
Tyger, *river* . . . E1
U.S. Dept. Of Energy Savannah River Site . . . C3
U.S. Naval Res. . . . E4
Waccamaw, *lake* . . . F2
Wateree, *lake* . . . D2
Wateree, *river* . . . D2

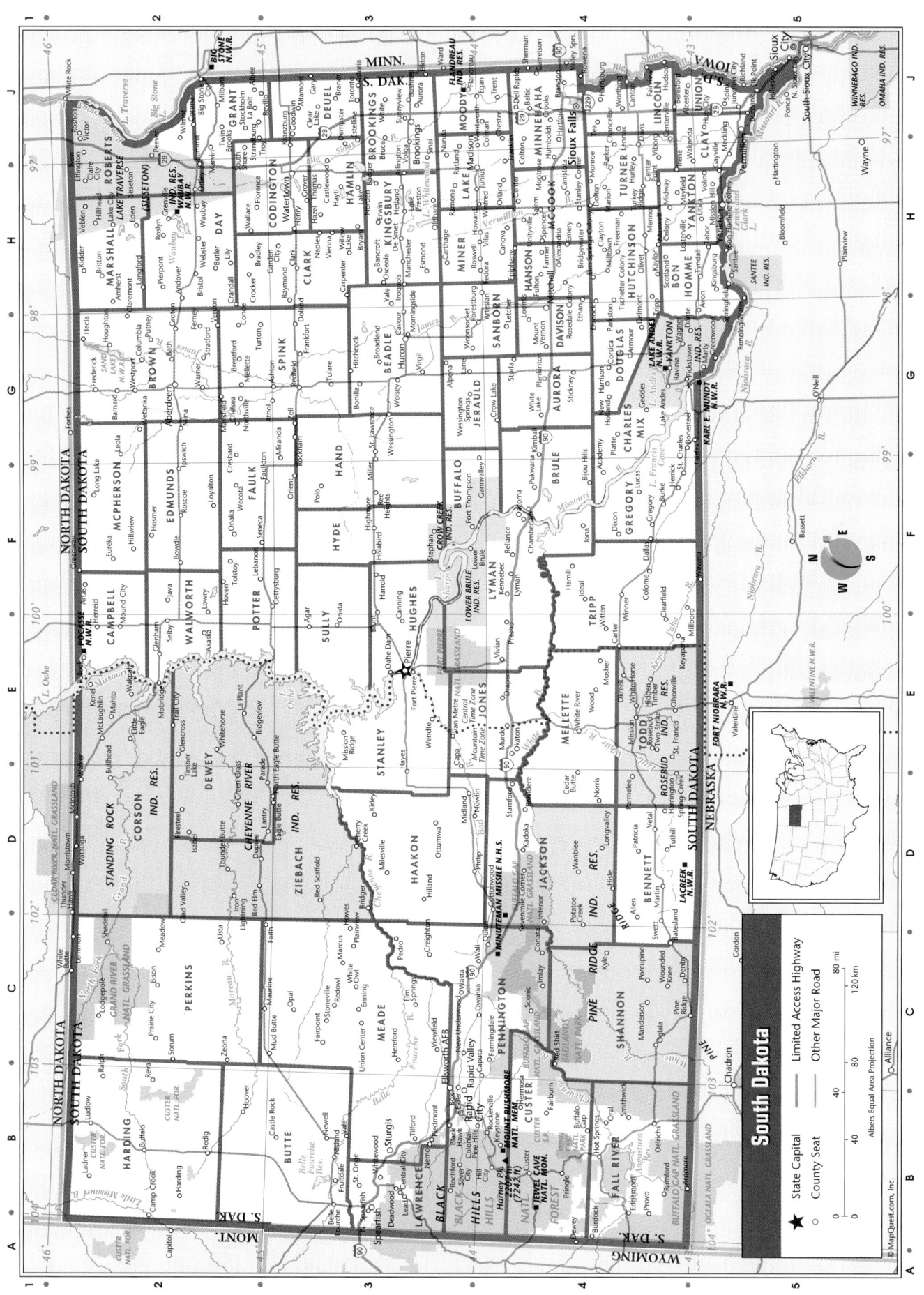

South Dakota

South Dakota

Capital: Pierre
Land Area: 75,896 sq. mi.
196,571 sq. km.
Population: 754,844 (2000 Census)
Largest City: Sioux Falls, 123,975
Highest Point: Harney Peak,
7,242 ft.
2,207 m.
Admitted to Union: November 2, 1889
Nickname: Coyote State,
Mount Rushmore State
State Flower: Pasqueflower
State Bird: Chinese Ring-necked
Pheasant

South Dakota:
Map Index

Counties

Aurora, **3,058** G4
Beadle, **17,023** G3
Bennett, **3,574** D4
Bon Homme, **7,260** H4
Brookings, **28,220** J3
Brown, **35,460** G2
Brule, **5,364** F4
Buffalo, **2,032** F3
Butte, **9,094** B3
Campbell, **1,782** E2
Charles Mix, **9,350** G4
Clark, **4,143** H3
Clay, **13,537** H5
Codington, **25,897** H3
Corson, **4,181** D2
Custer, **7,275** B4
Davison, **18,741** G4
Day, **6,267** H2
Deuel, **4,498** J3
Dewey, **5,972** D2
Douglas, **3,458** G4
Edmunds, **4,367** F2
Fall River, **7,453** B4
Faulk, **2,640** F2
Grant, **7,847** J2
Gregory, **4,792** F4
Haakon, **2,196** D3
Hamlin, **5,540** H3
Hand, **3,741** F3
Hanson, **3,139** H4
Harding, **1,353** B2
Hughes, **16,481** F3
Hutchinson, **8,075** H4
Hyde, **1,671** F3
Jackson, **2,930** D4
Jerauld, **2,295** G3
Jones, **1,193** E3
Kingsbury, **5,815** H3
Lake, **11,276** H3
Lawrence, **21,802** B3
Lincoln, **24,131** J4
Lyman, **3,895** F4
Marshall, **4,576** H2
McCook, **5,832** H4
McPherson, **2,904** F2
Meade, **24,253** C3
Mellette, **2,083** E4
Miner, **2,884** H3
Minnehaha, **148,281** J4
Moody, **6,595** J3
Pennington, **88,565** C4
Perkins, **3,363** C2
Potter, **2,693** F2
Roberts, **10,016** H2
Sanborn, **2,675** G4
Shannon, **12,466** C4
Spink, **7,454** G3
Stanley, **2,772** E3
Sully, **1,556** E3
Todd, **9,050** E4
Tripp, **6,430** F4
Turner, **8,849** H4
Union, **12,584** J5
Walworth, **5,974** E2
Yankton, **21,652** H4
Ziebach, **2,519** D3

Cities and Towns

Aberdeen, **24,658** G2
Academy F4
Agar, **82** E3
Akaska, **31** E2
Albee, **10** J2
Alcester, **880** J4
Alexandria, **563** H4
Allen, **419** D4
Alpena, **265** G3
Altamont, **34** J3
Amherst H2
Andover, **99** H2
Ardmore B4
Arlington, **992** H3
Armour, **782** G4
Artas, **13** F2
Artesian, **157** H4
Ashton, **152** G3
Astoria, **150** J3
Athol G2
Aurora, **500** J3
Avon, **561** G5
Badger, **144** H3
Baltic, **811** J4
Bancroft, **37** H3
Barnard, *60* G2
Batesland, **88** C4
Bath, *200* G2
Belle Fourche, **4,565** B3
Belvidere, **57** D4
Beresford, **2,006** J4
Big Stone City, **605** J2
Bijou Hills F4
Bison, **373** C2
Black Hawk, **2,432** B3
Blunt, **370** F3
Bonesteel, **297** G4
Bon Homme Colony, *50* H5
Bonilla G3
Bowdle, **571** F2
Box Elder, **2,841** B3
Bradley, **112** H2
Brandon, **5,693** J4
Brandt, **113** J3
Brentford, **65** G2
Bridger D3
Bridgewater, **607** H4
Bristol, **377** H2
Britton, **1,328** H2
Broadland, **38** G3
Brookings, **18,504** J3
Bruce, **272** J3
Bryant, **396** H3
Buffalo, **380** B2
Buffalo Gap, **164** B4
Bullhead, **308** D2
Burbank, *60* J5
Burdock B4
Burke, **676** F4
Bushnell, **75** J3
Butler, **17** H2
Camp Crook, **56** B2
Canistota, **700** H4
Canning E3
Canova, **140** H4
Canton, **3,110** J4
Capa E3
Caputa, *50* C4
Carpenter, *40* H3
Carter E4
Carthage, **187** H3
Castle Rock B3
Castlewood, **666** H3
Cavour, **141** G3
Cedar Butte D4
Center H4
Center Point H4
Centerville, **910** J4
Central City, **149** B3
Chamberlain, **2,338** F4
Chancellor, **328** J4
Chelsea, **33** G2
Cherry Creek, *350* D3
Chester, *275* J4
Claire City, **85** H2
Claremont, **130** G2
Clark, **1,285** H3
Clayton H4
Clearfield E4
Clear Lake, **1,335** J3
Colman, **572** J4
Colome, **340** F4
Colonial Pine Hills, **2,561** B3
Colton, **662** J4
Columbia, **140** G2
Conata C4
Conde, **187** G2
Corona, **112** J2
Corsica, **644** G4
Cottonwood, **6** D4
Crandall H2
Creighton C3
Cresbard, **143** G2
Crocker H2
Crooks, **859** J4
Crow Lake G4
Custer, **1,860** B4
Dallas, **144** F4
Dante, **82** G4
Davis, **104** J4
Deadwood, **1,380** B3
Dell Rapids, **2,980** J4
Delmont, **263** G4
Dempster, *40* J3
Denby C4
De Smet, **1,164** H3
Dewey A4
Dimock, **151** H4
Dixon F4
Doland, **297** G3
Dolton, **41** H4
Draper, **92** E4
Dupree, **434** D2
Eagle Butte, **619** D3
Eden, **97** H2
Edgemont, **867** B4
Egan, **265** J4
Elk Point, **1,714** J5
Elkton, **677** J3
Elm Springs C3
Elm Springs Colony, *80* H4
Emery, **439** H4
Enning, *40* C3
Epiphany, *60* H4
Erwin, **58** H3
Esmond H3
Estelline, **675** J3
Ethan, **330** G4
Eureka, **1,101** F2
Fairburn, **80** B4
Fairfax, **123** G4
Fairpoint C3
Fairview, **94** J4
Faith, **489** C2
Farmer, **18** H4
Farmingdale C4
Faulkton, **785** F2
Fedora, *40* H4
Ferney, *50* G2
Firesteel D2
Flandreau, **2,376** J3
Florence, **299** H2
Forbes G2
Forestburg, *70* G3
Fort Pierre, **1,991** E3
Fort Thompson, **1,375** F3
Frankfort, **166** G3
Franklin, *50* H4
Frederick, **255** G2
Freeman, **1,317** H4
Fruitdale, **62** B3
Fulton, **86** H4
Gannvalley F3
Garden City, **72** H3
Garretson, **1,165** J4
Gary, **231** J3
Gayville, **418** H5
Geddes, **252** G4
Gettysburg, **1,352** F2
Glad Valley D2
Glencross E2
Glenham, **139** E2
Goodwin, **160** J3
Green Grass, **58** D2
Greenway F2
Greenwood G5
Gregory, **1,342** F4
Grenville, **62** H2
Groton, **1,356** G2
Grover H3
Hamill, **11** F4
Harding B2
Harrington D4
Harrisburg, **958** J4
Harrison, **51** G4
Harrold, **209** F3
Hartford, **1,844** J4
Hayes D3
Hayti, **367** H3
Hazel, **105** H3
Hecla, **314** G2
Henry, **268** H3
Hereford C3
Hermosa, **315** B4
Herreid, **482** E2
Herrick, **105** F4
Hetland, **43** H3
Hidden Timber E4
Highmore, **851** F3
Hilland D3
Hill City, **780** B4
Hillhead H2
Hillsview, **3** F2
Hisle D4
Hitchcock, **108** G3
Holabird F3
Hoover B2
Hosmer, **287** F2
Hot Springs, **4,129** B4
Houghton, *60* G2
Hoven, **511** F2
Howard, **1,071** H3
Howes C3
Hub City, *40* J5
Hudson, **402** J4
Humboldt, **521** H4
Hurley, **426** H4
Huron, **11,893** G3
Ideal, *50* F4
Imlay C4
Interior, **77** D4
Iona F4
Ipswich, **943** F2
Irene, **432** H4
Iron Lightning, *90* D2
Iroquois, **278** H3
Isabel, **239** D2
Java, **197** F2
Jefferson, **586** J5
Junction City J5
Junius, *80* H3
Kadoka, **706** D4
Kaylor, **64** H4
Kenel, *90* E2
Kennebec, **286** F4
Keyapaha E4
Keystone, **311** B4
Kidder, *70* H2
Kimball, **745** G4
Kingsburg H5
Kirley D3
Kranzburg, **185** J3
Kyle, **970** C4
La Bolt, **86** J2
Ladner B2
Lake Andes, **819** G4
Lake City, **47** H2
Lake Norden, **432** H3
Lake Preston, **737** H3
Lane, **59** G3
Langford, **290** H2
Lantry D2
La Plant, **150** E2
Lead, **3,027** B3
Lebanon, **86** F2
Lemmon, **1,398** C2
Lennox, **2,037** J4
Leola, **462** G2
Lesterville, **158** H4
Letcher, **177** G4
Lily, **21** H2
Little Eagle, **370** E2
Lodgepole C2
Long Lake, **58** F2
Longvalley D4
Loomis, **47** G4
Lower Brule, **599** F3
Lowry, **10** F2
Loyalton F2
Lucas F4
Ludlow B2
Lyman F4
Madison, **6,540** H3
Mahto E2
Manchester H3
Manderson, **626** C4
Mansfield, *90* G2
Marcus C3
Marion, **892** H4
Martin, **1,106** D4
Marty, **421** G5
Marvin, **66** J2
Maurine C2
Maxwell Colony, *100* H4
Mayfield, *40* H4
McIntosh, **217** D2
McLaughlin, **775** E2
Meadow C2
Meckling, *100* H5
Mellette, **248** G2
Menno, **729** H4
Midland, **179** D3
Midway H4
Milbank, **3,640** J2
Milesville D3
Millboro F4
Miller, **1,530** G3
Milltown, **8** H4
Mina G2
Miranda G3
Mission, **904** E4
Mission Hill, **183** H5
Mission Ridge, *70* E3
Mitchell, **14,558** G4
Mobridge, **3,574** E2
Monroe, **163** H4
Montrose, **460** H4
Morningside, *125* G3
Morristown, **82** D2
Mosher E4
Mound City, **84** E2
Mount Vernon, **477** G4
Mud Butte C3
Murdo, **612** E4
Naples, **25** H3
Nemo B3
New Effington, **233** J2
Newell, **646** B3
New Holland, **78** G4
New Underwood, **616** C3
Nisland, **204** B3
Norris, *150* D4
North Eagle Butte, **2,163** D3
North Sioux City, **2,288** J5
North Spearfish, **2,306** B3
Northville, **124** G2
Nowlin, *80* D3
Nunda, **47** H3
Oacoma, **390** F4
Oahe Dam E3
Oelrichs, **145** B4
Oglala, **1,229** C4
Okaton, **29** E4
Okreek, *40* E4
Oldham, **206** H3
Olivet, **70** H4
Olsonville E4
Onaka, **30** F2
Onida, **740** E3
Opal, *70* C3
Oral B4
Orient, **57** F3
Orland H4
Ortley, **54** H2
Osceola H3
Ottumwa D3
Owanka C3
Parade, *40* D2
Parker, **1,031** H4
Parkston, **1,674** G4
Parmelee, **650** D4
Patricia D4
Pedro C3
Peever, **209** J2
Philip, **885** D3
Pickstown, **168** G4
Piedmont, *700* B3
Pierpont, **122** H2
Pierre, **13,876** E3
Pine Ridge, **3,171** C4
Plainview C3
Plankinton, **601** G4
Platte, **1,367** G4
Pollock, **339** E2
Polo F3
Porcupine, **407** C4
Potatoe Creek, *40* D4
Prairie City C2
Presho, **588** E4
Pringle, **125** B4
Provo B4
Pukwana, **287** F4
Putney G2
Quinn, **44** C4
Ralph B2
Ramona, **190** H3
Rapid City, **59,607** B3
Rapid Valley, **7,043** B3
Ravinia, **79** G4
Raymond, **86** H3
Red Elm D2
Redfield, **2,897** G3
Redig B2
Redowl C3
Red Scaffold, *80* D3
Red Shirt C4
Ree Heights, **85** F3
Reliance, **206** F4
Reva B2
Revillo, **147** J2
Richland, *80* J5
Ridgeview E2
Rochford B3
Rockerville, *50* B4
Rockham, **53** G3
Roscoe, **324** F2
Rosebud, **1,557** E4
Rosedale Colony, *90* H4
Rosholt, **419** J2
Roslyn, **225** H2
Roswell, **21** H3
Rowena, *100* J4
Rumford B4
Running Water G5
Rutland, *40* J3
St. Charles, **19** F4
St. Francis, **675** E4
St. Lawrence, **210** G3
St. Onge, *150* B3
Salem, **1,371** H4
Scenic C4
Scotland, **891** H4
Selby, **736** E2
Seneca, **58** F2
Sevenmile Corner D4
Shadehill C2
Sherman, **87** J4
Silver City, *50* B3
Sinai, **133** H3
Sioux Falls, **123,975** J4
Sisseton, **2,572** H2
Smithwick B4
Sorum C2
South Shore, **270** J2
Spearfish, **8,606** B3
Spencer, **157** H4
Spink, *60* J5
Spring Creek, **136** D4
Springfield, **792** H5
Stamford D4
Stanley Corner H4
Stephan F3
Stickney, **334** G4
Stockholm, **105** J2
Stoneville C3
Storla, **15** G4
Strandburg, **69** J2
Stratford, **96** G2
Sturgis, **6,442** B3
Summit, **281** H2
Sunnyview, *150* J3
Swett D4
Tabor, **417** H5
Tea, **1,742** J4
Thomas, *40* H3
Thunder Butte, *60* D2
Thunder Hawk D2
Tilford B3
Timber Lake, **443** D2
Tolstoy, **64** F2
Toronto, **202** J3
Trail City, *40* E2
Trent, **254** J4
Tripp, **711** H4
Troy J2
Tschetter Colony, *100* H4
Tulare, **221** G3
Turkey Ridge H4
Turton, **61** G2
Tuthill, *40* D4
Twin Brooks, **55** J2
Two Strike, **33** E4
Tyndall, **1,239** H5
Union Center, *50* C3
Unityville, *40* H4
Usta C2
Utica, **86** H5
Vale, *150* B3
Valley Springs, **792** J4
Van Metre E3
Veblen, **281** H2
Verdon, **6** G2
Vermillion, **9,765** J5
Vetal D4
Viborg, **832** H4
Victor J2
Vienna, **78** H3
Viewfield, *40* C3
Vilas, **19** H4
Virgil, **25** G3
Vivian, **131** E4
Volga, **1,435** J3
Volin, **207** H5
Wagner, **1,675** G4
Wakonda, **374** H4
Wakpala, *225* E2
Walker D2
Wall, **818** C3
Wallace, **86** H2
Wanblee, **641** D4
Ward, **41** J3
Warner, **419** G2
Wasta, **75** C3
Watauga D2
Watertown, **20,237** H3
Waubay, **662** H2
Webster, **1,952** H2
Wecota F2
Wendte E3
Wentworth, **188** J3
Wessington, **248** G3
Wessington Springs, **1,011** G3
Westport, **125** G2
Wetonka, **12** G2
Wewela F4
White, **530** J3
White Butte C2
Whitehorse, **141** E2
White Horse, **180** E4
White Lake, **405** G4
White Owl, *40* C3
White River, **598** E4
White Rock, **18** J2
Whitewood, **844** B3
Willow Lake, **294** H3
Wilmot, **543** J2
Winfred, **50** H4
Winner, **3,137** F4
Witten, **51** E4
Wolsey, **418** G3
Wood, **66** E4
Woonsocket, **720** G3
Worthing, **585** J4
Wounded Knee, **328** C4
Yale, **118** H3
Yankton, **13,528** H5
Zell, *70* G3
Zeona C2

Other Features

Andes, *lake* G4
Angostura, *reservoir* B4
Bad, *river* D3
Badlands Natl. Park C4
Belle Fourche, *river* B3
Belle Fourche, *reservoir* B3
Big Sioux, *river* H3, J4
Big Stone, *lake* J2
Big Stone N.W.R. J2
Black, *hills* B3
Black Hills Natl. Forest B3
Bois de Sioux, *river* J2
Buffalo Gap
Natl. Grassland B4, C4, D4
Cedar River Natl. Grassland D1
Cheyenne, *river* B4, D3
Cheyenne River Ind. Res. D2
Crow Creek Ind. Res. F3
Custer Natl. For. A2, B2
Custer S.P. B4
Elkhorn, *river* F5
Flandreau Ind. Res. J3
Fort Niobrara N.W.R. E5
Fort Pierre Natl. Grassland E3
Francis Case, *lake* G4
Grand, *river* D2
Grand River Natl. Grassland C2
Harney, *peak* B4
James, *river* G2, G3
Jewel Cave Natl. Mon. B4
Karl E. Mundt N.W.R. G5
Keya Paha, *river* E4
Lacreek N.W.R. D4
Lake Andes N.W.R. G4
Lake Traverse (Sisseton) Ind. Res. H2
Lewis and Clark, *lake* H5
Little Missouri, *river* B2
Little White, *river* E4
Lower Brule Ind. Res. F3
Minuteman Missile N.H.S. C4
Missouri, *river* E2, F4, J5
Moreau, *river* C2
Mount Rushmore Natl. Mem. B4
Nebraska Natl. For. B5
Niobrara, *river* F5, G5
North Fork C2
Oahe, *lake* E1, E3
Oglala Natl. Grassland B5
Omaha Ind. Res. J5
Pine, *ridge* C5
Pine Ridge Ind. Res. C4
Pocasse N.W.R. E2
Rosebud Ind. Res. D4
Sand Lake N.W.R. G2
Santee Ind. Res. H5
Sharpe, *lake* F3
South Fork B2
Standing Rock Ind. Res. D2
Traverse, *lake* J2
Valentine N.W.R. E5
Vermillion, *river* H4
Waubay, *lake* H2
Waubay N.W.R. H2
White, *river* C4, E4
Whitewood, *lake* H3
Wind Cave Natl. Park B4
Winnebago Ind. Res. J5
Yankton Ind. Res. G4

Tennessee

Capital: Nashville
Land Area: 41,219 sq. mi.
106,757 sq. km.
Population: 5,689,283 (2000 Census)
Largest City: Memphis, 650,100
Highest Point: Clingmans Dome, 6,643 ft. 2,025 m.
Admitted to Union: June 1, 1796
Nickname: Volunteer State
State Flower: Iris
State Bird: Mockingbird

Tennessee: Map Index

Counties

Anderson, 71,330 ....N2
Bedford, 37,586 ....J3
Benton, 16,537 ....E2
Bledsoe, 12,367 ....L3
Blount, 105,823 ....P3
Bradley, 87,965 ....M4
Campbell, 39,854 ....N2
Cannon, 12,826 ....J3
Carroll, 29,475 ....E3
Carter, 56,742 ....S2
Cheatham, 35,912 ....G2
Chester, 15,540 ....D4
Claiborne, 29,862 ....P2
Clay, 7,976 ....K2
Cocke, 33,565 ....Q3
Coffee, 48,014 ....J3
Crockett, 14,532 ....C3
Cumberland, 46,802 ....L3
Davidson, 569,891 ....H2
Decatur, 11,731 ....E3
DeKalb, 17,423 ....K3
Dickson, 43,156 ....G2
Dyer, 37,279 ....C2
Fayette, 28,806 ....C4
Fentress, 16,625 ....M2
Franklin, 39,270 ....J4
Gibson, 48,152 ....D2
Giles, 29,447 ....G4
Grainger, 20,659 ....P2
Greene, 62,909 ....R2
Grundy, 14,332 ....K4
Hamblen, 58,128 ....Q2
Hamilton, 307,896 ....L4
Hancock, 6,786 ....Q2
Hardeman, 28,105 ....C4
Hardin, 25,578 ....E4
Hawkins, 53,563 ....R2
Haywood, 19,797 ....C3
Henderson, 25,522 ....E3
Henry, 31,115 ....E2
Hickman, 22,295 ....G3
Houston, 8,088 ....F2
Humphreys, 17,929 ....F2
Jackson, 10,984 ....K2
Jefferson, 44,294 ....Q2
Johnson, 17,499 ....T2
Knox, 382,032 ....P3

Cities and Towns

Adams, 566 ....G1
Adamsville, 1,983 ....E4

Lake, 7,954 ....C2
Lauderdale, 27,101 ....B3
Lawrence, 39,926 ....G4
Lewis, 11,367 ....G3
Lincoln, 31,340 ....H4
Loudon, 39,086 ....N3
Macon, 20,386 ....K1
Madison, 91,837 ....D3
Marion, 27,776 ....K4
Marshall, 26,767 ....H4
Maury, 69,498 ....G3
McMinn, 49,015 ....M4
McNairy, 24,653 ....D4
Meigs, 11,086 ....M3
Monroe, 38,961 ....N4
Montgomery, 134,768 ....G2
Moore, 5,740 ....J4
Morgan, 19,757 ....M2
Obion, 32,450 ....C2
Overton, 20,118 ....L2
Perry, 7,631 ....F3
Pickett, 4,945 ....L1
Polk, 16,050 ....M4
Putnam, 62,315 ....L2
Rhea, 28,400 ....M3
Roane, 51,910 ....M3
Robertson, 54,433 ....H2
Rutherford, 182,023 ....J3
Scott, 21,127 ....M2
Sequatchie, 11,370 ....L4
Sevier, 71,170 ....Q3
Shelby, 897,472 ....B4
Smith, 17,712 ....K2
Stewart, 12,370 ....F1
Sullivan, 153,048 ....S1
Sumner, 130,449 ....H2
Tipton, 51,271 ....B3
Trousdale, 7,259 ....J2
Unicoi, 17,667 ....S2
Union, 17,808 ....P2
Van Buren, 5,508 ....L3
Warren, 38,276 ....K3
Washington, 107,198 ....R2
Wayne, 16,842 ....F4
Weakley, 34,895 ....D2
White, 23,102 ....L3
Williamson, 126,638 ....H3
Wilson, 88,809 ....J2

Alamo, 2,392 ....C3
Alcoa, 7,734 ....P3
Algood, 2,942 ....L2
Alexandria, 814 ....J2
Allardt, 642 ....L2
Allons, 125 ....L2
Alpine, 200 ....L2
Altamont, 1,136 ....K4
Ardmore, 1,082 ....H5
Arlington, 2,569 ....B4
Armona N3
Arthur, 1,100 ....P1
Ashland City, 3,641 ....G2
Ashport B3
Athens, 13,220 ....M4
Atoka, 3,235 ....B4
Atwood, 1,000 ....D3
Auburntown, 252 ....J3
Baileyton, 504 ....R2
Bakewell, 450 ....L4
Baneberry, 366 ....Q2
Banner Hill, 1,053 ....S2
Bartlett, 40,543 ....B4
Bath Springs, 50 ....E4
Baxter, 1,279 ....K2
Bean Station, 1,400 ....Q2
Beech Bluff, 250 ....D3
Beechgrove, 70 ....J3
Beersheba Springs, 553 ....K4
Belfast, 50 ....H4
Belinda City, 2,100 ....J2
Bell Buckle, 391 ....J3
Belle Meade, 2,943 ....H2
Bells, 2,171 ....C3
Belvidere, 200 ....J4
Benton, 1,138 ....M4
Berry Hill, 674 ....H2
Bethel Springs, 763 ....D4
Bethpage, 300 ....J1
Big Rock, 350 ....F1
Big Sandy, 518 ....E2
Blaine, 1,585 ....P2
Bloomingdale, 10,350 ....S1
Blountville, 2,959 ....S1
Bluff City, 1,559 ....S2
Bogota, 200 ....C2
Bold Spring, 70 ....F3
Bolivar, 5,802 ....C4
Bon Air, 375 ....L3
Boyds Creek P3
Braden, 271 ....B4
Bradford, 1,113 ....D2

Brentwood, 23,445 ....H2
Briceville, 650 ....N2
Brighton, 1,719 ....B4
Bristol, 24,821 ....S1
Brownsville, 10,748 ....C3
Bruceton, 1,554 ....E2
Brush Creek, 250 ....J2
Buchanan, 125 ....E2
Buena Vista, 100 ....E3
Buffalo Valley, 50 ....K2
Bulls Gap, 714 ....Q2
Bumpus Mills, 225 ....F1
Burlison, 453 ....B3
Burns, 1,366 ....G2
Byrdstown, 903 ....L1
Calhoun, 496 ....M4
Camden, 3,828 ....E2
Campaign, 450 ....K3
Campbellsville, 80 ....G4
Capleville, 60 ....B4
Carthage, 2,251 ....K2
Caryville, 2,243 ....N2
Castalian Springs, 250 ....J2
Cedar Grove, 150 ....D3
Cedar Hill, 298 ....G1
Celina, 1,379 ....K1
Centertown, 200 ....K3
Centerville, 3,793 ....G3
Central, 2,717 ....S3
Chapel Hill, 943 ....H3
Charleston, 630 ....M4
Charlotte, 1,153 ....G2
Chattanooga, 155,554 ....L4
Cherry, 100 ....B3
Chestnut Mound, 200 ....K2
Chewalla, 200 ....D4
Christiana, 350 ....J3
Church Hill, 5,916 ....R1
Clarkrange, 200 ....L2
Clarksburg, 285 ....E3
Clarksville, 103,455 ....G1
Cleveland, 37,192 ....M4
Clifton, 2,699 ....F4
Clinton, 9,409 ....N2
Coalmont, 948 ....K4
Collegedale, 6,514 ....L4
College Grove, 325 ....H3
Collierville, 31,872 ....B4
Collinwood, 1,024 ....F4
Colonial Heights, 7,067 ....S2
Columbia, 33,055 ....G3
Como, 150 ....D2

Conasauga, 125 ....M5
Cookeville, 23,923 ....K2
Copperhill, 511 ....N5
Cordova, 2,800 ....B4
Cornersville, 962 ....H4
Cottage Grove, 97 ....E2
Cottontown J2
Counce, 225 ....E4
Covington, 8,463 ....B3
Cowan, 1,770 ....J4
Crab Orchard, 838 ....M3
Cross Plains, 1,381 ....H1
Crossville, 8,981 ....L3
Crump, 1,521 ....E4
Culleoka, 1,000 ....H4
Cumberland City, 316 ....F2
Cumberland Furnace, 125 ....G2
Cumberland Gap, 204 ....P1
Cunningham, 150 ....G2
Cypress Inn, 80 ....F4
Dancyville, 80 ....C4
Dandridge, 2,078 ....Q2
Darden, 200 ....E3
Daus, 325 ....L4
Dayton, 6,180 ....L3
Decatur, 1,395 ....M3
Decaturville, 859 ....E3
Decherd, 2,246 ....J4
Delano, 425 ....M4
Dibrell, 150 ....K3
Dickson, 12,244 ....G2
Difficult K2
Dover, 1,442 ....F1
Dowelltown, 302 ....K2
Doyle, 525 ....K3
Dresden, 2,855 ....D2
Duck River, 80 ....G3
Ducktown, 427 ....N4
Dunlap, 4,173 ....L4
Dyer, 2,406 ....C2
Dyersburg, 17,452 ....C2
Eagan, 200 ....P1
Eagleton Village, 4,883 ....P3
Eagleville, 464 ....H3
East Cleveland, 1,729 ....M4
East Ridge, 20,640 ....L4
Eastview, 618 ....D4
Elizabethton, 13,372 ....S2
Elkton, 510 ....H4
Elk Valley, 400 ....N2
Elora, 500 ....J4
Englewood, 1,590 ....N4

Enville, 230 ....E4
Erin, 1,490 ....F2
Erwin, 5,610 ....S2
Estill Springs, 2,152 ....J4
Ethridge, 536 ....G4
Etowah, 3,663 ....N4
Eva, 300 ....E2
Evensville, 300 ....M3
Fairfield Glade, 4,885 ....M2
Fairview, 5,800 ....G3
Fall Branch, 1,313 ....R2
Farner, 300 ....N4
Farragut, 17,720 ....N3
Fayetteville, 6,994 ....H4
Finger, 350 ....D4
Five Points, 175 ....G4
Flatwoods, 40 ....F4
Flintville, 300 ....J4
Forest Hills, 4,710 ....H2
Fork Mountain N2
Fort Pillow, 650 ....B3
Fowlkes, 600 ....C2
Frankewing, 80 ....H4
Franklin, 41,842 ....H3
Friendship, 608 ....C3
Friendsville, 890 ....N3
Gadsden, 553 ....D3
Gainesboro, 879 ....K2
Gallatin, 23,230 ....J2
Gallaway, 666 ....B4
Garland, 309 ....B3
Gates, 901 ....C3
Gatlinburg, 3,382 ....P3
Germantown, 37,348 ....B4
Gibson, 305 ....D3
Gilt Edge, 489 ....B3
Gleason, 1,463 ....D2
Goodlettsville, 13,780 ....H1
Gordonsville, 1,066 ....K2
Grand Junction, 301 ....C4
Grandview, 100 ....M3
Granville, 70 ....K2
Gray, 1,273 ....S2
Graysville, 1,411 ....L3
Greenback, 954 ....N3
Greenbrier, 4,940 ....H1
Greeneville, 15,198 ....R2
Greenfield, 2,208 ....D2
Green Hill, 7,068 ....H2
Greenwood J2
Grimsley, 375 ....M2
Gruetli-Laager, 1,867 ....K4
Guys, 483 ....D4

Haletown, 300 ....K4
Halls (Knox Co.) P2
Halls (Lauderdale Co.), 2,311 ....C3
Halls Crossroads (Halls), 2,100 ....P2
Hampshire, 175 ....G3
Hampton, 1,300 ....S2
Hanging Limb, 100 ....L2
Harriman, 6,744 ....M3
Harrison, 7,630 ....L4
Harrogate (Harrogate-Shawnee), 2,865 ....P1
Hartford, 250 ....Q3
Hartsville, 2,395 ....J2
Helenwood, 846 ....M2
Henderson, 5,670 ....D4
Hendersonville, 40,620 ....H2
Henning, 970 ....B3
Henry, 520 ....E2
Henryville, 70 ....G4
Hermitage Springs, 150 ....K1
Hickory Valley, 136 ....C4
Hillsboro, 225 ....K4
Hohenwald, 3,754 ....F3
Holladay, 125 ....E3
Hollow Rock, 963 ....E2
Hopewell, 1,815 ....M4
Hornbeak, 435 ....C2
Hornsby, 306 ....D4
Howell, 175 ....H4
Humboldt, 9,467 ....D3
Hunter, 1,566 ....S2
Huntingdon, 4,349 ....E2
Huntland, 916 ....J4
Huntsville, 981 ....N2
Hurricane Mills, 125 ....F3
Indian Mound, 80 ....F1
Iron City, 368 ....F4
Jacksboro, 1,887 ....N2
Jackson, 59,643 ....D3
Jamestown, 1,839 ....M2
Jasper, 3,214 ....K4
Jefferson City, 7,760 ....P2
Jellico, 2,448 ....N1
Johnson City, 55,469 ....S2
Jonesborough, 4,168 ....S2
Karns, 1,500 ....N3
Kenton, 1,306 ....C2
Kimball, 1,312 ....K4
Kimmins, 70 ....F3

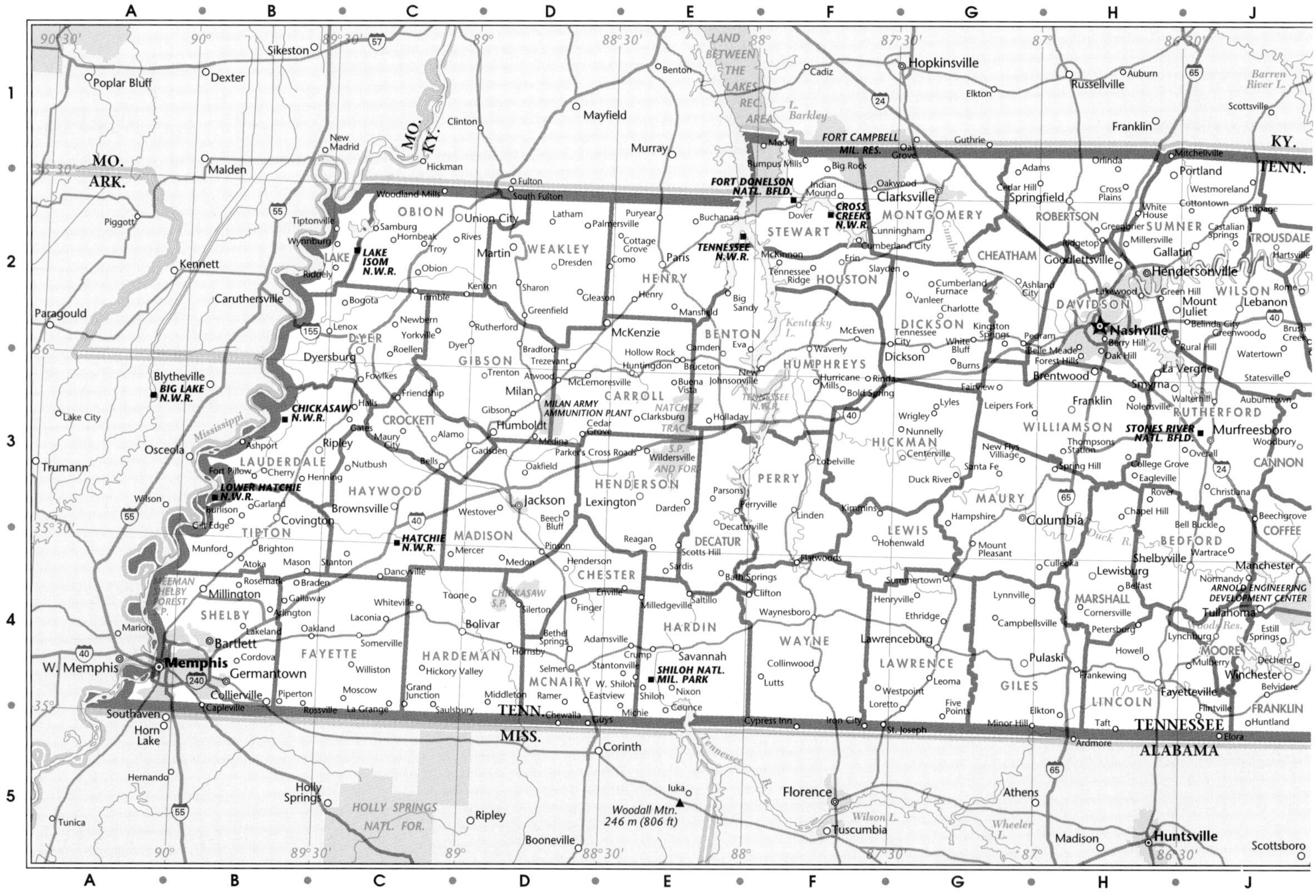

Kingsport, 44,905 . . . . .R1
Kingston, 5,264 . . . . .N3
Kingston Springs,
2,773 . . . . .G2
Kinzel Springs P3
Knoxville, 173,890 . . .P3
Laconia, 50 . . . . .C4
Lafayette, 3,885 . . . . .J1
La Follette, 7,926 . . . .P2
La Grange, 136 . . . . . .C4
Lake City, 1,888 . . . . .P2
Lakeland, 6,862 . . . . .B4
Lakesite, 1,845 . . . . . .L4
Lakewood, 2,341 . . . . .H2
Lancing, 150 . . . . . . .M2
Latham, 125 . . . . .D2
La Vergne, 18,687 . . . .H2
Lawrenceburg, 10,796 .G4
Lebanon, 20,235 . . . . .J2
Lee Valley Q2
Leipers Fork, 150 . . . .G3
Lenoir City, 6,819 . . . .N3
Lenox, 200 . . . . .C2
Leoma, 400 . . . . .G4
Lewisburg, 10,413 . . . .H4
Lexington, 7,393 . . . . .E3
Liberty, 367 . . . . .K3
Limestone, 550 . . . . . .R2
Linden, 1,015 . . . . . . .F3
Livingston, 3,498 . . . . .L2
Lobelville, 915 . . . . . . .F3
Lone Mountain, 275 . .P2
Lookout Mountain,
2,000 . . . . .L5
Loretto, 1,665 . . . . . . .G4
Loudon, 4,476 . . . . . .N3
Louisville, 2,001 . . . . .N3
Luttrell, 915 . . . . .P2
Lutts, 150 . . . . .F4
Lyles, 450 . . . . .G3
Lynchburg, 5,740 . . . . .J4
Lynnville, 345 . . . . . . .G4
Madisonville, 3,939 . . .N3
Manchester, 8,294 . . . .J4
Mansfield, 150 . . . . . . .E2
Martin, 10,515 . . . . . . .D2
Maryville, 23,120 . . . . .P3
Mascot, 2,119 . . . . . . .P2
Mason, 1,089 . . . . . . .B4
Maury City, 704 . . . . . .C3
Mayland, 150 . . . . .L2
Maynardville, 1,782 . . .P2
McEwen, 1,702 . . . . . .F2

McKenzie, 5,295 . . . . .D2
McKinnon, 40 . . . . . . .F2
McLemoresville, 259 . .D3
McMinnville, 12,749 . . .K3
Medina, 969 . . . . .D3
Medon, 191 . . . . .D4
Memphis, 650,100 . . . .A4
Mercer, 225 . . . . .C4
Michie, 647 . . . . .E4
Middleton, 602 . . . . . .D4
Middle Valley, 11,854 . .L4
Milan, 7,664 . . . . .D3
Milledgeville, 287 . . . .E4
Millersville, 5,308 . . . .H2
Milligan College, 275 . .S2
Millington, 10,433 . . . .B4
Milltown K2
Minor Hill, 437 . . . . . .G4
Mitchellville, 207 . . . . .H1
Model F1
Monteagle, 1,238 . . . .K4
Monterey, 2,717 . . . . .L2
Morrison, 684 . . . . . . .K3
Morristown, 24,965 . . .Q2
Moscow, 422 . . . . . . .C4
Mosheim, 1,749 . . . . .R2
Moss, 100 . . . . .K1
Mountain City, 2,383 . .T2
Mount Carmel, 4,795 . .R1
Mount Juliet, 12,366 . .H2
Mount Pleasant, 4,491 .G3
Mount Vernon, 225 . . .N4
Mulberry, 125 . . . . .J4
Munford, 4,708 . . . . . .B4
Murfreesboro, 68,816 . .J3
Nashville, 569,891 . . . .H2
Newbern, 2,988 . . . . .C2
New Flys Villiage G3
New Hope, 1,043 . . . . .K4
New Johnsonville,
1,905 . . . . .F2
New Market, 1,234 . . .P2
Newport, 7,242 . . . . . .Q3
New River, 175 . . . . . .M2
New Tazewell, 2,871 . .P2
Niota, 781 . . . . .M3
Nixon, 400 . . . . .E4
Nolensville, 3,099 . . . .H3
Norma, 80 . . . . .N2
Normandy, 141 . . . . . . .J4
Norris, 1,446 . . . . . . .N2
Nunnelly, 150 . . . . . . .G3
Nutbush, 125 . . . . . . .C3

Oakdale, 244 . . . . . . .M3
Oakfield, 100 . . . . . . .D3
Oak Grove, 4,072 . . . . .S2
Oak Hill, 4,493 . . . . . .H2
Oakland, 1,279 . . . . . .B4
Oakwood, 350 . . . . . . .F1
Obion, 1,134 . . . . . . .C2
Ocoee, 400 . . . . .M4
Oliver Springs, 3,303 . .N2
Oneida, 3,615 . . . . . . .M2
Ooltewah, 5,681 . . . . .L4
Orlinda, 594 . . . . .H1
Orme, 124 . . . . .K4
Overall, 800 . . . . .J3
Ozone, 125 . . . . .M3
Pall Mall, 175 . . . . . . .M1
Palmer, 726 . . . . .K4
Palmersville, 90 . . . . .D2
Paris, 9,763 . . . . .E2
Parker's Cross Roads,
241 . . . . .E3
Parrottsville, 207 . . . . .Q2
Parsons, 2,452 . . . . . .E3
Pegram, 2,146 . . . . . .G2
Perryville, 275 . . . . . . .E3
Petersburg, 580 . . . . .H4
Petros, 650 . . . . .N2
Philadelphia, 533 . . . .N3
Pigeon Forge, 5,083 . .P3
Pikeville, 1,781 . . . . . .L3
Pine Crest, 2,872 . . . . .S2
Pinson, 475 . . . . .D4
Pioneer, 40 . . . . .M2
Piperton, 589 . . . . . . .B4
Pittman Center, 477 . .Q3
Plainview, 1,866 . . . . .P2
Pleasant Hill, 544 . . . .L3
Portland, 8,458 . . . . . .H1
Powell, 7,500 . . . . . . .N2
Powells Crossroads,
1,286 . . . . .L4
Pruden, 60 . . . . .P1
Pulaski, 7,871 . . . . . .G4
Puryear, 667 . . . . .E2
Quebeck, 225 . . . . . . .K3
Ramer, 354 . . . . .D4
Reagan, 50 . . . . .E3
Red Bank, 12,418 . . . .L4
Red Boiling Springs,
1,023 . . . . .K1
Riceville, 650 . . . . . . .M4
Rickman, 475 . . . . . . .L2

Ridgely, 1,667 . . . . . . .C2
Ridgeside, 389 . . . . . . .L4
Ridgetop, 1,083 . . . . . .H2
Rinda F3
Ripley, 7,844 . . . . .B3
Rives, 331 . . . . .C2
Roan Mountain, 1,160 .S2
Robbins, 500 . . . . . . .M2
Rockford, 798 . . . . . . .P3
Rockwood, 5,774 . . . .N3
Rocky Fork, 100 . . . . . .R2
Roellen, 350 . . . . .C2
Rogersville, 4,240 . . . .Q2
Rome, 200 . . . . .J2
Rosedale, 50 . . . . .N2
Rosemark, 350 . . . . . .B4
Rossville, 380 . . . . . . .B4
Rover, 125 . . . . .H3
Rugby, 60 . . . . .M2
Rural Hill, 2,032 . . . . . .L4
Russellville, 1,000 . . . .Q2
Rutherford, 1,272 . . . .D2
Rutledge, 1,187 . . . . .Q2
Ryall Springs (East
Brainerd), 4,600 . . . .L4
Sadie, 325 . . . . .F4
St. Joseph, 829 . . . . . .F4
Sale Creek, 750 . . . . . .L4
Saltillo, 342 . . . . .E4
Samburg, 260 . . . . . . .C2
Santa Fe, 300 . . . . . . .G3
Sardis, 445 . . . . .E4
Saulsbury, 99 . . . . . . .C4
Savannah, 6,917 . . . . .E4
Scotts Hill, 894 . . . . . .E3
Selmer, 4,541 . . . . . . .D4
Sevierville, 11,757 . . . .P3
Sewanee, 2,361 . . . . .K4
Seymour, 8,850 . . . . .P3
Sharon, 988 . . . . .D2
Shawanee, 2,865 . . . .P1
Shelbyville, 16,105 . . . .J4
Sherwood, 150 . . . . . .K4
Shiloh, 175 . . . . .E4
Signal Mountain,
7,429 . . . . .L4
Silerton, 60 . . . . .D4
Silver Point K2
Slayden, 185 . . . . .G2
Smithville, 3,994 . . . . .K3
Smyrna, 25,569 . . . . .H3
Sneedville, 1,257 . . . . .Q1
Soddy-Daisy, 11,530 . .L4

Solway, 1,200 . . . . . . .N3
Somerville, 2,519 . . . .C4
South Carthage, 1,302 K2
South Cleveland,
6,216 . . . . .M4
South Fulton, 2,517 . . .C2
South Pittsburg, 3,295 .K4
Sparta, 4,599 . . . . . . .L3
Speedwell, 125 . . . . . .P2
Spencer, 1,713 . . . . . .L3
Spring City, 2,025 . . . .M3
Spring Hill, 7,715 . . . .H3
Springfield, 14,329 . . .H1
Spurgeon S2
Stanton, 615 . . . . . . .C4
Stantonville, 312 . . . . .E4
Statesville, 185 . . . . . .J2
Summertown, 800 . . . .G4
Summitville, 400 . . . . .K3
Sunbright, 577 . . . . . .M2
Surgoinsville, 1,800 . . .Q2
Sweetwater, 5,586 . . . .N3
Taft, 150 . . . . .H4
Talbott, 1,400 . . . . . . .Q2
Tallassee P3
Tazewell, 2,165 . . . . . .P2
Tellico Plains, 859 . . . .N4
Ten Mile, 40 . . . . .M3
Tennessee City, 175 . . .F2
Tennessee Ridge,
1,334 . . . . .F2
Thompsons Station,
1,283 . . . . .H3
Thornton
(see Farragut) N3
Three Points
(see Mascot) P2
Tiptonville, 2,439 . . . . .C2
Toone, 330 . . . . .D4
Townsend, 244 . . . . . .P3
Tracy City, 1,679 . . . . .K4
Trenton, 4,683 . . . . . .D3
Trezevant, 901 . . . . . .D2
Trimble, 728 . . . . .C2
Troy, 1,273 . . . . .C2
Tullahoma, 17,994 . . . .J4
Tusculum, 2,000 . . . . .R2
Unicoi, 3,519 . . . . .S2
Union City, 10,876 . . . .C2
Vanleer, 310 . . . . .G2
Victoria, 175 . . . . .K4
Viola, 129 . . . . .K3
Vonore, 1,162 . . . . . . .N3

Walden, 1,960 . . . . . . .L4
Walnut Hill, 2,756 . . . .S1
Walterhill, 1,523 . . . . . .J3
Wartburg, 890 . . . . . .M2
Wartrace, 548 . . . . .J3
Washburn, 125 . . . . . .P2
Watauga, 403 . . . . . . .S2
Watertown, 1,358 . . . . .J2
Waverly, 4,028 . . . . . . .F2
Waynesboro, 2,228 . . .F4
Westel, 375 . . . . .M3
Westmoreland, 2,093 . . .J1
Westover, 900 . . . . . . .D3
Westpoint, 250 . . . . . .F4
West Shiloh, 125 . . . . .E4
White Bluff, 2,142 . . . .G2
White House, 7,220 . . .H2
White Pine, 1,997 . . . .Q2
Whiteville, 3,148 . . . . .C4
Whitwell, 1,660 . . . . . .K4
Wilder L2
Wildersville, 225 . . . . .E3
Willette, 100 . . . . .K2
Williston, 341 . . . . . . .C4
Winchester, 7,329 . . . .J4
Winfield, 911 . . . . .N1
Witt, 500 . . . . .Q2
Woodbury, 2,428 . . . . .J3
Woodland Mills, 296 . .C2
Wrigley, 475 . . . . .G3
Wynnburg, 175 . . . . . .C2
Yorkville, 293 . . . . . . .C2

Other Features

Andrew Johnson
Natl. Hist. Site R2
Appalachian,
mountains N4
Appalachian N.S.T. . . .Q3
Arnold Engineering
Development Center .J4
Barkley, lake F1
Barren River, lake J1
Big Lake N.W.R. A3
Big South Fork Natl. River
and Rec. Area M1
Center Hill, lake K3
Chattahoochee Natl.
For. M5
Chatuge, lake P5
Cherokee, lake Q2
Cherokee Ind. Res. . . .Q4

Cherokee Natl. For.
. . . . .N4, R2
Chickamauga, lake . . .M3
Chickamauga and
Chattanooga Natl. Mil.
Park L5
Chickasaw N.W.R. B3
Chickasaw S.P. D4
Clinch, river Q2
Clingmans Dome,
peak Q3
Cross Creeks N.W.R. . .F2
Cumberland, lake L1
Cumberland, river G2
Cumberland Gap
Natl. Hist. Park P1
Dale Hollow, lake L1
Daniel Boone
Natl. For. N1
Douglas, lake Q3
Duck, river H3
Fall Creek Falls S.P. . . .L3
Fontana, lake P4
Fort Campbell
Mil. Res. F1
Fort Donelson
Natl. Bfld. F1
Frozen Head
St. Nat. Area N2
Great Smoky,
mountains P3
Great Smoky Mountains
Natl. Park P3
Hatchie N.W.R. C3
Hiwassee, lake N4
Holly Springs Natl. For. C5
Holston, river R2
Jefferson Natl. For. . . .R1
Kentucky, lake F2
Lake Isom N.W.R. C2
Land Between The Lakes
Rec. Area E1
Lower Hatchie N.W.R. . .B3
Meeman Shelby
Forest S.P. A4
Milan Army Ammunition
Plant D3
Mississippi, river B3
Mount Rogers Natl.
Rec. Area T1
Nantahala Natl. For. . . .P4
Natchez Trace S.P.
and For. E3

Norris, lake P2
Pisgah Natl. For. . .R4, T2
Prentice Cooper
St. For. L4
Roan, mountain S2
Rogers, mountain T1
Russell Cave Natl. Mon.K5
Savage Gulf St.
Nat. Area K4
Shiloh Natl. Mil. Park . .E4
Stones River Natl. Bfld. .J3
Sumter Natl. For. Q5
Tennessee, river . . .E5, K5
Tennessee N.W.R. .E2, F3
Watts Bar, lake M3
Wheeler, lake G5
Wilson, lake F5
Woodall, mountain E5
Woods, reservoir J4

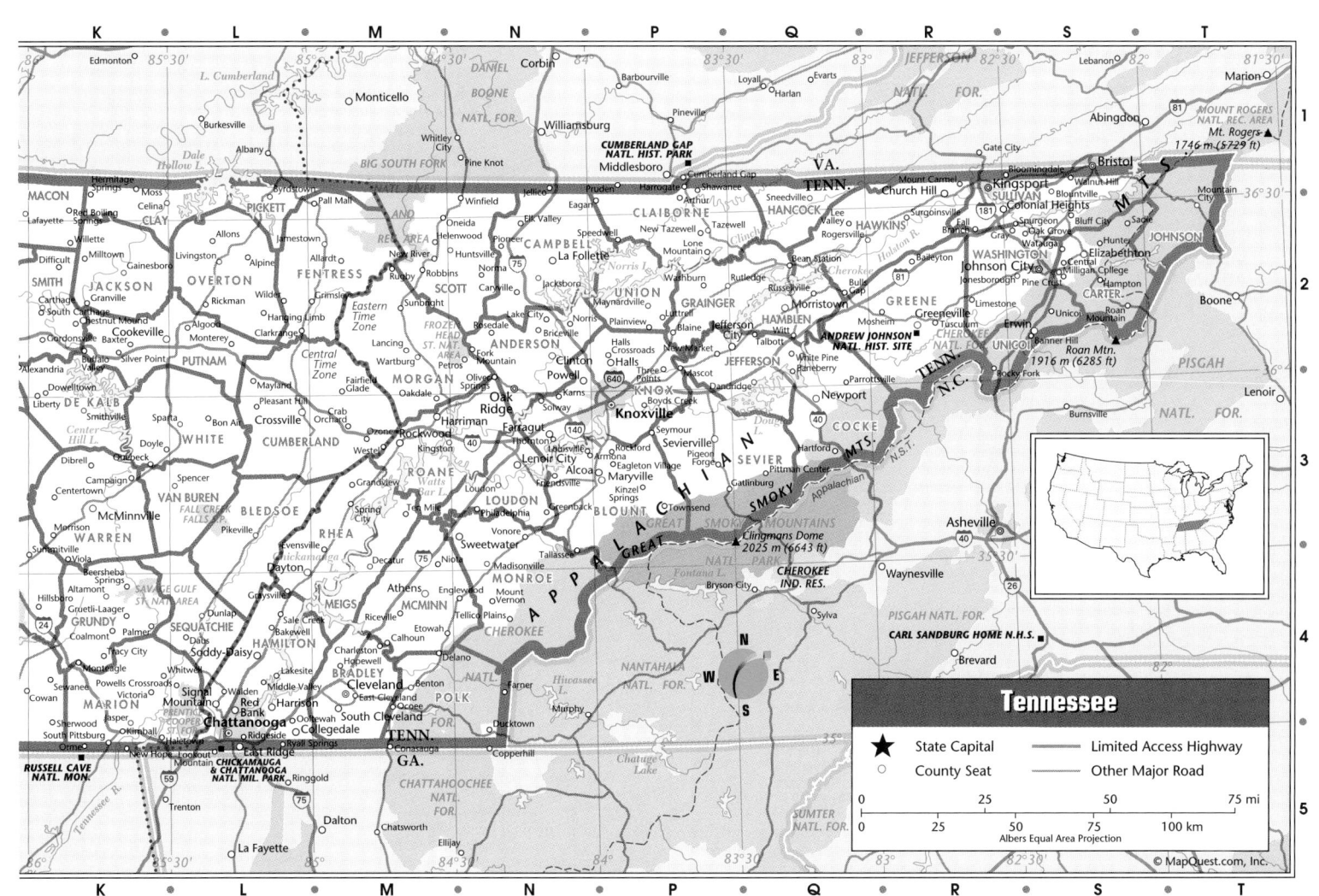

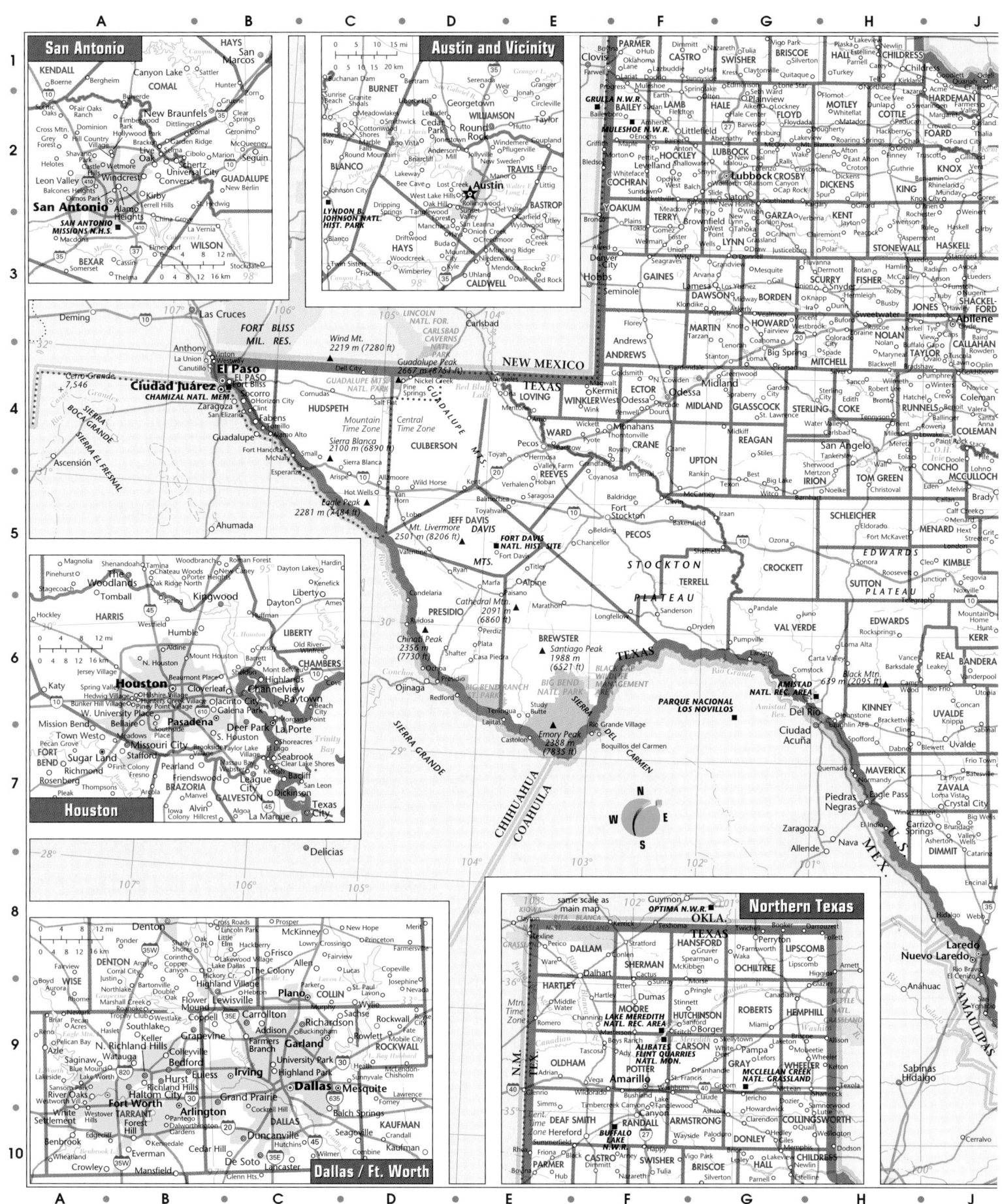

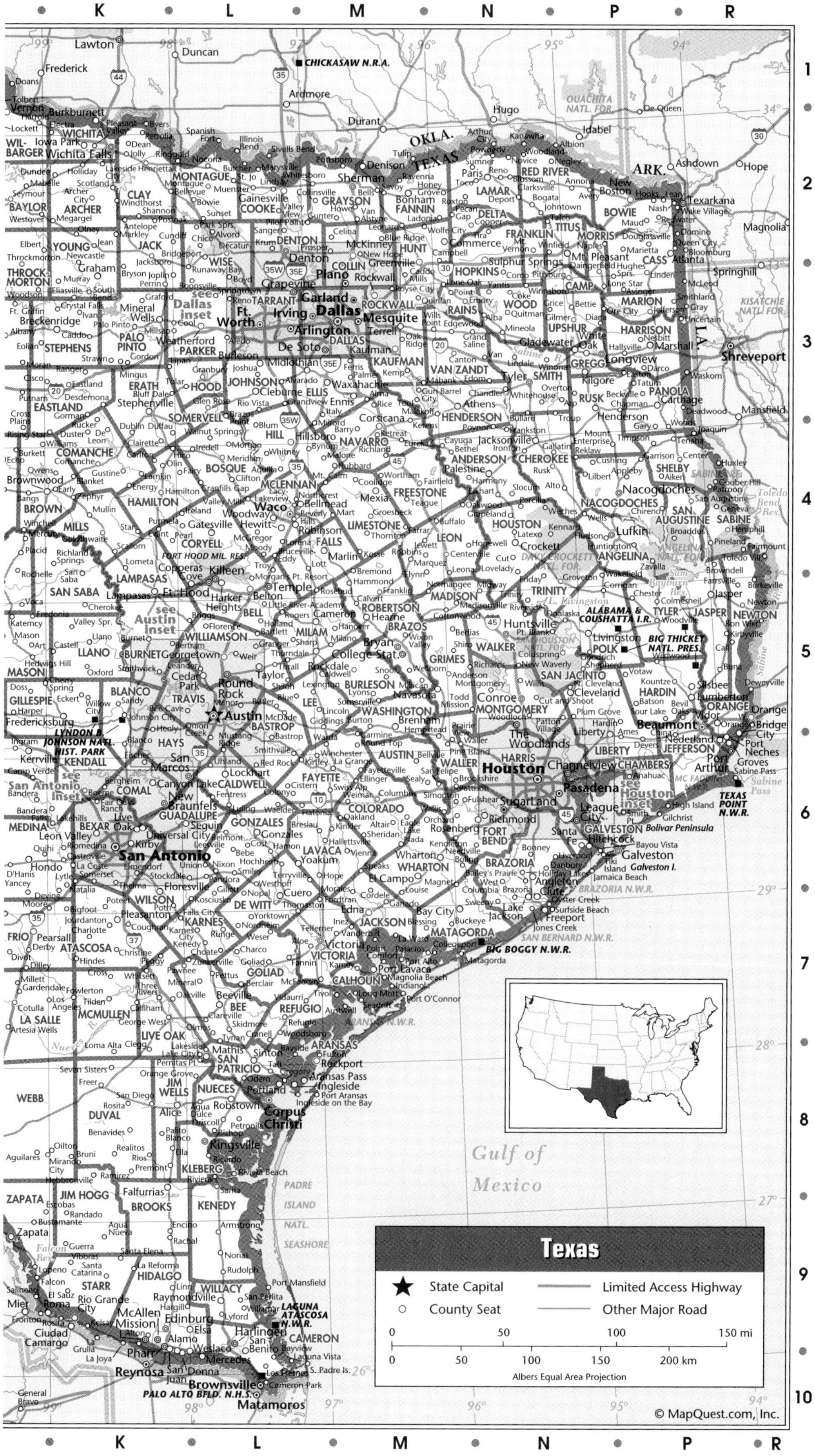

Texas

Capital:	Austin
Land Area:	261,914 sq. mi.
	678,358 sq. km.
Population:	20,851,820 (2000 Census)
Largest City:	Houston, 1,953,631
Highest Point:	Guadalupe Peak,
	8,749 ft.
	2,667 m.
Admitted to Union:	December 29, 1845
Nickname:	Lone Star State
State Flower:	Bluebonnet
State Bird:	Mockingbird

Texas:
Map Index

Counties

Anderson, 55,109 . . . . . . .N4
Andrews, 13,004 . . . . .F3
Angelina, 80,130 . . . . . . .P4
Aransas, 22,497 . . . . .L7
Archer, 8,854 . . . . .K2
Armstrong, 2,148 . . . . . . .F9
Atascosa, 38,628 . . . . . . .K7
Austin, 23,590 . . . . .M6
Bailey, 6,594 . . . . .F1
Bandera, 17,645 . . . . .J6
Bastrop, 57,733 . . . . .E2, L5
Baylor, 4,093 . . . . .J2
Bee, 32,359 . . . . .L7
Bell, 237,974 . . . . .L5
Bexar, 1,392,931 . . . . .A3, K6
Blanco, 8,418 . . . . . . .C2, K5
Borden, 729 . . . . .G3
Bosque, 17,204 . . . . .L4
Bowie, 89,306 . . . . .P2
Brazoria, 241,767 . . . .B7, N6
Brazos, 152,415 . . . . .M5
Brewster, 8,866 . . . . .E6
Briscoe, 1,790 . . . . .G1
Brooks, 7,976 . . . . .K8
Brown, 37,674 . . . . .J4
Burleson, 16,470 . . . . . . .M5
Burnet, 34,147 . . . . . .C1, K5
Caldwell, 32,194 . . . .D3, L6
Calhoun, 20,647 . . . . . . .M7
Callahan, 12,905 . . . . .J3
Cameron, 335,227 . . . . . .L9
Camp, 11,549 . . . . .P3
Carson, 6,516 . . . . .F9
Cass, 30,438 . . . . .P2
Castro, 8,285 . . . . .F1
Chambers, 26,031 . . . .C6, P6
Cherokee, 46,659 . . . . . . .N4
Childress, 7,688 . . . . .G1, H1
Clay, 11,006 . . . . .K2
Cochran, 3,730 . . . . .F2
Coke, 3,864 . . . . .H4
Coleman, 9,235 . . . . .J4
Collin, 491,675 . . . . . .C8, M2
Collingsworth, 3,206 . . . . .G9
Colorado, 20,390 . . . . . . .M6
Comal, 78,021 . . . . . .A1, K6
Comanche, 14,026 . . . . . .K4
Concho, 3,966 . . . . .J4
Cooke, 36,363 . . . . .L2
Coryell, 74,978 . . . . .L4
Cottle, 1,904 . . . . .H1
Crane, 3,996 . . . . .F4
Crockett, 4,099 . . . . .G5
Crosby, 7,072 . . . . .G2
Culberson, 2,975 . . . . . . .D4
Dallam, 6,222 . . . . .E9
Dallas, 2,218,899 . . . .C9, M3
Dawson, 14,985 . . . . .F3
Deaf Smith, 18,561 . . . . . .E9
Delta, 5,327 . . . . .N2
Denton, 432,976 . . . . .A8, L2
De Witt, 20,013 . . . . .L6
Dickens, 2,762 . . . . .H2
Dimmit, 10,248 . . . . .J7
Donley, 3,828 . . . . .G9
Duval, 13,120 . . . . .K8
Eastland, 18,297 . . . . .K3
Ector, 121,123 . . . . .F4
Edwards, 2,162 . . . . .H5
Ellis, 111,360 . . . . .M3
El Paso, 679,622 . . . . .B4
Erath, 33,001 . . . . .K3
Falls, 18,576 . . . . .M4
Fannin, 31,242 . . . . .M2
Fayette, 21,804 . . . . .L6
Fisher, 4,344 . . . . .H3
Floyd, 7,771 . . . . .G1
Foard, 1,622 . . . . .J1
Fort Bend, 354,452 . . . .A7, N6
Franklin, 9,458 . . . . .N2
Freestone, 17,867 . . . . . . .M4
Frio, 16,252 . . . . .J7
Gaines, 14,467 . . . . .F3
Galveston, 250,158 . . .B7, N6
Garza, 4,872 . . . . .G2
Gillespie, 20,814 . . . . .J5
Glasscock, 1,406 . . . . .G4
Goliad, 6,928 . . . . .L7
Gonzales, 18,628 . . . . .L6
Gray, 22,744 . . . . .G9
Grayson, 110,595 . . . . . . .M2
Gregg, 111,379 . . . . .P3
Grimes, 23,552 . . . . .M5
Guadalupe, 89,023 . . .B2, K6
Hale, 36,602 . . . . .G1
Hall, 3,782 . . . . .G1, H1
Hamilton, 8,229 . . . . .K4
Hansford, 5,369 . . . . .F8
Hardeman, 4,724 . . . . .J1
Hardin, 48,073 . . . . .P5
Harris, 3,400,578 . . . .A6, N6
Harrison, 62,110 . . . . .P3
Hartley, 5,537 . . . . .E8
Haskell, 6,093 . . . . .J2
Hays, 97,589 . . . . . .B1, D3, K5
Hemphill, 3,351 . . . . .G8
Henderson, 73,277 . . . . . .N3
Hidalgo, 569,463 . . . . . . .K9
Hill, 32,321 . . . . .L3
Hockley, 22,716 . . . . .F2
Hood, 41,100 . . . . .L3

Hopkins, 31,960 . . . . .N2
Houston, 23,185 . . . . .N4
Howard, 33,627 . . . . .G3
Hudspeth, 3,344 . . . . .C4
Hunt, 76,596 . . . . .M2
Hutchinson, 23,857 . . . . . .F9
Irion, 1,771 . . . . .G4
Jack, 8,763 . . . . .K2
Jackson, 14,391 . . . . .M7
Jasper, 35,604 . . . . .P5
Jeff Davis, 2,207 . . . . .D5
Jefferson, 252,051 . . . . . .P6
Jim Hogg, 5,281 . . . . .K8
Jim Wells, 39,326 . . . . . . .K8
Johnson, 126,811 . . . . . . .L3
Jones, 20,785 . . . . .H3
Karnes, 15,446 . . . . .L7
Kaufman, 71,313 . . . .D9, M3
Kendall, 23,743 . . . . .A1, K6
Kenedy, 414 . . . . .L8
Kent, 859 . . . . .H2
Kerr, 43,653 . . . . .J6
Kimble, 4,468 . . . . .J5
King, 356 . . . . .H2
Kinney, 3,379 . . . . .H6
Kleberg, 31,549 . . . . .L8
Knox, 4,253 . . . . .J2
Lamar, 48,499 . . . . .N2
Lamb, 14,709 . . . . .F1
Lampasas, 17,762 . . . . . . .K4
La Salle, 5,866 . . . . .J7
Lavaca, 19,210 . . . . .L6
Lee, 15,657 . . . . .L5
Leon, 15,335 . . . . .M4
Liberty, 70,154 . . . . . .C6, P6
Limestone, 22,051 . . . . . .M4
Lipscomb, 3,057 . . . . .G8
Live Oak, 12,309 . . . . .K7
Llano, 17,044 . . . . .K5
Loving, 67 . . . . .E4
Lubbock, 242,628 . . . . . . .G2
Lynn, 6,550 . . . . .G2
Madison, 12,940 . . . . .M5
Marion, 10,941 . . . . .P3
Martin, 4,746 . . . . .F3
Mason, 3,738 . . . . .J5
Matagorda, 37,957 . . . . . .M7
Maverick, 47,297 . . . . .H7
McCulloch, 8,205 . . . . .J4
McLennan, 213,517 . . . . . .L4
McMullen, 851 . . . . .K7
Medina, 39,304 . . . . .J6
Menard, 2,360 . . . . .J5
Midland, 116,009 . . . . . . .F4
Milam, 24,238 . . . . .L5
Mills, 5,151 . . . . .K4
Mitchell, 9,698 . . . . .H3
Montague, 19,117 . . . . . . .L2
Montgomery, 293,768 . . . .N5
Moore, 20,121 . . . . .F8
Morris, 13,048 . . . . .P2
Motley, 1,426 . . . . .H1
Nacogdoches, 59,203 . . . .P4
Navarro, 45,124 . . . . .M4
Newton, 15,072 . . . . .R5
Nolan, 15,802 . . . . .H3
Nueces, 313,645 . . . . .L8
Ochiltree, 9,006 . . . . .G8
Oldham, 2,185 . . . . .E9
Orange, 84,966 . . . . .P6
Palo Pinto, 27,026 . . . . . . .K3
Panola, 22,756 . . . . .P3
Parker, 88,495 . . . . .L3
Parmer, 10,016 . . . . . .E1, F1
Pecos, 16,809 . . . . .F5
Polk, 41,133 . . . . .P5
Potter, 113,546 . . . . .F9
Presidio, 7,304 . . . . .D5
Rains, 9,139 . . . . .N3
Randall, 104,312 . . . . .F9
Reagan, 3,326 . . . . .G4
Real, 3,047 . . . . .J6
Red River, 14,314 . . . . . . .N2
Reeves, 13,137 . . . . .E4
Refugio, 7,828 . . . . .L7
Roberts, 887 . . . . .G8
Robertson, 16,000 . . . . . . .M5
Rockwall, 43,080 . . . .D9, M3
Runnels, 11,495 . . . . .J4
Rusk, 47,372 . . . . .P3
Sabine, 10,469 . . . . .R4
San Augustine, 8,946 . . . .P4
San Jacinto, 22,246 . . . . . .N5
San Patricio, 67,138 . . . . .L7
San Saba, 6,186 . . . . .K4
Schleicher, 2,935 . . . . .H5
Scurry, 16,361 . . . . .H3
Shackelford, 3,302 . . . . . .J3
Shelby, 25,224 . . . . .P4
Sherman, 3,186 . . . . .F8
Smith, 174,706 . . . . .N3
Somervell, 6,809 . . . . .L3
Starr, 53,597 . . . . .K9
Stephens, 9,674 . . . . .K3
Sterling, 1,393 . . . . .G4
Stonewall, 1,693 . . . . .H2
Sutton, 4,077 . . . . .H5
Swisher, 8,378 . . . . . .F1, G1
Tarrant, 1,446,219 . . . .B1, L3
Taylor, 126,555 . . . . .H3
Terrell, 1,081 . . . . .F5
Terry, 12,761 . . . . .F2
Throckmorton, 1,850 . . . . .J2
Titus, 28,118 . . . . . . .F1, G1
Tom Green, 104,010 . . . . .H4
Travis, 812,280 . . . . . .E2, K5

Texas

★ State Capital   Limited Access Highway
○ County Seat   Other Major Road

0   50   100   150 mi
0   50   100   150   200 km

Albers Equal Area Projection

Trinity, 13,779 . . . . .N5
Tyler, 20,871 . . . . .P5
Upshur, 35,291 . . . . .N3
Upton, 3,404 . . . . .F4
Uvalde, 25,926 . . . . .J6
Val Verde, 44,856 . . . . .G5
Van Zandt, 48,140 . . . . . . .N3
Victoria, 84,088 . . . . .L7
Walker, 61,758 . . . . .N5
Waller, 32,663 . . . . .M6
Ward, 10,909 . . . . .E4
Washington, 30,373 . . . . . . .M5
Webb, 193,117 . . . . .J8
Wharton, 41,188 . . . . .M6
Wheeler, 5,284 . . . . .C9
Wichita, 131,664 . . . . .K2
Wilbarger, 14,676 . . . . .J2
Willacy, 20,082 . . . . .L9
Williamson, 249,967 . .D2, L5
Wilson, 32,408 . . . . . . .B3, K6
Winkler, 7,173 . . . . .E4
Wise, 48,793 . . . . .A9, L2
Wood, 36,752 . . . . .N3
Yoakum, 7,322 . . . . .F2
Young, 17,943 . . . . .K3
Zapata, 12,182 . . . . .J8
Zavala, 11,600 . . . . .J7

Cities and Towns

Abernathy, 2,839 . . . . .G2
Abilene, 115,930 . . . . .J3
Ackerly, 245 . . . . .G3
Acme J1
Addison, 14,166 . . . . .C9
Adrian, 159 . . . . .F8
Ady .E8
Afton, 60 . . . . .H2
Agua Dulce, 737 . . . . .L8
Agua Nueva, 20 . . . . .K9
Aguilares J8
Aiken (Floyd Co.), 40 . . . . .G1
Aiken (Shelby Co.), 80 . . . .P4
Alamo, 14,760 . . . . .K9
Alamo Alto, 70 . . . . .B4
Alamo Heights, 7,319 . . . . .A2
Alba, 430 . . . . .N3
Albany, 1,921 . . . . .J3
Albion, 80 . . . . .P2
Aldine, 13,979 . . . . .B6
Aledo, 1,726 . . . . .L3
Algoa, 90 . . . . .B7
Alice, 19,010 . . . . .K8
Allamoore D4
Allen, 43,554 . . . . .C8
Allison, 150 . . . . .H9
Allred, 70 . . . . .F3
Alma, 302 . . . . .M3
Aloe, 850 . . . . .L7
Alpine, 5,786 . . . . .E5
Altair, 125 . . . . .M6
Alto, 1,190 . . . . .N4
Alton, 4,384 . . . . .K9
Alvarado, 3,288 . . . . .L3
Alvin, 21,413 . . . . .B7
Alvord, 1,007 . . . . .L2
Amarillo, 173,627 . . . . .F9
Ames, 1,079 . . . . .C5, P5
Amherst, 791 . . . . .F2
Anahuac, 2,210 . . . . .P6
Anderson, 257 . . . . .N5
Anderson Mill D2
Andrews, 9,652 . . . . .F3
Angeles E4
Angleton, 18,130 . . . . .N6
Annona, 282 . . . . .J3
Anson, 2,556 . . . . .J3
Antelope, 50 . . . . .K2
Anton, 1,200 . . . . .F2
Appleby, 444 . . . . .P4
Aquilla, 136 . . . . .L4
Aransas Pass, 8,138 . . . . . . .L8
Arcade E4
Archer City, 1,848 . . . . .K2
Arcola, 1,048 . . . . .B7
Argyle, 2,365 . . . . .B8
Arispe, 100 . . . . .C4
Arlington, 332,969 . . . .B9, L3
Armstrong L9
Arney F10
Arno E4
Arp, 901 . . . . .N3
Artesia Wells, 50 . . . . .J7
Arthur City, 125 . . . . .N2
Arvana G3
Asherton, 1,342 . . . . .J7
Ashtola G9
Aspermont, 1,021 . . . . .H2
Athens, 11,297 . . . . .N3
Atlanta, 5,745 . . . . .P2
Aurora, 853 . . . . .A9
Austin, 656,562 . . . . . .D2, L5
Austwell, 192 . . . . .M7
Avery, 462 . . . . .P2
Avinger, 464 . . . . .P3
Avoca, 125 . . . . .J3
Azle, 9,600 . . . . .A9
Bacliff, 6,962 . . . . .C7
Baileyboro F1
Bailey's Prairie, 694 . . . . . .N6
Bainer F2
Baird, 1,623 . . . . .J4
Bakersfield F5
Balch, 50 . . . . .F2
Balch Springs, 19,375 . . . . .C9
Balcones Heights, 3,016 . . .A2
Baldridge F4
Ballinger, 4,243 . . . . .J4
Balmorhea, 527 . . . . .E4
Bandera, 957 . . . . .J6
Bandera Falls, 225 . . . . .K6
Bangs, 1,620 . . . . .J4
Barksdale H6
Barnhart, 100 . . . . .G4
Barrett, 2,872 . . . . .B6
Barry, 209 . . . . .M3
Bartlett, 1,675 . . . . .L5
Bartonville, 1,093 . . . . .B8
Barwise, 40 . . . . .G2
Bastrop, 5,340 . . . . .L5
Batesville, 1,298 . . . . .J7
Batson, 150 . . . . .P5
Bay City, 18,667 . . . . .N7
Bayou Vista, 1,644 . . . . .P6
Bayside, 360 . . . . .L7

Baytown, 66,430 . . . . .C6
Bayview, 323 . . . . .L9
Beach City, 1,645 . . . . .C6
Beaumont, 113,866 . . . . . . .P5
Bebe L6
Beckville, 752 . . . . .P3
Bedford, 47,152 . . . . .B9
Bedias, 350 . . . . .N5
Bee Cave, 656 . . . . . . .D2, K5
Beeville, 13,129 . . . . .L7
Belding, 350 . . . . .E5
Bellaire, 15,642 . . . . .A6
Bellevue, 386 . . . . .L2
Bellmead, 9,214 . . . . .L4
Bells, 1,190 . . . . .M2
Bellville, 3,794 . . . . .M6
Belmont, 20 . . . . .L6
Belton, 14,623 . . . . .L4
Benavides, 1,686 . . . . .K8
Benbrook, 20,208 . . . . . . .A10
Benjamin, 264 . . . . .J2
Benoit E8
Berclair, 150 . . . . .L7
Bergheim, 80 . . . . .A1, K6
Bertram, 1,122 . . . . . . .D1, K5
Best .G4
Bethel, 90 . . . . .N4
Bettie, 150 . . . . .P3
Beverly Hills, 2,113 . . . . . . .L4
Bevil Oaks, 1,346 . . . . .P5
Bigfoot, 304 . . . . .K6
Big Lake, 2,885 . . . . .G4
Big Spring, 25,233 . . . . .G3
Big Wells, 704 . . . . .J7
Bishop, 3,305 . . . . .L8
Black E10
Blackwell, 360 . . . . .H3
Blanco, 1,505 . . . . . . .C3, K5
Blanket, 402 . . . . .K4
Bledsoe, 175 . . . . .E2
Blessing, 861 . . . . .M7
Blewett H6
Bloomburg, 375 . . . . .P2
Blossom, 1,439 . . . . .N2
Blue, 90 . . . . .L5
Blue Mound, 2,388 . . . . . . .A9
Blue Ridge, 672 . . . . .M2
Bluff Dale, 80 . . . . .K3
Blum, 399 . . . . .L3
Boerne, 6,178 . . . . .A1, K6
Bogata, 1,396 . . . . .N2
Boling (Boling-Iago), 1,271 . .N6
Bonham, 9,990 . . . . .M2
Bonney, 384 . . . . .N6
Bon Wier, 800 . . . . .R5
Booker, 1,315 . . . . .G8
Boonsville, 40 . . . . .L2
Borger, 14,302 . . . . .G9
Bovina, 1,874 . . . . . . .E10, F1
Bowie, 5,219 . . . . .L2
Boyd, 1,099 . . . . .A9, L2
Boys Ranch, 600 . . . . .F8
Bracken, 150 . . . . .A2
Brackettville, 1,876 . . . . . . .H6
Bradshaw J3
Brady, 5,523 . . . . .J4
Brazoria, 2,787 . . . . .N6
Brazos Point, 60 . . . . .L3
Breckenridge, 5,868 . . . . . .K3
Bremond, 876 . . . . .M4
Brenham, 13,507 . . . . .M5
Breslau, 60 . . . . .M6
Briar, 5,350 . . . . .A9
Briarcliff, 895 . . . . .D2
Brice G1
Bridge City, 8,651 . . . . .R5
Bridgeport, 4,309 . . . . .L2
Briggs, 50 . . . . .L5
Briscoe G9
Broaddus, 389 . . . . .P4
Bronco E2
Bronson, 528 . . . . .Q4
Bronte, 1,076 . . . . .H4
Brookshire, 3,450 . . . . .N6
Brookside Village, 1,960 . . .B7
Browndell, 219 . . . . .R4
Brownfield, 9,488 . . . . .F2
Brownsboro, 796 . . . . .N3
Brownsville, 139,722 . . . . .L10
Brownwood, 18,813 . . . . . .K4
Bruceville-Eddy, 1,490 . . . . .L4
Brundage, 31 . . . . .J7
Bruni, 412 . . . . .K8
Bryan, 65,660 . . . . .M5
Bryson, 528 . . . . .K2
Buchanan Dam, 1,688 . . . . . .C1
Buckingham C9
Buckner M7
Buda, 2,404 . . . . .D3
Buffalo, 1,804 . . . . .M4
Buffalo Gap, 463 . . . . .J3
Buford L2
Bulcher L2
Bullard, 1,150 . . . . .N3
Bulverde, 3,761 . . . . .A2
Buna, 2,269 . . . . .R5
Bunker Hill Village, 3,654 . . .A6
Burkburnett, 10,927 . . . . . . .K1
Burkett J4
Burkeville, 500 . . . . .R5
Burleson, 20,976 . . . . .L3
Burnet, 4,735 . . . . .K5
Burton, 359 . . . . .M5
Busby H3
Bushland, 125 . . . . .F9
Bustamante J9
Butler, 300 . . . . .L5
Byers, 517 . . . . .K1
Bynum, 225 . . . . .M4
Cactus, 2,538 . . . . .F8
Caddo K3
Caddo Mills, 1,149 . . . . . . .M2
Caldwell, 3,449 . . . . .M5
Calf Creek J5
Call, 125 . . . . .R5
Callan J4
Calliham, 80 . . . . .K7
Calvert, 1,426 . . . . .M5
Camargo Park, 5,961 . . . . .L10
Campbell, 734 . . . . .N2
Camp Verde J6
Camp Wood, 822 . . . . .H6
Canadian, 2,233 . . . . .H9
Candelaria, 150 . . . . .D5
Canton, 3,292 . . . . .N3
Canutillo, 5,129 . . . . .B4
Canyon, 12,875 . . . . .F9

Canyon Lake, 16,870 . .A1, K6
Cap Rock G2
Caps, 100 . . . . .J3
Carey H1
Carlsbad, 250 . . . . .H4
Carlton, 90 . . . . .K4
Carmine, 228 . . . . .M5
Carrizo Springs, 5,655 . . . . .J7
Carrollton, 109,576 . . . . . . .C9
Carta Valley H6
Carthage, 6,664 . . . . .P3
Casa Piedra D6
Cassin, 475 . . . . .A3
Castell K5
Castle Hills, 4,202 . . . . .A2
Castolon E6
Castroville, 2,664 . . . . .K6
Catarina, 135 . . . . .J7
Cayuga, 50 . . . . .N4
Cedar Creek, 70 . . . . .L5
Cedar Hill, 32,093 . . . . . . .C10
Cedar Park, 26,049 . . . .D2, L5
Cee Vee H1
Celina, 1,861 . . . . .M2
Center, 5,678 . . . . .P4
Centerville, 903 . . . . .N4
Chalk H2
Chancellor, 175 . . . . .E5
Chandler, 2,099 . . . . .N3
Channelview, 29,685 . .B6, N6
Channing, 356 . . . . .F9
Chapman, 100 . . . . .P3
Charco, 40 . . . . .L7
Charlotte, 1,637 . . . . .K7
Chateau Woods A5
Cherokee K5
Cherry Spring, 40 . . . . .K5
Chester, 265 . . . . .P5
Chico, 947 . . . . .L2
Childress, 6,778 . . . . .H1
Chillicothe, 798 . . . . .J1
China, 1,112 . . . . .P5
China Grove, 1,247 . . . . . . .A2
Chireno, 405 . . . . .P4
Choate, 100 . . . . .L7
Christine, 436 . . . . .K7
Christoval, 422 . . . . .H4
Cibolo, 3,035 . . . . .B2
Circleville, 40 . . . . .E1
Cisco, 3,851 . . . . .J3
Cistern L6
Clairemont H2
Clairette, 50 . . . . .K3
Clarendon, 1,974 . . . . .G9
Clareville L7
Clarksville, 3,883 . . . . .N2
Claude, 1,313 . . . . .G9
Claytonville, 40 . . . . .G1
Clear Lake Shores, 1,205 . . .C7
Clear Springs, 300 . . . . .B2
Cleburne, 26,005 . . . . .L3
Clegg K7
Cleo, 50 . . . . .J5
Cleveland, 7,605 . . . . .N5
Clifton, 3,542 . . . . .L4
Cline H6
Clint, 980 . . . . .B4
Cloverleaf, 23,508 . . . . .B6
Clute, 10,424 . . . . .N6
Clyde, 3,345 . . . . .J3
Coahoma, 932 . . . . .G3
Cockrell Hill, 4,443 . . . . . . .C9
Coke, 70 . . . . .N3
Coldspring, 691 . . . . .N5
Coleman, 5,127 . . . . .J4
Collegeport, 325 . . . . .M7
College Station, 67,890 . . . .M5
Colleyville, 19,636 . . . . .B9
Collinsville, 1,235 . . . . .M2
Colmesneil, 638 . . . . .P5
Colony L6
Colorado City, 4,281 . . . . . .H3
Columbus, 3,916 . . . . .M6
Comal, 100 . . . . .A2
Comanche, 4,482 . . . . .K4
Combine, 1,788 . . . . .D10
Commerce, 7,669 . . . . .N2
Como, 621 . . . . .N2
Comstock, 250 . . . . .G6
Concan, 100 . . . . .J6
Cone, 70 . . . . .G2
Conlen F8
Conroe, 36,811 . . . . .N5
Converse, 11,508 . . . . .A2
Cool, 162 . . . . .L3
Coolidge, 848 . . . . .M4
Cooper, 2,150 . . . . .N2
Copeville, 848 . . . . .D8
Coppell, 35,958 . . . . .B9
Copperas Cove, 29,592 . . . .L4
Copper Canyon, 1,216 . . . . .B8
Cordele M6
Corinth, 11,325 . . . . .B8
Cornudas C4
Corpus Christi, 277,454 . . . .L8
Corral City, 89 . . . . .B8
Corrigan, 1,721 . . . . .P5
Corsicana, 24,485 . . . . .M3
Cost, 100 . . . . .L6
Cottonwood M5
Cottonwood Shores, 877 . . .C2
Cotulla, 3,614 . . . . .J7
Coughran K7
Coupland, 200 . . . . .L5
Cove, 323 . . . . .C6
Coyanosa, 138 . . . . .F4
Crandall, 2,774 . . . . .D10
Crane, 3,191 . . . . .F4
Cranell, 175 . . . . .L7
Cranfills Gap, 335 . . . . .L4
Creedmoor, 211 . . . . .D2
Crews J4
Crockett, 7,141 . . . . .N4
Crosby, 1,714 . . . . .B6
Crosbyton, 1,874 . . . . .G2
Cross J4
Cross Mountain, 1,524 . . . . .A2
Cross Plains, 1,068 . . . . .J3
Cross Roads, 603 . . . . .B8
Croton H2
Crowell, 1,141 . . . . .J2
Crowley, 7,467 . . . . .A10
Crystal City, 7,190 . . . . .J7
Crystal Falls K3
Cuero, 6,571 . . . . .L6
Cundiff, 70 . . . . .K2
Cushing, 637 . . . . .P4

Fentress, 250 . . . . .L6
Ferris, 2,175 . . . . .M3
Fieldton F1
Fife J4
Finney H2
First Colony A7
Fischer, 40 . . . . .C3, K6
Flatonia, 1,377 . . . . .L6
Florence, 1,054 . . . . .L5
Floresville, 5,868 . . . . .K6
Florey F3
Flower Mound, 50,702 . . . . .B9
Floydada, 3,676 . . . . .G2
Fluvanna, 80 . . . . .G3
Flynn, 40 . . . . .M4
Foard City J2
Follett, 412 . . . . .G8
Fordtran M6
Forest Hill, 12,949 . . . . . . .B10
Forney, 5,588 . . . . .D9
Forsan, 226 . . . . .G3
Fort Bliss, 8,264 . . . . .B4
Fort Davis, 1,050 . . . . .E5
Fort Griffin J3
Fort Hancock, 1,713 . . . . . .C4
Fort Hood, 33,711 . . . . .L4
Fort McKavett H5
Fort Stockton, 7,846 . . . . . . .F5
Fort Worth, 534,694 . . .A9, L3
Foster F2
Fowlerton, 62 . . . . .K7
Franklin, 1,470 . . . . .M4
Frankston, 1,209 . . . . .N3
Fredericksburg, 8,911 . . . . .K5
Fredonia, 40 . . . . .J5
Freeport, 12,708 . . . . .N7
Freer, 3,241 . . . . .K8
Fresno, 6,603 . . . . .B7
Friday, 50 . . . . .N4
Friendswood, 29,037 . . . . . .B7
Friona, 3,854 . . . . .E10
Frio Town J6
Frisco, 33,714 . . . . .C8
Fritch, 2,235 . . . . .F9
Fronton, 599 . . . . .J9
Fulshear, 716 . . . . .N6
Fulton, 1,553 . . . . .L7
Funston J3
Gail, 70 . . . . .G3
Gainesville, 15,538 . . . . . . .L2
Galena Park, 10,592 . . . . . .B6
Gallatin, 378 . . . . .N4
Galveston, 57,247 . . . . .P6
Ganado, 1,915 . . . . .M6
Garden City, 200 . . . . .G4
Gardendale (Ector Co.),
1,197 . . . . .F3
Gardendale (La Salle Co.),
250 . . . . .J7
Garden Ridge, 1,882 . . . . . .A2
Garfield, 1,660 . . . . .E2
Garland, 215,768 . . . . .C9, M3
Garrison, 844 . . . . .P4
Gary, 303 . . . . .P3
Gatesville, 15,591 . . . . .L4
Geneva, 80 . . . . .R4
Georgetown, 28,339 . . .D1, L5
George West, 2,524 . . . . . . .K7
Geronimo, 619 . . . . .B2
Giddings, 5,105 . . . . .M5
Gilchrist, 300 . . . . .P6
Giles G9
Gillett, 60 . . . . .L6
Gilliland, 70 . . . . .J2
Gilmer, 4,799 . . . . .P3
Gilpin H2
Girard, 62 . . . . .H2
Girvin, 40 . . . . .G5
Gladewater, 6,078 . . . . .P3
Glazier, 40 . . . . .G8
Glenn H3
Glenn Heights, 7,224 . . . . .C10
Glenrio E9
Glen Rose, 2,122 . . . . .L3
Goldsboro J3
Goldsmith, 253 . . . . .F4
Goldthwaite, 1,802 . . . . . . .K4
Goliad, 1,975 . . . . .L7
Gomez F2
Gonzales, 7,202 . . . . .L6
Goober Hill R4
Goodlett, 60 . . . . .J1
Goodrich, 243 . . . . .P5
Gordon (Lynn Co.) G2
Gordon (Palo Pinto Co.),
451 . . . . .K3
Goree, 321 . . . . .J2
Gorman, 1,236 . . . . .K3
Graford, 578 . . . . .K3
Graham (Garza Co.) G2
Graham (Young Co.), 8,716 . .K2
Granbury, 5,718 . . . . .L3
Grandfalls, 391 . . . . .F4
Grand Prairie, 127,427 . . . .B9
Grand Saline, 3,028 . . . . . . .N3
Grandview (Dawson Co.) . . .F3
Grandview (Johnson Co.),
1,358 . . . . .L3
Granger, 1,299 . . . . . . .E1, L5
Granite Shoals, 2,040 . . . . .C2
Grapeland, 1,451 . . . . .N4
Grapevine, 42,059 . . . .B9, L3
Grassland, 60 . . . . .G2
Gray, 40 . . . . .P3
Greenville, 23,960 . . . . .M2
Greenwood, 250 . . . . .G3
Gregory, 2,318 . . . . .L8
Grey Forest, 418 . . . . .A2
Grice, 40 . . . . .N3
Griffith, 40 . . . . .E2
Grit J5
Groesbeck, 4,291 . . . . .M4
Groom, 587 . . . . .G9
Groves, 15,733 . . . . .R6
Groveton, 1,107 . . . . .N4
Gruene, 175 . . . . .B2
Gruver, 1,162 . . . . .F8
Guadalupe, 175 . . . . .B4
Guerra, 8 . . . . .K9
Gun Barrel City, 5,145 . . . . .M3
Gunter, 1,230 . . . . .M2
Gustine, 457 . . . . .K4
Guthrie H2
Hackberry (Cottle Co.) H2
Hackberry (Denton Co.), 544 .B8

Hale Center, 2,263 . . . . .G1
Hallettsville, 2,345 . . . . .M6
Hallsville, 2,772 . . . . .P3
Haltom City, 39,018 . . . . . . .B9
Hamilton, 2,977 . . . . .K4
Hamlin, 2,248 . . . . .H3
Hammon, 40 . . . . .M4
Hamon L6
Hanover M5
Happy, 647 . . . . .F10
Hardin, 755 . . . . .C5, P5
Hargill, 900 . . . . .K9
Harker Heights, 17,308 . . . . .L4
Harlingen, 57,564 . . . . .L9
Harmony, 90 . . . . .N4
Harper, 1,006 . . . . .J5
Harrold, 125 . . . . .J1
Hart, 1,198 . . . . .F1
Hartley, 441 . . . . .F8
Haskell, 3,106 . . . . .J2
Haslet, 1,134 . . . . .A9
Hatchel J4
Hawley, 646 . . . . .J3
Hays .D2
Hearne, 4,690 . . . . .M5
Heath, 4,149 . . . . .D9
Hebbronville, 4,498 . . . . . . .K8
Hebron, 874 . . . . .C8
Hedley, 379 . . . . .G9
Hedwig Village J5
Helotes, 4,285 . . . . .A2
Hemphill, 1,106 . . . . .R4
Hempstead, 4,691 . . . . .M5
Henderson, 11,273 . . . . .P3
Henly, 60 . . . . .K5
Henrietta, 3,264 . . . . .K2
Hereford, 14,597 . . . . .F9
Hermleigh, 393 . . . . .H3
Hermosa E4
Hewitt, 11,085 . . . . .L4
Hext .J5
Hickory Creek, 2,078 . . . . . .B8
Hico, 1,341 . . . . .K4
Hidalgo, 7,322 . . . . .J8
Higgins, 425 . . . . .H8
High Island, 500 . . . . .P6
Highland Park, 8,842 . . . . . .C9
Highland Village, 12,173 . . .B8
Hill Country Village, 1,028 . .A2
Hillcrest, 722 . . . . .B7
Hillsboro, 8,232 . . . . .L3
Hilshire Village, 720 . . . . . . .A6
Hindes K7
Hitchcock, 6,386 . . . . .P6
Hoban E4
Hochheim L6
Hockley, 175 . . . . .A6
Holiday Lakes, 1,095 . . . . . .N6
Holland, 1,102 . . . . .L5
Holliday, 1,632 . . . . .K2
Hollywood Park, 2,983 . . . . .A2
Hondo, 7,897 . . . . .J6
Honey Grove, 1,746 . . . . . . .N2
Hooks, 2,973 . . . . .P2
Hope, 60 . . . . .M6
Hopewell N4
Horizon City, 5,833 . . . . . . .B4
Horseshoe Bay, 3,337 . . . . .C2
Hot Wells B4
Houston, 1,953,631 . . .B6, N6
Howardwick, 437 . . . . .G9
Howe, 2,478 . . . . .M2
Hub E10, F1
Hubbard, 1,586 . . . . .M4
Hudson, 3,792 . . . . .P4
Huffman, 475 . . . . .B6
Hughes Springs, 1,856 . . . . .P2
Humble, 14,579 . . . . .B6
Hunt, 275 . . . . .J5
Hunters Creek Village, 4,374 .A6
Huntington, 2,068 . . . . .P4
Huntsville, 35,078 . . . . .N5
Hurst, 36,273 . . . . .B9
Hutchins, 2,805 . . . . .C10
Hutto, 1,250 . . . . .E2
Huxley, 298 . . . . .R4
Idalou, 2,157 . . . . .G2
Illinois Bend, 10 . . . . .L2
Impact, 39 . . . . .J3
Imperial, 428 . . . . .F4
Indianola M7
Inez, 1,737 . . . . .L7
Ingleside, 9,388 . . . . .L8
Ingleside on the Bay, 659 . . .L8
Ingram, 1,740 . . . . .J5
Iowa Colony, 804 . . . . .B7
Iowa Park, 6,431 . . . . .K2
Ira, 90 . . . . .G3
Iraan, 1,238 . . . . .G5
Irby J2
Iredell, 360 . . . . .L4
Ireland L4
Ironton, 60 . . . . .N4
Irving, 191,615 . . . . . . .C9, M3
Italy, 1,993 . . . . .M3
Ivan .K3
Jacinto City, 10,302 . . . . . . .B6
Jacksboro, 4,533 . . . . .K2
Jacksonville, 13,868 . . . . . . .N4
Jamaica Beach, 1,075 . . . . . .P6
Jasper, 8,247 . . . . .R5
Jayton, 513 . . . . .H2
Jean, 80 . . . . .K2
Jefferson, 2,024 . . . . .P3
Jericho G9
Jersey Village, 6,880 . . . . . .A6
Jewett, 861 . . . . .M4
Joaquin, 925 . . . . .P4
Johnson City, 1,191 . . . .C2, K5
Johnstone, 50 . . . . .H6
Johntown, 125 . . . . .N2
Jolly, 188 . . . . .K2
Jollyville, 15,813 . . . . .D2
Jonah, 125 . . . . .E1
Jones Creek, 2,130 . . . . .N7
Jonestown, 1,681 . . . . .D2
Joplin K2
Josephine, 594 . . . . .D8
Joshua, 4,528 . . . . .L3
Jourdanton, 3,732 . . . . .K7
Juliff, 40 . . . . .B7
Junction, 2,618 . . . . .J5
Juno G5
Justiceburg, 40 . . . . .G2

Justin, 1,891 . . . . .A8
Kalgary G2
Kamey M7
Kanawha N2
Karnes City, 3,457 . . . . .L7
Katemcy, 40 . . . . .J5
Katy, 11,775 . . . . .N6
Kaufman, 6,490 . . . . .D10, M3
Keller, 27,345 . . . . .B9
Kelsay, 325 . . . . .K9
Kelton, 40 . . . . .H9
Kemah, 2,330 . . . . .C7
Kemp, 1,133 . . . . .M3
Kendleton, 466 . . . . .N6
Kenedy, 3,487 . . . . .L7
Kenefick, 667 . . . . .C5
Kennard, 317 . . . . .N4
Kennedale, 5,850 . . . . .B10
Kent, 40 . . . . .D4
Kerens, 1,681 . . . . .M3
Kermit, 5,714 . . . . .E4
Kerrick F8
Kerrville, 20,425 . . . . .J5
Kilgore, 11,301 . . . . .P3
Killeen, 86,911 . . . . .L4
Kingsville, 25,575 . . . . .L8
Kingwood, 37,400 . . . . .B5
Kinkler L6
Kirby, 8,673 . . . . .A2, K6
Kirbyville, 2,085 . . . . .R5
Kirkland H1
Kirtley, 50 . . . . .L6
Klondike, 60 . . . . .F3
Knapp G3
Knippa, 739 . . . . .J6
Knott, 60 . . . . .G3
Knox City, 1,219 . . . . .J2
Kosciusko, 100 . . . . .L6
Kosse, 497 . . . . .M4
Kountze, 2,115 . . . . .P5
Kress, 826 . . . . .G1
Krum, 1,979 . . . . .L2
Kyle, 5,700 . . . . .D3
La Coste, 1,255 . . . . .K6
Lacy-Lakeview, 5,764 . . . . . .L4
Ladonia, 667 . . . . .N2
Lago Vista, 4,507 . . . . .D2
La Grange, 4,478 . . . . .M6
La Grulla, 1,211 . . . . .K9
Laguna Vista, 1,658 . . . . . . .L9
Lajitas, 40 . . . . .E6
La Joya, 3,303 . . . . .K9
Lake City, 526 . . . . .L7
Lake Dallas, 6,166 . . . . .B8
Lakehills, 4,668 . . . . .K6
Lake Jackson, 26,386 . . . . . .N6
Lakeside (San Patricio Co.),
333 . . . . .L8
Lakeside (Tarrant Co.), 1,040 .A9
Lakeside City, 984 . . . . .K2
Lake Tanglewood, 825 . . . . .F9
Laketon G9
Lakeview (Floyd Co.) G2
Lakeview (Hall Co.) . . . .
152 . . . . .G10, H1
Lakeway, 8,002 . . . . .D2
Lakewood Village, 342 . . . . .B8
La Marque, 13,682 . . . . .C7
Lamesa, 9,952 . . . . .G3
Lamkin K4
Lampasas, 6,786 . . . . .L4
Lancaster, 25,894 . . . . .C10
Langtry G6
La Porte, 31,880 . . . . .C6
La Pryor, 1,491 . . . . .J7
Laredo, 176,576 . . . . .J8
Lariat, 60 . . . . .F1
Latexo, 272 . . . . .N4
La Vernia, 931 . . . . .B3
Lavon, 387 . . . . .D8
La Ward, 200 . . . . .M7
Lawn, 353 . . . . .J3
Lawrence D9
Lazare H1
Lazbuddie, 100 . . . . .F1
League City, 45,444 . . . .C7, N6
Leakey, 387 . . . . .J6
Leander, 7,596 . . . . .D2, L5
Leary, 555 . . . . .P2
Leesville, 70 . . . . .L6
Lefors, 559 . . . . .G9
Lenorah, 60 . . . . .G3
Leona, 181 . . . . .N4
Leonard, 1,846 . . . . .M2
Leon Valley, 9,239 . . . .A2, K6
Lesley G10
Levelland, 12,866 . . . . .F2
Lewisville, 77,737 . . . . .B9
Lexington, 1,178 . . . . .L5
Liberty, 8,033 . . . . .C5, P5
Liberty Hill, 1,409 . . . . .D1
Libert, 8 . . . . .P4
Lincoln, 60 . . . . .M5
Lincoln Park, 517 . . . . .B8
Lindale, 2,954 . . . . .N3
Linden, 2,256 . . . . .P3
Lindsay, 788 . . . . .L2
Linn, 958 . . . . .K9
Lipan, 430 . . . . .K3
Lipscomb, 44 . . . . .H8
Littig, 60 . . . . .E2
Little Elm, 3,646 . . . . .B8
Littlefield, 6,507 . . . . .F2
Little River-Academy, 1,645 . .L5
Live Oak, 9,156 . . . . . . .A2, K6
Liverpool, 404 . . . . .N6
Livingston, 5,433 . . . . .P5
Llano, 3,325 . . . . .K5
Lobo D5
Lockett, 100 . . . . .J1
Lockettville F2
Lockhart, 11,615 . . . . .L6
Lockney, 2,056 . . . . .G1
Lohn, 40 . . . . .J4
Loma Alta (McMullen Co.) . .K7
Loma Alta (Val Verde Co.) . .H6
Loma Vista, 50 . . . . .G3
Lomax G3
Lometa, 782 . . . . .K4
London, 50 . . . . .J5
Lone Oak, 521 . . . . .N2
Lone Star (Floyd Co.), 50 . . .G1
Lone Star (Morris Co.),
1,631 . . . . .P3
Longfellow F5

Texas 349

Long Mott M7
Longview, **73,344** P3
Lopeno, **140** J9
Loraine, **656** H3
Lorena, **1,433** L4
Lorenzo, **1,372** G2
Los Angeles K7
Los Fresnos, **4,512** L9
Lost Creek, **4,729** D2
Los Ybanez, **32** G3
Lott, **724** L4
Louise, **977** M6
Lovelady, **608** N4
Lowake H4
Lowry Crossing, **1,229** C8
Lubbock, **199,564** G2
Lucas, **2,890** C8
Lueders, **300** J3
Lufkin, **32,709** P4
Luling, **5,080** L6
Lumberton, **8,731** P5
Lutie H9
Lyford, **1,973** L9
Lyons, *80* M5
Lytle, **2,383** K6
Mabank, **2,151** M3
Mabelle J2
Macdona, *650* A3
Madisonville, **4,159** N5
Magnet M6
Magnolia, **1,111** A5
Magnolia Beach, *125* M7
Magwalt E4
Malakoff, **2,257** M3
Malone, **278** M4
Manchaca, *1,200* D2
Manor, **1,204** E2, L5
Mansfield, **28,031** B10
Manvel, **3,046** B7
Maple, *50* F2
Marathon, **455** E5
Marble Falls, **4,959** C2
Marfa, **2,121** D5
Margaret, *60* J1
Marietta, **112** P2
Marion, **1,099** B2
Markley K2
Marlin, **6,628** M4
Marquez, **220** M4
Marshall, **23,935** P3
Marshall Creek, **431** B9
Mart, **2,273** M4
Maryneal, *50* H3
Marysville L2
Mason, **2,134** J5
Masterson F9
Matador, **740** H1
Matagorda, *400* N7
Mathis, **5,034** L7
Maud, **1,028** P2
McAllen, **106,414** K9
McCamey, **1,805** F4
McCaulley, *100* H3
McCoy G2
McDade, *325* L5
McFaddin L7
McGregor, **4,727** L4
McKibben G8
McKinney, **54,369** C8, M2
McLean, **830** G9
McLendon-Chisholm, **914** . . D9
McLeod, *175* P3
McNary, *40* C4
McQueeney, **2,527** B2
Meadow, **658** F2
Meadowlakes, **1,293** C2
Meadows, **4,912** A7
Megargel, **248** K2
Melvin, **155** J4
Memphis, **2,479** G10
Menard, **1,653** J5
Mendoza, *80* D3
Mentone E4
Mercedes, **13,649** L9
Mercury J4
Mereta, *175* H4
Meridian, **1,491** L4
Merit, *175* D8
Merkel, **2,637** H3
Mertzon, **839** H4
Mesquite (Borden Co.) G3
Mesquite (Dallas Co.),
124,523 . . . . . C9, M3
Mexia, **6,563** M4
Miami, **588** G9
Middle Water E8
Midkiff, *100* G4
Midland, **94,996** F4
Midlothian, **7,480** M3
Midway (Dawson Co.) G3
Midway (Madison Co.), **288** N4
Milano, **400** M5
Miles, **850** H4
Milford, **685** M3
Millett J7
Millican, **108** M5
Millsap, **353** K3
Mineola, **4,550** N3
Mineral, *40* L7
Mineral Wells, **16,946** K3
Mingus, **246** K3
Mirando City, **493** K8
Mission, **45,408** K9
Mission Bend, **30,831** A6
Missouri City, **52,913** A7
Mobeetie, **107** G9
Mobile City, **196** D9
Monahans, **6,821** F4
Montague, *225* L2
Mont Belvieu, **2,324** C6
Montgomery, **489** N5
Moody, **1,400** L4
Moore, **644** J6
Morales M6
Moran, **233** J3
Morgan, **485** L4
Morgan's Point, **336** C6
Morgan's Pt. Resort, **2,989** . . L4
Morse, **172** F8
Morton, **2,249** F2
Mountain City, **671** D3
Mountain Home J5
Mount Blanco G2
Mount Calm, **310** M4
Mount Enterprise, **525** P4
Mount Houston, *4,400* B6
Mount Pleasant, **13,935** P2
Mount Vernon, **2,286** N2
Muenster, **1,556** L2
Muleshoe, **4,530** F1
Mullin, **175** K4
Munday, **1,527** J2
Murphy, **3,099** C9
Murray K2
Mustang Ridge, **785** D3, L5
Nacogdoches, **29,914** P4
Nada, *175* M6
Naples, **1,410** P2
Nash, **2,169** P2
Nassau Bay, **4,170** C7
Natalia, **1,663** K6
Navasota, **6,789** M5
Nazareth, **356** F1, F10
Nederland, **17,422** P6
Needville, **2,609** N6
Negley, **80** N2
Nesbitt, **302** P3
Nevada, **563** D8
Newark, **887** A9
New Berlin, **467** B2
New Boston, **4,808** P2
New Braunfels, **36,494** . . B2, K6
New Caney, *475* B5
Newcastle, **575** K2
New Deal, **708** G2
New Home, **320** G2
New Hope, **662** C8, M2
Newlin G10, H1
New Lynn G2
New Sweden, *100* E2
Newton, **2,459** R5
New Waverly, **950** N5
Nickel Creek D4
Niederwald, **584** D3
Nixon, **2,186** L6
Nocona, **3,198** L2
Noelke H4
Nolan H3
Nopal L6
Nordheim, **323** L7
Norias, *40* L9
Normandy, *70* H7
Normangee, **719** M4
North Cleveland, **263** N5
North Cowden F4
Northcrest, **1,700** L4
Northfield H1
North Houston, *4,900* A6
Northlake, **921** B8
North Richland Hills, **55,635** . A9
Novice (Coleman Co.), **142** . . J4
Novice (Lamar Co.) N2
Noxville J5
Nugent, *50* J3
Oak Hill, *400* D2
Oakland, *50* M6
Oak Point, **1,747** B8
Oak Ridge, **400** M3
Oak Ridge North, **2,991** A5
Oakville K7
Oakwood, **471** N4
O'Brien, **132** J2
Ochoa D6
Odell, *80* J1
Odem, **2,499** L8
Odessa, **90,943** F4
O'Donnell, **1,011** G3
Oilton, **310** K8
Oklahoma Lane F1
Old River-Winfree, **1,364** . . . C6
Olin K4
Olmos L7
Olmos Park, **2,343** A2
Olney, **3,396** K2
Olton, **2,288** F1
Onalaska, **1,174** N5
Onion Creek, **2,116** D2, L5
Opdyke West, **188** F2
Oplin J3
Orange, **18,643** R5
Orange Grove, **1,288** L8
Orchard, **408** N6
Ore City, **1,106** P3
Orient, *80* H4
Orla E4
Ovalo, *150* J3
Overton, **2,350** P3
Owens, *150* K4
Oxford K5
Oyster Creek, **1,192** N7
Ozona, **3,436** G5
Paducah, **1,498** H1
Paint Rock, **320** J4
Paisano E5
Palacios, **5,153** M7
Palestine, **17,598** N4
Palito Blanco, *70* K8
Palmer, **1,774** M3
Paloduro G9
Palo Pinto, *150* K3
Pampa, **17,887** G9
Pandale G5
Pandora, *70* L6
Panhandle, **2,589** G9
Pantego, **2,318** B10
Paris, **25,898** N2
Parker, **175** C8
Park Springs L2
Parnell G10, H1
Pasadena, **141,674** B6, N6
Patricia G3
Patroon R4
Pattison, **447** N6
Patton Village, **1,391** N5
Pawnee, **201** K7
Peacock, *40* H2
Pearl, *50* K4
Pearland, **37,640** B7
Pearsall, **7,157** J7
Pecan Acres A9
Pecan Gap, **214** N2
Pecan Grove, **13,551** A7
Pecos, **9,501** E4
Peggy K7
Pelican Bay, **1,505** A9
Penwell F4
Pep, *40* F2
Percilla, *90* N4
Perdiz E6
Perico E8
Pernitas Point, **269** L7
Perrin, *100* K2
Perryton, **7,774** G8
Petersburg, **1,262** G2
Petrolia, **782** K2
Petronila, **83** L8
Pettit, *40* F2
Pettus, **608** L7
Petty G2
Pflugerville, **16,335** E2
Pharr, **46,660** K9
Pilot Point, **3,538** M2
Pinehurst (Montgomery Co.),
4,266 . . . . . A5
Pine Island, **849** M5
Pineland, **980** R4
Pine Springs D4
Piney Point Village, **3,380** . . A6
Pittsburg, **4,347** P2
Placid J4
Plains, **1,450** F2
Plainview, **22,336** G1
Plano, **222,030** C8, M2
Plaska H1
Plata D6
Pleak, **947** A7
Pleasanton, **8,266** K7
Pleasant Valley, **408** K2
Plum Grove, **930** N5
Point, **792** N3
Point Blank, **559** N5
Point Comfort, **781** M7
Polar H2
Ponder, **507** A8
Port Alto M7
Port Aransas, **3,370** L8
Port Arthur, **57,755** R6
Porter Heights, **1,490** B5
Portland, **14,827** L8
Port Lavaca, **12,035** M7
Port Mansfield, **415** L9
Port Neches, **13,601** R6
Port O'Connor, *600* M7
Post, **3,708** G2
Postoak K2
Poteet, **3,305** K6
Poth, **1,850** K6
Pottsboro, **1,579** M2
Powderly, *175* N2
Poynor, **314** N3
Prairie View, **4,410** N5
Premont, **2,772** K8
Presidio, **4,167** D6
Princeton, **3,477** D8
Pringle, *50* F8
Progress, *125* F1
Prosper, **2,097** C8, L2
Pumphrey H3
Pumpville G6
Purmela L4
Putnam, **88** J3
Pyote, **131** E4
Quail, **33** G9
Quanah, **3,022** J1
Queen City, **1,613** P2
Quemado, **243** H7
Quihi, *40* J6
Quinlan, **1,370** M3
Quitaque, **432** G1
Quitman, **2,030** N3
Rachal, *80* K9
Radium J3
Ralls, **2,252** G2
Ramirez K8
Randado K8
Ranger, **2,584** K3
Rankin, **800** G4
Ransom Canyon, **1,011** G2
Ravenna, **215** M2
Rayland J1
Raymondville, **9,733** L9
Realitos, **209** K8
Redford, **132** D6
Red Rock, *100* E3, L6
Redwater, **872** P2
Refugio, **2,941** L7
Reklaw, **327** P4
Reno (Lamar Co.), **2,767** . . . N2
Reno (Parker Co.), **2,441** . A9, L3
Retreat, **339** M3
Rhea E10
Rhineland, *90* J2
Rhome, **551** A9
Ricardo, *450* L8
Rice, **798** M3
Richards, *275* N5
Richardson, **91,802** C9
Richland, **291** M4
Richland Hills, **8,132** B9
Richland Springs, **350** K4
Richmond, **11,081** A7, N6
Ringgold, *225* K2
Rio Bravo, **5,553** J8
Rio Frio, *100* J6
Rio Grande City, **11,923** . . . K9
Rio Grande Village, *250* . . . F6
Riomedina K6
Rios, *40* K8
Rio Vista, **656** L3
Rising Star, **835** K3
River Oaks, **6,985** A9
Riverside, **425** N5
Riviera, *550* L8
Riviera Beach L8
Roanoke, **2,810** B9
Roaring Springs, **265** H2
Robbins, *60* M4
Robert Lee, **1,171** H4
Robinson, **7,845** L4
Robstown, **12,727** L8
Roby, **673** H3
Rochelle J4
Rochester, **378** J2
Rockdale, **5,439** M5
Rockne, *150* E3
Rockport, **7,385** L7
Rocksprings, **1,285** H5
Rockwall, **17,976** D9, M3
Rogers, **1,117** L5
Rollingwood, **1,403** D2
Roma, **9,617** J9
Roman Forest, **1,279** B5
Romero E9
Roosevelt H5
Ropesville, **517** F2
Roscoe, **1,378** H3
Rosebud, **1,493** M4
Rosenberg, **24,043** A7, N6
Rosita (Duval Co.) K8
Rosita (Starr Co.), *500* K9
Rotan, **1,611** H3
Round Mountain, **111** C2
Round Rock, **61,136** D2, L5
Round Top, **77** M5
Rowden J3
Rowena, *350* H4
Rowlett, **44,503** D9
Roxton, **694** N2
Royalty F4
Royse City, **2,957** D9, M3
Rucker K3
Rudolph, *40* L9
Ruidosa, *40* D5
Rule, **698** J2
Runaway Bay, **1,104** L2
Runge, **1,080** L7
Rusk, **5,085** N4
Ryan, *40* D5
Sabinal, **1,586** J6
Sabine Pass, *40* R6
Sachse, **9,751** C9
Saginaw, **12,374** A9
St. Francis F9
St. Hedwig, **1,875** B2
St. Jo, **977** L2
St. Lawrence, *40* G4
St. Paul (Collin Co.), **630** . . C8
Salineno, **304** J9
Salt Flat C4
Samnorwood, **39** H9
San Angelo, **88,439** H4
San Antonio, **1,144,646** . A2, K6
San Augustine, **2,475** P4
San Benito, **23,444** L9
Sanco H3
Sanderson, **861** F5
San Diego, **4,753** K8
Sandy K5
San Elizario, **11,046** B4
San Felipe, **868** M6
Sanford, **203** F9
Sanger, **4,534** L2
San Juan, **26,229** K9
San Leanna, **384** D2
San Leon, **4,365** C7
San Marcos, **34,733** B1, L6
San Perlita, **680** L9
San Saba, **2,637** K4
Sansom Park, **4,181** A9
Santa Anna, **1,081** J4
Santa Catarina K9
Santa Elena, *40* K9
Santa Fe, **9,548** N6
San Ygnacio, *350* J8
Saragosa E4
Sarita L8
Sattler B1
Savoy, **850** M2
Scallorn, *40* K4
Scenic Oaks, **3,279** A2
Schertz, **18,694** A2
Scotland, **438** K2
Seabrook, **9,443** C7
Seadrift, **1,352** M7
Seagoville, **10,823** D10
Seagraves, **2,334** F3
Sealy, **5,248** M6
Segovia J5
Seguin, **22,011** B2, L6
Selma, **788** A2
Seminole, **5,910** F3
Serenada, **1,847** D1
Seth Ward, **1,926** G1
Seven Sisters, **60** K8
Seymour, **2,908** J2
Shady Shores, **1,461** B8
Shafter D6
Shallowater, **2,086** F2
Shamrock, **2,029** H9
Shannon K2
Sharp, *100* L5
Shavano Park, **1,754** A2
Sheffield, *225* G5
Sheldon, **1,831** B6
Shenandoah, **1,503** A5
Shepherd, **2,029** P5
Sheridan, *60* M6
Sherman, **35,082** M2
Sherwood, *90* H4
Shiloh L5
Shiro N5
Shoreacres, **1,488** C6
Sierra Blanca, **533** C4
Silsbee, **6,393** P5
Silver H3
Silverton, **771** G1, G10
Simms E9
Simonton, **718** N6
Sinton, **5,676** L7
Sivells Bend L2
Skellytown, **610** G9
Skidmore, **1,013** L7
Slaton, **6,109** G2
Slide G2
Slocum, *150* N4
Small C4
Smiley, **453** L6
Smithland, *175* P3
Smith Point P6
Smithville, **3,901** L5
Smithwick C2, K5
Smyer, **480** F2
Snook, **568** M5
Snyder, **10,783** H3
Socorro, **27,152** B4
Somerset, **1,550** A3, K6
Somerville, **1,704** M5
Sonora, **2,924** H5
Sour Lake, **1,667** P5
South Bend, *50* K3
South Houston, **15,833** B6
Southlake, **21,519** B9
Southland G2
South Padre Island, **2,422** . . L9
Southside Place, **1,546** B6
Spade H3
Spanish Fort, *60* L2
Speaks M6
Spearman, **3,021** G8
Spofford, **75** H6
Spraberry, *125* G4
Spring, **36,385** B5
Springlake, **135** F1
Springtown, **2,062** L3
Spring Valley, **3,611** A6
Spur, **1,088** H2
Stacy J4
Stafford, **15,681** A7
Stagecoach, **455** A5
Stamford, **3,636** J3
Stanton, **2,556** G3
Star, *60* K4
Stephenville, **14,921** K3
Sterling City, **1,081** H4
Stiles, *40* G4
Stinnett, **1,936** F8
Stockdale, **1,398** B3, L6
Stratford, **1,991** F8
Strawn, **739** K3
Streeter J5
Study Butte, **267** E6
Sudan, **1,039** F1
Sugarland, **63,328** N6
Sugar Land, **63,328** A7
Sulphur Springs, **14,551** . . . N2
Summerfield, *70* F10
Sumner, *60* N2
Sundown, **1,505** F2
Sunnyside, *70* F1
Sunnyvale, **2,693** D9
Sunray, **1,950** F8
Sunrise Beach, **704** C2
Sunset, **339** L2
Sunset Valley, **365** D2
Surfside Beach, **763** N7
Swearingen, **10** H1
Sweeny, **3,624** N6
Sweetwater, **11,415** H3
Swenson H2
Swiss Alp M6
Taft, **3,396** L8
Tahoka, **2,910** G2
Talco, **570** N2
Tamina, **304** A5
Tanglewood Forest D2
Tankersley, *150* H4
Tarzan G3
Tascosa, *175* F9
Tatum, **1,175** P3
Taylor, **13,575** E1, L5
Taylor Lake Village, **3,694** . . C7
Teague, **4,557** M4
Telegraph J5
Telferner, *550* M7
Tell, *40* H1
Temple, **54,514** L4
Tenaha, **1,046** P4
Tennyson H4
Terlingua, **267** E6
Terrell, **13,606** M3
Terrell Hills, **5,019** A2
Terryville L6
Texarkana, **34,782** P2
Texas City, **41,521** C7
Texhoma, **371** F8
Texline, **511** E8
Texola H9
Texon, *40* G4
Thalia, *40* J2
The Colony, **26,531** C8
Thelma, *375* A3, K6
The Woodlands, **55,649** . A5, N5
Thomaston, **30** L6
Thompsons, **236** A7
Thorndale, **1,278** L5
Thornton, **525** M4
Thorntonville, **442** F4
Thrall, **710** L5
Three Rivers, **1,878** K7
Throckmorton, **905** J2
Tiki Island, **1,016** P6
Tilden, **500** K7
Timbercreek Canyon, **406** . . . F9
Timberwood Park, **5,889** . . . A2
Timpson, **1,094** P4
Tira, **248** N2
Titley E5
Tivoli, *450* M7
Toco, **89** N2
Todd Mission, **146** N5
Tokio, *40* F2
Tolar, **504** L3
Tolbert J1
Toledo Village R4
Tomball, **9,089** A5
Tool, **2,275** M3
Tornillo, **1,609** B4
Town West A7
Toyah, **100** E4
Toyahvale E5
Trent, **318** H3
Trinity, **2,721** N5
Trophy Club, **6,350** B9
Troup, **1,949** N3
Troy, **1,378** L4
Truby J3
Truscott, *90* J2
Tulia, **5,117** F10, G1
Tulip M2
Turkey, **494** H1
Tuscola, **714** J3
Tuxedo J3
Twichell G8
Twin Sisters C3
Tye, **1,158** J3
Tyler, **83,650** N3
Tynan, **301** L7
Uhland, **386** D3, L6
Uncertain, **150** P3
Union (Scurry Co.), *100* G3
Union (Terry Co.) F2
Union (Wilson Co.), **30** L6
Universal City, **14,849** . . A2, K6
University Park, **23,324** C9
Utley E2
Utopia, **241** J6
Uvalde, **14,929** J6
Valentine, **187** D5
Valera J4
Valley Farm E4
Valley Mills, **1,123** L4
Valley Spring, *50* K5
Valley View, **737** L2
Valley Wells J7
Van, **2,362** N3
Van Alstyne, **2,502** M2
Vance H6
Vanderbilt, **411** M7
Vanderpool J6
Van Horn, **2,435** D4
Vealmoor G3
Vega, **936** F9
Vera, *100* J2
Verbena, *60* G2
Verhalen E4
Vernon, **11,660** J1
Viboras, *60* K9
Vick H4
Victoria, **60,603** M7
Vidaurri L7
Vidor, **11,440** P5
Vienna M6
View, *50* J3
Vigo Park F10, G1
Vincent G3
Vinton, **1,892** B4
Voca, *40* J5
Votaw, *90* P5
Waco, **113,726** L4
Waelder, **947** L6
Waka, *125* G8
Wake G2
Wakefield P4
Wake Village, **5,129** P2
Wall, *250* H4
Waller, **2,092** N5
Wallis, **1,172** M6
Walnut Springs, **755** L3
Warda M5
Ware E8
Washburn, *150* F9
Waskom, **2,068** P3
Watauga, **21,908** A9
Water Valley, *125* H4
Waxahachie, **21,426** M3
Wayside F9
Weatherford, **19,000** L3
Webb J8
Webster, **9,083** B7
Weches N4
Weimar, **1,981** M6
Weinert, **177** J2
Weir, **591** D1, L5
Welch, *275* F3
Wellborn, *300* M5
Wellington, **2,275** H9
Wellman, **203** F2
Wells (Cherokee), **769** P4
Wells (Lynn Co.) G2
Weser, *40* L7
Weslaco, **26,935** L9
Westbrook, **203** G3
West Columbia, **4,255** N6
Westfield, *1,700* B6
Westhoff, *175* L6
Westlake, **207** B9
West Lake Hills, **3,116** D2
West Odessa, **17,799** F4
West Orange, **4,111** R5
Westover J2
Westover Hills, **658** A10
West Point F2
West University Place, **14,211** B6
Westway, **3,829** B4
Westworth Village, **2,124** . . A9
Wetmore, *1,200* A2
Wharton, **9,237** M6
Wheatland, *80* A10
Wheeler, **1,378** H9
White Deer, **1,060** G9
Whiteface, **465** F2
Whiteflat H1
Whitehouse, **5,346** N3
White Oak, **5,624** P3
Whitesboro, **3,760** M2
White Settlement, **14,831** . . A10
Whitney, **1,833** L4
Whitsett, *50* K7
Wichita Falls, **104,197** K2
Wickett, **455** F4
Wild Horse D4
Wildorado, *150* F9
Wildwood, *550* P5
Willamar, **15** L9
Williams K3
Willis, **3,985** N5
Willow City K5
Wills Point, **3,496** M3
Wilmer, **3,393** C10
Wilmeth H4
Wilson, **532** G2
Wimberley, **3,797** D3
Winchell, *40* J4
Winchester, *80* M6
Windcrest, **5,105** A2
Windemere, **6,868** D2
Windthorst, **440** K2
Winfield, **499** N2
Wink, **919** E4
Winnsboro, **3,584** N3
Winona, **582** N3
Winter Haven J7
Winters, **2,880** J4
Witco, *90* G4
Wixon Valley, **235** M5
Wolfe City, **1,566** M2
Wolfforth, **2,554** G2
Woodbranch, **1,305** B5
Woodcreek, **1,274** D3
Woodland N2
Woodloch, **247** N5
Woods, *150* P3
Woodsboro, **1,685** L7
Woodson, **296** J2
Woodville, **2,415** P5
Woodway, **8,733** L4
Wortham, **1,082** M4
Wyldwood, **2,310** E2
Wylie, **15,132** D9
Yancey, *200* J6
Yantis, **321** N3
Yoakum, **5,731** L6
Yorktown, **2,271** L7
Zapata, **4,856** J9
Zavalla, **647** P4
Zephyr, *125* K4
Zorn, *70* B1
Zunkerville L7

Other Features

Alabama & Coushatta I.R. . . . P5
Alibates Flint Quarries
Natl. Mon. F9
Amistad, *reservoir* G6
Amistad Natl. Rec. Area G6
Angelina Natl. For. P4
Aransas N.W.R. M7
Benbrook, *lake* A10
Big Bend Natl. Park E6
Big Bend Ranch
St. Park D6
Big Boggy N.W.R. N7
Big Thicket Natl. Pres. P5
Black, *mountain* H6
Black Gap Wildlife
Management Area F6
Black Kettle Natl. Grassland . H8
Blanco, *river* C3
Bolivar, *peninsula* P6
Brazoria N.W.R. N6
Brazos, *river* A7
Buffalo Lake N.W.R. F9
Calaveras, *lake* B3
Canadian, *river* E9, G8
Canyon, *lake* B1, C3
Carlsbad Caverns Natl. Park . D3
Cathedral, *mountain* E5
Cerro Grande, *peak* A4
Chamizal Natl. Mem. B4
Chickasaw N.R.A. M1
Chinati, *peak* D6
Colorado, *river* D2
Davis, *mountains* D5
Davy Crockett Natl. For. . . . N4
Eagle, *peak* C5
Eagle Mtn., *lake* A9
Edwards, *plateau* H5
Emory, *peak* E6
Falcon, *reservoir* J9
Fort Bliss Mil. Res. B3
Fort Davis Natl. Hist. Site . . E5
Fort Hood Mil. Res. L4
Galveston, *island* P6
Granger, *lake* E1
Grapevine, *lake* A9
Guadalupe, *mountains* D4
Guadalupe, *peak* D3
Guadalupe, *river* A1
Guadalupe Mts. Natl. Park . . D4
Houston, *lake* B6
Kemp, *lake* J2
Kiowa Natl. Grassland E8
Kisatchie Natl. For. R3
Laguna Atascosa N.W.R. . . . L9
Lake Meredith Natl.
Rec. Area F9
Lavon, *lake* C8
Lewisville, *lake* C8
Lincoln Natl. For. D3
Livermore, *mountain* D5
Livingston, *lake* N5
Lyndon B. Johnson
Natl. Hist. Park C2, K5
McClellan Creek
Natl. Grassland G9
McFaddin N.W.R. P6
Medio, *creek* A3
Meredith, *lake* F9
Mexico, *gulf* N8
Nueces, *river* K7
O.H. Ivie, *lake* J4
Optima N.W.R. F8
Ouachita Natl. For. P2
Padre Island Natl. Seashore . . L8
Palo Alto Battlefield N.H.S. . L10
Parque Nacional
Los Novillos G6
Pecos, *river* F4
Pedernales, *river* C2
Punta de Agua E8
Ray Hubbard, *lake* D9
Red Bluff, *lake* D4
Rio Casas Grandes, *river* . . . A4
Rio Conchos, *river* D6
Rio Grande, *river* D5, G6
Rio Salado, *river* H8
Rita Blanca, *creek* E8
Rita Blanca Natl. Grassland . E8
Sabine, *pass* R6
Sabine, *river* N3, R5
Sabine N.F. R4
Sam Houston Natl. For. N5
Sam Rayburn, *reservoir* P4
San Antonio, *river* B2
San Antonio Missions N.H.P. . A3
San Bernard N.W.R. N7
San Gabriel, *river* D1
Santiago, *peak* E6
Sierra Blanca, *peak* C4
Sierra Boca Grande, *range* . . A4
Sierra Del Carmen, *range* . . . E6
Sierra El Fresnal, *range* . . . A4
Sierra Grande, *range* D6
Stockton, *plateau* F5
Texas Point N.W.R. R6
Toledo Bend, *reservoir* R4
Travis, *lake* D2
Trinity, *bay* C6
Trinity, *river* C5, C9, C10
Walter E. Long, *lake* E2
Washita, *river* G9
Wind, *mountain* C3
Worth, *lake* A9

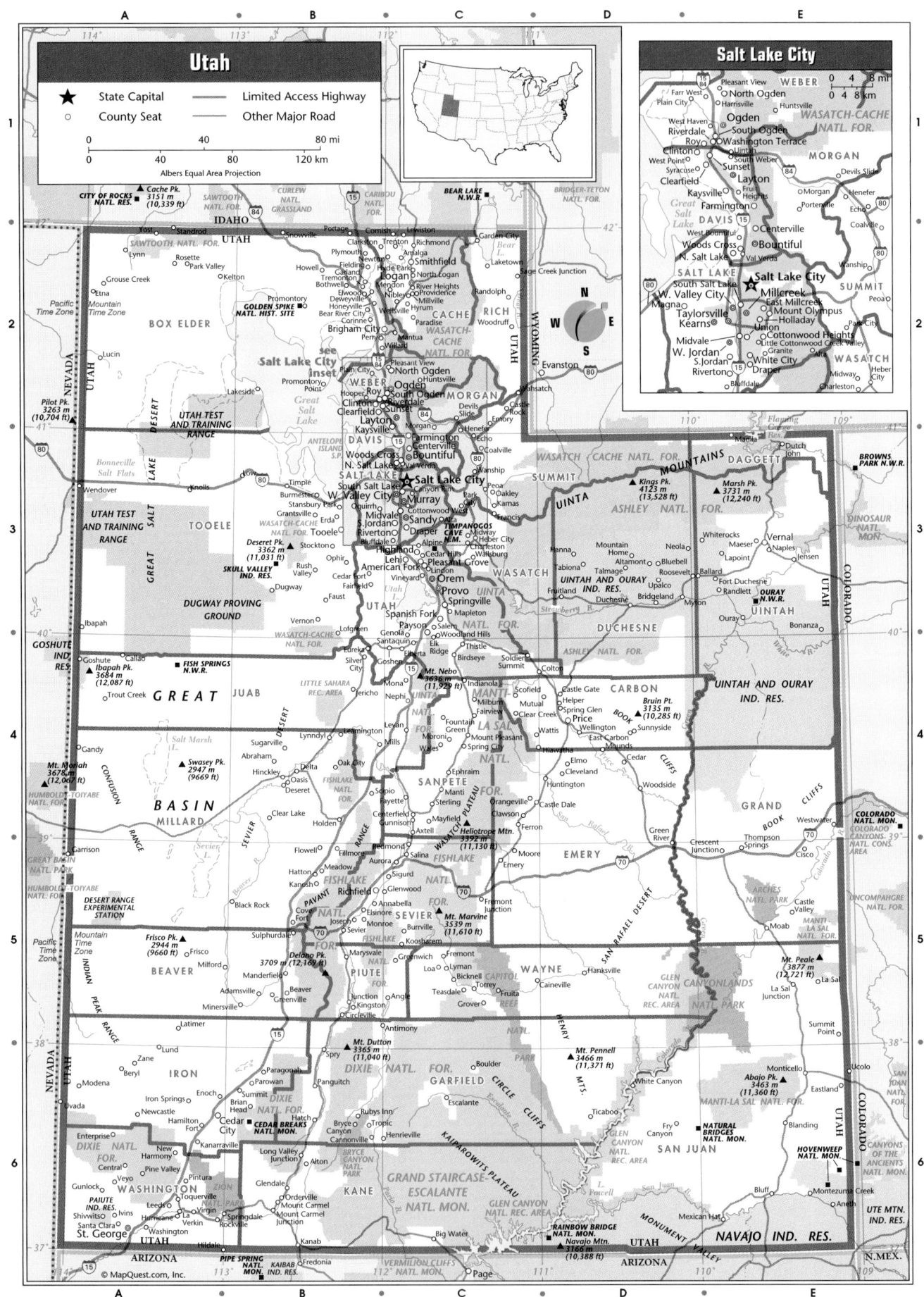

Utah

★ State Capital
○ County Seat
── Limited Access Highway
── Other Major Road

0   40   80 mi
0   40   80   120 km
Albers Equal Area Projection

Salt Lake City

0 4 8 mi
0 4 8 km

© MapQuest.com, Inc.

Utah

- **Capital:** Salt Lake City
- **Land Area:** 82,168 sq. mi. 212,815 sq. km.
- **Population:** 2,233,169 (2000 Census)
- **Largest City:** Salt Lake City, 181,743
- **Highest Point:** Kings Peak 13,528 ft. 4,123 m.
- **Admitted to Union:** January 4, 1896
- **Nickname:** Beehive State
- **State Flower:** Sego Lily
- **State Bird:** Seagull

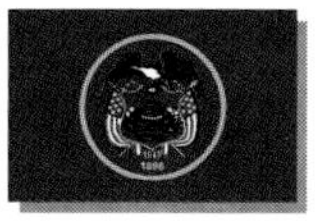

Utah: Map Index

Counties

- Beaver, **6,005** A5
- Box Elder, **42,745** A2
- Cache, **91,391** C2
- Carbon, **20,422** D4
- Daggett, **921** E3
- Davis, **238,994** B3, E1
- Duchesne, **14,371** D3
- Emery, **10,860** D5
- Garfield, **4,735** C6
- Grand, **8,485** E4
- Iron, **33,779** A6
- Juab, **8,238** B4
- Kane, **6,046** B6
- Millard, **12,405** A4
- Morgan, **7,129** C2, E1
- Piute, **1,435** B5
- Rich, **1,961** C2
- Salt Lake, **898,387** B3, E2
- San Juan, **14,413** D6
- Sanpete, **22,763** C4
- Sevier, **18,842** C5
- Summit, **29,736** D3, E2
- Tooele, **40,735** A3
- Uintah, **25,224** E3
- Utah, **368,536** B3
- Wasatch, **15,215** C3, E2
- Washington, **90,354** A6
- Wayne, **2,509** D5
- Weber, **196,533** B2, E1

Cities and Towns

- Abraham, *60* B4
- Adamsville B5
- Alpine, **7,146** C3
- Alta, **370** C3
- Altamont, **178** D3
- Alton, **134** B6
- Amalga, **427** C2
- American Fork, **21,941** C3
- Aneth, **598** E6
- Angle C5
- Annabella, **603** B5
- Antimony, **122** C5
- Aurora, **947** C5
- Axtell, *100* C4
- Ballard, **566** E3
- Bear River City, **750** B2
- Beaver, **2,454** B5
- Bennion E2
- Beryl, *125* A6
- Bicknell, **353** C5
- Big Water, **417** C6
- Birdseye, *175* C4
- Black Rock B5
- Blanding, **3,162** E6
- Bluebell, *150* D3
- Bluff, **320** E6
- Bluffdale, **4,700** C3, E2
- Bonanza E3
- Bothwell, *175* B2
- Boulder, **180** C6
- Bountiful, **41,301** C3, E2
- Brian Head, **118** B6
- Bridgeland D3
- Brigham City, **17,411** B2
- Bryce Canyon B6
- Burmester B3
- Burrville, *40* C5
- Caineville C5
- Callao A4
- Cannonville, **148** B6
- Canyon Rim, **10,428** C3
- Castle Dale, **1,657** C4
- Castle Gate D4
- Castle Rock C2
- Castle Valley, **349** E5
- Cedar D4
- Cedar City, **20,527** A6
- Cedar Fort, **341** B3
- Cedar Hills, **3,094** C3
- Centerfield, **1,048** C4
- Centerville, **14,585** C3, E2
- Central, *100* A6
- Charleston, **378** C3
- Circleville, **505** B5
- Cisco E5
- Clarkston, **688** B2
- Clawson, **153** C4
- Clear Creek C4
- Clearfield, **25,974** B2, E1
- Clear Lake B4
- Cleveland, **508** D4
- Clinton, **12,585** B2, E1
- Coalville, **1,382** C3, E2
- Colton D4
- Corinne, **621** B2
- Cornish, **259** C2
- Cottonwood Heights, **27,569** E2
- Cottonwood West, **18,727** C3
- Cove Fort B5
- Crescent Junction, *50* E5
- Delta, **3,209** B4
- Deseret, *100* B4
- Devils Slide, *50* C2, E1
- Deweyville, **278** B2
- Draper, **25,220** C3, E2
- Duchesne, **1,408** D3
- Dugway B3
- Dutch John, *125* E3
- East Carbon, **1,393** D4
- Eastland, *50* E6
- East Millcreek, **21,385** E2
- Echo, *50* C3, E1
- Elberta, **278** C4
- Elk Ridge, **1,838** C4
- Elmo, **368** D4
- Elsinore, **733** B5
- Elwood, **678** B2
- Emery, **308** C5
- Emory C2
- Enoch, **3,467** A6
- Enterprise, **1,285** A6
- Ephraim, **4,505** C4
- Erda, **2,473** B3
- Escalante, **818** C6
- Etna A2
- Eureka, **766** B4
- Fairfield, *90* B3
- Fairview, **1,160** C4
- Farmington, **12,081** C3, E1
- Farr West, **3,094** E1
- Faust B3
- Fayette, **204** C4
- Ferron, **1,623** C4
- Fielding, **448** B2
- Fillmore, **2,253** B5
- Flowell, *80* B5
- Fort Duchesne, **621** E3
- Fountain Green, **945** C4
- Francis, **698** C3
- Fremont, *125* C5
- Fremont Junction C5
- Frisco A5
- Fruita C5
- Fruit Heights, **4,701** E1
- Fruitland, *40* D3
- Fry Canyon, *40* D6
- Gandy A4
- Garden City, **357** C2
- Garland, **1,943** B2
- Garrison, *50* A5
- Genola, **965** C3
- Glendale, **355** B6
- Glenwood, **437** C5
- Goshen, **874** C4
- Goshute A4
- Granite, **2,018** E2
- Grantsville, **6,015** B3
- Green River, **973** D4
- Greenville B5
- Greenwich C5
- Grouse Creek A2
- Grover C5
- Gunlock, *70* A6
- Gunnison, **2,394** C4
- Hamilton Fort, *150* A6
- Hanksville, *125* D5
- Hanna, *100* D3
- Harrisville, **3,645** E1
- Hatch, **127** B6
- Hatton B5
- Heber City, **7,291** C3, E2
- Helper, **2,025** D4
- Henefer, **684** C2, E1
- Henrieville, **159** C6
- Hiawatha, **40** C4
- Highland, **8,172** C3
- Hildale, **1,895** A6
- Hinckley, **698** B4
- Holden, **400** B4
- Holladay, **14,561** E2
- Honeyville, **1,214** B2
- Hooper, **3,926** B2
- Howell, **221** B2
- Huntington, **2,131** D4
- Huntsville, **649** C2, E1
- Hurricane, **8,250** A6
- Hyde Park, **2,955** C2
- Hyrum, **6,316** C2
- Ibapah, *70* A3
- Indianola C4
- Iron Springs, *90* A6
- Ivins, **4,450** A6
- Jensen, *125* E3
- Jericho B4
- Joseph, **269** B5
- Junction, **177** B5
- Kamas, **1,274** C3
- Kanab, **3,564** B6
- Kanarraville, **311** A6
- Kanosh, **485** B5
- Kaysville, **20,351** C2, E1
- Kearns, **33,659** E2
- Kelton A2
- Kingston, **142** B5
- Knolls, *70* A3
- Koosharem, **276** C5
- Lakeside, *60* B2
- Laketown, **188** C2
- Lapoint, *175* E3
- La Sal, **339** E5
- La Sal Junction E5
- Latimer A5
- La Verkin, **3,392** A6
- Layton, **58,474** C2, E1
- Leamington, **217** B4
- Leeds, **547** A6
- Lehi, **19,028** C3
- Levan, **688** C4
- Lewiston, **1,877** C2
- Lindon, **8,363** C3
- Little Cottonwood Creek Valley, **7,221** E2
- Loa, **525** C5
- Lofgreen B3
- Logan, **42,670** C2
- Long Valley Junction B6
- Low, *70* B3
- Lucin A2
- Lund A6
- Lyman, **234** C5
- Lynn A2
- Lynndyl, **134** B4
- Maeser, **2,855** E3
- Magna, **22,770** D2
- Manderfield, *90* B5
- Manila, **308** E3
- Manti, **3,040** C4
- Mantua, **791** C2
- Mapleton, **5,809** C3
- Marysvale, **381** B5
- Mayfield, **420** C4
- Meadow, **254** B5
- Mendon, **898** C2
- Mexican Hat, **88** E6
- Midvale, **27,029** C3, E2
- Midway, **2,121** C3, E2
- Milburn C4
- Milford, **1,451** A5
- Millcreek, **30,377** E2
- Mills B4
- Millville, **1,507** C2
- Minersville, **817** B5
- Moab, **4,779** E5
- Modena A6
- Mona, **850** C4
- Monroe, **1,845** B5
- Montezuma Creek, **507** E6
- Monticello, **1,958** E6
- Moore C5
- Morgan, **2,635** C2, E1
- Moroni, **1,280** C4
- Mounds D4
- Mountain Home, *100* D3
- Mount Carmel, *50* B6
- Mount Carmel Junction, *40* B6
- Mount Olympus, **7,103** E2
- Mount Pleasant, **2,707** C4
- Murray, **34,024** C3
- Mutual D4
- Myton, **539** D3
- Naples, **1,300** E3
- Neola, **533** D3
- Nephi, **4,733** C4
- Newcastle, *90* A6
- New Harmony, **190** A6
- Newton, **699** C2
- Nibley, **2,045** C2
- North Logan, **6,163** C2
- North Ogden, **15,026** C2, E1
- North Salt Lake, **8,749** C3, E2
- Oak City, **650** B4
- Oakley, **948** C3
- Oasis, *125* B4
- Ogden, **77,226** C2, E1
- Ophir, **23** B3
- Oquirrh, **10,390** B3
- Orangeville, **1,398** C4
- Orderville, **596** B6
- Orem, **84,324** C3
- Ouray E3
- Panguitch, **1,623** B6
- Paradise, **759** C2
- Paragonah, **470** B6
- Park City, **7,371** C3, E2
- Park Valley, *80* A2
- Parowan, **2,565** B6
- Payson, **12,716** C3
- Peoa, *125* C3, E2
- Perry, **2,383** B2
- Pine Valley A6
- Pintura A6
- Plain City, **3,489** B2, E1
- Pleasant Grove, **23,468** C3
- Pleasant View, **5,632** C2, E1
- Plymouth, **328** B2
- Portage, **257** B2
- Porterville, *150* E1
- Price, **8,402** D4
- Promontory B2
- Promontory Point, *100* B2
- Providence, **4,377** C2
- Provo, **105,166** C3
- Randlett, **224** E3
- Randolph, **483** C2
- Redmond, **788** C5
- Richfield, **6,847** B5
- Richmond, **2,051** C2
- Riverdale, **7,656** C2, E1
- River Heights, **1,496** C2
- Riverton, **25,011** C3, E2
- Rockville, **247** A6
- Roosevelt, **4,299** D3
- Rosette, *70* A2
- Roy, **32,885** B2, E1
- Rubys Inn, *125* B6
- Rush Valley, **453** B3
- Sage Creek Junction, *50* C2
- St. George, **49,663** A6
- Salem, **4,372** C3
- Salina, **2,393** C5
- Salt Lake City, **181,743** C3, E2
- Sandy, **88,418** C3
- Santa Clara, **4,630** A6
- Santaquin, **4,834** C4
- Scipio, **290** B4
- Scofield, **28** C4
- Sevier, *40* B5
- Shivwits A6
- Sigurd, **430** C5
- Silver City B4
- Smithfield, **7,261** C2
- Snowville, **177** B2
- Soldier Summit C4
- South Jordan, **29,437** C3, E2
- South Ogden, **14,377** C2, E1
- South Salt Lake, **22,038** C3, E2
- South Weber, **4,260** E1
- Spanish Fork, **20,246** C3
- Spring City, **956** C4
- Springdale, **457** B6
- Spring Glen, *1,000* D4
- Springville, **20,424** C3
- Spry B6
- Standrod, *40* A2
- Stansbury Park, **2,385** B3
- Sterling, **235** C4
- Stockton, **443** B3
- Sugarville B4
- Sulphurdale B5
- Summit, *175* B6
- Summit Point E5
- Sunnyside, **404** D4
- Sunset, **5,204** C2, E1
- Syracuse, **9,398** E1
- Tabiona, **149** D3
- Talmage, *60* D3
- Taylorsville, **57,439** E2
- Teasdale, *100* C5
- Thistle C4
- Thompson Springs, *50* E5
- Ticaboo, *40* D6
- Timpie, *50* B3
- Tooele, **22,502** B3
- Toquerville, **910** A6
- Torrey, **171** C5
- Tremonton, **5,592** B2
- Trenton, **449** C2
- Tropic, **508** B6
- Trout Creek A4
- Ucolo E6
- Union E2
- Upalco D3
- Uvada, *60* A6
- Val Verda C3, E2
- Vernal, **7,714** E3
- Vernon, **236** B3
- Veyo, *200* A6
- Vineyard, **150** C3
- Virgin, **394** A6
- Wahsatch, **10** C2
- Wales, **219** C4
- Wallsburg, **274** C3
- Wanship, *175* C3, E2
- Washington, **8,186** A6
- Washington Terrace, **8,551** E1
- Wattis, *60* C4
- Wellington, **1,666** D4
- Wellsville, **2,728** C2
- Wendover, **1,537** A3
- West Bountiful, **4,484** E2
- West Haven, **3,976** E1
- West Jordan, **68,336** E2
- West Point, **6,033** E1
- West Valley City, **108,896** C3, E2
- Westwater E4
- White Canyon D6
- White City, **5,988** E2
- Whiterocks, **341** E3
- Willard, **1,630** B2
- Woodland Hills, **941** C3
- Woodruff, **194** C2
- Woods Cross, **6,419** C3, E2
- Woodside D4
- Yost A2
- Zane A6

Other Features

- Abajo, *peak* E6
- Antelope Island S.P. B3
- Arches Natl. Park E5
- Ashley Natl. For. D3, D4
- Bear, *lake* C2
- Bear, *river* C2
- Bear Lake N.W.R. C1
- Beaver, *river* B5
- Bonneville, *salt flats* A3
- Book , *cliffs* D4, E4
- Bridger-Teton Natl. For. D1
- Browns Park N.W.R. E3
- Bruin, *point* D4
- Bryce Canyon Natl. Park B6
- Cache, *peak* A1
- Canyonlands Natl. Park E5
- Capitol Reef Natl. Park C5
- Caribou Natl. For. B1
- Cedar Breaks Natl. Mon. B6
- Circle, *cliffs* C6
- City of Rocks Natl. Res. A1
- Colorado, *river* D6, E5
- Colorado Natl. Mon. E4
- Confusion Range A4
- Curlew Natl. Grassland B1
- Delano, *peak* B5
- Deseret, *peak* B3
- Deseret Test Center A3
- Desert Range Experimental Station A5
- Dinosaur Natl. Mon. E3
- Dixie Natl. For. A6, B6, C6
- Dugway Proving Ground A3
- Dutton, *mountain* B5
- Escalante, *river* C6
- Fishlake Natl. For. B4, B5, C5
- Fish Springs N.W.R. A4
- Flaming Gorge, *reservoir* E2
- Frisco, *peak* A5
- Glen Canyon Natl. Rec. Area C6, D5, D6
- Golden Spike Natl. Hist. Site B2
- Goshute Ind. Res. A4
- Grand Staircase-Escalante National Monument C6
- Great Basin A4
- Great Basin Natl. Park A5
- Great Salt, *lake* B2, D1
- Great Salt Lake Desert A3
- Green, *river* D4, E5
- Heliotrope Mtn. C4
- Henry Mts. D5
- Hovenweep Natl. Mon. E6
- Humboldt Natl. For. A4, A5
- Ibapah, *peak* A4
- Indian Peak, *range* A5
- Kaibab Ind. Res. B6
- Kaiparowits, *plateau* C6
- Kings, *peak* D3
- Little Sahara Rec. Area B4
- Manti-La Sal Natl. For. E5, C4, E6
- Marsh, *peak* E3
- Marvine, *mountain* C5
- Monument, *valley* D6
- Moriah, *mountain* A4
- Natural Bridges Natl. Mon. E6
- Navajo, *mountain* D6
- Navajo Ind. Res. E6
- Nebo, *mountain* C4
- Ouray N.W.R. E3
- Paiute Ind. Res. A6
- Paria, *river* C6
- Pavant, *range* B5
- Peale, *mountain* E5
- Pennell, *mountain* D6
- Pilot, *peak* A2
- Pipe Spring Natl. Mon. B6
- Powell, *lake* D6
- Price, *river* D4
- Rainbow Bridge Natl. Mon. D6
- Salt Marsh, *lake* A4
- San Juan, *river* D6
- San Juan Natl. For. E6
- San Rafael, *desert* D5
- San Rafael, *river* D4
- Sawtooth Natl. For. A1, A2
- Sevier, *desert* B4
- Sevier, *lake* A5
- Skull Valley Ind. Res. B3
- Strawberry, *river* D3
- Swasey, *peak* A4
- Timpanogos Cave N.M. C3
- Uinta, *mountains* D3
- Uintah and Ouray Ind. Res. D3, D4, E4
- Uinta Natl. For. C3, C4
- Uncompahgre Natl. For. E5
- Utah, *lake* C3
- Utah Test and Training Range A2, A3
- Ute Mtn. Ind. Res. E6
- Wasatch, *plateau* C5
- Wasatch-Cache Natl. For. C3, C2, B3, E1
- White, *river* E4
- Zion Natl. Park A6

Utah: Past & Present

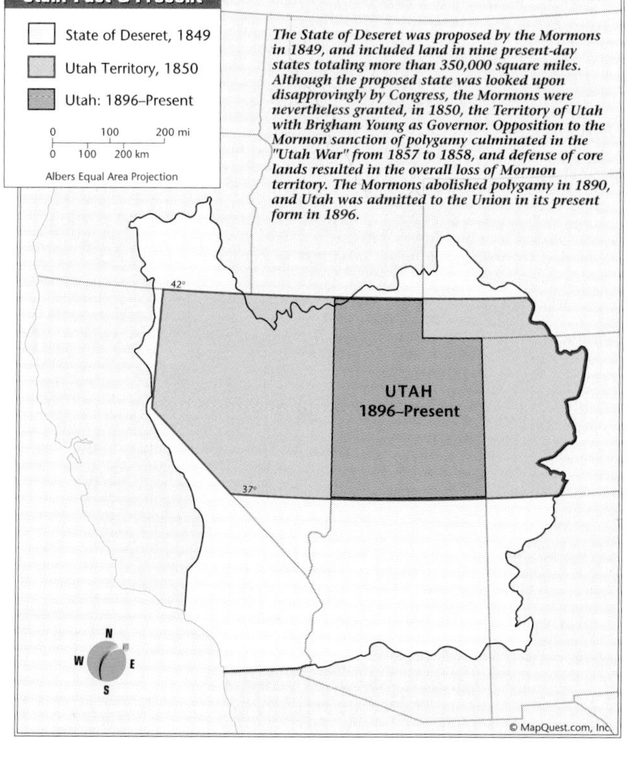
State of Deseret, 1849
Utah Territory, 1850
Utah: 1896–Present
0 100 200 mi
0 100 200 km
Albers Equal Area Projection
42°
37°
UTAH
1896–Present
N
W
E
S
© MapQuest.com, Inc.

The State of Deseret was proposed by the Mormons in 1849, and included land in nine present-day states totaling more than 350,000 square miles. Although the proposed state was looked upon disapprovingly by Congress, the Mormons were nevertheless granted, in 1850, the Territory of Utah with Brigham Young as Governor. Opposition to the Mormon sanction of polygamy culminated in the "Utah War" from 1857 to 1858, and defense of core lands resulted in the overall loss of Mormon territory. The Mormons abolished polygamy in 1890, and Utah was admitted to the Union in its present form in 1896.

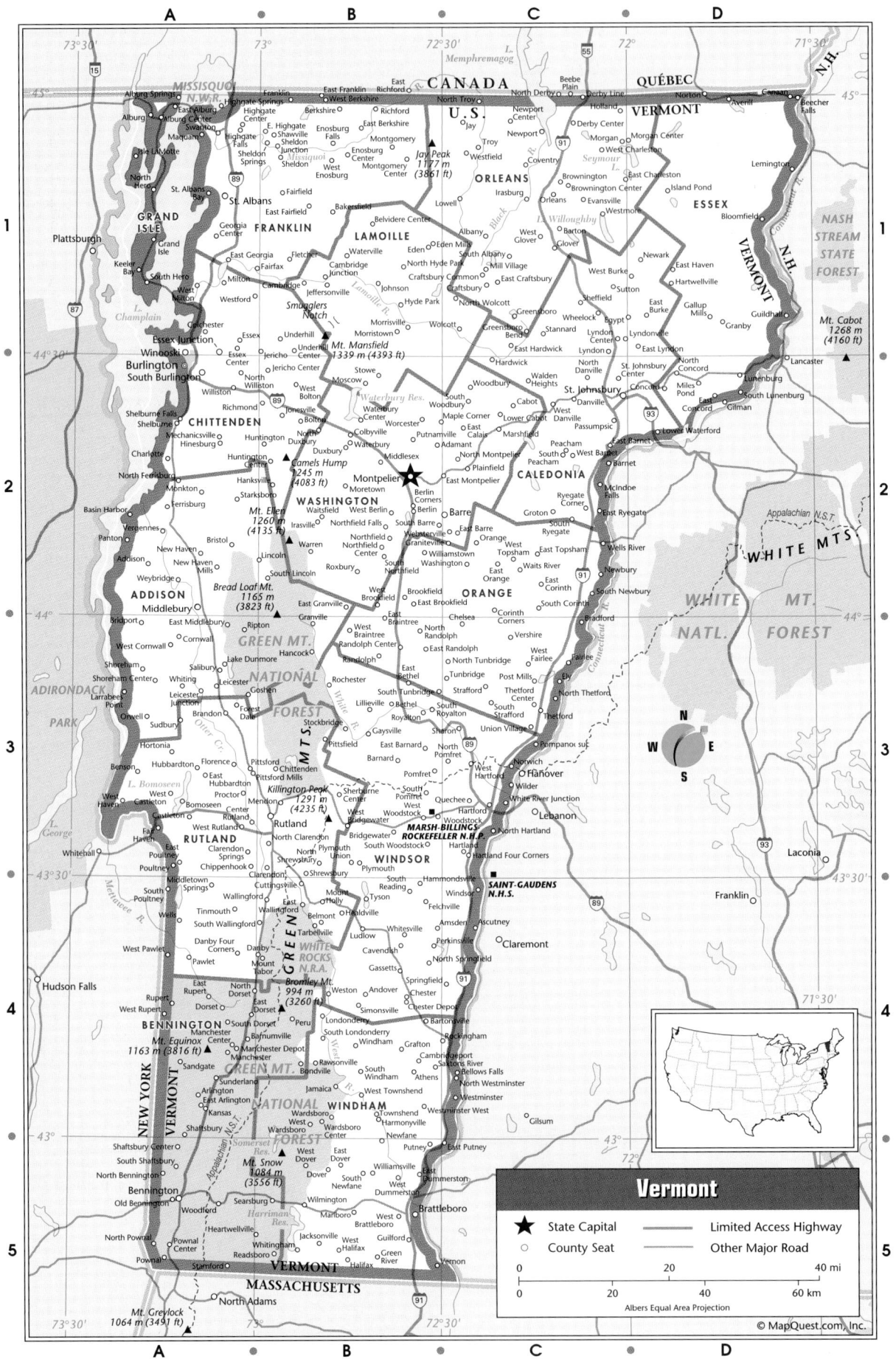

Vermont

★ State Capital
○ County Seat

Limited Access Highway
Other Major Road

0   20   40 mi
0   20   40   60 km
Albers Equal Area Projection

© MapQuest.com, Inc.

Vermont

Capital: Montpelier
Land Area: 9,249 sq. mi. / 23,955 sq. km.
Population: 608,827 (2000 Census)
Largest City: Burlington, 38,889
Highest Point: Mount Mansfield, 4,393 ft. / 1,339 m.
Admitted to Union: March 4, 1791
Nickname: Green Mountain State
State Flower: Red Clover
State Bird: Hermit Thrush

Vermont: Map Index

Counties

Addison, **35,974** ... A2
Bennington, **36,994** ... A4
Caledonia, **29,702** ... C2
Chittenden, **146,571** ... A2
Essex, **6,459** ... D1
Franklin, **45,417** ... B1
Grand Isle, **6,901** ... A1
Lamoille, **23,233** ... B1
Orange, **28,226** ... C2
Orleans, **26,277** ... C1
Rutland, **63,400** ... A3
Washington, **58,039** ... B2
Windham, **44,216** ... B4
Windsor, **57,418** ... B3

Cities and Towns

Cities and towns that are not labeled on the map are shown with an asterisk. They are included here only for population reference.

Addison, **1,393** ... A2
Albany, **840** ... C1
Alburg, **1,952** ... A1
Andover, **496** ... B4
Arlington, **2,397** ... A4
Athens, **340** ... B4
Averill, **8** ... D1
Bakersfield, **1,215** ... B1
Baltimore, **250** ... *
Barnard, **958** ... B3
Barnet, **1,690** ... C2
Barre (city), **9,291** ... C2
Barre (town), **7,602** ... C2
Barton, **2,780** ... C1
Belvidere, **294** ... *
Bennington, **15,737** ... A5
Benson, **1,039** ... A3
Berkshire, **1,388** ... B1
Berlin, **2,864** ... B2
Bethel, **1,968** ... B3
Bloomfield, **261** ... D1
Bolton, **971** ... B2
Bradford, **2,619** ... C3
Braintree, **1,194** ... *
Brandon, **3,917** ... A3
Brattleboro, **12,005** ... B5
Bridgewater, **980** ... B3
Bridport, **1,235** ... A3
Brighton, **1,260** ... *
Bristol, **3,788** ... A2
Brookfield, **1,222** ... B2
Brookline, **467** ... *
Brownington, **885** ... C1
Brunswick, **107** ... *
Buels Gore, **12** ... *
Burke, **1,571** ... *
Burlington, **38,889** ... A2
Cabot, **1,213** ... C2
Calais, **1,529** ... *
Cambridge, **3,186** ... B1
Canaan, **1,078** ... D1
Castleton, **4,367** ... A3
Cavendish, **1,470** ... B4
Charleston, **895** ... *
Charlotte, **3,569** ... A2
Chelsea, **1,250** ... C3
Chester, **3,044** ... B4
Chittenden, **1,182** ... B3
Clarendon, **2,811** ... B3
Colchester, **16,986** ... A1
Concord, **1,196** ... D2
Corinth, **1,461** ... *
Cornwall, **1,136** ... A3
Coventry, **1,014** ... C1
Craftsbury, **1,136** ... C1
Danby, **1,292** ... B4
Danville, **2,211** ... C2
Derby, **4,604** ... *
Dorset, **2,036** ... A4
Dover, **1,410** ... B5
Dummerston, **1,915** ... *
Duxbury, **1,289** ... B2
East Haven, **301** ... D1
East Montpelier, **2,578** ... C2
Eden, **1,152** ... B1
Elmore, **849** ... *
Enosburg, **2,788** ... *
Essex, **18,626** ... A1
Fairfax, **3,765** ... B1
Fairfield, **1,800** ... B1
Fair Haven, **2,928** ... A3
Fairlee, **967** ... C3
Fayston, **1,141** ... *
Ferdinand, **33** ... *
Ferrisburg, **2,657** ... A2
Fletcher, **1,179** ... B1
Franklin, **1,268** ... B1
Georgia, **4,375** ... *
Glastenbury, **16** ... *
Glover, **966** ... C1
Goshen, **227** ... A3
Grafton, **649** ... B4
Granby, **86** ... D1
Grand Isle, **1,955** ... A1
Granville, **303** ... B3
Greensboro, **770** ... C1
Groton, **876** ... C2
Guildhall, **268** ... D1
Guilford, **2,046** ... B5
Halifax, **782** ... B5
Hancock, **382** ... B3
Hardwick, **3,174** ... C2
Hartford, **10,367** ... C3
Hartland, **3,223** ... C3
Highgate, **3,397** ... *
Hinesburg, **4,340** ... A2
Holland, **588** ... C1
Hubbardton, **752** ... A3
Huntington, **1,861** ... B2
Hyde Park, **2,847** ... B1
Ira, **455** ... *
Irasburg, **1,077** ... C1
Isle La Motte, **488** ... A1
Jamaica, **946** ... B4
Jay, **426** ... C1
Jericho, **5,015** ... B1
Johnson, **3,274** ... B1
Killington (Sherburne), **1,095** ... *
Kirby, **456** ... *
Landgrove, **144** ... *
Leicester, **974** ... A3
Lemington, **107** ... D1
Lewis ... *
Lincoln, **1,214** ... B2
Londonderry, **1,709** ... B4
Lowell, **738** ... C1
Ludlow, **2,449** ... B4
Lunenburg, **1,328** ... D2
Lyndon, **5,448** ... C1
Maidstone, **105** ... *
Manchester, **4,180** ... A4
Marlboro, **978** ... B5
Marshfield, **1,496** ... C2
Mendon, **1,028** ... B3
Middlebury, **8,183** ... A2
Middlesex, **1,729** ... B2
Middletown Springs, **823** ... A4
Milton, **9,479** ... A1
Monkton, **1,759** ... A2
Montgomery, **992** ... B1
Montpelier, **8,035** ... B2
Moretown, **1,653** ... B2
Morgan, **669** ... C1
Morristown, **5,139** ... B1
Mount Holly, **1,241** ... B4
Mount Tabor, **203** ... B4
Newark, **470** ... D1
Newbury, **1,955** ... C2
Newfane, **1,680** ... B5
New Haven, **1,666** ... A2
Newport (city), **5,005** ... C1
Newport (town), **1,511** ... C1
Northfield, **5,791** ... B2
North Hero, **810** ... A1
Norton, **214** ... D1
Norwich, **3,544** ... C3
Orange, **965** ... C2
Orwell, **1,185** ... A3
Panton, **682** ... A2
Pawlet, **1,394** ... A4
Peacham, **665** ... C2
Peru, **416** ... B4
Pittsfield, **427** ... B3
Pittsford, **3,140** ... A3
Plainfield, **1,286** ... C2
Plymouth, **555** ... B3
Pomfret, **997** ... B3
Poultney, **3,633** ... A3
Pownal, **3,560** ... A5
Proctor, **1,877** ... A3
Putney, **2,634** ... B5
Randolph, **4,853** ... B3
Reading, **707** ... *
Readsboro, **809** ... B5
Richford, **2,321** ... B1
Richmond, **4,090** ... B2
Ripton, **556** ... A3
Rochester, **1,171** ... B3
Rockingham, **5,309** ... C4
Roxbury, **576** ... B2
Royalton, **2,603** ... B3
Rupert, **704** ... A4
Rutland (city), **17,292** ... B3
Rutland (town), **4,038** ... *B3
Ryegate, **1,150** ... *
St. Albans (city), **7,650** ... A1
St. Albans (town), **5,086** ... A1
St. George, **698** ... *
St. Johnsbury, **7,571** ... C2
Salisbury, **1,090** ... A3
Sandgate, **353** ... A4
Searsburg, **96** ... B5
Shaftsbury, **3,767** ... A4
Sharon, **1,411** ... C3
Sheffield, **727** ... C1
Shelburne, **6,944** ... A2
Sheldon, **1,990** ... B1
Shoreham, **1,222** ... A3
Shrewsbury, **1,108** ... B3
Somerset, **5** ... *
South Burlington, **15,814** ... A2
South Hero, **1,696** ... A1
Springfield, **9,078** ... C4
Stamford, **813** ... A5
Stannard, **185** ... C1
Starksboro, **1,898** ... A2
Stockbridge, **674** ... B3
Stowe, **4,339** ... B2
Strafford, **1,045** ... C3
Stratton, **136** ... *
Sudbury, **583** ... A3
Sunderland, **850** ... A4
Sutton, **1,001** ... C1
Swanton, **6,203** ... A1
Thetford, **2,617** ... C3
Tinmouth, **567** ... A4
Topsham, **1,142** ... *
Townshend, **1,149** ... B4
Troy, **1,564** ... C1
Tunbridge, **1,309** ... C3
Underhill, **2,980** ... B1
Vergennes, **2,741** ... A2
Vernon, **2,141** ... B5
Vershire, **629** ... C3
Victory, **97** ... *
Waitsfield, **1,659** ... B2
Walden, **782** ... *
Wallingford, **2,274** ... B4
Waltham, **479** ... *
Wardsboro, **854** ... B4
Warren, **1,681** ... B2
Warren's Gore, **10** ... *
Washington, **1,047** ... C2
Waterbury, **4,915** ... B2
Waterford, **1,104** ... *
Waterville, **697** ... B1
Weathersfield, **2,788** ... *
Wells, **1,121** ... A4
West Fairlee, **726** ... C3
Westfield, **503** ... C1
Westford, **2,086** ... A1
West Haven, **278** ... A3
Westminster, **3,210** ... C4
Westmore, **306** ... C1
Weston, **630** ... B4
West Rutland, **2,535** ... A3
West Windsor, **1,067** ... *
Weybridge, **824** ... A2
Wheelock, **621** ... C1
Whiting, **380** ... A3
Whitingham, **1,298** ... B5
Williamstown, **3,225** ... B2
Williston, **7,650** ... A2
Wilmington, **2,225** ... B5
Windham, **328** ... B4
Windsor, **3,756** ... C4
Winhall, **702** ... *
Winooski, **6,561** ... A1
Wolcott, **1,456** ... C1
Woodbury, **809** ... C2
Woodford, **414** ... A5
Woodstock, **3,232** ... C3
Worcester, **902** ... B2

Other Places

The city or town containing each entry is shown in italics. Village populations are given if available from the U.S. Census. See the "Cities and Towns" listing for total population.

Adamant *(Calais and East Montpelier)*, **150** ... B2
Alburg Center *(Alburg)*, **30** ... A1
Alburg Springs *(Alburg)*, **100** ... A1
Amsden *(Weathersfield)*, **175** ... B4
Ascutney *(Weathersfield)*, **450** ... C4
Barnumville ... A4
Bartonsville *(Rockingham)* ... B4
Basin Harbor *(Ferrisburg)*, **20** ... A2
Beebe Plain *(Derby)*, **200** ... C1
Beecher Falls *(Canaan)*, **100** ... D1
Bellows Falls *(Rockingham)*, **3,165** ... C4
Belmont *(Mount Holly)*, **90** ... B4
Belvidere Center *(Belvidere)*, **10** ... B1
Berlin Corners *(Berlin)*, **300** ... B2
Bomoseen *(Castleton)*, **90** ... A3
Bondville *(Winhall)*, **125** ... B4
Brownington Center *(Brownington)*, **125** ... C1
Cambridge Junction *(Cambridge)* ... B1
Cambridgeport *(Grafton and Rockingham)*, **125** ... B4
Center Rutland *(Rutland)*, **300** ... A3
Chester Depot *(Chester)*, **850** ... B4
Chippenhook *(Clarendon)* ... A3
Clarendon Springs *(Clarendon)*, **250** ... A3
Colbyville *(Waterbury)* ... B2
Corinth Corners *(Corinth)*, **90** ... C2
Craftsbury Common *(Craftsbury)*, **275** ... C1
Cuttingsville *(Shrewsbury)*, **175** ... B4
Danby Four Corners *(Danby)*, **80** ... A4
Derby Center *(Derby)*, **670** ... C1
Derby Line *(Derby)*, **776** ... C1
East Alburg *(Alburg)* ... A1
East Arlington *(Arlington)*, **750** ... A4
East Barnard *(Barnard)*, **50** ... B3
East Barnet *(Barnet)*, **70** ... C2
East Barre *(Barre [town])*, **2,136** ... C2
East Berkshire *(Berkshire)*, **175** ... B1
East Bethel *(Bethel)*, **175** ... B3
East Braintree *(Braintree)*, **150** ... B2
East Brookfield *(Brookfield)*, **225** ... B2
East Burke *(Burke)*, **175** ... D1
East Calais *(Calais)*, **275** ... C2
East Charleston *(Charleston)*, **70** ... D1
East Concord *(Concord)*, **80** ... D2
East Corinth *(Corinth)*, **175** ... C2
East Craftsbury *(Craftsbury)*, **125** ... C1
East Dorset *(Dorset)*, **250** ... A4
East Dover *(Dover)*, **150** ... B5
East Dummerston *(Dummerston)*, **175** ... B5
East Fairfield *(Fairfield)*, **200** ... B1
East Franklin *(Berkshire and Franklin)*, **125** ... B1
East Georgia *(Georgia)*, **200** ... A1
East Granville *(Granville)*, **50** ... B2
East Hardwick *(Hardwick)*, **300** ... C1
East Highgate *(Highgate)*, **175** ... B1
East Hubbardton *(Hubbardton)*, **90** ... A3
East Lyndon *(Lyndon)*, **100** ... D1
East Middlebury *(Middlebury)*, **650** ... A3
East Orange *(Orange)*, **80** ... C2
East Poultney *(Poultney)*, **400** ... A3
East Putney *(Putney)*, **350** ... C5
East Randolph *(Randolph)*, **200** ... B3
East Richford *(Richford)*, **20** ... B1
East Rupert *(Rupert)*, **90** ... A4
East Ryegate *(Ryegate)*, **150** ... C2
East Topsham *(Topsham)*, **90** ... C2
East Wallingford *(Wallingford)*, **200** ... B4
Eden Mills *(Eden)*, **175** ... B1
Egypt *(Bakersfield and Fairfield)* ... C1
Ely *(Fairlee)*, **100** ... C3
Enosburg Center *(Enosburg)* ... B1
Enosburg Falls *(Enosburg)*, **1,473** ... B1
Essex Center *(Essex)*, **2,700** ... A1
Essex Junction *(Essex)*, **8,591** ... A1
Evansville *(Brownington)*, **125** ... C1
Felchville *(Reading)*, **125** ... B4
Florence *(Pittsford)*, **275** ... A3
Forest Dale *(Brandon)*, **800** ... A3
Gallup Mills *(Victory)*, **30** ... D1
Gassetts *(Chester)*, **175** ... B4
Gaysville *(Stockbridge)*, **150** ... B3
Georgia Center *(Georgia)*, **375** ... A1
Gilman *(Lunenburg)*, **375** ... D2
Graniteville *(Barre)*, **2,136** ... C2
Green River *(Guilford)*, **100** ... B5
Greensboro Bend *(Greensboro)*, **350** ... C1
Hammondsville *(Reading)*, **70** ... B4
Hanksville *(Huntington)*, **70** ... B2
Harmonyville *(Townshend)*, **325** ... B4
Hartland Four Corners *(Hartland)* ... C3
Hartwellville, **175** ... D1
Healdville *(Mount Holly)*, **150** ... B4
Heartwellville *(Readsboro)*, **30** ... B5
Highgate Center *(Highgate)*, **600** ... A1
Highgate Falls *(Highgate)* ... A1
Highgate Springs *(Highgate)*, **125** ... A1
Hortonia *(Hubbardton)*, **125** ... A3
Huntington Center *(Huntington)*, **125** ... B2
Irasville *(Waitsfield)*, **150** ... B2
Island Pond *(Brighton)*, **849** ... D1
Jacksonville *(Whitingham)*, **237** ... B5
Jeffersonville *(Cambridge)*, **568** ... B1
Jericho Center *(Jericho)*, **375** ... B2
Jonesville *(Richmond)*, **375** ... B2
Kansas *(Sunderland)*, **80** ... A4
Keeler Bay *(South Hero)*, **250** ... A1
Lake Dunmore *(Leicester and Salisbury)*, **175** ... A3
Larrabees Point *(Shoreham)*, **30** ... A3
Leicester Junction *(Leicester)* ... A3
Lillieville *(Bethel)* ... B3
Lower Cabot *(Cabot)*, **125** ... C2
Lower Waterford *(Waterford)*, **80** ... D2
Lyndon Center *(Lyndon)*, **1,200** ... C1
Lyndonville *(Lyndon)*, **1,227** ... D1
Manchester Center *(Manchester)*, **2,065** ... A4
Manchester Depot *(Manchester)* ... A4
Maple Corner *(Calais)*, **125** ... C2
Maquam *(Swanton)*, **175** ... A1
McIndoe Falls *(Barnet)*, **200** ... C2
Mechanicsville *(Hinesburg)*, **500** ... A2
Miles Pond *(Concord)*, **20** ... D2
Mill Village *(Vershire)*, **125** ... C1
Montgomery Center *(Montgomery)*, **90** ... B1
Morgan Center *(Morgan)*, **60** ... D1
Morrisville *(Morristown)*, **2,009** ... B1
Moscow *(Stowe)*, **250** ... B2
New Haven Mills *(New Haven)*, **90** ... A2
Newport Center *(Newport)*, **300** ... C1
North Bennington *(Bennington)*, **1,428** ... A5
North Clarendon *(Clarendon)*, **700** ... B3
North Concord *(Concord)*, **175** ... D2
North Danville *(Danville)*, **225** ... C2
North Derby *(Derby)* ... C1
North Dorset *(Dorset)*, **30** ... A4
North Duxbury *(Duxbury)*, **30** ... B2
North Ferrisburg *(Ferrisburg)*, **500** ... A2
Northfield Center *(Northfield)* ... B2
Northfield Falls *(Northfield)*, **650** ... B2
North Hartland *(Hartland)*, **425** ... C3
North Hyde Park *(Hyde Park)*, **200** ... B1
North Montpelier *(East Montpelier)*, **275** ... C2
North Pomfret *(Pomfret)*, **175** ... C3
North Pownal *(Pownal)*, **300** ... A5
North Randolph *(Randolph)*, **100** ... B3
North Shrewsbury *(Shrewsbury)*, **40** ... B3
North Springfield *(Springfield)*, **1,100** ... B4
North Thetford *(Thetford)*, **250** ... C3
North Troy *(Troy)*, **593** ... C1
North Tunbridge *(Tunbridge)*, **125** ... C3
North Westminster *(Westminster)*, **271** ... C4
North Williston *(Williston)* ... A2
North Wolcott *(Wolcott)*, **200** ... C1
Old Bennington *(Bennington)*, **232** ... A5
Orleans *(Barton)*, **826** ... C1
Passumpsic *(Barnet)*, **150** ... C2
Perkinsville *(Weathersfield)*, **142** ... B4
Pittsford Mills ... A3
Plymouth Union *(Plymouth)*, **20** ... B3
Pompanoosuc *(Norwich)*, **125** ... C3
Post Mills *(Thetford)*, **300** ... C3
Pownal Center *(Pownal)*, **800** ... A5
Putnamville *(Middlesex)*, **90** ... B2
Quechee *(Hartford)*, **550** ... C3
Randolph Center *(Randolph)*, **850** ... B3
Rawsonville *(Jamaica)*, **60** ... B4
Ryegate Corner *(Ryegate)* ... C2
St. Albans Bay *(St. Albans)*, **425** ... A1
St. Johnsbury Center *(St. Johnsbury)*, **1,000** ... C2
Saxtons River *(Rockingham)*, **519** ... B4
Shaftsbury Center *(Shaftsbury)*, **250** ... A5
Shawville *(Sheldon)*, **200** ... B1
Shelburne Falls *(Shelburne)*, **1,700** ... A2
Sheldon Junction *(Sheldon)*, **125** ... B1
Sheldon Springs *(Sheldon)*, **200** ... B1
Sherburne Center *(Killington)*, **150** ... B3
Shoreham Center *(Shoreham)* ... A3
Simonsville *(Andover)*, **50** ... B4
South Albany *(Albany)*, **50** ... C1
South Barre *(Barre)*, **1,242** ... B2
South Corinth *(Corinth)*, **50** ... C2
South Dorset *(Dorset)*, **125** ... A4
South Lincoln *(Lincoln)*, **100** ... B2
South Londonderry *(Londonderry)*, **100** ... B4
South Lunenburg *(Lunenburg)*, **10** ... D2
South Newbury *(Newbury)*, **100** ... C2
South Newfane *(Newfane)*, **100** ... B5
South Northfield *(Northfield)* ... B2
South Peacham *(Peacham)*, **150** ... C2
South Pomfret *(Pomfret)*, **80** ... B3
South Poultney *(Poultney)*, **80** ... A4
South Reading *(Reading)*, **60** ... B4
South Royalton *(Royalton)*, **800** ... B3
South Ryegate *(Ryegate)*, **275** ... C2
South Shaftsbury *(Shaftsbury)*, **772** ... A5
South Strafford *(Strafford)*, **100** ... C3
South Tunbridge *(Tunbridge)*, **90** ... B3
South Wallingford *(Wallingford)*, **100** ... B4
South Windham *(Windham)*, **70** ... B4
South Woodbury *(Woodbury)*, **200** ... C2
South Woodstock *(Woodstock)*, **200** ... B3
Tarbellville *(Mount Holly)*, **100** ... B4
Thetford Center *(Thetford)* ... C3
Tyson *(Plymouth)*, **100** ... B4
Underhill Center *(Underhill)*, **500** ... B1
Union Village *(Norwich and Thetford)*, **125** ... C3
Waits River *(Topsham)*, **80** ... C2
Walden Heights *(Walden)*, **100** ... C2
Wardsboro Center *(Wardsboro)*, **125** ... B4
Waterbury Center *(Waterbury)*, **850** ... B2
Websterville *(Barre)*, **1,200** ... C2
Wells River *(Newbury)*, **325** ... C2
West Barnet *(Barnet)*, **225** ... C2
West Berkshire *(Berkshire)*, **125** ... B1
West Berlin *(Berlin)*, **150** ... B2
West Bolton *(Bolton)*, **150** ... B2
West Braintree *(Braintree)*, **70** ... B3
West Brattleboro *(Brattleboro)*, **3,222** ... B5
West Bridgewater *(Bridgewater and Killington)* ... B3
West Brookfield *(Brookfield)*, **60** ... B2
West Burke *(Burke)*, **364** ... D1
West Castleton *(Castleton)*, **20** ... A3
West Charleston *(Charleston)*, **150** ... C1
West Cornwall *(Cornwall)*, **150** ... A3
West Danville *(Danville)*, **125** ... C2
West Dover *(Dover)*, **175** ... B5
West Dummerston *(Dummerston)*, **325** ... B5
West Enosburg *(Enosburg)*, **100** ... B1
West Glover *(Glover)*, **90** ... C1
West Halifax *(Halifax)*, **175** ... B5
West Hartford *(Hartford)*, **375** ... C3
West Milton *(Milton)*, **600** ... A1
Westminster West *(Westminster)*, **80** ... B4
West Pawlet *(Pawlet)*, **40** ... A4
West Rupert *(Rupert)*, **125** ... A4
West Topsham *(Topsham)*, **175** ... C2
West Townshend *(Townshend)*, **150** ... B4
West Wardsboro *(Wardsboro)*, **125** ... B4
West Woodstock *(Woodstock)*, **300** ... B3
White River Junction *(Hartford)*, **2,569** ... C3
Whitesville *(Cavendish)* ... B4
Wilder *(Hartford)*, **1,636** ... C3
Williamsville *(Newfane)*, **200** ... B5

Other Features

Appalachian N.S.T. ... A5
Black, *river* ... C1
Bomoseen, *lake* ... A3
Bread Loaf, *mountain* ... B2
Bromley, *mountain* ... B4
Camels Hump, *mountain* ... B2
Champlain, *lake* ... A1
Connecticut, *river* ... C3, D1
Ellen, *mountain* ... B2
Equinox, *mountain* ... A4
Green, *mountains* ... B4
Green Mt. National Forest ... A4, B3
Harriman, *reservoir* ... B5
Jay, *peak* ... B1
Killington, *peak* ... B3
Lamoille, *river* ... B1
Mansfield, *mountain* ... B1
Marsh-Billings-Rockefeller N.H.P. ... B3
Memphremagog, *lake* ... C1
Mettawee, *river* ... A4
Missiquoi, *river* ... B1
Missisquoi N.W.R. ... A1
Otter, *creek* ... A3
Seymour, *lake* ... C1
Smugglers Notch, *pass* ... B1
Snow, *mountain* ... B5
Somerset, *reservoir* ... B5
Waterbury, *reservoir* ... B2
West, *river* ... B4
White, *river* ... B3
White Rocks N.R.A. ... B4
Willoughby, *lake* ... C1

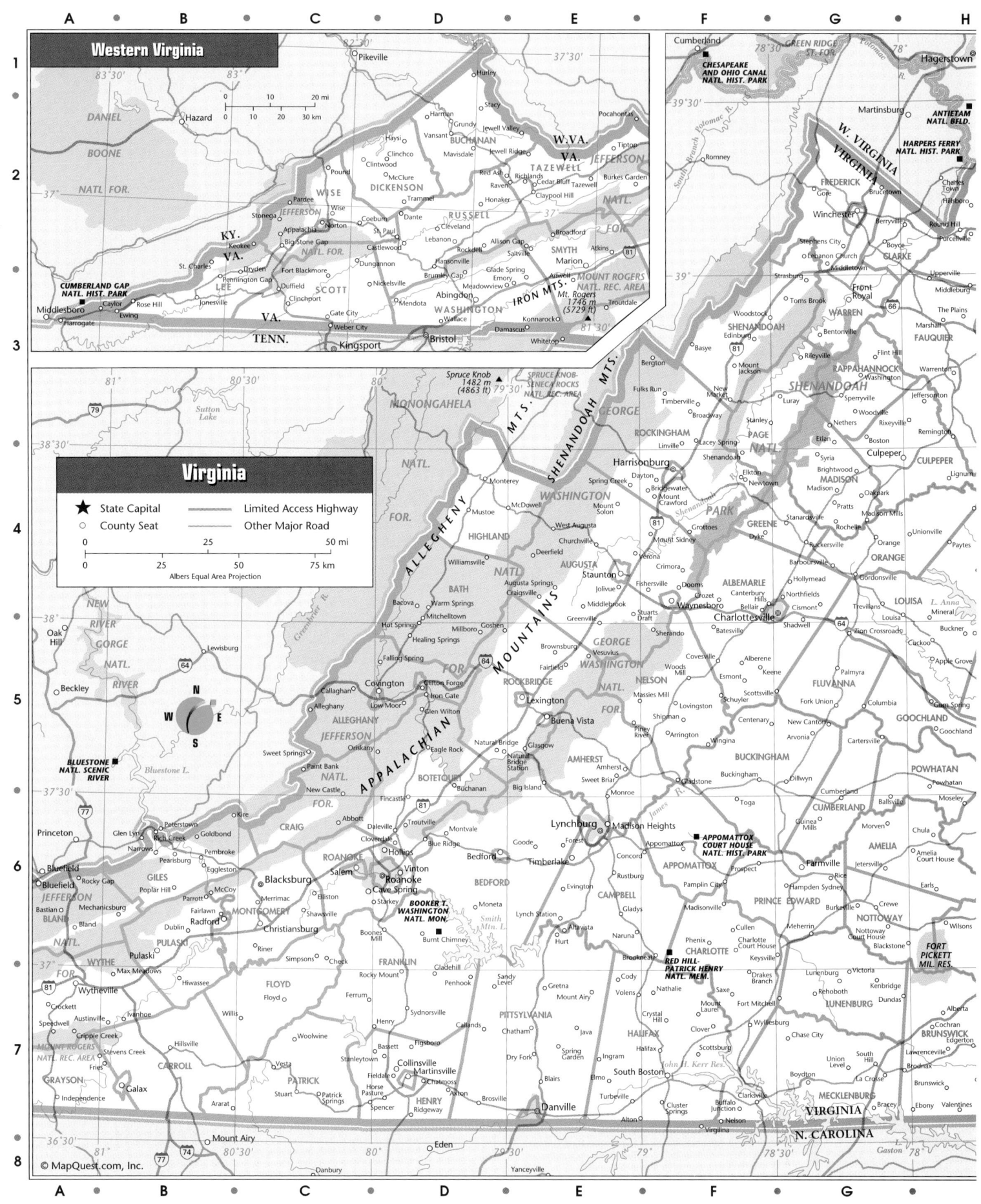

Western Virginia

0   10   20 mi
0 10 20 30 km

Virginia

★ State Capital —— Limited Access Highway
○ County Seat   —— Other Major Road

0   25   50 mi
0   25   50   75 km
Albers Equal Area Projection

© MapQuest.com, Inc.

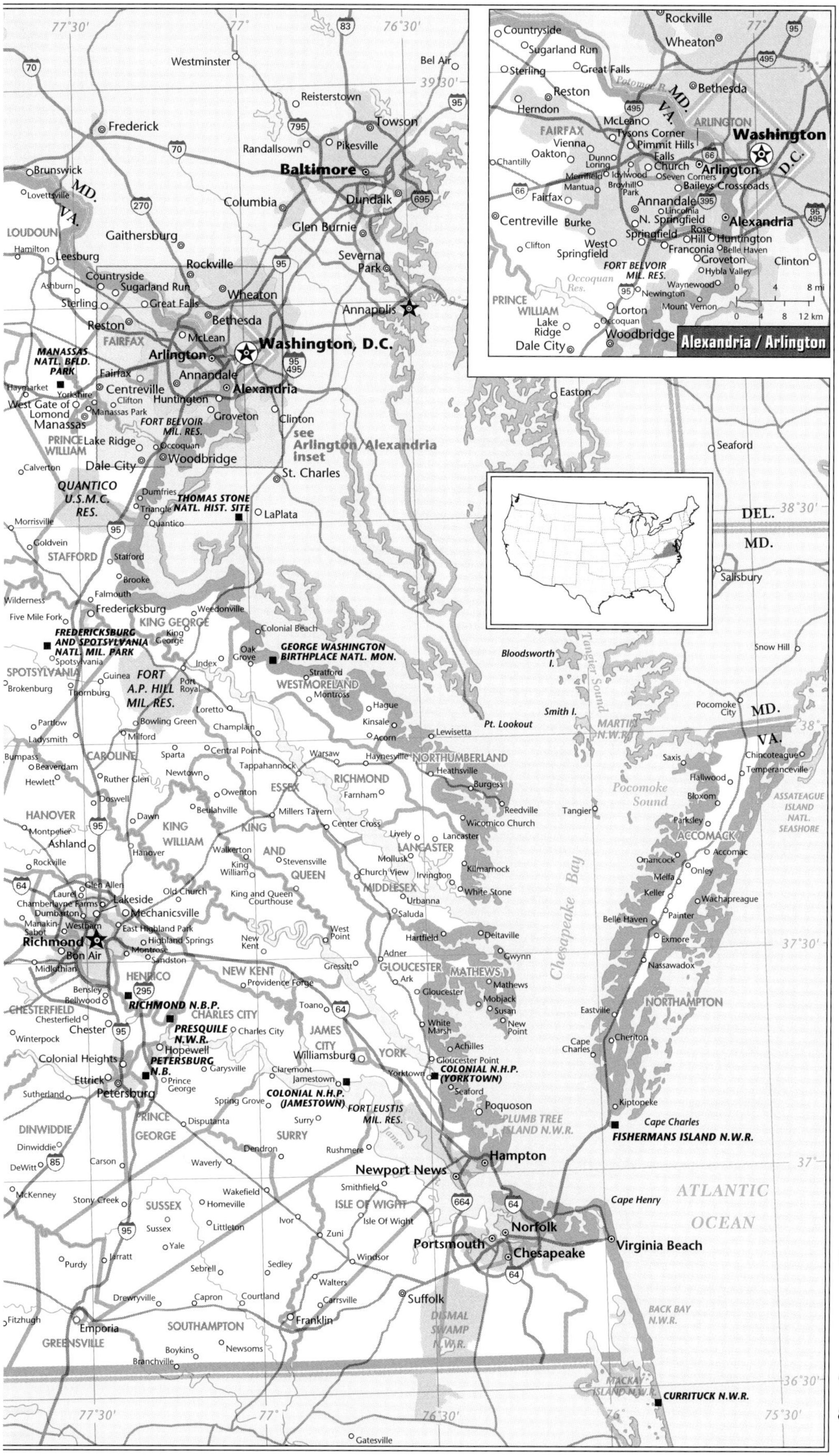

Virginia

Capital:	Richmond
Land Area:	39,598 sq. mi.
	102,559 sq. km.
Population:	7,078,515 (2000 Census)
Largest City:	Virginia Beach, 425,257
Highest Point:	Mount Rogers,
	5,729 ft.
	1,746 m.
Admitted to Union:	June 25, 1788
Nickname:	Old Dominion
State Flower:	Dogwood
State Bird:	Cardinal

Virginia:
Map Index

Counties

Accomack, 38,305 . . . . .M5
Albemarle, 79,236 . . . . .F4
Alleghany, 12,926 . . . . .C5
Amelia, 11,400 . . . . . . .G6
Amherst, 31,894 . . . . . .E5
Appomattox, 13,705 . . . .F6
Arlington, 189,453 . .J3, M2
Augusta, 65,615 . . . . . .E4
Bath, 5,048 . . . . .D4
Bedford, 60,371 . . . . . .D6
Bland, 6,871 . . . . .A6
Botetourt, 30,496 . . . . .D5
Brunswick, 18,419 . . . . .H7
Buchanan, 26,978 . . . . .D2
Buckingham, 15,623 . . . .F5
Campbell, 51,078 . . . . . .E6
Caroline, 22,121 . . . . . .J5
Carroll, 29,245 . . . . . . .B7
Charles City, 6,926 . . . . .J6
Charlotte, 12,472 . . . . . .F6
Chesterfield, 259,903 . . .H6
Clarke, 12,652 . . . . . . .G2
Craig, 5,091 . . . . .C6
Culpeper, 34,262 . . . . . .H4
Cumberland, 9,017 . . . . .G6
Dickenson, 16,395 . . . . .D2
Dinwiddie, 24,533 . . . . .H6
Essex, 9,989 . . . . .K5
Fairfax, 969,749 . . . .J3, L2
Fauquier, 55,139 . . . . . .H3
Floyd, 13,874 . . . . .C7
Fluvanna, 20,047 . . . . . .G5
Franklin, 47,286 . . . . . .D6
Frederick, 59,209 . . . . . .G2
Giles, 16,657 . . . . .B6
Gloucester, 34,780 . . . . .K6
Goochland, 16,863 . . . . .H5
Grayson, 17,917 . . . . . . .A7
Greene, 15,244 . . . . . . .F4
Greensville, 11,560 . . . . .H7
Halifax, 37,355 . . . . . . .E7
Hanover, 86,320 . . . . . .H5
Henrico, 262,300 . . . . . .J6
Henry, 57,930 . . . . .D7
Highland, 2,536 . . . . . . .D4
Isle of Wight, 29,728 . . .K7
James City, 48,102 . . . . .K6
King and Queen, 6,630 . .J5
King George, 16,803 . . . .J4
King William, 13,146 . . . .J5
Lancaster, 11,567 . . . . . .K5
Lee, 23,589 . . . . .B3
Loudoun, 169,599 . . . . .H2
Louisa, 25,627 . . . . . . .G4
Lunenburg, 13,146 . . . . .G7
Madison, 12,520 . . . . . .G4
Mathews, 9,207 . . . . . . .L6
Mecklenburg, 32,380 . . . .G7
Middlesex, 9,932 . . . . . .K5
Montgomery, 83,629 . . . .B6
Nelson, 14,445 . . . . . . .F5
New Kent, 13,462 . . . . . .J6
Northampton, 13,093 . . .M6
Northumberland,
12,259 . . . . .K5
Nottoway, 15,725 . . . . . .G6
Orange, 25,881 . . . . . . .G4
Page, 23,177 . . . . .F3
Patrick, 19,407 . . . . . . .C7
Pittsylvania, 61,745 . . . .E7
Powhatan, 22,377 . . . . . .H5
Prince Edward, 19,720 . .F6
Prince George, 33,047 . . .J6
Prince William,
280,813 . . . . . . .H3, L3
Pulaski, 35,127 . . . . . . .B6
Rappahannock, 6,983 . . .G3
Richmond, 8,809 . . . . . .K5
Roanoke, 85,778 . . . . . .C6
Rockbridge, 20,808 . . . . .E5
Rockingham, 67,725 . . . .F3
Russell, 30,308 . . . . . . .D2
Scott, 23,403 . . . . .C3
Shenandoah, 35,075 . . . .F3
Smyth, 33,081 . . . . .E2
Southampton, 17,482 . . .J7
Spotsylvania, 90,395 . . . .H4
Stafford, 92,446 . . . . . .H4
Surry, 6,829 . . . . .K6
Sussex, 12,504 . . . . .J7
Tazewell, 44,598 . . . . . .E2

Warren, 31,584 . . . . . . .G3
Washington, 51,103 . . .D3
Westmoreland, 16,718 .K4
Wise, 40,123 . . . . .C2
Wythe, 27,599 . . . . . . .A6
York, 56,297 . . . . .K6

Cities and Towns

Abbott, 70 . . . . .C6
Abingdon, 7,780 . . . . . .D3
Accomac, 547 . . . . . . .M5
Achilles, 650 . . . . .L6
Acorn, 60 . . . . .K4
Adner, 250 . . . . .K6
Adwolf, 1,457 . . . . .E3
Alberene, 175 . . . . .F5
Alberta, 306 . . . . .H7
Alexandria, 128,283 J3, M2
Alleghany, 40 . . . . .C5
Allison Gap, 900 . . . . . .E2
Altavista, 3,425 . . . . . . .E6
Alton, 60 . . . . .E7
Amelia Court House,
400 . . . . .H6
Amherst, 2,251 . . . . . . .E5
Annandale, 54,994 . J3, M2
Appalachia, 1,839 . . . . .C2
Apple Grove, 70 . . . . . .H5
Appomattox, 1,761 . . . .F6
Ararat, 275 . . . . .B7
Ark, 175 . . . . .K6
Arlington, 189,453 . .J3, M2
Arrington, 175 . . . . .F5
Arvonia, 325 . . . . .G5
Ashburn, 3,400 . . . . . . .J2
Ashland, 6,619 . . . . . . .J5
Atkins, 1,138 . . . . .E2
Augusta Springs, 300 . . .E4
Austinville, 273 . . . . . . .B7
Axton, 425 . . . . .D7
Bacova, 175 . . . . .D4
Baileys Crossroads,
23,166 . . . . .M2
Ballsville, 200 . . . . .G6
Barboursville, 200 . . . . .G4
Bassett, 1,338 . . . . .D7
Bastian, 350 . . . . .A6
Basye, 986 . . . . .F3
Batesville, 175 . . . . .F5
Beaverdam, 175 . . . . . .H5
Bedford, 6,299 . . . . . . .D6
Bellair, 3,700 . . . . .F4
Belle Haven (Accomack-
Northampton Cos.),
480 . . . . .M5
Belle Haven (Fairfax Co.),
6,269 . . . . .M2
Bellwood, 5,974 . . . . . .J6
Bensley, 5,435 . . . . .J6
Bentonville, 275 . . . . . .G3
Bergton F3
Berryville, 2,963 . . . . . .H2
Beulahville, 150 . . . . . . .J5
Big Island, 425 . . . . . . .E5
Big Stone Gap, 4,856 . . .C2
Blacksburg, 39,573 . . . .C6
Blackstone, 3,675 . . . . .G6
Blairs, 650 . . . . .E7
Bland, 500 . . . . .A6
Bloxom, 395 . . . . .M5
Bluefield, 5,078 . . . . . . .A6
Blue Ridge, 3,188 . . . . .D6
Bon Air, 16,213 . . . . . .H5
Boones Mill, 285 . . . . . .D6
Boston, 200 . . . . .G3
Bowling Green, 936 . . . .J4
Boyce, 426 . . . . .G2
Boydton, 454 . . . . .G7
Boykins, 620 . . . . .J7
Bracey, 90 . . . . .G7
Branchville, 123 . . . . . . .J7
Bridgewater, 5,203 . . . . .F4
Brightwood, 500 . . . . . .G4
Bristol, 17,367 . . . . . . .D3
Broadford, 150 . . . . .E2
Broadway, 2,192 . . . . . .F3
Brodnax, 317 . . . . .G7
Brokenburg, 200 . . . . . .H4
Brooke, 650 . . . . .J4
Brookneal, 1,259 . . . . . .F6
Brosville, 150 . . . . .D7
Brownsburg, 50 . . . . . . .E5
Broyhill Park, 17,000 . . .M2
Brucetown, 400 . . . . . . .G2
Brumley Gap, 100 . . . .D2

Brunswick, 70 . . . . .H7
Buchanan, 1,233 . . . . .D5
Buckingham, 175 . . . . .F5
Buckner, 250 . . . . .H5
Buena Vista, 6,349 . . . . .E5
Buffalo Junction, 125 . . . . . . .F7
Bumpass H5
Burgess, 300 . . . . .L5
Burke, 57,737 . . . . .M2
Burkes Garden E2
Burkeville, 489 . . . . .G6
Burnt Chimney, 200 . . . . .D6
Callaghan, 400 . . . . .D5
Callands, 60 . . . . .D7
Calverton, 125 . . . . .H3
Canterbury Hills F4
Cape Charles, 1,134 . . . . .L6
Capron, 167 . . . . .J7
Carrsville, 250 . . . . .K7
Carson, 150 . . . . .J6
Cartersville, 150 . . . . .G5
Castlewood, 2,036 . . . . .D2
Cave Spring, 24,941 . . . . .C6
Caylor, 225 . . . . .A3
Cedar Bluff, 1,085 . . . . .E2
Centenary, 100 . . . . .F5
Center Cross, 70 . . . . .K5
Central Point J5
Centreville, 48,661 . . . . . . .J3, L2
Chamberlayne Farms
  (Chamberlayne), 4,700 . . . .J5
Champlain, 90 . . . . .K4
Chantilly, 41,041 . . . . .L2
Charles City, 175 . . . . .J6
Charlotte Court House, 404 . . .F6
Charlottesville, 45,049 . . . . . .G4
Chase City, 2,457 . . . . .G7
Chatham, 1,338 . . . . .E7
Chatmoss, 1,742 . . . . .D7
Check, 225 . . . . .C6
Cheriton, 499 . . . . .M6
Chesapeake, 199,184 . . . . . . .L7
Chester, 17,890 . . . . .J6
Chesterfield, 3,558 . . . . .H6
Chincoteague, 4,317 . . . . .N5
Christiansburg, 16,947 . . . . . .C6
Chula, 250 . . . . .H6
Church View, 125 . . . . .K5
Churchville, 275 . . . . .E4
Cismont, 125 . . . . .G4
Claremont, 343 . . . . .K6
Clarksville, 1,329 . . . . .F7
Claypool Hill, 1,719 . . . . .E2
Cleveland, 148 . . . . .D2
Clifton, 185 . . . . .J3, L2
Clifton Forge, 4,289 . . . . .D5
Clinchco, 424 . . . . .D2
Clinchport, 77 . . . . .C3
Clintwood, 1,549 . . . . .C2
Clover, 200 . . . . .F7
Cloverdale, 2,986 . . . . .D6
Cluster Springs, 100 . . . . .F7
Cochran, 70 . . . . .H7
Cody, 60 . . . . .E7
Coeburn, 1,996 . . . . .C2
Collinsville, 7,777 . . . . .D7
Colonial Beach, 3,228 . . . . . . .K4
Colonial Heights, 16,897 . . . . .J6
Columbia, 49 . . . . .G5
Concord, 800 . . . . .F6
Countryside, 8,300 . . . . . .J2, L1
Courtland, 1,270 . . . . .J7
Covesville, 100 . . . . .F5
Covington, 6,303 . . . . .D5
Craigsville, 979 . . . . .E4
Crewe, 2,378 . . . . .G6
Crimora, 1,796 . . . . .F4
Cripple Creek, 60 . . . . .A7
Crockett, 150 . . . . .A7
Crozet, 2,820 . . . . .F4
Crystal Hill, 100 . . . . .F7
Cuckoo, 150 . . . . .H5
Cullen, 60 . . . . .F6
Culpeper, 9,664 . . . . .G4
Cumberland, 125 . . . . .G6
Dale City, 55,971 . . . . . . .J3, L3
Daleville, 1,454 . . . . .D6
Damascus, 981 . . . . .E3
Dante, 650 . . . . .D2
Danville, 48,411 . . . . .E7
Dawn, 100 . . . . .J5
Dayton, 1,344 . . . . .F4
Deerfield, 100 . . . . .E4
Deltaville, 800 . . . . .L5
Dendron, 297 . . . . .K6
DeWitt, 200 . . . . .H6
Dillwyn, 447 . . . . .G5
Dinwiddie, 350 . . . . .H6
Disputanta, 275 . . . . .J6
Dooms, 1,282 . . . . .F4
Doswell, 300 . . . . .J5
Drakes Branch, 504 . . . . .F7
Drewryville, 90 . . . . .J7
Dryden, 1,253 . . . . .B2
Dry Fork, 100 . . . . .E7
Dublin, 2,288 . . . . .B6
Duffield, 62 . . . . .C3
Dumbarton, 6,674 . . . . .H5
Dumfries, 4,937 . . . . .J3
Dundas, 125 . . . . .G7
Dungannon, 317 . . . . .C2
Dunn Loring, 7,861 . . . . .M2
Dyke, 125 . . . . .F4
Eagle Rock, 150 . . . . .D5
Earls, 60 . . . . .H6
East Highland Park, 12,488 . . .J5
Eastville, 203 . . . . .M6
Ebony, 125 . . . . .H7
Edgerton, 100 . . . . .H7
Edinburg, 813 . . . . .F3
Eggleston, 200 . . . . .B6
Elkton, 2,042 . . . . .F4

Elliston (Elliston-Lafayette),
  1,241 . . . . .C6
Elmo, 40 . . . . .E7
Emory (Emory-Meadow View),
  2,266 . . . . .E3
Emporia, 5,665 . . . . .H7
Esmont, 225 . . . . .F5
Etlan, 40 . . . . .G3
Ettrick, 5,627 . . . . .J6
Evington, 300 . . . . .E6
Ewing, 436 . . . . .B3
Exmore, 1,136 . . . . .M5
Fairfax, 21,498 . . . . .J3, L2
Fairfield, 225 . . . . .E5
Fairlawn, 2,211 . . . . .B6
Falling Spring, 200 . . . . .D5
Falls Church, 10,377 . . . . .M2
Falmouth, 3,624 . . . . .J4
Farmville, 6,845 . . . . .G6
Farnham, 250 . . . . .K5
Ferrum, 1,313 . . . . .C7
Fieldale, 929 . . . . .D7
Figsboro, 250 . . . . .D7
Fincastle, 359 . . . . .D6
Fishersville, 4,998 . . . . .E4
Fitzhugh, 50 . . . . .H7
Five Mile Fork H4
Flint Hill, 200 . . . . .G3
Floyd, 432 . . . . .C7
Forest, 8,006 . . . . .E6
Fork Union, 275 . . . . .G5
Fort Blackmore, 80 . . . . .C2
Fort Mitchell, 80 . . . . .G7
Franconia, 31,907 . . . . .M2
Franklin, 8,346 . . . . .K7
Fredericksburg, 19,279 . . . . . .J4
Fries, 614 . . . . .B7
Front Royal, 13,589 . . . . .G3
Fulks Run, 200 . . . . .F3
Galax, 6,837 . . . . .B7
Garysville J6
Gate City, 2,159 . . . . .C3
Gladehill, 125 . . . . .D7
Glade Spring, 1,374 . . . . .E3
Gladstone, 125 . . . . .F5
Gladys, 70 . . . . .E6
Glasgow, 1,046 . . . . .E5
Glen Allen, 12,562 . . . . .H5
Glen Lyn, 151 . . . . .B6
Glen Wilton, 175 . . . . .D5
Gloucester, 2,269 . . . . .K6
Gloucester Point, 9,429 . . . . . .L6
Goldbond, 80 . . . . .B6
Goldvein, 150 . . . . .H4
Goochland, 1,100 . . . . .H5
Goode, 125 . . . . .E6
Gordonsville, 1,498 . . . . .G4
Gore, 225 . . . . .G2
Goshen, 406 . . . . .D5
Great Falls, 8,549 . . . . . . .J2, M1
Greenville, 886 . . . . .E4
Gressitt, 80 . . . . .K6
Gretna, 1,257 . . . . .E7
Grottoes, 2,114 . . . . .F4
Groveton, 21,296 . . . . . . .J3, M2
Grundy, 1,105 . . . . .D2
Guinea, 125 . . . . .J4
Guinea Mills, 175 . . . . .G6
Gum Spring, 200 . . . . .H5
Gwynn, 600 . . . . .L5
Hague, 125 . . . . .K4
Halifax, 1,389 . . . . .F7
Hallwood, 290 . . . . .M5
Hamilton, 562 . . . . .H2
Hampden Sydney, 1,264 . . . . .G6
Hampton, 146,437 . . . . .L6
Hanover, 225 . . . . .J5
Hansonville, 80 . . . . .D2
Harman, 225 . . . . .D2
Harrisonburg, 40,468 . . . . . . .F4
Hartfield, 150 . . . . .L5
Haymarket, 879 . . . . .H3
Haynesville, 550 . . . . .K5
Haysi, 186 . . . . .D2
Healing Springs, 200 . . . . .D5
Heathsville L5
Henry, 100 . . . . .D7
Herndon, 21,655 . . . . .L2
Hewlett, 40 . . . . .H5
Highland Springs, 15,137 . . . . .J5
Hillsboro, 96 . . . . .H2
Hillsville, 2,607 . . . . .B7
Hiwassee, 275 . . . . .B7
Hollins, 14,309 . . . . .D6
Hollymead G4
Homeville, 80 . . . . .J7
Honaker, 945 . . . . .D2
Hopewell, 22,354 . . . . .J6
Horse Pasture, 2,255 . . . . .D7
Hot Springs, 300 . . . . .D5
Huntington, 8,325 . . . . . . .J3, M2
Hurley, 175 . . . . .D1
Hurt, 1,276 . . . . .E6
Hybla Valley, 16,721 . . . . .M2
Idylwood, 16,005 . . . . .M2
Independence, 971 . . . . .A7
Index, 150 . . . . .J4
Ingram, 90 . . . . .E7
Iron Gate, 404 . . . . .D5
Irvington, 673 . . . . .L5
Isle of Wight, 100 . . . . .K7
Ivanhoe, 300 . . . . .B7
Ivor, 320 . . . . .K7
Jamestown, 90 . . . . .K6
Jarratt, 589 . . . . .J7
Java, 175 . . . . .E7
Jeffersonton, 225 . . . . .H3
Jetersville, 60 . . . . .G6
Jewell Ridge, 325 . . . . .E2
Jewell Valley, 250 . . . . .E2
Jolivue, 1,037 . . . . .E4
Jonesville, 995 . . . . .B3

Keene, 60 . . . . .F5
Keller, 173 . . . . .M5
Kenbridge, 1,253 . . . . .G7
Keokee, 316 . . . . .C2
Keysville, 817 . . . . .G6
Kilmarnock, 1,244 . . . . .L5
King and Queen Courthouse,
  50 .K5
King George, 375 . . . . .J4
King William, 50 . . . . .J5
Kinsale, 250 . . . . .K4
Kiptopeke M6
Kire B6
Konnarock, 225 . . . . .E3
Lacey Spring, 400 . . . . .F3
La Crosse, 618 . . . . .G7
Ladysmith, 750 . . . . .H4
Lake Ridge, 30,404 . . . . . .J3, L3
Lakeside, 11,157 . . . . .J5
Lancaster, 100 . . . . .L5
Laurel, 14,875 . . . . .H5
Lawrenceville, 1,275 . . . . .H7
Lebanon, 3,273 . . . . .D2
Lebanon Church, 125 . . . . . . .G2
Leesburg, 28,311 . . . . .H2
Lewisetta, 100 . . . . .L4
Lexington, 6,867 . . . . .E5
Lignum, 225 . . . . .H4
Lincolnia, 15,788 . . . . .M2
Linville, 175 . . . . .F3
Littleton J7
Lively, 200 . . . . .K5
Loretto J4
Lorton, 17,786 . . . . .M3
Louisa, 1,401 . . . . .G4
Lovettsville, 853 . . . . .H2
Lovingston, 475 . . . . .F5
Low Moor, 367 . . . . .D5
Lunenburg, 40 . . . . .G7
Luray, 4,871 . . . . .G3
Lynchburg, 65,269 . . . . .E6
Lynch Station, 500 . . . . .E6
Madison, 210 . . . . .G4
Madison Heights, 11,584 . . . . .E6
Madison Mills, 125 . . . . .G4
Madisonville, 80 . . . . .F6
Manakin-Sabot, 90 . . . . .H5
Manassas, 35,135 . . . . .J3
Manassas Park, 10,290 . . . . . .J3
Mantua, 7,485 . . . . .M2
Marion, 6,349 . . . . .E2
Marshall, 1,200 . . . . .H3
Martinsville, 15,416 . . . . .D7
Massies Mill, 175 . . . . .E5
Mathews, 850 . . . . .L6
Mavisdale, 550 . . . . .D2
Max Meadows, 512 . . . . .B7
McClure, 350 . . . . .D2
McCoy, 90 . . . . .B6
McDowell, 30 . . . . .E4
McKenney, 441 . . . . .H7
McLean, 38,929 . . . . .J3, M2
Meadowview (Emory-
  Meadowview), 2,266 . . . . . .D3
Mechanicsburg, 80 . . . . .B6
Mechanicsville, 30,464 . . . . . .J5
Meherrin, 175 . . . . .G6
Melfa, 450 . . . . .M5
Mendota, 225 . . . . .D3
Merrifield, 11,170 . . . . .M2
Merrimac, 1,751 . . . . .C6
Middlebrook, 30 . . . . .E4
Middleburg, 632 . . . . .H3
Middletown, 1,015 . . . . .G2
Midlothian, 3,300 . . . . .H5
Milford, 375 . . . . .J4
Millboro, 150 . . . . .D5
Millers Tavern, 60 . . . . .K5
Mineral, 424 . . . . .H4
Mitchelltown, 250 . . . . .D4
Mobjack, 300 . . . . .L6
Mollusk, 300 . . . . .K5
Moneta, 225 . . . . .D6
Monroe, 1,200 . . . . .E5
Monterey, 158 . . . . .D4
Montpelier, 225 . . . . .H5
Montrose, 7,018 . . . . .J5
Montross, 315 . . . . .K4
Montvale, 375 . . . . .D6
Morrisville, 550 . . . . .H3
Morven, 125 . . . . .G6
Moseley, 275 . . . . .H6
Mount Airy, 90 . . . . .E7
Mount Crawford, 254 . . . . . . .F4
Mount Jackson, 1,664 . . . . . . .F3
Mount Laurel, 125 . . . . .F7
Mount Sidney, 750 . . . . .F4
Mount Solon, 100 . . . . .E4
Mount Vernon, 28,582 . . . . . .M3
Mustoe D4
Narrows, 2,111 . . . . .B6
Naruna, 175 . . . . .E6
Nassawadox, 572 . . . . .M6
Nathalie, 150 . . . . .F7
Natural Bridge, 100 . . . . .D5
Natural Bridge Station, 250 . . .D5
Nelson, 150 . . . . .F7
Nethers, 175 . . . . .G3
New Canton, 125 . . . . .G5
New Castle, 179 . . . . .C5
Newington, 19,784 . . . . .M2
New Kent, 175 . . . . .K5
New Market, 1,637 . . . . .F3
New Point, 325 . . . . .L6
Newport News, 180,150 . . . . . .L6
Newsoms, 282 . . . . .J7
Newtown (King and Queen Co.),
  40 .J5
Newtown (Rockingham Co.),
  750 . . . . .F4
Nickelsville, 448 . . . . .C3
Norfolk, 234,403 . . . . .L7

Northfields, 3,700 . . . . .G4
North Springfield, 9,173 . . . . .M2
Norton, 3,904 . . . . .C2
Nottoway Court House
  (Nottoway), 100 . . . . .G6
Oak Grove, 350 . . . . .J4
Oakpark, 125 . . . . .G4
Oakton, 29,348 . . . . .L2
Occoquan, 759 . . . . .J3, M3
Old Church, 150 . . . . .J5
Onancock, 1,525 . . . . .M5
Onley, 500 . . . . .M5
Orange, 4,123 . . . . .G4
Oriskany, 60 . . . . .D5
Owenton, 175 . . . . .J5
Paint Bank C5
Painter, 246 . . . . .M5
Palmyra, 100 . . . . .G5
Pamplin City, 199 . . . . .F6
Pardee, 50 . . . . .C2
Parksley, 837 . . . . .M5
Parrott, 225 . . . . .B6
Partlow, 200 . . . . .H4
Patrick Springs, 2,068 . . . . . . .C7
Paytes, 250 . . . . .H4
Pearisburg, 2,729 . . . . .B6
Pembroke, 1,134 . . . . .B6
Penhook, 726 . . . . .D7
Pennington Gap, 1,781 . . . . . .B3
Petersburg, 33,740 . . . . .J6
Phenix, 200 . . . . .F6
Pimmit Hills, 6,152 . . . . .M2
Piney River, 200 . . . . .E5
Pocahontas, 441 . . . . .E2
Poplar Hill B6
Poquoson, 11,566 . . . . .L6
Port Royal, 150 . . . . .J4
Portsmouth, 100,565 . . . . .L7
Pound, 1,089 . . . . .C2
Powhatan, 550 . . . . .H5
Pratts, 250 . . . . .G4
Prince George, 750 . . . . .J6
Prospect, 250 . . . . .F6
Providence Forge, 175 . . . . . . .J6
Pulaski, 9,473 . . . . .B6
Purcellville, 3,584 . . . . .H2
Purdy, 70 . . . . .H7
Quantico, 561 . . . . .J3
Radford, 15,859 . . . . .B6
Raven, 2,593 . . . . .E2
Red Ash, 100 . . . . .D2
Reedville, 600 . . . . .L5
Rehoboth G7
Remington, 624 . . . . .H3
Reston, 56,407 . . . . .J3, L2
Rice, 250 . . . . .G6
Rich Creek, 665 . . . . .B6
Richlands, 4,144 . . . . .E2
Richmond, 197,790 . . . . .J5
Ridgeway, 775 . . . . .D7
Rileyville, 275 . . . . .G3
Riner, 300 . . . . .C6
Rixeyville, 50 . . . . .H3
Roanoke, 94,911 . . . . .D6
Rochelle, 400 . . . . .G4
Rockdell, 70 . . . . .D7
Rockville, 450 . . . . .H5
Rocky Gap, 175 . . . . .A6
Rocky Mount, 4,066 . . . . .D7
Rose Hill (Fairfax Co.), 15,058 . M2
Rose Hill (Lee Co.), 714 . . . . . .B3
Round Hill, 500 . . . . .H2
Ruckersville, 100 . . . . .G4
Rushmere, 1,083 . . . . .K6
Rustburg, 1,271 . . . . .E6
Ruther Glen, 300 . . . . .J5
St. Charles, 159 . . . . .B2
St. Paul, 1,000 . . . . .D2
Salem, 24,747 . . . . .D6
Saltville, 2,204 . . . . .E2
Saluda, 575 . . . . .K5
Sandston, 3,400 . . . . .J5
Sandy Level, 50 . . . . .D7
Saxe, 70 . . . . .F7
Saxis, 337 . . . . .M5
Schuyler, 250 . . . . .F5
Scottsburg, 145 . . . . .F7
Scottsville, 555 . . . . .G5
Seaford, 2,000 . . . . .L6
Sebrell, 60 . . . . .J7
Sedley, 500 . . . . .K7
Seven Corners, 8,701 . . . . . . .M2
Shadwell, 150 . . . . .G4
Shawsville, 1,029 . . . . .C6
Shenandoah, 1,878 . . . . .F4
Sherando, 665 . . . . .F5
Shipman, 375 . . . . .F5
Simpsons, 125 . . . . .C6
Smithfield, 6,324 . . . . .K7
South Boston, 8,491 . . . . .F7
South Hill, 4,403 . . . . .G7
Sparta, 175 . . . . .A7
Speedwell, 450 . . . . .A7
Spencer, 175 . . . . .C7
Sperryville, 250 . . . . .G3
Spotsylvania (Spotsylvania
  Courthouse), 3,833 . . . . . . .H4
Spring Creek, 250 . . . . .E4
Springfield, 30,417 . . . . .M2
Spring Garden, 175 . . . . .E7
Spring Grove K6
Stacy, 275 . . . . .D2
Stafford, 3,000 . . . . .J4
Stanardsville, 476 . . . . .G4
Stanley, 1,326 . . . . .F4
Stanleytown, 1,515 . . . . .D7
Starkey, 600 . . . . .D6
Staunton, 23,853 . . . . .E4
Stephens City, 1,146 . . . . .G2
Sterling, 20,500 . . . . .J2, L1
Stevens Creek, 550 . . . . .B7
Stevensville, 40 . . . . .K5

Stonega, 475 . . . . .C2
Stony Creek, 202 . . . . .J7
Strasburg, 4,017 . . . . .G3
Stratford, 80 . . . . .K4
Stuart, 961 . . . . .C7
Stuarts Draft, 8,367 . . . . .E4
Suffolk, 63,677 . . . . .K7
Sugarland Run, 9,400 . . . . .J2, L1
Surry, 262 . . . . .K6
Susan, 475 . . . . .L6
Sussex, 125 . . . . .J7
Sutherland, 400 . . . . .H6
Sweet Briar, 750 . . . . .E5
Sydnorsville, 150 . . . . .D7
Syria G3
Tangier, 604 . . . . .M5
Tappahannock, 2,068 . . . . . . .K5
Tazewell, 4,206 . . . . .E2
Temperanceville, 275 . . . . . . .M5
The Plains, 266 . . . . .H3
Thornburg, 450 . . . . .H4
Timberlake, 10,683 . . . . .E6
Timberville, 1,739 . . . . .F3
Tiptop, 175 . . . . .E2
Toano, 1,400 . . . . .K6
Toga, 125 . . . . .F6
Toms Brook, 255 . . . . .G3
Trammel D2
Trevilians, 100 . . . . .G4
Triangle, 5,500 . . . . .J3
Troutdale, 1,230 . . . . .E3
Troutville, 432 . . . . .D6
Turbeville, 70 . . . . .E7
Tysons Corner, 18,540 . . . . . . .M2
Union Level, 125 . . . . .G7
Unionville, 175 . . . . .H4
Upperville, 150 . . . . .H3
Urbanna, 543 . . . . .K5
Valentines H7
Vansant, 989 . . . . .D2
Verona, 3,638 . . . . .E4
Vesta, 125 . . . . .C7
Vesuvius, 200 . . . . .E5
Victoria, 1,821 . . . . .G7
Vienna, 14,453 . . . . .M2
Vinton, 7,782 . . . . .D6
Virgilina, 159 . . . . .F7
Virginia Beach, 425,257 . . . . .M7
Volens, 80 . . . . .E7
Wachapreague, 236 . . . . .M5
Wakefield, 1,038 . . . . .K7
Walkerton, 175 . . . . .J5
Wallace, 550 . . . . .D3
Walters, 275 . . . . .K7
Warm Springs, 200 . . . . .D4
Warrenton, 6,670 . . . . .H3
Warsaw, 1,375 . . . . .K5
Washington, 183 . . . . .G3
Waverly, 2,309 . . . . .J6
Waynesboro, 19,520 . . . . .F4
Waynewood (part of Fort Hunt,
  pop. 12,923), 6,000 . . . . . . .M2
Weber City, 1,333 . . . . .C3
Weedonville, 450 . . . . .J4
West Augusta, 80 . . . . .E4
West Gate of Lomond, 7,493 . . .H3
Westham (part of Tuckahoe, pop.
  43,242) H5
West Point, 2,866 . . . . .K5
West Springfield, 28,378 . . . . .M2
White Marsh, 600 . . . . .K6
White Stone, 358 . . . . .L5
Whitetop, 175 . . . . .E3
Wicomico Church, 250 . . . . . . .L5
Wilderness, 300 . . . . .H4
Williamsburg, 11,998 . . . . .K6
Williamsville D4
Willis, 100 . . . . .C7
Wilsons, 100 . . . . .H6
Winchester, 23,585 . . . . .G2
Windsor, 916 . . . . .K7
Wingina F5
Winterpock, 125 . . . . .H6
Wise, 3,255 . . . . .C2
Woodbridge, 31,941 . . . . .J3, M3
Woods Mill, 50 . . . . .F5
Woodstock, 3,952 . . . . .F3
Woodville, 60 . . . . .G3
Woolwine, 175 . . . . .C7
Wylliesburg, 100 . . . . .F7
Wytheville, 7,804 . . . . .A7
Yale, 60 . . . . .J7
Yorkshire, 6,732 . . . . .J3

Yorktown, 203 . . . . .K6
Zion Crossroads, 375 . . . . .G5
Zuni, 200 . . . . .K7

Other Features

Allegheny, mountains D4
Anna, lake H4
Antietam Natl. Bfld. H2
Appalachian, mountains C5
Appomattox Court House
  Natl. Hist. Park F6
Assateague Island
  Natl. Seashore N5
Atlantic, ocean M7
Back Bay N.W.R. M7
Bloodsworth, island L4
Bluestone, lake B5
Bluestone Natl. Scenic River . . .A5
Booker T. Washington
  Natl. Mon. D6
Charles, cape M6
Chesapeake, bay L6
Chesapeake And Ohio Canal
  Natl. Hist. Park F1
Colonial Natl.
  Hist. Park K6, L6
Cumberland Gap
  Natl. Hist. Park A3
Currituck N.W.R. M8
Daniel Boone Natl. For. A2
Dismal Swamp N.W.R. L7
Fishermans Island N.W.R. M6
Fort A.P. Hill Mil. Res. J4
Fort Belvoir Mil. Res. J3, M2
Fort Eustis Mil. Res. K6
Fort Pickett Mil. Res. H6
Fredericksburg And Spotsylvania
  Natl. Mil. Park H4
Gaston, lake G8
George Washington Birthplace
  Natl. Mon. K4
George Washington
  Natl. For. E3, E5
Greenbrier, river C5
Green Ridge St. For. G1
Harpers Ferry Natl. Hist. Park . .H2
Henry, cape M7
Iron, mountains E3
James, river E6, K6
Jefferson Natl. For. A6, C2, C5, E2
John H. Kerr, reservoir F7
Lookout, point L4
Mackay Island N.W.R. M7
Manassas Natl. Bfld. Park H3
Martin N.W.R. M4
Monongahela Natl. For. D3
Mount Rogers
  Natl. Rec. Area A7, E3
New River Gorge Natl. River . . .A4
Occoquan, reservoir L2
Petersburg N.B. J6
Plumb Tree Island N.W.R. L6
Pocomoke, sound M5
Potomac, river F2, G1, K4, M2
Presquile N.W.R. J6
Quantico U.S.M.C. Res. J3
Rappahannock, river J4
Red Hill-Patrick Henry
  Natl. Mem. F6
Richmond N.B.P. J6
Rogers, mountain E3
Shenandoah, mountains E4
Shenandoah, river F4
Shenandoah Natl. Park G3
Smith, island L4
Smith Mtn., lake D6
Spruce Knob, mountain D3
Spruce Knob Seneca
  Rocks Natl. Rec. Area E3
Sutton, lake B3
Tangier, sound M4
York, river K6

Springtime in Shenandoah National Park

Washington

Capital:	Olympia
Land Area:	66,581 sq. mi.
	172,445 sq. km.
Population:	5,894,121 (2000 Census)
Largest City:	Seattle, 563,374
Highest Point:	Mount Rainier,
	14,410 ft.
	4,392 m.
Admitted to Union:	November 11, 1889
Nickname:	Evergreen State
State Flower:	Western Rhododendron
State Bird:	Willow Goldfinch

Washington:
Map Index

Counties

Adams, 16,428 . . . . .G2
Asotin, 20,551 . . . . .H3
Benton, 142,475 . . . . .F3
Chelan, 66,616 . . . . .E1
Clallam, 64,525 . . . . .B2
Clark, 345,238 . . . . .C4
Columbia, 4,064 . . . . .H3
Cowlitz, 92,948 . . . . .C3
Douglas, 32,603 . . . . .F2
Ferry, 7,260 . . . . .G1
Franklin, 49,347 . . . . .G3
Garfield, 2,397 . . . . .H3
Grant, 74,698 . . . . .F2
Grays Harbor, 67,194 . . . . .B2
Island, 71,558 . . . . .C1
Jefferson, 25,953 . . . . .B2
King, 1,737,034 . . . . . .B4, D2
Kitsap, 231,969 . . . . . .A4, C2
Kittitas, 33,362 . . . . .E2
Klickitat, 19,161 . . . . .E4
Lewis, 68,600 . . . . .C3
Lincoln, 10,184 . . . . .G2
Mason, 49,405 . . . . .B2
Okanogan, 39,564 . . . . . . .F1
Pacific, 20,984 . . . . .B3
Pend Oreille, 11,732 . . . . . .H1
Pierce, 700,820 . . . . .C2
San Juan, 14,077 . . . . . . .C1
Skagit, 102,979 . . . . .D1
Skamania, 9,872 . . . . .C3
Snohomish, 606,024 . .B4, D2
Spokane, 417,939 . . . . . . .H2
Stevens, 40,066 . . . . .H1
Thurston, 207,355 . . . . . . .C3
Wahkiakum, 3,824 . . . . . . .B3
Walla Walla, 55,180 . . . . . .G3
Whatcom, 166,814 . . . . . . .D1
Whitman, 40,740 . . . . .H3
Yakima, 222,581 . . . . .D3

Cities and Towns

Aberdeen, 16,461 . . . . . . .B2
Acme, 263 . . . . .C1
Addy, 175 . . . . .H1
Adna, 350 . . . . .B3
Aeneas, 40 . . . . .G1
Airway Heights, 4,500 . . . .H2
Albion, 616 . . . . .H3
Alder, 130 . . . . .C3
Alderdale F4
Alderwood Manor
 (Alderwood Manor-Bothell
 North), 15,329 . . . . . . .A4
Algona, 2,460 . . . . .C2
Allyn (Allyn-Grapeview),
 2,004 . . . . .C2
Almira, 302 . . . . .G2
Almota H3
Alstown F2
Altoona B3
Amanda Park, 100 . . . . . . .B2
Amber H2
Amboy, 2,085 . . . . .C4
Anacortes, 14,557 . . . . . . .C1
Anatone, 40 . . . . .H3
Arden, 250 . . . . .H1
Ardenvoir, 90 . . . . .E2
Ariel, 70 . . . . .C4
Arlington, 11,713 . . . . . . .C1
Artondale C2
Ashford, 267 . . . . .C3
Asotin, 1,095 . . . . .H3
Auburn, 40,314 . . . . .C2
Ault Field, 2,064 . . . . . . .C1
Ayer, 50 . . . . .G3
Azwell, 40 . . . . .F2
Bainbridge Island, 20,308 . .A4
Baring, 233 . . . . .D2
Basin City, 968 . . . . .F3
Battle Ground, 9,296 . . . . .C4
Bay Center, 174 . . . . .B3
Beaux Arts, 307 . . . . .A4
Beaver, 150 . . . . .A1
Belfair, 700 . . . . .C2
Bellevue, 109,569 . . . .A4, C2
Bellingham, 67,171 . . . . . .C1
Belmont H2
Belvedere, 100 . . . . .G1
Benge G3
Benton City, 2,624 . . . . . .F3

Berrydale, 850 . . . . .B4, C2
Beverly, 70 . . . . .F3
Bickleton, 113 . . . . .E4
Bingen, 672 . . . . .D4
Big Lake, 1,153 . . . . .C1
Birch Bay, 4,961 . . . . .C1
Black Diamond, 3,970 . . . .C2
Blaine, 3,770 . . . . .C1
Blanchard, 150 . . . . .C1
Blyn, 162 . . . . .B1
Boistfort B3
Bonney Lake, 9,687 . . . . . .C2
Boston Harbor, 450 . . . . . .B2
Bothell, 30,150 . . . . .A4
Bow, 425 . . . . .C1
Boyds G1
Bremerton, 37,259 . . .A4, C2
Brewster, 2,189 . . . . .F1
Briarwood (part of East
 Renton Highlands, pop.
 13,264) B4
Bridgeport, 2,059 . . . . . . .F2
Brier, 6,383 . . . . .A4
Brinnon, 803 . . . . .C2
Brooklyn, 50 . . . . .B3
Brownsville, 600 . . . . .A4
Brush Prairie, 2,384 . . . . . .C4
Bryant, 550 . . . . .C1
Buckley, 4,145 . . . . .C2
Bucoda, 628 . . . . .C3
Buena, 950 . . . . .E3
Burbank, 3,303 . . . . .F3
Burien, 31,881 . . . . . .A4, C2
Burley, 900 . . . . .C2
Burlington, 6,757 . . . . . . .C1
Camas, 12,534 . . . . .C4
Camden, 90 . . . . .H1
Carbonado, 621 . . . . .C2
Carlisle A2
Carlton, 60 . . . . .F1
Carnation, 1,893 . . .B4, D2
Carrolls, 300 . . . . .C3
Carson (Carson River Valley),
 1,200 . . . . .D4
Cascade Park East C4
Cascade Park West C4
Cascade Valley, 1,811 . . .F2
Cashmere, 2,965 . . . . . . .E2
Castle Rock, 2,130 . . . . . .C3
Cathan, 526 . . . . .C1
Cathlamet, 565 . . . . .B3
Cedar Falls, 500 . . . .B4, D2
Cedonia, 60 . . . . .G1
Centralia, 14,742 . . . . . . .C3
Central Park, 2,558 . . . . . .B2
Chattaroy, 550 . . . . .H2
Chehalis, 7,057 . . . . .C3
Chehalis Village, 346 . . . . .B3
Chelan, 3,522 . . . . .E2
Chelan Falls, 225 . . . . . . .F2
Chelatchie, 50 . . . . .C4
Cheney, 8,832 . . . . .H2
Chesaw, 50 . . . . .F1
Chewelah, 2,186 . . . . . . .H1
Chinook, 457 . . . . .B3
Cinebar, 60 . . . . .C3
Clallam Bay, 850 . . . . . . .A1
Clarkston, 7,337 . . . . .H3
Clarkston Heights (Clarkston
 Heights-Vineland),
 6,117 . . . . .H3
Clayton, 175 . . . . .H2
Cle Elum, 1,755 . . . . .E2
Cliffdell, 40 . . . . .D3
Clinton, 868 . . . . .C1
Clyde G3
Clyde Hill, 2,890 . . . . .A4
Colbert, 400 . . . . .H2
Colfax, 2,844 . . . . .H3
College Place, 7,818 . . . . . .G3
Colton, 386 . . . . .H3
Colville, 4,988 . . . . .H1
Conconully, 185 . . . . .F1
Concrete, 790 . . . . .D1
Connell, 2,956 . . . . .G3
Conway, 84 . . . . .C1
Copalis Beach, 489 . . . . . .A2
Copalis Crossing, 100 . . . . .A2
Cordell, 50 . . . . .F1
Cosmopolis, 1,595 . . . . . .B3
Cougar, 90 . . . . .C3
Coulee City, 600 . . . . .F2
Coulee Dam, 1,044 . . . . . .G2
Country Homes, 5,203 . . . .H2
Coupeville, 1,723 . . . . . . .C1
Covington (Covington-

Sawyer-Wilderness),
 13,783 . . . . .B4
Creston, 232 . . . . .G2
Cumberland, 250 . . . . . . .D2
Cunningham, 40 . . . . .G3
Curlew, 175 . . . . .G1
Cusick, 212 . . . . .H1
Custer, 299 . . . . .C1
Daisy G1
Dalkena, 80 . . . . .H1
Dallesport, 1,185 . . . . . . .D4
Danville, 70 . . . . .G1
Darrington, 1,136 . . . . . . .D1
Davenport, 1,730 . . . . . . .G2
Dayton, 2,655 . . . . .H3
Deep Creek, 275 . . . . .H2
Deer Park, 3,017 . . . . .H2
Deming, 210 . . . . .C1
Desert Aire, 1,124 . . . . . . .F3
Des Moines, 29,267 . . . . . .A4
Diablo, 50 . . . . .D1
Diamond Lake, 200 . . . . . .H1
Disautel, 40 . . . . .F1
Dishman, 10,031 . . . . . . .H2
Dixie, 220 . . . . .G3
Dockton, 375 . . . . .A4
Dodge H3
Donald, 175 . . . . .E3
Doris, 90 . . . . .E3
Doty, 325 . . . . .B3
Douglas F2
Dungeness, 425 . . . . .B1
Du Pont, 2,452 . . . . .C2
Dusty H3
Duvall, 4,616 . . . .B4, D2
East Farms (Otis Orchards-
 East Farms), 6,318 . . . .H2
Eastgate, 4,558 . . . . .B4
East Olympia, 900 . . . . . . .C3
Easton, 383 . . . . .D2
East Port Orchard, 5,116 .A4
Eastsound, 750 . . . . .C1
East Wenatchee, 5,757 . .E2
Eatonville, 2,012 . . . . .C3
Edgewood, 9,089 . . . . . . .C2
Edmonds, 39,515 . . . .A4, C2
Edwall, 40 . . . . .H2
Elbe, 21 . . . . .C3
Elberton H3
Eldon, 40 . . . . .B2
Electric City, 922 . . . . .F2
Elk, 175 . . . . .H1
Elk Plain, 15,697 . . . . . . .C2
Ellensburg, 15,414 . . . . . .E3
Ellisforde, 150 . . . . .F1
Ellisport, 1,200 . . . . .A4, C2
Ellsworth
 (Ellsworth South) C4
Ellsworth North C4
Elma, 3,049 . . . . .B2
Elmer City, 267 . . . . .G2
Eltopia, 80 . . . . .F3
Endicott, 621 . . . . .H3
Entiat, 957 . . . . .E2
Enumclaw, 11,116 . . . . . .D2
Ephrata, 6,808 . . . . .F2
Erlands Point (Erlands Point-
 Kitsap Lake), 2,723 . . . .C2
Esperance, 3,503 . . . . .A4
Eureka, 80 . . . . .G3
Evans, 125 . . . . .G1
Everett, 91,488 . . . . .C1
Everson, 2,035 . . . . .C1
Ewan H2
Fairfield, 494 . . . . .H2
Fairmount (part of Paine
 Field-Lake Stickney, pop.
 24,383) C2
Fairview
 (Fairview-Sumach) E3
Fairwood (King Co.,
 Cascade-Fairwood),
 34,580 . . . . .A4
Fairwood (Spokane Co.),
 6,764 . . . . .H2
Fall City, 1,638 . . . . .B4
Farmer F2
Farmington, 153 . . . . .H2
Federal Way, 83,259 . . . .C2
Felida, 5,683 . . . . .C4
Ferndale, 8,758 . . . . .C1
Fife, 4,784 . . . . .C2
Finley, 5,770 . . . . .F3
Fircrest, 5,868 . . . . .C2
Five Corners, 12,207 . . . .C4
Ford, 40 . . . . .H2
Fords Prairie, 1,961 . . . . . .B3
Forks, 3,120 . . . . .A2
Fort Lewis, 19,089 . . . . . .C2
Four Lakes, 400 . . . . .H2
Fox Island, 2,803 . . . . . . .C2
Frances, 70 . . . . .B3
Freeland, 1,313 . . . . .C1
Freeman, 80 . . . . .H2
Friday Harbor, 1,989 . . . . .B1
Fruitland G1
Fruitvale E3
Garfield, 641 . . . . .H2
Garrett, 1,022 . . . . .G3
Geneva, 2,257 . . . . .C1
George, 528 . . . . .F2
Gifford G1
Gig Harbor, 6,465 . . . . . . .C2
Glacier, 90 . . . . .D1
Gleed, 2,947 . . . . .E3
Glenoma, 225 . . . . .C3
Glenwood, 175 . . . . .D3
Gold Bar, 2,014 . . . .B4, D2
Goldendale, 3,760 . . . . . . .E4
Goodnoe Hills E4
Goose Prairie D3

Grand Coulee, 897 . . . . .F2
Grand Mound, 1,948 . . . . .B3
Grandview, 8,377 . . . . . . .F3
Granger, 2,530 . . . . .E3
Granite Falls, 2,347 . . .D1
Grayland, 1,002 . . . . .A3
Grays River, 90 . . . . .B3
Green Acres, 5,158 . . . . . .H2
Greenbank, 225 . . . . .C1
Greenwater, 100 . . . . .D2
Grisdale B2
Grotto D2
Hamilton, 309 . . . . .D1
Hansville, 100 . . . . .C1
Harbour Pointe C2
Harrah, 542 . . . . .E3
Harrington, 426 . . . . .G2
Hartline, 134 . . . . .F2
Hatton, 98 . . . . .G3
Havillah F1
Hay H3
Hayford, 150 . . . . .H2
Hazel Dell (Hazel Dell
 South), 6,605 . . . . . . .C4
Highland, 3,388 . . . . .F3
Hobart, 6,251 . . . .B4, D2
Holden, 60 . . . . .E1
Holly, 80 . . . . .C2
Home, 400 . . . . .C2
Hood, 80 . . . . .D4
Hoodsport, 200 . . . . .B2
Hooper G3
Hoquiam, 9,097 . . . . .B3
Humptulips, 216 . . . . .B2
Hunters, 125 . . . . .G1
Hunts Point, 443 . . . . .A4
Huntsville G3
Husum, 200 . . . . .D4
Hyak D2
Ilwaco, 950 . . . . .A3
Inchelium, 389 . . . . .G1
Index, 157 . . . . .D2
Indianola, 3,026 . . . . .A4
Inglewood (Inglewood-Finn
 Hill), 22,661 . . . . .A4
Ione, 479 . . . . .H1
Irby, 100 . . . . .G2
Issaquah, 11,212 . . .B4, C2
Johnson H3
Joyce, 90 . . . . .B1
Kahlotus, 214 . . . . .G3
Kalaloch, 40 . . . . .A2
Kalama, 1,783 . . . . .C3
Kapowsin, 200 . . . . .C3
Keller G1
Kelso, 11,895 . . . . .C3
Kenmore, 18,678 . . . . . . .A4
Kennewick, 54,693 . . . .F3
Kenroy (East Wenatchee
 Bench), 13,658 . . . . . .E2
Kent, 79,524 . . . . . .A4, C2
Kettle Falls, 1,527 . . . . . .G1
Kewa, 60 . . . . .G1
Kingsgate, 12,222 . . . . . . .A4
Kingston, 1,611 . . . . .A4
Kirkland, 45,054 . . . .A4, C2
Kitsap Lake (see Erlands
 Point) C2
Kittitas, 1,105 . . . . .E3
Klickitat, 417 . . . . .D4
Kooskooskie, 100 . . . . . . .G4
Krupp, 60 . . . . .G2
La Center, 1,654 . . . . .C4
La Conner, 761 . . . . .C1
La Crosse, 380 . . . . .H3
La Grande, 70 . . . . .C3
Lake Forest Park, 13,142 .A4
Lake Goodwin, 3,354 . . . .C1
Lake Shore, 6,670 . . . . . . .C4
Lake Stevens, 6,361 . . . . . .C1
Lakewood (Pierce Co.),
 58,211 . . . . .C2
Lakewood
 (Snohomish Co.), 350 . .C1
Lamona G2
Lamont, 106 . . . . .H2
Lancaster H2
Langley, 959 . . . . .C1
La Push, 225 . . . . .A2
Latah, 151 . . . . .H2
Laurel, 600 . . . . .C1
Laurier, 60 . . . . .G1
Leadpoint, 200 . . . . .H1
Leavenworth, 2,074 . . . . . .E2
Lebam, 176 . . . . .B3
Lester D2
Lexington, 325 . . . . .C3
Liberty E2
Liberty Lake, 4,660 . . . . . .H2
Lilliwaup, 125 . . . . .B2
Lincoln G2
Lind, 582 . . . . .G3
Littlerock, 250 . . . . .B3
Long Beach, 1,283 . . . . . . .A3
Longbranch, 90 . . . . .C2
Long Lake H2
Longmire D3
Longview, 34,660 . . . . . . .C3
Longview Heights, 3,513 .C3
Loomis, 125 . . . . .F1
Loon Lake, 400 . . . . .H1
Lopez, 200 . . . . .C1
Lost Creek, 100 . . . . .H1
Lucerne, 60 . . . . .E1
Lummi Island, 325 . . . . . . .C1
Lyle, 530 . . . . .D4
Lyman, 409 . . . . .C1
Lynden, 9,020 . . . . .C1
Lynnwood, 33,847 . .A4, C2
Mabana, 325 . . . . .C1
Mabton, 1,891 . . . . .F3

Malden, 215 . . . . .H2
Malo G1
Malott, 250 . . . . .F1
Maltby, 8,267 . . . . .C2
Manchester, 4,958 . . . . . .A4
Mansfield, 319 . . . . .F2
Manson, 900 . . . . .E2
Maple Falls, 277 . . . . .C1
Maple Valley, 14,209 . . . .B4
Marble H1
Marblemount, 251 . . . . . .D1
Marcellus G2
Marcus, 117 . . . . .G1
Marengo G3
Marietta (Marietta-
 Alderwood), 3,594 . . . .C1
Markham, 95 . . . . .B3
Marshall, 175 . . . . .H2
Martha Lake, 12,633 . . . .C2
Maryhill, 98 . . . . .E4
Marys Corner, 325 . . . . . .C3
Marysville, 25,315 . . . . . .C1
Matlock B2
Mattawa, 2,609 . . . . .F3
Mazama E1
McCleary, 1,454 . . . . .B2
McKenna, 800 . . . . .C3
McMurray, 150 . . . . .C1
Mead, 2,100 . . . . .H2
Meadow Glade, 2,225 . . . .C4
Medical Lake, 3,758 . . . . . .H2
Medina, 3,011 . . . . .A4
Menlo, 225 . . . . .B3
Mercer Island, 22,036 . . . .A4
Meridian Heights (part of
 East Hill-Meridian, pop.
 29,308) B4
Merritt E2
Mesa, 425 . . . . .G3
Metaline, 162 . . . . .H1
Metaline Falls, 223 . . . . . .H1
Methow, 100 . . . . .E1
Mica, 225 . . . . .H2
Midland, 7,414 . . . . .C2
Milan, 225 . . . . .H2
Miles G2
Mill Creek, 11,525 . . . . . . .A4
Milton, 5,795 . . . . .C2
Mineral, 250 . . . . .C3
Minnehaha, 7,689 . . . . . . .C4
Mirrormont, 3,804 . .B4, D2
Moclips, 615 . . . . .A2
Mohler G2
Molson F1
Mondovi G2
Monitor, 375 . . . . .E2
Monroe, 13,795 . . . .B4, D2
Monse F1
Montesano, 3,312 . . . . . . .B3
Morton, 1,045 . . . . .C3
Moses Lake, 14,953 . . . . .F2
Moses Lake North, 4,232 .F2
Mossyrock, 486 . . . . .C3
Mountlake Terrace,
 20,362 . . . . .A4
Mount Pleasant (part of Port
 Angeles East, pop.
 3,053) B1
Mount Vernon, 26,232 . . .C1
Moxee E3
Moxee City, 821 . . . . .E3
Mukilteo, 18,019 . . . . . . .C2
Naches, 643 . . . . .E3
Napavine, 1,361 . . . . .C3
Naselle, 377 . . . . .B3
Navy Yard City, 2,638 . . . .A4
Neah Bay, 794 . . . . .A1
Neilton, 345 . . . . .B2
Nemah B3
Nespelem, 212 . . . . .G1
Nespelem Community,
 290 . . . . .F1
Newcastle, 7,737 . . . .A4, C2
Newhalem, 60 . . . . .D1
New London, 90 . . . . .B2
Newport, 1,921 . . . . .H1
Nighthawk F1
Nine Mile Falls, 250 . . . . . .H2
Nisqually, 550 . . . . .C2
Nooksack, 851 . . . . .C1
Normandy Park, 6,392 . . .A4
North Bend, 4,746 . .B4, D2
North Bonneville, 593 . . . .D4
North Hill A4
North Lynnwood (Lake
 Serene-North
 Lynnwood) A4
North Marysville, 21,161 .C1
North Omak, 688 . . . . . . .F1
Northport, 336 . . . . .H1
North Yelm, 2,793 . . . . . . .C3
Oakesdale, 420 . . . . .H2
Oak Harbor, 19,795 . . . . . .C1
Oakville, 675 . . . . .B3
Ocean City, 217 . . . . .A2
Ocean Park, 1,459 . . . . . . .A3
Ocean Shores, 3,836 . . . . .A3
Odessa, 957 . . . . .G2
Okanogan, 2,484 . . . . . . .F1
Olga, 150 . . . . .C1
Olympia, 42,514 . . . . .C2
Omak, 4,721 . . . . .F1
Onalaska, 325 . . . . .C3
Opportunity, 25,065 . . . . .H2
Orcas, 150 . . . . .C1
Orchards (Orchards South),
 17,852 . . . . .C4
Orient, 80 . . . . .G1
Orondo, 175 . . . . .E2
Oroville, 1,653 . . . . .F1
Orting, 3,760 . . . . .C2

Ostrander, 275 . . . . .C3
Othello, 5,847 . . . . .F3
Otis Orchards (Otis
 Orchards-East Farms),
 6,318 . . . . .H2
Oysterville, 40 . . . . .A3
Pacific, 5,527 . . . . .C2
Pacific Beach, 375 . . . . . . .A2
Packwood, 550 . . . . .D3
Palisades, 50 . . . . .F2
Palouse, 1,011 . . . . .H3
Parker, 400 . . . . .E3
Parkland, 24,053 . . . . . . .C2
Park Rapids, 70 . . . . .H1
Parkwood, 7,213 . . . . . . .A4
Pasco, 32,066 . . . . .F3
Pataha, 60 . . . . .H3
Pateros, 643 . . . . .F1
Paterson F4
Pe Ell, 627 . . . . .B3
Peshastin, 650 . . . . .E2
Pine City H2
Pine Lake B4
Plain, 50 . . . . .E2
Plaza H2
Pleasant View G3
Plymouth, 175 . . . . .F4
Point Roberts, 375 . . . . . . .B1
Pomeroy, 1,517 . . . . .H3
Port Angeles, 18,397 . . . . .B1
Porter, 473 . . . . .B3
Port Gamble, 325 . .A4, C2
Port Hadlock, 3,476 . . . . .C1
Port Ludlow, 1,968 . . . . . .C1
Port Madison, 1,000 . . . . .A4
Port Orchard, 7,693 .A4, C2
Port Townsend, 8,334 . . . .C1
Poulsbo, 6,813 . . . . .A4, C2
Prescott, 314 . . . . .G3
Preston, 200 . . . . .B4
Priest Point, 779 . . . . .C1
Prosser, 4,838 . . . . .F3
Pullman, 24,675 . . . . .H3
Puyallup, 33,011 . . . . . . .C2
Queets, 175 . . . . .A2
Quilcene, 591 . . . . .C2
Quinault, 40 . . . . .B2
Quincy, 5,044 . . . . .F2
Rainier, 1,492 . . . . .C3
Ralston G3
Randle, 70 . . . . .D3
Ravensdale, 86 . . . . .B4
Raymond, 2,975 . . . . .B3
Reardan, 608 . . . . .H2
Redmond, 45,256 . . .B4, C2
Renton, 50,052 . . . . .A4, C2
Republic, 954 . . . . .G1
Revere H2
Rice, 70 . . . . .G1
Richardson, 80 . . . . .C1
Richland, 38,708 . . . . . . .F3
Ridgefield, 2,147 . . . . . . .C4
Rimrock D3
Ritzville, 1,736 . . . . .G2
Riverside, 348 . . . . .F1
Riverton Heights A4
Robe, 70 . . . . .D1
Rochester, 1,829 . . . . .B3
Rockford, 413 . . . . .H2
Rock Island, 863 . . . . .E2
Rockport, 102 . . . . .D1
Roosevelt, 79 . . . . .E4
Rosalia, 648 . . . . .H2
Rosario, 175 . . . . .C1
Rosburg, 40 . . . . .B3
Roslyn, 1,017 . . . . .E2
Roy, 250 . . . . .C3
Royal City, 1,823 . . . . . . .F3
Ruby, 80 . . . . .H1
Ruff G2
Ruston, 738 . . . . .C2
Ryderwood, 325 . . . . .B3
Sahalee B4, C2
St. John, 548 . . . . .H2
Salkum, 250 . . . . .C3
Salmon Creek, 16,767 . . . .C4
San de Fuca, 325 . . . . . . .C1
Sappho A1
Satsop, 746 . . . . .B3
Satus, 746 . . . . .E3
Sawyer, 200 . . . . .E3
Schrag G2
Seabeck, 325 . . . . .C2
SeaTac, 25,496 . . . . .A4
Seattle, 563,374 . . . .A4, C2
Sedro-Woolley, 8,658 . . . .C1
Selah, 6,310 . . . . .E3
Selleck, 225 . . . . .B4
Sequim, 4,334 . . . . .B1
Shaw Island, 70 . . . . .C1
Shelter Bay C1
Shelton, 8,442 . . . . .C2
Shoreline, 53,025 . . . .A4, C2
Silverdale, 15,816 . . . . . . .C2
Silver Lake (Cowlitz Co.),
 250 . . . . .C3
Silver Lake
 (Snohomish Co.) C2
Silverton D1
Similk Beach, 450 . . . . . . .C1
Skamokawa, 60 . . . . .B3
Skokomish, 616 . . . . .B2
Skykomish, 214 . . . . .D2
Skyway (Bryn Mawr-
 Skyway), 13,977 . . . . .A4
Smokey Point, 1,556 . . . . .C1
Smyrna, 230 . . . . .F3
Snake River G3
Snee Oosh C1
Snohomish, 8,494 . . . . . .C2
Snoqualmie, 1,631 . .B4, D2
Snoqualmie Pass, 201 . . .D2
Soap Lake, 1,733 . . . . . . .F2

South Bend, 1,807 . . . .B3
South Broadway E3
South Cle Elum, 457 . . . .E2
South Prairie, 382 . . . . . .C2
South Wenatchee, 1,991 .E2
Spanaway, 21,588 . . . . .C2
Spangle, 240 . . . . .H2
Spokane, 195,629 . . . . . .H2
Sprague, 490 . . . . .H2
Springdale, 283 . . . . .H1
Stanwood, 3,923 . . . . . . .C1
Starbuck, 130 . . . . .G3
Stehekin, 60 . . . . .E1
Steilacoom, 6,049 . . . . . .C2
Steptoe, 60 . . . . .H3
Stevenson, 1,200 . . . . . . .D4
Stimson Crossing, 773 . . . .C1
Stratford F2
Sudden Valley, 4,165 . . . .C1
Sultan, 3,344 . . . . .D2
Sumach E3
Sumas, 960 . . . . .C1
Sumner, 8,504 . . . . .C2
Sunnyside, 13,905 . . . . . .E3
Sunnyslope, 2,521 . . . . . .E2
Suquamish, 3,510 . . . . . . .A4
Synarep, 10 . . . . .F1
Tacoma, 193,556 . . . . . .C2
Tahlequah, 225 . . . . .C2
Taholah, 824 . . . . .A2
Tahuya, 225 . . . . .B2
Tampico, 150 . . . . .E3
Tanglewilde (Tanglewilde-
 Thompson Place),
 5,670 . . . . .C2
Tekoa, 826 . . . . .H2
Telma, 80 . . . . .E2
Tenino, 1,447 . . . . .C3
Terrace Heights, 6,447 . . . .E3
Thompson Place (see
 Tanglewild) C2
Thornton, 70 . . . . .H2
Thorp, 273 . . . . .E2
Thrashers Corner A4
Tieton, 1,154 . . . . .E3
Tiger H1
Tokeland, 194 . . . . .B3
Toledo, 653 . . . . .C3
Tonasket, 994 . . . . .F1
Toppenish, 8,946 . . . . . . .E3
Touchet, 396 . . . . .G3
Toutle, 125 . . . . .C3
Town and Country,
 4,452 . . . . .H2
Tracyton, 3,267 . . . . .A4
Trentwood, 4,388 . . . . . . .H2
Trout Lake, 494 . . . . .D4
Tukwila, 17,181 . . . . .A4
Tulalip, 1,561 . . . . .C1
Tumtum, 40 . . . . .H2
Tumwater, 12,698 . . . . . .C3
Turner H3
Twisp, 938 . . . . .E1
Tyler H2
Union, 375 . . . . .B2
Union Gap, 5,621 . . . . . . .E3
Uniontown, 345 . . . . .H3
University Place, 29,933 .C2
Usk, 100 . . . . .H1
Vader, 590 . . . . .C3
Vail, 225 . . . . .C3
Valley, 125 . . . . .H1
Vancouver, 143,560 . . . .C4
Vantage, 70 . . . . .F3
Van Zandt, 200 . . . . .C1
Vashon Heights, 1,100 . . . .A4
Vaughn, 400 . . . . .A4
Veradale, 9,387 . . . . .H2
Waitsburg, 1,212 . . . . . . .G3
Waldron B1
Walla Walla, 29,686 . . . . .G3
Walla Walla East, 2,479 .G3
Wallula, 197 . . . . .G3
Walnut Grove, 7,164 . . . . .C4
Wapato, 4,582 . . . . .E3
Warden, 2,544 . . . . .F3
Warm Beach, 2,040 . . . . . .C1
Washougal, 8,595 . . . . . . .C4
Washtucna, 260 . . . . .G3
Waterville, 1,163 . . . . . . .E2
Wauconda F1
Waukon H2
Waverly, 121 . . . . .H2
Wawawai, 60 . . . . .H3
Wellpinit, 60 . . . . .H1
Wenatchee, 27,856 . . . . .E2
West Clarkston (West
 Clarkston-Highland),
 4,707 . . . . .H3
West Lake Sammamish,
 5,937 . . . . .B4
West Lake Stevens,
 18,071 . . . . .C2
West Longview, 2,882 . . . .B3
West Pasco, 4,629 . . . . . .F3
Westport, 2,137 . . . . .A3
West Richland, 8,385 . . . .F3
West Wenatchee, 1,681 . . .E2
Wheeler, 20 . . . . .F2
White Center, 20,975 . . . .A4
White Salmon, 2,193 . . . . .D4
White Swan, 3,033 . . . . . .E3
Wickersham, 125 . . . . . . .C1
Wilbur, 914 . . . . .G2
Wiley City, 850 . . . . .E3
Wilkeson, 395 . . . . .C2
Wilson Creek, 227 . . . . . . .F2
Winchester, 70 . . . . .F2
Winlock, 1,166 . . . . .C3
Winona, 40 . . . . .H3
Winthrop, 349 . . . . .E1
Winton E2

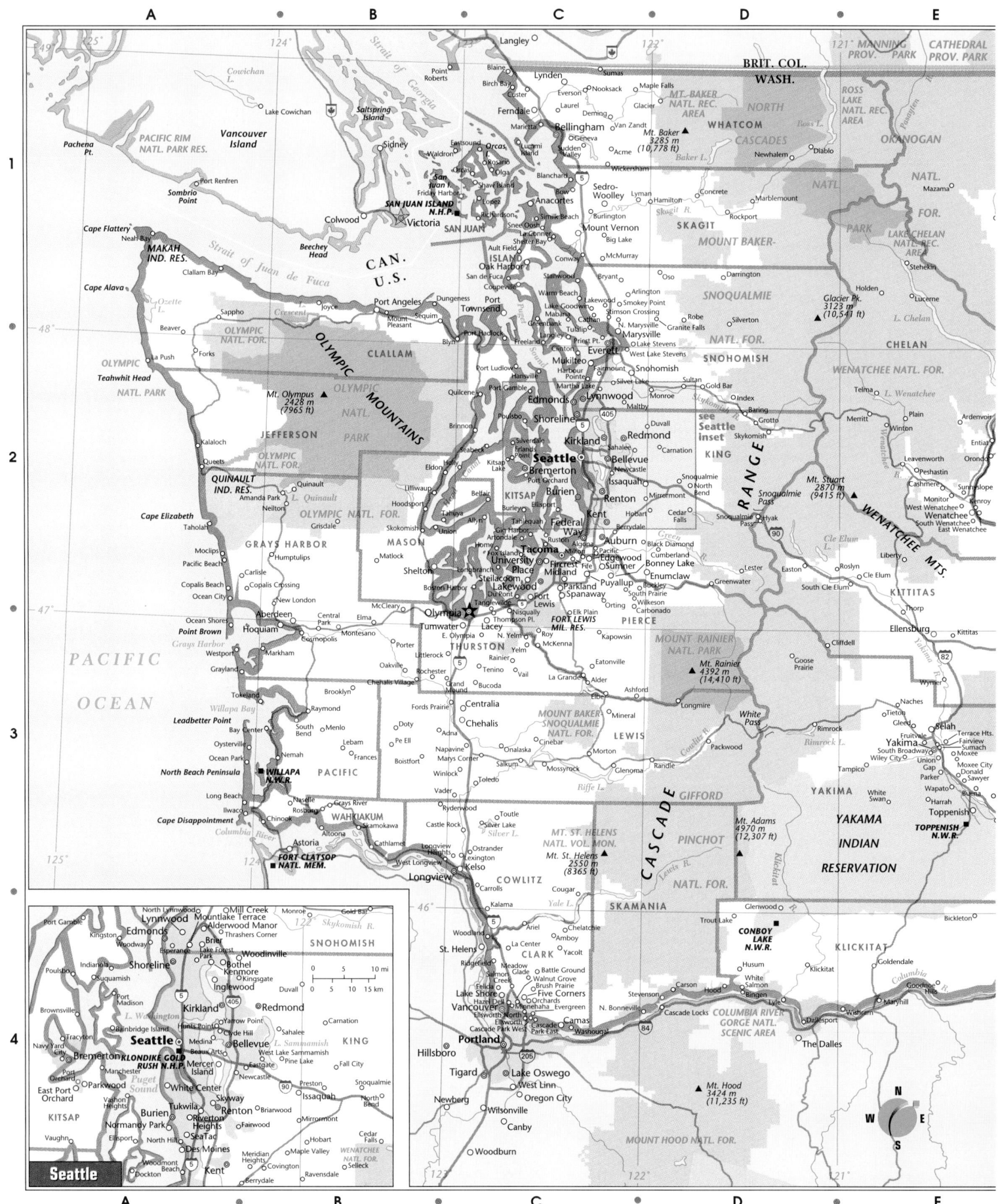

Seattle

Wishram, 324 . . . . .E4
Withrow F2
Woodinville, 9,194 . . . . . .A4
Woodland, 3,780 . . . . . . .C4
Woodmont Beach A4
Woodway, 936 . . . . .A4
Wymer E3
Yacolt, 1,055 . . . . .C4
Yakima, 71,845 . . . . .E3
Yarrow Point, 1,008 . . . . .A4
Yelm, 3,289 . . . . .C3
Zillah, 2,198 . . . . .E3

Other Features

Adams, mountain D3
Alava, cape A1
Baker, lake D1
Baker, mountain D1
Banks, lake F2
Beechey Head, cape B1
Blue, mountains H4
Boardman Bombing
   Range F4
Brown, point A3
Cascade, range D3
Cathedral Prov. Park E1
Chelan, lake E1
Chewuch, river E1
Christina, lake G1
Cle Elum, lake D2
Coeur d'Alene Ind. Res. . . .H2
Coeur d'Alene, lake H2
Cold Springs N.W.R. F4
Columbia, river
   . . . . . . A3, E4, F1, F3, H1
Columbia N.W.R. F3
Columbia River Gorge
   Natl. Scenic Area D4
Colville Indian
   Reservation G1
Colville Natl. For. . . .G1, H1
Conboy Lake N.W.R. D4
Copper, butte G1
Cowichan, lake A1
Cowlitz, river D3
Crescent, lake B1
Disappointment, cape . . .A3
Elizabeth, cape A2
Flattery, cape A1
Fort Clatsop Natl. Mem. . .B3
Fort Lewis Mil. Res. C2
Franklin D. Roosevelt,
   lake G1
Georgia, strait B1
Gifford Pinchot Natl. For. .D3
Glacier, peak D1
Grande Ronde, river H4
Grays, harbor A3
Green, river D2
Hanford Reach
   Natl. Mon. F3
Hood, canal B2
Hood, mountain D4
Juan de Fuca, strait A1
Kalispell Ind. Res. H1
Kaniksu Natl. For. H1
Kettle River, range G1
Klickitat, river D3
Lake Chelan Natl.
   Rec. Area E1
Lake Roosevelt Natl.
   Rec. Area G1, G2
Leadbetter, point A3
Lewis, river D3
Makah Ind. Res. A1
Manning Prov. Park E1
McKay Creek N.W.R. G4
Molybdenite, mountain . .H1
Mount Baker Natl. Rec.
   Area D1
Mount Baker-Snoqualmie
   Natl. For. C3, D1
Mount Hood Natl. For. . . .C4
Mount Rainier Natl. Park D3
Mount St. Helens Natl.
   Vol. Mon. C3

North Beach, peninsula . .A3
North Cascades
   Natl. Park D1
Okanogan, river F1
Okanogan Natl. For. . .E1, F1
Olympic, mountains B1
Olympic Natl. For. . .A1, B2
Olympic Natl. Park . .A2, B2
Olympus, mountain B2
Omak, mountain F1
Orcas, island C1
Oregon, butte H3
Ozette, lake A1
Pachena, point A1
Pacific, ocean A3
Pacific Rim Natl. Park . . .A1
Pasayten, river E1
Pend Oreille, river H1
Potholes, reservoir F3
Priest, lake H1
Priest Rapids, lake F3
Puget, sound A4, C1
Quinault, lake B2
Quinault Ind. Res. A2
Rainier, mountain D3
Riffe, lake C3
Rimrock, lake D3
Ross, lake D1
Ross Lake Natl. Rec. Area .E1
Sacajawea, lake G3
Saddle Mountain N.W.R. . .F3
St. Helens, mountain C3
Saltspring, island B1
Sammamish, lake B4
San Juan, island B1
Sanpoil, river G1
Selkirk, mountains H1
Silver, lake C3
Skagit, river D1
Skykomish, river B4, D2
Snake, river H3
Snoqualmie, pass D2
Sombrio, point A1
Spokane, river H2
Spokane Ind. Res. G2
Stuart, mountain E2
Teahwhit Head, cape A2
Toppenish N.W.R. E3
Turnbull N.W.R. H2
U.S. Dept. Of Energy
   Hanford Site F3
U.S. Mil. Res. Yakima
   Training Center E3
Umatilla, lake F4
Umatilla Ind. Res. G4
Umatilla N.W.R. F4
Vancouver, island B1
Wallowa-Whitman
   Natl. For. H4
Wallula, river F3
Washington, lake A4
Wenatchee, lake E2
Wenatchee, mountains . . .E2
Wenatchee, river E2
Wenatchee Natl. For. .E2, B4
White, pass D3
Whitman Mission
   Natl. Hist. Site G3
Willapa, bay A3
Willapa N.W.R. B3
Yakama Indian Res. E3
Yakima, river E3
Yale, lake C3

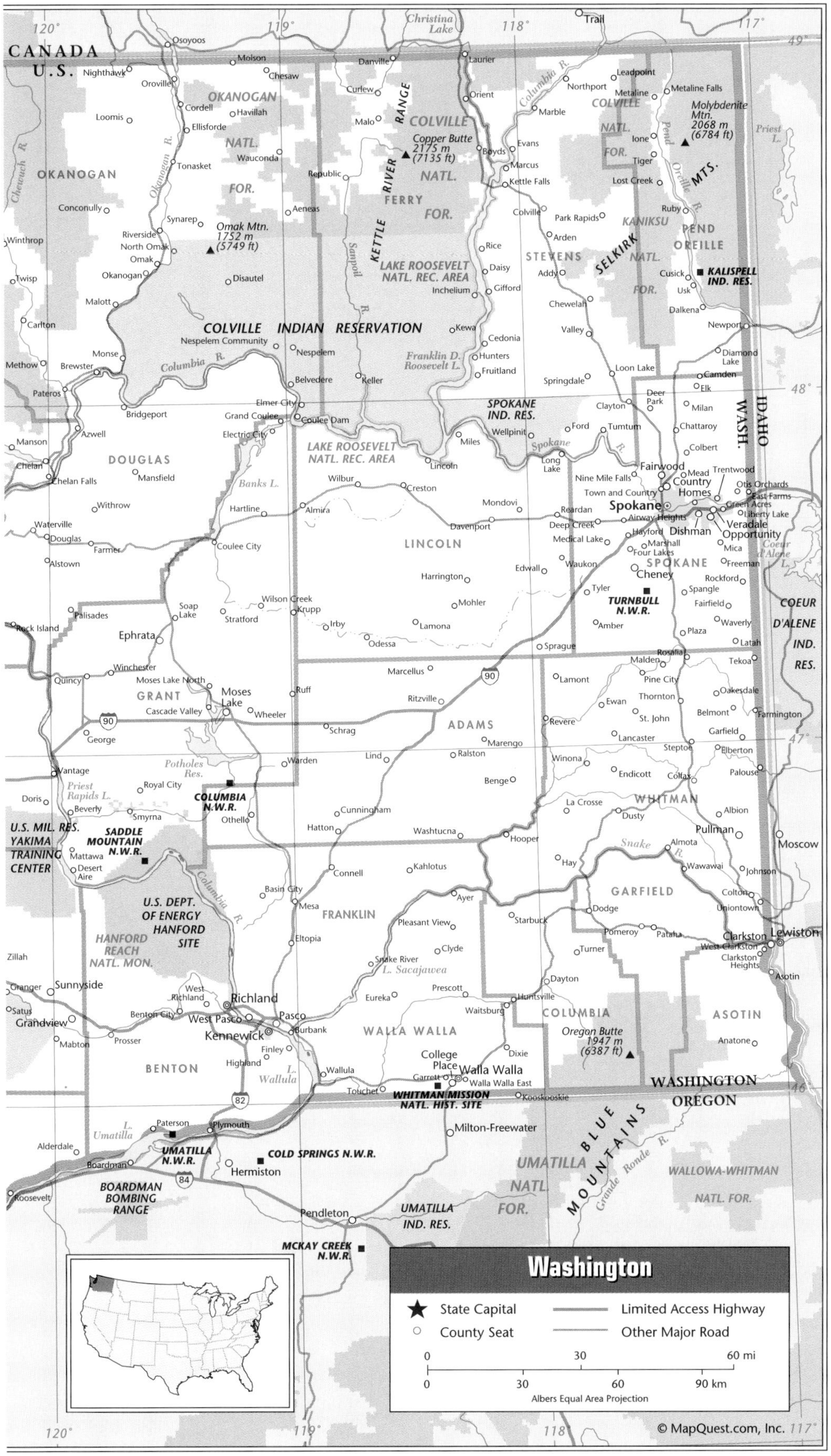

Washington

★ State Capital
○ County Seat
— Limited Access Highway
— Other Major Road

0   30   60 mi
0   30   60   90 km
Albers Equal Area Projection

© MapQuest.com, Inc.

Mount Rainier

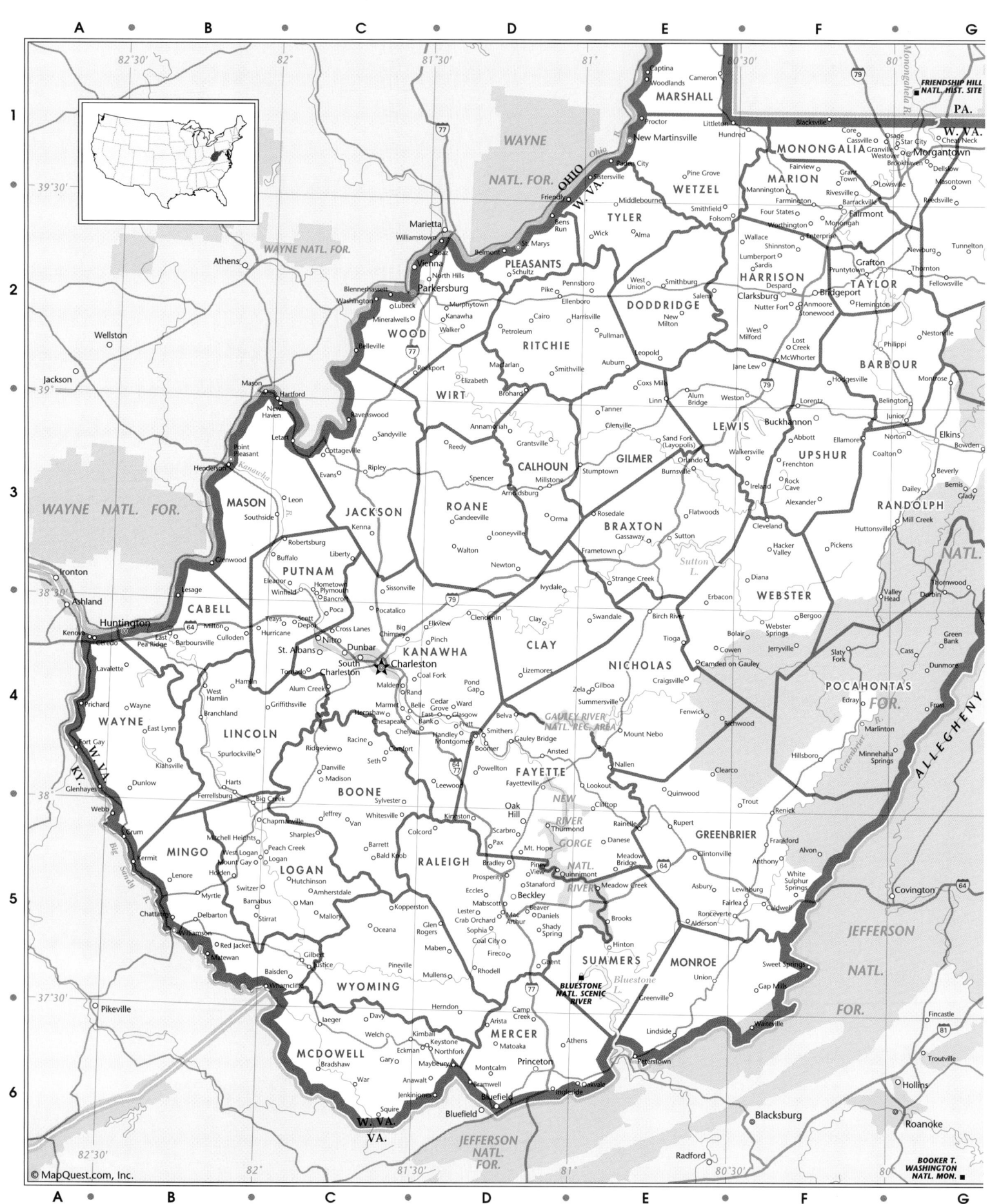

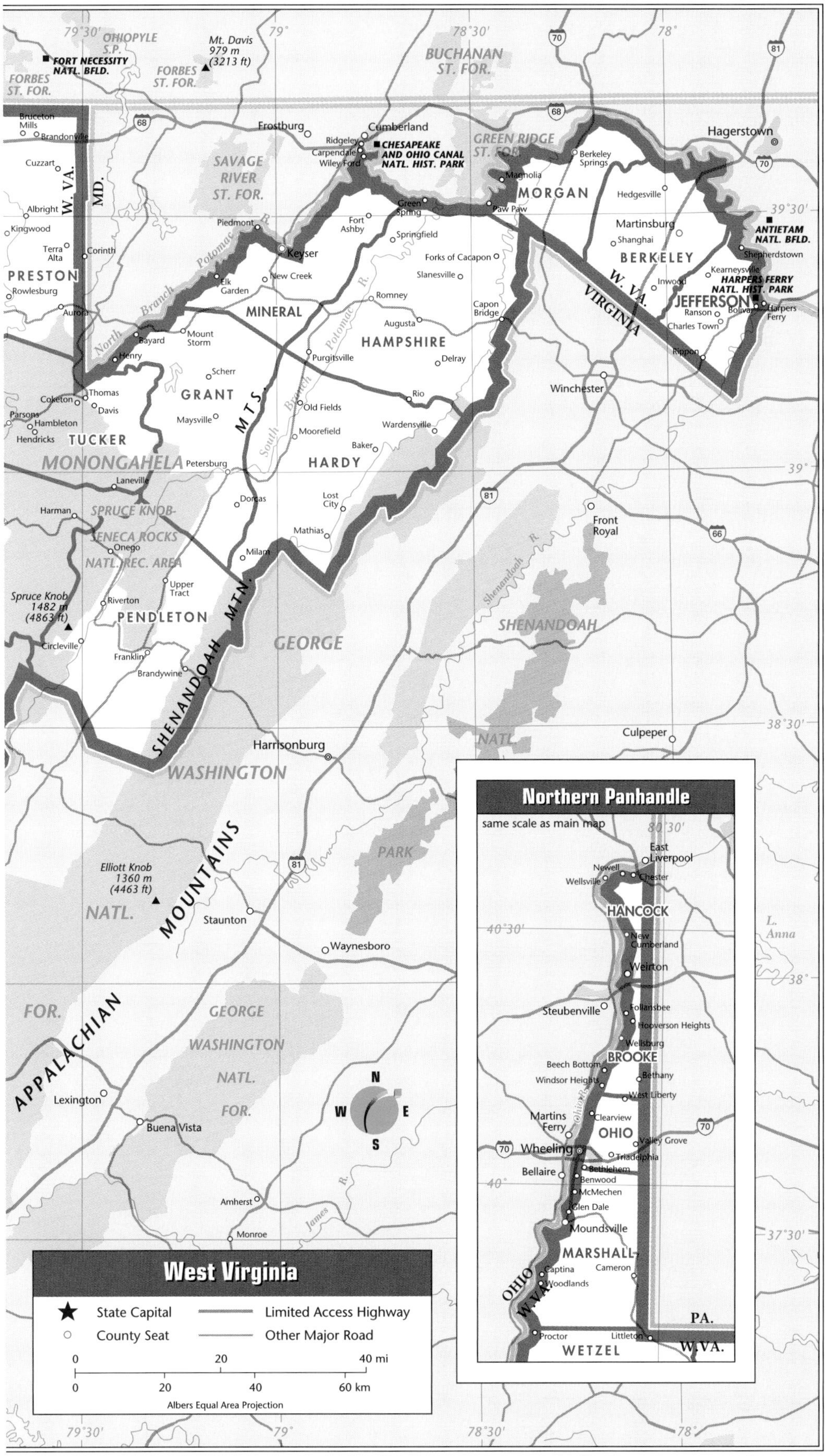

Map Labels (Main Map)

OHIOPYLE S.P.
Mt. Davis 979 m (3213 ft) ▲
BUCHANAN ST. FOR.
79°30'
79°
78°30'
78°
FORT NECESSITY NATL. BFLD. ■
FORBES NATL. BFLD. ■
FORBES ST. FOR.
Bruceton Mills
Brandonville
Frostburg
Ridgeley
Carpendale
Wiley Ford
Cumberland
CHESAPEAKE AND OHIO CANAL NATL. HIST. PARK ■
GREEN RIDGE ST. FOR.
Hagerstown
70
81
Cuzzart
Albright
Kingwood
Corinth
Piedmont
Fort Ashby
Green Spring
Magnolia
Paw Paw
Berkeley Springs
Hedgesville
Martinsburg
MORGAN
BERKELEY
39°30'
Terra Alta
Rowlesburg
Keyser
Springfield
Shanghai
Shepherdstown
ANTIETAM NATL. BFLD. ■
W. VA.
MD.
PRESTON
Aurora
New Creek
Elk Garden
Slanesville
Romney
Forks of Cacapon
Kearneysville
Inwood
HARPERS FERRY NATL. HIST. PARK
Bayard
Mount Storm
Henry
MINERAL
Augusta
Capon Bridge
JEFFERSON
Ranson
Bolivar Harpers Ferry
W. VA.
VIRGINIA
Scherr
Purgitsville
Delray
Charles Town
2
Coketon
Parsons
Thomas
Davis
Hambleton
Hendricks
Maysville
HAMPSHIRE
Rio
Old Fields
Winchester
Rippon
GRANT MTS.
TUCKER
MONONGAHELA
Laneville
Harman
Petersburg
Dorcas
Moorefield
Wardensville
Baker
HARDY
39°
SPRUCE KNOB-
SENECA ROCKS NATL. REC. AREA
Onego
Milam
Lost City
Mathias
81
Front Royal
66
Spruce Knob 1482 m (4863 ft) ▲
Riverton
Upper Tract
SHENANDOAH
3
Circleville
PENDLETON
Franklin
Brandywine
GEORGE
SHENANDOAH MTN.
SHENANDOAH R.
38°30'
Elliott Knob 1360 m (4463 ft) ▲
Harrisonburg
WASHINGTON
NATL.
Culpeper
L. Anna
MOUNTAINS
NATL.
PARK
Staunton
Waynesboro
40°30'
38°
4
APPALACHIAN
FOR.
GEORGE
WASHINGTON
NATL.
FOR.
Lexington
Buena Vista
Amherst
Monroe
James R.
N W E S
5
PA.
W.VA.

Northern Panhandle Inset

Northern Panhandle
same scale as main map
80°30'
East Liverpool
Newell
Wellsville
Chester
HANCOCK
New Cumberland
Weirton
Steubenville
Follansbee
Hooverson Heights
Wellsburg
BROOKE
Beech Bottom
Windsor Heights
Bethany
West Liberty
OHIO
Martins Ferry
Clearview
Valley Grove
Triadelphia
Wheeling
Bellaire
Bethlehem
Benwood
McMechen
Glen Dale
Moundsville
MARSHALL
Captina
Cameron
Woodlands
OHIO
W.VA.
Proctor
Littleton
WETZEL
40°
37°30'
70
PA.
W.VA.

Legend

West Virginia
★ State Capital
○ County Seat
Limited Access Highway
Other Major Road
0 20 40 mi
0 20 40 60 km
Albers Equal Area Projection

West Virginia

Capital: Charleston
Land Area: 24,087 sq. mi.
62,385 sq. km.
Population: 1,808,344 (2000 Census)
Largest City: Charleston, 53,421
Highest Point: Spruce Knob
4,861 ft.
1,482 m.
Admitted to Union: June 20, 1863
Nickname: Mountain State
State Flower: Big Rhododendron
State Bird: Cardinal

West Virginia: Map Index

Counties

Barbour, 15,557 ....F2
Berkeley, 75,905 ....K2
Boone, 25,535 ....C4
Braxton, 14,702 ....E3
Brooke, 25,447 ....K5
Cabell, 96,784 ....B4
Calhoun, 7,582 ....D3
Clay, 10,330 ....D4
Doddridge, 7,403 ....E2
Fayette, 47,579 ....D4
Gilmer, 7,160 ....E3
Grant, 11,299 ....H2
Greenbrier, 34,453 ....E5
Hampshire, 20,203 ....J2
Hancock, 32,667 ....K4
Hardy, 12,669 ....J2
Harrison, 68,652 ....F2
Jackson, 28,000 ....C3
Jefferson, 42,190 ....L2
Kanawha, 200,073 ....D4
Lewis, 16,919 ....E3
Lincoln, 22,108 ....B4
Logan, 37,710 ....C5
Marion, 56,598 ....F1
Marshall, 35,519 ....E1, K6
Mason, 25,957 ....B3
McDowell, 27,329 ....C6
Mercer, 62,980 ....D6
Mineral, 27,078 ....H2
Mingo, 28,253 ....B5
Monongalia, 81,866 ....F1
Monroe, 14,583 ....E5
Morgan, 14,943 ....K1
Nicholas, 26,562 ....E4
Ohio, 47,427 ....K5
Pendleton, 8,196 ....H3
Pleasants, 7,514 ....D2
Pocahontas, 9,131 ....F4
Preston, 29,334 ....G2
Putnam, 51,589 ....C3
Raleigh, 79,220 ....D5
Randolph, 28,262 ....G3
Ritchie, 10,343 ....D2
Roane, 15,446 ....D3
Summers, 12,999 ....E5
Taylor, 16,089 ....F2
Tucker, 7,321 ....H2
Tyler, 9,592 ....E2
Upshur, 23,404 ....F3
Wayne, 42,903 ....B4
Webster, 9,719 ....F3
Wetzel, 17,693 ....E1, K6
Wirt, 5,873 ....D2
Wood, 87,986 ....C2
Wyoming, 25,708 ....C5

Cities and Towns

Abbott, 80 ....F3
Albright, 247 ....G1
Alderson, 1,091 ....E5
Alexander, 40 ....F3
Alma, 60 ....E2
Alum Bridge, 100 ....E2
Alum Creek, 1,839 ....C4
Alvon, 50 ....F5
Amherstdale, 1,785 ....C5
Anawalt, 272 ....D6
Anmoore, 685 ....F2
Annamoriah, 90 ....D3
Ansted, 1,576 ....D4
Anthony, 60 ....F5
Arista, 225 ....D6
Arnoldsburg, 60 ....D3
Asbury, 50 ....E5
Athens, 1,102 ....D6
Auburn, 103 ....E2
Augusta, 450 ....J2
Aurora, 225 ....G2

Baisden..............................C5
Baker, *125*.........................J2
Bald Knob, *40*.....................C5
Bancroft, **367**....................C3
Barboursville, **3,183**.........B4
Barnabus, *175*...................B5
Barrackville, **1,288**...........F1
Barrett, *250*......................C5
Bayard, **299**....................H2
Beaver, **1,378**.................D5
Beckley, **17,254**..............D5
Belington, **1,788**.............G2
Belle, **1,259**...................C4
Belleville, *150*...................C2
Belmont, **1,036**..............D2
Belva, *225*.......................D4
Bemis..............................G3
Bens Run, *70*...................D2
Bergoo, *125*.....................F4
Berkeley Springs, **663**......K1
Beverly, **651**..................G3
Big Chimney, *600*.............C4
Big Creek, *425*.................B4
Birch River, *150*................E4
Blacksville, *175*................F1
Blennerhassett, **3,225**.....C2
Bluefield, **11,451**............D6
Boaz, **1,345**..................D2
Bolair, *225*......................F4
Bolivar, **1,045**................L2
Boomer, *1,100*.................D4
Bowden, *70*.....................G3
Bradley, **2,371**...............D5
Bradshaw, **289**...............C6
Bramwell, **426**................D6
Branchland, *350*...............B4
Brandonville, **102**...........G1
Brandywine.......................H3
Bridgeport, **7,306**...........F2
Brohard...........................D2
Brookhaven, **4,734**.........G1
Brooks, *225*.....................E5
Bruceton Mills, **74**..........G1
Buckhannon, **5,725**........F3
Buffalo, **1,171**................C3
Burnsville, **481**...............E3
Cairo, **263**.....................D2
Caldwell, *350*...................F5
Camden on Gauley, **157**...E4
Cameron, **1,212**........E1, K6
Camp Creek, *30*...............D6
Capon Bridge, **200**.........K2
Captina, *125*....................E1
Carpendale, **954**.............J1
Cass, *100*.......................G4
Cassville, **1,586**.............F1
Cedar Grove, **862**..........D4
Ceredo, **1,675**...............A4
Chapmanville, **1,211**.......B5
Charleston, **53,421**.........C4
Charles Town, **2,907**.......L2
Chattaroy, **1,136**...........B5
Cheat Neck, **950**............G1
Chelyan, *1,400*................D4
Chesapeake, **1,643**........C4
Chester, **2,592**..............K4
Circleville, *100*.................G3
Clarksburg, **16,743**.........F2
Clay, **593**......................D4
Clearco...........................E4
Clendenin, **1,116**...........D4
Cleveland, *60*..................F3
Clifftop, *70*......................E4
Clintonville, *125*...............E5
Coal City, **1,905**............D5
Coal Fork, **1,350**............C4
Coalton, **247**.................G3
Coketon, *100*..................G2
Colcord, *300*...................D5
Comfort, *150*...................C4
Core, *125*........................F1
Corinth, *275*....................H2
Cottageville, *750*..............C3
Cowen, **513**..................E4
Coxs Mills, *50*.................E2
Crab Orchard, **2,761**.......D5
Craigsville, **2,204**...........E4
Cross Lanes, **10,353**......C4
Crum, *125*.......................B5
Culloden, **2,940**.............B4
Cuzzart, *100*...................G1
Dailey, *350*......................G3
Danese, *350*....................E5
Daniels, **1,846**...............D5
Danville, *550*...................C4
Davis, **624**....................H2
Davy, **373**.....................C6
Delbarton, **474**..............B5
Dellslow, *375*..................G1
Delray, *90*.......................J2
Despard, **1,039**.............F2
Diana, *125*......................F3
Dorcas, *175*....................H3
Dunbar, **8,154**...............C4
Dunlow, *150*...................B4
Dunmore, *100*.................G4

Durbin, **262**...................G3
East Bank, **933**..............D4
East Lynn, *150*.................B4
East Pea Ridge, **6,363**....B4
Eccles, **700**...................D5
Eckman, *250*...................D6
Edray, *175*......................F4
Eleanor, **1,345**..............C3
Elizabeth, **994**...............D2
Elk Garden, **217**............H2
Elkins, **7,032**.................G3
Elkview, **1,182**...............D4
Ellamore, *150*..................F3
Ellenboro, **373**...............D2
Enterprise, **939**..............F2
Erbacon............................E3
Evans, *750*......................C3
Fairlea, **1,706**................F5
Fairmont, **19,097**...........F2
Fairview, **435**.................F1
Farmington, **387**............F1
Fayetteville, **2,754**..........D4
Fellowsville, *175*...............G2
Fenwick, **400**.................E4
Ferrellsburg, **500**............B4
Fireco.............................D5
Flatwoods, **348**..............E3
Flemington, **287**.............F2
Follansbee, **3,115**..........K5
Folsom, *175*....................E2
Forks of Cacapon, *90*.......K2
Fort Ashby, **1,354**...........J2
Fort Gay, **819**................A4
Four States, *625*..............F2
Frametown, *275*..............E3
Frankford, *100*.................F5
Franklin, **797**.................H3
Frenchton, *250*................F3
Friendly, **159**.................D1
Frost..............................G4
Gandeeville, *150*..............D3
Gap Mills...........................F5
Gary, **917**.....................C6
Gassaway, **901**..............E3
Gauley Bridge, **738**.........D4
Ghent, *325*......................D5
Gilbert, **417**...................C5
Gilboa, *275*.....................E4
Glady, *50*........................G3
Glasgow, **783**................D4
Glenhayes........................A4
Glen Rogers, *450*.............D5
Glenville, **1,544**..............E3
Glenwood, *225*................B3
Grafton, **5,489**...............F2
Grantsville, **565**..............D3
Grant Town, **657**............F1
Granville, **778**................G1
Green Bank, *200*..............G4
Green Spring, *150*............J1
Greenville, *70*..................E5
Griffithsville, *60*................C4
Hacker Valley, *70*.............F3
Hambleton, **246**.............G2
Hamlin, **1,119**................B4
Handley, **362**.................D4
Harman, *126*...................G3
Harpers Ferry, **307**.........L2
Harrisville, **1,842**............D2
Hartford, **519**.................C2
Harts, **2,361**..................B4
Hedgesville, **240**............K1
Henderson, **325**.............B3
Hendricks, **319**..............G2
Henry..............................H2
Herndon, *80*....................D6
Hernshaw, *250*................C4
Hillsboro, **243**................F4
Hinton, **2,880**................E5
Hodgesville, *225*..............F2
Holden, **1,105**...............B5
Hometown, **750**.............C3
Hooverson Heights, **2,909**...K5
Hundred, **344**................F1
Huntington, **51,475**.........B4
Hurricane, **5,222**............B4
Hutchinson, *350*...............C5
Huttonsville, **217**............G3
Iaeger, **358**...................C6
Ingleside, *90*....................D6
Inwood, **2,084**...............K2
Ireland, *150*.....................F3
Ivydale, *175*.....................D3
Jane Lew, **406**...............F2
Jeffrey, *300*.....................C5
Jenkinjones, *350*..............D6
Jerryville..........................F4
Junior, **450**...................G3
Justice, *325*.....................C5
Kanawha, *500*.................D2
Kearneysville, *650*............L2
Kenna, *100*.....................C3
Kenova, **3,485**..............A4
Kermit, **209**...................B5
Keyser, **5,303**................J2
Keystone, **453**...............D6

Kiahsville.........................B4
Kimball, **411**..................D6
Kingston, *60*....................D5
Kingwood, **2,944**...........G2
Kopperston, *500*..............C5
Laneville..........................H3
Lavalette, *850*..................B4
Leewood, *100*..................D4
Lenore, *225*....................B5
Leon, *132*.......................C3
Leopold, *50*.....................E2
Lesage, *125*....................B3
Lester, **322**...................D5
Letart, *125*......................C3
Lewisburg, **3,624**...........F5
Liberty, *150*.....................C3
Lindside, *275*...................E6
Linn, *125*........................E2
Littleton, **207**............E1, K6
Lizemores, *200*................D4
Logan, **1,630**................C5
Lookout, *175*...................E4
Looneyville, *50*................D3
Lorentz, *250*....................F2
Lost City, *50*....................J3
Lost Creek, **467**.............F2
Lowsville, *160*..................F1
Lubeck, **1,303**...............C2
Lumberport, **937**............F2
Maben, *60*......................D5
Mabscott, **1,403**............D5
MacArthur, **1,693**...........D5
Macfarlan, *70*..................D2
Madison, **2,677**.............C4
Magnolia..........................K1
Malden, *750*....................C4
Mallory, **1,143**...............C5
Man, **770**......................C5
Mannington, **2,124**.........F1
Marlinton, **1,204**............F4
Marmet, **1,693**..............C4
Martinsburg, **14,972**.......L2
Mason, **1,064**...............B2
Masontown, **647**............G1
Matewan, **498**...............B5
Mathias, *80*.....................J3
Matoaka, **317**................D6
Maybeury, *550*................D6
Maysville, *125*..................H2
McWhorter, *175*...............F2
Meadow Bridge, **321**......E5
Meadow Creek, *100*.........E5
Middlebourne, **870**.........E2
Milam.............................H3
Mill Creek, **662**..............G3
Millstone, *275*..................D3
Milton, **2,206**.................B4
Mineralwells, **1,860**.........C2
Minnehaha Springs.............G4
Mitchell Heights, **301**.......B5
Monongah, **939**.............F2
Montcalm, **885**..............D6
Montgomery, **1,942**........D4
Montrose, **156**...............G2
Moorefield, **2,375**...........J2
Morgantown, **26,809**......G1
Moundsville, **9,998**.........K5
Mount Gay, **2,623**..........B5
Mount Hope, **1,487**........D5
Mount Nebo, *300*............E4
Mount Storm, *150*...........H2
Mullens, **1,769**..............D5
Murphytown, *200*............D2
Myrtle.............................B5
Nallen, *125*.....................E4
Nestorville, *150*................G2
Newburg, **360**...............G2
New Creek, *275*...............H2
New Cumberland, **1,099**...K4
New Haven, **1,559**.........C3
New Martinsville, **5,984**...E1
New Milton, *40*................E2
Newton, *80*.....................D3
Nitro, **6,824**..................C4
Northfork, **519**...............D6
North Hills, **880**..............D2
Norton, *275*.....................G3
Nutter Fort, **1,686**..........F2
Oak Hill, **7,589**..............D5
Oakvale, **142**.................E6
Oceana, **1,550**..............C5
Old Fields, *90*...................J2
Onego, *80*......................H3
Orlando, *125*...................E3
Orma, *40*........................D3
Osage, *175*.....................F1
Paden City, **2,860**..........E1
Parkersburg, **33,099**.......C2
Parsons, **1,463**..............G2
Paw Paw, **524**...............K1
Pax, *174*........................D5
Peach Creek, *175*............C5
Pennsboro, **1,199**..........E2
Petersburg, **2,423**..........H2
Petersburg, **499**.............E6
Petroleum........................D2

Philippi, **2,870**...............F2
Pickens...........................F3
Piedmont, **1,014**............H2
Pike, *125*........................D2
Pinch, **2,811**.................D4
Pine Grove, **571**.............E1
Pineville, **715**.................C5
Piney View, **1,046**..........D5
Plymouth, *1,000*..............C3
Poca, **1,013**..................C4
Pocatalico, *425*................C4
Point Pleasant, **4,637**......B3
Pond Gap, *225*................D4
Powellton, **1,796**............D4
Pratt, **551**.....................D4
Prichard, *325*..................A4
Princeton, **6,347**............D6
Proctor, *100*...............E1, K6
Prosperity, **1,310**............D5
Pruntytown, *600*..............F2
Pullman, **169**.................E2
Purgitsville, *80*.................J2
Quinnimont, *40*................D5
Quinwood, **435**..............E4
Racine, *475*.....................C4
Rainelle, **1,545**..............E5
Rand, *2,300*....................C4
Ranson, **2,951**...............L2
Ravenswood, **4,031**........C3
Red Jacket, **728**.............B5
Reedsville, **517**...............G1
Reedy, **198**...................D3
Renick, *200*.....................F4
Rhodell, **234**..................D5
Richwood, **2,477**............E4
Ridgeley, **762**.................J1
Ridgeview, *375*................C4
Rio, *90*...........................J2
Ripley, **3,263**.................C3
Rippon, *200*....................L2
Riverton, *80*....................H3
Rivesville, **913**................F1
Robertsburg, *225*.............C3
Rock Cave, *300*...............F3
Rockport..........................C2
Romney, **1,940**..............J2
Ronceverte, **1,557**..........F5
Rosedale, *100*.................E3
Rowlesburg, **613**............G2
Rupert, **940**...................E5
St. Albans, **11,567**..........C4
St. Marys, **2,017**............D2
Salem, **2,006**................E2
Sand Fork (Layopolis), **176**...E3
Sandyville, **400**...............C3
Sardis, *200*.....................F2
Scarbro, *1,700*.................D5
Scherr, *40*.......................H2
Schultz, *125*....................D2
Scott Depot, **2,600**.........C4
Seth, *275*........................C4
Shady Spring, **2,078**.......D5
Shanghai, *100*.................K2
Sharples, *70*....................C5
Shepherdstown, **803**.......L2
Shinnston, **2,295**...........F2
Sissonville, **4,399**...........C3
Sistersville, **1,588**...........E1
Slanesville, *90*.................J2
Slaty Fork..........................F4
Smithburg, *350*................E2
Smithers, **904**................D4
Smithfield, **177**...............E2
Smithville, *90*...................D2
Sophia, **1,301**................D5
South Charleston, **13,390**...C4
Southside.........................C3
Spencer, **2,352**..............D3
Springfield, *400*................J2
Spurlockville, *150*.............B4
Squire, *100*.....................C6
Stanaford, **1,443**............D5
Star City, **1,366**..............G1
Stirrat, *90*.......................B5
Stonewood, **1,815**..........F2
Strange Creek, *80*............E3
Stumptown, *50*................E3
Summersville, **3,294**........E4
Sutton, **1,011**................E3
Swandale.........................E4
Sweet Springs, *150*..........F5
Switzer, **1,138**...............C5
Sylvester, **195**................C4
Tanner, *100*.....................E3
Teays, **2,400**.................C4
Terra Alta, **1,456**............G2
Thomas, **452**................H2
Thornton, *175*..................G2
Thornwood, *50*................G3
Thurmond, **7**.................D5
Tioga, *175*......................E4
Tornado, **1,111**.............C4
Trout, *50*........................F4
Tunnelton, **336**..............G2
Union, **548**....................E5
Upper Tract, *175*..............H3

Valley Head, *200*.............F3
Van, *250*........................C5
Vienna, **10,861**..............C2
Waiteville..........................F6
Walker, *80*......................D2
Walkersville, *50*................F3
Wallace, *150*...................F2
Walton, *250*....................D3
War, **788**......................C6
Ward, *90*........................D4
Wardensville, **246**..........J2
Washington, **1,170**.........C2
Wayne, **1,105**...............B4
Webb, *100*......................B5
Webster Springs, **808**......F4
Weirton, **20,411**............K4
Welch, **2,683**................C6
Wellsburg, **2,891**...........K5
West Hamlin, **696**..........B4
West Logan, **418**...........B5
West Milford, **651**...........F2
Weston, **4,317**..............F2
Westover, **3,941**............G1
West Union, **806**............E2
Wharncliffe, *150*...............C5
Wheeling, **31,419**..........K5
White Sulphur Springs, **2,315**...F5
Whitesville, **520**..............D4
Wick, *100*.......................E2
Wiley Ford, **1,095**...........J1
Williamson, **3,414**..........B5
Williamstown, **2,996**.......D2
Windsor Heights, **431**......K5
Winfield, **1,858**..............C3
Woodlands, *100*...............E1
Worthington, *170*.............F2
Zela, *200*........................E4

Other Features

Allegheny, *mountains*........G4
Anna, *lake*......................L4
Antietam Natl. Bfld..............L2
Appalachian, *mountains*.....G5
Appomattox Court House
  Natl. Hist. Park................J6
Big Sandy, *river*................B5
Bluestone, *lake*.................E5
Bluestone Natl. Scenic River....E5
Booker T. Washington
  Natl. Mon......................G6
Buchanan St. For................J1
Chesapeake And Ohio
  Canal Natl. Hist. Park........J1
Davis, *mountain*...............H1
Elliott Knob, *peak*.............H4
Forbes St. For...............G1, H1
Fort Necessity Natl. Bfld.......G1
Friendship Hill Natl. Hist. Site...G1
Gauley River Natl. Rec. Area...D4
George Washington Natl. For....H5
George Washington Natl. For....J3
Greenbrier, *river*...............F4
Green Ridge St. For.............K1
Harpers Ferry Natl. Hist. Park....L2
James, *river*....................H6
Jefferson Natl. For........D6, F5
Kanawha, *river*................B3
Monongahela Natl. For........G2
New River Gorge Natl. River....D4
Ohio, *river*................E1, K5
Ohiopyle S.P.....................H1
Potomac, *river*................J2
Savage River St. For...........H1
Shenandoah, *mountain*......H4
Shenandoah, *river*............K3
Shenandoah Natl. Park........K3
Spruce Knob, *peak*...........G3
Spruce Knob-Seneca Rocks
  Natl. Rec. Area...............H3
Sutton, *lake*....................E3
Wayne Natl. For........A3, B1, C2, D1

Wisconsin

Capital: Madison
Land Area: 54,314 sq. mi.
140,673 sq. km.
Population: 5,363,675 (2000 Census)
Largest City: Milwaukee, 596,974
Highest Point: Timms Hill
1,952 ft.
595 m.
Admitted to Union: May 29,1848
Nickname: Badger State
State Flower: Wood Violet
State Bird: Robin

Wisconsin: Map Index

Counties

Adams, 18,643 . . . D4
Ashland, 16,866 . . . C2
Barron, 44,963 . . . B3
Bayfield, 15,013 . . . B2
Brown, 226,778 . . . E4
Buffalo, 13,804 . . . B4
Burnett, 15,674 . . . A3
Calumet, 40,631 . . . E4
Chippewa, 55,195 . . . B3
Clark, 33,557 . . . C4
Columbia, 52,468 . . . D5
Crawford, 17,243 . . . C5
Dane, 426,526 . . . D6
Dodge, 85,897 . . . E1, E5
Door, 27,961 . . . F4
Douglas, 43,287 . . . B2
Dunn, 39,858 . . . B4
Eau Claire, 93,142 . . . B4
Florence, 5,088 . . . E3
Fond du Lac, 97,296 . . . E5
Forest, 10,024 . . . E3
Grant, 49,597 . . . C6
Green, 33,647 . . . D6
Green Lake, 19,105 . . . D5
Iowa, 22,780 . . . C5
Iron, 6,861 . . . C2
Jackson, 19,100 . . . C4
Jefferson, 74,021 . . . E6
Juneau, 24,316 . . . C5
Kenosha, 149,577 . . . E6
Kewaunee, 20,187 . . . F4
La Crosse, 107,120 . . . B5
Lafayette, 16,137 . . . C6
Langlade, 20,740 . . . D3
Lincoln, 29,641 . . . D3
Manitowoc, 82,887 . . . F5
Marathon, 125,834 . . . D4
Marinette, 43,384 . . . E3
Marquette, 15,832 . . . D5
Menominee, 4,562 . . . E4
Milwaukee, 940,164 . . . F2, F5
Monroe, 40,899 . . . C5
Oconto, 35,634 . . . E3
Oneida, 36,776 . . . D3
Outagamie, 160,971 . . . E4
Ozaukee, 82,317 . . . F1, F5
Pepin, 7,213 . . . B4
Pierce, 36,804 . . . A4
Polk, 41,319 . . . A3
Portage, 67,182 . . . D4
Price, 15,822 . . . C3
Racine, 188,831 . . . E6, F2
Richland, 17,924 . . . C5
Rock, 152,307 . . . D6
Rusk, 15,347 . . . B3
St. Croix, 63,155 . . . A3
Sauk, 55,225 . . . D5
Sawyer, 16,196 . . . B3
Shawano, 40,664 . . . E4
Sheboygan, 112,646 . . . F5
Taylor, 19,680 . . . C3
Trempealeau, 27,010 . . . B4
Vernon, 28,056 . . . C5
Vilas, 21,033 . . . D2
Walworth, 93,759 . . . E6
Washburn, 16,036 . . . B2
Washington, 117,493 . . . E5, F1
Waukesha, 360,767 . . . E6, F2
Waupaca, 51,731 . . . E4
Waushara, 23,154 . . . D4
Winnebago, 156,763 . . . E4
Wood, 75,555 . . . C4

Cities and Towns

Abbotsford, 1,956 . . . C4
Abrams, 350 . . . E4
Adams, 1,914 . . . D5
Adell, 517 . . . F5
Albany, 1,191 . . . D6
Algoma, 3,357 . . . F4
Allenton, 850 . . . E5
Allouez, 15,443 . . . E4
Alma, 942 . . . B4
Alma Center, 446 . . . C4
Almena, 720 . . . A3
Almond, 459 . . . D4
Alto, 250 . . . E5
Altoona, 6,698 . . . B4
Alvin . . . E3
Amberg, 225 . . . F3
Amery, 2,845 . . . A3
Amherst, 964 . . . D4
Amherst Jct., 305 . . . D4
Angelica, 150 . . . E4
Aniwa, 272 . . . D3
Anston, 275 . . . E4
Antigo, 8,560 . . . D3
Appleton, 70,087 . . . E4
Arbor Vitae, 90 . . . D3
Arcadia, 2,402 . . . B4
Arena, 685 . . . D5
Argonne, 175 . . . E3
Argyle, 823 . . . D6
Arkdale, 150 . . . D4
Arlington, 484 . . . D5
Arpin, 337 . . . C4
Ashippun, 500 . . . E1
Ashland, 8,620 . . . C2
Ashwaubenon, 17,634 . . . E4
Athelstane, 70 . . . E3
Athens, 1,095 . . . C3
Auburndale, 738 . . . C4
Augusta, 1,460 . . . B4
Aurora, 300 . . . E3
Auroraville, 100 . . . E4
Avalon, 150 . . . E6
Avoca, 608 . . . C5
Babcock, 125 . . . C4
Bagley, 339 . . . B6
Baileys Harbor, 200 . . . F3
Baldwin, 2,667 . . . A4
Balsam Lake, 950 . . . A3
Bancroft, 450 . . . D4
Bangor, 1,400 . . . C5
Baraboo, 10,711 . . . D5
Barksdale, 125 . . . C2
Barneveld, 1,088 . . . D5
Barron, 3,248 . . . B3
Barronett, 125 . . . B3
Bay City, 465 . . . A4
Bayfield, 611 . . . C2
Bayside, 4,518 . . . F1
Bear Creek, 415 . . . E4
Beaver, 100 . . . E3
Beaver Dam, 15,169 . . . E5
Beecher, 150 . . . F3
Beetown, 125 . . . C6
Belgium, 1,678 . . . F5
Bell Center, 116 . . . C5
Belleville, 1,908 . . . D6
Bellevue, 11,828 . . . F4
Belmont, 871 . . . C6
Beloit, 35,775 . . . D6
Bennett, 50 . . . B2
Benoit . . . B2
Benton, 976 . . . C6
Berlin, 5,305 . . . E5
Bevent, 50 . . . D4
Big Bend, 1,278 . . . F2
Big Falls, 85 . . . D4
Birch, 250 . . . C2
Birchwood, 518 . . . B3
Birnamwood, 795 . . . D4
Biron, 915 . . . D4
Black Creek, 1,192 . . . E4
Black Earth, 1,320 . . . D5
Black Hawk, 125 . . . D5
Black River Falls, 3,618 . . . C4
Blair, 1,273 . . . B4
Blanchardville, 806 . . . D6
Bloom City, 60 . . . C5
Bloomer, 3,347 . . . B3
Bloomington, 701 . . . C6
Bloomville, 125 . . . D3
Blue Mounds, 708 . . . D5
Blue River, 429 . . . C5
Boardman, 200 . . . A3
Boaz, 137 . . . C5
Bohners Lake, 1,952 . . . E6
Bonduel, 1,416 . . . E4
Borth, 175 . . . E4
Boscobel, 3,047 . . . C5
Bowler, 343 . . . E4
Boyceville, 1,043 . . . A3
Boyd, 680 . . . C4
Brackett, 150 . . . B4
Bradley, 150 . . . D3
Brandon, 912 . . . E5
Brantwood, 40 . . . C3
Breed, 80 . . . E3
Brice Prairie, 1,804 . . . B5
Bridgeport, 125 . . . B5
Briggsville, 250 . . . D5
Brill, 150 . . . B3
Brillion, 2,937 . . . E4
Brodhead, 3,180 . . . D6
Brokaw, 107 . . . D4
Brookfield, 38,649 . . . E5, F2
Brooklyn, 916 . . . D6
Brooks, 125 . . . D5
Brown Deer, 12,170 . . . F1, F5
Brownsville, 570 . . . E5
Browntown, 252 . . . D6
Bruce, 787 . . . B3
Brule, 200 . . . B2
Brussels, 275 . . . F4
Bryant, 90 . . . D3
Buena Park . . . E6
Buffalo, 1,040 . . . B4
Burlington, 9,936 . . . E6
Butler, 1,881 . . . F2
Butternut, 407 . . . C2
Cable, 200 . . . B2
Cadott, 1,345 . . . B4
Calamine, 80 . . . C6
Caledonia, 250 . . . F2
Cambria, 792 . . . D5
Cambridge, 1,101 . . . D5
Cameron, 1,546 . . . B3
Campbellsport, 1,913 . . . E5
Camp Douglas, 592 . . . C5
Campia, 175 . . . B3
Canton, 150 . . . B3
Carlsville, 175 . . . F4
Caryville, 80 . . . B4
Cascade, 666 . . . E5
Casco, 572 . . . F4
Cashton, 1,005 . . . C5
Cassville, 1,085 . . . C6
Cataract, 175 . . . C4
Catawba, 149 . . . C3
Cavour, 50 . . . E3
Cazenovia, 326 . . . C5
Cecil, 466 . . . E4
Cedarburg, 10,908 . . . F1, F5
Cedar Grove, 1,887 . . . F5
Centuria, 865 . . . A3
Chain O' Lakes (Chain O' Lakes-King), 2,215 . . . D4
Champion, 175 . . . F4
Chaseburg, 306 . . . B5
Chelsea, 125 . . . C3
Chenequa, 583 . . . E2
Chetek, 2,180 . . . B3
Chili, 275 . . . C4
Chilton, 3,708 . . . E4
Chippewa Falls, 12,925 . . . B4
Christie, 125 . . . C4
City Point . . . C4
Clam Falls, 70 . . . A3
Clam Lake, 50 . . . C2
Clayton, 507 . . . A3
Clear Lake, 1,051 . . . A3
Clearwater Lake, 200 . . . D3
Cleveland, 1,361 . . . F5
Clifton, 80 . . . C5
Clinton, 2,162 . . . E6
Clintonville, 4,736 . . . E4
Clyman, 388 . . . E5
Cobb, 442 . . . C6
Cochrane, 435 . . . B4
Colburn . . . B3
Colby, 1,616 . . . C4
Coleman, 716 . . . E3
Colfax, 1,136 . . . B4
Coloma, 461 . . . D4
Columbus, 4,479 . . . D5
Como, 1,870 . . . E6
Comstock, 150 . . . A3
Connorsville, 175 . . . A3
Conover . . . D2
Conrath, 98 . . . B3
Cooksville, 125 . . . D6
Coon Valley, 714 . . . B5
Cornell, 1,466 . . . B3
Cornucopia, 100 . . . B2
Cottage Grove, 4,059 . . . D5
Couderay, 96 . . . B3
Crandon, 1,961 . . . E3
Crescent, 90 . . . D3
Crivitz, 998 . . . F3
Cross Plains, 3,084 . . . D5
Cuba City, 2,156 . . . C6
Cudahy, 18,429 . . . G2
Cumberland, 2,280 . . . A3
Curtiss, 198 . . . C4
Cushing, 175 . . . A3
Dairyland . . . A2
Daleyville, 150 . . . D6
Dallas, 356 . . . B3
Dalton, 250 . . . D5
Danbury, 225 . . . A2
Dane, 799 . . . D5
Darien, 1,572 . . . E6
Darlington, 2,418 . . . C6
Dayton, 175 . . . D6
Deerbrook, 125 . . . D3
Deerfield, 1,971 . . . D5
Deer Park, 227 . . . A3
De Forest, 7,368 . . . D5
Delafield, 6,472 . . . E2
Delavan, 7,956 . . . E6
Dellwood, 175 . . . D5
Denmark, 1,958 . . . F4
De Pere, 20,559 . . . E4
De Soto, 366 . . . B5
Dexterville, 40 . . . C4
Diamond Bluff, 125 . . . A4
Dickeyville, 1,043 . . . C6
Dodge, 125 . . . B4
Dodgeville, 4,220 . . . C6
Doering, 40 . . . D3
Dorchester, 827 . . . C3
Dousman, 1,584 . . . E2
Downing, 257 . . . A3
Downsville, 200 . . . B4
Doylestown, 328 . . . D5
Dresser, 732 . . . A3
Drummond, 150 . . . B2
Dunbar, 70 . . . E3
Durand, 1,968 . . . B4
Dyckesville, 300 . . . F4
Eagle, 1,707 . . . E2
Eagle Lake, 1,320 . . . E6
Eagle River, 1,443 . . . D3
Eagleton, 150 . . . B3
Earl, 60 . . . B3
Eastman, 437 . . . B5
Easton, 150 . . . D5
East Troy, 3,564 . . . E6
Eau Claire, 61,704 . . . B4
Eau Galle, 175 . . . A4
Eden, 687 . . . E5
Edgar, 1,386 . . . D4
Edgerton, 4,933 . . . D6
Edgewater, 80 . . . B3
Egg Harbor, 250 . . . F3
Eland, 251 . . . D4
Elcho, 375 . . . D3
Elderon, 189 . . . D4
Eleva, 635 . . . B4
Elkhart Lake, 1,021 . . . E5
Elkhorn, 7,305 . . . E6
Elk Mound, 785 . . . B4
Ella . . . A4
Ellison Bay, 200 . . . F3
Ellsworth, 2,909 . . . A4
Elm Grove, 6,249 . . . F2
Elmwood, 841 . . . A4
Elmwood Park, 474 . . . F6
Elroy, 1,578 . . . C5
Elton, 50 . . . E3
Embarrass, 399 . . . E4
Endeavor, 440 . . . D5
Enterprise, 80 . . . D3
Ephraim, 353 . . . F3
Esofea . . . C5
Ettrick, 521 . . . B4
Euren, 175 . . . F4
Evansville, 4,039 . . . D6
Evergreen, 3,611 . . . D4
Exeland, 212 . . . B3
Fairchild, 564 . . . C4
Fairwater, 350 . . . E5
Fall Creek, 1,236 . . . B4
Fall River, 1,097 . . . D5
Falun, 125 . . . A3
Fence, 70 . . . E3
Fennimore, 2,387 . . . C6
Fenwood, 174 . . . C4
Ferryville, 174 . . . B5
Fifield, 250 . . . C3
Finley . . . C4
Fitchburg, 20,501 . . . D6
Florence, 750 . . . E3
Fond du Lac, 42,203 . . . E5
Fontana, 1,754 . . . E6
Footville, 788 . . . D6
Forest, 70 . . . A3
Forestville, 429 . . . F4
Fort Atkinson, 11,621 . . . E6
Foster, 125 . . . B4
Fountain City, 983 . . . B4
Foxboro . . . A2
Fox Lake, 1,454 . . . E5
Fox Point, 7,012 . . . F2
Francis Creek, 681 . . . F4
Franklin (Jackson Co.), 60 . . . B4
Franklin (Milwaukee Co.), 29,494 . . . E6, F2
Franksville, 1,789 . . . F2
Frederic, 1,262 . . . A3
Fredonia, 1,934 . . . F5
Freedom, 1,500 . . . E4
Fremont, 666 . . . E4
French Island, 4,410 . . . B5
Friendship, 698 . . . D5
Friesland, 298 . . . D5
Gagen . . . D3
Galesville, 1,427 . . . B4
Galloway, 125 . . . D4
Gays Mills, 625 . . . C5
Genoa, 263 . . . B5
Genoa City, 1,949 . . . E6
Germania, 70 . . . D5
Germantown, 18,260 . . . E5, F1
Gillett, 1,256 . . . E4
Gills Rock, 125 . . . F3
Gilman, 474 . . . C3
Gilmanton, 175 . . . B4
Gleason, 325 . . . D3
Glenbeulah, 378 . . . E5
Glendale, 13,367 . . . F2
Glen Flora, 93 . . . C3
Glen Haven, 50 . . . B6
Glenwood City, 1,183 . . . A3
Glidden, 650 . . . C2
Goodman, 275 . . . E3
Goodrich, 40 . . . C3
Gordon, 150 . . . B2
Gotham, 275 . . . C5
Grafton, 10,312 . . . F1, F5
Grand View, 125 . . . B2
Granton, 406 . . . C4
Grantsburg, 1,369 . . . A3
Gratiot, 252 . . . C6
Green Bay, 102,313 . . . F4
Greendale, 14,405 . . . F2
Greenfield, 35,476 . . . E6, F2
Green Lake, 1,100 . . . E5
Greenleaf, 650 . . . E4
Green Valley, 175 . . . E4
Greenwood, 1,079 . . . C4
Gresham, 575 . . . E4
Gurney . . . C2
Hager City, 300 . . . A4
Hales Corners, 7,765 . . . F2
Hamburg, 100 . . . D3
Hammond, 1,153 . . . A4
Hancock, 463 . . . D4
Hannibal, 40 . . . C3
Harmony Grove (part of Lake Wisconsin, pop. 3,493), 550 . . . D5
Harrison, 100 . . . D3
Harrisville, 125 . . . D5
Harshaw, 125 . . . D3
Hartford, 10,905 . . . E5, F1
Hartland, 7,905 . . . F2
Hatfield, 150 . . . C4
Hatley, 476 . . . D4
Haugen, 287 . . . B3
Haven, 200 . . . F5
Hawkins, 317 . . . C3
Hawthorne, 125 . . . B2
Hayward, 2,129 . . . B2
Hazel Green, 1,183 . . . C6
Hazelhurst, 250 . . . D3
Heafford Junction, 325 . . . D3
Herbster, 50 . . . B2
Hertel, 90 . . . A3
Hewitt, 670 . . . C4
High Bridge, 90 . . . C2
Highland, 855 . . . C5
Hilbert, 1,089 . . . E4
Hiles, 100 . . . E3
Hillsboro, 1,302 . . . C5
Hillsdale, 200 . . . B3
Hines, 125 . . . A2
Hixton, 446 . . . B4
Holcombe, 200 . . . B3
Hollandale, 283 . . . D6
Hollister . . . E3
Holmen, 6,200 . . . B5
Horicon, 3,775 . . . E5
Hortonville, 2,357 . . . E4
Howard, 13,546 . . . E4
Howards Grove, 2,792 . . . F5
Hudson, 8,775 . . . A4
Humbird, 225 . . . C4
Hurley, 1,818 . . . C2
Hustisford, 1,135 . . . E5
Hustler, 113 . . . C5
Independence, 1,244 . . . B4
Ingram, 76 . . . C3
Ino . . . B2
Institute, 250 . . . F4
Iola, 1,298 . . . D4
Irma, 125 . . . D3
Iron Belt, 225 . . . C2
Iron Ridge, 998 . . . E5
Iron River, 500 . . . B2
Ironton, 250 . . . C5
Island Lake, 80 . . . B3
Ixonia, 642 . . . E2
Jackson, 4,938 . . . F1
Jacksonport, 125 . . . F4
Janesville, 59,498 . . . D6
Jefferson, 7,338 . . . E5
Jim Falls, 325 . . . B3
Joel . . . A3
Johnsburg, 200 . . . E5
Johnson Creek, 1,581 . . . E5
Juda, 325 . . . D6
Jump River, 100 . . . C3
Junction City, 440 . . . D4
Juneau, 2,485 . . . E5
Kaukauna, 12,983 . . . E4
Kekoskee, 169 . . . E5
Kellner, 650 . . . D4
Kellnersville, 374 . . . F4
Kempster, 100 . . . D3
Kendall, 469 . . . C5
Kennan, 171 . . . C3
Kenosha, 90,352 . . . F6
Keshena, 1,394 . . . E4
Kewaskum, 3,274 . . . E5
Kewaunee, 2,806 . . . F4
Kiel, 3,450 . . . F5
Kimberly, 6,146 . . . E4
King (see Chain O'Lakes) . . . D4
Kingston, 288 . . . D5
Knapp, 421 . . . A4
Kohler, 1,926 . . . F5
Krakow, 275 . . . E4
Lac du Flambeau, 1,646 . . . D3
Lac La Belle, 329 . . . E2
La Crosse, 51,818 . . . B5
Ladysmith, 3,932 . . . B3
La Farge, 775 . . . C5
La Grange, 100 . . . E6
Lake Delton, 1,982 . . . D5
Lake Geneva, 7,148 . . . E6
Lake Mills, 4,843 . . . E5
Lake Nebagamon, 1,015 . . . B2
Lake Tomahawk, 325 . . . D3
Lake Wissota, 2,458 . . . B4
Lakewood, 200 . . . E3
Lampson, 80 . . . B3
Lancaster, 4,070 . . . C6
Land O' Lakes, 225 . . . D2
Langlade, 100 . . . E3
Lannon, 1,009 . . . F2
Laona, 700 . . . E3
La Pointe, 60 . . . C2
La Valle, 326 . . . C5
Lebanon, 275 . . . E5
Leland . . . D5
Lena, 510 . . . E4
Leon, 40 . . . C5
Lewis, 150 . . . A3
Leyden, 80 . . . D6
Liberty Pole, 125 . . . C5
Lily, 80 . . . E3
Lime Ridge, 169 . . . C5
Linden, 615 . . . C6
Little Chute, 10,476 . . . E4
Little Round Lake, 948 . . . B3
Little Suamico, 225 . . . E4
Livingston, 597 . . . C6
Lodi, 2,882 . . . D5
Loganville, 276 . . . C5
Lohrville, 408 . . . D4
Lomira, 2,233 . . . E5
Lone Rock, 929 . . . C5
Long Lake, 90 . . . E3
Longwood, 90 . . . C4
Loretta . . . C3
Lowell, 366 . . . E5
Loyal, 1,308 . . . C4
Loyd, 125 . . . C5
Lublin, 110 . . . C3
Luck, 1,210 . . . A3
Ludington, 150 . . . B4
Lugerville, 40 . . . C3
Luxemburg, 1,935 . . . F4
Lyndon Station, 458 . . . D5
Lynxville, 176 . . . B5
Lyons, 600 . . . E6
Mackville, 450 . . . E4
Madison, 208,054 . . . D5
Maiden Rock, 121 . . . A4
Manawa, 1,330 . . . E4
Manitowish . . . C2
Manitowoc, 34,053 . . . F4
Maple, 200 . . . B2
Maple Bluff, 1,358 . . . D5
Maplewood, 175 . . . F4
Marathon City, 1,640 . . . D4
Marengo, 225 . . . C2
Maribel, 264 . . . F4
Marinette, 11,749 . . . F3
Marion, 1,297 . . . E4
Markesan, 1,396 . . . E5
Marquette, 169 . . . D5
Marshall, 3,432 . . . D5
Marshfield, 18,800 . . . C4
Martell, 150 . . . A4
Mason, 72 . . . B2
Mather, 40 . . . C4
Mattoon, 466 . . . D3
Mauston, 3,740 . . . C5
Mayville, 4,902 . . . E5
Mazomanie, 1,485 . . . D5
McAllister . . . F3
McFarland, 6,416 . . . D5
McKinley, 100 . . . A3
McNaughton . . . D3
Medford, 4,350 . . . C3
Mellen, 845 . . . C2
Melrose, 529 . . . B4
Melvina, 93 . . . C5
Menasha, 16,331 . . . E4
Menomonee Falls, 32,647 . . . E5, F1
Menomonie, 14,937 . . . B4
Mequon, 21,823 . . . F1, F5
Mercer, 450 . . . C2
Meridean, 40 . . . B4
Merrill, 10,146 . . . D3
Merrillan, 585 . . . C4
Merrimac, 416 . . . D5
Merton, 1,926 . . . F2
Middle Inlet, 90 . . . E3
Middleton, 15,770 . . . D5
Mikana, 100 . . . B3
Milan, 200 . . . C4
Milladore, 268 . . . D4
Millston, 100 . . . C4
Milltown, 888 . . . A3
Milton, 5,132 . . . E6
Milwaukee, 596,974 . . . F2, F5
Mindoro, 200 . . . B4
Mineral Point, 2,617 . . . C6
Minocqua, 750 . . . D3
Minong, 531 . . . B2
Mishicot, 1,422 . . . F4
Modena, 40 . . . B4
Mole Lake, 275 . . . E3
Mondovi, 2,634 . . . B4
Monico, 175 . . . D3
Monona, 8,018 . . . E5
Monroe, 10,843 . . . D6
Monroe Center, 100 . . . D4
Montello, 1,397 . . . D5
Montfort, 663 . . . C6
Monticello, 1,146 . . . D6
Montreal, 838 . . . C2
Moose Junction . . . A2
Moquah, 40 . . . B2
Morse . . . C2
Mosinee, 4,063 . . . D4
Mountain, 200 . . . E3
Mount Calvary, 956 . . . E5
Mount Hope, 186 . . . C6
Mount Horeb, 5,860 . . . D5
Mount Sterling, 215 . . . C5
Mount Tabor, 80 . . . C5
Mount Zion, 50 . . . C5
Mukwonago, 6,162 . . . F2
Muscoda, 1,453 . . . C5
Muskego, 21,397 . . . E6, F2
Namekagon, 40 . . . B2
Nashotah, 1,266 . . . E2
Navarino, 100 . . . E4
Necedah, 888 . . . C4
Neenah, 24,507 . . . E4
Neillsville, 2,731 . . . C4
Nekoosa, 2,590 . . . D4
Nelma, 70 . . . E2
Nelson, 395 . . . A4
Nelsonville, 191 . . . D4
Neopit, 839 . . . E4
Neosho, 593 . . . E1, E5
Neshkoro, 453 . . . D5
Newald, 125 . . . E3
New Auburn, 562 . . . B3
New Berlin, 38,220 . . . E6, F2
Newburg, 1,119 . . . E5
New Diggings, 125 . . . C6
New Franken, 225 . . . F4
New Glarus, 2,111 . . . D6
New Holstein, 3,301 . . . E5
New Lisbon, 1,436 . . . C5
New London, 7,085 . . . E4
New Post, 367 . . . B3
New Richmond, 6,310 . . . A3
Newry, 60 . . . C5
Newton, 300 . . . F5
Niagara, 1,880 . . . F3
Nichols, 307 . . . E4
North Bay, 260 . . . F6, G2
North Bend, 100 . . . B4
North Cape, 300 . . . F2
Northfield, 90 . . . B4
North Fond du Lac, 4,557 . . . E5
North Freedom, 649 . . . D5
North Hudson, 3,463 . . . A3
North Prairie, 1,571 . . . E2
Norton . . . B3
Norwalk, 653 . . . C5
Oak Creek, 28,456 . . . F2, F6
Oakdale, 297 . . . C5
Oakfield, 1,012 . . . E5
Oconomowoc, 12,382 . . . E2, E5
Oconomowoc Lake, 564 . . . E2
Oconto, 4,708 . . . F4
Oconto Falls, 2,843 . . . E4
Odanah, 254 . . . C2
Ogdensburg, 224 . . . D4
Ogema, 250 . . . C3
Ojibwa . . . B3
Okauchee, 2,100 . . . E2
Oliver, 358 . . . A2
Omro, 3,177 . . . E4
Onalaska, 14,839 . . . B5
Ontario, 476 . . . C5
Oostburg, 2,660 . . . F5
Oregon, 7,514 . . . D6
Orfordville, 1,272 . . . D6
Osceola, 2,421 . . . A3
Oshkosh, 62,916 . . . E4
Osseo, 1,669 . . . B4
Owen, 936 . . . C4
Oxbo . . . C3
Oxford, 536 . . . D5
Paddock Lake, 3,012 . . . E6
Palmyra, 1,766 . . . E6
Pardeeville, 1,982 . . . D5
Park Falls, 2,793 . . . C3
Park Ridge, 488 . . . D4
Parrish . . . D3
Patch Grove, 166 . . . C6
Patzau, 80 . . . A2
Pearson, 80 . . . D3
Pelican Lake, 50 . . . D3
Pella, 125 . . . E4
Pell Lake, 2,988 . . . E6
Pembine, 175 . . . F3
Pensaukee, 125 . . . F4
Pepin, 878 . . . A4
Peru, 90 . . . D4
Peshtigo, 3,357 . . . F3
Pewaukee, 8,170 . . . F2
Phelps, 350 . . . D2
Phillips, 1,675 . . . C3
Phlox, 150 . . . D3
Pickerel, 100 . . . E3
Pickett, 200 . . . E5
Pigeon Falls, 388 . . . B4
Pilsen, 125 . . . F4
Pipe, 175 . . . E5
Pittsville, 866 . . . C4
Plain, 792 . . . C5
Plainfield, 899 . . . D4
Plainville, 150 . . . D5
Platteville, 9,989 . . . C6
Pleasant Prairie, 16,136 . . . F6
Plover, 10,520 . . . D4
Plum City, 574 . . . A4
Plymouth, 7,781 . . . F5
Polonia, 275 . . . D4
Poplar, 552 . . . B2
Portage, 9,728 . . . D5
Port Edwards, 1,944 . . . D4
Porterfield, 125 . . . F3
Port Washington, 10,467 . . . F5
Port Wing, 175 . . . B2
Poskin, 125 . . . B3
Postville . . . D6
Potosi, 711 . . . C6
Potter, 223 . . . E4
Pound, 355 . . . E3
Poynette, 2,266 . . . D5
Poy Sippi, 375 . . . E4
Prairie du Chien, 6,018 . . . B5
Prairie du Sac, 3,231 . . . D5
Prairie Farm, 508 . . . B3
Prentice, 626 . . . C3
Prescott, 3,764 . . . A4
Presque Isle, 70 . . . D2
Price . . . B4
Princeton, 1,504 . . . D5
Pulaski, 3,060 . . . E4
Racine, 81,855 . . . F6
Radisson, 222 . . . B3
Randolph, 1,869 . . . E5
Random Lake, 1,551 . . . F5
Range, 150 . . . A3
Readstown, 395 . . . C5
Red Cliff, 600 . . . C2
Redgranite, 1,040 . . . D4
Reedsburg, 7,827 . . . D5
Reedsville, 1,187 . . . F4
Reeseville, 703 . . . E5
Rewey, 311 . . . C6
Rhinelander, 7,735 . . . D3
Rib Falls, 150 . . . D4
Rib Lake, 878 . . . C3
Rice Lake, 8,320 . . . B3
Richfield, 500 . . . F1
Richford, 40 . . . D4
Richland Center, 5,114 . . . C5
Ridgeland, 265 . . . B3
Ridgeway, 689 . . . D5
Rio, 938 . . . D5
Rio Creek, 150 . . . F4
Riplinger, 125 . . . C4
Ripon, 6,828 . . . E5
River Falls, 12,560 . . . A4
River Hills, 1,631 . . . F1
Roberts, 969 . . . A4
Rochester, 1,149 . . . E6
Rockdale, 214 . . . D6
Rockfield, 125 . . . F1
Rockland, 628 . . . C5
Rock Springs, 425 . . . D5
Rosendale, 923 . . . E5
Rosholt, 518 . . . D4
Rothschild, 4,970 . . . D4
Roxbury, 200 . . . D5
Rozellville, 275 . . . C4
Rubicon, 350 . . . E1, E5
Rudolph, 423 . . . D4
Rush Lake, 175 . . . E5
Rusk, 90 . . . B4
St. Cloud, 497 . . . E5
St. Croix Falls, 2,033 . . . A3
St. Francis, 8,662 . . . F2
St. Germain, 225 . . . D3
St. Nazianz, 749 . . . F4
Sanborn, 60 . . . C2
Sand Creek, 175 . . . B3
Sarona, 100 . . . B3
Sauk City, 3,109 . . . D5
Saukville, 4,068 . . . F5
Saxeville, 200 . . . D4
Saxon, 125 . . . C2
Sayner, 175 . . . D3
Scandinavia, 349 . . . D4
Schofield, 2,117 . . . D4
Seeley, 100 . . . B2
Seneca, 125 . . . C5
Sextonville, 250 . . . C5
Seymour (Eau Claire Co.), 1,474 . . . B4
Seymour (Outagamie Co.), 3,335 . . . E4
Sharon, 1,549 . . . E6
Shawano, 8,298 . . . E4
Sheboygan, 50,792 . . . F5
Sheboygan Falls, 6,772 . . . F5
Sheldon, 256 . . . C3
Shell Lake, 1,309 . . . B3
Sheridan, 150 . . . D4
Sherwood, 1,550 . . . E4
Shiocton, 954 . . . E4
Shorewood, 13,763 . . . F2
Shorewood Hills, 1,732 . . . D5
Shullsburg, 1,246 . . . C6
Silver Lake (Kenosha Co.), 2,341 . . . E6
Silver Lake (Waushara Co.), 400 . . . D4
Siren, 988 . . . A3
Sister Bay, 886 . . . F3
Slinger, 3,901 . . . E5, F1
Sobieski, 150 . . . E4
Soldiers Grove, 653 . . . C5
Solon Springs, 576 . . . B2
Somers, 1,100 . . . F6
Somerset, 1,556 . . . A3
South Milwaukee, 21,256 . . . F6, G2
South Range, 250 . . . B2
South Wayne, 484 . . . D6
Sparta, 8,648 . . . C5
Spencer, 1,932 . . . C4
Spooner, 2,653 . . . B3
Spread Eagle, 250 . . . E3
Springbrook, 50 . . . B3
Spring Green, 1,444 . . . C5
Springstead, 60 . . . C2
Spring Valley, 1,189 . . . A4

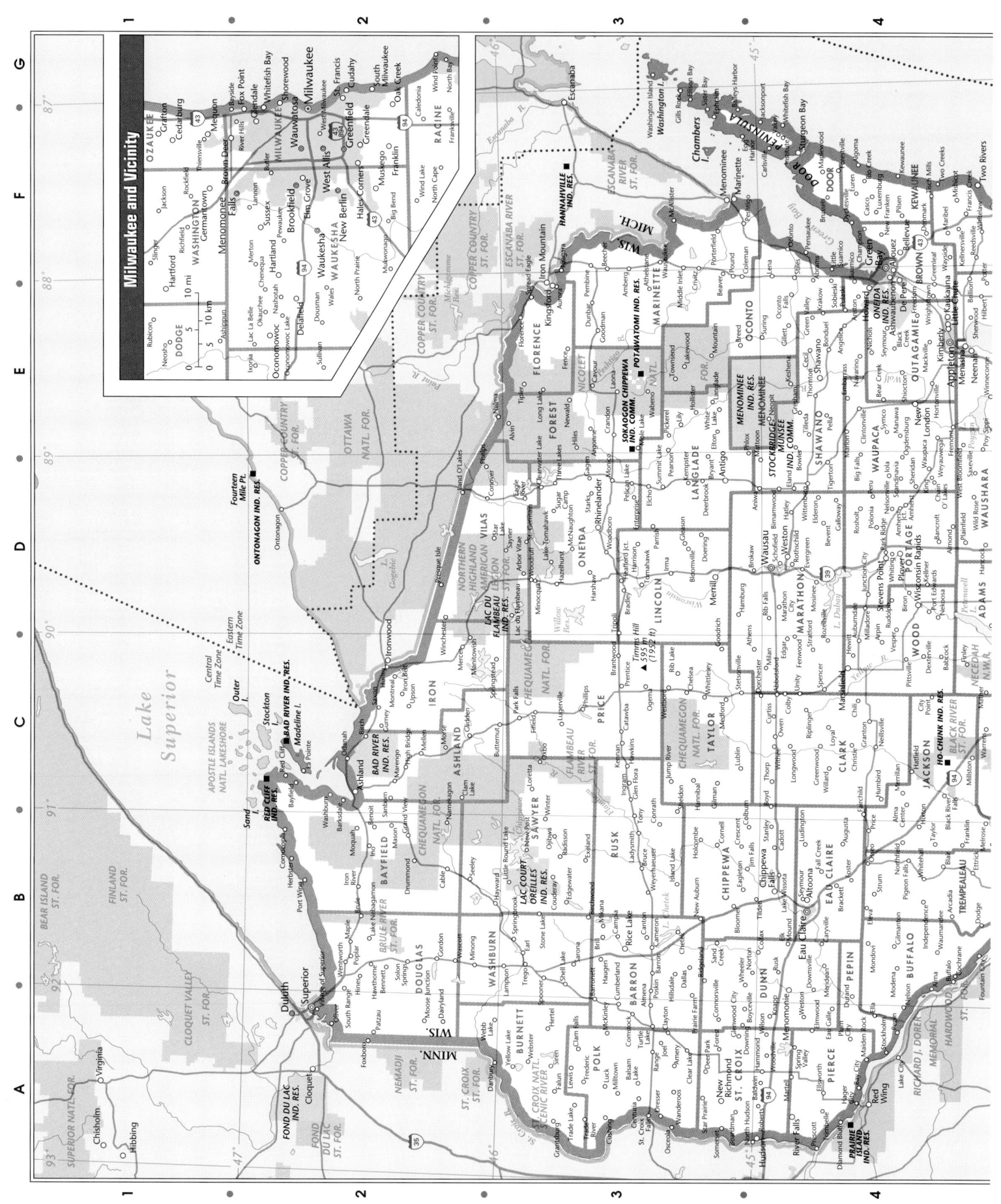

Milwaukee and Vicinity

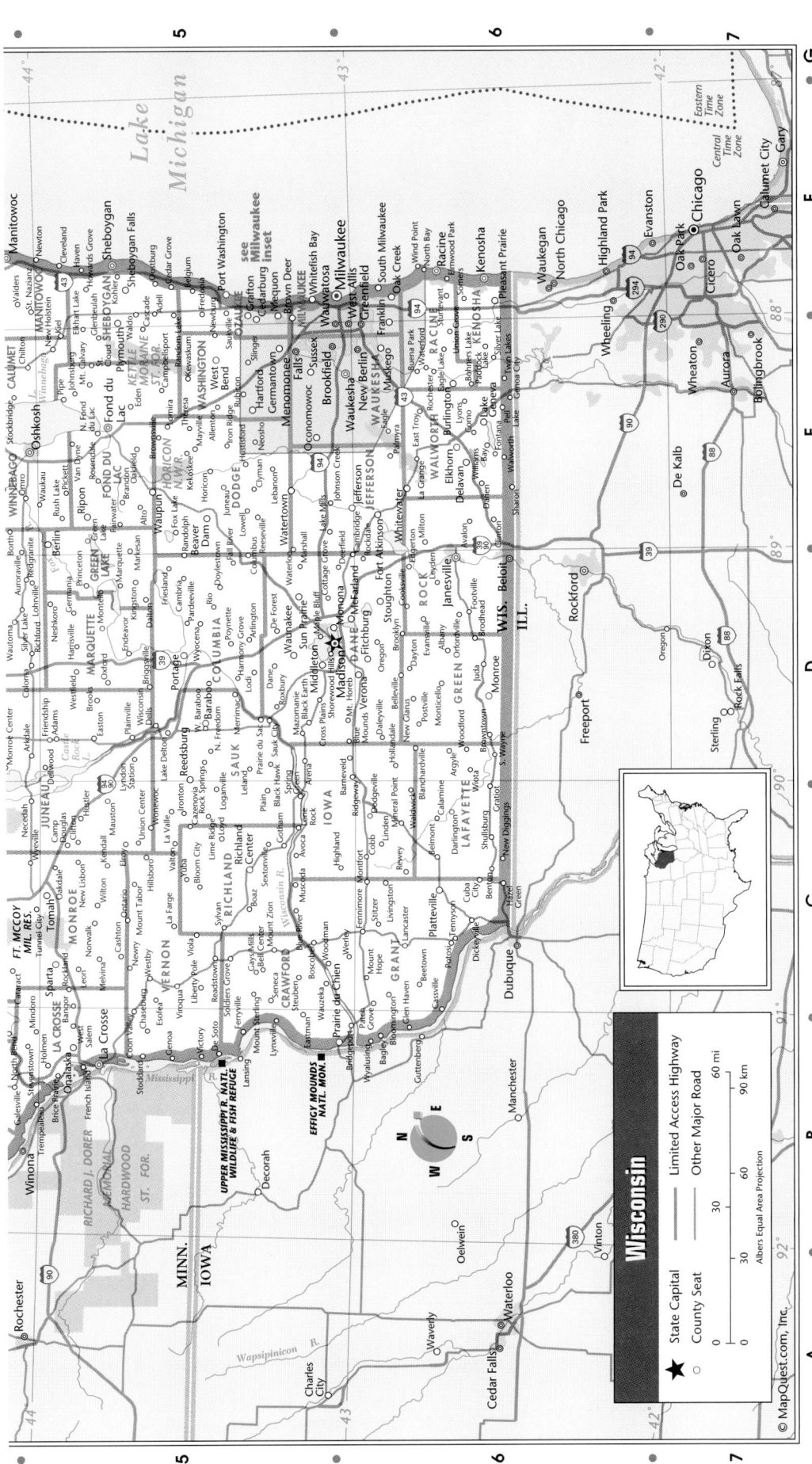

Wisconsin

State Capital
★

County Seat
○

Limited Access Highway
Other Major Road

0   30   60 mi
0   30   60   90 km

Albers Equal Area Projection

© MapQuest.com, Inc.

Stanley, 1,898 . . . . .B4
Starks, 90 . . . . .D3
Star Lake D2
Star Prairie, 574 . . . . .A3
Stetsonville, 563 . . . . .C3
Steuben, 177 . . . . .C5
Stevens Point, 24,551 . . . . .D4
Stevenstown, 80 . . . . .B4
Stiles, 200 . . . . .E4
Stitzer, 175 . . . . .C6
Stockbridge, 649 . . . . .E4
Stockholm, 97 . . . . .A4
Stoddard, 815 . . . . .B5
Stone Lake, 225 . . . . .B3
Stoughton, 12,354 . . . . . . .D6
Stratford, 1,523 . . . . .C4
Strum, 1,001 . . . . .B4
Sturgeon Bay, 9,437 . . . . . .F4
Sturtevant, 5,287 . . . . . . .F6
Suamico, 950 . . . . .E4
Sugar Camp, 90 . . . . .D3
Sullivan, 688 . . . . .E2
Summit Lake, 150 . . . . . . .D3
Sun Prairie, 20,369 . . . . . .D5
Suring, 605 . . . . .E3
Superior, 27,368 . . . . .A2
Sussex, 8,828 . . . . .E5, F2
Sylvan C5
Symco, 175 . . . . .E4
Taylor, 513 . . . . .B4
Tennyson, 370 . . . . .C6
Theresa, 1,252 . . . . .E5
Thiensville, 3,254 . . . . . . .F1
Thornton, 100 . . . . .E4
Thorp, 1,536 . . . . .C4
Three Lakes, 600 . . . . .D3
Tigerton, 764 . . . . .D4
Tilden, 250 . . . . .B3
Tilleda, 100 . . . . .D4
Tipler, 40 . . . . .E3
Tisch Mills, 275 . . . . .F4
Tomah, 8,419 . . . . .C5
Tomahawk, 3,770 . . . . .D3
Tony, 105 . . . . .B3
Townsend, 150 . . . . .E3
Trade Lake, 100 . . . . .A3
Trade River, 80 . . . . .A3
Trego, 200 . . . . .B3
Trempealeau, 1,319 . . . . . .B4
Trimbelle, 175 . . . . .A4
Tripoli, 40 . . . . .D3
Tunnel City, 225 . . . . .C4
Turtle Lake, 1,065 . . . . . . .A3
Twin Lakes, 5,124 . . . . . . .E6
Two Creeks, 125 . . . . .F4
Two Rivers, 12,639 . . . . . . .F4
Union Center, 214 . . . . . . .C5
Union Grove, 4,322 . . . . . . .E6
Unity, 368 . . . . .C4
Upson, 50 . . . . .C2
Valders, 948 . . . . .F4
Valmy, 150 . . . . .F4
Valton, 100 . . . . .C5
Van Dyne, 250 . . . . .E5
Verona, 7,052 . . . . .D6
Vesper, 541 . . . . .D4
Victory, 90 . . . . .B5
Village of Superior, 500 . . . .A2
Viola, 667 . . . . .C5
Viroqua, 4,335 . . . . .C5
Wabeno, 475 . . . . .E3
Waldo, 450 . . . . .F5
Waldwick, 80 . . . . .C6
Wales, 2,523 . . . . .E2
Walworth, 2,304 . . . . .E6
Wanderoos, 200 . . . . .A3
Warrens, 286 . . . . .C4
Wascott B2
Washburn, 2,280 . . . . .C2
Washington Island, 150 . . . .G3
Waterford, 4,048 . . . . .E6
Waterloo, 3,259 . . . . .D5
Watertown, 21,598 . . . . . . .E5
Waukau, 300 . . . . .E5
Waukesha, 64,825 . . . . .E5, F2
Waumandee B4
Waunakee, 8,995 . . . . .D5
Waupaca, 5,676 . . . . .D4
Waupun, 10,718 . . . . .E5
Wausau, 38,426 . . . . .D4
Wausaukee, 572 . . . . .F3
Wautoma, 1,998 . . . . .D4
Wauwatosa, 47,271 . . . .F2, F5
Wauzeka, 768 . . . . .C5
Wayside, 275 . . . . .F4
Webb Lake, 40 . . . . .A2
Webster, 653 . . . . .A3
Wentworth, 70 . . . . .B2
Werley, 40 . . . . .D6
West Allis, 61,254 . . . . .F2, F5
West Baraboo, 1,248 . . . . . .D5
West Bend, 28,152 . . . . . . .E5
West Bloomfield, 100 . . . . . .E4
Westboro, 200 . . . . .C3
Westby, 2,045 . . . . .C5
Westfield, 1,217 . . . . .D5
West Milwaukee, 4,201 . . . . .F2
Weston (Dunn Co.), 30 . . . . .A4
Weston (Marathon Co.),
  12,079 . . . . .D4
West Salem, 4,540 . . . . . . .B5
Weyauwega, 1,806 . . . . . . .E4
Weyerhaeuser, 353 . . . . . . .B3
Wheeler, 317 . . . . .B4
Whitefish Bay (Door Co.),
  50 . . . . .F4
Whitefish Bay (Milwaukee Co.),
  14,163 . . . . .F2, F5
Whitehall, 1,651 . . . . .B4
White Lake, 329 . . . . .E3
Whitelaw, 730 . . . . .F4
Whitewater, 13,437 . . . . . . .E6
Whiting, 1,760 . . . . .D4
Whittlesey, 125 . . . . .C3
Wild Rose, 765 . . . . .D4
Willard, 100 . . . . .C4
Williams Bay, 2,415 . . . . . .E6
Wilson, 176 . . . . .A4
Wilton, 519 . . . . .C5
Winchester, 100 . . . . .D2
Wind Lake, 5,202 . . . . .E6
Wind Point, 1,853 . . . . .F6, G2
Winneconne, 2,401 . . . . . . .E4
Winter, 344 . . . . .B3

Wiota, 80 . . . . .D6
Wisconsin Dells, 2,418 . . . . .D5
Wisconsin Rapids, 18,435 . . .D4
Withee, 508 . . . . .C4
Wittenberg, 1,177 . . . . . . .D4
Wonewoc, 834 . . . . .C5
Woodboro, 325 . . . . .D3
Woodford, 150 . . . . .D6
Woodman, 96 . . . . .C5
Woodruff, 1,300 . . . . .D3
Woodville, 1,104 . . . . .A4
Wrightstown, 1,934 . . . . . . .E4
Wyalusing B6
Wyeville, 146 . . . . .C4
Wyocena, 668 . . . . .D5
Yellow Lake, 90 . . . . .A3
Yuba, 92 . . . . .C5

Other Features

Abbaye, point E2
Apostle Islands Natl.
  Lakeshore C1
Bad River Ind. Res. C2
Bear Island St. For. B1
Black River St. For. C4
Brule River St. For. B2
Castle Rock, lake D5
Chambers, island F3
Chequamegon
  Natl. For. B2, C3
Chetek, lake B3
Chippewa, lake B3
Cloquet Valley St. For. A1
Copper Country
  St. For. E2, F2
Door, peninsula F4
Dubay, lake D4
Effigy Mounds Natl. Mon. . . .B5
Escanaba, river F2
Escanaba River St. For. . .F2, F3
Finland St. For. B1
Flambeau, river C3
Flambeau River St. For. C3
Fond Du Lac Ind. Res. A2
Fond Du Lac St. For. A2
Fourteen Mile, point D1
Fox, river D5
Ft. McCoy Mil. Res. C4
Gogebic, lake D2
Green, bay F4
Hannahville Ind. Res. F3
Ho-Chunk Ind. Res. C4
Horicon N.W.R. E5
Huron, mountains E2
Huron N.W.R. F2
K.I. Sawyer A.F.B. F2
Kettle Moraine St. For. E2
Keweenaw, bay E2
Keweenaw, peninsula E1
L'Anse Ind. Res. E2
Lac Court Oreilles Ind. Res. . .B3
Lac Du Flambeau Ind. Res. . .D2
Laughing Fish, point F2
Madeline, island C2
Menominee Ind. Res. E3
Michigamme, reservoir E2
Michigan, lake F5
Mississippi, river B5
Necedah N.W.R. C4
Nemadji St. For. A2
Nicolet Natl. For. E3
Northern Highland
  American Legion St. For. .D2
Oneida Ind. Res. E4
Ontonagon Ind. Res. D2
Ottawa Natl. For. E2
Outer, island C1
Paint, river E2
Peshtigo, river E3
Petenwell, lake D4
Potawatomi Ind. Res. F3
Poygan, lake E4
Prairie Island Ind. Res. A4
Red Cliff Ind. Res. C1
Richard J. Dorer Memorial
  Hardwood For. . . .A4, B5
St. Croix, river A3
St. Croix Natl.
  Scenic Riverway A3
St. Croix St. For. A2
Sand, island B2
Sokaogon Chippewa
  Ind. Comm. E3
Stockbridge-Munsee
  Ind. Comm. E4
Stockton, island C2
Superior, lake C1, F1
Superior Natl. For. A1
Timms, hill C3
Traverse, point E1
Upper Mississippi R. Natl.
  Wildlife & Fish Refuge . . .B5
Wapsipinicon, river A5
Washington, island G3
Willow, reservoir D3
Winnebago, lake E4
Wisconsin, river C5
Wisconsin, river D3
Wolf, river E4
Yellow, river C4

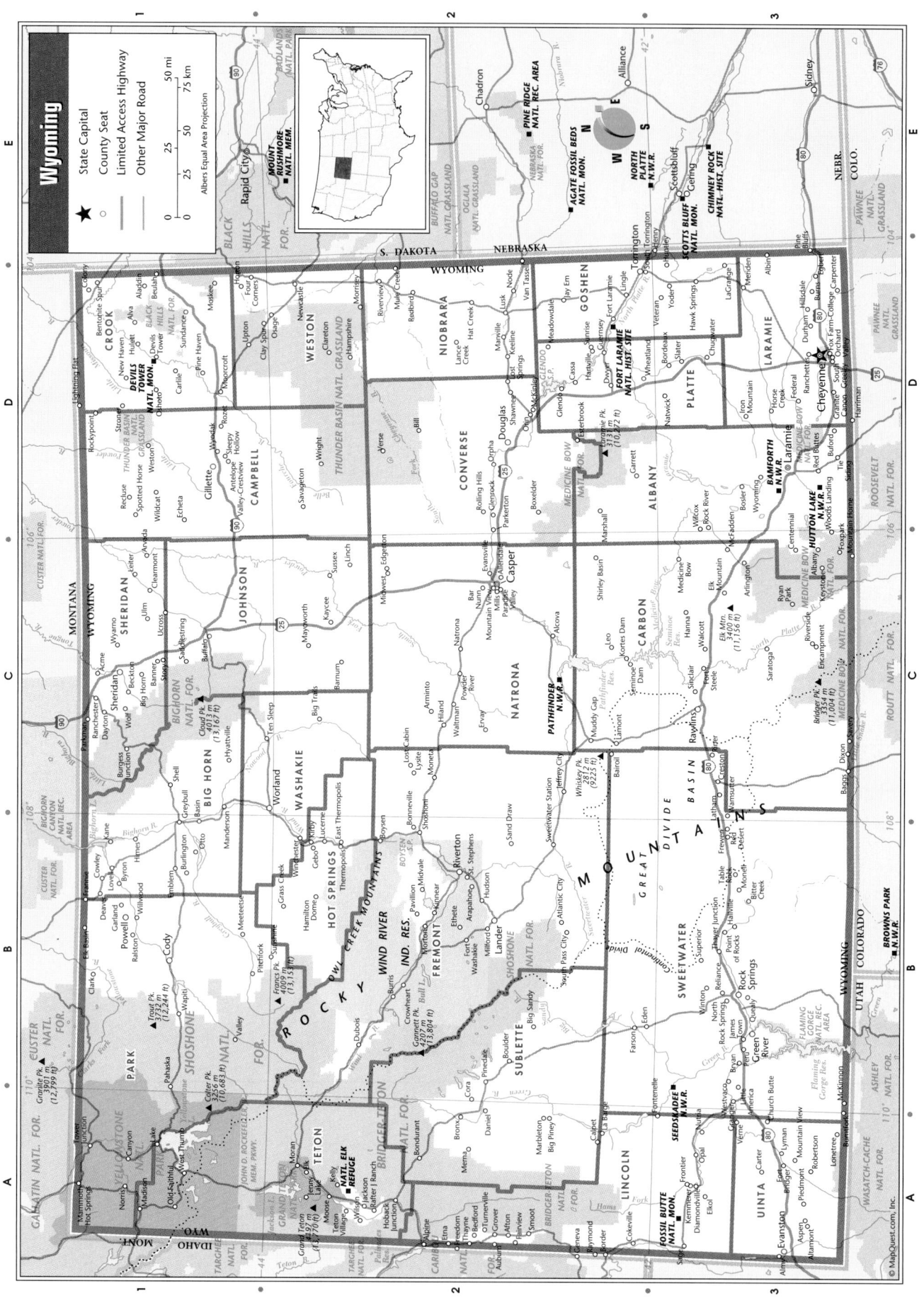

Wyoming

Capital:	Cheyenne
Land Area:	97,105 sq. mi.
	251,502 sq. km.
Population:	493,782 (2000 census)
Largest City:	Cheyenne, 53,011
Highest Point:	Gannett Peak
	13,804 ft.
	4,207 m.
Admitted to Union:	July 10, 1890
Nickname:	Equality State
State Flower:	Indian Paintbrush
State Bird:	Meadowlark

Wyoming:
Map Index

Counties

Albany, 32,014 .... D2
Big Horn, 11,461 .... C1
Campbell, 33,698 .... D1
Carbon, 15,639 .... D2
Converse, 12,052 .... D2
Crook, 5,887 .... D3
Fremont, 35,804 .... B2
Goshen, 12,538 .... D2
Hot Springs, 4,882 ..... B2
Johnson, 7,075 .... D3
Laramie, 81,607 .... A2
Lincoln, 14,573 .... A2
Natrona, 66,533 .... D2
Niobrara, 2,407 .... D2
Park, 25,786 .... C1
Platte, 8,807 .... D2
Sheridan, 26,560 ...... B2
Sublette, 5,920 .... A2
Sweetwater, 37,613 .... A2
Teton, 18,251 .... A3
Uinta, 19,742 .... A2
Washakie, 8,289 .... D2
Weston, 6,644 .... D2

Cities and Towns

Acme C1
Afton, 1,818 .... A2
Aladdin D1
Albany, 120 .... C3
Albin, 120 .... C2
Alcova, 20 .... C2
Allendale, 250 .... A3
Almy, 125 .... D1
Alpine, 550 .... A2
Altamont D1
Alva D1
Antelope Valley-Crestview,
 1,642 .... D1
Arapahoe, 1,766 .... B2
Arlington C3
Arminto C2
Arvada, 33 .... C1
Aspen A2
Atlantic City, 39 ..... A3
Auburn, 276 .... A2
Baggs, 348 .... D1
Bairoil, 97 .... C1
Banner C1
Bar Nunn, 936 .... C2
Basin, 1,238 .... B1
Beckton, 80 .... C1
Bedford, 169 .... A2
Bentonite Spur A3
Beulah, 40 .... D1
Big Horn, 198 .... C1
Big Piney, 408 .... A2
Big Sandy B2
Big Trails C2
Bill C2
Bitter Creek, 125 .... B3
Bondurant, 155 .... A2
Bonneville B2
Bordeaux D2
Border A2
Bosler C3
Boulder, 30 .... B2
Boxelder C2
Boysen B2
Bronx B3
Bryan A2
Buffalo, 3,900 .... C1
Burgess Junction C1
Burlington, 250 ...... B1

Burns, 285 .... D3
Burntfork A2
Burris B2
Byron, 557 .... B1
Calpet, 7 .... A2
Canyon A1
Carlile, 60 .... D1
Carpenter, 80 .... D3
Carter, 8 .... A3
Casper, 49,644 .... C2
Cassa D2
Centennial, 191 ...... C3
Cheyenne, 53,011 ..... D3
Chugwater, 244 .... D2
Church Butte A3
Clareton D2
Clark B1
Clay Spur, 90 .... D1
Clearmont, 115 .... C1
Cody, 8,835 .... B1
Cokeville, 506 .... A2
Colony D1
Cora, 76 .... A2
Cowley, 560 .... B1
Creston B3
Crowheart, 163 .... A2
Daniel, 89 .... A2
Dayton, 678 .... C1
Deaver, 177 .... B1
Devils Tower D1
Diamondville, 716 .... A3
Dixon, 79 .... C3
Douglas, 5,288 .... D2
Dubois, 962 .... B2
Durham D3
Dwyer D2
East Thermopolis, 274 B2
Echeta C1
Eden, 388 .... A3
Edgerton, 169 .... C2
Egbert D3
Elk A3
Elk Basin B1
Elk Mountain, 192 .... C3
Elkol A3
Emblem B1
Encampment, 443 ...... C3
Ervay C2
Esterbrook, 32 .... D2
Ethete, 1,455 .... B2
Etna, 123 .... A2
Evanston, 11,507 ..... A3
Evansville, 2,255 .... C2
Fairview, 277 .... A2
Farson, 242 .... B2
Federal D3
Fontenelle, 19 .... A2
Fort Bridger, 400 .... A3
Fort Laramie, 243 .... D2
Fort Steele C3
Fort Washakie, 1,477 B2
Four Corners D1
Fox Farm-College, 3,272 D3
Foxpark, 48 .... C3
Frannie, 209 .... B1
Freedom, 100 .... A2
Frontier, 50 .... A3
Garland, 95 .... B1
Garrett D2
Gebo B2
Geneva A2
Gillette, 19,646 ..... D1
Glendo, 229 .... D2
Glenrock, 2,231 ...... D2
Granger, 146 .... A3
Granite Canon D3
Grass Creek B2
Green River, 11,808 .. B3
Greybull, 1,815 ...... B1
Grover, 137 .... A2

Guernsey, 1,147 ...... D2
Hallville B3
Hamilton Dome B2
Hampshire C3
Hanna, 873 .... D3
Harriman D3
Hartville, 76 .... D2
Hawk Springs, 69 ..... D3
Hat Creek D2
Hiland C2
Hillsdale, 80 .... D3
Himes B1
Hoback Junction, 40 .. A2
Horse Creek D3
Horton D1
Hudson, 407 .... B2
Hulett, 408 .... D1
Huntley, 21 .... D3
Hyattville, 73 .... C1
Iron Mountain D3
James Town, 552 ...... A2
Jay Em D2
Jeffrey City, 106 .... C2
Jenny Lake A2
Kane B1
Kaycee, 249 .... C2
Keeline D2
Kelly A2
Kemmerer, 2,651 ...... A3
Keystone C3
Kinnear, 125 .... B2
Kirby, 57 .... B2
Kortes Dam C2
La Barge, 431 .... A2
Lagrange, 332 .... D3
Lake A1
Lamont C2
Lance Creek, 51 ...... D2
Lander, 6,867 .... B2
Laramie, 27,204 ...... C3
Latham C3
Leiter C1
Leo C2
Lightning Flat D1
Linch, 100 .... C2
Lingle, 510 .... D2
Little America, 56 ... A3
Lonetree, 61 .... A3
Lost Cabin C2
Lost Springs, 1 ...... D2
Lovell, 2,281 .... B1
Lucerne, 525 .... B2
Lusk, 1,447 .... D2
Lyman, 1,938 .... A3
Lysite C2
Madison A1
Mammoth Hot Springs, 275 A1
Manderson, 104 .... C1
Manville, 101 .... D2
Marbleton, 720 .... A2
Marshall B2
Mayoworth C2
McFadden C3
McKinnon, 49 .... A3
McKinley D3
Meadowdale D2
Medicine Bow, 274 .... C3
Meeteetse, 351 .... B1
Meriden D2
Merna A2
Midvale B2
Midwest, 408 .... C2
Milford B3
Mills, 2,591 .... C2
Monell A3
Moneta C2
Moorcroft, 807 .... D1
Moose, 80 .... A2
Moran A2
Morrisey C3
Morton, 209 .... B2
Moskee D1
Mountain Home D3
Mountain View (Natrona Co.),
 103 .... C2
Mountain View (Uinta Co.),
 1,153 .... A3
Muddy Gap C2
Mule Creek D1
Natrona C2
Newcastle, 3,065 ..... D1
New Haven D1
Node D2
Norris A1
North Rock Springs, 1,974 B3
Nutria A2

Old Faithful A1
Opal, 102 .... A3
Orchard Valley, 550 .. D3
Orin D2
Orpha D2
Osage, 215 .... D1
Oshoto D1
Otto, 40 .... B1
Pahaska B1
Paradise Valley, 270 . C2
Parkerton C2
Parkman, 137 .... C1
Pavillion, 165 .... B2
Peru D2
Piedmont A3
Pine Bluffs, 1,153 ... D3
Pinedale, 1,412 ...... A2
Pine Haven, 222 ...... D1
Pitchfork, 40 .... B1
Point of Rocks, 3 .... B3
Powder River, 51 ..... C2
Powell, 5,373 .... B1
Quealy, 80 .... A2
Rafter J Ranch, 1,138 A2
Ralston, 233 .... B1
Ranchester, 701 ...... C1
Ranchettes, 4,869 .... D3
Rawlins, 8,538 .... C3
Raymond A2
Recluse D1
Red Buttes D3
Red Desert B3
Redbird D2
Reliance, 665 .... B3
Riner C3
Riverside, 59 .... C3
Riverton, 9,310 ...... B2
Riverview, 59 .... C2
Robertson, 59 .... A3
Rock River, 235 ...... C3
Rock Springs, 18,708 . B3
Rockypoint D1
Rolling Hills, 449 ... D2
Rozet, 90 .... D1
Ryan Park C3
Saddlestring, 40 ..... C1
Sage A3
St. Stephens, 70 ..... B2
Sand Draw C2
Saratoga, 1,726 ...... C3
Savageton C2
Savery C3
Seminoe Dam C2
Shawnee D2
Shell, 70 .... B1
Sheridan, 15,804 ..... C1
Shirley Basin, 40 .... C2
Shoshoni, 635 .... B2
Sinclair, 423 .... C3
Slater, 82 .... D2
Sleepy Hollow, 1,177 . D3
Smoot, 182 .... A3
South Greeley, 4,201 . D3
South Pass City B2
South Torrington, 550 D2
Spotted Horse C1
Story, 887 .... C1
Stroner D1
Sundance, 1,161 ...... D1
Sunrise D2
Sunshine B2
Superior, 244 .... B3
Sussex, 70 .... C2
Sweetwater Station ... C2
Table Rock, 82 .... B3
Ten Sleep, 304 .... C2
Teton Village, 175 ... A2
Thayer Junction, 80 .. B3
Thayne, 341 .... A2
Thermopolis, 3,172 ... B2
Tie Siding C3
Torrington, 5,776 .... D2
Tower Junction A1
Turnerville, 155 ..... A2
Ucross C2
Ulm C2
Upton, 872 .... D1
Valley B1
Van Tassell, 18 ...... D2
Veteran, 28 .... D2
Verne C2
Verse D2
Walcott C3
Waltman C2
Wamsutter, 261 .... B3
Wapiti B1
Weston D1
West Thumb A1

Westvaco A1
Wheatland, 3,548 ..... D2
Wilcox D2
Wildcat D1
Willwood, 100 .... B1
Wilson, 1,294 .... A2
Winchester, 60 .... B1
Winton B3
Wolf, 40 .... C1
Woods Landing, 100 ... C3
Worland, 5,250 .... C2
Wright, 1,347 .... C1
Wyamo B2
Wyodak, 125 .... D1
Wyoming, 169 .... B2
Yoder, 169 .... D2

Other Features

Absaroka, range A1
Agate Fossil Beds Natl. Mon. B3
Ashley Natl. For. A2
Badlands Natl. Park .. B1
Bamforth N.W.R. A2
Belle Fourche, river . D1
Bighorn, lake B1
Bighorn, mountains ... C1
Bighorn, river C1
Bighorn Canyon Natl.Rec. Area B1
Bighorn Natl. For. ... C1
Big Sandy, river B2
Black Hills Natl. For. D1, E1
Boysen S.P. B2
Bridger, peak C3
Bridger-Teton Natl. For. A2
Browns Park N.W.R. ... A3
Buffalo Gap Natl. Grassland B2
Bull, lake B2
Caribou Natl. For. ... A2
Chimney Rock Natl. Hist. Site D3
Clarks Fork Yellowstone, river B1
Cloud, peak C1

Colter, peak A1
Continental Divide ... B3
Custer Natl. For. B1, C1
Devils Tower Natl. Mon. D1
Elk, mountain C3
Flaming Gorge, reservoir A3
Flaming Gorge Natl. Rec. Area B3
Fort Laramie Natl. Hist. Mon. D2
Fossil Butte Natl. Mon. A3
Francs, peak B2
Gannett, peak A1
Glendo S.P. D2
Grand Teton, peak A2
Grand Teton Natl. Park A2
Granite, peak B1
Great Divide, basin .. B2
Green, river B2, B3
Greybull, river B1
Hams Fork, river A2
Hutton Lake N.W.R. ... D3
Jackson, lake A2
Laramie, mountains ... D2
Laramie, peak D2
Laramie, river D3
Little Bighorn, river C1
Little Missouri, river D1
Little Powder, river . D1
Little Snake, river .. C3
Medicine Bow, river .. C3
Medicine Bow, river .. C3, D2, D3
Natl. Elk Refuge A2
Mount Rushmore Natl. Mem. E2
Nebraska Natl. For. .. E2
Niobrara, river C3, D2
North Platte, river .. D2
North Platte N.W.R. .. D2
Nowood, river C1
Oglala Natl. Grassland D3
Owl Creek Mountains .. B2
Palisades, reservoir . A2

Pathfinder, reservoir C2
Pathfinder N.W.R. C2
Pawnee Natl. Grassland D3, E3
Powder, river D1
Rocky, mountains D3
Roosevelt Natl. For. . C3
Routt Natl. For. C3
Scotts Bluff Natl. Mon. E3
Seedskadee N.W.R. B3
Shoshone Natl. For. .. B1, B2
South Fork Cheyenne, river C2
South Fork Powder, river C2
Sweetwater, river B2
Targhee Natl. For. ... A1, A2
Teton, river A2
Thunder Basin Natl.
 Grassland D1, C1
Tongue, river C1
Trout, peak B1
Wasatch-Cache Natl. For. A3
Whiskey, peak C2
Wind, river B2
Wind River, range B2
Wind River Ind. Res. . A1
Yellowstone, lake A1
Yellowstone Natl. Park A1

Yellowstone National Park

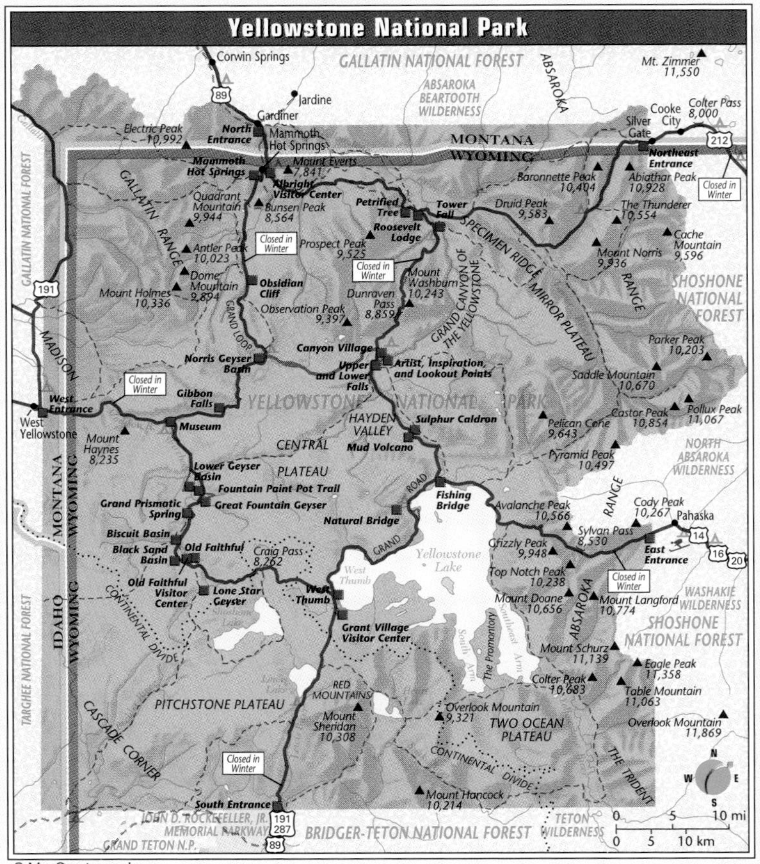

Boston

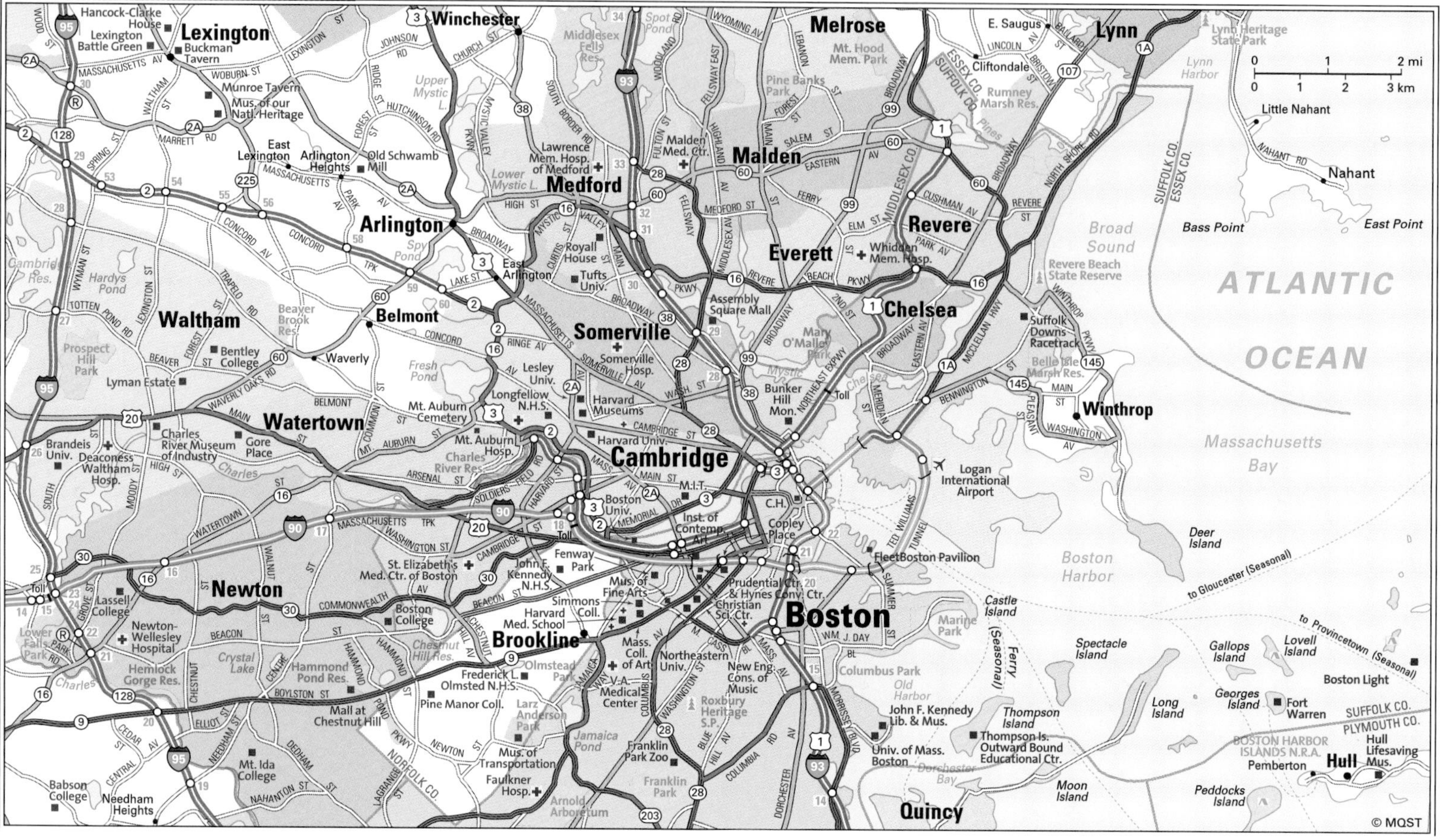

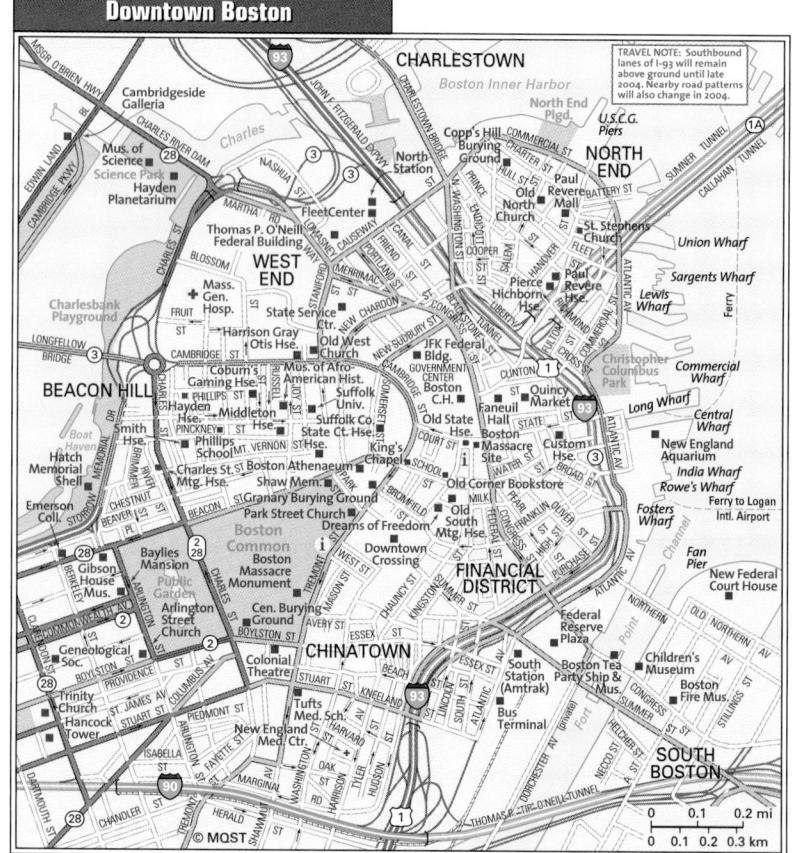

Downtown Boston

Main Gates to Boston Common, city landmark since 1634

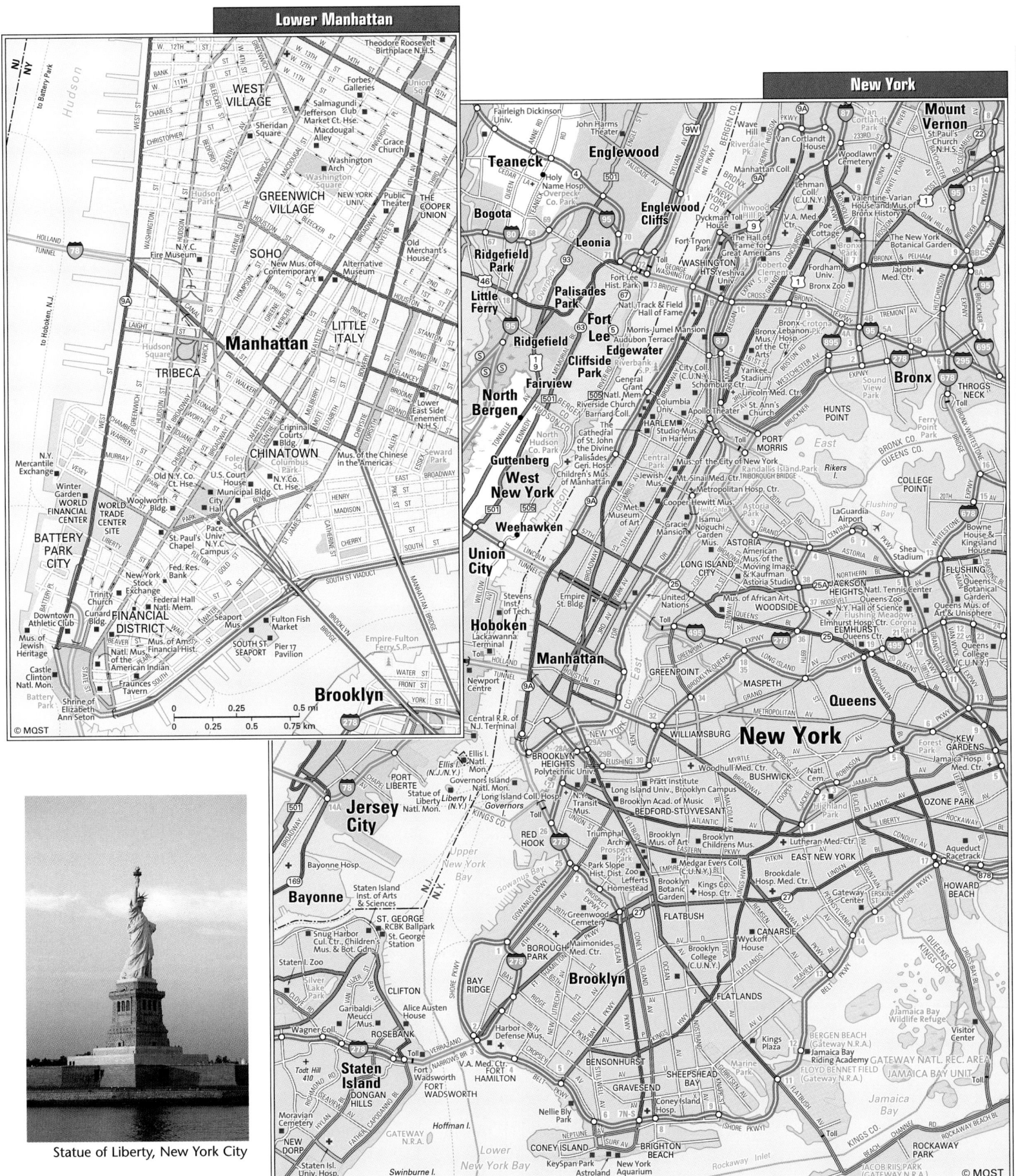

Statue of Liberty, New York City

Philadelphia

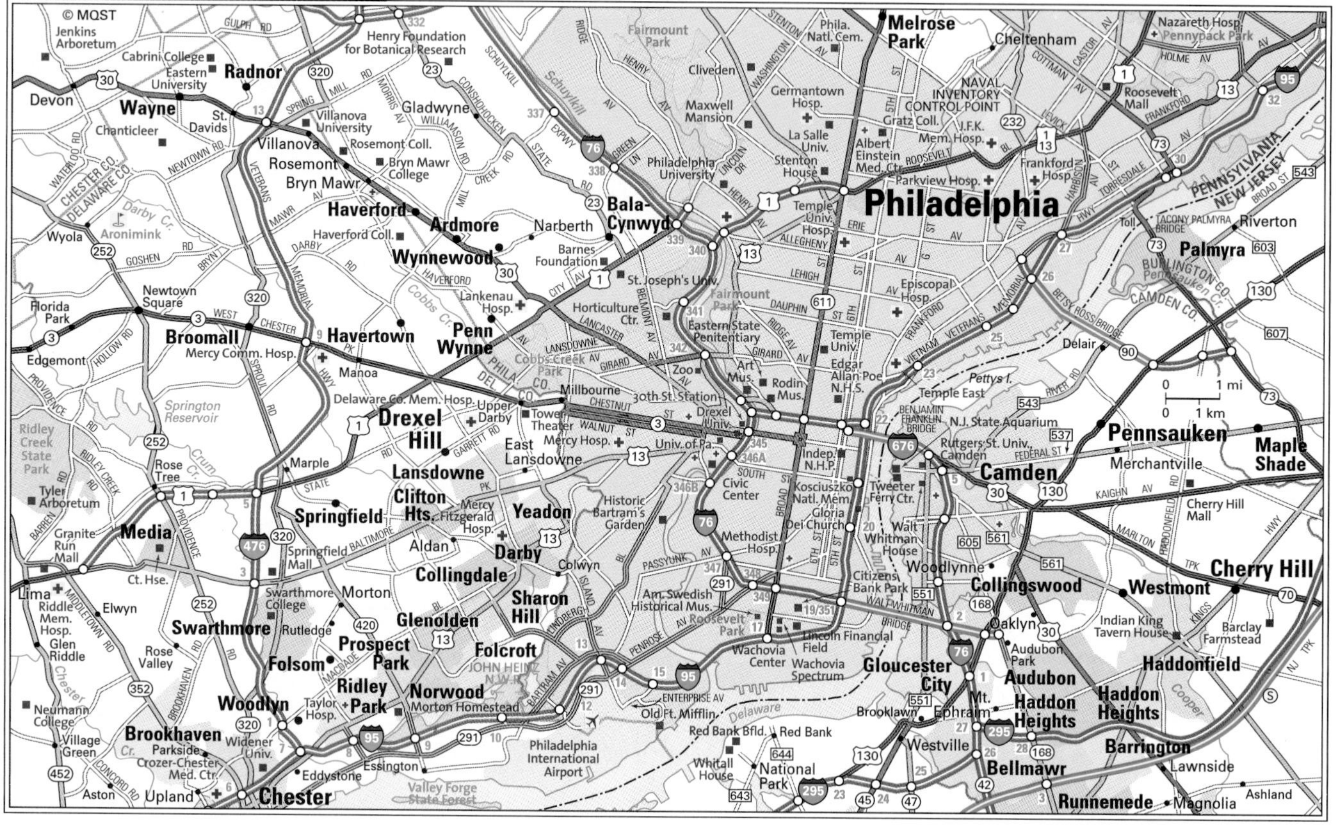

Pittsburgh

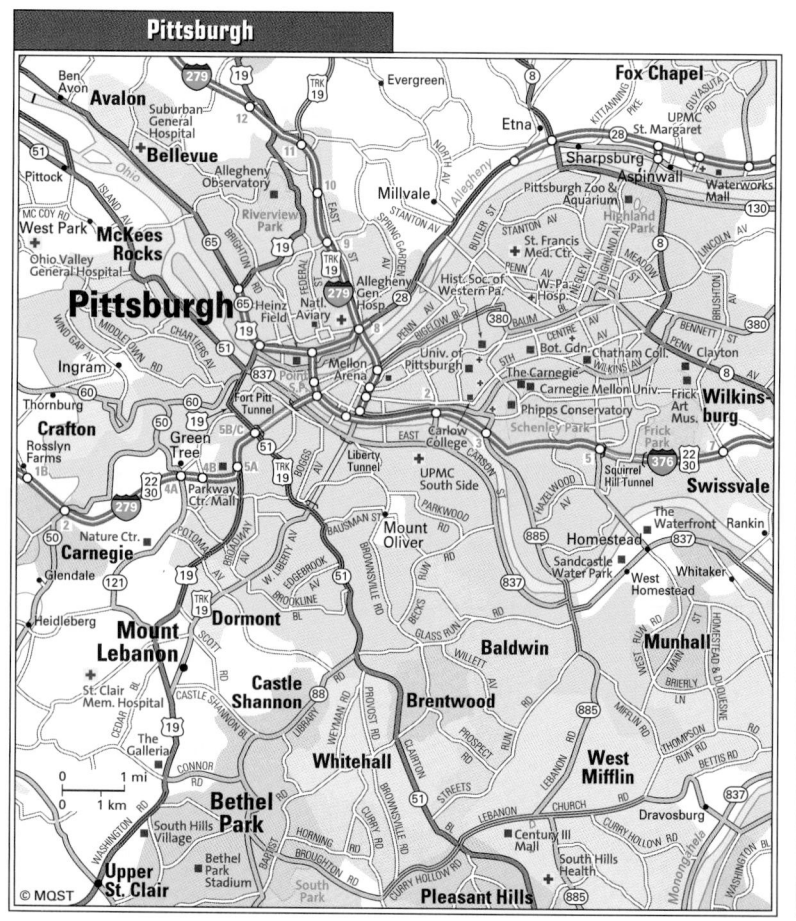

Baltimore

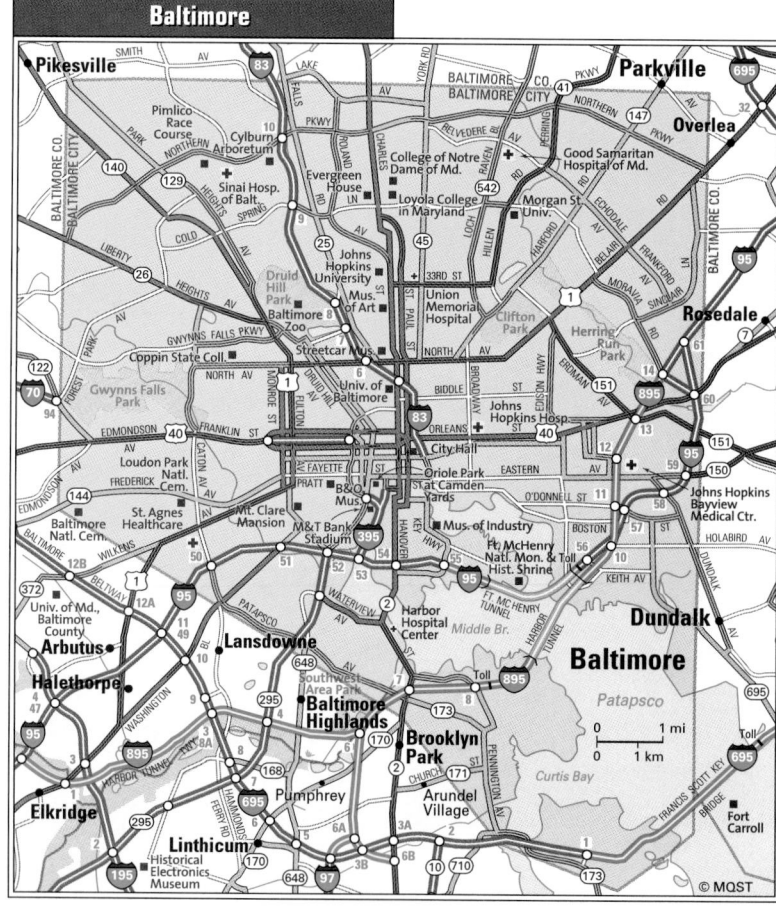

Washington, D.C.

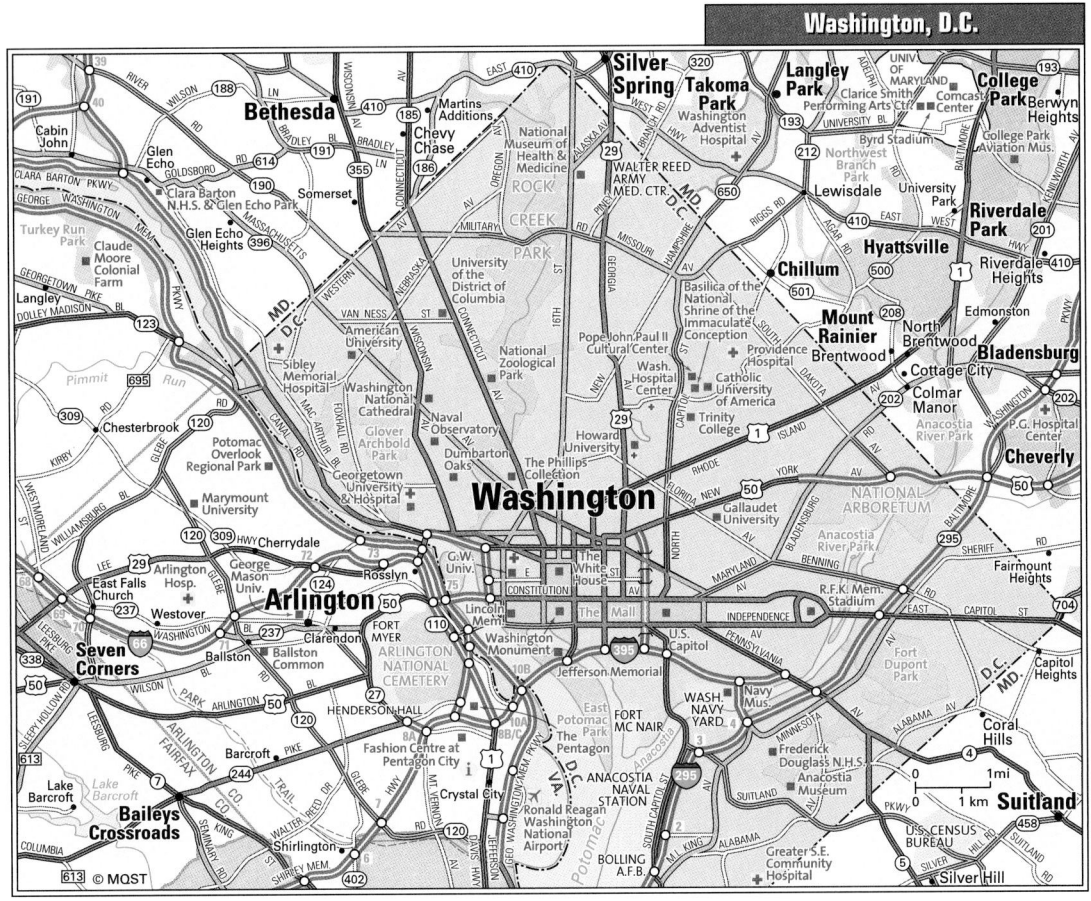

Downtown Washington, D.C.

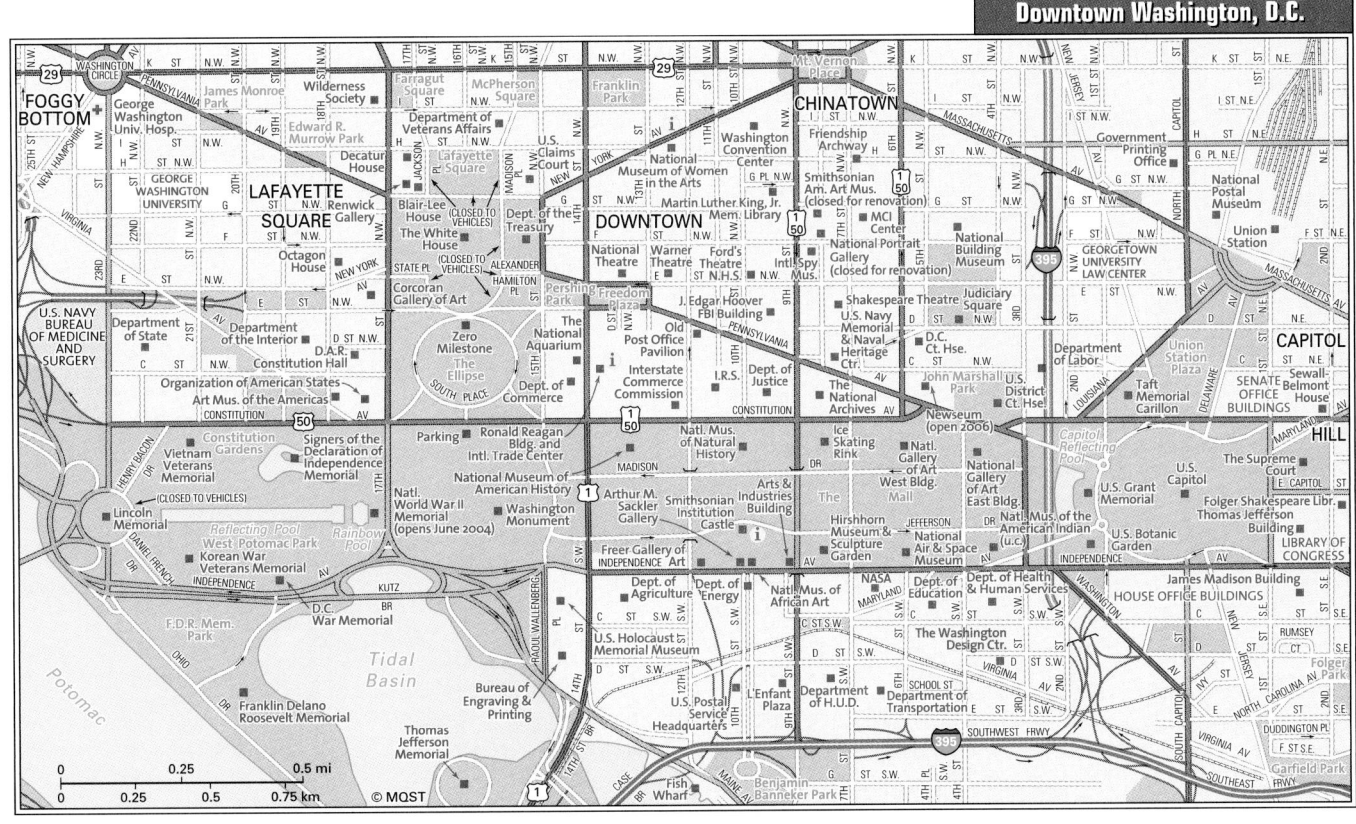

Atlanta

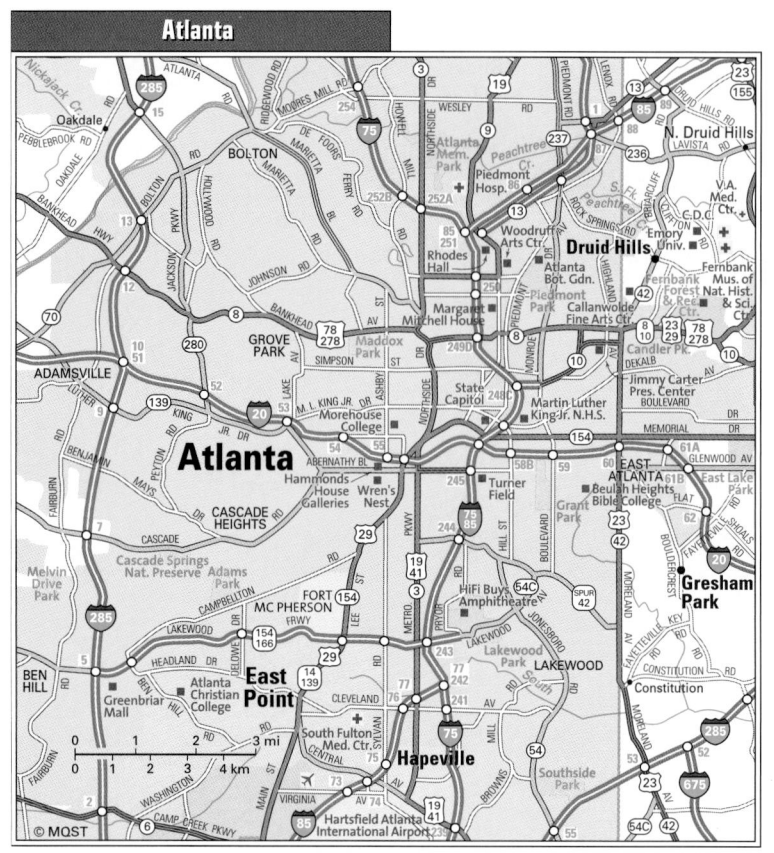

Downtown Atlanta

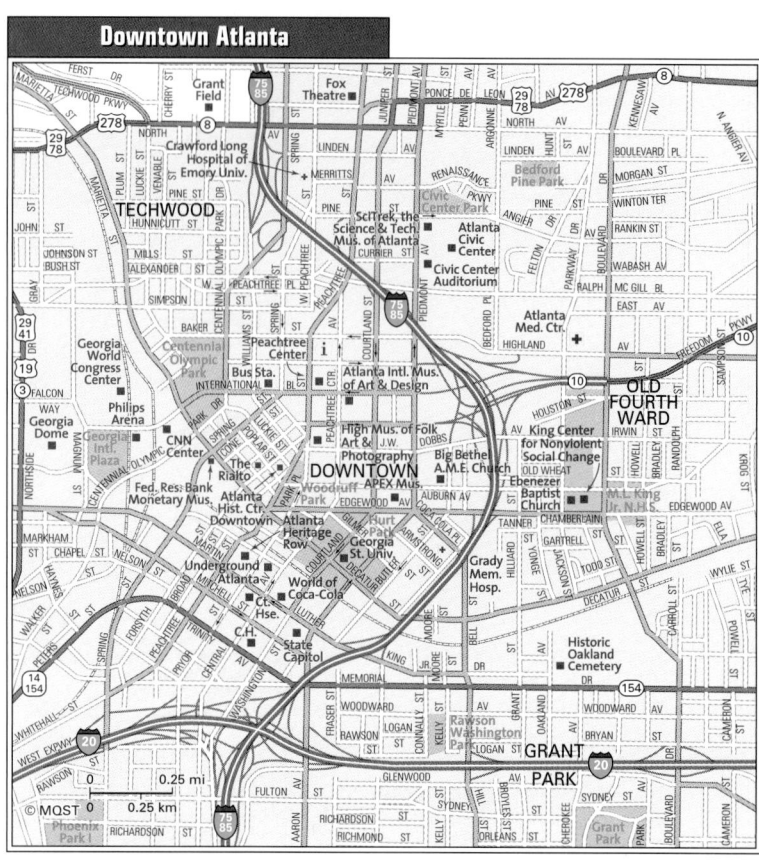

Tampa–St. Petersburg

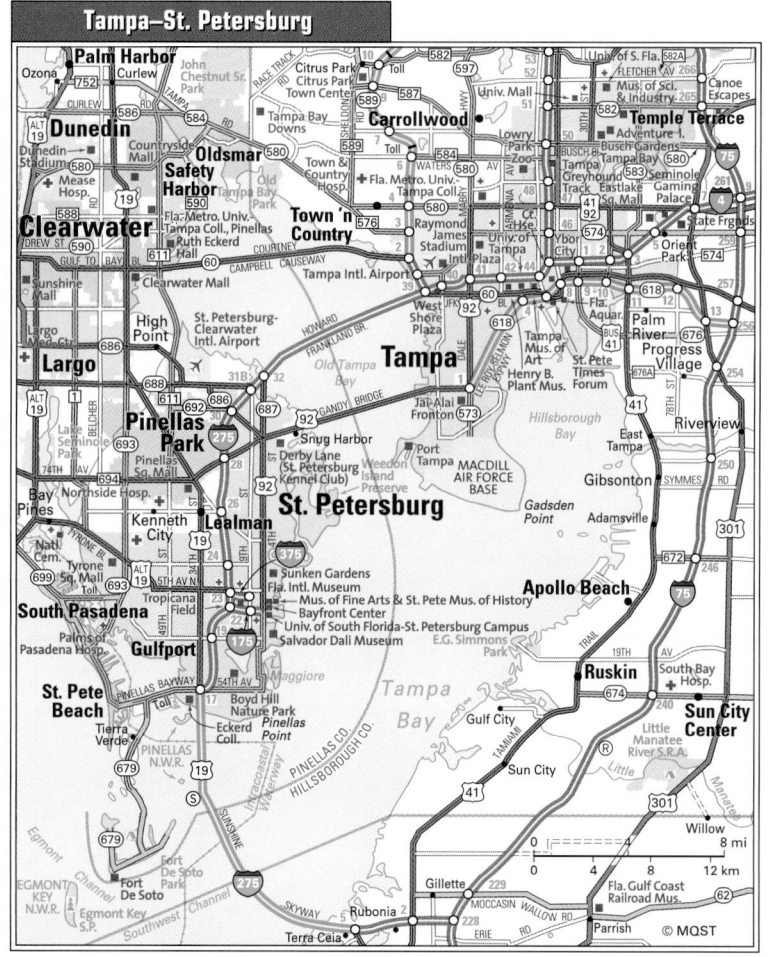

Orlando

Miami

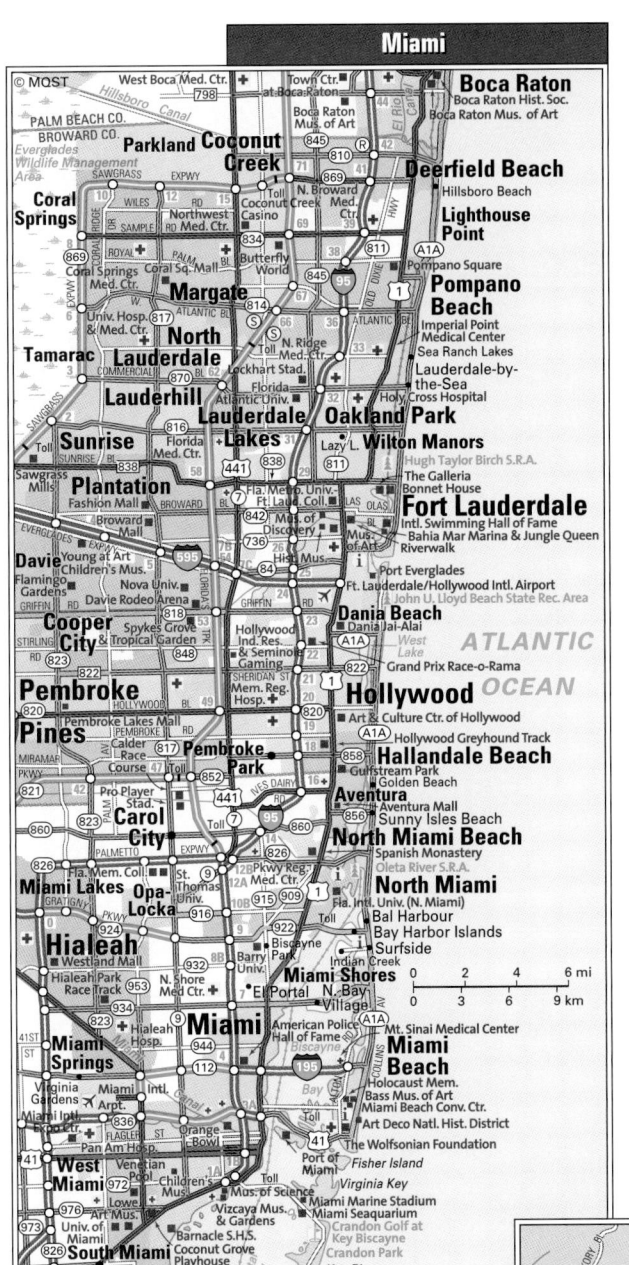

Memphis

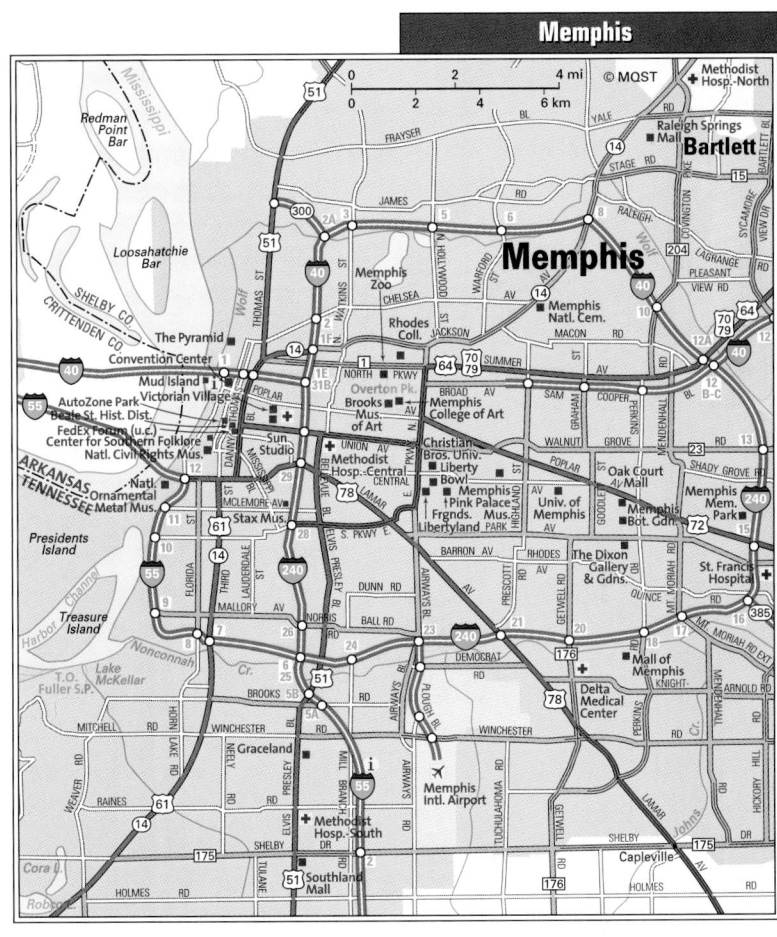

Nashville

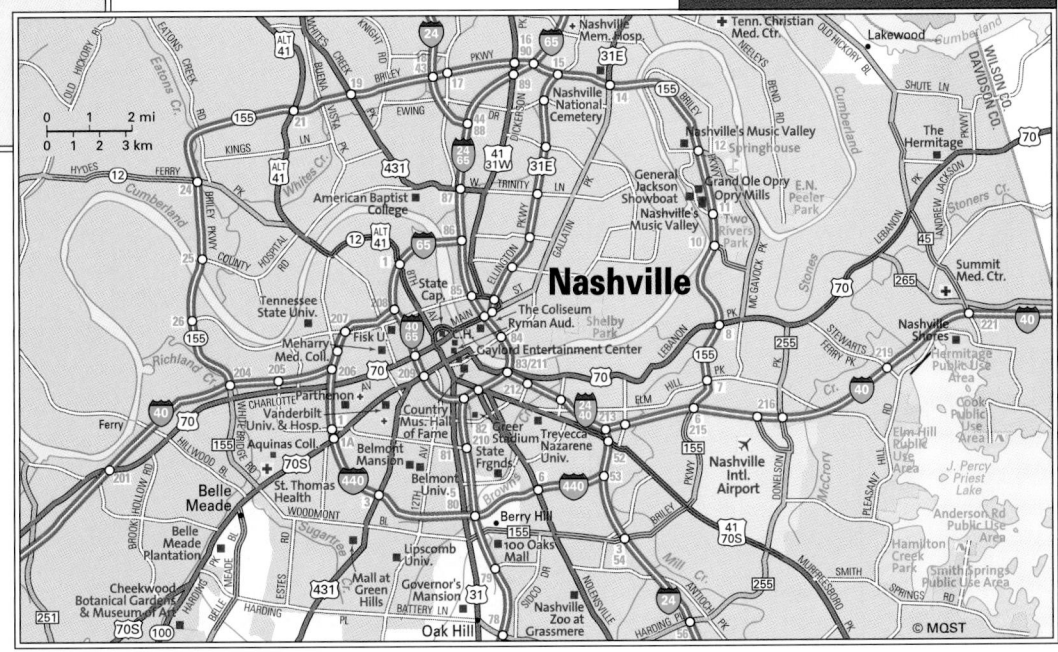

Cleveland

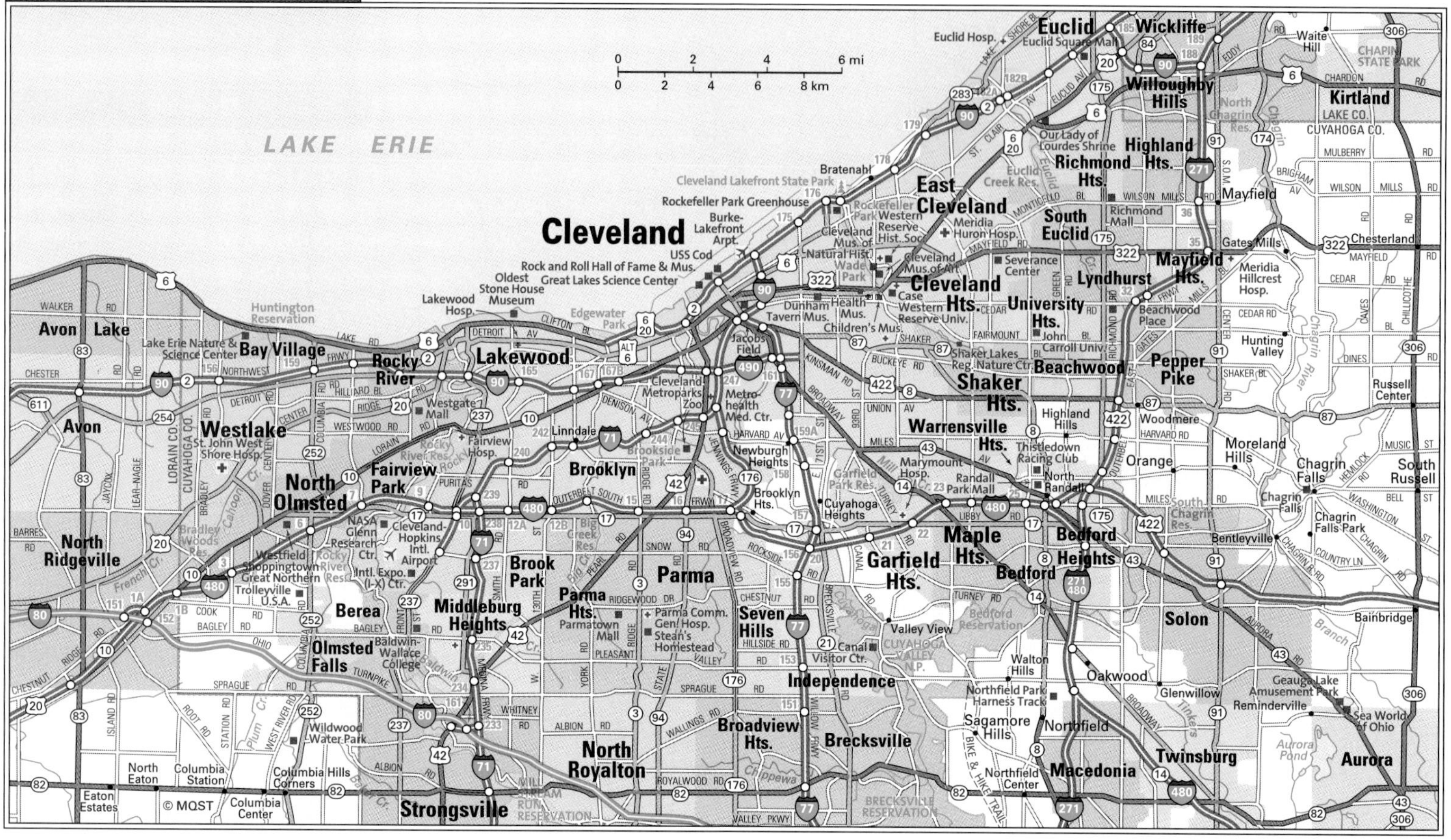

LAKE ERIE

Euclid · Wickliffe · Waite Hill · CHAPIN STATE PARK · Willoughby Hills · Kirtland · LAKE CO. · CUYAHOGA CO. · Highland Hts. · Richmond Hts. · Mayfield · Chesterland · East Cleveland · South Euclid · Mayfield Hts. · Lyndhurst · Cleveland · Cleveland Hts. · University Hts. · Beachwood · Pepper Pike · Hunting Valley · Russell Center · Shaker Hts. · Warrensville Hts. · Highland Hills · Orange · Moreland Hills · Chagrin Falls · South Russell · Bratenahl · Avon Lake · Bay Village · Rocky River · Lakewood · Avon · Westlake · Fairview Park · North Olmsted · Brooklyn · Newburgh Heights · Brooklyn Hts. · Cuyahoga Heights · Garfield Hts. · Maple Hts. · Bedford Hts. · Bedford · North Ridgeville · Berea · Middleburg Heights · Parma Hts. · Parma · Seven Hills · Independence · Solon · Bainbridge · Bentleyville · Olmsted Falls · Broadview Hts. · Brecksville · Walton Hills · Oakwood · Glenwillow · Twinsburg · Macedonia · Aurora · North Royalton · Strongsville · Northfield · Sagamore Hills · North Eaton · Columbia Station · Columbia Hills Corners · Columbia Center · Eaton Estates · Sea World of Ohio · Geauga Lake Amusement Park · Reminderville

© MQST

Cincinnati

Forest Park · Springdale · Loveland · Dallasburg · New Haven · Dunlap · New Baltimore · Greenhills · Glendale · Woodlawn · Evendale · Montgomery · Epworth Heights · Springvale · MIAMI WHITEWATER FOREST · Bevis · Northbrook · Mount Healthy · Wyoming · Lincoln Heights · Blue Ash · Indianview · Miamiville · Mulberry · Mt. Repose · Groesbeck · White Oak · North College Hill · Reading · Deer Park · Kenwood · The Village of Indian Hill · Taylors Creek · Monfort Heights · Finneytown · Elmwood Place · Golf Manor · Silverton · Madeira · Milford · Miamitown · Hooven · Dent · Arboretum · St. Bernard · Norwood · Amberley · Fairfax · Mariemont · Terrace Park · Day Heights · Bridgetown · Cheviot · Cincinnati · Mack · Addyston · North Bend · Cleves · Miami Heights · Covedale · Delhi Hills · Dayton · Bellevue · Newton · Turpin Hills · Mt. Carmel · Summerside · Gleneste · Willowville · Ludlow · Newport · Fort Thomas · Cherry Grove · Forestville · Withamsville · Francisville · Taylorsport · Bromley · Park Hills · Southgate · Wilder · Villa Hills · Ft. Wright · Fort Mitchell · Covington · Highland Hts. · Crescent Springs · Erlanger · Lakeside Park · Kenton Vale · Cold Spring · Crestview · Melbourne · Amelia · Burlington · Limaburg · Florence · Crestview Hills · Edgewood · Taylor Mill · Ross · New Palestine · Hamlet

© MQST

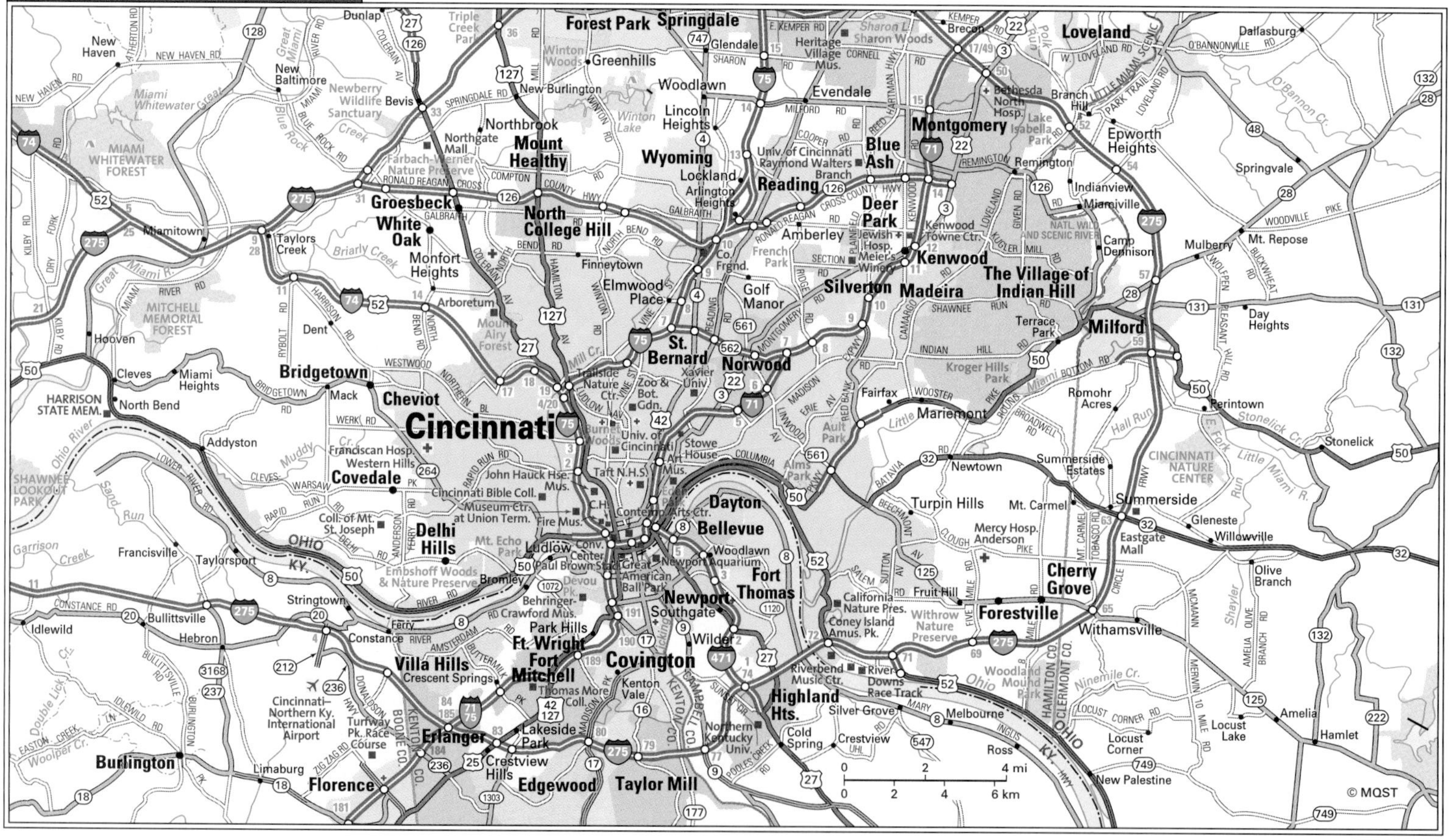

Detroit

Indianapolis

Milwaukee

Downtown Chicago

RIVER NORTH

NEAR NORTH

Jane Addams Mem. Park

Chicago Children's Museum

NAVY PIER

Terra Mus. of American Art

V.A. Med. Ctr.

Tribune Tower

River East Plaza

River Esplanade Park

Merchandise Mart

Wrigley Bldg

Centennial Fountain & Arc

James R. Thompson Ctr.

Ford Ctr. for the Perf. Arts

Chicago Theatre

Hellenic Museum & Cultural Center

City Hall

Daley Plaza

Chicago Cultural Ctr.

Mus. of Broadcast Communications

GREEK TOWN

Civic Opera House

THE LOOP

Chicago Atheneum

Shubert Theatre

Lakefront Millennium Park

Grant Park

Chicago Yacht Club

Chicago Mercantile Exchange

Sears Tower

Symphony Center

Art Inst. of Chicago

Petrillo Band Shell

Chicago Harbor

LAKE MICHIGAN

Union Station

Chicago Board of Trade

Monadnock Building

De Paul Center

Buckingham Fountain

Chicago Stock Exchange

Univ. of Illinois at Chicago

Harold Washington Library Center

Auditorium Building

Mus. of Contemporary Photography

PRINTER'S ROW

Spertus Mus.

Jane Addams' Hull House Museum

Chicago Main Post Office

Dearborn Station

Grant Park

Chicago Fire Marker

John G. Shedd Aquarium

Adler Planetarium & Astronomy Mus.

LITTLE ITALY

New Maxwell Street Market

The Field Mus.

Soldier Field

Burnham Park

Northerly Island Park

Northerly Island

12th Street Beach

Natl. Vietnam Veterans Art Museum

Prairie Av. Historic District

MERRILL C. MEIGS FIELD

© MQST

Chicago

Winnetka

Northfield

Glenview

Wilmette

Des Plaines

Park Ridge

Skokie

Morton Grove

Niles

Evanston

Lincolnwood

Schiller Park

Norridge

Harwood Hts.

Franklin Park

River Grove

Elmwood Park

Northlake

Stone Park

Melrose Park

Oak Park

Berkeley

Bellwood

River Forest

Hillside

Maywood

Forest Park

Broadview

Berwyn

La Grange Park

North Riverside

Cicero

Brookfield

Lyons

Stickney

Western Sprs.

La Grange

Countryside

Summit

Justice

Burbank

Bridgeview

Hickory Hills

Evergreen Park

Palos Hills

Oak Lawn

Chicago Ridge

Worth

Palos Park

Alsip

Blue Island

Calumet Park

Orland Park

Palos Heights

Robbins

Riverdale

Crestwood

Midlothian

Oak Forest

Harvey

Dolton

Calumet City

Orland Hills

Markham

Hazel Crest

S. Holland

Chicago

LAKE MICHIGAN

Whiting

East Chicago

Hammond

© MQST

Minneapolis–St. Paul

St. Louis

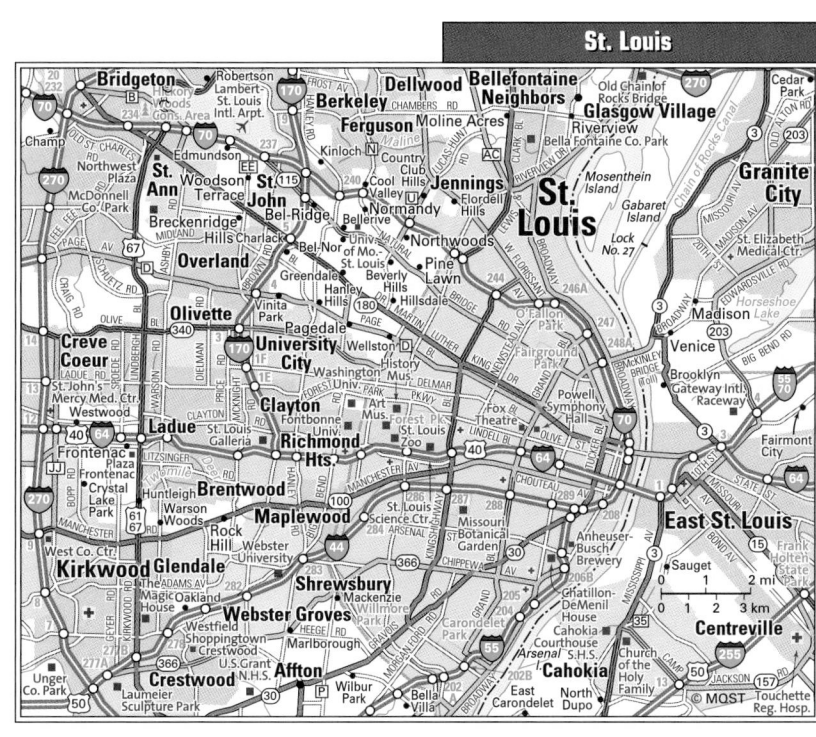

Kansas City

New Orleans

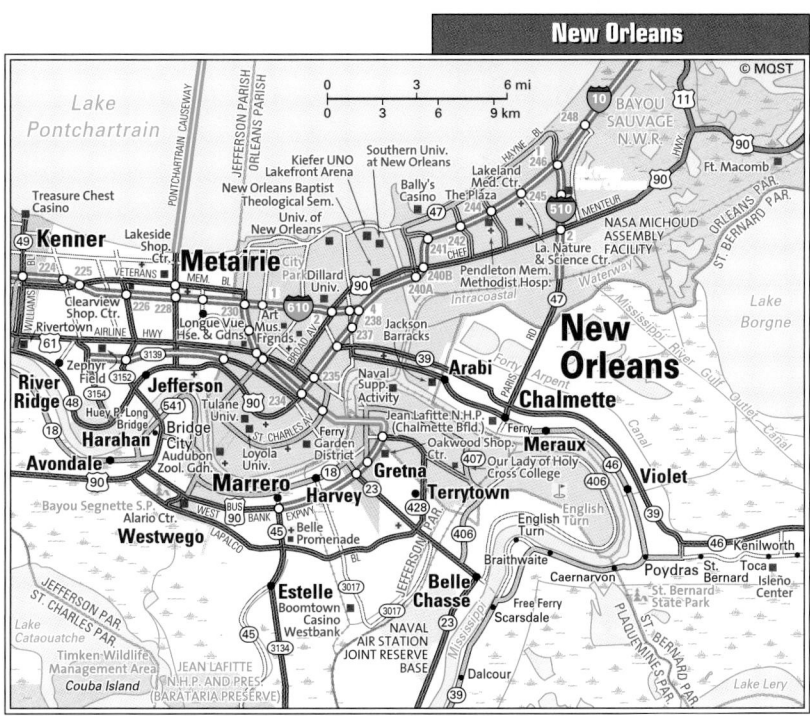

Dallas–Fort Worth

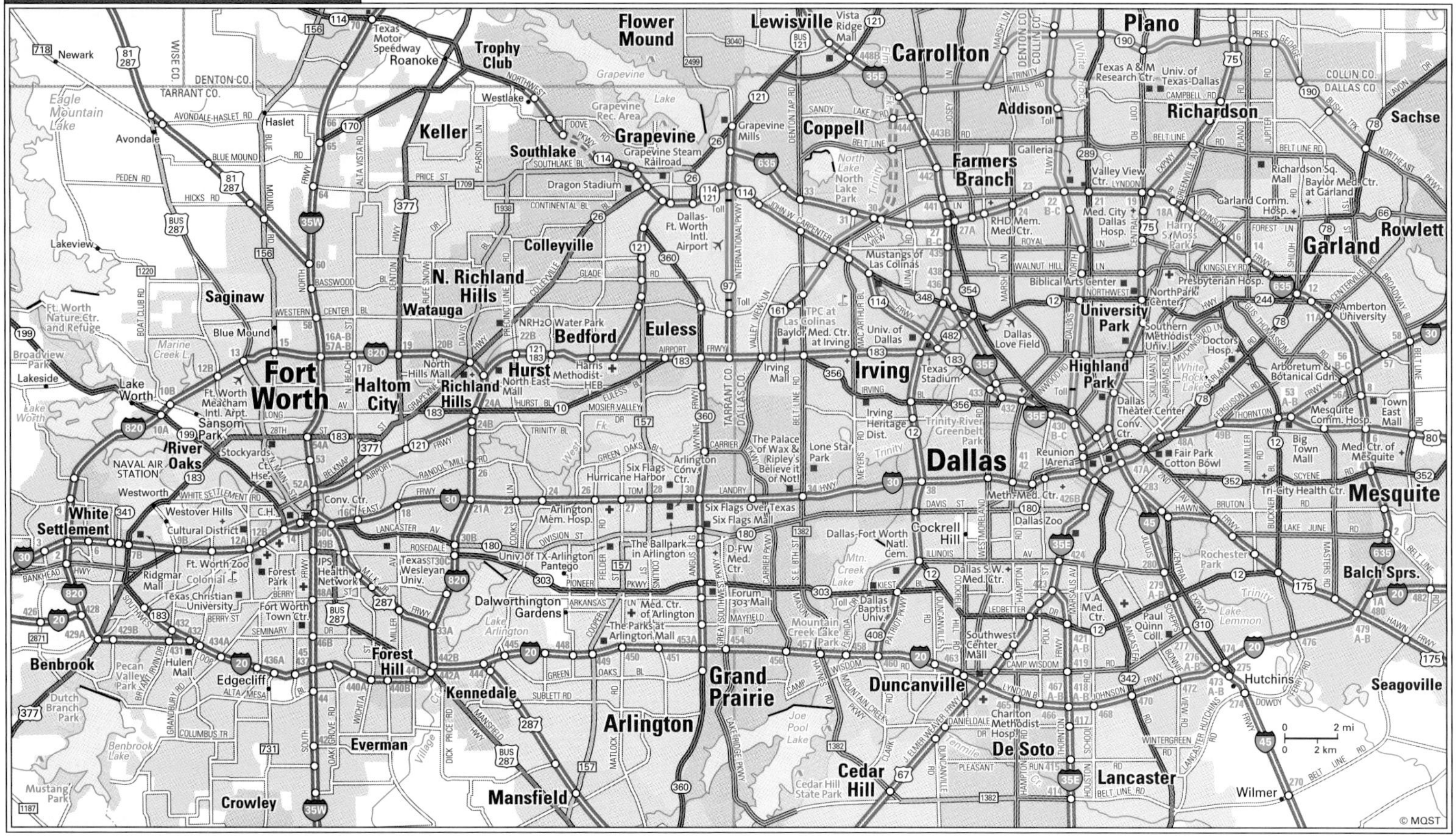

Newark, Denton Co., Tarrant Co., Avondale-Haslet Rd., Wise Co., Eagle Mountain Lake, Roanoke, Texas Motor Speedway, Trophy Club, Flower Mound, Lewisville, Vista Ridge Mall, Plano, Carrollton, Haslet, Westlake, Grapevine, Grapevine Mills, Coppell, Addison, Richardson, Sachse, Keller, Southlake, Grapevine Steam Railroad, Dallas-Ft. Worth Intl. Airport, Farmers Branch, Galleria, Valley View Mall, Collin Co., Dallas Co., Avondale, Lakeview, Saginaw, Colleyville, Dragon Stadium, Mustangs of Las Colinas, RHD Mem. Med. Ctr., Collin Co., N. Richland Hills, Watauga, Baylor Med. Ctr. at Irving, Univ. of Dallas, Dallas Love Field, University Park, Southern Methodist Univ., Rowlett, Garland, Blue Mound, Bedford, Euless, Lake Worth, Fort Worth, Ft. Worth Meacham Intl. Arpt., Haltom City, Richland Hills, Hurst, Harris Methodist HEB, Irving, Texas Stadium, Highland Park, White Rock Lake, Amberton University, Mesquite, River Oaks, Naval Air Station, Stockyards, Six Flags Over Texas, Hurricane Harbor, Arlington, Dallas, Reunion Arena, Dallas Zoo, Fair Park, Cotton Bowl, White Settlement, Westworth, Cultural District, Ft. Worth Zoo, Texas Christian University, The Ballpark in Arlington, Univ. of TX-Arlington, Forum 303 Mall, Dallas-Fort Worth Natl. Cem., Cockrell Hill, Benbrook, Edgecliff, Kennedale, Grand Prairie, Duncanville, Hutchins, Seagoville, Forest Hill, Arlington, Everman, Joe Pool Lake, De Soto, Balch Sprs., Crowley, Mansfield, Cedar Hill, Lancaster, Wilmer

Houston

Cypress Fairbanks Med. Ctr., Greenspoint Mall, Humble, Lake Houston, Satsuma, Sam Houston Race Park, Jersey Village, Aldine, Redstone, Crosby, Alexander Deussen Park, Dwight D. Eisenhower Park, Magnolia Gardens, Barrett, North Houston, Doctors Hosp. Airline, Houston Natl. Cem., Houston, Northline Mall, Sheldon, Highlands, Spring Branch Medical Center, Spring Valley, Hilshire Village, Hedwig Village, Northwest Mall, Antique Car Mus., Anheuser-Busch Brewery, LBJ Gen. Hosp., Beaumont Place, Memorial City Mall, Mem. Hosp.-Mem. City, Hunters Creek Village, Bunker Hill Village, Piney Point Village, Memorial Park, The Galleria, Compaq Center, Bayou Bend, Buffalo Soldiers Natl. Mus., Univ. of St. Thomas, Jacinto City, Cloverleaf, E. Houston Reg. Med. Ctr., Lynchburg, Baytown, Channelview, San Jacinto Battleground S.H.P., Battleship Texas, West Oaks Mall, West Houston Med. Ctr., Rosewood Med. Ctr., Bellaire Med. Center, W. Univ. Place, Mus. of Fine Arts, Rice Univ., Zoo, Texas Southern Univ., Galena Park, Port of Houston Turning Basin, Pasadena, Deer Park, Mission Bend, Four Corners, Sharpstown Center, Houston Baptist Univ., Adventure Bay, Bellaire, Mem. Hosp. S.W., Braeswood, Southside Place, Reliant Park, Mus. of Natural Science, Univ. of Houston, Pasadena Hist. Mus., Mem. Hosp.-Pasadena, Dow Park Botanical Gardens, La Porte, Meadows Place, Westwood Mall, Six Flags AstroWorld, South Houston, Pasadena, Bayshore Med. Ctr., Busch I., Sugar Land, Stafford, William P. Hobby Airport, Pasadena Fairground & Rodeo Grounds, Morgans Point, Atkinson Island, Shoreacres, Missouri City, Mercer Stadium, First Colony Mall, The Reef, Brookside Village, El Franco Lee Park, Ellington Field, Armand Bayou Nature Center, Galveston Bay, Seabrook, Pearland, Tom Bass Reg. Park, University of Houston-Clear Lake, Johnson Space Center, Taylor Lake Village, El Lago, Bay Area Park

© MQST

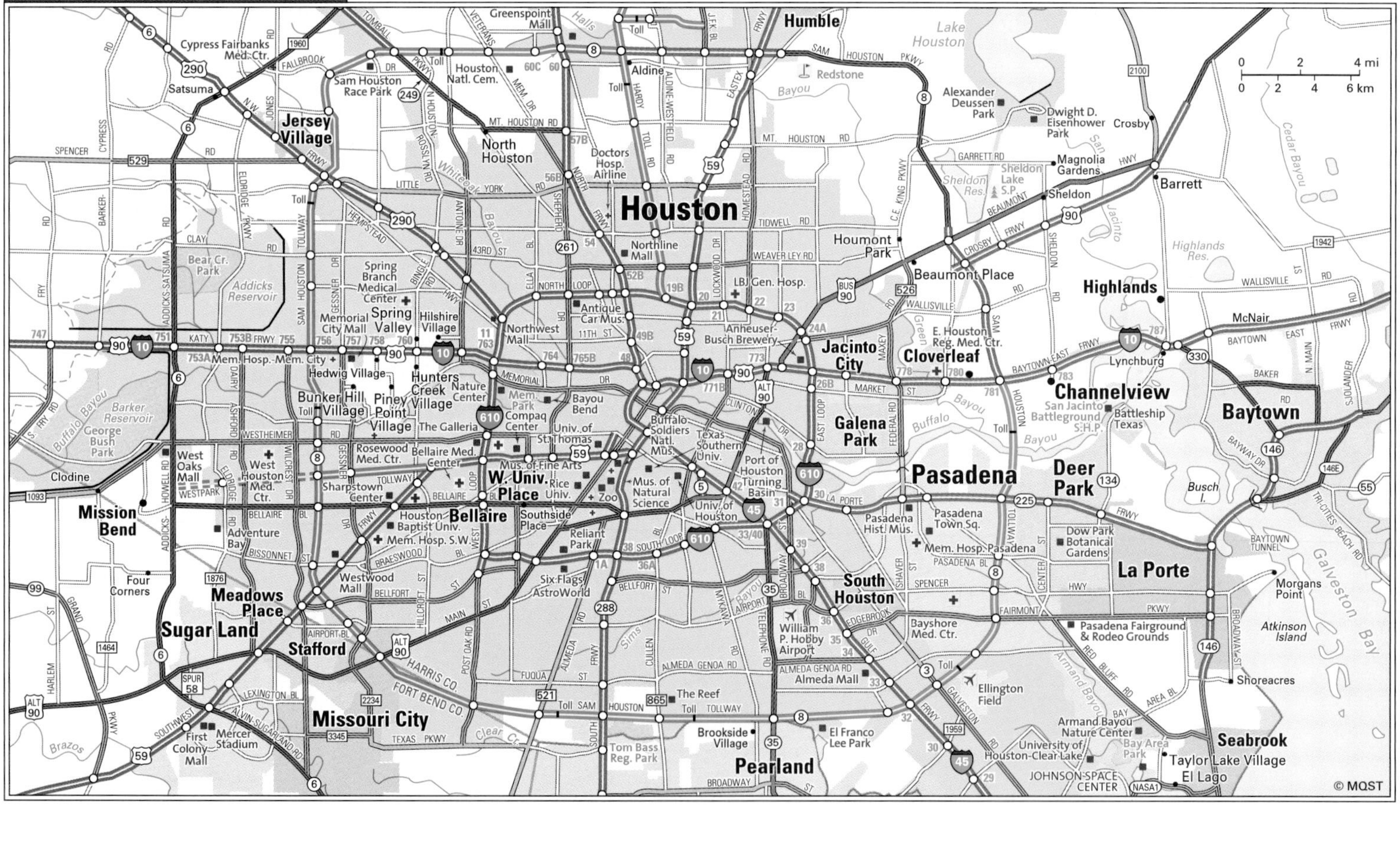

San Antonio

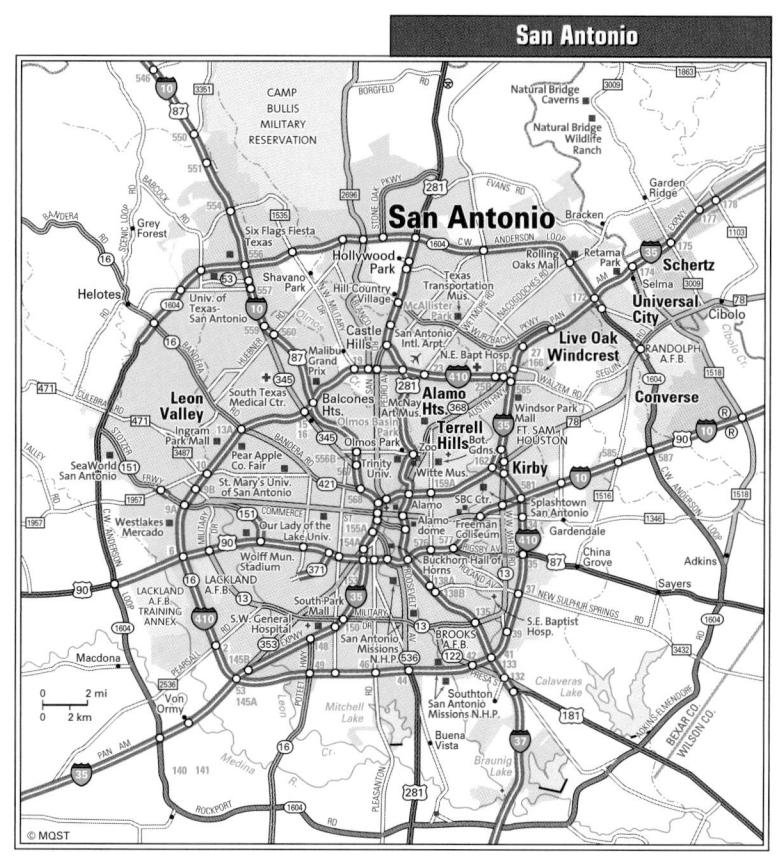

Denver

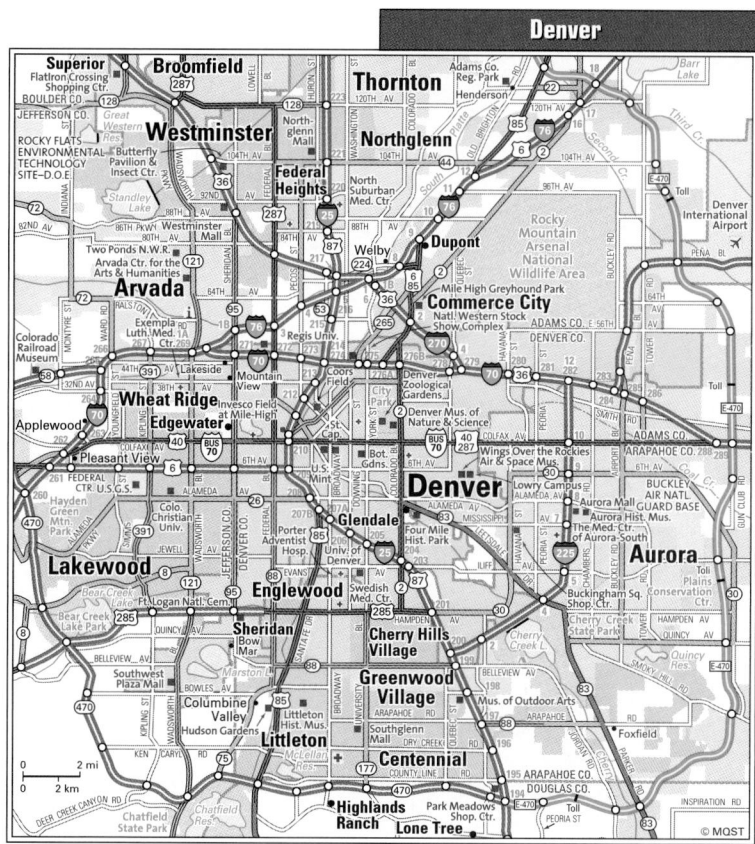

Phoenix

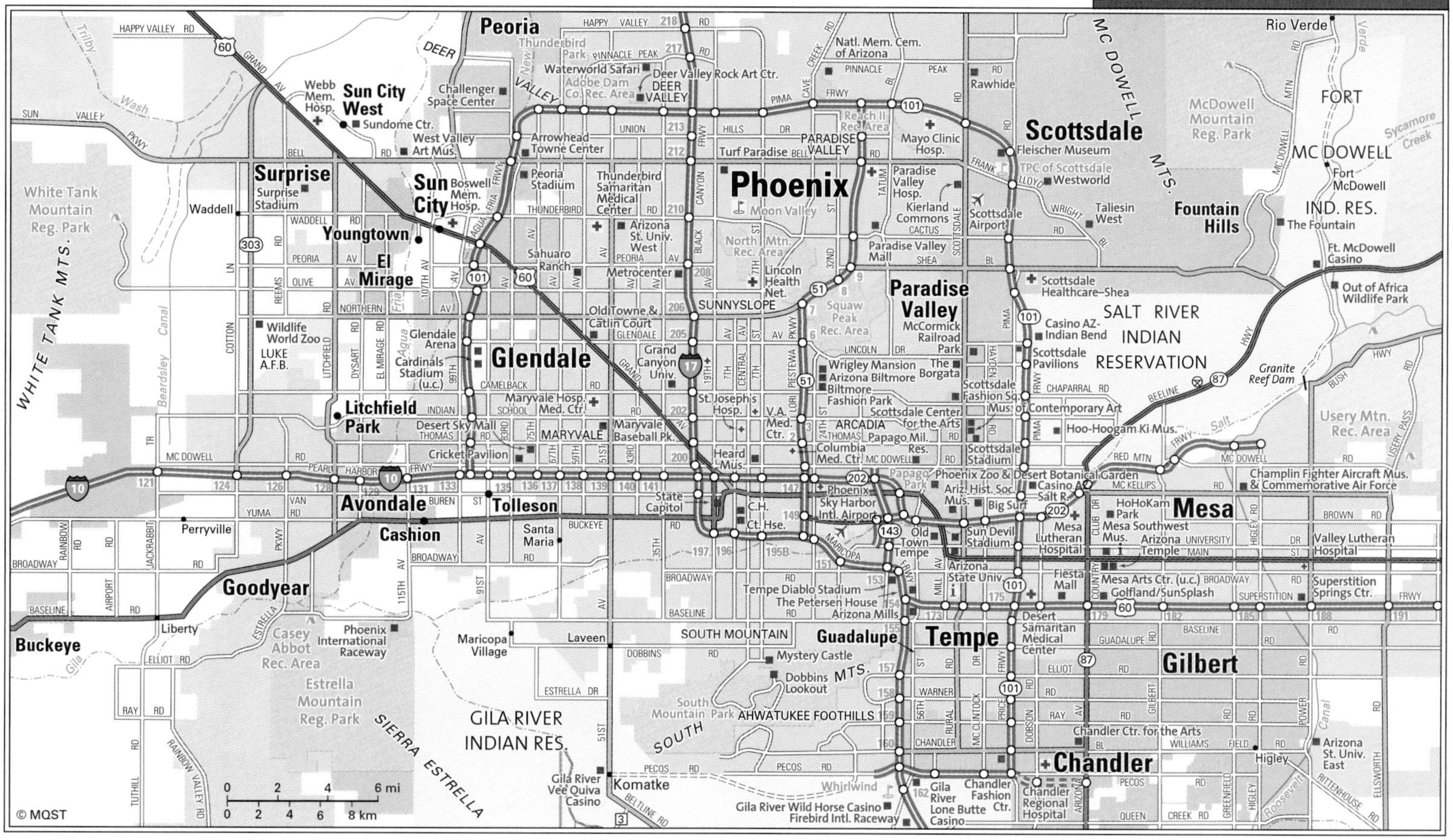

San Francisco cable car, bay, and Alcatraz

Golden Gate Bridge

San Francisco

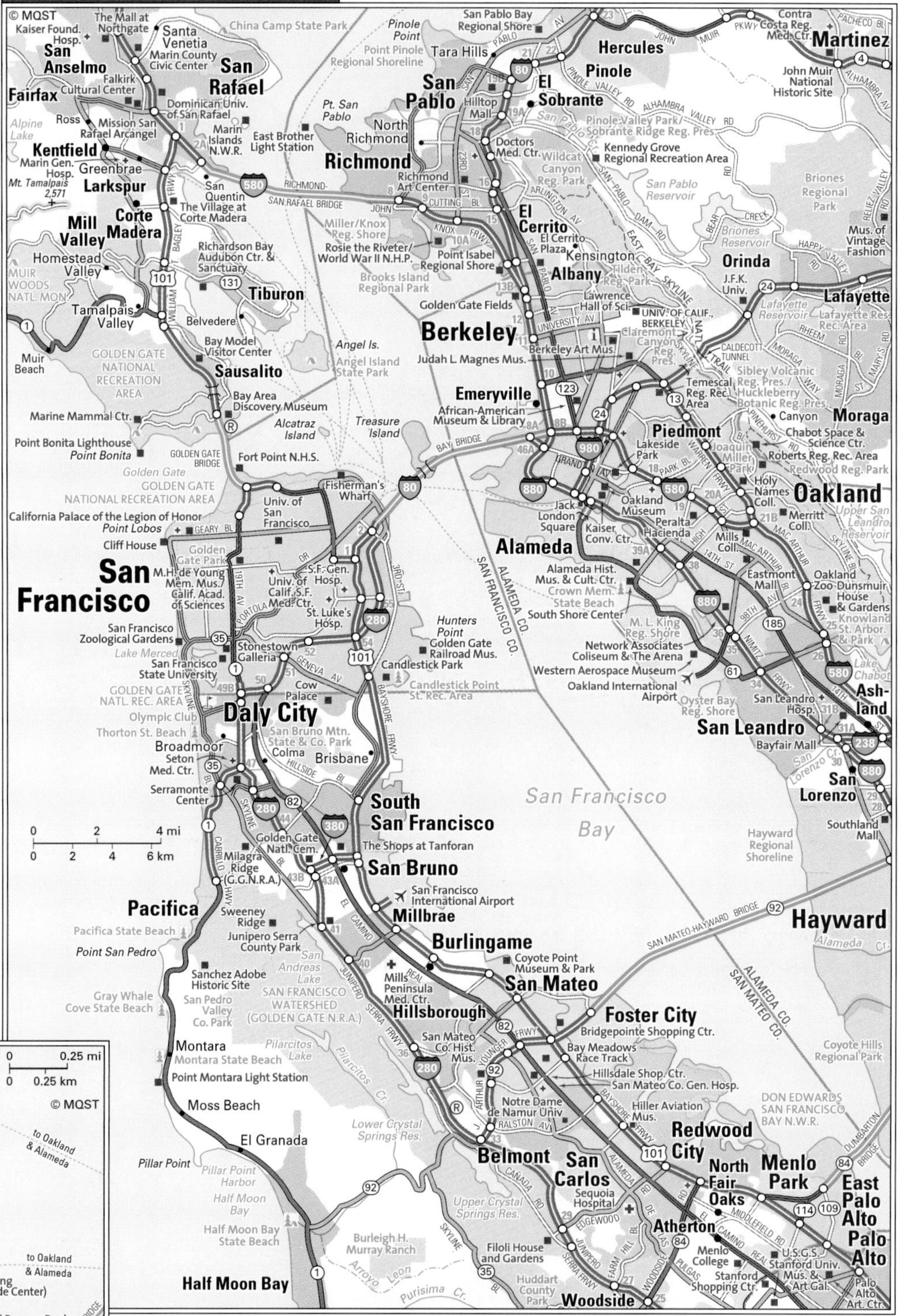

© MQST

Kaiser Found. Hosp.
The Mall at Northgate
Santa Venetia
Marin County Civic Center
China Camp State Park
San Anselmo
Fairfax
Falkirk Cultural Center
Ross
Alpine Lake
Mt. Tamalpais 2,571
Kentfield
Marin Gen. Hosp.
Greenbrae
Larkspur
Mill Valley
Corte Madera
Homestead Valley
MUIR WOODS NATL. MON.
Muir Beach
Tamalpais Valley
San Rafael
Dominican Univ. of San Rafael
Mission San Rafael Arcangel
Marin Islands N.W.R.
San Quentin
The Village at Corte Madera
Richardson Bay Audubon Ctr. & Sanctuary
Tiburon
Belvedere
Bay Model Visitor Center
Sausalito
Bay Area Discovery Museum
Marine Mammal Ctr.
Point Bonita Lighthouse
Point Bonita
GOLDEN GATE BRIDGE
Fort Point N.H.S.
GOLDEN GATE NATIONAL RECREATION AREA

Pt. San Pablo
East Brother Light Station
North Richmond
Richmond
Richmond Art Center
SAN RAFAEL BRIDGE
Miller/Knox Reg. Shore.
Rosie the Riveter/World War II N.H.P.
Point Isabel Regional Shore.
Brooks Island Regional Park
Golden Gate Fields
Angel Is.
Angel Island State Park
Treasure Island
Alcatraz Island
Fisherman's Wharf
BAY BRIDGE

Pinole Point
Point Pinole Regional Shoreline
Tara Hills
San Pablo Bay Regional Shore.
San Pablo
El Sobrante
El Cerrito
El Cerrito Plaza
Kensington
Albany
Berkeley
UNIV. OF CALIF. BERKELEY
Berkeley Art Mus.
Judah L. Magnes Mus.
African-American Museum & Library
Emeryville

Hercules
Pinole
Hilltop Mall
Doctors Med. Ctr.
Wildcat Canyon Reg. Park
Kennedy Grove Regional Recreation Area
San Pablo Reservoir
Lawrence Hall of Sci.
Claremont
Temescal Reg. Rec. Area
Tilden Reg. Park

Contra Costa Reg. Med.Ctr.
Martinez
John Muir National Historic Site
Briones Regional Park
Briones Reservoir
Mus. of Vintage Fashion
Orinda
J.F.K. Univ.
Lafayette
Lafayette Reservoir
Sibley Volcanic Reg. Pres.
Huckleberry Botanic Reg. Pres.
Moraga
Canyon
Chabot Space & Science Ctr.
Roberts Reg. Rec. Area
Redwood Reg. Park

San Francisco
California Palace of the Legion of Honor
Point Lobos
Cliff House
Golden Gate Park
M.H. de Young Mem. Mus.
Calif. Acad. of Sciences
San Francisco Zoological Gardens
Lake Merced
San Francisco State University
GOLDEN GATE NATL. REC. AREA
Olympic Club
Thorton St. Beach
Univ. of San Francisco
S.F. Gen. Hosp.
Univ. of Calif. S.F. Med. Ctr.
St. Luke's Hosp.
Stonestown Galleria
Cow Palace
Daly City
Broadmoor
Seton Med. Ctr.
Serramonte Center

Hunters Point
Golden Gate Railroad Mus.
Candlestick Park
Candlestick Point St. Rec. Area
San Bruno Mtn. State & Co. Park
Colma
Brisbane

Piedmont
Lakeside Park
Oakland Museum
Peralta Hacienda
Jack London Square
Merritt Coll.
Oakland
Mills Coll.
Alameda
Alameda Hist. Mus. & Cult. Ctr.
Crown Mem. State Beach
South Shore Center
Network Associates Coliseum & The Arena
Western Aerospace Museum
Oakland International Airport
M. L. King Reg. Shore.
Oyster Bay Reg. Shore.

Holy Names Coll.
Eastmont Mall
Oakland Zoo
Dunsmuir House & Gardens
Knowland Park
St. Arbor & Park
Ash-land
Lake Chabot Reg. Park
San Leandro
Bayfair Mall
San Lorenzo
Southland Mall
Hayward Regional Shoreline
Hayward

San Francisco Bay

0 2 4 mi
0 2 4 6 km

Milagra Ridge (G.G.N.R.A.)
Sweeney Ridge
Junipero Serra County Park
San Andreas Lake
SAN FRANCISCO WATERSHED (GOLDEN GATE N.R.A.)
Pacifica
Pacifica State Beach
Point San Pedro
Sanchez Adobe Historic Site
Gray Whale Cove State Beach
San Pedro Valley Co. Park
Montara
Montara State Beach
Point Montara Light Station
Moss Beach
El Granada
Pillar Point
Pillar Point Harbor
Half Moon Bay
Half Moon Bay State Beach
Burleigh H. Murray Ranch

South San Francisco
The Shops at Tanforan
San Bruno
San Francisco International Airport
Millbrae
Burlingame
Coyote Point Museum & Park
Hillsborough
Mills Peninsula Med. Ctr.
San Mateo
San Mateo Co. Hist. Mus.
Coyote Point Recreation Area
Foster City
Bridgepointe Shopping Ctr.
Bay Meadows Race Track
Hillsdale Shop. Ctr.
San Mateo Co. Gen. Hosp.
Hiller Aviation Mus.
Notre Dame de Namur Univ.
Belmont
San Carlos
Sequoia Hospital
Upper Crystal Springs Res.
Lower Crystal Springs Res.
Filoli House and Gardens
Huddart County Park
Woodside
Redwood City
North Fair Oaks
Atherton
Menlo College
Stanford Univ.
Stanford Shopping Ctr.
Menlo Park
East Palo Alto
Palo Alto
Stanford Univ. Mus. & Art Gal.
Palo Alto Art Ctr.
U.S.G.S.
DON EDWARDS SAN FRANCISCO BAY N.W.R.
Coyote Hills Regional Park
Don Edwards

Half Moon Bay

Downtown San Francisco

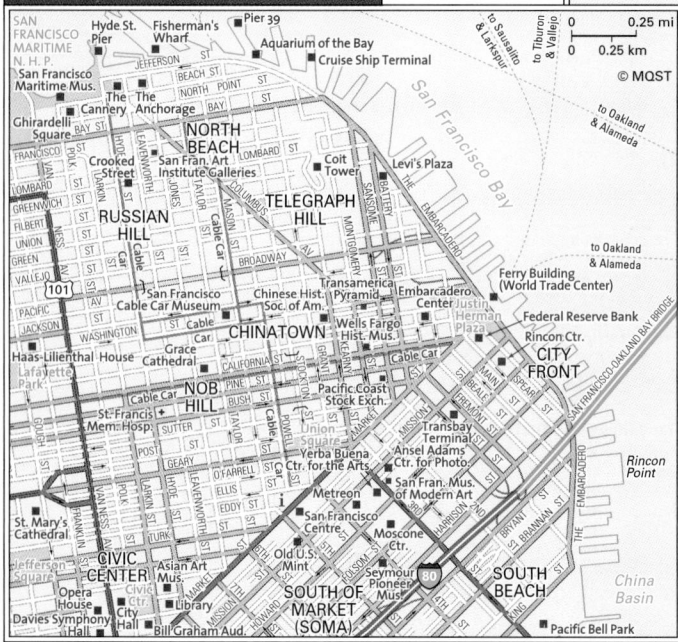

SAN FRANCISCO MARITIME N. H. P.
San Francisco Maritime Mus.
Ghirardelli Square
The Cannery
The Anchorage
Hyde St. Pier
Fisherman's Wharf
Pier 39
Aquarium of the Bay
Cruise Ship Terminal
Coit Tower
Levi's Plaza
NORTH BEACH
TELEGRAPH HILL
RUSSIAN HILL
Crooked Street
San Fran. Art Institute Galleries
Lombard St.
Transamerica Pyramid
Chinese Hist. Soc. of Am.
San Francisco Cable Car Museum
Haas-Lilienthal House
Lafayette Park
CHINATOWN
Wells Fargo Hist. Mus.
Grace Cathedral
NOB HILL
Pacific Coast Stock Exch.
St. Francis Mem. Hosp.
Union Square
Yerba Buena Ctr. for the Arts
Ansel Adams Ctr. for Photo.
St. Mary's Cathedral
Metreon
San Francisco Centre
San Fran. Mus. of Modern Art
Old U.S. Mint
Moscone Ctr.
CIVIC CENTER
Opera House
City Hall
Asian Art Mus.
Library
Davies Symphony Hall
Bill Graham Aud.
Seymour Pioneers Mus.
SOUTH OF MARKET (SOMA)
Pacific Bell Park
SOUTH BEACH
China Basin

Ferry Building (World Trade Center)
Embarcadero Center
Justin Herman Plaza
Federal Reserve Bank
Rincon Ctr.
CITY FRONT
Transbay Terminal
Rincon Point

San Francisco Bay

to Sausalito & Larkspur
to Tiburon & Vallejo
to Oakland & Alameda

0 0.25 mi
0 0.25 km
© MQST

San Francisco old and new

Los Angeles

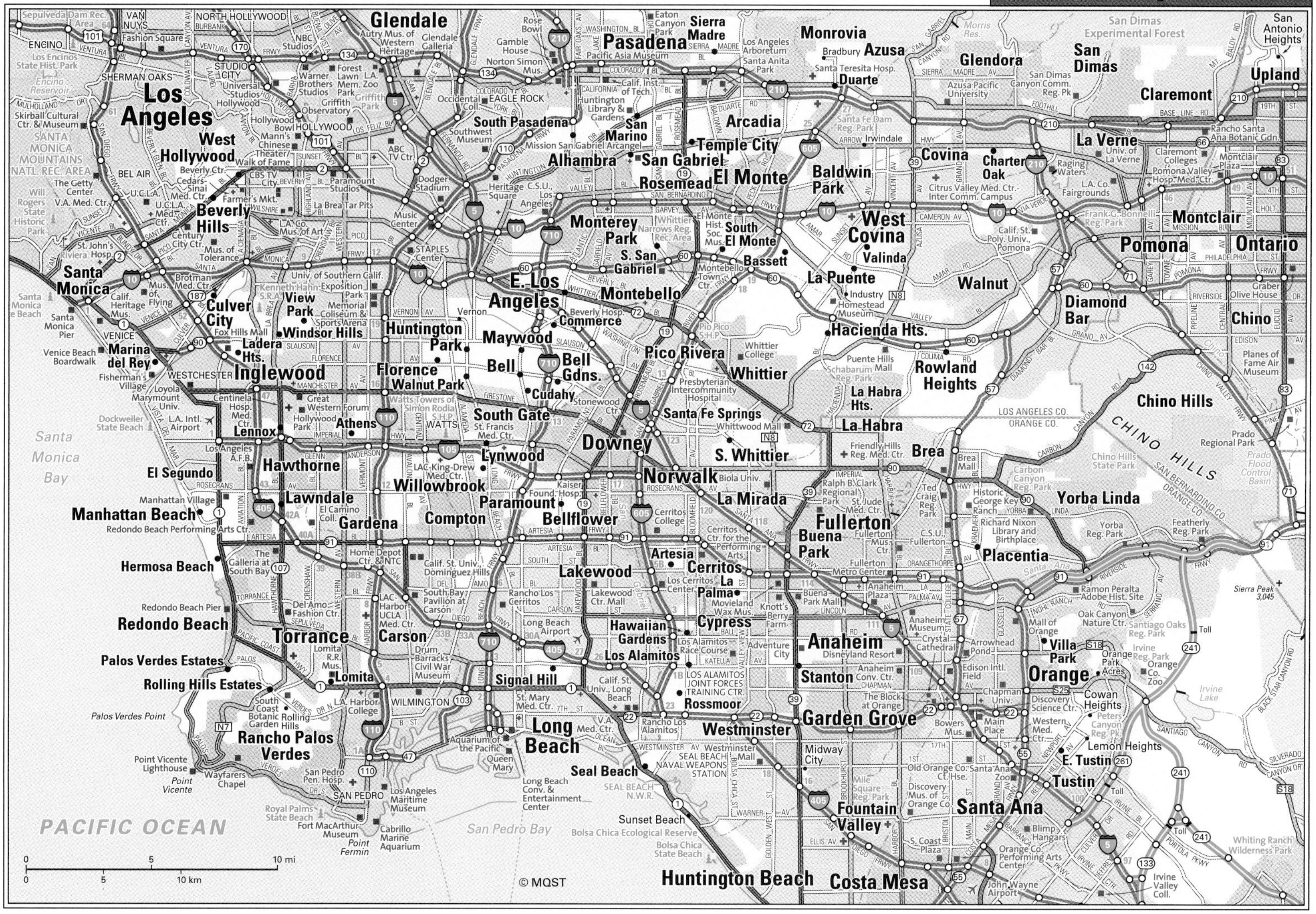

Downtown Los Angeles

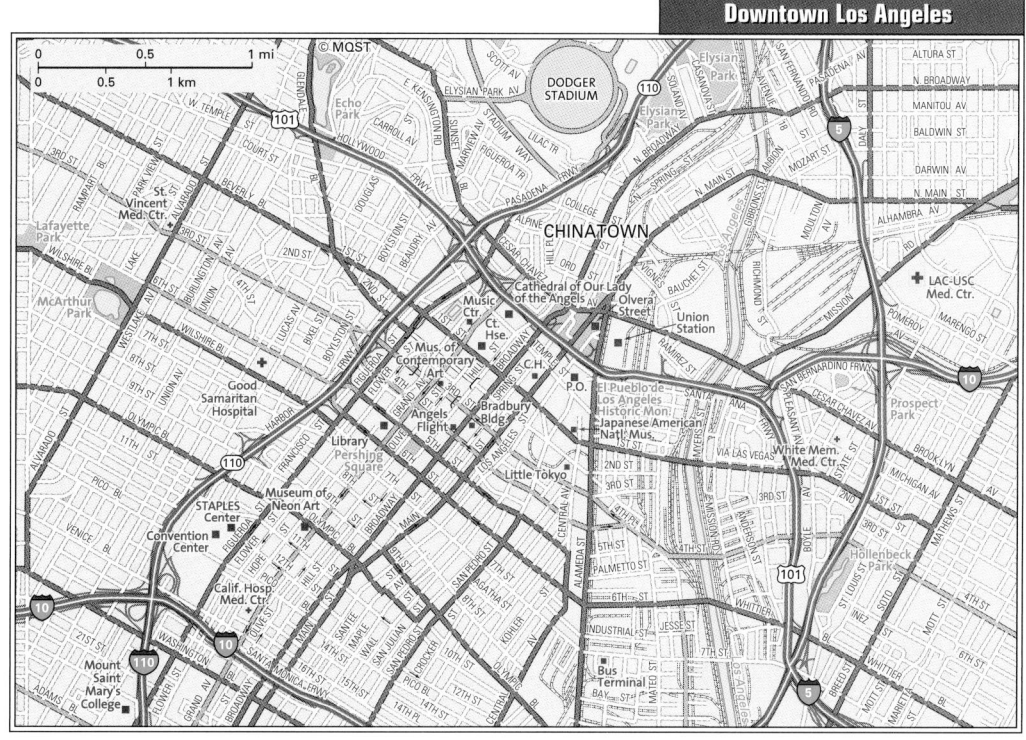

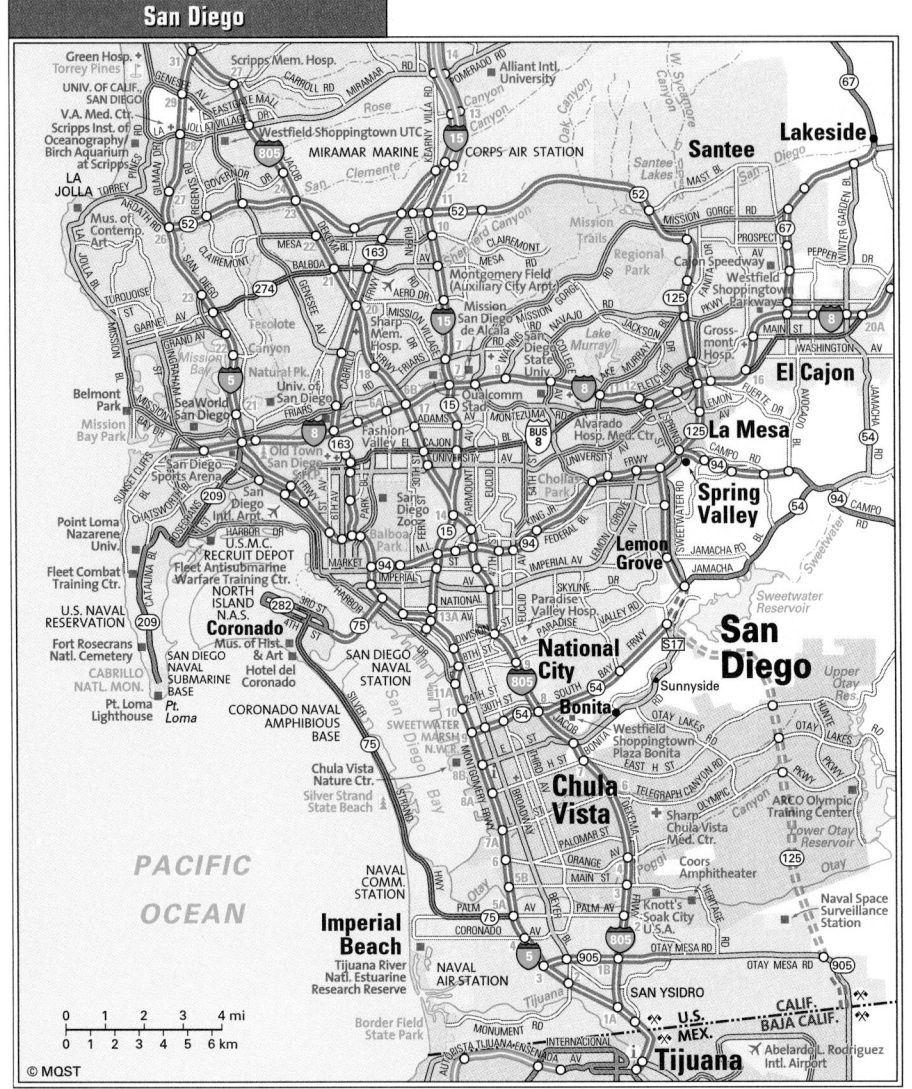

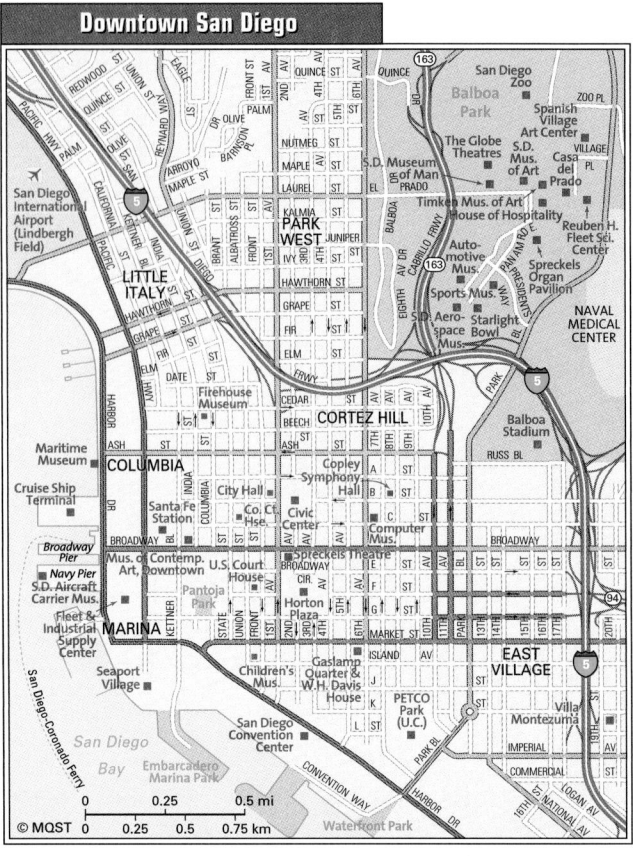

Waikiki, Hawaii

Portland, View from River Place Marina

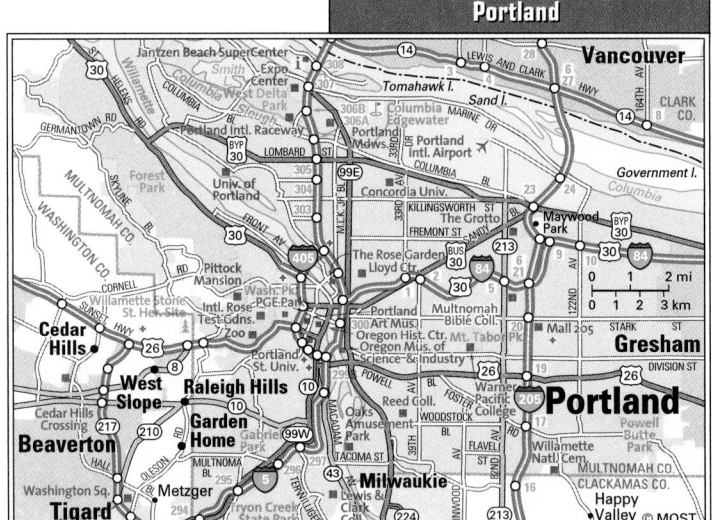

Seattle

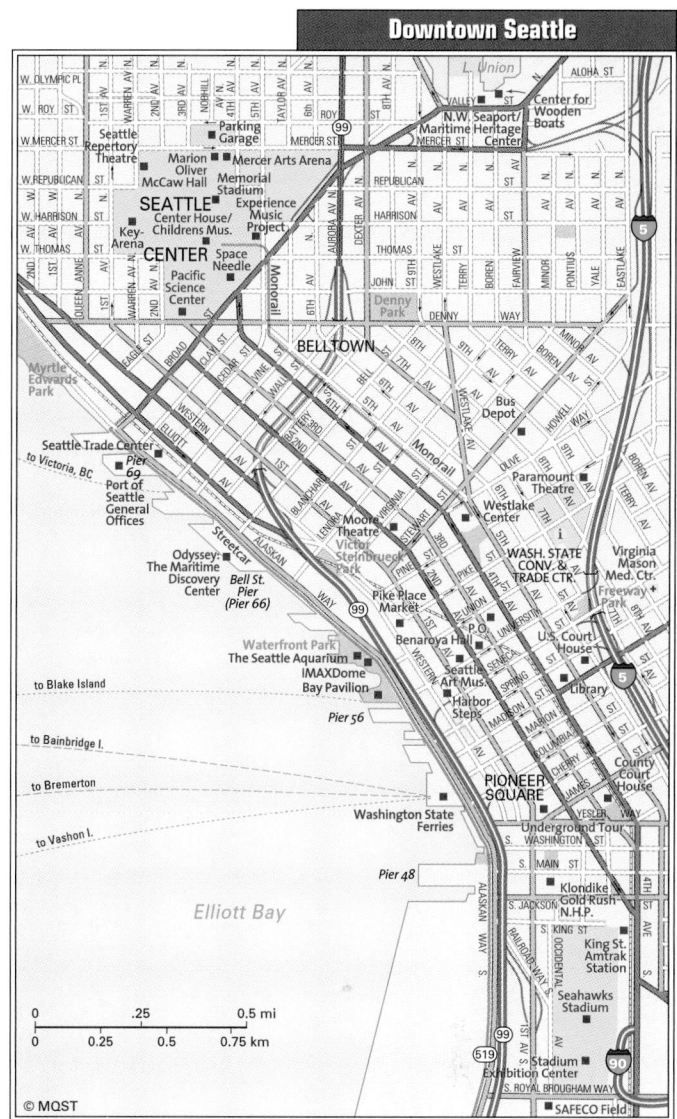

Downtown Seattle

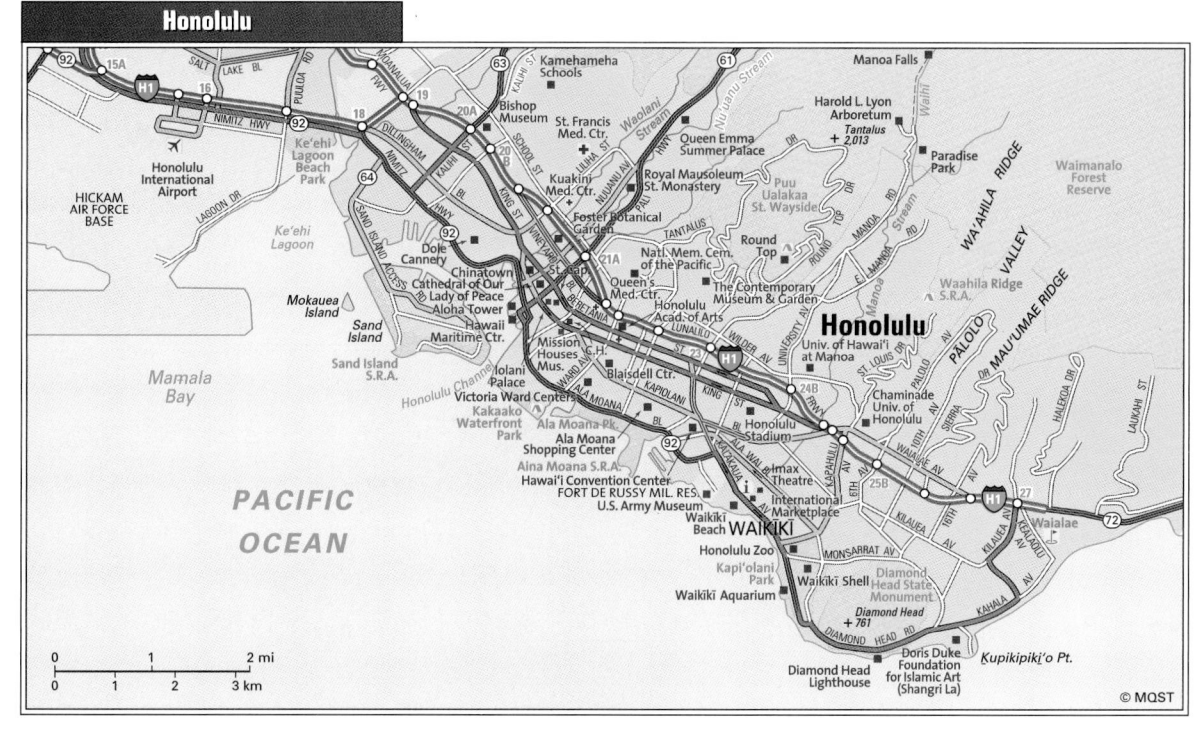

Honolulu

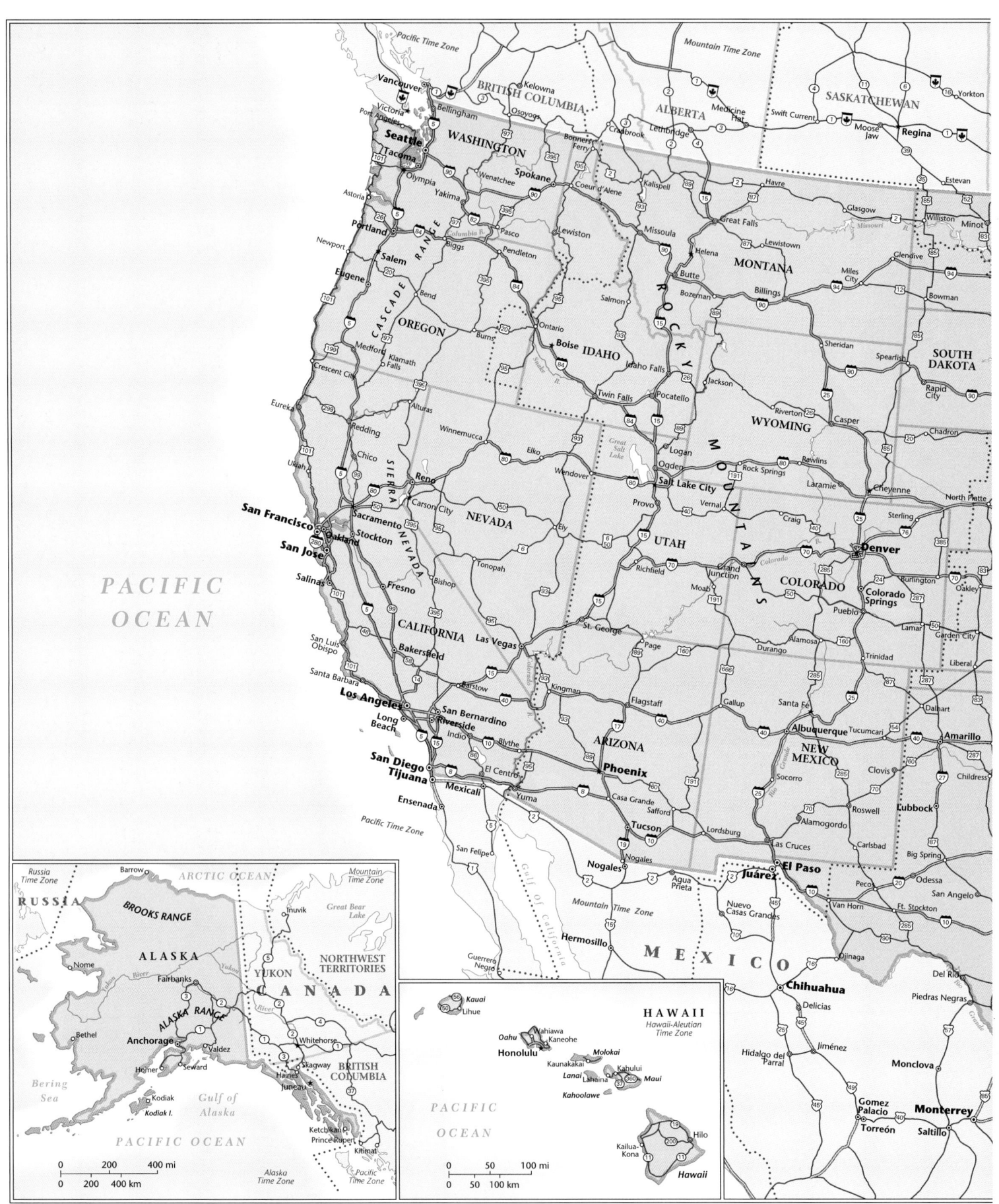

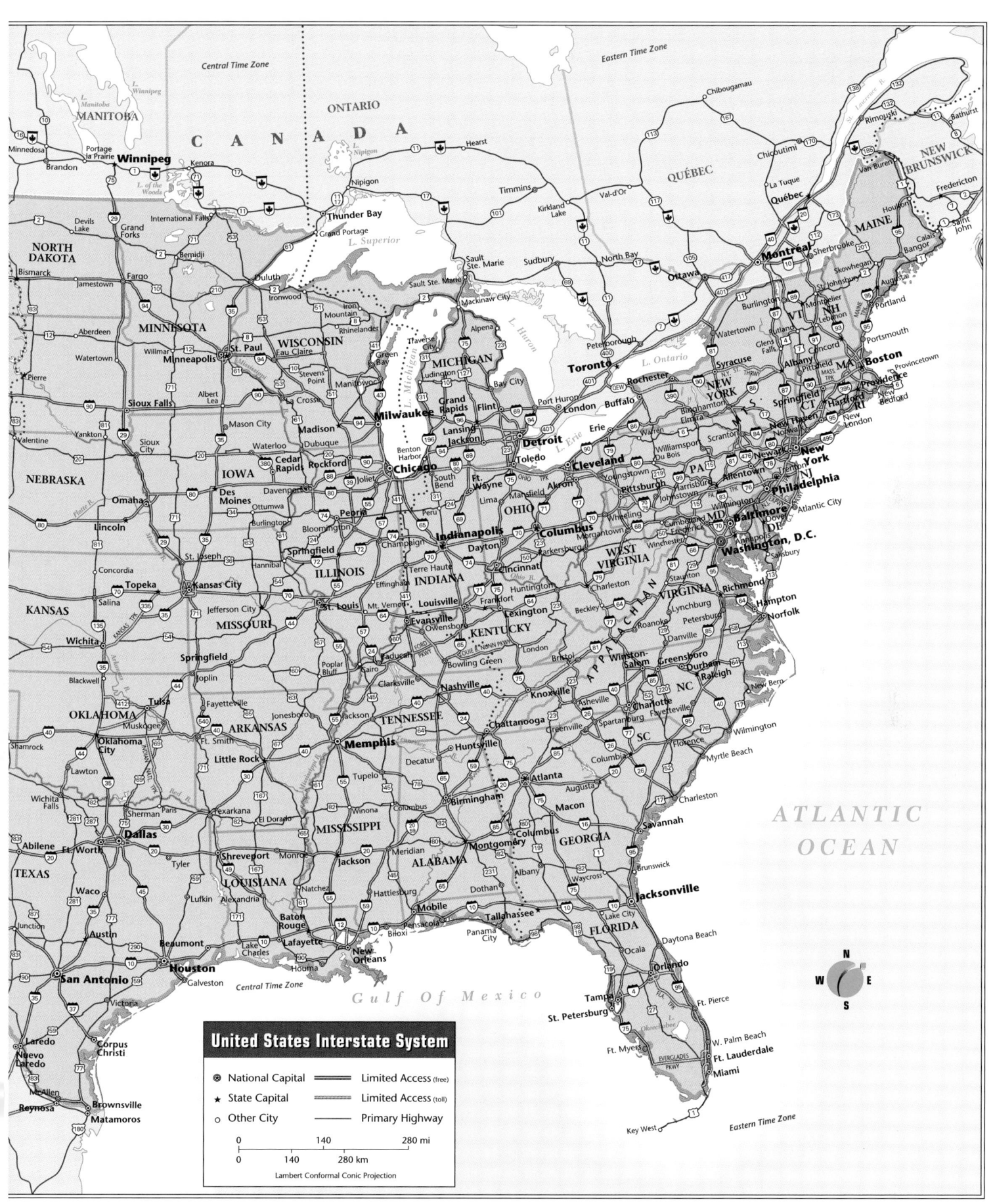

United States Interstate System

⊗ National Capital   ═══ Limited Access (free)
★ State Capital   ═══ Limited Access (toll)
○ Other City   ─── Primary Highway

0   140   280 mi
0   140   280 km

Lambert Conformal Conic Projection

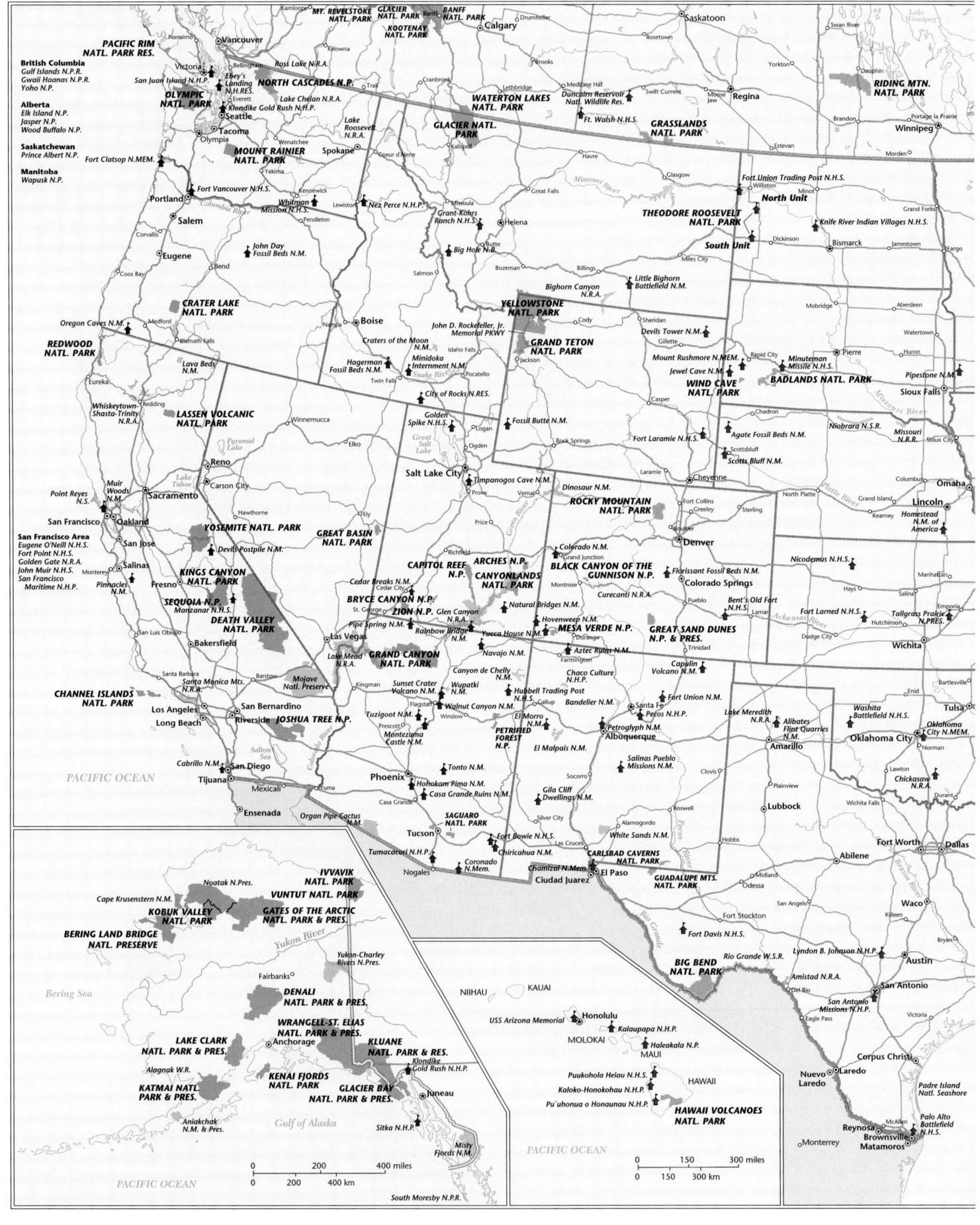

British Columbia
Gulf Islands N.P.R.
Gwaii Haanas N.P.R.
Yoho N.P.

Alberta
Elk Island N.P.
Jasper N.P.
Wood Buffalo N.P.

Saskatchewan
Prince Albert N.P.

Manitoba
Wapusk N.P.

San Francisco Area
Eugene O'Neill N.H.S.
Fort Point N.H.S.
Golden Gate N.R.A.
John Muir N.H.S.
San Francisco Maritime N.H.P.

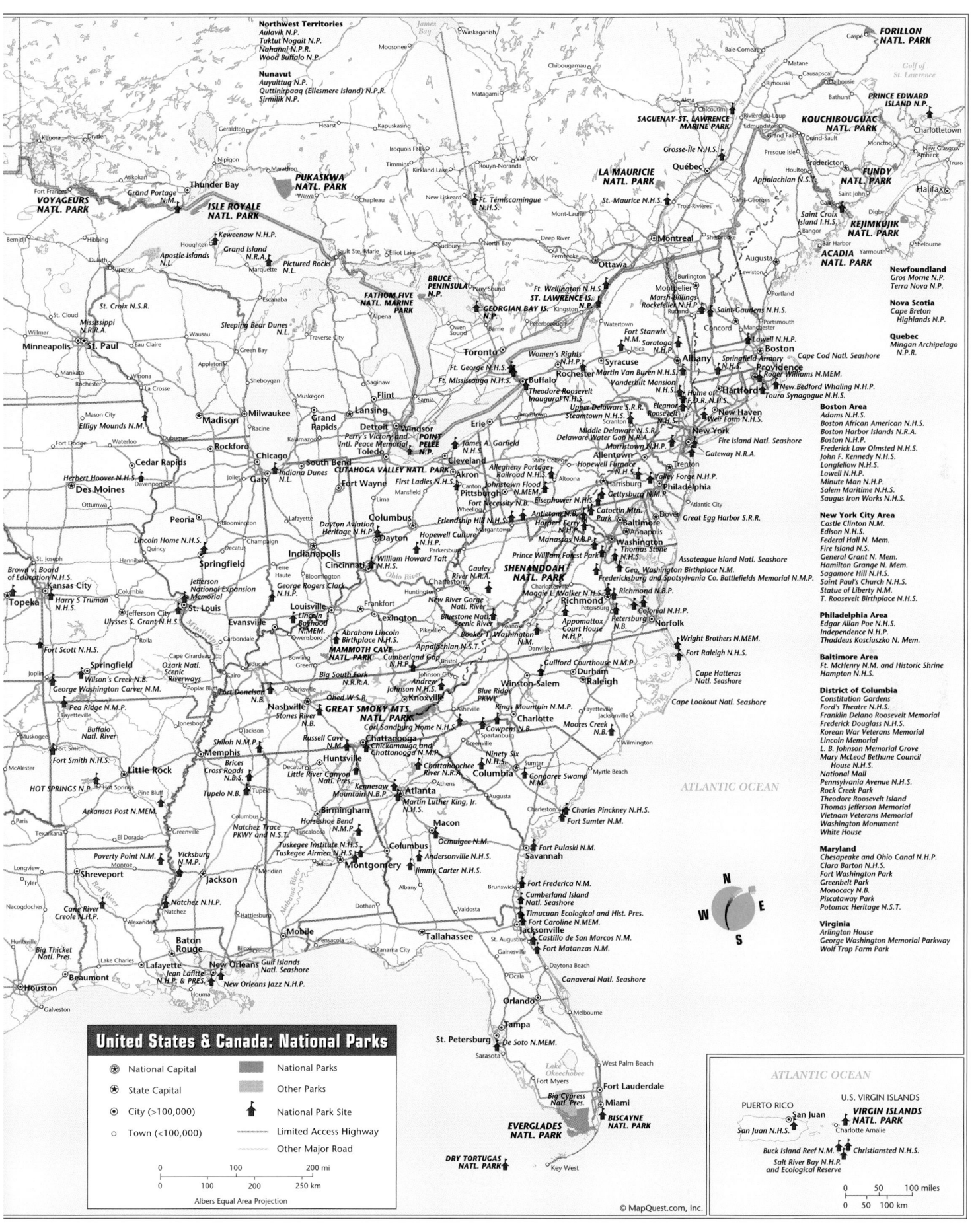

United States and Canada: National Parks

Northwest Territories
Aulavik N.P.
Tuktut Nogait N.P.
Nahanni N.P.R.
Wood Buffalo N.P.

Nunavut
Auyuittuq N.P.
Quttinirpaaq (Ellesmere Island) N.P.R.
Sirmilik N.P.

FORILLON NATL. PARK

PRINCE EDWARD ISLAND N.P.

KOUCHIBOUGUAC NATL. PARK

SAGUENAY-ST. LAWRENCE MARINE PARK

FUNDY NATL. PARK

LA MAURICIE NATL. PARK

Grosse-Ile N.H.S.

Appalachian N.S.T.

Saint Croix Island I.H.S.

KEJIMKUJIK NATL. PARK

ACADIA NATL. PARK

PUKASKWA NATL. PARK

VOYAGEURS NATL. PARK

ISLE ROYALE NATL. PARK

Keweenaw N.H.P.
Grand Island N.R.A.
Pictured Rocks N.L.

Apostle Islands N.L.

Newfoundland
Gros Morne N.P.
Terra Nova N.P.

Nova Scotia
Cape Breton Highlands N.P.

Quebec
Mingan Archipelago N.P.R.

St. Croix N.S.R.

Mississippi N.R.R.A.

Sleeping Bear Dunes N.L.

BRUCE PENINSULA N.P.

FATHOM FIVE NATL. MARINE PARK

GEORGIAN BAY IS. N.P.

Ft. Wellington N.H.S.
ST. LAWRENCE IS. N.P.

Marsh-Billings-Rockefeller N.H.P.

Saint-Gaudens N.H.S.

Effigy Mounds N.M.

Fort Stanwix N.M.
Saratoga N.H.P.

Women's Rights N.H.P.

Ft. George N.H.S.
Ft. Mississauga N.H.S.

Theodore Roosevelt Inaugural N.H.S.

Martin Van Buren N.H.S.
Vanderbilt Mansion N.H.S.

Home of F.D.R. N.H.S.
Eleanor Roosevelt N.H.S.

Springfield Armory N.H.S.

Cape Cod Natl. Seashore

Roger Williams N.MEM.

New Bedford Whaling N.H.P.
Touro Synagogue N.H.S.

Boston Area
Adams N.H.S.
Boston African American N.H.S.
Boston Harbor Islands N.R.A.
Boston N.H.P.
Frederick Law Olmsted N.H.S.
John F. Kennedy N.H.S.
Longfellow N.H.S.
Lowell N.H.P.
Minute Man N.H.P.
Salem Maritime N.H.S.
Saugus Iron Works N.H.S.

Upper Delaware S.R.R.
Steamtown N.H.S.
Middle Delaware N.S.R.
Delaware Water Gap N.R.A.

James A. Garfield N.H.S.

Perry's Victory and Intl. Peace Memorial N.M.

POINT PELEE N.P.

CUYAHOGA VALLEY NATL. PARK

Indiana Dunes N.L.

First Ladies N.H.S.

Allegheny Portage Railroad N.H.S.
Johnstown Flood N.MEM.

Hopewell Furnace N.H.S.

Fire Island Natl. Seashore

Gateway N.R.A.

New York City Area
Castle Clinton N.M.
Edison N.H.S.
Federal Hall N. Mem.
Fire Island N.S.
General Grant N. Mem.
Hamilton Grange N. Mem.
Sagamore Hill N.H.S.
Saint Paul's Church N.H.S.
Statue of Liberty N.M.
T. Roosevelt Birthplace N.H.S.

Valley Forge N.H.P.

Eisenhower N.H.S.
Gettysburg N.M.P.

Morristown N.H.P.

Friendship Hill N.H.S.

Dayton Aviation Heritage N.H.P.

Hopewell Culture N.H.P.

William Howard Taft N.H.S.

Catoctin Mtn. Park

Antietam N.B.
Harpers Ferry N.H.P.

Great Egg Harbor S.R.R.

Philadelphia Area
Edgar Allan Poe N.H.S.
Independence N.H.P.
Thaddeus Kosciuszko N. Mem.

Manassas N.B.P.

Washington Thomas Stone N.H.S.

Prince William Forest Park

SHENANDOAH NATL. PARK

Assateague Island Natl. Seashore

Geo. Washington Birthplace N.M.

Fredericksburg and Spotsylvania Co. Battlefields Memorial N.M.P.

Baltimore Area
Ft. McHenry N.M. and Historic Shrine
Hampton N.H.S.

Gauley River N.R.A.

Maggie L. Walker N.H.S.

New River Gorge Natl. River

Booker T. Washington N.M.

Bluestone Natl. Scenic River

Appalachian N.S.T.

Colonial N.H.P.
Appomattox Court House N.H.P.
Petersburg N.B.

District of Columbia
Constitution Gardens
Ford's Theatre N.H.S.
Franklin Delano Roosevelt Memorial
Frederick Douglass N.H.S.
Korean War Veterans Memorial
Lincoln Memorial
L. B. Johnson Memorial Grove
Mary McLeod Bethune Council House N.H.S.
National Mall
Pennsylvania Avenue N.H.S.
Rock Creek Park
Theodore Roosevelt Island
Thomas Jefferson Memorial
Vietnam Veterans Memorial
Washington Monument
White House

George Rogers Clark N.H.P.

Lincoln Boyhood N.MEM.

Abraham Lincoln Birthplace N.H.S.

MAMMOTH CAVE NATL. PARK

Cumberland Gap N.H.P.

Big South Fork N.R.R.A.

Johnson N.H.S.

Obed W.S.R.

Blue Ridge PKWY.

Guilford Courthouse N.M.P.

Cape Hatteras Natl. Seashore

Cape Lookout Natl. Seashore

Maryland
Chesapeake and Ohio Canal N.H.P.
Clara Barton N.H.S.
Fort Washington Park
Greenbelt Park
Monocacy N.B.
Piscataway Park
Potomac Heritage N.S.T.

Virginia
Arlington House
George Washington Memorial Parkway
Wolf Trap Farm Park

Ozark Natl. Scenic Riverways

Wilson's Creek N.B.

George Washington Carver N.M.

Pea Ridge N.M.P.

Fort Donelson N.B.

Kings Mountain N.M.P.

Cowpens N.B.

Moores Creek N.B.

Buffalo Natl. River

Fort Smith N.H.S.

HOT SPRINGS N.P.

GREAT SMOKY MTS. NATL. PARK

Stones River N.B.

Russell Cave N.M.

Carl Sandburg Home N.H.S.

Ninety Six N.H.S.

Shiloh N.M.P.

Brices Cross Roads N.B.S.

Little River Canyon Natl. Pres.

Chickamauga and Chattanooga N.M.P.

Chattahoochee River N.R.A.

Congaree Swamp N.M.

Charles Pinckney N.H.S.
Fort Sumter N.M.

Tupelo N.B.

Natchez Trace PKWY and N.S.T.

Horseshoe Bend N.M.P.

Tuskegee Institute N.H.S.
Tuskegee Airmen N.H.S.

Kennesaw Mountain N.B.P.

Martin Luther King, Jr. N.H.S.

Andersonville N.H.S.

Ocmulgee N.M.

Jimmy Carter N.H.S.

Poverty Point N.M.

Vicksburg N.M.P.

Fort Pulaski N.M.

ATLANTIC OCEAN

Cane River Creole N.H.P.

Natchez N.H.P.

Big Thicket Natl. Pres.

Jean Lafitte N.H.P. & PRES.

New Orleans Jazz N.H.P.

Gulf Islands Natl. Seashore

Fort Frederica N.M.

Cumberland Island Natl. Seashore

Timucuan Ecological and Hist. Pres.
Fort Caroline N.MEM.

Castillo de San Marcos N.M.
Fort Matanzas N.M.

De Soto N.MEM.

Canaveral Natl. Seashore

Big Cypress Natl. Pres.

BISCAYNE NATL. PARK

EVERGLADES NATL. PARK

DRY TORTUGAS NATL. PARK

United States & Canada: National Parks

⊛ National Capital
⊛ State Capital
◉ City (>100,000)
○ Town (<100,000)

National Parks
Other Parks
National Park Site
Limited Access Highway
Other Major Road

0   100   200 mi
0   100   200   250 km
Albers Equal Area Projection

ATLANTIC OCEAN

PUERTO RICO

San Juan
San Juan N.H.S.

U.S. VIRGIN ISLANDS

VIRGIN ISLANDS NATL. PARK

Charlotte Amalie

Buck Island Reef N.M.
Christiansted N.H.S.

Salt River Bay N.H.P. and Ecological Reserve

0   50   100 miles
0   50   100 km

© MapQuest.com, Inc.

AREA	PAGE
Afghanistan	413
AFRICA	420
Western Africa	421
Northeastern Africa	422
Central Africa	423
Southern Africa	424
Albania	407
Algeria	421
Andorra	404
Angola	423
Antarctica	390
Antigua and Barbuda	433
Arabian Peninsula	410
Argentina	429
Armenia	408
ASIA	409
Australia	419
Austria	405
Azerbaijan	408
Bahamas	433
Bahrain	410
Balkan States, The	407
Baltic States, The	401
Bangladesh	414
Barbados	435
Belarus	408
Belgium	403
Belize	432
Benin	421
Bhutan	414
Bolivia	428
Bosnia and Herzegovina	407
Botswana	424
Brazil	428
Bulgaria	407
Burkina Faso	421
Burundi	423
Cambodia	417
Cameroon	423
Canada	434
Alberta	437
British Columbia	437
Manitoba	438
New Brunswick	441
Newfoundland and Labrador	442
Northwest Territories	436
Nova Scotia	441
Nunavut	436
Ontario	439
Prince Edward Island	441
Quebec	440
Saskatchewan	438
Yukon	435
Central African Republic	423
Central America	432
Central Europe	405
Chad	422
Chile	429
China	415
Colombia	426
Comoros	424
Congo, Dem. Republic of the	423
Congo, Republic of the	423
Costa Rica	432
Côte d'Ivoire	421
Croatia	407
Cuba	433
Cyprus	411
Czech Republic	406
Denmark	401
Djibouti	422
Dominica	433
Dominican Republic	433
East Timor	417
Ecuador	426
Egypt	422
El Salvador	432
Equatorial Guinea	423
Eritrea	422
Estonia	401
Ethiopia	422
EUROPE	391
Fiji	418
Finland	401
France	403
French Guiana	427
Gabon	423
Gambia	421
Georgia	408
Germany	405
Ghana	421
Greece	407
Greenland	402
Grenada	433
Guatemala	432
Guinea	421
Guinea-Bissau	421
Guyana	427
Haiti	433
Honduras	432
Hungary	406
Iceland	402
India	414
Indian Subcontinent	414
Indonesia	417
Iran	413
Iraq	413
Ireland	400
Israel	412
Italy	407
Jamaica	433
Japan	416
Jordan	412
Kazakhstan	408
Kenya	423
Kiribati	418
Korea, North	416
Korea, South	416
Kuwait	410
Kyrgyzstan	408
Laos	417
Latvia	401
Lebanon	411
Lesotho	424
Liberia	421
Libya	422
Lithuania	401
Luxembourg	403
Macedonia	407
Madagascar	424
Malawi	423
Malaysia	417
Mali	421
Malta	407
Marshall Islands	418
Mauritania	421
Mexico	431
Micronesia, Federated States of	418
Moldova	407
Monaco	403
Mongolia	415
Morocco	421
Mozambique	424
Myanmar (Burma)	417
Namibia	424
Nauru	418
Nepal	414
Netherlands	403
New Zealand	419
Nicaragua	432
Niger	421
Nigeria	421
NORTH AMERICA	430
Norway	401
Oceania	418
Oman	410
Pakistan	413
Palau	418
Panama	432
Papua New Guinea	418
Paraguay	429
Peru	426
Philippines	417
Poland	406
Portugal	404
Qatar	410
Romania	407
Russia	408
Rwanda	423
St. Kitts and Nevis	433
St. Lucia	433
St. Vincent and the Grenadines	433
Samoa	418
Saudi Arabia	410
Scandinavia	401
Senegal	421
Serbia and Montenegro	407
Sierra Leone	421
Singapore	417
Slovakia	406
Slovenia	407
Solomon Islands	418
Somalia	423
South Africa	424
SOUTH AMERICA	425
Southeast Asia	417
Spain	404
Sri Lanka	414
Sudan	422
Suriname	427
Swaziland	424
Sweden	401
Switzerland	405
Syria	411
Taiwan	415
Tajikistan	408
Tanzania	423
Thailand	417
Togo	421
Tonga	418
Trinidad and Tobago	433
Tunisia	421
Turkey	411
Turkmenistan	408
Tuvalu	418
Uganda	423
Ukraine	408
United Arab Emirates	410
United Kingdom	392
East and West Midlands	394
East Anglia, London, Southeast	395
North England, Yorkshire/Humberside	393
Northern Ireland	399
Scotland	397
Southwest England	396
Wales	398
United States	443
Alabama	444
Alaska	445
Arizona	446
Arkansas	447
California	448
Colorado	449
Connecticut	450
Delaware	451
District of Columbia	463
Florida	452
Georgia	453
Hawaii	454
Idaho	455
Illinois	456
Indiana	457
Iowa	458
Kansas	459
Kentucky	460
Louisiana	461
Maine	462
Maryland	463
Massachusetts	464
Michigan	465
Minnesota	466
Mississippi	467
Missouri	468
Montana	469
Nebraska	470
Nevada	471
New Hampshire	472
New Jersey	473
New Mexico	474
New York	475
North Carolina	476
North Dakota	477
Ohio	478
Oklahoma	479
Oregon	480
Pennsylvania	481
Rhode Island	482
South Carolina	483
South Dakota	484
Tennessee	485
Texas	486
Utah	487
Vermont	488
Virginia	489
Washington	490
West Virginia	491
Wisconsin	492
Wyoming	493
Uruguay	429
Uzbekistan	408
Vanuatu	418
Venezuela	427
Vietnam	417
West Indies	433
WORLD	389
Yemen	410
Zambia	423
Zimbabwe	424

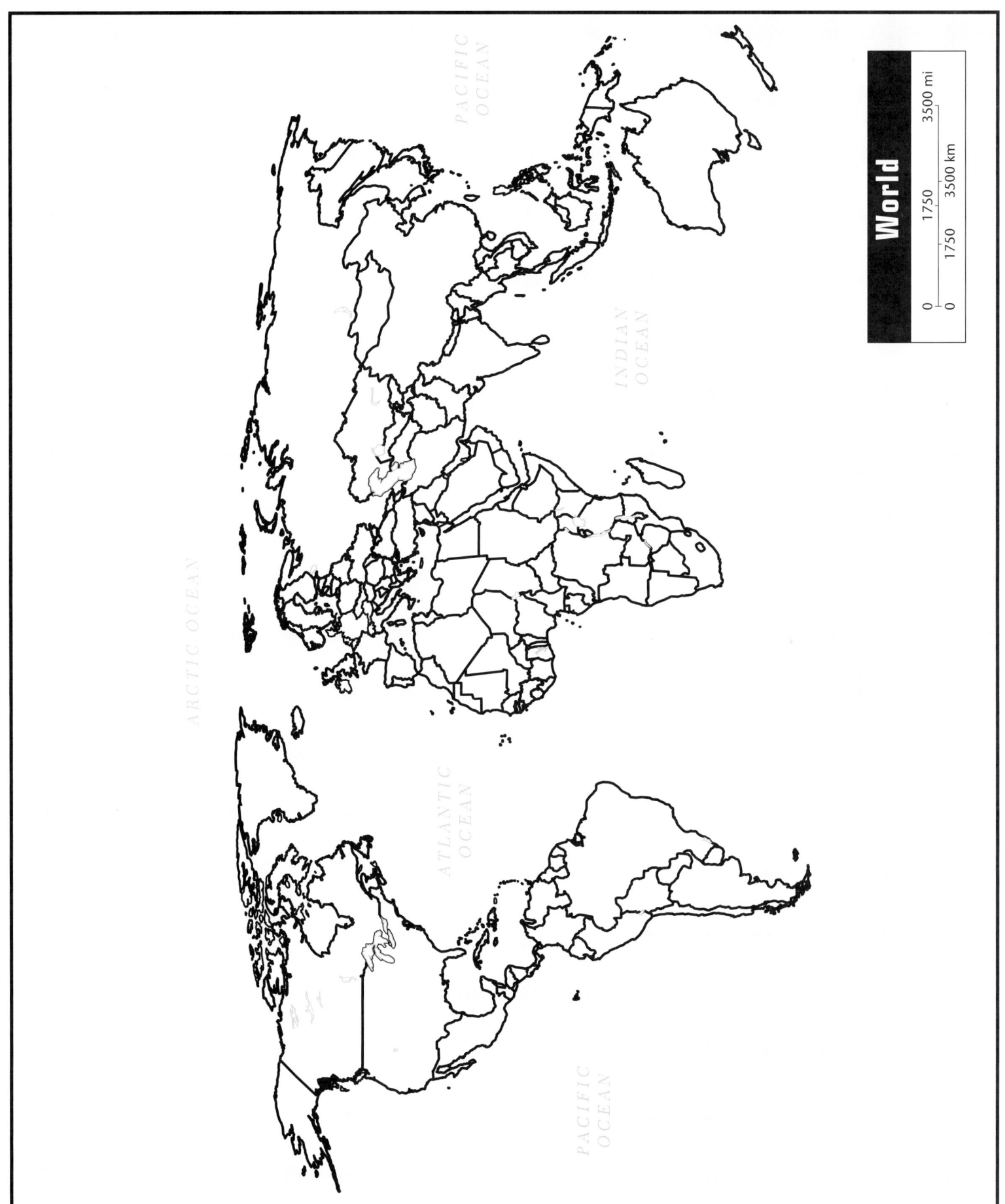

PACIFIC OCEAN

INDIAN OCEAN

ARCTIC OCEAN

ATLANTIC OCEAN

PACIFIC OCEAN

World

3500 mi

1750   3500 km

1750

0

0

Antarctica

0   400   800 mi
0   400   800 km

Bellingshausen
Sea

Amundsen
Sea

Weddell
Sea

Ross
Sea

ANTARCTICA

INDIAN OCEAN

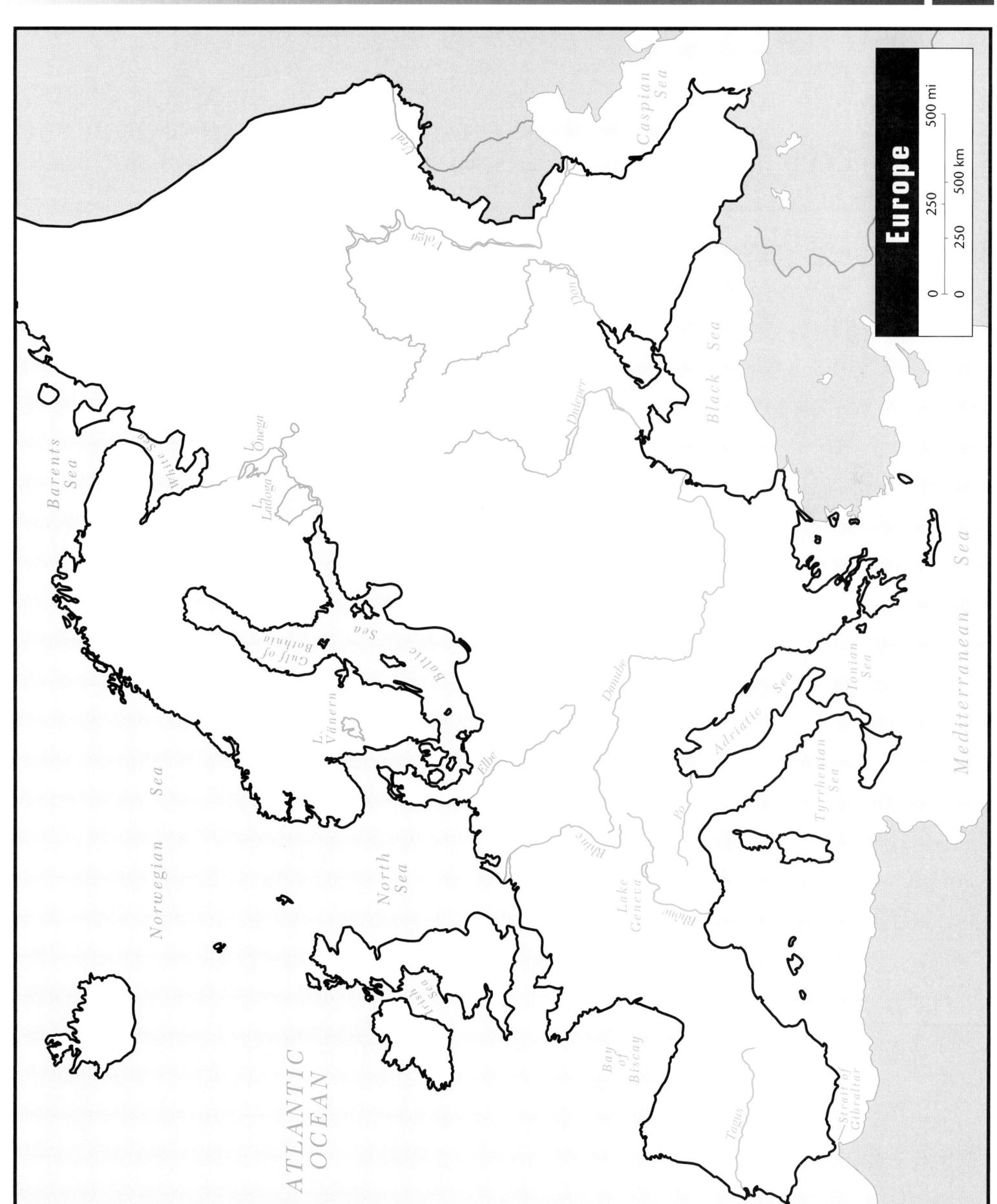

Caspian Sea

Ural

Volga

Don

Dnieper

Black Sea

Barents Sea

White Sea

Onega

L. Ladoga

L. Onega

Gulf of Bothnia

Baltic Sea

L. Vänern

Elbe

Danube

Adriatic Sea

Ionian Sea

Mediterranean Sea

Po

Rhône

Lake Geneva

Tyrrhenian Sea

Norwegian Sea

North Sea

Irish Sea

Bay of Biscay

Tagus

Strait of Gibraltar

ATLANTIC OCEAN

Europe

0   250   500 mi

0   250   500 km

United Kingdom and Ireland

0   100   200 mi
0   100   200 km

SHETLAND ISLANDS

ORKNEY ISLANDS

ATLANTIC OCEAN

SCOTLAND

North Sea

NORTHERN IRELAND

ISLE OF MAN (Britain)

Dublin

Irish Sea

IRELAND

UNITED KINGDOM

Celtic Sea

WALES

ENGLAND

London

Isle of Wight

BELGIUM

English Channel

CHANNEL ISLANDS

FRANCE

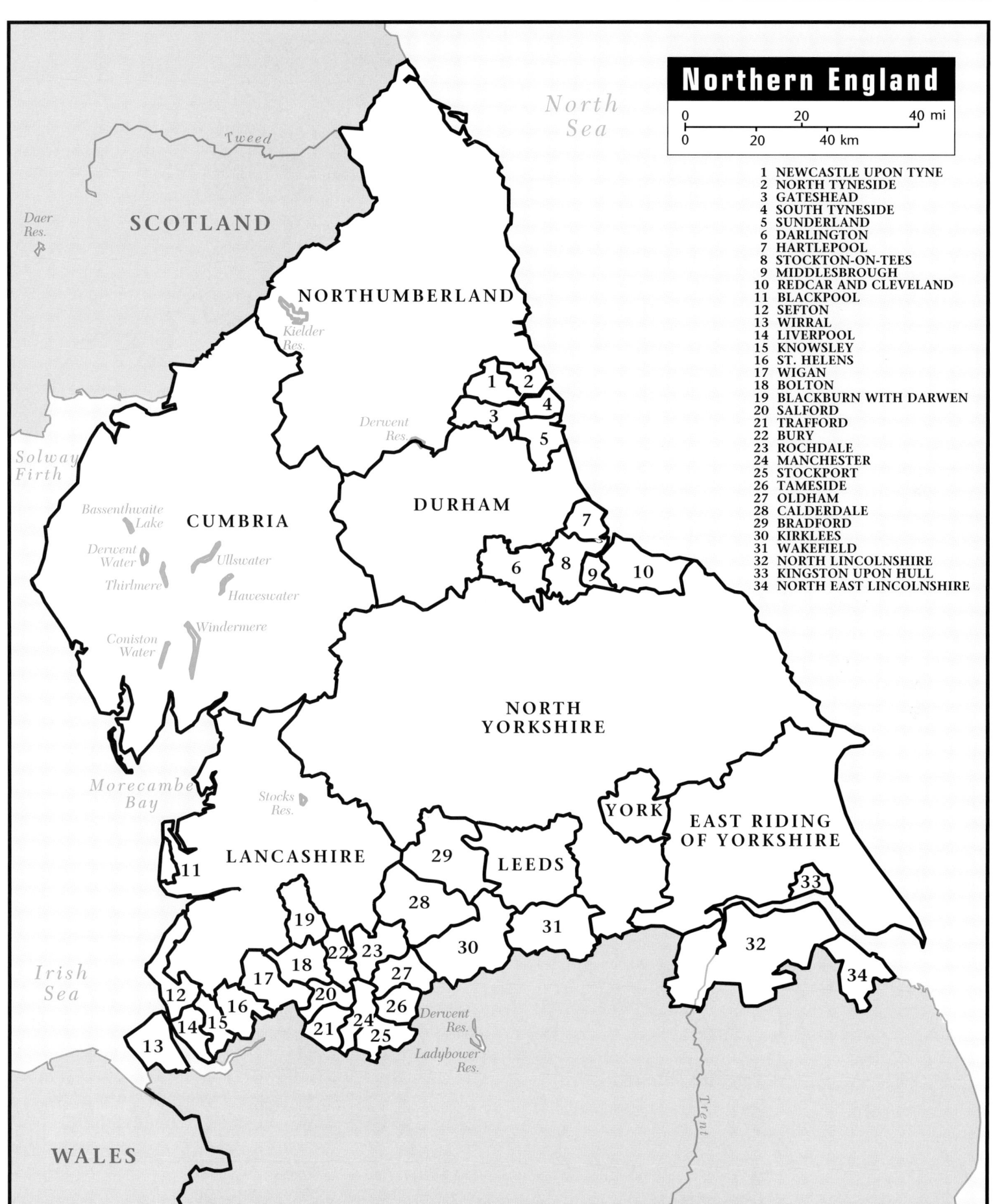

Northern England

0   20   40 mi
0   20   40 km

1   NEWCASTLE UPON TYNE
2   NORTH TYNESIDE
3   GATESHEAD
4   SOUTH TYNESIDE
5   SUNDERLAND
6   DARLINGTON
7   HARTLEPOOL
8   STOCKTON-ON-TEES
9   MIDDLESBROUGH
10 REDCAR AND CLEVELAND
11 BLACKPOOL
12 SEFTON
13 WIRRAL
14 LIVERPOOL
15 KNOWSLEY
16 ST. HELENS
17 WIGAN
18 BOLTON
19 BLACKBURN WITH DARWEN
20 SALFORD
21 TRAFFORD
22 BURY
23 ROCHDALE
24 MANCHESTER
25 STOCKPORT
26 TAMESIDE
27 OLDHAM
28 CALDERDALE
29 BRADFORD
30 KIRKLEES
31 WAKEFIELD
32 NORTH LINCOLNSHIRE
33 KINGSTON UPON HULL
34 NORTH EAST LINCOLNSHIRE

SCOTLAND

North Sea

Daer Res.

Tweed

NORTHUMBERLAND

Kielder Res.

Solway Firth

Derwent Res.

CUMBRIA

Bassenthwaite Lake

Derwent Water

Thirlmere

Ullswater

Haweswater

Coniston Water

Windermere

DURHAM

Morecambe Bay

Stocks Res.

LANCASHIRE

Irish Sea

NORTH YORKSHIRE

YORK

EAST RIDING OF YORKSHIRE

LEEDS

Derwent Res.

Ladybower Res.

WALES

Trent

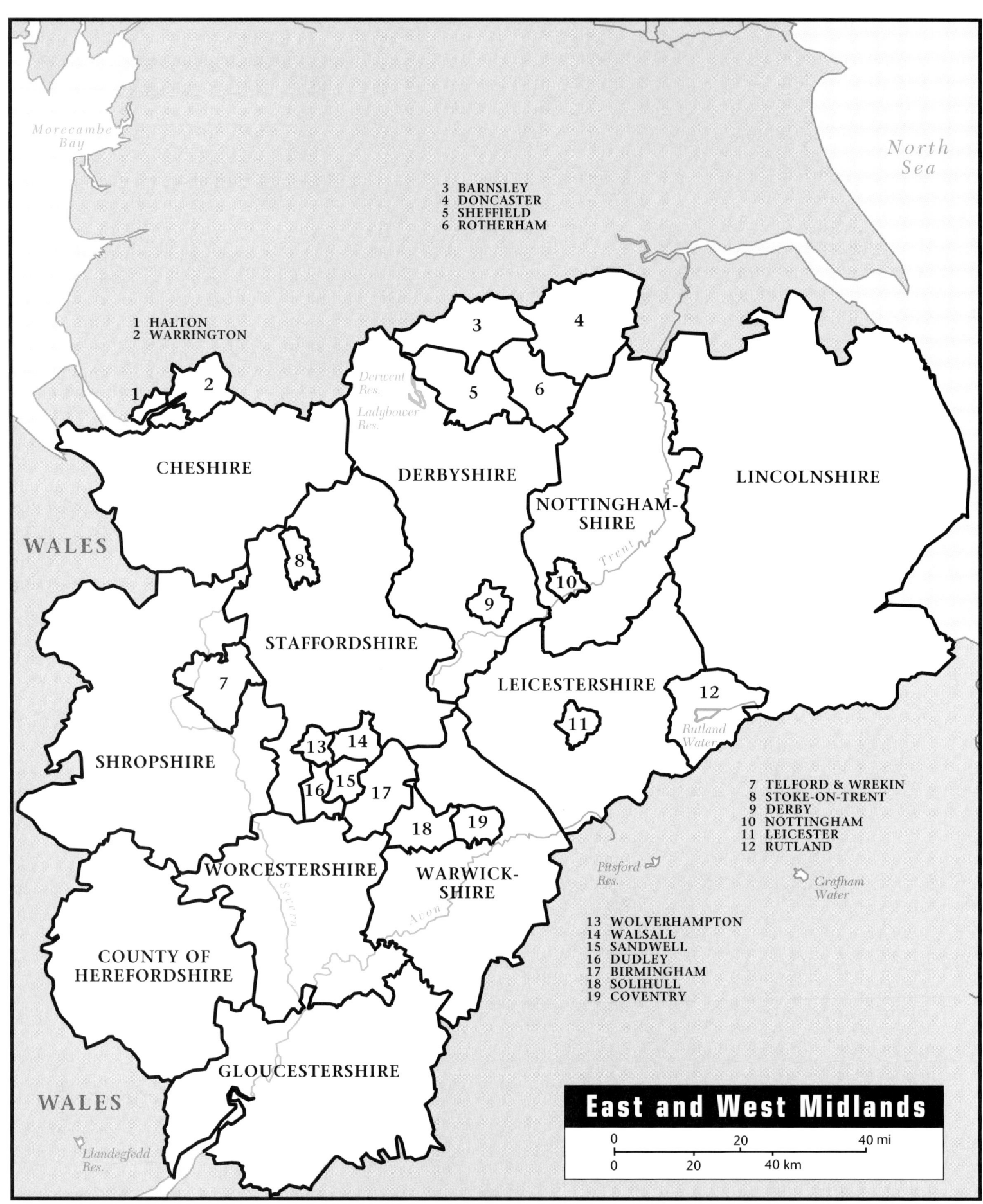

Morecambe Bay

North Sea

3 BARNSLEY
4 DONCASTER
5 SHEFFIELD
6 ROTHERHAM

1 HALTON
2 WARRINGTON

CHESHIRE

WALES

Derwent Res.

Ladybower Res.

DERBYSHIRE

LINCOLNSHIRE

NOTTINGHAM-
SHIRE

Trent

STAFFORDSHIRE

SHROPSHIRE

LEICESTERSHIRE

Rutland Water

7 TELFORD & WREKIN
8 STOKE-ON-TRENT
9 DERBY
10 NOTTINGHAM
11 LEICESTER
12 RUTLAND

Pitsford Res.

Grafham Water

WORCESTERSHIRE

WARWICK-
SHIRE

Severn

Avon

13 WOLVERHAMPTON
14 WALSALL
15 SANDWELL
16 DUDLEY
17 BIRMINGHAM
18 SOLIHULL
19 COVENTRY

COUNTY OF
HEREFORDSHIRE

GLOUCESTERSHIRE

WALES

Llandegfedd Res.

East and West Midlands

0   20   40 mi

0   20   40 km

1 PETERBOROUGH
2 MILTON KEYNES
3 LUTON
4 READING
5 WOKINGHAM
6 WINDSOR AND MAIDENHEAD
7 BRACKNELL FOREST
8 SLOUGH

The Wash

Rutland Water

Eyebrook Res.

NORFOLK

Great Ouse

1

Pitsford Res.

CAMBRIDGESHIRE

Grafham Water

SUFFOLK

NORTHAMPTON-SHIRE

2

BEDFORD-SHIRE

3

Abberton Res.

BUCKINGHAM-SHIRE

HERTFORD-SHIRE

ESSEX

OXFORDSHIRE

9 THURROCK
10 SOUTHEND-ON-SEA
11 MEDWAY

8

SEE PAGE 68
FOR THE SUBDIVISION
London

OF
GREATER
LONDON

9

10

Thames

6

11

4

WEST
BERKSHIRE

5

7

Medway

HAMPSHIRE

SURREY

KENT

Strait of Dover

12

WEST
SUSSEX

EAST
SUSSEX

13

14

12 SOUTHAMPTON
13 PORTSMOUTH
14 BRIGHTON AND HOVE

ISLE OF
WIGHT

English Channel

Southeastern England

0   20   40 mi
0   20   40 km

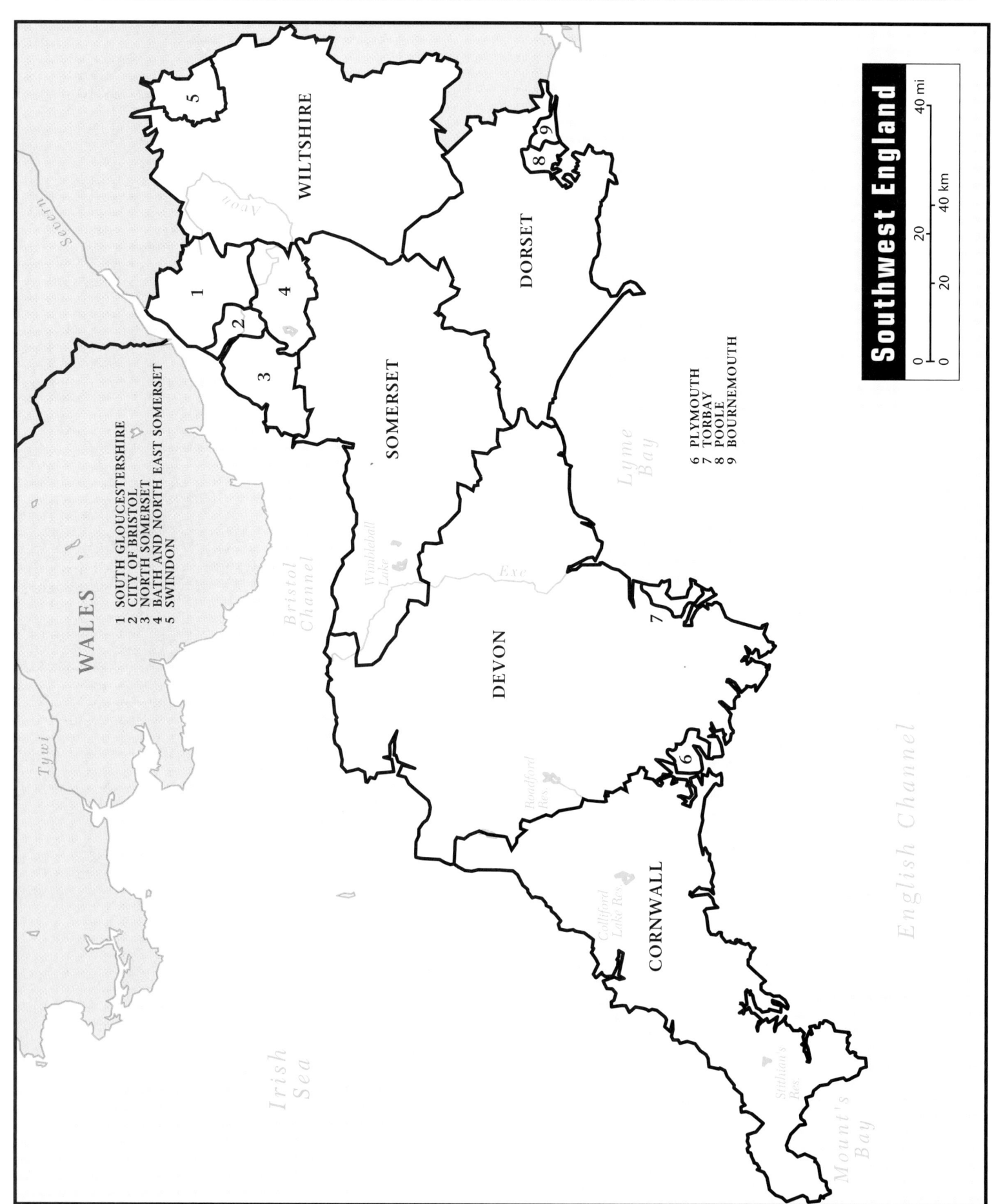

Southwest England

WALES

1 SOUTH GLOUCESTERSHIRE
2 CITY OF BRISTOL
3 NORTH SOMERSET
4 BATH AND NORTH EAST SOMERSET
5 SWINDON

6 PLYMOUTH
7 TORBAY
8 POOLE
9 BOURNEMOUTH

WILTSHIRE

DORSET

SOMERSET

DEVON

CORNWALL

Severn

Tywi

Irish Sea

Bristol Channel

Avon

Wimbleball Lake

Exe

Roadford Res.

Colliford Lake Res.

Stithian's Res.

Lyme Bay

English Channel

Mount's Bay

40 mi

40 km

20

20

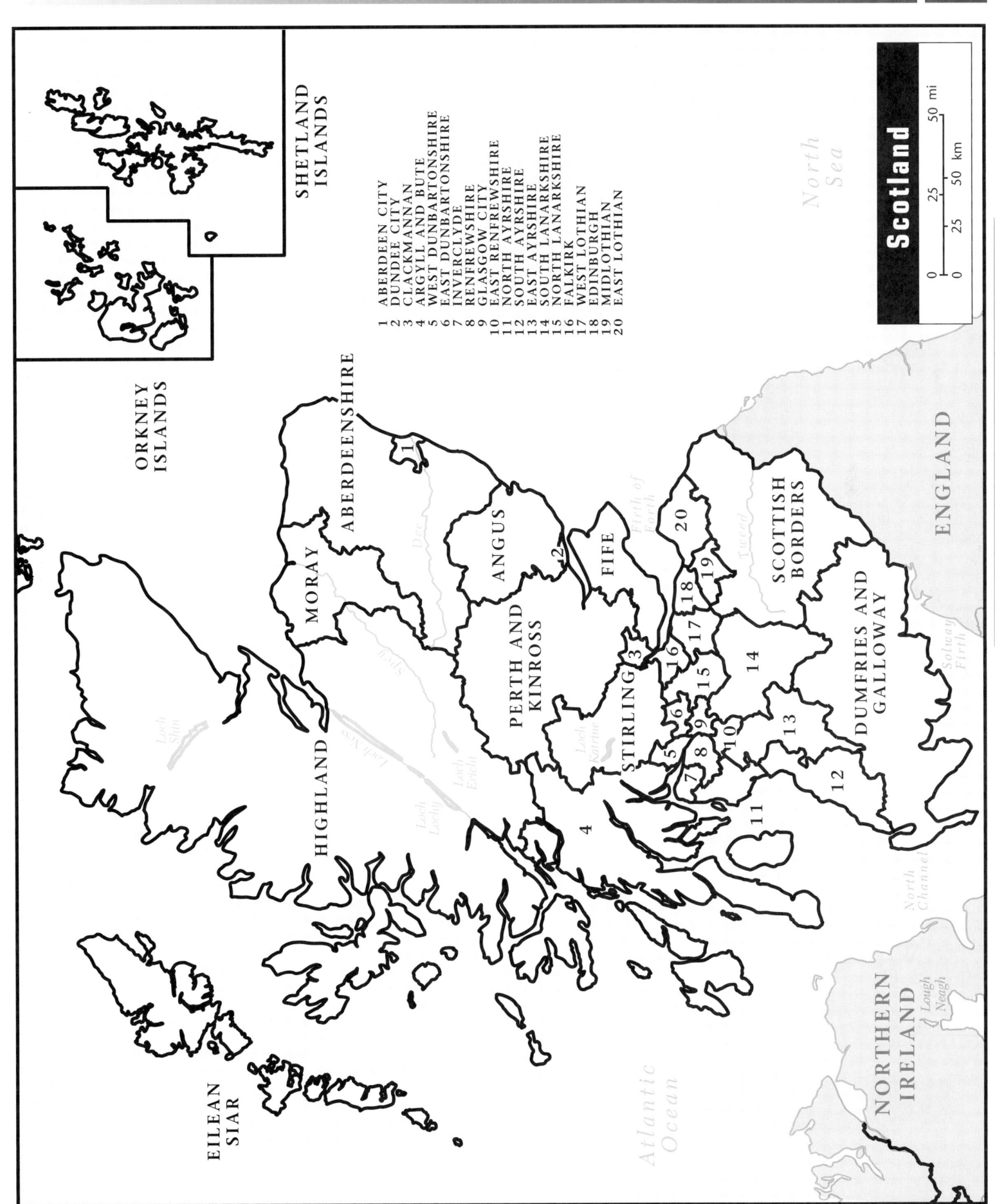

SHETLAND ISLANDS

ORKNEY ISLANDS

1 ABERDEEN CITY
2 DUNDEE CITY
3 CLACKMANNAN
4 ARGYLL AND BUTE
5 WEST DUNBARTONSHIRE
6 EAST DUNBARTONSHIRE
7 INVERCLYDE
8 RENFREWSHIRE
9 GLASGOW CITY
10 EAST RENFREWSHIRE
11 NORTH AYRSHIRE
12 SOUTH AYRSHIRE
13 EAST AYRSHIRE
14 SOUTH LANARKSHIRE
15 NORTH LANARKSHIRE
16 FALKIRK
17 WEST LOTHIAN
18 EDINBURGH
19 MIDLOTHIAN
20 EAST LOTHIAN

Scotland

50 mi
25
50 km
25

North Sea

ABERDEENSHIRE

MORAY

HIGHLAND

ANGUS

Dee

FIFE

Firth of Forth

Tweed

SCOTTISH BORDERS

ENGLAND

PERTH AND KINROSS

2

20
19
18
17
16
15

3
STIRLING

Loch Katrine

Loch Ericht

Loch Lochy

Loch Ness

Loch Shin

4

5 6 7 8 9 10
11

13
14

12

DUMFRIES AND GALLOWAY

Solway Firth

North Channel

NORTHERN IRELAND

Lough Neagh

Atlantic Ocean

EILEAN SIAR

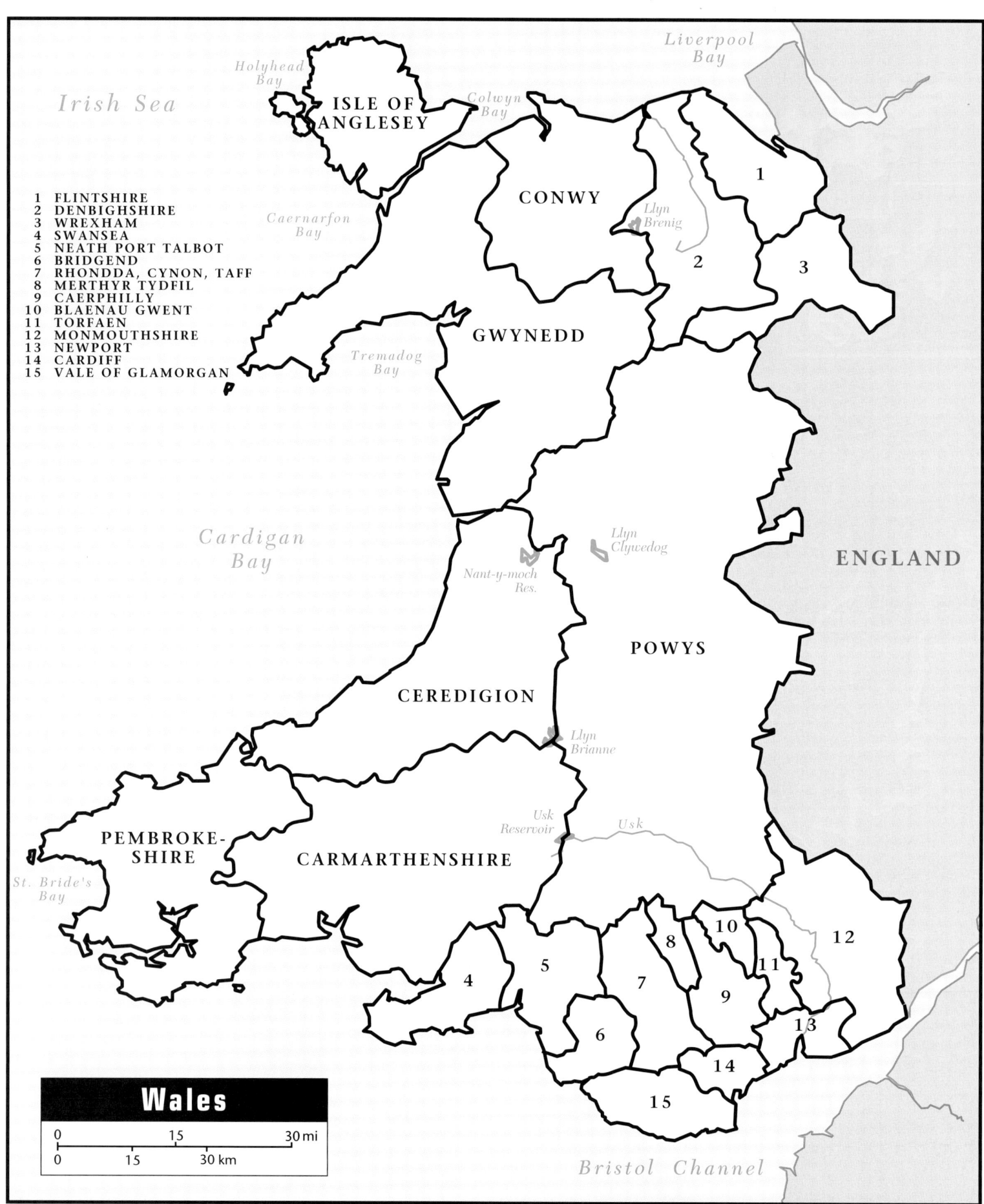

Irish Sea

Holyhead Bay

ISLE OF ANGLESEY

Colwyn Bay

Liverpool Bay

CONWY

Llyn Brenig

1

Caernarfon Bay

2

3

1 FLINTSHIRE
2 DENBIGHSHIRE
3 WREXHAM
4 SWANSEA
5 NEATH PORT TALBOT
6 BRIDGEND
7 RHONDDA, CYNON, TAFF
8 MERTHYR TYDFIL
9 CAERPHILLY
10 BLAENAU GWENT
11 TORFAEN
12 MONMOUTHSHIRE
13 NEWPORT
14 CARDIFF
15 VALE OF GLAMORGAN

GWYNEDD

Tremadog Bay

Cardigan Bay

Nant-y-moch Res.

Llyn Clywedog

ENGLAND

POWYS

CEREDIGION

Llyn Brianne

PEMBROKE-SHIRE

St. Bride's Bay

CARMARTHENSHIRE

Usk Reservoir

Usk

Usk

4

5

8

10

12

7

11

9

6

13

14

15

Wales

0   15   30 mi
0   15   30 km

Bristol Channel

1 LONDONDERRY
2 LIMAVADY
3 COLERAIN
4 BALLYMONEY
5 MAGHERAFELT
6 CARRICKFERGUS
7 NEWTOWNABBEY
8 BELFAST
9 NORTH DOWN
10 CASTLEREAGH
11 CRAIGAVON

SCOTLAND

Atlantic
Ocean

North
Channel

Lough
Foyle

MOYLE

3

2

4

1

BALLYMENA

STRABANE

5

LARNE

ANTRIM

7

6

Lough
Neagh

Lough
Derg

OMAGH

COOKSTOWN

8

9

ARDS

10

Lower
Lough
Erne

DUNGANNON

11

LISBURN

FERMANAGH

Blackwater

Strangford
Lough

Upper
Lough
Erne

ARMAGH

BANBRIDGE

DOWN

NEWRY
AND MOURNE

IRELAND

Irish Sea

Northern Ireland

0   15   30 mi

0   15   30 km

Belfast
Lough

Bann

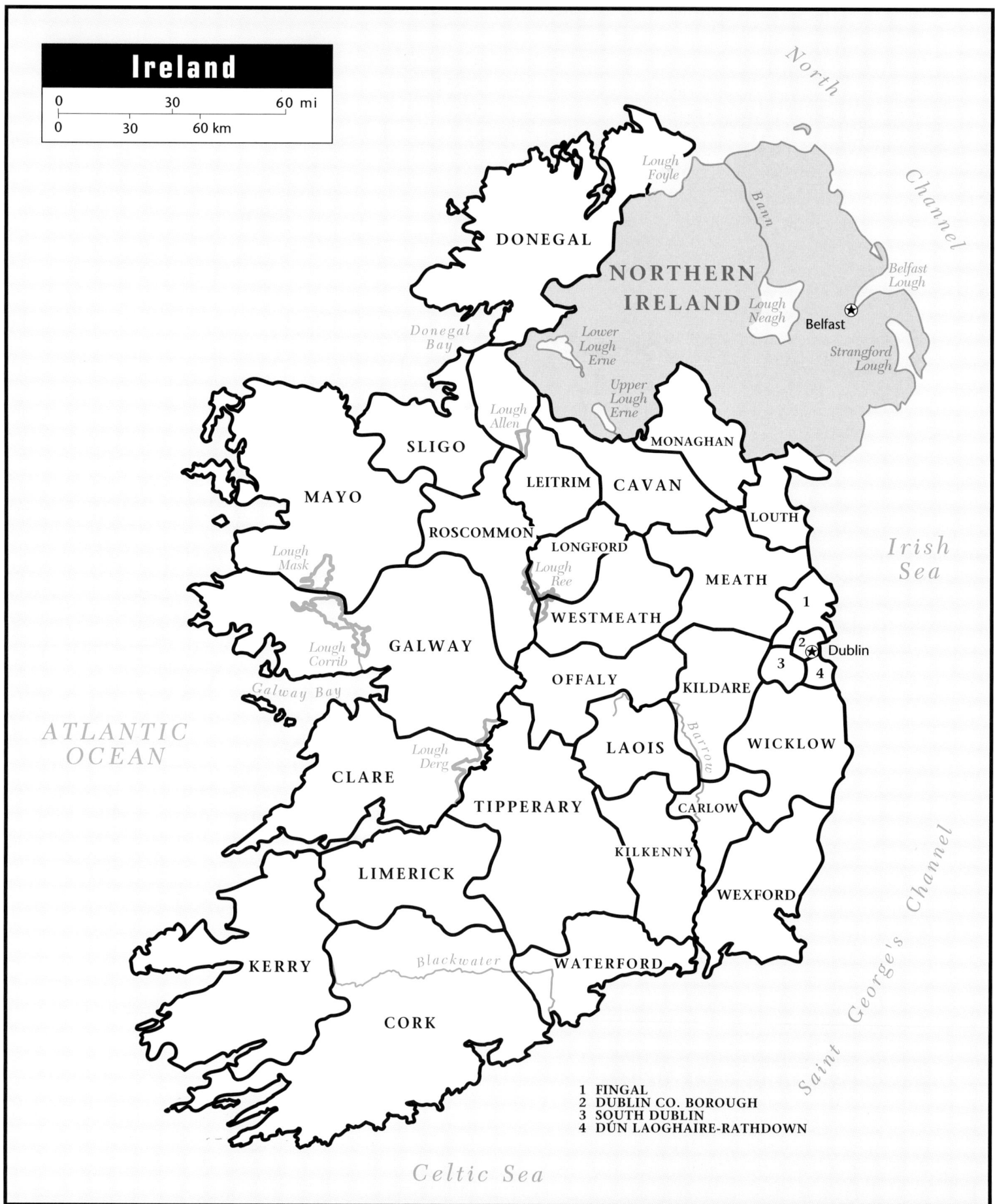

Ireland

0   30   60 mi
0 30 60 km

North Channel

Lough Foyle

DONEGAL

NORTHERN IRELAND

Bann

Belfast Lough

Lough Neagh

Belfast ★

Strangford Lough

Donegal Bay

Lower Lough Erne

Upper Lough Erne

MONAGHAN

Lough Allen

SLIGO

LEITRIM   CAVAN

LOUTH

MAYO

ROSCOMMON

LONGFORD

MEATH

Lough Mask

Lough Ree

1

Lough Corrib

GALWAY

WESTMEATH

2 ★ Dublin

3   4

Galway Bay

OFFALY

KILDARE

WICKLOW

ATLANTIC OCEAN

Lough Derg

LAOIS

Barrow

CLARE

TIPPERARY

CARLOW

LIMERICK

KILKENNY

WEXFORD

Irish Sea

Saint George's Channel

KERRY

Blackwater

WATERFORD

CORK

1 FINGAL
2 DUBLIN CO. BOROUGH
3 SOUTH DUBLIN
4 DÚN LAOGHAIRE-RATHDOWN

Celtic Sea

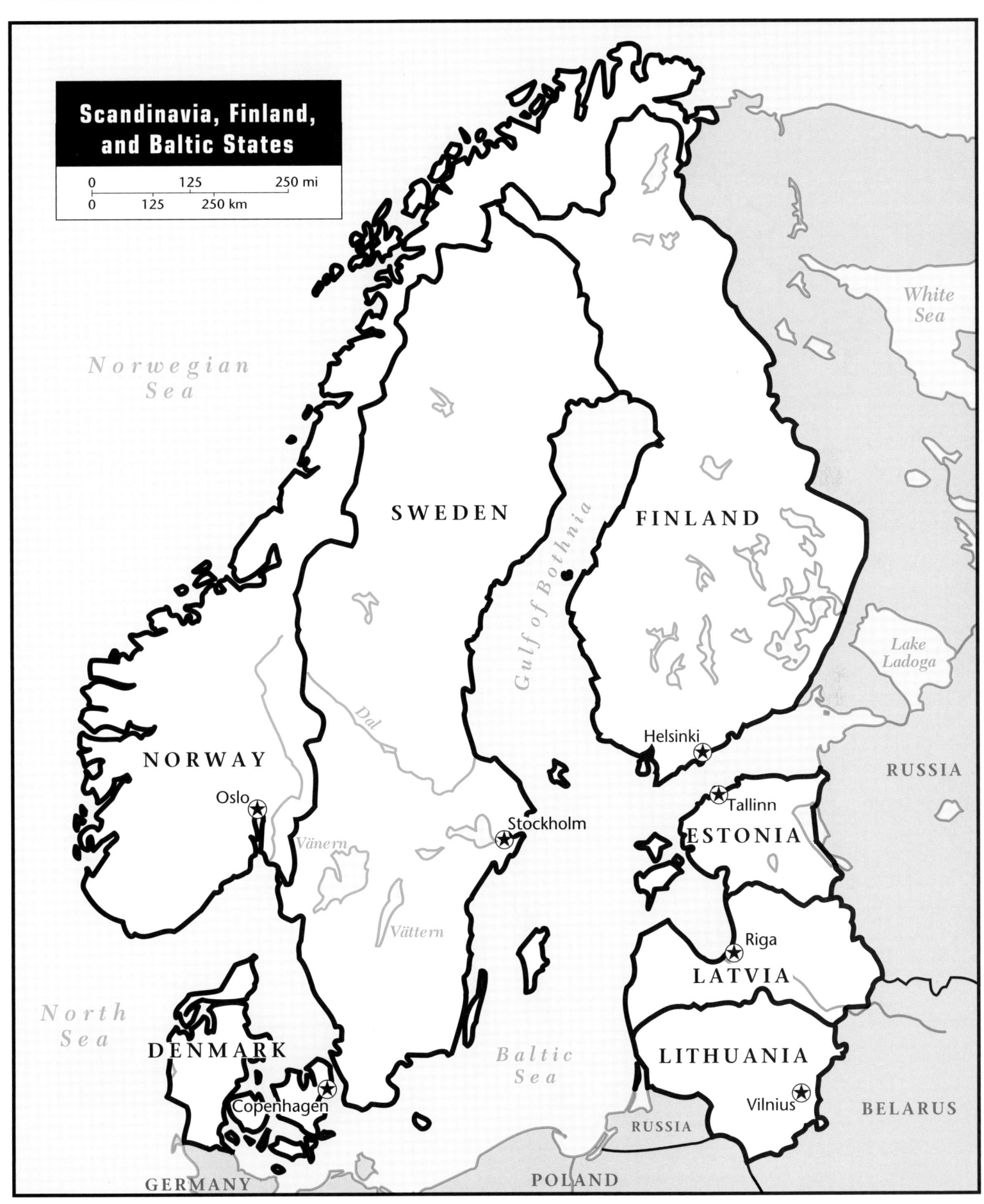

Scandinavia, Finland, and Baltic States

0   125   250 mi
0   125   250 km

Norwegian Sea

White Sea

SWEDEN

FINLAND

Gulf of Bothnia

Dal

RUSSIA

Lake Ladoga

NORWAY

Oslo

Helsinki

Vänern

Stockholm

Tallinn

ESTONIA

Vättern

Riga

LATVIA

North Sea

DENMARK

Baltic Sea

LITHUANIA

Copenhagen

Vilnius

BELARUS

RUSSIA

GERMANY

POLAND

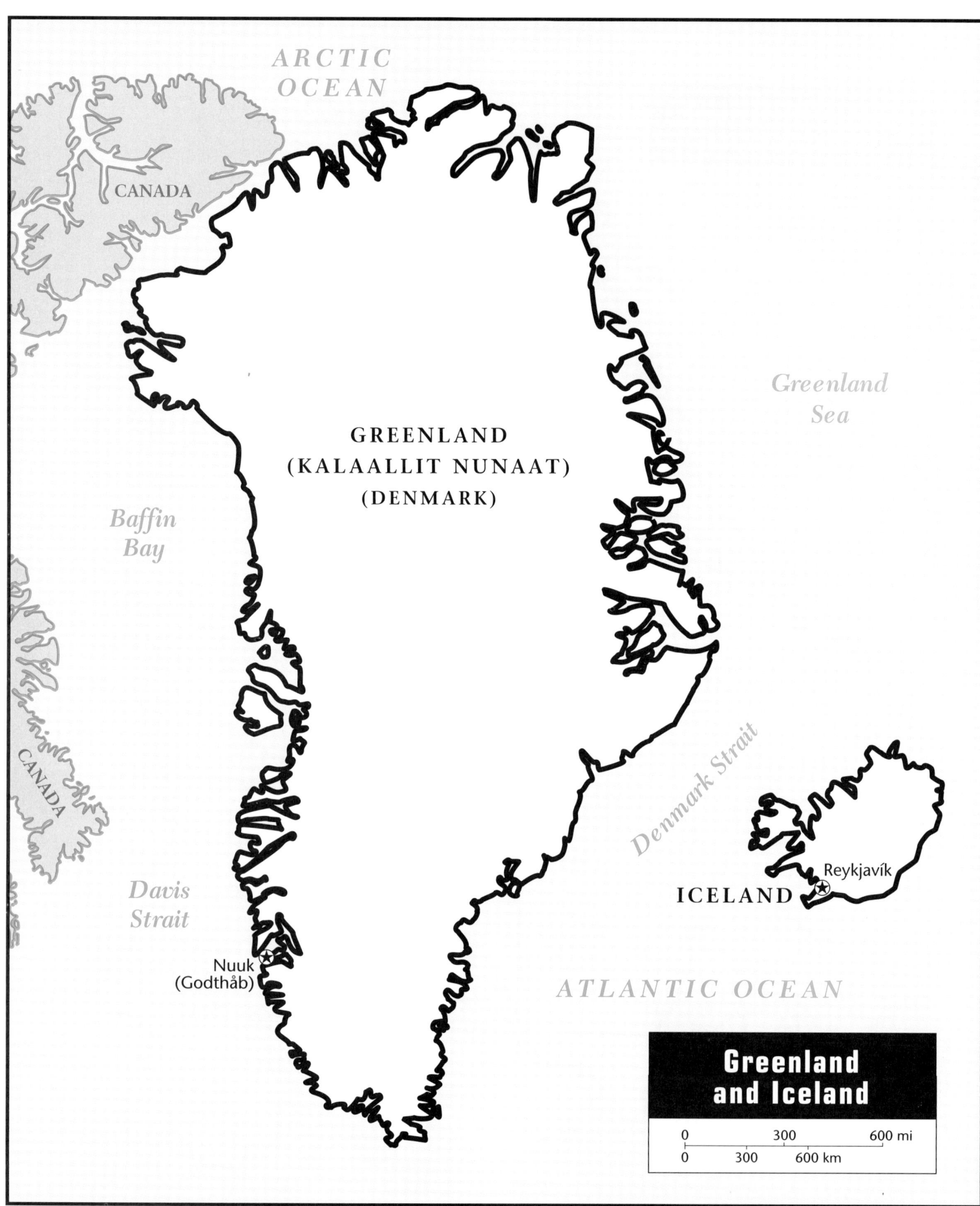

ARCTIC
OCEAN

CANADA

Greenland
Sea

GREENLAND
(KALAALLIT NUNAAT)
(DENMARK)

Baffin
Bay

CANADA

Denmark Strait

Davis
Strait

ICELAND   Reykjavík

Nuuk
(Godthåb)

ATLANTIC OCEAN

**Greenland
and Iceland**

| 0 | 300 | 600 mi |
| 0 | 300 | 600 km |

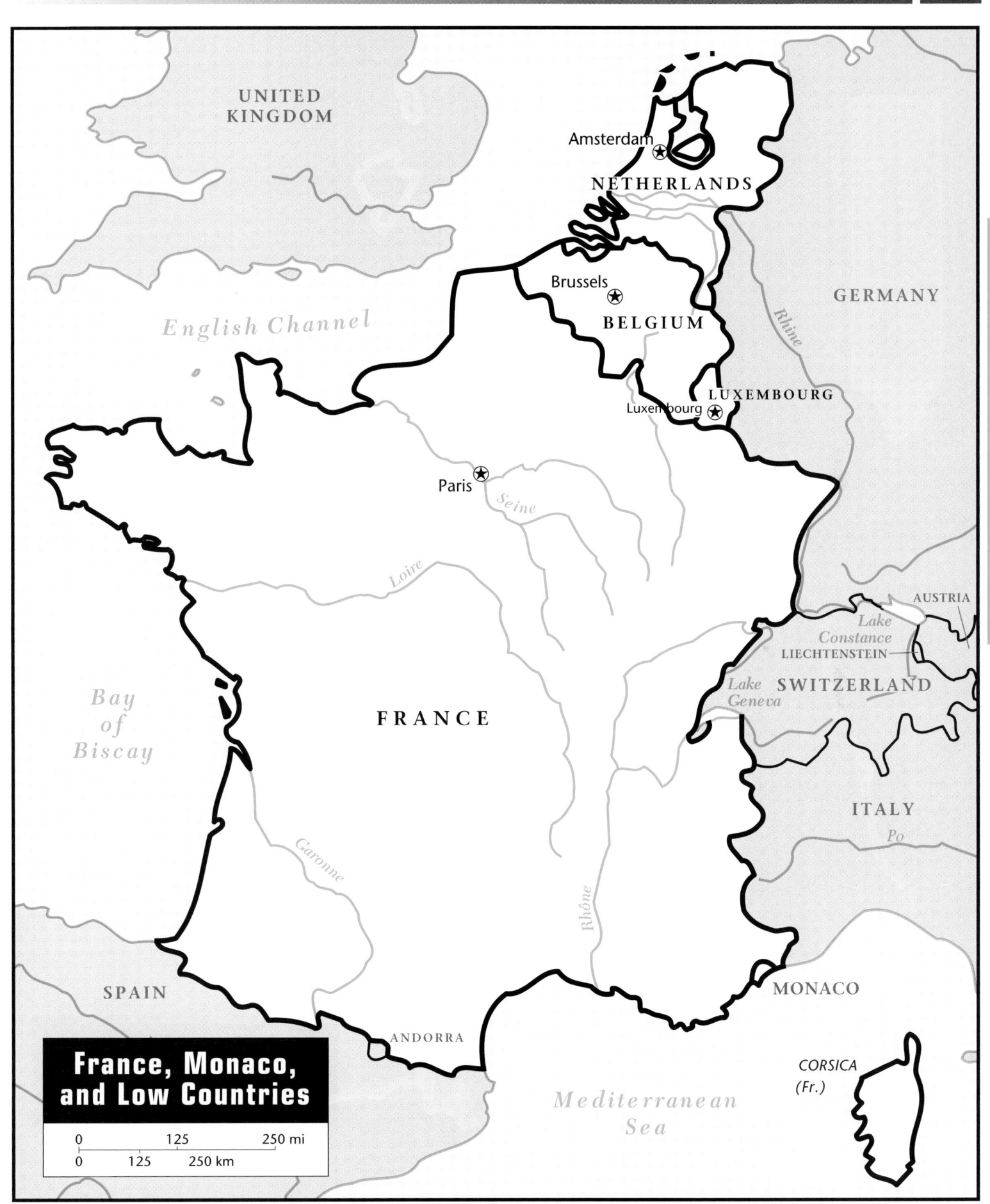

UNITED
KINGDOM

English Channel

Amsterdam ⭐

NETHERLANDS

Brussels ⭐

BELGIUM

GERMANY

Rhine

LUXEMBOURG

Luxembourg ⭐

Paris ⭐

Seine

Loire

FRANCE

Bay
of
Biscay

Garonne

Rhône

AUSTRIA

Lake
Constance

LIECHTENSTEIN

SWITZERLAND

Lake
Geneva

ITALY

Po

SPAIN

ANDORRA

MONACO

Mediterranean
Sea

CORSICA
(Fr.)

**France, Monaco,
and Low Countries**

| 0 | 125 | 250 mi |
| 0 | 125 | 250 km |

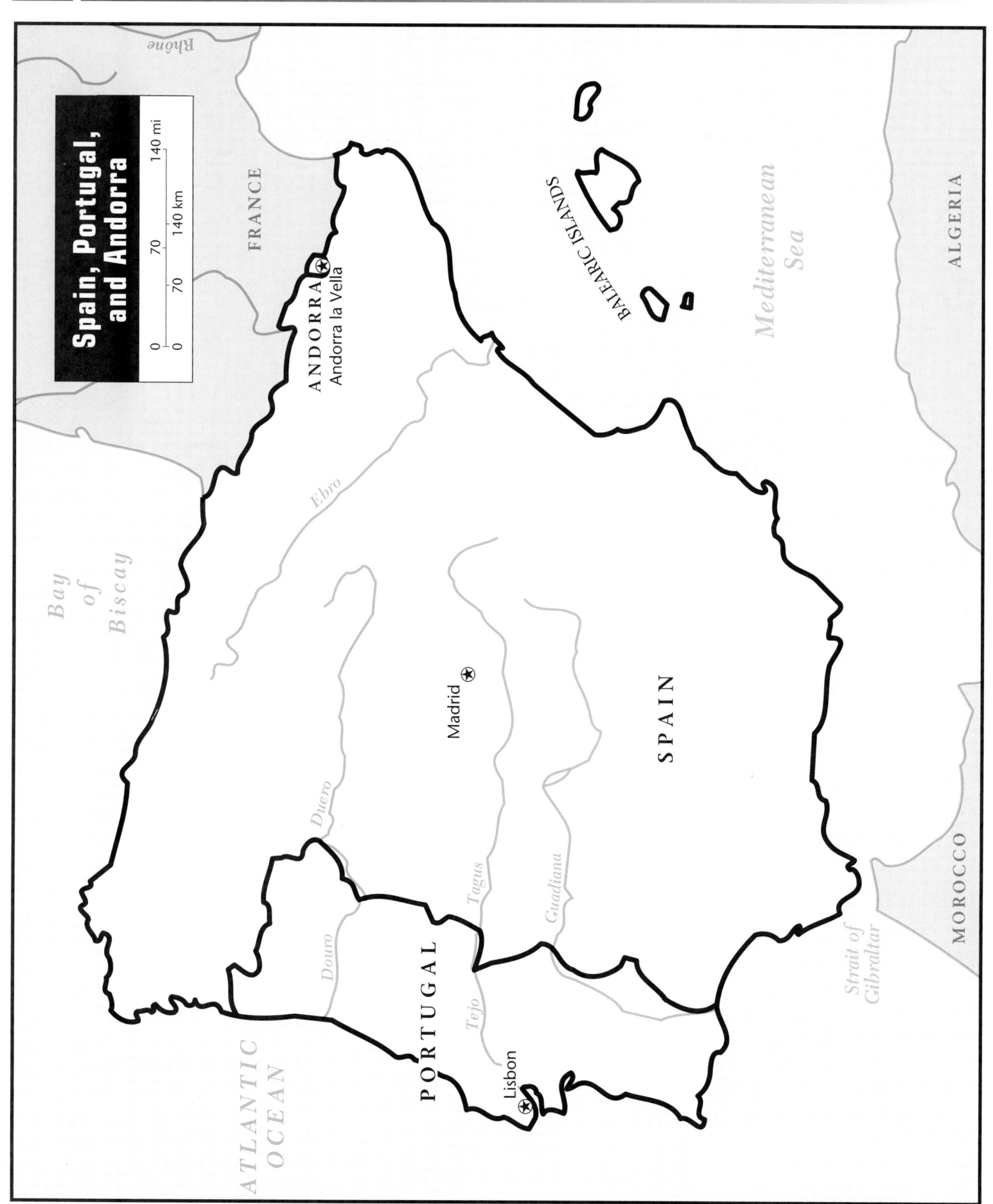

Spain, Portugal, and Andorra

140 mi

140 km

70

70

0

0

Rhône

FRANCE

ANDORRA
Andorra la Vella

BALEARIC ISLANDS

Mediterranean Sea

ALGERIA

Bay of Biscay

Ebro

Madrid

SPAIN

MOROCCO

Duero

ATLANTIC OCEAN

Douro

PORTUGAL

Tejo

Tagus

Guadiana

Lisbon

Strait of Gibraltar

North Sea

DENMARK

Baltic Sea

Central Europe

0   100   200 mi

0   100   200 km

Elbe

NETHERLANDS

⊛ Berlin

POLAND

Vistula

Oder

BELGIUM

GERMANY

Rhine

LUXEMBOURG

CZECH
REPUBLIC

Danube

SLOVAKIA

FRANCE

*Lake
Constance*

Vienna

⊛

Bern
⊛

Vaduz ⊛ LIECHTENSTEIN

AUSTRIA

*Lake
Balaton*

SWITZERLAND

*Lake
Geneva*

HUNGARY

ITALY

SLOVENIA

CROATIA

Poland, Czech. Rep., Slovakia and Hungary

0 275 550 mi
0 275 550 km

Baltic Sea

LITHUANIA

RUSSIA

BELARUS

Elbe

GERMANY

Oder

Vistula

Bug

Warsaw

POLAND

UKRAINE

Prague

CZECH REP.

SLOVAKIA

Danube

Bratislava

Tisza

Budapest

HUNGARY

AUSTRIA

Lake Balaton

ROMANIA

ITALY

SLOVENIA

CROATIA

SERBIA & MONTE.

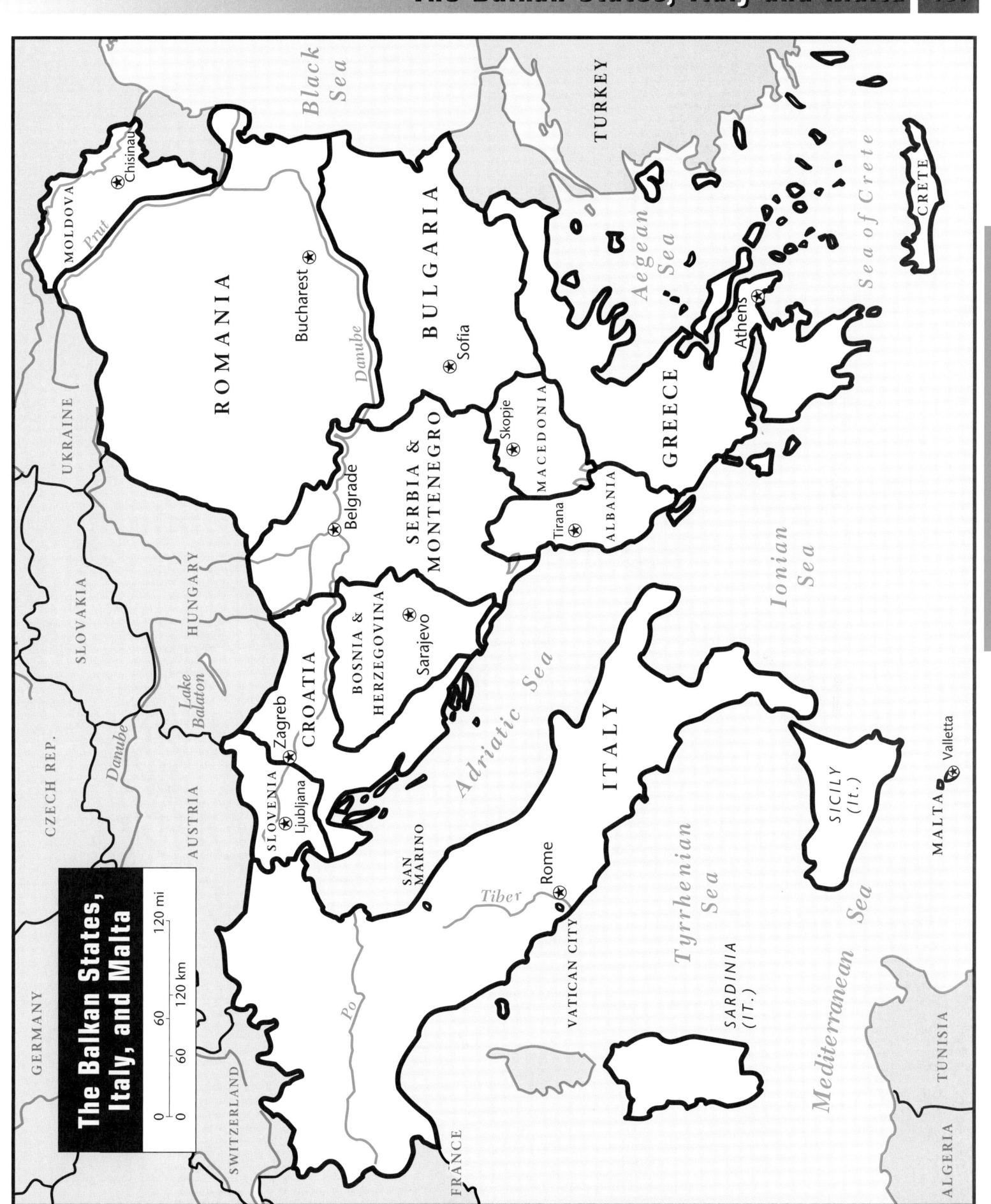

The Balkan States, Italy, and Malta

120 mi

120 km

60

60

0

0

GERMANY

CZECH REP.

SLOVAKIA

UKRAINE

MOLDOVA

Chisinau

Prut

Danube

ROMANIA

Bucharest

Black Sea

BULGARIA

Sofia

TURKEY

Aegean Sea

Sea of Crete

CRETE

Athens

GREECE

Skopje

MACEDONIA

SERBIA & MONTENEGRO

Belgrade

Tirana

ALBANIA

HUNGARY

Lake Balaton

Danube

AUSTRIA

SLOVAKIA

BOSNIA & HERZEGOVINA

Sarajevo

CROATIA

Zagreb

SLOVENIA

Ljubljana

SAN MARINO

Adriatic Sea

Ionian Sea

ITALY

Po

Tiber

Rome

VATICAN CITY

Tyrrhenian Sea

SARDINIA (IT.)

SICILY (IT.)

MALTA

Valletta

Mediterranean Sea

SWITZERLAND

FRANCE

TUNISIA

ALGERIA

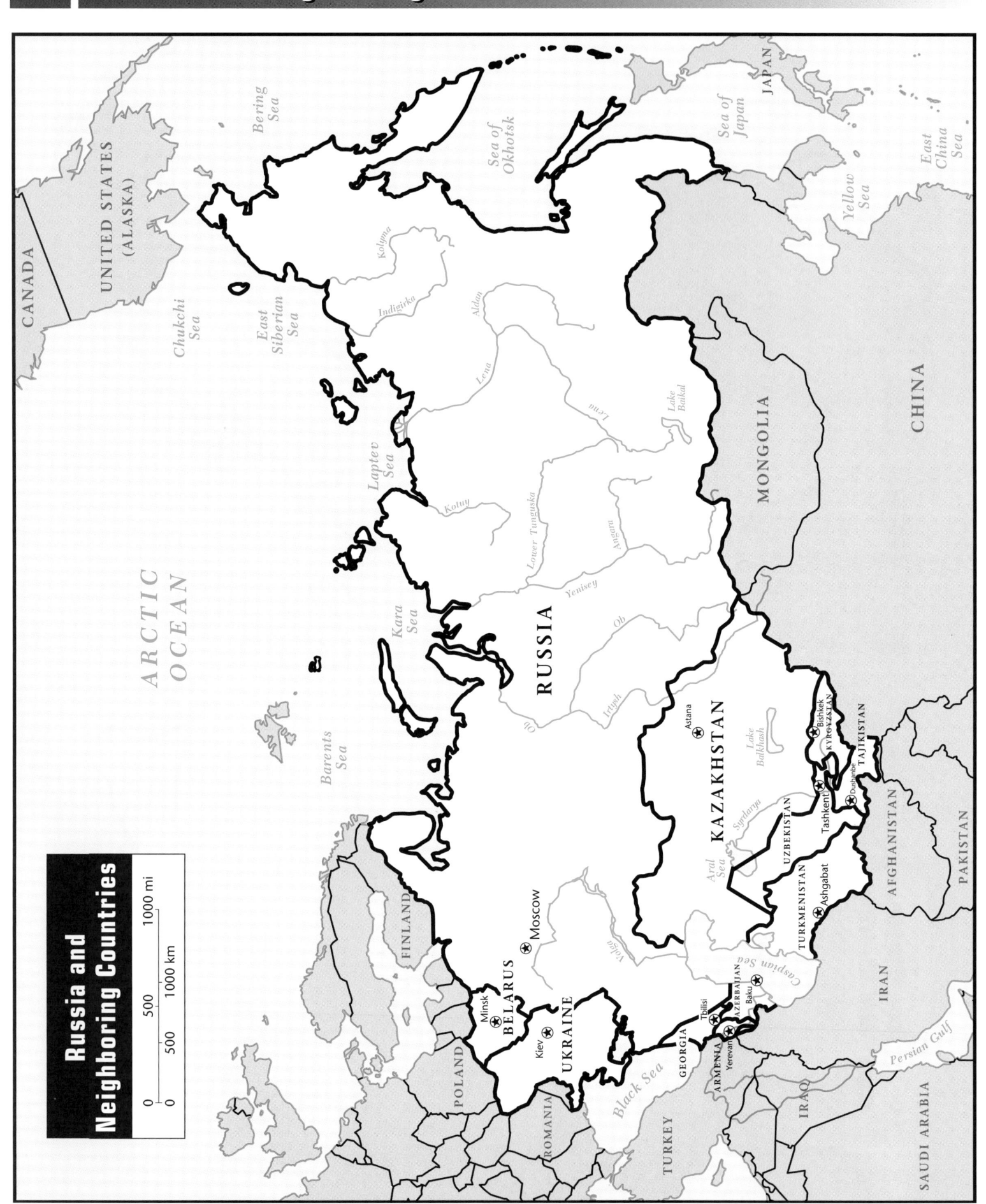

Russia and Neighboring Countries

0	500		1000 mi
0	500	1000 km	

CANADA

UNITED STATES (ALASKA)

Bering Sea

Chukchi Sea

East Siberian Sea

Kolyma

Indigirka

Aldon

Lena

Sea of Okhotsk

Sea of Japan

JAPAN

Yellow Sea

East China Sea

Laptev Sea

Kotuy

Lena

Lower Tunguska

Angara

Lake Baikal

MONGOLIA

CHINA

ARCTIC OCEAN

Kara Sea

Yenisey

Ob

RUSSIA

Irtish

Astana

KAZAKHSTAN

Lake Balkhash

Bishkek

KYRGYZSTAN

TAJIKISTAN

Dushanbe

AFGHANISTAN

PAKISTAN

Barents Sea

Ob

Tashkent

UZBEKISTAN

Syrdarya

Aral Sea

TURKMENISTAN

Ashgabat

IRAN

FINLAND

Moscow

Volga

Caspian Sea

AZERBAIJAN

Baku

Yerevan

ARMENIA

GEORGIA

Tbilisi

IRAQ

Minsk

BELARUS

Kiev

UKRAINE

Black Sea

TURKEY

POLAND

ROMANIA

SAUDI ARABIA

Persian Gulf

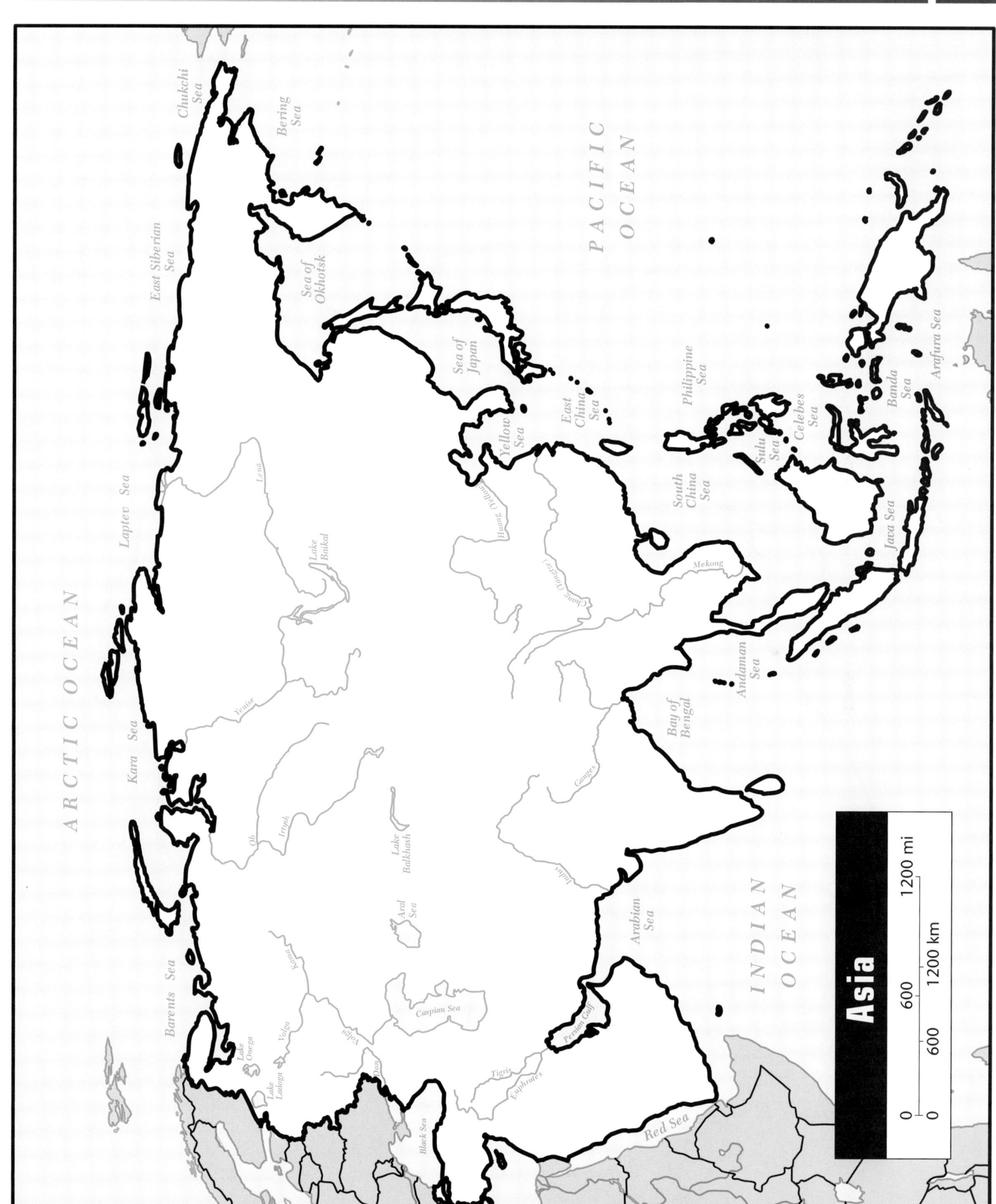

ARCTIC OCEAN

PACIFIC OCEAN

INDIAN OCEAN

Chukchi Sea

Bering Sea

East Siberian Sea

Sea of Okhotsk

Laptev Sea

Sea of Japan

East China Sea

Philippine Sea

Banda Sea

Arafura Sea

Yellow Sea

Sulu Sea

Celebes Sea

Kara Sea

South China Sea

Java Sea

Lena

Lake Baikal

Huang (Yellow)

Chang (Yangtze)

Mekong

Andaman Sea

Yenisei

Bay of Bengal

Barents Sea

Ob

Irtysh

Lake Balkhash

Ganges

Indus

Arabian Sea

Kama

Aral Sea

Lake Onega

Volga

Caspian Sea

Persian Gulf

Lake Ladoga

Volga

Don

Tigris

Euphrates

Black Sea

Red Sea

Asia

1200 mi

600   1200 km

600

0

0   600

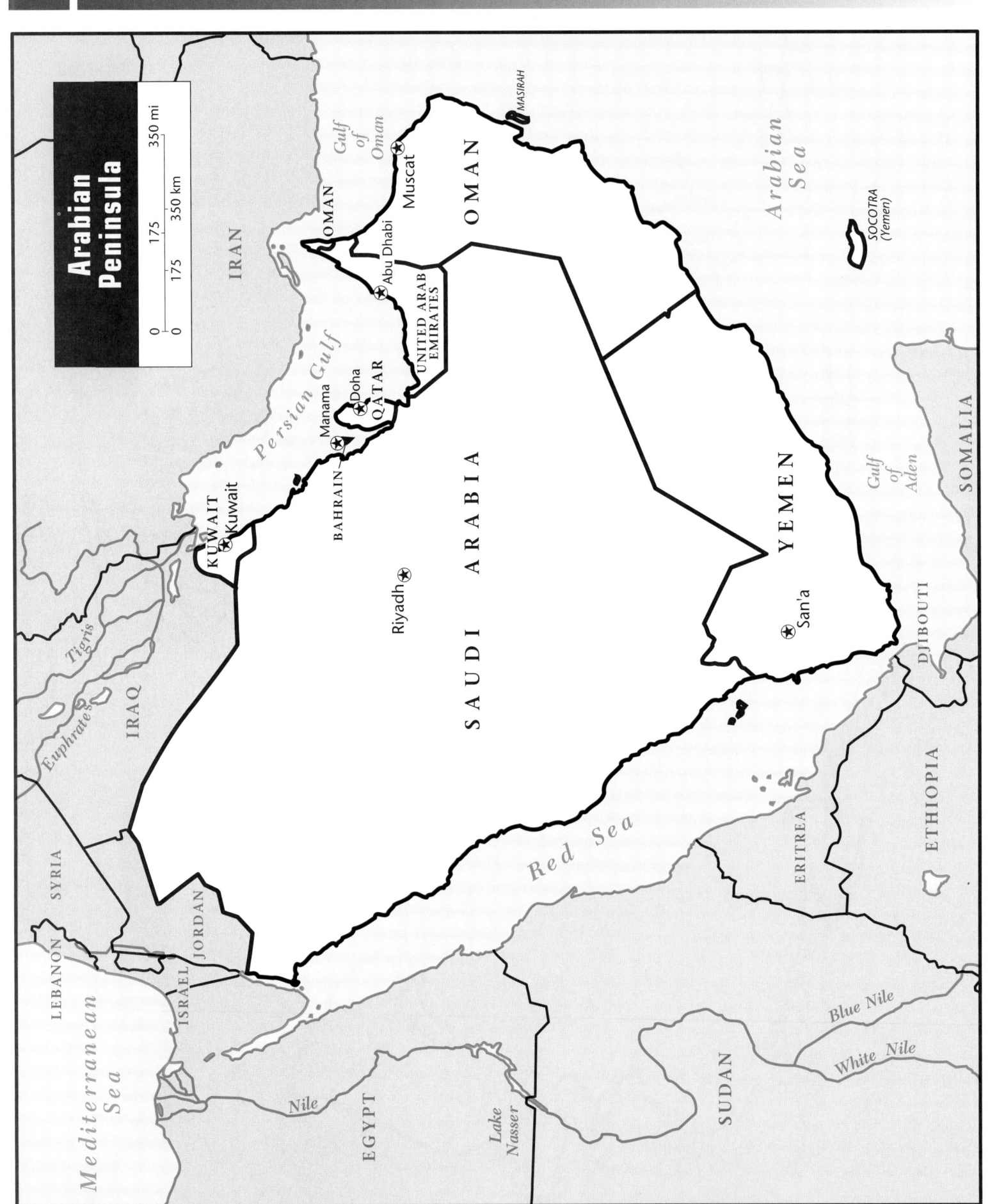

Arabian Peninsula

0	175	350 km	
0	175	350 mi	

IRAN

OMAN

Gulf of Oman

MASIRAH

Muscat

OMAN

Arabian Sea

SOCOTRA (Yemen)

Abu Dhabi

UNITED ARAB EMIRATES

Persian Gulf

Doha QATAR

Manama

BAHRAIN

SAUDI ARABIA

Riyadh

YEMEN

Gulf of Aden

San'a

DJIBOUTI

SOMALIA

KUWAIT

Kuwait

Tigris

Euphrates

IRAQ

SYRIA

LEBANON

ISRAEL

JORDAN

Mediterranean Sea

Red Sea

ERITREA

ETHIOPIA

EGYPT

Nile

Lake Nasser

SUDAN

Blue Nile

White Nile

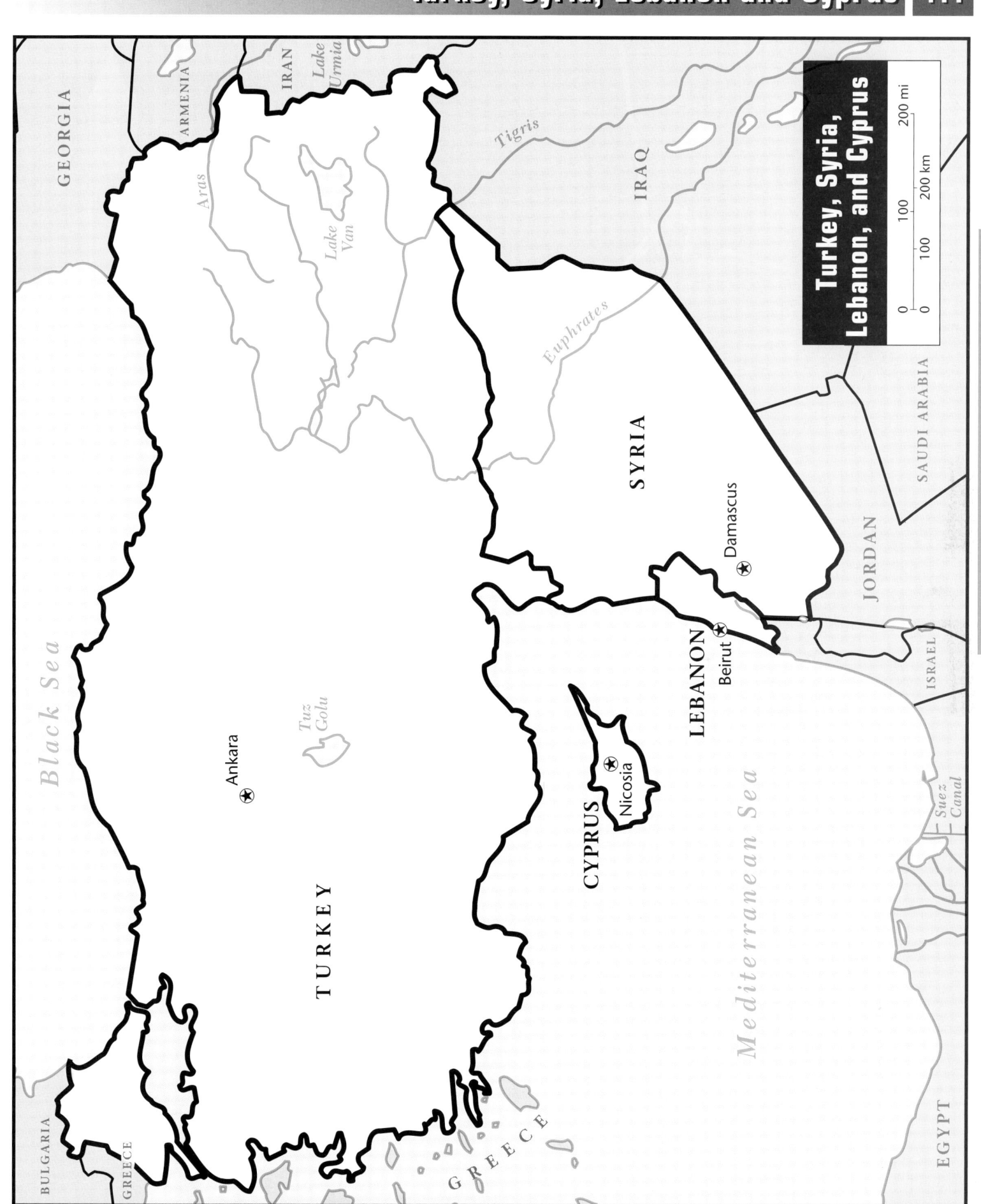

Turkey, Syria, Lebanon, and Cyprus

200 mi
200 km

BULGARIA

GEORGIA

ARMENIA

IRAN

Lake Urmia

Tigris

IRAQ

Aras

Lake Van

Euphrates

SYRIA

SAUDI ARABIA

Damascus

JORDAN

Black Sea

Tuz Golu

Ankara

TURKEY

LEBANON

Beirut

ISRAEL

CYPRUS

Nicosia

Mediterranean Sea

Suez Canal

GREECE

EGYPT

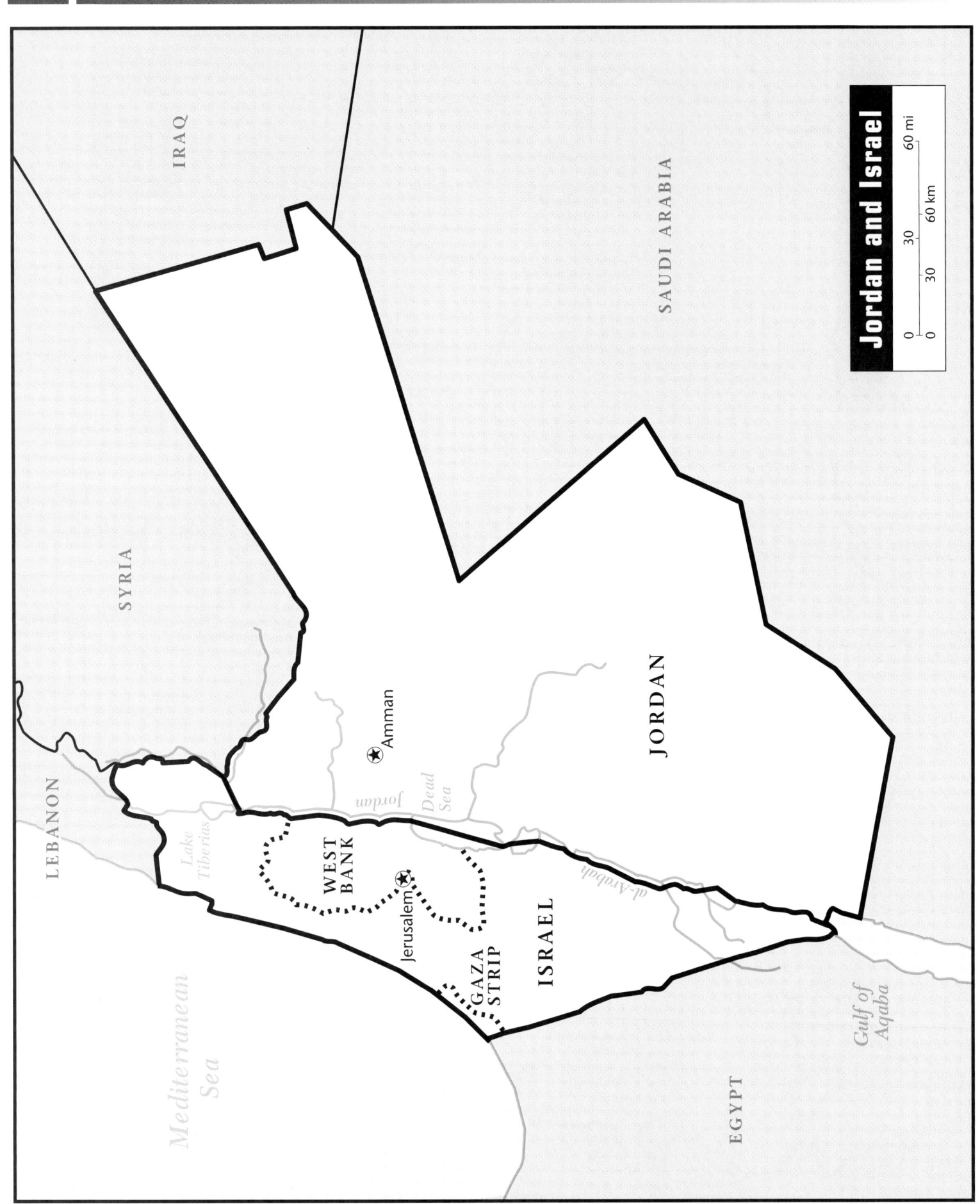

Jordan and Israel

IRAQ

SAUDI ARABIA

SYRIA

LEBANON

Mediterranean Sea

Amman

Lake Tiberias

Jordan

Dead Sea

WEST BANK

Jerusalem

GAZA STRIP

ISRAEL

JORDAN

al-ʿArabah

Gulf of Aqaba

EGYPT

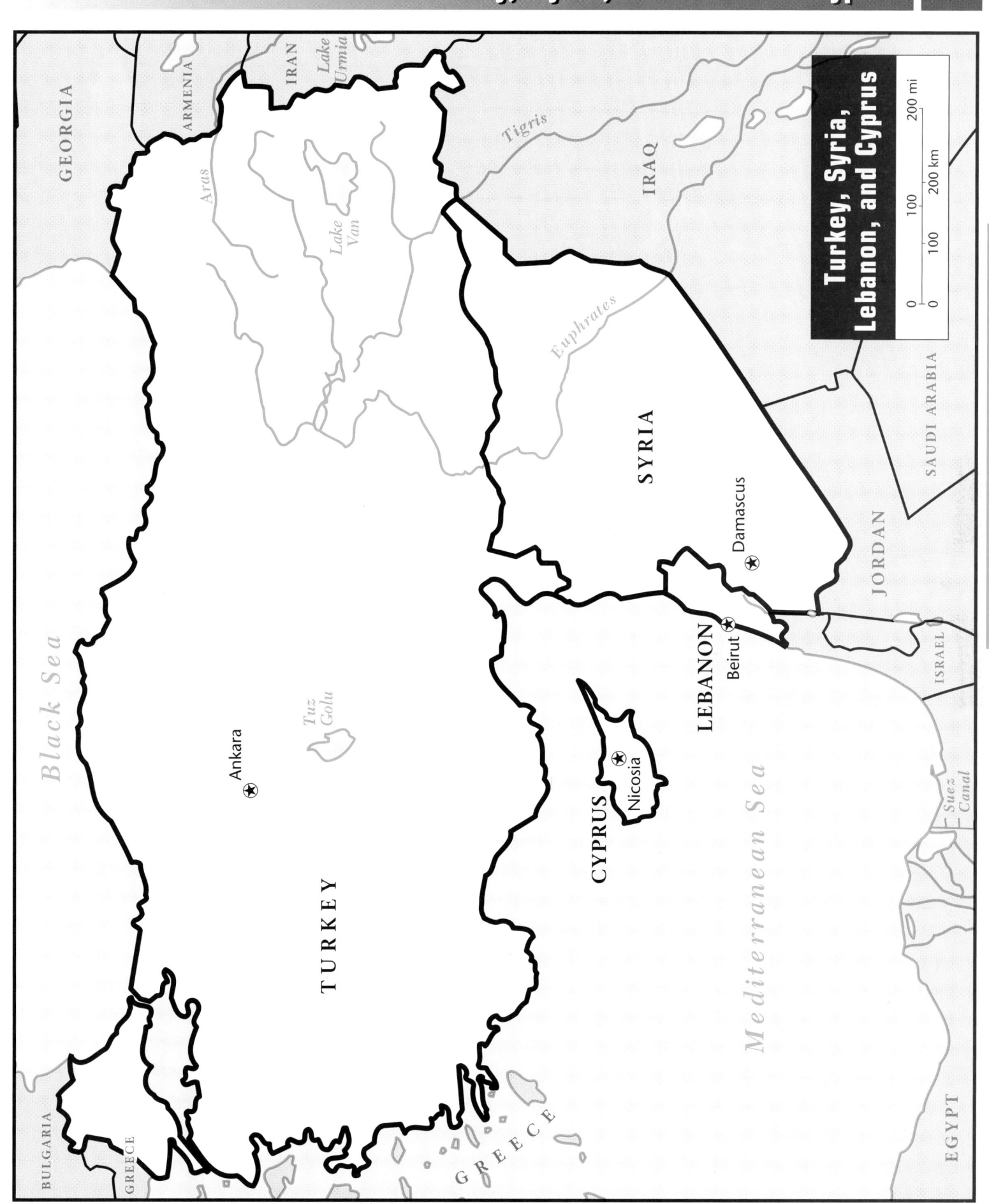

Turkey, Syria, Lebanon, and Cyprus

200 mi

200 km

GEORGIA

ARMENIA

IRAN

Lake Urmia

Aras

Lake Van

Tigris

IRAQ

Euphrates

SYRIA

SAUDI ARABIA

Damascus ✪

Black Sea

Tuz Golu

Ankara ✪

LEBANON

Beirut ✪

JORDAN

ISRAEL

Suez Canal

CYPRUS

Nicosia ✪

Mediterranean Sea

TURKEY

BULGARIA

GREECE

GREECE

EGYPT

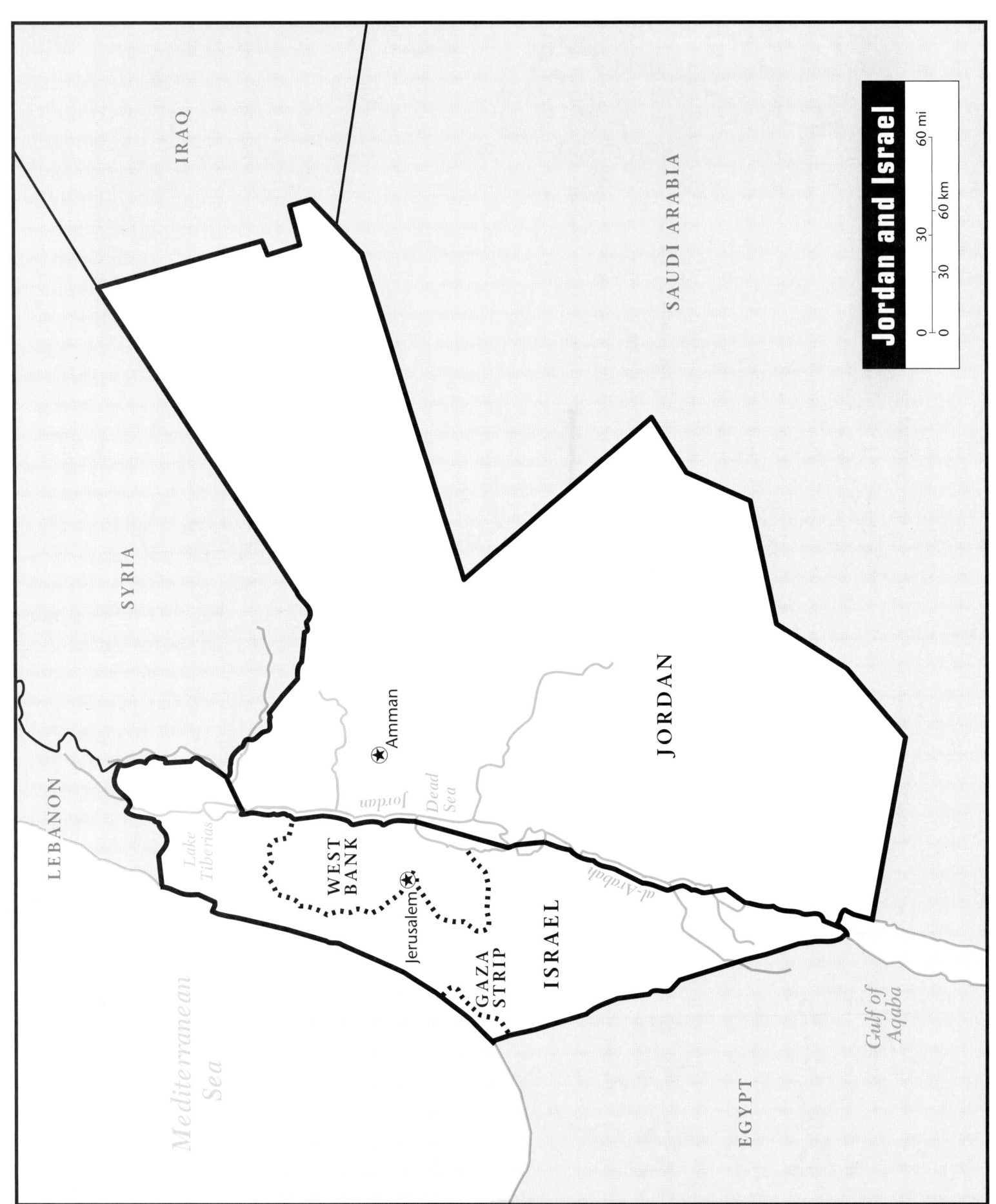

Jordan and Israel

IRAQ

SYRIA

LEBANON

SAUDI ARABIA

Mediterranean Sea

Lake Tiberius

Amman

Jordan

Dead Sea

WEST BANK

Jerusalem

GAZA STRIP

ISRAEL

JORDAN

al-Arabah

Gulf of Aqaba

EGYPT

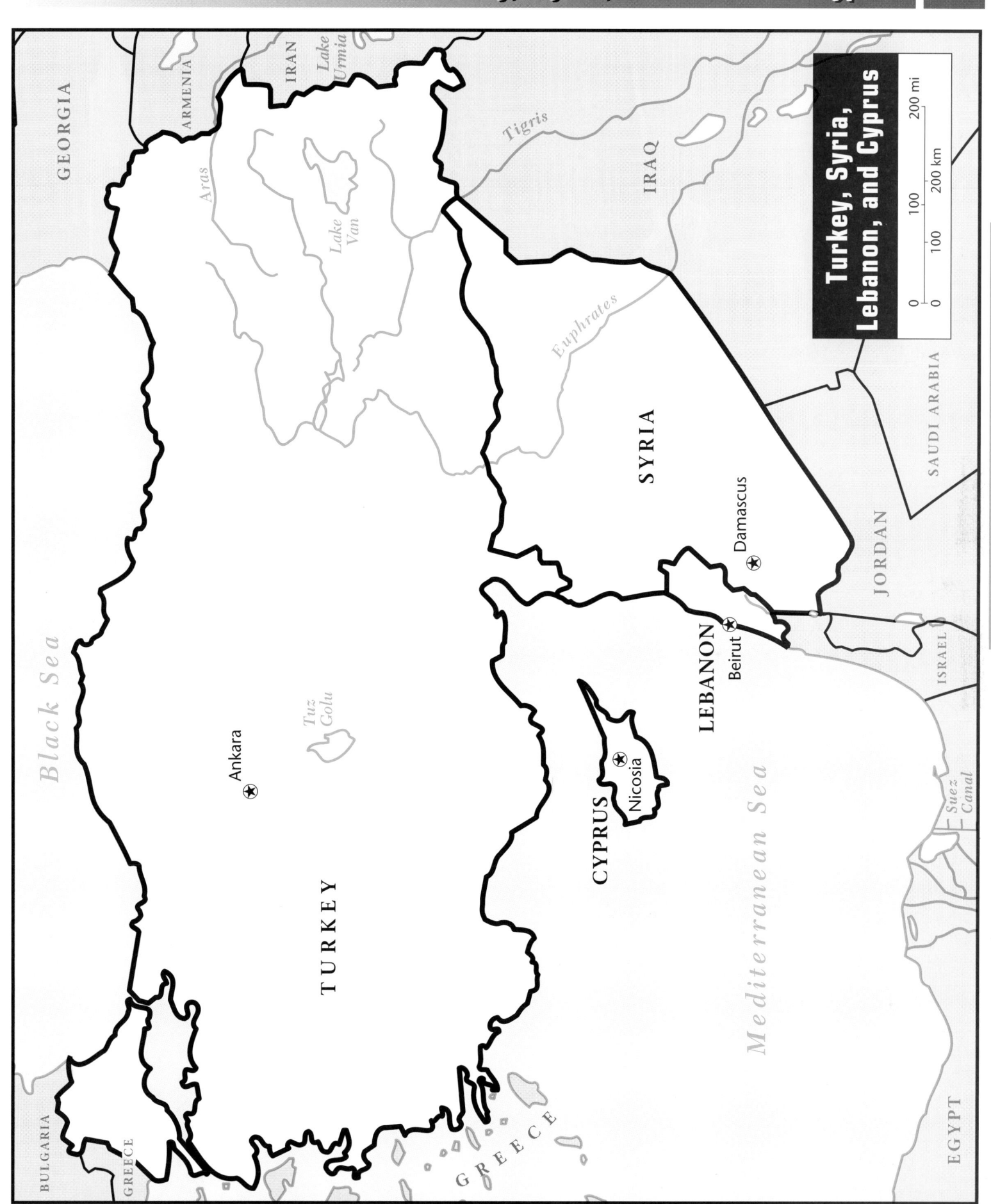

Turkey, Syria, Lebanon, and Cyprus

200 mi
200 km

GEORGIA
ARMENIA
IRAN
Lake Urmia
Aras
Lake Van
Tigris
IRAQ
Euphrates
SYRIA
Damascus
SAUDI ARABIA
JORDAN
LEBANON
Beirut
ISRAEL
Suez Canal
Black Sea
Tuz Golu
Ankara
CYPRUS
Nicosia
TURKEY
Mediterranean Sea
BULGARIA
GREECE
GREECE
EGYPT

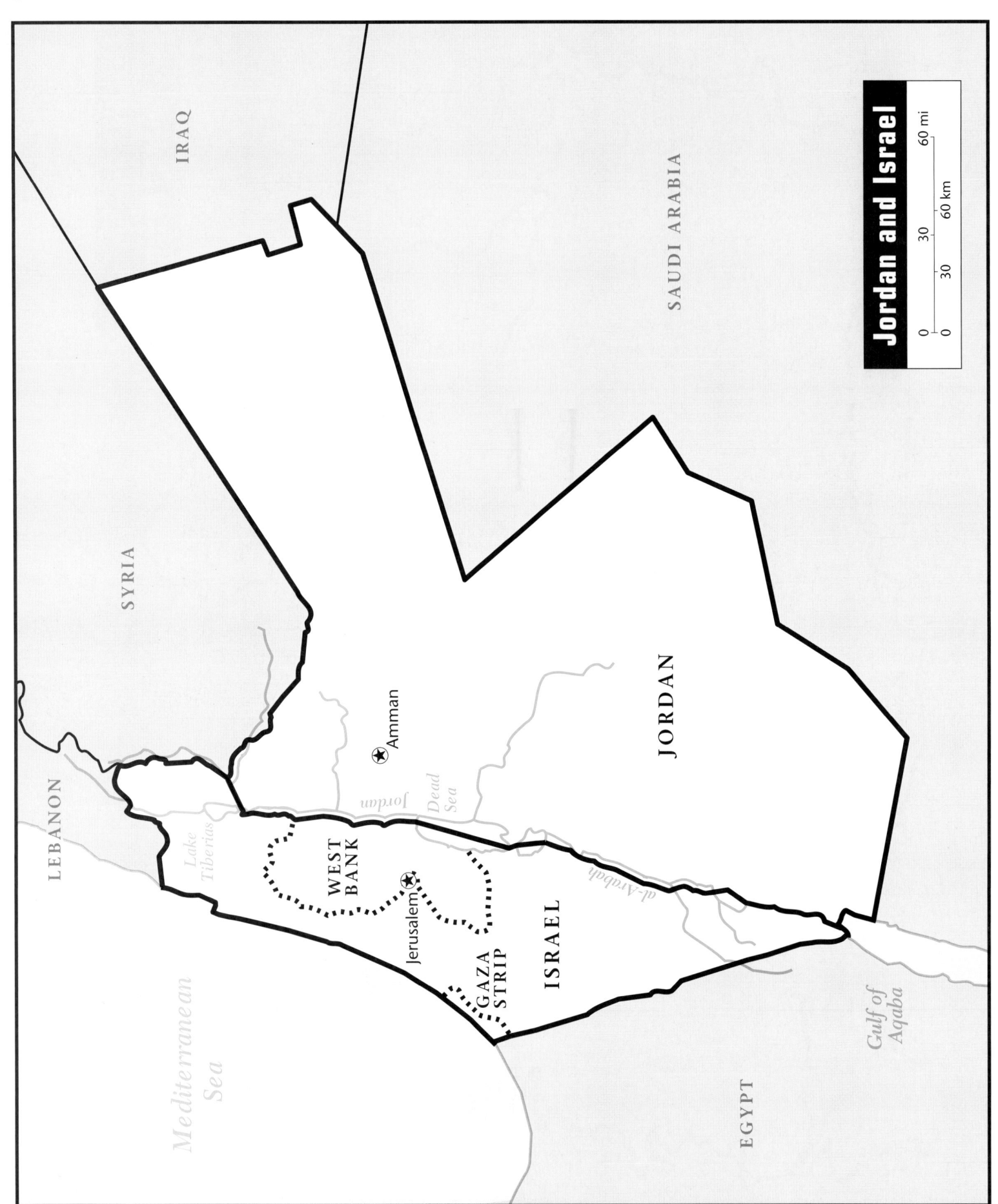

Jordan and Israel

0   30   60 mi
0   30   60 km

IRAQ

SAUDI ARABIA

SYRIA

JORDAN

Amman

Jordan

Dead Sea

LEBANON

Lake Tiberius

WEST BANK

Jerusalem

al-ʿArabah

GAZA STRIP

ISRAEL

Mediterranean Sea

Gulf of Aqaba

EGYPT

**Afghanistan, Iran,
Iraq, and Pakistan**

200 mi
200 km
100
200 km
100
100
0
0

KYRGYZSTAN

CHINA

INDIA

TAJIKISTAN

★ Islamabad

UZBEKISTAN

★ Kabul

AFGHANISTAN

PAKISTAN

Indus

KAZAKHSTAN

Aral
Sea

TURKMENISTAN

Arabian
Sea

Caspian Sea

IRAN

Gulf
of
Oman

OMAN

★ Tehran

OMAN

UNITED ARAB
EMIRATES

RUSSIA

Persian Gulf

QATAR

Don

GEORGIA

AZERBAIJAN

ARMENIA

KUWAIT

BAHRAIN

Baghdad ★

Tigris

TURKEY

Euphrates

IRAQ

SAUDI ARABIA

UKRAINE

Black
Sea

SYRIA

JORDAN

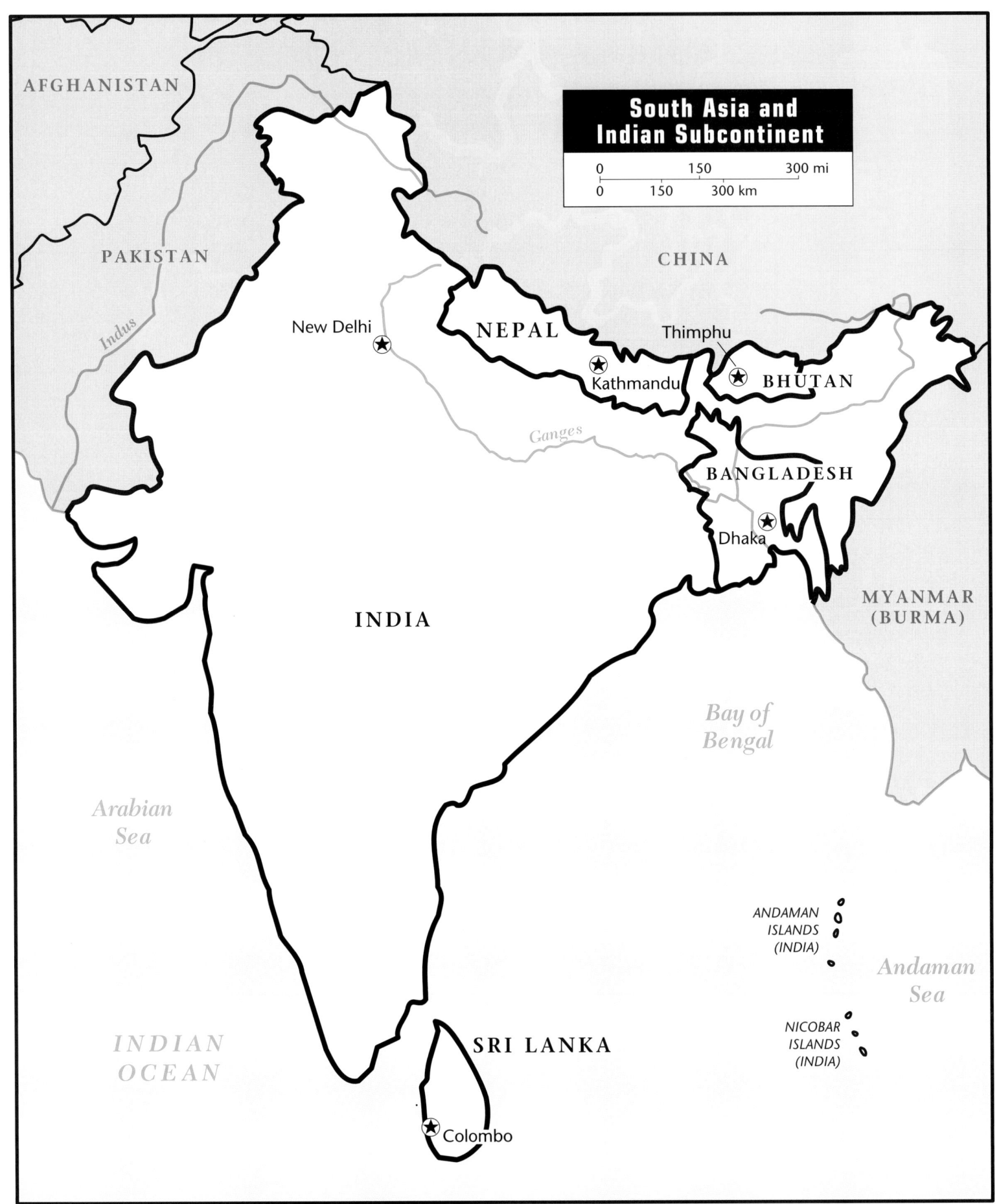

AFGHANISTAN

PAKISTAN

Indus

CHINA

New Delhi ★

NEPAL

Thimphu

Kathmandu ★

★ **BHUTAN**

Ganges

BANGLADESH

Dhaka ★

**MYANMAR
(BURMA)**

INDIA

*Arabian
Sea*

*Bay of
Bengal*

*ANDAMAN
ISLANDS
(INDIA)*

*Andaman
Sea*

*NICOBAR
ISLANDS
(INDIA)*

**INDIAN
OCEAN**

SRI LANKA

★ Colombo

**South Asia and
Indian Subcontinent**

0   150   300 mi
0   150   300 km

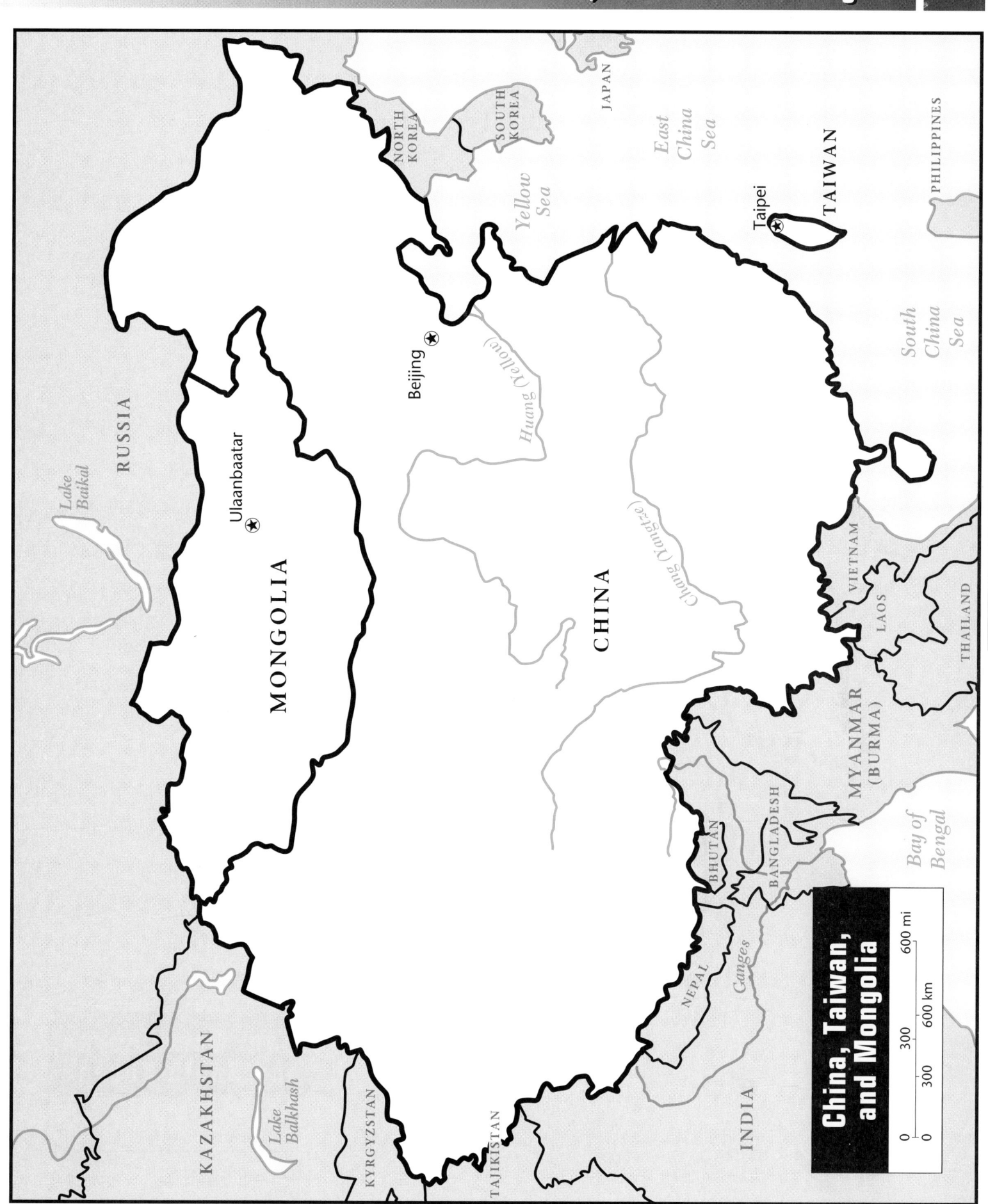

China, Taiwan, and Mongolia

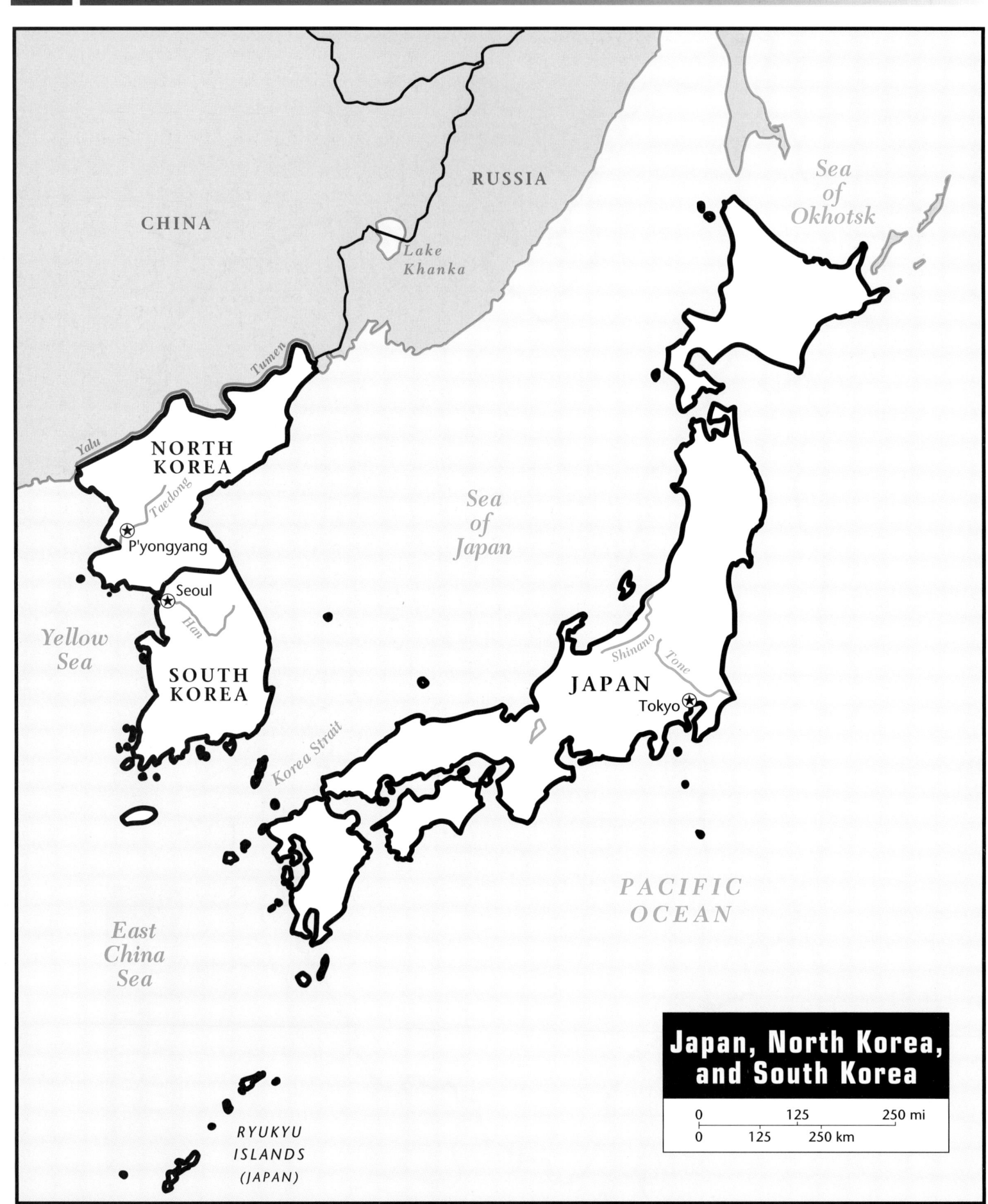

CHINA

RUSSIA

Lake
Khanka

Sea
of
Okhotsk

Tumen

Yalu

NORTH
KOREA

Taedong

⊛ P'yongyang

⊛ Seoul

Han

Yellow
Sea

SOUTH
KOREA

Sea
of
Japan

Shinano

Tone

JAPAN

Tokyo ⊛

Korea Strait

PACIFIC
OCEAN

East
China
Sea

RYUKYU
ISLANDS
(JAPAN)

**Japan, North Korea,
and South Korea**

0   125   250 mi

0   125   250 km

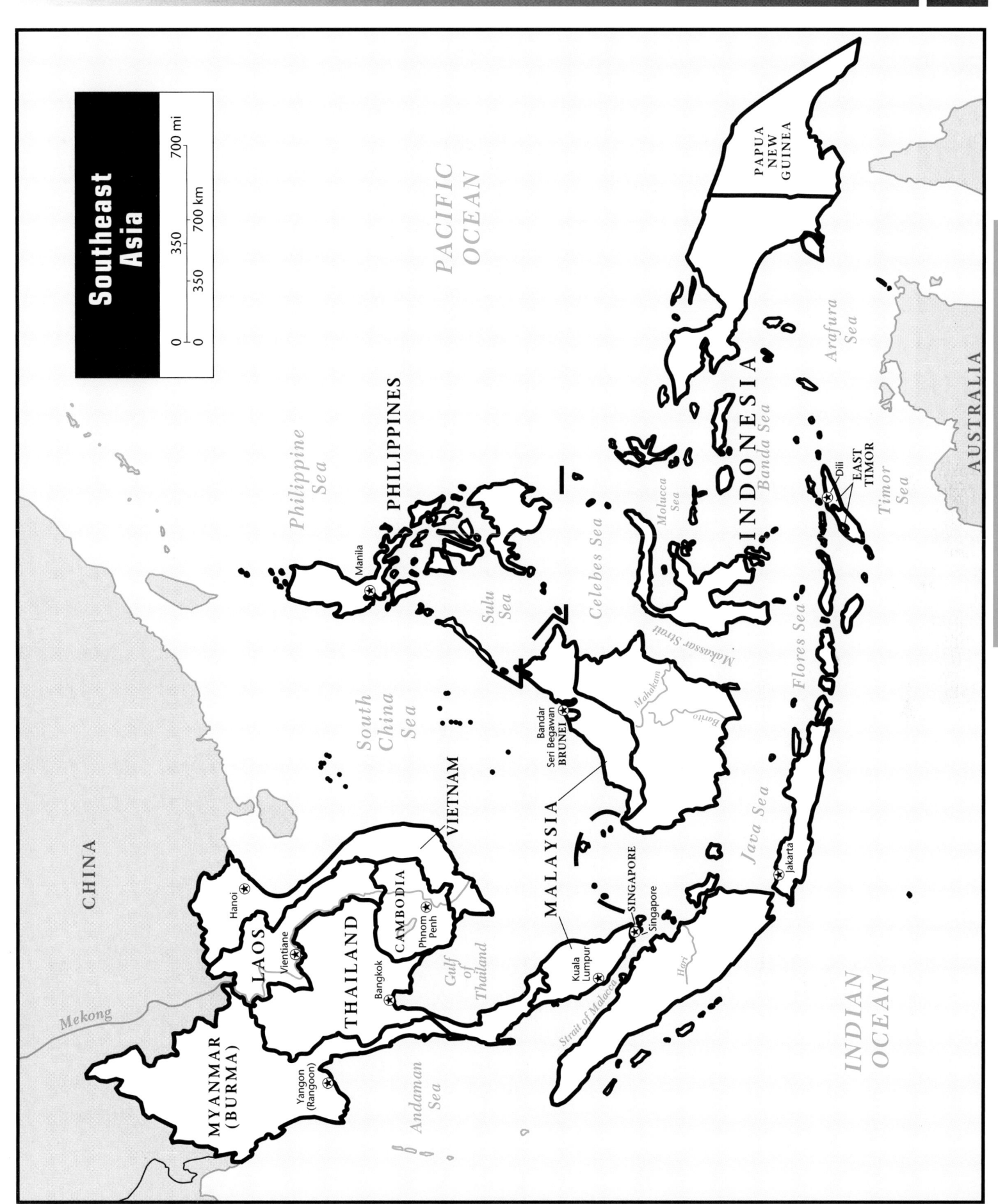

Southeast Asia

700 mi
350 | 700 km
350
0
0 | 350

PACIFIC OCEAN

PAPUA NEW GUINEA

Arafura Sea

AUSTRALIA

INDONESIA

Banda Sea

Philippine Sea

PHILIPPINES

Moluca Sea

East Timor

Dili

EAST TIMOR

Timor Sea

Manila

Celebes Sea

Sulu Sea

Macassar Strait

Flores Sea

South China Sea

VIETNAM

Mahakam

Barito

Java Sea

CHINA

Hanoi

LAOS

Vientiane

THAILAND

CAMBODIA

Phnom Penh

Bangkok

Gulf of Thailand

Bandar Seri Begawan

BRUNEI

MALAYSIA

SINGAPORE

Singapore

Kuala Lumpur

Jakarta

Hari

Mekong

MYANMAR (BURMA)

Yangon (Rangoon)

Andaman Sea

Strait of Malacca

INDIAN OCEAN

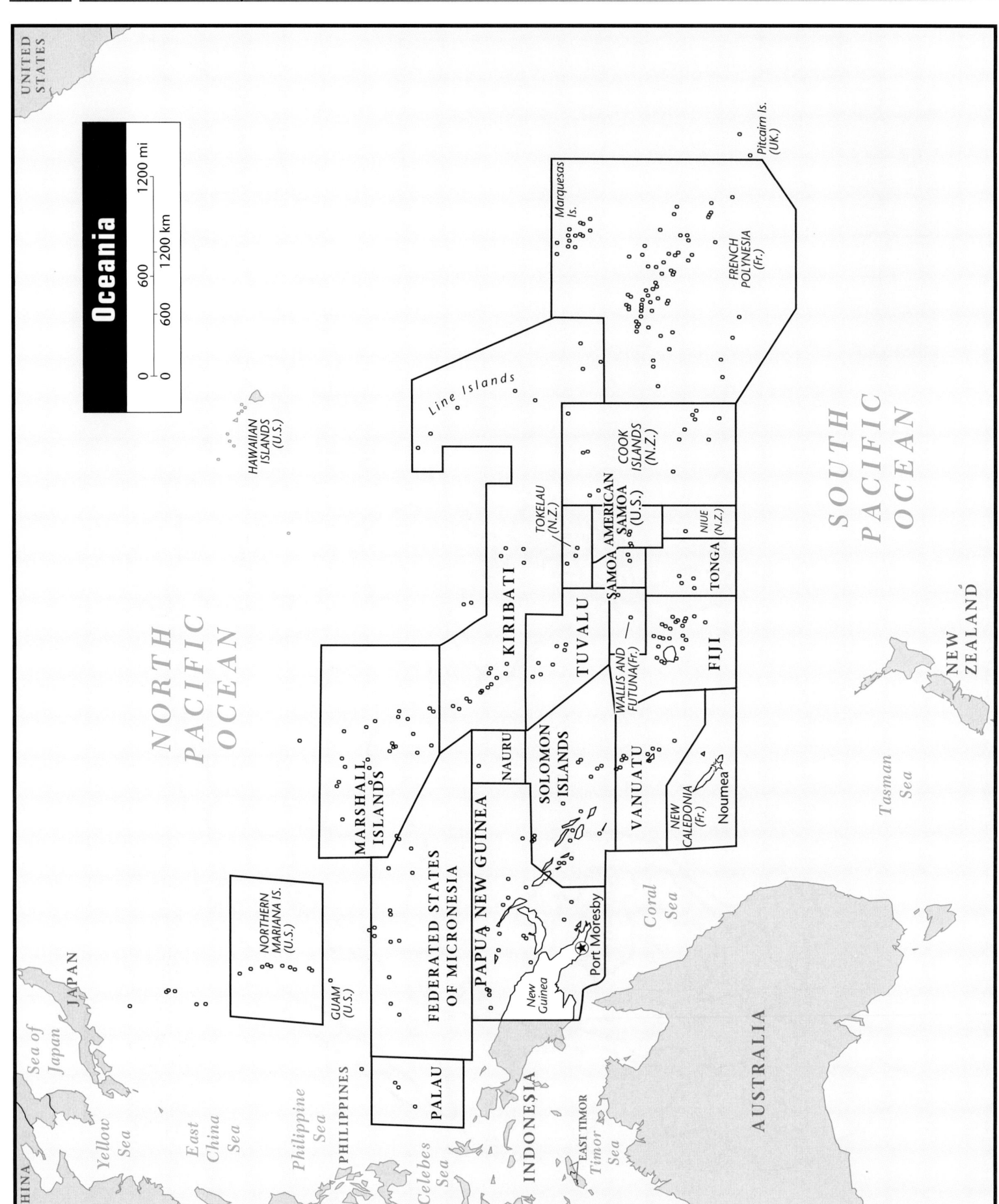

Oceania

| 0 | 600 | 1200 mi |
| 0 | 600 | 1200 km |

UNITED STATES

Pitcairn Is.
(UK.)

Marquesas
Is.

FRENCH
POLYNESIA
(Fr.)

Line Islands

HAWAIIAN
ISLANDS
(U.S.)

COOK
ISLANDS
(N.Z.)

SOUTH
PACIFIC
OCEAN

TOKELAU
(N.Z.)

SAMOA   AMERICAN
SAMOA
(U.S.)

NIUE
(N.Z.)

TONGA

NORTH
PACIFIC
OCEAN

KIRIBATI

TUVALU

WALLIS AND
FUTUNA(Fr.)

FIJI

MARSHALL
ISLANDS

NAURU

SOLOMON
ISLANDS

VANUATU

NEW
CALEDONIA
(Fr.)

Noumea

NEW
ZEALAND

NORTHERN
MARIANA IS.
(U.S.)

FEDERATED STATES
OF MICRONESIA

PAPUA NEW GUINEA

Port Moresby

New
Guinea

Coral
Sea

Tasman
Sea

AUSTRALIA

GUAM
(U.S.)

PALAU

PHILIPPINES

INDONESIA

EAST TIMOR
Timor
Sea

JAPAN

Sea of
Japan

Philippine
Sea

Celebes
Sea

CHINA

Yellow
Sea

East
China
Sea

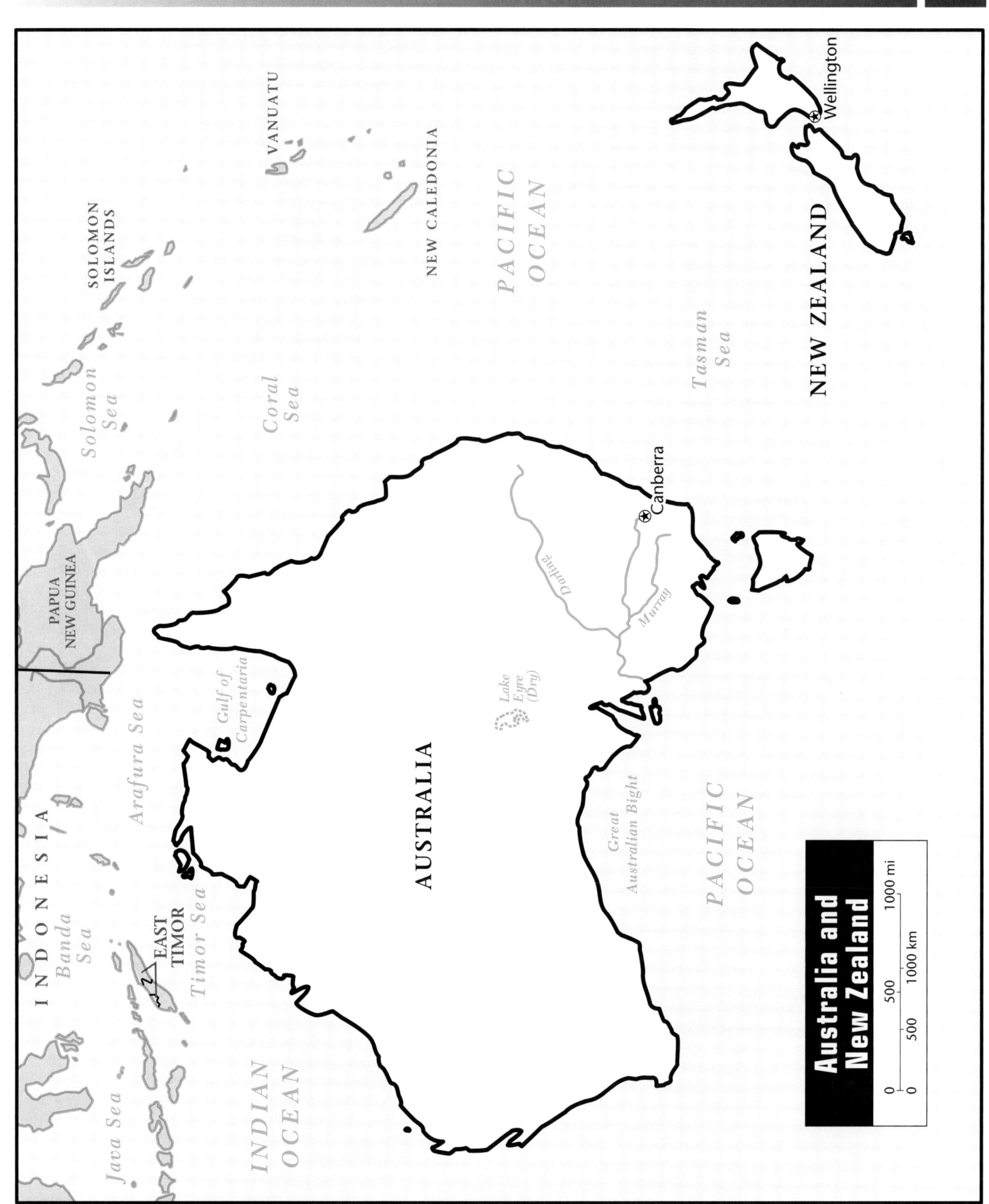

INDONESIA

Banda Sea

Java Sea

PAPUA NEW GUINEA

SOLOMON ISLANDS

Solomon Sea

VANUATU

NEW CALEDONIA

PACIFIC OCEAN

Coral Sea

Tasman Sea

NEW ZEALAND

Wellington

★ Canberra

Darling

Murray

Lake Eyre (Dry)

AUSTRALIA

Gulf of Carpentaria

Arafura Sea

EAST TIMOR

Timor Sea

INDIAN OCEAN

Great Australian Bight

PACIFIC OCEAN

Australia and New Zealand

| 0 | 500 | 1000 mi |
| 0 | 500 | 1000 km |

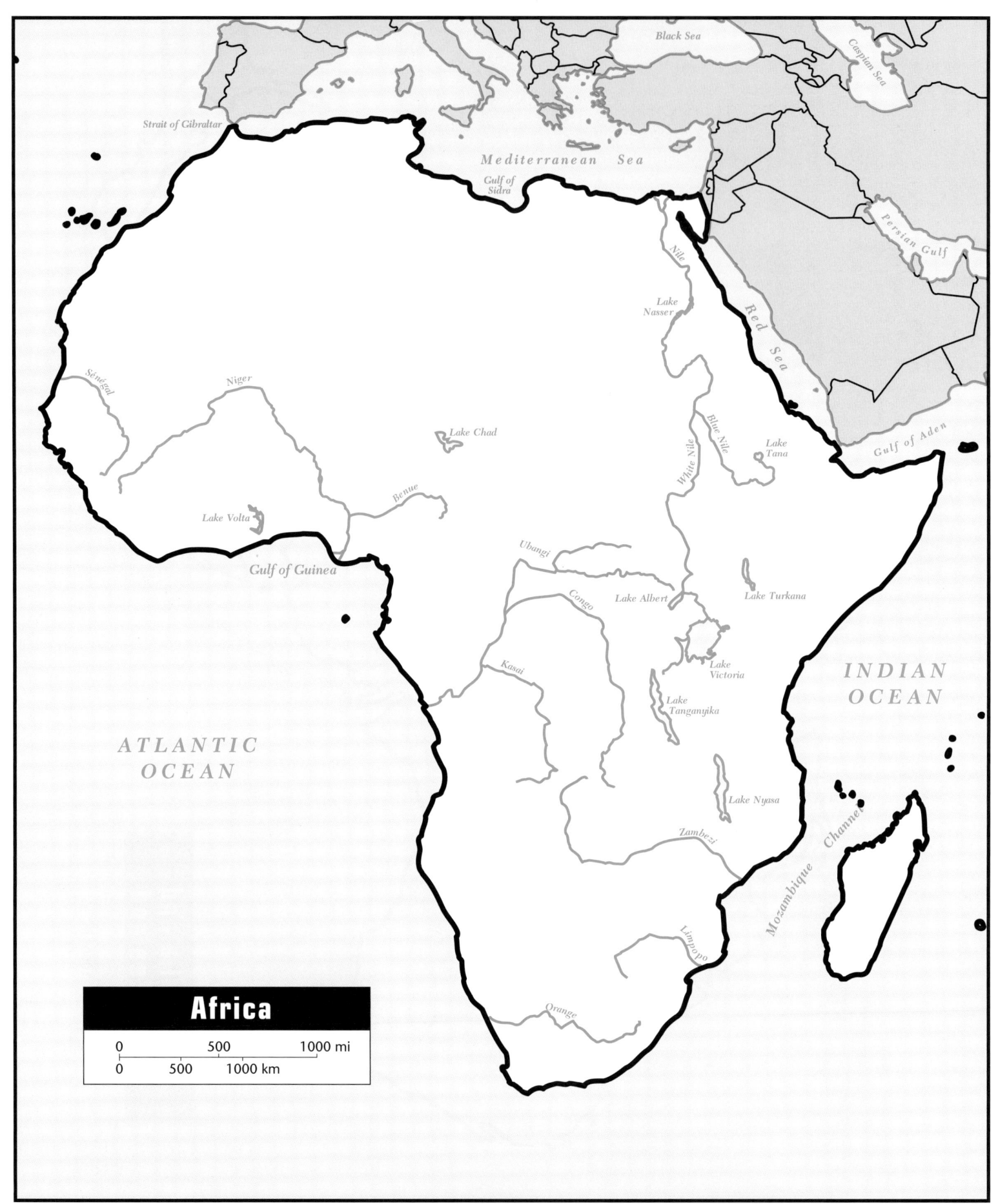

Black Sea

Caspian Sea

Strait of Gibraltar

Mediterranean Sea

Gulf of Sidra

Persian Gulf

Nile

Lake Nasser

Red Sea

Sénégal

Niger

Lake Chad

Blue Nile

Lake Tana

Gulf of Aden

Benue

White Nile

Lake Volta

Ubangi

Gulf of Guinea

Congo

Lake Albert

Lake Turkana

Kasai

INDIAN OCEAN

Lake Victoria

ATLANTIC OCEAN

Lake Tanganyika

Lake Nyasa

Mozambique Channel

Zambezi

Limpopo

Orange

Africa

0   500   1000 mi

0   500   1000 km

Western Africa

| 0 | 250 | 500 mi |
| 0 | 250 | 500 km |

ATLANTIC
OCEAN

FRANCE

ITALY

PORTUGAL
SPAIN

Mediterranean Sea

Strait of Gibraltar

⊛ Algiers

⊛ Tunis

⊛ Rabat

MOROCCO

TUNISIA

CANARY ISLANDS
(Sp.)

WESTERN
SAHARA
(Occupied by
Morocco)

ALGERIA

LIBYA

MAURITANIA

MALI

NIGER

⊛ Nouakchott

Sénégal

Niger

⊛ Dakar

SENEGAL

Banjul ⊛

GAMBIA

Bissau ⊛

GUINEA
BISSAU

Bamako ⊛

BURKINA
FASO

Niamey ⊛

CHAD

Lake Chad

NIGERIA

Abuja ⊛

Benue

Conakry ⊛

GUINEA

Ouagadougou ⊛

BENIN

⊛ Freetown

SIERRA
LEONE

CÔTE
D'IVOIRE

GHANA

TOGO

Monrovia ⊛

Yamoussoukro ⊛

Lake Volta

Porto-Novo ⊛

LIBERIA

Accra ⊛

Lomé ⊛

Gulf of Guinea

CENTRAL
AFRICAN
REPUBLIC

CAMEROON

EQUATORIAL
GUINEA

GABON

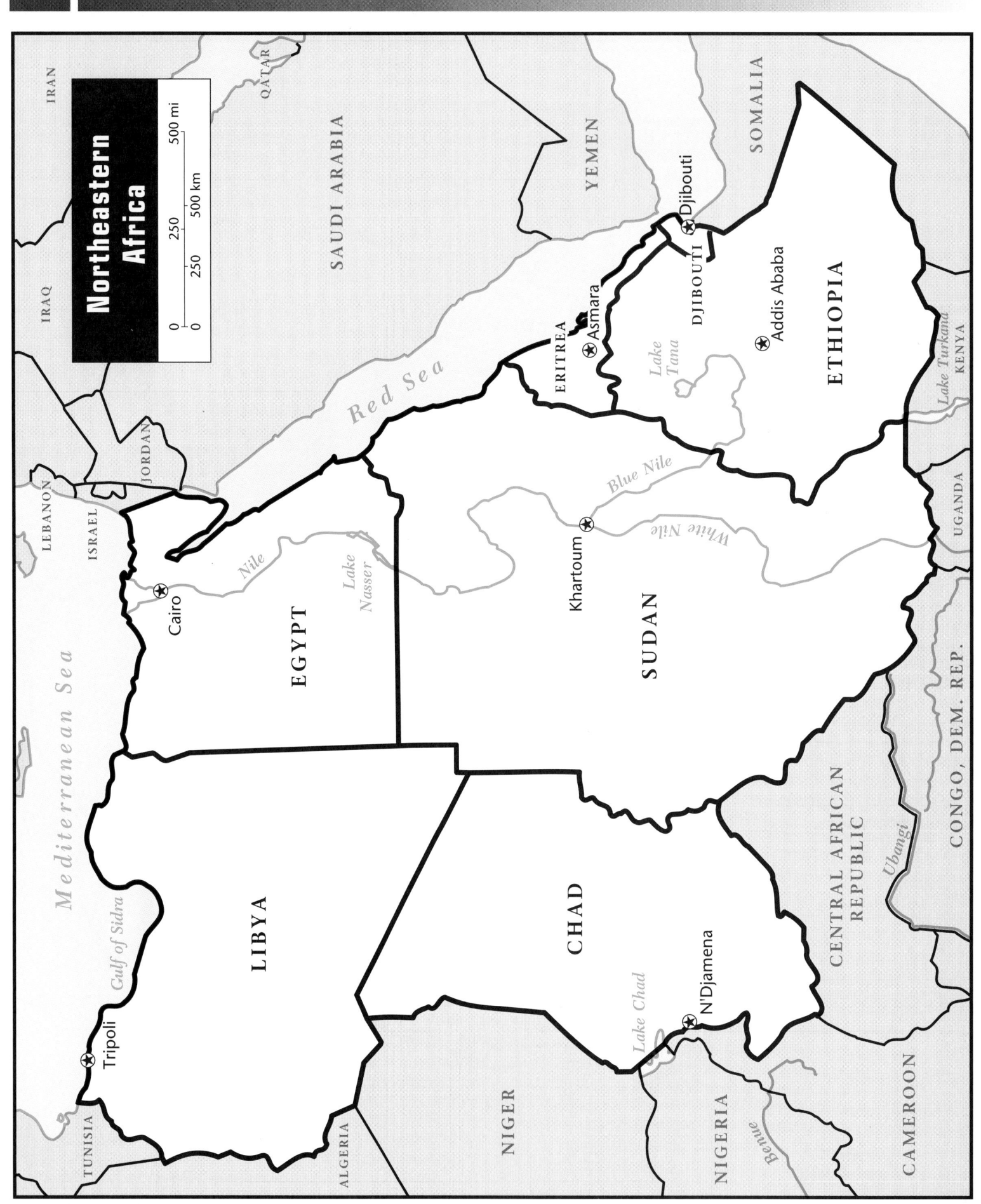

Northeastern Africa

500 mi
250
500 km
250
250
0
0

IRAN
IRAQ
QATAR
SAUDI ARABIA
YEMEN
SOMALIA
DJIBOUTI
⊛ Djibouti
ERITREA
⊛ Asmara
Lake Tana
Addis Ababa
ETHIOPIA
Red Sea
Blue Nile
White Nile
Lake Turkana
KENYA
UGANDA
JORDAN
LEBANON
ISRAEL
Mediterranean Sea
Nile
⊛ Cairo
EGYPT
Lake Nasser
Khartoum ⊛
SUDAN
CONGO, DEM. REP.
Ubangi
CENTRAL AFRICAN REPUBLIC
Gulf of Sidra
LIBYA
⊛ Tripoli
CHAD
Lake Chad
N'Djamena ⊛
NIGER
ALGERIA
TUNISIA
NIGERIA
Benue
CAMEROON

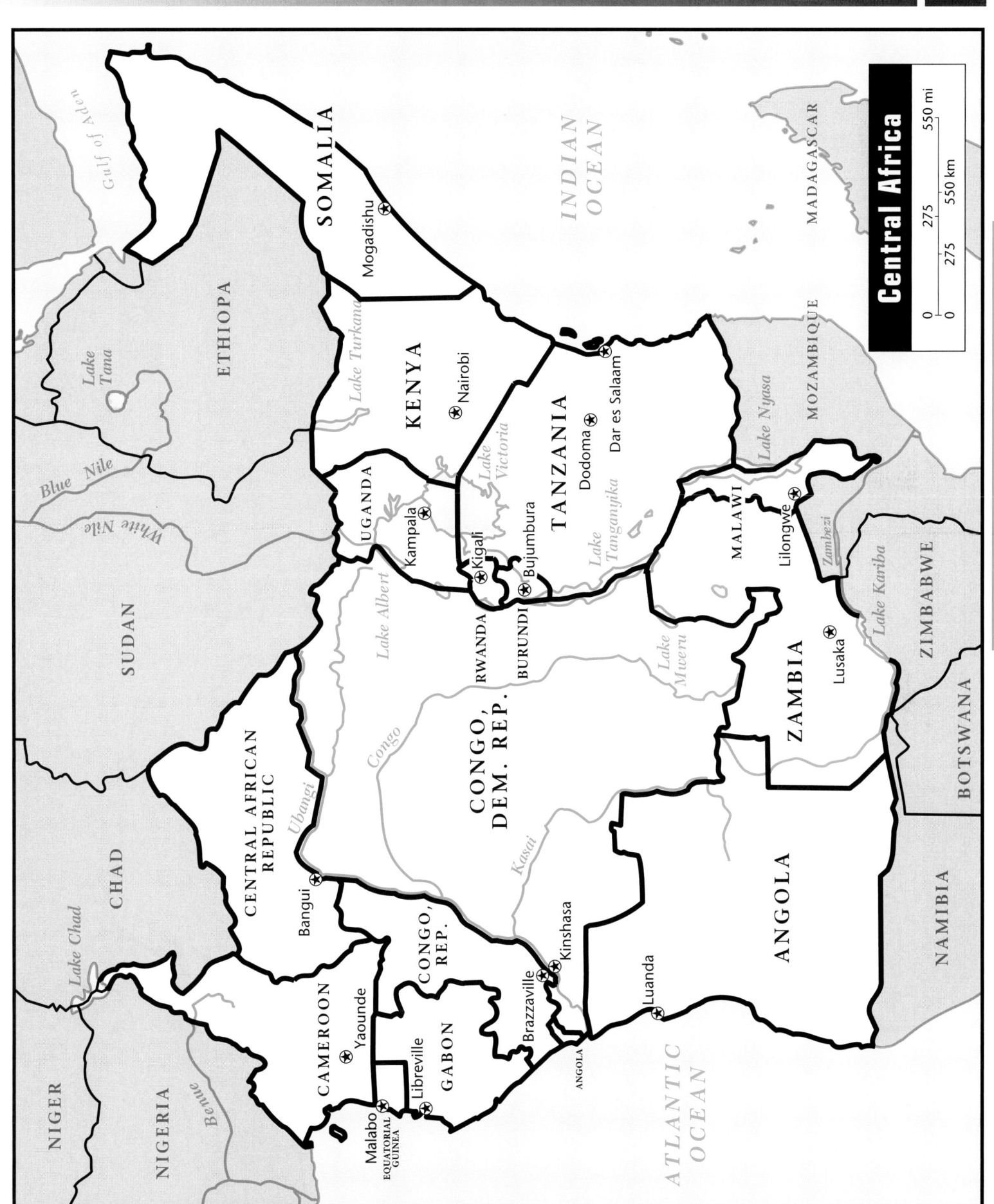

Central Africa

550 mi
275
0
550 km
275
0

Gulf of Aden

SOMALIA

Mogadishu

ETHIOPA

Lake Tana

INDIAN OCEAN

MADAGASCAR

MOZAMBIQUE

Lake Turkana

KENYA

Nairobi

TANZANIA

Dodoma

Dar es Salaam

Lake Victoria

Lake Nyasa

Blue Nile

White Nile

SUDAN

UGANDA

Kampala

Kigali

RWANDA

Bujumbura

BURUNDI

Lake Albert

Lake Tanganyika

MALAWI

Lilongwe

Zambezi

Lake Kariba

ZIMBABWE

Lake Mweru

ZAMBIA

Lusaka

CENTRAL AFRICAN REPUBLIC

CONGO, DEM. REP.

Congo

Ubangi

Kasai

BOTSWANA

NAMIBIA

CHAD

Lake Chad

Bangui

CONGO, REP.

Kinshasa

Brazzaville

ANGOLA

Luanda

ANGOLA

ATLANTIC OCEAN

NIGER

NIGERIA

Benue

CAMEROON

Yaounde

GABON

Libreville

Malabo

EQUATORIAL GUINEA

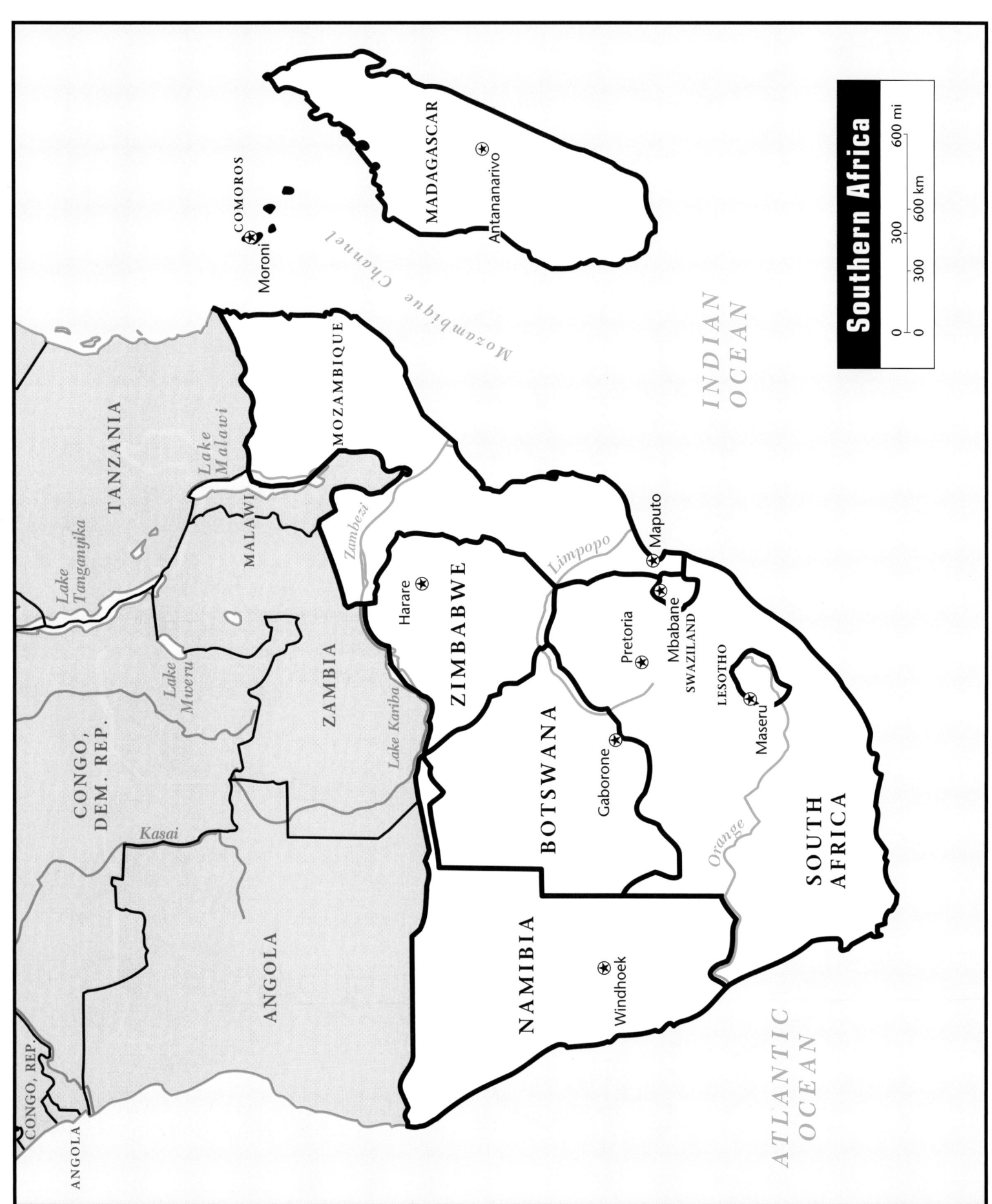

MADAGASCAR

⊛ Antananarivo

COMOROS
⊛
Moroni

Mozambique Channel

INDIAN
OCEAN

Southern Africa

600 mi

300

600 km

300

0

0

TANZANIA

Lake Malawi

MOZAMBIQUE

MALAWI

Zambezi

Lake Tanganyika

Lake Mweru

CONGO, DEM. REP.

Kasai

ZAMBIA

Lake Kariba

ZIMBABWE

Harare ⊛

Limpopo

Maputo ⊛

Pretoria ⊛
Mbabane ⊛
SWAZILAND

LESOTHO
Maseru ⊛

BOTSWANA

Gaborone ⊛

Orange

SOUTH
AFRICA

NAMIBIA

Windhoek ⊛

ANGOLA

CONGO, REP.

ANGOLA

ATLANTIC
OCEAN

Caribbean Sea

ATLANTIC
OCEAN

Lake Maracaibo

Magdalena

Meta

Orinoco

Orinoco

Caroni

Caquetá

Negro

Putumayo

Amazon

Marañón

Purus

Madeira

Tapajós

Xingu

Tocantins

Parnaíba

Ucayali

Guaporé

Lake Titicaca

Mamoré

Araguaia

São Francisco

Lake Poopó

Paraguay

Grande

Pilcomayo

Paraná

PACIFIC
OCEAN

Desaguadero

Salado

Uruguay

Paraná

Río de la Plata

Salado

ATLANTIC
OCEAN

Colorado

San Matías Gulf

Gulf of San Jorge

Bahía Grande

Strait of Magellan

South America

0	250	500	750 mi
0	250	500	750	1000 km

HONDURAS
EL SALVADOR
NICARAGUA

Caribbean Sea

COSTA RICA

PANAMA

VENEZUELA

Lake Maracaibo

Orinoco

Orinoco

Magdalena

⊛ Bogotá

COLOMBIA

⊛ Quito

ECUADOR

Negro

PACIFIC OCEAN

Amazon

Amazon

BRAZIL

Marañón

Madeira

PERU

Ucayali

Beni

⊛ Lima

Lake Titicaca

BOLIVIA

Lake Poopó

Peru, Ecuador, and Colombia

0   300   600 mi
0   300   600 km

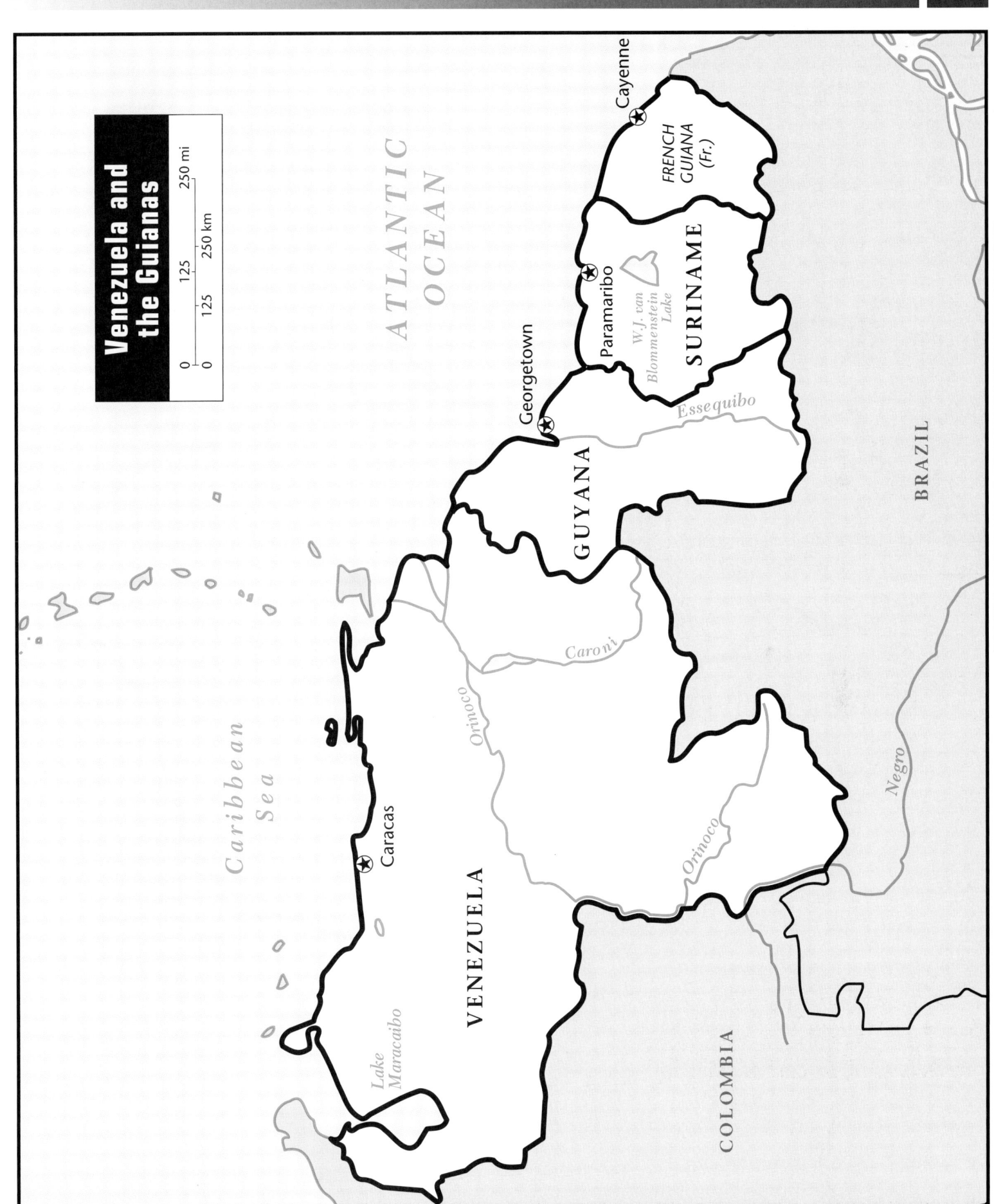

Venezuela and the Guianas

250 mi
125
0

250 km
125
0

ATLANTIC OCEAN

Cayenne

FRENCH GUIANA (Fr.)

SURINAME

Paramaribo

W.J. van Blommenstein Lake

Georgetown

Essequibo

GUYANA

Caribbean Sea

Caroni

Orinoco

Orinoco

BRAZIL

Negro

Caracas

Lake Maracaibo

VENEZUELA

COLOMBIA

Brazil and Bolivia

0   250   500 mi
0   250   500 km

Caribbean Sea

Lake Maracaibo

VENEZUELA

Orinoco

GUYANA

SURINAME

FRENCH GUIANA

COLOMBIA

ATLANTIC OCEAN

Negro

Amazon

BRAZIL

Madeira

Tocantins

Beni

BOLIVIA

Ucayali

PERU

Lake Titicaca

La Paz

Brasília

Lake Poopó

Paraguay

PACIFIC OCEAN

PARAGUAY

CHILE

ARGENTINA

Paraná

URUGUAY

ATLANTIC OCEAN

Río de la Plata

PERU

Lake Titicaca

Mamoré

BOLIVIA

Lake Poopó

Paraguay

BRAZIL

Grande

PARAGUAY

Pilcomayo

Paraná

⊛ Asunción

Salado

Desaguadero

PACIFIC OCEAN

Uruguay

Santiago ⊛

Salado

URUGUAY

ARGENTINA

Buenos Aires ⊛

⊛ Montevideo

Río de la Plata

CHILE

Colorado

Negro

San Matías Gulf

ATLANTIC OCEAN

Chubut

Chico

Gulf of San Jorge

Bahía Grande

FALKLAND ISLANDS (UK)

Strait of Magellan

Argentina, Chile, Paraguay, and Uruguay

0		250		500 mi
0	250		500 km	

RUSSIA

ARCTIC OCEAN

ICELAND

Bering
Strait

Beaufort
Sea

Baffin
Bay

Denmark
Strait

Bering
Sea

Yukon

Mackenzie

Davis Strait

Gulf of
Alaska

Great
Bear L.

Labrador
Sea

Great
Slave L.

L.
Athabasca

Hudson
Bay

Peace

Athabasca

Fraser

Saskatchewan

James
Bay

Columbia

L.
Winnipeg

St. Lawrence

PACIFIC
OCEAN

Missouri

Lake
Superior

Snake

L.
Michigan

L. Huron

L. Ontario

Great
Salt L.

L. Erie

Colorado

Platte

Ohio

ATLANTIC
OCEAN

Arkansas

Mississippi

Gulf of
California

Rio

Grande

Gulf of
Mexico

Bay of
Campeche

Caribbean Sea

North America

0	450	900 mi
0	450	900 km

VENEZUELA

COLOMBIA

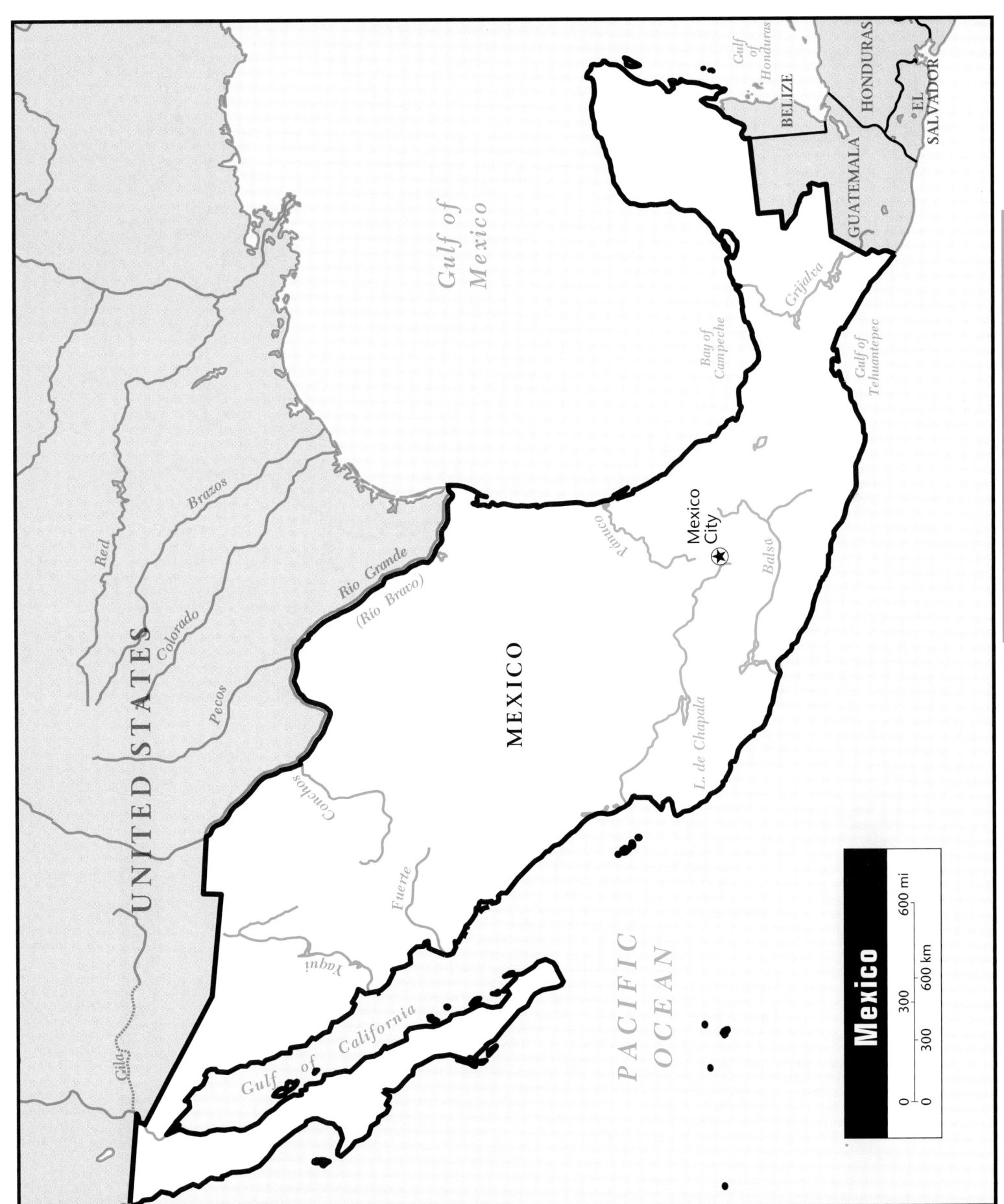

UNITED STATES

Gulf of Mexico

MEXICO

PACIFIC OCEAN

Red

Brazos

Colorado

Rio Grande
(Río Bravo)

Pecos

Conchos

Fuerte

Yaqui

Gila

Gulf of California

Bay of Campeche

Gulf of Honduras

BELIZE

GUATEMALA

HONDURAS

EL SALVADOR

Grijalva

Gulf of Tehuantepec

Pánuco

Mexico City

Balsa

L. de Chapala

Mexico

0	300		600 mi
0	300		600 km

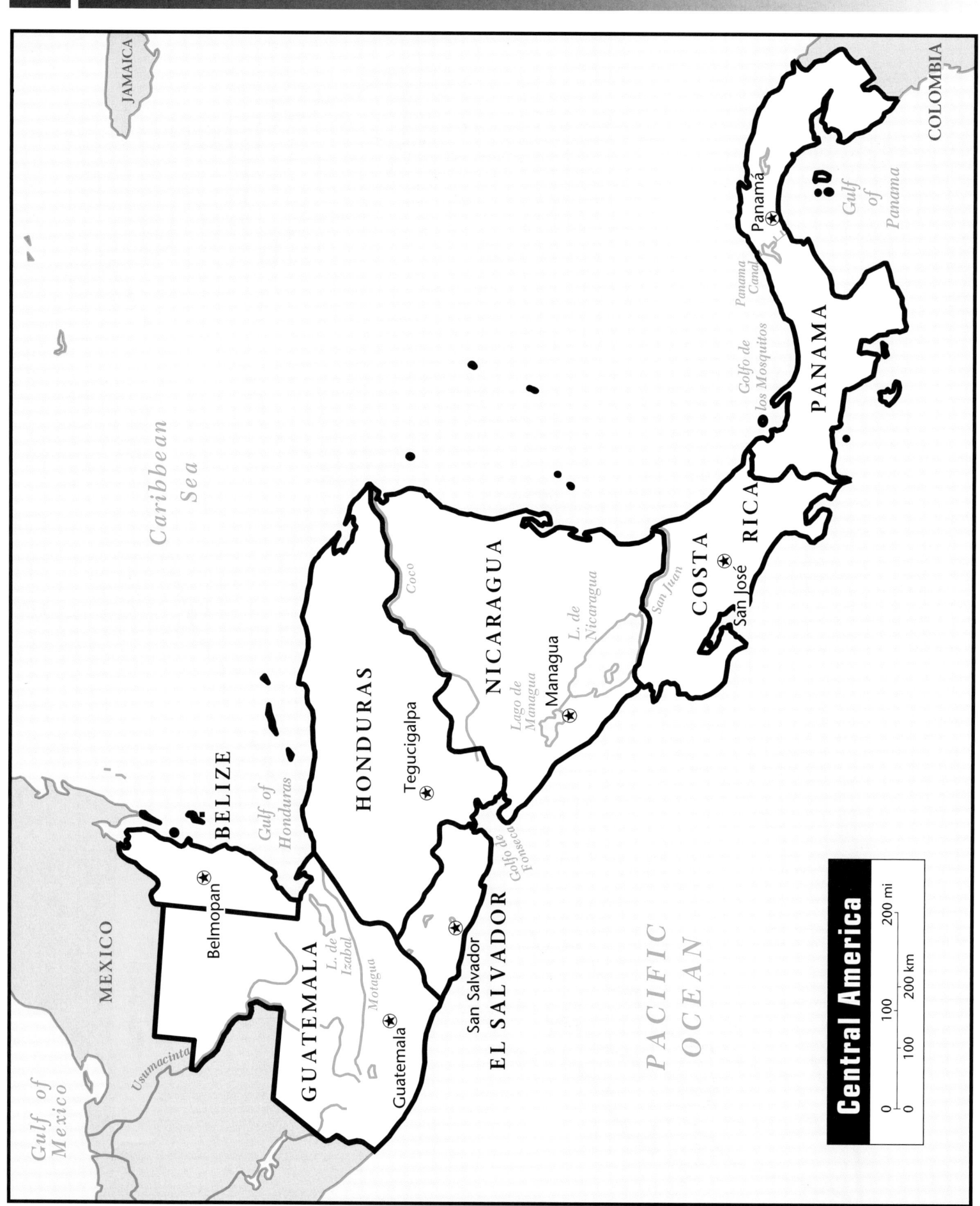

Central America

JAMAICA

COLOMBIA

Caribbean Sea

Gulf of Mexico

MEXICO

BELIZE

Belmopan ✪

Gulf of Honduras

GUATEMALA

L. de Izabal

Motagua

Usumacinta

Guatemala ✪

HONDURAS

Tegucigalpa ✪

San Salvador

EL SALVADOR

Coco

NICARAGUA

Golfo de Fonseca

Managua ✪

Lago de Managua

L. de Nicaragua

San Juan

COSTA RICA

San José ✪

Golfo de los Mosquitos

PANAMA

Panama Canal

Panamá ✪

Panama

Gulf of Panama

PACIFIC OCEAN

200 mi

100

200 km

100

0 100 200

0

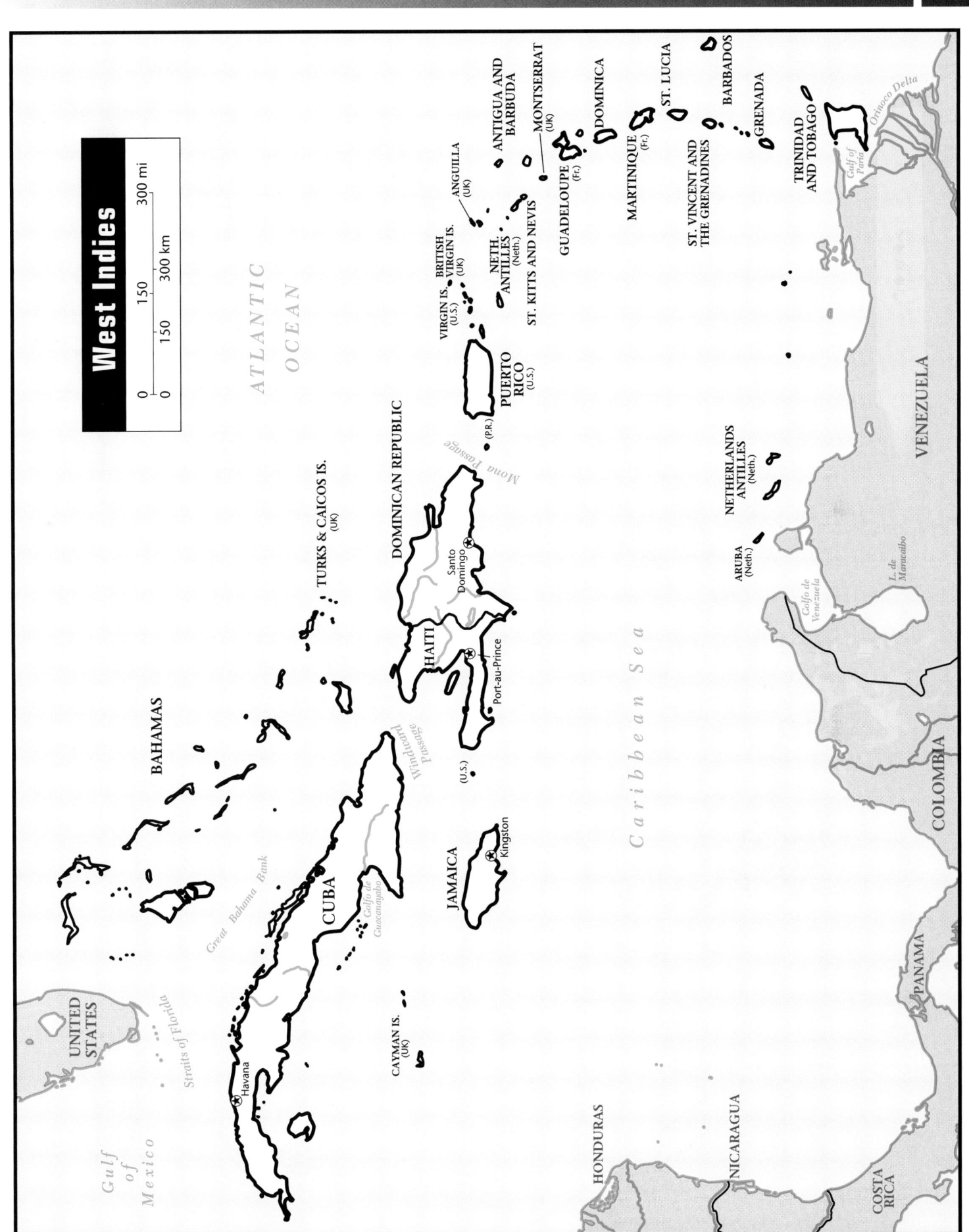

West Indies

300 mi

0   150   300 km

0   150   300 km

ATLANTIC OCEAN

ANGUILLA (UK)

ANTIGUA AND BARBUDA

MONTSERRAT (UK)

GUADELOUPE (Fr.)

DOMINICA

MARTINIQUE (Fr.)

ST. LUCIA

BARBADOS

ST. VINCENT AND THE GRENADINES

GRENADA

TRINIDAD AND TOBAGO

Orinoco Delta

Gulf of Paria

VIRGIN IS. (U.S.)

BRITISH VIRGIN IS. (UK)

NETH. ANTILLES (Neth.)

ST. KITTS AND NEVIS

PUERTO RICO (U.S.)

(P.R.)

Mona Passage

DOMINICAN REPUBLIC

Santo Domingo

HAITI

Port-au-Prince

Windward Passage

(U.S.)

TURKS & CAICOS IS. (UK)

BAHAMAS

NETHERLANDS ANTILLES (Neth.)

ARUBA (Neth.)

VENEZUELA

L. de Maracaibo

Golfo de Venezuela

Caribbean Sea

JAMAICA

Kingston

CUBA

Golfo de Guacanayabo

Great Bahama Bank

CAYMAN IS. (UK)

Havana

Straits of Florida

UNITED STATES

Gulf of Mexico

COLOMBIA

PANAMA

COSTA RICA

NICARAGUA

HONDURAS

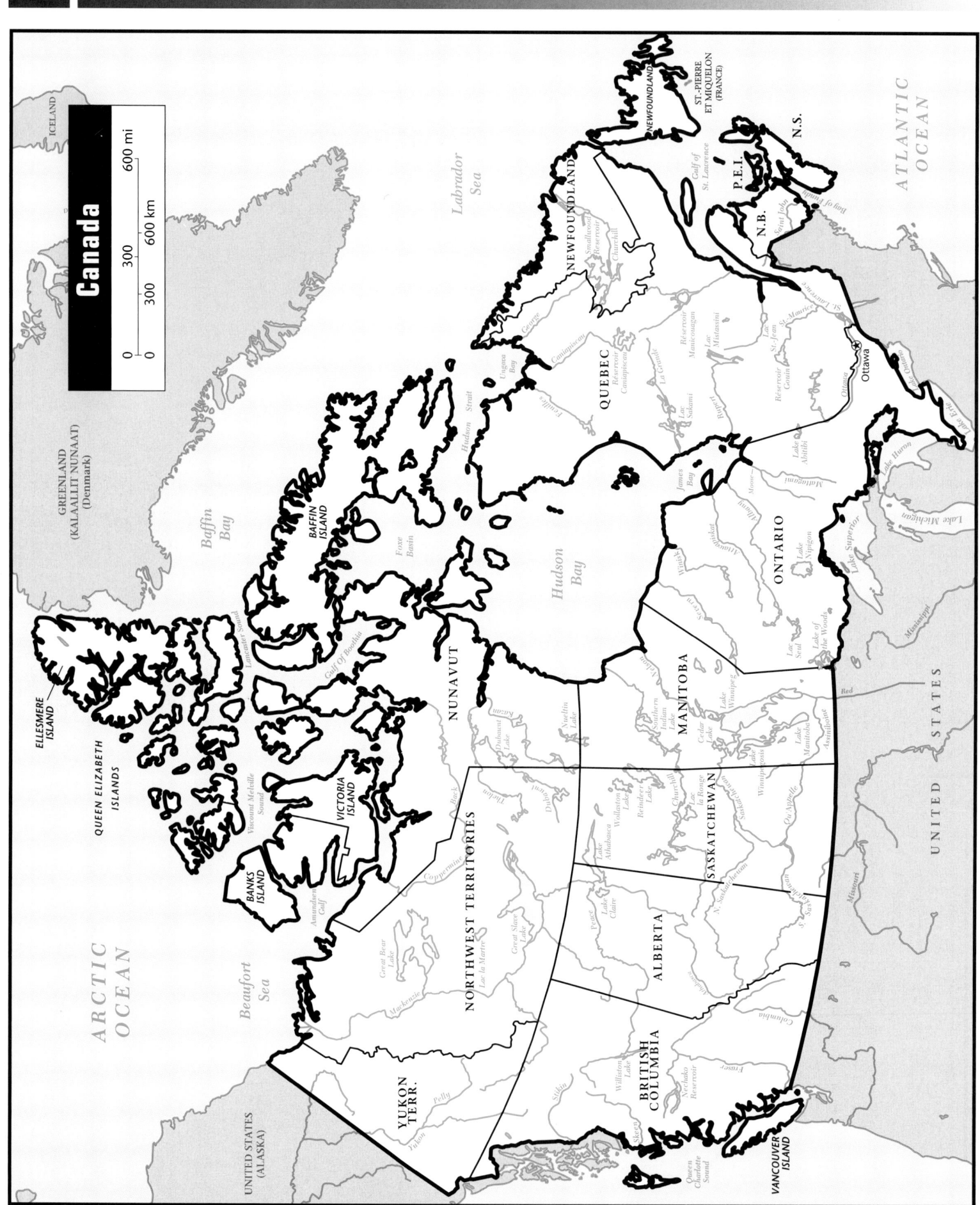

Canada

600 mi

0   300   600 km

0   300

ICELAND

ATLANTIC OCEAN

GREENLAND (KALAALLIT NUNAAT) (Denmark)

Labrador Sea

NEWFOUNDLAND

ST-PIERRE ET MIQUELON (FRANCE)

N.S.

P.E.I.

Gulf of St. Lawrence

N.B.

Baffin Bay

Smallwood Reservoir

Churchill

QUEBEC

Reservoir Caniapiscau

La Grande

Lac Mistassini

Reservoir Manicouagan

St-Maurice

Lake St-Jean

St. Lawrence

Ottawa

BAFFIN ISLAND

Foxe Basin

Hudson Strait

Ungava Bay

Feuilles

George

Caniapiscau

Rupert

Lac Sakami

Reservoir Gouin

Ottawa

Lac Abitibi

Ma Ontario

Lake Huron

ELLESMERE ISLAND

QUEEN ELIZABETH ISLANDS

Lancaster Sound

Gulf Of Boothia

Hudson Bay

James Bay

ONTARIO

Lake Superior

Lake Nipigon

Lake Michigan

VICTORIA ISLAND

Viscount Melville Sound

NUNAVUT

Back

Kazan

Dubawnt Lake

Nueltin Lake

MANITOBA

Southern Indian Lake

Lac Seul

Lake of the Woods

Mississippi

BANKS ISLAND

Amundsen Gulf

Coppermine

Thelon

Dubawnt

Lake Athabasca

Wollaston Lake

Reindeer Lake

Churchill

Lac la Ronge

SASKATCHEWAN

Saskatchewan

N. Saskatchewan

Lake Winnipeg

Cedar Lake

Winnipegosis

Lake Manitoba

Qu'Appelle

Assiniboine

Red

UNITED STATES

ARCTIC OCEAN

Beaufort Sea

Great Bear Lake

Lac la Martre

NORTHWEST TERRITORIES

Great Slave Lake

Mackenzie

Peace

Lake Claire

ALBERTA

Athabasca

S. Saskatchewan

Missouri

UNITED STATES (ALASKA)

YUKON TERR.

Pelly

Yukon

Polly

Stikine

BRITISH COLUMBIA

Williston Lake

Nechako Reservoir

Fraser

Columbia

Skeena

Queen Charlotte Sound

VANCOUVER ISLAND

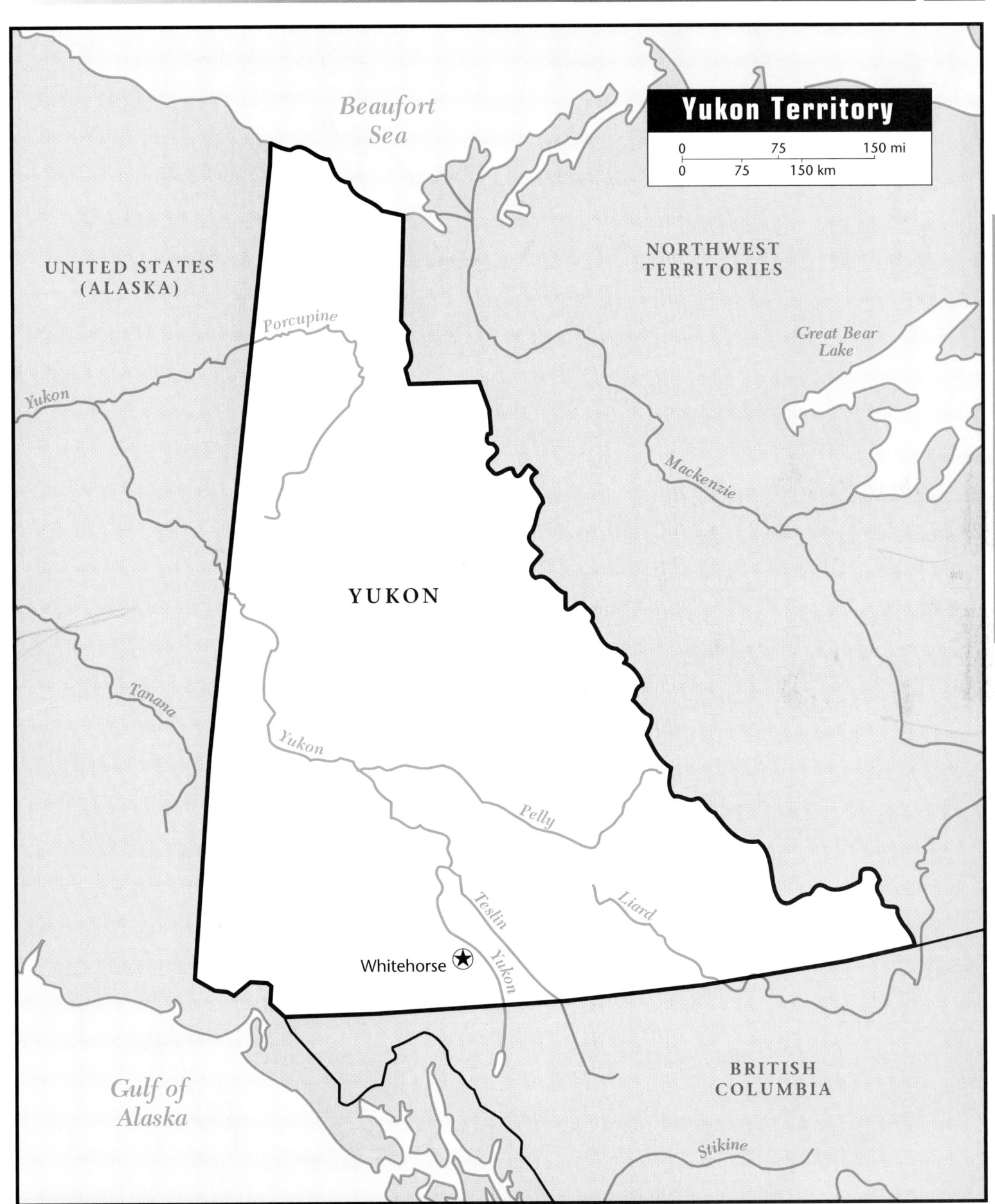

0   75   150 mi

0   75   150 km

Beaufort
Sea

UNITED STATES
(ALASKA)

NORTHWEST
TERRITORIES

Great Bear
Lake

Porcupine

Yukon

Mackenzie

YUKON

Tanana

Yukon

Pelly

Liard

Teslin

Yukon

Whitehorse ★

Gulf of
Alaska

BRITISH
COLUMBIA

Stikine

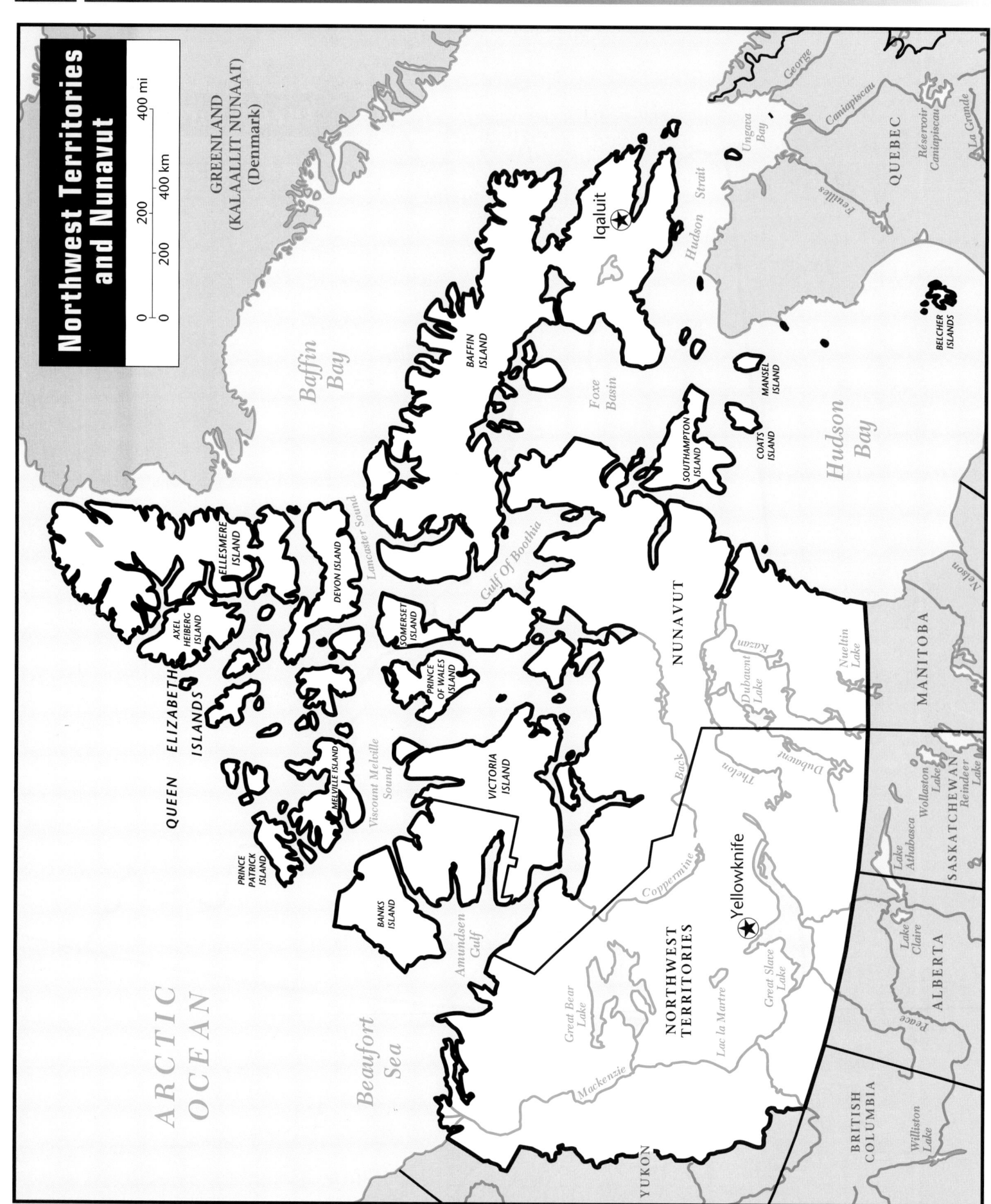

Northwest Territories and Nunavut

400 mi
400 km

ARCTIC OCEAN

GREENLAND (KALAALLIT NUNAAT) (Denmark)

Baffin Bay

Beaufort Sea

QUEEN ELIZABETH ISLANDS

ELLESMERE ISLAND

AXEL HEIBERG ISLAND

DEVON ISLAND

Lancaster Sound

BAFFIN ISLAND

Iqaluit

Hudson Strait

Foxe Basin

George

Ungava Bay

QUEBEC

Caniapiscau

Réservoir Caniapiscau

La Grande

Feuilles

BELCHER ISLANDS

MANSEL ISLAND

COATS ISLAND

SOUTHAMPTON ISLAND

Hudson Bay

Gulf Of Boothia

SOMERSET ISLAND

PRINCE OF WALES ISLAND

NUNAVUT

Nelson

MANITOBA

Nueltin Lake

Kazan

Dubawnt Lake

Thelon

Dubawnt

Back

Wollaston Lake

Lake Athabasca

SASKATCHEWAN

Reindeer Lake

PRINCE PATRICK ISLAND

MELVILLE ISLAND

Viscount Melville Sound

VICTORIA ISLAND

BANKS ISLAND

Amundsen Gulf

Coppermine

Yellowknife

NORTHWEST TERRITORIES

Great Bear Lake

Lac la Martre

Great Slave Lake

Mackenzie

Lake Claire

ALBERTA

Peace

YUKON

BRITISH COLUMBIA

Williston Lake

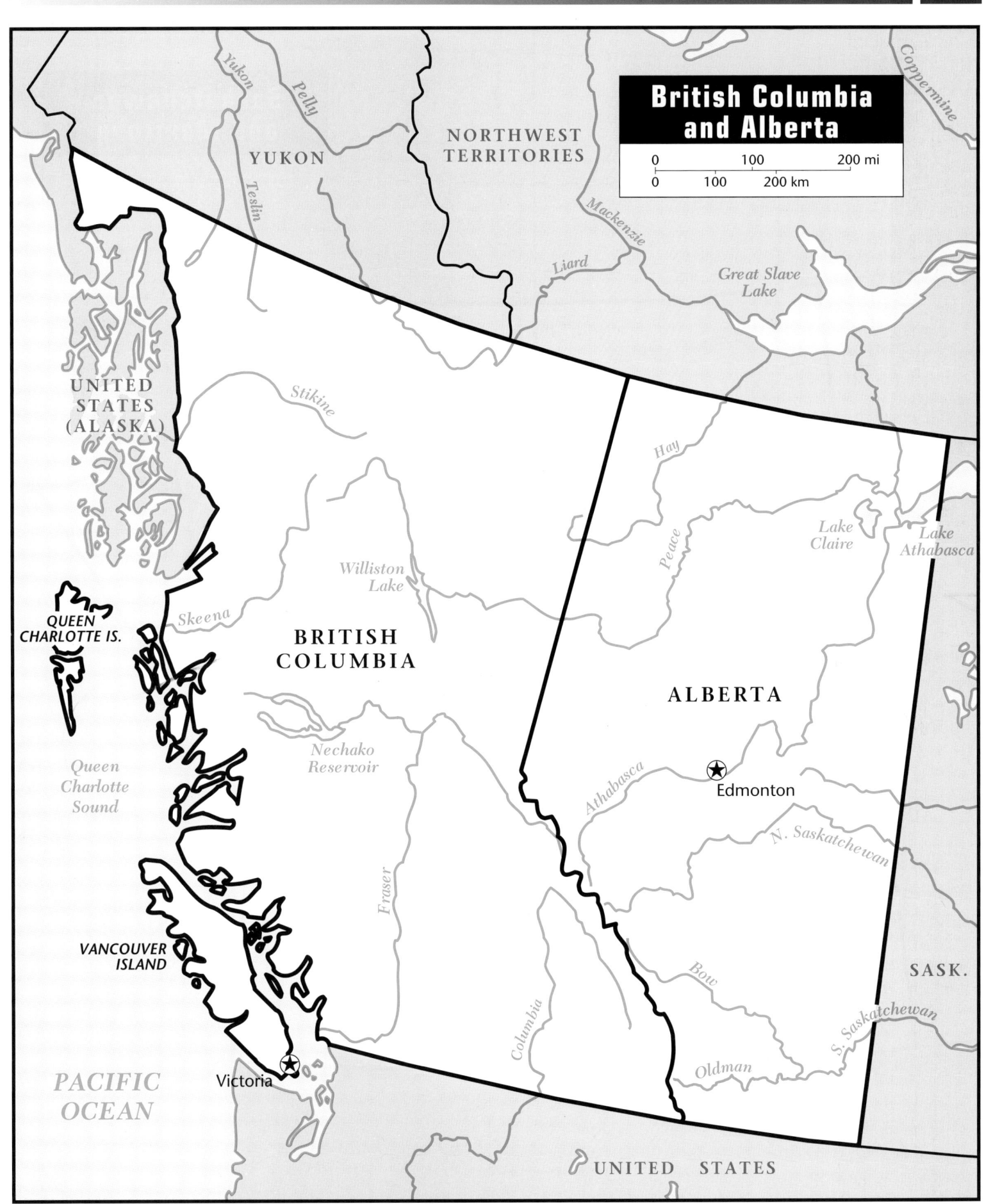

British Columbia and Alberta

0   100   200 mi

0   100   200 km

YUKON

NORTHWEST TERRITORIES

Yukon

Pelly

Teslin

Coppermine

Mackenzie

Liard

Great Slave Lake

UNITED STATES (ALASKA)

Stikine

Hay

Peace

Lake Claire

Lake Athabasca

QUEEN CHARLOTTE IS.

Williston Lake

Skeena

BRITISH COLUMBIA

ALBERTA

Queen Charlotte Sound

Nechako Reservoir

Athabasca

★ Edmonton

N. Saskatchewan

VANCOUVER ISLAND

Fraser

Bow

Columbia

SASK.

S. Saskatchewan

PACIFIC OCEAN

★ Victoria

Oldman

UNITED STATES

Saskatchewan and Manitoba

0   100   200 mi
0   100   200 km

Great Slave Lake

Thelon

Dubawnt Lake

Kazan

NORTHWEST TERRITORIES

Dubawnt

NUNAVUT

Nueltin Lake

Hudson Bay

Lake Claire

Lake Athabasca

ALBERTA

Wollaston Lake

Reindeer Lake

Southern Indian Lake

Nelson

MANITOBA

N. Saskatchewan

Churchill

Lac la Ronge

SASKATCHEWAN

Cedar Lake

Severn

Saskatchewan

Lake Winnipeg

Lac Seul

ONTARIO

S. Saskatchewan

Lake Winnipegosis

Qu'Appelle

Regina ⍟

Assiniboine

Lake Manitoba

Winnipeg ⍟

Lake of the Woods

Missouri

UNITED STATES

Red River of the North

Mississippi

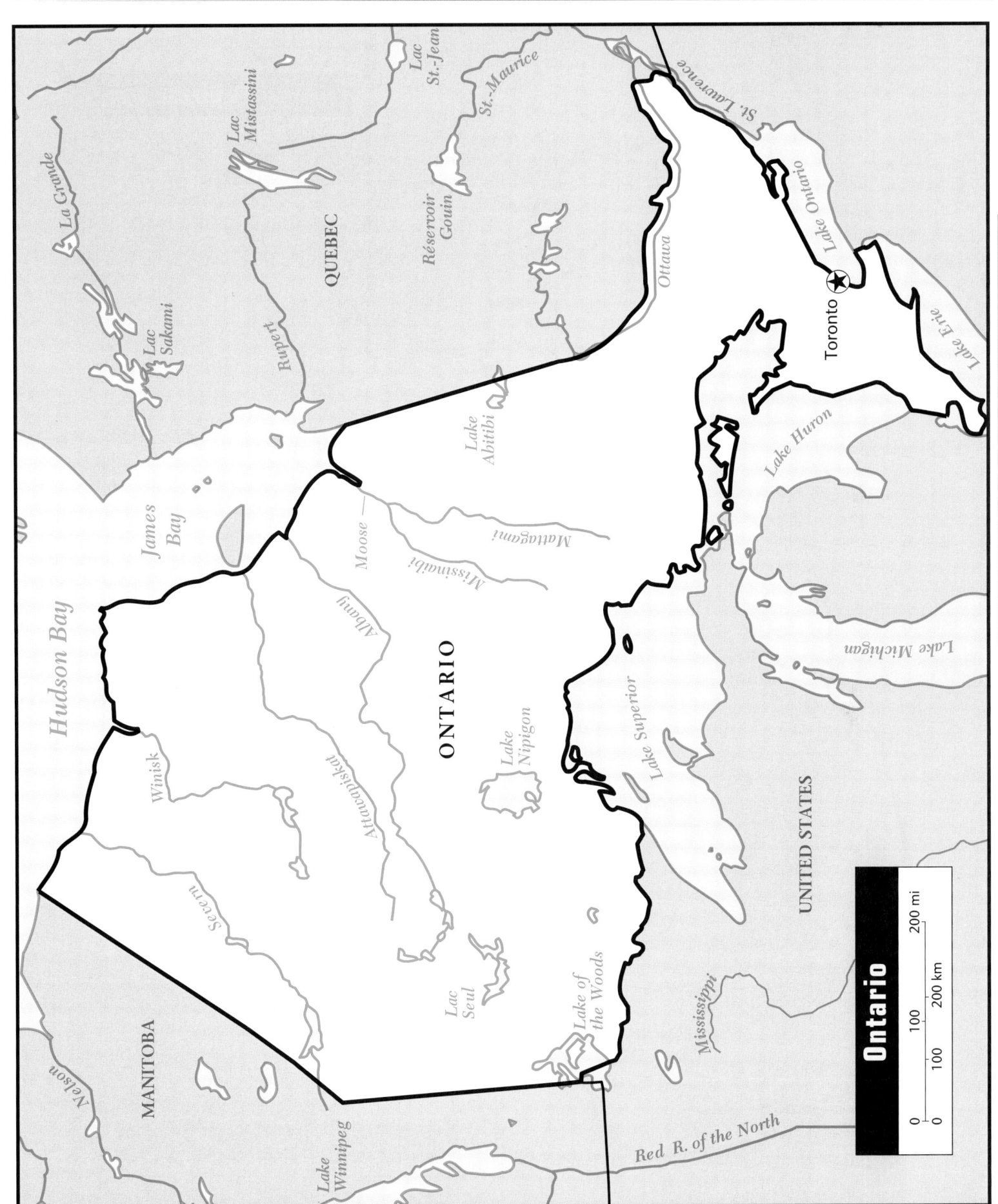

QUEBEC

La Grande

Lac Mistassini

Lac St-Jean

St.-Maurice

Réservoir Gouin

Lac Sakami

Rupert

St. Lawrence

Ottawa

Lake Ontario

Toronto

Lake Erie

Lake Abitibi

Lake Huron

James Bay

Moose

Mattagami

Missinaibi

Hudson Bay

Albany

Lake Michigan

ONTARIO

Winisk

Attawapiskat

Lake Nipigon

Lake Superior

UNITED STATES

Severn

Lac Seul

Lake of the Woods

MANITOBA

Nelson

Lake Winnipeg

Mississippi

Red R. of the North

Ontario

200 mi

200 km

100

100

0

0

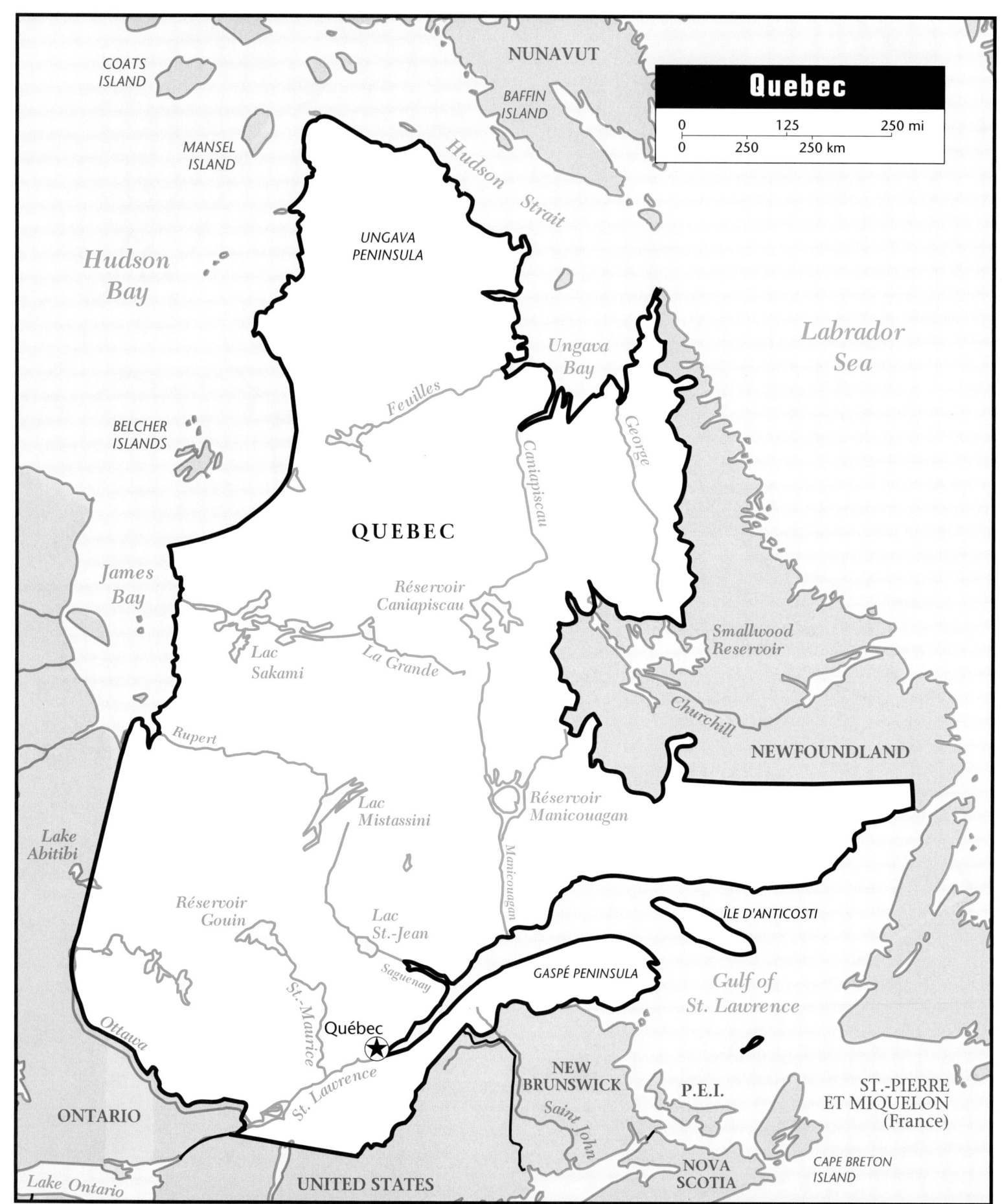

Quebec

0   125   250 mi
0   250   250 km

COATS ISLAND

NUNAVUT

BAFFIN ISLAND

MANSEL ISLAND

Hudson Strait

UNGAVA PENINSULA

Hudson Bay

Labrador Sea

BELCHER ISLANDS

Feuilles

Ungava Bay

Caniapiscau

George

QUEBEC

James Bay

Réservoir Caniapiscau

Smallwood Reservoir

Lac Sakami

La Grande

Churchill

NEWFOUNDLAND

Rupert

Réservoir Manicouagan

Lake Abitibi

Lac Mistassini

Manicouagan

Réservoir Gouin

Lac St.-Jean

ÎLE D'ANTICOSTI

Gulf of St. Lawrence

Saguenay

GASPÉ PENINSULA

St.-Maurice

Ottawa

Québec ★

St. Lawrence

NEW BRUNSWICK

P.E.I.

ST.-PIERRE ET MIQUELON (France)

ONTARIO

Saint John

Lake Ontario

UNITED STATES

NOVA SCOTIA

CAPE BRETON ISLAND

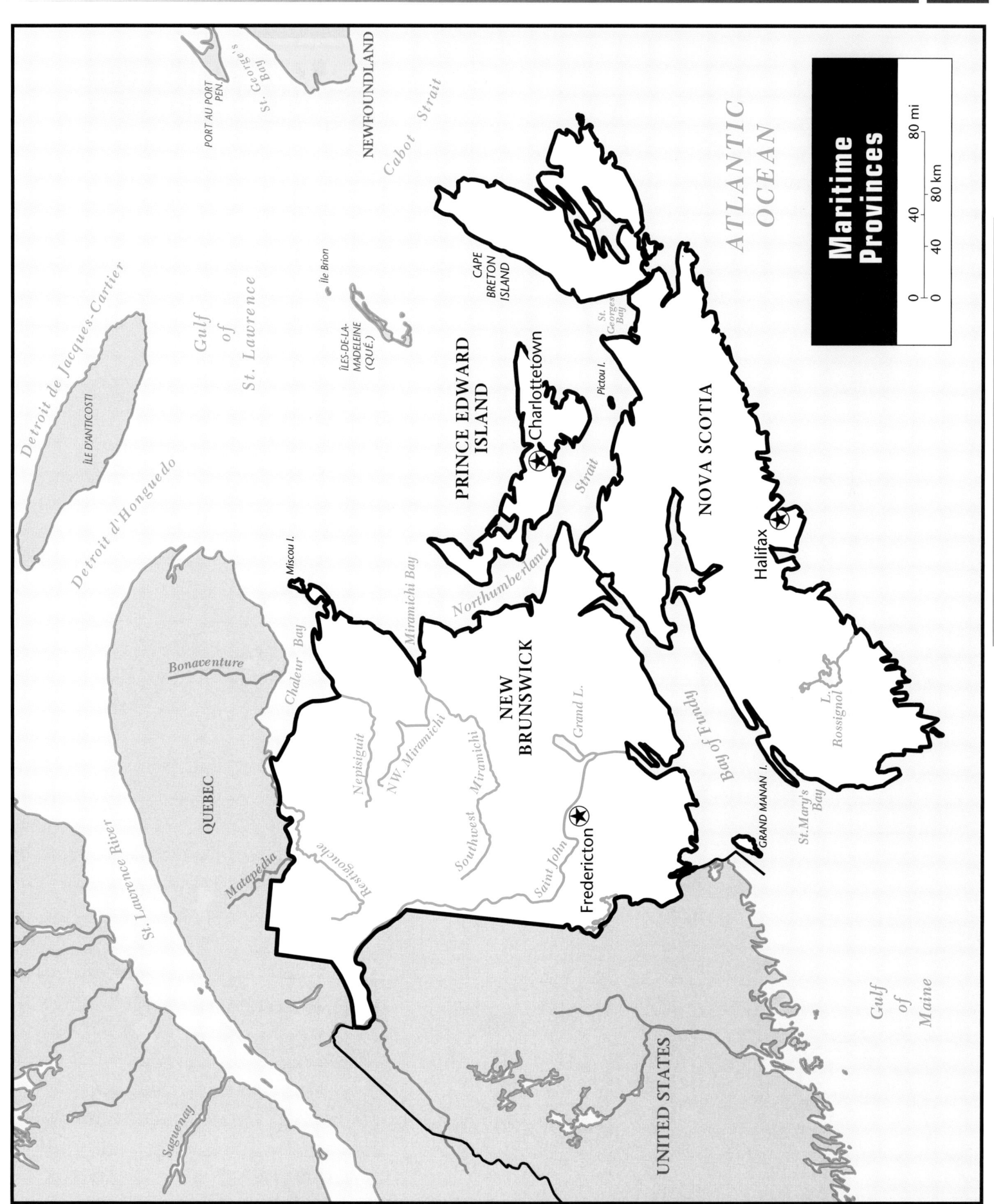

PORT AU PORT PEN.

St. George's Bay

NEWFOUNDLAND

Cabot Strait

ATLANTIC OCEAN

Île Brion

ÎLES-DE-LA-MADELEINE (QUÉ.)

CAPE BRETON ISLAND

St. George's Bay

Detroit de Jacques-Cartier

ÎLE D'ANTICOSTI

Gulf of St. Lawrence

Detroit d'Honguedo

Pictou I.

Charlottetown

PRINCE EDWARD ISLAND

Strait

NOVA SCOTIA

Halifax

Miscou I.

Northumberland

Chaleur Bay

Miramichi Bay

L. Rossignol

St. Lawrence River

QUEBEC

Bonaventure

Nepisiguit

NW. Miramichi

Southwest Miramichi

NEW BRUNSWICK

Grand L.

Bay of Fundy

Matapédia

Restigouche

Saint John

Fredericton

GRAND MANAN I.

St.Mary's Bay

Saguenay

UNITED STATES

Gulf of Maine

Maritime Provinces

80 mi
80 km
40
40
0
0

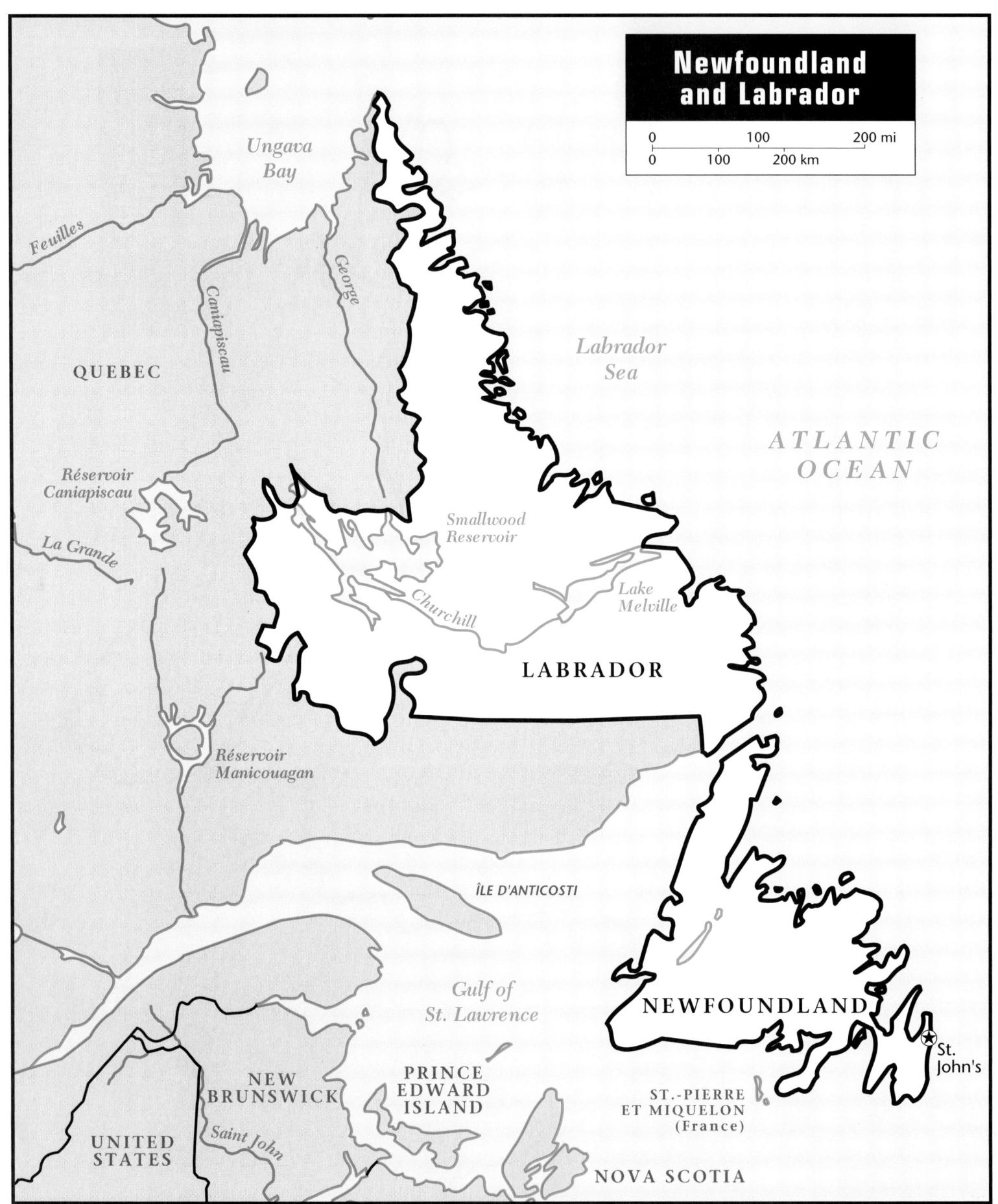

Newfoundland
and Labrador

| 0 | 100 | 200 mi |

| 0 | 100 | 200 km |

Ungava
Bay

Feuilles

Caniapiscau

George

QUEBEC

Labrador
Sea

Réservoir
Caniapiscau

ATLANTIC
OCEAN

La Grande

Smallwood
Reservoir

Lake
Melville

Churchill

LABRADOR

Réservoir
Manicouagan

ÎLE D'ANTICOSTI

Gulf of
St. Lawrence

NEWFOUNDLAND

NEW
BRUNSWICK

PRINCE
EDWARD
ISLAND

ST.-PIERRE
ET MIQUELON
(France)

St.
John's

UNITED
STATES

Saint John

NOVA SCOTIA

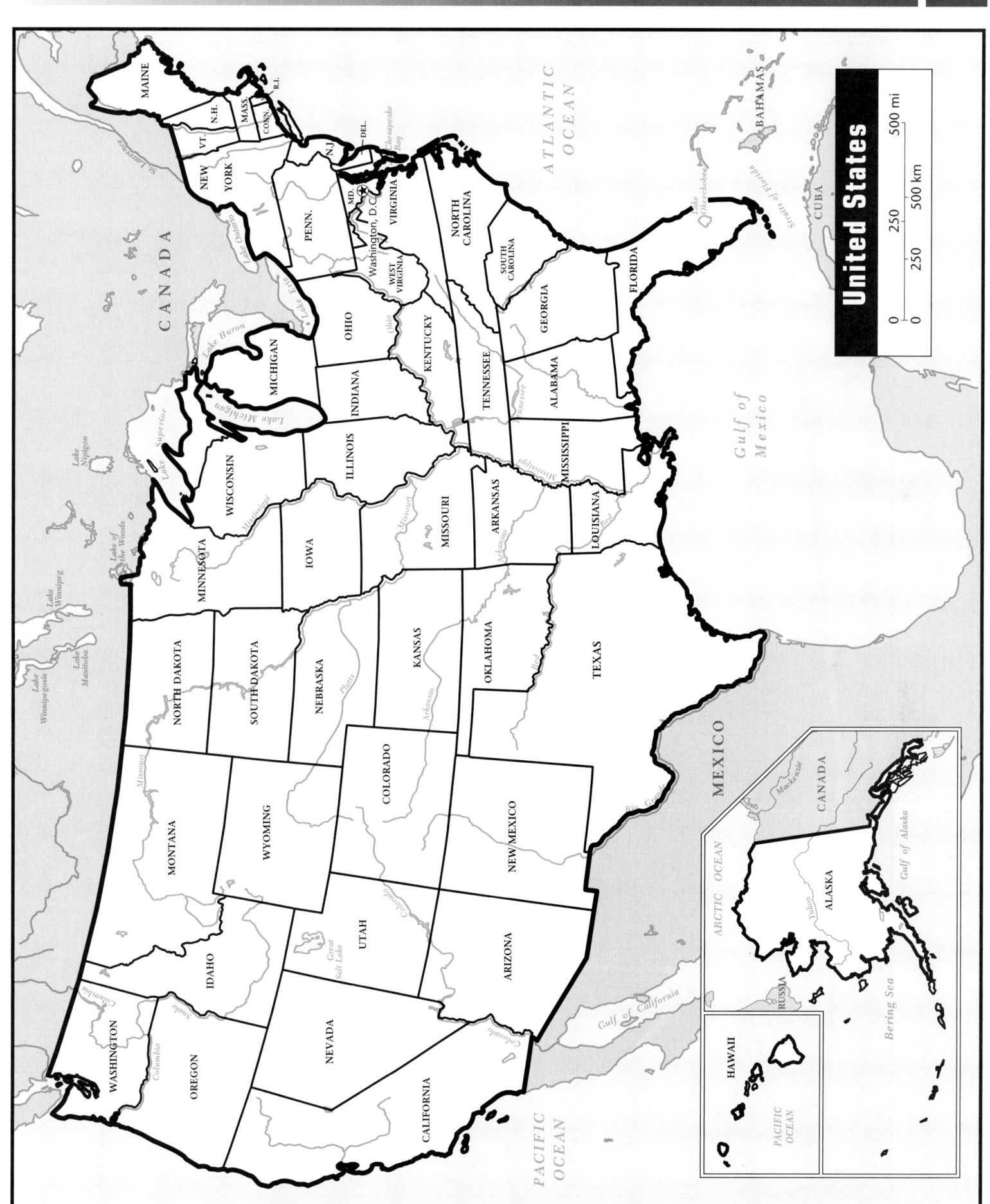

United States

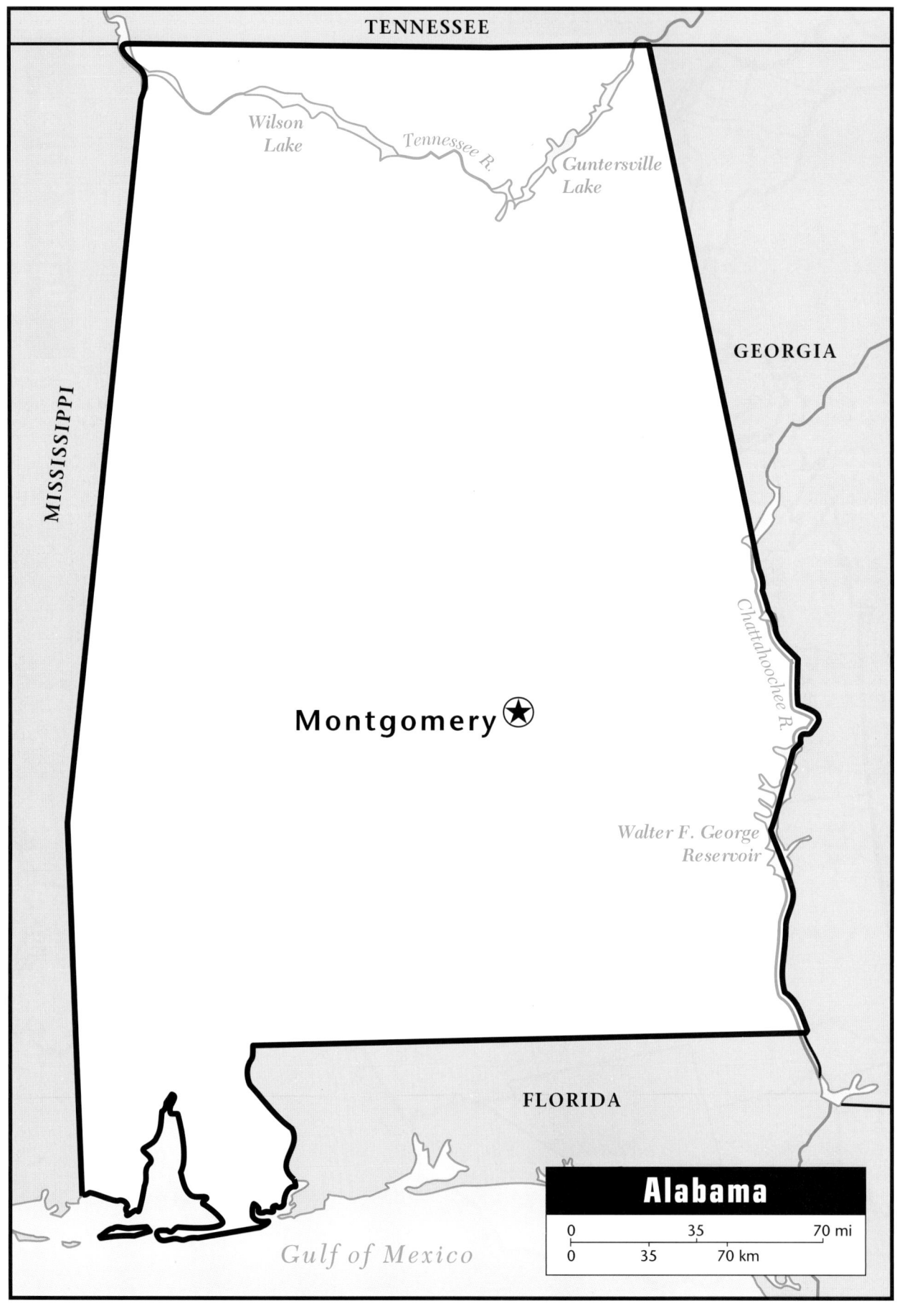

TENNESSEE

MISSISSIPPI

Wilson Lake

Tennessee R.

Guntersville Lake

GEORGIA

Chattahoochee R.

Montgomery ★

Walter F. George Reservoir

FLORIDA

Gulf of Mexico

Alabama

| 0 | 35 | 70 mi |
| 0 | 35 | 70 km |

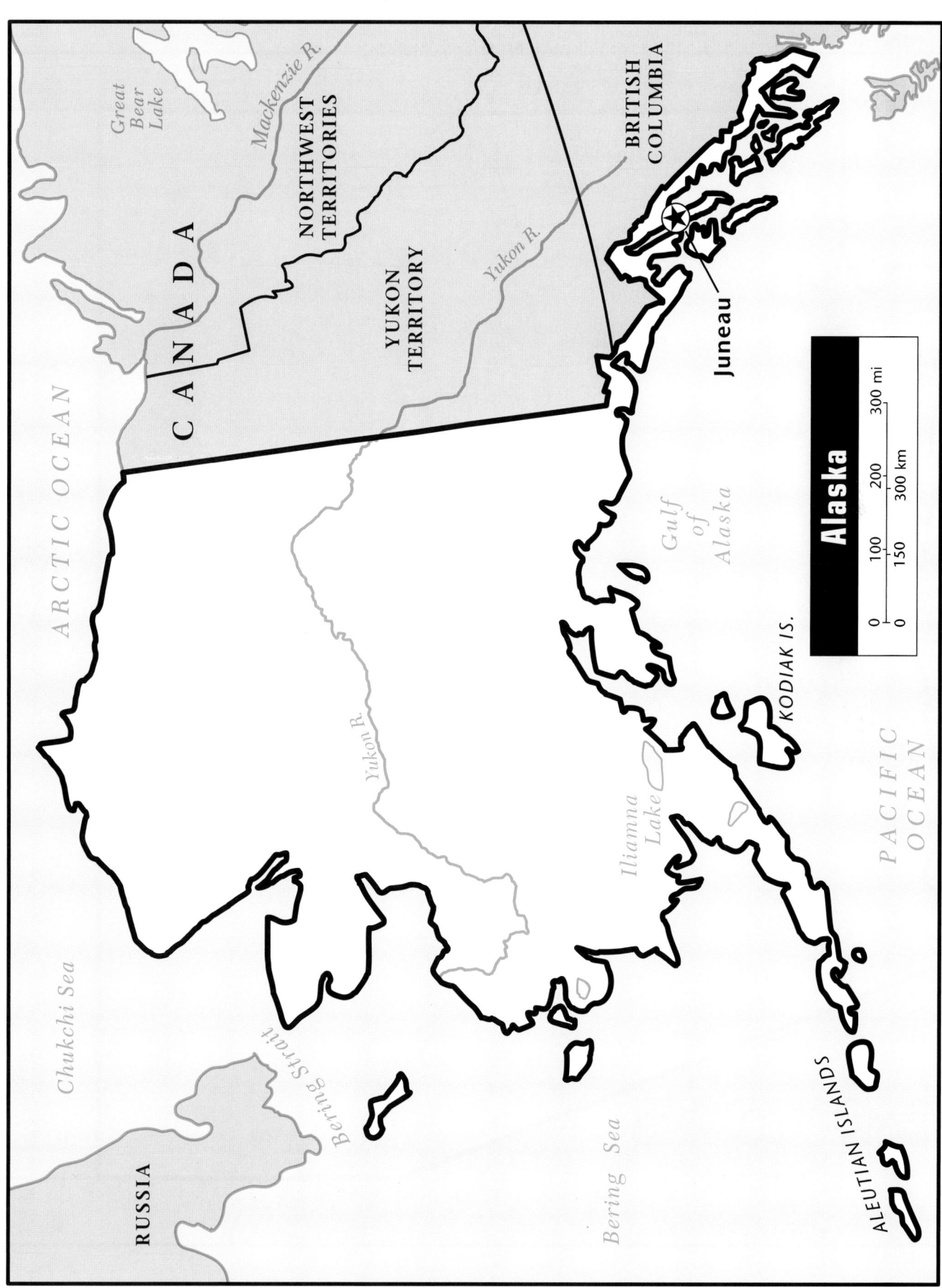

ARCTIC OCEAN

Great Bear Lake

Mackenzie R.

NORTHWEST TERRITORIES

C A N A D A

YUKON TERRITORY

Yukon R.

BRITISH COLUMBIA

Juneau

Gulf of Alaska

Chukchi Sea

Yukon R.

Bering Strait

Iliamna Lake

KODIAK IS.

PACIFIC OCEAN

RUSSIA

Bering Sea

ALEUTIAN ISLANDS

Alaska

| 0 | 100 | 200 | 300 mi |

| 0 | 150 | 300 km |

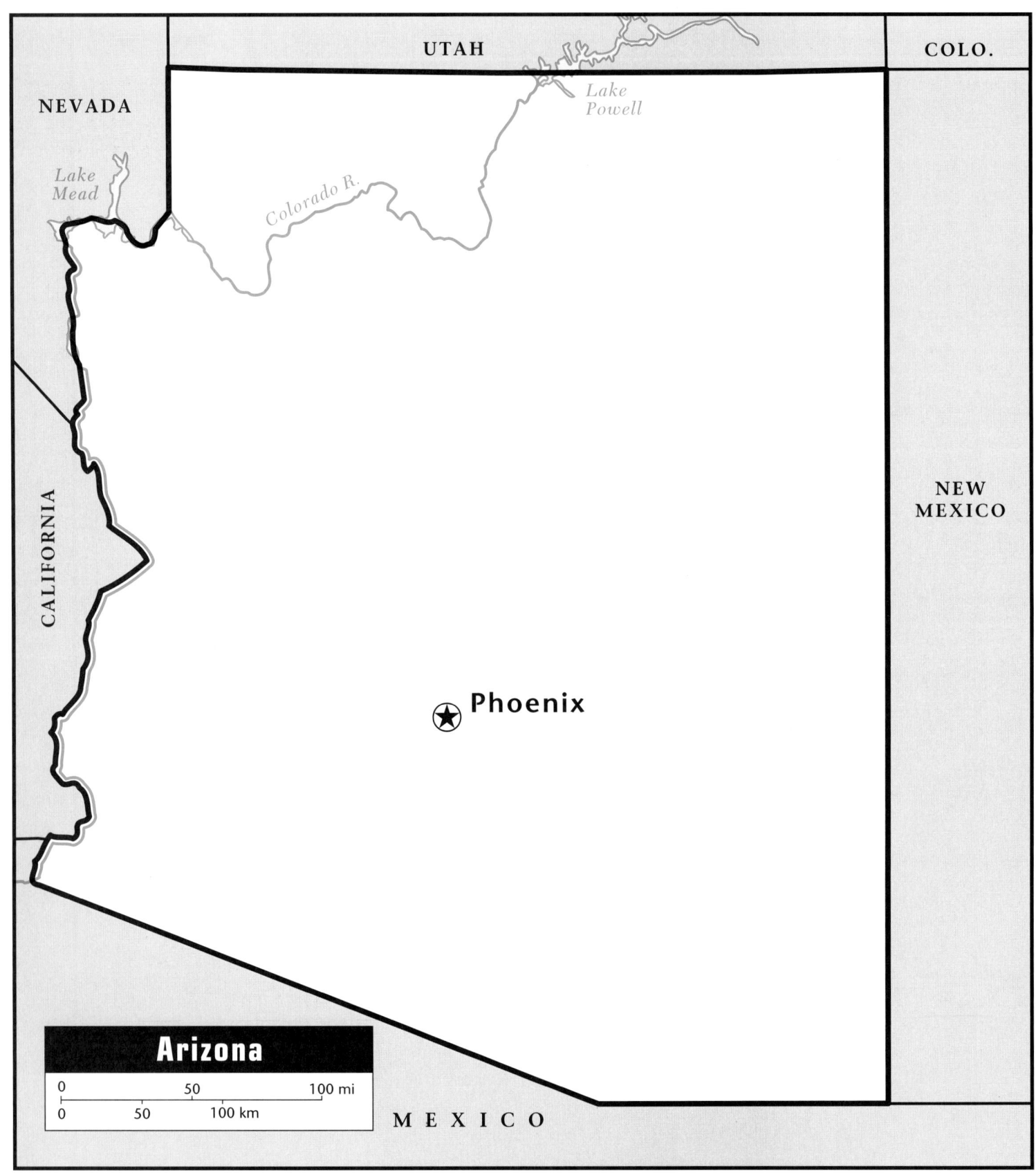

NEVADA

UTAH

COLO.

Lake Powell

Lake Mead

Colorado R.

CALIFORNIA

NEW MEXICO

★ Phoenix

Arizona

0   50   100 mi

0   50   100 km

M E X I C O

KANSAS

MISSOURI

OKLA.

TENN.

Arkansas

| 0 | | 35 | | 70 mi |
| 0 | 35 | | 70 km | |

Beaver
Lake

Bull Shoals
Lake

White R.

Lake
Dardanelle

Arkansas R.

Mississippi R.

Little Rock ★

MISSISSIPPI

TEXAS

LOUISIANA

OREGON

Klamath R.   Goose L.

UTAH

Sacramento R.

Pyramid L.

NEVADA

L. Tahoe

★ **Sacramento**

San Joaquin R.

PACIFIC
OCEAN

L. Mead

ARIZ.

Colorado R.

California

| 0 | 75 | 150 mi |
| 0 | 75 | 150 km |

CHANNEL ISLANDS

Salton
Sea

MEXICO

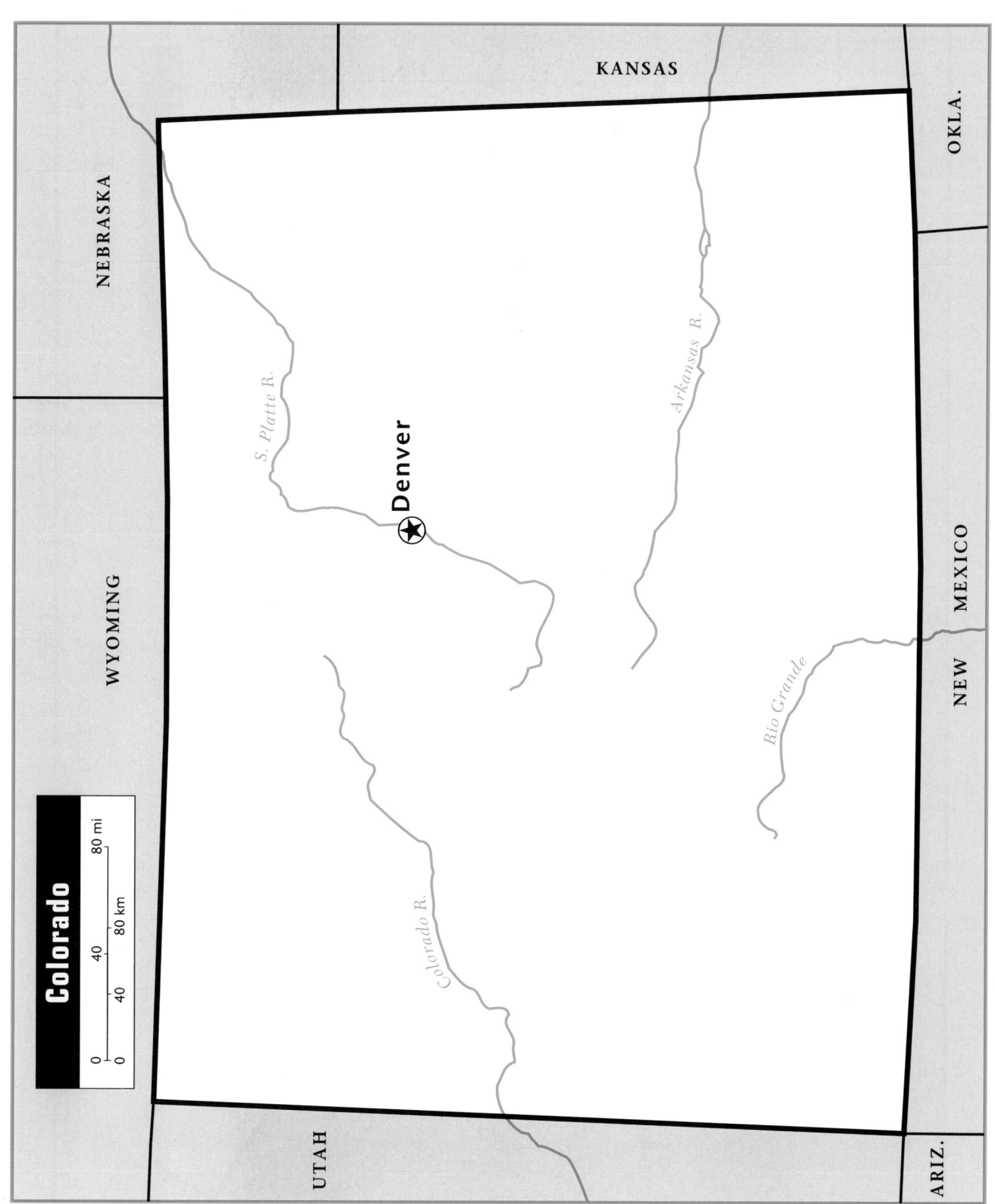

Colorado

KANSAS

OKLA.

NEBRASKA

S. Platte R.

Arkansas R.

Denver

WYOMING

Rio Grande

NEW MEXICO

Colorado R.

UTAH

ARIZ.

Colorado

80 mi

40

80 km

40

0

0

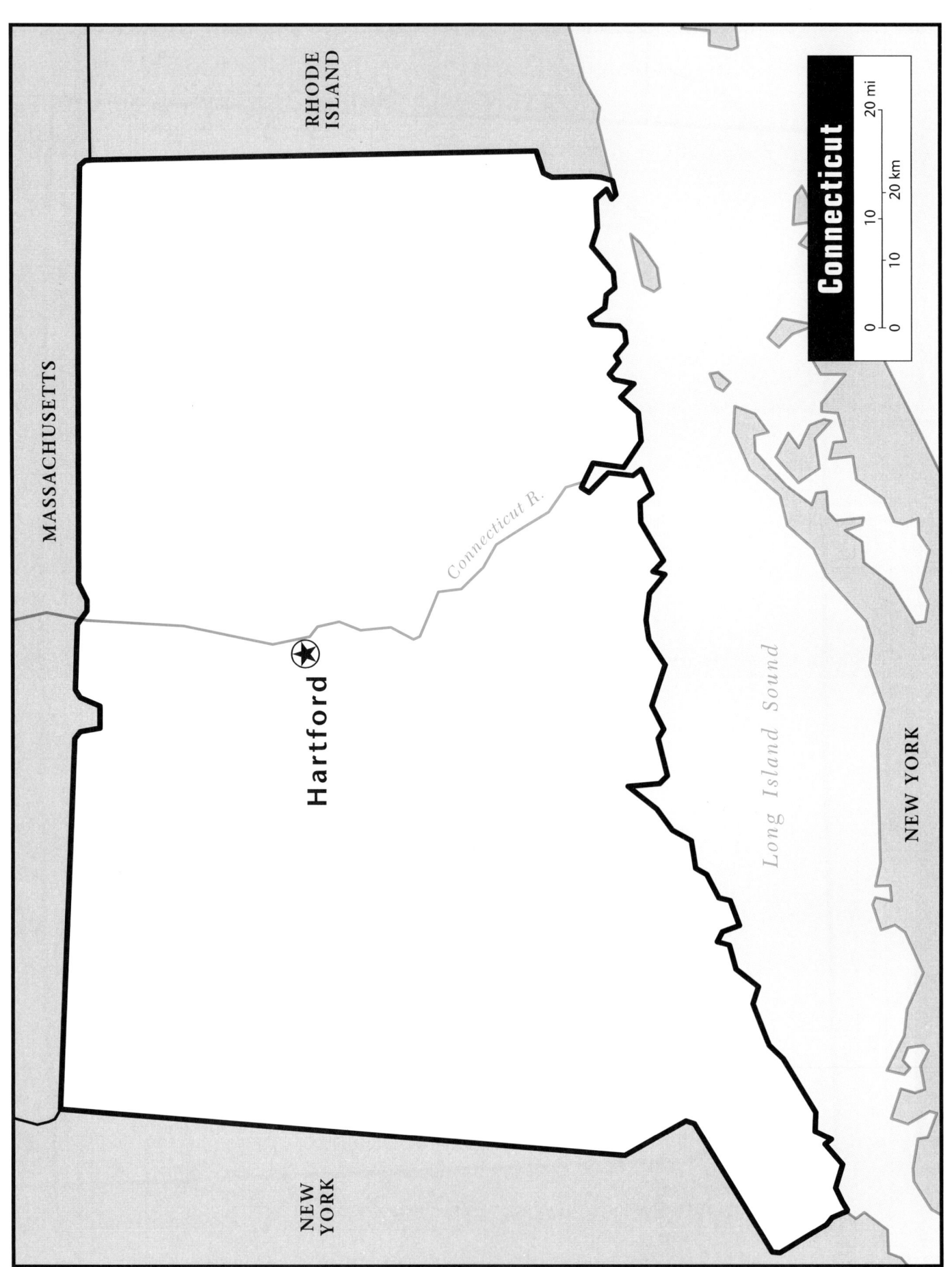

RHODE ISLAND

MASSACHUSETTS

Connecticut R.

Hartford

Long Island Sound

NEW YORK

NEW YORK

Connecticut

20 mi

20 km

10

10

0

0

10

10

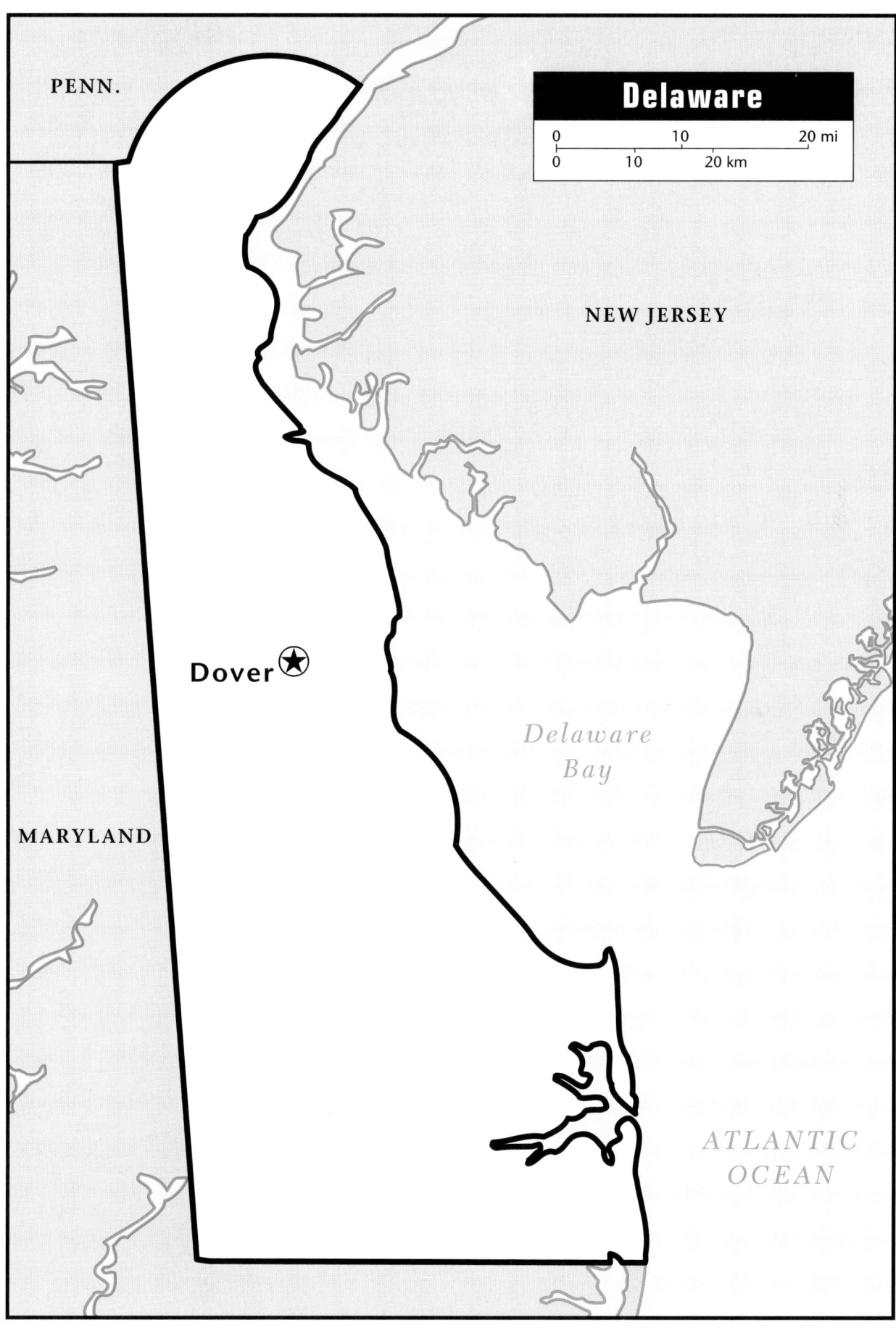

PENN.

NEW JERSEY

Dover ★

MARYLAND

Delaware Bay

ATLANTIC OCEAN

Delaware

0		10		20 mi
0	10		20 km	

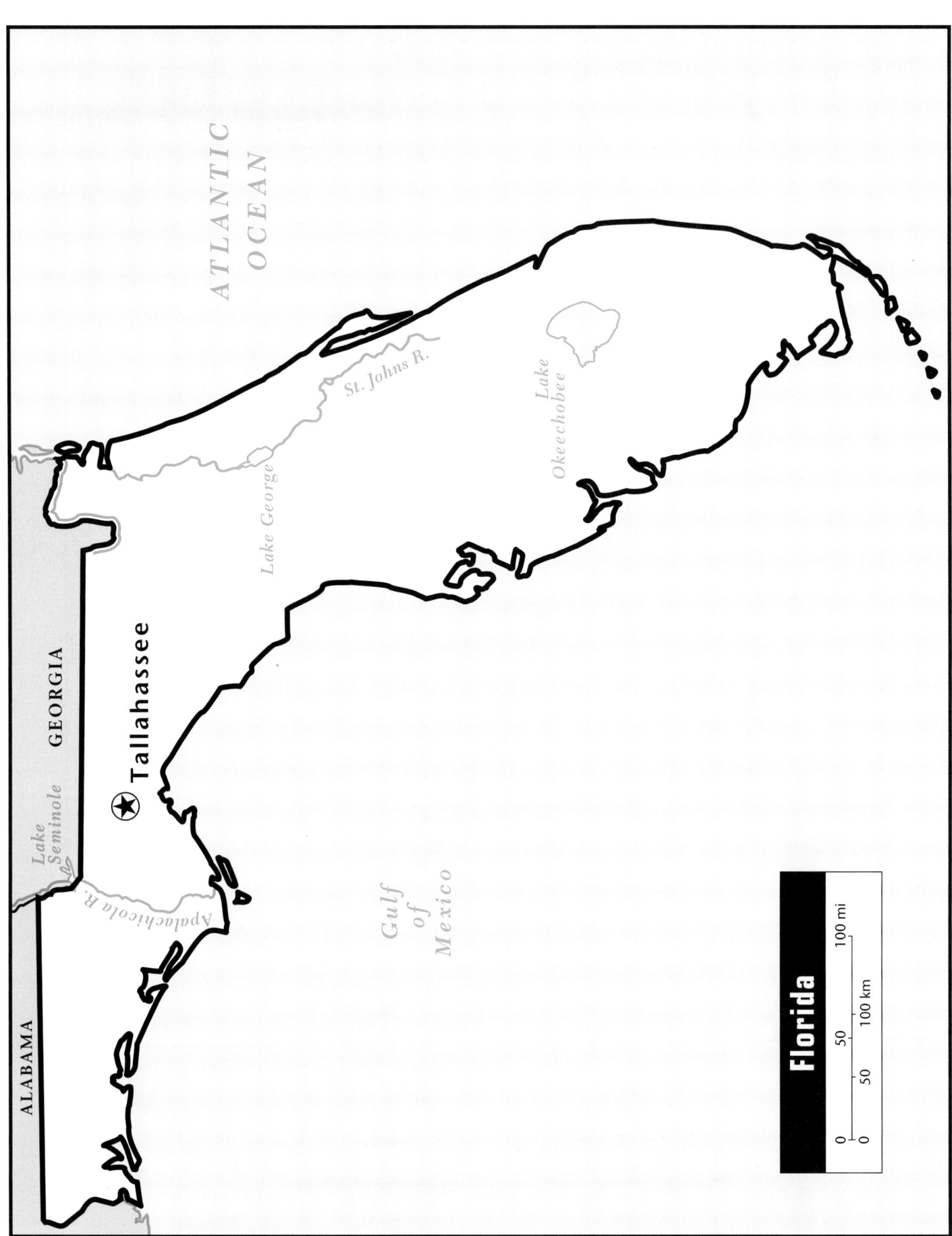

ATLANTIC OCEAN

St. Johns R.

Lake George

Lake Okeechobee

GEORGIA

ALABAMA

Lake Seminole

Apalachicola R.

⊛ Tallahassee

Gulf of Mexico

Florida

| 0 | 50 | 100 mi |
| 0 | 50 | 100 km |

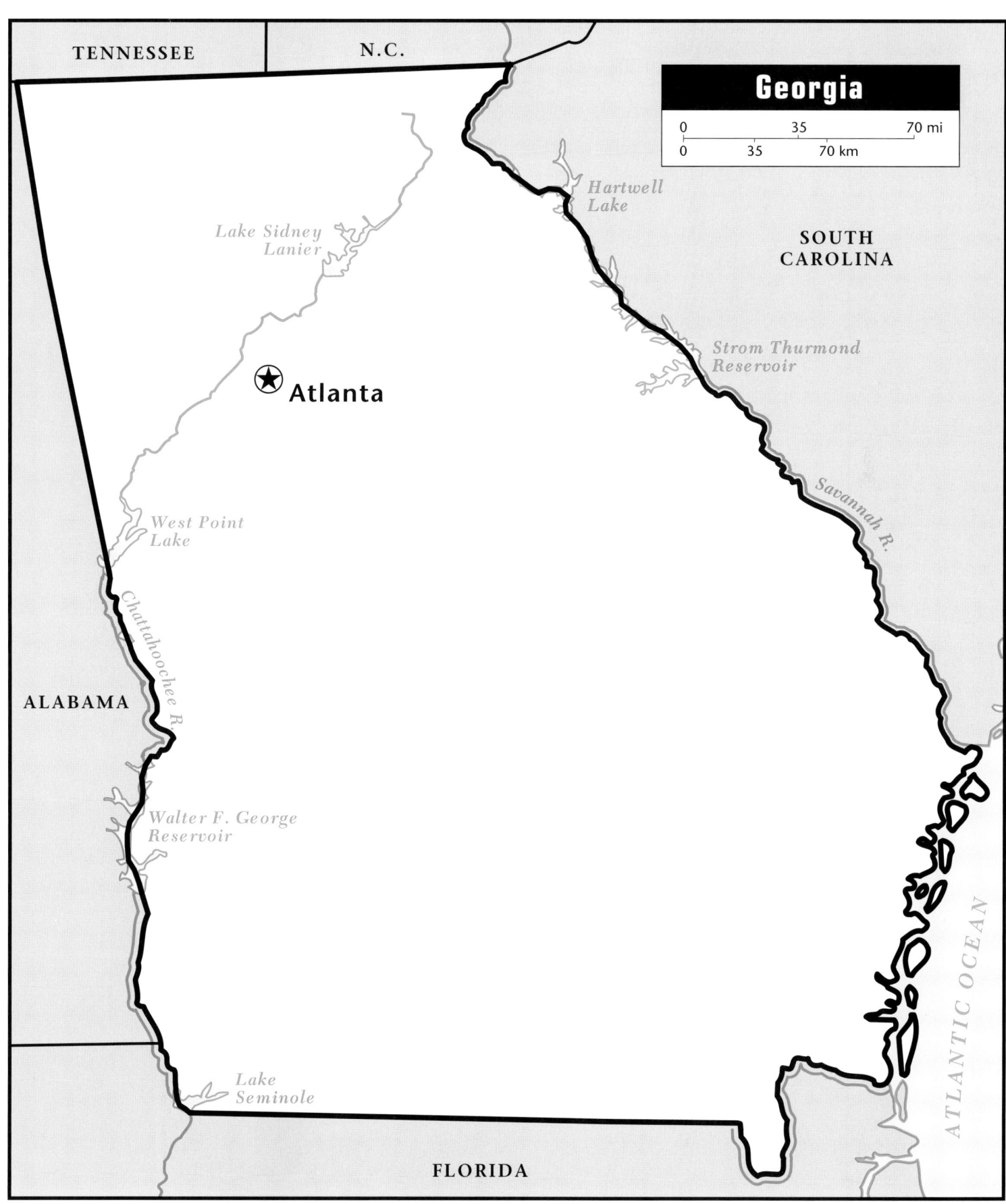

TENNESSEE

N.C.

SOUTH CAROLINA

Hartwell Lake

Lake Sidney Lanier

Strom Thurmond Reservoir

★ Atlanta

Savannah R.

West Point Lake

Chattahoochee R.

ALABAMA

Walter F. George Reservoir

ATLANTIC OCEAN

Lake Seminole

FLORIDA

Georgia

0   35   70 mi
0   35   70 km

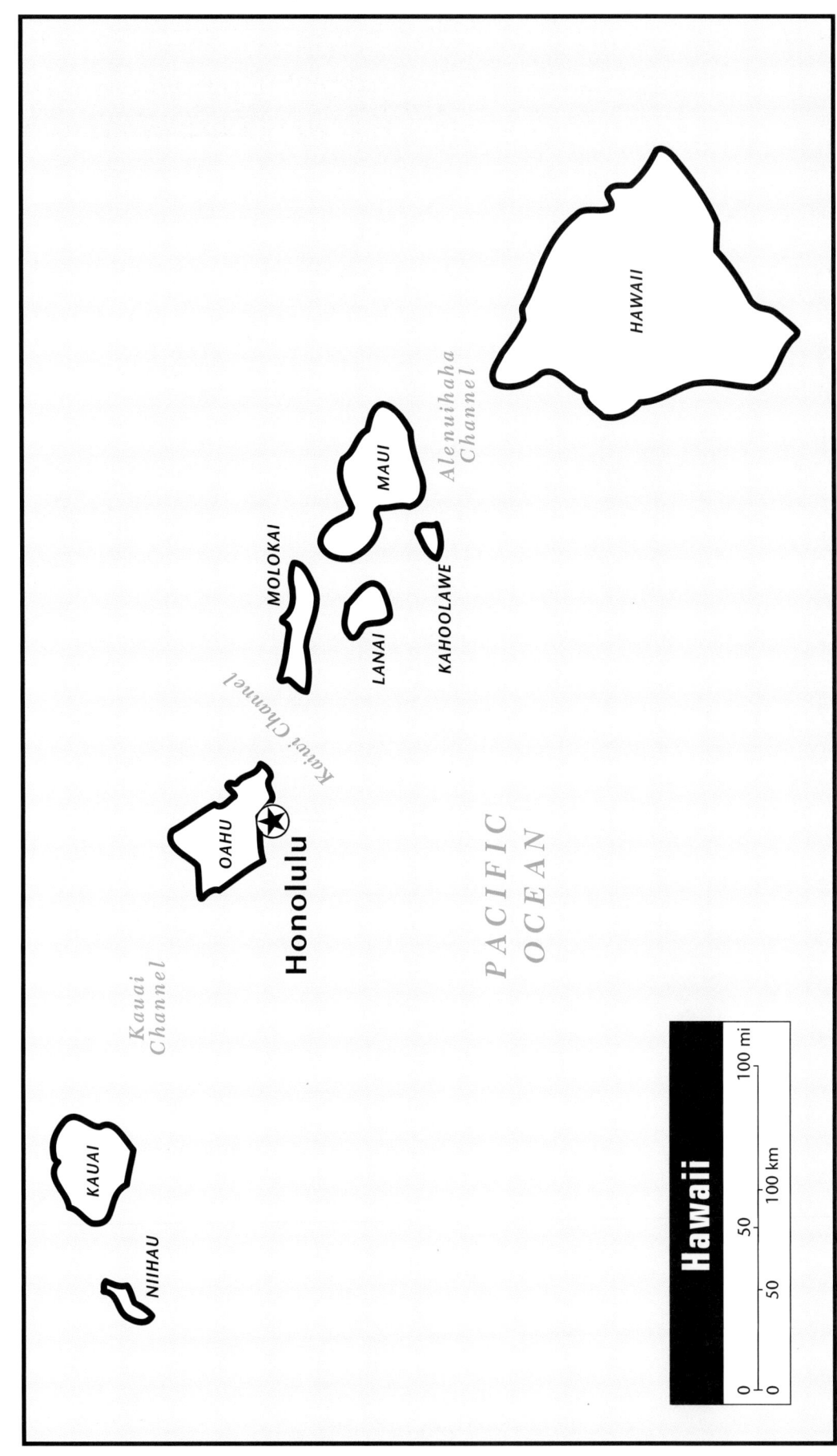

HAWAII

Alenuihaha Channel

MAUI

MOLOKAI

LANAI

KAHOOLAWE

Kalui Channel

OAHU

Honolulu

PACIFIC OCEAN

Kauai Channel

KAUAI

NIIHAU

Hawaii

0   50   100 km
0   50   100 mi

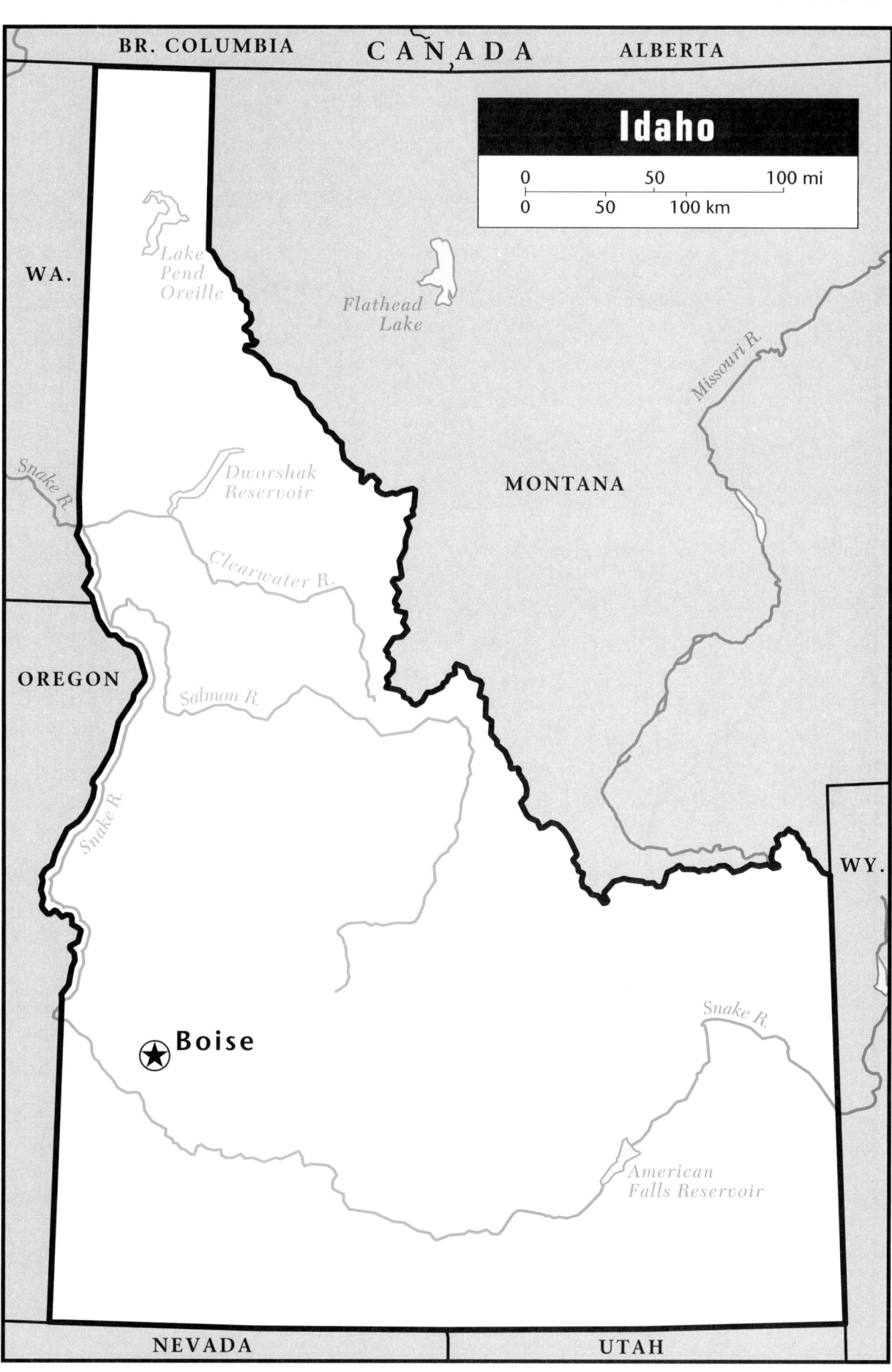

BR. COLUMBIA CANADA ALBERTA

WA.

Lake Pend Oreille

Flathead Lake

Missouri R.

MONTANA

Snake R.

Dworshak Reservoir

Clearwater R.

OREGON

Salmon R.

Snake R.

WY.

Snake R.

⭐ **Boise**

American Falls Reservoir

NEVADA UTAH

Idaho

0   50   100 mi

0   50   100 km

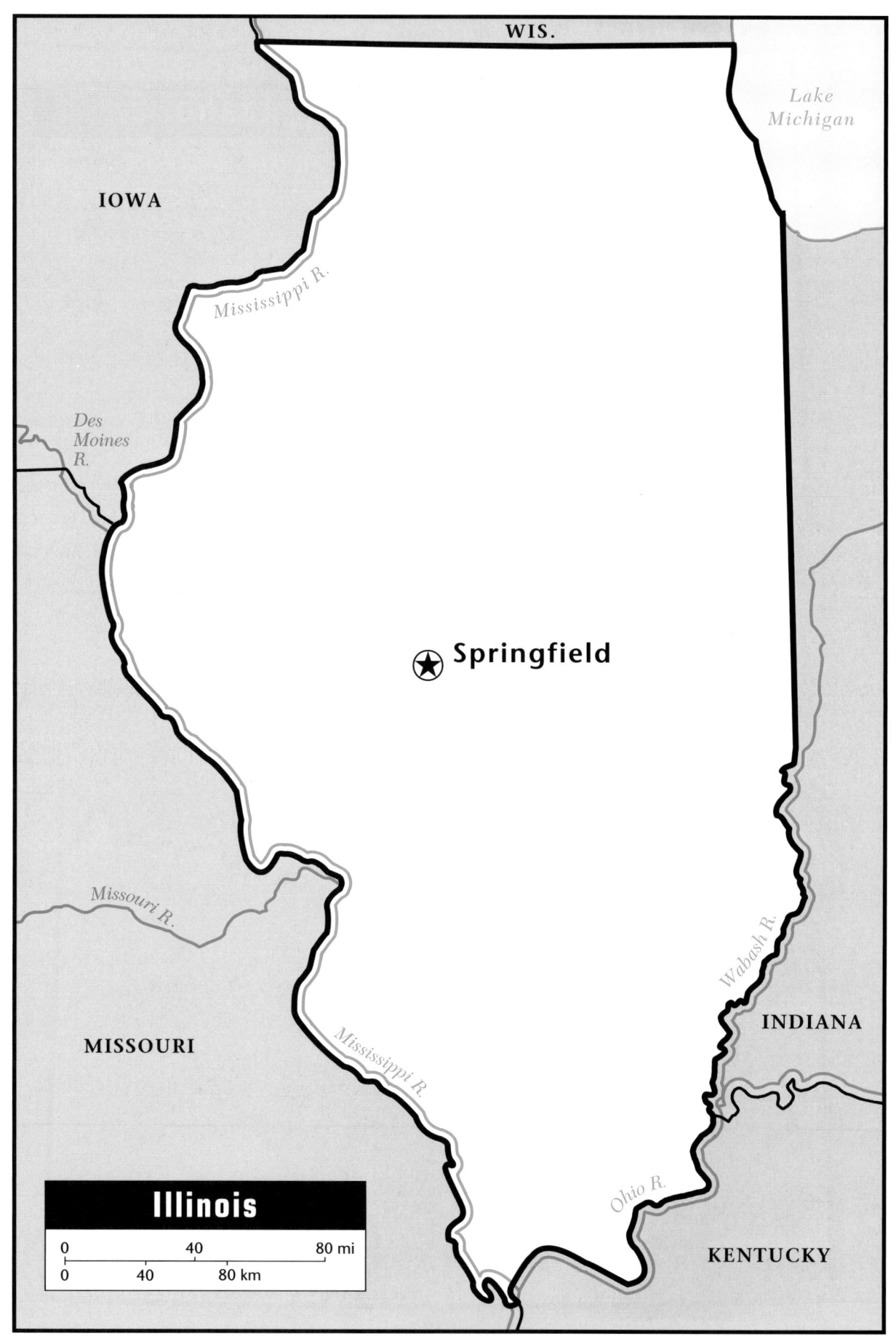

WIS.

Lake
Michigan

IOWA

Mississippi R.

*Des
Moines
R.*

★ **Springfield**

Missouri R.

Wabash R.

INDIANA

MISSOURI

Mississippi R.

Ohio R.

KENTUCKY

Illinois

0	40	80 mi
0	40	80 km

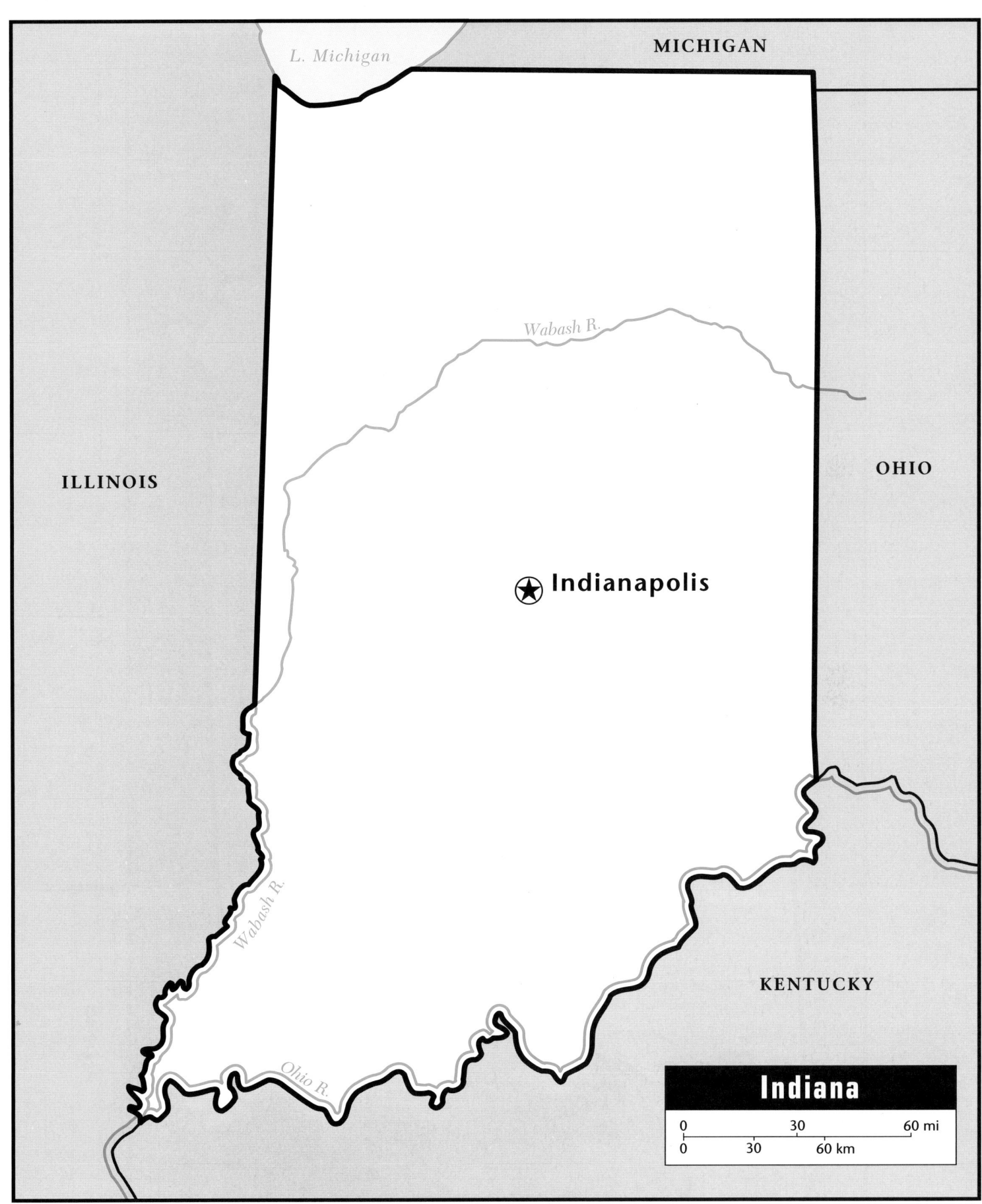

L. Michigan

MICHIGAN

ILLINOIS

Wabash R.

OHIO

★ Indianapolis

Wabash R.

KENTUCKY

Ohio R.

Indiana

0 30 60 mi

0 30 60 km

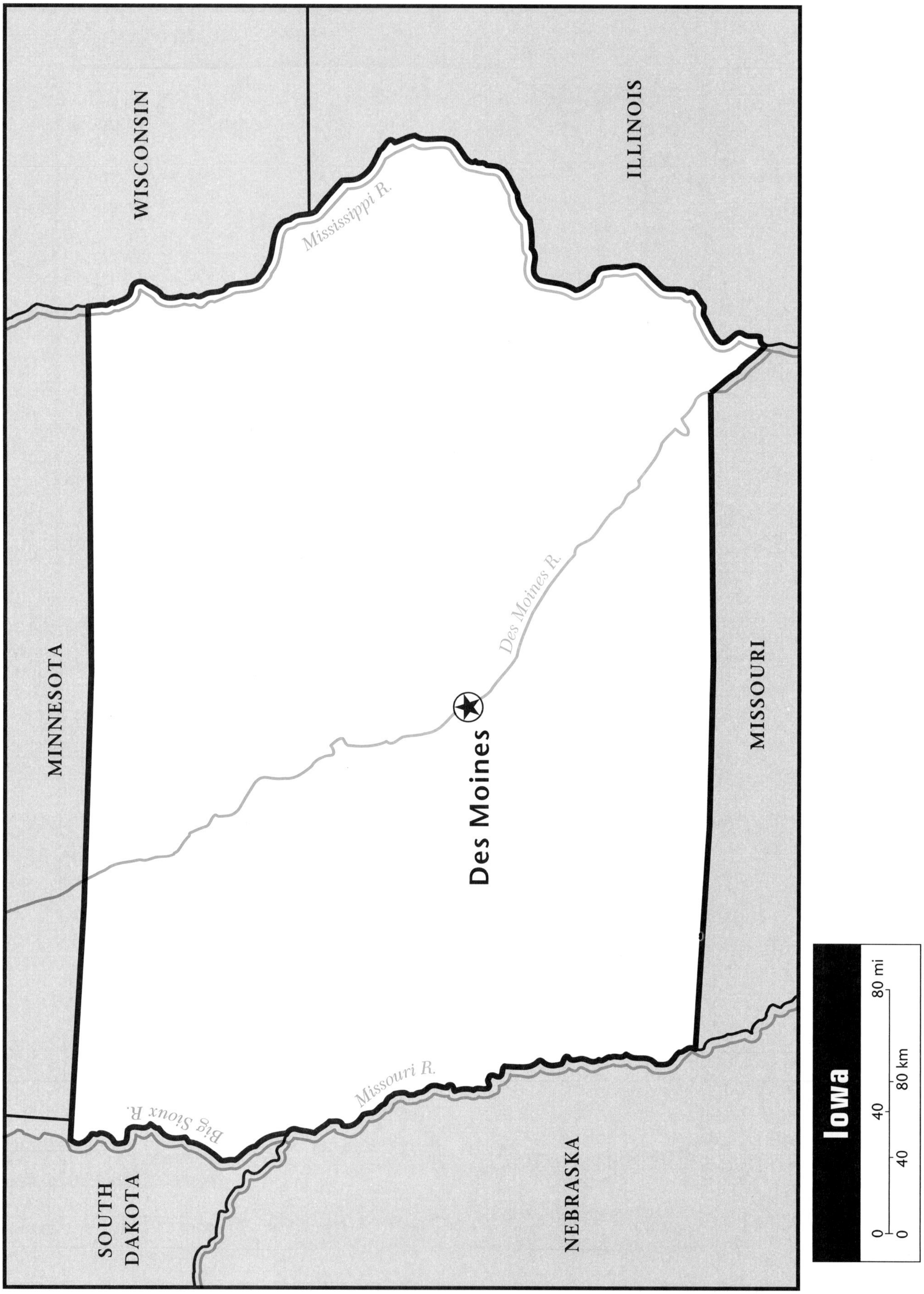

WISCONSIN

ILLINOIS

Mississippi R.

MINNESOTA

Des Moines R.

MISSOURI

⊛ **Des Moines**

SOUTH DAKOTA

Big Sioux R.

Missouri R.

NEBRASKA

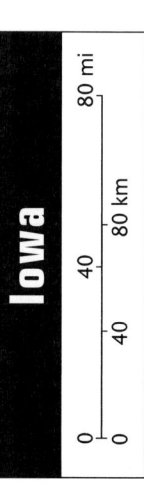

Iowa

| 0 | 40 | 80 km |
| 0 | 40 | 80 mi |

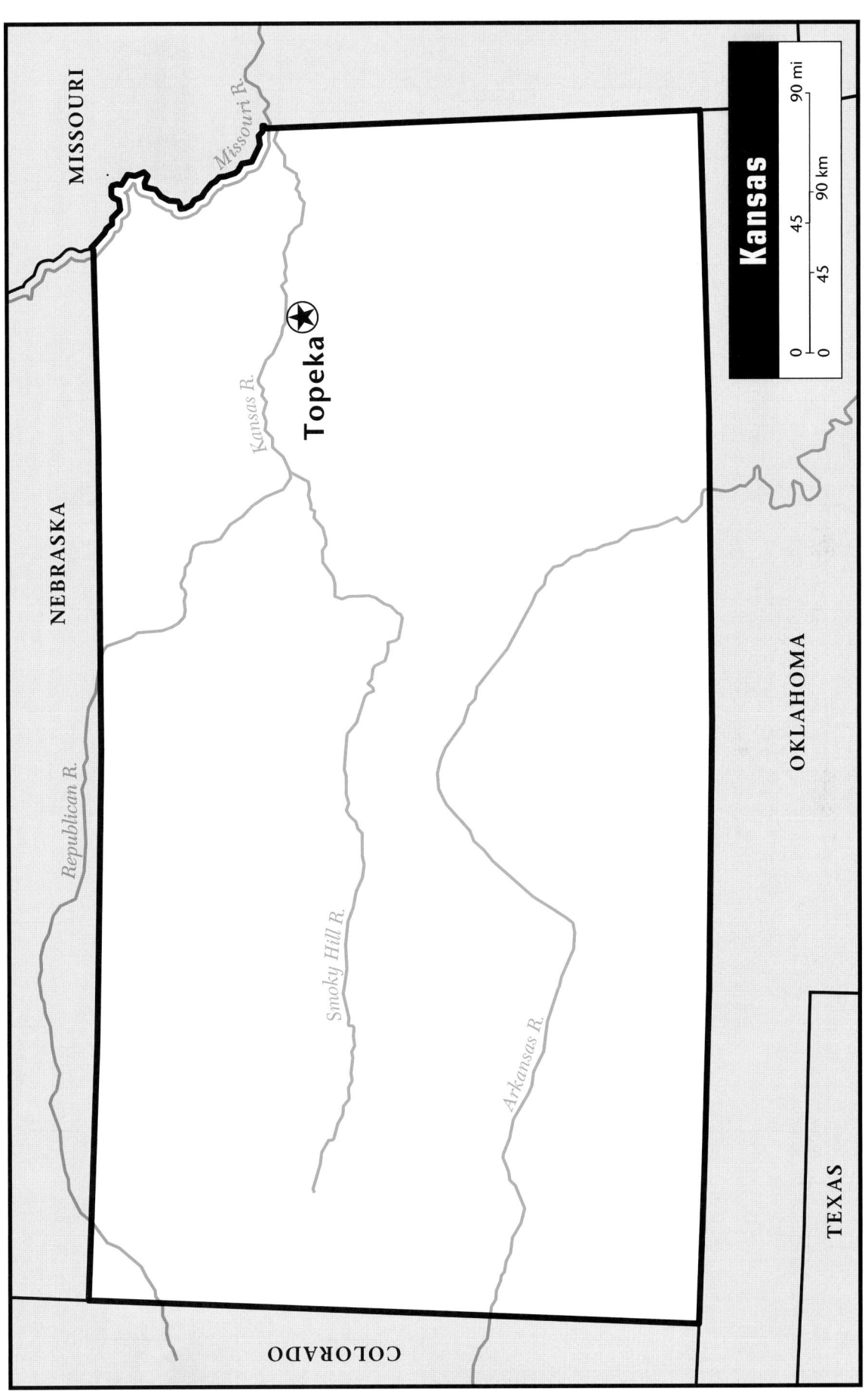

Kansas

MISSOURI

NEBRASKA

COLORADO

OKLAHOMA

TEXAS

Missouri R.

Kansas R.

Republican R.

Smoky Hill R.

Arkansas R.

★ Topeka

0   45   90 mi

0   45   90 km

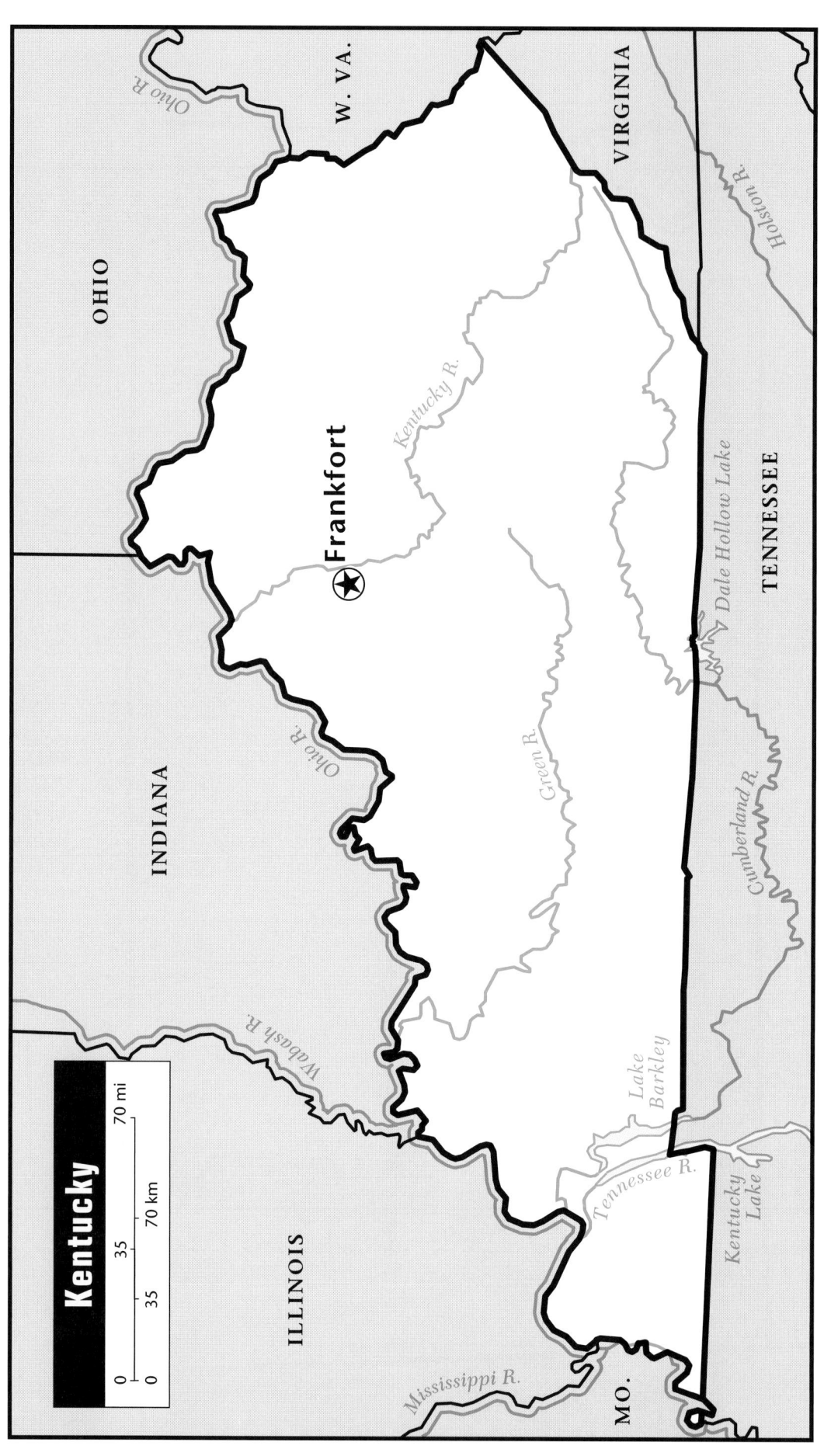

OHIO

Ohio R.

W. VA.

VIRGINIA

Holston R.

Kentucky R.

Dale Hollow Lake

★ Frankfort

TENNESSEE

INDIANA

Ohio R.

Green R.

Cumberland R.

Wabash R.

Lake Barkley

Kentucky Lake

Tennessee R.

ILLINOIS

MO.

Mississippi R.

Kentucky

| 0 | 35 | 70 mi |
| 0 | 35 | 70 km |

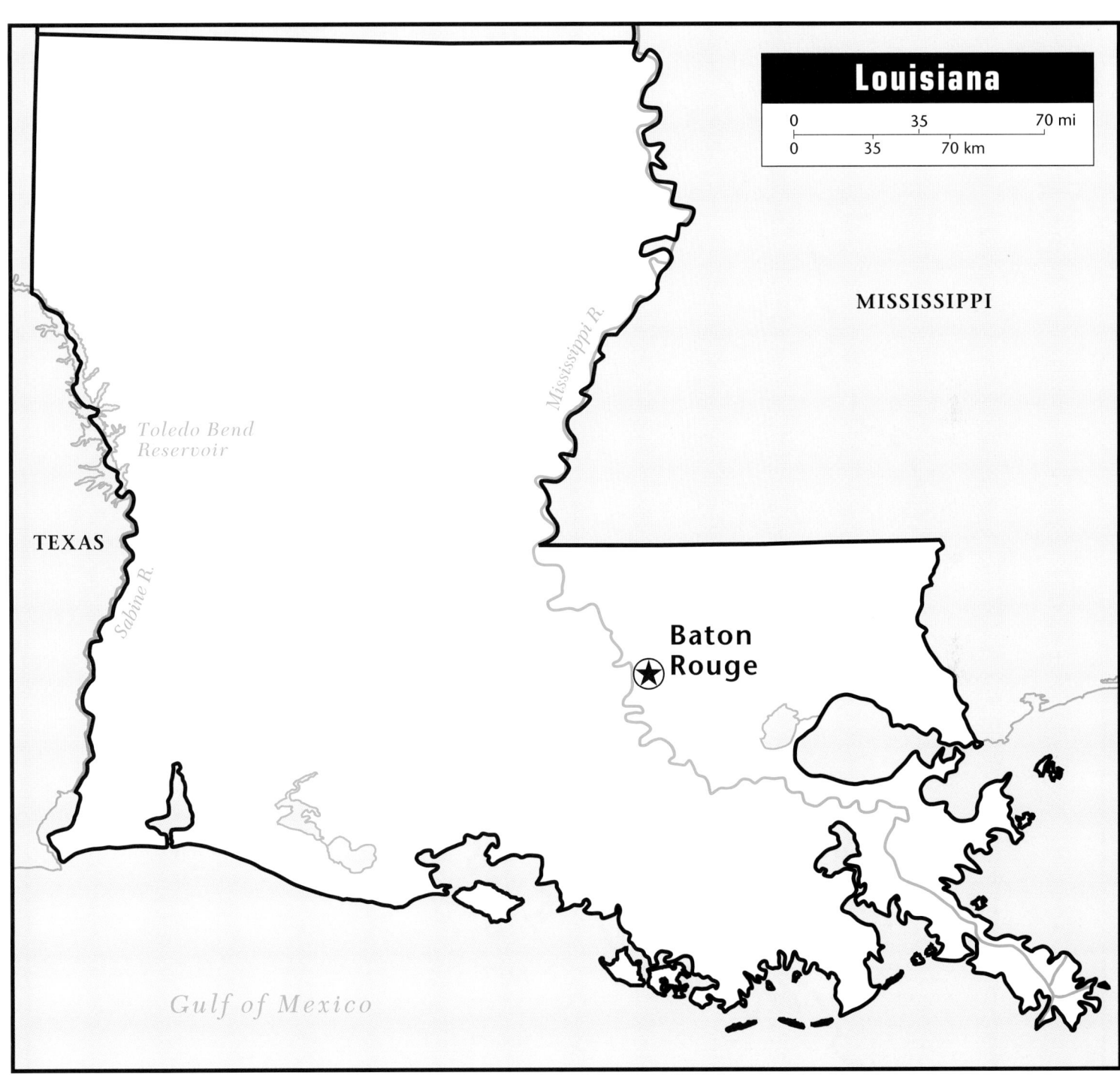

Louisiana

0	35	70 mi
0	35	70 km

MISSISSIPPI

TEXAS

Toledo Bend Reservoir

Sabine R.

Mississippi R.

★ Baton Rouge

Gulf of Mexico

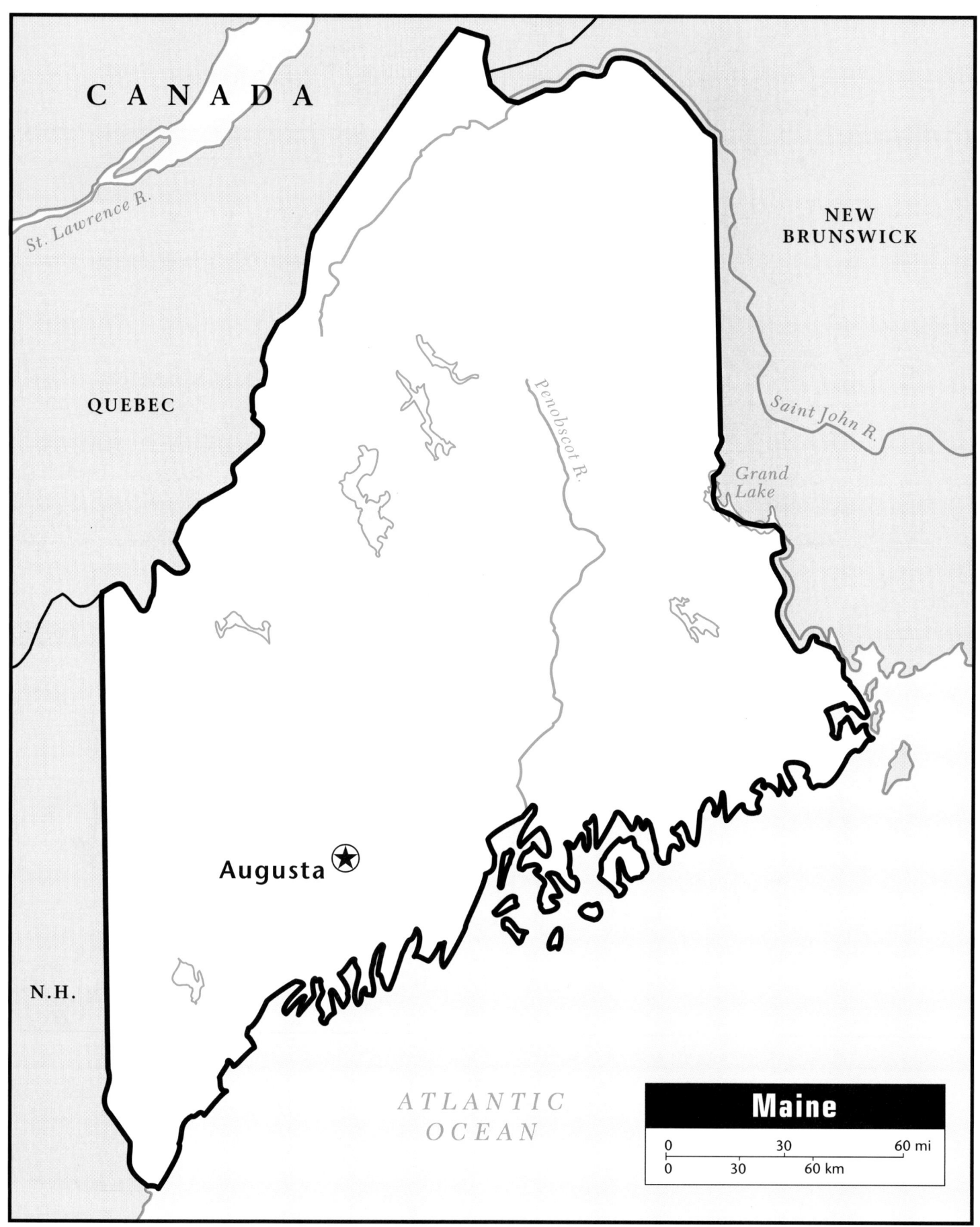

CANADA

St. Lawrence R.

NEW
BRUNSWICK

QUEBEC

Penobscot R.

Saint John R.

Grand
Lake

N.H.

Augusta ★

ATLANTIC
OCEAN

Maine

| 0 | 30 | 60 mi |
| 0 | 30 | 60 km |

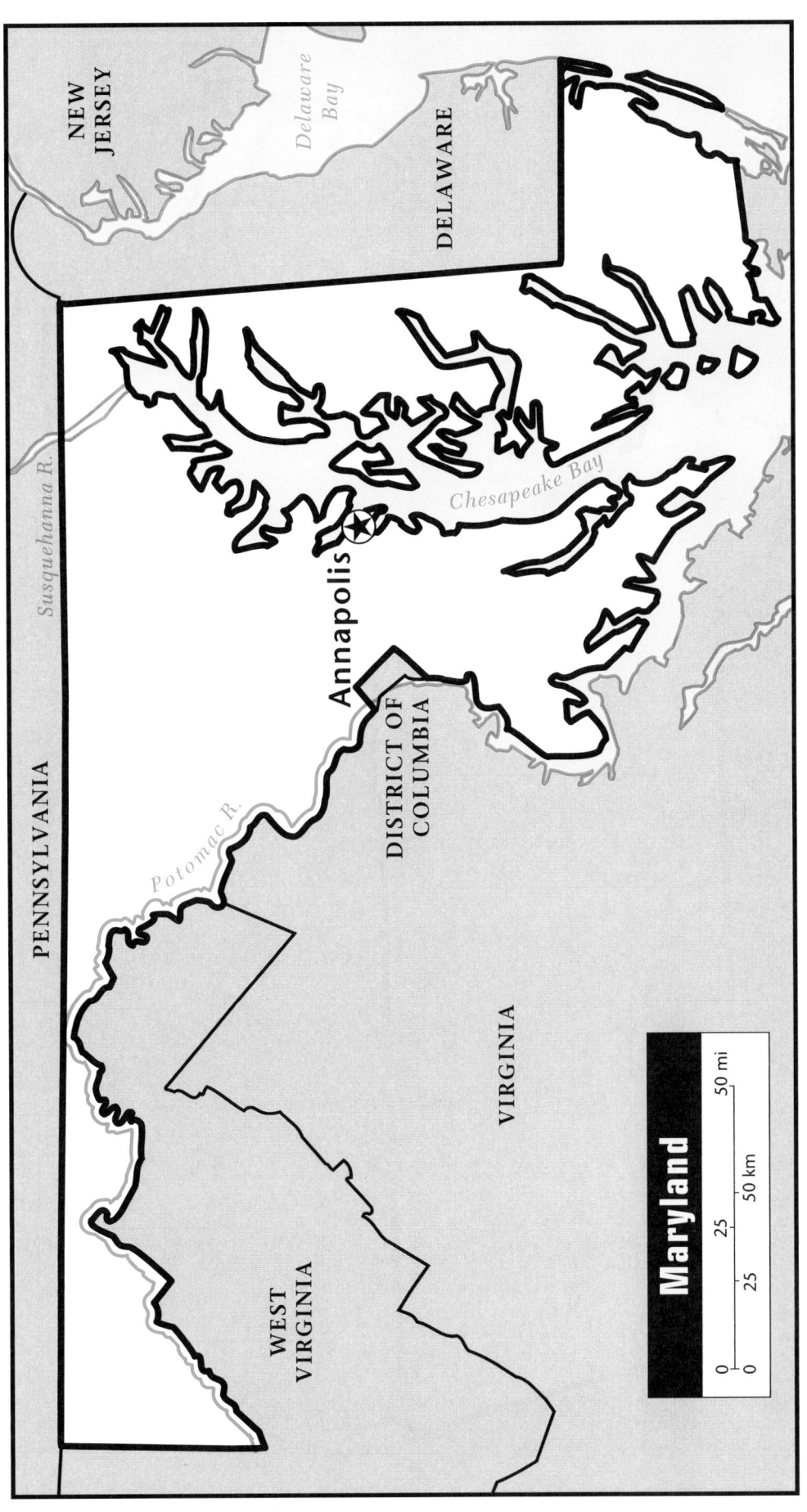

Maryland

NEW JERSEY

DELAWARE

Delaware Bay

PENNSYLVANIA

Susquehanna R.

Chesapeake Bay

Annapolis

Potomac R.

DISTRICT OF COLUMBIA

WEST VIRGINIA

VIRGINIA

VIRGINIA

50 mi
25
0

50 km
25
0

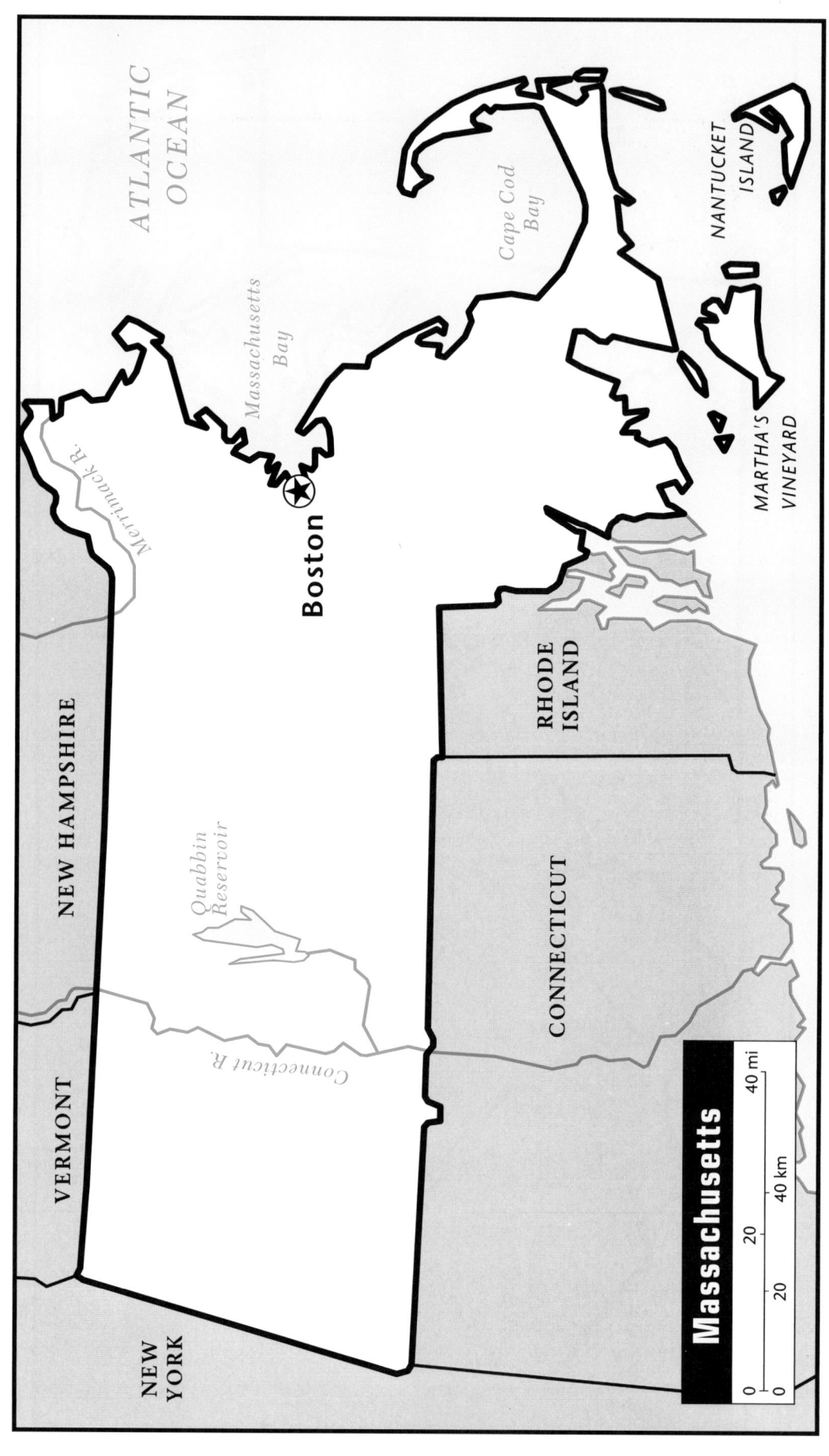

ATLANTIC OCEAN

Massachusetts Bay

Cape Cod Bay

NANTUCKET ISLAND

MARTHA'S VINEYARD

Merrimack R.

Boston

NEW HAMPSHIRE

VERMONT

NEW YORK

Quabbin Reservoir

Connecticut R.

CONNECTICUT

RHODE ISLAND

Massachusetts

40 mi

40 km

20

20

0

0

KEWEENAW
PENINSULA

Lake Superior

C A N A D A

ONTARIO

Menominee R.

Wisconsin R.

Green Bay

WISCONSIN

*Lake
Huron*

*L.
Winnebago*

Saginaw Bay

Muskegon R.

*Lake
Michigan*

Grand R.

⭐ **Lansing**

ILLINOIS

Michigan

0	50	100 mi
0	50	100 km

INDIANA

OHIO

*Lake
Erie*

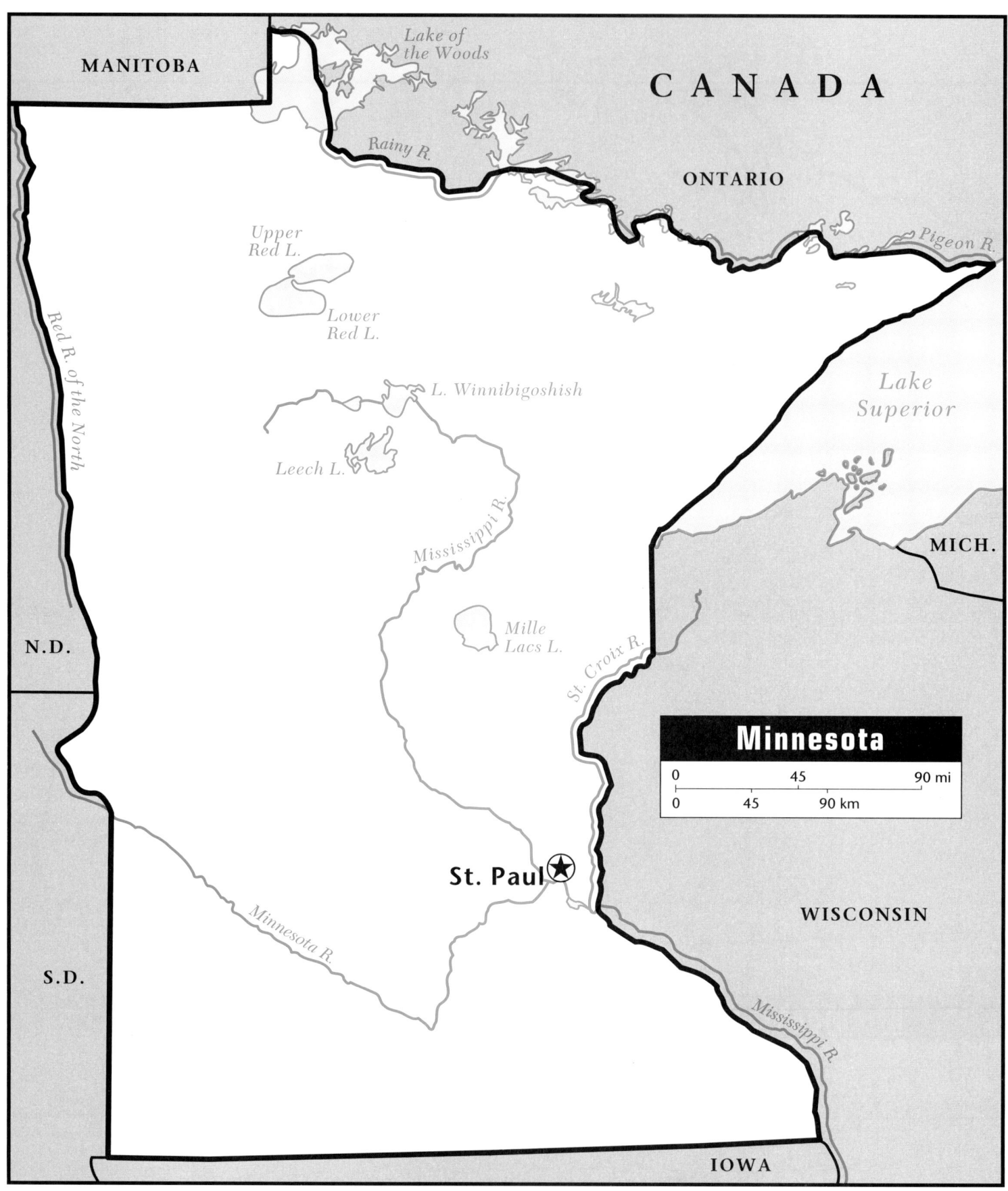

MANITOBA

CANADA

Lake of
the Woods

Rainy R.

ONTARIO

Pigeon R.

Upper
Red L.

Lower
Red L.

Red R. of the North

L. Winnibigoshish

Lake
Superior

Leech L.

Mississippi R.

MICH.

N.D.

Mille
Lacs L.

St. Croix R.

Minnesota

0	45	90 mi
0	45	90 km

St. Paul ✪

WISCONSIN

Minnesota R.

S.D.

Mississippi R.

IOWA

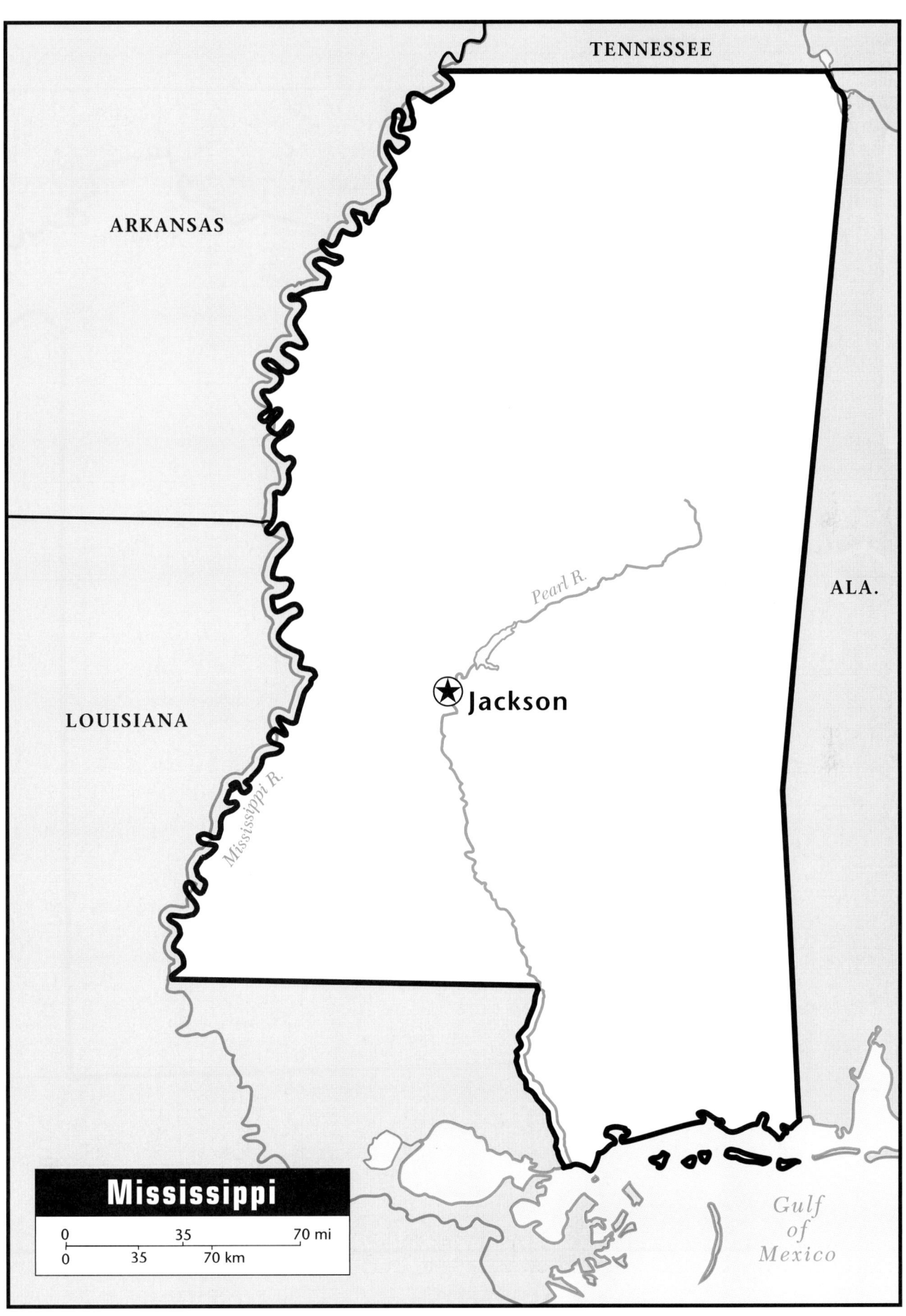

TENNESSEE

ARKANSAS

ALA.

Pearl R.

⊛ Jackson

LOUISIANA

Mississippi R.

Mississippi

| 0 | 35 | 70 mi |
| 0 | 35 | 70 km |

*Gulf
of
Mexico*

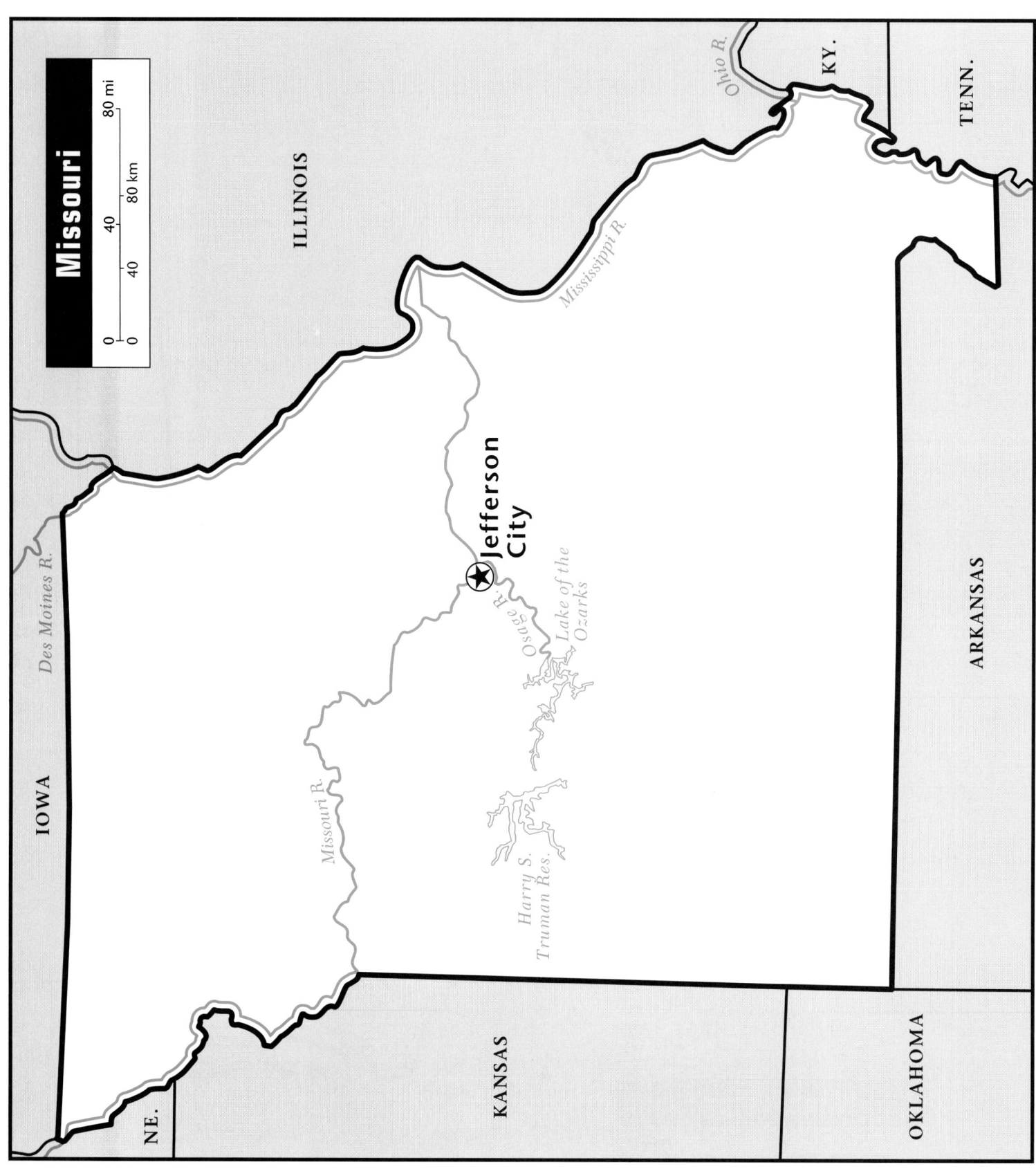

Missouri

80 mi
80 km
40
40
0
0

ILLINOIS

Ohio R.

KY.

TENN.

Mississippi R.

Des Moines R.

Jefferson
City

Osage R.

Lake of the
Ozarks

ARKANSAS

IOWA

Missouri R.

Harry S.
Truman Res.

KANSAS

OKLAHOMA

N.E.

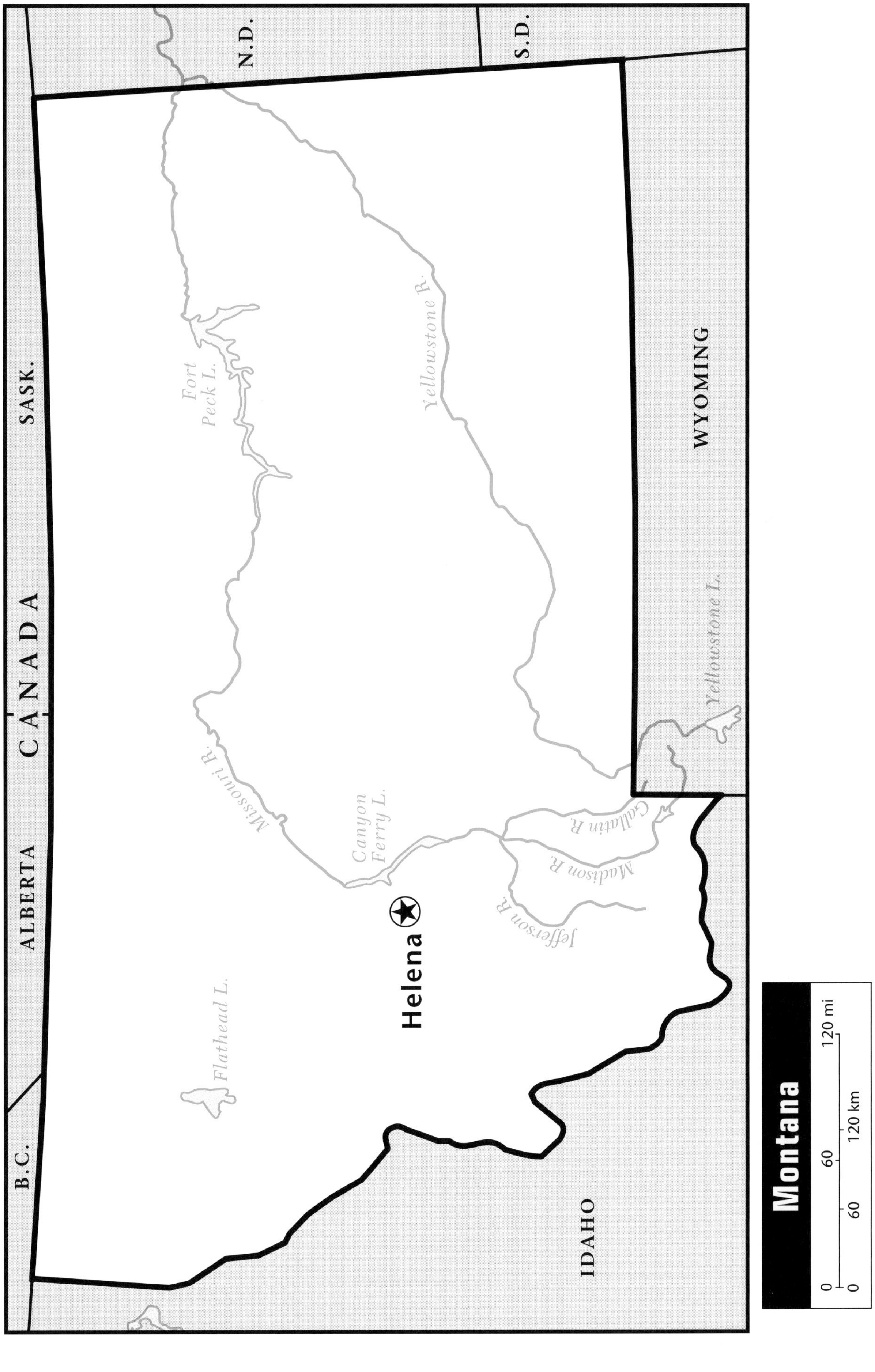

CANADA

B.C.

ALBERTA

SASK.

N.D.

S.D.

WYOMING

IDAHO

Flathead L.

Missouri R.

Fort Peck L.

Canyon Ferry L.

Yellowstone R.

Jefferson R.

Madison R.

Gallatin R.

Yellowstone L.

★ Helena

Montana

0	60	120 mi
0	60	120 km

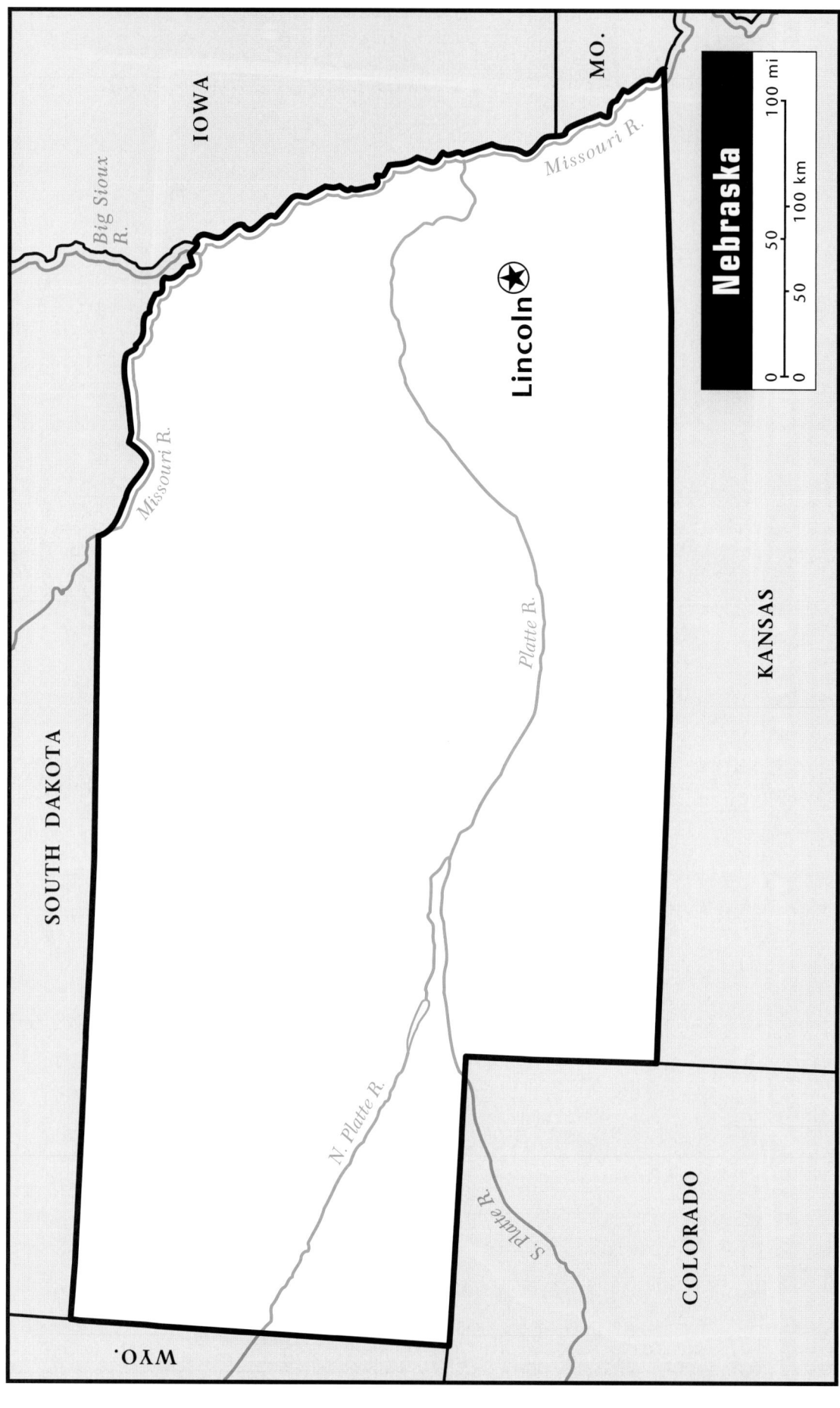

IOWA

MO.

Big Sioux R.

Missouri R.

Missouri R.

Lincoln ✪

Nebraska

0 50 100 mi

0 50 100 km

SOUTH DAKOTA

KANSAS

Platte R.

N. Platte R.

S. Platte R.

COLORADO

WYO.

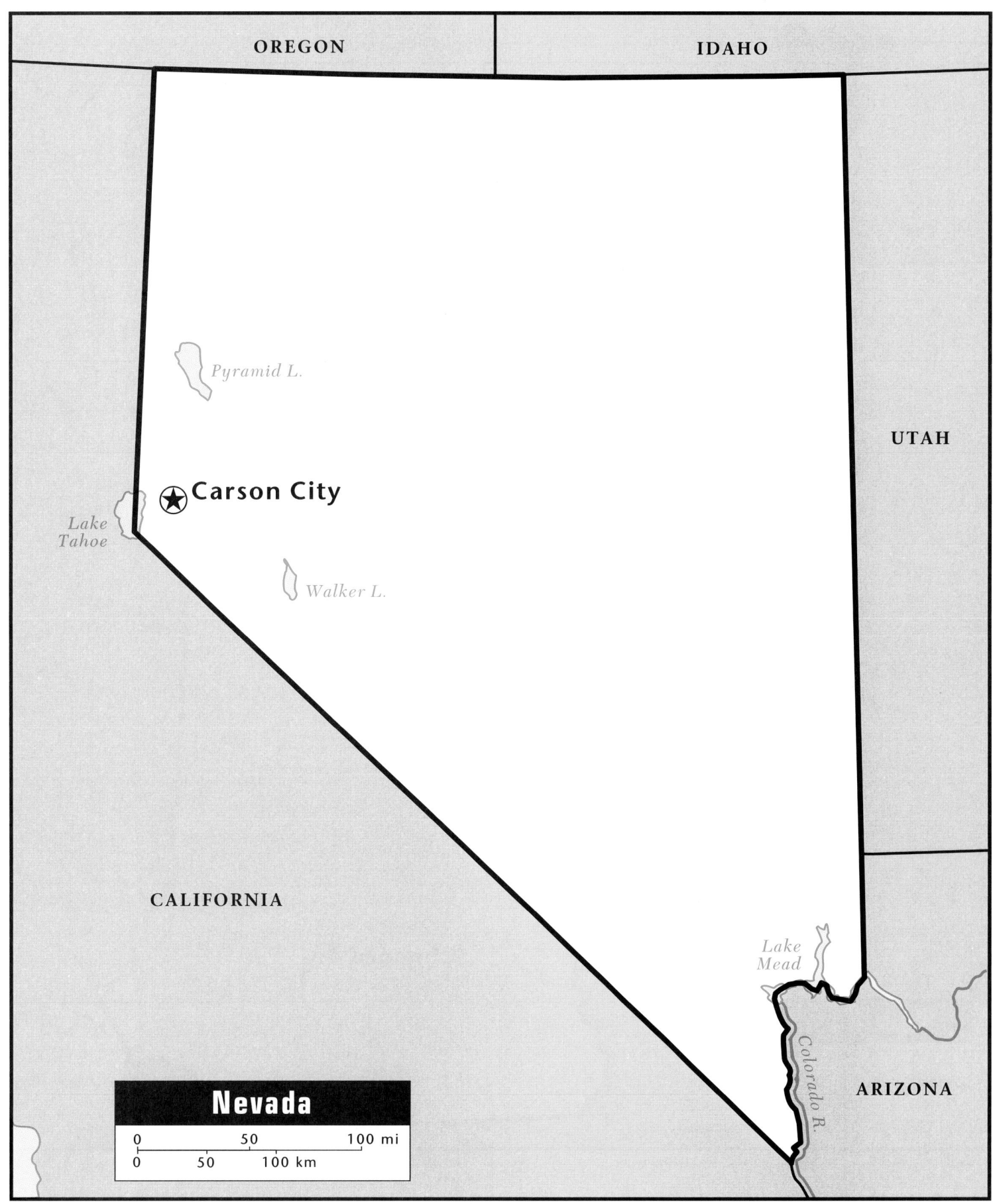

OREGON

IDAHO

UTAH

Pyramid L.

⭐**Carson City**

*Lake
Tahoe*

Walker L.

CALIFORNIA

*Lake
Mead*

Colorado R.

ARIZONA

Nevada

| 0 | 50 | 100 mi |

| 0 | 50 | 100 km |

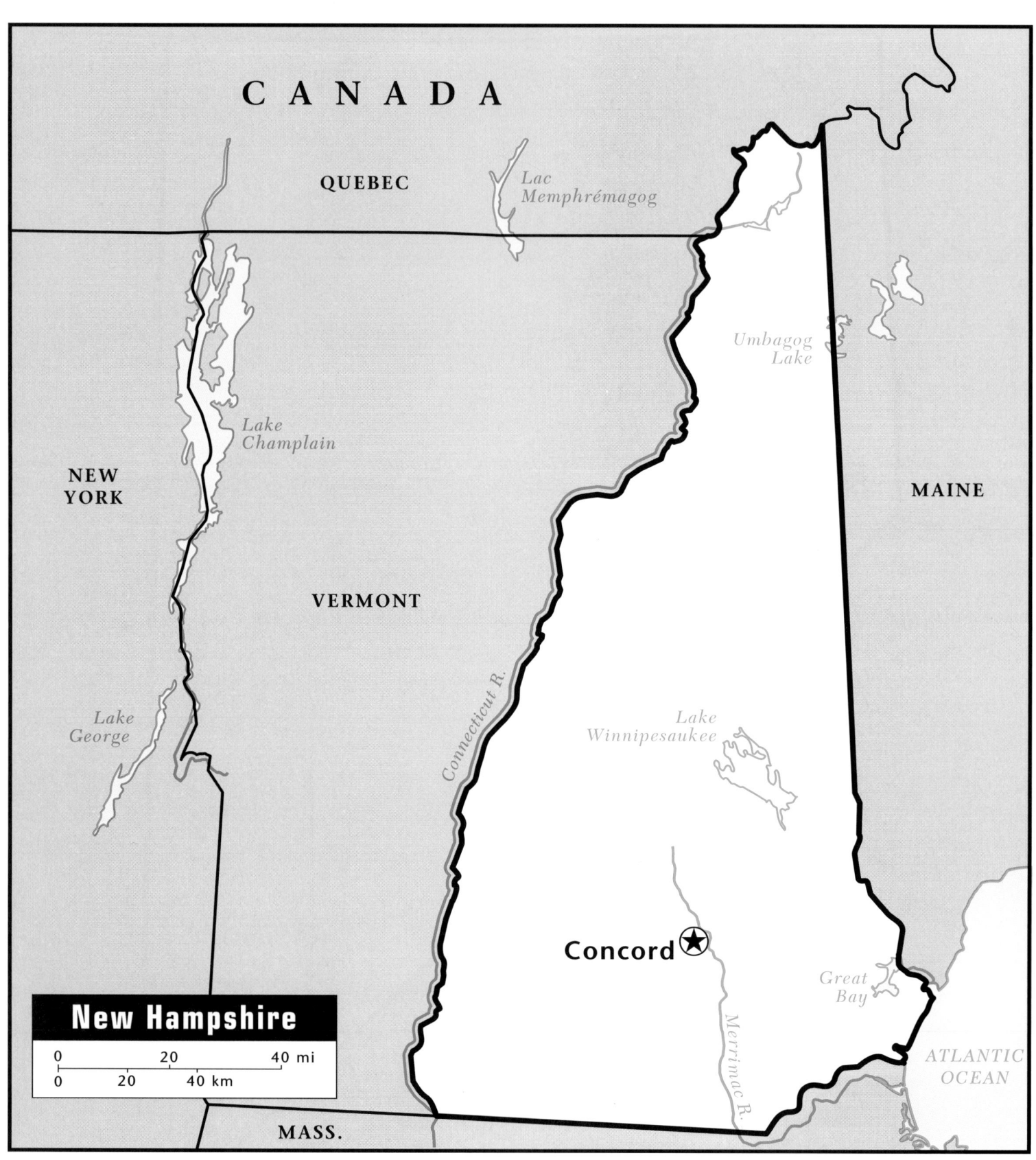

CANADA

QUEBEC

Lac Memphrémagog

NEW YORK

MAINE

Umbagog Lake

Lake Champlain

VERMONT

Lake George

Connecticut R.

Lake Winnipesaukee

Concord ★

Great Bay

Merrimac R.

ATLANTIC OCEAN

New Hampshire

| 0 | 20 | 40 mi |
| 0 | 20 | 40 km |

MASS.

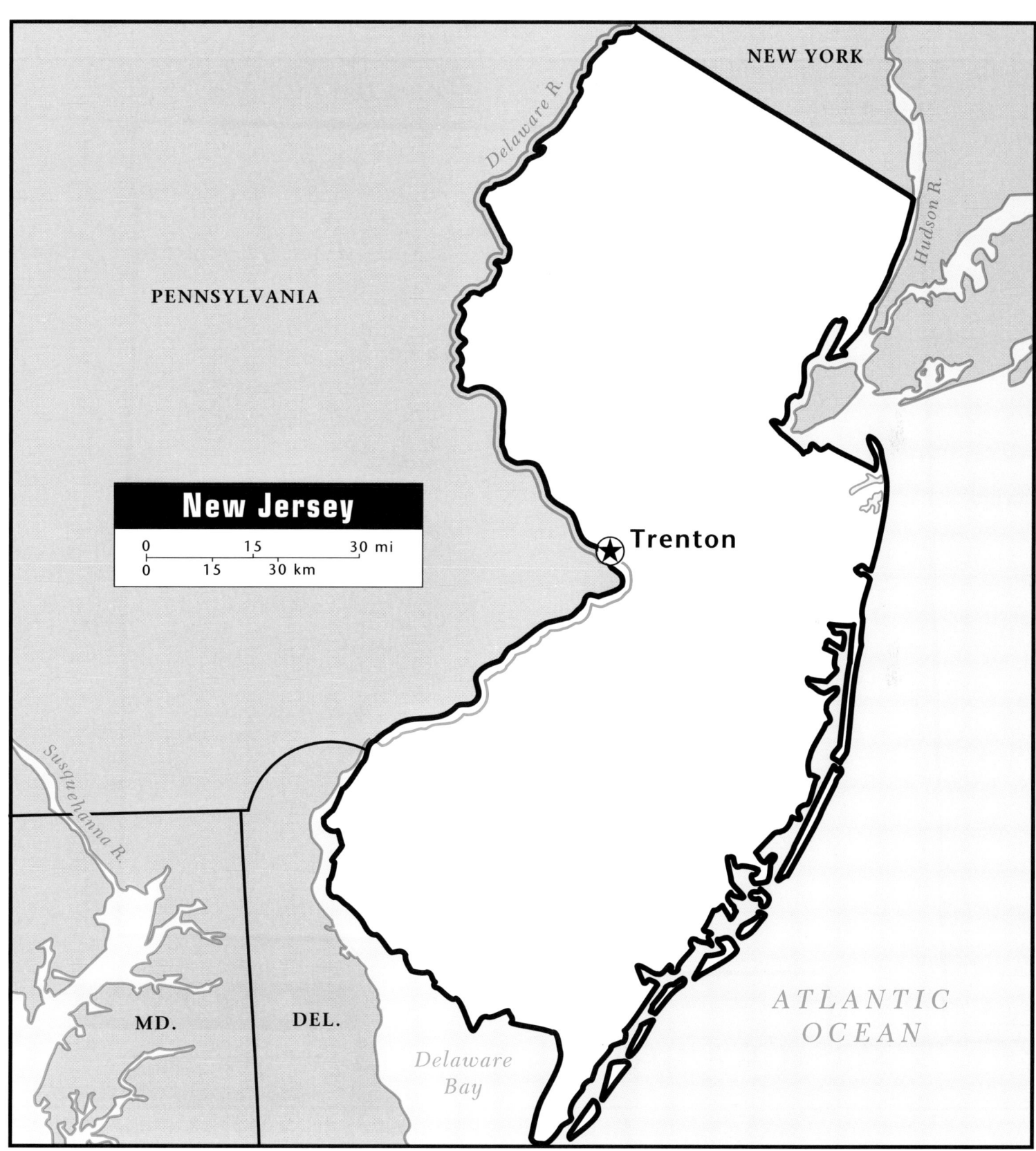

NEW YORK

PENNSYLVANIA

Delaware R.

Hudson R.

New Jersey

| 0 | 15 | 30 mi |
| 0 | 15 | 30 km |

★ Trenton

Susquehanna R.

MD.

DEL.

Delaware Bay

ATLANTIC OCEAN

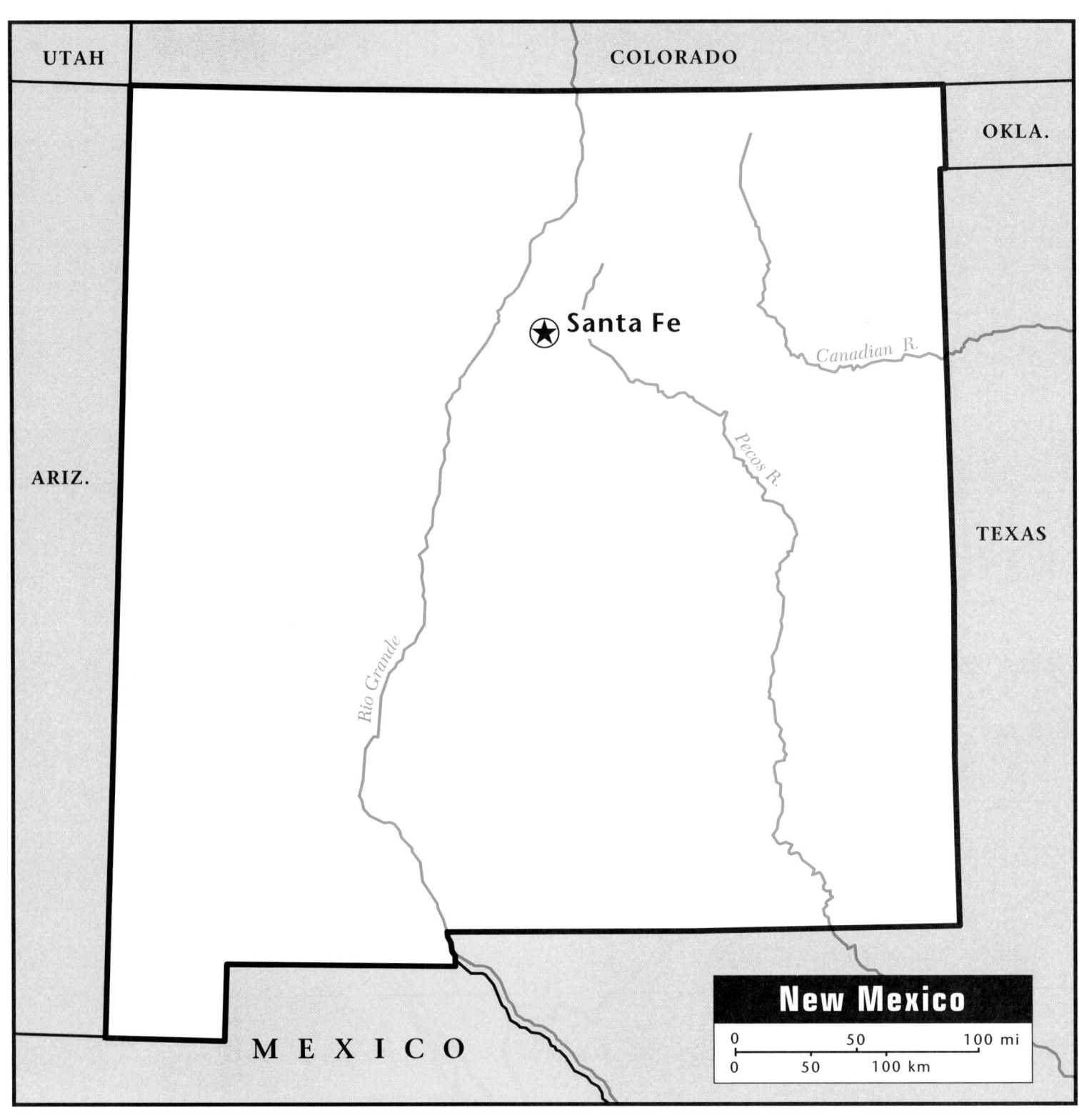

UTAH

COLORADO

OKLA.

★ Santa Fe

Canadian R.

ARIZ.

Pecos R.

TEXAS

Rio Grande

M E X I C O

New Mexico

| 0 | | 50 | | 100 mi |
| 0 | 50 | | 100 km | |

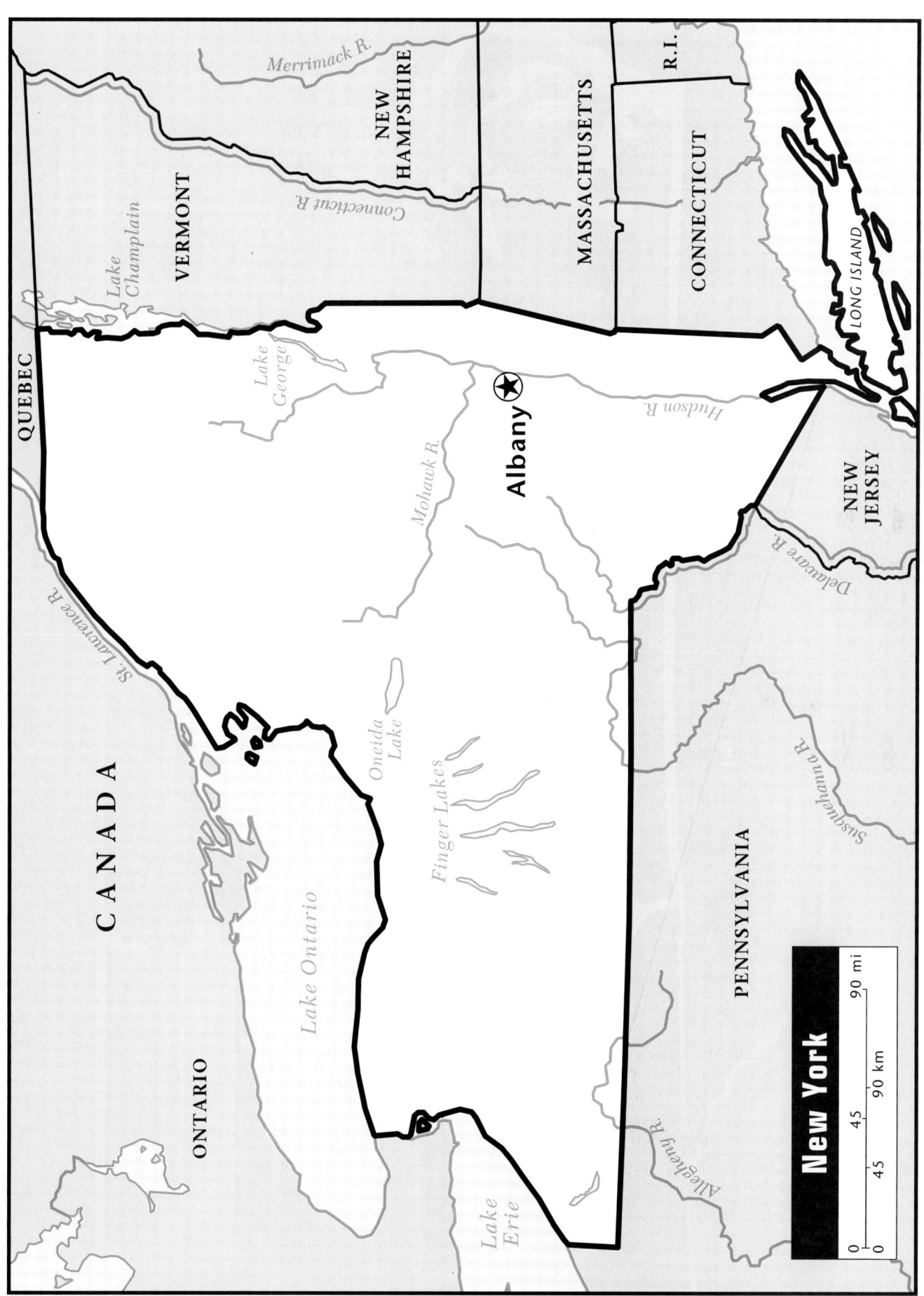

New York

QUEBEC

CANADA

ONTARIO

VERMONT

NEW HAMPSHIRE

MASSACHUSETTS

R.I.

CONNECTICUT

LONG ISLAND

NEW JERSEY

PENNSYLVANIA

Merrimack R.

Connecticut R.

Lake Champlain

Lake George

Mohawk R.

Hudson R.

Albany

St. Lawrence R.

Oneida Lake

Finger Lakes

Lake Ontario

Lake Erie

Allegheny R.

Susquehanna R.

Delaware R.

| 0 | 45 | 90 mi |
| 0 | 45 | 90 km |

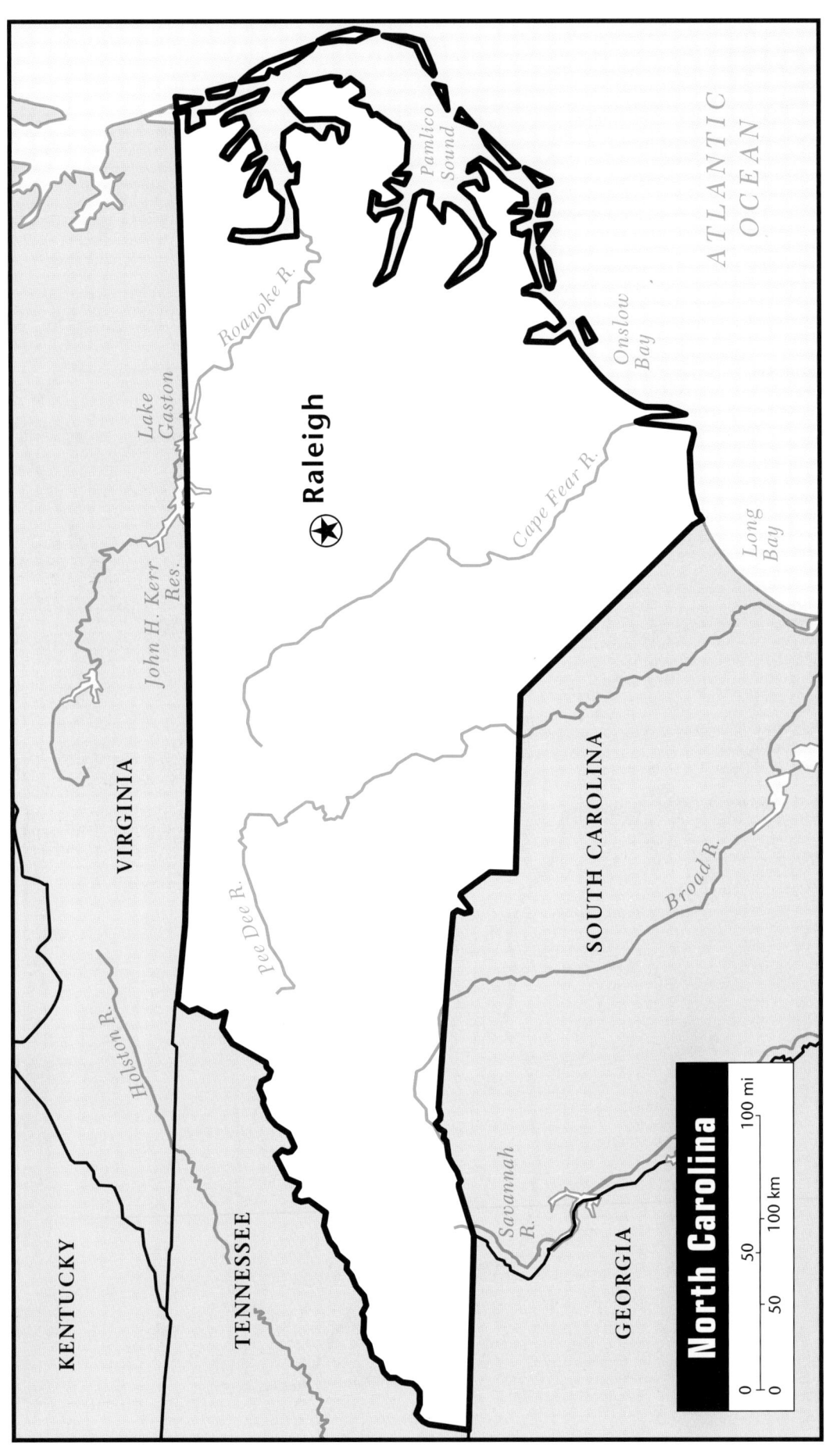

ATLANTIC OCEAN

Pamlico Sound

Onslow Bay

Long Bay

Roanoke R.

Lake Gaston

Raleigh

Cape Fear R.

John H. Kerr Res.

VIRGINIA

SOUTH CAROLINA

Broad R.

Pee Dee R.

Holston R.

KENTUCKY

TENNESSEE

GEORGIA

Savannah R.

North Carolina

100 mi

100 km

50

50

0

0

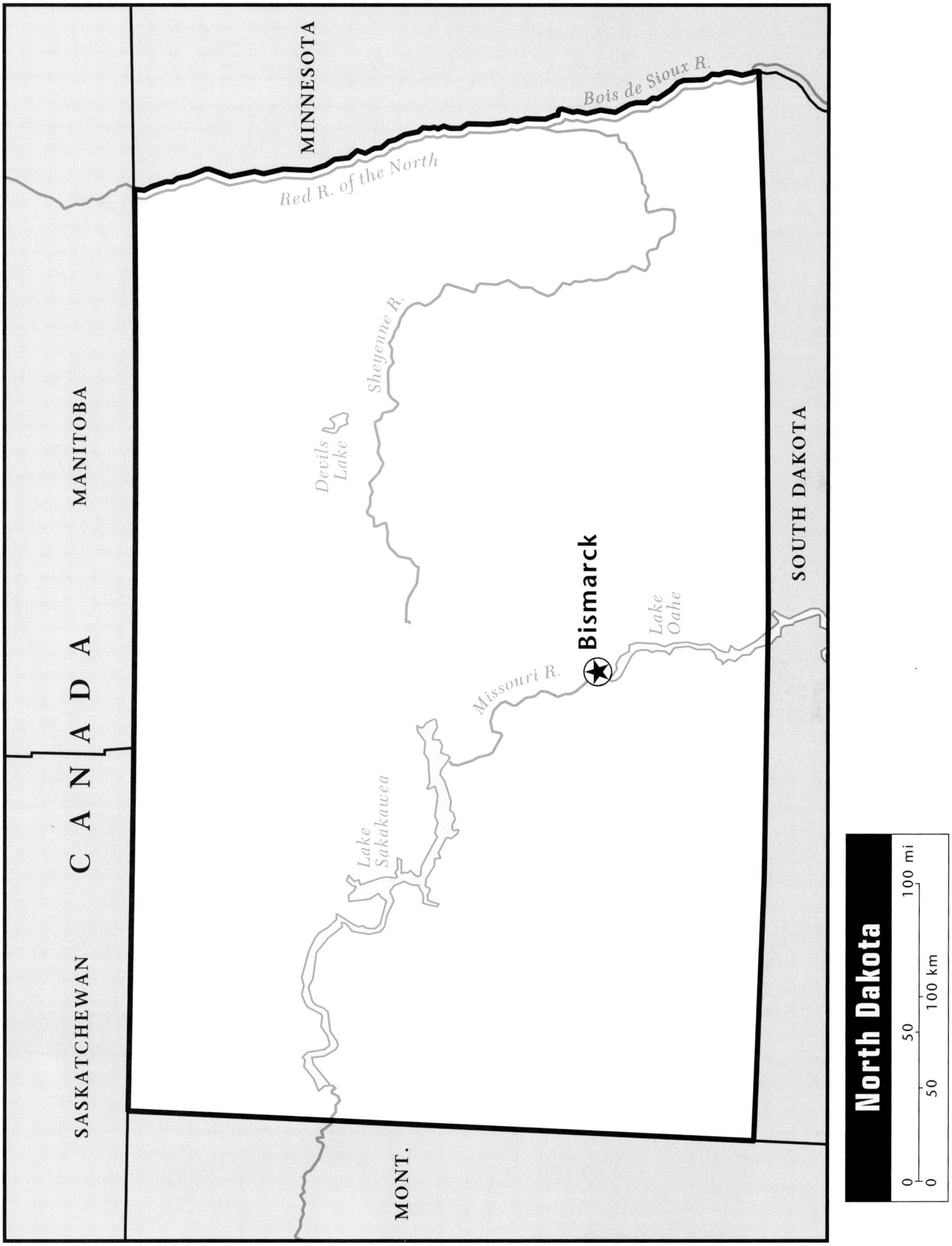

MINNESOTA

Bois de Sioux R.

Red R. of the North

Sheyenne R.

MANITOBA

Devils Lake

CANADA

SOUTH DAKOTA

★ **Bismarck**

Lake Oahe

Missouri R.

Lake Sakakawea

SASKATCHEWAN

MONT.

North Dakota

| 0 | 50 | 100 mi |
| 0 | 50 | 100 km |

MICHIGAN

CANADA

IND.

Sandusky R.

PA.

★ Columbus

WEST
VIRGINIA

Ohio R.

Ohio R.

KENTUCKY

Ohio

| 0 | 30 | 60 mi |
| 0 | 30 | 60 km |

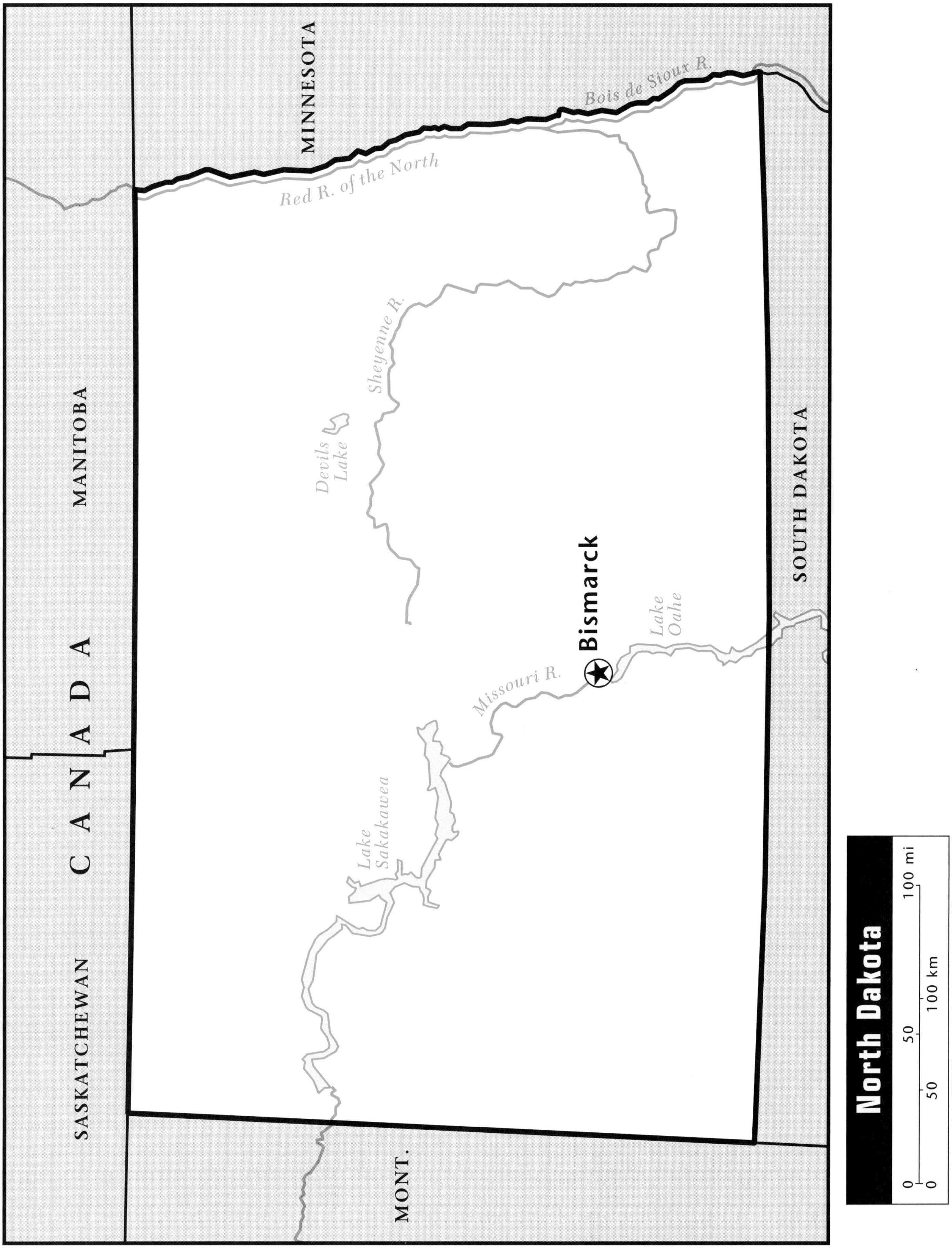

CANADA

SASKATCHEWAN

MANITOBA

MINNESOTA

SOUTH DAKOTA

MONT.

Bois de Sioux R.

Red R. of the North

Sheyenne R.

Devils Lake

Bismarck

Missouri R.

Lake Oahe

Lake Sakakawea

North Dakota

| 0 | 50 | 100 mi |
| 0 | 50 | 100 km |

CANADA

MICHIGAN

PA.

IND.

Sandusky R.

⭐ **Columbus**

WEST
VIRGINIA

Ohio R.

KENTUCKY

Ohio R.

Ohio

| 0 | 30 | 60 mi |
| 0 | 30 | 60 km |

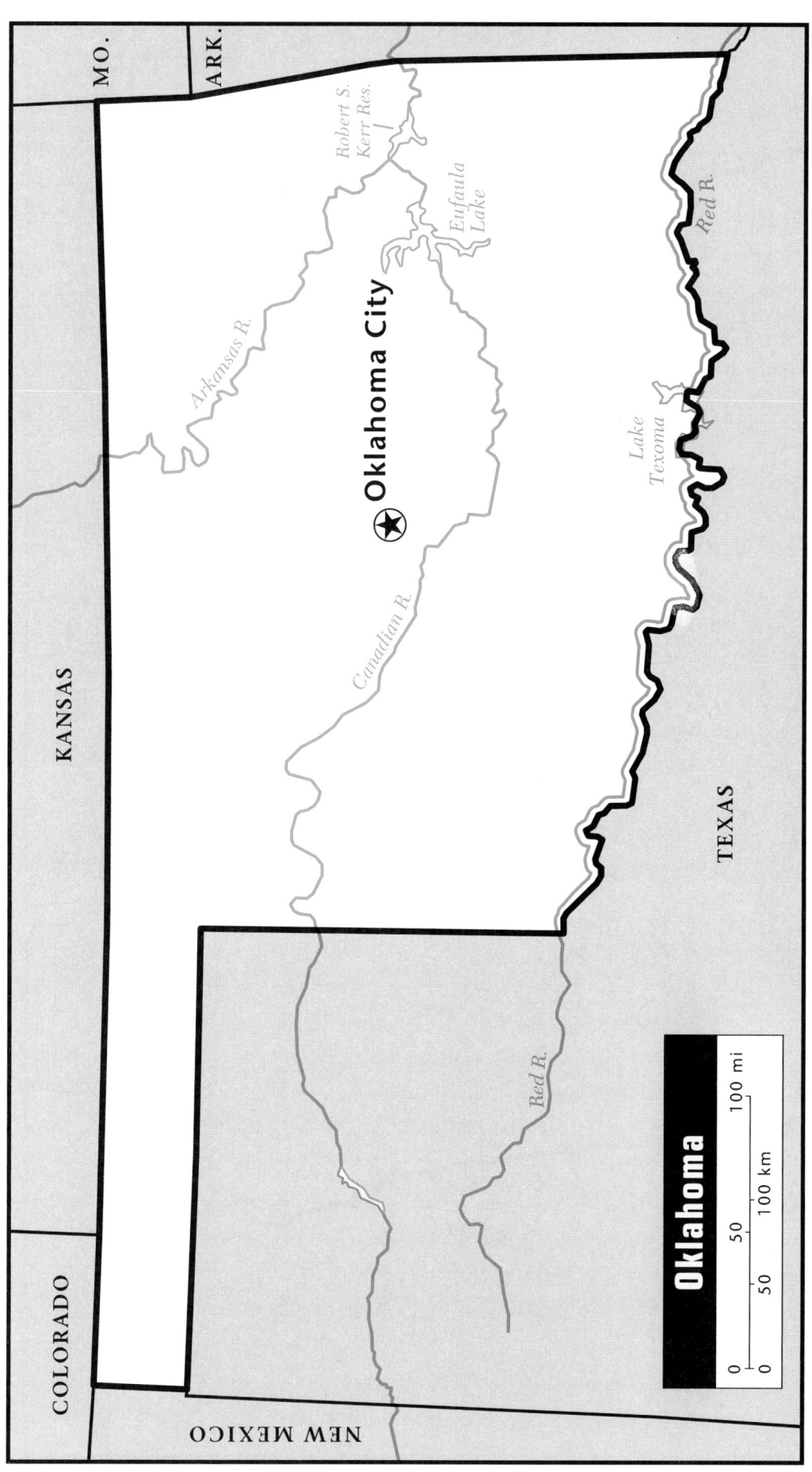

COLORADO

KANSAS

MO.

ARK.

Robert S. Kerr Res.

Eufaula Lake

Arkansas R.

⊛ **Oklahoma City**

Canadian R.

Red R.

Lake Texoma

Red R.

NEW MEXICO

TEXAS

Oklahoma

| 0 | 50 | 100 mi |

| 0 | 50 | 100 km |

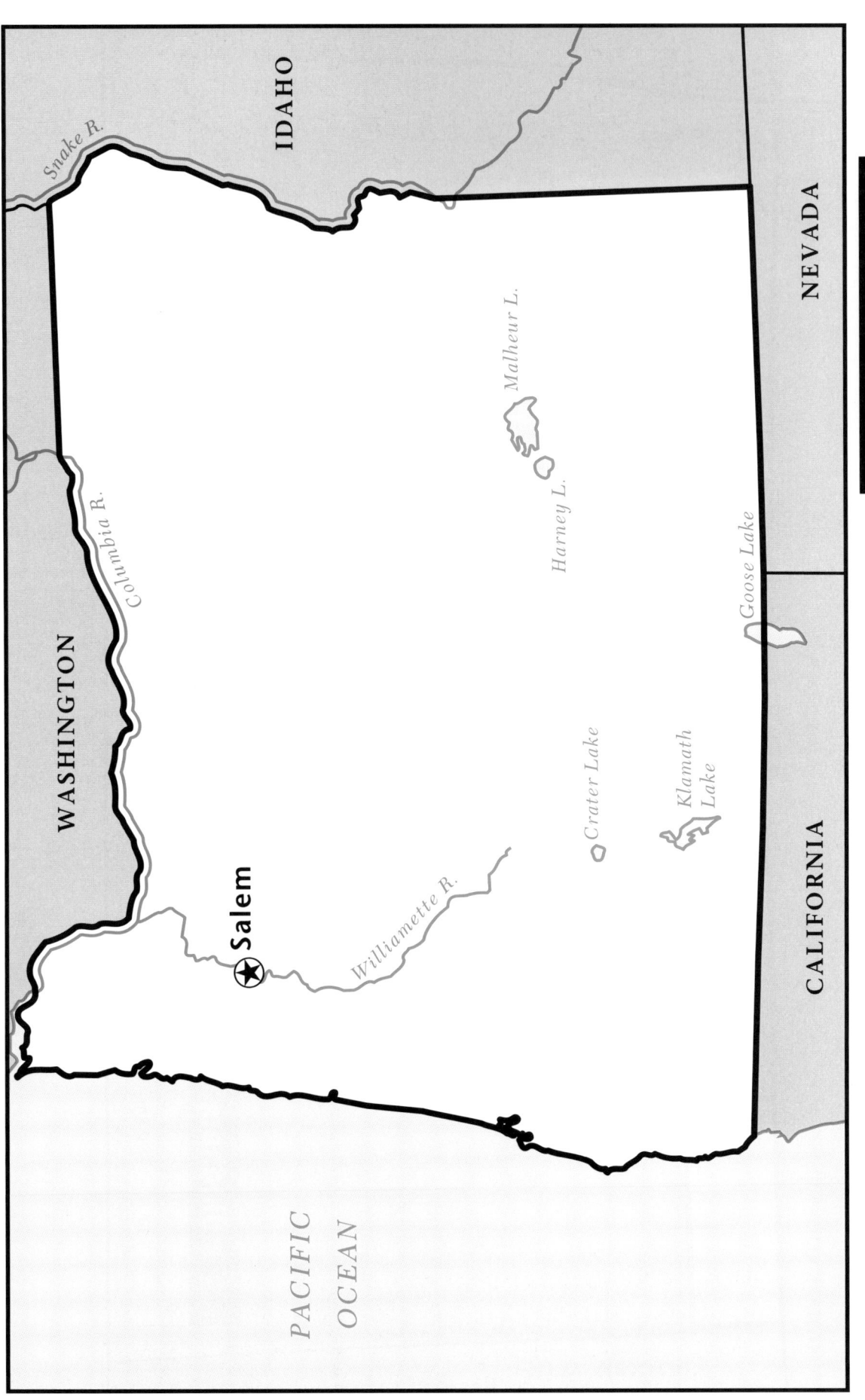

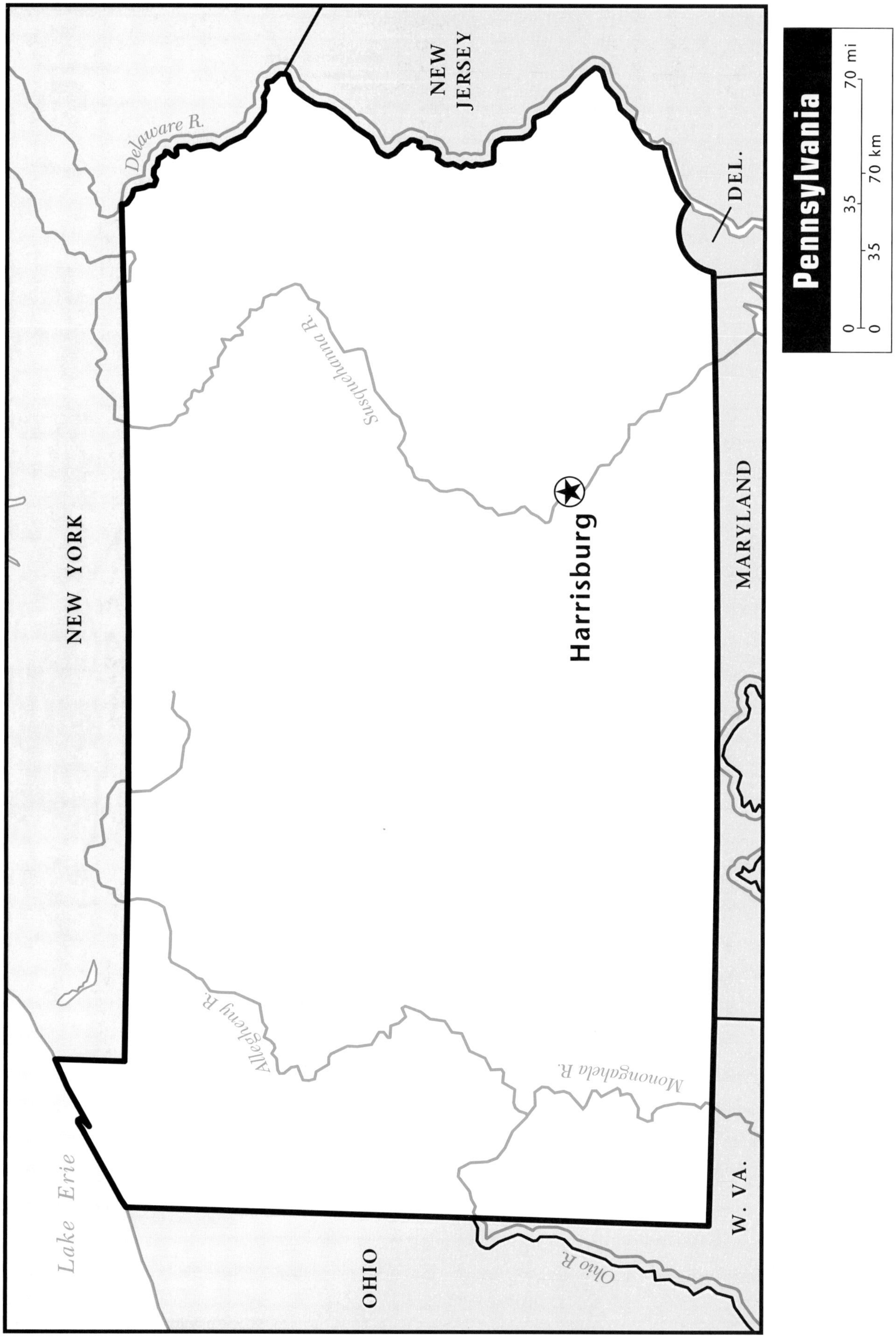

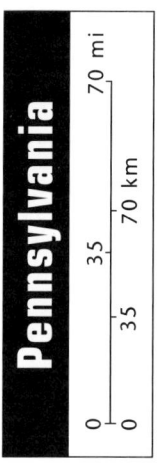

Pennsylvania

0   35   70 mi

0   35   70 km

NEW JERSEY

DEL.

Delaware R.

NEW YORK

Susquehanna R.

★ Harrisburg

MARYLAND

Allegheny R.

Monongahela R.

W. VA.

Lake Erie

OHIO

Ohio R.

MASSACHUSETTS

CONNECTICUT

Scituate Reservoir

Providence ★

Narragansett Bay

Rhode Island Sound

Block Island Sound

ATLANTIC OCEAN

Block Island

Rhode Island

| 0 | | 5 | | 10 mi |
| 0 | 5 | | 10 km | |

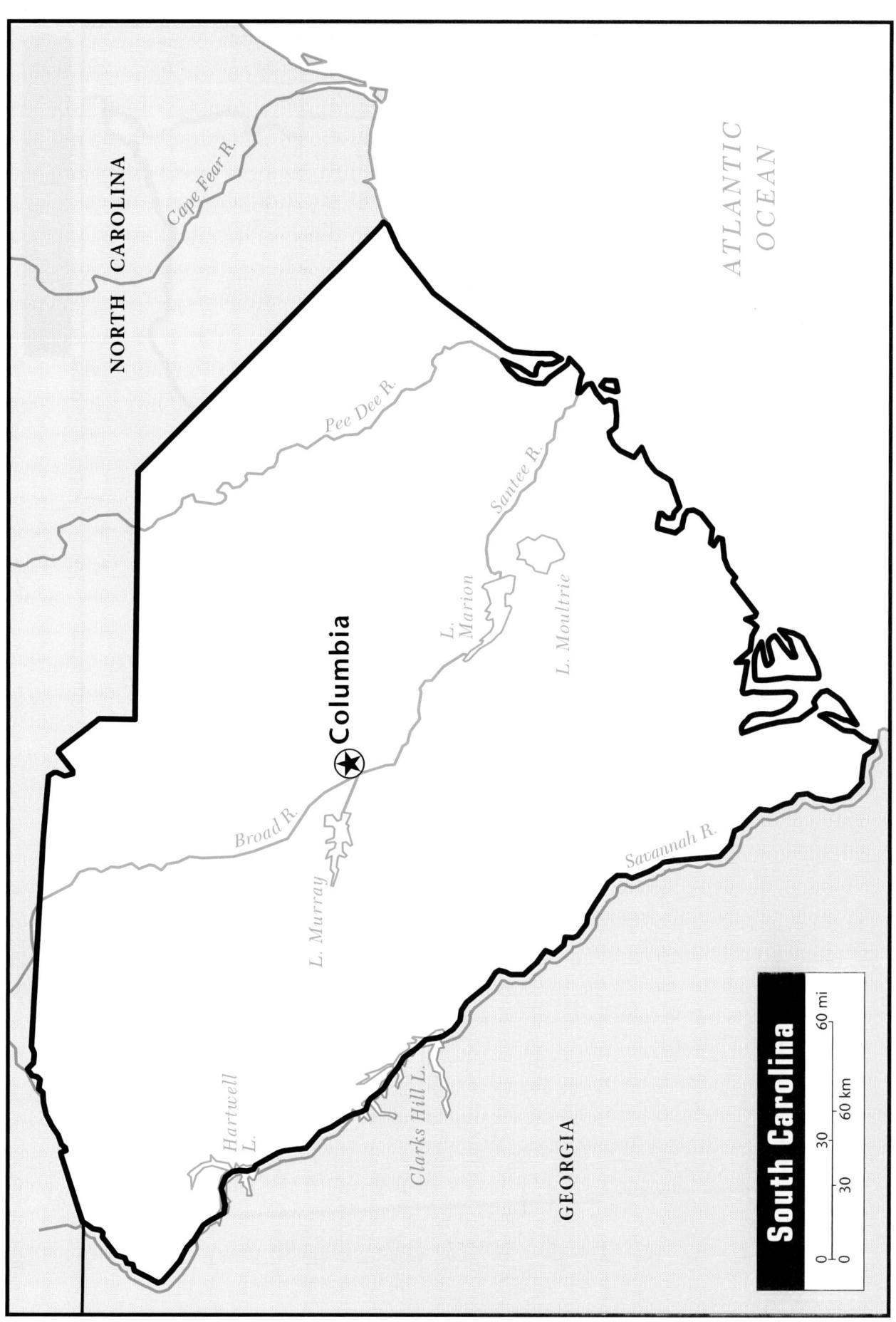

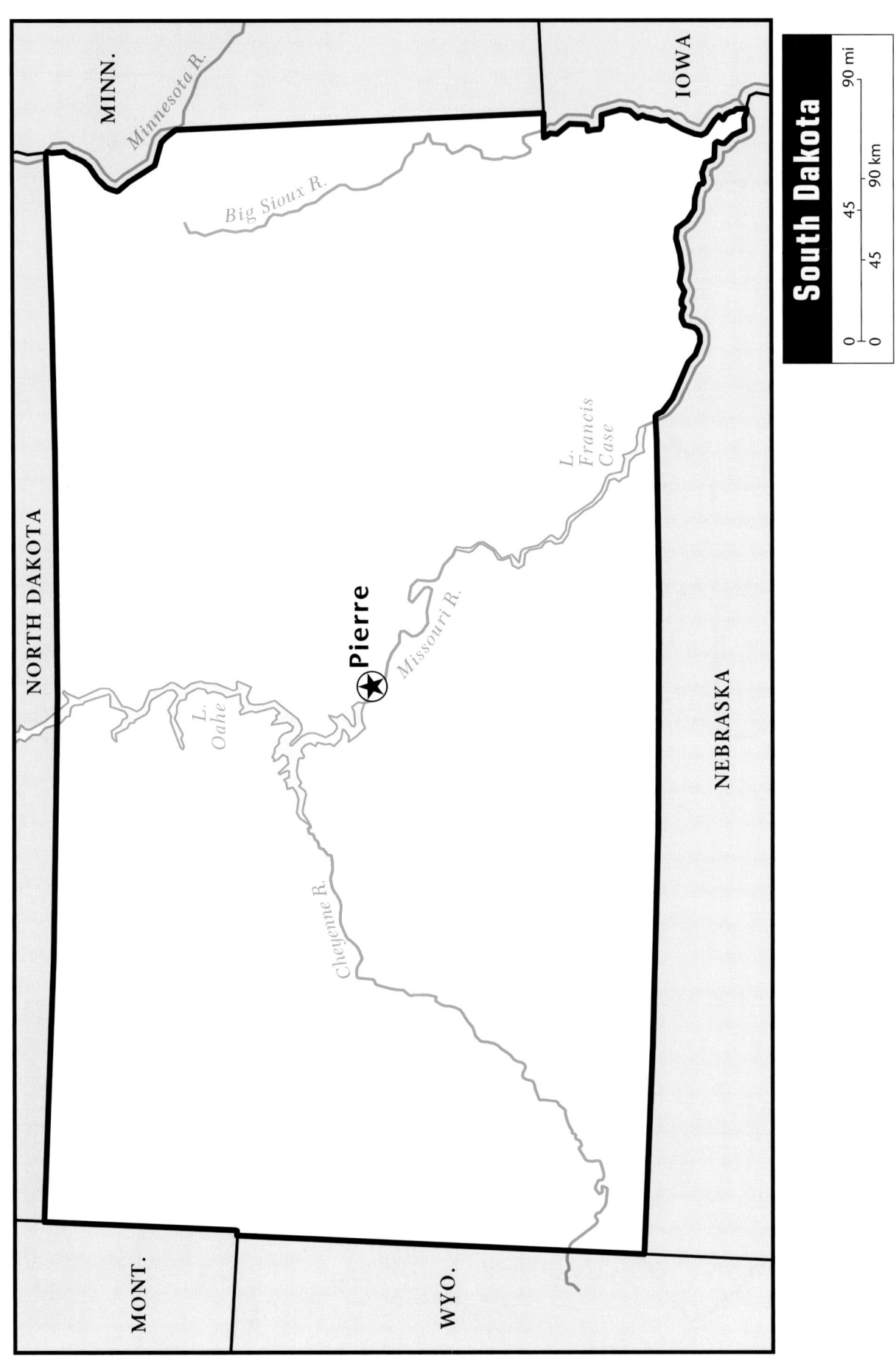

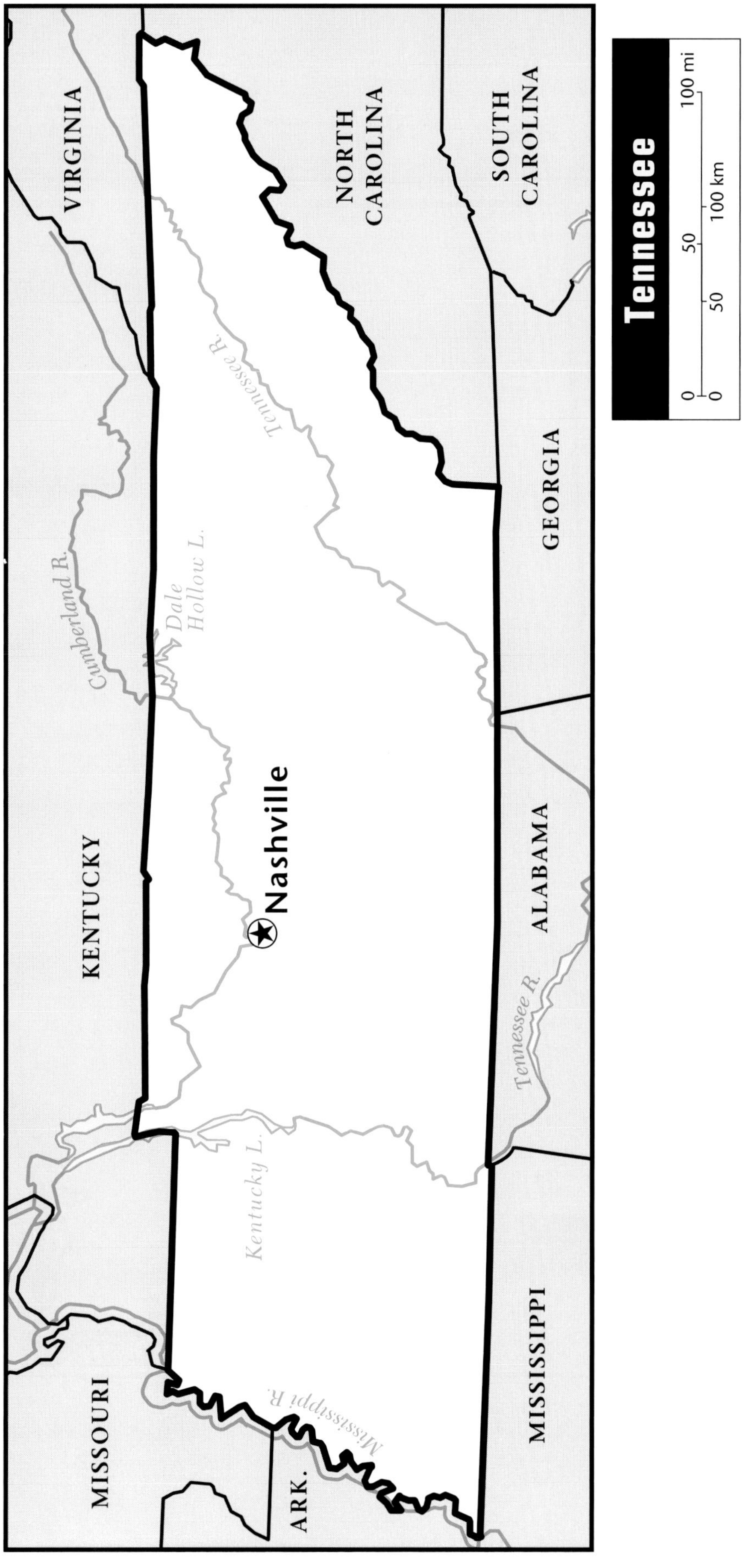

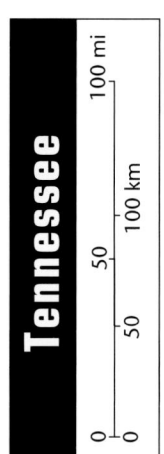

VIRGINIA

NORTH CAROLINA

SOUTH CAROLINA

KENTUCKY

Tennessee R.

Cumberland R.

Dale Hollow L.

GEORGIA

★ Nashville

ALABAMA

Tennessee R.

Kentucky L.

MISSOURI

Mississippi R.

ARK.

MISSISSIPPI

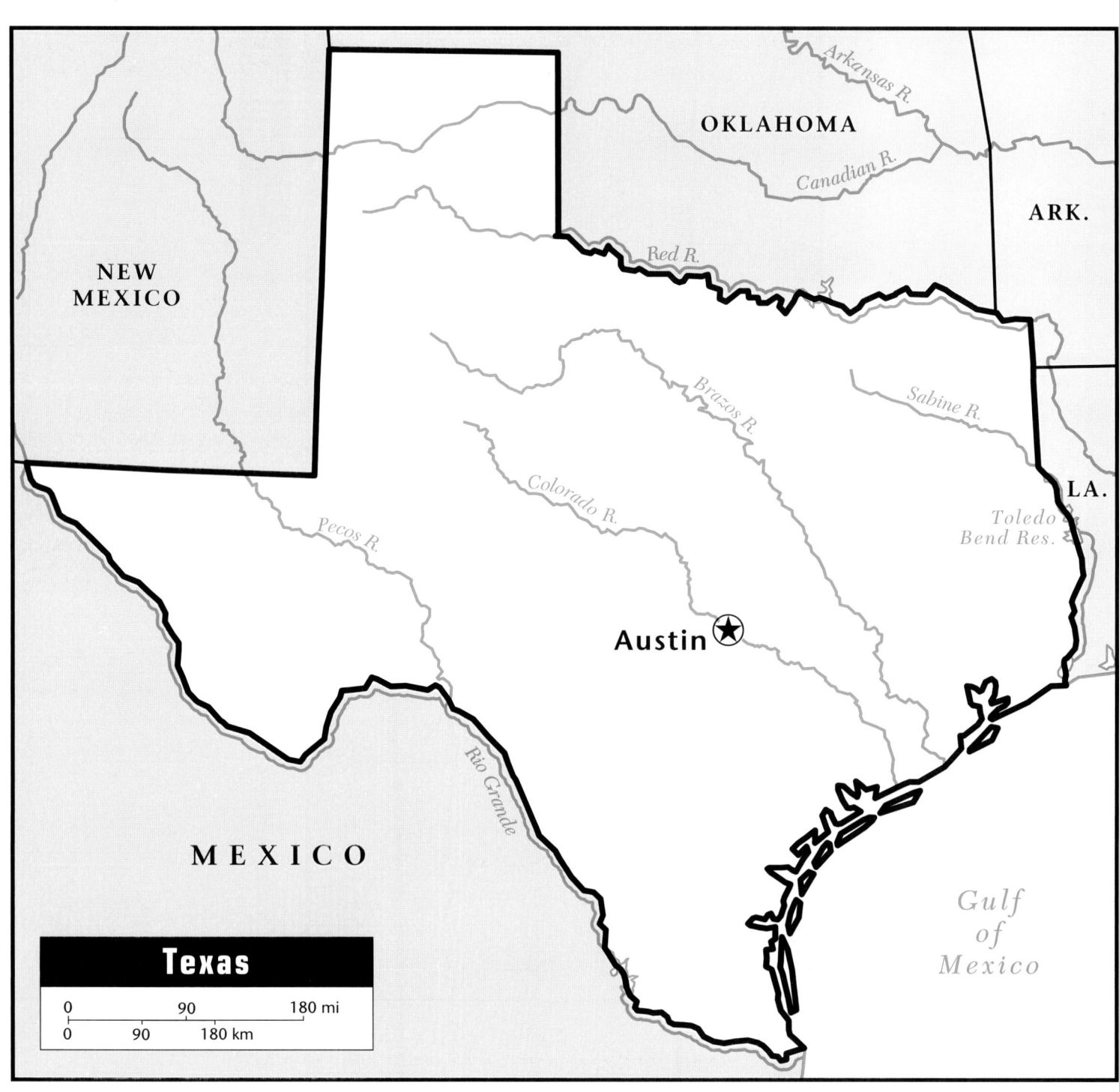

OKLAHOMA

Arkansas R.

ARK.

Canadian R.

NEW
MEXICO

Red R.

Brazos R.

Sabine R.

LA.

Colorado R.

*Toledo
Bend Res.*

Pecos R.

Austin ★

MEXICO

Rio Grande

Gulf
of
Mexico

Texas

0	90	180 mi
0	90	180 km

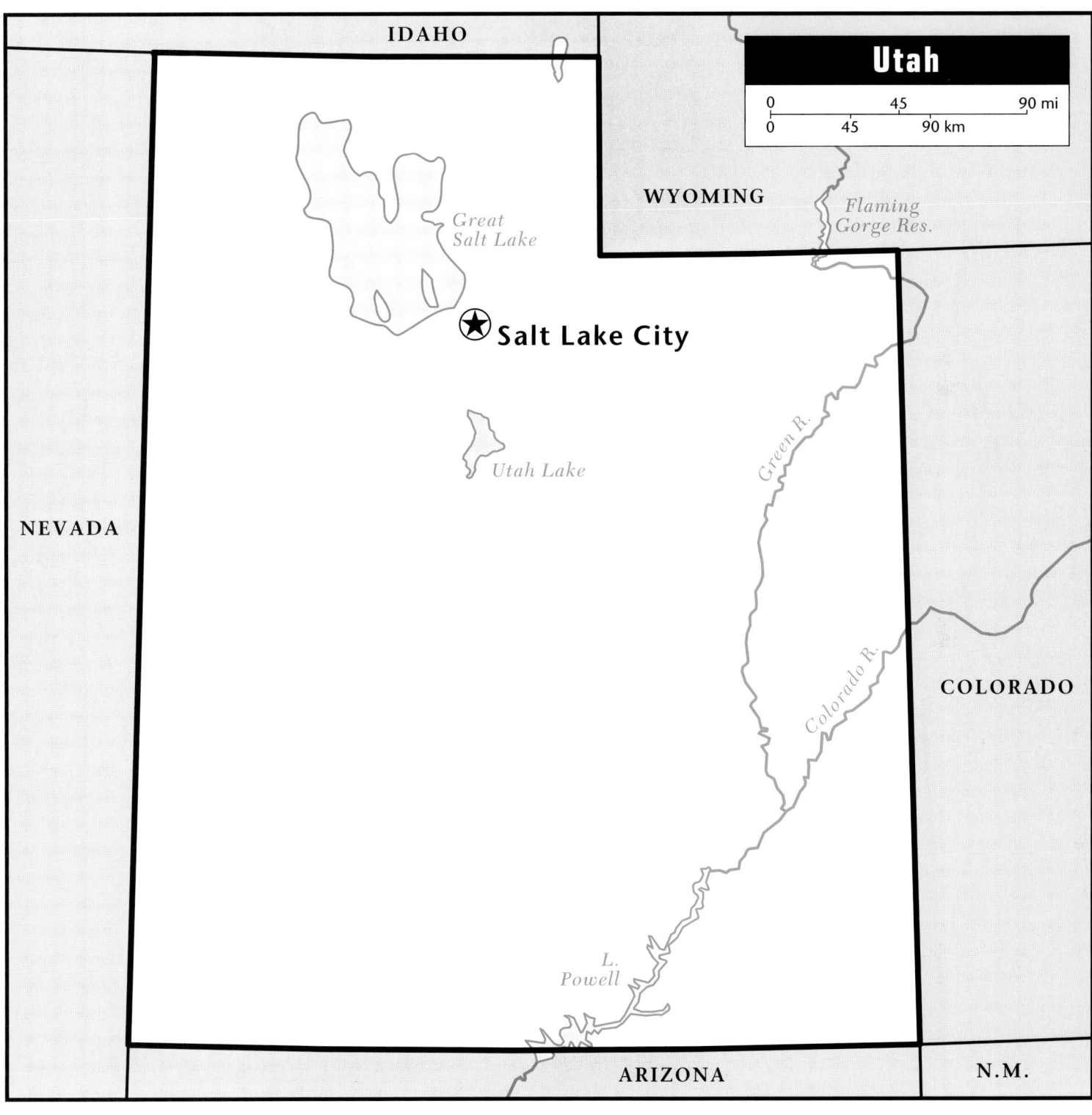

IDAHO

WYOMING

Utah

| 0 | 45 | 90 mi |
| 0 | 45 | 90 km |

Great
Salt Lake

Flaming
Gorge Res.

★ **Salt Lake City**

NEVADA

Utah Lake

Green R.

COLORADO

Colorado R.

L.
Powell

ARIZONA

N.M.

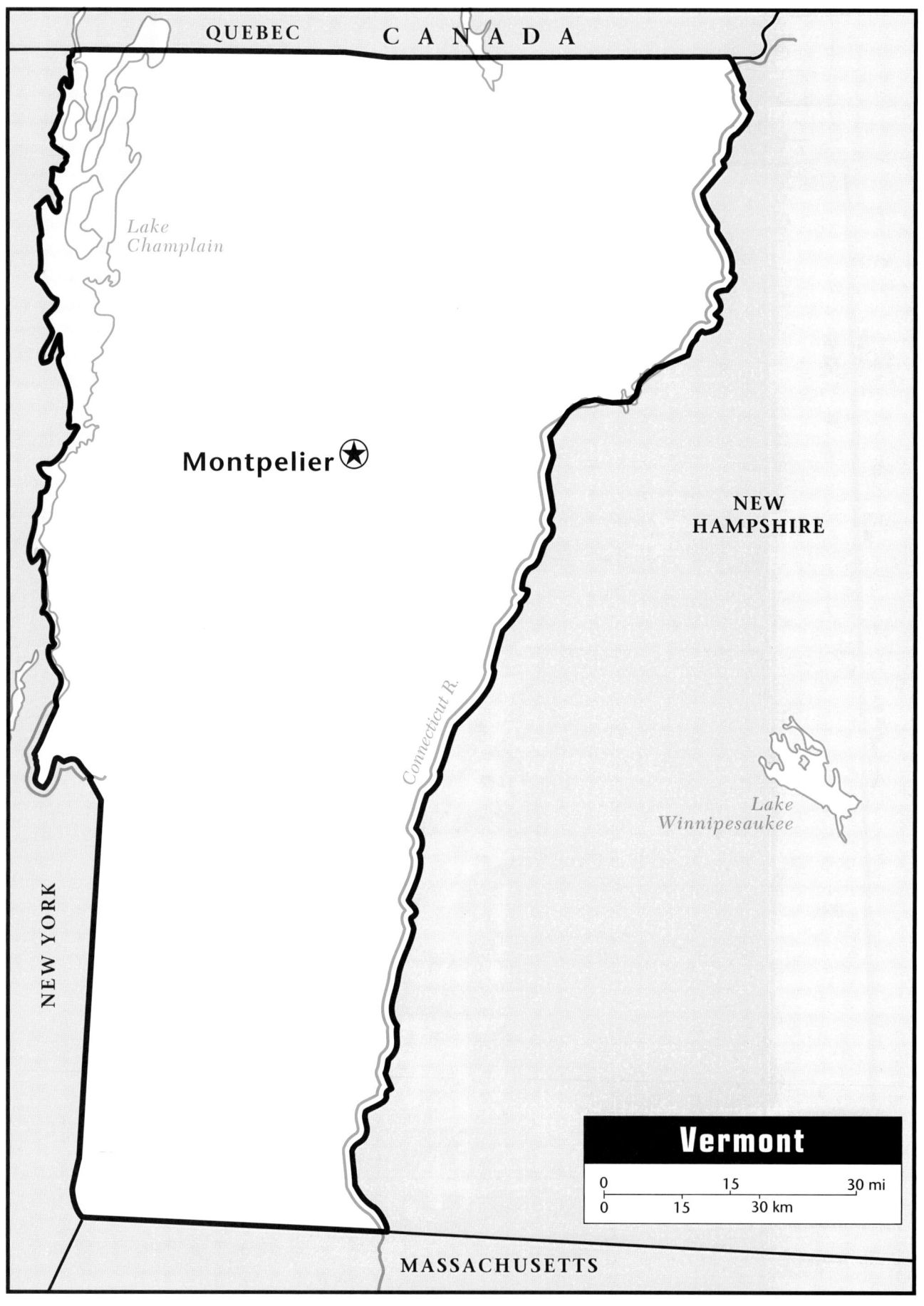

QUEBEC C A N A D A

Lake Champlain

Montpelier ★

NEW HAMPSHIRE

Connecticut R.

Lake Winnipesaukee

NEW YORK

Vermont

0		15		30 mi
0	15		30 km	

MASSACHUSETTS

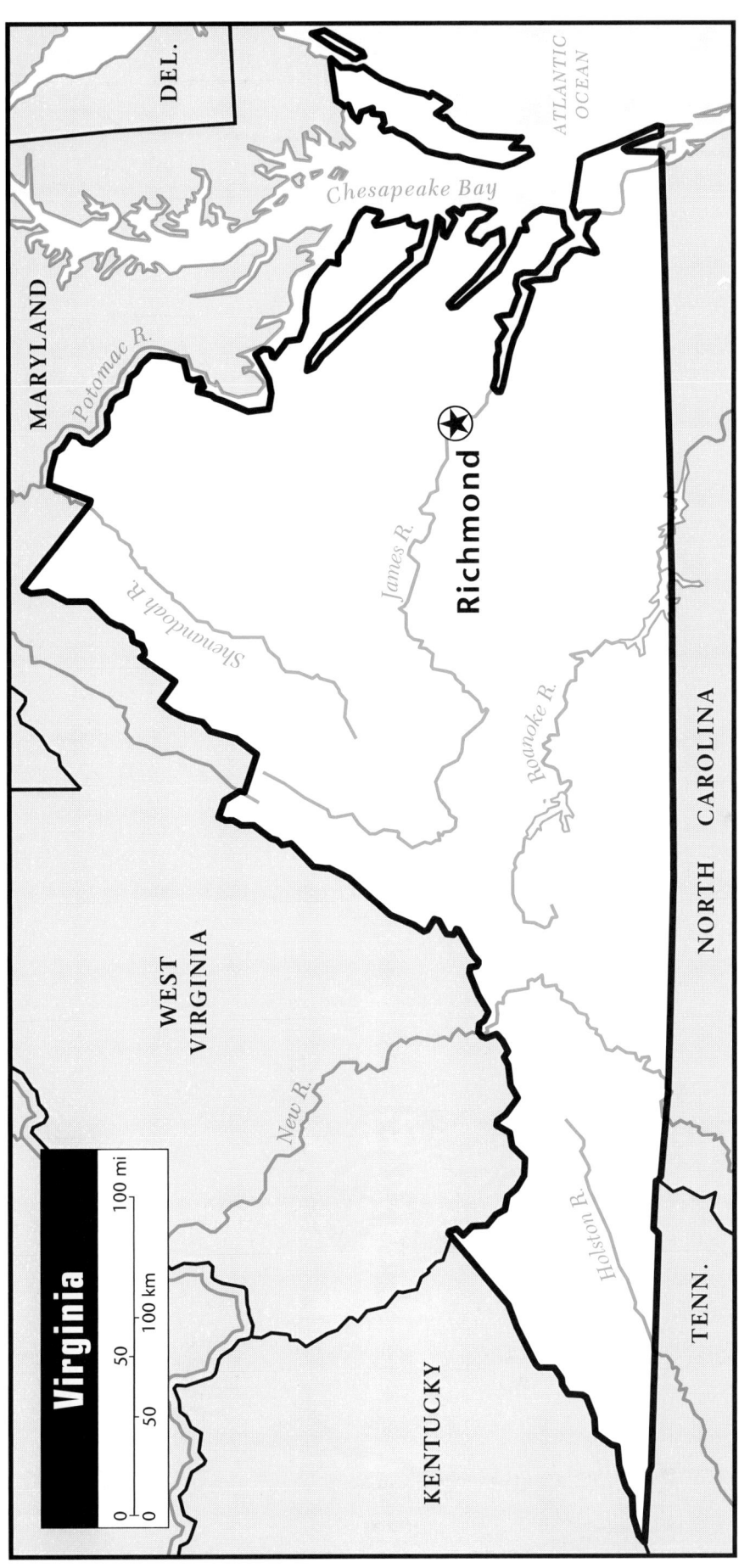

Virginia

100 mi

100 km

MARYLAND

DEL.

Chesapeake Bay

ATLANTIC OCEAN

Potomac R.

Shenandoah R.

Richmond

James R.

Roanoke R.

WEST VIRGINIA

NORTH CAROLINA

New R.

Holston R.

KENTUCKY

TENN.

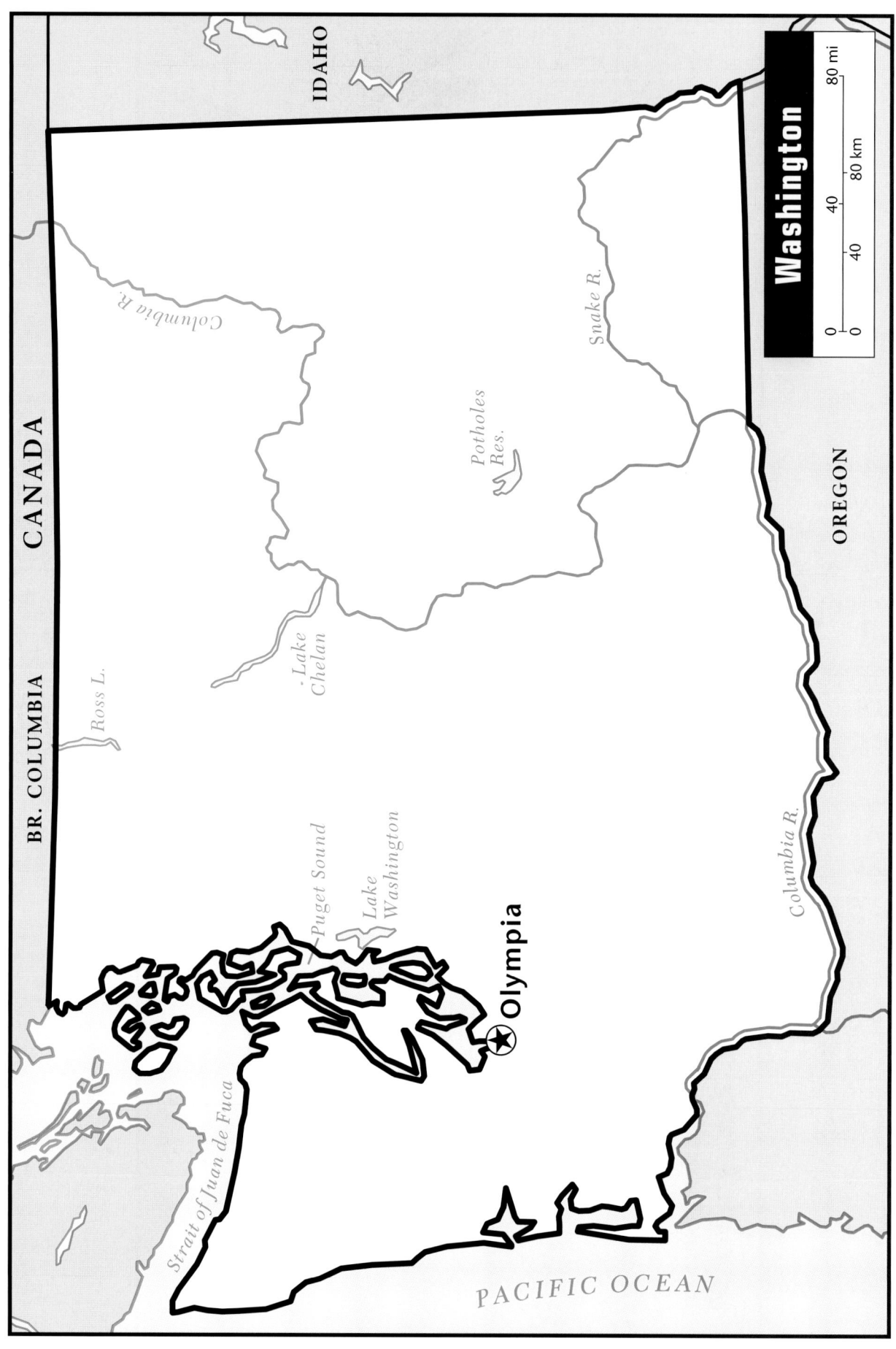

Washington

CANADA

BR. COLUMBIA

IDAHO

OREGON

PACIFIC OCEAN

Strait of Juan de Fuca

Puget Sound

Lake Washington

Olympia

Ross L.

Lake Chelan

Columbia R.

Potholes Res.

Snake R.

Columbia R.

80 mi
80 km
40
40
0
0

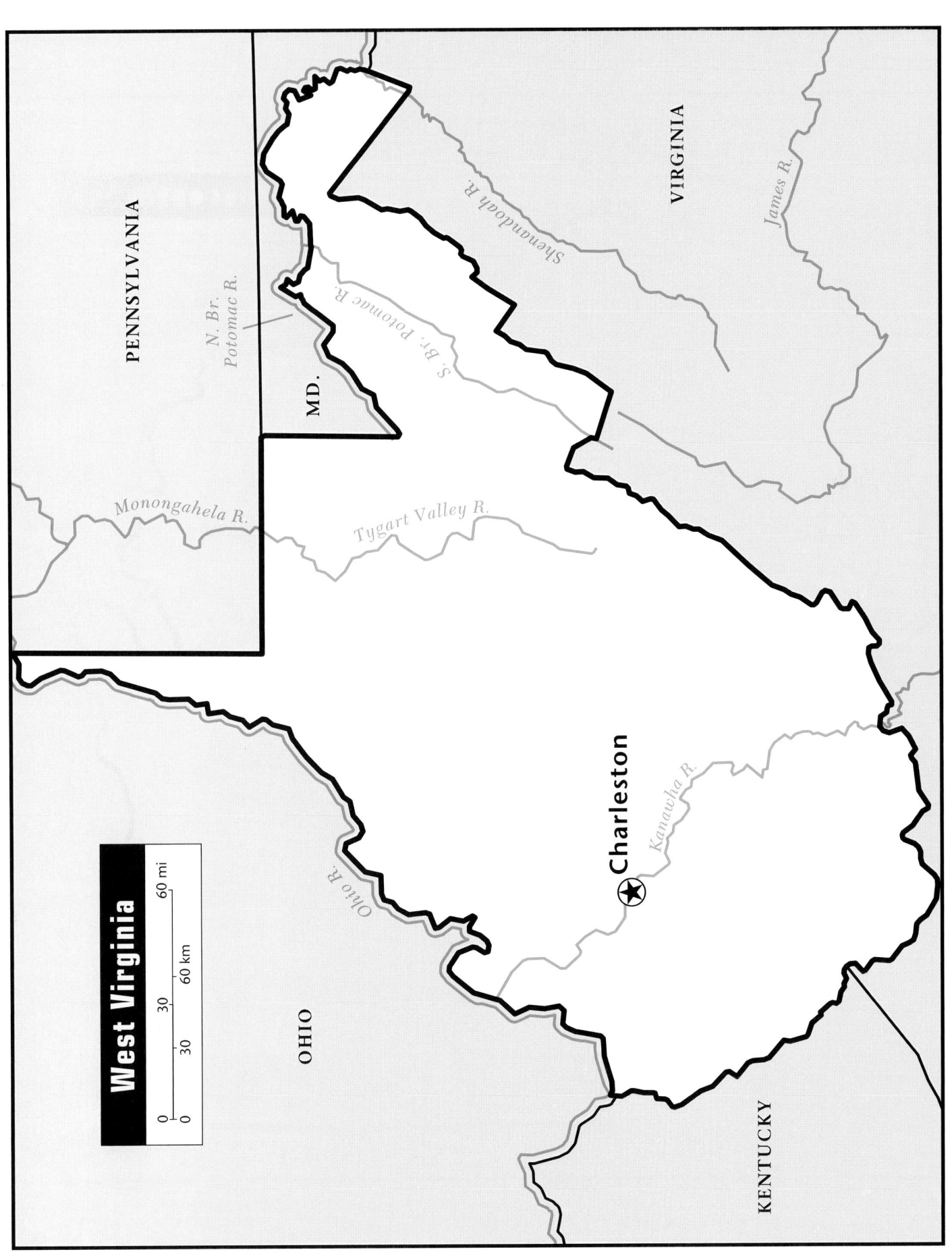

Wisconsin

0   35   70 mi
0   35   70 km

MICHIGAN

Lake Superior

St. Croix R.

Green Bay

Wisconsin R.

MINNESOTA

Mississippi R.

Petenwell L.

Castle
Rock L.

L. Winnebago

Lake
Michigan

IOWA

Iowa R.

★ Madison

ILLINOIS

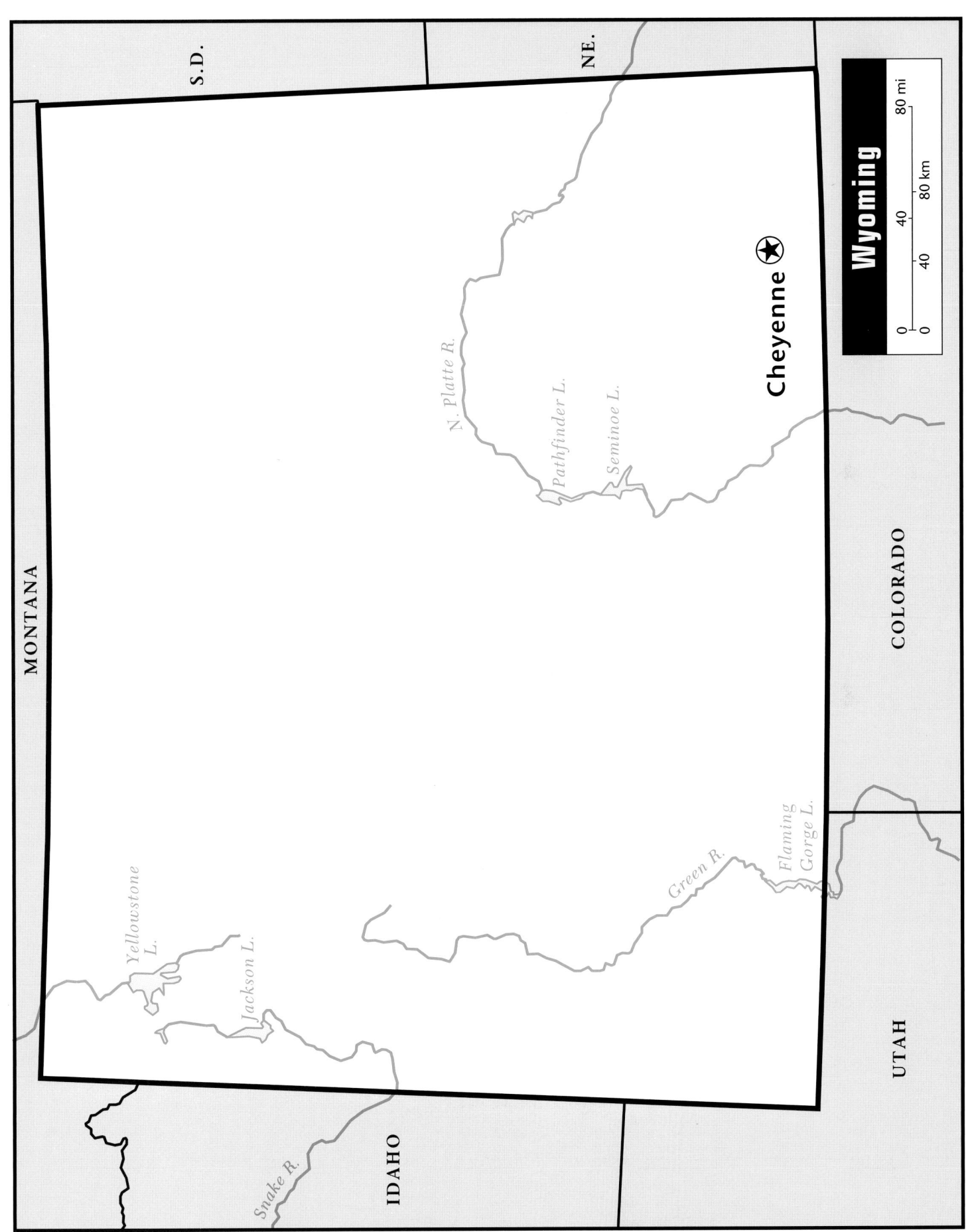

S.D.

N.E.

MONTANA

N. Platte R.

Pathfinder L.

Seminoe L.

Cheyenne ⍟

COLORADO

Yellowstone L.

Jackson L.

Green R.

Flaming Gorge L.

UTAH

IDAHO

Snake R.

Wyoming

| 0 | 40 | 80 mi |
| 0 | 40 | 80 km |

Elevation 496
Climate 498
Vegetation 500
Precipitation and Time Zones 502
January and July Temperatures 503
Plate Tectonics 504
Earthquakes 506
Vulcanism 507
Population 508
    Continent Projections
    Density by Country
Languages and Literacy .510
Religions 511
Life Expectancy 512
Youthful Population and Nutrition 513
Land Use, GDP and Employment 514
    Industrial and Agricultural Employment
Mining and Energy 516
Environmental Issues 518
    Forest Cover
    Deforestation

Rice Fields - Kaiko, Kawasaki City, Japan

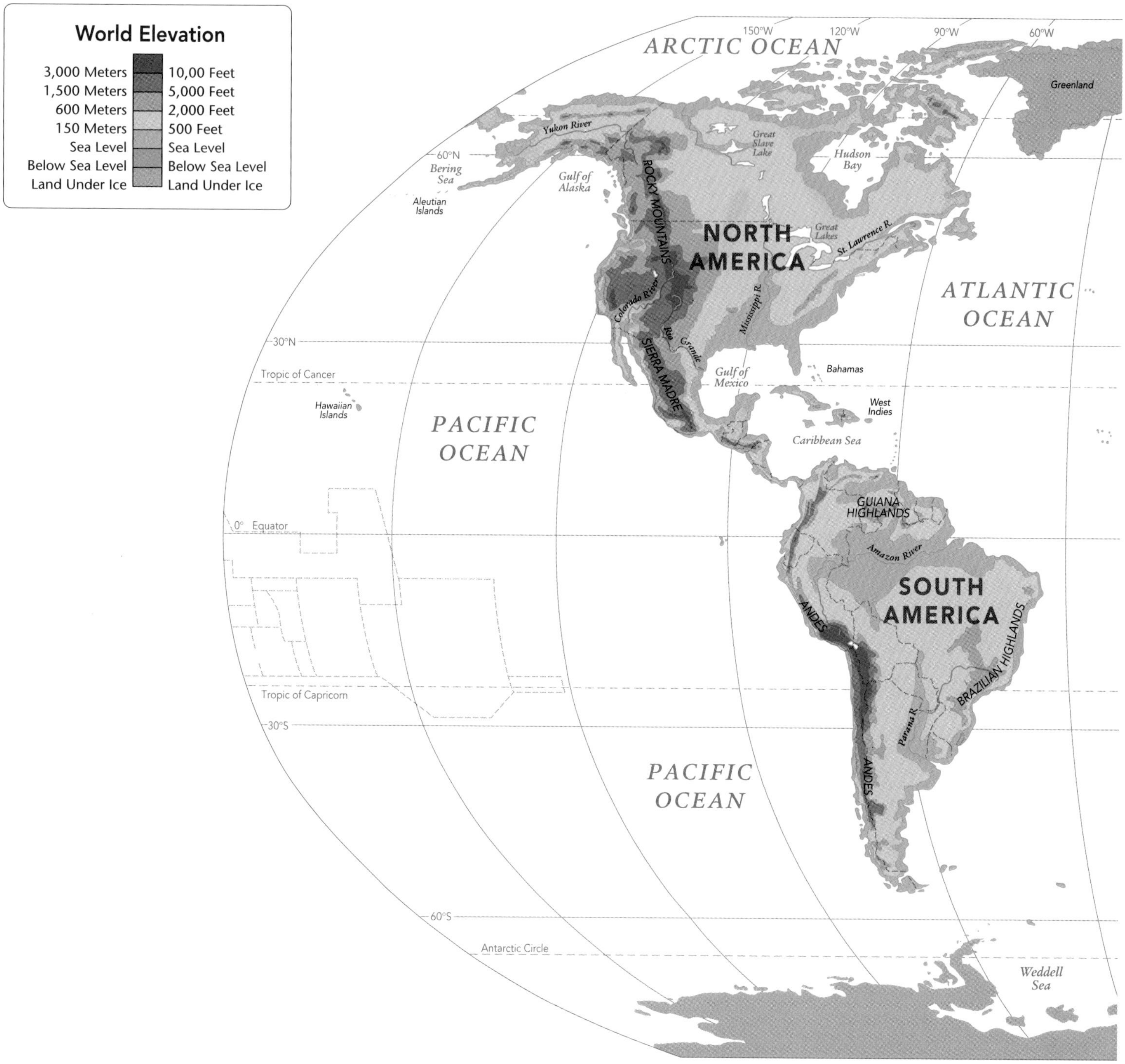

World Elevation

3,000 Meters	10,00 Feet
1,500 Meters	5,000 Feet
600 Meters	2,000 Feet
150 Meters	500 Feet
Sea Level	Sea Level
Below Sea Level	Below Sea Level
Land Under Ice	Land Under Ice

ARCTIC OCEAN

150°W   120°W   90°W   60°W

Greenland

Yukon River

60°N

Bering
Sea

Gulf of
Alaska

Great
Slave
Lake

Hudson
Bay

Aleutian
Islands

NORTH
AMERICA

ROCKY MOUNTAINS

Great
Lakes

St. Lawrence R.

ATLANTIC
OCEAN

Colorado River

Mississippi R.

30°N

Tropic of Cancer

SIERRA MADRE

Rio Grande

Hawaiian
Islands

PACIFIC
OCEAN

Gulf of
Mexico

Bahamas

West
Indies

Caribbean Sea

0° Equator

GUIANA
HIGHLANDS

Amazon River

SOUTH
AMERICA

ANDES

BRAZILIAN HIGHLANDS

Tropic of Capricorn

Paraná R.

30°S

PACIFIC
OCEAN

ANDES

60°S

Antarctic Circle

Weddell
Sea

Rocky Mountains, United States

Death Valley, United States

The Pampas, Argentina

PIERRE AUGER OBSERVATORY

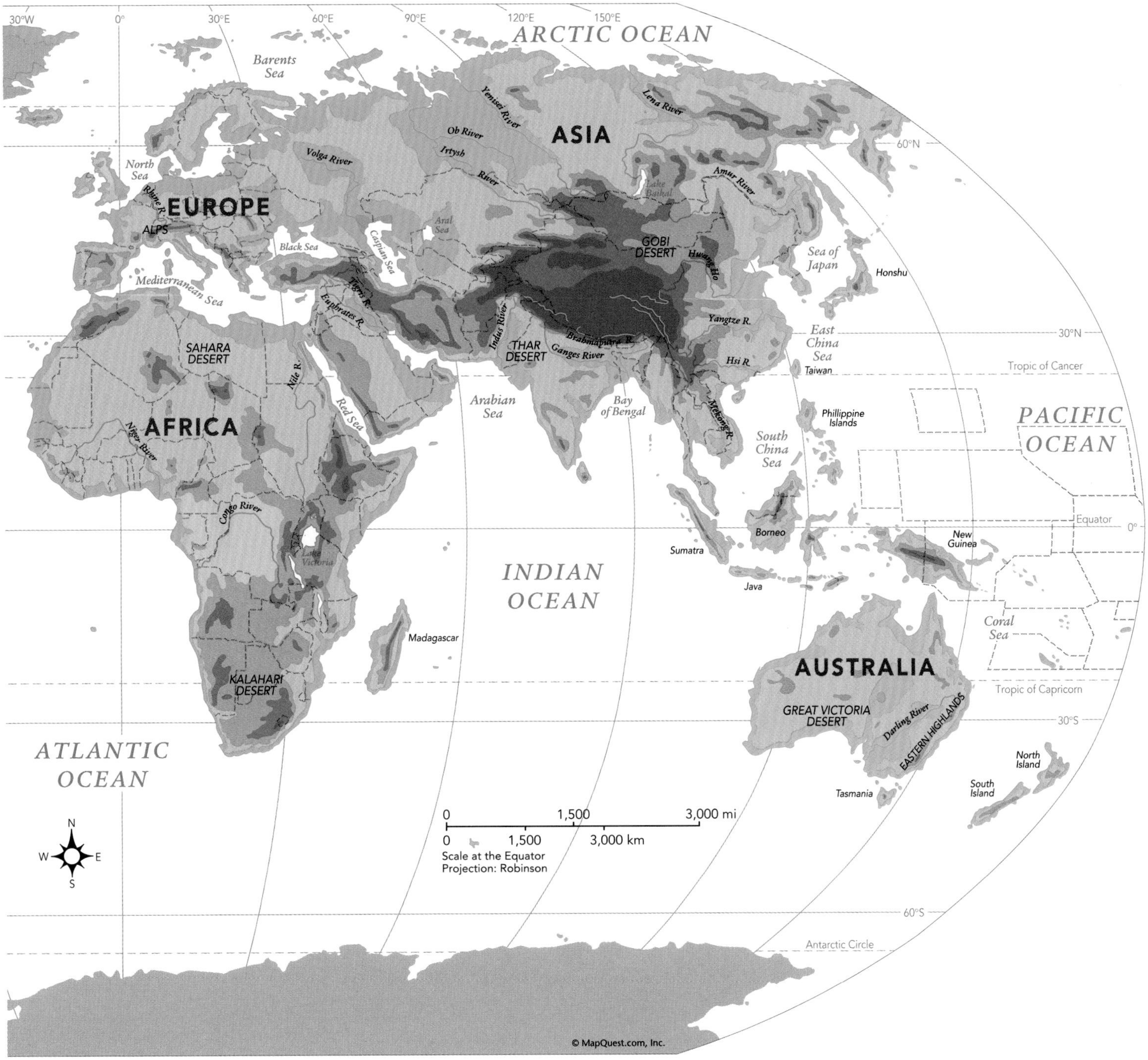

ARCTIC OCEAN

Barents
Sea

30°W 0° 30°E 60°E 90°E 120°E 150°E

Yenisei River

Lena River

ASIA

Ob River

Volga River

Irtysh
River

Amur River

60°N

North
Sea

EUROPE

ALPS

Lake
Baikal

GOBI
DESERT

Huang Ho

Sea of
Japan

Honshu

Aral
Sea

Black Sea

Caspian Sea

Rhine R.

Mediterranean Sea

Tigris R.

Euphrates R.

Indus River

Yangtze R.

East
China
Sea

30°N

SAHARA
DESERT

Nile R.

Red Sea

THAR
DESERT

Ganges River

Brahmaputra R.

Hsi R.

Taiwan

Tropic of Cancer

Arabian
Sea

Bay
of Bengal

Mekong R.

Phillippine
Islands

PACIFIC
OCEAN

AFRICA

Niger River

Congo River

Victoria

South
China
Sea

Sumatra

Borneo

New
Guinea

Equator 0°

INDIAN
OCEAN

Java

KALAHARI
DESERT

Madagascar

Coral
Sea

AUSTRALIA

Tropic of Capricorn

GREAT VICTORIA
DESERT

Darling River

EASTERN HIGHLANDS

30°S

ATLANTIC
OCEAN

North
Island

Tasmania

South
Island

0   1,500   3,000 mi

0   1,500   3,000 km

Scale at the Equator
Projection: Robinson

N
W   E
S

60°S

Antarctic Circle

© MapQuest.com, Inc.

Nile River, Egypt

The Himalayas, Nepal

Ayer's Rock, Australia

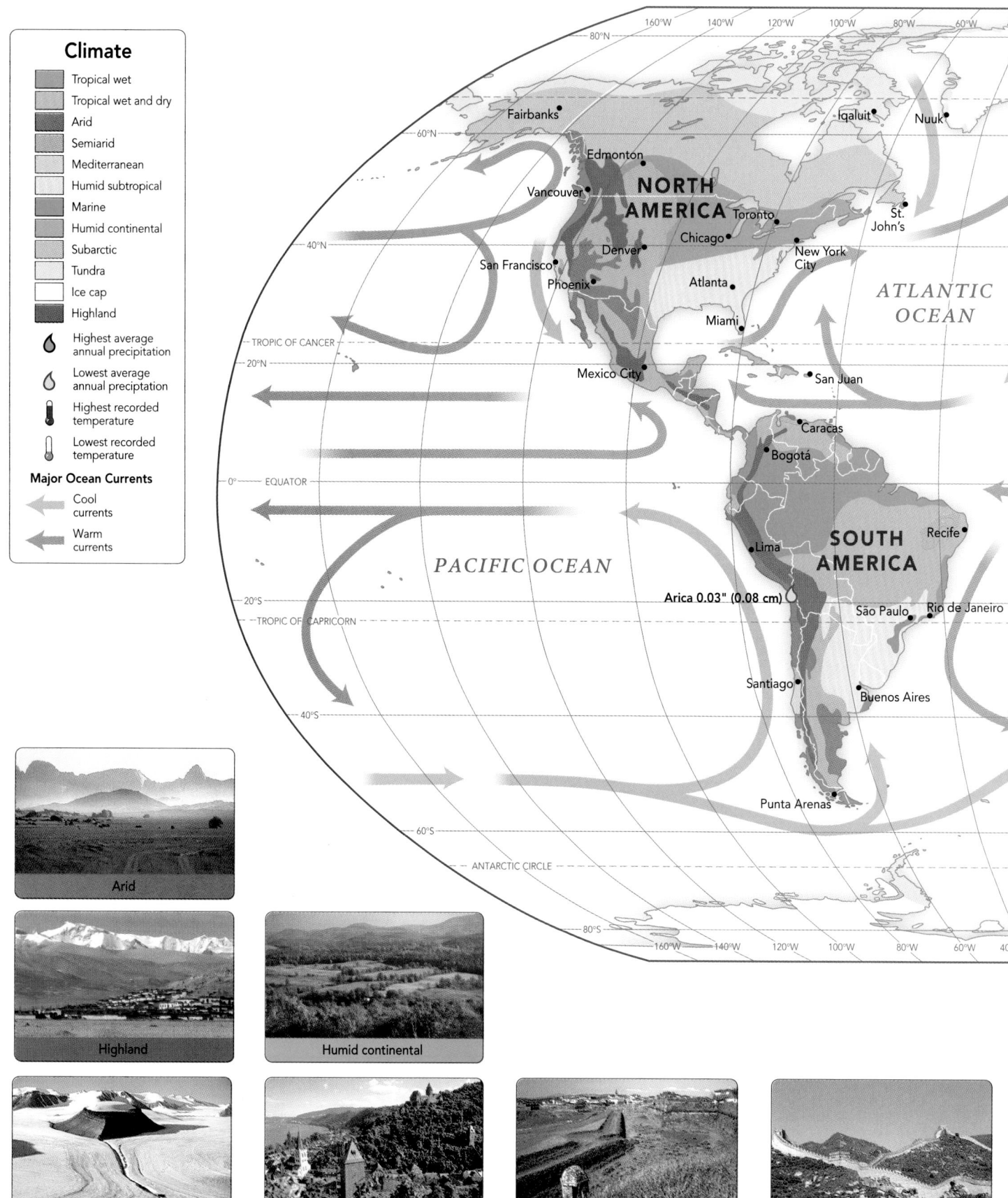

Climate

- Tropical wet
- Tropical wet and dry
- Arid
- Semiarid
- Mediterranean
- Humid subtropical
- Marine
- Humid continental
- Subarctic
- Tundra
- Ice cap
- Highland

- Highest average annual precipitation
- Lowest average annual precipitation
- Highest recorded temperature
- Lowest recorded temperature

Major Ocean Currents

- Cool currents
- Warm currents

Arica 0.03" (0.08 cm)

Arid

Highland

Humid continental

Icecap

Marine

Mediterranean

Semiarid

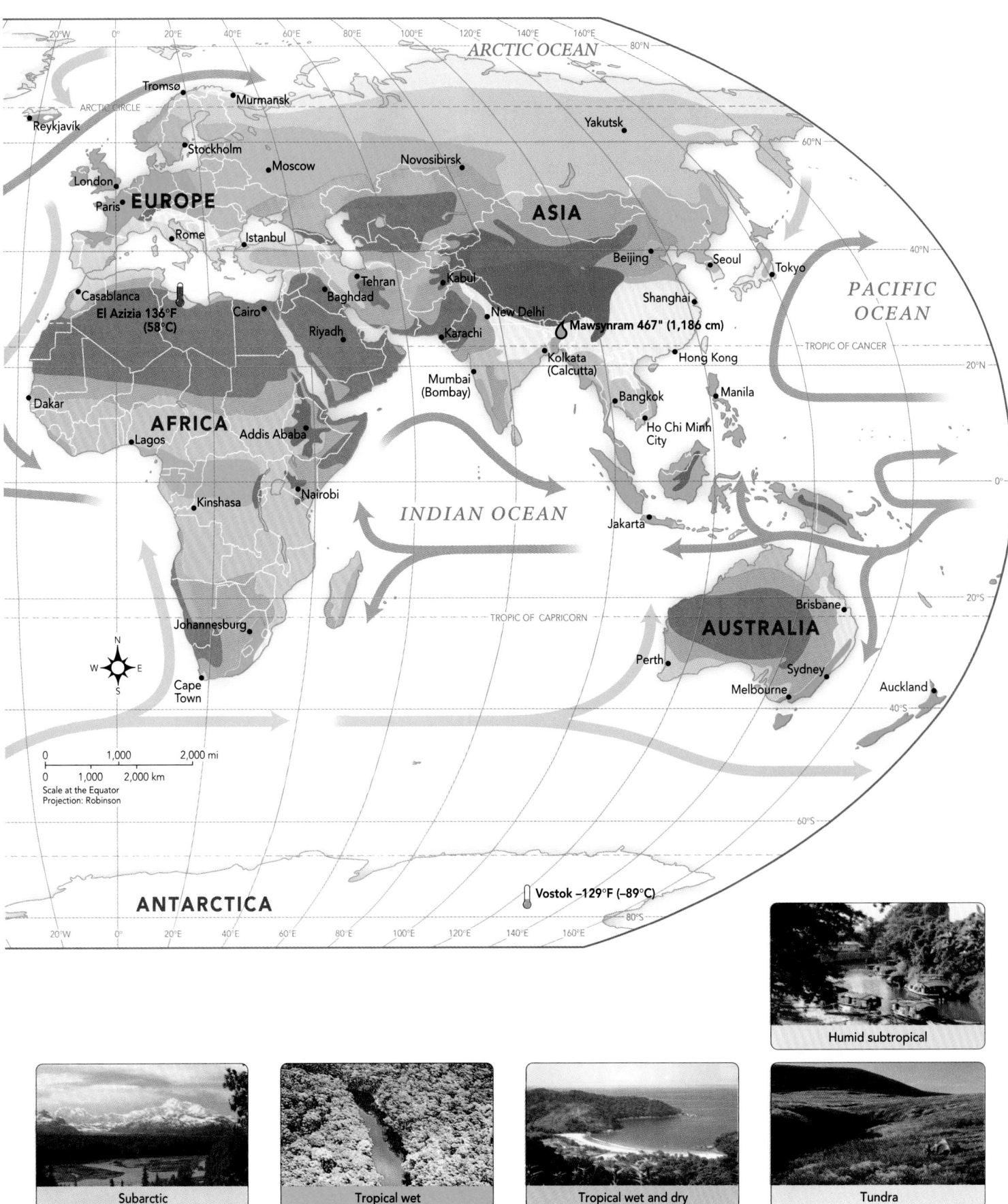

ARCTIC OCEAN

80°N

ARCTIC CIRCLE

Tromsø
Murmansk
Reykjavík
Yakutsk
Stockholm
60°N
Moscow
Novosibirsk
London
EUROPE
Paris
ASIA
Rome
Istanbul
40°N
Beijing
Seoul
Tokyo
Tehran
Kabul
Shanghai
PACIFIC
OCEAN
Casablanca
Baghdad
El Azizia 136°F
(58°C)
Cairo
New Delhi
Mawsynram 467" (1,186 cm)
Riyadh
Karachi
Kolkata
(Calcutta)
TROPIC OF CANCER
20°N
Hong Kong
Mumbai
(Bombay)
Dakar
Bangkok
Manila
AFRICA
Addis Ababa
Ho Chi Minh
City
Lagos
0°
Kinshasa
Nairobi
INDIAN OCEAN
Jakarta
20°S
Brisbane
TROPIC OF CAPRICORN
AUSTRALIA
Johannesburg
Perth
Sydney
Melbourne
Auckland
Cape
Town
40°S

0   1,000   2,000 mi
0   1,000   2,000 km
Scale at the Equator
Projection: Robinson

ANTARCTICA
Vostok –129°F (–89°C)
80°S

Humid subtropical

Subarctic

Tropical wet

Tropical wet and dry

Tundra

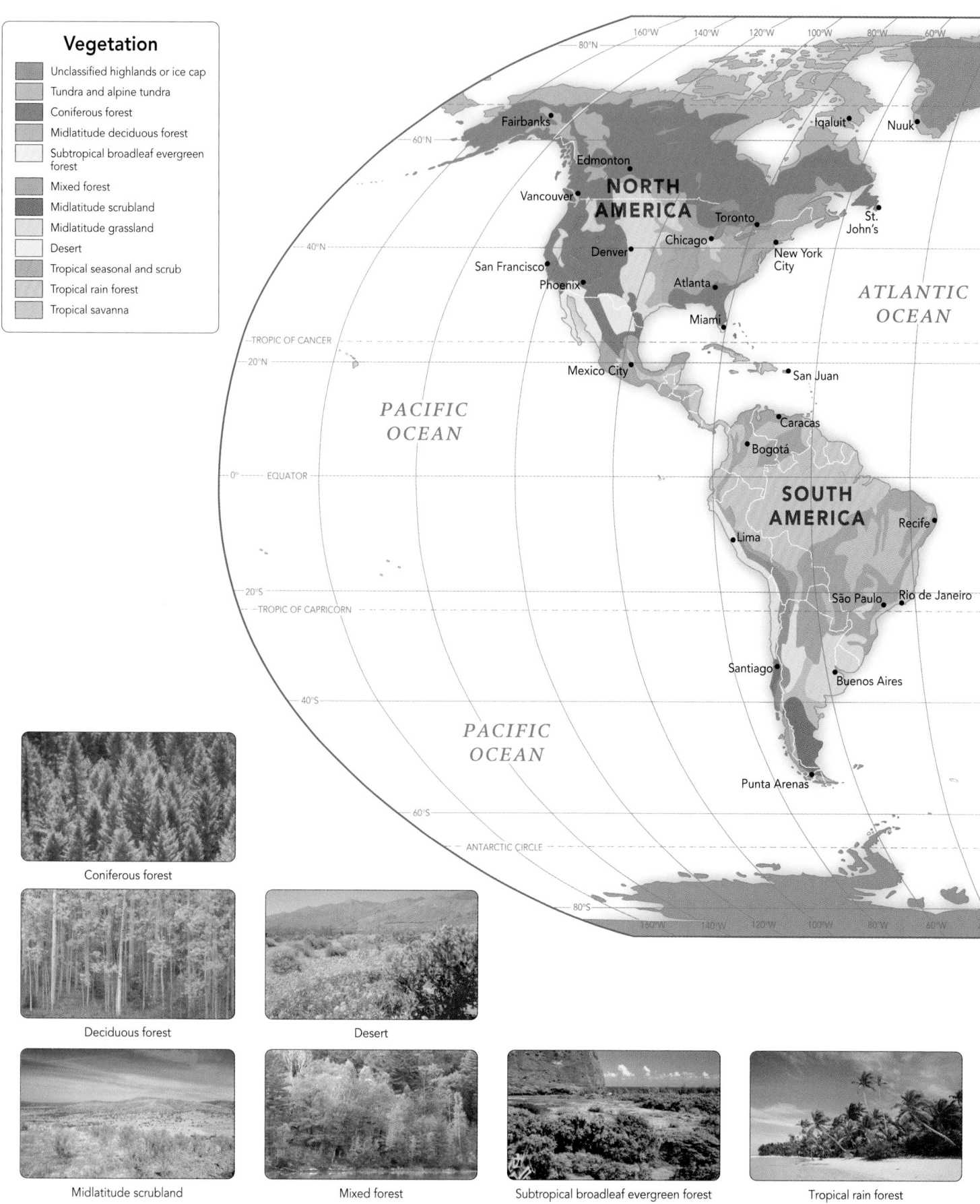

Vegetation

- Unclassified highlands or ice cap
- Tundra and alpine tundra
- Coniferous forest
- Midlatitude deciduous forest
- Subtropical broadleaf evergreen forest
- Mixed forest
- Midlatitude scrubland
- Midlatitude grassland
- Desert
- Tropical seasonal and scrub
- Tropical rain forest
- Tropical savanna

Coniferous forest

Deciduous forest

Desert

Midlatitude scrubland

Mixed forest

Subtropical broadleaf evergreen forest

Tropical rain forest

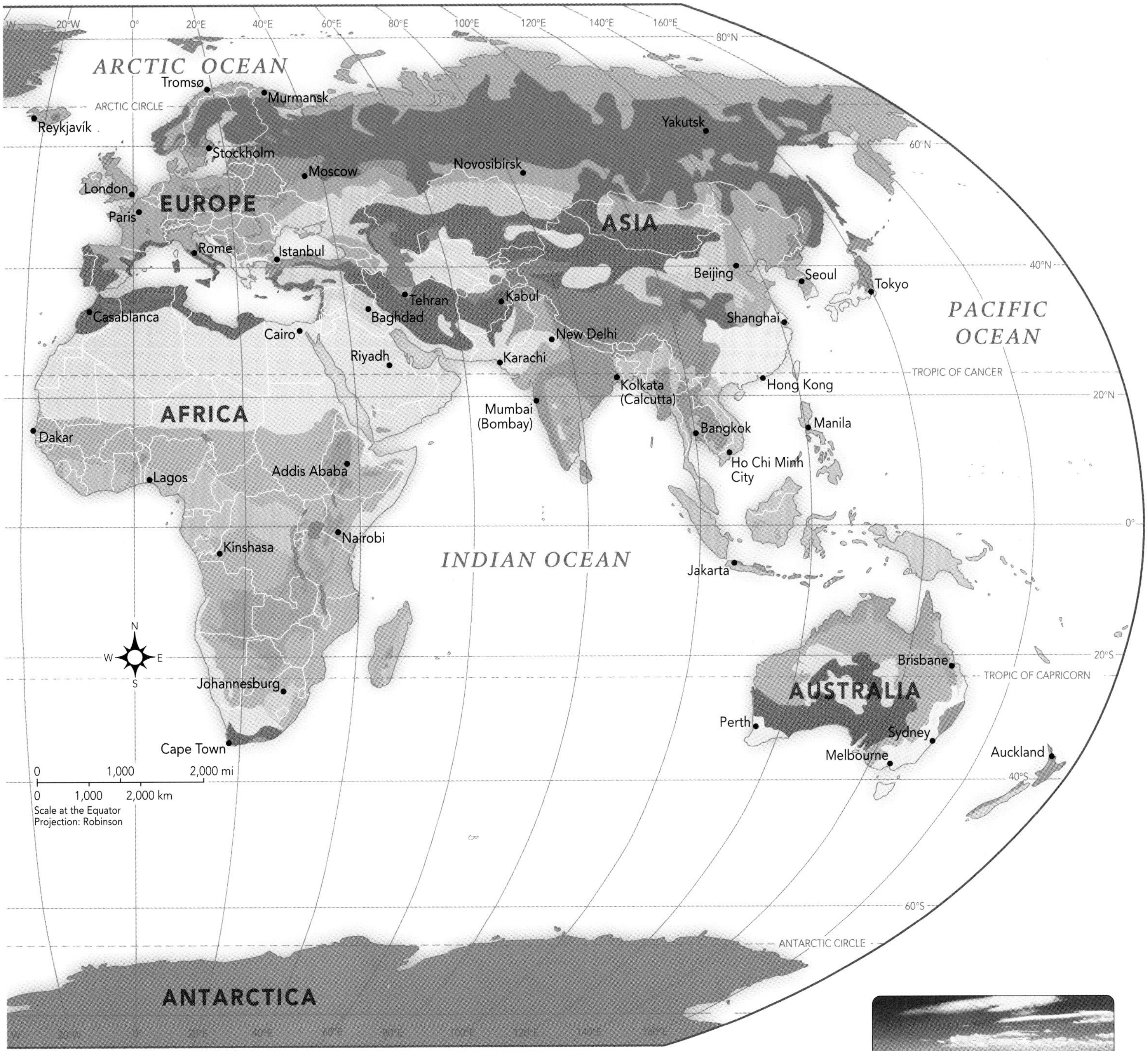
ARCTIC OCEAN
ARCTIC CIRCLE
Tromsø
Murmansk
Reykjavík
Stockholm
Moscow
Novosibirsk
Yakutsk
London
Paris
EUROPE
ASIA
Rome
Istanbul
Beijing
Seoul
Tokyo
PACIFIC OCEAN
Casablanca
Tehran
Kabul
Baghdad
Shanghai
Cairo
New Delhi
Riyadh
Karachi
TROPIC OF CANCER
Kolkata (Calcutta)
Hong Kong
Mumbai (Bombay)
AFRICA
Dakar
Manila
Bangkok
Ho Chi Minh City
Addis Ababa
Lagos
Nairobi
Kinshasa
INDIAN OCEAN
Jakarta
Brisbane
TROPIC OF CAPRICORN
AUSTRALIA
Johannesburg
Perth
Sydney
Cape Town
Auckland
Melbourne
0 1,000 2,000 mi
0 1,000 2,000 km
Scale at the Equator
Projection: Robinson
ANTARCTIC CIRCLE
ANTARCTICA
80°N
60°N
40°N
20°N
0°
20°S
40°S
60°S
20°W
0°
20°E
40°E
60°E
80°E
100°E
120°E
140°E
160°E
N
S
E
W

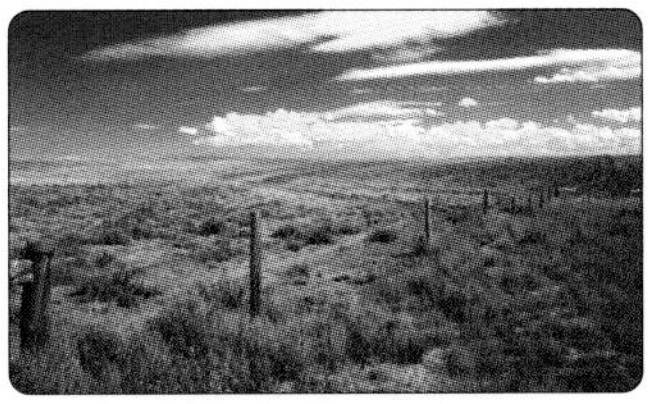
Midlatitude grassland

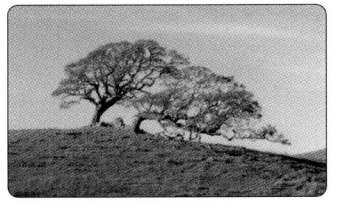

Tropical savanna

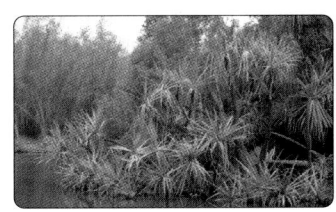

Tropical seasonal and scrub

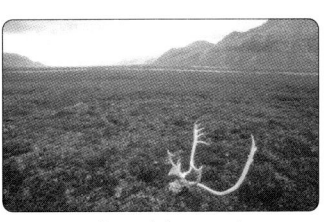

Tundra and alpine tundra

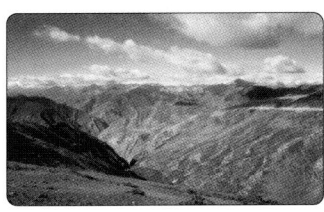

Unclassified highlands or ice cap

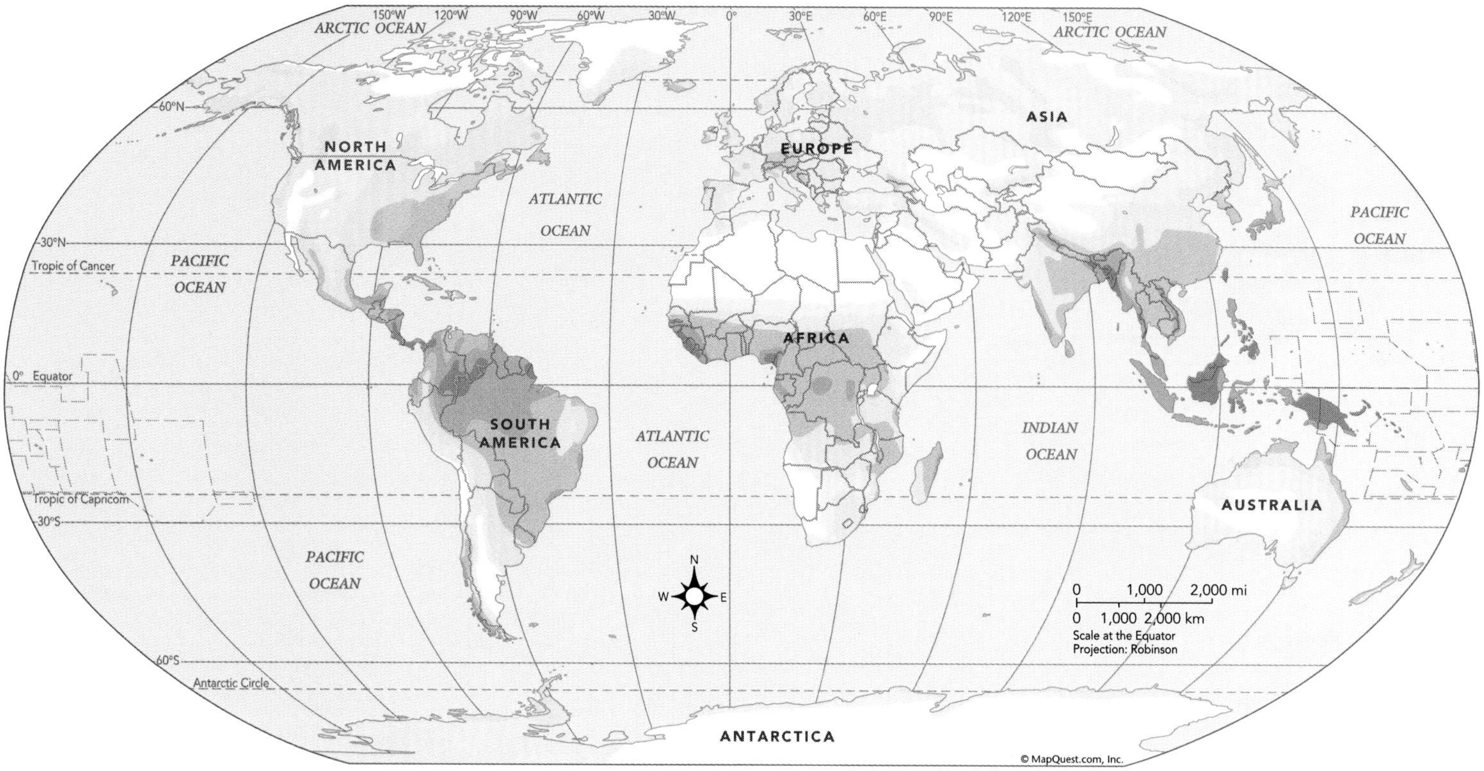

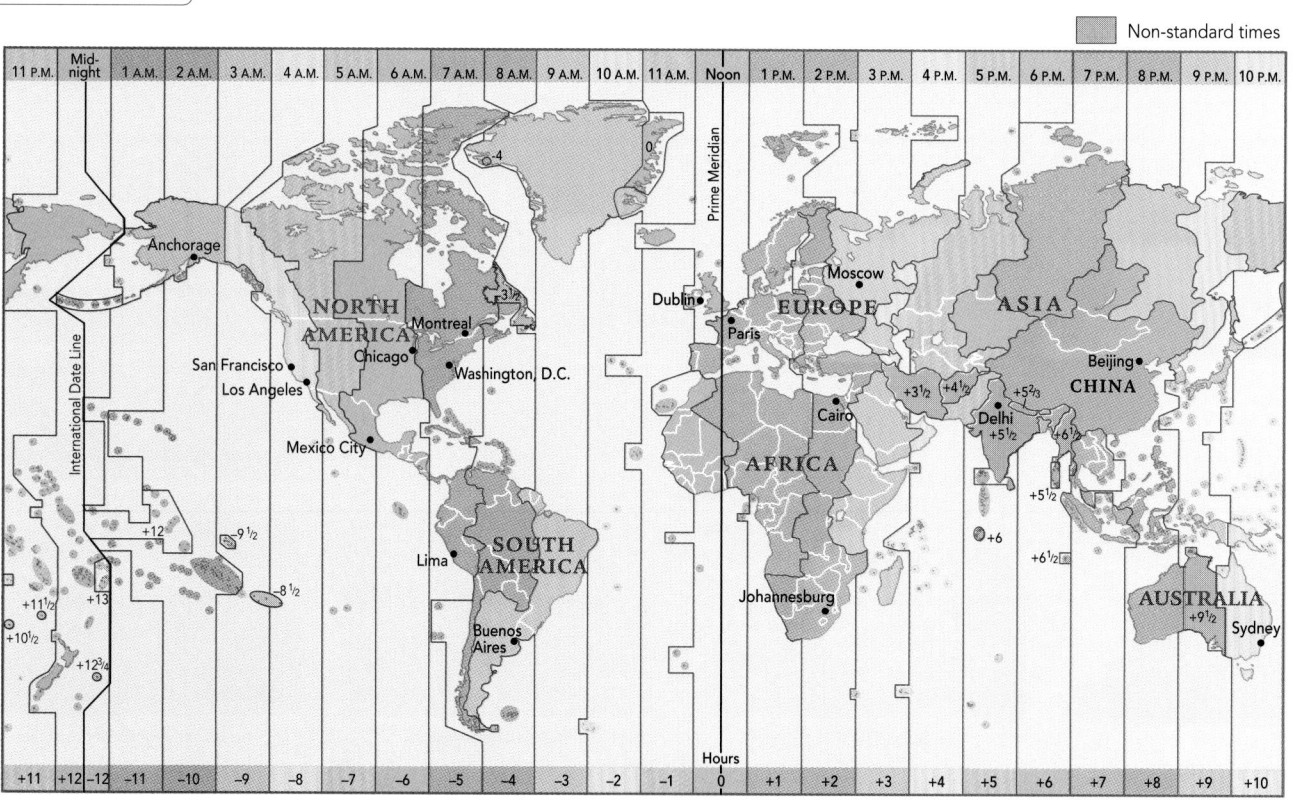

World Precipitation

World Precipitation

Inches	Millimeters
>120	>3000
80–120	2000–3000
40–80	1000–2000
20–40	500–1000
10–20	250–500
<10	<250

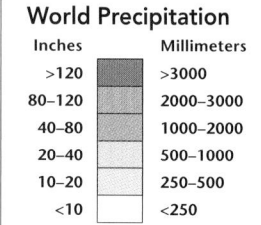

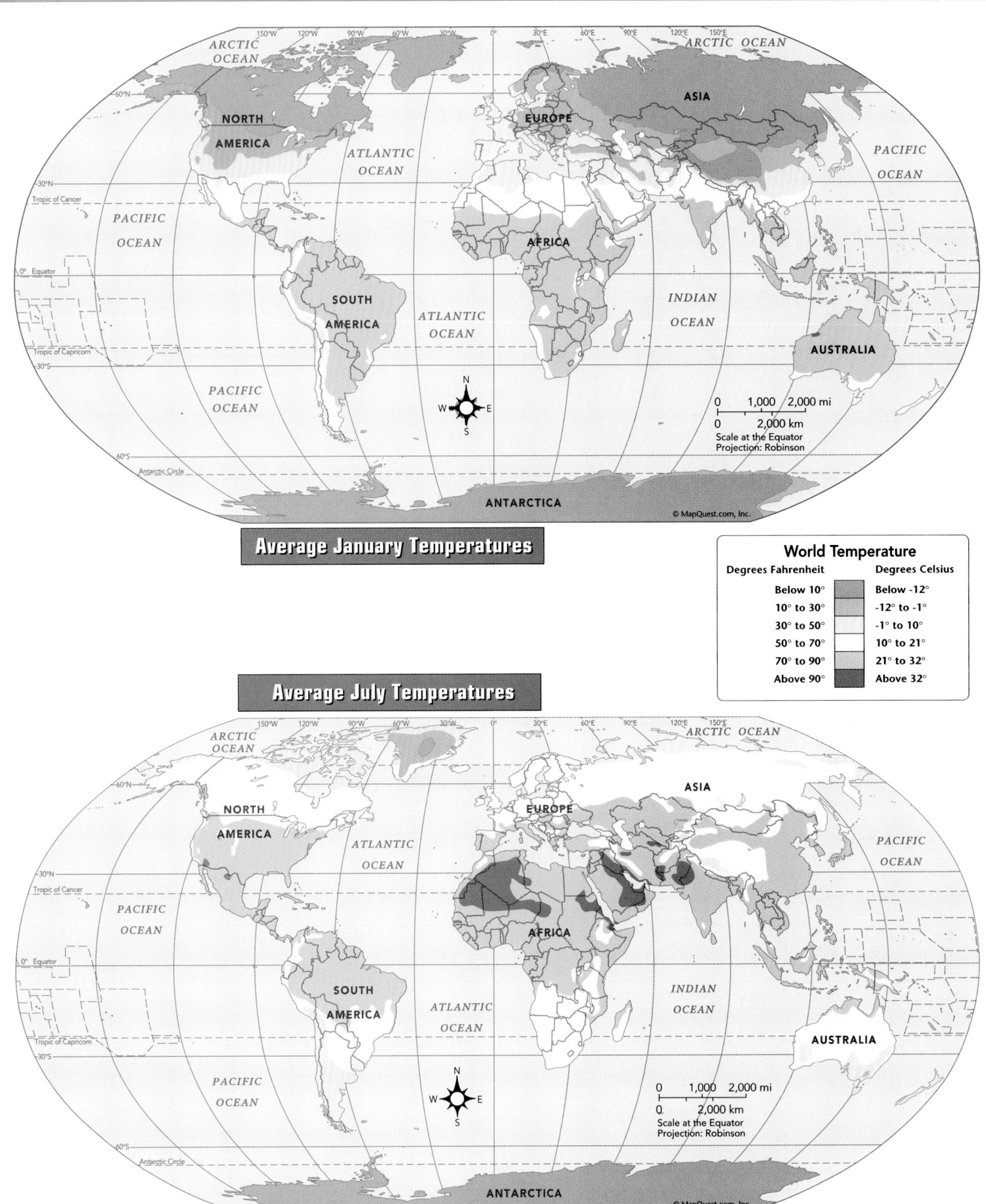

Average January Temperatures

Average July Temperatures

World Temperature

Degrees Fahrenheit	Degrees Celsius
Below 10°	Below -12°
10° to 30°	-12° to -1°
30° to 50°	-1° to 10°
50° to 70°	10° to 21°
70° to 90°	21° to 32°
Above 90°	Above 32°

237 Million Years Ago

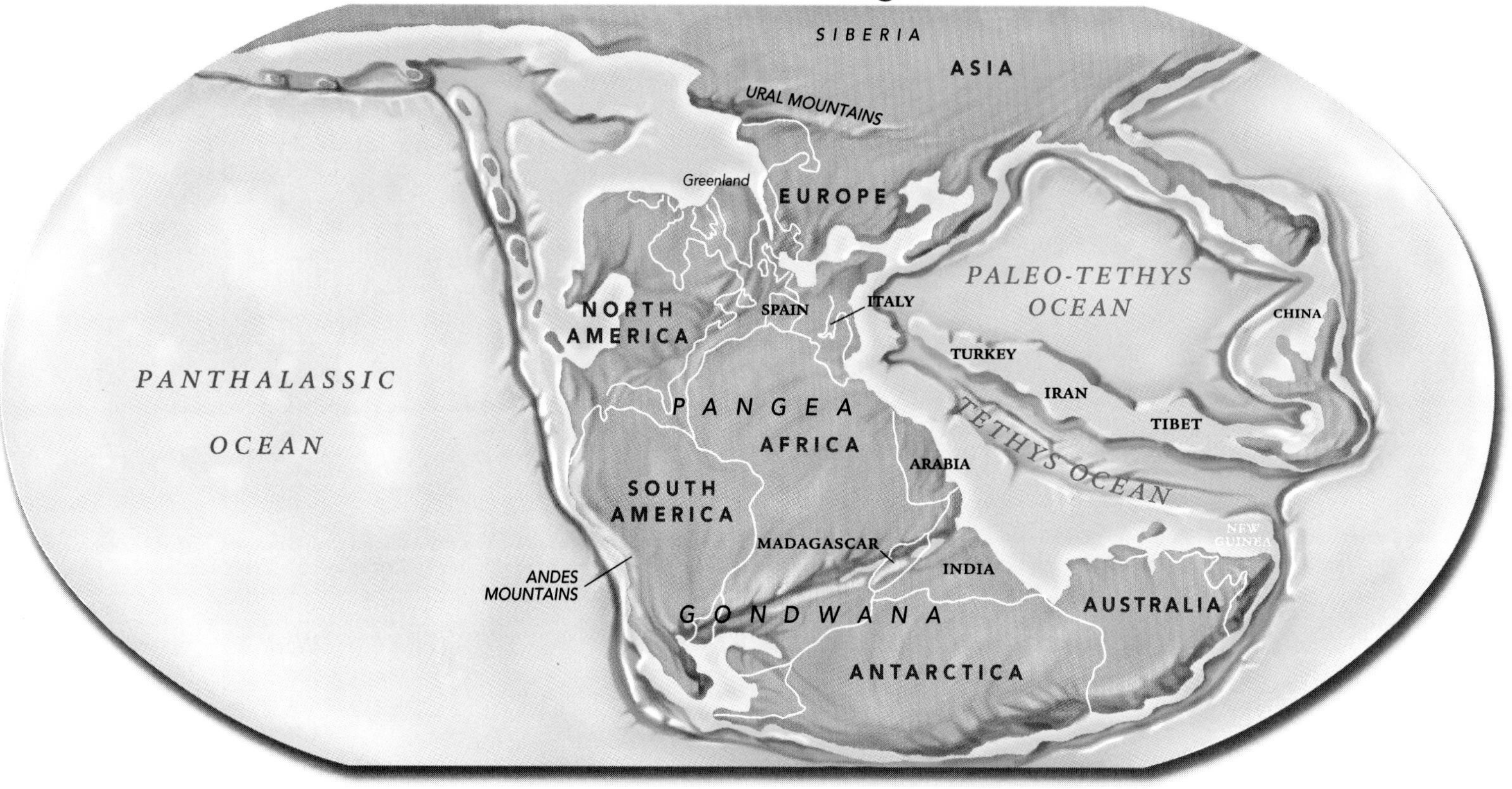

SIBERIA

ASIA

URAL MOUNTAINS

Greenland

EUROPE

PALEO-TETHYS
OCEAN

CHINA

NORTH
AMERICA

SPAIN

ITALY

TURKEY

IRAN

TIBET

PANTHALASSIC

OCEAN

P A N G E A

AFRICA

ARABIA

TETHYS OCEAN

SOUTH
AMERICA

MADAGASCAR

INDIA

NEW
GUINEA

ANDES
MOUNTAINS

G O N D W A N A

AUSTRALIA

ANTARCTICA

This peculiar—to our eyes—arrangement of continents with its unfamiliar oceans and seas, mountains and plains, and peninsulas and islands reminds us that the dinosaurs lived in a far different landscape than our own. As the last dinosaurs receded into memory, the future Atlantic Ocean and Mediterranean Sea were becoming more substantial and recognizable, and the continents, except for Australia and Antarctica, were nearing their present latitudes. Within the last 65 million years, most continents nestled unhurriedly into their current positions. However, the Indian sub-continent "sprinted" north, crashing into Asia and bulldozing up the Himalayas, earth's loftiest mountain range.

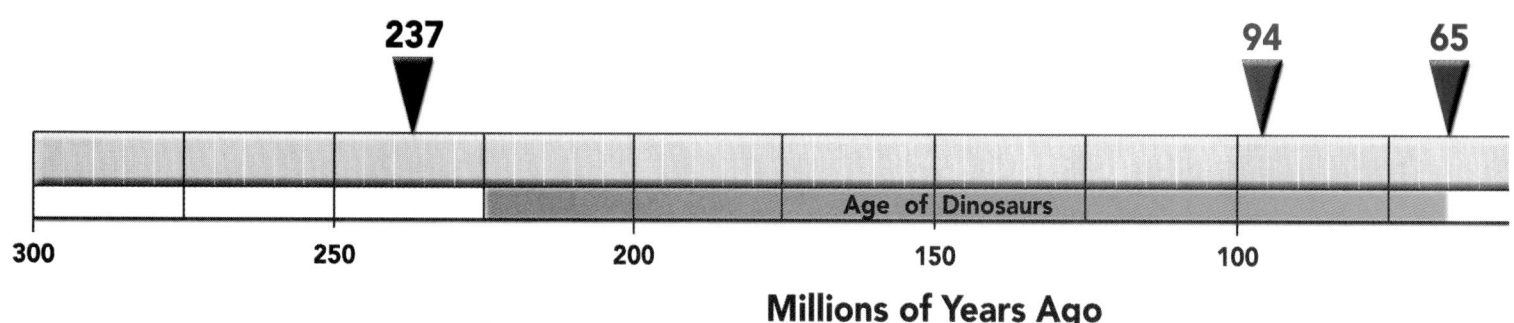

237

94

65

Age of Dinosaurs

300   250   200   150   100

Millions of Years Ago

94 Million Years Ago

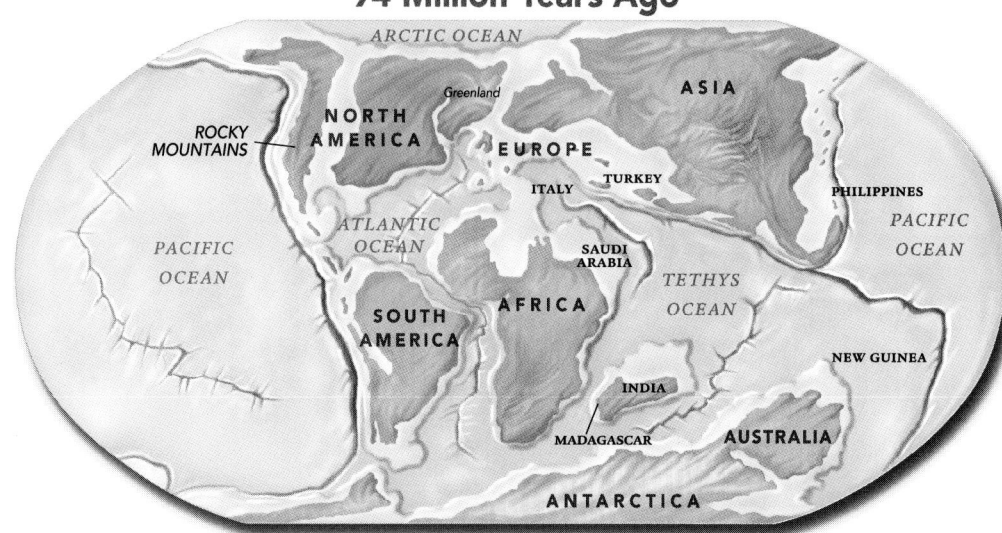

The highly controversial theory of Continental Drift was proposed in 1915 by Alfred Wegener to explain both geologic and fossil discoveries. Although supported by strong data and seemingly obvious visual evidence—most notably, the close fit of the coastlines of Africa and South America—the theory was rejected by other scientists. By the 1960s, further studies, especially those that discovered that some rocks contained a record of the alignment of the Earth's magnetic field, resurrected the theory, which was redefined under the term Plate Tectonics. Few scientists now dispute its general premise, that continental and oceanic plates move atop a layer of hot and semi-solid rock below them, although many details, particularly the causes and mechanics of the motion, are still not well understood.

65 Million Years Ago

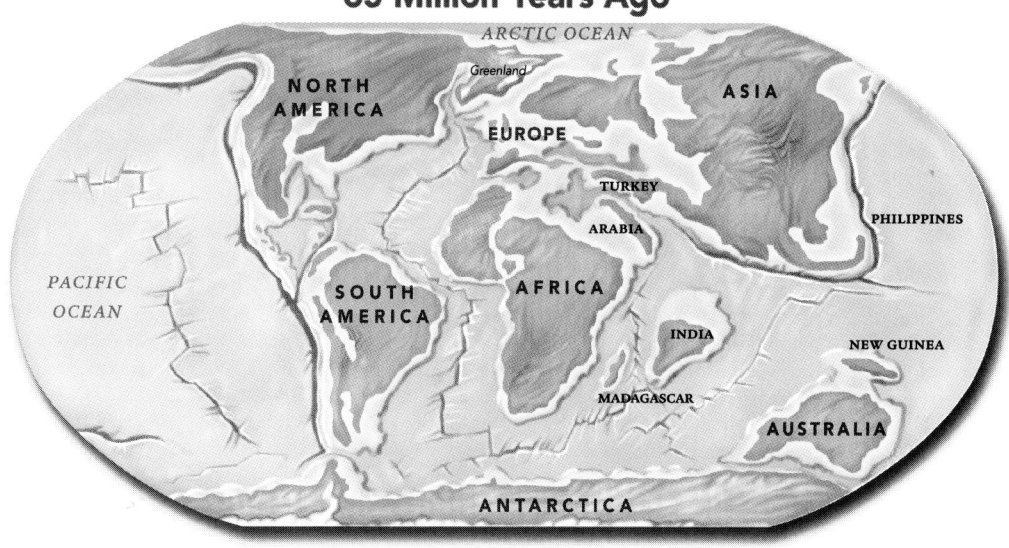

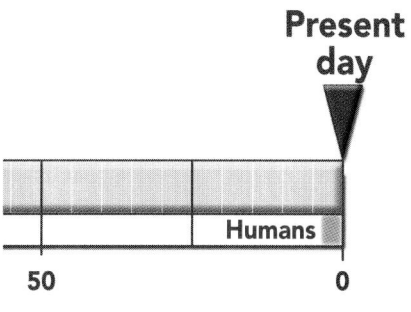

Present Day

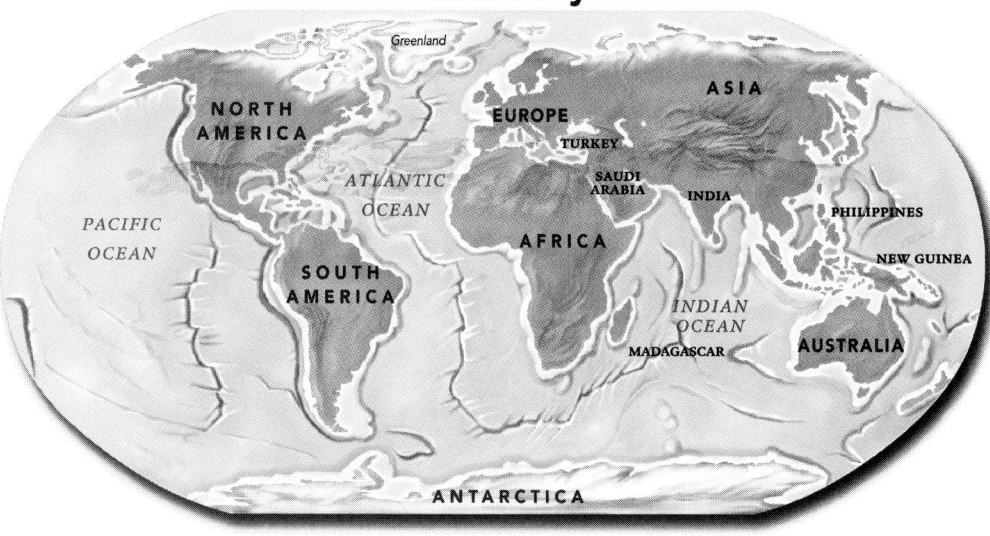

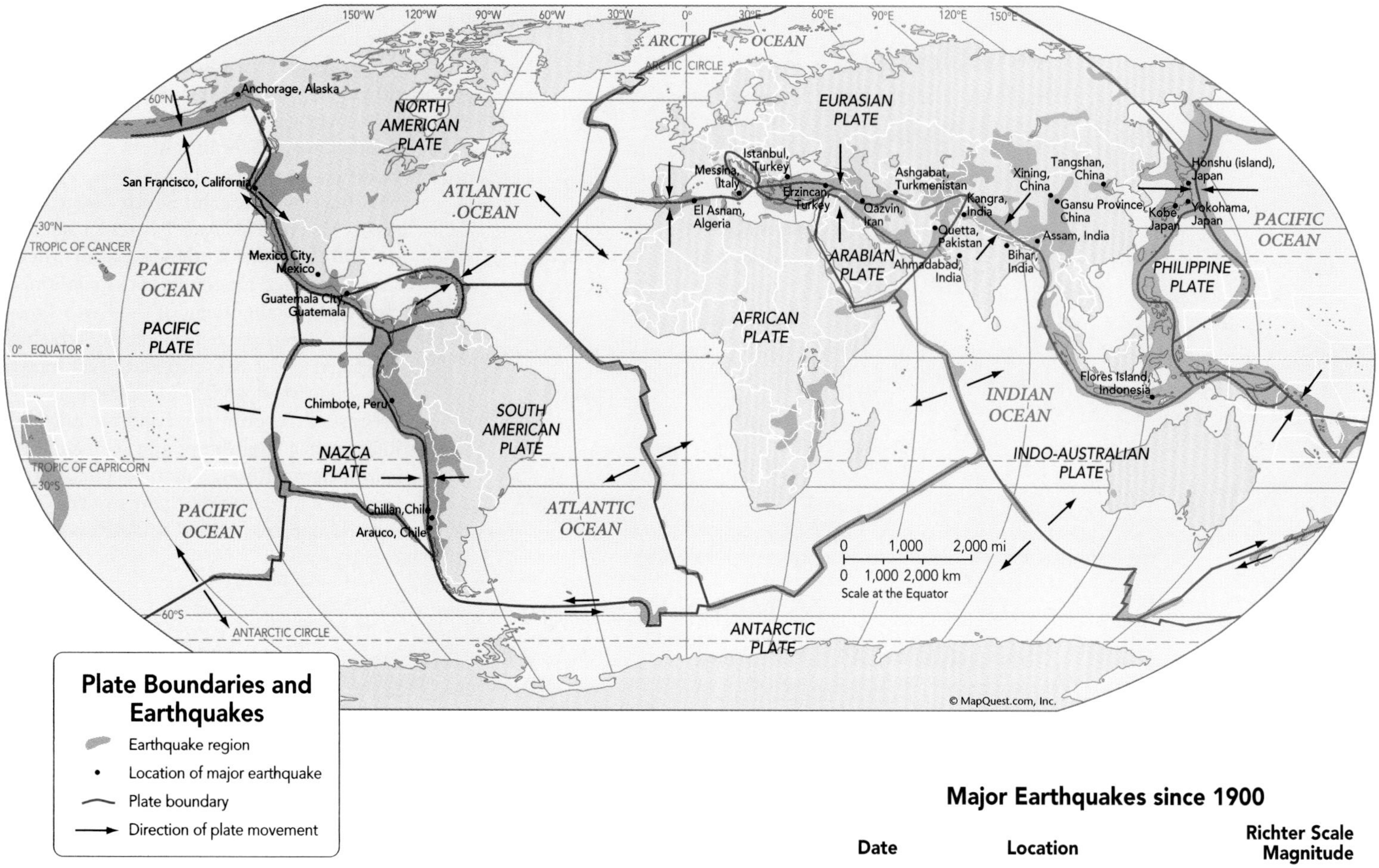

Plate Boundaries and Earthquakes

- Earthquake region
- • Location of major earthquake
- Plate boundary
- → Direction of plate movement

The movement of Earth's crustal plates causes the phenomena known as earthquakes. The surface of the Earth actually moves or quakes. An earthquake can have the destructive energy of an atomic bomb. However, thousands of earthquakes occur each day all over the world without most people realizing it.

The majority of earthquakes occur along a fault. A fault is usually a weak or broken area in the rocks beneath the surface of the Earth, but some, like the *San Andreas Fault* in California, can be seen on the surface.

The Richter Scale measures the energy of an earthquake. This measurement is obtained from the focus, or hypocenter, the spot where the first break in the rock layers occurs. The spot on the surface of the Earth, directly above the focus and nearest to the source of energy is called the epicenter.

Earthquake damage is caused by this energy, called seismic energy, moving through the rocks or along the surface. Many geographic factors, both physical and human, determine how much damage is done by these seismic waves of energy.

Major Earthquakes since 1900

Date	Location	Richter Scale Magnitude
April 4, 1905	Kangra, India	8.6
April 18, 1906	San Francisco, California	7.8
Dec. 28, 1908	Messina, Italy	7.5
Dec 16, 1920	Gansu Province, China	8.6
Sept. 1, 1923	Sagami Bay (near Yokohama), Japan	8.3
May 22, 1927	Xining, China	8.3
Dec. 25, 1932	Gansu Province, China	7.6
March 2, 1933	off northeast coast of Honshu, Japan	8.9
Jan. 15, 1934	Bihar, India/Nepal	8.4
May 30, 1935	Quetta, Pakistan	7.5
Jan. 25, 1939	Chillán, Chile	8.3
Dec. 26, 1939	Erzincan, Turkey	8.0
Dec. 21, 1946	Honshu, Japan	8.4
Oct. 5, 1948	Ashgabat, Turkmenistan	7.3
Aug. 15, 1950	Assam, India	8.7
May 22, 1960	Arauco, Chile	9.5
March 27, 1964	Anchorage, Alaska	9.2
May 31, 1970	Northern Peru, near Chimbote	7.8
Feb. 4, 1976	Guatemala City, Guatemala	7.5
July 28, 1976	Tangshan, China	8.0
Oct. 10, 1980	El Asnam, Algeria	7.7
Sept. 19, 1985	Mexico City, Mexico	8.1
June 20, 1990	Western Iran, near Qazvin	7.7
Dec. 12, 1992	Flores Island, Indonesia	7.5
Jan. 17, 1995	Kobe, Japan	6.9
Aug. 17, 1999	Istanbul, Turkey	7.4
Jan. 26, 2001	Ahmadabad, India	7.7

Source: National Earthquake Information Center, U.S.G.S

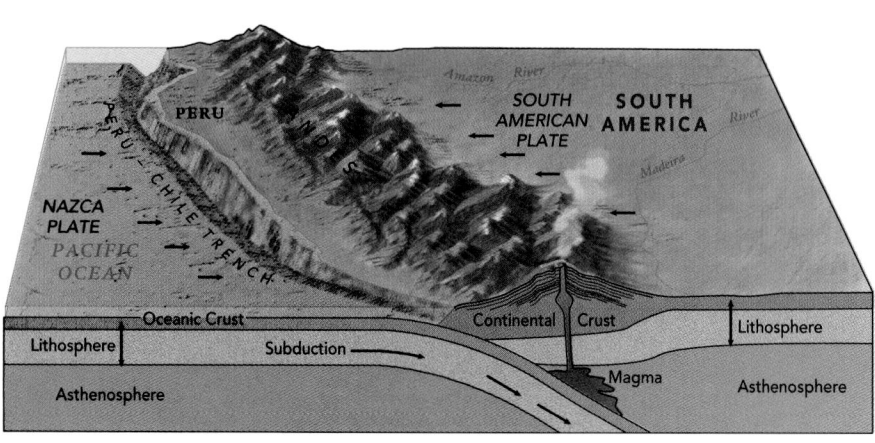

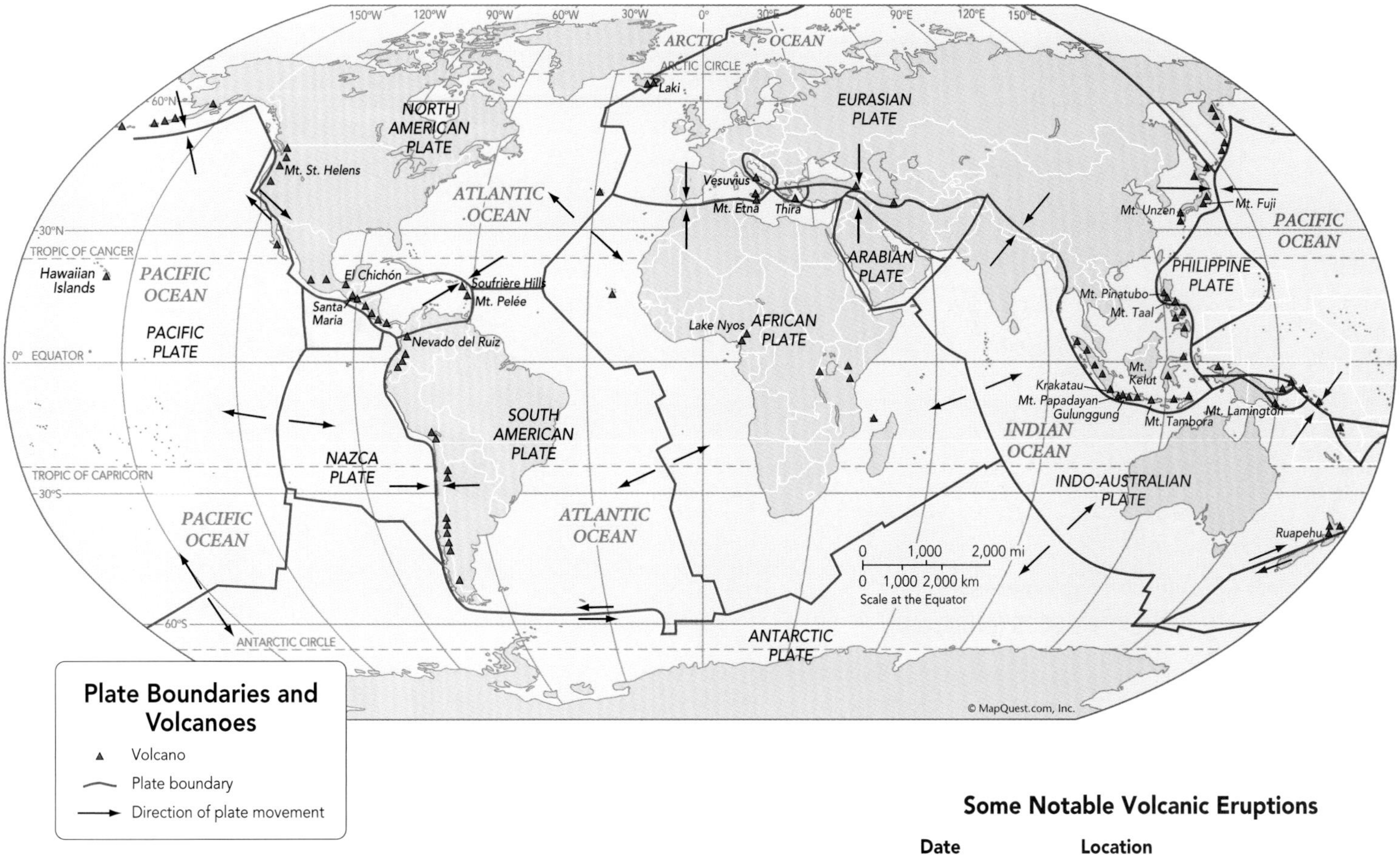

Plate Boundaries and Volcanoes

▲ Volcano

⌒ Plate boundary

→ Direction of plate movement

A volcano is an opening in the Earth's crust often capped by a cone-shaped hill or mountain formed from erupted lava and ash.

Volcanoes are associated with plate boundaries. Powerful forces occurring far beneath the surface at the edges of plates cause rock to melt and, at the same time, open cracks in the crust. An eruption occurs when magma (melted rock) flows, and many times explodes, through a weakness, such as a crack in the Earth's crust. Once magma is flowing on the Earth's surface it is called lava. Flowing lava can be several thousand degrees Fahrenheit.

In a few cases, volcanoes exist without being near the edge of a plate. In these cases, such as the Hawaiian Islands, a powerful and persistent flow of magma has broken through the crust.

Some Notable Volcanic Eruptions

Date	Location
1500 B.C.	Thira (Santorini), Greece
Aug. 24, A.D. 79	Vesuvius, Italy
1169	Mt. Etna, Italy
1586	Mt. Kelut, Java, Indonesia
Dec. 15, 1631	Vesuvius, Italy
March–July, 1669	Mt. Etna, Italy
Aug. 12, 1772	Mt. Papandayan, Java, Indonesia
June 8, 1783	Laki, Iceland
May 21, 1792	Mt. Unzen, Japan
Apr. 10–12, 1815	Mt. Tambora, Sumbawa, Indonesia
Oct. 8, 1822	Galunggung, Java, Indonesia
Aug. 26–28, 1883	Krakatau, Indonesia
Apr. 24, 1902	Santa Maria, Guatemala
May 8, 1902	Mt. Pelée, Martinique
Jan. 30, 1911	Mt. Taal, Philippines
May 19, 1919	Mt. Kelut, Java, Indonesia
Jan. 17–21, 1951	Mt. Lamington, New Guinea
May 18, 1980	Mt. St. Helens, United States
Mar. 28, 1982	El Chichon, Mexico
Nov. 13, 1985	Nevado del Ruiz, Colombia
Aug. 21, 1986	Lake Nyos, Cameroon
June 15, 1991	Mt. Pinatubo, Philippines
June–Sept., 1997	Soufrière Hills, Montserrat

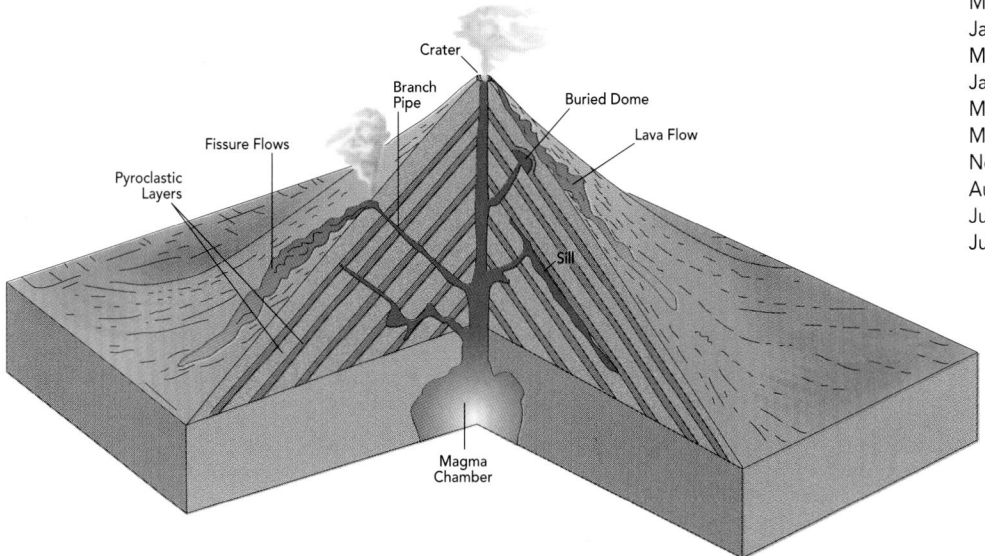

Population Density 2002

Persons per sq. mile	Persons per sq. km
Over 520	Over 200
260 to 519	100 to 199
130 to 259	50 to 99
25 to 129	10 to 49
1 to 24	1 to 9
0	0

● Urban agglomerations with over 10,000,000 inhabitants

World population total as of March 1, 2003: 6,277,603,768
(Every day it increases by about 202,500)

Source: International Programs Center, U.S. Bureau of the Census

Largest Cities (urban agglomerations)

	2000		2015 (projected)
1	Tokyo 26,444,000	1	Tokyo 26,444,000
2	Mexico City 18,131,000	2	Mumbai 26,138,000
3	Mumbai 18,066,000	3	Lagos 23,173,000
4	São Paulo 17,755,000	4	Dhaka 21,119,000
5	New York 16,640,000	5	São Paulo 20,397,000
6	Lagos 13,427,000	6	Karachi 19,211,000
7	Los Angeles 13,140,000	7	Mexico City 19,180,000
8	Kolkata 12,918,000	8	New York 17,432,000
9	Shanghai. 12,887,000	9	Jakarta 17,256,000
10	Buenos Aires . . . 12,560,000	10	Kolkata 17,252,000
11	Dhaka 12,317,000	11	Delhi 16,808,000
12	Karachi 11,794,000	12	Manila. 14,825,000
13	Delhi 11,695,000	13	Shanghai. 14,575,000
14	Jakarta 11,018,000	14	Los Angeles 14,080,000
15	Osaka. 11,013,000	15	Buenos Aires . . . 14,076,000

Source: United Nations Population Division

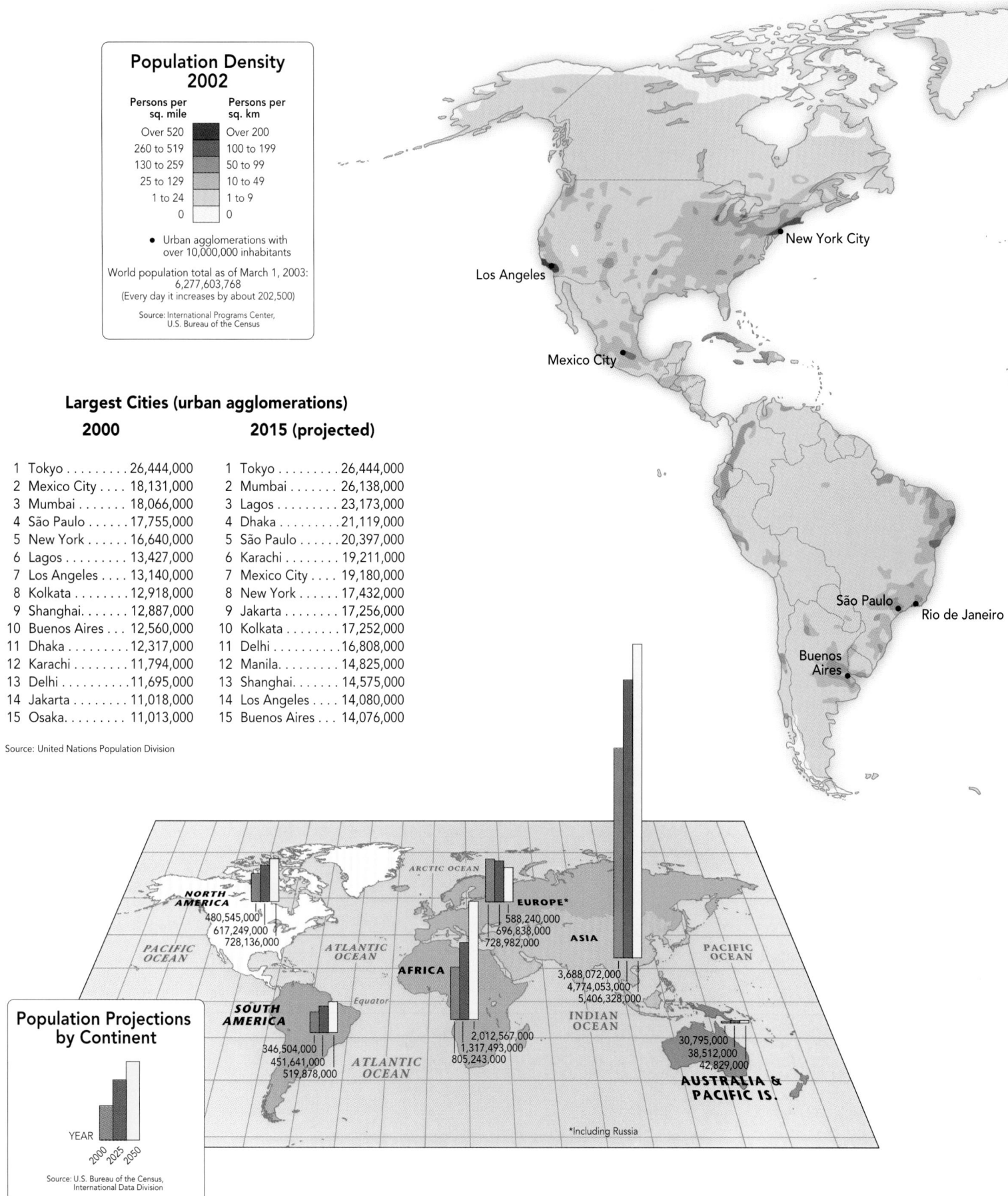

New York City
Los Angeles
Mexico City
São Paulo
Rio de Janeiro
Buenos Aires

NORTH AMERICA
480,545,000
617,249,000
728,136,000

EUROPE*
588,240,000
696,838,000
728,982,000

ASIA
3,688,072,000
4,774,053,000
5,406,328,000

AFRICA
2,012,567,000
1,317,493,000
805,243,000

SOUTH AMERICA
346,504,000
451,641,000
519,878,000

AUSTRALIA & PACIFIC IS.
30,795,000
38,512,000
42,829,000

ARCTIC OCEAN
PACIFIC OCEAN
ATLANTIC OCEAN
Equator
ATLANTIC OCEAN
INDIAN OCEAN
PACIFIC OCEAN

*Including Russia

Population Projections by Continent

YEAR
2000 2025 2050

Source: U.S. Bureau of the Census, International Data Division

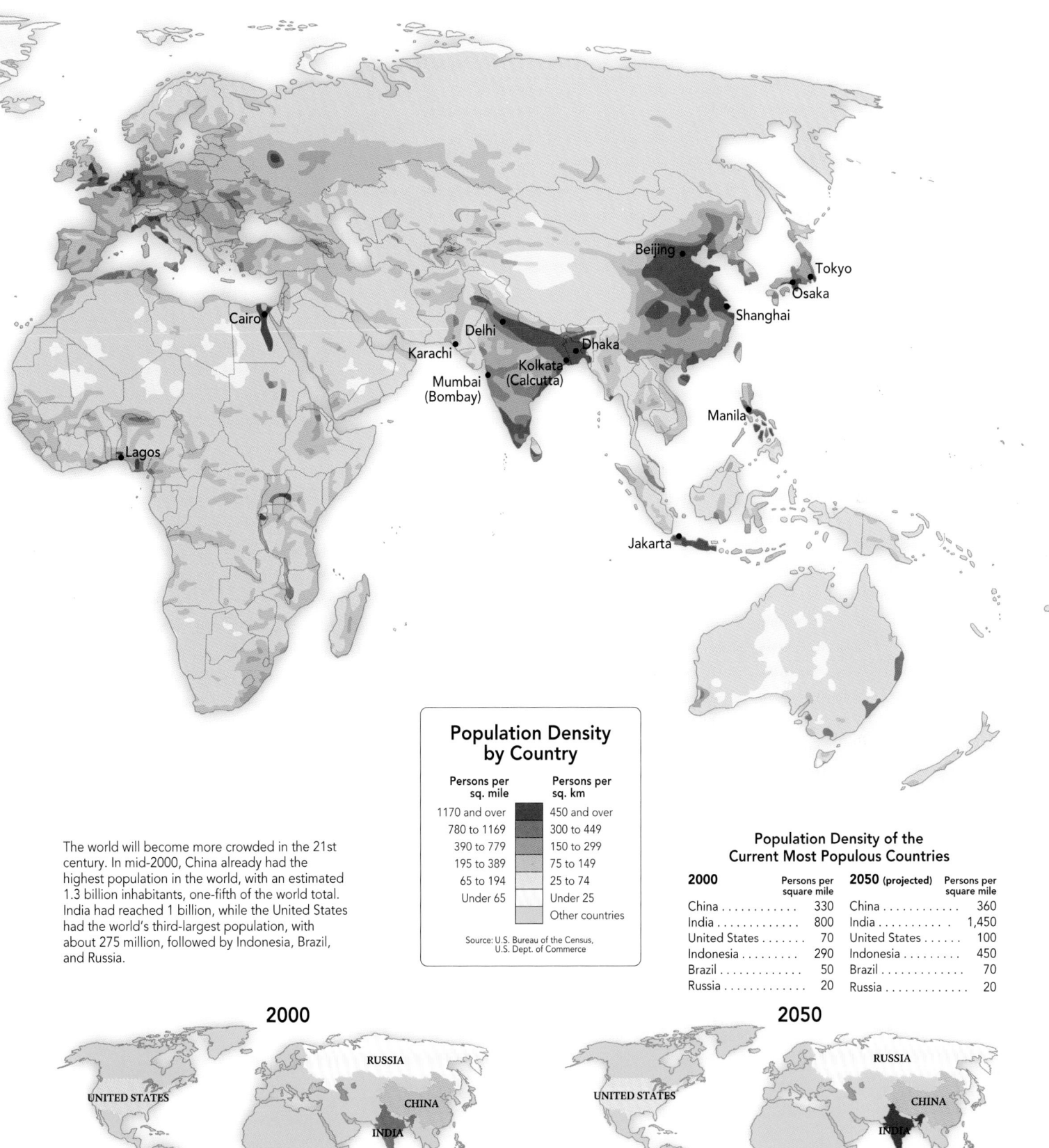

Population Density by Country

Persons per sq. mile	Persons per sq. km
1170 and over	450 and over
780 to 1169	300 to 449
390 to 779	150 to 299
195 to 389	75 to 149
65 to 194	25 to 74
Under 65	Under 25
	Other countries

Source: U.S. Bureau of the Census, U.S. Dept. of Commerce

The world will become more crowded in the 21st century. In mid-2000, China already had the highest population in the world, with an estimated 1.3 billion inhabitants, one-fifth of the world total. India had reached 1 billion, while the United States had the world's third-largest population, with about 275 million, followed by Indonesia, Brazil, and Russia.

Population Density of the Current Most Populous Countries

2000	Persons per square mile	2050 (projected)	Persons per square mile
China	330	China	360
India	800	India	1,450
United States	70	United States	100
Indonesia	290	Indonesia	450
Brazil	50	Brazil	70
Russia	20	Russia	20

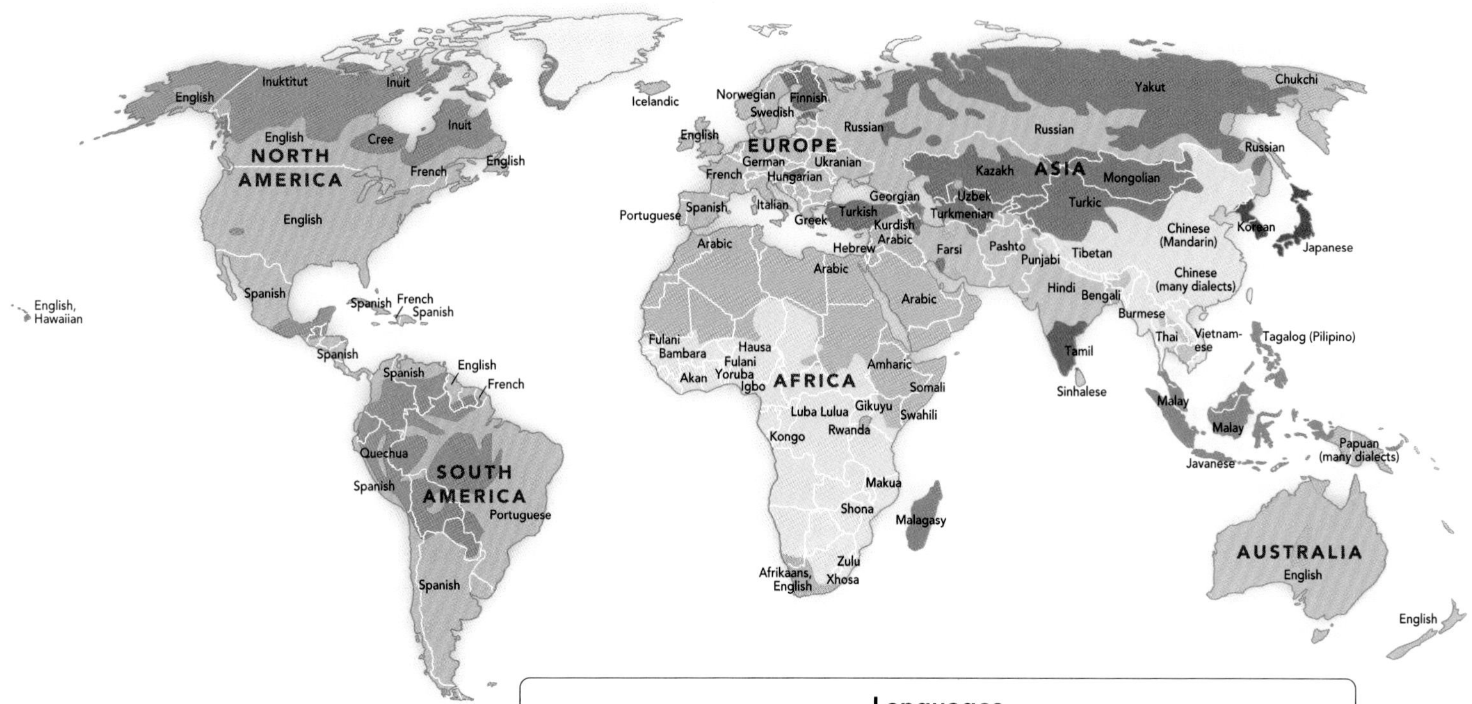
English
Inuktitut
Inuit
English
NORTH AMERICA
Cree
Inuit
French
English
English
Spanish
English, Hawaiian
Spanish
French
Spanish
Spanish
Spanish
English
French
Quechua
SOUTH AMERICA
Spanish
Portuguese
Spanish
Icelandic
Norwegian
Finnish
Swedish
English
EUROPE
Russian
German
Ukranian
French
Hungarian
Portuguese
Spanish
Italian
Greek
Turkish
Georgian
Kurdish
Arabic
Hebrew
Arabic
Arabic
Arabic
Fulani
Bambara
Hausa
Fulani
Akan
Yoruba
Igbo
AFRICA
Amharic
Somali
Luba Lulua
Gikuyu
Swahili
Kongo
Rwanda
Makua
Shona
Malagasy
Zulu
Afrikaans, English
Xhosa
Yakut
Chukchi
Russian
Russian
Kazakh
ASIA
Mongolian
Uzbek
Turkmenian
Turkic
Farsi
Pashto
Punjabi
Tibetan
Chinese (Mandarin)
Korean
Japanese
Hindi
Bengali
Chinese (many dialects)
Burmese
Thai
Vietnamese
Tagalog (Pilipino)
Tamil
Sinhalese
Malay
Malay
Papuan (many dialects)
Javanese
AUSTRALIA
English
English

Languages

- African (including Yoruba, Swahili)
- Afro-Asiatic (including Hebrew, Arabic)
- Amerindian (including Inuit, Iroquoian, Quechua)
- Dravidian
- Indo-European (including English, Spanish, Hindi)
- Japanese and Korean
- Malayo-Polynesian (including Hawaiian, Pilipino)
- Sino-Tibetan (including Chinese, Burmese)
- Ural-Asiatic (including Finnish, Hungarian, Turkish)
- Other
- Uninhabited
- French — Primary regional language

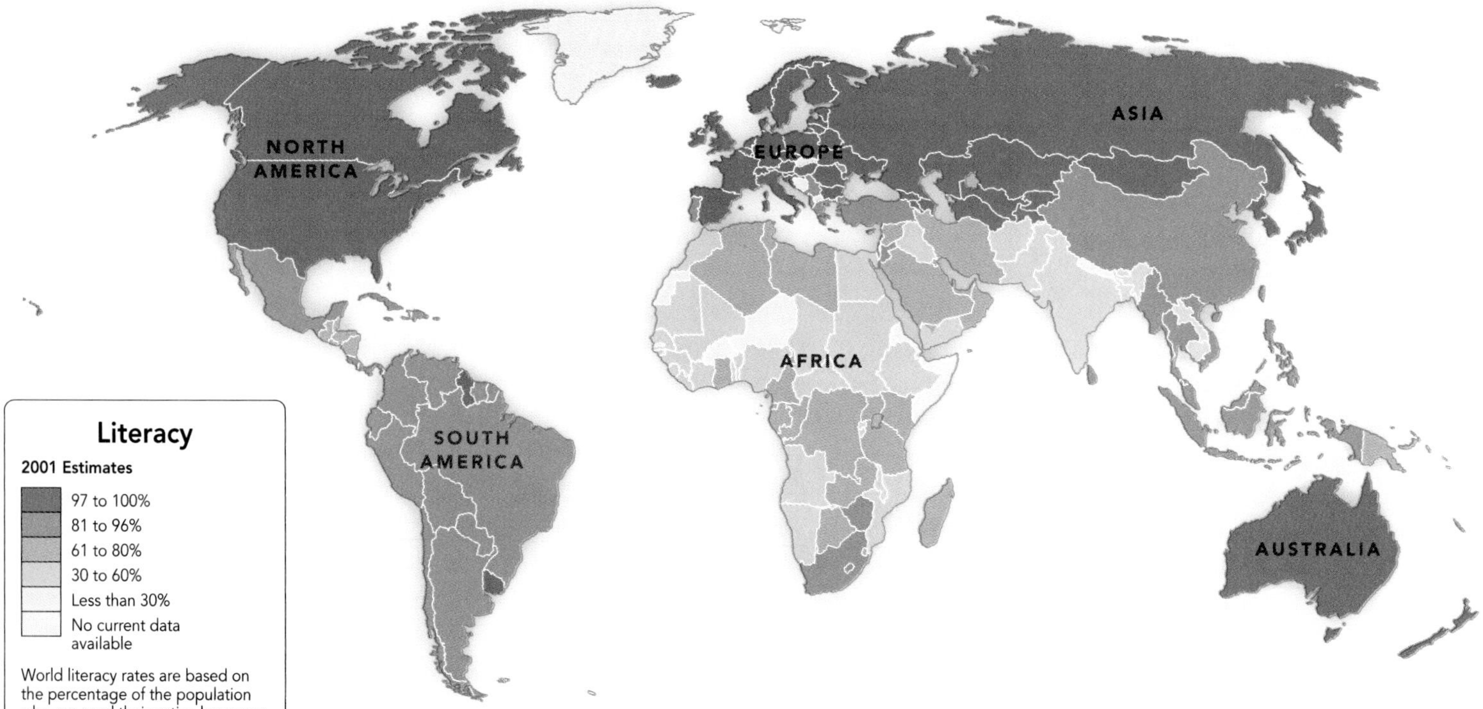
NORTH AMERICA
SOUTH AMERICA
EUROPE
ASIA
AFRICA
AUSTRALIA

Literacy

2001 Estimates

- 97 to 100%
- 81 to 96%
- 61 to 80%
- 30 to 60%
- Less than 30%
- No current data available

World literacy rates are based on the percentage of the population who can read their native language. The data varies between the years of 1989 to 2000.

Source: *World Factbook*, CIA, 2001

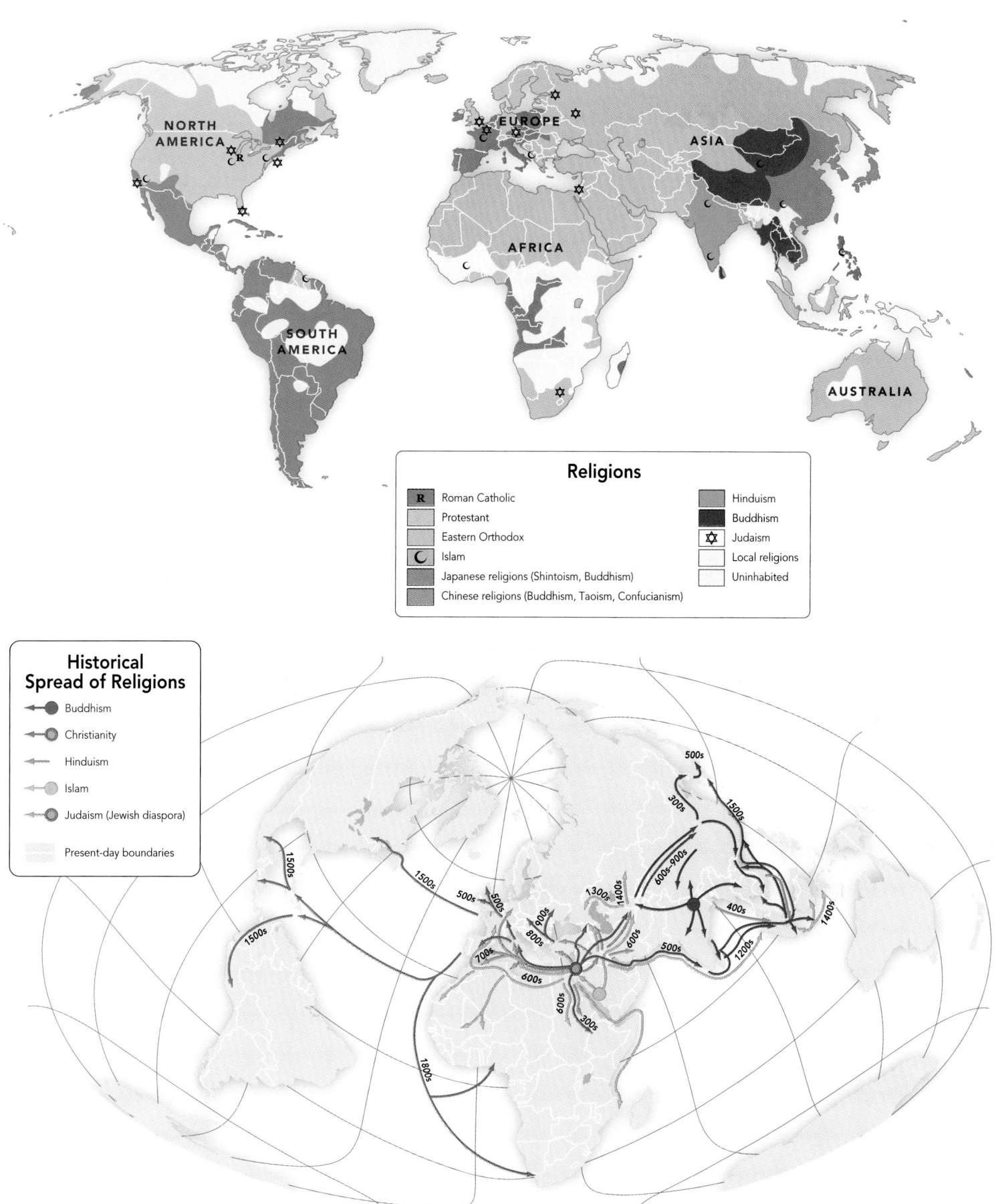

Religions

- **R** Roman Catholic
- Protestant
- Eastern Orthodox
- ☪ Islam
- Japanese religions (Shintoism, Buddhism)
- Chinese religions (Buddhism, Taoism, Confucianism)
- Hinduism
- Buddhism
- ✡ Judaism
- Local religions
- Uninhabited

Historical Spread of Religions

- Buddhism
- Christianity
- Hinduism
- Islam
- Judaism (Jewish diaspora)
- Present-day boundaries

Life expectancy at birth is a common measure of the number of years a person may expect to live. There are many factors, such as nutrition, sanitation, health and medical services, that contribute to helping people live longer.

As some of the above factors improve in the developing countries, life expectancy there should increase. But most of sub-Saharan Africa will have less than average life expectancies.

Although it is not included here, females almost always have a longer life expectancy than males.

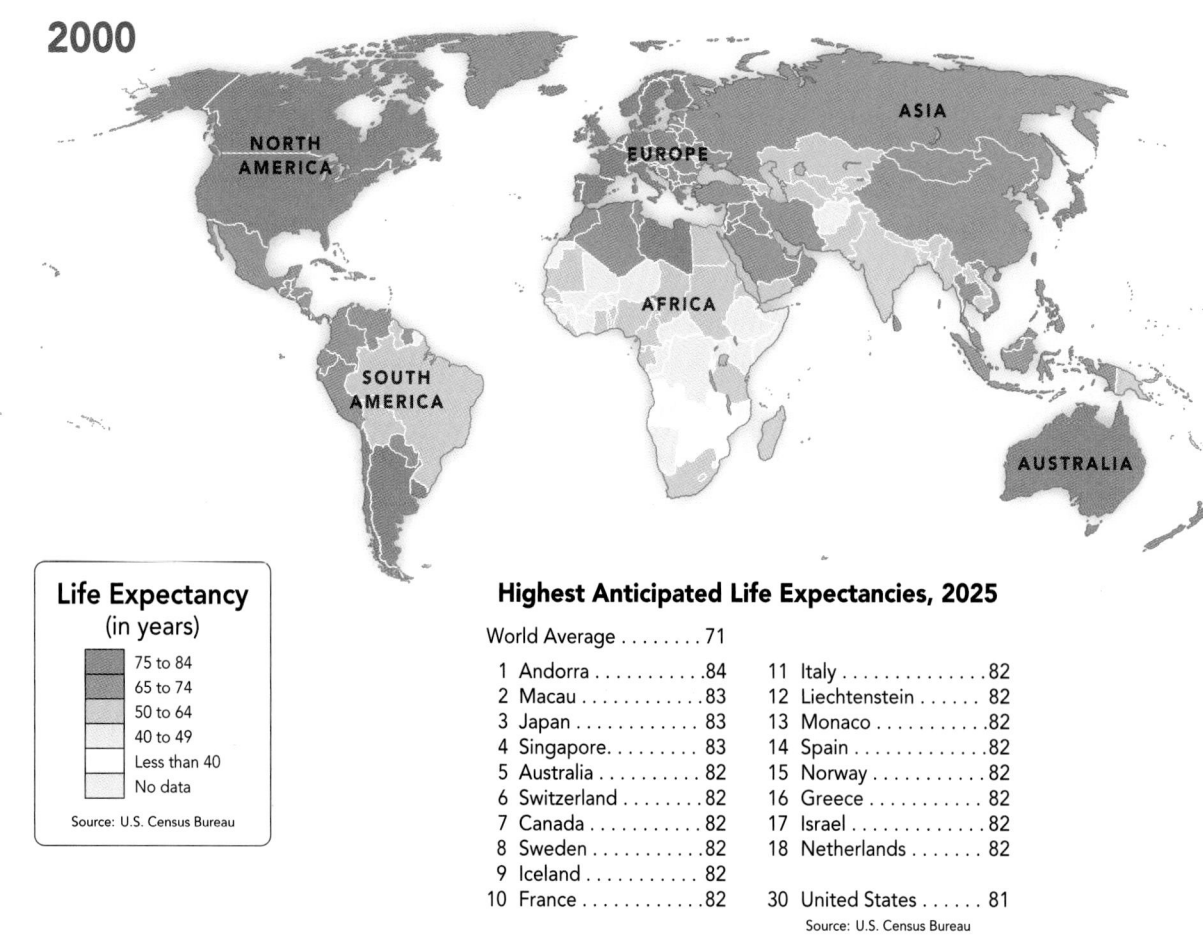

2000

Life Expectancy
(in years)

- 75 to 84
- 65 to 74
- 50 to 64
- 40 to 49
- Less than 40
- No data

Source: U.S. Census Bureau

Highest Anticipated Life Expectancies, 2025

World Average 71

1	Andorra 84	11	Italy 82
2	Macau 83	12	Liechtenstein 82
3	Japan 83	13	Monaco 82
4	Singapore. 83	14	Spain 82
5	Australia 82	15	Norway 82
6	Switzerland 82	16	Greece 82
7	Canada 82	17	Israel 82
8	Sweden 82	18	Netherlands 82
9	Iceland 82		
10	France 82	30	United States 81

Source: U.S. Census Bureau

2025

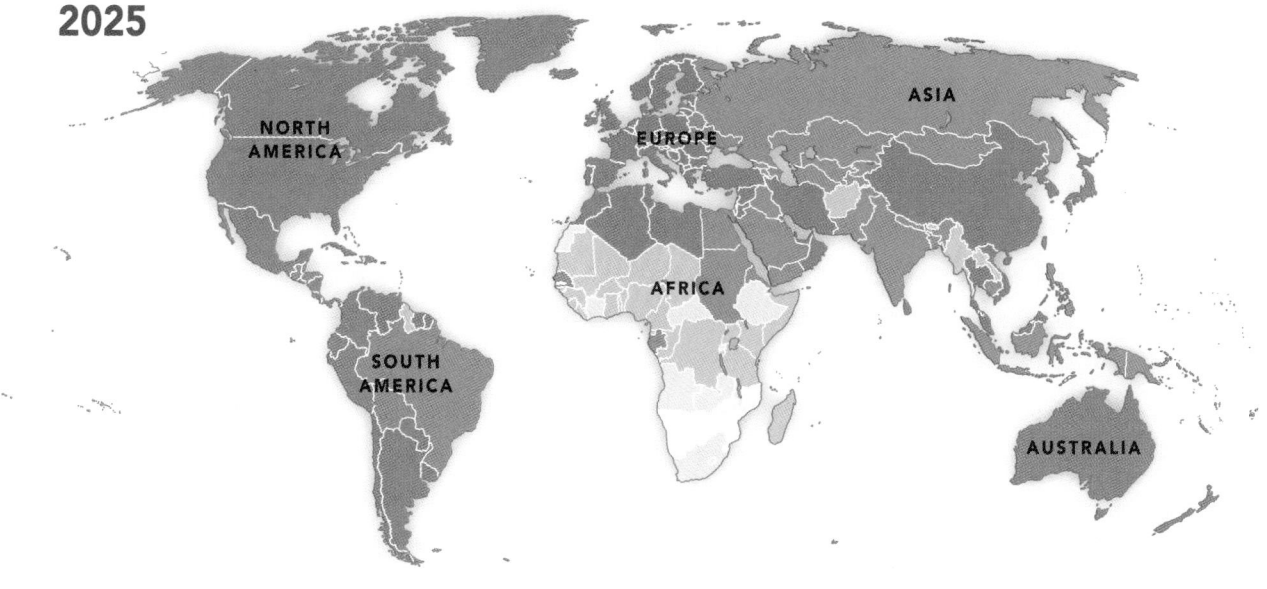

A country with a youthful population often reflects a high birthrate and a short life expectancy. The youthful component of a country's population should be the healthiest and the most energetic. In countries where there is a good system of education, the standards of living can only benefit from a large, educated youthful population. Furthermore, large numbers of young workers offer a means for provid-

ing financial and social support for the older members of the population. Unfortunately, a country's economic and physical resources may not be able to absorb a ballooning youthful population. A lack of opportunity in rural regions encourages migration to over-crowded cities where, in turn, a lack of jobs or space in schools leads to swelling numbers of unemployed.

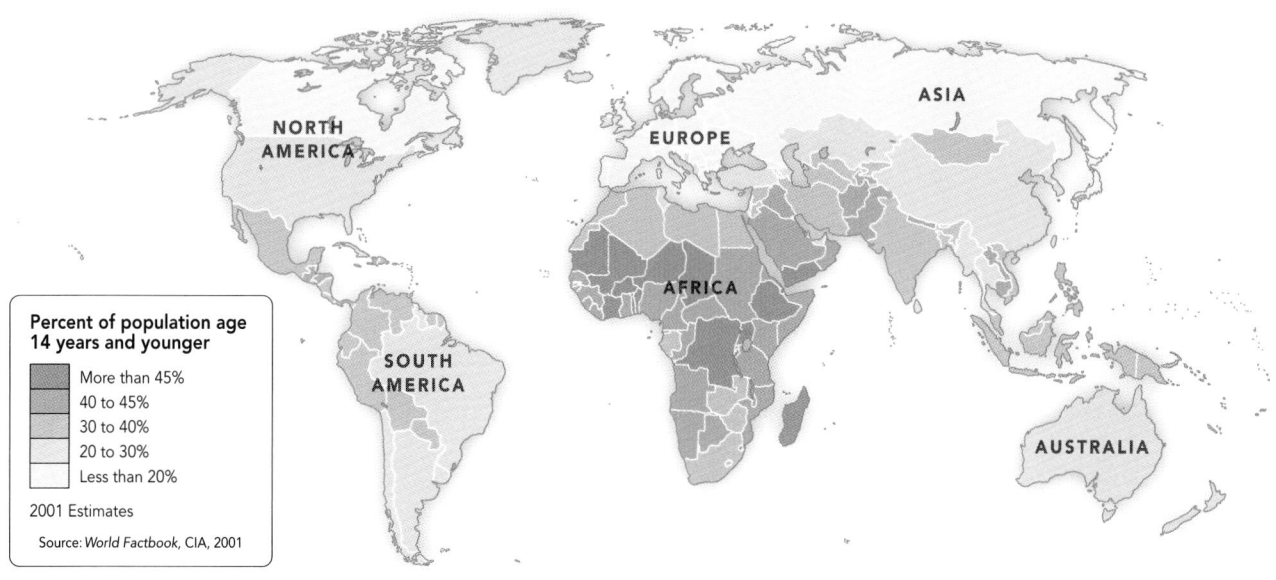

Percent of population age 14 years and younger

- More than 45%
- 40 to 45%
- 30 to 40%
- 20 to 30%
- Less than 20%

2001 Estimates

Source: *World Factbook*, CIA, 2001

There has been a general trend towards better nutrition, but sub-Saharan Africa remains a problem area: increasing numbers of people will be suffering from undernutrition.

On a worldwide basis, the food supply seems adequate. Unfortunately the availability of food and the distribution of people don't always match up.

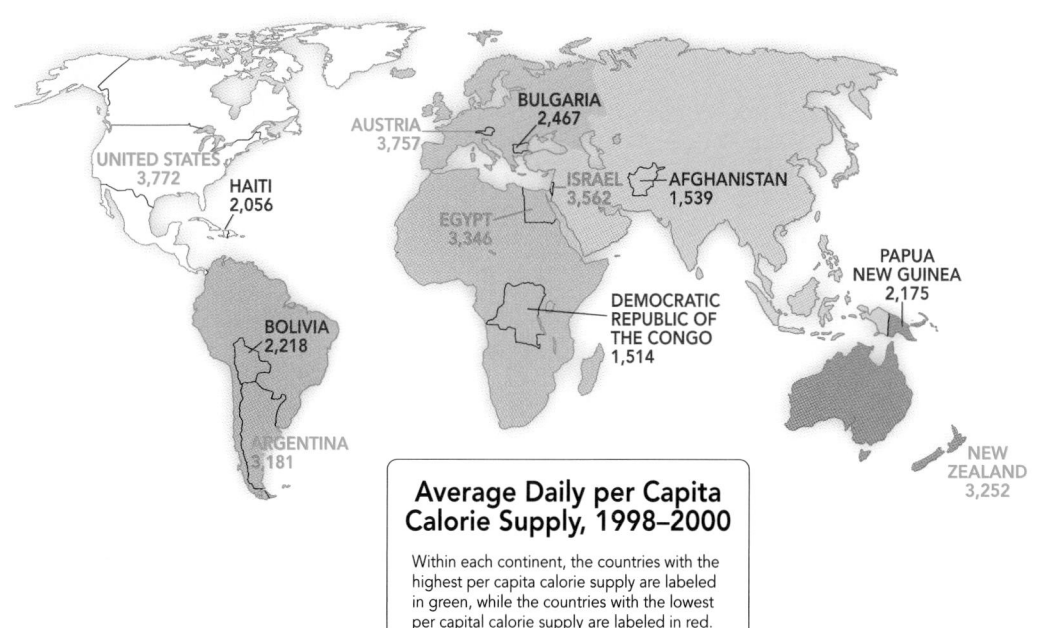

Average Daily per Capita Calorie Supply, 1998–2000

Within each continent, the countries with the highest per capita calorie supply are labeled in green, while the countries with the lowest per capital calorie supply are labeled in red.

Source: UN Food and Agriculture Organization

UNITED STATES 3,772
HAITI 2,056
BOLIVIA 2,218
ARGENTINA 3,181
AUSTRIA 3,757
BULGARIA 2,467
ISRAEL 3,562
EGYPT 3,346
AFGHANISTAN 1,539
DEMOCRATIC REPUBLIC OF THE CONGO 1,514
PAPUA NEW GUINEA 2,175
NEW ZEALAND 3,252

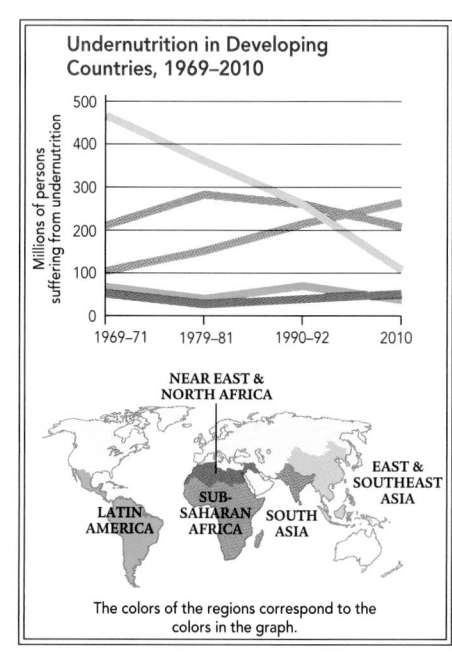

Undernutrition in Developing Countries, 1969–2010

Millions of persons suffering from undernutrition

1969–71 1979–81 1990–92 2010

NEAR EAST & NORTH AFRICA
LATIN AMERICA
SUB-SAHARAN AFRICA
SOUTH ASIA
EAST & SOUTHEAST ASIA

The colors of the regions correspond to the colors in the graph.

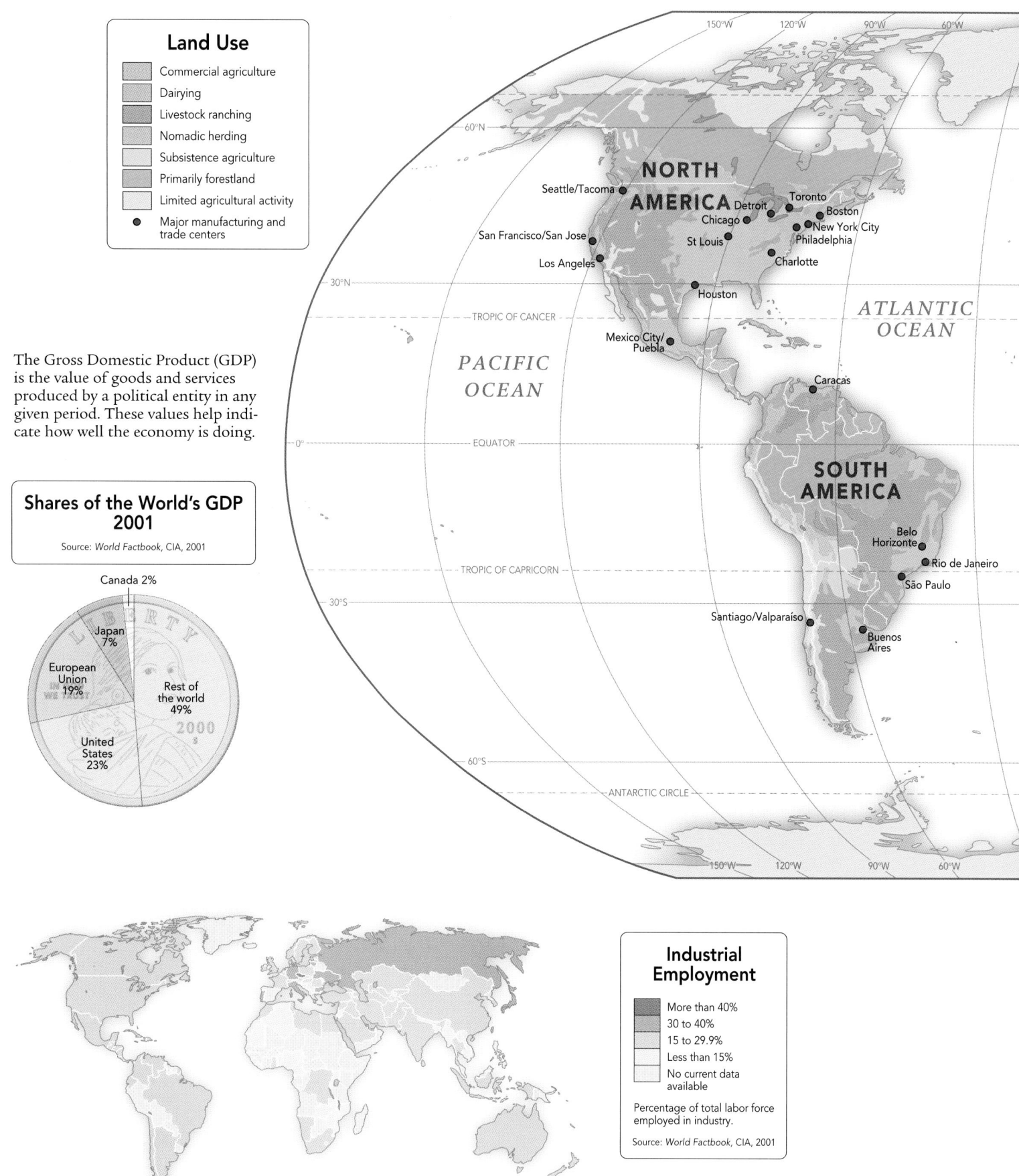

Land Use

- Commercial agriculture
- Dairying
- Livestock ranching
- Nomadic herding
- Subsistence agriculture
- Primarily forestland
- Limited agricultural activity
- ● Major manufacturing and trade centers

The Gross Domestic Product (GDP) is the value of goods and services produced by a political entity in any given period. These values help indicate how well the economy is doing.

Shares of the World's GDP 2001

Source: *World Factbook*, CIA, 2001

Canada 2%
Japan 7%
European Union 19%
United States 23%
Rest of the world 49%

Industrial Employment

- More than 40%
- 30 to 40%
- 15 to 29.9%
- Less than 15%
- No current data available

Percentage of total labor force employed in industry.

Source: *World Factbook*, CIA, 2001

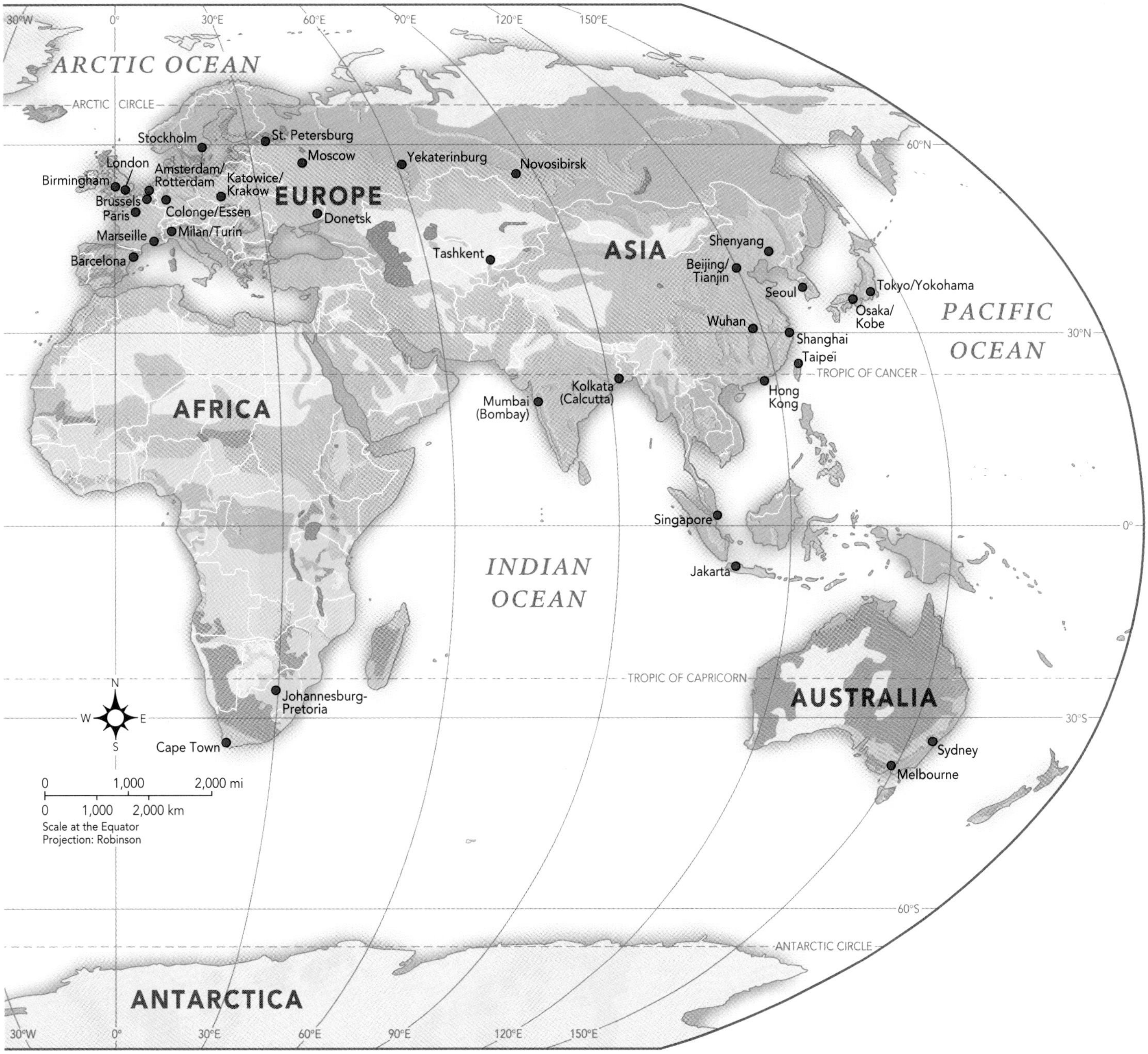

ARCTIC OCEAN

ARCTIC CIRCLE

60°N

Stockholm
St. Petersburg
London
Moscow
Yekaterinburg
Novosibirsk
Birmingham
Amsterdam/
Rotterdam
Katowice/
Krakow
EUROPE
Brussels
Colonge/Essen
Donetsk
Paris
Marseille
Milan/Turin
Shenyang
ASIA
Barcelona
Tashkent
Beijing/
Tianjin
Seoul
Tokyo/Yokohama
Osaka/
Kobe
PACIFIC
OCEAN
Wuhan
Shanghai
30°N
AFRICA
Taipei
TROPIC OF CANCER
Kolkata
(Calcutta)
Hong
Kong
Mumbai
(Bombay)

INDIAN
OCEAN

Singapore
0°

Jakarta

TROPIC OF CAPRICORN

AUSTRALIA

30°S

N
W   E
S

Johannesburg-
Pretoria

Cape Town

Sydney

Melbourne

| 0 | 1,000 | 2,000 mi |
| 0 | 1,000 | 2,000 km |

Scale at the Equator
Projection: Robinson

60°S

ANTARCTIC CIRCLE

ANTARCTICA

30°W   0°   30°E   60°E   90°E   120°E   150°E

Agricultural
Employment

- More than 80%
- 60 to 80%
- 30 to 59.9%
- 10 to 29.9%
- Less than 10%
- No current data available

Percent of total labor force
employed in agriculture.

Source: *World Factbook*, CIA, 2001

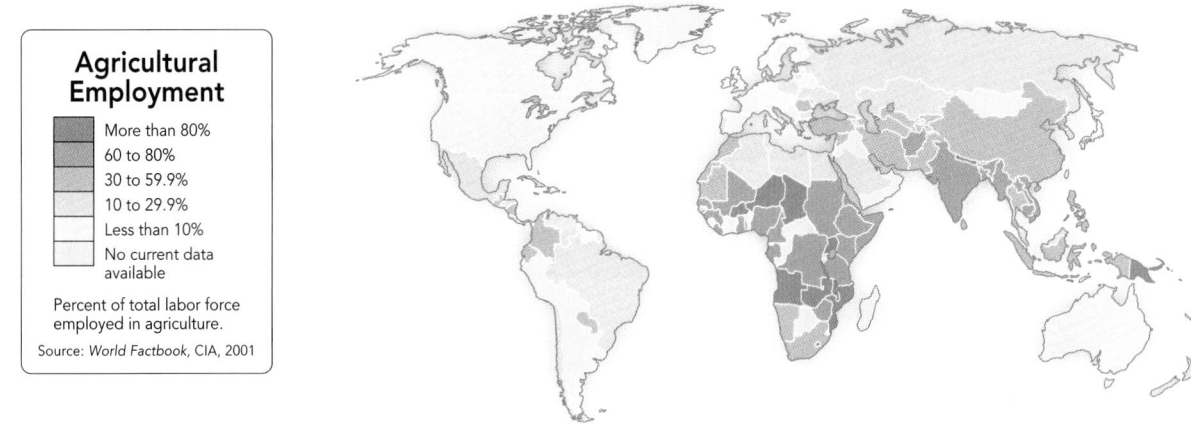

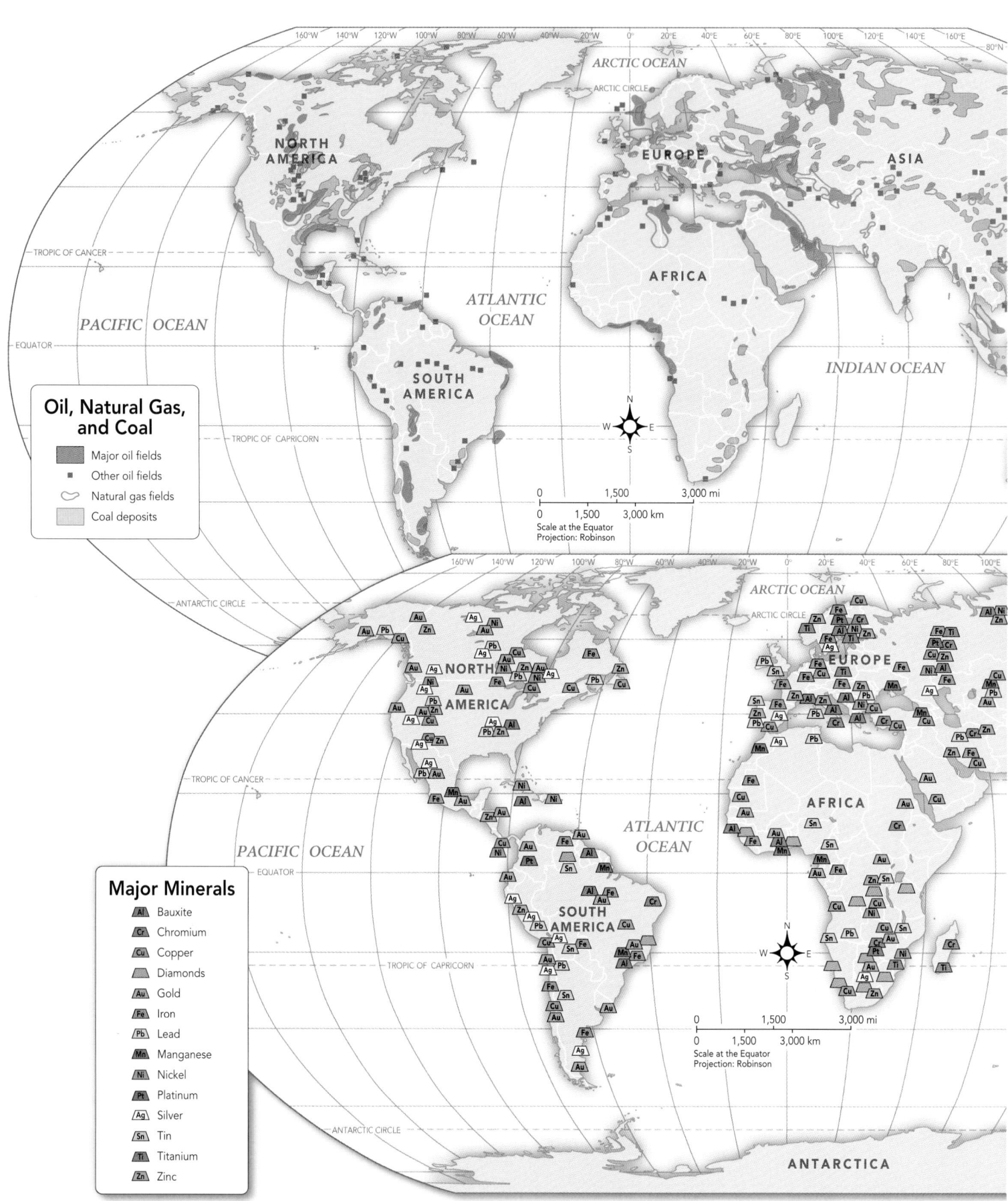

Oil, Natural Gas, and Coal

Major oil fields
Other oil fields
Natural gas fields
Coal deposits

Major Minerals

Al Bauxite
Cr Chromium
Cu Copper
Diamonds
Au Gold
Fe Iron
Pb Lead
Mn Manganese
Ni Nickel
Pt Platinum
Ag Silver
Sn Tin
Ti Titanium
Zn Zinc

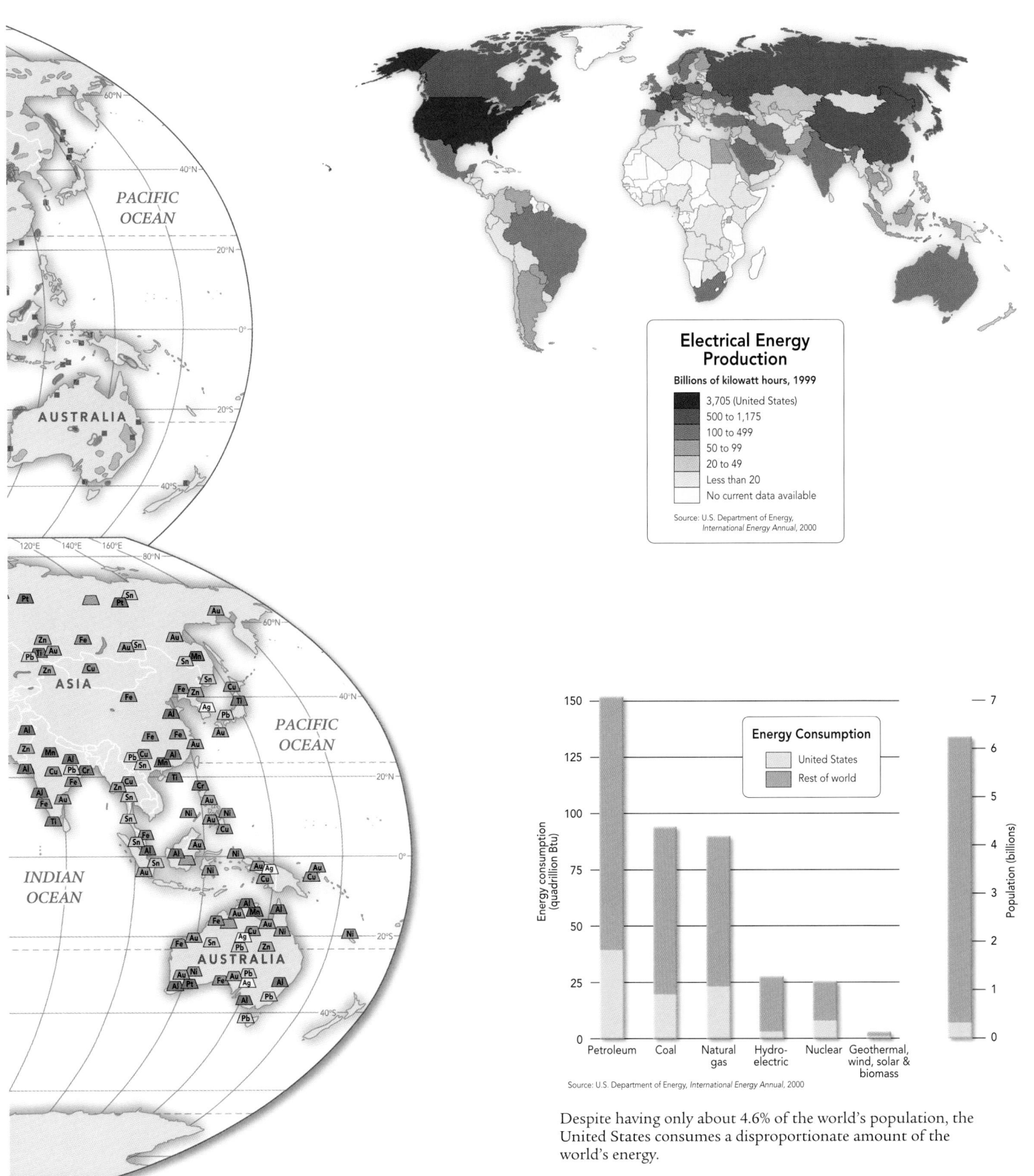

Electrical Energy Production

Billions of kilowatt hours, 1999

- 3,705 (United States)
- 500 to 1,175
- 100 to 499
- 50 to 99
- 20 to 49
- Less than 20
- No current data available

Source: U.S. Department of Energy, *International Energy Annual*, 2000

Energy Consumption

- United States
- Rest of world

Energy consumption (quadrillion Btu)

Population (billions)

Petroleum | Coal | Natural gas | Hydro-electric | Nuclear | Geothermal, wind, solar & biomass

Source: U.S. Department of Energy, *International Energy Annual*, 2000

Despite having only about 4.6% of the world's population, the United States consumes a disproportionate amount of the world's energy.

Forests help regulate climate by storing huge amounts of carbon dioxide, while providing habitats for countless animal and plant species. Environmentalists have voiced concern over a long-term decrease in forest cover, as forest lands have been cleared for such purposes as farming, logging, mining, and urban expansion.

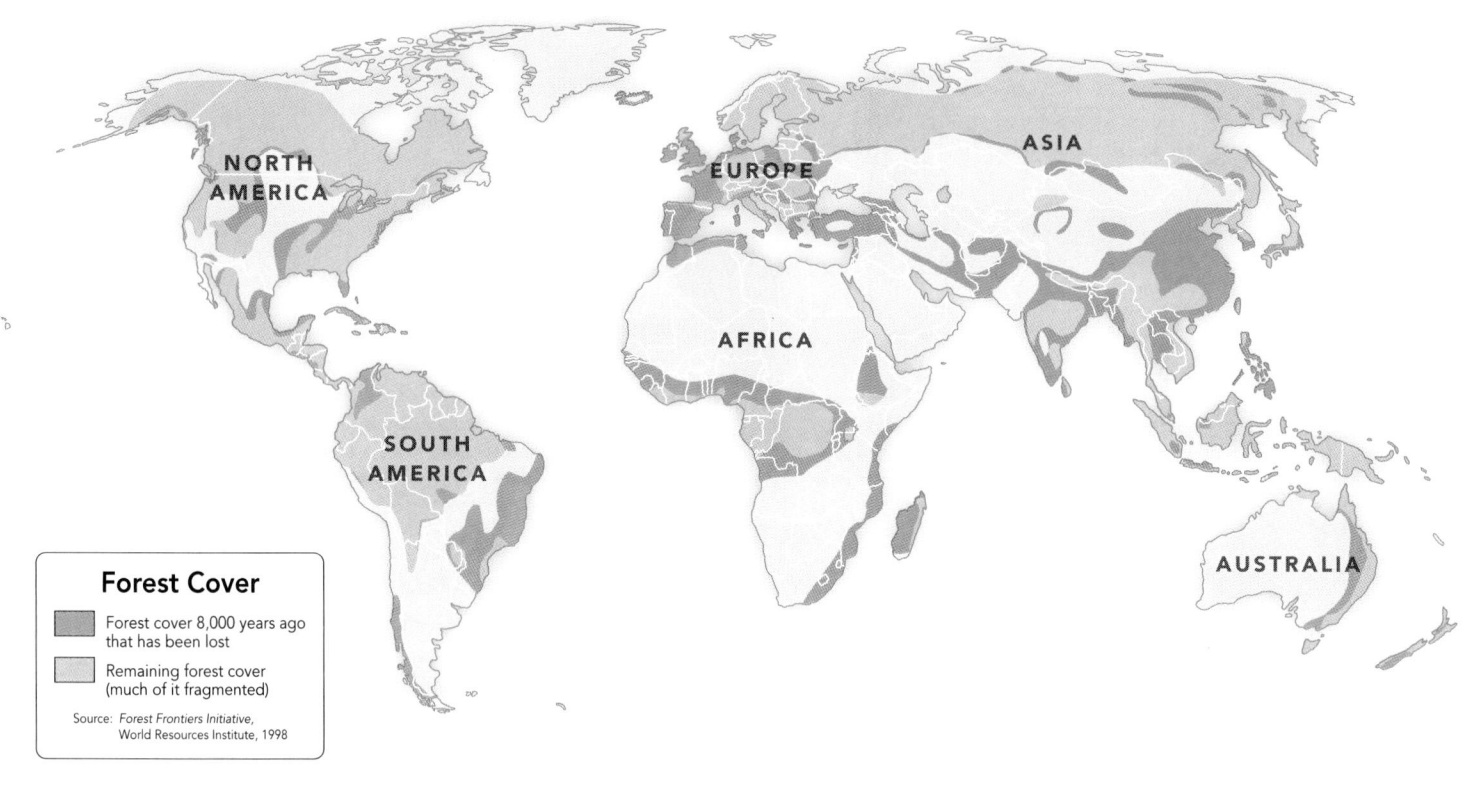

Forest Cover

■ Forest cover 8,000 years ago that has been lost

■ Remaining forest cover (much of it fragmented)

Source: *Forest Frontiers Initiative, World Resources Institute, 1998*

Annual Deforestation Rates

■ More than 0.9% deforested
■ 0.1 to 0.9% deforested
■ Stable or increased forest area
□ No current data available

Source: World Resources Institute

Tropical rain forests, found around the Earth within 10 degrees of the equator, contain more than half of all the world's plants and animal species, besides to being home to many indigenous peoples. They are vital to the balance of nature. In the past 40 years alone, about one-fifth of the acreage has been cleared for logging and other purposes. These rain forests, including the major forests pinpointed here, remain under serious threat.

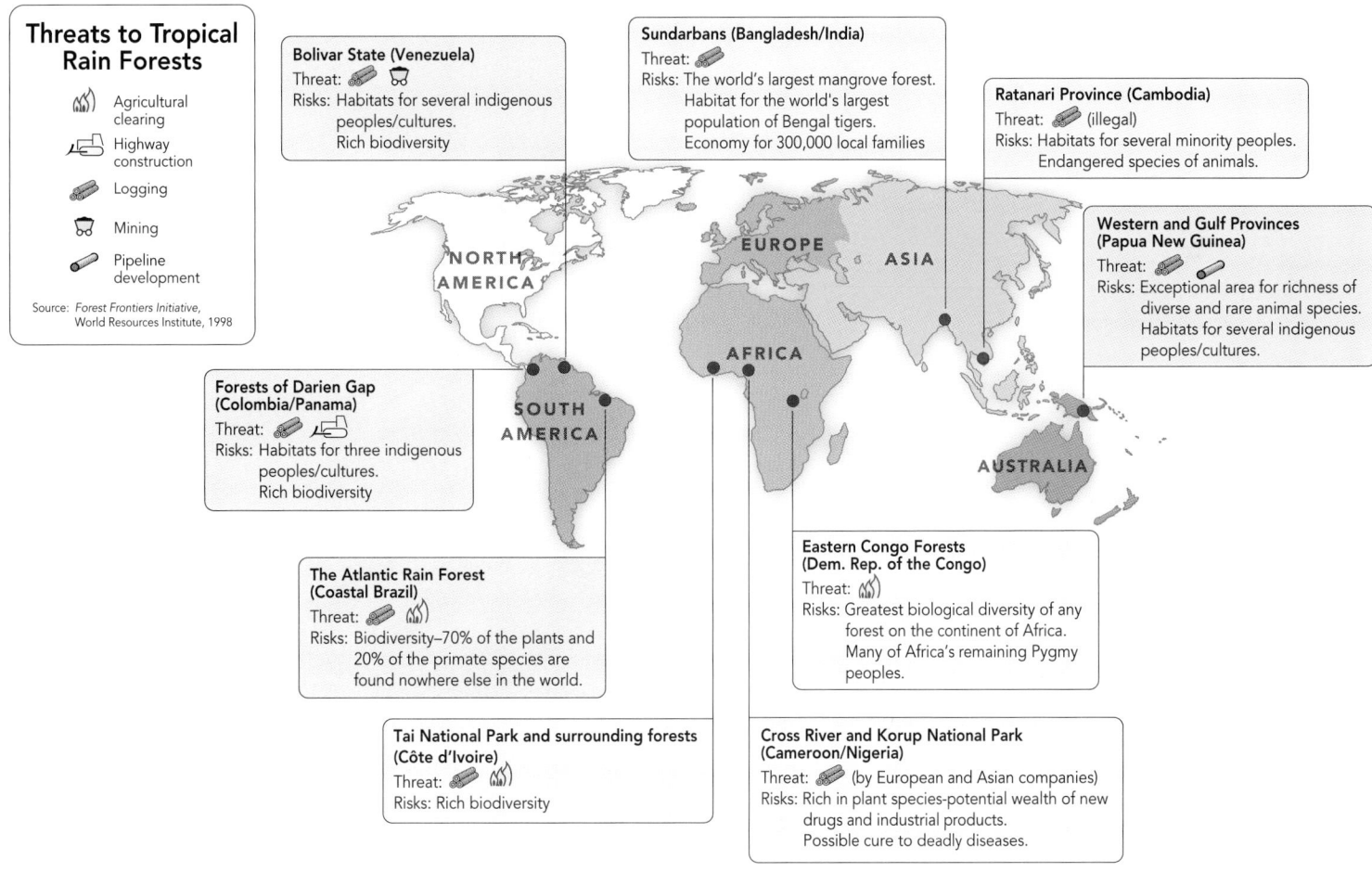

Threats to Tropical Rain Forests

- Agricultural clearing
- Highway construction
- Logging
- Mining
- Pipeline development

Source: *Forest Frontiers Initiative,* World Resources Institute, 1998

Bolivar State (Venezuela)
Threat:
Risks: Habitats for several indigenous peoples/cultures.
Rich biodiversity

Sundarbans (Bangladesh/India)
Threat:
Risks: The world's largest mangrove forest. Habitat for the world's largest population of Bengal tigers. Economy for 300,000 local families

Ratanari Province (Cambodia)
Threat: (illegal)
Risks: Habitats for several minority peoples. Endangered species of animals.

Western and Gulf Provinces (Papua New Guinea)
Threat:
Risks: Exceptional area for richness of diverse and rare animal species. Habitats for several indigenous peoples/cultures.

Forests of Darien Gap (Colombia/Panama)
Threat:
Risks: Habitats for three indigenous peoples/cultures. Rich biodiversity

The Atlantic Rain Forest (Coastal Brazil)
Threat:
Risks: Biodiversity–70% of the plants and 20% of the primate species are found nowhere else in the world.

Eastern Congo Forests (Dem. Rep. of the Congo)
Threat:
Risks: Greatest biological diversity of any forest on the continent of Africa. Many of Africa's remaining Pygmy peoples.

Tai National Park and surrounding forests (Côte d'Ivoire)
Threat:
Risks: Rich biodiversity

Cross River and Korup National Park (Cameroon/Nigeria)
Threat: (by European and Asian companies)
Risks: Rich in plant species-potential wealth of new drugs and industrial products. Possible cure to deadly diseases.

Afghanistan	Albania	Algeria	Andorra	Angola
Antigua and Barbuda	Argentina	Armenia	Australia	Austria
Azerbaijan	Bahamas	Bahrain	Bangladesh	Barbados
Belarus	Belgium	Belize	Benin	Bhutan
Bolivia	Bosnia and Herzegovina	Botswana	Brazil	Brunei
Bulgaria	Burkina Faso	Burundi	Cambodia	Cameroon
Canada	Cape Verde	Central African Republic	Chad	Chile
China	Colombia	Comoros	Congo, Dem. Rep.	Congo, Rep.
Costa Rica	Côte d'Ivoire	Croatia	Cuba	Cyprus

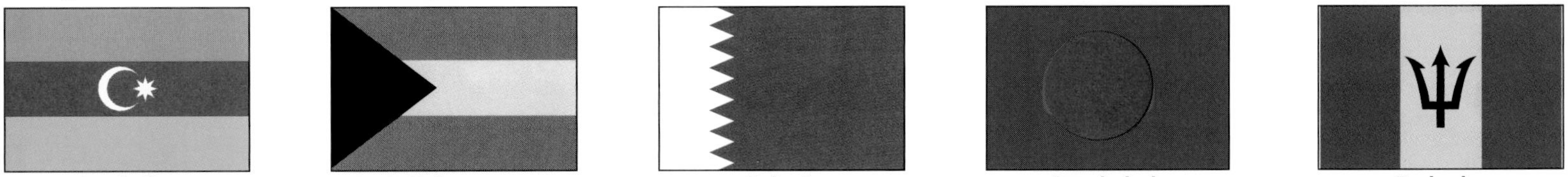

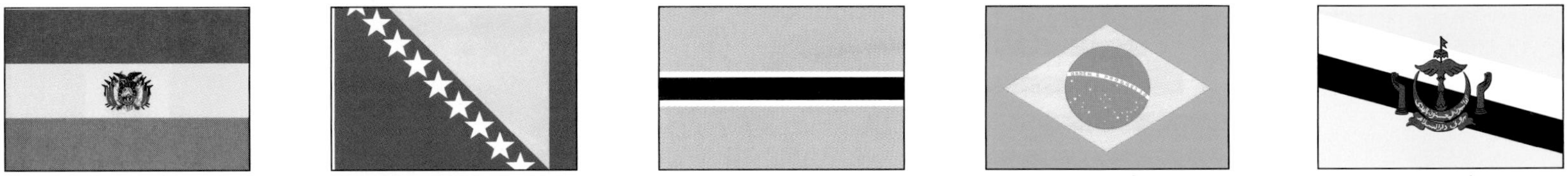

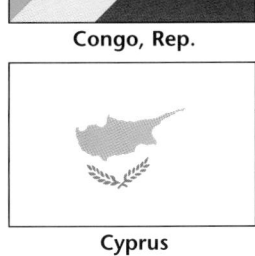

Czech Republic

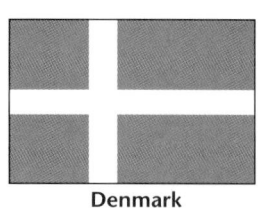

Denmark

Djibouti

Dominica

Dominican Republic

East Timor

Ecuador

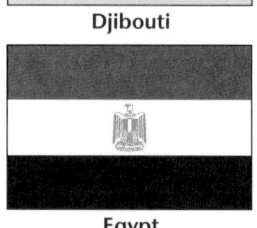

Egypt

El Salvador

Equatorial Guinea

Eritrea

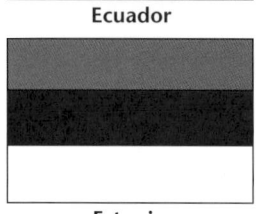

Estonia

Ethiopia

Fiji

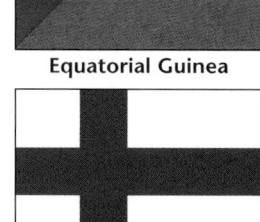

Finland

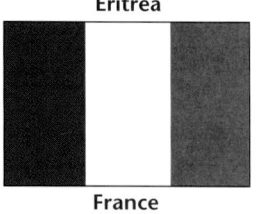

France

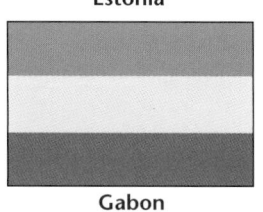

Gabon

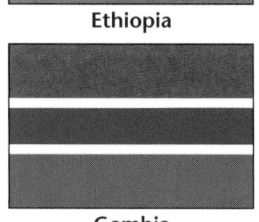

Gambia

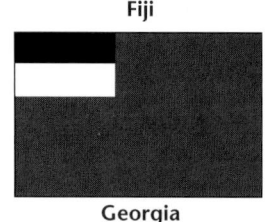

Georgia

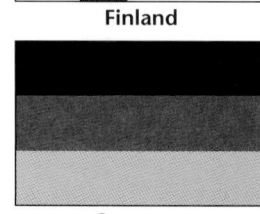

Germany

Ghana

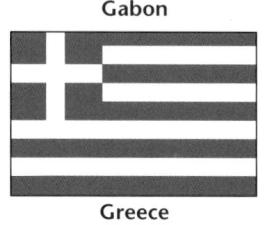

Greece

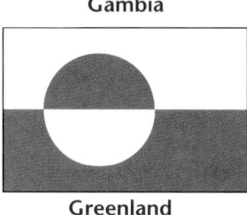

Greenland

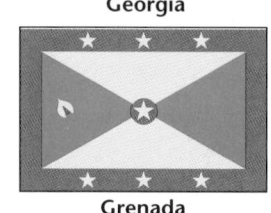

Grenada

Guatemala

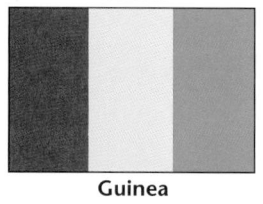

Guinea

Guinea Bissau

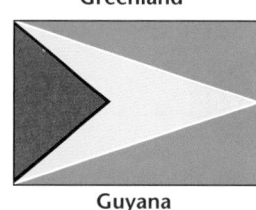

Guyana

Haiti

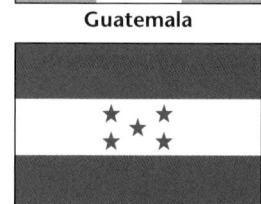

Honduras

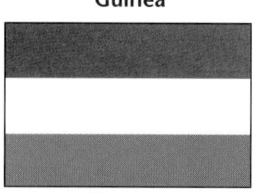

Hungary

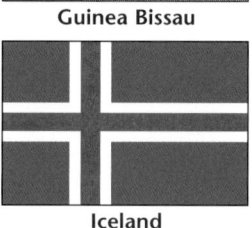

Iceland

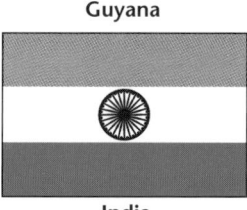

India

Indonesia

Iran

Iraq

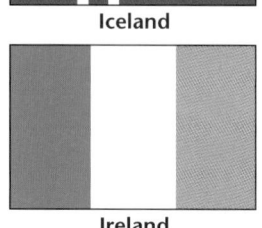

Ireland

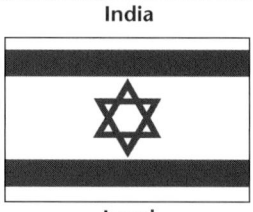

Israel

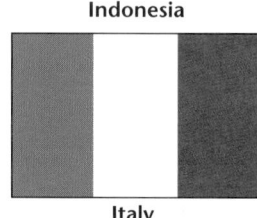

Italy

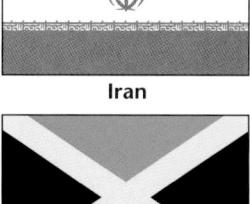

Jamaica

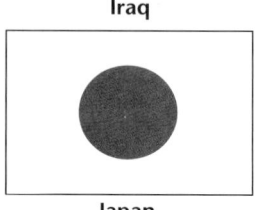

Japan

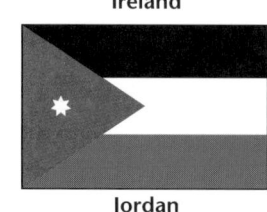

Jordan

Kazakhstan

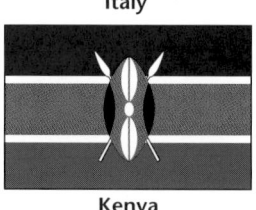

Kenya

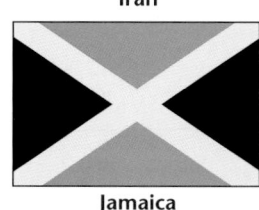

Kiribati

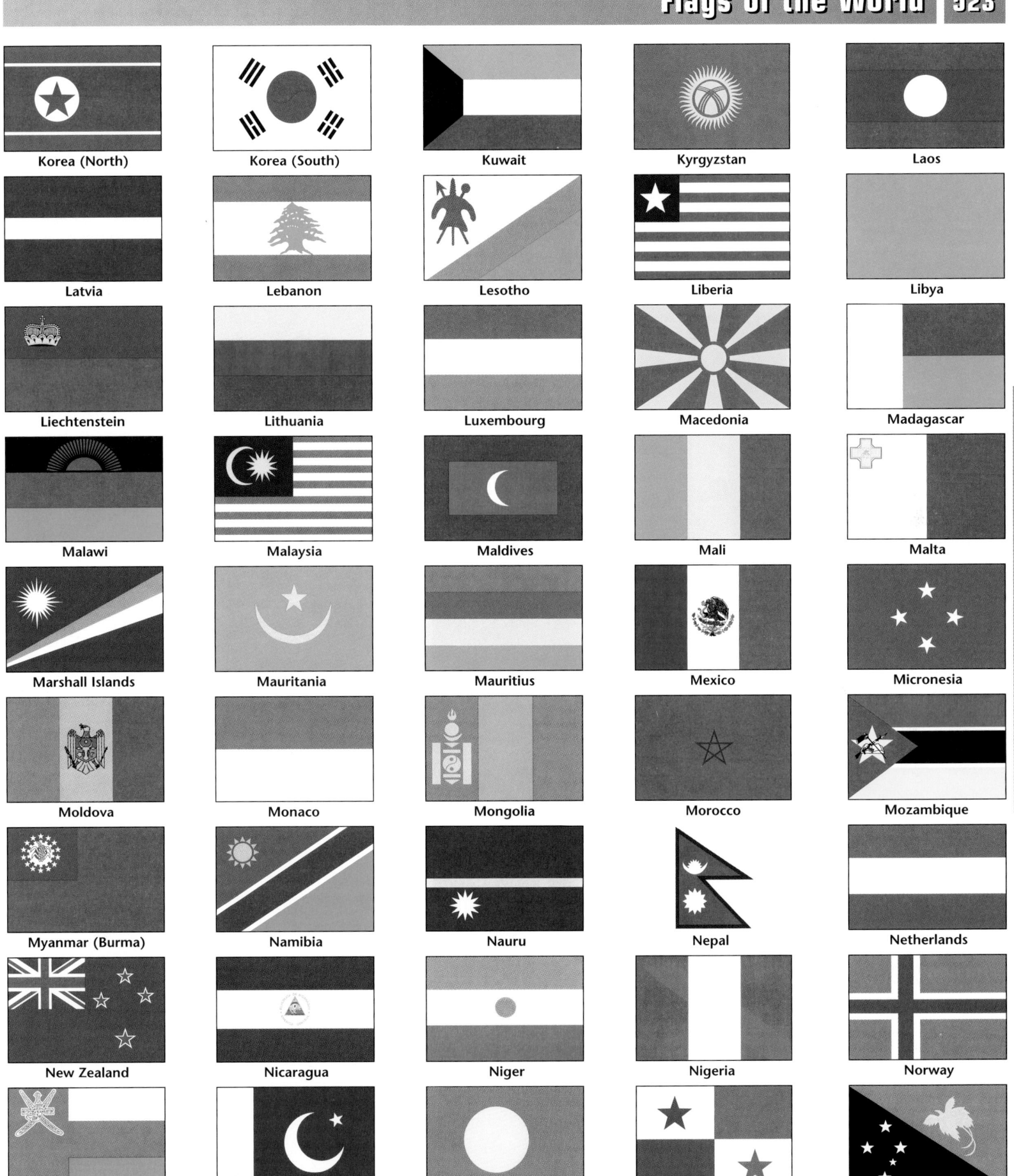

Korea (North)

Korea (South)

Kuwait

Kyrgyzstan

Laos

Latvia

Lebanon

Lesotho

Liberia

Libya

Liechtenstein

Lithuania

Luxembourg

Macedonia

Madagascar

Malawi

Malaysia

Maldives

Mali

Malta

Marshall Islands

Mauritania

Mauritius

Mexico

Micronesia

Moldova

Monaco

Mongolia

Morocco

Mozambique

Myanmar (Burma)

Namibia

Nauru

Nepal

Netherlands

New Zealand

Nicaragua

Niger

Nigeria

Norway

Oman

Pakistan

Palau

Panama

Papua New Guinea

Paraguay

Peru

Philippines

Poland

Portugal

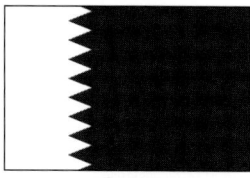
Qatar

Romania

Russia

Rwanda

St. Kitts and Nevis

St. Lucia

St. Vincent & the Grenadines

Samoa

San Marino

São Tomé & Príncipe

Saudi Arabia

Senegal

Serbia and Montenegro

Seychelles

Sierra Leone

Singapore

Slovakia

Slovenia

Solomon Islands

Somalia

South Africa

Spain

Sri Lanka

Sudan

Suriname

Swaziland

Sweden

Switzerland

Syria

Taiwan

Tajikistan

Tanzania

Thailand

Togo

Tonga

Trinidad and Tobago

Tunisia

Turkey

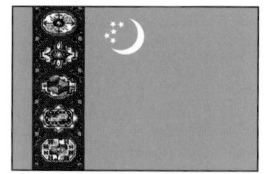
Turkmenistan

Tuvalu

Uganda

Ukraine

United Arab Emirates

United Kingdom

United States

Uruguay

Uzbekistan

Vanuatu

Vatican City

Venezuela

Vietnam

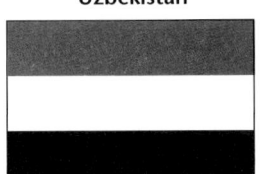

Yemen

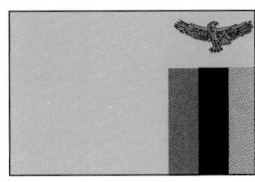

Zambia

Zimbabwe

Flags of the United Kingdom

United Kingdom
(also Northern Ireland)

England

Scotland

Wales

Flags of Canada

Canada

Alberta

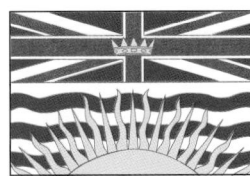

British Columbia

Manitoba

New Brunswick

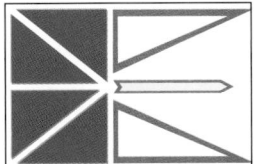

Newfoundland & Lab.

Nova Scotia

Northwest Territories

Nunavut

Ontario

Prince Edward Island

Québec

Saskatchewan

Yukon Territory

Alabama

Alaska

Arizona

Arkansas

California

Colorado

Connecticut

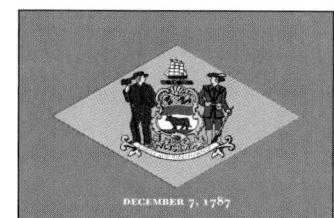

Delaware

District of Columbia

Florida

Georgia

Hawaii

Idaho

Illinois

Indiana

Iowa

Kansas

Kentucky

Louisiana

Maine

Maryland

Massachusetts

Michigan

Minnesota

Mississippi

Missouri

Montana

Nebraska

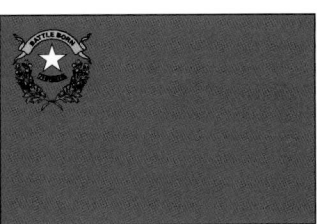

Nevada

New Hampshire

New Jersey

New Mexico

New York

North Carolina

North Dakota

Ohio

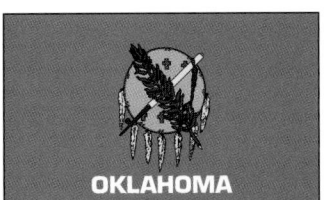

Oklahoma

Oregon

Pennsylvania

Rhode Island

South Carolina

South Dakota

Tennessee

Texas

Utah

Vermont

Virginia

Washington

West Virginia

Wisconsin

Wyoming

American Samoa

Guam

Northern Mariana Islands

Puerto Rico

Virgin Islands

INDEX OF THE WORLD

This index is an alphabetical listing of every subject area label found on the world reference maps in Volume 3. It is not necessary to know the country, state, or province where the feature is located in order to find the entry in this index. Each entry lists the name of the place or feature, followed by the name of the country, state or province that contains the feature. For all entries which are physical features, the type of feature is also provided. This allows the feature to be listed by its proper name. For example, the Gulf of Mexico will be listed as *Mexico, gulf.*

Each entry lists the page number and the map coordinate which can be used to pinpoint the location of the label on the map. After noting the page number and the coordinate, turn to the map page and refer to the letters and numbers found around the edge of the map. The place name or its associated symbol will be found in the square formed by latitude and longitude lines identified by the grid numbering system. Entries are indexed to all maps that show the place; therefore, some entries will show more than one page number or map coordinate.

Many of the city entries also include population information. These figures are from the United Nations and other official census agencies. For Canada, the United Kingdom and the United States, census information is as complete as possible. For other nations, populations for all cities above 100,000 people are included; other key cities with fewer than 100,000 people are listed if available. Because census practices vary widely throughout the world, comparisons of city populations from one nation to another can be problematic. In order to give a more realistic point of comparison, metropolitan populations are listed for many cities, and are identified with the abbreviation *metro.* For a full listing of all abbreviations used in this index, please see page 8.

Note that the terrain maps found on pages 26 to 46 have been indexed separately. That index is located on pages 47 to 49. The information in the terrain map index may not appear in this index of the world.

Aachen, Ger., 243,825 ....86/A3
Aalst, Belg., 76,382, (262,193 metro.) 85/C2
Aarau, Switz. 90/C1
Aare, Switz., river 86/B5
Aare, Switz., river 88/D3
Aare, Switz., river 90/B1, B2
Aargau, Switz., canton 90/C1
Aba, Nig. 152/D5
Abaco, Bah., island 207/B2
Abadan, Iran, 206,073 ....130/B3
Abaí, Para. 187/E4
Abajo, Utah, U.S., peak 350/E6
Abakaliki, Nig. 152/E4
Abakan, Russ., 168,047 ....104/F4
Abancay, Peru 185/C3
Abaya, Eth., lake 156/B3
Abbaye, Wisc., U.S., point 364/E2
Abbeville, Fr. 88/C1
Abbeville, Ala., U.S., 2,987 ....238/D4
Abbeville, Ga., U.S., 2,298 ....260/E8
Abbeville, La., U.S., 11,887 ....282/E7
Abbeville, Miss., U.S., 423 ....300/C1
Abbeville, S.C., U.S., 5,840 ....340/B2
Abbeville, S.C., U.S., county, 26,167 ....340/B2
Abbey, Sask., Can., 137 ....227/B10
Abbeytown, Eng., U.K. 66/B3
Abbey Wood, Eng., U.K. 70/E4
Abbots Bromley, Eng., U.K., 1,356 ....68/D4
Abbotsbury, Eng., U.K. 73/C3
Abbotsford, Br. Col., Can., 115,463 ....214/L6
Abbotsford, Wisc., U.S., 1,956 ....364/C4
Abbots Langley, Eng., U.K. 70/D3
Abbott, Ark., U.S., 50 ....244/A2
Abbott, N. Mex., U.S. 317/F1
Abbott, Va., U.S., 70 ....354/C6
Abbott, W. Va., U.S., 80 ....360/F3
Abbottsburg, N.C., U.S., 125 ....322/H5
Abbottstown, Penn., U.S., 905 ....336/G6
Abbot Vil., Maine, U.S., 60 ....286/C3
Abbyville, Kans., U.S., 128 ....276/D4
Abdali, Kuw. 136/B1
Abéché, Chad, 187,936 ....153/C4
Abemama, Kiri., island 175/A1
Abengourou, C. d'Iv. 150/E3
Abenrá, Den. 79/B3
Abeokuta, Nig. 152/B4
Aberaeron, Wales, U.K. 64/C3
Aberarth, Wales, U.K. 64/C3
Abercarn, (Abercarn/Newbridge), Wales, U.K.,
14,069 ....64/E4
Aberchirder, Scot., U.K., 1,149 ....62/L3
Abercraf, Wales, U.K. 64/D4
Abercrombie, N. Dak., U.S., 296 ....326/J3
Aberdare, Kenya, range 157/D4
Aberdare, Wales, U.K., 29,040 ....64/E4
Aberdaron, Wales, U.K. 64/B2
Aberdeen, Nun., Can., lake 208/H4
Aberdeen, H.K., China 117/B2
Aberdeen, Scot., U.K. 60/C1
Aberdeen, Scot., U.K., 184,788 ....62/M4
Aberdeen, City of, Scot., U.K., unitary authority,
212,125 ....62/N4
Aberdeen, Ida., U.S., 1,840 ....264/E7
Aberdeen, Md., U.S., 13,842 ....288/K2
Aberdeen, Miss., U.S., 6,415 ....300/D2
Aberdeen, N.C., U.S., 3,400 ....322/G4
Aberdeen, Ohio, U.S., 1,603 ....328/C8
Aberdeen, S. Dak., U.S., 24,658 ....342/G2
Aberdeen, Wash., U.S., 16,461 ....358/B2
Aberdeen Proving Grounds, Md., U.S. 288/K2
Aberdeenshire, Scot., U.K., unitary authority,
226,871 ....62/L3
Aberdyfi, Wales, U.K. 64/C2
Aberfeldy, Scot., U.K., 1,895 ....62/J5
Aberffraw, Wales, U.K. 64/C1
Aberfoil, Ala., U.S., 125 ....238/D3
Aberford, Eng., U.K. 66/F5
Aberfoyle, Scot., U.K., 576 ....62/H6
Abergavenny, Wales, U.K., 14,092 ....64/E4
Abergele, Wales, U.K., 7,373 ....64/D1
Aberkenfig, Wales, U.K. 64/C4
Aberkenfig, (Aberkenfig/Bryncoch), Wales, U.K.,
9,412 ....64/D4
Abermule, Wales, U.K. 64/E2
Abernant, Ala., U.S., 175 ....238/B2
Abernathy, Tex., U.S., 2,839 ....346/G2
Aberon, Azer., peninsula 103/C2
Aberporth, Wales, U.K., 1,431 ....64/B3
Abersoch, Wales, U.K. 64/B2
Abersychan, Wales, U.K. 64/E4
Abert, Oreg., U.S., lake 334/F5
Abertillery, Wales, U.K., 11,680 ....64/E4

Aberyscir, Wales, U.K. 64/E4
Aberystwyn, Wales, U.K. 60/B3
Aberystwyth, Wales, U.K., 11,154 ....64/C3
Abeytas, N. Mex., U.S., 60 ....317/D3
Abha, Sa. Arab. 136/B2
Abhe, Dji., lake 156/A2
Abhe, Eth., lake 156/C2
Abia, Eq. Gui., river 154/C3
Abia, Nig., state 152/D5
Abidjan, C. d'Iv., 1,929,079, (3,199,000 metro.) 150/D4
Abie, Nebr., U.S., 108 ....308/H2
Abilene, Kans., U.S., 6,543 ....276/E3
Abilene, Tex., U.S., 115,930, (126,555 metro.) ..346/J3
Abingdon, Eng., U.K., 35,234 ....68/E6
Abingdon, Eng., U.K., 35,234 ....70/B3
Abingdon, Ill., U.S., 3,612 ....266/C3
Abingdon, Iowa, U.S., 50 ....274/K5
Abingdon, Md., U.S., 950 ....288/J2
Abingdon, Va., U.S., 7,780 ....354/D3
Abington, Scot., U.K. 62/J8
Abington, Conn., U.S. 253/G2
Abington, Mass., U.S., 14,605 ....292/L4
Abiquiu, N. Mex., U.S., 225 ....317/D1
Abiquiu, N. Mex., U.S., reservoir 317/D1
Abita Sprs., La., U.S., 1,957 ....282/J6
Abkhazia, Geo., autonomous republic 103/A3
Abo, N. Mex., U.S., 60 ....317/D3
Aboisso, C. d'Iv. 150/E4
Aboite, Ind., U.S., 175 ....270/F5
Abomey, Ben., 66,695 ....151/A4
Abong Mbang, Came. 153/B3
Abou Deia, Chad 153/B5
Abovyan, Arm. 103/B2
Aboyne, Scot., U.K., 2,202 ....62/L4
Abraham, Utah, U.S., 60 ....350/B4
Abrams, Wisc., U.S., 350 ....364/E4
Abram-Village, P.E.I., Can., 342 ....224/A2
Abrantes, Port. 93/A3
Abruzzi, It., region 95/C2
Absaroka, Wyo., U.S., range 366/A1
Absarokee, Mont., U.S., 1,234 ....306/G4
Absecon, N.J., U.S., 7,638 ....314/E5
Abthorpe, Eng., U.K. 70/B2
Abu Dhabi, U.A.E., capital, 398,695 ....136/C2
Abuja, Nig., capital, 107,069, (371,674 metro.) 152/D3
Abuja Capital Terr., Nig., state 152/D3
Abu Kamal, Syria 134/B2
Abuná, Bol., river 186/A2
Academy, Calif., U.S., 40 ....246/F6
Academy, S. Dak., U.S. 342/F4
Academy of Sciences, Vat. 96/B1
Acadia, La., U.S., parish, 58,861 ....282/D6
Acadia N.P., Maine, U.S. 286/D4, E4
Acadia Valley, Alta., Can., 122 ....212/E5
Acadieville, N.B., Can. 217/D2
Acajutla, El. Salv. 203/A2
Acámbaro, Mex., 55,516, (110,718 metro.) ..200/D4
Acaponeta, Mex., 18,145, (36,512 metro.) ..200/C3
Acapulco, Mex., 620,656, (722,499 metro.) ..200/E4
Acaraí, Braz., range 188/C1
Acaraí, Guy., mountains 183/B5
Acaray, Para., river 187/E4
Acarigua, Ven., 188,607, (208,070 metro.) ..182/C2
Accident, Md., U.S., 353 ....288/A3
Accokeek, Md., U.S., 7,349 ....288/F5
Accokeek Acres, Md., U.S., 1,500 ....288/G5
Accomac, Va., U.S., 547 ....354/M5
Accomack, Va., U.S., county, 38,305 ....354/M5
Accord, Mass., U.S., 2,300 ....292/L4
Accra, Gha., capital, 859,640,
(1,904,000 metro.) 150/B4
Accrington, Eng., U.K., 36,466, (70,442 metro.) ..66/D5
Accrington, Eng., U.K., 36,466, (70,442 metro.) ..68/C2
Ace Basin N.W.R., S.C., U.S. 340/D4
Aceh, Indon., province 122/A1
Aceitunos, P.R. 206/A2
Acequia, Ida., U.S., 144 ....264/D7
Achallader, Scot., U.K. 62/G5
Acharn, Scot., U.K. 62/H5
Achavanich, Scot., U.K. 62/K2
Achfary, Scot., U.K. 62/G2
Achill, Ire., island 76/A2
Achille, Okla., U.S., 506 ....330/F4
Achilles, Va., U.S., 650 ....354/L6
Achiltibuie, Scot., U.K. 62/F3
Achinsk, Russ., 121,419, (122,800 metro.) ..104/F4
Achmore, Scot., U.K. 62/C2
Achnacroish, Scot., U.K. 62/E5
Achnasheen, Scot., U.K. 62/G2
Achwa, Ug., river 157/C2
Ackerly, Tex., U.S., 245 ....346/G3
Ackerman, Miss., U.S., 1,696 ....300/C2

Ackley, Iowa, U.S., 1,809 ....274/H2
Acklins, Bah., island 204/C2
Acklins, Bah., island 207/C4
Ackworth, Iowa, U.S., 85 ....274/H5
Ackworth Moor Top, Eng., U.K., 5,851 ....66/F5
Ackworth Moor Top, Eng., U.K., 5,851 ....68/E2
Acme, Alta., Can., 648 ....212/D5
Acme, La., U.S., 100 ....282/F4
Acme, Mich., U.S., 650 ....294/D5
Acme, Wash., U.S., 263 ....358/C1
Acme, Wyo., U.S. 366/C1
Acoaxet, Mass., U.S., 175 ....292/K6
Acolman, Mex. 200/Inset
Acoma, Nev., U.S. 310/C3
Acoma Indian Res., N. Mex., U.S. 317/C3
Acoma Pueblo, N. Mex., U.S., 40 ....317/C3
Acomita, N. Mex., U.S., 288 ....317/C3
Acomita Lake, N. Mex., U.S., 312 ....317/C2
Aconcagua, Arg., mountain 191/A3
Aconibe, Eq. Gui. 154/C3
Acorn, N.Y., U.S. 354/K4
A Coruña, Sp., 236,379 ....94/B1
A Coruña, Sp., Province 94/B1
Acquaviva, S. Mar. 97/A1
Acra, N.Y., U.S., 550 ....320/N6
Acre, Braz., state 188/A2
Acre, (Akko), Isr. 135/B1
Acree, Ga., U.S., 212/ 260/C8
Acton, N.B., Can. 217/C3
Acton, Ont., Can., 7,767 ....223/E4
Acton, Calif., U.S., 2,390 ....246/G8
Acton, Maine, U.S., 2,145 ....286/B5
Acton, Mass., U.S., 20,331 ....292/J3
Acton, Mont., U.S., 50 ....306/H4
Acton Vale, Que., Can., 7,299 ....226/D6
Açúcar, Braz., mountain ....188/Inset I
Acurenam, Eq. Gui. 154/C3
Acushnet, Mass., U.S., 10,161 ....292/L6
Acworth, Ga., U.S., 13,422 ....260/B3, G1
Acworth, N.H., U.S., 50 ....312/B5
Ada, Ida., U.S., county, 300,904 ....264/A6
Ada, Kans., U.S., 100 ....276/E2
Ada, La., U.S., 325 ....282/C1
Ada, Minn., U.S., 1,657 ....298/A3
Ada, Ohio, U.S., 5,582 ....328/C4
Ada, Okla., U.S., 15,691 ....330/F3
Adair, Ill., U.S., 250 ....266/C3
Adair, Iowa, U.S., 839 ....274/E4
Adair, Iowa, U.S., county, 8,243 ....274/F5
Adair, Ky., U.S., county, 17,244 ....280/E3
Adair, Mo., U.S., county, 24,977 ....302/D1
Adair, Okla., U.S., 704 ....330/G1
Adair, Okla., U.S., county, 21,038 ....330/H2
Adairsville, Ga., U.S., 2,542 ....260/B3
Adair Vil., Oreg., U.S., 536 ....334/C3
Adairville, Ky., U.S., 920 ....280/D4
Adak, (Adak Sta), Alaska, U.S., 316 ....240/Inset
Adak, Alaska, U.S., island 240/Inset
Adamant, Vt., U.S., 150 ....352/B2
Adamawa, Came., massif 153/B2
Adamawa, Came., Province 153/B2
Adamawa, Nig., massif 152/E5
Adamawa, Nig., state 152/G3
Adams, Br. Col., Can., lake 214/N5
Adams, Sri Lan., peak 126/B4
Adams, Colo., U.S., county, 348,618 ....250/A3, F2
Adams, Ida., U.S., county, 3,476 ....264/A5
Adams, Ill., U.S., county, 68,277 ....266/B4
Adams, Ind., U.S., 325 ....270/E6
Adams, Iowa, U.S., county, 33,625 ....270/C3
Adams, Iowa, U.S., county, 4,482 ....274/E5
Adams, Ky., U.S., 60 ....280/H2
Adams, Mass., U.S., 8,809 ....292/B2
Adams, Mich., U.S., point 294/F4
Adams, Minn., U.S., 800 ....298/E7
Adams, Miss., U.S., county, 34,340 ....300/A4
Adams, Nebr., U.S., 489 ....308/H3
Adams, Nebr., U.S., county, 31,151 ....308/F3
Adams, N.Y., U.S., 1,624 ....320/K3
Adams, N. Dak., U.S., 203 ....326/G1
Adams, N. Dak., U.S., county, 2,593 ....326/C3
Adams, Ohio, U.S., county, 27,330 ....328/C8
Adams, Okla., U.S., 175 ....330/A1, C4
Adams, Oreg., U.S., 297 ....334/H2
Adams, Penn., U.S., county, 91,292 ....336/G6
Adams, Tenn., U.S., 566 ....344/G1
Adams, Wash., U.S., county, 16,428 ....358/G2
Adams, Wash., U.S., mountain 358/D3
Adams, Wisc., U.S., 1,914 ....364/D5
Adams, Wisc., U.S., county, 18,643 ....364/D4
Adams Bridge, Sri Lan., shoal 126/A3

Adams Ctr., N.Y., U.S., 1,500 ....320/K3
Adams-McGill, Nev., U.S., reservoir 310/C2
Adamston, N.J., U.S., 4,900 ....314/E3
Adamstown, Md., U.S., 650 ....288/E2
Adamstown, Penn., U.S., 1,203 ....336/J5
Adamsville, Ala., U.S., 4,965 ....238/C2, D1
Adamsville, Del., U.S., 90 ....255/B5
Adamsville, Mass., U.S., 212/ 292/D2
Adamsville, Ohio, U.S., 127 ....328/G5
Adamsville, R.I., U.S., 550 ....339/F4
Adamsville, Tenn., U.S., 1,983 ....344/E4
Adamsville, Utah, U.S. 350/B5
Adana, Tur., 1,130,710 ....133/C3
Adana, Tur., province 133/C3
Ad Dahna, Sa. Arab., desert 136/B1
Ad Dakhla, W. Sah. 147/A2
ad-Damazin, Sudan 145/C3
Ad Damman, Sa. Arab. 136/C1
Ad Damur, Leb. 134/A2
Adderbury, Eng., U.K., 2,348 ....68/E5
Adderley, Eng., U.K. 68/B4
Adderstone, Eng., U.K. 66/E1
Addeville, Ill., U.S., 267 ....266/D5
Addingham, Eng., U.K., 2,769 ....66/E5
Addingham, Eng., U.K., 2,769 ....68/D2
Addington, Eng., U.K. 70/D4
Addington, Okla., U.S., 117 ....330/E3
Addis, La., U.S., 2,238 ....282/G6
Addis Ababa, Eth., capital, 2,424,000 ....156/C2
Addis Ababa, Eth., state 156/C2
Addison, Ala., U.S., 723 ....238/B1
Addison, Ill., U.S., 35,914 ....266/B5
Addison, Maine, U.S., 1,209 ....286/E4
Addison, Mich., U.S., 627 ....294/E7
Addison, N.Y., U.S., 1,797 ....320/G6
Addison, Ohio, U.S., 225 ....328/F8
Addison, Penn., U.S., 214 ....336/C6
Addison, Tex., U.S., 14,166 ....346/C2
Addison, Vt., U.S., 1,393 ....352/A2
Addison, Vt., U.S., county, 35,974 ....352/A2
Ad Diwaniyah, Iraq 130/C2
Addu, Mald., atoll 127/A5
Ad Duqm, Oman 137/C2
Addy, Wash., U.S., 175 ....358/H1
Addyston, Ohio, U.S., 1,010 ....328/A9
Adel, Ga., U.S., 5,307 ....260/E9
Adel, Iowa, U.S., 3,435 ....274/F4
Adel, Mont., U.S. 306/F2
Adel, Oreg., U.S., 90 ....334/G5
Adelaide, Antar., island 192/C11
Adelaide, S.A., Austl., state capital,
(1,043,909 metro.) ....170/C3, Inset II
Adelanto, Calif., U.S., 18,130 ....246/H8
Adeline, Ill., U.S., 139 ....266/D1
Adelino, N. Mex., U.S., 2,211 ....317/D3
Adelphi, Md., U.S., 14,998 ....288/C6
Adelphi, Ohio, U.S., 371 ....328/E7
Adelphia, N.J., U.S., 700 ....314/E3
Aden, Alta., Can. 212/F4
Aden, Dji., gulf 156/C2
Aden, Som., gulf 157/B2
Aden, Yemen, (400,783 metro.) 137/B2
Aden, Yemen, gulf 137/B2
Adena, Ohio, U.S., 815 ....328/J5
Adgateville, Ga., U.S. 260/D5
Adige, It., river 95/B1
Adi Keyih, Erit. 156/B2
Adirondack, N.Y., U.S., mountains 320/M2
Adirondack Park, N.Y., U.S. 320/N2
Adi Ugri, Erit. 156/B2
Adiyaman, Tur., 212,500 ....133/D3
Adiyaman, Tur., province 133/D3
Adjuntas, P.R. 206/B2
Adlestrop, Eng., U.K. 70/A3
Adlington, Eng., U.K., 8,556 ....66/C5
Adlington, Eng., U.K., 8,556 ....68/B2
Admiralty, P.N.G., islands 172/A2
Admiralty Island Natl. Mon., Alaska, U.S. 240/J3
Admire, Kans., U.S., 177 ....276/E3
Adna, Wash., U.S., 350 ....358/B3
Adona, Ark., U.S., 187 ....244/C2
Adour, Fr., river 88/B3
Adrar, Alg. 146/B2
Adrár, Maur., region 147/B2

Adrar des Ifôghas, Mali, *massif* 150/D2
Adrian, Ga., U.S., 579 . . . . .260/F6
Adrian, Mich., U.S., 21,574 . . . . .298/B7
Adrian, Minn., U.S., 1,234 . . . . .298/B7
Adrian, Mo., U.S., 1,780 . . . . .302/B3
Adrian, Oreg., U.S., 147 . . . . .334/J4
Adrian, Tex., U.S., 159 . . . . .346/E9
Adriatic, Alb., *sea* .99/A2
Adriatic, It., *sea* 95/C2
Adriatic, Serb.-Mont., *sea* 99/A4
Adriatic, Slove., *sea* 98/A3
Advance, Ind., U.S., 562 . . . . .270/C5
Advance, Mo., U.S., 1,244 . . . . .302/G4
Advance, N.C., U.S., 250 . . . . .322/E3
Advocate Harbour, N.S., Can. 221/C2
Adwa, Eth. 156/C1
Adwick le Street, Eng., U.K., 10,288 . . . . .68/E2
Adwolf, Va., U.S., 1,457 . . . . .354/E3
Ady, Tex., U.S. 346/F9
Adygeya, Russ., *region* 104/D5
Adzopé, C. d'Iv. 150/C3
Ae, Eng., U.K., *forest* 66/A2
Aegean, Gr., *sea* .100/C2
Aegean, Tur., *sea* 133/A3
Aeneas, Wash., U.S., 40 . . . . .358/G1
Ærø, Den., *island* .79/C4
Aetna, Alta., Can. 212//J6
Aetna, Kans., U.S. .276/D4
Afadjoto, Gha., *mountain* 150/C3
Afar, Eth., *state* 156/C1
Affric, Scot., U.K., *River* 62/F4
Affton, Mo., U.S., 20,535 . . . . .302/H3
Afghanistan, *nation* 125
Afikpo, Nig. 152/D5
Afram, Gha., *river* 150/B3
Africa, *continent* 136
Afton, Iowa, U.S., 917 . . . . .274/F5
Afton, La., U.S., 40 . . . . .282/G2
Afton, Mich., U.S., 100 . . . . .294/E4
Afton, Minn., U.S., 2,839 . . . . .298/E6
Afton, N.Y., U.S., 836 . . . . .320/K6
Afton, N.C., U.S., 212/ 322//J2
Afton, Okla., U.S., 1,118 . . . . .330/H1
Afton, Tex., U.S., 60 . . . . .346/H2
Afton, Wyo., U.S., 1,818 . . . . .366/A2
Afula, Isr. 135/B1
Afyon, Tur. 133/B2
Afyon, Tur., *province* 133/B2
Agadez, Niger 152/D2
Agadir, Mor., 137,000 . . . . .147/B2
Agar, S. Dak., U.S., 82 . . . . .342/E3
Agartala, India 128/F4
Agassiz N.W.R., Minn., U.S. 298/B2
Agate, Colo., U.S., 60 . . . . .250/G2
Agate Fossil Beds N.M., Nebr., U.S. 308/A1
Agattu, Alaska, U.S., *island* 240/Inset
Agawam, Mass., U.S., 28,144 . . . . .306/D2
Agawam, Mont., U.S. 306/D2
Agawam, Okla., U.S., 70 . . . . .330/E3
Agboville, C. d'Iv. .150/D4
Açcabâdi, Azer. 103/B2
Ağdam, Azer. 103/B3
Agen, Fr. 88/C4
Agency, Iowa, U.S., 622 . . . . .274/K6
Agency, Mo., U.S., 599 . . . . .302/B2
Agenda, Kans., U.S., 81 . . . . .276/E2
Aghalee, N. Ire., U.K., 480 . . . . .65/E2
Aginskiy Buryat, Russ., *autonomous okrug* . .104/G4
Aginskoye, Russ. 104/Inset
Agios Dimitrios, Gr. 298/F2
Agnes, Ont., Can., *lake* 334/B5
Agness, Oreg., U.S. 334/B5
Agnew, Mich., U.S., 275 . . . . .294/C7
Agnew, Nebr., U.S., 100 . . . . .308/H2
Agnos, Ark., U.S., 50 . . . . .244/D1
Agou, Togo, *mountain* 151/B3
Agoura Hills, Calif., U.S., 20,537 . . . . .246/G8
Agra, India, 1,259,979, (1,321,410 *metro.*) . .128/C3
Agra, Kans., U.S., 306 . . . . .276/C2
Agra, Okla., U.S., 356 . . . . .330/F2
Ağri, Tur. 133/E2
Ağri, Tur., *province* 133/E2
Agricola, Kans., U.S. 276/G3
Agricola, Miss., U.S., 212/ 300/D5
Agrigento, It. 95/C3
Agrinion, Gr. 100/B2
Ağstafa, Azer. 103/A2
Agua Caliente, Ariz., U.S., 50 . . . . .242/B4
Aguada, P.R. 206/A2
Aguada de Cachinal, Chile 190/C2
Aguadilla, P.R., (146,424 *metro.*) 206/A2
Aguadulce, Pan. 203/B2
Agua Dulce, Tex., U.S., 737 . . . . .346/L8
Agua Fria, Ariz., U.S., *river* 242/C4
Agua Fria, N. Mex., U.S., 2,051 . . . . .317/D2
Agua Fria Natl. Mon., Ariz., U.S. 202/B2
Aguán, Hond., *river* 246//J9
Aguanga, Calif., U.S., 300 . . . . .246/J9
Agua Nueva, Tex., U.S. 346/K9
Agua Prieta, Mex., 60,420, (61,944 *metro.*) .200/C1
Aguas Blancas, Chile 190/C2
Aguas Buenas, P.R. 206/C2
Aguascalientes, Mex., *state capital*, 594,092,
  (643,419 *metro.*) 200/D3
Aguascalientes, Mex., *state* 200/D3
Aguilar, Colo., U.S., 593 . . . . .250/F4
Aguilares, Tex., U.S. 346//J8
Aguilas, Sp. 94/F4
Aguilita, P.R. 206/B2
Agulhas, S. Afr., *cape* 162/B3
Agung, Indon., *volcano* 122/C4
Agusan, Phil., *river* 120/C4
Ahaggar, Alg., *mountains* 146/B2
Ahal, Turkm., *province* 132/C2
Ahloso, Okla., U.S., 175 . . . . .330/F3
Ahmadabad, India, 3,515,361,
  (4,519,278 *metro.*) 128/B4
Ahmic Harbour, Ont., Can. 223/F2
Aghoghill, N. Ire., U.K., 2,260 . . . . .65/H2
Ahoskie, N.C., U.S., 4,523 . . . . .322/N4
Ahsahka, Ida., U.S., 600 . . . . .264/A3
Ahuachapán, El Salv, 83,885 . . . . .203/A2
Ahuimanu, Hawaii, U.S., 8,506 . . . . .262/J2
Ahvaz, Iran, 804,980 . . . . .130/B3
Ahvenanmaa, Fin., *province* 81/A2
Ahwahnee, Calif., U.S., 475 . . . . .246/F5
Ahwar, Yemen 137/B2
Aibonito, P.R. 206/C2
Aichi, Jap., *prefecture* 114/C3
Aid, Ohio, U.S., 125 . . . . .328/F8
Aiea, Hawaii, U.S., 9,019 . . . . .262/F1, J2
Aigaleo, Gr., *mountains* 100/Inset
Aiken, S.C., U.S., 25,337 . . . . .340/C3
Aiken, S.C., U.S., *county*, 142,552 . . . . . . .340/C3
Aiken, (Floyd County), Tex., U.S. 346/G1
Aiken, (Shelby County), Tex., U.S. 346/P4
Aikers, Scot., U.K. 62/L1, M2
Aikton, Eng., U.K. .66/B3
Aileu, E. Timor 122/B1
Aileu, E. Timor, *province* 122/B1
Ailey, Ga., U.S., 394 . . . . .260/F7

Ailinglapalap, Marsh. Is., *island* 173/B2
Aillik, Nfld., Can. 206/B1
Ailsa Craig, Scot., U.K., *island* 62/F8
Ailuk, Marsh. Is., *island* 173/B1
Ain, Fr., *department* 88/D3
Ainaro, E. Timor 122/B2
Ainaro, E. Timor, *province* 122/B2
Ainstable, Eng., U.K. 66/C3
Ainsworth, Iowa, U.S., 524 . . . . .274/L5
Ainsworth, Nebr., U.S., 1,862 . . . . .308/E1
Aiquile, Bol. 186/A3
Air, Niger, *massif* 152/B2
Airdrie, Alta., Can., 20,382 . . . . .212//C5
Airdrie, Scot., U.K., 36,326 . . . . .62//J7
Air Force, Nun., U.S., *island* 320/A1
Airmont, N.Y., U.S., 7,799 . . . . .320/A1
Airport Drive, Mo., U.S., 622 . . . . .302/B4
Air Ronge, Sask., Can., 955 . . . . .227/E5
Airton, Eng., U.K. 66/D4
Airway Hts., Wash., U.S., 4,500 . . . . .358/H2
Aishihik, Yukon, Can., *lake* 228/B5
Aisne, Fr., *department* 88/C2
Aisne, Fr., *river* 88/D2
Aith, (Orkney Islands), Scot., U.K. 62/L2
Aith, (Shetland Islands), Scot., U.K. 62/P2
Aitkin, Minn., U.S., 1,984 . . . . .298/D4
Aitkin, Minn., U.S., *county*, 15,301 . . . . . . .298/D4
Aitnoch, Scot., U.K. 62//J4
Aiwo, Nauru 174/A2
Aix-en-Provence, Fr. 88/D5
Aix-les-Bains, Fr. 88/D4
Aiyina, Gr., *island* 100/B3
Aizawl, India 128/F4
Aizuwakamatsu, Jap. 114/C2
Ajaccio, Fr. . . . . .88//Inset I
Ajaria, Geo., *autonomous republic* 103/A4
Ajdabiya, Lib. 145/D1
Ajka, Hun. 91/A2
'Ajlūn, Jor., *governorate* 134/A1
Ajman, U.A.E. 136/C2
Ajmer, India 128/B3
Ajo, Ariz., U.S., 3,705 . . . . .158/C1
Akagera, Rwa., *national park* 158/C1
Akagera, Rwa., *river* 158/C1, C2
Akanyaru, Rwa., *river* 158/B2
Akashi, Jap., 293,000 . . . . .114/B3
Ak-Chin, Ariz., U.S., 150 . . . . .242/C4
Ak Chin, Ariz., U.S., 150 . . . . .242/D5
Akanyaru, Rwa., *river* 158/B2
Akeld, Eng., U.K. 66/D1
Akeley, Eng., U.K. .68/F5
Akeley, Minn., U.S., 412 . . . . .298/C3
Akers, La., U.S., 70 . . . . .282//J6
Akershus, Nor., *province* 80/C3
Akhalkalak'i, Geo. .103/B4
Akhalts'ikhe, Geo. .103/B4
Akharnai, Gr. .100//Inset
Akheloos, Gr., *river* 100/B2
Akhiok, Alaska, U.S., 80 . . . . .240/E3
Akhmeta, Geo. 103/C3
Akhuryan, Arm., *river* 103/A2
Akin, Ill., U.S., 225 .266/E6
Akita, Jap., 318,000 . . . . .114/D2
Akita, Jap., *prefecture* 114/D2
Akjoujt, Maur. 147/B3
Aklavik, N.W. Terr., Can., 632 . . . . .208/A3
Akobo, Eth., *river* 156/A3
Akobo, Sudan, *river* 145/C3
Akola, India 128/C4
Akbrdat, Erit. 156/A2
Akosombo, Gha., *dam* 150/C3
Akpatok, Nun., Can., *island* 208/P4
Akra, N. Dak., U.S., 50 . . . . .326/H1
Akranes, Ice., 5,433 . . . . .79/A2
Akron, Ala., U.S., 521 . . . . .238/B3
Akron, Colo., U.S., 1,711 . . . . .250/C1
Akron, Ind., U.S., 1,076 . . . . .270/D2
Akron, Iowa, U.S., 1,489 . . . . .274/A2
Akron, Kans., U.S. .276/E4
Akron, Mich., U.S., 461 . . . . .294/F6
Akron, N.Y., U.S., 3,085 . . . . .320/E4
Akron, Ohio, U.S., 217,074 . . . . .328/G3
Akron, Penn., U.S., 4,046 . . . . .336//J5
Akrotiri, Cyp., *bay* 133/B2
Aksaray, Tur. 133/C2
Aksaray, Tur., *province* 133/C2
Aksu, China 119/B1
Aktau, Kaz., 143,396 . . . . .131/B1
Aktobe, Kaz., 253,088 . . . . .131/B1
Aktobe, Kaz., *oblast* 131/B1
Akulivik, Que., Can. 225/A1
Akure, Nig. 152/C4
Akureyri, Ice., 15,396 . . . . .79/B2
Akuseki, Jap., *island* 114/A4
Akutan, Alaska, U.S., 713 . . . . .240/B4
Akwa Ibom, Nig., *State* 152/E5
Alabam, Ark., U.S., 40 . . . . .244/B1
Alabama, U.S., *state* 226
Alabama, Ala., U.S., *river* 238/B3, B4
Alabama & Coushatta Ind. Res., Tex., U.S. . . .346/P5
Alabaster, Ala., U.S., 22,619 . . . . .238/C2
Alabaster, Mich., U.S., 40 . . . . .294/F5
Alachua, Fla., U.S., 6,098 . . . . .256/F2
Alachua, Fla., U.S., *county*, 217,955 . . . . . .256/F2
Aladdin, Wyo., U.S. 366/D1
Alagoas, Braz., *state* 188/E3
Alagoinhas, Braz. 188/E3
Al Ahmadi, Kuw. 136/C2
Al Ahsa, Sa. Arab., *region* 136/C1
Alajuela, C.R., 188,274 . . . . .203/B2
Alajuela, C.R., *province* 203/B2
Alakanuk, Alaska, U.S., 652 . . . . .240/C2
Alalakeiki, Hawaii, U.S., *channel* 262/B4
Al Alamayn, Egy. .144/A1
Alamance, N.C., U.S., 310 . . . . .322/G2
Alamance, N.C., U.S., *county*, 130,800 . . . .322/G3
Al Amarah, Iraq 227/H11
Alameda, Sask., Can., 311 . . . . .227/H11
Alameda, Calif., U.S., 72,259 . . . . .246//J2
Alameda, Calif., U.S., *county*, 1,443,741 .246/D5, L2
Alameda, N. Mex., U.S., 4,212/ 317/D2
Alamo, Ariz., U.S., *lake* 242/B3
Alamo, Calif., U.S., 15,626 . . . . .246/K2
Alamo, Ga., U.S., 1,943 . . . . .260/F7
Alamo, Ind., U.S., 137 . . . . .270/B5
Alamo, Mich., U.S., 275 . . . . .294/D7
Alamo, Nev., U.S. .310/C3
Alamo, N. Mex., U.S., 1,183 . . . . .317/C3
Alamo, N. Dak., U.S., 51 . . . . .326/B1
Alamo, Tenn., U.S., 2,392 . . . . .346/K9
Alamo, Tex., U.S., 14,760 . . . . .346/K9
Alamo Alto, Tex., U.S., 70 . . . . .346/B4
Alamo Band Navajo Ind. Res., N. Mex., U.S. . .317/C3
Alamogordo, N. Mex., U.S., 35,582 . . . . .317/E5
Alamo Hts., Tex., U.S., 7,319 . . . . .346/A5
Alamosa, Colo., U.S., 7,960 . . . . .250/E4
Alamosa, Colo., U.S., *county*, 14,966 . . . . . .250/E4
Alamosa East, Colo., U.S., 1,528 . . . . .250/E4
Alamosa N.W.R., Colo., U.S. 250/E4

Alamota, Kans., U.S. 276/B3
Alampur, India . . . . .128//Inset II
Åland, Fin., *autonomous province* 81/A2
Åland, Fin., *islands* 81/A2
Alanson, Mich., U.S., 785 . . . . .294/E4
Alaotra, Madag., *lake* 163/B2
Alapaha, Ga., U.S., 682 . . . . .260/E9
Alapaha, Ga., U.S., *river* 260/E9
Alappuzha, India 128/C7
Al Aqabah, Jor. 134/A3
Al 'Aqabah, Jor., *governorate* 134/A3
Alarcón, Sp., *reservoir* 94/E3
Al Arish, Egy. 144/B1
Alaska, U.S., *state* 193/C11
Alaska, U.S., *state* 228
Alaska, Alaska, U.S., *gulf* 240/F3
Alaska, Alaska, U.S., *peninsula* 240/C3
Alaska, Alaska, U.S., *range* 240/E2
Alaska Maritime N.W.R., Alaska, U.S. 240/B4
Alaska Peninsula N.W.R., Alaska, U.S. 240/D3
Alât, Azer. 103/C4
Alava, Sp., *province* 94/E1
Alava, Wash., U.S., *cape* 358/A1
Alaverdi, Arm. 103/B1
Alaw, Wales, U.K., *river* 64/B1
Alawa-Ngandji, Austl., *aboriginal land* 170/C1
Alay, Kyrg., *mountains* 131/B3
Alay, Taj., *mountains* 132/B1
Alayli Dadda, Dji. 156/B1
Al Ayn, U.A.E. 136/C2
Alazani, Geo., *river* 103/C4
Alba, Rom., *county* 101/B2
Alba, Mich., U.S., 325 . . . . .294/E5
Alba, Mo., U.S., 588 . . . . .302/B4
Alba, Penn., U.S., 186 . . . . .336/H2
Alba, Tex., U.S., 430 . . . . .346/N3
Albacete, Sp., 148,934 . . . . .94/F3
Albacete, Sp., *province* 94/E3
Al Bahah, Sa. Arab. 136/B2
Al Bahah, Sa. Arab., *emirate* 136/B2
Alba Iulia, Rom. 101/B2
Al Balqa', Jor., *Governorate* 134/A1
Alban, Ont., Can., 1,084 . . . . .223/E1
Albania, *nation* 97
Albany, W.A., Austl. 170/A3
Albany, P.E.I., Can. 224/B2
Albany, Ont., Can., *river* 222/C2
Albany, Calif., U.S., 16,444 . . . . .246/J1
Albany, Ga., U.S., 76,939, (120,822 *metro.*) .260/C8
Albany, Ill., U.S., 895 . . . . .266/C2
Albany, Ind., U.S., 2,368 . . . . .270/F4
Albany, Ky., U.S., 2,220 . . . . .280/H4
Albany, La., U.S., 865 . . . . .282/H5
Albany, Minn., U.S., 1,796 . . . . .298/C5
Albany, Mo., U.S., 1,937 . . . . .302/B1
Albany, N.H., U.S., 654 . . . . .312/D4
Albany, N.Y., U.S., *county*, 294,565 . . . . . .320/N5
Albany, N.Y., U.S., *state capital*, 95,658,
  (875,583 *metro.*) 320/P5
Albany, Ohio, U.S., 808 . . . . .328/F7
Albany, Okla., U.S., 80 . . . . .330/F4
Albany, Oreg., U.S., 40,852 . . . . .334/C3
Albany, Tex., U.S., 1,921 . . . . .346//J3
Albany, Vt., U.S., 840 . . . . .352/C1
Albany, Wisc., U.S., 1,191 . . . . .364/D6
Albany, Wyo., U.S., 80 . . . . .366/C3
Albany, Wyo., U.S., *county*, 32,014 . . . . . . .366/D2
Al Batinah, Oman, *region* 137/C1
Al Batrun, Leb. 134/A1
Al Bawiti, Egy. 144/A2
Al Bayda, Lib. 145/D1
Al Bayda, Yemen .137/B2
Albee, S. Dak., U.S. 342//J2
Albemarle, N.C., U.S., 15,680 . . . . .322/E4
Albemarle, N.C., U.S., *sound* 322/N2
Albemarle, Va., U.S., *county*, 79,236 . . . . . .354/F4
Alberene, Va., U.S. .354/F5
Alberhill, Calif., U.S. 246/G10
Albers, Ill., U.S., 878 . . . . .266/D5
Albert, Belg., *canal* 85/C1
Albert, N.B., Can., *county* 217/E3
Albert, Congo, D.R., *lake* 155/C1
Albert, Ug., *lake* .157/B3
Albert, Kans., U.S., 181 . . . . .276/C3
Albert, Okla., U.S., 100 . . . . .330/D2
Alberta, Can., *province* 212/
Alberta, Ala., U.S., 175 . . . . .238/B3
Alberta, Mich., U.S., 150 . . . . .294/A3
Alberta, Minn., U.S., 142 . . . . .298/A5
Alberta, Va., U.S., 306 . . . . .354/H7
Albert City, Iowa, U.S., 709 . . . . .298/D7
Albert Lea, Minn., U.S., 18,356 . . . . .298/D7
Albert Nile, Ug., *river* 157/B2
Alberton, P.E.I., Can., 1,115 . . . . .224/A2
Alberton, Mont., U.S., 374 . . . . .306/B2
Albertville, Ala., U.S., 17,247 . . . . .238/C1
Albertville, Minn., U.S., 3,621 . . . . .298/D5
Albi, Fr. 88/C5
Albia, Iowa, U.S., 3,706 . . . . .274//J5
Albin, Miss., U.S., 40 . . . . .300/B2
Albin, Wyo., U.S., 120 . . . . .366/D3
Albina, Sur. 183/B2
Albion, Calif., U.S., 150 . . . . .246/B3
Albion, Ida., U.S., 262 . . . . .264/D7
Albion, Ill., U.S., 1,933 . . . . .266/E5
Albion, Ind., U.S., 2,284 . . . . .270/F2
Albion, Iowa, U.S., 592 . . . . .274//J3
Albion, Maine, U.S., 1,946 . . . . .286/C4
Albion, Mich., U.S., 9,144 . . . . .294/E7
Albion, Mont., U.S. 306/M4
Albion, Nebr., U.S., 1,797 . . . . .308/E1
Albion, N.Y., U.S., 7,438 . . . . .320/E4
Albion, Okla., U.S., 143 . . . . .330/G3
Albion, Penn., U.S., 1,607 . . . . .336/A2
Albion, R.I., U.S., 80 . . . . .346/P2
Albion, Wash., U.S., 616 . . . . .358/H3
Alboran, Sp., *Sea* .79/B1
Ålborg, Den., 119,996, (156,614 *metro.*) . . .79/C2
Ålborg, Den., *bay* 79/C2
Alborn, Minn., U.S., 60 . . . . .298/E4
Albright, W. Va., U.S., 262 . . . . .360/G1
Albrighton, Eng., U.K., 6,135 . . . . .68/C4
Albuquerque, Col., *Cays* 184/Inset
Albuquerque, N. Mex., U.S., 448,607,
  (712,738 *metro.*) 317/D2
Alburg, Vt., U.S., 1,952 . . . . .352/A1
Alburg Ctr., Vt., U.S. 352/A1
Alburg Sprs., Vt., U.S., 100 . . . . .352/A1
Alburnett, Iowa, U.S., 559 . . . . .274/L3
Albury, N.S.W., Austl. 170/D3
Alcalá de Henares, Sp., 176,434 . . . . . . .94//Inset II
Alcalde, N. Mex., U.S., 377 . . . . .317/D1
Alcañiz, Sp. 94/F2
Alcántara, Sp., *reservoir* 94/C3
Alcázar de San Juan, Sp. 94/E3
Alcester, Eng., U.K., 6,282 . . . . .68/D5
Alcester, S. Dak., U.S., 880 . . . . .342//J4
Alco, Ark., U.S., 50 . . . . .244/C2
Alcoa, Tenn., U.S., 7,734 . . . . .348/P3
Alcobendas, Sp. . . . . .94//Inset II

Alcolu, S.C., U.S., 375 . . . . .340/D3
Alcona, Mich., U.S., 40 . . . . .294/F5
Alcona, Mich., U.S., *county*, 11,719 . . . . . . .294/F5
Alcorcón, Sp., 153,100 . . . . .94/E2, Inset II
Alcorn, Miss., U.S., 1,212/ 300/A4
Alcorn, Miss., U.S., *county*, 34,558 . . . . . . .300/D1
Alcova, Wyo., U.S. 366/C2
Alcoy, Sp. 94/F3
Alda, Nebr., U.S., 652 . . . . .308/E3
Aldabra, Sey., *islands* 163/A2
Aldan, Russ. 104/H4
Aldan, Russ., *river* 104/H4
Aldborough, Eng., U.K. 66/H5
Aldeburgh, Eng., U.K., 2,654 . . . . .70/H2
Alden, Iowa, U.S., 904 . . . . .274/H2
Alden, Kans., U.S., 168 . . . . .276/D3
Alden, Mich., U.S., 150 . . . . .294/D5
Alden, Minn., U.S., 652 . . . . .298/D7
Alden, N.Y., U.S., 2,666 . . . . .320/E5
Alden, Okla., U.S. .330/D3
Alden Bridge, La., U.S., 40 . . . . .282/B1
Alder, Mont., U.S., 116 . . . . .306/D4
Alder, Wash., U.S., 150 . . . . .358/C4
Alder Creek, N.Y., U.S., 212/ 320/L4
Alderdale, Wash., U.S. 358/F4
Alder Flats, Alta., Can., 133 . . . . .212//C5
Alderley Edge, Eng., U.K., 5,280 . . . . .66/D6
Alderley Edge, Eng., U.K., 5,280 . . . . .68/C3
Aldermaston, Eng., U.K. 70/B4
Alderminster, Eng., U.K. 70/A2
Alderney, Fr., *department* . . . . .60//Inset II
Alderney, U.K., *island* 73/J4
Aldershot, Eng., U.K., 51,356 . . . . .70/C4
Alderson, Okla., U.S., 261 . . . . .330/G3
Alderson, W. Va., U.S., 1,091 . . . . .360/C3
Alder Sprs., Calif., U.S. 246/C3
Alderwood Manor, (Alderwood Manor-Bothell North),
  Wash., U.S., 15,329 . . . . .358/A4
Aldford, Eng., U.K. .68/B3
Aldine, N.J., U.S., 150 . . . . .314/C4
Aldine, Tex., U.S., 13,979 . . . . .346/B6
Aldingham, Eng., U.K. 66/B4
Aldino, Md., U.S., 375 . . . . .288/K1
Aldora, Ga., U.S., 98 . . . . .260/C5
Aldrich, Minn., U.S., 53 . . . . .298/C4
Aldrich, Mo., U.S., 75 . . . . .302/C4
Aldridge, Eng., U.K., 16,862 . . . . .68/D4
Aldwincle, Eng., U.K. 70/C2
Alean, Eng., U.K. 66/C2
Aledo, Ill., U.S., 3,613 . . . . .266/C3
Aledo, Tex., U.S., 1,726 . . . . .346/L3
Aleg, Maur. 147/B3
Alegres, N. Mex., U.S., *mountain* 317/B3
Aleknagik, Alaska, U.S., 221 . . . . .240/D3
Alençon, Fr. 88/C2
Alenuihaha, Hawaii, U.S., *channel* 262/D6
Alert, Can. 193/A15
Alert, Nun., Can. 208/Q1
Alès, Fr. 88/D4
Alessandria, It. 95/B1
Ålesund, Nor. 80/B3
Aleutian, Alaska, U.S., *islands* . . . . . .240/A4, Inset
Alewa Hts., Hawaii, U.S. 262/F2
Alex, Okla., U.S., 635 . . . . .330/E3
Alexander, Antar., *island* 192/B11
Alexander, Man., Can. 215/A4
Alexander, Alaska, U.S., *archipelago* 240/H3
Alexander, Ark., U.S., 614 . . . . .244/C3
Alexander, Ga., U.S., 125 . . . . .260/H5
Alexander, Ill., U.S., *county*, 9,590 . . . . . . .266/D6
Alexander, Iowa, U.S., 165 . . . . .274/H2
Alexander, Kans., U.S., 75 . . . . .276/C3
Alexander, Maine, U.S., 514 . . . . .286/E3
Alexander, N.Y., U.S., 481 . . . . .320/E5
Alexander, N.C., U.S., *county*, 33,603 . . . . .322/C3
Alexander, N. Dak., U.S., 217 . . . . .326/B2
Alexander, W. Va., U.S., 40 . . . . .360/F3
Alexander City, Ala., U.S., 15,008 . . . . .238/D3
Alexander Graham Bell Natl. Hist. Park,
  N.S., Can. 221/G1
Alexander Mills, N.C., U.S. 322/B4
Alexandra, N.Z. 171/A4
Alexandra, Ont., Can., 3,369 . . . . .223/L2
Alexandria, Egy., 3,339,076 . . . . .144/A1
Alexandria, Rom. .101/C4
Alexandria, Ind., U.S., 6,260 . . . . .270/E4
Alexandria, Ky., U.S., 8,286 . . . . .280/F2
Alexandria, La., U.S., 46,342, (126,337 *metro.*) .282/E4
Alexandria, Minn., U.S., 8,820 . . . . .298/B5
Alexandria, Mo., U.S., 216 . . . . .302/E1
Alexandria, N.H., U.S., 1,329 . . . . .312/C4
Alexandria, Ohio, U.S., 85 . . . . .328/E5
Alexandria, Penn., U.S., 401 . . . . .336/E4
Alexandria, S. Dak., U.S., 563 . . . . .342/H4
Alexandria, Tenn., U.S., 814 . . . . .344//J2
Alexandria, Va., U.S., 128,283 . . . . .354//J3, M2
Alexandria Bay, N.Y., U.S., 1,088 . . . . .320/K2
Alexandroupolis, Gr. 100/C1
Alexis, Ill., U.S., 863 . . . . .266/C2
Alexis Creek, Br. Col., Can., 162 . . . . .214/L5
Alfalfa, Okla., U.S., 40 . . . . .330/D2
Alfalfa, Okla., U.S., *county*, 6,105 . . . . .334/E3
Alfalfa, Oreg., U.S., 90 . . . . .334/E4
Al Fallujah, Iraq 130/B2
Al Fashir, Sudan, 141,884 . . . . .144/B2
Al Fayyum, Egy., 261,000 . . . . .144/B2
Alfios, Gr., *river* 66//J6
Alford, Eng., U.K., 2,989 . . . . .68/H3
Alford, Eng., U.K., 2,989 . . . . .68/H3
Alford, Scot., U.K., 1,925 . . . . .62/L4
Alford, Fla., U.S., 466 . . . . .256/C1
Alford, Mass., U.S., 399 . . . . .292/A4
Alfordsville, Ind., U.S., 112 . . . . .270/C7
Alfred, Ont., Can., 1,348 . . . . .223/L2
Alfred, Maine, U.S., 2,497 . . . . .286/B5
Alfred, N. Dak., U.S. 326/G3
Alfreton, Eng., U.K., 22,822 . . . . .68/E3
Al Fuhayhil, Kuw. .136/C2
Al Fujayrah, U.A.E. 136/C2
Algarrobo, Chile .190/Inset
Algarve, Port., *region* 93/A4
Algeciras, Sp., 101,468 . . . . .94/D4
Alger, Mich., U.S., *county*, 9,862 . . . . .294/C3
Alger, Ohio, U.S., 888 . . . . .328/C4
Algeria, *nation* 140
Al Ghaydah, Yemen 137/C1
Algiers, Alg., *capital*, 1,507,241,
  (1,904,499 *metro.*) 146/B1
Algoa, Iowa, U.S., 900 . . . . .346/B7
Algodones, N. Mex., U.S., 688 . . . . .317/D2
Algoma, Ont., Can., *county* 223/B1
Algoma, Ont., Can., *county* 223/B1
Algoma, Ida., U.S. .264/A1
Algoma, Miss., U.S., 508 . . . . .300/C1
Algoma, Oreg., U.S. 334/E5
Algoma, Wisc., U.S., 3,357 . . . . .364/F4
Algoma, Iowa, U.S., 5,741 . . . . .274/F1
Algona, Wash., U.S., 2,460 . . . . .358/C2

Algonac, Mich., U.S., 4,613 . . . . .294/G7
Algonquin, Ill., U.S., 23,276 . . . . .266/A5
Algonquin Prov. Park, Ont., Can. 223/G2
Algonquin St. For., Conn., U.S. 253/C2
Algood, Tenn., U.S., 2,942 . . . . .344/L2
Al Hadithah, Iraq 130/B2
Al Ha'it, Sa. Arab. 136/B1
Alhambra, Calif., U.S., 85,804 . . . . .246/C9
Alhambra, Ill., U.S., 630 . . . . .266/B3
Al Hasakah, Syria, 119,798, (143,844 metro.) .134/B1
Al Hawtah, Yemen 137/A2
Al Hazm, Yemen 137/A1
Al Hillah, Iraq .130/B2
Al Hillah, Sa. Arab. 136/B2
Al Hirmil, Leb. .134/B1
Al Hoceima, Mor. 147/D1
Al Hudaydah, Yemen, (246,068 metro.) 137/A2
Al Hufuf, Sa. Arab. 136/C1
Ali Adde, Dji. 156/C2
Aliakmon, Gr., river 100/B1
Alibates Flint Quarries Natl. Mon., Tex., U.S. .346/F9
Ali Bayramli, Azer. 103/C3
Alibori, Ben., river 151/B2
Alicante, Sp., 284,580 . . . . .94/F3
Alicante, Sp., province 94/F3
Alice, S. Afr. 162/C3
Alice, N. Dak., U.S. 326/H3
Alice, Tex., U.S., 19,010 . . . . .346/K8
Alice Arm, Br. Col., Can. 214/H3
Alice Sprs., N.T., Austl. 170/C2
Alice Town, Bah. 207/B2
Aliceville, Ala., U.S., 2,567 . . . . .238/A2
Aliceville, Kans., U.S., 60 . . . . .276/G3
Aliceville, Miss., U.S., lake 300/D2
Ali Chuk, Ariz., U.S., 450 . . . . .242/C6
Alicia, Ark., U.S., 145 . . . . .244/D2
Alida, Minn., U.S. 298/B3
Aligarh, India .128/C3
Alika Cone, Hawaii, U.S., mountain 262/G6
Alima, Congo, river 155/D4
Aline, Okla., U.S., 214 . . . . .330/D1
Aliquippa, Penn., U.S., 11,734 . . . . .336/A4
Ali Sabih, Dji. .156/C2
Al Ismailiyah, Egy. 144/B1
Aliso Viejo, Calif., U.S., 40,166 . . . . .246/E11
Aliwal North, S. Afr. 162/C3
Alix, Alta., Can., 825 . . . . .212//D5
Alix, Ark., U.S., 212/ 244/B2
Al Jafr, Jor. 134/B2
Al Jaghbub, Lib. 145/D2
Al Jahrah, Kuw., 111,222 . . . . .136/B2
Al Jawf, Lib. 145/D3
Al Jawf, Sa. Arab. 136/A1
Al Jawf, Sa. Arab., emirate 136/A1
Al Jazirah, Syria, region 134/B1
Al Jubayl, Sa. Arab. 136/C1
Al Jumayliyah, Qatar 137/C2
Al Junaynah, Sudan 145/C2
Alkabo, N. Dak., U.S. 326/B1
Alkali Lake, Oreg., U.S. 334/G5
Al Karak, Jor. 134/A2
Al Karak, Jor., governorate 134/A2
Alkborough, Eng., U.K. 66/G5
Al Khaluf, Oman 137/C2
Alkham, Eng., U.K. 70/G4
Al Kharijah, Egy. 144/B2
Al Kharj, Sa. Arab. 136/B1
Al Khawr, Qatar 137/D2
Al Khiran, Kuw. 136/C3
Al Khums, Lib. .145/B1
Al Khurmah, Sa. Arab. 136/B2
Alkmaar, Neth. .84/B2
Al Kut, Iraq 130/C2
Al Ladhiqiyah, (Latakia), Syria, 311,784,
    (357,562 metro.) 134/A2
Allagash, Maine, U.S., 277 . . . . .286/C1
Allagash Wilderness Waterway, Maine, U.S. . .286/C2
Allahabad, India, 990,298, (1,049,579 metro.) .128/D3
Allakaket, Alaska, U.S., 97 . . . . .240/E1
Allamakee, Iowa, U.S., county, 14,675 . . . . .274/M1
Allamoore, Tex., U.S. 346/D4
Allamuchy, N.J., U.S., 3,877 . . . . .314/D2
Allanton, Scot., U.K., 1,251 . . . . .62/M7
Allardt, Tenn., U.S., 642 . . . . .344/M2
Allardville, N.B., Can., 463 . . . . .217/D1
Allatoona, Ga., U.S., lake 260/C3
Alleene, Ark., U.S., 80 . . . . .244/A4
Allegan, Mich., U.S., 4,838 . . . . .294/D7
Allegan, Mich., U.S., county, 105,665 . . . . . .294/C7
Allegany, Md., U.S., county, 74,930 . . . . . . .288/A1, D3
Allegany, N.Y., U.S., 1,883 . . . . .320/F6
Allegany, N.Y., U.S., county, 49,927 . . . . . . .320/F6
Allegany, Oreg., U.S., 212/ 334/B4
Allegany Ind. Res., N.Y., U.S. 320/D6
Allegany St. Park, N.Y., U.S. 320/D6
Alleghany, N.C., U.S., county, 10,677 . . . . . .322/C2
Alleghany, Va., U.S., 40 . . . . .354/C5
Alleghany, Va., U.S., county, 12,926 . . . . . . .354/C5
Allegheny, Penn., U.S., county, 1,281,666 . . .336/A5, E7
Allegheny, Penn., U.S., reservoir 336/D2
Allegheny, Penn., U.S., river 336/B3, D7
Allegheny, Va., U.S., mountains 354/C4
Allegheny, W. Va., U.S., mountains 360/G4
Allegheny Front, Md., U.S., ridge 288/B4
Allegheny Natl. For., Penn., U.S. 336/C2
Allegheny Natl. Rec. Area, Penn., U.S. 336/D2
Allegheny Portage Railroad Natl. Hist. Site,
    Penn., U.S. 336/D5
Allegre, Ky., U.S., 100 . . . . .280/C4
Alleman, Iowa, U.S., 439 . . . . .274/G4
Allen, Ire., lake .76/B3
Allen, Ind., U.S., county, 331,849 . . . . .270/C4
Allen, Kans., U.S., 211 . . . . .276/F3
Allen, Kans., U.S., county, 14,385 . . . . .276/G4
Allen, Ky., U.S., 150 . . . . .280/H3
Allen, Ky., U.S., county, 17,800 . . . . .280/B4
Allen, La., U.S., parish 25,440 . . . . .282/C3
Allen, Md., U.S., 212/ 288/M6
Allen, Mich., U.S., 225 . . . . .294/E8
Allen, Nebr., U.S., 411 . . . . .308/H1
Allen, Ohio, U.S., county, 108,473 . . . . .328/B4
Allen, Okla., U.S., 951 . . . . .330/F3
Allen, S. Dak., U.S., 419 . . . . .342/D4
Allen, Tex., U.S., 43,554 . . . . .346/C8
Allendale, Ill., U.S., 528 . . . . .266/F5
Allendale, Mich., U.S., 11,555 . . . . .294/D7
Allendale, Mo., U.S., 54 . . . . .302/F1
Allendale, N.J., U.S., 6,699 . . . . .314/B1, E1
Allendale, S.C., U.S., 4,052 . . . . .340/C3
Allendale, S.C., U.S., county, 11,211 . . . . . . .340/C4
Allendale, Wyo., U.S. 366/C2
Allenford, Ont., Can. 223/B2
Allenheads, Eng., U.K. 66/D3
Allenhurst, Ga., U.S., 788 . . . . .260/D4
Allenhurst, N.J., U.S., 718 . . . . .314/F3
Allen Park, Mich., U.S., 29,376 . . . . .294/A7
Allenport, Penn., U.S., 549 . . . . .336/B5
Allens Mills, Penn., U.S., 275 . . . . .286/B4
Allenspark, Colo., U.S., 496 . . . . .250/E1
Allensville, Ky., U.S., 189 . . . . .280/C4
Allensville, Ohio, U.S., 100 . . . . .328/E7

Allensville, Penn., U.S., 500 . . . . .336/F4
Allenton, R.I., U.S., 1,400 . . . . .339/D4
Allenton, Wisc., U.S., 850 . . . . .364/E5
Allentown, Fla., U.S., 40 . . . . .256/A1
Allentown, Ga., U.S., 287 . . . . .260/E6
Allentown, N.J., U.S., 1,882 . . . . .314/D3
Allentown, Penn., U.S., 106,632,
    (637,958 metro.) 336/L4
Allenville, Ill., U.S., 154 . . . . .266/E4
Allenville, Mo., U.S., 104 . . . . .302/G4
Allerton, Ill., U.S., 293 . . . . .266/F4
Allerton, Iowa, U.S., 559 . . . . .274/H6
Allgood, Ala., U.S., 629 . . . . .238/C2
Allgreave, Eng., U.K. 68/C3
Allhallows, Eng., U.K. 70/F4
Alliance, Alta., Can., 171 . . . . .212//E5
Alliance, Nebr., U.S., 8,959 . . . . .308/B1
Alliance, N.C., U.S., 781 . . . . .322/M4
Alliance, Ohio, U.S., 23,253 . . . . .328/H4
Allier, Fr., department 88/C3
Allier, Fr., river .88/C3
Alligator, Miss., U.S., 220 . . . . .300/B1
Alligator, N.C., U.S., lake 322/N3
Alligator, N.C., U.S., river 322/N3
Alligator Pond, Jam. 206/B3
Alligator River N.W.R., N.C., U.S. 322/P3
Allington, Eng., U.K. 56/
Allison, Colo., U.S., 125 . . . . .250/C4
Allison, Iowa, U.S., 1,006 . . . . .274//J2
Allison, N. Mex., U.S., 125 . . . . .317/B2
Allison, Tex., U.S., 150 . . . . .346/H9
Allison Gap, Va., U.S., 900 . . . . .354/F2
Alloa, Scot., U.K., 18,989 . . . . .62/J6
Allonby, Eng., U.K. 66/B3
Allons, Tenn., U.S., 125 . . . . .344/L2
Allouez, Mich., U.S., 225 . . . . .294/A2
Allouez, Wisc., U.S., 15,443 . . . . .364/E4
Alloway, N.J., U.S., 2,774 . . . . .314/C4
Allport, Ark., U.S., 127 . . . . .244/D3
Allred, Tex., U.S., 70 . . . . .346/F3
Allsbrook, S.C., U.S., 250 . . . . .340/F2
Alluvial City, La., U.S., 300 . . . . .282/K7
Allyn, (Allyn-Grapeview), Wash., U.S., 2,004 . .358/C2
Alma, N.B., Can., 290 . . . . .217/E3
Alma, Que., Can., 25,918 . . . . .225/B4
Alma, Que., Can., 25,918 . . . . .226/B4
Alma, Ala., U.S., 250 . . . . .238/B4
Alma, Ark., U.S., 4,160 . . . . .244/A2
Alma, Colo., U.S., 179 . . . . .250/D2
Alma, Ga., U.S., 3,236 . . . . .260/G8
Alma, Ill., U.S., 386 . . . . .266/E5
Alma, Mich., U.S., 9,275 . . . . .294/E6
Alma, Mo., U.S., 399 . . . . .302/C2
Alma, Nebr., U.S., 1,214 . . . . .308/E3
Alma, N. Mex., U.S., 60 . . . . .317/B4
Alma, Tex., U.S., 302 . . . . .346/M4
Alma, W. Va., U.S., 60 . . . . .360/E2
Alma, Wisc., U.S., 942 . . . . .364/B4
Alma Ctr., Wisc., U.S., 446 . . . . .364/C4
Almada, Port. 93/A3
Almadén, Sp. 94/D3
Al Mafraq, Jor. .134/B1
Al Mafraq, Jor., governorate 134/C1
Al Mahallah al Kubra, Egy., 395,000 . . . . . . .144/B1
Al Mahbas, W. Sah. 147/C1
Al Mamtalah, Bahr. 137/B2
Almanor, Calif., U.S. 246/D2
Almanor, Calif., U.S., lake 246/D2
Almansa, Sp. 94/F3
Al Mansurah, Egy., 369,000 . . . . .144/B1
Al Marj, Lib. 145/D1
Almelo, Neth. 84/D2
Almena, Kans., U.S., 469 . . . . .276/C2
Almena, Wisc., U.S., 720 . . . . .364/A3
Almendra, Sp., reservoir 94/C2
Almendralejo, Sp. 94/C3
Almería, Sp., 166,328 . . . . .94/E4
Almería, Sp., province 94/E4
Almena, Nebr., U.S. 308/E2
Al Minya, Egy., 201,000 . . . . .144/B2
Almira, Wash., U.S., 302 . . . . .358/G2
Almirante, Pan. .203/A2
Almo, Ida., U.S., 40 . . . . .264/D7
Almo, Ky., U.S., 225 . . . . .280/B4
Almon, Ga., U.S., 1,000 . . . . .260/D4
Almond, Ark., U.S., 50 . . . . .244/D2
Almond, N.Y., U.S., 461 . . . . .320/F6
Almond, N.C., U.S. 322/C6
Almond, Wisc., U.S., 459 . . . . .364/D4
Almont, Colo., U.S. 250/D3
Almont, Mich., U.S., 2,803 . . . . .294/F7
Almont, N. Dak., U.S., 89 . . . . .326/D3
Almonte, Ont., Can., 4,659 . . . . .223//J2
Almora, Minn., U.S., 50 . . . . .298/B4
Almota, Wash., U.S. 358/H3
Al Mudawwarah, Jor. 134/B3
Al Muharraq, Bahr., island 137/B1
Al Mukalla, Yemen 137/B2
Al Mukha, (Mocha), Yemen 137/A2
Almy, Wyo., U.S., 125 . . . . .366/A3
Almyra, Ark., U.S., 319 . . . . .244/D3
Alna, Maine, U.S., 675 . . . . .286/C4
Alness, Scot., U.K., 5,186 . . . . .62/H3
Alnham, Eng., U.K. 66/C2
Alnwick, Eng., U.K., 7,419 . . . . .66/E2
Aloe, Tex., U.S., 850 . . . . .346/L7
Aloha, Mich., U.S., 175 . . . . .294/E4
Aloha, Oreg., U.S., 41,741 . . . . .334/A2
Alonsa, Man., Can. 215/B4
Alor, Indon., island 122/D2
Alor Setar, Malay., 124,412, (164,444 metro.) .121/A1
Alorton, Ill., U.S., 2,749 . . . . .266/A3
Alotau, P.N.G. .172/B3
Aloys, Nebr., U.S., 50 . . . . .308/H2
Alpaugh, Calif., U.S., 761 . . . . .246/F7
Alpena, Ark., U.S., 371 . . . . .244/B1
Alpena, Mich., U.S., 11,304 . . . . .294/F4
Alpena, Mich., U.S., county, 31,314 . . . . . . .294/F4
Alpena, S. Dak., U.S., 265 . . . . .342/G3
Alpes-de-Haute-Provence, Fr., department . .88/D4
Alpes-Maritimes, Fr., department 88/D4
Alpha, Ill., U.S., 726 . . . . .266/C2
Alpha, Mich., U.S., 198 . . . . .294/A3
Alpha, Minn., U.S., 125 . . . . .298/C7
Alpha, N.J., U.S., 2,482 . . . . .314/C2
Alpharetta, Ga., U.S., 34,854 . . . . .260//C3, J1
Alpine, Ariz., U.S. 242/F4
Alpine, Ark., U.S., 80 . . . . .244/B3
Alpine, Calif., U.S., county, 1,208 . . . . .246/F4
Alpine, Calif., U.S., 350 . . . . .270/F5
Alpine, Ky., U.S., 80 . . . . .280/F4
Alpine, N.J., U.S., 2,183 . . . . .314/C1
Alpine, N.Y., U.S., 275 . . . . .320/H6
Alpine, Tenn., U.S., 212/ 344/L2
Alpine, Tex., U.S., 5,786 . . . . .346/E5
Alpine, Utah, U.S., 7,146 . . . . .350/C3

Alpine, Wyo., U.S., 550 . . . . .366/A2
Alps, Aus., range 91/B3
Alps, Fr., range .88/D4
Alps, It., mountains 95/A1, B1
Alps, Liech., range 90/A2
Alps, Switz., mountains 90/B2
Al Qadarif, Sudan, 191,164 . . . . .145/C2
Al Qamishli, Syria, 144,286, (188,825 metro.) .134/B1
Al Qaryah ash Sharqiyah, Lib. 145/B1
Al Qatranah, Jor. 134/B2
Al Qayyarah, Iraq 130/B1
Al Qubbayat, Leb. 134/B1
Alquina, Ind., U.S., 125 . . . . .270/F5
Al Qunaytirah, Syria 134/A3
Al Qunfudhah, Sa. Arab. 136/A2
Al Qurayyat, Sa. Arab. 136/A1
Alrewas, Eng., U.K., 2,907 . . . . .68/D4
Alsace, Fr., region 88/D2
Alsager, Eng., U.K., 13,435 . . . . .68/C3
Alsask, Sask., Can., 178 . . . . .227/A9
Alsatia, La., U.S., 70 . . . . .282/C1
Alsea, Oreg., U.S., 125 . . . . .334/C3
Alsen, La., U.S., 950 . . . . .282/G5
Alsen, N. Dak., U.S., 68 . . . . .326/G1
Alsey, Ill., U.S., 246 . . . . .266/C4
Alsip, Ill., U.S., 19,725 . . . . .266/B6
Alsted Ctr., N.H., U.S., 60 . . . . .312/B5
Alston, Ga., U.S., 159 . . . . .260/G7
Alstown, Wash., U.S. 358/F2
Alta, Nor. 80/E1
Alta, Iowa, U.S., 1,865 . . . . .274/D2
Alta, Utah, U.S., 370 . . . . .350/C3
Altadena, Calif., U.S., 42,610 . . . . .246/C9
Altair, Tex., U.S., 125 . . . . .346/M6
Altamaha, Ga., U.S., river 260/G8
Altamahaw, (Altamahaw-Ossipee),
    N.C., U.S., 996 . . . . .322/F2
Altamira, Braz., 24,846, (120,556 metro.) . . .188/C2
Altamira, Chile .190/C3
Altamont, Ill., U.S., 2,283 . . . . .266/E4
Altamont, Kans., U.S., 1,092 . . . . .276/G4
Altamont, Mo., U.S., 218 . . . . .302/C2
Altamont, N.Y., U.S., 1,737 . . . . .320/N5
Altamont, Oreg., U.S., 19,603 . . . . .334/E5
Altamont, S. Dak., U.S. 342//J3
Altamont, Tenn., U.S., 1,136 . . . . .344/K4
Altamont, Utah, U.S., 178 . . . . .350/D3
Altamont, Wyo., U.S. 366/A3
Altamonte Sprs., Fla., U.S., 41,212/ 256/C4, G3
Altario, Alta., Can. 212//E5
Altarnun, Eng., U.K. 73/B2
Alta Vista, Iowa, U.S., 286 . . . . .274/K1
Alta Vista, Kans., U.S., 442 . . . . .276/F3
Altavista, Va., U.S., 3,425 . . . . .354/E5
Altay, China 119/B1
Altay, China, mountains 119/B1
Altay, Mong. 118/B2
Altay, Mong., mountains 118/B2
Altay, Russ., region 104/F4
Altdorf, Switz. 90/C2
Altenburg, Mo., U.S., 309 . . . . .302/G4
Altha, Fla., U.S., 506 . . . . .256/C1
Altheimer, Ark., U.S., 1,192 . . . . .244/D3
Altiplano, Bol., plateau 186/A3
Altmar, N.Y., U.S., 351 . . . . .320/K3
Altnaharra, Scot., U.K. 62/H2
Alto, Ga., U.S., 876 . . . . .260/D3
Alto, La., U.S., 80 . . . . .282/F2
Alto, Mich., U.S., 300 . . . . .294/D7
Alto, N. Mex., U.S., 80 . . . . .317/E4
Alto, Tex., U.S., 1,190 . . . . .346/N4
Alto, Wisc., U.S., 250 . . . . .364/E5
Alton, Eng., U.K., 16,005 . . . . .68/D4
Alton, Eng., U.K., 16,005 . . . . .70/C4
Alton, Fla., U.S., 80 . . . . .256/E1
Alton, Ill., U.S., 30,496 . . . . .266/A3, C5
Alton, Ind., U.S., 53 . . . . .270/D8
Alton, Iowa, U.S., 1,095 . . . . .274/B2
Alton, Kans., U.S., 117 . . . . .276/D2
Alton, Ky., U.S., 225 . . . . .280/F2
Alton, Mo., U.S., 668 . . . . .302/E5
Alton, N.H., U.S., 4,502 . . . . .312/D5
Alton, N.Y., U.S., 475 . . . . .320/H4
Alton, R.I., U.S., 350 . . . . .339/B5
Alton, Tex., U.S., 4,384 . . . . .346/K9
Alton, Utah, U.S., 134 . . . . .350/B6
Altona, Vic., Austl. . . . . .170/Inset V
Altona, Man., Can., 3,434 . . . . .215/C4
Altona, Ill., U.S., 570 . . . . .266/C2
Altona, Ind., U.S., 198 . . . . .270/F2
Altona, Nebr., U.S., 40 . . . . .308/G1
Altona, N.Y., U.S., 1,056 . . . . .320/P1
Alton Bay, N.H., U.S., 400 . . . . .312/D5
Altoona, Ala., U.S., 984 . . . . .238/C1
Altoona, Fla., U.S., 88 . . . . .256/C3
Altoona, Iowa, U.S., 10,345 . . . . .274/H4
Altoona, Kans., U.S., 485 . . . . .276/G4
Altoona, Penn., U.S., 49,523, (129,144 metro.) .336/E4
Altoona, Wash., U.S. 358/B3
Altoona, Wisc., U.S., 6,698 . . . . .364/B4
Alto Paraguay, Para., department 187/C2
Alto Paraná, Para., department 187/E4
Alto Pass, Ill., U.S., 388 . . . . .266/D6
Altrincham, Eng., U.K., 40,042 . . . . .66/D6
Altrincham, Eng., U.K., 40,042 . . . . .68/C3
Altun Shan, China, mountains 119/B2
Altura, Minn., U.S., 417 . . . . .298/F6
Alturas, Calif., U.S., 2,892 . . . . .246/E1
Altus, Ark., U.S., 817 . . . . .244/B2
Altus, Okla., U.S., 21,447 . . . . .330/C3
Al Ubayyid, Sudan, 229,425 . . . . .145/C2
Alüksne, Lat. 82/D2
Alum, Ohio, U.S., river 328/E10
Alum Bridge, W. Va., U.S., 100 . . . . .360/E2
Alum Creek, W. Va., U.S., 1,839 . . . . .360/C4
Alum Rock, Calif., U.S., 13,479 . . . . .246/K3
Al Uwaynat, Lib. 145/B2
Alva, Scot., U.K., 5,181 . . . . .62/J6
Alva, Fla., U.S., 2,182 . . . . .256/E5
Alva, Ky., U.S., 150 . . . . .280/D1
Alva, Okla., U.S., 5,288 . . . . .330/D1
Alva, Wyo., U.S. 366/D1
Alvarado, Minn., U.S., 371 . . . . .298/A2
Alvarado, Tex., U.S., 3,288 . . . . .346/L3
Alvaro Obregón, Mex. 200/Inset
Alvaston, Eng., U.K. 70/B1
Alvaton, Ga., U.S., 125 . . . . .260/B5
Alvaton, Ky., U.S., 375 . . . . .280/D4
Alvechurch, Eng., U.K., 3,317 . . . . .68/D5
Alverno, Mich., U.S., 225 . . . . .294/E4
Alves, Scot., U.K. 62/K3
Alvescot, Eng., U.K. 70/A3
Aveston, Eng., U.K., 2,525 . . . . .73/G1
Alvie, Scot., U.K. 62/J4
Alvin, Ill., U.S., 316 . . . . .266/F3
Alvin, Tex., U.S., 21,413 . . . . .346/R2
Alvin, Wisc., U.S. 364/E3
Alvinston, Ont., Can. 223/D3
Alvo, Nebr., U.S., 142 . . . . .308/H3
Alvon, W. Va., U.S., 50 . . . . .360/F5
Alvord, Iowa, U.S., 187 . . . . .274/B1

Alvord, Oreg., U.S., lake 334/H5
Alvord, Tex., U.S., 1,007 . . . . .346/L2
Alvordton, Ohio, U.S., 305 . . . . .328/B3
Alvwood, Minn., U.S. 298/C3
Al Wafrah, Kuw. 136/C3
Al Wajh, Sa. Arab. 136/A1
Al Wakrah, Qatar 137/D3
Alwen, Wales, U.K., reservoir 64/D1
Alyth, Scot., U.K., 2,301 . . . . .62/K5
Alytus, Lith. 82/C3
Alzada, Mont., U.S., 50 . . . . .306/M4
Al Zarqa', Jor., governorate 134/B1
Alzette, Lux., river 85/B2
Alzira, Sp. 94/F3
Amadjuak, Nun., Can., lake 208/G4
Amado, Ariz., U.S., 275 . . . . .242/D6
Amador, Calif., U.S., county, 35,100 . . . . . . .246/E4, L5
Amadora, Port., 175,872 . . . . .93/A3
Amador City, Calif., U.S., 196 . . . . .246/L6
Amagansett, N.Y., U.S., 1,067 . . . . .320/Q5
Amagasaki, Jap., 466,000 . . . . .114/B3
Amagon, Ark., U.S., 95 . . . . .244/D2
Amahai, Indon. .122/D2
Amakusa, Jap., islands 114/A3
Amalga, Utah, U.S., 427 . . . . .350/C2
Amalia, N. Mex., U.S., 100 . . . . .317/E1
Amambay, Para., department 187/E3
Amambay, Para., mountains 187/E3
Amami, Jap., island . . . . .114/Inset II
Amami, Jap., islands . . . . .114/Inset II
Amana, Iowa, U.S., 700 . . . . .274/L4
Amanda, Ohio, U.S., 707 . . . . .328/E6
Amanda Park, Wash., U.S., 100 . . . . .358/B2
Amapá, Braz., state 188/C1
Amapala, Hond. 202/B3
Amaranth, Man., Can. 215/B4
Amargosa, Calif., U.S., range 246//J6
Amargosa, Calif., U.S., river 246//J7
Amargosa Valley, Nev., U.S. 310/B3
Amarillo, Tex., U.S., 173,627, (217,858 metro.) .346/F9
Amasa, Mich., U.S., 212/ 294/A3
Amasia, Arm. 103/A2
Amasya, Tur. 133/C2
Amasya, Tur., province 133/C2
Amazon, Braz., basin 188/B2
Amazon, Braz., river 188/B2
Amazon, Col., river 184/C5
Amazon, Peru, river 185/C1
Amazonas, Braz., state 188/B2
Amazonas, Col., department 184/B5
Amazonas, Peru, department 185/B2
Amazonas, Ven., state 182/C3
Amazonia, Mo., U.S., 277 . . . . .302/B2
Ambato, Ecua., 124,166 . . . . .185/B3
Ambatolampy, Madag. 163/B2
Ambatondrazaka, Madag. 163/B2
Amber, Iowa, U.S., 125 . . . . .274/M3
Amber, Okla., U.S., 490 . . . . .330/E2
Amber, Wash., U.S. 358/H2
Amberg, Ger. 86/B4
Amberg, Wisc., U.S., 225 . . . . .364/F3
Ambergris, Bel., cay 201/C2
Ambergris, T.-C. Is., cay 207/D4
Amberley, Ont., Can. 223/B3
Amberley, Eng., U.K. 70/C5
Amberley, Ohio, U.S., 3,425 . . . . .328/B9
Ambia, Ind., U.S., 197 . . . . .270/D4
Ambino, E. Timor, province 122/A2
Amble, Eng., U.K., 5,639 . . . . .66/E2
Ambler, Alaska, U.S., 309 . . . . .240/D1
Ambler, Penn., U.S., 6,426 . . . . .336/L6
Ambleside, Eng., U.K., 2,905 . . . . .66/C4
Ambon, Indon. .122/D2
Ambositra, Madag. 163/B3
Amboy, Calif., U.S. 246/K8
Amboy, Ill., U.S., 2,561 . . . . .266/D2
Amboy, Ind., U.S., 360 . . . . .270/E3
Amboy, Minn., U.S., 575 . . . . .298/C7
Amboy, Wash., U.S., 2,085 . . . . .358/C4
Ambre, Madag., cape 163/B1
Ambre, Mauritius, island 163/C2
Ambridge, Penn., U.S., 7,769 . . . . .336/A4
Ambrose, Ga., U.S., 320 . . . . .260/F8
Ambrose, N. Dak., U.S. 326/B1
Ambrosia Lake, N. Mex., U.S. 317/C2
Ambrym, Van., island 173/C3
Amchitka, Alaska, U.S., island 240/Inset
Amcotts, Eng., U.K. 66/G5
Amdanga, India . . . . .128/Inset II
Ameca, Mex., 34,703, (56,681 metro.) 200/D3
Ameland, Neth., island 84/C1
Amelia, Fla., U.S., island 256/G1
Amelia, La., U.S., 2,423 . . . . .282/G7
Amelia, Nebr., U.S. 308/E1
Amelia, Ohio, U.S., 2,752 . . . . .328/B7
Amelia, Va., U.S., county, 11,400 . . . . .354/G6
Amelia City, Fla., U.S., 1,300 . . . . .256/G1
Amelia C.H., Va., U.S., 400 . . . . .354/H6
Amenia, N.Y., U.S., 1,115 . . . . .320/P7
Amenia, N. Dak., U.S., 89 . . . . .326/H2
American Canyon, Calif., U.S., 9,774 . . . . . . .246/J1
American Falls, Ida., U.S., 4,111 . . . . .264/E7
American Falls, Ida., U.S., reservoir 264/E7
American Fork, Utah, U.S., 21,941 . . . . .350/C3
American Highland, Antar., region 192/B1
American Samoa, U.S., dependency 161
Americus, Ga., U.S., 17,013 . . . . .260/C7
Americus, Kans., U.S., 938 . . . . .276/F3
Americus, Mo., U.S., 100 . . . . .302/E3
Amersfoort, Neth., 124,755, (153,373 metro.) .84/C2
Amersham, Eng., U.K., 21,711 . . . . .68/F6
Amersham, Eng., U.K., 21,711 . . . . .70/C3
Amery, Wisc., U.S., 2,845 . . . . .364/A3
Amery Ice Shelf, Antar., glacier 192/C18
Ames, Iowa, U.S., 50,731 . . . . .274/G3
Ames, Kans., U.S., 50 . . . . .276/E2
Ames, N.Y., U.S., 173 . . . . .320/M5
Ames, Okla., U.S., 199 . . . . .330/D1
Ames, Tex., U.S., 1,079 . . . . .346/C5, P5
Amesbury, Eng., U.K., 6,333 . . . . .73//J2
Amesbury, Mass., U.S., 16,450 . . . . .292/L1
Ameville, Ohio, U.S., 184 . . . . .328/G7
Amhara, Eth., state 156/B2
Amherst, N.S., Can., 9,470 . . . . .221/C2
Amherst, Colo., U.S., 70 . . . . .221//G1
Amherst, Maine, U.S., 230 . . . . .286/D4
Amherst, Mass., U.S., 34,874 . . . . .292/D3
Amherst, Nebr., U.S., 277 . . . . .308/E3
Amherst, N.H., U.S., 10,769 . . . . .312/C6
Amherst, N.Y., U.S., 13,212/ 320/D5
Amherst, Ohio, U.S., 11,797 . . . . .328/F3
Amherst, S. Dak., U.S. 342/H2
Amherst, Tex., U.S. 346/F2
Amherst, Va., U.S., 2,251 . . . . .354/E5
Amherst, Va., U.S., county, 31,894 . . . . .354/E5
Amherst, Wisc., U.S., 964 . . . . .364/D4
Amherstburg, Ont., Can., 20,339 . . . . .223/B5
Amherstdale, W. Va., U.S., 1,785 . . . . .360/C5
Amherst Jct., Wisc., U.S., 305 . . . . .364/D4
Amidon, N. Dak., U.S. 326/B3
Amiens, Fr., 139,210, (160,815 metro.) 88/C2

Amindivi, India, *islands* 128/B6
Amirante, Sey., *islands* 163/B2
Amiret, Minn., U.S., 70 ....298/B6
Amisk, Alta., Can., 181 ....212/E5
Amisk, Sask., Can., *lake* 227/H6
Amistad, N. Mex., U.S. 317/G2
Amistad, Tex., U.S., *reservoir* 346/G6
Amistad Natl. Rec. Area, Tex., U.S. 346/G6
Amite, La., U.S., 4,110 ....282/J5
Amite, Miss., U.S., *county*, 13,599 ....300/B4
Amity, Ark., U.S., 762 ....244/B3
Amity, Ind., U.S., 250 ....270/E6
Amity, Mo., U.S., 70 ....302/B2
Amity, Oreg., U.S., 1,478 ....334/C2
Amityville, N.Y., U.S., 9,441 ....320/D2
Amlamé, Togo 151/B3
Amlia, Alaska, U.S., *island* 240/Inset
Amlwch, Wales, U.K., 3,519 ....64/C1
Amman, Jor., *capital*, 1,147,447 ....134/A2
Amman, Jor., *governorate* 134/B2
Ammanford, Wales, U.K., 12,106 ....64/D4
Ammassalik, Grld. 193/C2
Ammersee, Ger., *lake* 86/B4
Ammon, Ida., U.S., 6,187 ....264/F6
Ammon, N.C., U.S., 40 ....322/H5
Amo, Ind., U.S., 414 ....270/C5
Amoret, Mo., U.S., 211 ....302/B3
Amorita, Okla., U.S., 44 ....330/D1
Amory, Miss., U.S., 6,956 ....300/D2
Amos, Que., Can., 13,044 ....225/A4
Ampanihy, Madag. 163/A3
Ampara, Sri Lan. 126/C4
Ampleforth, Eng., U.K. 66/F4
Ampthill, Eng., U.K., 6,230 ....68/G5
Ampthill, Eng., U.K., 6,230 ....70/D2
Amqui, Que., Can., 6,473 ....226/J3
Amran, Yemen 137/A1
Amravati, India 128/C4
Amritsar, India, (1,011,327 *metro.*) 128/B2
Amsden, Ohio, U.S., 175 ....328/D3
Amsden, Vt., U.S., 175 ....352/B4
Amsterdam, Neth., *capital*, 734,000, (1,000,307 *metro.*) 84/B2
Amsterdam, Mo., U.S., 281 ....302/B3
Amsterdam, Mont., U.S., 727 ....306/E4
Amsterdam, N.Y., U.S., 18,355 ....320/N5
Amsterdam, Ohio, U.S., 568 ....328/J5
Amstetten, Aus. 91/D2
Am Timan, Chad 153/C2
Amu Darya, Afg., *river* 129/B1
Amu Darya, Taj., *river* 132/A2
Amu Darya, Turkm., *river* 132/D2
Amu Darya, Uzb., *river* 132/B2
Amund Ringnes, Nun., Can., *island* 208/J1
Amundsen, Antar., *sea* 192/B9
Amundsen, N.W. Terr., Can., *gulf* 208/C2
Amur, Russ., *river* 104/H4
Amy, Ark., U.S., 100 ....244/C4
Amy, Kans., U.S. 276/B3
Amyun, Leb. 134/A1
Anabar, Nauru 174/C1
Anaco, Ven. 182/D2
Anacoco, La., U.S., 866 ....282/C4
Anaconda, Mont., U.S., 9,417 ....306/K3
Anacortes, Wash., U.S., 14,557 ....358/C1
Anadarko, Okla., U.S., 6,645 ....330/D2
Anadyr', Russ. 104/J3
Anadyr', Russ., *gulf* 104/K3
Anagance, N.B., Can. 217/D3
Anaheim, Calif., U.S., 328,014 ....246/E10, H9
Anahim Lake, Br. Col., Can., 163 ....214/K5
Anahola, Hawaii, U.S., 1,932 ....262/D1
Anáhuac, Mex., 15,976, (18,524 *metro.*) 200/D3
Anahuac, Tex., U.S., 2,210 ....346/P6
Anaktuvuk Pass, Alaska, U.S., 282 ....240/E1
Ana María, Cuba, *gulf* 204/D2
Anambas, Indon., *islands* 122/B1
Anambra, Nig., *state* 152/D4
Anamoose, N. Dak., U.S., 282 ....326/E2
Anamosa, Iowa, U.S., 5,494 ....274/M3
Anandale, La., U.S., 100 ....282/E4
Anápolis, Braz., 160,520, (239,047 *metro.*) 188/D3
Añasco, P.R. 206/A2
Añasco, P.R., *beach* 206/A2
Anatolia, Tur., *region* 133/B2
Anatom, Van., *island* 173/C5
Anatone, Wash., U.S., 40 ....358/H3
Anawalt, W. Va., U.S., 272 ....360/D6
Anceney, Mont., U.S. 306/E4
Ancho, N. Mex., U.S. 317/E4
Ancho, Ill., U.S., 175 ....266/E3
Anchorage, U.S. 193/C11
Anchorage, Alaska, U.S., 260,283, (260,283 *metro.*) 240/F2
Anchorage, Ky., U.S., 2,264 ....280/B4
Anchor Bay, Calif., U.S., 80 ....246/B4
Anchor Pt., Alaska, U.S., 1,845 ....240/E3
Anchorville, Mich., U.S., 3,212/ 294/G7
Ancient Oaks, Penn., U.S., 3,161 ....336/K4
Ancona, It. 95/C4
Ancud, Chile 190/B6
An Daimh, Scot., U.K., *lake* 62/C5
Andale, Kans., U.S., 766 ....276/D4, E4
Andalusia, Sp., *autonomous community* 94/D4
Andalusia, Ala., U.S., 8,794 ....238/C4
Andalusia, Ill., U.S., 1,050 ....266/C2
Andaman, India, *islands* 128/F6
Andaman, Mya., *sea* 125/B3
Andaman and Nicobar Islands, India, *territory* 128/F6
Anderlecht, Belg. 85/C2
Anderson, N.W. Terr., Can., *river* 208/C3
Anderson, Ala., U.S., 354 ....238/B1
Anderson, Alaska, U.S., 367 ....240/F2
Anderson, Calif., U.S., 9,022 ....246/C2
Anderson, Ind., U.S., 59,734 ....270/C6
Anderson, Iowa, U.S., 80 ....274/C6
Anderson, Kans., U.S., *county* 8,110 ....276/V3
Anderson, Ky., U.S., *county*, 19,111 ....280/E3
Anderson, Mo., U.S., 1,856 ....302/B5
Anderson, N.J., U.S., 500 ....314/D2
Anderson, S.C., U.S., 25,514 ....340/B2
Anderson, S.C., U.S., *county*, 165,740 ....340/B2
Anderson, Tenn., U.S., *county*, 71,330 ....344/N2
Anderson, Tex., U.S., 257 ....346/N5
Anderson, Tex., U.S., *county*, 55,109 ....346/N4
Anderson Mill, Tex., U.S. 346/Q2
Andersonville, Ga., U.S., 331 ....260/C7
Andersonville, Ind., U.S., 275 ....270/F6
Andersonville, Ohio, U.S., 800 ....328/D7
Andersonville Natl. Historic Site, Ga., U.S. 260/C7
Andes, Arg., *mountains* 191/A6-B1
Andes, Chile, *mountains* 190/B7, C4
Andes, Col., *range* 184/A4
Andes, Ecua., *mountains* 184/A4
Andes, Peru, *mountains* 185/B1, C3
Andes, Mont., U.S. 306/M2
Andes, N.Y., U.S., 289 ....320/M6
Andes, S. Dak., U.S., *lake* 342/G4
Andheri, India ....128/Inset I
Andhra Pradesh, India, *state* 128/C5
Andijon, Uzb., 323,900 ....132/D2

Andijon, Uzb., *province* 132/D2
Anding, Miss., U.S., 225 ....300/B3
Andoany, Madag. 163/B1
Andong, S. Kor., 188,443 ....116/C4
Andorra, *nation* 91
Andorra la Vella, And., *capital*, 20,787 ....93/B1
Andover, Eng., U.K., 34,647 ....70/B4
Andover, Conn., U.S., 3,036 ....253/F3
Andover, Ill., U.S., 594 ....266/C2
Andover, Iowa, U.S., 87 ....274/P4
Andover, Kans., U.S., 6,698 ....276/E4
Andover, Maine, U.S., 864 ....286/B4
Andover, Mass., U.S., 31,247 ....292/K2
Andover, Minn., U.S., 26,588 ....298/D5
Andover, N.H., U.S., 2,109 ....312/C5
Andover, N.J., U.S., *borough*, 658 ....314/D2
Andover, N.J., U.S., *township*, 6,033 ....314/D2
Andover, N.Y., U.S., 1,073 ....320/F6
Andover, Ohio, U.S., 1,269 ....328/J2
Andover, S. Dak., U.S., 99 ....342/H2
Andover, Vt., U.S., 496 ....352/B4
Andrade, Calif., U.S., 100 ....246/L10
Andreanof, Alaska, U.S., *islands* 240/Inset
Andreas, Cyp., *cape* 133/C1
Andreas, Eng., U.K. 66/B5
Andrew, Alta., Can., 485 ....212/D4
Andrew, Iowa, U.S., 460 ....274/N3
Andrew, La., U.S., 125 ....282/E6
Andrew, Mo., U.S., *county*, 16,492 ....302/B2
Andrew Johnson Natl. Hist. Site, Tenn., U.S. 344/R4
Andrews, Fla., U.S., *bay* 256/C1
Andrews, Ind., U.S., 1,290 ....270/E3
Andrews, Md., U.S., 70 ....288/K6
Andrews, N.C., U.S., 1,602 ....322/C8
Andrews, Oreg., U.S., 100 ....334/H5
Andrews, S.C., U.S., 3,068 ....340/E3
Andrews, Tex., U.S., 9,652 ....346/F3
Andrews, Tex., U.S., *county*, 13,004 ....346/F3
Andrewville, Del., U.S., 150 ....255/B5
Andrix, Colo., U.S. 250/G4
Andros, Bah., *island* 204/B1
Andros, Bah., *island* 207/A3
Andros, Gr., *island* 100/C3
Androscoggin, Maine, U.S., *county*, 103,793 ....286/B4
Androscoggin, Maine, U.S., *river* 286/A4
Androth, India, *island* 128/B6
Anegam, Ariz., U.S., 175 ....242/C5
Aného, Togo 151/B3
Anelghowhat, Van. 173/C5
Aneta, N. Dak., U.S., 284 ....326/H2
Anetan, Nauru 174/B1
Aneth, Utah, U.S., 598 ....350/E6
Aneto, Sp., *mountain* 94/G1
Angara, Russ., *river* 104/F4
Angarsk, Russ., 265,410, (270,750 *metro.*) 104/G4
Angaur, Palau, *island* 172/B4
Angel, Ven., *falls* 182/D2
Angela, Mont., U.S. 306/K3
Angeles, Phil., 263,971 ....120/B3
Angeles, Tex., U.S. 346/E4
Angeles Natl. For., Calif., U.S. 246/C8
Angeles Natl. For., Calif., U.S. 246/H8
Angel Fire, N. Mex., U.S., 1,048 ....317/E1
Angelica, N.Y., U.S., 903 ....320/E6
Angelica, Wisc., U.S., 150 ....364/E4
Angelina, Tex., U.S., *county*, 80,130 ....346/P4
Angelina Natl. For., Tex., U.S. 346/P4
Angels Camp, Calif., U.S., 3,004 ....246/E4
Angelus, Kans., U.S., 40 ....276/B2
Angermanälven, Swe., *river* 80/C2
Angers, Fr., 156,327, (226,843 *metro.*) 88/B3
Angie, La., U.S., 240 ....282/K5
Angier, N.C., U.S., 3,419 ....322/H3
Angikuni, Nun., Can., *lake* 208/H4
Angkor Thom, Camb., *ruins* 124/B2
Angkor Wat, Camb., *ruins* 124/B2
Angle, Wales, U.K. 64/A4
Angle, Utah, U.S. 350/C5
Angle Inlet, Minn., U.S. 298/B1
Anglesey, Wales, U.K., *island* 60/B3
Anglesey, Wales, U.K., *island* 64/C1
Angleton, Tex., U.S., 18,130 ....346/N6
Anglo Tignish, P.E.I., Can. 224/C1
Angoche, Moz. 161/C3
Angol, Chile 190/B5
Angola, *nation* 153
Angola, Ind., U.S., 7,344 ....270/G1
Angola, Kans., U.S. 276/C4
Angola, N.Y., U.S., 2,135 ....320/C5
Angola on the Lake, N.Y., U.S., 1,771 ....320/C5
Angoon, Alaska, U.S., 572 ....240/J3
Angora, Minn., U.S. 298/E3
Angora, Nebr., U.S. 308/A2
Angostura, S. Dak., U.S., *reservoir* 342/B4
Angoulême, Fr., 46,324, (103,746 *metro.*) 88/C4
Angra do Heroísmo, Port. ....93/Inset II
Anguilla, U.K., *dependency* 204/F3
Anguilla, Miss., U.S., 907 ....300/B3
Angus, Ont., Can., 9,722 ....223/F3
Angus, Scot., U.K., *unitary authority*, 108,400 ....62/K5
Angus, Minn., U.S., 40 ....298/A2
Angus, Nebr., U.S. 308/G3
Angus, N. Mex., U.S., 50 ....317/E4
Anholt, Den., *island* 79/C2
Anhui, China, *province* 119/E2
Aniak, Alaska, U.S., 572 ....240/D2
Aniakchak Natl. Mon. and Pres., Alaska, U.S. 240/D3
Anibare, Nauru 174/B2
Anibare, Nauru, *bay* 174/B2
Anié, Togo 151/B3
Animas, Colo., U.S., *river* 250/C4
Animas, N. Mex., U.S., 125 ....317/B6
Añisoc, Eq. Gui. 154/C3
Anita, Iowa, U.S., 1,049 ....274/E5
Anita, Penn., U.S., 550 ....336/D3
Anita Sta., Ariz., U.S. 242/C2
Aniwa, Wisc., U.S., 272 ....364/D3
Anjou, Que., Can., 38,015 ....226/I5
Anju, N. Kor. 116/A3
Ankang, China 119/D2
Ankara, Tur., *capital*, 3,203,362 ....133/C2
Ankara, Tur., *province* 133/C2
Ankaratra, Madag., *mountains* 163/B2
Ankeny, Iowa, U.S., 27,117 ....274/G4
Ankeny N.W.R., Oreg., U.S. 334/C3
Ankobra, Gha., *river* 150/A4
Anmoore, W. Va., U.S., 685 ....360/F2
Ann, Mass., U.S., *cape* 292/M2
Ann, Nauru, U.S., *cape* 174/B1
Anna, Ill., U.S., 5,136 ....266/D6
Anna, Ohio, U.S., 1,319 ....328/B5
Anna, Va., U.S., *lake* 354/H4
Annaba, Alg., 270,773 ....146/B1
An Nabatiyah at Tahta, Leb. 134/A2
An Nabk, Syria 134/A2
Anabella, Utah, U.S., 603 ....350/B5
An Nafud, Sa. Arab., *desert* 136/B1
An Najaf, Iraq 130/B2
Annalong, N. Ire., U.K., 1,937 ....65/F3
Annam, Viet., *mountains* 123/A2

Anna Maria, Fla., U.S., 1,814 ....256/F4
Annamoriah, W. Va., U.S., 90 ....360/D3
Annan, Scot., U.K., 8,389 ....62/F6
Annandale, P.E.I., Can. 224/C2
Annandale, Eng., U.K., *valley* 66/A2
Annandale, Minn., U.S., 2,684 ....298/C5
Annandale, N.J., U.S., 1,276 ....314/D2
Annandale, Va., U.S., 54,994 ....354/J3, M2
Annapolis, N.S., Can., *county* 221/B3
Annapolis, Calif., U.S., 50 ....246/B4
Annapolis, Ill., U.S., 70 ....266/F4
Annapolis, Md., U.S., *state capital*, 35,838 ....288/J4
Annapolis, Mo., U.S., 310 ....302/F4
Annapolis Royal, N.S., Can., 550 ....221/B3
Annapurna, Nepal, *mountain* 126/B2
Ann Arbor, Mich., U.S., 114,024 ....294/F7
An Nashshash, U.A.E. 136/C3
An Nasiriyah, Iraq 130/C2
Annawan, Ill., U.S., 868 ....266/D2
Annbank, Scot., U.K., 854 ....62/H8
Anne Arundel, Md., U.S., *county*, 489,656 ....288/D5, H4
Annecy, Fr., 52,100, (136,815 *metro.*) 88/D4
Anneta, Ky., U.S., 175 ....280/D3
Anniston, Ala., U.S., 24,276, (112,249 *metro.*) 238/D2
Anniston, Mo., U.S., 285 ....302/G5
Anniston Army Depot, Ala., U.S. 238/D2
Annona, Tex., U.S., 282 ....346/P2
An Nuhud, Sudan 145/B2
Annville, Ky., U.S., 589 ....280/G3
Anoka, Minn., U.S., 18,076 ....298/D5, E5
Anoka, Minn., U.S., *county*, 298,084 ....298/D5, F5
Anqing, China 119/E2
An Ruathair, Scot., U.K., *lake* 62/F3
Ansbach, Ger. 86/B4
Anse-à-Galets, Haiti 205/C2
Anse-Bleue, N.B., Can., 409 ....217/D1
Anse Boileau, Sey. 163/Inset
Anselmo, Nebr., U.S., 159 ....308/E2
Anse Royale, Sey. 163/Inset
Anshan, China, 1,195,580, (2,517,080 *metro.*) 119/F1
Ansley, Ala., U.S. 238/C4
Ansley, La., U.S. 282/D2
Ansley, Miss., U.S., 70 ....300/C5
Ansley, Nebr., U.S., 520 ....308/E2
Anson, Kans., U.S., 70 ....276/E4
Anson, Maine, U.S., 2,583 ....286/C4
Anson, N.C., U.S., *county*, 25,275 ....322/E5
Anson, Tex., U.S., 2,556 ....346/J3
Ansongo, Mali 150/D2
Ansonia, Conn., U.S., 18,554 ....253/C4
Ansonia, Ohio, U.S., 1,145 ....328/A5
Ansonville, N.C., U.S., 636 ....322/E4
Ansted, W. Va., U.S., 1,576 ....360/D4
Anstey, Eng., U.K., 6,192 ....68/E4
Anstey, Eng., U.K., 6,192 ....70/B1
Anston, (Anston/Dinnington), Eng., U.K., 17,691 ....66/F6
Anston, (Anston/Dinnington), Eng., U.K., 17,691 ....68/E3
Anston, Wisc., U.S., 275 ....364/E4
Anstruther, Scot., U.K., 3,442 ....62/L6
Antalaha, Madag. 163/C1
Antalya, Tur., 572,100 ....133/B3
Antalya, Tur., *gulf* 133/B3
Antalya, Tur., *province* 133/B3
Antananarivo, Madag., *capital*, 1,103,304 ....163/B2
Antarctic, Antar., *peninsula* 192/C12
Antarctica 182
An Teallach, Scot., U.K., *hill* 62/F3
Antelope, Kans., U.S. 276/F3
Antelope, Mont., U.S., 43 ....306/M1
Antelope, Nebr., U.S., *county*, 7,452 ....308/F1
Antelope, Oreg., U.S., 59 ....334/F3
Antelope, Oreg., U.S., *reservoir* 334/J5
Antelope, Tex., U.S. 346/K2
Antelope Island St. Park, Utah, U.S. 350/B3
Antelope Valley-Crestview, Wyo., U.S., 1,642 ....366/D1
Antequera, Sp. 94/D4
Anthon, Iowa, U.S., 687 ....274/C3
Anthony, Fla., U.S., 1,600 ....256/F2
Anthony, Kans., U.S., 2,440 ....276/D4
Anthony, N. Mex., U.S., 7,904 ....317/D6
Anthony, R.I., U.S. 339/C3
Anthony, W. Va., U.S., 60 ....360/F5
Anthoston, Ky., U.S., 350 ....280/C3
Anti Atlas, Mor., *ranges* 147/B2
Anticosti, Que., Can., *island* 225/D4
Antietam, Md., U.S., 275 ....288/D2
Antietam Natl. Bfld., Md., U.S. 288/C2
Antigo, Wisc., U.S., 8,560 ....364/D3
Antigonish, N.S., Can., 4,754 ....221/F2
Antigonish, N.S., Can., *county* 221/E1
Antigua, Ant.-Bar., *island* 204/F3
Antigua, Ant.-Bar., *island* 207/D4
Antigua and Barbuda, *nation* 204/F3
Antigua and Barbuda, *nation* 195
Antigua Guatemala, Guat. 201/C5
Anti Lebanon, Leb., *mountains* 134/B1
Anti Lebanon, Syria, *mountains* 134/A3
Antimony, Utah, U.S., 122 ....350/C5
Antioch, Calif., U.S., 90,532 ....246/M4, E1
Antioch, Ill., U.S., 8,788 ....266/F4, E1
Antioch, Nebr., U.S. 308/B1
Antioch, Ohio, U.S., 89 ....328/H6
Antioch, Okla., U.S., 70 ....330/E3
Antioquia, Col., *department* 184/B3
Antler, Sask., Can., *river* 326/D1
Antler, N. Dak., U.S., 47 ....326/D1
Antlers, Okla., U.S., 2,552 ....330/G3
Antofagasta, Chile, 239,854 ....190/B2
Antofagasta, Chile, *region* 190/C2
Antoine, Ark., U.S., 156 ....244/B3
Anton, Colo., U.S. 250/C2
Anton, Ky., U.S., 300 ....280/C3
Anton, Tex., U.S., 1,212/ 346/F2
Anton Chico, N. Mex., U.S., 212/ 317/E2
Antonino, Kans., U.S. 276/C3
Antonito, Colo., U.S., 873 ....250/D4
Antrim, N. Ire., U.K., 20,878 ....65/E2
Antrim, N. Ire., U.K., *mountains* 60/A4
Antrim, N. Ire., U.K., *mountains* 76/C1
Antrim, N. Ire., U.K., *unitary authority*, 48,366 ....65/E2
Antrim, Mich., U.S., *county*, 23,110 ....294/D4
Antrim, N.H., U.S., 2,449 ....312/C5
Antrim, Ohio, U.S., 175 ....328/H5
Antrim, Penn., U.S., 175 ....336/G2
Antsirabe, Madag. 163/B2
Antsiranana, Madag., 54,418 ....163/B1
Antsohihy, Madag. 163/B1
Antwerp, Belg., 448,709, (935,381 *metro.*) 85/C1
Antwerp, Belg., *province* 85/C1
Antwerp, N.Y., U.S., 716 ....320/K2
Antwerp, Ohio, U.S., 1,740 ....328/A3
Anuradhapura, Sri Lan. 126/B3
Anvik, Alaska, U.S., 104 ....240/C2
Anyang, China 119/D2
Anyang, S. Kor., 591,106 ....116/A4
Anyos, And. 93/B2
Anza, Calif., U.S., 48 ....246/J9
Anzoátegui, Ven., *state* 182/D2
Aoba, Van., *island* 173/B2
Aomori, Jap., 298,000 ....114/D1

Aomori, Jap., *prefecture* 114/D1
Aosta, It. 95/A1
Aozou, Chad 153/B2
Apa, Para., *river* 187/D3
Apache, Ariz., U.S. 242/F6
Apache, Ariz., U.S., *county*, 69,423 ....242/D4
Apache, Ariz., U.S., *lake* 242/D4
Apache, Okla., U.S., 1,616 ....330/D3
Apache Creek, N. Mex., U.S. 317/B4
Apache Jct., Ariz., U.S., 31,814 ....242/D4
Apache N.F., Ariz., U.S. 242/F4
Apache N.F., N. Mex., U.S. 317/A4, B4
Apalachee, Fla., U.S., *bay* 256/D5
Apalachee, Ga., U.S., 100 ....260/E4
Apalachicola, Fla., U.S., 2,334 ....256/D7
Apalachicola, Fla., U.S., *bay* 256/D2
Apalachicola, Fla., U.S., *river* 256/C1
Apalachicola Natl. For., Fla., U.S. 256/D1
Apalachin, N.Y., U.S., 1,126 ....320/H6
Apaporis, Col., *river* 184/C4
Aparan, Arm. 103/B2
Apatity, Russ. 104/C3
Apatou, Fr. Gui. 183/A1
Apeldoorn, Neth., 153,061 ....84/C2
Apennines, It., *range* 95/B1
Apetina, Sur. 183/B3
Apex, N.C., U.S., 20,212 ....322/H3
Apgar, Mont., U.S. 306/C1
Api, Nepal, *mountain* 126/A2
Apia, Sam., *capital*, (34,126 *metro.*) 175/C2
Apishapa, Colo., U.S., *river* 250/F4
Aplin, Ark., U.S., 50 ....244/C3
Aplington, Iowa, U.S., 1,054 ....274/J2
Apo, Phil., *volcano* 120/C5
Apoera, Sur. 183/A2
Apohaqui, N.B., Can. 217/D3
Apollo Beach, Fla., U.S., 7,444 ....256/D7, F4
Apopka, Fla., U.S., 26,642 ....256/C4, G3
Apostle Islands Natl. Lakeshore, Wisc., U.S. 364/C1
Apostolic Palace, Vat. 96/B2
Appalachia, Va., U.S., 1,839 ....354/C2
Appalachian, Que., Can., *mountains* 286/A3
Appalachian, Ga., U.S., *mountains* 260/D3
Appalachian, Maine, U.S., *mountains* 286/A3
Appalachian, Tenn., U.S., *mountains* 336/F5
Appalachian, Tenn., U.S., *mountains* 344/N4
Appalachian, Va., U.S., *mountains* 354/C5
Appalachian Natl. Scenic Trail, Conn., U.S. 253/B2
Appalachian N.S.T. Md., U.S. 288/D1
Appalachian N.S.T. N.Y., U.S. 320/A1, Q6
Appalachian N.S.T. Vt., U.S. 352/A5, D2
Appam, N. Dak., U.S. 326/B1
Appanoose, Iowa, U.S., *county*, 13,721 ....274/J6
Appenzell Ausser-Rhoden, Switz., *canton* 90/D1
Appenzell Inner-Rhoden, Switz., *canton* 90/D1
Appleby, Eng., U.K., 2,570 ....66/E5
Appleby, Tex., U.S., 2,570 ....68/F2
Appleby-in-Westmorland, Eng., U.K. 66/C3
Apple Creek, Ohio, U.S., 999 ....328/G4
Appledore, Eng., U.K., 2,187 ....70/F4
Appleford, Eng., U.K. 70/B3
Applegate, Mich., U.S., 287 ....294/G6
Apple Grove, Va., U.S. 354/H5
Apple River, N.S., Can. 221/C2
Appleton, Ark., U.S., 212/ 244/C2
Appleton, Maine, U.S., 1,271 ....286/C4
Appleton, Minn., U.S., 2,871 ....298/A5
Appleton, Wisc., U.S., 70,087, (358,365 *metro.*) 364/E4
Appleton City, Mo., U.S., 1,314 ....302/B3
Appletrewick, Eng., U.K. 66/E4
Apple Valley, Calif., U.S., 54,239 ....246/H8
Apple Valley, Minn., U.S., 45,527 ....298/D6
Applewood, Penn., U.S., 356 ....336/B4
Applewood, Colo., U.S., 7,123 ....250/A3
Appling, Ga., U.S., 225 ....260/G4
Appling, Ga., U.S., *county*, 17,419 ....260/G8
Appomattox, Va., U.S., 1,761 ....354/F6
Appomattox, Va., U.S., *county*, 13,705 ....354/F6
Appomattox C.H. Natl. Hist. Park, Va., U.S. 354/F6
Appomattox C.H. Natl. Hist. Park, Va., U.S. 360/J6
Apsley, Ont., Can. 223/G3
Aptos, Calif., U.S., 9,396 ....246/M4
Apua, Hawaii, U.S., *point* 262/J6
Apuila, (Puglia), It., *region* 95/C2
Apure, Ven., *river* 182/C2
Apure, Ven., *state* 182/C2
Apurimac, Peru, *department* 185/C3
Apurímac, Peru, *river* 185/C3
Apuseni, Rom., *mountains* 101/B2
Aqaba, Egy., *gulf* 144/B2
Aqaba, Isr., *gulf* 135/B3
Aqaba, Jor., *gulf* 134/A3
Aqaba, Sa. Arab., *gulf* 134/A3
Aqmola, Kaz., *oblast* 131/D1
Aquasco, Md., U.S., 250 ....288/H5
Aqueboque, N.Y., U.S., 2,254 ....320/F1
Aquila, Ariz., U.S., 90 ....242/B4
Aquileia, It. 95/B1
Aquilla, Ohio, U.S., 372 ....328/H2, J8
Aquilla, Tex., U.S., 136 ....346/L4
Aquinnah, (Gay Head), Mass., U.S., 344 ....292/L7
Aquitaine, Fr., *region* 88/B4
Aquone, N.C., U.S., 125 ....322/C8
Ara, India 128/D3
Arab, Ala., U.S., 7,174 ....238/C1
Arabah, Wadi al, Isr., *river* 135/B2
Arabah, Wadi al, Jor., *river* 317/E4
Arabi, Ga., U.S., 456 ....260/D8
Arabi, La., U.S., 8,093 ....282/K3
Arabia, Ohio, U.S. 328/F8
Arabian, India, *sea* ....128/A5, Inset I
Arabian, Oman, *sea* 137/C3
Arabian, Pak., *sea* 129/B6
Arabian, Yemen, *sea* 137/C2
Aracaju, Braz., 461,949 ....188/E3
Arachon, Fr. 88/B4
Arad, Rom., 182,846 ....101/A2
Arad, Rom., *county* 101/B2
Aradah, U.A.E. 136/C3
Arafura, Austl., *sea* 70/C1
Arafura, Indon., *sea* 122/E2
Aragats, Arm., *mountain* 103/B2
Aragatsotn, Arm., *district* 103/A2
Aragón, Sp., *autonomous community* 94/F2
Aragon, Ga., U.S., 1,039 ....260/A3
Aragon, N. Mex., U.S., 150 ....317/B4
Aragua, Ven., *state* 182/C2
Araguaia, Braz., *river* 188/C3
Arak, Iran, 380,755 ....130/B3
Arakabesan, Palau, *island* 172/B3
Arakan Yoma, Mya., *mountains* 125/B2
Aral, Kaz. 131/C2
Aral, Kaz., *sea* 132/A2
Aral, Uzb., *sea* 132/A2
Aran, Ire., *islands* 76/B2
Aranda de Duero, Sp. 94/E2

Aranjuez, Sp. 94/E2
Aransas, Tex., U.S., *county, 22,497* ...346/L7
Aransas N.W.R., Tex., U.S. 346/M7
Aransas Pass, Tex., U.S., 8,138 ....346/L8
Aranyaprathet, Thai. 125/C3
Arapaho, Okla., U.S., 748 ....330/D2
Arapahoe, Colo., U.S., 80 ....250/H3
Arapahoe, Colo., U.S., *county, 487,967* ...250/A3, F2
Arapahoe, Nebr., U.S., 1,028 ....308/E3
Arapahoe, N.C., U.S., 436 ....322/M4
Arapaho, Wyo., U.S., 1,766 ....366/B2
Arapaho Natl. For., Colo., U.S. 250/D1, E2
Arapaho N.R.A., Colo., U.S. 250/E1
Arapaho N.W.R., Colo., U.S. 250/D1
Arapey Grande, Uru., *river* 187/B1
Ar'ar, Sa. Arab. 136/B3
Ararat, Arm. 103/B3
Ararat, Arm., *district* 103/B2
Ararat, (Ağrı Dağı), Tur., *mountain* ...133/F2
Ararat, Va., U.S., 275 ....354/B7
Aras, Arm., *river* 103/B3
Aras, Azer., *river* 103/B3
Aras, Iran, *river* 130/B2
Aras, Tur., *river* 133/E2
Arauca, Col., 69,000 ....184/C3
Arauca, Col., *department* 184/C3
Arauca, Ven., *river* 182/C2
Aravalli, India, *range* 128/B3
Arawa, P.N.G. 172/B2
Arba Minch, Eth. 156/B3
Arbela, Mo., U.S. 302/D1
Arboe, N. Ire., U.K. 65/D2
Arboles, Colo., U.S., 232 ....250/C4
Arbon, Ida., U.S. 264/E7
Arborfield, Sask., Can., 411 ....227/G7
Arborg, Man., Can., 959 ....215/C4
Arbor Hill, Iowa, U.S. 274/F5
Arbor Vitae, Wisc., U.S., 90 ....364/D3
Arbuckle, Calif., U.S., 2,332 ......246/C3
Arbutus, Md., U.S., 20,116 ....288/H3
Arbyrd, Mo., U.S., 528 ....302/F5
Arcade, Calif., U.S., 96,025 ....246/K5
Arcade, Ga., U.S., 1,643 ....260/D3
Arcade, N.Y., U.S., 2,026 ....320/E5
Arcade, Tex., U.S. 346/F4
Arcadia, Calif., U.S., 53,054 ......246/D9
Arcadia, Fla., U.S., 6,604 ....256/D6
Arcadia, Ind., U.S., 1,747 ....270/D4
Arcadia, Iowa, U.S., 443 ....274/D3
Arcadia, Kans., U.S., 391 ....276/H4
Arcadia, La., U.S., 3,041 ....282/D1
Arcadia, Mich., U.S., 325 ....294/C5
Arcadia, Nebr., U.S., 359 ....308/E2
Arcadia, Ohio, U.S., 357 ....328/C3
Arcadia, Okla., U.S., 279 ....330/B3, E2
Arcadia, Penn., U.S., 250 ....336/D4
Arcadia, R.I., U.S., 150 ....339/B4
Arcadia, Wisc., U.S., 2,402 ....364/B4
Arcadia Lakes, S.C., U.S., 882 .....340/A3
Arcanum, Ohio, U.S., 2,076 ....328/A6
Arcata, Calif., U.S., 16,651 ....246/A2
Arc Dome, Nev., U.S., *peak* 310/B2
Arch, N. Mex., U.S. 317/G3
Archbald, Penn., U.S., 6,220 ....336/J6, K2
Archbold, Ohio, U.S., 4,290 ....328/B2
Arch Cape, Oreg., U.S., 40 ....334/C2
Archdale, N.C., U.S., 9,014 ....322/F3
Archer, Fla., U.S., 1,289 ....256/F2
Archer, Iowa, U.S., 126 ....274/C1
Archer, Nebr., U.S., 90 ....308/E2
Archer, Tex., U.S., *county, 8,854* .346/K2
Archer City, Tex., U.S., 1,848 .....346/K2
Archerwill, Sask., Can., 215 ....227/G8
Arches Natl. Park, Utah, U.S. 350/E5
Archibald, La., U.S., 325 ....282/F2
Archie, La., U.S. 282/F3
Archie, Mo., U.S., 890 ....302/B3
Archuleta, Colo., U.S., *county, 9,898* ...250/C4
Archuleta, N. Mex., U.S., 50 ....317/C1
Arcid Green, Eng., U.K. 66/G5
Arco, Ida., U.S., 1,026 ....264/D6
Arco, Minn., U.S., 100 ....298/A6
Arcola, Sask., Can., 532 ....227/H11
Arcola, Ill., U.S., 2,652 ....266/E4
Arcola, Ind., U.S., 225 ....270/F2
Arcola, Miss., U.S., 563 ....300/B2
Arcola, Mo., U.S., 45 ....302/C4
Arcola, Tex., U.S., 1,048 ....346/B7
Arctic Bay, Nun., Can., 646 ....208/L2
Arctic N.W.R., Alaska, U.S. 240/G1
Arctic Vil., Alaska, U.S., 152 .....240/F1
Arda, Bul., *river* 101/C4
Ardabil, Iran, 340,386 ....130/B2
Ardabil, Iran, *province* 130/B2
Ardara, Ire. 76/B1
Ardbeg, Ont., Can. 223/E2
Ardbeg, Scot., U.K. 62/D7
Arddleen, Wales, U.K. 64/E2
Ardean, N. Ire., U.K. 65/E2
Ardèche, Fr., *department* 88/D4
Arden, Ark., U.S. 244/A4
Arden, (Arden-Arcade), Calif., U.S., 96,025 ...246/K5
Arden, Del., U.S., 474 ....255/C1
Arden, Nev., U.S. 310/C3
Arden, Wash., U.S., 250 ....358/H1
Ardencroft, Del., U.S., 267 ....255/C1
Arden Hills, Minn., U.S., 9,652 ....298/F5
Ardennes, Belg., *forest* 85/D2
Ardennes, Fr., *department* 88/D2
Ardennes, Fr., *region* 88/D1
Ardennes, Lux., *plateau* 85/A1
Arden-on-the-Severn, Md., U.S., 1,971 ...288/H3
Ardentown, Del., U.S., 300 ....255/C1
Ardenvoir, Wash., U.S., 90 ....358/E2
Ardeonaig, Scot., U.K. 62/H6
Ardgay, Scot., U.K. 62/H3
Ardglass, N. Ire., U.K., 1,651 .....65/F3
Ardleigh, Eng., U.K. 70/F3
Ardley, Eng., U.K. 68/E6
Ardlussa, Scot., U.K. 62/E6
Ardminish, Scot., U.K. 62/E7
Ardmore, Ala., U.S., 1,034 ....238/C1
Ardmore, Okla., U.S., 23,711 ....330/E3
Ardmore, Penn., U.S., 12,616 ....336/L7
Ardmore, S. Dak., U.S. 342/B4
Ardmore, Tenn., U.S., 1,082 ....344/H5
Ardno, Scot., U.K. 62/G6
Ardoch, N. Dak., U.S., 61 ....326/H1
Ardoch N.W.R., N. Dak., U.S. 326/H1
Ardrishaig, Scot., U.K., 1,283 .....62/F7
Ardrossan, Scot., U.K., 10,952 .....62/G7
Ards, N. Ire., U.K., *unitary authority, 73,244* ...65/F2
Ardsley, N.Y., U.S., 4,269 ....320/B1
Ardvourlie, Scot., U.K. 62/E3
Arecibo, P.R. 206/B2
Aredale, Iowa, U.S., 89 ....274/J2
Arekalong, Palau, *peninsula* 172/C2
Arena, Calif., U.S., *point* 246/B4

Arena, Wisc., U.S., 685 ....364/D5
Arenac, Mich., U.S., *county, 17,269* ...294/F5
Arenal, C.R., *lake* 203/B2
Arenal, P.R., *point* 206/D2
Arendal, Nor. 80/B4
Arendtsville, Penn., U.S., 848 .....336/G6
Arenig Fawr, Wales, U.K., *hill* ...64/D2
Arenzville, Ill., U.S., 419 ....266/C4
Arequipa, Peru, 93,502, (830,034 metro.) ...185/C4
Arequipa, Peru, *department* 185/C4
Arezzo, It. 95/B2
Argenta, Ill., U.S., 921 ....266/E4
Argenteuil, Fr. ....88/Inset II
Argentia, Nfld., Can. 206/D5
Argentina, *nation* 181
Argentine, Mich., U.S., 2,285 ......294/F7
Argentino, Arg., *lake* 191/A7
Argeş, Rom., *county* 101/C3
Argeş, Rom., *river* 101/C3
Arghandab, Afg., *river* 127/A3
Argo, Ala., U.S., 1,780 ....238/C2
Argo, Ky., U.S. 280/H3
Argonia, Kans., U.S., 534 ....276/E4
Argonne, Fr., *region* 88/D2
Argonne, Wisc., U.S., 175 ....364/E3
Argos, Gr. 100/B3
Argos, Ind., U.S., 1,613 ....270/D2
Argos Corner, Del., U.S., 550 ......255/C5
Arguello, Calif., U.S., *point* 246/E8
Argusville, N. Dak., U.S., 147 .....326/J2
Argyle, Man., Can. 215/C4
Argyle, Ont., Can. 223/F3
Argyle, Ga., U.S., 151 ....260/F9
Argyle, Iowa, U.S., 212/ 274/L6
Argyle, Maine, U.S., 253 ....286/D3
Argyle, Mich., U.S., 125 ....294/G6
Argyle, Minn., U.S., 656 ....298/A2
Argyle, Mo., U.S., 164 ....302/D3
Argyle, N.Y., U.S., 289 ....320/Q4
Argyle, Tex., U.S., 2,365 ....346/B8
Argyle, Wisc., U.S., 823 ....364/D6
Argyll and Bute, Scot., U.K., *unitary authority, 91,306* ...62/F6
Århus, Den., 218,380, (267,873 metro.) ...79/C2
Århus, Den., *county* 79/C2
Ari, Mald., *atoll* 127/A3
Arial, S.C., U.S., 2,607 ....340/B2
Ariana, Tun. 146/C1
Arica, Chile, 175,879 ....190/B1
Arichat, N.S., Can. 221/F2
Ariège, Fr., *department* 88/C5
Ariel, Wash., U.S., 70 ....358/C4
Arikaree, Colo., U.S., *river* 250/G2
Arileod, Scot., U.K. 62/C5
Arima, Trin.-To., 27,955 ....209/A2
Arimo, Ida., U.S., 348 ....264/E7
Arinsal, And. 93/A2
Arion, Iowa, U.S., 136 ....274/D4
Aripeka, Fla., U.S., 650 ....256/F3
Aripine, Ariz., U.S. 242/E3
Aripuanã, Braz., *river* 188/C2
Arispe, Iowa, U.S., 89 ....274/F6
Arispe, Tex., U.S. 346/C4
Arista, W. Va., U.S., 225 ....360/D6
Ariton, Ala., U.S., 772 ....238/D4
Arivaca, Ariz., U.S., 100 ....242/D6
Arizola, Ariz., U.S., 550 ....242/D5
Arizona, U.S., *state* 230
Arizona City, Ariz., U.S., 4,385 ...242/D5
Ark, Va., U.S., 175 ....354/K6
Arkabutla, Miss., U.S., *lake* 300/D1
Arkadelphia, Ala., U.S., 100 ....238/C2
Arkadelphia, Ark., U.S., 10,912 ....244/C3
Arkaig, Scot., U.K., *lake* 62/F4
Arkalyk, Kaz. 131/C1
Arkansas, U.S., *state* 232
Arkansas, Ark., U.S., *county, 20,749* ...244/D3
Arkansas, Ark., U.S., *river* 244/D3
Arkansas, Colo., U.S., *river* 244/D3
Arkansas, Kans., U.S., *river* 276/A4, D3
Arkansas, Okla., U.S., *river* 330/F1, H2
Arkansas City, Ark., U.S., 589 .....244/D4
Arkansas City, Kans., U.S., 11,963 .276/E4
Arkansas Jct., N. Mex., U.S. 317/G5
Arkansas Post Natl. Mem., Ark., U.S. ...244/D3
Arkdale, Wisc., U.S., 150 ....364/D4
Arkhangel'sk, Russ., 364,985, (372,212/ metro.) ...104/D3
Arkhangel'sk, Russ. 193/C3
Arkinda, Ark., U.S. 76/C2
Arkoe, Mo., U.S., 58 ....302/B1
Arkoma, Okla., U.S., 2,180 ....330/H2
Arkona, Ont., Can., 598 ....223/D4
Arkport, N.Y., U.S., 832 ....320/F6
Arlee, Mont., U.S., 602 ....306/B2
Arles, Fr. 88/D5
Arlesey, Eng., U.K., 4,374 ....68/G6
Arlesey, Eng., U.K., 4,374 ....70/D3
Arley, Ala., U.S., 290 ....238/B1
Arlingham, Eng., U.K. 66/G4
Arlington, Ariz., U.S., 90 ....242/C4
Arlington, Colo., U.S. 250/G3
Arlington, Ga., U.S., 1,602 ....260/B9
Arlington, Ill., U.S., 211 ....266/D2
Arlington, Iowa, U.S., 490 ....274/L2
Arlington, Kans., U.S., 459 ....276/D4
Arlington, Ky., U.S., 395 ....280/A4
Arlington, La., U.S. 282/G6
Arlington, Mass., U.S., 42,389 .....292/C7, K3
Arlington, Minn., U.S., 2,048 ......298/C6
Arlington, Nebr., U.S., 1,197 ......308/H2
Arlington, N.Y., U.S., 12,481 ......320/P7
Arlington, N.C., U.S., 795 ....322/D2
Arlington, Ohio, U.S., 1,351 ....328/C3
Arlington, Oreg., U.S., 524 ....334/F2
Arlington, S. Dak., U.S., 992 ......342/H3
Arlington, Tenn., U.S., 2,569 ......344/B4
Arlington, Tex., U.S., 332,969 .....346/B9, L3
Arlington, Vt., U.S., 2,397 ....352/A4
Arlington, Va., U.S., 189,453 ......354/J3, M2
Arlington, Va., U.S., *county, 189,453* ...342
Arlington, Wash., U.S., 11,713 .....358/C1
Arlington, Wisc., U.S., 484 ....364/D5
Arlington, Wyo., U.S. 366/C3
Arlington Hts., Ill., U.S., 76,031 .266/B5
Arlington Hts., Penn., U.S., 5,132 .336/L3
Arlit, Niger 152/B2
Arlon, Belg. 85/D3
Arm, Miss., U.S., 125 ....300/B4
Arma, Kans., U.S., 1,529 ....276/H4
Armada, Mich., U.S., 1,573 ....294/G7
Armadale, W.A., Austl. ....170/Inset I
Armagh, N. Ire., U.K. 60/A4
Armagh, N. Ire., U.K., 14,640 ......65/D3
Armagh, N. Ire., U.K., *unitary authority, 54,263* ...65/D3
Armagh, Penn., U.S., 131 ....336/C5
Armarvir, Arm. 103/A2
Armarvir, Arm., *district* 103/A2
Armenia, *nation* 101
Armenia, Col., 284,000 ....184/B3
Armidale, N.S.W., Austl. 170/E3
Armijo, N. Mex., U.S., 9,500 ....317/D2
Armington, Ill., U.S., 368 ....266/D3

Arminton, Mont., U.S., 150 ....306/F2
Arminto, Wyo., U.S. 366/C2
Armona, Calif., U.S., 3,239 ....246/F6
Armona, Tenn., U.S. 344/N3
Armorel, Ark., U.S., 100 ....244/F2
Armour, S. Dak., U.S., 782 ....342/G4
Armourdale, N. Dak., U.S. 326/F1
Armoy, N. Ire., U.K., 560 ....65/E1
Armstrong, Br. Col., Can., 4,256 ...214/N6
Armstrong, Ont., Can., 250 ....222/C2
Armstrong, Ill., U.S., 275 ....266/F3
Armstrong, Iowa, U.S., 979 ....274/F1
Armstrong, Okla., U.S., 141 ....330/F3
Armstrong, Penn., U.S., *county, 72,392* ...336/C4
Armstrong, Tex., U.S., *county, 2,148* ...346/F9
Armstrong Mills, Ohio, U.S. 328/J6
Arnaud, Que., Can., *river* 225/B2
Arnaudville, La., U.S., 1,398 ......282/F6
Arnauti, Cyp., *cape* 133/A1
Arncliffe, Eng., U.K. 66/D4
Arnegard, N. Dak., U.S., 105 ....326/B2
Arnes, Man., Can. 215/C4
Arnesby, Eng., U.K. 70/B1
Arnett, (Ellis County), Okla., U.S., 520 ...330/C1
Arnett, (Harmon County), Okla., U.S. ...330/C3
Arney, Tex., U.S. 346/F10
Arnhem, Austl., *cape* 170/C1
Arnhem, Neth., 137,688, (139,032 metro.) ...84/C3
Arnhem Land, Austl., *region* 170/C1
Arnisdale, Scot., U.K. 62/E4
Arno, It., *river* 95/B2
Arno, Marsh. Is., *island* 173/C2
Arno, Tex., U.S. 346/E4
Arnold, Eng., U.K., 37,646 ....68/E4
Arnold, Eng., U.K., 37,646 ....70/B1
Arnold, Calif., U.S., 4,218 ....246/E4
Arnold, Kans., U.S., 60 ....276/B3
Arnold, Md., U.S., 23,422 ....288/H3
Arnold, Mich., U.S. 294/B3
Arnold, Minn., U.S., 3,032 ....298/E4
Arnold, Mo., U.S., 19,965 ....302/F3
Arnold, Nebr., U.S., 630 ....308/D2
Arnold, Penn., U.S., 5,667 ....336/B4
Arnold Engineering Development Ctr., Tenn., U.S. ...344/J4
Arnold Line, Miss., U.S., 1,800 ....300/C4
Arnoldsburg, W. Va., U.S., 160 .....360/D3
Arnolds Cove, Nfld., Can., 1,024 ...206/D5
Arnolds Park, Iowa, U.S., 1,162 ....274/D1
Arnoldsville, Ga., U.S., 312 ....260/E4
Arnot, Penn., U.S., 300 ....336/G2
Arnprior, Ont., Can., 7,192 ....223/J2
Arnprior, Scot., U.K. 62/H6
Arnsberg, Ger. 86/B3
Arnsberg, Ger., *department* 86/A3
Arnside, Eng., U.K., 1,627 ....66/C4
Arnside and Silverdale, Eng., U.K. .66/B4
Arock, Oreg., U.S. 334/J5
Aroma Park, Ill., U.S., 821 ....266/F2
Aromas, Calif., U.S., 2,797 ....246/D6
Arona, Penn., U.S., 407 ....336/B5
Aroostook, N.B., Can., 380 ....217/B2
Aroostook, Maine, U.S., *county, 73,938* ...286/D2
Aroostook, Maine, U.S., *river* 286/D2
Arorae, Kiri., *island* 175/A2
Aroya, Colo., U.S. 250/G3
Arp, Tex., U.S., 901 ....346/N3
Arpa, Arm., *river* 103/C3
Arpajon, Fr. ....88/Inset II
Arpelar, Okla., U.S., 50 ....330/G3
Arpin, Wisc., U.S., 337 ....364/C4
Ar Ramadi, Iraq 130/B2
Ar Ramtha, Jor. 134/B1
Arran, Scot., U.K., *island* 62/F7
Arran, Scot., U.K., *island* 62/F7
Ar Raqqah, Syria, 165,195, (201,114 metro.) ...134/B2
Arras, Fr. 88/C1
Ar Rawdatayn, Kuw. 136/B2
Arreton, Eng., U.K. 70/B5
Arrey, N. Mex., U.S., 150 ....317/C5
Arriba, Colo., U.S., 244 ....250/G2
Arrington, Kans., U.S. 276/G2
Arrington, Va., U.S., 175 ....354/F5
Arriola, Colo., U.S., 40 ....250/B4
Arrochar, Scot., U.K. 62/G6
Arrow Creek, Mont., U.S. 306/F2
Arrow Rock, Mo., U.S., 79 ....302/D2
Arrowsic, Maine, U.S., 477 ....286/C5
Arrowsmith, Ill., U.S., 298 ....266/E3
Arrowwood N.W.R., N. Dak., U.S. 326/G2
Arroyo, P.R. 206/C3
Arroyo Grande, Calif., U.S., 15,851 ...246/E7
Arroyo Hondo, N. Mex., U.S., 1,500 .317/E1
Arroyo Seco, N. Mex., U.S., 1,149 ..317/E1
Ar Rutbah, Iraq 130/B2
Ar Ruways, Qatar 137/C1
Ar Ruways, U.A.E. 136/B2
Art, Tex., U.S. 346/J5
Arta, Dji. 156/B2
Artas, S. Dak., U.S. 342/F1
Artashat, Arm. 103/B3
Artemisa, Cuba 204/B2
Artesia, Ariz., U.S., 212/ 242/F5
Artesia, Calif., U.S., 16,380 ......246/D10
Artesia, Miss., U.S., 498 ....300/D3
Artesia, N. Mex., U.S., 10,692 .....317/F5
Artesian, S. Dak., U.S., 157 ....342/H4
Artesia Wells, Tex., U.S., 50 ......346/J7
Art Gallery, Vat. 96/B1
Arthog, Wales, U.K. 64/D2
Arthur, Ont., Can., 2,284 ....223/E4
Arthur, Ill., U.S., 2,203 ....266/E4
Arthur, Iowa, U.S., 245 ....274/D3
Arthur, Nebr., U.S. 308/C2
Arthur, Nebr., U.S., *county, 444* .308/C2
Arthur, Nev., U.S., 60 ....310/C1
Arthur, N. Dak., U.S., 402 ....326/H2
Arthur, Tenn., U.S., 1,100 ....344/P1
Arthur City, Tex., U.S., 125 ....346/N2
Arthurette, N.B., Can. 217/B2
Arthur's Town, Bah. 207/B3
Artibonite, Haiti, *department* 205/C1
Artibonite, Haiti, *river* 205/C1
Artigas, Uru. 187/B1
Artigas, Uru., *department* 187/B1
Art'ik, Arm. 103/A2
Artois, Calif., U.S., 150 ....246/C3
Artondale, Wash., U.S., 8,630 ......358/C2
Artsakh, (Nagorno Karabakh), Azer., *region* ...103/B2
Artsvashen, Arm. 103/C2
Artvin, Tur. 133/E2
Artvin, Tur., *province* 133/E2
Aru, Indon., *islands* 122/E2
Arua, Ug., 45,883 ....157/B2
Aruba, Neth. 204/D4
Arun, Nepal, *river* 126/D2
Arunachal Pradesh, India, *state* ..128/F3
Arundel, Eng., U.K., 3,033 ....70/C5
Arundel, Maine, U.S., 3,571 ....286/B5
Arundel Vil., Md., U.S., 8,000 .....288/H3
Arusha, Tan., 134,708 ....158/C1

Arusha, Tan., *region* 158/C1
Aruvi, Sri Lan., *river* 126/D3
Aruwimi, Congo, D.R., *river* 154/D1
Arvada, Colo., U.S., 102,153 ....250/A3, G1
Arvada, Wyo., U.S. 366/C1
Arvana, Tex., U.S. 346/G3
Arvayheer, Mong. 118/C2
Arviat, Nun., Can., 1,899 ....208/K4
Arvin, Calif., U.S., 12,956 ....246/G7
Arvon, Mich., U.S., *mountain* 294/A3
Arvonia, Va., U.S., 325 ....354/G5
Asaba, Nig. 152/D4
Asad, Buhayrat al, Syria, *reservoir* ...134/B1
Asadabad, Afg. 129/C2
Asahi dake, Jap., *volcano* ....114/Inset I
Asahikawa, Jap., 360,000 ....114/Inset I
Asal, Dji., *lake* 156/B2
Asama yama, Jap., *volcano* 114/C2
Asansol, India, (1,090,171 metro.) .128/E4
Asau, Sam. 175/A2
Asbestos, Que., Can., 6,580 ....226/E6
Asbury, Iowa, U.S., 2,450 ....274/N2
Asbury, Mo., U.S., 218 ....302/B4
Asbury, N.J., U.S., 550 ....314/C2
Asbury, W. Va., U.S., 50 ....360/E5
Asbury Park, N.J., U.S., 16,930 ....314/E3
Ascension, U.K., *island* 136/A5
Ascension, La., U.S., *parish, 76,627* ...282/M6
Ascoli Piceno, It. 95/C2
Ascutney, Vt., U.S., 450 ....352/C4
Aseb, Erit., 50,000 ....156/B3
As Ela, Dji. 156/B2
Asela, Eth. 156/C3
Asenovgrad, Bul. 101/C3
Ash, Eng., U.K., 2,024 ....70/G4
Ash, Oreg., U.S., 40 ....334/C4
Asharoken, N.Y., U.S., 625 ....320/D2
Ashaway, R.I., U.S., 1,537 ....339/B5
Ashbourne, Eng., U.K., 6,300 ....68/D3
Ashburn, Ga., U.S., 4,419 ....260/D8
Ashburn, Mo., U.S., 51 ....302/D2
Ashburn, Va., U.S., 3,400 ....354/J2
Ashburnham, Mass., U.S., 5,546 .....292/G2
Ashburton, Austl., *river* 170/A2
Ashburton, Eng., U.K., 3,660 ....73/E3
Ashbury, Eng., U.K. 70/A3
Ashby, Ala., U.S., 125 ....238/C2
Ashby, Mass., U.S., 2,845 ....292/G2
Ashby, Minn., U.S., 472 ....298/B4
Ashby, Nebr., U.S. 308/C1
Ashbyburg, Ky., U.S., 40 ....280/C3
Ashby-de-la-Zouch, Eng., U.K., 10,595 ...68/E4
Ashby-de-la-Zouch, Eng., U.K., 10,595 ...70/B1
Ashcott, Eng., U.K. 66/F5
Ashcroft, Br. Col., Can., 1,788 ....214/M6
Ashdod, Isr., 146,900 ....135/B2
Ashdod, Mass., U.S. 292/L4
Ashdown, Ark., U.S., 4,781 ....244/A4
Ashe, N.C., U.S., *county, 24,384* .322/C2
Asheboro, N.C., U.S., 21,672 ....322/F3
Asher, Okla., U.S., 419 ....330/F3
Ashern, Man., Can. 215/B3
Asherton, Tex., U.S., 1,342 ....346/J7
Asherville, Kans., U.S., 60 ....276/E2
Asheville, N.C., U.S., 68,889, (225,965 metro.) ...322/EF4
Asheweig, Ont., Can., *river* 222/C2
Ashfield, Eng., U.K. 70/G2
Ashfield, Mass., U.S., 1,800 ....292/C2
Ash Flat, Ark., U.S., 977 ....244/D1
Ashford, Eng., U.K., 52,002 ....70/F4
Ashford, Ala., U.S., 1,853 ....238/D4
Ashford, Wash., U.S., 267 ....358/C3
Ashford Hollow, N.Y., U.S., 100 ....320/D6
Ashford in the Water, Eng., U.K. ...68/D3
Ash Fork, Ariz., U.S., 457 ....242/C2
Ashgabat, Turkm., *capital*, 407,000 ...132/C3
Ash Grove, Kans., U.S. 276/D2
Ash Grove, Mo., U.S., 1,430 ....302/C4
Ashikaga, Jap. 114/C2
Ashington, Eng., U.K., 27,962 ......66/E2
Ashippun, Wisc., U.S., 500 ....364/E1
Ashizuri, Jap., *cape* 114/B3
Ashkirk, Scot., U.K. 62/L6
Ashkum, Ill., U.S., 724 ....266/F3
Ashland, Ala., U.S., 1,965 ....238/C2
Ashland, Calif., U.S., 20,793 ......246/J2
Ashland, Ill., U.S., 1,361 ....266/C4
Ashland, Kans., U.S., 975 ....276/C4
Ashland, Ky., U.S., 21,981 ....280/H2
Ashland, La., U.S., 291 ....282/C2
Ashland, Maine, U.S., 1,474 ....286/D2
Ashland, Mass., U.S., 14,674 ....292/J3
Ashland, Miss., U.S., 577 ....300/C1
Ashland, Mo., U.S., 1,869 ....302/D3
Ashland, Mont., U.S. 306/K4
Ashland, Nebr., U.S., 2,262 ....308/H2
Ashland, N.H., U.S., 1,955 ....352/D3
Ashland, Ohio, U.S., 21,249 ....328/E9, F4
Ashland, Ohio, U.S., *county, 52,523* ...328/F4
Ashland, Okla., U.S., 53 ....330/F3
Ashland, Oreg., U.S., 19,522 ....334/D5
Ashland, Penn., U.S., 3,283 ....336/J4
Ashland, Va., U.S., 6,619 ....354/J5
Ashland, Wisc., U.S., 8,620 ....364/C2
Ashland, Wisc., U.S., *county, 16,866* ...364/C2
Ashland City, Tenn., U.S., 3,641 ...344/G2
Ashley, Eng., U.K. 70/E2
Ashley, Ark., U.S., *county, 24,209* ...244/D4
Ashley, Ill., U.S., 613 ....266/D5
Ashley, Ind., U.S., 1,010 ....270/F1
Ashley, Mich., U.S., 526 ....294/E6
Ashley, Mo., U.S., 80 ....302/E3
Ashley, N. Dak., U.S., 882 ....326/F3
Ashley, Ohio, U.S., 1,216 ....328/E5
Ashley, Penn., U.S., 2,866 ....336/G7, K3
Ashley Falls, Mass., U.S., 450 .....292/A4
Ashley Natl. For., Utah, U.S. 350/D3, D4
Ash Meadows N.W.R., Nev., U.S. 310/B3
Ashmont, Alta., Can. 212/F4
Ashmore and Cartier, Austl., *Islands* ...170/A1
Ashots'k', Arm. 103/A1
Ashport, Tenn., U.S. 344/B3
Ashqelon, Isr. 135/B2
Ash Sha'm, U.A.E. 136/D1
Ash Sharawrah, Sa. Arab. 136/B2
Ash Sprs., Nev., U.S. 310/C3
Ashtabula, Ohio, U.S., 20,962 ......328/J2
Ashtabula, Ohio, U.S., *county, 102,728* ...328/J2
Ashtarak, Arm. 103/B2
Ashtead, Eng., U.K. 70/D4
Ashtola, Wisc., U.S. 364/E3
Ashton, St. Vin.-Gren. 208/A4
Ashton, Eng., U.K. 73/H2
Ashton, Ida., U.S., 1,129 ....264/F5
Ashton, Ill., U.S., 1,142 ....266/D2
Ashton, Iowa, U.S., 461 ....274/C1
Ashton, Kans., U.S. 276/E4
Ashton, (Ashton-Sandy Sprs), Md., U.S., 3,437 ...288/F3
Ashton, Mich., U.S., 212 ....294/D6

Ashton, Nebr., U.S., 237 . . . . .308/E2
Ashton, R.I., U.S., 2,600 . . . . .339/D2
Ashton, S.C., U.S., 100 . . . . .340/D3
Ashton, S. Dak., U.S., 152 . . . . .336/D4
Ashton-in-Makersfield, Eng., U.K., 28,105 . . . . .66/C5
Ashton-in-Makersfield, Eng., U.K., 28,105 . . . . .68/B3
Ashton-under-Lyne, Eng., U.K., 43,906 . . . . . . .66/D6
Ashton-under-Lyne, Eng., U.K., 43,906 . . . . . . .68/C3
Ashuapmushuan, Que., Can., river 226/C2
Ashuapmushuan Prov. Reserve, Que., Can. 226/C2
Ashuelot, N.H., U.S., 375 . . . . .312/B6
Ashurst, (Ashurst/Netley Marsh),
  Eng., U.K., 2,541 .70/E4
Ashville, Ala., U.S., 2,260 . . . . .238/C2
Ashville, Fla., U.S., 90 . . . . .256/E1
Ashville, Ohio, U.S., 3,174 . . . . .328/E6
Ashville, Penn., U.S., 279 . . . . .336/D4
Ashwater, Eng., U.K. 73/D3
Ashwaubenon, Wisc., U.S., 17,634 . . . . .364/E4
Ashwell, Eng., U.K., 1,629 . . . . .68/G5
Ashwell, Eng., U.K. .70/D2
Ashwood, Oreg., U.S., 40 . . . . .334/F3
Asia, continent 109
Asinara, It., island .95/B2
Asipovichy, Bela. 82/D3
Asir, Sa. Arab., emirate 136/B2
Asir, Sa. Arab., region 136/B2
Askar, Bahr. 137/B1
Askern, Eng., U.K., 5,862 . . . . .66/F5
Askern, Eng., U.K., 5,862 . . . . .68/C2
Askerville, N.C., U.S., 180 . . . . .322/N12
Askin, N.C., U.S., 125 . . . . .322/L4
Askov, Minn., U.S., 368 . . . . .298/E4
Askrigg, Eng., U.K. 66/D4
Asmara, Erit., capital, 358,100, (514,000 metro.) 156/B2
Asosa, Eth. 156/B2
Aso san, Jap., volcano 114/A3
Asotin, Wash., U.S., 1,095 . . . . .358/H3
Asotin, Wash., U.S., county, 20,551 . . . . .358/H3
Aspatria, Eng., U.K., 2,219 . . . . .66/B3
Aspen, Colo., U.S., 5,914 . . . . .250/D2
Aspen, Wyo., U.S. .366/A3
Aspen Hill, Md., U.S., 50,228 . . . . .288/B5, F3
Aspermont, Tex., U.S., 1,021 . . . . .346/H2
Aspinwall, Iowa, U.S., 58 . . . . .274/D4
Aspinwall, Penn., U.S., 2,960 . . . . .336/E7
Aspiring, N.Z., mountain 171/A3
Aspropyrgos, Gr. .100/Inset
Aspy, N.S., Can., bay 221/G1
Asquith, N.S.W., Austl. . . . . .170/Inset IV
Asquith, Sask., Can., 574 . . . . .227/C8
As Sallum, Egy. 144/A1
As Salt, Jor. 134/A1
Assam, India, state 128/F3
As Samawah, Iraq 130/C2
Assaria, Kans., U.S., 438 . . . . .276/E3
Assateague, Md., U.S., island 288/P7
Assateague Island Natl. Seashore, Md., U.S. . .288/P7
Assateague Island Natl. Seashore, Va., U.S. . . .354/N5
Assawoman, Md., U.S., bay 288/P6
Assawompset, Mass., U.S., pond 292/L5
Assen, Neth. 84/D2
Assiniboia, Sask., Can., 2,483 . . . . .227/D11
Assiniboine, Br. Col., Can., mountain 214/F6
Assiniboine, Man., Can., river 215/A4
Assiniboine, Sask., Can., river 227/J10
Assinica Prov. Reserve, Que., Can. 226/A1
Assinippi, Mass., U.S., 2,700 . . . . .292/L4
Assonet, Mass., U.S., 1,212/ 292/K5
As Sukhnah, Syria .134/B2
As Sulaybikhat, Kuw. 136/B2
As Sulaymaniyah, Iraq 130/C1
As Sulayyi, Sa. Arab. 136/B2
Assumption, Ill., U.S., 1,261 . . . . .266/D4
Assumption, La., U.S., parish, 23,388 . . . . . .282/G7
Assumption, Nebr., U.S., 70 . . . . .308/E3
As Suwar, Syria 134/B2
As Suwayda, Syria 134/A3
Assynt, Scot., U.K., lake 62/F2
Assynt-Coigach N.P. Scot., U.K. 62/F2
Assyria, Mich., U.S., 275 . . . . .294/D7
Astana, Kaz., capital, 312,965,
  (319,324 metro.) 131/D1
Astana City, Kaz., oblast 131/D1
Astara, Azer. 103/C3
Astatula, Fla., U.S., 1,298 . . . . .256/C3, G3
Asti, It. 95/B1
Astipalaia, Gr., island 100/C3
Astle, N.B., Can. 217/C2
Aston, Eng., U.K. 68/B3
Aston Clinton, Eng., U.K., 3,467 . . . . .70/C3
Aston on Clun, Eng., U.K. 68/B5
Astor, Fla., U.S., 1,487 . . . . .256/G2
Astorga, Sp. 94/C1
Astoria, Ill., U.S., 1,193 . . . . .266/C4
Astoria, Oreg., U.S., 9,813 . . . . .334/C1
Astoria, S. Dak., U.S., 150 . . . . .342/H2
Astrakhan', Russ., 482,402 . . . . .104/D5
Asturias, Sp., autonomous community 94/C1
Astwood, Eng., U.K. 70/C2
Astwood Bank, Eng., U.K. 68/D5
Asunción, Para., capital, 513,399,
  (1,130,000 metro.) 187/D4
Asunción, Para., department 187/D4
Aswad, Al Haruj al, Lib., hills 145/C2
Aswan, Egy., 219,541 . . . . .144/B3
Aswan High, Egy., dam 144/B3
Aswarby, Eng., U.K. 70/D1
Asyut, Egy., 343,000 . . . . .144/B2
Atacama, Chile, desert 190/C2
Atacama, Chile, region 190/B3
Atakora, Ben., mountains 151/A2
Atakpamé, Togo 151/B3
Atalissa, Iowa, U.S., 283 . . . . .274/M4
Ataq, Yemen 137/B2
Atâr, Maur. 147/B2
Atascadero, Calif., U.S., 26,411 . . . . .246/E7
Atascosa, Tex., U.S., county, 38,628 . . . . . . .346/K7
Atatürk, Tur., reservoir 133/D3
Atbara, Eth., river .156/B1
Atbara, Sudan 145/C2
Atbara, Sudan, river 131/C2
Atbasar, Kaz. 131/D2
At-Bashy, Kyrg. 131/D2
Atchafalaya, La., U.S., bay 282/F8
Atchafalaya, La., U.S., river 282/F5
Atchafalaya N.W.R., La., U.S. 282/F6
Atchison, Kans., U.S., 10,232 . . . . .276/F2
Atchison, Kans., U.S., county, 16,774 . . . . . . .276/G2
Atchison, Mo., U.S., county, 6,430 . . . . .302/A1
Atco, N.J., U.S., 4,500 . . . . .314/D4
Atglen, Penn., U.S., 1,217 . . . . .336/K6
Ath, Belg. 85/B2
Athabasca, Alta., Can., 2,415 . . . . .212/D4
Athabasca, Alta., Can. 212//B4, D3, E2
Athabasca, Sask., Can., lake 212//E1
Athabasca, Sask., Can., river 227/A1
Athalia, Ohio, U.S., 328 . . . . .328/F8
Athelstan, Iowa, U.S. 274/E6
Athelstane, Wisc., U.S., 70 . . . . .364/E3
Athena, Fla., U.S. .256/C5
Athena, Oreg., U.S., 1,221 . . . . .334/H2

Athens, Gr., capital, 745,514,
  (3,112,000 metro.) . . . . .100/B3, Inset
Athens, Ala., U.S., 18,967 . . . . .238/B1
Athens, Ga., U.S., 101,489, (153,444 metro.) .260/E4
Athens, Ill., U.S., 1,726 . . . . .266/D4
Athens, La., U.S., 262 . . . . .282/C1
Athens, Maine, U.S., 847 . . . . .286/C4
Athens, Mich., U.S., 1,111 . . . . .294/D7
Athens, N.Y., U.S., 1,695 . . . . .320/P6
Athens, Ohio, U.S., 21,342 . . . . .328/F7
Athens, Ohio, U.S., county, 62,223 . . . . .328/G7
Athens, Penn., U.S., 3,415 . . . . .336/H2
Athens, Tenn., U.S., 13,220 . . . . .344/M4
Athens, Tex., U.S., 11,297 . . . . .346/N3
Athens, Vt., U.S., 340 . . . . .352/B4
Athens, W. Va., U.S., 1,102 . . . . .360/D6
Athens, Wisc., U.S., 1,095 . . . . .364/C3
Atherstone, Eng., U.K., 10,677 . . . . .68/D4
Atherstone, Eng., U.K., 10,677 . . . . .70/A1
Atherton, Eng., U.K., 21,696 . . . . .66/C6
Atherton, Eng., U.K., 21,696 . . . . .68/C2
Atherton, Calif., U.S., 7,194 . . . . .246/J3
Athertonville, Ky., U.S., 60 . . . . .280/E3
Athi, Kenya, river .157/E5
Athlone, Ire., 7,479 . . . . .76/C2
Athol, Ida., U.S., 676 . . . . .264/A2
Athol, Kans., U.S., 51 . . . . .276/D2
Athol, Mass., U.S., 11,299 . . . . .292/F2
Athol, S. Dak., U.S. 342/G2
Athol, Scot., U.K., forest 62/H5
Atholville, N.B., Can., 1,381 . . . . .217/C1
Ath Thawrah, Syria 134/B2
Ati, Chad 153/B4
Atiak, Ug. 157/C2
Atikaki Prov. Wilderness Park, Man., Can. 215/D3
Atikameg, Alta., Can. 212//C3
Atikameg Lake, Man., Can. 215/A2
Atikokan, Ont., Can., 3,560 . . . . .222/B3
Atitlán, Guat., lake 201/B5
Atka, Alaska, U.S., 92 . . . . .240/Inset
Atka, Alaska, U.S., island 240/Inset
Atkins, Ark., U.S., 2,878 . . . . .244/C2
Atkins, Iowa, U.S., 977 . . . . .274/L3
Atkins, Va., U.S., 1,138 . . . . .354/E2
Atkinson, Ga., U.S., 100 . . . . .260/H9
Atkinson, Ga., U.S., county, 7,609 . . . . .260/F9
Atkinson, Ill., U.S., 1,001 . . . . .266/C2
Atkinson, Minn., U.S., 50 . . . . .298/E4
Atkinson, Nebr., U.S., 1,244 . . . . .308/E1
Atkinson, N.H., U.S., 6,178 . . . . .312/D6
Atkinson, N.C., U.S., 236 . . . . .322/J5
Atkinson Corner, Maine, U.S., 70 . . . . .286/C3
Atlanta, Ark., U.S. .244/A1
Atlanta, Ga., U.S., state capital, 416,474,
  (4,112,198 metro.) 260/C4, H3
Atlanta, Ida., U.S. .264/B6
Atlanta, Ill., U.S., 1,649 . . . . .266/D4
Atlanta, Ind., U.S., 761 . . . . .270/D4
Atlanta, Kans., U.S., 255 . . . . .276/F4
Atlanta, La., U.S., 150 . . . . .282/D3
Atlanta, Mich., U.S., 757 . . . . .294/D4
Atlanta, Mo., U.S., 450 . . . . .302/D2
Atlanta, Nebr., U.S., 130 . . . . .308/E3
Atlanta, Nev., U.S. .310/C2
Atlanta, N.Y., U.S., 650 . . . . .320/G5
Atlanta, Tex., U.S., 5,745 . . . . .346/P2
Atlantic, N. Ire., U.K., ocean 65/B1
Atlantic, Scot., U.K., ocean 62/B6
Atlantic, Del., U.S., ocean 255/E6
Atlantic, Fla., U.S., ocean 256/B4, H3
Atlantic, Ga., U.S., ocean 260//10
Atlantic, Iowa, U.S., 7,257 . . . . .274/D5
Atlantic, Maine, U.S., 125 . . . . .286/D4
Atlantic, Maine, U.S., ocean 286/C5
Atlantic, Md., U.S., ocean 288/P7
Atlantic, Mass., U.S., ocean 292/J8, N2
Atlantic, N.H., U.S., ocean 312/E6
Atlantic, N.J., U.S., county, 252,552 . . . . . . .314/D5
Atlantic, N.J., U.S., ocean 314/E5
Atlantic, N.Y., U.S., ocean 320/G2
Atlantic, N.C., U.S., 400 . . . . .322/N5
Atlantic, N.C., U.S., ocean 322/L7
Atlantic, S.C., U.S., ocean 340/F4
Atlantic, Va., U.S., ocean 354/M7
Atlantic Beach, Fla., U.S., 13,368 . . . . .256/G1
Atlantic Beach, N.Y., U.S., 1,986 . . . . .320/C3
Atlantic Beach, N.C., U.S., 1,781 . . . . .322/M5
Atlantic Beach, S.C., U.S., 351 . . . . .340/F3
Atlantic City, N.J., U.S., 40,517 . . . . .314/E5
Atlantic City, Wyo., U.S. 366/B2
A.C. Expressway, N.J., U.S. 314/D4
Atlantic Highlands, N.J., U.S., 4,705 . . . . .314/E3
Atlántico, Col., department 184/B2
Atlántico Norte, Nicar., autonomous region . . .202/B1
Atlántico Sur, Nicar., autonomous region 202/B2
Atlantida, Hond., department 202/B2
Atlantis, Fla., U.S., 2,005 . . . . .256/B5
Atlas, Alg., Mor., mountains 146/A1
Atlas, Mor., mountains 146/A1
Atlas, Tun., mountains 146/A1
Atlin, Br. Col., Can. 214/F1
Atlin, Br. Col., Can., lake 214/F1
Atlin Prov. Park, Br. Col., Can. 214/F1
Atmore, Alta., Can. 212//D4
Atmore, Ala., U.S., 7,676 . . . . .238/B4
Atoka, N. Mex., U.S., 150 . . . . .317/F5
Atoka, Okla., U.S., 2,988 . . . . .330/F3
Atoka, Okla., U.S., county, 13,879 . . . . .330/C3
Atoka, Tenn., U.S., 3,235 . . . . .344/B4
Atolia, Calif., U.S. .246/H7
Atomic City, Ida., U.S. 264/E6
Atqasuk, Alaska, U.S., 228 . . . . .240/D1
Atrai, Bangl., river .127/B4
Atrak, Iran, river 130/D2
Atrato, Col., river 184/A3
Atsion, N.J., U.S. 314/D4
At Tafilah, Jor. 134/A1
At Tafilah, Jor., governorate 134/A1
At Ta'if, Sa. Arab. .136/B2
Attalla, Miss., U.S., county, 19,661 . . . . .300/C2
Attalla, Ala., U.S., 6,592 . . . . .238/C1
Attapulgus, Ga., U.S., 492 . . . . .260/C1
Attawapiskat, Ont., Can., 1,293 . . . . .222/D2
Attawapiskat, Ont., Can., river 222/C2
Attawaugan, Conn., U.S., 950 . . . . .253/H2
Attica, Gr., region .100/C3
Attica, Ind., U.S., 3,491 . . . . .270/C4
Attica, Iowa, U.S., 125 . . . . .274/H5
Attica, Kans., U.S., 636 . . . . .276/D4
Attica, Mich., U.S., 700 . . . . .294/F6
Attica, N.Y., U.S., 2,597 . . . . .320/E5
Attica, Ohio, U.S., 955 . . . . .328/E3
Attleboro, Mass., U.S., 42,068 . . . . .292/J5
Attleborough, Eng., U.K., 6,530 . . . . .70/G1
Attlebridge, Eng., U.K. 70/G1
Attu, Alaska, U.S. 240/Inset
Attu, Alaska, U.S., island 240/Inset
At Tur, Egy. 144/B2
Atwater, Calif., U.S., 23,113 . . . . .246/F5
Atwater, Minn., U.S., 1,079 . . . . .298/C5
Atwater, Ohio, U.S., 950 . . . . .328/H3

Atwood, Colo., U.S., 195 . . . . .250/G1
Atwood, Ill., U.S., 1,290 . . . . .266/E4
Atwood, Kans., U.S., 1,279 . . . . .276/A2
Atwood, Mich., U.S., 90 . . . . .294/D4
Atwood, Okla., U.S., 113 . . . . .330/F3
Atwood, Tenn., U.S., 1,000 . . . . .344/D3
Atyraü, Kaz., 142,497 . . . . .131/B2
Atyraü, Kaz., oblast 131/B2
Auau, Hawaii, U.S., channel 263/G5
Aube, Fr., department 88/C2
Aube, Fr., river 88/D3
Auberry, Calif., U.S., 2,053 . . . . .246/F5
Aubrey, Kans., U.S. 276/H3
Aubry, N.S.W., Austl. . . . . .170/Inset IV
Auburn, Ala., U.S., 42,987, (115,092 metro.) .238/D3
Auburn, Calif., U.S., 12,462 . . . . .246/D4, L4
Auburn, Ga., U.S., 6,904 . . . . .260/D3
Auburn, Ill., U.S., 4,317 . . . . .266/D4
Auburn, Ind., U.S., 12,074 . . . . .270/F2
Auburn, Iowa, U.S., 296 . . . . .274/D4
Auburn, Kans., U.S., 1,121 . . . . .276/G3
Auburn, Ky., U.S., 1,444 . . . . .280/D4
Auburn, Maine, U.S., 23,203 . . . . .286/B4
Auburn, Mass., U.S., 15,901 . . . . .292/G4
Auburn, Mich., U.S., 2,011 . . . . .294/E6
Auburn, Miss., U.S. 300/B4
Auburn, Nebr., U.S., 3,350 . . . . .308/J3
Auburn, N.H., U.S., 4,682 . . . . .312/D6
Auburn, N.J., U.S., 550 . . . . .314/C4
Auburn, N.Y., U.S., 28,574 . . . . .320/H5
Auburn, Penn., U.S., 839 . . . . .336/J4
Auburn, Wash., U.S., 40,314 . . . . .358/C2
Auburn, W. Va., U.S., 103 . . . . .360/E4
Auburn, Wyo., U.S., 270 . . . . .366/A2
Auburndale, Fla., U.S., 11,032 . . . . .256/G3
Auburndale, Wisc., U.S., 738 . . . . .364/C3
Auburn Hills, Mich., U.S., 19,837 . . . . . .294/A6, F7
Auburntown, Tenn., U.S., 252 . . . . .344/J3
Auch, Fr. 88/C5
Auchallater, Scot., U.K. 62/K5
Auchencairn, Scot., U.K. 62/J9
Auchmull, Scot., U.K. 62/M4
Auchnagatt, Scot., U.K. 62/N4
Auchterarder, Scot., U.K., 3,945 . . . . .62/J6
Auchtermuchty, Scot., U.K., 2,010 . . . . .62/K6
Auchtertyre, Scot., U.K. 62/E4
Aucilla, Fla., U.S., river 256/E1
Auckland, N.Z., 367,737, (1,074,507 metro.) .171/B2
Auckland, N.Z., region 171/B2
Aude, Fr., department 88/C5
Audenshaw, Eng., U.K. 68/B4
Audley, Eng., U.K., 6,180 . . . . .68/C3
Audrain, Mo., U.S., county, 25,853 . . . . .302/D2
Audubon, Iowa, U.S., 2,382 . . . . .274/E4
Audubon, Iowa, U.S., county, 6,830 . . . . .274/E4
Audubon, Minn., U.S., 445 . . . . .298/B4
Audubon, N.J., U.S., 9,182 . . . . .314/B3
Audubon, Penn., U.S., 6,549 . . . . .336/L5
Audubon N.W.R., N. Dak., U.S. 326/D2
Audubon Park, Ky., U.S., 1,545 . . . . .280/A2
Audubon Park, N.J., U.S., 1,102 . . . . .314/B3
Augher, N. Ire., U.K., 597 . . . . .65/D3
Aughnacloy, N. Ire., U.K., 430 . . . . .65/C3
Auglaize, Ohio, U.S., county, 46,611 . . . . . . .328/B4
Au Gres, Mich., U.S., 1,028 . . . . .294/F5
Au Gres, Mich., U.S., point 294/F6
Augsburg, Ger., 254,867 . . . . .86/B4
August, Calif., U.S., 7,808 . . . . .246/D4
Augusta, Ark., U.S., 2,665 . . . . .244/D2
Augusta, Ga., U.S., 199,775, (477,441 metro.) .260/H5
Augusta, Ill., U.S., 657 . . . . .266/C4
Augusta, Kans., U.S., 8,423 . . . . .276/F4
Augusta, Ky., U.S., 1,204 . . . . .280/F2
Augusta, Maine, U.S., state capital, 18,560 . . .286/C4
Augusta, Mich., U.S., 899 . . . . .294/D7
Augusta, Mo., U.S., 218 . . . . .302/F3
Augusta, Mont., U.S., 284 . . . . .306/D2
Augusta, N.J., U.S., 300 . . . . .314/D1
Augusta, Wisc., U.S., county, 65,615 . . . . . . .354/E4
Augusta, W. Va., U.S., 450 . . . . .360/J2
Augusta, Wisc., U.S., 1,460 . . . . .364/B4
Augusta Sprs., Va., U.S., 300 . . . . .354/E4
Auki, Sol. Is. 173/B1
Aulac, N.B., Can. 217/E3
Aulander, N.C., U.S., 888 . . . . .322/L2
Aullville, Mo., U.S., 86 . . . . .302/C2
Aulne, Kans., U.S., 50 . . . . .276/E3
Ault, Colo., U.S., 1,432 . . . . .250/F1
Ault Field, Wash., U.S., 2,064 . . . . .358/C1
Aumsville, Oreg., U.S., 3,003 . . . . .334/D3
Auob, Nam., river .160/C3
Auob, S. Afr., river .162/B2
Aur, Marsh. Is., island 173/C2
Aura, Mali, U.S., 150 . . . . .294/A3
Aurangabad, India, 572,034, (592,052 metro.) .128/C3
Aurelia, Iowa, U.S., 1,062 . . . . .274/D2
Aurillac, Fr. 88/C4
Aurora, Ont., Can., 40,167 . . . . .223/F3
Aurora, Colo., U.S., 276,393 . . . . .250/A3, F2
Aurora, Ill., U.S., 142,990 . . . . .266/A6, E2
Aurora, Ind., U.S., 3,965 . . . . .270/G6
Aurora, Iowa, U.S., 194 . . . . .274/L4
Aurora, Kans., U.S., 79 . . . . .276/E2
Aurora, Ky., U.S., 150 . . . . .280/B4
Aurora, Maine, U.S., 121 . . . . .286/D4
Aurora, Minn., U.S., 1,850 . . . . .298/E3
Aurora, Mo., U.S., 7,014 . . . . .302/C5
Aurora, Nebr., U.S., 4,225 . . . . .308/E3
Aurora, N. Mex., U.S. 317/E2
Aurora, N.Y., U.S., 720 . . . . .320/H5
Aurora, N.C., U.S., 583 . . . . .322/M4
Aurora, Ohio, U.S., 13,556 . . . . .328/H3, J9
Aurora, Oreg., U.S., 655 . . . . .334/D2
Aurora, S. Dak., U.S., 500 . . . . .342/J3
Aurora, S. Dak., U.S., county, 3,058 . . . . .342/G4
Aurora, Tex., U.S., 853 . . . . .346/A9
Aurora, Utah, U.S., 947 . . . . .350/C5
Aurora, W. Va., U.S., 225 . . . . .360/G2
Auroraville, Wisc., U.S., 100 . . . . .364/E4
Ausa, S. Mar., river 97/C1
Au Sable, Mich., U.S., 1,533 . . . . .294/F5
Au Sable, Mich., U.S., point 294/C3, F5
Au Sable, Mich., U.S., river 294/E5
Au Sable Forks, N.Y., U.S., 670 . . . . .320/P2
Auskerry, Scot., U.K., island 62/N2
Aust-Agder, Nor., province 80/B4
Austell, Ga., U.S., 5,359 . . . . .260/B4, G2
Austin, Ark., U.S., 605 . . . . .244/D3
Austin, Ind., U.S., 4,724 . . . . .270/E7
Austin, Man., Can. .215/B4
Austin, Minn., U.S., 23,314 . . . . .298/E7
Austin, Mont., U.S. 306/D3
Austin, Nev., U.S., 600 . . . . .310/B2
Austin, Penn., U.S., 623 . . . . .336/F2
Austin, Tex., U.S., county, 23,590 . . . . .346/M6
Austin, Tex., U.S., state capital, 656,562,
  (1,249,763 metro.) 346/D2, L5

Austinburg, Ohio, U.S., 450 . . . . .328/J2
Austintown, Ohio, U.S., 31,627 . . . . .328/J3
Austinville, Va., U.S., 275 . . . . .354/B7
Australia, nation 162
Australian Alps, Austl., mountains 170/D3
Australian Capital Terr., Austl. 170/D3
Austria, nation 89
Austwell, Tex., U.S., 192 . . . . .346/M7
Austwick, Eng., U.K. 66/D4
Autauga, Ala., U.S., county, 43,671 . . . . .238/C3
Autaugaville, Ala., U.S., 820 . . . . .238/C3
Autlán, Mex., 39,310, (50,846 metro.) 200/D4
Autryville, N.C., U.S., 196 . . . . .322/H5
Auvergne, Fr., region 88/C4
Auvergne, Ark., U.S., 80 . . . . .244/D2
Aux Barques, Mich., U.S., point 294/G5, C4
Auxerre, Fr. 88/C3
Auxvasse, Mo., U.S., 901 . . . . .302/E2
Auyuittuq Natl. Park, Nun., Can. 208/P3
Ava, Ill., U.S., 662 .266/D6
Ava, Mo., U.S., 3,021 . . . . .302/D5
Ava, Ohio, U.S., 250 . . . . .328/G6
Avalon, Nfld., Can., peninsula 206/E5
Avalon, Calif., U.S., 3,127 . . . . .246/G9
Avalon, Ga., U.S., 278 . . . . .260/E2
Avalon, Miss., U.S. .300/B2
Avalon, Mo., U.S., 100 . . . . .302/C2
Avalon, N.J., U.S., 2,143 . . . . .314/D5
Avalon, Penn., U.S., 5,294 . . . . .336/D7
Avalon, Wisc., U.S., 150 . . . . .364/E6
Avant, Okla., U.S., 372 . . . . .330/F1
Avard, Okla., U.S. .330/D1
Avawam, Ky., U.S., 450 . . . . .280/G3
Avebury, Eng., U.K. 73/J2
Aveiro, Port. 93/A2
Avella, Penn., U.S., 750 . . . . .336/A5
Avellaneda, Arg., 344,024 . . . . .191/D3
Avellino, It. 95/C2
Avenal, Calif., U.S., 14,674 . . . . .246/E6
Avenel, N.J., U.S., 17,552 . . . . .314/E2
Avening, Eng., U.K. .68/C6
Avenue, Md., U.S., 475 . . . . .288/G6
Avera, Ga., U.S., 217 . . . . .260/F5
Averill, Minn., U.S. .298/A4
Averill Park, N.Y., U.S., 1,517 . . . . .320/P5
Avery, Ida., U.S. 264/B2
Avery, Iowa, U.S., 125 . . . . .274/J5
Avery, N.C., U.S., county, 17,167 . . . . .322/B4
Avery, Okla., U.S., 60 . . . . .330/F2
Avery, Tex., U.S., 462 . . . . .346/P2
Avery Creek, N.C., U.S., 1,405 . . . . .322/E8
Avery Island, La., U.S., 225 . . . . .282/F7
Aveyron, Fr., department 88/C4
Aviemore, Scot., U.K. 60/B1
Aviemore, Scot., U.K., 2,397 . . . . .62/J4
Aviero, Port., district 93/A2
Avignon, Fr., 88,312, (253,580 metro.) 88/D5
Avila, Sp., 49,712 .94/C2
Avila, Sp., province 94/C2
Avila Beach, Calif., U.S., 500 . . . . .246/E7
Avilés, Sp., 83,185 . . . . .94/B1
Avilla, Ind., U.S., 2,049 . . . . .270/F2
Avilla, Mo., U.S., 137 . . . . .302/B4
Avinger, Tex., U.S., 464 . . . . .346/P3
Avis, Penn., U.S., 1,492 . . . . .336/G3
Avison, Ill., U.S., 1,231 . . . . .266/D5
Avoca, Ark., U.S., 423 . . . . .244/A1
Avoca, Iowa, U.S., 1,610 . . . . .274/D5
Avoca, Mich., U.S., 325 . . . . .294/G6
Avoca, Minn., U.S., 146 . . . . .298/B7
Avoca, Nebr., U.S., 270 . . . . .308/H3
Avoca, N.Y., U.S., 1,008 . . . . .320/G6
Avoca, Penn., U.S., 2,851 . . . . .336/H7
Avoca, Tex., U.S., 125 . . . . .346/J3
Avoca, Wisc., U.S., 608 . . . . .364/C5
Avon, Eng., U.K., river 60/C3
Avon, Ala., U.S., 466 . . . . .238/D4
Avon, Colo., U.S., 5,561 . . . . .250/D2
Avon, Conn., U.S., 15,832 . . . . .266/C3
Avon, Ill., U.S., 915 . . . . .266/C3
Avon, Ind., U.S., 6,248 . . . . .270/D5
Avon, Maine, U.S., 504 . . . . .286/B4
Avon, Mass., U.S., 4,443 . . . . .292/K4
Avon, Minn., U.S., 1,242 . . . . .298/C5
Avon, Mont., U.S., 124 . . . . .306/D3
Avon, N.Y., U.S., 2,977 . . . . .320/F5
Avon, N.C., U.S., 550 . . . . .322/Q4
Avon, Ohio, U.S., 11,446 . . . . .328/F9
Avon, S. Dak., U.S., 561 . . . . .342/G5
Avon-by-the-Sea, N.J., U.S., 2,244 . . . . .314/E3
Avondale, Ariz., U.S., 35,883 . . . . .242/C4
Avondale, Colo., U.S., 500 . . . . .250/F3
Avondale, La., U.S., 5,441 . . . . .282/K3
Avondale, Mo., U.S., 529 . . . . .302/H5
Avondale, Penn., U.S., 1,108 . . . . .336/K6
Avondale, R.I., U.S., 425 . . . . .339/A6
Avondale Estates, Ga., U.S., 2,609 . . . . .260//3
Avonia, Penn., U.S., 1,331 . . . . .336/A1
Avon Lake, Ohio, U.S., 18,145 . . . . .328/F9
Avonmore, Penn., U.S., 820 . . . . .336/C4
Avonmouth, Eng., U.K. 73/G1
Avon Park, Fla., U.S., 8,542 . . . . .256/G4
Avon Park A.F. Range, Fla., U.S. 256/E4
Aoyelles, La., U.S., parish, 41,481 . . . . .282/E4
Awaji, Jap. 114/B3
Awaji, Jap., island .114/B3
Awasa, Eth. 156/C3
Awash, Eth., river .156/C2
Awaso, Gha. 150/A3
Awbari, Lib. 145/B2
Awbari Sand Sea, Lib. 145/B2
Awe, Scot., U.K., lake 62/F6
Awendaw, S.C., U.S., 1,195 . . . . .340/E3
Awka, Nig. 152/D4
Awwali, Leb., river .134/A2
Axbridge, Eng., U.K. 73/G2
Axel Heiberg, Nun., Can., island 208/K1
Axford, Eng., U.K. .68/F3
Axial, Colo., U.S. 250/C1
Axim, Gha. 150/A4
Axis, Ala., U.S., 400 . . . . .238/A5
Axminster, Eng., U.K., 3,472 . . . . .73/G3
Axson, Ga., U.S., 90 . . . . .260/F9
Axtell, Kans., U.S., 445 . . . . .276/F2
Axtell, Nebr., U.S., 696 . . . . .308/E3
Axtell, Utah, U.S., 100 . . . . .350/C4
Axton, Va., U.S., 425 . . . . .354/D7
Ayacucho, Peru, 88,262 . . . . .185/C3
Ayacucho, Peru, department 185/C3
Ayaköz, Kaz. 131/E2
Ayame, C. d'Iv., lake 150/E4
Aycock, La., U.S. 282/C1
Ayden, N.C., U.S., 4,622 . . . . .322/L4
Aydin, Tur. 133/B3
Aydin, Tur., province 133/B3
Ayer, Mass., U.S., 7,287 . . . . .292/H2
Ayer, Wash., U.S., 50 . . . . .358/G3
Ayer Chawan, Sing., island 123/A1
Ayers, Maine, U.S. .286/E4

Ayers Cliff, Que., Can., 1,102 . . . . .226/D6
Ayeyarwady, Mya., *division* 125/B3
Aylburton, Eng., U.K. .68/B6
Ayle, Eng., U.K. 66/D3
Aylesbury, Eng., U.K. . . . . .60/Inset III
Aylesbury, Eng., U.K., 58,058 . . . . .70/C3
Aylesham, Eng., U.K., 4,044 . . . . .70/G4
Aylmer, N.W. Terr., Can., *lake* 208/U4
Aylmer, Ont., Can., 7,126 . . . . .223/E5
Aylmer, Que., Can., 36,085 . . . . .226/A6
Aylmer, Que., Can., *lake*, 36,085 . . . . .226/E6
Aylmer, N. Dak., U.S. 326/E2
Aylsham, Eng., U.K., 4,910 . . . . .70/G1
Aynho, Eng., U.K. 70/B3
Aynor, S.C., U.S., 587 . . . . .340/E3
Ayoûn el Atroûs, Maur. 147/C3
Ayr, Scot., U.K. 60/B2
Ayr, Scot., U.K., 46,431 . . . . .62/G8
Ayr, Nebr., U.S. 308/E3
Ayr, N. Dak., U.S. .326/H2
Ayrshire, Iowa, U.S., 202 . . . . .274/E1
Aysgarth, Eng., U.K. .66/D4
Ayton, Eng., U.K. 66/H4
Aytos, Bul. 101/F3
Azad Kashmir, Pak., *province* 129/D2
Azalia, Ind., U.S., 225 . . . . .270/C6
Azaouâd, Mali, *region* 150/C2
Azare, Nig. 152/F2
A'zaz, Syria 134/A1
Azcapotzalco, Mex. 200/Inset
Azerbaijan, *nation* 101
Aziscohos, Maine, U.S., *lake* 286/B3
Azle, Tex., U.S., 9,600 . . . . .346/A9
Azogues, Ecua. 185/B4
Azov, Russ., *sea* 104/C5
Azov, Ukr., *sea* 102/D3
Azraq ash Shishan, Jor. 134/B2
Aztec, Ariz., U.S. 242/B5
Aztec, Ariz., U.S., *peak* 242/E4
Aztec, N. Mex., U.S., 6,378 . . . . .31/C1
Aztec Ruins N.M., Colo., U.S. 250/B4
Aztec Ruins N.M., N. Mex., U.S. 317/C1
Azua, Dom. Rep. 205/B2
Azua, Dom. Rep., *province* 205/B2
Azuay, Ecua., *province* 185/B4
Azuero, Pan., *peninsula* 203/B3
Azusa, Calif., U.S., 44,712 . . . . .246/E9
Azwell, Wash., U.S., 40 . . . . .358/F2
Az Zarqā', Jor., 428,623 . . . . .134/B1
Az Zarqā', Jor., *governorate* 134/B1
Ba, Viet., *river* 123/B3
Baalbek, Leb. 134/B1
Babahoyo, Ecua. 185/B3
Bab al Mandab, Dji., *strait* 156/C1
Bab al Mandab, Erit., *strait* 156/D3
Babanusah, Sudan 145/B3
Babar, Indon., *island* 122/D2
Babb, Mont., U.S. .306/C1
Babbacombe, Eng., U.K. 73/E4
Babbage, Yukon, Can., *river* 228/B1
Babbie, Ala., U.S., 627 . . . . .238/C4
Babbitt, Minn., U.S., 1,670 . . . . .298/F3
Babbs, Okla., U.S. .330/C3
Babcock, Fla., U.S., 50 . . . . .256/G5
Babcock, Wisc., U.S., 125 . . . . .364/C4
B'abda, Leb. 134/A2
Babelthuap, Palau, *island* 172/C3
Babine, Br. Col., Can., *lake* 214/J4
Babine, Br. Col., Can., *river* 214/J3
Babruysk, Bela. 82/D3
Babson Park, Fla., U.S., 1,182 . . . . .256/G5
Babu Bheri, India . . . . .128/Inset II
Babuyan, Phil., *channel* 120/B2
Babuyan, Phil., *islands* 120/B2
Babylon, Iraq, *ruins* 130/B2
Babylon, N.Y., U.S., 12,615 . . . . .320/D2
Baca, Colo., U.S., *county*, 4,517 . . . . .250/H4
Bacabal, Braz. 188/D3
Bacău, Rom., 207,573 . . . . .101/D2
Bacău, Rom., *county* 101/D2
Bach, Mich., U.S., 90 . . . . .294/F6
Back, Nun., Can., *river* 208/H3
Bačka Palanka, Serb.-Mont. 99/A2
Back Bay, N.B., Can. 217/C3
Back Bay N.W.R., Va., U.S. 354/M7
Backbone, Md., U.S., *mountain* 288/A4
Back Gate, Ark., U.S., 70 . . . . .244/D4
Backus, Minn., U.S., 311 . . . . .298/C4
Bac Lieu, Viet. 123/A5
Bacliff, Tex., U.S., 6,962 . . . . .346/C7
Bacolod, Phil., 429,076 . . . . .120/B4
Bacon, Ga., U.S., *county*, 10,103 . . . . .260/F8
Baconton, Ga., U.S., 804 . . . . .260/C9
Bacova, W.Va., U.S., 175 . . . . .354/D4
Bács-Kiskun, Hun., *county* 91/B2
Bacton, (Bacton/Walcott), Eng., U.K., 1,435 . . .70/G1
Bacup, Eng., U.K., 13,682 . . . . .66/D5
Bacup, Eng., U.K., 13,682 . . . . .68/C2
Bad, S. Dak., U.S., *river* 342/D3
Badajoz, Sp., 133,519 . . . . .94/C3
Badajoz, Sp., *province* 94/C3
Badakhshan, Afg., *region* 129/B2
Badakhshoni Kuni, Taj., *autonomous oblast* . .132/B2
Badalona, Sp., 205,836 . . . . .94/H2
Badas, Bru. 121/A2
Bad Axe, Mich., U.S., 3,462 . . . . .294/G6
Badby, Eng., U.K. 70/B2
Baddeck, N.S., Can., 907 . . . . .217/C3
Bad Ems, Ger. 86/A3
Baden, Aus. 91/E2
Baden, Man., Can. 215/A3
Baden, Switz. 90/C1
Baden, Md., U.S., 225 . . . . .288/G5
Baden, Penn., U.S., 4,377 . . . . .336/A4
Baden-Baden, Ger. .86/B4
Badenscoth, Scot., U.K. 62/M4
Baden-Württemberg, Ger., *state* 86/B4
Badenyon, Scot., U.K. 62/K4
Badgastein, Aus. 91/E2
Badger, Man., Can. 215/D4
Badger, Nfld., Can., 906 . . . . .206/C5
Badger, Iowa, U.S., 610 . . . . .274/F2
Badger, Minn., U.S., 470 . . . . .298/A2
Badger, S. Dak., U.S., 144 . . . . .342/H3
Badin, N.C., U.S., 1,154 . . . . .322/E4
Bad Ischl, Aus. 91/E2
Bad Kreuznach, Ger. 86/A4
Badlands Natl. Park, S. Dak., U.S. 342/C4
Badou, Togo 151/B3
Bad Reichenhall, Ger. 86/C5
Bad River Ind. Res., Wisc., U.S. 364/C2
Bafatá, Gui.-B. 149/C1
Baffin, Nun., Can., *bay* 193/C15
Baffin, Nun., Can., *island* 208/M2
Baffin, Grnld., *bay* 193/B15
Baffin, Grnld., *bay* 193/B2
Bafilo, Togo 151/B2
Bafing, Guin., *river* 149/C2
Bafoulabé, Mali 150/A3
Bafoussam, Came., 113,000 . . . . .153/B2
Bagdad, Ariz., U.S., 1,578 . . . . .242/B3

Bagdad, Calif., U.S., 60 . . . . .246/K8
Bagdad, Fla., U.S., 1,490 . . . . .256/A1
Bagdad, Ky., U.S., 150 . . . . .280/E2
Baggs, Wyo., U.S., 348 . . . . .366/C3
Baghdad, Iraq, *capital*, 3,841,268,
  (4,689,000 *metro.*) 130/B2
Baghlan, Afg., 39,228 . . . . .129/B1
Bagley, Iowa, U.S., 354 . . . . .274/F4
Bagley, Minn., U.S., 1,235 . . . . .298/B3
Bagley, Wisc., U.S., 339 . . . . .364/B6
Baglung, Nepal 126/D2
Bagmati, Nepal, *river* 126/C2
Bago, Mya., *division* 125/B3
Bagoé, C. d'Iv., *river* 150/B3
Bagshot, Eng., U.K., 5,190 . . . . .70/C4
Baguio, Phil., 252,386 . . . . .120/B2
Bagwy Llydiart, Eng., U.K. 68/B6
Bagzane, Niger, *mountain* 152/B2
Bahama, N.C., U.S., 550 . . . . .322/H2
Bahamas, *nation* .204/C1
Bahamas, *nation* 195
Bahawalpur, Pak., 408,395 . . . . .129/D4
Bahia, Braz., *state* 188/D3
Bahía Blanca, Arg., 260,096 . . . . .191/C4
Bahía Honda, Cuba 204/A2
Bahir Dar, Eth. 156/B2
Bahrain, *nation* 133
Bahrain, Bahr., *gulf* 137/A2
Bahr al Arab, Sudan, *river* 145/B3
Bahr al Ghazal, Sudan, *river* 154/A2
Bahr Aouk, C.A.R., *river* 154/A2
Bahr el Ghazal, Chad, *river* 153/B4
Bahriyah, Egy., *oasis* 144/A2
Bahr Salamat, Chad, *river* 153/B5
Baia Mare, Rom., 149,780 . . . . .101/B2
Baicheng, China 119/F1
Baidoa, Som. 157/B3
Baidyabati, India . . . . .128/Inset II
Baie-Comeau, Que., Can., 23,079 . . . . .225/C4
Baie-Comeau, Que., Can., 23,079 . . . . .226/H2
Baie-des-Sables, Que., Can., 654 . . . . .226/J3
Baie de Wasai, Mich., U.S. 294/E3
Baie-Ste-Anne, N.B., Can., 1,600 . . . . .217/E1
Baie-Ste-Catherine, Que., Can., 273 . . . . . . .226/G3
Baie-St-Paul, Que., Can., 7,290 . . . . .226/F4
Baie Verte, N.B., Can., 413 . . . . .217/E2
Baie Verte, Nfld., Can., 1,492 . . . . .206/C4
Bailey, Colo., U.S., 175 . . . . .250/E2
Bailey, Miss., U.S., 475 . . . . .300/D3
Bailey, N.C., U.S., 670 . . . . .322/J3
Bailey, Tex., U.S., *county*, 6,594 . . . . .346/F1
Baileyboro, Tex., U.S. 346/F1
Bailey Island, Maine, U.S., 400 . . . . .286/B5
Bailey Lakes, Ohio, U.S., 397 . . . . .328/F4
Baileys Crossroads, Va., U.S., 23,166 . . . . . .354/M2
Baileys Harbor, Wisc., U.S., 212/ 364/F3
Bailey's Prairie, Tex., U.S., 694 . . . . .346/N6
Baileys Switch, Ky., U.S., 400 . . . . .280/G4
Baileyton, Ala., U.S., 684 . . . . .238/C1
Baileyton, Tenn., U.S., 504 . . . . .344/R2
Baileyville, Ill., U.S., 275 . . . . .266/D1
Baileyville, Kans., U.S., 212/ 276/F2
Bailieboro, Ont., Can. 223/G3
Bainbridge, Eng., U.K. 66/D4
Bainbridge, Ga., U.S., 11,722 . . . . .260/B1
Bainbridge, Ind., U.S., 765 . . . . .270/C5
Bainbridge, N.Y., U.S., 1,365 . . . . .320/L6
Bainbridge, (Geauga County), Ohio, U.S., 3,417 . .328/J9
Bainbridge, (Ross County), Ohio, U.S., 1,012 . . .328/D7
Bainbridge Island, Wash., U.S., 20,308 . . . . .358/A4
Bainer, Tex., U.S. 346/F2
Bains, La., U.S., 150 . . . . .282/G5
Bainsville, Ont., Can. 223/K2
Bainville, Mont., U.S., 153 . . . . .306/M1
Ba'ir, Jor. 134/B2
Baird, Miss., U.S. .300/B2
Baird, Tex., U.S., 1,623 . . . . .346/J3
Bairdstown, Ohio, U.S., 130 . . . . .328/C3
Bairoil, Wyo., U.S., 97 . . . . .366/C2
Baisden, W. Va., U.S. 360/C5
Baiti, Nauru 174/B1
Baizetown, Ky., U.S., 40 . . . . .280/D3
Baja, Hun. 91/B2
Baja California, Mex., *state* 200/A1
Baja California Sur, Mex., *state* 200/B2
Bajadero, P.R. 206/B2
Baj Baj, India . . . . .128/Inset II
Bajo Boquete, Pan. 203/A2
Bajram Curri, Alb. 99/B1
Bakel, Sen. 148/C2
Baker, Nun., Can., *lake* 208/J4
Baker, U.S., *island* .161
Baker, Calif., U.S., 350 . . . . .246/J7
Baker, Fla., U.S., 300 . . . . .256/B1
Baker, Fla., U.S., *county*, 22,259 . . . . .256/F1
Baker, Ga., U.S., *county*, 4,074 . . . . .260/C9
Baker, Ida., U.S., 70 . . . . .264/D4
Baker, Ill., U.S., 80 . . . . .266/E2
Baker, La., U.S., 13,793 . . . . .282/G5
Baker, Minn., U.S., 80 . . . . .298/A4
Baker, Mo., U.S. 302/G5
Baker, Mont., U.S., 1,695 . . . . .306/M3
Baker, Nev., U.S., 50 . . . . .310/C2
Baker, N. Dak., U.S. 326/F1
Baker, Okla., U.S., 60 . . . . .330/A1, C4
Baker, Okla., U.S., *county*, 16,741 . . . . .334/I3
Baker, Wash., U.S., *lake* 358/D1
Baker, Wash., U.S., *mountain* 360/D1
Baker, W. Va., U.S., 125 . . . . .360/H1
Baker Brook, N.B., Can., 599 . . . . .217/A1
Baker City, Oreg., U.S., 9,860 . . . . .334/J3
Baker Hill, Ala., U.S., 90 . . . . .238/D4
Baker Lake, Nun., Can., 1,507 . . . . .208/J4
Bakersfield, Calif., U.S., 247,057,
  (661,645 *metro.*) 246/G7
Bakersfield, Mo., U.S., 285 . . . . .302/D5
Bakersfield, Tex., U.S. 346/F5
Bakersfield, Vt., U.S., 1,215 . . . . .352/B1
Bakers Mills, N.Y., U.S., 60 . . . . .320/N3
Bakersville, Conn., U.S., 475 . . . . .253/C2
Bakersville, N.C., U.S., 357 . . . . .322/A2, F6
Bakewell, Eng., U.K., 3,818 . . . . .68/D3
Bakewell, Tenn., U.S., 450 . . . . .344/L4
Bakhardok, Turkm. 132/C2
Bakony, Hun., *mountains* 91/A2
Bakouma, C.A.R. .154/B2
Baku, Azer., *capital*, 1,792,300 . . . . .103/C2
Bala, Ont., Can. 223/F2
Bala, Wales, U.K., 1,922 . . . . .64/D2
Bala, Wales, U.K., *lake* 60/B3
Bala, Kans., U.S. 276/E2
Balabac, Phil., *island* 120/A5
Balabac, Phil., *strait* 120/A5
Balakän, Azer. 62/C2
Balallan, Scot., U.K. 62/E2
Balance Rock, Calif., U.S. 246/G7
Balaton, Hun., *lake* 91/A2
Balaton, Minn., U.S., 637 . . . . .298/B6
Balboa, Pan. 203/C2
Balcarres, Sask., Can., 622 . . . . .227/G10
Balcatta, W.A., Austl. . . . . .170/Inset I

Balch, Tex., U.S., 50 . . . . .346/F2
Balch Sprs., Tex., U.S., 19,375 . . . . .346/C9
Balcom, Ill., U.S., 150 . . . . .266/D6
Balcones Hts., Tex., U.S., 3,016 . . . . .346/A2
Bald, Fla., U.S., *point* 256/D2
Bald Creek, N.C., U.S., 125 . . . . .322/E7
Bald Eagle St. For., Penn., U.S. 336/G4
Balderton, Eng., U.K. 70/C1
Bald Head Island, N.C., U.S., 173 . . . . .322/K7
Bald Hills, Qnsld., Austl. . . . . .170/Inset III
Bald Knob, Ark., U.S., 3,210 . . . . .244/D2
Bald Knob, W. Va., U.S., 40 . . . . .360/C5
Baldock, Eng., U.K., 9,232 . . . . .68/G6
Baldock, Eng., U.K., 9,232 . . . . .70/D3
Baldridge, Tex., U.S. 346/F4
Baldur, Man., Can. 215/B4
Baldwin, Ala., U.S., *county*, 140,415 . . . . . .238/B5
Baldwin, Fla., U.S., 1,634 . . . . .256/G1
Baldwin, Ga., U.S., 2,425 . . . . .260/D3
Baldwin, Ga., U.S., *county*, 44,700 . . . . . . .260/E5
Baldwin, Ill., U.S., 3,627 . . . . .266/D5
Baldwin, Iowa, U.S., 127 . . . . .274/N3
Baldwin, La., U.S., 2,497 . . . . .282/F7
Baldwin, Md., U.S., 850 . . . . .288/J2
Baldwin, Mich., U.S., 1,107 . . . . .294/D6
Baldwin, N. Dak., U.S., 50 . . . . .326/E2
Baldwin, Penn., U.S., 19,999 . . . . .336/E7
Baldwin, Wisc., U.S., 2,667 . . . . .364/A4
Baldwin City, Kans., U.S., 3,400 . . . . .276/G3
Baldwin Park, Calif., U.S., 75,837 . . . . .246/D9
Baldwinsville, N.Y., U.S., 7,053 . . . . .320/J4
Baldwinville, Mass., U.S., 1,852 . . . . .292/F2
Baldwyn, Miss., U.S., 3,321 . . . . .300/D1
Baldy, Man., Can., *mountain* 215/A3
Baldy, Ariz., U.S., *mountain* 242/F4
Baldy, N. Mex., U.S., *mountain* 317/E1
Balearic, Sp., *islands* 94/G3
Balearic, Sp., *sea* .94/G2
Balearic Islands, Sp., *autonomous community* . .94/G3
Baleia, Braz., *point* 188/E3
Baleine, Que., Can., *river* 225/C2
Baleine, St. Vin.-Gren., *bay* 208/B1
Balesville, N.J., U.S., 475 . . . . .314/D1
Balfour, Scot., U.K. 62/M2
Balfour, N.C., U.S., 1,212/ 322/E8
Balfour, N. Dak., U.S. 326/E2
Balgonie, Sask., Can., 1,239 . . . . .227/F10
Balhaf, Yemen 137/B2
Balho, Dji. 156/C1
Bali, Indon., *island* 122/C2
Bali, Indon., *province* 122/C2
Baliceaux, St. Vin.-Gren., *island* 208/B3
Balikesir, Tur. 133/A2
Balikesir, Tur., *province* 133/B2
Balikpapan, Indon. 122/C2
Balintore, Scot., U.K., 1,087 . . . . .62/J3
Balivanich, Scot., U.K. 62/B4
Balkan, Bul., *mountains* 101/B2
Balkan, Serb.-Mont., *mountains* 99/C3
Balkan, Turkm., *province* 132/B2
Balkh, Afg. 129/B1
Balkhash, Kaz. 131/D2
Balkhash, Kaz., *lake* 131/D2
Balko, Okla., U.S., 40 . . . . .330/B1, D4
Ball, La., U.S., 3,681 . . . . .282/E4
Ballajora, Eng., U.K. 66/A2
Ballancourt-sur-Essonne, Fr. . . . . .88/Inset II
Ballantine, Mont., U.S., 346 . . . . .306/H4
Ballantrae, Scot., U.K. 62/F8
Ballard, Ky., U.S., *county*, 8,286 . . . . .280/B4
Ballard, Mo., U.S., 60 . . . . .302/B3
Ballard, Utah, U.S., 566 . . . . .350/E3
Ballardvale, Mass., U.S., 3,500 . . . . .292/K2
Ballasalla, Eng., U.K. 66/A5
Ballater, Scot., U.K., 1,446 . . . . .62/K4
Ballaugh, Eng., U.K. 66/B5
Ball Bluff, Minn., U.S. 298/D3
Ball Club, Minn., U.S., 80 . . . . .298/D3
Ballenger Creek, Md., U.S., 13,518 . . . . .288/F2
Ballentine, S.C., U.S., 850 . . . . .340/A3, C2
Ballemy, Antar., *islands* 192/C5
Ball Ground, Ga., U.S., 730 . . . . .260/C3
Ball Hill, Eng., U.K. 70/B2
Ballina, Ire. 76/B1
Ballinamallard, N. Ire., U.K., 1,068 . . . . .65/D3
Ballinger, Tex., U.S., 4,243 . . . . .346/H4
Ballinluig, Scot., U.K. 62/J5
Ballintoy, N. Ire., U.K., 184 . . . . .65/E1
Ballouville, Conn., U.S., 950 . . . . .253/H2
Balls Cross, Eng., U.K. 70/C4
Ballston Spa, N.Y., U.S., 5,556 . . . . .320/P5
Ballsville, Va., U.S., 212/ 354/C6
Balltown, Iowa, U.S., 73 . . . . .274/N2
Balltown, Ky., U.S., 250 . . . . .280/E3
Ballville, Ohio, U.S., 3,255 . . . . .328/D3
Ballwin, Mo., U.S., 31,283 . . . . .302/G3
Bally, India . . . . .128/Inset II
Bally, Penn., U.S., 1,062 . . . . .336/K5
Ballycarry, N. Ire., U.K., 1,010 . . . . .65/F2
Ballycastle, N. Ire., U.K., 4,005 . . . . .65/D1
Ballyclare, N. Ire., U.K., 7,761 . . . . .65/F2
Ballygalley, N. Ire., U.K., 496 . . . . .65/F2
Ballygawley, N. Ire., U.K., 655 . . . . .65/C3
Ballygowan, N. Ire., U.K., 2,384 . . . . .65/F3
Ballyhaugh, Scot., U.K. 62/C5
Ballyhornan, N. Ire., U.K. 65/F3
Ballykelly, N. Ire., U.K., 2,277 . . . . .65/C1
Ballymagorry, N. Ire., U.K., 493 . . . . .65/C2
Ballymartin, N. Ire., U.K., 472 . . . . .65/F4
Ballymena, N. Ire., U.K. 60/A2
Ballymena, N. Ire., U.K., 28,717 . . . . .65/E2
Ballymena, N. Ire., U.K., *unitary authority*, 58,610 .65/E2
Ballymoney, N. Ire., U.K., 8,242 . . . . .65/E1
Ballymoney, N. Ire., U.K., *unitary authority*,
  26,894 . . . . .65/E1
Ballynahinch, N. Ire., U.K., 5,196 . . . . .65/F3
Ballynure, N. Ire., U.K., 368 . . . . .65/F2
Ballyronan, N. Ire., U.K. 65/D2
Ballyroney, N. Ire., U.K. 65/E3
Ballyvoy, N. Ire., U.K. 65/E1
Ballywalter, N. Ire., U.K., 1,162 . . . . .65/G2
Ballyward, N. Ire., U.K. 65/E3
Balmaceda, Chile .190/B7
Balmaha, Scot., U.K. 62/G6
Balmedie, Scot., U.K., 1,653 . . . . .62/M4
Balmertown, Ont., Can. 222/B2
Balmoral, N.B., Can., 1,836 . . . . .217/C1
Balmorhea, Tex., U.S., 527 . . . . .346/E4
Balnacra, Scot., U.K. 62/F4
Balnaguard, Scot., U.K. 62/J5
Balsall Common, Eng., U.K. 62/D5
Balsam, Fla., U.S. .322/D8
Balsam Lake, Wisc., U.S., 950 . . . . .364/A3
Balsas, Mex., *river* 200/D4
Balsham, Eng., U.K. 70/E2
Balta, N. Dak., U.S., 73 . . . . .326/E1
Baltasound, Scot., U.K. 62/Q1

Bălți, Mol., 156,000 . . . . .102/A2
Baltic, *sea* 80/E4
Baltic, Den., *sea* .193/D5
Baltic, Den., *sea* 79/D3
Baltic, Est., *sea* 81/A1
Baltic, Fin., *sea* 81/B3
Baltic, Ger., *sea* 86/C5
Baltic, Lat., *sea* 82/A2
Baltic, Lith., *sea* 82/A2
Baltic, Pol., *sea* 83/B1
Baltic, Russ., *sea* 104/B4
Baltic, Swe., *sea* .80/C3
Baltic, Conn., U.S., 1,500 . . . . .253/G3
Baltic, Ohio, U.S., 743 . . . . .328/G5
Baltic, S. Dak., U.S., 811 . . . . .342/J4
Baltimore, Md., U.S., 651,154 . . . . .288/H2
Baltimore, Md., U.S., *county*, 754,292 . . . . .288/H1
Baltimore, Ohio, U.S., 2,881 . . . . .328/E6
Baltimore City, Md., U.S., *county*, 651,154 . .288/H2
Baltimore Highlands, Md., U.S., 15,724 . . . . .288/H3
Baluchistan, Pak., *province* 129/B4
Balvicar, Scot., U.K. 62/E6
Balwina, Austl., *aboriginal land* 170/B2
Balykchy, Kyrg. 131/E1
Balzers, Liech. 90/B2
Bam, Iran 130/D4
Bamako, Mali, *capital*, 1,178,977 . . . . .150/B3
Bamangachi, India . . . . .128/Inset II
Bambadinca, Gui.-B. 149/C1
Bambana, Nicar., *river* 202/B2
Bambari, C.A.R., 43,000 . . . . .154/B2
Bamberg, Ger. 86/B4
Bamberg, S.C., U.S., 3,733 . . . . .340/C3
Bamberg, S.C., U.S., *county*, 16,658 . . . . . .340/C3
Bamburgh, Eng., U.K. 66/E1
Bamenda, Came., 110,000 . . . . .153/B2
Bamford, Eng., U.K. 66/E6
Bamforth N.W.R., Wyo., U.S. 366/D3
Bamian, Afg. 129/B2
Bampton, Eng., U.K., 2,459 . . . . .68/D6
Bampton, Eng., U.K., 2,459 . . . . .70/A3
Banaba, Kiri., *island* 175
Banana, Congo, D.R. 155/A2
Banana, S.L., *island* 149/A1
Bananga, India 128/F7
Banat, Rom., *region* 101/A2
Banbridge, N. Ire., U.K., 12,529 . . . . .65/E3
Banbridge, N. Ire., U.K., *unitary authority*,
  41,392 . . . . .65/E3
Banbury, Eng., U.K. 60/C3
Banbury, Eng., U.K., 39,906 . . . . .68/E5
Banbury, Eng., U.K., 39,906 . . . . .70/B2
Banchory, Scot., U.K., 6,034 . . . . .62/M4
Bancroft, Ont., Can., 4,089 . . . . .223/H2
Bancroft, Ida., U.S., 382 . . . . .264/F7
Bancroft, Iowa, U.S., 808 . . . . .274/F1
Bancroft, Ky., U.S., 536 . . . . .280/B2
Bancroft, La., U.S., 60 . . . . .282/B5
Bancroft, Maine, U.S., 61 . . . . .286/D4
Bancroft, Mass., U.S., 125 . . . . .292/B3
Bancroft, Mich., U.S., 616 . . . . .294/F7
Bancroft, Nebr., U.S., 520 . . . . .308/H1
Bancroft, S. Dak., U.S. 342/H3
Bancroft, W. Va., U.S., 367 . . . . .360/C3
Bancroft, Wisc., U.S., 450 . . . . .364/D4
Banda, Indon., *sea* 122/D2
Banda Aceh, Indon. 122/A1
Bandama, C. d'Iv., *river* 150/B3
Bandama Blanc, C. d'Iv., *river* 150/C2
Bandama Rouge, C. d'Iv., *river* 150/B3
Bandana, Ky., U.S., 150 . . . . .280/B3
Bandarbeyla, Som. 157/C2
Bandar-e Abbas, Iran, 273,578 . . . . .130/D4
Bandar-e Anzali, Iran 130/C2
Bandar-e Bushehr, Iran 130/C4
Bandar-e Khomeyni, Iran 130/B3
Bandar-e Torkeman, Iran 130/C2
Bandar Lampung, Indon. 122/B2
Bandar Seri Begawan, Bru., *capital*, 49,902,
  (85,000 *metro.*) 121/B2
Bandeira, Braz., *mountain* 188/D4
Bandelier N.M., N. Mex., U.S. 317/D2
Bandera, Tex., U.S., 957 . . . . .346/J6
Bandera, Tex., U.S., *county*, 17,645 . . . . . . .346/J6
Bandera Falls, Tex., U.S., 225 . . . . .346/K6
Bandon, Oreg., U.S., 2,833 . . . . .334/B4
Bandra, India . . . . .128/Inset I
Bandundu, Congo, D.R. 155/B2
Bandundu, Congo, D.R., *region* 155/B2
Bandung, Indon., 5,920,000 . . . . .122/B2
Baneberry, Tenn., U.S., 366 . . . . .344/Q2
Banff, Alta., Can., 7,135 . . . . .212/C5
Banff, Scot., U.K., 3,991 . . . . .62/M4
Banff Natl. Park, Alta., Can. 212/B5
Banff Natl. Park, Alta., Can. 214/G5
Bangalore, India, 4,292,233, (5,686,844 *metro.*) .128/C6
Bangar, Bru. 121/B2
Bangassou, C.A.R. 154/B3
Bangi, Malay., *island* 121/D1
Banghazi, Lib., 800,000 . . . . .145/D1
Banghiang, Laos, *river* 124/C3
Bangka, Indon., *island* 122/B2
Bangladesh, *nation* 123
Bangor, N. Ire., U.K. 60/B2
Bangor, N. Ire., U.K., 52,437 . . . . .65/F2
Bangor, Wales, U.K. 60/B3
Bangor, Wales, U.K., 12,330 . . . . .64/C1
Bangor, Maine, U.S., 31,473, (90,864 *metro.*) .286/D4
Bangor, Mich., U.S., 1,933 . . . . .294/C7
Bangor, Penn., U.S., 5,319 . . . . .336/L4
Bangor, Wisc., U.S., 1,400 . . . . .364/C5
Bangs, Tex., U.S., 1,620 . . . . .346/J4
Bangui, C.A.R., *capital*, 451,691,
  (622,000 *metro.*) 154/A2
Bangweulu, Zam., *lake* 159/B2
Bani, Dom. Rep. 205/B2
Bani, Mali, *river* .150/B3
Banida, Ida., U.S., 100 . . . . .264/F7
Bani Suwayf, Egy., 172,000 . . . . .144/B2
Bani Walid, Lib. 145/B1
Baniyas, Syria 134/A2
Banja Luka, Bos.-Her., 195,994 . . . . .98/B1
Banjarmasin, Indon. 122/C2
Banjul, Gam., *capital*, 42,326, (270,540 *metro.*) .148/B2
Bankend, Scot., U.K. 62/K9
Bankfoot, Scot., U.K., 1,136 . . . . .62/K6
Banks, Can., *island* 193/G2
Banks, Br. Col., Can., *island* 214/G4
Banks, N.W. Terr., Can., *island* 208/D2
Banks, N.Z., *peninsula* 171/B3
Banks, Ala., U.S., 224 . . . . .238/C4
Banks, Ark., U.S., 125 . . . . .244/D4
Banks, Ga., U.S., *county*, 14,422 . . . . .260/D3
Banks, Ida., U.S., 40 . . . . .264/B5
Banks, Miss., U.S. .300/B1
Banks, Oreg., U.S., 1,286 . . . . .334/C2
Banks, Wash., U.S., *lake* 358/F2
Banks, Van., *islands* 173/B1
Banks Lake N.W.R., Ga., U.S. 260/D10
Banks Odee, Md., U.S. 288/G6
Bankston, Ala., U.S., 80 . . . . .238/B2

Bankston, Iowa, U.S. 274/N2
Bankstown, N.S.W., Austl. .....170/Inset IV
Bann, N. Ire., U.K., river 60/A2
Bann, N. Ire., U.K., river 65/E2
Bann, N. Ire., U.K., river 76/C1
Bannack, Mont., U.S. 306/D4
Banner, Ark., U.S. 244/D2
Banner, Ill., U.S., 149 .....266/D3
Banner, Miss., U.S., 90 .....300/C1
Banner, Nebr., U.S., county, 819 .....308/A2
Banner, Wyo., U.S. 366/C1
Banner Elk, N.C., U.S., 811 .....322/B2
Banner Hill, Tenn., U.S., 1,053 .....344/S2
Bannertown, N.C., U.S., 950 .....322/D2
Bannock, Ida., U.S., county, 75,565 .....264/E7
Bannockburn, Ont., Can. 223/H3
Bannockburn, Ill., U.S., 1,429 .....266/B5
Ban Phai, Thai. 125/C2
Bansang, Gam. 148/D2
Bansbaria, India .....128/Inset II
Banská Bystrica, Slvk., 111,984 .....92/B3
Banskobystrický, Slvk., region 92/B2
Banstead, (Banstead/Tadworth),
Eng., U.K., 37,245 .....70/D4
Bantam, Conn., U.S., 802 .....253/C3
Bantam, Conn., U.S., lake 253/C3
Bantry, Ire. 76/B3
Bantry, Ire., bay 76/B3
Bantry, N. Dak., U.S. 326/E1
Banwell, Eng., U.K., 1,850 .....73/G2
Banyo, Came. 153/B2
Baoding, China 119/E2
Baoruco, Dom. Rep., mountains 205/A2
Baoruco, Dom. Rep., province 205/A2
Baoshan, China 119/C3
Baotou, China, 1,075,920, (1,592,940 metro.) 119/E1
Baoulé, C. d'Iv., river 150/C1
Baoulé, Mali, river 150/B3
Bapchule, Ariz., U.S., 70 .....242/D4
Baptistown, N.J., U.S., 275 .....314/C2
Baqubah, Iraq 130/B2
Bar, Serb.-Mont. 99/A3
Baraawe, Som. 157/A3
Barabinsk, Russ. 104/E4
Baraboo, Wisc., U.S., 10,711 .....364/D5
Barachois, N.B., Can. 217/E2
Barachois, Que., Can. 226/M3
Baracoa, Cuba 204/F3
Barada, Nebr., U.S. 308/J3
Baraga, Mich., U.S., 1,285 .....294/A3
Baraga, Mich., U.S., county, 8,746 .....294/A3
Barahona, Dom. Rep. 205/A2
Barahona, Dom. Rep., province 205/A2
Barakaldo, Sp., 94,478 .....94/E1
Baraki Barak, Afg. 129/B2
Barakpur, India .....128/Inset II
Baram, Malay., river 121/D2
Barama, Guy., river 183/B2
Baranagar, India .....128/Inset II
Baranavichy, Bela. 82/C3
Baranya, Hun., county 91/B3
Barasat, India .....128/Inset II
Barataria, La., U.S., 1,333 .....282/J7, K4
Barataria, La., U.S., bay 282/K8
Barbados, nation 204/G4
Barbados, nation 197
Barbeau, Mich., U.S. 294/E3
Barber, Kans., U.S., county, 5,307 .....276/D4
Barber, Mont., U.S. 306/G3
Barbers, Hawaii, U.S. 262/H3
Barbers Pt. Naval Air Sta., Hawaii, U.S. 262/J2
Barberton, Ohio, U.S., 27,899 .....328/G4
Barberville, Fla., U.S., 212/ 256/G2
Barbon, Eng., U.K. 66/C4
Barbour, Ala., U.S., county, 29,038 .....238/D4
Barbour, W. Va., U.S., county, 15,557 .....360/F2
Barbours, Penn., U.S. 336/H3
Barboursville, Va., U.S., 212/ 354/C4
Barboursville, W. Va., U.S., 3,183 .....360/B4
Barbourville, Ky., U.S., 3,589 .....280/G4
Barbuda, Ant.-Bar., island 204/F3
Barbuda, Ant.-Bar., island 207/E3
Barcaldine, Scot., U.K. 62/F5
Barcelona, Sp., 1,503,884 .....94/H2
Barcelona, Sp., province 94/G2
Barcelona, Ven., 222,466, (405,103 metro.) 182/D1
Barceloneta, P.R. 206/B2
Barclay, Md., U.S., 143 .....288/L3
Barclay, Nev., U.S. 310/C3
Barco, N.C., U.S., 300 .....322/P2
Bard, Calif., U.S., 150 .....246/L10
Bard, N. Mex., U.S., 50 .....317/G2
Bárda, Azer. 103/B2
Bardai, Chad 153/B2
Bardejov, Slvk. 92/C2
Bardley, Mo., U.S., 40 .....302/E5
Bardney, Eng., U.K. 68/G3
Bardolph, Ill., U.S., 253 .....266/C3
Bardsea, Eng., U.K. 66/B4
Bardsey, Wales, U.K., island 64/B2
Bardstown, Ky., U.S., 10,374 .....280/E3
Bardwell, Ky., U.S., 799 .....280/B4
Bareilly, India, 583,473, (607,652 metro.) 128/C3
Barentu, Erit. 156/B4
Barents, sea 193/B22
Barents, Nor., sea 80/D1
Barents, Nor., sea 80/D1
Barents, Russ., sea 104/C2
Bargachia, India .....128/Inset II
Bargersville, Ind., U.S., 2,120 .....270/D5
Bargrennan, Scot., U.K. 62/G8
Barham, Eng., U.K. 70/G4
Bar Harbor, Maine, U.S., 4,820 .....286/D4
Bar Hill, Eng., U.K., 4,397 .....68/H5
Bar Hill, Eng., U.K., 4,397 .....70/E2
Bari, It. 95/D2
Baril, Alta., Can., river 212/E2
Barinas, Ven., 163,034, (176,336 metro.) 182/B2
Barinas, Ven., state 182/C2
Baring, Bangl., region 127/B4
Baring, Maine, U.S., 255 .....286/E3
Baring, Mo., U.S., 159 .....302/D1
Baring, Wash., U.S., 233 .....358/D2
Baris, Egy. 144/B3
Barisal, Bangl., 163,481 .....127/D6
Barisal, Bangl., division 127/D6
Bark, Ont., Can., lake 223/H2
Barker, N.Y., U.S., 577 .....320/D4
Barker Hts., N.C., U.S., 1,237 .....322/E8
Barker Ten Mile, N.C., U.S., 976 .....322/H5
Barkerville, Br. Col., Can. 214/M4
Barkeyville, Penn., U.S., 237 .....336/B3
Barkhamsted, Conn., U.S., reservoir 253/D2
Barking, (Barking and Dagenham),
Eng., U.K., 143,180 .....70/E3
Barking and Dagenham, Eng., U.K.,
unitary authority, 163,944 .....70/E3
Barking Sands Pacific Missile Range Facility,
Hawaii, U.S. 262/B1
Barkley, Ky., U.S., lake 280/C4
Barkly, Austl., tableland 170/C1

Bark River, Mich., U.S., 425 .....294/B4
Barksdale, Tex., U.S. 346/H6
Barksdale, Wisc., U.S., 125 .....364/C2
Barkston, Eng., U.K. 70/C1
Barkway, Eng., U.K. 68/H6
Barlaston, Eng., U.K., 2,119 .....68/C4
Barlby, Eng., U.K., 2,432 .....66/F5
Barlby, Eng., U.K., 2,432 .....66/H5
Bar-le-Duc, Fr. 88/D2
Barlestone, Eng., U.K., 2,547 .....68/E4
Barlestone, Eng., U.K., 2,547 .....70/B1
Barletta, It. 95/D2
Barley, Eng., U.K. 70/E2
Barling, Ark., U.S., 4,176 .....244/A2
Barlow, Eng., U.K. 66/E6
Barlow, Ky., U.S., 715 .....280/A3
Barlow, N. Dak., U.S., 40 .....326/F2
Barmby Moor, Eng., U.K. 68/F2
Barmouth, Wales, U.K., 2,306 .....64/C2
Barnston, Eng., U.K. 66/H4
Barnabus, W. Va., U.S., 175 .....360/B5
Barnaby River, N.B., Can. 217/D2
Barnack, Eng., U.K. 70/D1
Barnard, Kans., U.S., 123 .....276/D2
Barnard, Mo., U.S., 257 .....302/B1
Barnard, S. Dak., U.S., 60 .....342/G2
Barnard, Vt., U.S., 958 .....352/B3
Barnard Castle, Eng., U.K., 6,084 .....66/E3
Barnard Mill, Ill., U.S. 266/E1
Barnby Moor, Eng., U.K. 66/G6
Barnegat, N.J., U.S., 15,270 .....314/E4
Barnegat Light, N.J., U.S., 764 .....314/E4
Barnegat Pines, N.J., U.S., 1,300 .....314/E4
Barnes, Nun., Can., ice cap 208/O3
Barnes, Kans., U.S., 152 .....276/F2
Barnes, N. Dak., U.S., county, 11,775 .....326/G3
Barnesboro, Penn., U.S. 336/D4
Barnes City, Iowa, U.S., 201 .....274/K4
Barnes Corners, N.Y., U.S., 50 .....320/K3
Barnes Lake-Millers Lake, Mich., U.S., 1,187 .....294/F6
Barneston, Nebr., U.S., 122 .....308/H3
Barnesville, Colo., U.S. 250/F1
Barnesville, Ga., U.S., 5,972 .....260/C5
Barnesville, Md., U.S., 161 .....288/J3
Barnesville, Minn., U.S., 2,173 .....298/A4
Barnesville, Ohio, U.S., 4,225 .....328/H6
Barnet, Eng., U.K., 292,783 .....70/D3
Barnet, Eng., U.K., unitary authority, 314,561 .....70/D3
Barnet, Vt., U.S., 1,690 .....352/C2
Barnetby le Wold, Eng., U.K. 66/H5
Barnet Friern Barnet, Eng., U.K. 68/G6
Barnett, Miss., U.S., 125 .....300/D4
Barnett, Mo., U.S., 207 .....302/D3
Barneveld, N.Y., U.S., 332 .....320/L4
Barneveld, Wisc., U.S., 1,088 .....364/D5
Barney, Eng., U.K. 70/F1
Barney, Ga., U.S., 300 .....260/D9
Barney, N. Dak., U.S., 69 .....326/H3
Barnham, Eng., U.K. 70/F2
Barnhart, Tex., U.S., 100 .....346/G4
Barnhill, Ill., U.S., 90 .....266/E5
Barnhill, Ohio, U.S., 364 .....328/H5
Barningham, Eng., U.K. 66/E4
Barnoldswick, Eng., U.K., 10,038 .....66/D5
Barnoldswick, Eng., U.K., 10,038 .....68/C2
Barnsboro, N.J., U.S., 2,500 .....314/C4
Barnsdall, Okla., U.S., 1,325 .....330/F1
Barnsley, Eng., U.K., 75,120, (211,448 metro.) 66/F5
Barnsley, Eng., U.K., 75,120, (211,448 metro.) 68/D2
Barnsley, Eng., U.K. 68/E2
Barnsley, Eng., U.K., unitary authority, 218,062 .....66/E5
Barnsley, Eng., U.K., unitary authority, 218,062 .....68/D2
Barnstable, Mass., U.S., 47,821,
(162,582 metro.) 292/N6
Barnstable, Mass., U.S., county, 222,230 .....292/N6
Barnstaple, Eng., U.K. 60/B3
Barnstaple, Eng., U.K., 27,691 .....73/D2
Barnstead, N.H., U.S., 3,886 .....312/D5
Barnum, Iowa, U.S., 195 .....274/F2
Barnum, Minn., U.S., 525 .....298/E4
Barnum, Wyo., U.S. 366/G2
Barnumville, Vt., U.S. 352/A4
Bar Nunn, Wyo., U.S., 936 .....366/G2
Barnwell, Alta., Can., 548 .....212//D6
Barnwell, S.C., U.S., 5,035 .....340/C3
Barnwell, S.C., U.S., county, 23,478 .....340/C3
Baro, Eth., river 156/B2
Baroda, Mich., U.S., 858 .....294/C8
Baron, Okla., U.S., 70 .....330/H2
Barons, Alta., Can., 284 .....212//D6
Barquisimeto, Ven., 895,989 .....182/C1
Barr, Ra's al, Bahr., cape 137/B2
Barr, Scot., U.K. 62/G8
Barra, Scot., U.K., island 60/A5
Barra, Scot., U.K., island 62/A3
Barracks of the Swiss Guard, Vat. 96/B1
Barrackville, W. Va., U.S., 1,288 .....360/H1
Barrancabermeja, Col. 184/B3
Barranquilla, Col., 1,549,197 .....184/B3
Barranquitas, P.R. 206/C2
Barrapol, Scot., U.K. 62/C5
Barre, Mass., U.S., 5,113 .....292/F3
Barre, Vt., U.S., city, 9,291 .....352/C2
Barre, Vt., U.S., town, 7,602 .....352/C2
Barreiro, Port. 93/A3
Barren, Ky., U.S., county, 38,033 .....280/E4
Barren, Ky., U.S., river 280/D3
Barren River, Ky., U.S., lake 280/D4
Barre Plains, Mass., U.S., 1,212/ 292/F3
Barrett, Minn., U.S., 355 .....298/B5
Barrett, Tex., U.S., 2,872 .....346/N6
Barrett, W. Va., U.S., 250 .....360/C5
Barretts, Ga., U.S., 550 .....260/E9
Barrhead, Alta., Can., 4,213 .....212//C4
Barrhead, Scot., U.K., 17,244 .....62/H7
Barrhill, Scot., U.K. 62/G8
Barrie, Ont., Can., 103,710 .....223/F3
Barrie, Ont., Can., island 294/G4
Barrier, Ky., U.S., 150 .....280/F4
Barriere, Br. Col., Can. 214/M5
Barrineau Park, Fla., U.S., 60 .....256/A1
Barrington, N.S., Can. 221/B4
Barrington, Ill., U.S., 10,168 .....266/A5
Barrington, N.H., U.S., 7,475 .....312/D5
Barrington, N.J., U.S., 7,084 .....314/B3, C4
Barrington, R.I., U.S., 16,819 .....339/E3
Barrington Hills, Ill., U.S., 3,915 .....266/A5
Barro, Gui.-B. 149/B1
Barron, Wisc., U.S., 3,248 .....364/B3
Barron, Wisc., U.S., county, 44,963 .....364/B3
Barron, Wisc., U.S., 125 .....364/C2
Barrouallie, St. Vin.-Gren. 208/B2
Barrow, Ire., river 76/C2
Barrow, Eng., U.K. 70/F2
Barrow, U.S. 193/B11
Barrow, Alaska, U.S., 4,581 .....240/D1
Barrow, Alaska, U.S., point 193/B11
Barrow, Alaska, U.S., point 240/D1
Barrow, Ga., U.S., county, 46,144 .....260/D3
Barrowby, Eng., U.K., 2,084 .....68/F4

Barrowby, Eng., U.K., 2,084 .....70/C1
Barrowford, Eng., U.K., 5,212 .....66/D5
Barrowford, Eng., U.K., 5,212 .....68/C2
Barrow-in-Furness, Eng., U.K. 60/B2
Barrow-in-Furness, Eng., U.K., 48,947 .....66/B4
Barrows, Minn., U.S., 80 .....298/C4
Barrow upon Humber, Eng., U.K., 2,161 .....66/H5
Barrow upon Humber, Eng., U.K., 2,161 .....68/G2
Barry, Wales, U.K., 49,887 .....64/E5
Barry, Ill., U.S., 1,368 .....266/B4
Barry, Mo., U.S., county, 56,755 .....294/D7
Barry, Minn., U.S. 298/A5
Barry, Mo., U.S., county, 34,010 .....302/C5
Barry, Tex., U.S., 209 .....346/M3
Barry M. Goldwater A.F. Range, Ariz., U.S. 242/B5
Barrys Bay, Ont., Can., 1,259 .....223/H2
Barryton, Mich., U.S., 381 .....294/D6
Barryville, N.Y., U.S., 125 .....320/M8
Barstow, Calif., U.S., 21,119 .....246/J8
Barstow, Md., U.S., 750 .....288/H5
Barstow, Tex., U.S., 406 .....346/E4
Bartang, Taj., river 132/B1
Bartelso, Ill., U.S., 593 .....266/D5
Bartholomew, Ind., U.S., county, 71,435 .....270/E6
Bartibog Bridge, N.B., Can., 255 .....217/D1
Bartica, Guy. 183/B2
Bartlesville, Okla., U.S., 34,748 .....330/F1
Bartlett, Ariz., U.S., reservoir 242/D4
Bartlett, Colo., U.S. 250/H4
Bartlett, Ill., U.S., 36,706 .....266/A5
Bartlett, Iowa, U.S. 274/C6
Bartlett, Kans., U.S., 124 .....276/G4
Bartlett, N.H., U.S., 128 .....308/E2
Bartlett, N.H., U.S., 2,705 .....312/D3
Bartlett, Ohio, U.S., 100 .....328/G7
Bartlett, Tenn., U.S., 40,543 .....344/B4
Bartlett, Tex., U.S., 1,675 .....346/L5
Bartley, Eng., U.K. 70/B5
Bartley, Nebr., U.S., 355 .....308/D3
Barton, Ark., U.S., 355 .....244/E3
Barton, Kans., U.S., county, 28,205 .....276/D3
Barton, Md., U.S., 478 .....288/B3
Barton, Mo., U.S., county, 12,541 .....302/B4
Barton, N. Dak., U.S. 326/E1
Barton, Ohio, U.S., 800 .....328/J5
Barton, Vt., U.S., 2,780 .....352/C1
Barton City, Mich., U.S., 250 .....294/F5
Barton Hills, Mich., U.S., 335 .....294/F7
Barton-le-Clay, Eng., U.K. 70/D3
Barton Mills, Eng., U.K. 70/F2
Bartonsville, (Linganore-Bartonsville),
Md., U.S., 12,529 .....288/E2
Bartonville, Vt., U.S. 352/B4
Barton-under-Needwood, Eng., U.K., 4,327 .....68/D4
Barton-upon-Humber, Eng., U.K., 9,422 .....66/H5
Barton-upon-Humber, Eng., U.K., 9,422 .....68/G2
Bartonville, Ill., U.S., 6,310 .....266/D3
Bartow, Fla., U.S., 15,340 .....256/G4
Bartow, Ga., U.S., 223 .....260/G5
Bartow, Ga., U.S., county, 76,019 .....260/B3
Barú, Pan., volcano 203/A2
Baruta, Ven., 189,166, (249,115 metro.) 182/C1
Baruun-Urt, Mong. 118/D2
Barvas, Scot., U.K. 62/C2
Barwick, Ga., U.S., 444 .....260/D1
Barwise, Tex., U.S., 40 .....346/G2
Basalt, Colo., U.S., 2,681 .....250/C2
Basalt, Ida., U.S., 419 .....264/E6
Basalt, Nev., U.S. 310/A2
Basarabeasca, Mol. 102/A2
Bas-Caraquet, N.B., Can., 1,689 .....217/E1
Basco, Ill., U.S., 107 .....266/B3
Bas-Congo, Congo, D.R., region 155/A2
Bascuñán, Chile, cape 190/B3
Basehor, Kans., U.S., 2,238 .....276/G1, H2
Basel, Switz., 164,850, (402,950 metro.) 90/B1
Basel-Land, Switz., canton 90/B1
Basel-Stadt, Switz., canton 90/B1
Bashaw, Alta., Can., 825 .....212//D5
Bashi, Phil., channel 120/B1
Bashi, Ala., U.S. 238/B4
Bashkortostan, Russ., region 104/D4
Basilan, Phil., island 120/B5
Basildon, Eng., U.K. .....60/Inset III
Basildon, Eng., U.K., 100,924 .....70/E3
Basile, La., U.S., 1,660 .....282/D5
Basilicata, It., region 95/C2
Basin, Mont., U.S., 255 .....306/D3
Basin, Wyo., U.S., 1,238 .....366/B1
Basin City, Wash., U.S., 968 .....358/F3
Basinger, Fla., U.S., 50 .....256/G4
Basingstoke, Eng., U.K., 77,837 .....70/B4
Basin Harbor, Vt., U.S. 352/A2
Baskahegan, Maine, U.S., lake 286/E3
Baskatong, Que., Can., reservoir 226/A5
Baskett, Ky., U.S., 550 .....280/C3
Baskett Slough N.W.R., Oreg., U.S. 334/C3
Baskin, La., U.S., 188 .....282/F2
Basking Ridge, N.J., U.S., 3,600 .....314/C2
Baslow, Eng., U.K., 1,184 .....68/D3
Basque, Oreg., U.S. 334/J5
Basque Country, Sp., autonomous community 94/E1
Basra, Iraq, 406,296 .....130/C2
Bas-Rhin, Fr., department 88/D2
Bass, Austl., strait 170/D3
Bassano, Alta., Can., 1,320 .....212//D6
Bassar, Togo 151/B2
Bassein, (Pathein), Mya., 144,096 .....125/B3
Basse-Normandie, Fr., region 88/B2
Bassenthwaite, Eng., U.K. 66/B3
Bassenthwaite, Eng., U.K., lake 66/B3
Basse Santa Su, Gam. 148/D2
Basse-Terre, Guad., capital, 12,410 .....204/F3
Basseterre, St. K.-Nevis, capital 204/F3
Basseterre, St. K.-Nevis, capital, 12,605 .....207/B2
Bassett, Ark., U.S., 168 .....244/E2
Bassett, Iowa, U.S., 74 .....274/J1
Bassett, Kans., U.S. 276/G4
Bassett, Nebr., U.S., 743 .....308/E1
Bassett, Va., U.S., 1,338 .....354/D7
Bassfield, Miss., U.S., 315 .....300/C4
Bass Harbor, Maine, U.S., 600 .....286/D4
Bassila, Ben. 151/A3
Bassingham, Eng., U.K. 68/F3
Bass Lake, Ind., U.S., 1,249 .....270/C2
Bass River, N.B., Can. 217/D2
Bass Rock, Scot., U.K., islet 60/C2
Basswood, Minn., U.S., 80 .....298/B4
Bastia, Fr. .....88/Inset I
Bastogne, Belg. 85/D2
Bastrop, La., U.S., 12,988 .....282/F1
Bastrop, Tex., U.S., 5,340 .....346/L5
Bastrop, Tex., U.S., county, 57,733 .....346/E2, L5
Basye, W. Va., U.S., 986 .....354/F3
Bata, Eq. Gui. 154/B3
Bataan, Phil., peninsula 120/B2
Batabanó, Cuba, gulf 204/B2
Batan, Phil., islands 120/B1
Batang, China 119/C3

Batangafo, C.A.R. 154/A2
Batangas, Phil., 247,588 .....120/B3
Batava, Duri, Bru. 121/C2
Batavia, Ill., U.S., 23,866 .....266/A6, E2
Batavia, Iowa, U.S., 500 .....274/K5
Batavia, N.Y., U.S., 16,256 .....320/E4
Batavia, Ohio, U.S., 1,617 .....328/B7, C10
Bat Cave, N.C., U.S., 125 .....322/A4, F8
Batchelor, La., U.S., 212/ 282/F5
Batchtown, Ill., U.S., 218 .....266/C4
Bâtdâmbâng, Camb. 124/B2
Bate, Austl., bay .....170/Inset IV
Batéké, Congo, plateau 155/C5
Bates, Ark., U.S., 125 .....244/A3
Bates, Mo., U.S., county, 16,653 .....302/B3
Bates, Oreg., U.S. 334/H3
Batesburg-Leesville, S.C., U.S., 5,517 .....340/C3
Bates City, Mo., U.S., 245 .....302/B2
Batesland, S. Dak., U.S., 88 .....342/C4
Batesville, Ala., U.S. 238/D3
Batesville, Ark., U.S., 9,445 .....244/D2
Batesville, Ind., U.S., 6,033 .....270/F6
Batesville, Miss., U.S., 7,113 .....300/C1
Batesville, Ohio, U.S., 100 .....328/H6
Batesville, Tex., U.S., 1,298 .....354/K5
Batesville, Va., U.S., 175 .....354/F5
Bath, N.B., Can., 592 .....217/B2
Bath, St. K.-Nevis 207/C3
Bath, Eng., U.K. 60/C3
Bath, Eng., U.K., 85,202 .....73/H2
Bath, Ill., U.S., 310 .....266/C3
Bath, Ky., U.S., county, 11,085 .....280/G2
Bath, Maine, U.S., 9,266 .....286/C5
Bath, Mich., U.S., 1,212/ 294/E7
Bath, N.C., U.S., 893 .....312/C3
Bath, N.Y., U.S., 5,641 .....320/G6
Bath, N.C., U.S., 275 .....322/M4
Bath, Penn., U.S., 2,678 .....336/L4
Bath, S. Dak., U.S., 1,212/ 342/G2
Bath, Va., U.S., county, 5,048 .....354/D4
Batha, Chad, river 153/C2
Bath and North East Somerset, Eng., U.K.,
unitary authority, 169,045 .....73/H2
Batheaston, Eng., U.K. 73/H2
Bathgate, N. Dak., U.S., 66 .....326/H1
Bathsheba, Barb. 209/B3
Bath Sprs., Tenn., U.S., 50 .....344/E4
Bathurst, N.B., Can., 12,924 .....217/D1
Bathurst, Nun., Can., island 208/J1
Bathurst Mines, N.B., Can. 217/D1
Batin, Wadi al, Kuw., river 136/A2
Batken, Kyr., province 131/B3
Batley, Eng., U.K., 48,030 .....66/E5
Batley, Eng., U.K., 48,030 .....68/D2
Batman, Tur., 212,700 .....133/E3
Batman, Tur., province 133/E2
Batna, Alg., 242,514 .....146/B1
Batoche N.H.S., Sask., Can. 227/D8
Baton Rouge, La., U.S., state capital, 227,818,
(602,894 metro.) 282/G6
Batouri, Came. 153/B3
Batson, Tex., U.S., 150 .....346/P5
Batsto, N.J., U.S., 175 .....314/D4
Batteau, Nfld., Can. 206/D2
Batticaloa, Sri Lan. 126/C4
Battle, Alta., Can., river 212/F5
Battle, Sask., Can., river 227/A7
Battle, Eng., U.K., 5,235 .....70/E5
Battleboro, N.C., U.S. 322/K2
Battle Creek, Iowa, U.S., 743 .....274/C3
Battle Creek, Mich., U.S., 53,364 .....294/D7
Battle Creek, Nebr., U.S., 1,158 .....308/G2
Battlefield, Mo., U.S., 2,385 .....302/C4
Battleford, Sask., Can., 3,820 .....227/B8
Battle Ground, Ind., U.S., 1,323 .....270/C3
Battle Ground, Wash., U.S., 9,296 .....358/C4
Battle Lake, Minn., U.S., 686 .....298/B4
Battlement Mesa, Colo., U.S., 3,497 .....250/B2
Battle Mtn., Nev., U.S., 2,871 .....310/B1
Battles, Miss., U.S., 175 .....300/D4
Battleview, N. Dak., U.S. 326/C1
Battle, Geo., 136,000 .....103/A4
Ba'tumi, Geo., 136,000 .....103/A4
Batu Pahat, Malay. 121/B2
Baubau, Indon. 122/D2
Bauchi, Nig. 152/E2
Bauchi, Nig., state 152/F2
Baudette, Minn., U.S., 1,104 .....298/C2
Baukau, E. Timor 122/C1
Baukau, E. Timor, province 122/C1
Baumber, Eng., U.K. 68/G6
Baumton, Eng., U.K. 68/D6
Bauria, India .....128/Inset II
Bauru, Braz., 178,861, (260,382 metro.) 188/D4
Bautzen, Lat. 82/C2
Bautzen, Ger. 86/C3
Bauxite, Ark., U.S., 432 .....244/C3
Bavaria, Ger., state 86/B4
Bavaria, Kans., U.S., 90 .....276/E3
Bavarian Alps, Aus., range 91/B3
Bavarian Alps, Ger., mountains 86/B5
Bawburgh, Eng., U.K. 70/G1
Bawcomville, (Brownville-Bawcomville),
La., U.S., 7,616 .....282/E2
Bawdeswell, Eng., U.K. 70/G1
Bawdsey, Eng., U.K. 70/G2
Bawku, Gha. 150/B1
Bawlf, Alta., Can., 362 .....212//D5
Bawtry, Eng., U.K., 2,696 .....66/F6
Bawtry, Eng., U.K., 2,696 .....68/E3
Baxley, Ga., U.S., 4,150 .....260/G8
Baxter, Ark., U.S., county, 38,386 .....244/C1
Baxter, Iowa, U.S., 1,052 .....274/H4
Baxter, Minn., U.S., 5,555 .....298/C4
Baxter, Tenn., U.S., 1,279 .....344/K2
Baxter Sprs., Kans., U.S., 4,602 .....276/H4
Baxter St. Park, Maine, U.S. 286/C3
Baxterville, Miss., U.S., 125 .....300/C4
Bay, Hond., islands 202/B1
Bay, Ark., U.S., 1,800 .....244/E2
Bay, Fla., U.S., county, 148,217 .....256/C1
Bay, Mich., U.S., county, 110,157 .....294/E6
Bayamo, Cuba, 144,000 .....204/E3
Bayamón, P.R. 206/C2
Bayamón, P.R., river 206/C2
Bayan Har Shan, China, range 119/C2
Bayanhongor, Mong. 118/C2
Bayano, Pan., lake 203/C2
Bayard, Iowa, U.S., 536 .....274/E4
Bayard, Nebr., U.S., 1,247 .....317/B5
Bayard, N. Mex., U.S., 2,534 .....317/B5
Bayard, W. Va., U.S., 299 .....360/H2
Bayble, Scot., U.K. 62/C2
Bayboro, N.C., U.S., 741 .....322/M4
Bayboro, S.C., U.S. 340/E2
Bay Bridge, Ohio, U.S. 328/E3
Bay Bulls, Nfld., Can., 1,014 .....206/E5
Bayburt, Tur. 133/E2
Bayburt, Tur., province 133/E2
Bay Ctr., Wash., U.S., 174 .....358/B3
Bay City, Ill., U.S. 266/E6

Bay City, Mich., U.S., 36,817 . . . . .294/F6
Bay City, Oreg., U.S., 1,149 . . . . .334/C2
Bay City, Tex., U.S., 18,667 . . . . .346/N7
Bay City, Wisc., U.S., 465 . . . . .364/A4
Bay de Verde, Nfld., Can., 534 . . . . .206/E5
Bay du Vin, N.B., Can. 217/D1
Bayerischer Wald, Ger., mountains 86/C4
Bayeux, Fr. 88/B2
Bayfield, Ont., Can., 909 . . . . .223/D4
Bayfield, Colo., U.S., 1,549 . . . . .250/C4
Bayfield, Wisc., U.S., 611 . . . . .364/C2
Bayfield, Wisc., U.S., county, 15,013 . . . . . . .364/B2
Bagorria, Uru., lake 187/B2
Bayhead, Scot., U.K. 62/B3
Bay Head, N.J., U.S., 1,238 . . . . .314/E3
Bay Hill, Fla., U.S., 5,177 . . . . .256/C4
Baykal, Russ., lake 104/G4
Baykonyr, Kaz. 131/C2
Baykonyr, Kaz., oblast 131/C2
Bay Lake, (Lake County), Fla., U.S., 100 . . . . .256/G3
Bay Lake, (Orange County), Fla., U.S. 256/C4
Bay Lake, Minn., U.S., 50 . . . . .298/D4
Baylis, Ill., U.S., 265 . . . . .266/C4
Baylor, Tex., U.S., county, 4,093 . . . . .346/J2
Bay Mills Ind. Res., Mich., U.S. 294/E3
Bay Minette, Ala., U.S., 7,820 . . . . .238/B5
Bay of Plenty, N.Z., region 171/C2
Bayonet Pt., Fla., U.S., 23,577 . . . . .256/F3
Bayonne, Fr., 41,778, (178,965 metro.) 88/B5
Bayonne, N.J., U.S., 61,842 . . . . .314/B3, E2
Bayou Cane, La., U.S., 17,046 . . . . .282/H7
Bayou Chicot, La., U.S., 212/ 282/E5
Bayou Cocodrie N.W.R., La., U.S. 282/F3
Bayou Current, La., U.S., 60 . . . . .282/F5
Bayou Goula, La., U.S., 750 . . . . .282/G6
Bayou La Batre, Ala., U.S., 2,313 . . . . .238/A5
Bayou Sauvage N.W.R., La., U.S. 282/K6
Bayou Sauvage N.W.R., La., U.S. 271/L2
Bayou Sorrel, La., U.S., 350 . . . . .282/G6
Bayou Vista, La., U.S., 4,351 . . . . .282/G7
Bayou Vista, Tex., U.S., 1,644 . . . . .346/P6
Bay Pt., N.J., U.S. 314/C5
Bayport, N.S., Can. 221/C3
Bayport, Fla., U.S. 256/F3
Bay Port, Mich., U.S., 500 . . . . .294/F6
Bayport, N.Y., U.S., 8,662 . . . . .320/E2
Bayqongyr, Kaz. 131/C2
Bayqongyr City, Kaz., oblast 131/C2
Bayramaly, Turkm. 132/D3
Bayreuth, Ger. 86/B4
Bay Ridge, Md., U.S., 2,300 . . . . .288/J4
Bay Roberts, Nfld., Can., 5,237 . . . . .206/E5
Bays, Ont., Can., lake 223/F2
Bay St. Lawrence, N.S., Can. 221/G1
Bay St. Louis, Miss., U.S., 8,209 . . . . .300/C5
Bay Shore, Mich., U.S., 550 . . . . .294/D4
Bayshore, N.C., U.S., 2,512 . . . . .322/K6
Bayside, N.J., U.S., 1,800 . . . . .314/C5
Bay Side, N.J., U.S., 1,800 . . . . .314/E4
Bayside, Tex., U.S., 360 . . . . .346/L7
Bayside, Wisc., U.S., 4,518 . . . . .364/F1
Bay Sprs., Fla., U.S., 50 . . . . .256/A1
Bay Sprs., Miss., U.S., 2,097 . . . . .300/C4
Bayston Hill, Eng., U.K., 5,462 . . . . .68/B4
Bayswater, W.A., Austl. . . . . .170/Inset I
Baytown, Tex., U.S., 66,430 . . . . .346/C6
Bayview, Ida., U.S., 350 . . . . .264/C4
Bay View, Ohio, U.S., 692 . . . . .328/E3
Bayview, Tex., U.S., 323 . . . . .346/L9
Bayview Gardens, Ill., U.S., 366 . . . . .266/D3
Bay Vil., Ohio, U.S., 16,087 . . . . .328/F9
Bayville, N.J., U.S., 4,700 . . . . .314/E4
Bayville, N.Y., U.S., 7,135 . . . . .320/C2
Baza, Sp. 94/E4
Bazaar, Kans., U.S. 276/F3
Bazardüzü Dağı, Azer., mountain 103/B2
Bazile Mills, Nebr., U.S. 308/G1
Bazin, Que., Can., river 226/B4
Bazine, Kans., U.S., 311 . . . . .276/C3
Beach, N. Dak., U.S., 1,116 . . . . .326/A3
Beachampton, Eng., U.K. 70/C2
Beach City, Ohio, U.S., 1,137 . . . . .328/G4
Beach City, Tex., U.S., 1,645 . . . . .346/C6
Beach Haven, N.J., U.S., 1,278 . . . . .314/E4
Beach Haven Gardens, N.J., U.S., 1,212/ 314/E4
Beach Haven Hts., N.J., U.S., 125 . . . . .314/E4
Beach Haven Terrace, N.J., U.S., 1,100 . . . . . . .314/E4
Beach Haven West, N.J., U.S., 4,444 . . . . .314/E4
Beach Lake, Penn., U.S., 450 . . . . .336/L2
Beach Park, Ill., U.S., 10,072 . . . . .266/B4
Beachside, Nfld., Can., 174 . . . . .206/D4
Beachville, Md., U.S., 225 . . . . .288/J7
Beachwood, N.J., U.S., 10,375 . . . . .314/E4
Beachwood, Ohio, U.S., 12,186 . . . . .328/H9
Beachy Head, Eng., U.K., cape 70/E5
Beacon, Iowa, U.S., 518 . . . . .274/J5
Beacon, N.Y., U.S., 13,808 . . . . .320/P7
Beacon End, Eng., U.K. 70/F4
Beacon Falls, Conn., U.S., 5,246 . . . . .253/C4
Beacon Hill, Fla., U.S., 500 . . . . .256/C2
Beaconsfield, Eng., U.K., 12,292 . . . . .70/C3
Beaconsfield, Iowa, U.S. 274/F6
Beadle, S. Dak., U.S., county, 17,023 . . . . . . .342/H2
Beadnell, Eng., U.K. 66/E1
Beagle, Arg., channel 191/B7
Beagle, Kans., U.S., 125 . . . . .276/H3
Beal, Ind., U.S., 80 . . . . .270/A7
Beal City, Mich., U.S., 345 . . . . .294/E6
Beallsville, Md., U.S., 150 . . . . .288/E3
Beallsville, Ohio, U.S., 423 . . . . .328/H6
Beallsville, Penn., U.S., 511 . . . . .336/A5
Beals, Maine, U.S., 618 . . . . .286/E4
Beaman, Iowa, U.S., 210 . . . . .274/J3
Bean Island, N.H., U.S. 312/D5
Bean Sta., Tenn., U.S., 1,400 . . . . .344/Q2
Bear, Ida., U.S., lake 264/F7
Bear, Ida., U.S., river 264/F7
Bear, Utah, U.S., lake 350/C2
Bear, Utah, U.S., river 350/C2
Bear Creek, Ala., U.S., 1,053 . . . . .238/B1
Bear Creek, Ala., U.S., reservoir 238/B1
Bearcreek, Mont., U.S., 83 . . . . .306/G4
Bear Creek, Wisc., U.S., 415 . . . . .364/E4
Bear Creek Vil., Penn., U.S., 284 . . . . .336/K3
Bearden, Ark., U.S., 1,125 . . . . .244/D4
Bearden, Okla., U.S., 140 . . . . .330/F2
Beardsley, Ariz., U.S. 242/C4
Beardsley, Kans., U.S. 276/A2
Beardsley, Minn., U.S., 262 . . . . .298/A5
Beardstown, Ill., U.S., 5,766 . . . . .266/C5
Bear Grass, N.C., U.S., 53 . . . . .322/L6
Bear Lake, Br. Col., Can., 227 . . . . .214/L4
Bear Lake, Ida., U.S., county, 6,411 . . . . .264/F7
Bear Lake, Mich., U.S., 318 . . . . .294/C6
Bear Lake, Penn., U.S., 193 . . . . .336/C2
Bear Lake N.W.R., Ida., U.S. 264/F7
Bearmouth, Mont., U.S. 306/C3
Bear River, P.E.I., Can. 224/C2
Bear River, Minn., U.S. 298/D3
Bear River City, Utah, U.S., 750 . . . . .350/B2

Bear Valley N.W.R., Oreg., U.S. 334/E5
Bear Valley Sprs., Calif., U.S., 4,232 . . . . . . .246/G7
Beata, Dom. Rep., cape 204/D3
Beata, Dom. Rep., cape 205/A3
Beata, Dom. Rep., island 205/A3
Beaton, Br. Col., Can. 214/O6
Beaton, Br. Col., Can., river 212//A3
Beatrice, Ala., U.S., 412 . . . . .238/B4
Beatrice, Nebr., U.S., 12,496 . . . . .308/H3
Beattie, Kans., U.S., 277 . . . . .276/F2
Beattock, Scot., U.K. 62/K8
Beatty, Miss., U.S. 300/C3
Beatty, Nev., U.S., 1,154 . . . . .310/B3
Beatty, Oreg., U.S., 60 . . . . .334/E5
Beattyville, Ky., U.S., 1,193 . . . . .280/G3
Beatyestown, N.J., U.S., 3,223 . . . . .314/D2
Beau Bassin, Mauritius, 103,872 . . . . .163/B2
Beauceville, Que., Can., 6,261 . . . . .226/F5
Beauchamp Roding, Eng., U.K. 70/E3
Beaufort, sea 193/B12
Beaufort, Yukon, Can., sea 228/B1
Beaufort, Alaska, U.S., sea 240/H1
Beaufort, N.C., U.S., 3,771 . . . . .322/M5
Beaufort, N.C., U.S., county, 44,958 . . . . .322/M4
Beaufort, S.C., U.S., 12,950 . . . . .340/D4
Beaufort, S.C., U.S., county, 120,937 . . . . . . .340/D4
Beaufort West, S. Afr. 162/B3
Beaulac, Que., Can. 226/E6
Beaulieu, Eng., U.K. 70/B5
Beaulieu, Minn., U.S. 298/B3
Beauly, Scot., U.K., 1,164 . . . . .62/H4
Beaumaris, Wales, U.K., 1,561 . . . . .64/C1
Beaumont, Alta., Can., 7,006 . . . . .212//D4
Beaumont, Kans., U.S., 90 . . . . .276/F4
Beaumont, Ky., U.S., 225 . . . . .280/E4
Beaumont, Miss., U.S., 977 . . . . .300/D4
Beaumont, Tex., U.S., 113,866, (385,090 metro.) . .346/P5
Beaumont Place, Tex., U.S., 4,500 . . . . .346/B6
Beaumont, Que., Can., 72,813 . . . . .226/F5
Beaupré, Que., Can., 2,761 . . . . .226/F4
Beauregard, La., U.S., parish, 32,986 . . . . . . .282/C5
Beauregard, Ala., U.S., 265 . . . . .300/B4
Beauséjour, Man., Can., 2,772 . . . . .215/C4
Beauvais, Fr. 88/C2
Beauval, Sask., Can., 843 . . . . .227/C5
Beaux Arts, Wash., U.S., 307 . . . . .358/A4
Beaver, Sask., Can., river 227/A6
Beaver, Yukon, Can., river 228/D5
Beaver, Alaska, U.S., 84 . . . . .240/F1
Beaver, Ark., U.S., 85 . . . . .244/B1
Beaver, Ark., U.S., lake 244/B1
Beaver, Colo., U.S., creek 250/G2
Beaver, Iowa, U.S., 53 . . . . .274/F3
Beaver, Kans., U.S., 50 . . . . .276/D3
Beaver, Kans., U.S., creek 276/A2
Beaver, Mich., U.S., island 294/D4
Beaver, Ohio, U.S., 464 . . . . .328/D7
Beaver, Okla., U.S., 1,570 . . . . .330/B1, D1
Beaver, Okla., U.S., county, 5,857 . . . . .330/B1, A4
Beaver, Oreg., U.S., 145 . . . . .334/C2
Beaver, Penn., U.S., 4,775 . . . . .336/A4
Beaver, Penn., U.S., county, 181,412 . . . . .336/A4
Beaver, Utah, U.S., 2,454 . . . . .350/B5
Beaver, Utah, U.S., county, 6,005 . . . . .350/A5
Beaver, Utah, U.S., river 350/B5
Beaver, W. Va., U.S., 1,378 . . . . .360/D5
Beaver, Wisc., U.S., 100 . . . . .364/E3
Beaver Bay, Minn., U.S., 175 . . . . .298/F3
Beaver City, Nebr., U.S., 641 . . . . .308/E3
Beaver Cove, Maine, U.S., 91 . . . . .286/C3
Beaver Creek, Yukon, Can., 88 . . . . .228/A4
Beaver Creek, Minn., U.S., 250 . . . . .298/A7
Beavercreek, Ohio, U.S., 37,984 . . . . .328/B6, G2
Beaver Crossing, Nebr., U.S., 457 . . . . .308/G3
Beaver Dam, Ky., U.S., 3,033 . . . . .280/D3
Beaverdam, Ohio, U.S., 356 . . . . .328/C4
Beaverdam, Va., U.S., 175 . . . . .354/H5
Beaver Dam, Wisc., U.S., 15,169 . . . . .364/E4
Beaver Falls, Penn., U.S., 9,920 . . . . .336/A4
Beaver Harbour, N.S., Can. 221/E3
Beaverhead, Mont., U.S., county, 9,202 . . . . . . .306/D4
Beaverhead-Deerlodge N.F.,
   Mont., U.S. 306/C4, D3, D4, E5
Beaver Hill, Man., Can., lake 215/D2
Beaver Lake, N.J., U.S. 314/D1
Beaverlick, Ky., U.S., 212/ 280/F2
Beaverlodge, Alta., Can., 2,110 . . . . .212//A3
Beaver Marsh, Oreg., U.S., 40 . . . . .334/E4
Beaver Meadows, Penn., U.S., 968 . . . . .336/K4
Beaver Mines, Ont., Can., 3,065 . . . . .223/F3
Beaverton, Ala., U.S., 226 . . . . .238/A2
Beaverton, Mich., U.S., 1,106 . . . . .294/E6
Beaverton, Mont., U.S. 306/J1
Beaverton, Oreg., U.S., 76,129 . . . . .334/A2, D2
Beavertown, Penn., U.S., 870 . . . . .336/G4
Beaverville, Ill., U.S., 391 . . . . .266/F3
Beaworthy, Eng., U.K. 73/D3
Bebe, Tex., U.S. 346/L6
Bebington, Eng., U.K., 60,148 . . . . .66/C6
Bebington, Eng., U.K., 60,148 . . . . .68/B3
Bécancour, Que., Can., 11,051 . . . . .226/D5
Beccles, Eng., U.K., 10,337 . . . . .70/H2
Becej, Serb.-Mont. 99/B2
Bécharof, Alaska, U.S., lake 146/A1
Becharof, Alaska, U.S., lake 240/D3
Becharof N.W.R., Alaska, U.S. 240/D3
Bechtelsville, Penn., U.S., 931 . . . . .336/K5
Bechyn, Minn., U.S., 40 . . . . .298/B6
Becida, Minn., U.S., 50 . . . . .298/B3
Beckemeyer, Ill., U.S., 1,043 . . . . .266/D5
Beckenham, Eng., U.K. 70/D4
Becker, Fla., U.S., 40 . . . . .256/G1
Becker, Minn., U.S., 2,673 . . . . .298/D5
Becker, Minn., U.S., county, 30,000 . . . . .298/B3
Becker, Miss., U.S., 225 . . . . .300/D2
Beckermet, Eng., U.K. 66/A4
Becket, Mass., U.S., 1,755 . . . . .292/B3
Becket Ctr., Mass., U.S., 100 . . . . .292/B3
Beckett, N.J., U.S., 4,726 . . . . .314/C4
Beckham, Okla., U.S., county, 19,799 . . . . .330/C2
Beckingham, Eng., U.K. 66/G6
Beckley, W. Va., U.S., 17,254 . . . . .360/D5
Beckton, Wyo., U.S., 80 . . . . .366/C1
Beckville, Tex., U.S., 752 . . . . .346/P3
Beda, Ky., U.S., 250 . . . . .280/D3
Bedale, Eng., U.K., 2,828 . . . . .66/E4
Beddau, Wales, U.K., 7,105 . . . . .64/C1
Beddgelert, Wales, U.K. 64/C1
Beddingham, Eng., U.K. 70/D4
Beddington, Maine, U.S. 286/D4
Bedeque, P.E.I., Can., 154 . . . . .224/B2
Bedeque, P.E.I., Can., bay 224/B2
Bedfield, Eng., U.K. 70/G2
Bedford, Que., Can., 2,667 . . . . .226/D6
Bedford, Eng., U.K. 60/C3
Bedford, Eng., U.K., 73,917 . . . . .68/G5
Bedford, Eng., U.K., 73,917 . . . . .70/D2
Bedford, Ind., U.S., 13,768 . . . . .270/D7

Bedford, Iowa, U.S., 1,620 . . . . .274/E6
Bedford, Ky., U.S., 677 . . . . .280/E2
Bedford, Mass., U.S., 12,595 . . . . .292/B6, J3
Bedford, Mich., U.S., 600 . . . . .294/D7
Bedford, N.H., U.S., 18,274 . . . . .312/C6
Bedford, N.Y., U.S., 1,724 . . . . .320/C1
Bedford, Ohio, U.S., 14,214 . . . . .328/H9
Bedford, Penn., U.S., 3,141 . . . . .336/E5
Bedford, Penn., U.S., county, 49,984 . . . . .336/D6
Bedford, Tenn., U.S., county, 37,586 . . . . .344/J3
Bedford, Tex., U.S., 47,152 . . . . .346/B9
Bedford, Va., U.S., 6,299 . . . . .354/D6
Bedford, Va., U.S., county, 60,371 . . . . .354/D6
Bedford, Wyo., U.S., 169 . . . . .366/A2
Bedford Hts., Ohio, U.S., 11,375 . . . . .328/H9
Bedford Park, Ill., U.S., 574 . . . . .266/B6
Bedfordshire, Eng., U.K., unitary authority,
   381,571 .68/G5
Bedfordshire, Eng., U.K., unitary authority,
   381,571 .70/D2
Bedias, Tex., U.S., 350 . . . . .346/N5
Bedlington, Eng., U.K., 15,430 . . . . .66/E2
Bedok, Sing. .123/B1
Bedrock, Colo., U.S. 250/B3
Bedwas, Wales, U.K., 8,488 . . . . .64/E4
Bedworth, Eng., U.K., 31,932 . . . . .68/E5
Bedworth, Eng., U.K., 31,932 . . . . .70/B2
Bee, Nebr., U.S., 223 . . . . .308/G2
Bee, Tex., U.S., county, 32,359 . . . . .346/L7
Beebe, Ark., U.S., 4,930 . . . . .244/D2
Beebe Plain, Vt., U.S., 212/ 352/C1
Beebe River, N.H., U.S., 175 . . . . .312/C4
Bee Branch, Ark., U.S., 60 . . . . .244/C2
Beeby, Eng., U.K. 70/B1
Bee Cave, Tex., U.S., 656 . . . . .346/D2, K5
Beech, Eng., U.K. 70/B4
Beech Bluff, Tenn., U.S., 250 . . . . .344/D3
Beech Creek, Penn., U.S., 717 . . . . .336/F3
Beecher, Ill., U.S., 2,033 . . . . .266/F2
Beecher, Mich., U.S., 12,793 . . . . .294/F6
Beecher, Wisc., U.S., 150 . . . . .364/F3
Beecher City, Ill., U.S., 493 . . . . .266/E4
Beecher Falls, Vt., U.S., 100 . . . . .352/D1
Beecher Island, Colo., U.S. 250/H2
Beechey Head, Br. Col., Can., cape 358/B1
Beech Grove, Ind., U.S., 14,880 . . . . .270/C6
Beech Grove, Ky., U.S., 250 . . . . .280/C3
Beechgrove, Tenn., U.S., 70 . . . . .344/J3
Beech Mtn., N.C., U.S., 310 . . . . .322/B2
Beechwood, N.B., Can. 217/B2
Beechwood, Ky., U.S., 125 . . . . .280/F2
Beechwood, (Iron County), Mich., U.S., 90 . . . . .294/A3
Beechwood, (Ottawa County), Mich., U.S.,
   2,963 . . . . .294/C7
Beechwood Vil., Ky., U.S., 1,173 . . . . .280/F2
Beechy, Sask., Can., 295 . . . . .227/C10
Beedeville, Ark., U.S., 105 . . . . .244/D2
Beekman, La., U.S., 125 . . . . .282/F1
Beeler, Kans., U.S. 276/B3
Beemer, Nebr., U.S., 773 . . . . .308/H2
Beemerville, N.J., U.S., 600 . . . . .314/D1
Beenleigh, Qnsld., Austl. . . . . .170/Inset III
Beer, Eng., U.K. 73/F3
Bee Ridge, Fla., U.S., 8,744 . . . . .256/F4
Beersheba, Isr., 160,300 . . . . .135/B2
Beersheba Sprs., Tenn., U.S., 553 . . . . .344/K4
Beesleys Pt., N.J., U.S., 1,400 . . . . .314/D5
Bee Spr., Ky., U.S., 225 . . . . .280/D3
Beeston, (Beeston and Stapleford), Eng., U.K.,
   66,626 . . . . .68/E4
Beeston, (Beeston and Stapleford), Eng., U.K.,
   66,626 . . . . .70/B1
Beeswing, Scot., U.K. 62/J9
Beetham, Eng., U.K. 66/C4
Beetown, Wisc., U.S., 125 . . . . .364/C6
Beeville, Tex., U.S., 13,129 . . . . .346/L7
Beg, N. Ire., U.K., lake 65/E2
Beggs, Okla., U.S., 1,364 . . . . .330/F2
Beguildy, Wales, U.K. 64/E3
Behala, India . . . . .128/Inset II
Bei'an, China 119/F1
Beihai, China 119/D3
Beijing, China, capital, 7,362,426 . . . . .119/E2
Beijing, China, independent municipality 119/E1
Beinn Alligin, Scot., U.K., hill 62/E3
Beinn Dearg, Scot., U.K., hill 62/G3
Beinn Dearg, Scot., U.K., hill 62/J5
Beinn Dhorain, Scot., U.K., hill 62/J2
Beinn Eighe, Scot., U.K., hill 62/F3
Beinn Mhor, Scot., U.K., hill 62/B4
Beinn Mhor, Scot., U.K., hill 62/C3
Beira, Moz., (412,588 metro.) 161/B3
Beira, Ark., U.S. 244/B4
Beirut, Leb., capital, 474,870, (938,940 metro.) .134/A2
Beiseker, Alta., Can., 838 . . . . .212//D5
Beja, Port. .93/B3
Beja, Port., district 93/A4
Béja, Tun. 146/B1
Bejaïa, Alg., 117,162 . . . . .146/B1
Bejaïa, Alg., gulf, 147,076 . . . . .146/B1
Béjar, Sp. 94/D2
Bejou, Minn., U.S., 94 . . . . .298/B3
Bekaa, Leb., valley 134/A2
Békés, Hun., county 91/C2
Békéscsaba, Hun. 91/C2
Beklabito, N. Mex., U.S., 70 . . . . .317/A1
Bela, Pak. 129/C4
Bela, Barb. .209/B4
Belair, Bru. .121/B3
Bel Air, Md., U.S., 10,080 . . . . .288/J1
Bel Aire, Kans., U.S., 5,836 . . . . .276/E4
Bel Alton, Md., U.S., 425 . . . . .288/G6
Belapurpada, India . . . . .128/Inset I
Belarus, nation 80
Belarus, nation 193/D2
Belasica, Mac., mountains 100/C2
Belcamp, Md., U.S., 1,900 . . . . .288/K2
Belchatów, Pol. 91/C2
Belcher, La., U.S., 272 . . . . .282/B1
Belchertown, Mass., U.S., 12,968 . . . . .292/E3
Belcoo, N. Ire., U.K., 327 . . . . .65/B3
Belcourt, N. Dak., U.S., 2,440 . . . . .326/F1
Belcoville, N.J., U.S., 425 . . . . .314/D5
Belden, Calif., U.S. 246/C2
Belden, Miss., U.S. 300/D1
Belden, Nebr., U.S., 131 . . . . .308/H1
Belden, N. Dak., U.S. 326/C1
Belding, Mich., U.S., 5,877 . . . . .294/D6
Belding, Tex., U.S. 346/K5
Beledweyne, Som. 157/B3
Belém, Braz., 1,279,861, (1,815,812 metro.) 188/D2
Belen, Miss., U.S., 125 . . . . .300/B1
Belen, N. Mex., U.S., 6,901 . . . . .317/D3
Belfair, Wash., U.S., 700 . . . . .358/C2
Belfast, N. Ire., U.K., administrative capital,
   277,391 .60/B2
Belfast, N. Ire., U.K., administrative capital,
   277,391 .65/F2
Belfast, N. Ire., U.K., bay 76/D1
Belfast, N. Ire., U.K., unitary authority, 277,391 .65/F2
Belfast, Ark., U.S. 244/C3

Belfast, Maine, U.S., 6,381 . . . . .286/C4
Belfast, N.Y., U.S., 800 . . . . .320/E6
Belfast, Penn., U.S., 1,301 . . . . .336/L4
Belfast, Tenn., U.S., 50 . . . . .344/H4
Belfast Lough, N. Ire., U.K., lake 65/F2
Belfield, N. Dak., U.S., 866 . . . . .326/B3
Belford, Eng., U.K. 66/E1
Belford, N.J., U.S., 1,340 . . . . .314/E3
Belford Roxo, Braz. . . . . .188/Inset I
Belfort, Fr. .88/D3
Belfort, Fr., department 88/D3
Belfort, Fr., gap 88/D3
Belfry, Mont., U.S., 219 . . . . .306/H4
Belgaum, India, 325,639, (401,609 metro.) 128/B5
Belgium, nation 83
Belgium, Ill., U.S., 466 . . . . .266/F3
Belgium, Wisc., U.S., 1,678 . . . . .364/F5
Belgrade, (Beograd), Serb.-Mont., capital,
   1,619,244 . . . . .99/B2
Belgrade, Maine, U.S., 2,978 . . . . .286/C4
Belgrade, Minn., U.S., 750 . . . . .298/B5
Belgrade, Mo., U.S., 125 . . . . .302/F4
Belgrade, Mont., U.S., 5,728 . . . . .306/F4
Belgrade, Nebr., U.S., 134 . . . . .308/F2
Belgrade Lakes, Maine, U.S., 350 . . . . .286/C4
Belgreen, Ala., U.S., 150 . . . . .238/B1
Belhaven, N.C., U.S., 1,968 . . . . .322/M3
Belin, Fla., U.S., 349 . . . . .256/C6
Bell, Ky., U.S., county, 30,060 . . . . .280/G4
Bell, Tex., U.S., county, 237,974 . . . . .346/L5
Bella Coola, Br. Col., Can., 167 . . . . .214/J5
Bellaghy, N. Ire., U.K., 1,041 . . . . .65/D2
Bellaire, Mich., U.S., 1,164 . . . . .294/D5
Bellaire, Minn., U.S. 298/F5
Bellaire, Ohio, U.S., 4,892 . . . . .328/J5
Bellaire, Tex., U.S., 15,642 . . . . .346/A6
Bellamy, Ala., U.S., 600 . . . . .238/A3
Bellary, India 128/C5
Bella Unión, Uru. 187/B1
Bella Villa, Mo., U.S., 687 . . . . .302/H3
Bella Vista, Ark., U.S., 16,582 . . . . .244/A1
Bellbrook, Ohio, U.S., 7,009 . . . . .328/G2
Bell Buckle, Tenn., U.S., 391 . . . . .344/J3
Bellburns, Nfld., Can., 80 . . . . .206/C4
Bell Ctr., Wisc., U.S., 116 . . . . .364/C5
Bell City, Ky., U.S., 40 . . . . .280/B4
Bell City, La., U.S., 125 . . . . .282/D6
Bell City, Mo., U.S., 461 . . . . .302/G4
Belle, Nfld., Can., island 206/C3
Belle, Fr., island 88/B3
Belle, W. Va., U.S., 1,344 . . . . .302/E3
Bellw, W. Va., U.S., 1,259 . . . . .360/C4
Belleair, Fla., U.S., 4,067 . . . . .256/C6
Belleair Beach, Fla., U.S., 1,751 . . . . .256/C6
Belleair Bluffs, Fla., U.S., 2,243 . . . . .256/C6
Belleair Shore, Fla., U.S. 256/C6
Belle-Anse, Haiti 205/C2
Belle Ctr., Ohio, U.S., 807 . . . . .328/C5
Belle Chasse, La., U.S., 9,848 . . . . .282/K3, K7
Bellechester, Minn., U.S., 172 . . . . .298/E6
Belledune, N.B., Can., 1,923 . . . . .217/D1
Belleek, N. Ire., U.K., 550 . . . . .65/A3
Belleek, N. Ire., U.K., 189 . . . . .65/E3
Bellefont, Kans., U.S. 276/C4
Bellefontaine, Miss., U.S., 80 . . . . .300/D2
Bellefontaine, Ohio, U.S., 13,069 . . . . .328/C5
Bellefontaine Neighbors, Mo., U.S., 11,271 . . . . .302/J2
Bellefonte, Ark., U.S., 400 . . . . .244/B1
Bellefonte, Del., U.S., 1,249 . . . . .255/C1
Bellefonte, Ky., U.S., 837 . . . . .280/H2
Bellefonte, Penn., U.S., 6,395 . . . . .336/F4
Belle Fourche, Mont., U.S., river 306/L5
Belle Fourche, S. Dak., U.S., 4,565 . . . . .342/B3
Belle Fourche, S. Dak., U.S., reservoir 342/B3
Belle Fourche, S. Dak., U.S., river 342/B3
Belle Fourche, Wyo., U.S., river 366/D2
Belle Glade, Fla., U.S., 14,906 . . . . .256/H5
Belle Haven, (Accomack-Northampton Counties),
   Va., U.S., 480 . . . . .354/M5
Belle Haven, (Fairfax County), Va., U.S., 6,269 . .354/M2
Belleheiglash, Scot., U.K. 62/K4
Belle Isle, Fla., U.S., 5,531 . . . . .256/C4
Belle Isle, Nfld., Can., strait 206/C3
Belle Mead, N.J., U.S., 550 . . . . .314/D3
Bellemeade, Ky., U.S., 871 . . . . .280/B2
Belle Meade, Tenn., U.S., 2,943 . . . . .344/H2
Bellemont, Ariz., U.S. 242/D4
Belleplain, N.J., U.S., 425 . . . . .314/D5
Belle Plaine, Iowa, U.S., 2,878 . . . . .274/K4
Belle Plaine, Kans., U.S., 1,708 . . . . .276/E4
Belle Plaine, Minn., U.S., 3,789 . . . . .298/D6
Belle Prairie City, Ill., U.S., 60 . . . . .266/E5
Belle Rive, Ill., U.S., 371 . . . . .266/E5
Belle Rose, La., U.S., 1,944 . . . . .282/G6
Belle Terre, N.Y., U.S., 832 . . . . .320/E1
Belle Valley, Ohio, U.S., 263 . . . . .328/G6
Belle Vernon, Penn., U.S., 1,211 . . . . .336/B5
Belleview, Man., Can. 215/A4
Belleview, Fla., U.S., 3,478 . . . . .256/F2
Belleview, Mo., U.S., 125 . . . . .302/F4
Belleville, Ont., Can., 45,986 . . . . .222/F4
Belleville, Ont., Can., 45,986 . . . . .223/H3
Belleville, Ark., U.S., 371 . . . . .244/B2
Belleville, Ill., U.S., 41,410 . . . . .266/A3, D5
Belleville, Kans., U.S., 2,239 . . . . .276/E2
Belleville, Mich., U.S., 3,997 . . . . .294/A7, F7
Belleville, N.J., U.S., 35,928 . . . . .314/B2
Belleville, Penn., U.S., 1,386 . . . . .336/F4
Belleville, W. Va., U.S., 150 . . . . .360/C2
Belleville, Wisc., U.S., 1,908 . . . . .364/E6
Bellevue, Ida., U.S., 1,876 . . . . .264/C6
Bellevue, Ill., U.S., 1,887 . . . . .266/D3
Bellevue, Iowa, U.S., 2,350 . . . . .274/P3
Bellevue, Ky., U.S., 6,480 . . . . .280/C1
Bellevue, Mich., U.S., 175 . . . . .288/K5
Bellevue, Mich., U.S., 1,365 . . . . .294/D7
Bellevue, Nebr., U.S., 44,382 . . . . .308/J2
Bellevue, Ohio, U.S., 8,193 . . . . .328/E3
Bellevue, Penn., U.S., 8,770 . . . . .336/D7
Bellevue, Tex., U.S., 386 . . . . .346/K2
Bellevue, Wash., U.S., 109,569 . . . . .358/A4, C4
Bellevue, Wisc., U.S., 11,828 . . . . .364/F4
Bellevue St. Park, Del., U.S. 255/C1
Bellflower, Calif., U.S., 72,878 . . . . .246/D10
Bellflower, Ill., U.S., 408 . . . . .266/E4

Bellflower, Mo., U.S., 427 . . . . .302/E3
Bell Gardens, Calif., U.S., 44,054 . . . . . .246/C9
Bellingham, Br. Col., Can. 214/L7
Bellingham, Mass., U.S., 15,314 . . . . . . .292/J4
Bellingham, Minn., U.S., 205 . . . . .298/A5
Bellingham, Wash., U.S., 67,171,
   (166,814 metro.) 358/C1
Bellingshausen, Antar., sea 90/D2
Bellinzona, Switz. 192/B10
Bellmawr, N.J., U.S., 11,262 . . . . . .314/B3, C4
Bellmead, Tex., U.S., 9,214 . . . . .346/L4
Bellmont, Ill., U.S., 297 . . . . .266/F5
Bellona, Sol. Is., island 173/A2
Bellows Falls, Vt., U.S., 3,165 . . . . .352/C4
Bellport, N.Y., U.S., 2,363 . . . . .320/E2
Bell Ranch, N. Mex., U.S., 40 . . . . .317/F2
Bell Rock, (Inchcape), Scot., U.K., reef 60/C2
Bells, Tenn., U.S., 2,171 . . . . .344/C3
Bells, Tex., U.S., 1,190 . . . . .346/M2
Bellshill, Eng. U.K. 66/C1
Belltown, Del., U.S. 255/D5
Belluno, It. 95/C1
Bellview, N. Mex., U.S. 317/G3
Bellville, S. Afr. 162/A3
Bellville, Ga., U.S., 130 . . . . .260/H7
Bellville, Ohio, U.S., 1,773 . . . . .328/E4
Bellville, Tex., U.S., 3,794 . . . . .346/M6
Bellvue, Colo., U.S., 500 . . . . .250/E1
Bellwood, Fla., U.S., 450 . . . . .256/H3
Bellwood, Ill., U.S., 20,535 . . . . .266/B6
Bellwood, La., U.S., 40 . . . . .282/C3
Bellwood, Nebr., U.S., 446 . . . . .308/G2
Bellwood, Penn., U.S., 2,016 . . . . .336/E4
Bellwood, Va., U.S., 5,974 . . . . .354/J6
Belmar, N.J., U.S., 6,045 . . . . .314/E3
Belmond, Iowa, U.S., 2,560 . . . . .274/G2
Belmont, W.A., Austl. . . . . .170/Inset I
Belmont, Man., Can. 215/B4
Belmont, Scot., U.K. 62/Q1
Belmont, Calif., U.S., 25,123 . . . . .246/J2
Belmont, Kans., U.S. 276/E4
Belmont, Ky., U.S., 425 . . . . .280/E3
Belmont, La., U.S., 125 . . . . .282/B3
Belmont, Mass., U.S., 24,194 . . . . .292/C7
Belmont, Miss., U.S., 1,961 . . . . .300/D1
Belmont, Mont., U.S. 306/H3
Belmont, N.H., U.S., 6,716 . . . . .312/D5
Belmont, N.Y., U.S., 952 . . . . .320/E6
Belmont, N.C., U.S., 8,705 . . . . .322/C4
Belmont, Ohio, U.S., 532 . . . . .328/H5
Belmont, Ohio, U.S., county, 70,226 . . . .328/H6
Belmont, Tex., U.S. 346/L6
Belmont, Vt., U.S., 90 . . . . .352/B4
Belmont, Wash., U.S. 358/H2
Belmont, W. Va., U.S., 1,036 . . . . .360/D2
Belmont, Wisc., U.S., 871 . . . . .364/C6
Belmont Corner, Maine, U.S., 375 . . . . . .286/C4
Belmopan, Bel., capital, 8,130 . . . . .201/B2
Belmore, Ohio, U.S., 171 . . . . .328/C3
Bel-Nor, Mo., U.S., 1,598 . . . . .302/H3
Beloeil, Que., Can. 226/C6
Belo Horizonte, Braz., 2,229,697,
   (4,799,878 metro.) 188/D3
Beloit, Kans., U.S., 4,019 . . . . .276/D2
Beloit, Ohio, U.S., 1,024 . . . . .328/H4
Beloit, Wisc., U.S., 35,775 . . . . .364/D6
Belomorsk, Russ. 104/C3
Belper, Eng., U.K., 18,213 . . . . .68/E3
Belpre, Kans., U.S., 104 . . . . .276/C4
Belpre, Ohio, U.S., 6,660 . . . . .328/G7
Bel Ridge, Mo., U.S., 3,082 . . . . .302/H3
Belsay, Eng., U.K. 66/E2
Belshaw, Ind., U.S., 21/ 270/B2
Belt, Mont., U.S., 633 . . . . .306/G5
Belton, Eng., U.K., 2,300 . . . . .66/C5
Belton, Eng., U.K., 2,300 . . . . .68/F2
Belton, Ky., U.S., 500 . . . . .280/C3
Belton, Mo., U.S., 21,730 . . . . .302/B3, H5
Belton, S.C., U.S., 4,461 . . . . .340/C3
Belton, Tex., U.S., 14,623 . . . . .346/L4
Belton-in-Rutland, Eng., U.K. 70/C1
Beltrami, Minn., U.S., 101 . . . . .298/A3
Beltrami, Minn., U.S., county, 39,650 . . . .298/B2
Beltsville, Md., U.S., 15,690 . . . . . .288/C6, G3
Belva, Okla., U.S. 330/D1
Belva, W. Va., U.S., 225 . . . . .360/D4
Belvedere, Calif., U.S., 2,125 . . . . .246/J1
Belvedere, Calif., U.S., 11,100 . . . . .260/C4, J3
Belvedere, Maine, U.S., 70 . . . . .286/D2
Belvedere, S.C., U.S., 5,631 . . . . .340/C3
Belvedere Hts., Md., U.S., 7,900 . . . . . . .288/H3
Belvidere, Ill., U.S., 20,820 . . . . .266/E1
Belvidere, Kans., U.S. 276/C4
Belvidere, Nebr., U.S., 98 . . . . .308/G3
Belvidere, N.J., U.S., 2,771 . . . . .314/C2
Belvidere, S. Dak., U.S. 342/D4
Belvidere, Tenn., U.S., 212/ 344/J4
Belvidere Ctr., Vt., U.S. 352/B1
Belview, Minn., U.S., 412 . . . . .298/B6
Belville, N.C., U.S., 285 . . . . .322/K6
Belvoir, Eng., U.K. 70/C1
Belvue, Kans., U.S., 228 . . . . .276/F2
Belwood, N.C., U.S., 925 . . . . .322/B4
Belzoni, Miss., U.S., 2,663 . . . . .300/B2
Bemaraha, Madag., plateau 163/A2
Bembridge, Eng., U.K., 3,397 . . . . .70/B5
Bement, Ill., U.S., 1,784 . . . . .266/E4
Bemidji, Minn., U.S., 11,917 . . . . .298/C3
Bemis, W. Va., U.S. 360/G3
Bemiss, Ga., U.S., 1,500 . . . . .260/E1
Bemus Pt., N.Y., U.S., 340 . . . . .320/C6
Bena, Minn., U.S., 110 . . . . .298/C3
Ben Aden, Scot., U.K., hill 62/F4
Ben Alder, Scot., U.K., hill 62/H5
Benavente, Sp. 94/D1
Benavides, Tex., U.S., 1,686 . . . . .346/K8
Ben Avon, Penn., U.S., 1,917 . . . . .336/D6
Ben Avon Hts., Penn., U.S., 392 . . . . . . .336/D6
Benbecula, Scot., U.K., island 62/B4
Benbrook, Tex., U.S., 20,208 . . . . .346/A10
Benbrook, Tex., U.S., lake 346/A10
Benburb, N. Ire., U.K., 287 . . . . .65/D3
Benchland, Mont., U.S. 306/F2
Bend, Oreg., U.S., 52,029 . . . . .334/E3
Bendavis, Mo., U.S., 80 . . . . .302/D4
Bender, (Tighina), Mol., 133,000 . . . . . .102/B2
Bendersville, Penn., U.S., 576 . . . . .336/G6
Bendigo, Vic., Austl. 170/D3
Benedict, Kans., U.S., 103 . . . . .276/G4
Benedict, Md., U.S., 450 . . . . .288/H5
Benedict, Minn., U.S., 150 . . . . .298/C3
Benedict, Nebr., U.S., 278 . . . . .308/G2
Benedict, N. Dak., U.S., 53 . . . . .326/D2
Benedicta, Maine, U.S., 50 . . . . .286/D3
Ben Eoin, N.S., Can. 221/G2
Beneshangul Gumuz, Eth., state 156/B2
Benevento, It. 95/C2
Benevolence, Ga., U.S., 40 . . . . .260/B8
Benewah, Ida., U.S., county, 9,171 . . . . .264/A2
Benezette, Penn., U.S., 60 . . . . .336/E3
Bengal, Bangl., bay 127/D7

Bengal, India, bay 128/E5
Bengal, Mya., bay 125/B3
Bengal, Sri Lan., bay 126/C3
Bengal, Ind., U.S., 125 . . . . .270/E6
Benge, Wash., U.S. 358/G3
Bengkulu, Indon. 122/B2
Bengkulu, Indon., province 122/B2
Bengo, Ang., province 159/B3
Bengough, Sask., Can., 401 . . . . .227/E11
Benguela, Ang., 155,000 . . . . .159/B4
Benguela, Ang., province 159/B4
Benham, Ky., U.S., 599 . . . . .280/H4
Ben Hill, Ga., U.S., county, 17,484 . . . . .260/E8
Ben Hope, Scot., U.K., hill 62/G2
Ben Hur, Ark., U.S. 244/C2
Beni, Bol., department 186/A2
Beni, Bol., river 186/A2
Benicia, Calif., U.S., 26,865 . . . . .246/J1
Benidorm, Sp., 51,873 . . . . .94/F3
Beni Mellal, Mor., 139,000 . . . . .147/C1
Benin, nation 145
Benin, Nig., bight 152/B5
Benin, Togo, bight 151/B4
Benin City, Nig. 152/C4
Benítez, P.R. 206/B2
Benito, Man., Can., 415 . . . . .215/A3
Benjamin, Tex., U.S., 264 . . . . .346/J2
Benkelman, Nebr., U.S., 1,006 . . . . .308/C3
Ben Klibreck, Scot., U.K., hill 62/H2
Benld, Ill., U.S., 1,541 . . . . .266/B3, D4
Benllech, Wales, U.K., 1,858 . . . . .64/C1
Ben Lomond, N.B., Can. 217/D3
Ben Lomond, Ark., U.S., 126 . . . . .244/A4
Ben Lomond, Calif., U.S., 2,364 . . . . . . .246/J3
Ben Macdhui, Scot., U.K., hill 62/J4
Benmore, Scot., U.K. 62/G6
Benndale, Miss., U.S., 100 . . . . .300/D5
Bennet, Nebr., U.S., 570 . . . . .308/H3
Bennett, Colo., U.S., 2,021 . . . . .250/F2
Bennett, Iowa, U.S., 395 . . . . .274/N4
Bennett, N. Mex., U.S., 50 . . . . .317/G5
Bennett, N.C., U.S., 250 . . . . .322/F3
Bennett, S. Dak., U.S., county, 3,574 . . . .342/D4
Bennett, Wisc., U.S., 50 . . . . .364/B2
Bennettsville, S.C., U.S., 9,425 . . . . .340/E2
Ben Nevis, Scot., U.K., hill 60/B2
Ben Nevis, Scot., U.K., hill 62/F5
Ben Nevis and Glen Coe N.P., Scot., U.K. . .62/G5
Bennington, Kans., U.S., 623 . . . . .276/E2
Bennington, Nebr., U.S., 937 . . . . .308/H2
Bennington, N.H., U.S., 1,401 . . . . .312/C6
Bennington, Okla., U.S., 289 . . . . .330/F5
Bennington, Vt., U.S., 15,737 . . . . .352/A5
Bennington, Vt., U.S., county, 36,994 . . . .352/A4
Benoit, Miss., U.S., 611 . . . . .300/B2
Benoit, Wisc., U.S. 364/B2
Benoits Cove, Nfld., Can. 206/B5
Benoni, S. Afr. 162/C2
Bensalem, Penn., U.S., 175 . . . . .336/M5
Bensenville, Ill., U.S., 20,703 . . . . .266/B5
Bensley, Va., U.S., 5,435 . . . . .354/J6
Benson, Sask., Can., 95 . . . . .227/G11
Benson, Eng., U.K., 4,796 . . . . .70/B3
Benson, Ariz., U.S., 4,711 . . . . .242/E6
Benson, Ill., U.S., 408 . . . . .266/D3
Benson, La., U.S., 80 . . . . .282/B3
Benson, Md., U.S., 950 . . . . .288/J1
Benson, Minn., U.S., 3,376 . . . . .298/B5
Benson, N.C., U.S., 2,923 . . . . .322/H4
Benson, N. Dak., U.S., county, 6,964 . . . .326/F2
Benson, N.C., U.S., 194 . . . . .336/D5
Benson, Vt., U.S., 1,039 . . . . .352/A3
Bens Run, W. Va., U.S., 70 . . . . .360/D2
Bent, Colo., U.S., county, 5,998 . . . . . . .250/G4
Bent, N. Mex., U.S. 317/E4
Bent Creek, N.C., U.S., 1,389 . . . . .322/E7
Bentiaba, Ang. 159/B4
Bentley, Alta., Can., 1,035 . . . . .212/D5
Bentley, Eng., U.K., 32,675 . . . . .66/F5
Bentley, Eng., U.K., 32,675 . . . . .68/E2
Bentley, Eng., U.K., 32,675 . . . . .70/C4
Bentley, Ill., U.S., 43 . . . . .266/B3
Bentley, Iowa, U.S. 274/C5
Bentley, Kans., U.S., 368 . . . . .276/E4
Bentley, La., U.S., 150 . . . . .282/C3
Bentley, Mich., U.S., 175 . . . . .294/E6
Bentley Sprs., Md., U.S. 288/H1
Bentley Subglacial Trench, Antar. 192/A9
Bentleyville, Ohio, U.S., 947 . . . . .328/H9
Bentleyville, Penn., U.S., 2,502 . . . . .336/K5
Benton, B.C., Can., 109 . . . . .217/B3
Benton, Ala., U.S., 47 . . . . .238/C3
Benton, Ark., U.S., 21,906 . . . . .244/C3
Benton, Ark., U.S., county, 153,406 . . . . .244/A1
Benton, Calif., U.S., 70 . . . . .246/G5
Benton, Ill., U.S., 6,880 . . . . .266/E6
Benton, Ind., U.S., county, 9,421 . . . . . .270/B3
Benton, Iowa, U.S., 40 . . . . .274/K3
Benton, Iowa, U.S., county, 25,308 . . . . .274/K3
Benton, Kans., U.S., 827 . . . . .276/E4
Benton, Ky., U.S., 4,197 . . . . .280/B4
Benton, La., U.S., 2,035 . . . . .282/B1
Benton, Maine, U.S., 2,557 . . . . .286/C4
Benton, Minn., U.S., county, 34,226 . . . .298/C5
Benton, Miss., U.S., 275 . . . . .300/B3
Benton, Miss., U.S., county, 8,026 . . . . . .300/C1
Benton, Mo., U.S., 732 . . . . .302/G4
Benton, Mo., U.S., county, 17,180 . . . . . .302/C3
Benton, N.H., U.S., 314 . . . . .312/C3
Benton, Oreg., U.S., county, 78,153 . . . . .334/C3
Benton, Penn., U.S., 955 . . . . .336/J3
Benton, Tenn., U.S., 1,138 . . . . .344/M4
Benton, Tenn., U.S., county, 16,537 . . . . .344/F2
Benton, Wash., U.S., county, 142,475 . . . .358/F3
Benton, Wisc., U.S., 976 . . . . .364/C6
Benton City, Mo., U.S., 122 . . . . .302/E2
Benton City, Wash., U.S., 2,624 . . . . .358/F3
Benton Harbor, Mich., U.S., 11,182,
   (162,453 metro.) 294/C7
Benton Hts., Mich., U.S., 5,458 . . . . .294/C7
Bentonia, Miss., U.S., 500 . . . . .300/B3
Bentonite Spur, Wyo., U.S. 366/D1
Benton Ridge, Ohio, U.S., 315 . . . . .328/C3
Bentonsport, Iowa, U.S. 274/L6
Bentonville, Ark., U.S., 19,730 . . . . .244/A1
Bentonville, Ohio, U.S., 250 . . . . .328/C8
Bentonville, Va., U.S., 275 . . . . .354/G3
Bentpath, Scot., U.K. 62/K8
Bents Old Fort Natl. Hist. Site, Colo., U.S. . .250/G4
Benue, Came., river 153/B2
Benue, Nig., river 152/E3
Benue, Nig., state 152/E4
Benwee Head, Ire., cape 76/B1
Benwick, Eng., U.K. 70/D2
Benxi, China, 773,730, (1,412,120 metro.) . .119/F1
Benzdorp, Sur. 183/B3
Benzie, Mich., U.S., county, 15,998 . . . . .294/D5
Benzonia, Mich., U.S., 519 . . . . .294/C5
Beowawe, Nev., U.S., 60 . . . . .310/B1
Beqa, Fiji, island 174/B3

Bequia, St. Vin.-Gren., island 208/B2
Beragh, N. Ire., U.K., 564 . . . . .65/C2
Berat, Alb., 40,112 . . . . .99/A3
Berbera, Som. 157/B1
Berbérati, C.A.R., 47,000 . . . . .154/A3
Berbice, Guy., river 183/B3
Berclair, Tex., U.S., 150 . . . . .346/L7
Berdians'k, Ukr. 102/D3
Berdoba, Chad 153/C4
Berea, Ky., U.S., 9,851 . . . . .280/F3
Berea, Nebr., U.S., 70 . . . . .308/A1
Berea, Ohio, U.S., 18,970 . . . . .328/G8
Berea, N.C., U.S., 225 . . . . .322/H2
Berea, S.C., U.S., 14,158 . . . . .340/B2, E2
Bere Alston, Eng., U.K., 2,362 . . . . .73/D4
Berekua, Dom. 208/B4
Berenda, Calif., U.S. 246/E5
Berens, Man., Can., island 215/C3
Berens, Man., Can., river 215/C3
Berens River, Man., Can., 42 . . . . .215/C3
Bere Regis, Eng., U.K., 1,767 . . . . .73/H3
Beresford, N.B., Can., 4,414 . . . . .217/D1
Beresford, S. Dak., U.S., 2,006 . . . . .342/J4
Berezniki, Russ., 182,900, (185,150 metro.) . .104/D4
Bergamo, It. .95/B1
Bergen, Nor., 233,291 . . . . .80/B3
Bergen, Minn., U.S., 40 . . . . .298/C7
Bergen, N.J., U.S., county, 884,118 . . .314/B1, E2
Bergen, N.Y., U.S., 1,240 . . . . .320/F4
Bergen, N. Dak., U.S. 326/E2
Bergenfield, N.J., U.S., 26,247 . . . . .314/C2
Bergen op Zoom, Neth. 84/B3
Berger, Mo., U.S., 206 . . . . .302/E3
Bergerac, Fr. .88/C4
Bergheim, Tex., U.S., 80 . . . . .346/A1, K6
Bergholz, Ohio, U.S., 769 . . . . .328/J4
Bergisch Gladbach, Ger., 106,150 . . . . . .86/A3
Bergman, Ark., U.S., 407 . . . . .244/C1
Bergoo, W. Va., U.S., 125 . . . . .360/F4
Bergton, Va., U.S. 354/F3
Bergville, Minn., U.S. 298/C3
Bering, sea .193/D10
Bering, strait 193/C10
Bering, Russ., sea 104/K4
Bering, Russ., strait 104/K3
Bering, Alaska, U.S., sea 240/B3
Bering, Alaska, U.S., strait 240/B2
Bering Land Bridge Natl. Pres., Alaska, U.S. . .240/C1
Berino, N. Mex., U.S., 900 . . . . .317/D5
Berkeley, Calif., U.S., 102,743 . . . . .246/C5, J2
Berkeley, Ill., U.S., 5,245 . . . . .266/B6
Berkeley, Mo., U.S., 10,063 . . . . .302/H2
Berkeley, R.I., U.S., 2,800 . . . . .339/D2
Berkeley, W. Va., U.S., county, 75,905 . . .360/K2
Berkeley, W. Va., U.S., county, 142,651 . . .340/E3
Berkeley, W. Va., U.S., county, 75,905 . . .360/K2
Berkeley Hts., N.J., U.S., 13,407 . . . . . . .314/A3
Berkeley Lake, Ga., U.S., 1,695 . . . .260/C4, J2
Berkeley Sprs., W. Va., U.S., 663 . . . . . . .360/K1
Berkey, Ohio, U.S., 265 . . . . .328/C2
Berkhamsted, Eng., U.K., 18,044 . . . . . . .70/C3
Berkley, Iowa, U.S. 274/F4
Berkley, Mass., U.S., 5,749 . . . . .292/K5
Berkley, Mich., U.S., 15,531 . . . . . .294/A6, F7
Berks, Penn., U.S., county, 373,638 . . . . .336/J5
Berkshire, Conn., U.S., 950 . . . . .253/B4
Berkshire, Mass., U.S., 400 . . . . .292/B2
Berkshire, Mass., U.S., county, 134,953 . . .292/A3
Berkshire, Mass., U.S., hills 292/B4
Berkshire, N.Y., U.S., 300 . . . . .320/J6
Berkshire, Vt., U.S., 1,388 . . . . .352/B1
Berlin, Ger., capital, 3,382,212/ 86/C2
Berlin, Ger., state 86/C2
Berlin, Conn., U.S., 18,215 . . . . .253/E3
Berlin, Ga., U.S., 595 . . . . .260/D9
Berlin, Ill., U.S., 140 . . . . .266/D4
Berlin, Md., U.S., 3,491 . . . . .288/C7
Berlin, Mass., U.S., 2,380 . . . . .292/H3
Berlin, N.H., U.S., 10,331 . . . . .312/D3
Berlin, N.J., U.S., borough, 6,149 . . .314/B4, D3
Berlin, N. Dak., U.S. 326/G3
Berlin, Ohio, U.S., 1,300 . . . . .328/G4
Berlin, Okla., U.S. 330/C2
Berlin, Penn., U.S., 2,192 . . . . .336/D6
Berlin, Vt., U.S., 2,864 . . . . .352/B2
Berlin, Wisc., U.S., 5,305 . . . . .364/E5
Berlin Corners, Vt., U.S., 300 . . . . .352/B2
Berlin Hts., Ohio, U.S., 685 . . . . .328/F3
Bermejo, Arg., river 191/C2
Bermuda, U.K., island 186/C6
Bern, Switz., canton 90/B2
Bern, Kans., U.S., 204 . . . . .276/G2
Bern, Switz., capital, 122,469, (317,136 metro.) . .90/B2
Bernal, N. Mex., U.S. 317/F2
Bernalillo, N. Mex., U.S., 6,611 . . . . .317/D2
Bernalillo, N. Mex., U.S., county, 556,678 . .317/D3
Bernard, Iowa, U.S., 97 . . . . .274/N3
Bernard, Maine, U.S., 600 . . . . .286/D4
Bernardo, N. Mex., U.S. 317/D3
Bernardston, Mass., U.S., 2,155 . . . . .292/D2
Bernardsville, N.J., U.S., 7,345 . . . . .314/D2
Bernburg, Ger. 86/B3
Berne, Ind., U.S., 4,150 . . . . .270/G3
Berner, Minn., U.S. 298/B3
Berneray, Scot., U.K., island 62/B3
Bernese Alps, Switz., mountains 90/B2
Bernice, La., U.S., 1,809 . . . . .282/C1
Bernice, Okla., U.S., 504 . . . . .330/H1
Bernie, Mo., U.S., 1,777 . . . . .302/G5
Bernières, Que., Can. 226/K6
Bernstadt, Ky., U.S., 475 . . . . .280/F3
Bernville, Penn., U.S., 865 . . . . .336/J5
Beroun, Minn., U.S. 298/E5
Berounka, Czh. Rep., river 92/A3
Berriedale, Scot., U.K. 62/K2
Berrien, Ga., U.S., county, 16,235 . . . . . .260/E9
Berrien, Mich., U.S., county, 162,453 . . . .294/C7
Berrien Sprs., Mich., U.S., 1,862 . . . . . . .294/C8
Berriew, Wales, U.K. 64/E2
Berry, Ala., U.S., 1,238 . . . . .238/B2
Berry, Ky., U.S., 310 . . . . .280/F2
Berrydale, Fla., U.S., 50 . . . . .256/A1
Berrydale, Wash., U.S. 358/B4, C2
Berry Hill, Eng., U.K. 68/B6
Berry Hill, Tenn., U.S., 674 . . . . .344/H2
Berry Mills, Maine, U.S., 225 . . . . .286/B4
Berrysburg, Penn., U.S., 363 . . . . .336/H4
Berryville, Ark., U.S., 4,433 . . . . .244/B1
Berryville, Va., U.S., 2,963 . . . . .354/H2
Bertha, Minn., U.S., 470 . . . . .298/B4
Berthierville, Que., Can., 3,939 . . . . .226/C5
Berthold, N. Dak., U.S., 466 . . . . .326/D1
Berthoud, Colo., U.S., 4,839 . . . . .250/E1
Bertie, N.C., U.S., county, 19,773 . . . . . .322/K3
Bertoua, Came., 18,254 . . . . .153/B3
Bertram, Iowa, U.S., 681 . . . . .274/L4
Bertram, Tex., U.S., 1,122 . . . . .346/D1, K5
Bertrand, N.B., Can., 1,269 . . . . .217/D1
Bertrand, Mich., U.S., 1,700 . . . . .294/C8
Bertrand, Mo., U.S., 740 . . . . .302/G5
Bertrand, Nebr., U.S., 786 . . . . .308/E3

Bertrandville, La., U.S., 212/ 282/K4, K7
Bertwell, Sask., Can. 227/H8
Berville, Mich., U.S., 425 . . . . .294/G7
Berwick, Vic., Austl. . . . . .170/Inset V
Berwick, N.B., Can. 217/D3
Berwick, N.S., Can., 2,282 . . . . .221/C2
Berwick, Iowa, U.S. 274/G4
Berwick, La., U.S., 4,418 . . . . .282/C7
Berwick, Maine, U.S., 6,353 . . . . .286/B5
Berwick, N. Dak., U.S., 10,774 . . . . .336/J3
Berwick-upon-Tweed, Eng., U.K., 13,544 . . .60/C2
Berwick-upon-Tweed, Eng., U.K., 13,544 . . .66/E1
Berwyn, Ill., U.S., 54,016 . . . . .266/B6
Berwyn, Nebr., U.S., 134 . . . . .308/E2
Berwyn, Penn., U.S., 5,067 . . . . .336/K7
Berwyn Hts., Md., U.S., 2,942 . . . . .288/C6
Beryl, Utah, U.S., 125 . . . . .350/A6
Besançon, Fr., 122,308, (134,376 metro.) . .88/D3
Beskids, Pol., mountains 83/D4
Beskidy, Slvk., mountains 92/B2
Besnard, Sask., Can., lake 227/D5
Besor, Isr., river 135/B2
Bessemer, Ala., U.S., 29,672 . . . . . .238/C2, D1
Bessemer, Mich., U.S., 2,148 . . . . .294/C2
Bessemer, Penn., U.S., 1,172 . . . . .336/A4
Bessemer City, N.C., U.S., 5,119 . . . . . . .322/C4
Bessie, Okla., U.S., 190 . . . . .330/D2
Best, Tex., U.S. 346/G4
Betances, P.R. 206/A2
Bete Grise, Mich., U.S. 294/B2
Bethalto, Ill., U.S., 9,454 . . . . .266/A3
Bethania, N.C., U.S., 354 . . . . .322/E2
Bethanien, Nam. 160/C4
Bethany, Man., Can. 215/B4
Bethany, Conn., U.S., 5,040 . . . . .253/C4
Bethany, Ill., U.S., 1,287 . . . . .266/E4
Bethany, Ind., U.S., 94 . . . . .270/D5
Bethany, Mo., U.S., 3,087 . . . . .302/B1
Bethany, Okla., U.S., 20,307 . . . . . .330/B4, E2
Bethany, Penn., U.S., 292 . . . . .336/L2
Bethany Beach, Del., U.S., 903 . . . . .255/D6
Betheden, Miss., U.S. 300/D2
Bethel, Alaska, U.S., 5,471 . . . . .240/C2
Bethel, Conn., U.S., 18,067 . . . . .253/B4
Bethel, Del., U.S., 184 . . . . .255/B6
Bethel, Maine, U.S., 2,411 . . . . .286/B4
Bethel, Minn., U.S., 443 . . . . .298/D5
Bethel, Mo., U.S., 121 . . . . .302/D2
Bethel, N.C., U.S., 1,681 . . . . .322/J3
Bethel, Ohio, U.S., 2,637 . . . . .328/B8
Bethel, Okla., U.S., 70 . . . . .330/H3
Bethel, Penn., U.S., 650 . . . . .336/J5
Bethel, Tex., U.S., 90 . . . . .346/N4
Bethel, Vt., U.S., 1,968 . . . . .352/B3
Bethel Acres, Okla., U.S., 2,735 . . . . . . .330/E2
Bethel Hts., Ark., U.S., 714 . . . . .244/A1
Bethel Hill, N.C., U.S., 175 . . . . .322/H1
Bethel Island, Calif., U.S., 2,312 . . . . . . .246/L1
Bethel Sprs., Tenn., U.S., 763 . . . . .344/D4
Bethesda, Wales, U.K., 3,558 . . . . .64/C1
Bethesda, Ark., U.S., 150 . . . . .244/D2
Bethesda, Md., U.S., 55,277 . . . . . .288/A6, F4
Bethesda, Ohio, U.S., 1,413 . . . . .328/H5
Bethlehem, S. Afr. 162/C2
Bethlehem, Conn., U.S., 3,422 . . . . .253/C3
Bethlehem, Ga., U.S., 716 . . . . .260/D4
Bethlehem, Md., U.S., 600 . . . . .288/L5
Bethlehem, N.H., U.S., 2,199 . . . . .312/C3
Bethlehem, N.C., U.S., 3,713 . . . . .322/C3
Bethlehem, Penn., U.S., 71,329 . . . . .336/L4
Bethpage, Tenn., U.S., 300 . . . . .344/J2
Bethune, Colo., U.S., 225 . . . . .250/H2
Bethune, S.C., U.S., 352 . . . . .340/D2
Béticos, Sp., mountains 94/D4
Bétou, Congo 155/E2
Betpakdala, Kaz., desert 131/C2
Betsham, Eng., U.K. 70/E4
Betsiamites, Que., Can., 1,625 . . . . .226/H3
Betsiamites, Que., Can., river, 1,625 . . . . .226/G2
Betsiboka, Madag., river 163/B2
Betsie, Mich., U.S., point 294/C5
Bette, Lib., mountain 145/C3
Bettendorf, Iowa, U.S., 31,275 . . . . .274/P4
Bettervia, Calif., U.S. 246/E8
Betterton, Md., U.S., 376 . . . . .288/K2
Bettie, Tex., U.S., 150 . . . . .346/P3
Bettles, Alaska, U.S., 43 . . . . .240/E1
Bettsville, Ohio, U.S., 784 . . . . .328/D3
Bettyhill, Scot., U.K. 62/H1
Between, Ga., U.S., 148 . . . . .260/D4
Betws-y-Coed, Wales, U.K. 64/D1
Beulah, Man., Can. 215/A4
Beulah, Colo., U.S., 1,164 . . . . .250/F3
Beulah, Kans., U.S., 60 . . . . .276/H4
Beulah, Ky., U.S., 212/ 280/G3
Beulah, Md., U.S., 125 . . . . .288/C5
Beulah, Mich., U.S., 363 . . . . .294/C5
Beulah, Miss., U.S., 473 . . . . .300/B2
Beulah, N. Dak., U.S., 3,152 . . . . .326/D2
Beulah, Oreg., U.S. 334/H4
Beulah, Wyo., U.S., 40 . . . . .366/D1
Beulahville, Va., U.S., 150 . . . . .354/J5
Beulaville, N.C., U.S., 1,067 . . . . .322/K5
Bevent, Wisc., U.S., 50 . . . . .364/D4
Beverley, Eng., U.K., 23,632 . . . . .66/H5
Beverley, Eng., U.K., 23,632 . . . . .68/G2
Beverly, Ill., U.S., 40 . . . . .266/C4
Beverly, Kans., U.S., 199 . . . . .276/D2
Beverly, Mass., U.S., 39,862 . . . . .292/L2
Beverly, N.J., U.S., 2,643 . . . . .314/D3
Beverly, Ohio, U.S., 1,282 . . . . .328/G6
Beverly, Wash., U.S., 70 . . . . .358/F3
Beverly, W. Va., U.S., 651 . . . . .360/G3
Beverly Beach, Fla., U.S., 547 . . . . .256/G2
Beverly Beach, Md., U.S., 1,600 . . . . . . .288/H4
Beverly Hills, Calif., U.S., 33,784 . . . . . . .246/F9
Beverly Hills, Fla., U.S., 8,317 . . . . .256/F3
Beverly Hills, Mich., U.S., 10,437 . . . . . .294/A6
Beverly Hills, Tex., U.S., 2,113 . . . . .346/L4
Beverly Shores, Ind., U.S., 708 . . . . .270/C1
Beverston, Eng., U.K. 68/C6
Bevier, Mo., U.S., 723 . . . . .302/D2
Bevil Oaks, Tex., U.S., 1,346 . . . . .346/P5
Bevington, Iowa, U.S., 58 . . . . .274/G5
Bevis, Ohio, U.S., 5,700 . . . . .328/A9
Bexar, Ala., U.S., 60 . . . . .238/A1
Bexar, Ark., U.S., 50 . . . . .244/D2
Bexar, Tex., U.S., county, 1,392,931 . . .346/A3, K6
Bexhill, Eng., U.K., 38,905 . . . . .70/E5
Bexley, Eng., U.K., unitary authority, 218,307 . .70/E4
Bexley, Ohio, U.S., 13,203 . . . . .328/E9
Beyehir Gölü, Tur., lake 133/B3
Beyla, Guin. .149/D3
Beyne, Kaz. .131/B2
Bezanson, Alta., Can., 81 . . . . .212/A3
Béziers, Fr. 88/C4

Bhadrakh, India 128/E4
Bhadreswar, India . . . . .128/Inset II
Bhagalpur, India .128/E3
Bhairahawa, Nepal 126/B2
Bhaktapur, Nepal, 61,122 . . . . .126/C2
Bhamapur, India .128/D5
Bhamo, Mya. 125/C1
Bhandup, India . . . . .128/Inset I
Bharatpur, India .128/C3
Bhatapara, India .128/D4
Bhatpara, India . . . . .128/Inset II
Bhavnagar, India, 400,636, (403,521 metro.) . .128/B4
Bhayandar, India . . . . .128/Inset I
Bheri, Nepal, river 126/B2
Bhima, India, river 128/C5
Bhimpur, India . . . . .128/Inset II
Bhiwandi, India, 378,546, (391,670 metro.) .128/Inset I
Bhopal, India, 1,433,875, (1,454,830 metro.) . .128/C4
Bhubaneswar, India 128/E4
Bhuj, India 128/A4
Bhunya, Swaz. 161/B2
Bhutan, nation 122
Biabou, St. Vin.-Gren. 208/B2
Biafra, Came., bight 153/A3
Biafra, Eq. Gui., bight 154/B1
Biak, Indon., island 122/E2
Biała Podlaska, Pol. 83/F2
Białystok, Pol., 284,404 . . . . .83/F2
Biankouma, C. d'Iv. 150/C3
Biarritz, Fr. 88/B5
Bibb, Ala., U.S., county, 20,826 . . . . .238/D4
Bibb, Ga., U.S., county, 153,887 . . . . .260/D6
Bibb City, Ga., U.S., 510 . . . . .260/B6
Bibury, Eng., U.K. .68/D6
Bicaz, Rom., reservoir 101/D2
Bicester, Eng., U.K., 22,128 . . . . .68/E6
Bicester, Eng., U.K., 22,128 . . . . .70/B3
Biche, Alta., Can., lake 212//E4
Bickington, Eng., U.K. 73/E3
Bickleigh, Eng., U.K. 73/E3
Bickleton, Wash., U.S., 113 . . . . .358/E4
Bickley Moss, Eng., U.K. 68/B3
Bicknell, Ind., U.S., 3,378 . . . . .270/B7
Bicknell, Utah, U.S., 353 . . . . .350/C5
Bicknor, Eng., U.K. 70/F4
Bicol, Phil., region 120/B3
Bida, Nig. 152/D3
Bidahochi, Ariz., U.S. 242/E2
Biddeford, Maine, U.S., 20,942 . . . . .286/B5
Biddeford Pool, Maine, U.S. 286/B5
Biddenden, Eng., U.K. 70/F4
Biddle, Mont., U.S. 306/L4
Biddulph, Eng., U.K., 16,725 . . . . .68/C3
Biddulph Moor, Eng., U.K. 68/C3
Bideford, Eng., U.K., 14,326 . . . . .73/D2
Bié, Ang., plateau 159/C4
Bié, Ang., province 159/C4
Bieber, Calif., U.S., 225 . . . . .246/D1
Biehle, Mo., U.S. 302/G4
Biel, Switz. 90/B1
Bielefeld, Ger., 321,125 . . . . .86/B2
Biele Karpaty, Czh. Rep., mountains 92/A3
Biele Karpaty, Slvk., mountains 92/A2
Bieler See, Switz., lake 90/B1
Bielsko-Biała, Pol., 180,158 . . . . .83/D4
Bien Hoa, Viet. 123/B4
Bienville, Que., Can., lake 225/B2
Bienville, La., U.S., 262 . . . . .282/C2
Bienville, La., U.S., parish, 15,752 . . . . .282/C2
Bienville Natl. For., Miss., U.S. 300/C3
Big, Nfld., Can., river 206/B2
Big, Nun., Can., island 208/O4
Big, Maine, U.S., lake 286/E3
Big Arm, Mont., U.S., 131 . . . . .306/B2
Big Bar, Calif., U.S., 40 . . . . .246/B2
Big Bay, Mich., U.S., 265 . . . . .294/B3
Big Bay de Noc, Mich., U.S. 294/C4
Big Bear Lake, Calif., U.S., 5,438 . . . . .246/J8
Big Beaver, Sask., Can. 227/E11
Big Beaver, Penn., U.S., 2,186 . . . . .336/A4
Bigbee Valley, Miss., U.S., 175 . . . . .300/D2
Big Bend, Swaz. .161/B2
Big Bend, La., U.S. 282/F4
Big Bend, Wisc., U.S., 1,278 . . . . .364/F2
Big Bend City, Minn., U.S., 100 . . . . .298/B5
Big Bend Natl. Park, Tex., U.S. 346/E6
Big Bend Ranch St. Park, Tex., U.S. 346/D6
Big Black, Miss., U.S., river 300/B3
Big Blue, Ind., U.S., river 270/E5
Big Blue, Kans., U.S., river 276/F2
Big Blue, Nebr., U.S., river 308/G2, H3
Big Boggy N.W.R., Tex., U.S. 346/N7
Big Bow, Kans., U.S., 50 . . . . .276/A4
Bigbury-on-Sea, Eng., U.K. 73/E4
Big Cabin, Okla., U.S., 293 . . . . .330/G1
Big Cedar, Okla., U.S. 330/H3
Big Chimney, W. Va., U.S., 600 . . . . .360/C4
Big Clifty, Ky., U.S., 250 . . . . .280/D3
Big Creek, Br. Col., Can. 214/L5
Big Creek, Ida., U.S. 264/R4
Big Creek, Miss., U.S., 127 . . . . .300/C2
Big Creek, W. Va., U.S., 425 . . . . .360/B4
Big Cypress, Fla., U.S., swamp 256/G5
Big Cypress Ind. Res., Fla., U.S. 256/H5
Big Cypress Natl. Pres., Fla., U.S. 256/G5
Big Delta, Alaska, U.S., 749 . . . . .240/F2
Bigelow, Ark., U.S., 329 . . . . .244/C3
Bigelow, Maine, U.S., 40 . . . . .286/B3
Bigelow, Minn., U.S., 231 . . . . .298/B7
Bigelow, Mo., U.S. 302/A1
Big Falls, Minn., U.S., 264 . . . . .298/D2
Big Falls, Wisc., U.S., 85 . . . . .364/D4
Big Fish, Yukon, Can., river 228/B1
Big Flat, Ark., U.S., 104 . . . . .244/C1
Big Flats, N.Y., U.S., 2,482 . . . . .320/H6
Bigfoot, Tex., U.S., 304 . . . . .346/K6
Big Fork, Ark., U.S., 60 . . . . .244/B3
Bigfork, Minn., U.S., 469 . . . . .298/D3
Big Fork, Minn., U.S., river 298/D2
Bigfork, Mont., U.S., 1,421 . . . . .306/B1
Biggar, Sask., Can., 2,243 . . . . .227/C8
Biggar, Scot., U.K., 2,098 . . . . .62//J7
Biggers, Ark., U.S., 355 . . . . .244/E1
Biggersville, Miss., U.S., 175 . . . . .300/D1
Biggin Hill, Eng., U.K., 14,107 . . . . .70/E4
Biggleswade, Eng., U.K., 12,350 . . . . .68/G5
Biggleswade, Eng., U.K., 12,350 . . . . .70/D2
Biggs, Calif., U.S., 1,793 . . . . .246/D3
Biggs, Oreg., U.S. 334/F2
Biggsville, Ill., U.S., 343 . . . . .266/C3
Big Gull, Ont., Can., lake 223/J3
Big Hole Natl. Bfld., Mont., U.S. 306/C4
Big Horn, Ariz., U.S., mountains 242/B4
Bighorn, Mont., U.S. 306/J3
Big Horn, Mont., U.S., county, 12,671 . . . . .306/J4
Bighorn, Mont., Wyo., U.S., river 306/H5, J4
Big Horn, Wyo., U.S., 198 . . . . .366/C1
Big Horn, Wyo., U.S., county, 11,461 . . . . . .366/B1
Bighorn, Wyo., U.S. 366/C1
Bighorn, Wyo., U.S., mountains 366/C1
Bighorn, Wyo., U.S., river 366/B1

Bighorn Canyon Natl. Rec. Area, Mont., U.S. . . .306/H4
Bighorn Natl. For., Wyo., U.S. 366/C1
Big Island, Va., U.S., 425 . . . . .354/E5
Big Lake, Minn., U.S., 6,063 . . . . .298/D5
Big Lake, Mo., U.S., 127 . . . . .302/A1
Big Lake, Tex., U.S., 2,885 . . . . .346/G4
Big Lake, Wash., U.S., 1,153 . . . . .358/C1
Big Lake N.W.R., Ark., U.S. 244/E2
Biglerville, Penn., U.S., 1,101 . . . . .336/G6
Big Lost, Ida., U.S., river 264/D6
Big Moose, N.Y., U.S. 320/M3
Big Muddy, Sask., Can., lake 227/F11
Bignona, Sen. 148/A3
Big Oak Flat, Calif., U.S., 3,388 . . . . .246/E5
Big Pine, Calif., U.S., 1,350 . . . . .246/G5
Big Pine Key, Fla., U.S., 5,032 . . . . .256/G7
Big Piney, Wyo., U.S., 408 . . . . .366/A2
Big Plain, Ohio, U.S., 212/ 328/D6
Big Pt., Mich., U.S., 115 . . . . .300/D5
Big Pool, Md., U.S., 212/ 288/B1
Big Rapids, Mich., U.S., 10,849 . . . . .294/D6
Big Rideau, Ont., Can., lake 320/J1
Big River, Sask., Can., 741 . . . . .227/C7
Big River, Calif., U.S., 1,266 . . . . .246/L8
Big Rock, Tenn., U.S., 350 . . . . .344/F1
Big Run, Penn., U.S., 686 . . . . .336/D4
Big Sable, Mich., U.S., point 294/C5
Big Sandy, Colo., U.S., creek 250/G3
Big Sandy, Mont., U.S., 703 . . . . .306/F1
Big Sandy, Tenn., U.S., 518 . . . . .344/F2
Big Sandy, Wyo., U.S. 366/B2
Big Sandy, Wyo., U.S., river 366/B2
Big Sky, Mont., U.S., 1,221 . . . . .306/E4
B. Sk. Fork Natl. River and Rec. Area, Ky., U.S. . . .280/F4
Big Spr., Ky., U.S., 70 . . . . .280/D3
Bigspring, Mo., U.S., 212/ 302/E3
Big Spr., Tex., U.S., 25,233 . . . . .346/G3
Big Sprs., Kans., U.S. 276/G3
Big Sprs., Miss., U.S., lake 300/D1
Big Sprs., Nebr., U.S., 418 . . . . .308/B2
Bigstone, Man., Can., river 215/D1
Big Stone, Minn., U.S., county, 5,820 . . . . . .298/A5
Big Stone City, S. Dak., U.S., 605 . . . . .342//J2
Big Stone Gap, Va., U.S., 4,856 . . . . .354/C2
Big Stone N.W.R., Minn., U.S. 298/A5
Big Sunflower, Miss., U.S., river 300/B2
Big Sur, Calif., U.S., 1,000 . . . . .246/D6
Big Thicket Natl. Pres., Tex., U.S. 346/P5
Big Timber, Mont., U.S., 1,650 . . . . .306/G4
Big Trails, Wyo., U.S. 366/C2
Big Trout Lake, Ont., Can. 222/C2
Big Valley, Alta., Can., 340 . . . . .212//D5
Big Water, Utah, U.S., 417 . . . . .350/C6
Big Wells, Tex., U.S., 704 . . . . .346//J7
Big Woods, Minn., U.S., 50 . . . . .298/A2
Bihać, Bos.-Her. 98/A1
Bihar, India 128/E3
Bihar, India, state 128/E4
Bihor, Rom., county 101/C2
Bihor, Rom., mountains 149/A2
Bijagós, Gui.-B., archipelago 149/B2
Bijapur, India 128/C5
Bijeljina, Bos.-Her. 98/C1
Bijou, Colo., U.S., creek 250/F2
Bijou Hills, S. Dak., U.S. 342/F4
Bikaner, India 128/B3
Bikar, Marsh. Is., island 173/C1
Bikini, Marsh. Is., island 173/B1
Bilaspur, India 128/D4
Biläsuvar, Azer. 103/C3
BilaTserkva, Ukr., 212,640 . . . . .102/C2
Bilauktaung, Thai., range 125/C3
Bilauktaung, Thai., range 125/B3
Bilbao, Sp., 349,972 . . . . .94/E1
Bildeston, Eng., U.K. 70/F2
Bilecik, Tur., province 133/B2
Bill, Wyo., U.S. 366/D2
Billerica, Mass., U.S., 38,981 . . . . .292/B6, J2
Billericay, Eng., U.K., 33,377 . . . . .70/E3
Billett, Ill., U.S., 150 . . . . .266/F5
Billingham, Eng., U.K., 36,869 . . . . .66/F3
Billings, Braz., reservoir . . . . .188/Inset II
Billings, Mo., U.S., 1,091 . . . . .302/C4
Billings, Mont., U.S., 89,847, (129,352 metro.) . .306/H4
Billings, N. Dak., U.S., county, 888 . . . . . . .326/B2
Billings, Okla., U.S., 436 . . . . .330/E1
Billingshurst, Eng., U.K., 4,980 . . . . .70/D4
Billingsley, Ala., U.S., 116 . . . . .238/C3
Billington Hts., N.Y., U.S., 1,691 . . . . .320/D5
Billockby, Eng., U.K. 70/H1
Bill Williams, Ariz., U.S., river 242/A3
Bilma, Niger 152/C2
Biloku, Guy. 183/B5
Biloxi, Miss., U.S., 50,644, (363,988 metro.) . .300/D5
Bilsborrow, Eng., U.K. 66/C5
Biltine, Chad 153/C4
Biltmore Forest, N.C., U.S., 1,440 . . . . .322/E7
Bimbila, Gha. 150/C2
Bimini, Bah., islands 204/B1
Binbrook, Eng., U.K. 66/H6
Binche, Belg. 85/C2
Bindloss, Alta., Can. 212//E6
Bindura, Zimb. 160/B1
Binegar, Eng., U.K. 73/C2
Binford, N. Dak., U.S., 201 . . . . .326/G2
Binga, Moz., mountain 161/B3
Bingen, Ger. 86/A4
Bingen, Ark., U.S., 100 . . . . .244/B4
Bingen, Wash., U.S., 672 . . . . .358/D4
Binger, Okla., U.S., 708 . . . . .330/D2
Bingham, Eng., U.K., 7,057 . . . . .68/F4
Bingham, Ida., U.S., county, 41,735 . . . . . . .264/E6
Bingham, Ill., U.S., 117 . . . . .266/D4
Bingham, Iowa, U.S., 60 . . . . .274/D6
Bingham, Maine, U.S., 989 . . . . .286/C3
Bingham, Nebr., U.S. 308/B1
Bingham, N. Mex., U.S., 50 . . . . .317/D4
Bingham Farms, Mich., U.S., 1,030 . . . . . . .294/A6
Bingham Lake, Minn., U.S., 167 . . . . .298/B7
Binghamton, N.Y., U.S., 47,380, (252,320 metro.) 320/K6
Bingley, Eng., U.K., 19,585 . . . . .66/D1
Bingley, Eng., U.K., 19,585 . . . . .68/D2
Bingo, Maine, U.S. 286/E3
Bingöl, Tur. 133/E2
Bingöl, Tur., province 133/E2
Binham, Eng., U.K. 70/F1
Binscarth, Man., Can., 445 . . . . .215/A4
Bintang, Gam. 148/B2
Bint Jubayl, Leb. .134/A2
Bío-Bío, Chile, region 190/B5
Bío-Bío, Chile, river 190/B5
Bioko, Eq. Gui., island 154/A1
Bippus, Ind., U.S., 300 . . . . .270/E3
Birak, Lib. 145/B2
Birao, C.A.R. 154/B1
Biratnagar, Nepal, 130,129 . . . . .126/D3
Birch, Alta., Can., mountains 212//D2
Birch, Wisc., U.S., 250 . . . . .364/C2
Birch Bay, Wash., U.S., 4,961 . . . . .358/C1
Birch Cliff, Ont., Can. 223/K5
Birchdale, Minn., U.S. 298/C2

Birch Green, Eng., U.K. 70/F3
Birchgrove, Wales, U.K. 64/E4
Birch Harbor, Maine, U.S., 175 . . . . .286/D4
Birch Hills, Sask., Can., 957 . . . . .227/E7
Birchington, Eng., U.K. 70/G4
Birch River, Man., Can. 215/A3
Birch River, W. Va., U.S., 150 . . . . .360/E4
Birch Run, Mich., U.S., 1,653 . . . . .294/E6
Birch Tree, Mo., U.S., 634 . . . . .302/E5
Birchwood, Wisc., U.S., 518 . . . . .364/B3
Birchwood Vil., Minn., U.S., 968 . . . . .298/F5
Birchy Bay, Nfld., Can., 612 . . . . .206/D4
Bird, Gren., island 209/B2
Bird City, Kans., U.S., 482 . . . . .276/A2
Bird Island, Minn., U.S., 1,195 . . . . .298/C6
Birdlip, Eng., U.K. .68/C6
Birds, Ill., U.S., 51 . . . . .266/F5
Birdsall, Eng., U.K. 66/G4
Birdsboro, Penn., U.S., 5,064 . . . . .336/K5
Birdseye, Ind., U.S., 465 . . . . .270/C8
Birdseye, Utah, U.S., 175 . . . . .350/C4
Birds Landing, Calif., U.S. 246/K1
Birdsong, Ark., U.S., 40 . . . . .244/E2
Birdsville, Ky., U.S., 40 . . . . .280/B3
Birendranagar, Nepal 126/B2
Bir Gandouz, W. Sah. 147/A2
Birganj, Nepal 126/C2
Birjand, Iran 130/D3
Birkat Qarun, Egy., lake 144/C2
Birkenhead, Eng., U.K. 60/B3
Birkenhead, Eng., U.K., 93,087 . . . . .66/B6
Birkenhead, Eng., U.K., 93,087 . . . . .68/A3
Birkirkara, Malta 97/B2
Birland, Rom. 101/D2
Birmingham, Eng., U.K. 60/C3
Birmingham, Eng., U.K., 977,091, (2,555,596 metro.) . . .68/D5
Birmingham, Eng., U.K., unitary authority, 977,091 . . . . .68/D4
Birmingham, Ala., U.S., 242,820, (921,106 metro.) 238/C2, E1
Birmingham, Iowa, U.S., 423 . . . . .274/L6
Birmingham, Kans., U.S., 50 . . . . .276/G2
Birmingham, Mich., U.S., 19,291 . . . . .294/A6
Birmingham, Mo., U.S., 214 . . . . .302//J5
Birmingham, Penn., U.S., 91 . . . . .336/E4
Bir Morqrein, Maur. 147/C1
Birnamwood, Wisc., U.S., 795 . . . . .364/D4
Birney, Mont., U.S., 108 . . . . .306/K4
Birnie, Man., Can. 215/B4
Birnin Kebbi, Nig. 152/C1
Birni Nkonni, Niger 152/B3
Birni N'konni, Niger 152/C1
Birobizhan, Russ. 104/H5
Biron, Wisc., U.S., 915 . . . . .364/D4
Birstall, Eng., U.K., 11,770 . . . . .68/E4
Birstall, Eng., U.K., 11,770 . . . . .70/B1
Birtle, Man., Can., 715 . . . . .215/A4
Biržai, Lith. 82/C1
Birzebbuga, Malta 97/C3
Bisbee, Ariz., U.S., 6,090 . . . . .242/F6
Bisbee, N. Dak., U.S., 167 . . . . .326/F1
Biscay, Fr., bay 88/B4
Biscay, Sp., bay 94/D1
Biscay, Minn., U.S., 114 . . . . .298/C6
Biscayne, Fla., U.S., bay 256/B7, H6
Biscayne Natl. Park, Fla., U.S. 256/B7, H6
Biscoe, Ark., U.S., 476 . . . . .244/D3
Biscoe, N.C., U.S., 1,700 . . . . .322/F4
Bishah, Sa. Arab. 136/B2
Bishkek, Kyrg., capital, 753,400 . . . . .131/D1
Bishkek, Kyrg., province 131/D1
Bishnupur, India . . . . .128/Inset II
Bishop, Calif., U.S., 3,575 . . . . .246/G5
Bishop, Ga., U.S., 146 . . . . .260/E4
Bishop, Md., U.S., 212/ 288/P6
Bishop, Tex., U.S., 3,305 . . . . .346/L8
Bishop Auckland, Eng., U.K., 23,154 . . . . . .66/E3
Bishop Burton, Eng., U.K. 68/G2
Bishop Hill, Ill., U.S., 125 . . . . .266/C2
Bishop Norton, Eng., U.K. 66/G6
Bishop's Castle, Eng., U.K. 68/B5
Bishop's Cleeve, Eng., U.K., 10,098 . . . . . . .68/C6
Bishops Falls, Nfld., Can., 3,688 . . . . .206/D4
Bishop's Lydeard, Eng., U.K. 73/F2
Bishop's Stortford, Eng., U.K., 28,403 . . . . .70/E3
Bishop's Tawton, Eng., U.K. 73/D2
Bishopstone, Eng., U.K. 73/J1
Bishop Sutton, Eng., U.K. 73/G2
Bishopswood, Eng., U.K. 73/F2
Bishopthorpe, Eng., U.K., 3,148 . . . . .66/F5
Bishopthorpe, Eng., U.K., 3,148 . . . . .66/E2
Bishopville, Md., U.S., 300 . . . . .288/P6
Bishopville, S.C., U.S., 3,670 . . . . .340/D2
Bishop Wilton, Eng., U.K. 66/G5
Biskra, Alg., 170,956 . . . . .146/B1
Bislig, Phil. 120/C4
Bismarck, P.N.G., archipelago 172/A2
Bismarck, P.N.G., range 172/A2
Bismarck, P.N.G., sea 172/A2
Bismarck, Ark., U.S., 225 . . . . .244/B3
Bismarck, Ill., U.S., 542 . . . . .266/F3
Bismarck, Mo., U.S., 1,470 . . . . .302/F4
Bismarck, N. Dak., U.S., state capital, 55,532, (94,719 metro.) . . .326/E3
Bismuna, Nic., lagoon 202/C1
Bison, Alta., Can., lake 212/B2
Bison, Kans., U.S., 235 . . . . .276/C3
Bison, Okla., U.S., 100 . . . . .330/E1
Bison, S. Dak., U.S., 373 . . . . .342/C2
Bissau, Gui.-B., capital, 109,214, (274,000 metro.) 149/B2
Bissell, Miss., U.S. 300/D1
Bissett, Man., Can., 243 . . . . .215/D3
Bissorã, Gui.-B. .149/B1
Bistcho, Alta., Can., lake 212//A1
Bistcho, Alta., Can., lake 214/N1
Bistineau, La., U.S., lake 282/C2
Bistrița, Rom. 101/C2
Bistrița, Rom., river 101/C2
Bistrița-Năsăud, Rom., county 101/C2
Bitam, Gabon 155/A1
Bitely, Mich., U.S., 125 . . . . .294/D6
Bithlo, Fla., U.S., 4,626 . . . . .256/D4, G3
Bitlis, Tur. 133/E2
Bitlis, Tur., province 133/E2
Bitola, Mac., 108,203 . . . . .100/B2
Bitter Creek, Wyo., U.S., 125 . . . . .366/B3
Bitter Lake N.W.R., N. Mex., U.S. 317/F4
Bitterroot, Ida., U.S., range 264/B3, D4
Bitterroot, Mont., U.S., river 306/B4
Bitterroot Natl. For., Mont., U.S. 306/B4
Bitter Sprs., Ariz., U.S., 547 . . . . .242/D1
Bitterwater, Calif., U.S. 246/E6
Bitumount, Alta., Can. 212//E2
Biu, Nig. 152/D2
Bivalve, Md., U.S., 450 . . . . .288/L6
Biwa, Jap., lake 114/B3
Biwabik, Minn., U.S., 954 . . . . .298/E3
Bixby, Minn., U.S., 60 . . . . .298/D7
Bixby, Mo., U.S., 125 . . . . .302/E4

Bixby, Okla., U.S., 13,336 . . . . .330/G2
Bixter, Scot., U.K. .62/P2
Biysk, Russ., 224,493, (236,250 metro.) 104/F4
Bizard, Que., Can., island 226/H5
Bizerte, Tun., 105,520 . . . . .146/B1
Bjorne, Nun., Can., peninsula 208/L1
Blaby, Eng., U.K., 6,538 . . . . .68/E4
Blaby, Eng., U.K., 6,538 . . . . .70/B1
Blachly, Oreg., U.S., 175 . . . . .334/C3
Black, Sask., Can., lake 227/E1
Black, Ger., forest .86/A4
Black, Russ., sea 104/C5
Black, Tur., sea 133/C1
Black, Ukr., sea .102/C3
Black, Eng., U.K., mountains 68/A6
Black, Wales, U.K., mountain 64/E4
Black, Wales, U.K., mountains 64/E4
Black, Ala., U.S., 202 . . . . .238/D4
Black, Ariz., U.S., mesa 242/E1
Black, Ariz., U.S., river 242/E4
Black, Calif., U.S., point 246/B4
Black, Ky., U.S., mountain 280/H4
Black, La., U.S., river 282/F3
Black, Miss., U.S., creek 300/C4
Black, N. Mex., U.S., range 317/C4
Black, N.Y., U.S., lake 320/K2
Black, N.Y., U.S., river 320/L3
Black, Okla., U.S., mesa 330/B4
Black, S. Dak., U.S., hills 342/B3
Black, Tex., U.S. .346/E10
Black, Tex., U.S., mountain 346/H6
Black, Vt., U.S., river 352/C1
Black, (Đà), Viet., river 123/A2
Blackacre, Scot. 62/K8
Blackbeard Island N.W.R., Ga., U.S. 260/J8
Blackberry, Minn., U.S., 100 . . . . .298/D3
Blackbird, Del., U.S., 700 . . . . .255/B3
Blackbird St. For., Del., U.S. 255/B3
Blackbrook, Eng., U.K. 68/C4
Blackburn, Eng., U.K. 60/C3
Blackburn, Eng., U.K., 105,994 . . . . .66/D5
Blackburn, Eng., U.K., 105,994 . . . . .68/C2
Blackburn, Scot., U.K. 62/M4
Blackburn, Alaska, U.S., mountain 240/G2
Blackburn, Mo., U.S., 284 . . . . .302/C2
Blackburn, Okla., U.S., 102 . . . . .330/F1
Blackburn with Darwen, Eng., U.K., unitary authority, 137,471 . . . . . .66/D5
Blackburn with Darwen, Eng., U.K., unitary authority, 137,471 . . . . . .68/C2
Black Canyon City, Ariz., U.S., 2,697 . . . . .242/C3
Black Canyon of the Gunnison N.P., Colo., U.S. . .250/C3
Black Coulee N.W.R., Mont., U.S. 306/H1
Black Country, Eng., U.K., region 60/C3
Black Creek, Br. Col., Can., 714 . . . . .322/K3
Black Creek, Wisc., U.S., 1,192 . . . . .364/E4
Black Diamond, Alta., Can., 1,866 . . . . . . .212//C6
Black Diamond, Wash., U.S., 3,970 . . . . . .358/C2
Black Dog, Eng., U.K. 73/E2
Blackduck, Minn., U.S., 696 . . . . .298/C3
Black Eagle, Mont., U.S., 914 . . . . .306/E2
Black Earth, Wisc., U.S., 1,320 . . . . .364/D5
Blackey, Ky., U.S., 153 . . . . .280/H3
Blackfeet Ind. Res., Mont., U.S. 306/C1
Blackfield, Eng., U.K. 70/B5
Blackfoot, Ida., U.S., 10,419 . . . . .264/E6
Blackfoot, Ida., U.S., reservoir 264/F7
Blackfoot, Ida., U.S., river 264/F6
Blackfoot, Mont., U.S. 306/D1
Blackford, Scot., U.K., 556 . . . . .62//J6
Blackford, Ind., U.S., county, 14,048 . . . . . .270/F3
Black Forest, Colo., U.S., 13,247 . . . . .250/F2
Black Fork, Ark., U.S. 244/A3
Black Fort, N. Ire., U.K. 65/D2
Black Gap Wildlife Management Area, Tex., U.S. . .346/F6
Black Hawk, Colo., U.S., 118 . . . . .250/E2
Black Hawk, Iowa, U.S., county, 128,012 . . .274/K4
Black Hawk, La., U.S. 282/F4
Black Hawk, Miss., U.S., 70 . . . . .300/C2
Black Hawk, S. Dak., U.S., 2,432 . . . . .342/B3
Black Hawk, Wisc., U.S., 125 . . . . .364/D5
Blackheath, Eng., U.K. 68/C5
Black Jack, Mo., U.S., 6,792 . . . . .302//J2
Black Kettle Natl. Grassland, Okla., U.S. . . .330/C2
Black Lake, Sask., Can. 227/E1
Black Lake, N. Mex., U.S. 317/E1
Black Lick, Penn., U.S., 1,438 . . . . .336/C5
Blackman, Fla., U.S. 256/B1
Blackmans, Barb. 209/B2
Black Mtn., N.C., U.S., 7,511 . . . . .322/A3, E7
Black Oak, Ark., U.S., 286 . . . . .244/E2
Black Pt., Conn., U.S., 300 . . . . .253/G4
Blackpool, Eng., U.K. 60/C3
Blackpool, Eng., U.K., 146,262, (261,355 metro.) . . .66/A5
Blackpool, Eng., U.K., 146,262, (261,355 metro.) . . .68/A2
Blackpool, Eng., U.K., unitary authority, 142,284 . . .66/B5
Blackpool, Eng., U.K., unitary authority, 142,284 . . .68/A2
Black River, N.B., Can. 217/D3
Black River, Jam. 206/B2
Black River, Mich., U.S., 100 . . . . .294/F5
Black River, N.Y., U.S., 1,285 . . . . .320//J3
Black River Falls, Wisc., U.S., 3,618 . . . . . .364/C4
Black River St. For., Wisc., U.S. 364/C4
Black River Vil., N. Mex., U.S. 317/F5
Blackrock, Wales, U.K. 64/E4
Black Rock, Ark., U.S., 717 . . . . .244/D1
Black Rock, N. Mex., U.S., desert 310/A1
Black Rock, N. Mex., U.S., 1,252 . . . . .317/B2
Black Rock, Utah, U.S. 350/B5
Black Rock Desert-High Rock Canyon Emigrant Trails Natl. Cons. Area, Nev., U.S. . .310/A1
Blacksburg, S.C., U.S., 1,880 . . . . .340/C1
Blacksburg, Va., U.S., 39,573 . . . . .354/C6
Blacks Ferry, Ky., U.S. 280/F4
Blackshear, Ga., U.S., 3,283 . . . . .260/G9
Blackshear, Ga., U.S., lake 260/D8
Blacksher, Ala., U.S. 238/B4
Black Sprs., Ark., U.S., 114 . . . . .244/B3
Black Sprs., Nev., U.S. 310/A2
Blackstone, Yukon, Can., river 228/B3
Blackstone, Ill., U.S., 70 . . . . .266/E2
Blackstone, Mass., U.S., 8,804 . . . . .292/A3
Blackstone, Va., U.S., 3,675 . . . . .354/C6
Blacksville, Ga., U.S. 260/C5
Blacksville, W. Va., U.S., 175 . . . . .360/F1
Blackthorn, Eng., U.K. 68/E6
Black Tickle, Nfld., Can., 249 . . . . .206/D2
Blackton, Ark., U.S., 70 . . . . .244/D3
Blacktown, N.S.W., Austl. . . . . .170/Inset IV
Blackville, N.B., Can., 1,015 . . . . .217/D2
Blackville, S.C., U.S., 2,973 . . . . .340/C3
Black Volta, Burkina, river 151/B3
Black Volta, Gha., river 150/A2
Black Warrior, Ala., U.S., river 238/B3
Blackwater, Ire., river 76/B2
Blackwater, Ire., river 76/C1
Blackwater, Mo., U.S., 199 . . . . .302/D3

Blackwater, N.H., U.S., *reservoir* 312/C5
Blackwaterfoot, Scot., U.K. 62/F8
Blackwater N.W.R., Md., U.S. 288/K6
Blackwell, Ark., U.S., 125 . . . . .244/C2
Blackwell, Okla., U.S., 7,668 . . . . .330/E1
Blackwell, Penn., U.S., 40 . . . . .336/G2
Blackwell, Tex., U.S., 360 . . . . .346/H3
Blackwells, La., U.S., 2,212/ 260/B3, H1
Blackwells Corner, Calif., U.S. 246/F7
Blackwood, N.J., U.S., 4,692 . . . . .314/B4, C4
Bladen, Nebr., U.S., 291 . . . . .308/E3
Bladen, N.C., U.S., *county*, 32,278 . . . . .322/H5
Bladenboro, N.C., U.S., 1,718 . . . . .322/H5
Bladen Lakes St. For., N.C., U.S. 322/H5
Bladen Lakes St. For., N.C., U.S. 340/F2
Bladensburg, Md., U.S., 7,661 . . . . .288/C7
Bladensburg, Ohio, U.S., 250 . . . . .328/G5
Blades, Del., U.S., 956 . . . . .255/B6
Bladon, Eng., U.K. 68/E6
Blaenau Ffestiniog, Wales, U.K., 4,546 . . . . . .64/D2
Blaenau Gwent, Wales, U.K., *unitary authority*,
70,058 . . . . .64/E4
Blaenavon, Wales, U.K., 6,066 . . . . .64/E4
Blaenplwyf, Wales, U.K. 64/C3
Blagdon, Eng., U.K. 73/C2
Blagoevgrad, Bul. 101/B4
Blagoevgrad, Bul., *oblast* 101/B4
Blagoveshchensk, Russ., 220,102,
(223,500 *metro.*) 104/D4, H4
Blaich, Scot., U.K. 62/F5
Blain, Penn., U.S., 252 . . . . .336/F5
Blaina, Wales, U.K. .64/E4
Blaine, Ida., U.S., *county*, 18,991 . . . . .264/C6
Blaine, Ky., U.S., 245 . . . . .280/H2
Blaine, Maine, U.S., 806 . . . . .286/E2
Blaine, Minn., U.S., 44,942 . . . . .298/F5
Blaine, Miss., U.S., 100 . . . . .300/B2
Blaine, Mont., U.S., *county*, 7,009 . . . . .306/G1
Blaine, Nebr., U.S., *county*, 583 . . . . .308/D2
Blaine, Okla., U.S., *county*, 11,976 . . . . .330/D2
Blaine, Tenn., U.S., 1,585 . . . . .344/P2
Blaine, Wash., U.S., 3,770 . . . . .358/C1
Blaine Lake, Sask., Can., 508 . . . . .227/D8
Blainville, Que., Can., 36,029 . . . . .226/H5
Blair, Nebr., U.S., 7,512 . . . . .308/H2
Blair, N.H., U.S., 225 . . . . .312/C4
Blair, Okla., U.S., 894 . . . . .330/C3
Blair, Penn., U.S., *county*, 129,144 . . . . .336/E5
Blair, Wisc., U.S., 1,273 . . . . .364/B4
Blair Atholl, Scot., U.K. 62/J5
Blairgowrie, Scot., U.K., 7,965 . . . . .62/J5
Blairmore, Alta., Can., 1,993 . . . . .212/C6
Blairnarrow, Scot., U.K. 62/K4
Blairs, Va., U.S., 650 . . . . .354/E7
Blairsburg, Iowa, U.S., 235 . . . . .274/G3
Blairsden, Calif., U.S., 50 . . . . .246/E3
Blairstown, Iowa, U.S., 682 . . . . .274/K4
Blairstown, Mo., U.S., 141 . . . . .302/C3
Blairstown, N.J., U.S., 5,747 . . . . .314/D2
Blairsville, Ga., U.S., 659 . . . . .260/D2
Blairsville, Penn., U.S., 3,607 . . . . .336/C5
Blaisdell, Ariz., U.S. 242/A5
Blaisdell, N. Dak., U.S. 326/C6
Blakeley, Minn., U.S., 50 . . . . .298/D6
Blakely, Ga., U.S., 5,696 . . . . .260/B9
Blakely, Penn., U.S., 7,027 . . . . .336/H6, K3
Blakeman, Kans., U.S. 276/A2
Blakenhall, Eng., U.K. 68/C3
Blakesburg, Iowa, U.S., 374 . . . . .274/J6
Blakeslee, Ohio, U.S., 130 . . . . .328/A2
Blalock, Oreg., U.S., 40 . . . . .334/F2
Blanc, Que., Can., *reservoir* 226/C4
Blanc, Fr., *mountain* 88/D4
Blanc, It., *mountain* 95/A1
Blanca, Arg., *bay* .191/C4
Blanca, Colo., U.S., 391 . . . . .250/E4
Blanca, Colo., U.S., *peak* 250/E4
Blanchard, Ida., U.S., 90 . . . . .264/A1
Blanchard, Iowa, U.S., 61 . . . . .274/D6
Blanchard, La., U.S., 2,050 . . . . .282/B1
Blanchard, Maine, U.S., 83 . . . . .286/C3
Blanchard, Mich., U.S., 350 . . . . .294/D6
Blanchard, N. Dak., U.S., 70 . . . . .326/H2
Blanchard, Okla., U.S., 2,816 . . . . .330/E2
Blanchard, Penn., U.S., 621 . . . . .336/F3
Blanchard, Wash., U.S., 150 . . . . .358/C1
Blanchardville, Wisc., U.S., 806 . . . . .364/D6
Blanche, Ala., U.S. .238/D1
Blanchester, Ohio, U.S., 4,220 . . . . .328/C7
Blanco, N. Mex., U.S., 40 . . . . .317/C1
Blanco, Okla., U.S., 90 . . . . .330/C3
Blanco, Oreg., U.S., *cape* 334/B5
Blanco, Tex., U.S., 1,505 . . . . .346/C3, K5
Blanco, Tex., U.S., *county*, 8,418 . . . . . .346/C3, K5
Blanco, Tex., U.S., *river* 346/C2
Blanco Trading Post, N. Mex., U.S., 70 . . . . . .317/C1
Blanc-Sablon, Que., Can., 1,201 . . . . .225/E3
Bland, Mo., U.S., 565 . . . . .302/E3
Bland, Va., U.S., 500 . . . . .354/A6
Bland, Va., U.S., *county*, 6,871 . . . . .354/A6
Blanda, Ice., *river* .79/B2
Blandburg, Penn., U.S., 425 . . . . .336/E4
Blandford, Mass., U.S., 1,214 . . . . .292/C4
Blandford Forum, Eng., U.K., 8,880 . . . . .73/H3
Blanding, Utah, U.S., 3,162 . . . . .350/E6
Blandinsville, Ill., U.S., 777 . . . . .266/B4
Blandville, Ky., U.S., 99 . . . . .280/B4
Blaney, N. Ire., U.K. 65/B3
Blaney Park, Mich., U.S. 294/D3
Blanket, Tex., U.S., 402 . . . . .346/K4
Blanquilla, Ven., *island* 204/E5
Blanton, Fla., U.S., 212/ 256/C6
Blantyre, Mal., 502,053, (2,000,000 *metro.*) .159/B4
Blarney, Ire. 76/B3
Blarney, Ire., *castle* 76/B3
Blasdell, N.Y., U.S., 2,718 . . . . .320/D5
Blatec, Mac. 100/C2
Blawenberg, N.J., U.S., 1,300 . . . . .314/D3
Blawnox, Penn., U.S., 1,550 . . . . .336/B5, E7
Blaxton, Eng., U.K. .66/G6
Bleadon, Eng., U.K. 73/G2
Bleaklow, Eng., U.K., *hill* 68/D3
Bleasby, Eng., U.K. .68/F3
Bleckley, Ga., U.S., *county*, 11,666 . . . . . . .260/E7
Bledington, Eng., U.K. 70/A3
Bledsoe, Tenn., U.S., *county*, 12,367 . . . . . .344/L3
Bledsoe, Tex., U.S., 175 . . . . .346/E2
Bleecker, Ala., U.S., 150 . . . . .238/D3
Blekinge, Swe., *county* 80/C3
Blencoe, Iowa, U.S., 231 . . . . .274/B4
Blenheim, Ont., Can., 4,795 . . . . .223/D5
Blenheim, N.Z. 171/B3
Blenheim, S.C., U.S., 137 . . . . .340/E2
Blennerhassett, W. Va., U.S., 3,225 . . . . .360/C2
Blessing, Tex., U.S., 861 . . . . .346/M7
Bletchingley, Eng., U.K., 2,558 . . . . .70/D4
Bletchley, Eng., U.K., 41,435 . . . . .68/F6
Bletchley, Eng., U.K., 41,435 . . . . .70/B3
Blevins, Ark., U.S., 365 . . . . .244/B4
Blewbury, Eng., U.K., 1,479 . . . . .70/B3
Blewett, Tex., U.S. .346/H6

Blida, Alg., 153,083 . . . . .146/B1
Blidworth, Eng., U.K., 4,215 . . . . .68/E3
Bligh Water, Fiji, *sound* 174/B2
Blind Bay, Br. Col., Can., 2,464 . . . . .214/N6
Blindley Heath, Eng., U.K. 70/D4
Blind River, Ont., Can., 3,969 . . . . .223/C1
Bliss, Ida., U.S., 275 . . . . .264/C7
Bliss, Mich., U.S., 70 . . . . .294/E4
Bliss, N.Y., U.S., 375 . . . . .320/E5
Bliss Corner, Mass., U.S., 5,466 . . . . .292/L6
Blissfield, N.B., Can. 217/C2
Blissfield, Mich., U.S., 3,223 . . . . .294/F8
Blissfield, Ohio, U.S., 150 . . . . .328/G5
Blissville, N.B., Can. 217/C3
Blitchton, Ga., U.S., 212/ 260/J7
Blitta, Togo 151/B2
Blocher, Ind., U.S., 600 . . . . .270/E7
Block, R.I., U.S., *island* 339/C6
Blocker, Okla., U.S., 60 . . . . .330/G2
Block Island, R.I., U.S., 150 . . . . .339/C7
Block Island, R.I., U.S., *sound* 339/B6
Block Island N.W.R., R.I., U.S. 339/C6
Blockley, Eng., U.K. 68/D5
Blockton, Iowa, U.S., 192 . . . . .274/F6
Blodgett, Mo., U.S., 265 . . . . .302/G5
Blodgett Landing, N.H., U.S. 312/B5
Bloemfontein, S. Afr., *judicial capital* 162/C2
Bloemhof, S. Afr., *reservoir* 162/C2
Blofield, Eng., U.K. .70/G1
Blomkest, Minn., U.S., 186 . . . . .298/B6
Bloodsworth, Md., U.S., *island* 288/K7
Bloodsworth, Va., U.S., *island* 354/L4
Bloodvein, Man., Can., *river* 215/C3
Bloom, Kans., U.S., 60 . . . . .276/C4
Bloomburg, Tex., U.S., 375 . . . . .346/P2
Bloom City, Wisc., U.S., 60 . . . . .364/C5
Bloomdale, Ohio, U.S., 724 . . . . .328/C3
Bloomer, Wisc., U.S., 3,347 . . . . .364/B3
Bloomfield, N.B., Can. 217/D3
Bloomfield, Ont., Can., 643 . . . . .223/H4
Bloomfield, Conn., U.S., 19,587 . . . . .253/E2
Bloomfield, Ind., U.S., 2,542 . . . . .270/C6
Bloomfield, Iowa, U.S., 2,601 . . . . .274/K6
Bloomfield, Ky., U.S., 855 . . . . .280/E3
Bloomfield, Mo., U.S., 1,952 . . . . .302/G5
Bloomfield, Mont., U.S. 306/M2
Bloomfield, N.J., U.S., 47,683 . . . . .314/B2, G1
Bloomfield, N. Mex., U.S., 6,417 . . . . .317/C1
Bloomfield, N.Y., U.S., 1,267 . . . . .320/E5
Bloomfield, Vt., U.S., 261 . . . . .352/D1
Bloomfield Hills, Mich., U.S., 3,940 . . . . .294/A6, F7
Bloomfield Township, Mich., U.S., 43,021 . . . .294/A6
Bloomingburg, N.Y., U.S., 353 . . . . .320/N7
Bloomingburg, Ohio, U.S., 874 . . . . .328/D6
Bloomingdale, Fla., U.S., 19,839 . . . . .256/D6
Bloomingdale, Ga., U.S., 2,665 . . . . .260/J7
Bloomingdale, Ill., U.S., 21,675 . . . . .266/B5
Bloomingdale, Ind., U.S., 319 . . . . .270/B5
Bloomingdale, Mich., U.S., 528 . . . . .294/D7
Bloomingdale, N.J., U.S., 7,610 . . . . .314/A1, E1
Bloomingdale, Ohio, U.S., 221 . . . . .328/J5
Bloomingdale, Tenn., U.S., 10,350 . . . . .344/S1
Blooming Prairie, Minn., U.S., 1,933 . . . . . . .298/D7
Bloomington, Ida., U.S., 250 . . . . .264/F7
Bloomington, Ill., U.S., 64,808, (150,433 *metro.*) 266/E3
Bloomington, Ind., U.S., 69,291,
(120,563 *metro.*) 270/C6
Bloomington, Kans., U.S. 276/F2
Bloomington, Minn., U.S., 85,172 . . . . . . .298/D6, F6
Bloomington, Nebr., U.S., 124 . . . . .308/E3
Bloomington, Wisc., U.S., 701 . . . . .364/C6
Blooming Valley, Penn., U.S., 378 . . . . .336/A2
Bloomsburg, Penn., U.S., 12,375 . . . . .336/J4
Bloomsbury, N.J., U.S., 886 . . . . .314/C2
Bloomsdale, Mo., U.S., 419 . . . . .302/F3
Bloomville, Ohio, U.S., 1,045 . . . . .328/D3
Bloomville, Wisc., U.S., 125 . . . . .364/D3
Blossburg, Mont., U.S. 306/D3
Blossburg, Penn., U.S., 1,480 . . . . .336/G2
Blossom, Tex., U.S., 1,439 . . . . .346/N2
Blossom Park, Ont., Can. 223/H6
Blount, Ala., U.S., *county*, 51,024 . . . . .238/C2
Blount, Tenn., U.S., *county*, 105,823 . . . . . .344/P3
Blountstown, Fla., U.S., 2,444 . . . . .256/C1
Blountsville, Ala., U.S., 1,768 . . . . .238/C1
Blountsville, Ind., U.S., 166 . . . . .270/F4
Blountville, Tenn., U.S., 2,959 . . . . .344/S1
Blow, Yukon, Can., *river* 228/B1
Blowing Rock, N.C., U.S., 1,418 . . . . .322/B2
Blowing Wind Cave N.W.R., Ala., U.S. 238/C1
Bloxham, Eng., U.K., 2,356 . . . . .68/E5
Bloxham, Eng., U.K., 2,356 . . . . .70/B2
Bloxham, Fla., U.S., 425 . . . . .256/D1
Bloxom, Va., U.S., 395 . . . . .354/M5
Bloxwich, Eng., U.K. 68/C3
Blubberhouses, Eng., U.K. 66/E4
Blue, Austl., *mountains* 170/E3
Blue, Jam., *mountains* 206/C2
Blue, Ariz., U.S. 242/F4
Blue, N.H., U.S., *mountain* 312/D2
Blue, Oreg., U.S., *mountains* 334/H3
Blue, Tex., U.S., 90 . . . . .346/L5
Blue Anchor, N.J., U.S., 1,500 . . . . .314/D4
Blue Ash, Ohio, U.S., 12,513 . . . . .328/B9
Blue Ball, Ark., U.S., 50 . . . . .244/B3
Bluebell, Utah, U.S., 150 . . . . .350/D3
Blue Diamond, Nev., U.S., 282 . . . . .310/C3
Blue Earth, Minn., U.S., 3,621 . . . . .298/C7
Blue Earth, Minn., U.S., *county*, 55,941 . . . .298/C7
Blue Eye, Ark., U.S. 244/B1
Blue Eye, Mo., U.S., 129 . . . . .302/C5
Bluefield, Va., U.S., 5,078 . . . . .354/A6
Bluefield, W. Va., U.S., 11,451 . . . . .360/D6
Bluefields, Nicar. .202/C3
Blue Grass, Iowa, U.S., 1,169 . . . . .274/N4
Blue Grass, Minn., U.S., 50 . . . . .298/C4
Blue Grass Army Depot, Ky., U.S. 280/F3
Blue Hill, Maine, U.S., 2,390 . . . . .286/D4
Blue Hill, Nebr., U.S., 867 . . . . .308/E3
Blue Hill Falls, Maine, U.S., 40 . . . . .286/D4
Blue Hills, Conn., U.S., 3,020 . . . . .253/E2
Blue Island, Ill., U.S., 23,463 . . . . .266/C6
Bluejacket, Okla., U.S., 274 . . . . .330/G1
Blue Lake, Calif., U.S., 1,135 . . . . .246/B2
Blue Mesa, Colo., U.S., *reservoir* 250/C3
Blue Mound, Ill., U.S., 1,129 . . . . .266/D4
Blue Mound, Kans., U.S., 277 . . . . .276/G3
Blue Mound, Tex., U.S., 2,388 . . . . .346/A9
Blue Mounds, Wisc., U.S., 708 . . . . .364/D5
Blue Mtn., Jam., *peak* 206/C2
Blue Mtn., Ala., U.S., 233 . . . . .238/D2
Blue Mtn., Ark., U.S., 132 . . . . .244/B2
Blue Mtn., Colo., U.S., 50 . . . . .250/B1
Blue Mtn., Miss., U.S., 670 . . . . .300/C1
Blue Mtn., Oreg., U.S., *pass* 334/J5
Blue Nile, Eth., *river* 156/B2
Blue Nile, Sudan, *river* 145/C2
Bluenose, Nun., Can., *lake* 208/E3

Blue Rapids, Kans., U.S., 1,088 . . . . .276/F2
Blue Ridge, Alta., Can., 230 . . . . .212/C4
Blue Ridge, Ala., U.S., 1,331 . . . . .238/C3
Blue Ridge, Ga., U.S., 1,210 . . . . .260/C2
Blue Ridge, Ga., U.S., *mountains* 260/C2
Blue Ridge, Tex., U.S., 672 . . . . .346/M2
Blue Ridge, Va., U.S., 3,188 . . . . .354/D6
Blue Ridge Manor, Ky., U.S., 623 . . . . .280/B2
Blue River, Br. Col., Can. 214/N5
Blue River, Colo., U.S., 685 . . . . .250/D2
Blue River, Oreg., U.S., 70 . . . . .334/D3
Blue River, Wisc., U.S., 429 . . . . .364/C5
Blue Sprs., Ala., U.S., 121 . . . . .238/D4
Blue Sprs., Miss., U.S., 144 . . . . .300/C1
Blue Sprs., Mo., U.S., 48,080 . . . . .302/B2, J5
Blue Sprs., Nebr., U.S., 383 . . . . .308/H3
Bluestone, Va., U.S., *lake* 354/A5
Bluestone, W. Va., U.S., *lake* 360/E5
Bluestone Natl. Scenic River, Va., U.S. 354/A5
Bluestone Natl. Scenic River, W. Va., U.S. . . .360/E5
Bluewater, Calif., U.S., 265 . . . . .246/L8
Bluewater, N. Mex., U.S., 90 . . . . .317/C2
Bluff, Utah, U.S., 320 . . . . .350/E6
Bluff City, Ark., U.S., 158 . . . . .244/B4
Bluff City, Ill., U.S., 212/ 266/D5
Bluff City, Kans., U.S., 80 . . . . .276/E4
Bluff City, Tenn., U.S., 1,559 . . . . .344/S2
Bluff Dale, Tex., U.S., 80 . . . . .346/K3
Bluffdale, Utah, U.S., 4,700 . . . . .350/C3, E2
Bluffs, Ill., U.S., 748 . . . . .266/C4
Bluffton, Alta., Can., 127 . . . . .212//C5
Bluffton, Ark., U.S. 244/B3
Bluffton, Ga., U.S., 118 . . . . .260/B8
Bluffton, Ind., U.S., 9,536 . . . . .270/F4
Bluffton, Iowa, U.S., 80 . . . . .274/L1
Bluffton, Minn., U.S., 210 . . . . .298/B4
Bluffton, Ohio, U.S., 3,896 . . . . .328/C4
Bluffton, S.C., U.S., 1,275 . . . . .340/D4
Bluford, Ill., U.S., 785 . . . . .266/E5
Blum, Tex., U.S., 399 . . . . .346/L3
Blundeston, Eng., U.K. 70/H1
Blunt, S. Dak., U.S., 370 . . . . .342/F3
Bly, Oreg., U.S., 250 . . . . .334/E5
Blyn, Wash., U.S., 162 . . . . .358/B1
Blyth, Ont., Can., 987 . . . . .223/D4
Blyth, Eng., U.K., 35,327 . . . . .66/E2
Blyth, Eng., U.K., 35,327 . . . . .68/E2
Blythe, Calif., U.S., 12,155 . . . . .246/L9
Blythe, Ga., U.S., 718 . . . . .260/G5
Blythe Bridge, Eng., U.K. 68/C4
Blythedale, Mo., U.S., 233 . . . . .302/C1
Blytheville, Ark., U.S., 18,272 . . . . .244/F2
Blythewood, S.C., U.S., 170 . . . . .340/D2
Bo, S.L. 149/A2
Bō, Scot., U.K., *lake* 62/E6
Boaco, Nicar. 202/B2
Boaco, Nicar., *department* 202/B2
Boalsburg, Penn., U.S., 3,578 . . . . .336/F4
Board Camp, Ark., U.S., 40 . . . . .244/A3
Boardman, N.C., U.S., 202 . . . . .322/H6
Boardman, Ohio, U.S., 37,215 . . . . .328/J3
Boardman, Oreg., U.S., 2,855 . . . . .334/G2
Boardman Bridge, Conn., U.S., 600 . . . . .253/B3
Boarhills, Scot., U.K. 62/L6
Boatman, Okla., U.S., 325 . . . . .330/G1
Boa Vista, Braz., 43,131, (142,813 *metro.*) . .188/B1
Boa Vista, C.V., *island* 148/D2
Boaz, Ala., U.S., 7,411 . . . . .238/C1
Boaz, W. Va., U.S., 1,345 . . . . .360/D2
Boaz, Wisc., U.S., 137 . . . . .364/C5
Bobcaygeon, Ont., Can., 2,854 . . . . .223/G3
Bobo, Miss., U.S., 212/ 300/B1
Bobo-Dioulasso, Burkina, 268,926 . . . . .151/B3
Bobonaro, E. Timor, *province* 122/B1
Bobtown, Penn., U.S., 1,000 . . . . .336/B6
Boca Chica, Fla., U.S., *key* 256/G7
Boca Grande, Fla., U.S., 700 . . . . .256/F5
Boca Raton, Fla., U.S., 74,764 . . . . .256/B5, H5
Bocas del Toro, Pan. 203/A2
Bocas del Toro, Pan., *province* 203/A2
Bocay, Nicar. 202/B2
Bocay, Nicar., *river* 202/B2
Bocholt, Ger. 86/A3
Bochum, Ger., 392,830 . . . . .86/A3
Bock, Minn., U.S., 106 . . . . .298/D5
Bodaybo, Russ. 104/G4
Bodcaw, Ark., U.S., 154 . . . . .244/B4
Bode, Iowa, U.S., 327 . . . . .274/F2
Bodega Bay, Calif., U.S., 1,423 . . . . .246/B4
Bodélé, Chad, *depression* 153/B3
Bodfari, Wales, U.K. 66/E1
Bodfish, Calif., U.S., 1,823 . . . . .246/G7
Bodfish, Maine, U.S. 286/C3
Bodfuan, Wales, U.K. 64/C2
Bodicote, Eng., U.K. 68/E5
Bodie, N.C., U.S., *island* 322/P3
Bodmin, Eng., U.K., 12,553 . . . . .73/C4
Bodmin, Eng., U.K., *moor* 73/C3
Bodney, Eng., U.K. .70/F1
Bodo, Alta., Can. .212//E5
Bodø, Nor. 80/C2
Boelus, Nebr., U.S., 221 . . . . .308/E2
Boende, Congo, D.R. 155/B2
Boerne, Tex., U.S., 6,178 . . . . .346/A2, K6
Boffa, Guin. 149/A2
Bogalusa, La., U.S., 13,365 . . . . .282/K5
Bogard, Mo., U.S., 234 . . . . .302/C2
Bogart, Ga., U.S., 1,049 . . . . .260/D4
Bogata, Tex., U.S., 1,396 . . . . .346/N2
Bogend, Scot., U.K. 62/G7
Boger City, N.C., U.S., 554 . . . . .322/C4
Boggeragh, Ire., *mountains* 76/B2
Boggy, Ant.-Bar., *peak* 207/D5
Bogia, Pap. N.G. 124/C3
Bogniebrae, Scot., U.K. 62/L4
Bognor Regis, Eng., U.K., 56,744 . . . . .70/C5
Bogor, Indon., 5,000,000 . . . . .116/C5
Bogotá, Col., *capital*, 6,422,198 . . . . .184/B3
Bogota, Ill., U.S., 900 . . . . .266/E5
Bogota, N.J., U.S., 8,249 . . . . .314/B2
Bogota, Tenn., U.S., 212/ 344/C2
Bogra, Bangl. 127/C4
Bogue, Kans., U.S., 179 . . . . .276/C2
Bogue, N.C., U.S., 590 . . . . .322/L6
Bogue Chito N.W.R., La., U.S. 282/K5
Bogue Chitto, (Lincoln County), Miss., U.S., 375 .300/B4
Bogue Chitto, (Neshoba County), Miss., U.S.,
533 . . . . .300/D3
Bogue Chitto, Miss., U.S., *river* 300/B4
Bo Hai, China, *gulf* 119/E2
Bohemia, Czh. Rep., *region* 92/A3
Bohemian, Czh. Rep., *forest* 92/A3
Bohemian, Ger., *forest* 86/C4
Bohners Lake, Wisc., U.S., 1,952 . . . . .364/E6
Bohol, Phil., *island* 120/C4
Bohol, Phil., *sea* .120/C4
Bohon, Ky., U.S., 60 . . . . .280/F3
Boicourt, Kans., U.S. 276/H3
Boiestown, N.B., Can. 217/C2
Boiling, Dom., *lake* 208/B3

Boiling Spr. Lakes, N.C., U.S., 2,972 . . . . . . .322/J6
Boiling Sprs., N.C., U.S., 3,866 . . . . .322/B4
Boiling Sprs., Penn., U.S., 2,769 . . . . .336/G5
Boiling Sprs., S.C., U.S., 4,544 . . . . .340/C1, F1
Boilleau, Que., Can. 226/F3
Bois Blanc, Mich., U.S., *island* 294/E4
Bois D'Arc, Mo., U.S., 300 . . . . .302/C4
Bois-des-Filion, Que., Can. 226/H5
Bois de Sioux, S. Dak., U.S., *river* 342/J2
Boise, Ida., U.S., *county*, 6,670 . . . . .264/B5
Boise, Ida., U.S., *state capital*, 185,787,
(432,345 *metro.*) 264/A6
Boise City, Okla., U.S., 1,483 . . . . .330/B4
Boise Natl. For., Ida., U.S. 264/B5
Boise Natl. For., Oreg., U.S. 334/K3
Boissevain, Man., Can., 1,495 . . . . .215/A4
Boistfort, Wash., U.S. 358/B3
Bokchito, Okla., U.S., 564 . . . . .330/F3
Boké, Guin. 149/A2
Bokeelia, Fla., U.S., 1,997 . . . . .256/F5
Bokhoma, Okla., U.S., 100 . . . . .330/H4
Boknafjord, Nor., *fjord* 80/B4
Boksburg, S. Afr. 162/C2
Bokoshe, Okla., U.S., 450 . . . . .330/H2
Bol, Chad 153/A4
Bolair, W. Va., U.S., 225 . . . . .360/F4
Bolama, Gui.-B. 149/B2
Bolans, Ant.-Bar. .207/D5
Bolckow, Mo., U.S., 234 . . . . .302/B1
Boldon, Eng., U.K., 12,420 . . . . .66/F3
Bold Spr., Tenn., U.S., 70 . . . . .344/F3
Bole, Gha. 150/A2
Boles, Ark., U.S., 100 . . . . .244/A3
Boles Acres, N. Mex., U.S., 1,172 . . . . .317/E5
Boley, Okla., U.S., 1,126 . . . . .330/F2
Bolgatanga, Gha. .150/B1
Boligee, Ala., U.S., 369 . . . . .238/A3
Bolinas, Calif., U.S., 1,246 . . . . .246/H1
Boling, (Boling-Iago), Tex., U.S., 1,271 . . . . .346/N6
Bolingbroke, Ga., U.S., 250 . . . . .260/D6
Bolingbrook, Ill., U.S., 56,321 . . . . .266/B6, E2
Bolinger, La., U.S., 212/ 282/B1
Bolívar, Col., *department* 184/B2
Bolívar, Ecua., *province* 185/B3
Bolivar, La., U.S., 150 . . . . .282/J5
Bolivar, Miss., U.S., 60 . . . . .300/A4
Bolivar, Miss., U.S., *county*, 40,633 . . . . . . .300/B2
Bolivar, Mo., U.S., 9,143 . . . . .302/C4
Bolivar, N.Y., U.S., 1,173 . . . . .320/E6
Bolivar, Ohio, U.S., 894 . . . . .328/H4
Bolivar, Penn., U.S., 501 . . . . .336/C5
Bolivar, Tenn., U.S., 5,802 . . . . .344/D4
Bolivar, Tex., U.S., *peninsula* 346/P6
Bolivar, W. Va., U.S., 1,045 . . . . .360/L2
Bolívar, Ven., *mountain* 182/B2
Bolívar, Ven., *state* 182/D2
Bolivia, *nation* 176
Bolivia, N.C., U.S., 148 . . . . .322/J6
Bolligen, Switz. 90/B2
Bollinger, Mo., U.S., *county*, 12,029 . . . . . . .302/F4
Bolnhurst, Eng., U.K. 70/D2
Bolnisi, Geo. 103/C4
Bolobo, Congo, D.R. 155/B2
Bologna, It., 369,955 . . . . .95/B1
Bolovens, Laos, *plateau* 115/D4
Bolsena, It., *lake* .95/B2
Bolsón de Mapimí, Mex., *depression* 200/D2
Bolsover, Eng., U.K., 11,743 . . . . .68/E3
Bolton, Ont., Can., 20,553 . . . . .223/F4
Bolton, Eng., U.K. .60/C3
Bolton, Eng., U.K., 139,020 . . . . .66/D5
Bolton, Eng., U.K., 139,020 . . . . .68/C2
Bolton, Eng., U.K., *unitary authority*, 261,035 .66/D5
Bolton, Eng., U.K., *unitary authority*, 261,035 .68/C2
Bolton, Scot., U.K. .62/L7
Bolton, Conn., U.S., 5,017 . . . . .253/F2
Bolton, Mass., U.S., 4,148 . . . . .292/H3
Bolton, Miss., U.S., 629 . . . . .300/B3
Bolton, N.C., U.S., 494 . . . . .322/J6
Bolton, Vt., U.S., 971 . . . . .352/B2
Bolton Abbey, Eng., U.K. 66/E5
Bolton-le-Sands, Eng., U.K., 6,772 . . . . .68/B1
Bolu, Tur. 133/B2
Bolu, Tur., *province* 133/B2
Bolzano, It. 95/B1
Boma, Congo, D.R. 155/A2
Bombay, India, *harbor* . . . . .128/Inset I
Bombay, N.Y., U.S., 325 . . . . .320/M1
Bombay Beach, Calif., U.S., 366 . . . . .246/K9
Bombay Hook N.W.R., Del., U.S. 255/C3
Bom Jesus da Lapa, Braz. 188/D3
Bomoseen, Vt., U.S., 90 . . . . .352/A3
Bomoseen, Vt., U.S., *lake* 352/A3
Bomu, Congo, D.R., *river* 155/C1
Bon, Tun., *cape* .146/C1
Bon Accord, N.B., Can. 217/B2
Bon Air, Ala., U.S., 96 . . . . .238/C2
Bon Air, Tenn., U.S., 375 . . . . .344/L3
Bon Air, Va., U.S., 16,213 . . . . .354/H5
Bonaire, Neth. Ant., *island* 204/D4
Bonaire, Ga., U.S., 800 . . . . .260/D6
Bonanza, Ark., U.S., 514 . . . . .244/A2
Bonanza, Ga., U.S. 250/D3
Bonanza, Ga., U.S., 2,904 . . . . .260/C5
Bonanza, Oreg., U.S., 415 . . . . .334/E5
Bonanza, Utah, U.S. 350/E3
Bonao, Dom. Rep. .205/B2
Bonaparte, Iowa, U.S., 458 . . . . .274/L6
Bonaventure, Que., Can., 2,756 . . . . .226/L3
Bonaventure, Que., Can., *river*, 2,756 . . . . .226/L3
Bonasila, Nfld., Can., 4,021 . . . . .206/E5
Bonavista, Nfld., Can., *bay* 206/E5
Boncarbo, Colo., U.S. 250/F4
Bond, Colo., U.S., 80 . . . . .250/D2
Bond, Ill., U.S., *county*, 17,633 . . . . .266/D5
Bond, Miss., U.S., 375 . . . . .300/C5
Bondad, Colo., U.S. 250/C4
Bond Mill Park, (W. Laurel), Md., U.S., 3,400 .288/C5
Bondo, Congo, D.R. 155/B1
Bondoukou, C. d'Iv. 150/E2
Bonds Corner, Calif., U.S., 60 . . . . .246/K10
Bondsville, Mass., U.S., 1,876 . . . . .292/E4
Bond Swamp N.W.R., Ga., U.S. 260/D6
Bonduel, Wisc., U.S., 1,416 . . . . .364/E4
Bondurant, Iowa, U.S., 1,846 . . . . .274/H4
Bondurant, Ky., U.S. 280/A4
Bondurant, Wyo., U.S., 155 . . . . .366/A2
Bondville, Ill., U.S., 425 . . . . .266/E3
Bondville, Vt., U.S., 125 . . . . .352/B4
Bondy, Fr. . . . . .88/Inset II
Bone, Ida., U.S. 264/F6
Bone Gap, Ill., U.S., 252 . . . . .266/F5
Bo'ness, Scot., U.K., 13,961 . . . . .62/J6
Bonesteel, S. Dak., U.S., 297 . . . . .342/G4
Bonetraill, N. Dak., U.S. 326/B1
Bonfield, Ill., U.S., 364 . . . . .266/E2
Bong, Liber., *range* 149/A2
Bongor, Chad, 196,713 . . . . .153/A5

Bongos, C.A.R., *massif* 154/B2
Bonham, Tex., U.S., 9,990 . . . . .346/M2
Bon Homme, S. Dak., U.S., *county*, 7,260 . .342/H4
Bon Homme Colony, S. Dak., U.S. 342/H5
Bonifay, Fla., U.S., 4,078 . . . . .256/C1
Bonilla, S. Dak., U.S. 342/G3
Bonin, Jap., *islands* . . . . .114/Inset III
Bonita, Ariz., U.S. 242/F5
Bonita, La., U.S., 335 . . . . .282/F1
Bonita Sprs., Fla., U.S., 32,797 . . . . .256/G5
Bonlee, N.C., U.S., 325 . . . . .322/G3
Bonn, Ger., 302,212/ 86/A3
Bonneau, S.C., U.S., 354 . . . . .340/E3
Bonneauville, Penn., U.S., 1,378 . . . . .336/G6
Bonner, Ida., U.S., *county*, 36,835 . . . . . . .264/A1
Bonner, (Bonner-W. Riverside), Mont., U.S., 1,693 306/C3
Bonners Ferry, Ida., U.S., 2,515 . . . . .264/A1
Bonne Terre, Mo., U.S., 4,039 . . . . .302/F4
Bonnet Plume, Yukon, Can., *river* 228/C3
Bonnet Shores, R.I., U.S., 2,212/ 339/D5
Bonneville, Ida., U.S., *county*, 82,522 . . . .264/F6
Bonneville, Utah, U.S., *salt flats* 350/A3
Bonneville, Wyo., U.S. 366/B2
Bonney, Tex., U.S., 384 . . . . .346/N6
Bonney Lake, Wash., U.S., 9,687 . . . . .358/C2
Bonnie, Ill., U.S., 424 . . . . .266/E5
Bonnie Doone, N.C., U.S., 3,900 . . . . .322/H4
Bonnieville, Ky., U.S., 354 . . . . .280/E3
Bonny, Nig. 152/D5
Bonny, Colo., U.S., *reservoir* 250/H2
Bonny River, N.B., Can., 415 . . . . .217/C3
Bonnyville, Alta., Can., 5,709 . . . . .212/E4
Bono, Ark., U.S., 1,512 . . . . .244/E2
Bon Pays, Lux., *region* 85/B2
Bon Secour, Ala., U.S., *bay* 238/B5
Bonshaw, P.E.I., Can. 224/C2
Bonthe, S.L. 149/A2
Bon Wier, Tex., U.S., 300 . . . . .346/R5
Boody, Ill., U.S., 300 . . . . .266/D4
Book, Colo., U.S., *cliffs* 250/A2
Book, Utah, U.S., *cliffs* 350/D4, E4
Booker, Tex., U.S., 1,315 . . . . .264/C8
Booker T. Washington Natl. Mon., Va., U.S. . .354/D6
Booles, Eng., U.K. 66/D6
Boomer, N.C., U.S., 425 . . . . .322/C2
Boomer, W. Va., U.S., 1,100 . . . . .360/D4
Boon, Mich., U.S., 150 . . . . .294/D5
Boone, Ark., U.S., *county*, 33,948 . . . . . . .244/B1
Boone, Colo., U.S., 323 . . . . .250/F3
Boone, Ill., U.S., *county*, 41,786 . . . . .266/E1
Boone, Ind., U.S., *county*, 46,107 . . . . . . .270/D4
Boone, Iowa, U.S., 12,803 . . . . .274/G3
Boone, Iowa, U.S., *river* 274/G2
Boone, Ky., U.S., 275 . . . . .280/F3
Boone, Ky., U.S., *county*, 85,991 . . . . .280/F2, G1
Boone, Mo., U.S., *county*, 135,454 . . . . . .302/D2
Boone, Nebr., U.S., 50 . . . . .308/G2
Boone, Nebr., U.S., *county*, 6,259 . . . . . . .308/F2
Boone, N.C., U.S., 13,472 . . . . .322/B2
Boone, Okla., U.S., 100 . . . . .330/D3
Boone, W. Va., U.S., *county*, 25,535 . . . . .360/C4
Boones Mill, Va., U.S., 285 . . . . .354/D6
Booneville, Ark., U.S., 4,117 . . . . .244/B2
Booneville, Ky., U.S., 111 . . . . .280/G3
Booneville, Miss., U.S., 8,625 . . . . .300/D1
Boonsboro, Md., U.S., 2,803 . . . . .288/D1
Boonville, Tex., U.S., 40 . . . . .346/L2
Boonville, N.J., U.S., *town* 8,496 . . . . .314/E2
Bööntsagaan, Mong., *lake* 118/B2
Boonville, Calif., U.S., 600 . . . . .246/B4
Boonville, Ind., U.S., 6,834 . . . . .270/B8
Boonville, Mo., U.S., 8,202 . . . . .302/D3
Boonville, N.Y., U.S., 2,138 . . . . .320/L4
Boonville, N.C., U.S., 1,138 . . . . .322/D2
Boosaaso, Som. .157/B1
Booth, Ala., U.S., 80 . . . . .238/C3
Boothbay, Maine, U.S., 2,960 . . . . .286/C5
Boothbay Harbor, Maine, U.S., 2,334 . . . . .286/C5
Boothia, Nun., Can., *gulf* 208/K2
Boothia, Nun., Can., *peninsula* 208/K2
Boothville, (Boothville-Venice), La., U.S., 2,220 . .282/L8
Boothwyn, Penn., U.S., 5,206 . . . . .336/K7
Bootjack, Calif., U.S., 1,588 . . . . .246/F5
Bootle, Eng., U.K., 65,454 . . . . .66/B4
Bootle, Eng., U.K. 66/C6
Bootle, Eng., U.K., 65,454 . . . . .68/B3
Booué, Gabon .155/A2
Boquerón, P.R. .206/A2
Boquerón, Para., *department* 187/B3
Bor, Serb.-Mont. .99/C2
Bora, Scot., U.K., *lake* 62/H2
Borah, Ida., U.S., *peak* 264/D5
Borås, Swe., 97,347 . . . . .80/B3
Bordeaux, Fr., 218,948, (753,931 *metro.*) 88/B4
Bordeaux, Wyo., U.S. 366/D3
Bordelonville, La., U.S., 100 . . . . .282/F4
Borden, N.W. Terr., Can., *island* 208/F1
Borden, Nun., Can., *peninsula* 208/M2
Borden, P.E.I., Can., 798 . . . . .224/B2
Borden, Sask., Can., 225 . . . . .227/C8
Borden, Eng., U.K. 70/F4
Borden, Tex., U.S., *county*, 729 . . . . .346/G3
Borden Sprs., Ala., U.S. 238/D2
Bordentown, N.J., U.S., *city*, 3,969 . . . . . .314/D3
Border, Minn., U.S., 40 . . . . .298/C2
Border, Wyo., U.S. 366/A2
Borduluc, N. Dak., U.S. 326/G2
Boreham, Eng., U.K., 3,170 . . . . .70/F3
Borehamwood, Eng., U.K., 29,837 . . . . .70/D3
Boreland, Scot., U.K. 62/K8
Boreray, Scot., U.K., *island* 62/B3
Borger, Tex., U.S., 14,302 . . . . .346/C9
Borgne, La., U.S., *lake* 282/K6, L3
Borgo Maggiore, S. Mar. 97/B1
Boring, Md., U.S., 550 . . . . .288/G1
Boring, Oreg., U.S., 1,000 . . . . .334/B2
Borivli, India . . . . .128/Inset I
Borjomi, Geo. 103/B4
Borneo, Indon., *island* 122/C1
Bornholm, Den., *county* 79/E3
Bornholm, Den., *island* 79/E3
Borno, Nig., *state* 152/G1
Boron, Calif., U.S., 2,025 . . . . .246/H8
Boroughbridge, Eng., U.K., 1,903 . . . . .66/F4
Boroughbridge, Eng., U.K., 1,903 . . . . .68/E1
Borough Green, Eng., U.K., 4,373 . . . . .70/E4
Boroy, Den., *island* 79/Inset
Borrego Sprs., Calif., U.S., 2,535 . . . . . .246/Inset
Borrowash, Eng., U.K., 7,092 . . . . .66/F6
Borrowash, Eng., U.K., 7,092 . . . . .70/B1
Borrowby, Eng., U.K. 66/F4
Borsod-Abaúj-Zemplén, Hun., *county* 91/C2
Borth, Wales, U.K., 1,289 . . . . .64/C3
Borth, Wisc., U.S., 175 . . . . .364/E4
Borton, Ill., U.S., 80 . . . . .266/F4
Borup, Minn., U.S., 91 . . . . .298/A3
Borwick, Eng., U.K. 66/E4
Bosanska Gradiška, Bos.-Her. 98/A1
Bosanska Krupa, Bos.-Her. 98/A1
Bosbury, Eng., U.K. 68/C5

Boscastle, Eng., U.K. 73/C3
Boscawen, N.H., U.S., 3,672 . . . . .312/C5
Bosco, La., U.S. .282/E2
Boscobel, Wisc., U.S., 3,047 . . . . .364/C5
Bosham, Eng., U.K., 2,270 . . . . .70/B4
Bosherston, Wales, U.K. 64/B4
Bosler, Wyo., U.S. 366/D3
Bosley, Eng., U.K. 68/C3
Bosna, Bos.-Her., *river* 98/B1
Bosnia and Herzegovina, *nation* 96
Boso, Jap., *peninsula* 114/D3
Bosporus, Tur., *strait* 133/B2
Bosque, Ariz., U.S., 100 . . . . .242/C5
Bosque, Tex., U.S., *county*, 17,204 . . . . . .346/L4
Bosque del Apache N.W.R., N. Mex., U.S. . .317/D3
Bosque Farms, N. Mex., U.S., 3,931 . . . . . .302/E4
Boss, Mo., U.S., 80 . . . . .306/J1
Bossangoa, C.A.R. 154/A2
Bossier, La., U.S., *parish*, 98,310 . . . . . . .282/B1
Bossier City, La., U.S., 56,461 . . . . .282/B1
Bosten, China, *lake* 119/B1
Bostic, N.C., U.S., 328 . . . . .322/B4
Boston, Eng., U.K. 60/C3
Boston, Eng., U.K., 34,606 . . . . .68/G4
Boston, Eng., U.K., 34,606 . . . . .70/D1
Boston, Ga., U.S., 1,417 . . . . .260/D1
Boston, Ind., U.S., 177 . . . . .270/C5
Boston, Ky., U.S., 375 . . . . .280/E3
Boston, Mass., U.S., *harbor* 292/B2
Boston, Mass., U.S., *state capital*, 589,141,
   (5,819,100 *metro.*) 292/C7, K3
Boston, Va., U.S., 212/ 354/G3
Boston Bar, Br. Col., Can., 233 . . . . .214/M6
Boston Harbor, Wash., U.S., 450 . . . . .358/B2
Boston Harbor Islands N.R.A., Mass., U.S. . .292/D8
Boston Hts., Ohio, U.S., 1,186 . . . . .328/H10
Boston Mountains, Ark., U.S. 244/A2
Boston N.H.P., Mass., U.S. 292/D7
Bostwick, Fla., U.S., 350 . . . . .256/C6
Bostwick, Ga., U.S., 322 . . . . .260/D4
Bostwick, Nebr., U.S. 308/E3
Boswell, Br. Col., Can. 214/O6
Boswell, Ark., U.S. 244/C1
Boswell, Ind., U.S., 827 . . . . .270/C3
Boswell, Okla., U.S., 703 . . . . .330/G3
Boswell, Penn., U.S., 1,364 . . . . .336/C5
Bosworth, Mo., U.S., 382 . . . . .302/D2
Botany, Austl., *bay* . . . . .170/Inset IV
Botany, N.S.W., Austl. . . . . .170/Inset IV
Boteti, Bots., *river* 160/A2
Botetourt, Va., U.S., *county*, 30,496 . . . . . .354/D5
Botha, Alta., Can., 186 . . . . .212//D5
Bothel, Eng., U.K. 66/B3
Bothel, Wash., U.S., 30,150 . . . . .358/A4
Bothnia, Fin., *gulf* 81/B2
Bothnia, Fin., Swe., *gulf* 80/D2, D3, E3
Bothwell, P.E.I., Can. 224/C2
Bothwell, Utah, U.S. 350/B2
Botijas, P.R. 206/C2
Botkinburg, Ark., U.S., 50 . . . . .244/C2
Botkins, Ohio, U.S., 1,205 . . . . .328/B5
Botley, Eng., U.K., 2,297 . . . . .68/G6
Botley, Eng., U.K., 2,297 . . . . .70/B3
Botley, Eng., U.K. 70/B5
Botna, Mol., *river* 102/B2
Botna, Iowa, U.S. 274/H4
Botosani, Rom., 126,621 . . . . .101/D2
Botosani, Rom., *county* 101/D1
Botrange, Belg., *mountain* 85/E2
Botsford, Conn., U.S., 1,000 . . . . .253/B4
Botswana, *nation* .154
Botte Donato, It., *mountain* 95/D3
Bottesford, Eng., U.K., 2,619 . . . . .68/F4
Bottineau, N. Dak., U.S., 2,336 . . . . .326/E1
Bottineau, N. Dak., U.S., *county*, 7,149 . . .326/E1
Bottisham, Eng., U.K., 1,784 . . . . .68/H5
Bottisham, Eng., U.K., 1,784 . . . . .70/E2
Botto, Ky., U.S., 550 . . . . .280/G3
Bottrop, Ger., 121,097 . . . . .86/A3
Botwood, Nfld., Can., 3,221 . . . . .206/D4
Bouaflé, C. d'Iv. .150/D3
Bouaké, C. d'Iv., 329,850 . . . . .150/D3
Bouar, C.A.R., 43,000 . . . . .154/A2
Boucherville, Que., Can. 226/J5
Bouches-du-Rhône, Fr., *department* 88/D5
Bouctouche, N.B., Can., 2,426 . . . . .217/E2
Boudreaux, La., U.S., 350 . . . . .282/H8
Bougainville, P.N.G., *island* 172/B2
Boughton, P.E.I., Can., *bay* 224/C2
Boughton, (Boughton/Ollerton),
   Eng., U.K., 10,441 . . . . .68/F3
Bougouni, Mali .150/B3
Boujdour, W. Sah. 147/B1
Boukra, W. Sah. 147/B1
Boulder, Colo., U.S., 94,673 . . . . .250/A2, E1
Boulder, Colo., U.S., *county*, 269,814 . .250/A2, E1
Boulder, Ill., U.S., 70 . . . . .266/D5
Boulder, Mont., U.S., 1,300 . . . . .306/D4
Boulder, Utah, U.S., 180 . . . . .350/C6
Boulder, Wyo., U.S. 366/B2
Boulder City, Nev., U.S., 14,966 . . . . .310/C4
Boulder Creek, Calif., U.S., 4,081 . . . . .246/J3
Boulder Hill, Ill., U.S., 8,169 . . . . .266/A6
Boulogne, Fla., U.S., 150 . . . . .256/C6
Boulogne-Billancourt, Fr. . . . . .88/Inset II
Boulogne-sur-Mer, Fr. . . . . .88/Inset II
Bouna, C. d'Iv. .150/E2
Boundary, Ida., U.S., *county*, 9,871 . . . . . .264/A1
Boundary, Nev., U.S., *peak* 310/A3
Bound Brook, N.J., U.S., 10,155 . . . . .314/C2
Bountiful, Utah, U.S., 41,301 . . . . . . .350/C3, E2
Bourbon, Ill., U.S., 100 . . . . .266/E4
Bourbon, Ind., U.S., 1,691 . . . . .270/D2
Bourbon, Kans., U.S., *county*, 15,379 . . . .276/H4
Bourbon, Ky., U.S., *county*, 19,360 . . . . . .280/F2
Bourbon, Miss., U.S., 40 . . . . .300/B2
Bourbon, Mo., U.S., 1,348 . . . . .302/E3
Bourbonnais, Ill., U.S., 15,256 . . . . .266/F2
Bourem, Mali 150/C2
Bourg-en-Bresse, Fr. 88/D3
Bourges, Fr. 88/C3
Bourgogne, Fr., *region* 88/C3
Burke, N.S.W., Austl. 170/D3
Bourne, Eng., U.K., 8,777 . . . . .68/G4
Bourne, Eng., U.K., 8,777 . . . . .70/D1
Bourne, Ky., U.S., 80 . . . . .280/F3
Bourne, Mass., U.S., 18,721 . . . . .292/M6
Bourne, Oreg., U.S. 334/D2
Bourne End, (Bourne End/Flackwell Heath),
   Eng., U.K., 13,562 . . . . .70/C3
Bournemouth, Eng., U.K., 155,488,
   (358,321 *metro.*) 73/J3
Bournemouth, Eng., U.K., *unitary authority*,
   163,441 . . . . .73/J3
Bourton, Eng., U.K. 68/B4
Bourton-on-the-Water, Eng., U.K., 2,239 . . . .68/D6
Bouse, Ariz., U.S., 615 . . . . .242/B4
Bousso, Chad 153/B5
Bouton, Iowa, U.S., 136 . . . . .274/F4
Boutte, La., U.S., 2,181 . . . . .282/J3, J7
Bovey, Minn., U.S., 662 . . . . .298/D3

Bovey Tracey, Eng., U.K., 3,492 . . . . .73/E3
Bovill, Ida., U.S., 305 . . . . .264/A3
Bovina, Colo., U.S. 250/G2
Bovina, Tex., U.S., 1,874 . . . . .346/E10, F1
Bow, Alta., Can., *river* 212//D6
Bow, Sask., Can., *river* 227/E6
Bow, Eng., U.K. .73/E3
Bow, Scot., U.K. .62/M2
Bowbells, N. Dak., U.S., 406 . . . . .326/C1
Bow City, Alta., Can. 212//D6
Bowden, Alta., Can., 1,174 . . . . .212//D5
Bowden, W. Va., U.S., 70 . . . . .360/G3
Bowdle, S. Dak., U.S., 571 . . . . .342/F2
Bowdoin, Maine, U.S., 2,727 . . . . .286/C4
Bowdoin, Mont., U.S. 306/J1
Bowdoinham, Maine, U.S., 2,612 . . . . .286/C4
Bowdoin N.W.R., Mont., U.S. 306/J1
Bowdon, Ga., U.S., 1,959 . . . . .260/A4
Bowdon, N. Dak., U.S., 139 . . . . .326/F2
Bowdon Jct., Ga., U.S., 600 . . . . .260/A4
Bowen, Qnsld., Austl. 170/D2
Bowen, Ill., U.S., 535 . . . . .266/B3
Bowerbank, Maine, U.S., 123 . . . . .286/C3
Bowers Beach, Del., U.S., 305 . . . . .255/C4
Bowerston, Ohio, U.S., 414 . . . . .328/H5
Bowersville, Ga., U.S., 334 . . . . .260/E3
Bowersville, Ohio, U.S., 290 . . . . .328/C6
Bowesmont, N. Dak., U.S., 40 . . . . .326/H1
Bowie, Ariz., U.S., 550 . . . . .242/F5
Bowie, Colo., U.S. 250/C3
Bowie, Md., U.S., 50,269 . . . . .288/D6, H4
Bowie, Tex., U.S., 5,219 . . . . .346/L2
Bowie, Tex., U.S., *county*, 89,306 . . . . . . .346/P2
Bow Island, Alta., Can., 1,704 . . . . .212//E6
Bowie, Ariz., U.S. 242/F5
Bowkerville, N.H., U.S., 450 . . . . .312/B6
Bowland, Eng., U.K., *forest* 66/C4
Bowland, Eng., U.K., *forest* 68/B1
Bowlegs, Okla., U.S., 371 . . . . .330/F2
Bowler, Wisc., U.S., 343 . . . . .364/E4
Bowley Quarters, Md., U.S., 6,314 . . . . .288/J2
Bowling Green, Fla., U.S., 2,892 . . . . .256/G4
Bowling Green, Mo., U.S., 3,260 . . . . .302/E2
Bowling Green, Ohio, U.S., 29,636 . . . . . . .328/C3
Bowling Green, Va., U.S., 936 . . . . .354/J4
Bowlus, Minn., U.S., 260 . . . . .298/C5
Bowman, Calif., U.S., 150 . . . . .246/D4
Bowman, Ga., U.S., 898 . . . . .260/E3
Bowman, N. Dak., U.S., 1,600 . . . . .326/B3
Bowman, N. Dak., U.S., *county*, 3,242 . . . .326/B3
Bowman, S.C., U.S., 1,198 . . . . .340/D3
Bowmanstown, Penn., U.S., 895 . . . . .336/K4
Bow Mar, Colo., U.S., 847 . . . . .250/A3
Bow Mills, N.H., U.S., 650 . . . . .312/C5
Bowmont, Ida., U.S., 125 . . . . .264/A6
Bowmore, Scot., U.K., 862 . . . . .62/D7
Bowness-on-Solway, Eng., U.K. 66/B3
Bowness-on-Windermere, Eng., U.K. 66/C4
Bowring, Okla., U.S., 40 . . . . .330/F1
Bowron Lake Prov. Pk., Br. Col., Can. 212//A4
Bowron Lake Prov. Pk., Br. Col., Can. 214/M4
Bowser, Br. Col., Can., *lake* 214/H3
Bowsman, Man., Can., 320 . . . . .215/A3
Bowstring, Minn., U.S., 40 . . . . .298/D3
Bow Valley, Nebr., U.S., 125 . . . . .308/G1
Box, Eng., U.K. .73/H2
Boxborough, Mass., U.S., 4,868 . . . . .292/H2
Box Butte, Nebr., U.S., *county*, 12,158 . . . .308/A1
Box Elder, Mont., U.S., 794 . . . . .306/F1
Box Elder, S. Dak., U.S., 2,841 . . . . .342/B3
Box Elder, Utah, U.S., *county*, 42,745 . . . . .350/A2
Boxelder, Wyo., U.S. 366/D2
Boxford, Eng., U.K. 70/F2
Boxford, Mass., U.S., 7,921 . . . . .292/L2
Boxgrove, Eng., U.K. 70/C5
Box Hill, Vic., Austl. . . . . .170/Inset V
Boxhill North, (Bel Air South), Md., U.S., 2,900 . .288/J1
Boxholm, Iowa, U.S., 215 . . . . .274/F3
Boxian, Md., U.S. 70/F4
Boyaca, Col., *department* 184/B3
Boyce, La., U.S., 1,190 . . . . .282/D4
Boyce, Va., U.S., 426 . . . . .354/G2
Boyceville, Wisc., U.S., 1,043 . . . . .364/A3
Boyd, Ala., U.S., 125 . . . . .238/A3
Boyd, Fla., U.S., 175 . . . . .256/E1
Boyd, Ky., U.S., *county*, 49,752 . . . . .280/H2
Boyd, Minn., U.S., 210 . . . . .298/B6
Boyd, Mont., U.S. 306/G4
Boyd, Nebr., U.S., *county*, 2,438 . . . . .308/F1
Boyd, Okla., U.S. 330/B1, D4
Boyd, Tex., U.S., 1,099 . . . . .346/A9, L2
Boyd, Wisc., U.S., 680 . . . . .364/C4
Boydell, Ark., U.S. 244/D4
Boyden, Iowa, U.S., 672 . . . . .274/B1
Boyds, Wash., U.S. 358/G1
Boyds Cove, Nfld., Can., 258 . . . . .206/D4
Boyds Creek, Tenn., U.S. 344/P3
Boydsville, Ark., U.S., 90 . . . . .244/E1
Boydton, Va., U.S., 454 . . . . .354/G7
Boyer, Iowa, U.S. 274/H4
Boyero, Colo., U.S. 250/G3
Boyers, Penn., U.S., 400 . . . . .336/B3
Boyertown, Penn., U.S., 3,940 . . . . .336/K5
Boyes, Mont., U.S. 306/L4
Boyes Hot Sprs., Calif., U.S., 6,665 . . . . . . .246/J1
Boyette, Fla., U.S., 5,895 . . . . .256/G6
Boykin, Ga., U.S., 125 . . . . .260/B9
Boykins, Va., U.S., 620 . . . . .354/J7
Boyle, Alta., Can., 836 . . . . .212//D4
Boyle, Ky., U.S., *county*, 27,697 . . . . .280/F3
Boyle, Miss., U.S., 720 . . . . .300/B3
Boyne, Man., Can., *river* 215/B4
Boyne, Ire., *river* .76/C2
Boyne City, Mich., U.S., 3,503 . . . . .294/D4
Boyne Falls, Mich., U.S., 370 . . . . .294/E4
Boynton, Okla., U.S., 274 . . . . .330/G2
Boynton Beach, Fla., U.S., 60,389 . . . .256/B5, H5
Boy River, Minn., U.S. 298/C3
Boysen, Wyo., U.S. 366/B2
Boysen St. Park, Wyo., U.S. 366/B2
Boys Ranch, Tex., U.S., 600 . . . . .346/F9
Boys Town, Nebr., U.S., 818 . . . . .308/H2
Boyton, Eng., U.K. 70/G2
Bozeat, Eng., U.K., 1,864 . . . . .68/F5
Bozeat, Eng., U.K., 1,864 . . . . .70/C2
Bozeman, Mont., U.S., 27,509 . . . . .306/E4
Bozoum, C.A.R. .154/A2
Brabant, Sask., Can. 227/G1
Brabant Lake, Sask., Can., 66 . . . . .227/G1
Brabourne Lees, Eng., U.K., 1,925 . . . . .70/F4
Brać, Cro., *island* 98/C3
Bracciano, It., *lake* 95/C2
Bracebridge, Ont., Can., 13,751 . . . . .223/F2
Braceville, Ill., U.S., 792 . . . . .266/E2
Bracey, Va., U.S., 90 . . . . .354/G7
Bracken, Ky., U.S., *county*, 8,279 . . . . . . .280/F2
Bracken, Tex., U.S., 150 . . . . .346/A2
Brackett, Wisc., U.S., 150 . . . . .364/B4

Brackettville, Tex., U.S., 1,876 . . . . .346/H6
Brackley, Eng., U.K., 9,113 . . . . .68/E5
Brackley, Eng., U.K., 9,113 . . . . .70/B2
Brackley Beach, P.E.I., Can. 224/B2
Bracknell, Eng., U.K., 60,895 . . . . .70/C4
Bracknell Forest, Eng., U.K., *unitary authority*,
   109,606 . . . . .70/C4
Bradbury, Calif., U.S., 855 . . . . .246/D9
Bradbury, Maine, U.S., 100 . . . . .286/D1
Braddock, N. Dak., U.S., 43 . . . . .326/E3
Braddock, Penn., U.S., 2,912 . . . . .336/E7
Braddock Hts., Md., U.S., 4,627 . . . . .288/D2
Braddock Hills, Penn., U.S., 1,998 . . . . .336/E7
Braddyville, Iowa, U.S., 176 . . . . .274/D6
Braden, Tenn., U.S., 271 . . . . .344/B4
Bradenham, Eng., U.K. 70/C3
Bradenton, Fla., U.S., 49,504 . . . . .256/F4
Bradenton Beach, Fla., U.S., 1,482 . . . . . . .256/F4
Bradfield Green, Eng., U.K. 68/C3
Bradford, Eng., U.K. 60/C3
Bradford, Eng., U.K., 289,376 . . . . .66/F5
Bradford, Eng., U.K., 289,376 . . . . .68/D2
Bradford, Eng., U.K., *unitary authority*, 467,668 . .66/F5
Bradford, Eng., U.K., *unitary authority*, 467,668 . .68/D2
Bradford, Ark., U.S., 800 . . . . .244/D2
Bradford, Fla., U.S., *county*, 26,088 . . . . . .256/F2
Bradford, Ill., U.S., 787 . . . . .266/D2
Bradford, Iowa, U.S., 150 . . . . .274/H2
Bradford, Maine, U.S., 1,186 . . . . .286/D3
Bradford, Minn., U.S., 271 . . . . .298/D5
Bradford, N.H., U.S., 1,454 . . . . .312/C5
Bradford, Ohio, U.S., 1,859 . . . . .328/B5
Bradford, Penn., U.S., 9,175 . . . . .336/D2
Bradford, Penn., U.S., *county*, 62,761 . . . .336/H2
Bradford, R.I., U.S., 1,497 . . . . .339/D5
Bradford, Tenn., U.S., 1,113 . . . . .344/D2
Bradford, Vt., U.S., 2,619 . . . . .352/C3
Bradford Ctr., Maine, U.S., 175 . . . . .286/D3
Bradford-on-Avon, Eng., U.K., 8,815 . . . . . .73/H2
Bradfordville, Ky., U.S., 304 . . . . .280/E3
Bradfordville, Fla., U.S., 1,100 . . . . .256/B2
Bradford Woods, Penn., U.S., 1,149 . . . . . . .336/M4
Bradgate, Iowa, U.S., 101 . . . . .274/F2
Brading, Eng., U.K., 2,077 . . . . .70/B5
Bradley, Ala., U.S., 40 . . . . .238/C4
Bradley, Ark., U.S., 563 . . . . .244/B4
Bradley, Ark., U.S., *county*, 12,600 . . . . . .244/C4
Bradley, Calif., U.S., 120 . . . . .246/E7
Bradley, Ill., U.S., 12,784 . . . . .266/F2
Bradley, Maine, U.S., 1,242 . . . . .286/D4
Bradley, Okla., U.S., 182 . . . . .330/E3
Bradley, S.C., U.S., 171 . . . . .340/B2
Bradley, S. Dak., U.S., 112 . . . . .342/H2
Bradley, Tenn., U.S., *county*, 87,965 . . . . .344/M4
Bradley, W. Va., U.S., 2,371 . . . . .360/D5
Bradley, Wisc., U.S., 150 . . . . .364/D3
Bradley Beach, N.J., U.S., 4,793 . . . . .314/E3
Bradleyville, Mo., U.S., 50 . . . . .302/C5
Bradner, Ohio, U.S., 1,171 . . . . .328/D3
Bradshaw, Nebr., U.S., 336 . . . . .308/G3
Bradshaw, Tex., U.S. 346/J3
Bradshaw, W. Va., U.S., 289 . . . . .360/C6
Bradwell, (Essex), Eng., U.K. 70/F3
Bradwell, (Norfolk), Eng., U.K. 70/H1
Bradwell Waterside, Eng., U.K. 70/F3
Bradworthy, Eng., U.K. 73/D3
Brady, Mont., U.S., 150 . . . . .306/E1
Brady, Nebr., U.S., 366 . . . . .308/D3
Brady, Tex., U.S., 5,523 . . . . .346/J4
Brady Lake, Ohio, U.S., 513 . . . . .328/H3
Brae, Scot., U.K., 660 . . . . .62/Q2
Braedownie, Scot., U.K. 62/K5
Braemar, Scot., U.K. 62/K5
Braeriach, Scot., U.K., *hill* 62/J4
Braeswick, Scot., U.K. 62/N1
Braga, Port., 164,192 . . . . .93/A2
Braga, Port., *district* 93/A2
Bragança, Port. 93/B2
Bragança, Port., *district* 93/B2
Braggadocio, Mo., U.S., 212/ 302/G5
Bragg City, Mo., U.S., 189 . . . . .302/G5
Bragg Creek, Alta., Can., 678 . . . . .212//C6
Braggs, Ala., U.S., 80 . . . . .238/C3
Braggs, Okla., U.S., 301 . . . . .330/G2
Braham, Minn., U.S., 1,276 . . . . .298/D5
Brahmanbaria, Bangl. 127/E5
Brahmaputra, Bangl., *river* 127/D3
Brahmaputra, China, *river* 119/B3
Brahmaputra, India, *river* 128/E3
Braich-y-Pwll, Wales, U.K., *point* 64/B2
Braidwood, Ill., U.S., 5,203 . . . . .266/E2
Brăila, Rom., 230,962 . . . . .101/D3
Brăila, Rom., *county* 101/D3
Brailes, Eng., U.K. 70/A2
Brailsford, Eng., U.K. 68/D4
Brainard, Nebr., U.S., 351 . . . . .308/H2
Brainards, N.J., U.S., 225 . . . . .314/C2
Brainerd, Minn., U.S., 13,178 . . . . .298/C4
Braintree, Eng., U.K. . . . . .60/Inset III
Braintree, Eng., U.K., 33,229 . . . . .70/F2
Braintree, Mass., U.S., 33,828 . . . . .292/K4
Brakpan, S. Afr. .162/C2
Bralorne, Br. Col., Can. 214/L6
Bramalea, Ont., Can. 223/H5
Braman, Okla., U.S., 244 . . . . .330/E1
Bramley, Eng., U.K., 2,278 . . . . .70/B4
Brampton, Ont., Can., 325,428 . . . . .222/E4
Brampton, Ont., Can., 325,428 . . . . .223/H5
Brampton, (Cumbria), Eng., U.K., 3,957 . . . .66/C3
Brampton, (Lincolnshire), Eng., U.K. 66/G6
Brampton, Mich., U.S., 4,673 . . . . .70/D2
Brampton, Mich., U.S., 80 . . . . .294/B4
Brampton, N. Dak., U.S. 326/H4
Bramshall, Eng., U.K. 68/D4
Bramwell, W. Va., U.S., 426 . . . . .360/D6
Brancaster, Eng., U.K. 70/F1
Branch, Nfld., Can., 318 . . . . .206/D5
Branch, Ark., U.S., 357 . . . . .244/B2
Branch, La., U.S., 275 . . . . .282/E6
Branch, Mich., U.S., 150 . . . . .294/C6
Branch, Mich., U.S., *county*, 45,787 . . . . . .294/E8
Branchland, W. Va., U.S., 350 . . . . .360/B4
Branchport, N.Y., U.S., 375 . . . . .320/G5
Branchville, Ala., U.S., 825 . . . . .238/C2
Branchville, N.J., U.S., 845 . . . . .314/D1
Branchville, S.C., U.S., 1,083 . . . . .340/D3
Branchville, Va., U.S., 123 . . . . .354/J7
Branco, Braz., *river* 188/D3
Brandberg, Nam., *mountain* 160/B2
Brandenberg, Mont., U.S. 306/K4
Brandenburg, Ger. 86/C2
Brandenburg, Ger., *state* 86/C2
Brandenburg, Ky., U.S., 2,049 . . . . .280/E3
Brandesburton, Eng., U.K. 66/H5
Brandon, Man., Can., 39,716 . . . . . . .215/B4, C2
Brandon, Eng., U.K., 9,162 . . . . .66/F3
Brandon, Eng., U.K., 7,804 . . . . .70/F2
Brandon, Colo., U.S. 250/C3
Brandon, Fla., U.S., 77,895 . . . . .256/D6, F4
Brandon, Iowa, U.S., 311 . . . . .274/K3
Brandon, Minn., U.S., 450 . . . . .298/B5
Brandon, Miss., U.S., 16,436 . . . . .300/C4

Brandon, Nebr., U.S. 308/C3
Brandon, Ohio, U.S., 212/ 328/F5
Brandon, S. Dak., U.S., 5,693 ....342/J4
Brandon, Vt., U.S., 3,917 ....352/A3
Brandon, Wisc., U.S., 912 ....364/E5
Brandonville, W. Va., U.S., 102 ....360/G1
Brandreth, N.Y., U.S. 320/M3
Brandsby, Eng., U.K. 66/F4
Brandsville, Mo., U.S., 174 ....302/E5
Brandt, S. Dak., U.S., 113 ....342/J3
Brandywine, Md., U.S., 1,410 ....288/G5
Brandywine, W. Va., U.S. 360/H3
Branford, Conn., U.S., 28,683 ....253/D4
Branford, Fla., U.S., 695 ....256/F2
Bransgore, Eng., U.K., 3,843 ....73/J3
Branson, Colo., U.S., 77 ....250/G4
Branson, Mo., U.S., 6,050 ....302/C5
Branson West, Mo., U.S., 408 ....302/C5
Branston, Eng., U.K., 3,350 ....68/F4
Branston, Eng., U.K. 68/G3
Branston, Eng., U.K., 3,350 ....70/C1
Brant, Alta., Can. 212//D6
Brant, Ont., Can. 223/E4
Brant, Ont., Can., county 223/E4
Brant Beach, N.J., U.S., 800 ....314/E4
Brantford, Ont., Can., 86,417 ....223/E4
Brantford, N. Dak., U.S. 326/G2
Brantley, Ala., U.S., 920 ....238/C4
Brantley, Ga., U.S., county, 14,629 ....260/H9
Brant Rock, Mass., U.S., 5,100 ....292/M4
Brantwood, Wisc., U.S., 40 ....364/C3
Bras d'Or, N.S., Can. 221/G1
Braselton, Ga., U.S., 1,206 ....260/D3
Brasher, Mo., U.S., 280 ....302/D1
Brasher Falls, (Brasher Falls-Winthrop),
  N.Y., U.S., 1,140 ....320/M1
Brasília, Braz., capital, 2,043,169,
  (2,941,957 metro.) 188/D3
Braşov, Rom., 309,671 ....101/C3
Braşov, Rom., county 101/C3
Brass Castle, N.J., U.S., 1,507 ....314/C2
Brasstown Bald, Ga., U.S., mountain 260/D2
Brassua, Maine, U.S. 286/C3
Braswell, Ga., U.S., 80 ....260/B4
Bratenahl, Ohio, U.S., 1,337 ....328/H8
Bratislava, Slvk., capital, 428,672 ....92/A2
Bratislavský, Slvk., region 92/A2
Bratsk, Russ., 279,664 ....104/C4
Bratt, Fla., U.S., 225 ....256/A1
Brattleboro, Vt., U.S., 12,005 ....352/B5
Bratton, Eng., U.K. 73/H2
Bratton Clovelly, Eng., U.K. 73/D3
Braunau, Aus. 91/C2
Braunschweig, Ger., 246,322 ....86/B2
Braunschweig, Ger., department 86/B2
Braunston, Eng., U.K., 1,669 ....68/E5
Braunston, Eng., U.K., 1,669 ....70/B2
Braunstone, Eng., U.K. 70/B1
Braunton, Eng., U.K., 9,227 ....73/D2
Brava, C.V., island 148/B4
Brava, Sp., coast 94/H2
Brave, Penn., U.S., 212/ 336/A6
Brawley, Calif., U.S., 22,052 ....246/K10
Braxton, Miss., U.S., 181 ....300/C3
Braxton, W. Va., U.S., county, 14,702 ....360/E3
Bray, Calif., U.S. 246/D1
Bray, Okla., U.S., 1,035 ....330/E3
Braymer, Mo., U.S., 910 ....302/C2
Brayton, Iowa, U.S., 145 ....274/E4
Brazil, nation 178
Brazil, Ind., U.S., 8,188 ....270/B5
Brazil, Miss., U.S., 60 ....300/B1
Brazilian, Braz., highlands 188/D3
Brazilton, Kans., U.S., 60 ....276/H4
Brazoria, Tex., U.S., 2,787 ....346/N6
Brazoria, Tex., U.S., county, 241,767 ....346/B7, N6
Brazoria N.W.R., Tex., U.S. 346/N6
Brazos, N. Mex., U.S., 150 ....317/D1
Brazos, Tex., U.S., county, 152,415 ....346/M5
Brazos, Tex., U.S., river 346/A7
Brazos Pt., Tex., U.S., 60 ....346/L3
Brazzaville, Congo, capital, 596,212/,
  (1,187,000 metro.) 155/C6
Brea, P.R., point 206/B3
Brea, Calif., U.S., 35,410 ....246/E10
Bread Loaf, Vt., U.S., mountain 352/B2
Bream, Eng., U.K., 2,704 ....68/B6
Breasclete, Scot., U.K. 62/C2
Breathitt, Ky., U.S., county, 16,100 ....280/G3
Breaux Bridge, La., U.S., 7,281 ....282/F6
Brechfa, Wales, U.K. 64/C4
Brechin, Scot., U.K., 7,199 ....62/L5
Breckenridge, Colo., U.S., 2,408 ....250/D2
Breckenridge, Mich., U.S., 1,339 ....294/E6
Breckenridge, Minn., U.S., 3,559 ....298/A4
Breckenridge, Mo., U.S., 454 ....302/C2
Breckenridge, Okla., U.S., 239 ....330/E3
Breckenridge, Tex., U.S., 5,868 ....346/K3
Breckenridge Hills, Mo., U.S., 4,817 ....302/L5
Breckinridge, Ky., U.S., county, 18,648 ....280/D3
Breckinridge Ctr., Ky., U.S., 1,874 ....280/C3
Brecksville, Ohio, U.S., 13,382 ....328/H1
Břeclav, Czh. Rep. 92/C4
Brecon, Wales, U.K., 7,523 ....64/E4
Brecon Beacons, Wales, U.S., mountains 60/B4
Brecon Beacons N.P., Wales, U.K. 64/D4
Breda, Neth., 159,829 ....84/B3
Breda, Iowa, U.S., 477 ....274/E3
Bredenbury, Sask., Can., 354 ....227/H10
Bredon, Eng., U.K., 2,008 ....68/C5
Breed, Wisc., U.S., 80 ....364/E3
Breedsville, Mich., U.S., 235 ....294/C7
Breen, Colo., U.S. 250/B4
Breese, Ill., U.S., 4,048 ....266/D5
Breezewood, Penn., U.S., 300 ....336/E5
Breezy Pt., Md., U.S., 800 ....288/H5
Breezy Pt., Minn., U.S., 979 ....298/C4
Bregalnica, Mac., river 100/C2
Bregenz, Aus. 91/A3
Breiðafjörður, Ice., fjord 79/A2
Breien, N. Dak., U.S. 326/G3
Bremen, Ger., 540,330 ....86/B2
Bremen, Ger., state 86/B2
Bremen, Ala., U.S., 250 ....238/C2
Bremen, Ga., U.S., 4,579 ....260/A4
Bremen, Ind., U.S., 4,486 ....270/B3
Bremen, Ky., U.S., 365 ....280/C3
Bremen, Maine, U.S., 782 ....286/C4
Bremen, N. Dak., U.S., 40 ....326/F2
Bremen, Ohio, U.S., 1,265 ....328/F6
Bremer, Iowa, U.S., 90 ....274/K2
Bremer, Iowa, U.S., county, 23,325 ....274/K2
Bremer, Ger., 122,735 ....86/B2
Bremerhaven, Wash., U.S., 37,259 ....358/A4, C2
Bremond, Tex., U.S., 876 ....346/M4
Brenda, Ariz., U.S., 50 ....242/B4
Brendon, Eng., U.K. 73/E2
Brenham, Tex., U.S., 13,507 ....346/M5
Brenig, Wales, U.K., lake 64/D1
Brenish, Scot., U.K. 62/B2
Brenner, Aus., pass 91/B3
Brenner, It., pass 95/B1
Brennyville, Minn., U.S., 100 ....298/D5
Brent, Eng., U.K., 243,025 ....70/D3
Brent, Eng., U.K., unitary authority, 263,463 ....70/D3
Brent, Ala., U.S., 4,024 ....238/B3
Brentford, S. Dak., U.S., 65 ....342/G2
Brentwood, Eng., U.K. ....60/Inset III
Brentwood, Eng., U.K., 49,463 ....70/E3
Brentwood, Ark., U.S., 50 ....244/A2
Brentwood, Calif., U.S., 23,302 ....246/L1
Brentwood, Md., U.S., 2,844 ....288/C7
Brentwood, Mo., U.S., 7,693 ....302/H3
Brentwood, N.H., U.S., 3,197 ....312/D6
Brentwood, N.Y., U.S., 53,917 ....320/D2
Brentwood, Penn., U.S., 10,466 ....336/P2
Brentwood, Tenn., U.S., 23,445 ....344/H2
Brentwood Corners, N.H., U.S. 312/D5
Brereton Green, Eng., U.K. 68/C3
Brescia, It. 95/B1
Breslau, Tex., U.S., 60 ....346/M6
Bressay, Scot., U.K., island 62/Q2
Brest, Bela., 300,400 ....82/A3
Brest, Bela., oblast 82/B3
Brest, Fr., 156,217, (210,005 metro.) 88/A2
Bretagne, Fr., region 88/B2
Bretforton, Eng., U.K. 68/D5
Brethren, Mich., U.S., 275 ....294/C5
Breton, Alta., Can., 573 ....212//C4
Breton, La., U.S., islands 282/L8
Breton, La., U.S., sound 282/L7
Breton Bay, Md., U.S., 750 ....288/H6
Breton N.W.R., La., U.S. 282/L7, M7
Bretton Woods, N.H., U.S. 312/D3
Brevard, Fla., U.S., county, 476,230 ....256/H4
Brevard, N.C., U.S., 6,789 ....322/E8
Brevig Mission, Alaska, U.S., 276 ....240/B1
Brevik, Minn., U.S., 50 ....298/C3
Brevort, Mich., U.S. 294/D3
Brewer, Maine, U.S., 8,987 ....286/D4
Brewer, Miss., U.S., 225 ....300/D4
Brewerton, N.Y., U.S., 3,453 ....320/J4
Brewster, Kans., U.S., 285 ....276/A2
Brewster, Mass., U.S., 10,094 ....292/P5
Brewster, Minn., U.S., 502 ....298/B7
Brewster, Nebr., U.S. 308/E2
Brewster, N.Y., U.S., 2,162 ....320/P8
Brewster, Ohio, U.S., 2,324 ....328/G4
Brewster, Tex., U.S., county, 8,866 ....346/E6
Brewster, Wash., U.S., 2,189 ....358/F1
Brewster Hill, N.Y., U.S., 2,226 ....320/P8
Brewton, Ala., U.S., 5,498 ....238/C4
Brewton, Ga., U.S., 150 ....260/F6
Breynat, Alta., Can. 212//D3
Bria, C.A.R. 154/B2
Briançon, Fr. 88/D4
Brian Head, Utah, U.S., 118 ....350/B6
Brianne, Wales, U.K., lake 64/D3
Briar, Mo., U.S. 302/F5
Briar, Tex., U.S., 5,350 ....346/L2
Briarcliff, Tex., U.S., 895 ....346/D2
Briarcliffe Acres, S.C., U.S., 470 ....340/F3
Briarcliff Manor, N.Y., U.S., 7,696 ....320/B1
Briar Creek, Penn., U.S., 651 ....336/J3
Briartown, Okla., U.S., 150 ....330/G2
Briarwood, Ky., U.S., 554 ....280/B2
Briarwood, N. Dak., U.S., 78 ....326/J3
Briarwood, (part of E. Renton Highlands),
  Wash., U.S. 358/B4
Briarwood Beach, Mass., U.S. 292/M6
Briarwood Beach, Ohio, U.S. 328/G3
Brice, Ohio, U.S., 70 ....328/E9
Brice, Tex., U.S. 346/G10
Briceland, Calif., U.S., 80 ....246/B2
Bricelyn, Minn., U.S., 379 ....298/C6
Briceni, Mol. 102/A1
Brice Prairie, Wisc., U.S., 1,804 ....364/B5
Brices Cross Roads N.B.S., Miss., U.S. 300/D1
Briceville, Tenn., U.S., 650 ....344/N2
Brick, N.J., U.S., 76,119 ....314/E4
Brickerville, Penn., U.S., 1,287 ....336/J5
Brickeys, Ark., U.S. 244/E3
Briddletown, Md., U.S. 288/P6
Bridestowe, Eng., U.K. 73/D3
Bridge, Eng., U.K. 70/G4
Bridge, Ida., U.S. 264/D7
Bridgeboro, Ga., U.S., 212/ 260/D9
Bridgeboro, N.J., U.S., 250 ....314/D3
Bridge City, La., U.S., 8,323 ....282/K3
Bridge City, Tex., U.S., 8,651 ....346/R5
Bridgehampton, N.Y., U.S., 1,381 ....320/G1
Bridge Lake, Br. Col., Can. 214/M5
Bridgeland, Utah, U.S. 350/D3
Bridgend, Scot., U.K., 765 ....62/D7
Bridgend, Wales, U.K., 35,841 ....64/D4
Bridgend, Wales, U.K., unitary authority,
  128,650 ....64/D4
Bridge of Balgie, Scot., U.K. 62/H5
Bridge of Cally, Scot., U.K. 62/K5
Bridge of Don, Scot., U.K. 62/M4
Bridge of Dye, Scot., U.K. 62/M5
Bridge of Forss, Scot., U.K. 62/J1
Bridge of Orchy, Scot., U.K. 62/G6
Bridgeport, Ala., U.S., 2,728 ....238/D1
Bridgeport, Ariz., U.S. 242/C3
Bridgeport, Calif., U.S., 212/ 246/F4
Bridgeport, Conn., U.S., 139,529 ....253/C5
Bridgeport, Ill., U.S., 2,168 ....266/F5
Bridgeport, Kans., U.S., 100 ....276/E3
Bridgeport, Md., U.S., 2,700 ....288/D1
Bridgeport, Mich., U.S., 7,849 ....294/F6
Bridgeport, Nebr., U.S., 1,594 ....308/A2
Bridgeport, N.J., U.S., 600 ....314/C4
Bridgeport, N.Y., U.S., 1,665 ....320/J4
Bridgeport, Ohio, U.S., 2,186 ....328/J5
Bridgeport, Okla., U.S., 109 ....330/D2
Bridgeport, Oreg., U.S. 334/J3
Bridgeport, Penn., U.S., 4,371 ....336/L5
Bridgeport, Tex., U.S., 4,309 ....346/L2
Bridgeport, Wash., U.S., 2,059 ....358/F2
Bridgeport, W. Va., U.S., 7,306 ....360/F2
Bridgeport, Wisc., U.S., 125 ....364/B5
Bridger, Mont., U.S., 745 ....306/H4
Bridger, S. Dak., U.S. 342/B3
Bridger, Wyo., U.S., peak 366/C3
Bridger-Teton Natl. For., Wyo., U.S. 366/A2
Bridges, Eng., U.K. 68/B4
Bridgeton, Ind., U.S., 125 ....270/B5
Bridgeton, Mo., U.S., 15,550 ....302/H2
Bridgeton, N.J., U.S., 22,771 ....314/C5
Bridgeton, N.C., U.S., 328 ....322/L4
Bridgetown, Barb., capital, 5,928,
  (133,000 metro.) 204/G4
Bridgetown, Barb., capital, 5,928,
  (133,000 metro.) 209/A4
Bridgetown, N.S., Can., 1,035 ....221/B3
Bridgetown, Md., U.S., 100 ....288/L3
Bridgeview, Ill., U.S., 15,335 ....266/B6
Bridgeville, Calif., U.S. 246/B2
Bridgeville, Del., U.S., 1,436 ....255/B6
Bridgeville, Penn., U.S., 5,341 ....336/D7
Bridgewater, N.S., Can., 7,621 ....221/C3
Bridgewater, Conn., U.S., 1,824 ....253/B3
Bridgewater, Iowa, U.S., 178 ....274/E5
Bridgewater, Maine, U.S., 612 ....286/E2
Bridgewater, Mass., U.S., 25,185 ....292/L5
Bridgewater, Mich., U.S., 175 ....294/F7
Bridgewater, N.H., U.S., 974 ....312/C4
Bridgewater, N.J., U.S., 42,940 ....314/D2
Bridgewater, N.Y., U.S., 579 ....320/L5
Bridgewater, S. Dak., U.S., 607 ....342/H4
Bridgewater, Vt., U.S., 980 ....352/B3
Bridgewater, Va., U.S., 5,203 ....354/F4
Bridgman, Mich., U.S., 2,428 ....294/C8
Bridgnorth, Eng., U.K., 11,229 ....68/C4
Bridgton, Maine, U.S., 4,883 ....286/B4
Bridgwater, Eng., U.K., 34,610 ....73/F2
Bridlington, Eng., U.K., 31,334 ....66/H4
Bridlington, Eng., U.K., 31,334 ....68/G1
Bridport, Eng., U.K., 11,667 ....73/G3
Brielle, N.J., U.S., 4,893 ....314/E3
Briensburg, Ky., U.S., 400 ....280/B4
Brienzersee, Switz., lake 90/B2
Brier, Wash., U.S., 6,383 ....358/A4
Brierfield, Eng., U.K., 9,567 ....66/D5
Brierfield, Eng., U.K., 9,567 ....68/C2
Brier Hill, N.Y., U.S., 212/ 320/K1
Brierley Hill, Eng., U.K. 68/D4
Brigantine, N.J., U.S., 12,594 ....314/E5
Brigg, Eng., U.K., 5,768 ....66/H5
Brigg, Eng., U.K., 5,768 ....68/F2
Briggs, Tex., U.S., 50 ....346/L5
Briggsdale, Colo., U.S., 80 ....250/F1
Briggsville, Ark., U.S., 50 ....244/B3
Briggsville, Wisc., U.S., 250 ....364/D5
Brigham City, Utah, U.S., 17,411 ....350/B2
Brighouse, Eng., U.K., 32,198 ....66/E5
Brighouse, Eng., U.K., 32,198 ....68/D2
Bright, Ind., U.S., 5,405 ....270/G6
Brightlingsea, Eng., U.K., 7,441 ....70/G3
Brighton, Ind. Res., Fla., U.S. 256/G4
Brightwood, Oreg., U.S., 80 ....334/D2
Brightwood, Va., U.S., 500 ....354/G4
Brig O'Turk, Scot., U.K. 62/H6
Brikama, Gam. 148/B3
Brill, Eng., U.K. 70/D2
Brill, Wisc., U.S., 150 ....364/B3
Brilliant, Ala., U.S., 762 ....238/B1
Brilliant, Ohio, U.S., 1,600 ....328/J5
Brillion, Wisc., U.S., 2,937 ....364/E4
Brimfield, Ill., U.S., 933 ....266/D3
Brimfield, Mass., U.S., 3,339 ....292/F4
Brimfield St. For., Conn., U.S. 253/G1
Brimley, Mich., U.S., 450 ....294/E3
Brimson, Minn., U.S. 298/F3
Brimson, Mo., U.S., 63 ....302/C1
Brinckerhoff, N.Y., U.S., 2,734 ....320/P7
Brindisi, It. 95/D2
Brinkhaven, Ohio, U.S., 143 ....328/F5
Brinkley, Ark., U.S., 3,940 ....244/D3
Brinkman, Okla., U.S. 330/C2
Brinnon, Wash., U.S., 803 ....358/C2
Brinsmade, N. Dak., U.S. 326/F1
Brinson, Ga., U.S., 225 ....260/D6
Brinton, Mich., U.S., 100 ....294/D6
Brinyan, Scot., U.K. 62/M1
Briny Breezes, Fla., U.S., 411 ....256/B5
Brisbane, Austl., river ....170/Inset III
Brisbane, Qnsld., Austl., state capital,
  (1,608,820 metro.) ....170/E2, Inset III
Brisbane, Calif., U.S., 3,597 ....246/J2
Brisbin, Penn., U.S., 413 ....336/E4
Briscoe, Tex., U.S. 346/G9
Briscoe, Tex., U.S., county, 1,790 ....346/G1
Bristol, N.B., Can., 719 ....217/B2
Bristol, Eng., U.K. 60/C3
Bristol, Eng., U.K., 407,992, (522,784 metro.) 73/G2
Bristol, Eng., U.K., channel 60/B3
Bristol, Eng., U.K., channel 73/E2
Bristol, Eng., U.K., channel 73/E2
Bristol, City of, Eng., U.K., unitary authority,
  380,615 ....73/G2
Bristol, Wales, U.K., channel 64/C3
Bristol, Alaska, U.S., bay 240/C3
Bristol, Colo., U.S., 70 ....250/H3
Bristol, Conn., U.S., 60,062 ....253/C3
Bristol, Fla., U.S., 845 ....256/D1
Bristol, Ind., U.S., 1,382 ....270/E1
Bristol, Mass., U.S., county, 534,678 ....292/K5
Bristol, Mich., U.S. 294/D5
Bristol, N.H., U.S., 3,033 ....312/C4
Bristol, Penn., U.S., 9,923 ....336/M5
Bristol, R.I., U.S., 22,469 ....339/E3
Bristol, R.I., U.S., county, 50,648 ....339/E3
Bristol, S. Dak., U.S., 377 ....342/H2
Bristol, Tenn., U.S., 24,821 ....344/S1
Bristol, Vt., U.S., 3,788 ....352/A2
Bristol, Va., U.S., 17,367 ....355/D3
Briston, Eng., U.K., 2,184 ....70/G1
Bristow, Iowa, U.S., 202 ....274/J2
Bristow, Nebr., U.S., 88 ....308/E1
Bristow, Okla., U.S., 4,325 ....330/F2
Britannia, Nfld., Can. 206/E5
Brithdir, Wales, U.K. 64/D2
British Columbia, Can., province 202
British Virgin Islands, U.K., dependency 204/F3
Britt, Ont., Can., 367 ....223/E2
Britt, Iowa, U.S., 2,052 ....274/G1
Britt, Minn., U.S., 125 ....298/E3
Brittany Farms, (Brittany Farms-Highlands),
  Penn., U.S., 3,268 ....336/M5
Britton, Mich., U.S., 699 ....294/F8
Britton, S. Dak., U.S., 1,328 ....342/H2
Brive-la-Gaillarde, Fr. 88/C3
Brixey, Mo., U.S. 302/D5
Brixham, Eng., U.K., 15,865 ....73/E4
Brize Norton, Eng., U.K. 68/D6
Brko, Bos.-Her. 98/B1
Brno, Czh. Rep., 379,185 ....92/C3
Broad, Scot., U.K., bay 62/D2
Broad, Del., U.S., creek 255/B6
Broad, Mass., U.S., sound 292/D7
Broadalbin, N.Y., U.S., 1,411 ....320/N4
Broadbent, Oreg., U.S., 100 ....334/B4
Broad Brook, Conn., U.S., 3,469 ....253/E2
Broadclyst, Eng., U.K. 73/F3
Broaddus, Tex., U.S., 189 ....346/P4
Broad Fields, Ky., U.S., 250 ....280/D2
Broadford, Scot., U.K. 62/E4
Broad Haven, Wales, U.K. 64/A4
Broadhurst, Ga., U.S. 260/H9
Broadkill, Del., U.S., river 255/C5
Broadkill Beach, Del., U.S., 70 ....255/D5
Broadland, Ill., U.S., 312 ....342/G3
Broadlands, Ill., U.S., 312 ....266/E4
Broadmayne, Eng., U.K. 73/H3
Broadmeadows, Vic., Austl. ....170/Inset V
Broadmoor, Calif., U.S., 4,026 ....246/H2
Broad Oak, Eng., U.K., 1,764 ....68/B6
Broad Oak, Eng., U.K., 1,764 ....70/F5
Broadstairs, Eng., U.K., 22,116 ....70/G4
Broadstone, Eng., U.K. 73/H3
Broad Top City, Penn., U.S., 384 ....336/E5
Broadus, Mont., U.S., 451 ....306/L4
Broadview, Sask., Can., 669 ....227/H10
Broadview, Ill., U.S., 8,264 ....266/B6
Broadview, Mont., U.S., 150 ....306/H3
Broadview, N. Mex., U.S., 40 ....317/G3
Broadview Hts., Ohio, U.S., 15,967 ....328/G9
Broadwater, Mont., U.S., county, 4,385 ....306/E3
Broadwater, Nebr., U.S., 140 ....308/B2
Broadway, Eng., U.K., 2,328 ....68/D5
Broadway, Eng., U.K., 2,328 ....73/G3
Broadway, N.J., U.S., 700 ....314/C2
Broadway, N.C., U.S., 1,015 ....322/G4
Broadway, Ohio, U.S., 225 ....328/D5
Broadway, Va., U.S., 2,192 ....354/F3
Broadwell, Ill., U.S., 169 ....266/D3
Broadwey, Eng., U.K. 73/H3
Broadwindsor, Eng., U.K. 73/G3
Brochet, Man., Can., 226 ....215/C1
Brock, N.W. Terr., Can., island 208/F1
Brock, Nebr., U.S., 162 ....308/J3
Brockenhurst, Eng., U.K., 3,048 ....70/A5
Brocket, Alta., Can. 212//D6
Brocket, N. Dak., U.S., 65 ....326/G1
Brockford Street, Eng., U.K. 70/G2
Brock Hall, (Greater Upper Marlboro),
  Md., U.S. 288/D7, G4
Brockley Green, Eng., U.K. 70/F2
Brockport, N.Y., U.S., 8,103 ....320/F4
Brockport, Penn., U.S., 550 ....336/D3
Brockton, Mass., U.S., 94,304 ....292/K4
Brockton, Mont., U.S., 245 ....306/M1
Brockville, Ont., Can., 21,375 ....223/K3
Brockway, N.B., Can. 217/B3
Brockway, Mont., U.S. 306/L2
Brockway, Penn., U.S., 2,182 ....336/D3
Brockwell, Ark., U.S., 60 ....244/D1
Brockworth, Eng., U.K. 68/C6
Brocton, Ill., U.S., 322 ....266/F4
Brocton, N.Y., U.S., 1,547 ....320/C6
Brodhead, Ky., U.S., 1,193 ....280/F3
Brodhead, Wisc., U.S., 3,180 ....364/D6
Brodnax, Va., U.S., 317 ....354/G7
Brogan, Oreg., U.S. 334/J3
Brogden, N.C., U.S., 2,907 ....322/J4
Brohard, W. Va., U.S. 360/D2
Brohman, Mich., U.S., 175 ....294/D6
Brokaw, Wisc., U.S., 107 ....364/D3
Broken Arrow, Okla., U.S., 74,859 ....330/G1
Broken Bow, Nebr., U.S., 3,491 ....308/E2
Broken Bow, Okla., U.S., 4,230 ....330/H3
Broken Bow, Okla., U.S., lake 330/H3
Brokenburg, Va., U.S. 354/H4
Broken Cross, Eng., U.K. 68/C3
Broken Hill, N.S.W., Austl. 170/G3
Brokopondo, Sur. 183/B2
Brome, Eng., U.K. 70/G2
Bromham, Eng., U.K., 3,909 ....70/C2
Bromide, Okla., U.S., 163 ....330/F3
Bromley, Eng., U.K., 275,841 ....70/E4
Bromley, Eng., U.K., unitary authority, 295,530 ....70/E4
Bromley, Ky., U.S., 838 ....280/G1
Bromley, Vt., U.S., mountain 352/B4
Bromptonville, Que., Can., 5,571 ....226/E6
Bromsgrove, Eng., U.K., 26,366 ....68/C5
Bromyard, Eng., U.K., 3,117 ....68/B5
Bronaugh, Mo., U.S., 245 ....302/B4
Bronco, Tex., U.S. 346/E2
Bronson, Fla., U.S., 964 ....256/F2
Bronson, Iowa, U.S., 269 ....274/B3
Bronson, Kans., U.S., 346 ....276/G4
Bronson, Mich., U.S., 2,421 ....294/D8
Bronte, Tex., U.S., 1,076 ....346/H4
Bronwood, Ga., U.S., 513 ....260/C8
Bronx, (see New York), N.Y., U.S. 320/B2
Bronx, N.Y., U.S., county, 1,332,650 ....320/B2
Bronx, Wyo., U.S. 366/A2
Bronxville, N.Y., U.S., 6,543 ....320/B2
Brook, (Hampshire), Eng., U.K. 70/A4
Brook, (Isle of Wight), Eng., U.K. 70/B5
Brook, (Surrey), Eng., U.K. 70/D4
Brook, Ind., U.S., 1,062 ....270/B3
Brookdale, Man., Can. 215/B4
Brookdale, S.C., U.S., 4,724 ....340/D3
Brooke, (Leicestershire), Eng., U.K. 70/C1
Brooke, (Norfolk), Eng., U.K. 70/G1
Brooke, Va., U.S., 650 ....354/J4
Brooke, W. Va., U.S., county, 25,447 ....360/K5
Brookeborough, N. Ire., U.K., 541 ....65/C3
Brooker, Fla., U.S., 352 ....256/F2
Brookeville, Md., U.S., 120 ....288/F3
Brookfield, Conn., U.S., 15,664 ....253/B4
Brookfield, Ga., U.S., 375 ....260/E9
Brookfield, Ill., U.S., 19,085 ....266/B6
Brookfield, Mass., U.S., 3,051 ....292/F4
Brookfield, Mo., U.S., 4,769 ....302/C2
Brookfield, Vt., U.S., 1,322 ....352/B2
Brookfield, Wisc., U.S., 38,649 ....364/E5, F2
Brookfield Ctr., Conn., U.S., 1,800 ....253/B4
Brookford, N.C., U.S., 434 ....322/C3
Brookhaven, Miss., U.S., 9,861 ....300/B4
Brookhaven, Penn., U.S., 7,985 ....336/L7
Brookhaven, W. Va., U.S., 4,734 ....360/F2
Brookings, Oreg., U.S., 5,447 ....334/B5
Brookings, S. Dak., U.S., 18,504 ....342/J3
Brookings, S. Dak., U.S., county, 28,220 ....342/J3
Brookland, Eng., U.K. 70/F5
Brookland, Ark., U.S., 1,332 ....244/F2
Brooklandville, (Mays Chapel), Md., U.S., 2,212/ 288/H2
Brooklawn, N.J., U.S., 2,354 ....314/D3
Brooklet, Ga., U.S., 1,113 ....260/H7
Brooklin, Maine, U.S., 841 ....286/D4
Brookline, Mass., U.S., 57,107 ....292/C8, K3
Brookline, Mo., U.S. 302/C4
Brookline, N.H., U.S., 4,181 ....312/C6
Brooklyn, Ala., U.S. 238/C4
Brooklyn, Conn., U.S., 7,173 ....253/H2
Brooklyn, Ga., U.S. 260/B7
Brooklyn, Ill., U.S., 676 ....266/A3
Brooklyn, Ind., U.S., 1,545 ....270/D5

Brooklyn, Iowa, U.S., 1,367 . . . . .274/K4
Brooklyn, Ky., U.S., 70 . . . . .280/D3
Brooklyn, Mich., U.S., 1,176 . . . . .294/E7
Brooklyn, Miss., U.S., 350 . . . . .300/C4
Brooklyn, (see New York), N.Y., U.S. 320/B2
Brooklyn, Ohio, U.S., 11,586 . . . . .328/G9
Brooklyn, Penn., U.S., 325 . . . . .336/K2
Brooklyn, Wash., U.S., 50 . . . . .358/B3
Brooklyn, Wisc., U.S., 916 . . . . .364/D6
Brooklyn Ctr., Minn., U.S., 29,172 . . . . .298/E5
Brooklyn Hts., Ohio, U.S., 1,558 . . . . . . .328/G9
Brooklyn Park, Minn., U.S., 67,388 . . . .298/D5, E5
Brookmont, Md., U.S., 3,202 . . . . . .288/A7, F4
Brookneal, Va., U.S., 1,259 . . . . .354/F6
Brook Park, Minn., U.S., 156 . . . . .298/D5
Brook Park, Ohio, U.S., 21,218 . . . . .328/G9
Brookport, Ill., U.S., 1,054 . . . . .266/E6
Brooks, Alta., Can., 11,604 . . . . .212/E66
Brooks, U.S., range 193/C11
Brooks, Alaska, U.S., range 240/D1
Brooks, Ga., U.S., 553 . . . . .260/C5
Brooks, Ga., U.S., county, 16,450 . . . . . .260/D1
Brooks, Iowa, U.S., 100 . . . . .274/E6
Brooks, Ky., U.S., 2,678 . . . . .280/E2
Brooks, Maine, U.S., 1,022 . . . . .286/C4
Brooks, Minn., U.S., 141 . . . . .298/A3
Brooks, Tex., U.S., county, 7,976 . . . . . .346/K8
Brooks, W. Va., U.S., 225 . . . . .360/E5
Brooks, Wisc., U.S., 125 . . . . .364/D5
Brooksburg, Ind., U.S., 74 . . . . .270/F7
Brookshire, Tex., U.S., 3,450 . . . . .346/N6
Brookside, Ala., U.S., 1,393 . . . . .238/D1
Brookside, Colo., U.S., 219 . . . . .250/E3
Brookside, Del., U.S., 14,806 . . . . .255/B2
Brookside, Ohio, U.S., 100 . . . . .328/J5
Brookside, (part of Northwest Harborcreek),
Penn., U.S. 336/B1
Brookside Vil., Tex., U.S., 1,960 . . . . . . .346/B7
Brookston, Ind., U.S., 1,717 . . . . .270/C3
Brookston, Minn., U.S., 98 . . . . .298/E4
Brooksville, Ala., U.S., 100 . . . . .238/C1
Brooksville, Fla., U.S., 7,264 . . . . .256/F3
Brooksville, Ky., U.S., 589 . . . . .280/F2
Brooksville, Maine, U.S., 911 . . . . .286/D4
Brooksville, Miss., U.S., 1,182 . . . . .300/D2
Brooksville, Okla., U.S., 90 . . . . .330/F2
Brookthorpe, Eng., U.K. 68/C6
Brookton, Maine, U.S., 50 . . . . .286/E3
Brookvale, Colo., U.S. 250/A3
Brookview, Md., U.S., 65 . . . . .288/L5
Brookville, Ind., U.S., 2,652 . . . . .270/F6
Brookville, Ind., U.S., lake 270/G6
Brookville, Kans., U.S., 259 . . . . .276/E3
Brookville, N.J., U.S., 90 . . . . .314/E4
Brookville, N.Y., U.S., 2,126 . . . . .320/C2
Brookville, Ohio, U.S., 5,289 . . . . .328/B6
Brookville, Penn., U.S., 4,230 . . . . .336/C3
Brookwood, Ala., U.S., 1,483 . . . . .238/B2
Broom, Scot., U.K., lake 62/G3
Broomall, Penn., U.S., 11,046 . . . . .336/L7
Broome, W.A., Austl. 170/A1
Broome, Eng., U.K. 70/G2
Broome, N.Y., U.S., county, 212/,536 . . .320/K6
Broomes Island, Md., U.S., 425 . . . . . . .288/H6
Broomfield, Ind., U.S. 70/E3
Broomfield, Colo., U.S., 38,272 . . . . .250/A3, E2
Broomfield, Colo., U.S., county, 38,272 238
Broomhill, Man., Can. 215/A4
Broomhill, Eng., U.K. 66/E2
Brooten, Minn., U.S., 649 . . . . .298/B6
Brora, Scot., U.K., 1,140 . . . . .62/J2
Broseley, Eng., U.K., 5,089 . . . . .68/C4
Broseley, Mo., U.S., 250 . . . . .302/F5
Brossard, Que., Can., 65,026 . . . . .226/J6
Brosville, Va., U.S., 150 . . . . .354/D7
Brothers, Oreg., U.S. 334/F4
Brothers, Yemen, islands 137/C2
Brothertoft, Eng., U.K. 68/G4
Brotmanville, N.J., U.S., 500 . . . . .314/C4
Brotton, Eng., U.K., 4,735 . . . . .66/G3
Broughshane, N. Ire., U.K., 1,873 . . . . . .65/E2
Broughton, (Hampshire), Eng., U.K. 70/A4
Broughton, (Humberside), Eng., U.K., 4,448 . . .68/F5
Broughton, (Northamptonshire), Eng., U.K., 2,005 . .68/F5
Broughton, (Northamptonshire), Eng., U.K., 2,005 . .68/F5
Broughton, Eng., U.K., 4,448 . . . . .66/G5
Broughton, Ill., U.S., 193 . . . . .266/E6
Broughton, Kans., U.S. 276/E2
Broughton, Ohio, U.S., 166 . . . . .328/A3
Broughton in Furness, Eng., U.K. 66/B4
Broughton Poggs, Eng., U.K. 68/D6
Broughtown, Scot., U.K. 62/N1
Broussard, La., U.S., 5,874 . . . . .282/F6
Brove, Scot., U.K. 62/B3
Broward, Fla., U.S., county, 1,623,018 . .256/A6, H5
Browerville, Minn., U.S., 735 . . . . .298/C4
Brown, Ill., U.S., county, 6,950 . . . . .266/C4
Brown, Ind., U.S., county, 14,957 . . . . . .270/D6
Brown, Kans., U.S., county, 10,724 . . . . .276/G2
Brown, Minn., U.S., county, 26,911 . . . . .298/C6
Brown, Nebr., U.S., county, 3,525 . . . . . .308/E1
Brown, Ohio, U.S., county, 42,285 . . . . . .328/C8
Brown, S. Dak., U.S., county, 35,460 . . . .342/G2
Brown, Tex., U.S., county, 37,674 . . . . . .346/J4
Brown, Wash., U.S., point 358/A3
Brown, Wisc., U.S., county, 226,778 . . . .364/E4
Brownbranch, Mo., U.S. 302/D5
Brown City, Mich., U.S., 1,334 . . . . .294/G6
Brown Deer, Wisc., U.S., 12,170 . . . . . .364/F1, F5
Browndell, Tex., U.S., 219 . . . . .346/R4
Brownell, Kans., U.S., 48 . . . . .276/C3
Brownfield, Maine, U.S., 1,251 . . . . .286/B5
Brownfield, Tex., U.S., 9,488 . . . . .346/F2
Brownfields, La., U.S., 5,222 . . . . .282/G5
Brownhills, Eng., U.K., 18,159 . . . . .68/D4
Browning, Ill., U.S., 130 . . . . .266/C3
Browning, Mo., U.S., 317 . . . . .302/C1
Browning, Mont., U.S., 1,065 . . . . .306/C1
Browningston, Mo., U.S., 119 . . . . .302/C3
Brownington, Vt., U.S., 885 . . . . .352/C1
Brownington Ctr., Vt., U.S., 125 . . . . . . .352/C1
Brownlee, La., U.S. 282/C1
Brownlee, Nebr., U.S. 308/D1
Brownlee Park, Mich., U.S., 2,588 . . . . . .294/D7
Brown Plains, Qnsld., Austl. . . . . . . .170/inset III
Browns, Ala., U.S. 238/B3
Browns, Ill., U.S., 175 . . . . .266/F5
Brownsboro Farm, Ky., U.S., 676 . . . . . .280/B1
Brownsburg, Ind., U.S., 14,520 . . . . .270/D5
Brownsburg, Va., U.S., 50 . . . . .354/E5
Brownsdale, Minn., U.S., 718 . . . . .298/E7
Browns Mills, N.J., U.S., 11,257 . . . . . . .314/D4
Brownson, Nebr., U.S. 308/A2
Browns Park N.W.R., Colo., U.S. 250/B1
Brownstown, Ill., U.S., 705 . . . . .266/E4
Brownstown, Ind., U.S., 2,978 . . . . .270/D7
Brownstown, Penn., U.S., 883 . . . . .336/C5
Browns Valley, Ky., U.S., 100 . . . . .280/C3
Browns Valley, Minn., U.S., 690 . . . . . . .298/A5
Brownsville, Ky., U.S., 921 . . . . .280/D3
Brownsville, Md., U.S., 325 . . . . .288/K3
Brownsville, Minn., U.S., 517 . . . . .298/F7

Brownsville, Miss., U.S., 70 . . . . .300/B3
Brownsville, Oreg., U.S., 1,449 . . . . .334/D3
Brownsville, Penn., U.S., 2,804 . . . . .336/B5
Brownsville, S.C., U.S., 90 . . . . .340/E2
Brownsville, Tenn., U.S., 10,748 . . . . . . .344/C3
Brownsville, Tex., U.S., 139,722,
(335,227 metro.) 346/L10
Brownsville, Wash., U.S., 600 . . . . .358/A4
Brownsville, Wisc., U.S., 570 . . . . .364/E5
Brownton, Minn., U.S., 807 . . . . .298/C6
Browntown, Wisc., U.S., 252 . . . . .364/D6
Brownville, Ala., U.S. 238/B2
Brownville, (see Bawcomville), La., U.S., 7,616 . .282/E2
Brownville, Maine, U.S., 1,259 . . . . .286/C3
Brownville, Nebr., U.S. 308/J3
Brownville, N.Y., U.S., 1,022 . . . . .320/K2
Brownville Jct., Maine, U.S., 750 . . . . . . .286/C3
Brown vs. Board of Education N.H.S., Kans., U.S. .276/C22
Brown Willy, Eng., U.K., hill 73/C3
Brownwood, Mo., U.S., 150 . . . . .302/G4
Brownwood, Tex., U.S., 18,813 . . . . .346/K4
Broxbourne, Eng., U.K. 70/D3
Broxton, Eng., U.K. 68/B3
Broxton, Ga., U.S., 1,428 . . . . .260/F8
Broxton, Okla., U.S. 330/D3
Broyhill Park, Va., U.S., 17,000 . . . . .354/M2
Bruce, Alta., Can. 212/D4
Bruce, Ont., Can. 223/D3
Bruce, Ont., Can., county 223/D3
Bruce, Miss., U.S., 2,097 . . . . .300/C2
Bruce, N.C., U.S., 80 . . . . .322/D3
Bruce, S. Dak., U.S., 787 . . . . .342/J3
Bruce, Wisc., U.S., 787 . . . . .364/B3
Bruce Crossing, Mich., U.S., 225 . . . . . . .294/A3
Bruce Mines, Ont., Can., 627 . . . . .223/B1
Bruce Peninsula N.P., Ont., Can. 223/D2
Bruceton, Tenn., U.S., 1,554 . . . . .344/E2
Bruceton Mills, W. Va., U.S., 74 . . . . .360/G1
Brucetown, Va., U.S. 354/G2
Bruce Vale, Barb., river 209/B3
Bruceville, Ind., U.S., 469 . . . . .270/B7
Bruceville-Eddy, Tex., U.S., 1,490 . . . . . .346/L4
Bruchsal, Scot., U.K., lake 62/G4
Bruin, Ky., U.S., 175 . . . . .280/G2
Bruin, Penn., U.S., 534 . . . . .336/B3
Bruin, Utah, U.S., point 350/D4
Bruie, Minn., U.S., lake 298/E2
Brule, Nebr., U.S., 372 . . . . .308/C2
Brule, S. Dak., U.S., county, 5,364 . . . . . .342/F4
Brule, Wisc., U.S., 212/ 364/B2
Brûlé, Alta., Can., 162 . . . . .212/B4
Brule River St. For., Wisc., U.S. 364/B2
Brumley, Mo., U.S., 102 . . . . .302/D3
Brumley Gap, Va., U.S. 354/B2
Brundage, Tex., U.S. 346/J7
Brundall, Eng., U.K., 6,076 . . . . .70/G1
Brundidge, Ala., U.S., 2,341 . . . . .238/D4
Brundish, Eng., U.K. 70/G2
Bruneau, Ida., U.S. 264/B7
Bruneau, Ida., U.S., river 264/B7
Brunei, nation 117
Brunei, Bru., bay 121/C1
Brunei, Bru., river 121/B2
Bruner, Mo., U.S., 175 . . . . .302/D4
Brunersburg, Ohio, U.S., 325 . . . . .328/B3
Bruni, Tex., U.S., 412 . . . . .346/K8
Bruning, Nebr., U.S., 300 . . . . .308/G3
Bruno, Minn., U.S., 102 . . . . .298/E4
Bruno, Nebr., U.S., 112 . . . . .308/H2
Bruno, Okla., U.S., 80 . . . . .330/F3
Brunson, S.C., U.S., 589 . . . . .340/C4
Brunswick, Iowa, U.S., 146 . . . . .274/B2
Brunswick, Chile, peninsula 190/B8
Brunswick, Ga., U.S., 15,600 . . . . .260/J9
Brunswick, Maine, U.S., 21,172 . . . . .286/C5
Brunswick, Md., U.S., 4,894 . . . . .288/D2
Brunswick, Minn., U.S., 225 . . . . .298/D5
Brunswick, Mo., U.S., 925 . . . . .302/C2
Brunswick, Nebr., U.S., 179 . . . . .308/G1
Brunswick, N.C., U.S., 360 . . . . .322/H6
Brunswick, N.C., U.S., county, 73,143 . . .322/H6
Brunswick, Ohio, U.S., 33,388 . . . . . .328/G3, G10
Brunswick, Va., U.S., 70 . . . . .354/H7
Brunswick, Va., U.S., county, 18,419 . . . .354/H7
Brusett, Mont., U.S. 306/J2
Brush, Colo., U.S., 5,117 . . . . .250/G1
Brush Creek, Tenn., U.S., 250 . . . . .344/F2
Brush Prairie, Wash., U.S., 2,384 . . . . . . .358/C4
Brushton, N.Y., U.S., 479 . . . . .320/M1
Brushvale, Minn., U.S. 298/A4
Brushy, Okla., U.S., 787 . . . . .330/H2
Brusly, La., U.S., 2,020 . . . . .282/G6
Brussels, Belg., capital, 136,730,
(978,384 metro.) 85/C2
Brussels, Ont., Can., 1,143 . . . . .223/D4
Brussels, Ill., U.S., 141 . . . . .266/C5
Brussels, Wisc., U.S., 275 . . . . .364/F4
Brussels Capital Region, Belg., region 85/C2
Bruton, Eng., U.K., 2,111 . . . . .73/H2
Brutus, Mich., U.S., 175 . . . . .294/E4
Bryan, Ga., U.S., county, 23,417 . . . . . . .260/H7
Bryan, Ohio, U.S., 8,333 . . . . .328/A3
Bryan, Okla., U.S., county, 36,534 . . . . . .330/F3
Bryan, Tex., U.S., 65,660, (152,415 metro.) .346/M5
Bryan, Wyo., U.S. 366/D3
Bryansk, Russ., 455,158, (477,450 metro.) . . .104/C4
Bryans Road, Md., U.S., 4,912 . . . . .288/F5
Bryant, Ark., U.S., 9,764 . . . . .244/C3
Bryant, Ill., U.S., 255 . . . . .266/C3
Bryant, Ind., U.S., 272 . . . . .270/G3
Bryant, S. Dak., U.S., 396 . . . . .342/H3
Bryant, Wash., U.S., 550 . . . . .358/C1
Bryant, Wisc., U.S., 90 . . . . .364/D3
Bryantown, (Charles County), Md., U.S. . .288/G5
Bryantown, (Queen Annes County), Md., U.S. .288/K4
Bryant Pond, Maine, U.S., 250 . . . . .286/B4
Bryants Store, Ky., U.S. 280/G4
Bryantsville, Ky., U.S., 300 . . . . .280/F3
Bryantville, Mass., U.S., 2,600 . . . . .292/L4
Bryce Canyon, Utah, U.S. 350/B6
Bryce Canyon Natl. Park, Utah, U.S. 350/B6
Bryceland, La., U.S., 114 . . . . .282/D2
Bryher, Eng., U.K., island 73/A1
Brynamman, (Brynmawr/Gwaun cae Gurwen),
Wales, U.K., 5,911 . . . . .64/D4
Bryn Athyn, Penn., U.S., 1,351 . . . . .336/M6
Bryncir Garn Dolbenmaen, Wales, U.K. . . .64/C2
Bryngwyn, Wales, U.K. 64/E4
Brynmawr, Wales, U.K., 14,581 . . . . .64/E4
Bryn Mawr, Penn., U.S., 4,382 . . . . .336/L7
Brynwood, (part of W. Augusta), Ga., U.S. .260/G5
Bryson, Tex., U.S., 528 . . . . .346/K2
Bryson City, N.C., U.S., 1,411 . . . . .322/C8
Bsharri, Leb. 134/B1
Bua, Mal., river 159/B2
Buada, Nauru .174/B2
Buada, Nauru, lagoon 174/B2
Buala, Sol. Is. .173/A1
Bualintur, Scot., U.K. 62/D4
Buba, Gui.-B. 149/C2

Bubanza, Bur. .158/B2
Bubaque, Gui.-B. 149/B2
Bubbenhall, Eng., U.K. 70/B2
Bubiyan, Kuw., island 66/G5
Bubwith, Eng., U.K. 66/G5
Bucaramanga, Col., 521,000 . . . . .184/B3
Buchanan, Sask., Can., 233 . . . . .227/H9
Buchanan, Liber. 149/C3
Buchanan, Ga., U.S., 941 . . . . .260/A4
Buchanan, Iowa, U.S., county, 21,093 . . .274/L2
Buchanan, Mich., U.S., 4,681 . . . . .294/C8
Buchanan, Mo., U.S., county, 85,998 . . . .302/B2
Buchanan, N.Y., U.S., 2,189 . . . . .320/B1
Buchanan, N. Dak., U.S., 77 . . . . .326/H2
Buchanan, Oreg., U.S. 334/H4
Buchanan, Tenn., U.S., 125 . . . . .344/E2
Buchanan, Va., U.S., county, 26,978 . . . . .354/D5
Buchanan, Va., U.S., 1,234 . . . . .354/E5
Buchanan Dam, Tex., U.S., 1,688 . . . . . .346/C1
Buchanan St. For., Penn., U.S. 336/D6, E5
Buchans, Nfld., Can., 877 . . . . .206/C5
Buchanty, Scot., U.K. 62/J6
Bucharest, Rom., capital, 2,009,212/ 101/D3
Bucharest Municipality, Rom., county 101/D3
Buchtel, Ohio, U.S., 574 . . . . .328/F7
Buckatunna, Miss., U.S., 300 . . . . .300/D4
Buck Creek, Alta., Can. 212//C4
Buckden, Eng., U.K., 2,534 . . . . .66/C4
Buckeye, Ariz., U.S., 6,537 . . . . .242/C4
Buckeye, Iowa, U.S., 110 . . . . .274/H3
Buckeye, N. Mex., U.S. 317/G5
Buckeye, Tex., U.S. 346/M7
Buckeye Lake, Ohio, U.S., 3,049 . . . . . . .328/E6
Buckeystown, Md., U.S., 425 . . . . .288/E2
Buckfastleigh, Eng., U.K., 2,786 . . . . .73/E4
Buckfield, Maine, U.S., 1,723 . . . . .286/B4
Buck Grove, Iowa, U.S., 49 . . . . .274/D4
Buckhannon, W. Va., U.S., 5,725 . . . . . . .360/F3
Buckhaven, Scot., U.K., 16,391 . . . . .62/L6
Buckhead, Ga., U.S., 205 . . . . .260/E4
Buckhead Ridge, Fla., U.S., 1,390 . . . . . .256/H4
Buckhorn, Ky., U.S., 144 . . . . .280/G3
Buckhorn, Ky., U.S., lake 280/G3
Buckhorn, N. Mex., U.S. 317/B4
Buckie, Scot., U.K., 8,059 . . . . .62/L5
Buckingham, Que., Can., 11,668 . . . . . . .226/A6
Buckingham, Eng., U.K., 10,168 . . . . .68/F6
Buckingham, Eng., U.K., 10,168 . . . . .70/C3
Buckingham, Colo., U.S. 250/G1
Buckingham, Ill., U.S., 237 . . . . .266/E2
Buckingham, Iowa, U.S., 70 . . . . .274/K3
Buckingham, Tex., U.S. 346/C9
Buckingham, Va., U.S., 175 . . . . .354/F5
Buckingham, Va., U.S., county, 15,623 . . .354/F5
Buckinghamshire, Eng., U.K.,
unitary authority, 479,028 . . . . .68/E6
Buckinghamshire, Eng., U.K.,
unitary authority, 479,028 . . . . .70/C3
Buck Lake, Alta., Can., 79 . . . . .212//C5
Buckland, Eng., U.K. 68/D6
Buckland, Eng., U.K. 70/D3
Buckland, Alaska, U.S., 406 . . . . .240/C1
Buckland, Mass., U.S., 1,991 . . . . .292/C2
Buckland, Ohio, U.S., 255 . . . . .328/B5
Bucklers Hard, Eng., U.K. 70/B5
Buckley, Wales, U.K., 17,753 . . . . .64/E1
Buckley, Ill., U.S., 593 . . . . .266/E3
Buckley, Mich., U.S., 550 . . . . .294/D5
Buckley, Wash., U.S., 4,145 . . . . .358/C2
Bucklin, Kans., U.S., 725 . . . . .276/C4
Bucklin, Mo., U.S., 524 . . . . .302/D2
Buckman, Minn., U.S., 208 . . . . .298/C5
Bucknall, Eng., U.K. 68/C3
Bucknell, Eng., U.K. 68/B5
Buckner, Ark., U.S., 396 . . . . .244/B4
Buckner, Ill., U.S., 479 . . . . .266/D6
Buckner, Ky., U.S., 4,000 . . . . .280/B1
Buckner, Mo., U.S., 2,725 . . . . .302/J5
Buckner, Va., U.S. 354/H5
Bucks, Ala., U.S., 40 . . . . .238/A4
Bucks, Penn., U.S., county, 597,635 . . . .336/L5, M6
Bucks Cross, Eng., U.K. 73/D3
Bucks Green, Eng., U.K. 70/D4
Bucks Harbor, Maine, U.S., 212/ 286/E4
Bucks Hill, Eng., U.K. 70/E3
Bucksport, Maine, U.S., 4,908 . . . . .286/D4
Bucksport, S.C., U.S., 1,117 . . . . .340/E5
Bucksport Ctr., Maine, U.S., 650 . . . . . . .286/D4
Bucktail, Nebr., U.S. 308/C2
Bucktown, Ind., U.S., 80 . . . . .270/C7
Bucktown, Md., U.S. 288/K6
Buckworth, Eng., U.K. 70/D2
Bucoda, Wash., U.S., 628 . . . . .358/C3
Bucyrus, Kans., U.S., 250 . . . . .276/H3
Bucyrus, Mo., U.S. 302/D4
Bucyrus, N. Dak., U.S. 326/C3
Bucyrus, Ohio, U.S., 13,224 . . . . .328/E4
Buda, Ill., U.S., 592 . . . . .266/D2
Buda, Tex., U.S., 2,404 . . . . .346/D3
Budapest, Hun. 91/B2
Budapest, Hun., capital, 1,825,153 . . . . . .91/B2
Budd Lake, N.J., U.S., 8,100 . . . . .314/D2
Buddtown, N.J., U.S., 150 . . . . .314/D4
Bude, Eng., U.K., 3,681 . . . . .73/C3
Bude, Miss., U.S., 1,037 . . . . .300/B4
Budeleigh Salterton, Eng., U.K., 3,759 . . . .73/F3
Buea, Came., 29,953 . . . . .153/A3
Bueche, La., U.S., 125 . . . . .282/G5
Buechel, Ky., U.S., 7,272 . . . . .280/B2, E2
Buell, Mo., U.S., 100 . . . . .302/E2
Buellton, Calif., U.S., 3,828 . . . . .246/E8
Buena, N.J., U.S., 3,873 . . . . .314/D4
Buena, Wash., U.S., 950 . . . . .358/E3
Buena Park, Calif., U.S., 78,282 . . . . . . .246/D10
Buena Park, Wisc., U.S. 364/E6
Buenaventura, Col. 184/A4
Buena Ventura Lakes, Fla., U.S., 14,100 . .256/C4
Buena Vista, Col. 184/A4
Buena Vista, Colo., U.S., 2,195 . . . . .250/D3
Buena Vista, Ga., U.S., 1,664 . . . . .260/B7
Buena Vista, Ind., U.S., 80 . . . . .270/E6
Buena Vista, Iowa, U.S., county, 20,411 . .274/D2
Buena Vista, Mich., U.S., 7,845 . . . . .294/F6
Buena Vista, N. Mex., U.S., 70 . . . . .317/E2
Buena Vista, Ohio, U.S., 150 . . . . .328/D7
Buena Vista, Tenn., U.S., 100 . . . . .344/E3
Buena Vista, Va., U.S., 6,349 . . . . .354/E5
Buena Vista, Va., U.S., river 94/E2
Buendia, Sp., reservoir 94/E2
Buene, Alb., river 99/A2
Buenos Aires, Arg., capital, 2,965,403,
(11,298,030 metro.) 191/D3
Buenos Aires, Arg., lake 191/A6
Buenos Aires, Arg., province 191/C4
Buenos Aires, Chile, lake 190/B7
Buenos Aires N.W.R., Ariz., U.S. 242/D6
Bueyeros, N. Mex., U.S. 317/G2
Buffalo, Alta., Can. 212/F6
Buffalo, Alta., Can., lake 212/D5
Buffalo, Ark., U.S., river 244/B1
Buffalo, Ill., U.S., 491 . . . . .266/D4

Buffalo, Ind., U.S., 672 . . . . .270/C3
Buffalo, Kans., U.S., 1,321 . . . . .274/N5
Buffalo, Kans., U.S., 284 . . . . .276/G4
Buffalo, Minn., U.S., 475 . . . . .280/E3
Buffalo, Minn., U.S., 10,097 . . . . .298/D5
Buffalo, Minn., U.S., river 298/A4
Buffalo, Mo., U.S., 2,781 . . . . .302/C4
Buffalo, Nebr., U.S., county, 42,259 . . . . .308/E3
Buffalo, N.Y., U.S., 292,648,
(1,170,111 metro.) 320/D5
Buffalo, N. Dak., U.S., 209 . . . . .326/H3
Buffalo, Okla., U.S., 1,212/ 330/C1
Buffalo, S.C., U.S., 1,426 . . . . .340/C2
Buffalo, S. Dak., U.S., 380 . . . . .342/B2
Buffalo, Tex., U.S., 1,804 . . . . .346/M4
Buffalo, W. Va., U.S., 1,171 . . . . .360/C3
Buffalo, Wisc., U.S., 1,040 . . . . .364/B4
Buffalo, Wisc., U.S., county, 13,804 . . . . .364/B4
Buffalo, Wyo., U.S., 3,900 . . . . .366/C1
Buffalo Ctr., Iowa, U.S., 963 . . . . .274/G1
Buffalo Creek, Colo., U.S., 50 . . . . .250/E2
Buffalo Gap, S. Dak., U.S., 164 . . . . .342/B3
Buffalo Gap, Tex., U.S., 463 . . . . .346/J3
Buffalo Gap Natl. Grassland,
S. Dak., U.S. 342/B4, C4, D4
Buffalo Grove, Ill., U.S., 42,909 . . . . .266/B5
Buffalo Jct., Va., U.S., 125 . . . . .354/F7
Buffalo Lake, Minn., U.S., 768 . . . . .298/C6
Buffalo Lake N.W.R., N. Dak., U.S. 326/H1
Buffalo Narrows, Sask., Can., 1,137 . . . . .227/B5
Buffalo Natl. River, Ark., U.S. 244/C2
Buffalo Prairie, Ill., U.S., 60 . . . . .266/C2
Buffalo Valley, Tenn., U.S., 50 . . . . .344/K2
Buford, Colo., U.S. 250/C1
Buford, Ga., U.S., 10,668 . . . . .260/C3, K1
Buford, N. Dak., U.S. 326/B1
Buford, Ohio, U.S., 100 . . . . .328/C7
Buford, Tex., U.S. 346/H3
Buford, Wyo., U.S. 366/G3
Bug, Bela., river 82/A3
Bug, Pol., river 83/E2, F3
Bug, Ukr., river 102/A1
Bugbrooke, Eng., U.K., 2,711 . . . . .68/E5
Bugbrooke, Eng., U.K., 2,711 . . . . .70/B2
Bugeac, Mol., region 102/B3
Bugle, (Bugle/Stenalees), Eng., U.K., 2,695 .73/C4
Bugojno, Bos.-Her. 98/B1
Buhl, Ida., U.S., 3,985 . . . . .264/C7
Buhl, Minn., U.S., 983 . . . . .298/E3
Buhler, Kans., U.S., 1,358 . . . . .276/E3
Buhta, N.C., U.S., 125 . . . . .322/G5
Buies Creek, N.C., U.S., 2,215 . . . . .322/H4
Builth Wells, Wales, U.K., 2,474 . . . . . . .64/E3
Buin, Chile, 8,581 . . . . .264/F7
Bujumbura, Bur., capital, 235,440,
(321,000 metro.) 158/B2
Buka, P.N.G., island 172/B2
Bukavu, Congo, D.R., 201,569 . . . . .155/C2
Bukhoro, Uzb., 237,900 . . . . .132/B3
Bukhoro, Uzb., province 132/B2
Bukit Pagon, Bru., mountain 121/C1
Bukit Panjang, Sing. 123/B1
Bukit Timah, Sing. 123/B1
Bükk, Hun., mountains 91/C1
Bukoba, Tan. 158/B2
Bukum, Sing., island 123/B2
Bula, Gui.-B. 149/B1
Buladean, N.C., U.S., 212/ 322/A2
Bulawayo, Zimb., 621,742 . . . . .160/B2
Bulby, Eng., U.K. 70/D1
Bulcher, Tex., U.S. 346/L2
Bulembu, Swaz. 161/B1
Bulera, Rwa., lake 158/B1
Bulgan, Mong. 118/C2
Bulgaria, nation 99
Bulkeley, Eng., U.K. 68/B3
Bull, Mont., U.S., mountains 306/H3
Bull, S.C., U.S., island 340/E4
Bull, Wyo., U.S., lake 366/B2
Bullard, Ga., U.S., 80 . . . . .260/E6
Bullard, Tex., U.S., 1,150 . . . . .346/N3
Bull Bay, Wales, U.K. 64/C1
Bull Creek, Mo., U.S., 225 . . . . .302/C5
Bulle, Switz. 90/B2
Bullhead, S. Dak., U.S., 308 . . . . .342/D2
Bullhead City, Ariz., U.S., 33,769 . . . . . . .242/A2
Bullion, Calif., U.S., mountains 246/E8
Bullitt, Ky., U.S., county, 61,236 . . . . . . .280/E3
Bulloch, Ga., U.S., county, 55,983 . . . . . .260/H7
Bullock, Ala., U.S., county, 11,714 . . . . . .238/D3
Bulls, S.C., U.S., bay 340/E4
Bulls Gap, Tenn., U.S., 714 . . . . .344/Q2
Bull Shoals, Ark., U.S., 2,000 . . . . .244/C1
Bull Shoals, Mo., U.S., lake 302/D5
Bull Valley, Ill., U.S., 726 . . . . .266/F1
Bulphan, Eng., U.K. 70/E3
Bulpitt, Ill., U.S., 206 . . . . .266/D4
Bulverde, Tex., U.S., 3,761 . . . . .346/A2
Bulwick, Eng., U.K. 70/C1
Bumba, Congo, D.R. 155/B1
Bumble Bee, Ariz., U.S. 242/C3
Bumpass, Va., U.S. 354/H5
Bumpus Mills, Tenn., U.S., 225 . . . . .344/F1
Buna, Tex., U.S., 2,269 . . . . .346/R5
Bunbury, W.A., Austl. 170/A5
Bunbury, Eng., U.K. 68/B3
Bunceton, Mo., U.S., 368 . . . . .302/D3
Bunch, Okla., U.S., 40 . . . . .330/H2
Buncombe, N.C., U.S., 186 . . . . .266/E6
Buncombe, N.C., U.S., county, 206,330 . .322/F7
Bundaberg, Qnsld., Austl., 49,513,
(51,000 metro.) 170/G2
Bunessan, Scot., U.K. 62/D6
Bungay, Eng., U.K., 3,393 . . . . .70/G2
Bungo, Jap., channel 114/B3
Bunia, Congo, D.R. 155/C1
Bunker, Mo., U.S., 427 . . . . .302/E4
Bunker Hill, Ill., U.S., 1,801 . . . . .266/A3, D4
Bunker Hill, Ind., U.S., 987 . . . . .270/D3
Bunker Hill, Kans., U.S., 101 . . . . .276/D3
Bunker Hill, Oreg., U.S., 1,462 . . . . .334/B4
Bunker Hill Vil., Tex., U.S., 3,654 . . . . . . .346/A6
Bunkie, La., U.S., 4,662 . . . . .282/E5
Bunn, Ark., U.S. 244/C3
Bunn, N.C., U.S., 357 . . . . .322//J3
Bunnell, Fla., U.S., 2,122 . . . . .256/G2
Bunnlevel, N.C., U.S., 300 . . . . .322/H4
Bunnvale, N.J., U.S., 950 . . . . .314/D2
Bunny, Eng., U.K. 70/B1
Buon Ma Thuot, Viet., 282,095 . . . . .123/B4
Buqayq, Sa. Arab. 136/C1
Buras, (Buras-Triumph), La., U.S., 3,358 . .282/K8
Buraydah, Sa. Arab. 68/D3
Burbage, Eng., U.K., 1,246 . . . . .70/D3

Cimarron Natl. Grassland, Kans., U.S. 276/A4
Cimone, It., *mountain* 95/B1
Cincinnati, Iowa, U.S., 428 ......274/J6
Cincinnati, Ohio, U.S., 331,285,
  (1,979,202 *metro.*) 328/A7, B10
Cincinnatus, N.Y., U.S., 600 .....320/K5
Cinderford, Eng., U.K., 9,566 ......68/B6
Cinebar, Wash., U.S., 60 .....358/C3
Cinnaminson, N.J., U.S., 14,595 ......314/D4
Circle, Alaska, U.S., 100 ......240/G1
Circle, Mont., U.S., 644 ......306/L2
Circle, Utah, U.S., *cliffs* 350/C6
Circle Pines, Minn., U.S., 4,663 ......298/F5
Circleville, Kans., U.S., 185 ......276/G2
Circleville, Ohio, U.S., 13,485 ......328/E6
Circleville, Tex., U.S. 346/L1
Circleville, Utah, U.S., 505 ......350/B5
Circleville, W. Va., U.S., 100 ......360/C3
Cirebon, Indon. 122/B2
Cirencester, Eng., U.K., 15,221 ......68/D6
Cisco, Ga., U.S., 450 ......260/B2
Cisco, Ill., U.S., 264 ......266/E3
Cisco, Tex., U.S., 3,851 ......346/J3
Cisco, Utah, U.S. 350/E5
Cismont, Va., U.S., 125 ......354/G4
Cisne, Ill., U.S., 673 ......266/E5
Cissna Park, Ill., U.S., 811 ......266/F3
Cistern, Tex., U.S. 346/L6
Citra, Fla., U.S., 800 ......256/F2
Citronelle, Ala., U.S., 3,659 ......238/A4
Citrus, Fla., U.S., *county*, 118,085 ......256/F3
Citrus Hts., Calif., U.S., 85,071 ......246/D4, K5
Citrus Sprs., Fla., U.S., 4,157 ......256/F2
City Beach, W.A., Austl. ......170/Inset I
City of Rocks Natl. Res., Ida., U.S. 264/D7
City Pt., Maine, U.S. 286/C4
City Pt., Wisc., U.S. 364/C4
City View, Ont., Can. 223/G6
City View, S.C., U.S., 1,254 ......340/E2
Cd. Acuña, Mex., 108,159, (110,487 *metro.*) 200/D2
Cd. Adolfo López Mateos, Mex., 467,544 ......200/Inset
Cd. Bolivar, Ven., 230,001 ......182/D2
Cd. Camargo, Mex., 37,456, (45,852 *metro.*) 200/C2
Cd. Constitución, Mex., 35,589 ......200/B3
Cd. de la Habana, Cuba, *province* 204/B1
Cd. del Carmen, Mex., 126,024,
  (172,076 *metro.*) 200/F4
Cd. del Este, Para., 223,350 ......187/E4
Cd. Guayana, Ven., 465,738 ......182/D2
Cd. Juárez, Mex., 1,187,275, (1,218,817 *metro.*) 200/C1
Cd. Mante, Mex., 80,533, (112,602 *metro.*) 200/E3
Cd. Obregón, Mex., 250,790, (356,290 *metro.*) 200/C2
Cd. Real, Sp., 63,251 ......94/E3
Cd. Real, Sp., *province* 94/D3
Cd. Rodrigo, Sp. 94/C2
Cd. Valles, Mex., 105,721, (146,604 *metro.*) 200/E3
Cd. Victoria, Mex., *state capital*, 249,029,
  (263,063 *metro.*) 200/E3
Ciudadela, Sp. 94/H2
Civil Administration Building, Vat. 96/A2
Civitavecchia, It. 95/B2
Clachan, Scot., U.K. 62/G6
Clackamas, Oreg., U.S., 5,177 ......334/C3
Clackamas, Oreg., U.S., *county*, 338,391 ......334/B3, D2
Clackamas, Oreg., U.S., *river* 334/D2
Clackmannan, Scot., U.K.,
  unitary authority, 48,077 ......62/J6
Clacton-on-Sea, Eng., U.K., 45,065 ......70/G3
Cladich, Scot., U.K. 62/F6
Claerwen, Wales, U.K., *reservoir* 64/D3
Claflin, Kans., U.S., 705 ......276/D3
Claggettsville, Md., U.S., 250 ......288/F2
Claiborne, Ala., U.S., 40 ......238/B4
Claiborne, La., U.S., 9,830 ......282/E1
Claiborne, La., U.S., *parish*, 16,851 ......282/C1
Claiborne, Md., U.S., 225 ......288/J4
Claiborne, Miss., U.S., *county*, 11,831 ......300/B4
Claiborne, Tenn., U.S., *county*, 29,862 ......344/P2
Claigan, Scot., U.K. 62/C4
Clair, N.B., Can., 863 ......217/A1
Claire, Alta., U.S., *lake* 212/D2
Claire City, S. Dak., U.S., 85 ......342/H1
Clairemont, Tex., U.S. 346/H2
Clair Engle, Calif., U.S., *lake* 246/C1
Clairette, Tex., U.S., 50 ......346/K3
Clairsholm, Alta., Can. 212/D6
Clairton, Penn., U.S., 8,491 ......336/B5
Clallam, Wash., U.S., *county*, 64,525 ......358/A2
Clallam Bay, Wash., U.S., 850 ......358/A1
Clam Falls, Wisc., U.S., 70 ......364/A3
Clam Lake, Wisc., U.S., 50 ......364/C2
Clanabogan, N. Ire., U.K. 65/C2
Clancy, Mont., U.S., 1,406 ......306/E3
Clandeboye, Man., Can. 215/C4
Clanfield, Eng., U.K. 70/A3
Clanton, Ala., U.S., 7,800 ......238/C2
Claonaig, Scot., U.K. 62/F7
Clapham, Eng., U.K., 3,501 ......68/F5
Clapperton, Ont., Can., *island* 294/E3
Clara, Ire. 76/C2
Clara, Miss., U.S., 375 ......300/D4
Clara City, Minn., U.S., 1,393 ......298/B6
Clare, Ire., *county* 76/B2
Clare, Iowa, U.S., 190 ......274/F2
Clare, Mich., U.S., 3,173 ......294/E6
Clare, Mich., U.S., *county*, 31,252 ......294/E6
Claremont, Calif., U.S., 33,998 ......246/H8
Claremont, Ill., U.S., 212 ......266/F5
Claremont, Minn., U.S., 620 ......298/E6
Claremont, N.H., U.S., 13,151 ......312/B5
Claremont, N.C., U.S., 1,038 ......322/C3
Claremont, S. Dak., U.S., 130 ......342/G2
Claremont, Va., U.S., 343 ......354/K6
Claremore, Okla., U.S., 15,873 ......330/G1
Clarinda, Iowa, U.S., 5,690 ......274/D6
Clarington, Ohio, U.S., 444 ......328/J6
Clarion, Iowa, U.S., 2,968 ......274/G2
Clarion, Penn., U.S., 6,185 ......336/C3
Clarion, Penn., U.S., *county*, 41,765 ......336/C3
Clarion, Penn., U.S., *river* 336/C3
Clarissa, Minn., U.S., 609 ......298/C4
Clarita, Okla., U.S., 80 ......330/F3
Clark, Ark., U.S., *county*, 23,546 ......244/B3
Clark, Colo., U.S., 40 ......250/D1
Clark, Ida., U.S., *county*, 1,022 ......264/E5

Clark, Ill., U.S., *county*, 17,008 ......266/F4
Clark, Ind., U.S., *county*, 96,472 ......270/E7
Clark, Kans., U.S., *county*, 2,390 ......276/C4
Clark, Ky., U.S., 33,144 ......280/F3
Clark, Mo., U.S., 275 ......302/D2
Clark, Mo., U.S., *county*, 7,416 ......302/E1
Clark, Nev., U.S., *county*, 1,375,765 ......310/C3
Clark, N.J., U.S., 14,597 ......314/A3
Clark, Ohio, U.S., *county*, 144,742 ......328/C6
Clark, Penn., U.S., 633 ......336/A3
Clark, S. Dak., U.S., 1,285 ......342/H3
Clark, S. Dak., U.S., *county*, 4,143 ......342/H3
Clark, Wash., U.S., *county*, 345,238 ......358/C4
Clark, Wisc., U.S., *county*, 33,557 ......364/C4
Clark, Wyo., U.S. 366/B1
Clark Ctr., Ill., U.S., 100 ......266/F4
Clarkdale, Ariz., U.S., 3,422 ......242/C3
Clarke, Ala., U.S., *county*, 27,867 ......238/B4
Clarke, Ga., U.S., *county*, 101,489 ......260/E4
Clarke, Iowa, U.S., *county*, 9,133 ......274/G6
Clarke, Miss., U.S., *county*, 17,955 ......300/D3
Clarke, Va., U.S., *county*, 12,652 ......354/G2
Clarkedale, Ark., U.S., 80 ......244/E2
Clarkesville, Ga., U.S., 1,248 ......260/D2
Clarkfield, Minn., U.S., 944 ......298/B6
Clark Fork, Ida., U.S., 530 ......264/A1
Clark Fork, Mont., U.S., *river* 306/A2
Clarkia, Ida., U.S. 264/A2
Clark Island, Maine, U.S., 212/ 286/C5
Clarklake, Mich., U.S., 250 ......294/E7
Clark Mills, N.Y., U.S., 1,424 ......320/L4
Clarkrange, Tenn., U.S., 212/ 344/L2
Clarks, La., U.S., 1,071 ......282/E2
Clarks, Nebr., U.S., 361 ......308/G2
Clarksboro, N.J., U.S., 2,600 ......314/C4
Clarksburg, Calif., U.S., 475 ......246/K5
Clarksburg, Ind., U.S., 125 ......270/F6
Clarksburg, Md., U.S., 1,834 ......288/F3
Clarksburg, Mass., U.S., 1,686 ......292/B2
Clarksburg, Mo., U.S., 375 ......302/D3
Clarksburg, N.J., U.S., 450 ......314/E3
Clarksburg, Ohio, U.S., 516 ......328/D6
Clarksburg, Tenn., U.S., 285 ......344/F3
Clarksburg, W. Va., U.S., 16,743 ......360/F2
Clarksdale, Miss., U.S., 20,645 ......300/B1
Clarksdale, Mo., U.S., 351 ......302/B2
Clarks Falls, Conn., U.S., 275 ......253/H4
Clarksfield, Ohio, U.S., 425 ......328/F3
Clark Fork Yellowstone, Wyo., U.S., *river* 366/B1
Clarks Green, Penn., U.S., 1,630 ......336/H6
Clarks Grove, Minn., U.S., 734 ......298/D7
Clarks Harbour, N.S., Can., 944 ......221/B4
Clarks Hill, Ind., U.S., 680 ......270/C4
Clarks Mills, Maine, U.S., 450 ......286/B5
Clarkson, Okla., U.S., 794 ......330/B1, D4
Clarkson, Nebr., U.S., 685 ......308/G2
Clarkson Valley, Mo., U.S., 2,675 ......302/G3
Clarks Pt., Alaska, U.S., 75 ......240/D3
Clarks Summit, Penn., U.S., 5,126 ......336/H6, K3
Clarkston, Ga., U.S., 7,231 ......260/C4, J2
Clarkston, Utah, U.S., 688 ......350/B2
Clarkston, Wash., U.S., 7,337 ......358/H3
Clarkston Hts., (Clarkston Hts.-Vineland),
  Wash., U.S., 6,117 ......358/H3
Clarksville, Ark., U.S., 7,719 ......244/B2
Clarksville, Del., U.S., 900 ......255/D6
Clarksville, Ind., U.S., 21,400 ......270/E8
Clarksville, Iowa, U.S., 1,441 ......274/J2
Clarksville, Md., U.S., 900 ......288/G3
Clarksville, Mich., U.S., 317 ......294/D7
Clarksville, Mo., U.S., 490 ......302/F2
Clarksville, N.J., U.S. 314/D3
Clarksville, Ohio, U.S., 497 ......328/C7
Clarksville, Penn., U.S., 234 ......336/A6
Clarksville, Tenn., U.S., 103,455,
  (207,033 *metro.*) 344/G1
Clarksville, Tex., U.S., 3,883 ......346/N2
Clarksville, Va., U.S., 1,329 ......354/F7
Clarkton, Mo., U.S., 1,330 ......302/G5
Clarkton, N.C., U.S., 705 ......322/H6
Clarkville, Colo., U.S. 250/H1
Clarno, Oreg., U.S. 334/F3
Claryville, Ky., U.S., 2,588 ......280/F2
Clashmore, Scot., U.K. 62/H3
Clatonia, Nebr., U.S., 275 ......308/H3
Clatskanie, Oreg., U.S., 1,528 ......334/C1
Clatsop, Oreg., U.S., *county*, 35,630 ......334/C1
Claude, Tex., U.S., 1,313 ......346/G9
Claudell, Kans., U.S. 276/C2
Claudy, N. Ire., U.K., 970 ......65/C2
Claughton, Eng., U.K. 66/C4
Claunch, N. Mex., U.S. 317/E3
Claverdon, Eng., U.K. 68/D5
Clavering, Eng., U.K. 70/E3
Clawdd-newydd, Wales, U.K. 64/E1
Clawson, Mich., U.S., 12,732 ......294/B6, F7
Clawson, Utah, U.S., 153 ......350/C4
Claxton, Ga., U.S., 2,276 ......260/H7
Clay, Ala., U.S., 4,947 ......238/E1
Clay, Ala., U.S., *county*, 14,254 ......238/D2
Clay, Ark., U.S., *county*, 17,609 ......244/E1
Clay, Calif., U.S., 225 ......246/L6
Clay, Fla., U.S., *county*, 140,814 ......256/G2
Clay, Ga., U.S., *county*, 3,357 ......260/B8
Clay, Ill., U.S., *county*, 14,560 ......266/E5
Clay, Ind., U.S., *county*, 26,556 ......270/B6
Clay, Iowa, U.S., *county*, 17,372 ......274/D2
Clay, Kans., U.S., *county*, 8,822 ......276/F3
Clay, Ky., U.S., 1,179 ......280/C3
Clay, Ky., U.S., *county*, 24,556 ......280/D3
Clay, La., U.S., 50 ......282/D2
Clay, Minn., U.S., *county*, 51,229 ......298/A3
Clay, Miss., U.S., *county*, 21,979 ......300/D2
Clay, Mo., U.S., *county*, 184,006 ......302/B2, J4
Clay, Nebr., U.S., *county*, 7,039 ......308/G3
Clay, N.C., U.S., *county*, 8,775 ......322/C8
Clay, S. Dak., U.S., *county*, 13,537 ......342/H5
Clay, Tenn., U.S., *county*, 7,976 ......344/K2
Clay, Tex., U.S., *county*, 11,006 ......346/K2
Clay, W. Va., U.S., 593 ......360/D4
Clay, W. Va., U.S., *county*, 10,330 ......360/D4
Clay Ctr., Kans., U.S., 4,564 ......276/E2
Clay Ctr., Nebr., U.S., 861 ......308/G3
Clay Ctr., Ohio, U.S., 294 ......328/D2
Clay City, Ill., U.S., 1,000 ......266/E5
Clay City, Ind., U.S., 1,019 ......270/B6
Clay City, Ky., U.S., 1,303 ......280/G3
Claycomo, Mo., U.S., 1,267 ......302/J5
Clay Cross, (Clay Cross/N. Wingfield),
  Eng., U.K., 24,271 ......68/E3
Claydon, Eng., U.K. 70/G2
Clayhatchee, Ala., U.S., 501 ......238/D4
Claymont, Del., U.S., 9,220 ......255/C1
Claypole, Eng., U.K. 70/C1
Claypool, Ariz., U.S., 1,794 ......242/E4
Claypool, Ind., U.S., 311 ......270/E3
Claypool Hill, Va., U.S., 1,719 ......354/E2
Claysburg, Penn., U.S., 1,503 ......336/E5
Clay Sprs., Ariz., U.S., 250 ......242/E3
Clay Spur, Wyo., U.S., 90 ......366/D1

Claysville, Ohio, U.S., 225 ......328/G6
Claysville, Penn., U.S., 724 ......336/A5
Clayton, Ala., U.S., 1,475 ......238/D4
Clayton, Calif., U.S., 10,762 ......246/K1
Clayton, Del., U.S., 1,273 ......255/B3
Clayton, Ga., U.S., 2,019 ......260/E2
Clayton, Ga., U.S., *county*, 236,517 ......260/C4, H3
Clayton, Ida., U.S. 264/C5
Clayton, Ill., U.S., 904 ......266/C3
Clayton, Ind., U.S., 693 ......270/C5
Clayton, Iowa, U.S., 55 ......274/M2
Clayton, Iowa, U.S., *county*, 18,678 ......274/M1
Clayton, Kans., U.S., 66 ......276/B2
Clayton, La., U.S., 858 ......282/F3
Clayton, Mass., U.S., 50 ......292/A4
Clayton, Mich., U.S., 326 ......294/E8
Clayton, Mo., U.S., 12,825 ......302/H3
Clayton, N.J., U.S., 7,139 ......314/C4
Clayton, N. Mex., U.S., 2,524 ......317/G1
Clayton, N.Y., U.S., 1,821 ......320/J3
Clayton, N.C., U.S., 6,973 ......322/J3
Clayton, Ohio, U.S., 13,347 ......328/B6
Clayton, Okla., U.S., 719 ......330/G3
Clayton, S. Dak., U.S. 342/H4
Clayton, Wash., U.S., 175 ......358/H2
Clayton, Wisc., U.S., 507 ......364/A3
Clayton Lake, Maine, U.S. 286/C2
Clayton-le-Moors, Eng., U.K., 6,961 ......66/D5
Clayton-le-Moors, Eng., U.K., 6,961 ......68/C2
Claytonville, Tex., U.S., 40 ......346/G1
Clay Vil., Ky., U.S., 90 ......280/E2
Clayville, N.Y., U.S., 445 ......320/L5
Clayville, R.I., U.S., 250 ......339/B3
Cleadale, Scot., U.K. 62/D5
Clear, Ire., *cape* 76/B3
Clear, Calif., U.S., *lake* 246/C3
Clear, Iowa, U.S., *lake* 274/H1
Clearbrook, Minn., U.S., 551 ......298/B3
Clearco, W. Va., U.S. 360/E4
Clear Creek, Ont., Can. 223/E5
Clear Creek, Calif., U.S., 100 ......246/B1
Clear Creek, Colo., U.S., *county*, 9,322 ......250/E2
Clear Creek, Ind., U.S., 1,800 ......270/C6
Clear Creek, Utah, U.S. 350/C4
Clearfield, Iowa, U.S., 371 ......274/F6
Clearfield, Penn., U.S., 6,631 ......336/E3
Clearfield, Penn., U.S., *county*, 83,382 ......336/D4
Clearfield, S. Dak., U.S. 342/E4
Clearfield, Utah, U.S., 25,974 ......350/B2, E1
Clearlake, Calif., U.S., 13,142 ......246/C4
Clear Lake, Calif., U.S., *reservoir* 246/D1
Clear Lake, Ill., U.S., 267 ......266/D4
Clear Lake, Ind., U.S., 244 ......270/G1
Clear Lake, Iowa, U.S., 8,161 ......274/H1
Clear Lake, Minn., U.S., 266 ......298/D4
Clear Lake, S. Dak., U.S., 1,335 ......342/J3
Clear Lake, Utah, U.S. 350/B4
Clear Lake, Wisc., U.S., 1,051 ......364/A3
Clearlake Oaks, Calif., U.S., 2,402 ......246/C3
Clear Lake Shores, Tex., U.S., 1,205 ......346/C2
Clearmont, Mo., U.S., 191 ......302/A1
Clearmont, Wyo., U.S., 115 ......366/C1
Clear Spr., Md., U.S., 455 ......288/C1
Clear Sprs., Tex., U.S. 346/B2
Clearview, Okla., U.S., 56 ......330/F2
Clearwater, Br. Col., Can. 214/M5
Clearwater, Sask., Can., *river* 227/A4
Clearwater, Fla., U.S., 108,787 ......256/C6, F4
Clearwater, Ida., U.S., *county*, 8,930 ......264/B3
Clearwater, Ida., U.S., *mountains* 264/A3
Clearwater, S. Fork, Ida., U.S., *river* 264/A3
Clearwater, Ida., U.S., *river* 264/B3, B4
Clearwater, Kans., U.S., 2,178 ......276/E4
Clearwater, Minn., U.S., 858 ......298/C5
Clearwater, Minn., U.S., *county*, 8,423 ......298/B3
Clearwater, Minn., U.S., *river* 298/B3
Clearwater, Nebr., U.S., 384 ......308/E1
Clearwater, Tex., U.S., 26,005 ......346/L3
Clearwater Beach, Fla., U.S. 256/C6
Clearwater Lake, Wisc., U.S., 212/ 364/D3
Clearwater Lake Prov. Park, Man., Can. 215/A2
Clearwater Natl. For., Ida., U.S. 264/B3
Clearwater River Prov. Park, Sask., Can. 212/F3
Clearwater River Prov. Park, Sask., Can. 227/A4
Cleat, Scot., U.K. 62/L1, M2
Cleaton, Ky., U.S., 500 ......280/C3
Cleator, Ariz., U.S. 242/C3
Cleator Moor, Eng., U.K., 6,410 ......66/B3
Cleburne, Ala., U.S., *county*, 14,123 ......238/D2
Cleburne, Ark., U.S., *county*, 24,046 ......244/C2
Cleburne, Tex., U.S., 26,005 ......346/L3
Cleckheaton, (Cleckheaton and Liversedge),
  Eng., U.K., 27,151 ......66/E5
Cleckheaton, (Cleckheaton and Liversedge),
  Eng., U.K., 27,151 ......68/D2
Cleedownton, Eng., U.K. 68/C5
Cle Elum, Wash., U.S., 1,755 ......358/E2
Cle Elum, Wash., U.S., *lake* 358/D2
Cleethorpes, Eng., U.K., 32,719 ......66/H5
Cleethorpes, Eng., U.K., 32,719 ......68/G2
Clegg, Tex., U.S. 346/K7
Cleghorn, Iowa, U.S., 250 ......274/C2
Clem, Ga., U.S., 275 ......260/A4
Clementon, N.J., U.S., 4,986 ......314/B4
Clements, Kans., U.S. 276/F3
Clements, Md., U.S., 150 ......288/H6
Clements, Minn., U.S., 191 ......298/B6
Clementson, Minn., U.S., 40 ......298/C2
Clementsport, N.S., Can. 221/B3
Clemmons, N.C., U.S., 13,827 ......322/E2
Clemons, Iowa, U.S., 148 ......274/H3
Clemson, S.C., U.S., 11,939 ......340/B2
Clendenin, W. Va., U.S., 1,116 ......360/D4
Clendening, Ohio, U.S., *lake* 328/H5
Cleo, Tex., U.S., 50 ......346/J5
Cleobury Mortimer, Eng., U.K., 2,164 ......68/C5
Cleona, Penn., U.S., 2,148 ......336/G5
Cleo Sprs., Okla., U.S., 326 ......330/D1
Clermont, Que., Can., 3,078 ......226/F4
Clermont, Fla., U.S., 9,333 ......256/C4, G3
Clermont, Ga., U.S., 564 ......260/D3
Clermont, Ind., U.S., 1,477 ......270/D5
Clermont, Iowa, U.S., 716 ......274/L1
Clermont-Ferrand, Fr., 141,004, (258,541 *metro.*) 88/C4
Clervaux, Lux. 85/B1
Clerve, Lux., *river* 85/B1
Clevedon, Eng., U.K., 21,670 ......73/G2
Cleveland, Qnsld., Austl. ......170/Inset III
Cleveland, Ala., U.S., 1,241 ......238/C2
Cleveland, Ark., U.S. 244/C4
Cleveland, Ark., U.S., *county*, 8,571 ......244/C4
Cleveland, Fla., U.S., 3,268 ......256/D2
Cleveland, Ga., U.S., 1,907 ......260/D2
Cleveland, Ill., U.S., 253 ......266/D3
Cleveland, Kans., U.S. 276/D4
Cleveland, Minn., U.S., 673 ......298/D6
Cleveland, Miss., U.S., 13,841 ......300/B2
Cleveland, Mo., U.S., 592 ......302/B3
Cleveland, Mont., U.S., *mountain* 306/C1

Cleveland, N. Mex., U.S., 175 ......317/E1
Cleveland, N.Y., U.S., 758 ......320/K4
Cleveland, N.C., U.S., 808 ......322/D3
Cleveland, N.C., U.S., *county*, 96,287 ......322/B3
Cleveland, N. Dak., U.S., 112 ......326/F3
Cleveland, Ohio, U.S., 478,403,
  (2,945,831 *metro.*) 328/G3, G9
Cleveland, Okla., U.S., 3,282 ......330/F1
Cleveland, Okla., U.S., *county*, 208,016 ......330/E2
Cleveland, S.C., U.S., 150 ......340/B1
Cleveland, Tenn., U.S., 37,192 ......344/M4
Cleveland, Tex., U.S., 7,605 ......346/N5
Cleveland, Utah, U.S., 508 ......350/D4
Cleveland, Va., U.S., 148 ......354/D2
Cleveland, W. Va., U.S., 60 ......360/F3
Cleveland, Wisc., U.S., 1,361 ......364/F5
Cleveland Hts., Ohio, U.S., 49,958 ......328/G2, H9
Cleveland Natl. For., Calif., U.S. 246/F10, J10, J9
Cleveleys, Eng., U.K. 66/B5
Clever, Mo., U.S., 1,010 ......302/C4
Cleves, Ohio, U.S., 2,790 ......328/A9
Clewiston, Fla., U.S., 6,460 ......256/H5
Cley next the Sea, Eng., U.K. 70/G1
Clichy, Fr. ......88/Inset II
Clifden, Ire. 76/A2
Cliff, N. Mex., U.S., 175 ......317/B5
Cliffdell, Wash., U.S., 40 ......358/D3
Cliff End, Eng., U.K. 70/F5
Clifford, Ont., Can., 792 ......223/E4
Clifford, Ind., U.S., 291 ......270/E6
Clifford, Mass., U.S. 292/L6
Clifford, Mich., U.S., 324 ......294/F6
Clifford, N. Dak., U.S., 51 ......326/H2
Cliffside, N.C., U.S., 600 ......322/B4
Cliffside Park, N.J., U.S., 23,007 ......314/C2, F2
Clifftop, W. Va., U.S., 70 ......360/E4
Cliffwood Beach, N.J., U.S., 3,538 ......314/E3
Clifton, Ariz., U.S., 2,596 ......242/F4
Clifton, Colo., U.S., 17,345 ......250/B2
Clifton, Ida., U.S., 213 ......264/F7
Clifton, Ill., U.S., 1,317 ......266/F3
Clifton, Kans., U.S., 557 ......276/E2
Clifton, La., U.S., 100 ......282/E5
Clifton, Maine, U.S., 743 ......286/D4
Clifton, N.J., U.S., 78,672 ......314/B2, E2
Clifton, Ohio, U.S., 179 ......328/C6
Clifton, Tenn., U.S., 2,699 ......344/F4
Clifton, Tex., U.S., 3,542 ......346/L4
Clifton, Va., U.S., 185 ......354/J3, L2
Clifton, Wisc., U.S., 80 ......364/C5
Clifton City, Mo., U.S. 302/C3
Clifton Forge, Va., U.S., 4,289 ......354/D5
Clifton Hampden, Eng., U.K. 70/B3
Clifton Hts., Penn., U.S., 6,779 ......336/J7
Clifton Hill, Mo., U.S., 124 ......302/D2
Clifton Park, N.Y., U.S., 4,600 ......320/P5
Clifton Sprs., N.Y., U.S., 2,223 ......320/G5
Cliftonville, Eng., U.K. 70/G4
Clifty, Ark., U.S., 100 ......244/B1
Clifty, Ky., U.S., 80 ......280/C4
Climax, Sask., Can., 206 ......227/B11
Climax, Colo., U.S., 40 ......250/D2
Climax, Ga., U.S., 297 ......260/C8
Climax, Kans., U.S., 64 ......276/F4
Climax, Mich., U.S., 791 ......294/D7
Climax, Minn., U.S., 243 ......298/A3
Climax Sprs., Mo., U.S., 80 ......302/C3
Climbing Hill, Iowa, U.S. 274/B3
Climping, Eng., U.K. 70/C5
Clinch, Ga., U.S., *county*, 6,878 ......260/F1
Clinch, Tenn., U.S., *river* 344/Q2
Clinchco, Va., U.S., 424 ......354/D2
Clinchport, Va., U.S., 77 ......354/C3
Cline, Tex., U.S. 346/H6
Cline River, Alta., Can. 212/B5
Clines Corners, N. Mex., U.S., 100 ......317/E2
Clingmans Dome, N.C., U.S., *peak* 322/C7
Clint, Tex., U.S., 980 ......346/B4
Clinton, Br. Col., Can., 621 ......214/M5
Clinton, Ont., Can., 3,117 ......223/D4
Clinton, Ala., U.S., 175 ......238/B3
Clinton, Ark., U.S., 2,283 ......244/C2
Clinton, Conn., U.S., 13,094 ......253/E4
Clinton, Ill., U.S., 7,485 ......266/E3
Clinton, Ill., U.S., *county*, 35,535 ......266/D5
Clinton, Ill., U.S., *lake* 266/E3
Clinton, Ind., U.S., 5,126 ......270/B5
Clinton, Ind., U.S., *county*, 33,866 ......270/C4
Clinton, Iowa, U.S., 27,772 ......274/P4
Clinton, Iowa, U.S., *county*, 50,149 ......274/P4
Clinton, Kans., U.S., 80 ......276/G3
Clinton, Kans., U.S., *lake* 276/G3
Clinton, Ky., U.S., 1,415 ......280/B4
Clinton, Ky., U.S., *county*, 9,634 ......280/E4
Clinton, La., U.S., 1,998 ......282/C5
Clinton, Maine, U.S., 3,340 ......286/C4
Clinton, Md., U.S., 26,064 ......288/G4
Clinton, Mass., U.S., 13,435 ......292/H3
Clinton, (Lenawee County), Mich., U.S., 2,294 ......294/F7
Clinton, (Macomb County), Mich., U.S., 95,648 ......294/B6
Clinton, Mich., U.S., *county*, 64,753 ......294/E7
Clinton, Minn., U.S., 453 ......298/A5
Clinton, Miss., U.S., 23,347 ......300/C3
Clinton, Mo., U.S., 9,311 ......302/C3
Clinton, Mo., U.S., *county*, 18,979 ......302/B2
Clinton, Mont., U.S., 549 ......306/C3
Clinton, Nebr., U.S. 308/B1
Clinton, N.J., U.S., *town*, 2,632 ......314/D2
Clinton, N.Y., U.S., 1,952 ......320/L4
Clinton, N.Y., U.S., *county*, 79,894 ......320/P1
Clinton, N.C., U.S., 8,600 ......322/J5
Clinton, Ohio, U.S., 1,337 ......328/G4
Clinton, Ohio, U.S., *county*, 40,543 ......328/C7
Clinton, Okla., U.S., 8,833 ......330/D2
Clinton, Penn., U.S., *county*, 37,914 ......336/F3
Clinton, S.C., U.S., 8,091 ......340/C2
Clinton, Tenn., U.S., 9,409 ......344/N2
Clinton, Utah, U.S., 12,585 ......350/B2, E1
Clinton, Wash., U.S., 868 ......358/C2
Clinton, Wisc., U.S., 2,162 ......364/E6
Clinton Colden, NW Terr., Can., *lake* 208/G4
Clintondale, N.Y., U.S., 1,424 ......320/N7
Clintonville, Penn., U.S., 528 ......336/B3
Clintonville, W. Va., U.S., 125 ......360/E5
Clintonville, Wisc., U.S., 4,736 ......364/E4
Clintwood, Va., U.S., 1,549 ......354/C2
Clio, Ala., U.S., 2,206 ......238/D4
Clio, Iowa, U.S., 91 ......274/H6
Clio, Mich., U.S., 2,483 ......294/F6
Clio, S.C., U.S., 774 ......340/E2
Clipsham, Eng., U.K. 70/C1
Clitherall, Minn., U.S., 118 ......298/B4
Clitheroe, Eng., U.K., 13,548 ......66/D5
Clitheroe, Eng., U.K., 13,548 ......68/C2
Clive, Iowa, U.S., 12,855 ......274/G4
Clogher, N. Ire., U.K., 578 ......65/C3
Cloghy, N. Ire., U.K., 647 ......65/D2
Clonelly, N. Ire., U.K. 65/B2
Clonmel, Ire. 76/C2
Clontarf, Minn., U.S., 173 ......298/B5

Clophill, Eng., U.K., 2,372 . . . . .68/G5
Clophill, Eng., U.K., 2,372 . . . . .70/D2
Clopton, Ala., U.S. .238/D4
Cloquet, Minn., U.S., 11,201 . . . . .298/E4
Cloquet, Minn., U.S., river 298/F3
Cloridorme, Que., Can. 226/M2
Closplint, Ky., U.S., 50 . . . . .280/G4
Closter, N.J., U.S., 8,383 . . . . .314/C1, F2
Clotho, Minn., U.S. .298/M4
Cloud, Kans., U.S., county, 10,268 . . . . .276/E2
Cloud, Wyo., U.S., peak 366/C1
Cloudcroft, N. Mex., U.S., 749 . . . . .317/E5
Cloud Lake, Fla., U.S., 167 . . . . .256/B4
Clough, N. Ire., U.K., 205 . . . . .65/F3
Clough, N. Ire., U.K., 236 . . . . .65/F3
Cloughton, Eng., U.K. 66/H4
Cloutierville, La., U.S., 225 . . . . .282/D3
Clovelly, Eng., U.K. .73/D2
Clover, S.C., U.S., 4,014 . . . . .340/C1
Clover, Va., U.S., 212/ 354/E7
Cloverdale, N.B., Can. 217/B2
Cloverdale, Ala., U.S., 150 . . . . .238/B1
Cloverdale, Calif., U.S., 6,831 . . . . .246/B4
Cloverdale, Ind., U.S., 2,243 . . . . .270/C5
Cloverdale, Iowa, U.S., 40 . . . . .274/C1
Cloverdale, Mich., U.S., 400 . . . . .294/D7
Cloverdale, Minn., U.S., 70 . . . . .298/E4
Cloverdale, N. Mex., U.S. 317/B6
Cloverdale, Ohio, U.S., 201 . . . . .328/B3
Cloverdale, Oreg., U.S., 242 . . . . .334/C2
Cloverdale, Va., U.S., 2,986 . . . . .354/D6
Clover Hill, Md., U.S., 3,260 . . . . .288/C2
Cloverleaf, Tex., U.S., 23,508 . . . . .346/B6
Cloverport, Ky., U.S., 1,256 . . . . .280/D3
Cloverton, Minn., U.S. 298/E4
Clovis, Calif., U.S., 68,468 . . . . .246/F6
Clovis, N. Mex., U.S., 32,667 . . . . .317/G5
Clow, Ark., U.S. 244/B4
Clowne, Eng., U.K., 7,234 . . . . .66/F6
Clowne, Eng., U.K., 7,234 . . . . .68/E3
Clows Top, Eng., U.K. 68/C5
Cloyne, Ont., Can. .223/H3
Cluanie, Scot., U.K. .62/F4
Cluanie, Scot., U.K., lake 62/F4
Cluff Lake Mine, Sask., Can. 227/A2
Cluj, Rom., county .101/B2
Cluj-Napoca, Rom., 329,310 . . . . .101/B2
Clun, Eng., U.K. 68/A5
Clun, Eng., U.K., forest 68/A5
Cluny, Alta., Can. 212/D6
Cluny, Fr. 88/D3
Cluster Sprs., Va., U.S., 100 . . . . .354/F7
Clute, Tex., U.S., 10,424 . . . . .346/N6
Clutha, N.Z., river .171/A4
Clutier, Iowa, U.S., 229 . . . . .274/K3
Clyattville, Ga., U.S., 450 . . . . .260/E1
Clydach, Wales, U.K. 64/D4
Clyde, Alta., Can., 491 . . . . .212/D4
Clyde, Scot., U.K., estuary 60/B2
Clyde, Scot., U.K., river 60/B2
Clyde, Kans., U.S., 740 . . . . .276/E2
Clyde, Mo., U.S., 74 . . . . .302/B1
Clyde, N.Y., U.S., 2,269 . . . . .320/H4
Clyde, N.C., U.S., 1,324 . . . . .322/D7
Clyde, N. Dak., U.S. 326/G1
Clyde, Ohio, U.S., 6,064 . . . . .328/E3
Clyde, Okla., U.S. 330/E1
Clyde, Tex., U.S., 3,345 . . . . .346/J3
Clyde, Wash., U.S. .358/G3
Clydebank, Scot., U.K. 60/B2
Clydebank, Scot., U.K., 29,858 . . . . .62/H7
Clyde Hill, Wash., U.S., 2,890 . . . . .358/A4
Clyde Park, Mont., U.S., 310 . . . . .306/F4
Clyde River, N.S., Can. 221/B4
Clyde River, Nun., Can., 785 . . . . .208/P2
Clyman, Wisc., U.S., 388 . . . . .364/E5
Clymer, Penn., U.S., 1,547 . . . . .336/C4
Clyo, Ga., U.S., 300 . . . . .260/J7
Clyro, Wales, U.K. 64/E3
Clywedog, Wales, U.K., lake 64/D3
Coacalco, Mex. 200/Inset
Coachella, Calif., U.S., 22,724 . . . . .246/J9
Coagh, N. Ire., U.K., 616 . . . . .65/F2
Coahoma, Miss., U.S., 325 . . . . .300/B1
Coahoma, Miss., U.S., county, 30,622 . . . . . .300/B1
Coahoma, Tex., U.S., 932 . . . . .346/G3
Coahuila, Mex., state 200/D2
Coal, Yukon, Can., river 228/D5
Coal, Mo., U.S., 60 .302/C3
Coal, Okla., U.S., county, 6,031 . . . . .330/F3
Coal Branch, N.B., Can. 217/D2
Coal City, Ill., U.S., 4,797 . . . . .266/E2
Coal City, Ind., U.S., 150 . . . . .270/B6
Coal City, W. Va., U.S., 1,905 . . . . .360/D5
Coal Creek, Colo., U.S., 303 . . . . .250/E3
Coaldale, Alta., Can., 6,008 . . . . .212/D6
Coaldale, Colo., U.S., 40 . . . . .250/D3
Coaldale, Nev., U.S. 310/B2
Coaldale, (Bedford County), Penn., U.S., 146 .336/E5
Coaldale, (Schuylkill County), Penn., U.S., 2,295 .336/K4
Coal Fork, W. Va., U.S., 1,350 . . . . .360/D4
Coalgate, Okla., U.S., 2,005 . . . . .330/F3
Coal Grove, Ohio, U.S., 2,027 . . . . .328/E8
Coal Hill, Ark., U.S., 1,001 . . . . .244/B2
Coaling, Ala., U.S., 1,115 . . . . .238/B2
Coalinga, Calif., U.S., 11,668 . . . . .246/E6
Coalisland, N. Ire., U.K., 3,802 . . . . .65/E1
Coalmont, Colo., U.S. 250/D1
Coalmont, Ind., U.S., 425 . . . . .270/B6
Coalmont, Penn., U.S., 128 . . . . .336/E5
Coalmont, Tenn., U.S., 948 . . . . .344/K4
Coal Mtn., Ga., U.S., 700 . . . . .260/G3
Coalport, Penn., U.S., 490 . . . . .336/D4
Coalridge, Mont., U.S., 50 . . . . .306/M1
Coal River, Br. Col. Can. 214/J1
Coal Run, Ohio, U.S., 325 . . . . .328/G6
Coal Run Vil., Ky., U.S., 577 . . . . .280/H3
Coalspur, Alta., Can. 212/B4
Coalton, Ill., U.S., 307 . . . . .266/D4
Coalton, Ohio, U.S., 545 . . . . .328/E7
Coalton, W. Va., U.S., 247 . . . . .360/G3
Coal Valley, Ill., U.S., 3,606 . . . . .266/C2
Coalville, Eng., U.K., 30,408 . . . . .68/E4
Coalville, Eng., U.K., 30,408 . . . . .70/B1
Coalville, Utah, U.S., 1,382 . . . . .350/C3, E2
Coalwood, Mont., U.S. 306/L4
Coamo, P.R. 206/C4
Coamo Hot Sprs., P.R. 206/C2
Coarsegold, Calif., U.S., 275 . . . . .246/F5
Coast, Can., mountains 193/D12
Coast, Br. Col., Can., mountains 214/F2, J5
Coast, Kenya, province 157/G5
Coast, Calif., U.S., ranges 246/B2, D6
Coast, Oreg., U.S., ranges 334/B5, C2
Coatbridge, Scot., U.K., 41,170 . . . . .62/J7
Coates, Minn., U.S., 163 . . . . .298/D6
Coatesville, Ind., U.S., 516 . . . . .270/C5
Coatesville, Penn., U.S., 10,838 . . . . .336/K6
Coatham, Eng., U.K. .66/F3
Coaticook, Que., Can., 8,988 . . . . .226/E6
Coatopa, Ala., U.S. .238/A3
Coats, Nun., Can., island 208/M4

Coats, Kans., U.S., 112 . . . . .276/D4
Coats, N.C., U.S., 1,845 . . . . .322/H4
Coatsburg, Ill., U.S., 226 . . . . .266/B3
Coats Land, Antar., region 192/B13
Coatzacoalcos, Mex., 225,973, (267,212 metro.) .200/D4
Cobalt, Ida., U.S. 264/C5
Cobalt City, Mo., U.S., 189 . . . . .302/F4
Cobán, Guat. 201/C4
Cobb, Ant.-Bar., cove 207/E1
Cobb, Calif., U.S., 1,638 . . . . .246/C4
Cobb, Ga., U.S., county, 607,751 . . . .260/B4, G2
Cobb, Ky., U.S., 50 .280/C4
Cobb, Wisc., U.S., 442 . . . . .364/C6
Cobb Island, Md., U.S., 750 . . . . .288/G6
Cobble Mtn. Res., Mass., U.S. 292/C4
Cobbtown, Ga., U.S., 311 . . . . .260/G7
Cobden, Ont., Can. .223/J2
Cobden, Ill., U.S., 1,116 . . . . .266/D6
Cobden, Minn., U.S., 61 . . . . .298/C6
Cóbh, Ire. 76/B3
Cobham, Man., Can., river 215/D2
Cobija, Bol. 186/A2
Cobleskill, N.Y., U.S., 4,533 . . . . .320/N5
Cobourg, Ont., Can., 17,172 . . . . .223/G4
Cobre, Nev., U.S. 310/C1
Coburg, Ger. 86/B3
Coburg, Iowa, U.S. .274/D6
Coburg, Mont., U.S. 306/H1
Coburg, Oreg., U.S., 969 . . . . .334/C3
Coburn, Penn., U.S., 145 . . . . .336/G4
Coburn Gore, Maine, U.S. 286/B3
Cocagne, N.B., Can., 2,659 . . . . .217/E2
Cochabamba, Bol., 517,024 . . . . .186/A3
Cochabamba, Bol., department 186/A3
Cochise, Ariz., U.S., 40 . . . . .242/F5
Cochise, Ariz., U.S., county, 117,755 . . . . . . .242/F6
Cochiti, N. Mex., U.S., 507 . . . . .317/D2
Cochiti Ind. Res., N. Mex., U.S. 317/D2
Cochituate, Mass., U.S., 6,768 . . . . .292/J3
Cochran, Ga., U.S., 4,455 . . . . .260/E7
Cochran, Tex., U.S., county, 3,730 . . . . .346/F2
Cochran, Va., U.S. 354/H7
Cochrane, Alta., Can., 11,798 . . . . .212/C5
Cochrane, Ont., Can., 5,690 . . . . .222/D3
Cochrane, Sask., Can., river 227/H2
Cochrane, Ala., U.S. 238/A2
Cochrane, Wisc., U.S., 435 . . . . .364/B4
Cochranton, Penn., U.S., 1,148 . . . . .336/A2
Cockaponset St. For., Conn., U.S. 253/E4
Cockburn, Ont., Can., island 223/B2
Cockburn, Ont., Can., island 294/F4
Cockburn Harbour, T.-C. Is. 207/D4
Cockburnspath, Scot., U.K. 62/M7
Cocke, Tenn., U.S., county, 33,565 . . . . .344/Q3
Cockermouth, Eng., U.K., 7,702 . . . . .66/B3
Cockfield, Eng., U.K., 1,537 . . . . .70/F2
Cockley Cley, Eng., U.K. 70/F1
Cockrell Hill, Tex., U.S., 4,443 . . . . .346/C9
Cockrum, Miss., U.S., 175 . . . . .300/C1
Coclé, Pan., province 203/B2
Coclé del Norte, Pan. 203/B2
Coco, Hond., river 202/C2
Coco, Mya., islands .125/B3
Coco, Nicar., river 202/A2, C1
Coco, P.R. 206/C2
Cocoa, Fla., U.S., 16,412 . . . . .256/H3
Cocoa Beach, Fla., U.S., 12,482 . . . . .256/H3
Cocodrie, La., U.S., 225 . . . . .282/H8
Cocolalla, Ida., U.S., 90 . . . . .264/A1
Coconino, Ariz., U.S., county, 116,320 . . . . . .242/D2
Coconino Natl. For., Ariz., U.S. 242/D2
Coconut Creek, Fla., U.S., 43,566 . . . . .256/B5
Cocotitlán, Mex. 200/Inset
Cod, Mass., U.S., cape 292/P4
Codell, Kans., U.S., 50 . . . . .276/C2
Codington, S. Dak., U.S., county, 25,897 . . . . .342/H3
Codnor, Eng., U.K. 70/B1
Codorus, Penn., U.S. 336/H6
Codrington, Antar., mountain 192/C17
Codrington, Ant.-Bar. 207/E2
Codrington, Ant.-Bar., lagoon 207/D1
Cody, Nebr., U.S., 149 . . . . .308/C1
Cody, Va., U.S., 60 .354/E7
Cody, Wyo., U.S., 8,835 . . . . .366/G3
Codys, N.B., Can. 217/D3
Codyville, Maine, U.S. 286/E3
Coe, Ind., U.S., 80 .270/B8
Coeburn, Va., U.S., 1,996 . . . . .354/C2
Coedpoeth, Wales, U.K., 5,300 . . . . .64/E1
Coeroeni, Sur., river 183/A3
Coeur d'Alene, Ida., U.S., 34,514 . . . . .264/A2
Coeur d'Alene Ind. Res., Ida., U.S. 264/A2
Coeur d'Alene Natl. For., Ida., U.S. 264/B2
Coffee, Ala., U.S., county, 43,615 . . . . .238/C4
Coffee, Ga., U.S., county, 37,413 . . . . .260/F9
Coffee, Tenn., U.S., county, 48,014 . . . . .344/J3
Coffee Creek, Mont., U.S. 306/F2
Coffeen, Ill., U.S., 709 . . . . .266/D4
Coffee Sprs., Ala., U.S., 251 . . . . .238/C4
Coffeeville, Ala., U.S., 360 . . . . .238/A4
Coffeeville, Miss., U.S., 930 . . . . .300/C2
Coffey, Kans., U.S., county, 8,865 . . . . .276/G3
Coffey, Mo., U.S., 140 . . . . .302/B1
Coffeyville, Kans., U.S., 11,021 . . . . .276/G4
Coffman, Mo., U.S., 50 . . . . .302/F4
Coffman Cove, Alaska, U.S., 199 . . . . .240/J3
Cofield, N.C., U.S., 347 . . . . .322/M2
Cogalnic, Mol., river 102/D2
Cogar, Okla., U.S. 330/D2
Cogdell, Ga., U.S., 40 . . . . .260/F9
Coggon, Iowa, U.S., 745 . . . . .274/L3
Cognac, Fr. 88/B4
Cogo, Eq. Gui. 154/B3
Cogswell, N. Dak., U.S., 165 . . . . .326/H3
Cohagen, Mont., U.S. 306/K2
Cohansey, N.J., U.S., 212/ 314/C4
Cohasset, Mass., U.S., 7,261 . . . . .292/L4
Cohasset, Minn., U.S., 2,481 . . . . .298/D3
Cohoctah, Mich., U.S., 275 . . . . .294/D7
Cohocton, N.Y., U.S., 854 . . . . .320/H5
Cohoes, N.Y., U.S., 15,521 . . . . .320/P5
Cohutta, Ga., U.S., 582 . . . . .260/B6
Coiba, Pan., island .203/B3
Coihaique, Chile 190/B4
Coila, Miss., U.S. 300/C2
Coimbatore, India, 853,402, (1,446,034 metro.) .128/C3
Coimbra, Port., 148,443 . . . . .93/A2
Coimbra, Port., district 93/A3
Coin, Iowa, U.S., 252 . . . . .274/D6
Cojedes, Ven., river .182/C2
Cojedes, Ven., state .182/C2
Cokato, Minn., U.S., 2,727 . . . . .298/C5
Coke, Tex., U.S., 70 . . . . .346/N3
Coke, Tex., U.S., county, 3,864 . . . . .346/H4
Cokedale, Colo., U.S., 139 . . . . .250/F4
Coker, Ala., U.S., 808 . . . . .238/B2

Cokesbury, Md., U.S., 212/ 288/M7
Cokesbury, N.J., U.S., 850 . . . . .314/D2
Coketon, W. Va., U.S., 100 . . . . .360/G2
Cokeville, Wyo., U.S., 506 . . . . .366/A2
Col, (Coll), Scot., U.K., 1,087 . . . . .62/D2
Colbert, Ala., U.S., county, 54,984 . . . . .238/B1
Colbert, Ga., U.S., 488 . . . . .260/E3
Colbert, Okla., U.S., 1,065 . . . . .330/F4
Colbert, Wash., U.S., 400 . . . . .358/H2
Colburn, Ida., U.S., 175 . . . . .264/A1
Colburn, Ind., U.S., 325 . . . . .270/C3
Colby, Kans., U.S., 5,450 . . . . .276/A2
Colby, Maine, U.S., 212/ 286/D2
Colby, Wisc., U.S., 1,616 . . . . .364/C4
Colbyville, Vt., U.S., 1,235 . . . . .352/B2
Colca, Peru, river 185/C4
Colchester, N.S., Can., county 221/D2
Colchester, Eng., U.K. 60/D3
Colchester, Eng., U.K., 96,063 . . . . .70/F3
Colchester, Conn., U.S., 14,551 . . . . .253/F3
Colchester, Ill., U.S., 1,493 . . . . .266/C3
Colchester, Vt., U.S., 16,986 . . . . .352/A1
Colcord, Okla., U.S., 819 . . . . .330/H1
Colcord, W. Va., U.S., 300 . . . . .360/D5
Cold Ashby, Eng., U.K. 70/B2
Cold Brook, N.Y., U.S., 336 . . . . .320/L4
Coldeast, Eng., U.K. .73/E3
Colden, N.Y., U.S., 700 . . . . .320/D5
Cold Lake, Alta., Can., 11,520 . . . . .212/E4
Cold Spr., Ky., U.S., 3,806 . . . . .280/G1
Cold Spr., Mass., U.S. 292/B4
Cold Spr., Minn., U.S., 2,975 . . . . .298/C5
Cold Spr., N.J., U.S., 950 . . . . .314/D6
Cold Spr., N.Y., U.S., 1,983 . . . . .320/P8
Cold Sprs., Nev., U.S. 310/C3
Cold Sprs., Okla., U.S. 330/C3
Cold Sprs. N.W.R., Oreg., U.S. 334/G2
Coldstream, N.B., Can., 134 . . . . .217/B2
Coldstream, Scot., U.K., 1,813 . . . . .62/M7
Coldstream, Ky., U.S., 956 . . . . .280/B1
Coldwater, Mich., U.S., 12,697 . . . . .294/D8
Coldwater, Miss., U.S., 1,674 . . . . .300/C1
Coldwater, Miss., U.S., river 300/B1
Coldwater, Mo., U.S., 2 . . . . .302/F4
Coldwater, Ohio, U.S., 4,482 . . . . .328/A5
Coldwells, Scot., U.K. 62/N4
Cole, Mo., U.S., county, 71,397 . . . . .302/D3
Cole, Okla., U.S., 473 . . . . .330/E2
Colebrook, Conn., U.S., 1,471 . . . . .253/C2
Colebrook, N.H., U.S., 2,321 . . . . .312/D2
Cole Camp, Mo., U.S., 1,028 . . . . .302/C3
Coleford, (Gloucestershire), Eng., U.K., 9,567 ..68/B6
Coleharbor, N. Dak., U.S., 106 . . . . .326/D2
Coleman, Fla., U.S., 647 . . . . .256/F3
Coleman, Ga., U.S., 149 . . . . .260/B8
Coleman, Md., U.S., 250 . . . . .288/K2
Coleman, Mich., U.S., 1,296 . . . . .294/E6
Coleman, Okla., U.S., 150 . . . . .330/F3
Coleman, Tex., U.S., 5,127 . . . . .346/J4
Coleman, Tex., U.S., county, 9,235 . . . . .346/J4
Coleman, Wisc., U.S., 716 . . . . .364/E3
Coleman's Hatch, Eng., U.K. 71/J4
Colerain, N.C., U.S., 221 . . . . .322/M2
Coleraine, N. Ire., U.K. 60/A2
Coleraine, N. Ire., U.K., 20,721 . . . . .65/D1
Coleraine, N. Ire., U.K., unitary authority, 56,315 .65/D2
Coleraine, Minn., U.S., 1,110 . . . . .298/D3
Coleridge, Nebr., U.S., 541 . . . . .308/G1
Coleridge, N.C., U.S., 212/ 322/F3
Coles, Ill., U.S., county, 53,196 . . . . .266/E4
Coles, Miss., U.S., 125 . . . . .300/A4
Colesbourne, Eng., U.K. 68/D6
Colesburg, Iowa, U.S., 412 . . . . .274/M2
Colesburg, Ky., U.S., 50 . . . . .280/E3
Coleshill, Eng., U.K., 6,324 . . . . .68/D5
Coleshill, Eng., U.K. .68/D6
Coleshill, Eng., U.K., 6,324 . . . . .70/A1
Coles Island, N.B., Can. 217/D3
Colesville, Md., U.S., 19,810 . . . . .288/B6, F3
Colesville, N.J., U.S., 400 . . . . .314/D1
Coleta, Ill., U.S., 155 . . . . .266/D2
Coleville, Sask., Can., 313 . . . . .227/A9
Coleville, Calif., U.S. 246/F4
Colfax, Calif., U.S., 1,496 . . . . .246/E3
Colfax, Ill., U.S., 989 . . . . .266/E3
Colfax, Ind., U.S., 768 . . . . .270/C4
Colfax, Iowa, U.S., 2,223 . . . . .274/H4
Colfax, Ky., U.S. 280/G2
Colfax, La., U.S., 1,659 . . . . .282/D3
Colfax, Nebr., U.S., county, 10,441 . . . . .308/G2
Colfax, N. Mex., U.S., county, 14,189 . . . . . . .317/F1
Colfax, N. Dak., U.S. 326/J3
Colfax, Wash., U.S., 2,844 . . . . .358/H4
Colfax, Wisc., U.S., 1,136 . . . . .364/B4
Colgate, N. Dak., U.S., 40 . . . . .326/H2
Colhaut, Dom. 208/A2
Colima, Mex., state capital, 119,639, (129,958 metro.) .200/D4
Colima, Mex., state .200/D4
Colina, Chile 190/Inset
Coll, Scot., U.K., island 60/A2
Coll, Scot., U.K., island 62/C5
Collafirth, Scot., U.K. 62/P2
Collbran, Ala., U.S., 50 . . . . .238/D1
Collbran, Colo., U.S., 408 . . . . .250/C2
College, Alaska, U.S., 11,402 . . . . .240/F2
College City, Ark., U.S., 269 . . . . .244/E1
College Corner, Ohio, U.S., 424 . . . . .328/A6
Collegedale, Tenn., U.S., 6,514 . . . . .344/L4
College Grove, Tenn., U.S., 325 . . . . .344/H3
College Park, Ga., U.S., 20,382 . . . . .260/C4, H3
College Park, Md., U.S., 24,657 . . . . .288/C6, G4
College Place, Wash., U.S., 7,818 . . . . .358/G3
Collegeport, Tex., U.S., 325 . . . . .346/M7
College Sprs., Iowa, U.S., 248 . . . . .274/D6
College Sta., Tex., U.S., 67,890 . . . . .346/M5
Collegeville, Penn., U.S., 865 . . . . .270/B3
Collegeville, Penn., U.S., 8,032 . . . . .336/L5
Colleton, S.C., U.S., county, 38,264 . . . . .340/D4
Collette, N.B., Can., 522 . . . . .217/D2
Collettsville, N.C., U.S., 175 . . . . .322/B3
Colleyville, Tex., U.S., 19,636 . . . . .346/B9
Collier, Fla., U.S., county, 251,377 . . . . .256/G5
Collierville, Tenn., U.S., 31,872 . . . . .344/B4
Colliford Lake, Eng., U.K., reservoir 73/C3
Collin, Tex., U.S., county, 491,675 . . . . . .346/C8, M2
Collingbourne Ducis, Eng., U.K. 70/A4
Collingbourne Kingston, Eng., U.K. 73/J2
Collingdale, Penn., U.S., 8,664 . . . . .336/L7
Collingham, (Nottinghamshire), Eng., U.K., 2,801 .68/F3
Collingham, (W. Yorkshire), Eng., U.K., 2,714 . .66/F5
Collings Lakes, N.J., U.S., 1,726 . . . . .314/D4
Collingswood, N.J., U.S., 14,326 . . . . . .314/B3, C4
Collingsworth, Tex., U.S., county, 3,206 . . . . . .346/G9
Collingwood, Ont., Can., 16,039 . . . . .223/E3
Collingwood, N.Z. 171/B3

Collins, Ark., U.S., 40 . . . . .244/D4
Collins, Ga., U.S., 528 . . . . .260/G7
Collins, Iowa, U.S., 499 . . . . .274/H4
Collins, Miss., U.S., 2,683 . . . . .300/C4
Collins, Mo., U.S., 176 . . . . .302/C4
Collins, Mont., U.S. .306/E2
Collins, Ohio, U.S., 450 . . . . .328/E3
Collins Park, Del., U.S., 8,300 . . . . .255/B2
Collinston, La., U.S., 327 . . . . .282/F1
Collinsville, Ala., U.S., 1,644 . . . . .238/D1
Collinsville, Conn., U.S., 2,686 . . . . .253/D2
Collinsville, Ill., U.S., 24,707 . . . . .266/A3, D5
Collinsville, Miss., U.S., 1,823 . . . . .300/D3
Collinsville, Okla., U.S., 4,077 . . . . .330/G1
Collinsville, Tex., U.S., 1,235 . . . . .346/D7
Collinsville, Va., U.S., 7,777 . . . . .354/D7
Collinwood, Tenn., U.S., 1,024 . . . . .344/F4
Collis, Minn., U.S. 298/A5
Collison, Ill., U.S., 100 . . . . .266/F3
Collyer, Kans., U.S., 133 . . . . .276/B2
Colma, Calif., U.S., 1,191 . . . . .246/J2
Colman, S. Dak., U.S., 572 . . . . .342/J4
Colmar, Fr. 88/D2
Colmar, Ky., U.S., 125 . . . . .280/G4
Colmar Manor, Md., U.S., 1,257 . . . . .288/C7
Colmesneil, Tex., U.S., 638 . . . . .346/P5
Colmor, N. Mex., U.S. 317/F1
Colne, Eng., U.K., 18,776 . . . . .68/C2
Colne Engaine, Eng., U.K. 70/F3
Cologne, Iowa, U.S., 868 . . . . .274/H3
Cologne, (Köln) Ger., 962,900 . . . . .86/A3
Cologne, Minn., U.S., 1,012 . . . . .298/D6
Cologne, N.J., U.S., 800 . . . . .314/D4
Coloma, Calif., U.S., 325 . . . . .246/L5
Coloma, Mich., U.S., 1,595 . . . . .294/C7
Coloma, Wisc., U.S., 461 . . . . .364/D4
Colombia, nation 174
Colombier, Que., Can., 890 . . . . .226/H3
Colombo, Sri Lan., capital, 642,163, (1,221,904 metro.) 126/A5
Colome, S. Dak., U.S., 340 . . . . .342/F4
Colon, Mich., U.S., 1,227 . . . . .294/D8
Colon, Nebr., U.S., 138 . . . . .308/H2
Colon, N.C., U.S., 300 . . . . .322/G3
Colón, Cuba 204/C2
Colón, Hond., department 202/C2
Colón, Pan., 42,133 .203/C2
Colón, Pan., province 203/C2
Colona, Colo., U.S., 50 . . . . .250/C3
Colona, Ill., U.S., 5,173 . . . . .266/C2
Colonia, Micr., 3,456 . . . . .172/A2
Colonia, N.J., U.S., 17,811 . . . . .314/E2
Colonia, Uru., department 187/B3
Colonia del Sacramento, Uru. 187/B3
Colonial Beach, Va., U.S., 3,228 . . . . .354/K4
Colonial Hts., Tenn., U.S., 7,067 . . . . .344/S2
Colonial Hts., Va., U.S., 16,897 . . . . .354/J6
Colonial Natl. Hist. Park, Va., U.S. 354/K6, L6
Colonial Park, Penn., U.S., 13,259 . . . . .336/H5
Colonial Pine Hills, S. Dak., U.S., 2,561 . . . . .342/B3
Colonia Nueva Guinea, Nicar. 202/B3
Colonias, N. Mex., U.S. 317/F2
Colonie, N.Y., U.S., 7,916 . . . . .320/P5
Colonsay, Sask., Can., 426 . . . . .227/E9
Colonsay, Scot., U.K., island 60/A2
Colonsay, Scot., U.K., island 62/D6
Colony, Ala., U.S., 385 . . . . .238/C2
Colony, Kans., U.S., 397 . . . . .276/G3
Colony, Okla., U.S., 147 . . . . .330/D2
Colony, Tex., U.S. 346/L6
Colony, Wyo., U.S. .366/M1
Colorado, Arg., river 191/B4
Colorado, C.R. 203/C2
Colorado, U.S., state 238
Colorado, Ariz., Nev., U.S., river 310/C3, C4
Colorado, Ariz., U.S., river 242/A2, A4, B1, D1
Colorado, Calif., U.S., desert 246/J9
Colorado, Calif., U.S., river 246/L7, L9
Colorado, Colo., U.S., plateau 250/A4
Colorado, Colo., U.S., river 250/A4, C2
Colorado, Tex., U.S., county, 20,390 . . . . .346/M6
Colorado, Tex., U.S., river 346/D2
Colorado, Utah, U.S., river 350/D6, E5
Colorado Canyons Natl. Cons. Area, Colo., U.S. .250/B2
Colorado City, Ariz., U.S., 3,334 . . . . .242/C1
Colorado City, Colo., U.S., 2,018 . . . . .250/F4
Colorado City, Tex., U.S., 4,281 . . . . .346/H3
Colorado N.M., Colo., U.S. 250/B2
Colorado River Ind. Res., Ariz., U.S. 242/A4
Colorado Sprs., Colo., U.S., 360,890, (516,929 metro.) 250/F3
Colp, Ill., U.S., 224 .266/D6
Colpy, Scot., U.K. 62/L4
Colquitt, Ga., U.S., 1,939 . . . . .260/B9
Colquitt, Ga., U.S., county, 42,053 . . . . .260/D9
Colquitt, La., U.S. 282/D1
Colrain, Mass., U.S., 1,813 . . . . .292/D1
Colson, Ky., U.S., 175 . . . . .280/H3
Colsterworth, Eng., U.K. 70/C1
Colston Bassett, Eng., U.K. 70/C1
Colstrip, Mont., U.S., 2,346 . . . . .306/K4
Colt, Ark., U.S., 368 . . . . .244/E2
Colter, Wyo., U.S., peak 366/A1
Coltishall, Eng., U.K., 1,992 . . . . .70/G1
Colton, Nebr., U.S. .308/B2
Colton, N.Y., U.S., 450 . . . . .320/M1
Colton, S. Dak., U.S., 662 . . . . .342/J4
Colton, Utah, U.S. 350/D4
Colton, Wash., U.S., 386 . . . . .358/H3
Colton Pt., Md., U.S., 375 . . . . .288/G7
Columbia, Br. Col., Can., mountains 214/M4
Columbia, Br. Col., Can., river 214/N5
Columbia, Ala., U.S., 804 . . . . .238/D4
Columbia, Ark., U.S., county, 25,603 . . . . .244/B4
Columbia, Calif., U.S., 2,405 . . . . .246/E4
Columbia, Conn., U.S., 4,971 . . . . .253/F3
Columbia, Fla., U.S., 550 . . . . .256/F1
Columbia, Fla., U.S., county, 56,513 . . . . .256/F1
Columbia, Ga., U.S., county, 89,288 . . . . .260/G4
Columbia, Ill., U.S., 7,922 . . . . .266/A4, D5
Columbia, Iowa, U.S., 125 . . . . .274/H5
Columbia, Ky., U.S., 4,014 . . . . .280/E3
Columbia, La., U.S., 477 . . . . .282/E2
Columbia, Maine, U.S., 459 . . . . .286/F4
Columbia, Md., U.S., 88,254 . . . . .288/C3
Columbia, Miss., U.S., 6,603 . . . . .300/C4
Columbia, Mo., U.S., 84,531, (135,454 metro.) .302/D3
Columbia, N.J., U.S., 375 . . . . .314/C2
Columbia, N.Y., U.S., county, 63,094 . . . . .320/P6
Columbia, N.C., U.S., 819 . . . . .322/N3
Columbia, Oreg., U.S., county, 43,560 . . . . . . .334/D2
Columbia, Oreg., U.S., river 334/A2, B1, F2
Columbia, Penn., U.S., 10,311 . . . . .336/J5
Columbia, Penn., U.S., county, 64,151 . . . . . . .336/J3
Columbia, S.C., U.S., state capital, 116,278, (536,691 metro.) 340/A3, C2
Columbia, S. Dak., U.S., 140 . . . . .342/G2
Columbia, Tenn., U.S., 33,055 . . . . .344/G3
Columbia, Va., U.S., 49 . . . . .354/G5
Columbia, Wash., U.S., county, 4,064 . . . . . . .358/H3
Columbia, Wash., U.S., river 358/A3, E4, F1, F3, H1

Columbia, Wisc., U.S., *county*, 52,468 . . . . .364/D5
Columbia Beach, Md., U.S., 700 . . . . .288/H4
Columbia City, Ind., U.S., 7,077 . . . . .270/E2
Columbia City, Oreg., U.S., 1,571 . . . . .334/D2
Columbia Falls, Maine, U.S., 599 . . . . .286/E4
Columbia Falls, Mont., U.S., 3,645 . . . . .306/B1
Columbia Hts., Minn., U.S., 18,520 . . . . .298/F5
Columbiana, Ala., U.S., 3,316 . . . . .238/C2
Columbiana, Ohio, U.S., *county*, 112,075 . . . . . .328/J4
Columbia N.W.R., Wash., U.S. 358/F3
Columbia River Gorge Natl. Scenic Area,
   Oreg., U.S. 334/E2
Columbia River Gorge Natl. Scenic Area,
   Wash., U.S. 358/D4
Columbiaville, Mich., U.S., 815 . . . . .294/F6
Columbine, Colo., U.S. .250/D1
Columbine Valley, Colo., U.S., 1,132 . . . . .250/A3, E2
Columbus, Ala., U.S., *lake* 238/A2
Columbus, Ga., U.S., 186,291,
   (274,624 *metro*.) 260/B7
Columbus, Ill., U.S., 112 . . . . .266/B4
Columbus, Ind., U.S., 39,059 . . . . .270/E6
Columbus, Kans., U.S., 3,396 . . . . .276/H4
Columbus, Ky., U.S., 229 . . . . .280/A4
Columbus, Miss., U.S., 25,944 . . . . .300/D2
Columbus, Miss., U.S., *lake* 300/D2
Columbus, Mont., U.S., 1,748 . . . . .306/G4
Columbus, Nebr., U.S., 20,971 . . . . .308/G2
Columbus, N.J., U.S., 750 . . . . .314/D3
Columbus, N. Mex., U.S., 1,765 . . . . .317/C6
Columbus, N.C., U.S., 992 . . . . .322/A4, F8
Columbus, N.C., U.S., *county*, 54,749 . . . . .322/H6
Columbus, N. Dak., U.S., 151 . . . . .326/C1
Columbus, Ohio, U.S., *state capital*, 711,470,
   (1,540,157 *metro*.) 328/D6, D9
Columbus, Penn., U.S., 550 . . . . .336/B2
Columbus, Tex., U.S., 3,916 . . . . .346/M6
Columbus, Wisc., U.S., 4,479 . . . . .364/D5
Columbus City, Iowa, U.S., 376 . . . . .274/M5
Columbus Grove, Ohio, U.S., 2,212/ 328/B4
Columbus Jct., Iowa, U.S., 1,900 . . . . .274/M5
Colusa, Calif., U.S., 5,402 . . . . .246/D3
Colusa, Calif., U.S., *county*, 18,804 . . . . .246/C3
Colvend, Scot., U.K. 62/J9
Colver, Penn., U.S., 1,035 . . . . .336/D4
Colville, Alaska, U.S., *river* 240/E1
Colville, Wash., U.S., 4,988 . . . . .358/H1
Colville Ind. Res., Wash., U.S. 358/G1, H1
Colville Natl. For., Wash., U.S. 358/G1, H1
Colwell, Eng., U.K. 66/D2
Colwell, Iowa, U.S., 76 .274/J1
Colwich, Kans., U.S., 1,229 . . . . .276/E4
Colwyn, Penn., U.S., 2,453 . . . . .336/L7
Colwyn Bay, Wales, U.K., 29,883 . . . . .64/D1
Colyton, Eng., U.K., 1,684 . . . . .73/F3
Comal, Tex., U.S. 346/B2
Comal, Tex., U.S., *county*, 78,021 . . . . . . .346/A1, K6
Comanche, Kans., U.S., *county*, 1,967 . . . . .276/C4
Comanche, Mont., U.S. 306/H3
Comanche, Okla., U.S., 1,556 . . . . .330/E3
Comanche, Okla., U.S., *county*, 114,996 . . . . . .330/D3
Comanche, Tex., U.S., 4,482 . . . . .346/K4
Comanche, Tex., U.S., *county*, 14,026 . . . . .346/K4
Comanche Natl. Grassland, Colo., U.S. 250/G4, H4
Coma Pedrosa, And., *mountain* 93/A1
Comayagua, Hond., 52,300 . . . . .202/B2
Comayagua, Hond., *department* 202/B2
Comayagua, Hond., *mountains* 202/B2
Combe Martin, Eng., U.K., 2,453 . . . . .73/D2
Comber, N. Ire., U.K., 8,516 . . . . .65/F2
Combermere, Ont., Can. 223/H2
Comberton, Eng., U.K., 2,311 . . . . .68/H5
Comberton, Eng., U.K., 2,311 . . . . .70/E2
Combine, Tex., U.S., 1,788 . . . . .346/D10
Comendador, Dom. Rep. 205/A2
Comer, Ala., U.S., 40 . . . . .238/D3
Comer, Ga., U.S., 1,052 . . . . .260/E3
Comerio, P.R. 206/C2
Comertown, Mont., U.S. 306/M1
Comfort, N.C., U.S., 212/ 322/K4
Comfort, W. Va., U.S., 150 . . . . .360/C4
Comfrey, Minn., U.S., 367 . . . . .298/C6
Comilla, Bangl., 143,282 . . . . .127/E5
Comino, (Kemmuna), Malta, *island* 97/B1
Cominotto, Malta, *island* 97/B1
Comins, Mich., U.S., 150 . . . . .294/E5
Comitán, Mex., 70,311, (105,210 *metro*.) 200/F4
Commack, N.Y., U.S., 36,367 . . . . .320/D2
Commerce, Calif., U.S., 12,568 . . . . .246/C9
Commerce, Ga., U.S., 5,292 . . . . .260/E3
Commerce, Mo., U.S., 110 . . . . .302/G4
Commerce, Okla., U.S., 2,645 . . . . .330/H1
Commerce, Tex., U.S., 7,669 . . . . .346/N2
Commerce City, Colo., U.S., 20,991 . . . . . .250/A3, F2
Commercial Pt., Ohio, U.S., 776 . . . . .328/D6
Committee, Nun., Can., *bay* 208/L3
Como, It. 95/B1
Como, It., *lake* 95/B1
Como, Colo., U.S. 250/E2
Como, Miss., U.S., 1,310 . . . . .300/C1
Como, N.C., U.S., 78 . . . . .322/L2
Como, Tenn., U.S., 150 . . . . .344/D2
Como, Tex., U.S., 621 . . . . .346/N2
Como, Wisc., U.S., 1,870 . . . . .364/E6
Comobabi, Ariz., U.S., 50 . . . . .242/D5
Comodoro Rivadavia, Arg., 124,104 . . . . .191/B6
Comorin, India, *cape* 128/C7
Comoros, *nation* 157
Comox, Br. Col., Can., 11,172 . . . . .214/K6
Compass Lake, Fla., U.S., 212/ 256/C1
Compeer, Alta., Can. 212//E5
Competition, Mo., U.S. .302/D4
Compiègne, Fr. 88/C2
Comptche, Calif., U.S., 90 . . . . .246/B3
Compton, Que., Can. 226/E6
Compton, (Compton/Otterbourne),
   Eng., U.K., 1,609 . . . . .70/B3
Compton, Eng., U.K. 70/C5
Compton, Ark., U.S. 244/B1
Compton, Calif., U.S., 93,493 . . . . .246/C10
Compton, Ill., U.S., 347 . . . . .266/D2
Comrat, Mol. 102/B2
Comstock, Mich., U.S., 4,472 . . . . .294/D7
Comstock, Minn., U.S., 123 . . . . .298/A4
Comstock, Nebr., U.S., 110 . . . . .308/E2
Comstock, Tex., U.S., 250 . . . . .346/G6
Comstock, Wisc., U.S., 150 . . . . .364/A3
Comstock Park, Mich., U.S., 10,674 . . . . .294/D6
Comunas, P.R. 206/D2
Conakry, Guin., *capital*, 705,000,
   (1,764,000 *metro*.) .149/B3
Conasauga, Tenn., U.S., 125 . . . . .344/M5
Conata, S. Dak., U.S. 342/C4
Conboy Lake N.W.R., Wash., U.S. 358/D4
Concan, Tex., U.S., 100 . . . . .346/J6
Concepción, Chile, 214,505 . . . . .190/B5
Concepción, Chile, *bay* 190/B5
Concepción, Para. 187/D3
Concepción, Para., *department* 187/D3
Concepción del Oro, Mex., 6,475,
   (11,728 *metro*.) 200/D3
Conception, Calif., U.S., *point* 246/E8

Conception Jct., Mo., U.S., 202 . . . . .302/B1
Conchalí, Chile 190/Inset
Conchas, N. Mex., U.S., *lake* 317/F2
Conchas Dam, N. Mex., U.S. 317/F2
Conche, Nfld., Can., 263 . . . . .206/D4
Concho, Ariz., U.S. 242/F3
Concho, Tex., U.S., *county*, 3,966 . . . . .346/J4
Conchos, Mex., *river* 200/C2
Conconully, Wash., U.S., 185 . . . . .358/F1
Concord, Ark., U.S., 255 . . . . .244/D2
Concord, Calif., U.S., 121,780 . . . . .246/C5, K1
Concord, Ga., U.S., 336 . . . . .260/B5
Concord, Ill., U.S., 176 .266/C4
Concord, (Lewis County), Ky., U.S. 280/C2
Concord, (McCracken County), Ky., U.S. 280/B3
Concord, Mass., U.S., 16,993 . . . . .292/J3
Concord, Mich., U.S., 1,101 . . . . .294/E7
Concord, (Callaway County), Mo., U.S. 302/E2
Concord, (St. Louis County), Mo., U.S., 16,689 . .302/H3
Concord, Nebr., U.S., 160 . . . . .308/H1
Concord, N.H., U.S., *state capital*, 40,687 . . . . .312/C5
Concord, N.C., U.S., 55,977 . . . . .322/D4
Concord, Vt., U.S., 1,196 . . . . .352/D2
Concord, Va., U.S., 800 . . . . .354/E6
Concordia, Arg., 116,485 . . . . .191/D3
Concordia, Kans., U.S., 5,714 . . . . .276/E2
Concordia, Ky., U.S., 50 . . . . .280/D2
Concordia, La., U.S., *parish*, 20,247 . . . . .282/F4
Concordia, Mo., U.S., 2,360 . . . . .302/C3
Concordia, N.J., U.S., 3,658 . . . . .314/E3
Concrete, Wash., U.S., 790 . . . . .358/D1
Conda, Ida., U.S. 264/F7
Conde, S. Dak., U.S., 187 . . . . .342/G2
Condit, Ohio, U.S., 325 . . . . .328/E5
Condon, Mont., U.S., 60 . . . . .306/C2
Condon, Oreg., U.S., 759 . . . . .334/F2
Condor, Alta., Can. 212//C5
Cone, Tex., U.S., 70 . . . . .346/G2
Conecuh, Ala., U.S., *county*, 14,089 . . . . .238/C4
Conecuh, Ala., U.S., *river* 238/C4
Conecuh Natl. For., Ala., U.S. 238/C4
Conehatta, Miss., U.S., 997 . . . . .300/C3
Conejos, Colo., U.S., 125 . . . . .250/D4
Conejos, Colo., U.S., *county*, 8,400 . . . . .250/D4
Conemaugh, Penn., U.S., *river* 336/C4
Conesville, Iowa, U.S., 424 . . . . .274/M5
Conesville, Ohio, U.S., 364 . . . . .328/G5
Conetoe, N.C., U.S., 365 . . . . .322/L3
Conflans-Ste-Honorine, Fr. . . . . .88/Inset II
Confluence, Penn., U.S., 834 . . . . .336/C6
Confusion Range, Utah, U.S. 350/A4
Congaree Swamp Natl. Mon., S.C., U.S. 340/D3
Conger, Minn., U.S., 133 . . . . .298/D7
Congerville, Ill., U.S., 466 . . . . .266/D3
Congleton, Eng., U.K., 24,897 . . . . .68/C3
Congo, *nation* 149
Congo, (Zaire), Congo, D.R., *river* 155/B1
Congo, Congo, *basin* 155/D3
Congo, Congo, *river* 155/D4
Congo Basin, Congo, D.R., *region* 155/B1
Congresbury, Eng., U.K., 3,435 . . . . .73/G2
Congress, Ariz., U.S., 1,717 . . . . .242/C3
Congress, Ohio, U.S., 192 . . . . .328/F4
Conifer, Colo., U.S., 325 . . . . .250/E2
Coningsby, Eng., U.K., 5,126 . . . . .68/G3
Coniston, Eng., U.K. 66/B4
Coniston Water, Eng., U.K., *lake* 66/B4
Conklin, Alta., Can., 166 . . . . .212//E3
Conklin, N.Y., U.S., 850 . . . . .320/K6
Conlen, Tex., U.S. 346/F8
Conley, Ga., U.S., 6,188 . . . . .260/J3
Conn, Ire., U.S., *lake* 76/B1
Connah's Quay, Wales, U.K., 14,443 . . . . .64/E1
Connaught, Ire., *province* 76/B2
Conneaut, Ohio, U.S., 12,485 . . . . .328/J2
Conneaut Lake, Penn., U.S., 708 . . . . .336/A2
Conneaut Lake Park, Penn., U.S., 2,502 . . . . . . .336/A2
Conneautville, Penn., U.S., 848 . . . . .336/A2
Connecticut, U.S., *state* 241
Connecticut, Conn., U.S., *river* 253/E3
Connecticut, Mass., U.S., *river* 292/E2
Connecticut, N.H., U.S., *river* 312/B4, C2
Connecticut, Vt., U.S., *river* 352/C3, D1
Connel, Scot., U.K. 62/F6
Connell, Wash., U.S., 2,956 . . . . .358/G3
Connellsville, Penn., U.S., 9,146 . . . . .336/B5
Connelly Sprs., N.C., U.S., 1,814 . . . . .322/B3
Connemara, Ire., *region* 76/B2
Conner, Mont., U.S., 40 . . . . .306/B4
Connersville, Ind., U.S., 15,411 . . . . .270/F5
Connerville, Okla., U.S., 80 . . . . .330/F3
Connoquenessing, Penn., U.S., 564 . . . . .336/A4
Connor, Maine, U.S., 424 . . . . .286/D2
Connors, N.B., Can. 217/A1
Connorsville, Wisc., U.S., 175 . . . . .364/A3
Connorville, Mich., U.S. 294/C2
Conor, N. Ire., U.K., 114 . . . . .65/E2
Conover, N.C., U.S., 6,604 . . . . .322/C3
Conover, Wisc., U.S. 364/D2
Conovertown, N.J., U.S., 1,000 . . . . .314/E5
Conrad, Iowa, U.S., 1,055 . . . . .274/J3
Conrad, Mont., U.S., 2,753 . . . . .306/D1
Conrath, Wisc., U.S., 98 . . . . .364/B3
Conroe, Tex., U.S., 36,811 . . . . .346/N5
Conroy, Iowa, U.S., 175 . . . . .274/L4
Consecon, Ont., Can. 223/H4
Consett, Eng., U.K., 20,148 . . . . .66/E3
Conshohocken, Penn., U.S., 7,589 . . . . .336/L6
Con Son, Viet., *islands* .123/B5
Consort, Alta., Can., 634 . . . . .212//E5
Constableville, N.Y., U.S., 305 . . . . .320/L3
Constance, Ger. 86/B5
Constance, Ger., *lake* .91/A3
Constance, (Bodensee), Switz., *lake* 90/D1
Constance, Switz., *lake* 86/B5
Constanța, Rom., 337,216 . . . . .101/E3
Constanța, Rom., *county* 101/E3
Constantia, N.J., U.S., 1,107 . . . . .320/J4
Constantine, Alg., 563,505 . . . . .146/B1
Constantine, Mich., U.S., 2,095 . . . . .294/D8
Constellation, Ariz., U.S., 100 . . . . .242/C3
Constitución, Chile 190/B5
Constitution, Barb., *river* 209/B4
Consul, Sask., Can., 91 . . . . .227/A11
Contact, Nev., U.S. 310/C1
Contin, Scot., U.K. 62/G3
Continental, Ariz., U.S. .242/E6
Continental, Ohio, U.S., 1,188 . . . . .328/B3
Continental Divide, Colo., U.S. 250/C1, D3
Continental Divide, Mont., U.S. 306/D2
Continental Divide, N. Mex., U.S., 70 . . . . .317/B2
Continental Divide, N. Mex., U.S., 70 . . . . .317/C2
Continental Divide, Wyo., U.S. 366/B3
Contoocook, N.H., U.S., 1,444 . . . . .312/C5
Contra Costa, Calif., U.S., *county*, 948,816 . .246/K2, D5
Contrecoeur, Que., Can., 5,222 . . . . .226/C6
Contwoyto, Nun., Can., *lake* 208/G3
Convent, La., U.S., 250 . . . . .282/H6
Converse, Ind., U.S., 1,137 . . . . .270/E3
Converse, La., U.S., 400 . . . . .282/B3

Converse, Tex., U.S., 11,508 . . . . .346/A2
Converse, Wyo., U.S., *county*, 12,052 . . . . .366/D2
Convoy, Ohio, U.S., 1,110 . . . . .328/A4
Conway, Ark., U.S., 43,167 . . . . .244/C2
Conway, Ark., U.S., *county*, 20,336 . . . . .244/C2
Conway, Iowa, U.S., 63 . . . . .274/E6
Conway, Ky., U.S., 225 .280/F3
Conway, Mass., U.S., 1,809 . . . . .292/D2
Conway, Mich., U.S., 275 . . . . .294/E4
Conway, Mo., U.S., 743 . . . . .302/D4
Conway, N.H., U.S., 8,604 . . . . .312/D4
Conway, N.C., U.S., 734 . . . . .322/L2
Conway, N. Dak., U.S. .326/H1
Conway, Penn., U.S., 2,290 . . . . .336/A4
Conway, S.C., U.S., 11,788 . . . . .340/E3
Conway, Wash., U.S., 84 . . . . .358/C1
Conway Sprs., Kans., U.S., 1,322 . . . . .276/E4
Conwy, Wales, U.K. 60/B3
Conwy, Wales, U.K., 3,627 . . . . .64/D1
Conwy, Wales, U.K., *bay* 64/D1
Conwy, Wales, U.K., *unitary authority*, 109,597 . .64/D1
Conyers, Ga., U.S., 10,689 . . . . .260/C4, K3
Conyngham, Penn., U.S., 1,958 . . . . .336/J4
Coober Pedy, S.A., Austl. 170/C2
Cook, Alaska, U.S., *inlet* 240/E3
Cook, N.Z., *strait* 171/B3
Cook, Ga., U.S., *county*, 15,771 . . . . .260/E9
Cook, Ill., U.S., *county*, 5,376,741 . . . . . .266/C6, F2
Cook, Minn., U.S., 622 .298/E3
Cook, Minn., U.S., *county*, 5,168 . . . . .298/F2, F3
Cook, Nebr., U.S., 322 .308/H3
Cooke, Tex., U.S., *county*, 36,363 . . . . .346/L2
Cooke City, Mont., U.S., 140 . . . . .306/G4
Cooke's, N. Mex., U.S., *peak* 317/C5
Cookeville, Tenn., U.S., 23,923 . . . . .344/K2
Cookietown, Okla., U.S. 330/D3
Cook Islands, N.Z., *dependency* 161
Cooks, Mich., U.S., 100 . . . . .294/C4
Cooks Hammock, Fla., U.S. 256/E2
Cooks Harbour, Nfld., Can., 226 . . . . .206/D3
Cookshire, Que., Can., 1,543 . . . . .226/E6
Cooks Mills, Maine, U.S., 325 . . . . .286/B5
Cook Sta., Mo., U.S. 302/E4
Cookstown, Ont., Can. .223/F3
Cookstown, N. Ire., U.K., 10,472 . . . . .65/D2
Cookstown, N. Ire., U.K.,
   unitary authority, 32,581 . . . . .65/D2
Cooksville, Ill., U.S., 213 . . . . .266/E3
Cooksville, Md., U.S., 125 . . . . .288/F2
Cooksville, Wisc., U.S., 125 . . . . .364/D6
Cool, Tex., U.S., 162 . . . . .346/L3
Cooleemee, N.C., U.S., 905 . . . . .322/D3
Coolham, Eng., U.K. 70/D5
Coolidge, Ariz., U.S., 7,786 . . . . .242/D5
Coolidge, Ga., U.S., 552 . . . . .260/D9
Coolidge, Kans., U.S., 86 . . . . .276/A3
Coolidge, N. Mex., U.S., 50 . . . . .317/B2
Coolidge, Tex., U.S., 848 . . . . .346/M4
Coolin, Ida., U.S., 100 .264/A1
Cool Sprs., Ky., U.S. 280/D3
Cool Valley, Mo., U.S., 1,081 . . . . .302/H3
Coolin, Ida., U.S., 100 .328/C7
Coon Rapids, Iowa, U.S., 1,305 . . . . .274/E4
Coon Rapids, Minn., U.S., 61,607 . . . . .298/D5, E5
Coon Valley, Wisc., U.S., 714 . . . . .364/B5
Cooper, Ala., U.S., 250 .238/C3
Cooper, Iowa, U.S., 50 .274/F4
Cooper, Ky., U.S., 100 .280/F4
Cooper, Mo., U.S., *county*, 16,670 . . . . .302/D3
Cooper, Tex., U.S., 2,150 . . . . .346/N2
Co-Operative, Ky., U.S. .280/F4
Cooper City, Fla., U.S., 27,939 . . . . .256/A6
Cooperdale, Ohio, U.S., 175 . . . . .328/F5
Cooper Hts., Ga., U.S., 175 . . . . .260/A2
Cooper Road, La., U.S., 175 . . . . .282/B1
Coopersburg, Penn., U.S., 2,582 . . . . .336/L4
Coopers Mills, Maine, U.S., 350 . . . . .286/C4
Coopers Plains, Qnsld., Austl. . . . . .170/Inset III
Cooperstown, N.Y., U.S., 2,032 . . . . .320/M5
Cooperstown, N. Dak., U.S., 1,053 . . . . .326/G2
Cooperstown, Penn., U.S., 460 . . . . .336/B2
Coopersville, Mich., U.S., 3,910 . . . . .294/D6
Cooperton, Okla., U.S. .330/D3
Coos, N.H., U.S., *county*, 33,111 . . . . .312/D2
Coos, Oreg., U.S., *bay* 334/C4
Coos, Oreg., U.S., *county*, 62,779 . . . . .334/C4
Coosa, Ala., U.S., *county*, 12,202 . . . . .238/C3
Coosa, Ala., U.S., *river* 238/D1
Coosa, Ga., U.S. 260/A3
Coosa, Ga., U.S., *river* 260/D2
Coosada, Ala., U.S., 1,382 . . . . .238/C3
Coosawhatchie, S.C., U.S., 150 . . . . .340/D4
Coos Bay, Oreg., U.S., 15,374 . . . . .334/B4
Cooter, Mo., U.S., 440 .302/G5
Copalis Beach, Wash., U.S., 489 . . . . .358/A2
Copalis Crossing, Wash., U.S., 100 . . . . .358/A2
Copán, Hond., *department* 202/A2
Copán, Hond., *ruins* 202/A2
Copan, Okla., U.S., 796 . . . . .330/G1
Copco, Calif., U.S. 246/C1
Copdock, Eng., U.K. 70/G2
Cope, Colo., U.S., 50 . . . . .250/H2
Cope, S.C., U.S., 107 . . . . .340/C3
Copeland, N. Ire., U.K., *island* 65/F2
Copeland, Fla., U.S., 80 . . . . .256/G6
Copeland, Kans., U.S., 339 . . . . .276/B4
Copemish, Mich., U.S., 232 . . . . .294/D5
Copenhagen, Den., *capital*, 500,531,
   (1,084,556 *metro*.) 79/D3
Copenhagen, Den., *capital* 193/D1
Copenhagen, N.Y., U.S., 865 . . . . .320/K3
Copiah, Miss., U.S., *county*, 28,757 . . . . .300/B4
Copiapó, Chile, 100,946 . . . . .190/B3
Copiapó, Chile, *river* 190/B3
Coplay, Penn., U.S., 3,387 . . . . .336/K4
Coplin, Maine, U.S., 135 . . . . .286/B3
Coppell, Tex., U.S., 35,958 . . . . .346/B9
Coppename, Sur., *river* 183/A2
Copper, Alaska, U.S., *river* 240/G2
Copper, Wash., U.S., *butte* 358/G1
Copperas Cove, Tex., U.S., 29,592 . . . . .346/L4
Copperbelt, Zam., *province* 159/B2
Copper Canyon, Tex., U.S., 1,216 . . . . .346/B8
Copper City, Alaska, U.S., 362 . . . . .240/F2
Copper Ctr., Alaska, U.S., 205 . . . . .294/A2
Copperfield, Nev., U.S. .310/A2
Copper Harbor, Mich., U.S., 50 . . . . .294/B2
Copperhill, Tenn., U.S., 511 . . . . .344/N5
Coppermine, N.W. Terr., Can., *river* 208/F3
Copper Mtn., Colo., U.S., 150 . . . . .250/D2
Copplestone, Eng., U.K. 73/E3
Coppock, Iowa, U.S., 57 . . . . .274/L5
Copthorne, Eng., U.K., 3,930 . . . . .70/D4
Coquí, P.R. 206/C3
Coquille, Oreg., U.S., 4,184 . . . . .334/B4
Coquimbo, Chile 190/B3
Coquimbo, Chile, *region* 190/B4
Cora, Wyo., U.S., 76 . . . . .366/B2

Coral, Austl., *sea* 170/E1
Coral, P.N.G., *sea* 172/A3
Coral, Van., *sea* 173/B3
Coral Gables, Fla., U.S., 42,249 . . . . .256/A6, H6
Coral Harbour, Nun., Can., 712 . . . . .208/N4
Coral Hills, Md., U.S., 10,720 . . . . .288/C7
Coral Sprs., Fla., U.S., 117,549 . . . . .256/A5, H5
Coralville, Iowa, U.S., 15,123 . . . . .274/L4
Coralville, Iowa, U.S., *lake* 274/L4
Coram, Mont., U.S., 337 . . . . .306/B1
Coram, N.Y., U.S., 34,923 . . . . .320/E2
Corantijn, Sur., *river* 183/A2
Coraopolis, Penn., U.S., 6,131 . . . . .336/A4
Corapeake, N.C., U.S., 350 . . . . .322/M1
Corazón, P.R. 206/C3
Corbeil-Essonnes, Fr. . . . . .88/Inset II
Corbett, Okla., U.S., 125 . . . . .330/E3
Corbin, Kans., U.S., 60 .276/E4
Corbin, Ky., U.S., 7,742 . . . . .280/F4
Corbin, La., U.S. 282/H6
Corbin, Mont., U.S., 100 . . . . .306/D3
Corbin City, N.J., U.S., 468 . . . . .314/D5
Corby, Eng., U.K., 2,719 . . . . .66/D3
Corby, Eng., U.K., 49,053 . . . . .68/F5
Corby, Eng., U.K., 49,053 . . . . .70/C1
Corby Glen, Eng., U.K. .70/C1
Corcoran, Calif., U.S., 14,458 . . . . .246/F6
Corcoran, Minn., U.S., 5,630 . . . . .298/D5
Corcovado, Braz., *mountain* . . . . .188/Inset I
Corcovado, Chile, *gulf* .190/B6
Cord, Ark., U.S., 70 . . . . .244/D2
Cordele, Ga., U.S., 11,608 . . . . .260/D8
Cordele, Tex., U.S. 346/M6
Cordell, Okla., U.S., 2,867 . . . . .330/D2
Cordell, Wash., U.S., 50 . . . . .358/F1
Corder, Mo., U.S., 427 .302/C2
Cordillera, Para., *department* 187/D4
Cordillera Administrative Region, Phil., *region* . .120/B2
Cordillera Central, Bol., *mountains* 186/A3
Cordillera Central, Col., *range* 184/A4
Cordillera Central, Phil., *mountains* 120/B2
Cordillera Central, P.R., *mountains* 206/B2
Cordillera Occidental, Bol., *mountains* 186/A3
Cordillera Occidental, Col., *range* 184/A4
Cordillera Occidental, Ecua., *mountains* 185/B4
Cordillera Oriental, Bol., *mountains* 186/A4
Cordillera Oriental, Col., *range* 184/B4
Cordillera Oriental, Ecua., *mountains* 185/C4
Cordillera Real, Bol., *mountains* 186/A3
Córdoba, Sp., 308,072 .94/D4
Córdoba, Sp., *province* 94/D3
Córdoba, Arg., 1,157,507, (1,208,554 *metro*.) . .191/C3
Córdoba, Arg., *province* 191/C3
Córdoba, Arg., *range* 191/B3
Córdoba, Col., *department* 184/B2
Cordova, Ala., U.S., 2,423 . . . . .238/B2
Cordova, Alaska, U.S., 2,454 . . . . .240/F2
Cordova, Ill., U.S., 633 .266/C2
Cordova, Md., U.S., 592 . . . . .288/L4
Cordova, Nebr., U.S., 127 . . . . .308/G3
Cordova, N. Mex., U.S., 225 . . . . .317/E1
Cordova, N.C., U.S., 1,100 . . . . .322/F5
Cordova, S.C., U.S., 157 . . . . .340/D3
Cordova, Tenn., U.S., 2,800 . . . . .344/B4
Core, W. Va., U.S., 125 .360/F1
Corea, Maine, U.S., 450 . . . . .286/E4
Corfe, Eng., U.K. 73/F3
Corfe Castle, Eng., U.K. 73/H3
Corfu, N.Y., U.S., 795 . . . . .320/E5
Corgarff, Scot., U.K. 62/K4
Corinna, Maine, U.S., 2,145 . . . . .286/C4
Corinne, Utah, U.S., 621 . . . . .350/B2
Corinth, Gr. 100/B3
Corinth, Gr., *gulf* 100/B2
Corinth, Gr., *isthmus* .100/B3
Corinth, Ark., U.S., 65 .244/B2
Corinth, Ga., U.S., 213 .260/B5
Corinth, (Grant County), Ky., U.S., 181 . . . . .280/F2
Corinth, (Logan County), Ky., U.S., 50 . . . . .280/D4
Corinth, Miss., U.S., 14,054 . . . . .300/D1
Corinth, N.Y., U.S., 2,474 . . . . .320/P4
Corinth, Tex., U.S., 11,325 . . . . .346/B8
Corinth, W. Va., U.S., 275 . . . . .360/H2
Corinth Corners, Vt., U.S., 90 . . . . .352/C2
Corinto, Nicar. 202/A2
Corisco, Eq. Gui., *bay* .154/B4
Corisco, Eq. Gui., *island* 154/B4
Cork, Ire., 123,338 . . . . .76/B3
Cork, Ire., *county* 76/B3
Cork County Borough, Ire., *county* 76/B3
Cormack, Br. Col., N.W. Terr., Can., *lake* 214/M1
Cormack, Nfld., Can., 675 . . . . .206/C4
Cormierville, N.B., Can. 217/E2
Cormoran, Palau, *reef* .172/B2
Cormorant, Man., Can., 400 . . . . .215/A2
Cormorant, Man., Can., *lake* 215/A2
Cormorant, Minn., U.S., 70 . . . . .298/A4
Corn, Okla., U.S., 591 .330/D2
Cornelia, Ga., U.S., 3,674 . . . . .260/D2
Cornelia, Iowa, U.S., 150 . . . . .274/G2
Cornelius, N.C., U.S., 11,969 . . . . .322/D4
Cornell, Ill., U.S., 511 . . . . .266/E3
Cornell, Mich., U.S., 90 . . . . .294/B4
Cornell, Wisc., U.S., 1,466 . . . . .364/B3
Cornellà de Llogregat, Sp., 79,979 . . . . .94/G2
Corner Brook, Nfld., Can., 20,103 . . . . .206/C5
Cornersville, Ark., U.S. .244/D3
Cornersville, Md., U.S., 175 . . . . .288/K5
Cornersville, Tenn., U.S., 962 . . . . .344/H4
Cornerville, Ark., U.S., 100 . . . . .244/D4
Cornerstone, Ark., U.S. 244/D3
Cornettsville, Ind., U.S., 70 . . . . .270/B7
Cornettsville, Ky., U.S., 125 . . . . .280/G3
Cornhill, Scot., U.K. 217/D3
Cornhill, Scot., U.K. 62/K4
Corning, Ark., U.S., 3,679 . . . . .244/E1
Corning, Calif., U.S., 6,741 . . . . .246/C3
Corning, Iowa, U.S., 1,783 . . . . .274/E6
Corning, Kans., U.S., 170 . . . . .276/F2
Corning, Mo., U.S. 302/A1
Corning, N.Y., U.S., 10,842 . . . . .320/G6
Corning, Ohio, U.S., 593 . . . . .328/F6
Cornish, Colo., U.S. 250/F1
Cornish, Maine, U.S., 1,269 . . . . .286/B5
Cornish, Okla., U.S., 172 . . . . .330/E3
Cornish, Utah, U.S., 259 . . . . .350/C2
Cornish City, N.H., U.S., 1,661 . . . . .312/B5
Cornish Flat, N.H., U.S., 325 . . . . .312/B5
Cornlea, Nebr., U.S., 41 . . . . .308/G2
Corno Grande, It., *mountain* 95/C2
Cornucopia, Wisc., U.S., 100 . . . . .364/B1
Cornudas, Tex., U.S. 346/C4
Cornville, Ariz., U.S., 3,335 . . . . .242/D3
Cornville, Maine, U.S., 1,208 . . . . .286/C4
Cornwall, Nun., Can., *island* 208/K1
Cornwall, Ont., Can., 45,640 . . . . .223/J2
Cornwall, P.E.I., Can., 4,412 . . . . .224/B2
Cornwall and Isles of Scilly, Eng., U.K.,
   unitary authority, 501,267 . . . . .73/A3, B4
Cornwall, Conn., U.S., 1,434 . . . . .253/B2
Cornwall, Penn., U.S., 3,486 . . . . .336/J5

Cornwall, Vt., U.S., 1,136 ...352/A3
Cornwall Bridge, Conn., U.S., 125 ...253/B2
Cornwallis, Nun., Can., island ...208/J1
Cornwall on Hudson, N.Y., U.S., 3,058 ...320/N8
Cornwell, Fla., U.S., 70 ...256/G4
Cornwell, S.C., U.S., 125 ...340/C2
Coro, Ven., 125,183, (136,379 metro.) ...182/C1
Corolla, N.C., U.S. ...322/P2
Coromandel, India, coast ...128/D6
Coromandel, N.Z., peninsula ...171/C2
Corona, Calif., U.S., 124,966 ...246/F10
Corona, N. Mex., U.S., 165 ...317/E3
Corona, S. Dak., U.S., 112 ...342/J2
Coronaca, S.C., U.S., 170 ...340/B2
Coronach, Sask., Can., 822 ...227/E11
Coronado, C.R., bay ...203/B3
Coronado, Calif., U.S., 24,100 ...246/H10
Coronado Natl. For., Ariz., U.S. ...242/D6, E5, E6, F6
Coronado Natl. For., N. Mex., U.S. ...317/A6
Coronado Natl. Mem., Ariz., U.S. ...242/E6
Coronation, Alta., Can., 902 ...212/J5
Coronation, Nun., Can., gulf ...208/F3
Coronel Oviedo, Para. ...187/D4
Coropuna, Peru, mountain ...185/C4
Corovodë, Alb. ...99/B3
Corozal, Bel., 7,888 ...201/B1
Corozal, P.R. ...206/C2
Corpus Christi, Tex., U.S., 277,454, (380,783 metro.) ...346/L8
Corral, Ida., U.S. ...264/C6
Corral City, Tex., U.S., 89 ...346/B8
Corrales, N. Mex., U.S., 7,334 ...317/D2
Corralitos, Calif., U.S., 2,431 ...246/K4
Corran, Scot., U.K. ...62/F5
Correctionville, Iowa, U.S., 851 ...274/C3
Corregidor, Phil., island ...120/B3
Correll, Minn., U.S., 47 ...298/A5
Correo, N. Mex., U.S. ...317/C3
Corrèze, Fr., department ...88/C4
Corrib, Ire., lake ...76/B2
Corrientes, Arg., 258,103 ...191/D2
Corrientes, Arg., province ...191/D2
Corrigan, Tex., U.S., 1,721 ...346/P5
Corriganville, Md., U.S., 1,000 ...288/C3
Corringham, Eng., U.K. ...66/G6
Corris Uchaf, Wales, U.K. ...64/D2
Corry, Penn., U.S., 6,834 ...336/B2
Corse, Fr., territorial collectivity ...88/Inset I
Corse-du-Sud, Fr., department ...88/Inset I
Corsica, Fr., island ...88/Inset I
Corsica, Penn., U.S., 354 ...336/C3
Corsica, S. Dak., U.S., 644 ...342/G4
Corsicana, Tex., U.S., 24,485 ...346/M3
Corsock, Scot., U.K. ...62/J8
Corson, S. Dak., U.S., county, 4,181 ...342/D2
Corston, Eng., U.K. ...73/J1
Cortachy, Scot., U.K. ...62/L5
Cortaro, Ariz., U.S., 1,700 ...242/D5
Corte Madera, Calif., U.S., 9,100 ...246/H1
Cortés, Hond., department ...202/A2
Cortez, Colo., U.S., 7,977 ...250/B4
Cortina d'Ampezzo, It. ...95/C1
Cortland, Ill., U.S., 2,066 ...266/E2
Cortland, Nebr., U.S., 488 ...308/H3
Cortland, N.Y., U.S., 18,740 ...320/J5
Cortland, N.Y., U.S., county, 48,599 ...320/J5
Cortland, Ohio, U.S., 6,830 ...328/J3
Corton, Eng., U.K. ...70/H1
Cortona, It. ...95/C3
Corubal, Gui.-B., river ...149/D1
Çoruh, Tur., river ...133/E2
Çorum, Tur. ...133/C2
Çorum, Tur., province ...133/C2
Corum, Okla., U.S., 40 ...330/D3
Corumbá, Braz., 75,235, (88,290 metro.) ...188/C3
Corumbau, Braz., point ...188/E3
Coruna, Ind., U.S., 254 ...270/F2
Corunna, Mich., U.S., 3,381 ...294/E6, G7
Corvallis, Mont., U.S., 443 ...306/B3
Corvallis, Oreg., U.S., 49,322, (78,153 metro.) ...334/C3
Corwen, Wales, U.K. ...64/E2
Corwin, Kans., U.S. ...276/D4
Corwin, Ohio, U.S., 256 ...328/B6
Corwin Sprs., Mont., U.S. ...306/F4
Corwith, Iowa, U.S., 350 ...274/G2
Cory, Ind., U.S., 175 ...270/B6
Corydon, Ind., U.S., 2,715 ...270/D8
Corydon, Iowa, U.S., 1,591 ...274/H6
Corydon, Ky., U.S., 744 ...280/C3
Corydon Jct., Ind., U.S., 650 ...270/D8
Coryell, Tex., U.S., county, 74,978 ...346/L4
Coryville, Penn., U.S., 212/ ...336/E2
Cosby, Mo., U.S., 143 ...302/B2
Cosenza, It. ...95/D3
Cosham, Eng., U.K. ...70/B5
Coshocton, Ohio, U.S., 11,682 ...328/G5
Coshocton, Ohio, U.S., county, 36,655 ...328/G5
Cosigüina, Nicar., point ...202/A2
Cosigüina, Nicar., volcano ...202/A2
Coslada, Sp. ...94/Inset II
Cosmoledo, Sey., island group ...163/A2
Cosmopolis, Wash., U.S., 1,595 ...358/B3
Cosmos, Minn., U.S., 582 ...298/C6
Coso Jct., Calif., U.S. ...246/H6
Cost, Tex., U.S., 100 ...346/L6
Costa Mesa, Calif., U.S., 108,724 ...246/E11
Costa Rica, nation ...191
Costen, Md., U.S., 80 ...288/M7
Costessey, Eng., U.K., 2,203 ...70/G1
Costigan, Maine, U.S., 100 ...286/D3
Costilla, Colo., U.S., county, 3,663 ...250/E4
Costilla, N. Mex., U.S., 100 ...317/E1
Cosumnes, Calif., U.S., river ...246/L5
Cotabato, Phil., 163,849 ...120/C5
Cotati, Calif., U.S., 6,471 ...246/C4
Coteau, N. Dak., U.S. ...
Coteau Holmes, La., U.S., 175 ...282/F6
Côte d'Ivoire, nation ...144
Côte-d'Or, Fr., department ...88/D3
Cotentin, Fr., peninsula ...88/B2
Côtes-du-Nord, Fr., department ...88/B2
Cotesfield, Nebr., U.S., 66 ...308/E2
Cotgrave, Eng., U.K., 7,364 ...70/B1
Cotia, Braz. ...188/Inset II
Cotilla, Cuba, caves ...204/B2
Coto de Caza, Calif., U.S., 13,057 ...246/F11
Coto Laurel, P.R. ...206/B2
Coto Norte, P.R. ...206/C2
Cotonou, Ben., 650,660 ...145/F4
Cotopaxi, Ecua., province ...185/B3
Cotopaxi, Ecua., volcano ...185/B3
Cotopaxi, Colo., U.S. ...250/D3
Cotswold, Eng., U.K., hills ...60/C6
Cotswold, Eng., U.K., hills ...68/C6
Cottage City, Md., U.S., 1,136 ...288/C7
Cottage Grove, Minn., U.S., 30,582 ...298/F6
Cottage Grove, Oreg., U.S., 8,445 ...334/C4
Cottage Grove, Tenn., U.S., 97 ...344/B2
Cottage Grove, Wisc., U.S., 4,059 ...364/D5
Cottage Hill, Fla., U.S., 1,300 ...256/A1
Cottageville, S.C., U.S., 707 ...340/D4
Cottageville, W. Va., U.S., 750 ...360/C3

Cottbus, Ger., 110,894 ...86/C3
Cottenham, Eng., U.K., 4,486 ...68/H5
Cottenham, Eng., U.K., 4,486 ...70/E2
Cotter, Ark., U.S., 921 ...244/C1
Cotter, Iowa, U.S., 48 ...274/M5
Cottingham, Eng., U.K. ...66/H5
Cottisford, Eng., U.K. ...70/B3
Cottle, Tex., U.S., county, 1,904 ...346/H1
Cottleville, Mo., U.S., 1,928 ...302/G2
Cotton, Eng., U.K. ...70/F2
Cotton, Ga., U.S., 80 ...260/C9
Cotton, Minn., U.S., 70 ...298/E3
Cotton City, N. Mex., U.S., 100 ...317/B5
Cotton, Okla., U.S., county, 6,614 ...330/D3
Cottondale, Ala., U.S., 2,000 ...238/B2
Cottondale, Fla., U.S., 869 ...256/C1
Cotton Ground, St. K.-Nevis ...207/C1
Cotton Plant, Ark., U.S., 960 ...244/D2
Cottonport, La., U.S., 2,316 ...282/E5
Cottonton, Ala., U.S. ...238/D3
Cottonwood (Apache County), Ariz., U.S. ...242/F1
Cottonwood (Yavapai County), Ariz., U.S., 9,179 ...242/D3
Cottonwood, Calif., U.S., 2,960 ...246/C2
Cottonwood, Ida., U.S., 944 ...264/A3
Cottonwood, Ill., U.S., 60 ...266/E6
Cottonwood, Minn., U.S., 1,148 ...298/B6
Cottonwood, Minn., U.S., county, 12,167 ...298/B6
Cottonwood, S. Dak., U.S. ...342/D4
Cottonwood, Tex., U.S. ...346/M5
Cottonwood Cove, Nev., U.S., 100 ...310/C4
Cottonwood Heights, Utah, U.S., 27,569 ...350/E2
Cottonwood Shores, Tex., U.S., 877 ...346/C2
Cottonwood West, Utah, U.S., 18,727 ...350/C3
Cotuí, Dom. Rep. ...205/B1
Cotuit, Mass., U.S., 2,400 ...292/N6
Cotulla, Tex., U.S., 3,614 ...346/J7
Coubert, Fr. ...88/Inset II
Couch, Mo., U.S. ...302/E5
Couchwood, La., U.S., 100 ...282/C1
Couderay, Wisc., U.S., 96 ...364/B3
Coudersport, Penn., U.S., 2,650 ...336/E2
Cougar, Wash., U.S., 90 ...358/C3
Coughran, Tex., U.S. ...346/K7
Coulee, N. Dak., U.S. ...326/C1
Coulee City, Wash., U.S., 600 ...358/F2
Coulee Dam, Wash., U.S., 1,044 ...358/G2
Coulter, Scot., U.K. ...62/J7
Coulter, Iowa, U.S., 262 ...274/H2
Coulterville, Calif., U.S., 100 ...246/E5
Coulterville, Ill., U.S., 1,230 ...266/D5
Counce, Tenn., U.S., 225 ...344/E4
Council, Ga., U.S. ...260/F1
Council, Ida., U.S., 816 ...264/A5
Council, N.C., U.S., 60 ...322/J6
Council Bluffs, Iowa, U.S., 58,268 ...274/C5
Council Grove, Kans., U.S., 2,321 ...276/F3
Council Hill, Okla., U.S., 129 ...330/G2
Counselor, N. Mex., U.S., 50 ...317/C1
Country Club, Calif., U.S., 9,462 ...246/L1
Country Club Estates, Ga., U.S., 7,594 ...260/D9
Country Club Hts., Ind., U.S., 91 ...270/E4
Country Club Hills, Ill., U.S., 16,169 ...266/B6
Country Club Vil., Mo., U.S., 1,846 ...302/A2
Country Homes, Wash., U.S., 5,203 ...358/H2
Country Knolls, N.Y., U.S., 2,155 ...320/P5
Country Lake Estates, N.J., U.S., 4,012 ...314/D4
Country Life Acres, Mo., U.S., 81 ...302/H3
Countryside, Ill., U.S., 5,991 ...266/B6
Countryside, Kans., U.S., 295 ...276/H1
Countryside, Va., U.S., 8,300 ...354/J2, L1
County Line (Blount County), Ala., U.S., 257 ...238/C2
County Line (Covington County), Ala., U.S., 125 ...238/C4
County Line, Okla., U.S., 212/ ...330/E3
Coupar Angus, Scot., U.K., 2,190 ...62/K5
Coupeville, Wash., U.S., 1,723 ...358/C1
Coupland, Tex., U.S., 212/ ...346/E2
Courantyne, Guy., river ...183/B3
Courland, Lith., lagoon ...82/A2
Courtdale, Penn., U.S., 791 ...336/G2
Courtenay, Br. Col., Can., 18,304 ...214/K6
Courtenay, N. Dak., U.S., 53 ...326/G2
Courtland, Ala., U.S., 769 ...238/C1
Courtland, Calif., U.S., 375 ...246/D4, K6, L1
Courtland, Kans., U.S., 334 ...276/F2
Courtland, Minn., U.S., 538 ...298/C6
Courtland, Miss., U.S., 460 ...300/C1
Courtland, Va., U.S., 1,270 ...354/J7
Courtney, Okla., U.S. ...330/E4
Courtsend, Eng., U.K. ...70/F3
Courval, Sask., Can. ...227/D10
Coushatta, La., U.S., 2,299 ...282/C2
Coutts, Alta., Can., 364 ...212/J6
Couva, Trin.-To. ...209/A2
Cove, Eng., U.K. ...70/C4
Cove, Eng., U.K. ...73/F3
Cove, Scot., U.K. ...62/E3
Cove, Ariz., U.S., 125 ...242/F1
Cove, Ark., U.S., 383 ...244/A3
Cove, Oreg., U.S., 594 ...334/J2
Cove, Tex., U.S., 323 ...346/C6
Cove City, N.C., U.S., 433 ...322/L4
Cove Fort, Utah, U.S. ...350/B5
Covelo, Calif., U.S., 1,175 ...246/B3
Coveney, Eng., U.K. ...70/E2
Coventry, Eng., U.K. ...60/C3
Coventry, Eng., U.K., 299,316, (495,367 metro.) ...68/C5
Coventry, Eng., U.K., (495,367 metro.) ...70/B2
Coventry, Eng., U.K., unitary authority, 300,844 ...68/D5
Coventry, Eng., U.K., unitary authority, 300,844 ...70/A2
Coventry, Conn., U.S., 11,504 ...253/F2
Coventry, Vt., U.S., 1,014 ...352/C1
Coventry Ctr., R.I., U.S., 850 ...339/C3
Cove Pt., Md., U.S., 275 ...288/J6
Coverack, Eng., U.K. ...73/B4
Coverdale, Ga., U.S., 50 ...260/D8
Covered Wells, Ariz., U.S., 60 ...242/C5
Covert, Kans., U.S. ...276/D2
Covert, Mich., U.S., 650 ...294/C7
Covesville, Va., U.S., 100 ...354/F5
Covilh, Port. ...93/B2
Covina, Calif., U.S., 46,837 ...246/E9
Covington, Ala., U.S., county, 37,631 ...238/C4
Covington, Ga., U.S., 11,547 ...260/D4
Covington, Ind., U.S., 2,565 ...270/B4
Covington, Ky., U.S., 43,370 ...280/G1
Covington, La., U.S., 8,483 ...282/J6
Covington, Mich., U.S., 40 ...294/A3
Covington, Miss., U.S., county, 19,407 ...300/C4
Covington, Ohio, U.S., 2,559 ...328/B5
Covington, Okla., U.S., 553 ...330/E1
Covington, Tenn., U.S., 8,463 ...344/B3
Covington, Va., U.S., 6,303 ...354/D5
Covington (Covington-Sawyer-Wilderness), Wash., U.S., 13,783 ...358/B4
Cowan, Man., Can. ...215/A3
Cowan, Ky., U.S., 212/ ...280/G2

Cowan, Tenn., U.S., 1,770 ...344/J4
Cowan Hts., (part of Tustin Foothills), Calif., U.S., 4,700 ...246/E10
Cowansville, Que., Can., 12,032 ...226/D6
Coward, S.C., U.S., 650 ...340/E3
Cowarts, Ala., U.S., 1,546 ...238/D4
Cowbridge, Wales, U.K., 3,682 ...64/E5
Cowden, Eng., U.K. ...70/E4
Cowden, Ill., U.S., 612 ...266/E4
Cowdrey, Colo., U.S. ...250/D1
Cowen, W. Va., U.S., 513 ...360/E4
Cowes, Eng., U.K. ...60/C4
Cowes, Eng., U.K., 16,335 ...70/B5
Coweta, Ga., U.S., county, 89,215 ...260/B5
Coweta, Okla., U.S., 7,139 ...330/G2
Cowfold, Eng., U.K., 1,564 ...70/D5
Cowgill, Mo., U.S., 247 ...302/C2
Cow Green, Eng., U.K., reservoir ...66/D3
Cowichan, Br. Col., Can., lake ...358/A1
Cowie, Scot., U.K., 2,387 ...62/J6
Cowles, Nebr., U.S., 48 ...308/E3
Cowles, N. Mex., U.S. ...317/E2
Cowley, Eng., U.K. ...68/E6
Cowley, Kans., U.S., county, 36,291 ...276/F4
Cowley, Wyo., U.S., 560 ...366/B1
Cowlic, Ariz., U.S., 100 ...242/C6
Cowlington, Okla., U.S., 133 ...330/H2
Cowlitz, Wash., U.S., county, 92,948 ...358/C3
Cowlitz, Wash., U.S., river ...358/D3
Cowold, Eng., U.K. ...66/F4
Cowpens, S.C., U.S., 2,279 ...340/C1, F1
Cowpens Natl. Bfld., S.C., U.S. ...340/C1
Cowshill, Eng., U.K. ...66/D3
Cow Sprs., Ariz., U.S., 225 ...242/E1
Cox, Ga., U.S., 60 ...260/H9
Cox City, Okla., U.S. ...330/E3
Coxhoe, Eng., U.K., 2,395 ...66/E3
Coxsackie, N.Y., U.S., 2,895 ...320/P6
Coxs Bazar, Bangl. ...127/E7
Cox Cove, Nfld., Can., 719 ...206/B4
Coxs Mills, W. Va., U.S., 50 ...360/E2
Coy, Ark., U.S., 116 ...244/D3
Coyah, Guin. ...149/B3
Coyanosa, Tex., U.S., 138 ...346/E4
Coyle, Okla., U.S., 337 ...330/E2
Coylton, Scot., U.K., 2,409 ...62/H8
Coylumbridge, Scot., U.K. ...62/J4
Coyoacán, Mex. ...200/Inset
Coyote, (Lincoln County), N. Mex., U.S. ...317/E4
Coyote, (Rio Arriba County), N. Mex., U.S., 80 ...317/D1
Coyote Canyon, N. Mex., U.S., 40 ...317/B2
Coyville, Kans., U.S., 71 ...276/G4
Cozad, Nebr., U.S., 4,163 ...308/E3
Cozumel, Mex., island ...200/G3
Crab Orchard, Ill., U.S., lake ...266/D6
Crab Orchard, Ky., U.S., 842 ...280/F3
Crab Orchard, Nebr., U.S., 49 ...308/H3
Crab Orchard, Tenn., U.S., 838 ...344/M3
Crab Orchard, W. Va., U.S., 2,761 ...360/D5
Crab Orchard N.W.R., Ill., U.S. ...266/D6
Crabtree, Ark., U.S., 70 ...244/C2
Crabtree, Oreg., U.S., 350 ...334/D3
Crackenthorpe, Eng., U.K. ...66/C3
Crackington Haven, Eng., U.K. ...73/C3
Cradock, S. Afr. ...162/C3
Crafton, Penn., U.S., 6,706 ...336/D7
Craftsbury, Vt., U.S., 1,136 ...352/C1
Craftsbury Common, Vt., U.S., 275 ...352/C1
Cragford, Ala., U.S., 90 ...238/D2
Craig, Alaska, U.S., 1,397 ...240/J3
Craig, Colo., U.S., 9,189 ...250/C1
Craig, Iowa, U.S., 102 ...274/B2
Craig, Mo., U.S., 309 ...302/A1
Craig, Mont., U.S., 60 ...306/E2
Craig, Nebr., U.S., 241 ...308/H2
Craig, Okla., U.S., county, 14,950 ...330/G1
Craig, Va., U.S., county, 5,091 ...354/C6
Craigavon, N. Ire., U.K., 9,201 ...65/D3
Craigavon, N. Ire., U.K., unitary authority, 80,671 ...65/E3
Craig Beach, Ohio, U.S., 1,254 ...328/H3
Craigellachie, Scot., U.K. ...62/K4
Craig Goch, Wales, U.K., reservoir ...64/D3
Craighead, Ark., U.S., county, 82,148 ...244/E2
Craigmont, Ida., U.S., 556 ...264/A3
Craigmyle, Alta., Can. ...212/J5
Craig Penllyn, Wales, U.K. ...64/E5
Craigsville, Va., U.S., 979 ...354/E4
Craigsville, W. Va., U.S., 2,204 ...360/E4
Craigtown, Md., U.S., 550 ...288/K1
Craigville, Minn., U.S. ...298/D3
Craik, Sask., Can., 418 ...227/E9
Crail, Scot., U.K., 1,695 ...62/L6
Crailsheim, Ger. ...86/B4
Craiova, Rom., 312,358 ...101/B3
Cramerton, N.C., U.S., 2,976 ...322/C4
Cramlington, Eng., U.K., 26,238 ...66/E2
Cranagh, N. Ire., U.K. ...65/C2
Cranberry, N.Y., U.S., lake ...320/M2
Cranberry Isles, Maine, U.S., 128 ...286/D4
Cranberry Portage, Man., Can. ...215/A2
Cranbourne, Vic., Austl. ...170/Inset V
Cranbrook, Br. Col., Can., 18,476 ...214/P6
Cranbrook, Eng., U.K. ...70/F4
Cranbury, N.J., U.S., 3,227 ...314/D3
Crandall, Ind., U.S., 131 ...270/D8
Crandall, Miss., U.S. ...
Crandall, S. Dak., U.S. ...342/H2
Crandall, Tex., U.S., 2,774 ...346/D10
Crandon, Wisc., U.S., 1,961 ...364/E3
Crandon Lakes, N.J., U.S., 1,180 ...314/D1
Crane, Ind., U.S., 203 ...270/C7
Crane, Mo., U.S., 1,390 ...302/C5
Crane, Mont., U.S., 40 ...306/M2
Crane, Oreg., U.S., 70 ...334/H4
Crane, Tex., U.S., 3,191 ...346/F4
Crane, Tex., U.S., county, 3,996 ...346/F4
Crane Lake, Minn., U.S. ...298/E2
Cranell, Tex., U.S., 175 ...346/L7
Crane Neck, Conn., U.S., point ...253/C5
Crane River, Man., Can., 161 ...215/B3
Cranesville, Penn., U.S., 600 ...336/A2
Crane Valley, Sask., Can., 40 ...227/E11
Cranfield, Eng., U.K., 4,142 ...68/F5
Cranfield, Eng., U.K., 4,142 ...70/C2
Cranfills Gap, Tex., U.S., 335 ...346/L3
Cranford, N.J., U.S., 22,578 ...314/A3
Cranford St. John, Eng., U.K. ...70/D4
Cranleigh, Eng., U.K., 9,574 ...70/D4
Cranshaws, Scot., U.K. ...62/M7
Cranstal, Eng., U.K. ...66/B4
Cranston, Ky., U.S., 40 ...280/G2
Cranston, R.I., U.S., 79,269 ...339/D3
Cranworth, Eng., U.K. ...70/F1
Crapaud, P.E.I., Can., 382 ...224/D3
Crapo, Md., U.S., 70 ...288/K6
Crary, N. Dak., U.S., 149 ...326/G1
Craster, Eng., U.K. ...66/E2
Crater, Oreg., U.S., lake ...334/D5
Crater Lake Natl. Park, Oreg., U.S. ...334/D5
Craters of the Moon Natl. Mon., Ida., U.S. ...264/D6

Craven, N.C., U.S., county, 91,436 ...322/L4
Craven Arms, Eng., U.K. ...68/C5
Cravens, La., U.S., 225 ...282/C5
Cravo Norte, Col. ...184/C3
Crawford, Scot., U.K. ...62/J8
Crawford, Ala., U.S., 275 ...238/D3
Crawford, Ark., U.S., county, 53,247 ...244/A2
Crawford, Colo., U.S., 366 ...250/C3
Crawford, Ga., U.S., 807 ...260/A3
Crawford, Ga., U.S., county, 12,495 ...260/C6
Crawford, Ill., U.S., county, 20,452 ...266/F5
Crawford, Ind., U.S., county, 10,743 ...270/D8
Crawford, Iowa, U.S., county, 16,942 ...274/C3
Crawford, Kans., U.S., county, 38,242 ...276/H4
Crawford, Maine, U.S., 108 ...286/E3
Crawford, Mich., U.S., county, 14,273 ...294/E5
Crawford, Miss., U.S., 655 ...300/D2
Crawford, Mo., U.S., county, 22,804 ...302/E4
Crawford, Nebr., U.S., 1,107 ...308/A1
Crawford, Ohio, U.S., county, 46,966 ...328/E4
Crawford, Okla., U.S. ...330/C2
Crawford, Penn., U.S., county, 90,366 ...336/A2
Crawford, Wisc., U.S., county, 17,243 ...364/C5
Crawford Bay, Br. Col., Can., 328 ...214/O6
Crawford House, N.H., U.S. ...312/D3
Crawfordjohn, Scot., U.K. ...62/J8
Crawfordsville, Ark., U.S., 514 ...244/E2
Crawfordsville, Ind., U.S., 15,243 ...270/C4
Crawfordsville, Iowa, U.S., 295 ...274/L5
Crawfordsville, Oreg., U.S., 125 ...334/D3
Crawfordville, Fla., U.S., 750 ...256/D1
Crawfordville, Ga., U.S., 572 ...260/D4
Crawley, Eng., U.K. ...60/Inset III
Crawley, Eng., U.K., 88,203 ...70/D4
Crawley Down, Eng., U.K., 4,993 ...70/D4
Creag Meagaidh, Scot., U.K., hill ...62/G5
Creagorry, Scot., U.K. ...62/B4
Creal Sprs., Ill., U.S., 702 ...266/E6
Cream Ridge, N.J., U.S., 400 ...314/D3
Crean, Sask., Can., lake ...227/D6
Creaton, Eng., U.K. ...70/C2
Credenhill, Eng., U.K., 2,013 ...68/B5
Crediton, Eng., U.K., 6,142 ...73/B3
Cree, Sask., Can., lake ...227/D3
Cree, Scot., U.K., river ...62/H8
Creede, Colo., U.S., 377 ...250/D3
Creedman Coulee N.W.R., Mont., U.S. ...306/G1
Creedmoor, N.C., U.S., 2,232 ...322/H2
Creedmoor, Tex., U.S., 211 ...346/D2
Creek, Okla., U.S., county, 67,367 ...330/F2
Creekside, Penn., U.S., 323 ...336/C4
Cree Lake, Sask., Can. ...227/D3
Creelsboro, Ky., U.S., 40 ...280/E4
Creetown, Scot., U.K., 685 ...62/H9
Creggan, N. Ire., U.K. ...65/C2
Creighton, Mo., U.S., 322 ...302/B3
Creighton, Nebr., U.S., 1,270 ...308/G1
Creighton, S. Dak., U.S. ...342/E2
Cremona, Alta., Can., 415 ...212/G5
Cremona, It. ...95/B1
Crenshaw, Ala., U.S., county, 13,665 ...238/C4
Crenshaw, Miss., U.S., 916 ...300/B1
Creola, Ala., U.S., 2,002 ...238/A5
Creola, Ohio, U.S., 60 ...328/F7
Creole, La., U.S., 175 ...282/C7
Cres, Cro., island ...98/B3
Cresaptown (Cresaptown-Bel Air), Md., U.S., 5,884 ...288/C3
Cresbard, S. Dak., U.S., 143 ...342/G2
Crescent, Iowa, U.S., 537 ...274/C5
Crescent, Okla., U.S., 1,281 ...330/E2
Crescent, Oreg., U.S., 175 ...334/E4
Crescent, Oreg., U.S., lake ...334/E4
Crescent, Wash., U.S., lake ...358/B1
Crescent Beach, Fla., U.S., 985 ...256/G2
Crescent City, Calif., U.S., 4,006 ...246/A1
Crescent City, Fla., U.S., 1,776 ...256/G2
Crescent City, Ill., U.S., 631 ...266/F4
Crescent Jct., Utah, U.S., 50 ...350/E5
Crescent Lake, Oreg., U.S. ...334/E4
Crescent Lake N.W.R., Nebr., U.S. ...308/B2
Crescent Park, Ky., U.S. ...280/G2
Crescent Sprs., Ky., U.S., 3,931 ...280/G2
Crescent Valley, Nev., U.S., 50 ...310/B1
Cresco, Iowa, U.S., 3,905 ...274/K1
Cressage, Eng., U.K. ...68/B4
Cressday, Alta., Can. ...212/E6
Cresselly, Wales, U.K. ...64/B4
Cresskill, N.J., U.S., 7,746 ...314/C2, F2
Cresson, Penn., U.S., 1,631 ...336/D5
Cressona, Penn., U.S., 1,635 ...336/F4
Creste Butte, Colo., U.S., 1,529 ...250/D3
Crest Hill, Ill., U.S., 13,329 ...266/B6
Crestline, Kans., U.S., 150 ...276/H4
Crestline, Nev., U.S. ...310/C3
Crestline, Ohio, U.S., 5,088 ...328/E4
Creston, Br. Col., Can., 4,795 ...214/O6
Creston, Ill., U.S., 543 ...266/E2
Creston, Iowa, U.S., 7,597 ...274/F5
Creston, Kans., U.S., 125 ...282/C3
Creston, Mont., U.S., 125 ...306/B1
Creston, Nebr., U.S., 215 ...308/G2
Creston, Ohio, U.S., 2,161 ...328/G4
Creston, Wash., U.S., 232 ...358/G2
Creston, Wyo., U.S. ...366/C3
Crestone, Colo., U.S., 73 ...250/E4
Crestone, Colo., U.S., peak ...250/E4
Crestview, Fla., U.S., 14,766 ...256/B1
Crestview, Hawaii, U.S. ...262/E1, J2
Crestview, Ky., U.S., 471 ...280/G1
Crestview Hills, Ky., U.S., 2,889 ...280/G1
Crestwood, Ill., U.S., 11,251 ...266/B6
Crestwood, Ky., U.S. ...280/B1, E2
Crestwood, Mo., U.S., 11,863 ...302/H3
Crestwood Vil., N.J., U.S., 8,392 ...314/E4
Creswell, Eng., U.K., 4,655 ...68/E3
Creswell, N.C., U.S., 278 ...322/N3
Creswell, Oreg., U.S., 3,579 ...334/C4
Creta, Okla., U.S. ...330/C3
Crete, Gr., island ...100/C4
Crete, Gr., region ...100/C4
Crete, Gr., sea ...100/C4
Crete, Ill., U.S., 7,346 ...266/F2
Crete, Nebr., U.S., 6,028 ...308/H3
Crete, N. Dak., U.S., 50 ...326/H3
Créteil, Fr. ...88/Inset II
Creuse, Fr., department ...88/C4
Creve Coeur, Ill., U.S., 5,448 ...266/D3
Creve Coeur, Mo., U.S., 16,500 ...302/H3
Crew, N. Ire., U.K. ...65/B2
Crewe, Eng., U.K. ...60/C3
Crewe, Va., U.S., 2,378 ...354/G6
Crewkerne, Eng., U.K., 7,142 ...73/G3
Crews, Tex., U.S. ...346/J4
Crianlarich, Scot., U.K. ...62/G6
Criccieth, Wales, U.K., 1,720 ...64/C2
Crich, Eng., U.K. ...68/E3
Crick, Eng., U.K., 1,314 ...68/E5

Crick, Eng., U.K., 1,314 . . . . .70/B2
Crickadarn, Wales, U.K. 64/E3
Cricket, N.C., U.S., 2,053 . . . . .322/C2
Crickhowell, Wales, U.K. 64/E4
Cricklade, Eng., U.K., 3,808 . . . . .68/D6
Crider, Ky., U.S., 50 . . . . .280/C3
Cridersville, Ohio, U.S., 1,817 . . . . .328/M4
Crieff, Scot., U.K., 6,579 . . . . .62/J6
Crimea, (Krym), Ukr., autonomous republic . . .102/C3
Crimean, Ukr., mountains 102/C4
Crimean, Ukr., peninsula 102/C3
Crimora, Va., U.S., 1,796 . . . . .354/F4
Criner, Okla., U.S. 330/E3
Cringleford, Eng., U.K., 2,190 . . . . .70/G1
Cripple Creek, Colo., U.S., 1,115 . . . . .250/E3
Cripple Creek, Va., U.S., 60 . . . . .354/A7
Cripp's Corner, Eng., U.K. 70/F5
Crisfield, Md., U.S., 2,723 . . . . .288/L7
Crisp, Ga., U.S., county, 21,996 . . . . .260/D8
Cristal, Gabon, mountains 155/A1
Cristobal Colón, Col., peak 184/B2
Crittenden, Ark., U.S., county, 50,866 . . . . . .244/E2
Crittenden, Ky., U.S., 2,401 . . . . .280/F2
Crittenden, Ky., U.S., county, 9,384 . . . . .280/B3
Crivitz, Wisc., U.S., 998 . . . . .364/F3
Crna, Mac., river 100/B2
Crna Gora, Mac., mountains 100/B1
Crna Gora, Serb.-Mont., mountains 99/B3
Croatan Natl. For., N.C., U.S. 322/L5
Croatia, nation 96
Crocker, Malay., range 121/D2
Crocker, Mo., U.S., 1,033 . . . . .302/D4
Crocker, S. Dak., U.S. 342/H2
Crockerton, Eng., U.K. 73/H2
Crockett, Calif., U.S., 3,194 . . . . .246/I1
Crockett, Ky., U.S. 280/G4
Crockett, Tenn., U.S., county, 14,532 . . . . . . .344/C3
Crockett, Tex., U.S., 7,141 . . . . .346/N4
Crockett, Tex., U.S., county, 4,099 . . . . .346/G5
Crockett, Va., U.S. 354/A7
Crocketts Bluff, Ark., U.S., 40 . . . . .244/D3
Crockham Hill, Eng., U.K. 70/E4
Crocodile Lake N.W.R., Fla., U.S. 256/H6
Croesgoch, Wales, U.K. 64/A4
Croft, Kans., U.S. 276/D4
Croft, Penn., U.S. 336/E3
Crofton, Ky., U.S., 838 . . . . .280/C3
Crofton, Md., U.S., 20,091 . . . . .288/H3
Crofton, Nebr., U.S., 754 . . . . .308/G1
Croggan, Scot., U.K. 62/E6
Croghan, N.Y., U.S., 665 . . . . .320/L3
Cromarty, Scot., U.K., 719 . . . . .62/H3
Cromberg, Calif., U.S., 290 . . . . .246/E3
Cromdale, Scot., U.K. 62/J4
Cromer, Man., Can. 215/A4
Cromer, Eng., U.K., 7,267 . . . . .70/G1
Cromra, Scot., U.K. 62/H5
Cromwell, Ala., U.S. 238/A4
Cromwell, Conn., U.S., 12,871 . . . . .253/E3
Cromwell, Ind., U.S., 452 . . . . .270/E2
Cromwell, Iowa, U.S., 120 . . . . .274/F5
Cromwell, Ky., U.S., 175 . . . . .280/D3
Cromwell, Minn., U.S., 143 . . . . .298/E4
Cromwell, Okla., U.S., 265 . . . . .330/F2
Cronulla, N.S.W., Austl. . . . . .170/Inset IV
Crook, Eng., U.K., 8,246 . . . . .66/E3
Crook, Colo., U.S., 128 . . . . .250/H1
Crook, Oreg., U.S., county, 19,182 . . . . .334/E3
Crook, Wyo., U.S., county, 5,887 . . . . .366/D1
Crooked, Bah., island 204/C2
Crooked, Bah., island 207/C4
Crooked, Br. Col., Can., river 214/L4
Crooked, Fla., U.S., island 256/C2
Crooked, Kans., U.S., creek 276/B4
Crooked, Oreg., U.S., river 334/F3
Crooked Island, Bah., passage 207/C4
Crooked River, Sask., Can., 64 . . . . .227/G8
Crooked River Natl. Grassland, Oreg., U.S. . . .334/E3
Crooks, S. Dak., U.S., 859 . . . . .342/J4
Crookston, Minn., U.S., 8,192 . . . . .298/A3
Crookston, Nebr., U.S., 98 . . . . .308/D1
Crooksville, Ohio, U.S., 2,483 . . . . .328/F6
Cropper, Ky., U.S., 100 . . . . .280/E2
Cropsey, Ill., U.S., 50 . . . . .266/E3
Crosby, (Cumbria), Eng., U.K., 52,869 . . . . . .66/B3
Crosby, (Merseyside), Eng., U.K. 68/A3
Crosby, Eng., U.K., 52,869 . . . . .66/B6
Crosby, Md., U.S., 300 . . . . .288/K3
Crosby, Minn., U.S., 2,299 . . . . .298/D4
Crosby, Miss., U.S., 360 . . . . .300/A4
Crosby, N. Dak., U.S., 1,089 . . . . .326/B1
Crosby, Penn., U.S., 125 . . . . .336/E2
Crosby, Tex., U.S., 1,714 . . . . .346/B6
Crosby, Tex., U.S., county, 7,072 . . . . .346/G2
Crosby Ravensworth, Eng., U.K. 66/C3
Crosbyton, Tex., U.S., 1,874 . . . . .346/G2
Cross, Man., U.S., lake 215/C2
Cross, Nig., river 152/N4
Cross, Ark., U.S., county, 19,526 . . . . .244/E2
Cross, Maine, U.S., island 286/E4
Cross, S.C., U.S., 250 . . . . .340/D3
Cross, Tex., U.S. 346/K7
Cross Anchor, S.C., U.S., 325 . . . . .340/C2
Cross Ash, Wales, U.K. 64/F4
Cross Bush, Eng., U.K. 70/C5
Cross City, Fla., U.S., 1,775 . . . . .256/E2
Cross Creek, N.B., Can. 217/C2
Cross Creeks N.W.R., Tenn., U.S. 344/F2
Crossett, Ark., U.S., 6,097 . . . . .244/D4
Cross Fell, Eng., U.K., hill 66/C3
Crossfield, Alta., Can., 2,389 . . . . .212//C5
Cross Fork, Penn., U.S. 336/F3
Crossgar, N. Ire., U.K., 1,406 . . . . .65/F3
Crossgare, N. Ire., U.K. 65/D1
Crossgates, Wales, U.K. 64/E3
Cross Hands, Wales, U.K., 9,520 . . . . .64/C4
Cross Hill, S.C., U.S., 601 . . . . .340/C2
Cross Inn, Wales, U.K. 64/C3
Cross Keys, N.J., U.S., 3,600 . . . . .314/C4
Cross Lake, Man., Can., 294 . . . . .215/C2
Cross Lake, Minn., U.S., 1,893 . . . . .298/C4
Cross Lanes, Eng., U.K. 66/F4
Cross Lanes, W. Va., U.S., 10,353 . . . . .360/C4
Crosslee, Scot., U.K. 62/K8
Crossmaglen, N. Ire., U.K., 1,586 . . . . .65/D3
Cross Mtn., Tex., U.S., 1,524 . . . . .346/A2
Crossnore, N.C., U.S., 242 . . . . .322/B2
Cross Plains, Ind., U.S., 150 . . . . .270/F7
Cross Plains, Tenn., U.S., 1,381 . . . . .344/H1
Cross Plains, Tex., U.S., 1,068 . . . . .346/J3
Cross Plains, Wisc., U.S., 3,084 . . . . .364/D5
Cross River, Nig., state 152/N5
Crossroads, Miss., U.S., 90 . . . . .300/C5
Crossroads, N. Mex., U.S. 317/G4
Cross Roads, Penn., U.S., 518 . . . . .336/H6
Cross Roads, Tex., U.S., 603 . . . . .346/B8
Cross Timbers, Mo., U.S., 185 . . . . .302/C3
Cross Vil., Mich., U.S., 70 . . . . .294/D4
Crossville, (De Kalb County), Ala., U.S., 1,431 . .238/B2
Crossville, (Lamar County), Ala., U.S., 150 . . .238/B2
Crossville, Ill., U.S., 782 . . . . .266/E5
Crossville, Tenn., U.S., 8,981 . . . . .344/L3

Crossway, Wales, U.K. 64/F4
Crosswicks, N.J., U.S., 900 . . . . .314/D3
Crostwick, Eng., U.K. 70/G1
Croswell, Mich., U.S., 2,467 . . . . .294/G6
Crothersville, Ind., U.S., 1,570 . . . . .270/E7
Croton, Iowa, U.S. 274/L6
Croton, Mich., U.S., 275 . . . . .294/D6
Croton, N.J., U.S., 400 . . . . .314/D2
Croton, Tex., U.S. 346/H2
Crotone, It. 95/D3
Croton-on-Hudson, N.Y., U.S., 7,606 . . . . . .320/B1
Crouch, Ida., U.S., 154 . . . . .264/B5
Crouse, N.C., U.S., 475 . . . . .322/C4
Crouseville, Maine, U.S., 275 . . . . .286/D2
Crow, Colo., U.S., creek 250/F1
Crow Agency, Mont., U.S., 1,552 . . . . .306/J4
Crowborough, Eng., U.K., 19,563 . . . . .70/E4
Crowcombe, Eng., U.K. 73/F2
Crow Creek Ind. Res., S. Dak., U.S. 342/F3
Crowder, Miss., U.S., 766 . . . . .300/B1
Crowder, Okla., U.S., 436 . . . . .330/G2
Crowders, N.C., U.S., 212/ 322/C4
Crowell, Tex., U.S., 1,141 . . . . .346/J2
Crowfield, Eng., U.K. 70/G2
Crowheart, Wyo., U.S., 163 . . . . .366/B2
Crow Hill, Eng., U.K. 68/B6
Crow Indian Res., Mont., U.S. 306/H4
Crow Lake, S. Dak., U.S. 342/G4
Crowland, Eng., U.K., 3,172 . . . . .68/G4
Crowland, Eng., U.K., 3,172 . . . . .70/D1
Crowle, Eng., U.K., 2,916 . . . . .68/G5
Crowle, Eng., U.K., 2,916 . . . . .68/B3
Crowley, Colo., U.S., 187 . . . . .250/G3
Crowley, Colo., U.S., county, 5,518 . . . . .250/G3
Crowley, La., U.S., 14,225 . . . . .282/E6
Crowley, Oreg., U.S. 334/J4
Crowley, Tex., U.S., 7,467 . . . . .346/A10
Crown, Minn., U.S., 80 . . . . .298/D5
Crown City, Ohio, U.S., 411 . . . . .328/F8
Crown Hts., N.Y., U.S., 2,992 . . . . .320/P7
Crownhill, Eng., U.K. 73/B6
Crown King, Ariz., U.S., 60 . . . . .242/C3
Crown Pt., Ind., U.S., 19,806 . . . . .270/B2
Crown Pt., La., U.S., 650 . . . . .282//7, K4
Crownpoint, N. Mex., U.S., 2,630 . . . . .317/B1
Crownsville, Md., U.S., 1,670 . . . . .288/H3
Crow River, Minn., U.S., 40 . . . . .298/C5
Crows Nest, Ind., U.S., 96 . . . . .270/D5
Crowthorne, Eng., U.K., 21,500 . . . . .70/C4
Crowville, La., U.S., 225 . . . . .282/F2
Crow Wing, Minn., U.S., county, 55,099 . . . .298/C4
Croxton, Eng., U.K. 70/F2
Croxton Kerrial, Eng., U.K. 70/C1
Croyde, Eng., U.K. 73/D2
Croydon, Eng., U.K., 298,486 . . . . .70/D4
Croydon, Eng., U.K., unitary authority, 330,688 . .70/D4
Croydon, N.H., U.S., 661 . . . . .312/B5
Croydon, Penn., U.S., 9,993 . . . . .336/M5
Croydon Flat, N.H., U.S., 250 . . . . .312/B5
Crozet, Va., U.S., 2,820 . . . . .354/F4
Crudgington, Eng., U.K. 68/B4
Cruger, Miss., U.S., 449 . . . . .300/B2
Crulivig, Scot., U.K. 62/C2
Crum, W. Va., U.S., 125 . . . . .360/B5
Crumlin, N. Ire., U.K., 2,697 . . . . .65/E2
Crump, Mich., U.S., 275 . . . . .294/E6
Crump, Oreg., U.S., lake 334/G5
Crump, Tenn., U.S., 1,521 . . . . .344/E4
Crumpton, Md., U.S., 500 . . . . .288/L3
Crumstown, Ind., U.S., 350 . . . . .270/D1
Cruso, N.C., U.S., 100 . . . . .322/E8
Crutchfield, Ky., U.S., 150 . . . . .280/B4
Crux Easton, Eng., U.K. 70/B4
Cruz, Cuba, cape 204/B3
Cruz, Cuba, cape 204/D3
Cruzeiro do Sul, Braz. 188/A2
Cruzville, N. Mex., U.S. 317/B4
Crynant, Wales, U.K. 64/D4
Crystal, Maine, U.S., 285 . . . . .286/D2
Crystal, Mich., U.S., lake 294/C5
Crystal, Minn., U.S., 22,698 . . . . .298/E5
Crystal, Nev., U.S. 310/B3
Crystal, N.H., U.S., 100 . . . . .312/D2
Crystal, N. Mex., U.S., 347 . . . . .317/B1
Crystal, N. Dak., U.S., 167 . . . . .326/H1
Crystal, Okla., U.S., 60 . . . . .330/G3
Crystal Bay, Nev., U.S., 9,952 . . . . .310/A2
Crystal Beach, Fla., U.S., 4,000 . . . . .256/C6
Crystal City, Man., Can., 414 . . . . .215/B4
Crystal City, Mo., U.S., 4,247 . . . . .302/F3
Crystal City, Tex., U.S., 7,190 . . . . .346/J7
Crystal Falls, Mich., U.S., 1,791 . . . . .294/A3
Crystal Falls, Tex., U.S. 346/K3
Crystal Hill, Va., U.S., 100 . . . . .354/F7
Crystal Lake, Conn., U.S., 1,459 . . . . .253/E2
Crystal Lake, Fla., U.S. 256/C1
Crystal Lake, Ill., U.S., 38,000 . . . . .266/AS, E1
Crystal Lake, Iowa, U.S., 285 . . . . .274/G1
Crystal Lake Park, Mo., U.S., 457 . . . . .302/H3
Crystal Lakes, Mo., U.S., 383 . . . . .302/J4
Crystal Lawns, Ill., U.S., 2,933 . . . . .266/A6
Crystal River, Fla., U.S., 3,485 . . . . .256/F3
Crystal Sprs., Ark., U.S. 244/C3
Crystal Sprs., Fla., U.S., 1,175 . . . . .256/D6, F3
Crystal Sprs., Kans., U.S., 50 . . . . .276/D4
Crystal Sprs., Miss., U.S., 5,873 . . . . .300/B3
Crystal Sprs., N. Dak., U.S. 326/F3
Crystal Valley, Mich., U.S., 175 . . . . .294/C6
Crystola, Colo., U.S. 250/E3
Csongrád, Hun., county 91/C2
Cuajimalpa, Mex. 200/Inset
Cuamba, Moz. .161/C2
Cuando, Ang., river 159/D4
Cuando, Zam., river 159/A3
Cuando Cubango, Ang., province 159/D5
Cuango, Ang., river 159/D2
Cuanza, Ang., river 159/C3
Cuanza Norte, Ang., province 159/B2
Cuanza Sul, Ang., province 159/B3
Cuareim, Uru., river 187/B1
Cuauhtémoc, Mex., 85,387, (124,378 metro.) . .200/C2
Cuautitlán, Mex. 200/Inset
Cuautitlán Izcalli, Mex., 433,830 . . . . . . .200/Inset
Cuba, nation 204/B2
Cuba, nation 192
Cuba, Ala., U.S., 363 . . . . .238/A3
Cuba, Ill., U.S., 1,418 . . . . .266/C3
Cuba, Kans., U.S., 231 . . . . .276/E2
Cuba, Mo., U.S., 3,230 . . . . .302/E3
Cuba, N. Mex., U.S., 590 . . . . .317/D1
Cuba, N.Y., U.S., 1,633 . . . . .320/E6
Cuba, Ohio, U.S., 325 . . . . .328/C7
Cuba City, Wisc., U.S., 2,156 . . . . .364/C6
Cubal, Ang., river 159/B4
Cubango, Ang., river . . . . .188/Inset II
Cubatão, Braz. . . . . .188/Inset II
Cubero, N. Mex., U.S., 150 . . . . .317/C2
Cuchara, Colo., U.S., 40 . . . . .250/E4
Cucharas, Colo., U.S., river 250/F4
Cuchillo, N. Mex., U.S., 60 . . . . .317/C4
Cuckfield, Eng., U.K., 2,879 . . . . .70/D4

Cucklebur, Ariz., U.S., 150 . . . . .242/D5
Cuckoo, Va., U.S., 150 . . . . .354/H5
Cúcuta, Col., 624,000 . . . . .184/B3
Cudahy, Calif., U.S., 24,208 . . . . .246/C10
Cudahy, Wisc., U.S., 18,429 . . . . .364/F2
Cuddalore, India .128/C6
Cudworth, Sask., Can., 766 . . . . .227/E8
Cudworth, Eng., U.K., 11,715 . . . . .66/F5
Cudworth, Eng., U.K., 11,715 . . . . .68/B4
Cuenca, Ecua., 194,981 . . . . .185/B4
Cuenca, Sp., 46,341 . . . . .94/E2
Cuenca, Sp., province 94/E3
Cuernavaca, Mex., state capital, 327,162,
    (338,706 metro.) 200/E4
Cuero, Tex., U.S., 6,571 . . . . .346/L6
Cuervo, N. Mex., U.S. 317/F2
Cuffley, Eng., U.K., 4,887 . . . . .70/D3
Cuiabá, Braz., 483,346 . . . . .188/C3
Cuileagh, N. Ire., U.K., mountain 65/B3
Cuillin, Scot., U.K., hills 62/D4
Cuito, Ang., river 159/D4
Cuito Cuanavale, Ang. 159/D5
Cukorova, Tur., plain 133/C3
Cu Lao Thu, Viet., island 123/B4
Culberson, N.C., U.S., 70 . . . . .322/B8
Culberson, Tex., U.S., county, 2,975 . . . . . . .346/D4
Culbertson, Mont., U.S., 716 . . . . .306/M1
Culbertson, Nebr., U.S., 594 . . . . .308/D3
Cul de Sac, St. Luc., river 208/B2
Culdesac, Ida., U.S., 378 . . . . .264/A3
Culebra, P.R., island 206/E2
Culebrinas, P.R., river 206/A2
Culford, Eng., U.K. 70/F2
Culgaith, Eng., U.K. 66/C3
Culiacán, Mex., state capital, 540,823,
    (745,537 metro.) 200/C3
Culkein, Scot., U.K. 62/F2
Cullen, La., U.S., 1,296 . . . . .282/C1
Cullen, Va., U.S., 60 . . . . .354/F6
Culleoka, Tenn., U.S., 450 . . . . .344/H4
Cullion, N. Ire., U.K. 65/C2
Cullison, Kans., U.S., 98 . . . . .276/D4
Cullivoe, Scot., U.K. 62/Q1
Cullman, Ala., U.S., 13,995 . . . . .238/C1
Cullman, Ala., U.S., county, 77,483 . . . . . . .238/C1
Culloch, Scot., U.K. 62//J6
Culloden, Ga., U.S., 223 . . . . .260/C6
Culloden, W. Va., U.S., 2,940 . . . . .360/B4
Cullom, Ill., U.S., 563 . . . . .266/E3
Cullomburg, Ala., U.S., 175 . . . . .238/A4
Cullowhee, N.C., U.S., 3,579 . . . . .322/D8
Cullyhanna, N. Ire., U.K., 199 . . . . .65/D3
Culmstock, Eng., U.K. 73/F3
Culnacraig, Scot., U.K. 62/F3
Culp Creek, Oreg., U.S., 375 . . . . .334/D4
Culpeper, Va., U.S., 9,664 . . . . .354/G4
Culpeper, Va., U.S., county, 34,262 . . . . . . .354/H4
Culswick, Scot., U.K. 62/P3
Culver, Ind., U.S., 1,539 . . . . .270/D2
Culver, Kans., U.S., 164 . . . . .276/E3
Culver, Minn., U.S., 40 . . . . .298/E4
Culver, Oreg., U.S., 802 . . . . .334/E3
Culver City, Calif., U.S., 38,816 . . . . .246/B9
Culvers Lake, N.J., U.S. 314/D1
Culverton, Ga., U.S., 80 . . . . .260/F5
Cumaná, Ven., 222,116, (246,247 metro.) . . .182/D1
Cumberland, Br. Col., Can., 2,618 . . . . .214/K6
Cumberland, Man., Can., lake 215/A2
Cumberland, N.S., Can., county 221/C2
Cumberland, Nun., Can., peninsula 208/P3
Cumberland, Nun., Can., sound 208/P3
Cumberland, Sask., Can., lake 227/H6
Cumberland, Ala., U.S., plateau 238/C1
Cumberland, Ga., U.S., island 260/J10
Cumberland, Ga., U.S., plateau 260/B2
Cumberland, Ill., U.S., county, 11,253 . . . . . .266/E4
Cumberland, Ind., U.S., 5,500 . . . . .270/E5
Cumberland, Iowa, U.S., 281 . . . . .274/E5
Cumberland, Ky., U.S., 2,611 . . . . .280/H4
Cumberland, Ky., U.S., county, 7,147 . . . . . .280/D4
Cumberland, Ky., U.S., lake 280/F4
Cumberland, Ky., U.S., mountains 280/G4
Cumberland, Ky., U.S., river 280/F4
Cumberland, Maine, U.S., county, 265,612 . . .286/B5
Cumberland, Md., U.S., 21,518,
    (102,008 metro.) 288/C3
Cumberland, N.J., U.S., 225 . . . . .314/D5
Cumberland, N.J., U.S., county, 146,438 . . . .314/C5
Cumberland, N.C., U.S., 4,400 . . . . .322/H4
Cumberland, N.C., U.S., county, 302,963 . . . .322/H5
Cumberland, Ohio, U.S., 402 . . . . .328/G6
Cumberland, Penn., U.S., county, 213,674 . . .336/G5
Cumberland, Tenn., U.S., county, 46,802 . . . .344/L3
Cumberland, Tenn., U.S., river 344/G2
Cumberland, Va., U.S., 125 . . . . .354/G6
Cumberland, Va., U.S., county, 9,017 . . . . . .354/G6
Cumberland, Wash., U.S., 250 . . . . .358/D2
Cumberland, Wisc., U.S., 2,280 . . . . .364/A3
Cumberland Bay, N.B., Can. 217/D2
Cumberland Ctr., Maine, U.S., 2,596 . . . . . . .286/B5
Cumberland City, Ky., U.S., 125 . . . . .280/C3
Cumberland City, Tenn., U.S., 316 . . . . .344/F2
Cumberland Foreside, Maine, U.S., 500 . . . . .286/B5
Cumberland Furnace, Tenn., U.S., 125 . . . . . .344/G2
Cumberland Gap, Tenn., U.S., 204 . . . . .344/P1
Cumberland Gap N.H.P., Ky., U.S. 280/G4
Cumberland Hill, R.I., U.S., 7,738 . . . . .339/D2
Cumberland House, Sask., Can., 632 . . . . . . .227/H7
Cumberland Island Natl. Seashore, Ga., U.S. . .260/J10
Cumbernauld, Scot., U.K., 49,664 . . . . .62/H7
Cumbria, Eng., U.K., unitary authority, 487,607 . .60/C3
Cumbrian, Eng., U.K., mountains 60/B2
Cuming, Nebr., U.S., county, 10,203 . . . . . . .308/H1
Cumming, Ga., U.S., 4,220 . . . . .260/D3
Cumming, Iowa, U.S., 162 . . . . .274/G5
Cummings, Calif., U.S. 246/B3
Cummings, Kans., U.S., 80 . . . . .276/G2
Cummings, N. Dak., U.S., 60 . . . . .326/H2
Cummings, S.C., U.S., 250 . . . . .340/D4
Cummington, Mass., U.S., 978 . . . . .292/C3
Cumnock, Scot., U.K., 9,358 . . . . .62/H8
Cumrew, Eng., U.K. 66/C3
Cumwhinton, Eng., U.K. 66/C3
Cundiff, Ky., U.S., 175 . . . . .280/E3
Cundiff, Tex., U.S., 70 . . . . .346/K2
Cundinamarca, Col., department 184/B3
Cunene, Ang., province 159/C5
Cunene, Ang., river 159/B5, C4
Cuneo, It. 95/A1
Cunningham, Kans., U.S., 514 . . . . .276/D4
Cunningham, Tenn., U.S., 150 . . . . .344/G2
Cunningham, Wash., U.S., 40 . . . . .358/G3
Cunninsburgh, Scot., U.K. 62/Q3
Cupar, Sask., Can., 602 . . . . .227/F10
Cupar, Scot., U.K. 62//J6
Cupar, Scot., U.K., 8,506 . . . . .62/L6
Cupertino, Calif., U.S., 50,546 . . . . .246/C5, K3
Cuprum, Ida., U.S. 264/A4
Curaçao, Neth. Ant., island 204/D4
Curaray, Ecua., river 185/C3

Curecanti N.R.A., Colo., U.S. 250/C3
Curepipe, Mauritius, 78,920 . . . . .163/C3
Curicó, Chile 190/B4
Curitiba, Braz., 1,586,898, (2,725,505 metro.) . .188/D4
Curlew, Fla., U.S., 5,900 . . . . .256/C6
Curlew, Wash., U.S., 62 . . . . .274/E2
Curlew, Wash., U.S., 175 . . . . .358/G1
Curlew Natl. Grassland, Ida., U.S. 264/E7
Curral Velho, C.V. 148/D3
Curran, Mich., U.S., 40 . . . . .294/F5
Currant, Nev., U.S. 310/C2
Currie, N.B., Can. 217/B2
Currie, Scot., U.K. 62/K7
Currie, Minn., U.S., 225 . . . . .298/B6
Currie, Nev., U.S. 310/C1
Currie, N.C., U.S., 250 . . . . .322/J6
Currituck, N.C., U.S. 322/N2
Currituck, N.C., U.S., county, 18,190 . . . . . . .322/N2
Curry, Ala., U.S., 125 . . . . .238/C2
Curry, N. Mex., U.S., county, 45,044 . . . . . . .317/G3
Curry, Oreg., U.S., county, 21,137 . . . . .334/B5
Curryville, Mo., U.S., 251 . . . . .302/E2
Curtis, Ark., U.S., 350 . . . . .244/B3
Curtis, Mich., U.S., 250 . . . . .294/D3
Curtis, Nebr., U.S., 832 . . . . .308/D3
Curtis, Okla., U.S., 50 . . . . .330/C1
Curtiss, Ariz., U.S., 40 . . . . .242/E6
Curtiss, Wisc., U.S., 198 . . . . .364/C4
Curtisville, Mich., U.S., 50 . . . . .294/F5
Curuzú Cuatiá, Arg. 191/D2
Curwensville, Penn., U.S., 2,650 . . . . .336/D4
Cushendall, N. Ire., U.K., 1,399 . . . . .65/E1
Cushendun, N. Ire., U.K., 347 . . . . .65/E1
Cushing, Iowa, U.S., 246 . . . . .274/C3
Cushing, Maine, U.S., 1,322 . . . . .286/C4
Cushing, Minn., U.S., 40 . . . . .298/C4
Cushing, Nebr., U.S. 308/E2
Cushing, Okla., U.S., 8,371 . . . . .330/F2
Cushing, Tex., U.S., 637 . . . . .346/P4
Cushing, Wisc., U.S., 175 . . . . .364/A3
Cushman, Ark., U.S., 461 . . . . .244/D2
Cushman, Mont., U.S. 306/G3
Cushman, Oreg., U.S., 125 . . . . .334/B4
Cusick, Wash., U.S., 212 . . . . .358/H1
Cusseta, Ala., U.S., 125 . . . . .238/D3
Cusseta, Ga., U.S., 1,196 . . . . .260/B7
Cusson, Minn., U.S. 298/E2
Custar, Ohio, U.S., 208 . . . . .328/C3
Custer, Colo., U.S., county, 3,503 . . . . .250/E3
Custer, Ida., U.S., county, 4,342 . . . . .264/C5
Custer, Ky., U.S., 70 . . . . .280/D3
Custer, Mich., U.S., 318 . . . . .294/C6
Custer, Mont., U.S., 145 . . . . .306/J3
Custer, Mont., U.S., county, 11,696 . . . . .306/L3
Custer, Nebr., U.S., county, 11,793 . . . . .308/D2
Custer, Okla., U.S., county, 26,142 . . . . .330/D2
Custer, S. Dak., U.S., 1,860 . . . . .342/B4
Custer, S. Dak., U.S., county, 7,275 . . . . . . .342/B4
Custer, Wash., U.S., 299 . . . . .358/C1
Custer City, Okla., U.S., 393 . . . . .330/D2
Custer Natl. For., Mont., U.S. 306/G4, H4, K4, M4
Custer St. Park, S. Dak., U.S. 342/B4
Cut, Tex., U.S., 125 . . . . .346/N4
Cut and Shoot, Tex., U.S., 1,158 . . . . .346/N5
Cut Bank, Mont., U.S., 3,105 . . . . .306/D1
Cutchogue, N.Y., U.S., 2,849 . . . . .320/F1
Cuthbert, Ga., U.S., 3,731 . . . . .260/B8
Cut Knife, Sask., Can., 556 . . . . .227/A8
Cutler, Fla., U.S., 17,390 . . . . .256/A7
Cutler, Ill., U.S., 543 . . . . .266/D5
Cutler, Maine, U.S., 623 . . . . .286/E4
Cutler, Minn., U.S. 298/D4
Cutler, Ohio, U.S., 125 . . . . .328/G7
Cutler Ridge, Fla., U.S., 24,781 . . . . .256/A7
Cutlerville, Mich., U.S., 15,114 . . . . .294/D7
Cutnall Green, Eng., U.K. 68/C5
Cut Off, La., U.S., 5,635 . . . . .282/J7
Cuttack, India, 403,418, (439,273 metro.) . . .128/E4
Cutten, Calif., U.S., 2,933 . . . . .246/A2
Cutter, Ariz., U.S. 242/E4
Cuttingsville, Vt., U.S., 175 . . . . .352/B4
Cuxhaven, Ger. 86/B2
Cuyahoga, Ohio, U.S., county, 1,393,978 . .328/G3, G9
Cuyahoga, Ohio, U.S., river 328/H9
Cuyahoga Falls, Ohio, U.S., 49,374 . . . . .328/H3
Cuyahoga Hts., Ohio, U.S., 599 . . . . .328/G9
Cuyahoga Valley N.P., Ohio, U.S. 328/G3, H10
Cuyama, Calif., U.S., 40 . . . . .246/F8
Cuyamungue, N. Mex., U.S., 421 . . . . .317/E2
Cuyo, Phil., islands 120/B4
Cuyuna, Minn., U.S., 231 . . . . .298/D4
Cuyuni, Guy., river 183/A2
Cuzco, Peru, 100,572, (319,422 metro.) 185/C3
Cuzco, Peru, department 185/C3
Cuzco, Ind., U.S. 270/C8
Cuzzart, W. Va., U.S., 100 . . . . .360/G1
Cwellyn, Wales, U.K., lake 64/C1
Cwmbach, Wales, U.K., 4,065 . . . . .64/E4
Cwmbran, Wales, U.K., 46,021 . . . . .64/E4
C.W. McConaughy, Nebr., U.S., lake 308/C2
Cwmcoy, Wales, U.K. 64/C4
Cwmdu, Wales, U.K. 64/E4
Cwmduad, Wales, U.K. 64/C4
Cyangugu, Rwa. .158/A2
Cyclades, Gr., islands 100/C3
Cyclone, Penn., U.S., 225 . . . . .336/D2
Cyffylliog, Wales, U.K. 64/E1
Cyfronydd, Wales, U.K. 64/E2
Cygnet, Ohio, U.S., 564 . . . . .328/C3
Cylinder, Iowa, U.S., 110 . . . . .274/E1
Cymmer, Wales, U.K. 64/D4
Cynthiana, Ind., U.S., 693 . . . . .270/A8
Cynthiana, Ky., U.S., 6,258 . . . . .280/F2
Cynwyd, Wales, U.K. 64/E2
Cynwyl Elfed, Wales, U.K. 64/C4
Cypress, Calif., U.S., 46,229 . . . . .246/D10
Cypress, Ill., U.S., 271 . . . . .266/D6
Cypress, La., U.S., 40 . . . . .282/C3
Cypress Hills Interprov. Park, Sask., Can. 212//E6
Cypress Hills Interprov. Park, Sask., Can. 227/A11
Cypress Inn, Tenn., U.S., 80 . . . . .344/F4
Cypress River, Man., Can. 215/B4
Cyprus, nation 129
Cyr, Maine, U.S., 117 . . . . .286/E1
Cyrenaica, Lib., region 145/D1
Cyril, Okla., U.S., 1,168 . . . . .330/D3
Cyrus, Minn., U.S., 303 . . . . .298/B5
Czar, Alta., Can., 205 . . . . .212//E5
Czech Republic, nation 90
Częstochowa, Pol., 257,171 . . . . .83/D3
Dabakala, C. d'Iv. 150/C3
Dabney, Va., U.S. 346/H6
Dabola, Guin. 149/C2
Dachang, China .119/D3
Dachau, Ger. 86/B4
Dachstein, Aus., mountain 91/C3
Dacoma, Okla., U.S., 148 . . . . .330/D1
Dacono, Colo., U.S., 3,015 . . . . .250/A2, F1
Da Costa, N.J., U.S. 314/D4
Dacotah, Man., Can. 215/C4

Dacula, Ga., U.S., 3,848 . . . . .260/D4
Dade, Fla., U.S., county, 15,154 . . . . . .260/A2
Dade, Mo., U.S., county, 7,923 . . . . . . .302/C4
Dade City, Fla., U.S., 6,188 . . . . .256/F3
Dadeldhura, Nepal 128/C2
Dades, Mor., river 147/C2
Dadeville, Ala., U.S., 3,212 . . . . .238/D3
Dadeville, Mo., U.S., 224 . . . . .302/C4
Dadra and Nagar Haveli, India, territory . .128/B4
Dadu, Pak., 102,550 . . . . .129/C4
Daegu, S. Kor., 2,449,420 . . . . .116/C5
Daegu, S. Kor., province 116/C5
Daejeon, S. Kor., 1,272,121 . . . . .116/B4
Daejeon, S. Kor., province 116/B4
Daer, Eng., U.K., reservoir 62/H8
Dafni, Gr. 100/Inset
Dafoe, Sask., Can. 227/F9
Dafter, Mich., U.S., 250 . . . . .294/C4
Dagenham, Eng., U.K. 70/E3
Dagestan, Russ., region 104/D5
Daggett, Mich., U.S., 270 . . . . .294/B4
Daggett, Utah, U.S., county, 921 . . . . . .350/E3
Dagmar, Mont., U.S. 306/M1
Dagnall, Eng., U.K. 70/C3
Dagsboro, Del., U.S., 519 . . . . .255/C6
Daguao, P.R. 206/D2
Dagupan, Phil., 130,321 . . . . .120/B2
Dahlak, Erit., archipelago 156/C2
Dahlen, N. Dak., U.S., 40 . . . . .326/H1
Dahlgren, Ill., U.S., 514 . . . . .266/E5
Dahlia, N. Mex., U.S. 317/E2
Dahlonega, Ga., U.S., 3,638 . . . . .260/D2
Dahomey N.W.R., Miss., U.S. 300/B2
Dahuk, Iraq 130/B1
Daigle, Maine, U.S., 50 . . . . .286/D1
Dailey, Colo., U.S. 250/H1
Dailey, W. Va., U.S., 350 . . . . .360/G3
Dailly, Scot., U.K., 908 . . . . .62/G8
Daingerfield, Tex., U.S., 2,517 . . . . . . .346/P2
Dairsie, Scot., U.K. 62/L6
Dairy, Oreg., U.S., 50 . . . . .334/E5
Dairyland, Wisc., U.S. 364/A2
Daisy, Ark., U.S., 118 . . . . .244/B3
Daisy, Ga., U.S., 126 . . . . .260/H7
Daisy, Wash., U.S. 358/G1
Daisytown, Penn., U.S., 356 . . . . .336/D5
Dajabón, Dom. Rep. 205/A1
Dajabón, Dom. Rep., province 205/A1
Daka, Gha., river 150/B2
Dakar, Sen., capital, 879,703,
  (1,976,533 metro.) 148/A2
Dakhilah, Egy., oasis 144/A2
Dakota, Ga., U.S., 80 . . . . .260/D8
Dakota, Ill., U.S., 499 . . . . .266/D1
Dakota, Minn., U.S., 329 . . . . .298/F7
Dakota, Minn., U.S., county, 355,904 . .298/D6, F6
Dakota, Nebr., U.S., county, 20,253 . . . .308/H1
Dakota City, Iowa, U.S., 911 . . . . .274/F2
Dakota City, Nebr., U.S., 1,821 . . . . . .308/H1
Đakovica, Serb.-Mont. 99/B3
Dalälven, Swe., river 80/C2
Dalandzadgad, Mong. 118/C3
Dalark, Ark., U.S. 244/C3
Dalarna, Swe., county 80/B2
Da Lat, Viet., 106,409 . . . . .123/B4
Dalbeattie, Scot., U.K., 4,289 . . . . .62/H9
Dalblair, Scot., U.K. 62/H8
Dalbo, Minn., U.S., 80 . . . . .298/D5
Dalby, Eng., U.K. 66/A5
Dale, Wales, U.K. 64/A4
Dale, Ala., U.S., county, 49,129 . . . . . .238/D4
Dale, Ind., U.S., 1,568 . . . . .270/D8
Dale, Minn., U.S., 50 . . . . .298/A4
Dale, Okla., U.S., 212/ 330/E2
Dale, Oreg., U.S., 50 . . . . .334/H3
Dale, Tex., U.S., 212/ 346/E3
Dale City, Va., U.S., 55,971 . . . . .354/J3, L3
Dale Hollow, Tenn., U.S., lake 344/L1
Dales, Calif., U.S. 246/C2
Daleville, Ala., U.S., 4,653 . . . . .238/D4
Daleville, Ind., U.S., 1,658 . . . . .270/E4
Daleville, Miss., U.S., 175 . . . . .300/D3
Daleville, Va., U.S., 1,454 . . . . .354/D6
Daleyville, Wisc., U.S., 150 . . . . .364/D6
Dalham, Eng., U.K. 70/F2
Dalhart, Tex., U.S., 7,237 . . . . .346/F8
Dalhousie, N.B., Can., 3,975 . . . . .217/C1
Dali, China 119/E3
Dalian, China, 1,480,240, (4,619,060 metro.) . .119/F2
Daliburgh, Scot., U.K. 62/B4
Dalkeith, Scot., U.K., 11,566 . . . . .62/K7
Dalkena, Wash., U.S., 80 . . . . .358/H1
Dallam, Tex., U.S., county, 6,222 . . . . .346/E8
Dallas, Man., Can., 65 . . . . .215/C3
Dallas, Ala., U.S., county, 46,365 . . . . .238/B3
Dallas, Ark., U.S., county, 9,210 . . . . . .244/C4
Dallas, Ga., U.S., 5,056 . . . . .260/C4
Dallas, Iowa, U.S., county, 40,750 . . . . .274/F4
Dallas, Maine, U.S., 250 . . . . .286/B4
Dallas, Mo., U.S., county, 15,661 . . . . .302/C4
Dallas, N.C., U.S., 3,402 . . . . .322/C4
Dallas, Oreg., U.S., 12,459 . . . . .334/C2
Dallas, Penn., U.S., 2,557 . . . . .336/G7, K3
Dallas, S. Dak., U.S., 144 . . . . .342/F4
Dallas, Tex., U.S., 1,188,580,
  (5,221,801 metro.) 346/C9, M3
Dallas, Tex., U.S., county, 2,218,899 . .346/C9, M3, F3
Dallas, Wisc., U.S., 356 . . . . .364/B3
Dallas City, Ill., U.S., 1,055 . . . . .266/B3
Dallastown, Penn., U.S., 4,087 . . . . . . .336/H6
Dalesport, Wash., U.S., 1,185 . . . . . . .358/D4
Dallol Bosso, Niger, river 152/A3
Dalmally, Scot., U.K. 62/G6
Dalmatia, Cro., region 98/B3
Dalmellington, (Dalmellington and Burnton),
  Scot., U.K., 1,407 . . . . .62/H8
Dalnaspidal Lodge, Scot., U.K. 62/H5
Dalnavie, Scot., U.K. 62/H3
Daloa, C. d'Iv., 121,842, (127,923 metro.) . .150/C3
Dalry, Scot., U.K., 5,398 . . . . .62/G7
Dalrymple, Scot., U.K., 1,281 . . . . .62/G8
Dalswinton, Scot., U.K. 62/J8
Dalton, Eng., U.K. 66/F4
Dalton, Ark., U.S. 244/D1
Dalton, Ga., U.S., 27,912 . . . . .260/B2
Dalton, Ky., U.S., 100 . . . . .280/C3
Dalton, Mass., U.S., 6,892 . . . . .292/B3
Dalton, Minn., U.S., 258 . . . . .298/B4
Dalton, Mo., U.S. 302/D2
Dalton, Nebr., U.S., 332 . . . . .308/B2
Dalton, N.H., U.S., 927 . . . . .312/C3
Dalton, Ohio, U.S., 1,605 . . . . .328/G4
Dalton, Penn., U.S., 1,294 . . . . .336/K2
Dalton, Wisc., U.S., 250 . . . . .364/D5
Dalton City, Ill., U.S., 581 . . . . .266/E4
Dalton Gardens, Ida., U.S., 2,278 . . . . .358/H1
Dalton-in-Furness, Eng., U.K., 7,550 . . .66/B4
Dalvík, Ice. 79/B2
Dalworthington Gardens, Tex., U.S., 2,186 . .346/B10
Daly, Austl., river 170/C1

Daly City, Calif., U.S., 103,621 . . . . . . .246/J2
Daly River, Austl., aboriginal land 170/B1
Dalzell, Ill., U.S., 717 . . . . .266/D2
Dalzell, S.C., U.S., 2,260 . . . . .340/D2
Daman, India 128/B4
Daman and Diu, India, territory 128/B4
Damanhur, Egy., 212,000 . . . . .144/B1
Damar, Kans., U.S., 155 . . . . .276/C2
Damariscotta, Maine, U.S., 2,041 . . . . .286/C4
Damascus, Syria, capital, 1,394,322 . . .134/A3
Damascus, Ark., U.S., 306 . . . . .244/C2
Damascus, Ga., U.S., 277 . . . . .260/B9
Damascus, Md., U.S., 11,430 . . . . .288/F2
Damascus, Va., U.S., 981 . . . . .354/E3
Damaturu, Nig. 152/F2
Damavand, Iran, mountain 130/C2
Dame-Marie, Haiti 205/A2
Damerham, Eng., U.K. 73/J3
Dames Ferry, Ga., U.S., 70 . . . . .260/D5
Dames Quarter, Md., U.S., 188 . . . . . . .288/L7
Damiansville, Ill., U.S., 368 . . . . .266/D5
Damietta, Egy. 144/B1
Damietta, Egy., river 144/B1
Damon, Okla., U.S., 50 . . . . .330/G3
Dampier, W.A., Austl. 170/A2
Dan, Ky., U.S., 50 . . . . .280/C3
Dan, N.C., U.S., river 322/F2
Dana, Calif., U.S., 50 . . . . .246/D1
Dana, Ill., U.S., 171 . . . . .266/E3
Dana, Ind., U.S., 662 . . . . .270/B5
Dana, Iowa, U.S., 84 . . . . .274/F3
Danané, C. d'Iv. 150/B3
Da Nang, Viet., 679,741 . . . . .123/B3
Dana Pt., Calif., U.S., 35,110 . . . . .246/E11
Danbury, Conn., U.S., 74,848 . . . . .253/B4
Danbury, Iowa, U.S., 384 . . . . .274/C3
Danbury, Nebr., U.S., 127 . . . . .308/D3
Danbury, N.H., U.S., 1,071 . . . . .312/C4
Danbury, N.C., U.S., 108 . . . . .322/E2
Danbury, Tex., U.S., 1,611 . . . . .346/N6
Danbury, Wisc., U.S., 225 . . . . .364/A2
Danby, Eng., U.K. 66/G4
Danby, Vt., U.S., 1,292 . . . . .352/B4
Danby Four Corners, Vt., U.S., 80 . . . . .352/A4
Dancy, Ala., U.S., 100 . . . . .238/A2
Dancyville, Tenn., U.S., 80 . . . . .344/C4
Dand, Man., Can. 215/A4
Dande, Ang., river 159/B2
Dandenong, Vic., Austl. . . . . .170/Inset V
Dandong, China, 545,180, (2,574,020 metro.) . .119/F1
Dandridge, Tenn., U.S., 2,078 . . . . . . .344/Q2
Dane, Wisc., U.S., 799 . . . . .364/D5
Dane, Wisc., U.S., county, 426,526 . . . .364/D6
Danebridge, Eng., U.K. 68/C3
Danehill, Eng., U.K. 70/E4
Danese, W. Va., U.S., 350 . . . . .360/E5
Danforth, Ill., U.S., 587 . . . . .266/F3
Danforth, Maine, U.S., 629 . . . . .286/E3
Dangara, Taj. 132/A1
Dangme, Bhu., river 126/C2
Dangrek, Camb., mountains 124/B1
Dangrek, Thai., mountains 125/C3
Dangriga, Bel., 8,814 . . . . .201/B2
Dania, Fla., U.S., 20,061 . . . . .256/B6
Daniel, Md., U.S., 650 . . . . .288/F2
Daniel, Wyo., U.S., 89 . . . . .366/A2
Daniel Boone Natl. For., Ky., U.S. 280/G3
Daniels, Mont., U.S., county, 2,017 . . . .306/L1
Daniels, W. Va., U.S., 1,846 . . . . .360/D5
Daniels Harbour, Nfld., Can., 350 . . . . .206/C4
Danielson, Conn., U.S., 4,265 . . . . . . .253/H2
Danielsville, Ga., U.S., 457 . . . . .260/E3
Danjiangkou, China 119/E2
Danli, Hond., 43,300 . . . . .202/B2
Dannebrog, Nebr., U.S., 352 . . . . .308/E2
Dannemora, N.Y., U.S., 4,129 . . . . .320/P1
Dansville, Mich., U.S., 429 . . . . .294/E7
Dansville, N.Y., U.S., 4,832 . . . . .320/F5
Dante, S. Dak., U.S., 82 . . . . .342/G4
Dante, Va., U.S., 650 . . . . .354/D2
Danube, Bul., river 101/B2
Danube, Ger., river 86/B4, C4
Danube, Ger., river 91/D2
Danube, Hun., river 91/A2, B2
Danube, Rom., river 101/B3, D3, E3
Danube, Serb.-Mont., river 99/A2, B2
Danube, Slvk., river 91/B2
Danube, Minn., U.S., 529 . . . . .298/B6
Danvers, Ill., U.S., 1,183 . . . . .266/E3
Danvers, Mass., U.S., 25,212 . . . . .292/D6, L2
Danvers, Minn., U.S., 108 . . . . .298/B5
Danvers, Mont., U.S. 306/G2
Danville, Que., Can., 4,301 . . . . .226/D6
Danville, Ark., U.S., 2,392 . . . . .244/B2
Danville, Calif., U.S., 41,715 . . . . .246/K2
Danville, Ga., U.S., 373 . . . . .260/E6
Danville, Ill., U.S., 33,904 . . . . .266/F3
Danville, Ind., U.S., 6,418 . . . . .270/D5
Danville, Iowa, U.S., 914 . . . . .274/M6
Danville, Kans., U.S., 59 . . . . .276/E4
Danville, Ky., U.S., 15,477 . . . . .280/F3
Danville, La., U.S. 282/D2
Danville, Maine, U.S., 125 . . . . .286/B4
Danville, N.H., U.S., 4,023 . . . . .312/D6
Danville, Ohio, U.S., 1,104 . . . . .328/F5
Danville, Penn., U.S., 4,897 . . . . .336/H4
Danville, Vt., U.S., 2,211 . . . . .352/C2
Danville, Va., U.S., 48,411, (110,156 metro.) . .354/E7
Danville, Wash., U.S., 70 . . . . .358/G1
Danville, W. Va., U.S., 691 . . . . .360/C4
Dao Phu Quoc, Viet., island 123/A4
Daoura, Alg., river 146/A2
Dapaong, Togo 151/B1
Daphne, Ala., U.S., 16,581 . . . . .238/B5
Dapp, Alta., Can. 212/D4
Dara, Sen. 148/A2
Dar'a, Syria 134/A3
Đaravica, Serb.-Mont., mountain 99/B3
Darbhanga, India 128/C3
Darbonne N.W.R., La., U.S. 282/E1
Darby, Mont., U.S., 710 . . . . .306/B3
Darby, Penn., U.S., 10,299 . . . . .336/L7
Darbyville, Ohio, U.S., 293 . . . . .328/D6
Darco, Tex., U.S., 70 . . . . .346/P3
Dardanelle, Ark., U.S., 4,228 . . . . .244/B2
Dardanelle, Calif., U.S. 246/F4
Dardanelle Res., Ark., U.S. 244/A2
Darden, Tenn., U.S., 212/ 344/K3
Dardenne Prairie, Mo., U.S., 4,384 . . . .302/F3
Dare, N.C., U.S., county, 29,967 . . . . . .322/P3
Dares Beach, Md., U.S., 1,400 . . . . . . .288/H5
Dar es Salaam, Tan., capital, 1,360,850 . .158/C2
Dar es Salaam, Tan., region 158/C2
Daretown, N.J., U.S. 314/C4
Darfield, Eng., U.K., 7,723 . . . . .66/F5
Darfield, Eng., U.K., 7,723 . . . . .66/B4
Darfur, Minn., U.S., 137 . . . . .298/C6
Dargan, Md., U.S., 350 . . . . .288/D2
Dargaville, N.Z. 171/B2
Darhan, Mong., 89,900 . . . . .118/C2

Darién, Pan., mountains 203/D2
Darien, Pan., province 203/C3
Darien, Conn., U.S., 19,607 . . . . .253/B5
Darien, Ill., U.S., 1,719 . . . . .260/J9
Darien, Ill., U.S., 22,860 . . . . .266/B6
Darien, Wisc., U.S., 1,572 . . . . .364/E6
Darjiling, India 128/C3
Darke, Ohio, U.S., county, 53,309 . . . . .328/A5
Darling, Austl., range 170/A3
Darling, Austl., river 170/D3
Darling, Miss., U.S., 325 . . . . .300/B1
Darlington, Eng., U.K. 60/C2
Darlington, Eng., U.K., 86,767 . . . . .66/E3
Darlington, Eng., U.K., unitary authority, 97,822 . .66/E3
Darlington, Fla., U.S., 175 . . . . .256/H1
Darlington, Ida., U.S., 60 . . . . .264/D6
Darlington, Ind., U.S., 854 . . . . .270/C4
Darlington, La., U.S., 50 . . . . .282/H5
Darlington, Md., U.S., 350 . . . . .288/K1
Darlington, Mo., U.S., 113 . . . . .302/B1
Darlington, Penn., U.S., 299 . . . . .336/A4
Darlington, S.C., U.S., 6,720 . . . . .340/E2
Darlington, S.C., U.S., county, 67,394 . .340/E2
Darlington, Wisc., U.S., 2,418 . . . . .364/C6
Darlove, Miss., U.S. 300/B2
Darlowo, Pol. 83/C1
Darmstadt, Ger., 137,776 . . . . .86/B4
Darmstadt, Ger., department 86/A3
Darmstadt, Ind., U.S., 1,313 . . . . .270/A8
Darnah, Lib. 145/D1
Darnell, La., U.S., 80 . . . . .282/C1
Darnley, P.E.I., Can. 224/B2
Darr, Nebr., U.S. 308/E3
Darragh, Mich., U.S., 212/ 294/D5
Darras Hall, Eng., U.K. 66/E2
Darrington, Wash., U.S., 1,136 . . . . . . .358/D1
Darrouzett, Tex., U.S., 303 . . . . .346/G8
Dartford, Eng., U.K., 59,411 . . . . .70/E4
Dartmoor, Eng., U.K., forest 60/B4
Dartmoor Natl. Park, Eng., U.K. 73/E3
Dartmouth, N.S., Can. 221/D3
Dartmouth, Eng., U.K., 5,676 . . . . .73/E4
Dartmouth, Mass., U.S., 30,666 . . . . . .292/K6
Daru, P.N.G. 172/A2
Darwen, Eng., U.K., 29,864 . . . . .66/D5
Darwen, Eng., U.K., 29,864 . . . . .68/C2
Darwin, N.T., Austl., territorial capital . . .170/C1
Darwin, Calif., U.S., 54 . . . . .246/H6
Darwin, Ill., U.S., 80 . . . . .266/F4
Darwin, Minn., U.S., 276 . . . . .298/C5
Dasher, Ga., U.S., 834 . . . . .260/E1
Dashhowuz, Turkm., 114,000 . . . . .132/C2
Dashhowuz, Turkm., province 132/C2
Dassel, Minn., U.S., 1,233 . . . . .298/C5
Date, Ariz., U.S. 242/C3
Dateland, Ariz., U.S., 70 . . . . .242/B5
Datil, N. Mex., U.S., 60 . . . . .317/C2
Datong, China 119/E1
Datto, Ark., U.S., 97 . . . . .244/E1
Daua, Kenya, river 157/F1
Daufuskie Island, S.C., U.S. 340/D4
Daugavpils, Lat., 114,980 . . . . .82/D3
Daule, Ecua., river 185/B3
Dauntsey, Eng., U.K. 73/H1
Dauphin, Man., Can., 8,085 . . . . .215/A3
Dauphin, Man., Can., lake 215/B3
Dauphin, St. Luc. 208/B1
Dauphin, Ala., U.S., island 238/A5
Dauphin, Penn., U.S., 773 . . . . .336/H5
Dauphin, Penn., U.S., county, 251,798 . .336/H5
Dauphin Island, Ala., U.S., 1,371 . . . . .238/A5
Dauphin Island, Ala., U.S. 238/A5
Dauphin River, Man., Can. 215/B3
Daus, Tenn., U.S., 325 . . . . .344/L4
Davant, La., U.S., 212/ 282/K7
Davao, Phil., 1,147,116 . . . . .120/C5
Davao, Phil., gulf 120/C5
Davenham, Eng., U.K. 68/B3
Davenport, Calif., U.S. 246/J4
Davenport, Fla., U.S., 1,924 . . . . .256/G5
Davenport, Iowa, U.S., 98,359,
  (359,062 metro.) 274/N4
Davenport, Nebr., U.S., 339 . . . . .308/G3
Davenport, N.Y., U.S., 60 . . . . .320/M6
Davenport, N. Dak., U.S., 261 . . . . . . .326/H3
Davenport, Okla., U.S., 881 . . . . .330/F2
Davenport, Wash., U.S., 1,730 . . . . . . .358/G2
Daventry, Eng., U.K., 18,099 . . . . .68/E5
Daventry, Eng., U.K., 18,099 . . . . .70/B2
Davey, Nebr., U.S., 153 . . . . .308/H3
David, Pan. 203/A2
David, Ky., U.S., 300 . . . . .280/H3
David City, Nebr., U.S., 2,597 . . . . . . .308/G2
Davidson, Sask., Can., 1,035 . . . . .227/D9
Davidson, Maine, U.S. 286/D3
Davidson, N.C., U.S., 7,139 . . . . .322/D3
Davidson, N.C., U.S., county, 147,246 . .322/E3
Davidson, Okla., U.S., 375 . . . . .330/C3
Davidson, Tenn., U.S., county, 569,891 . .344/H2
Davie, Fla., U.S., 75,720 . . . . .256/B6, H5
Davie, N.C., U.S., county, 34,835 . . . . . .322/D3
Daviess, Ind., U.S., county, 29,820 . . . . .270/B7
Daviess, Ky., U.S., county, 91,545 . . . . .280/B2
Daviess, Mo., U.S., county, 8,016 . . . . .302/B2
Daviot, Scot., U.K. 62/H4
Davis, Nun., Can., strait 208/R3
Davis, Grld., strait 193/B2
Davis, Calif., U.S., 60,308 . . . . .246/K5
Davis, Ill., U.S., 662 . . . . .266/D1
Davis, Iowa, U.S., county, 8,541 . . . . . .274/K6
Davis, Okla., U.S., 2,610 . . . . .330/E3
Davis, Oreg., U.S., lake 334/E4
Davis, S. Dak., U.S., 104 . . . . .342/J4
Davis, Tex., U.S., mountains 346/E4
Davis, Utah, U.S., county, 238,994 . . . .350/B3, E1
Davis, W. Va., U.S., 624 . . . . .360/H2
Davisboro, Ga., U.S., 1,544 . . . . .260/F6
Davis City, Iowa, U.S., 275 . . . . .274/G6
Davis Creek, Calif., U.S., 70 . . . . .246/E1
Davis Inlet, Nfld., Can. 206/C2
Davis Jct., Ill., U.S., 491 . . . . .266/D1
Davison, Mich., U.S., 5,536 . . . . .294/F6
Davison, S. Dak., U.S., county, 18,741 . .342/G4
Daviston, Ala., U.S., 267 . . . . .238/D2
Davisville, Mo., U.S. 302/E4
Davisville, N.H., U.S., 225 . . . . .312/C5
Davos, Switz. 90/D2
Davy, W. Va., U.S., 373 . . . . .360/C6
Davy Crockett Natl. For., Tex., U.S. 346/P4
Dawa, Eth., river 156/C3
Dawes, Nebr., U.S., county, 9,060 . . . . .308/A1
Dawkah, Oman 137/B2
Dawlah, Eng., U.K., 9,648 . . . . .73/F3
Dawn, Va., U.S., 100 . . . . .354/J5
Dawna, Thai., range 125/B2
Dawson, Man., Can., bay 215/A2
Dawson, Yukon, Can., 1,251 . . . . .228/B3
Dawson, Ga., U.S., 5,058 . . . . .260/C7
Dawson, Ga., U.S., county, 15,999 . . . . .260/C3
Dawson, Ill., U.S., 466 . . . . .266/D4

Dawson, Iowa, U.S., 155 . . . . .274/F4
Dawson, Minn., U.S., 1,539 . . . . .298/A6
Dawson, Mo., U.S., 50 . . . . .302/D4
Dawson, Mont., U.S., county, 9,059 . . . .306/L2
Dawson, Nebr., U.S., 209 . . . . .308/J3
Dawson, Nebr., U.S., county, 24,365 . . .308/E3
Dawson, N. Dak., U.S., 75 . . . . .326/F3
Dawson, Penn., U.S., 451 . . . . .336/B5
Dawson Creek, Br. Col., Can., 10,754 . . .214/M3
Dawson Sprs., Ky., U.S., 2,980 . . . . . . .280/C3
Dawsonville, N.B., Can. 217/C1
Dawsonville, Ga., U.S., 619 . . . . .260/C3
Day, Fla., U.S., 90 . . . . .256/E1
Day, Minn., U.S. 298/D5
Day, S. Dak., U.S., county, 6,267 . . . . . .342/H2
Day Hts., Ohio, U.S., 2,823 . . . . .328/C9
Daykin, Nebr., U.S., 177 . . . . .308/G3
Daymán, Uru., river 187/B1
Dayr az Zawr, Syria, 140,459, (201,306 metro.) . .134/B2
Days Creek, Oreg., U.S., 100 . . . . .334/C5
Daysland, Alta., Can., 779 . . . . .212/D5
Daysville, Ky., U.S., 90 . . . . .280/C4
Dayton, Ala., U.S., 60 . . . . .238/B3
Dayton, Ida., U.S., 444 . . . . .264/E7
Dayton, Ind., U.S., 1,120 . . . . .270/C4
Dayton, Iowa, U.S., 884 . . . . .274/F3
Dayton, Ky., U.S., 5,966 . . . . .280/F1, G1
Dayton, Md., U.S., 600 . . . . .288/G3
Dayton, Minn., U.S., 4,699 . . . . .298/D5
Dayton, Mont., U.S., 95 . . . . .306/B2
Dayton, Nev., U.S., 5,907 . . . . .310/A2
Dayton, N.J., U.S., 6,235 . . . . .314/F3
Dayton, N. Mex., U.S. 317/F5
Dayton, Ohio, U.S., 166,179,
  (950,558 metro.) 328/B6, F2
Dayton, Oreg., U.S., 2,119 . . . . .334/C2
Dayton, Penn., U.S., 543 . . . . .336/C4
Dayton, Tenn., U.S., 6,180 . . . . .344/L3
Dayton, Tex., U.S., 5,709 . . . . .346/C5
Dayton, Va., U.S., 1,344 . . . . .354/F4
Dayton, Wash., U.S., 2,655 . . . . .358/H3
Dayton, Wisc., U.S., 175 . . . . .364/D6
Dayton, Wyo., U.S., 678 . . . . .366/C1
Daytona Beach, Fla., U.S., 64,112,
  (493,175 metro.) 256/G2
Daytona Beach Shores, Fla., U.S., 4,299 . .256/H2
Dayton Aviation Heritage N.H.P., Ohio, U.S. . .328/C5
Dayton Lakes, Tex., U.S., 101 . . . . . . .346/C5
Day Valley, Calif., U.S., 3,587 . . . . . . .246/K4
Dayville, Conn., U.S., 1,600 . . . . .253/H2
Dayville, Oreg., U.S., 138 . . . . .334/G3
Dazey, N. Dak., U.S., 91 . . . . .326/G2
De Aar, S. Afr. 162/B3
Dead, Isr., sea 135/B2
Deadman, Fla., U.S., bay 256/E2
Dead Sea, Jor., lake 134/A2
Deadwood, S. Dak., U.S., 1,380 . . . . . .342/B3
Deaf Smith, Tex., U.S., county, 18,561 . .346/E9
Deal, Eng., U.K., 28,504 . . . . .70/G4
Deal, N.J., U.S., 1,070 . . . . .314/F3
Deale, Md., U.S., 4,796 . . . . .288/H4
Deal Island, Md., U.S., 578 . . . . .288/L7
Dean, Br. Col., Can., channel 214/J5
Dean, Br. Col., Can., river 214/K5
Dean, Mont., U.S. 306/G4
Dean, Tex., U.S., 341 . . . . .346/K2
De Ann, Ark., U.S., 50 . . . . .244/B4
Deanshanger, Eng., U.K., 2,724 . . . . . .68/F5
Deanshanger, Eng., U.K., 2,724 . . . . . .70/B2
Dearborn, Ind., U.S., county, 46,109 . . .270/F6
Dearborn, Mich., U.S., 97,775 . . . . . . .294/A7
Dearborn, Mo., U.S., 529 . . . . .302/B2
Dearborn Hts., Mich., U.S., 58,264 . . . .294/A7
Dearing, Ga., U.S., 441 . . . . .260/G5
Dearing, Kans., U.S., 415 . . . . .276/G4
Deary, Ida., U.S., 552 . . . . .264/C3
Dease Lake, Br. Col., Can. 214/G2
Death, Calif., U.S., valley 246/G6
Death Valley, Calif., U.S. 246/G6
Death Valley Jct., Calif., U.S. 246/G6
Death Valley Natl. Park, Calif., U.S. 246/G6
Deatsville, Ala., U.S., 340 . . . . .238/C3
Deauville, Fr. 88/C2
Deaver, Wyo., U.S., 177 . . . . .366/B1
De Baca, N. Mex., U.S., county, 2,240 . .317/F3
Debar, Mac. 100/A2
De Bary, Fla., U.S., 15,559 . . . . .256/G3
Debden, Sask., Can., 355 . . . . .227/D7
Debden, Eng., U.K. 70/E2
Debec, N.B., Can., 135 . . . . .217/B2
Debed, Arm., river 103/B2
De Beque, Colo., U.S., 451 . . . . .250/B2
DeBolt, Alta., Can., 124 . . . . .212//A3
Deblois, Maine, U.S., 49 . . . . .286/D4
Debre Birhan, Eth. 156/C2
Debrecen, Hun., 204,340 . . . . .91/C2
Debrecen, Hun. 91/C2
Debre Markos, Eth. 156/C2
Debs, Minn., U.S. 298/B3
Decatur, Ala., U.S., 53,929, (145,867 metro.) . .238/C1
Decatur, Ark., U.S., 1,314 . . . . .244/A1
Decatur, Ga., U.S., 18,147 . . . . .260/C4, J3
Decatur, Ga., U.S., county, 28,240 . . . . .260/B9
Decatur, Ill., U.S., 81,860, (114,706 metro.) . .266/D4
Decatur, Ind., U.S., 9,528 . . . . .270/G3
Decatur, Ind., U.S., county, 24,555 . . . .270/E6
Decatur, Iowa, U.S., county, 8,689 . . . . .274/G6
Decatur, Kans., U.S., county, 3,472 . . . .276/C2
Decatur, Miss., U.S., 1,838 . . . . .294/C7
Decatur, Miss., U.S., 1,426 . . . . .300/C3
Decatur, Nebr., U.S., 618 . . . . .308/H1
Decatur, Ohio, U.S., 150 . . . . .328/C8
Decatur, Tenn., U.S., 1,395 . . . . .344/M3
Decatur, Tenn., U.S., county, 11,731 . . .344/F3
Decatur, Tex., U.S., 5,201 . . . . .346/L2
Decatur City, Iowa, U.S., 199 . . . . .274/G6
Decaturville, Mo., U.S. 302/D4
Decaturville, Tenn., U.S., 859 . . . . .344/E3
Deccan, India, plateau 128/C5
Decherd, Tenn., U.S., 2,246 . . . . .344/J4
Decker, Ind., U.S., 283 . . . . .270/B7
Decker, Mont., U.S. 306/K4
Deckers, Colo., U.S. 250/E2
Deckerville, Ark., U.S., 60 . . . . .244/D2
Deckerville, Mich., U.S., 944 . . . . .294/G6
Declo, Ida., U.S., 338 . . . . .264/D7
Decorah, Iowa, U.S., 8,172 . . . . .274/L1
Decoy, Ky., U.S. 280/G3
Dedham, Iowa, U.S., 260 . . . . .274/E4
Dedham, Mass., U.S., 23,464 . . . . .292/K4
Dédougou, Burkina 151/C2
Dedza, Mal. 159/B2
Dee, Scot., U.K., river 60/C1
Dee, Wales, U.K., river 60/B3
Dee, Wales, U.K., river 64/F1
Dee, Oreg., U.S., 212/ 334/F2
Deemer, Miss., U.S., 350 . . . . .300/C3
Deemston, Penn., U.S., 809 . . . . .336/B5
Deenwood, Ga., U.S., 1,836 . . . . .260/E9
Deep, Nfld., Can., inlet 206/B1
Deep, H.K., China, bay 117/A

Deep, N.C., U.S., *river* 322/F3
Deep Creek, Md., U.S., *lake* 288/A3
Deep Creek, Wash., U.S., 275 ....358/H2
Deepdale, Man., Can. 215/A3
Deep Gap, N.C., U.S., 212/ 322/C2
Deephaven, Minn., U.S., 3,853 ....298/D6
Deeping St. Nicholas, Eng., U.K. 70/D1
Deep River, Ont., Can., 4,135 ....223/H1
Deep River, Conn., U.S., 4,610 ....253/F4
Deep River, Iowa, U.S., 288 ....274/K4
Deep Run, N.C., U.S., 300 ....322/K4
Deep Sprs., Calif., U.S. 246/H5
Deepstep, Ga., U.S., 132 ....260/F5
Deepwater, Mo., U.S., 507 ....302/C3
Deepwater, N.J., U.S., 1,700 ....314/C4
Deer, Nfld., Can., *lake* 206/C4
Deer, Ark., U.S., 100 ....244/B2
Deerbrook, Wisc., U.S., 125 ....364/D3
Deer Creek, Ill., U.S., 605 ....266/D3
Deer Creek, Ind., U.S., 250 ....270/D3
Deer Creek, Minn., U.S., 328 ....298/B4
Deer Creek, Okla., U.S., 147 ....330/E1
Deer Creek Ind. Res., Minn., U.S. 298/D3
Deerfield, Ill., U.S., 18,420 ....266/B5
Deerfield, Kans., U.S., 884 ....276/A4
Deerfield, Mass., U.S., 4,750 ....292/D2
Deerfield, Mich., U.S., 1,005 ....294/F8
Deerfield, Mo., U.S., 75 ....302/B4
Deerfield, N.H., U.S., 3,678 ....312/D5
Deerfield, N.J., U.S., 2,927 ....314/C4
Deerfield, Ohio, U.S., 300 ....328/H3
Deerfield, Va., U.S., 100 ....354/E4
Deerfield, Wisc., U.S., 1,971 ....364/D5
Deerfield Beach, Fla., U.S., 64,583 ....256/B5, H5
Deerfield Ctr., N.H., U.S., 275 ....312/D5
Deer Grove, Ill., U.S., 48 ....266/D2
Deering, Alaska, U.S., 136 ....240/C1
Deering, N.H., U.S., 1,875 ....312/C5
Deering, N. Dak., U.S., 118 ....326/D1
Deer Isle, Maine, U.S., 1,876 ....286/D4
Deer Isle, Maine, U.S., *island* 286/D4
Deer Lake, Nfld., Can., 4,769 ....206/C4
Deer Lake, Penn., U.S., 528 ....336/J4
Deer Lodge, Mont., U.S., 3,421 ....306/D3
Deer Lodge, Mont., U.S., *county*, 9,417 ....306/C3
Deer Park, Ala., U.S. 238/A4
Deer Park, Fla., U.S., 60 ....256/H3
Deer Park, Ill., U.S., 3,102 ....266/B5
Deer Park, Md., U.S., 405 ....288/A4
Deer Park, Mich., U.S. 294/D3
Deer Park, N.Y., U.S., 28,316 ....320/D2
Deer Park, Ohio, U.S., 5,982 ....328/B9
Deer Park, Tex., U.S., 28,520 ....346/B6
Deer Park, Wash., U.S., 3,017 ....358/H2
Deer Park, Wisc., U.S., 227 ....364/A3
Deer River, Minn., U.S., 903 ....298/D3
Deersville, Ohio, U.S., 82 ....328/H5
Deerton, Mich., U.S. 294/B3
Deer Trail, Colo., U.S., 598 ....250/F2
Deerwood, Minn., U.S., 590 ....298/D4
Deeson, Miss., U.S. 300/B1
Deeth, Nev., U.S. 310/C1
Dee Why, N.S.W., Austl. ....170/Inset IV
Deferiet, N.Y., U.S., 309 ....320/K2
Defford, Eng., U.K. 68/C5
Defiance, Iowa, U.S., 346 ....274/D4
Defiance, Ohio, U.S., 16,465 ....328/B3
Defiance, Ohio, U.S., *county*, 39,500 ....328/A3
Deford, Mich., U.S., 325 ....294/F6
DeForest, (Bolindale), Ohio, U.S., 2,800 ....328/J3
De Forest, Wisc., U.S., 7,368 ....364/D5
De Funiak Sprs., Fla., U.S., 5,089 ....256/B1
Defynnog, Wales, U.K. 64/D4
Degeh Bur, Eth. 156/D2
Dégelis, Que., Can., 3,317 ....226/H4
De Graff, Minn., U.S., 133 ....298/B5
De Graff, Ohio, U.S., 1,212 ....328/C5
Degray, Ark., U.S., *lake* 244/B3
Dehiwala-Mt. Lavinia, Sri Lan., 209,787 ....128/C2
Dehra Dun, India 128/C2
Deighton, Eng., U.K. 66/F4
Déïn, Czh. Rep. 92/B2
Dej, Rom. 101/B2
De Kalb, Ala., U.S., *county*, 64,452 ....238/D1
De Kalb, Ga., U.S., *county*, 665,865 ....260/C4, J3
De Kalb, Ill., U.S., 39,018 ....266/E2
De Kalb, Ill., U.S., *county*, 88,969 ....266/E2
De Kalb, Ind., U.S., *county*, 40,285 ....270/G2
De Kalb, Miss., U.S., 972 ....300/D3
De Kalb, Mo., U.S., 257 ....302/B2
De Kalb, Mo., U.S., *county*, 11,597 ....302/B2
De Kalb, Tenn., U.S., *county*, 17,423 ....344/K3
De Kalb Jct., N.Y., U.S., 450 ....320/L2
Dekle Beach, Fla., U.S. 256/E2
Dekoven, Ky., U.S., 225 ....280/B3
Delabole, Eng., U.K. 73/C3
Delacour, Alta., Can. 212/D5
Delacroix, La., U.S. 282/K7, L4
Delafield, Ill., U.S., 40 ....266/E5
Delafield, Wisc., U.S., 6,472 ....364/E2
De Lancey, N.Y., U.S., 150 ....320/M6
Delanco, N.J., U.S., 3,237 ....314/D3
De Land, Fla., U.S., 20,904 ....256/G2
De Land, Ill., U.S., 475 ....266/E3
Delano, Calif., U.S., 38,824 ....246/E7
Delano, Minn., U.S., 3,837 ....298/D6
Delano, Tenn., U.S., 425 ....344/M4
Delano, Utah, U.S., *peak* 350/B5
Delanson, N.Y., U.S., 385 ....320/N5
Delaplaine, Ark., U.S., 127 ....244/E1
Delaps Cove, N.S., Can. 221/B3
Delaronde, Sask., Can., *lake* 227/C6
Delavan, Ill., U.S., 1,825 ....266/D3
Delavan, Kans., U.S., 40 ....276/F3
Delavan, Minn., U.S., 223 ....298/C7
Delavan, Wisc., U.S., 7,956 ....364/E6
Delaware, U.S., *state* 243
Delaware, Ark., U.S., 125 ....244/B2
Delaware, Del., U.S., *bay* 255/D4
Delaware, Del., U.S., *river* 255/B2
Delaware, Ind., U.S., *county* 118,769 ....270/F4
Delaware, Iowa, U.S., 188 ....274/M3
Delaware, Iowa, U.S., *county*, 18,404 ....274/M3
Delaware, Mich., U.S. 294/A2
Delaware, N.J., U.S., 4,478 ....314/C2
Delaware, N.J., U.S., *bay* 314/C5
Delaware, N.J., U.S., *river* 314/B5, D3
Delaware, N.Y., U.S., *county*, 48,055 ....320/L6
Delaware, Ohio, U.S., 25,243 ....328/D5
Delaware, Ohio, U.S., *county*, 109,989 ....328/D8, D5
Delaware, Okla., U.S., 456 ....330/G1
Delaware, Okla., U.S., *county*, 37,077 ....330/H1
Delaware, Penn., U.S., *county*, 550,864 ....336/K6, K7
Delaware, Penn., U.S., *river* 336/L2, L7
Delaware City, Del., U.S., 1,453 ....255/B2
Delaware Seashore St. Park, Del., U.S. 255/D6
Delaware St. For., Penn., U.S. 336/L3
Delaware Water Gap, Penn., U.S., 744 ....336/L4
Delbarton, W. Va., U.S., 474 ....360/B5
Del Bonita, Alta., Can. 212//D6
Delburne, Alta., Can., 719 ....212//D5

Delcambre, La., U.S., 2,168 ....282/F7
Del City, Okla., U.S., 22,128 ....330/B4
Delco, N.C., U.S., 275 ....322/J6
Deleau, Man., Can. 215/A4
De Leon, Tex., U.S., 2,433 ....346/K3
De Leon Sprs., Fla., U.S., 2,358 ....256/G2
Delevan, N.Y., U.S., 1,089 ....320/E6
Delft, Neth. 84/B3
Delft, Sri Lan., *island* 126/A2
Delft, Minn., U.S., 90 ....298/B7
Delfzijl, Neth. 84/D1
Delgado, El. Salv. 203/A2
Del Haven, N.J., U.S., 1,212/ 314/D5
Delhi, Ont., Can., 4,002 ....223/E5
Delhi, India, 9,817,439, (12,791,458 metro.) 128/C3
Delhi, India, *territory* 128/C3
Delhi, Calif., U.S., 8,022 ....246/E5
Delhi, Colo., U.S. 250/F4
Delhi, Iowa, U.S., 458 ....274/M3
Delhi, La., U.S., 3,066 ....282/G2
Delhi, Minn., U.S., 69 ....298/B6
Delhi, N.Y., U.S., 2,583 ....320/M6
Delhi, Okla., U.S. 330/C2
Delia, Kans., U.S., 179 ....276/G2
Delicias, Mex. 98,615, (116,426 metro.) 200/C2
Delight, Ark., U.S., 311 ....244/B3
Deline, N.W. Terr., Can., 536 ....208/D3
Delisle, Sask., Can., 884 ....227/C9
De Lisle, Miss., U.S., 800 ....300/C5
Dell, Ark., U.S., 251 ....244/E2
Dell, Mont., U.S. 306/D5
Dell City, Tex., U.S., 413 ....346/C4
Dell Rapids, S. Dak., U.S., 2,980 ....342/J4
Dellroy, Ohio, U.S., 294 ....328/H4
Dellslow, W. Va., U.S., 375 ....360/F2
Dellvale, Kans., U.S. 276/B2
Dellview, N.C., U.S. 322/C4
Dellwood, Fla., U.S., 125 ....256/C1
Dellwood, Minn., U.S., 1,053 ....298/F5
Dellwood, Mo., U.S., 255 ....302/H2
Dellwood, Wisc., U.S., 175 ....364/D5
Del Mar, Calif., U.S., 4,389 ....246/H10
Delmar, Del., U.S., 1,407 ....255/B7
Delmar, Iowa, U.S., 514 ....274/N3
Delmar, Md., U.S., 1,859 ....288/M6
Delmar, N.Y., U.S., 8,292 ....320/P5
Delmont, N.J., U.S., 80 ....314/C5
Delmont, Penn., U.S., 2,497 ....336/B5
Delmont, S. Dak., U.S., 263 ....342/G4
Del Norte, Calif., U.S., *county*, 27,507 ....246/A1
Del Norte, Colo., U.S., 1,705 ....250/D4
Deloit, Iowa, U.S., 288 ....274/D3
Delong, Ind., U.S., 450 ....270/D2
Deloraine, Man., Can., 1,026 ....215/A4
Delos, Gr., *island* 100/C3
Delphi, Ind., U.S., 3,015 ....270/D3
Delphia, Mont., U.S. 306/H3
Delphos, Iowa, U.S. 274/F4
Delphos, Kans., U.S., 469 ....276/E2
Delphos, Ohio, U.S., 6,944 ....328/B4
Delray, W. Va., U.S., 90 ....360/J2
Delray Beach, Fla., U.S., 60,020 ....256/B5, H5
Delrey, Ill., U.S. 266/E3
Del Rey Oaks, Calif., U.S., 1,650 ....246/D6
Del Rio, Fla., U.S. 256/D6
Del Rio, Tex., U.S., 33,867 ....346/H6
Delson, Que., Can. 226/J6
Delta, Nig., *state* 152/C5
Delta, Ala., U.S., 90 ....238/D2
Delta, Colo., U.S., 6,400 ....250/B3
Delta, Colo., U.S., *county*, 27,834 ....250/C3
Delta, Iowa, U.S., 410 ....274/K5
Delta, La., U.S., 239 ....282/H2
Delta, Mich., U.S., *county*, 38,520 ....294/C3
Delta, Mo., U.S., 517 ....302/G4
Delta, Ohio, U.S., 2,930 ....328/B2
Delta, Penn., U.S., 741 ....336/J6
Delta, Tex., U.S., *county*, 5,327 ....346/N2
Delta, Utah, U.S., 3,209 ....350/B4
Delta Amacuro, Ven., *state* 182/D2
Delta Beach, Man., Can. 215/B4
Delta City, Miss., U.S., 100 ....300/B2
Delta Jct., Alaska, U.S., 840 ....240/F2
Delta Natl. For., Miss., U.S. 300/B3
Delta N.W.R., La., U.S. 282/L8
Deltaville, Va., U.S., 800 ....354/L5
Deltona, Fla., U.S., 69,543 ....256/G3
Del Valle, Tex., U.S., 1,300 ....346/D2
Demarest, N.J., U.S., 4,845 ....314/C1
Demerara, Guy., *river* 183/B3
Deming, N. Mex., U.S., 14,116 ....317/C5
Deming, Wash., U.S., 210 ....358/C1
Demmitt, Alta., Can. 212/A3
Demopolis, Ala., U.S., 7,540 ....238/B3
Demorest, Ga., U.S., 1,465 ....260/D2
Demotte, Ind., U.S., 3,234 ....270/B2
Dempsey, Okla., U.S. 330/C2
Dempster, S. Dak., U.S. 342/J3
Denakil, Erit., *desert* 156/C2
Denakil, Eth., *desert* 156/C1
Denali Natl. Park and Preserve, Alaska, U.S. 240/E2
Denare Beach, Sask., Can., 784 ....227/H6
Denbigh, Ont., Can. 223/H2
Denbigh, Wales, U.K., 8,529 ....64/E1
Denbigh, N. Dak., U.S. 326/E1
Denbighshire, Wales, U.K.,
  unitary authority, 93,092 ....64/E1
Denby, S. Dak., U.S. 342/C4
Denby Dale, Eng., U.K., 2,282 ....66/E5
Denby Dale, Eng., U.K., 2,282 ....68/E5
Dencross, Man., Can. 215/C4
Dender, Belg., *river* 85/B2
Dendron, Va., U.S., 297 ....354/K6
Denham, Ind., U.S., 125 ....270/C2
Denham, Minn., U.S., 40 ....298/E4
Denham, Miss., U.S. 300/D4
Denham Sprs., La., U.S., 8,757 ....282/H5
Den Helder, Neth. 84/B2
Denhoff, N. Dak., U.S. 326/E2
Denholm, Scot., U.K., 608 ....62/L8
Denigomodu, Nauru 174/A2
Denio, Nev., U.S., 40 ....310/A1
Denio Jct., Nev., U.S. 310/A1
Denison, Iowa, U.S., 7,339 ....274/D3
Denison, Kans., U.S., 231 ....276/G2
Denison, Tex., U.S., 22,773 ....346/M2
Denizli, Tur., 233,700 ....133/B3
Denizli, Tur., *province* 133/B3
Denman, Nebr., U.S. 308/E3
Denmark, *nation* 193/D1
Denmark, *nation* 77
Denmark, *strait* 193/C17
Denmark, Grld., *strait* 193/C17
Denmark, Ga., U.S., 150 ....260/D7
Denmark, Iowa, U.S., 400 ....274/M6
Denmark, Kans., U.S. 276/D2
Denmark, Maine, U.S., 1,004 ....286/B5
Denmark, Miss., U.S., 80 ....300/C1
Denmark, Oreg., U.S., 70 ....334/B5
Denmark, S.C., U.S., 3,328 ....340/C3
Denmark, Wisc., U.S., 1,958 ....364/F4
Denmead, Eng., U.K., 5,626 ....70/B5

Denmore, Scot., U.K. 62/M4
Dennard, Ark., U.S., 150 ....244/C2
Dennehotso, Ariz., U.S., 734 ....242/F1
Dennery, St. Luc. 208/B2
Denning, Ark., U.S., 270 ....244/B2
Dennis, Kans., U.S., 150 ....276/G4
Dennis, Mass., U.S., 15,973 ....292/P6
Dennis, Miss., U.S., 250 ....300/D1
Dennison, Ill., U.S., 125 ....266/F4
Dennison, Minn., U.S., 168 ....298/D6
Dennison, Ohio, U.S., 2,992 ....328/H5
Dennis Port, Mass., U.S., 3,612 ....292/P6
Dennistown, Maine, U.S. 286/B3
Dennisville, N.J., U.S., 350 ....314/D5
Denny, Scot., U.K., 9,797 ....62/J6
Dennysville, Maine, U.S., 319 ....286/E4
Denpasar, Indon. 122/D3
Dent, Eng., U.K. 66/D4
Dent, Minn., U.S., 192 ....298/B4
Dent, Mo., U.S., *county*, 14,927 ....302/E4
Dent, Ohio, U.S., 7,612 ....328/B9
Denton, Eng., U.K. 68/F5
Denton, Eng., U.K., 37,785 ....70/C2
Denton, Ga., U.S., 269 ....260/F8
Denton, Kans., U.S., 186 ....276/G2
Denton, Md., U.S., 2,960 ....288/L4
Denton, Mont., U.S., 301 ....306/G2
Denton, Nebr., U.S., 189 ....308/H3
Denton, N.C., U.S., 1,450 ....322/E3
Denton, Tex., U.S., 80,537 ....346/B8, L2
Denton, Tex., U.S., *county*, 432,976 ....346/A8, L2
D'Entrecasteaux, P.N.G., *islands* 172/B2
Dentsville, S.C., U.S., 13,009 ....340/A3
Dentville, Miss., U.S. 300/B4
Denver, Colo., U.S., *county*, 554,636 ....250/A3, F2
Denver, Colo., U.S., *state capital*, 554,636,
  (2,581,506 metro.) 250/A3, F2
Denver, Ind., U.S., 54 ....270/D3
Denver, Iowa, U.S., 1,627 ....274/K2
Denver, Mo., U.S., 40 ....302/B1
Denver, Penn., U.S., 3,332 ....336/J5
Denver City, Tex., U.S., 3,985 ....346/F3
Denville, N.J., U.S., 15,824 ....314/E2
Denzil, Sask., Can., 161 ....227/B9
Deokjeok, S. Kor., *islands* 116/A4
Deopham Green, Eng., U.K. 70/G1
Deora, Colo., U.S. 250/H4
Depauw, Ind., U.S., 250 ....270/D8
Dependencias Federales, Ven. 182/D2
De Pere, Wisc., U.S., 20,559 ....364/E4
Depew, N.Y., U.S., 16,629 ....320/D5
Depew, Okla., U.S., 564 ....330/F2
Depoe Bay, Oreg., U.S., 1,174 ....334/B3
Deport, Tex., U.S., 718 ....346/N2
Deposit, N.Y., U.S., 1,699 ....320/L6
Depue, Ill., U.S., 1,842 ....266/D2
De Queen, Ark., U.S., 5,765 ....244/A3
De Quincy, La., U.S., 3,398 ....282/C6
De Quincy Vil., Sey. 163/Inset
Dera Ghazi Khan, Pak., 190,542 ....129/D3
Dera Ismail Khan, Pak. 129/D3
Derby, Eng., U.K. 60/C3
Derby, Eng., U.K., 223,836 ....68/E4
Derby, Eng., U.K., 223,836 ....70/B1
Derby, Eng., U.K., *unitary authority*, 221,716 ....68/E4
Derby, Eng., U.K., *unitary authority*, 221,716 ....70/B1
Derby, Conn., U.S., 12,391 ....253/C4
Derby, Ind., U.S. 270/C8
Derby, Iowa, U.S., 131 ....274/H6
Derby, Kans., U.S., 17,807 ....276/E4
Derby, Miss., U.S., 225 ....300/C5
Derby, N.Y., U.S., 900 ....320/D5
Derby, Tex., U.S. 346/J7
Derby Acres, Calif., U.S., 376 ....246/F7
Derby Ctr., Vt., U.S. 352/C1
Derby Line, Vt., U.S., 776 ....352/C1
Derbyshire, Eng., U.K., *unitary authority*, 734,581 ....66/B6
Derbyshire, Eng., U.K., *unitary authority*, 734,581 ....68/D3
Derbyshire, Eng., U.K., *unitary authority*, 734,581 ....70/A1
Dereham, Eng., U.K. 70/F1
Derg, Ire., *lake* 78/B2
De Ridder, La., U.S., 9,808 ....282/C5
Dering Harbor, N.Y., U.S. 320/D5
Derma, Miss., U.S., 1,023 ....300/C2
Dermott, Ark., U.S., 3,292 ....244/D3
Dermott, Tex., U.S. 346/H3
Derrick, St. Vin.-Gren. 208/B3
Derrick City, Penn., U.S., 350 ....336/D4
Derry, N. Ire., U.K., *unitary authority*, 105,066 ....65/C2
Derry, N.H., U.S., 34,021 ....312/D6
Derry, N. Mex., U.S., 212/ 317/C5
Derry, Penn., U.S., 2,991 ....336/C5
Derrylin, N. Ire., U.K., 321 ....65/B3
Derrytrasna, N. Ire., U.K., 209 ....65/E2
Dersingham, Eng., U.K., 3,761 ....70/F1
DeRuyter, N.Y., U.S., 531 ....320/K5
Dervaig, Scot., U.K. 62/D5
Derventa, Bos.-Her. 98/B1
Derwent, Alta., Can., 111 ....212/E4
Derwent, Eng., U.K., *reservoir* 66/D3
Derwent, Eng., U.K., *reservoir* 66/E6
Derwent, Eng., U.K., *reservoir* 66/F3
Derwent Water, Eng., U.K., *lake* 66/B3
Derwood, Md., U.S., 2,000 ....288/A5
Desaguadero, Arg., *river* 191/B2
Desaguadero, Bol., *river* 186/A3
Des Allemands, La., U.S., 2,500 ....282/H3, J7
Des Arc, Ark., U.S., 1,933 ....244/D3
Des Arc, Mo., U.S., 187 ....302/F4
De Sart, N. Dak., U.S. 326/C3
Desberats, Ont., Can. 294/C1
Deschaillons, (Deschaillons-Sur-St-Laurent),
  Que., Can. 226/D5
Deschambault, Sask., Can., *lake* 227/G6
Deschambault Lake, Sask., Can., 896 ....227/G6
Deschutes, Oreg., U.S., *county*, 115,367 ....334/E4
Deschutes, Oreg., U.S., *river* 334/E4
Deschutes Natl. For., Oreg., U.S. 334/E4
Deschutes River Woods, Oreg., U.S., 4,631 ....334/E4
Desdemona, Tex., U.S., 150 ....346/K3
Dese, Eth. 156/C2
Deseado, Arg., *river* 191/B6
Deselm, Ill., U.S., 80 ....266/F2
Deseret, Utah, U.S., 100 ....350/B3
Deseret, Utah, U.S., *peak* 350/B3
Deseret Test Ctr., Utah, U.S. 350/A3
Deseronto, Ont., Can., 1,796 ....223/H3
Desert, Calif., U.S., 70 ....246/K7
Desert, Nev., U.S., *valley* 310/A1
Desert Aire, Wash., U.S., 1,124 ....358/F3
Desert Ctr., Calif., U.S., 60 ....246/K9
Desert Grande, Port., *island* ....93/Inset I
Desert Hot Sprs., Calif., U.S., 16,582 ....246/J9
Desert Natl. Wildlife Range, Nev., U.S. 310/C3
Desert Range Experimental Sta., Utah, U.S. 350/A5
Desert Shores, Calif., U.S., 792 ....246/J9
Desert View, Ariz., U.S. 242/D1
Desert View Highlands, Calif., U.S., 2,337 ....246/G8

Desha, Ark., U.S., 650 ....244/D2
Desha, Ark., U.S., *county*, 15,341 ....244/D4
Deshler, Nebr., U.S., 879 ....308/G3
Deshler, Ohio, U.S., 1,831 ....328/C3
De Lacs, N. Dak., U.S., 209 ....326/D1
Des Lacs N.W.R., N. Dak., U.S. 326/D1
Desloge, Mo., U.S., 4,802 ....302/F4
De Smet, S. Dak., U.S., 1,164 ....342/H3
Des Moines, Iowa, U.S., *county*, 42,351 ....274/M6
Des Moines, Iowa, U.S., *river* 274/F2, K6
Des Moines, Iowa, U.S., *state capital*,
  198,682, (456,022 metro.) 274/G4
Des Moines, Wash., U.S., 29,267 ....358/A4
Desna, Ukr., *river* 102/C1
Desolación, Chile, *island* 190/B8
De Soto, Fla., U.S., *county*, 32,209 ....256/G4
De Soto, Ga., U.S., 214 ....260/C8
De Soto, Ill., U.S., 1,653 ....266/D6
De Soto, Iowa, U.S., 1,009 ....274/F4
De Soto, Kans., U.S., 4,561 ....276/G1, H3
De Soto, La., U.S., *parish*, 25,494 ....282/B2
De Soto, Miss., U.S., *county*, 107,199 ....300/C1
De Soto, Mo., U.S., 6,375 ....302/F3
De Soto, Tex., U.S., 37,646 ....346/C10, M3
De Soto, Wisc., U.S., 366 ....364/B5
De Soto City, Fla., U.S., 550 ....256/G4
De Soto Natl. For., Miss., U.S. 300/D4, D5
De Soto Natl. Mem., Fla., U.S. 256/F4
Despard, W. Va., U.S., 1,039 ....360/F2
Des Peres, Mo., U.S., 8,592 ....302/H3
Des Plaines, Ill., U.S., 58,720 ....266/B5
Des Plaines, Ill., U.S., *river* 266/B6
Desruisseau, St. Luc. 208/B3
Dessau, Ger. 86/C3
Dessau, Ger., *department* 86/C3
Destin, Fla., U.S., 11,119 ....256/B1
Destrehan, La., U.S., 11,260 ....282/J3, J7
Destruction Bay, Yukon, Can., 43 ....228/B5
Detmold, Ger. 86/B3
Detmold, Ger., *department* 86/B3
Detonti, Ark., U.S. 244/C3
Detour, Mich., U.S., *point* 294/C4
De Tour Vil., Mich., U.S., 421 ....294/F4
Detroit, Ala., U.S., 247 ....238/A1
Detroit, Maine, U.S., 816 ....286/C4
Detroit, Mich., U.S., 951,270,
  (5,456,428 metro.) 294/B7, F7
Detroit, Oreg., U.S., 262 ....334/D3
Detroit Beach, Mich., U.S., 2,289 ....294/F8
Detroit Lakes, Minn., U.S., 7,348 ....298/B4
Detroit, Nebr., U.S., *county*, 2,098 ....308/B2
Deuel, S. Dak., U.S., *county*, 4,498 ....342/J3
Deux-Montagnes, Que., Can. 226/H5
Deux Rivieres, Ont., Can. 223/G1
Deux-Sèvres, Fr., *department* 88/B3
Deva, Rom. 101/B2
De Valls Bluff, Ark., U.S., 783 ....244/D3
Deventer, Neth. 84/D2
Devault, Wales, U.K. 64/F4
Devereux, Ga., U.S., 100 ....260/E5
Devers, Tex., U.S., 416 ....346/P5
Deville, La., U.S., 1,007 ....282/E4
Devil's, Fr. Gui., *island* 183/B1
Devils, N. Dak., U.S., *lake* 326/G1
Devils Den, Calif., U.S. 246/F7
Devils Hole, (Death Valley Natl. Park), Nev., U.S. 310/E7
Devils Lake, N. Dak., U.S., 7,222 ....326/G1
Devils Playground, Calif., U.S. 246/K8
Devils Postpile N.M., Calif., U.S. 246/F6
Devils Slide, Utah, U.S., 50 ....350/C2, E1
Devils Tower, Wyo., U.S. 366/F0
Devils Tower Natl. Mon., Wyo., U.S. 366/F0
Devine, Colo., U.S., 500 ....250/F3
Devine, Tex., U.S., 4,140 ....346/K6
Devizes, Eng., U.K., 13,205 ....73/J2
Devol, Okla., U.S., 150 ....330/D3
Devola, Ohio, U.S., 2,771 ....328/H7
Devon, Alta., *river* 99/B3
Devon, Alta., Can., 4,969 ....212/D4
Devon, Eng., U.K., *island* 208/L1
Devon, Eng., U.K., *unitary authority*, 704,499 ....73/E2
Devon, Kans., U.S., 80 ....276/H4
Devon, Mont., U.S. 306/E1
Devon, (Devon-Berwyn), Penn., U.S., 5,067 ....336/K7
Devonport, Tas., Austl. 170/D4
Devonshire, N.J., U.S., 475 ....314/D4
Dewar, Okla., U.S., 919 ....330/G2
Dewberry, Alta., Can., 212/ 212/E4
Deweese, Miss., U.S. 300/D3
Deweese, Nebr., U.S., 80 ....308/E3
Dewey, P.R. 206/E2
Dewey, (Dewey-Humboldt), Ariz., U.S., 6,295 ....242/C3
Dewey, Mont., U.S., 40 ....306/D4
Dewey, Okla., U.S., 3,179 ....330/G1
Dewey, Okla., U.S., *county*, 4,743 ....330/D2
Dewey, S. Dak., U.S. 342/A4
Dewey, S. Dak., U.S., *county*, 5,972 ....342/D2
Dewey Beach, Del., U.S., 301 ....255/D6
Deweyville, Tex., U.S., 1,190 ....346/R5
Deweyville, Utah, U.S., 278 ....350/B2
De Witt, Ark., U.S., 3,552 ....244/D3
De Witt, Ill., U.S., 188 ....266/E3
De Witt, Ill., U.S., *county*, 16,798 ....266/E3
De Witt, Iowa, U.S., 5,049 ....274/N4
De Witt, Mich., U.S., 4,702 ....294/E7
De Witt, Mo., U.S., 120 ....302/C2
De Witt, Nebr., U.S., 572 ....308/H3
De Witt, N.Y., U.S., 8,212/ 320/J4
De Witt, Tex., U.S., *county*, 20,013 ....346/L6
DeWitt, Va., U.S. 354/H6
Dewsbury, Eng., U.K., 50,168 ....66/E5
Dewsbury, Eng., U.K., 50,168 ....68/F5
Dewy Rose, Ga., U.S., 225 ....260/F3
Dexter, Ga., U.S., 509 ....260/E7
Dexter, Iowa, U.S., 689 ....274/F4
Dexter, Kans., U.S., 364 ....276/F4
Dexter, Ky., U.S., 375 ....280/B4
Dexter, Maine, U.S., 3,890 ....286/C3
Dexter, Mich., U.S., 2,338 ....294/F7
Dexter, Minn., U.S., 333 ....298/E7
Dexter, Miss., U.S., 90 ....300/C4
Dexter, Mo., U.S., 7,356 ....302/G5
Dexter, N. Mex., U.S., 1,235 ....317/F4
Dexter, N.Y., U.S., 1,120 ....320/J2
Dexter, Ohio, U.S., 70 ....328/G7
Dexter, Oreg., U.S., 750 ....334/D4
Dexter City, Ohio, U.S., 166 ....328/H6
Dexterville, Wisc., U.S., 40 ....364/C4
Dezful, Iran, 202,639 ....130/B3
Dhahran, Sa. Arab. 136/C1
Dhaka, Bangl., *capital*, 4,232,034,
  (11,276,000 metro.) 127/D5
Dhaka, Bangl., *division* 127/D4
Dhamar, Yemen 137/A2
Dhanbad, India, (1,064,357 metro.) 128/E4
Dhangadhi, Nepal 126/A2
D'Hanis, Tex., U.S. 346/J6

Dhankuta, Nepal 126/D2
Dharan, Nepal .126/D3
Dhaulagiri, Nepal, *mountain* 126/B2
Dhofar, Oman, *region* 137/B3
Dhulagarh, India . . . . .128/Inset II
Dhuusamareeb, Som. 157/B2
Diable, Mauritius, *point* 163/D3
Diablo, (part of Blackhawk), Calif., U.S., 988 . .246/K2
Diablo, Wash., U.S., 50 . . . . .358/D1
Diadema, Braz. . . . . .188/Inset II
Diagonal, Iowa, U.S., 312 . . . . .274/F6
Dialakoto, Sen. 148/C3
Diamond, Gren., *island* 209/B1
Diamond, Ill., U.S., 1,393 . . . . .266/E2
Diamond, Mo., U.S., 807 . . . . .302/B5
Diamond, Oreg., U.S. 334/H4
Diamond, Oreg., U.S., *peak* 334/D4
Diamond Bar, Calif., U.S., 56,287 . . . . . .246/E9
Diamond Bluff, Wisc., U.S., 125 . . . . .364/A4
Diamond City, Ark., U.S., 730 . . . . .244/C1
Diamond Head, Hawaii, U.S., *point* 262/G3
Diamondhead, Miss., U.S., 5,912 . . . . . . .300/C5
Diamond Head State Mon., Hawaii, U.S. . .262/G3, J3
Diamond Hill, R.I., U.S., 1,100 . . . . .339/D2
Diamond Lake, Oreg., U.S., 100 . . . . .334/D4
Diamond Lake, Wash., U.S., 212/ 358/H1
Diamond Sprs., Calif., U.S., 4,888 . . . . . .246/E4
Diamondville, Wyo., U.S., 716 . . . . .366/A3
Diana, Ill., U.S., 425 . . . . .346/P3
Diana, W. Va., U.S., 125 . . . . .360/F3
Diaz, Ark., U.S., 1,284 . . . . .244/D2
Dibble, Okla., U.S., 289 . . . . .330/E2
D'Iberville, Miss., U.S., 7,608 . . . . .300/D5
Dibrell, Tenn., U.S., 150 . . . . .344/K3
Dibrugarh, India 128/F3
Dickens, Iowa, U.S., 202 . . . . .274/D1
Dickens, Nebr., U.S. 308/D3
Dickens, Tex., U.S., 332 . . . . .346/H2
Dickens, Tex., U.S., *county, 2,762* 346/H2
Dickenson, Va., U.S., *county, 16,395* 354/D2
Dickerson, Md., U.S., 250 . . . . .288/E3
Dickey, Maine, U.S. 286/C1
Dickey, N. Dak., U.S., 57 . . . . .326/G3
Dickey, N. Dak., U.S., *county, 5,757* 326/G3
Dickeyville, Wisc., U.S., 1,043 . . . . .364/C6
Dickinson, Ala., U.S., 250 . . . . .238/B4
Dickinson, Iowa, U.S., *county, 16,424* 274/D1
Dickinson, Kans., U.S., *county, 19,344* . . .276/E3
Dickinson, Mich., U.S., *county, 27,472* . . .294/B3
Dickinson, N. Dak., U.S., 16,010 . . . . . . .326/C3
Dickinson, Tex., U.S., 17,093 . . . . .346/C7
Dickson, Okla., U.S., 1,139 . . . . .330/E2
Dickson, Tenn., U.S., 12,244 . . . . .344/G2
Dickson, Tenn., U.S., *county, 43,156* 344/G2
Dickson City, Penn., U.S., 6,205 . . . . .336/H7, K3
Didcot, Eng., U.K., 17,691 . . . . .70/B3
Didley, Eng., U.K. 68/B6
Didsbury, Alta., Can., 3,932 . . . . .212/C5
Diefenbaker, Sask., Can., *lake* 227/C10
Diehlstadt, Mo., U.S., 163 . . . . .302/G5
Diekirch, Lux. 85/B2
Diekirch, Lux., *district* 85/B2
Dien Bien, Viet. 123/A2
Dieppe, N.B., Can., 14,951 . . . . .217/E2
Dieppe, Fr. 88/C2
Dieppe Bay Town, St. K.-Nevis 207/B1
Dierks, Ark., U.S., 1,230 . . . . .244/A3
Dieterich, Ill., U.S., 591 . . . . .266/E4
Dietrich, Ida., U.S., 150 . . . . .264/C7
Diffa, Niger 152/C3
Differdange, Lux., 17,700 . . . . .85/A2
Difficult, Tenn., U.S. 344/K2
Digby, N.S., Can., 2,111 . . . . .221/B3
Digby, N.S., Can., *county, 2,111* 221/B3
Diggins, Mo., U.S., 298 . . . . .302/D4
Dighton, Kans., U.S., 1,261 . . . . .276/B3
Dighton, Mass., U.S., 6,175 . . . . .292/K5
Dighton, Mich., U.S., 100 . . . . .294/D5
Digne, Fr. 88/D4
Digul, Indon., *river* 122/E2
Dihewyd, Wales, U.K. 64/C3
Dijon, Fr., 153,815, (236,953 *metro.*) 88/D3
Dike, Iowa, U.S., 944 . . . . .274/J3
Dikhil, Dji. 156/B2
Dikson, Russ. 104/F2
Dikson, Russ. 193/B5
Dili, E. Timor, *capital, 140,000* 122/B1
Dili, E. Timor, *province* 122/B1
Dilia, N. Mex., U.S. 317/E2
Dilijan, Arm. 103/B2
Dilkon, Ariz., U.S., 1,265 . . . . .242/E2
Dillard, Ga., U.S., 198 . . . . .260/E2
Dillard, Mo., U.S. 302/E4
Dillard, Oreg., U.S., 500 . . . . .334/C4
Dill City, Okla., U.S., 526 . . . . .330/C2
Diller, Nebr., U.S., 287 . . . . .308/H3
Dilley, Tex., U.S., 3,674 . . . . .346/J7
Dillia, Niger, *river* 152/C2
Dillingham, Alaska, U.S., 2,466 . . . . .240/D3
Dillingham, N.C., U.S., 90 . . . . .322/E7
Dillon, Sask., Can. 227/B5
Dillon, Colo., U.S., 802 . . . . .250/D2
Dillon, Mont., U.S., 3,752 . . . . .306/D4
Dillon, S.C., U.S., 6,316 . . . . .340/E2
Dillon, S.C., U.S., *county, 30,722* 340/E2
Dillonvale, Ohio, U.S., 781 . . . . .328/J5
Dillsboro, Ind., U.S., 1,436 . . . . .270/F6
Dillsboro, N.C., U.S., 205 . . . . .322/D8
Dillsburg, Penn., U.S., 2,063 . . . . .336/G5
Dillwyn, Va., U.S., 447 . . . . .354/G5
Dilolo, Congo, D.R. 155/B3
Dilworth, Minn., U.S., 3,001 . . . . .298/A4
Dimbokro, C. d'Iv. 150/D3
Dimbovita, Rom., *county* 101/C3
Dimitrovgrad, Bul. 101/D3
Dimlang, Nig., *mountain* 152/F3
Dimmit, Tex., U.S., *county, 10,248* 346/J7
Dimmitt, Tex., U.S., 4,375 . . . . .346/F1, F10
Dimock, S. Dak., U.S., 151 . . . . .342/G4
Dimona, Isr. 135/B2
Dimondale, Mich., U.S., 1,342 . . . . .294/E7
Dimple, Ky., U.S., 100 . . . . .280/D3
Dinagat, Phil., *island* 120/C4
Dinajpur, Bangl., 126,189 . . . . .127/B3
Dinant, Belg. 85/C2
Dinara, Bos.-Her., *mountain* 98/A2
Dinara, Cro., *mountain* 98/C3
Dinaric Alps, Bos.-Her., *mountains* 98/A1
Dinaric Alps, Cro., *mountains* 99/A3
Dinaric Alps, Serb.-Mont., *mountains* 99/A3
Dinas, Wales, U.K. 64/B4
Dinas Mawddwy, Wales, U.K. 64/D2
Dinder, Eth., *river* 156/B1
Dingle, Ire. 78/A2
Dingle, Ire., *bay* 78/A2
Dingle, Ida., U.S., 100 . . . . .264/F7
Dingli, Malta 97/B2
Dingmans Ferry, Penn., U.S. 336/M3
Dinguiraye, Guin. 149/C2
Dingus, Ky., U.S. 280/G3
Dingwall, Scot., U.K., 5,026 . . . . .62/H3
Dinkey Creek, Calif., U.S. 246/F5

Dinnet, Scot., U.K. 62/L4
Dinnington, Eng., U.K., 1,722 . . . . .66/E2
Dinosaur, Colo., U.S., 319 . . . . .250/A1
Dinosaur Natl. Mon., Colo., U.S. 250/B1
Dinsmore, Sask., Can., 337 . . . . .227/C9
Dinuba, Calif., U.S., 16,844 . . . . .246/F6
Dinwiddie, Va., U.S., 350 . . . . .354/H6
Dinwiddie, Va., U.S., *county, 24,533* 354/H6
Diomede, Alaska, U.S., 146 . . . . .240/B1
Diourbel, Sen. 148/A2
Dipolog, Phil., 99,862 . . . . .120/B4
Dire Dawa, Eth., 208,456 . . . . .156/D2
Dire Dawa, Eth., *state* 156/D2
Diriamba, Nicar. 202/A3
Disappointment, Wash., U.S., *cape* 358/A3
Disautel, Wash., U.S., 40 . . . . .358/F1
Discovery Bay, Calif., U.S., 8,981 . . . . . . .246/K2
Dishforth, Eng., U.K. 66/F4
Dishman, Wash., U.S., 10,031 . . . . .358/H2
Disney, Okla., U.S., 226 . . . . .330/G1
Dispur, India 128/F3
Disputanta, Va., U.S., 275 . . . . .354/J6
Diss, Eng., U.K., 6,538 . . . . .70/G2
Disston, Oreg., U.S., 212/ 334/D4
District Hts., Md., U.S., 5,958 . . . . . . .288/C7, G4
District of Columbia, U.S., *district* 276
Distrito Federal, Arg., *province* 191/D3
Distrito Federal, Mex., *state* . . . . . .200/E4, Inset
Distrito Federal, Ven. 182/C1
Distrito Nacional, Dom. Rep., *province* . . .205/B2
Dittlinger, Tex., U.S. 346/B2
Ditton, Eng., U.K. 70/E4
Diu, India 128/B4
Divata, Phil., *mountains* 120/C4
Divernon, Ill., U.S., 1,201 . . . . .266/D4
Divide, Colo., U.S., 40 . . . . .250/D3
Divide, Mont., U.S. 306/D4
Divide, N. Dak., U.S., *county, 2,283* 326/B1
Dividing Creek, N.J., U.S., 475 . . . . .314/C5
Divo, C. d'Iv. 150/D4
Divriği, Tur. 133/D2
Dix, Ill., U.S., 494 . . . . .266/E5
Dix, Nebr., U.S., 267 . . . . .308/A2
Dixfield, Maine, U.S., 2,514 . . . . .286/B4
Dixie, Ark., U.S. 244/D2
Dixie, Fla., U.S., *county, 13,827* 256/E2
Dixie, Ga., U.S., 125 . . . . .260/D1
Dixie, Ida., U.S. .264/B4
Dixie, Wash., U.S., 220 . . . . .358/G3
Dixie Inn, La., U.S., 352 . . . . .282/C1
Dixie Natl. For., Utah, U.S. 350/A6, B6, C6
Dixie Union, Ga., U.S., 125 . . . . .260/G9
Dixie Valley, Nev., U.S. 310/A2
Dixmont, Maine, U.S., 1,065 . . . . .286/C4
Dixmoor, Ill., U.S., 3,934 . . . . .266/C6
Dixon, Calif., U.S., 16,103 . . . . .246/K4
Dixon, Ill., U.S., 15,941 . . . . .266/D2
Dixon, Iowa, U.S., 276 . . . . .274/N4
Dixon, Ky., U.S., 632 . . . . .280/C3
Dixon, Mo., U.S., 1,570 . . . . .302/D4
Dixon, Mont., U.S., 216 . . . . .306/B2
Dixon, Nebr., U.S., 108 . . . . .308/H1
Dixon, Nebr., U.S., *county, 6,339* 308/H1
Dixon, N. Mex., U.S., 275 . . . . .317/E1
Dixon, N.C., U.S., 125 . . . . .322/L5
Dixon, S. Dak., U.S. 342/F4
Dixon, Wyo., U.S., 79 . . . . .366/C3
Dixon Entrance, Br. Col., U.S., *channel* . . .214/F4
Dixons Mills, Ala., U.S., 400 . . . . .238/B3
Dixonville, Alta., Can., 97 . . . . .212/B3
Dixonville, Ala., U.S. 238/B4
Dixville Notch, N.H., U.S., 40 . . . . .312/D2
Diyala, Iraq, *river* 130/C2
Diyarbakir, Tur., 511,600 . . . . .133/E3
Diyarbakir, Tur., *province* 133/E3
Dizney, Ky., U.S., 300 . . . . .280/G4
Dja, Came., *river* 153/B3
Djado, Niger 152/C1
Djado, Niger, *plateau* 152/C1
Djambala, Congo 155/C5
Djanet, Alg. 146/B2
Djelfa, Alg., 154,265 . . . . .146/B1
Djéma, C.A.R. 154/C2
Djenné, Mali 150/C3
Djerba, Tun., *island* 146/C3
Djerid, Tun., *salt marsh* 146/B3
Djibouti, *nation* .150
Djibouti, Dji., *capital, 62,000, (523,000 metro.)* .156/C2
Djoua, Gabon, *river* 155/B1
Djougou, Ben., 132,192 . . . . .151/A3
D'Lo, Miss., U.S., 394 . . . . .300/C4
Dnepr, *river* 193/D2
Dnieper, Bela., *river* 82/E3
Dnieper, Russ., *river* 104/C4
Dnieper, Ukr., *river* 102/C1, C3
Dnieper-Bug, Bela., *canal* 82/B3
Dniester, Mol., *river* 102/B2
Dniester, Ukr., *river* 102/B2
Dniprodzerzhyns'k, Ukr., 270,757 . . . . . . .102/C2
Dniprodzerzhyns'k, Ukr., *reservoir* 102/C2
Dnipropetrovs'k, Ukr., 1,108,682 . . . . .102/D2
Dnipropetrovs'k, Ukr., *oblast* 102/D2
Doagh, N. Ire., U.K., 961 . . . . .65/E2
Doaktown, N.B., Can., 955 . . . . .217/C2
Doans, Tex., U.S. 346/J1
Doba, Chad, 185,461 . . . . .153/B5
Dobbins Hts., N.C., U.S., 936 . . . . .322/F5
Dobbs Ferry, N.Y., U.S., 10,622 . . . . .320/B1
Doboj, Bos.-Her. .98/B1
Dobrich, Bul., 100,400 . . . . .101/F2
Dobrich, Bul., *oblast* 101/F2
Dobruja, Bul., *region* 101/F2
Dobruja, Rom., *region* 191/D1
Dobson, N.C., U.S., 1,457 . . . . .322/D2
Dobwalls, Eng., U.K. 73/C4
Dock Jct., Ga., U.S., 6,951 . . . . .260/H9
Docklow, Eng., U.K. 68/B5
Dockray, Eng., U.K. 66/C3
Dockton, Wash., U.S., 375 . . . . .358/A4
Doctor Pedro P. Peña, Para. 187/A3
Doctor Phillips, Fla., U.S., 9,548 . . . . .256/C4
Doctortown, Ga., U.S. 260/H8
Dodburn, Scot., U.K. 62/L8
Dodd, Tex., U.S. 346/F1
Doddington, (Deddington/Wimblington), Eng., U.K., 2,810 . . . . .68/H5
Doddington, (Deddington/Wimblington), Eng., U.K., 2,810 . . . . .70/E4
Doddington, Eng., U.K. 70/F4
Doddridge, Ark., U.S., 40 . . . . .244/B4
Doddridge, W. Va., U.S., *county, 7,403* . . .360/E2
Doddsville, Miss., U.S., 108 . . . . .300/B2
Dodecanese, Gr., *islands* 100/C3
Dodge, Ga., U.S., *county, 19,171* 260/E7
Dodge, Minn., U.S., *county, 17,731* 298/E7
Dodge, Nebr., U.S., 700 . . . . .308/H2
Dodge, Nebr., U.S., *county, 36,160* 308/H2
Dodge, N. Dak., U.S., 125 . . . . .326/C2

Dodge, Wash., U.S. 358/H3
Dodge, Wisc., U.S., 125 . . . . .364/B4
Dodge, Wisc., U.S., *county, 85,897* . . .364/E1, E5
Dodge Ctr., Minn., U.S., 2,226 . . . . .298/E7
Dodge City, Ala., U.S., 612 . . . . .238/C1
Dodge City, Kans., U.S., 25,176 . . . . .276/B4
Dodge Park, Md., U.S. 288/C7
Dodgeville, Wisc., U.S., 4,220 . . . . .364/C6
Dodoma, Tan., 203,833 . . . . .158/C2
Dodoma, Tan., *region* 158/C2
Dodsland, Sask., Can., 211 . . . . .227/B9
Dodson, La., U.S., 357 . . . . .282/D2
Dodson, Mont., U.S., 122 . . . . .306/H1
Dodson, Tex., U.S., 115 . . . . .346/H10
Dodsonville, Ohio, U.S., 275 . . . . .328/C7
Doering, Wisc., U.S., 40 . . . . .364/D3
Doerun, Ga., U.S., 828 . . . . .260/D9
Doetinchem, Neth. 84/D3
Dog, Fla., U.S., *island* 256/D2
Dog, Ga., U.S., *island* 260/B11
Dogo, Jap., *island* 114/B2
Dogondoutchi, Niger 152/A3
Doha, Qatar, *capital, 264,009* 137/D3
Doiran, Gr., Mac., *lake* 100/C2
Doland, S. Dak., U.S., 297 . . . . .342/G3
Dolan Sprs., Ariz., U.S., 1,867 . . . . .242/A2
Dolbeau, Que., Can., 14,879 . . . . .226/D3
Dôle, Fr. 88/D3
Doles, Ga., U.S., 100 . . . . .260/D8
Dolgarrog, Wales, U.K. 64/D1
Dolgellau, Wales, U.K., 2,396 . . . . .64/D2
Dolgeville, N.Y., U.S., 2,166 . . . . .320/M4
Dolisie, Congo, 83,605 . . . . .155/B6
Dolj, Rom., *county* 101/B3
Dollar, Scot., U.K., 2,877 . . . . .62/J6
Dollar Bay, Mich., U.S., 950 . . . . .294/A2
Dolliver, Iowa, U.S., 77 . . . . .274/E1
Dolnoślaskie, Pol., *province* 83/C3
Dolomite, Ala., U.S. 238/D1
Dolomites, It., *range* 95/B1
Dolores, Colo., U.S., 857 . . . . .250/B4
Dolores, Colo., U.S., *county, 1,844* 250/B4
Dolores, Colo., U.S., *river* 250/B3
Dolphinholme, Eng., U.K. 66/C5
Dolphinton, Scot., U.K. 62/K7
Dolton, Ill., U.S., 25,614 . . . . .266/C6
Dolton, S. Dak., U.S., 41 . . . . .342/H4
Domagnano, S. Mar. 97/B1
Dome, Ariz., U.S. 242/A5
Domestic, Ind., U.S. 270/F3
Domingo, N. Mex., U.S., 70 . . . . .317/D2
Dominica, *nation* 204/F4
Dominica, *nation* 196
Dominica, Dom., *passage* 208/A1
Dominican Republic, *nation* 204/D3
Dominican Republic, *nation* 193
Dominion, Md., U.S., 600 . . . . .288/J4
Dominion City, Man., Can. 215/C4
Domino, Tex., U.S., 52 . . . . .346/P2
Domont, Fr. . . . . .88/Inset II
Domremy, Sask., Can., 135 . . . . .227/E8
Domuyo, Arg., *volcano* 191/A4
Doña Ana, N. Mex., U.S., 1,379 . . . . .317/D5
Doña Ana, N. Mex., U.S., *county, 174,682* .317/D5
Donagh, N. Ire., U.K., 230 . . . . .65/C3
Donaghadee, N. Ire., U.K., 4,799 . . . . .65/F2
Donaghmore, N. Ire., U.K., 768 . . . . .65/D2
Donahue, Iowa, U.S., 293 . . . . .274/N4
Doña Juana, P.R., *mountain* 206/C2
Donald, Wash., U.S., 175 . . . . .358/E3
Donalda, Alta., Can., 230 . . . . .212/D5
Donalds, S.C., U.S., 354 . . . . .340/B2
Donaldson, Ark., U.S., 326 . . . . .244/C3
Donaldson, Minn., U.S., 41 . . . . .298/A2
Donaldson, La., U.S., 7,605 . . . . .282/H6
Donald Sta., Br. Col., Can. 214/D5
Donaldsonville, Ga., U.S., 2,796 . . . . .260/B9
Don Benito, Sp. .94/D3
Doncaster, Vic., Austl. . . . . .170/Inset V
Doncaster, Eng., U.K. 60/C3
Doncaster, Eng., U.K., 71,595, (128,847 *metro.*) .66/F5
Doncaster, Eng., U.K., 71,595, (128,847 *metro.*) .68/E2
Doncaster, Eng., U.K., *unitary authority, 286,865* .66/F5
Doncaster, Eng., U.K., *unitary authority, 286,865* .68/E2
Dondo, Ang. 159/B3
Dondra Head, Sri Lan., *cape* 126/B6
Donegal, Ire. 78/B1
Donegal, Ire., *bay* 78/B1
Donegal, Ire., *county* 78/B1
Donegal, Penn., U.S., 165 . . . . .336/C5
Donets, Ukr., *basin* 102/D2
Donets, Ukr., *river* 102/D2
Donets'k, Ukr., 1,050,369 . . . . .102/D2
Donets'k, Ukr., *oblast* 102/D2
Dong Hoi, Viet. .123/B3
Dong Nai, Viet., *river* 123/B4
Dongola, Ill., U.S., 806 . . . . .266/D6
Dongting, China, *lake* 119/E3
Dongwe, Zam., *river* 159/A2
Donington, Eng., U.K., 2,569 . . . . .68/G4
Donington, Eng., U.K., 2,569 . . . . .70/D1
Doniphan, Kans., U.S., 50 . . . . .276/G2
Doniphan, Kans., U.S., *county, 8,249* 276/G2
Doniphan, Mo., U.S., 1,932 . . . . .302/F5
Doniphan, Nebr., U.S., 763 . . . . .308/E3
Donken, Mich., U.S. 294/A3
Donley, Tex., U.S., *county, 3,828* 346/G9
Donna, Tex., U.S., 14,768 . . . . .346/K9
Donnacona, Que., Can., 5,479 . . . . .226/E5
Donnan, Iowa, U.S. 274/L2
Donnellson, Ill., U.S., 243 . . . . .266/D4
Donnellson, Iowa, U.S., 963 . . . . .274/L6
Donnelly, Ida., U.S., 138 . . . . .264/A5
Donnelly, Minn., U.S., 254 . . . . .298/B5
Donnelsville, Ohio, U.S., 293 . . . . .328/C6
Donnington, Eng., U.K., 275 . . . . .282/H7
Donnington, Eng., U.K. 68/C4
Donnybrook, N. Dak., U.S., 90 . . . . .326/D1
Donora, Penn., U.S., 5,653 . . . . .336/B5
Donostia-San Sebastián, Sp., 178,377 . . . .94/F1
Donovan, Ill., U.S., 50 . . . . .266/F6
Donovan, Ill., U.S., 351 . . . . .266/F6
Dooish, N. Ire., U.K. 65/C2
Doole, Tex., U.S. 346/J4
Dooling, Ga., U.S., 163 . . . . .260/D7
Doolittle, Mo., U.S., 644 . . . . .302/E4
Dooly, Ga., U.S., *county, 11,525* 260/D7
Dooms, Va., U.S., 1,282 . . . . .354/F4
Door, La., U.S., *point* 282/L6
Door, Wisc., U.S., *county, 27,961* 364/F4
Door, Wisc., U.S., *peninsula* 364/F4
Dor, Sask., Can., *lake* 227/C6
Dora, Ala., U.S., 2,413 . . . . .238/B1
Dora, Mo., U.S. .302/D5
Dora, N. Mex., U.S., 130 . . . . .317/F3
Dora, Oreg., U.S. 334/C4
Dorado, P.R. 206/C2
Doran, Minn., U.S., 59 . . . . .298/A4
Doraville, Ga., U.S., 9,862 . . . . .260/C4, J2

Dorcas, W. Va., U.S., 175 . . . . .360/H3
Dorchester, N.B., Can., 954 . . . . .217/E3
Dorchester, Eng., U.K. 60/C4
Dorchester, Eng., U.K., 15,037 . . . . .68/E6
Dorchester, Eng., U.K., 15,037 . . . . .70/B3
Dorchester, Eng., U.K., 15,037 . . . . .73/H3
Dorchester, Ill., U.S., 142 . . . . .266/A3
Dorchester, Iowa, U.S., 80 . . . . .274/M1
Dorchester, Md., U.S., *county, 30,674* . . .288/K6
Dorchester, Nebr., U.S., 615 . . . . .308/G3
Dorchester, N.J., U.S., 600 . . . . .314/D5
Dorchester, S.C., U.S., 212/ 340/D3
Dorchester, S.C., U.S., *county, 96,413* . . .340/D3
Dorchester, Wisc., U.S., 827 . . . . .364/C3
Dordogne, Fr., *river* 88/C4
Dordrecht, Neth., 119,642, (240,829 *metro.*) .84/B3
Dore, N. Dak., U.S., 40 . . . . .326/A2
Dore Lake, Sask., Can. 227/C6
Dorena, Oreg., U.S., 375 . . . . .334/D4
Dörgön, Mong., *lake* 118/B2
Dori, Burkina 151/D1
Dorintosh, Sask., Can., 125 . . . . .227/B6
Doris, Wash., U.S., 90 . . . . .358/E3
Dorking, Eng., U.K. . . . . .60/Inset III
Dorking, Eng., U.K., 15,658 . . . . .70/D4
Dormont, Penn., U.S., 9,305 . . . . .336/D7
Dornbirn, Aus. 91/A3
Dornoch, Scot., U.K. 60/B1
Dornoch, Scot., U.K., 1,206 . . . . .62/H3
Dornoch, Scot., U.K., *estuary* 60/B1
Dornoch, Scot., U.K., *estuary* 62/J3
Dornsife, Penn., U.S., 212/ 336/H4
Dorohoi, Rom. 101/D2
Dorothy, Alta., Can. 212/D5
Dorothy, Minn., U.S. 298/A3
Dorothy, N.J., U.S., 600 . . . . .314/D5
Dorr, Mich., U.S., 2,800 . . . . .294/D7
Dorra, Dji. 156/B1
Dorrance, Kans., U.S., 205 . . . . .276/D3
Dorris, Calif., U.S., 886 . . . . .246/D1
Dorset, Eng., U.K., *unitary authority, 390,986* .73/H3
Dorset, Minn., U.S., 100 . . . . .298/B4
Dorset, Ohio, U.S., 225 . . . . .328/J2
Dorset, Vt., U.S., 2,036 . . . . .352/A4
Dorsey, Ill., U.S., 150 . . . . .266/A3, C5
Dorsey, Md., U.S., 1,000 . . . . .288/G3
Dorstone, Eng., U.K. 68/B5
Dortches, N.C., U.S., 809 . . . . .322/K2
Dortmund, Ger., 590,213 . . . . .86/A3
Dorton, Ky., U.S., 250 . . . . .280/H3
Dorval, Que., Can., 17,706 . . . . .226/H6
Dos Cabezas, Ariz., U.S. 242/F5
Dos Hermanas, Sp., 101,988 . . . . .94/D4
Dos Palos, Calif., U.S., 4,581 . . . . .246/E6
Dosquet, Que., Can., 889 . . . . .226/E5
Dos Rios, Calif., U.S., 40 . . . . .246/B3
Doss, Tex., U.S. .346/J5
Dosso, Niger 152/A3
Dossville, Miss., U.S., 70 . . . . .300/C3
Doswell, Va., U.S., 300 . . . . .354/J5
Dothan, Ala., U.S., 57,737, (137,916 *metro.*) .238/D4
Doty, Wash., U.S., 325 . . . . .358/B3
Douai, Fr., (518,727, *metro.*) 88/C1
Douala, Came., 810,000, (1,320,000, *metro.*) .153/A3
Double Adobe, Ariz., U.S., 125 . . . . .242/F6
Double Oak, Tex., U.S., 2,179 . . . . .346/B8
Double Sprs., Ala., U.S., 1,003 . . . . .238/B1
Doubs, Switz., *river* 90/A1
Doubs, Md., U.S., 750 . . . . .288/E2
Douds, Iowa, U.S., 165 . . . . .274/K6
Dougherty, Ga., U.S., *county, 96,065* 260/C9
Dougherty, Iowa, U.S., 80 . . . . .274/H2
Dougherty, Okla., U.S., 224 . . . . .330/E3
Dougherty, Tex., U.S., 150 . . . . .346/G2
Douglas, Br. Col., Can., *channel* 214/H4
Douglas, Isle of Man, U.K., *territorial capital* .60/B2
Douglas, Isle of Man, U.K., *territorial capital* .66/B5
Douglas, Alta., Can., 530 . . . . .238/C1
Douglas, Ariz., U.S., 14,312 . . . . .242/F6
Douglas, Colo., U.S., *county, 175,766* . . .250/E2
Douglas, Ga., U.S., 10,639 . . . . .260/F8
Douglas, Ga., U.S., *county, 92,174* . .260/B4, G3
Douglas, Ill., U.S., *county, 19,922* 266/E4
Douglas, Kans., U.S., *county, 99,962* 276/G3
Douglas, Mass., U.S., 7,045 . . . . .292/H4
Douglas, Mich., U.S., 1,214 . . . . .294/C7
Douglas, Minn., U.S., 175 . . . . .298/E6
Douglas, Minn., U.S., *county, 32,821* 298/B5
Douglas, Mo., U.S., *county, 13,084* 302/D5
Douglas, Nebr., U.S., 231 . . . . .308/H3
Douglas, Nebr., U.S., *county, 463,585* . . .308/H2
Douglas, Nev., U.S., *county, 41,259* 310/A2
Douglas, N. Dak., U.S. 326/D2
Douglas, Okla., U.S. 330/E1
Douglas, Oreg., U.S., *county, 100,399* . . .334/D4
Douglas, S. Dak., U.S., *county, 3,458* . . .342/G4
Douglas, Tenn., U.S., *lake* 344/Q3
Douglas, Wash., U.S. 358/F2
Douglas, Wash., U.S., *county, 32,603* . . .358/F2
Douglas, Wisc., U.S., *county, 43,287* 364/B2
Douglas, Wyo., U.S., 5,288 . . . . .366/D2
Douglas City, Calif., U.S., 212/ 246/C2
Douglass, Kans., U.S., 1,813 . . . . .276/F4
Douglass Hills, Ky., U.S., 5,718 . . . . .280/B2
Douglass, Wash., U.S., 175 . . . . .358/F2
Douglastown, N.B., Can. 217/D1
Douglastown, Que., Can. 226/M3
Douglasville, Ga., U.S., 20,065 . . . . .260/B4
Dounby, Scot., U.K. 62/M2
Doune, Scot., U.K., 1,635 . . . . .62/J5
Dourados, Braz., 76,838, (135,779, *metro.*) .188/C4
Douro, Port., *river* 93/B2
Douro, Tex., U.S. 346/F4
Dousman, Wisc., U.S., 1,584 . . . . .364/E6
Dove Creek, Colo., U.S., 698 . . . . .250/B4
Dove Holes, Eng., U.K. 68/D3
Dover, Fr., *strait* 88/C1
Dover, Eng., U.K. .60/D3
Dover, Eng., U.K., 34,179 . . . . .70/G4
Dover, Eng., U.K., *strait* 60/D4
Dover, Eng., U.K., *strait* 70/G5
Dover, Ark., U.S., 1,329 . . . . .244/B2
Dover, Del., U.S., *state capital, 32,135, (126,697, metro.)* 255/B4
Dover, Fla., U.S., 2,798 . . . . .256/C4
Dover, Ida., U.S., 342 . . . . .264/A1
Dover, Ill., U.S., 172 . . . . .266/C2
Dover, Ind., U.S., 100 . . . . .270/C4
Dover, Kans., U.S., 125 . . . . .276/G3
Dover, Ky., U.S., 316 . . . . .280/G2
Dover, Mass., U.S., 5,558 . . . . .292/J4
Dover, Minn., U.S., 438 . . . . .298/F7
Dover, Mo., U.S., 108 . . . . .302/C2
Dover, N.H., U.S., 26,884 . . . . .312/E5
Dover, N.J., U.S., *town, 18,188* 314/D2
Dover, N.C., U.S., 443 . . . . .322/L4
Dover, Ohio, U.S., 12,210 . . . . .328/H4
Dover, Okla., U.S., 367 . . . . .330/E2
Dover, Penn., U.S., 1,815 . . . . .336/H5
Dover, Tenn., U.S., 1,442 . . . . .344/F2
Dover, Vt., U.S., 1,410 . . . . .352/B5
Dover A.F.B., Del., U.S. 255/C4

Dover-Foxcroft, Maine, U.S., 4,211 . . . . .286/C3
Doveridge, Eng., U.K. .68/D4
Dover Plains, N.Y., U.S., 1,996 . . . . .320/P7
Dovray, Minn., U.S., 67 . . . . .298/B6
Dovrefjell, Nor., mountains 80/B3
Dow, Ill., U.S., 300 . . . . .266/C4
Dowagiac, Mich., U.S., 6,147 . . . . .294/C7
Dowally, Scot., U.K. 62/J5
Dow City, Iowa, U.S., 503 . . . . .274/D4
Dowell, Ill., U.S., 441 .266/D6
Dowell, Md., U.S., 750 . . . . .288/J6
Dowelltown, Tenn., U.S., 302 . . . . .344/K2
Dowling, Mich., U.S., 150 . . . . .294/D7
Dowling Park, Fla., U.S., 650 . . . . .256/E1
Down, N. Ire., U.K., unitary authority, 63,828 . . . .65/F3
Downer, Minn., U.S. 298/A4
Downers Grove, Ill., U.S., 48,724 . . . . .266/B6
Downey, Calif., U.S., 107,323 . . . . .246/D10
Downey, Ida., U.S., 613 . . . . .264/E7
Downey, Iowa, U.S., 125 . . . . .274/M4
Downham Market, Eng., U.K., 5,841 . . . . .70/E1
Downhill, N. Ire., U.K. .65/D1
Downieville, Calif., U.S., 80 . . . . .246/E3
Downing, Mo., U.S., 396 . . . . .302/D1
Downing, Wisc., U.S., 257 . . . . .364/A3
Downingtown, Penn., U.S., 7,589 . . . . .336/K6
Downpatrick, N. Ire., U.K. 60/B2
Downpatrick, N. Ire., U.K., 10,257 . . . . .65/F3
Downs, Ill., U.S., 776 .266/E3
Downs, Kans., U.S., 1,038 . . . . .276/D2
Downsville, La., U.S., 118 . . . . .282/E1
Downsville, Md., U.S., 175 . . . . .288/C1
Downsville, N.Y., U.S., 325 . . . . .320/L6
Downsville, Wisc., U.S., 200 . . . . .364/B4
Dows, Iowa, U.S., 675 . . . . .274/G2
Dowsby, Eng., U.K. 70/D1
Doyle, Calif., U.S., 225 . . . . .246/E2
Doyle, Ga., U.S., 40 . . . . .260/C7
Doyle, Tenn., U.S., 525 . . . . .344/K3
Doylestown, Ohio, U.S., 2,799 . . . . .328/C4
Doylestown, Penn., U.S., 8,227 . . . . .336/L5
Doylestown, Wisc., U.S., 328 . . . . .364/D5
Doyleville, Colo., U.S. 250/D3
Doyline, La., U.S., 841 . . . . .282/C1
Doyon, N. Dak., U.S., 40 . . . . .326/G1
Dozen, Jap., island 114/B2
Dozier, Ala., U.S., 391 . . . . .238/C4
Dozier, Tex., U.S. 346/G9
Drâa, Alg., Mor., river 146/A1
Drâa, Mor., river 147/B2, C2
Dracut, Mass., U.S., 28,562 . . . . .292/J2
Dragoon, Ariz., U.S., 70 . . . . .242/E5
Draguignan, Fr. 88/D5
Drain, Oreg., U.S., 1,021 . . . . .334/C4
Drake, Sask., Can., 248 . . . . .227/E9
Drake, Ariz., U.S., 50 . . . . .242/C3
Drake, Colo., U.S. 250/E1
Drake, Mo., U.S. 302/E3
Drake, N. Dak., U.S., 322 . . . . .326/E2
Drakensberg, Leso., mountains 161/B3
Drakensberg, S. Afr., mountains 162/C3
Drakesboro, Ky., U.S., 627 . . . . .280/C3
Drakes Branch, Va., U.S., 504 . . . . .354/F7
Drakesville, Iowa, U.S., 185 . . . . .274/K6
Draketown, Ga., U.S., 300 . . . . .260/A4
Drammen, Nor. 80/C4
Draper, S. Dak., U.S., 92 . . . . .342/E4
Draper, Utah, U.S., 25,220 . . . . .350/C3, E2
Draperstown, N. Ire., U.K., 1,409 . . . . .65/D2
Drasco, Ark., U.S., 100 . . . . .244/D2
Drava, Aus., river 91/C4
Drava, Cro., river 98/C2
Drava, Hun., river 91/A2
Drava, Slove., river 98/C2
Dravosburg, Penn., U.S., 2,015 . . . . .336/E7
Draw, Tex., U.S. 346/G2
Drax, Eng., U.K. 66/G5
Draycote Water, Eng., U.K., lake 68/E5
Draycote Water, Eng., U.K., lake 70/B2
Drayton, Eng., U.K., 2,240 . . . . .68/E6
Drayton, Eng., U.K. 68/E6
Drayton, Eng., U.K., 2,240 . . . . .70/B2
Drayton, N. Dak., U.S., 913 . . . . .326/H1
Drayton Valley, Alta., Can., 5,801 . . . . .212/C4
Drefach, Wales, U.K. 64/C3
Drenthe, Neth., province 84/D2
Drenthe, Mich., U.S., 325 . . . . .294/D7
Dresden, Ont., Can., 2,582 . . . . .223/C5
Dresden, Ger., 477,800 . . . . .86/C3
Dresden, Ger., department 86/C3
Dresden, Kans., U.S., 51 . . . . .276/B2
Dresden, Mo., U.S., 175 . . . . .302/C3
Dresden, N.Y., U.S., 307 . . . . .320/H5
Dresden, Ohio, U.S., 1,423 . . . . .328/F5
Dresden, Tenn., U.S., 2,855 . . . . .344/D2
Dresser, Wisc., U.S., 732 . . . . .364/A3
Dreux, Fr. 88/C2
Drew, Ark., U.S., county, 18,723 . . . . .244/D4
Drew, Miss., U.S., 2,434 . . . . .300/B2
Drew, Oreg., U.S., 100 . . . . .334/D5
Drewryville, Va., U.S., 90 . . . . .354/J7
Drewsey, Oreg., U.S. .334/H4
Drewsville, N.H., U.S., 175 . . . . .212/B3
Drexel, Mo., U.S., 1,090 . . . . .302/B3
Drexel, N.C., U.S., 1,938 . . . . .322/B3
Drexel Hill, Penn., U.S., 29,364 . . . . .336/L6, L7
Driffield, Eng., U.K. 66/H4
Drifton, Fla., U.S., 200 . . . . .256/E1
Driftwood, Okla., U.S. 330/D1
Driftwood, Penn., U.S., 103 . . . . .336/E3
Driftwood, Tex., U.S., 200 . . . . .346/D2
Driggs, Ark., U.S., 100 . . . . .244/B2
Driggs, Ida., U.S., 1,100 . . . . .264/F6
Drimsallie, Scot., U.K. .62/F5
Drin, Alb., river 99/A1
Drina, Bos.-Her., river 98/C1
Drina, Serb.-Mont., river 99/A2
Dripping Sprs., Tex., U.S., 1,548 . . . . .346/D2
Drip Rock, Ky., U.S., 100 . . . . .280/G3
Driscoll, N. Dak., U.S., 100 . . . . .326/E3
Driscoll, Tex., U.S., 825 . . . . .346/L8
Driskill, La., U.S., mountain 282/C2
Driver, Ark., U.S., 80 .244/E2
Drobeta-Turnu Severin, Rom., 115,979 . . . . . . .101/B3
Drogheda, Ire., 28,308 . . . . .78/C2
Droitwich Spa, Eng., U.K., 20,966 . . . . .68/C5
Dromara, N. Ire., U.K., 511 . . . . .65/F3
Drôme, Fr., department .88/D4
Dromore, N. Ire., U.K., 3,708 . . . . .65/C2
Dromore, N. Ire., U.K., 655 . . . . .65/E3
Dronfield, Eng., U.K., 22,985 . . . . .66/F6
Dronfield, Eng., U.K., 22,985 . . . . .68/E3
Druid Hills, Ga., U.S., 12,741 . . . . .260/J3
Drum, N.C., U.S., inlet 322/N5
Drumaness, N. Ire., U.K., 1,026 . . . . .65/F3
Drumbadmeen, N. Ire., U.K. 65/B3
Drumbeg, Scot., U.K. 62/F2
Drumdallagh, N. Ire., U.K. 65/E1
Drumheller, Alta., U.S., 7,785 . . . . .212/D5
Drummond, N.B., Can., 932 . . . . .217/B2
Drummond, Ida., U.S. .264/F5
Drummond, Mich., U.S., 200 . . . . .294/F3

Drummond, Mich., U.S., island 294/F4
Drummond, Mont., U.S., 318 . . . . .306/C3
Drummond, Okla., U.S., 405 . . . . .330/D1
Drummond, Wisc., U.S., 150 . . . . .364/B2
Drummondville, Que., Can., 46,599 . . . . .225/B4
Drummondville, Que., Can., 46,599 . . . . .226/D6
Drummore, Scot., U.K. .62/G9
Drumnadrochit, Scot., U.K., 813 . . . . .62/H4
Drumphail, Scot., U.K. .62/G9
Drum Pt., Md., U.S., 11,503 . . . . .288/J6
Drumquin, N. Ire., U.K., 558 . . . . .65/C2
Drumright, Okla., U.S., 2,905 . . . . .330/F2
Drury, Mass., U.S., 100 . . . . .292/C2
Drury, Mo., U.S., 50 . . . . .302/D5
Druskininkai, Lith. 82/B2
Dry, Nev., U.S., lake 310/A1
Drybrook, Eng., U.K. 68/B6
Dry Creek, La., U.S. 282/C5
Dryden, Ont., Can., 8,198 . . . . .222/B3
Dryden, Mich., U.S., 815 . . . . .294/F7
Dryden, N.Y., U.S., 1,832 . . . . .320/J6
Dryden, Tex., U.S. 346/F5
Dryden, Va., U.S., 1,253 . . . . .354/E7
Dry Fork, Va., U.S., 100 . . . . .354/E7
Dry Lake, Nev., U.S. 310/D3
Drymen, Scot., U.K., 681 . . . . .62/H6
Drynob, Mo., U.S. 302/D4
Dry Prong, La., U.S., 421 . . . . .282/D3
Dry Ridge, Ky., U.S., 1,995 . . . . .280/F2
Dry Run, Penn., U.S., 325 . . . . .336/F5
Drysdale River Natl. Park, Austl. 170/D1
Dry Tortugas Natl. Park, Fla., U.S. 256/D7
Dschang, Came. 153/B2
Duarte, Dom. Rep., mountain 204/D3
Duarte, Dom. Rep., mountain 205/B1
Duarte, Dom. Rep., province 205/C1
Duarte, Calif., U.S., 21,486 . . . . .246/D9
Dūba, Sa. Ar. 136/A1
Dubach, La., U.S., 800 . . . . .282/D1
Dubai, U.A.E., 669,181 . . . . .136/C2
Dubăsari, Mol. 102/B2
Dubawnt, N.W. Terr., Can., river 220/H4
Dubawnt, Nun., Can., lake 220/H4
Dubay, Wisc., U.S., lake 364/D4
Dubberly, La., U.S., 290 . . . . .282/C1
Dubbo, N.S.W., Austl. 170/D3
Dubbs, Miss., U.S. 300/B1
Dube, Liber., river 149/C3
Dublin, Ire., capital, 495,101,
   (1,122,600, metro.) . . . . .78/C2, metro)
Dublin, Calif., U.S., 29,973 . . . . .246/K2
Dublin, Ga., U.S., 15,857 . . . . .260/F6
Dublin, Ind., U.S., 697 . . . . .270/F5
Dublin, Ky., U.S., 175 .280/B4
Dublin, Md., U.S., 650 . . . . .288/J1
Dublin, Miss., U.S., 70 . . . . .300/B1
Dublin, N.H., U.S., 1,476 . . . . .212/B6
Dublin, N.C., U.S., 250 . . . . .322/H5
Dublin, Ohio, U.S., 31,392 . . . . .328/C5, D9
Dublin, Penn., U.S., 2,083 . . . . .336/L5
Dublin, Tex., U.S., 3,754 . . . . .346/K3
Dublin, Va., U.S., 2,288 . . . . .354/B6
Dublin County Borough, Ire., county 78/C2
Dubois, Ida., U.S., 647 . . . . .264/E5
Du Bois, Ill., U.S., 222 . . . . .266/D6
Dubois, Ind., U.S., 425 . . . . .270/C8
Dubois, Ind., U.S., county, 39,674 . . . . .270/C8
Dubois, Nebr., U.S., 166 . . . . .308/H3
DuBois, Penn., U.S., 8,123 . . . . .336/D3
Dubois, Wyo., U.S., 962 . . . . .366/B2
Duboistown, Penn., U.S., 1,280 . . . . .336/G3
Dubrovnik, Cro., 30,436 . . . . .98/D4
Dubuque, Iowa, U.S., 57,686, (89,143, metro.) . . .274/N2
Dubuque, Iowa, U.S., county, 89,143 . . . . .274/N3
Dubysa, Lith., river 82/B2
Duchally, Scot., U.K. 62/G2
Duchénier Prov. Reserve, Que., Can. 226/H3
Duchesne, Utah, U.S., 1,408 . . . . .350/D3
Duchesne, Utah, U.S., county, 14,371 . . . . .350/D3
Duchess, Alta., Can., 836 . . . . .212/E6
Duck, Tenn., U.S., river 344/H3
Duck Bay, Man., Can., 454 . . . . .215/A3
Duck Hill, Miss., U.S., 746 . . . . .300/C2
Duck Lake, Sask., Can., 624 . . . . .227/D8
Duck Mtn. Natl. Park, Man., Can. 215/A3
Duck Mtn. Prov. Park, Sask., Can. 227/J9
Duck River, Tenn., U.S., 80 . . . . .344/G3
Ducktown, Tenn., U.S., 427 . . . . .344/N4
Duck Valley Ind. Res., Ida., U.S. 264/A7
Duck Valley Ind. Res., Nev., U.S. 310/B1
Duckwater, Nev., U.S. 310/C2
Duckwater Ind. Res., Nev., U.S. 310/C2
Ducor, Calif., U.S., 504 . . . . .246/F7
Duddington, Eng., U.K. .70/C1
Dudinka, Russ. 104/F3
Dudley, (W. Dudley), Eng., U.K., 192,171 . . . . . . .68/C4
Dudley, Eng., U.K. 60/C5
Dudley, Eng., U.K., unitary authority, 305,164 . . . .68/C5
Dudley, Ga., U.S., 447 . . . . .260/E6
Dudley, Mass., U.S., 10,036 . . . . .292/G4
Dudley, Mo., U.S., 289 . . . . .302/F5
Dudley, Penn., U.S., 192 . . . . .336/F5
Dudleyville, Ariz., U.S., 1,454 . . . . .242/E5
Duelm, Minn., U.S., 100 . . . . .298/D5
Duero, Sp., river 88/B4
Duero, Sp., river 94/D2
Duette, Fla., U.S. 256/F4
Due West, S.C., U.S., 1,209 . . . . .340/B2
Duffau, Tex., U.S., 80 .346/K3
Duffee, Miss., U.S., 60 . . . . .300/D3
Dufferin, Ont., Can. 223/E3
Dufferin, Ont., Can., county 223/E3
Duffield, Eng., U.K., 4,514 . . . . .68/E4
Duffield, Eng., U.K., 4,514 . . . . .70/B1
Duffield, Va., U.S., 62 . . . . .354/C3
Dufftown, Scot., U.K., 1,454 . . . . .62/K4
Dufourspitze, Switz., mountain 90/B3
Dufrost, Man., Can. 215/C4
Dufur, Oreg., U.S., 588 . . . . .334/E2
Dugald, Man., Can. 215/C4
Dugger, Ind., U.S., 955 . . . . .270/B6
Duggleby, Eng., U.K. 66/G4
Dugway, Utah, U.S. 350/B3
Dugway Proving Ground, Utah, U.S. 350/A3
Duich, Scot., U.K., lake 62/F4
Duisburg, Ger., 519,793 . . . . .86/A3
Duke, Okla., U.S., 445 . . . . .330/C3
Dukes, Fla., U.S., 70 .256/F2
Dukes, Miss., U.S., county, 14,987 . . . . .292/M7
Dukhān, Qatar 137/B3
Dulac, La., U.S., 2,458 . . . . .282/H8
Dulce, C.R., gulf 203/C4
Dulce, N. Mex., U.S., 2,623 . . . . .317/C1
Dulnain Bridge, Scot., U.K. 62/J4
Duluth, Ga., U.S., 22,122 . . . . .260/C3, J2
Duluth, Kans., U.S., 50 . . . . .276/F2
Duluth, Minn., U.S., 86,918, (243,815, metro.) . . .298/E4
Duma, Leb. 134/A1
Dumaguete, Phil. 120/B4
Dumai, Indon. 122/B1
Dumas, Ark., U.S., 5,238 . . . . .244/D4

Dumas, Miss., U.S., 452 . . . . .300/D1
Dumas, Tex., U.S., 13,747 . . . . .346/F8
Dumbarton, Scot., U.K., 20,527 . . . . .62/G7
Dumbarton, Va., U.S., 6,674 . . . . .354/H5
Dumbás, Nor. 80/B3
Dum-Dum, India .128/Inset II
Dumfries, Scot., U.K. 60/B2
Dumfries, Scot., U.K., 31,146 . . . . .62/J8
Dumfries, Va., U.S., 4,937 . . . . .354/J3
Dumfries and Galloway, Scot., U.K.,
   unitary authority, 147,765 . . . . .62/H9
Dumjor, India . . . . .128/Inset II
Dumont, Colo., U.S., 364 . . . . .250/E2
Dumont, Iowa, U.S., 676 . . . . .274/J2
Dumont, Minn., U.S., 122 . . . . .298/A5
Dumont, N.J., U.S., 17,503 . . . . .314/C2
Dunaújváros, Hun. 91/B2
Dunbar, Scot., U.K., 6,354 . . . . .62/M7
Dunbar, Iowa, U.S., 100 . . . . .274/J4
Dunbar, Nebr., U.S., 237 . . . . .308/H3
Dunbar, Penn., U.S., 1,219 . . . . .336/B6
Dunbar, W. Va., U.S., 8,154 . . . . .360/C4
Dunbar, Wisc., U.S., 70 . . . . .364/E3
Dunbarton, La., U.S., 50 . . . . .282/F3
Dunbarton Ctr., N.H., U.S., 200 . . . . .212/C5
Dunbeath, Scot., U.K. .62/K2
Dunblane, Scot., U.K., 7,911 . . . . .62/J6
Duncan, Br. Col., Can., 4,699 . . . . .214/L7
Duncan, Ariz., U.S., 812 . . . . .242/F5
Duncan, Ky., U.S., 100 . . . . .280/F3
Duncan, Miss., U.S., 578 . . . . .300/B1
Duncan, Nebr., U.S., 359 . . . . .308/G2
Duncan, Okla., U.S., 22,505 . . . . .330/E3
Duncan, S.C., U.S., 2,870 . . . . .340/F2
Duncan Falls, Ohio, U.S., 950 . . . . .328/G6
Duncannon, Penn., U.S., 1,508 . . . . .336/G5
Duncans Bridge, Mo., U.S., 50 . . . . .302/D2
Duncansby, Scot., U.K., cape 60/B1
Duncansville, Penn., U.S., 1,238 . . . . .336/E5
Duncanville, Ala., U.S., 175 . . . . .238/B2
Duncanville, Ill., U.S., 125 . . . . .266/F5
Duncanville, Tex., U.S., 36,081 . . . . .346/C10
Dunchurch, Eng., U.K., 2,251 . . . . .68/E5
Dunchurch, Eng., U.K., 2,251 . . . . .70/B2
Duncombe, Iowa, U.S., 474 . . . . .274/F3
Dundalk, Ire., 27,399 . . . . .78/C2
Dundalk, Md., U.S., 62,306 . . . . .288/H2
Dundarrach, N.C., U.S., 62 . . . . .322/G5
Dundas, P.E.I., Can. 224/C2
Dundas, Ill., U.S., 225 . . . . .266/E5
Dundas, Minn., U.S., 547 . . . . .298/D6
Dundas, Va., U.S., 125 . . . . .354/G7
Dundee, Scot., U.K. 60/C2
Dundee, Scot., U.K., 154,674 . . . . .62/L6
Dundee, City of, Scot., U.K.,
   unitary authority, 145,663 . . . . .62/L5
Dundee, Iowa, U.S., 179 . . . . .274/L2
Dundee, Kans., U.S., 100 . . . . .276/D3
Dundee, Ky., U.S., 50 .280/D3
Dundee, Mich., U.S., 3,522 . . . . .294/F8
Dundee, Minn., U.S., 102 . . . . .298/B7
Dundee, Miss., U.S., 125 . . . . .300/B1
Dundee, N.Y., U.S., 1,690 . . . . .320/H5
Dundee, Oreg., U.S., 2,598 . . . . .334/D2
Dundee, Tex., U.S. 346/K2
Dundgovĭ, Mong. 118/B2
Dundonald, N. Ire., U.K., 12,943 . . . . .65/F2
Dundrod, N. Ire., U.K. .65/E2
Dundrum, N. Ire., U.K., 1,131 . . . . .65/F3
Dundrum, N. Ire., U.K., bay 65/F3
Dundurn, Sask., Can., 596 . . . . .227/D9
Dundy, Nebr., U.S., county, 2,292 . . . . .308/C3
Dune Acres, Ind., U.S., 213 . . . . .270/B1
Dunean, S.C., U.S., 4,158 . . . . .340/E2
Dunedin, N.Z., 114,342, (107,088, metro.) 171/B4
Dunedin, Fla., U.S., 35,691 . . . . .256/C6, F3
Dunellen, N.J., U.S., 6,823 . . . . .314/C2
Dunes City, Oreg., U.S., 1,241 . . . . .334/B4
Dunfermline, Scot., U.K. 60/B2
Dunfermline, Scot., U.K., 39,229 . . . . .62/K6
Dunfermline, Ill., U.S., 262 . . . . .266/C3
Dungannon, N. Ire., U.K., 9,420 . . . . .65/D3
Dungannon, N. Ire., U.K., unitary authority,
   47,735 . . . . .65/D3
Dungannon, Va., U.S., 317 . . . . .354/C2
Dungarvan, Ire. 78/C2
Dungeness, Eng., U.K., cape 70/F5
Dungeness, Wash., U.S., cape 358/B1
Dungiven, N. Ire., U.K., 2,812 . . . . .65/D2
Dunken, N. Mex., U.S. 317/E5
Dunkerton, Iowa, U.S., 749 . . . . .274/K2
Dunkinsville, Ohio, U.S., 90 . . . . .328/D8
Dunkirk, (Dunkerque), Fr., 72,333,
   (191,173, metro.) .88/C1
Dunkirk, Eng., U.K., 2,705 . . . . .70/F4
Dunkirk, Ind., U.S., 2,646 . . . . .270/F4
Dunkirk, Md., U.S., 2,363 . . . . .288/H5
Dunkirk, Mont., U.S. .306/E1
Dunkirk, N.Y., U.S., 13,131 . . . . .320/C6
Dunkirk, Ohio, U.S., 952 . . . . .328/C4
Dunklin, Mo., U.S., county, 33,155 . . . . .302/F5
Dunlap, Ill., U.S., 926 .266/D3
Dunlap, Ind., U.S., 5,887 . . . . .270/E1
Dunlap, Iowa, U.S., 1,139 . . . . .274/C4
Dunlap, Kans., U.S., 81 . . . . .276/F3
Dunlap, Tenn., U.S., 4,173 . . . . .344/L4
Dunleith, Del., U.S., 9,100 . . . . .255/B2
Dunlop, Man., Can. 215/B2
Dunlow, W. Va., U.S., 150 . . . . .360/B4
Dunloy, N. Ire., U.K., 1,119 . . . . .65/E2
Dunmor, Ky., U.S., 250 . . . . .280/D3
Dunmore, Penn., U.S., 14,018 . . . . .336/H7, K3
Dunmore, W. Va., U.S., 100 . . . . .360/G4
Dunn, La., U.S., 125 . . . . .282/F2
Dunn, N.C., U.S., 9,196 . . . . .322/H4
Dunn, N. Dak., U.S., county, 3,600 . . . . .326/C3
Dunn, Tex., U.S., 100 .346/H3
Dunn, Wisc., U.S., county, 39,858 . . . . .364/B4
Dunnamanagh, N. Ire., U.K., 675 . . . . .65/C2
Dunn Ctr., N. Dak., U.S., 122 . . . . .326/C3
Dunn Corner, R.I., U.S. 339/B5
Dunneason, Mo., U.S., 125 . . . . .302/C4
Dunnell, Minn., U.S., 197 . . . . .298/C7
Dunnellon, Fla., U.S., 1,898 . . . . .256/F2
Dunnigan, Calif., U.S., 150 . . . . .246/D4
Dunnigan, W. Va., U.S., 109 . . . . .308/D2
Dunn Loring, Va., U.S., 7,861 . . . . .354/M2
Dunns, Maine, U.S., 300 . . . . .286/B5
Dunnstown, Penn., U.S., 1,365 . . . . .336/G3
Dunnville, Ont., Can., 5,686 . . . . .223/F5
Dunnville, Ky., U.S., 40 . . . . .280/F3
Dunoon, Scot., U.K., 8,251 . . . . .62/G7
Dunphy, Nev., U.S. 310/B1
Dunqulah, Sudan 145/C1

Dunragit, Scot., U.K. 62/G9
Duns, Scot., U.K., 2,594 . . . . .62/M7
Dunscore, Scot., U.K. 62/J8
Dunseith, N. Dak., U.S., 739 . . . . .326/E1
Dunsfold, Eng., U.K. 70/C4
Dunsinane, Scot., U.K., mountain 60/B2
Dunstable, Eng., U.K. . . . . .60/Inset III
Dunstable, Eng., U.K., 49,666 . . . . .70/C3
Dunstable, Mass., U.S., 2,829 . . . . .292/J2
Dunster, Br. Col., Can. 214/N4
Dunster, Eng., U.K. 73/F2
Dunton, Colo., U.S. 68/C4
Dunton Bassett, Eng., U.K. 68/E4
Duntroe, Scot., U.K. 62/G8
Dunvilla, Minn., U.S., 50 . . . . .298/A4
Dunvegan, N.S., Can. .221/F1
Dunwich, Eng., U.K. 70/H2
Dunwoody, Ga., U.S., 32,808 . . . . .260/C4, J2
Du Page, Ill., U.S., county, 904,161 . . . . . . .266/A6, E2
Dupleix, N.C., U.S., county, 49,063 . . . . .322/K5
Dupo, Ill., U.S., 3,933 .266/A3
Dupont, (Derby), Colo., U.S., 4,500 . . . . .250/A3
Dupont, Ga., U.S., 139 . . . . .260/F1
Dupont, Ind., U.S., 392 . . . . .270/E7
Dupont, La., U.S., 50 .282/F5
Dupont, Ohio, U.S., 268 . . . . .328/B3
Dupont, Penn., U.S., 2,719 . . . . .336/H7
Du Pont, Wash., U.S., 2,452 . . . . .358/C2
Dupree, S. Dak., U.S., 434 . . . . .342/D2
Dupuyer, Mont., U.S., 40 . . . . .306/D2
Duque, P.R. 206/D2
Duque de Caxias, Braz., 775,456 . . . . .188/Inset I
Duquesne, Iowa, U.S. .242/E6
Duquesne, Mo., U.S., 1,640 . . . . .302/B4
Duquesne, Penn., U.S., 7,332 . . . . .336/E7
Duquette, Minn., U.S., 60 . . . . .298/E4
Du Quoin, Ill., U.S., 6,448 . . . . .266/D6
Duquoin, Kans., U.S. .276/D4
Duran, N. Mex., U.S. .317/E3
Durance, Fr., river 88/D5
Durand, Ga., U.S., 175 . . . . .260/B6
Durand, Ill., U.S., 1,081 . . . . .266/D1
Durand, Mich., U.S., 3,933 . . . . .294/F7
Durand, Wisc., U.S., 1,968 . . . . .364/B4
Durango, Mex., state capital, 427,135,
   (491,436, metro.) .200/D3
Durango, Mex., state .200/D3
Durango, Colo., U.S., 13,922 . . . . .250/C4
Durango, Iowa, U.S. 274/N2
Durant, Iowa, U.S., 1,677 . . . . .274/N4
Durant, Miss., U.S., 2,932 . . . . .300/C2
Durant, Okla., U.S., 13,549 . . . . .330/F4
Durazno, Uru. 187/B2
Durazno, Uru., department 187/C2
Durban, S. Afr., 669,242, (2,992,386, metro.) . .162/D2
Durbin, Fla., U.S. 256/G1
Durbin, W. Va., U.S., 262 . . . . .360/G3
Durham, Ont., Can., 2,709 . . . . .223/E3
Durham, Ont., Can., 2,709 . . . . .223/G3
Durham, Ont., Can., county 223/G3
Durham, Eng., U.K. 60/C2
Durham, Eng., U.K., 36,937 . . . . .66/E3
Durham, Eng., U.K., unitary authority, 493,470 . .66/D3
Durham, Scot., U.K. 62/J8
Durham, Ark., U.S., 80 . . . . .244/B2
Durham, Calif., U.S., 5,200 . . . . .246/D3
Durham, Conn., U.S., 6,627 . . . . .253/E4
Durham, Kans., U.S., 114 . . . . .276/E3
Durham, Maine, U.S., 3,381 . . . . .286/B5
Durham, N.H., U.S., 12,664 . . . . .212/F5
Durham, N.C., U.S., 187,035 . . . . .322/H2
Durham, N.C., U.S., county, 223,314 . . . . .322/H2
Durham, Okla., U.S. 330/C2
Durham, Oreg., U.S., 1,382 . . . . .334/A3
Durham, Wyo., U.S. 366/D3
Durisdeer, Scot., U.K. 62/J8
Durkee, Oreg., U.S. 334/J3
Durley, Eng., U.K. 70/B5
Durmitor, Serb.-Mont., mountains 99/A3
Durness, Scot., U.K. 62/G1
Durrës, Alb., 99,546 . . . . .99/A2
Dursley, Eng., U.K., 13,331 . . . . .68/C6
Duryea, Penn., U.S., 4,634 . . . . .336/H7
Dushanbe, Taj., capital, 528,600 . . . . .132/A1
Dushore, Penn., U.S., 663 . . . . .336/J2
Duson, La, U.S., 1,672 . . . . .282/E6
Düsseldorf, Ger., 568,855 . . . . .86/A3
Düsseldorf, Ger., department 86/A3
Duster, Tex., U.S. 346/K3
Dustin, Okla., U.S., 452 . . . . .330/F2
Dusty, Wash., U.S. 358/H3
Dutchess, N.Y., U.S., county, 280,150 . . . . .320/P7
Dutch Harbor, Alaska, U.S. 240/B4
Dutch John, Utah, U.S. 350/E3
Dutch Neck, N.J., U.S., 4,400 . . . . .314/D3
Dutchtown, Mo., U.S., 99 . . . . .302/G4
Duton Hill, Eng., U.K. 70/E3
Dutton, Ala., U.S., 310 . . . . .238/D1
Dutton, Mont., U.S., 389 . . . . .306/E2
Dutton, Utah, U.S., mountain 350/B5
Duval, Fla., U.S., county, 778,879 . . . . .256/G1
Duval, Tex., U.S., county, 13,120 . . . . .346/K8
Duvall, Wash., U.S., 4,616 . . . . .358/B4, D3
Duxbury, Mass., U.S., 14,248 . . . . .292/M4
Duxbury, Vt., U.S., 1,289 . . . . .352/B2
Dwarf, Ky., U.S., 525 .280/G3
Dwight, Ill., U.S., 4,363 . . . . .266/E3
Dwight, Kans., U.S., 330 . . . . .276/F3
Dwight, Nebr., U.S., 259 . . . . .308/G2
Dwight, N. Dak., U.S., 75 . . . . .326/J3
Dworshak, Ida., U.S., reservoir 264/A3
Dwyer, N. Mex., U.S. .317/C5
Dwyer, Wyo., U.S. 366/D3
Dyce, Man., Can. 215/A2
Dyce, Scot., U.K., 5,661 . . . . .62/M4
Dyckesville, Wisc., U.S., 300 . . . . .364/F4
Dycusburg, Ky., U.S. 280/B3
Dyer, Ark., U.S., 585 .244/A2
Dyer, Ind., U.S., 13,895 . . . . .270/A1
Dyer, Ky., U.S., 175 . . . . .280/C3
Dyer, Nev., U.S. 310/A3
Dyer, Tenn., U.S., 2,406 . . . . .344/C2
Dyer, Tenn., U.S., county, 37,279 . . . . .344/C2
Dyer Brook, Maine, U.S., 199 . . . . .286/D2
Dyer Cove, Maine, U.S., 600 . . . . .286/C5
Dyersburg, Tenn., U.S., 17,452 . . . . .344/C2
Dyersville, Iowa, U.S., 4,035 . . . . .274/M3
Dyess, Ark., U.S., 515 . . . . .244/E2
Dyffryn Ardudwy, (Dyffryn Ardudwy/Tal-y-bont),
   Wales, U.K., 1,452 .64/C2
Dyje, Czh. Rep., river 92/B4
Dyke, Scot., U.K. 62/J3
Dyke, Va., U.S., 125 .354/F4
Dykends, Scot., U.K. 62/K5
Dymchurch, Eng., U.K., 2,951 . . . . .70/G4
Dymock, Eng., U.K. 68/C6

Dysart, Iowa, U.S., 1,303 . . . . .274/K3
Dysartville, N.C., U.S., 100 . . . . .322/B3
Dyserth, Wales, U.K., 2,394 . . . . .64/E1
Dzavhan, Mong., river 118/B2
Dzhugdzhur, Russ., range 104/H4
Dzungarian, China, basin 119/B1
Dzyarzhynskaya Hara, Bela., mountain 82/C3
Eads, Colo., U.S., 747 . . . . .250/H3
Eagan, Minn., U.S., 63,557 . . . . .298/F6
Eagan, Tenn., U.S., 200 . . . . .344/P2
Eagar, Ariz., U.S., 4,033 . . . . .242/F3
Eagarville, Ill., U.S., 128 . . . . .266/B3
Eagle, Nfld., Can., river 218/B2
Eagle, Yukon, Can., river 228/B2
Eagle, Alaska, U.S., 129 . . . . .240/G2
Eagle, Calif., U.S. 246/E2
Eagle, Calif., U.S., peak 246/E1
Eagle, Colo., U.S., 3,032 . . . . .250/D2
Eagle, Colo., U.S., county, 41,659 . . . . .250/D2
Eagle, Ida., U.S., 11,085 . . . . .264/A6
Eagle, Minn., U.S., mountain 294/E7
Eagle, Nebr., U.S., 1,105 . . . . .298/H3
Eagle, Tex., U.S., peak 346/C5
Eagle, Wisc., U.S., 1,707 . . . . .364/E6
Eagle Bend, Minn., U.S., 595 . . . . .298/B4
Eagle Bend, Miss., U.S., 80 . . . . .300/A3
Eagle Butte, S. Dak., U.S., 619 . . . . .342/D3
Eagle City, Okla., U.S., 60 . . . . .330/D2
Eagle Grove, Iowa, U.S., 3,712 . . . . .274/G2
Eagle Harbor, Md., U.S., 55 . . . . .288/H5
Eagle Harbor, Mich., U.S. 294/A2
Eagle Lake, Fla., U.S., 2,496 . . . . .256/G4
Eagle Lake, Maine, U.S., 815 . . . . .286/D1
Eagle Lake, Minn., U.S., 1,787 . . . . .298/D6
Eagle Lake, Tex., U.S., 3,664 . . . . .346/M6
Eagle Lake, Wisc., U.S., 1,320 . . . . .364/E6
Eagle Mills, Ark., U.S., 60 . . . . .244/C4
Eagle Mills, Ohio, U.S., 50 . . . . .328/E7
Eagle Mtn., Calif., U.S., 125 . . . . .246/K9
Eagle Mtn., Tex., U.S., lake 346/A9
Eagle Nest, N. Mex., U.S., 306 . . . . .317/E1
Eagle Pass, Tex., U.S., 22,413 . . . . .346/H7
Eagle Pitcher Mine, Nev., U.S. 310/A1
Eagle Pt., Oreg., U.S., 4,797 . . . . .334/D5
Eagleport, Ohio, U.S., 300 . . . . .328/G6
Eagle River, Mich., U.S. 294/A2
Eagle River, Wisc., U.S., 1,443 . . . . .364/D3
Eagle Rock, Va., U.S. 354/D5
Eaglesfield, Scot., U.K., 616 . . . . .62/K8
Eaglesham, Scot., U.K., 3,127 . . . . .62/H7
Eagles Mere, Penn., U.S., 153 . . . . .336/H3
Eagleton, Ark., U.S. 244/A3
Eagleton, Mont., U.S. 306/G2
Eagleton, Wisc., U.S., 150 . . . . .364/B3
Eagleton Vil., Tenn., U.S., 4,883 . . . . .344/P3
Eagletown, Okla., U.S., 475 . . . . .330/H3
Eagleville, Calif., U.S. 246/E1
Eagleville, Conn., U.S., 500 . . . . .253/F2
Eagleville, Mo., U.S., 321 . . . . .302/B1
Eagleville, Ohio, U.S., 175 . . . . .328/J2
Eagleville, Penn., U.S., 4,458 . . . . .336/L6
Eagleville, Tenn., U.S., 464 . . . . .344/H3
Eakly, Okla., U.S., 276 . . . . .330/D2
Ealing, Eng., U.K., 275,257 . . . . .70/D3
Ealing, Eng., U.K., unitary authority, 300,947 . .70/D3
Earby, Eng., U.K., 4,957 . . . . .66/D5
Earby, Eng., U.K., 4,957 . . . . .68/C2
Ear Falls, Ont., Can. 222/B2
Earl, N.C., U.S., 234 . . . . .322/B4
Earl, Wisc., U.S., 60 . . . . .364/B3
Earle, Ark., U.S., 3,036 . . . . .244/E2
Earle, N.J., U.S., 550 . . . . .314/E3
Earles, Ky., U.S., 60 . . . . .280/C3
Earleville, Md., U.S., 125 . . . . .288/L2
Earlham, Iowa, U.S., 1,298 . . . . .274/F5
Earlimart, Calif., U.S., 6,583 . . . . .246/F7
Earling, Iowa, U.S., 471 . . . . .274/D4
Earlington, Ky., U.S., 1,649 . . . . .280/C3
Earl Park, Ind., U.S., 485 . . . . .270/B3
Earls, Va., U.S., 60 . . . . .354/H6
Earls Barton, Eng., U.K., 4,917 . . . . .68/F5
Earls Barton, Eng., U.K., 4,917 . . . . .70/C2
Earlsboro, Okla., U.S., 633 . . . . .330/F2
Earlsferry, Scot., U.K. 62/L6
Earl Shilton, Eng., U.K., 18,083 . . . . .68/E4
Earl Shilton, Eng., U.K., 18,083 . . . . .70/B1
Earl Stonham, Eng., U.K. 70/G2
Earlton, Kans., U.S., 80 . . . . .276/G4
Earlville, Ill., U.S., 1,778 . . . . .266/E2
Earlville, Iowa, U.S., 900 . . . . .274/M3
Earlville, N.Y., U.S., 791 . . . . .320/M5
Early, Ga., U.S., county, 12,354 . . . . .260/B9
Early, Iowa, U.S., 605 . . . . .274/D3
Early, Tex., U.S., 2,588 . . . . .346/K4
Early Branch, S.C., U.S., 80 . . . . .340/D4
Earp, Calif., U.S. .246/L8
Earsham, Eng., U.K. 70/G2
Earth, Tex., U.S., 1,109 . . . . .346/F1
Eartham, Eng., U.K. 70/C5
Easebourne, Eng., U.K. 70/C5
Easington, (Durham Co), Eng., U.K., 7,593 . . .66/F3
Easington, (East Riding of Yorkshire), Eng., U.K. .66/J5
Easington, (East Riding of Yorkshire), Eng., U.K. .68/H2
Easingwold, Eng., U.K., 2,816 . . . . .68/E1
Easley, S.C., U.S., 17,754 . . . . .340/D4
Eason, Okla., U.S., 50 . . . . .330/E2
East, Came., province 153/B3
East, P.E.I., Can., point 224/C2
East, N.Z., cape .171/C2
E. Afton, Tex., U.S. 346/H2
E. Alburg, Vt., U.S. 352/A1
E. Alstead, N.H., U.S., 175 . . . . .212/B5
E. Alton, Ill., U.S., 6,830 . . . . .266/A3
E. Amana, Iowa, U.S., 90 . . . . .274/L4
E. Andover, Maine, U.S., 150 . . . . .286/B4
E. Andover, N.H., U.S., 300 . . . . .212/C5
E. Angus, Que., Can., 3,570 . . . . .226/C6
E. Antarctica, Antar. 192/B1
E. Arcadia, N.C., U.S., 524 . . . . .322/J6
E. Arlington, Vt., U.S., 750 . . . . .352/A4
E. Aurora, N.Y., U.S., 6,673 . . . . .320/D5
East Ayrshire, Scot., U.K., unitary authority,
  120,235 . . . . .62/H8
East Azerbaijan, Iran, province 130/B2
E. Baldwin, Maine, U.S., 225 . . . . .286/B5
E. Bangor, Penn., U.S., 979 . . . . .336/L4
E. Bank, W. Va., U.S., 933 . . . . .360/D4
E. Barkwith, Eng., U.K. 66/H6
E. Barnard, Vt., U.S. 352/B3
E. Barnet, Vt., U.S., 70 . . . . .352/C2
E. Barre, Vt., U.S., 2,136 . . . . .352/C2
E. Barrington, N.H., U.S., 400 . . . . .212/D5
E. Barsham, Eng., U.K. 70/F1
East Baton Rouge, La., U.S., parish, 412,852 . .282/H5
E. Bend, N.C., U.S., 659 . . . . .322/D4
E. Bergholt, Eng., U.K. 70/G3
E. Berkshire, Vt., U.S., 175 . . . . .352/B1
E. Berlin, Penn., U.S., 1,365 . . . . .336/H6
E. Bernstadt, Ky., U.S., 774 . . . . .280/F3
E. Bethel, Minn., U.S., 10,941 . . . . .298/D5
E. Bethel, Vt., U.S., 175 . . . . .352/B3

E. Blackstone, Mass., U.S., 1,600 . . . . .292/H4
E. Blythe, Calif., U.S. 246/L9
Eastborough, Kans., U.S., 826 . . . . .276/E4
Eastbourne, Eng., U.K. 60/D4
Eastbourne, Eng., U.K., 94,793 . . . . .70/E5
E. Brady, Penn., U.S., 1,038 . . . . .336/M4
E. Braintree, Man., Can. 215/D4
E. Braintree, Mass., U.S., 150 . . . . .352/B2
E. Branch, N.Y., U.S., 250 . . . . .320/L7
E. Brewster, Mass., U.S., 850 . . . . .292/P5
E. Brewton, Ala., U.S., 2,496 . . . . .238/B4
E. Bridgewater, Mass., U.S., 12,974 . . . . .292/L4
Eastbrook, Maine, U.S., 370 . . . . .286/D4
E. Brookfield, Mass., U.S., 2,097 . . . . .292/F4
E. Brookfield, Vt., U.S., 225 . . . . .352/B2
E. Brooklyn, Conn., U.S., 1,473 . . . . .253/H2
E. Brooklyn, Ill., U.S., 123 . . . . .266/E2
E. Brunswick, N.J., U.S., 46,756 . . . . .314/E3
E. Burke, Vt., U.S., 175 . . . . .352/D1
E. Butler, Penn., U.S., 679 . . . . .336/B4
E. Calais, Vt., U.S., 275 . . . . .352/C2
E. Camden, Ark., U.S., 902 . . . . .244/C4
E. Candia, N.H., U.S. 212/D5
E. Canton, Ohio, U.S., 1,629 . . . . .328/H4
E. Cape Girardeau, Ill., U.S., 437 . . . . .266/D6
E. Carbon, Utah, U.S., 1,393 . . . . .350/D4
E. Carondelet, Ill., U.S., 267 . . . . .266/A3
East Carroll, La., U.S., parish, 9,421 . . . . . . .282/G1
E. Cayuga Hts., N.Y., U.S. 320/J6
E. Challow, Eng., U.K. 70/B3
E. Charleston, Vt., U.S., 70 . . . . .352/D1
E. Chicago, Ind., U.S., 32,414 . . . . .270/B1
East China, China, sea 119/F3
E. Claridon, Ohio, U.S., 325 . . . . .328/H2
E. Cleveland, Ohio, U.S., 27,217 . . . . . . .328/G2, H9
E. Cleveland, Tenn., U.S., 1,729 . . . . .344/M4
E. Coast Bays, N.Z. 171/B2
E. Concord, Vt., U.S., 80 . . . . .352/D2
E. Conemaugh, Penn., U.S., 1,291 . . . . .336/D5
E. Corinth, Maine, U.S., 125 . . . . .286/C4
E. Corinth, Vt., U.S., 175 . . . . .352/C2
E. Coulee, Alta., Can., 156 . . . . .212/D5
E. Craftsbury, Vt., U.S., 125 . . . . .352/C1
E. Croachy, Scot., U.K. 62/H4
E. Dean, Eng., U.K., 1,487 . . . . .70/C5
E. Dean, Eng., U.K. 70/E5
E. Dennis, Mass., U.S., 3,299 . . . . .292/P6
E. Derry, N.H., U.S., 550 . . . . .292/L6
E. Dixfield, Maine, U.S., 125 . . . . .286/B4
E. Dorset, Vt., U.S., 250 . . . . .352/A4
E. Douglas, Mass., U.S., 2,319 . . . . .292/H4
E. Dover, Maine, U.S., 40 . . . . .286/C3
E. Dover, Vt., U.S., 150 . . . . .352/B5
E. Dublin, Ga., U.S., 2,484 . . . . .260/F6
E. Dubuque, Ill., U.S., 1,995 . . . . .266/C1
E. Dummerston, Vt., U.S., 175 . . . . .352/B5
East Dunbartonshire, Scot., U.K.,
  unitary authority, 108,243 . . . . .62/H7
E. Dundee, Ill., U.S., 2,955 . . . . .266/A5
E. Dunseith, N. Dak., U.S., 219 . . . . .326/E1
E. Eddington, Maine, U.S., 300 . . . . .286/D4
E. Ellijay, Ga., U.S., 707 . . . . .260/C4
Eastend, Sask., Can., 576 . . . . .227/B11
Easter Balmoral, Scot., U.K. 62/K4
Easter Compton, Eng., U.K. 73/G1
Eastern, Egy., desert 144/B2
Eastern, Kenya, province 157/E3
Eastern, Sri Lan., province 126/C4
Eastern, Zam., province 159/C2
Eastern Finland, Fin., province 81/C2
Eastern Ghats, India, mountains 128/C6
Eastern Macedonia and Thrace, Gr., region . .100/C1
Eastern Neck N.W.R., Md., U.S. 288/K3
Eastern Province, Sa. Arab., emirate 136/C2
Eastern Visayas, Phil., region 120/C4
Eastertown, Eng., U.K. 73/G2
Easterville, Man., Can., 80 . . . . .215/B2
E. Fairfield, Vt., U.S., 200 . . . . .352/B1
E. Falmouth, Mass., U.S., 6,615 . . . . .292/M6
E. Farms, Wash., U.S., 6,318 . . . . .358/H2
East Feliciana, La., U.S., parish, 21,360 . . . . .282/H5
Eastfield, Eng., U.K., 9,708 . . . . .66/H4
East Flanders, Belg., province 85/B2
E. Flat Rock, N.C., U.S., 4,151 . . . . .322/E8
E. Foothills, Calif., U.S., 8,133 . . . . .246/K3
Eastford, Conn., U.S., 1,618 . . . . .253/G2
E. Fork, Ariz., U.S. 242/F4
E. Franklin, Vt., U.S., 125 . . . . .352/B1
E. Freehold, N.J., U.S., 4,936 . . . . .314/E3
E. Freetown, Mass., U.S., 1,200 . . . . .292/L5
East Frisian, Ger., islands 84/D1
East Frisian, Ger., islands 86/A2
E. Galesburg, Ill., U.S., 839 . . . . .266/C3
Eastgate, Wash., U.S., 4,558 . . . . .358/B4
E. Georgia, Vt., U.S., 200 . . . . .352/A1
E. Germantown, Ind., U.S., 243 . . . . .270/F5
E. Gillespie, Ill., U.S., 234 . . . . .266/B2
E. Glacier Park, Mont., U.S., 396 . . . . .306/C1
E. Glastonbury, Conn., U.S., 1,400 . . . . .253/E3
E. Glenville, N.Y., U.S., 6,064 . . . . .320/P5
E. Grafton, Eng., U.K. 70/A4
E. Grafton, N.H., U.S., 100 . . . . .212/C4
E. Granby, Conn., U.S., 4,745 . . . . .253/D2
E. Grand Forks, Minn., U.S., 7,501 . . . . .298/A3
E. Grand Rapids, Mich., U.S., 10,764 . . . . . . .294/D7
E. Granville, Vt., U.S., 50 . . . . .352/B2
E. Greenbush, N.Y., U.S., 4,085 . . . . .320/P5
E. Greenville, Penn., U.S., 3,103 . . . . .336/K5
E. Greenwich, R.I., U.S., 12,948 . . . . .339/D4
E. Griffin, Ga., U.S., 1,635 . . . . .260/C5
E. Grinstead, Eng., U.K., 27,058 . . . . .70/E4
E. Gull Lake, Minn., U.S., 978 . . . . .298/C4
Eastham, Mass., U.S., 5,453 . . . . .292/Q5
E. Hampden, Maine, U.S., 800 . . . . .286/D4
E. Hampstead, N.H., U.S., 1,400 . . . . .212/D6
E. Hampton, Conn., U.S., 13,352 . . . . .253/E3
Easthampton, Mass., U.S., 15,994 . . . . .292/D3
E. Hampton, N.Y., U.S., 1,334 . . . . .320/G1
E. Hampton North, N.Y., U.S., 3,587 . . . . . . .320/G1
E. Hanover, N.J., U.S., 11,393 . . . . .314/E2
E. Hardwick, Vt., U.S., 300 . . . . .352/C1
E. Hartford, Conn., U.S., 49,575 . . . . .253/E2
E. Hartford Gardens, Conn., U.S. 253/E3
E. Hartland, Conn., U.S., 500 . . . . .253/D2
E. Harwich, Mass., U.S., 4,744 . . . . .292/P6
E. Haven, Conn., U.S., 28,189 . . . . .253/D4
E. Haven, Vt., U.S., 301 . . . . .352/D1
E. Haverhill, N.H., U.S., 60 . . . . .212/C4
E. Hazel Crest, Ill., U.S., 1,607 . . . . .266/C6
E. Hebron, N.H., U.S., 90 . . . . .212/C4
E. Helena, Mont., U.S., 1,642 . . . . .306/E3
E. Highgate, Vt., U.S., 175 . . . . .352/B1
E. Highland Park, Va., U.S., 12,488 . . . . .354/J5
E. Hills, N.Y., U.S., 6,842 . . . . .320/C2
E. Hiram, Maine, U.S. 286/B5
E. Hodge, La., U.S., 366 . . . . .282/D2
E. Holden, Maine, U.S., 475 . . . . .286/D4
E. Holderness, N.H., U.S., 175 . . . . .212/C4
E. Hope, Ida., U.S., 200 . . . . .264/A1

E. Hubbardton, Vt., U.S., 90 . . . . .352/A3
E. Hyde, Eng., U.K. 70/D3
Eastington, Eng., U.K. 68/C6
East Java, Indon., province 122/C2
E. Jordan, Mich., U.S., 2,507 . . . . .294/D4
East Kalimantan, Indon., province 122/C1
East Kazakhstan, Kaz., oblast 131/E2
E. Keansburg, N.J., U.S. 314/E3
E. Kilbride, Scot., U.K., 73,796 . . . . .62/H7
E. Killingly, Conn., U.S., 350 . . . . .253/H2
E. Kingston, N.H., U.S., 1,784 . . . . .212/D6
Eastlake, Colo., U.S. 250/A3
Eastlake, Mich., U.S., 441 . . . . .294/C5
E. Lake, N.C., U.S., 100 . . . . .322/P3
Eastlake, Ohio, U.S., 20,255 . . . . .328/H8
E. Lake Ainslie, N.S., Can. 221/F1
Eastland, Tex., U.S., 3,769 . . . . .346/K3
Eastland, Tex., U.S., county, 18,297 . . . . .346/K3
East Land, Utah, U.S., 50 . . . . .350/E6
E. Langton, Eng., U.K. 70/C1
E. Lansdowne, Penn., U.S., 2,586 . . . . .336/L7
E. Lansing, Mich., U.S., 46,525 . . . . .294/E7
Las Vegas, Nev., U.S. 310/C3
E. Laurinburg, N.C., U.S., 295 . . . . .322/C5
E. Lebanon, Maine, U.S., 650 . . . . .286/B5
Eastleigh, Eng., U.K., 49,934 . . . . .70/B5
E. Lempster, N.H., U.S., 175 . . . . .212/B5
E. Leroy, Mich., U.S., 275 . . . . .294/D7
E. Leverett, Mass., U.S., 275 . . . . .292/E3
E. Linton, Scot., U.K., 1,744 . . . . .62/L7
E. Litchfield, Conn., U.S., 250 . . . . .253/C2
E. Liverpool, Ohio, U.S., 13,089 . . . . .328/J4
East Loch, Hawaii, U.S., harbor 262/E1
E. London, S. Afr. 162/C3
E. Longmeadow, Mass., U.S., 14,100 . . . . . . .292/D4
E. Los Angeles, Calif., U.S., 124,283 . . . . . . .246/C9
E. Lothian, Scot., U.K., unitary authority, 90,088 .62/M6
Lyme, Conn., U.S., 18,118 . . . . .253/G4
E. Lyndon, Vt., U.S., 100 . . . . .352/D1
E. Lynn, W. Va., U.S., 150 . . . . .360/B4
E. Lynne, Mo., U.S., 300 . . . . .302/B3
E. Machias, Maine, U.S., 1,298 . . . . .286/E4
E. Madison, Maine, U.S., 125 . . . . .286/C4
E. Madison, N.H., U.S. 212/C4
Eastmain, Que., Can. 225/A3
Eastmain, Que., Can., river 225/B3
Eastman, Que., Can., 5,440 . . . . .260/E7
Eastman, Wisc., U.S., 437 . . . . .364/B5
E. Marion, Mass., U.S., 550 . . . . .292/L6
E. Markham, Eng., U.K. 68/F3
E. McKeesport, Penn., U.S., 2,343 . . . . .336/E7
E. Meon, Eng., U.K. 70/B5
E. Meredith, N.Y., U.S., 150 . . . . .320/M6
E. Mersea, Eng., U.K. 70/F3
E. Middlebury, Vt., U.S., 650 . . . . .352/A3
E. Millcreek, Utah, U.S., 21,385 . . . . .350/E2
E. Millinocket, Maine, U.S., 1,828 . . . . .286/D3
E. Moline, Ill., U.S., 20,333 . . . . .266/C2
E. Montpelier, Vt., U.S., 2,578 . . . . .352/C2
E. Moriches, N.Y., U.S., 4,550 . . . . .320/F2
E. Naples, Fla., U.S., 23,000 . . . . .256/G5
E. Newark, N.J., U.S., 2,377 . . . . .314/B2
E. New Market, Md., U.S., 167 . . . . .288/L5
E. Newnan, Ga., U.S., 1,305 . . . . .260/B5
E. Newport, Maine, U.S., 175 . . . . .286/C4
E. New Portland, Maine, U.S., 70 . . . . .286/B4
E. Northfield, Mass., U.S., 150 . . . . .292/E2
East Nusa Tenggara, Indon., province 122/D2
E. Oakley, Kans., U.S. 70/B4
Eastoft, Eng., U.K. 66/G5
Eastoke, Eng., U.K. 70/C5
E. Olympia, Wash., U.S., 900 . . . . .358/C3
Easton, (Easton/Weston), Eng., U.K., 7,631 . . .68/F4
Easton, Conn., U.S., 7,272 . . . . .253/B5
Easton, Ill., U.S., reservoir 253/B4
Easton, Ill., U.S., 373 . . . . .266/D3
Easton, Kans., U.S., 362 . . . . .276/G2
Easton, La., U.S., 150 . . . . .282/E5
Easton, Maine, U.S., 1,249 . . . . .286/E2
Easton, Md., U.S., 11,708 . . . . .288/K4
Easton, Minn., U.S., 214 . . . . .298/D7
Easton, Mo., U.S., 258 . . . . .302/B2
Easton, N.H., U.S., 256 . . . . .212/C3
Easton, Penn., U.S., 26,263 . . . . .336/L4
Easton, Tex., U.S., 524 . . . . .346/P3
Easton, Wash., U.S., 383 . . . . .358/D2
Easton, Wisc., U.S., 150 . . . . .364/D5
E. Orange, N.J., U.S., 69,824 . . . . .314/B2, E2
E. Orange, Vt., U.S., 80 . . . . .352/C2
E. Orland, Maine, U.S., 250 . . . . .286/D4
E. Orleans, Mass., U.S., 1,800 . . . . .292/Q5
E. Otis, Mass., U.S., 200 . . . . .292/B4
Eastover, N.C., U.S., 1,376 . . . . .322/H4
Eastover, S.C., U.S., 830 . . . . .340/D3
E. Palestine, Ohio, U.S., 4,917 . . . . .328/J4
E. Palo Alto, Calif., U.S., 29,506 . . . . .246/J3
E. Parsonsfield, Maine, U.S., 200 . . . . .286/B5
E. Pasadena, Calif., U.S., 6,045 . . . . .246/D9
E. Pea Ridge, W. Va., U.S., 6,363 . . . . .360/B4
E. Peoria, Ill., U.S., 22,638 . . . . .266/D3
E. Pepperell, Mass., U.S., 2,034 . . . . .292/H2
E. Peru, Iowa, U.S., 133 . . . . .274/G5
E. Peru, Maine, U.S., 225 . . . . .286/B4
E. Petersburg, Penn., U.S., 4,450 . . . . .336/J5
E. Pittsburgh, Penn., U.S., 2,017 . . . . .336/E7
E. Plainfield, N.H., U.S., 125 . . . . .212/B4
Eastpoint, Fla., U.S., 2,158 . . . . .256/D2
E. Point, Ga., U.S., 39,595 . . . . .260/C4, H3
Eastpointe, Mich., U.S., 34,077 . . . . .294/B6
E. Portal, Colo., U.S., 70 . . . . .250/B2
E. Port Orchard, Wash., U.S., 5,116 . . . . .358/A4
E. Poultney, Vt., U.S., 400 . . . . .352/A3
E. Prairie, Mo., U.S., 3,227 . . . . .302/G5
E. Preston, Eng., U.K. 70/D5
E. Princeton, Mass., U.S., 300 . . . . .292/G3
E. Prospect, Penn., U.S., 678 . . . . .336/H6
E. Providence, R.I., U.S., 48,688 . . . . .339/D3
E. Putney, Vt., U.S., 350 . . . . .352/C5
E. Quantoxhead, Eng., U.K. 73/F2
E. Quincy, Calif., U.S., 2,398 . . . . .246/E3
E. Quoque, N.Y., U.S., 4,265 . . . . .320/F2
E. Randolph, N.Y., U.S., 630 . . . . .320/D6
E. Randolph, Vt., U.S., 200 . . . . .352/C3
East Renfrewshire, Scot., U.K.,
  unitary authority, 89,311 . . . . .62/H7
E. Richford, Vt., U.S. 352/B1
E. Ridge, Tenn., U.S., 20,640 . . . . .344/L4
East Riding of Yorkshire, Eng., U.K.,
  unitary authority, 314,076 . . . . .66/G5
East Riding of Yorkshire, Eng., U.K.,
  unitary authority, 314,076 . . . . .68/G2

E. Rindge, N.H., U.S., 600 . . . . .212/C6
Eastrington, Eng., U.K. 66/G5
E. Rochester, N.Y., U.S., 6,650 . . . . .320/F4
E. Rockaway, N.Y., U.S., 10,414 . . . . .320/C2
E. Rockingham, N.C., U.S., 3,885 . . . . .322/F5
E. Rupert, Vt., U.S., 90 . . . . .352/A4
E. Ruston, Eng., U.K. 70/G1
E. Rutherford, N.J., U.S., 8,716 . . . . .314/B2, E2
Eastry, Eng., U.K., 2,273 . . . . .70/G4
E. Ryegate, Vt., U.S., 150 . . . . .352/C2
E. St. Louis, Ill., U.S., 31,542 . . . . .266/A3, C5
E. Sandwich, Mass., U.S., 3,720 . . . . .292/N6
E. Shoreham, Vt., U.S., 5,809 . . . . .320/E1
East Siberian, sea .193/B9
E. Side, Penn., U.S., 290 . . . . .336/K3
E. Smithfield, Penn., U.S., 375 . . . . .336/H2
Eastsound, Wash., U.S., 750 . . . . .358/C1
E. Sparta, Ohio, U.S., 806 . . . . .328/H4
E. Spencer, N.C., U.S., 1,755 . . . . .322/E3
E. Stewartry Coast N.P., Eng., U.K. 66/A3
E. Stoneham, Maine, U.S., 150 . . . . .286/B4
E. Stroudsburg, Penn., U.S., 9,888 . . . . .336/L3
E. Studdal, Eng., U.K. 70/G4
E. Sullivan, N.H., U.S., 225 . . . . .212/B6
E. Sumter, S.C., U.S., 1,220 . . . . .340/D3
East Sussex, Eng., U.K., unitary authority,
  492,324 . . . . .70/E5
E. Swanzey, N.H., U.S., 475 . . . . .212/B6
E. Syracuse, N.Y., U.S., 3,178 . . . . .320/J4
E. Tavaputs Plateau, Colo., U.S. 250/A2
E. Tawas, Mich., U.S., 2,951 . . . . .294/F5
E. Templeton, Mass., U.S., 1,200 . . . . .292/F2
E. Thermopolis, Wyo., U.S., 274 . . . . .366/B2
E. Thirston, Eng., U.K. 66/E2
E. Thompson, Conn., U.S., 275 . . . . .253/H1
E. Tilbury, Eng., U.K. 70/E4
East Timor, nation .118
E. Tisted, Eng., U.K. 70/C4
E. Topsham, Vt., U.S., 90 . . . . .352/C2
E. Troy, Penn., U.S., 250 . . . . .336/H2
E. Troy, Wisc., U.S., 3,564 . . . . .364/E6
E. Uniontown, Penn., U.S., 2,760 . . . . .336/B6
E. Unity, N.H., U.S., 60 . . . . .212/B5
Eastvale, Penn., U.S., 293 . . . . .336/A4
E. Vandergrift, Penn., U.S., 742 . . . . .336/B4
E. Vassalboro, Maine, U.S., 300 . . . . .286/C4
Eastview, Md., U.S., 650 . . . . .288/G1
Eastview, Tenn., U.S., 618 . . . . .344/D4
E. Village, Conn., U.S., 1,500 . . . . .253/C4
Eastville, Va., U.S., 203 . . . . .354/M6
E. Wallingford, Vt., U.S., 200 . . . . .352/B4
E. Walton, Eng., U.K. 70/F1
E. Wareham, Mass., U.S., 1,700 . . . . .292/M5
E. Washington, N.H., U.S., 125 . . . . .212/B5
E. Washington, Penn., U.S., 1,930 . . . . .336/A5
E. Waterboro, Maine, U.S., 275 . . . . .286/B5
E. Wenatchee, Wash., U.S., 5,757 . . . . .358/E2
E. Wilson, N.Y., U.S., 175 . . . . .320/D4
E. Winch, Eng., U.K. 70/E1
E. Windsor, Mass., U.S., 80 . . . . .292/C3
E. Winn, Maine, U.S., 100 . . . . .286/D3
E. Wittering, Eng., U.K., 4,630 . . . . .70/C5
E. Wolfeboro, N.H., U.S., 80 . . . . .212/D4
Eastwood, Eng., U.K., 19,363 . . . . .68/E3
Eastwood, Eng., U.K., 19,363 . . . . .70/B1
Eastwood, Eng., U.K. 70/F3
Eastwood, La., U.S., 3,374 . . . . .282/B1
Eastwood, Mich., U.S., 6,265 . . . . .294/D7
Eastwood, Mo., U.S. 302/E5
E. Woodstock, Conn., U.S., 450 . . . . .253/H1
E. York, Ont., Can. 223/K5
E. York, Penn., U.S., 8,782 . . . . .336/H6
Eaton, Colo., U.S., 2,690 . . . . .250/F1
Eaton, Ind., U.S., 1,603 . . . . .270/F4
Eaton, Maine, U.S. 286/E3
Eaton, Mich., U.S., county, 103,655 . . . . .294/E7
Eaton, Ohio, U.S., 8,133 . . . . .328/A6
Eaton Ctr., N.H., U.S., 80 . . . . .212/D4
Eaton Estates, Ohio, U.S., 1,409 . . . . .328/F9
Eatonia, Sask., Can., 474 . . . . .227/A9
Eaton Rapids, Mich., U.S., 5,330 . . . . .294/E7
Eatons Neck, Conn., U.S., point 253/B5
Eaton Socon, Eng., U.K., 12,370 . . . . .68/G5
Eatonton, Ga., U.S., 6,764 . . . . .260/E5
Eatontown, N.J., U.S., 14,008 . . . . .314/E3
Eatonville, Fla., U.S., 2,432 . . . . .256/C4
Eatonville, Wash., U.S., 2,012 . . . . .358/C3
Eau Claire, Mich., U.S., 656 . . . . .294/C7
Eau Claire, Penn., U.S., 355 . . . . .336/B3
Eau Claire, Wisc., U.S., 61,704,
  (148,337, metro.) 364/B4
Eau Claire, Wisc., U.S., county, 93,142 . . . . . .364/B4
Eau Galle, Wisc., U.S., 175 . . . . .364/A4
Eauripik, Micr., atoll 172/B2
Ebbw Vale, Wales, U.K., 19,484 . . . . .64/E4
Ebchester, Eng., U.K. 66/E3
Ebebiyín, Eq. Gui. 154/D2
Ebenezer, Miss., U.S., 80 . . . . .300/B3
Eben Jct., Mich., U.S., 200 . . . . .294/C3
Ebensburg, Penn., U.S., 3,091 . . . . .336/D5
Eberswalde, Ger. .86/C2
Ebolowa, Came., 22,222 . . . . .153/B3
Ebon, Marsh. Is., island 173/B3
Ebony, W. Va., U.S., 125 . . . . .354/H7
Ebor, Man., Can. .215/A4
Ebro, Sp., river 88/C2
Ebro, Sp. 94/F1
Ebro, Fla., U.S., 250 . . . . .256/C1
Ebro, Minn., U.S., 60 . . . . .298/B3
Ecatepec, Mex., 1,621,827 . . . . .200/Inset
Ecclaw, Scot., U.K. 62/M7
Eccles, Eng., U.K., 36,000 . . . . .70/E4
Eccles, Scot., U.K. 62/M7
Eccles, W. Va., U.S., 700 . . . . .360/D5
Ecclesfield, Eng., U.K. 66/F6
Eccleshall, Eng., U.K., 2,748 . . . . .68/C4
Echeta, Wyo., U.S. 366/D1
Echo, Ala., U.S., 50 . . . . .238/D4
Echo, La., U.S., 250 . . . . .282/E4
Echo, Minn., U.S., 278 . . . . .298/B6
Echo, Oreg., U.S., 650 . . . . .334/G2
Echo, Tex., U.S. .346/L4
Echo, Utah, U.S., 50 . . . . .350/C3, E1
Echo Bay, N.W. Terr., Can. 220/E3
Echo Bay, Ont., Can. 223/A1
Echols, Ga., U.S., county, 3,754 . . . . .260/E1
Echternach, Lux. 85/B2
Ecija, Sp. 94/D4
Eckerman, Mich., U.S., 50 . . . . .294/D3
Eckert, Tex., U.S. .346/K5
Eckford, Scot., U.K. 62/M7
Eckington, (Derbyshire Co), Eng., U.K., 7,167 . .66/F6
Eckington, (Derbyshire Co), Eng., U.K., 7,167 . .68/E3
Eckington, (Hereford & Worcester Co), Eng., U.K. .68/D5
Eckley, Colo., U.S., 278 . . . . .250/H1
Eckman, N. Dak., U.S. 326/D1
Eckman, W. Va., U.S., 1,037 . . . . .360/D6
Eclectic, Ala., U.S., 1,037 . . . . .238/C3
Economy, Ind., U.S., 200 . . . . .270/F5
Economy, Penn., U.S., 9,363 . . . . .336/A4
Ecorse, Mich., U.S., 11,229 . . . . .294/B7, F7

Ecru, Miss., U.S., 947 .300/C1
Ector, Tex., U.S., county, 121,123 . . . . .346/F4
Ecuador, nation 175
Ed, Erit. 156/C3
Edam, Sask., Can., 429 . . . . .227/B7
Edam, Neth. 84/C2
Eday, Scot., U.K., island 62/N1
Eddiceton, Miss., U.S., 80 . . . . .300/B4
Eddies Cove, Nfld., Can. 218/C3
Eddy, N. Mex., U.S., county, 51,658 . . . . . . .317/F5
Eddy, N. Dak., U.S., county, 2,757 . . . . .326/G2
Eddystone, Man., Can. 215/B3
Eddystone, Penn., U.S., 2,442 . . . . .336/L7
Eddyville, Ill., U.S., 153 . . . . .274/J5
Eddyville, Iowa, U.S., 1,064 . . . . .274/J5
Eddyville, Ky., U.S., 2,350 . . . . .280/B3
Eddyville, Nebr., U.S., 96 . . . . .308/E2
Ede, Neth. 84/C2
Ede, Nig. 152/C4
Edéa, Came. 153/B3
Eden, Ariz., U.S., 70 . . . . .242/F5
Eden, Ida., U.S., 411 . . . . .264/C7
Eden, Md., U.S., 793 . . . . .288/M6
Eden, Miss., U.S., 126 . . . . .300/B3
Eden, N.Y., U.S., 3,579 . . . . .320/D5
Eden, N.C., U.S., 15,908 . . . . .322/F2
Eden, S. Dak., U.S., 97 . . . . .342/H2
Eden, Tex., U.S., 2,561 . . . . .346/J4
Eden, Vt., U.S., 1,152 . . . . .352/B1
Eden, Wisc., U.S., 687 . . . . .364/E5
Eden, Wyo., U.S., 388 . . . . .366/B2
Edenbridge, Eng., U.K., 7,196 . . . . .70/E4
Eden Mills, Vt., U.S., 175 . . . . .352/B1
Eden Prairie, Minn., U.S., 54,901 . . . . .298/D6
Edenton, N.C., U.S., 5,394 . . . . .322/M4
Eden Valley, Minn., U.S., 866 . . . . .298/C5
Edenville, Mich., U.S., 200 . . . . .294/E6
Edenville, N.Y., U.S., 650 . . . . .320/A1
Ederney, N. Ire., U.K., 626 . . . . .65/B2
Edesville, Md., U.S., 275 . . . . .288/K3
Edgar, Ill., U.S., 40 . . . . .266/F4
Edgar, Ill., U.S., county, 19,704 . . . . .266/F4
Edgar, Mont., U.S., 125 . . . . .306/H4
Edgar, Nebr., U.S., 539 . . . . .308/G3
Edgar, Wisc., U.S., 1,386 . . . . .364/C4
Edgard, La., U.S., 2,637 . . . . .282/H6
Edgar Sprs., Mo., U.S., 190 . . . . .302/E4
Edgartown, Mass., U.S., 3,779 . . . . .292/M7
Edgecliff, Tex., U.S., 2,550 . . . . .346/A10
Edgecomb, Maine, U.S., 1,090 . . . . .286/C5
Edgecombe, N.C., U.S., county, 55,606 . . .322/K3
Edgefield, Eng., U.K. 70/G1
Edgefield, La., U.S., 190 . . . . .282/C2
Edgefield, S.C., U.S., 4,449 . . . . .340/C3
Edgefield, S.C., U.S., county, 24,595 . . . . .340/C3
Edge Hill, Ga., U.S. 260/F5
Edgeley, N. Dak., U.S., 637 . . . . .326/G3
Edgemere, Md., U.S., 9,248 . . . . .288/J3
Edgemont, S. Dak., U.S., 867 . . . . .342/B4
Edgemont Park, Mich., U.S., 2,442 . . . . . . .294/E7
Edgemoor, Del., U.S., 5,992 . . . . .255/B1
Edgemoor, S.C., U.S., 450 . . . . .340/D2
Edgerly, La., U.S., 225 . . . . .282/B6
Edgerton, Alta., Can., 403 . . . . .212/E5
Edgerton, Kans., U.S., 1,440 . . . . .276/F3, G3
Edgerton, Minn., U.S., 1,033 . . . . .298/A7
Edgerton, Mo., U.S., 533 . . . . .302/B2
Edgerton, Ohio, U.S., 2,117 . . . . .328/A3
Edgerton, Va., U.S., 100 . . . . .354/H7
Edgerton, Wisc., U.S., 4,933 . . . . .364/D6
Edgerton, Wyo., U.S., 169 . . . . .366/C2
Edgewater, Colo., U.S., 5,445 . . . . .250/A3
Edgewater, Fla., U.S., 18,668 . . . . .256/H3
Edgewater, Md., U.S., 2,600 . . . . .288/H4
Edgewater, N.J., U.S., 7,677 . . . . .314/C2, F2
Edgewater, N.Y., U.S. 320/D4
Edgewater, Wisc., U.S., 80 . . . . .364/B3
Edgewater Park, N.J., U.S., 7,864 . . . . .314/D3
Edgewood, Fla., U.S., 1,901 . . . . .256/C6
Edgewood, Ill., U.S., 527 . . . . .266/E5
Edgewood, (Madison County), Ind., U.S., 1,988 . .270/E4
Edgewood, (Marion County), Ind., U.S. 270/D5
Edgewood, Iowa, U.S., 923 . . . . .274/M2
Edgewood, Ky., U.S., 9,400 . . . . .280/F1, G1
Edgewood, Md., U.S., 23,378 . . . . .288/J2
Edgewood, Mich., U.S., 100 . . . . .294/E6
Edgewood, N. Mex., U.S., 1,893 . . . . .317/D2
Edgewood, Ohio, U.S., 4,762 . . . . .328/J2
Edgewood, (Allegheny County), Penn., U.S., 3,311 336/E7
Edgewood, (Northumberland County),
   Penn., U.S., 2,619 . . . . .336/H4
Edgewood, Tex., U.S., 1,348 . . . . .346/N3
Edgewood, Wash., U.S., 9,089 . . . . .358/C2
Edgeworth, Penn., U.S., 1,730 . . . . .336/A4
Edgmond, Eng., U.K., 1,376 . . . . .68/C4
Edina, Minn., U.S., 47,425 . . . . .298/D6, B6
Edina, Mo., U.S., 1,233 . . . . .302/D1
Edinbane, Scot., U.K. 62/D4
Edinboro, Penn., U.S., 6,950 . . . . .336/A2
Edinburg, Ill., U.S., 1,135 . . . . .266/D4
Edinburg, Maine, U.S., 98 . . . . .286/D3
Edinburg, Miss., U.S., 100 . . . . .300/C3
Edinburg, N.J., U.S., 900 . . . . .314/D3
Edinburg, N. Dak., U.S., 252 . . . . .326/H1
Edinburg, Tex., U.S., 48,465 . . . . .346/K9
Edinburg, Va., U.S., 813 . . . . .354/F3
Edinburgh, Scot., U.K., administrative capital,
   430,082 . . . . .60/B2
Edinburgh, Scot., U.K., administrative capital,
   430,082 . . . . .62/K7
Edinburgh, Scot., U.K., administrative capital,
   430,082 . . . . .193/D18
Edinburgh, City of, Scot., U.K., unitary authority,
   430,082 . . . . .62/K7
Edinburgh, Ind., U.S., 4,505 . . . . .270/E6
Edington, Eng., U.K. 73/G2
Edirne, Tur. 133/A2
Edirne, Tur., province 133/A2
Edison, Calif., U.S., 375 . . . . .246/G7
Edison, Ga., U.S., 1,340 . . . . .260/D6
Edison, Nebr., U.S., 154 . . . . .308/E3
Edison, N.J., U.S., 97,687 . . . . .314/E2
Edison, Ohio, U.S., 437 . . . . .328/B6
Edison N.H.S., N.J., U.S. 314/B2
Edisto, S.C., U.S., 2,632 . . . . .340/D3
Edisto, S.C., U.S., river 340/D3
Edisto Beach, S.C., U.S., 641 . . . . .340/D4
Edisto Island, S.C., U.S., 90 . . . . .340/D4
Edith, Tex., U.S. 346/H4
Ed Jenkins N.R.A., Ga., U.S. 260/C2
Edler, Colo., U.S. 250/H4
Edmeston, N.Y., U.S., 550 . . . . .320/L5
Edmond, Kans., U.S., 47 . . . . .276/C4
Edmond, Okla., U.S., 68,315 . . . . .330/B3, E2
Edmonds, Wash., U.S., 39,515 . . . . . . .358/A4, C2
Edmonson, Ark., U.S. 244/F2
Edmonson, Tex., U.S., county, 11,644 . . . . .280/D3
Edmonson, Tex., U.S., 123 . . . . .346/G1
Edmonston, Md., U.S., 959 . . . . .288/C7
Edmonton, Alta., Can., 666,104,
   (967,200, metro.) 212/D4
Edmonton, Ky., U.S., 1,586 . . . . .280/E4

Edmore, Mich., U.S., 1,244 . . . . .294/D6
Edmore, N. Dak., U.S., 256 . . . . .326/G1
Edmunds, S. Dak., U.S., county, 4,367 . . . .342/F2
Edmundson, Mo., U.S., 840 . . . . .302/H2
Edmundston, N.B., Can., 17,373 . . . . .217/A1
Edna, Iowa, U.S. .274/B1
Edna, Kans., U.S., 423 . . . . .276/G4
Edna, La., U.S., 90 . . . . .282/D6
Edna, Tex., U.S., 5,899 . . . . .346/M7
Ednor, Md., U.S. .288/G3
Edo, Nig., state .152/D4
Edom, Tex., U.S., 322 . . . . .346/N3
Edon, Ohio, U.S., 898 . . . . .328/A2
Edouard, Que., Can., lake 226/D3
Edrans, Man., Can. 215/B4
Edray, W. Va., U.S., 175 . . . . .212/B4
Edson, Alta., Can., 7,585 . . . . .212/B4
Edson, Kans., U.S., 50 . . . . .276/A2
Edwall, Wash., U.S., 40 . . . . .358/H2
Edward, Ont., Can., island 294/A1
Edward, Congo, D.R., lake 155/C2
Edward, Ug., lake 157/A4
Edward, N.C., U.S., 250 . . . . .322/M4
Edwards, Colo., U.S., 8,257 . . . . .250/D2
Edwards, Ill., U.S., county, 6,971 . . . . .266/E5
Edwards, Kans., U.S., county, 3,449 . . . . . .276/C4
Edwards, Miss., U.S., 1,347 . . . . .300/B3
Edwards, Mo., U.S. 302/C3
Edwards, N.Y., U.S., 465 . . . . .320/L2
Edwards, Tex., U.S., county, 2,162 . . . . . . .346/H5
Edwards, Tex., U.S., plateau 346/H5
Edwards A.F.B., Calif., U.S. 246/H8
Edwardsburg, Mich., U.S., 1,147 . . . . .294/C8
Edwardsport, Ind., U.S., 363 . . . . .270/B7
Edwardsville, Ala., U.S., 186 . . . . .238/D2
Edwardsville, Ill., U.S., 21,491 . . . . . .266/A3, D5
Edwardsville, Kans., U.S., 4,146 . . . . .276/H1
Edwardsville, Penn., U.S., 4,984 . . . . .336/G7, K3
Edwin B. Forsythe N.W.R., (Barnegat Division),
   N.J., U.S. 314/E4
Edwin B. Forsythe N.W.R., (Brigantine Division),
   N.J., U.S. 314/E4
Edworth, Eng., U.K. 68/G5
Edzell, Scot., U.K., 783 . . . . .62/L5
Eek, Alaska, U.S., 280 . . . . .240/C2
Eel, Calif., U.S., river 246/B2
Eel, Ind., U.S., river 270/E3
Eel River Crossing, N.B., Can., 1,335 . . . . .217/C1
Eems, Neth., river 84/D1
Éfaté, Van., island 173/C3
Effie, La., U.S., 250 . . . . .282/E4
Effie, Minn., U.S., 91 . . . . .298/D3
Effigy Mounds N.M., Iowa, U.S. 274/M1
Effingham, Ga., U.S., county, 37,535 . . . . . .260/J7
Effingham, Ill., U.S., 12,384 . . . . .266/E4
Effingham, Ill., U.S., county, 34,264 . . . . . .266/E4
Effingham, Kans., U.S., 588 . . . . .276/G2
Effingham, N.H., U.S., 1,273 . . . . .212/E4
Effingham, S.C., U.S., 200 . . . . .340/E2
Effingham Falls, N.H., U.S., 175 . . . . .212/D4
Efland, N.C., U.S. 322/G2
Efyrnwy, Wales, U.K., lake 64/E2
Egadi, It., islands .95/C3
Egan, La., U.S., 325 . . . . .282/E6
Egan, Nev., U.S., range 310/C2
Egan, S. Dak., U.S., 265 . . . . .342/J4
Eganville, Ont., Can., 1,230 . . . . .223/H2
Egbert, Wyo., U.S. 366/D3
Egegik, Alaska, U.S., 116 . . . . .240/D3
Egeland, N. Dak., U.S., 49 . . . . .326/F1
Eger, Hun. 91/C2
Egersund, Nor. 80/B4
Egerton, Eng., U.K. 70/F4
Eggesford, Eng., U.K. 73/E3
Egg Harbor, Wisc., U.S., 250 . . . . .364/F3
Egg Harbor City, N.J., U.S., 4,545 . . . . .314/D4
Egg Island, N.J., U.S., point 314/C5
Eggleston, Eng., U.K. 66/D3
Eggleston, Va., U.S., 200 . . . . .354/B6
Egham, Eng., U.K., 23,816 . . . . .70/C4
Eglin A.F.B., Fla., U.S. 256/B1
Eglinton, N.W. Terr., Can., island 220/E1
Eglwysbach, Wales, U.K. 64/B3
Eglwyswrw, Wales, U.K. 64/B3
Egmont, P.E.I., Can., bay 224/A2
Egmont, N.Z., cape 171/B2
Egmont, N.Z., mountain 171/B2
Egmont Key N.W.R., Fla., U.S. 256/F4
Egnar, Colo., U.S. 250/B4
Egremont, Eng., U.K., 6,581 . . . . .66/A4
Eğridir Gölü, Tur., lake 133/B2
Egypt, nation 138
Egypt, Ark., U.S., 101 . . . . .244/E2
Egypt, Ga., U.S., 70 . . . . .260/J7
Egypt, Miss., U.S., 40 . . . . .300/D2
Egypt, Vt., U.S. .352/C1
Egypt Lake, Fla., U.S. 256/D6
Ehime, Jap., prefecture 114/B3
Ehrenberg, Ariz., U.S., 1,357 . . . . .242/A4
Ehrenfeld, Penn., U.S., 234 . . . . .336/D5
Ehrhardt, S.C., U.S., 614 . . . . .340/C3
Eifel, Ger., plateau 86/A3
Eigg, Scot., U.K., island 60/D4
Eigg, Scot., U.K., island 62/D5
Eil, Scot., U.K., lake 62/F5
Eildon and Leaderfoot N.P., Eng., U.K. 66/C1
Eilean Siar, Scot., U.K., unitary authority, 26,502 .62/C2
Eindhoven, Neth., 203,200, (300,981, metro.) . .84/C3
Einsiedeln, Switz. 160/D2
Eiseb, Nam., river 160/D2
Eisenach, Ger. 86/B3
Eisenerz, Aus. 91/D3
Eisenhower N.H.S., Penn., U.S. 336/G6
Eisenhüttenstadt, Ger. 86/C2
Eisenstadt, Aus. 91/E3
Eisleben, Ger. 86/B3
Eitzen, Minn., U.S., 229 . . . . .298/F7
Ejmiatsin, Arm. .103/B2
Ejura, Gha. 150/B3
Ekalaka, Mont., U.S., 410 . . . . .306/M4
Ekibastuz, Kaz., 127,197 . . . . .131/D1
Ekron, Ky., U.S., 170 . . . . .280/D3
Ekwan, Ont., Can., river 222/D2
Ekwok, Alaska, U.S., 130 . . . . .240/D3
Elaine, Ark., U.S., 865 . . . . .244/F3
Eland, Wisc., U.S., 251 . . . . .364/D4
Elat, Isr. 135/B3
Elâziğ, Tur., 250,500 . . . . .133/D2
Elâziğ, Tur., province 133/D2
Elba, It., island 95/B2
Elba, Ala., U.S., 4,185 . . . . .238/C4
Elba, Ida., U.S. 264/D7
Elba, La., U.S. 282/F5
Elba, Minn., U.S., 214 . . . . .298/E6
Elba, Nebr., U.S., 243 . . . . .308/E2
Elba, N.Y., U.S., 696 . . . . .320/E4
Elbasan, Alb., 87,797 . . . . .99/B2
Elbe, Ger., river 86/B2, C3
Elbe, Wash., U.S. 358/C3
Elberfeld, Ind., U.S., 636 . . . . .270/B8
Elberon, Iowa, U.S., 245 . . . . .274/K3
Elbert, Colo., U.S., 100 . . . . .250/F2

Elbert, Colo., U.S., county, 19,872 . . . . . . .250/F2
Elbert, Ga., U.S., county, 20,511 . . . . .260/F3
Elbert, Tex., U.S., 56 . . . . .346/J2
Elberta, Ala., U.S., 552 . . . . .238/B5
Elberta, Mich., U.S., 457 . . . . .294/C5
Elberta, Utah, U.S., 288 . . . . .350/C4
Elberton, Ga., U.S., 4,743 . . . . .260/F3
Elberton, Wash., U.S. 358/H3
Elbing, Kans., U.S., 218 . . . . .276/E3
Elbląg, Pol., 129,816 . . . . .83/D1
Elbow Lake, Minn., U.S., 1,275 . . . . .298/B5
Elbow, Sask., Can., 298 . . . . .227/D9
Elbridge, N.Y., U.S., 1,103 . . . . .320/J4
Elburn, Ill., U.S., 2,756 . . . . .266/E2
Elburz, Iran, mountains 130/C2
El Cajon, Calif., U.S., 94,869 . . . . .246/J10
El Campo, Tex., U.S., 10,945 . . . . .346/M6
El Cañuelo, P.R., ruins 206/C2
El Cenizo, Tex., U.S., 3,545 . . . . .346/J8
El Centro, Calif., U.S., 37,835 . . . . .246/K10
El Cerrito, (Contra Costa County), Calif., U.S.,
   23,171 . . . . .246/J1
El Cerrito, (Riverside County), Calif., U.S.,
   23,171 . . . . .246/F10
El Cerro del Aripo, Trin.-To., mountain 209/A2
Elche, Sp., 194,767 . . . . .94/F3
Elcho, Wisc., U.S., 375 . . . . .364/D3
Elco, Ill., U.S., 60 . . . . .266/D6
El Dara, Ill., U.S., 89 . . . . .266/C4
Eldena, Ill., U.S., 175 . . . . .266/D2
Elderon, Wisc., U.S., 189 . . . . .364/D4
Eldersburg, Md., U.S., 27,741 . . . . .288/G2
Elderton, Penn., U.S., 358 . . . . .336/C4
El Djouf, Mali, desert 150/B1
El Djouf, Maur., desert 147/C3
Eldon, P.E.I., Can. 224/C2
Eldon, Iowa, U.S., 998 . . . . .274/K6
Eldon, Mo., U.S., 4,895 . . . . .302/D3
Eldon, Okla., U.S., 991 . . . . .330/H2
Eldon, Wash., U.S., 40 . . . . .358/B2
Eldora, Colo., U.S., 170 . . . . .250/E2
Eldora, Iowa, U.S., 3,035 . . . . .274/H3
Eldorado, Ariz., U.S., 150 . . . . .314/D5
El Dorado, Ark., U.S., 21,530 . . . . .244/C4
El Dorado, Calif., U.S., county, 156,299 . .246/E4, L5
El Dorado, Kans., U.S., 12,057 . . . . .276/F4
Eldorado, Ill., U.S., 4,534 . . . . .266/E6
Eldorado, Md., U.S., 60 . . . . .288/L5
Eldorado, Nebr., U.S. 308/G3
Eldorado, Ohio, U.S., 543 . . . . .328/A6
Eldorado, Okla., U.S., 527 . . . . .330/C3
Eldorado, Tex., U.S., 1,951 . . . . .346/H5
Eldorado at Santa Fe, N. Mex., U.S., 5,799 . .317/E2
El Dorado Hills, Calif., U.S., 18,016 . . . . . .246/L5
Eldorado Natl. For., Calif., U.S. 246/E4, L5
El Dorado Sprs., Mo., U.S., 3,775 . . . . .302/B4
Eldorendo, Ga., U.S., 100 . . . . .260/B9
Eldoret, Kenya, 104,900 . . . . .157/C3
Eldred, Ill., U.S., 211 . . . . .266/C4
Eldred, Minn., U.S., 50 . . . . .298/A3
Eldred, N.Y., U.S., 375 . . . . .320/M7
Eldred, Penn., U.S., 858 . . . . .336/E2
Eldridge, Ala., U.S., 184 . . . . .238/B2
Eldridge, Iowa, U.S., 4,159 . . . . .274/N4
Eldridge, Mo., U.S., 80 . . . . .302/D4
Eldridge, N. Dak., U.S., 45 . . . . .326/G3
Eleanor, W. Va., U.S., 1,345 . . . . .360/C3
Eleanor Roosevelt N.H.S., N.Y., U.S. 321/P7
Electra, Tex., U.S., 3,168 . . . . .346/K1
Electric City, Wash., U.S., 922 . . . . .358/F2
Electric Mills, Miss., U.S., 40 . . . . .300/D3
Eleele, Hawaii, U.S., 2,040 . . . . .262/C2
El Encanto, Col. .184/B5
Elephant, Antar., island 192/C12
Elephanta, India, island . . . . .128/Inset I
Elephant Butte, N. Mex., U.S., 1,390 . . . . . .317/C4
Elephant Butte, N. Mex., U.S., reservoir 317/C4
Eleusis, Gr. 100/Inset
Eleusis, Gr., bay 100/Inset
Eleuthera, Bah., island 204/B1
Eleuthera, Bah., island 207/B2
Eleva, Wisc., U.S., 635 . . . . .364/B4
Eleven Pt., Mo., U.S., river 302/E5
Elfers, Fla., U.S., 13,161 . . . . .256/F3
Elfrida, Ariz., U.S., 475 . . . . .242/F6
Elfros, Sask., Can., 161 . . . . .227/G9
Elgin, Man., Can. .215/A4
Elgin, N.B., Can., 220 . . . . .217/D3
Elgin, Ont., Can. .223/D5
Elgin, Ont., Can., county 223/D5
Elgin, Scot., U.K. .60/B1
Elgin, Scot., U.K., 20,829 . . . . .62/K3
Elgin, Ariz., U.S., 309 . . . . .242/E6
Elgin, Ill., U.S., 94,487 . . . . .266/A5, E1
Elgin, Iowa, U.S., 676 . . . . .274/L2
Elgin, Kans., U.S., 82 . . . . .276/F4
Elgin, Minn., U.S., 826 . . . . .298/E6
Elgin, Nebr., U.S., 735 . . . . .308/E2
Elgin, Nev., U.S. .310/C3
Elgin, N. Dak., U.S., 659 . . . . .326/D3
Elgin, Ohio, U.S., 50 . . . . .328/B4
Elgin, Okla., U.S., 1,210 . . . . .330/D3
Elgin, Oreg., U.S., 1,654 . . . . .334/J2
Elgin, Penn., U.S., 236 . . . . .336/B2
Elgin, (Kershaw County), S.C., U.S., 806 . . .340/D2
Elgin, (Lancaster County), S.C., U.S., 2,426 . .340/D2
Elgin, Tex., U.S., 5,700 . . . . .346/E2
Elgol, Scot., U.K. .62/D4
El Golea, Alg. 146/D2
Elgon, Ug., mountain 157/D3
El Granada, Calif., U.S., 5,724 . . . . .246/H2
Elham, Eng., U.K., 1,429 . . . . .70/G4
El Hamra, W. Sah., river 147/B1
Eli, Nebr., U.S. 308/C1
Eliasville, Tex., U.S., 40 . . . . .346/K3
Elida, Ohio, U.S., 183 . . . . .317/C4
Elida, Ohio, U.S., 1,917 . . . . .328/B4
Elie, Man., Can. 215/C4
Elihu, Ky., U.S., 650 . . . . .280/F3
Elim, Alaska, U.S., 313 . . . . .240/C2
Eli Malk, Palau, island 172/B3
Elimsport, Penn., U.S., 275 . . . . .336/G3
El Indio, Tex., U.S., 263 . . . . .346/H7
Elista, Russ., 102,189, (106,150, metro.) . . .104/D3
Elizabeth, S.A., Austl. . . . . .170/Inset II
Elizabeth, Colo., U.S., 1,434 . . . . .250/F2
Elizabeth, Ill., U.S., 685 . . . . .266/C1
Elizabeth, Ind., U.S., 137 . . . . .270/E8
Elizabeth, La., U.S., 574 . . . . .282/D5
Elizabeth, Maine, U.S., cape 286/C5
Elizabeth, Mass., U.S., islands 292/L7
Elizabeth, Minn., U.S., 172 . . . . .298/A4
Elizabeth, N.J., U.S., 120,568 . . . . .314/B3, E2
Elizabeth, Penn., U.S., 1,609 . . . . .336/B5
Elizabeth, Wash., U.S., cape 358/A2
Elizabeth, W. Va., U.S., 994 . . . . .360/D2
Elizabeth City, N.C., U.S., 17,188 . . . . .322/N2
Elizabethton, Tenn., U.S., 13,372 . . . . .344/S2
Elizabethtown, Ill., U.S., 348 . . . . .266/E6
Elizabethtown, Ind., U.S., 391 . . . . .270/E6
Elizabethtown, Ky., U.S., 22,542 . . . . .280/E3

Elizabethtown, N.Y., U.S., 750 . . . . .320/P2
Elizabethtown, N.C., U.S., 3,698 . . . . .322/H5
Elizabethtown, Penn., U.S., 11,887 . . . . . . .336/H5
Elizaville, Penn., U.S., 1,344 . . . . .336/H4
Elizaville, Ky., U.S., 150 . . . . .270/D4
El Jadida, Mor., 125,000 . . . . .147/B1
El Jebel, Colo., U.S., 4,488 . . . . .250/C2
Ełk, Pol. 83/F2
Elk, Ala., U.S., river 238/C1
Elk, Calif., U.S., 60 . . . . .246/B3
Elk, Kans., U.S., county 276/F4
Elk, N. Mex., U.S. 317/E5
Elk, Penn., U.S., county, 35,112 . . . . .336/D3
Elk, Wash., U.S., 175 . . . . .358/H1
Elk, Wyo., U.S. 366/C3
Elk, Wyo., U.S., mountain 366/C3
Elkader, Iowa, U.S., 1,465 . . . . .274/M2
Elkatawa, Ky., U.S., 40 . . . . .280/G3
Elk Basin, Wyo., U.S. 366/B1
Elk City, Ida., U.S., 150 . . . . .264/B4
Elk City, Kans., U.S., 305 . . . . .276/G4
Elk City, Nebr., U.S. 308/H2
Elk City, Okla., U.S., 10,510 . . . . .330/C2
Elk Creek, Ky., U.S., 150 . . . . .280/E2
Elk Creek, Mo., U.S. 302/D4
Elk Creek, Nebr., U.S., 112 . . . . .308/H3
El Kef, Tun. 146/B1
Elk Falls, Kans., U.S., 112 . . . . .276/F4
Elkford, Br. Col., Can., 2,589 . . . . .214/P6
Elk Garden, W. Va., U.S., 217 . . . . .360/H2
Elk Grove, Calif., U.S., 59,984 . . . . .246/K5
Elk Grove Vil., Ill., U.S., 34,727 . . . . .266/B5
Elkhart, Ill., U.S., 443 . . . . .266/D3
Elkhart, Ind., U.S., 51,874, (182,791, metro.) . .270/E1
Elkhart, Ind., U.S., county, 182,791 . . . . . .270/E1
Elkhart, Iowa, U.S., 362 . . . . .274/G4
Elkhart, Kans., U.S., 2,233 . . . . .276/A4
Elkhart, Tex., U.S., 1,215 . . . . .346/N4
Elkhart Lake, Wisc., U.S., 1,021 . . . . .364/E5
Elkhorn, Man., Can., 470 . . . . .215/A4
Elkhorn, Calif., U.S., 1,591 . . . . .246/D6
Elk Horn, Iowa, U.S., 649 . . . . .274/D4
Elk Horn, Ky., U.S., 60 . . . . .280/E3
Elkhorn, Mont., U.S. 306/E3
Elkhorn, Nebr., U.S., 6,062 . . . . .308/E1, H2
Elkhorn, Oreg., U.S. 334/D3
Elkhorn, Wisc., U.S., 7,305 . . . . .364/E6
Elkhorn City, Ky., U.S., 1,060 . . . . .280/H3
Elkhovo, Bul. 101/E3
Elkin, N.C., U.S., 4,109 . . . . .322/D2
Elkins, Ark., U.S., 1,251 . . . . .244/A1
Elkins, N.H., U.S. .212/C5
Elkins, N. Mex., U.S. 317/F4
Elkins, W. Va., U.S., 7,032 . . . . .360/F3
Elk Island Natl. Park, Alta., Can. 212/D4
Elkland, Penn., U.S., 1,786 . . . . .336/G2
Elkmont, Ala., U.S., 470 . . . . .238/C1
Elk Mound, Wisc., U.S., 785 . . . . .364/B4
Elk Mtn., Wyo., U.S., 192 . . . . .366/C3
Elko, Br. Col., Can. 214/P6
Elko, Ga., U.S., 175 . . . . .260/D7
Elko, Minn., U.S., 472 . . . . .298/D6
Elko, Nev., U.S., 16,708 . . . . .310/C1
Elko, Nev., U.S., county, 45,291 . . . . .310/C1
Elko, S.C., U.S., 212 . . . . .340/C3
Elkol, Wyo., U.S. .366/A3
Elk Park, N.C., U.S., 459 . . . . .322/B2
Elk Plain, Wash., U.S., 15,697 . . . . .358/C2
Elk Pt., Alta., Can., 1,440 . . . . .212/E4
Elk Pt., S. Dak., U.S., 1,714 . . . . .342/J5
Elkport, Iowa, U.S., 88 . . . . .274/M2
Elk Rapids, Mich., U.S., 1,700 . . . . .294/D5
Elkridge, Md., U.S., 22,042 . . . . .288/G3
Elk Ridge, Utah, U.S., 1,838 . . . . .350/C4
Elk River, Ida., U.S., 156 . . . . .264/A3
Elk River, Minn., U.S., 16,447 . . . . .298/D5
Elk Run Hts., Iowa, U.S., 1,052 . . . . .274/K3
Elk Sprs., Colo., U.S. 250/B1
Elk St. For., Penn., U.S. 336/D2, E3
Elkton, Ky., U.S., 1,984 . . . . .280/C4
Elkton, Md., U.S., 11,893 . . . . .288/L1
Elkton, Mich., U.S., 863 . . . . .294/F6
Elkton, Minn., U.S., 149 . . . . .298/E7
Elkton, Mo., U.S., 60 . . . . .302/C4
Elkton, Ohio, U.S., 325 . . . . .328/J4
Elkton, Oreg., U.S., 147 . . . . .334/C4
Elkton, S. Dak., U.S., 677 . . . . .342/J3
Elkton, Tenn., U.S., 510 . . . . .344/H4
Elkton, Va., U.S., 2,042 . . . . .354/F4
Elk Valley, Tenn., U.S., 400 . . . . .344/N2
Elkview, W. Va., U.S., 1,182 . . . . .360/D4
Elkville, Ill., U.S., 1,001 . . . . .266/D6
Elkwater, Alta., Can., 50 . . . . .212/E6
Ella, Tex., U.S., 50 . . . . .346/K8
Ella, Wisc., U.S. .364/A4
Ellabell, Ga., U.S., 425 . . . . .260/J7
El Lago, Tex., U.S., 3,075 . . . . .346/C7
Ellamore, W. Va., U.S., 150 . . . . .360/F3
Ellastone, Eng., U.K. 68/D4
Ellaville, Fla., U.S. 256/E1
Ellaville, Ga., U.S., 1,609 . . . . .260/C7
Ellef Ringnes, Nun., Can., island 220/L1
Ellemford, Scot., U.K. 62/M7
Ellen, Vt., U.S., mountain 352/B2
Ellenboro, N.C., U.S., 479 . . . . .322/B4
Ellenboro, W. Va., U.S., 373 . . . . .360/D2
Ellenburg Depot, N.Y., U.S., 300 . . . . .320/P1
Ellendale, Del., U.S., 327 . . . . .255/C5
Ellendale, Minn., U.S., 590 . . . . .298/D7
Ellendale, N. Dak., U.S., 1,559 . . . . .326/G3
Ellensburg, Wash., U.S., 15,414 . . . . .358/E3
Ellenton, Ga., U.S., 336 . . . . .260/D9
Ellenville, N.Y., U.S., 4,130 . . . . .320/N7
Ellerbe, N.C., U.S., 1,021 . . . . .322/F4
Ellerby, Eng., U.K. 66/G4
Ellerslie, Md., U.S., 600 . . . . .288/A3
Ellerts de Haan, Sur., mountains 183/A3
Ellesmere, Can., island 193/B15
Ellesmere, Eng., U.K., 3,600 . . . . .220/M1
Ellesmere, Eng., U.K., 2,967 . . . . .68/B4
Ellesmere Island Natl. Park Reserve, Nun., Can. .220/O1
Ellesmere Port, Eng., U.K., 64,504 . . . . . . .66/C4
Ellesmere Port, Eng., U.K., 64,504 . . . . . . .68/B3
Elletsville, Ind., U.S., 5,078 . . . . .270/C6
El Libertador General Bernardo O'Higgins, Chile,
   region 190/B4
Ellice, Nun., Can., river 220/G3
Ellicott, Colo., U.S., 80 . . . . .250/F3
Ellicott, N.Y., U.S., 2,200 . . . . .320/D5
Ellicott City, Md., U.S., 56,397 . . . . .288/G2
Ellicottville, N.Y., U.S., 472 . . . . .320/D6
Ellijay, Ga., U.S., 1,584 . . . . .260/C2
Ellinger, Tex., U.S. 346/M6
Ellington, Eng., U.K., 2,253 . . . . .68/G5
Ellington, Conn., U.S., 12,921 . . . . .253/F2
Ellington, Mo., U.S., 1,045 . . . . .302/F4
Ellington, N.Y., U.S., 300 . . . . .320/C6
Ellinikon, Gr. .100/Inset
Ellinwood, Kans., U.S., 2,164 . . . . .276/D3

Elliot Lake, Ont., Can., 11,956 . . . . .223/C1
Elliott, Ark., U.S., 150 . . . . .244/C4
Elliott, Fla., U.S., key 256/B7, H6
Elliott, Ill., U.S., 341 . . . . .266/E3
Elliott, Iowa, U.S., 402 . . . . .274/D5
Elliott, Ky., U.S., county, 6,748 . . . . .280/G2
Elliott, Md., U.S. 288/K6
Elliott, Miss., U.S., 175 . . . . .300/C2
Elliott, N. Dak., U.S., 44 . . . . .326/H3
Elliott, S.C., U.S., 425 . . . . .340/D2
Elliott Knob, W. Va., U.S., peak 360/H4
Elliotts Bluff, Ga., U.S. 260/H1
Ellis, Ida., U.S. 264/C5
Ellis, Kans., U.S., 1,873 . . . . .276/C3
Ellis, Kans., U.S., county, 27,507 . . . . .276/C2
Ellis, Nebr., U.S. 308/H3
Ellis, Okla., U.S., county, 4,075 . . . . .330/C1
Ellis, Tex., U.S., county, 111,360 . . . . .346/M3
Ellisburg, N.Y., U.S., 269 . . . . .320/J3
Ellisforde, Wash., U.S., 150 . . . . .358/F1
Ellis Grove, Ill., U.S., 381 . . . . .266/D6
Ellis Island N.M., N.Y., U.S. 314/B2
Ellis Island N.M., N.Y., U.S. 320/A2
Ellison Bay, Wisc., U.S., 200 . . . . .364/F3
Ellisport, Wash., U.S., 1,200 . . . . . .358/A4, C2
Ellisras, S. Afr. 162/C1
Elliston, Mont., U.S., 225 . . . . .306/D3
Elliston, (Elliston-Lafayette), Va., U.S., 1,241 . . . .354/C6
Ellistown, Miss., U.S., 175 . . . . .300/D1
Ellisville, Ill., U.S., 87 . . . . .266/C3
Ellisville, Miss., U.S., 3,465 . . . . .300/C4
Ellisville, Mo., U.S., 9,104 . . . . .302/G3
Ellon, Scot., U.K., 8,754 . . . . .62/M4
Elloree, S.C., U.S., 742 . . . . .340/D3
Ellport, Penn., U.S., 1,148 . . . . .336/A4
Ellsinore, Mo., U.S., 363 . . . . .302/F5
Ellston, Iowa, U.S., 57 . . . . .274/F6
Ellsworth, Antar., mountains 192/B10
Ellsworth, Ill., U.S., 271 . . . . .266/E3
Ellsworth, Iowa, U.S., 531 . . . . .274/G3
Ellsworth, Kans., U.S., 2,965 . . . . .276/D3
Ellsworth, Kans., U.S., county, 6,525 . . . . .276/D3
Ellsworth, Maine, U.S., 6,456 . . . . .286/D4
Ellsworth, Mich., U.S., 483 . . . . .294/D4
Ellsworth, Minn., U.S., 540 . . . . .298/A7
Ellsworth, Nebr., U.S. 308/B1
Ellsworth, Penn., U.S., 1,083 . . . . .336/A5
Ellsworth, (Ellsworth South), Wash., U.S. 358/C4
Ellsworth Falls, Maine, U.S. 286/D4
Ellsworth Land, Antar., region 192/B10
Ellsworth North, Wash., U.S. 358/C4
Ellwood City, Penn., U.S., 8,688 . . . . .336/A4
Elizey, Fla., U.S., 60 . . . . .256/F2
Elma, Man., Can. .215/D4
Elma, Iowa, U.S., 598 . . . . .274/K1
Elma, N.Y., U.S., 2,491 . . . . .320/D5
Elma, Wash., U.S., 3,049 . . . . .358/C4
El Macao, Dom. Rep. 205/D2
El Malpais Natl. Mon. and Cons. Area,
N. Mex., U.S. 317/B3
El Mangó, P.R. 206/D2
Elm City, N.C., U.S., 1,165 . . . . .322/K3
Elm Creek, Man., Can. 215/C4
Elm Creek, Nebr., U.S., 894 . . . . .308/E3
Elmdale, Kans., U.S., 50 . . . . .276/F3
Elmdale, Minn., U.S., 107 . . . . .298/C5
Elmendorf, Tex., U.S., 664 . . . . . .346/A3, K6
Elmer, Minn., U.S., 50 . . . . .298/E3
Elmer, Mo., U.S., 98 . . . . .302/D2
Elmer, N.J., U.S., 1,384 . . . . .314/C4
Elmer, Okla., U.S., 96 . . . . .330/C3
Elmer City, Wash., U.S., 267 . . . . .358/G2
Elm Grove, La., U.S. 282/B2
Elm Grove, Ohio, U.S., 200 . . . . .328/D7
Elm Grove, Wisc., U.S., 6,249 . . . . .364/F2
Elmhurst, Ill., U.S., 42,762 . . . . .266/B6
Elmina, Gha. 150/B4
Elmira, Ont., Can., 8,155 . . . . .223/E4
Elmira, P.E.I., Can. 224/C2
Elmira, Ida., U.S., 60 . . . . .264/A1
Elmira, Mich., U.S., 200 . . . . .294/E4
Elmira, Mo., U.S., 82 . . . . .302/B2
Elmira, N.Y., U.S., 30,940, (91,070, metro.) . .320/H6
El Mirage, Ariz., U.S., 7,609 . . . . .242/C4
Elmira Hts., N.Y., U.S., 4,170 . . . . .320/H6
Elmo, Kans., U.S., 50 . . . . .276/E3
Elmo, Mo., U.S., 166 . . . . .302/A1
Elmo, Mont., U.S., 143 . . . . .306/B2
Elmo, Utah, U.S., 368 . . . . .350/D4
Elmo, Va., U.S., 40 . . . . .354/E7
Elmodel, Ga., U.S. 260/C9
Elmont, Kans., U.S., 425 . . . . .276/G2
Elmont, N.Y., U.S., 32,657 . . . . .320/C2
El Monte, Calif., U.S., 115,965 . . . . .246/D9
Elmora, Penn., U.S. 336/D4
Elmore, Ala., U.S., 199 . . . . .238/C3
Elmore, Ala., U.S., county 65,874 . . . . .238/C3
Elmore, Ida., U.S., county, 29,130 . . . . .264/B6
Elmore, Minn., U.S., 735 . . . . .298/C7
Elmore, Ohio, U.S., 1,426 . . . . .328/D3
Elmore City, Okla., U.S., 756 . . . . .330/E3
El Moro, Colo., U.S., 70 . . . . .250/F4
El Morro, N. Mex., U.S., 60 . . . . .317/B2
El Morro N.M., N. Mex., U.S. 317/B3
Elmsdale, P.E.I., Can. 224/A2
Elms Spring, N.Y., U.S., 4,676 . . . . .320/B1
Elm Sprs., Ark., U.S., 1,044 . . . . .244/A1
Elm Sprs., S. Dak., U.S. 342/C3
Elm Sprs. Colony, S. Dak., U.S. 342/H4
Elmvale, Ont., Can., 2,176 . . . . .223/F3
Elmville, Conn., U.S., 1,300 . . . . .253/H2
Elmwood, Ill., U.S., 1,945 . . . . .266/D3
Elmwood, Nebr., U.S., 668 . . . . .308/H3
Elmwood, Okla., U.S. 330/B1, D4
Elmwood, Wisc., U.S., 841 . . . . .364/A4
Elmwood Park, Ill., U.S., 25,405 . . . . .266/B5
Elmwood Park, N.J., U.S., 18,925 . . . . .314/A2
Elmwood Park, Wisc., U.S., 474 . . . . .364/F6
Elmwood Place, Ohio, U.S., 2,681 . . . . .328/B9
El Nido, Calif., U.S., 325 . . . . .246/E5
Elnora, Alta., Can., 290 . . . . .212/D5
Elnora, Ind., U.S., 721 . . . . .270/B7
Elo, Mich., U.S., 70 . . . . .294/A3
Elobey, Eq. Gui., islands 154/A3
Elon College, N.C., U.S., 6,738 . . . . .322/F2
Elora, Tenn., U.S., 500 . . . . .344/J4
El Oro, Ecua., province 185/B4
Eloy, Ariz., U.S., 10,375 . . . . .242/D5
El Paraíso, Hond., department 202/B3
El Paso, Ark., U.S., 150 . . . . .244/C2
El Paso, Colo., U.S., county, 516,929 . . . . .250/F3
El Paso, Ill., U.S., 2,695 . . . . .266/D3
El Paso, Tex., U.S., 563,662, (679,622, metro.) . .346/B4
El Paso, Tex., U.S., county, 679,622 . . . . . .346/B4
Elphin, Scot., U.K. 62/F2
El Pital, El Salv., mountain 203/A1
El Portal, Calif., U.S., 200 . . . . .246/F5
El Portal, Fla., U.S., 2,505 . . . . .256/B6
El Porvenir, Pan. .203/D2
El Porvenir, Pan., province 203/C2
El Porvenir, N. Mex., U.S. 317/E2

El Prado, N. Mex., U.S., 400 . . . . .317/E1
El Progreso, Hond., 156,554 . . . . .202/B2
Elqui, Chile, river .190/B3
El Reno, Okla., U.S., 16,212 . . . . .330/E2
El Rito, N. Mex., U.S., 425 . . . . .317/D1
Elrod, Ala., U.S., 150 . . . . .238/A3
Elrod, N.J., U.S. 280/F3
Elrosa, Minn., U.S., 166 . . . . .298/C5
Elrose, Sask., Can., 517 . . . . .227/B9
Elroy, N.C., U.S., 3,896 . . . . .322/K4
Elroy, Wisc., U.S., 1,578 . . . . .364/C5
Elsa, Yukon, Can. 228/B4
Elsa, Tex., U.S., 5,549 . . . . .346/L9
Elsah, Ill., U.S., 635 . . . . .266/C5
El Salvador, nation 191
El Sauz, Tex., U.S. 346/K9
Elsberry, Mo., U.S., 2,047 . . . . .302/F2
El Segundo, Calif., U.S., 16,033 . . . . .246/B10
El Seibo, Dom. Rep. 205/C2
El Seibo, Dom. Rep., province 205/C2
Elsenham, Eng., U.K. 70/E3
El Serrat, And. 93/B1
Elsey, Mo., U.S., 150 . . . . .302/C5
Elsham, Eng., U.K. 66/H5
Elsie, Mich., U.S., 1,055 . . . . .294/E6
Elsie, Nebr., U.S., 139 . . . . .308/C3
Elsie, Oreg., U.S. .334/C2
Elsinore, Calif., U.S., lake 246/G11
Elsinore, Utah, U.S., 733 . . . . .350/B5
Elsmere, Del., U.S., 5,800 . . . . .255/B1
Elsmere, Ky., U.S., 8,139 . . . . .280/G1
Elsmere, Nebr., U.S. 308/D1
Elsmore, Kans., U.S., 73 . . . . .276/G4
Elsrickle, Scot., U.K. 62/K7
Elstead, Eng., U.K., 2,436 . . . . .70/C4
Elsted, Eng., U.K. .70/C5
El Tabo, Chile 190/Inset
Eltham, Vic., Austl. . . . . .170/Inset V
El Tigre, Ven. 182/D2
Elton, Eng., U.K. 70/D1
Elton, La., U.S., 1,261 . . . . .282/D6
Elton, Wisc., U.S., 50 . . . . .364/E3
Eltopia, Wash., U.S., 80 . . . . .358/F3
El Toro, P.R., mountain 206/D2
El Toro Sta., Calif., U.S. 246/E11
Eltrut, Ont., Can., lake 298/E1
Elva, Man., Can. .215/A4
El Vado, N. Mex., U.S. 317/D1
Elvas, Port. 93/B3
Elvaston, Ill., U.S., 152 . . . . .266/B3
El Verano, Calif., U.S., 3,954 . . . . .246/J1
Elverson, Penn., U.S., 959 . . . . .336/K5
Elvington, Eng., U.K. 66/G5
Elwell, Mich., U.S., 300 . . . . .294/E6
Elwell, Mont., U.S., lake 306/E1
Elwood, Ill., U.S., 1,620 . . . . .266/E2
Elwood, Ind., U.S., 9,737 . . . . .270/E4
Elwood, Kans., U.S., 1,145 . . . . .276/H2
Elwood, Mo., U.S. 302/C4
Elwood, Nebr., U.S., 761 . . . . .308/E3
Elwood, N.J., U.S., 1,392 . . . . .314/D4
Elwood, Utah, U.S., 678 . . . . .350/B2
Ely, Eng., U.K. 60/D3
Ely, Eng., U.K., 10,329 . . . . .68/H5
Ely, Eng., U.K., 10,329 . . . . .70/E2
Ely, Wales, U.K., 10,329 . . . . .64/E5
Ely, Iowa, U.S., 1,149 . . . . .274/L4
Ely, Minn., U.S., 3,724 . . . . .298/F3
Ely, Nev., U.S., 4,041 . . . . .310/C2
Ely, Vt., U.S., 100 . . . . .352/C3
Elyria, Kans., U.S., 90 . . . . .276/E3
Elyria, Nebr., U.S., 54 . . . . .308/E2
Elyria, Ohio, U.S., 55,953 . . . . .328/F3
Elysburg, Penn., U.S., 2,067 . . . . .336/H4
Elysian, Minn., U.S., 486 . . . . .298/D6
Emanuel, Ga., U.S., county, 21,837 . . . . . . .260/G6
Emba, Kaz. 131/B2
Embarcación, Arg. 191/C1
Embarras Portage, Alta., Can. 212/E2
Embarrass, Minn., U.S., 70 . . . . .298/E3
Embarrass, Wisc., U.S., 399 . . . . .364/E4
Embden, Maine, U.S., 881 . . . . .286/C3
Embden, N. Dak., U.S., 70 . . . . .326/H3
Emblem, Wyo., U.S. 366/B1
Embleton, Eng., U.K. 66/E2
Embu, Kenya 157/D4
Embudo, N. Mex., U.S., 70 . . . . .317/E1
Emden, Ger. 86/A2
Emden, Ill., U.S., 515 . . . . .266/D3
Emden, Mo., U.S., 70 . . . . .302/E2
Emelle, Ala., U.S. .238/A3
Emerado, N. Dak., U.S., 510 . . . . .326/H2
Emerald, Qnsld., Austl. 170/D2
Emerald, N.W. Terr., Can., island 220/F1
Emerald Beach, Mo., U.S., 250 . . . . .302/C5
Emerald Isle, N.C., U.S., 3,488 . . . . .322/M5
Emerson, Man., Can., 655 . . . . .215/C4
Emerson, Ark., U.S., 359 . . . . .244/B4
Emerson, Ga., U.S., 1,092 . . . . .260/B3
Emerson, Iowa, U.S., 480 . . . . .274/D5
Emerson, Ky., U.S., 80 . . . . .280/G2
Emerson, Nebr., U.S., 817 . . . . .308/H1
Emerson, N.J., U.S., 7,197 . . . . .314/B1, E2
Emery, S. Dak., U.S., 439 . . . . .342/H4
Emery, Utah, U.S., 308 . . . . .350/C5
Emery, Utah, U.S., county, 10,860 . . . . .350/D5
Emery Mills, Maine, U.S., 350 . . . . .286/B5
Emeryville, Calif., U.S., 6,882 . . . . .246/J2
Emida, Ida., U.S., 70 . . . . .264/A2
Emigrant, Mont., U.S. 306/F4
Emigsville, Penn., U.S., 2,467 . . . . .336/H5
Emi Koussi, Chad, mountain 153/B3
Emilia-Romagna, It., region 95/B1
Emily, Minn., U.S., 847 . . . . .298/D4
Eminence, Ind., U.S., 275 . . . . .270/C5
Eminence, Ky., U.S., 2,231 . . . . .280/E2
Eminence, Mo., U.S., 548 . . . . .302/E4
Emington, Ill., U.S., 120 . . . . .266/E3
Emlembe, Swaz., mountain 161/B1
Emlenton, Penn., U.S., 784 . . . . .336/B3
Emma, Ind., U.S., 325 . . . . .270/E1
Emma, Mo., U.S., 243 . . . . .302/C3
Emmalane, La., U.S., 125 . . . . .260/G6
Emmaus, Penn., U.S., 11,313 . . . . .336/L4
Emmeloord, Neth. 84/C2
Emmen, Neth., 105,735 . . . . .84/D2
Emmeram, Kans., U.S. 276/C3
Emmet, Ark., U.S., 506 . . . . .244/B4
Emmet, Iowa, U.S., county, 11,027 . . . . . . .274/E1
Emmet, Mich., U.S., county, 31,437 . . . . . . .294/E4
Emmet, Nebr., U.S., 77 . . . . .308/E1
Emmetsburg, Iowa, U.S., 3,958 . . . . .274/E1
Emmett, Ida., U.S., 5,490 . . . . .264/A6
Emmett, Kans., U.S., 277 . . . . .276/F2
Emmett, Mich., U.S., 251 . . . . .294/G6
Emmitsburg, Md., U.S., 2,290 . . . . .288/E1
Emmonak, Alaska, U.S., 767 . . . . .240/C2
Emmons, Minn., U.S., 432 . . . . .298/D7
Emmons, N. Dak., U.S., county, 4,331 . . . . .326/E3
Emmorton, Md., U.S., 4,000 . . . . .288/J2
Emory, Tex., U.S., 1,021 . . . . .346/N3

Emory, Tex., U.S., peak 346/E6
Emory, Va., U.S. 354/C6
Emory, (Emory-Meadow View), Va., U.S., 2,266 . .354/E3
Empingham, Eng., U.K. 70/C1
Empire, Colo., U.S., 355 . . . . .250/A3
Empire, Ga., U.S., 450 . . . . .260/E7
Empire, La., U.S., 2,211 . . . . .282/K8
Empire, Mich., U.S., 378 . . . . .294/C5
Empire, Nev., U.S., 499 . . . . .310/A1
Empire, Ohio, U.S., 300 . . . . .328/J4
Empire City, Okla., U.S., 734 . . . . .330/D3
Emporia, Kans., U.S., 26,760 . . . . .276/F3
Emporia, Va., U.S., 5,665 . . . . .354/H7
Emporium, Penn., U.S., 2,526 . . . . .336/E2
Empress, Alta., Can., 171 . . . . .212/E6
Empshott, Eng., U.K. 70/C4
Ems, Ger., river 86/A2
Emsworth, (Emsworth/Southbourne),
Eng., U.K., 18,310 . . . . .70/C5
Emsworth, Penn., U.S., 2,598 . . . . .336/C6
Encampment, Wyo., U.S., 443 . . . . .366/C3
Encarnación, Para., 69,769 . . . . .187/E5
Enchant, Alta., Can. 212/D6
Encinal, Tex., U.S., 629 . . . . .346/J7
Encinitas, Calif., U.S., 58,014 . . . . .246/H9
Encino, N. Mex., U.S., 94 . . . . .317/E3
Encino, Tex., U.S., 177 . . . . .346/K9
Ende, Indon. 122/D2
Endeavor, Wisc., U.S., 440 . . . . .364/D5
Endee, N. Mex., U.S. 317/G2
Enderbury, Kiri., island 175/B2
Enderby, Br. Col., Can., 2,818 . . . . .214/N6
Enderby Land, Antar., region 192/C17
Enderlin, N. Dak., U.S., 947 . . . . .326/H3
Enders, Nebr., U.S., 70 . . . . .308/C3
Endiang, Alta., Can. 212/D5
Endicott, Nebr., U.S., 139 . . . . .308/G3
Endicott, N.Y., U.S., 13,038 . . . . .320/J6
Endicott, Wash., U.S., 621 . . . . .358/H3
Endon, Eng., U.K. 68/C3
Endwell, N.Y., U.S., 11,706 . . . . .320/J6
Energy, Ill., U.S., 1,175 . . . . .266/D6
Energy, Tex., U.S. .346/K4
Enewetak, Marsh. Is., island 173/A1
Enfield, S.A., Austl. . . . . .170/Inset II
Enfield, Eng., U.K., 256,664 . . . . .68/G6
Enfield, Eng., U.K., 256,664 . . . . .70/D3
Enfield, Eng., U.K., unitary authority, 273,563 . .70/D3
Enfield, Conn., U.S., 45,212 . . . . .253/E2
Enfield, Ill., U.S., 625 . . . . .266/E5
Enfield, Maine, U.S., 1,616 . . . . .286/D3
Enfield, N.H., U.S., 4,618 . . . . .212/B4
Enfield, N.C., U.S., 2,347 . . . . .322/K2
Enfield Ctr., N.H., U.S., 600 . . . . .212/B4
Engadine, Switz., valley 90/D2
Engadine, Mich., U.S., 275 . . . . .294/D3
Engaño, Dom. Rep., cape 205/D2
Engelhard, N.C., U.S., 425 . . . . .322/P3
Enggano, Indon., island 122/B2
England, (Midlands), U.K., country 66
England, (North), U.K., country 64
England, (Southeastern), U.K., country 68
England, (Southwestern), U.K., country 71
England, Ark., U.S., 2,972 . . . . .244/D3
Engle, N. Mex., U.S. 317/C4
Englee, Nfld., Can., 694 . . . . .218/C4
Englevale, Kans., U.S., 50 . . . . .276/H4
Englewood, Colo., U.S., 31,727 . . . . . . .250/A3, F2
Englewood, Fla., U.S., 16,196 . . . . .256/F5
Englewood, Kans., U.S., 109 . . . . .276/C4
Englewood, N.J., U.S., 26,203 . . . . .314/C2
Englewood, Ohio, U.S., 12,235 . . . . .328/H1
Englewood, Tenn., U.S., 1,590 . . . . .344/N4
Englewood Cliffs, N.J., U.S., 5,322 . . . . .314/C2, D2
English, Fr., channel 88/B2
English, Eng., U.K., channel 60/C4
English, Eng., U.K., channel 70/E5
English, Ind., U.S., 673 . . . . .270/D8
English Ctr., Penn., U.S. 336/G3
English Creek, N.J., U.S., 550 . . . . .314/D5
Englishtown, N.S., Can. 221/G1
Englishtown, N.J., U.S., 1,764 . . . . .314/E3
Enguri, Geo., river 103/A3
Enid, Ark., U.S., lake 244/F3
Enid, Miss., U.S., 225 . . . . .300/C1
Enid, Miss., U.S., lake 300/C1
Enid, Mont., U.S. .306/M2
Enid, Okla., U.S., 47,045, (57,813, metro.) . .330/E1
Enigma, Ga., U.S., 869 . . . . .260/E9
Enilda, Alta., Can., 154 . . . . .212/B3
Enka, N.C., U.S., 1,500 . . . . .322/E7
Enmore, P.E.I., Can. 224/A2
Enna, It. 95/C3
Ennadai, Nun., Can., lake 220/H4
Ennedi, Chad, plateau 153/C3
Ennerdale Water, Eng., U.K., lake 66/B4
Enneri Ké, Chad, river 153/B3
Ennis, Ire., 18,977 . . . . .78/B2
Ennis, Mont., U.S., 840 . . . . .306/E4
Ennis, Tex., U.S., 16,045 . . . . .346/M3
Enniskillen, N. Ire., U.K., 11,436 . . . . .65/H3
Ennistymon, Ire. 78/B2
Enns, Aus., river 91/D3
Enoch, Utah, U.S., 3,467 . . . . .350/A6
Enochs, Tex., U.S. .346/F2
Enochville, N.C., U.S., 2,851 . . . . .322/D3
Enola, Ark., U.S., 188 . . . . .244/C2
Enola, Penn., U.S., 275 . . . . .336/H5
Enon, Ohio, U.S., 2,638 . . . . .328/C6
Enoree, S.C., U.S., 700 . . . . .340/C2
Enoree, S.C., U.S., river 340/F2
Enos, Ind., U.S., 60 . . . . .270/B2
Enosburg Ctr., Vt., U.S. 352/B1
Enosburg Falls, Vt., U.S., 1,473 . . . . .352/B1
Enriquillo, Dom. Rep., lake 204/D3
Enriquillo, Dom. Rep., lake 205/A2
Enschede, Neth., 149,160 . . . . .84/D2
Ensenada, Mex., 223,492, (370,730, metro.) . .200/A1
Ensenada, N. Mex., U.S., 80 . . . . .317/D1
Ensenguly, Turkm. 132/A2
Ensign, Kans., U.S., 203 . . . . .276/B4
Ensign, Mich., U.S., 40 . . . . .294/C3
Ensley Ctr., Mich., U.S., 175 . . . . .294/D6
Ensor, Ky., U.S., 500 . . . . .280/D3
Enstone, Eng., U.K. 70/B3
Entebbe, Ug., 57,518 . . . . .157/C3
Enterprise, Ala., U.S., 21,178 . . . . .238/D4
Enterprise, Kans., U.S., 836 . . . . .276/E3
Enterprise, La., U.S., 125 . . . . .282/F3
Enterprise, Miss., U.S., 474 . . . . .300/D4
Enterprise, Nev., U.S., 14,676 . . . . .310/C3
Enterprise, Okla., U.S. 330/G2
Enterprise, Oreg., U.S., 1,895 . . . . .334/J2
Enterprise, Utah, U.S., 1,285 . . . . .350/A6
Enterprise, W. Va., U.S., 939 . . . . .360/F3
Enterprise, Wisc., U.S., 80 . . . . .364/D3
Entiat, Wash., U.S., 957 . . . . .358/F2
Entrance to Museums, Vat. 96/B1
Entre Ríos, Arg., province 191/D2
Entwistle, Alta., Can. 212/C4

Enugu, Nig. 152/D4
Enugu, Nig., state 152/D4
Enumclaw, Wash., U.S., 11,116 . . . . .358/D2
Enville, Eng., U.K. .68/C5
Enville, Tenn., U.S., 230 . . . . .344/E4
Eola, Tex., U.S., 125 . . . . .346/H4
Eolia, Ky., U.S., 50 . . . . .280/H3
Eolia, Mo., U.S., 435 . . . . .302/E2
Eoline, Ala., U.S., 70 . . . . .238/B3
Eolus, Colo., U.S., mountain 250/C4
Epes, Ala., U.S., 206 . . . . .238/A3
Ephesus, Ga., U.S., 388 . . . . .260/A5
Ephraim, Utah, U.S., 4,505 . . . . .350/C4
Ephraim, Wisc., U.S., 353 . . . . .364/F3
Ephrata, Penn., U.S., 13,213 . . . . .336/J5
Ephrata, Wash., U.S., 6,808 . . . . .358/F2
Epi, Van., island 173/C3
Epinal, Fr. 88/D2
Epiphany, S. Dak., U.S., 60 . . . . .342/H4
Epirus, Gr., region 100/B2
Episkopi, Cyp. 133/A2
E Plantation, Maine, U.S. 286/C2
Epleys, Ky., U.S., 275 . . . . .280/D4
Epoufette, Mich., U.S., 40 . . . . .294/D3
Epping, N.S.W., Austl. . . . . .170/Inset IV
Epping, Eng., U.K., 9,922 . . . . .70/E3
Epping, N.H., U.S., 5,476 . . . . .212/D5
Epping, N. Dak., U.S., 79 . . . . .326/B1
Epps, La., U.S., 1,153 . . . . .282/G1
Epsie, Mont., U.S. 306/L4
Epsilon, Mich., U.S., 200 . . . . .294/E4
Epsom, (Epsom and Ewell), Eng., U.K., 64,405 . .70/D4
Epsom, Eng., U.K. . . . . .60/Inset III
Epsom, N.H., U.S., 4,021 . . . . .212/D5
Epsom, N.C., U.S., 275 . . . . .322/J2
Epsom Four Corners, N.H., U.S. 212/D5
Epworth, Eng., U.K., 3,359 . . . . .66/G5
Epworth, Eng., U.K., 3,359 . . . . .68/F2
Epworth, Iowa, U.S., 1,428 . . . . .274/N3
Epworth Hts., Ohio, U.S., 3,300 . . . . .328/C9
Equality, Ala., U.S., 60 . . . . .238/C3
Equality, Ill., U.S., 721 . . . . .266/E6
Equateur, Congo, D.R., region 155/B1
Equatorial, Mald., channel 127/A5
Equatorial Guinea, nation 148
Equinox, Vt., U.S., mountain 352/A4
Erath, La., U.S., 2,187 . . . . .282/E7
Erath, Tex., U.S., county, 33,001 . . . . .346/K3
Erbacon, W. Va., U.S. 360/E3
Erciyas Daği, Tur., mountain 133/C2
Erd, Hun. 91/B2
Erda, Utah, U.S., 2,473 . . . . .350/B3
Erdahl, Minn., U.S. 298/B5
Erdenet, Mong., 65,600 . . . . .118/C2
Erebus, Antar., mountain 192/B5
Erenhot, China 119/E1
Erenköy, (Kokkina), Cyp. 133/A1
Erfurt, Ger., 201,267 . . . . .86/B3
Erg Chech, Alg., desert 146/A2
Erg Chech, Mali, desert 150/C1
Erg Iguidi, Alg., desert 146/A2
Erg Iguidi, Maur., desert 147/D1
Erhard, Minn., U.S., 150 . . . . .298/A4
Erial, N.J., U.S., 6,200 . . . . .314/C4
Ericht, Scot., U.K., lake 62/H5
Erick, Okla., U.S., 1,023 . . . . .330/C2
Erickson, Man., Can., 448 . . . . .215/B3
Ericsburg, Minn., U.S., 60 . . . . .298/D2
Ericson, Nebr., U.S., 104 . . . . .308/E2
Erie, Ill., U.S., 40 .266/C2
Erie, Ont., Can., lake 223/E5
Erie, N.Y., U.S., Ont., U.S., Can., lake 320/B3
Erie, Colo., U.S., 6,291 . . . . .250/A2, F1
Erie, Ill., U.S., 1,589 . . . . .266/C2
Erie, Kans., U.S., 1,211 . . . . .276/G4
Erie, Mich., U.S., lake 294/G8
Erie, Minn., U.S. 298/D3
Erie, N.Y., U.S., canal 320/E4, K4
Erie, N.Y., U.S., county, 950,265 . . . . .320/D5
Erie, N. Dak., U.S. 326/H2
Erie, Ohio, U.S., county, 79,551 . . . . .328/E3
Erie, Penn., U.S., 103,717, (280,843, metro.) . .336/A1
Erie, Ohio, U.S. county, 280,843 . . . . . .328/G8, H2
Erie, Penn., U.S., lake 336/A1
Erie NW.R., Penn., U.S. 336/B2
Eriksdale, Man., Can. 215/B4
Erimo, Jap., cape .114/Inset I
Erin, Tenn., U.S., 1,490 . . . . .344/F2
Erin Sprs., Okla., U.S., 114 . . . . .330/E3
Eriskay, Scot., U.K., island 62/B4
Eriswell, Eng., U.K. 70/F2
Erith, Eng., U.K. 70/E4
Eritrea, nation 150
Erlands Pt., (Erlands Point-Kitsap Lake),
Wash., U.S., 2,723 . . . . .358/C2
Erlangen, Ger., 100,750 . . . . .86/B4
Erlanger, Ky., U.S., 16,676 . . . . .280/G1
Erling, Ark., U.S., lake 244/B4
Erma, N.J., U.S., 2,088 . . . . .314/D6
Ermelo, S. Afr. 162/C2
Ermera, E. Timor .122/B1
Ermera, E. Timor, province 122/B1
Ermine, Ky., U.S., 300 . . . . .280/H3
Erne, Ire., river 78/B1
Erne, N. Ire., U.K., lake 60/A2
Erne, N. Ire., U.K., lake 78/C1
Erne, N. Ire., U.K., river 60/A2
Ernest, Penn., U.S., 501 . . . . .336/C4
Ernul, N.C., U.S., 425 . . . . .322/L4
Eros, La., U.S., 202 . . . . .282/F2
Erose, Ky., U.S., 100 . . . . .280/G4
Erpingham, Eng., U.K. 70/G1
Er Rachidia, Mor. .147/C2
Er Rif, Mor., range 147/C1
Errigal, Ire., mountain 78/B1
Errol, N.H., U.S., 298 . . . . .212/D2
Erromango, Van., island 173/C3
Erskeë, Alb. 99/B3
Erskine, Minn., U.S., 437 . . . . .298/A3
Ervay, Wyo., U.S. .366/C2
Erving, Mass., U.S., 1,467 . . . . .292/E2
Erwin, N.C., U.S., 4,537 . . . . .322/H4
Erwin, S. Dak., U.S., 70 . . . . .342/H3
Erwin, Tenn., U.S., 5,610 . . . . .344/S2
Erwinville, La., U.S., 700 . . . . .282/G5
Erzen, Alb., river 99/A2
Erzgebirge, Ger., mountains 86/C3
Erzgebirge, Czh. Rep., mountains 92/A2
Erzincan, Tur. 133/D2
Erzincan, Tur., province 133/E2
Erzurum, Tur., 298,700 . . . . .133/E2
Erzurum, Tur., province 133/E2
Esbjerg, Den., 73,046 . . . . .79/B3
Esbon, Kans., U.S., 148 . . . . .276/D2
Escabosa, N. Mex., U.S. 317/D3
Escalante, Utah, U.S., 818 . . . . .350/C6
Escalante, Utah, U.S., river 350/C6
Escalon, Calif., U.S., 5,963 . . . . .246/D5
Escambia, Ala., U.S., county, 38,440 . . . . . .238/B4

Escambia, Fla., U.S., *county*, 294,410 . . . . .256/A1
Escanaba, Mich., U.S., 13,140 . . . . .294/B4
Escanaba, Mich., U.S., *river* 294/B3
Escanbia, Fla., U.S., *river* 256/A1
Eschen, Liech. 85/A2
Esch-sur-Alzette, Lux., 25,400 . . . . .85/A2
Escobas, Tex., U.S. 346/J8
Escondida, N. Mex., U.S., 150 . . . . .317/D3
Escondido, Nicar., *river* 202/B2
Escondido, Calif., U.S., 133,559 . . . . .246/H9
Escrick, Eng., U.K. 66/F5
Escuintla, Guat., 70,000 . . . . .201/C5
Escuminac, N.B., Can., 252 . . . . .217/E1
Escuminac, Que., Can., 604 . . . . .226/K3
Eséka, Came. 153/B3
Esfahan, Iran, 1,266,072 . . . . .130/C3
Esfahan, Iran, *province* 130/C3
Esher, (Esher/Molesey), Eng., U.K., 46,599 . . . .66/E3
Esh Winning, Eng., U.K., 3,643 . . . . .66/E3
Esil, Kaz. 131/C1
Eskdale, Eng., U.K., *valley* 66/B2
Eskdalemuir, Scot., U.K. 62/K8
Esker, Nfld., Can. 218/D3
Eskişehir, Tur., 454,500 . . . . .133/B2
Eskişehir, Tur., *province* 133/B2
Eskifjördur, Ice. .79/C2
Eskilstuna, Swe. .80/C3
Esko, Minn., U.S., 1,300 . . . . .298/E4
Eskridge, Kans., U.S., 589 . . . . .276/F3
Esla, Sp., *river* .94/D2
Esmeralda, Nev., U.S., *county*, 971 . . . . .310/B3
Esmeraldas, Ecua., 98,558 . . . . .185/B2
Esmeraldas, Ecua., *province* 185/B2
Esmond, Ill., U.S., 100 . . . . .266/E1
Esmond, N. Dak., U.S., 159 . . . . .326/F1
Esmond, S. Dak., U.S. 342/H3
Esmont, Va., U.S., 225 . . . . .354/F5
Esofea, Wisc., U.S. 364/C5
Esom Hill, Ga., U.S., 125 . . . . .260/A4
Espaillat, Dom. Rep., *province* 205/B1
Española, Ont., Can., 5,449 . . . . .223/D1
Española, Ecua., *island* 185/Inset
Española, Fla., U.S., 40 . . . . .256/G5
Española, N. Mex., U.S., 9,688 . . . . .317/D1
Espanong, N.J., U.S., 2,700 . . . . .314/D2
Esparto, Calif., U.S., 1,858 . . . . .246/C4
Esperance, W.A., Austl. 170/B3
Esperance, N.Y., U.S., 380 . . . . .320/N5
Esperance, Wash., U.S., 3,503 . . . . .358/A4
Esperanza, P.R. .206/E2
Esperanza, Tex., U.S. 346/C4
Espichel, Port., *cape* 93/A3
Espírito Santo, Braz., *state* 188/D3
Espíritu Santo, Van., *island* 173/B2
Espoo, Fin., 213,271 . . . . .81/B2
Espy, Penn., U.S., 1,428 . . . . .336/J3
Esquel, Arg. 191/A5
Essaouira, Mor. .147/B2
Es Semara, W. Sah. 147/B1
Essen, Ger., 599,515 . . . . .86/A3
Essendon, Vic., Austl. . . . . .170/Inset V
Essequibo, Guy., *river* 183/B3, B5
Essex, Ont., Can., 20,085 . . . . .223/C5
Essex, Ont., Can., 20,085 . . . . .223/C5
Essex, Ont., Can., *county* 223/C5
Essex, Eng., U.K., *unitary authority*, 1,310,922 . .70/E3
Essex, Calif., U.S. 246/K8
Essex, Conn., U.S., 6,505 . . . . .253/F4
Essex, Ill., U.S., 554 . . . . .266/E2
Essex, Iowa, U.S., 884 . . . . .274/D6
Essex, Md., U.S., 39,078 . . . . .288/J2
Essex, Mass., U.S., 3,267 . . . . .292/L2
Essex, Mass., U.S., *county*, 723,419 . . . .292/D6, L2
Essex, Mo., U.S., 524 . . . . .302/G5
Essex, Mont., U.S. 306/C1
Essex, N.J., U.S., *county*, 793,633 . . . . .314/B2, E2
Essex, N.Y., U.S., 175 . . . . .320/Q2
Essex, N.Y., U.S., *county*, 38,851 . . . . .320/P2
Essex, Vt., U.S., 18,626 . . . . .352/A1
Essex, Vt., U.S., *county*, 6,459 . . . . .352/D1
Essex, Va., U.S., *county*, 9,989 . . . . .354/K5
Essex Ctr., Vt., U.S., 2,700 . . . . .352/A1
Essex Fells, N.J., U.S., 2,162 . . . . .314/A2
Essex Jct., Vt., U.S., 8,591 . . . . .352/A1
Essexville, Mich., U.S., 3,766 . . . . .294/F6
Esslingen, Ger. .86/B4
Essonne, Fr. .88/Inset II
Essonne, Fr., *department* 88/C2
Estacada, Oreg., U.S., 2,371 . . . . .334/D2
Estados, Arg., *island* 191/C7
Estaire, Ont., Can. 223/E1
Estancia, N. Mex., U.S., 1,584 . . . . .317/D3
Estany d'Engolasters, And., *lake* 93/B2
Este, P.R., *point* 206/E2
Estelí, Nicar. 202/A2
Estelí, Nicar., *department* 202/A2
Estelle, La., U.S., 15,880 . . . . .282/J7, K3
Estelline, S. Dak., U.S., 675 . . . . .342/J3
Estelline, Tex., U.S., 168 . . . . .346/G10, H1
Estell Manor, N.J., U.S., 1,585 . . . . .314/D5
Esterbrook, Wyo., U.S. 366/D2
Esterhazy, Sask., Can., 2,348 . . . . .227/H10
Estero, Calif., U.S., *bay* 246/E7
Estero, Fla., U.S., 9,503 . . . . .256/G5
Estes Park, Colo., U.S., 5,413 . . . . .250/E1
Estevan, Sask., Can., 10,242 . . . . .227/G11
Estey, Mich., U.S., 150 . . . . .294/E6
Esther, Alta., Can. 212/E5
Esther, La., U.S. 282/E7
Estherville, Iowa, U.S., 6,656 . . . . .274/E1
Estherwood, La., U.S., 807 . . . . .282/E6
Estill, Ky., U.S., *county*, 15,307 . . . . .280/F3
Estill, Miss., U.S., 70 . . . . .300/B1
Estill, S.C., U.S., 2,425 . . . . .340/C4
Estill Sprs., Tenn., U.S., 2,152 . . . . .344/J4
Eston, Sask., Can., 1,048 . . . . .227/B9
Estonia, *nation* .79
Estonia, *nation* 193/D2
Estoril, Port. 93/A3
Estral Beach, Mich., U.S., 486 . . . . .294/F7
Estrela, Port., *mountain* 93/B2
Estrela, Port., *mountains* 93/B2
Estrella, Colo., U.S. 250/E4
Esztergom, Hun. 91/B2
Etchemin, Que., Can., *river* 226/L6
Etchingham, Eng., U.K. 70/E4
Etchison, Md., U.S., 325 . . . . .288/F2
Etelä-Savo, Fin., *region* 81/C2
Ethan, S. Dak., U.S., 330 . . . . .342/G4
Ethel, Ark., U.S. 244/D3
Ethel, La., U.S., 125 . . . . .282/G5
Ethel, Miss., U.S., 452 . . . . .300/C2
Ethel, Mo., U.S., 100 . . . . .302/D2
Ethelbert, Man., Can., 335 . . . . .215/A3
Ethelsville, Ala., U.S., 81 . . . . .238/A2
Ethete, Wyo., U.S., 1,455 . . . . .366/B2
Ethiopia, *nation* 150
Ethiopia, Eth., *plateau* 156/C2
Ethiopian Seminary, Vat. 96/A2
Ethridge, Mont., U.S. 306/D1
Ethridge, Tenn., U.S., 536 . . . . .344/G4

Etive, Scot., U.K., *lake* 62/F6
Etlan, Va., U.S., 40 . . . . .354/G4
Etna, It., *mountain* 95/C3
Etna, Calif., U.S., 781 . . . . .246/C1
Etna, Maine, U.S., 1,012 . . . . .286/C4
Etna, Minn., U.S., 40 . . . . .298/E7
Etna, N.H., U.S., 275 . . . . .212/B4
Etna, Penn., U.S., 3,924 . . . . .336/E6
Etna, Utah, U.S. 350/A2
Etna, Wyo., U.S., 123 . . . . .366/A2
Etna Green, Ind., U.S., 663 . . . . .270/D2
Etobicoke, Ont., Can. 223/J5
Eton, Eng., U.K. 70/C4
Eton, Ga., U.S., 319 . . . . .260/B3
Etosha, Nam., *pan* 160/B1
Etowah, Ala., U.S., *county*, 103,459 . . . . .238/D2
Etowah, Ark., U.S., 366 . . . . .244/E2
Etowah, Ga., U.S., *river* 260/B3
Etowah, N.C., U.S., 2,766 . . . . .322/E8
Etowah, Okla., U.S., 122 . . . . .330/E2
Etowah, Tenn., U.S., 3,663 . . . . .344/M4
Etrechy, Fr. .88/Inset II
Etrek, Turkm., *river* 132/B3
Etta, Miss., U.S., 50 . . . . .300/C1
Ettelbruck, Lux. .85/B2
Etter, Tex., U.S., 150 . . . . .346/F8
Etteridge, Scot., U.K. 62/H5
Ettington, Eng., U.K. 70/A2
Ettrick, Va., U.S., 5,627 . . . . .354/J6
Ettrick, Wisc., U.S., 521 . . . . .364/B4
Ettrick Pen, Eng., U.K., *hill* 66/B2
Etzikom, Alta., Can. 212/E6
Eua, Tonga, *island* 175/C4
Eubank, Ky., U.S., 358 . . . . .280/F3
Euboea, Gr., *island* 100/B2
Eucha, Okla., U.S., 300 . . . . .330/H1
Euclid, Minn., U.S., 70 . . . . .298/A3
Euclid, Ohio, U.S., 52,717 . . . . .328/G2, H8
Eudora, Ark., U.S., 2,819 . . . . .244/D4
Eudora, Kans., U.S., 4,307 . . . . .276/F3, G3
Eufaula, Ala., U.S., 13,908 . . . . .238/D4
Eufaula, Okla., U.S., 2,639 . . . . .330/G2
Eufaula N.W.R., Ala., U.S. 238/D3
Eugene, Mo., U.S., 175 . . . . .302/D3
Eugene, Oreg., U.S., 137,893, (322,959, *metro.*) .334/C3
Eugenia, Mex., *point* 200/A2
Euharlee, Ga., U.S., 3,208 . . . . .260/B3
Euless, Tex., U.S., 46,005 . . . . .346/B9
Eulonia, Ga., U.S., 70 . . . . .260/J8
Eunice, La., U.S., 11,499 . . . . .282/E6
Eunice, Mo., U.S., 50 . . . . .302/E4
Eunice, N. Mex., U.S., 2,562 . . . . .317/G5
Eunola, Ala., U.S., 182 . . . . .238/D4
Euphrates, Iraq, *river* 130/C2
Euphrates, (Al Furat), Syria, *river* 134/B2
Euphrates, Tur., *river* 133/D2
Eupora, Miss., U.S., 2,326 . . . . .300/C2
Eure, Fr., *department* 88/C2
Eure-et-Loir, Fr., *department* 88/C2
Eureka, Calif., U.S., 26,128 . . . . .246/A2
Eureka, Ill., U.S., 4,871 . . . . .266/D3
Eureka, Kans., U.S., 2,914 . . . . .276/F4
Eureka, Mich., U.S., 300 . . . . .294/E6
Eureka, Mo., U.S., 7,676 . . . . .302/F3
Eureka, Mont., U.S., 1,017 . . . . .306/A1
Eureka, Nev., U.S., 550 . . . . .310/C2
Eureka, Nev., U.S., *county*, 1,651 . . . . .310/B2
Eureka, N.C., U.S., 244 . . . . .322/K5
Eureka, S.C., U.S., 200 . . . . .340/C3
Eureka, S. Dak., U.S., 1,101 . . . . .342/F2
Eureka, Tex., U.S., 340 . . . . .346/M4
Eureka, Utah, U.S., 766 . . . . .350/B4
Eureka, Wash., U.S., 80 . . . . .358/G5
Eureka Mill, S.C., U.S., 1,737 . . . . .340/C2
Eureka River, Alta., Can. 212/A3
Eureka Sprs., Ark., U.S., 2,278 . . . . .244/B1
Euren, Wisc., U.S., 175 . . . . .364/F4
Europe, *continent* 57
Eustis, Fla., U.S., 15,106 . . . . .256/C3, G3
Eustis, Maine, U.S., 685 . . . . .286/B3
Eustis, Mont., U.S. 306/F4
Eustis, Nebr., U.S., 464 . . . . .308/D3
Eutaw, Ala., U.S., 1,878 . . . . .238/B3
Eutawville, S.C., U.S., 344 . . . . .340/D3
Eutsuk, Br. Col., Can., *lake* 214/J4
Eva, Ala., U.S., 491 . . . . .238/C1
Eva, La., U.S., 225 . . . . .282/F4
Eva, Okla., U.S. .330/C4
Eva, Tenn., U.S., 300 . . . . .344/F2
Evan, Minn., U.S., 91 . . . . .298/C6
Evandale, N.B., Can. 217/C3
Evangeline, La., U.S., 150 . . . . .282/D6
Evangeline, La., U.S., *parish*, 35,434 . . . . . . .282/D5
Evans, Colo., U.S., 9,514 . . . . .250/F1
Evans, Colo., U.S., *mountain* 250/E2
Evans, Ga., U.S., 17,727 . . . . .260/G4
Evans, Ga., U.S., *county*, 10,495 . . . . .260/H7
Evans, Iowa, U.S., 90 . . . . .274/J5
Evans, La., U.S., 100 . . . . .282/C5
Evans, Mich., U.S., 225 . . . . .294/D6
Evans, Wash., U.S., 125 . . . . .358/G1
Evans, W. Va., U.S., 750 . . . . .360/C3
Evans City, Penn., U.S., 2,009 . . . . .336/A4
Evansdale, Iowa, U.S., 4,526 . . . . .274/K3
Evans Mills, N.Y., U.S., 605 . . . . .320/K2
Evanston, Ill., U.S., 74,239 . . . . .266/B5, F1
Evanston, Wyo., U.S., 11,507 . . . . .366/A3
Evanston, Ont., Can. 223/C2
Evansville, Ark., U.S., 100 . . . . .244/A2
Evansville, Ga., U.S., 50 . . . . .260/A5
Evansville, Ill., U.S., 724 . . . . .266/D5
Evansville, Ind., U.S., 121,582, (296,195, *metro.*) 270/A9
Evansville, Minn., U.S., 566 . . . . .298/B4
Evansville, Miss., U.S., 60 . . . . .300/B1
Evansville, Vt., U.S., 125 . . . . .352/C1
Evansville, Wisc., U.S., 4,039 . . . . .364/D6
Evant, Tex., U.S., 393 . . . . .346/K4
Evaro, Mont., U.S., 329 . . . . .306/B2
Evart, Mich., U.S., 1,738 . . . . .294/D6
Evarts, Ky., U.S., 1,101 . . . . .280/G4
Eveleth, Minn., U.S., 3,865 . . . . .298/E3
Evelyn, La., U.S., 50 . . . . .282/C3
Evendale, Ohio, U.S., 3,090 . . . . .328/B9
Evening Shade, (Hempstead County),
   Ark., U.S., 100 . . . . .244/B4
Evening Shade, (Sharp County), Ark., U.S., 465 . .244/D1
Evenkia, Russ., *autonomous okrug* 104/F3
Evensville, Tenn., U.S., 300 . . . . .344/M3
Evercreech, Eng., U.K., 1,821 . . . . .73/H2
Everdell, Minn., U.S. 298/A4
Everest, Nepal, *mountain* 126/C2
Everest, Kans., U.S., 314 . . . . .276/G2
Everett, N.B., Can. 217/B1
Everett, Ga., U.S., 70 . . . . .260/H9
Everett, Mass., U.S., 38,037 . . . . .292/D7, K3
Everett, Penn., U.S., 1,905 . . . . .336/F5
Everett, Wash., U.S., 91,488 . . . . .358/C1
Everetts, N.C., U.S., 175 . . . . .322/L3
Everglades, Fla., U.S., *swamp* 256/H6
Everglades City, Fla., U.S., 479 . . . . .256/G6
Everglades Natl. Park, Fla., U.S. 256/A7, H6

Evergreen, Ala., U.S., 3,630 . . . . .238/C4
Evergreen, Colo., U.S., 9,216 . . . . .250/E2
Evergreen, La., U.S., 314 . . . . .282/E5
Evergreen, Minn., U.S., 40 . . . . .298/B4
Evergreen, Mont., U.S., 6,215 . . . . .306/B1
Evergreen, N.C., U.S., 325 . . . . .322/H6
Evergreen, Wash., U.S. 358/C4
Evergreen Park, Ill., U.S., 20,821 . . . . .266/B6
Everingham, Eng., U.K. 66/G5
Everittstown, N.J., U.S., 275 . . . . .314/C2
Everly, Iowa, U.S., 647 . . . . .274/D1
Everman, Tex., U.S., 5,836 . . . . .346/B10
Evershot, Eng., U.K. 73/G3
Eversley Cross, Eng., U.K. 70/C4
Everson, Penn., U.S., 842 . . . . .336/B5
Everson, Wash., U.S., 2,035 . . . . .358/C1
Everton, Eng., U.K. 68/F3
Everton, Ark., U.S., 170 . . . . .244/C1
Everton, Mo., U.S., 322 . . . . .302/C4
Evesboro, N.J., U.S., 2,400 . . . . .314/B3, D4
Evesham, Eng., U.K., 17,823 . . . . .68/D5
Evesham, Eng., U.K., *valley* 68/D5
Evinayong, Eq. Gui. 154/C3
Evington, Va., U.S., 300 . . . . .354/E6
Évora, Port., 56,519 . . . . .93/B3
Évora, Port., *district* 93/B3
Évreux, Fr. 88/C2
Evry, Fr. . . . . .88/Inset II
Ewry, Nauru 174/B1
Ewa, Hawaii, U.S. 262/D2, J2
Ewa Beach, Hawaii, U.S., 14,650 . . . . . . .262/E2, J3
Ewa Forest Reserve, Hawaii, U.S. 262/F1
Ewan, Wash., U.S. 358/H2
Ewell, Eng., U.K. . . . . .60/Inset III
Ewell, Eng., U.K. 70/D4
Ewell, Md., U.S., 364 . . . . .288/K7
Ewen, Mich., U.S., 175 . . . . .294/D2
Ewerby, Eng., U.K. 70/D1
Ewing, Ill., U.S., 310 . . . . .266/E5
Ewing, Ky., U.S., 278 . . . . .280/G2
Ewing, Mo., U.S., 464 . . . . .302/E2
Ewing, Nebr., U.S., 433 . . . . .308/E1
Ewing, N.J., U.S., 35,707 . . . . .314/D3
Ewing, Va., U.S., 436 . . . . .354/B3
Ewingville, Md., U.S., 150 . . . . .288/L3
Ewo, Congo 155/C4
Excel, Ala., U.S., 582 . . . . .238/B4
Excello, Mo., U.S., 40 . . . . .302/D2
Excelsior, Minn., U.S., 2,393 . . . . .298/D6
Excelsior, Mo., U.S., 263 . . . . .302/B2
Excelsior Estates, Mo., U.S. 302/J4
Excelsior Sprs., Mo., U.S., 10,847 . . . . .302/J4
Exebridge, Eng., U.K. 73/F2
Exeland, Wisc., U.S., 212 . . . . .364/B3
Exeter, Ont., Can., 4,562 . . . . .223/D4
Exeter, Eng., U.K. 60/B4
Exeter, Eng., U.K., 94,717 . . . . .73/E3
Exeter, Calif., U.S., 9,168 . . . . .246/F6
Exeter, Ill., U.S., 70 . . . . .266/C4
Exeter, Mo., U.S., 707 . . . . .302/C5
Exeter, Nebr., U.S., 712 . . . . .308/G3
Exeter, N.H., U.S., 14,058 . . . . .212/D7
Exeter, Penn., U.S., 5,955 . . . . .336/H7, K3
Exeter, R.I., U.S., 6,045 . . . . .339/C4
Exeter Corners, Maine, U.S., 100 . . . . .286/C4
Exford, Eng., U.K. 73/E2
Exira, Iowa, U.S., 810 . . . . .274/F4
Exline, Iowa, U.S., 191 . . . . .274/J6
Exmoor, Eng., U.K., *forest* 60/B3
Exmoor Natl. Park, Eng., U.K. 73/E2
Exmore, Va., U.S., 1,136 . . . . .354/M5
Exmouth, Eng., U.K., 28,414 . . . . .73/F3
Experiment, Ga., U.S., 3,233 . . . . .260/C5
Export, Penn., U.S., 895 . . . . .336/B5
Exshaw, Alta., Can., 231 . . . . .212/C5
Extension, La., U.S., 40 . . . . .282/F3
Extaan, Penn., U.S. 336/K5
Extremadura, Sp., *autonomous community* 94/C3
Extreme-North, Came., *province* 153/B1
Exton, Penn., U.S., 4,267 . . . . .336/K5
Exton, Eng., U.K. 73/E2
Exuma, Bah., *sound* 207/B3
Eyam, Eng., U.K. 66/F6
Eyasi, Tan., *lake* 152/B1
Eye, (Cambridgeshire), Eng., U.K., 3,010 . . . . . .68/G4
Eye, (Cambridgeshire), Eng., U.K., 3,010 . . . . . .70/D1
Eye, (Suffolk), Eng., U.K., 1,741 . . . . .70/G2
Eyebrook, Eng., U.K., *reservoir* 70/C1
Eyebrow, Sask., Can., 136 . . . . .227/D10
Eyemouth, Scot., U.K., 3,383 . . . . .62/M7
Eyhorne Street, Eng., U.K. 70/F4
Eyl, Som. 157/B2
Eynsham, Eng., U.K., 4,764 . . . . .68/E6
Eynsham, Eng., U.K., 4,764 . . . . .70/B3
Eyota, Minn., U.S., 1,644 . . . . .298/E7
Eyre, Austl., *lake* 170/C2
Eyre, Austl., *peninsula* 170/C3
Eysturoy, Den., *island* 79/Inset
Eyüp, Tur. 133/B2
Ezel, Ky., U.S., 225 . . . . .280/G3
Eyüp, Tur. 133/B2

Faadhippolhu, Mald., *atoll* 127/A2
Fabens, Tex., U.S., 8,043 . . . . .346/B4
Fabius, N.Y., U.S., 355 . . . . .320/K5
Fabyan, Alta., Can. 212/E5
Fabyan, N.H., U.S. 212/D3
Faceville, Ga., U.S., 70 . . . . .260/B1
Fackler, Ala., U.S., 175 . . . . .238/D1
Factoryville, Penn., U.S., 1,144 . . . . .336/K2
Fada, Chad 153/C3
Faenza, It. 95/B1
Fagamalo, Sam. .175/B1
Fagus, Mo., U.S., 60 . . . . .302/F5
Faial, Port., *island* . . . . .93/Inset II
Fair, Scot., U.K., *island* . . . . .60/Inset I
Fairacres, N. Mex., U.S., 1,100 . . . . .317/D3
Fairbank, Ariz., U.S. 242/E6
Fairbank, Iowa, U.S., 1,041 . . . . .274/K2
Fairbanks, U.S. .193/C11
Fairbanks, Alaska, U.S., 30,224 . . . . .240/F2
Fairbanks, Fla., U.S., 750 . . . . .256/G2
Fairbanks, Ind., U.S., 175 . . . . .270/A6
Fairbanks, La., U.S., 50 . . . . .282/E1
Fairbanks, Minn., U.S. 298/F3
Fair Bluff, N.C., U.S., 1,181 . . . . .322/G6
Fairborn, Ohio, U.S., 32,052 . . . . .328/B6, G1
Fairbourne, Wales, U.K. 64/C2
Fairbrook, Penn., U.S., 600 . . . . .336/G5
Fairburn, Ga., U.S., 5,464 . . . . .260/B4, H3
Fairburn, S. Dak., U.S., 80 . . . . .342/B4
Fairbury, Ill., U.S., 3,968 . . . . .266/E3
Fairbury, Nebr., U.S., 4,262 . . . . .308/G3
Fairchance, Penn., U.S., 2,174 . . . . .336/B6
Fairchild, Wisc., U.S., 564 . . . . .364/A4
Fairdale, Ky., U.S., 7,658 . . . . .280/A2
Fairdale, N. Dak., U.S., 51 . . . . .326/G1
Fairdealing, Mo., U.S., 225 . . . . .302/F5
Fairfax, Calif., U.S., 7,319 . . . . .246/H1
Fairfax, (see Talleyville), Del., U.S., 2,300 . . . . .255/B1
Fairfax, Iowa, U.S., 889 . . . . .274/L4
Fairfax, Minn., U.S., 1,295 . . . . .298/C6
Fairfax, Mo., U.S., 645 . . . . .302/A1
Fairfax, Ohio, U.S., 1,938 . . . . .328/B9

Fairfax, Okla., U.S., 1,555 . . . . .330/F1
Fairfax, S.C., U.S., 3,206 . . . . .340/C4
Fairfax, S. Dak., U.S., 123 . . . . .342/G4
Fairfax, Vt., U.S., 3,765 . . . . .352/B1
Fairfax, Va., U.S., 21,498 . . . . .354/J3, L2
Fairfax, Va., U.S., *county*, 969,749 . . . . .354/J3, L2
Fairfax, N.S.W., Austl. . . . . .170/Inset IV
Fairfield, (Covington County), Ala., U.S., 60 . . . .238/C4
Fairfield, (Jefferson County), Ala., U.S.,
   12,381 . . . . .238/C2, E1
Fairfield, Calif., U.S., 96,178 . . . . .246/D4, K1
Fairfield, Conn., U.S., 57,340 . . . . .253/B5
Fairfield, Conn., U.S., *county*, 882,567 . . . . . .253/B5
Fairfield, Ida., U.S., 395 . . . . .264/D3
Fairfield, Ill., U.S., 5,421 . . . . .266/E5
Fairfield, Iowa, U.S., 9,509 . . . . .274/L5
Fairfield, Ky., U.S., 72 . . . . .280/E3
Fairfield, Maine, U.S., 6,573 . . . . .286/C4
Fairfield, Mo., U.S. 302/C3
Fairfield, Mont., U.S., 659 . . . . .306/D2
Fairfield, Nebr., U.S., 467 . . . . .308/E3
Fairfield, (Essex County), N.J., U.S., 7,063 .314/A2, E2
Fairfield, N.C., U.S., 125 . . . . .322/N3
Fairfield, N. Dak., U.S. 326/B2
Fairfield, Ohio, U.S., 42,097 . . . . .328/A7, B9
Fairfield, Ohio, U.S., *county*, 122,759 . . .328/E1, E6
Fairfield, (Adams County), Penn., U.S., 486 . . . .336/G6
Fairfield, (Erie County), Penn., U.S. 336/B1
Fairfield, S.C., U.S., *county*, 23,454 . . . . .340/C2
Fairfield, Tex., U.S., 3,094 . . . . .346/M4
Fairfield, Utah, U.S., 90 . . . . .350/B3
Fairfield, Vt., U.S., 1,800 . . . . .352/B1
Fairfield, Va., U.S., 225 . . . . .354/E5
Fairfield, Wash., U.S., 494 . . . . .358/H2
Fairfield Bay, Ark., U.S., 2,460 . . . . .244/C2
Fairfield Beach, Ohio, U.S., 1,163 . . . . .328/F6
Fairfield Ctr., Maine, U.S., 500 . . . . .286/C4
Fairfield Glade, Tenn., U.S., 4,885 . . . . .344/M2
Fairford, Man., Can. 215/B3
Fairford, Eng., U.K., 2,633 . . . . .68/D6
Fairford, Eng., U.K., 2,633 . . . . .73/J1
Fairgrange, Ill., U.S., 80 . . . . .266/E4
Fairgrove, Mich., U.S., 627 . . . . .294/F6
Fair Grove, Mo., U.S., 1,107 . . . . .302/C4
Fairhaven, Mass., U.S., 16,159 . . . . .292/L6
Fair Haven, Mich., U.S., 1,500 . . . . .294/G7
Fair Haven, N.J., U.S., 5,937 . . . . .314/E3
Fair Haven, N.Y., U.S., 884 . . . . .320/H4
Fair Haven, Vt., U.S., 2,928 . . . . .352/A3
Fair Head, N. Ire., U.K., *cape* 65/E1
Fair Hill, Md., U.S. 288/L1
Fairhope, Ala., U.S., 12,480 . . . . .238/B5
Fairland, Ind., U.S., 1,275 . . . . .270/E5
Fairland, Ind., U.S., 21,738 . . . . .288/C6, G3
Fairland, Okla., U.S., 1,025 . . . . .330/H1
Fair Lawn, N.J., U.S., 31,637 . . . . .314/B2, E2
Fairlawn, Ohio, U.S., 7,307 . . . . .328/G3
Fairlea, W. Va., U.S., 1,706 . . . . .360/F5
Fairlee, Md., U.S., 250 . . . . .288/K3
Fairlee, Vt., U.S., 967 . . . . .352/C3
Fairless Hills, Penn., U.S., 8,365 . . . . .336/M5
Fairlie, Scot., U.K., 1,510 . . . . .62/G7
Fairlight, Eng., U.K., 1,605 . . . . .70/F5
Fairmont, Ill., U.S., 2,563 . . . . .266/B6
Fairmont, Minn., U.S., 10,889 . . . . .298/C7
Fairmont, Nebr., U.S., 691 . . . . .308/G3
Fairmont, N.C., U.S., 2,604 . . . . .322/G5
Fairmont, Okla., U.S., 147 . . . . .330/E1
Fairmont, W. Va., U.S., 19,097 . . . . .360/F2
Fairmont City, Ill., U.S., 2,436 . . . . .266/A3
Fairmont Hot Sprs., Br. Col., Can., 429 . . . . . . .214/P6
Fairmount, Ga., U.S., 745 . . . . .260/B3
Fairmount, Ill., U.S., 640 . . . . .266/F3
Fairmount, Ind., U.S., 2,992 . . . . .270/E4
Fairmount, Kans., U.S., 250 . . . . .276/G2, H2
Fairmount, N.J., U.S., 300 . . . . .314/D2
Fairmount, N.Y., U.S., 10,795 . . . . .320/J4
Fairmount, N. Dak., U.S., 406 . . . . .326/J3
Fairmount, Tex., U.S., 125 . . . . .346/R4
Fairmount, (part of Paine Field-Lake Stickney),
   Wash., U.S. .358/C4
Fairmount Hts., Md., U.S., 1,508 . . . . .288/C7
Fair Oaks, Ark., U.S., 150 . . . . .244/D2
Fair Oaks, Calif., U.S., 28,008 . . . . .246/L5
Fair Oaks, Ga., U.S., 8,443 . . . . .260/B4, H2
Fair Oaks, Ind., U.S., 175 . . . . .270/B2
Fair Oaks, Okla., U.S., 122 . . . . .330/G1
Fair Oaks Ranch, Tex., U.S., 4,695 . . . . . .346/A2, K6
Fair Plain, Mich., U.S., 7,828 . . . . .294/C7
Fairplains, N.C., U.S., 2,051 . . . . .322/C2
Fairplay, Colo., U.S., 610 . . . . .250/E2
Fair Play, Mo., U.S., 418 . . . . .302/C4
Fair Play, S.C., U.S., 375 . . . . .340/B2
Fairpoint's, S. Dak., U.S. 342/C3
Fairport, Iowa, U.S., 175 . . . . .274/N5
Fairport, Kans., U.S. 276/C2
Fairport, Mich., U.S., 125 . . . . .294/C4
Fairport, Mo., U.S., 80 . . . . .302/B2
Fairport, N.Y., U.S., 5,740 . . . . .320/F4
Fairport Harbor, Ohio, U.S., 3,180 . . . . .328/H2
Fairstead, (Essex), Eng., U.K. 70/F3
Fairstead, (Norfolk), Eng., U.K. 70/G1
Fairton, N.J., U.S., 2,253 . . . . .314/C5
Fairvale, N.B., Can. 217/C3
Fairview, Alta., Can., 3,150 . . . . .212/A3
Fairview, Ala., U.S., 522 . . . . .238/C1
Fairview, Calif., U.S., 9,470 . . . . .246/K2
Fairview, Ga., U.S., 6,601 . . . . .260/A2
Fairview, Ida., U.S. 264/F7
Fairview, Ill., U.S., 493 . . . . .266/C4
Fairview, Kans., U.S., 271 . . . . .276/G2
Fairview, (Christian County), Ky., U.S., 150 . . . .280/C4
Fairview, (Fleming County), Ky., U.S., 70 . . . . . .280/G2
Fairview, (Kenton County), Ky., U.S., 156 . . . . .280/G1
Fairview, Mich., U.S., 600 . . . . .294/E5
Fairview, Miss., U.S., 150 . . . . .300/M5
Fairview, Mo., U.S., 395 . . . . .302/B5
Fairview, Mont., U.S., 709 . . . . .306/M2
Fairview, (Bergen County), N.J., U.S., 13,255 .314/C2, F2
Fairview, N.Y., U.S., 5,421 . . . . .320/P7
Fairview, N.C., U.S., 2,495 . . . . .322/E7
Fairview, Ohio, U.S., 81 . . . . .328/B6
Fairview, Okla., U.S., 2,733 . . . . .330/D1
Fairview, (Coos County), Oreg., U.S., 60 . . . . . .334/B4
Fairview, (Multnomah County),
   Oreg., U.S., 7,561 . . . . .334/B2
Fairview, (Butler County), Penn., U.S., 220 . . . . .336/B3
Fairview, (Erie County), Penn., U.S. 336/A1
Fairview, (Northumberland County, Fairview-Ferndale)
   Penn., U.S., 2,411 . . . . .336/H4
Fairview, S. Dak., U.S., 94 . . . . .342/J4
Fairview, Tenn., U.S., 5,800 . . . . .344/G3
Fairview, (Collin County), Tex., U.S., 2,644 . . . . .346/C8
Fairview, (Howard County), Tex., U.S. 346/A4
Fairview, (Wise County), Tex., U.S., 877 . . . . . .346/A8
Fairview, Utah, U.S., 1,160 . . . . .350/C4
Fairview, (Fairview-Sumach), Wash., U.S. 358/E3
Fairview, W. Va., U.S., 435 . . . . .360/F1
Fairview, Wyo., U.S., 277 . . . . .366/A2
Fairview Hts., Ill., U.S., 15,034 . . . . .266/A3

Fairview Park, Ind., U.S., 1,496 . . . . .270/B5
Fairview Park, Ohio, U.S., 17,572 . . . . .328/G9
Fairwater, Wisc., U.S., 350 . . . . .364/E5
Fairway, Kans., U.S., 3,952 . . . . .276/H1
Fairweather, Br. Col., Can., *mountain* 214/D1
Fairweather, Alaska, U.S., *mountain* 240/H3
Fairwood, (King County, Cascade-Fairwood),
   Wash., U.S., 34,580 . . . . .358/A4
Fairwood, (Spokane County), Wash., U.S., 6,764 .358/H2
Fairy, Tex., U.S. 346/L4
Faisalabad, Pak., 2,008,861 . . . . .129/D3
Faison, N.C., U.S., 744 . . . . .322/J4
Faith, Ark., U.S., 125 . . . . .244/C3
Faith, Minn., U.S., 50 . . . . .298/A3
Faith, N.C., U.S., 695 . . . . .322/E3
Faith, S. Dak., U.S., 489 . . . . .342/C2
Faithorn, Mich., U.S. 294/B4
Faizabad, India 128/D3
Fajardo, P.R. 206/D2
Fakenham, Eng., U.K., 6,471 . . . . .70/F1
Fakfak, Indon. 122/E2
Falciano, S. Mar. 97/C1
Falcon, Ark., U.S. .244/B4
Falcon, Colo., U.S., 225 . . . . .250/F3
Falcon, Ky., U.S., 225 . . . . .280/H3
Falcon, Miss., U.S., 317 . . . . .300/B1
Falcon, Mo., U.S., 50 . . . . .302/D4
Falcon, N.C., U.S., 328 . . . . .322/H4
Falcon, Oreg., U.S., *cape* 334/B2
Falcon, Tex., U.S., 150 . . . . .346/J9
Falcon, Tex., U.S., *reservoir* 346/J9
Falcón, Ven., *state* 182/B1
Falconer, N.Y., U.S., 2,540 . . . . .320/C6
Falcon Hts., Minn., U.S., 5,572 . . . . .298/F5
Falcon Lake, Man., Can. 215/D4
Faldingworth, Eng., U.K. 66/H6
Faelatai, Sam. 175/B2
Faelima, Sam. 175/A2
Falémé, Sen., *river* 148/C3
Fălești, Mol. 102/A2
Falfurrias, Tex., U.S., 5,297 . . . . .346/K8
Falher, Alta., Can., 1,109 . . . . .212/B3
Falkirk, Scot., U.K., *unitary authority*, 145,191 .62/J7
Falkirk, N. Dak., U.S. 326/D2
Falkland, U.K., *islands* 191/C7
Falkland, N.C., U.S., 112 . . . . .322/K3
Falkner, Miss., U.S., 212 . . . . .300/D1
Falköping, Swe. 80/B3
Falkville, Ala., U.S., 1,202 . . . . .238/C1
Fall, Kans., U.S., *river* 276/F4
Fall Branch, Tenn., U.S., 1,313 . . . . .344/R2
Fallbrook, Calif., U.S., 29,100 . . . . .246/H9
Fall City, Wash., U.S., 1,638 . . . . .358/B4
Fall Creek, Ill., U.S. 266/B4
Fall Creek, Wisc., U.S., 1,236 . . . . .364/B4
Fall Creek Falls St. Park, Tenn., U.S. 344/L3
Falling Spr., Va., U.S., 200 . . . . .354/D5
Fallis, Okla., U.S. .330/E2
Fallon, Mont., U.S., 138 . . . . .306/L3
Fallon, Mont., U.S., *county*, 2,837 . . . . .306/M3
Fallon, Nev., U.S., 7,536 . . . . .310/A2
Fallon Ind. Res., Nev., U.S. 310/A2
Fallon N.W.R., Nev., U.S. 310/A2
Fallon N.A.S., Nev., U.S. 310/A2
Fallon Sta., Nev., U.S., 1,265 . . . . .310/A2
Fall River, Kans., U.S., 156 . . . . .276/F4
Fall River, Mass., U.S., 91,938 . . . . .292/K6
Fall River, S. Dak., U.S., *county*, 7,453 . . . . . .342/B4
Fall River, Wisc., U.S., 1,097 . . . . .364/D5
Falls, Penn., U.S., 500 . . . . .336/G7, K3
Falls, Tex., U.S., *county*, 18,576 . . . . .346/M4
Fallsburg, Ky., U.S., 175 . . . . .280/H2
Falls Church, Va., U.S., 10,377 . . . . .354/M2
Falls City, Nebr., U.S., 4,671 . . . . .308/J3
Falls City, Tex., U.S., 591 . . . . .346/K7
Falls Creek, Penn., U.S., 983 . . . . .336/D3
Falls Lake, N.C., U.S., *reservoir* 322/H3
Fallston, Md., U.S., 8,427 . . . . .288/J1
Fallston, N.C., U.S., 603 . . . . .322/C4
Falls Vil., Conn., U.S., 500 . . . . .253/B2
Fallsville, Ark., U.S., 50 . . . . .244/B2
Falmer, Eng., U.K. .70/D5
Falmouth, Ant.-Bar. 207/E5
Falmouth, Jam. 206/B2
Falmouth, Eng., U.K., 20,297 . . . . .73/B4
Falmouth, Fla., U.S. 256/E1
Falmouth, Ky., U.S., 2,058 . . . . .280/F2
Falmouth, Maine, U.S., 10,310 . . . . .286/B5
Falmouth, Mass., U.S., 32,660 . . . . .292/M6
Falmouth, Mich., U.S., 275 . . . . .294/D5
Falmouth, Va., U.S., 3,624 . . . . .354/J4
Falmouth Foreside, Maine, U.S., 1,964 . . . . . . .286/B5
False Divi, India, *point* 128/D5
False Pass, Alaska, U.S., 64 . . . . .240/C4
Falster, Den., *island* 79/D4
Falstone, Eng., U.K. .66/D2
Falun, Swe., 54,601 . . . . .80/C2
Falun, Kans., U.S., 125 . . . . .276/E3
Falun, Wisc., U.S., 125 . . . . .364/A3
Famagusta, Cyp., *bay* 133/C1
Famoso, Calif., U.S. 246/F7
Fancy Farm, Ky., U.S., 500 . . . . .280/B4
Fangfoss, Eng., U.K. 66/G5
Fangliao, Tai. 117/B2
Fannettsburg, Penn., U.S., 375 . . . . .336/F5
Fannich, Scot., U.K., *lake* 62/F3
Fannin, Ga., U.S., *county*, 19,798 . . . . .260/C2
Fannin, Tex., U.S. .346/L7
Fannin, Tex., U.S., *county*, 31,242 . . . . .346/M2
Fanning, Kans., U.S., 40 . . . . .276/G2
Fanning Sprs., Fla., U.S., 737 . . . . .256/F2
Fanø, Den., *island* .79/B3
Fanshawe, Okla., U.S., 384 . . . . .330/H3
Fan Si Pan, Viet., *mountain* 123/A1
Fanwood, N.J., U.S., 7,174 . . . . .314/E2
Farafangana, Madag. 163/B3
Farafenni, Gam. 148/C2
Farafirah, Egy., *oasis* 144/A2
Farah, Afg., 19,800 . . . . .129/A2
Farah, Afg., *river* .129/A2
Fargo, Ark., U.S., 118 . . . . .244/D3
Fargo, Ga., U.S., 380 . . . . .260/F1
Fargo, N. Dak., U.S., 90,599, (174,367, *metro.*) .326/J3
Fargo, Okla., U.S., 326 . . . . .330/C1
Far Hills, N.J., U.S., 859 . . . . .314/D2
Faribault, Minn., U.S., 20,818 . . . . .298/D6
Faribault, Minn., U.S., *county*, 16,181 . . . . . .298/D7
Faridpur, Bangl. 127/C5
Farim, Gui.-B. 149/B1
Farina, Ill., U.S., 558 . . . . .266/E5

Faringdon, Eng., U.K., 5,235 . . . . .68/D6
Faringdon, Eng., U.K., 5,235 . . . . .70/A3
Faringdon, Eng., U.K., 5,235 . . . . .73/J1
Farisita, Colo., U.S. 250/E4
Farley, Iowa, U.S., 1,334 . . . . .274/M3
Farley, Mass., U.S., 200 . . . . .292/E2
Farley, N. Mex., U.S. 317/F1
Farlin, Iowa, U.S., 40 . . . . .274/F3
Farlington, Kans., U.S., 125 . . . . .276/H4
Farmer, Ohio, U.S., 150 . . . . .328/A3
Farmer, S. Dak., U.S. 342/H4
Farmer, Wash., U.S. 358/F2
Farmer City, Ill., U.S., 2,055 . . . . .266/E3
Farmers Branch, Tex., U.S., 27,508 . . . . .266/C9
Farmersburg, Ind., U.S., 1,180 . . . . .270/B6
Farmersburg, Iowa, U.S., 300 . . . . .274/M2
Farmers Valley, Tex., U.S. 346/J1
Farmersville, Calif., U.S., 8,737 . . . . .246/F6
Farmersville, Ill., U.S., 768 . . . . .266/D4
Farmersville, Ohio, U.S., 980 . . . . .328/B6
Farmersville, Tex., U.S., 3,118 . . . . .346/D8
Farmerville, La., U.S., 3,808 . . . . .282/E1
Farmingdale, Maine, U.S., 2,804 . . . . .286/C4
Farmingdale, N.J., U.S., 1,587 . . . . .314/E3
Farmingdale, S. Dak., U.S. 342/C4
Farmington, Br. Col., Can. 214/M3
Farmington, Ark., U.S., 3,605 . . . . .244/A1
Farmington, Calif., U.S., 262 . . . . .246/E5
Farmington, Conn., U.S., 23,641 . . . . .253/D3
Farmington, Conn., U.S., *river* 253/D3
Farmington, Del., U.S., 75 . . . . .255/B5
Farmington, Ga., U.S., 250 . . . . .260/E4
Farmington, Ill., U.S., 2,601 . . . . .266/C3
Farmington, Iowa, U.S., 756 . . . . .274/L6
Farmington, Kans., U.S. 276/G2
Farmington, Ky., U.S., 225 . . . . .280/B4
Farmington, Maine, U.S., 7,410 . . . . .286/B4
Farmington, Md., U.S., 375 . . . . .288/K1
Farmington, Mich., U.S., 10,423 . . . . .294/A6
Farmington, Minn., U.S., 12,365 . . . . .298/E6
Farmington, Mo., U.S., 13,924 . . . . .302/F4
Farmington, Mont., U.S. 306/D2
Farmington, N.H., U.S., 5,774 . . . . .212/D5
Farmington, N. Mex., U.S., 37,844 . . . . .317/B1
Farmington, N.Y., U.S., 475 . . . . .320/G5
Farmington, N.C., U.S., 125 . . . . .322/D2
Farmington, Penn., U.S., 650 . . . . .336/B6
Farmington, Utah, U.S., 12,081 . . . . .350/C3, E1
Farmington, Wash., U.S., 153 . . . . .358/H2
Farmington, W. Va., U.S., 387 . . . . .360/F1
Farmington Falls, Maine, U.S., 225 . . . . .286/B4
Farmington Hills, Mich., U.S., 82,111 . . . . .294/A6
Farmland, Ind., U.S., 1,456 . . . . .270/F4
Farmoor, Eng., U.K. .68/E6
Farmville, N.C., U.S., 4,302 . . . . .322/K3
Farmville, Va., U.S., 6,845 . . . . .354/G6
Farnam, Nebr., U.S., 223 . . . . .308/D3
Farnborough, Eng., U.K., 52,535 . . . . .70/B3
Farndon, (Cheshire Co), Eng., U.K. 68/B3
Farndon, (Nottinghamshire Co), Eng., U.K. 68/F3
Farne, Eng., U.K., *islands* 66/E1
Farner, Tenn., U.S., 300 . . . . .344/N4
Farnham, Que., Can. . . . . .60/Inset III
Farnham, Eng., U.K., 36,178 . . . . .70/C4
Farnham, N.Y., U.S., 322 . . . . .320/C5
Farnham, Va., U.S., 250 . . . . .354/K5
Farnhamville, Iowa, U.S., 430 . . . . .274/F3
Farnsworth, Tex., U.S., 150 . . . . .346/G8
Farnworth, Eng., U.K., 25,053 . . . . .66/D5
Farnworth, Eng., U.K., 25,053 . . . . .68/C2
Faro, Yukon, Can., 313 . . . . .228/C4
Faro, Port., 58,051 .93/B4
Faro, Port., *district* 93/A4
Faroe, Den., *islands* 79/Inset
Farquhar, Sey., *island group* 163/B3
Farragut, Iowa, U.S., 509 . . . . .274/D6
Farragut, Tenn., U.S., 17,720 . . . . .344/N3
Farrandsville, Penn., U.S., 40 . . . . .336/F3
Farrar, Tex., U.S., 100 . . . . .346/M4
Farrell, Miss., U.S., 200 . . . . .300/B1
Farrell, Penn., U.S., 6,050 . . . . .336/A3
Farrellton, Que., Can. 226/A6
Farrington, N.C., U.S., 100 . . . . .322/G3
Farris, Okla., U.S., 80 . . . . .330/G3
Farristown, Ky., U.S., 200 . . . . .280/F3
Farrsville, Tex., U.S. 346/R5
Farr West, Utah, U.S., 3,094 . . . . .350/E1
Fars, Iran, *province* 130/C4
Farson, Wyo., U.S., 242 . . . . .366/B2
Fartak, Ra's, Yemen, *cape* 137/C1
Farwell, Mich., U.S., 855 . . . . .294/E6
Farwell, Minn., U.S., 57 . . . . .298/B5
Farwell, Nebr., U.S., 148 . . . . .308/E2
Farwell, Tex., U.S., 1,364 . . . . .346/E1
Fate, Tex., U.S., 497 . . . . .346/D9
Father Marquette Natl. Mem., Mich., U.S. 294/E4
Fathom Five Natl. Marine Park, Ont., Can. 223/C2
Fatick, Sen. 148/A2
Fatoto, Gam. 148/E2
Faucett, Mo., U.S., 300 . . . . .302/B2
Faulk, S. Dak., U.S., *county*, 2,640 . . . . .342/F2
Faulkner, Ark., U.S., *county*, 86,014 . . . . . . .244/C2
Faulkner, Iowa, U.S., 60 . . . . .274/H2
Faulkner, Kans., U.S., 40 . . . . .276/G4
Faulkner, Md., U.S., 250 . . . . .288/G6
Faulkton, S. Dak., U.S., 785 . . . . .342/F2
Faunsdale, Ala., U.S., 87 . . . . .238/B3
Fauquier, Br. Col., Can., 219 . . . . .214/N6
Fauquier, Va., U.S., *county*, 55,139 . . . . .354/H3
Faust, Alta., Can., 365 . . . . .212/C3
Faust, Utah, U.S. .350/B3
Faversham, Eng., U.K., 17,070 . . . . .70/F4
Favoretta, Fla., U.S., 650 . . . . .256/G2
Fawcett, Alta., Can., 102 . . . . .212/C4
Fawfieldhead, Eng., U.K. 68/D3
Fawley, Eng., U.K., 13,034 . . . . .70/B3
Fawn Grove, Penn., U.S., 463 . . . . .336/J6
Faxaflói, Ice., *bay* .79/A2
Faxälven, Swe. 80/C2
Faxfleet, Eng., U.K. .66/G5
Faxon, Okla., U.S., 134 . . . . .330/D3
Fay, Okla., U.S., 100 . . . . .330/D2
Fayette, Ala., U.S., 4,922 . . . . .238/B2
Fayette, Ala., U.S., *county*, 18,495 . . . . .238/B2
Fayette, Ga., U.S., *county*, 91,263 . . . . .260/B5, H4
Fayette, Ill., U.S., *county*, 21,802 . . . . .266/D4
Fayette, Ind., U.S., *county*, 25,588 . . . . .270/F5
Fayette, Iowa, U.S., 1,300 . . . . .274/L2
Fayette, Iowa, U.S., *county*, 22,008 . . . . .274/L2
Fayette, Ky., U.S., *county*, 260,512 . . . . .280/F3
Fayette, Mich., U.S., 1,040 . . . . .286/B4
Fayette, Mich., U.S. 294/C4
Fayette, Miss., U.S., 2,242 . . . . .300/A4
Fayette, Mo., U.S., 2,793 . . . . .302/D3
Fayette, N.Y., U.S., 275 . . . . .320/H5
Fayette, Ohio, U.S., 1,340 . . . . .328/B2
Fayette, Ohio, U.S., *county*, 28,433 . . . . .328/D7
Fayette, Penn., U.S., *county*, 148,644 . . . . . .336/B6
Fayette, Tenn., U.S., *county*, 28,806 . . . . . . .344/C4
Fayette, Tex., U.S., *county*, 21,804 . . . . .346/L6
Fayette, Utah, U.S., 204 . . . . .350/C4

Fayette, W. Va., U.S., *county*, 47,579 . . . . . . .360/D4
Fayette City, Penn., U.S., 714 . . . . .336/B5
Fayetteville, Ala., U.S., 200 . . . . .238/C2
Fayetteville, Ark., U.S., 58,047, (311,121, *metro.*) 244/A1
Fayetteville, Ga., U.S., 11,148 . . . . .260/C5
Fayetteville, Ill., U.S., 384 . . . . .266/B4
Fayetteville, Mo., U.S., 90 . . . . .302/C3
Fayetteville, N.Y., U.S., 4,190 . . . . .320/K4
Fayetteville, N.C., U.S., 121,015,
   (302,963, *metro.*) 322/H4
Fayetteville, Ohio, U.S., 372 . . . . .328/C7
Fayetteville, Penn., U.S., 2,774 . . . . .336/F6
Fayetteville, Tenn., U.S., 6,994 . . . . .344/H4
Fayetteville, Tex., U.S., 261 . . . . .346/M6
Fayetteville, W. Va., U.S., 2,754 . . . . .360/D4
Faygate, Eng., U.K. .70/C4
Faylakah, Kuw., *island* 136/C2
Fdérik, Maur. 147/B2
Feagaville, Md., U.S., 600 . . . . .288/E2
Fear, N.C., U.S., *cape* 322/K7
Fearisville, Ky., U.S., 150 . . . . .280/C2
Fearnmore, Scot., U.K. 62/E3
Fearrington Post, (Fearrington), N.C., U.S., 903 .322/G3
Feasterville, (Feasterville-Trevose),
   Penn., U.S., 6,525 . . . . .336/M6
Feather Sound, Fla., U.S., 3,597 . . . . .256/C6
Featherville, Ida., U.S. 264/B6
Federal, Wyo., U.S. 366/D3
Federal Dam, Minn., U.S., 101 . . . . .298/C3
Federal District, Braz. 188/D3
Federal Hts., Colo., U.S., 12,065 . . . . .250/A3, E2
Federally Administrated Tribal Areas, Pak. 129/C3
Federalsburg, Md., U.S., 2,620 . . . . .288/L5
Federal Way, Wash., U.S., 83,259 . . . . .358/C2
Fedora, S. Dak., U.S., 40 . . . . .342/H4
Feeding Hills, Mass., U.S. 292/E2
Feeny, N. Ire., U.K., 583 . . . . .65/C2
Feetham, Eng., U.K. 66/D4
Fehmarn, Ger., *island* 86/B1
Fehmarn, Ger., *strait* 79/C4
Fehmarn, Ger., *island* 86/B1
Fejér, Hun., *county* 91/B2
Feira de Santana, Braz., 480,949 . . . . .188/E3
Felch, Mich., U.S., 80 . . . . .294/B4
Felchville, Vt., U.S., 125 . . . . .352/B4
Felda, Fla., U.S., 300 . . . . .256/G5
Feldkirch, Aus. 91/A3
Felicity, Ohio, U.S., 922 . . . . .328/B8
Felida, Wash., U.S., 5,683 . . . . .358/C4
Felidhu, Mald., *atoll* 127/A3
Felixstowe, Eng., U.K. 60/D1
Felixstowe, Eng., U.K., 28,606 . . . . .70/G3
Felixville, La., U.S., 70 . . . . .282/H5
Fellowship, N.J., U.S., 4,900 . . . . .314/B3
Fellowsville, W. Va., U.S., 175 . . . . .360/G2
Fellsburg, Kans., U.S. 276/C4
Fellsmere, Fla., U.S., 3,813 . . . . .256/H4
Felmersham, Eng., U.K. 68/F5
Felpham, Eng., U.K. 70/C5
Felsenthal, Ark., U.S., 152 . . . . .244/C4
Felsenthal N.W.R., Ark., U.S. 244/C4
Felsted, Eng., U.K. .70/E3
Felt, Ida., U.S., 40 .264/F6
Felt, Okla., U.S., 100 . . . . .330/B4
Felton, Ark., U.S., 70 . . . . .244/E3
Felton, Calif., U.S., 1,051 . . . . .246/J4
Felton, Del., U.S., 784 . . . . .255/B4
Felton, Ga., U.S., 275 . . . . .260/A4
Felton, Minn., U.S., 216 . . . . .298/A3
Felton, Penn., U.S., 449 . . . . .336/H6
Feltwell, Eng., U.K., 2,931 . . . . .70/E2
Fen, China, *river* .119/E2
Fence, Wisc., U.S., 70 . . . . .364/E3
Fence Lake, N. Mex., U.S. 317/B5
Fenelon Falls, Ont., Can., 1,874 . . . . .223/G3
Fengshan, Tai. 117/B2
Fengyüan, Tai. 117/B1
Fenholloway, Fla., U.S. 256/E1
Feni, P.N.G., *islands* 172/B2
Fenn, Calif., U.S. 264/A4
Fenner, Calif., U.S. .246/K8
Fennimore, Wisc., U.S., 2,387 . . . . .364/C6
Fennville, Mich., U.S., 1,459 . . . . .294/C7
Fenny Stratford, Eng., U.K. 68/F3
Fens, The, Eng., U.K., *region* 60/D3
Fens, The, Eng., U.K., *region* 68/G4
Fenton, Ill., U.S., 150 . . . . .266/C2
Fenton, Iowa, U.S., 317 . . . . .274/F1
Fenton, La., U.S., 380 . . . . .282/D6
Fenton, Mich., U.S., 10,582 . . . . .294/F6
Fenton, Mo., U.S., 4,360 . . . . .302/H3
Fentress, Tenn., U.S., *county*, 16,625 . . . . . .344/M2
Fentress, Tex., U.S., 250 . . . . .346/L6
Fenwick, Conn., U.S., 52 . . . . .253/F4
Fenwick, W. Va., U.S., 400 . . . . .360/E4
Fenwick Island, Del., U.S., 342 . . . . .255/D7
Fenwood, Wisc., U.S., 174 . . . . .364/C4
Feodosiia, Ukr. 102/D3
Feolin Ferry, Scot., U.K. 62/D7
Ferdinand, Ida., U.S., 145 . . . . .264/A3
Ferdinand, Ind., U.S., 2,277 . . . . .270/C8
Fergus, Ont., Can., 16,732 . . . . .223/E4
Fergus, Mont., U.S. 306/G2
Fergus, Mont., U.S., *county*, 11,893 . . . . . . .306/G2
Fergus Falls, Minn., U.S., 13,471 . . . . .298/A4
Ferguson, Iowa, U.S., 126 . . . . .274/J4
Ferguson, Ky., U.S., 881 . . . . .280/F3
Ferguson, Mo., U.S., 22,406 . . . . .302/H2
Ferkessédougou, C. d'Iv. 149/D2
Ferlo, Sen., *region* 148/B2
Ferlo, Sen., *river* .148/B2
Fermanagh, N. Ire., U.K., *unitary authority*,
   57,527 . . . . .65/B3
Ferme-Neuve, Que., Can., 2,947 . . . . .226/A5
Fernald, Iowa, U.S., 125 . . . . .274/H3
Fernandina, Ecua., *island* 185/Inset
Fernandina Beach, Fla., U.S., 10,549 . . . . . . .256/G1
Fernando, Minn., U.S., 50 . . . . .298/C6
Fernan Lake Vil., Ida., U.S., 186 . . . . .264/A2
Fern Cave N.W.R., Ala., U.S. 238/C1
Fern Creek, Ky., U.S., 17,870 . . . . .280/B2
Ferndale, Wales, U.K., 17,341 . . . . .64/E4
Ferndale, Ark., U.S., 80 . . . . .244/C3
Ferndale, Calif., U.S., 1,382 . . . . .246/A3
Ferndale, Fla., U.S., 233 . . . . .256/C4
Ferndale, Md., U.S., 16,056 . . . . .288/H3
Ferndale, Mich., U.S., 22,105 . . . . .294/B6
Ferndale, (Cambria County), Penn., U.S., 1,834 .336/D5
Ferndale, (Northumberland County),
   Penn., U.S., 2,411 . . . . .336/H4
Ferndale, Wash., U.S., 8,758 . . . . .358/C1
Ferney, S. Dak., U.S., 50 . . . . .342/G2
Fernham, Eng., U.K. 70/A3
Fernhurst, Eng., U.K. 70/C4
Fernie, Br. Col., Can., 4,611 . . . . .214/P6
Fernlee, Eng., U.K. .68/E6
Fernley, Nev., U.S., 8,543 . . . . .310/A2
Ferntree Gully, Vic., Austl. . . . . .170/Inset V
Fernwood, Fla., U.S., 200 . . . . .264/A2
Fernwood, Miss., U.S., 325 . . . . .300/B4
Fernwood, N.Y., U.S. 320/P4
Fernworthy, Eng., U.K., *reservoir* 73/D3

Ferny Grove, Qnsld., Austl. . . . . .170/Inset III
Ferrara, It. 95/B1
Ferrell, N.J., U.S., 1,100 . . . . .314/C4
Ferrellsburg, W. Va., U.S., 500 . . . . .360/B4
Ferrelview, Mo., U.S., 593 . . . . .302/B2, H4
Ferriday, La., U.S., 3,723 . . . . .282/G3
Ferring, Eng., U.K. 70/D5
Ferris, Ill., U.S., 168 . . . . .266/B3
Ferris, Tex., U.S., 2,175 . . . . .346/M3
Ferrisburg, Vt., U.S., 2,657 . . . . .352/A2
Ferrol, Sp. 94/B1
Ferron, Utah, U.S., 1,623 . . . . .350/C4
Ferrum, Va., U.S., 1,313 . . . . .354/C7
Ferry, Mich., U.S., 250 . . . . .294/C6
Ferry, Wash., U.S., *county*, 7,260 . . . . .358/G1
Ferryden, Scot., U.K., 929 . . . . .62/M5
Ferryhill, Eng., U.K., 11,610 . . . . .66/E3
Ferryland, Nfld., Can., 607 . . . . .218/E5
Ferrysburg, Mich., U.S., 3,040 . . . . .294/C6
Ferryside, Wales, U.K. 64/C4
Ferryville, Wisc., U.S., 174 . . . . .364/B5
Fertile, Iowa, U.S., 360 . . . . .274/H1
Fertile, Minn., U.S., 893 . . . . .298/A3
Fessenden, N. Dak., U.S., 625 . . . . .326/F2
Festus, Mo., U.S., 9,660 . . . . .302/F3
Fetești, Rom. 101/D3
Fethiye, Tur. 133/B3
Fetlar, Scot., U.K., *island* 62/G2
Fetters Hot Sprs., (Fetters Hot Sprs.-Agua Caliente),
   Calif., U.S., 2,505 . . . . .246/J4
Feuilles, Que., U.S., *river* 225/B2
Fewston, Eng., U.K. 66/E5
Feyzabad, Afg., 9,098 . . . . .129/C1
Fez, Mor., 564,000 . . . . .147/C1
Fezzan, Lib., *region* 145/B2
Ffarmers, Wales, U.K. 64/D3
Ffestiniog, Wales, U.K. 64/D2
Ffostrasol, Wales, U.K. 64/C3
Fiag Lodge, Scot., U.K. 62/G2
Fianarantsoa, Madag., 109,248 . . . . .163/B3
Fiche, Mich., U.S. .294/E3
Fichtelberg, Ger., *mountain* 86/C3
Fichtelgebirge, Ger., *mountains* 86/B4
Fidelity, Ill., U.S., 105 . . . . .266/A2
Field, Br. Col., Can. 214/O5
Field, Ont., Can. 223/E1
Field, N. Mex., U.S. 317/G3
Fieldale, Va., U.S., 929 . . . . .354/D7
Fielding, Utah, U.S., 448 . . . . .350/B2
Fieldon, Ill., U.S., 271 . . . . .266/C4
Fields, La., U.S. 282/B5
Fields, Oreg., U.S., 40 . . . . .334/H5
Fieldsboro, N.J., U.S., 522 . . . . .314/D3
Fieldton, Tex., U.S. 346/F1
Fier, Alb., 56,297 . . . . .99/A3
Fiery, N.J., U.S. 317/B5
Fife, Sask., Can., *lake* 227/E11
Fife, Scot., U.K., *unitary authority*, 349,429 . . .62/L6
Fife, Mont., U.S. 306/F2
Fife, Tex., U.S. 346/J4
Fife, Wash., U.S., 4,784 . . . . .358/C2
Fife Lake, Mich., U.S., 466 . . . . .294/D5
Fifield, Eng., U.K. 70/A3
Fifield, Wisc., U.S., 250 . . . . .364/C3
Fifty Lakes, Minn., U.S., 392 . . . . .298/C4
Fifty-Six, Ark., U.S., 163 . . . . .244/C2
Figgs Landing, Md., U.S. 288/N7
Figsboro, Va., U.S., 250 . . . . .354/D7
Fig Tree, St. K.-Nevis 207/C3
Figueira da Foz, Port. 93/A2
Figueres, Sp. 94/H1
Figuig, Mor. 147/D1
Fiji, *nation* 166
Filadelfia, Para. 187/B3
Filchner Ice Shelf, Antar., *glacier* 192/B12
Filer, Ida., U.S., 1,620 . . . . .264/C6
Filey, Eng., U.K., 6,044 . . . . .66/H4
Filfla, Malta, *island* 97/B3
Filion, Mich., U.S., 225 . . . . .294/F6
Filkins, Eng., U.K. 70/A3
Filleigh, Eng., U.K. .73/E2
Filley, Nebr., U.S., 174 . . . . .308/H3
Fillmore, Sask., Can., 246 . . . . .227/C11
Fillmore, Calif., U.S., 13,643 . . . . .246/G8
Fillmore, Ill., U.S., 362 . . . . .266/D4
Fillmore, Ind., U.S., 545 . . . . .270/C5
Fillmore, Minn., U.S., *county*, 21,122 . . . . . . .298/E7
Fillmore, Mo., U.S., 211 . . . . .302/B1
Fillmore, Nebr., U.S., *county*, 6,634 . . . . . . .308/G3
Fillmore, N.Y., U.S., 450 . . . . .320/E6
Fillmore, N. Dak., U.S. 326/F1
Fillmore, Utah, U.S., 2,253 . . . . .350/B5
Fillongley, Eng., U.K. 70/A2
Fimbul Ice Shelf, Antar., *glacier* 192/B14
Fincastle, Ky., U.S., 825 . . . . .280/B1
Fincastle, Va., U.S., 359 . . . . .354/D6
Fincham, Eng., U.K. 70/E2
Finchford, Iowa, U.S., 125 . . . . .274/J2
Finchingfield, Eng., U.K. 70/E3
Finchley, Eng., U.K. 70/D3
Finchville, Ky., U.S., 200 . . . . .280/E2
Findhorn, Scot., U.K., 885 . . . . .62/J3
Findhorn, Scot., U.K., *river* 62/J4
Findlay, Ill., U.S., 723 . . . . .266/E4
Findlay, Ohio, U.S., 38,967 . . . . .328/C4
Findon, Eng., U.K., 1,776 . . . . .70/D5
Fine, N.Y., U.S., 200 . . . . .320/L2
Finedon, Eng., U.K., 4,051 . . . . .68/F4
Finedon, Eng., U.K., 4,051 . . . . .70/C2
Finesville, N.J., U.S., 400 . . . . .314/C2
Fingal, Ire., *county* 78/C2
Fingal, N. Dak., U.S., 133 . . . . .326/H3
Finger, Tenn., U.S., 350 . . . . .344/D4
Finger Lakes Natl. For., N.Y., U.S. 320/H5
Finistère, Fr., *department* 88/B2
Finland, *nation* 79
Finland, *nation* 193/C2
Finland, Est., U.S., *gulf* 81/C1
Finland, Fin., *gulf* .80/D3
Finland, Minn., U.S., 80 . . . . .298/F3
Finlay, Br. Col., Can., *river* 214/J2
Finlayson, Minn., U.S., 314 . . . . .298/E4
Finley, N. Dak., U.S., 515 . . . . .326/H2
Finley, Okla., U.S., 40 . . . . .330/G3
Finley, Wash., U.S., 5,770 . . . . .358/F4
Finley, Wisc., U.S. .364/B5
Finley Pt., Mont., U.S., 493 . . . . .306/B2
Finleyville, Penn., U.S., 459 . . . . .336/A5
Finmere, Eng., U.K. 68/E4
Finn, Ire., *river* 78/C1
Finnegan, Alta., Can. 212/D4
Finney, Kans., U.S., *county*, 40,523 . . . . . . .346/H2
Finney, Tex., U.S. .346/H2
Finningley, Eng., U.K. 66/G6
Finningley, Eng., U.K., 3,624 . . . . .68/F3
Finnmark, Nor., *plateau* 80/E2
Finnmark, Nor., *province* 80/E1
Finstown, Scot., U.K. 62/M2
Fintona, N. Ire., U.K., 1,523 . . . . .65/C3
Fintry, Scot., U.K. 62/H6

Fionn, Scot., U.K., *lake* 62/E3
Fiordland Prov. Rec. Area, Br. Col., Can. 214/H5
Fircrest, Wash., U.S. 358/C2
Firebag, Sask., Can., *river* 227/A3
Firebaugh, Calif., U.S., 5,743 . . . . . . 246/E6
Firebrick, Ky., U.S., 300 . . . . 280/G2
Fireco, W. Va., U.S. 360/D5
Fire Island Natl. Seashore, N.Y., U.S. 320/C2
Fireside, Br. Col., Can. 214/J1
Firesteel, S. Dak., U.S. 342/D2
Firestone, Colo., U.S., 1,908 . . . . . 250/A2, F1
First Colony, Tex., U.S. 346/A7
First Connecticut, N.H., U.S., *lake* 212/D1
First Ladies N.H.S., Ohio, U.S. 250/H3
Firstview, Colo., U.S. 250/H3
Firth, Yukon, Can., *river* 228/A1
Firth, Nebr., U.S., 564 . . . . 308/H3
Firth, Ida., U.S., 408 . . . . 264/E6
Fischer, Tex., U.S., 40 . . . . . . 346/C3, K6
Fish, Nam., *river* 160/C4
Fish, Mich., U.S., *point* 294/F6
Fisher, Ark., U.S., 265 . . . . 244/E2
Fisher, Ill., U.S., 1,647 . . . . 266/E3
Fisher, La., U.S., 268 . . . . 282/C3
Fisher, Minn., U.S., 435 . . . . 298/A3
Fisher, Tex., U.S., *county*, 4,344 . . . . . 346/H3
Fisher Branch, Man., Can. 215/C3
Fishermans Island N.W.R., Va., U.S. 270/D5
Fishers, Ind., U.S., 37,835 . . . . . . 270/D5
Fishers, N.Y., U.S., *island* 320/H1
Fishersville, Va., U.S., 4,998 . . . . . 354/E4
Fisherton, Man., Can. 215/C3
Fisherville, N.Y., U.S., 400 . . . . . . 320/H6
Fishguard, Wales, U.K. 60/B3
Fishguard, Wales, U.K., 2,679 . . . . . . 64/B4
Fish Haven, Ida., U.S. 264/F7
Fishing, Md., U.S., *bay* 288/L6
Fishing Creek, Md., U.S., 300 . . . . . 288/K6
Fishkill, N.Y., U.S., 1,735 . . . . . . 320/P7
Fish Lake Natl. For., Utah, U.S. . . . 350/B4, B5, C5
Fish Sprs. N.W.R., Utah, U.S. 350/A4
Fishtail, Mont., U.S., 60 . . . . 306/G4
Fishtrap, Ky., U.S., *lake* 280/H3
Fisk, Mo., U.S., 363 . . . . 302/F5
Fiskdale, Mass., U.S., 2,156 . . . . . . 292/F4
Fiskeville, R.I., U.S. 339/C3
Fisterra, Sp., *cape* 94/B1
Fitchburg, Mass., U.S., 39,102 . . . . . 292/G2
Fitchburg, Wisc., U.S., 20,501 . . . . . 364/D6
Fitchville, Conn., U.S., 612 . . . . . . 253/G3
Fitchville, Ohio, U.S., 750 . . . . . . 328/F3
Fithian, Ill., U.S., 506 . . . . 266/F3
Fitler, Miss., U.S. 300/A3
Fittleton, Eng., U.K. 73/J2
Fittleworth, Eng., U.K. 70/C5
Fittstown, Okla., U.S., 175 . . . . . . 330/F3
Fitzgerald, Alta., Can. 212/E1
Fitzgerald, Ga., U.S., 8,758 . . . . . . 260/E8
Fitzhugh, Ark., U.S. 244/D2
Fitzhugh, Okla., U.S., 204 . . . . . . 330/F3
Fitzhugh, Va., U.S., 50 . . . . 354/H7
Fitzroy, Arg., *mountain* 191/A6
Fitzroy, Austl., *river* 170/B1
Fitzroy, Chile, *mountain* 190/B7
Fitzwilliam, N.H., U.S., 2,141 . . . . . 212/B6
Fitzwilliam Depot, N.H., U.S., 450 . . . . 212/B6
Five Ashes, Eng., U.K. 70/E4
Five Corners, Mass., U.S., 2,100 . . . . 292/K4
Five Corners, Wash., U.S., 12,207 . . . . 358/C4
Five Islands, N.S., Can. 221/C2
Five Islands, Maine, U.S. 286/C5
Five Mile Fork, Va., U.S. 354/H4
Fivemiletown, N. Ire., U.K., 1,107 . . . . 65/C3
Five Pts., Ala., U.S., 146 . . . . . . 238/D2
Five Pts., N.J., U.S. 314/D5
Five Pts., Tenn., U.S., 175 . . . . . . 344/G4
Fladdabister, Scot., U.K. 62/Q2
Flagler, Colo., U.S., 612 . . . . 250/G2
Flagler, Fla., U.S., *county*, 49,832 . . . 256/G2
Flagler Beach, Fla., U.S., 4,954 . . . . 256/G2
Flagstaff, Ariz., U.S., 52,894, (122,366, *metro.*) . . . 242/D2
Flagstaff, Maine, U.S., *lake* 286/B3
Flagtown, N.J., U.S., 3,000 . . . . . . 314/D2
Flaherty, Ky., U.S., 175 . . . . 280/D3
Flambeau, Wisc., U.S., *river* 364/C3
Flambeau River St. For., Wisc., U.S. . . . 364/C3
Flamborough, Eng., U.K., 1,741 . . . . . 66/H4
Flamborough, Eng., U.K., 1,741 . . . . . 68/G1
Flaming Gorge, Wyo., U.S., *reservoir* . . . 366/B3
Flaming Gorge Natl. Rec. Area, Wyo., U.S. . . . 366/B3
Flamingo, Fla., U.S., 200 . . . . 256/H6
Flanagan, Ill., U.S., 1,083 . . . . . . 266/E3
Flanders, Belg., *region* 85/B1
Flanders, Conn., U.S., 200 . . . . . . 253/B3
Flanders, N.J., U.S., 3,300 . . . . . . 314/D2
Flanders, N.Y., U.S., 3,646 . . . . . . 320/F2
Flandreau, S. Dak., U.S., 2,376 . . . . . 342/J3
Flandreau Ind. Res., S. Dak., U.S. 342/J3
Flanigan, Nev., U.S. 310/A1
Flannan, Scot., U.K., *islands* 62/A2
Flansham, Eng., U.K. 70/C5
Flash, Eng., U.K. 68/D3
Flasher, N. Dak., U.S., 285 . . . . . . 326/D3
Flat, Mauritius, *island* 163/C1
Flat, Alaska, U.S. 202/E4
Flat, Mo., U.S., 90 . . . . 302/E4
Flatbrookville, N.J., U.S. 314/D1
Flatbush, Alta., Can. 212/C4
Flatgap, Ky., U.S., 200 . . . . 280/H3
Flathead, Mont., U.S., *county*, 74,471 . . . 306/B1
Flathead, Mont., U.S., *lake* 306/B2
Flathead, Clark Fork, Mont., U.S., *river* . . . 264/B2
Flathead, N. Fork, Mont., U.S., *river* . . . 264/B2, C1
Flathead, S. Fork, Mont., U.S., *river* . . . 264/C2
Flathead, Mont., U.S., *river* 306/B1
Flathead Ind. Res., Mont., U.S. 306/B2
Flathead, Middle Fork, Mont., U.S., *river* . . . 264/C2
Flathead Natl. For., Mont., U.S. . . . 306/B1, C2
Flat Lick, Ky., U.S., 700 . . . . 280/C4
Flatonia, Tex., U.S., 1,377 . . . . . . 346/L6
Flat Rock, Ala., U.S., 175 . . . . . . 238/D1
Flat Rock, Ill., U.S., 415 . . . . . . 266/F5
Flat Rock, Ind., U.S., 325 . . . . . . 270/E6
Flat Rock, Mich., U.S., 8,488 . . . . . 294/A7, F7
Flat Rock, N.C., U.S., 1,690 . . . . . 322/D1
Flat Rock, Ohio, U.S., 400 . . . . . . 328/E3
Flats, Nebr., U.S. 308/C2
Flattery, Wash., U.S., *cape* 358/A4
Flatwillow, Mont., U.S. 306/H3
Flatwood, Ala., U.S. 238/B3
Flatwoods, Ky., U.S., 7,605 . . . . . . 280/H2
Flatwoods, La., U.S., 125 . . . . 282/D4
Flatwoods, Tenn., U.S. 344/F4
Flatwoods, W. Va., U.S., 348 . . . . . . 360/E3
Flaxcombe, Sask., Can., 128 . . . . . . 227/A9
Flaxton, N. Dak., U.S., 73 . . . . . . 326/C1
Flaxville, Mont., U.S., 87 . . . . . . 306/L1
Fleckney, Eng., U.K., 4,295 . . . . . . 68/E4
Flecknoe, Eng., U.K. 70/B2
Fleet, Alta., Can. 212/E5
Fleet, (Hampshire), Eng., U.K., 30,391 . . . 70/C4
Fleet, (Lincolnshire), Eng., U.K. 70/E1

Fleet, Eng., U.K., 30,391 . . . . 68/H4
Fleetwood, Eng., U.K. 60/C3
Fleetwood, Eng., U.K., 27,227 . . . . . 66/B5
Fleetwood, Eng., U.K., 27,227 . . . . . 68/A2
Fleetwood, Penn., U.S., 4,018 . . . . . 336/K5
Fleischmanns, N.Y., U.S., 351 . . . . . 320/M6
Fleming, Man., Can. 215/A4
Fleming, Colo., U.S., 426 . . . . 250/H1
Fleming, Ky., U.S., *county*, 13,792 . . . 280/G2
Fleming, Mo., U.S., 122 . . . . 302/B2
Fleming-Neon, Ky., U.S., 840 . . . . . . 280/H3
Flemingsburg, Ky., U.S., 3,010 . . . . . 280/G2
Flemington, Ga., U.S., 369 . . . . . . 260/J8
Flemington, Mo., U.S., 124 . . . . . . 302/C4
Flemington, N.J., U.S., 4,200 . . . . . 314/D3
Flemington, Penn., U.S., 1,319 . . . . . 336/G3
Flemington, W. Va., U.S., 287 . . . . . 360/F2
Flemish Brabant, Belg., *province* 85/C2
Flensburg, Ger. 86/B1
Flensburg, Minn., U.S., 244 . . . . . . 298/C5
Flesherton, Ont., Can., 617 . . . . . . 223/E3
Fletcher, Ky., U.S. 280/G3
Fletcher, N.C., U.S., 4,185 . . . . . . 322/E8
Fletcher, Ohio, U.S., 510 . . . . 328/B5
Fletcher, Okla., U.S., 1,022 . . . . . 330/D3
Fletcher, Vt., U.S., 1,179 . . . . . . 352/B1
Fleur de Lys, Nfld., Can., 348 . . . . . 218/C4
Flevoland, Neth., *polder* 84/C2
Flevoland, Neth., *province* 84/C2
Flimby, Eng., U.K., 1,775 . . . . 66/B3
Flimwell, Eng., U.K. 70/E4
Flinders, Austl., *range* 170/C3
Flinders, Austl., *river* 170/D1
Flin Flon, Man., Can., 6,000 . . . . . 215/A2, C2
Flint, Kiri., U.S., *island* 175/D3
Flint, Wales, U.K., 11,737 . . . . . . 64/E1
Flint, Ga., U.S., *river* 260/C6, C9
Flint, Kans., U.S., *hills* 276/F4
Flint, Mich., U.S., 124,943 . . . . . . 294/F6
Flintham, Eng., U.K. 70/C1
Flint Hill, Mo., U.S., 379 . . . . . . 302/F3
Flint Hill, Va., U.S., 200 . . . . . . 354/G3
Flint Hills N.W.R., Kans., U.S. 276/C3
Flintshire, Wales, U.K., *unitary authority*, 148,565 . . . 64/E1
Flintstone, Md., U.S., 275 . . . . . . 288/D3
Flintville, Tenn., U.S., 300 . . . . . 344/J4
Flippen, Ga., U.S. 260/C5, J4
Flippin, Ark., U.S., 1,357 . . . . . . 244/C1
Flitcham, Eng., U.K. 70/F1
Flitwick, Eng., U.K., 11,063 . . . . . 68/F5
Flitwick, Eng., U.K., 11,063 . . . . . 70/D3
Flixborough, Eng., U.K. 66/G5
Flixton, Eng., U.K. 70/G2
Flohrville, Md., U.S., 950 . . . . . . 288/G2
Flom, Minn., U.S., 60 . . . . 298/A3
Flomaton, Ala., U.S., 1,588 . . . . . . 238/B4
Flomot, Tex., U.S. 346/H1
Floodwood, Minn., U.S., 503 . . . . . . 298/E4
Flora, Ill., U.S., 5,086 . . . . 266/E5
Flora, Ind., U.S., 2,227 . . . . 270/C3
Flora, La., U.S. 282/C3
Flora, Miss., U.S., 1,546 . . . . 300/B3
Flora, Oreg., U.S. 334/J2
Flora, Ark., U.S., 125 . . . . 244/D2
Florala, Ala., U.S., 1,964 . . . . . . 238/C4
Floral Park, N.Y., U.S., 15,967 . . . . 320/C2
Floraville, Ill., U.S., 200 . . . . . . 266/A4
Flora Vista, N. Mex., U.S., 1,383 . . . . 317/B1
Florence, Ala., U.S., 36,264, (142,950, *metro.*) . . . 238/B1
Florence, Ariz., U.S., 17,054 . . . . . 242/D4
Florence, Ark., U.S., 60 . . . . 244/D4
Florence, (Florence-Graham), Calif., U.S., 60,197 . . . 246/C10
Florence, Colo., U.S., 3,653 . . . . . 250/E3
Florence, (Pike County), Ill., U.S., 71 . . . 266/C4
Florence, (Stephenson County), Ill., U.S., 125 . . . 266/D1
Florence, Kans., U.S. 276/F3
Florence, Ky., U.S., 23,551 . . . . . . 280/F2, G1
Florence, Minn., U.S., 61 . . . . 298/A6
Florence, Miss., U.S., 2,396 . . . . . 300/B3
Florence, Mo., U.S., 125 . . . . 302/D3
Florence, Mont., U.S., 901 . . . . . . 306/B3
Florence, N.J., U.S., 10,746 . . . . . 314/D3
Florence, N.C., U.S., 175 . . . . 322/M4
Florence, Oreg., U.S., 7,263 . . . . . 334/B4
Florence, S.C., U.S., 30,248, (125,761, *metro.*) . . . 340/E2
Florence, S.C., U.S., *county*, 125,761 . . . 340/E2
Florence, S. Dak., U.S., 299 . . . . . 342/H2
Florence, Tex., U.S., 1,054 . . . . . . 346/L5
Florence, Vt., U.S., 275 . . . . 352/A3
Florence, Wisc., U.S., *county*, 5,088 . . . 364/E3
Florence Jct., Ariz., U.S., 275 . . . . 242/D4
Florence Lake N.W.R., N. Dak., U.S. . . . 326/E2
Florenceville, N.B., Can., 762 . . . . . 217/B2
Florencia, Col., 115,000 . . . . 184/B4
Florenton, Minn., U.S., 125 . . . . . . 298/E3
Flores, Guat. 201/D3
Flores, Indon., *island* 122/D2
Flores, Indon., *sea* 122/C2
Flores, Port., *island* . . . . 93/Inset II
Flores, Uru., *department* 187/B2
Floreşti, Mol. 102/B2
Floresville, Tex., U.S., 5,868 . . . . . 346/K6
Florey, Tex., U.S. 346/F3
Florham Park, N.J., U.S., 8,857 . . . . 314/E2
Floriano, Braz. 188/D2
Florianópolis, Braz., 153,547, (254,944, *metro.*) . . . 188/D4
Florida, Cuba 204/D2
Florida, Cuba, *straits* 204/B1
Florida, P.R. 206/B2
Florida, U.S., *state* 244
Florida, Fla., U.S., *bay* 256/H6
Florida, Fla., U.S., *keys* 256/H7
Florida, Fla., U.S., *straits* 256/H7
Florida, Mass., U.S., 676 . . . . 292/B2
Florida, Mo., U.S. 302/E2
Florida, N.Y., U.S., 2,571 . . . . . . 320/A1
Florida, Ohio, U.S., 246 . . . . 328/B3
Florida, Uru. 187/B3
Florida, Uru., *department* 187/B2
Florida City, Fla., U.S., 7,843 . . . . 256/A7, H6
Florida Panther N.W.R., Fla., U.S. . . . 256/G5
Floridas Turnpike, Fla., U.S. 256/G3
Florien, La., U.S., 692 . . . . 282/C4
Florin, Calif., U.S., 27,653 . . . . . 246/K5
Floris, Iowa, U.S., 153 . . . . 274/H4
Floris, Okla., U.S. 330/B1, D4
Florissant, Colo., U.S., 60 . . . . . . 250/E3
Florissant, Mo., U.S., 50,497 . . . . . 302/H2
Florissant Fossil Beds N.M., Colo., U.S. . . . 250/E3
Florø, Nor. 80/A3
Flossmoor, Ill., U.S., 9,301 . . . . . 266/C6
Flotta, Scot., U.K., *island* 62/M2
Flourtown, Penn., U.S., 4,669 . . . . . 336/L6
Flovilla, Ga., U.S., 652 . . . . 260/D5
Flowell, Utah, U.S., 80 . . . . 350/B5
Floweree, Mont., U.S. 306/E2
Flower Mound, Tex., U.S., 50,702 . . . . 346/B9

Flowery Branch, Ga., U.S., 1,806 . . . . 260/D3
Flowood, Miss., U.S., 4,750 . . . . . . 300/B3
Floyd, Ga., U.S., *county*, 90,565 . . . . 260/A3
Floyd, Ind., U.S., *county*, 70,823 . . . . 270/E8
Floyd, Iowa, U.S., 361 . . . . 274/J1
Floyd, Iowa, U.S., *county*, 16,900 . . . . 274/J2
Floyd, Iowa, U.S., *river* 274/B2
Floyd, Ky., U.S., *county*, 42,441 . . . . 280/H3
Floyd, Tex., U.S., *county*, 7,771 . . . . 346/G1
Floyd, Va., U.S., 432 . . . . 354/C7
Floyd, Va., U.S., *county*, 13,874 . . . . 354/C7
Floydada, Tex., U.S., 3,676 . . . . . . 346/G2
Floydale, S.C., U.S. 340/E2
Fluker, La., U.S., 150 . . . . 282/H5
Flushing, Mich., U.S., 8,348 . . . . . 294/F6
Flushing, Ohio, U.S., 900 . . . . 328/H5
Fluvanna, Tex., U.S., 80 . . . . 346/G3
Fluvanna, Va., U.S., *county*, 20,047 . . . 354/G5
Fly, P.N.G., *river* 172/A2
Flying H, N. Mex., U.S. 317/E4
Flynn, Tex., U.S., 40 . . . . 346/M4
Foa, Bos.-Her. 98/B2
Foam Lake, Sask., Can., 1,218 . . . . . 227/G9
Foard, Tex., U.S., *county*, 1,622 . . . . 346/J2
Foard City, Tex., U.S. 346/J2
Fochabers, Scot., U.K., 1,499 . . . . . 62/K3
Focşani, Rom., 96,930 . . . . 101/D3
Foggia, It. 95/C2
Fogo, Nfld., Can., 803 . . . . 218/D4
Fogo, C.V., *island* 148/B4
Foinaven, Scot., U.K., *hill* 62/G2
Foix, Fr. 88/C5
Folcroft, Penn., U.S., 6,978 . . . . . 336/L7
Foley, Ala., U.S., 7,590 . . . . 238/B5
Foley, Minn., U.S., 2,154 . . . . 298/D5
Foley, Mo., U.S., 178 . . . . 302/F2
Folkestone, Eng., U.K. 60/D3
Folkestone, Eng., U.K. 70/G4
Folkingham, Eng., U.K. 70/D1
Folkston, Ga., U.S., 2,178 . . . . . . 260/G1
Follansbee, W. Va., U.S., 3,115 . . . . 360/K5
Follett, Tex., U.S., 412 . . . . 346/H8
Folletts, Iowa, U.S., 150 . . . . 274/P4
Folly Beach, S.C., U.S., 2,116 . . . . . 340/E4
Folsom, Calif., U.S., 51,884 . . . . . 246/D4, L5
Folsom, Calif., U.S., *lake* 246/L5
Folsom, La., U.S., 525 . . . . 282/J5
Folsom, N.J., U.S., 1,972 . . . . 314/D4
Folsom, N. Mex., U.S., 75 . . . . 317/C1
Folsom, Penn., U.S., 8,072 . . . . . . 336/L7
Folsom, W. Va., U.S., 175 . . . . 360/E2
Fomboni, Com., 5,600 . . . . 163/A2
Fonda, Iowa, U.S., 648 . . . . 274/E2
Fonda, N.Y., U.S., 810 . . . . 320/N5
Fond d'Or, St. Luc., *river* 208/B2
Fond du Lac, Sask., Can., *river* . . . 227/F2
Fond du Lac, Wisc., U.S., 42,203 . . . . 364/E5
Fond du Lac, Wisc., U.S., *county*, 97,296 . . . 364/E5
Fond du Lac Ind. Res., Minn., U.S. . . . 298/E4
Fonde, Ky., U.S., 80 . . . . 280/G4
Fonseca, El. Salv., *gulf* 203/C2
Fonseca, Hond., *gulf* 202/B3
Fonseca, Nicar., *gulf* 202/A2
Fontainebleau, Fr. 88/C2
Fontana, Calif., U.S., 128,929 . . . . . 246/H8
Fontana, Kans., U.S., 149 . . . . 276/H3
Fontana, N.C., U.S., *lake* 322/C8
Fontana, Wisc., U.S., 1,754 . . . . . . 364/E6
Fontana Vil., N.C., U.S., 175 . . . . . 322/C8
Fontanelle, Iowa, U.S., 692 . . . . . . 274/E5
Fontas, Br. Col., Can. 214/M2
Fontenelle, Wyo., U.S. 366/A3
Fontmell Magna, Eng., U.K. 73/H3
Fontvieille, Mon., *district* 97/B2
Fontvieille, Mon., *port* 97/B2
Fontwell, Eng., U.K. 70/C5
Fonuafo'ou, (Falcon) Tonga, *island* . . . 175/B3
Fonualei, Tonga, *island* 175/C2
Foosland, Ill., U.S., 90 . . . . 266/E3
Foothill Farms, Calif., U.S., 17,426 . . . 246/K5
Footville, Wisc., U.S., 788 . . . . . . 364/D6
Forada, Minn., U.S., 197 . . . . 298/B5
Foraker, Okla., U.S. 330/F1
Forbes, Minn., U.S., 50 . . . . 298/E3
Forbes, N. Dak., U.S., 64 . . . . 326/G4
Forbes St. For., Penn., U.S. 336/B6, C5, C6
Forbing, La., U.S., 250 . . . . 282/B2
Forcett, Eng., U.K. 66/E4
Ford, (Gloucester), Eng., U.K. 68/D6
Ford, (Shropshire), Eng., U.K. 68/D1
Ford, Eng., U.K. 66/D1
Ford, Scot., U.K. 62/F6
Ford, Hawaii, U.S., *island* 262/E1
Ford, Ill., U.S., *county*, 14,241 . . . . 266/E3
Ford, Kans., U.S., 314 . . . . 276/C4
Ford, Kans., U.S., *county*, 32,458 . . . . 276/C4
Ford, Wash., U.S., 40 . . . . 358/G2
Ford City, Calif., U.S., 3,512 . . . . . 246/F7
Ford City, Mo., U.S. 302/B1
Ford City, Penn., U.S., 3,451 . . . . . 336/B4
Ford Cliff, Penn., U.S., 412 . . . . . 336/B4
Forden, Wales, U.K. 64/E2
Ford End, Eng., U.K. 70/E2
Fordham, (Cambridgeshire), Eng., U.K., 2,206 . . . 70/E2
Fordham, (Essex), Eng., U.K. 70/F3
Fordland, Mo., U.S., 684 . . . . 302/D4
Fordoche, La., U.S., 933 . . . . 282/F5
Ford River, Mich., U.S., 150 . . . . . 294/B4
Fords, N.J., U.S., 15,032 . . . . 314/E2
Fords Prairie, Wash., U.S., 1,961 . . . . 358/B3
Fordsville, Ky., U.S., 531 . . . . . . 280/D3
Fordtran, Tex., U.S. 346/M6
Fordville, N. Dak., U.S., 266 . . . . . 326/H1
Fordyce, Ark., U.S., 4,799 . . . . . . 244/C4
Fordyce, Nebr., U.S., 182 . . . . 308/G1
Forécariah, Guin. 149/B3
Foreman, Ark., U.S., 1,125 . . . . . . 244/A4
Foremost, Alta., Can., 531 . . . . . . 212/E6
Forepaugh, Ariz., U.S., 60 . . . . . . 242/B4
Forest, Ont., Can., 2,857 . . . . 223/D4
Forest, La., U.S., 275 . . . . 282/E3
Forest, Maine, U.S., 80 . . . . 300/A3
Forest, Miss., U.S., 5,987 . . . . . . 300/C3
Forest, Ohio, U.S., 1,488 . . . . 328/C4
Forest, Penn., U.S., *county*, 4,946 . . . 336/C3
Forest, Va., U.S., 8,006 . . . . 354/E6
Forest, Wisc., U.S. 364/A3
Forest, Wisc., U.S., *county*, 10,024 . . . 364/E3
Forest Acres, S.C., U.S., 10,558 . . . . 340/A3, D2
Forestbrook, S.C., U.S., 3,391 . . . . . 340/F3
Forestburg, Alta., Can., 870 . . . . . 212/D5
Forestburg, S. Dak., U.S., 70 . . . . . 342/G3
Forest Ctr., Minn., U.S. 298/F3
Forest City, Ill., U.S., 287 . . . . . 266/D3
Forest City, Iowa, U.S., 4,362 . . . . . 274/G1

Forest City, Maine, U.S. 286/E3
Forest City, Minn., U.S., 125 . . . . . 298/C5
Forest City, Mo., U.S., 338 . . . . . . 302/A2
Forest City, N.C., U.S., 7,549 . . . . . 322/B4
Forest City, Penn., U.S., 1,855 . . . . 336/L2
Forestdale, Ala., U.S., 10,509 . . . . . 238/E1
Forestdale, Mass., U.S., 3,992 . . . . . 292/N6
Forest Dale, Vt., U.S., 800 . . . . . . 352/A3
Forest Glen, Calif., U.S. 246/B2
Forest Green, Eng., U.K. 70/D4
Forest Grove, Penn., U.S., 3,800 . . . . 336/C7
Forest Hts., Md., U.S., 2,585 . . . . . 288/B7
Forest Hill, La., U.S., 456 . . . . . . 282/D4
Forest Hill, Tex., U.S., 12,949 . . . . 346/B10
Forest Hills, Ky., U.S., 494 . . . . . 280/B2
Forest Hills, Mich., U.S., 20,942 . . . . 294/D7
Forest Hills, Penn., U.S., 6,831 . . . . 336/E7
Forest Hills, Tenn., U.S., 4,710 . . . . 344/H2
Forest Home, Ala., U.S. 238/C4
Forest Home, N.Y., U.S., 941 . . . . . 320/J6
Forest Knoll, Calif., U.S., 1,835 . . . . 246/C4
Forest Lake, Ill., U.S., 1,530 . . . . . 266/B5
Forest Lake, Md., U.S. 294/C3
Forest Lake, Minn., U.S., 6,798 . . . . 298/E5
Forest Lakes, Ariz., U.S., 90 . . . . . 242/E3
Forest Oaks, N.C., U.S., 3,241 . . . . . 322/F3
Foreston, Minn., U.S., 389 . . . . . . 298/D5
Foreston, S.C., U.S., 100 . . . . 340/D3
Forest Park, Ga., U.S., 21,447 . . . . . 260/C4, H3
Forest Park, Ill., U.S., 15,688 . . . . 266/B6
Forest Park, Ohio, U.S., 19,463 . . . . 328/A7, B9
Forest Park, Okla., U.S., 1,066 . . . . 330/B4, E2
Forest River, N. Dak., U.S., 154 . . . . 326/H1
Forest Row, Eng., U.K., 3,508 . . . . . 70/E4
Forest View, Ill., U.S., 778 . . . . . 266/B6
Forestville, Que., Can., 3,748 . . . . . 225/D4
Forestville, Md., U.S., 12,707 . . . . . 288/C7
Forestville, Mich., U.S., 127 . . . . . 294/G6
Forestville, N.Y., U.S., 770 . . . . . 320/C6
Forestville, Ohio, U.S., 10,978 . . . . 328/B10
Forestville, Wisc., U.S., 429 . . . . . 364/F4
Forfar, Scot., U.K., 13,206 . . . . . . 62/L5
Forgan, Okla., U.S., 532 . . . . 330/B1, D4
Forge Vil., Mass., U.S., 2,300 . . . . . 292/H2
Forillon Natl. Park, Que., Can. 225/D4
Forillon Natl. Park, Que., Can. 226/M3
Forked Island, La., U.S., 325 . . . . . 282/E7
Forked River, N.J., U.S., 4,914 . . . . 314/E4
Forkhill, N. Ire., U.K., 343 . . . . . 65/C3
Forkland, Ala., U.S., 629 . . . . 238/B3
Fork Mtn., Tenn., U.S. 344/N2
Fork River, Man., Can. 215/A3
Forks, Wash., U.S., 3,120 . . . . 358/A2
Forks of Cacapon, W. Va., U.S., 90 . . . 360/K2
Forks of Salmon, Calif., U.S. 246/B1
Forksville, Penn., U.S., 147 . . . . . 336/H2
Fork Union, Va., U.S., 275 . . . . . . 354/G5
Forkville, Miss., U.S. 300/C3
Forlì, It. 95/C1
Forman, N. Dak., U.S., 506 . . . . . . 326/H3
Formby, Eng., U.K., 25,356 . . . . . . 66/B5
Formby, Eng., U.K., 25,356 . . . . . . 68/A2
Formentera, Sp., *island* 94/C3
Formosa, Arg., 147,636 . . . . 191/D2
Formosa, Arg., *province* 191/D1
Formosa, Ark., U.S., 150 . . . . 244/C2
Formoso, Kans., U.S., 129 . . . . 276/E2
Forney, Ala., U.S. 238/D1
Forney, Tex., U.S., 5,588 . . . . 346/D9
Foros, Ukr. 102/C4
Forres, Scot., U.K., 8,967 . . . . . . 62/J3
Forrest, Ill., U.S., 1,225 . . . . . . 266/E3
Forrest, Miss., U.S., *county*, 72,604 . . . 300/C4
Forrest, N. Mex., U.S. 317/G3
Forrest City, Ark., U.S., 14,774 . . . . 244/D2
Forreston, Ill., U.S., 1,469 . . . . . 266/D1
Forsan, Tex., U.S., 226 . . . . 346/G3
Forsinard, Scot., U.K. 62/J2
Forsyth, Ga., U.S., 3,776 . . . . 260/C5
Forsyth, Ga., U.S., *county*, 98,407 . . . 260/C3, J1
Forsyth, Ill., U.S., 2,434 . . . . . . 266/E4
Forsyth, Mo., U.S., 1,686 . . . . 302/C5
Forsyth, Mont., U.S., 1,944 . . . . . . 306/K3
Forsyth, N.C., U.S., *county*, 306,067 . . . 322/E2
Ft. Adams, Miss., U.S. 300/A4
Ft. Albany, Ont., Can. 222/D2
Fortaleza, Braz., 2,138,234, (2,974,919, *metro.*) . . . 188/E2
Ft. Ann, N.Y., U.S., 471 . . . . 320/Q4
Ft. Anne Natl. Hist. Park, N.S., Can. . . . 221/B3
Ft. Apache, Ariz., U.S., 100 . . . . . 242/F4
Ft. Apache Ind. Res., Ariz., U.S. 242/E3
Ft. A.P. Hill Mil. Res., Va., U.S. 354/J4
Ft. Ashby, W. Va., U.S., 1,354 . . . . . 360/J2
Ft. Assiniboine, Alta., Can. 212/C4
Ft. Atkinson, Iowa, U.S., 389 . . . . . 274/L1
Ft. Atkinson, Wisc., U.S., 11,621 . . . . 364/E6
Ft. Augustus, Scot., U.K., 508 . . . . . 62/G4
Ft. Barnwell, N.C., U.S., 250 . . . . . 322/L4
Ft. Basinger, Fla., U.S. 256/G4
Ft. Battleford N.H.S., Sask., Can. . . . 227/B8
Ft. Belknap Agency, Mont., U.S., 1,262 . . . 306/H1
Ft. Belknap Indian Res., Mont., U.S. . . . 306/H1
Ft. Belvoir Mil. Res., Va., U.S. 354/J3, M2
Ft. Bend, Tex., U.S., *county*, 354,452 . . . 346/A7, N6
Ft. Benning Mil. Res., Ga., U.S. 260/B7
Ft. Benton, Mont., U.S., 1,594 . . . . . 306/F2
Ft. Berthold Ind. Res., N. Dak., U.S. . . . 326/C2
Ft. Bidwell, Calif., U.S., 80 . . . . . 246/E1
Ft. Bidwell Ind. Res., Calif., U.S. . . . 246/E1
Ft. Blackmore, Va., U.S., 80 . . . . . 354/C2
Ft. Bliss, Tex., U.S., 8,264 . . . . . 346/B4
Ft. Bliss Mil. Res., N. Mex., U.S. 317/D5
Ft. Bowie N.H.S., Ariz., U.S. 242/F5
Ft. Bragg, Calif., U.S., 7,026 . . . . . 246/B3
Ft. Bragg, N.C., U.S., 29,183 . . . . . 322/H4
Ft. Bragg Mil. Res., N.C., U.S. 322/G4
Ft. Bragg Mil. Res., S.C., U.S. 340/E1
Ft. Branch, Ind., U.S., 2,320 . . . . . 270/A8
Ft. Bridger, Wyo., U.S., 400 . . . . . 366/A3
Ft. Calhoun, Nebr., U.S., 856 . . . . . 308/H2
Ft. Caroline Natl. Mem., Fla., U.S. . . . 256/G1
Ft. Carson Mil. Res., Colo., U.S. 250/F3, G4
Ft. Chaffee Maneuver Train. Ctr., Ark., U.S. . . . 244/A2
Ft. Chipewyan, Alta., Can., 902 . . . . 212/E2
Ft. Clark, N. Dak., U.S. 326/D2
Ft. Clatsop Natl. Mem., Oreg., U.S. . . . 334/C1
Ft. Cobb, Okla., U.S., 657 . . . . . . 330/D2
Ft. Collins, Colo., U.S., 118,652, (251,494, *metro.*) . . . 250/E1
Ft. Covington, N.Y., U.S., 700 . . . . . 320/N1
Ft. Davis, Ala., U.S., 80 . . . . 238/D3
Ft. Davis, Tex., U.S., 1,050 . . . . . 346/E5
Ft. Davis Natl. Hist. Site, Tex., U.S. . . . 346/E5
Ft. Defiance, Ariz., U.S., 4,061 . . . . 242/F2
Fort-de-France, Mart., *capital* 204/F4
Ft. Delaware St. Park, Del., U.S. 255/B2
Ft. Deposit, Ala., U.S., 1,270 . . . . . 238/C4
Ft. Dick, Calif., U.S., 300 . . . . . . 246/A1
Ft. Dodge, Iowa, U.S., 25,136 . . . . . 274/F2
Ft. Dodge, Kans., U.S., 550 . . . . . . 276/C4

Ft. Donelson Natl. Bfld., Tenn., U.S. 344/F1
Ft. Douglas, Ark., U.S. .244/B2
Ft. Drum, Fla., U.S., 150 . . . . .256/H4
Ft. Drum Mil. Res., N.Y., U.S. 320/K2
Ft. Duchesne, Utah, U.S., 621 . . . . .350/E3
Forteau, Nfld., Can., 477 . . . . .218/C3
Ft. Edward, N.Y., U.S., 3,141 . . . . .320/P4
Ft. Erie, Ont., Can., 28,143 . . . . .223/G5
Fortescue, Mo., U.S., 51 . . . . .302/A1
Fortescue, N.J., U.S., 225 . . . . .314/C5
Ft. Eustis Mil. Res., Va., U.S. 354/K6
Forteviot, Scot., U.K. 62/K6
Ft. Fairfield, Maine, U.S., 3,579 . . . . .286/E2
Ft. Foote Vil., (Ft. Washington), Md., U.S. 288/F5
Ft. Frances, Ont., Can., 8,315 . . . . .222/B3
Ft. Fraser, Br. Col., Can., 308 . . . . .214/K4
Ft. Frederica N.M., U.S. 260/J9
Ft. Gaines, Ga., U.S., 1,110 . . . . .260/A8
Ft. Garland, Colo., U.S., 432 . . . . .250/E4
Ft. Gay, W. Va., U.S., 819 . . . . .360/A4
Ft. George, Scot., U.K. .62/H3
Ft. Gibson, Okla., U.S., 4,054 . . . . .330/G2
Ft. Gibson, Okla., U.S., lake 330/G1
Ft. Good Hope, N.W. Terr., Can., 549 . . . . .220/C3
Ft. Grant, Ariz., U.S., 800 . . . . .242/F5
Ft. Green, Fla., U.S., 40 . . . . .256/G4
Ft. Griffin, Tex., U.S. 346/J3
Forth, Scot., U.K., estuary 60/C2
Forth, Scot., U.K., estuary 62/L6
Forth, Scot., U.K., river 60/B2
Ft. Hall, Ida., U.S., 3,193 . . . . .264/E6
Ft. Hall Ind. Res., Ida., U.S. 264/E6, E7
Ft. Hancock, Tex., U.S., 1,713 . . . . .346/C4
Ft. Hood, Tex., U.S., 33,711 . . . . .346/L4
Ft. Hood Mil. Res., Tex., U.S. 346/L4
Ft. Huachuca Mil. Res., Ariz., U.S. 242/E6
Fortín Conde de Mirasol, (fort), P.R. 206/E2
Fortine, Mont., U.S., 169 . . . . .306/B1
Fortingall, Scot., U.K. .62/H5
Fortín Ravelo, Bol. 186/B3
Ft. Irwin Natl. Training Ctr., Calif., U.S. 246/J7
Ft. Jackson Mil. Res., S.C., U.S. 340/A3, D2
Ft. Jefferson, Fla., U.S. 256/F7
Ft. Jennings, Ohio, U.S., 432 . . . . .328/B4
Ft. Jesup, La., U.S., 200 . . . . .282/C3
Ft. Johnson, N.Y., U.S., 491 . . . . .320/N5
Ft. Jones, Calif., U.S., 660 . . . . .246/C1
Ft. Kent, Maine, U.S., 4,233 . . . . .286/D1
Ft. Kent Mills, Maine, U.S., 325 . . . . .286/D1
Ft. Klamath, Oreg., U.S., 80 . . . . .334/E5
Ft. Knox Mil. Res., Ky., U.S. 280/E3
Ft. Landing, N.C., U.S., 40 . . . . .322/N3
Ft. Laramie, Wyo., U.S., 243 . . . . .366/D2
Ft. Laramie Natl. Hist. Site, Wyo., U.S. 366/D2
Ft. Larned N.H.S., Kans., U.S. 276/C3
Ft. Lauderdale, Fla., U.S., 152,397 . . . . . .256/B6, H5
Ft. Lawn, S.C., U.S., 864 . . . . .340/D2
Ft. Leavenworth Mil. Res., Kans., U.S. 276/H2
Ft. Lee, N.J., U.S., 35,461 . . . . .314/C2, F2
Ft. Leonard Wood Mil. Res., Mo., U.S. 302/D4
Ft. Lewis, Wash., U.S., 19,089 . . . . .358/C2
Ft. Lewis Mil. Res., Wash., U.S. 358/C2
Ft. Liard, N.W. Terr., Can., 530 . . . . .220/D4
Ft. Loramie, Ohio, U.S., 1,344 . . . . .328/B5
Ft. Loudon, Penn., U.S., 500 . . . . .336/F6
Ft. Lupton, Colo., U.S., 6,787 . . . . .250/A2, F1
Ft. MacKay, Alta., Can., 437 . . . . .212/E2
Ft. Macleod, Alta., Can., 2,990 . . . . .212/D6
Ft. Madison, Iowa, U.S., 10,715 . . . . .274/M6
Ft. Matanzas N.M., Fla., U.S. 256/G2
Ft. McCoy Mil. Res., Wisc., U.S. 364/C4
Ft. McDermitt Ind. Res., Nev., U.S. 310/A1, B1
Ft. McDermitt Ind. Res., Oreg., U.S. 334/H6, J5
Ft. McDowell Ind. Res., Ariz., U.S. 242/D4
Ft. McHenry N.M., Md., U.S. 288/H2
Ft. McKavett, Tex., U.S. 346/H5
Ft. McKinley, Ohio, U.S., 3,989 . . . . .328/F1
Ft. McMurray, Alta., Can., 38,667 . . . . .212/E3
Ft. McPherson, N.W. Terr., Can., 761 . . . . .220/B3
Ft. Meade, Fla., U.S., 5,691 . . . . .256/G4
Ft. Mill, S.C., U.S., 7,587 . . . . .340/D1
Ft. Mitchell, Ala., U.S., 200 . . . . .238/D3
Ft. Mitchell, Ky., U.S., 8,089 . . . . .280/F1, G1
Ft. Mitchell, Va., U.S., 80 . . . . .354/G7
Ft. Mohave Ind. Res., Ariz., U.S. 242/A3
Ft. Morgan, Ala., U.S., 350 . . . . .238/A5
Ft. Morgan, Colo., U.S., 11,034 . . . . .250/G1
Ft. Motte, S.C., U.S., 100 . . . . .340/D3
Ft. Myers, Fla., U.S., 48,208, (440,888, metro.) .256/G5
Ft. Myers Beach, Fla., U.S., 6,561 . . . . .256/G5
Ft. Myers Villas, (Villas), Fla., U.S., 11,346 . . . .256/G5
Ft. Necessity Natl. Bfld., Penn., U.S. 336/B6
Ft. Nelson, Br. Col., Can., 4,188 . . . . .214/L2
Ft. Nelson, Br. Col., Can., river 212/A1
Ft. Nelson, Br. Col., Can., river 214/L1
Ft. Niobrara N.W.R., Nebr., U.S. 308/D1
Ft. Niobrara N.W.R., S. Dak., U.S. 342/E5
Ft. Ogden, Fla., U.S., 225 . . . . .256/G4
Ft. Oglethorpe, Ga., U.S., 6,940 . . . . .260/A2
Ft. Payne, Ala., U.S., 12,938 . . . . .238/D1
Ft. Peck, Mont., U.S., 240 . . . . .306/K2
Ft. Peck, Mont., U.S., lake 306/K2
Ft. Peck Indian Res., Mont., U.S. 306/K2
Ft. Pickett Mil. Res., Va., U.S. 354/H6
Ft. Pierce, Fla., U.S., 37,516, (319,426, metro.) .256/H4
Ft. Pierre, S. Dak., U.S., 1,991 . . . . .342/E3
Ft. Pierre Natl. Grassland, S. Dak., U.S. 342/E3
Ft. Pillow, Tenn., U.S., 650 . . . . .344/B3
Ft. Plain, N.Y., U.S., 2,288 . . . . .320/M5
Ft. Polk Mil. Res., La., U.S. 282/C4
Ft. Portal, Ug., 40,605 . . . . .157/B3
Ft. Providence, N.W. Terr., Can., 753 . . . . .220/E4
Ft. Pulaski N.M., Ga., U.S. 260/K7
Ft. Qu'Appelle, Sask., Can., 1,940 . . . . . . .227/G10
Ft. Raleigh Natl. Hist. Site, N.C., U.S. 322/P3
Ft. Ransom, N. Dak., U.S., 79 . . . . .326/H3
Ft. Recovery, Ohio, U.S., 1,273 . . . . .328/A5
Ft. Resolution, N.W. Terr., Can. 220/F4
Fortress of Louisbourg N.H.P., N.S., Can. 221/H2
Ft. Rice, N. Dak., U.S. .326/E3
Ft. Riley Mil. Res., Kans., U.S. 276/F2
Ft. Ripley, Minn., U.S., 74 . . . . .298/C4
Ft. Robinson, Nebr., U.S. 308/A1
Ft. Rock, Oreg., U.S. 334/E4
Fortrose, (Fortrose and Rosemarkie), Scot., U.K.,
  1,174 . . . . .62/H3
Ft. Rucker Mil. Res., Ala., U.S. 238/D4
Ft. St. James, Br. Col., Can., 1,927 . . . . .214/K4
Ft. St. John, Br. Col., Can., 16,034 . . . . .214/M3
Ft. Saskatchewan, Alta., Can., 13,121 . . . . .212/D4
Ft. Scott, Kans., U.S., 8,297 . . . . .276/H4
Ft. Scott N.H.S., Kans., U.S. 276/H4
Ft. Severn, Ont., Can. .222/C1
Ft. Shafter Mil. Res., Hawaii, U.S. 262/F1
Ft. Shaw, Mont., U.S., 274 . . . . .306/E2
Ft. Shawnee, Ohio, U.S., 3,855 . . . . .328/B4
Ft. Sill, Okla., U.S. 330/D3
Ft. Sill Mil. Res., Okla., U.S. 330/D3
Ft. Simpson, N.W. Terr., Can., 1,163 . . . . .220/D4
Ft. Smith, N.W. Terr., Can., 2,185 . . . . .220/F4
Ft. Smith, Ark., U.S., 80,268, (207,290, metro.) .244/A2
Ft. Smith, Mont., U.S., 122 . . . . .306/J4

Ft. Smith Natl. Hist. Site, Ark., U.S. 244/A2
Fortsonia, Ga., U.S., 125 . . . . .260/F3
Ft. Stanton, N. Mex., U.S., 150 . . . . .317/E4
Ft. Stanwix Natl. Mon., N.Y., U.S. 320/L4
Ft. Steele, Br. Col., Can. 214/P6
Ft. Steele, Wyo., U.S. .366/C3
Ft. Stewart Mil. Res., Ga., U.S. 260/H7
Ft. Stockton, Tex., U.S., 7,846 . . . . .346/F5
Ft. Sumner, N. Mex., U.S., 1,249 . . . . .317/F3
Ft. Sumter Natl. Mon., S.C., U.S. 342/F4
Ft. Supply, Okla., U.S., 328 . . . . .330/C1
Ft. Thomas, Ariz., U.S., 125 . . . . .242/F4
Ft. Thomas, Ky., U.S., 16,495 . . . . .280/F1, G1
Ft. Thompson, S. Dak., U.S., 1,375 . . . . .342/F3
Ft. Totten, N. Dak., U.S., 952 . . . . .326/F2
Ft. Towson, Okla., U.S., 611 . . . . .330/G3
Fortuna, Calif., U.S., 10,497 . . . . .246/A2
Fortuna, Mo., U.S., 225 . . . . .302/D3
Fortuna, N. Dak., U.S. .326/B1
Fortuna Foothills, Ariz., U.S. 242/A5
Fortune, Nfld., Can., 1,615 . . . . .218/D5
Fortune, Nfld., Can., bay 218/D5
Fortune Bridge, P.E.I., Can. 224/C2
Fortuneswell, Eng., U.K., 4,584 . . . . .73/H3
Ft. Union N.M., N. Mex., U.S. 317/F2
Ft. Union Trading Post Natl. Hist. Site,
  N. Dak., U.S. 326/A2
Ft. Union Trading Post N.H.S., N. Dak., U.S. . . .306/M2
Ft. Valley, Ga., U.S., 8,005 . . . . .260/D6
Ft. Vancouver N.H.S., Wash., U.S. 334/A2
Ft. Vermilion, Alta., Can., 818 . . . . .212/C2
Fortville, Ind., U.S., 3,444 . . . . .270/E5
Ft. Walsh N.H.S., Sask., Can. 227/A11
Ft. Walton Beach, Fla., U.S., 19,973,
  (170,498, metro.) 256/B1
Ft. Washakie, Wyo., U.S., 1,477 . . . . .366/B2
Ft. Washington, Penn., U.S., 3,680 . . . . .336/L6
Ft. Washington Forest, Md., U.S. 288/G5
Ft. Wayne, Ind., U.S., 205,727, (502,141, metro.) 270/F2
Ft. White, Fla., U.S., 409 . . . . .256/F2
Ft. William, Scot., U.K. .60/B2
Ft. William, Scot., U.K., 9,908 . . . . .62/F5
Ft. Wingate, N. Mex., U.S., 550 . . . . .317/B2
Ft. Worth, Tex., U.S., 534,694 . . . . .346/A9, L3
Ft. Wright, Ky., U.S., 5,681 . . . . .280/F1, G1
Ft. Yates, N. Dak., U.S., 228 . . . . .326/E3
Forty Fort, Penn., U.S., 4,579 . . . . .336/G7
Ft. Yukon, Alaska, U.S., 595 . . . . .240/F1
Fosdyke, Eng., U.K. 70/D1
Foss, Okla., U.S., 127 .330/C2
Fossebridge, Eng., U.K. 68/D6
Fossil, Oreg., U.S., 469 . . . . .334/F3
Fossil, Oreg., U.S., lake 334/F4
Fossil Butte Natl. Mon., Wyo., U.S. 366/A3
Fosston, Minn., U.S., 1,575 . . . . .298/B3
Fossum, Minn., U.S. 298/A3
Foster, Sask., Can., river 227/E4
Foster, Ind., U.S., 125 .270/B4
Foster, Ky., U.S., 70 . . . . .280/F2
Foster, Mo., U.S., 130 .302/B3
Foster, Mont., U.S. 306/J4
Foster, Nebr., U.S., 63 .308/G1
Foster, N. Dak., U.S., county, 3,759 . . . . .326/G2
Foster, Ohio, U.S. 328/C9
Foster, Okla., U.S., 50 .330/E3
Foster, Oreg., U.S., 175 . . . . .334/D3
Foster, Tex., U.S. 346/F2
Foster, Wisc., U.S., 125 . . . . .364/B4
Foster Ctr., R.I., U.S., 500 . . . . .339/B3
Foster City, Calif., U.S., 28,803 . . . . .246/J2
Foster City, Mich., U.S., 60 . . . . .294/B4
Foster Vil., Hawaii, U.S. 262/F1, J2
Fosterville, N.B., Can. .217/B3
Fostoria, Iowa, U.S., 230 . . . . .274/B4
Fostoria, Kans., U.S., 800 . . . . .276/F2
Fostoria, Mich., U.S., 600 . . . . .294/F6
Fostoria, Ohio, U.S., 13,931 . . . . .328/D3
Fouke, Ark., U.S., 814 .244/B4
Foula, Scot., U.K., island 62/N2
Foulness, Eng., U.K., island 70/F3
Foulridge, Eng., U.K. 66/D5
Foumban, Came. 153/B2
Foumbouni, Com. 163/A1
Fount, Ky., U.S. 280/G4
Fountain, Ala., U.S., 50 . . . . .238/B4
Fountain, Colo., U.S., 15,197 . . . . .250/F3
Fountain, Fla., U.S., 225 . . . . .256/C1
Fountain, Ind., U.S., county, 17,954 . . . . .270/B4
Fountain, Mich., U.S., 175 . . . . .294/C5
Fountain, Minn., U.S., 343 . . . . .298/F7
Fountain, (Duplin County), N.C., U.S. 322/K5
Fountain, (Pitt County), N.C., U.S., 533 . . . . . . .322/K3
Fountain City, Ind., U.S., 735 . . . . .270/G5
Fountain City, Wisc., U.S., 983 . . . . .364/B4
Fountain Green, Utah, U.S., 945 . . . . .350/C4
Fountainhall, Scot., U.K. 62/L7
Fountain Head, (Long Meadow), Md., U.S. 288/D1
Fountain Hill, Ark., U.S., 159 . . . . .244/D4
Fountain Hill, Penn., U.S., 4,614 . . . . .336/L4
Fountain Hills, Ariz., U.S., 20,235 . . . . .242/D4
Fountain Inn, S.C., U.S., 6,017 . . . . .340/B2
Fountain Run, Ky., U.S., 236 . . . . .280/E4
Fountain Valley, Calif., U.S., 54,978 . . . . .246/D11
Four Bears Vil., N. Dak., U.S., 364 . . . . .326/C2
Four Buttes, Mont., U.S. 306/L1
Fourche, Ark., U.S., 59 . . . . .244/C3
Four Corners, Calif., U.S. 246/H8
Four Corners, Oreg., U.S., 13,922 . . . . .334/D3
Four Corners, Wyo., U.S. 366/D1
Four Crosses, Wales, U.K. 64/E2
Four Falls, N.B., U.S. 217/B2
Four Lakes, Wash., U.S., 400 . . . . .358/H2
Four Mile, N.J., U.S., 900 . . . . .314/D5
Four Oaks, Eng., U.K. .70/F5
Four Oaks, N.C., U.S., 1,424 . . . . .322/J4
Four States, W. Va., U.S. 360/F2
Fourteen Mile, Mich., U.S., point 294/A2
Fourtown, Minn., U.S. .298/B2
Fouta Djallon, Guin., plateau 149/B2
Fovant, Eng., U.K. 73/H2
Foveaux, N.Z., strait 171/A4
Fowey, Eng., U.K., 1,939 . . . . .73/C4
Fowlblesburg, Md., U.S., 600 . . . . .288/G1
Fowler, Calif., U.S., 3,979 . . . . .246/F6
Fowler, Colo., U.S., 1,206 . . . . .250/F3
Fowler, Ind., U.S., 2,415 . . . . .270/B3
Fowler, Kans., U.S., 567 . . . . .276/B4
Fowler, Mich., U.S., 1,136 . . . . .294/E6
Fowler, N.Y., U.S., 300 . . . . .320/L2
Fowlerton, Ind., U.S., 298 . . . . .270/E4
Fowlerton, Tex., U.S., 62 . . . . .346/K7
Fowlerville, Mich., U.S., 2,972 . . . . .294/E7
Fowlis Wester, Scot., U.K. 62/J6
Fowlkes, Tenn., U.S., 60 . . . . .344/C3
Fowlstown, Ga., U.S., 275 . . . . .260/B9
Fox, Ill., U.S., river 266/A5, E2
Fox, Iowa, U.S., river 274/K6
Fox, Minn., U.S., 125 . . . . .298/B2
Fox, Mo., U.S., river 302/E1
Fox, Okla., U.S., 225 . . . . .330/E3

Fox, Oreg., U.S. 334/G3
Fox, Wisc., U.S., river .364/D5
Foxboro, Mass., U.S., 16,246 . . . . .292/K4
Foxboro, Wisc., U.S. 364/A2
Foxburg, Penn., U.S., 275 . . . . .336/B3
Fox Chapel, Penn., U.S., 5,436 . . . . .336/B4
Fox Chase, Ky., U.S., 476 . . . . .280/E2
Fox Creek, Alta., Can., 2,337 . . . . .212/B4
Fox Creek, Colo., U.S. .250/A4
Fox Creek, Ky., U.S., 100 . . . . .280/F3
Foxe, Nun., Can., basin 220/N3
Foxe, Nun., Can., channel 220/M3
Foxe, Nun., Can., peninsula 220/N4
Fox Farm-College, Wyo., U.S., 3,272 . . . . .366/D3
Foxfield, Colo., U.S., 746 . . . . .250/A3
Foxfire, N.C., U.S., 474 . . . . .322/H4
Foxholes, Eng., U.K. 66/H4
Foxhome, Minn., U.S., 143 . . . . .298/A4
Fox Island, N.S., Can. .221/F2
Fox Island, Wash., U.S., 2,803 . . . . .358/C2
Fox Lake, Alta., Can. 212/C2
Fox Lake, Ill., U.S., 9,178 . . . . .266/A4, E1
Fox Lake, Wisc., U.S., 1,454 . . . . .364/E5
Fox Lake Hills, Ill., U.S., 2,561 . . . . .266/A4
Foxpark, Wyo., U.S., 50 . . . . .366/C3
Fox Pt., Wisc., U.S., 7,012 . . . . .364/F2
Fox River Grove, Ill., U.S., 4,862 . . . . .266/A5
Fox River Valley Gardens, Ill., U.S., 788 . . . . . . .266/A5
Foxton, Colo., U.S., 70 .250/E2
Fox Valley, Sask., Can., 326 . . . . .227/A10
Foxworth, Miss., U.S., 500 . . . . .300/C4
Foyers, Scot., U.K. 62/G3
Foyil, Okla., U.S., 234 .330/G1
Foyle, Ire., inlet 78/C1
Foyle, N. Ire., U.K., lake 60/A2
Foyle, N. Ire., U.K., lake 65/C1
Foz, Braz., river 188/C1
Foz do Iguaçu, Braz., 93,619, (188,190, metro.) .188/C4
Frýdek-Místek, Czh. Rep. 92/D3
Frackville, Penn., U.S., 4,361 . . . . .336/H4
Framcesville, Ind., U.S., 905 . . . . .270/C3
Framingham, Mass., U.S., 66,910 . . . . .292/J3
Framlingham, Eng., U.K., 2,697 . . . . .70/G2
Frampton, Eng., U.K. 73/G3
France, nation 86
Frances, Yukon, Can., lake 228/D3
Frances, Ky., U.S., 125 . . . . .280/B3
Frances, Wash., U.S., 70 . . . . .358/B3
Francestown, N.H., U.S., 1,480 . . . . .212/C6
Franceville, Gabon, 30,541 . . . . .155/B2
Franche-Comté, Fr., region 88/D3
Francis, Sask., Can., 172 . . . . .227/G10
Francis, Mont., U.S. 306/F3
Francis, Okla., U.S., 332 . . . . .330/F3
Francis, Utah, U.S., 698 . . . . .350/C3
Francis Case, S. Dak., U.S., lake 342/G4
Francisco, Ind., U.S., 543 . . . . .270/B8
Francisco Morazán, Hond., department 202/B2
Francis Creek, Wisc., U.S., 681 . . . . .364/F4
Francis Marion Natl. For., S.C., U.S. 340/E3
Francistown, Bots., 92,516 . . . . .160/B2
François, Br. Col., Can., lake 214/K4
François, Nfld., Can., 162 . . . . .218/C5
Franconia, N.H., U.S., 924 . . . . .212/C5
Franconia, W. Va., U.S., 31,907 . . . . .354/M2
Franconian Jura, Ger., mountains 86/B4
Franconia Notch, N.H., U.S., pass 212/C3
Francs, Wyo., U.S., peak 366/B2
Frankenmuth, Mich., U.S., 4,838 . . . . .294/F6
Frankenwald, Ger., mountains 86/B3
Frankewing, Tenn., U.S., 80 . . . . .344/H4
Frankford, Ont., Can., 2,487 . . . . .223/H3
Frankford, Del., U.S., 714 . . . . .255/D6
Frankford, Mo., U.S., 351 . . . . .302/E2
Frankford, W. Va., U.S., 100 . . . . .360/F5
Frankfort, Ill., U.S., 10,391 . . . . .266/B6, F2
Frankfort, Ind., U.S., 16,662 . . . . .270/C4
Frankfort, Kans., U.S., 855 . . . . .276/F2
Frankfort, Ky., U.S., state capital, 27,741 . . . . . .280/E2
Frankfort, Maine, U.S., 1,041 . . . . .286/D4
Frankfort, Mich., U.S., 1,513 . . . . .294/C5
Frankfort, N.Y., U.S., 2,537 . . . . .320/L4
Frankfort, Ohio, U.S., 1,011 . . . . .328/D7
Frankfort, S. Dak., U.S., 166 . . . . .342/G3
Frankfort Sprs., Penn., U.S., 130 . . . . .336/A5
Frankfurt am Main, Ger., 646,300 . . . . .86/B3
Frankfurt an der Oder, Ger. 86/C2
Franklin, Nun., Can., strait 220/J2
Franklin, (Macon County), Ala., U.S., 149 . . . . .238/D3
Franklin, (Monroe County), Ala., U.S. 238/B4
Franklin, Ala., U.S., county, 31,223 . . . . .238/B1
Franklin, Ariz., U.S., 100 . . . . .242/F5
Franklin, Ark., U.S., 184 . . . . .244/D1
Franklin, Ark., U.S., county, 17,771 . . . . .244/B2
Franklin, Conn., U.S., 1,835 . . . . .253/G3
Franklin, Fla., U.S., county, 11,057 . . . . .256/C2
Franklin, Ga., U.S., 902 . . . . .260/A5
Franklin, Ga., U.S., county, 20,285 . . . . .260/E3
Franklin, Ida., U.S., 641 . . . . .264/F7
Franklin, Ida., U.S., county, 11,329 . . . . .264/F7
Franklin, Ill., U.S., 586 .266/C4
Franklin, Ill., U.S., county, 39,018 . . . . .266/E6
Franklin, Ind., U.S., 19,463 . . . . .270/D6
Franklin, Ind., U.S., county, 22,151 . . . . .270/F6
Franklin, Iowa, U.S., 136 . . . . .274/H2
Franklin, Iowa, U.S., county, 10,704 . . . . .274/H2
Franklin, Kans., U.S., 475 . . . . .276/H4
Franklin, Kans., U.S., county, 24,784 . . . . .276/G3
Franklin, Ky., U.S., 7,996 . . . . .280/D4
Franklin, Ky., U.S., county, 47,687 . . . . .280/F2
Franklin, La., U.S., 8,354 . . . . .282/F7
Franklin, La., U.S., parish, 21,263 . . . . .282/F2
Franklin, Maine, U.S., 1,370 . . . . .286/E4
Franklin, Maine, U.S., county, 29,467 . . . . .286/B4
Franklin, Mass., U.S., 29,560 . . . . .292/J4
Franklin, Minn., U.S., county, 71,535 . . . . .292/C2
Franklin, Minn., U.S., 2,937 . . . . .294/A6, F7
Franklin, (Renville County), Minn., U.S., 498 . . .298/B6
Franklin, Miss., U.S., county, 8,448 . . . . .300/B4
Franklin, Mo., U.S., 112 . . . . .302/D2
Franklin, Mo., U.S., county, 93,807 . . . . .302/E3
Franklin, Mont., U.S. 306/G3
Franklin, Nebr., U.S., 1,026 . . . . .308/E3
Franklin, Nebr., U.S., county, 3,574 . . . . .308/F3
Franklin, N.H., U.S., 8,405 . . . . .212/C5
Franklin, (Sussex County), N.J., U.S., 5,160 . . .314/D1
Franklin, N.Y., U.S., 402 . . . . .320/L6
Franklin, N.Y., U.S., 3,490 . . . . .322/C8
Franklin, N.Y., U.S., county, 51,134 . . . . .320/N1
Franklin, N.C., U.S., 3,490 . . . . .322/C8
Franklin, N.C., U.S., county, 47,260 . . . . .322/J2
Franklin, Ohio, U.S., 11,396 . . . . .328/C6
Franklin, Ohio, U.S., county, 1,068,978 . . . .328/E5, D7
Franklin, (Cambria County), Penn., U.S., 442 . . .336/D5
Franklin, (Venango County), Penn., U.S., 7,212 .336/B3
Franklin, Penn., U.S., county, 129,313 . . . . .336/F6
Franklin, S. Dak., U.S. .342/H4
Franklin, Tenn., U.S., 41,842 . . . . .344/H3
Franklin, Tenn., U.S., county, 39,270 . . . . .344/G4
Franklin, Tex., U.S., 1,470 . . . . .346/M4
Franklin, Tex., U.S., county, 9,458 . . . . .346/N2
Franklin, Vt., U.S., 1,268 . . . . .352/B1

Franklin, Vt., U.S., county, 45,417 . . . . .352/B1
Franklin, Va., U.S., 8,346 . . . . .354/K7
Franklin, Va., U.S., county, 47,286 . . . . .354/D6
Franklin, Wash., U.S., county, 49,347 . . . . .358/G3
Franklin, W. Va., U.S., 797 . . . . .360/H4
Franklin, (Jackson County), Wisc., U.S. 364/B4
Franklin, (Milwaukee County), Wisc., U.S.,
  29,494 . . . . .364/E6, F2
Franklin D. Roosevelt, Wash., U.S., lake 358/G1
Franklin Furnace, Ohio, U.S., 1,537 . . . . .328/E8
Franklin Grove, Ill., U.S., 1,052 . . . . .266/D2
Franklin Lakes, N.J., U.S., 10,422 . . . . .314/B1
Franklin Park, Ill., U.S., 19,434 . . . . .266/B5
Franklin Park, Penn., U.S., 11,364 . . . . .336/A4
Franklin Sprs., Ga., U.S., 762 . . . . .260/E3
Franklin Square, N.Y., U.S., 29,342 . . . . .320/B2
Franklinton, La., U.S., 3,657 . . . . .282/J5
Franklinton, N.C., U.S., 1,745 . . . . .322/J2
Franklinville, N.J., U.S., 1,500 . . . . .314/C4
Franklinville, N.Y., U.S., 1,855 . . . . .320/E6
Franklinville, N.C., U.S., 1,258 . . . . .322/H3
Frankston, Vic., Austl. . . . . .170/Inset V
Frankston, Tex., U.S., 1,209 . . . . .346/N3
Franksville, Wisc., U.S., 1,789 . . . . .364/F2
Frankton, Ala., U.S., 1,905 . . . . .270/E4
Franktown, Colo., U.S., 99 . . . . .250/A4
Frankville, Ala., U.S., 125 . . . . .238/A4
Frankville, Iowa, U.S., 125 . . . . .274/L2
Frannie, Wyo., U.S., 209 . . . . .366/B1
Franquelin, Que., Can. .226/J2
Franz Josef Land, Russ., island 193/B3
Franz Josef Land, Russ., islands 104/D1
Fraser, Br. Col., Can. 214/E1
Fraser, Br. Col., Can., river 212/A4
Fraser, Br. Col., Can., river 214/L5, M4
Fraser, Colo., U.S., 910 . . . . .250/E2
Fraser, Iowa, U.S., 137 . . . . .274/G3
Fraser, Mich., U.S., 15,297 . . . . .294/B6, G7
Fraserburgh, Scot., U.K. 60/C1
Fraserburgh, Scot., U.K., 12,454 . . . . .62/N3
Fraserdale, Ont., Can. .222/D2
Fraser Lake, Br. Col., Can., 1,268 . . . . .214/K4
Fraserwood, Man., Can. 215/C4
Fray Bentos, Uru. 187/A2
Frazee, Minn., U.S., 1,377 . . . . .298/B4
Frazer, Mont., U.S., 452 . . . . .306/K1
Frazeysburg, Ohio, U.S., 1,201 . . . . .328/F5
Frazier Park, Calif., U.S., 2,348 . . . . .246/G8
Frazier Park, N.J., U.S., 225 . . . . .314/C3
Freckleton, (Freckleton/Warton), Eng., U.K., 8,273 66/C5
Freckleton, (Freckleton/Warton), Eng., U.K., 8,273 68/B2
Fred, La., U.S., 125 . . . . .282/C5
Freda, Mich., U.S., 50 .294/A2
Freda, N. Dak., U.S. 326/D3
Frederic, Mich., U.S., 425 . . . . .294/E5
Frederic, Wisc., U.S., 1,262 . . . . .364/A3
Frederica, Del., U.S., 648 . . . . .255/C4
Fredericia, Den. 79/B3
Frederick, Colo., U.S., 2,467 . . . . .250/A2
Frederick, Kans., U.S. .276/D3
Frederick, Md., U.S., 52,767 . . . . .288/E2
Frederick, Md., U.S., county, 195,277 . . . . .288/F1
Frederick, Okla., U.S., 4,637 . . . . .330/D3
Frederick, S. Dak., U.S., 255 . . . . .342/G2
Frederick, Va., U.S., county, 59,209 . . . . .354/G2
Fredericksburg, Ind., U.S., 92 . . . . .270/D8
Fredericksburg, Iowa, U.S., 984 . . . . .274/K2
Fredericksburg, Ohio, U.S., 487 . . . . .328/G4
Fredericksburg, (Crawford County), Penn., U.S.,
  1,140 . . . . .336/A2
Fredericksburg, (Lebanon County), Penn., U.S.,
  987 . . . . .336/J5
Fredericksburg, Va., U.S., 8,911 . . . . .346/K5
Fredericksburg, Va., U.S., 19,279 . . . . .354/J4
Fredericksburg and Spotsylvania Natl. Mil. Park,
  Va., U.S. 354/H4
Fredericktown, Jct., N.B., Can., 692 . . . . .217/C3
Fredericktown, Mo., U.S., 3,928 . . . . .302/F4
Fredericktown, Ohio, U.S., 2,428 . . . . .328/E5
Fredericton, N.B., Can., 47,560 . . . . .217/C3
Fredericton, P.E.I., Can. 224/B2
Frederika, Iowa, U.S., 199 . . . . .274/K2
Frederiksberg, Den. 79/D3
Frederiksborg, Den., county 79/D2
Frederikshavn, Den. 79/C1
Fredonia, Ariz., U.S., 1,036 . . . . .242/C1
Fredonia, Iowa, U.S., 251 . . . . .274/M5
Fredonia, Kans., U.S., 2,600 . . . . .276/G4
Fredonia, Ky., U.S., 10,706 . . . . .320/E6
Fredonia, N. Dak., U.S., 51 . . . . .326/F3
Fredonia, Penn., U.S., 652 . . . . .336/A3
Fredonia, Tex., U.S., 40 . . . . .346/J4
Fredonia, Wisc., U.S., 1,934 . . . . .364/F5
Fredrikstad, Nor., 93,273 . . . . .80/C4
Freeborn, Minn., U.S., 305 . . . . .298/D7
Freeborn, Minn., U.S., county, 32,584 . . . . .298/D7
Freeburg, Ill., U.S., 3,872 . . . . .266/A4, D5
Freeburg, Mo., U.S., 423 . . . . .302/E3
Freeburg, Penn., U.S., 584 . . . . .336/H4
Freedhem, Minn., U.S. .298/C4
Freedom, Calif., U.S., 6,000 . . . . .246/K4
Freedom, Ind., U.S., 150 . . . . .270/C6
Freedom, Maine, U.S., 645 . . . . .286/C4
Freedom, N.H., U.S., 1,303 . . . . .212/D4
Freedom, Okla., U.S., 271 . . . . .330/C1
Freedom, Penn., U.S., 1,763 . . . . .336/A4
Freedom, Wisc., U.S., 1,500 . . . . .364/E4
Freedom, Wyo., U.S., 100 . . . . .366/A2
Freehold, N.J., U.S., borough, 10,976 . . . . .314/E3
Free Home, Ga., U.S., 550 . . . . .260/C3
Freeland, P.E.I., Can. 224/B2
Freeland, Mich., U.S., 5,147 . . . . .294/E6
Freeland, Penn., U.S., 3,643 . . . . .336/K3
Freeland, Wash., U.S., 1,313 . . . . .358/C1
Freeman, Mo., U.S., 521 . . . . .302/B3
Freeman, S. Dak., U.S., 1,317 . . . . .342/H4
Freeman, Wash., U.S., 80 . . . . .358/H2
Freemansburg, Penn., U.S., 1,897 . . . . .336/L4
Freemanspur, W. Va., U.S., 273 . . . . .336/C6
Freemanville, Ala., U.S., 450 . . . . .238/B4
Freeport, Bah., 45,000 .204/B1
Freeport, Bah., 45,000 .207/A2
Freeport, N.S., Can., 345 . . . . .221/A3
Freeport, Fla., U.S., 1,190 . . . . .256/B1
Freeport, Ill., U.S., 26,443 . . . . .266/D1
Freeport, Kans., U.S. 276/E4
Freeport, Maine, U.S., 7,800 . . . . .286/B5
Freeport, Mich., U.S., 444 . . . . .294/D7
Freeport, Minn., U.S., 454 . . . . .298/C5
Freeport, N.Y., U.S., 43,783 . . . . .320/H5
Freeport, Ohio, U.S., 398 . . . . .328/H5
Freer, Tex., U.S., 3,241 . . . . .346/K8
Freesoil, Mich., U.S., 177 . . . . .294/C5
Freestone, Tex., U.S., county, 17,867 . . . . .346/M4
Freethorpe, Eng., U.K. .70/H1
Freetown, Ant.-Bar. 207/E5
Freetown, S.L., capital, 469,776 . . . . .149/A1
Freetown, Ind., U.S., 600 . . . . .270/D7

Freeville, N.Y., U.S., 505 ....320/J5
Freewood Acres, N.J., U.S., 3,100 ....314/E3
Freiberg, Ger. 86/C3
Freiburg, Ger., 202,455 ....86/A5
Freiburg, Ger., department 86/A5
Freirina, Chile 190/B3
Freistatt, Mo., U.S., 184 ....302/C4
Fréjus, Fr. 88/D5
Fremantle, W.A., Austl. ....170/A3, Inset I
Fremington, Eng., U.K., 3,727 ....73/D2
Fremont, Calif., U.S., 203,413 ....246/D5, K2
Fremont, Colo., U.S., county, 46,145 ....250/E2
Fremont, Ida., U.S., county, 11,819 ....270/C1
Fremont, Ind., U.S., 1,696 ....274/K5
Fremont, Iowa, U.S., 704 ....274/C6
Fremont, Iowa, U.S., county, 8,010 ....274/C6
Fremont, Ky., U.S., 325 ....280/B4
Fremont, Mich., U.S., 4,224 ....294/D6
Fremont, Mo., U.S., 125 ....302/E5
Fremont, Nebr., U.S., 25,174 ....308/H2
Fremont, N.H., U.S., 3,510 ....212/D6
Fremont, N.C., U.S., 1,463 ....322/K3
Fremont, Ohio, U.S., 17,375 ....328/D3
Fremont, Utah, U.S., 125 ....350/C5
Fremont, Wisc., U.S., 666 ....364/E4
Fremont, Wyo., U.S., county, 35,804 ....366/B2
Fremont Hills, Mo., U.S., 597 ....302/C5
Fremont Jct., Utah, U.S. 350/C5
Fremont Natl. For., Oreg., U.S. 334/E4, F5
French, Ont., Can., river 223/E1
Frenchboro, Maine, U.S. 286/D4
Frenchburg, Ky., U.S., 551 ....280/G3
French Camp, Calif., U.S., 4,109 ....246/L2
French Camp, Miss., U.S., 393 ....300/C2
Frenchglen, Oreg., U.S. 334/H5
French Guiana, dependency 173
French Island, Wisc., U.S., 4,410 ....364/B5
French Lick, Ind., U.S., 1,941 ....270/C7
Frenchman, Sask., Can., river 227/B11
Frenchman, Nebr., U.S., creek 308/C3
Frenchman, Nev., U.S. 310/A2
French Polynesia, Fr., dependency 161
French River, Ont., Can. 223/E1
French River, Minn., U.S., 325 ....298/F4
French Settlement, La., U.S., 945 ....282/H6
Frenchton, W. Va., U.S., 250 ....360/F3
Frenchtown, Mont., U.S., 883 ....306/B3
Frenchtown, N.J., U.S., 1,488 ....314/C2
Frenchville, Maine, U.S., 1,225 ....286/D1
Frensham, Eng., U.K. 70/C4
Freshwater, (Freshwater/Totland),
  Eng., U.K., 7,317 ....70/A5
Fresnal Canyon, Ariz., U.S. 242/D6
Fresnillo, Mex., 97,023 (183,236, metro.) 200/D3
Fresno, Calif., U.S., 427,652, (922,516, metro.) .246/E6
Fresno, Calif., U.S., county, 799,407 ....246/E6
Fresno, Mont., U.S. 306/G1
Fresno, Mont., U.S., reservoir 306/F1
Fresno, Ohio, U.S., 225 ....328/G5
Fresno, Tex., U.S., 6,603 ....346/B7
Freswick, Scot., U.K. 62/K1
Frewen, Wyo., U.S. 366/B3
Frewsburg, N.Y., U.S., 1,965 ....320/C6
Fria, Guin. 149/B2
Friars Pt., Miss., U.S., 1,480 ....300/B1
Fribourg, Switz. 90/B2
Fribourg, Switz., canton 90/B2
Friday, Tex., U.S., 50 ....346/N4
Friday Bridge, Eng., U.K. 70/E1
Friday Harbor, Wash., U.S., 1,989 ....358/B1
Fridaythorpe, Eng., U.K. 66/G4
Fridley, Minn., U.S., 27,449 ....298/E5
Friedens, Penn., U.S., 1,673 ....336/C5
Friedrichshafen, Ger. 86/B5
Friend, Kans., U.S. 276/B3
Friend, Nebr., U.S., 1,174 ....308/G3
Friendly, Md., U.S., 10,938 ....288/G4
Friendly, W. Va., U.S., 159 ....360/D1
Friendly Corners, Ariz., U.S. 242/D5
Friendship, Ark., U.S., 206 ....244/B3
Friendship, Ga., U.S. 260/C7
Friendship, Maine, U.S., 1,204 ....286/C5
Friendship, Md., U.S., 425 ....288/H5
Friendship, N.J., U.S. 314/A2
Friendship, N.Y., U.S., 1,176 ....320/E6
Friendship, Okla., U.S., 70 ....330/C3
Friendship, Tenn., U.S., 608 ....344/C3
Friendship, Wisc., U.S., 698 ....364/D5
Friendship Hill Natl. Hist. Site, Penn., U.S. 336/B6
Friendsville, Md., U.S., 539 ....288/A3
Friendsville, Penn., U.S., 91 ....336/J2
Friendsville, Tenn., U.S., 890 ....344/N3
Friendswood, Tex., U.S., 29,037 ....346/B7
Friern Barnet, Eng., U.K. 70/B3
Fries, Va., U.S., 614 ....354/B7
Friesland, Neth., province 84/C1
Friesland, Wisc., U.S., 298 ....364/D5
Fries Mill, N.J., U.S., 600 ....314/C4
Frigate, Gren., island 209/C1
Frilford, Eng., U.K. 70/B3
Frimley, Eng., U.K. 70/C4
Frink, Fla., U.S. 256/C1
Frinton-on-Sea, (Frinton and Walton),
  Eng., U.K., 15,043 ....70/G3
Frio, C.R., river 203/B2
Frio, Tex., U.S., county, 16,252 ....346/I7
Frio, Tex., U.S., river 62/L5
Friockheim, Scot., U.K., 820 ....62/L5
Friona, Tex., U.S., 3,854 ....346/E10
Frio Town, Tex., U.S. 346/I6
Frisa, Scot., U.K., lake 62/D5
Frisches Haff, Pol., bay 83/D1
Frisco, Colo., U.S., 2,443 ....250/D2
Frisco, Tex., U.S., 33,714 ....346/C8
Frisco, Utah, U.S. 350/A5
Frisco, Utah, U.S., peak 350/A5
Frisco City, Ala., U.S., 1,460 ....238/B4
Friskney, Eng., U.K. 68/H3
Fristoe, Mo., U.S. 302/C3
Fritch, Tex., U.S., 2,235 ....346/F9
Frithville, Eng., U.K. 68/H3
Fritton, Eng., U.K. 70/H1
Fritz, Ky., U.S., 80 ....280/G3
Friuli-Venezia Giulia, It., region 95/C1
Frizington, Eng., U.K., 2,472 ....66/B3
Frobisher, Sask., Can., lake 227/C4
Frodsham, Eng., U.K., 8,903 ....66/C6
Frodsham, Eng., U.K., 8,903 ....68/B3
Frog, Alta., Can., lake 212/E4
Froghall, Eng., U.K. 68/D3
Frogmore, La., U.S. 282/F3
Frohna, Mo., U.S., 192 ....302/G4
Froid, Mont., U.S., 195 ....306/M1
Fromberg, Mont., U.S., 486 ....306/H4
Frome, Austl., lake 170/D2
Frome, Eng., U.K., 23,159 ....73/D2
Fron-goch, Wales, U.K. 64/D2
Front, Colo., U.S., range 250/E1
Frontenac, Ont., Can. 223/J3
Frontenac, Ont., Can., county 223/J3
Frontenac, Kans., U.S., 2,996 ....276/H4
Frontenac, Minn., U.S., 3,483 ....302/H3
Frontenac Prov. Park, Ont., Can. 223/J3

Frontenac Prov. Park, Que., Can. 226/E6
Frontier, Sask., Can., 302 ....227/B11
Frontier, Mich., U.S., 250 ....294/E8
Frontier, Nebr., U.S., county, 3,099 ....308/D3
Frontier, N. Dak., U.S., 273 ....326/J3
Frontier, Wyo., U.S., 50 ....366/A3
Fronton, Tex., U.S., 599 ....346/J9
Front Royal, Va., U.S., 13,589 ....354/G3
Frosinone, It. 95/C2
Frost, Minn., U.S., 251 ....298/D7
Frost, W. Va., U.S. 360/G4
Frostburg, Md., U.S., 7,873 ....288/C3
Frostproof, Fla., U.S., 2,975 ....256/C4
Foxfield, Eng., U.K. 70/A4
Frozen Head St. Nat. Area, Tenn., U.S. 344/N2
Fruita, Colo., U.S., 6,478 ....250/B2
Fruita, Utah, U.S. 350/C5
Fruitdale, Ala., U.S., 125 ....238/A4
Fruitdale, Ohio, U.S., 80 ....328/D7
Fruitdale, (Harbeck-Fruitdale), Oreg., U.S., 3,780 334/C5
Fruitdale, S. Dak., U.S., 62 ....342/B3
Fruit Hts., Utah, U.S., 4,701 ....350/E1
Fruithurst, Ala., U.S., 270 ....238/D2
Fruitland, Ida., U.S., 3,805 ....264/A5
Fruitland, Iowa, U.S., 703 ....274/M5
Fruitland, Md., U.S., 3,774 ....288/M6
Fruitland, N. Mex., U.S., 650 ....317/B1
Fruitland, Utah, U.S., 40 ....350/D3
Fruitland, Wash., U.S. 358/G1
Fruitport, Mich., U.S., 1,124 ....294/C6
Fruitvale, Colo., U.S., 6,936 ....250/B2
Fruitvale, Ida., U.S., 175 ....264/A5
Fruitvale, Wash., U.S. 358/E3
Fruška Gora, Serb.-Mont., mountains 99/A2
Frutigen, Switz. 90/B2
Fryburg, N. Dak., U.S. 326/B3
Fryburg, Penn., U.S., 350 ....336/C3
Fry Canyon, Utah, U.S., 40 ....350/D6
Frye, Maine, U.S., 90 ....286/B4
Fryeburg, La., U.S., 716 ....282/C2
Fryeburg, Maine, U.S., 3,083 ....286/A4
Fua'amotu, Tonga 175/B4
Fuahmulah, Mald., atoll 127/A5
Fuenlabrada, Sp., 182,705 ....94/Inset II
Fuerte, Mex., river 200/C2
Fuerte Olimpo, Para. 187/D2
Fuerteventura, Sp., island ....94/Inset I
Fuji, Jap., volcano 114/C3
Fujian, China, province 114/C3
Fujisawa, Jap., 379,000 ....114/A3
Fukae, Jap. 114/A3
Fukae, Jap., island 114/A3
Fukue, Jap. 114/A3
Fukue, Jap., island 114/A3
Fukui, Jap., 252,000 ....114/C2
Fukui, Jap., prefecture 114/C2
Fukuoka, Jap., 1,341,470 ....114/A3
Fukuoka, Jap., prefecture 114/A3
Fukushima, Jap., 291,000 ....114/D2
Fukushima, Jap., prefecture 114/C2
Fukuyama, Jap., 379,000 ....114/B3
Fulacunda, Gui.-B. 149/B2
Fuladi, Kuh-e, Afg., mountain 129/B2
Fulbourn, Eng., U.K., 3,896 ....68/H5
Fulbourn, Eng., U.K., 3,896 ....70/E2
Fulda, Ger. 86/B3
Fulda, Ger., river 86/B3
Fulda, Minn., U.S., 1,283 ....298/B7
Fulking, Eng., U.K. 70/D5
Fulks Run, Va., U.S., 200 ....354/F3
Fullarton, Trin.-To. 209/A2
Fullerton, Eng., U.K. 70/B4
Fullerton, Calif., U.S., 126,003 ....246/D10, H9
Fullerton, Ky., U.S. 280/H2
Fullerton, La., U.S., 90 ....282/D5
Fullerton, Md., U.S., 10,100 ....288/H2
Fullerton, Nebr., U.S., 1,378 ....308/G2
Fullerton, N. Dak., U.S., 85 ....326/G3
Fulshear, Tex., U.S., 716 ....346/N6
Fulton, Ala., U.S., 308 ....238/B4
Fulton, Ark., U.S., 245 ....244/B4
Fulton, Ark., U.S., county, 11,642 ....244/D2
Fulton, Ga., U.S., county, 816,006 ....260/B4, G3
Fulton, Ill., U.S., 3,881 ....266/C2
Fulton, Ill., U.S., county, 38,250 ....266/C3
Fulton, Ind., U.S. 270/D3
Fulton, Ind., U.S., county, 20,511 ....270/D2
Fulton, Iowa, U.S., 100 ....274/N3
Fulton, Kans., U.S., 184 ....276/H4
Fulton, Ky., U.S., 2,775 ....280/B4
Fulton, Ky., U.S., county, 7,752 ....280/A4
Fulton, Md., U.S., 850 ....288/G3
Fulton, Mich., U.S., 350 ....294/D7
Fulton, Miss., U.S., 3,882 ....300/D1
Fulton, Mo., U.S., 12,128 ....302/E3
Fulton, N.Y., U.S., 11,855 ....320/J4
Fulton, N.Y., U.S., county, 55,073 ....320/N4
Fulton, Ohio, U.S., 264 ....328/E5
Fulton, Ohio, U.S., county, 42,084 ....328/B2
Fulton, Penn., U.S., county, 14,261 ....336/E6
Fulton, S. Dak., U.S., 86 ....342/H4
Fulton, Tex., U.S., 1,553 ....346/L7
Fultondale, Ala., U.S., 6,595 ....238/C2, E1
Fultonham, Ohio, U.S., 151 ....328/F6
Fultonville, N.Y., U.S., 265 ....320/N5
Fults, Ill., U.S. 266/C5
Fulwood, (Lancashire Co,) Eng., U.K. 66/C5
Fulwood, (Lancashire Co,) Eng., U.K. 68/B2
Fulwood, (Sheffield Co,) Eng., U.K. 66/E6
Funabashi, Jap., 550,000 ....114/D3
Funafuti, Tuv., capital, 3,839 ....174/C3
Funafuti, Tuv., island 174/C3
Funchal, Port. ....93/Inset I
Fundy, N.B., Can., bay 217/D3
Fundy, N.S., Can., bay 221/A3
Fundy Natl. Park, N.B., Can. 217/D3
Funk, Nebr., U.S., 204 ....308/E3
Funkley, Minn., U.S. 298/C3
Funkstown, Md., U.S., 983 ....288/D1
Funston, Ga., U.S., 426 ....260/D9
Funston, La., U.S., 50 ....282/A2
Funston, Tex., U.S. 346/J3
Funtley, Eng., U.K. 70/B5
Funzie, Scot., U.K. 62/R1
Fuquay-Varina, N.C., U.S., 7,898 ....322/H3
Furley, Eng., U.K. 70/E4
Furman, Ala., U.S. 238/C3
Furman, S.C., U.S., 286 ....340/C4
Furnace, Scot., U.K. 62/F6
Furnace, Ky., U.S., 50 ....280/G3
Furnas, Braz., reservoir 188/D4
Furnas, Nebr., U.S., county, 5,324 ....308/E3
Fürstenfeld, Aus. 91/E3
Fürth, Ger., 109,771 ....86/B4
Fushun, China, 1,184,940, (2,045,150, metro.) ...119/F1
Futuna, Van., island 173/C4
Fuxin, China, 646,580, (1,693,380, metro.) 119/F1
Fuzhou, China, 1,111,550, (1,651,500, metro.) ...119/E3
Fyfett, Eng., U.K. 73/D2
Fyffe, Ala., U.S., 971 ....238/D1
Fyfield, Eng., U.K. 70/A4
Fyn, Den., county 79/C3
Fyn, Den., island 79/C3

Fyne, Scot., U.K., lake 62/F6
Fyvie, Scot., U.K. 62/M4
Gaalkacyo, Som. 157/B2
Gaastra, Mich., U.S., 339 ....294/A3
Gabarus, N.S., Can. 221/G2
Gabbs, Nev., U.S., 318 ....310/B2
Gabès, Tun., 104,950 ....146/C2
Gabès, Tun., gulf 146/C2
Gabon, nation 149
Gaborone, Bots., capital, 186,007 ....160/B3
Gabriel, Mauritius, island 101/D3
Gabrovo, Bul. 101/D3
Gabrovo, Bul., oblast 101/D2
Gabú, Gui.-B. 149/C1
Gackle, N. Dak., U.S., 335 ....326/F3
Gacko, Bos.-Her. 98/B2
Gadsden, Ala., U.S., 38,978, (103,459, metro.) ..238/C1
Gadsden, Ariz., U.S., 953 ....242/A5
Gadsden, Fla., U.S., county, 45,087 ....256/C6
Gadsden, S.C., U.S., 550 ....340/D3
Gadsden, Tenn., U.S., 553 ....344/D3
Gaeta, It. 95/C2
Gaffney, S.C., U.S., 12,968 ....340/C1
Gafsa, Tun. 146/B2
Gage, Nebr., U.S., county, 22,993 ....308/H3
Gage, N. Mex., U.S. 317/B5
Gage, Okla., U.S., 429 ....330/C1
Gagen, Wisc., U.S. 364/D3
Gage Lake, Ill., U.S., 10,415 ....266/B4
Gagetown, N.B., Can., 682 ....217/C3
Gagetown, Mich., U.S., 389 ....294/F6
Gaggade, Dji., plain 156/C2
Gagingwell, Eng., U.K. 68/E6
Gagnoa, C. d'Iv. 150/C2
Gagnon, Que., Can. 225/C3
Gagra, Geo. 103/A2
Gahanna, Ohio, U.S., 32,636 ....328/E5, E9
Gaick Lodge, Scot., U.K. 62/H5
Gail, Tex., U.S., 70 ....346/G3
Gaillard, Conn., U.S., lake 253/D4
Gaines, Mich., U.S., 366 ....294/F7
Gaines, Penn., U.S., 125 ....336/F2
Gaines, Tex., U.S., county, 14,467 ....346/F3
Gainesboro, Tenn., U.S., 879 ....344/K2
Gainesville, Ala., U.S., 220 ....238/A2
Gainesville, Ark., U.S., 125 ....244/F1
Gainesville, Fla., U.S., 95,447, (217,955, metro.) 256/F2
Gainesville, Ga., U.S., 25,578 ....260/D3
Gainesville, Mo., U.S., 632 ....302/D5
Gainesville, N.Y., U.S., 304 ....320/E5
Gainesville, Tex., U.S., 15,538 ....346/L2
Gainesville Mills, Ga., U.S. 260/D3
Gainsborough, Sask., Can., 286 ....227/J11
Gainsborough, Eng., U.K., 19,704 ....66/G6
Gainsborough, Eng., U.K., 19,704 ....68/F3
Gairdner, Austl., lake 170/C3
Gairloch, Scot., U.K. 62/E3
Gairlochy, Scot., U.K. 62/F5
Gaithersburg, Md., U.S., 52,613 ....288/F3
Gaizina Kalns, Lat., mountain 82/C2
Galahad, Alta., Can., 161 ....212/E5
Galana, Kenya, river 157/E5
Galápagos, Ecua., islands 185/Inset
Galápagos, Ecua., province 185/Inset
Galashiels, Scot., U.K., 14,361 ....62/L7
Galata, Mont., U.S. 306/E1
Galatea, Colo., U.S. 250/G3
Galaţi, Rom., 326,956 ....101/E3
Galaţi, Rom., county 101/D3
Galatia, Ill., U.S., 1,013 ....266/E6
Galatia, Kans., U.S., 61 ....276/D3
Galax, Va., U.S., 6,837 ....354/B7
Galbraith, La., U.S., 80 ....282/D4
Galchutt, N. Dak., U.S., 50 ....326/J3
Galena, Alaska, U.S., 675 ....240/D2
Galena, Ill., U.S., 3,460 ....266/C1
Galena, Ind., U.S., 1,831 ....270/E8
Galena, Kans., U.S., 3,287 ....276/H4
Galena, Md., U.S., 428 ....288/J3
Galena, Mo., U.S., 451 ....302/C5
Galena, Ohio, U.S., 305 ....328/E5
Galena, Oreg., U.S. 334/H3
Galena Bay, Br. Col., Can. 214/O6
Galena Park, Tex., U.S., 10,592 ....346/B6
Galera, Ecua., point 185/A2
Galesburg, Ill., U.S., 33,706 ....266/C3
Galesburg, Kans., U.S., 150 ....276/G4
Galesburg, Mich., U.S., 1,988 ....294/D7
Galesburg, N. Dak., U.S., 157 ....326/H2
Gales Ferry, Conn., U.S., 2,400 ....253/G4
Galestown, Md., U.S., 101 ....288/M5
Galesville, Md., U.S., 600 ....288/H4
Galesville, Wisc., U.S., 1,427 ....364/B4
Galeton, Colo., U.S., 150 ....250/F1
Galeton, Penn., U.S., 1,325 ....336/F2
Galgate, Eng., U.K. 66/C5
Galice, Oreg., U.S. 334/C5
Galicia, Sp., autonomous community 94/C1
Galien, Mich., U.S., 593 ....294/C8
Galilee, Isr., region 135/B1
Galilee, R.I., U.S., 700 ....339/C5
Galion, La., U.S. 282/F1
Galion, Ohio, U.S., 11,341 ....328/E4
Galisteo, N. Mex., U.S. 317/E2
Galite, Tun., island 146/B1
Galivants Ferry, S.C., U.S., 70 ....340/E2
Gallatin, Ky., U.S., county, 7,870 ....280/F2
Gallatin, Mo., U.S., 1,789 ....302/C2
Gallatin, Mont., U.S., county, 67,831 ....306/E4
Gallatin, Tenn., U.S., 23,230 ....344/J2
Gallatin, Tex., U.S., 378 ....346/N4
Gallatin Gateway, Mont., U.S., 350 ....306/E4
Gallatin Natl. For., Mont., U.S. 306/F4
Gallaway, Tenn., U.S., 666 ....344/B4
Galle, Sri Lan., 90,934 ....126/B5
Gallegos, Arg., river 191/A7
Galleywood, Eng., U.K. 70/E3
Gallia, Ohio, U.S., county, 31,069 ....328/F8
Gallina, N. Mex., U.S., 175 ....317/D1
Gallinas, Col., point 184/C1
Gallinas, N. Mex., U.S., 40 ....317/E3
Gallinas, N. Mex., U.S., peak 317/E3
Gallion, Ala., U.S., 100 ....238/B3
Gallipolis, Ohio, U.S., 4,180 ....328/F8
Gallitzin, Penn., U.S., 1,756 ....336/D5
Gallitzin St. For., Penn., U.S. 336/D5
Gällivare, Swe. 80/E2
Gallman, Miss., U.S., 275 ....300/B4
Galloo, N.Y., U.S., island 320/J3
Galloway, Wisc., U.S., 125 ....364/D4
Galloway Forest Park, Scot., U.K. 62/H7
Gallup, Ky., U.S. 280/H2
Gallup, N. Mex., U.S., 20,209 ....317/B2
Gallup Mills, Vt., U.S. 352/D2
Galoa, Fiji 174/C4
Galt, Calif., U.S., 19,472 ....246/D4, K6, L1
Galt, Iowa, U.S. 274/G2
Galt, Mo., U.S., 275 ....302/C1
Galva, Ill., U.S., 2,758 ....266/C3
Galva, Iowa, U.S., 368 ....274/D2

Galva, Kans., U.S., 701 ....276/E3
Galveston, Ind., U.S., 1,532 ....270/D3
Galveston, Ky., U.S., 450 ....280/H3
Galveston, Tex., U.S., 57,247 ....346/P6
Galveston, Tex., U.S., county, 250,158 ....346/B7, N6
Galveston, Tex., U.S., island 346/P6
Galway, Ire., 65,774 ....78/B2
Galway, Ire., bay 78/B2
Galway, Ire., county 78/B2
Galway, N.Y., U.S., 214 ....320/N4
Galway County Borough, Ire., county 78/B2
Gam, Viet., river 123/A1
Gamaliel, Ark., U.S., 175 ....244/C1
Gamaliel, Ky., U.S., 439 ....280/E4
Gambell, Alaska, U.S., 649 ....240/A2
Gambela, Eth., state 156/A2
Gamber, Md., U.S., 1,000 ....288/G2
Gambia, The, nation 142
Gambia, Gam., river 148/D2
Gambia, Guin., river 149/B2
Gambia, Sen., river 148/C3
Gambier, Ohio, U.S., 1,871 ....328/F5
Gambo, Nfld., Can., 2,084 ....218/D5
Gambrill, Iowa, U.S., 175 ....274/N4
Gamerco, N. Mex., U.S., 300 ....317/B2
Gamewell, N.C., U.S., 3,644 ....322/B3
Gamlingay, Eng., U.K., 3,391 ....68/G5
Gamlingay, Eng., U.K., 3,391 ....70/D2
Gamprin, Liech. 90/B1
Gan, China, river 119/E3
Ganado, Ariz., U.S., 1,505 ....242/F2
Ganado, Tex., U.S., 1,915 ....346/M6
Gananoque, Ont., Can., 5,167 ....223/J3
Gäncä, Azer., 298,600 ....103/B2
Gandeeville, W. Va., U.S., 150 ....360/D3
Gander, Nfld., Can., 9,651 ....218/D5
Gander Bay, Nfld., Can., 315 ....218/D4
Gandhinagar, India 128/B4
Gandy, Nebr., U.S. 308/D2
Gandy, Utah, U.S. 350/A4
Ganganagar, India 128/B3
Ganges, Bangl., river 127/B4
Ganges, India, river 128/E3
Ganghwa, S. Kor., bay 116/A4
Gang Mills, N.Y., U.S., 3,304 ....320/G6
Gangneung, S. Kor., 220,403 ....116/C4
Gangtok, India 128/E3
Gangwon, S. Kor., province 116/B4
Ganllwyd, Wales, U.K. 64/C2
Gannett, Ida., U.S. 264/C6
Gannett, Wyo., U.S., peak 366/B2
Gannvalley, S. Dak., U.S. 342/F3
Gans, Okla., U.S., 208 ....330/H2
Gansevoort, N.Y., U.S., 800 ....320/P4
Gansu, China, province 119/C1, D2
Gantt, Ala., U.S., 241 ....238/C4
Gantt, S.C., U.S., 13,962 ....340/B2, D2
Ganzhou, China 119/E3
Gao, Mali 150/D2
Gaoua, Burkina 151/C3
Gaoual, Guin. 149/B2
Gap, Fr. 88/D4
Gap, Penn., U.S., 1,611 ....336/J6
Gapland, Md., U.S., 325 ....288/D2
Gap Mills, W. Va., U.S. 360/F5
Garabil, Turkm., plateau 132/C3
Garabogazköl, Turkm., lake 132/A2
Garagum, Turkm., canal 132/D3
Garagum, Turkm., desert 132/C2
Garber, Iowa, U.S., 103 ....274/M2
Garber, Okla., U.S., 845 ....330/E1
Garberville, Calif., U.S., 300 ....246/B2
Garcia, Colo., U.S. 250/E4
Gard, Fr., department 88/D4
Garda, It., lake 95/B1
Gardar, N. Dak., U.S., 50 ....326/H1
Garden, Austl., island ....170/Inset I
Garden, Ont., Can., river 223/A1
Garden, Mich., U.S., 240 ....294/C4
Garden, Mich., U.S., island 294/D4
Garden, Nebr., U.S., county, 2,292 ....308/B2
Gardena, Calif., U.S., 57,746 ....246/C10
Gardena, N. Dak., U.S., 40 ....326/E1
Garden Acres, Calif., U.S., 9,747 ....246/L1
Garden City, Ala., U.S., 564 ....238/C1
Garden City, Colo., U.S., 357 ....250/F1
Garden City, Ga., U.S., 11,289 ....260/J7
Garden City, Ida., U.S., 10,624 ....264/A6
Garden City, Iowa, U.S., 150 ....274/H3
Garden City, Kans., U.S., 28,451 ....276/B4
Garden City, La., U.S., 275 ....282/G7
Garden City, Mich., U.S., 30,047 ....294/A7, F7
Garden City, Minn., U.S., 275 ....298/C6
Garden City, Miss., U.S., 80 ....300/A4
Garden City, Mo., U.S., 1,500 ....302/B3
Garden City, S.C., U.S., 9,357 ....340/F3
Garden City, S. Dak., U.S., 72 ....342/H3
Garden City, Tex., U.S., 200 ....346/G4
Garden City, Utah, U.S., 357 ....350/E1
Gardendale, Ala., U.S., 11,626 ....238/C2, E1
Gardendale, Mich., U.S., 800 ....294/G6
Gardendale, (Ector County), Tex., U.S., 1,197 ...346/F3
Gardendale, (La Salle County), Tex., U.S. 346/I7
Garden Grove, Calif., U.S., 165,196 ....246/D10
Garden Grove, Iowa, U.S., 250 ....274/G4
Garden Hill, Man., Can. 215/D2
Garden Home, (Garden Home-Whitford),
  Oreg., U.S., 6,931 ....334/A2
Garden Plain, Kans., U.S., 797 ....276/E4
Garden Reach, India ....128/Inset II
Garden Ridge, Tex., U.S., 1,882 ....346/A2
Garden St. Parkway, N.J., U.S. 314/D4, D5, E1
Gardenton, Man., Can. 215/C4
Garden Valley, Ida., U.S. 264/B5
Garden View, Penn., U.S., 2,679 ....336/G3
Gardere, La., U.S., 8,992 ....282/G6
Garderhouse, Scot., U.K. 62/P2
Gardeyz, Afg. 129/B2
Gardi, Ga., U.S., 150 ....260/H8
Gardiner, Maine, U.S., 6,198 ....286/C4
Gardiner, Mont., U.S., 851 ....306/F4
Gardiner, Oreg., U.S., 325 ....334/B4
Gardiners, N.Y., U.S., island 320/H1
Gardiner, Br. Col., Can., canal 214/N4
Gardner, Colo., U.S., 70 ....250/E4
Gardner, Fla., U.S. 256/C4
Gardner, Ill., U.S., 1,406 ....266/C2
Gardner, Kans., U.S., 9,396 ....276/H3
Gardner, La., U.S., 125 ....282/D5
Gardner, Mass., U.S., 20,770 ....292/G2
Gardner, N. Dak., U.S., 80 ....326/J2
Gardnerville, Nev., U.S., 3,357 ....310/A2
Gardnerville Ranchos, Nev., U.S., 11,054 ....310/A2
Garelochhead, Scot., U.K., 1,265 ....62/G6
Garfield, Ark., U.S., 490 ....244/B1
Garfield, Colo., U.S. 250/D3
Garfield, Colo., U.S., county, 43,791 ....250/B2
Garfield, Ga., U.S., 152 ....260/G6
Garfield, Kans., U.S., 198 ....276/C3
Garfield, Maine, U.S., 86 ....286/D2
Garfield, Minn., U.S., 281 ....298/B5

Garfield, Mont., U.S., *county*, 1,279 . . . . .306/K2
Garfield, Nebr., U.S., *county*, 1,902 . . . . .308/E2
Garfield, N.J., U.S., 29,786 . . . . .314/B2, E2
Garfield, N. Mex., U.S., 175 . . . . .317/C5
Garfield, Okla., U.S., *county*, 57,813 . . . . .330/E1
Garfield, Tex., U.S., 1,660 . . . . .346/E2
Garfield, Utah, U.S., *county*, 4,735 . . . . .350/C6
Garfield, Wash., U.S., 641 . . . . .358/H2
Garfield, Wash., U.S., *county*, 2,397 . . . . .358/H5
Garfield Hts., Ohio, U.S., 30,734 . . . . .328/G3, H9
Garforth, Eng., U.K., 15,250 . . . . .66/E5
Garforth, Eng., U.K., 15,250 . . . . .68/E2
Garibaldi, Oreg., U.S., 899 . . . . .334/C2
Garibaldi Prov. Park, Br. Col., Can. 214/L6
Garissa, Kenya, 31,319 . . . . .157/E4
Garland, Man., Can. .215/A3
Garland, Ala., U.S., 40 . . . . .238/C4
Garland, Ark., U.S., 352 . . . . .244/B4
Garland, Ark., U.S., *county*, 88,068 . . . . .244/B3
Garland, Kans., U.S., 100 . . . . .276/H4
Garland, Maine, U.S., 990 . . . . .286/C3
Garland, Mo., U.S., 100 . . . . .302/C3
Garland, Mont., U.S. 306/L3
Garland, Nebr., U.S., 247 . . . . .308/G3
Garland, N.C., U.S., 808 . . . . .322/J5
Garland, Penn., U.S., 225 . . . . .336/C2
Garland, Tenn., U.S. 344/D3
Garland, Tex., U.S., 215,768 . . . . .346/C9, M3
Garland, Utah, U.S., 1,943 . . . . .350/B2
Garland, Wyo., U.S., 95 . . . . .366/B1
Garlandville, Miss., U.S., 50 . . . . .300/C3
Garlin, Ky., U.S., 325 . . . . .280/E3
Garlock, Calif., U.S. 246/H7
Garlogie, Scot., U.K. .62/M4
Garmisch-Partenkirchen, Ger. 86/B5
Garnavillo, Iowa, U.S., 754 . . . . .274/M2
Garneill, Mont., U.S. 306/G3
Garner, Ark., U.S., 284 . . . . .244/D2
Garner, Iowa, U.S., 2,922 . . . . .274/G1
Garner, Ky., U.S., 600 . . . . .280/H3
Garner, N.C., U.S., 17,757 . . . . .322/H3
Garnet, Mich., U.S., 40 . . . . .294/D3
Garnett, Kans., U.S., 3,368 . . . . .276/G3
Garnett, S.C., U.S., 80 . . . . .340/C4
Garnish, Nfld., Can., 665 . . . . .218/D5
Garo, Colo., U.S. 250/E2
Garoowe, Som. 157/B2
Garoua, Came., 142,000 . . . . .153/B2
Garreston, Ky., U.S., *county*, 14,792 . . . . .280/F3
Garretson, S. Dak., U.S., 1,165 . . . . .342/J4
Garrett, Ill., U.S., 198 . . . . .266/E4
Garrett, Ind., U.S., 5,803 . . . . .270/F2
Garrett, Md., U.S., *county*, 29,846 . . . . .288/A3
Garrett, Penn., U.S., 449 . . . . .336/C6
Garrett, Wash., U.S., 1,022 . . . . .358/G3
Garrett, Wyo., U.S. .366/D2
Garrett Park, Md., U.S., 917 . . . . .288/B6
Garrettsville, Ohio, U.S., 2,262 . . . . .328/H3
Garrison, N. Ire., U.K., 325 . . . . .65/A3
Garrison, Iowa, U.S., 413 . . . . .274/K3
Garrison, Ky., U.S., 950 . . . . .280/G2
Garrison, Md., U.S., 7,969 . . . . .288/G2
Garrison, Minn., U.S., 213 . . . . .298/D4
Garrison, Mo., U.S., 40 . . . . .302/C5
Garrison, Mont., U.S., 112 . . . . .306/D3
Garrison, Nebr., U.S., 67 . . . . .308/G2
Garrison, N. Mex., U.S. 317/C4
Garrison, N. Dak., U.S., 1,318 . . . . .326/D2
Garrison, Tex., U.S., 844 . . . . .346/P4
Garrison, Utah, U.S., 50 . . . . .350/A5
Garron, N. Ire., U.K., *point* 65/F1
Garrow, Scot., U.K. 62/J5
Garry, Nun., Can., *lake* 220/H3
Garry, Scot., U.K., *lake* 62/G4
Garryowen, Mont., U.S. 306/J4
Garsdale Head, Eng., U.K. 66/D4
Garske, N. Dak., U.S. 326/G1
Garson Lake, Sask., Can. 227/A4
Garstang, Eng., U.K., 5,697 . . . . .66/C5
Garstang, Eng., U.K., 5,697 . . . . .68/B2
Garth, Wales, U.K. 64/D3
Garthorpe, Eng., U.K. .66/G5
Gartmore, Scot., U.K. .62/H6
Garton-on-the-Wolds, Eng., U.K. 66/G4
Garulia, India . . . . .128/Inset II
Garvagh, N. Ire., U.K., 1,091 . . . . .65/D2
Garve, Scot., U.K. 62/G3
Garvin, Minn., U.S., 159 . . . . .298/B6
Garvin, Okla., U.S., 143 . . . . .330/H4
Garvin, Okla., U.S., *county*, 27,210 . . . . .330/E3
Garwin, Iowa, U.S., 565 . . . . .274/J3
Garwood, Mo., U.S. 302/F4
Garwood, N.J., U.S., 4,153 . . . . .314/A3
Gary, Ind., U.S., 102,746 . . . . .270/B1
Gary, Minn., U.S., 215 . . . . .298/A3
Gary, S. Dak., U.S., 231 . . . . .342/J3
Gary, Tex., U.S., 303 . . . . .346/P3
Gary, W. Va., U.S., 917 . . . . .360/C6
Garysburg, N.C., U.S., 1,254 . . . . .322/K2
Garyville, La., U.S., 90 . . . . .354/J6
Garza, Tex., U.S., *county*, 4,872 . . . . .346/G2
Gas, Kans., U.S., 556 . . . . .276/G4
Gas City, Ind., U.S., 5,940 . . . . .270/E4
Gascon, N. Mex., U.S. 317/E2
Gasconade, Mo., U.S., 267 . . . . .302/E3
Gasconade, Mo., U.S., *county*, 15,342 . . . . .302/E3
Gascoyne, N. Dak., U.S. 326/B3
Gascoyne *river*, Austl. 170/A2
Gash, Erit., U.S., *river* 156/B2
Gaskin, Fla., U.S., 80 . . . . .256/B1
Gasparilla, Fla., U.S., *island* 256/F5
Gaspé, Que., Can., 14,932 . . . . .225/D4
Gaspé, Que., Can., 14,932 . . . . .226/M3
Gaspé, Que., Can., *peninsula*, 14,932 . . . . .226/L3
Gasper, Ky., U.S., 125 . . . . .280/E3
Gaspereau Forks, N.B., Can. 217/D2
Gaspereaux, P.E.I., Can. 224/C2
Gaspésie Prov. Park, Que., Can. 226/K3
Gasport, N.Y., U.S., 1,248 . . . . .320/E4
Gasque, Ala., U.S., 350 . . . . .238/B6
Gasquet, Calif., U.S., 300 . . . . .246/B1
Gassaway, W. Va., U.S., 901 . . . . .360/E4
Gassetts, Vt., U.S., 175 . . . . .352/B4
Gassoway, La., U.S. .282/G1
Gassville, Ark., U.S., 1,706 . . . . .244/C1
Gaston, Ind., U.S., 1,010 . . . . .270/E4
Gaston, N.C., U.S., 973 . . . . .322/K2
Gaston, N.C., U.S., *county*, 190,365 . . . . .322/C4
Gaston, N.C., U.S., *lake* 322/K1
Gaston, Oreg., U.S., 600 . . . . .334/C2
Gaston, S.C., U.S., 1,304 . . . . .340/C3
Gastonia, N.C., U.S., 66,277 . . . . .322/C4
Gata, Cyp., *cape* .133/B2
Gata, Sp., *cape* 94/E4
Gatcombe, Eng., U.K. .70/B5
Gate, Okla., U.S., 112 . . . . .330/B1
Gate City, Va., U.S., 2,159 . . . . .354/C3
Gatehouse, Eng., U.K. .66/D2
Gatehouse of Fleet, Scot., U.K., 892 . . . . .62/H9
Gates, N.Y., U.S., 15,138 . . . . .320/F4

Gates, N.C., U.S., 300 . . . . .322/M1
Gates, N.C., U.S., *county*, 10,516 . . . . .322/M2
Gates, Oreg., U.S., 471 . . . . .334/D3
Gates, Tenn., U.S., 901 . . . . .344/C3
Gateshead, Eng., U.K. .60/C2
Gateshead, Eng., U.K., 83,159 . . . . .66/E3
Gateshead, Eng., U.K., *unitary authority*,
191,151 . . . . .66/E3
Gates Mills, Ohio, U.S., 2,493 . . . . .328/H9
Gates of the Arctic Natl. Park and Preserve,
Alaska, U.S. 240/E1
Gatesville, Miss., U.S., 70 . . . . .300/B3
Gatesville, N.C., U.S., 281 . . . . .322/M2
Gatesville, Tex., U.S., 15,591 . . . . .346/L4
Gateway, Ark., U.S., 116 . . . . .244/B1
Gateway, Colo., U.S. 250/B3
Gateway Natl. Rec. Area, N.Y., U.S. 320/B3
Gatewood, Mo., U.S., 50 . . . . .302/E5
Gatico, Chile 190/B2
Gatineau, Que., Can., 102,898 . . . . .226/A6
Gatineau, Que., Can., *park*, 102,898 . . . . .225/A4
Gatineau, Que., Can., *river*, 102,898 . . . . .226/A4, A5
Gatineau Park, Que., Can. 226/A4
Gatliff, Ky., U.S., 90 . . . . .280/F4
Gatlinburg, Tenn., U.S., 3,382 . . . . .344/F3
Gattman, Miss., U.S., 114 . . . . .300/D2
Gatún, Pan., *lake* .203/C2
Gau, Fiji, *island* .174/B3
Gauley Bridge, W. Va., U.S., 738 . . . . .360/D4
Gauley River Natl. Rec. Area, W. Va., U.S. 360/D4
Gaultois, Nfld., Can., 321 . . . . .218/D5
Gautier, Miss., U.S., 11,681 . . . . .300/D5
Gavarr, Arm. 103/C2
Gavilan, N. Mex., U.S., 60 . . . . .317/C1
Gaviota, Calif., U.S. 246/E8
Gävle, Swe., 91,233 . . . . .80/C2
Gävleborg, Swe., *county* 80/C2
Gawthorpe, Eng., U.K. .66/D4
Gay, Ga., U.S., 149 .260/B5
Gay, Mich., U.S., 40 .294/A2
Gay, Okla., U.S., 100 . . . . .330/G4
Gaya, India 128/E4
Gaya, Niger 152/A3
Gayhurst, Eng., U.K. .68/F5
Gayle Mill, S.C., U.S., 1,094 . . . . .340/C1
Gaylesville, Ala., U.S., 140 . . . . .238/D1
Gaylord, Kans., U.S., 145 . . . . .276/D2
Gaylord, Mich., U.S., 3,681 . . . . .294/E4
Gaylord, Minn., U.S., 2,279 . . . . .298/C6
Gaylord, Oreg., U.S. 334/B5
Gaylordsville, Conn., U.S., 750 . . . . .253/B3
Gays, Ill., U.S., 259 . . . . .266/E4
Gays Mills, Wisc., U.S., 625 . . . . .364/C5
Gaysville, Vt., U.S., 150 . . . . .352/B3
Gayville, S. Dak., U.S., 418 . . . . .342/H5
Gaza, Iowa, U.S., 70 . . . . .274/C1
Gaza, N.Y., U.S., 100 . . . . .212/C4
Gazanjyk, Turkm. 132/B2
Gazelle, P.N.G., *peninsula* 172/B2
Gaziantep, Tur., 712,800 . . . . .133/D3
Gaziantep, Tur., *province* 133/D3
Gazimağusa, (Famagusta), Cyp. 133/B1
Gbarnga, Liber. 149/B2
Gdańsk, Pol., 455,464 .83/D1
Gdańsk, Pol., *gulf* .83/D1
Gdynia, Pol., 254,034 . . . . .83/D1
Gearhart, Oreg., U.S., 995 . . . . .334/C1
Gearhart, Oreg., U.S., *mountain* 334/F5
Geary, N.B., Can. 217/C3
Geary, Kans., U.S., *county*, 27,947 . . . . .276/F3
Geary, Okla., U.S., 1,258 . . . . .330/D2
Geauga, Ohio, U.S., *county*, 90,895 . . . . .328/H3, J9
Gêba, Gui.-B., *river* 149/C1
Gebo, Wyo., U.S. 366/B2
Geddes, S. Dak., U.S., 252 . . . . .342/G4
Gedney Drove End, Eng., U.K. 70/E1
Geelong, Vic., Austl. 170/D3
Gees Gwardafuy, Som., *cape* 157/C1
Geeville, Miss., U.S., 40 . . . . .300/D1
Geff, Ill., U.S., 366 . . . . .266/E5
Gege, Swaz. 161/B2
Geghark'unik', Arm., *district* 103/C2
Geidam, Nig. 152/F1
Geiger, Ala., U.S., 161 . . . . .238/A3
Geikie, Sask., Can., *river* 227/F3
Geismar, La., U.S., 80 . . . . .282/G6
Gejiu, China 119/D3
Gela, It. 95/C3
Gelderland, Neth., *province* 84/D2
Gelibolu, Tur. 133/A2
Gelligaer, Wales, U.K., 15,906 . . . . .64/E4
Gelsenkirchen, Ger., 281,979 . . . . .86/E3
Gem, Alta., Can. 212/D6
Gem, Ida., U.S. 264/B2
Gem, Ida., U.S., *county*, 15,181 . . . . .264/A5
Gem, Kans., U.S., 96 . . . . .276/B2
Gembloux, Belg. 85/C2
Gemena, Congo, D.R. .155/B1
Gemmell, Minn., U.S. 298/C3
Gem Vil., Colo., U.S., 175 . . . . .250/C4
Genale, Eth., *river* 156/C3
General, C.R., *river* 203/C3
General Eugenio A. Garay, Para. 187/A2
General Santos, Phil., 411,822 . . . . .120/C5
Genesee, Alta., Can. 212/C4
Genesee, Ida., U.S., 946 . . . . .264/A3
Genesee, Mich., U.S., 1,800 . . . . .294/F6
Genesee, Mich., U.S., *county*, 436,141 . . . . .294/F6
Genesee, N.Y., U.S., *county*, 60,370 . . . . .320/E5
Genesee, N.Y., U.S., *river* 320/E5
Genesee, Penn., U.S., 425 . . . . .336/F2
Geneseo, Ill., U.S., 6,480 . . . . .266/C2
Geneseo, Kans., U.S., 272 . . . . .276/D3
Geneseo, N.Y., U.S., 7,579 . . . . .320/F5
Geneva, Fr., Ger., *lake* 88/D3
Geneva, Switz., 175,998, (450,592, *metro.*) 90/A2
Geneva, Switz., *canton* 90/A2
Geneva, Switz., *lake* 90/A2
Geneva, Ala., U.S., 4,388 . . . . .238/D4
Geneva, Ala., U.S., *county*, 25,764 . . . . .238/D4
Geneva, Fla., U.S., 2,601 . . . . .256/D3
Geneva, Ga., U.S., 114 . . . . .260/B6
Geneva, Ida., U.S. .264/F7
Geneva, Ill., U.S., 19,515 . . . . .266/A6, E2
Geneva, Ind., U.S., 1,368 . . . . .270/G3
Geneva, Iowa, U.S., 171 . . . . .274/H2
Geneva, Minn., U.S., 449 . . . . .298/D7
Geneva, Nebr., U.S., 2,226 . . . . .308/G3
Geneva, N.Y., U.S., 13,617 . . . . .320/H5
Geneva, Ohio, U.S., 6,595 . . . . .328/J2
Geneva, Tex., U.S. .346/R4
Geneva, Wash., U.S., 2,257 . . . . .358/C1
Geneva, Wyo., U.S. .366/A2
Geneva-on-the-Lake, Ohio, U.S., 1,545 . . . . .328/J2
Genk, Belg. 85/D2
Gennargentu, It., *mountains* 95/B2
Genoa, It. 95/B1
Genoa, It., *gulf* 95/B1
Genoa, Ark., U.S., 250 . . . . .244/B4
Genoa, Colo., U.S., 211 . . . . .250/G2
Genoa, Fla., U.S., 50 . . . . .256/F1

Genoa, Ill., U.S., 4,169 . . . . .266/E1
Genoa, Nebr., U.S., 981 . . . . .308/G2
Genoa, Nev., U.S., 250 . . . . .310/A2
Genoa, Ohio, U.S., 2,230 . . . . .328/D2
Genoa, Wisc., U.S., 263 . . . . .364/B5
Genoa City, Wisc., U.S., 1,949 . . . . .364/E6
Genola, Minn., U.S., 71 . . . . .298/C5
Genola, Utah, U.S., 965 . . . . .350/C3
Gentilly, Fr. .88/Inset II
Gentilly, Minn., U.S., 100 . . . . .298/A3
Gentofte, Den. 79/D3
Gentry, Ark., U.S., 2,165 . . . . .244/A1
Gentry, Mo., U.S., 101 . . . . .302/B1
Gentry, Mo., U.S., *county*, 6,861 . . . . .302/B1
Gentryville, Ind., U.S., 262 . . . . .270/B8
Gentryville, Mo., U.S. 302/D5
Geoje-do, S. Kor., *island* 116/C5
George, Que., Can., *river* 218/D3
George, Que., Can., *river* 225/C2
George, S. Afr. 162/B3
George, Ug., *lake* .157/B4
George, Fla., U.S., *lake* 256/G2
George, Iowa, U.S., 1,051 . . . . .274/B1
George, Miss., U.S., *county*, 19,144 . . . . .300/D5
George, N.Y., U.S., *lake* 320/P3
George, S.C., U.S., 125 . . . . .322/L2
George, Wash., U.S., 528 . . . . .358/F2
George Rogers Clark N.H.P., Ind., U.S. 270/A7
Georges, Fr. .88/Inset II
Georges Mills, N.H., U.S., 300 . . . . .212/B5
Georgetown, P.E.I., Can., 721 . . . . .224/C2
George Town, Cay. Is., *capital* 204/A3
Georgetown, Gam. 148/D2
Georgetown, Guy., *capital*, 72,049,
(275,000, *metro.*) 183/B2
George Town, Malay., 219,603 . . . . .121/A2
Georgetown, St. Vin.-Gren. 208/B2
Georgetown, Ala., U.S., 300 . . . . .238/A5
Georgetown, Ark., U.S., 126 . . . . .244/D2
Georgetown, Calif., U.S., 962 . . . . .246/L5
Georgetown, Colo., U.S., 1,088 . . . . .250/E2
Georgetown, Conn., U.S., 1,650 . . . . .253/B5
Georgetown, Del., U.S., 4,643 . . . . .255/C6
Georgetown, Fla., U.S., 450 . . . . .256/G2
Georgetown, Ga., U.S., 973 . . . . .260/A8
Georgetown, Ill., U.S., 538 . . . . .264/F7
Georgetown, Ill., U.S., 3,628 . . . . .266/F4
Georgetown, (Floyd County), Ind., U.S., 2,227 . . . . . . .270/E8
Georgetown, (St. Joseph County), Ind., U.S.,
4,497 . . . . .270/D1
Georgetown, Ky., U.S., 18,080 . . . . .280/F2
Georgetown, La., U.S., 301 . . . . .282/E3
Georgetown, Mass., U.S., 7,377 . . . . .292/L2
Georgetown, Minn., U.S., 125 . . . . .298/A3
Georgetown, Miss., U.S., 344 . . . . .300/B4
Georgetown, N.J., U.S., 550 . . . . .314/D3
Georgetown, Ohio, U.S., 3,691 . . . . .328/C8
Georgetown, Penn., U.S., 182 . . . . .336/A4
Georgetown, S.C., U.S., 8,950 . . . . .340/E3
Georgetown, S.C., U.S., *county*, 55,797 . . . . .340/E3
Georgetown, Tex., U.S., 28,339 . . . . .346/D1, L5
George Washington Birthplace Natl. Mon.,
Va., U.S. 354/K4
George Washington Natl. For., Va., U.S. 354/E3, E5
George West, Tex., U.S., 2,524 . . . . .346/K7
Georgia, *nation* 101
Georgia, Br. Col., Can., *strait* 358/B1
Georgia, U.S., *state* 248
Georgia Ctr., Vt., U.S., 375 . . . . .352/A1
Georgian, Ont., Can., *bay* 222/D3
Georgian, Ont., Can., *bay* 223/E2
Georgiana, Ala., U.S., 1,737 . . . . .238/C4
Georgian Bay Islands Natl. Park, Ont., Can. 223/F3
Gera, Ger., 114,718 .86/C3
Geral, Braz., *range* 188/C4
Gerald, Man., Can. .215/A4
Gerald, Mo., U.S., 1,171 . . . . .302/E3
Gerald, Ohio, U.S., 150 . . . . .328/B3
Geraldine, Ala., U.S., 786 . . . . .238/C1
Geraldine, Mont., U.S., 284 . . . . .306/F3
Geraldton, W.A., Austl. 170/A2
Geraldton, Ont., Can., 2,224 . . . . .222/C3
Gerard, Maine, U.S. .286/B3
Gerber, (Gerber-Las Flores), Calif., U.S., 1,389 . . . . .246/C2
Gerber, Oreg., U.S., *reservoir* 334/E5
Gering, Nebr., U.S., 7,751 . . . . .308/A2
Gerlach, Nev., U.S., 499 . . . . .310/A1
Gerlachovský Štít, Slvk., *mountain* 92/C2
Germania, N.J., U.S., 750 . . . . .314/D4
Germania, Penn., U.S., 80 . . . . .336/F2
Germania, Wisc., U.S., 70 . . . . .364/D5
Germann, Ariz., U.S. 242/D4
Germantown, Ill., U.S., 1,118 . . . . .266/D5
Germantown, Iowa, U.S., 100 . . . . .274/C2
Germantown, Ky., U.S., 190 . . . . .280/G2
Germantown, Md., U.S., 55,419 . . . . .288/E3
Germantown, Tenn., U.S., 37,348 . . . . .344/B4
Germantown, Wisc., U.S., 18,260 . . . . .364/E5, F1
Germantown Hills, Ill., U.S., 2,111 . . . . .266/D3
German Valley, Ill., U.S., 481 . . . . .266/D1
Germany, *nation* 84
Germfask, Mich., U.S., 125 . . . . .294/D3
Germiston, S. Afr. .162/C2
Gernika-Lumo, Sp. 94/E1
Geronimo, Ariz., U.S. 242/E4
Geronimo, Okla., U.S., 959 . . . . .330/D3
Geronimo, Tex., U.S., 619 . . . . .346/B3
Gerrards Cross, Eng., U.K. 70/C3
Gerry, Maine, U.S., 40 . . . . .286/D3
Gers, Fr., *department* 88/C5
Gerster, Mo., U.S. .302/C4
Gerton, N.C., U.S., 175 . . . . .322/A4
Gerty, Okla., U.S., 101 . . . . .330/F3
Gervais, Oreg., U.S., 2,009 . . . . .334/D2
Gessie, Ind., U.S., 100 . . . . .270/A5
Getafe, Sp., 151,479 . . . . .94/E2, Inset II
Gettysburg, Ohio, U.S., 558 . . . . .328/A5
Gettysburg, Penn., U.S., 7,490 . . . . .336/G6
Gettysburg, S. Dak., U.S., 1,352 . . . . .342/F2
Gettysburg Natl. Mil. Park, Penn., U.S. 336/G6
Geuda Sprs., Kans., U.S., 212 . . . . .276/E4
Geum, S. Kor., *river* 116/B4
Gevgelija, Mac. 100/C2
Geylegphug, Bhu. 126/B3
Geyser, Mont., U.S., 40 . . . . .306/F3
Geyserville, Calif., U.S., 700 . . . . .246/C4
Ghabah, Oman 137/C2
Ghadamis, Lib. 145/A1
Ghaghara, India, *river* 128/D3
Ghana, *nation* 144
Ghanzi, Bots. 160/A2
Ghardaïa, Alg. 146/B1
Gharyan, Lib. 145/B3
Ghat, Lib. 145/B3
Ghatkopar, India . . . . .128/Inset I
Ghazni, Afg. 129/B2
Gheen, Minn., U.S. .298/E3
Ghent, Belg., 226,220, (498,631, *metro.*) 85/B1
Ghent, Ky., U.S., 371 . . . . .280/E2
Ghent, Minn., U.S., 315 . . . . .298/B6
Ghent, Ohio, U.S., 5,261 . . . . .328/G3
Ghent, W. Va., U.S., 325 . . . . .360/D5

Gheorghe Gheorghiu-Dej, Rom. 101/D2
Gholson, Miss., U.S. 300/D3
Giant's Causeway, N. Ire., U.K. 65/D1
Giant Sequoia Natl. Mon. (N. Unit), Calif., U.S. 246/G6
Giant Sequoia Natl. Mon. (S. Unit), Calif., U.S. 246/G6
Giants Neck, Conn., U.S., 1,000 . . . . .253/E4
Gibbon, Minn., U.S., 808 . . . . .298/C6
Gibbon, Nebr., U.S., 1,759 . . . . .308/E3
Gibbon, Oreg., U.S. .334/H2
Gibbonsville, Ida., U.S. 264/D4
Gibbs, Mo., U.S., 100 . . . . .302/D1
Gibbsboro, N.J., U.S., 2,435 . . . . .314/B3, D4
Gibbstown, N.J., U.S., 3,758 . . . . .314/C4
Gibraltar, Mor., *strait* 147/C1
Gibraltar, Sp., *dependency* 94/D5
Gibraltar, Mich., U.S., 4,264 . . . . .294/B7, F7
Gibsland, La., U.S., 1,119 . . . . .282/C1
Gibson, Austl., *desert* 170/B2
Gibson, (Craighead County), Ark., U.S., 60 . . . . .244/E2
Gibson, (Pulaski County), Ark., U.S., 4,678 . . . . .244/C3
Gibson, Ga., U.S., 694 . . . . .260/F5
Gibson, Ind., U.S., *county*, 32,500 . . . . .270/A8
Gibson, Iowa, U.S., 92 . . . . .274/K5
Gibson, La., U.S., 475 . . . . .282/H7
Gibson, Md., U.S., 650 . . . . .288/J1
Gibson, N.C., U.S., 584 . . . . .322/F5
Gibson, Tenn., U.S., 305 . . . . .344/D3
Gibson, Tenn., U.S., *county*, 48,152 . . . . .344/D2
Gibsonburg, Ohio, U.S., 2,506 . . . . .328/D3
Gibson City, Ill., U.S., 3,373 . . . . .266/E3
Gibsonton, Fla., U.S., 8,752 . . . . .256/D6, F4
Gibsonville, N.C., U.S., 4,372 . . . . .322/F2
Giddings, Tex., U.S., 5,105 . . . . .346/M5
Gideon, Mo., U.S., 1,113 . . . . .302/G5
Giessen, Ger. 86/B3
Giessen, Ger., *department* 86/B3
Gifford, Nun., Can., *river* 220/M2
Gifford, Ark., U.S., 250 . . . . .244/C3
Gifford, Fla., U.S., 7,599 . . . . .256/H4
Gifford, Ida., U.S. .264/A3
Gifford, Ill., U.S., 815 . . . . .266/E3
Gifford, Ind., U.S., 80 . . . . .270/B2
Gifford, Iowa, U.S., 70 . . . . .274/H3
Gifford, S.C., U.S., 370 . . . . .340/C4
Gifford, Wash., U.S. 358/G1
Gifford Pinchot Natl. For., Wash., U.S. 358/D3
Gift Lake, Alta., Can., 809 . . . . .212/C3
Gifu, Jap., 403,000 .114/C3
Gifu, Jap., *prefecture* 114/C3
Giggleswick, Eng., U.K. 68/C1
Gigha, Scot., U.K., *island* 62/E7
Gig Harbor, Wash., U.S., 6,465 . . . . .358/C2
Giglio, It., *island* 95/B2
Gijón, Sp., 266,419 .94/D1
Gikongoro, Rwa. 152/B2
Gila, Ariz., U.S., *county*, 51,335 . . . . .242/E4
Gila, Ariz., U.S., *river* 242/B5, D4, F4
Gila, N. Mex., U.S., 90 . . . . .317/B5
Gila, N. Mex., U.S., *river* 317/B4, B5
Gila Bend, Ariz., U.S., 1,980 . . . . .242/C5
Gila Box Riparian Natl. Cons. Area, Ariz., U.S. 242/F4
Gila Cliff Dwellings N.M., N. Mex., U.S. 317/B4
Gilan, Iran, *province* 130/C2
Gila Natl. For., N. Mex., U.S. 317/B4, B5
Gilark, La., U.S. 282/C1
Gilbert, Austl., *river* 170/D1
Gilbert, Kiri., *islands* 175/A1
Gilbert, Ariz., U.S., 109,697 . . . . .242/D4
Gilbert, Ark., U.S. .244/C1
Gilbert, Iowa, U.S., 987 . . . . .274/G3
Gilbert, La., U.S., 561 . . . . .282/F2
Gilbert, Minn., U.S., 1,847 . . . . .298/E3
Gilbert, S.C., U.S., 500 . . . . .340/C3
Gilbert, W. Va., U.S., 417 . . . . .360/C5
Gilberton, Penn., U.S., 867 . . . . .336/J4
Gilbert Plains, Man., Can., 757 . . . . .215/A3
Gilberts, Ill., U.S., 1,279 . . . . .266/E1
Gilbertsville, Ky., U.S., 375 . . . . .320/L6
Gilbertville, Iowa, U.S., 767 . . . . .274/K3
Gilbertville, Mass., U.S., 1,000 . . . . .292/F3
Gilboa, Ohio, U.S., 170 . . . . .328/C3
Gilboa, W. Va., U.S., 275 . . . . .360/E4
Gilby, N. Dak., U.S., 243 . . . . .326/H1
Gilchrist, Fla., U.S., *county*, 14,437 . . . . .256/C2
Gilchrist, Mich., U.S. 294/D3
Gilchrist, Oreg., U.S., 450 . . . . .334/E4
Gilchrist, Tex., U.S., 300 . . . . .346/P6
Gilcrest, Colo., U.S., 1,162 . . . . .250/F1
Gildford, Mont., U.S., 185 . . . . .306/F1
Gilead, Conn., U.S., 325 . . . . .253/F3
Gilead, Maine, U.S., 156 . . . . .286/A4
Gilead, Nebr., U.S., 40 . . . . .308/G3
Giles, Tenn., U.S., *county*, 29,447 . . . . .344/G4
Giles, Tex., U.S. 346/G9
Giles, Va., U.S., *county*, 16,657 . . . . .354/B6
Gilford, N. Ire., U.K., 1,639 . . . . .65/E3
Gilford, N.H., U.S., 6,803 . . . . .312/D4
Gilford Park, N.J., U.S., 8,700 . . . . .314/E4
Gilgit, Pak. 129/E2
Gill, Colo., U.S., 250 . . . . .250/F1
Gill, Mass., U.S., 1,363 . . . . .292/E2
Gillam, Man., Can., 1,178 . . . . .215/D1
Gillespie, Ill., U.S., 3,412 . . . . .266/B3, D4
Gillespie, Tex., U.S., *county*, 20,814 . . . . .346/J5
Gillett, Ark., U.S., 819 . . . . .244/D3
Gillett, Penn., U.S., 375 . . . . .336/H2
Gillett, Tex., U.S., 60 . . . . .346/K6
Gillett, Wisc., U.S., 1,256 . . . . .364/E4
Gillette, Wyo., U.S., 19,646 . . . . .366/D2
Gillett Grove, Iowa, U.S., 55 . . . . .274/D1
Gilham, Ark., U.S., 188 . . . . .244/A3
Gilliam, La., U.S., 178 . . . . .282/B1
Gilliam, Mo., U.S., 229 . . . . .302/D2
Gilliam, Oreg., U.S., *county*, 1,915 . . . . .334/F2
Gilliland, Tex., U.S., 70 . . . . .346/J2
Gillingham, Eng., U.K. 60/D4
Gillingham, Eng., U.K., 94,923 . . . . .70/F4
Gillingham, Eng., U.K., 6,404 . . . . .73/H2
Gillis, La., U.S. 282/C6
Gilsburg, Miss., U.S. 300/B4
Gills Rock, Wisc., U.S., 125 . . . . .364/F3
Gillsville, Ga., U.S., 195 . . . . .260/D3
Gilman, Colo., U.S. .250/D2
Gilman, Conn., U.S., 275 . . . . .253/G3
Gilman, Ill., U.S., 1,793 . . . . .266/F3
Gilman, Iowa, U.S., 600 . . . . .274/J4
Gilman, Minn., U.S., 215 . . . . .298/D5
Gilman, Vt., U.S., 375 . . . . .352/D2
Gilman, Wisc., U.S., 474 . . . . .364/C3
Gilman City, Mo., U.S., 380 . . . . .302/C1
Gilmanton, N.H., U.S., 3,060 . . . . .312/D5
Gilmanton, Wisc., U.S., 175 . . . . .364/B4
Gilmanton Ironworks, N.H., U.S., 225 . . . . .312/D5
Gilmer, Ga., U.S., *county*, 23,456 . . . . .260/C2
Gilmer, Tex., U.S., 4,799 . . . . .346/P3
Gilmer, W. Va., U.S., *county*, 7,160 . . . . .360/E3
Gilmore, Ark., U.S., 292 . . . . .244/E2
Gilmore City, Iowa, U.S., 556 . . . . .274/F2
Gilpin, Colo., U.S., *county*, 4,757 . . . . .250/E2

Gilpin, Ky., U.S., 40 . . . . .280/F3
Gilpin, Tex., U.S. 294/H2
Gilroy, Calif., U.S., 41,464 . . . . . .246/D5, L4
Gilsum, N.H., U.S., 777 . . . . .312/B5
Gilt Edge, Tenn., U.S., 489 . . . . . .344/B3
Giltner, Nebr., U.S., 389 . . . . .308/E3
Gilwern, Wales, U.K., 2,311 . . . . . .64/E4
Gimcheon, S. Kor. 116/C4
Gimie, St. Luc., mountain 208/A2
Gimli, Man., Can., 1,657 . . . . .215/C4
Girard, Ga., U.S., 227 . . . . .260/H5
Girard, Ill., U.S., 2,245 . . . . .266/D4
Girard, Kans., U.S., 2,773 . . . . . . .276/H4
Girard, Mich., U.S., 275 . . . . .294/D7
Girard, Ohio, U.S., 10,902 . . . . . . .328/J3
Girard, Penn., U.S., 3,164 . . . . . . .336/A2
Girard, Tex., U.S., 62 . . . . .346/H2
Girardville, Penn., U.S., 1,742 . . . . .336/J4
Girdletree, Md., U.S., 117 . . . . . . .288/N7
Giresun, Tur. 133/D2
Giresun, Tur., province 133/D2
Girista, Scot., U.K. 62/Q2
Girne, (Kyrenia), Cyp. 133/B1
Girona, Sp., 74,879 . . . . .94/H2
Girona, Sp., province 94/H2
Gironde, Fr., department 88/B4
Gironde, Fr., river 88/B4
Girouxville, Alta., Can., 306 . . . . . .212/B3
Girvan, Scot., U.K., 6,992 . . . . . . .62/G8
Girvin, Tex., U.S., 60 . . . . .346/F4
Gisborne, N.Z., (31,719, metro.) . . .171/C2
Gisborne, N.Z., region 171/C2
Gisburn, Eng., U.K. 66/D5
Gisela, Ariz., U.S., 532 . . . . .242/D3
Gisenyi, Rwa. 152/B2
Gishingham, Eng., U.K. 152/B2
Gitarama, Rwa. 152/B2
Gitega, Bur., 102,000 . . . . .152/F2
Giurgiu, Rom. 101/C4
Giurgiu, Rom., county 101/C3
Giza, Egy., 2,221,817 . . . . .144/B2
Gizo, Sol. Is. 173/A1
Gjirokastër, Alb., 20,630 . . . . .99/B3
Gjoa Haven, Nun., Can., 960 . . . . .220/J3
Gjøvik, Nor. 80/C3
Glace Bay, N.S., Can., 21,187 . . . . .221/H1
Glacier, Mont., U.S., county, 13,247 .306/D1
Glacier, Wash., U.S., 90 . . . . .358/D1
Glacier, Wash., U.S., peak 358/D1
Glacier Bay Natl. Park and Preserve, Alaska, U.S. .240/H3
Glacier Natl. Park, Br. Col., Can. . . .212/B5
Glacier Natl. Park, Br. Col., Can. . . .214/O5
Glacier Natl. Park, Mont., U.S. 306/C1
Gladbrook, Iowa, U.S., 1,015 . . . . .274/J3
Gladden, Ariz., U.S., 400 . . . . .242/B4
Gladden, Mo., U.S. 302/E4
Glade, Kans., U.S., 114 . . . . .276/C2
Gladehill, Va., U.S., 125 . . . . .354/D7
Glade Park, Colo., U.S., 125 . . . . . .250/B3
Glades, Fla., U.S., county, 10,576 . . .256/C5
Glade Spr., Va., U.S., 1,374 . . . . . . .354/E3
Gladewater, Tex., U.S., 6,078 . . . . .346/P3
Gladiola, N. Mex., U.S. 317/G4
Gladstone, Qnsld., Austl., 33,447, (34,000, metro.) 170/E2
Gladstone, Man., Can., 848 . . . . . . .215/B4
Gladstone, Colo., U.S. 250/C4
Gladstone, Ill., U.S., 284 . . . . .266/C4
Gladstone, Mich., U.S., 5,032 . . . . .294/B4
Gladstone, Mo., U.S., 26,365 . . . . .302/B2, H4
Gladstone, N.J., U.S., 2,433 . . . . . . .314/D2
Gladstone, N. Mex., U.S. 317/G1
Gladstone, N. Dak., U.S., 284 . . . . .326/C3
Gladstone, Oreg., U.S., 11,438 . . . . .334/A3
Gladstone, Va., U.S., 125 . . . . .354/F5
Glad Valley, S. Dak., U.S. 342/D2
Gladwin, Mich., U.S., 3,001 . . . . . .294/E6
Gladwin, Mich., U.S., county, 26,023 .294/E5
Glady, W. Va., U.S., 50 . . . . .360/G3
Gladys, Va., U.S., 70 . . . . .354/E6
Glais, Wales, U.K. 64/D4
Glåma, Nor., river 80/B2
Glåma, Nor., river 80/B2
Glamis, Scot., U.K. 62/L5
Glamis, Calif., U.S. 246/K10
Glanaman, Wales, U.K., 4,244 . . . . .64/D4
Glancy, Miss., U.S. 300/B4
Glandorf, Ohio, U.S., 919 . . . . .328/B3
Glanvillia, Dom. 208/A2
Glarus, Switz., canton 90/D2
Glascarnoch, Scot., U.K., lake 62/G3
Glasco, Kans., U.S., 536 . . . . .276/E2
Glasco, N.Y., U.S., 1,692 . . . . .320/P6
Glascock, Ga., U.S., county, 2,556 . . .260/F5
Glascoed, Wales, U.K. 64/F4
Glasford, Ill., U.S., 1,076 . . . . .266/D4
Glasgo, Conn., U.S., 500 . . . . .253/H3
Glasgow, Scot., U.K., 629,501 . . . . .60/B2
Glasgow, Scot., U.K., 629,501 . . . . .62/H7
Glasgow, City of, Scot., U.K., unitary authority, 629,501 . . . . .62/H7
Glasgow, Del., U.S., 12,840 . . . . . . .255/B2
Glasgow, Ill., U.S., 170 . . . . .266/C4
Glasgow, Iowa, U.S., 40 . . . . .274/L6
Glasgow, Ky., U.S., 13,019 . . . . . . .280/E3
Glasgow, Mo., U.S., 1,263 . . . . . . .302/D2
Glasgow, Mont., U.S., 3,253 . . . . . .306/K1
Glasgow, Penn., U.S., 63 . . . . .336/A4
Glasgow, Va., U.S., 1,046 . . . . .354/E5
Glasgow, W. Va., U.S., 783 . . . . . . .360/D4
Glasgow Vil., Mo., U.S., 5,234 . . . . .302/J2
Glaslyn, Sask., Can., 375 . . . . .227/B7
Glas Maol, Scot., U.K., hill 62/K5
Glass, Scot., U.K., lake 62/G3
Glassboro, N.J., U.S., 19,068 . . . . . .314/C4
Glasscock, Tex., U.S., county, 1,406 . .346/G4
Glasshouses, Eng., U.K. 66/E4
Glassmanor, Md., U.S., 35,355 . . . . .288/B7, F4
Glasson, Eng., U.K. 66/C5
Glassport, Penn., U.S., 4,993 . . . . . .336/D7
Glassville, N.B., Can., 108 . . . . .217/B2
Glastonbury, Eng., U.K. 60/C3
Glastonbury, Eng., U.K., 7,747 . . . . .73/G2
Glastonbury, Conn., U.S., 31,876 . . .253/E3
Glazeley, Eng., U.K. 68/C5
Glazier, Tex., U.S., 40 . . . . .346/H8
Gleason, Tenn., U.S., 1,463 . . . . . . .344/D2
Gleason, Wisc., U.S., 325 . . . . .364/D3
Gleed, Wash., U.S., 2,947 . . . . .358/E3
Gleeson, Ariz., U.S. 242/F6
Gleichen, Alta., Can., 408 . . . . .212/D6
Glen, Mich., U.S., lake 294/D5
Glen, Minn., U.S., 50 . . . . .298/C4
Glen, Miss., U.S., 286 . . . . .300/D1
Glen, Mont., U.S. 306/D4
Glen, N.H., U.S., 200 . . . . .312/D3
Glen Affric N.P., Scot., U.K. 62/G4
Glenaire, Mo., U.S., 553 . . . . .302/J4
Glen Allan, Miss., U.S., 400 . . . . . . .300/A2
Glen Allen, Ala., U.S., 442 . . . . .238/B2
Glenallen, Mo., U.S., 145 . . . . .302/F4
Glen Allen, Va., U.S., 12,562 . . . . . .354/H5

Glen Alpine, N.C., U.S., 1,090 . . . . .322/B3
Glen Arbor, Mich., U.S., 200 . . . . . .294/C5
Glenarden, Md., U.S., 6,318 . . . . . . .288/C7, G4
Glenariff, N. Ire., U.K., 371 . . . . . . .65/E1
Glenarm, N. Ire., U.K., 603 . . . . . . .65/F2
Glen Arm, Md., U.S., 500 . . . . .288/J2
Glenavy, N. Ire., U.K., 497 . . . . . . .65/E2
Glenbar, Ariz., U.S. 242/F5
Glenbeulah, Wisc., U.S., 378 . . . . . .364/E5
Glenboro, Man., Can., 656 . . . . .215/B4
Glenburn, N. Dak., U.S., 374 . . . . . .326/D1
Glen Burnie, Md., U.S., 38,922 . . . . .288/H3
Glen Campbell, Penn., U.S., 306 . . . .336/D4
Glen Canyon, Ariz., U.S., dam 242/D1
Glen Canyon Natl. Rec. Area, Utah, U.S. 350/C6, D5, D6
Glen Carbon, Ill., U.S., 10,425 . . . . .266/A3
Glencliff, N.H., U.S., 40 . . . . .312/C4
Glencoe, Ont., Can., 2,152 . . . . .223/D5
Glencoe, Scot., U.K. 62/F5
Glencoe, Ala., U.S., 5,152 . . . . .238/D2
Glencoe, Ark., U.S., 100 . . . . .244/D1
Glencoe, Ill., U.S., 8,762 . . . . .266/B5
Glencoe, Ky., U.S., 251 . . . . .280/F2
Glencoe, Md., U.S., U.S. 288/H1
Glencoe, Minn., U.S., 5,453 . . . . . . .298/C6
Glencoe, N. Mex., U.S. 317/E4
Glencoe, Okla., U.S., 583 . . . . .330/F1
Glen Cove, Maine, U.S., 375 . . . . . .286/C4
Glen Cove, N.Y., U.S., 26,622 . . . . .320/C2
Glencross, S. Dak., U.S. 342/E2
Glendale, Ariz., U.S., 218,812 . . . . .242/C4
Glendale, Ark., U.S., 200 . . . . .244/D4
Glendale, Calif., U.S., 194,973 . . . . .246/C9, G8
Glendale, Colo., U.S., 4,547 . . . . . . .250/A3
Glendale, Fla., U.S., 80 . . . . .256/B1
Glendale, Ind., U.S., 50 . . . . .270/B7
Glendale, Kans., U.S. 276/E3
Glendale, Ky., U.S., 350 . . . . .280/D3
Glendale, Mass., U.S., 250 . . . . .292/A3
Glendale, Mich., U.S., 300 . . . . .294/D7
Glendale, Mo., U.S., 5,767 . . . . .302/H3
Glendale, Nev., U.S. 310/C3
Glendale, N.H., U.S., 700 . . . . .312/D4
Glendale, Ohio, U.S., 2,188 . . . . . . .328/B9
Glendale, Oreg., U.S., 855 . . . . .334/C5
Glendale, R.I., U.S., 800 . . . . .339/C2
Glendale, Utah, U.S., 355 . . . . .350/B6
Glendale, Wisc., U.S., 13,367 . . . . . .364/F2
Glendale Hts., Ill., U.S., 31,765 . . . . .266/B5
Glendale Sprs., N.C., U.S., 225 . . . . .322/C2
Glen Dean, Ky., U.S. 280/D3
Glendevey, Colo., U.S. 250/E1
Glendive, Mont., U.S., 4,729 . . . . . .306/M2
Glendo, Wyo., U.S., 229 . . . . .366/F2
Glendon, Alta., Can., 459 . . . . .212/E4
Glendon, N.C., U.S. 322/G4
Glendon, Penn., U.S., 367 . . . . .336/L4
Glendora, Calif., U.S., 49,415 . . . . . .246/E9
Glendora, Mich., U.S., 325 . . . . .294/C8
Glendora, Miss., U.S., 285 . . . . .300/B3
Glendora, N.J., U.S., 4,907 . . . . .314/B3, C4
Glendo St. Park, Wyo., U.S. 366/F2
Glen Echo, Md., U.S., 242 . . . . .288/A6
Glen Elder, Kans., U.S., 439 . . . . . . .276/D2
Glenelg, S.A., Austl. . . . . .170/Inset II
Glenella, Man., Can. 215/B4
Glen Ellyn, Ill., U.S., 26,999 . . . . . . .266/B6
Glenfield, Eng., U.K. 70/B1
Glenfield, N.Y., U.S., 475 . . . . .320/L3
Glenfield, N. Dak., U.S., 134 . . . . . .326/G2
Glen Flora, Wisc., U.S., 93 . . . . .364/C3
Glenford, Ohio, U.S., 198 . . . . .328/F6
Glen Forrest, W.A., Austl. . . . . .170/Inset I
Glen Gardner, N.J., U.S., 1,902 . . . . .314/D2
Glengolly, Scot., U.K. 62/J1
Glenham, S. Dak., U.S., 139 . . . . . . .342/E2
Glen Haven, Colo., U.S. 250/E1
Glen Haven, Wisc., U.S., 50 . . . . . . .364/B6
Glenhayes, W. Va., U.S. 360/A4
Glenholme, N.S., Can. 221/D2
Glen Hope, Penn., U.S., 149 . . . . . . .336/D4
Glenkerry, Scot., U.K. 62/K8
Glen Lyn, Va., U.S., 151 . . . . .354/B6
Glen Margaret, N.S., Can. 221/D3
Glenmaye, Eng., U.K. 66/A5
Glen Mills, Mass., U.S., 750 . . . . . . .292/L1
Glenmont, Ohio, U.S., 283 . . . . .328/F4
Glenmoor, Ohio, U.S., 2,192 . . . . . . .328/J4
Glenmora, La., U.S., 1,558 . . . . .282/D5
Glenn, Calif., U.S., county, 26,453 . . .246/C3
Glenn, Mich., U.S., 325 . . . . .294/C7
Glenn, Tex., U.S. 346/H2
Glennallen, Alaska, U.S., 554 . . . . . .240/F2
Glenn Dale, Md., U.S., 12,609 . . . . .288/D6
Glenn Hts., Tex., U.S., 7,224 . . . . . .346/C10
Glennie, Mich., U.S., 90 . . . . .294/F5
Glenns Ferry, Ida., U.S., 1,611 . . . . .264/B7
Glennville, Ga., U.S., 3,641 . . . . . . .260/H8
Glenolden, Penn., U.S., 7,476 . . . . . .336/L7
Glenoma, Wash., U.S., 225 . . . . .358/C3
Glen Park, N.Y., U.S., 487 . . . . .320/K2
Glenpool, Okla., U.S., 8,123 . . . . . . .330/G2
Glen Raven, N.C., U.S., 2,750 . . . . . .322/G2
Glen Ridge, Fla., U.S., 276 . . . . .256/B4
Glen Ridge, N.J., U.S., 7,271 . . . . . . .314/B2, E2
Glenrio, N. Mex., U.S. 317/G2
Glenrio, Tex., U.S. 346/E9
Glen Rock, N.J., U.S., 11,546 . . . . . .314/B1, E2
Glen Rock, Penn., U.S., 1,809 . . . . . .336/H6
Glenrock, Wyo., U.S., 2,231 . . . . . . .366/D2
Glen Rogers, W. Va., U.S., 450 . . . . .360/D5
Glen Rose, Tex., U.S., 2,122 . . . . . . .346/L3
Glen St. Mary, Fla., U.S., 473 . . . . . .256/G1
Glensboro, Ky., U.S., 70 . . . . .280/E2
Glens Falls, N.Y., U.S., 14,354, (124,345, metro.) .320/P4
Glenside, Penn., U.S., 7,914 . . . . . . .336/M6
Glen Strathfarrar N.P., Scot., U.K. . . .62/G4
Glentana, Mont., U.S. 306/K1
Glentham, Eng., U.K. 68/G3
Glentrool, Scot., U.K., forest 62/G8
Glen Ullin, N. Dak., U.S., 865 . . . . .326/D3
Glenview, Ill., U.S., 41,847 . . . . .266/B5
Glenview, Ky., U.S., 558 . . . . .280/B1
Glenview, N.C., U.S., 150 . . . . .322/K2
Glenvil, Nebr., U.S., 332 . . . . .308/E3
Glenville, Ala., U.S. 238/D3
Glenville, Ky., U.S., 150 . . . . .280/C3
Glenville, Minn., U.S., 720 . . . . .298/D7
Glenville, N.C., U.S., 200 . . . . .322/D8
Glenville, W. Va., U.S., 1,544 . . . . . .360/E3
Glen Wilton, Va., U.S., 150 . . . . . . .354/D5
Glenwood, Nfld., Can., 845 . . . . .218/D5
Glenwood, Ala., U.S., 191 . . . . .238/C4
Glenwood, Ark., U.S., 1,751 . . . . . . .244/B3
Glenwood, Ga., U.S., 884 . . . . .260/F7
Glenwood, Hawaii, U.S. 262/J6
Glenwood, Ida., U.S., 60 . . . . .264/B3

Glenwood, Ill., U.S., 9,000 . . . . .266/C6
Glenwood, Ind., U.S., 318 . . . . .270/F5
Glenwood, Iowa, U.S., 5,358 . . . . . .274/C5
Glenwood, Maine, U.S. 286/D3
Glenwood, Md., U.S., 650 . . . . .288/B5
Glenwood, Minn., U.S., 2,594 . . . . . .298/B5
Glenwood, Mo., U.S., 203 . . . . .302/D1
Glenwood, N. Mex., U.S., 80 . . . . . .317/B4
Glenwood, N.C., U.S., 475 . . . . .322/B3
Glenwood, Oreg., U.S., 60 . . . . .334/C2
Glenwood, Utah, U.S., 437 . . . . .350/C5
Glenwood, Wash., U.S., 175 . . . . . . .358/D3
Glenwood, W. Va., U.S., 225 . . . . . . .360/B3
Glenwood City, Wisc., U.S., 1,183 . . .364/A3
Glenwood Park, Nebr., U.S., 500 . . . .308/E3
Glenwood Sprs., Colo., U.S., 7,736 . . .250/C2
Glidden, Sask., Can. 227/A9
Glidden, Iowa, U.S., 1,253 . . . . .274/E3
Glidden, Wisc., U.S., 650 . . . . .364/C2
Glide, Oreg., U.S., 1,690 . . . . .334/C4
Glinton, Eng., U.K., 1,663 . . . . .68/G4
Glinton, Eng., U.K. 70/D1
Glittertinden, Nor., mountain 80/B3
Gliwice, Pol., 211,676 . . . . .83/D3
Globe, Ariz., U.S., 7,486 . . . . .242/E4
Głogów, Pol. 83/C3
Gloria Glens Park, Ohio, U.S., 538 . . .328/G3
Glorieta, N. Mex., U.S., 859 . . . . . . .317/E2
Glossop, (Glossop/Hollingworth), Eng., U.K., 30,771 . . . . .66/E6
Glossop, (Glossop/Hollingworth), Eng., U.K., 30,771 . . . . .68/D3
Gloster, Miss., U.S., 1,073 . . . . .300/A4
Gloucester, N.B., Can., county 217/D1
Gloucester, Ont., Can. 223/K2
Gloucester, Eng., U.K. 60/C3
Gloucester, Eng., U.K., 114,003, (126,149, metro.) 68/C6
Gloucester, Mass., U.S., 30,273 . . . . .292/M2
Gloucester, N.J., U.S., county, 254,673 .314/A4, C4
Gloucester, Va., U.S., 2,269 . . . . . . .354/K6
Gloucester, Va., U.S., county, 34,780 . .354/K6
Gloucester City, N.J., U.S., 11,484 . . .314/B3, C4
Gloucester Pt., Va., U.S., 9,429 . . . . .354/L6
Gloucestershire, Eng., U.K., unitary authority, 564,559 . . . . .68/C6
Gloucestershire, Eng., U.K., unitary authority, 564,559 . . . . .73/H1
Glouster, Ohio, U.S., 1,972 . . . . . . .328/F6
Glover, Mo., U.S. 302/F4
Glover, Vt., U.S., 966 . . . . .352/C1
Glovers, Bel., reef 201/C3
Gloversville, N.Y., U.S., 15,413 . . . . .320/N4
Glovertown, Nfld., Can., 2,163 . . . . .218/D5
Gloverville, S.C., U.S., 2,805 . . . . . .340/E2
Gluck, S.C., U.S., 300 . . . . .340/B2
Gluek, Minn., U.S., 40 . . . . .298/B6
Glusburn, Eng., U.K., 6,859 . . . . . . .66/E5
Glusburn, Eng., U.K., 6,859 . . . . . . .68/D2
Glyfada, Gr. 100/Inset
Glympton, Eng., U.K. 70/B3
Glyncorrwg, Wales, U.K. 64/D4
Glyndon, Md., U.S., 1,200 . . . . .288/G2
Glyndon, Minn., U.S., 1,049 . . . . . . .298/A4
Glyndyfrdwy, Wales, U.K. 64/E2
Glynn, Ga., U.S., county, 67,568 . . . .260/H9
Glynn, La., U.S., 275 . . . . .282/G5
Glyn Neath, Wales, U.K., 4,616 . . . . .64/D4
Gmünd, Aus. 91/D2
Gmunden, Aus. 91/C3
Gnadenhutten, Ohio, U.S., 1,280 . . . .328/H5
Goa, India, state 128/B5
Goat, Ant.-Bar., point 207/D1
Goathland, Eng., U.K. 66/G4
Goba, Eth. 156/C3
Gobabis, Nam. 160/C2
Gobernador, N. Mex., U.S., 60 . . . . .317/C1
Gobi, China, desert 119/D3
Gobi, Mong., desert 118/C3
Godavari, India, river 128/C5
Godbout, Que., Can. 226/J2
Goddard, Kans., U.S., 2,037 . . . . . . .276/E4
Goderich, Ont., Can., 7,604 . . . . . . .223/D4
Godfrey, Ont., Can. 223/J3
Godfrey, Ga., U.S., 100 . . . . .260/D5
Godfrey, Ill., U.S., 16,286 . . . . .266/A3, C5
Godley, Ill., U.S., 594 . . . . .266/E2
Godmanchester, Eng., U.K., 5,243 . . .68/G5
Godmanchester, Eng., U.K., 5,243 . . .70/D2
Godoy Cruz, Arg. 191/B3
Gods, Man., Can., lake 215/D2
Godstone, Eng., U.K., 2,399 . . . . . . .70/D4
Godwin, N.C., U.S., 112 . . . . .322/H4
Goehner, Nebr., U.S., 186 . . . . .308/G3
Goële, Fr. . . . . .88/Inset II
Goessel, Kans., U.S., 565 . . . . .276/E3
Goetzville, Mich., U.S., 70 . . . . .294/E3
Goff, Kans., U.S., 181 . . . . .276/G2
Goffs, Calif., U.S. 246/K8
Goffstown, N.H., U.S., 16,929 . . . . . .312/C5
Gogama, Ont., Can., 467 . . . . .222/D3
Gogebic, Mich., U.S., county, 17,370 . .294/D2
Gogebic, Mich., U.S., lake 294/D2
Goginan, Wales, U.K. 64/D3
Goiânia, Braz., 1,093,007 . . . . .188/D3
Goiás, Braz., state 188/D3
Golan Heights, Syria, occupied territory .134/A3
Golconda, Ill., U.S., 726 . . . . .266/E6
Golconda, Nev., U.S., 175 . . . . .310/B1
Gold, Penn., U.S., 125 . . . . .336/F2
Gold Bar, Wash., U.S., 2,014 . . . . . .358/B4, D2
Gold Beach, Oreg., U.S., 1,897 . . . . .334/B5
Goldbond, Va., U.S., 80 . . . . .354/B6
Goldcliff, Wales, U.K. 64/F4
Gold Coast, Qnsld., Austl., 266,000, (290,000, metro.) 170/E2
Goldcreek, Mont., U.S., 40 . . . . .306/D3
Golden, Br. Col., Can., 4,020 . . . . . .214/O5
Golden, Colo., U.S., 17,159 . . . . . . .250/A3, E2
Golden, Ida., U.S. 264/B4
Golden, Ill., U.S., 629 . . . . .266/B3
Golden, Miss., U.S., 201 . . . . .300/D1
Golden, N. Mex., U.S. 317/D2
Golden, Okla., U.S., 125 . . . . .330/H3
Golden Beach, Fla., U.S., 919 . . . . . .256/B6
Golden Beach, Md., U.S., 2,665 . . . . .288/H6
Golden Bridge, N.Y., U.S., 1,578 . . . .320/D1
Golden City, Mo., U.S., 884 . . . . . . .302/B4
Golden Cross, Eng., U.K. 70/E5
Goldendale, Wash., U.S., 3,760 . . . . .358/E4
Golden Ears Prov. Park, Br. Col., Can. .214/L6
Golden Gate, Fla., U.S., 20,951 . . . . .256/C5
Golden Gate N.R.A., Calif., U.S. 246/C5, H1
Golden Hills, Calif., U.S., 7,434 . . . . .246/G7
Golden Lake, Ont., Can. 223/H2
Golden Meadow, La., U.S., 2,193 . . . .282/J8
Goldenrod, Fla., U.S., 12,871 . . . . . . .256/D4
Golden Spike Natl. Hist. Site, Utah, U.S. .350/B2

Golden Valley, Minn., U.S., 20,281 . . .298/E5
Golden Valley, Mont., U.S., county, 1,042 .306/G3
Golden Valley, N. Dak., U.S., 183 . . . .326/C2
Golden Valley, N. Dak., U.S., county, 1,924 .326/B3
Goldfield, Iowa, U.S., 680 . . . . .274/G2
Goldfield, Nev., U.S., 175 . . . . .310/B3
Goldhanger, Eng., U.K. 70/F3
Goldman, La., U.S. 282/G3
Goldonna, La., U.S., 457 . . . . .282/D2
Gold Pt., Nev., U.S. 310/B3
Goldsboro, Md., U.S., 216 . . . . .288/L3
Goldsboro, N.C., U.S., 39,043, (113,329, metro.) 322/J4
Goldsboro, Penn., U.S., 939 . . . . . . .336/H5
Goldsboro, Tex., U.S. 346/J3
Goldsby, Okla., U.S., 1,204 . . . . .330/E2
Goldsmith, Tex., U.S., 253 . . . . .346/F4
Goldston, N.C., U.S., 319 . . . . .322/G3
Goldthwaite, Tex., U.S., 1,802 . . . . . .346/K4
Goldvein, Va., U.S., 150 . . . . .354/H4
Goldville, Ala., U.S. 238/D2
Golf, Fla., U.S., 230 . . . . .256/B5
Golf, Ill., U.S., 451 . . . . .266/B5
Golfito, C.R. 203/C4
Golf Manor, Ohio, U.S., 3,999 . . . . .328/B9
Golfview, Fla., U.S., 150 . . . . .256/B4
Goliad, Tex., U.S., 1,975 . . . . .346/L7
Goliad, Tex., U.S., county, 6,928 . . . .346/L7
Golmud, China 119/C2
Golovin, Alaska, U.S., 144 . . . . .240/C2
Golspie, Scot., U.K., 1,404 . . . . .62/J3
Goltry, Okla., U.S., 268 . . . . .330/D1
Golva, N. Dak., U.S., 106 . . . . .326/B3
Golyama Kamchiya, Bul., river 101/E2
Goma, Congo, D.R., 109,094 . . . . . .155/C2
Gombe, Nig. 152/F2
Gomera, Sp., island . . . . .94/Inset I
Gomez, Tex., U.S. 346/F2
Gómez Palacio, Mex., 210,113, (273,315, metro.) 200/D2
Gonaïves, Haiti, 63,291 . . . . .205/B1
Gonâve, Haiti, gulf 205/B1
Gonâve, Haiti, island 204/C3
Gonâve, Haiti, island 205/B2
Gonder, Eth., 142,328 . . . . .156/B1
Gondola Pt., N.B., Can. 217/C3
Gongola, Nig., river 152/F2
Gonvick, Minn., U.S., 294 . . . . .298/B3
Gonzales, Calif., U.S., 7,525 . . . . . . .246/D6
Gonzales, La., U.S., 8,156 . . . . .282/H6
Gonzales, Tex., U.S., 7,202 . . . . . . .346/L6
Gonzales, Tex., U.S., county, 18,628 . .346/L6
Gonzalez, Fla., U.S., 11,365 . . . . . . .256/A1
Goober Hill, Tex., U.S. 346/R4
Goobies, Nfld., Can., 108 . . . . .218/E5
Goochland, Va., U.S., 1,100 . . . . . . .354/H5
Goochland, Va., U.S., county, 16,863 . .354/H5
Goode, Va., U.S., 125 . . . . .354/E6
Goodell, Iowa, U.S., 174 . . . . .274/G2
Goodenow, Ill., U.S. 266/F2
Goodfield, Ill., U.S., 686 . . . . .266/D3
Good Hart, Mich., U.S., 50 . . . . .294/D4
Good Hope, S. Afr., cape 162/A3
Good Hope, Ala., U.S., 1,966 . . . . . .238/C1
Good Hope, Ga., U.S., 210 . . . . .260/D4
Good Hope, Ill., U.S., 415 . . . . .266/C3
Good Hope, Ohio, U.S., 275 . . . . . . .328/D7
Goodhue, Minn., U.S., 778 . . . . .298/E6
Goodhue, Minn., U.S., county, 44,127 . .298/E6
Gooding, Ida., U.S., 3,384 . . . . .264/C7
Gooding, Ida., U.S., county, 14,155 . . .264/B6
Goodings Grove, Ill., U.S., 17,084 . . .266/B6
Goodland, Ind., U.S., 1,096 . . . . .270/B3
Goodland, Kans., U.S., 4,948 . . . . . . .276/A2
Goodland, Minn., U.S., 60 . . . . .298/D3
Goodlands, Man., Can. 215/A4
Goodlands, Mauritius 163/G2
Goodlett, Tex., U.S., 60 . . . . .346/J1
Goodlettsville, Tenn., U.S., 13,780 . . .344/H2
Goodman, Miss., U.S., 1,252 . . . . . . .300/C3
Goodman, Mo., U.S., 1,183 . . . . . . .302/B5
Goodman, Wisc., U.S., 275 . . . . .364/E3
Goodna, Qnsld., Austl. . . . . .170/Inset III
Goodnews Bay, Alaska, U.S., 230 . . . .240/C3
Goodnoe Hills, Wash., U.S. 358/E4
Goodrich, Colo., U.S. 250/F1
Goodrich, Kans., U.S., 90 . . . . .276/H3
Goodrich, Maine, U.S., 40 . . . . .286/E2
Goodrich, Mich., U.S., 1,353 . . . . . . .294/F7
Goodrich, N. Dak., U.S., 163 . . . . . . .326/E2
Goodrich, Tex., U.S., 243 . . . . .346/P5
Goodrich, Wisc., U.S., 40 . . . . .364/D3
Goodrich Hts., Conn., U.S. 253/E3
Goodridge, Minn., U.S., 98 . . . . .298/B2
Goodsoil, Sask., Can., 284 . . . . .227/A6
Goodsprings, Nev., U.S., 232 . . . . . .310/C4
Good Thunder, Minn., U.S., 592 . . . . .298/C6
Goodview, Minn., U.S., 3,373 . . . . . .298/F6
Goodwater, Ala., U.S., 1,633 . . . . . . .238/C2
Goodwater, Okla., U.S., 70 . . . . .330/H4
Goodwell, Okla., U.S., 1,192 . . . . . . .330/C4
Goodwick, Wales, U.K., 1,933 . . . . . .64/B3
Goodwill, Md., U.S., 150 . . . . .288/N7
Goodwin, Ark., U.S., 100 . . . . .244/D4
Goodwin, S. Dak., U.S., 160 . . . . . . .342/J3
Goodwine, Ill., U.S., 80 . . . . .266/F3
Goodwood, Eng., U.K. 70/C5
Goodyear, Ariz., U.S., 18,911 . . . . . .242/C4
Goole, Eng., U.K., 19,410 . . . . .66/G5
Goole, Eng., U.K., 19,410 . . . . .68/F2
Goonhavern, Eng., U.K. 73/B4
Goose, Calif., U.S., lake 246/E1
Goose, Oreg., U.S., lake 334/F5
Goose Creek, S.C., U.S., 29,208 . . . . .340/D3
Goose Lake, Iowa, U.S., 232 . . . . . . .274/P4
Goose Prairie, Wash., U.S. 358/D3
Goose Rocks Beach, Maine, U.S., 250 . .286/B5
Göppingen, Ger. 86/B4
Goražde, Bos.-Her. 98/B2
Gorakhpur, India 128/D3
Gordo, Ala., U.S., 1,677 . . . . .238/B2
Gordon, Alta., Can., lake 212/E3
Gordon, Scot., U.K. 62/L7
Gordon, Ala., U.S., 408 . . . . .238/D4
Gordon, Ga., U.S., 2,152 . . . . .260/E6
Gordon, Ga., U.S., county, 44,104 . . . .260/A3
Gordon, Kans., U.S., 60 . . . . .276/F4
Gordon, Nebr., U.S., 1,756 . . . . .308/B1
Gordon, Ohio, U.S., 190 . . . . .328/A6
Gordon, Penn., U.S., 781 . . . . .336/J4
Gordon, (Lynn County), Tex., U.S. . . .346/G2
Gordon, (Palo Pinto County), Tex., U.S., 451 .346/K3
Gordon, Wisc., U.S., 150 . . . . .364/B2
Gordondale, Alta., Can. 212/A2
Gordonsville, Miss., U.S., 318 . . . . . .238/C3
Gordonsville, Tenn., U.S., 1,066 . . . . .344/H2
Gordonsville, Va., U.S., 1,498 . . . . . .354/G4
Gordonville, Mo., U.S., 425 . . . . . . .302/G4

Gordonville, Penn., U.S., 800 . . . . .336/J5
Gordy, Ga., U.S., 125 .260/D9
Gore, Eth. 156/B2
Gore, N.Z. 171/A4
Gore, Okla., U.S., 850 . . . . .330/G2
Gore, Va., U.S., 225 . . . . .354/G2
Gore Bay, Ont., Can., 898 . . . . .223/C2
Goree, Tex., U.S., 321 . . . . .346/J2
Goreville, Ill., U.S., 938 . . . . .266/E6
Gorgas, Ala., U.S., 40 .238/B2
Gorham, Ill., U.S., 256 . . . . .266/D6
Gorham, Kans., U.S., 360 . . . . .276/C3
Gorham, Maine, U.S., 14,141 . . . . .286/B5
Gorham, N.H., U.S., 2,895 . . . . .312/D3
Gorham, N.Y., U.S., 650 . . . . .320/G5
Gori, Geo., 59,000 . . . . .103/C4
Goring, Eng., U.K. 70/B3
Goring-by-Sea, Eng., U.K. 70/D5
Goris, Arm. 103/D3
Gorizia, It. 95/C1
Gorj, Rom., county 101/B3
Gorleston-on-Sea, Eng., U.K. 70/H1
Görlitz, Ger. 86/C3
Gorman, Calif., U.S. 246/G8
Gorman, N.C., U.S., 1,002 . . . . .322/H2
Gorman, Tex., U.S., 1,236 . . . . .346/K3
Gorno-Altaysk, Russ. .104/F4
Goroka, P.N.G. 172/A2
Gorontalo, Indon. 122/D1
Gorra Haven, Eng., U.K. 73/C4
Gorseinon, Wales, U.K., 18,917 . . . . .64/C4
Gorsty Common, Eng., U.K. 68/B5
Gortin, N. Ire., U.K., 226 . . . . .65/C2
Gorum, La., U.S., 60 . . . . .282/D4
Gorzów Wielkopolski, Pol., 126,172 . . . . .83/B2
Gosberton, Eng., U.K., 1,785 . . . . .68/G4
Gosberton, Eng., U.K., 1,785 . . . . .70/D1
Gosford, N.S.W., Austl. 170/E3
Gosforth, Eng., U.K., 23,315 . . . . .66/B4
Goshen, N.S., Can. 221/F2
Goshen, Ala., U.S., 300 . . . . .238/C4
Goshen, Ark., U.S., 752 . . . . .244/B1
Goshen, Conn., U.S., 2,697 . . . . .253/C2
Goshen, Ind., U.S., 29,383 . . . . .270/E1
Goshen, Ky., U.S., 907 . . . . .280/E2
Goshen, Md., U.S., 1,300 . . . . .288/F3
Goshen, Mass., U.S., 921 . . . . .292/C3
Goshen, N.H., U.S., 741 . . . . .312/B5
Goshen, N.J., U.S., 350 . . . . .314/D5
Goshen, N.Y., U.S., 5,676 . . . . .320/N8
Goshen, Utah, U.S., 874 . . . . .350/C4
Goshen, Vt., U.S., 227 . . . . .352/A3
Goshen, Va., U.S., 406 . . . . .354/D5
Goshen, Wyo., U.S., county, 12,538 . . . . .366/D2
Goshute, Nev., U.S., lake 310/C1
Goshute, Utah, U.S. 350/A4
Goshute Ind. Res., Nev., U.S. 310/C2
Goslar, Ger. 86/B3
Gosnell, Ark., U.S., 3,968 . . . . .244/F2
Gosnells, W.A., Austl. . . . . .170/Inset I
Gosper, Nebr., U.S., county, 2,143 . . . . .308/E3
Gospić, Cro. 98/B3
Gosport, Eng., U.K. 60/C4
Gosport, Eng., U.K., 67,802 . . . . .70/B5
Gosport, Ind., U.S., 715 . . . . .270/D6
Goss, Miss., U.S., 125 .300/C4
Gossville, N.H., U.S., 600 . . . . .312/D5
Göta, Swe., canal 80/B3
Gotebo, Okla., U.S., 272 . . . . .330/D2
Göteborg, Swe., 471,267, (803,941, metro.) . .80/B3
Gotha, Ger. 86/B3
Gotham, Wisc., U.S., 275 . . . . .364/C5
Gothenburg, Nebr., U.S., 3,619 . . . . .308/D3
Gotland, Swe., county .80/C3
Gotland, Swe., island 80/C3
Gotsu, Jap. 114/B3
Göttingen, Ger., 124,775 . . . . .86/B3
Gouda, Neth. 84/B2
Goudeau, La., U.S., 150 . . . . .282/E5
Goudhurst, Eng., U.K. 70/E4
Goudiri, Sen. 148/C2
Gough, Ga., U.S., 225 .260/G5
Gouin, Que., Can., reservoir 225/A4
Gouin, Que., Can., reservoir 226/B3
Goulceby, Eng., U.K. 66/H6
Gould, Ark., U.S., 1,305 . . . . .244/D4
Gould, Colo., U.S. 250/D1
Gould, Okla., U.S., 206 . . . . .330/C3
Gould City, Mich., U.S., 80 . . . . .294/D3
Goulds, Fla., U.S., 7,453 . . . . .256/A7, H6
Gouldsboro, Maine, U.S., 1,941 . . . . .286/D4
Gouldtown, N.J., U.S., 2,300 . . . . .314/C5
Goundam, Mali 150/C2
Gouré, Niger 152/C3
Gouverneur, N.Y., U.S., 4,263 . . . . .320/L2
Govan, Que., Can., 274 . . . . .227/C9
Govan, S.C., U.S., 67 .340/C3
Cove, Kans., U.S., county, 3,068 . . . . .276/B3
Governador Valadares, Braz., 173,699,
(230,487, metro.) .188/D3
Government, Mich., U.S., peak 294/D1
Govt. Camp, Oreg., U.S., 150 . . . . .334/E2
Gowan, Minn., U.S. 298/E4
Gowanda, N.Y., U.S., 2,842 . . . . .320/D6
Gowen, Okla., U.S., 175 . . . . .330/G3
Gower, Wales, U.K., peninsula 64/C4
Gower, Mo., U.S., 1,399 . . . . .302/B2
Gowrie, Iowa, U.S., 1,038 . . . . .274/F3
Göyçay, Azer. 103/B3
Gozo (Ghawdex), Malta, island 97/Inset
Graaf-Reinet, S. Afr. 162/B3
Grabill, Ind., U.S., 1,113 . . . . .270/G2
Gračanica, Bos.-Her. 98/B1
Grace, Ida., U.S., 990 .264/F7
Grace, Mich., U.S., 40 . . . . .294/E4
Grace, Miss., U.S., 125 . . . . .300/B3
Grace City, N. Dak., U.S., 71 . . . . .326/G2
Graceham, Md., U.S., 475 . . . . .288/E1
Gracemont, Okla., U.S., 336 . . . . .330/D2
Graceton, Minn., U.S. .298/C2
Graceville, Fla., U.S., 2,402 . . . . .256/C1
Graceville, Minn., U.S., 605 . . . . .298/A5
Gracewood, Ga., U.S., 550 . . . . .260/G5
Gracey, Ky., U.S., 125 .280/C4
Gracias, Hond. 202/A2
Gracias a Dios, Hond., department 202/C2
Gracias a Dios, Nicar., cape 202/C1
Graciosa, Port., island . . . . .93/Inset II
Grady, Ala., U.S., 100 .238/C4
Grady, Ark., U.S., 523 .244/D3
Grady, Ga., U.S., county, 23,659 . . . . .260/C9
Grady, N. Mex., U.S., 98 . . . . .317/G3
Grady, Okla., U.S. 330/E3
Grady, Okla., U.S., county, 45,516 . . . . .330/E2
Gradyville, Ky., U.S., 70 . . . . .280/E3
Graettinger, Iowa, U.S., 900 . . . . .274/F1
Graf, Iowa, U.S., 73 . . . . .274/N2
Grafham, Eng., U.K. 70/D2
Graford, Tex., U.S., 578 . . . . .346/K3
Grafton, N.S.W., Austl. 170/E4
Grafton, N.B., Can. 217/B2
Grafton, Ill., U.S., 609 . . . . .266/C5

Grafton, Iowa, U.S., 290 . . . . .274/H1
Grafton, Mass., U.S., 14,894 . . . . .292/H4
Grafton, Nebr., U.S., 152 . . . . .308/G3
Grafton, N.H., U.S., 1,138 . . . . .312/C4
Grafton, N.H., U.S., county, 81,743 . . . . .312/C4
Grafton, N. Dak., U.S., 4,516 . . . . .326/H1
Grafton, Ohio, U.S., 2,302 . . . . .328/F3, F10
Grafton, Vt., U.S., 649 . . . . .352/B4
Grafton, W. Va., U.S., 5,489 . . . . .360/F2
Grafton, Wisc., U.S., 10,312 . . . . .364/F1, F5
Grafton Ctr., N.H., U.S., 150 . . . . .312/C4
Grafton Underwood, Eng., U.K. 70/C2
Graham, Br. Col., Can., island 214/F4
Graham, Nun., Can., island 220/K1
Graham, Ariz., U.S., county, 33,489 . . . . .242/E5
Graham, Ga., U.S., 312 . . . . .260/G8
Graham, Kans., U.S., county, 2,946 . . . . .276/C2
Graham, Ky., U.S., 475 . . . . .280/C3
Graham, Mo., U.S., 191 . . . . .302/A1
Graham, N.C., U.S., 12,833 . . . . .322/B8
Graham, N.C., U.S., county, 7,993 . . . . .322/B8
Graham, Okla., U.S., 50 . . . . .330/E3
Graham, (Garza County), Tex., U.S. 346/G2
Graham, (Young County), Tex., U.S., 8,716 . . .346/K2
Graham Land, Antar., region 192/C11
Grahamstown, S. Afr. .162/C3
Grain, Eng., U.K. 70/F4
Grainfield, Kans., U.S., 327 . . . . .276/B2
Grainger, Tenn., U.S., county, 20,659 . . . . . . .344/P2
Grainola, Okla., U.S. 330/F1
Granton, Nebr., U.S. 308/C3
Grain Valley, Mo., U.S., 5,160 . . . . .302/J5
Grama, N. Mex., U.S., 70 . . . . .317/C5
Grambling, La., U.S., 4,693 . . . . .282/D1
Gramercy, La., U.S., 3,066 . . . . .282/H6
Grampian, Scot., U.K., mountains 60/B2
Grampian, Penn., U.S., 441 . . . . .336/D4
Gramsh, Alb. 99/B3
Granada, Nicar., 96,996 . . . . .202/B3
Granada, Nicar., department 202/B3
Granada, Sp., 240,661 .94/E4
Granada, Sp., province .94/E4
Granada, Colo., U.S., 640 . . . . .250/H3
Granada, Minn., U.S., 317 . . . . .298/C7
Granborough, Eng., U.K. 70/C3
Granbury, Tex., U.S., 5,718 . . . . .346/K3
Granby, Que., Can., 44,121 . . . . .226/D6
Granby, Eng., U.K. 70/C1
Granby, Colo., U.S., 1,525 . . . . .250/E1
Granby, Conn., U.S., 10,347 . . . . .253/E1
Granby, Mass., U.S., 6,132 . . . . .292/D3
Granby, Mo., U.S., 2,121 . . . . .302/B5
Granby, Vt., U.S., 86 . . . . .352/D1
Gran Canaria, Sp., island . . . . .94/Inset I
Gran Chaco, Arg., region 191/C1
Gran Chaco, Bol., region 186/B4
Gran Chaco, Para., region 187/B3
Grand, N.B., Can., lake 217/D2
Grand, N.B., Can., lake 286/E3
Grand, Nfld., Can., lake 218/C4
Grand, Ont., Can., river 320/B4
Grand, Dom., bay 208/B4
Grand, Ire., canal 78/C2
Grand, Malta, harbor 97/C2
Grand, Mauritius, river 163/C3
Grand, Ariz., U.S., canyon 242/C1
Grand, Colo., U.S., county, 12,442 . . . . .250/D1
Grand, La., U.S., lake 282/D7
Grand, Maine, U.S., lake 286/E3
Grand, Mich., U.S., island 294/C3
Grand, Mo., U.S., river .302/B1
Grand, S. Dak., U.S., river 342/D2
Grand, Utah, U.S., county, 8,485 . . . . .350/E4
Grand-Aldouane, N.B., Can. 217/E2
Grand' Anse, Haiti, department 205/B2
Grand Anse, St. Luc. 208/B1
Grand Bahama, Bah., island 204/B1
Grand Bahama, Bah., island 207/A2
Grand Bale, Mauritius 163/C2
Grand Bank, Nfld., Can., 2,841 . . . . .218/D5
Grand Bay, N.B., Can., 4,949 . . . . .217/C3
Grand Bay, Gren. 209/C1
Grand Bay, Ala., U.S., 3,918 . . . . .238/A5
Grand Bay N.W.R., Ala., U.S. 238/A5
Grand Bay N.W.R., Miss., U.S. 300/D5
Grand Bayou, La., U.S., 40 . . . . .282/C2
Grand Beach, Mich., U.S., 221 . . . . .294/C8
Grand Bend, Ont., Can., 1,949 . . . . .223/D4
Grand Blanc, Mich., U.S., 8,242 . . . . .294/F7
Grand Bruit, Nfld., Can., 44 . . . . .218/B5
Grand Cane, La., U.S., 191 . . . . .282/B2
Grand Canyon, Ariz., U.S., 1,460 . . . . .242/C1
Grand Canyon Natl. Park, Ariz., U.S. 242/B2, C1
Grand Canyon-Parashant Natl. Mon., Ariz., U.S. .242/B1
Grand Cayman, Cay. Is., island 204/A3
Grand Ctr., Alta., Can., 11,780 . . . . .212/E4
Grand Cess, Liber. 149/B3
Grand Chain, Ill., U.S. .266/D6
Grand Chenier, La., U.S., 125 . . . . .282/D7
Grand Coteau, La., U.S., 1,040 . . . . .282/E6
Grand Coulee, Wash., U.S., 897 . . . . .358/F2
Grand Detour, Ill., U.S., 550 . . . . .266/D2
Grande, Arg., bay 191/B7
Grande, Bol., river 186/B3
Grande, Braz., river 188/D3
Grande, C.R., river 203/B3
Grande, Uru., range 187/C2
Grande-Anse, N.B., Can., 853 . . . . .217/D1
Grande Baleine, Que., Can., river 225/A2
Grande Cache, Alta., Can., 3,828 . . . . .212/A4
Grand Ecore, La., U.S. .282/C3
Grande de Añasco, P.R., river 206/A2
Grande de Manatí, P.R., river 206/C2
Grande de Matagalpa, Nicar., river 202/B2
Grande Prairie, Alta., Can., 36,983 . . . . .212/A3
Grand Erg de Bilma, Chad, desert 153/A3
Grand Erg de Bilma, Niger, desert 152/C2
Grand Erg Occidental, Alg., desert 146/B1
Grand Erg Oriental, Alg., desert 146/B2
Grand Erg Oriental, Tun., dune 146/B3
Grande-Rivière, Que., Can. 226/M3
Grande-Etang, N.S., Can. 221/F1
Grande-Vallée, Que., Can. 226/M2
Grand Falls, N.B., Can., 5,858 . . . . .217/B1
Grand Falls, Minn., U.S. 298/D2
Grandfalls, Tex., U.S., 391 . . . . .346/F4
Grand Falls Plaza, Mo., U.S. 302/B4
Grand Falls-Windsor, Nfld., Can., 13,340 . . . . .218/D5
Grandfather, N.C., U.S., 73 . . . . .322/B2
Grandfield, Okla., U.S., 1,110 . . . . .330/D3
Grand Forks, Br. Col., Can., 4,054 . . . . .214/N6
Grand Forks, N. Dak., U.S., 49,321,
(97,478, metro.) 326/H2
Grand Forks, N. Dak., U.S., county, 66,109 . . .326/H2
Grand Gulf, Miss., U.S. 300/A3
Grand Haven, Mich., U.S., 11,168 . . . . .294/C6
Grandin, Mo., U.S., 236 . . . . .302/F5
Grandin, N.J., U.S., 1,800 . . . . .314/D2
Grandin, N. Dak., U.S., 181 . . . . .326/J2
Grand Island, Nebr., U.S., 42,940 . . . . .308/E3
Grand Island N.R.A., Mich., U.S. 294/C3

Grand Isle, La., U.S., 1,541 . . . . .282/K8
Grand Isle, Maine, U.S., 518 . . . . .286/D1
Grand Isle, Vt., U.S., 1,955 . . . . .352/A1
Grand Isle, Vt., U.S., county, 6,901 . . . . .352/A1
Grand Jct., Colo., U.S., 41,986,
(116,255, metro.) .250/B2
Grand Jct., Iowa, U.S., 964 . . . . .274/F3
Grand Jct., Mich., U.S., 325 . . . . .294/C7
Grand Jct., Tenn., U.S., 301 . . . . .344/C4
Grand Lake, Colo., U.S., 447 . . . . .250/E1
Grand Lake, La., U.S., 40 . . . . .282/C6
Grand Lake Matagamon, Maine, U.S., lake . . .286/D2
Grand Lake Seboeis, Maine, U.S., lake 286/D2
Grand Lake Stream, Maine, U.S., 150 . . . . . . .286/E3
Grand Lake Towne, Okla., U.S., 65 . . . . .330/G1
Grand Ledge, Mich., U.S., 7,813 . . . . .294/E7
Grand Manan, N.B., Can., 2,610 . . . . .217/C4
Grand Manan, N.B., Can., island 217/C4
Grand Marais, Man., Can. 215/C4
Grand Marais, Mich., U.S., 300 . . . . .294/D3
Grand Marais, Minn., U.S., 1,353 . . . . .298/F2
Grand Meadow, Minn., U.S., 945 . . . . .298/E7
Grand Mesa, Colo., U.S. 250/C2
Grand Mesa Natl. For., Colo., U.S. 250/B3, C2
Grand Mound, Iowa, U.S., 676 . . . . .274/N4
Grand Mound, Wash., U.S., 1,948 . . . . .358/B3
Grand Narrows, N.S., Can. 221/G2
Grândola, Port. 93/A3
Grand Pass, Mo., U.S., 53 . . . . .302/C2
Grand Portage, Minn., U.S., 100 . . . . .298/F2
Grand Portage Ind. Res., Minn., U.S. 298/F2
Grand Portage N.M., Minn., U.S. 298/F2
Grand Portage St. For., Minn., U.S. 298/F2
Grand Prairie, Tex., U.S., 127,427 . . . . .346/B9
Grand Pré, N.S., Can. .221/C2
Grand Rapids, Man., Can., 355 . . . . .215/B2
Grand Rapids, Mich., U.S., 197,800,
(1,088,514, metro.) 294/D7
Grand Rapids, Minn., U.S., 7,764 . . . . .298/D3
Grand Rapids, N. Dak., U.S. 326/G3
Grand Rapids, Ohio, U.S., 1,002 . . . . .328/C3
Grand-Remous, Que., Can., 1,216 . . . . .226/A5
Grand Ridge, Fla., U.S., 792 . . . . .256/C1
Grand Ridge, Ill., U.S., 546 . . . . .266/E2
Grand River, Iowa, U.S., 225 . . . . .274/G6
Grand River, Ohio, U.S., 345 . . . . .328/H2, J8
Grand River Natl. Grassland, S. Dak., U.S. 342/C2
Grand Rivers, Ky., U.S., 343 . . . . .280/B3
Grand Ronde, Oreg., U.S., 271 . . . . .334/C2
Grand Roy, Gren. 209/B2
Grand Saline, Tex., U.S., 3,028 . . . . .346/N3
Grand Santi, Fr. Gui. 183/A1
Grands Jardins Prov. Park, Que., Can. 226/F4
Grand Staircase-Escalante Natl. Mon., Utah, U.S. .350/C6
Grand Strand, The, S.C., U.S., beach 322/H8
Grand Teton, Wyo., U.S., peak 366/A2
Grand Teton Natl. Park, Wyo., U.S. 366/A2
Grand Tower, Ill., U.S., 624 . . . . .266/D6
Grand Traverse, Mich., U.S., bay 294/D4
Grand Traverse, Mich., U.S., county, 77,654 . .294/D5
Grand Turk, T.-C. Is., capital 204/D2
Grand Turk, T.-C. Is., capital 207/D4
Grand Turk, T.-C. Is., island 207/D4
Grand Valley, Ont., Can., 1,757 . . . . .223/E4
Grandview, Man., Can., 814 . . . . .215/A3
Grandview, Colo., U.S., 600 . . . . .250/C4
Grand View, Ida., U.S., 470 . . . . .264/A7
Grandview, (Edgar County), Ill., U.S., 80 . . . . .266/D4
Grandview, (Sangamon County), Ill., U.S., 1,537 .266/D4
Grandview, Ind., U.S., 696 . . . . .270/C9
Grandview, Iowa, U.S., 600 . . . . .274/M5
Grandview, Mo., U.S., 24,881 . . . . .302/B3, H5
Grandview, Tenn., U.S., 100 . . . . .344/M3
Grandview, (Dawson County), Tex., U.S. 346/G4
Grandview, (Johnson County), Tex., U.S., 1,358 .346/L3
Grandview, Wash., U.S., 8,377 . . . . .358/F3
Grand View, Wisc., U.S., 125 . . . . .364/B2
Grandview Hts., Ohio, U.S., 6,695 . . . . . .328/D6, D9
Grandview Park, Penn., U.S. 336/D3
Grandview Plaza, Kans., U.S., 1,184 . . . . .276/F2
Grandville, Mich., U.S., 16,263 . . . . .294/D7
Grandy, Minn., U.S., 175 . . . . .298/D5
Grandy, N.C., U.S., 1,000 . . . . .322/P2
Grange, S.A., Austl. . . . . .170/Inset II
Grange, Ga., U.S. 260/F5
Grangeburg, Ala., U.S. .238/D4
Grangemont, Ida., U.S. 264/A3
Grange-over-Sands, Eng., U.K., 4,473 . . . . .66/C4
Granger, Ind., U.S., 28,284 . . . . .270/D1
Granger, Iowa, U.S., 583 . . . . .274/G4
Granger, Minn., U.S., 50 . . . . .298/E7
Granger, Mo., U.S. 302/E1
Granger, Tex., U.S., 1,299 . . . . .346/E1, L5
Granger, Tex., U.S., lake 346/E1
Granger, Wash., U.S., 2,530 . . . . .358/E3
Granger, Wyo., U.S., 146 . . . . .366/B3
Grangeville, Ida., U.S., 3,228 . . . . .264/A4
Granisle, Br. Col., Can., 353 . . . . .214/J4
Granite, Colo., U.S. 250/D2
Granite, Mont., U.S., county, 2,830 . . . . .306/C3
Granite, (highest point), Mont., U.S., peak . . .306/C4
Granite, Mont., U.S., peak 306/D4
Granite, N.H., U.S., 90 . . . . .312/D4
Granite, Okla., U.S., 1,844 . . . . .330/C3
Granite, Oreg., U.S. 334/H3
Granite, Utah, U.S., 2,018 . . . . .350/E2
Granite Canon, Wyo., U.S. 366/D3
Granite City, Ill., U.S., 31,301 . . . . .266/A3, C5
Granite Falls, Minn., U.S., 3,070 . . . . .298/B6
Granite Falls, N.C., U.S., 4,612 . . . . .322/C4
Granite Falls, Wash., U.S., 2,347 . . . . .358/D1
Granite Quarry, N.C., U.S., 2,175 . . . . .322/E3
Granite Shoals, Tex., U.S., 2,040 . . . . .346/C2
Graniteville, Vt., U.S., 2,136 . . . . .352/C2
Granma, Cuba, province 204/E3
Grannis, Ark., U.S., 575 . . . . .244/A3
Grano, N. Dak., U.S. 326/D1
Gran Quivira, N. Mex., U.S. 317/D3
Grant, Ala., U.S., 665 .238/C1
Grant, Ark., U.S., county, 16,464 . . . . .244/C3
Grant, Colo., U.S., 60 .250/E2
Grant, Fla., U.S., 275 .256/H4
Grant, Ind., U.S., county, 73,403 . . . . .270/E3
Grant, Iowa, U.S., 102 . . . . .274/E5
Grant, Kans., U.S., county, 7,909 . . . . .276/A4
Grant, Ky., U.S., county, 22,384 . . . . .280/E2
Grant, La., U.S. 282/D5
Grant, La., U.S., parish, 18,698 . . . . .282/D3
Grant, Mich., U.S., 881 . . . . .294/D6
Grant, Minn., U.S., county, 6,289 . . . . .298/A5
Grant, Mont., U.S. 306/C4
Grant, Nebr., U.S., 1,225 . . . . .308/C2
Grant, Nebr., U.S., county, 747 . . . . .308/C2
Grant, Nev., U.S., mountain 310/A2
Grant, Nev., U.S., range 310/C2
Grant, N. Mex., U.S., county, 31,002 . . . . .317/B5
Grant, N. Mex., U.S., county, 2,841 . . . . .326/D3
Grant, Ohio, U.S., 125 . . . . .328/C4
Grant, Okla., U.S., 300 . . . . .330/G4
Grant, Okla., U.S., county, 5,144 . . . . .330/E1
Grant, Oreg., U.S., county, 7,935 . . . . .334/H3

Grant, S. Dak., U.S., county, 7,847 . . . . .342/J2
Grant, Wash., U.S., county, 74,698 . . . . .358/F2
Grant, W. Va., U.S., county, 11,299 . . . . .360/H2
Grant, Wisc., U.S., county, 49,597 . . . . .364/C6
Grant Ctr., Iowa, U.S. .274/B3
Grant City, Mo., U.S., 926 . . . . .302/B1
Grantfork, Ill., U.S., 254 . . . . .266/B3
Grantham, Eng., U.K. 60/C3
Grantham, Eng., U.K., 33,243 . . . . .68/F4
Grantham, N.H., U.S., 2,167 . . . . .312/B5
Grantham, N.C., U.S., 100 . . . . .322/J4
Grant-Kohrs Ranch Natl. Historic Site,
Mont. 306/D3
Granton, Wisc., U.S., 406 . . . . .364/C4
Grantown-on-Spey, Scot., U.K., 2,166 . . . . . . .62/B1
Grant Park, Ill., U.S., 1,358 . . . . .266/F2
Grants, Maine, U.S. 286/B3
Grants, N. Mex., U.S., 8,806 . . . . .317/C2
Grantsburg, Wisc., U.S., 1,369 . . . . .364/A3
Grantsdale, Mont., U.S., 750 . . . . .306/B3
Grants Pass, Oreg., U.S., 23,003 . . . . .334/C5
Grantsville, Md., U.S., 619 . . . . .288/B3
Grantsville, Utah, U.S., 6,015 . . . . .350/B3
Grantsville, W. Va., U.S., 565 . . . . .360/F1
Grant Town, W. Va., U.S., 657 . . . . .360/F1
Grantville, Ga., U.S., 1,309 . . . . .260/B5
Grantville, Kans., U.S., 250 . . . . .276/G2
Grantville, Penn., U.S., 1,000 . . . . .336/H5
Grantwood Vil., Mo., U.S., 883 . . . . .302/Q2
Granum, Alta., Can., 392 . . . . .212/D6
Granville, Ill., U.S., 1,414 . . . . .266/D2
Granville, Iowa, U.S., 325 . . . . .274/C2
Granville, Mass., U.S.1,521 . . . . .292/C4
Granville, N.Y., U.S., 2,644 . . . . .320/Q4
Granville, N.C., U.S., county, 48,498 . . . . .322/H2
Granville, N. Dak., U.S., 286 . . . . .326/E1
Granville, Ohio, U.S., 3,167 . . . . .328/E5
Granville, Tenn., U.S., 70 . . . . .344/K2
Granville, Vt., U.S., 303 . . . . .352/B3
Granville, W. Va., U.S., 778 . . . . .360/G1
Granville Lake, Man., Can., 69 . . . . .215/A1
Grapeland, Tex., U.S., 1,451 . . . . .346/N4
Grapevine, Ark., U.S. .244/C3
Grapevine, Calif., U.S., 42,059 . . . . .346/B9, L3
Grapevine, Tex., U.S., lake 346/A9
Gras, N.W. Terr., Can., lake 220/F4
Grasmere, Eng., U.K. 66/B4
Grasmere, Ida., U.S. 264/B7
Grasmere, N.H., U.S., 1,100 . . . . .312/C5
Grasonville, Md., U.S., 2,193 . . . . .288/K4
Grass, Man., Can., river 215/A3, M1
Grass Creek, Ind., U.S., 100 . . . . .270/D3
Grass Creek, Wyo., U.S. 366/B2
Grassflat, Penn., U.S., 650 . . . . .336/E3
Grass Lake, Mich., U.S., 1,082 . . . . .294/E7
Grassland, Alta., Can., 101 . . . . .212/D4
Grassland, Tex., U.S., 60 . . . . .346/G2
Grasslands Natl. Park, Sask., Can. 227/C11
Grasslands Natl. Park, Sask., Can. 306/J1
Grassmoor, Eng., U.K. .68/E3
Grassrange, Mont., U.S., 149 . . . . .306/H2
Grass River Prov. Park, Man., Can. 215/A2
Grasston, Minn., U.S., 105 . . . . .298/D5
Grass Valley, Calif., U.S., 10,922 . . . . .246/E3
Grass Valley, Oreg., U.S., 171 . . . . .334/F2
Grassy, Mo., U.S., 50 . . . . .302/F4
Grassy Butte, N. Dak., U.S. 326/B2
Grassy Creek, Ky., U.S., 100 . . . . .280/G3
Gratiot, Ohio, U.S., 187 . . . . .328/F6
Gratiot, Mich., U.S., county, 42,285 . . . . .294/E6
Gratiot, Ohio, U.S., 187 . . . . .328/F6
Gratiot, Wisc., U.S., 252 . . . . .364/C6
Gratis, Ohio, U.S., 934 . . . . .328/A6
Gratz, Ky., U.S., 89 . . . . .280/F2
Gratz, Penn., U.S., 676 . . . . .336/H4
Graubünden, Switz., canton 90/D2
Grauspitz, Liech., mountain 90/B2
Gravelbourg, Sask., Can., 1,187 . . . . .227/D11
Gravelford, Oreg., U.S. 334/B4
Gravelly, Ark., U.S., 60 . . . . .244/B3
Gravel Ridge, Ark., U.S., 3,232 . . . . .244/C3
Gravel Switch, Ky., U.S., 125 . . . . .280/E3
Gravenhurst, Ont., Can., 10,899 . . . . .223/F3
Gravenmacher, Lux., district 85/B2
Gravenor, Ant.-Bar., bay 207/E2
Graves, Ky., U.S., county, 37,028 . . . . .280/B4
Gravesend, Eng., U.K. . . . . .60/Inset III
Gravesend, Eng., U.K., 51,435 . . . . .70/E4
Gravette, Ark., U.S., 1,810 . . . . .244/A1
Gravity, Iowa, U.S., 218 . . . . .274/E6
Gravois Mills, Mo., U.S., 208 . . . . .302/D3
Grawn, Mich., U.S., 1,600 . . . . .294/D5
Gray, Ga., U.S., 1,811 .260/D5
Gray, Iowa, U.S., 82 . . . . .274/E4
Gray, Kans., U.S., county, 5,904 . . . . .276/B4
Gray, Ky., U.S., 650 . . . . .280/F4
Gray, La., U.S., 4,958 .282/H7
Gray, Maine, U.S., 6,820 . . . . .286/B5
Gray, Okla., U.S. 330/B1, D4
Gray, Tenn., U.S., 1,273 . . . . .344/S2
Gray, Tex., U.S., 40 . . . . .346/P3
Gray, Tex., U.S., county, 22,744 . . . . .346/G9
Gray Court, S.C., U.S., 1,021 . . . . .340/B2
Gray Hawk, Ky., U.S., 250 . . . . .280/G3
Grayland, Wash., U.S., 1,002 . . . . .358/A3
Grayling, Alaska, U.S., 194 . . . . .240/C2
Grayling, Mich., U.S., 1,952 . . . . .294/E5
Grayling, Mont., U.S. 306/E5
Graymoor-Devondale, Ky., U.S., 2,925 . . . . . . .280/B2
Gray Mtn., Ariz., U.S. 242/D2
Grayridge, Mo., U.S., 150 . . . . .302/G5
Grays, Eng., U.K., 59,145 . . . . .70/E4
Grays, Ark., U.S. 244/D2
Grays, Ida., U.S., lake .264/F6
Grays, S.C., U.S. 340/C4
Grays, Wash., U.S., harbor 358/A3
Grays Branch, Ky., U.S., 225 . . . . .280/H2
Grays Harbor, Wash., U.S., county, 67,194 . . .358/B2
Grayslake, Ill., U.S., 18,506 . . . . .266/B4
Grayson, Ga., U.S., 100 . . . . .238/B1
Grayson, Ga., U.S., 765 . . . . .260/D4
Grayson, Ky., U.S., 3,877 . . . . .280/H2
Grayson, Ky., U.S., county, 24,053 . . . . .280/D3
Grayson, La., U.S., 531 . . . . .282/E2
Grayson, Okla., U.S., 134 . . . . .330/G2
Grayson, Tex., U.S., county, 110,595 . . . . .346/M2
Grayson, Va., U.S., county, 17,917 . . . . .354/A7
Grays River, Wash., U.S., 90 . . . . .358/B3
Gray Summit, Mo., U.S., 2,640 . . . . .302/P4
Graysville, Ala., U.S., 2,344 . . . . .238/D1
Graysville, Ind., U.S., 125 . . . . .270/A6
Graysville, Ohio, U.S., 113 . . . . .328/H6
Graysville, Tenn., U.S., 1,411 . . . . .344/L4
Grayville, Ill., U.S., 1,725 . . . . .266/E5
Graz, Aus., 226,892 . . . . .91/D3
Greaney, Minn., U.S. 298/D3
Greasewood, Ariz., U.S., 581 . . . . .242/F2
Great, Mass., U.S., point 292/P7
Great, N.H., U.S., bay .312/E5

Great, N.J., U.S., bay ...314/E5
Great, N.C., U.S., lake ...322/L5
Great Abaco, Bah., island ...204/B4
Great Alföld, Hun., plain ...91/B2
Great Alne, Eng., U.K. ...68/D5
Great Artesian, Austl., basin ...170/D2
Great Australian, Austl., bight ...170/B3
Great Ayton, Eng., U.K., 3,592 ...66/F3
Great Bahama, bank ...204/B2
Great Bahama, Bah., bank ...207/B4
Great Barford, Eng., U.K., 1,754 ...68/G5
Great Barford, Eng., U.K., 1,754 ...70/D2
Great Barrier, Austl., reef ...170/D1
Great Barrier, N.Z., island ...171/C2
Great Barrington, Mass., U.S., 7,527 ...292/A4
Great Basin, Nev., U.S. ...310/B2
Great Basin, Utah, U.S. ...350/A4
Great Basin N.P., Nev., U.S. ...310/C2
Great Bear, Can., lake ...193/C12
Great Bear, N.W. Terr., Can., lake ...220/D3
Great Bedwyn, Eng., U.K. ...70/A4
Great Bedwyn, Eng., U.K. ...73/J2
Great Bend, Kans., U.S., 15,345 ...276/D3
Great Bend, N. Dak., U.S., 118 ...326/I3
Great Bend, Penn., U.S., 700 ...336/K2
Great Bircham, Eng., U.K. ...70/F1
Great Bookham, Eng., U.K. ...70/D4
Great Broughton, Eng., U.K. ...66/F4
Great Casterton, Eng., U.K. ...70/C1
Great Clifton, Eng., U.K. ...66/A3
Great Cubley, Eng., U.K. ...68/C4
Great Divide, Colo., U.S. ...250/C1
Great Divide, Wyo., U.S., basin ...366/A3
Great Dividing, Austl., range ...170/D1, D3
Great Duck, Ont., Can., island ...294/G4
Great Dunmow, Eng., U.K., 4,907 ...70/E3
Greater Antilles, islands ...204/B3
Greater Hinggan, China, range ...119/F1
Greater Manchester, Eng., U.K.,
  unitary authority, 2,482,352 ...68/C2
Greater Sunda, Indon., islands ...122/B3
Greaterville, Ariz., U.S., 60 ...242/E6
Great Exuma, Bah., island ...204/B2
Great Exuma, Bah., island ...207/B3
Great Falls, Man., Can. ...215/C4
Great Falls, Mont., U.S., 56,690,
  (80,357, metro.) ...306/E2
Great Falls, S.C., U.S., 2,194 ...340/D2
Great Falls, Va., U.S., 8,549 ...354/J2, M1
Great Fish, S. Afr., river ...162/C3
Great Gable, Eng., U.K., hill ...66/B4
Great Gaddesden, Eng., U.K. ...70/C3
Great Gidding, Eng., U.K. ...70/D2
Great Gransden, Eng., U.K. ...70/D2
Great Harwood, Eng., U.K., 10,562 ...66/D5
Great Harwood, Eng., U.K., 10,562 ...68/C2
Great Haseley, Eng., U.K. ...70/B3
Great Horkesley, Eng., U.K. ...70/F3
Great Horwood, Eng., U.K. ...70/C3
Great Inagua, Bah., island ...204/C2
Great Inagua, Bah., island ...207/C4
Great Indian, India, desert ...128/B3
Qreat Karroo, S. Afr., plateau ...162/B3
Great Livermere, Eng., U.K. ...70/F2
Great Malvern, Eng., U.K., 31,537 ...68/C5
Great Massingham, Eng., U.K. ...70/F1
Great Meadows, N.J., U.S., 1,264 ...314/D2
Great Meadows N.W.R., Mass., U.S. ...292/J3
Great Miami, Ohio, U.S., river ...328/A9, F2
Great Mills, Md., U.S., 2,600 ...288/J7
Great Mitton, Eng., U.K. ...68/C2
Great Neck, N.Y., U.S., 9,538 ...320/C2
Great Neck Plaza, N.Y., U.S., 6,433 ...320/C2
Great Nicobar, India, island ...128/F7
Great Ormes Head, Wales, U.K., cape ...64/D1
Great Orton, Eng., U.K. ...66/B3
Great Ouse, Eng., U.K., river ...60/D3
Great Ouse, Eng., U.K., river ...70/E2
Great Palgrave, Eng., U.K. ...70/F1
Great Pond, Maine, U.S., 47 ...286/D4
Great Ponton, Eng., U.K. ...70/C1
Great Quittacus, Mass., U.S., pond ...292/L5
Great Rift, Eth., valley ...156/C3
Great Rift, Kenya, valley ...157/C3
Great Rift, Mal., valley ...159/B3
Great Rift, Tan., valley ...152/B2, C1
Great Rissington, Eng., U.K. ...68/D6
Great Ruaha, Tan., river ...152/C2
Great Sacandaga, N.Y., U.S., lake ...320/N4
Great Saling, Eng., U.K. ...70/E3
Great Salt, St. K.-Nevis, pond ...207/C2
Great Salt, Utah, U.S., lake ...350/B2, D1
Great Salt Lake Desert, Utah, U.S. ...350/A3
Great Sampford, Eng., U.K. ...70/E3
Great Sand Dunes N.P., Colo., U.S. ...250/E4
Great Sand Dunes Natl. Pres., Colo., U.S. ...250/E4
Great Sandy, Austl., desert ...170/B2
Great Scarcies, S.L., river ...149/A1
Great Sea, Fiji, reef ...174/B1
Great Shefford, Eng., U.K. ...70/B4
Great Shelford, Eng., U.K., 6,522 ...68/H5
Great Shelford, Eng., U.K., 6,522 ...70/E2
Great Slave, N.W. Terr., Can., lake ...214/P1
Great Slave, N.W. Terr., Can., lake ...220/F4
Great Smeaton, Eng., U.K. ...66/F4
Great Smoky, Tenn., U.S., mountains ...344/P3
Great Smoky Mountains Natl. Park, Tenn., U.S. ...344/P3
Greatstone-on-Sea, Eng., U.K. ...70/F5
Great Strickland, Eng., U.K. ...66/C3
Great Tew, Eng., U.K. ...70/B3
Great Tey, Eng., U.K. ...70/F3
Great Torrington, Eng., U.K., 4,073 ...73/D3
Great Totham, Eng., U.K. ...70/F3
Great Victoria, Austl., desert ...170/B2
Great Wakering, Eng., U.K. ...70/F3
Great Wall of China, China ...119/D2
Great Walsingham, Eng., U.K. ...70/F1
Great Wass, Maine, U.S., island ...286/E4
Great White Heron N.W.R., Fla., U.S. ...256/G7
Great Whittington, Eng., U.K. ...66/E2
Great Witley, Eng., U.K. ...68/C5
Great Works, Maine, U.S. ...286/D4
Great Wratting, Eng., U.K. ...70/E2
Great Yarmouth, Eng., U.K. ...60/D3
Great Yarmouth, Eng., U.K., 56,190,
  (64,260, metro.) ...70/H1
Great Yeldham, Eng., U.K., 1,513 ...70/F2
Great Zab, Iraq, river ...130/B1
Great Zab, Tur., river ...133/E3
Gréboun, Niger, mountain ...152/B1
Greco, Cyp., cape ...94/D2
Gredos, Sp., mountains ...90/C1
Greece, nation ...98
Greece, N.Y., U.S., 14,614 ...320/F4
Greeley, Colo., U.S., 76,930 ...250/F1
Greeley, Iowa, U.S., 276 ...274/M2
Greeley, Kans., U.S., 327 ...276/G3
Greeley, Kans., U.S., county, 1,534 ...276/A3
Greeley, Nebr., U.S., 531 ...308/F2
Greeley, Nebr., U.S., county, 2,714 ...308/F2
Greeley, Penn., U.S., 250 ...336/L3
Greeleyville, S.C., U.S., 452 ...340/E3

Greely, Nun., Can., fjord ...220/L1
Green, P.N.G., islands ...172/B2
Green, Colo., U.S., river ...250/A1
Green, Kans., U.S., 147 ...276/E2
Green, Ky., U.S., county, 11,518 ...280/E3
Green, Ky., U.S., river ...280/C3, E3
Green, Mich., U.S., 80 ...294/D1
Green, N. Dak., U.S., river ...326/B3
Green, Ohio, U.S., 22,817 ...328/H4
Green, Oreg., U.S., 6,174 ...334/C4
Green, Utah, U.S., river ...350/D4, E5
Green, Vt., U.S., mountains ...352/B4
Green, Wash., U.S., river ...358/D2
Green, Wisc., U.S., bay ...364/F4
Green, Wisc., U.S., county, 33,647 ...364/D6
Greenacres, Calif., U.S., 7,400 ...246/F7
Greenacres, Fla., U.S., 27,569 ...256/B5, H5
Green Acres, Wash., U.S., 5,158 ...358/H2
Greenback, Tenn., U.S., 954 ...344/N3
Green Bank, N.J., U.S., 125 ...314/D4
Greenbank, Wash., U.S., 225 ...358/C1
Green Bank, W. Va., U.S., 200 ...360/G4
Green Bay, Wisc., U.S., 102,313,
  (226,778, metro.) ...364/F4
Greenbelt, Md., U.S., 21,456 ...288/C6, G3
Greenbrier, Ark., U.S., 3,042 ...244/C2
Greenbrier, Tenn., U.S., 4,940 ...344/H2
Greenbrier, W. Va., U.S., county, 34,453 ...360/E5
Greenbrier, W. Va., U.S., river ...354/C5
Greenbrier, W. Va., U.S., river ...360/F4
Greenbush, Maine, U.S., 1,421 ...286/D3
Greenbush, Mass., U.S., 550 ...292/L4
Greenbush, Mich., U.S., 225 ...294/F5
Greenbush, Minn., U.S., 784 ...298/A2
Green Camp, Ohio, U.S., 342 ...328/D4
Greencastle, Ind., U.S., 9,880 ...270/C5
Greencastle, Ind., U.S., 308 ...302/D1
Greencastle, Penn., U.S., 3,722 ...336/F6
Green City, Mo., U.S., 688 ...302/D1
Green Cove Sprs., Fla., U.S., 5,378 ...256/G2
Green Creek, N.J., U.S., 1,300 ...314/D5
Greendale, Ind., U.S., 4,296 ...270/G6
Greendale, Wisc., U.S., 14,405 ...364/F2
Greendell, N.J., U.S., 550 ...314/D2
Greene, Ala., U.S., county, 9,974 ...238/A3
Greene, Ark., U.S., county, 37,331 ...244/E1
Greene, Ga., U.S., county, 14,406 ...260/E4
Greene, Ill., U.S., county, 14,761 ...266/A2, C4
Greene, Ind., U.S., county, 33,157 ...270/B7
Greene, Iowa, U.S., 1,099 ...274/J2
Greene, Iowa, U.S., county, 10,366 ...274/F4
Greene, Maine, U.S., 4,076 ...286/B4
Greene, Miss., U.S., county, 13,299 ...300/D4
Greene, Mo., U.S., county, 240,391 ...302/C4
Greene, N.Y., U.S., 1,701 ...320/K6
Greene, N.Y., U.S., county, 48,195 ...320/N6
Greene, N.C., U.S., county, 18,974 ...322/K4
Greene, Ohio, U.S., county, 147,886 ...328/C6, G2
Greene, Penn., U.S., county, 40,672 ...336/A6
Greene, Tenn., U.S., county, 62,909 ...344/R3
Greene, Va., U.S., county, 15,244 ...354/F4
Greenevers, N.C., U.S., 560 ...322/K5
Greeneville, Tenn., U.S., 15,198 ...344/R2
Greenfield, Ark., U.S., 125 ...244/F2
Greenfield, Calif., U.S., 12,583 ...246/D6
Greenfield, Ill., U.S., 1,179 ...266/C4
Greenfield, Ind., U.S., 14,600 ...270/E5
Greenfield, Iowa, U.S., 2,129 ...274/F5
Greenfield, Maine, U.S. ...286/D3
Greenfield, Mass., U.S., 18,168 ...292/D2
Greenfield, Minn., U.S., 2,544 ...298/D5
Greenfield, Mo., U.S., 1,358 ...302/C4
Greenfield, N.H., U.S., 1,657 ...312/C6
Greenfield, N. Mex., U.S., 175 ...317/F4
Greenfield, Ohio, U.S., 4,906 ...328/D7
Greenfield, Okla., U.S., 123 ...330/D2
Greenfield, Tenn., U.S., 2,208 ...344/D2
Greenfield, Wisc., U.S., 35,476 ...364/E6, F2
Green Forest, Ark., U.S., 2,717 ...244/B1
Green Grass, S. Dak., U.S., 58 ...342/D2
Green Harbor, Mass., U.S., 2,397 ...292/M4
Green Haven, Md., U.S., 17,415 ...288/H3
Greenhill, Md., U.S., 50 ...288/L6
Greenhill, (W. Canton), N.C., U.S. ...322/D7
Green Hill, R.I., U.S., 275 ...339/C5
Green Hill, Tenn., U.S., 7,068 ...344/H2
Greenhills, Ohio, U.S., 4,103 ...328/B9
Green Hills, Penn., U.S. ...336/A5
Greenhorn, Oreg., U.S. ...334/H3
Greenhow Hill, Eng., U.K. ...66/F2
Greenland, N. Ire., U.K., 4,967 ...65/F2
Green Island, Iowa, U.S., 50 ...274/P3
Green Island, N.Y., U.S., 2,278 ...320/P5
Green Isle, Minn., U.S., 334 ...298/D6
Green Lake, Sask., Can., 498 ...227/C6
Green Lake, Maine, U.S., 70 ...286/D4
Green Lake, Wisc., U.S., 1,100 ...364/E5
Green Lake, Wisc., U.S., county, 19,105 ...364/D5
Greenland, (Kalaallit Nunaat), dependency ...193/B16
Greenland, sea ...193/B18
Greenland, Grld., sea ...193/D2
Greenland, Ice., sea ...79/B1
Greenland, Ark., U.S., 907 ...244/A2
Greenland, Mich., U.S., 325 ...294/A3
Greenland, N.H., U.S., 3,208 ...312/E5
Greenland, Penn., U.S., 584 ...336/L5
Greenlaw, Scot., U.K., 579 ...62/M7
Greenleaf, Ida., U.S., 862 ...264/A6
Greenleaf, Kans., U.S., 357 ...276/F2
Greenleaf, Minn., U.S., 40 ...298/C5
Greenleaf, Wisc., U.S., 650 ...364/E4
Greenleafton, Minn., U.S., 125 ...298/E7
Greenlee, Ariz., U.S., county, 8,547 ...242/F4
Green Level, N.C., U.S. ...322/H3
Greenmount, Md., U.S., 600 ...288/C1
Green Mtn. Falls, Colo., U.S., 773 ...250/F3
Green Mount Natl. For., Vt., U.S. ...352/A4, B3
Green Oaks, Ill., U.S., 3,572 ...266/B5
Greenock, Scot., U.K. ...60/B2
Greenock, Scot., U.K., 45,467 ...62/G7
Greenodd, Eng., U.K. ...66/B4
Greenough, Mont., U.S. ...306/C3
Green Peter, Oreg., U.S., lake ...334/D3
Green Pond, N.J., U.S., 1,400 ...314/E1
Green Pond, S.C., U.S., 175 ...340/D4
Greenport, N.Y., U.S., 2,048 ...320/G1
Green Ridge, Mo., U.S., 445 ...302/C3
Green Ridge St. For., Md., U.S. ...288/A1, D3
Green River, Ky., U.S., lake ...280/E3
Green River, Utah, U.S., 973 ...350/D4
Green River, Wyo., U.S., 100 ...352/B5
Green River, Wyo., U.S., 11,808 ...366/B3
Greensboro, Ala., U.S., 2,731 ...238/B3
Greensboro, Fla., U.S., 619 ...256/D1
Greensboro, Ga., U.S., 3,238 ...260/E4
Greensboro, Ind., U.S., 174 ...270/E5
Greensboro, Md., U.S., 1,632 ...288/L4
Greensboro, N.C., U.S., 223,891,
  (1,251,509, metro.) ...322/F2
Greensboro, Penn., U.S., 295 ...336/B6
Greensboro, Vt., U.S., 770 ...352/C1
Greensboro Bend, Vt., U.S., 350 ...352/C1

Greensburg, Ind., U.S., 10,260 ...270/F6
Greensburg, Kans., U.S., 1,574 ...276/C4
Greensburg, Ky., U.S., 2,396 ...280/E3
Greensburg, La., U.S., 631 ...282/H5
Greensburg, Penn., U.S., 15,889 ...336/B5
Green Sea, S.C., U.S., 150 ...340/F2
Greens Fork, Ind., U.S., 371 ...270/F5
Greenslopes, Qnsld., Austl. ...170/Inset III
Green Spr., Ky., U.S., 759 ...280/B1
Green Spr., W. Va., U.S., 150 ...360/J1
Greensville, Va., U.S., county, 11,560 ...354/H7
Greentop, Mo., U.S., 427 ...302/D1
Greentown, Ind., U.S., 2,546 ...270/E4
Green Tree, Penn., U.S., 4,719 ...336/D7
Greenup, Ill., U.S., 1,532 ...266/E4
Greenup, Ky., U.S., 1,198 ...280/H2
Greenup, Ky., U.S., county, 36,891 ...280/G2
Green Valley, Ariz., U.S., 17,283 ...242/E6
Green Valley, Ill., U.S., 728 ...266/D3
Green Valley, Md., U.S., 12,262 ...288/E2
Green Valley, Minn., U.S., 150 ...298/B6
Green Valley, Wisc., U.S., 175 ...364/E4
Greenview, Calif., U.S., 200 ...246/C1
Greenview, Ill., U.S., 862 ...266/D3
Greenview, Minn., U.S. ...298/A3
Greenville, Liber. ...149/B3
Greenville, Ala., U.S., 7,228 ...238/C4
Greenville, Calif., U.S., 1,160 ...246/E2
Greenville, Fla., U.S., 837 ...256/E1
Greenville, Ga., U.S., 946 ...260/B5
Greenville, Ill., U.S., 6,955 ...266/D5
Greenville, Ind., U.S., 591 ...270/E8
Greenville, Iowa, U.S., 93 ...274/D1
Greenville, Ky., U.S., 4,398 ...280/C3
Greenville, Maine, U.S., 1,623 ...286/C3
Greenville, Mich., U.S., 7,935 ...294/D6
Greenville, Miss., U.S., 41,633 ...300/A2
Greenville, Mo., U.S., 451 ...302/F4
Greenville, N.H., U.S., 2,224 ...312/C6
Greenville, N.Y., U.S., 493 ...320/N6
Greenville, N.C., U.S., 60,476, (133,798, metro.) ...322/L3
Greenville, Ohio, U.S., 13,294 ...328/A5
Greenville, Penn., U.S., 6,380 ...336/A3
Greenville, R.I., U.S., 8,626 ...339/C2
Greenville, S.C., U.S., 56,002,
  (962,441, metro.) ...340/B2, E2
Greenville, S.C., U.S., county, 379,616 ...340/B2, E1
Greenville, Tex., U.S., 23,960 ...346/M2
Greenville, Utah, U.S. ...350/B5
Greenville, Va., U.S., 886 ...354/E4
Greenville, W. Va., U.S., 70 ...360/E5
Greenville Jct., Maine, U.S., 850 ...286/C3
Greenwald, Minn., U.S., 201 ...298/C5
Greenwater, Wash., U.S., 91 ...358/D2
Greenway, Ark., U.S., 244 ...244/E1
Greenway, S. Dak., U.S. ...342/F2
Greenwich, Eng., U.K., unitary authority,
  214,540 ...70/E4
Greenwich, Conn., U.S., 61,101 ...253/A5
Greenwich, (Cumberland County), N.J., U.S., 847 ...314/C5
Greenwich, N.Y., U.S., 1,902 ...320/Q4
Greenwich, Ohio, U.S., 1,525 ...328/E3
Greenwich, Utah, U.S. ...350/C5
Greenwood, Br. Col., Can., 666 ...214/N6
Greenwood, Ark., U.S., 7,112 ...244/A2
Greenwood, (Custer County), Colo., U.S. ...250/E3
Greenwood, (Pueblo County), Colo., U.S. ...250/F4
Greenwood, Del., U.S., 837 ...255/B5
Greenwood, Fla., U.S., 735 ...256/C1
Greenwood, Ill., U.S. ...266/E1
Greenwood, Ind., U.S., 36,037 ...270/D5
Greenwood, Kans., U.S., county, 7,673 ...276/F4
Greenwood, Ky., U.S., 50 ...280/F4
Greenwood, La., U.S., 2,458 ...282/B2
Greenwood, Maine, U.S., 802 ...286/B4
Greenwood, Miss., U.S., 18,425 ...300/B2
Greenwood, Mo., U.S., 3,952 ...302/J3
Greenwood, N.Y., U.S., 325 ...320/F6
Greenwood, S.C., U.S., 22,071 ...340/B2
Greenwood, S.C., U.S., county, 66,271 ...340/B2
Greenwood, S.C., U.S., lake ...340/C2
Greenwood, S. Dak., U.S. ...342/G5
Greenwood, Tenn., U.S. ...344/J2
Greenwood, Tex., U.S., 250 ...346/G3
Greenwood, Wisc., U.S., 1,079 ...364/C4
Greenwood Lake, N.Y., U.S., 3,411 ...320/A1
Greenwood Sprs., Miss., U.S., 50 ...300/D2
Greenwood Vil., Colo., U.S., 11,035 ...250/A3, F2
Greer, Ariz., U.S. ...242/F3
Greer, Ida., U.S. ...264/A3
Greer, Mo., U.S., 50 ...302/E4
Greer, Okla., U.S., county, 6,061 ...330/C3
Greer, S.C., U.S., 16,843 ...340/B2, F2
Greers Ferry, Ark., U.S., 930 ...244/C2
Greers Ferry, Ark., U.S., lake ...244/C2
Greeson, Ark., U.S., lake ...244/B3
Greetham, Eng., U.K. ...70/C1
Gregg, Tex., U.S., county, 111,379 ...346/P3
Gregory, Mich., U.S., 70 ...294/D7
Gregory, Mich., U.S., 500 ...294/E7
Gregory, S. Dak., U.S., 1,342 ...342/F4
Gregory, S. Dak., U.S., county, 4,792 ...342/F4
Gregory, Tex., U.S., 2,318 ...346/L8
Gregory Natl. Park, Austl. ...170/C1
Greifswald, Ger. ...86/C1
Greilickville, Mich., U.S., 1,415 ...294/D5
Grená, Den. ...79/C2
Grenada, nation ...204/F4
Grenada, nation ...197
Grenada, Gren., island ...209/B2
Grenada, Calif., U.S., 351 ...246/C1
Grenada, Miss., U.S., 14,879 ...300/C2
Grenada, Miss., U.S., county, 23,263 ...300/C2
Grenada, Miss., U.S., lake ...300/C2
Grenadines, Gren., island group ...209/B1, C1
Grenadines, St. Vin.-Gren., islands ...208/A3
Grenfell, Sask., Can., 1,067 ...227/H10
Grenoble, Fr., 156,203, (419,334, metro.) ...88/D4
Grenola, Kans., U.S., 231 ...276/F4
Grenora, N. Dak., U.S., 202 ...326/B1
Grenville, N. Mex., U.S. ...317/G1
Grenville, S. Dak., U.S., 62 ...342/H2
Grenville and Leeds, Ont., Can. ...223/K3
Grenville and Leeds, Ont., Can., county ...223/K3
Gresford, Wales, U.K., 4,915 ...64/F1
Gresham, Nebr., U.S., 270 ...308/G2
Gresham, Oreg., U.S., 90,205 ...334/A2
Gresham, S.C., U.S., 125 ...340/E3
Gresham, Wisc., U.S., 575 ...364/E4
Gresham Park, Ga., U.S., 9,215 ...260/C4, J3
Gressenhall, Eng., U.K. ...70/F1
Gressitt, Va., U.S., 80 ...354/K6
Gresston, Ga., U.S., 275 ...260/D5
Gretna, Man., Can., 563 ...215/C4
Gretna, Fla., U.S., 1,709 ...256/C1
Gretna, La., U.S., 17,423 ...282/J7, K3
Gretna, Nebr., U.S., 2,355 ...308/H2
Gretna, Va., U.S., 1,257 ...354/E7

Gretton, Eng., U.K. ...70/C1
Greve, Den. ...79/D3
Grevenmacher, Lux. ...85/B2
Grey, Austl., range ...170/D2
Grey, Nfld., Can., river ...218/C5
Grey, Ont., Can. ...223/E3
Grey, Ont., Can., county ...223/E3
Greyabbey, N. Ire., U.K., 697 ...65/F2
Greybull, Wyo., U.S., 1,815 ...366/B1
Greybull, Wyo., U.S., river ...366/B1
Greycliff, Mont., U.S., 56 ...306/G4
Grey Eagle, Minn., U.S., 335 ...298/C5
Grey Forest, Tex., U.S., 418 ...346/A2
Greylock, Mass., U.S., mountain ...292/B2
Greymouth, N.Z. ...171/B3
Grey River, Nfld., Can., 169 ...218/C5
Greystone, Colo., U.S. ...250/B1
Greystones, C.A.R., river ...154/A2
Gribingui, C.A.R., river ...154/A2
Grice, Tex., U.S., 40 ...346/N3
Grider, Ark., U.S. ...244/F2
Gridley, Calif., U.S., 5,382 ...246/D3
Gridley, Ill., U.S., 1,411 ...266/E3
Gridley, Kans., U.S., 372 ...276/G3
Grier, Mont., U.S. ...317/G3
Griffin, Sask., Can. ...227/G11
Griffin, Ga., U.S., 23,451 ...260/C5
Griffin, Ind., U.S., 160 ...270/A8
Griffith, N.S.W., Austl. ...170/D3
Griffith, Ind., U.S., 17,334 ...270/B1
Griffith, Tex., U.S., 40 ...346/E2
Griffithsville, W. Va., U.S., 60 ...360/C4
Griffithville, Ark., U.S., 262 ...244/D2
Grifton, N.C., U.S., 2,073 ...322/L4
Griggs, N. Dak., U.S., county, 2,754 ...326/G2
Griggs, Okla., U.S. ...330/B4
Griggsville, Ill., U.S., 1,258 ...266/C4
Grigston, Kans., U.S. ...276/B3
Grijalva, Mex., river ...200/F4
Grimari, C.A.R. ...154/A2
Grimes, Ala., U.S., 459 ...238/D4
Grimes, Iowa, U.S., 5,098 ...274/G4
Grimes, Okla., U.S. ...330/C2
Grimes, Tex., U.S., county, 23,552 ...346/M5
Grimesland, N.C., U.S., 440 ...322/L3
Grimes Mill, Maine, U.S. ...286/E2
Grimoldby, Eng., U.K. ...66/J6
Grimsby, Eng., U.K. ...60/C3
Grimsby, Eng., U.K., 90,703, (145,364, metro.) ...66/H5
Grimsby, Eng., U.K., 90,703, (145,364, metro.) ...68/G2
Grimscote, Eng., U.K. ...70/B2
Grimsey, Ice., island ...79/B1
Grimshaw, Alta., Can., 2,435 ...212/B3
Grimsley, Tenn., U.S., 375 ...344/M2
Grimsthorpe, Eng., U.K. ...70/C1
Grimston, Eng., U.K. ...70/F1
Grindleton, Eng., U.K. ...66/D5
Grindstone, Maine, U.S. ...286/D3
Grind Stone City, Mich., U.S., 100 ...294/F5
Grinnell, Nun., Can., peninsula ...220/J1
Grinnell, Iowa, U.S., 9,105 ...274/J4
Grinnell, Kans., U.S., 329 ...276/B2
Griqualand East, S. Afr., region ...162/C3
Griqualand West, S. Afr., region ...162/B2
Griquatown, S. Afr. ...162/B2
Grisdale, Wash., U.S. ...358/B2
Grise Fiord, Nun., Can., 163 ...220/M1
Griswold, Man., Can. ...215/A4
Griswold, Iowa, U.S., 1,039 ...274/D5
Griswoldville, Mass., U.S., 150 ...292/D2
Grit, Tex., U.S. ...346/J5
Groesbeck, Tex., U.S., 4,291 ...346/M4
Groningen, Neth., 172,166, (190,752, metro.) ...84/D1
Groningen, Neth., province ...84/D1
Groningen, Sur. ...183/B2
Gronlid, Sask., Can., 70 ...227/F7
Groom, Tex., U.S., 587 ...346/C9
Groom Creek, Ariz., U.S., 250 ...242/C3
Groote Eylandt, Austl., island ...170/C1
Grootfontein, Nam. ...160/C1
Grootvloer, S. Afr., pan ...162/B2
Gros Cap, Mich., U.S., 90 ...294/E4
Gros Islet, St. Luc. ...208/B1
Gros-Morne, Que., Can. ...226/L2
Gros Morne Natl. Park, Nfld., Can. ...218/C4
Gross, Nebr., U.S. ...308/E1
Grosse Ile, Mich., U.S., 10,894 ...294/B7
Grosse Pointe, Mich., U.S., 5,670 ...294/B7
Grosse Pointe Farms, Mich., U.S., 9,764 ...294/B7
Grosse Pointe Park, Mich., U.S., 12,443 ...294/B7
Grosse Pointe Shores, Mich., U.S., 2,823 ...294/B6, G7
Grosse Pointe Woods, Mich., U.S., 17,080 ...294/B7
Grosse Tete, La., U.S., 670 ...282/G6
Grosseto, It. ...95/B2
Grossglockner, Aus., mountain ...91/C3
Grosvenor Dale, Conn., U.S., 700 ...253/G4
Groton, Conn., U.S., 39,907 ...253/G4
Groton, Mass., U.S., 9,547 ...292/H2
Groton, N.H., U.S., 456 ...312/C4
Groton, N.Y., U.S., 2,470 ...320/J5
Groton, S. Dak., U.S., 1,356 ...342/G2
Groton, Vt., U.S., 876 ...352/C2
Groton Long Pt., Conn., U.S., 667 ...253/G4
Grotto, Wash., U.S. ...358/D2
Grottoes, Va., U.S., 2,114 ...354/F4
Grotto of the Redemption, Iowa, U.S. ...274/F2
Grouard Mission, Alta., Can., 436 ...212/B3
Groundbirch, Br. Col., Can. ...214/M3
Grouse Creek, Utah, U.S. ...350/A2
Grovania, Ga., U.S. ...260/D7
Grove, Eng., U.K., 7,504 ...70/B4
Grove, Kans., U.S. ...276/G2
Grove, Maine, U.S., 70 ...286/E4
Grove, Md., U.S. ...288/L4
Grove, Okla., U.S., 5,131 ...330/H1
Grove Ctr., Ky., U.S., 90 ...280/B3
Grove City, Fla., U.S., 2,092 ...256/F5
Grove City, Minn., U.S., 608 ...298/C5
Grove City, Ohio, U.S., 27,075 ...328/D6, D10
Grove City, Penn., U.S., 8,024 ...336/A3
Grove Hill, Ala., U.S., 1,438 ...238/B4
Grove Lake, Minn., U.S., 50 ...298/B5
Groveland, (Groveland-Big Oak Flat),
  Calif., U.S., 3,388 ...246/E5
Groveland, Fla., U.S., 2,360 ...256/B4
Groveland, Ga., U.S., 100 ...260/H7
Groveland, Mass., U.S., 6,038 ...292/K1
Groveport, Ohio, U.S., 3,865 ...328/E10
Grover, Colo., U.S., 153 ...250/F1
Grover, N.C., U.S., 698 ...322/C4
Grover, S.C., U.S., 250 ...340/D3
Grover, S. Dak., U.S. ...342/H3
Grover, Utah, U.S. ...350/C5
Grover, Wyo., U.S., 137 ...366/A2
Grover Beach, Calif., U.S., 13,067 ...246/E7
Grover Hill, Ohio, U.S., 412 ...328/B3
Grovertown, Ind., U.S., 350 ...270/C2
Groves, Tex., U.S., 15,733 ...346/R6
Grovespring, Mo., U.S., 125 ...302/D4
Groveton, N.H., U.S., 1,197 ...312/C2
Groveton, Tex., U.S., 1,107 ...346/N4
Groveton, Va., U.S., 21,296 ...354/J3, M2
Grovetown, Ga., U.S., 6,089 ...260/G5

Groveville, Maine, U.S. 286/B5
Groveville, N.J., U.S., 9,208 . . . . .314/D3
Grow, Tex., U.S. .346/H2
Groznyy, Russ. 104/D5
Grubbs, Ark., U.S., 438 . . . . .244/D2
Gruene, Tex., U.S. 346/B2
Gruetli-Laager, Tenn., U.S., 1,867 . . . . . . .344/K4
Grulla N.W.R., N. Mex., U.S. 317/G3
Grundisburgh, Eng., U.K. 70/G2
Grundy, Ill., U.S., county, 37,535 . . . . .266/E2
Grundy, Iowa, U.S., county, 12,369 . . . . . .274/J3
Grundy, Mo., U.S., county, 10,432 . . . . . . .302/C1
Grundy, Tenn., U.S., county, 14,332 . . . . . .344/K4
Grundy, Va., U.S., 1,105 . . . . .354/D2
Grundy Ctr., Iowa, U.S., 2,596 . . . . .274/J3
Grundy Lake Prov. Park, Ont., Can. 223/E2
Grunthal, Man., Can. 215/C4
Gruver, Iowa, U.S., 106 . . . . .274/E1
Gruver, Tex., U.S., 1,162 . . . . .346/G8
Grygla, Minn., U.S., 228 . . . . .298/B2
Guacanayabo, Cuba, gulf 204/B2
Guacanayabo, Cuba, gulf 204/D3
Guadalajara, Mex., state capital, 1,646,319,
     (3,349,465, metro.) 200/D3
Guadalajara, Sp., 68,248 . . . . .94/E2
Guadalajara, Sp., province 94/E2
Guadalcanal, Sol. Is., island 173/A1
Guadalquivir, Sp., river 94/D4
Guadalupe, Mex., reservoir 200/Inset
Guadalupe, Ariz., U.S., 5,228 . . . . .242/D4
Guadalupe, Calif., U.S., 5,659 . . . . .246/E8
Guadalupe, N. Mex., U.S., county, 4,680 . . .317/F3
Guadalupe, N. Mex., U.S., mountains 317/E5
Guadalupe, Tex., U.S., 175 . . . . .346/B4
Guadalupe, Tex., U.S., county, 89,023 . .346/B2, K6
Guadalupe, Tex., U.S., mountains 346/D4
Guadalupe, Tex., U.S., peak 346/D3
Guadalupe, Tex., U.S., river 346/A1
Guadalupe Mountains Natl. Park, Tex., U.S. .346/D4
Guadalupita, N. Mex., U.S. 317/E1
Guadarrama, Sp., mountains 94/D2
Guadeloupe, Fr., overseas department 204/F3
Guadiana, Port., river 93/B3
Guadiana, Sp., river 94/C3
Guage, Ky., U.S., 80 . . . . .280/C3
Guaillabamba, Ecua., river 185/B2
Guainía, Col., department 184/C4
Guainía, Col., river 184/C4
Guainía, Ven., river 182/C3
Guairá, Para., department 187/D4
Guajará Mirim, Braz. 188/B3
Guajataca Forest Reserve, P.R. 206/B2
Guajira, Col., peninsula 184/C1
Gualachulain, Scot., U.K. 62/F5
Gualala, Calif., U.S., 275 . . . . .246/B4
Guam, U.S., territory 172/B1
Guanacaste, C.R., province 203/A2
Guanacaste, C.R., range 203/A2
Guanaja, Hond., island 202/C1
Guanajuato, Mex., state capital, 74,874,
     (141,196, metro.) 200/D3
Guanajuato, Mex., state 200/D3
Guanare, Ven., 98,597, (120,118, metro.) . .182/C2
Guandu, Braz., river . . . . .188/Inset I
Guangdong, China, province 119/E3
Guangxi, China, autonomous region 119/D3
Guangzhou, China, 3,935,193 . . . . .119/E3
Guánica, P.R. 206/B3
Guánica Forest Reserve, P.R. 206/B3
Guantánamo, Cuba 204/C2
Guantánamo, Cuba, 207,000 . . . . .204/E3
Guantánamo, Cuba, province 204/E3
Guaporé, Bol., river 186/B2
Guaporé, Braz., river 186/A3
Guaqui, Bol. 186/A3
Guaranda, Ecua. .185/B3
Guarda, Port. 93/B2
Guarda, Port., district 93/B2
Guárico, Ven., state 182/C2
Guarujá, Braz., 67,730, (203,386, metro.) .188/Inset II
Guarulhos, Braz., 1,072,717 . . . . .188/Inset II
Guasave, Mex., 62,801, (277,402, metro.) .200/C2
Guatemala, nation .189
Guatemala City, Guat., capital, 1,006,954,
     (3,119,000, metro.) 201/C5
Guaviare, Col., department 184/C4
Guaviare, Col., river 184/C4
Guayabal, P.R. 206/C2
Guayaguayare, Trin.-To. 209/A2
Guayama, P.R. 206/C3
Guayambre, Hond., river 202/B2
Guayanilla, P.R. .206/B2
Guayape, Hond., river 202/B2
Guayaquil, Ecua., 2,117,553 . . . . .185/B4
Guayaquil, Ecua., gulf 185/A4
Guayaquil, Peru, gulf 185/A1
Guayas, Ecua., province 185/A4
Guayas, Ecua., river 185/B4
Guaymas, Mex., 97,593, (130,329, metro.) .200/B2
Guaynabo, P.R. .206/C2
Guben, Ger. 86/C3
Gudaut'a, Geo. 103/A2
Gudená, Den., river 79/B2
Guecho, Sp. 94/E1
Guéckédou, Guin. 149/C3
Guelph, Ont., Can., 106,170 . . . . .223/E4
Guelph, N. Dak., U.S. 326/G3
Gueltat Zemmour, W. Sah. 147/B1
Guerette, Maine, U.S., 50 . . . . .286/D1
Guernsey, Eng., U.K., island . . . . .60/Inset II
Guernsey, Eng., U.K., island 73/G4
Guernsey, Iowa, U.S., 70 . . . . .274/K4
Guernsey, Ohio, U.S., county, 40,792 . . . .328/H5
Guernsey, Wyo., U.S., 1,147 . . . . .366/D2
Guerra, Tex., U.S. 346/K9
Guerrero, Mex., state 200/D4
Guerrero Negro, Mex., 10,235 . . . . .200/B2
Guestwick, Eng., U.K. 70/G1
Gueydan, La., U.S., 1,598 . . . . .282/E6
Guffey, Colo., U.S. 250/E3
Guiana, Braz., highlands 188/B1
Guide Rock, Nebr., U.S., 245 . . . . .308/E3
Guiers, Sen., lake 148/B1
Guilarte, P.R., mountain 206/B2
Guilarte Forest Reserve, P.R. 206/C3
Guildford, Eng., U.K. 60/C3
Guildford, Eng., U.K., 65,998 . . . . .70/C4
Guildhall, Vt., U.S., 268 . . . . .352/D1
Guilford, Conn., U.S., 21,398 . . . . .253/E4
Guilford, Ind., U.S., 100 . . . . .270/G6
Guilford, Maine, U.S., 1,531 . . . . .286/C3
Guilford, Md., U.S., 12,918 . . . . .288/G3
Guilford, Mo., U.S., 87 . . . . .302/B1
Guilford, N.C., U.S., county, 421,048 . . . . .322/F2
Guilford, Vt., U.S., 2,046 . . . . .352/B5
Guilford Courthouse N.M.P., N.C., U.S. 322/F2
Guilford Hills, (Guilford), Pa., U.S., 2,100 . .336/F6
Guilin, China, 432,410, (686,170, metro.) . .119/E3
Guimaräes, Port. .93/A2
Guin, Ala., U.S., 2,389 . . . . .238/B2

Guinda, Calif., U.S., 100 . . . . .246/C4
Guinea, nation 143
Guinea, Ben., gulf 151/A4
Guinea, C. d'Iv., gulf 150/D4
Guinea, Eq. Gui., gulf 154/A3
Guinea, Gha., gulf 150/C4
Guinea, Nig., gulf 152/B5
Guinea, Va., U.S., 125 . . . . .354/J4
Guinea-Bissau, nation 143
Guinea Mills, Va., U.S., 175 . . . . .354/G6
Guion, Ark., U.S., 90 . . . . .244/D2
Guipúzcoa, Sp., province 94/E1
Güiria, Ven. 182/D1
Guisborough, Eng., U.K., 18,156 . . . . .66/F3
Guiseley (Guiseley/Yeadon), Eng., U.K., 31,104 .66/E5
Guiseley (Guiseley/Yeadon), Eng., U.K., 31,104 .68/D2
Guiyang, China 119/D3
Guizhou, China, province 119/D3
Gujarat, India, state 128/B4
Gujranwala, Pak., 1,132,509 . . . . .129/E3
Gujrat, Pak., 251,792 . . . . .129/E3
Gulbarga, India 128/C5
Gulbene, Lat. 82/D2
Gulf, Fla., U.S., county, 13,332 . . . . .256/C2
Gulf Breeze, Fla., U.S., 5,665 . . . . .256/A1
Gulf Crest, Ala., U.S., 90 . . . . .238/A4
Gulf Hammock, Fla., U.S., 40 . . . . .256/F2
Gulf Hills, Miss., U.S., 5,900 . . . . .300/D5
Gulf Island Natl. Seashore, Miss., U.S. 300/D5
Gulf Islands Natl. Seashore, Ala., U.S. 238/A5
Gulf Islands Natl. Seashore, Fla., U.S. 256/B1
Gulf Park Estates, Miss., U.S., 4,272 . . . . .300/D5
Gulfport, Fla., U.S., 12,527 . . . . .256/C7
Gulfport, Ill., U.S. 266/B4
Gulfport, Miss., U.S., 71,127 . . . . .300/C5
Gulf Shores, Ala., U.S., 5,044 . . . . .238/B5
Gulf Stream, Fla., U.S., 716 . . . . .256/B5
Guliston, Uzb. 132/C2
Gulivoire Park, Ind., U.S., 2,974 . . . . .270/D1
Gulkana, Alaska, U.S., 88 . . . . .240/F2
Gull, Alta., U.S., lake 212/C5
Gull, Minn., U.S., lake 298/C4
Gullane, Scot., U.K., 2,172 . . . . .62/L6
Gulliver, Mich., U.S., 90 . . . . .294/C3
Gull Lake, Sask., Can., 1,016 . . . . .227/B10
Gull Rock, N.C., U.S. 322/N4
Gully, Minn., U.S., 106 . . . . .298/B3
Gulnare, Colo., U.S. 250/F4
Gulnare, Ky., U.S., 100 . . . . .280/H3
Gulu, Ug., 113,144 . . . . .157/C2
Gumboro, Del., U.S., 275 . . . . .255/C7
Gum Branch, Ga., U.S., 273 . . . . .260/H8
Gumdag, Turkm. .132/B2
Gumlog, Ga., U.S., 2,025 . . . . .260/E3
Gumma, Jap., prefecture 114/C2
Gummi, Nig. 152/C1
Gum Neck, N.C., U.S., 150 . . . . .322/N3
Gum Spr., Va., U.S., 200 . . . . .354/H5
Gum Sprs., Ark., U.S., 194 . . . . .244/B3
Gümüshane, Tur. .133/D2
Gümüshane, Tur., province 133/D2
Gun Barrel City, Tex., U.S., 5,145 . . . . .346/M3
Gunder, Iowa, U.S., 50 . . . . .274/L2
Gunisao, Man., Can., river 215/C2
Gunlock, Utah, U.S., 70 . . . . .350/A6
Gunnbjørn Fjeld, Grld., mountain 193/D2
Gunn City, Mo., U.S., 85 . . . . .302/B3
Gunnerside, Eng., U.K. 66/D4
Gunners Quoin, Mauritius, island 163/C1
Gunnison, Colo., U.S., 5,409 . . . . .250/D3
Gunnison, Colo., U.S., county, 13,956 . . . . .250/D3
Gunnison, Colo., U.S., mountain 250/C3
Gunnison, Colo., U.S., river 250/B3
Gunnison, Miss., U.S., 633 . . . . .300/B2
Gunnison, Utah, U.S., 2,394 . . . . .350/C3
Gunnison Gorge Natl. Cons. Area, Colo., U.S. .250/C3
Gunnison Natl. For., Colo., U.S. 250/C3, D3
Gunsan, S. Kor., 266,569 . . . . .116/B5
Gunsight, Ariz., U.S., 200 . . . . .242/C5
Gunter, Oreg., U.S. 334/C4
Gunter, Tex., U.S., 1,230 . . . . .346/M2
Guntersville, Ala., U.S., 7,395 . . . . .238/C1
Guntersville, Ala., U.S., lake 238/C1
Gunton, Man., Can. 215/C4
Guntown, Miss., U.S., 1,183 . . . . .300/D1
Guntur, India 128/C5
Gu Oidak, Ariz., U.S., 150 . . . . .242/C6
Gurabo, P.R. 206/D2
Gurabo, Ark., U.S., 2,276 . . . . .244/B4
Guri, Ven., reservoir 182/D2
Gurley, Ala., U.S., 876 . . . . .238/C1
Gurley, Nebr., U.S., 228 . . . . .308/B2
Gurleyville, Conn., U.S., 100 . . . . .253/G2
Gurnee, Ill., U.S., 28,834 . . . . .266/B4
Gurney, Wisc., U.S. 364/C2
Gusau, Nig. 152/C1
Gushgy, Turkm. .132/D3
Gushgy, Turkm., river 132/D3
Gushikawa, Jap. . . . . .114/Inset II
Gustavo A. Madero, Mex. 200/Inset
Gustavus, Alaska, U.S., 429 . . . . .240/H3
Gustavus, Ohio, U.S., 275 . . . . .328/J3
Gustine, Calif., U.S., 4,698 . . . . .246/D5
Gustine, Tex., U.S., 457 . . . . .346/K4
Güstrow, Ger. 86/C2
Gutcher, Scot., U.K. 62/U1
Guthrie, Ariz., U.S. 242/F5
Guthrie, Iowa, U.S., county, 11,353 . . . . . .274/K4
Guthrie, Ky., U.S., 1,469 . . . . .280/C4
Guthrie, Minn., U.S., 50 . . . . .298/C3
Guthrie, N. Dak., U.S. 326/E2
Guthrie, Okla., U.S., 9,925 . . . . .330/E2
Guthrie, Tex., U.S. 346/H2
Guthrie Ctr., Iowa, U.S., 1,668 . . . . .274/K4
Guttenberg, Iowa, U.S., 1,987 . . . . .274/M2
Guttenberg, N.J., U.S., 10,807 . . . . . . .314/C2, E2
Gu Vo, Ariz., U.S., 175 . . . . .242/C5
Guwahati, India .128/F3
Gu-Win, Ala., U.S., 204 . . . . .238/B2
Guy, Alta., Can. .212/B3
Guy, Ark., U.S., 202 . . . . .244/C2
Guyana, nation 173
Guyhirn, Eng., U.K. 70/E1
Guymon, Okla., U.S., 10,472 . . . . .330/C4
Guys, Tenn., U.S., 483 . . . . .344/D4
Guysborough, N.S., Can., 462 . . . . .221/F2
Guysborough, N.S., Can., county 221/F2
Guy's Head, Eng., U.K. 70/E1
Guyton, Ga., U.S., 917 . . . . .260/J7
Güzelyurt, (Morphou), Cyp. 133/A1
Gwadar, Pak. 129/B3
Gwai, Zimb., river 160/A2
Gwalchmai, Wales, U.K. 64/C1
Gwalior, India, 692,982, (720,068, metro.) .128/C3
Gwangju, S. Kor., 1,257,636 . . . . .116/B5
Gwangju, S. Kor., province 116/B5
Gwbert-on-Sea, Wales, U.K. 64/B3
G.W. Carver N.M., Mo., U.S. 302/B5
Gwenddwr, Wales, U.K. 64/E3
Gweru, Zimb., 128,037 . . . . .160/B2
Gwillim Lake Prov. Park, Br. Col., Can. 212/A3

Gwillim Lake Prov. Park, Br. Col., Can. 214/M3
Gwinn, Mich., U.S., 1,965 . . . . .294/B3
Gwinner, N. Dak., U.S., 717 . . . . .326/H3
Gwinnett, Ga., U.S., county, 588,448 . . .260/C3, J2
Gwyddelwern, Wales, U.K. 64/E1
Gwyddgrug, Wales, U.K. 64/C4
Gwynedd, Wales, U.K., unitary authority,
     116,838 . . . . .64/D2
Gwynn, Va., U.S., 600 . . . . .354/L5
Győr, Hun., 127,000 . . . . .91/A2
Győr-Moson-Sopron, Hun., county 91/A2
Gyda, Russ., peninsula 104/E2
Gyeonggi, S. Kor., province 116/B4
Gyeongju, S. Kor., 272,968 . . . . .116/C5
Gympie, Qnsld., Austl. 170/E2
Gyöngyös, Hun. 91/B2
Gypsum, Colo., U.S., 3,654 . . . . .250/D2
Gypsum, Kans., U.S., 414 . . . . .276/E3
Gypsumville, Man., Can. 215/B3
Gyumri, Arm., 211,600 . . . . .103/A2
Gyzylarbat, Turkm. 132/B2

Haakon, S. Dak., U.S., county, 2,196 . . . . . .342/D3
Haapai, Tonga, island group 175/B3
Haapsalu, Est. 81/B2
Haarlem, Neth., 148,373, (190,999, metro.) .84/B2
Haast, N.Z. 171/A3
Haasts Bluff, Austl., aboriginal land 170/C2
Habarut, Yemen 137/C1
Habay, Alta., Can. 212/A2
Habersham, Ga., U.S., county, 35,902 . . . . .260/D2
Haboro, Jap. .114/Inset I
Hachijo, Jap., island 114/C3
Hachinohe, Jap. .114/D1
Hachioji, Jap., 536,000 . . . . .114/C3
Hachita, N. Mex., U.S. 317/B6
Hacienda Hts., Calif., U.S., 53,122 . . . . . . .246/D9
Hackamore, Calif., U.S. 246/D1
Hackberry, Ariz., U.S. 242/B2
Hackberry, La., U.S., 1,699 . . . . .282/C6
Hackberry, (Cottle County), Tex., U.S. 346/H2
Hackberry, (Denton County), Tex., U.S., 544 .346/B8
Hackensack, Minn., U.S., 285 . . . . .298/C3
Hackensack, N.J., U.S., 42,677 . . . . . . .314/B2, E2
Hacker Valley, W. Va., U.S., 70 . . . . .360/F3
Hackett, Ark., U.S., 694 . . . . .244/A2
Hackettstown, N.J., U.S., 10,403 . . . . .314/D2
Hackland, Scot., U.K. 62/M2
Hackleburg, Ala., U.S., 1,527 . . . . .238/B1
Hackney, Eng., U.K., unitary authority, 202,819 .71/E4
Hackney, Kans., U.S. 276/E4
Hack Pt., Md., U.S., 400 . . . . .288/L2
Hacoda, Ala., U.S., 50 . . . . .238/C4
Hadar, Nebr., U.S., 312 . . . . .308/G1
Haddam, Conn., U.S., 7,157 . . . . .253/E4
Haddam, Kans., U.S., 169 . . . . .276/E2
Haddam Neck, Conn., U.S., 300 . . . . .253/E3
Haddenham, (Cambridgeshire), Eng., U.K., 2,556 .68/E2
Haddenham, (Cambridgeshire), Eng., U.K., 2,556 .70/E2
Haddington, Scot., U.K., 8,851 . . . . .62/L7
Haddock, Ga., U.S., 475 . . . . .260/E5
Haddonfield, N.J., U.S., 11,659 . . . . . . .314/B3, C4
Haddon Hts., N.J., U.S., 7,547 . . . . .314/B3
Hadejia, Nig., river 152/D1
Hadera, Isr. 135/B1
Haderslev, Den. 79/B3
Hadhdhunmathi, Mald., atoll 127/A4
Hadiboh, Yemen .137/C2
Hadleigh, Eng., U.K., 6,595 . . . . .70/F2
Hadleigh, Eng., U.K. 70/F3
Hadley, Mass., U.S., 4,793 . . . . .292/D3
Hadley, Mich., U.S., 450 . . . . .294/F7
Hadley, Minn., U.S., 81 . . . . .298/B6
Hadley, N.Y., U.S., 2,240 . . . . .320/P4
Hadlow, Eng., U.K., 3,137 . . . . .70/E4
Hadlyme, Conn., U.S., 300 . . . . .253/F4
Hadramawt, Yemen, region 137/B1
Haedo, Uru., range 187/B2
Haeju, N. Kor. 116/A3
Haena, Hawaii, U.S. 262/C1, J5
Hafar al Batin, Sa. Arab. 136/B1
Hafford, Sask., Can., 401 . . . . .227/C8
Hafnarfjör...ur, Ice., 19,644 . . . . .79/A3
Hafnarfjör...ur, Ice., 19,644 . . . . .79/A3
Hagagman, N.Y., U.S., 1,357 . . . . .320/N5
Hagan, Ga., U.S., 898 . . . . .260/H7
Hagarville, Ark., U.S., 50 . . . . .244/B2
Hagen, Ger., 205,201 . . . . .86/A3
Hager City, Wisc., U.S., 300 . . . . .364/A4
Hagerhill, Ky., U.S., 900 . . . . .280/H3
Hagerman, Ida., U.S., 656 . . . . .264/C7
Hagerman, N. Mex., U.S., 1,168 . . . . .317/F4
Hagerman Fossil Beds Natl. Mon., Ida., U.S. .264/C7
Hagerstown, Ind., U.S., 1,768 . . . . .270/F5
Hagerstown, Md., U.S., 36,687 . . . . .288/D1
Hagewood, La., U.S., 225 . . . . .282/C3
Haggerston, Eng., U.K. 66/E1
Hagley, Eng., U.K., 5,417 . . . . .68/C5
Hague, Fr., cape 88/B2
Hague, N.Y., U.S., 150 . . . . .320/P3
Hague, N. Dak., U.S., 91 . . . . .326/F3
Hague, Va., U.S., 125 . . . . .354/K4
Haha, Jap., U.S. . . . . .114/Inset III
Hahira, Ga., U.S., 1,626 . . . . .260/E1
Hahns Peak, Colo., U.S., 40 . . . . .250/D1
Hahnville, La., U.S., 2,792 . . . . .282/J3, J7
Haikou, China 119/E4
Haiku, (Haiku-Pauwela), Hawaii, U.S., 6,578 .262/C3
Ha'il, Sa. Arab. 136/B1
Ha'il, Sa. Arab., emirate 136/B1
Hailar, China 119/E1
Haile, La., U.S., 60 . . . . .282/C1
Hailey, Eng., U.K. .70/A3
Hailey, Ida., U.S., 6,200 . . . . .264/C6
Haileyville, Okla., U.S., 891 . . . . .330/G3
Hailsham, Eng., U.K., 18,426 . . . . .70/E5
Hailstone N.W.R., Mont., U.S. 306/G3
Hainan, China, province 119/D4
Hainaut, Belg., province 85/B2
Haines, Alaska, U.S., 1,811 . . . . .240/H3
Haines, Oreg., U.S., 426 . . . . .334/J3
Hainesburg, N.J., U.S., 400 . . . . .314/C2
Haines City, Fla., U.S., 13,174 . . . . .256/C3
Haines Jct., Yukon, Can., 531 . . . . .228/B5
Haines Landing, Maine, U.S., 40 . . . . .286/B4
Hainesville, Ill., U.S., 2,129 . . . . .266/B4
Hainesville, N.J., U.S., 400 . . . . .314/D1
Haiphong, Viet., 783,133 . . . . .123/B2
Hairé Lao, Sen. 148/B1
Haiti, nation 204/C3
Haiti, nation 193
Haivana Nakya, Ariz., U.S., 200 . . . . .242/D5
Hajdú-Bihar, Hun., county 91/C2
Hajdúböszörmény, Hun. 91/C2
Haji Ibrahim, Iraq, mountain 130/B1
Hajjah, Yemen 137/A1
Haka, Mya. 125/B2
Hakalau, Hawaii, U.S. 262/J4
Hakkâri, Tur. 133/E3

Hakkâri, Tur., province 133/E3
Hakodate, Jap., 288,000 . . . . .114/D1, Inset I
Halab, (Aleppo), Syria, 1,582,930,
     (1,813,355, metro.) 134/A1
Halaib, Sudan 145/D1
Halalii, Hawaii, U.S., lake 262/A3
Halaula, Hawaii, U.S., 495 . . . . .262/G3
Halawa, Hawaii, U.S., 13,891 . . . . .262/B3
Halawa, Hawaii, U.S., bay 262/B3
Halawa, Hawaii, U.S., cape 262/B3
Halawa Hts., Hawaii, U.S. 262/F1, J2
Halba, Leb. 134/B1
Halberstadt, Ger. .86/B3
Halbur, Iowa, U.S., 202 . . . . .274/E3
Haldane, Ill., U.S., 125 . . . . .266/D1
Haldeman, Ky., U.S., 350 . . . . .280/G2
Haldimand, Ont., Can. 223/F5
Haldimand-Norfolk, Ont., Can. 223/E5
Haldimand-Norfolk, Ont., Can., county 223/E5
Hale, Ala., U.S., county, 17,185 . . . . .238/B3
Hale, Colo., U.S. .250/H2
Hale, Iowa, U.S., 60 . . . . .274/M3
Hale, Mich., U.S., 600 . . . . .294/F5
Hale, Mo., U.S., 473 . . . . .302/C2
Hale, Tex., U.S., county, 36,602 . . . . .346/G1
Haleakala Natl. Park, Hawaii, U.S. 262/C4, D6
Haleburg, Ala., U.S., 108 . . . . .238/D4
Hale Ctr., Tex., U.S., 2,263 . . . . .346/G1
Haledon, N.J., U.S., 8,252 . . . . .314/B2, E2
Haleiwa, Hawaii, U.S., 2,225 . . . . .262/H1
Halelea Forest Reserve, Hawaii, U.S. 262/C1
Hales Corners, Wisc., U.S., 7,765 . . . . .364/F2
Halesowen, Eng., U.K., 57,918 . . . . .68/C5
Halesworth, Eng., U.K., 4,575 . . . . .70/G2
Halethorpe, Md., U.S., 150 . . . . .288/H3
Haletown, Tenn., U.S., 300 . . . . .344/K4
Haley, N. Dak., U.S. 326/B4
Haleyville, Ala., U.S., 4,182 . . . . .238/B1
Haleyville, N.J., U.S., 250 . . . . .314/C5
Halfa, Iowa, U.S. .274/E1
Halfbreed Lake N.W.R., Mont., U.S. 306/G4
Half Moon, N.C., U.S., 6,645 . . . . .322/L5
Halfmoon Bay, Br. Col., Can., 358 . . . . .214/L6
Half Moon Bay, Calif., U.S., 11,842 . . . . . . .246/J3
Halford, Eng., U.K. 70/A2
Halford, Kans., U.S. 276/B2
Halfway, Wales, U.K. 64/D4
Halfway, Ky., U.S., 40 . . . . .280/D4
Halfway, Md., U.S., 10,065 . . . . .288/C1
Half Way, Mo., U.S., 176 . . . . .302/C4
Halfway, Oreg., U.S., 337 . . . . .334/J3
Haliburton, Ont., Can. 223/G2
Haliburton, Ont., Can., county 223/G2
Halifax, N.S., Can., 359,111, (363,200, metro.) .221/D3
Halifax, N.S., Can., county 221/D3
Halifax, Eng., U.K. 60/C3
Halifax, Eng., U.K., 91,069 . . . . .66/E5
Halifax, Eng., U.K., 91,069 . . . . .68/D5
Halifax, Mass., U.S., 7,500 . . . . .292/L5
Halifax, N.C., U.S., 344 . . . . .322/K2
Halifax, N.C., U.S., county, 57,370 . . . . . . .322/K2
Halifax, Penn., U.S., 875 . . . . .336/H5
Halifax, Vt., U.S., 782 . . . . .352/B5
Halifax, Va., U.S., 1,389 . . . . .354/F7
Halifax, Va., U.S., county, 37,355 . . . . .354/F7
Haliimaile, Hawaii, U.S., 895 . . . . .262/C3
Halil, Iran, river 130/D4
Halisahar, India . . . . .128/Inset II
Hall, Nun., Can., peninsula 220/P4
Hall, Ga., U.S., county, 139,277 . . . . .260/D3
Hall, Ky., U.S., 225 . . . . .280/F5
Hall, Mont., U.S., 150 . . . . .306/C3
Hall, Nebr., U.S., county, 53,534 . . . . .308/F3
Hall, Tex., U.S., county, 3,782 . . . . .346/G1, H1
Hallam, Nebr., U.S., 276 . . . . .308/H3
Hallam, Penn., U.S., 1,532 . . . . .336/H5
Halland, Swe., county 80/B3
Hallandale, Fla., U.S., 34,282 . . . . . . .256/B6, H6
Halla-san, S. Kor., mountain 116/Inset
Hallatton, Eng., U.K. 68/F4
Hallbankgate, Eng., U.K. 66/C3
Hall Beach, Nun., Can., 609 . . . . .220/M3
Hallboro, Man., Can. 215/B4
Halle, Belg. 85/C2
Halle, Ger., 254,360 . . . . .86/B3
Halle, Ger., department 86/B3
Halleck, Nev., U.S. 310/C1
Hallett, Okla., U.S., 168 . . . . .330/F1
Hallettsville, Tex., U.S., 2,345 . . . . .346/M6
Halley, Ark., U.S., 90 . . . . .244/D4
Hall Green, Eng., U.K. 68/D5
Halliday, Ark., U.S., 100 . . . . .244/C5
Halliday, N. Dak., U.S., 227 . . . . .326/C2
Hallingdal, Nor., valley 80/B3
Hallock, Minn., U.S., 1,196 . . . . .298/A2
Halloran Sprs., Calif., U.S., 350 . . . . .246/K7
Hallowell, Maine, U.S., 2,467 . . . . .286/C4
Hall Park, Okla., U.S., 1,088 . . . . .330/E2
Hall Quarry, Maine, U.S., 125 . . . . .286/D4
Halls, (Knox County), Tenn., U.S. 344/P2
Halls, (Lauderdale County), Tenn., U.S., 2,311 .344/P2
Halls Crossroads, (Halls), Tenn., U.S. 344/P2
Halls Gap, Ky., U.S., 450 . . . . .280/E3
Halls Summit, Kans., U.S. 276/G3
Hallstead, Penn., U.S., 1,216 . . . . .336/K2
Hall Summit, La., U.S., 264 . . . . .282/C2
Hallsville, Mo., U.S., 978 . . . . .302/D2
Hallsville, Tex., U.S., 2,772 . . . . .346/P3
Hallthwaites, Eng., U.K. 66/B4
Halltown, Mo., U.S., 189 . . . . .302/C4
Hallville, Wyo., U.S. 366/B3
Hallwood, Va., U.S., 290 . . . . .354/M5
Hallworthy, Eng., U.K. 73/C3
Halma, Minn., U.S., 78 . . . . .298/A2
Halmahera, Indon., island 122/D1
Halmstad, Swe., 85,742 . . . . .80/B3
Halsell, Ala., U.S. 238/A3
Halsey, Nebr., U.S., 59 . . . . .308/D2
Halsey, Oreg., U.S., 724 . . . . .334/C3
Halstad, Minn., U.S., 622 . . . . .298/A3
Halstead, Eng., U.K., 9,775 . . . . .70/F3
Halstead, Kans., U.S., 1,873 . . . . .276/E4
Haltiatunturi, Fin., mountain 81/B1
Halton City, Tex., U.S., 39,018 . . . . .346/B9
Halton, Ont., Can. 223/F4
Halton, Ont., Can., county 223/F4
Halton, Eng., U.K., unitary authority, 118,215 .66/C6
Halton, Eng., U.K., unitary authority, 118,215 .68/B3
Halton Gill, Eng., U.K. 66/D4
Halton Hills, Ont., Can. 223/F4
Halton Lea Gate, Eng., U.K. 66/D3
Haltwhistle, Eng., U.K., 3,773 . . . . .66/D3
Halwell, Eng., U.K. 73/D5
Hamadan, Iran, 401,281 . . . . .130/B3
Hamadan, Iran, province 130/B2
Hamah, Syria, 264,348, (343,279, metro.) . .134/A2
Hamakua, Hawaii, U.S., coast 262/H4
Hamakua Forest Reserve, Hawaii, U.S. 262/H4
Hamamatsu, Jap., 582,000 . . . . .114/C3
Hamar, Nor. 80/C3
Hambantota, Sri Lan. 126/C5
Hamberg, N. Dak., U.S. 326/F2

Hartfield 571

Hamber Prov. Park, Br. Col., Can. 214/O5
Hamblen, Tenn., U.S., *county*, 58,128 344/Q2
Hambleton, W. Va., U.S., 246 360/G2
Hamburg, Ger., 1,715,400 86/B2
Hamburg, Ger., *state* 86/B2
Hamburg, Ark., U.S., 3,039 244/D4
Hamburg, Calif., U.S., 50 246/B1
Hamburg, Conn., U.S., 125 253/F4
Hamburg, Ill., U.S., 126 266/C4
Hamburg, Iowa, U.S., 1,240 274/C6
Hamburg, La., U.S., 60 282/F4
Hamburg, Minn., U.S., 538 298/D6
Hamburg, Miss., U.S., 90 300/A4
Hamburg, N.J., U.S., 3,105 314/D1
Hamburg, N.Y., U.S., 10,116 320/D5
Hamburg, Penn., U.S., 4,114 336/K4
Hamburg, Wisc., U.S., 100 364/D3
Hamd, Wadi al, Sa. Arab. 136/A1
Hamden, Conn., U.S., 56,913 253/D4
Hamden, Ohio, U.S., 871 328/E7
Häme, Fin., *region* 81/B2
Hämeenlinna, Fin., 46,108 81/B2
Hamel, Ill., U.S., 570 266/B3
Hameln, Ger. 86/B2
Hamer, Ida., U.S. 264/E6
Hamersley, Austl., *range* 170/A2
Hamersville, Ohio, U.S., 515 328/C8
Hamerton, Eng., U.K. 70/D2
Hamgyŏng Sanmaek, N. Kor., *mountains* 116/C2
Hamhŭng, N. Kor., 709,730 116/B3
Hami, China 119/C1
Hamill, S. Dak., U.S. 342/F4
Hamilton, Nfld., Can., *inlet* 218/B2
Hamilton, Ont., Can., 490,268, (686,900, *metro.*) 222/E4
Hamilton, Ont., Can., 490,268, (686,900, *metro.*) 223/F4
Hamilton, N.Z., 114,921, (166,128, *metro.*) 171/C2
Hamilton, Scot., U.K. 60/B2
Hamilton, Scot., U.K., 48,546 62/J7
Hamilton, Ala., U.S., 6,786 238/B1
Hamilton, Ark., U.S., *lake* 244/B3
Hamilton, Colo., U.S. 250/C1
Hamilton, Fla., U.S., *county*, 13,327 256/F1
Hamilton, Ga., U.S., 307 260/B6
Hamilton, Ill., U.S., 3,029 266/B3
Hamilton, Ill., U.S., *county*, 8,621 266/E5
Hamilton, Ind., U.S., 1,233 270/G1
Hamilton, Ind., U.S., *county*, 182,740 270/D4
Hamilton, Iowa, U.S., 144 274/J5
Hamilton, Iowa, U.S., *county*, 16,438 274/G3
Hamilton, Kans., U.S., 334 276/F4
Hamilton, Kans., U.S., *county*, 2,670 276/A3
Hamilton, Mass., U.S., 8,315 292/L2
Hamilton, Mich., U.S., 1,300 294/C7
Hamilton, Mo., U.S., 1,813 302/B2
Hamilton, Mont., U.S., 3,705 306/B3
Hamilton, Nebr., U.S., *county*, 9,403 308/F3
Hamilton, N.Y., U.S., 3,509 320/K5
Hamilton, N.Y., U.S., *county*, 5,379 320/M3
Hamilton, N.C., U.S., 516 322/L3
Hamilton, N. Dak., U.S., 73 326/H1
Hamilton, Ohio, U.S., 60,690 328/A7
Hamilton, Ohio, U.S., *county*, 845,303 328/A1, A7
Hamilton, Oreg., U.S. 334/G3
Hamilton, R.I., U.S., 2,500 339/D4
Hamilton, Tenn., U.S., *county*, 307,896 344/L4
Hamilton, Tex., U.S., 2,977 346/K4
Hamilton, Tex., U.S., *county*, 8,229 346/K4
Hamilton, Va., U.S., 562 354/H2
Hamilton, Wash., U.S., 309 358/D1
Hamilton City, Calif., U.S., 1,903 246/C3
Hamilton Dome, Wyo., U.S. 366/B2
Hamilton Fort, Utah, U.S., 150 350/A6
Hamilton Square, N.J., U.S., 26,419 314/D3
Hamilton-Wentworth, Ont., Can. 223/F4
Hamilton-Wentworth, Ont., Can., *county* 223/F4
Hamiota, Man., Can., 858 215/A4
Hamir, Tuwayyir al, Qatar, *hill* 137/C4
Ham Lake, Minn., U.S., 12,710 298/D5
Hamler, Ohio, U.S., 650 328/B3
Hamlet, Ind., U.S., 820 270/C2
Hamlet, Nebr., U.S., 54 308/C3
Hamlet, N.C., U.S., 6,018 322/F5
Hamletsburg, Ill., U.S., 90 266/E6
Hamlin, Iowa, U.S., 70 274/E4
Hamlin, Kans., U.S., 53 276/G2
Hamlin, Maine, U.S., 257 286/E1
Hamlin, Mich., U.S., *lake* 294/C5
Hamlin, Penn., U.S., 300 336/L3
Hamlin, S. Dak., U.S., *county*, 5,540 342/H3
Hamlin, Tex., U.S., 2,248 346/H3
Hamlin, W. Va., U.S., 1,119 360/B4
Hamm, Ger., 181,804 86/A3
Hammamet, Tun. 146/C1
Hammamet, Tun., *gulf* 146/C1
Hammerfest, Nor. 80/E1
Hammerfest, Nor. 193/B2
Hammersley Fork, Penn., U.S. 336/F3
Hammersmith, (Hammersmith and Fulham), Eng., U.K., 148,502 70/D4
Hammersmith and Fulham, Eng., U.K., *unitary authority*, 165,243 70/D4
Hammett, Ida., U.S., 300 264/B7
Hammon, Okla., U.S., 469 330/C2
Hammonasset, Conn., U.S., *river* 253/E4
Hammond, Ill., U.S., 518 266/E4
Hammond, Ind., U.S., 83,048 270/A1
Hammond, Kans., U.S. 276/H4
Hammond, La., U.S., 17,639 282/J5
Hammond, Mich., U.S., *bay* 294/E4
Hammond, Minn., U.S., 198 298/E6
Hammond, Mont., U.S. 306/M4
Hammond, N.Y., U.S., 302 320/K2
Hammond, Tex., U.S., 40 346/M4
Hammond, Wisc., U.S., 1,153 364/A4
Hammonds Plains, N.S., Can. 221/D3
Hammondsport, N.Y., U.S., 731 320/G6
Hammondsville, Vt., U.S., 70 352/B4
Hammondvale, N.B., Can. 217/D3
Hammondville, Ala., U.S., 486 238/D1
Hammonton, N.J., U.S., 12,604 314/D4
Hamnavoe, Scot., U.K. 62/P2
Hamon, Tex., U.S. 346/L6
Hampden, Nfld., Can., 544 218/C4
Hampden, Maine, U.S., 6,327 286/D4
Hampden, Mass., U.S., 5,171 292/E4
Hampden, Mass., U.S., *county*, 456,228 292/C4
Hampden, N. Dak., U.S., 60 326/G1
Hampden Highlands, Maine, U.S. 286/D4
Hampden Park, Eng., U.K. 70/E5
Hampden Sydney, Va., U.S., 1,264 354/G6
Hampshire, Eng., U.K., *unitary authority*, 1,240,032 70/B4
Hampshire, Eng., U.K., *unitary authority*, 1,240,032 73/J3
Hampshire, Ill., U.S., 2,900 266/E1
Hampshire, Mass., U.S., *county*, 152,251 292/C3
Hampshire, Tenn., U.S., 175 344/G3
Hampshire, W. Va., U.S., *county*, 20,203 360/J2
Hampshire, Wyo., U.S. 366/D2
Hampstead, N.B., Can., 312 217/C3
Hampstead, Que., Can., 6,974 226/J5
Hampstead, Md., U.S., 5,060 288/G1
Hampstead, N.H., U.S., 8,297 312/D6
Hampstead, N.C., U.S., 475 322/K6
Hampton, N.B., Can., 3,997 217/D3
Hampton, Ark., U.S., 1,579 244/C4
Hampton, Conn., U.S., 1,758 253/G2
Hampton, Fla., U.S., 431 256/F2
Hampton, Ga., U.S., 3,857 260/C5
Hampton, Ill., U.S., 1,626 266/C2
Hampton, Iowa, U.S., 4,218 274/H2
Hampton, Ky., U.S., 100 280/B3
Hampton, Md., U.S., 5,004 288/H2
Hampton, Minn., U.S., 434 298/D6
Hampton, Nebr., U.S., 439 308/G3
Hampton, N.H., U.S., 14,937 312/E6
Hampton, (Hunterdon County), N.J., U.S., 1,546 314/D2
Hampton, Oreg., U.S. 334/F4
Hampton, S.C., U.S., 2,837 340/C4
Hampton, S.C., U.S., *county*, 21,386 340/C4
Hampton, Tenn., U.S., 1,300 344/S2
Hampton, Va., U.S., 146,437 354/L6
Hampton Bays, N.Y., U.S., 12,236 320/F2
Hampton Beach, N.H., U.S., 1,800 312/E6
Hampton Bishop, Eng., U.K. 68/B5
Hampton Falls, N.H., U.S., 1,880 312/E6
Hampton Heath, Eng., U.K. 68/B3
Hampton Manor, N.Y., U.S., 2,525 320/P5
Hampton Sprs., Fla., U.S., 40 256/E1
Hamra, Al Hamadah al, Lib., *plateau* 145/B1
Hams Fork, Wyo., U.S., *river* 366/A2
Hamstead, Eng., U.K. 70/B5
Hamsterley, Eng., U.K. 66/E3
Hamtramck, Mich., U.S., 22,976 294/B7, F7
Han, China, *river* 119/E2
Han, S. Kor., *river* 116/B4
Hana, Hawaii, U.S., 709 262/D4
Hana, Hawaii, U.S., *bay* 262/D4
Hana Forest Reserve, Hawaii, U.S. 262/D4
Hanahan, S.C., U.S., 12,937 340/D4
Hanalei, Hawaii, U.S., 478 262/C1
Hanalei N.W.R., Hawaii, U.S. 262/C1
Hanamanioa, Hawaii, U.S., *cape* 262/C4
Hanamaulu, Hawaii, U.S., 3,272 262/D1
Hanapepe, Hawaii, U.S., 2,153 262/C2
Hanau, Ger. 86/B3
Hanbury, Eng., U.K. 68/C5
Hanceville, Ala., U.S., 2,951 238/C1
Hancock, Ga., U.S., *county*, 10,076 260/E5
Hancock, Ill., U.S., *county*, 20,121 266/B3
Hancock, Ind., U.S., *county*, 55,391 270/E5
Hancock, Iowa, U.S., 207 274/D5
Hancock, Iowa, U.S., *county*, 12,100 274/G1
Hancock, Ky., U.S., *county*, 8,392 280/D3
Hancock, Maine, U.S., 2,147 286/D4
Hancock, Maine, U.S., *county*, 51,791 286/D4
Hancock, Md., U.S., 1,725 288/B1
Hancock, Mass., U.S., 721 292/A2
Hancock, Mich., U.S., 4,323 294/A2
Hancock, Minn., U.S., 717 298/B5
Hancock, Miss., U.S., *county*, 42,967 300/C5
Hancock, N.H., U.S., 1,739 312/C6
Hancock, N.Y., U.S., 1,189 320/L7
Hancock, Ohio, U.S., *county*, 71,295 328/C3
Hancock, Tenn., U.S., *county*, 6,786 344/Q2
Hancock, Vt., U.S., 382 352/B3
Hancock, W. Va., U.S., *county*, 32,667 360/K4
Hancock, Wisc., U.S., 463 364/D4
Hancocks Bridge, N.J., U.S., 350 314/C4
Hand, S. Dak., U.S., *county*, 3,741 342/F3
Handan, China 119/E2
Handforth, Eng., U.K. 66/D6
Handley, W. Va., U.S., 362 360/D4
Handshoe, Ky., U.S. 280/H3
Handsworth, Eng., U.K. 68/D4
Handy Brake N.W.R., La., U.S. 282/F1
Hanford, Calif., U.S., 41,686 246/F6
Hanford, Maine, U.S. 286/D2
Hanford Brook, N.B., Can. 217/D3
Hanford Reach Natl. Mon., Wash., U.S. 358/F3
Hangayn, Mong., *mountains* 118/B2
Hanging Limb, Tenn., U.S., 100 344/L2
Hanging Rock, Ohio, U.S., 279 328/E8
Hangö, Fin. 81/B3
Hangzhou, China, 1,171,450, (5,234,150, *metro.*) 119/F2
Hankinson, N. Dak., U.S., 1,058 326/J3
Hanks, N. Dak., U.S. 326/B1
Hanksville, Utah, U.S., 125 350/D5
Hanksville, Vt., U.S., 70 352/B2
Hanley, Sask., Can., 495 227/D9
Hanley Falls, Minn., U.S., 323 298/B6
Hanlontown, Iowa, U.S., 229 274/H1
Hanna, Alta., Can., 2,986 212/E5
Hanna, Ind., U.S., 500 270/C2
Hanna, La., U.S. 282/C3
Hanna, Okla., U.S., 133 330/G2
Hanna, Utah, U.S., 100 350/D3
Hanna, Wyo., U.S., 873 366/C3
Hanna City, Ill., U.S., 1,013 266/D3
Hannaford, N. Dak., U.S., 181 326/G2
Hannagan Meadow, Ariz., U.S. 242/F4
Hannah, N. Dak., U.S. 326/G1
Hannah, S.C., U.S., 100 340/E3
Hannawa Falls, N.Y., U.S., 550 320/M1
Hannibal, Mo., U.S., 17,757 302/E2
Hannibal, N.Y., U.S., 542 320/H4
Hannibal, Ohio, U.S., 300 328/J6
Hannibal, Wisc., U.S., 40 364/C3
Hannover, Ger., 514,718 86/B2
Hannover, Ger., *department* 86/B2
Hannover, N. Dak., U.S., 40 326/D2
Hanoi, Viet., *capital*, 2,464,100 123/A2
Hanover, Ont., Can., 6,869 223/D3
Hanover, Ark., U.S., 50 244/C2
Hanover, Conn., U.S., 700 253/G3
Hanover, Ill., U.S., 836 266/C1
Hanover, Ind., U.S., 2,834 270/F7
Hanover, Kans., U.S., 653 276/F2
Hanover, Maine, U.S., 251 286/B4
Hanover, Mass., U.S., 13,164 292/L4
Hanover, Mich., U.S., 424 294/E7
Hanover, Minn., U.S., 1,355 298/D5
Hanover, Mont., U.S. 306/G2
Hanover, N.H., U.S., 10,850 312/B4
Hanover, N.J., U.S., 12,898 314/E2
Hanover, N. Mex., U.S. 317/B5
Hanover, Ohio, U.S., 885 328/F5
Hanover, Penn., U.S., 14,535 336/H6
Hanover, Tex., U.S. 346/M5
Hanover, Va., U.S., 225 354/J5
Hanover, Va., U.S., *county*, 86,320 354/H5
Hanover Ctr., N.H., U.S., 225 312/B4
Hanover Park, Ill., U.S., 38,278 266/A5
Hanoverton, Ohio, U.S., 387 328/J4
Hansboro, N. Dak., U.S. 326/F1
Hansell, Iowa, U.S., 96 274/H2
Hansen, Ida., U.S., 970 264/C7
Hansen, Nebr., U.S., 90 308/E3
Hansford, Tex., U.S., *county*, 5,369 346/F8
Hanska, Minn., U.S., 443 298/C6
Hanson, Fla., U.S., 175 256/E1
Hanson, Ky., U.S., 625 280/C3
Hanson, Mass., U.S., 9,495 292/L4
Hanson, S. Dak., U.S., *county*, 3,139 342/H4
Hansonville, Va., U.S., 80 354/D2
Hanston, Kans., U.S., 259 276/C3
Hansville, Wash., U.S., 100 358/C2
Hants, N.S., Can., *county* 221/C3
Hantzsch, Nun., Can., *river* 220/O3
Hanzhong, China 119/D2
Haora, India, 1,008,704 128/E4, Inset II
Haparanda, Swe. 80/D2
Hapeville, Ga., U.S., 6,180 260/C4, H3
Happy, Tex., U.S., 647 346/F10
Happy Corner, N.H., U.S. 312/D1
Happy Jack, Ariz., U.S. 242/D3
Happy Jack, La., U.S., 250 282/K7
Happy's Inn, Mont., U.S. 306/A1
Happy Valley, Oreg., U.S., 4,519 334/A2
Happy Valley-Goose Bay, Nfld., Can., 7,969 218/A2, E4
Haql, Sa. Arab. 136/A1
Harad, Sa. Arab. 136/C1
Harahan, La., U.S., 9,885 282/J7, K3
Haralson, Ga., U.S., 144 260/B5
Haralson, Ga., U.S., *county*, 25,690 260/A4
Harare, Zimb., *capital*, 1,189,103 160/B1
Harbel, Liber. 149/A2
Harbert, Mich., U.S., 1,619 294/C8
Harbeson, Del., U.S., 375 255/C6
Harbin, China 119/F1
Harbine, Nebr., U.S., 56 308/H3
Harbor, Oreg., U.S., 2,622 334/B5
Harbor Beach, Mich., U.S., 1,837 294/G6
Harbor Creek, Penn., U.S. 336/B1
Harborside, Maine, U.S. 286/D4
Harbor Sprs., Mich., U.S., 1,567 294/D4
Harbor View, Ohio, U.S., 99 328/D2
Harbour, Bah., *island* 207/B2
Hbr. Breton, Nfld., Can., 2,079 218/D5
Hbr. Deep, Nfld., Can. 218/C4
Hbr. Pointe, Wash., U.S. 358/C2
Harbourton, N.J., U.S., 250 314/D3
Harcourt, N.B., Can. 217/D2
Harcourt, Iowa, U.S., 340 274/F3
Harcuvar, Ariz., U.S., 40 242/B4
Harcuvar, Ariz., U.S., *mountains* 242/B4
Hardangerfjord, Nor., *fjord* 80/B4
Hardangervidda, Nor., *plateau* 80/B3
Hardaway, Ala., U.S., 40 238/D3
Hardee, Fla., U.S., *county*, 26,938 256/G4
Hardeeville, S.C., U.S., 1,793 340/C4
Hardeman, Tenn., U.S., *county*, 28,105 344/C4
Hardeman, Tex., U.S., *county*, 4,724 346/J1
Hardesty, Okla., U.S., 277 330/A1, C4
Hardin, Ill., U.S., 959 266/C4
Hardin, Ill., U.S., *county*, 4,800 266/E6
Hardin, Iowa, U.S., *county*, 18,812 274/H3
Hardin, Ky., U.S., 564 280/B4
Hardin, Ky., U.S., *county*, 94,174 280/D3
Hardin, Mo., U.S., 614 302/C2
Hardin, Mont., U.S., 3,384 306/J4
Hardin, Ohio, U.S., *county*, 31,945 328/C4
Hardin, Tenn., U.S., *county*, 25,578 344/E4
Hardin, Tex., U.S., 755 346/C5, P5
Hardin, Tex., U.S., *county*, 48,073 346/P5
Harding, Kans., U.S. 276/H4
Harding, Minn., U.S., 105 298/C4
Harding, N. Mex., U.S., *county*, 810 317/G2
Harding, S. Dak., U.S. 342/B2
Harding, S. Dak., U.S., *county*, 1,353 342/B2
Harding Lakes, N.J., U.S., 1,900 314/D5
Hardinsburg, Ind., U.S., 244 270/D8
Hardinsburg, Ky., U.S., 2,345 280/D3
Hardisty, Alta., Can., 743 212/E5
Hardman, Oreg., U.S. 334/G2
Hardtner, Kans., U.S., 199 276/D4
Hardwick, Eng., U.K., 2,461 70/G2
Hardwick, Ga., U.S., 5,135 260/E5
Hardwick, Mass., U.S., 2,622 292/F3
Hardwick, Minn., U.S., 222 298/A7
Hardwick, Vt., U.S., 3,174 352/C2
Hardwood Lake, Ont., Can. 223/H2
Hardwood Ridge, N.B., Can. 217/C2
Hardy, Ark., U.S., 578 244/D1
Hardy, Iowa, U.S., 57 274/F2
Hardy, Mont., U.S., 50 306/E2
Hardy, Nebr., U.S., 179 308/G3
Hardy, Okla., U.S. 330/F1
Hardy, W. Va., U.S., *county*, 12,669 360/J2
Hare Bay, Nfld., Can., 1,065 218/D5
Harer, Eth. 156/D2
Harer, Eth., *state* 156/D2
Harewood Park, Md., U.S., 3,400 288/J2
Harford, Md., U.S., *county*, 218,590 288/J1
Hargett, Ky., U.S., 40 280/F3
Hargeysa, Som. 157/A2
Harghita, Rom., *county* 101/C2
Hargill, Tex., U.S., 900 346/K9
Hargis, Ky., U.S. 280/F4
Hargrave, Man., Can. 215/A4
Haringey, Eng., U.K., *unitary authority*, 216,510 70/D4
Harirud, Afg., *river* 129/A2
Harker Hts., Tex., U.S., 17,308 346/L4
Harkers Island, N.C., U.S., 1,525 322/M5
Harlan, Iowa, U.S., 5,282 274/D4
Harlan, Kans., U.S. 276/D2
Harlan, Ky., U.S., 2,081 280/G4
Harlan, Ky., U.S., *county*, 33,202 280/G4
Harlan, Nebr., U.S., *county*, 3,786 308/E3
Harlan, Oreg., U.S., 40 334/C3
Harlan County, Nebr., U.S., *lake* 308/E3
Harlech, Wales, U.K., 1,233 64/C2
Harlem, Fla., U.S., 2,730 256/H5
Harlem, Ga., U.S., 1,814 260/G5
Harlem, Ill., U.S. 266/D1
Harlem, Mont., U.S., 848 306/H1
Harleston, Eng., U.K., 3,717 70/G2
Harleysville, Penn., U.S., 8,795 336/L5
Harleyville, S.C., U.S., 594 340/D3
Harlingen, Tex., U.S., 57,564 346/L9
Harlow, Eng., U.K. 60/Inset III
Harlow, Eng., U.K., 74,629 70/E3
Harlow, N. Dak., U.S., 50 326/F1
Harlowton, Mont., U.S., 1,062 306/G3
Harman, Va., U.S., 225 354/D2
Harman, W. Va., U.S., 126 360/G3
Harmersville, N.J., U.S., 125 314/C5
Harmon, Ill., U.S., 149 266/D2
Harmon, La., U.S., 80 282/C2
Harmon, Okla., U.S. 330/C1
Harmon, Okla., U.S., *county*, 3,283 330/C3
Harmontown, Miss., U.S., 60 300/C1
Harmony, Ark., U.S., 50 244/B2
Harmony, Calif., U.S. 246/E7
Harmony, Ind., U.S., 589 270/B5
Harmony, Maine, U.S., 954 286/C4
Harmony, Minn., U.S., 1,080 298/E7
Harmony, N.J., U.S., 2,729 314/C2
Harmony, N.C., U.S., 526 322/D3
Harmony, Penn., U.S., 937 336/A4
Harmony, R.I., U.S., 850 339/C2
Harmony, Tex., U.S. 346/N4
Harmony Grove, Wisc., U.S., 550 364/D5
Harmonyville, Vt., U.S., 325 352/B4
Harmston, Eng., U.K. 68/F3
Harnett, N.C., U.S., *county*, 91,025 322/H4
Harney, Nev., U.S. 310/B1
Harney, Oreg., U.S. 334/H4
Harney, Oreg., U.S., *basin* 334/G4
Harney, Oreg., U.S., *county*, 7,609 334/G4
Harney, Oreg., U.S., *lake* 334/G4
Harney, S. Dak., U.S., *peak* 342/B4
Härnösand, Swe. 80/C2
Harold, Ky., U.S., 1,400 280/H3
Haroldswick, Scot., U.K. 62/Q1
Harpenden, Eng., U.K., 28,097 70/D3
Harper, Liber. 149/C3
Harper, Iowa, U.S., 134 274/K5
Harper, Kans., U.S., 1,567 276/D4
Harper, Kans., U.S., *county*, 6,536 276/D4
Harper, Okla., U.S., *county*, 3,562 330/C1
Harper, Oreg., U.S., 70 334/J4
Harper, Tex., U.S., 1,006 346/J5
Harpers Ferry, Iowa, U.S., 330 274/M1
Harpers Ferry, W. Va., U.S., 307 360/L2
Harpers Ferry Natl. Hist. Park, W. Va., U.S. 354/H2
Harpers Ferry Natl. Hist. Park, W. Va., U.S. 360/L2
Harpersville, Ala., U.S., 1,620 238/C2
Harperville, Miss., U.S., 250 300/C3
Harper Woods, Mich., U.S., 14,254 294/B7
Harpley, Eng., U.K. 70/F1
Harpole, Eng., U.K. 68/E5
Harpster, Ida., U.S., 40 264/B4
Harpster, Ohio, U.S., 203 328/D4
Harpur Hill, Eng., U.K. 68/D3
Harrah, Okla., U.S., 4,719 330/B4, E2
Harrah, Wash., U.S., 542 358/E3
Harrell, Ark., U.S., 293 244/C4
Harrells, N.C., U.S., 187 322/J5
Harrellsville, N.C., U.S., 102 322/M2
Harriet, Ark., U.S., 60 244/C2
Harrietsham, Eng., U.K. 70/F4
Harrietta, Mich., U.S., 169 294/D5
Harriman, N.Y., U.S., 2,252 320/A1
Harriman, Tenn., U.S., 6,744 344/M3
Harriman, Vt., U.S., *reservoir* 352/B5
Harriman, Wyo., U.S. 366/D3
Harriman St. Park, N.Y., U.S. 320/A1
Harrington, Del., U.S., 3,174 255/B5
Harrington, Maine, U.S., 882 286/E4
Harrington, S. Dak., U.S. 342/D4
Harrington, Wash., U.S., 426 358/G2
Harrington Park, N.J., U.S., 4,740 314/C1
Harris, Sask., Can., 232 227/C9
Harris, Scot., U.K. 62/D5
Harris, Scot., U.K., *island* 62/B3
Harris, Ga., U.S., *county*, 23,695 260/A6
Harris, Iowa, U.S., 200 274/D1
Harris, Kans., U.S., 53 276/G3
Harris, Minn., U.S., 1,121 298/E5
Harris, Mo., U.S., 105 302/C1
Harris, Okla., U.S., 80 330/H4
Harris, Tex., U.S., *county*, 3,400,578 346/A6, N6
Harrisburg, Ark., U.S., 2,192 244/E2
Harrisburg, Ill., U.S., 9,860 266/E6
Harrisburg, Mo., U.S., 184 302/D2
Harrisburg, Nebr., U.S., 75 308/A2
Harrisburg, N.C., U.S., 4,493 322/D4
Harrisburg, Ohio, U.S., 332 328/D6
Harrisburg, Oreg., U.S., 2,795 334/C3
Harrisburg, Penn., U.S., *state capital*, 48,950, (629,401, *metro.*) 336/H5
Harrisburg, S. Dak., U.S., 958 342/J4
Harris Hill, N.Y., U.S., 4,881 320/D5
Harris Neck N.W.R., Ga., U.S. 260/J8
Harrison, Ark., U.S., 12,152 244/B1
Harrison, Ga., U.S., 509 260/F6
Harrison, Ida., U.S., 267 264/A2
Harrison, Ind., U.S., *county*, 34,325 270/D8
Harrison, Iowa, U.S., *county*, 15,666 274/C4
Harrison, Ky., U.S., *county*, 17,983 280/F2
Harrison, Maine, U.S., 2,315 286/B4
Harrison, (Clare County), Mich., U.S., 2,108 294/E5
Harrison, (Macomb County), Mich., U.S., 24,461 294/B6
Harrison, Miss., U.S., *county*, 189,601 300/C5
Harrison, Mo., U.S., *county*, 8,850 302/B1
Harrison, Mont., U.S., 162 306/E4
Harrison, Nebr., U.S., 279 308/A1
Harrison, (Hudson County), N.J., U.S., 14,424 314/B2
Harrison, N.Y., U.S., 24,154 320/C1
Harrison, Ohio, U.S., 7,487 328/A7
Harrison, Ohio, U.S., *county*, 15,856 328/H5
Harrison, S. Dak., U.S., 51 342/G4
Harrison, Tenn., U.S., 7,630 344/L4
Harrison, Tex., U.S., *county*, 62,110 346/P3
Harrison, W. Va., U.S., *county*, 68,652 360/F2
Harrison, Wisc., U.S., 100 364/D3
Harrisonburg, La., U.S., 746 282/F3
Harrisonburg, Va., U.S., 40,468 354/F4
Harrison Valley, Penn., U.S., 250 336/F2
Harrisonville, Mo., U.S., 8,946 302/B3
Harrisonville, N.J., U.S., 325 314/C4
Harrisonville, Ohio, U.S., 150 328/F7
Harriston, Miss., U.S., 60 300/A4
Harristown, Ill., U.S., 1,338 266/D4
Harrisville, (Carroll County), Md., U.S., 475 288/F2
Harrisville, (Cecil County), Md., U.S., 600 288/K1
Harrisville, Mich., U.S., 514 294/F5
Harrisville, Miss., U.S., 175 300/B4
Harrisville, N.H., U.S., 1,075 312/B6
Harrisville, N.Y., U.S., 653 320/L2
Harrisville, Ohio, U.S., 259 328/J5
Harrisville, Penn., U.S., 883 336/A3
Harrisville, R.I., U.S., 1,561 339/B2
Harrisville, Utah, U.S., 3,645 350/E1
Harrisville, W. Va., U.S., 1,842 360/D2
Harrisville, Wisc., U.S., 125 364/D5
Harrod, Ohio, U.S., 491 328/C4
Harrodsburg, Ind., U.S., 375 270/C6
Harrodsburg, Ky., U.S., 8,014 280/F3
Harrogate, Eng., U.K. 60/C2
Harrogate, Eng., U.K., 66,178 66/E5
Harrogate, Eng., U.K., 66,178 68/D2
Harrogate, (Harrogate-Shawnee), Tenn., U.S., 2,865 344/P1
Harrold, Eng., U.K. 70/C2
Harrold, S. Dak., U.S., 209 342/F3
Harrold, Tex., U.S., 125 346/J1
Harrow, Eng., U.K., 198,562 70/D3
Harrow, Eng., U.K., *unitary authority*, 207,389 70/D3
Harrowden, Eng., U.K. 70/D2
Harry S Truman, Mo., U.S., *reservoir* 302/C3
Harry S Truman N.H.S., Mo., U.S. 303/J5
Harshaw, Wisc., U.S., 125 364/D3
Harstad, Nor. 80/D2
Hart, Br. Col., Can., *ranges* 214/L3
Hart, Yukon, Can., *river* 228/B3
Hart, Ga., U.S., *county*, 22,997 260/E3
Hart, Ky., U.S., *county*, 17,445 280/E3
Hart, Mich., U.S., 1,950 294/C6
Hart, Tex., U.S., 1,198 346/F1
Hartburn, Eng., U.K. 66/E2
Hart Fell, Eng., U.K., *hill* 66/B2
Hartfield, Va., U.S., 150 354/L5

Hartford, Eng., U.K. 70/D2
Hartford, Ala., U.S., 2,369 . . . . .238/D4
Hartford, Ark., U.S., 772 . . . . .244/A2
Hartford, Conn., U.S., county, 857,183 . . . . .253/E2
Hartford, Conn., U.S., state capital, 121,578,
   (1,183,110, metro.) 253/E3
Hartford, Ill., U.S., 1,545 . . . . .266/A3
Hartford, Iowa, U.S., 759 . . . . .274/H5
Hartford, Kans., U.S., 500 . . . . .276/G3
Hartford, Ky., U.S., 2,571 . . . . .280/D3
Hartford, Mich., U.S., 2,476 . . . . .294/C7
Hartford, Ohio, U.S., 412 . . . . .328/E5
Hartford, S. Dak., U.S., 1,844 . . . . .342/J4
Hartford, Tenn., U.S., 250 . . . . .344/Q3
Hartford, W. Va., U.S., 519 . . . . .360/C2
Hartford, Wisc., U.S., 10,905 . . . . .364/E5, F1
Hartford City, Ind., U.S., 6,928 . . . . .270/F4
Hartington, Eng., U.K. 68/D3
Hartington, Nebr., U.S., 1,640 . . . . .308/G1
Hartland, N.B., Can., 902 . . . . .217/B2
Hartland, Eng., U.K. 73/D3
Hartland, Eng., U.K., point 73/C2
Hartland, Ill., U.S. 266/E1
Hartland, Maine, U.S., 1,816 . . . . .286/C4
Hartland, Mich., U.S., 375 . . . . .294/F7
Hartland, Minn., U.S., 288 . . . . .298/D7
Hartland, N. Dak., U.S. 326/D1
Hartland, Vt., U.S., 3,223 . . . . .352/C3
Hartland, Wisc., U.S., 7,905 . . . . .364/F2
Hartland Four Corners, Vt., U.S. 352/C3
Hartlebury, Eng., U.K. 68/C5
Hartlepool, Eng., U.K., 87,310 . . . . .66/F3
Hartlepool, Eng., U.K., unitary authority, 88,629 .66/F3
Hartleton, Penn., U.S., 260 . . . . .336/G4
Hartley, Eng., U.K. 70/E4
Hartley, Iowa, U.S., 1,733 . . . . .274/D1
Hartley, Tex., U.S., 441 . . . . .346/E8
Hartley, Tex., U.S., county, 5,537 . . . . .346/E8
Hartley Bay, Br. Col., Can. 214/H4
Hartline, Wash., U.S., 134 . . . . .358/F2
Hartly, Del., U.S., 78 . . . . .255/B4
Hartman, Ark., U.S., 596 . . . . .244/B2
Hartman, Colo., U.S., 111 . . . . .250/H3
Hart Mtn. Natl. Antelope Refuge, Oreg., U.S. . .334/G5
Hartney, Man., Can., 446 . . . . .215/A4
Hartpury, Eng., U.K. 68/C6
Harts, W. Va., U.S., 2,361 . . . . .360/B4
Hartsburg, Ill., U.S., 358 . . . . .266/D3
Hartsburg, Mo., U.S., 108 . . . . .302/D3
Hartsel, Colo., U.S., 40 . . . . .250/E2
Hartselle, Ala., U.S., 12,019 . . . . .238/C1
Hartshore, Eng., U.K. 70/A1
Hartshorn, Mo., U.S., 70 . . . . .302/E4
Hartshorne, Okla., U.S., 2,102 . . . . .330/G3
Hartsville, Ind., U.S., 376 . . . . .270/E6
Hartsville, Mass., U.S. 292/B4
Hartsville, S.C., U.S., 7,556 . . . . .340/D2
Hartsville, Tenn., U.S., 2,395 . . . . .344/J2
Hartville, Mo., U.S., 607 . . . . .302/D4
Hartville, Ohio, U.S., 2,174 . . . . .328/H4
Hartville, Wyo., U.S., 76 . . . . .366/D2
Hartwell, (Northamptonshire), Eng., U.K., 1,780 .68/F5
Hartwell, (Northamptonshire), Eng., U.K., 1,780 .70/C2
Hartwell, Ga., U.S., 4,188 . . . . .260/F3
Hartwell, Ga., U.S., lake 260/F2
Hartwell, Mo., U.S. 302/C3
Hartwell, S.C., U.S., lake 340/A2
Hartwellville, Vt., U.S., 175 . . . . .352/D1
Hartwick, Iowa, U.S., 83 . . . . .274/K4
Hartwick, N.Y., U.S., 550 . . . . .320/L5
Har Us, Mong., lake 118/B2
Harvard, Ida., U.S., 125 . . . . .264/A3
Harvard, Ill., U.S., 7,996 . . . . .266/E1
Harvard, Mass., U.S., 5,981 . . . . .292/H2
Harvard, Nebr., U.S., 998 . . . . .308/E3
Harvel, Ill., U.S., 235 . . . . .266/D4
Harvest, Ala., U.S., 3,054 . . . . .238/C1
Harvey, N.B., Can., 349 . . . . .217/C3
Harvey, Ark., U.S., 40 . . . . .244/B3
Harvey, Ill., U.S., 30,000 . . . . .266/C6
Harvey, Iowa, U.S., 277 . . . . .274/J5
Harvey, Kans., U.S., county, 32,869 . . . . . . .276/G3
Harvey, La., U.S., 22,226 . . . . .282/K3
Harvey, Mich., U.S. 286/E2
Harvey, Mich., U.S., 1,321 . . . . .294/B3
Harvey, N. Dak., U.S., 1,989 . . . . .326/F2
Harvey Cedars, N.J., U.S., 359 . . . . .314/E4
Harveysburg, Ohio, U.S., 563 . . . . .328/B6
Harveys Lake, Penn., U.S., 2,888 . . . . . .336/G7, J3
Harveyville, Kans., U.S., 267 . . . . .276/G3
Harvington, Eng., U.K. 68/D5
Harwell, Eng., U.K., 2,236 . . . . .70/B3
Harwich, Eng., U.K., 18,436 . . . . .70/G3
Harwich, Mass., U.S., 12,386 . . . . .292/P6
Harwich Port, Mass., U.S., 1,809 . . . . .292/P6
Harwill, Man., Can. 215/C3
Harwinton, Conn., U.S., 5,283 . . . . .253/C2
Harwood, Eng., U.K. 66/D3
Harwood, Mo., U.S., 90 . . . . .302/B4
Harwood, N. Dak., U.S., 607 . . . . .326/J3
Harwood Hts., Ill., U.S., 8,297 . . . . .266/B6
Harworth, (Harworth/Bircotes), Eng., U.K., 7,813 .68/F6
Harworth, (Harworth/Bircotes), Eng., U.K., 7,813 .68/E3
Haryana, India, state 128/C3
Harz, Ger., mountains 86/B3
Hasbrouck Hts., N.J., U.S., 11,662 . . . . .314/B2
Hascombe, Eng., U.K. 70/C4
Haskell, Ark., U.S., 2,645 . . . . .244/C3
Haskell, Kans., U.S., county, 4,307 . . . . .276/B4
Haskell, N.J., U.S. 314/A1
Haskell, Okla., U.S., 1,765 . . . . .330/G2
Haskell, Okla., U.S., county, 11,792 . . . . . . .330/G2
Haskell, Tex., U.S., 3,106 . . . . .346/J2
Haskell, Tex., U.S., county, 6,093 . . . . .346/J2
Haskins, Ohio, U.S., 638 . . . . .328/C3
Haskovo, Bul., oblast 101/D4
Haslemere, Eng., U.K. . . . . .60/Inset III
Haslemere, Eng., U.K., 12,218 . . . . .70/C4
Haslet, Tex., U.S., 1,134 . . . . .346/A9
Haslett, Mich., U.S., 11,283 . . . . .294/E7
Haslingden, Eng., U.K., 15,024 . . . . .66/D5
Haslingden, Eng., U.K., 15,024 . . . . .66/D3
Hassell, N.C., U.S., 72 . . . . .322/J3
Hasselt, Belg., 68,771, (386,283, metro.) 85/D2
Hassman, Minn., U.S. 298/D4
Hassocks, Eng., U.K. 70/D5
Hastingleigh, Eng., U.K. 70/F4
Hastings, Ont., Can., 1,208 . . . . .223/H3
Hastings, Ont., Can., 1,208 . . . . .223/H3
Hastings, Ont., Can., county 223/H3
Hastings, N.Z. 171/C2
Hastings, Eng., U.K., 81,139, (120,044, metro.) .70/F5
Hastings, Fla., U.S., 2 . . . . .256/G2
Hastings, Iowa, U.S., 214 . . . . .274/D4
Hastings, Mich., U.S., 7,095 . . . . .294/D7
Hastings, Minn., U.S., 18,204 . . . . .298/E6
Hastings, Nebr., U.S., 24,064 . . . . .308/E3
Hastings, Okla., U.S., 155 . . . . .330/D3
Hastings, Penn., U.S., 1,398 . . . . .336/D4

Hastings-on-Hudson, N.Y., U.S., 7,648 . . . . . .320/B1
Hasty, Colo., U.S., 200 . . . . .250/H3
Hasty, Minn., U.S., 225 . . . . .298/D5
Haswell, Colo., U.S., 84 . . . . .250/G3
Hatay (Antakya), Tur. 133/D3
Hatay, Tur., province 133/D3
Hatboro, Penn., U.S., 7,393 . . . . .336/M6
Hatch, N. Mex., U.S., 1,673 . . . . .317/C5
Hatch, Utah, U.S., 127 . . . . .350/B6
Hatchbend, Fla., U.S., 50 . . . . .256/F2
Hatchechubbee, Ala., U.S., 40 . . . . .238/D3
Hatchel, Tex., U.S. 346/J4
Hatchie N.W.R., Tenn., U.S. 344/C3
Hat Creek, Calif., U.S., 40 . . . . .246/D2
Hat Creek, Wyo., U.S. 366/D2
Hatfield, (Hertfordshire), Eng., U.K., 31,104 . . . .70/D3
Hatfield, (S. Yorkshire), Eng., U.K., 14,067 . . . .68/E2
Hatfield, Eng., U.K., 14,067 . . . . .66/F5
Hatfield, Ark., U.S., 402 . . . . .244/A3
Hatfield, Ind., U.S., 1,000 . . . . .270/B9
Hatfield, Mass., U.S., 3,249 . . . . .292/H3
Hatfield, Minn., U.S., 47 . . . . .298/A7
Hatfield, Penn., U.S., 2,605 . . . . .336/L5
Hatfield, Wisc., U.S., 150 . . . . .364/C4
Hatfield Heath, Eng., U.K. 70/E3
Hatfield Pt., N.B., Can. 217/D3
Hathaway, La., U.S., 275 . . . . .282/D6
Hathaway, Mont., U.S. 306/K3
Hatherleigh, Eng., U.K. 73/D3
Hathersage, Eng., U.K. 66/E6
Hatherton, Eng., U.K. 69/G4
Hatillo, P.R. 206/B2
Hatley, Ga., U.S., 60 . . . . .260/D8
Hatley, Miss., U.S., 476 . . . . .300/C3
Hatley, Wisc., U.S., 476 . . . . .364/D4
Hato Mayor, Dom. Rep. 205/C2
Hato Mayor, Dom. Rep., province 205/C2
Hatteras, N.C., U.S., 650 . . . . .322/P4
Hatteras, N.C., U.S., cape 322/P4
Hatteras, N.C., U.S., inlet 322/P4
Hattiesburg, Miss., U.S., 44,779,
   (111,674, metro.) 300/C4
Hattieville, Ark., U.S., 60 . . . . .244/C2
Hattingley, Eng., U.K. 70/B4
Hatton, Ala., U.S., 400 . . . . .238/B1
Hatton, N. Dak., U.S., 707 . . . . .326/H2
Hatton, Utah, U.S. 350/B5
Hatton, Wash., U.S., 98 . . . . .358/G3
Hatton Heath, Eng., U.K. 68/B3
Hat Yai, Thai. 125/B5
Haubstadt, Ind., U.S., 1,529 . . . . .270/A8
Haugan, Mont., U.S. 306/A2
Haugen, Wisc., U.S., 287 . . . . .364/B3
Haugesund, Nor. .80/B4
Haughton, La., U.S., 2,792 . . . . .282/C1
Haultain, Sask., Can., river 227/D4
Haupu Forest Reserve, Hawaii, U.S. 262/J1
Hauraki, N.Z., gulf 171/A3
Hauser, Ida., U.S., 668 . . . . .264/A2
Hauser, Oreg., U.S., 475 . . . . .334/B4
Haute-Corse, Fr., department . . . . .88/Inset I
Haute-Garonne, Fr., department 88/C4
Haute-Loire, Fr., department 88/C4
Haute-Marne, Fr., department 88/D3
Haute-Normandie, Fr., region 88/C2
Hautes-Alpes, Fr., department 88/D4
Haute-Saône, Fr., department 88/D3
Haute-Savoie, Fr., department 88/D3
Hautes-Pyrénées, Fr., department 88/C5
Haute-Vienne, Fr., department 88/C3
Haut-Rhin, Fr., department 88/D3
Hauts-de-Seine, Fr., department 88/C2
Hauts Plateaux, Alg., plateau 146/B1
Hauula, Hawaii, U.S., 3,651 . . . . .262/J1
Hauula Forest Reserve, Hawaii, U.S. 262/J1
Havana, Cuba, capital 204/A2
Havana, Cuba, capital, 2,192,321 . . . . .204/A2
Havana, Ark., U.S., 392 . . . . .244/B2
Havana, Fla., U.S., 1,713 . . . . .256/D1
Havana, Ill., U.S., 3,577 . . . . .266/C3
Havana, Kans., U.S., 86 . . . . .276/G4
Havana, N. Dak., U.S., 94 . . . . .326/H4
Havana, Ohio, U.S., 90 . . . . .328/E3
Havant, Eng., U.K., 46,510 . . . . .70/C5
Havasu, Ariz., U.S., lake 242/A3
Havasu Lake, Calif., U.S., 125 . . . . .246/L8
Havasu N.W.R., Ariz., U.S. 242/A3
Havasupai Ind. Res., Ariz., U.S. 242/C1
Havel, Ger., river .86/C2
Havelock, N.B., Can., 380 . . . . .217/D2
Havelock, Ont., Can., 1,328 . . . . .223/H3
Havelock, Iowa, U.S., 177 . . . . .274/E2
Havelock, N.C., U.S., 22,442 . . . . .322/M5
Havelock, N. Dak., U.S. 326/C3
Haven, Kans., U.S., 1,175 . . . . .276/E4
Haven, Wisc., U.S., 200 . . . . .364/F5
Havens, Nebr., U.S. 308/G2
Havensville, Kans., U.S., 146 . . . . .276/F2
Haverfordwest, Wales, U.K., 13,454 . . . . .64/C4
Haverhill, Eng., U.K., 19,086 . . . . .70/E2
Haverhill, Fla., U.S., 1,454 . . . . .256/B4
Haverhill, Iowa, U.S., 170 . . . . .274/J4
Haverhill, Mass., U.S., 58,969 . . . . .292/K1
Haverhill, N.H., U.S., 4,416 . . . . .312/B3
Haverigg, Eng., U.K. 66/B4
Havering, Eng., U.K., 228,879 . . . . .70/E3
Havering, Eng., U.K., unitary authority, 224,248 .70/E3
Haverstraw, N.Y., U.S., 10,117 . . . . .320/B1
Havilah, Calif., U.S. 246/G7
Haviland, Kans., U.S., 612 . . . . .276/C4
Haviland, Ohio, U.S., 180 . . . . .328/A3
Havillah, Wash., U.S. 358/F1
Havířov, Czh. Rep., 88,000 . . . . .92/D3
Havre, Mont., U.S., 9,621 . . . . .306/G1
Havre de Grace, Md., U.S., 11,331 . . . . .288/K1
Havre-St-Pierre, Que., Can., 3,291 . . . . .225/D3
Hawaii, U.S., state 250
Hawaii, Hawaii, U.S., county, 148,677 . .262/E7, G5
Hawaii, Hawaii, U.S., island 262/E6, G5
Hawaiian Gardens, Calif., U.S., 14,779 . . . . .246/D10
Hawaii Volcanoes Natl. Park, Hawaii, U.S. . .262/E7, H6
Hawalli, Kuw., 82,238 . . . . .136/C2
Hawar, Bahr., islands 137/B2
Hawarden, Iowa, U.S., 2,478 . . . . .274/B1
Hawea, N.Z., lake 171/A3
Hawesville, Ky., U.S., 971 . . . . .280/D3
Haweswater, Eng., U.K., lake 66/C3
Hawf, Yemen 137/C1
Hawi, Hawaii, U.S., 938 . . . . .262/G5
Hawick, Scot., U.K. 60/C2
Hawick, Scot., U.K., 14,573 . . . . .62/L8
Hawick, Scot., U.K., 125 . . . . .298/C5
Hawke, N.Z., bay 171/C2
Hawke Harbour, Nfld., Can. 218/D2
Hawkes Bay, Nfld., Can., 445 . . . . .218/C4
Hawkes Bay, N.Z., region 171/C3
Hawkesbury, Ont., Can., 10,314 . . . . .223/L2
Hawkeye, Iowa, U.S., 489 . . . . .274/L2
Hawkhurst, Eng., U.K., 3,463 . . . . .70/F4
Hawkinge, Eng., U.K., 2,224 . . . . .70/G4
Hawkins, Tenn., U.S., county, 53,563 . . . . . .344/R2
Hawkins, Wisc., U.S., 317 . . . . .364/C3

Hawkinsville, Ga., U.S., 3,280 . . . . .260/E7
Hawk Pt., Mo., U.S., 459 . . . . .302/E2
Hawks, Mich., U.S., 80 . . . . .294/F4
Hawkshead, Eng., U.K. 66/C4
Hawk Sprs., Wyo., U.S., 69 . . . . .366/D4
Hawksworth, Eng., U.K. 70/C1
Hawkwell, Eng., U.K. 70/E4
Hawley, Colo., U.S., 80 . . . . .250/G4
Hawley, Mass., U.S., 336 . . . . .292/G2
Hawley, Minn., U.S., 1,882 . . . . .298/A4
Hawley, Penn., U.S., 1,303 . . . . .336/L3
Hawley, Tex., U.S., 646 . . . . .346/J3
Hawley Lake, Ariz., U.S. 242/F4
Hawleyville, Conn., U.S., 800 . . . . .253/B4
Hawnby, Eng., U.K. 66/F4
Haworth, Eng., U.K., 4,956 . . . . .66/D2
Haworth, Eng., U.K., 4,956 . . . . .68/C2
Haworth, N.J., U.S., 3,390 . . . . .314/C1
Haworth, Okla., U.S., 354 . . . . .330/H4
Haw River, N.C., U.S., 1,908 . . . . .322/G2
Hawthorn, Penn., U.S., 587 . . . . .336/C3
Hawthorne, Calif., U.S., 84,112 . . . . .246/C10
Hawthorne, Fla., U.S., 1,415 . . . . .256/F2
Hawthorne, Nev., U.S., 3,311 . . . . .310/A2
Hawthorne, N.J., U.S., 18,218 . . . . .314/B1, E2
Hawthorne, Wisc., U.S., 125 . . . . .364/B2
Hawthorne Ammunition Depot, Calif., U.S. . .246/G4
Hawthorne Army Depot, Nev., U.S. 310/A2
Hawthorn Woods, Ill., U.S., 6,002 . . . . .266/B5
Haxby, Mont., U.S. 306/K2
Haxey, Eng., U.K. 68/G2
Haxtun, Colo., U.S., 982 . . . . .250/H1
Hay, Br. Col., Can., river 212/A2, B1
Hay, Br. Col., Can., river 214/M2
Hay, N.W. Terr., Can., river 220/E4
Hay, Wash., U.S. .358/H3
Hay Creek, Minn., U.S., 90 . . . . .298/E6
Hayden, Ala., U.S., 470 . . . . .238/C2
Hayden, Ariz., U.S., 892 . . . . .242/E4
Hayden, Colo., U.S., 1,634 . . . . .250/C1
Hayden, Ida., U.S., 9,159 . . . . .264/A2
Hayden, Ind., U.S., 550 . . . . .270/E7
Hayden, N. Mex., U.S. 317/G2
Hayden Lake, Ida., U.S., 494 . . . . .264/A2
Haydenville, Mass., U.S., 700 . . . . .292/D3
Haydenville, Ohio, U.S., 475 . . . . .328/F7
Haydon Bridge, Eng., U.K., 1,784 . . . . .66/D3
Hayes, Man., Can., river 215/D1, D2
Hayes, Eng., U.K. 70/D3
Hayes, La., U.S., 750 . . . . .282/D6
Hayes, Nebr., U.S., county, 1,068 . . . . .308/C3
Hayes, S. Dak., U.S. 342/D3
Hayes Ctr., Nebr., U.S., 240 . . . . .308/C3
Hayesville, Iowa, U.S., 64 . . . . .274/K5
Hayesville, Ohio, U.S., 348 . . . . .328/F4
Hayesville, Oreg., U.S., 18,222 . . . . .334/B3
Hayfield, Eng., U.K., 2,293 . . . . .66/E6
Hayfield, Eng., U.K., 2,293 . . . . .68/D3
Hayfield, Iowa, U.S., 60 . . . . .274/G1
Hayfield, Minn., U.S., 1,325 . . . . .298/E7
Hayford, Wash. .358/H2
Hayfork, Calif., U.S., 2,315 . . . . .246/B2
Hayle, Eng., U.K., 7,034 . . . . .73/B4
Hayma, Oman 137/C2
Haymarket, Va., U.S., 879 . . . . .354/H3
Haynes, Ark., U.S., 214 . . . . .244/E3
Haynes, N. Dak., U.S. 326/C4
Haynesville, La., U.S., 2,679 . . . . .282/C1
Haynesville, Maine, U.S., 122 . . . . .286/F3
Haynesville, Va., U.S., 550 . . . . .354/K5
Hayneville, Ala., U.S., 1,177 . . . . .238/C3
Hayneville, Ga., U.S., 400 . . . . .260/D7
Hay-on-Wye, Wales, U.K., 1,407 . . . . .64/E3
Hays, Kans., U.S., 20,013 . . . . .276/C3
Hays, Mont., U.S., 702 . . . . .306/H2
Hays, N.C., U.S., 1,731 . . . . .322/C2
Hays, Tex., U.S., 233 . . . . .346/D2
Hays, Tex., U.S., county, 97,589 . . .346/B1, D3, K5
Haysi, Va., U.S., 186 . . . . .354/D2
Hay Sprs., Nebr., U.S., 622 . . . . .308/B1
Haysville, Kans., U.S., 8,502 . . . . .276/E4
Hayter, Alta., Can. 212/E5
Hayti, Mo., U.S., 3,207 . . . . .302/G5
Hayti, S. Dak., U.S., 367 . . . . .342/H3
Hayti Hts., Mo., U.S., 771 . . . . .302/G5
Hayton, Eng., U.K. 66/G5
Hayward, Calif., U.S., 140,030 . . . . .246/C5, K2
Hayward, Minn., U.S., 249 . . . . .298/D7
Hayward, Mo., U.S., 123 . . . . .302/G5
Hayward, Wisc., U.S., 2,129 . . . . .364/B2
Haywards Heath, Eng., U.K., 28,923 . . . . . . .70/D4
Haywood, N.C., U.S., 475 . . . . .322/G3
Haywood, N.C., U.S., county, 54,033 . . . . . . .322/D7
Haywood, Okla., U.S., 80 . . . . .330/G3
Haywood, Tenn., U.S., county, 19,797 . . . . . .344/C3
Haywood City, Mo., U.S., 239 . . . . .302/G5
Hazard, Ky., U.S., 4,806 . . . . .280/G3
Hazard, Nebr., U.S., 66 . . . . .308/E2
Hazardville, Conn., U.S., 4,900 . . . . .253/E2
Hazel, Ky., U.S., 440 . . . . .280/B4
Hazel, S. Dak., U.S., 105 . . . . .342/H3
Hazel Crest, Ill., U.S., 14,816 . . . . .266/C6
Hazel Dell, Ill., U.S., 125 . . . . .266/E4
Hazel Dell, Wash., U.S., 6,605 . . . . .358/C4
Hazel Green, Ala., U.S., 3,805 . . . . .238/C1
Hazel Green, Ky., U.S., 275 . . . . .280/G3
Hazel Green, Wisc., U.S., 1,183 . . . . .364/C6
Hazel Hurst, Penn., U.S., 200 . . . . .336/D2
Hazelhurst, Wisc., U.S., 250 . . . . .364/D3
Hazel Park, Mich., U.S., 18,963 . . . . .294/B6
Hazel Run, Minn., U.S., 64 . . . . .298/B6
Hazelton, Br. Col., Can., 345 . . . . .214/J3
Hazelton, Br. Col., Can., mountains 214/H3
Hazelton, Ida., U.S., 687 . . . . .264/C7
Hazelton, Kans., U.S., 144 . . . . .276/D4
Hazelton, N. Dak., U.S., 237 . . . . .326/E3
Hazelwood, Mo., U.S., 26,206 . . . . .302/H2
Hazelwood, N.C., U.S. 322/D8
Hazelwood, Oreg., U.S. 334/A2
Hazen, Ala., U.S., 60 . . . . .238/B3
Hazen, Ark., U.S., 1,637 . . . . .244/D3
Hazen, Nev., U.S. 310/A2
Hazen, N. Dak., U.S., 2,457 . . . . .326/D2
Hazen, N. Dak., U.S., lake 326/D2
Hazlehurst, Ga., U.S., 3,787 . . . . .260/F8
Hazlehurst, Miss., U.S., 4,400 . . . . .300/B4
Hazlemere, (Hazlemere/Tylers Green),
   Eng., U.K., 20,843 . . . . .68/F6
Hazlet, Sask., Can., 126 . . . . .227/B10
Hazleton, Ind., U.S., 288 . . . . .270/A8
Hazleton, Iowa, U.S., 950 . . . . .274/L2
Hazleton, Penn., U.S., 23,329 . . . . .336/K4
Hazlettville, Del., U.S., 450 . . . . .255/B4
Heacham, Eng., U.K., 4,064 . . . . .70/E1
Headcorn, Eng., U.K., 2,295 . . . . .70/F4
Headland, Ala., U.S., 3,523 . . . . .238/D4
Headley, Eng., U.K., 5,176 . . . . .70/C4
Head of Grassy, Ky., U.S., 40 . . . . .280/G2
Head of the Harbor, N.Y., U.S., 1,447 . . . . . .320/D2
Headquarters, Ida., U.S. 264/B3

Headrick, Okla., U.S., 130 . . . . .330/C3
Heads, Miss., U.S. 300/B2
Head Tide, Maine, U.S. 286/C4
Heafford Jct., Wisc., U.S., 325 . . . . .364/D3
Healdsburg, Calif., U.S., 10,722 . . . . .246/C4
Healdton, Okla., U.S., 2,786 . . . . .330/E3
Healdville, Vt., U.S., 150 . . . . .352/B4
Healing Sprs., Va., U.S., 200 . . . . .354/F3
Healy, Eng., U.K. .66/E4
Healy, Alaska, U.S., 1,000 . . . . .240/V2
Healy, Kans., U.S., 250 . . . . .276/B3
Heanor, Eng., U.K., 22,180 . . . . .68/E3
Heanor, Eng., U.K., 22,180 . . . . .70/B1
Heard, Ga., U.S., county, 11,012 . . . . .260/A5
Hearne, Tex., U.S., 4,690 . . . . .346/M5
Hearst, Ont., Can., 5,825 . . . . .222/E1
Heart Butte, Mont., U.S., 698 . . . . .306/D1
Hearts Content, Nfld., Can., 495 . . . . .218/E5
Heartwell, Nebr., U.S., 80 . . . . .308/E3
Heartwellville, Vt., U.S. 352/B5
Heaslip, Man., Can. 215/A4
Heath, Ala., U.S., 249 . . . . .238/C4
Heath, Mass., U.S., 805 . . . . .292/C2
Heath, Mont., U.S. 306/G3
Heath, Ohio, U.S., 8,527 . . . . .328/F5
Heath, Tex., U.S., 4,149 . . . . .346/M8
Heathcote, N.J., U.S., 4,755 . . . . .314/D3
Heathfield, Eng., U.K., 6,629 . . . . .70/E5
Heath Sprs., S.C., U.S., 864 . . . . .340/D2
Heaton, N. Dak., U.S. 326/F2
Heavener, Okla., U.S., 3,201 . . . . .330/H3
Hebardville, Ohio, U.S., 200 . . . . .328/F7
Hebbardsville, Ky., U.S., 175 . . . . .280/C3
Hebbronville, Tex., U.S., 4,498 . . . . .346/K8
Hebbville, (Milford Mill), Md., U.S., 10,900 . . .288/C2
Hebden Bridge, Eng., U.K., 3,681 . . . . .66/D5
Hebden Bridge, Eng., U.K., 3,681 . . . . .70/C1
Hebei, China, province 119/E2
Hebei, (Heber-Overgaard), Ariz., U.S., 2,722 . .242/E3
Heber, Calif., U.S., 2,988 . . . . .246/K10
Heber City, Utah, U.S., 7,291 . . . . .350/C3, E2
Heber Sprs., Ark., U.S., 6,432 . . . . .244/C2
Hebo, Oreg., U.S., 231 . . . . .334/C2
Hebrides, Scot., U.K., sea 60/A4
Hebron, Nfld., Can. 218/B3
Hebron, Conn., U.S., 8,610 . . . . .253/F3
Hebron, Ill., U.S., 1,038 . . . . .266/E1
Hebron, Ind., U.S., 3,596 . . . . .270/B2
Hebron, Ky., U.S., 1,300 . . . . .280/F1
Hebron, Maine, U.S., 1,053 . . . . .286/B4
Hebron, N. Mex., U.S. 288/M6
Hebron, Nebr., U.S., 1,565 . . . . .308/G3
Hebron, N.H., U.S., 459 . . . . .312/C4
Hebron, N. Dak., U.S., 803 . . . . .326/C3
Hebron, Ohio, U.S., 2,034 . . . . .328/F6
Hebron, Tex., U.S., 874 . . . . .346/C8
Hebron Estates, Ky., U.S., 1,104 . . . . .280/E2
Hecate, Br. Col., Can., strait 214/G4
Hecker, Ill., U.S., 475 . . . . .266/C6
Heckington, Eng., U.K., 2,723 . . . . .68/G4
Heckington, Eng., U.K., 2,723 . . . . .70/D1
Hecla, Man., Can. 215/C3
Hecla, S. Dak., U.S., 314 . . . . .342/H2
Hecla and Griper, N.W. Terr., Can., bay 220/F1
Hecla Prov. Park, Man., Can. 215/C3
Hector, Ark., U.S., 506 . . . . .244/C2
Hector, Minn., U.S., 1,166 . . . . .298/C6
Hedding, N.J., U.S., 475 . . . . .314/D4
Hedger House, N.J., U.S. 314/D4
Hedgesville, Mont., U.S. 306/G3
Hedgesville, W. Va., U.S., 240 . . . . .360/K1
Hedley, Br. Col., Can., 272 . . . . .214/M6
Hedley, Tex., U.S., 379 . . . . .346/G9
Hedmark, Nor., province 80/C3
Hedon, Eng., U.K., 6,646 . . . . .66/H5
Hedon, Eng., U.K., 6,646 . . . . .68/G2
Hedrick, Iowa, U.S., 837 . . . . .274/K5
Hedville, Kans., U.S., 100 . . . . .276/E3
Hedwigs Hill, Tex., U.S. 346/J5
Hedwig Vil., Tex., U.S., 2,334 . . . . .346/A6
Heeia, Hawaii, U.S., 4,944 . . . . .262/G1, K2
Heerenveen, Neth. 84/C2
Heerlen, Neth., (218,448, metro.) 84/C4
Hefei, China, 795,420, (1,541,250, metro.) . . .119/E2
Heflin, Ala., U.S., 3,002 . . . . .238/D2
Heflin, La., U.S., 245 . . . . .282/C1
Hegang, China 119/G1
Heha, Bur., mountain 152/B2
Heiberger, Ala., U.S. 238/B3
Heidelberg, Vic., Austl. . . . . .170/Inset V
Heidelberg, Ger., 139,672 . . . . .86/B4
Heidelberg, Minn., U.S., 72 . . . . .298/D6
Heidelberg, Miss., U.S., 840 . . . . .300/D4
Heidelberg, Penn., U.S., 1,225 . . . . .336/D7
Heidenheim, Ger. 86/B4
Heidrick, Ky., U.S., 275 . . . . .280/G4
Heil, N. Dak., U.S. 326/D3
Heilbronn, Ger., 119,526 . . . . .86/B4
Heilong, (Amur), China, river 119/F1
Heilongjiang, China, province 119/F1
Heimaey, Ice., island 79/A3
Heimdal, N. Dak., U.S., 40 . . . . .326/F2
Heinsburg, Alta., Can. 212/E4
Heisker or Monarch, Scot., U.K., islands 62/A4
Heisler, Alta., Can., 183 . . . . .212/D5
Heislerville, N.J., U.S., 275 . . . . .314/D5
Heizer, Kans., U.S., 80 . . . . .276/D3
Hejaz, Sa. Arab., region 136/A1
Hekla, Ice., volcano 79/B3
Hel, Pol. 83/D1
Helen, Palau, reef 172/A4
Helen, Ga., U.S., 430 . . . . .260/D2
Helen, Md., U.S., 500 . . . . .288/H4
Helena, Ala., U.S., 10,296 . . . . .238/C2
Helena, Ark., U.S., 6,323 . . . . .244/E3
Helena, Ga., U.S., 2,307 . . . . .260/F7
Helena, Ky., U.S., 125 . . . . .280/G2
Helena, Mont., U.S., state capital, 25,780 . . .306/D3
Helena, N.Y., U.S., 40 . . . . .320/L1
Helena, Ohio, U.S., 236 . . . . .328/D3
Helena, Okla., U.S., 443 . . . . .330/D1
Helena Natl. For., Mont., U.S. 306/D3, E3
Helendale, Calif., U.S., 250 . . . . .246/H8
Helensburgh, Scot., U.K., 14,626 . . . . .62/G7
Helenwood, Tenn., U.S., 846 . . . . .344/M2
Helford, Eng., U.K. 73/B4
Helgoland, Ger., island 86/A1
Helhoughton, Eng., U.K. 70/F1
Heliotrope Mtn., Utah, U.S. 350/C4
Helix, Oreg., U.S., 183 . . . . .334/H2
Hellertown, Penn., U.S., 5,606 . . . . .336/L4
Hellidon, Eng., U.K. 70/B2
Hellifield, Eng., U.K. 66/D4
Hellin, Sp. 94/F3
Hells, Ida., U.S., canyon 264/A5
Hells, Oreg., U.S., canyon 334/K3
Hells Canyon Natl. Rec. Area, Oreg., U.S. . . .334/K2

Helm, Calif., U.S., 60 ....246/E6
Helmand, Afg., *river* 129/A2
Helmer, Ida., U.S. 264/A3
Helmer, Mich., U.S. 294/D3
Helmetta, N.J., U.S., 1,825 ....314/E3
Helmsdale, Alta., Can. 212/E5
Helmsdale, Scot., U.K. 62/J2
Helmsley, Eng., U.K. 66/F4
Helmville, Mont., U.S. 306/D3
Helotes, Tex., U.S., 4,285 ....346/A2
Helper, Utah, U.S., 2,025 ....350/D4
Helps, Mich., U.S. 294/B4
Helsby, Eng., U.K., 4,538 ....66/C6
Helsby, Eng., U.K., 4,538 ....68/B3
Helsingborg, Swe., 118,512 ....80/B3
Helsingør, Den. 79/D2
Helsinki, Fin., *capital*, 559,718,
   (964,960, *metro*.) 81/B2
Helsinki, Fin., *capital*, 559,718,
   (964,960, *metro*.) 193/C2
Helston, Eng., U.K., 8,505 ....73/B4
Helton, Ky., U.S. 280/G4
Heltonville, Ind., U.S., 225 ....270/D7
Hemby Acres, (Hemby Bridge), N.C., U.S. 322/D4
Hemel Hempstead, Eng., U.K., 79,235 ....70/D3
Hemet, Calif., U.S., 58,812 ....246/I9
Hemingford, Nebr., U.S., 993 ....308/A1
Heming Lake, Man., Can. 215/A2
Hemington, Eng., U.K. 68/G5
Hemingway, S.C., U.S., 573 ....340/E3
Hemlock, Mich., U.S., 1,585 ....294/E6
Hemlock, Ohio, U.S., 142 ....328/F6
Hemmingbrough, Eng., U.K. 66/G5
Hemphill, Tex., U.S., 1,106 ....346/R4
Hemphill, Tex., U.S., *county*, 3,351 ....346/G8
Hempstead, (Essex), Eng., U.K. 70/E2
Hempstead, (Norfolk), Eng., U.K. 70/H1
Hempstead, N.Y., U.S., *county*, 23,587 ....244/B4
Hempstead, N.Y., U.S., 56,554 ....320/C2
Hempstead, Tex., U.S., 4,691 ....346/M5
Hemsby, Eng., U.K., 5,109 ....70/H1
Hemsworth, Eng., U.K., 9,401 ....68/E2
Hemsworth, Eng., U.K., 9,401 ....66/E2
Hemyock, Eng., U.K. 73/F3
Henagar, Ala., U.S., 2,400 ....238/D1
Henan, China, *province* 119/E2
Henashi, Jap., *cape* 114/C1
Henderson, Ark., U.S., 60 ....244/C1
Henderson, Colo., U.S., 250 ....250/A3
Henderson, Ga., U.S., 125 ....260/D7
Henderson, Ill., U.S., 319 ....266/C4
Henderson, Ill., U.S., *county*, 8,213 ....266/C3
Henderson, Iowa, U.S., 171 ....274/D5
Henderson, Ky., U.S., *county*, 44,829 ....280/C3
Henderson, La., U.S., 1,531 ....282/F6
Henderson, Md., U.S., 118 ....288/L3
Henderson, Minn., U.S., 910 ....298/D6
Henderson, Nebr., U.S., 986 ....308/G3
Henderson, Nev., U.S., 175,381 ....310/C3
Henderson, N.C., U.S., 16,095 ....322/J2
Henderson, N.C., U.S., *county*, 89,173 ....322/E8
Henderson, Tenn., U.S., 5,670 ....344/E3
Henderson, Tenn., U.S., *county*, 25,522 ....344/E3
Henderson, Tex., U.S., 11,273 ....346/P3
Henderson, Tex., U.S., *county*, 73,277 ....346/N3
Henderson, W. Va., U.S., 325 ....360/D6
Hendersonville, N.C., U.S., 10,420 ....322/E8
Hendersonville, S.C., U.S., 100 ....340/D4
Hendersonville, Tenn., U.S., 40,620 ....344/H2
Hendley, Nebr., U.S. 308/F2
Hendon, Eng., U.K. 70/D3
Hendricks, Ind., U.S., *county*, 104,093 ....270/C5
Hendricks, Ky., U.S., 125 ....280/C3
Hendricks, Minn., U.S., 725 ....298/A6
Hendricks, W. Va., U.S., 319 ....360/G2
Hendrik Verwoerd, S. Afr., *reservoir* 162/C3
Hendrix, Ala., U.S., 175 ....238/C1
Hendrix, Okla., U.S., 79 ....330/F4
Hendron, Ky., U.S., 4,239 ....280/B3
Hendrum, Minn., U.S., 315 ....298/A3
Hendry, Fla., U.S., *county*, 36,210 ....256/G5
Henefer, Utah, U.S., 684 ....350/C2, E1
Henfield, Eng., U.K., 4,111 ....70/D5
Hengch'un, Tai. 117/B2
Hengelo, Neth. 84/D2
Hengoed, Wales, U.K. 64/E4
Hengyang, China 119/E3
Henley, Eng., U.K. 68/B5
Henley, Eng., U.K. 73/G2
Henley Harbour, Nfld., Can. 218/D3
Henley-in-Arden, Eng., U.K., 2,803 ....68/D5
Henley-on-Thames, Eng., U.K., 10,558 ....70/C3
Henllan, Wales, U.K. 64/E1
Henlopen, Del., U.S., *cape* 255/D5
Henlopen Acres, Del., U.S., 139 ....255/D6
Henlow, (Henlow/Shefford), Eng., U.K., 11,391 ....68/G5
Henlow, (Henlow/Shefford), Eng., U.K., 11,391 ....70/D2
Henly, Tex., U.S., 60 ....346/K5
Hennepin, Ill., U.S., 707 ....266/D4
Hennepin, Minn., U.S., *county*, 1,116,200 ....298/D5, E6
Hennessey, Okla., U.S., 2,058 ....330/E1
Hennepin, Okla., U.S., 125 ....330/E1
Henniker, N.H., U.S., 4,433 ....312/C5
Henning, Ill., U.S., 241 ....266/F3
Henning, Minn., U.S., 719 ....298/B4
Henning, Tenn., U.S., 970 ....344/B3
Henrico, Va., U.S., *county*, 262,300 ....354/C4
Henrietta, Mo., U.S., 457 ....302/C2
Henrietta, N.Y., U.S., 6,600 ....320/F4
Henrietta, Tex., U.S., 3,264 ....346/K2
Henriette, Minn., U.S., 101 ....298/D5
Henrieville, Utah, U.S., 159 ....350/C6
Henry, Ala., U.S., *county*, 16,310 ....238/D4
Henry, Ga., U.S., *county*, 119,341 ....260/C5, J4
Henry, Ida., U.S. 264/F7
Henry, Ill., U.S., 2,540 ....266/D2
Henry, Ill., U.S., *county*, 51,020 ....266/C2
Henry, Ind., U.S., *county*, 48,508 ....270/F5
Henry, Iowa, U.S., *county*, 20,336 ....274/L5
Henry, Ky., U.S., *county*, 15,060 ....280/E2
Henry, La., U.S., 275 ....282/E7
Henry, Mo., U.S., *county*, 21,997 ....302/D3
Henry, Nebr., U.S., 162 ....308/A2
Henry, Nev., U.S. 310/C1
Henry, Ohio, U.S., *county*, 29,210 ....328/B3
Henry, S. Dak., U.S., 268 ....342/H3
Henry, Tenn., U.S., 520 ....344/E2
Henry, Tenn., U.S., *county*, 31,115 ....344/E2
Henry, Utah, U.S., *mountains* 350/D5
Henry, Va., U.S., 100 ....354/D7
Henry, Va., U.S., *cape* 354/M7
Henry, Va., U.S., *county*, 57,930 ....354/D7
Henry, W. Va., U.S. 360/H2
Henryetta, Okla., U.S., 6,096 ....330/F2
Henryville, Ind., U.S., 1,545 ....270/E7
Hensall, Ont., Can., 1,194 ....223/D4
Hensel, N. Dak., U.S., 42 ....326/H1
Henshaw, Ky., U.S., 125 ....280/B3
Hensler, N. Dak., U.S., 60 ....326/D2
Henstridge, Eng., U.K. 73/H3

Henzada, (Hinthada), Mya. 125/B3
Hepburn, Eng., U.K. 66/E1
Hepburn, Iowa, U.S. 274/D6
Hepburn, Ohio, U.S., 300 ....328/D4
Hephzibah, Ga., U.S., 3,880 ....260/G5
Hepler, Kans., U.S., 154 ....276/H4
Hepple, Eng., U.K. 66/D2
Heppner, Oreg., U.S., 1,395 ....334/G2
Herald, Ill., U.S., 60 ....266/E6
Herald Harbor, Md., U.S., 2,313 ....288/H3
Herat, Afg., 177,300 ....129/A2
Hérault, Fr., *department* 88/C5
Herbert, Sask., Can., 812 ....227/C10
Herbert Hoover N.H.S., Iowa, U.S. 274/M4
Herb Lake, Man., Can. 215/B2
Herbster, Wisc., U.S., 50 ....364/B2
Herculaneum, Mo., U.S., 2,805 ....302/F3
Hercules, Calif., U.S., 19,488 ....246/J1
Herd, Okla., U.S. 330/F1
Heredia, C.R. 203/B2
Heredia, C.R., *province* 203/B2
Hereford, Eng., U.K. 60/C3
Hereford, Eng., U.K., 54,326 ....68/B5
Hereford, (part of Sierra Vista Southeast),
   Ariz., U.S. 242/E6
Hereford, Colo., U.S., 50 ....250/F1
Hereford, Md., U.S., 550 ....288/H1
Hereford, Oreg., U.S. 334/H3
Hereford, S. Dak., U.S. 342/C3
Hereford, Tex., U.S., 14,597 ....346/F9
Herefordshire, (County of), Eng., U.K.,
   unitary authority, 174,844 ....68/B5
Herington, Kans., U.S., 2,563 ....276/F3
Heriot, Scot., U.K. 62/L7
Heriot Bay, Br. Col., Can., 625 ....214/K6
Herkimer, Kans., U.S., 100 ....276/F2
Herkimer, N.Y., U.S., 7,498 ....320/M4
Herkimer, N.Y., U.S., *county*, 64,427 ....320/M4
Herm, Eng., U.K., *island* 73/G4
Herman, Mich., U.S., 60 ....294/A3
Herman, Minn., U.S., 452 ....298/A5
Herman, Nebr., U.S., 310 ....308/H2
Herman, Mo., U.S., 2,674 ....302/E3
Hermansville, Mich., U.S., 325 ....294/B4
Hermantown, Minn., U.S., 7,448 ....298/C4
Hermanville, Md., U.S., 1,100 ....288/J6
Hermanville, Miss., U.S., 125 ....300/B4
Hermiston, Oreg., U.S., 13,154 ....334/G2
Hermitage, Eng., U.K., 1,557 ....70/B4
Hermitage, Scot., U.K. 62/L8
Hermitage, Ark., U.S., 769 ....244/C4
Hermitage, Tex., U.S., 375 ....282/G5
Hermitage, Mo., U.S., 406 ....302/C4
Hermitage, Penn., U.S., 16,157 ....336/A3
Hermitage-Sandyville, Nfld., Can., 602 ....218/K1
Hermitage Sprs., Tenn., U.S., 150 ....344/K1
Hermleigh, Tex., U.S., 393 ....346/H3
Hermon, Leb., *mountain* 134/C3
Hermon, Syria, *mountain* 134/A3
Hermon, Maine, U.S., 4,437 ....286/D4
Hermon, N.Y., U.S., 402 ....320/L2
Hermosa, Colo., U.S., 700 ....250/C4
Hermosa, S. Dak., U.S., 315 ....342/B4
Hermosa, Tex., U.S. 346/E4
Hermosa Beach, Calif., U.S., 18,566 ....246/B10
Hermosillo, Mex., *state capital*, 545,928,
   (609,829, *metro*.) 200/D4
Hernád, Hun., *river* 91/C1
Hernandez, N. Mex., U.S., 600 ....317/D1
Hernando, Fla., U.S., 8,253 ....256/F3
Hernando, Fla., U.S., *county*, 130,802 ....256/F3
Hernando, Miss., U.S., 6,812 ....300/B1
Herndon, Kans., U.S., 149 ....276/B2
Herndon, Ky., U.S., 70 ....280/C4
Herndon, Penn., U.S., 383 ....336/H4
Herndon, Va., U.S., 21,655 ....354/L2
Herndon, W. Va., U.S., 80 ....360/D6
Herne, Ger., 175,661 ....86/A3
Herne, Eng., U.K. 70/G4
Herne Bay, Eng., U.K., 31,861 ....70/G4
Herning, Den. 79/B2
Henshaw, W. Va., U.S., 250 ....360/C4
Herod, Ga., U.S., 40 ....260/C8
Herod, Ill., U.S. 266/E6
Heron, Mont., U.S., 149 ....306/A1
Heron Bay, Ala., U.S., 550 ....238/A5
Heron Lake, Minn., U.S., 768 ....298/B7
Herreid, S. Dak., U.S., 482 ....342/E2
Herrera, Pan., *province* 203/B3
Herriard, Eng., U.K. 70/B4
Herrick, Ill., U.S., 524 ....266/E4
Herrick, S. Dak., U.S., 105 ....342/F4
Herrin, Ill., U.S., 11,298 ....266/E6
Herring, Okla., U.S. 330/C2
Herrings, N.Y., U.S., 129 ....320/K2
Herscher, Ill., U.S., 1,523 ....266/E2
Hersden, Eng., U.K. 70/G4
Hersey, Maine, U.S., 63 ....286/D2
Hersey, Mich., U.S., 374 ....294/D6
Hershey, Nebr., U.S., 572 ....308/D2
Hershey, Penn., U.S., 12,771 ....336/H5
Herstmonceux, Eng., U.K. 70/E5
Hertel, Wisc., U.S., 90 ....364/A3
Hertford, Eng., U.K. ....60/Inset III
Hertford, Eng., U.K., 21,665 ....70/D3
Hertford, N.C., U.S., 2,070 ....322/N2
Hertford, N.C., U.S., *county*, 22,601 ....322/L2
Hertfordshire, Eng., U.K., *unitary authority*,
   1,033,977 ....68/G6
Hertfordshire, Eng., U.K., *unitary authority*,
   1,033,977 ....70/D3
Herzliyya, Isr. 135/B1
Hesler, Ky., U.S., 60 ....280/F2
Hesperia, Calif., U.S., 62,582 ....246/H8
Hesperia, Mich., U.S., 954 ....294/C6
Hesperus, Colo., U.S. 250/B4
Hess, Yukon, Can., *river* 228/C4
Hess, Okla., U.S. 330/C3
Hesse, Ger., *state* 86/B3
Hessel, Mich., U.S., 200 ....294/E3
Hessle, Eng., U.K. 66/H5
Hessmer, La., U.S., 642 ....282/E4
Hesston, Kans., U.S., 3,509 ....276/E3
Hest Bank, Eng., U.K. 66/C4
Hester, Okla., U.S. 330/C3
Heswall, Eng., U.K., 31,093 ....66/B6
Heswall, Eng., U.K., 31,093 ....68/A3
Hetauda, Nepal 126/C2
Heth, Ark., U.S. 244/E2
Hethersgill, Eng., U.K. 66/C3
Hetland, S. Dak., U.S., 43 ....342/H3
Hettick, Ill., U.S., 182 ....266/C4
Hettinger, N. Dak., U.S., 1,307 ....326/C3
Hettinger, N. Dak., U.S., *county*, 2,715 ....326/C3
Hetton-le-Hole, Eng., U.K., 13,538 ....66/F1
Heuksan, S. Kor., *islands* 116/A5
Heuvelton, N.Y., U.S., 804 ....320/L1
Heveningham, Eng., U.K. 70/G2
Heves, Hun., *county* 91/C2
Hevingham, Eng., U.K. 70/G1
Hewins, Kans., U.S. 276/F4
Hewitt, Minn., U.S., 267 ....298/B4

Hewitt, N.J., U.S., 50 ....314/E1
Hewitt, Tex., U.S., 11,085 ....346/L4
Hewitt, Wisc., U.S., 670 ....364/C4
Hewitt Lake N.W.R., Mont., U.S. 306/J1
Hewlett, Va., U.S., 40 ....354/H5
Hext, Okla., U.S. 330/C2
Hext, Tex., U.S. 346/J5
Heyburn, Ida., U.S., 2,899 ....264/D7
Heysham, Eng., U.K. 66/C4
Heywood, Eng., U.K., 29,286 ....66/D5
Heywood, Eng., U.K., 29,286 ....66/C2
Heyworth, Ill., U.S., 2,431 ....266/E3
Hialeah, Fla., U.S., 226,419 ....256/B6, H6
Hialeah Gardens, Fla., U.S., 19,297 ....256/A6
Hiatikulu, Swaz. 161/B2
Hiattville, Kans., U.S., 60 ....276/H4
Hiawassee, Ga., U.S., 808 ....260/D2
Hiawatha, Colo., U.S. 250/B1
Hiawatha, Iowa, U.S., 6,480 ....274/L3
Hiawatha, Kans., U.S., 3,417 ....276/G2
Hiawatha, Utah, U.S., 40 ....350/D4
Hiawatha Natl. For., Mich., U.S. 294/C3, E3
Hibbing, Minn., U.S., 17,071 ....298/E3
Hibernia, N.J., U.S., 175 ....314/E2
Hickam Air Force Base, Hawaii, U.S. 262/E2
Hickiwan, Ariz., U.S. 242/C5
Hickling, Eng., U.K. 70/H1
Hickman, Del., U.S. 255/B5
Hickman, Ky., U.S., 2,560 ....280/A4
Hickman, Ky., U.S., *county*, 5,262 ....280/A4
Hickman, Md., U.S. 288/M4
Hickman, Nebr., U.S., 1,084 ....308/H3
Hickman, Tenn., U.S., *county*, 22,295 ....344/G3
Hickok, Kans., U.S., 50 ....276/A4
Hickory, Ky., U.S., 250 ....280/B4
Hickory, Miss., U.S., 499 ....300/C3
Hickory, N.C., U.S., 37,222, (341,851, *metro*.) 322/C3
Hickory, Okla., U.S., 87 ....330/F3
Hickory Creek, Tex., U.S., 2,078 ....346/B8
Hickory Flat, Miss., U.S., 565 ....300/C1
Hickory Grove, (Horry County), S.C., U.S. 340/C2
Hickory Grove, (York County), S.C., U.S., 337 ....340/F3
Hickory Hills, Ill., U.S., 13,926 ....266/B6
Hickory Plains, Ark., U.S., 80 ....244/D3
Hickory Ridge, Ark., U.S., 384 ....244/E2
Hickory Run St. Park, Penn., U.S. 336/K3
Hickory Valley, Tenn., U.S., 136 ....344/C4
Hickox, Ga., U.S., 200 ....260/H9
Hicks, La., U.S., 225 ....282/D4
Hicks Bay, N.Z. 171/C2
Hickson, N. Dak., U.S., 80 ....326/J3
Hicksville, Ohio, U.S., 3,649 ....328/A3
Hico, La., U.S. 282/D1
Hico, Tex., U.S., 1,341 ....346/K4
Hidaka, Jap., *mountains* ....114/Inset I
Hidalgo, Mex., *state* 200/E3
Hidalgo, Ill., U.S., 123 ....266/E4
Hidalgo, N. Mex., U.S., *county*, 5,932 ....317/B6
Hidalgo, Tex., U.S., 7,322 ....346/J8
Hidalgo, Tex., U.S., *county*, 569,463 ....346/K9
Hidalgo del Parral, Mex., 98,876,
   (100,821, *metro*.) 200/C3
Hiddenite, N.C., U.S., 650 ....322/C3
Hidden Timber, S. Dak., U.S. 342/E4
Hidden Valley, Ind., U.S., 4,417 ....270/G6
Hide Creek, Ariz., U.S., *mountain* 242/C3
Hieflau, Aus. 91/D3
Hierro, Sp., *island* ....94/Inset I
Higashiosaka, Jap., 515,000 ....114/B3
Higbee, Mo., U.S., 623 ....302/D2
Higbie, Ark., U.S., 101 ....244/C2
Higganum, Conn., U.S., 1,671 ....253/E4
Higgins, Mich., U.S., *lake* 294/E5
Higgins, Okla., U.S. 330/G3
Higgins, Tex., U.S., 425 ....346/H8
Higgins Bay, N.Y., U.S. 320/M4
Higgins Beach, Maine, U.S., 800 ....286/B5
Higgins Lake, Mich., U.S., 60 ....294/E5
Higginson, Ark., U.S., 378 ....244/D2
Higginsport, Ohio, U.S., 291 ....328/D8
Higginsville, Mo., U.S., 4,682 ....302/C2
Higgston, Ga., U.S., 316 ....260/G7
High, Mich., U.S., *island* 294/D4
Higham, Eng., U.K., 2,670 ....68/E3
Higham Ferrers, Eng., U.K., 5,345 ....68/F5
Higham Ferrers, Eng., U.K., 5,345 ....70/C2
Highampton, Eng., U.K. 73/D3
High Atlas, Mor., *ranges* 147/B2
High Bank, P.E.I., Can. 224/C3
High Bentham, Eng., U.K., 2,538 ....68/C1
Highbridge, Eng., U.K. 73/G2
High Bridge, N.H., U.S., 300 ....312/C6
High Bridge, N.J., U.S., 3,776 ....314/D2
High Bridge, Wisc., U.S., 90 ....364/C2
Highclere, Eng., U.K., 2,905 ....70/B4
Highcliff, Eng., U.K. 70/A5
Highcliff, Eng., U.K. 73/J3
High Ercall, Eng., U.K. 68/B4
Highest Pt. in Florida, Fla., U.S. 256/B1
Highest Pt. in Indiana, Ind., U.S. 270/B6
Highest Pt. in Iowa, Iowa, U.S. 274/C1
Highest Pt. in Nebraska, Nebr., U.S. 308/A2
Highfill, Ark., U.S., 379 ....244/A1
High Garrett, Eng., U.K. 70/F3
Highgate Ctr., Vt., U.S., 600 ....352/A1
Highgate Falls, Vt., U.S. 352/A1
Highgate Sprs., Vt., U.S., 125 ....352/A1
High Halden, Eng., U.K. 70/F4
High Hawsker, Eng., U.K. 66/G4
High Hesket, Eng., U.K. 66/C3
High Hill, Mo., U.S., 231 ....302/E3
High Island, Tex., U.S., 500 ....346/P6
Highland, Scot., U.K., *unitary authority*, 208,914 ....62/G2
Highland, Ark., U.S., 90 ....244/B3
Highland, Calif., U.S., 44,605 ....246/H8
Highland, Fla., U.S., 80 ....256/F1
Highland, Ill., U.S., 8,438 ....266/B3, D5
Highland, (Lake County), Ind., U.S., 23,546 ....270/B1
Highland, (Vanderburgh County),
   Ind., U.S., 4,107 ....270/A8
Highland, Kans., U.S., 976 ....276/G2
Highland, Md., U.S., 800 ....288/G3
Highland, (Fillmore County), Minn., U.S., 40 ....298/F7
Highland, (Lake County), Minn., U.S. 298/F3
Highland, N.Y., U.S., 5,060 ....320/P7
Highland, Ohio, U.S., 283 ....328/C7
Highland, Ohio, U.S., *county*, 40,875 ....328/D7
Highland, Utah, U.S., 8,172 ....350/C3
Highland, Va., U.S., *county*, 2,536 ....354/F3
Highland, Wash., U.S., 3,388 ....358/F3
Highland Beach, Fla., U.S., 3,775 ....256/B5
Highland Beach, Md., U.S., 109 ....288/J4
Highland Ctr., Iowa, U.S. 274/K5
Highland Falls, N.Y., U.S., 3,678 ....320/B1
Highland Hts., Ky., U.S., 6,554 ....280/G1
Highland Hts., Ohio, U.S., 8,082 ....328/H8
Highland Hills, Ohio, U.S., 1,618 ....328/H9
Highland Home, Ala., U.S., 125 ....238/C4

High Landing, Minn., U.S. 298/B2
Highland Lake, Ala., U.S., 408 ....238/C2
Highland Lakes, N.J., U.S., 5,051 ....314/E1
Highland Mills, N.Y., U.S., 3,468 ....320/A1
Highland Park, Ill., U.S., 31,365 ....266/B5, F1
Highland Park, Mich., U.S., 16,746 ....294/B7
Highland Park, N.J., U.S., 13,999 ....314/E3
Highland Park, Penn., U.S., 1,446 ....336/F4
Highland Park, Tex., U.S., 8,842 ....346/C9
Highlands, Calif., U.S. 246/J2
Highlands, Fla., U.S., *county*, 87,366 ....256/C4
Highlands, N.J., U.S., 5,097 ....314/F3
Highlands, N.C., U.S., 909 ....322/D8
Highlands, Tex., U.S., 7,089 ....346/C6
Highland Sprs., Va., U.S., 15,137 ....354/J5
Highlands Ranch, Colo., U.S., 70,931 ....250/F2
Highland View, Fla., U.S., 450 ....256/C2
Highland Vil., Tex., U.S., 12,173 ....346/B8
Highlandville, Iowa, U.S. 274/L1
Highlandville, Mo., U.S., 872 ....302/C5
High Lane, Eng., U.K., 4,861 ....68/C5
High Level, Alta., Can., 3,444 ....212/B2
High Lorton, Eng., U.K. 66/B3
Highmore, S. Dak., U.S., 851 ....342/F3
Highpoint, Miss., U.S., 150 ....300/C2
High Pt., Mo., U.S., 80 ....302/D3
High Pt., N.J., U.S., *hill* 314/D1
High Pt., N.Y., U.S., 85,839 ....314/D1
High Pt. St. Park, N.J., U.S. 314/D1
High Prairie, Alta., Can., 2,737 ....212/B3
High River, Alta., Can., 9,345 ....212/D6
Highrock, Man., Can. 215/A1
Highrock, Man., Can., *lake* 215/A1
High Rock, N.C., U.S., 90 ....322/E3
High Rolls, N. Mex., U.S., 425 ....317/E5
High Shoals, N.C., U.S., 729 ....322/C4
Highspire, Penn., U.S., 2,720 ....336/H5
High Sprs., Fla., U.S., 3,863 ....256/F2
High Tatra, Pol., *mountains* 91/C2
Hightowers, N.C., U.S., 225 ....322/G2
Hightown, Eng., U.K. 68/C3
Hightstown, N.J., U.S., 5,216 ....314/D3
Highview, Ky., U.S., 15,161 ....280/B2
Highway, N. Mex., U.S. 317/G4
Highwood, Ill., U.S., 4,143 ....266/B5
Highwood, Mont., U.S., 189 ....306/F2
Highworth, Eng., U.K., 8,259 ....68/D6
Highworth, Eng., U.K., 8,259 ....73/J1
High Wycombe, Eng., U.K. ....60/Inset III
High Wycombe, Eng., U.K., 71,718,
   (116,361, *metro*.) 68/F6
High Wycombe, Eng., U.K., 71,718,
   (116,361, *metro*.) 70/C3
Higley, Ariz., U.S., 425 ....242/D4
Higuey, Dom. Rep. 205/D2
Hiiumaa, Est., *island* 81/B2
Hiko, Nev., U.S., 100 ....310/C3
Hiland, Wyo., U.S. 366/C2
Hilbert, Wisc., U.S., 1,089 ....364/E4
Hilborough, Eng., U.K. 70/F1
Hilda, Alta., Can., 55 ....212/E6
Hilda, S.C., U.S., 436 ....340/C3
Hildale, Utah, U.S., 1,895 ....350/A6
Hildebran, N.C., U.S., 1,472 ....322/C3
Hilden, N.S., Can. 221/D2
Hilden, Ger., 56,000 ....70/84
Hilderstone, Eng., U.K. 68/C4
Hildesheim, Ger., 104,013 ....86/B2
Hildreth, Nebr., U.S., 370 ....308/E3
Hiles, Wisc., U.S., 100 ....364/D3
Hilgard, Oreg., U.S. 334/H2
Hilger, Mont., U.S., 70 ....306/G2
Hill, Mont., U.S. 306/E1
Hill, Mont., U.S., *county*, 16,673 ....306/G1
Hill, N. Mex., U.S., 175 ....317/D5
Hill, Tex., U.S., *county*, 32,321 ....346/L3
Hillaby, Barb., *mountain* 209/A3
Hilland, S. Dak., U.S. 342/D3
Hilandale, Md., U.S., 3,054 ....288/B6
Hill Bank, Bel. 201/B2
Hillburn, N.Y., U.S., 881 ....320/A1
Hill Ctr., N.H., U.S. 312/C4
Hill City, Ida., U.S. 264/B6
Hill City, Kans., U.S., 1,604 ....276/C2
Hill City, Minn., U.S., 479 ....298/D4
Hill City, S. Dak., U.S., 780 ....342/B4
Hill Country Vil., Tex., U.S., 1,028 ....346/B2
Hillcrest, Ill., U.S., 1,158 ....266/D2
Hillcrest, Tex., U.S., 722 ....346/B7
Hillcrest Hts., Fla., U.S., 266 ....256/G4
Hillcrest Hts., Md., U.S., 16,359 ....288/C7
Hillsmann, Ark., U.S. 244/D2
Hillerød, Den. 79/D3
Hill Head, Eng., U.K. 70/B5
Hillhead, S. Dak., U.S. 342/H2
Hillhouse, Miss., U.S. 300/B1
Hilliard, Fla., U.S., 2,702 ....256/F1
Hilliard, Ohio, U.S., 24,230 ....328/D5, D9
Hilliards, Penn., U.S., 175 ....336/B3
Hilliard's Cross, Eng., U.K. 68/D4
Hillingdon, Eng., U.K., 231,288 ....70/D3
Hillingdon, Eng., U.K., *unitary authority*,
   242,435 ....70/D3
Hillington, Eng., U.K. 70/F1
Hillman, Mich., U.S., 685 ....294/F4
Hillman, Minn., U.S. 298/D4
Hillrose, Colo., U.S., 254 ....250/G1
Hills, Iowa, U.S., 679 ....274/L4
Hills, Minn., U.S., 565 ....298/A7
Hills and Dales, Ky., U.S., 153 ....280/B1
Hills and Dales, Ohio, U.S., 260 ....328/H4
Hillsboro, Ala., U.S., 608 ....238/B1
Hillsboro, Ga., U.S., 50 ....260/D5
Hillsboro, Ill., U.S., 4,359 ....266/D4
Hillsboro, Ind., U.S., 489 ....270/B4
Hillsboro, Iowa, U.S., 205 ....274/L6
Hillsboro, Kans., U.S., 2,854 ....276/F3
Hillsboro, Ky., U.S., 250 ....280/G2
Hillsboro, Md., U.S., 163 ....288/L4
Hillsboro, Miss., U.S., 300 ....300/C3
Hillsboro, Mo., U.S., 1,675 ....302/F3
Hillsboro, Mont., U.S. 306/H4
Hillsboro, N.H., U.S., 4,928 ....312/C5
Hillsboro, N. Mex., U.S., 50 ....317/C5
Hillsboro, N. Dak., U.S., 1,563 ....326/H2
Hillsboro, Ohio, U.S., 6,368 ....328/C7
Hillsboro, Oreg., U.S., 70,186 ....334/D2
Hillsboro, Tenn., U.S., 225 ....344/K4
Hillsboro, Tex., U.S., 8,232 ....346/L3
Hillsboro, Va., U.S., 96 ....354/H4
Hillsboro, Wisc., U.S., 243 ....364/C5
Hillsboro, Wisc., U.S., 1,302 ....364/C5
Hillsboro Beach, Fla., U.S., 2,163 ....256/B5
Hillsborough, N.B., Can., 1,288 ....217/E3
Hillsborough, P.E.I., Can., *bay* 224/B2
Hillsborough, Gren. 209/C1
Hillsborough, N. Ire., U.K., 2,407 ....65/E3
Hillsborough, Calif., U.S., 10,825 ....246/J2
Hillsborough, Fla., U.S., *county*, 998,948 ....256/D6, F4
Hillsborough, N.H., U.S., *county*, 380,841 ....312/C5
Hillsborough, N.C., U.S., 5,446 ....322/G2

Hillsborough Ctr., N.H., U.S. .312/C5
Hillsborough Lower Vil., N.H., U.S., 400 .312/C5
Hillsborough Upper Vil., N.H., U.S., 225 .312/C5
Hillsdale, Ill., U.S., 588 .266/C2
Hillsdale, Ind., U.S., 300 .270/B5
Hillsdale, Kans., U.S., 275 .276/H3
Hillsdale, Mich., U.S., 8,233 .294/E8
Hillsdale, Mich., U.S., county, 46,527 .294/E8
Hillsdale, N.J., U.S., 1,477 .302/H3
Hillsdale, N.J., U.S., 10,087 .314/B1, E1
Hillsdale, N.Y., U.S., 375 .320/P6
Hillsdale, Okla., U.S., 101 .330/D1
Hillsdale, Wisc., U.S., 200 .364/B3
Hillsdale, Wyo., U.S., 80 .366/D3
Hillside, Ariz., U.S., 100 .242/C3
Hillside, Colo., U.S. .250/E3
Hillside, Ill., U.S., 8,155 .266/B6
Hillside, N.J., U.S., 21,747 .314/B3
Hillside Lake, N.Y., U.S., 2,022 .320/P7
Hillside N.W.H. Miss., U.S. .300/B2
Hillsmere Shores, Md., U.S., 2,977 .288/J4
Hillsview, S. Dak., U.S. .342/F2
Hillsville, Va., U.S., 2,607 .354/B7
Hillswick, Scot., U.K. .62/P2
Hilltonia, Ga., U.S., 421 .260/H6
Hill Top, Eng., U.K. .70/B5
Hilltop, Ariz., U.S. .242/F5
Hill Top, Ky., U.S., 100 .280/G2
Hilltop, Minn., U.S., 766 .298/F5
Hilltown, N. Ire., U.K., 982 .65/J3
Hillview, Ill., U.S., 179 .266/C4
Hillview, Ky., U.S., 7,037 .280/E2
Hillview, Minn., U.S. .298/M4
Hilmar, Calif., U.S., 4,807 .246/E5
Hilo, Hawaii, U.S., 40,759 .262/E7, J5
Hilo, Hawaii, U.S., bay .262/J5
Hilo Forest Reserve, Hawaii, U.S. .262/J5
Hilo Intl. Airport, Hawaii, U.S. .262/J5
Hilshire Vil., Tex., U.S., 720 .346/M6
Hilt, Calif., U.S. .246/C1
Hilton, Eng., U.K., 1,755 .68/C4
Hilton, Eng., U.K. .68/D4
Hilton, Eng., U.K., 1,755 .70/A1
Hilton, N.Y., U.S., 5,856 .320/F4
Hilton Beach, Ont., Can., 174 .223/B1
Hilton Head Island, S.C., U.S., 33,862 .340/D4
Hilversum, Neth. .84/C2
Himachal Pradesh, India, state .128/C2
Himalayas, Bhu., mountains .126/B1
Himalayas, China, mountains .119/B3
Himalayas, India, mountains .128/C2, E3
Himalayas, Nepal, mountains .126/B1
Himeji, Jap., 478,000 .114/B3
Himes, Wyo., U.S. .366/B1
Hims, (Homs), Syria, 540,133, (659,282, metro.) .134/A2
Hinchcliff, Miss., U.S. .300/B1
Hinche, Haiti .205/C1
Hinckley, Eng., U.K., 40,608 .68/C4
Hinckley, Eng., U.K., 40,608 .70/B1
Hinckley, Ill., U.S., 1,994 .266/E2
Hinckley, Maine, U.S., 125 .286/C4
Hinckley, Minn., U.S., 1,291 .298/E4
Hinckley, N.Y., U.S., reservoir .320/L4
Hinckley, Utah, U.S., 698 .350/B4
Hindelang, Ger. .86/B5
Hindes, Tex., U.S. .346/K7
Hindhead, Eng., U.K., 7,473 .70/C4
Hindley, Eng., U.K., 22,581 .66/C5
Hindley, Eng., U.K., 22,581 .68/B2
Hindman, Ky., U.S., 787 .280/H3
Hindon, Eng., U.K. .73/H2
Hindringham, Eng., U.K. .70/F1
Hinds, Miss., U.S., county, 250,800 .300/B3
Hindsboro, Ill., U.S., 361 .266/E4
Hindsville, Ark., U.S., 75 .244/B1
Hindu Kush, Afg., range .129/B1
Hindu Kush, Pak., mountains .129/D2
H-Nella, Mali, 1,029 .314/B3
Hines, Fla., U.S. .256/E2
Hines, Minn., U.S., 50 .298/C3
Hines, Oreg., U.S., 1,623 .334/G4
Hines, Wisc., U.S. .364/A2
Hinesburg, Vt., U.S., 4,340 .352/A2
Hines Creek, Alta., Can., 437 .212/A3
Hineston, La., U.S., 175 .282/D4
Hinesville, Ga., U.S., 30,392 .260/H8
Hingham, Eng., U.K., 1,995 .70/F1
Hingham, Mass., U.S., 19,882 .292/L4
Hingham, Mont., U.S., 157 .306/F1
Hino, Jap., cape .114/B4
Hinsdale, Colo., U.S., county, 790 .250/C4
Hinsdale, Ill., U.S., 17,349 .266/B6
Hinsdale, Mass., U.S., 1,872 .292/B3
Hinsdale, Mont., U.S., 225 .306/J1
Hinsdale, N.H., U.S., 4,082 .312/B6
Hinson, Fla., U.S., 750 .256/D1
Hinton, Alta., Can., 9,405 .212/B4
Hinton, Iowa, U.S., 808 .274/B2
Hinton, Ky., U.S., 100 .280/F2
Hinton, Okla., U.S., 2,175 .330/D2
Hinton, W. Va., U.S., 2,880 .360/E5
Hinwick, Eng., U.K. .70/C2
Hirakata, Jap., 403,000 .114/B3
Hirakud, India, reservoir .128/D4
Hiram, Ark., U.S. .244/D2
Hiram, Ga., U.S., 1,361 .260/B4
Hiram, Maine, U.S., 1,423 .286/B5
Hiram, Ohio, U.S., 1,242 .328/H3
Hirara, Jap. .114/Inset II
Hirnant, Wales, U.K. .64/E2
Hirosake, Jap. .114/D1
Hiroshima, Jap., 1,126,282 .114/B3
Hiroshima, Jap., prefecture .114/B3
Hirtshals, Den. .79/B1
Hisabpur, India .128/Inset II
Hiseville, Ky., U.S., 224 .280/E3
Hisle, S. Dak., U.S. .342/D4
Hispaniola, island .204/C3
Hitachi, Jap. .114/D2
Hitcham, Eng., U.K. .70/D2
Hitchcock, Nebr., U.S., county, 3,111 .308/C3
Hitchcock, Okla., U.S., 141 .330/D2
Hitchcock, S. Dak., U.S., 108 .342/G3
Hitchcock, Tex., U.S., 6,386 .346/P6
Hitchin, Eng., U.K., 32,221 .70/D3
Hitchins, Ky., U.S., 475 .280/H2
Hitchita, Okla., U.S., 113 .330/G2
Hiteman, Iowa, U.S., 60 .274/J5
Hitschmann, Kans., U.S. .276/D3
Hitterdal, Minn., U.S., 201 .298/A4
Hi Vista, Calif., U.S., 40 .246/H8
Hiwannee, Miss., U.S., 90 .300/D4
Hiwasse, Ark., U.S., 325 .244/A1
Hiwassee, N.C., U.S., lake .322/B8
Hiwassee, Va., U.S., 275 .354/B7
Hiwassee Dam, N.C., U.S. .322/B8
Hixon, Br. Col., Can., 264 .214/L4
Hixton, Wisc., U.S., 446 .364/B4
Hixville, Mass., U.S., 500 .292/K6
Hjørring, Den. .79/B1
Hkakabo Razi, Mya., mountain .125/C1
Ho, Gha. .150/C3

Hoa Binh, Viet. .123/A2
Hoagland, Ind., U.S., 550 .270/G3
Hoback Jct., Wyo., U.S., 40 .366/A2
Hoban, Tex., U.S. .346/E4
Hobart, Tas., Austl., state capital, 127,106, (179,020, metro.) .170/D4
Hobart, Ind., U.S., 25,363 .270/B1
Hobart, N.Y., U.S., 390 .320/M6
Hobart, Okla., U.S., 3,997 .330/C2
Hobart, Wash., U.S., 6,251 .358/B4, D2
Hobart Lake N.W.R., N. Dak., U.S. .326/G2
Hobbs, Ind., U.S., 150 .288/L4
Hobbs, N. Mex., U.S., 28,657 .317/G5
Hoberg, Mo., U.S., 60 .302/C4
Hobe Sound, Fla., U.S., 11,376 .256/B4, H4
Hobe Sound N.W.R., Fla., U.S. .256/B4, H4
Hobgood, N.C., U.S., 404 .322/L2
Hobkirk, Scot., U.K. .62/L8
Hoboken, Ga., U.S., 463 .260/G9
Hoboken, N.J., U.S., 38,577 .314/B2, E2
Hobson, Ky., U.S., 100 .280/E3
Hobson, Mont., U.S., 244 .306/G3
Hobsons, Austl., bay .170/Inset V
Hobucken, N.C., U.S., 225 .322/M4
Hoby, Eng., U.K. .70/C1
Hobyo, Som. .157/B2
Hochheim, Tex., U.S. .346/L6
Ho Chi Minh City, Viet., 4,989,703 .123/B4
Ho-Chunk Ind. Res., Wisc., U.S. .364/C4
Hockering, Eng., U.K. .70/G1
Hockessin, Del., U.S., 12,902 .255/B1
Hocking, Ohio, U.S., county, 28,241 .328/E7
Hocking, Ohio, U.S., river .328/F7
Hockley, Tex., U.S., 175 .346/A6
Hockley, Tex., U.S., county, 22,716 .346/F2
Hockliffe, Eng., U.K. .70/C3
Hockwold cum Wilton, Eng., U.K. .70/F2
Hoddesdon, Eng., U.K., 36,883 .70/D3
Hodgdon, Maine, U.S., 1,240 .286/E2
Hodgdon Corners, Maine, U.S., 300 .286/E2
Hodge, Calif., U.S., 100 .246/H8
Hodge, La., U.S., 492 .282/D2
Hodgeman, Kans., U.S., county, 2,085 .276/C4
Hodgenville, Ky., U.S., 2,874 .280/E3
Hodges, Ala., U.S., 261 .238/B1
Hodges, Mont., U.S. .306/M3
Hodges, S.C., U.S., 158 .340/B3
Hodgesville, W. Va., U.S., 225 .360/F2
Hodgeville, Sask., Can., 175 .227/D10
Hodgkins, Ill., U.S., 2,134 .266/B6
Hodgson, Man., Can. .215/C3
Hódmezővásárhely, Hun. .91/C2
Hodnet, Eng., U.K. .68/B4
Hoehne, Colo., U.S., 90 .250/F4
Hoeryŏng, N. Kor. .116/C1
Hof, Ger. .86/B3
Hoffman, Ill., U.S., 460 .266/D5
Hoffman, Minn., U.S., 672 .298/B5
Hoffman, N.C., U.S., 624 .322/F4
Hoffman, Okla., U.S., 148 .330/G2
Hoffman Estates, Ill., U.S., 49,495 .266/A5
Hoffmeister, N.Y., U.S., 40 .320/M4
Hofmann Forest, N.C., U.S. .322/L5
Höfn, Ice. .79/C2
Hog, Mich., U.S., island .294/D4
Hogansburg, N.Y., U.S., 450 .320/M1
Hogansville, Ga., U.S., 2,774 .260/B5
Hogeland, Mont., U.S. .306/H1
Hohenwald, Tenn., U.S., 3,754 .344/F3
Hohe Tauern, Aus., mountains .91/C3
Hohhot, China, 754,120, (1,206,290, metro.) .119/E1
Ho-Ho-Kus, N.J., U.S., 4,060 .314/B1
Hoisington, Kans., U.S., 2,975 .276/D3
Hokah, Minn., U.S., 614 .298/F7
Hoke, N.C., U.S., county, 33,646 .322/G4
Hokes Bluff, Ala., U.S., 4,149 .238/C2
Hokkaido, Jap., island .114/D1, Inset I
Hokkaido, Jap., prefecture .114/D1, Inset I
Hoktemberyan, Arm. .103/B2
Holabird, S. Dak., U.S. .342/F3
Holbæk, Den. .79/C3
Holbeach, Eng., U.K., 6,088 .68/H4
Holbeach, Eng., U.K., 6,088 .70/E1
Holbeach Drove, Eng., U.K. .70/D1
Holbeach St. Mark's, Eng., U.K. .70/E1
Holberrow Green, Eng., U.K. .68/D5
Holbrook, Eng., U.K. .70/G3
Holbrook, Ariz., U.S., 4,917 .242/E3
Holbrook, Idaho, U.S., 60 .264/E7
Holbrook, Mass., U.S., 10,785 .292/K4
Holbrook, Nebr., U.S., 225 .308/D3
Holbrook, N.Y., U.S., 27,512 .320/P8
Holcomb, Kans., U.S., 2,026 .276/B4
Holcomb, Miss., U.S., 250 .300/C2
Holcomb, Mo., U.S., 696 .302/F5
Holcombe, Wisc., U.S., 200 .364/B3
Holden, Alta., Can., 374 .212/D4
Holden, Mass., U.S., 15,621 .292/G3
Holden, Mo., U.S., 2,510 .302/C3
Holden, Utah, U.S., 400 .350/B4
Holden, Wash., U.S., 60 .358/E1
Holden, W. Va., U.S., 1,105 .360/B5
Holden Beach, N.C., U.S., 787 .322/J7
Holden Hts., Fla., U.S., 3,856 .256/C4
Holdenville, Okla., U.S., 4,732 .330/F2
Holder, Fla., U.S., 225 .256/F3
Holder, Ill., U.S., 60 .266/E3
Holderness, N.H., U.S., 1,930 .312/C4
Holdfast, Sask., Can., 190 .227/E10
Holdingford, Minn., U.S., 736 .298/C5
Holdrege, Nebr., U.S., 5,636 .308/E3
Holeb, Maine, U.S. .286/B3
Holetown, Barb. .209/A3
Holford, Eng., U.K. .73/F2
Holgate, Ohio, U.S., 1,194 .328/B3
Holguin, Cuba .204/E3
Holguin, Cuba, 236,425 .204/E3
Holhol, Dji. .156/B2
Holiday, Fla., U.S., 21,904 .256/C6, F3
Holiday City, N.J., U.S. .314/E3
Holiday City at Berkeley, N.J., U.S., 13,884 .314/E4
Holiday City South, N.J., U.S., 4,047 .314/E4
Holiday Hills, Ill., U.S., 831 .266/A5
Holiday Lakes, Tex., U.S., 1,095 .346/N6
Holkham, Eng., U.K. .70/F1
Holla Bend N.W.R., Ark., U.S. .244/D3
Holladay, Tenn., U.S., 125 .344/E3
Holladay, Utah, U.S., 14,561 .350/D2
Holland, Man., Can. .215/B4
Holland, Scot., U.K. .62/N2
Holland, Ark., U.S., 577 .244/C2
Holland, Ga., U.S., 90 .260/A3
Holland, Ind., U.S., 695 .270/B8
Holland, Iowa, U.S., 250 .274/J3
Holland, Mass., U.S., 2,407 .292/F4
Holland, Mich., U.S., 35,048 .294/C7
Holland, Minn., U.S., 215 .298/A6
Holland, Mo., U.S., 246 .302/F5
Holland, N.Y., U.S., 1,261 .320/E5
Holland, Ohio, U.S., 1,306 .328/C2
Holland, Tex., U.S., 1,102 .346/L5

Holland, Vt., U.S., 588 .352/C1
Hollandale, Minn., U.S., 292 .298/D7
Hollandale, Miss., U.S., 3,437 .300/B2
Hollandale, Wisc., U.S., 283 .364/D6
Holland-on-Sea, Eng., U.K. .70/E3
Holland Park, Qnsld., Austl. .170/Inset III
Holland Patent, N.Y., U.S., 461 .320/L4
Hollandsburg, Ind., U.S., 125 .270/B5
Hollansburg, Ohio, U.S., 214 .328/A5
Hollenberg, Kans., U.S. .276/F2
Hollene, N. Mex., U.S. .317/G3
Holley, Fla., U.S., 650 .256/B1
Holley, N.Y., U.S., 1,802 .320/F4
Holliday, Kans., U.S. .276/H1
Holliday, Mo., U.S., 129 .302/D2
Holliday, Tex., U.S., 1,632 .346/K2
Hollidaysburg, Penn., U.S., 5,368 .336/E5
Hollinger, Nebr., U.S. .308/E3
Hollins, Va., U.S., 14,309 .354/D6
Hollis, Ark., U.S., 70 .244/B3
Hollis, Kans., U.S. .276/E2
Hollis, N.H., U.S., 7,015 .312/C6
Hollis, Okla., U.S., 2,264 .330/C3
Hollis Crossroads, Ala., U.S., 225 .238/D2
Hollister, Calif., U.S., 34,413 .246/D4
Hollister, Ida., U.S., 237 .264/C7
Hollister, Mo., U.S., 3,867 .302/C5
Hollister, N.C., U.S., 600 .322/K2
Hollister, Okla., U.S., 60 .330/D3
Hollister, Wisc., U.S. .364/E3
Holliston, Mass., U.S., 13,801 .292/J4
Holloman A.F.B., N. Mex., U.S. .317/D5
Holloway, Minn., U.S., 112 .298/B5
Holloway, Ohio, U.S., 345 .328/H5
Hollowayville, W. Va., U.S., 90 .266/D2
Hollow Creek, Ky., U.S., 815 .280/B2
Hollow Rock, Tenn., U.S., 963 .344/E2
Holly, Colo., U.S., 1,048 .250/G3
Holly, Mich., U.S., 6,135 .294/F7
Holly, Wash., U.S., 80 .358/C2
Holly Beach, La., U.S., 60 .282/C7
Holly Bluff, Miss., U.S., 200 .300/B3
Holly Grove, Ark., U.S., 722 .244/D3
Holly Hill, Fla., U.S., 12,119 .256/G2
Holly Hill, S.C., U.S., 1,281 .340/D3
Hollyhill, Ky., U.S., 80 .280/F4
Holly Park, N.J., U.S., 2,200 .314/E4
Holly Pond, Ala., U.S., 645 .238/C1
Holly Ridge, N.C., U.S., 831 .322/K6
Holly Sprs., Ark., U.S., 70 .244/C4
Holly Sprs., Ga., U.S., 3,195 .260/C3
Holly Sprs., Miss., U.S., 7,957 .300/C1
Holly Sprs., N.C., U.S., 9,192 .322/H3
Holly Sprs. Natl. For., Miss., U.S. .300/C1
Hollyvilla, Ky., U.S., 481 .280/E2
Hollywood, Ala., U.S., 950 .238/D1
Hollywood, Ark., U.S., 80 .244/B3
Hollywood, Fla., U.S., 139,357 .256/B6, H5
Hollywood, Ga., U.S., 400 .260/E2
Hollywood, Md., U.S., 500 .288/H6
Hollywood, Miss., U.S., 150 .300/B1
Hollywood Park, Tex., U.S., 3,946 .340/D4
Hollywood Park, Tex., U.S., 2,983 .346/A2
Holman, N.W. Terr., Can., 398 .220/E2
Holman, N. Mex., U.S., 175 .317/E1
Holmdel, N.J., U.S., 15,781 .314/E3
Holme, Eng., U.K. .70/D2
Holmen, Wisc., U.S., 6,200 .364/B5
Holme next the Sea, Eng., U.K. .70/F1
Holmes, Fla., U.S., county, 18,564 .256/C1
Holmes, Miss., U.S., county, 21,609 .300/B2
Holmes, Ohio, U.S., county, 38,943 .328/G4
Holmes Beach, Fla., U.S., 4,966 .256/F4
Holmes Chapel, Eng., U.K., 5,465 .68/C3
Holmes City, Minn., U.S., 100 .298/B5
Holmesville, Nebr., U.S., 90 .308/H3
Holmesville, Ohio, U.S., 386 .328/G4
Holme upon Spalding Moor, Eng., U.K., 2,629 .66/G5
Holme upon Spalding Moor, Eng., U.K., 2,629 .68/F2
Holmfirth, (Holmfirth/Honley), Eng., U.K., 21,979 .66/D5
Holmfirth, (Holmfirth/Honley), Eng., U.K., 21,979 .68/D2
Holmrook, Eng., U.K. .66/B4
Holmwood, La., U.S., 90 .282/C6
Holon, Isr., 162,900 .135/B1
Holopaw, Fla., U.S., 425 .256/G3
Holroyd, N.S.W., Austl. .170/Inset IV
Holstebro, Den. .79/B2
Holstein, Iowa, U.S., 1,470 .274/C3
Holstein, Nebr., U.S., 229 .308/E3
Holston, Tenn., U.S., river .344/R2
Holsworthy, Eng., U.K., 1,892 .73/E3
Holt, Wales, U.K., 2,972 .64/F1
Holt, Ala., U.S., 4,103 .238/B2
Holt, Fla., U.S., 125 .256/B1
Holt, Mich., U.S., 11,315 .294/E7
Holt, Minn., U.S., 89 .298/A2
Holt, Mo., U.S., 405 .302/B2
Holt, Mo., U.S., county, 5,351 .302/A1
Holt, Nebr., U.S., county, 11,551 .308/F1
Holter Dam, Mont., U.S. .306/D3
Holt Heath, Eng., U.K. .68/C5
Holton, Nfld., Can. .218/C2
Holton, Ind., U.S., 407 .270/F6
Holton, Kans., U.S., 3,353 .276/G2
Holton, Mich., U.S., 600 .294/C6
Holts Summit, Mo., U.S., 2,935 .302/D3
Holtoltville, Calif., U.S., 5,612 .246/K10
Holtwood, Penn., U.S., 325 .336/J6
Holualoa, Hawaii, U.S., 6,107 .262/G5
Holy, Eng., U.K., island .66/C1
Holy, Scot., U.K., island .62/F7
Holy, Wales, U.K., island .64/B1
Holybourne, Eng., U.K. .70/C4
Holy Cross, Alaska, U.S., 227 .240/D2
Holy Cross, Iowa, U.S., 339 .274/M2
Holyhead, Wales, U.K. .64/B1
Holyhead, Wales, U.K., 11,796 .64/B1
Holyhead, Wales, U.K., bay .64/B1
Holyoke, Colo., U.S., 2,261 .250/H1
Holyoke, Mass., U.S., 39,838 .292/D4
Holyoke, Minn., U.S., 100 .298/E4
Holyrood, Nfld., Can., 1,906 .218/E5
Holyrood, Kans., U.S., 464 .276/D3
Holywell, Wales, U.K., 7,531 .64/E1
Holywood, N. Ire., U.K. .65/F2
Holywood, N. Ire., U.K., 9,252 .65/F2
Homathko, Br. Col., Can., river .214/K5
Hombori Tondo, Mali, mountain .150/C2
Home, Kans., U.S., 175 .276/F2
Home, Wash., U.S., 400 .358/B4
Homecroft, Ind., U.S., 751 .270/D5
Homedale, Ida., U.S., 2,528 .264/A6
Home Gardens, Calif., U.S., 9,461 .246/F10
Homeland, Fla., U.S., 325 .256/G4
Homeland, Ga., U.S., 765 .260/C1
Homeland Park, S.C., U.S., 6,337 .340/B2
Home of FDR N.H.S., N.Y., U.S. .320/N7
Homer, Alaska, U.S., 3,946 .240/E3
Homer, Ga., U.S., 950 .260/D3

Homer, Ill., U.S., 1,200 .266/F3
Homer, La., U.S., 3,788 .282/C1
Homer, Mich., U.S., 1,851 .294/E7
Homer, Nebr., U.S., 590 .308/H1
Homer, N.Y., U.S., 3,368 .320/J5
Homer City, Penn., U.S., 1,844 .336/C4
Homerville, Ga., U.S., 2,803 .260/F9
Homer Youngs Mont., U.S., peak .306/C4
Homestead, Fla., U.S., 31,909 .256/A7, H6
Homestead, Mo., U.S., 181 .302/A4
Homestead, Mont., U.S. .306/M1
Homestead, Okla., U.S., 80 .330/D1
Homestead, Oreg., U.S. .334/K3
Homestead, Penn., U.S., 3,569 .336/E7
Homestead N.M., Kans., U.S. .276/F1
Homestead N.M., Nebr., U.S. .308/H3
Homestead Valley, (Tamalpais-Homestead Valley), Calif., U.S., 10,691 .246/H1
Homestown, Mo., U.S., 181 .302/A4
Hometown, Ill., U.S., 4,467 .266/B6
Hometown, W. Va., U.S., 750 .360/C3
Homeville, Va., U.S., 80 .354/J7
Homewood, Ala., U.S., 25,043 .238/C2, E1
Homewood, Ill., U.S., 19,543 .266/C6
Homewood, Kans., U.S., 100 .276/G3
Homewood, Pa., U.S., 147 .336/A4
Homington, Eng., U.K. .73/J2
Hominy, Okla., U.S., 2,584 .330/F1
Homo, Van, bay .173/B2
Homochitto, Miss., U.S., river .300/A4
Homochitto Natl. For., Miss., U.S. .300/A4
Homosassa, Fla., U.S., bay .256/F3
Homosassa Sprs., Fla., U.S., 12,458 .256/F3
Homyel', Bela., 503,700 .82/D4
Homyel', Bela., oblast .82/D4
Hon, Ark., U.S., 150 .244/A3
Honaker, Va., U.S., 945 .354/D2
Honalo, Hawaii, U.S., 1,987 .262/G6
Honaunau, (Honaunau-Napoopoo), Hawaii, U.S., 2,414 .262/G6
Honaunau Forest Reserve, Hawaii, U.S. .201/B1
Hondo, Bel., river .201/B1
Hondo, Alta., Can. .212/C3
Hondo, N. Mex., U.S. .317/E4
Hondo, Tex., U.S., 7,897 .346/J6
Honduras, nation .190
Honduras, Guat., gulf .201/C3
Honduras, Hond., gulf .202/A1
Honea Path, S.C., U.S., 3,504 .340/B2
Honeoye, N.Y., U.S., 800 .320/F5
Honeoye Falls, N.Y., U.S., 2,595 .320/F5
Honesdale, Penn., U.S., 4,874 .336/L2
Honey, Calif., U.S., lake .246/E2
Honey Brook, Penn., U.S., 1,287 .336/K5
Honeydew, Calif., U.S., 60 .246/A2
Honey Grove, Tex., U.S., 1,746 .346/N2
Honey Hill, Eng., U.K. .70/G4
Honey Hill, S.C., U.S., 90 .340/E3
Honeyville, Fla., U.S., 60 .256/C1
Honeyville, Utah, U.S., 1,214 .350/B2
Honga, Md., U.S., 225 .288/K6
Hon Gai, Viet., 127,484 .123/B2
Hong Kong, China, special administrative region, 6,708,389 .113
Hong Kong, H.K., China, island .117/B2
Hongze, China, lake .119/E2
Honiara, Sol. Is., capital, 49,107, (60,719, metro.) .173/A1
Honingham, Eng., U.K. .70/G1
Honington, Eng., U.K. .70/C1
Honiton, Eng., U.K., 7,859 .73/F3
Honobia, Okla., U.S., 50 .330/H3
Honokaa, Hawaii, U.S., 2,233 .262/H4
Honokahua, Hawaii, U.S. .262/B3
Honokai Hale, Hawaii, U.S. .262/H2
Honokohau, Hawaii, U.S. .262/A3
Honokowai, (Napili-Honokowai), Hawaii, U.S., 6,788 .262/B3
Honolua, Hawaii, U.S., bay .262/B3
Honolulu, Hawaii, U.S., county, 876,156 .262/C5, D2, K1
Honolulu, Hawaii, U.S., state capital, 371,657, (876,156, metro.) .262/C5, F2, J2
Honolulu Intl. Airport, Hawaii, U.S. .262/F2
Honolununi, Hawaii, U.S., bay .262/C3
Honolulu Watershed Forest Reserve, Hawaii, U.S. .262/J1
Honomu, Hawaii, U.S., 541 .262/J4
Honor, Mich., U.S., 299 .294/C5
Honoraville, Ala., U.S., 90 .238/C2
Honorine, Fr. .88/Inset I
Honouliuli, Hawaii, U.S. .262/D1, J2
Honshu, Jap., island .114/C2
Honuapo, Hawaii, U.S. .262/H7
Honuaula Forest Reserve, Hawaii, U.S. .262/G5
Hood, Oreg., U.S., mountain .334/E2
Hood, Tex., U.S., county, 41,100 .346/L3
Hood, Wash., U.S. .358/D4
Hood, Wash., U.S., canal .358/C4
Hood River, Oreg., U.S., 5,831 .334/E2
Hood River, Oreg., U.S., county, 20,411 .334/E2
Hoodsport, Wash., U.S., 200 .358/B2
Hoogeveen, Neth. .84/D2
Hook, Eng., U.K., 6,471 .70/C4
Hookdale, Ill., U.S., 40 .266/D5
Hookena, Hawaii, U.S. .262/G6
Hooker, Nebr., U.S., county, 783 .308/C2
Hooker, Okla., U.S., 1,788 .330/A1, C4
Hookerton, N.C., U.S., 467 .322/K4
Hookgate, Eng., U.K. .68/C4
Hook Norton, Eng., U.K., 1,913 .68/E6
Hook Norton, Eng., U.K., 1,913 .70/B2
Hooks, Tex., U.S., 2,973 .346/P2
Hooksett, N.H., U.S., 11,721 .312/D5
Hookstown, Penn., U.S., 152 .336/A4
Hoolehua, Hawaii, U.S. .262/A3
Hoomaluhia Botanical Gardens, Hawaii, U.S. .262/G1
Hoonah, Alaska, U.S., 860 .240/H3
Hoopa, Calif., U.S., 300 .246/B1
Hoopa Valley Ind. Res., Calif., U.S. .246/B1
Hooper, Colo., U.S. .250/E4
Hooper, Nebr., U.S., 827 .308/H2
Hooper, Utah, U.S., 3,926 .350/B2
Hooper, Wash., U.S. .358/G3
Hooper Bay, Alaska, U.S., 1,014 .240/B2
Hoopeston, Ill., U.S., 5,965 .266/F3
Hoople, N. Dak., U.S., 292 .326/H1
Hooppole, Ill., U.S., 162 .266/D2
Hoorn, Neth. .84/C2
Hoosick Falls, N.Y., U.S., 3,436 .320/Q5
Hoosier Natl. For., Ind., U.S. .270/C7, D6
Hoot Owl, Okla., U.S. .330/G1
Hoover, Ala., U.S., 62,742 .238/C2, E1
Hoover, Ariz., U.S., dam .242/A1
Hoover, S. Dak., U.S. .342/B2
Hooversön Hts., W. Va., U.S., 2,909 .360/K5
Hooversville, Penn., U.S., 779 .336/E5
Hop, Conn., U.S., river .253/F3
Hopatcong, N.J., U.S., 15,888 .314/D2
Hop Bottom, Penn., U.S., 335 .336/K2
Hope, Br. Col., Can., 6,184 .214/M6
Hope, Eng., U.K. .66/E6
Hope, Scot., U.K., lake .62/G3

Hope, (Hope/Caergrwrle), Wales, U.K., 4,554 . . . .64/E1
Hope, Ariz., U.S. 242/B4
Hope, Ark., U.S., 10,616 . . . . .244/B4
Hope, Ida., U.S., 79 .264/A1
Hope, Ind., U.S., 2,140 . . . . .270/E6
Hope, Kans., U.S., 372 . . . . .276/E3
Hope, Maine, U.S., 1,310 . . . . .286/C4
Hope, Mich., U.S., 200 . . . . .294/E6
Hope, Minn., U.S., 125 . . . . .298/D7
Hope, N.J., U.S., 1,891 . . . . .314/D2
Hope, N. Mex., U.S., 107 . . . . .317/F5
Hope, N. Dak., U.S., 303 . . . . .326/H2
Hope, R.I., U.S., 1,900 . . . . .339/C3
Hope, Tex., U.S., 60 .346/M6
Hope Bay, Jam. 206/C2
Hope Bowdler, Eng., U.K. 68/B4
Hopedale, Nfld., Can., 559 . . . . .218/A1, E3
Hopedale, Ill., U.S., 929 . . . . .266/D3
Hopedale, Mass., U.S., 5,907 . . . . .292/H4
Hopedale, Ohio, U.S., 984 . . . . .328/J5
Hopeful, Ga., U.S., 40 . . . . .260/C9
Hopeman, Scot., U.K., 1,624 . . . . .62/K3
Hope Mills, N.C., U.S., 11,237 . . . . .322/H5
Hopeton, Okla., U.S., 40 . . . . .330/D1
Hope-under-Dinmore, Eng., U.K. 68/B5
Hope Valley, Alta., Can. 212/E5
Hope Valley, R.I., U.S., 1,649 . . . . .339/B5
Hopewell, Ill., U.S., 396 . . . . .266/D3
Hopewell, Kans., U.S. 276/D4
Hopewell, Md., U.S., 550 . . . . .288/L7
Hopewell, Miss., U.S., 150 . . . . .300/B4
Hopewell, (borough, Mercer County),
  N.J., U.S., 2,035 .314/D3
Hopewell, Penn., U.S., 222 . . . . .336/E5
Hopewell, Tenn., U.S., 1,815 . . . . .344/M4
Hopewell, Tex., U.S. 346/N4
Hopewell, Va., U.S., 22,354 . . . . .354/J6
Hopewell Cape, N.B., Can. 217/E3
Hopewell Culture Natl. Hist. Park, Ohio, U.S. . .328/E7
Hopewell Furnace N.H.S., Penn., U.S. 337/K5
Hopewell Jct., N.Y., U.S., 2,610 . . . . .320/P7
Hopi Ind. Res., Ariz., U.S. 242/E2
Hopkins, Ky., U.S., county, 46,519 . . . . .280/C3
Hopkins, Mich., U.S., 592 . . . . .294/D7
Hopkins, Minn., U.S., 17,145 . . . . .298/E6
Hopkins, Mo., U.S., 579 . . . . .302/B1
Hopkins, S.C., U.S., 600 . . . . .340/A3, D3
Hopkins, Tex., U.S., county, 31,960 . . . . .346/N2
Hopkins Park, Ill., U.S., 711 . . . . .266/F2
Hopkinton, Iowa, U.S., 681 . . . . .274/M3
Hopkinton, Mass., U.S., 13,346 . . . . .292/H4
Hopkinton, N.H., U.S., 5,399 . . . . .312/C5
Hopkinton, R.I., U.S., 7,836 . . . . .339/B5
Hopland, Calif., U.S., 300 . . . . .246/B4
Hopper, Ark., U.S., 40 . . . . .244/B3
Hopton, Eng., U.K. .70/F2
Hopwood, Penn., U.S., 2,006 . . . . .336/B6
Hoquiam, Wash., U.S., 9,097 . . . . .358/B3
Horace, Kans., U.S., 143 . . . . .276/A3
Horace, N. Dak., U.S., 915 . . . . .326/J3
Horam, Eng., U.K., 1,962 . . . . .70/E5
Horatio, Ark., U.S., 997 . . . . .244/A4
Horatio, S.C., U.S., 100 . . . . .340/D2
Horbling, Eng., U.K. 70/D1
Hord, Ill., U.S., 90 . . . . .266/E5
Hordaland, Nor., province 80/A3
Hordville, Nebr., U.S., 150 . . . . .308/G2
Horgèn, Switz. 90/C1
Horham, Eng., U.K. .70/G2
Horicon, Wisc., U.S., 3,775 . . . . .364/E5
Horicon N.W.R., Wisc., U.S. 364/E4
Horizon City, Tex., U.S., 5,253 . . . . .346/B4
Horley, (Oxfordshire), Eng., U.K., 19,267 . . . . .70/B2
Horley, (Surrey), Eng., U.K. 70/D4
Horley, Eng., U.K., 19,267 . . . . .68/E5
Horlivka, Ukr. 102/D2
Hormigueros, P.R. 206/A2
Hormozgan, Iran, province 130/D4
Hormuz, Iran, strait .130/D4
Hormuz, Oman, strait 137/C1
Hormuz, U.A.E., strait 136/D1
Horn, Chile, cape 190/C8
Horn, Ice., cape 79/A1
Horn, Ariz., U.S., 150 . . . . .242/B5
Horn, Miss., U.S., island 300/D5
Hornad, Slvk., river .92/C2
Hornavan, Swe. 80/C1
Hornavan, Swe., lake 80/C2
Hornbeak, Tenn., U.S., 435 . . . . .344/C2
Hornbeck, La., U.S., 435 . . . . .282/C4
Hornbrook, Calif., U.S., 286 . . . . .246/C1
Hornby, Eng., U.K. .66/C4
Horncastle, Eng., U.K., 4,994 . . . . .68/G3
Horndean, Eng., U.K. 70/B5
Hornell, N.Y., U.S., 9,019 . . . . .320/F6
Hornepayne, Ont., Can., 1,312 . . . . .222/D3
Hornersville, Mo., U.S., 686 . . . . .302/F5
Horn Hill, Ala., U.S., 150 . . . . .238/C4
Hornick, Iowa, U.S., 253 . . . . .274/B3
Horningtoft, Eng., U.K. 70/F1
Horn Lake, Miss., U.S., 14,099 . . . . .300/B1
Horns, Ga., U.S., 200 . . . . .260/C6
Hornsby, N.S.W., Austl. . . . . .170/Inset IV
Hornsby, Tenn., U.S., 306 . . . . .344/D4
Hornsea, Eng., U.K., 7,573 . . . . .66/H5
Hornsea, Eng., U.K., 7,573 . . . . .68/G2
Horrel Hill, S.C., U.S. 340/A3, D3
Horry, S.C., U.S., county, 196,629 . . . . .340/E3
Horsburgh, Mald., atoll 127/A2
Horse, Alta., Can., river 212/D3
Horse, Colo., U.S., creek 250/G3
Horse Branch, Ky., U.S., 250 . . . . .280/D3
Horse Cave, Ky., U.S., 2,252 . . . . .280/E3
Horse Creek, Calif., U.S. 246/C1
Horse Creek, Wyo., U.S. 366/J3
Horseheads, N.Y., U.S., 6,452 . . . . .320/H6
Horsehouse, Eng., U.K. 66/E4
Horsens, Den., 48,837 . . . . .79/B3
Horse Pasture, Va., U.S., 2,255 . . . . .354/D7
Horseshoe, Ariz., U.S., reservoir 242/D4
Horseshoe, Mo., U.S., lake 302/J3
Horseshoe Bay, Tex., U.S., 3,337 . . . . .346/C2
Horseshoe Beach, Fla., U.S., 206 . . . . .256/E2
Horseshoe Bend, Ark., U.S., 2,278 . . . . .244/D1
Horseshoe Bend, Ida., U.S., 770 . . . . .264/A6
Horseshoe Bend Natl. Mil. Park, Ala., U.S. 238/E3
Horseshoe Lake, Ark., U.S., 321 . . . . .244/E3
Horsford, Eng., U.K., 2,255 . . . . .70/G1
Horsforth, Eng., U.K., 18,593 . . . . .66/E5
Horsforth, Eng., U.K., 18,593 . . . . .68/F2
Horsham, Eng., U.K., 42,552 . . . . .70/D4
Horsham, Penn., U.S., 14,779 . . . . .336/M6
Horsington, Eng., U.K. 68/G3
Horsley, Eng., U.K. .66/E3
Horsted Keynes, Eng., U.K. 70/D4
Horta, Port. . . . . .93/Inset II
Hortense, Ga., U.S., 225 . . . . .260/H9
Horton, N.W. Terr., Can., river 220/D3
Horton, Eng., U.K. .70/C2
Horton, Kans., U.S., 1,967 . . . . .276/G2
Horton, Mo., U.S., 40 . . . . .302/B4
Horton, Mont., U.S. .306/K3

Horton, Wyo., U.S. .366/D1
Hortonia, Vt., U.S., 125 . . . . .352/A3
Horton in Ribblesdale, Eng., U.K. 66/D4
Hortonville, Mass., U.S., 850 . . . . .292/K5
Hortonville, Wisc., U.S., 2,357 . . . . .364/E4
Horwich, Eng., U.K., 18,017 . . . . .66/C5
Horwich, Eng., U.K., 18,017 . . . . .68/B2
Hoschton, Ga., U.S., 1,070 . . . . .260/D3
Hosford, Fla., U.S., 450 . . . . .256/D1
Hoskins, Nebr., U.S., 283 . . . . .308/G1
Hoskinston, Ky., U.S., 90 . . . . .280/G4
Hosmer, S. Dak., U.S., 287 . . . . .342/F2
Hospah, N. Mex., U.S. 317/C2
Hospers, Iowa, U.S., 672 . . . . .274/C1
Hosston, La., U.S., 387 . . . . .282/B1
Hoste, Chile, island 190/C8
Hotan, China 119/A2
Hotchkiss, Alta., Can. 212/B2
Hotchkiss, Colo., U.S., 968 . . . . .250/E3
Hotchkissville, Conn., U.S., 1,200 . . . . .253/C3
Hot Coffee, Miss., U.S., 150 . . . . .300/C4
Hotevilla, Ariz., U.S., 767 . . . . .242/E2
Hotham, Eng., U.K. .66/G5
Hot Spr., Ark., U.S., county, 30,353 . . . . .244/C3
Hot Spr., Ida., U.S., 60 . . . . .264/B7
Hot Sprs., Ark., U.S., 35,750 . . . . .244/B3
Hot Sprs., Mont., U.S., 531 . . . . .306/B2
Hot Sprs., N.C., U.S., 645 . . . . .322/D7
Hot Sprs., S. Dak., U.S., 4,129 . . . . .342/A4
Hot Sprs., Va., U.S., 300 . . . . .354/D5
Hot Sprs., Wyo., U.S., county, 4,882 . . . . .366/B2
Hot Sprs. Natl. Park, Ark., U.S. 244/B3
Hot Sprs. Vil., Ark., U.S., 8,397 . . . . .244/C3
Hot Sulphur Sprs., Colo., U.S., 521 . . . . .250/F1
Hottah, N.W. Terr., Can., lake 220/E3
Hot Wells, Tex., U.S. 346/C4
Houayxay, Laos 124/A1
Houbie, Scot., U.K. .62/Q1
Houck, Ariz., U.S., 1,087 . . . . .242/F2
Hough, Okla., U.S. .330/C4
Houghton, Iowa, U.S., 130 . . . . .274/L6
Houghton, Maine, U.S. 286/E4
Houghton, Mich., U.S., 7,010 . . . . .294/A2
Houghton, Mich., U.S., county, 36,016 . . . . . . .294/A3
Houghton, Mich., U.S., lake 294/E5
Houghton, N.Y., U.S., 1,748 . . . . .320/E6
Houghton, S. Dak., U.S., 60 . . . . .342/G2
Houghton Lake, Mich., U.S., 3,749 . . . . .294/E5
Houlton, Maine, U.S., 6,476 . . . . .286/E2
Houma, La., U.S., 32,393, (194,477, metro.) . . .282/H7
Houmt Souk, Tun. 146/C3
Hounslow, Eng., U.K., 204,397 . . . . .70/D4
Hounslow, Eng., U.K., unitary authority, 212,344 .70/D4
Hourn, Scot., U.K., lake 62/H3
Housatonic, Conn., Mass., U.S., river 292/A4, A5
Housatonic, Conn., U.S., river 253/B3
Housatonic, Mass., U.S., 1,335 . . . . .292/A3
Housatonic St. For., Conn., U.S. 253/B2
House, N. Mex., U.S., 72 . . . . .317/G3
Houston, Br. Col., Can., 3,577 . . . . .214/J4
Houston, Ala., U.S., county, 88,787 . . . . .238/D4
Houston, Alaska, U.S., 1,202 . . . . .240/F2
Houston, Ark., U.S., 159 . . . . .244/C2
Houston, Del., U.S., 430 . . . . .255/B5
Houston, Fla., U.S., 125 . . . . .256/F1
Houston, Ga., U.S., county, 110,765 . . . . .260/D7
Houston, Minn., U.S., 1,020 . . . . .298/F7
Houston, Minn., U.S., county, 19,718 . . . . .298/F7
Houston, Miss., U.S., 4,079 . . . . .300/D2
Houston, Mo., U.S., 1,992 . . . . .302/E4
Houston, Penn., U.S., 1,314 . . . . .336/A5
Houston, Tenn., U.S., county, 8,088 . . . . .344/F2
Houston, Tex., U.S., 1,953,631,
  (4,669,571, metro.) 346/B6, N6
Houston, Tex., U.S., county, 23,185 . . . . .346/N4
Houston, Tex., U.S., lake 346/B6
Houston Acres, Ky., U.S., 491 . . . . .280/B2
Houstonia, Mo., U.S., 275 . . . . .302/C3
Houston Lake, Mo., U.S., 284 . . . . .302/H5
Houtzdale, Penn., U.S., 941 . . . . .336/E4
Hovd, Mong., river .118/B2
Hove, Eng., U.K. 60/C4
Hove, Eng., U.K., 67,602 . . . . .70/D5
Hove Mobile Park, N. Dak., U.S. 326/G1
Hoven, S. Dak., U.S., 511 . . . . .342/F2
Hovenweep N.M., Colo., U.S. 250/B4
Hoverla, Ukr., mountain 102/A2
Hovland, Minn., U.S. 298/F2
Hövsgöl, Mong., lake 118/C1
Howard, N.B., Can. .217/D2
Howard, Ark., U.S., county, 14,300 . . . . .244/A3
Howard, Colo., U.S., 80 . . . . .250/E3
Howard, Ga., U.S., 60 . . . . .260/C6
Howard, Ind., U.S., county, 84,964 . . . . .270/E4
Howard, Iowa, U.S., county, 9,932 . . . . .274/K1
Howard, Md., U.S., county, 247,842 . . . . .288/G2
Howard, Miss., U.S. 300/B4
Howard, Mo., U.S., county, 10,212 . . . . .302/D2
Howard, Nebr., U.S., county, 6,567 . . . . .308/F2
Howard, Penn., U.S., 699 . . . . .336/F3
Howard, S. Dak., U.S., 1,071 . . . . .342/H3
Howard, Tex., U.S., county, 33,627 . . . . .346/G3
Howard, Wisc., U.S., 13,546 . . . . .364/E4
Howard City, Mich., U.S., 1,585 . . . . .294/D6
Howardian, Eng., U.K., hills 66/F4
Howard Lake, Minn., U.S., 1,853 . . . . .298/C5
Howards Grove, Wisc., U.S., 2,792 . . . . .364/F5
Howardstown, Ky., U.S. 280/E3
Howardsville, N.J., U.S. 314/E4
Howardville, Mo., U.S., 342 . . . . .302/G5
Howardwick, Tex., U.S., 437 . . . . .346/G9
Howden, Eng., U.K., 3,673 . . . . .66/G5
Howden, Eng., U.K., 3,673 . . . . .68/F2
Howe, Ida., U.S., 70 . . . . .264/E6
Howe, Ind., U.S., 850 . . . . .270/F1
Howe, Nebr., U.S., 50 . . . . .308/J3
Howe, Okla., U.S., 697 . . . . .330/H3
Howe, Tex., U.S., 2,478 . . . . .346/M2
Howe Bay, P.E.I., Can. 224/C2
Howe Brook, Maine, U.S. 286/D2
Howe Green, Eng., U.K. 70/F3
Howell, Ark., U.S. 244/C3
Howell, Ga., U.S., 40 . . . . .260/E1
Howell, Kans., U.S., 40 . . . . .276/B4
Howell, Mich., U.S., 9,232 . . . . .294/F7
Howell, Mo., U.S., county, 37,238 . . . . .302/E5
Howell, Tenn., U.S., 175 . . . . .344/H4
Howell, Utah, U.S., 221 . . . . .350/B2
Howells, Nebr., U.S., 632 . . . . .308/G2
Howes, S. Dak., U.S. 342/C3
Howes Mill, Mo., U.S. 302/E4
Howesville, Ind., U.S., 80 . . . . .270/B6
Howey, Wales, U.K. .64/C3
Howey-in-the-Hills, Fla., U.S., 956 . . . . .256/C3
Howick, Miss., U.S., 100 . . . . .300/C5
Howland, U.S., island 161
Howland, Maine, U.S., 1,362 . . . . .286/D3
Howley, Nfld., Can., 271 . . . . .218/C4
Hoxeyville, Mich., U.S., 40 . . . . .294/D5
Hoxie, Ark., U.S., 2,817 . . . . .244/E1
Hoxie, Kans., U.S., 1,244 . . . . .276/B2

Hoxne, Eng., U.K. 70/G2
Hoy, Scot., U.K., island . . . . .60/Inset I
Hoy, Scot., U.K., island 62/L2
Hoylake, (Hoylake/W. Kirby), Eng., U.K., 25,554 .66/B6
Hoyleton, Ill., U.S., 520 . . . . .266/D5
Hoyt, N.B., Can. 217/C3
Hoyt, Colo., U.S. 250/F1
Hoyt, Kans., U.S., 571 . . . . .276/G2
Hoyt, Mont., U.S. 306/M3
Hoyt, Okla., U.S., 70 . . . . .330/G2
Hoyt Lakes, Minn., U.S., 2,082 . . . . .298/E3
Hoytville, Ohio, U.S., 296 . . . . .328/C3
Hradec Králové, Czh. Rep., 100,000 . . . . .92/B2
Hrazdan, Arm. 103/B2
Hrazdan, Arm., river 103/B2
Hrodna, Bela., 308,900 . . . . .82/A3
Hrodna, Bela., oblast 82/B3
Hron, Slvk., river 92/B2
Hsinchu, Tai. 117/B1
Hsinchuang, Tai. 117/B1
Hsintien, Tai. 117/B1
Hsinying, Tai. 117/B2
Huacho, Peru 185/B3
Huachuca City, Ariz., U.S., 1,751 . . . . .242/E6
Hua Hin, Thai. 125/B3
Huai, China, river 119/E2
Huainan, China, 1,029,220, (1,519,420, metro.) .119/E2
Huajuapan de León, Mex., 43,073,
  (53,219, metro.) .200/E4
Hualalai, Hawaii, U.S., mountain 262/G5
Hualapai, Ariz., U.S., peak 242/B2
Hualapai Ind. Res., Ariz., U.S. 242/B2
Huallága, Peru, river 185/B2
Huambo, Ang., (400,000, metro.) 159/C4
Huambo, Ang., province 159/C4
Huancavelica, Peru .185/B3
Huancavelica, Peru, department 185/B3
Huancayo, Peru 185/B3
Huang, (Yellow), China, river 119/D2, E2
Huánuco, Peru 185/B2
Huánuco, Peru, department 185/B2
Huapí, Nicar., mountains 202/B2
Huaraz, Peru, 55,349 . . . . .185/B2
Huascarán, Peru, mountain 185/B2
Hub, Tex., U.S. 346/E10, I1
Hubbard, Iowa, U.S., 885 . . . . .274/H3
Hubbard, Mich., U.S., lake 294/F5
Hubbard, Minn., U.S., 200 . . . . .298/B4
Hubbard, Minn., U.S., county, 18,376 . . . . .298/C3
Hubbard, Nebr., U.S., 234 . . . . .308/H1
Hubbard, Ohio, U.S., 8,284 . . . . .328/J3
Hubbard, Oreg., U.S., 2,483 . . . . .334/D2
Hubbard, Tex., U.S., 1,586 . . . . .346/M4
Hubbard Lake, Mich., U.S., 993 . . . . .294/F5
Hubbards, N.S., Can. 221/D3
Hubbardston, Mass., U.S., 3,909 . . . . .292/G3
Hubbardston, Mich., U.S., 394 . . . . .294/E6
Hubbardton, Vt., U.S., 752 . . . . .352/A3
Hubbell, Mich., U.S., 1,105 . . . . .294/A2
Hubbell, Nebr., U.S., 73 . . . . .308/G3
Hubbell Trading Post N.H.S., Ariz., U.S. 242/F2
Hub City, S. Dak., U.S., 40 . . . . .342/J5
Hubei, China, province 119/E2
Huber Hts., Ohio, U.S., 38,212 . . . . . . .328/B6, J10
Huber Ridge, Ohio, U.S., 4,883 . . . . . . .328/E5, E9
Hubley, N.S., Can. 221/D3
Hubli, India 128/C5
Huby, Eng., U.K. 66/E5
Hucknall, Eng., U.K., 29,160 . . . . .68/C2
Hucknall, Eng., U.K., 29,160 . . . . .70/B1
Huddersfield, Eng., U.K. 66/C5
Huddersfield, Eng., U.K., 143,726 . . . . .66/E5
Huddersfield, Eng., U.K., 143,726 . . . . .68/F2
Huddy, Ky., U.S., 900 . . . . .280/H3
Hudiksvall, Swe. 80/C2
Hudson, Nun., Can., bay 220/L4
Hudson, Nun., Can., strait 220/O4
Hudson, Ont., Can., bay 222/D1
Hudson, Que., Can., bay 225/A2
Hudson, Colo., U.S., 1,565 . . . . .250/F1
Hudson, Fla., U.S., 12,765 . . . . .256/F3
Hudson, Ill., U.S., 1,510 . . . . .266/E3
Hudson, Ind., U.S., 596 . . . . .270/F1
Hudson, Iowa, U.S., 2,117 . . . . .274/K3
Hudson, Kans., U.S., 133 . . . . .276/D3
Hudson, Ky., U.S., 100 . . . . .280/D3
Hudson, La., U.S., 50 . . . . .282/D2
Hudson, Maine, U.S., 1,393 . . . . .286/D4
Hudson, Md., U.S., 275 . . . . .288/J5
Hudson, Mass., U.S., 18,113 . . . . .292/H3
Hudson, Mich., U.S., 2,499 . . . . .294/E8
Hudson, N.H., U.S., 22,928 . . . . .312/D6
Hudson, N.J., U.S., county, 608,975 . . . . .314/B2, E2
Hudson, N.Y., U.S., 7,524 . . . . .320/P5
Hudson, N.Y., U.S., river 320/B1, N3, P6
Hudson, N.C., U.S., 3,078 . . . . .322/C3
Hudson, S. Dak., U.S., 402 . . . . .342/J4
Hudson, Tex., U.S., 3,792 . . . . .346/P4
Hudson, Wisc., U.S., 8,775 . . . . .364/A4
Hudson, Wyo., U.S., 407 . . . . .366/B2
Hudson Bay, Sask., Can., 1,783 . . . . .227/H8
Hudson Falls, N.Y., U.S., 6,927 . . . . .320/P4
Hudson's Hope, Br. Col., Can., 1,039 . . . . .214/M3
Hudson Vil., Ohio, U.S., 22,439 . . . . . . .328/H3, H10
Hudsonville, Mich., U.S., 7,160 . . . . .294/D7
Hudsonville, Miss., U.S., 70 . . . . .300/C1
Hudspeth, Tex., U.S., county, 3,344 . . . . .346/C4
Hue, Viet., 291,818 .123/B3
Hueco, Mex., mountains 317/D6
Huehue, Hawaii, U.S. 262/F5
Huehuetenango, Guat. 202/A1
Huelo, Hawaii, U.S. .262/D3
Huelva, Sp., 142,284 . . . . .94/C4
Huelva, Sp., province 94/C4
Huerfano, Colo., U.S., county, 7,862 . . . . .250/F4
Huesca, Sp., 46,243 . . . . .94/F1
Huesca, Sp., province 94/F2
Huetter, Ida., U.S., 96 . . . . .264/A2
Huey, Ill., U.S., 196 .266/D5
Hueytown, Ala., U.S., 15,364 . . . . .238/B2, D1
Huffman, Tex., U.S., 475 . . . . .346/B6
Huger, S.C., U.S. 340/E3
Huggate, Eng., U.K. .66/G5
Hughenden, Alta., Can., 235 . . . . .212/E5
Hughes, Alaska, U.S., 78 . . . . .240/E1
Hughes, Ark., U.S., 1,867 . . . . .244/E3
Hughes, La., U.S., 70 . . . . .282/B3
Hughes, Okla., U.S., county, 14,154 . . . . .330/F2
Hughes, S. Dak., U.S., county, 16,481 . . . . . . .342/F3
Hughestown, Penn., U.S., 1,541 . . . . .336/G7
Hughesville, Md., U.S., 1,537 . . . . .288/G5
Hughesville, Mo., U.S., 174 . . . . .302/C3
Hughesville, Mont., U.S. 306/F2
Hughesville, Penn., U.S., 2,220 . . . . .336/H3
Hughson, Calif., U.S., 3,980 . . . . .246/D3
Hugh Town, Eng., U.K. 73/A3
Hugli, India, river . . . . .128/Inset II
Hugli-Chunchura, India . . . . .128/Inset II
Hugo, Colo., U.S., 885 . . . . .250/G2

Hugo, Minn., U.S., 6,363 . . . . .298/F5
Hugo, Okla., U.S., 5,536 . . . . .330/G3
Hugo, Okla., U.S., lake 330/G3
Hugoton, Kans., U.S., 3,708 . . . . .276/A4
Huguley, Ala., U.S., 2,953 . . . . .238/D3
Hŭich'ŏn, N. Kor. 116/B2
Huila, Ang., province 159/B4
Huila, Col., department 184/A4
Huila, Col., mountain 184/A4
Hulaco, Ala., U.S., 400 . . . . .238/C1
Hulah, Okla., U.S. 330/F1
Hulbert, Mich., U.S., 80 . . . . .294/D3
Hulbert, Okla., U.S., 543 . . . . .330/G2
Hulcott, Eng., U.K. 70/C3
Hulen, Ky., U.S., 350 . . . . .280/G4
Hulett, Wyo., U.S., 408 . . . . .366/D1
Hull, Que., Can., 66,246 . . . . .225/A4
Hull, Que., Can., 66,246 . . . . .226/A6
Hull, Ga., U.S., 160 .260/E3
Hull, Iowa, U.S., 1,960 . . . . .274/B1
Hull, Mass., U.S., 11,050 . . . . .292/L3
Hullbridge, Eng., U.K., 6,630 . . . . .70/F3
Hulmeville, Penn., U.S., 893 . . . . .336/M5
Hulun Nur, China, lake 119/E1
Hulwan, Egy., 372,000 . . . . .144/B2
Humacao, P.R. 206/D2
Humansville, Mo., U.S., 946 . . . . .302/C4
Humarock, Mass., U.S., 2,000 . . . . .292/M4
Humber, Eng., U.K., estuary 60/D3
Humber, Eng., U.K., river 66/H5
Humber, Eng., U.K., river 68/G2
Humberston, Eng., U.K., 6,877 . . . . .66/H5
Humberston, Eng., U.K., 6,877 . . . . .68/G2
Humbie, Scot., U.K. .62/L7
Humbird, Wisc., U.S., 225 . . . . .364/C4
Humble, Tex., U.S., 14,579 . . . . .346/B6
Humble City, N. Mex., U.S., 90 . . . . .317/G5
Humboldt, Sask., Can., 5,161 . . . . .227/E8
Humboldt, (Dewey-Humboldt), Ariz., U.S., 6,295 .242/C3
Humboldt, Calif., U.S., bay 246/A2
Humboldt, Calif., U.S., county, 126,518 . . . . . .246/B2
Humboldt, Ill., U.S., 481 . . . . .266/F4
Humboldt, Iowa, U.S., 4,452 . . . . .274/F2
Humboldt, Iowa, U.S., county, 10,381 . . . . .274/F2
Humboldt, Kans., U.S., 1,999 . . . . .276/G4
Humboldt, Minn., U.S., 61 . . . . .298/A2
Humboldt, Nebr., U.S., 941 . . . . .308/J3
Humboldt, Nev., U.S., 500 . . . . .310/A1
Humboldt, Nev., U.S., county, 16,106 . . . . .310/A1
Humboldt, Nev., U.S., river 310/B1
Humboldt, S. Dak., U.S., 521 . . . . .342/H4
Humboldt, Tenn., U.S., 9,467 . . . . .344/D3
Humboldt-Toiyabe N.F., Nev., U.S. 310/B1, C1, C2
Hume, Ill., U.S., 382 .266/F4
Hume, Mo., U.S., 337 . . . . .302/B3
Humenné, Slvk. 92/C2
Humeston, Iowa, U.S., 543 . . . . .274/G6
Humfreville, Ariz., U.S., 280 . . . . .244/D3
Humphrey, Ark., U.S., 806 . . . . .244/D3
Humphrey, Ida., U.S. 264/E5
Humphrey, Nebr., U.S., 786 . . . . .308/G2
Humphreys, Ariz., U.S., peak 242/D2
Humphreys, Miss., U.S., county, 11,206 . . . . . .300/B2
Humphreys, Mo., U.S., 164 . . . . .302/C1
Humphreys, Okla., U.S., 70 . . . . .330/C3
Humphreys, Tenn., U.S., county, 17,929 . . . . . .344/F2
Humptulips, Wash., U.S., 216 . . . . .358/B2
Humuya, Hond., river 202/B2
Húnaflói, Ice., bay 79/A2
Hunan, China, province 119/E3
Hundred, W. Va., U.S., 344 . . . . .354/B1
Hunedoara, Rom. 101/B3
Hunedoara, Rom., county 101/B3
Hungary, nation 89
Hungerford, Eng., U.K., 5,046 . . . . .70/A4
Hŭngnam, N. Kor. 116/B3
Hungry Horse, Mont., U.S., 934 . . . . .306/M1
Hungry Horse Res., Mont., U.S. 306/C1
Hunker, Penn., U.S., 329 . . . . .336/B5
Hunmanby, Eng., U.K., 3,068 . . . . .66/H4
Hunnewell, Kans., U.S., 83 . . . . .276/E4
Hunnewell, Mo., U.S., 227 . . . . .302/E2
Hünsruck, Ger., mountains 86/A4
Hunstanton, Eng., U.K., 4,634 . . . . .70/F1
Hunston, Eng., U.K. .70/C5
Hunt, Tex., U.S., 275 . . . . .346/J5
Hunt, Tex., U.S., county, 76,596 . . . . .346/M2
Hunter, Ark., U.S., 152 . . . . .244/D2
Hunter, Kans., U.S., 77 . . . . .276/D2
Hunter, Mo., U.S. 302/F5
Hunter, N.Y., U.S., 490 . . . . .320/N6
Hunter, N. Dak., U.S., 326 . . . . .326/H2
Hunter, Okla., U.S., 173 . . . . .330/E1
Hunter, Tenn., U.S., 1,566 . . . . .344/S2
Hunter, Tex., U.S., 150 . . . . .346/B1
Hunterdon, N.J., U.S., county, 121,989 . . . . . . .314/C2
Hunter Liggett Mil. Res., Calif., U.S. 246/D7
Hunter River, P.E.I., Can. 224/B2
Hunters, Wash., U.S., 125 . . . . .358/G1
Hunters Creek Vil., Tex., U.S., 4,374 . . . . .346/A6
Hunters Hollow, Ky., U.S., 372 . . . . .280/E2
Hunters Pt., Ariz., U.S., 400 . . . . .242/F2
Huntersville, Minn., U.S. 298/C4
Huntersville, N.C., U.S., 24,960 . . . . .322/D4
Huntertown, Ind., U.S., 1,771 . . . . .270/F2
Huntingburg, Ind., U.S., 5,598 . . . . .270/C8
Huntingdon, Eng., U.K., 15,575 . . . . .68/G5
Huntingdon, Eng., U.K., 15,575 . . . . .70/D2
Huntingdon, Penn., U.S., county, 45,586 . . . . . .336/F4
Huntingdon, Tenn., U.S., 4,349 . . . . .344/E2
Huntington, Ark., U.S., 688 . . . . .244/A2
Huntington, Ind., U.S., 17,450 . . . . .270/F3
Huntington, Ind., U.S., county, 38,075 . . . . . . .270/E3
Huntington, Iowa, U.S., 50 . . . . .274/K4
Huntington, Mass., U.S., 2,174 . . . . .292/C4
Huntington, Oreg., U.S., 515 . . . . .334/J3
Huntington, Tex., U.S., 2,068 . . . . .346/P4
Huntington, Utah, U.S., 2,131 . . . . .350/D4
Huntington, Vt., U.S., 1,861 . . . . .352/A2
Huntington, Va., U.S., 8,325 . . . . .354/J3, M2
Huntington, W. Va., U.S., 51,475,
  (315,538, metro.) 360/B4
Huntington Bay, N.Y., U.S., 1,496 . . . . .320/D2
Huntington Beach, Calif., U.S., 189,594 . . . . . .246/D11
Huntington Ctr., Vt., U.S., 125 . . . . .352/B2
Huntington Park, Calif., U.S., 61,348 . . . . .246/C9
Huntington Sta., N.Y., U.S., 29,910 . . . . .320/D2
Huntington Woods, Mich., U.S., 6,151 . . . . . . .294/B6
Huntingtown, Md., U.S., 2,436 . . . . .288/H5
Huntington Valley, Ohio, U.S., 735 . . . . .328/H9
Huntland, Tenn., U.S., 916 . . . . .344/J4
Huntleigh, Mo., U.S., 323 . . . . .302/H3
Huntley, Ill., U.S., 5,730 . . . . .266/E1
Huntley, Minn., U.S., 150 . . . . .298/C7
Huntley, Mont., U.S., 411 . . . . .306/H4
Huntley, Nebr., U.S., 67 . . . . .308/E3
Huntley, Wyo., U.S. .366/D3
Huntly, Scot., U.K., 4,412 . . . . .62/L4
Hunts Pt., Wash., U.S., 443 . . . . .358/A4

Huntsville, Ont., Can., 17,338 . . . . .223/F2
Huntsville, Ala., U.S., 158,216,
 (342,376, metro.) 238/C1
Huntsville, Ark., U.S., 1,931 . . . . .244/B1
Huntsville, Mo., U.S., 150 . . . . .280/D3
Huntsville, Mo., U.S., 1,553 . . . . .302/D2
Huntsville, N.J., U.S., 250 . . . . .314/D2
Huntsville, Ohio, U.S., 454 . . . . .328/C5
Huntsville, Tenn., U.S., 981 . . . . .344/N2
Huntsville, Tex., U.S., 35,078 . . . . .346/N5
Huntsville, Utah, U.S., 649 . . . . .350/C2, E1
Huntsville, Wash., U.S. 358/G3
Hunyani, Zimb., river 160/B1
Huon, P.N.G., peninsula 172/A2
Hurdland, Mo., U.S., 239 . . . . .302/D1
Hurdle Mills, N.C., U.S., 225 . . . . .322/G2
Hurdsfield, N. Dak., U.S., 91 . . . . .326/F2
Hurlford, Scot., U.K. 62/F7
Hurleville, Egy. 144/B2
Hurley, Miss., U.S., 985 . . . . .300/D5
Hurley, Mo., U.S., 157 . . . . .302/C5
Hurley, N. Mex., U.S., 1,464 . . . . .317/B5
Hurley, N.Y., U.S., 3,561 . . . . .320/N7
Hurley, S. Dak., U.S., 426 . . . . .342/H4
Hurley, Va., U.S., 175 . . . . .354/D1
Hurley, Wisc., U.S., 1,818 . . . . .364/C2
Hurliness, Scot., U.K. 62/K1, M2
Hurlock, Md., U.S., 1,874 . . . . .288/L5
Hurn, Eng., U.K. 73/J3
Huron, Ont., Can. 223/D4
Huron, Ont., Can., county 222/D4
Huron, Ont., Can., lake 223/C4
Huron, Ont., Can., lake 223/C4
Huron, Calif., U.S., 6,306 . . . . .246/E6
Huron, Ind., U.S., 200 . . . . .270/C7
Huron, Kans., U.S., 87 . . . . .276/C2
Huron, Mich., U.S., bay 294/A3
Huron, Mich., U.S., county, 36,079 . . . . . . .294/G6
Huron, Mich., U.S., lake 294/G5
Huron, Mich., U.S., mountains 294/A3
Huron, Ohio, U.S., 7,958 . . . . .328/E3
Huron, Ohio, U.S., county, 59,487 . . . . .328/E3
Huron, S. Dak., U.S., 11,893 . . . . .342/G3
Huron, Wisc., U.S., mountains 364/C2
Huron Beach, Mich., U.S., 225 . . . . .294/D4
Huron Natl. For., Mich., U.S. 294/E5, F5
Huron N.W.R., Mich., U.S. 294/B3
Huron N.W.R., Wisc., U.S. 364/F2
Hurricane, Utah, U.S., 8,250 . . . . .350/A6
Hurricane, W. Va., U.S., 5,222 . . . . .360/B4
Hurricane Mills, Tenn., U.S., 125 . . . . .344/F3
Hursley, Eng., U.K. 70/B4
Hurst, Ill., U.S., 805 . . . . .266/D6
Hurst, Tex., U.S., 36,273 . . . . .346/B9
Hurstbourne, Ky., U.S., 3,884 . . . . .280/B2
Hurstbourne Acres, Ky., U.S., 1,504 . . . . . . .280/B2
Hurstbourne Tarrant, Eng., U.K. 70/E4
Hurst Green, Eng., U.K. 73/N4
Hurstville, N.S.W., Austl. . . . . .170/Inset IV
Hurstville, Iowa, U.S., 100 . . . . .274/N3
Hurt, Va., U.S., 1,276 . . . . .354/E6
Hurtsboro, Ala., U.S., 592 . . . . .238/D3
Huscher, Kans., U.S. 276/E2
Hushinish, Scot., U.K. 62/B3
Hushpuckena, Miss., U.S. 300/B1
Huslia, Alaska, U.S., 293 . . . . .240/D1
Huson, Mont., U.S., 125 . . . . .306/B2
Hussar, Alta., Can., 181 . . . . .212/D5
Husser, La., U.S., 150 . . . . .282/J5
Hustisford, Wisc., U.S., 1,135 . . . . .364/E5
Hustler, Wisc., U.S., 113 . . . . .364/C5
Hustontown, Penn., U.S., 400 . . . . .336/E5
Hustonville, Ky., U.S., 347 . . . . .280/F3
Husum, Wash., U.S., 200 . . . . .358/D4
Hutchins, Tex., U.S., 2,805 . . . . .346/C10
Hutchinson, Kans., U.S., 40,787 . . . . .276/E3
Hutchinson, Minn., U.S., 13,080 . . . . .298/C6
Hutchinson, S. Dak., U.S., county, 8,075 . . . .342/H4
Hutchinson, Tex., U.S., county, 23,857 . . . . .346/F9
Hutchinson, W. Va., U.S. 360/C5
Hutsonville, Ill., U.S., 568 . . . . .266/F4
Huttig, Ark., U.S., 731 . . . . .244/C4
Hutto, Tex., U.S., 1,250 . . . . .346/E2
Hutton, La., U.S. 282/C4
Hutton Cranswick, Eng., U.K. 66/H5
Hutton Lake N.W.R., Wyo., U.S. 366/D3
Huttonsville, W. Va., U.S., 217 . . . . .360/D4
Huvadhu, Mald., atoll 127/A4
Huxford, Ala., U.S. 238/B4
Huxley, Iowa, U.S., 2,316 . . . . .274/G4
Huxley, Tex., U.S., 298 . . . . .346/R4
Hvannadalshnúkur, Ice., mountain 79/B3
Hvar, Cro., island 98/C3
Hvítá, Ice., river 79/A2
Hwange, Zimb. 160/A2
Hyak, Wash., U.S. 358/D2
Hyampom, Calif., U.S., 60 . . . . .246/B2
Hyannis, Mass., U.S., 14,100 . . . . .292/N6
Hyannis, Nebr., U.S., 287 . . . . .308/C2
Hyannis Port, Mass., U.S., 3,100 . . . . .292/N6
Hyargas, Mong., lake 118/B2
Hyattstown, Md., U.S., 60 . . . . .288/E2
Hyattsville, Md., U.S., 14,733 . . . . . . .288/C6, G4
Hyattville, Wyo., U.S., 73 . . . . .366/C1
Hybart, Ala., U.S. 238/B4
Hybla Valley, Va., U.S., 16,721 . . . . .354/M2
Hyco, N.C., U.S., lake 322/G2
Hydaburg, Alaska, U.S., 382 . . . . .240/J3
Hyde, Eng., U.K., 30,666 . . . . .66/D6
Hyde, Eng., U.K., 30,666 . . . . .68/C3
Hyde, Colo., U.S. 250/H1
Hyde, Mich., U.S., 275 . . . . .294/R4
Hyde, N.C., U.S., county, 5,826 . . . . .322/N3
Hyde, Penn., U.S., 1,491 . . . . .336/D3
Hyde, S. Dak., U.S., county, 1,671 . . . . . . .342/F3
Hyden, Ky., U.S., 204 . . . . .280/G3
Hyde Park, N.Y., U.S., 2,900 . . . . .320/P7
Hyde Park, Penn., U.S., 513 . . . . .336/M4
Hyde Park, Utah, U.S., 2,955 . . . . .350/C2
Hyde Park, Vt., U.S., 2,847 . . . . .352/B1
Hyder, Alaska, U.S., 97 . . . . .240/J3
Hyder, Ariz., U.S., 40 . . . . .242/B4
Hyderabad, India, 3,449,878,
 (5,533,640, metro.) 128/C5
Hyderabad, Pak., 1,166,894 . . . . .129/C3
Hydesville, Calif., U.S., 1,209 . . . . .246/A2
Hydetown, Penn., U.S., 605 . . . . .336/B2
Hydra, Gr., island 100/B3
Hydro, Okla., U.S., 1,060 . . . . .330/D2
Hyesan, N. Kor. 116/C2
Hygiene, Colo., U.S., 450 . . . . .250/E1
Hyland, Yukon, Can., river 228/D5
Hyland Post, Br. Col., Can. 214/H2
Hylo, Alta., Can. 212/D4
Hymer, Kans., U.S. 276/F3
Hymera, Ind., U.S., 833 . . . . .270/B6
Hyndman, Ida., U.S., peak 264/C6
Hyndman, Penn., U.S., 1,005 . . . . .336/D6
Hynish, Scot., U.K. 62/C6
Hyogo, Jap., prefecture 114/B2
Hypoluxo, Fla., U.S., 2,015 . . . . .256/B5
Hyrum, Utah, U.S., 6,316 . . . . .350/C2

Hysham, Mont., U.S., 330 . . . . .306/J3
Hythe, Alta., Can., 582 . . . . .212/A3
Hythe, Eng., U.K., 14,569 . . . . .70/G4
Hytop, Ala., U.S., 315 . . . . .238/C1
Hyvinkää, Fin., 42,545 . . . . .81/B2
Iaeger, W. Va., U.S., 358 . . . . .360/C6
Ialomiţa, Rom., county 101/D3
Ialomiţa, Rom., river 101/D3
Ialpug, Mol., river 102/B2
Iantha, Mo., U.S., 125 . . . . .302/B4
Iaşi, Rom., 345,795 . . . . .101/D2
Iaşi, Rom., county 101/D2
Iatan, Mo., U.S., 54 . . . . .302/B2
Ibadan, Nig., 1,835,300 . . . . .152/B4
Ibagué, Col., 420,000 . . . . .184/B3
Ibapah, Utah, U.S., 70 . . . . .350/A3
Ibapah, Utah, U.S., peak 350/A4
Ibar, Serb.-Mont., river 99/B3
Ibaraki, Jap., 261,000 . . . . .114/B3
Ibaraki, Jap., prefecture 114/D2
Ibarra, Ecua. 185/B2
Ibb, Yemen 137/A2
Iberia, La., U.S., parish, 73,266 . . . . .282/F7
Iberia, Mo., U.S., 605 . . . . .302/D3
Ibérico, Sp., mountains 94/E1
Iberville, La., U.S., parish, 33,320 . . . . . .282/F6
Ibiza, (Eivissa), Sp. 94/G3
Ibiza, (Eivissa), Sp., island 94/G3
Iboundji, Gabon, mountain 155/A2
Ibrahim, Leb., river 134/A1
Ibri, Oman 137/C1
Ibstock, Eng., U.K., 5,243 . . . . .68/E4
Ibstock, Eng., U.K., 5,243 . . . . .70/B1
Içá, Braz., river 188/B2
Ica, Peru, 125,577 . . . . .185/B3
Ica, Peru, department 185/B3
Icacos, P.R., key 206/D2
Icard, N.C., U.S., 2,734 . . . . .322/C3
Ice Cap, Grld. 193/C2
İçel, (Mersin), Tur. 133/C3
İçel, Tur., province 133/C3
Iceland, nation 77
Iceland, nation 193/C17
Ichihara, Jap., 278,000 . . . . .114/D3
Ichikawa, Jap., 449,000 . . . . .114/D2
Ichiko, Bol., river 186/B3
Ichinomiya, Jap., 274,000 . . . . .114/C3
Ich'ŏn, N. Kor. 116/B3
Ickesburg, Penn., U.S., 425 . . . . .336/G5
Icklesham, Eng., U.K. 70/F5
Icklingham, Eng., U.K. 70/F2
Iconium, Iowa, U.S. 274/J6
Ida, Ark., U.S., 100 . . . . .244/D2
Ida, Iowa, U.S., county, 7,837 . . . . .274/D3
Ida, La., U.S., 258 . . . . .282/B1
Ida, Mich., U.S., 1,100 . . . . .294/F8
Idabel, Okla., U.S., 6,952 . . . . .330/H4
Ida Grove, Iowa, U.S., 2,350 . . . . .274/D3
Idaho, U.S., state 252
Idaho, Ida., U.S., county, 15,511 . . . . .264/B3
Idaho City, Ida., U.S., 458 . . . . .264/B6
Idaho Falls, Ida., U.S., 50,730 . . . . .264/E6
Idaho Natl. Engineering and Environmental Lab.,
 Ida., U.S. 264/E6
Idaho Sprs., Colo., U.S., 1,889 . . . . .250/E2
Idalia, Colo., U.S., 90 . . . . .250/H2
Idalou, Tex., U.S., 2,157 . . . . .346/G2
Idamay, Ky., U.S., 90 . . . . .280/G3
Idana, Kans., U.S., 70 . . . . .276/E2
Idanha, Oreg., U.S., 232 . . . . .334/D3
Iddesleigh, Alta., Can. 212/E6
Ideal, Ga., U.S., 518 . . . . .260/C7
Ideal, S. Dak., U.S., 50 . . . . .342/F4
Iden, Eng., U.K. 70/F5
Ider, Ala., U.S., 664 . . . . .238/D1
Idfu, Egy. 144/B3
Idington, Minn., U.S., 50 . . . . .298/E3
Idlewild, Mich., U.S., 350 . . . . .294/D6
Idleyld Park, Oreg., U.S., 200 . . . . .334/C4
Idlib, Syria 134/A2
Idrija, Slove., 11,943 . . . . .98/B2
Idylwood, Va., U.S., 16,005 . . . . .354/M2
Ife, Nig. .152/C4
Ifield, Eng., U.K. 70/D4
Igarka, Russ. 104/F3
Ightfield, Eng., U.K. 68/B4
Igloolik, Nun., Can., 1,286 . . . . .220/M3
Ignacio, Colo., U.S., 669 . . . . .250/C4
Igombe, Tan., river 152/B1
Iguaçu, Arg., river 191/E4
Iguala, Mex., 104,759, (123,960, metro.) 200/E4
Iguazú, Arg., river 191/E2
Iguazú, Braz., falls 188/C4
Iguazú, Para., falls 187/E4
Ihavandhippolhu, Mald., atoll 127/A1
Ih Bogd Uul, Mong., mountain 118/C3
Ihema, Rwa., lake 152/C1
Ihlen, Minn., U.S., 107 . . . . .298/A7
Ihosy, Madag. 163/B3
Iian, Tai. 117/B1
Iijoki, Fin., river 81/C1
Iisalmi, Fin. 81/C2
Ijamsville, Md., U.S., 225 . . . . .288/E2
Ijevan, Arm. 103/C2
Ijssel, Neth., river 84/C2
Ijsselmeer, Neth., sea 84/C2
Ijuw, Nauru 174/C2
Ikaria, Gr., island 100/C3
Ikeja, Nig. 152/B4
Ikela, Congo, D.R. 155/B4
Iki, Jap., island 114/A4
Ikorodu, Nig. 152/B4
Iksan, S. Kor. 116/B5
Ila, Nig. .152/C3
Ila, Ga., U.S., 328 . . . . .260/E3
Ilam, Iran 130/B3
Ilam, Iran, province 130/B3
Ilam, Nepal 126/D3
Ilam, Eng., U.K. 68/D3
Ilchester, Eng., U.K., 1,733 . . . . .73/G3
Île, Kaz., river 131/D2
Île-à-la-Crosse, Sask., Can., 1,268 . . . . . . .227/C5
Île-à-la-Crosse, Sask., Can., lake 227/C5
Ilebo, Congo, D.R. 155/B2
Île-de-France, Fr., region 88/C2
Île d'Orléans, Que., Can., island 286/B2
Île d'Orléans, Que., Can., island 286/B2
Îles-de-Boucherville Prov. Park, Que., Can. . . .226/J5
Ilesha, Nig. 152/C4
Ilfeld, N. Mex., U.S., 100 . . . . .317/E2
Ilford, Man., Can., 143 . . . . .215/D1
Ilford, Eng., U.K. 70/E3
Ilfov, Rom., county 101/D3
Ilfracombe, Eng., U.K., 10,429 . . . . .73/D3
Ilhéu de Baixo, Port., island . . . . . . .93/Inset I
Ilhéu de Bugio, Port., island . . . . . . .93/Inset I
Ilhéus, Braz., 71,240, (223,352, metro.) 188/E3
Iliad, Mont., U.S. 306/G2
Iliamna, Alaska, U.S., lake 240/D3
Iliff, Colo., U.S., 213 . . . . .250/G1
Iligan, Phil., 285,061 . . . . .120/C4
Ilio, Hawaii, U.S., point 262/A3

Ilion, N.Y., U.S., 8,610 . . . . .320/L4
Ilkeston, Eng., U.K., 35,134 . . . . .68/E4
Ilkeston, Eng., U.K., 35,134 . . . . .70/B1
Ilkley, Eng., U.K., 13,530 . . . . .66/E5
Ilkley, Eng., U.K., 13,530 . . . . .68/D2
Illampu, Bol., mountain 186/A3
Illapel, Chile 190/B4
Ille-et-Vilaine, Fr., department 88/B2
Illgen City, Minn., U.S. 298/F3
Illimani, Bol., mountain 186/A3
Illinois, U.S., state 254
Illinois, Ill., U.S., river 266/C3, C4, E2
Illinois, Okla., U.S., river 330/H1
Illinois Bend, Tex., U.S. 346/L2
Illinois City, Ill., U.S., 200 . . . . .266/C2
Illiopolis, Ill., U.S., 916 . . . . .266/D4
Ilmington, Eng., U.K. 68/D5
Ilminster, Eng., U.K., 4,162 . . . . .73/G3
Ilo, Peru .185/C4
Ilocos, Phil., region 120/B2
Iloilo, Phil., 365,820 . . . . .120/B4
Ilorin, Nig. 152/C3
Ilwaco, Wash., U.S., 950 . . . . .358/A3
Imatra, Fin. 81/C2
Imbabura, Ecua., province 185/B2
Imbariê, Braz. . . . . .188/Inset I
Imbéry, P.R. 206/B2
Imbler, Oreg., U.S., 284 . . . . .334/J2
Imi, Eth. .156/D3
Imin, N. Kor., river 116/B3
Imlay, Nev., U.S., 300 . . . . .310/A1
Imlay, S. Dak., U.S. 342/C4
Imlay City, Mich., U.S., 3,869 . . . . .294/F6
Imlaystown, N.J., U.S., 175 . . . . .314/D3
Imlili, W. Sah. 147/A2
Immingham, Eng., U.K., 12,278 . . . . .66/H5
Immingham, Eng., U.K., 12,278 . . . . .68/G2
Immokalee, Fla., U.S., 19,763 . . . . .256/G5
Imnaha, Oreg., U.S., 50 . . . . .334/K2
Imo, Nig., state 152/D5
Imogene, Iowa, U.S., 66 . . . . .274/D6
Impact, Tex., U.S. 346/J3
Imperatriz, Braz., 111,818, (276,450, metro.) . .188/D2
Imperial, Sask., Can., 339 . . . . .227/E9
Imperial, Calif., U.S., 7,560 . . . . .246/K10
Imperial, Calif., U.S., county, 142,361 . . . . .246/L9
Imperial, Calif., U.S., valley 246/K9
Imperial, Mo., U.S., 4,373 . . . . .302/F3
Imperial, Nebr., U.S., 1,982 . . . . .308/C3
Imperial, (Imperial-Enlow), Penn., U.S., 3,514 . .336/A5
Imperial, Tex., U.S., 428 . . . . .346/F4
Imperial Beach, Calif., U.S., 26,992 . . . . . .246/H10
Imperial Mills, Alta., Can. 212/E4
Imperial N.W.R., Ariz., U.S. 242/A4
Imperial Sand Dunes Rec. Area, Calif., U.S. . . .246/K10
Impfondo, Congo 155/D3
Imphal, India, 196,268, (200,615, metro.) 128/F4
Ina, Ill., U.S., 2,455 . . . . .266/E5
Inala, Qnsld., Austl. . . . . .170/Inset III
I-n-Amenas, Alg. 146/B2
I-n-Amguel, Alg. 146/B2
Inari, Fin., lake 81/C1
Inavale, Nebr., U.S., 150 . . . . .308/E3
Inchelium, Wash., U.S., 389 . . . . .358/G1
Incheon, S. Kor., 2,466,338 . . . . .116/B4
Incheon, S. Kor., province 116/B4
Inchgrundle, Scot., U.K. 62/L5
Inchnadamph, Scot., U.K. 62/G2
Inchture, Scot., U.K., 735 . . . . .62/K6
Incline Vil., Nev., U.S., 9,952 . . . . .310/A2
Indalsälven, Swe. 80/B2
Independence, Ark., U.S., county, 34,233 . . . .244/D2
Independence, Calif., U.S., 574 . . . . .246/G6
Independence, Iowa, U.S., 6,014 . . . . .274/L3
Independence, Kans., U.S., 9,846 . . . . .276/G4
Independence, Ky., U.S., 14,982 . . . . .280/F2
Independence, La., U.S., 1,724 . . . . .282/H5
Independence, Minn., U.S., 40 . . . . .298/E4
Independence, Miss., U.S., 350 . . . . .300/C2
Independence, Mo., U.S., 113,288 . . . . . .302/B2, J5
Independence, Nev., U.S., mountains 310/C1
Independence, Ohio, U.S., 7,109 . . . . .328/H9
Independence, Oreg., U.S., 6,035 . . . . .334/C3
Independence, Va., U.S., 971 . . . . .354/A7
Independence, Wisc., U.S., 1,244 . . . . .364/B4
Independence N.H.P., Penn., U.S. 337/M7
Independencia, Dom. Rep., province 205/A2
Index, Va., U.S. 354/J4
Index, Wash., U.S., 157 . . . . .358/E2
India, nation 124
Indiahoma, Okla., U.S., 374 . . . . .330/D3
Indian, Fla., U.S., river 256/R1
Indian, Mich., U.S., lake 294/C3, G2
Indian, N.H., U.S., river 312/D1
Indian, N.Y., U.S., lake 320/N3
Indiana, U.S., state 258
Indiana, Penn., U.S., 14,895 . . . . .336/C4
Indiana, Penn., U.S., county, 89,605 . . . . . .336/C4
Indiana Dunes Natl. Lakeshore, Ind., U.S. 270/B1
Indianapolis, Ind., U.S., state capital, 791,926,
 (1,607,486, metro.) 270/E5
Indian Bay, Man., Can. 215/D3
Indian Beach, Del., U.S. 255/D6
Indian Beach, N.C., U.S., 95 . . . . .322/M5
Indian Brook, N.S., Can. 221/G1
Indian Cabins, Alta., Can. 212/B1
Indian Creek, Ill., U.S., 194 . . . . .266/C5
Indian Falls, Calif., U.S. 246/E2
Indian Fields, Ky., U.S., 90 . . . . .280/G3
Indian Harbour, N.C., Can. 221/D3
Indian Harbour Beach, Fla., U.S., 8,152 . . . . .256/H3
Indian Head, Sask., Can., 1,758 . . . . .227/G10
Indian Head, Md., U.S., 3,422 . . . . .288/F5
Indian Head Park, Ill., U.S., 3,685 . . . . . . .266/B6
Indian Hts., Ind., U.S., 3,274 . . . . .270/D4
Indian Hill, Ohio, U.S. 328/B7, C9
Indian Hills, Ky., U.S., 2,882 . . . . .280/A2
Indian Hills, Nev., U.S., 4,407 . . . . .310/A2
Indian Hills Cherokee Section, Ky., U.S. 280/B2
Indian Island, N.B., Can. 217/E2
Indian Lake, N.Y., U.S., 325 . . . . .320/N3
Indian Lake, Penn., U.S., 450 . . . . .336/C6
Indian Lake Estates, Fla., U.S., 250 . . . . . .256/G4
Indian Mills, N.J., U.S., 300 . . . . .314/D4
Indian Mound, Tenn., U.S., 80 . . . . .344/F1
Indian Neck, Conn., U.S., 3,400 . . . . .253/D5
Indianola, Ill., U.S., 207 . . . . .266/F4
Indianola, Iowa, U.S., 12,998 . . . . .274/G5
Indianola, Miss., U.S., 12,066 . . . . .300/B3
Indianola, Nebr., U.S., 642 . . . . .308/D3
Indianola, Okla., U.S., 191 . . . . .330/G3
Indianola, Tex., U.S. 346/M7
Indianola, Utah, U.S. 350/C4
Indianola, Wash., U.S., 3,026 . . . . .358/A4
Indian Peak, Utah, U.S., range 350/A5
Indian Pt., Mo., U.S., 588 . . . . .302/C5
Indian River, Del., U.S., bay 255/D6
Indian River, Fla., U.S., county, 112,947 . . . .256/H4
Indian River, Maine, U.S., 50 . . . . .286/C4
Indian River, Mich., U.S., 2,008 . . . . .294/E4

Indian River Shores, Fla., U.S., 3,448 . . . . .256/H4
Indian Rocks Beach, Fla., U.S., 5,072 . . . .256/C6, F4
Indian Shores, Fla., U.S., 1,705 . . . . .256/C6
Indian Sprs., Ga., U.S., 1,982 . . . . .260/C2
Indian Sprs., Ind., U.S., 100 . . . . .270/C7
Indian Sprs., Nev., U.S., 1,302 . . . . .310/C3
Indian Sprs. Vil., Ala., U.S., 2,225 . . . .238/C2, E1
Indiantown, Fla., U.S., 5,588 . . . . .256/A4, H4
Indiantown, Md., U.S. 288/N7
Indiantown, Mich., U.S., 1,158 . . . . .294/F6
Indian Trail, N.C., U.S., 11,905 . . . . .322/D4
Indian Valley, Ida., U.S., 60 . . . . .264/A5
Indian Vil., Ind., U.S., 144 . . . . .270/D1
Indian Vil., La., U.S., 100 . . . . .282/D6
Indigirka, Russ., river 104/I3
Indio, Calif., U.S., 49,116 . . . . .246/J9
Indispensable, Sol. Is., reefs 173/B2
Indonesia, nation 118
Indore, India, 1,597,441, (1,639,044, metro.) . .128/C4
Indre, Fr., department 88/C3
Indre-et-Loire, Fr., department 88/C3
Indrio, Fla., U.S., 550 . . . . .256/H4
Indus, China, river 119/A2
Indus, India, river 128/C2
Indus, Pak., river 129/C4, E2
Indus, Minn., U.S. 298/D2
Industry, Ill., U.S., 540 . . . . .266/C3
Industry, Kans., U.S., 40 . . . . .276/E2
Industry, Tex., U.S., 1,921 . . . . .336/A4
Inez, Ky., U.S., 466 . . . . .280/H3
Ingalls, Ark., U.S., 1,787 . . . . .346/N7
Ingalls, Ark., U.S., 60 . . . . .244/C4
Ingalls, Ind., U.S., 1,168 . . . . .270/E5
Ingalls, Kans., U.S., 328 . . . . .276/B4
Ingalls, Mich., U.S., 175 . . . . .294/B4
Ingalls Park, Ill., U.S., 3,082 . . . . .266/B6
Inger, Minn., U.S., 100 . . . . .298/D3
Ingersoll, Okla., U.S. 330/D1
Ingham, Eng., U.K. 70/F2
Ingham, Mich., U.S., county, 279,320 . . . . . .294/E7
Ingleside, Ont., Can. 223/K3
Ingleside, Md., U.S., 125 . . . . .288/L3
Ingleside, Tex., U.S., 9,388 . . . . .346/L8
Ingleside, W. Va., U.S., 90 . . . . .360/D6
Ingleside on the Bay, Tex., U.S., 659 . . . . . .346/L8
Ingleton, Eng., U.K., 1,979 . . . . .66/D4
Ingleton, Eng., U.K., 1,979 . . . . .68/C1
Inglewood, Calif., U.S., 112,580 . . . . .246/C10
Inglewood, Nebr., U.S., 382 . . . . .308/H2
Inglewood, Wash., U.S., 22,661 . . . . .358/A4
Inglis, Fla., U.S., 1,491 . . . . .256/F2
Ingoe, Eng., U.K. 66/E2
Ingoldmells, Eng., U.K., 2,874 . . . . .68/H3
Ingolstadt, Ger., 114,826 . . . . .86/B4
Ingomar, Miss., U.S., 400 . . . . .300/C1
Ingomar, Mont., U.S. 306/J3
Ingonish, N.S., Can. 221/G1
Ingonish Beach, N.S., Can. 221/G1
Ingot, Calif., U.S., 250 . . . . .246/C2
Ingraham, Ill., U.S., 150 . . . . .266/E5
Ingram, Penn., U.S., 3,712 . . . . .336/M7
Ingram, Tex., U.S., 1,740 . . . . .346/J5
Ingram, Va., U.S., 90 . . . . .354/E7
Ingram, Wisc., U.S., 76 . . . . .364/C3
Inguadona, Minn., U.S. 298/C4
Ingushetia, Russ., region 104/G5
Inhambane, Moz. 161/B5
Inhomirim, Braz. . . . . .188/Inset I
Ink, Ark., U.S., 125 . . . . .244/A3
Inkerman, N.B., Can., 936 . . . . .217/E1
Inkom, Ida., U.S., 738 . . . . .264/A7
Inkster, Mich., U.S., 30,115 . . . . .294/A7, F7
Inkster, N. Dak., U.S., 102 . . . . .326/H1
Inland, Jap., sea 114/B3
Inland, Nebr., U.S., 70 . . . . .308/E3
Inlet, N.Y., U.S., 70 . . . . .320/M3
Inman, Ga., U.S., 650 . . . . .260/C5
Inman, Kans., U.S., 1,142 . . . . .276/E3
Inman, Nebr., U.S., 148 . . . . .308/E1
Inman, S.C., U.S., 1,884 . . . . .340/B1, F1
Inn, Aus., river 91/B3, J7
Inn, Ger., river 86/C4
Inn, Switz., river 90/D2
Innellan, Scot., U.K., 1,188 . . . . .62/F7
Inner Hebrides, Scot., U.K., islands 60/A2
Innerleithen, Scot., U.K., 2,586 . . . . .62/K7
Inner Mongolia, China, autonomous region 119/E1
Innis, N.S., Can., 175 . . . . .282/F5
Innisfail, Alta., Can., 6,928 . . . . .212/D5
Innisfail, Ont., Can. 223/F3
Innisfree, Alta., Can., 219 . . . . .212/E4
Inniswold, La., U.S., 4,944 . . . . .282/G6
Innoko N.W.R., Alaska, U.S. 240/D2
Innsbruck, Aus., 113,826 . . . . .91/B3
Innviertel, Aus., region 91/C2
Ino, Wisc., U.S. 364/B2
Inola, Okla., U.S., 1,589 . . . . .330/G1
I-n-Salah, Alg. 146/B2
Insch, Scot., U.K., 1,523 . . . . .62/L4
Inside Passage, Alaska, U.S., waterway 240/J3
Institute, Wisc., U.S., 250 . . . . .364/F4
Inta, Russ. 104/K3
Intake, Mont., U.S. 306/M2
Interior, S. Dak., U.S., 77 . . . . .342/D4
Interlachen, Fla., U.S., 1,475 . . . . .256/G2
Interlaken, Switz. 90/B2
Interlaken, Calif., U.S., 7,328 . . . . .246/K4
Interlaken, Mass., U.S., 225 . . . . .292/A3
Interlaken, N.J., U.S., 900 . . . . .314/E2
Interlaken, N.Y., U.S., 674 . . . . .320/H5
Interlaken, Mich., U.S., 600 . . . . .294/B4
International Falls, Minn., U.S., 6,703 . . . . .298/D2
Intl. Peace Garden, N. Dak., U.S. 326/E1
Intervale, N.H., U.S., 200 . . . . .312/D3
Inthanon, Thai., mountain 125/B2
Intibucá, Hond., department 202/A2
Intracoastal City, La., U.S. 282/E7
Inukjuak, Que., Can. 225/D2
Inuvik, N.W. Terr., Can., 2,894 . . . . . . .193/C12
Inuvik, N.W. Terr., Can., 2,894 . . . . .220/B3
Inverallochy, Scot., U.K. 62/N3
Inveran, Scot., U.K. 62/H3
Inveraray, Scot., U.K. 62/F6
Inverarnan, Scot., U.K. 62/G6
Inverbervie, Scot., U.K., 2,094 . . . . .62/M5
Invercargill, N.Z., 49,830, (46,305, metro.) . .171/A4
Inverclyde, Scot., U.K., unitary authority,
 84,203 . . . . .62/F7
Invergarry, Scot., U.K. 62/G4
Invergeldie, Scot., U.K. 62/H6
Invergordon, Scot., U.K., 3,890 . . . . .62/H3
Inver Grove Hts., Minn., U.S., 29,751 . . . . . .298/F6
Invergowrie, Scot., U.K. 62/K6
Invermoriston, Scot., U.K. 62/G4
Inverness, N.S., Can., 1,702 . . . . .221/F1
Inverness, N.S., Can., county 221/F1
Inverness, Scot., U.K. 60/B1

Jamestown, Va. 577

Inverness, Scot., U.K., 40,949 62/H4
Inverness, Ala., U.S. 238/E1
Inverness, Calif., U.S., 1,421 246/C4
Inverness, Fla., U.S., 6,789 256/F3
Inverness, Ill., U.S., 6,749 266/A5
Inverness, Miss., U.S., 1,153 300/B2
Inverness, Mont., U.S., 103 306/F1
Inveruglas, Scot., U.K. 62/G6
Inverurie, Scot., U.K., 10,882 62/M4
Inwood, Man., Can. 215/C4
Inwood, Iowa, U.S., 875 274/B1
Inwood, W. Va., U.S., 2,084 360/K2
Inyangani, Zimb., *mountain* 160/C2
Inyo, Calif., U.S., *county*, 17,945 246/H6
Inyo, Calif., U.S., *mountains* 246/H6
Inyokern, Calif., U.S., 984 246/H7
Inyo Natl. For., Calif., U.S. 246/G5, G6
Ioannina, Gr. 100/B2
Iola, Ill., U.S., 171 266/E5
Iola, Kans., U.S., 6,302 276/G4
Iola, Wisc., U.S., 1,298 364/D4
Iona, Scot., U.K., *island* 62/D6
Iona, Ida., U.S., 1,201 264/F6
Iona, Ind., U.S., 50 270/B7
Iona, Minn., U.S., 173 298/B7
Iona, N.J., U.S. 314/C4
Iona, S. Dak., U.S. 342/F4
Ione, Calif., U.S., 7,129 246/E4, L6
Ione, Colo., U.S., 40 250/A2, F1
Ione, Nev., U.S., 50 310/B2
Ione, Oreg., U.S., 321 334/G2
Ione, Wash., U.S., 479 358/H1
Ionia, Iowa, U.S., 277 274/K1
Ionia, Kans., U.S., 60 276/D2
Ionia, Mich., U.S., 10,569 294/D6
Ionia, Mich., U.S., *county*, 61,518 294/D7
Ionia, Mo., U.S., 108 302/C3
Ionian, Alb., *sea* 99/A4
Ionian, Gr., *islands* 100/B2
Ionian, Gr., *sea* 100/A2
Ionian, It., *sea* 95/D3
Ionian Islands, Gr., *region* 100/B2
Iori, Geo., *river* 103/C4
Iosco, Mich., U.S., *county*, 27,339 294/F5
Iota, La., U.S., 1,376 282/E6
Iowa, U.S., *state* 262
Iowa, Iowa, U.S., *county*, 15,671 274/K4
Iowa, Iowa, U.S., *river* 274/K4, M5
Iowa, La., U.S., 2,663 282/C6
Iowa, Wisc., U.S., *county*, 22,780 364/C5
Iowa City, Iowa, U.S., 62,220, (111,006, *metro.*) 274/L4
Iowa Colony, Tex., U.S., 804 346/B7
Iowa Falls, Iowa, U.S., 5,193 274/H2
Iowa Ind. Res., Kans., U.S. 276/G2
Iowa Ind. Res., Nebr., U.S. 308/J3
Iowa Park, Tex., U.S., 6,431 346/K2
Iowa Pt., Kans., U.S., 40 276/G2
Ipava, Ill., U.S., 506 266/C3
Ipel', Slvk., *river* 92/B2
Ipiíba, Braz. 188/Inset I
Ipoh, Malay., 382,853, (468,841, *metro.*) 121/A2
Ipoly, Hun., *river* 91/B1
Ippy, C.A.R. 154/B2
Ipswich, Qnsld., Austl. 170/Inset III
Ipswich, Eng., U.K. 60/D3
Ipswich, Eng., U.K., 130,157 70/G2
Ipswich, Mass., U.S., 12,987 292/L2
Ipswich, S. Dak., U.S., 943 342/F2
Iqaluit, Nun., Can., 5,236 220/P4
Iquique, Chile, 156,149 190/B2
Iquitos, Peru, 169,707 185/C1
Ira, Iowa, U.S., 100 274/H4
Ira, Tex., U.S., 90 346/G3
Iraan, Tex., U.S., 1,238 346/G5
Iracoubo, Fr. Gui. 183/B1
Iraklion, Gr., 102,398, (110,958, *metro.*) 100/C4
Iran, *nation* 126
Iranshahr, Iran 130/E4
Irapuato, Mex., 319,148, (440,134, *metro.*) 200/D3
Iraq, *nation* 126
Irasburg, Vt., U.S., 1,077 352/C1
Irasville, Vt., U.S., 150 352/B2
Irazú, C.R., *volcano* 203/C3
Irbe, Est., *strait* 81/A3
Irbid, Jor., 247,275 134/A1
Irbid, Jor., *governorate* 134/A1
Irby, Tex., U.S. 346/J2
Irby, Wash., U.S., 100 358/G2
Iredell, N.C., U.S., *county*, 122,660 322/D3
Iredell, Tex., U.S., 360 346/L4
Ireland, *nation* 76
Ireland, *nation* 193/D18
Ireland, Tex., U.S. 346/L4
Ireland, W. Va., U.S., 150 360/F3
Ireleth, Eng., U.K. 66/B4
Irene, S. Dak., U.S., 432 342/H4
Ireton, Iowa, U.S., 585 274/B2
Irian Jaya, Indon., *province* 122/E2
Iringa, Tan. 152/C2
Iringa, Tan., *region* 152/C2
Iriomote, Jap., *island* 114/Inset II
Irion, Tex., U.S., *county*, 1,771 346/G4
Iriona, Hond. 202/C2
Irish, Ire., *sea* 78/D2
Irish, Eng., U.K., *sea* 60/B3
Irish, Eng., U.K., *sea* 66/B5
Irish, Eng., U.K., *sea* 73/B3
Irish, N. Ire., U.K., *sea* 65/F3
Irishtown, N.B., Can. 217/E2
Irkutsk, Russ., 591,047 104/G4
Irma, Alta., Can., 435 212/E5
Irma, Wisc., U.S., 125 364/D3
Irmo, S.C., U.S., 11,039 340/A3
Irmo, S.C., U.S., 11,039 340/C2
Iron, Fla., U.S., *mountain* 256/G4
Iron, Mich., U.S., *county*, 13,138 294/A3
Iron, Mo., U.S., *county*, 10,697 302/E4
Iron, Utah, U.S., *county*, 33,779 350/A6
Iron, Va., U.S., *mountains* 354/E3
Iron, Wisc., U.S., *county*, 6,861 364/C2
Iron Belt, Wisc., U.S., 225 364/C2
Ironbridge, Ont., Can., 826 223/B1
Ironbridge, Eng., U.K., 2,184 68/C4
Iron City, Ga., U.S., 321 260/B9
Iron City, Tenn., U.S., 368 344/F4
Irondale, Ala., U.S., 9,813 238/C2, E1
Irondale, Ga., U.S., 7,727 260/C5, H4
Irondale, Mo., U.S., 437 302/F4
Irondale, Ohio, U.S., 418 328/J4
Irondequoit, N.Y., U.S., 52,354 320/F4
Iron Gate, Rom., *reservoir* 101/B3
Iron Gate, Va., U.S., 404 354/D5
Iron Gates, Mo., U.S. 302/B4
Iron Hill, Ky., U.S., 70 280/G2
Iron Jct., Minn., U.S., 93 298/E3
Iron Lightning, S. Dak., U.S., 90 342/D2
Iron Mtn., Mich., U.S., 8,154 294/A4
Iron Mtn., Wyo., U.S. 366/D3
Iron Mtn. Lake, Mo., U.S., 693 302/F4
Iron Ridge, Wisc., U.S., 998 364/E5
Iron River, Alta., Can. 212/E4
Iron River, Mich., U.S., 3,386 294/A3
Iron River, Wisc., U.S., 500 364/B2
Irons, Mich., U.S., 90 294/D5
Ironshire, Md., U.S., 225 288/P6
Ironside, Oreg., U.S. 334/J3
Iron Sprs., Ariz., U.S. 242/C3
Iron Sprs., Ark., U.S., 3,499 244/C3
Iron Sprs., Utah, U.S., 90 350/A6
Iron Sta., N.C., U.S., 450 322/C4
Ironton, Mich., U.S., 200 294/D4
Ironton, Minn., U.S., 498 298/D4
Ironton, Mo., U.S., 1,471 302/F4
Ironton, Ohio, U.S., 11,211 328/E8
Ironton, Tex., U.S., 60 346/N4
Ironton, Wisc., U.S., 250 364/C5
Ironwood, Mich., U.S., 6,293 294/C2
Ironwood Forest Natl. Mon., Ariz., U.S. 242/D5
Iroquois, Ill., U.S., 207 266/F3
Iroquois, Ill., U.S., *county*, 31,334 266/F3
Iroquois, S. Dak., U.S., 278 342/H3
Iroquois Falls, Ont., Can., 5,217 222/D3
Iroquois N.W.R., N.Y., U.S. 320/E4
Iroquois Pt., Hawaii, U.S., 2,462 262/E2, J2
Irrawaddy, Mya., *river* 125/B2
Irricana, Alta., Can., 1,038 212/D5
Irrigon, Oreg., U.S., 1,702 334/G2
Irtysh, (Ertis), Kaz., *river* 131/D1
Irtysh, Russ., *river* 104/E4
Irvine, Alta., Can. 212/E6
Irvine, Scot., U.K., 33,090 62/G7
Irvine, Calif., U.S., 143,072 246/E11, H9
Irvine, Ky., U.S., 2,843 280/G3
Irvinestown, N. Ire., U.K., 1,906 65/B3
Irving, Ill., U.S., 2,484 266/D4
Irving, Tex., U.S., 191,615 346/C9, M3
Irvington, Ill., U.S., 736 266/D5
Irvington, Iowa, U.S., 40 274/F1
Irvington, Ky., U.S., 1,257 280/D3
Irvington, Nebr., U.S., 950 308/H2
Irvington, N.J., U.S., 60,695 314/B2, E2
Irvington, N.Y., U.S., 6,631 320/B1
Irvington, Va., U.S., 673 354/L5
Irvona, Penn., U.S., 680 336/D4
Irwin, Ga., U.S., *county*, 9,931 260/E8
Irwin, Ida., U.S., 157 264/F6
Irwin, Ill., U.S., 92 266/F2
Irwin, Iowa, U.S., 372 274/D4
Irwin, Mo., U.S., 50 302/B4
Irwin, Penn., U.S., 4,366 336/B5
Irwin, S.C., U.S., 1,343 340/D2
Irwindale, Calif., U.S., 1,446 246/D9
Irwinton, Ga., U.S., 587 260/E6
Irwinville, Ga., U.S., 125 260/E8
Isabel, Kans., U.S., 108 276/D4
Isabel, S. Dak., U.S., 239 342/D2
Isabela, Ecua., *island* 185/Inset
Isabela, Phil. 120/B5
Isabela, P.R. 206/A1
Isabelia, Nicar., *mountains* 202/B2
Isabella, Mich., U.S., 40 294/C4
Isabella, Mich., U.S., *county*, 63,351 294/E6
Isabella, Minn., U.S. 298/F3
Isabella, Okla., U.S., 150 330/D1
Isabella Ind. Res., Mich., U.S. 294/E6, F6
Isabel Segunda, P.R. 206/E2
Ísafjörður, Ice., 2,635 79/A1
Isangel, Van. 173/C4
Isanti, Minn., U.S., 2,324 298/D5
Isanti, Minn., U.S., *county*, 31,287 298/D5
Isar, Ger., *river* 86/C4
Isbell, Ala., U.S., 200 238/B1
Ischia, It., *island* 95/C2
Ise, Jap. 114/C3
Ise, Jap., *bay* 114/C3
Iselin, N.J., U.S., 16,698 314/E2
Isère, Fr., *department* 88/D4
Isère, Fr., *river* 88/D4
Isernia, It. 95/C2
Iseyin, Nig. 152/B4
Isherton, Guy. 183/B4
Ishigaki, Jap., *island* 114/Inset II
Ishikari, Jap., *river* 114/Inset I
Ishikawa, Jap., *prefecture* 114/C2
Ishim, (Esil), Kaz., *river* 131/C1
Ishim, Russ. 104/E4
Ishinomaki, Jap. 114/D2
Ishinomaki, Jap., *bay* 114/D2
Ishizuchi-san, Jap., *mountain* 114/B3
Ishpeming, Mich., U.S., 6,686 294/B3
Isiro, Congo, D.R. 155/C1
İskenderun, Tur., *gulf* 133/C3
İskenderun, Tur. 133/D3
Iskur, Bul., *river* 101/C2
Isla de la Juventud, Cuba, *special municipality* 204/B2
Islamabad, Pak., *capital*, 529,180 129/D3
Islamabad Capital, Pak., *territory* 129/D3
Islamorada, Fla., U.S., 6,846 256/H7
Island, Man., Can., *lake* 215/D2
Island, Ky., U.S., 435 280/C3
Island, Wash., U.S., *county*, 71,558 358/C1
Island Bay N.W.R., Fla., U.S. 256/F5
Island Beach, N.J., U.S., 60 314/E4
Island City, Ky., U.S., 70 280/G3
Island City, Oreg., U.S., 916 334/H2
Island Falls, Maine, U.S., 793 286/D3
Island Hts., N.J., U.S., 1,751 314/E4
Islandia, Fla., U.S. 256/H6
Islandia, N.Y., U.S., 3,057 320/D2
Island Lake, Man., Can., 59 215/D2
Island Lake, Ill., U.S., 8,153 266/A5
Island Lake, (Beltrami County), Minn., U.S., 40 298/B3
Island Lake, (St. Louis County), Minn., U.S., 40 298/E3
Island Lake, Wisc., U.S., 80 364/B3
Island Mtn., Calif., U.S. 246/B2
Island Park, Ida., U.S., 215 264/F5
Island Park, N.Y., U.S., 4,732 320/C3
Island Pond, Vt., U.S., 849 352/D1
Islandstown, N. Ire., U.K. 65/E2
Islandton, S.C., U.S., 50 340/D4
Island View, Minn., U.S., 150 298/D2
Islas de la Bahía, Hond., *department* 202/B1
Isla Vista, Calif., U.S., 18,344 246/F8
Islay, Scot., U.K., *island* 60/A2
Islay, Scot., U.K., *island* 62/D7
Isle, Minn., U.S., 707 298/D4
Isle au Haut, Maine, U.S., 79 286/D4
Isle au Haut, Maine, U.S., *island* 286/D4
Isle aux Morts, Nfld., Can., 813 218/B5
Isleham, Eng., U.K., 1,953 70/E2
Isle La Motte, Vt., U.S., 488 352/A1
Islen, Nev., U.S. 310/C3
Isle of Anglesey, Wales, U.K., *unitary authority*, 66,828 64/C1
Isle of Hope, (Isle of Hope-Dutch Island), Ga., U.S., 2,605 260/J8
Isle of Palms, S.C., U.S., 4,583 340/E4
Isle of Sheppey, Eng., U.K., *island* 70/F4
Isle of Whithorn, Scot., U.K. 62/H9
Isle of Wight, Eng., U.K., *island* 70/B5
Isle of Wight, Eng., U.K., *unitary authority*, 132,719 70/B5
Isle of Wight, Va., U.S., 100 354/K7
Isle of Wight, Va., U.S., *county*, 29,728 354/K7
Isleornsay, Scot., U.K. 62/E4
Isle Royale, Mich., U.S., *island* 294/A1
Isle Royale Natl. Park, Mich., U.S. 294/A2
Islesboro, Maine, U.S., 603 286/D4
Islesboro, Maine, U.S., *island* 286/D4
Isleta, N. Mex., U.S., 496 317/D3
Isleta Indian Res., N. Mex., U.S. 317/D3
Isleta Pueblo, N. Mex., U.S. 317/D3
Isleton, Calif., U.S., 828 246/L1
Islington, Ont., Can. 223/J6
Islington, Eng., U.K., 164,686 70/D3
Islington, Eng., U.K., *unitary authority*, 175,787 70/D3
Islip, Eng., U.K. 70/B3
Ismail Semani, Taj., *peak* 132/B1
Ismay, Mont., U.S. 306/M3
Isna, Egy. 144/B2
Isoka, Zam. 159/C2
Isola, Miss., U.S., 768 300/B2
Isparta, Tur. 133/B3
Isparta, Tur., *province* 133/B3
Israel, *nation* 131
Issaquah, Wash., U.S., 11,212 358/B4, C2
Issaquena, Miss., U.S., *county*, 2,274 300/B3
Istachatta, Fla., U.S., 65 256/F3
İstanbul, Tur., 8,803,468 133/B2
İstanbul, Tur., *province* 133/B2
Istokpoga, Fla., U.S., *lake* 256/G4
Istria, Cro., *peninsula* 98/A2
Itabira, Braz. 188/D3
Itabuna, Braz., 129,938, (185,180, *metro.*) 188/E3
Itaipu, Braz. 188/Inset I
Itaipú, Braz., *reservoir* 188/C4
Itaipú, Para., *reservoir* 187/E4
Itajaí, Braz., 78,867, (119,583, *metro.*) 188/D4
Italia, Fla., U.S. 256/G1
Italy, *nation* 93
Italy, Tex., U.S., 1,993 346/M3
Itanagar, India 128/F3
Itapecerica da Serra, Braz. 188/Inset II
Itapeva, Braz. 188/Inset II
Itapúa, Para., *department* 187/E5
Itaquaquecetuba, Braz. 188/Inset II
Itasca, Ill., U.S., 8,302 266/B5
Itasca, Minn., U.S., *county*, 43,992 298/D3
Itasca St. Park, Minn., U.S. 298/B3
Itä-Uusimaa, Fin., *region* 81/C2
Itawamba, Miss., U.S., *county*, 22,770 300/D1
Itchen Abbas, Eng., U.K. 70/B4
Iténez, Bol., *river* 186/B2
Ithaca, Gr., *island* 100/B2
Ithaca, Mich., U.S., 3,098 294/E6
Ithaca, Nebr., U.S., 168 308/H2
Ithaca, N.Y., U.S., 29,287 320/J6
Ithaca, Ohio, U.S., 102 328/A6
Itta Bena, Miss., U.S., 2,208 300/B2
Itton, Wales, U.K. 64/F4
Ittoqqortoormiit, (Scoresbysund), Grld. 193/D2
Ituna, Sask., Can., 709 227/G9
Iuka, Ill., U.S., 598 266/E5
Iuka, Kans., U.S., 185 276/D4
Iuka, Miss., U.S., 3,059 300/D1
Iva, S.C., U.S., 1,156 340/B2
Ivalo, Fin. 81/C1
Ivan, Ark., U.S., 90 244/C4
Ivan, Tex., U.S. 346/K3
Ivanhoe, Minn., U.S., 679 298/A6
Ivanhoe, Va., U.S., 500 354/B7
Ivano-Frankivs'k, Ukr., 234,256 102/D2
Ivano-Frankivs'k, Ukr., *oblast* 102/B2
Ivanovo, Russ., 458,531 104/D4
Ivanpah, Calif., U.S. 246/K7
Iver, (Iver/Iver Heath), Eng., U.K., 7,134 70/C3
Ivesdale, Ill., U.S., 288 266/E4
Ivey, Ga., U.S., 1,100 260/E6
Ivindo, Gabon, *river* 155/B1
Ivins, Utah, U.S., 4,450 350/A6
Ivor, Va., U.S., 320 354/K7
Ivujivik, Que., Can., 298 225/A1
Ivvavik Natl. Park, Yukon, Can. 228/B1
Ivybridge, Eng., U.K., 9,179 73/E4
Ivychurch, Eng., U.K. 70/F4
Ivydale, W. Va., U.S., 175 360/D3
Ivyland, Penn., U.S., 492 336/M6
Iwaki, Jap., 360,000 114/D2
Iwakuni, Jap. 114/B3
Iwate, Jap., *prefecture* 114/D2
Iwilei, Hawaii, U.S. 262/F2
Iwo, Nig. 152/C4
Iwo Jima, Jap., *island* 114/Inset III
Ixelles, Belg. 85/C2
Ixonia, Wisc., U.S., 642 364/E2
Ixtapa, Mex., 4,953 200/D4
Ixtapaluca, Mex. 200/Inset
Ixworth, Eng., U.K., 2,011 70/F2
Izabal, Guat., *lake* 201/E4
Izagora, Fla., U.S., 80 256/C1
Izard, Ark., U.S., *county*, 13,249 244/C1
Izembek N.W.R., Alaska, U.S. 240/C3
Izhevsk, Russ., 653,691 104/D4
Izki, Oman 137/C1
Izmail, Ukr. 102/B3
İzmir, Tur., 2,232,265 133/A2
İzmir, Tur., *province* 133/A2
Iztacalco, Mex. 200/Inset
Iztapalapa, Mex. 200/Inset
Izu, Jap., *islands* 114/C3
Izu, Jap., *peninsula* 114/C3
Izuhara, Jap. 114/A3
Jabalpur, India, 739,961, (1,117,200, *metro.*) 128/C4
Jabal Zuqar, Yemen, *island* 137/A2
Jaboatão, Braz., 67,120, (482,434, *metro.*) 188/E2
Jacareacanga, Braz. 188/C2
Jacinto City, Tex., U.S., 10,302 346/B6
Jack, Ala., U.S., 90 238/C4
Jack, Tex., U.S., *county*, 8,763 346/K2
Jack Creek, Nev., U.S., 50 310/B1
Jackhead, Man., Can. 215/C3
Jackman, Maine, U.S., 718 286/B3
Jackman Sta., Maine, U.S., 750 286/B3
Jackpot, Nev., U.S., 1,100 310/C1
Jackrabbit, Ariz., U.S. 242/D5
Jacksboro, Tenn., U.S., 1,887 344/N2
Jacksboro, Tex., U.S., 4,533 346/K2
Jackson, Austl., *port* 170/Inset IV
Jackson, Ala., U.S., 5,419 238/B4
Jackson, Ala., U.S., *county*, 53,926 238/C1
Jackson, Ark., U.S., *county*, 18,418 244/D2
Jackson, Calif., U.S., 3,989 246/E4, L6
Jackson, Colo., U.S., *county*, 1,577 250/D1
Jackson, Fla., U.S., *county*, 46,755 256/C1
Jackson, Ga., U.S., 3,934 260/D5
Jackson, Ga., U.S., *county*, 41,589 260/D3
Jackson, Ga., U.S., *lake* 260/D5
Jackson, Ill., U.S., *county*, 59,612 266/D6
Jackson, Ind., U.S., *county*, 41,335 270/D7
Jackson, Iowa, U.S., *county*, 20,296 274/N3
Jackson, Kans., U.S., *county*, 12,657 276/G2
Jackson, Ky., U.S., 2,490 280/G3
Jackson, Ky., U.S., *county*, 13,495 280/F3
Jackson, La., U.S., 4,130 282/G5
Jackson, La., U.S., *parish*, 15,397 282/D2
Jackson, Maine, U.S., 506 286/C4
Jackson, Mich., U.S., 36,316, (158,422, *metro.*) 294/E7
Jackson, Mich., U.S., *county*, 158,422 294/E7
Jackson, Minn., U.S., 3,501 298/B7
Jackson, Minn., U.S., *county*, 11,268 298/B7
Jackson, Miss., U.S., *county*, 131,420 300/D5
Jackson, Miss., U.S., *state capital*, 184,256, (440,801, *metro.*) 300/B3
Jackson, Mo., U.S., 11,947 302/G4
Jackson, Mo., U.S., *county*, 654,880 302/B3, J5
Jackson, Mont., U.S. 306/C4
Jackson, Nebr., U.S., 205 308/H1
Jackson, N.H., U.S., 835 312/D3
Jackson, N.C., U.S., 695 322/L2
Jackson, N.C., U.S., *county*, 33,121 322/B8
Jackson, Ohio, U.S., 6,184 328/E7
Jackson, Ohio, U.S., *county*, 32,641 328/E8
Jackson, Okla., U.S., *county*, 28,439 330/C3
Jackson, Oreg., U.S., *county*, 181,269 334/D5
Jackson, S.C., U.S., 1,625 340/C3
Jackson, S. Dak., U.S., *county*, 2,930 342/D4
Jackson, Tenn., U.S., 59,643, (107,377, *metro.*) 344/D3
Jackson, Tenn., U.S., *county*, 10,984 344/K2
Jackson, Tex., U.S., *county*, 14,391 346/M7
Jackson, W. Va., U.S., *county*, 28,000 360/C3
Jackson, Wisc., U.S., 4,938 364/F1
Jackson, Wisc., U.S., *county*, 19,100 364/C4
Jackson, Wyo., U.S., 8,647 366/A2
Jackson, Wyo., U.S., *lake* 366/A2
Jacksonburg, Ohio, U.S., 67 328/A6
Jackson Ctr., Ohio, U.S., 1,369 328/B5
Jackson Ctr., Penn., U.S., 221 336/A3
Jackson Jct., Iowa, U.S., 60 274/K1
Jacksonport, Ark., U.S., 235 244/D2
Jacksonport, Wisc., U.S., 125 364/F4
Jacksons Arm, Nfld., Can., 420 218/C4
Jacksons Gap, Ala., U.S., 761 238/D3
Jacksonville, Ala., U.S., 8,404 238/D2
Jacksonville, Ark., U.S., 29,916 244/C3
Jacksonville, Fla., U.S., 735,617, (1,100,491, *metro.*) 256/G1
Jacksonville, Ga., U.S., 118 260/F8
Jacksonville, Ill., U.S., 18,940 266/C4
Jacksonville, Maine, U.S., 350 286/E4
Jacksonville, Md., U.S., 900 288/H1
Jacksonville, Mo., U.S., 163 302/D2
Jacksonville, N.J., U.S., 500 314/D3
Jacksonville, N.C., U.S., 66,715, (150,355, *metro.*) 322/L5
Jacksonville, Ohio, U.S., 544 328/F7
Jacksonville, Oreg., U.S., 2,235 334/D5
Jacksonville, Penn., U.S., 675 336/C4
Jacksonville, Tex., U.S., 13,868 346/N4
Jacksonville, Vt., U.S., 237 352/B5
Jacksonville Beach, Fla., U.S., 20,990 256/G1
Jackstown, Ky., U.S., 40 280/F2
Jacktown, Okla., U.S. 330/E2
Jacmel, Haiti 205/C2
Jacob Lake, Ariz., U.S. 242/C1
Jacobs, Fla., U.S., 281 256/C1
Jacobson, Minn., U.S., 50 298/D4
Jacobstown, N.J., U.S., 950 314/D3
Jacobsville, Mich., U.S. 294/A3
Jacobus, Penn., U.S., 1,203 336/H6
Jaconita, N. Mex., U.S., 343 317/D2
Jacques-Cartier, Que., Can., *river* 226/E4
Jacques Cartier Prov. Park, Que., Can. 226/E4
Jacquet River, N.B., Can. 217/C1
Jadabpur, India 128/Inset II
Jaén, Sp., 112,590 94/E4
Jaén, Sp., *province* 94/E4
Jaffna, Sri Lan., 129,000 126/B2
Jaffna, Sri Lan., *lagoon* 126/B2
Jaffrey, N.H., U.S., 5,476 312/B6
Jagdalpur, India 128/D5
Jagual, P.R. 206/C2
Jaipur, India, 2,324,319, (2,324,319, *metro.*) 128/C3
Jaipurhat, Bangl. 127/B3
Jajce, Bos.-Her. 98/B1
Jakarta, Indon., *capital*, 9,373,900, (10,620,000, *metro.*) 122/B2
Jakarta, Indon., *province* 122/B2
Jakes Corner, Ariz., U.S. 242/D3
Jakin, Ga., U.S., 157 260/B9
Jakobstad, Fin. 81/B2
Jakupica, Mac., *mountains* 100/B2
Jal, N. Mex., U.S., 1,996 317/G5
Jalalabad, Afg., 53,915 129/C2
Jalal-Abad, Kyrg., 74,200 131/C2
Jalal-Abad, Kyrg., *province* 131/B2
Jalandhar, India 128/C2
Jalingo, Nig. 152/F3
Jalisco, Mex., *state* 200/D4
Jalu, Lib. 145/D2
Jaluit, Marsh. Is., *island* 173/B2
Jamaame, Som. 157/A3
Jamaica, *nation* 204/B3
Jamaica, *nation* 194
Jamaica, Ill., U.S., 80 266/F4
Jamaica, Iowa, U.S., 237 274/F4
Jamaica, (see New York), N.Y., U.S. 320/B2
Jamaica, Vt., U.S., 946 352/B4
Jamaica Beach, Tex., U.S., 1,075 346/P6
Jamalpur, Bangl., 101,242 127/C4
Jambi, Indon. 122/B2
Jambi, Indon., *province* 122/B2
Jambol, Bul. 101/E3
Jambol, Bul., *oblast* 101/E3
James, Ont., Can., *bay* 222/D2
James, Que., Can., *bay* 225/A3
James, Ga., U.S., 150 260/E6
James, Miss., U.S., 90 300/A2
James, N. Dak., U.S., *river* 326/F2, G3, G4
James, S. Dak., U.S., *river* 342/G2, G3
James, Va., U.S., *river* 354/F6, K6
James, W. Va., U.S., *river* 360/H6
James A. Garfield N.H.S., Ohio, U.S. 328/H2, J8
Jamesburg, Ill., U.S., 70 266/F3
Jamesburg, N.J., U.S., 6,025 314/E3
James Campbell N.W.R., Hawaii, U.S. 262/J1
James City, N.C., U.S., 5,420 322/L4
James City, Penn., U.S., 200 336/D2
James City, Va., U.S., *county*, 48,102 354/K6
Jameson, Mo., U.S., 120 302/C1
Jamesport, Mo., U.S., 505 302/C2
Jamesport, N.Y., U.S., 1,526 320/F1
Jamestown, Colo., U.S., 205 250/E1
Jamestown, Ind., U.S., 886 270/C5
Jamestown, Kans., U.S., 399 276/E2
Jamestown, Ky., U.S., 1,624 280/E4
Jamestown, La., U.S., 149 282/C2
Jamestown, Mich., U.S., 750 294/D7
Jamestown, Mo., U.S., 382 302/D3
Jamestown, N.Y., U.S., 31,730, (139,750, *metro.*) 320/C6
Jamestown, N.C., U.S., 3,088 322/F3
Jamestown, N. Dak., U.S., 15,527 326/G3
Jamestown, Ohio, U.S., 1,917 328/C6
Jamestown, Okla., U.S. 330/G1
Jamestown, Penn., U.S., 636 336/A3
Jamestown, R.I., U.S., 5,622 339/D5
Jamestown, S.C., U.S., 97 340/E3
Jamestown, Tenn., U.S., 1,839 344/M2
Jamestown, Va., U.S., 90 354/K6

James Town, Wyo., U.S., 552 . . . . .366/B3
Jamestown Res., N. Dak., U.S. 326/G2
Jamesville, N.Y., U.S., 550 . . . . .320/J5
Jamesville, N.C., U.S., 502 . . . . .322/M3
Jamieson, Oreg., U.S., 40 . . . . .334/J3
Jamison, Iowa, U.S. 274/G5
Jammu, India, 206,135 (223,361, metro.) . . .128/C2
Jammu and Kashmir, India, state 128/C2
Jamnagar, India, 325,475, (365,464, metro.) .128/B4
Jampur, India .128/Inset II
Jämsä, Fin. 81/C2
Jamshedpur, India, 461,212, (1,101,804, metro.) 128/E4
Jämtland, Swe., county 80/B2
Jamuna, Bangl., river 127/C4
Janai, India . . . . .128/Inset II
Janakpur, Nepal 126/C3
Jane, Mo., U.S., 200 . . . . .302/B5
Jane Lew, W. Va., U.S., 406 . . . . .360/F2
Janesville, Calif., U.S., 550 . . . . .246/E2
Janesville, Iowa, U.S., 829 . . . . .274/K2
Janesville, Minn., U.S., 2,109 . . . . .298/D6
Janesville, Wisc., U.S., 59,498, (152,307, metro.) 364/D6
Janeville, N.B., Can. 217/D1
Jangy-Bazar, Kyrg. .131/B2
Janice, Miss., U.S. .300/C4
Jan Lake, Sask., Can. 227/H6
Jansen, Colo., U.S., 125 . . . . .250/F4
Jansen, Nebr., U.S., 143 . . . . .308/G3
Japan, nation 110
Japan, Jap., sea 114/B2
Japan Alps, Jap., mountains 114/B2
Japeri, Braz. . . . . .188/Inset I
Japton, Ark., U.S., 60 . . . . .244/B2
Japurá, Braz., river .188/B2
Jarales, N. Mex., U.S., 1,434 . . . . .317/D3
Jarama, Sp., river . . . . .94/Inset II
Jarash, Jor. 134/A1
Jarash, Jor., governorate 134/B1
Jarbidge, Nev., U.S. 310/C1
Jardine, Mont., U.S. 306/F4
Jari, Braz., river 188/C1
Jaroso, Colo., U.S. .250/E4
Jarratt, Va., U.S., 589 . . . . .354/J7
Jarrettsville, Md., U.S., 2,756 . . . . .288/J1
Jarvie, Alta., Can., 112 . . . . .212/D4
Jarvis, Ont., Can., 2,180 . . . . .223/E5
Jarvisburg, N.C., U.S., 200 . . . . .322/P2
Jask, Iran 130/D4
Jasonville, Ind., U.S., 2,490 . . . . .270/B6
Jasper, Alta., Can., 3,716 . . . . .212/A5
Jasper, Ala., U.S., 14,052 . . . . .238/B2
Jasper, Ark., U.S., 498 . . . . .244/B1
Jasper, Fla., U.S., 1,780 . . . . .256/F1
Jasper, Ga., U.S., 2,167 . . . . .260/C3
Jasper, Ga., U.S., county, 11,426 . . . . .260/D5
Jasper, Ill., U.S., county, 10,117 . . . . .266/E4
Jasper, Ind., U.S., 12,100 . . . . .270/C8
Jasper, Ind., U.S., county, 30,043 . . . . .270/C8
Jasper, Iowa, U.S., county, 37,213 . . . . .274/H4
Jasper, Mich., U.S., 400 . . . . .294/E8
Jasper, Minn., U.S., 597 . . . . .298/A7
Jasper, Miss., U.S., county, 18,149 . . . . .300/C4
Jasper, Mo., U.S., 1,011 . . . . .302/B4
Jasper, Mo., U.S., county, 104,686 . . . . .302/B4
Jasper, N.Y., U.S., 325 . . . . .320/G6
Jasper, Ohio, U.S., 350 . . . . .328/D7
Jasper, Oreg., U.S., 700 . . . . .334/D4
Jasper, S.C., U.S., county, 20,678 . . . . .340/C4
Jasper, Tenn., U.S., 3,214 . . . . .344/K4
Jasper, Tex., U.S., 8,247 . . . . .346/K5
Jasper, Tex., U.S., county, 35,604 . . . . .346/P5
Jasper Natl. Park, Alta., Can. 212/B5
Jasper Natl. Park, Alta., Can. 214/O5
Jastrebac, Serb.-Mont., mountains 99/B3
Jászberény, Hun. 91/B2
Jász-Nagykun-Szolnok, Hun., county 91/C2
Java, Indon., island 122/C2
Java, Indon., sea 122/C2
Java, S. Dak., U.S., 197 . . . . .342/E3
Java, Va., U.S., 175 . . . . .354/E7
Java Ctr., N.Y., U.S., 225 . . . . .320/E5
Javari, Braz., river .188/B3
Jawhar, Som. 157/B3
Jay, Fla., U.S., 579 .256/A1
Jay, Fla., U.S., county, 21,806 . . . . .270/G4
Jay, N.Y., U.S., 350 . . . . .320/P2
Jay, Okla., U.S., 2,482 . . . . .330/H1
Jay, Vt., U.S., 426 .352/C1
Jay, Vt., U.S., peak .352/B1
Jaya, Puncak, Indon., mountain 122/F2
Jayapura, Indon. 122/F2
Jay Em, Wyo., U.S. 366/A2
Jayess, Miss., U.S., 175 . . . . .300/B4
Jayton, Tex., U.S., 513 . . . . .346/H2
Jayuya, P.R. 206/C2
Jaz Murian, Hamun-e, Iran, lake 130/D4
Jazzin, Leb. 134/A2
J. Clark Salyer N.W.R., N. Dak., U.S. 326/E1
Jean, Nev., U.S. 310/C4
Jean, Tex., U.S., 80 . . . . .346/K2
Jeanerette, La., U.S., 5,997 . . . . .282/F7
Jean Lafitte, La., U.S., 2,137 . . . . .282/J7, K4
Jean Lafitte Natl. Hist. Park and Pres.,
   La., U.S. 282/J7, K3
Jeannette, Penn., U.S., 10,654 . . . . .336/B5
Jebba, Nig. 152/C3
Jebel Toubkal, Mor., mountain 147/C2
Jecheon, S. Kor. 116/C4
Jedburgh, Scot., U.K., 4,090 . . . . .62/L8
Jeddito, Ariz., U.S., 390 . . . . .242/C3
Jeddo, Penn., U.S., 144 . . . . .336/K3
Jeddore, Nfld., Can., lake 218/D5
Jeff Davis, Ga., U.S., county, 12,684 . . . . . . .260/F8
Jeff Davis, Tex., U.S., county, 2,207 . . . . .346/D5
Jeffers, Minn., U.S., 396 . . . . .298/B6
Jeffers, Mont., U.S., 70 . . . . .306/E4
Jefferson, Ala., U.S., county, 662,047 . . .238/C2, K4
Jefferson, Ark., U.S., 175 . . . . .244/C3
Jefferson, Ark., U.S., county, 84,278 . . . . . . .244/C3
Jefferson, Colo., U.S. 250/D2
Jefferson, Colo., U.S., county, 525,507 . .250/A3, E2
Jefferson, Fla., U.S., county, 12,902 . . . . .256/E1
Jefferson, Ga., U.S., 3,825 . . . . .260/D5
Jefferson, Ga., U.S., county, 17,266 . . . . .260/D5
Jefferson, Ida., U.S., county, 19,155 . . . . . . .264/E6
Jefferson, Ill., U.S., county, 40,045 . . . . .266/E5
Jefferson, Ind., U.S., county, 31,705 . . . . . . .270/E7
Jefferson, Iowa, U.S., 4,626 . . . . .274/F3
Jefferson, Iowa, U.S., county, 16,181 . . . . . . .274/K5
Jefferson, Kans., U.S., 70 . . . . .276/G4
Jefferson, Kans., U.S., county, 18,426 . . . . . .276/G2
Jefferson, La., U.S., 11,843 . . . . .282/K3
Jefferson, La., U.S., parish, 455,466 . . . .282/J7, K3
Jefferson, Maine, U.S., 2,388 . . . . .286/C4
Jefferson, Mass., U.S., 1,600 . . . . .292/G3
Jefferson, Miss., U.S., 9,740 . . . . .300/A3
Jefferson, Mo., U.S., county, 198,099 . . .302/F3, G4
Jefferson, Mont., U.S., county, 10,049 . . . . . .306/D3
Jefferson, Nebr., U.S., county, 8,333 . . . . . . .308/G3
Jefferson, Nev., U.S., mountain 310/D2
Jefferson, N.H., U.S., 1,006 . . . . .312/D3

Jefferson, N.J., U.S., 19,717 . . . . .314/C4
Jefferson, N.Y., U.S., county, 111,738 . . . . . .320/K2
Jefferson, N.C., U.S., 1,422 . . . . .322/C2
Jefferson, Ohio, U.S., 3,572 . . . . .328/J2
Jefferson, Ohio, U.S., county, 73,894 . . . . . . .328/J5
Jefferson, Okla., U.S., 230 . . . . .330/E1
Jefferson, Okla., U.S., county, 6,818 . . . . . . .330/E3
Jefferson, Oreg., U.S., 2,487 . . . . .334/D3
Jefferson, Oreg., U.S., 19,009 . . . . .334/E3
Jefferson, Oreg., U.S., mountain 334/E3
Jefferson, (Allegheny County), Penn., U.S., 9,666 336/B5
Jefferson, (Greene County), Penn., U.S., 337 . .336/A6
Jefferson, (York County), Penn., U.S., 631 . . .336/H6
Jefferson, Penn., U.S., county, 45,932 . . . . . .336/D3
Jefferson, S.C., U.S., 704 . . . . .340/D2
Jefferson, S. Dak., U.S., 586 . . . . .342/J5
Jefferson, Tenn., U.S., county, 44,294 . . . . . .344/Q2
Jefferson, Tex., U.S., 2,024 . . . . .346/P3
Jefferson, Tex., U.S., county, 252,051 . . . . . .346/P6
Jefferson, Wash., U.S., county, 25,953 . . . . . .358/B2
Jefferson, W. Va., U.S., county, 42,190 . . . . . .360/L2
Jefferson, Wisc., U.S., 7,338 . . . . .364/E5
Jefferson, Wisc., U.S., county, 74,021 . . . . . .364/E6
Jefferson City, Mo., U.S., state capital, 39,636 .302/D3
Jefferson City, Tenn., U.S., 7,760 . . . . .344/P2
Jefferson Davis, La., U.S., parish, 31,435 . . . .282/D6
Jefferson Davis, Miss., U.S., county, 13,962 . .300/C4
Jefferson Hts., N.Y., U.S., 1,104 . . . . .320/P6
Jefferson Natl. For., Va., U.S. . . .354/A6, C2, C5, E2
Jeffersonton, Va., U.S., 225 . . . . .354/H3
Jeffersontown, Ky., U.S., 26,633 . . . . .280/B2
Jefferson Valley, N.Y., U.S., 14,891 . . . . .320/B1
Jeffersonville, Ga., U.S., 1,209 . . . . .260/E6
Jeffersonville, Ind., U.S., 27,362 . . . . .270/E8
Jeffersonville, Ky., U.S., 1,804 . . . . .280/G3
Jeffersonville, N.Y., U.S., 420 . . . . .320/M7
Jeffersonville, Ohio, U.S., 1,288 . . . . .328/C6
Jeffersonville, Vt., U.S., 568 . . . . .352/B1
Jeffrey, W. Va., U.S., 300 . . . . .360/C5
Jeffrey City, Wyo., U.S., 106 . . . . .366/C2
Jeiseyville, Ill., U.S., 128 . . . . .266/D4
Jeju, S. Kor., 258,511 . . . . .116/Inset
Jeju, S. Kor., province 116/Inset
Jeju, S. Kor., strait 116/Inset
Jeju-do, S. Kor., island 116/Inset
Jejuí-Guazú, Para., river 187/D4
Jejur, India . . . . .128/Inset II
Jēkabpils, Lat. 82/C2
Jekyll, Ga., U.S., island 260/J9
Jelenia Góra, Pol. 83/B3
Jelgava, Lat., 71,004 . . . . .82/B2
Jellico, Tenn., U.S., 2,448 . . . . .344/N1
Jelloway, Ohio, U.S., 175 . . . . .328/F4
Jemez Ind. Res., N. Mex., U.S. 317/D2
Jemez Pueblo, N. Mex., U.S., 1,953 . . . . .317/D2
Jemez Sprs., N. Mex., U.S., 375 . . . . .317/D2
Jemison, Ala., U.S., 2,248 . . . . .238/C3
Jemseg, N.B., Can. 217/C3
Jena, Ger. 86/B3
Jena, Fla., U.S., 400 . . . . .256/E2
Jena, La., U.S., 2,971 . . . . .282/E3
Jenera, Ohio, U.S., 235 . . . . .328/C4
Jengish Chokusu, Kyrg., mountain 131/G1
Jenifer, Ala., U.S., 550 . . . . .238/D2
Jenison, Mich., U.S., 17,211 . . . . .294/D7
Jenkinjones, W. Va., U.S., 350 . . . . .360/D6
Jenkins, Ga., U.S., county, 8,575 . . . . .260/G6
Jenkins, Ky., U.S., 2,401 . . . . .280/H3
Jenkins, Minn., U.S., 287 . . . . .298/C4
Jenkins, Mo., U.S., 50 . . . . .302/C5
Jenkins, N.J., U.S. .314/D4
Jenkinsburg, Ga., U.S., 203 . . . . .260/C5
Jenkins Neck, N.J., U.S. 314/D4
Jenkintown, Penn., U.S., 4,478 . . . . .336/M6
Jenks, Okla., U.S., 9,557 . . . . .330/G1
Jenner, Alta., Can. .212/E6
Jenner, Calif., U.S., 50 . . . . .246/B3
Jenners, Penn., U.S., 850 . . . . .336/C5
Jennerstown, Penn., U.S., 714 . . . . .336/C5
Jennette, Ark., U.S., 124 . . . . .244/E2
Jennie, Ark., U.S., 40 . . . . .244/D4
Jennings, Fla., U.S., 833 . . . . .256/E1
Jennings, Ind., U.S., county, 27,554 . . . . .270/E6
Jennings, Kans., U.S., 146 . . . . .276/B2
Jennings, La., U.S., 10,986 . . . . .282/D6
Jennings, Mo., U.S., 15,469 . . . . .302/J3
Jennings, Okla., U.S., 373 . . . . .330/F1
Jennings Lodge, Oreg., U.S., 7,036 . . . . .334/A3
Jenny Lake, Wyo., U.S. 366/A2
Jenny Lind, Ark., U.S., 650 . . . . .244/A2
Jenpeg, Man., Can. 215/B2
Jensen, Utah, U.S., 125 . . . . .350/D1
Jensen Beach, Fla., U.S., 11,100 . . . . . .256/A3, H4
Jeongju, S. Kor., 531,376 . . . . .116/B4
Jeonju, S. Kor., 563,153 . . . . .116/B5
Jerauld, S. Dak., U.S., county, 2,295 . . . . . . .342/G3
Jérémie, Haiti, 43,277 . . . . .205/A2
Jerez de la Frontera, Sp., 183,273 . . . . .94/C4
Jericho, Ark., U.S., 184 . . . . .244/E2
Jericho, Tex., U.S. .346/G9
Jericho, Utah, U.S. .350/B4
Jericho, Vt., U.S., 5,015 . . . . .352/B1
Jericho Ctr., Vt., U.S., 375 . . . . .352/B2
Jerico, Iowa, U.S. .274/K1
Jerico Sprs., Mo., U.S., 259 . . . . .302/B4
Jerimoth, R.I., U.S., hill 339/B2
Jermyn, Penn., U.S., 2,287 . . . . .336/K2
Jerome, Ariz., U.S., 329 . . . . .242/C3
Jerome, Ark., U.S., 46 . . . . .244/D4
Jerome, Fla., U.S., 40 . . . . .256/G6
Jerome, Ida., U.S., 7,780 . . . . .264/C7
Jerome, Ida., U.S., county, 18,342 . . . . .264/C7
Jerome, Ill., U.S., 1,414 . . . . .266/D4
Jerome, Penn., U.S., 1,068 . . . . .336/C5
Jeromesville, Ohio, U.S., 478 . . . . .328/F4
Jerry City, Ohio, U.S., 453 . . . . .328/C3
Jerryville, W. Va., U.S. 360/F4
Jersey, U.K., island . . . . .60/Inset II
Jersey, Ark., U.S. 244/C4
Jersey, Ga., U.S., 163 . . . . .260/D5
Jersey, Ill., U.S., county, 21,668 . . . . . . .266/A3, C4
Jersey City, N.J., U.S., 240,055 . . . . . .314/B2, E2
Jersey Shore, Penn., U.S., 4,482 . . . . .336/G3
Jersey Vil., Tex., U.S., 6,880 . . . . .346/A6
Jerseyville, Ill., U.S., 7,984 . . . . .266/C4
Jerseyville, N.J., U.S., 1,000 . . . . .314/E3
Jerudong, Bru. 121/B2
Jerusalem, Isr., capital, 627,900 . . . . .135/B2
Jerusalem, Isr., district 135/B2
Jerusalem, Ark., U.S., 150 . . . . .244/C2
Jerusalem, Ohio, U.S., 152 . . . . .328/H6
Jerusalem, R.I., U.S., 800 . . . . .339/C5
Jesenice, Slove., 21,386 . . . . .98/B3
Jessamine, Ky., U.S., county, 39,041 . . . . . . .280/F3
Jessie, N. Dak., U.S., 50 . . . . .326/G2
Jessietown, Ky., U.S., 175 . . . . .280/G4
Jessieville, Ark., U.S., 200 . . . . .244/B3
Jessore, Bangl., 160,198 . . . . .127/C5
Jessup, Md., U.S., 7,865 . . . . .288/J2

Jessup, Penn., U.S., 4,718 . . . . .336/J7
Jesterville, Md., U.S., 225 . . . . .288/L6
Jesup, Ga., U.S., 9,279 . . . . .260/H8
Jesup, Iowa, U.S., 2,212 . . . . .274/K3
Jésus, Que., Can., island 226/J3
Jet, Okla., U.S., 230 . . . . .330/D1
Jetait, Man., Can. 215/A1
Jetersville, Va., U.S., 60 . . . . .354/G6
Jewel Cave Natl. Mon., S. Dak., U.S. 342/B4
Jewell, Iowa, U.S., 1,239 . . . . .274/G3
Jewell, Kans., U.S., 483 . . . . .276/D2
Jewell, Kans., U.S., county, 3,791 . . . . .276/D2
Jewell, Ohio, U.S., 150 . . . . .328/B3
Jewell Ridge, Va., U.S., 325 . . . . .354/B5
Jewell Valley, Va., U.S., 250 . . . . .354/E2
Jewett, Ill., U.S., 232 . . . . .266/E4
Jewett, Ohio, U.S., 784 . . . . .328/H5
Jewett, Tex., U.S., 861 . . . . .346/M4
Jewett City, Conn., U.S., 3,053 . . . . .253/F3
Jezreel, Isr., valley .135/B1
Jhang Sadar, Pak., 293,366 . . . . .129/D3
Jhansi, India 128/C3
Jhelum, Pak., 147,392 . . . . .129/D3
Jhelum, Pak., river .129/D3
Jiamusi, China 119/G1
Ji'an, China 119/E2
Jiangsu, China, province 119/E2
Jiangxi, China, province 119/E3
Jicarilla Apache Ind. Res., N. Mex., U.S. 317/C1
Jiddah, Bahr., island 137/C1
Jiddah, Sa. Arab., 2,046,251 . . . . .136/A2
Jigawa, Nig., state .152/E1
Jigger, La., U.S., 90 . . . . .282/F2
Jiggs, Nev., U.S. 310/C1
Jihlava, Czh. Rep., 53,000 . . . . .92/B3
Jihočeský, Czh. Rep., region 92/B3
Jihomoravský, Czh. Rep., region 92/C4
Jilib, Som. 157/A3
Jilin, China, 1,088,420, (3,974,260, metro.) . .119/F1
Jilin, China, province 119/F1
Jima, Eth., 119,717 . . . . .156/B3
Jimaní, Dom. Rep. .205/A2
Jiménez, Mex., 31,195, (38,323, metro.) 200/D2
Jim Falls, Wisc., U.S., 325 . . . . .364/B3
Jim Hogg, Tex., U.S., county, 5,281 . . . . .346/K8
Jimmy Carter Natl. Historic Site, Ga., U.S. . . .260/C7
Jim Thorpe, Penn., U.S., 4,804 . . . . .336/K4
Jimtown, Del., U.S., 175 . . . . .255/D6
Jim Wells, Tex., U.S., county, 39,326 . . . . . . .346/K8
Jinan, China, 1,359,130, (3,375,830, metro.) .119/E2
Jingdezhen, China .119/E3
Jingo, Kans., U.S. .276/H3
Jinhae, S. Kor. 116/C5
Jining, China 119/E2
Jinja, Ug., 86,520 .157/C3
Jinju, S. Kor., 329,886 . . . . .116/C5
Jinotega, Nicar. 202/B2
Jinotega, Nicar., department 202/B2
Jinotepe, Nicar. 202/A3
Jinsha, (Yangtze), China, river 119/C2
Jinzhou, China, 599,490, (4,448,460, metro.) .119/F1
Ji-Paraná, Braz. 188/B3
Jipijapa, Ecua. 185/A3
Jirgatol, Taj. 132/B1
Jiu, Rom., river 101/B3
Jiujiang, China 119/E3
Jixi, China 119/G1
Jizan, Sa. Arab. 136/B2
Jizan, Sa. Arab., emirate 136/B2
Jizzakh, Uzb. 132/C2
Jizzakh, Uzb., province 132/C3
Joanna, S.C., U.S., 1,609 . . . . .340/C2
Joaquin, Tex., U.S., 925 . . . . .346/P4
Jobos, P.R. 206/C3
Jobstown, N.J., U.S., 250 . . . . .314/D3
Jo Daviess, Ill., U.S., county, 22,289 . . . . . . .266/C1
Jodhpur, India 128/B3
Joe Batts Arm, Nfld., Can., 889 . . . . .218/D4
Joel, Wisc., U.S. 364/A3
Joensuu, Fin., 51,758 . . . . .81/C2
Joes, Colo., U.S., 100 . . . . .250/H2
Joetsu, Jap. 114/C2
Joggins, N.S., Can. 221/C2
Johannesburg, S. Afr., 752,349,
   (2,884,817, metro.) 162/C2
Johannesburg, Calif., U.S., 176 . . . . .246/H7
Johannesburg, Mich., U.S., 80 . . . . .294/E5
John Day, Oreg., U.S., 1,821 . . . . .334/H3
John Day, Oreg., U.S., river 334/F2
John Day Fossil Beds Natl. Mon., Oreg., U.S. .334/F3, G3
John dor Prairie, Alta., Can. 212/C2
Johnetta, Ky., U.S. .280/F3
John F. Kennedy N.H.S., Mass., U.S. 292/C8
John F. Kennedy Space Ctr., Fla., U.S. 256/H3
John H. Kerr, N.C., Va., U.S., reservoir 322/H1
John H. Kerr, Va., U.S., reservoir 354/F7
John Martin, Colo., U.S., reservoir 250/G3
John O'Groats, Scot., U.K. 62/K1, M2
Johns, Miss., U.S., 175 . . . . .300/C3
Johnsburg, Ill., U.S., 5,391 . . . . .266/A4
Johnsburg, N.Y., U.S., 375 . . . . .320/N3
Johnsburg, Wisc., U.S., 200 . . . . .364/E5
Johnson, Ark., U.S., 2,319 . . . . .244/A1
Johnson, Ga., U.S., county, 8,560 . . . . .260/F6
Johnson, Ill., U.S., county, 12,878 . . . . .266/E6
Johnson, Iowa, U.S., county, 111,006 . . . . . . .274/J4
Johnson, Kans., U.S., county, 451,086 . . .276/H1, H3
Johnson, Ky., U.S., county, 23,445 . . . . .280/H3
Johnson, Minn., U.S. 298/A5
Johnson, Mo., U.S., county, 48,258 . . . . .302/C3
Johnson, Nebr., U.S., 280 . . . . .308/H3
Johnson, Nebr., U.S., county, 4,488 . . . . .308/H3
Johnson, Okla., U.S., 223 . . . . .330/F2
Johnson, Tenn., U.S., county, 17,499 . . . . . . .344/T2
Johnson, Tex., U.S., county, 126,811 . . . . . . .346/L3
Johnson, Vt., U.S., 3,274 . . . . .352/B1
Johnson, Wash., U.S. 358/H3
Johnson, Wyo., U.S., county, 7,075 . . . . .366/C1
Johnsonburg, N.J., U.S., 375 . . . . .314/D2
Johnsonburg, Penn., U.S., 3,003 . . . . .336/D3
Johnson City, Kans., U.S., 1,528 . . . . .276/A4
Johnson City, N.Y., U.S., 15,535 . . . . .320/K6
Johnson City, Oreg., U.S., 634 . . . . .334/A3
Johnson City, Tenn., U.S., 55,469,
   (480,091, metro.) 344/S2
Johnson City, Tex., U.S., 1,191 . . . . .346/C2, K5
Johnson Creek, Wisc., U.S., 1,581 . . . . .364/E5
Johnson Lake N.W.R., N. Dak., U.S. 326/G2
Johnson Lane, Nev., U.S., 4,837 . . . . .310/A2
Johnsons Bayou, La., U.S., 500 . . . . .282/C7
Johnsonville, Ill., U.S., 69 . . . . .266/E5
Johnsonville, S.C., U.S., 1,418 . . . . .340/E3
Johnston, Iowa, U.S., 8,649 . . . . .274/G4
Johnston, Miss., U.S. 300/B4
Johnston, N.C., U.S., county, 121,965 . . . . . .322/J3
Johnston, S.C., U.S., 2,362 . . . . .340/C3
Johnston, S.C., U.S., county, 10,513 . . . . . . .330/D1

Johnston City, Ill., U.S., 3,557 . . . . .266/E6
Johnstone, Tex., U.S., 50 . . . . .346/H6
Johnstonville, Calif., U.S., 450 . . . . .246/E2
Johnstown, Colo., U.S., 3,827 . . . . .250/E1
Johnstown, Nebr., U.S., 53 . . . . .308/D1
Johnstown, N.Y., U.S., 8,511 . . . . .320/N4
Johnstown, Ohio, U.S., 3,440 . . . . .328/E6
Johnstown, Penn., U.S., 23,906,
   (232,621, metro.) 336/D5
Johnstown Flood Natl. Mem., Penn., U.S. 336/D5
Johntown, Tex., U.S., 125 . . . . .346/N2
Johor, Sing., strait .123/B1
Johor Bahru, Malay., 328,436, (441,703, metro.) .121/B2
Joice, Iowa, U.S., 231 . . . . .274/H1
Joiner, Ark., U.S., 540 . . . . .244/E2
Joinville, Antar. 192/C12
Joinville, Braz., 429,604 . . . . .188/D4
Joka, India . . . . .128/Inset II
Joliet, Ill., U.S., 106,221 . . . . .266/B6, B6
Joliet, Mont., U.S., 575 . . . . .306/H4
Joliette, Que., Can., 17,837 . . . . .226/C5
Joliette, N. Dak., U.S. 326/H1
Jolivue, Va., U.S., 1,037 . . . . .354/E4
Jolley, Iowa, U.S., 54 . . . . .274/E3
Jolly, Tex., U.S., 188 . . . . .346/D2
Jollyville, Tex., U.S., 15,813 . . . . .346/D2
Jolo, Phil. 120/B5
Jolo, Phil., island 120/B5
Jonah, Tex., U.S. 346/E1
Jonancy, Ky., U.S., 350 . . . . .280/H3
Jonava, Lith. 82/C2
Jones, Nun., Can., sound 220/L1
Jones, Ala., U.S., 70 . . . . .238/C3
Jones, Ga., U.S., county, 23,639 . . . . .260/D6
Jones, Iowa, U.S., county, 20,221 . . . . .274/M3
Jones, La., U.S. 282/F1
Jones, Mich., U.S., 450 . . . . .294/D8
Jones, Miss., U.S., county, 64,958 . . . . .300/C4
Jones, N.C., U.S., county, 10,381 . . . . .322/L4
Jones, Okla., U.S., 2,517 . . . . .330/B3, G2
Jones, S. Dak., U.S., county, 1,193 . . . . .342/E3
Jones, Tex., U.S., county, 20,785 . . . . .346/H3
Jonesboro, Ark., U.S., 55,515, (82,148, metro.) .244/E2, J4
Jonesboro, Ga., U.S., 3,829 . . . . .260/C4, J4
Jonesboro, Ill., U.S., 1,853 . . . . .266/D6
Jonesboro, Ind., U.S., 1,887 . . . . .270/E4
Jonesboro, La., U.S., 3,914 . . . . .282/D2
Jonesboro, Maine, U.S., 594 . . . . .286/E4
Jonesborough, N. Ire., U.K., 460 . . . . .65/E3
Jonesborough, Tenn., U.S., 4,168 . . . . .344/S2
Jonesburg, Mo., U.S., 695 . . . . .302/E3
Jones Chapel, Ala., U.S., 50 . . . . .238/B1
Jones Creek, Tex., U.S., 2,130 . . . . .346/N7
Jones Mills, Penn., U.S., 375 . . . . .336/C5
Jonesport, Maine, U.S., 1,408 . . . . .286/E4
Jonestown, Ky., U.S. 280/F3
Jonestown, Md., U.S., 475 . . . . .288/C5
Jonestown, Miss., U.S., 1,701 . . . . .300/B1
Jonestown, Penn., U.S., 1,028 . . . . .336/J5
Jonestown, Tex., U.S., 1,681 . . . . .346/D2
Jonesville, Ind., U.S., 220 . . . . .270/E6
Jonesville, Ky., U.S., 225 . . . . .280/F2
Jonesville, La., U.S., 2,469 . . . . .282/F3
Jonesville, Mich., U.S., 2,337 . . . . .294/E7
Jonesville, N.C., U.S., 1,464 . . . . .322/D2
Jonesville, S.C., U.S., 982 . . . . .340/C2
Jonesville, Va., U.S., 375 . . . . .352/B2
Jonesville, Va., U.S., 995 . . . . .354/B3
Jong, S.L., river 149/A2
Jönköping, Swe., 117,896 . . . . .80/B3
Jönköping, Swe., county 80/B3
Jonquière, Que., Can. 226/E3
Joplin, Mo., U.S., 45,504, (157,322, metro.) . .302/B4
Joplin, Mont., U.S., 210 . . . . .306/H4
Joplin, Tex., U.S. 346/K2
Joppa, Ill., U.S., 409 . . . . .266/E6
Joppatowne, Md., U.S., 11,391 . . . . .288/J2
Jordan, nation 130
Jordan, Jor., river 134/A2
Jordan, Ala., U.S., lake 238/C3
Jordan, Iowa, U.S., 60 . . . . .274/G3
Jordan, Minn., U.S., 3,833 . . . . .298/D6
Jordan, Mont., U.S., 364 . . . . .306/L3
Jordan, N. Mex., U.S. 317/G3
Jordan, N.Y., U.S., 1,314 . . . . .320/J4
Jordan Valley, Oreg., U.S., 239 . . . . .334/J5
Jornada del Muerto, N. Mex., U.S. 317/D4
Jos, Nig. 152/E3
Jos, Nig., plateau 152/E2
Joseph, Oreg., U.S., 1,054 . . . . .334/J2
Joseph, Utah, U.S., 269 . . . . .350/B5
Joseph City, Ariz., U.S., 1,000 . . . . .242/E2
Josephine, Oreg., U.S., county, 75,726 . . . . . .334/C5
Josephine, Tex., U.S., 594 . . . . .346/D8
Josephine, Mo., U.S., 270 . . . . .302/F3
Joshua, Tex., U.S., 4,528 . . . . .346/L3
Joshua Tree, Calif., U.S., 4,207 . . . . .246/J8
Joshua Tree Natl. Park, Calif., U.S. 246/K8
Joslin, Ill., U.S., 60 .266/C2
Jotunheimen, Nor., mountains 80/B3
Jou, São T.-Prínc. 154/C4
Jourdanton, Tex., U.S., 3,732 . . . . .346/K7
Joussard, Alta., Can., 219 . . . . .212/C3
Joy, Ill., U.S., 373 . . . . .266/C2
Joy, Okla., U.S., 100 . . . . .330/D3
Joyce, La., U.S., 200 . . . . .282/D3
Joyce, Wash., U.S., 90 . . . . .358/B1
J. Strom Thurmond, Ga., U.S., lake 260/G4
J. Strom Thurmond, S.C., U.S., lake 340/B3
Juab, Utah, U.S., county, 8,238 . . . . .350/B4
Juana Díaz, P.R. 206/B2
Juan de Fuca, Br. Col., Can., strait 214/I7
Juan de Fuca, Wash., U.S., strait 358/A1
Juan Fernández, Chile 178/A6
Juanita, La., U.S., 150 . . . . .282/C5
Juanita, N. Dak., U.S. 326/G2
Juàzeiro, Braz., 60,940, (128,378, metro.) . . .188/D2
Juàzeiro do Norte, Braz., 125,248,
   (173,304, metro.) 188/E2
Juba, Sudan, 114,980 . . . . .145/C4
Jubayl, Leb. 134/A1
Jubba, Som., river .157/A3
Jubilee, Nfld., Can., lake 218/D5
Júcar, Sp., river 94/F3
Juchitán de Zaragoza, Mex., 64,642,
   (78,512, metro.) 200/F4
Jud, N. Dak., U.S., 76 . . . . .326/G3
Juda, Wisc., U.S., 325 . . . . .364/D6
Judique, N.S., Can. 221/F2
Judith Basin, Mont., U.S., county, 2,329 . . . . .306/F3
Judith Gap, Mont., U.S., 164 . . . . .306/G3
Judson, Ind., U.S. .270/C6
Judson, Minn., U.S., 70 . . . . .298/C6
Judson, S.C., U.S. .326/D3
Judson, S.C., U.S., 2,456 . . . . .340/B2, G2
Judsonia, Ark., U.S., 1,982 . . . . .244/D2
Judyville, Ind., U.S., 50 . . . . .270/B4
Juigalpa, Nicar. 202/B2
Juiz de Fora, Braz., 456,796 . . . . .188/D4
Jujuy, Arg., province 191/B3
Julesburg, Colo., U.S., 1,467 . . . . .250/H1
Juliaca, Peru, 198,553 . . . . .185/C4

Juliaetta, Ida., U.S., 609 . . . . .264/A3
Julian, Calif., U.S., 1,621 . . . . .246/J9
Julian, Nebr., U.S., 63 . . . . .308/J3
Julian, N.C., U.S., 600 . . . . .322/F3
Julian Alps, Slove., mountains 98/A2
Juliana Top, Sur., mountain 183/A3
Juliette, Ga., U.S., 200 . . . . .260/D5
Juliff, Tex., U.S., 40 .346/B7
Juliustown, N.J., U.S., 450 . . . . .314/D3
Jumla, Nepal 126/B2
Jumpertown, Miss., U.S., 404 . . . . .300/D1
Jump River, Wisc., U.S., 100 . . . . .364/C3
Junagadh, India 128/B4
Juncos, P.R. 206/D2
Junction, Ill., U.S., 139 . . . . .266/E6
Junction, La., U.S., 175 . . . . .282/C5
Junction, Tex., U.S., 2,618 . . . . .346/J5
Junction, Utah, U.S., 177 . . . . .350/B5
Junction City, Ark., U.S., 721 . . . . .244/C4
Junction City, Ga., U.S., 179 . . . . .260/C6
Junction City, Ill., U.S., 559 . . . . .266/D6
Junction City, Kans., U.S., 18,886 . . . . .276/F2
Junction City, Ky., U.S., 2,184 . . . . .280/F3
Junction City, La., U.S., 652 . . . . .282/D1
Junction City, Mo., U.S., 319 . . . . .302/F4
Junction City, Ohio, U.S., 818 . . . . .328/F6
Junction City, Oreg., U.S., 4,721 . . . . .334/C3
Junction City, S. Dak., U.S. 342/J5
Junction City, Wisc., U.S. 364/D4
Jundiaí, Braz., 210,015, (312,517, metro.) 188/D4
Juneau, U.S. 193/D12
Juneau, Alaska, U.S., state capital, 30,711 . . . . .240/J3
Juneau, Wisc., U.S., 2,485 . . . . .364/E5
Juneau, Wisc., U.S., county, 24,316 . . . . .364/C5
June Lake, Calif., U.S., 300 . . . . .246/F5
Jungfrau, Switz., mountain 90/B2
Jungo, Nev., U.S. 310/A1
Juniata, Nebr., U.S., 693 . . . . .308/E3
Juniata, Penn., U.S., county, 22,821 . . . . .336/G4
Juniata, Penn., U.S., river 336/F5
Juniata Terrace, Penn., U.S., 502 . . . . .336/F4
Junín, Peru, department 185/B3
Junior, W. Va., U.S., 450 . . . . .360/G3
Juniper, N.B., Can. .217/B2
Juniper, Ga., U.S. 260/B6
Juniper, Ida., U.S. 264/E7
Junius, S. Dak., U.S., 80 . . . . .342/H3
Juniyah, Leb. 134/A2
Juno, Ga., U.S., 100 . . . . .260/C3
Juno, Tex., U.S. 346/G5
Juno Beach, Fla., U.S., 3,262 . . . . .256/B4, H5
Juntura, Oreg., U.S. 334/H4
Juozapinės Kalnas, Lith., hill 82/C2
Jupiter, Fla., U.S., 39,328 . . . . .256/B4, H5
Jupiter Inlet Colony, Fla., U.S., 368 . . . . .256/B4
Jupiter Island, Fla., U.S., 620 . . . . .256/B4
Jura, Fr., department .88/D3
Jura, Fr., mountains .88/D3
Jūra, Lith., river 82/A2
Jura, Switz., canton .90/B1
Jura, Switz., mountains 90/A2
Jura, Scot., U.K., island 60/B2
Jura, Scot., U.K., island 62/E6
Jura N.P., Scot., U.K. 62/D7
Jurbarkas, Lith. 82/B2
Jūrmala, Lat., 58,975 . . . . .82/B2
Jurong, Sing. 123/A1
Juruá, Braz., river 188/B2
Juruena, Braz., river 188/C3
Justice, Ill., U.S., 12,193 . . . . .266/B6
Justice, N.C., U.S., 150 . . . . .322/J2
Justice, W. Va., U.S., 325 . . . . .360/C5
Justiceburg, Tex., U.S., 40 . . . . .346/G2
Justin, Tex., U.S., 1,891 . . . . .346/A8
Jutiapa, Guat. 201/D5
Juticalpa, Hond., 25,600 . . . . .202/B2
Jutland, Den., peninsula 79/B3
Juventud, Cuba, island 204/A3
Juventud, Cuba, island 204/B2
Južna, Serb.-Mont., river 99/B3
Jvari, Geo. 103/B3
Jwaneng, Bots. 160/B3
Jyväskylä, Fin., 78,996 . . . . .81/C2
K2, (Godwin Austen), China, mountain 119/A2
K2, (Godwin Austen), Pak., mountain 129/E2
Ka, Nig., river 152/C2
Kaaawa, Hawaii, U.S., 1,324 . . . . .262/J1
Kaala, Hawaii, U.S., mountain 262/H1
Kaalaea, Hawaii, U.S. 262/J2
Kaanapali, Hawaii, U.S., 1,375 . . . . .262/B3
Kabala, S.L. 149/B1
Kabale, Ug., 45,757 . . . . .157/A4
Kabalo, Congo, D.R. 155/C2
Kabardino-Balkaria, Russ., region 104/D5
Kabekona, Minn., U.S., 40 . . . . .298/C3
Kabelebo, Sur., river 183/A2
Kabetogama, Minn., U.S., 40 . . . . .298/D2
Kabir, Leb., river 134/B1
Kabompo, Zam., river 159/A2
Kabul, Afg., capital, 1,526,971 . . . . .129/B2
Kabul, Afg., river 129/B2
Kabwe, Zam., 233,197 . . . . .159/B2
Kachin, Mya., state 125/C1
Kackley, Kans., U.S. 276/E2
Ka Dake, Swaz. 161/B2
Kadavu, Fiji, island .174/B3
Kadavu, Fiji, passage 174/A3
Kadéï, C.A.R., river 154/A3
Kadıköy, Tur. 133/A2
Kadoka, S. Dak., U.S., 706 . . . . .342/D4
Kadoma, Zimb. 160/B2
Kaduna, Nig. 152/D2
Kaduna, Nig., river 152/D2
Kaduna, Nig., state 152/D2
Kadugli, Sudan 145/B3
Kaédi, Maur., 107,309, (metro.) 148/A2
Kaélé, Came. 153/B1
Kaena, Hawaii, U.S., point 262/B5, H1
Kaeo, N.Z. 171/B2
Kaesŏng, N. Kor. 116/B4
Kaesŏng, N. Kor., province 116/B3
Kaffrine, Sen. 148/B2
Kafr ad Dawwar, Egy., 232,000 . . . . .144/B1
Kafu, Ug., river 157/B3
Kafue, Zam. 159/B3
Kafue, Zam., river .159/B2
Kaga Bandoro, C.A.R. 154/A2
Kagawa, Jap., prefecture 114/B3
Kagawong, Ont., Can. 222/D3
Kagera, Tan., river .152/C1
Kagera, Tan., river .152/B1
Kagera, Ug., river .157/B4
Kagitumba, Rwa. 152/C1
Kagoshima, Jap., 552,000 . . . . .114/A4
Kagoshima, Jap., prefecture 114/A4
Kahakuloa, Hawaii, U.S. 262/B3
Kahala, Hawaii, U.S. 262/G3
Kahaluu, Hawaii, U.S., 2,414 . . . . .262/F5, J2
Kahaluu Forest Reserve, Hawaii, U.S. 262/J1
Kahana, Hawaii, U.S. 262/B3, J1
Kahana, Hawaii, U.S., bay 262/J1
Kahayan, Indon., river 122/C2

Kahemba, Congo, D.R. 155/B2
Kahikinui Forest Reserve, Hawaii, U.S. 262/C4
Kahiu, Hawaii, U.S., point 262/A3
Kahlotus, Wash., U.S., 214 . . . . .358/G3
Kahnawake, Que., Can. 226/H6
Kahntah, Br. Col., Can. 214/M2
Kahoka, Mo., U.S., 2,241 . . . . .302/E1
Kahoolawe, Hawaii, U.S., island 262/B4, D6
Kahraman Maraş, Tur., province 133/D2
Kahua, Hawaii, U.S. 262/G4
Kahuku, Hawaii, U.S. 262/G7, J1
Kahuku, Hawaii, U.S., point 262/C1, J1
Kahuku Forest Reserve, Hawaii, U.S. 262/J1
Kahului, Hawaii, U.S., 20,146 . . . . .262/C3, D5
Kahului, Hawaii, U.S., bay 262/C3
Kai, Indon., islands 122/E2
Kaibab, Ariz., U.S., 275 . . . . .242/C1
Kaibab Ind. Res., Ariz., U.S. 242/C1
Kaibab Natl. For., Ariz., U.S. 242/C1, C2, D2
Kaibito, Ariz., U.S., 1,607 . . . . .242/D1
Kaieteur, Guy., falls 183/B3
Kaifeng, China 119/E2
Kaihon Kug, Ariz., U.S. 242/D1
Kaikipaula, Hawaii, U.S., mountain 262/H4
Kakoura, N.Z. 171/B3
Kailahun, Guin. 149/C3
Kailahun, Guin. 149/B1
Kailio, Hawaii, U.S., point 262/C4
Kailua, (Honolulu County), Hawaii,
    U.S., 36,513 . . . . .262/C5, K2
Kailua, Hawaii, U.S., bay 262/C3
Kailua-Kona, (Hawaii County,Kailua),
    Hawaii, U.S., 9,870 . . . . .262/D7, F5
Kaimu, Hawaii, U.S., point 262/F6
Kaimuki, Hawaii, U.S. 262/G2
Kaindisoy, Taj. 132/A1
Kainji, Nig., lake 152/C2
Kainuu, Fin., region .81/C2
Kaipapau Forest Reserve, Hawaii, U.S. 262/J1
Kaiparowits, Utah, U.S., plateau 350/C6
Kairouan, Tun., 110,280 . . . . .146/C2
Kaiser, Mo., U.S., 500 . . . . .302/D3
Kaiserslautern, Ger., 100,025 . . . . .86/A4
Kaitaia, N.Z. 171/B2
Kaiwi, Hawaii, U.S., channel 262/C5, K3
Kajaani, Fin. 81/C2
Kaka, Ariz., U.S., 175 . . . . .242/C5
Kaka, Hawaii, U.S., point 262/B4
Kakadu Natl. Park, Austl. 170/C1
Kakamega, Kenya, 58,862 . . . . .157/C3
Kakata, Liber. 149/A2
Kake, Alaska, U.S., 710 . . . . .240/J3
Kakeroma, Jap., island . . . . .114/Inset V
Kakhovka, Ukr. 102/C3
Kakhovka, Ukr., reservoir 102/C3
Kakinada, India 128/D5
Kaktovik, Alaska, U.S., 293 . . . . .240/G1
Kakwa Prov. Rec. Area, Alta., Can. 212/A4
Kaladar, Ont., Can. 223/H3
Ka Lae, (S. Cape), Hawaii, U.S., cape 262/D7, G7
Kalahari, Bots., desert 160/A2
Kalahari, Nam., desert 160/C3
Kalahari, S. Afr., desert 162/B2, B3
Kalaheo, Hawaii, U.S., 3,913 . . . . .262/A2
Kaloloch, Wash., U.S., 40 . . . . .358/A2
Kalalua, Hawaii, U.S., mountain 262/J6
Kalama, Wash., U.S., 1,783 . . . . .358/A5
Kalamakion, Gr. 100/Inset
Kalamata, Gr. 100/B3
Kalamazoo, Mich., U.S., 77,145,
    (452,851, metro.) 294/D7
Kalamazoo, Mich., U.S., county, 238,603 . . . .294/D7
Kalamunda, W.A., Austl. . . . . .170/Inset II
Kalaoa, Hawaii, U.S., 6,794 . . . . .262/F5
Kalapana, Hawaii, U.S. 262/J6
Kalaupapa, Hawaii, U.S. 262/A3
Kalaupapa, Hawaii, U.S., peninsula 262/B3
Kalaupapa Natl. Hist. Park, Hawaii, U.S. 262/B3
Kalawao, Hawaii, U.S., county, 147 . . . . .262/B3, D5
Kalb, Ra's al, Yemen, cape 137/B2
Kälbäcär, Azer. 103/B2
Kalemie, Congo, D.R. 155/C2
Kalepa Forest Reserve, Hawaii, U.S. 262/D1
Kaleva, Mich., U.S., 509 . . . . .294/D5
Kalgary, Tex., U.S. 346/G2
Kalgoorlie, W.A., Austl. 170/B3
Kali, Guin. 149/C1
Kali, Nepal, river .126/B2
Kalida, Ohio, U.S., 1,031 . . . . .328/B4
Kalihi Kai, Hawaii, U.S. 262/F2
Kalihiwai, Hawaii, U.S., 717 . . . . .262/C1
Kalilli, Hawaii, U.S. 262/F2
Kalimantan, Indon., region 122/C2
Kaliningrad, Russ., 425,089 . . . . .104/A4
Kalispell, Mont., U.S., 14,223 . . . . .306/B1
Kalispell Ind. Res., Wash., U.S. 358/H1
Kalisz, Pol., 106,553 . . . . .83/C3
Kalixälven, Swe. 80/D1
Kalkaska, Mich., U.S., 2,226 . . . . .294/D5
Kalkaska, Mich., U.S., county, 16,571 . . . . . . .294/D5
Kallithea, Gr., 114,233 . . . . .100/Inset
Kalmar, Swe., 59,787 . . . . .80/C3
Kalmar, Swe., county 80/C3
Kalmykia, Russ., region 104/D5
Kalohi, Hawaii, U.S., channel 262/A3
Koloko-Honokohau Natl. Hist. Park, Hawaii, U.S. .262/F5
Kaloli, Hawaii, U.S., point 262/K5
Kalona, Iowa, U.S., 2,293 . . . . .274/L5
Kalpeni, India, island 128/B7
Kaltag, Alaska, U.S., 230 . . . . .240/D2
Kalu, Sri Lan., river 126/B5
Kalundborg, Den. .79/C3
Kalutara, Sri Lan. .126/A5
Kalvesta, Kans., U.S. 276/A5
Kalwa, India .128/Inset I
Kamalii, Hawaii, U.S. 262/K6
Kamakou, Hawaii, U.S., mountain 262/B3
Kamakwie, S.L. 149/A1
Kamalino, Hawaii, U.S. 262/A2
Kamalo, Hawaii, U.S. 262/B3
Kaman, India . . . . .128/Inset I
Kamaole, Hawaii, U.S. 262/C4
Kamaran, Yemen, island 137/A1
Kamarhati, India . . . . .128/Inset II
Kamas, Utah, U.S., 1,274 . . . . .350/C3
Kambia, S.L. 149/A1
Kamchatka, Russ., peninsula 104/J4
Kamchatka, Russ., peninsula 193/D9
Kamchiya, Bul., river 101/F2
Kamehameha Hts., Hawaii, U.S. 262/F2
Kamehameha I Birthsite State Mon., Hawaii, U.S. .262/G3
Kamela, Oreg., U.S. 334/H2
Kamensk-Ural'skiy, Russ., 190,352,
    (192,000, metro.) 104/E4
Kames, Scot., U.K. 62/F7
Kamet, India, mountain 128/C2
Kamey, Tex., U.S. .346/M7
Kamiah, Ida., U.S., 1,160 . . . . .264/A3
Kamina, Congo, D.R. 155/C3
Kaminak, Nun., Can., lake 220/J4
Kamloops, Br. Col., Can., 77,281 . . . . .214/M6
Kamooloa, Hawaii, U.S. 262/H1

Kampala, Ug., capital, 1,208,544 . . . . .157/C3
Kâmpóng Cham, Camb. 124/D4
Kâmpóng Chhnăng, Camb. 124/C3
Kâmpóng Saôm, Camb. 124/C5
Kâmpóng Thum, Camb. 124/C3
Kâmpôt, Camb. 124/C5
Kampsville, Ill., U.S., 302 . . . . .266/C4
Kamrar, Iowa, U.S., 229 . . . . .274/G3
Kamsack, Sask., Can., 2,009 . . . . .227/J9
Kamsar, Guin. 149/A2
Kamui, Jap., cape . . . . .114/Inset I
Kanab, Ariz., U.S., creek 242/C1
Kanab, Utah, U.S., 3,564 . . . . .350/B6
Kanabec, Minn., U.S., county, 14,996 . . . . . . .298/D5
Kanaga, Alaska, U.S., island 240/Inset
Kanagawa, Jap., prefecture 114/C3
Kananga, Congo, D.R., 393,030 . . . . .155/B2
Kanapou, Hawaii, U.S., bay 262/B4
Kanaranzi, Minn., U.S., 80 . . . . .298/A7
Kanarraville, Utah, U.S., 311 . . . . .350/A6
Kanawha, Iowa, U.S., 739 . . . . .274/G2
Kanawha, W. Va., U.S., 500 . . . . .360/D2
Kanawha, W. Va., U.S., county, 200,073 . . . . . .360/D4
Kanawha, W. Va., U.S., river 328/G8
Kanawha, W. Va., U.S., river 360/D3
Kanazawa, Jap., 456,000 . . . . .114/C2
Kanchenjunga, India, mountain 128/E3
Kanchenjunga, Nepal, mountain 126/D2
Kanchipuram, India 128/C6
Kanchrapara, India . . . . .128/Inset II
Kandi, Ben., 73,138 . . . . .151/B2
Kandiyohi, Minn., U.S., 555 . . . . .298/C5
Kandiyohi, Minn., U.S., county, 41,203 . . . . . .298/B5
Kandy, Sri Lan., 110,049 . . . . .126/B4
Kane, Nun., Can., basin 220/P1
Kane, Ill., U.S., 459 . . . . .266/C4
Kane, Ill., U.S., county 404,119 . . . . .266/A6, E2
Kane, Penn., U.S., 4,126 . . . . .336/D2
Kane, Utah, U.S., county, 6,046 . . . . .350/B6
Kane, Wyo., U.S. .366/F1
Kaneohe, Hawaii, U.S., 34,970 . . . . . .262/C5, G1, K2
Kaneohe Bay Marine Corps Air Sta., Hawaii, U.S. .262/K2
Kaneohe Forest Preserve, Hawaii, U.S. 262/G1, J2
Kaneville, Ill., U.S., 375 . . . . .266/E2
Kangaroo, Austl., island 170/C3
Kangen, Sudan, river 145/C3
Kanggye, N. Kor. .116/B2
Kanghwa, N. Kor., bay 116/A4
Kangiqsualujjuaq, Que., Can. 225/C2
Kangiqsujuaq, Que., Can. 225/B1
Kangirsuk, Que., Can. 225/B1
Kangley, Ill., U.S., 287 . . . . .266/E3
Kangshan, Tai. 117/B2
Kangwŏn, N. Kor., province 116/B3
Kaniahiku Vil., Hawaii, U.S. 262/K6
Kaniksu Natl. For., Ida., U.S. 264/A1, B2
Kaniksu Natl. For., Mont., U.S. 306/A1
Kaniksu Natl. For., Wash., U.S. 358/H1
Kankakee, Ill., U.S., 27,491 . . . . .266/F2
Kankakee, Ill., U.S., county, 103,833 . . . . . . .266/F2
Kankakee, Ind., U.S., river 270/C2
Kankakee, Ill., U.S., river 266/E2
Kankan, Guin., 89,000 . . . . .149/D2
Kannapolis, N.C., U.S., 36,910 . . . . .322/D4
Kano, Nig., 2,166,554 . . . . .152/E1
Kano, Nig., state .152/E2
Kanona, Kans., U.S. 276/B2
Kanopolis, Kans., U.S., 543 . . . . .276/D3
Kanopolis, Kans., U.S., lake 276/D3
Kanorado, Kans., U.S., 248 . . . . .276/A2
Kanosh, Utah, U.S., 485 . . . . .350/B5
Kanpur, India, 2,532,138, (2,690,486, metro.) .128/D3
Kansaripara, India . . . . .128/Inset II
Kansas, U.S., state 264
Kansas, Ill., U.S., 842 . . . . .266/G5
Kansas, Kans., U.S., river 276/F2, G1
Kansas, Mo., U.S., river 302/H1
Kansas, Okla., U.S., 685 . . . . .330/H1
Kansas, Vt., U.S., 80 . . . . .352/A4
Kansas City, Kans., U.S., 146,866 . . . . .276/H1
Kansas City, Mo., U.S., 441,545,
    (1,776,062, metro.) 302/B2, H5
Kansas Settlement, Ariz., U.S. 242/F5
Kansay, Taj. 132/A1
Kansk, Russ., 108,063 . . . . .104/F4
Kanté, Togo 151/B2
Kanton, Kiri., island 175/B2
Kanuku, Guy., mountains 183/B4
Kanuti NWR., Alaska, U.S. 240/E1
Kanye, Bots., 35,515 . . . . .160/B3
Kaohsiung, Tai., 1,386,723 . . . . .117/B2
Kaoko Veld, Nam., mountains 160/A1
Kaolack, Sen., (227,915, metro.) 148/A2
Kaoma, Zam. 159/A2
Kaop'ing, Tai., river 117/A2
Kapaa, Hawaii, U.S., 9,472 . . . . .262/A5, D1
Kapaa Beach Park, Hawaii, U.S. 262/G3
Kapaau, Hawaii, U.S., 1,159 . . . . .262/G3
Kapahulu, Hawaii, U.S. 262/G3
Kapan, Arm. 103/D3
Kapapala Forest Reserve, Hawaii, U.S. 262/H6
Kapfenberg, Aus. .91/D3
Kapingamarangi, Micr., atoll 172/C2
Kapiskau, Ont., Can., river 222/D2
Kaplan, La., U.S., 5,177 . . . . .282/E6
Kapoho, Hawaii, U.S. 262/K6
Kaposvár, Hun. 91/A2
Kapowsin, Wash., U.S., 200 . . . . .358/C3
Kappa, Ill., U.S., 170 . . . . .266/D3
Kapulena, Hawaii, U.S. 262/H4
Kapuskasing, Ont., Can., 9,238 . . . . .222/D3
Kara, Russ., sea 193/B4
Kara, Russ., sea 104/E2
Kara, Togo 151/B2
Karabakh, Azer., canal 103/B2
Karachay-Cherkessia, Russ., region 104/D5
Karachi, Pak., 9,339,023 . . . . .129/C5
Karaj, Iran, 940,968 . . . . .130/C2
Karakalpakstan, Uzb., republic 132/A2
Karakol, Kyrg. 131/F1
Karakoram, India, range 128/C1
Karakoram, Pak., range 129/E2
Karaman, Tur. 133/C3
Karaman, Tur., province 133/C3
Kara-Say, Kyrg. 131/F2
Karasburg, Nam. .160/C4
Karasuk, Russ. 104/F4
Karawanken, Aus., range 91/A4
Karbala, Iraq 130/B2
Karcag, Hun. 91/C2
Kardiva, Mald., channel 127/A2
Kärdla, Est. 81/B1
Kardzhali, Bul., oblast 101/D4
Karelia, Russ., region 104/C3
Kariba, Zam., lake 159/B3
Kariba, Zimb. 160/B1
Karibib, Nam. 160/B2
Karisimbi, Rwa., volcano 155/C2
Karkar, P.N.G., island 172/A2
Karkinit, Ukr., bay .102/C3
Karl E. Mundt N.W.R., S. Dak., U.S. 342/G5

Karlin, Mich., U.S., 100 . . . . .294/D5
Karlovac, Cro. 98/B2
Karlovarský, Czh. Rep., region 92/A2
Karlovy Vary, Czh. Rep., 55,000 . . . . .92/A2
Karlskrona, Swe., 60,596 . . . . .80/C3
Karlsruhe, Ger., 277,204 . . . . .86/B4
Karlsruhe, Ger., department 86/B4
Karlsruhe, N. Dak., U.S., 119 . . . . .326/E1
Karlstad, Swe., 80,748 . . . . .80/B3
Karlstad, Minn., U.S., 794 . . . . .298/A2
Karnak, Ill., U.S., 619 . . . . .266/E6
Karnali, Nepal, river 126/B2
Karnaphuli, Bangl., reservoir 127/F6
Karnaphuli, Bangl., river 127/F6
Karnataka, India, state 128/C6
Karnes, Tex., U.S., county, 15,446 . . . . .346/L7
Karnes City, Tex., U.S., 3,457 . . . . .346/L7
Karns, Tenn., U.S., 1,500 . . . . .344/N3
Karns City, Penn., U.S., 244 . . . . .336/B3
Karonga, Mal. 159/B1
Karpas, Cyp., peninsula 133/C1
Kárpathos, Gr., island 100/C4
Kars, Tur. 133/E2
Kars, Tur., province 133/E2
Kartala, Com., volcano 163/A1
Karthaus, Penn., U.S., 300 . . . . .336/E3
Kartung, Gam. 148/B2
Karun, Iran, river .130/B3
Karuzi, Bur. 152/C2
Karval, Colo., U.S. 250/G3
Karviná, Czh. Rep. 92/D3
Kasai, Ang., river .159/E2
Kasai, Congo, D.R., river 155/B2
Kasai-Occidental, Congo, D.R., region 155/B2
Kasai-Oriental, Congo, D.R., region 155/B2
Kasama, Zam. 159/C2
Kasane, Bots. 160/B1
Kasba, N.W. Terr., Can., lake 220/H4
Kasha-Katuwe Tent Rocks Natl. Mon.,
    N. Mex., U.S. .317/D2
Kashan, Iran 130/C3
Kashi, China 119/A2
Kashiwa, Jap., 328,000 . . . . .114/D3
Kasigluk, Alaska, U.S., 543 . . . . .240/C2
Kasinathpur, India . . . . .128/Inset II
Kaskaskia, Ill., U.S. 266/D6
Kaskaskia, Ill., U.S., river 266/D4
Kaslo, Br. Col., Can., 1,032 . . . . .214/O6
Kasota, Minn., U.S., 680 . . . . .298/D6
Kassala, Sudan, 234,622 . . . . .145/C3
Kassel, Ger., 196,211 . . . . .86/B3
Kassel, Ger., department 86/B3
Kasserine, Tun. 146/B2
Kasson, Ind., U.S., 1,500 . . . . .270/A8
Kasson, Minn., U.S., 4,398 . . . . .298/E7
Kastamonu, Tur. .133/C2
Kastamonu, Tur., province 133/C2
Kastoria, Gr. 100/A1
Kastrup, Den. 79/D3
Kasugai, Jap., 288,000 . . . . .114/C3
Kasungu, Mal. 159/B1
Kasur, Pak., 245,321 . . . . .129/E3
Katagum, Nig., river 152/E2
Katahdin, Maine, U.S., mountain 288/C3
Katama, Mass., U.S., 125 . . . . .292/M7
Katanga, Congo, D.R., plateau 155/B3
Katanga, Congo, D.R., region 155/C3
Katemcy, Tex., U.S., 40 . . . . .346/J5
Katerini, Gr. 100/A1
Katesbridge, N. Ire., U.K., 174 . . . . .65/E3
Kates Needle, Br. Col., Can., mountain 214/F2
Katherine, N.T., Austl. 170/C1
Kathgodam, India 128/C2
Kathiawar, India, peninsula 128/B4
Kathleen, Alta., U.S. 212/B3
Kathleen, Fla., U.S., 3,280 . . . . .256/F3
Kathleen, Ga., U.S., 650 . . . . .260/D7
Kathmandu, Nepal, capital, 421,258 . . . . . . .126/C2
Kathmandu, Nepal, valley 126/C2
Kathryn, N. Dak., U.S., 63 . . . . .326/H3
Katmai Natl. Park and Preserve, Alaska, U.S. . .240/D3
Katowice, Pol., 344,844 . . . . .83/D3
Katrine, Scot., U.K., lake 60/B2
Katsina, Nig. 152/D1
Katsina, Nig., state 152/D2
Kattegat, Den., strait 79/C2
Kattegat, Den., Swe., strait 80/B3
Katy, Tex., U.S., 11,775 . . . . .346/A6
Kau, Hawaii, U.S., desert 262/H6
Kauai, Hawaii, U.S., channel 262/B5, D2
Kauai, Hawaii, U.S., county, 58,463 . . . . .262/A5, B1
Kauai, Hawaii, U.S., island 262/A5, B1
Kaufbeuren, Ger. .86/B5
Kaufman, Tex., U.S., 6,490 . . . . .346/D10, M3
Kaufman, Tex., U.S., county, 71,313 . . . . .346/D9, M3
Kau Forest Reserve, Hawaii, U.S. 262/G7
Kaukauna, Wisc., U.S., 12,983 . . . . .364/E4
Kaukau Veld, Nam., region 160/C2
Kaulakahi, Hawaii, U.S., channel 262/A5, B1
Kaumakani, Hawaii, U.S., 607 . . . . .262/A2
Kaumalapau, Hawaii, U.S. 262/A4
Kauna, Hawaii, U.S., point 262/D7, G7
Kaunakakai, Hawaii, U.S., 2,726 . . . . .262/B3
Kaunas, Lith., 414,174 . . . . .82/B2
Kaupakulua, Hawaii, U.S. 262/C3
Kaupo, Hawaii, U.S. 262/C4
Kaupulehu Forest Reserve, Hawaii, U.S. 262/G5
Kaura-Namoda, Nig. 152/D1
Kau-Ur, Gam. 148/C2
Kavadarci, Mac. 100/C2
Kavajë, Alb., 24,817 . . . . .99/A2
Kavala, Gr. 100/C1
Kavaratti, India, island 128/B6
Kavieng, P.N.G. 172/B2
Kavir, Dasht-e, Iran, desert 130/D3
Kaw, Fr. Gui. 183/B1
Kaw, Okla., U.S., lake 330/F1
Kawagoe, Jap., 331,000 . . . . .114/C3
Kawaguchi, Jap., 460,000 . . . . .114/C3
Kawaihae, Hawaii, U.S., point 262/A2, A5
Kawaihoa, Hawaii, U.S., point 262/H1
Kawaikini, Hawaii, U.S., mountain 262/H1
Kawailoa, Hawaii, U.S. 262/H1
Kawailoa Beach, Hawaii, U.S. 262/H1
Kawailoa Forest Reserve, Hawaii, U.S. 262/J1
Kawasaki, Jap., 1,249,905 . . . . .114/C3
Kawawachikamach, Que., Can. 225/C2
Kaw City, Okla., U.S., 372 . . . . .262/J1
Kawela, (Kawela Bay), Hawaii, U.S., 410 . . . . .262/J1
Kawhia, N.Z. 171/B2
Kawkawlin, Mich., U.S., 1,600 . . . . .294/F6
Kawnipi, Minn., U.S., lake 298/F2
Kawthoung, Mya. .144/A3
Kay, Okla., U.S., county, 48,080 . . . . .330/E1
Kaya, Burkina, 25,799 . . . . .151/D2
Kayah, Mya., state 125/C2
Kayangel, Palau, islands 172/C2
Kaycee, Wyo., U.S., 249 . . . . .366/G2
Kayenta, Ariz., U.S., 4,922 . . . . .242/E1
Kayes, Mali 150/A3

Kayin, Mya., *state* 125/C3
Kaylor, S. Dak., U.S., 64 ....342/H4
Kayser, Sur., *mountains* 183/A3
Kayseri, Tur., 498,200 ....133/C2
Kayseri, Tur., *province* 133/D2
Kaysville, Utah, U.S., 20,351 ....350/C2, E1
Kazakhstan, *nation* 127
Kazakh Upland region, Kaz. 131/C2
Kazan', Russ., 1,091,656, (1,092,150, *metro.*) 104/D4
Kazanlŭk, Bul. 101/D3
Kazincbarcika, Hun. 91/C1
Keaau, Hawaii, U.S., 2,010 ....262/J5
Keady, N. Ire., U.K., 2,467 ....65/D3
Keahi, Hawaii, U.S., *point* 262/E2
Keahole, Hawaii, U.S., *point* 262/D7, F5
Kealaikahiki, Hawaii, U.S., *channel* 262/B4
Kealaikahiki, Hawaii, U.S., *point* 262/B4
Kealakekua, Hawaii, U.S., 1,645 ....262/G5
Kealia, Hawaii, U.S. 262/D1, G6
Kealia Forest Reserve, Hawaii, U.S. 262/D1
Keams Canyon, Ariz., U.S., 260 ....242/E2
Keanae, Hawaii, U.S. 262/C3
Keanapapa, Hawaii, U.S., *point* 262/A3
Keansburg, N.J., U.S., 10,732 ....314/E3
Kearney, Ont., Can., 773 ....223/F2
Kearney, Mo., U.S., 5,472 ....302/J4
Kearney, Nebr., U.S., 27,431 ....308/E3
Kearney, Nebr., U.S., *county*, 6,882 ....308/E3
Kearneysville, W. Va., U.S., 650 ....360/L2
Kearns, Utah, U.S., 33,659 ....350/E2
Kearny, Ariz., U.S., 2,249 ....242/E4
Kearny, Kans., U.S., *county*, 4,531 ....276/A3
Kearny, N.J., U.S., 40,513 ....314/B2, E2
Kearsarge, N.H., U.S., 325 ....312/D3
Kearsarge, N.H., U.S., *mountain* 312/C5
Keatchie, La., U.S., 323 ....282/B2
Keating, Oreg., U.S. 334/J3
Keaton Beach, Fla., U.S., 80 ....256/E2
Keats, Kans., U.S., 150 ....276/F2
Keauhou, (Kahaluu-Keauhou), Hawaii, U.S., 2,414 ....262/G5
Keavy, Ky., U.S., 450 ....280/F3
Keban, Tur., *reservoir* 133/D2
Kebbi, Nig., *state* 152/C2
Kebili, Tun. 146/B3
Kebnekaise, Swe., *mountain* 80/C1
Kechi, Kans., U.S., 1,038 ....276/E4
Kechika, Br. Col., Can., *river* 214/J2
Kecskemét, Hun., 105,000 ....91/B2
Kecskemét, Hun. 91/B2
Kedainiai, Lith. 68/C4
Kedgwick, N.B., Can., 1,184 ....217/B1
Kedgwick River, N.B., Can. 217/B1
Kediri, Indon. 122/C2
Kédougou, Sen. 148/C3
Kedron, Ark., U.S., 175 ....244/C3
Keedysville, Md., U.S., 482 ....288/D2
Keefeton, Okla., U.S., 225 ....330/G2
Keegan, Maine, U.S., 550 ....286/E1
Keego Harbor, Mich., U.S., 2,769 ....294/A6, F7
Keehi, Hawaii, U.S., *lagoon* 262/E2
Keei, Hawaii, U.S. 262/G6
Keele, N.W. Terr., Can., *river* 220/C4
Keele, Eng., U.K. 68/C4
Keeler, Calif., U.S., 66 ....246/H6
Keeler Bay, Vt., U.S., 250 ....352/A1
Keeley, Sask., Can., *lake* 227/B6
Keeline, Wyo., U.S. 366/D2
Keene, Ky., U.S., 225 ....280/F3
Keene, Nebr., U.S. 308/E3
Keene, N.H., U.S., 22,563 ....312/B6
Keene, N.Y., U.S., 100 ....320/P2
Keene, N. Dak., U.S., 50 ....326/C2
Keene, Ohio, U.S., 200 ....328/G5
Keene, Va., U.S., 60 ....354/F5
Keener, Ala., U.S., 150 ....238/D1
Keener, K.C., U.S., 508 ....322/J4
Keenes, Ill., U.S., 99 ....266/E5
Keenesburg, Colo., U.S., 855 ....250/F1
Keeneyville, Penn., U.S., 80 ....336/G2
Keensburg, Ill., U.S., 252 ....266/F5
Keeseville, N.Y., U.S., 1,850 ....320/Q1
Keetmanshoop, Nam., 15,032 ....160/C4
Keewatin, Minn., U.S., 1,164 ....298/D3
Kefallinia, Gr., *island* 100/B2
Keflavík, Ice., 7,823 ....79/A3
Keg River, Alta., Can. 212/D2
Kegworth, Eng., U.K., 3,405 ....68/E4
Kegworth, Eng., U.K., 3,405 ....70/B1
Kehena, Hawaii, U.S. 262/K6
Keighley, Eng., U.K., 49,567 ....66/E5
Keighley, Eng., U.K., 49,567 ....68/D2
Keila, Est. 81/C1
Keillmore, Scot., U.K. 62/E7
Keilor, Vic., Austl. ....170/Inset V
Keiser, Ark., U.S., 808 ....244/E2
Keiss, Scot., U.K. 62/K1
Keith, Scot., U.K., 4,491 ....62/L3
Keith, Nebr., U.S., *county*, 8,875 ....308/C2
Keithsburg, Ga., U.S., 300 ....260/C3
Keithsburg, Ill., U.S., 714 ....266/C2
Keithville, La., U.S., 550 ....282/B2
Keizer, Oreg., U.S., 32,203 ....334/C3
Kejimkujik N.P., (Seaside Adjunct), N.S., Can. 221/A4
Kejimkujik Natl. Park, N.S., Can. 221/B3
Kekaha, Hawaii, U.S., 3,175 ....262/B2
Kékes, Hun., *mountain* 91/C2
Kekoskee, Wisc., U.S., 169 ....364/E5
Kelang, Malay., 243,355, (368,379, *metro.*) 121/A2
Kelani, Sri Lan., *river* 126/B4
Kelford, N.C., U.S., 245 ....322/L2
Kelham, Eng., U.K. 68/F3
Kell, Ill., U.S., 231 ....266/E5
Kellas, (Grampian), Scot., U.K. 62/K3
Kellas, (Tayside), Scot., U.K. 62/L5
Keller, Ga., U.S., 80 ....260/J8
Keller, Tex., U.S., 27,345 ....346/B9
Keller, Va., U.S., 173 ....354/M5
Keller, Wash., U.S. 358/G1
Kellerton, Iowa, U.S., 372 ....274/F6
Kelley, Iowa, U.S., 300 ....274/G4
Kelleyland, Maine, U.S. 286/E1
Kelleys, Mich., U.S., *island* 294/G8
Kelleys, Ohio, U.S., *island* 328/E2
Kelleys Island, Ohio, U.S., 367 ....328/E2
Kelliher, Sask., Can., 317 ....227/G9
Kelliher, Minn., U.S., 294 ....298/C3
Kellner, Wisc., U.S., 650 ....364/D4
Kellnersville, Wisc., U.S., 374 ....364/F4
Kellogg, Ida., U.S., 2,395 ....264/A2
Kellogg, Iowa, U.S., 606 ....274/J4
Kellogg, Minn., U.S., 439 ....298/F6
Kellogg, Oreg., U.S. 334/C4
Kells, N. Ire., U.K., 1,130 ....65/E2
Kelly, Del., U.S., *island* 255/C4
Kelly, Kans., U.S., 50 ....276/F2
Kelly, Ky., U.S., 125 ....280/C4
Kelly, La., U.S., 125 ....282/E3
Kelly, N.C., U.S., 454 ....322/J6
Kelly, Wyo., U.S., 125 ....366/A2
Kellys Slough N.W.R., N. Dak., U.S. 326/H2
Kellyville, N.H., U.S. 312/B5
Kellyville, Okla., U.S., 906 ....330/F2

Kelmarsh, Eng., U.K. 70/C2
Kelmscott, W.A., Austl. ....170/Inset I
Kelowna, Br. Col., Can., 96,288 ....214/N6
Kelsall, Eng., U.K., 2,394 ....68/B3
Kelsay, Tex., U.S., 325 ....346/K9
Kelsey, Man., Can. 215/C1
Kelsey, Minn., U.S., 40 ....298/E3
Kelseyville, Calif., U.S., 2,928 ....246/C4
Kelso, Scot., U.K., 5,116 ....62/M7
Kelso, Ark., U.S., 80 ....244/C4
Kelso, Calif., U.S. 246/K7
Kelso, Mo., U.S., 527 ....302/G4
Kelso, Wash., U.S., 11,895 ....358/C3
Kelton, Tex., U.S., 40 ....346/H9
Kelton, Utah, U.S. 350/A2
Keluang, Malay. 121/B2
Kelvedon Hatch, Eng., U.K., 2,738 ....68/H6
Kelvedon Hatch, Eng., U.K., 2,738 ....70/E3
Kelvin, Ariz., U.S., 150 ....242/E4
Kelvin, N. Dak., U.S. 326/E1
Kelvington, Sask., Can., 1,007 ....227/G8
Kemah, Tex., U.S., 2,330 ....346/C7
Kemano, Br. Col., Can. 214/J4
Kemble, Eng., U.K. 68/C6
Kemerovo, Russ., 492,240, (532,200, *metro.*) 104/F4
Kemi, Fin. 81/B1
Kemijärvi, Fin. 81/C1
Kemijoki, Fin., *river* 81/C1
Kemijoki, Swe., *river* 80/F2
Kemmerer, Wyo., U.S., 2,651 ....366/A3
Kemnay, Man., Can. 215/A4
Kemp, Okla., U.S., 144 ....330/F4
Kemp, Tex., U.S., 1,133 ....346/M3
Kemp, Tex., U.S., *lake* 346/K2
Kempenland, Belg., *region* 85/D1
Kemper, Miss., U.S., *county*, 10,453 ....300/D3
Kemps Bay, Bah. 207/B3
Kempsey, Eng., U.K., 3,147 ....68/C5
Kempster, Wisc., U.S., 100 ....364/D3
Kempston, Eng., U.K., 18,233 ....68/F5
Kempston, Eng., U.K., 18,233 ....70/D2
Kempt, Que., Can., *lake* 226/B4
Kempten, Ger. 86/B5
Kempton, Ill., U.S., 235 ....266/E3
Kempton, Ind., U.S., 380 ....270/D4
Kempton, N. Dak., U.S. 326/H2
Kemptown, Md., U.S. 288/F2
Kemptville, Ont., Can., 4,004 ....223/K2
Kenai, Alaska, U.S., 6,942 ....240/E2
Kenai, Alaska, U.S., *peninsula* 240/E2
Kenai Fjords Natl. Park, Alaska, U.S. 240/E3
Kenai N.W.R., Alaska, U.S. 240/E2
Kenansville, Fla., U.S. 256/H4
Kenansville, N.C., U.S., 1,149 ....322/K5
Kenaston, Sask., Can., 282 ....227/D9
Kenbridge, Va., U.S., 1,253 ....354/G7
Kenchester, Eng., U.K. 68/B5
Kendal, Eng., U.K. 60/C2
Kendal, Eng., U.K., 25,461 ....66/C2
Kendall, Fla., U.S., 75,226 ....256/A7, H6
Kendall, Ill., U.S., *county*, 54,544 ....266/A6, E2
Kendall, Kans., U.S. 276/A4
Kendall, N.Y., U.S., 750 ....320/F4
Kendall, Tex., U.S., *county*, 23,743 ....346/A1, K6
Kendall, Wisc., U.S., 469 ....364/C5
Kendall Park, N.J., U.S., 9,006 ....314/D3
Kendallville, Ind., U.S., 9,616 ....270/F2
Kendari, Indon., 70,700, (488,471, *metro.*) 122/D2
Kendleton, Tex., U.S., 466 ....346/N6
Kendrick, Ida., U.S., 369 ....264/A3
Kendrick, Okla., U.S., 138 ....330/F2
Kenduskeag, Maine, U.S., 1,171 ....286/D4
Kenedy, Tex., U.S., 3,487 ....346/L7
Kenedy, Tex., U.S., *county*, 414 ....346/L8
Kenefic, Okla., U.S., 192 ....330/F3
Kenefick, Tex., U.S., 667 ....346/C5
Kenel, S. Dak., U.S., 90 ....342/E2
Kenema, S.L. 149/B2
Kenesaw, Nebr., U.S., 873 ....308/E3
Kengtung, Mya. 125/C2
Kenhorst, Penn., U.S., 2,679 ....336/K5
Kenilworth, Eng., U.K. 60/C1
Kenilworth, Eng., U.K., 21,623 ....68/D5
Kenilworth, Eng., U.K., 21,623 ....70/A2
Kenilworth, Ill., U.S., 2,494 ....266/B5
Kenilworth, N.J., U.S., 7,675 ....314/A3, E2
Kenilworth, Penn., U.S., 1,576 ....336/K5
Kenitra, Mor., 234,000 ....147/C1
Kenknock, Scot., U.K. 62/H6
Kenly, N.C., U.S., 1,569 ....322/J3
Kenmare, N. Dak., U.S., 1,081 ....326/C1
Kenmore, N.Y., U.S., 16,426 ....320/D5
Kenmore, Wash., U.S., 18,678 ....358/A4
Kenna, N. Mex., U.S. 317/G4
Kenna, W. Va., U.S., 100 ....360/C3
Kennacraig, Scot., U.K. 62/F7
Kennan, Wisc., U.S., 171 ....364/C3
Kennard, Ind., U.S., 455 ....270/E5
Kennard, Nebr., U.S., 371 ....308/H2
Kennard, Tex., U.S., 317 ....346/N4
Kennebago Lake, Maine, U.S. 286/B4
Kennebec, Maine, U.S., 225 ....286/E4
Kennebec, Maine, U.S., *county*, 117,114 ....286/C3
Kennebec, S. Dak., U.S., 286 ....342/F4
Kennebec, S. Dak., U.S., *river* 286/C3
Kennebunk, Maine, U.S., 10,476 ....286/B5
Kennebunk Beach, Maine, U.S., 800 ....286/B5
Kennebunkport, Maine, U.S., 3,720 ....286/B5
Kennedale, Tex., U.S., 5,850 ....346/B10
Kennedy, Ala., U.S., 541 ....238/B2
Kennedy, Minn., U.S., 255 ....298/A2
Kennedyville, Md., U.S., 175 ....288/L2
Kenner, La., U.S., 70,517 ....282/J3, J6
Kennesaw, Ga., U.S., 21,675 ....260/B3, G2
Kennesaw Mtn. Natl. Bfld. Park, Ga., U.S. 260/G2
Kennet, Eng., U.K., *river* 70/B4
Kennetcook, N.S., Can. 221/D2
Kenneth, Minn., U.S., 61 ....298/A4
Kenneth City, Fla., U.S., 4,400 ....256/C6
Kennett, Mo., U.S., 11,260 ....302/F5
Kennett Square, Penn., U.S., 5,273 ....336/K6
Kennewick, Wash., U.S., 54,693 ....358/F3
Kenney, Ill., U.S., 374 ....266/D3
Kenninghall, Eng., U.K. 70/F2
Kennington, Eng., U.K., 4,290 ....68/E6
Kennington, Eng., U.K., 4,290 ....70/C1
Keno, Yukon, Can. 228/B4
Keno, Oreg., U.S., 650 ....334/E5
Kenora, Ont., Can., 15,838 ....222/B3
Kenosha, Wisc., U.S., 90,352 ....364/F6
Kenosha, Wisc., U.S., *county*, 149,577 ....364/F6
Kenova, W. Va., U.S., 3,485 ....360/A4
Kenroy, (East Wenatchee Bench), Wash., U.S. 358/E2
Kensal, N. Dak., U.S., 161 ....326/G2
Kensaleyre, Scot., U.K. 62/D4
Kensett, Ark., U.S., 1,791 ....244/D2
Kensett, Iowa, U.S., 280 ....274/H1
Kensington, P.E.I., Can., 1,385 ....224/B2
Kensington, Calif., U.S., 4,936 ....246/J1
Kensington, Conn., U.S., 8,541 ....253/D3
Kensington, Kans., U.S., 529 ....276/C2
Kensington, Md., U.S., 1,873 ....288/B6

Kensington, Minn., U.S., 286 ....298/B5
Kensington and Chelsea, Eng., U.K., unitary authority, 158,922 ....70/D3
Kent, N.B., Can., *county* 217/D2
Kent, Ont., Can. 223/C5
Kent, Ont., Can., *county* 223/C5
Kent, Eng., U.K., *downs* 70/F4
Kent, Eng., U.K., *unitary authority, 1,329,653* 70/F4
Kent, Ala., U.S., 175 ....238/D3
Kent, Ark., U.S., 90 ....244/C4
Kent, Conn., U.S., 2,858 ....253/B3
Kent, Del., U.S., *county*, 126,697 ....255/B4
Kent, Del., U.S., *island* 255/C4
Kent, Iowa, U.S., 52 ....274/F6
Kent, Md., U.S., *county*, 19,197 ....288/L2
Kent, Md., U.S., *island* 288/J4
Kent, Minn., U.S., 120 ....298/A4
Kent, Ohio, U.S., 27,906 ....328/H3
Kent, Oreg., U.S. 334/F2
Kent, R.I., U.S., *county*, 167,090 ....339/C4
Kent, Tex., U.S., 40 ....346/D4
Kent, Tex., U.S., *county*, 859 ....346/H2
Kent, Wash., U.S., 79,524 ....358/A4, C2
Kent Acres, Del., U.S., 1,637 ....255/B4
Kentchurch, Eng., U.K. 68/B6
Kent City, Mich., U.S., 1,061 ....294/D6
Kentfield, Calif., U.S., 6,351 ....246/H1
Kentford, Eng., U.K. 70/F2
Kent Jct., N.B., Can. 217/D2
Kentland, Ind., U.S., 1,822 ....270/B3
Kentland, Md., U.S. 288/C7
Kentmore Park, Md., U.S. 288/L2
Kenton, Man., Can. 215/A4
Kenton, Eng., U.K. 73/F3
Kenton, Del., U.S., 237 ....255/B4
Kenton, Ga., U.S., 375 ....280/F2
Kenton, Ky., U.S., *county*, 151,464 ....280/F2, J1
Kenton, Mich., U.S. 294/A3
Kenton, Ohio, U.S., 8,336 ....328/C4
Kenton, Tenn., U.S., 1,306 ....344/C2
Kenton Vale, Ky., U.S., 156 ....280/G1
Kents Hills, Maine, U.S., 375 ....286/C4
Kentucky, U.S., *state* 280/E2
Kentucky, Ky., U.S., *river* 280/E2, F3
Kentucky, Tenn., U.S., *lake* 344/F2
Kentville, N.S., Can., 5,610 ....221/C2
Kentwood, La., U.S., 2,205 ....282/J5
Kentwood, Mich., U.S., 45,255 ....294/D7
Kenvil, N.J., U.S., 12,569 ....314/D2
Kenville, Man., Can. 215/A3
Kenwood, Ark., U.S. 90 ....244/C2
Kenwood, Ohio, U.S., 7,423 ....328/B9
Kenwood Beach, Md., U.S., 600 ....288/H6
Kenya, *nation* 151
Kenya, Kenya, *mountain* 157/D4
Kenyon, Minn., U.S., 1,661 ....298/E6
Keo, Ark., U.S., 235 ....244/D3
Keokea, Hawaii, U.S. 262/C4, G6
Keokea Beach Park, Hawaii, U.S. 262/G3
Keokee, Va., U.S., 316 ....354/C2
Keokradong, Bangl., *mountain* 127/F7
Keokuk, Iowa, U.S., 11,427 ....274/N7
Keokuk, Iowa, U.S., *county*, 11,400 ....274/K5
Keomah Vil., Iowa, U.S., 97 ....274/J5
Keosauqua, Iowa, U.S., 1,066 ....274/L6
Keota, Colo., U.S. 250/F1
Keota, Iowa, U.S., 1,025 ....274/L5
Keota, Okla., U.S., 517 ....330/H2
Keowee, Ga., U.S., *lake* 260/B2
Keowee, S.C., U.S., *lake* 340/B2
Keppel, Sing., *harbor* 123/B2
Kepuhi, Hawaii, U.S., *point* 262/H2
Kerala, India, *state* 128/C6
Kerangan Nyatan, Bru. 121/B3
Keratsinion, Gr. 100/Inset
Kerby, Oreg., U.S., 450 ....334/C5
Kerch, Ukr. 167,222 ....102/D3
Kerch, Ukr., *strait* 102/D3
Kerema, P.N.G. 172/A2
Keremeos, Br. Col., Can., 1,197 ....214/N6
Keren, Erit., 40,000 ....156/B2
Kerens, Tex., U.S., 1,681 ....346/M3
Kerewan, Gam. 148/B2
Kerhonkson, N.Y., U.S., 1,732 ....157/C4
Kericho, Kenya 157/C4
Kerinci, Indon., *volcano* 122/B2
Kerkennah, Tun., *islands* 146/C2
Kerkhoven, Minn., U.S., 759 ....298/B5
Kerki, Turkm. 132/D3
Kerkyra, Gr. 100/A2
Kerkyra, (Corfu), Gr., *island* 100/A2
Kermadec, N.Z., *islands* 161
Kerman, Iran, 384,991 ....130/D3
Kerman, Iran, *province* 130/D3
Kerman, Calif., U.S., 8,551 ....246/E6
Kermanshah, Iran, 692,986 ....130/B3
Kermanshahan, Iran, *province* 130/B3
Kermit, Tex., U.S., 5,714 ....346/E4
Kermit, W. Va., U.S., 209 ....360/B5
Kern, Calif., U.S., *county*, 661,645 ....246/G6
Kern, Calif., U.S., *river* 246/G6
Kernersville, N.C., U.S., 17,126 ....322/E2
Kernville, Calif., U.S., 1,736 ....246/G7
Kernville, Oreg., U.S., 125 ....334/C3
Kérouané, Guin. 149/D3
Kerr, Tex., U.S., *county*, 43,653 ....346/J6
Kerrick, Minn., U.S., 71 ....298/E4
Kerrick, Tex., U.S. 328/B2
Kerrobert, Sask., Can., 1,111 ....227/A9
Kerrville, Tex., U.S., 20,425 ....346/J5
Kerry, Ire., *county* 78/B2
Kerry's Gate, Eng., U.K. 68/B6
Kersall, Eng., U.K. 68/F3
Kersbrook, S.A., Austl. ....170/Inset II
Kersey, Colo., U.S., 1,389 ....250/F1
Kersey, Penn., U.S., 750 ....336/D3
Kershaw, S.C., U.S., 1,645 ....340/D2
Kershaw, S.C., U.S., *county*, 52,647 ....340/D2
Kershopefoot, Eng., U.K. 66/C1
Kerulen, Mong., *river* 118/D2
Kesgrave, Eng., U.K. 70/G2
Keshena, Wisc., U.S., 1,394 ....364/E4
Kesley, Iowa, U.S., 150 ....274/J2
Kessingland, Eng., U.K., 3,167 ....70/H2
Keswick, Eng., U.K., 4,836 ....66/B3
Keswick, Iowa, U.S., 295 ....274/K5
Keswick, Oreg., U.S. 314/E4
Keswick Ridge, N.B., Can., 1,331 ....217/C2
Keszthely, Hun. 91/A2
Keta, Gha. 150/C4
Ketchikan, Alaska, U.S., 7,922 ....240/J3
Ketchum, Ida., U.S., 3,003 ....264/C6
Ketchum, Okla., U.S., 286 ....330/G1
Kettering, Eng., U.K., 47,186 ....68/F5
Kettering, Eng., U.K., 47,186 ....70/C2
Kettering, Md., U.S. 288/D7, G4
Kettering, Ohio, U.S., 57,502 ....328/B6, G2
Kettle Falls, Wash., U.S., 1,527 ....358/G1
Kettleman City, Calif., U.S., 1,499 ....246/F6
Kettle Moraine St. For., Wisc., U.S. 364/E5
Kettle River, Minn., U.S., 168 ....298/E4

Kettle River, Wash., U.S., *range* 358/G1
Kettlersville, Ohio, U.S., 175 ....328/B5
Kettlewell, Eng., U.K. 66/D2
Ketton, Eng., U.K., 1,708 ....68/F4
Ketton, Eng., U.K., 1,708 ....70/C1
Keuka, N.Y., U.S., 100 ....320/G5
Keuka, N.Y., U.S., *lake* 320/G5
Keuka, Ky., U.S., 574 ....280/B3
Kevin, Mont., U.S., 178 ....306/E1
Kewa, Wash., U.S. 358/G1
Kewanee, Ill., U.S., 12,944 ....266/D2
Kewanee, Mo., U.S., 175 ....302/G5
Kewanna, Ind., U.S., 614 ....270/D2
Kewaskum, Wisc., U.S., 3,274 ....364/E5
Kewaunee, Wisc., U.S., 2,806 ....364/F4
Kewaunee, Wisc., U.S., *county*, 20,187 ....364/F4
Keweenaw, Mich., U.S., *bay* 294/A2
Keweenaw, Mich., U.S., *county*, 2,301 ....294/A2
Keweenaw, Mich., U.S., *peninsula* 294/A2
Keweenaw, Mich., U.S., *point* 294/B2
Keweenaw, Wisc., U.S., *bay* 364/E2
Keweenaw, Wisc., U.S., *peninsula* 364/E1
Keweenaw Bay, Mich., U.S., 150 ....294/A2
Keyano, Que., Can. 225/B3
Keya Paha, Nebr., U.S., *county*, 983 ....308/E1
Keyapaha, S. Dak., U.S. 342/E4
Keya Paha, S. Dak., U.S., *river* 342/E4
Key Biscayne, Fla., U.S., 10,507 ....256/B6
Key Colony Beach, Fla., U.S., 788 ....256/G7
Keyes, Calif., U.S., 4,575 ....246/E5
Keyes, Okla., U.S., 410 ....330/B4
Keyesport, Ill., U.S., 481 ....266/C5
Key Haven, Fla., U.S. 256/B4
Key Lake Mine, Sask., Can. 227/E3
Key Largo, Fla., U.S., 11,886 ....256/H6
Keymar, Md., U.S., 350 ....288/E1
Keynsham, Eng., U.K., 15,193 ....73/G2
Keyport, N.J., U.S., 7,568 ....314/E3
Keyser, W. Va., U.S., 5,303 ....360/F2
Keysers Ridge, Md., U.S. 288/A3
Keystone, Eng., U.K. 70/D2
Keystone, Colo., U.S., 825 ....250/E2
Keystone, Iowa, U.S., 687 ....274/K4
Keystone, Nebr., U.S., 60 ....308/C2
Keystone, Okla., U.S., *lake* 330/F1
Keystone, S. Dak., U.S., 311 ....342/B4
Keystone, W. Va., U.S., 453 ....360/D6
Keystone, Wyo., U.S. 366/C3
Keystone Hts., Fla., U.S., 1,349 ....256/B7
Keysville, Ga., U.S., 180 ....260/C5
Keysville, Md., U.S., 80 ....288/E1
Keysville, Mo., U.S. 302/E4
Keysville, Va., U.S., 817 ....354/G6
Keytesville, Mo., U.S., 533 ....302/D2
Key West, Fla., U.S., 25,478 ....256/G6
Key West N.W.R., Fla., U.S. 256/F7
Keyworth, Eng., U.K., 7,467 ....68/E4
Keyworth, Eng., U.K., 7,467 ....70/B1
Kezar Falls, Maine, U.S., 750 ....286/B5
Khabarovsk, Russ., 608,853 ....104/H5
Khabur, Syria, *river* 134/B1
Khakasia, Russ. 104/F4
Khalandrion, Gr. 100/Inset
Khambhat, India, *gulf* 128/B4
Khamis Mushayt, Sa. Arab. 136/B2
Khanaqin, Iraq 130/C2
Khanka, China, *lake* 119/G1
Khan-Tengri, Kaz., *mountain* 131/E2
Khanthabouli, Laos 124/C3
Khanty-Mansia, Russ., *autonomous okrug* 104/E3
Khanty-Mansiysk, Russ. 104/E3
Kharagpur, India 128/E3
Kharg, Iran, *island* 130/C4
Kharijah, Egy., *oasis* 144/B2
Kharkiv, Ukr., 1,494,235 ....102/D1
Kharkiv, Ukr., *oblast* 102/D2
Khartoum, Sudan, *capital*, 947,483 ....145/C2
Khartoum North, Sudan, 700,887 ....145/C2
Khash, Dasht-e, Afg., *desert* 129/A2
Khashm al Qirbah, Sudan 145/C2
Khashuri, Geo. 103/B4
Khasi, India, *hills* 128/F3
Khaskovo, Bul., 100,600 ....101/D4
Khaskovo, Bul., *oblast* 101/D4
Khatanga, Russ. 104/G2
Khatlon, Taj., *province* 132/A2
Khatt Atoui, W. Sah., *river* 147/A2
Kherson, Ukr., 354,243 ....102/C3
Kherson, Ukr., *oblast* 102/C3
Khe Sanh, Viet. 123/B3
Khmel'nyts'kyi, Ukr., 258,237 ....102/B2
Khmel'nyts'kyi, Ukr., *oblast* 102/B2
Khojak, Afg., *pass* 129/B2
Khojak, Pak., *pass* 129/B2
Khon Kaen, Thai., (223,300, *metro.*) 125/C2
Khor Angar, Dji. 156/C1
Khorasan, Iran, *province* 130/D3
Khorat, Thai., *plateau* 125/C2
Khorazm, Uzb., *province* 132/B2
Khorixas, Nam. 160/B2
Khorramabad, Iran, 272,815 ....130/B3
Khorramshahr, Iran, 105,636 ....130/C3
Khorugh, Taj. 132/B2
Khouribga, Mor., 190,000 ....147/C1
Khowst, Afg. 129/B2
Khujand, Taj. 132/A1
Khŭjayli, Uzb. 132/A2
Khulna, Bangl., 545,849, (1,071,000, *metro.*) 127/C6
Khulna, Bangl., *division* 127/C6
Khuriya Muriya, Oman, *islands* 137/C3
Khust, Ukr. 102/A2
Khuzdar, Pak. 129/C4
Khuzestan, Iran, *province* 130/B3
Khvoy, Iran 130/A2
Khyber, Afg., *pass* 129/C2
Khyber, Pak., *pass* 129/C2
Kiahsville, W. Va., U.S. 360/B4
Kiana, Alaska, U.S., 388 ....240/C1
Kiawah Island, S.C., U.S., 1,163 ....340/D4
Kiblah, Ark., U.S., 60 ....244/B3
Kibler, Ark., U.S., 969 ....244/A2
Kibungo, Rwa. 152/B2
Kibuye, Rwa. 152/B2
Kickapoo Ind. Res., Kans., U.S. 276/G2
Kicking Horse, Mont., U.S., 80 ....306/B2
Kidal, Mali 150/D2
Kidder, Mo., U.S., 271 ....302/J3
Kidder, N. Dak., U.S., *county*, 2,753 ....326/F3
Kidder, S. Dak., U.S., 70 ....342/H2
Kidderminster, Eng., U.K., 54,644 ....68/C5
Kidsgrove, Eng., U.K., 27,702 ....68/C4
Kidwelly, Wales, U.K., 2,664 ....64/C4
Kief, N. Dak., U.S. 326/E2
Kiefer, Okla., U.S., 1,026 ....330/F2
Kiel, Ger., 233,795 ....86/B4
Kiel, Ger., *bay* 86/B1
Kiel, Wisc., U.S., 3,450 ....364/E5

Kielce, Pol., 212,180 . . . . .83/E3
Kielder Water, Eng., U.K., *lake* 66/C2
Kiester, Minn., U.S., 540 . . . . .298/D7
Kiev, (Kyiv), Ukr., *capital*, 2,589,541 . . . . .102/C1
Kiev, (Kyiv), Ukr., *oblast* 102/C2
Kiev, Ukr., *reservoir* 102/C1
Kievo, Mac. 100/A2
Kiffa, Maur. 147/C3
Kifisia, Gr. 100/Inset
Kifissos, Gr., *river* 100/Inset
Kigali, Rwa., *capital*, 234,274 . . . . .152/B1
Kigoma, Tan. 152/A1
Kigoma, Tan., *region* 152/A1
Kihei, Hawaii, U.S., 16,749 . . . . .262/C4, D6
Kiholo, Hawaii, U.S., *bay* 262/G4
Kii, Jap., *channel* 114/B3
Kii, Jap., *peninsula* 114/B3
Kii Landing, Hawaii, U.S. 262/A2
Kikepa, Hawaii, U.S., *point* 262/A1
Kikinda, Serb.-Mont. 99/B2
Kikkertavak, Nfld., Can., *island* 218/B2
Kikwit, Congo, D.R., 182,142 . . . . .155/B2
Kila, Mont., U.S., 225 . . . . .306/B1
Kilauea, Hawaii, U.S., 2,092 . . . . .262/C1
Kilauea, Hawaii, U.S., *crater* 262/C1
Kilauea, Hawaii, U.S., *point* 262/C1
Kilbourne, Ill., U.S., 375 . . . . .266/C3
Kilbourne, La., U.S., 436 . . . . .282/C1
Kilbourne, Ohio, U.S., 275 . . . . .328/E5
Kilbride, Scot., U.K. 62/B4
Kilburn, N.B., Can. 217/B2
Kilby, Eng., U.K. .70/B1
Kilby Corner, Md., U.S. 288/K1
Kilchattan, Scot., U.K. 62/F7
Kilchenzie, Scot., U.K. 62/E8
Kilchrenan, Scot., U.K. 62/F6
Kilchu, N. Kor. 116/C2
Kildare, Ire. 78/C2
Kildare, Ire., *county* 78/C2
Kildare, Okla., U.S., 92 . . . . .330/E1
Kildary (Milton and Kildary), Scot., U.K., 604 . .62/H3
Kildavanan, Scot., U.K. 62/F7
Kildeer, Ill., U.S., 3,460 . . . . .266/B5
Kildonan, Scot., U.K. 62/F8
Kilfinan, Scot., U.K. 62/F7
Kilgetty, Wales, U.K. 64/B4
Kilgore, Ida., U.S. 264/F5
Kilgore, Nebr., U.S. 308/D1
Kilgore, Tex., U.S., 11,301 . . . . .346/P3
Kilham, Eng., U.K. 66/H4
Kilimanjaro, Tan., *mountain* 152/C1
Kilimanjaro, Tan., *region* 152/C1
Kilinochchi, Sri Lan. 126/B2
Kilkee, Ire. 78/B2
Kilkeel, N. Ire., U.K., 6,123 . . . . .65/F3
Kilkenny, Ire., 8,594 . . . . .78/C2
Kilkenny, Ire., *county* 78/C2
Kilkenny, Minn., U.S., 148 . . . . .298/D6
Kilkenny, N.C., U.S., 50 . . . . .322/N3
Kilkhampton, Eng., U.K. 73/D3
Killagan Fork, N. Ire., U.K. 65/E1
Killala, Ire., *bay* .78/B1
Killaloe, Ont., Can., 661 . . . . .223/H2
Killaloo, N. Ire., U.K. 65/C1
Killaloo, N. Ire., U.K. 65/C2
Killam, Alta., Can., 1,004 . . . . .212/E5
Killarney, Man., Can., 2,221 . . . . .215/B4
Killarney, Ont., Can., 428 . . . . .223/D1
Killarney, Ire. 78/B2
Killarney Lake, Alta., Can. 212/E5
Killarney Prov. Park, Ont., Can. 223/D1
Killbuck, Ohio, U.S., 839 . . . . .328/G5
Killdeer, Sask., Can. 227/D11
Killdeer, N. Dak., U.S., 713 . . . . .326/C2
Kill Devil Hills, N.C., U.S., 5,897 . . . . . . .322/P2
Killduff, Iowa, U.S., 150 . . . . .274/J4
Killean, Scot., U.K. 62/E7
Killearn, Scot., U.K., 1,781 . . . . .62/H6
Killeen, Tex., U.S., 86,911, (312,952, *metro.*) .346/L4
Killen, Ala., U.S., 1,119 . . . . .238/B1
Killian, La., U.S., 1,053 . . . . .282/H6
Killichonan, Scot., U.K. 62/G5
Killiecrankie, Scot., U.K. 62/J5
Killin, Scot., U.K., 666 . . . . .62/H6
Killinghall, Eng., U.K. 66/E4
Killington, Vt., U.S., *peak* 352/B3
Killingworth, Conn., U.S., 6,018 . . . . .253/E4
Killylea, N. Ire., U.K., 293 . . . . .65/F3
Killyleagh, N. Ire., U.K., 2,221 . . . . .65/F3
Kilmaluag, Scot., U.K. 62/D3
Kilmarnock, Scot., U.K. 60/B2
Kilmarnock, Scot., U.K., 43,588 . . . . .60/B2
Kilmarnock, Va., U.S., 1,244 . . . . .354/L5
Kilmeston, Eng., U.K. 70/B4
Kilmichael, Miss., U.S., 830 . . . . .300/C2
Kilmington, Eng., U.K. 73/F3
Kilmory, (Highland), Scot., U.K. 62/D4
Kilmory, (N. Ayrshire), Scot., U.K. 62/F8
Kiln, Miss., U.S., 2,040 . . . . .300/C5
Kilninver, Scot., U.K. 62/E6
Kilohana, Hawaii, U.S., *crater* 262/C2
Kilombero, Tan., *river* 152/C2
Kilough, N. Ire., U.K., 779 . . . . .65/F3
Kilrea, N. Ire., U.K., 1,405 . . . . .65/D2
Kilrenny, Scot., U.K. 62/L6
Kilsyth, Scot., U.K., 9,816 . . . . .62/H7
Kilwa Kivinje, Tan. 152/C2
Kilwaughter, N. Ire., U.K. 65/F2
Kilwinning, Scot., U.K., 15,908 . . . . .62/G7
Kim, Colo., U.S., 65 . . . . .250/G4
Kimball, Kans., U.S., 60 . . . . .276/G4
Kimball, Minn., U.S., 635 . . . . .298/C5
Kimball, Nebr., U.S., 2,559 . . . . .308/A2
Kimball, Nebr., U.S., *county*, 4,089 . . . . .308/A2
Kimball, Ohio, U.S., 150 . . . . .328/E4
Kimball, S. Dak., U.S., 745 . . . . .342/G4
Kimball, Tenn., U.S., 1,312 . . . . .344/K4
Kimball, W. Va., U.S., 411 . . . . .360/D6
Kimballton, Iowa, U.S., 342 . . . . .274/D4
Kimbe, P.N.G. 172/B2
Kimberley, Austl., *plateau* 170/B1
Kimberley, Br. Col., Can., 6,484 . . . . .214/O6
Kimberley, Ont., Can. 223/E3
Kimberley, S. Afr. 162/B2
Kimberley, Eng., U.K., 10,488 . . . . .70/G1
Kimberling City, Mo., U.S., 2,253 . . . . . . .302/C5
Kimberly, Ala., U.S., 1,801 . . . . .238/C2
Kimberly, Ida., U.S., 2,614 . . . . .264/C7
Kimberly, Minn., U.S. 298/D4
Kimberly, Oreg., U.S., 50 . . . . .334/G3
Kimberly, Wisc., U.S., 6,146 . . . . .364/E4
Kimble, Tex., U.S., *county*, 4,468 . . . . . .346/J5
Kimbolton, Eng., U.K. 328/G5
Kimbolton, Ohio, U.S., 190 . . . . .328/G5
Kimbrough, Ala., U.S., 70 . . . . .238/B3
Kimch'aek, N. Kor. 116/C2
Kimmeridge, Eng., U.K. 73/H3
Kimmins, Tenn., U.S., 70 . . . . .344/F3
Kimmirut, Nun., Can., 433 . . . . .220/O4
Kimmswick, Mo., U.S., 94 . . . . .302/F2
Kimper, Ky., U.S., 50 . . . . .280/H3
Kimpton, Eng., U.K., 2,247 . . . . .70/D3

Kinabalu, Malay., *mountain* 121/D1
Kinabatangan, Malay., *river* 121/D2
Kinard, Fla., U.S. 256/C1
Kinards, S.C., U.S., 125 . . . . .340/C2
Kinau, Hawaii, U.S., *cape* 262/C4
Kinbasket, Br. Col., Can., *lake* 212/B5
Kinbasket, Br. Col., Can., *lake* 214/O5
Kinbrace, Scot., U.K. 62/J2
Kinbrae, Minn., U.S. 298/B7
Kinbuck, Scot., U.K. 62/J6
Kincaid, Sask., Can., 161 . . . . .227/C11
Kincaid, Ill., U.S., 1,441 . . . . .266/D4
Kincaid, Kans., U.S., 178 . . . . .276/C3
Kincardine, Ont., Can., 6,410 . . . . .223/D3
Kinde, Mich., U.S., 534 . . . . .294/G6
Kinder, La., U.S., 2,148 . . . . .282/D5
Kinderhook, Ill., U.S., 249 . . . . .266/B4
Kinderhook, Mich., U.S., 350 . . . . .294/D8
Kinderhook, N.Y., U.S., 1,275 . . . . .320/P6
Kindersley, Sask., Can., 4,548 . . . . .227/A9
Kindia, Guin., 80,000 . . . . .149/B2
Kindred, N. Dak., U.S., 614 . . . . .326/H3
Kindu, Congo, D.R. 155/C2
Kineo, Maine, U.S. 286/C3
Kineton, Eng., U.K., 2,079 . . . . .68/D6
King, Iowa, U.S., 450 . . . . .274/N3
King, N.C., U.S., 5,952 . . . . .322/N4
King, Tex., U.S., *county*, 356 . . . . .346/H2
King, Wash., U.S., *county*, 1,737,034 . .358/B4, D2
King, Wisc., U.S., 2,215 . . . . .364/D4
King and Queen, Va., U.S., *county*, 6,630 . .354/J4
King and Queen Courthouse, Va., U.S., 50 . .354/K5
Kingarth, Scot., U.K. 62/F7
King Christian X, Grld., *land* 193/D2
King City, Calif., U.S., 11,094 . . . . .246/D6
King City, Mo., U.S., 1,012 . . . . .302/B1
King City, Oreg., U.S., 1,949 . . . . .334/A3
King Cove, Alaska, U.S., 792 . . . . .240/C3
Kingdom City, Mo., U.S., 121 . . . . .302/E3
Kingfield, Maine, U.S., 1,103 . . . . .286/B4
Kingfisher, Okla., U.S., 4,380 . . . . .330/E2
Kingfisher, Okla., U.S., *county*, 13,926 . .330/E2
King Frederik VIII, Grld., *land* 193/D2
King George, Va., U.S. 354/J4
King George, Va., U.S., *county*, 16,803 . .354/J4
King Hill, Ida., U.S., 150 . . . . .264/B6
King Leopold, Austl., *range* 170/B1
Kingman, U.S., *reef* 161
Kingman, Ariz., U.S., 20,069 . . . . .242/A2
Kingman, Ind., U.S., 538 . . . . .270/B5
Kingman, Kans., U.S., 3,387 . . . . .276/D4
Kingman, Kans., U.S., *county*, 8,673 . . . .276/D4
Kingman, Maine, U.S., 213 . . . . .286/D3
King of Prussia, Penn., U.S., 18,511 . . .336/L5, L6
Kings, N.B., Can., *county* 217/B3
Kings, N.S., Can., *county* 221/C3
Kings, P.E.I., Can., *county* 224/C2
Kings, Calif., U.S., *county*, 129,461 . . . .246/E7
Kings, Calif., U.S., *river* 246/F6
Kings, Ill., U.S., 150 . . . . .266/D1
Kings, N.Y., U.S., *county*, 2,465,326 . . .320/B2
Kings, Utah, U.S., *peak* 350/D3
King Salmon, Alaska, U.S., 442 . . . . .240/D3
Kingsbarns, Scot., U.K. 62/L6
Kingsboro, P.E.I., Can. 224/C2
Kingsbridge, Eng., U.K., 5,258 . . . . .73/E4
King's Bromley, Eng., U.K. 68/D4
Kingsburg, Calif., U.S., 9,199 . . . . .246/F6
Kingsbury, S. Dak., U.S. 342/H5
Kingsbury, Ind., U.S., 229 . . . . .270/C1
Kingsbury, Maine, U.S. 286/C3
Kingsbury, Nev., U.S., 2,624 . . . . .310/A2
Kingsbury, S. Dak., U.S., *county*, 5,815 . .342/H3
Kings Canyon, Colo., U.S. 250/G5
Kings Canyon Natl. Park, Calif., U.S. 246/G5
Kings Cove, Nfld., Can., 159 . . . . .218/E5
Kingsdale, Minn., U.S. 298/E4
Kingsdown, Eng., U.K. 70/G4
Kingsdown, Kans., U.S., 50 . . . . .276/C4
Kingsfold, Eng., U.K. 70/D4
Kingsford, Mich., U.S., 5,549 . . . . .294/A4
Kingsford Hts., Ind., U.S., 1,453 . . . . .270/C2
Kingsgate, Wash., U.S., 12,222 . . . . .358/C4
Kingshouse, Scot., U.K. 62/H6
Kingskerswell, Eng., U.K., 3,672 . . . . .73/E4
Kingsland, Ark., U.S., 449 . . . . .244/C4
Kingsland, Ga., U.S., 10,506 . . . . .260/H5
Kings Landing, N.B., Can. 217/B3
Kings Langley, Eng., U.K., 8,144 . . . . .70/D3
Kingsley, Eng., U.K. 70/C4
Kingsley, Fla., U.S., 425 . . . . .256/G2
Kingsley, Iowa, U.S., 1,245 . . . . .274/C2
Kingsley, Ky., U.S., 428 . . . . .280/A2
Kingsley, Mich., U.S., 1,469 . . . . .294/D5
King's Lynn, Eng., U.K. 60/D3
King's Lynn, Eng., U.K., 41,281 . . . . .70/E1
Kings Mtn., N.C., U.S., 9,693 . . . . .322/C4
Kings Mtn. Natl. Mil. Park, S.C., U.S. 340/C1
Kingsnorth, Eng., U.K. 70/F4
King's Norton, Eng., U.K. 70/C1
King's Nympton, Eng., U.K. 73/E3
Kings Pt., Nfld., Can., 771 . . . . .218/C4
Kingsport, Tenn., U.S., 44,905 . . . . .344/N1
King's Sutton, Eng., U.K., 2,073 . . . . .68/E5
King's Sutton, Eng., U.K., 2,073 . . . . .70/B2
Kingston, N.B., Can. 217/D3
Kingston, N.S., Can., 3,009 . . . . .221/C3
Kingston, Ont., Can., 114,195 . . . . .223/J3
Kingston, Jam., *capital* 204/B3
Kingston, Jam., *capital*, 97,424,
(577,623, *metro.*) 206/C3
Kingston, Eng., U.K. 70/B5
Kingston, Eng., U.K. 73/H3
Kingston, Ark., U.S., 60 . . . . .244/B1
Kingston, Ga., U.S., 659 . . . . .260/B3
Kingston, Ida., U.S., 650 . . . . .264/A2
Kingston, Ill., U.S., 980 . . . . .266/E1
Kingston, Ky., U.S., 600 . . . . .280/F3
Kingston, Md., U.S., 175 . . . . .288/M7
Kingston, Mass., U.S., 11,780 . . . . .292/M5
Kingston, Mich., U.S., 450 . . . . .294/F6
Kingston, Minn., U.S., 120 . . . . .298/C5
Kingston, Mo., U.S., 287 . . . . .302/B2
Kingston, N.H., U.S., 5,862 . . . . .312/D6
Kingston, N.J., U.S., 1,292 . . . . .314/D3
Kingston, N. Mex., U.S., 125 . . . . .317/C5
Kingston, N.Y., U.S., 23,456 . . . . .320/P7
Kingston, Ohio, U.S., 1,032 . . . . .328/E7
Kingston, Okla., U.S., 1,390 . . . . .330/F3
Kingston, Penn., U.S., 13,855 . . . . . . .336/G7, K3
Kingston, R.I., U.S., 5,446 . . . . .339/C5
Kingston, Tenn., U.S., 5,264 . . . . .344/N3
Kingston, Utah, U.S., 142 . . . . .350/B5
Kingston, W. Va., U.S., 1,611 . . . . .358/A4
Kingston, W. Va., U.S., 60 . . . . .360/D5
Kingston, Wash., U.S., 288 . . . . .364/B5
Kingston Bagpuize, Eng., U.K., 2,098 . . . .68/E6
Kingston Bagpuize, Eng., U.K., 2,098 . . . .70/B3
Kingstone, Eng., U.K. 68/B5
Kingston Mines, Ill., U.S., 259 . . . . .266/D3
Kingston Seymour, Eng., U.K. 73/G2

Kingston Sprs., Tenn., U.S., 2,773 . . . . . .344/G2
Kingston upon Hull, Eng., U.K. 60/C3
Kingston upon Hull, Eng., U.K., 310,636 . . .66/H5
Kingston upon Hull, Eng., U.K., 310,636 . . .68/G2
Kingston upon Hull, City of, Eng., U.K.,
unitary authority, 243,595 . . . . .66/H5
Kingston upon Hull, City of, Eng., U.K.,
unitary authority, 243,595 . . . . .68/G2
Kingston upon Thames, Eng., U.K. . . .60/Inset III
Kingston upon Thames, Eng., U.K., 132,206 . .70/D4
Kingston upon Thames, Eng., U.K.,
unitary authority, 147,295 . . . . .70/D4
Kingstown, St. Vin.-Gren., *capital*, 15,466 . .204/F4
Kingstown, St. Vin.-Gren., *capital*, 15,466 . .208/B2
Kingstown, Md., U.S., 1,644 . . . . .288/K3
Kingstown, N.C., U.S., 845 . . . . .322/K5
Kingstree, S.C., U.S., 3,496 . . . . .340/E3
Kings Valley, Oreg., U.S. 334/C3
Kingsville, N.S., Can. 221/F2
Kingsville, Ont., Can., 19,619 . . . . .223/C5
Kingsville, Md., U.S., 4,214 . . . . .288/J2
Kingsville, Mo., U.S., 257 . . . . .302/B3
Kingsville, Tex., U.S., 25,575 . . . . .346/L8
Kingswear, Eng., U.K. 73/E4
Kingswinford, Eng., U.K. 68/C5
Kingswood, (Buckinghamshire),
Eng., U.K., 60,192 . . . . .70/C3
Kingswood, (Surrey), Eng., U.K. 70/D4
Kingswood, Eng., U.K., 60,192 . . . . .68/F6
Kingswood, Eng., U.K., 60,192 . . . . .73/G2
Kingussie, Scot., U.K., 1,410 . . . . .62/H4
King William, Nun., Can., *island* 220/I3
King William, Va., U.S., 50 . . . . .354/J5
King William, Va., U.S., *county*, 13,146 . .354/J5
King William's Town, S. Afr. 162/C3
Kingwood, N.J., U.S., 3,782 . . . . .314/C3
Kingwood, Tex., U.S., 37,400 . . . . .346/B5
Kingwood, W. Va., U.S., 2,944 . . . . .360/G2
Kininvie, Sask., Can., 702 . . . . .227/E8
Kinkala, Congo .155/C6
Kinkler, Tex., U.S. 346/M6
Kinkony, Madag., *lake* 163/B2
Kinkora, P.E.I., Can., 315 . . . . .224/B2
Kinlichee, Ariz., U.S. 242/F2
Kinloch, Scot., U.K. 62/D4
Kinloch, Mo., U.S., 449 . . . . .302/H2
Kinlochbervie, Scot., U.K. 62/F2
Kinloch Hourn, Scot., U.K. 62/F4
Kinlochleven, Scot., U.K., 897 . . . . .62/H5
Kinloch Rannoch, Scot., U.K. 62/H5
Kinloss, Ont., Can. 223/D3
Kinmount, Ont., Can. 223/G3
Kinmundy, Ill., U.S., 892 . . . . .266/E5
Kinnairds, Scot., U.K., *cape* 60/C1
Kinnear, Wyo., U.S., 125 . . . . .366/B2
Kinnelon, N.J., U.S., 9,365 . . . . .314/E2
Kinnersley, Eng., U.K. 68/A5
Kinney, Minn., U.S., 199 . . . . .298/E3
Kinney, Tex., U.S., *county*, 3,379 . . . . . .346/H6
Kinnota, Man., Can. 215/B4
Kinross, Scot., U.K., 4,681 . . . . .62/K6
Kinross, Iowa, U.S., 80 . . . . .274/L5
Kinross, Mich., U.S., 175 . . . . .294/E3
Kinsale, Va., U.S., 250 . . . . .354/K4
Kinsarvik, Nor. 80/B3
Kinsella, Alta., Can. 212/E5
Kinsey, Ala., U.S., 1,796 . . . . .238/D4
Kinsey, Mont., U.S. 306/L3
Kinshasa, Congo, D.R., *capital*, 4,657,061 . .155/C2
Kinshasa, Congo, D.R., *region* 155/B2
Kinsley, Kans., U.S., 1,658 . . . . .276/C4
Kinsman, Ill., U.S., 109 . . . . .266/E2
Kinsman, Ohio, U.S., 800 . . . . .328/J3
Kinston, Ala., U.S., 602 . . . . .238/C4
Kinston, N.C., U.S., 23,688 . . . . .322/K4
Kinta, Okla., U.S., 243 . . . . .330/G2
Kintail N.P., Scot., U.K. 62/F4
Kintbury, Eng., U.K., 2,072 . . . . .70/B4
Kintocher, Scot., U.K. 62/L4
Kintore, Scot., U.K., 1,696 . . . . .62/M4
Kintyre, N. Dak., U.S. 326/F3
Kinuso, Alta., Can., 231 . . . . .212/C3
Kinyeti, Sudan, *mountain* 145/C4
Kinzia, Oreg., U.S. 334/F3
Kioa, Fiji, *island* 174/C2
Kiosk, Ont., Can. 223/G1
Kiowa, Colo., U.S., 581 . . . . .250/G3
Kiowa, Colo., U.S., *county*, 1,622 . . . . . .250/G3
Kiowa, Colo., U.S., *creek* 250/F2
Kiowa, Kans., U.S., 1,055 . . . . .276/D4
Kiowa, Kans., U.S., *county*, 3,278 . . . . . .276/C4
Kiowa, Mont., U.S. 306/C1
Kiowa, Okla., U.S., 693 . . . . .330/G3
Kiowa, Okla., U.S., *county*, 10,227 . . . . .330/D3
Kiowa Natl. Grassland, N. Mex., U.S. . .317/F1, G1
Kipahulu, Hawaii, U.S. 262/D4
Kipahulu Forest Reserve, Hawaii, U.S. . . .262/C4
Kipengere, Tan., *range* 152/B2
Kipihigan, Sask., Can., *lake* 227/H10
Kipling, Sask., Can., 1,037 . . . . .227/H10
Kipling, M.D., U.S., 300 . . . . .294/B4
Kipp, Kans., U.S., 100 . . . . .276/E3
Kipton, Ohio, U.S., 265 . . . . .328/F3
Kiptopeke, Va., U.S. 354/M6
Kipuka Puaulu, Hawaii, U.S., *mountain* . .262/H6
Kırşehir, Tur. 133/C2
Kırşehir, Tur., *province* 133/C2
Kirakira, Sol. Is. .173/B2
Kirbister, Scot., U.K. 62/M2
Kirby, Ark., U.S., 225 . . . . .244/B3
Kirby, Miss., U.S. 300/B4
Kirby, Mont., U.S. 306/K4
Kirby, Ohio, U.S., 132 . . . . .328/D4
Kirby, S.C., U.S., 8,673 . . . . .346/N2, K6
Kirby, Wyo., U.S., 57 . . . . .366/B2
Kirby Bedon, Eng., U.K. 70/G1
Kirby Cane, Eng., U.K. 70/H2
Kirby Cross, Eng., U.K. 70/G3
Kirby Grindalythe, Eng., U.K. 68/F1
Kirby Muxloe, Eng., U.K., 7,780 . . . . .68/E4
Kirbyville, Tex., U.S., 2,085 . . . . .346/R5
Kircubbin, N. Ire., U.K., 1,098 . . . . .65/F3
Kire, Va., U.S. 354/B4
Kirensk, Russ. 104/G4
Kiribati, *nation* 167
Kırıkkale, Tur. 133/C2
Kırıkkale, Tur., *province* 133/C2
Kiritimati, (Christmas), Kiri., *island* 175/D1
Kirk, Colo., U.S., 100 . . . . .250/H4
Kirk, Oreg., U.S., 80 . . . . .334/E5
Kirkabister, Scot., U.K. 62/Q2
Kirkbride, Eng., U.K. 66/B3
Kirkburn, Eng., U.K. 66/H5
Kirkburton, Eng., U.K., 4,121 . . . . .66/E5
Kirkburton, Eng., U.K., 4,121 . . . . .68/D2
Kirkby, Eng., U.K., 43,017 . . . . .66/C6
Kirkby, Eng., U.K., 43,017 . . . . .68/B3
Kirkby in Ashfield, Eng., U.K., 27,014 . . . . .68/E3
Kirkby Lonsdale, Eng., U.K. 66/C4

Kirkby Malzeard, Eng., U.K. 66/E4
Kirkbymoorside, Eng., U.K., 2,650 . . . . . . .66/G4
Kirkby Stephen, Eng., U.K., 1,619 . . . . . . .66/D4
Kirkcaldy, Scot., U.K. 60/B2
Kirkcaldy, Scot., U.K., 46,912 . . . . .62/K6
Kirkcolm, Scot., U.K. 62/F9
Kirkcudbright, Scot., U.K., 3,477 . . . . .62/H9
Kirkenes, Nor. 80/F2
Kirkersville, Ohio, U.S., 520 . . . . .328/E6
Kirkfield, Ont., Can. 223/G3
Kirkham, Eng., U.K., 9,038 . . . . .66/C5
Kirkham, Eng., U.K., 9,038 . . . . .68/B2
Kirkinner, Scot., U.K. 62/H9
Kirkintilloch, Scot., U.K., 20,281 . . . . .62/H7
Kirk Ireton, Eng., U.K. 68/D3
Kirkland, Ga., U.S. 260/F9
Kirkland, Ill., U.S., 1,166 . . . . .266/E1
Kirkland, Tex., U.S. 346/H1
Kirkland, Wash., U.S., 45,054 . . . . .358/A4, C2
Kirkland Jct., Ariz., U.S. 242/C3
Kirkland Lake, Ont., Can., 8,616 . . . . .222/D3
Kirk Langley, Eng., U.K. 70/A1
Kirklareli, Tur. 133/A2
Kirklareli, Tur., *province* 133/A2
Kirklees, Eng., U.K., *unitary authority*, 388,576 . .66/E5
Kirklees, Eng., U.K., *unitary authority*, 388,576 . .68/D2
Kirklin, Ind., U.S., 766 . . . . .270/D4
Kirkman, Iowa, U.S., 76 . . . . .274/D4
Kirkmansville, Ky., U.S., 50 . . . . .280/C3
Kirk Michael, Eng., U.K. 66/A5
Kirkoswald, Scot., U.K. 62/G8
Kirkpatrick, Antar., *mountain* 192/A5
Kirksanton, Eng., U.K. 66/B4
Kirksey, Ky., U.S., 175 . . . . .280/B4
Kirksey, S.C., U.S., 40 . . . . .340/B2
Kirksville, Mo., U.S., 16,988 . . . . .302/D1
Kirkton, Scot., U.K. 62/L8
Kirkuk, Iraq, 418,624 . . . . .130/B1
Kirkville, Iowa, U.S., 214 . . . . .274/J5
Kirkville, Miss., U.S., 40 . . . . .300/D1
Kirkwall, Scot., U.K. . . . . .60/Inset I
Kirkwall, Scot., U.K., 6,206 . . . . .62/M2
Kirkwhelpington, Eng., U.K. 66/F2
Kirkwood, Del., U.S., 1,800 . . . . .255/B2
Kirkwood, Ill., U.S., 794 . . . . .266/C3
Kirkwood, Ky., U.S. 280/F3
Kirkwood, Mo., U.S., 27,324 . . . . .302/F3, H3
Kirley, S. Dak., U.S. 342/D3
Kirn, Iowa, U.S., 273 . . . . .274/D3
Kirov, Russ., 465,628, (508,150, *metro.*) . .104/D4
Kirovohrad, Ukr., 266,856 . . . . .102/C2
Kirovohrad, Ukr., *oblast* 102/C2
Kirriemuir, Scot., U.K., 5,963 . . . . .62/L5
Kirthar, Pak., *range* 129/C4
Kirtland, N. Mex., U.S., 6,190 . . . . .317/B1
Kirtland, Ohio, U.S., 6,670 . . . . .328/H2, J8
Kirtland Hills, Ohio, U.S., 597 . . . . .328/J8
Kirtley, Tex., U.S., 50 . . . . .346/L6
Kirtlington, Eng., U.K. 70/B3
Kirton, Eng., U.K., 2,588 . . . . .68/G4
Kirton, Eng., U.K., 2,588 . . . . .70/D1
Kirton in Lindsey, Eng., U.K., 2,773 . . . . . .66/G6
Kirton in Lindsey, Eng., U.K., 2,773 . . . . . .68/F3
Kiruna, Swe. 80/D1
Kirwin, Kans., U.S., 229 . . . . .276/C2
Kirwin, Kans., U.S., *reservoir* 276/C2
Kirwin N.W.R., Kans., U.S. 276/C2
Kiryas Joel, N.Y., U.S., 13,138 . . . . .320/A1
Kisangani, Congo, D.R., 317,581 . . . . . . .155/C1
Kisatchie, La., U.S. 282/D5
Kisatchie Natl. For., La., U.S. . .282/C1, C4, C5, D1-4
K.I. Sawyer A.F.B., Wisc., U.S. 364/F2
Kishi, Nig. 152/B3
Kiska, Alaska, U.S., *island* 240/Inset
Kiskitto, Man., Can., *lake* 215/B2
Kiskőrei-víztároló, Hun., *lake* 91/C2
Kiskunhalas, Hun. 91/B2
Kislingbury, Eng., U.K. 70/C2
Kismaayo, Som. .157/A4
Kismet, Kans., U.S., 484 . . . . .276/B4
Kissidougou, Guin. 149/C3
Kissimmee, Fla., U.S., 47,814 . . . . . . .256/C4, G3
Kissimmee, Fla., U.S., *lake* 256/C4
Kississing, Man., Can., *lake* 215/A1
Kistler, Pa., U.S., 344 . . . . .336/F5
Kisumu, Kenya, 185,100 . . . . .157/C2
Kita, Jap., *island* . . . . .114/Inset II
Kita, Mali 150/B3
Kitakami, Jap., *river* 114/D2
Kitakyushu, Jap., 1,011,471 . . . . .114/A3
Kitale, Kenya 157/C2
Kitami, Jap. .114/Inset I
Kitami, Jap., *mountains* . . . . .114/Inset I
Kit Carson, Calif., U.S. 246/E4
Kit Carson, Colo., U.S. 250/H3
Kit Carson, Colo., U.S., 253 . . . . .250/H3
Kit Carson, Colo., U.S., *county*, 8,011 . . .250/H2
Kitchel, Ind., U.S., 70 . . . . .270/G5
Kitchener, Ont., Can., 190,399,
(438,000, *metro.*) 222/D4
Kitchener, Ont., Can., 190,399,
(438,000, *metro.*) 223/E4
Kite, Ga., U.S., 241 . . . . .260/F6
Kitgum, Ug., 42,929 . . . . .157/C2
Kitimat, Br. Col., Can., 10,285 . . . . .214/H4
Kitsap, Wash., U.S., *county*, 231,969 . .358/A4, C2
Kitsap Lake, Wash., U.S., 2,723 . . . . .358/C2
Kitscoty, Alta., Can., 671 . . . . .212/E4
Kittanning, Penn., U.S., 4,787 . . . . .336/B4
Kittatinny Lake, N.J., U.S. 314/D1
Kittery, Maine, U.S., 9,543 . . . . .286/B5
Kittery Pt., Maine, U.S., 1,135 . . . . .286/B5
Kittitas, Wash., U.S., 1,105 . . . . .358/E3
Kittitas, Wash., U.S., *county*, 33,362 . . . .358/E2
Kittrell, N.C., U.S., 148 . . . . .322/J2
Kitts Hill, Ohio, U.S., 650 . . . . .328/E8
Kitts Hummock, Del., U.S., 250 . . . . .255/C4
Kittson, Minn., U.S., *county*, 5,285 . . . . .298/A2
Kitty Hawk, N.C., U.S., 2,991 . . . . .322/P2
Kitwanga, Br. Col., Can. 214/H3
Kitwe, Zam., 467,084 . . . . .159/B2
Kitzbühel, Aus. 91/C3
Kitzmiller, Md., U.S., 302 . . . . .288/B4
Kiva, Mich., U.S., 50 . . . . .294/B3
Kivalina, Alaska, U.S., 377 . . . . .240/C1
Kiveton Park, Eng., U.K. 66/F6
Kivi, Fin., *lake* 81/C2
Kivu, Congo, D.R., *lake* 155/C2
Kivu, Rwa., *lake* 152/B1
Kızılırmak, Tur., *river* 133/C2
Kjølen, Swe., *mountains* 80/C1
Kjustendil, Bul., *oblast* 101/A3
Kladno, Czh. Rep. 92/B2
Klagenfurt, Aus., 89,502, (138,558, *metro.*) . .91/C4
Klagetoh, Ariz., U.S., 50 . . . . .242/F2
Klaipeda, Lith., 202,528 . . . . .82/A2
Klamath, Calif., U.S., 651 . . . . .246/A1
Klamath, Calif., U.S., *mountains* 246/B1
Klamath, Oreg., U.S., *county*, 63,775 . . .334/E5
Klamath, Oreg., U.S., *river* 246/B1
Klamath, Oreg., U.S., *mountains* 334/B5

Klamath Falls, Oreg., U.S., 19,462 . . . . .334/E5
Klamath Forest N.W.R., Oreg., U.S. 334/E5
Klamath Natl. For., Calif., U.S. 246/B1, D1
Klamath River, Calif., U.S. 246/C1
Klarälven, Swe., river 80/B2
Klatovy, Czh. Rep. 92/A3
Klawock, Alaska, U.S., 854 . . . . .240/J3
Kleberg, Tex., U.S., county, 31,549 . . . . .346/L8
Klein, Mont., U.S., 188 . . . . .306/H3
Kleinburg, Ont., Can. 223/J5
Klemme, Iowa, U.S., 593 . . . . .274/C1
Klemtu, Br. Col., Can. .214/H5
Kleve, Ger. 86/A3
Klickitat, Wash., U.S., 417 . . . . .358/D4
Klickitat, Wash., U.S., county, 19,161 . . . . .358/E4
Klickitat, Wash., U.S., river 358/D3
Kline, Colo., U.S., 100 .250/B4
Kline, S.C., U.S., 238 . . . . .340/C3
Klondike, Tex., U.S., 60 . . . . .346/F3
Klondike Gold Rush N.H.P., Alaska, U.S. 240/H3
Klondike Gold Rush N.H.P., Wash., U.S. 358/A4
Klondyke, Ariz., U.S., 50 . . . . .242/E5
Klossner, Minn., U.S., 100 . . . . .298/C6
Kloten, N. Dak., U.S., 40 . . . . .326/C2
Kloulklubed, Palau 172/B3
Kluane, Yukon, Can., lake 228/B5
Kluane Natl. Park Res., Yukon, Can. 228/B5
Klyuchevskaya Sopka, Russ., mountain 193/D9
Knapdale N.P., Scot., U.K. 62/E7
Knapp, Tex., U.S. 346/G3
Knapp, Wisc., U.S., 421 . . . . .364/A4
Knappa, Oreg., U.S., 275 . . . . .334/C1
Knapton, Eng., U.K. 70/C1
Knaresborough, Eng., U.K., 13,380 . . . . .66/F4
Knaresborough, Eng., U.K., 13,380 . . . . .68/E1
Knarsdale, Eng., U.K. 70/D2
Knayton, Eng., U.K. 66/F4
Knebworth, Eng., U.K., 4,025 . . . . .70/D3
Knee, Man., Can., lake .215/D1
Kneeland, Calif., U.S., 70 . . . . .246/B2
Kneesworth, Eng., U.K. .70/D2
Knierim, Iowa, U.S., 70 . . . . .274/F3
Knife, N. Dak., U.S., river 326/C2
Knife River, Minn., U.S., 300 . . . . .298/F4
Knife River Indian Vil.s Natl. Hist. Site,
   N. Dak., U.S. 326/D2
Knifley, Ky., U.S., 225 .280/E3
Knight, Br. Col., Can., inlet 214/K6
Knight, La., U.S. 282/C5
Knightdale, N.C., U.S., 5,958 . . . . .322/I3
Knighton, Wales, U.K., 2,972 . . . . .64/E3
Knights Corner, Mass., U.S., 50 . . . . .292/E3
Knights Landing, Calif., U.S., 1,000 . . . . .246/K5
Knights Landing, Maine, U.S. 286/A2
Knightstown, Ind., U.S., 2,148 . . . . .270/E5
Knightsville, Ind., U.S., 624 . . . . .270/B5
Knightwick, Eng., U.K. .68/C5
Kniman, Ind., U.S., 175 . . . . .270/B2
Knippa, Tex., U.S., 739 . . . . .346/I6
Knittelfeld, Aus. 91/D3
Kniverton, Eng., U.K. 70/A1
Knobel, Ark., U.S., 358 . . . . .280/E1
Knob Lick, Ky., U.S., 150 . . . . .280/E3
Knob Lick, Mo., U.S., 200 . . . . .302/F4
Knob Noster, Mo., U.S., 2,462 . . . . .302/C3
Knockboy, Ire., mountain 78/B3
Knockholt Pound, Eng., U.K. 70/E4
Knockin, Eng., U.K. 68/A4
Knocklayd, N. Ire., U.K., hill 65/E1
Knocksharry, Eng., U.K. 66/A5
Knoke, Iowa, U.S., 60 .274/E2
Knokke-Heist, Belg. 85/B1
Knollcrest, Conn., U.S., 1,300 . . . . .253/B4
Knolls, Utah, U.S., 70 .350/A3
Knollwood, Conn., U.S., 2,500 . . . . .253/F4
Knook, Eng., U.K. 73/H2
Knossington, Eng., U.K. 70/C1
Knott, Ky., U.S., county, 17,649 . . . . .280/H3
Knott, Tex., U.S., 60 . . . . .346/G3
Knottingley, Eng., U.K., 14,690 . . . . .66/F5
Knottingley, Eng., U.K., 14,690 . . . . .68/E2
Knotts Island, N.C., U.S., 175 . . . . .322/P1
Knowles, N. Mex., U.S. 317/G5
Knowles, Okla., U.S. 330/B1
Knowles Corner, Maine, U.S. 286/D2
Knowl Hill, Eng., U.K. 70/C3
Knowlton, Mont., U.S. .306/L3
Knowsley, Eng., U.K., unitary authority, 150,468 . .66/C6
Knowsley, Eng., U.K., unitary authority, 150,468 . .68/B3
Knox, Ill., U.S., county 55,836 . . . . .266/C3
Knox, Ind., U.S., 3,721 .270/C2
Knox, Ind., U.S., county, 39,256 . . . . .270/B7
Knox, Ky., U.S., county, 31,795 . . . . .280/G4
Knox, Maine, U.S., county, 39,618 . . . . .286/C4
Knox, Mo., U.S., county, 4,361 . . . . .302/D1
Knox, Nebr., U.S., county, 9,374 . . . . .308/G1
Knox, N. Dak., U.S., 59 . . . . .326/F1
Knox, Ohio, U.S., county, 54,500 . . . . .328/F5
Knox, Penn., U.S., 1,176 . . . . .336/B3
Knox, Tenn., U.S., county, 382,032 . . . . .344/P3
Knox, Tex., U.S., county, 4,253 . . . . .346/J2
Knox City, Mo., U.S., 223 . . . . .302/D1
Knox City, Tex., U.S., 1,219 . . . . .346/J2
Knoxville, Ala., U.S. 238/B3
Knoxville, Ark., U.S., 511 . . . . .244/B2
Knoxville, Ga., U.S., 60 . . . . .260/D6
Knoxville, Ill., U.S., 3,183 . . . . .266/C3
Knoxville, Iowa, U.S., 7,731 . . . . .274/H5
Knoxville, Mo., U.S., 50 . . . . .302/B2
Knoxville, Penn., U.S., 617 . . . . .336/G2
Knoxville, Tenn., U.S., 173,890,
   (687,249, metro.) 344/P3
Knoydart N.P., Scot., U.K. 62/E4
Knud Rasmussen, Grld., land 193/B2
Knutsford, Eng., U.K., 13,352 . . . . .66/D6
Knutsford, Eng., U.K., 13,352 . . . . .68/C3
Kožuf, Mac., mountains 100/C2
Koani, Mac. 100/C2
Kobe, Jap., 1,493,595 .114/B3
København, Den., county 79/D3
Koblenz, Ger., 108,003 .86/A3
Koblenz, Ger., department 86/A3
Kobuk, Alaska, U.S., 109 . . . . .240/D1
Kobuk, Alaska, U.S., river 240/D1
Kobuk Valley Natl. Park, Alaska, U.S. 240/D1
K'obulet'i, Geo. 103/A4
Kocaeli, (Izmit), Tur. 133/B2
Kocaeli, Tur., province .133/B2
Kočevje, Slove., 16,071 .99/B3
Ko Chang, Thai., island 125/C3
Kochi, India, 564,038, (1,355,406, metro.) 128/C7
Kochi, Jap., 331,000 . . . . .114/B3
Kochi, Jap., prefecture .114/B3
Kodiak, Alaska, U.S., 6,334 . . . . .240/E3
Kodiak, Alaska, U.S., island 240/E3
Kodiak N.W.R., Alaska, U.S. 240/E3
Kofa N.W.R., Ariz., U.S. 242/B4
Kofarnihon, Taj., river .132/A2
Köflach, Aus. 91/D3
Koforidua, Gha. 150/B3
Kofu, Jap. 114/C2
Køge, Den. 79/D3

Kogi, Nig., state 152/D4
Kohala, Hawaii, U.S., coast 262/F5
Kohala, Hawaii, U.S., mountain 262/G4
Kohala, Hawaii, U.S., mountains 262/G4
Kohala Forest Reserve, Hawaii, U.S. 262/G4
Kohatk, Ariz., U.S., 150 . . . . .242/C5
Kohima, India 128/F3
Kohkiluyeh and Buyer Ahmadi, Iran, province . . .130/C3
Kohler, Wisc., U.S., 1,926 . . . . .364/F5
Kohtla-Järve, Est., 47,679 . . . . .81/D1
Koindu, S.L. 149/B1
Kokadjo, Maine, U.S. 286/C3
Kokanee Glacier Prov. Park, Br. Col., Can. 214/O6
Kokkola, Fin. 81/B2
Koko Head, Hawaii, U.S., point 262/K3
Kokomo, Ind., U.S., 46,113, (101,541, metro.) . . .270/D3
Kokomo, Miss., U.S., 125 . . . . .300/C4
Kökshetaū, Kaz., 123,389 . . . . .131/C1
Ko Kut, Thai., island 125/C4
Kola, Man., Can. 215/A4
Kola, Russ., peninsula .104/C3
Kola, Russ., peninsula .193/C2
Kolar, India, gold fields 128/C6
Kolari, Fin. 81/B1
Kolda, Sen. 148/B3
Kolding, Den., 53,687 . . . . .79/B3
Koleen, Ind., U.S., 70 .270/C7
Kolekole Beach Park, Hawaii, U.S. 262/J4
Kolhapur, India, 405,118, (417,286, metro.) 128/B5
Kolhumadulu, Mald., atoll 127/A3
Koliganek, Alaska, U.S., 182 . . . . .240/D3
Kolín, Czh. Rep. 92/B2
Kolin, La., U.S., 600 . . . . .282/E4
Kolin, Mont., U.S. 306/G2
Kolkata (Calcutta), India, 4,580,544,
   (13,216,546, metro.) . . . . .128/E4 Inset II
Kolshet, India . . . . .128/Inset I
Kolwezi, Congo, D.R., 417,810 . . . . .155/C3
Kolyma, Russ., range 104/J3
Kolyma, Russ., range 193/C9
Kolyma, Russ., river 104/J3
Kolyma, Russ., river 193/C8
Komadugu Gana, Nig., river 152/F2
Komadugu Yobe, Niger, river 152/F1
Komadugu Yobe, Nig., river 152/F1
Komalty, Okla., U.S. 330/D2
Kománro, Slvk., 108,556 . . . . .92/B3
Komárom, Hun. 91/B2
Komárom-Esztergom, Hun., county 91/B2
Komati, Swaz., river 161/B2
Komatke, Ariz., U.S., 1,100 . . . . .242/C4
Komatsu, Jap. 114/C2
Komi, Russ., region 104/D3
Komi-Permyakia, Russ., autonomous okrug 104/D3
Komoé, C. d'Iv., river .150/E3
Komotini, Gr. 100/C1
Komsomol'sk-na-Amure, Russ., 294,268 . . . . . .104/H4
Kona, Hawaii, U.S., coast 262/F6
Konahuanui, Hawaii, U.S., mountain 262/G2, K2
Konar, Afg., river 129/B1
Konar, Pak., river 129/D2
Konawa, Okla., U.S., 1,479 . . . . .330/F3
Konduz, Afg. 129/B1
Konduz, Afg., river 129/B1
Kong, Laos, river 124/D4
Konibodom, Taj. 132/B1
Konin, Pol. 83/D2
Konnagar, India . . . . .128/Inset II
Konnarock, Va., U.S., 125 . . . . .354/E3
Konotop, Ukr. 102/C1
Kontagora, Nig. 152/C2
Kon Tum, Viet. 125/B3
Konya, Tur., 623,000 . . . . .133/C3
Konya, Tur., province 133/C2
Koocanusa, Mont., U.S., lake 306/A1
Koochiching, Minn., U.S., county, 14,355 . . . . . .298/D2
Koolau Forest Reserve, Hawaii, U.S. 262/C4
Koolau Range, Hawaii, U.S., mountains 262/F1, J1
Koontz Lake, Ind., U.S., 1,554 . . . . .270/C2
Koosharem, Utah, U.S., 276 . . . . .350/C5
Kooskia, Ida., U.S., 675 . . . . .264/B3
Kooskooskie, Wash., U.S., 100 . . . . .358/G4
Kootenai, Ida., U.S., 441 . . . . .264/A1
Kootenai, Ida., U.S., county, 108,685 . . . . .264/A2
Kootenai, Ida., U.S., river 264/A1, B1
Kootenai Mont., U.S., river 306/A1
Kootenai Natl. For., Mont., U.S. 306/A1
Kootenai N.W.R., Ida., U.S. 264/A1
Kootenay, Br. Col., Can., lake 214/O6
Kootenay, Br. Col., Can., river 214/P6
Kootenay Natl. Park, Br. Col., Can. 212/B6, C6
Kootenay Natl. Park, Br. Col., Can. 214/O5
Kopaonik, Serb.-Mont., mountains 99/B3
Kópavogur, Ice., 23,527 . . . . .79/A2
Koper, Slove., 46,757 . . . . .98/A3
Kopet, Iran, mountains 130/D2
Kopet, Turkm., mountains 132/B2
Ko Phangan, Thai., island 125/B4
Koppel, Penn., U.S., 856 . . . . .336/A4
Kopperston, W. Va., U.S., 500 . . . . .360/C5
Koprivnica, Cro. 98/C2
Korab, Alb., mountain 99/A2
Korab, Mac., mountain 100/A2
Korçë, Alb., 55,130 . . . . .99/B3
Korčula, Cro., island 98/C4
Kordestan, Iran, province 130/B2
Korea, (North), nation 112
Korea, (South), nation 112
Korea, Jap., strait 114/A3
Korea, N. Kor., bay 116/A3
Korea, S. Kor., strait 116/C5
Korhogo, C. d'Iv., 109,445 . . . . .150/D2
Koriyama, Jap., 335,000 . . . . .114/D2
Korla, China 119/B1
Kormakiti, Cyp., cape 133/A1
Kornegay, N.C., U.S. 322/K4
Kornman, Colo., U.S., 100 . . . . .250/H3
Koro, Fiji, island 174/B2
Koro, Fiji, sea 174/B2
Korona, Fla., U.S., 40 .256/G2
Koror, Palau, capital, 13,303 . . . . .172/B3
Koror, Palau, island 172/B3
Körös, Hun., river 91/C2
Korosten', Ukr. 102/B1
Koro Toro, Chad 153/B4
Kortes Dam, Wyo., U.S. 366/G2
Kortrijk, Belg., 76,081, (114,371, metro.) 85/B2
Koryak, Russ., range 104/K3
Koryakia, Russ., autonomous okrug 104/J3
Kos, Gr., island 100/C3
Ko Samui, Thai., island 125/B4
Kosciusko, Austl., mountain 170/D3
Kosciusko, Ind., U.S., county, 74,057 . . . . .270/E2
Kosciusko, Miss., U.S., 7,372 . . . . .300/C2
Kosciusko, Tex., U.S., 100 . . . . .346/L6
Koshigaya, Jap., 308,000 . . . . .114/C3
Koshiki, Jap., islands 114/A4

Koshkonong, Mo., U.S., 205 . . . . .302/E5
Kosi, Nepal, river 126/C3
Košice, Slvk., 236,093 . . . . .92/C2
Košický, Slvk., region 92/C2
Kosŏng, N. Kor. 116/C3
Kosovo, Serb.-Mont., autonomous province 99/B3
Kosovska Mitrovica, Serb.-Mont. 99/B3
Kosrae, Micr. 172/D2
Kosrae, Micr., island 172/D2
Kosrae, Micr., state 172/D2
Koss, Mich., U.S., 80 . . . . .294/B4
Kosse, Tex., U.S., 497 .346/M4
Kossol, Palau, passage 172/C2
Kossol, Palau, reef 172/C2
Kossou, C. d'Iv., lake 150/D3
Kossuth, Iowa, U.S., county, 17,163 . . . . .274/F1
Kossuth, Miss., U.S., 170 . . . . .300/D1
Koszalin, Pol., 112,344 .83/C1
Koszta, Iowa, U.S., 70 .274/K4
Kota, India 126/B3
Kotayk', Arm., district .103/B2
Kotcho, Br. Col., Can., lake 212/A1
Kotcho, Br. Col., Can., lake 214/H1
Kotka, Fin., 54,846 . . . . .81/C2
Kotlas, Russ. 104/D3
Kotlik, Alaska, U.S., 591 . . . . .240/C2
Kotor, Serb.-Mont., gulf .99/A3
Kotovs'k, Ukr. 102/B2
Kotte, Sri Lan. 126/A5
Kotto, C.A.R., river 154/B2
Kotzebue, Alaska, U.S., 3,082 . . . . .240/C1
Kotzebue, Alaska, U.S., sound 240/C1
Kouango, C.A.R. 154/A2
Kouchibouguac, N.B., Can. 217/D2
Kouchibouguac Natl. Park, N.B., Can. 217/E2
Koudougou, Burkina, 105,000 . . . . .151/C2
Kouffo, Ben., river 151/C3
Koulamoutou, Gabon 155/B2
Koulikoro, Mali 150/B3
Koulountou, Sen., river 148/C3
Koundara, Guin. 149/B1
Koungheul, Sen. 148/B2
Kountze, Tex., U.S., 2,115 . . . . .346/P5
Kourou, Fr. Gui., 19,107 . . . . .183/B1
Kouroussa, Guin. 149/D2
Kousséri, Came. 153/B1
Koutiala, Mali 150/B3
Kouto, C. d'Iv. 150/C2
Kouts, Ind., U.S., 1,698 . . . . .270/B2
Kouvola, Fin. 81/C2
Kova-Lima, E. Timor, province 122/B2
Kovel', Ukr. 102/A1
Kowloon, H.K., China 117/B2
Kowŏn, N. Kor. 116/B3
Kowt-e Ashrow, Afg. 129/B2
Koyuk, Alaska, U.S., 297 . . . . .240/C2
Koyukuk, Alaska, U.S., 101 . . . . .240/D2
Koyukuk, Alaska, U.S., river 240/D1
Koyukuk N.W.R., Alaska, U.S. 240/D1
Kozani, Gr. 100/B1
Kozhikode, India, 419,531, (800,913, metro.) . . .128/C6
Kozloduy, Bul. 101/B2
Kozu, Jap., island 114/C3
Kpalimé, Togo 151/B3
Kpandu, Gha. 150/C3
Kpémé, Togo 151/B3
Kra, Thai., isthmus 125/B4
Kráchéh, Camb. 124/E3
Kraemer, La., U.S., 325 . . . . .282/H7
Kragnes, Minn., U.S., 40 . . . . .298/A4
Kragujevac, Serb.-Mont., 180,882 . . . . .99/B2
Krakatau, Indon., island 122/B2
Kraków, Pol., 740,737 . . . . .83/D3
Krakow, Wisc., U.S., 275 . . . . .364/E4
Kraljevo, Serb.-Mont., 125,269 . . . . .99/B3
Královehradecký, Czh. Rep., region 92/B2
Kramators'k, Ukr., 187,476 . . . . .102/D2
Kramer, Nebr., U.S., 80 . . . . .308/H3
Kramer, N. Dak., U.S., 44 . . . . .326/F1
Kranj, Slove., 50,825 . . . . .98/B2
Kranji, Sing. 123/B1
Kranzburg, S. Dak., U.S., 185 . . . . .342/J3
Krasnodar, Russ., 639,917, (757,150, metro.) . . .104/C5
Krasnoyarsk, Russ., 876,418 . . . . .104/F4
Krebs, Okla., U.S., 2,051 . . . . .330/G3
Krefeld, Ger., 241,769 . . . . .86/A3
Kremenchuk, Ukr., 238,757 . . . . .102/C2
Kremenchuk, Ukr., reservoir 102/C2
Kremlin, Mont., U.S., 126 . . . . .306/F1
Kremlin, Okla., U.S., 240 . . . . .330/E1
Kremmling, Colo., U.S., 1,578 . . . . .250/D1
Krems an der Donau, Aus. 91/D2
Kress, Tex., U.S., 826 .346/G1
Kretinga, Lith. 82/A2
Kribi, Came. 153/A3
Krishna, India, river 128/C5
Kristiansand, Nor. 80/B4
Kristianstad, Swe., 74,518 . . . . .80/B3
Kristiansund, Nor. 80/B3
Kristinehamn, Swe. 80/B3
Krk, Cro., island 98/B2
Krka, Slove., river 98/B3
Kronborg, Nebr., U.S., 40 . . . . .308/G2
Krŏng Kaôh Kŏng, Camb. 124/A4
Kronoberg, Swe., county 80/B3
Kroonstad, S. Afr. 162/C2
Krosno, Pol. 83/E4
Krotz Sprs., La., U.S., 1,219 . . . . .282/F5
Krško, Slove., 27,215 . . . . .98/C3
Kruger Natl. Park, S. Afr. 162/D1
Krugersdorp, S. Afr. 162/C2
Krujë, Alb. 99/A2
Krum, Tex., U.S., 1,979 . . . . .346/L2
Krupp, Wash., U.S., 60 . . . . .358/G2
Kruševac, Serb.-Mont., 137,330 . . . . .99/B3
Kruševo, Mac. 100/B2
Krychaw, Bela. 82/E3
Kryvyi Rih, Ukr., 704,817 . . . . .102/C2
Kuala Abang, Bru. 121/A2
Kuala Belait, Bru., 21,163 . . . . .121/A2
Kuala Lumpur, Malay., capital, 1,379,310 . . . . . .121/B2
Kualapuu, Hawaii, U.S., 1,936 . . . . .262/A3
Kuala Terengganu, Malay., 228,119 . . . . .121/B2
Kuantan, Malay., 199,484, (202,445, metro.) . . .121/B2
Kuaokala Forest Reserve, Hawaii, U.S. 262/H1
Kuching, Malay. 121/C2
Kuchino, Jap., island 114/A4
Kuykmar, Russ. 104/E4
Kuee Ruins, Hawaii, U.S. 262/H7
Kufstein, Aus. 91/C3
Kuikui, Hawaii, U.S., point 262/B4
Kuito, Ang. 159/C4
Kujawsko-Pomorskie, Pol., province 83/D2
Kükës, Alb. 99/B2
Kukuihaele, Hawaii, U.S., 317 . . . . .262/H4
Kukuiula, Hawaii, U.S. .262/B4
Kul, Iran, river 130/D4
Kula, Hawaii, U.S. 262/C4
Kula Kangri, Bhu., mountain 126/B1

Kulani, Hawaii, U.S., mountain 262/H5
Kuldīga, Lat. 82/A2
Kulm, N. Dak., U.S., 422 . . . . .326/G3
Kulmbach, Ger. 86/B3
Kŭlob, Taj. 132/A2
Kulpawn, Gha., river 150/B3
Kulpmont, Penn., U.S., 2,985 . . . . .336/J4
Kulpsville, Penn., U.S., 8,005 . . . . .336/K5
Kumamoto, Jap., 662,000 . . . . .114/A3
Kumamoto, Jap., prefecture 114/A3
Kumanovo, Mac., 71,853 . . . . .100/B1
Kumasi, Gha., 348,880, (488,991, metro.) 150/B3
Kume, Jap., island . . . . .114/Inset II
Kumo, Nig. 152/E2
Kumukahi, Hawaii, U.S., cape 262/E7, K5
Kuna, Ida., U.S., 5,382 . . . . .264/A6
Kunda, Est. 81/D1
Kunene, Nam., river 160/A1
Kunia, Hawaii, U.S. 262/H2
Kunkle, Ohio, U.S., 400 . . . . .328/B2
Kunlun Shan, China, mountains 119/B2
Kunming, China, 1,418,640,
   (1,975,820, metro.) .119/D3
Kuntaur, Gam. 148/D2
Kuopio, Fin., 86,651 . . . . .81/C2
Kupa, Slove., river 98/B3
Kupang, Indon. 122/D3
Kupikipikio, Hawaii, U.S., point 262/G3, K3
Kür, Azer., river 103/A2, C2
Kura, Tur., river 133/E2
Kür-Aras, Azer., lowland 103/B2
Kurashiki, Jap., 430,000 . . . . .114/B3
Kuraymah, Sudan 145/C1
Kurdzhali, Bul. 101/A3
Kurdzhali, Bul., oblast .101/A4
Kure, Jap. 114/B3
Kure Beach, N.C., U.S., 1,507 . . . . .322/K7
Kuressaare, Est. 81/B2
Kurgan, Russ., 364,211 . . . . .104/E4
Kuri, Abd al, Yemen, island 137/C2
Kuril, Russ., islands 104/I5
Kurinwás, Nicar., river .148/C3
Kurla, India . . . . .128/Inset I
Kurnool, India 128/C5
Kuršėnai, Lith. 82/B1
Kursk, Russ., 440,208 .104/C4
Kurthwood, La., U.S., 60 . . . . .282/C4
Kurtistown, Hawaii, U.S., 1,157 . . . . .262/J5
Kurtz, Ind., U.S., 200 . . . . .270/D7
Kuru, Bhu., river 126/C2
Kuruman, S. Afr. 162/B2
Kurume, Jap. 114/A3
Kurunegala, Sri Lan. 126/B4
Kusawa, Yukon, Can., lake 214/D1
Kushiro, Jap. . . . . .114/Inset I
Kushtia, Bangl. 127/C5
Kuskokwim, Alaska, U.S., bay 240/C3
Kuskokwim, Alaska, U.S., mountains 240/D2
Kuskokwim, Alaska, U.S., river 240/D2
Kusŏng, N. Kor. 116/A3
Kusti, Sudan, 173,599 .145/C2
Kütahya, Tur. 133/B2
Kütahya, Tur., province 133/B2
K'ut'aisi, Geo., 240,000 . . . . .103/B3
Kutch, India, gulf 128/A4
Kutch, Colo., U.S. 250/G3
Kutno, Pol. 83/D2
Kuttawa, Ky., U.S., 596 . . . . .280/B3
Kutztown, Penn., U.S., 5,067 . . . . .336/K4
Kuujjuaq, Que., Can., 1,932 . . . . .225/C2
Kuujjuarapik, Que., Can., 555 . . . . .225/A2
Kuwait, nation 132
Kuwait, Kuw., bay 136/B2
Kuwait, Kuw., capital, 192,974,
   (385,675, metro.) 136/B2
Kwa, Congo, D.R., river 155/B2
Kwahu, Gha., plateau 150/B3
Kwajalein, Marsh. Is., island 173/B2
Kwango, Congo, D.R., river 155/B2
Kwara, Nig., state 152/C3
Kwekwe, Zimb. 160/B2
Kwethluk, Alaska, U.S., 713 . . . . .240/C2
Kwinana, W.A., Austl. . . . . .170/Inset I
Kwinana Beach, W.A., Austl. . . . . .170/Inset I
Kyaukpyu, Mya. 125/B2
Kyburz, Calif., U.S., 80 . . . . .246/E4
Kykotsmovi, Ariz., U.S., 776 . . . . .242/E2
Kyle, Sask., Can., 478 . . . . .227/B10
Kyle, S. Dak., U.S., 970 . . . . .342/C4
Kyle, Tex., U.S., 5,314 .346/D3
Kyleakin, Scot., U.K. 62/E4
Kyle of Lochalsh, Scot., U.K. 62/E4
Kyle of Lochalsh, Scot., U.K., 739 . . . . .62/E4
Kyle of Tongue N.P., Scot., U.K. 62/G1
Kylerhea, Scot., U.K. 62/E4
Kylestrome, Scot., U.K. .62/F2
Kymenlaakso, Fin., region 81/C2
Kyoga, Ug., lake 157/C3
Kyoto, Jap., 1,467,705 . . . . .114/B3
Kyoto, Jap., prefecture 114/B3
Kyrenia, Cyp., range 133/B1
Kyrgyzstan, nation 127
Kythira, Gr., island 100/B3
Kyushu, Jap., island 114/A3
Kyustendil, Bul. 101/A3
Kyustendil, Bul., oblast 101/A3
Kyzyl, Russ. 104/F4
Kyzylkum, Uzb., desert 132/B2
Kyzylorda, Kaz., 157,364 . . . . .131/C2
Kyzylorda, Kaz., oblast 131/C2
Kyzyl-Kyya, Kyrg. 131/D2
Kyzyl-Suu, Kyrg., river 131/E2
La Altagracia, Dom. Rep., province 205/D2
La Araucanía, Chile, region 190/B5
La Asunción, Ven. 182/C1
Laau, Hawaii, U.S., point 262/A3, C5
Laayoune, W. Sah., 159,000 . . . . .147/B1
Labadie, Mo., U.S., 225 . . . . .302/F3
Labadieville, La., U.S., 1,811 . . . . .282/H7
La Baie, Que., Can., 19,940 . . . . .226/F3
La Barge, Wyo., U.S., 431 . . . . .366/A2
Labasa, Fiji, 24,187 . . . . .174/B2
Labe, (Elbe), Czh. Rep., river 92/B2
Labé, Guin., 65,000, (110,000, metro.) 149/B2
Labelle, N.S., Can. 221/C3
La Belle, Fla., U.S., 4,210 . . . . .256/G5
La Belle, Mo., U.S., 669 . . . . .302/E1
Laberge, Yukon, Can., lake 228/B5
Labette, Kans., U.S., 68 . . . . .276/G4
Labette, Kans., U.S., county, 22,835 . . . . .276/G4
Labi, Bru. 121/A2
La Bolt, S. Dak., U.S., 86 . . . . .342/J2
Laborec, Slvk., river 92/C2
Laborie, St. Luc. 208/B3
Labrador City, Nfld., Can., 7,744 . . . . .218/D3
La Branche, Man., Can. 215/C4
Labrieville, Que., Can. .226/G2
La Broquerie, Man., Can. 215/C4
Labu, Bru. 121/A2
Labuan, Malay., island .121/D2
Laç, Alb. 99/A2

Lac Albanel, Mistassini & Waconichi Prov.
  Reserve, Que., Can. ...226/B1
La Canada Flintridge, Calif., U.S., 20,318 ...246/C8
Lacassine N.W.R., La., U.S. ...282/D7
Lac-aux-Sables, Que., Can., 1,313 ...226/D5
Lac-Baker, N.B., Can., 226 ...217/A1
Lac-Bouchette, Que., Can., 1,370 ...226/D3
Laccadive, India, islands ...128/B6
Lac Court Oreilles Ind. Res., Wisc., U.S. ...364/B3
Lac-des-Aigles, Que., Can., 657 ...226/H4
Lac-des-Îles, Que., Can. ...226/A5
Lac du Bonnet, Man., Can., 1,089 ...215/C4
Lac du Flambeau, Wisc., U.S., 1,646 ...364/D3
Lac du Flambeau Ind. Res., Mich., U.S. ...294/D2
Lac du Flambeau Ind. Res., Wisc., U.S. ...364/D2
Laceby, Eng., U.K., 2,666 ...68/H5
Laceby, Eng., U.K., 2,666 ...68/G2
Lac-Édouard, Que., Can., 137 ...226/D4
La Ceiba, Hond., 117,318 ...202/B2
La Ctr., Ky., U.S., 1,038 ...280/A3
La Ctr., Wash., U.S., 1,654 ...358/C4
Lac-Etchemin, Que., Can., 2,276 ...226/F5
Lacey, Ark., U.S., 90 ...244/D4
Lacey, Iowa, U.S., 70 ...274/J5
Lacey, Okla., U.S. ...330/D1
Lacey, Wash., U.S., 31,226 ...358/C3
Lacey Spr., Ala., U.S., 750 ...238/C1
Laceyville, Penn., U.S., 396 ...336/J2
La Chaux-de-Fonds, Switz. ...90/A1
Lachenaie, Que., Can. ...226/J5
Lachine, Que., Can., 40,222 ...226/H6
Lachine, Mich., U.S., 225 ...294/F4
Lachute, Que., Can., 11,628 ...226/B6
La Cienega, N. Mex., U.S., 3,007 ...317/D2
La Cienegas Natl. Cons. Area, Ariz., U.S. ...242/E6
Lackawanna, N.Y., U.S., 19,064 ...320/D5
Lackawanna, Penn., U.S., county, 213,295 ...336/H7, K2
Lackford, Eng., U.K. ...70/F2
Lac La Belle, Wisc., U.S., 329 ...364/E2
Lac La Biche, Alta., Can., 2,776 ...212/E4
Lac La Hache, Br. Col., Can., 396 ...214/M5
Lac La Ronge Prov. Park, Sask., Can. ...227/F5
Laclede, Ida., U.S., 150 ...264/A1
La Clede, Ill., U.S., 100 ...266/E5
Laclede, Mo., U.S., 415 ...302/C2
Laclede, Mo., U.S., county, 32,513 ...302/D4
Lac-Mégantic, Que., Can., 5,897 ...226/F6
Lac-Nominingue, Que., Can., 2,064 ...226/A5
La Coma, And., river ...93/B1
Lacomb, Oreg., U.S., 350 ...334/D3
Lacombe, Alta., Can., 9,384 ...212/D5
Lacombe, La., U.S., 7,518 ...282/K6
Lacon, Ill., U.S., 1,979 ...266/D2
Lacona, Iowa, U.S., 360 ...274/H5
Lacona, N.Y., U.S., 590 ...320/J3
La Conception, Que., Can., 1,050 ...226/B5
La Condamine, Mon., district ...97/B1
Laconia, Ind., U.S. ...270/D8
Laconia, N.H., U.S., 16,411 ...312/D4
Laconia, Tenn., U.S., 50 ...344/C4
La Conner, Wash., U.S., 761 ...358/C1
La Coste, Tex., U.S., 1,255 ...346/K6
Lac qui Parle, Minn., U.S., 50 ...298/B6
Lac qui Parle, Minn., U.S., county, 8,067 ...298/A6
Lacreek N.W.R., S. Dak., U.S. ...342/D4
La Crescent, Minn., U.S., 4,923 ...298/F7
La Crescenta, (La Crescenta-Montrose),
  Calif., U.S., 18,532 ...246/C8
La Crete, Alta., Can., 1,783 ...212/B2
La Croft, Ohio, U.S., 1,307 ...328/J4
La Croix Maingot, St. Luc. ...208/A2
La Crosse, Fla., U.S., 143 ...256/F2
La Crosse, Ind., U.S., 561 ...270/C2
La Crosse, Kans., U.S., 1,376 ...276/C3
La Crosse, Va., U.S., 618 ...354/G7
La Crosse, Wash., U.S., 380 ...358/H3
La Crosse, Wisc., U.S., 51,818,
  (126,838, metro.) ...364/B5
La Crosse, Wisc., U.S., county, 107,120 ...364/B5
La Cruz, C.R. ...203/A1
Lac-Saguay, Que., Can., 382 ...226/A5
La Cueva, N. Mex., U.S., 40 ...317/E2
La Cygne, Kans., U.S., 1,115 ...276/H3
Lacy-Lakeview, Tex., U.S., 5,764 ...346/L4
Ladd, Ark., U.S., 90 ...244/D3
Ladd, Ill., U.S., 1,313 ...266/D2
Ladder, Kans., U.S., creek ...276/A3
Laddonia, Mo., U.S., 620 ...302/E2
Ladelle, Ark., U.S., 50 ...244/D4
Ladera Hts., Calif., U.S., 6,568 ...246/B9
Ladiesburg, Md., U.S., 275 ...288/C1
La Digue, Sey., island ...163/C1
Ladner, S. Dak., U.S. ...342/B2
Ladoga, Fin., lake ...81/D2
Ladoga, Russ., lake ...104/C3
Ladoga, Russ., lake ...193/C2
Ladoga, Ind., U.S., 1,047 ...270/C5
Ladonia, Ala., U.S., 3,229 ...238/D3
Ladonia, Tex., U.S., 667 ...346/N2
Ladora, Iowa, U.S., 287 ...274/K4
La Doré, Que., Can. ...226/D3
Ladson, S.C., U.S., 13,264 ...340/D4
La Due, Mo., U.S., 8,645 ...302/C3
Ladue, Mo., U.S., 8,645 ...302/H3
Ladybank, Scot., U.K., 1,487 ...68/K6
Ladybower, Eng., U.K., reservoir ...68/D3
Lady Lake, Fla., U.S., 11,828 ...256/G3
Ladysmith, S. Afr. ...162/C2
Ladysmith, Va., U.S., 750 ...354/H4
Ladysmith, Wisc., U.S., 3,932 ...364/B3
Ladywood, Man., Can. ...215/C4
Lae, Marsh. Is., island ...173/B2
Lae, P.N.G. ...172/A2
Laem, Thai., mountain ...125/B3
Læsø, Den., island ...79/C1
La Esperanza, Hond. ...202/A2
La Esperanza, P.R. ...206/B2
La Estrelleta, Dom. Rep., province ...205/A1
La Farge, Wisc., U.S. ...364/C5
La Fargeville, N.Y., U.S., 588 ...320/K2
Lafayette, Ala., U.S., 3,234 ...238/D3
Lafayette, Ark., U.S., county, 8,559 ...244/B4
Lafayette, Calif., U.S., 23,908 ...246/K2
Lafayette, Colo., U.S., 23,197 ...250/A2, E1
Lafayette, Colo., U.S., county, 7,022 ...256/E2
Lafayette, Ga., U.S., 6,702 ...260/A2
La Fayette, Ill., U.S., 227 ...266/D2
Lafayette, Ind., U.S., 56,397, (182,821, metro.) ...270/C4
La Fayette, Ky., U.S., 193 ...280/C4
Lafayette, La., U.S., 110,257, (385,647, metro.) ...282/E6
Lafayette, La., U.S., parish, 190,503 ...282/E6
Lafayette, Minn., U.S., 529 ...298/C5
Lafayette, Miss., U.S., county, 38,744 ...300/C1
Lafayette, Mo., U.S., county, 32,960 ...302/C3
Lafayette, N.J., U.S., 2,300 ...314/D1
Lafayette, (Allen County), Ohio, U.S. ...328/C4
Lafayette, (Madison County), Ohio, U.S., 304 ...328/D6
Lafayette, Oreg., U.S., 2,586 ...334/C2
Lafayette, Tenn., U.S., 3,885 ...344/J1
Lafayette, Wisc., U.S., county, 16,137 ...364/C6
Lafayette Sprs., Miss., U.S., 100 ...300/C1

Lafe, Ark., U.S., 385 ...244/E1
Laffan, Ra's, Qatar, cape ...137/D2
Lafia, Nig. ...152/E3
Lafitte, La., U.S., 1,576 ...282/J7
Lafleche, Sask., Can., 446 ...227/D11
Laflin, Penn., U.S., 1,502 ...336/H7
La Follette, Tenn., U.S., 7,926 ...344/N2
Lafond, Alta., Can. ...212/E4
La Fontaine, Ind., U.S., 900 ...270/E3
Lafontaine, Kans., U.S., 90 ...276/G4
Lafourche, La., U.S., parish, 89,974 ...282/J7
Laga Bor, Kenya, river ...157/E2
Lagan, N. Ire., U.K., river ...78/C1
La Garita, Colo., U.S., 40 ...250/D4
Lagdo, Came., reservoir ...153/B2
Lages, Nev., U.S. ...310/C1
Laggan, Scot., U.K. ...62/H4
Laggan, Scot., U.K., lake ...62/H5
Laghouat, Alg. ...146/B1
La Glace, Alta., Can., 213 ...212/A3
Lagodekhi, Geo. ...103/D4
Lagos, Nig., 5,195,247 ...152/B4
Lagos, Nig., state ...152/B4
Lagos, Port. ...93/A4
Lagouira, W. Sah. ...147/A2
La Goulette, Tun. ...146/C1
Lago Vista, Tex., U.S., 4,507 ...346/D2
La Grande, Que., Can., river ...225/B3
La Grande, Oreg., U.S., 12,327 ...334/H2
La Grande, Wash., U.S., 70 ...358/C3
LaGrange, Ark., U.S., 122 ...244/E3
LaGrange, Ga., U.S., 25,998 ...260/A5
La Grange, Ill., U.S., 15,608 ...266/B6
Lagrange, Ind., U.S., 2,919 ...270/F1
Lagrange, Ind., U.S., county, 34,909 ...270/F1
La Grange, Ky., U.S., 5,676 ...280/E2
Lagrange, Maine, U.S., 747 ...286/D3
La Grange, Mo., U.S., 1,000 ...302/E1
La Grange, N.C., U.S., 2,844 ...322/K4
La Grange, Ohio, U.S., 1,815 ...328/F3
La Grange, Tex., U.S., 4,478 ...346/M6
La Grange, Wisc., U.S., 100 ...364/E6
Lagrange, Wyo., U.S., 332 ...366/D3
La Grange Park, Ill., U.S., 13,295 ...266/B6
La Gran Sabana, Ven., plain ...182/C1
Lagro, Ind., U.S., 454 ...270/E3
La Grulla, Tex., U.S., 1,211 ...346/K9
La Guadeloupe, Que., Can., 1,716 ...226/F6
La Guaira Maiquetía, Ven. ...182/C1
La Guajira, Col., department ...184/B2
Laguna, Calif., U.S., 34,309 ...246/K5
Laguna, N. Mex., U.S., 423 ...317/C2
Laguna Atascosa N.W.R., Tex., U.S. ...346/L9
Laguna Beach, Calif., U.S., 23,727 ...246/E11
Laguna Beach, Fla., U.S., 2,909 ...256/C1
Laguna de Bay, Phil., lake ...120/B3
Laguna Hills, Calif., U.S., 31,178 ...246/E11
Laguna Ind. Res., N. Mex., U.S. ...317/C3
Laguna Niguel, Calif., U.S., 61,891 ...246/E11
Laguna Vista, Tex., U.S., 1,658 ...346/L9
Lagunitas, (Lagunitas-Forest Knolls),
  Calif., U.S., 1,835 ...246/H1
La Habana, Cuba, province ...204/B2
La Habra, Calif., U.S., 58,974 ...246/D10
La Habra Hts., Calif., U.S., 5,712 ...246/D9
Lahaina, Hawaii, U.S., 9,118 ...262/B3, D6
La Harpe, Ill., U.S., 1,385 ...266/C3
La Harpe, Kans., U.S., 706 ...276/G4
La Have, (La Have Islands), N.S., Can. ...221/C3
Lahave, N.S., Can., river ...221/C3
Lahilahi, Hawaii, U.S., point ...262/H2
Lahn, Ger., river ...86/B3
Lahoma, Okla., U.S., 577 ...330/D1
Lahore, Pak., 5,143,495 ...129/E3
Lahti, Fin., 96,921 ...81/C2
Lai, Chad ...153/B5
Laide, Scot., U.K. ...62/E3
Laie, Hawaii, U.S., 4,585 ...262/C5, J1
La Hawaii, U.S., point ...262/J1
Laingsburg, Mich., U.S., 1,223 ...294/E7
Lair, Ky., U.S., 100 ...280/F2
Laird, Colo., U.S., 60 ...250/H1
Lairg, Scot., U.K. ...60/B1
Lairg, Scot., U.K. ...62/H2
La Jara, Colo., U.S., 877 ...250/E4
La Jara, N. Mex., U.S., 209 ...317/D1
Lajas, P.R. ...206/A2
Lajes, Braz., 108,768, (150,866, metro.) ...188/C4
Lajitas, Tex., U.S., 40 ...346/E6
La Joya, N. Mex., U.S., 70 ...317/D3
La Joya, Tex., U.S., 3,303 ...346/K9
La Junta, Colo., U.S., 7,568 ...250/G4
Lakatoro, Van. ...173/B3
Lake, Eng., U.K., district ...69/B2
Lake, Calif., U.S., county, 58,309 ...246/C3
Lake, Colo., U.S., county, 7,812 ...250/D2
Lake, Fla., U.S., county, 210,528 ...256/C4, G3
Lake, Ill., U.S., county, 644,356 ...266/B5, E1
Lake, Ind., U.S., county, 484,564 ...270/B2
Lake, Mich., U.S., 475 ...294/D6
Lake, Mich., U.S., county, 11,333 ...294/D6
Lake, Minn., U.S., county, 11,058 ...298/F3
Lake, Miss., U.S., 408 ...300/C3
Lake, Mont., U.S., county, 26,507 ...306/D2
Lake, Ohio, U.S., county, 227,511 ...328/H2, J8
Lake, Oreg., U.S., county, 7,422 ...334/F4
Lake, S. Dak., U.S., county, 11,276 ...342/H3
Lake, Tenn., U.S., county, 7,954 ...344/B1
Lake, Wyo., U.S. ...366/A1
Lake Alice N.W.R., N. Dak., U.S. ...326/F1
Lake Alma, Sask., Can. ...227/F11
Lake Alpine, Calif., U.S. ...246/F4
Lake Aluma, Okla., U.S., 97 ...330/B3
Lake Andes, S. Dak., U.S., 819 ...342/G4
Lake Andes N.W.R., S. Dak., U.S. ...342/G4
Lake Angelus, Mich., U.S., 326 ...294/A6
Lake Ann, Mich., U.S., 276 ...294/D5
Lake Annette, Mo., U.S., 163 ...302/B3
Lake Ariel, Penn., U.S., 1,000 ...336/L3
Lake Arthur, La., U.S., 3,007 ...282/D6
Lake Arthur, N. Mex., U.S., 432 ...317/F5
Lakeba, Fiji, island ...174/C3
Lakeba, Fiji, passage ...174/C3
Lake Barrington, Ill., U.S., 4,757 ...266/A5
Lake Benton, Minn., U.S., 703 ...298/A6
Lake Bird, Fla., U.S. ...256/E1
Lake Bluff, Ill., U.S., 6,056 ...266/B5
Lake Bronson, Minn., U.S., 246 ...298/A2
Lake Buena Vista, Fla., U.S. ...256/C4, G3
Lake Burrell, Penn., U.S. ...336/M4
Lake Butler, Fla., U.S., 1,927 ...256/F1
Lake Carmel, Ill., U.S., 8,663 ...320/P8
Lake Catherine, Ill., U.S., 1,490 ...266/A4
Lake Charles, La., U.S., 71,757,
  (183,577, metro.) ...282/C6
Lake Charlotte, N.S., Can. ...221/E3
Lake Chelan Natl. Rec. Area, Wash., U.S. ...358/E1
Lake City, Ark., U.S., 1,956 ...244/E1
Lake City, Calif., U.S., 50 ...246/E1
Lake City, Colo., U.S., 375 ...250/C3
Lake City, Fla., U.S., 9,980 ...256/F1

Lake City, Ga., U.S., 2,886 ...260/C4, J3
Lake City, Iowa, U.S., 1,787 ...274/E3
Lake City, Kans., U.S. ...276/D4
Lake City, Mich., U.S., 923 ...294/D5
Lake City, Minn., U.S., 4,950 ...298/E6
Lake City, Penn., U.S., 2,811 ...336/A1
Lake City, S.C., U.S., 6,478 ...340/E3
Lake City, S. Dak., U.S., 47 ...342/H2
Lake City, Tenn., U.S., 1,888 ...344/N2
Lake City, Tex., U.S., 526 ...346/L7
Lake Clarke Shores, Fla., U.S., 3,451 ...256/B5
Lake Clark Natl. Park and Preserve, Alaska, U.S. ...240/E2
Lake Clear Jct., N.Y., U.S., 100 ...320/N2
Lake Cormorant, Miss., U.S., 150 ...300/B1
Lakecreek, Oreg., U.S. ...334/D5
Lake Crystal, Minn., U.S., 2,420 ...298/C6
Lake Dalecarlia, Ind., U.S., 1,285 ...270/B2
Lake Dallas, Tex., U.S., 6,166 ...346/B8
Lake Delton, Wisc., U.S., 1,982 ...364/D5
Lake District Natl. Park, Eng., U.K. ...66/B4
Lake Dunmore, Vt., U.S., 175 ...352/A3
Lake Edward, N.B., Can. ...217/B2
Lake Elmo, Minn., U.S., 6,863 ...298/F5
Lake Elsinore, Calif., U.S., 28,928 ...246/G11
Lake End, La., U.S., 50 ...282/C3
Lake Erie Beach, N.Y., U.S., 4,499 ...320/C5
Lake Fenton, Mich., U.S., 4,876 ...294/F7
Lakefield, Ont., Can., 2,734 ...223/G3
Lakefield, Minn., U.S., 1,721 ...298/B7
Lakefield Natl. Park, Austl. ...170/D1
Lake Forest, Calif., U.S., 58,707 ...246/E11
Lake Forest, Ill., U.S., 20,059 ...266/B5
Lake Forest Park, Wash., U.S., 13,142 ...358/A4
Lake Fork, Ida., U.S., 50 ...264/A5
Lake Fork, Ill., U.S., 100 ...266/D4
Lake Geneva, Wisc., U.S., 7,148 ...364/E6
Lake George, Colo., U.S., 50 ...250/E3
Lake George, Mich., U.S., 400 ...294/E6
Lake George, Minn., U.S., 150 ...298/C3
Lake George, N.Y., U.S., 985 ...320/P4
Lake George N.W.R., N. Dak., U.S. ...326/F3
Lake Goodwin, Wash., U.S., 3,354 ...358/C1
Lake Grove, N.Y., U.S., 10,250 ...320/E2
Lake Hamilton, Ark., U.S., 1,609 ...244/B3
Lake Harbor, Fla., U.S., 195 ...256/H5
Lake Hart, Fla., U.S., 250 ...270/D5
Lake Havasu City, Ariz., U.S., 41,938 ...242/A3
Lakehead, Calif., U.S., 549 ...246/C2
Lake Helen, Fla., U.S., 2,743 ...256/G3
Lake Henry, Minn., U.S., 90 ...298/C5
Lakehills, Tex., U.S., 4,668 ...346/K6
Lakehurst, N.J., U.S., 2,522 ...314/E3
Lake Ilo N.W.R., N. Dak., U.S. ...326/C2
Lake in the Hills, Ill., U.S., 23,152 ...266/A5
Lake Isabella, Calif., U.S., 3,315 ...246/G7
Lake Isom N.W.R., Tenn., U.S. ...344/C2
Lake Itasca, Minn., U.S. ...298/B3
Lake Jackson, Tex., U.S., 26,386 ...346/N6
Lake Junaluska, N.C., U.S., 2,675 ...322/D7
Lake Katrine, N.Y., U.S., 2,396 ...320/P7
Lake Lafayette, Mo., U.S., 346 ...302/C3
Lakeland, Fla., U.S., 78,452, (483,924, metro.) ...256/G3
Lakeland, Ga., U.S., 2,730 ...260/E9
Lakeland, La., U.S., 375 ...282/G5
Lakeland, Minn., U.S., 1,917 ...298/E6
Lakeland, Mo., U.S. ...302/D3
Lakeland, Tenn., U.S., 6,862 ...344/B4
Lakeland Vil., Calif., U.S., 5,626 ...246/G11
Lake Lenore, Sask., Can., 314 ...227/F8
Lake Lillian, Minn., U.S., 257 ...298/C6
Lake Linden, Mich., U.S., 1,081 ...294/A2
Lakeline, Ohio, U.S., 165 ...328/H8
Lake Linganore, (Linganore-Bartonsville),
  Md., U.S. ...288/E2
Lake Lotawana, Mo., U.S., 1,872 ...302/J5
Lake Louise, Alta., Can., 1,041 ...212/B5
Lakelse Lake, Br. Col., Can. ...214/H4
Lake Lure, N.C., U.S., 1,027 ...322/A4, F8
Lake Luzerne, (Lake Luzerne-Hadley),
  N.Y., U.S., 2,240 ...320/P4
Lake Mackay, Austl., aboriginal land ...170/B2
Lake Magdalene, Fla., U.S., 28,755 ...256/D6
Lake Mary, Fla., U.S., 11,458 ...256/D3, G3
Lake Mason N.W.R., Mont., U.S. ...306/H3
Lake McDonald, Mont., U.S. ...306/C2
Lake Mead Natl. Rec. Area, Ariz., U.S. ...242/A1, A2, B1
Lake Meredith Natl. Rec. Area, Tex., U.S. ...346/F9
Lake Miami, Ohio, U.S., river ...328/C9, G2
Lake Michigan Beach, Mich., U.S., 1,509 ...294/C7
Lake Mills, Iowa, U.S., 2,140 ...274/G1
Lake Mills, Wisc., U.S., 4,843 ...364/E5
Lake Mohawk, N.J., U.S., 1,500 ...314/D1
Lake Monroe, Fla., U.S. ...256/D3
Lakemont, Ga., U.S., 325 ...260/E2
Lakemont, Penn., U.S., 1,600 ...336/E5
Lake Montezuma, Ariz., U.S., 3,344 ...242/D3
Lakemoor, Ill., U.S., 2,788 ...266/A4
Lakemore, Ohio, U.S., 2,561 ...328/H3
Lake Moxie, Maine, U.S. ...286/C3
Lake Mykee, Mo., U.S., 326 ...302/D3
Lake Nacimiento, Calif., U.S., 2,176 ...246/E7
Lake Nebagamon, Wisc., U.S., 1,015 ...364/D2
Lake Nettie N.W.R., N. Dak., U.S. ...326/E2
Lakenham, Eng., U.K. ...70/G1
Lakenheath, Eng., U.K., 9,226 ...70/F2
Lake Norden, S. Dak., U.S., 432 ...342/H3
Lake Odessa, Mich., U.S., 2,272 ...294/D7
Lake of the Ozarks, Mo., U.S., lake ...302/D3
Lake of the Woods, Ill., U.S., 3,026 ...266/E3
Lake of the Woods, Minn., U.S., county, 4,522 ...298/C2
Lake of the Woods, Minn., U.S., lake ...298/C1
Lake Ophelia N.W.R., La., U.S. ...282/F4
Lake Orion, Mich., U.S., 2,715 ...294/A6, F7
Lake Oswego, Oreg., U.S., 35,278 ...334/A2, D2
Lake Ozark, Mo., U.S., 1,489 ...302/D3
Lake Panasoffkee, Fla., U.S., 3,413 ...256/F3
Lake Park, Fla., U.S., 8,721 ...256/B4
Lake Park, Ga., U.S., 549 ...260/E1
Lake Park, Iowa, U.S., 1,023 ...274/D1
Lake Park, Minn., U.S., 782 ...298/A4
Lake Park, N.C., U.S., 2,093 ...322/D4
Lake Parlin, Maine, U.S. ...286/B3
Lake Placid, Fla., U.S., 1,668 ...256/G4
Lake Placid, N.Y., U.S., 2,638 ...320/N2
Lake Pleasant, Mass., U.S., 350 ...292/D2
Lake Pleasant, N.Y., U.S., 100 ...320/N4
Lake Pocotopaug, Conn., U.S., 3,169 ...253/E3
Lakeport, Calif., U.S., 4,820 ...246/C3
Lakeport, Mich., U.S., 700 ...294/G6
Lake Preston, S. Dak., U.S., 537 ...342/H3
Lake Providence, La., U.S., 5,104 ...282/G1
Lake Purdy, Ala., U.S., 5,799 ...238/B3
Lake Ridge, Va., U.S., 30,404 ...354/J3, L3
Lake Roosevelt Natl. Rec. Area, Wash., U.S. ...359/G1, G2
Lake St. Louis, Mo., U.S., 10,169 ...302/F3
Lake St. Peter, Ont., Can. ...223/G3
Lakeshire, Mo., U.S., 1,375 ...302/H3
Lakeshore, Calif., U.S. ...246/F5
Lake Shore, Md., U.S., 13,065 ...288/J3
Lake Shore, Minn., U.S., 966 ...298/C4
Lakeshore, Miss., U.S., 225 ...300/C5

Lake Shore, Wash., U.S., 6,670 ...358/C4
Lakeside, Calif., U.S., 19,560 ...246/J10
Lakeside, Colo., U.S. ...250/A3, E2
Lakeside, (Litchfield County), Conn., U.S., 275 ...253/C3
Lakeside, (New Haven County), Conn., U.S., 275 ...253/C4
Lakeside, Iowa, U.S., 484 ...274/D2
Lakeside, Mass., U.S., 300 ...292/K6
Lakeside, Mo., U.S. ...302/D3
Lakeside, Mont., U.S., 1,679 ...306/B1
Lakeside, Nebr., U.S. ...308/B1
Lakeside, Ohio, U.S., 1,000 ...328/E2
Lakeside, Oreg., U.S., 1,371 ...334/B4
Lakeside, (San Patricio County), Tex., U.S., 333 ...346/L7
Lakeside, (Tarrant County), Tex., U.S., 1,040 ...346/A9
Lakeside, Utah, U.S. ...350/B2
Lakeside, Va., U.S., 11,157 ...354/J5
Lakeside City, Tex., U.S., 984 ...346/K2
Lakeside Park, Ky., U.S., 2,869 ...280/G1
Lakesite, Tenn., U.S., 1,845 ...344/L4
Lakes of the Four Seasons, Ind., U.S., 7,291 ...270/B2
Lake Spr., Mo., U.S. ...302/E4
Lake Sta., Ind., U.S., 13,948 ...270/B1
Lake Stevens, Wash., U.S., 6,361 ...358/C1
Lake Stockholm, N.J., U.S. ...314/D1
Lake Success, N.Y., U.S., 2,797 ...320/C2
Lake Summerset, Ill., U.S., 2,061 ...266/D1
Lake Tanglewood, Tex., U.S., 825 ...346/F9
Lake Telemark, N.J., U.S., 843 ...302/J5
Lake Telemark, N.J., U.S., 1,202 ...314/D2
Lake Thibadeau N.W.R., Mont., U.S. ...306/G1
Lake Tomahawk, Wisc., U.S., 325 ...364/D3
Laketon, Ill., U.S., 700 ...270/E3
Laketown, Utah, U.S., 188 ...350/D2
Lake Traverse I.R., (Sisseton I.R.), N. Dak., U.S. ...326/H4
Lake Traverse I.R., (Sisseton I.R.), S. Dak., U.S. ...342/H2
Lake Valley, N. Mex., U.S., 60 ...317/B1
Lakeview, Ala., U.S., 163 ...238/D1
Lake View, Ark., U.S., 763 ...244/C1
Lakeview, Calif., U.S., 80 ...246/E7
Lakeview, Ga., U.S., 4,820 ...260/A2
Lakeview, Ida., U.S. ...264/A2
Lake View, Iowa, U.S., 1,278 ...274/D3
Lakeview, Mich., U.S., 1,112 ...294/D6
Lakeview, Mont., U.S. ...306/E5
Lake View, N.Y., U.S., 2,100 ...320/D5
Lakeview, Ohio, U.S., 1,074 ...328/C5
Lakeview, Oreg., U.S., 2,474 ...334/F5
Lakeview, Tex., U.S., 789 ...340/G2
Lakeview, (Floyd County), Tex., U.S. ...346/G2
Lakeview, (Hall County), Tex., U.S., 152 ...346/G10, H1
Lakeview Estates, Ga., U.S., 2,637 ...260/K3
Lakeview Hts., Ky., U.S., 251 ...280/G2
Lake Villa, Ill., U.S., 5,864 ...266/A4
Lake Vil., Ark., U.S., 2,823 ...244/D4
Lake Vil., Ind., U.S., 855 ...270/B2
Lakeville, N.B., Can., 381 ...217/B2
Lakeville, Conn., U.S., 900 ...253/B2
Lakeville, Ind., U.S., 567 ...270/D1
Lakeville, Mass., U.S., 9,821 ...292/L5
Lakeville, Minn., U.S., 43,128 ...298/D6
Lake Waccamaw, N.C., U.S., 1,411 ...322/H6
Lake Wales, Fla., U.S., 10,194 ...256/G4
Lake Waukomis, Mo., U.S., 917 ...302/H4
Lakeway, Tex., U.S., 8,002 ...346/D2
Lake Williams, N. Dak., U.S. ...326/F2
Lake Wilson, Minn., U.S., 270 ...298/B6
Lake Winnebago, Mo., U.S., 902 ...302/B3, J5
Lake Wissota, Wisc., U.S., 2,458 ...364/B4
Lakewood, Calif., U.S., 79,345 ...246/D10
Lakewood, Colo., U.S., 144,126 ...250/A3, E2
Lakewood, (McHenry County), Ill., U.S., 2,337 ...266/C6
Lakewood, (Shelby County), Ill., U.S., 125 ...266/E4
Lakewood, Maine, U.S., 225 ...286/C4
Lakewood, Md., U.S. ...288/M6
Lakewood, N.J., U.S., 60,352 ...314/E3
Lakewood, N. Mex., U.S., 70 ...317/F5
Lakewood, N.Y., U.S., 3,258 ...320/C6
Lakewood, Ohio, U.S., 56,646 ...328/G3, J9
Lakewood, Tenn., U.S., 2,341 ...344/N2
Lakewood, (Pierce County), Wash., U.S., 58,211 ...358/C2
Lakewood, (Snohomish County), Wash., U.S. ...358/C1
Lakewood, Wisc., U.S., 200 ...364/E3
Lakewood Club, Mich., U.S., 1,006 ...294/C6
Lakewood Park, N. Dak., U.S., 425 ...326/G1
Lakewood Shores, Ill., U.S., 1,487 ...266/E2
Lakewood Vil., Tex., U.S., 342 ...346/B8
Lake Worth, Fla., U.S., 35,133 ...256/B5, H5
Lake Worth, Tex., U.S., 4,618 ...346/A9
Lake Wylie, S.C., U.S., 3,061 ...340/C1
Lake Wynonah, Penn., U.S., 1,961 ...336/J4
Lake Zahl N.W.R., N. Dak., U.S. ...306/M1
Lake Zahl N.W.R., N. Dak., U.S. ...326/B1
Lake Zurich, Ill., U.S., 18,104 ...266/A5
Lakhpat, India ...128/A4
Laki, Ice., volcano ...79/B2
Lakin, Kans., U.S., 2,316 ...276/A4
Lakota, Iowa, U.S., 255 ...274/F1
Lakota, N. Dak., U.S., 781 ...326/G1
Lakselv, Nor. ...80/F1
Lakshadweep, India, territory ...128/B6
La Laguna, Sp., 128,822 ...94/Inset I
La Libertad, Ecua. ...185/A4
La Libertad, Guat. ...201/C3
La Libertad, Peru, department ...185/B2
Lalitpur, Nepal, 117,203 ...126/C2
La Loche, Sask., Can., 2,136 ...227/A4
La Loche, Sask., Can., lake, 2,136 ...212/E3
La Louvière, Belg., 76,535, (174,801, metro.) ...85/C2
La Luz, N. Mex., U.S., 1,615 ...317/E5
La Madera, N. Mex., U.S., 40 ...317/D1
La Malbaie, Que., Can., 9,143 ...226/F4
Lamaline, Nfld., Can., 346 ...218/D5
Lamap, Van. ...173/B3
Lamar, Ala., U.S., county, 15,904 ...238/A2
Lamar, Ark., U.S., 1,415 ...244/B2
Lamar, Colo., U.S., 8,869 ...250/H3
Lamar, Ga., U.S., county, 15,912 ...260/C8
Lamar, Ill., U.S., 150 ...270/C8
Lamar, Miss., U.S., 175 ...300/C1
Lamar, Miss., U.S., county, 39,070 ...300/C4
Lamar, Mo., U.S., 4,425 ...302/B4
Lamar, Nebr., U.S. ...308/C3
Lamar, Okla., U.S., 172 ...330/F3
Lamar, Penn., U.S., 600 ...336/F3
Lamar, S.C., U.S., 1,015 ...340/D2
Lamar, S.C., U.S., county, 48,499 ...346/N2
Lamar Hts., Mo., U.S., 216 ...302/B4
La Marque, Tex., U.S., 13,682 ...346/C7
La Martre, N.W. Terr., Can., lake ...220/E4
La Mauricie Natl. Park, Que., Can. ...225/B4
La Mauricie Natl. Park, Que., Can. ...226/C5
Lamb, Tex., U.S., county, 14,709 ...346/F1
Lambaréné, Gabon, 25,033 ...155/A2
Lambayeque, Peru, department ...185/A2
Lamberhurst, Eng., U.K. ...70/E4
Lambert, Miss., U.S., 1,967 ...300/B1
Lambert, Mo., U.S., 49 ...302/G4
Lambert, Mont., U.S., 150 ...306/M2

Lambert, Okla., U.S. ...330/D1
Lambert Lake, Maine, U.S. 859 ...286/E3
Lamberton, Minn., U.S., 859 ...298/B6
Lambertville, Mich., U.S., 9,299 ...294/F8
Lambertville, N.J., U.S., 3,868 ...314/D3
Lambeth, Eng., U.K., 244,834 ...70/D4
Lambeth, Eng., U.K., unitary authority, 266,170 ...266/D3
Lamboglia, P.R. ...206/D3
Lambourn, Eng., U.K., 2,850 ...70/A3
Lambrook, Ark., U.S. ...244/E3
Lambs Grove, Iowa, U.S., 225 ...274/H4
Lambton, Ont., Can. ...223/C5
Lambton, Ont., Can., county ...223/C5
Lambton, Que., Can., 1,525 ...226/E6
Lane Deer, Mont., U.S., 2,018 ...306/K4
Lamèque, N.B., Can., 1,580 ...217/E1
Lamèque, N.B., Can., island, 1,580 ...217/E1
Lamerton, Eng., U.K. ...73/D3
La Mesa, Calif., U.S., 54,749 ...246/H10
La Mesa, N. Mex., U.S., 800 ...317/C4
Lamesa, Tex., U.S., 9,952 ...346/G3
Lamesteer N.W.R., Mont., U.S. ...306/M3
Lami, Fiji ...174/B3
Lamia, Gr. ...100/B2
Lamine, Mo., U.S. ...302/D3
Lamington, Scot., U.K. ...62/J7
Lamington, N.J., U.S. ...314/D2
La Mirada, Calif., U.S., 46,783 ...246/D10
Lamison, Ala., U.S., 50 ...238/B3
Lamkin, Tex., U.S. ...346/K4
Lamlash, Scot., U.K., 1,010 ...62/F7
Lammermuir, Scot., U.K., hills ...60/C2
La Moille, Ill., U.S., 773 ...266/D2
Lamoille, Minn., U.S., 60 ...298/F7
Lamoille, Nev., U.S., 60 ...310/C1
Lamoille, Vt., U.S., county, 23,233 ...352/B1
Lamoille, Vt., U.S., river ...352/B1
Lamoine, Calif., U.S. ...246/C2
Lamoine Beach, Maine, U.S. ...286/D4
Lamon, Phil., bay ...120/B3
Lamona, Wash., U.S. ...358/G2
Lamoni, Iowa, U.S., 2,444 ...274/G6
Lamont, Alta., Can., 1,692 ...212/D4
Lamont, Ark., U.S. ...244/C3
Lamont, Calif., U.S., 13,296 ...246/G7
Lamont, Fla., U.S., 125 ...256/E1
Lamont, Ida., U.S. ...264/F6
Lamont, Iowa, U.S., 503 ...274/L2
Lamont, Kans., U.S., 60 ...276/F3
Lamont, Miss., U.S., 275 ...300/A2
Lamont, Okla., U.S., 465 ...330/E1
Lamont, Wash., U.S., 106 ...358/H2
Lamont, Wyo., U.S. ...366/C2
La Montaña, Peru, region ...185/C2
La Monte, Mo., U.S., 1,064 ...302/C3
La Motte, Iowa, U.S., 272 ...274/N3
La Moure, N. Dak., U.S., 944 ...326/G3
La Moure, N. Dak., U.S., county, 4,701 ...326/G3
Lamourie, La., U.S., 100 ...282/E4
Lampa, Chile ...190/Inset
Lampang, Thai. ...125/B2
Lam Pao, Thai., reservoir ...125/C2
Lampasas, Tex., U.S., 6,786 ...346/K4
Lampasas, Tex., U.S., county, 17,762 ...346/K4
Lampeter, Wales, U.K. ...60/B3
Lampeter, Wales, U.K., 1,989 ...64/C3
Lamphey, Wales, U.K. ...64/B4
Lamphun, Thai. ...125/B2
Lampman, Sask., Can., 650 ...227/H11
Lamport, Eng., U.K. ...70/D2
Lampson, Wisc., U.S., 80 ...364/B3
Lampung, Indon., province ...122/B2
Lamu, Kenya ...157/F5
Lamy, N. Mex., U.S., 137 ...317/E2
Lan, Tai., island ...117/B2
Lanagan, Mo., U.S., 411 ...302/B5
Lanai, Hawaii, U.S., island ...262/B3, C6
Lanai City, Hawaii, U.S., 3,164 ...262/B3
Lanaihale, Hawaii, U.S., mountain ...262/B3
Lanark, Ont., Can., 869 ...223/J2
Lanark, Ont., Can., 869 ...223/J2
Lanark, Ont., Can., county ...223/J2
Lanark, Scot., U.K., 8,253 ...62/J7
Lanark, Ill., U.S., 1,584 ...266/D1
Lanark Vil., Fla., U.S., 550 ...256/D2
Lancashire, Eng., U.K., unitary authority, 1,134,976 ...66/C5
Lancashire, Eng., U.K., unitary authority, 1,134,976 ...68/B2
Lancaster, Ont., Can., 797 ...223/L2
Lancaster, Eng., U.K. ...60/C2
Lancaster, Eng., U.K., 44,497, (91,154, metro.) ...66/C4
Lancaster, Eng., U.K., 44,497, (91,154, metro.) ...68/B1
Lancaster, Calif., U.S., 118,718 ...246/G8
Lancaster, Ill., U.S., 100 ...266/F5
Lancaster, Kans., U.S., 291 ...276/G2
Lancaster, Ky., U.S., 3,734 ...280/F3
Lancaster, Mass., U.S., 7,380 ...292/H3
Lancaster, Minn., U.S., 363 ...298/A2
Lancaster, Mo., U.S., 737 ...302/D1
Lancaster, Nebr., U.S., county, 250,291 ...308/H3
Lancaster, N.H., U.S., 3,280 ...312/C3
Lancaster, N.Y., U.S., 11,188 ...320/D5
Lancaster, Ohio, U.S., 35,335 ...328/E6
Lancaster, Penn., U.S., 56,348, (470,658, metro.) ...336/J5
Lancaster, Penn., U.S., county, 470,658 ...336/J6
Lancaster, S.C., U.S., 8,177 ...340/D2
Lancaster, S.C., U.S., county, 61,351 ...340/D2
Lancaster, Tex., U.S., 25,894 ...346/C10
Lancaster, Va., U.S., 100 ...354/L5
Lancaster, Va., U.S., county, 11,567 ...354/K5
Lancaster, Wash., U.S. ...358/H2
Lancaster, Wisc., U.S., 4,070 ...364/C6
Lance Creek, Wyo., U.S., 51 ...366/F2
Lanchester, Eng., U.K., 3,599 ...66/E3
L'Ancienne-Lorette, Que., Can., 15,929 ...226/K5
Lancing, Tenn., U.S., 150 ...344/M2
Landa, N. Dak., U.S. ...326/E1
Land Between the Lakes Rec. Area, Ky., U.S. ...280/B4
Landeck, Aus. ...91/B3
Lander, Nev., U.S., county, 5,794 ...310/B1
Lander, Wyo., U.S., 6,867 ...366/B2
Landers, Calif., U.S., 90 ...246/J8
Landersville, Ala., U.S., 150 ...238/B1
Landes, Fr., department ...88/B5
Landes, Fr., region ...88/B5
Landfall, Minn., U.S., 700 ...298/F6
Landingville, Penn., U.S., 175 ...336/J4
Landis, Sask., Can., 161 ...227/B8
Landis, Ark., U.S. ...244/C2
Landis, N.C., U.S., 2,996 ...322/D3
Landisburg, Penn., U.S., 195 ...336/G5
Landisville, N.J., U.S., 500 ...314/D4
Landisville, Penn., U.S., 4,771 ...336/J5
Lando, S.C., U.S., 250 ...340/C1
Land O' Lakes, Fla., U.S., 20,971 ...256/F3
Land O' Lakes, Wisc., U.S., 225 ...364/D2
Landover, Md., U.S., 22,900 ...288/C7
Landover Hills, Md., U.S., 1,534 ...288/C7
Landrum, S.C., U.S., 2,472 ...340/B1
Land's End, Eng., U.K., promontory ...60/B4
Land's End, Eng., U.K., promontory ...73/A4
Landshut, Ger. ...86/C4
Landusky, Mont., U.S., 200 ...306/H2
Lane, Kans., U.S., 256 ...276/G3
Lane, Kans., U.S., county, 2,155 ...276/B3
Lane, Nev., U.S. ...310/C2
Lane, Okla., U.S., 300 ...330/G3
Lane, Oreg., U.S., county, 322,959 ...334/D4
Lane, S.C., U.S., 585 ...340/E3
Lane, S. Dak., U.S., 59 ...342/G3
Laneburg, Ark., U.S., 50 ...244/B4
Lanesboro, Iowa, U.S., 152 ...274/E3
Lanesboro, Mass., U.S., 2,990 ...292/B2
Lanesboro, Minn., U.S., 788 ...298/F7
Lanesville, Conn., U.S., 3,100 ...253/B3
Lanesville, Ind., U.S., 614 ...270/E8
Lanett, Ala., U.S., 7,897 ...238/D3
Laneville, W. Va., U.S. ...360/H3
Lanfair, Calif., U.S., valley ...246/K7
Langavat, Scot., U.K., lake ...62/C2
Langdon, Iowa, U.S., 125 ...274/D1
Langdon, Kans., U.S., 72 ...276/D4
Langdon, N.H., U.S., 586 ...312/B5
Langdon, N. Dak., U.S., 2,101 ...326/G1
Langdon Beck, Eng., U.K. ...66/D3
Langdon Place, Ky., U.S., 974 ...280/B2
Langeberg, S. Afr., mountains ...162/B3
Langeland, Den., island ...79/C4
Langeli Valley, Oreg., U.S. ...334/E5
Langenburg, Sask., Can., 1,107 ...227/J10
Langenhoe, Eng., U.K. ...70/F3
Langford, Eng., U.K., 2,760 ...68/F3
Langford, Eng., U.K., 2,760 ...70/F3
Langford, S. Dak., U.S., 290 ...342/H2
Langham, Sask., Can., 1,145 ...227/D8
Langham, Eng., U.K. ...70/C1
Langholm, Scot., U.K., 2,311 ...62/L8
Langhorne, Penn., U.S., 1,981 ...336/M5
Langhorne Manor, Penn., U.S., 927 ...336/M5
Langkawi, Malay., island ...121/A1
Langkawi, Wisc., U.S., 100 ...364/E3
Langlade, Wisc., U.S., county, 20,740 ...364/D3
Langley, Br. Col., Can., 23,643 ...214/L6
Langley, (Hertfordshire), Eng., U.K. ...70/D3
Langley, (Kent), Eng., U.K. ...70/F4
Langley, Eng., U.K. ...66/D6
Langley, Ark., U.S., 90 ...244/B3
Langley, Kans., U.S. ...276/E3
Langley, Ky., U.S., 375 ...280/H3
Langley, Wash., U.S., 959 ...358/C1
Langley, Okla., U.S., 669 ...330/G1
Langley Park, Md., U.S., 16,214 ...288/B6, G4
Langlois, Oreg., U.S., 50 ...334/B5
Langold, Eng., U.K., 2,802 ...66/E1
Langold, Eng., U.K., 2,802 ...68/E3
Langrick, Eng., U.K. ...70/D1
Langruth, Man., Can. ...215/B4
Langsa, Indon. ...122/A1
Langskaill, Scot., U.K. ...62/M1
Lang Son, Viet. ...123/B2
Langstaff, Ont., Can. ...223/K5
Langston, Ala., U.S., 254 ...238/C1
Langston, Mich., U.S., 300 ...294/D6
Langston, Okla., U.S., 1,670 ...330/E2
Langtoft, Eng., U.K. ...66/H4
Langton, Ont., Can. ...223/E5
Langton, Eng., U.K. ...66/G4
Langton, Eng., U.K. ...68/F1
Langtry, Tex., U.S. ...346/G6
Languedoc-Roussillon, Fr., region ...88/C5
Langworthy, Iowa, U.S., 90 ...274/M3
Lanham, (Lanham-Seabrook), Md., U.S., 18,190 ...288/C6
Lanham, Nebr., U.S., 40 ...308/H3
Lanier, Ga., U.S., county, 7,241 ...260/E9
Lanigan, Sask., Can., 1,289 ...227/E9
Lanín, Arg., volcano ...191/A4
Lanín, Chile, volcano ...190/B5
Länkäran, Azer. ...103/C3
Lankin, N. Dak., U.S., 131 ...326/H1
Lannon, Wisc., U.S., 1,009 ...364/F2
L'Annonciation, Que., Can., 1,984 ...226/B5
Lanoka Harbor, N.J., U.S., 3,800 ...314/E4
Lanreath, Eng., U.K. ...73/C4
Lansdale, Penn., U.S., 16,071 ...336/L5
Lansdowne, Ont., Can. ...223/J3
Lansdowne, (Lansdowne-Baltimore Hts), Md., U.S., 15,724 ...288/H3
Lansdowne, Penn., U.S., 11,044 ...336/L7
Lansdowne House, Ont., Can., 270 ...222/C2
L'Anse, Mich., U.S., 2,107 ...294/A3
L'Anse-à-Valleau, Que., Can. ...226/M3
L'Anse aux Meadows Natl. Hist. Site, Nfld., Can. ...218/D3
L'Anse Ind. Res., Mich., U.S. ...364/E2
L'Anse-St-Jean, Que., Can., 1,155 ...226/F3
Lansford, N. Dak., U.S., 253 ...326/D1
Lansford, Penn., U.S., 4,230 ...336/K4
Lansing, Ill., U.S., 28,332 ...266/C6
Lansing, Iowa, U.S., 1,012 ...274/M1
Lansing, Kans., U.S., 9,199 ...276/G1, H2
Lansing, Mich., U.S., state capital, 119,128, (447,728, metro.) ...294/E7
Lansing, Minn., U.S., 225 ...298/E7
Lansing, N.Y., U.S., 3,417 ...320/J5
Lansing, N.C., U.S., 151 ...322/C1
Lantana, Fla., U.S., 9,437 ...256/B5, H5
Lantau, H.K., China, island ...117/A2
Lanton, Mo., U.S., 70 ...302/E5
Lantry, S. Dak., U.S. ...342/D2
Lanús, Arg., 468,561 ...191/D3
Lanyon, Iowa, U.S., 100 ...274/F3
Lanzarote, Sp., island ...94/Inset I
Lanzhou, China, 1,364,480, (2,339,750, metro.) ...119/D2
Laoag, Phil. ...120/B2
Laoang, Phil. ...120/C3
Lao Cai, Viet. ...123/A1
Laois, Ire., county ...78/C2
Laon, Fr. ...88/C2
Laona, Wisc., U.S., 700 ...364/E3
La Oroya, Peru ...185/B3
Laos, nation ...120
Laotto, Ind., U.S., 425 ...270/F2
La Palma, Pan. ...203/C2
La Palma, Sp., island ...94/Inset I
La Palma, Ariz., U.S. ...242/D5
La Palma, Calif., U.S., 15,408 ...246/D10
La Pampa, Arg., province ...191/B4
La Parguera, P.R. ...206/A3
La Paz, Bol., administrative capital, 793,293, (1,484,328, metro.) ...186/A3
La Paz, Bol., department ...186/A2
La Paz, Hond. ...202/B2
La Paz, Hond., department ...202/B2
La Paz, Mex., state capital, 162,954, (196,907, metro.) ...200/B3
La Paz, Ariz., U.S., county, 19,715 ...242/A4
La Paz, Ind., U.S., 489 ...270/D2
Lapeer, Mich., U.S., 9,072 ...294/F6
Lapeer, Mich., U.S., county, 87,904 ...294/F6
Lapel, Ind., U.S., 1,855 ...270/D5
La Perouse, N.S.W., Austl. ...170/Inset IV
La Pérouse, Man., Can. ...215/B1
La Perouse, Jap., strait ...114/Inset I
La Pica, P.R. ...206/B2
La Pine, Oreg., U.S., 5,799 ...334/E4
Laplace, La., U.S., 27,684 ...282/H3, J6
Lapland, Fin., province ...81/C1
Lapland, Fin., region ...81/B1
Lapland, Fin., region ...193/C1
Lapland, Nor., Swe., region ...80/C1, D1
La Plant, S. Dak., U.S., 150 ...342/E2
La Plata, Arg., 521,936, (642,979, metro.) ...191/D4
La Plata, P.R., river ...206/C2
La Plata, Colo., U.S., county, 43,941 ...250/C4
La Plata, Md., U.S., 6,551 ...288/G5
La Plata, Mo., U.S., 1,486 ...302/D1
La Plata, N. Mex., U.S., 60 ...317/B1
LaPlatte, Nebr., U.S. ...308/J2
La Plena, P.R. ...206/C2
La Plonge, Sask., Can., lake ...227/C5
La Pocatière, Que., Can. ...226/F4
Lapoint, Utah, U.S., 175 ...350/E3
La Pointe, Wisc., U.S., 60 ...364/C2
La Porte, Calif., U.S., 43 ...246/E3
La Porte, Ind., U.S., 21,621 ...270/C1
La Porte, Ind., U.S., county, 110,106 ...270/C1
Laporte, Minn., U.S., 145 ...298/C3
Laporte, Ohio, U.S., 1,600 ...328/F3, F9
Laporte, Penn., U.S., 290 ...336/H3
La Porte, Tex., U.S., 31,880 ...346/C6
La Porte City, Iowa, U.S., 2,275 ...274/K3
Lappeenranta, Fin., 58,041 ...81/C2
La Prairie, Que., Can., 18,896 ...226/J6
La Prairie, Ill., U.S., 60 ...266/B3
La Prairie, Minn., U.S., 605 ...298/D3
La Pryor, Tex., U.S., 1,491 ...346/J7
Lapta, (Lapithos), Cyp. ...133/B1
Laptev, sea ...193/B7
Laptev, Russ., sea ...104/H2
La Puente, Calif., U.S., 41,063 ...246/D9
La Puente, N. Mex., U.S., 175 ...317/D1
La Push, Wash., U.S., 225 ...358/A2
Lapwai, Ida., U.S., 1,134 ...264/A3
L'Aquila, It. ...95/C2
La Quinta, Calif., U.S., 23,694 ...246/J9
Lara, Ven., state ...182/B1
Larache, Mor. ...147/C1
Laramie, Colo., U.S., mountains ...250/E1
Laramie, Colo., U.S., river ...250/E1
Laramie, Wyo., U.S., 27,204 ...366/D3
Laramie, Wyo., U.S., county, 81,607 ...366/F2
Laramie, Wyo., U.S., mountains ...366/D2
Laramie, Wyo., U.S., peak ...366/D3
Laramie, Wyo., U.S., river ...366/D3
Larchmont, N.Y., U.S., 6,485 ...320/C2
Larchwood, Iowa, U.S., 788 ...274/B1
Laredo, Mo., U.S., 250 ...302/C1
Laredo, Mont., U.S. ...306/G1
Laredo, Tex., U.S., 176,576, (193,117, metro.) ...346/J8
La Reforma, Tex., U.S., 50 ...346/K9
Lares, P.R. ...206/B2
Large, Gren., island ...209/C1
Largo, Fla., U.S., 69,371 ...256/C6, F4
Largo, Fla., U.S., key ...256/H6
Largo, Md., U.S., 8,408 ...288/D7
Largs, Scot., U.K., 11,241 ...62/G7
Lariat, Tex., U.S. ...346/F1
Larimer, Colo., U.S., county, 251,494 ...250/E1
Larimore, N. Dak., U.S., 1,433 ...326/H2
La Rioja, Arg. ...191/B2
La Rioja, Arg., province ...191/B2
La Rioja, Sp., autonomous community ...94/E1
Larisa, Gr., 112,777 ...100/B2
Lark, N. Dak., U.S. ...326/D3
Larkana, Pak., 270,283 ...129/C4
Larkhall, Man., Can. ...215/C4
Lark Harbour, Nfld., Can., 613 ...218/B4
Larkhill, Eng., U.K., 2,108 ...73/J2
Larkspur, Calif., U.S., 12,014 ...246/H1
Larkspur, Colo., U.S., 234 ...250/F2
Larksville, Penn., U.S., 4,694 ...336/G7
Larnaca, Cyp., 115,266 ...133/B2
Larne, N. Ire., U.K. ...60/B2
Larne, N. Ire., U.K., 17,575 ...65/F2
Larne, N. Ire., U.K., unitary authority, 30,832 ...65/F2
Larned, Kans., U.S., 4,236 ...276/C3
La Roche, Sask., Can., lake ...227/A4
La Rochelle, Fr., 80,055, (116,157, metro.) ...88/B3
La-Roche-sur-Yon, Fr. ...88/B3
Larochette, Lux. ...85/B2
La Roda, Sp. ...94/E3
La Romana, Dom. Rep., 136,000 ...205/D2
La Romana, Dom. Rep., province ...205/D2
La Ronge, Sask., Can., 2,727 ...227/E5
La Ronge, Sask., Can., lake, 2,727 ...227/E6
La Rose, Ill., U.S., 159 ...266/D3
Larose, La., U.S., 7,306 ...282/J7
La Rosita, Nicar. ...202/B2
Larrabee, Iowa, U.S., 149 ...274/C2
Larrabees Pt., Vt., U.S. ...352/A3
Larrys River, N.S., Can. ...221/F2
Larsen Bay, Alaska, U.S., 115 ...240/E3
Larsen Ice Shelf, Antar., glacier ...192/C12
Larslan, Mont., U.S. ...306/K1
Larsmont, Minn., U.S., 100 ...298/F4
Lartington, Eng., U.K. ...66/E3
Larto, La., U.S., 225 ...282/F4
Larue, Ky., U.S., county, 13,373 ...280/E3
La Rue, Ohio, U.S., 775 ...328/D4
La Russell, Mo., U.S., 138 ...302/B4
Larwill, Ind., U.S., 282 ...270/E2
La Sal, Utah, U.S., 339 ...350/E5
La Sal Jct., Utah, U.S. ...350/E5
La Salle, Man., Can. ...215/C4
LaSalle, Que., Can., 73,983 ...226/J6
La Salle, Colo., U.S., 1,849 ...250/F1
La Salle, Ill., U.S., 9,796 ...266/D2
La Salle, Ill., U.S., county, 111,509 ...266/E2
La Salle, La., U.S., parish, 14,282 ...282/F4
La Salle, Mich., U.S., 350 ...294/F8
La Salle, Minn., U.S., 90 ...298/C6
La Salle, Tex., U.S., county, 5,866 ...346/J7
Las Animas, Colo., U.S., 2,758 ...250/G3
Las Animas, Colo., U.S., county, 15,207 ...250/F4
L'Ascension, (L'Ascension-de-Patapedia), Que., Can. ...226/B5
La Scie, Nfld., Can., 1,063 ...218/D4
Las Cruces, Calif., U.S. ...246/E8
Las Cruces, N. Mex., U.S., 74,267, (174,682, metro.) ...317/D5
La Serena, Chile, 120,548 ...190/B3
Lasham, Eng., U.K. ...70/B4
Lashburn, Sask., Can., 783 ...227/A7
Lashio, Myan. ...125/C2
Lashkar Gah, Afg. ...129/A2
Lasker, N.C., U.S., 103 ...322/L2
Las Lomas, Calif., U.S., 3,078 ...246/D6
Las Marías, P.R. ...206/A2
Las Marías, P.R. ...206/B2
Las Minas, Hond., mountain ...202/A2
Las Nutrias, (Rio Arriba County), N. Mex., U.S. ...317/D1
Las Nutrias, (Socorro County), N. Mex., U.S., 70 ...317/D3
Las Palmas, Sp., 354,863 ...94/Inset I
Las Palmas, Sp., province ...94/Inset I
Las Palomas, N. Mex., U.S., 100 ...317/C4
La Spezia, It. ...95/B1
Las Piedras, P.R. ...206/D2
Las Piedras, Uru. ...187/B3
Lassen, Calif., U.S., county, 33,828 ...246/E2
Lassen, Calif., U.S., peak ...246/D2
Lassen Natl. For., Calif., U.S. ...246/D2, E2
Lassen Volcanic Natl. Park, Calif., U.S. ...246/D2
Las Tablas, Pan. ...203/B3
Last Chance, Colo., U.S. ...250/G2
Last Mtn., Sask., Can., lake ...227/E9
Las Trampas, N. Mex., U.S., 100 ...317/E1
Lastrup, Minn., U.S., 99 ...298/C4
Las Tunas, Cuba, 134,000 ...204/C3
Las Tunas, Cuba, province ...204/E2
Las Vegas, Nev., U.S., 478,434, (1,563,282, metro.) ...310/C3
Las Vegas, N. Mex., U.S., 14,565 ...317/E2
Las Vegas N.W.R., N. Mex., U.S. ...317/E2
Latacunga, Ecua. ...185/B3
Latah, Ida., U.S., county, 34,935 ...264/A3
Latah, Wash., U.S., 151 ...358/H2
Latanier, La., U.S., 90 ...282/E4
Latchingdon, Eng., U.K. ...70/F3
Late, Tonga, island ...175/C2
Latexo, Tex., U.S., 272 ...346/N4
Latham, Ill., U.S., 371 ...266/D4
Latham, Kans., U.S., 164 ...276/F4
Latham, Tenn., U.S., 125 ...344/D2
Latham, Wyo., U.S. ...366/C3
Latham Park, Ill., U.S. ...266/D1
Latheron, Scot., U.K. ...62/K2
Lathrop, Calif., U.S., 10,445 ...246/L2
Lathrop, Mo., U.S., 2,092 ...302/B2
Lathrup Vil., Mich., U.S., 4,236 ...294/A6, F7
Latimer, Eng., U.K. ...70/C3
Latimer, Iowa, U.S., 535 ...274/H2
Latimer, Kans., U.S. ...276/F3
Latimer, Miss., U.S., 4,288 ...300/D5
Latimer, Okla., U.S., county, 10,692 ...330/G3
Latimer, Utah, U.S. ...350/A5
Latina, It. ...95/C2
Latium, It., region ...95/C2
Laton, Calif., U.S., 1,236 ...246/F6
Latonia Lakes, Ky., U.S., 325 ...280/F2
La Tortuga, Ven., island ...182/C1
La Tour, Mo., U.S., 65 ...302/B3
Latrobe, Penn., U.S., 8,994 ...336/C5
Latta, Okla., U.S., 800 ...330/F3
Latta, S.C., U.S., 1,410 ...340/E2
Latsburg, Ohio, U.S., 275 ...328/F4
Lattimore, N.C., U.S., 419 ...322/B4
Lattingtown, N.Y., U.S., 1,860 ...320/C2
Latty, Ohio, U.S., 200 ...328/B3
La Tuque, Que., Can., 11,298 ...226/D4
Latvia, nation ...80
Latvia, nation ...193/D2
Lau, Fiji, island group ...174/C2
Lauada, N.C., U.S., 125 ...322/C8
Laucala, Fiji, island ...174/C2
Laud, Ind., U.S., 250 ...270/F2
Laudat, Dom. ...208/B3
Lauder, Man., Can. ...215/A4
Lauder, Scot., U.K., 1,081 ...62/L7
Lauderdale, Eng., U.K., valley ...66/C1
Lauderdale, Ala., U.S., county, 87,966 ...238/B1
Lauderdale, Minn., U.S., 2,364 ...298/E6
Lauderdale, Miss., U.S., 325 ...300/D3
Lauderdale, Miss., U.S., county, 78,161 ...300/D4
Lauderdale, Tenn., U.S., county, 27,101 ...344/B3
Lauderdale-by-the-Sea, Fla., U.S., 2,563 ...256/B5
Lauderdale Lakes, Fla., U.S., 31,705 ...256/B5
Lauderhill, Fla., U.S., 57,585 ...256/B5
Laughing Fish, Mich., U.S., point ...294/C3
Laughing Fish, Wisc., U.S., point ...364/F2
Laughlin, Nev., U.S., 7,076 ...310/C4
Launceston, Tas., Austl. ...170/D4
Launceston, Eng., U.K. ...60/B4
Launceston, Eng., U.K., 6,466 ...73/D3
La Unión, N. Mex., U.S., 850 ...317/D6
La Unión, Chile ...190/B6
La Unión, El. Salv., 36,927 ...203/C2
Laupahoehoe, Hawaii, U.S., 473 ...262/J4
Laura, Ky., U.S., 600 ...280/H3
Laura, Ohio, U.S., 487 ...328/B5
Laurel, Del., U.S., 3,668 ...255/B6
Laurel, Fla., U.S., 8,393 ...256/F4
Laurel, Ind., U.S., 579 ...270/F5
Laurel, Iowa, U.S., 266 ...274/J4
Laurel, Ky., U.S., county, 52,715 ...280/F3
Laurel, Md., U.S., 19,960 ...288/C5, G3
Laurel, Miss., U.S., 18,393 ...300/C4
Laurel, Mont., U.S., 6,255 ...306/H4
Laurel, Nebr., U.S., 986 ...308/G1
Laurel, N.Y., U.S., 1,188 ...320/F1
Laurel, Va., U.S., 14,875 ...354/H5
Laurel, Wash., U.S., 600 ...358/C1
Laurel Bay, S.C., U.S., 6,625 ...340/D4
Laureldale, N.J., U.S., 800 ...314/D5
Laureldale, Penn., U.S., 3,759 ...336/K5
Laurel Hill, Fla., U.S., 549 ...256/B1
Laurel Hill, N.C., U.S. ...282/C5
Laurel Hill, N.C., U.S., 1,524 ...322/F6
Laurel Mtn., Penn., U.S., 185 ...336/C5
Laurel Park, N.C., U.S., 1,835 ...322/E8
Laurel Run, Penn., U.S., 723 ...336/G7
Laurel Sprs., N.J., U.S., 1,970 ...314/B4
Laurelton, Penn., U.S., 475 ...336/G4
Laurelville, Ohio, U.S., 533 ...328/E7
Laurence Harbor, N.J., U.S., 6,227 ...314/E3
Laurencekirk, Scot., U.K., 1,808 ...62/M5
Laurens, Ga., U.S., county, 44,874 ...260/E6
Laurens, Iowa, U.S., 1,476 ...274/E2
Laurens, N.Y., U.S., 277 ...320/L5
Laurens, S.C., U.S., 9,916 ...340/C2
Laurens, S.C., U.S., county, 69,567 ...340/B2
Laurentides Prov. Reserve, Que., Can. ...226/E3
Laurie, Mo., U.S., 663 ...302/D3
Laurie, Wash., U.S., 60 ...358/G1
Laurier, Man., Can. ...215/B4
Laurinburg, N.C., U.S., 15,874 ...322/G5
Laurium, Mich., U.S., 2,126 ...294/A2
Lausanne, Switz., 115,638, (285,350, metro.) ...90/A2
Lautem, E. Timor, province ...122/D1
Lautoka, Fiji, 42,917 ...174/A2
Lava Beds Natl. Mon., Calif., U.S. ...246/D1
Lavaca, Ark., U.S., 1,825 ...244/A2
Lavaca, Tex., U.S., county, 19,210 ...346/L6
Lava Hot Sprs., Ida., U.S., 521 ...264/F7
Laval, Que., Can., 343,005 ...226/C6, J5
Laval, Fr. ...88/B2
La Vale, Md., U.S., 4,613 ...288/C3
Lavalette, W. Va., U.S., 850 ...360/B4
La Valle, Wisc., U.S., 326 ...364/C5
Lavalleja, Uru., department ...187/C2
Lavallette, N.J., U.S., 2,665 ...314/E4

Lava Tree State Mon., Hawaii, U.S. 262/K5
Laveen, Ariz., U.S., 850 . . . . .242/C4
La Vega, Dom. Rep., 189,000 . . . . .205/B1
La Vega, Dom. Rep., *province* 205/B2
Lavendon, Eng., U.K. .70/C2
Lavenham, Man., Can. 215/B4
Lavenham, Eng., U.K., 1,231 . . . . .70/F2
La Vergne, Tenn., U.S., 18,687 . . . . .344/H2
La Verkin, Utah, U.S., 3,392 . . . . .350/A6
La Verne, Calif., U.S., 31,638 . . . . .246/H8
Laverne, Okla., U.S., 1,097 . . . . .330/C1
La Vernia, Tex., U.S., 931 . . . . .346/B3
La Veta, Colo., U.S., 924 . . . . .250/F4
Lavillette, N.B., Can. 217/D1
Lavina, Mont., U.S., 209 . . . . .306/H3
Lavinia, Minn., U.S., 100 . . . . .298/C3
La Virtud, Hond. 202/A2
La Vista, Nebr., U.S., 11,699 . . . . .308/H2
Lavon, Tex., U.S., 387 . . . . .346/D8
Lavon, Tex., U.S., *lake* 346/C8
Lavonia, Ga., U.S., 1,827 . . . . .260/E3
Lavoy, Alta., Can. 212/E4
Lavumisa, Swaz. 161/B3
Lawa, Fr. Gui., *river* 183/A2
Lawa, Sur., *river* .183/B2
Lawai, Hawaii, U.S., 1,984 . . . . .262/C2
La Ward, Tex., U.S., 200 . . . . .346/M7
Lawen, Oreg., U.S. .334/H4
Lawers, Scot., U.K. 62/H5
Lawler, Iowa, U.S., 461 . . . . .274/K1
Lawler, Minn., U.S. 298/C4
Lawley, Ala., U.S., 125 . . . . .238/C3
Lawn, Nfld., Can., 779 . . . . .218/D5
Lawn, Tex., U.S., 353 . . . . .346/J3
Lawndale, Calif., U.S., 31,711 . . . . .246/C10
Lawndale, Ill., U.S., 150 . . . . .266/D3
Lawndale, Minn., U.S. 298/A4
Lawndale, N.C., U.S., 642 . . . . .322/B4
Lawnside, N.J., U.S., 2,692 . . . . .314/B3
Lawrence, Ala., U.S., *county*, 34,803 . . . . . . .238/B1
Lawrence, Ark., U.S., *county*, 17,774 . . . . . . .244/D1
Lawrence, Ill., U.S., 350 . . . . .266/E1
Lawrence, Ill., U.S., *county*, 15,452 . . . . .266/F5
Lawrence, Ind., U.S., 38,915 . . . . .270/D5
Lawrence, Ind., U.S., *county*, 45,922 . . . . . . .270/D7
Lawrence, Kans., U.S., 80,098, (99,962, *metro.*) .276/C3
Lawrence, Ky., U.S., *county*, 15,569 . . . . . . .280/H2
Lawrence, Mass., U.S., 72,043 . . . . .292/K2
Lawrence, Mich., U.S., 1,059 . . . . .294/C7
Lawrence, Miss., U.S., *county*, 13,258 . . . . . . .300/B4
Lawrence, Mo., U.S., *county*, 35,204 . . . . . . .302/C4
Lawrence, Nebr., U.S., 312 . . . . .308/E3
Lawrence, N.Y., U.S., 6,522 . . . . .320/C3
Lawrence, Ohio, U.S., *county*, 62,319 . . . . . . .328/E8
Lawrence, Penn., U.S., *county*, 94,643 . . . . . .336/A3
Lawrence, S. Dak., U.S., *county*, 21,802 . . . . .342/B3
Lawrence, Tenn., U.S., *county*, 39,926 . . . . . .344/G4
Lawrence, Tex., U.S. 346/D9
Lawrenceburg, Ind., U.S., 4,685 . . . . .270/C6
Lawrenceburg, Ky., U.S., 9,014 . . . . .280/F2
Lawrenceburg, Tenn., U.S., 10,796 . . . . .344/G4
Lawrence Creek, Okla., U.S., 119 . . . . .330/F1
Lawrence Park, Penn., U.S., 4,048 . . . . .336/A1
Lawrence Sta., N.B., Can. 217/B3
Lawrenceville, Ga., U.S., 22,397 . . . . . . .260/D4, K2
Lawrenceville, Ill., U.S., 4,745 . . . . .266/F5
Lawrenceville, N.J., U.S., 4,081 . . . . .314/D3
Lawrenceville, Ohio, U.S., 302 . . . . .328/C5
Lawrenceville, Penn., U.S., 627 . . . . .336/G2
Lawrenceville, Va., U.S., 1,275 . . . . .354/H7
Lawrenny, Wales, U.K. 64/B4
Lawson, Ark., U.S., 100 . . . . .244/C4
Lawson, Mo., U.S., 2,336 . . . . .302/B2
Lawsonia, Md., U.S., 1,300 . . . . .288/L7
Lawtell, La., U.S., 850 . . . . .282/E5
Lawtey, Fla., U.S., 656 . . . . .256/F1
Lawton, Iowa, U.S., 697 . . . . .274/B3
Lawton, Kans., U.S. 276/H4
Lawton, Mich., U.S., 1,859 . . . . .294/D7
Lawton, N. Dak., U.S., 42 . . . . .326/G1
Lawton, Okla., U.S., 92,757, (114,996, *metro.*) .330/D3
Laxey, Eng., U.K. 66/B5
Laxford Bridge, Scot., U.K. 62/F2
Laxton, (East Riding of Yorkshire), Eng., U.K. . . .68/F2
Laxton (Nottinghamshire Co), Eng., U.K. 250/C1
Lay, Colo., U.S., 40 . . . . .136/B2
Layla, S. Arab. 136/B2
Layland, Man., U.K. 215/B4
Layou, Dom., *river* 208/B3
Laysville, Conn., U.S., 1,100 . . . . .253/F4
Layton, Fla., U.S., 186 . . . . .256/H7
Layton, N.J., U.S., 225 . . . . .314/D1
Layton, Utah, U.S., 58,474 . . . . .350/C2, E1
Laytonsville, Md., U.S., 277 . . . . .288/F3
Laytonville, Calif., U.S., 1,301 . . . . .246/B3
Lazare, Tex., U.S. .346/H1
Lázaro Cárdenas, Mex. 200/D4
Lazbuddie, Tex., U.S., 100 . . . . .346/F1
Lazear, Colo., U.S., 200 . . . . .66/C3
Lazonby, Eng., U.K. .66/C3
Lazy Lake, Fla., U.S. 256/B5
Lea, Eng., U.K. 68/C6
Lea, N. Mex., U.S., *county*, 55,511 . . . . .317/C3
Leaburg, Oreg., U.S., 300 . . . . .334/D3
Leachville, Ark., U.S., 1,981 . . . . .244/E2
Leacock, (Leacock-Leola-Bareville),
  Penn., U.S., 6,625 . . . . .336/J5
Lead, S. Dak., U.S., 3,027 . . . . .342/B3
Leadbetter, Wash., U.S., *point* 358/A3
Leadenham, Eng., U.K. 68/F3
Leader, Sask., Can., 914 . . . . .227/A10
Leader, Minn., U.S. 298/C4
Leadgate, Eng., U.K., 4,736 . . . . .66/D3
Lead Hill, Ark., U.S., 287 . . . . .244/C1
Leadhills, Scot., U.K. 62/J8
Leading Tickles, Nfld., Can., 453 . . . . .218/D4
Leadington, Mo., U.S., 206 . . . . .302/F4
Leadore, Ida., U.S., 90 . . . . .264/D5
Leadpoint, Wash., U.S., 200 . . . . .358/H1
Leadville, Colo., U.S., 2,821 . . . . .250/D2
Leadwood, Mo., U.S., 1,160 . . . . .302/F4
Leaf, Miss., U.S., 100 . . . . .300/D4
Leaf, Miss., U.S., *river* 300/C4
Leafield, Eng., U.K. .70/A3
Leaf Rapids, Man., Can., 1,309 . . . . .215/D1
Leaf River, Ill., U.S., 555 . . . . .266/D2
League City, Tex., U.S., 45,444 . . . . . . .346/C7, N6
Leake, Miss., U.S., *county*, 20,940 . . . . .300/C3
Leakesville, Miss., U.S., 1,026 . . . . .300/D4
Leakey, Tex., U.S., 387 . . . . .346/J6
Leal, N. Dak., U.S. 326/G2
Leamington, Ont., Can., 27,138 . . . . .223/C5
Leamington, Utah, U.S., 217 . . . . .350/B4
Leander, La., U.S., 100 . . . . .282/D4
Leander, Tex., U.S., 7,596 . . . . .346/D2, L5
Learned, Miss., U.S., 50 . . . . .300/B3
Leary, Ga., U.S., 666 . . . . .260/C9
Leary, Tex., U.S., 555 . . . . .346/P2
Leasburg, Mo., U.S., 323 . . . . .302/E3
Leasburg, N.C., U.S., 300 . . . . .322/G2
Leatherhead, Eng., U.K., 42,903 . . . . .70/D4
Leatherwood, Ky., U.S., 125 . . . . .280/G3

Leaton, Eng., U.K. 68/B4
L'Eau Claire, Que., Can., *lake* 225/B2
Leavening, Eng., U.K. 66/G4
Leavenworth, Ind., U.S., 353 . . . . .270/D8
Leavenworth, Kans., U.S., 35,420 . . . . .276/H2
Leavenworth, Kans., U.S., *county*, 68,691 . .276/G1, G2
Leavenworth, Minn., U.S. 298/C6
Leavenworth, Wash., U.S., 2,074 . . . . .358/E2
Leawood, Kans., U.S., 27,656 . . . . .276/H1
Lebam, Wash., U.S., 176 . . . . .358/B3
Lebanon, *nation* .130
Lebanon, Leb., *mountains* 134/B1
Lebanon, Conn., U.S., 6,907 . . . . .253/G3
Lebanon, (see Rising Sun), Del., U.S., 2,458 . . .255/F5
Lebanon, Fla., U.S. 256/F2
Lebanon, Ill., U.S., 3,523 . . . . .266/B3
Lebanon, Ind., U.S., 14,222 . . . . .270/D4
Lebanon, Kans., U.S., 303 . . . . .276/D2
Lebanon, Ky., U.S., 5,718 . . . . .280/E3
Lebanon, Mo., U.S., 12,155 . . . . .302/D4
Lebanon, Nebr., U.S., 70 . . . . .308/D3
Lebanon, N.H., U.S., 12,568 . . . . .312/B4
Lebanon, N.J., U.S., *borough*, 1,065 . . . . . . .314/D2
Lebanon, Ohio, U.S., 16,962 . . . . .328/B7
Lebanon, Okla., U.S., 125 . . . . .330/F4
Lebanon, Oreg., U.S., 12,950 . . . . .334/D3
Lebanon, Penn., U.S., 24,461 . . . . .336/J5
Lebanon, Penn., U.S., *county*, 120,327 . . . . .336/J5
Lebanon, S. Dak., U.S., 86 . . . . .342/F2
Lebanon, Tenn., U.S., 20,235 . . . . .344/J2
Lebanon, Va., U.S., 3,273 . . . . .354/D2
Lebanon, Wisc., U.S., 275 . . . . .364/E5
Lebanon Church, Va., U.S., 125 . . . . .354/G2
Lebanon Jct., Ky., U.S., 1,801 . . . . .280/E3
Lebanon St. For., N.J., U.S. 314/D4
Lebap, Turkm., *province* 132/D2
Lebeau, La., U.S. .282/F5
Lebec, Calif., U.S., 1,285 . . . . .246/G8
Le Bic, Que., Can., 2,872 . . . . .226/H3
Le Blanc, La., U.S., 50 . . . . .282/D5
Lebo, Kans., U.S., 961 . . . . .276/G3
Lebombo, Moz., *mountains* 161/A4
Lebombo, S. Afr., *mountains* 162/D1
Lebombo, Swaz., *mountains* 161/C2
Lebrazhd, Alb. 99/B2
Lebu, Chile 190/B5
Lecanto, Fla., U.S., 5,161 . . . . .256/F3
Lecce, It. 95/D2
Le Center, Minn., U.S., 2,240 . . . . .298/D6
Lech, Aus. 91/B3
Lech, Ger., *river* 86/B4
Lechlade, Eng., U.K., 1,638 . . . . .68/D6
Lechlade, Eng., U.K., 1,638 . . . . .73/J1
Lechtal Alps, Aus., *range* 91/B3
Leckhampstead, Eng., U.K. 70/B4
Le Claire, Iowa, U.S., 2,847 . . . . .274/P4
Lecompte, La., U.S., 1,366 . . . . .282/E4
Lecompton, Kans., U.S., 608 . . . . .276/G2
Leconfield, Eng., U.K., 1,436 . . . . .66/H5
Leconfield, Eng., U.K., 1,436 . . . . .68/G2
Le Creusot, Fr. 88/D3
Ledbetter, Ky., U.S., 1,700 . . . . .280/B3
Ledbury, Eng., U.K., 6,216 . . . . .68/C5
Ledford, Ill., U.S., 475 . . . . .266/E6
Ledger, Mont., U.S. 306/F1
Ledger, N.C., U.S., 500 . . . . .322/A3, F6
Ledgewood, N.J., U.S., 1,100 . . . . .314/D2
Ledmore Jct., Scot., U.K. 62/G2
Ledoux, La., U.S., 250 . . . . .282/E5
Ledoux, N. Mex., U.S., 60 . . . . .317/E2
Ledyard, Iowa, U.S., 147 . . . . .274/F1
Ledyard Ctr., Conn., U.S., 800 . . . . .253/G4
Lee, Ire., *river* 78/B3
Lee, Scot., U.K., *lake* 62/L5
Lee, Ala., U.S., *county*, 115,092 . . . . .238/C3
Lee, Ark., U.S., *county*, 12,580 . . . . .244/E3
Lee, Fla., U.S., 352 . . . . .256/F1
Lee, Fla., U.S., *county*, 440,888 . . . . .256/E5
Lee, Ga., U.S., *county*, 24,757 . . . . .260/C8
Lee, Ill., U.S., 313 .266/D2
Lee, Ill., U.S., *county*, 36,062 . . . . .266/D2
Lee, Ind., U.S., 70 .270/C3
Lee, Iowa, U.S., *county*, 38,052 . . . . .274/N6
Lee, Ky., U.S., *county*, 7,916 . . . . .280/G3
Lee, Maine, U.S., 845 . . . . .286/D3
Lee, Mass., U.S., 5,985 . . . . .292/B3
Lee, Miss., U.S., *county*, 75,755 . . . . .300/D1
Lee, Nev., U.S., 40 . . . . .310/C1
Lee, N.H., U.S., 4,145 . . . . .312/D5
Lee, N.C., U.S., *county*, 49,040 . . . . .322/G4
Lee, S.C., U.S., *county*, 20,119 . . . . .340/D2
Lee, Tex., U.S., *county*, 15,657 . . . . .346/L5
Lee, Va., U.S., *county*, 23,589 . . . . .354/A2
Lee Bayou, La., U.S., 60 . . . . .282/F3
Leebotwood, Eng., U.K. 68/B4
Leech, Minn., U.S., *lake* 298/C3
Leechburg, Penn., U.S., 2,386 . . . . .336/B4
Leech Lake Ind. Res., Minn., U.S. 298/C3
Lee City, Ky., U.S., 100 . . . . .280/G3
Lee Clump, Eng., U.K. 70/C3
Lee Creek, Ark., U.S. 244/A2
Leedey, Okla., U.S., 345 . . . . .330/C2
Leeds, Eng., U.K. 60/C3
Leeds, Eng., U.K., 715,404, (2,079,217, *metro.*) .66/E5
Leeds, Eng., U.K., 715,404, (2,079,217, *metro.*) .68/D2
Leeds, Eng., U.K., *unitary authority*, 715,404 . .66/E5
Leeds, Eng., U.K., *unitary authority*, 715,404 . .68/D2
Leeds, Ala., U.S., 10,455 . . . . .238/C2
Leeds, Maine, U.S., 2,001 . . . . .286/B4
Leeds, N. Dak., U.S., 464 . . . . .326/F1
Leeds, Utah, U.S., 547 . . . . .350/A6
Leeds Pt., N.J., U.S., 350 . . . . .314/E5
Leedy, Miss., U.S., 175 . . . . .300/D1
Leek, Eng., U.K., 18,167 . . . . .66/E6
Leelanau, Mich., U.S., *county*, 21,119 . . . . . .294/D5
Lee Metcalf N.W.R., Mont., U.S. 306/D3
Lee-on-the-Solent, Eng., U.K., 7,259 . . . . .70/B5
Leeper, Mo., U.S., 60 . . . . .302/F4
Leeper, Penn., U.S., 225 . . . . .336/C3
Leesburg, Ala., U.S., 799 . . . . .238/D1
Leesburg, Fla., U.S., 15,956 . . . . .256/F3
Leesburg, Ga., U.S., 2,633 . . . . .260/C8
Leesburg, Ind., U.S., 625 . . . . .270/E2
Leesburg, Ky., U.S., 250 . . . . .280/F2
Leesburg, N.J., U.S., 350 . . . . .314/D5
Leesburg, Ohio, U.S., 1,253 . . . . .328/C7
Leesburg, Va., U.S., 28,311 . . . . .354/H2
Lees Ferry, Ariz., U.S., 100 . . . . .242/D1
Leesport, Penn., U.S., 1,805 . . . . .336/K5
Lee's Summit, Mo., U.S., 70,700 . . . . . .302/B3, J5
Leesville, Calif., U.S. 246/C3
Leesville, La., U.S., 6,753 . . . . .282/C4
Leesville, (Carroll County), Ohio, U.S., 184 . . . .328/H5
Leesville, (Crawford County), Ohio, U.S. 328/E4
Leesville, Tex., U.S., 70 . . . . .346/C6
Leeton, Mo., U.S., 619 . . . . .302/C3
Leetonia, Minn., U.S., 40 . . . . .298/E3
Leetonia, Ohio, U.S., 2,043 . . . . .328/J4
Leetsdale, Penn., U.S., 1,232 . . . . .336/A4
Leeuwarden, Neth. .84/C1
Leeuwin, Austl., *cape* 170/A3

Lee Valley, Tenn., U.S. 344/Q2
Leeville, La., U.S., 80 . . . . .282/J8
Lee Vining, Calif., U.S., 175 . . . . .246/F5
Leeward, *islands* .204/F3
Leeward Group, C.V. 148/B3
Leewood, W. Va., U.S., 100 . . . . .360/D4
Lefke, (Lefka), Cyp. 133/A1
Leflore, Miss., U.S., 50 . . . . .300/B2
Leflore, Miss., U.S., *county*, 37,947 . . . . . . .300/B2
Le Flore, Okla., U.S., 168 . . . . .330/H3
Le Flore, Okla., U.S., *county*, 48,109 . . . . . . .330/H3
Lefor, N. Dak., U.S., 40 . . . . .326/C3
Lefors, Tex., U.S., 559 . . . . .346/G9
Legal, Alta., Can., 1,058 . . . . .212/D4
Leganés, Sp., 173,584 . . . . .94/Inset II
Legaspi, Phil., 157,010 . . . . .120/B3
Leggett, Calif., U.S. 246/B3
Leggett, N.C., U.S., 77 . . . . .322/K3
Le Grand, Calif., U.S., 1,760 . . . . .246/E5
Le Grand, Iowa, U.S., 883 . . . . .274/J3
Le Havre, Fr., 193,259, (248,547, *metro.*) 88/C2
Lehi, Utah, U.S., 19,028 . . . . .350/C3
Lehigh, Iowa, U.S., 497 . . . . .274/F3
Lehigh, Kans., U.S., 215 . . . . .276/E3
Lehigh, Okla., U.S., 315 . . . . .330/F3
Lehigh, Penn., U.S., *county*, 312,090 . . . . . .336/K4
Lehigh, Penn., U.S., *river* 336/J7, K3
Lehighton, Penn., U.S., 5,537 . . . . .336/K4
Lehr, N. Dak., U.S., 114 . . . . .326/F3
Lehua, Hawaii, U.S., *island* 262/A1
Leicester, Eng., U.K. 60/C3
Leicester, Eng., U.K., 318,518, (416,601, *metro.*) .68/E4
Leicester, Eng., U.K., 318,518, (416,601, *metro.*) .70/B1
Leicester, Eng., U.K., *unitary authority*, 279,923 .68/E4
Leicester, Eng., U.K., *unitary authority*, 279,923 .70/B1
Leicester, Mass., U.S., 10,471 . . . . .292/G3
Leicester, N.Y., U.S., 469 . . . . .320/F5
Leicester, Vt., U.S., 974 . . . . .352/A3
Leicester Jct., Vt., U.S. 352/A3
Leicestershire, Eng., U.K., *unitary authority*,
  609,579 . . . . .68/E4
Leicestershire, Eng., U.K., *unitary authority*,
  609,579 . . . . .70/C1
Leichhardt, Austl., *river* 170/D1
Leichhardt, N.S.W., Austl. . . . . .170/Inset IV
Leiden, Neth., 117,290, (249,812, *metro.*) 84/B2
Leie, Belg., *river* .85/B2
Leigh, Eng., U.K., 43,150 . . . . .66/C6
Leigh, Eng., U.K., 43,150 . . . . .68/B3
Leigh, Eng., U.K., 43,150 . . . . .70/E4
Leigh, Nebr., U.S., 442 . . . . .308/G2
Leigh Sinton, Eng., U.K. 68/C5
Leighton, Ala., U.S., 849 . . . . .238/B1
Leighton, Iowa, U.S., 153 . . . . .274/J5
Leighton Buzzard, Eng., U.K., 32,610 . . . . . . .70/C3
Leikanger, Nor. 80/B3
Leinster, Ire., *province* 78/C2
Leintwardine, Eng., U.K. 68/B5
Leipers Fork, Tenn., U.S., 150 . . . . .344/H2
Leipsic, Del., U.S., 203 . . . . .255/B4
Leipsic, Ohio, U.S., 2,236 . . . . .328/C3
Leipzig, Ger., 493,200 . . . . .86/C3
Leipzig, Ger., *department* 86/C3
Leiria, Port. 93/A3
Leiria, Port., *district* 93/A3
Leiston, Eng., U.K., 5,950 . . . . .70/H2
Leisure City, Fla., U.S., 22,152 . . . . .256/A7
Leisuretowne, N.J., U.S., 2,535 . . . . .314/D4
Leisure Vil., N.J., U.S., 4,443 . . . . .314/E3
Leisure Vil. West, N.J., U.S., 11,085 . . . . .314/E3
Leitchfield, Ky., U.S., 6,139 . . . . .280/D3
Leiter, Wyo., U.S. .366/C1
Leitersburg, Md., U.S., 523 . . . . .288/D2
Leith, N. Dak., U.S. 326/D3
Leith, (Leith-Hatfield), Penn., U.S., 2,820 . . . . .336/B6
Leitholm, Scot., U.K. 62/M7
Leitrim, Ont., Can. 223/H6
Leitrim, Ire., *county* 78/B1
Lékéti, Congo, *mountains* 155/C5
Leland, Ill., U.S., 970 . . . . .266/F2
Leland, Iowa, U.S., 258 . . . . .274/G1
Leland, Mich., U.S., 350 . . . . .294/D4
Leland, Miss., U.S., 5,502 . . . . .300/B2
Leland, N.C., U.S., 1,938 . . . . .322/J6
Leland, Oreg., U.S., 40 . . . . .334/C5
Leland, Wisc., U.S. 364/D5
Leland Grove, Ill., U.S., 1,592 . . . . .266/D4
Leleiwi, Hawaii, U.S., *point* 262/J5
Lélouma, Guin. 149/B2
Le Loup, Kans., U.S., 125 . . . . .276/G2
Lelystad, Neth. 84/C2
Le Mans, Fr., 150,605, (194,825, *metro.*) 88/C2
Le Mars, Iowa, U.S., 9,237 . . . . .274/B2
Lemay, Mo., U.S., 17,215 . . . . .302/H3
Lemhi, Ida., U.S. .264/D5
Lemhi, Ida., U.S., *county*, 7,806 . . . . .264/C4
Lemhi, Ida., U.S., *river* 264/D4
Lemington, Vt., U.S., 107 . . . . .352/D1
Lemitar, N. Mex., U.S., 400 . . . . .317/D3
Lemmon, S. Dak., U.S., 1,398 . . . . .342/C1
Lemmon Valley, Nev., U.S., 6,855 . . . . .310/A2
Lemon, Ind., U.S., *lake* 270/C4
Lemon Grove, Calif., U.S., 24,918 . . . . .246/H10
Lemont, Ill., U.S., 13,098 . . . . .266/B6
Lemoore, Calif., U.S., 19,712 . . . . .246/F6
Lemoore Naval Air Sta., Calif., U.S. 246/E6
Le Moyen, La., U.S. 282/E5
Lemoyne, Nebr., U.S., 60 . . . . .308/C2
Lempa, El Salv., *river* 203/A1, B2
Lempira, Hond., *department* 202/A2
Lempster, N.H., U.S., 971 . . . . .312/B5
Lemreway, Scot., U.K. 62/D2
Lena, Russ., *river* 104/H3
Lena, Russ., *river* 193/C7
Lena, Ill., U.S., 2,887 . . . . .266/D1
Lena, La., U.S. 282/D4
Lena, Miss., U.S., 167 . . . . .300/C3
Lena, Wisc., U.S., 510 . . . . .364/E4
Lenapah, Okla., U.S., 298 . . . . .330/G1
Lenawee, Mich., U.S., *county*, 98,890 . . . . . .294/F8
Lendalfoot, Scot., U.K. 62/G8
Lenexa, Kans., U.S., 40,238 . . . . .276/H1, H3
Lengby, Minn., U.S., 79 . . . . .298/B3
Lenghu, China 119/C2
Lengoué, Congo, *river* 155/C3
Lenhartsville, Penn., U.S., 173 . . . . .336/K4
Leninobod, Taj., *province* 132/A1
Lennep, Mont., U.S., 40 . . . . .306/F3
Lennon, Mich., U.S., 517 . . . . .294/F6
Lennox, S. Dak., U.S., 2,037 . . . . .342/J4
Lennox and Addington, Ont., Can. 223/J6
Lennox and Addington, Ont., Can., *county* . . .223/J6
Lennox Island, P.E.I., Can. 224/B2
Lenoir, N.C., U.S., 16,793 . . . . .322/B3
Lenoir, N.C., U.S., *county*, 59,648 . . . . .322/K3
Lenoir City, Tenn., U.S., 6,819 . . . . .344/N3
Lenola, N.J., U.S., 13,860 . . . . .314/D4
Lenora, Kans., U.S., 306 . . . . .276/C2

Lenora, Okla., U.S. 330/C1
Lenorah, Tex., U.S., 60 . . . . .346/G3
Lenore, Man., Can. 215/A4
Lenore, W. Va., U.S., 225 . . . . .360/B5
Lenox, Ga., U.S., 889 . . . . .260/E9
Lenox, Iowa, U.S., 1,401 . . . . .274/E6
Lenox, Mass., U.S., 5,077 . . . . .292/A3
Lenox, Mo., U.S., 125 . . . . .302/E4
Lenox, Tenn., U.S., 200 . . . . .344/C2
Lenoxburg, Ky., U.S., 125 . . . . .280/F2
Lenox Dale, Mass., U.S., 1,100 . . . . .292/B3
Lens, Fr. 88/C1
Lensk, Russ. 104/G3
Lenwade, Eng., U.K. 70/G1
Lenzburg, Ill., U.S., 577 . . . . .266/C5
Léo, Burkina 151/C3
Leo, Wyo., U.S. 366/G3
Leoben, Aus. 91/D3
Leo-Cedarville, Ind., U.S., 2,782 . . . . .270/F2
Léogâne, Haiti 205/C2
Leola, Ark., U.S., 515 . . . . .244/C3
Leola, Penn., U.S., 6,625 . . . . .336/J5
Leola, S. Dak., U.S., 462 . . . . .342/G2
Leoma, Tenn., U.S., 400 . . . . .344/G4
Leominster, Eng., U.K., 9,543 . . . . .68/B5
Leominster, Mass., U.S., 41,303 . . . . .292/G2
León, Sp., 130,916 . . . . .94/D1
León, Sp., *province* 94/D1
León, Sp., *province*, 239,452 . . . . .256/D1
León, Iowa, U.S., 1,983 . . . . .274/G6
Leon, Kans., U.S., 645 . . . . .276/F4
Leon, Okla., U.S., 40 . . . . .330/E4
Leon, Tex., U.S., *county*, 15,335 . . . . .346/M4
Leon, W. Va., U.S., 132 . . . . .360/C4
Leon, Wisc., U.S., 40 . . . . .364/C5
León, Mex., 1,020,818, (1,134,842, *metro.*) . .200/D3
León, Nicar., 161,530 . . . . .202/A2
León, Nicar., *department* 202/A2
Leona, Kans., U.S., 88 . . . . .276/G2
Leona, Tex., U.S., 181 . . . . .346/N4
Leonard, Mich., U.S., 332 . . . . .294/F6
Leonard, Minn., U.S. 298/B3
Leonard, Mo., U.S., 66 . . . . .302/D2
Leonard, N. Dak., U.S., 255 . . . . .326/H3
Leonard, Okla., U.S., 325 . . . . .330/G2
Leonard, Tex., U.S., 1,846 . . . . .346/M2
Leonardo, N.J., U.S., 2,823 . . . . .314/E3
Leonardsville, N.Y., U.S., 275 . . . . .320/L5
Leonardtown, Md., U.S., 1,896 . . . . .288/H6
Leonardville, Kans., U.S., 398 . . . . .276/F2
Leonia, Fla., U.S., 40 . . . . .256/B1
Leonia, N.J., U.S., 8,914 . . . . .314/C2
Leonidas, Minn., U.S., 60 . . . . .298/E3
Leonore, Ill., U.S., 110 . . . . .266/E2
Leon Valley, Tex., U.S., 9,239 . . . . .346/A2, K6
Leopold, Ind., U.S., 90 . . . . .270/C8
Leopold, W. Va., U.S., 50 . . . . .360/D2
Leota, Minn., U.S., 230 . . . . .298/A7
Leoti, Kans., U.S., 1,598 . . . . .276/A3
Leova, Mol. 102/B2
Leoville, Sask., Can., 343 . . . . .227/C7
Leoville, Kans., U.S., 50 . . . . .276/B2
Lepanto, Ark., U.S., 2,133 . . . . .244/E2
Lepontine Alps, Switz., *mountains* 90/C2
Lepreau, N.B., Can. 217/C3
Lepsi, Kaz. 131/D2
Le Puy, Fr. 88/C4
Lequire, Okla., U.S., 125 . . . . .330/G2
Le Raysville, Penn., U.S., 318 . . . . .336/J2
Leribe, Leso. 161/B1
Lerna, Ill., U.S., 322 . . . . .266/E4
Le Roy, Ill., U.S., 3,332 . . . . .266/E3
Le Roy, Iowa, U.S. 274/G6
Le Roy, Kans., U.S., 593 . . . . .276/G3
Le Roy, Mich., U.S., 267 . . . . .294/D5
Le Roy, Minn., U.S., 925 . . . . .298/E7
Leroy, Mont., U.S., 40 . . . . .306/G2
Le Roy, N.Y., U.S., 4,462 . . . . .320/F5
Leroy, N. Dak., U.S. 326/H1
Le Roy, Penn., U.S., 175 . . . . .60/Inset I
Lerwick, Scot., U.K., 6,830 . . . . .60/Inset I
Lerwick, Scot., U.K., 6,830 . . . . .62/G2
Lery, La., U.S., *lake* 282/L3
Lesage, W. Va., U.S., 125 . . . . .360/B3
Lesbury, Eng., U.K. .66/E2
Les Cayes, Haiti, 45,904 . . . . .205/B2
Les Cheneaux, Mich., U.S., *islands* 294/E4
Les Éboulements, Que., Can., 1,027 . . . . .226/F4
Les Escaldes, And. .93/B2
Les Escoumins, Que., Can., 2,009 . . . . .226/G3
Leshara, Nebr., U.S., 111 . . . . .308/H2
Les Islets-Caribou, Que., Can. 226/J2
Lesley, Tex., U.S. 346/G10
Leskovac, Serb.-Mont., 162,278 . . . . .99/B3
Leslie, Ark., U.S., 482 . . . . .244/C2
Leslie, Ga., U.S., 455 . . . . .260/C8
Leslie, Ida., U.S. 264/D6
Leslie, Ky., U.S., *county*, 12,401 . . . . .280/G3
Leslie, Mich., U.S., 2,044 . . . . .294/E7
Leslie, Mo., U.S., 87 . . . . .302/E3
Lesmahagow, Scot., U.K., 3,685 . . . . .62/J7
Les Méchins, Que., Can., 1,220 . . . . .226/K3
Lesosibirsk, Russ. .104/F4
Lesotho, *nation* .155
Lesser Antilles, *islands* 204/E4, F4
Lesser Caucasus, Arm., *mountains* 103/B1
Lesser Caucasus, Azer., *range* 103/A2
Lesser Caucasus, Geo., *mountains* 103/B4
Lesser Hinggan, China, *range* 119/F1
Lesser Slave, Alta., Can., *lake* 212/C3
Lesser Slave, Alta., Can., *lake* 214/P3
Lesser Slave Lake Prov. Park, Alta., Can. 212/C3
Lesser Sunda, Indon., *islands* 122/C2
Lessley, Miss., U.S. 300/A4
Lesslie, S.C., U.S., 2,268 . . . . .340/D1
Les Tantes, Gren., *island* 209/B1
Lester, Ala., U.S., 107 . . . . .238/B1
Lester, Iowa, U.S., 251 . . . . .274/B1
Lester, Wash., U.S. 358/D2
Lester, W. Va., U.S., 322 . . . . .360/D5
Lester Prairie, Minn., U.S., 1,377 . . . . .298/C6
Lesterville, Mo., U.S., 225 . . . . .302/F4
Lesterville, S. Dak., U.S., 158 . . . . .342/H4
Lestock, Sask., Can. 227/G9
Le Sueur, Minn., U.S., 3,922 . . . . .298/D6
Le Sueur, Minn., U.S., *county*, 25,426 . . . . . .298/D6
Les Ulis, Fr. . . . . .88/Inset II
Lesvos, (Mitilini), Gr., *island* 100/C2
Leszno, Pol. 83/C3
Letart, W. Va., U.S., 125 . . . . .360/C3
Letcher, Ky., U.S., 425 . . . . .280/H3
Letcher, Ky., U.S., *county*, 25,277 . . . . .280/H3
Letcher, S. Dak., U.S., 177 . . . . .342/G4
Letchworth, Eng., U.K., 31,418 . . . . .70/D3
Letchworth St. Park, N.Y., U.S. 320/F5
Letcombe Regis, Eng., U.K. 70/B3
Letete, N.B., Can. .217/C3
Letha, Ida., U.S., 70 . . . . .264/A6

Lethbridge, Alta., Can., 67,374 .....212/D6
Lethbridge, Nfld., Can. 218/E5
Lethem, Guy. 183/B4
Leticia, Col., 30,000 .....184/C6
Letlhakeng, Bots. 160/B3
Letohatchee, Ala., U.S., 175 .....238/C3
Leton, La., U.S., 50 .....282/C1
Letona, Ark., U.S., 201 .....244/D2
Le Tourneau, Miss., U.S., 200 .....300/B3
Letterbreen, N. Ire., U.K. 65/B3
Letterkenny, Ire. 78/C1
Letterston, Wales, U.K. 64/B4
Letts, Ind., U.S., 150 .....270/E6
Letts, Iowa, U.S., 392 .....274/M5
Lettsworth, La., U.S., 150 .....282/F5
Leuchars, Scot., U.K., 2,518 .....62/L6
Leupp, Ariz., U.S., 970 .....242/F2
Leupp Corner, Ariz., U.S., 100 .....242/F2
Leuven, Belg., 89,152, (459,451, metro.) 85/C2
Levack, Ont., Can. 223/D1
Levallois-Perret, Fr. .....88/Inset II
Levan, Utah, U.S., 688 .....350/C4
Levant, Kans., U.S., 90 .....276/A2
Levant, Maine, U.S., 2,171 .....286/D4
Levasy, Mo., U.S., 108 .....302/B2, J5
Levelland, Tex., U.S., 12,866 .....346/F2
Level Park, Mich., U.S., 3,605 .....294/D7
Level Plains, Ala., U.S., 1,544 .....238/D4
Leven, Eng., U.K., 2,036 .....66/H5
Leven, Eng., U.K., 2,036 .....68/G2
Leven, Scot., U.K., 8,051 .....62/L6
Levenwick, Scot., U.K. 62/Q3
Leveque, Austl., cape 170/B1
Leverett, Mass., U.S., 1,663 .....292/D3
Levering, Mich., U.S., 300 .....294/E4
Leverkusen, Ger., 160,841 .....86/A3
Levice, Slvk., 120,021 .....92/D3
Lévis, (Lévis-Lauzon), Que., Can., 40,926 .....226/E5, L6
Levittown, P.R. 206/C2
Levittown, N.Y., U.S., 53,067 .....320/C2
Levittown, Penn., U.S., 53,966 .....336/M5
Levy, Fla., U.S., county, 34,450 .....256/F2
Levy, N. Mex., U.S. 317/F1
Lew, Eng., U.K. 70/A3
Lewdown, Eng., U.K. 73/D3
Lewellen, Nebr., U.S., 282 .....308/B2
Lewes, Eng., U.K. 60/D4
Lewes, Eng., U.K., 15,376 .....70/D5
Lewes, Del., U.S., 2,932 .....255/D5
Lewis, Scot., U.K. 60/A1
Lewis, Scot., U.K., island 62/E3
Lewis, Colo., U.S., 125 .....250/B4
Lewis, Ida., U.S., county, 3,747 .....264/A3
Lewis, Ind., U.S., 225 .....270/B6
Lewis, Iowa, U.S., 438 .....274/J3
Lewis, Kans., U.S., 486 .....276/C4
Lewis, Ky., U.S., county, 14,092 .....280/G2
Lewis, Mo., U.S., county, 10,494 .....302/E1
Lewis, N.Y., U.S., county, 26,944 .....320/K3
Lewis, Tenn., U.S., county, 11,367 .....344/G3
Lewis, Wash., U.S., county, 68,600 .....358/C4
Lewis, Wash., U.S., river 358/D3
Lewis, W. Va., U.S., county, 16,919 .....360/E3
Lewis, Wisc., U.S., 150 .....364/A3
Lewis and Clark, Mo., U.S., 155 .....302/A2
Lewis and Clark, Mont., U.S., county, 55,716 .....306/D2
Lewis and Clark Natl. For., Mont., U.S. 306/D2, F2, F3
Lewisberry, Penn., U.S., 385 .....336/H5
Lewisburg, (Logan County), Ky., U.S., 903 .....280/D4
Lewisburg, (Mason County), Ky., U.S., 225 .....280/G2
Lewisburg, La., U.S., 425 .....282/E6
Lewisburg, Ohio, U.S., 1,798 .....328/A6
Lewisburg, Penn., U.S., 5,620 .....336/H4
Lewisburg, Tenn., U.S., 10,413 .....344/H4
Lewisburg, W. Va., U.S., 3,624 .....360/F5
Lewis Ctr., Ohio, U.S., 500 .....328/D5
Lewisetta, Va., U.S. 354/L4
Lewisham, Eng., U.K., 231,175 .....70/D4
Lewisham, Eng., U.K., unitary authority, 248,924 .....70/D4
Lewisport, Ky., U.S., 1,639 .....280/D3
Lewisporte, Nfld., Can., 3,312 .....218/D4
Lewis Run, Penn., U.S., 577 .....336/D2
Lewis Smith, Ala., U.S., lake 238/B2
Lewiston, Calif., U.S., 1,305 .....246/C2
Lewiston, Ida., U.S., 30,904 .....264/A3
Lewiston, Maine, U.S., 35,690, (90,830, metro.) 286/B4
Lewiston, Mich., U.S., 990 .....294/E5
Lewiston, Minn., U.S., 1,484 .....298/F7
Lewiston, Nebr., U.S., 86 .....308/H3
Lewiston, N.Y., U.S., 2,781 .....320/C4
Lewiston, Utah, U.S., 1,877 .....350/C2
Lewiston Woodville, N.C., U.S., 613 .....322/L2
Lewistown, Ill., U.S., 2,522 .....266/C3
Lewistown, (Frederick County), Md., U.S., 600 .....288/E1
Lewistown, (Talbot County), Md., U.S., 175 .....288/L4
Lewistown, Mo., U.S., 595 .....302/E1
Lewistown, Mont., U.S., 5,813 .....306/G2
Lewistown, Penn., U.S., 8,998 .....336/F4
Lewisville, Ark., U.S., 1,285 .....244/B4
Lewisville, Ida., U.S., 467 .....264/E6
Lewisville, Ind., U.S., 395 .....270/F5
Lewisville, Minn., U.S., 274 .....298/C7
Lewisville, N.C., U.S., 8,826 .....322/E2
Lewisville, Ohio, U.S., 233 .....328/H6
Lewisville, Tex., U.S., 77,737 .....346/B9
Lewisville, Tex., U.S., lake 346/C8
Lewknor, Eng., U.K. 70/B3
Lexa, Ark., U.S., 331 .....244/E3
Lexie, Miss., U.S., 125 .....300/B4
Lexington, Ala., U.S., 840 .....238/B1
Lexington, Ga., U.S., 239 .....260/E4
Lexington, Ill., U.S., 1,912 .....266/E3
Lexington, Ind., U.S., 325 .....270/E7
Lexington, Ky., U.S., 260,512, (479,198, metro.) 280/F2
Lexington, Mass., U.S., 30,355 .....292/B7, K3
Lexington, Mich., U.S., 1,104 .....294/G6
Lexington, Minn., U.S., 2,214 .....298/F5
Lexington, Miss., U.S., 2,025 .....300/B2
Lexington, Mo., U.S., 4,453 .....302/C2
Lexington, Nebr., U.S., 10,011 .....308/E3
Lexington, N.C., U.S., 19,953 .....322/E3
Lexington, Ohio, U.S., 4,165 .....328/E4
Lexington, Okla., U.S., 2,086 .....330/E3
Lexington, Oreg., U.S., 263 .....334/G2
Lexington, S.C., U.S., 9,793 .....340/C3
Lexington, S.C., U.S., county, 216,014 .....340/A3, C3
Lexington, Tenn., U.S., 7,393 .....344/E3
Lexington, Tex., U.S., 1,178 .....346/L5
Lexington, Va., U.S., 6,867 .....354/E5
Lexington, Wash., U.S., 325 .....358/C3
Lexington Hts., Mich., U.S., 1,000 .....294/G6
Lexington Park, Md., U.S., 11,021 .....288/J6
Leyba, N. Mex., U.S., 70 .....317/E2
Leyburn, Eng., U.K., 1,716 .....66/E4
Leyden, Mass., U.S., 772 .....292/D3
Leyland, Wisc., U.S., 80 .....364/D6
Leyland, Eng., U.K., 37,331 .....66/C5
Leyland, Eng., U.K. 68/D3
Leysdown-on-Sea, Eng., U.K., 2,483 .....70/F4
Leyte, Phil., island 120/C4
Lezhë, Alb. 99/A2
Lhanbryde, Scot., U.K., 1,845 .....62/K3

Lhasa, China, 375,968 .....119/C3
Lhobrak, Bhu., river 126/C2
Lhokseumawe, Indon. 122/A1
L'Hospitalet de Llobregat, Sp., 239,019 .....94/H2
Lhuntshi, Bhu. 126/C2
Lianyungang, China 119/E2
Liao, China, river 119/F1
Liaoning, China, province 119/F1
Liaoyang, China, 470,020, (1,611,850, metro.) 119/F1
Liaoyuan, China 119/F1
Liard, Br. Col., Yukon, Can., river 214/H1, K1
Liard, N.W. Terr., Can., river 220/D4
Liard, Yukon, Can., river 228/C5
Liard River, Br. Col., Can. 214/I1
Libanus, Wales, U.K. 64/E4
Libau, Man., Can. 215/C4
Libby, Minn., U.S. 298/D4
Libby, Mont., U.S., 2,626 .....306/A1
Liberal, Kans., U.S., 19,666 .....276/B4
Liberal, Mo., U.S., 779 .....302/B4
Liberec, Czh. Rep., 100,000 .....92/B2
Liberecký, Czh. Rep., region 92/B2
Liberia, nation 143
Liberia, C.R. 203/A2
Liberty, Ariz., U.S., 250 .....242/C4
Liberty, Fla., U.S., 50 .....256/B1
Liberty, Fla., U.S., county, 7,021 .....256/D1
Liberty, Ga., U.S., county, 61,610 .....260/H8
Liberty, Ill., U.S., 519 .....266/B4
Liberty, Ind., U.S., 2,061 .....270/G6
Liberty, Kans., U.S., 95 .....276/G4
Liberty, Ky., U.S., 1,850 .....280/F3
Liberty, Maine, U.S., 927 .....286/C4
Liberty, Md., U.S., reservoir 288/G2
Liberty, Miss., U.S., 633 .....300/B4
Liberty, Mont., U.S., county, 2,158 .....306/E1
Liberty, Nebr., U.S., 86 .....308/H3
Liberty, N.Y., U.S., 3,975 .....320/M7
Liberty, N.C., U.S., 2,661 .....322/F3
Liberty, Okla., U.S., 184 .....330/G2
Liberty, (Allegheny County), Penn., U.S., 2,670 .....336/E7
Liberty, (Tioga County), Penn., U.S., 230 .....336/G4
Liberty, S.C., U.S., 3,009 .....340/B2
Liberty, Tenn., U.S., 367 .....344/K3
Liberty, Tex., U.S., 8,033 .....346/C5, P5
Liberty, Tex., U.S., county, 70,154 .....346/C6, P6
Liberty, Wash., U.S. 358/E2
Liberty, W. Va., U.S., 150 .....360/C3
Liberty Ctr., Ohio, U.S., 1,109 .....328/C3
Liberty Corner, N.J., U.S., 1,700 .....314/D2
Liberty Hill, Conn., U.S., 300 .....253/F3
Liberty Hill, S.C., U.S. 340/D2
Liberty Hill, Tex., U.S., 1,409 .....346/D1
Liberty Lake, Wash., U.S., 4,660 .....358/H2
Liberty Pole, Wisc., U.S., 125 .....364/C5
Libertytown, Md., U.S., 275 .....288/F2
Libertyville, Ala., U.S., 106 .....238/C4
Libertyville, Ill., U.S., 20,742 .....266/B5
Libertyville, Ind., U.S., 225 .....270/A5
Libertyville, Iowa, U.S., 325 .....274/K6
Libertyville, Mo., U.S., 70 .....302/F4
Libono, Leso. 161/B1
Library, (part of S. Park Township), Penn., U.S. 336/A5
Libreville, Gabon, capital, 419,596 .....155/A1
Libuse, La., U.S., 475 .....282/E4
Libya, nation 139
Libyan, Egy., desert 144/A2
Libyan, Egy., plateau 144/A1
Libyan, Lib., desert 145/D2
Libyan, Sudan, desert 145/B1
Lichfield, Eng., U.K. 60/C3
Lichfield, Eng., U.K., 28,666 .....68/D4
Lichinga, Moz. 161/B2
Licking, Ky., U.S., river 280/G2
Licking, Mo., U.S., 1,471 .....302/E4
Licking, Ohio, U.S., county, 145,491 .....328/F5
Lida, Bela. 82/B3
Lida, Nev., U.S. 310/B3
Lidderdale, Iowa, U.S., 186 .....274/E3
Lidgate, Eng., U.K. 70/E2
Lidgerwood, N. Dak., U.S., 738 .....326/H3
Liebenthal, Kans., U.S., 111 .....276/C3
Liechtenstein, nation 88
Liège, Belg., 185,131, (585,726, metro.) 85/D2
Liège, Belg., province 85/D2
Lieksa, Fin. 81/D2
Lienz, Aus. 91/C4
Liepāja, Lat., 95,427 .....82/A2
Lièvre, Que., Can., river 226/A5
Lifford, Ire. 78/C1
Lifton, Eng., U.K. 73/D3
Lifuka, Tonga, island 175/C3
Lighthouse Pt., Fla., U.S., 10,767 .....256/D5
Lightning Flat, Wyo., U.S. 366/D1
Light Oak, N.C., U.S., 779 .....322/C4
Lightwater, Eng., U.K., 6,432 .....70/C4
Lignite, N. Dak., U.S., 174 .....326/C1
Lignum, Va., U.S., 225 .....354/H4
Ligon, Ky., U.S., 150 .....280/H3
Ligonier, Ind., U.S., 4,357 .....270/E2
Ligonier, Penn., U.S., 1,695 .....336/C5
Liguria, It., region 95/B1
Ligurian, It., sea 95/B2
Ligurta, Ariz., U.S. 242/A5
Lihir, P.N.G., group 172/C2
Lihue, Hawaii, U.S., 5,674 .....262/A5, D2
Lihue Koloa Forest Reserve, Hawaii, U.S. 262/C1
Likasi, Congo, D.R., 299,118 .....155/C3
Likely, Calif., U.S., 100 .....246/E1
Likiep, Marsh. Is., island 173/B1
Lilbert, Tex., U.S., 60 .....346/P4
Lilbourn, Mo., U.S., 1,303 .....302/G5
Lilburn, Ga., U.S., 11,307 .....260/C4, J2
Lilesville, N.C., U.S., 459 .....322/F5
Lille, Den., strait 79/B3
Lille, Fr., 191,164, (1,000,900, metro.) 88/C1
Lille, Maine, U.S., 150 .....286/D1
Lillehammer, Nor. 80/C3
Lillian, Ala., U.S., 350 .....238/B5
Lillie, La., U.S., 139 .....282/D2
Lilliesville, Vt., U.S. 352/B3
Lillington, N.C., U.S., 2,915 .....322/H4
Lilliwaup, Wash., U.S., 125 .....358/B2
Lilly, Ga., U.S., 221 .....260/D7
Lilongwe, Mal., capital, 440,471, (1,000,000, metro.) 159/B2
Lily, Ky., U.S., 1,200 .....280/F3
Lily, S. Dak., U.S. 342/H2
Lily, Wisc., U.S., 80 .....364/E3
Lily Bay, Maine, U.S. 286/C2
Lilydale, Vic., Austl. .....170/Inset V
Lilydale, Minn., U.S., 552 .....298/F6
Lily Lake, Ill., U.S., 825 .....266/E2
Lima, Peru, capital, 345,898, (6,987,984, metro.) 185/B3
Lima, Peru, department 185/B3
Lima, Port., river 93/A2
Lima, Ill., U.S., 159 .....266/B3

Lima, Mont., U.S., 242 .....306/D5
Lima, N.Y., U.S., 2,459 .....320/F5
Lima, Ohio, U.S., 40,081, (155,084, metro.) 328/B4
Lima, Okla., U.S., 74 .....330/F2
Lima, Penn., U.S., 3,225 .....336/K7
Limassol, Cyp., 94,628 .....133/C3
Limavady, N. Ire., U.K., 10,764 .....65/D1
Limavady, N. Ire., U.K., unitary authority, 32,422 .....65/D2
Limaville, Ohio, U.S., 193 .....328/H4
Limbaži, Lat. 82/C2
Limbe, Came. 153/A3
Limbourg, Belg. 85/D1
Limburg, Belg., province 85/D1
Limburg, Neth., province 84/C3
Lime, Oreg., U.S. 334/J3
Lime Creek, Minn., U.S., 50 .....298/B7
Lime Lake, (Lime Lake-Machias), N.Y., U.S., 1,422 .....320/E6
Limerick, Ire., 54,058 .....78/B2
Limerick, Ire., county 78/B2
Limerick, Maine, U.S., 2,240 .....286/B5
Limerick County Borough, Ire., county 78/B2
Lime Ridge, Wisc., U.S., 169 .....364/C5
Lime Rock, Conn., U.S. 253/B2
Lime Sprs., Iowa, U.S., 496 .....274/K1
Limestone, Ala., U.S., county, 65,676 .....238/C1
Limestone, Ark., U.S., 50 .....244/B3
Limestone, Fla., U.S. 256/C4
Limestone, Ky., U.S., 275 .....280/G2
Limestone, Maine, U.S., 2,361 .....286/E2
Limestone, Mont., U.S. 306/G4
Limestone, N.Y., U.S., 411 .....320/D6
Limestone, Tenn., U.S., 550 .....344/R2
Limestone, Tex., U.S., county, 22,051 .....346/M4
Lime Vil., Alaska, U.S. 240/D2
Limfjorden, Den., channel 79/B2
Limington, Maine, U.S., 3,403 .....286/B5
Limmen, Gr., island 100/C3
Limoges, Fr., 137,502, (173,299, metro.) 88/C4
Limon, Colo., U.S., 2,071 .....250/G2
Limón, C.R., province 203/C3
Limours, Fr. .....88/Inset II
Limpopo, Bots., river 160/B2
Limpopo, Moz., river 161/B4
Limpopo, S. Afr., river 162/C1
Limpopo, Zimb., river 160/B3
Linares, Chile 190/B5
Linares, Mex., 53,681, (69,205, metro.) 200/E3
Linares, Sp., 57,578 .....94/E3
Linby, Iowa, U.S. 274/K5
Linch, Wyo., U.S., 100 .....366/C2
Linchester, Md., U.S. 288/L5
Linchmere, Eng., U.K. 70/C4
Lincoln, Eng., U.K. 60/D3
Lincoln, Eng., U.K., 80,281, (97,996, metro.) 66/G6
Lincoln, Eng., U.K., 80,281, (97,996, metro.) 68/F3
Lincoln, Ala., U.S., 4,577 .....238/C2
Lincoln, Ark., U.S., 1,752 .....244/A2
Lincoln, Ark., U.S., county, 14,492 .....244/D4
Lincoln, Calif., U.S., 11,205 .....246/D4, L4
Lincoln, Colo., U.S., county, 6,087 .....250/G3
Lincoln, Del., U.S., 950 .....255/C5
Lincoln, Ga., U.S., county, 8,348 .....260/F4
Lincoln, Ida., U.S., 2,800 .....264/F6
Lincoln, Ida., U.S., county, 4,044 .....264/C6
Lincoln, Ill., U.S., 15,369 .....266/D3
Lincoln, Iowa, U.S., 182 .....274/J3
Lincoln, Kans., U.S., 1,349 .....276/D2
Lincoln, Kans., U.S., county, 3,578 .....276/D2
Lincoln, Ky., U.S., county, 23,361 .....280/F3
Lincoln, La., U.S., parish, 42,509 .....282/D1
Lincoln, Maine, U.S., 46 .....286/D3
Lincoln, Maine, U.S., county, 33,616 .....286/C4
Lincoln, Mass., U.S., 8,056 .....292/B7, J3
Lincoln, Mich., U.S., 364 .....294/F5
Lincoln, Minn., U.S., 40 .....298/A6
Lincoln, Minn., U.S., county, 6,429 .....298/A6
Lincoln, Miss., U.S., county, 33,166 .....300/B4
Lincoln, Mo., U.S., 1,026 .....302/C3
Lincoln, Mo., U.S., county, 38,944 .....302/E2
Lincoln, Mont., U.S., 1,100 .....306/D3
Lincoln, Mont., U.S., county, 18,837 .....306/A1
Lincoln, Nebr., U.S., county, 34,632 .....308/D3
Lincoln, Nebr., U.S., state capital, 225,581, (250,291, metro.) 308/H3
Lincoln, Nev., U.S., county, 4,165 .....310/C3
Lincoln, N.H., U.S., 1,271 .....312/C3
Lincoln, N. Mex., U.S., 150 .....317/E4
Lincoln, N. Mex., U.S., county, 19,411 .....317/E4
Lincoln, N.C., U.S., county, 63,780 .....322/C3
Lincoln, N. Dak., U.S., 1,730 .....326/E3
Lincoln, Okla., U.S., county, 32,080 .....330/F2
Lincoln, Penn., U.S., 1,218 .....336/B5
Lincoln, S. Dak., U.S., county, 24,131 .....342/J4
Lincoln, Tenn., U.S., county, 31,340 .....344/H4
Lincoln, Tex., U.S., 60 .....346/M5
Lincoln, Vt., U.S., 1,214 .....352/B2
Lincoln, Wash., U.S. 358/G2
Lincoln, W. Va., U.S., county, 22,108 .....360/B4
Lincoln, Wisc., U.S., county, 29,641 .....364/D3
Lincoln, Wyo., U.S., county, 14,573 .....366/A2
Lincoln Beach, Oreg., U.S., 2,078 .....334/B3
Lincoln Birthplace Natl. Hist. Site, Ky., U.S. 280/E3
Lincoln Boyhood Natl. Mem., Ind., U.S. 270/D6
Lincoln Ctr., Maine, U.S., 275 .....286/D3
Lincoln City, Ind., U.S., 150 .....270/B8
Lincoln City, Oreg., U.S., 7,437 .....334/B3
Lincoln Hts., Ohio, U.S., 4,113 .....328/B9
Lincoln Home Natl. Historic Site, Ill., U.S. 266/D4
Lincolnia, Va., U.S., 15,788 .....355/M4
Lincoln Natl. For., N. Mex., U.S. 317/E4, E5
Lincoln Park, Colo., U.S., 3,904 .....250/E3
Lincoln Park, Mich., U.S., 40,008 .....294/B7, F6
Lincoln Park, N.J., U.S., 10,930 .....314/A2
Lincoln Park, Tex., U.S., 517 .....346/B9
Lincolnshire, Eng., U.K., unitary authority, 646,646 .....66/H6
Lincolnshire, Eng., U.K., unitary authority, 646,646 .....68/G3
Lincolnshire, Eng., U.K. 70/D1
Lincolnshire, Ill., U.S., 6,108 .....266/B5
Lincolnshire, Ky., U.S., 154 .....280/B2
Lincolnshire Wolds, Eng., U.K., hills 66/H6
Lincolnshire Wolds, Eng., U.K., hills 68/G3
Lincolnton, Ga., U.S., 1,595 .....260/G4
Lincolnton, N.C., U.S., 9,965 .....322/C4
Lincoln Vil., Calif., U.S., 4,216 .....246/L1
Lincoln Vil., Ohio, U.S., 9,482 .....328/D9
Lincolnville, Kans., U.S., 225 .....276/F3
Lincolnville, Maine, U.S., 2,042 .....286/D4
Lincolnville, S.C., U.S., 904 .....340/D3
Lincolnville Ctr., Maine, U.S., 325 .....286/D4
Lincolnwood, Ill., U.S., 12,359 .....266/B5
Lincroft, N.J., U.S., 6,255 .....314/E3
Lind, Wash., U.S., 582 .....358/G3
Linda, Calif., U.S., 13,474 .....246/D4
Lindale, Ga., U.S., 4,088 .....260/A3

Lindale, Tex., U.S., 2,954 .....346/N3
Lindbergh, Alta., Can. 212/E4
Linden, N.S., Can. 221/D2
Linden, Guy. 183/B3
Linden, Ala., U.S., 2,424 .....238/B3
Linden, Ariz., U.S., 60 .....242/E3
Linden, Calif., U.S., 1,103 .....246/D4
Linden, Ind., U.S., 700 .....270/C4
Linden, Iowa, U.S., 226 .....274/F4
Linden, Mich., U.S., 2,861 .....294/F7
Linden, N.J., U.S., 39,394 .....314/B3, E2
Linden, N.C., U.S., 127 .....322/H4
Linden, Tenn., U.S., 1,015 .....344/F3
Linden, Tex., U.S., 2,256 .....346/P3
Linden, Wisc., U.S., 615 .....364/C6
Lindenhurst, Ill., U.S., 12,539 .....266/B4
Lindenhurst, N.Y., U.S., 27,819 .....320/D2
Lindenwold, N.J., U.S., 17,414 .....314/B4, C4
Lindenwood, Ill., U.S., 275 .....266/C1
Lindford, Eng., U.K. 70/C4
Lindford, Minn., U.S. 298/D2
Lindi, Tan. 152/C2
Lindi, Tan., region 152/C2
Lindley, N.Y., U.S., 225 .....320/G6
Lindon, Colo., U.S. 250/G2
Lindon, Utah, U.S., 8,363 .....350/C3
Lindrith, N. Mex., U.S., 125 .....317/C1
Lindsay, N.B., Can. 221/F2
Lindsay, Ont., Can., 17,757 .....223/C3
Lindsay, Calif., U.S., 10,297 .....246/F6
Lindsay, La., U.S. 282/G5
Lindsay, Mont., U.S. 306/L2
Lindsay, Nebr., U.S., 276 .....308/G2
Lindsay, Okla., U.S., 2,889 .....330/E3
Lindsay, Tex., U.S., 788 .....346/L2
Lindsborg, Kans., U.S., 3,321 .....276/E3
Lindsey, Ohio, U.S., 504 .....328/D3
Lindseyville, Ky., U.S., 175 .....280/D3
Lindside, W. Va., U.S., 275 .....360/E6
Lindstrom, Minn., U.S., 3,015 .....298/E5
Lindy, Nebr., U.S. 308/G1
Line, Kiri., islands 175/D1
Linesville, Penn., U.S., 1,155 .....336/A2
Lineville, Ala., U.S., 2,401 .....238/D2
Lineville, Iowa, U.S., 273 .....274/G6
Lingague, Eng., U.K. 66/A5
Lingayen, Phil., gulf 120/B2
Lingfield, Eng., U.K., 2,691 .....70/E4
Lingga, Indon., island 122/B2
Lingle, Wyo., U.S., 510 .....366/G2
Lingo, N. Mex., U.S. 317/G4
Lingshi, Bhu. 126/A2
Linguere, Sen. 148/B2
Linketter, P.E.I., Can., 332 .....224/B2
Linköping, Swe., 134,039 .....80/C3
Linlithgow, Scot., U.K., 13,370 .....62/I7
Linn, Iowa, U.S., county, 191,701 .....274/L3
Linn, Kans., U.S., 425 .....276/E2
Linn, Kans., U.S., county, 9,570 .....276/H3
Linn, Mo., U.S., 1,354 .....302/E3
Linn, Mo., U.S., county, 13,754 .....302/C2
Linn, Oreg., U.S., county, 103,069 .....334/D3
Linn, Tex., U.S., 958 .....346/K9
Linn, W. Va., U.S., 125 .....360/E2
Linn Creek, Mo., U.S., 280 .....302/D3
Linndale, Ohio, U.S., 117 .....328/G9
Linneus, Maine, U.S., 892 .....286/E2
Linneus, Mo., U.S., 369 .....302/C2
Linn Grove, Iowa, U.S., 211 .....274/D2
Linnhe, Scot., U.K., lake 60/B2
Linnhe, Scot., U.K., lake 62/F5
Linntown, Penn., U.S., 1,542 .....336/H4
Lino Lakes, Minn., U.S., 16,791 .....298/F5
Linslade, Eng., U.K. 70/C3
Linthicum, Md., U.S., 7,539 .....288/H3
Linthicum Hts., Md., U.S. 288/H3
Linton, Eng., U.K., 3,959 .....68/H5
Linton, Eng., U.K., 3,959 .....70/E2
Linton, Ga., U.S., 150 .....260/E5
Linton, Ind., U.S., 5,774 .....270/C6
Linton, Ky., U.S. 280/C4
Linton, N. Dak., U.S., 1,321 .....326/E3
Linvanti, Bots., river 160/A1
Linville, La., U.S., 80 .....282/E1
Linville, N.C., U.S., 300 .....322/B3
Linville, Va., U.S., 175 .....354/F3
Linwood, N.S., Can. 221/F2
Linwood, Ind., U.S., 700 .....270/E4
Linwood, Kans., U.S., 374 .....276/G2
Linwood, Ky., U.S., 90 .....280/E3
Linwood, Mich., U.S., 1,200 .....294/F6
Linwood, Nebr., U.S., 118 .....308/H2
Linwood, N.J., U.S., 7,172 .....314/C5
Linwood, Penn., U.S., 3,374 .....336/K7, L6
Linz, Aus., 186,266 .....91/D3
Lion, Fr., gulf 88/D5
Lionel, Scot., U.K. 62/D2
Lionel Town, Jam. 206/B3
Lions Head, Ont., Can., 500 .....223/D3
Lionville, (Lionville-Marchwood), Penn., U.S., 6,298 .....336/K5
Lipa, Phil., 218,447 .....120/B3
Lipan, Tex., U.S., 425 .....346/K3
Lipari, It., islands 95/C3
Lipetsk, Russ., 518,926 .....104/C4
Liphook, Eng., U.K., 5,374 .....70/C4
Lippstadt, Ger. 86/B3
Lipscomb, Ala., U.S., 2,458 .....238/D1
Lipscomb, Tex., U.S., 44 .....346/G8
Lipscomb, Tex., U.S., county, 3,057 .....346/G8
Lipton, Sask., Can., 331 .....227/G10
Liptovský Mikuláš, Slvk. 92/B2
Liquica, E. Timor 122/D4
Liquica, E. Timor, province 122/B1
Lira, Ug., 89,871 .....157/C2
Lisala, Congo, D.R. 155/B1
L'Isalo, Madag., massif 163/B3
Lisbellaw, N. Ire., U.K., 632 .....65/B3
Lisbon, Port., capital, 564,657, (1,947,261, metro.) 93/A3
Lisbon, Port., district 93/A3
Lisbon, Ill., U.S., 248 .....266/E2
Lisbon, Iowa, U.S., 1,898 .....274/M4
Lisbon, Maine, U.S., 9,077 .....286/B4
Lisbon, N.H., U.S., 1,587 .....312/C3
Lisbon, N.Y., U.S., 400 .....320/L1
Lisbon, N. Dak., U.S., 2,292 .....326/H3
Lisbon, Ohio, U.S., 2,788 .....328/J4
Lisbon Falls, Maine, U.S., 4,420 .....286/B5
Lisburn, N. Ire., U.K. 65/E2
Lisburn, N. Ire., U.K., unitary authority, 108,694 .....65/E2
Lisburne, Alaska, U.S., cape 240/C1
Lisco, Nebr., U.S. 308/B2
Liscomb, Iowa, U.S., 272 .....274/H3
Liskeard, Eng., U.K., 7,044 .....73/D4
Lisle, Ill., U.S., 21,182 .....266/B6
Lisle, N.Y., U.S., 302 .....320/J6

Lislea, N. Ire., U.K. 65/E3
L'Isle-Adam, Fr. . . . . .88/Inset II
L'Isle-Verte, Que., Can., 1,519 . . . . .226/G3
Lisman, Ala., U.S., 653 . . . . .238/A3
Lisman, Ky., U.S., 100 . . . . .280/C3
Lismore, N.S.W., Austl. 170/E2
Lismore, Scot., U.K., island 62/E6
Lismore, Minn., U.S., 238 . . . . .298/B7
Lisnaskea, N. Ire., U.K., 2,457 . . . . .65/C3
Liss, Eng., U.K., 6,148 . . . . .70/C4
Listowel, Ont., Can., 5,905 . . . . .223/E4
Litani, Fr. Gui., river 183/A2
Litani, Leb., river 134/A2
Litani, Sur., river 183/B3
Litcham, Eng., U.K. 70/F1
Litchfield, Eng., U.K. 70/B4
Litchfield, Conn., U.S., 8,316 . . . . .253/C3
Litchfield, Conn., U.S., county, 182,193 . . . .253/C2
Litchfield, Ill., U.S., 6,815 . . . . .266/B2, D4
Litchfield, Maine, U.S., 3,110 . . . . .286/C4
Litchfield, Mich., U.S., 1,458 . . . . .294/E7
Litchfield, Minn., U.S., 6,562 . . . . .298/C5
Litchfield, Nebr., U.S., 280 . . . . .308/E2
Litchfield, N.H., U.S., 7,360 . . . . .312/D6
Litchfield, Ohio, U.S., 650 . . . . .328/F3
Litchfield Park, Ariz., U.S., 3,810 . . . . . . .242/C4
Litchville, N. Dak., U.S., 191 . . . . .326/G3
Literberry, Ill., U.S., 125 . . . . .266/C4
Litherland, Eng., U.K., 20,905 . . . . .66/B6
Lithia, Mass., U.S., 60 . . . . .292/C3
Lithia Sprs., Ga., U.S., 2,072 . . . . . . .260/B4, G2
Lithium, Mo., U.S. 302/G4
Lithonia, Ga., U.S., 2,187 . . . . .260/C4, K3
Lithopolis, Ohio, U.S., 600 . . . . .328/E6, E10
Lithuania, nation .80
Lithuania, nation 193/D2
Lititz, Penn., U.S., 9,029 . . . . .336/J5
Litlington, Eng., U.K. 70/D2
Littig, Tex., U.S. 346/E2
Little, Eng., U.K. 68/G5
Little, La., U.S., river 282/D2
Little, Okla., U.S., 125 . . . . .330/F2
Little Alföld, Hun., plain 91/A2
Little America, Wyo., U.S., 56 . . . . .366/B3
Little Andaman, India, island 128/F6
Little Barningham, Eng., U.K. 70/G1
Little Bay, Nfld., Can. 218/B5
Little Bighorn, Wyo., U.S., river 366/C1
Little Bighorn Battlefield N.M., Mont., U.S. . .306/J4
Little Blue, Nebr., U.S., river 308/G3
Little Boars Head, N.H., U.S. 312/E6
Littleborough, Eng., U.K., 13,638 . . . . .66/D5
Littleborough, Eng., U.K., 13,638 . . . . .68/C4
Little Bras d'Or, N.S., Can. 221/G1
Little Canada, Minn., U.S., 9,771 . . . . .298/F5
Little Chute, Wisc., U.S., 10,476 . . . . .364/E4
Little City, Okla., U.S., 100 . . . . .330/F3
Little Colorado, Ariz., U.S., river 242/D2
Little Common, Eng., U.K. 70/E5
Little Compton, Eng., U.K. 68/D6
Little Compton, R.I., U.S., 3,593 . . . . .339/E5
Little Cottonwood Creek Valley, Utah, U.S., 7,221 .350/C2
Little Creek, Del., U.S., 195 . . . . .255/C4
Little Creek, La., U.S., 40 . . . . .282/C4
Little Current, Ont., Can., 1,564 . . . . .223/D2
Little Downham, Eng., U.K., 1,728 . . . . .68/H5
Little Downham, Eng., U.K., 1,728 . . . . .70/E2
Little Eagle, S. Dak., U.S., 370 . . . . .342/E2
Little Elm, Tex., U.S., 3,646 . . . . .346/B8
Little Falls, Minn., U.S., 7,719 . . . . .298/C5
Little Falls, N.J., U.S., 10,855 . . . . . . .314/B2, G2
Little Falls, N.Y., U.S., 5,188 . . . . .320/M4
Little Ferry, N.J., U.S., 10,800 . . . . .314/B2
Littlefield, Ariz., U.S. 242/B1
Littlefield, Tex., U.S., 6,507 . . . . .346/F2
Little Flock, Ark., U.S., 2,585 . . . . .244/A1
Littlefork, Minn., U.S., 680 . . . . .298/D2
Little Fork, Minn., U.S., river 298/D2
Little Fort, Br. Col., Can. 214/M5
Little Fransham, Eng., U.K. 70/F1
Little Gaddesden, Eng., U.K. 70/C3
Little Grand Rapids, Man., Can. 215/D3
Littlehampton, Eng., U.K., 50,408 . . . . .70/C5
Little Heaven, Del., U.S., 1,400 . . . . .255/C4
Little Inagua, Bah., island 204/C3
Little Inagua, Bah., island 207/C4
Little Kanawha, W. Va., U.S., river 328/G7
Little Lake, Mich., U.S., 225 . . . . .294/B3
Little Marais, Minn., U.S. 298/F3
Little Meadows, Penn., U.S., 290 . . . . .336/J2
Little Milton, Eng., U.K. 70/B3
Little Missouri, Ark., U.S., river 244/B4
Little Missouri, N. Dak., U.S., river 326/B3
Little Missouri, S. Dak., U.S., river 342/B2
Little Missouri Natl. Grassland,
 N. Dak., U.S. 326/B1, B2, B3
Little Mtn., S.C., U.S., 255 . . . . .340/C2
Littleport, Eng., U.K., 5,780 . . . . .68/H5
Littleport, Eng., U.K., 5,780 . . . . .70/E2
Littleport, Iowa, U.S. 274/M2
Little Powder, Wyo., U.S., river 366/D1
Little Ridge, N.B., Can. 217/B3
Little River, Ark., U.S., county, 13,628 . . . . .244/A4
Little River, Calif., U.S., 70 . . . . .246/B3
Little River, Kans., U.S., 536 . . . . .276/D3
Little River, S.C., U.S., 7,027 . . . . .340/F3
Little River-Academy, Tex., U.S., 1,645 . . . .346/L5
Little River Canyon Natl. Pres., Ala., U.S. . . .238/D1
Little River N.W.R., Okla., U.S. 330/H4
Little Rock, Ark., U.S., state capital, 183,133,
 (583,845, metro.) 244/C3
Littlerock, Calif., U.S., 1,402 . . . . .246/H8
Little Rock, Iowa, U.S., 489 . . . . .274/C1
Little Rock, Ky., U.S., 100 . . . . .280/C2
Little Rock (Beltrami County), Minn., U.S., 1,055 .298/B3
Little Rock, (Morrison County), Minn., U.S., 50 .298/C3
Little Rock, Miss., U.S., 150 . . . . .300/C3
Little Rock, Tex., U.S., 325 . . . . .340/E2
Littlerock, Wash., U.S., 250 . . . . .358/B3
Little Rock Central H.S. N.H.S., Ark., U.S. . . .244/C3
Little Round Lake, Wisc., U.S., 948 . . . . . . .364/B3
Little Sable, Mich., U.S., point 294/C6
Little Sahara Rec. Area, Utah, U.S. 350/B4
Little St. Bernard, Fr., pass 88/D4
Little Salmon, Yukon, Can., lake 228/C5
Little Sauk, Minn., U.S., 125 . . . . .298/C5
Little Scarcies, S.L., river 149/A1
Little Seldom, (Seldom-Little Seldom), Nfld., Can. 218/D4
Little Silver, N.J., U.S., 6,170 . . . . .314/E3
Little Sioux, Iowa, U.S., 217 . . . . .274/B4
Little Sioux, Iowa, U.S., river 274/D2
Little Smoky, Alta., Can., river 212/B4
Little Smoky, Alta., Can. 212/A4
Little Snake, Colo., U.S., river 250/B1
Little Snake, Wyo., U.S., river 366/C3
Little Staughton, Eng., U.K. 70/D2
Little Steeping, Eng., U.K. 68/H3
Little Stukeley, Eng., U.K. 70/D2
Little Suamico, Wisc., U.S., 225 . . . . .364/E4
Littleton, Colo., U.S., 40,340 . . . . .250/A3, F2

Littleton, Ill., U.S., 197 . . . . .266/C3
Littleton, Maine, U.S., 955 . . . . .286/E2
Littleton, Mass., U.S., 8,184 . . . . .292/H2
Littleton, N.H., U.S., 5,845 . . . . .312/C3
Littleton, N.C., U.S., 692 . . . . .322/K2
Littleton, Va., U.S. 354/J7
Littleton, W. Va., U.S., 207 . . . . .360/E1, K6
Littleton Common, Mass., U.S., 2,816 . . . . .292/J2
Little Tucson, Ariz., U.S. 242/D6
Little Valley, Calif., U.S. 246/D2
Little Valley, N.Y., U.S., 1,130 . . . . .320/D6
Little Valley, N.Y., U.S., county, 17,044 . . . .320/D6
Littleville, Ala., U.S., 978 . . . . .238/B1
Little Waltham, Eng., U.K. 70/E3
Little Wappinger, Conn., U.S., creek 253/A1
Little White, S. Dak., U.S., river 342/F4
Little York, Ill., U.S., 269 . . . . .266/C2
Little York, Ind., U.S., 185 . . . . .270/E7
Little York, N.J., U.S., 300 . . . . .314/C2
Little Zab, Iraq, river 130/B1
Littoral, Came., province 153/A3
Liuzhou, China 119/D3
Lively, Va., U.S., 200 . . . . .354/K5
Live Oak, (Santa Cruz County), Calif., U.S.,
 16,628 . . . . .246/K4
Live Oak, (Sutter County), Calif., U.S., 6,229 .246/D3
Live Oak, Fla., U.S., 6,480 . . . . .256/F1
Live Oak, Tex., U.S., 9,156 . . . . .346/A2, K6
Live Oak, Tex., U.S., county, 12,309 . . . . . .346/K7
Livermore, Calif., U.S., 73,345 . . . . .246/K4
Livermore, Colo., U.S. 250/F1
Livermore, Iowa, U.S., 431 . . . . .274/F2
Livermore, Ky., U.S., 1,482 . . . . .280/C3
Livermore, Maine, U.S., 2,106 . . . . .286/B4
Livermore, Tex., U.S., mountain 346/D5
Livermore Falls, Maine, U.S., 3,227 . . . . . .286/B4
Livermore Falls, N.H., U.S., 350 . . . . .312/C4
Liverpool, N.S.W., Austl. . . . . .170/Inset IV
Liverpool, N.S., Can., 2,888 . . . . .221/C3
Liverpool, Eng., U.K. 60/C3
Liverpool, Eng., U.K., 439,476,
 (1,362,034, metro.) 66/C6
Liverpool, Eng., U.K., 439,476,
 (1,362,034, metro.) 68/B3
Liverpool, Eng., U.K., unitary authority, 439,476 .66/C6
Liverpool, Eng., U.K., unitary authority, 439,476 .60/B3
Liverpool, Wales, U.K., bay 64/E1
Liverpool, Eng., U.K., bay 60/B3
Liverpool, Ill., U.S., 119 . . . . .266/C3
Liverpool, N.Y., U.S., 2,505 . . . . .320/J4
Liverpool, Penn., U.S., 876 . . . . .336/H4
Liverpool, Tex., U.S., 404 . . . . .346/N6
Livia, Ky., U.S., 125 . . . . .280/C3
Livingston, Scot., U.K., 50,826 . . . . .62/J7
Livingston, Ala., U.S., 3,297 . . . . .238/A3
Livingston, Calif., U.S., 10,473 . . . . .246/E5
Livingston, Ill., U.S., 825 . . . . .266/B3, D5
Livingston, Ill., U.S., county, 39,678 . . . . . .266/E3
Livingston, Ky., U.S., 228 . . . . .280/F3
Livingston, Ky., U.S., county, 9,804 . . . . . .280/D5
Livingston, La., U.S., 1,342 . . . . .282/H5
Livingston, La., U.S., parish, 91,814 . . . . . .282/D5
Livingston, Mich., U.S., county, 156,951 . . .294/F7
Livingston, Mo., U.S., county, 14,558 . . . . .302/C2
Livingston, Mont., U.S., 6,851 . . . . .306/F4
Livingston, N.J., U.S., 27,391 . . . . . . .314/A2, G2
Livingston, N.Y., U.S., county, 64,328 . . . . .320/F5
Livingston, S.C., U.S., 148 . . . . .340/C3
Livingston, Tenn., U.S., 3,498 . . . . .344/L2
Livingston, Tex., U.S., 5,433 . . . . .346/P5
Livingston, Tex., U.S., lake 346/N5
Livingston, Wisc., U.S., 597 . . . . .364/C6
Livingstone, Zam. 159/C4
Livingston Manor, N.Y., U.S., 1,355 . . . . . .320/M7
Livno, Bos.-Her. 98/B2
Livona, N. Dak., U.S. 326/E3
Livonia, Ind., U.S., 112 . . . . .270/D7
Livonia, La., U.S., 1,339 . . . . .282/F5
Livonia, Mich., U.S., 100,545 . . . . . . .294/A7, F7
Livonia, Mo., U.S., 114 . . . . .302/D1
Livonia, N.Y., U.S., 1,373 . . . . .320/F5
Livorno, It. 95/C3
Lizard, Eng., U.K. 73/B5
Lizard, Eng., U.K., point 73/B5
Lizella, Ga., U.S., 600 . . . . .260/D6
Lizemores, W. Va., U.S., 200 . . . . .360/D4
Lizton, Ind., U.S., 352 . . . . .270/C5
Ljubljana, Slove., capital, 264,269,
 (331,235, metro.) 98/B2
Ljusnaälven, Swe. 80/B2
Llallagua, Bol. .186/A3
Llanaelhaearn, Wales, U.K. 64/C2
Llanarmon Dyffryn Ceiriog, Wales, U.K. 64/E2
Llanarth, Wales, U.K. 64/C3
Llanasa, Wales, U.K. 64/E1
Llanbadarn Fynydd, Wales, U.K. 64/E3
Llanbedr, Wales, U.K. 64/C2
Llanbedr, Wales, U.K. 64/C2
Llanbedrog, Wales, U.K. 64/C2
Llanberis, Wales, U.K., 1,859 . . . . .64/C1
Llanbister, Wales, U.K. 64/E3
Llanbrynmair, Wales, U.K. 64/D2
Llanderfel, Wales, U.K. 64/D2
Llanddewi Brefi, Wales, U.K. 64/D3
Llandeilo, Wales, U.K., 1,666 . . . . .64/D4
Llandeilo Graban, Wales, U.K. 64/E3
Llandewi, Wales, U.K. 64/E3
Llandinabo, Eng., U.K. 68/B6
Llandissilio, Wales, U.K. 64/B4
Llandogo, Wales, U.K. 64/F4
Llandovery, Wales, U.K., 2,037 . . . . .64/D4
Llandre, Wales, U.K. 64/C3
Llandrillo, Wales, U.K. 64/E2
Llandrindod Wells, Wales, U.K. 60/B3
Llandrindod Wells, Wales, U.K., 4,362 . . . . .64/D3
Llandudno, Wales, U.K., 14,576 . . . . .64/D1
Llandwrog, Wales, U.K. 64/C1
Llandybie, Wales, U.K., 2,833 . . . . .64/C4
Llandysul, Wales, U.K. 64/C3
Llanegwad, Wales, U.K. 64/C4
Llanelidan, Wales, U.K. 64/E2
Llanelli, Wales, U.K., 44,953 . . . . .64/C4
Llanelwedd, Wales, U.K. 64/E3
Llanerch, Penn., U.S. 336/L7
Llanerchymedd, Wales, U.K. 64/C1
Llanfachraeth, Wales, U.K. 64/C1
Llanfaelog, Wales, U.K. 64/C1
Llanfair Caereinion, Wales, U.K. 64/E2
Llanfairfechan, Wales, U.K., 3,338 . . . . .64/D1
Llanfair Talhaiarn, Wales, U.K. 64/D1
Llanfarian, Wales, U.K. 64/C3
Llanfihangel Nant Bran, Wales, U.K. 64/D3
Llanfrothen, Wales, U.K. 64/E4
Llanfrynach, Wales, U.K. 64/E4
Llanfyllin, Wales, U.K. 64/E2
Llangadfan, Wales, U.K. 64/E2
Llangadog, Wales, U.K. 64/D4
Llangefni, Wales, U.K., 4,643 . . . . .64/C1
Llangeinor, Wales, U.K. 64/D1
Llangernyw, Wales, U.K. 64/D1
Llanglydwen, Wales, U.K. 64/B4
Llangollen, Wales, U.K., 3,267 . . . . .64/E2
Llangollen Estates, Del., U.S., 5,600 . . . . . .255/B2

Llangorse, Wales, U.K. 64/E4
Llangranog, Wales, U.K. 64/C3
Llangurig, Wales, U.K. 64/D3
Llangybi, Wales, U.K. 64/F4
Llangynidr, Wales, U.K. 64/E4
Llangynog, Wales, U.K. 64/E2
Llanharan, Wales, U.K., 5,107 . . . . .64/E4
Llanidloes, Wales, U.K., 2,616 . . . . .64/D3
Llanmaes, Wales, U.K. 64/E4
Llano, Tex., U.S., 3,325 . . . . .346/K5
Llano, Tex., U.S., county, 17,044 . . . . .346/K5
Llano Estacado, N. Mex., U.S., plains 317/G4
Llanos, Col., prairie 184/C3
Llanquihue, Chile, lake 190/B6
Llanrhaeadr, Wales, U.K. 64/E1
Llanrhaeadr-ym-Mochnant, Wales, U.K. 64/E2
Llanrhidian, Wales, U.K. 64/C4
Llanrhystud, Wales, U.K. 64/C3
Llanrug, Wales, U.K., 2,092 . . . . .64/C1
Llanrwst, Wales, U.K., 3,012 . . . . .64/D1
Llansannan, Wales, U.K. 64/D1
Llansantffraid, Wales, U.K. 64/E2
Llansawel, Wales, U.K. 64/C4
Llanstephan, Wales, U.K. 64/C4
Llanthony, Wales, U.K. 64/E4
Llantwit Major, Wales, U.K., 12,909 . . . . . .64/E5
Llanuwchllyn, Wales, U.K. 64/D2
Llanvetherine, Wales, U.K. 64/F4
Llanwddyn, Wales, U.K. 64/E2
Llanwnda, Wales, U.K. 64/C1
Llanwrda, Wales, U.K. 64/D4
Llanwrtyd Wells, Wales, U.K. 64/D3
Llanybydder, Wales, U.K. 64/C3
Llanycefn, Wales, U.K. 64/B4
Llanymawddwy, Wales, U.K. 64/D2
Llanystumdwy, Wales, U.K. 64/C2
Llaves, N. Mex., U.S., 175 . . . . .317/D1
Lleyn, Wales, U.K., peninsula 60/B3
Lloc, Wales, U.K. 64/E1
Llorts, And. 93/B1
Llowes, Wales, U.K. 64/E3
Lloyd, Sask., Can., lake 227/B3
Lloyd, Conn., U.S., point 253/B5
Lloyd, Fla., U.S., 200 . . . . .256/F1
Lloyd, Mont., U.S., 60 . . . . .306/G1
Lloyd Harbor, N.Y., U.S., 3,675 . . . . .320/C2
Lloydminster, Alta., Can., 13,148 . . . . .212/E4
Lloydminster, Sask., Can., 7,840 . . . . .227/A7
Lloyds, Nfld., Can., river 218/C5
Llullaillaco, Arg., volcano 191/B1
Llullaillaco, Chile, volcano 190/C2
Llwyngwril, Wales, U.K. 64/C2
Llynclys, Eng., U.K. 68/A4
Llyswen, Wales, U.K. 64/E3
Llysworney, Wales, U.K. 64/E4
Lo, Viet., river .123/A1
Loa, Chile, river 190/C2
Loa, Utah, U.S., 525 . . . . .350/C5
Loachapoka, Ala., U.S., 165 . . . . .238/D3
Loami, Ill., U.S., 804 . . . . .266/D4
Loanhead, Scot., U.K., 6,384 . . . . .62/K7
Lobamba, Swaz. 161/B2
Lobatse, Bots., 26,052 . . . . .160/B3
Lobaye, C.A.R., river 154/A2
Lobeco, S.C., U.S., 125 . . . . .340/D4
Lobelville, Tenn., U.S., 915 . . . . .344/F3
Lobethal, S.A., Austl. . . . . .170/Inset II
Lobito, Ang., 150,000 . . . . .159/B4
Lobo, Tex., U.S. 346/D5
Locarno, Switz. .90/C2
Locate, Mont., U.S. 306/L3
Lochan Fada, Scot., U.K., lake 62/F3
Lochawe, Scot., U.K. 62/F6
Lochbuie, Scot., U.K. 62/F6
Lochbuie, Colo., U.S., 2,049 . . . . .250/A2, F1
Lochcarron, Scot., U.K. 62/F4
Lochearn, Md., U.S., 25,269 . . . . .288/H2
Lochearnhead, Scot., U.K. 62/H6
Lochgelly, Scot., U.K., 6,749 . . . . .62/K6
Lochgilphead, Scot., U.K. 62/F6
Lochgoilhead, Scot., U.K. 62/G6
Lochiel, Ariz., U.S. 242/E6
Lochindorb, Scot., U.K., lake 62/J4
Lochinver, Scot., U.K. 62/F2
Lochloosa, Fla., U.S., lake 256/G2
Loch Lynn Hts., Md., U.S., 469 . . . . .288/A4
Loch na Keal Isle of Mull N.P., Scot., U.K. . .62/D6
Lochsa, Ida., U.S., river 264/B3
Lochside, Scot., U.K. 62/M5
Lochton, Scot., U.K. 62/M4
Lochy, Scot., U.K., lake 62/G5
Lockbourne, Ohio, U.S., 280 . . . . .328/E6, E10
Locke, N.Y., U.S., 550 . . . . .320/J5
Lockeford, Calif., U.S., 3,179 . . . . .246/D4, L6
Locke Mills, Maine, U.S., 150 . . . . .286/B4
Lockeport, N.S., Can., 701 . . . . .221/B4
Lockerbie, Scot., U.K., 4,009 . . . . .62/K8
Lockesburg, Ark., U.S., 711 . . . . .244/A4
Lockett, Tex., U.S., 100 . . . . .346/J1
Lockettville, Tex., U.S. 346/F2
Lockhart, Ala., U.S., 548 . . . . .238/C4
Lockhart, Calif., U.S., 50 . . . . .246/H7
Lockhart, La., U.S. 282/D1
Lockhart, Minn., U.S. 298/A3
Lockhart, S.C., U.S. 340/C2
Lockhart, Tex., U.S., 11,615 . . . . .346/L6
Lock Haven, Penn., U.S., 9,149 . . . . .336/G3
Lockington, Ohio, U.S., 208 . . . . .328/B5
Lockmere, N.H., U.S., 600 . . . . .312/C5
Lockney, Tex., U.S., 2,056 . . . . .346/G1
Lockport, Man., Can. 215/C4
Lockport, Ill., U.S., 15,191 . . . . .266/B6
Lockport, La., U.S., 2,624 . . . . .282/H7
Lockport, N.Y., U.S., 22,279 . . . . .320/D4
Lockridge, Iowa, U.S., 275 . . . . .274/L6
Lock Sprs., Mo., U.S., 69 . . . . .302/C2
Locks Vil., Mass., U.S., 225 . . . . .292/G2
Lockton, Eng., U.K. 66/G4
Locktown, N.J., U.S., 400 . . . . .314/D3
Lockwood, Calif., U.S., 150 . . . . .246/D7
Lockwood, Mo., U.S., 989 . . . . .302/C4
Lockwood, Mont., U.S., 4,306 . . . . .306/H4
Loco, Okla., U.S., 111 . . . . .330/E3
Loco Hills, N. Mex., U.S., 80 . . . . .317/G5
Locust, N.C., U.S., 2,416 . . . . .322/E4
Locust Fork, Ala., U.S., 1,016 . . . . .238/C2
Locust Grove, Ark., U.S., 150 . . . . .244/D3
Locust Grove, Ga., U.S., 2,322 . . . . .260/C5
Locust Grove, Ohio, U.S., 225 . . . . .328/D8
Locust Grove, Okla., U.S., 1,366 . . . . .330/J3
Lod, (Lydda), Isr. 135/B2
Łódź, Pol., 786,526 . . . . .83/D3
Łódzkie, Pol., province 83/D3
Loda, Ill., U.S., 419 . . . . .266/E3
Loddington, Eng., U.K. 70/C2
Loddon, Eng., U.K., 2,901 . . . . .70/G2
Lodge, Ill., U.S., 125 . . . . .266/E3
Lodge, S.C., U.S., 114 . . . . .340/D3
Lodge Corner, Ark., U.S. 244/D3
Lodge Grass, Mont., U.S., 510 . . . . .306/J4

Lodgepole, Alta., Can., 165 . . . . .212/C4
Lodgepole, Colo., U.S., creek 250/G1
Lodgepole, Mont., U.S., 214 . . . . .306/H1
Lodgepole, Nebr., U.S., 348 . . . . .308/B2
Lodgepole, Nebr., U.S., river 308/A2
Lodgepole, S. Dak., U.S. 342/C2
Lodi, Calif., U.S., 56,999 . . . . .246/D4, K6, L1
Lodi, Mo., U.S. 302/F4
Lodi, N.J., U.S., 23,971 . . . . .314/B2
Lodi, N.Y., U.S., 338 . . . . .320/H5
Lodi, Ohio, U.S., 3,061 . . . . .328/F3
Lodi, Wisc., U.S., 2,882 . . . . .364/D5
Lodja, Congo, D.R. 155/B2
Lodoga, Calif., U.S. 246/C3
Lodwar, Kenya 157/C2
Loei, Thai. 125/B2
Lofgreen, Utah, U.S. 350/B3
Lofoten, Nor., islands 66/E4
Lofthouse, Eng., U.K. 66/E4
Loftus, Eng., U.K., 5,931 . . . . .66/G3
Logan, Austl., river . . . . .170/Inset III
Logan, Qnsld., Austl. . . . . .170/Inset III
Logan, Yukon, Can., mountain 228/A5
Logan, Alaska, U.S., mountain 240/G2
Logan, Ark., U.S., county, 22,486 . . . . .244/B2
Logan, Colo., U.S., county, 20,504 . . . . . . .250/G1
Logan, Ill., U.S., 55 . . . . .266/E6
Logan, Ill., U.S., county, 31,183 . . . . .266/D3
Logan, Iowa, U.S., 1,545 . . . . .274/C4
Logan, Kans., U.S., 603 . . . . .276/C2
Logan, Kans., U.S., county, 3,046 . . . . .276/A3
Logan, Ky., U.S., county, 26,573 . . . . .280/D4
Logan, Mont., U.S., 90 . . . . .306/E4
Logan, Nebr., U.S., county, 774 . . . . .308/D2
Logan, N. Mex., U.S., 1,094 . . . . .317/G2
Logan, N. Dak., U.S., county, 2,308 . . . . . .326/F3
Logan, Ohio, U.S., 6,704 . . . . .328/F6
Logan, Ohio, U.S., county, 46,005 . . . . . . .328/C5
Logan, Okla., U.S. 330/B1
Logan, Okla., U.S., county, 33,924 . . . . . . .330/E2
Logan, Utah, U.S., 42,670 . . . . .350/C2
Logan, W. Va., U.S., 1,630 . . . . .360/C5
Logan, W. Va., U.S., county, 37,710 . . . . . .360/C5
Logandale, Nev., U.S., 800 . . . . .310/C3
Logan Morgan, Ala., U.S., lake 238/C2
Logansport, Ind., U.S., 19,684 . . . . .270/D3
Logansport, La., U.S., 1,630 . . . . .282/B3
Loganton, Penn., U.S., 453 . . . . .336/G3
Loganville, Ga., U.S., 5,435 . . . . .260/D4
Loganville, Penn., U.S., 908 . . . . .336/H6
Loganville, Wisc., U.S., 276 . . . . .364/C5
Log Cabin, La., U.S., 325 . . . . .282/F1
Loggieville, N.B., Can. 217/D1
Logie Coldstone, Scot., U.K. 62/L4
Log Lane Vil., Colo., U.S., 1,006 . . . . .250/G1
Logone, Came., river 153/C1
Logone, Chad, river 153/A5
Logroño, Sp., 133,058 . . . . .94/E1
Logroño, Sp., province 94/E1
Logsden, Oreg., U.S., 125 . . . . .334/C3
Lohman, Mo., U.S., 168 . . . . .302/D3
Lohman, Mont., U.S., 40 . . . . .306/G1
Lohn, Tex., U.S., 40 . . . . .346/J4
Lohrville, Iowa, U.S., 431 . . . . .274/E3
Lohrville, Wisc., U.S., 408 . . . . .364/D4
Loikaw, Mya. .125/C2
Loire, Fr., department 88/C4
Loire, Fr., river .88/C3
Loire-Atlantique, Fr., department 88/B3
Loiret, Fr., department 88/C3
Loir-et-Cher, Fr., department 88/C3
Loiza, P.R. 206/D2
Loja, Ecua., 94,305 . . . . .185/B4
Loja, Ecua., province 185/B5
Loja, Sp. 94/D4
Lokka, Fin., reservoir 81/C1
Lokoja, Nig. 152/D4
Lokossa, Ben., 52,909 . . . . .151/A4
Lol, Sudan, river 145/B3
Lola, Ky., U.S., 150 . . . . .280/B3
Loleta, Calif., U.S., 600 . . . . .246/A2
Lolland, Den., island 79/C4
Lolo, Mont., U.S., 3,388 . . . . .306/B3
Lolo Hot Sprs., Mont., U.S. 306/B3
Lolo Natl. For., Mont., U.S. 306/A2, B2, C2, C3
Lom, Bul. 101/B2
Lomża, Pol. 83/F2
Loma, S.L., mountains 149/B1
Loma, Colo., U.S. 250/B2
Loma, Mont., U.S., 92 . . . . .306/F2
Loma, Nebr., U.S., 60 . . . . .308/H2
Loma, N. Dak., U.S. 326/G1
Loma Alta, (McMullen County), Tex., U.S. . . .346/K7
Loma Alta, (Val Verde County), Tex., U.S. . . .346/H6
Loma Mansa, S.L., mountain 149/B1
Lomami, Congo, D.R., river 155/B2
Loman, Minn., U.S. 50 . . . . .298/D2
Loma Rica, Calif., U.S., 2,075 . . . . .246/D3
Lomas de Zamora, Arg., 574,330 . . . . .191/D4
Loma Vista, Tex., U.S., 50 . . . . .346/J7
Lomawai, Fiji .174/A3
Lomax, Ala., U.S., 150 . . . . .238/C3
Lomax, Ill., U.S., 477 . . . . .266/B3
Lomax, Tex., U.S. 346/G3
Lombard, Ill., U.S., 42,322 . . . . .266/B6
Lombard, Mont., U.S. 223/J3
Lombardy, It., plain 95/B1
Lombardy, It., region 95/B1
Lombok, Indon., island 122/C2
Lome, Togo, capital, 450,000 . . . . .151/B3
Lometa, Tex., U.S., 782 . . . . .346/K4
Lomira, Wisc., U.S., 2,233 . . . . .364/E5
Lomita, Calif., U.S., 20,046 . . . . .246/C10
Lomond, Alta., Can., 171 . . . . .212/D6
Lomond, Scot., U.K., lake 60/B2
Lomond, Scot., U.K., lake 62/G6
Lompoc, Calif., U.S., 41,103 . . . . .246/E8
Lonaconing, Md., U.S., 1,205 . . . . .288/C3
London, Ont., Can., 336,539, (427,300, metro.) .222/D4
London, Ont., Can., 336,539, (427,300, metro.) .223/D5
London, Eng., U.K., capital . . . . .60/U, Inset III
London, Eng., U.K., capital, 7,172,036 . . . . .70/D4
London, City of, Eng., U.K., unitary authority,
 7,172,036 . . . . .70/D3
London, Ark., U.S., 925 . . . . .244/B2
London, Calif., U.S., 1,848 . . . . .246/F6
London, Ky., U.S., 5,692 . . . . .280/D3
London, Minn., U.S. 298/D7
London, Ohio, U.S., 8,771 . . . . .328/D6
London, Oreg., U.S., 150 . . . . .334/C4
London, Tex., U.S., 50 . . . . .346/J5
Londonderry, N. Ire., U.K. 60/A2
Londonderry, N. Ire., U.K., 72,334 . . . . .65/C1
Londonderry, N.H., U.S., 23,236 . . . . .312/D5
Londonderry, Ohio, U.S., 200 . . . . .328/E7
Londonderry, Vt., U.S., 1,709 . . . . .352/B4
London Mills, Ill., U.S., 419 . . . . .266/C3
Londontown, (Londontowne), Md., U.S., 7,595 .288/H4
Londrina, Braz., 447,065 . . . . .188/C4
Lone Butte, Br. Col., Can., 266 . . . . .214/M5
Lone Chimney, Okla., U.S., 50 . . . . .330/F1
Lonedell, Mo., U.S., 300 . . . . .302/F3

Lone Elm, Kans., U.S. 276/G3
Lone Grove, Okla., U.S., 4,631 ......330/E3
Lone Jack, Mo., U.S., 528 ....302/J5
Lone Mtn., Tenn., U.S., 275 ....344/P2
Lone Oak, Ga., U.S., 104 ....260/B5
Lone Oak, Ky., U.S., 454 ....280/B3
Lone Oak, Tex., U.S., 521 ....346/N3
Lone Pine, Calif., U.S., 1,655 ......246/G6
Lonepine, Mont., U.S., 137 ....306/B2
Lone Rock, Iowa, U.S., 157 ....274/F1
Lonerock, Oreg., U.S. 334/G2
Lone Rock, Wisc., U.S., 929 ....364/C5
Lone Star, Kans., U.S., 50 ....276/G3
Lone Star (Iberville Par.), La., U.S., 80 ...282/G6
Lone Star (St. Charles Par.), La., U.S., 1,400 ...282/J3
Lone Star, S.C., U.S., 90 ....340/F3
Lone Star (Floyd County), Tex., U.S. ...346/G1
Lone Star (Morris County), Tex., U.S., 1,631 ...346/N3
Lone Tree, Iowa, U.S., 1,151 ....274/M5
Lonetree, Wyo., U.S., 61 ....366/A3
Lone Wolf, Okla., U.S., 500 ....330/C3
Long, Bah., island 207/C3
Long, Conn., U.S., island 253/D5
Long, Ga., U.S., county, 10,304 .....260/H8
Long, Maine, U.S., island 286/D4
Long, Mass., U.S., pond 292/L5
Long, N.J., U.S., island 314/C3, F2
Long, N.Y., U.S., island 320/G2
Long, N.Y., U.S., lake 320/N3
Long, N.C., U.S., bay 322/J7
Long, N. Dak., U.S., lake 326/C1
Long, S.C., U.S., bay 340/F3
Long Ashton, Eng., U.K., 4,080 ......68/C5
Long Beach, Calif., U.S., 461,522 ...246/C10, G9
Long Beach, Ind., U.S., 1,559 ....270/C1
Long Beach, Maine, U.S., 300 ....286/B5
Long Beach (see Calvert Beach), Md., U.S., 2,487 .288/J6
Long Beach, Minn., U.S., 271 ....298/B5
Long Beach, Miss., U.S., 17,320 .....300/C5
Long Beach, N.J., U.S., 3,329 ....314/E4
Long Beach, N.Y., U.S., 35,462 .....320/C3
Long Beach, N.C., U.S. 322/J7
Long Beach, Wash., U.S., 1,283 .....358/A3
Longboat Key, Fla., U.S., 7,603 .....256/F4
Long Branch, N.J., U.S., 31,340 .....314/F3
Longbranch, Wash., U.S., 90 ....358/C2
Longbridge, Eng., U.K. 68/D5
Long Bridge, La., U.S. 282/E4
Long Buckby, Eng., U.K., 3,428 ......68/E5
Long Buckby, Eng., U.K., 3,428 ......70/B2
Longburton, Eng., U.K. 73/H3
Long Clawson, Eng., U.K. 70/C1
Long Compton, Eng., U.K. 68/D6
Long Creek, Ill., U.S., 1,364 ....266/E4
Long Creek, Oreg., U.S., 228 ....334/G3
Long Crendon, Eng., U.K., 2,505 .....68/E6
Longdale, Okla., U.S., 310 ....330/D1
Longdon (Hereford & Worcester Co), Eng., U.K. ...68/C5
Longdon (Staffordshire Co), Eng., U.K. 68/D5
Longdown, Eng., U.K. 73/E3
Long Eaton, Eng., U.K., 44,826 ......68/E4
Long Eaton, Eng., U.K., 44,826 ......70/B1
Long Eddy, N.Y., U.S., 100 ....320/L7
Longfellow, Tex., U.S. 346/F5
Longfellow N.H.S., Mass., U.S. 292/C7
Longfield (Longfield/New Ash Green), Eng., U.K., 17,234 ....70/L4
Longford, Ire., 6,899 ....78/C2
Longford, Ire., county 78/C2
Longford, Kans., U.S., 94 ....276/E2
Long Green, Md., U.S., 1,000 ....288/H2
Long Grove, Ill., U.S., 6,735 ....266/B5
Long Grove, Iowa, U.S., 597 ....274/N4
Longhorsley, Eng., U.K. 66/E2
Longhoughton, Eng., U.K. 66/E2
Long Island, Conn., U.S., sound 253/C5
Long Island, Kans., U.S., 155 ....276/C2
Long Island, N.Y., U.S., sound 320/D1
Longlac, Ont., Can., 1,748 ....222/C3
Long Lake, Man., Can. 215/D4
Long Lake, Ill., U.S., 3,356 ....266/A4
Long Lake, Mich., U.S., 200 ....294/F5
Long Lake, Minn., U.S., 1,842 ......298/D6
Long Lake, N.Y., U.S., 325 ....320/N3
Long Lake, S. Dak., U.S., 58 ....342/F2
Long Lake, Wash., U.S. 358/H2
Long Lake, Wisc., U.S., 90 ....364/C3
Long Lake N.W.R., N. Dak., U.S. 326/E3
Long Lawford, Eng., U.K., 2,501 .....68/E5
Long Lawford, Eng., U.K., 2,501 .....70/B2
Long Marston, Eng., U.K. 66/F4
Longmeadow, Mass., U.S., 15,633 ...292/D4
Long Melford, Eng., U.K., 2,808 .....70/F2
Longmire, Wash., U.S. 358/D3
Longmont, Colo., U.S., 71,093 ...250/A2, E1
Long Mott, Tex., U.S. 346/M7
Longnor, Eng., U.K. 68/D3
Long Pine, Nebr., U.S., 341 ....308/E1
Long Pt., Ill., U.S., 247 ....266/E2
Long Pond, Maine, U.S. 286/B3
Long Pond, Mass., U.S., 1,500 ......292/M5
Longport, N.J., U.S., 1,054 ....314/E5
Long Prairie, Minn., U.S., 3,040 ....298/C5
Long Preston, Eng., U.K. 66/D4
Long Range, Nfld., Can., mountains ..218/B5, C4
Longreach, Qnsld., Austl. 170/D2
Longridge, Eng., U.K., 7,351 ....66/C5
Longridge, Eng., U.K., 7,351 ....68/B2
Long Ridge, Ky., U.S., 90 ....280/F2
Longridge, Md., U.S., 40 ....288/M6
Longrun, Mo., U.S. 302/G6
Longs, Colo., U.S., peak 250/E1
Longs, S.C., U.S., 375 ....340/F3
Longsdon, Eng., U.K. 68/C3
Longstreet, La., U.S., 163 ....282/B2
Long Sutton, Eng., U.K., 4,185 ......68/H4
Long Sutton, Eng., U.K., 4,185 ......70/C4
Long Sutton, Eng., U.K. 70/E1
Long Sutton, Eng., U.K., 4,185 ......73/G2
Longton, Kans., U.S., 394 ....276/F4
Longtown, Eng., U.K., 2,548 ....66/C2
Longtown, Eng., U.K. 68/B6
Longtown, Okla., U.S., 2,397 ....330/G2
Longueuil, Que., Can., 128,016 .....226/P13
Longvale, Calif., U.S., 50 ....246/B3
Long Valley, N.J., U.S., 1,818 ......314/D2
Longvalley, S. Dak., U.S. 342/D4
Long Valley Jct., Utah, U.S. 350/B6
Longview, Alta., Can., 300 ....212/C6
Longview, Ill., U.S., 153 ....266/E4
Longview, Miss., U.S., 350 ....300/D2
Longview, Mo., U.S., reservoir 302/H5
Long View, N.C., U.S., 4,722 ....322/D4
Longview, Tex., U.S., 73,344, (208,780, metro.) ...346/P3
Longview Beach, Md., U.S. 288/G6
Longview Hts., Wash., U.S., 3,513 ...358/C6
Longville, La., U.S., 225 ....282/C5
Longville, Minn., U.S., 180 ....298/C4
Longville in the Dale, Eng., U.K. 68/B4
Long Whatton, Eng., U.K. 70/B1
Longwick, Eng., U.K. 70/C3

Longwood, Fla., U.S., 13,745 ....256/D3
Longwood, N.C., U.S., 375 ....322/H6
Longwood, Wisc., U.S., 90 ....364/C4
Longwoods, Md., U.S., 250 ....288/K4
Long Xuyen, Viet., 132,681 ....123/A4
Longyester, Scot., U.K. 62/C7
Lono, Ark., U.S., 100 ....244/C3
Lonoke, Ark., U.S., 4,287 ....244/D3
Lonoke, Ark., U.S., county, 52,828 ..244/D3
Lonsdale, Ark., U.S., 118 ....244/C3
Lonsdale, Minn., U.S., 1,491 ....298/D6
Lonsdale, R.I., U.S. 339/D2
Looe, Eng., U.K., 5,022 ....73/C4
Loogootee, Ind., U.S., 2,741 ....270/C7
Lookeba, Okla., U.S., 131 ....330/D2
Lookout, Ala., U.S., mountain 238/D1
Lookout, Calif., U.S. 246/D1
Lookout, Md., U.S., point 288/J7
Lookout, Mich., U.S., point 294/F5
Lookout, N.C., U.S., cape 322/M5
Lookout, Oreg., U.S., cape 334/B2
Lookout, Penn., U.S., 80 ....336/L2
Lookout, Va., U.S., point 354/L4
Lookout, W. Va., U.S., 175 ....360/E4
Lookout Mtn., Ga., U.S., 1,617 .....260/A2
Lookout Mtn., Tenn., U.S., 2,000 ...344/L5
Loomis, Calif., U.S., 6,260 ....246/L5
Loomis, Nebr., U.S., 397 ....308/E3
Loomis, S. Dak., U.S., 47 ....342/G4
Loomis, Wash., U.S., 125 ....358/F1
Looneyville, W. Va., U.S., 50 ......360/F2
Loon Lake, Alta., Can., 399 ....212/C3
Loon Lake, Sask., Can., 318 ....227/A6
Loon Lake, Maine, U.S. 286/B3
Loon Lake, N.Y., U.S. 320/N1
Loon Lake, Wash., U.S., 400 ....358/H1
Loop Head, Ire., cape 78/B2
Loose, Eng., U.K. 70/F4
Loose Creek, Mo., U.S., 80 ....302/E3
Lop Buri, Thai. 125/B3
Lopcombe Corner, Eng., U.K. 70/A4
Lopcombe Corner, Eng., U.K. 73/J2
Lopeno, Tex., U.S., 140 ....346/J9
Lopez, Gabon, cape 155/A2
Lopez, Calif., U.S., county 246/D6
Lopez, Wash., U.S., 200 ....358/C1
Lop Nur, China, lake 119/C1
Lorain, Ohio, U.S., 68,652 ....328/E1
Lorain, Ohio, U.S., county, 284,664 .328/F1, F3
Lorain, Penn., U.S., 747 ....336/D5
Loraine, Calif., U.S., 125 ....246/G7
Loraine, Ill., U.S., 363 ....266/B3
Loraine, N. Dak., U.S. 326/D1
Loraine, Tex., U.S., 656 ....346/H3
Lorane, Oreg., U.S., 125 ....334/C4
Loranger, La., U.S., 425 ....282/J5
Lorbottle, Eng., U.K. 66/E2
Lorca, Sp., 77,477 ....94/F4
Lordsburg, N. Mex., U.S., 3,379 ....317/B5
Lords Cove, N.B., Can. 217/C4
Lordstown, Ohio, U.S., 3,633 ......328/J3
Loreauville, La., U.S., 938 ....282/F6
Loreburn, Sask., Can., 143 ....227/D9
Lore City, Ohio, U.S., 305 ....328/H6
Lorella, Oreg., U.S. 334/E5
Lorena, Tex., U.S., 1,433 ....346/L4
Lorengau, P.N.G. 172/A2
Lorentz, W. Va., U.S., 250 ....360/F2
Lorenzo, Ida., U.S., 275 ....264/F6
Lorenzo, Nebr., U.S., 40 ....308/A2
Lorenzo, Tex., U.S., 1,372 ....346/G2
Lorestan, Iran, province 130/B3
Loreto, Mex., 10,010 ....200/B2
Loreto, Peru, department 185/B1
Loretta, Kans., U.S. 276/C3
Loretta, Wisc., U.S. 364/C3
Lorette, Man., Can. 215/C4
Loretteville, Que., Can., 13,737 ...226/K5
Loretto, Ky., U.S., 623 ....280/E3
Loretto, Mich., U.S., 150 ....294/B4
Loretto, Nebr., U.S. 308/E2
Loretto, Penn., U.S., 1,190 ....336/D4
Loretto, Tenn., U.S., 1,665 ....344/G4
Loretto, Va., U.S. 354/J4
Lorian, Kenya, swamp 157/E3
Lorida, Fla., U.S., 375 ....256/C4
Lorient, Fr., 61,844, (116,174, metro.) ..88/B3
L'Orignal, Ont., Can. 223/L2
Lorimor, Iowa, U.S., 427 ....274/F5
Loring, Mont., U.S. 306/J1
Loris, S.C., U.S., 2,079 ....340/F2
Lorman, Miss., U.S., 50 ....300/A4
Lorne, N.B., Can. 217/C1
Lorne, Scot., U.K., estuary 60/A2
Lorraine, Que., Can. 226/N5
Lorraine, Fr., region 88/D2
Lorraine, Kans., U.S., 136 ....276/D3
Lorri, Arm., district 103/B2
Lorton, Nebr., U.S. 308/H3
Lorton, Va., U.S., 17,786 ....354/M3
Los, Guin., islands 149/A3
Los Alamitos, Calif., U.S., 11,536 ..246/D10
Los Alamos, Calif., U.S., 1,372 ....246/E8
Los Alamos, N. Mex., U.S., 11,909 ..317/D2
Los Alamos, N. Mex., U.S., county, 18,343 ...317/D2
Los Altos, Calif., U.S., 27,693 ....246/J3
Los Altos Hills, Calif., U.S., 7,902 .246/J3
Los Andes, Chile 190/B4
Los Angeles, Calif., U.S., 3,694,820, (16,373,645, metro.) ...246/C9, G9
Los Angeles, Calif., U.S., county, 9,519,338 ..246/B9, G8
Los Angeles, Chile 190/B4
Losantville, Ind., U.S., 280 ....270/C6
Los Banos, Calif., U.S., 25,869 ....246/E5
Los Cerrillos, N. Mex., U.S., 229 ..317/D2
Los Chavez, N. Mex., U.S., 5,033 ..317/D3
Los Chiles, C.R. 203/B1
Los Fresnos, Tex., U.S., 4,512 .....346/L9
Los Gatos, Calif., U.S., 28,592 ....246/K3
Losier Settlement, N.B., Can. 217/E1
Los Lagos, Chile, region 190/B5
Los Llanos, P.R. 206/C2
Los Lunas, N. Mex., U.S., 10,034 ..317/D3
Los Mochis, Mex., 200,906, (359,146, metro.) ..200/C2
Los Molinos, Calif., U.S., 1,952 ...246/C2
Los Montoyas, N. Mex., U.S., 275 ..317/E2
Los Olivos, Calif., U.S., 950 ......246/E8
Los Osos (Baywood-Los Osos), Calif., U.S., 14,351 ...246/E7
Los Padillas, N. Mex., U.S., 1,800 .317/D3
Los Padres Natl. For., Calif., U.S. .246/D6, E8
Los Palos, E. Timor 122/C1
Los Pinos, N. Mex., U.S. 317/D1
Los Ranchos de Albuquerque, N. Mex., U.S., 5,092 ...317/D2
Los Reyes, Mex. 200/Inset
Los Ríos, Ecua., province 185/B3
Los Santos, Pan., province 203/B3
Los Serranos, Calif., U.S. 246/E9
Lossiemouth, Scot., U.K., 6,803 ....62/K3
Lostant, Ill., U.S., 486 ....266/D2
Lost Cabin, Wyo., U.S. 366/C2

Lost City, W. Va., U.S., 50 ....360/J3
Lost Creek, Ky., U.S., 425 ....280/G3
Lost Creek, Tex., U.S., 4,729 ......346/D2
Lost Creek, Wash., U.S., 100 ......358/H1
Lost Creek, W. Va., U.S., 467 ......360/F2
Los Teques, Ven., 147,055, (179,062, metro.) ..182/C1
Lost Hills, Calif., U.S., 1,938 .....246/F7
Lostine, Oreg., U.S., 263 ....334/J2
Lost Nation, Iowa, U.S., 497 ......274/N4
Lost River, Ida., U.S. 264/D6
Los Trujillo, N. Mex., U.S., 2,166 ..317/D3
Lost Sprs., Kans., U.S., 71 ....276/F3
Lost Sprs., Wyo., U.S. 366/F2
Lostwithiel, Eng., U.K., 2,452 .....73/C4
Lostwood, N. Dak., U.S. 326/C1
Lostwood N.W.R., N. Dak., U.S. 326/C1
Los Ybanez, Tex., U.S. 346/G3
Lot, Fr., department 88/C4
Lot, Fr., river 88/C4
Lot-et-Garonne, Fr., department 88/C4
Lothair, Mont., U.S. 306/E1
Lotikipi, Kenya, plain 157/C1
Lotsee, Okla., U.S. 330/F1
Lott, Tex., U.S., 724 ....346/L4
Louangnamtha, Laos 124/A1
Louangphabang, Laos, 68,399 ....124/B2
Louangphabang, Laos, range 124/A3
Louann, Ark., U.S., 195 ....244/C4
Loudon, N.H., U.S., 4,481 ....312/D5
Loudon, Tenn., U.S., 4,476 ....344/N3
Loudon, Tenn., U.S., county, 39,086 .344/N3
Loudonville, N.Y., U.S., 10,800 ....320/P5
Loudonville, Ohio, U.S., 2,906 .....328/G4
Loudoun, Va., U.S., county, 169,599 .354/H2
Louellen, Ky., U.S., 80 ....280/G4
Louga, Sen. 148/A2
Loughborough, Eng., U.K., 46,867 ...68/E4
Loughborough, Eng., U.K., 46,867 ...70/B1
Loughbrickland, N. Ire., U.K., 674 ..65/B3
Lougheed, Nun., Can., island 220/G1
Loughermore, N. Ire., U.K., hill 65/C1
Louin, Miss., U.S., 339 ....300/C3
Louisa, Ky., U.S., county, 12,183 ..274/M5
Louisa, Ky., U.S., 2,018 ....280/H2
Louisa, Va., U.S., 1,401 ....354/G4
Louisa, Va., U.S., county, 25,627 ..354/G4
Louisbourg, N.S., Can., 1,071 .....221/H2
Louisburg, Kans., U.S., 2,576 .....276/H3
Louisburg, Minn., U.S. 298/A5
Louisburg, Mo., U.S., 147 ....302/C4
Louisburg, N.C., U.S., 3,111 ......322/J2
Louisdale, N.S., Can. 221/F2
Louise, Miss., U.S., 315 ....300/B3
Louise, Tex., U.S., 977 ....346/M6
Louisiade, P.N.G., archipelago 172/B3
Louisiana, U.S., state 270
Louisiana, Mo., U.S., 3,863 ....302/E2
Louisville, Ala., U.S., 612 ....238/D4
Louisville, Colo., U.S., 18,937 ...250/A2, E2
Louisville, Ga., U.S., 2,712 ....260/G5
Louisville, Ill., U.S., 1,242 ......266/E6
Louisville, Kans., U.S., 209 ....276/G2
Louisville, Ky., U.S., 256,231, (1,025,598, metro.) ..280/A2
Louisville, Miss., U.S., 7,006 .....300/C2
Louisville, Nebr., U.S., 1,046 .....308/H3
Louisville, Ohio, U.S., 8,904 ......328/H4
Louisville, Tenn., U.S., 2,001 .....344/N3
Loup, Nebr., U.S., county, 712 .....308/E2
Loup, Nebr., U.S., river 308/F2
Loup City, Nebr., U.S., 996 ....308/F2
Lourdes, Fr. 88/B5
Lourdes, Iowa, U.S. 274/K1
Louri, Bhu. 126/C2
Louth, Ire., county 78/C2
Louth, Eng., U.K., 14,248 ....66/H6
Louth, Eng., U.K., 14,248 ....68/H3
Louviers, Colo., U.S., 237 ....250/F6
Louvres, Fr. ....88/Inset II
Love, Okla., U.S., county, 8,831 ...330/E4
Lovech, Bul. 101/C2
Lovech, Bul., oblast 101/C2
Lovejoy, Ga., U.S., 2,495 ....260/C5
Lovelady, Tex., U.S., 608 ....346/N4
Loveland, Colo., U.S., 50,608 .....250/E1
Loveland, Ohio, U.S., 11,677 ......328/C9
Loveland, Okla., U.S. 330/D3
Loveland Park, Ohio, U.S., 1,799 ..328/C9
Lovell, Maine, U.S., 974 ....286/B4
Lovell, Okla., U.S., 50 ....330/E1
Lovell, Wyo., U.S., 2,281 ....366/B1
Lovells, Mich., U.S., 80 ....294/E5
Lovell Vil., St. Vin.-Gren. 208/B3
Lovelock, Nev., U.S., 2,003 ....310/A1
Love Pt., Md., U.S. 288/J3
Loves Park, Ill., U.S., 20,044 .....266/D1
Lovett, Ga., U.S., 70 ....260/F6
Lovett, Ind., U.S., 80 ....270/E7
Lovettsville, Va., U.S., 853 ....354/H2
Love Valley, N.C., U.S. 322/D3
Loveville, Md., U.S., 650 ....288/H6
Lovilia, Iowa, U.S., 583 ....274/J5
Loving, N. Mex., U.S., 1,326 ......317/F5
Loving, Tex., U.S., county, 67 .....346/E4
Lovington, Va., U.S. 354/F5
Lovington, Ill., U.S., 1,222 ....266/E4
Lovington, N. Mex., U.S., 9,471 ...317/G5
Low, Utah, U.S., 70 ....350/B3
Lowake, Tex., U.S. 346/H4
Low Bentham, Eng., U.K. 66/C4
Low Brunton, Eng., U.K. 66/D2
Lowden, Iowa, U.S., 794 ....274/N4
Lowe Farm, Man., Can. 215/C4
Lowell, Ark., U.S., 5,013 ....244/A1
Lowell, Ida., U.S. 264/B3
Lowell, Ind., U.S., 7,505 ....270/B2
Lowell, Iowa, U.S., 100 ....274/M6
Lowell, Maine, U.S., 291 ....286/D3
Lowell, Mass., U.S., 105,167 ......292/J2
Lowell, Mich., U.S., 4,013 ....294/D7
Lowell, N.C., U.S., 2,662 ....322/C4
Lowell, Ohio, U.S., 628 ....328/G6
Lowell, Oreg., U.S., 857 ....334/D4
Lowell, Vt., U.S., 738 ....352/C1
Lowell, Wisc., U.S., 366 ....364/E5
Lowell N.H.P., Mass., U.S. 292/J2
Lowelltown, Maine, U.S. 286/B3
Lowellville, Ohio, U.S., 1,281 .....328/J3
Lowemont, Kans., U.S., 125 ....276/G2
Lower Arrow, Br. Col., Can., lake ..214/N6
Lower Assendon, Eng., U.K. 70/C3
Lower Austria, Aus., state 91/D2
Lower Bank, N.J., U.S., 70 ....314/D4
Lower Beeding, Eng., U.K. 70/D4
Lower Brule, S. Dak., U.S., 599 ...342/F3
Lower Brule Ind. Res., S. Dak., U.S. .342/F3
Lower Bullingham, Eng., U.K. 68/B5

Lower Cabot, Vt., U.S., 125 ....352/C2
Lower Chapel, Wales, U.K. 64/E3
Lower Colonias, N. Mex., U.S. 317/E2
Lower Debert, N.S., Can. 221/D2
Lower Five Islands, N.S., Can. 221/D2
Lower Hainesville, N.B., Can. 217/B2
Lower Hatchie N.W.R., Ark., U.S. ...244/F2
Lower Hatchie N.W.R., Tenn., U.S. ..344/B3
Lower Heyford, Eng., U.K. 70/B3
Lower Hutt, N.Z. 171/B3
Lower Kalskag, Alaska, U.S., 267 ...240/C2
Lower Lake, Calif., U.S., 1,755 ....246/C4
Lower Lough Erne, N. Ire., U.K., lake .65/B3
Lower Manitou, Ont., Can., lake 298/E1
Lower Marlboro, Md., U.S., 450 .....288/H5
Lower Montague, P.E.I., Can. 224/C2
Lower Moor, Eng., U.K. 68/C5
Lower Paia, Hawaii, U.S. 262/C3
Lower Peach Tree, Ala., U.S., 100 ..238/B4
Lower Peover, Eng., U.K. 68/C3
Lower Post, Br. Col., Can. 214/H1
Lower Red, Minn., U.S., lake 298/B3
Lower Rideau, Ont., Can., lake 320/J1
Lower Salem, Ohio, U.S., 109 ......328/H6
Lower San Francisco Plaza, N. Mex., U.S., 275 .317/B4
Lower Saxony, Ger., state 86/B2
Lower Suwannee N.W.R., Fla., U.S. ..256/C6
Lower Tunguska, Russ., river 104/F3
Lower Waterford, Vt., U.S., 80 .....352/D2
Lower Whitefish, Minn., U.S., lake ..298/C4
Lower Winchendon, Eng., U.K. 70/C3
Lower Woods Harbour, N.S., Can. ...221/B4
Lowes, Ky., U.S., 175 ....280/B4
Lowestoft, Eng., U.K. 60/D3
Lowestoft, Eng., U.K., 62,907 ......70/H2
Lowesville, N.C., U.S., 1,440 ......322/C4
Lowgap, N.C., U.S., 475 ....322/E2
Lowick, Eng., U.K. 66/B4
Lowland, N.C., U.S., 200 ....322/M4
Lowman, Ida., U.S. 264/B5
Low Moor, Iowa, U.S., 240 ....274/P4
Low Moor, Va., U.S., 367 ....354/D5
Low Mtn., Ariz., U.S., 175 ....242/E2
Lowndes, Ala., U.S., county, 13,473 .238/C3
Lowndes, Ga., U.S., county, 92,115 .260/E1
Lowndes, Miss., U.S., county, 61,586 .300/D2
Lowndesboro, Ala., U.S., 140 ......238/C3
Lowndesville, S.C., U.S., 166 ......340/B2
Lowry, Ark., U.S. 244/B1
Lowry, Minn., U.S., 271 ....298/B5
Lowry, S. Dak., U.S. 342/F2
Lowry City, Mo., U.S., 728 ....302/C3
Lowry Crossing, Tex., U.S., 1,229 ..346/C8
Lowrys, S.C., U.S., 207 ....340/C2
Low Street, Eng., U.K. 70/G1
Lowsville, W. Va., U.S. 360/F1
Lowville, N.Y., U.S., 3,476 ....320/K3
Loxa, Ill., U.S., 50 ....266/F4
Loxahatchee N.W.R., Fla., U.S. 256/A5, H5
Loxhill, Eng., U.K. 70/C4
Loxley, Ala., U.S., 1,348 ....238/B5
Loyada, Dji. 156/C2
Loyal, Scot., U.K., lake 62/H2
Loyal, Okla., U.S., 81 ....330/D2
Loyal, Wisc., U.S., 1,308 ....364/C4
Loyall, Ky., U.S., 766 ....280/G4
Loyalsockville, Penn., U.S., 375 ...336/H3
Loyalton, Calif., U.S., 862 ....246/E3
Loyalton, S. Dak., U.S. 342/F2
Loyd, Wisc., U.S., 125 ....364/C5
Loyne, Scot., U.K., lake 62/G4
Loyola, Calif., U.S., 3,478 ....246/J3
Loyoro, Ug. 157/D2
Loysburg, Penn., U.S., 275 ....336/E5
Loysville, Penn., U.S., 450 ....336/G5
Lozeau, Mont., U.S. 306/B2
Lozère, Fr., department 88/C4
Lü, Tai., island 117/B2
Lualaba, Congo, D.R., river 155/C2
Lualualei Naval Res., Hawaii, U.S. ..262/H2
Lua Makika, Hawaii, U.S., mountain ..262/B4
Luana, Iowa, U.S., 249 ....274/M1
Luanda, Ang., capital, (1,822,407 metro.) .159/B2
Luanda, Ang., province 159/B3
Luang, Thai., mountain 125/B4
Luangwa, Zam. 159/C3
Luangwa, Zam., river 159/C2
Luanshya, Zam., 186,372 ....159/B2
Luapula, Congo, D.R., river 155/C3
Luapula, Zam., province 159/B2
Luapula, Zam., river 159/B2
Luau, Ang. 159/C3
Luba, Eq. Gui. 154/A1
Lubango, Ang., 105,000 ....159/B3
Lubbock, Tex., U.S., 199,564, (242,628 metro.) .346/G2
Lubbock, Tex., U.S., county, 242,628 ..346/G2
Lubec, Maine, U.S., 1,652 ....286/F4
Lubec, W. Va., U.S., 1,303 ....360/C2
Lübeck, Ger., 213,326 ....86/B2
Lubelskie, Pol., province 83/F3
Lubenham, Eng., U.K. 70/C2
Lubicon, Alta., Can., lake 212/C3
Lublin, Pol., 356,468 ....83/F3
Lublin, Wisc., U.S. 364/C3
Lubumbashi, Congo, D.R., 564,830 ..155/C3
Lucama, N.C., U.S., 847 ....322/J3
Lucan, Minn., U.S., 226 ....298/C6
Lucapa, Ang. 159/D2
Lucas, Iowa, U.S., 243 ....274/H6
Lucas, Iowa, U.S., county, 9,422 ..274/H6
Lucas, Kans., U.S., 436 ....276/D2
Lucas, Ky., U.S., 200 ....280/D4
Lucas, Ohio, U.S., 620 ....328/F4
Lucas, Ohio, U.S., county, 455,054 .328/C2
Lucas, S. Dak., U.S. 342/F4
Lucas, Tex., U.S., 2,890 ....346/C8
Lucasville, Ohio, U.S., 1,588 .....328/E7
Lucca, It. 95/B2
Lucca, N. Dak., U.S. 326/H3
Luce, Mich., U.S., county, 7,024 ..294/B3
Lucea, Jam. 206/A2
Lucedale, Miss., U.S., 2,458 ......300/D5
Lucena, Phil. 120/B3
Lucena, Sp. 94/B3
Lucena, Sp. 92/B2
Lucerne, Slvk. 92/B2
Lucerne, Switz., 57,374, (180,536 metro.) ..90/C1
Lucerne, Switz., canton 90/C1
Lucerne, Switz., lake 90/C2
Lucerne, Calif., U.S., 2,870 ......246/C3
Lucerne, Colo., U.S., 175 ....250/F1
Lucerne, Mo., U.S., 92 ....302/C1
Lucerne, Wash., U.S., 60 ....358/E2
Lucerne, Wyo., U.S., 525 ....366/B2
Lucernemines, Penn., U.S., 951 ....336/C4
Lucia, Calif., U.S., 90 ....246/D6
Lucie, Sur., river 183/A3
Lucien, Okla., U.S., 100 ....330/E1
Lucile, Ga., U.S. 260/E1
Lucile, Ida., U.S. 264/A4
Lucin, Utah, U.S. 350/A2

Madrid, Sp. 589

Lucinda, Penn., U.S., 600 .336/C3
Luck, Wisc., U.S., 1,210 .364/A3
Luckenwalde, Ger. .86/C2
Luckey, Ohio, U.S., 998 .328/D3
Lucknow, Ont., Can., 1,207 .223/D4
Lucknow, India, 2,207,340, (2,266,933 *metro.*) .128/D3
Lucky, La., U.S., 355 .282/D2
Lucky Lake, Sask., Can., 354 .227/C9
Luda Kamchiya, Bul., *river* .101/E3
Ludborough, Eng., U.K. .66/H6
Ludden, N. Dak., U.S. .326/G3
Lude, Minn., U.S., 60 .298/C2
Ludell, Kans., U.S., 80 .276/B2
Lüderitz, Nam. .160/B4
Ludgershall, Eng., U.K., 3,664 .68/E6
Ludgershall, Eng., U.K., 3,664 .70/A4
Ludgershall, Eng., U.K. .70/B3
Ludham, Eng., U.K. .70/H1
Ludhiana, India, 1,395,053 .128/C2
Ludington, Mich., U.S., 8,357 .294/C6
Ludington, Wisc., U.S., 150 .364/B4
Ludlow, N.B., Can. .217/C2
Ludlow, Eng., U.K., 9,040 .68/B5
Ludlow, Calif., U.S. .246/J8
Ludlow, Colo., U.S. .250/F4
Ludlow, Ill., U.S., 324 .266/E3
Ludlow, Ky., U.S., 4,409 .280/G1
Ludlow, Maine, U.S., 402 .286/D2
Ludlow, Mass., U.S., 21,209 .292/E4
Ludlow, Miss., U.S., 250 .300/C3
Ludlow, Mo., U.S., 204 .302/C2
Ludlow, Penn., U.S., 250 .336/D2
Ludlow, S. Dak., U.S. .342/B2
Ludlow, Vt., U.S., 2,449 .352/B4
Ludlow City, Mass., U.S., 375 .292/E4
Ludlow Falls, Ohio, U.S., 210 .328/B5
Ludlowville, N.Y., U.S., 600 .320/H5
Ludogorie, Bul., *region* .101/E2
Ludowici, Ga., U.S., 1,440 .260/H8
Ludville, Ga., U.S., 200 .260/B3
Ludwigsburg, Ger. .86/B4
Ludwigshafen am Rhein, Ger., 163,771 .86/B4
Lueders, Tex., U.S., 300 .334/J3
Luella, Ga., U.S., 125 .260/C5
Luena, Ang. .159/D3
Lufkin, Tex., U.S., 32,709 .346/P4
Lugano, It., *lake* .95/B1
Lugano, Switz. .90/C3
Lugano, Switz., *lake* .90/C3
Luganville, Van. .173/B2
Lugenda, Moz., *river* .161/C2
Lugert, Okla., U.S. .330/C3
Lugerville, Wisc., U.S., 40 .364/C3
Lugo, Sp., 88,414 .94/C1
Lugo, Sp., *province* .94/C1
Lugoff, S.C., U.S., 6,278 .340/D2
Lugoj, Rom. .101/A3
Luhans'k, Ukr., 467,356 .102/D2
Luhans'k, Ukr., *oblast* .102/D2
Luhondo, Rwa., *lake* .158/B1
Luing, Scot., U.K., *island* .62/E6
Luis Cintrón, P.R. .206/D2
Luis Lopez, N. Mex., U.S., 125 .317/D4
Lukachukai, Ariz., U.S., 1,565 .242/F1
Luke, Md., U.S., 80 .288/B4
Lukeville, Ariz., U.S., 125 .242/C6
Lukuga, Congo, D.R., *river* .155/C2
Lula, Ga., U.S., 1,438 .260/D3
Lula, Miss., U.S., 370 .300/B1
Lula, Okla., U.S., 60 .330/F3
Lulea, Swe., 71,952 .80/D1
Luleälven, Swe., *river* .80/D1
Luleälven, Swe., *river* .80/E2
Luling, La., U.S., 11,512 .282/J3, J7
Luling, Tex., U.S., 5,080 .346/L6
Lulu, Fla., U.S., 90 .256/F1
Lum, Mich., U.S., 500 .294/F6
Lumber Bridge, N.C., U.S., 118 .322/G5
Lumber City, Ga., U.S., 1,247 .260/F8
Lumber City, Penn., U.S., 86 .336/D4
Lumberport, W. Va., U.S., 937 .360/F2
Lumberton, Miss., U.S., 2,228 .300/C5
Lumberton, N.J., U.S., 10,461 .314/D4
Lumberton, N. Mex., U.S., 80 .317/D1
Lumberton, N.C., U.S., 20,795 .322/G5
Lumberton, Tex., U.S., 8,731 .346/P5
Lummi Island, Wash., U.S., 325 .346/C1
Lumphăt, Camb. .124/F2
Lumpkin, Ga., U.S., 1,369 .260/B7
Lumpkin, Ga., U.S., *county*, 21,016 .260/C2
Lumsden, Nfld., Can., 622 .218/E4
Lumsden, Sask., Can., 1,581 .227/F10
Lumsden, Scot., U.K. .62/L4
Lumut, Bru. .121/A2
Luna, La., U.S., 70 .282/E2
Luna, N. Mex., U.S. .317/B4
Luna, N. Mex., U.S., *county*, 25,016 .317/C5
Lunan, Scot., U.K. .62/M5
Luna Pier, Mich., U.S., 1,483 .294/F8
Luncarty, Scot., U.K., 1,265 .62/K6
Lund, Br. Col., Can. .214/K6
Lund, Swe., 99,622 .80/B3
Lund, Eng., U.K. .66/G5
Lund, Nev., U.S., 60 .310/C2
Lund, Utah, U.S. .350/A6
Lunda Norte, Ang., *province* .159/D2
Lundar, Man., Can. .215/B4
Lunda Sul, Ang., *province* .159/D3
Lundazi, Zam. .159/C2
Lundbreck, Alta., Can., 263 .212/C6
Lundi, Zimb., *river* .160/B2
Lundy, Eng., U.K., *island* .73/C2
Lüneburg, Ger. .86/B2
Lüneburg, Ger., *department* .86/B2
Lüneburger Heide, Ger., *region* .86/B2
Lünen, Ger. .86/A3
Lunenburg, N.S., Can., 2,568 .221/C3
Lunenburg, N.S., Can., *county* .221/C3
Lunenburg, Mass., U.S., 9,401 .292/H2
Lunenburg, Vt., U.S., 1,328 .352/D2
Lunenburg, Va., U.S., 40 .354/G7
Lunenburg, Va., U.S., *county*, 13,146 .354/G7
Lunga, Zam., *river* .159/B2
Lungwebungu, Zam., *river* .159/A2
Luning, Nev., U.S., 100 .310/A2
Lunsar, S.L. .149/A1
Luoyang, China .119/E2
Lupeni, Rom. .101/B3
Luperón, Dom. Rep. .205/B1
Lupton, Ariz., U.S., 375 .242/F2
Lupton, Mich., U.S., 350 .294/E5
Lupus, Mo., U.S. .302/D3
Luquillo, P.R. .206/D2
Luraville, Fla., U.S. .256/E1
Luray, Kans., U.S., 203 .276/D2
Luray, Mo., U.S., 102 .302/E1
Luray, S.C., U.S., 115 .340/C4
Luray, Va., U.S., 4,871 .354/G3
Luremo, Ang. .159/C2
Lurgan, N. Ire., U.K., 21,905 .65/E3
Lúrio, Moz., *river* .161/C2
Lurton, Ark., U.S., 50 .244/B2
Lusaka, Zam., *capital*, 1,269,848 .159/B3
Lusaka, Zam., *province* .159/B2
Lusambo, Congo, D.R. .155/B2
Lusby, Eng., U.K. .68/H3
Lusby, Md., U.S., 1,666 .288/J6
Luseland, Sask., Can., 602 .227/A8
Lushnjë, Alb., 32,580 .99/A3
Lushton, Nebr., U.S. .308/G3
Lusk, Wyo., U.S., 1,447 .366/D2
Luss, Scot., U.K. .62/G6
Lusta, Scot., U.K. .62/C3
Lustre, Mont., U.S. .306/L1
Lusutfu, Swaz., *river* .161/B2
Lut, Dasht-e, Iran, *desert* .130/D3
Lutcher, La., U.S., 3,735 .282/H6
Lutes Mtn., N.B., Can. .217/E2
Luther, Iowa, U.S., 158 .274/G4
Luther, Mich., U.S., 339 .294/D5
Luther, Mont., U.S., 50 .306/G4
Luther, Okla., U.S., 612 .330/B3, E2
Luthersburg, Penn., U.S., 375 .336/D3
Luthersville, Ga., U.S., 783 .260/B5
Lutherville, (Lutherville-Timonium), Md., U.S., 15,814 .288/H2
Lutie, Okla., U.S., 80 .330/G3
Lutie, Tex., U.S. .346/H9
Luton, Eng., U.K. .60/C3
Luton, Eng., U.K., 171,671, (221,337 *metro.*) .70/D3
Luton, Eng., U.K., *unitary authority*, 184,390 .70/D3
Luton, Iowa, U.S. .274/B3
Łutselk'e, N.W. Terr., Can., 248 .220/F4
Lutsen, Minn., U.S., 100 .298/E2
Luts'k, Ukr., 216,100 .102/B1
Lutterworth, Eng., U.K., 7,380 .68/E5
Lutterworth, Eng., U.K., 7,380 .70/B2
Luttrell, Tenn., U.S., 915 .344/P2
Lutts, Tenn., U.S. .344/F4
Lutz, Fla., U.S., 17,081 .256/D6, F3
Lützow-Holm, Antar., *bay* .192/C16
Luuq, Som. .157/A3
Luverne, Ala., U.S., 2,635 .238/C4
Lu Verne, Iowa, U.S., 299 .274/F2
Luverne, Minn., U.S., 4,617 .298/A7
Luverne, N. Dak., U.S., 44 .326/H2
Luvua, Congo, D.R., *river* .155/C2
Luvua, Congo, D.R., *river* .159/B1
Luwegu, Tan., *river* .158/C2
Luxembourg, *nation* .83
Luxembourg, Belg., *province* .85/D3
Luxembourg, Lux., *capital*, 76,688 .85/B2
Luxembourg, Lux., *district* .85/B2
Luxemburg, Iowa, U.S., 246 .274/M2
Luxemburg, Wisc., U.S., 1,935 .364/F4
Luxor, Egy., 361,000 .144/B2
Luxora, Ark., U.S., 1,317 .244/F2
Luzarches, Fr. .88/Inset II
Luzerne, Iowa, U.S., 105 .274/K4
Luzerne, Mich., U.S., 275 .294/E5
Luzerne, Penn., U.S., 2,952 .336/G7
Luzerne, Penn., U.S., *county*, 319,250 .336/H7, J3
Luzhou, China .119/D3
Luzon, Phil., *island* .120/B3
Luzon, Phil., *strait* .120/B2
Luzon, Tai., *strait* .117/B3
L'viv, Ukr., 786,147 .102/A2
L'viv, Ukr., *oblast* .102/A2
Lybster, Scot., U.K. .62/K2
Lycan, Colo., U.S. .250/H4
Lycoming, Penn., U.S., *county*, 120,044 .336/G3
Lydbury North, Eng., U.K. .68/B5
Lydd, Eng., U.K., 3,173 .70/F5
Lyddal, Man., Can. .215/B1
Lydd-on-Sea, Eng., U.K. .70/F5
Lydham, Eng., U.K. .68/A4
Lydia, Kans., U.S. .276/A3
Lydia, La., U.S., 1,079 .282/F7
Lydia, S.C., U.S., 550 .340/D2
Lydick, Ind., U.S., 1,300 .270/D1
Lyerly, Ga., U.S., 488 .260/A3
Lyford, Tex., U.S., 1,973 .346/L9
Lykens, Penn., U.S., 1,937 .336/H4
Lyle, Minn., U.S., 566 .298/E7
Lyle, Wash., U.S., 530 .358/D4
Lyles, Tenn., U.S., 450 .344/G3
Lyman, Iowa, U.S., 125 .274/E5
Lyman, Maine, U.S., 3,795 .286/B5
Lyman, Nebr., U.S., 421 .308/A2
Lyman, N.H., U.S., 487 .312/C3
Lyman, S.C., U.S., 2,659 .340/B2, F2
Lyman, S. Dak., U.S. .342/F4
Lyman, S. Dak., U.S., *county*, 3,895 .342/F4
Lyman, Utah, U.S., 234 .350/C5
Lyman, Wash., U.S., 409 .358/C1
Lyman, Wyo., U.S., 1,938 .366/A3
Lyme, Eng., U.K., *bay* .60/C4
Lyme, Eng., U.K., *bay* .73/G3
Lyme, N.H., U.S., 1,679 .312/B4
Lyme Ctr., N.H., U.S., 175 .312/B4
Lyme Regis, Eng., U.K., 3,851 .73/G3
Lymington, Eng., U.K., 13,508 .70/A5
Lyminster, Eng., U.K. .70/C5
Lymm, Eng., U.K., 9,721 .66/D6
Lymm, Eng., U.K., 9,721 .68/C3
Lympne, Eng., U.K. .70/F4
Lympstone, Eng., U.K., 1,855 .73/F3
Lynbrook, N.Y., U.S., 19,911 .320/C2
Lynch, Ky., U.S., 900 .280/H4
Lynch, Md., U.S., 200 .288/K2
Lynch, Nebr., U.S., 269 .308/E1
Lynch, Penn., U.S. .336/C2
Lynchburg, Miss., U.S., 2,959 .300/B1
Lynchburg, Mo., U.S. .302/D4
Lynchburg, Ohio, U.S., 1,350 .328/C7
Lynchburg, S.C., U.S., 588 .340/E2
Lynchburg, Tenn., U.S., 5,740 .344/J4
Lynchburg, Va., U.S., 65,269, (214,911 *metro.*) .354/E6
Lynches, S.C., U.S., *river* .340/D2
Lynch Hts., Del., U.S., 550 .255/C5
Lynch Sta., Va., U.S., 500 .354/E6
Lyncourt, N.Y., U.S., 4,268 .320/J4
Lynd, Minn., U.S., 346 .298/B6
Lyndeborough, N.H., U.S., 1,585 .312/C6
Lynden, Wash., U.S., 9,020 .358/C1
Lyndhurst, Eng., U.K., 2,381 .70/A5
Lyndhurst, N.J., U.S., 19,383 .314/B2
Lyndhurst, Ohio, U.S., 15,279 .328/H9
Lyndon, Ill., U.S., 566 .266/D2
Lyndon, Ky., U.S., 9,369 .280/B2, E2
Lyndon, Vt., U.S., 5,448 .352/C1
Lyndon B. Johnson Natl. Hist. Park, Tex., U.S. .346/C2, K5
Lyndon Ctr., Vt., U.S., 1,200 .352/C1
Lyndon Sta., Wisc., U.S., 458 .364/D5
Lyndonville, N.Y., U.S., 862 .320/E4
Lyndonville, Vt., U.S., 1,227 .352/D1
Lyndora, Penn., U.S., 6,685 .336/B4
Lyneham, Eng., U.K., 4,747 .73/J1
Lynemouth, Eng., U.K., 2,024 .66/E2
Lyness, Scot., U.K. .62/M2
Lyng, Eng., U.K. .73/G2
Lynmouth, Eng., U.K. .73/E2
Lynn, Ala., U.S., 597 .238/B1
Lynn, Alaska, U.S., *canal* .240/J3
Lynn, Ark., U.S., 315 .244/D1
Lynn, Ind., U.S., 1,143 .270/G4
Lynn, Mass., U.S., 89,050 .292/D7, L3
Lynn, Tex., U.S., *county*, 6,550 .346/G2
Lynn, Utah, U.S. .350/A2
Lynndyl, Utah, U.S., 134 .350/B4
Lynne, Fla., U.S., 300 .256/G2
Lynnfield, Mass., U.S., 11,542 .292/D6, K2
Lynn Grove, Ky., U.S., 225 .280/B4
Lynn Haven, Fla., U.S., 12,451 .256/C1
Lynn Lake, Man., Can., 699 .215/C1
Lynn of Lorn N.P., Scot., U.K. .62/F5
Lynnview, Ky., U.S., 965 .280/A2
Lynnville, Ill., U.S., 137 .266/C4
Lynnville, Ind., U.S., 781 .270/B8
Lynnville, Iowa, U.S., 366 .274/J4
Lynnville, Ky., U.S., 100 .280/B4
Lynnville, Tenn., U.S., 345 .344/G4
Lynnwood, Wash., U.S., 33,847 .358/A4, C2
Lynton, Eng., U.K. .73/E2
Lynwood, Calif., U.S., 69,845 .246/C10
Lynwood, Ill., U.S., 7,377 .266/C6
Lynx, Ohio, U.S., 350 .328/D8
Lynxville, Wisc., U.S., 176 .364/B5
Lyon, Fr., 453,187, (1,348,832 *metro.*) .88/D4
Lyon, Scot., U.K., *lake* .62/G6
Lyon, Iowa, U.S., *county*, 11,763 .274/B1
Lyon, Kans., U.S., *county*, 35,935 .276/F3
Lyon, Ky., U.S., *county*, 8,080 .280/B4
Lyon, Minn., U.S., *county*, 25,425 .298/B6
Lyon, Miss., U.S., 418 .300/B1
Lyon, Nev., U.S., *county*, 34,501 .310/A2
Lyon Mtn., N.Y., U.S., 458 .320/P1
Lyons, Colo., U.S., 1,585 .250/E1
Lyons, Ga., U.S., 4,169 .260/G7
Lyons, Ill., U.S., 10,255 .266/B6
Lyons, Ind., U.S., 748 .270/B7
Lyons, Kans., U.S., 3,732 .276/D3
Lyons, Mich., U.S., 726 .294/E7
Lyons, Nebr., U.S., 963 .308/H2
Lyons, N.Y., U.S., 3,695 .320/H4
Lyons, Ohio, U.S., 559 .328/B2
Lyons, Oreg., U.S., 1,008 .334/D3
Lyons, Penn., U.S., 504 .336/K5
Lyons, Tex., U.S., 80 .346/M5
Lyons, Wisc., U.S., 600 .364/E6
Lyons Falls, N.Y., U.S., 591 .320/L3
Lyons Plain, Conn., U.S., 2,100 .253/B5
Lysite, Wyo., U.S. .366/C2
Lysychans'k, Ukr. .102/D2
Lytham St. Anne's, Eng., U.K., 40,866 .66/C5
Lytham St. Anne's, Eng., U.K., 40,866 .68/B2
Lytle, Tex., U.S., 2,383 .346/K6
Lytton, Br. Col., Can., 319 .214/M6
Lytton, Iowa, U.S., 305 .274/E3
Ma, Viet., *river* .123/A2
Maalaea, Hawaii, U.S., 454 .262/C4
Maalaea, Hawaii, U.S., *bay* .262/C4
Maamakunudhoo, Mald., *atoll* .127/A1
Ma'an, Jor. .134/A2
Ma'an, Jor., *governorate* .134/B2
Maas, Belg., *river* .85/D2
Maas, Belg., *river* .86/A3
Maas, Neth., *river* .84/C3, D3
Maastricht, Neth., 121,775 .84/C4
Mabana, Wash., U.S., 325 .358/C1
Mabank, Tex., U.S., 2,151 .346/M3
Mabaruma, Guy. .183/B1
Mabel, Minn., U.S., 766 .298/F7
Mabelle, Tex., U.S. .346/J2
Maben, Miss., U.S., 803 .300/C2
Maben, W. Va., U.S., 60 .360/D5
Maberly, Ont., Can. .223/J3
Mabla, Dji., *mountains* .156/B2
Mablethorpe, (Mablethorpe/Sutton on Sea), Eng., U.K., 9,719 .66/J6
Mablethorpe, (Mablethorpe/Sutton on Sea), Eng., U.K., 9,719 .68/H3
Mableton, Ga., U.S., 29,733 .260/B4, H2
Mabou, N.S., Can. .221/F1
Mabscott, W. Va., U.S., 1,403 .360/D5
Mabton, Wash., U.S., 1,891 .358/F3
MacAlpine, Nun., Can., *lake* .220/H3
Macao, China, 436,686 .119/E3
Macapá, Braz., 95,798, (179,609 *metro.*) .188/C1
MacArthur, W. Va., U.S., 1,693 .360/D5
Macas, Ecua. .185/B4
Maccan, N.S., Can. .221/C2
Macclenny, Fla., U.S., 4,459 .256/F1
Macclesfield, Eng., U.K., 50,270, (53,616 *metro.*) .66/D6
Macclesfield, Eng., U.K., 50,270, (53,616 *metro.*) .68/C3
Macclesfield, N.C., U.S., 458 .322/K3
Macdoel, Calif., U.S., 140 .246/C1
Macdona, Tex., U.S., 650 .346/A3
Macdonnell, Austl., *ranges* .170/C2
Macduff, Scot., U.K., 3,767 .62/M3
Macedon, N.Y., U.S., 1,496 .320/G4
Macedonia, *nation* .98
Macedonia, Ark., U.S., 125 .244/B4
Macedonia, Ill., U.S., 51 .266/E5
Macedonia, Iowa, U.S., 325 .274/D5
Macedonia, N.J., U.S. .314/E3
Macedonia, Ohio, U.S., 9,224 .328/G3, H9
Maceió, Braz., 797,759 .188/E2
Macenta, Guin. .149/D3
Maceo, Ky., U.S., 400 .280/D3
Macerata, It. .95/C2
Maces Bay, N.B., Can. .217/C3
Macfarlan, W. Va., U.S., 70 .360/D2
Macfarlane, Sask., Can., *river* .227/C2
Macgregor, Man., Can., 882 .215/B4
Machakos, Kenya, 116,100 .157/D4
Machala, Ecua., 144,197 .185/B4
Machen, Wales, U.K. .64/E4
Machens, Mo., U.S. .302/H2
Machesney Park, Ill., U.S., 20,759 .266/D1
Machias, Maine, U.S., 2,353 .286/E4
Machias, (see Lime Lake), N.Y., U.S., 1,422 .320/E6
Machiasport, Maine, U.S., 1,160 .286/E4
Machida, Jap., 378,000 .114/C3
Machrihanish, Scot., U.K. .62/E8
Machu Picchu, Peru, *ruins* .185/C3
Machynlleth, Wales, U.K. .64/D2
Mack, Colo., U.S., 150 .250/B2
Mack, Ohio, U.S., 8,900 .328/A9
Mackamp, Maine, U.S. .286/B3
Mackan, N. Ire., U.K. .65/B3
Mackay, Qnsld., Austl. .170/D2
MacKay, N.W. Terr., Can., *lake* .220/F4
Mackay, Ida., U.S., 566 .264/D6
Mackay Island N.W.R., N.C., U.S. .322/P1
Mackenzie, Can., *mountain* .193/C12
Mackenzie, Can., *river* .193/C12
Mackenzie, Br. Col., Can., 5,206 .214/L3
Mackenzie, N.W. Terr., Can., *mountains* .220/C4
Mackenzie, N.W. Terr., Can., *river* .220/B3, D4
Mackenzie, Yukon, Can., *bay* .228/B1
Mackenzie, Mo., U.S., 137 .302/H3
Mackenzie King, N.W. Terr., Can., *island* .220/F1
Mackey, Ont., Can. .223/H1
Mackey, Ind., U.S., 142 .270/B8
Mackeys, N.C., U.S., 225 .322/M3
Mackinac, Mich., U.S., *county*, 11,943 .294/E3
Mackinac, Mich., U.S., *straits* .294/E4
Mackinac Island, Mich., U.S., 523 .294/E4
Mackinaw, Ill., U.S., 1,452 .266/D3
Mackinaw City, Mich., U.S., 859 .294/E4
Macklin, Sask., Can., 1,330 .227/A8
Macksburg, Iowa, U.S., 142 .274/F5
Macksburg, Ohio, U.S., 202 .328/H6
Macks Creek, Mo., U.S., 267 .302/D4
Macksville, Kans., U.S., 514 .276/D4
Mackville, Ky., U.S., 206 .280/E3
Mackville, Wisc., U.S., 450 .364/E4
Maclean, Nun., Can., *strait* .220/G1
Macmillan, Yukon, Can., *river* .228/C4
Macomb, Ill., U.S., 18,558 .266/C3
Macomb, Mich., U.S., *county*, 788,149 .294/B6, G7
Macomb, Okla., U.S., 61 .330/E2
Mâcon, Fr. .88/D3
Macon, Ala., U.S., *county*, 24,105 .238/D3
Macon, Ark., U.S., 1,100 .244/C3
Macon, Ga., U.S., 97,255, (322,549 *metro.*) .260/D6
Macon, Ga., U.S., *county*, 14,074 .260/C7
Macon, Ill., U.S., 1,213 .266/E4
Macon, Ill., U.S., *county*, 114,706 .266/E4
Macon, Miss., U.S., 2,461 .300/D2
Macon, Mo., U.S., 5,538 .302/D2
Macon, Mo., U.S., *county*, 15,762 .302/D2
Macon, Nebr., U.S., 40 .308/E3
Macon, N.C., U.S., 115 .322/J2
Macon, N.C., U.S., *county*, 29,811 .322/C8
Macon, Ohio, U.S., 250 .328/C8
Macon, Tenn., U.S., *county*, 20,386 .344/K1
Macoupin, Ill., U.S., *county*, 49,019 .266/A2, D4
Mac. Robertson Land, Antar., *region* .192/B18
Mac Tier, Ont., Can. .223/F2
Macungie, Penn., U.S., 3,039 .336/K4
Macwahoc, Maine, U.S., 98 .286/D3
Macy, Ind., U.S., 248 .270/D3
Macy, Nebr., U.S., 956 .308/H1
Mad, Calif., U.S., *river* .246/B2
Mādabā, Jor. .134/A2
Mādabā, Jor., *governorate* .134/A2
Madagascar, *nation* .157
Madaket, Mass., U.S., 125 .292/P7
Madan, Bul. .101/C4
Madang, P.N.G. .172/A2
Madawaska, N.B., Can., *county* .217/A1
Madawaska, Ont., Can., 407 .223/G2
Madawaska, Maine, U.S., 4,534 .286/D1
Madbury, N.H., U.S., 1,509 .312/E5
Madden, Alta., Can. .212/C5
Madden, Miss., U.S. .300/C3
Maddock, N. Dak., U.S., 498 .326/F2
Maddox, Md., U.S., 225 .288/G6
Madehurst, Eng., U.K. .70/C5
Madeira, Braz., *river* .188/B2
Madeira, Ohio, U.S., 8,923 .328/B7, B9
Madeira Beach, Fla., U.S., 4,511 .256/C6
Madeley, (Shropshire), Eng., U.K., 17,909 .68/C4
Madeley, (Staffordshire), Eng., U.K., 2,254 .68/C4
Madelia, Minn., U.S., 2,340 .298/C6
Madeline, Calif., U.S. .246/E1
Madeline, Wisc., U.S., *island* .364/C2
Madera, Calif., U.S., 43,207 .246/E6
Madera, Calif., U.S., *county*, 123,109 .246/F5
Madera, Penn., U.S., 425 .336/E4
Madera Canyon, Ariz., U.S., 70 .242/E6
Madhumati, Bangl., *river* .127/C5
Madhupur Tract, Bangl., *region* .127/D4
Madhya Pradesh, India, *state* .128/C4
Madiera Island, Port., *island* .93/Inset I
Madill, Okla., U.S., 3,410 .330/F3
Madison, Ala., U.S., 29,329 .238/C1
Madison, Ala., U.S., *county*, 276,700 .238/C1
Madison, Ark., U.S., 987 .244/E2
Madison, Ark., U.S., *county*, 14,243 .244/B1
Madison, Conn., U.S., 17,858 .253/E4
Madison, Fla., U.S., 3,061 .256/E1
Madison, Fla., U.S., *county*, 18,733 .256/E1
Madison, Ga., U.S., 3,636 .260/E4
Madison, Ga., U.S., *county*, 25,730 .260/E3
Madison, Ida., U.S., *county*, 27,467 .264/F6
Madison, Ill., U.S., 4,545 .266/A3
Madison, Ill., U.S., *county*, 258,941 .266/A3, D5
Madison, Ind., U.S., 12,004 .270/F7
Madison, Ind., U.S., *county*, 133,358 .270/E4
Madison, Iowa, U.S., *county*, 14,019 .274/F5
Madison, Kans., U.S., 857 .276/F3
Madison, Ky., U.S., *county*, 70,872 .280/F3
Madison, La., U.S., *parish*, 13,728 .282/G2
Madison, Maine, U.S., 4,523 .286/C4
Madison, Md., U.S., 70 .288/K5
Madison, Minn., U.S., 1,768 .298/A5
Madison, Miss., U.S., 14,692 .300/B3
Madison, Miss., U.S., *county*, 74,674 .300/C3
Madison, Mo., U.S., 586 .302/D2
Madison, Mo., U.S., *county*, 11,800 .302/F4
Madison, Mont., U.S., *county*, 6,851 .306/E4
Madison, Mont., U.S., *river* .306/E4
Madison, Nebr., U.S., 2,367 .308/G2
Madison, Nebr., U.S., *county*, 35,226 .308/G2
Madison, N.H., U.S., 1,984 .312/D4
Madison, N.J., U.S., 16,530 .314/E2
Madison, N.Y., U.S., 315 .320/K5
Madison, N.Y., U.S., *county*, 69,441 .320/K5
Madison, N.C., U.S., 2,262 .322/F2
Madison, N.C., U.S., *county*, 19,635 .322/E7
Madison, Ohio, U.S., 2,921 .328/H2
Madison, Ohio, U.S., *county*, 40,213 .328/D6
Madison, Penn., U.S., 510 .336/B5
Madison, S. Dak., U.S., 6,540 .342/H3
Madison, Tenn., U.S., *county*, 91,837 .344/D3
Madison, Tex., U.S., *county*, 12,940 .346/M5
Madison, Va., U.S., 210 .354/G4
Madison, Va., U.S., *county*, 12,520 .354/G4
Madison, W. Va., U.S., 2,677 .360/C4
Madison, Wisc., U.S., *state capital*, 208,054, (426,526 *metro.*) .364/D5
Madison, Wyo., U.S. .366/A1
Madison Hts., Mich., U.S., 31,101 .294/B6
Madison Hts., Va., U.S., 11,584 .354/E6
Madison Lake, Minn., U.S., 837 .298/D6
Madison Mills, Ohio, U.S., 150 .328/D6
Madison Mills, Va., U.S., 125 .354/G4
Madison-on-the-Lake, Ohio, U.S., 3,900 .328/H2
Madisonville, Ky., U.S., 19,307 .280/C3
Madisonville, La., U.S., 677 .282/J6
Madisonville, Tenn., U.S., 3,939 .344/N3
Madisonville, Tex., U.S., 4,159 .346/N5
Madisonville, Va., U.S., 80 .354/F6
Madiun, Indon. .122/C2
Madoc, Ont., Can., 1,730 .223/H3
Madoc, Mont., U.S. .306/L1
Madrakah, Ra's al, Oman, *cape* .137/C2
Madras, Ga., U.S., 350 .260/B5
Madras, Oreg., U.S., 5,078 .334/E3
Madre de Dios, Bol., *river* .186/A2
Madre de Dios, Chile, *island* .190/A8
Madre de Dios, Peru, *department* .185/C3
Madre de Dios, Peru, *river* .185/C3
Madrid, Sp., *autonomous community* .94/E2

Madrid, Sp., *capital*, 2,938,723 . . . . .94/E2, Inset II
Madrid, Sp., *province* 94/D2
Madrid, Ala., U.S., 303 . . . . .238/D4
Madrid, Iowa, U.S., 2,264 . . . . .274/C4
Madrid, Maine, U.S., 173 . . . . .286/B4
Madrid, Nebr., U.S., 265 . . . . .308/C3
Madrid, N. Mex., U.S., 149 . . . . .317/D2
Madrid, N.Y., U.S., 650 . . . . .320/L1
Madriu, And. 93/B3
Madriz, Nicar., *department* 202/A2
Madura, Indon., *island* 122/C2
Madurai, India, 951,696, (1,194,655 metro.) . .128/C7
Maebashi, Jap., 284,000 . . . . .114/C2
Mae Klong, Thai., *river* 125/B3
Maentwrog, Wales, U.K. 64/D2
Maerdy, Wales, U.K. .64/C3
Maes, N. Mex., U.S. 31/F2
Maeser, Utah, U.S., 2,855 . . . . .350/E3
Maesteg, Wales, U.K., 20,576 . . . . .64/D4
Maestra, Cuba, *mountains* 204/B3
Maéwo, Van., *island* 173/C2
Maeystown, Ill., U.S., 148 . . . . .266/C5
Mafeking, Man., Can. 215/A3
Mafeteng, Leso., 12,667 . . . . .161/A2
Mafia, Tan., *island* .158/C2
Mafikeng, S. Afr. 162/C2
Mafra, Port. 93/A3
Magadalena de Kino, Mex., 22,023,
   (24,447 metro.) 200/B1
Magadan, Russ., 121,330, (130,450 metro.) . .104/I4
Magadi, Kenya, Indon. 157/D4
Magalia, Calif., U.S., 10,569 . . . . .246/D3
Magallanes y Antártica Chilena, Chile, *region* .190/B8
Magalloway, Maine, U.S. 286/A4
Magazine, Ark., U.S., 915 . . . . .244/B2
Magazine, Ark., U.S., *mountain* 244/B2
Magburaka, S.L. 149/B1
Magdagachi, Russ. 104/H4
Magdalena, Bol. 186/B2
Magdalena, Chile, *island* 190/B6
Magdalena, Col., *department* 184/B2
Magdalena, Col., *river* 184/B3
Magdalena, N. Mex., U.S., 913 . . . . .317/C3
Magdalena Contreras, Mex. 200/Inset
Magdeburg, Ger., 235,073 . . . . .86/B2
Magdeburg, Ger., *department* 86/B2
Magee, Miss., U.S., 4,200 . . . . .300/C4
Magelang, Indon. 122/C2
Magellan, Arg., *strait* 191/B7
Magellan, Chile, *strait* 190/B8
Maggie Valley, N.C., U.S., 607 . . . . .322/D7
Maggiore, It., *lake* 95/B1
Maggiore, Switz., *lake* 90/C2
Maggy's Leap, N. Ire., U.K. 65/F3
Maghera, N. Ire., U.K., 129 . . . . .65/D2
Magherafelt, N. Ire., U.K., 7,143 . . . . .65/D2
Magherafelt, N. Ire., U.K., *unitary authority*,
   39,780 . . . . .65/D2
Magheragall, N. Ire., U.K. 65/E2
Maghery, N. Ire., U.K., 223 . . . . .65/D2
Maghull, (Maghull/Lydiate), Eng., U.K., 29,206 .66/C5
Maghull, (Maghull/Lydiate), Eng., U.K., 29,206 .68/B5
Magna, Utah, U.S., 22,770 . . . . .350/D2
Magness, Ark., U.S., 191 . . . . .244/D2
Magnet, Nebr., U.S., 79 . . . . .308/G1
Magnet, Tex., U.S. 346/M6
Magnetawan, Ont., Can., 244 . . . . .223/F2
Magnetic Sprs., Ohio, U.S., 323 . . . . .328/D5
Magnitogorsk, Russ., 426,866, (427,300 metro.) .104/D4
Magnolia, Ark., U.S., 10,858 . . . . .244/B4
Magnolia, Del., U.S., 226 . . . . .255/C4
Magnolia, Ill., U.S., 279 . . . . .266/D2
Magnolia, Iowa, U.S., 200 . . . . .274/C4
Magnolia, Ky., U.S., 425 . . . . .280/E3
Magnolia, Minn., U.S., 221 . . . . .298/A7
Magnolia, Miss., U.S., 2,071 . . . . .300/B4
Magnolia, N.J., U.S., 4,409 . . . . .314/B3
Magnolia, N.C., U.S., 932 . . . . .322/J5
Magnolia, Ohio, U.S., 931 . . . . .328/H4
Magnolia, Tex., U.S., 1,111 . . . . .346/A5
Magnolia, W. Va., U.S. 360/K1
Magnolia Beach, Tex., U.S., 125 . . . . .346/M7
Magoffin, Ky., U.S., *county* 13,332 . . . . .280/G3
Magog, Que., Can., 14,283 . . . . .226/D6
Magrath, Alta., Can., 1,993 . . . . .212/D6
Maguiresbridge, N. Ire., U.K., 645 . . . . .65/C3
Magwalt, Tex., U.S. .346/E4
Magway, Mya. 125/B2
Magway, Mya., *division* 125/B2
Mahabharat, Nepal, *range* 126/D2
Mahaffey, Penn., U.S., 402 . . . . .336/D4
Mahahoe, Hawaii, U.S., *point* 262/J1
Mahajamba, Madag., *river* 163/B2
Mahajanga, Madag., 100,807 . . . . .163/B2
Mahalapye, Bots., 39,719 . . . . .160/B2
Mahanadi, India, *river* 128/D4
Mahanoy City, Penn., U.S., 4,647 . . . . .336/J4
Maharashtra, India, *state* 128/B5
Mahaska, Alta., Can. 212/C4
Mahaska, Iowa, U.S., *county* 22,335 . . . . . . .274/E5
Mahaska, Kans., U.S., 107 . . . . .276/E2
Mahaweli, Sri Lan., *river* 126/C3, C4
Mahdia, Guy. 183/C3
Mahdia, Tun. 146/C2
Mahé, Sey., *island group* 163/B1
Mahé, Sey., *island* . . . . .163/C1, Inset
Mahébourg, Mauritius 163/C3
Maher, Colo., U.S., 70 . . . . .250/C3
Mahilyou, Bela., 371,300 . . . . .82/E3
Mahilyow, Bela., *oblast* 82/D3
Mahim, India, *bay* . . . . .128/Inset I
Mahnomen, Minn., U.S., 1,202 . . . . .298/B3
Mahnomen, Minn., U.S., *county*, 5,190 . . . . .298/B3
Mahomet, Ill., U.S., 4,877 . . . . .266/E3
Mahón, (Maó), Sp. 94/J3
Mahoning, Ohio, U.S., *county*, 257,555 . . . . .328/J4
Mahopac, N.Y., U.S., 8,478 . . . . .320/C1, P8
Mahto, S. Dak., U.S. .342/E2
Mahtomedi, Minn., U.S., 7,563 . . . . .298/F5
Mahtowa, Minn., U.S., 80 . . . . .298/E4
Mahwah, N.J., U.S., 24,062 . . . . .314/B1, E1
Maida, N. Dak., U.S. .326/G1
Maiden, N.C., U.S., 3,282 . . . . .322/C3
Maidenhead, Eng., U.K., 59,605 . . . . .70/C3
Maiden Newton, Eng., U.K. 73/C3
Maiden Rock, Wisc., U.S., 121 . . . . .364/A4
Maidford, Eng., U.K. .70/B2
Maidstone, Sask., Can., 995 . . . . .227/A7
Maidstone, Eng., U.K. 60/D3
Maidstone, Eng., U.K., 90,878 . . . . .70/F4
Maiduguri, Nig. 152/G2
Maili, Hawaii, U.S., 5,943 . . . . .262/H2
Maili, Hawaii, U.S., *point* 262/H2
Main, Ger., *river* 86/B4
Main, N. Ire., U.K., *river* 78/C1
Main-à-Dieu, N.S., Can. 221/H1
Main Brook, Nfld., Can., 357 . . . . .218/C3
Main-Danube, Ger., *canal* 86/B4
Mai-Ndombe, Congo, D.R., *lake* 155/B2
Maine, U.S., *state* 273
Maine, Maine, U.S., *gulf* 286/C5
Maine, N.Y., U.S., 1,000 . . . . .320/J6

Maine-et-Loire, Fr., *department* 88/B3
Maineville, Ohio, U.S., 885 . . . . .328/B7, C9
Mainland, Scot., U.K., *island* . . . . .60/Inset I
Mainland, Scot., U.K., *island* 62/M2
Mainland, Scot., U.K., *island* 62/Q2
Maintirano, Madag. .163/A2
Mainz, Ger., 183,134 . . . . .86/B4
Maio, C.V., *island* 148/C3
Maipo, Chile, *river* . . . . .190/B4, Inset
Maipú, Chile 190/Inset
Maiquetía, Ven. 182/C1
Maisemore, Eng., U.K. 68/C6
Maisí, Cuba, *cape* .204/F3
Maisonnette, N.B., Can., 605 . . . . .217/D1
Maisons-Laffitte, Fr. . . . . .88/Inset II
Maitland, Fla., U.S., 12,019 . . . . .256/C4
Maitland, Mo., U.S., 342 . . . . .302/A1
Maitland Bridge, N.S., Can. 221/B3
Maiz, Nicar., *islands* 202/C2
Maize, Kans., U.S., 1,868 . . . . .276/E4
Maizuru, Jap. 114/B3
Majé, Braz., 37,597, (91,359 metro.) . . . .188/Inset I
Majenica, Ind., U.S., 175 . . . . .270/F3
Majestic, Ky., U.S. 280/H3
Major, Okla., U.S., *county*, 7,545 . . . . .330/D1
Majorca, (Mallorca), Sp., *island* 94/H3
Majors Place, Nev., U.S. 310/C2
Majuro, Marsh. Is., *capital*, 18,308,
   (33,000 metro.) 173/C2
Majuro, Marsh. Is., *island* 173/C2
Makaha, Hawaii, U.S., 7,753 . . . . .262/H2
Makah Ind. Res., Wash., U.S. 358/A1
Makahuena, Hawaii, U.S., *point* 262/C1
Makakilo City, Hawaii, U.S., 13,156 . . . . .262/H2
Makaleha, Hawaii, U.S., *mountains* 262/C1
Makamba, Bur. 158/B3
Makanda, Ill., U.S., 419 . . . . .266/D6
Makapala, Hawaii, U.S. 262/G3
Makapuu, Hawaii, U.S., *point* 262/E2, K2
Makassar, (Ujungpandang), Indon., 1,153,900 .122/C2
Makassar, Indon., *strait* 122/C2
Makawao, Hawaii, U.S., 6,327 . . . . .262/C3
Makena, (Wailea-Makena), Hawaii, U.S., 5,671 .262/C4
Makeni, S.L. 149/B1
Makgadikgadi, Bots., *salt pans* 160/B2
Makhachkala, Russ., 330,942, (378,650 metro.) .104/D5
Makhaleng, Leso., *river* 161/A2
Makiki Hts., Hawaii, U.S. 262/G2
Makin, Kiri., *island* .175/A1
Makinen, Minn., U.S., 60 . . . . .298/E4
Makiyivka, Ukr., 387,657 . . . . .102/D2
Makkovik, Nfld., Can., 384 . . . . .218/B1
Makokou, Gabon 155/B1
Makona, Liber., *river* 149/A1
Makoti, N. Dak., U.S., 145 . . . . .326/D2
Makoua, Congo 155/C4
Makran Coast, Pak., *range* 129/B5
Makua Keeau Forest Reserve, Hawaii, U.S. . . .262/H2
Makua Mil. Res., Hawaii, U.S. 262/H2
Makundu, Mald., *atoll* 127/A1
Makung, Tai. 117/A2
Makurdi, Nig. 152/E4
Mala, Pan., *point* 203/B3
Malabar, India, *coast* 128/B6
Malabar, India, *point* . . . . .128/Inset I
Malabar, Fla., U.S., 2,622 . . . . .256/H3
Malabo, Eq. Gui., *capital*, 30,418 . . . . .154/A1
Malacca, Indon., *strait* 122/A1
Malacca, Malay., *strait* 121/A2
Malacca, Thai., *strait* 125/B5
Malad, India . . . . .128/Inset I
Malad City, Ida., U.S., 2,158 . . . . .264/E7
Maladzyechna, Bela. 82/C2
Málaga, Sp., 524,414 . . . . .94/D4
Málaga, Sp., *province* 94/D4
Malaga, N.J., U.S., 1,700 . . . . .314/C4
Malaga, N. Mex., U.S., 100 . . . . .317/F5
Malagarasi, Tan., *river* 158/B1
Malaita, Sol. Is., *island* 173/B1
Malakal, Sudan 145/C3
Malakoff, Tex., U.S., 2,257 . . . . .346/M3
Malakula, Van., *island* 173/B3
Malang, Indon., 3,170,000 . . . . .122/C2
Malanje, Ang., 31,559 . . . . .159/C3
Malanje, Ang., *province* 159/C2
Malanville, Ben. 145/B2
Mälaren, Swe. 83/G2
Malaspina, Alaska, U.S., *glacier* 240/G3
Malatya, Tur., 400,200 . . . . .133/D2
Malatya, Tur., *province* 133/D2
Malawi, *nation* 153
Malawi, (Nyasa), Mal., *lake* 159/B2
Malay, Malay., *peninsula* 121/A1
Malay, Thai., *peninsula* 125/B4
Malaysia, *nation* 117
Malbaie, Que., Can., *river* 226/F4
Malbun, Liech. 90/B2
Malcolm, Nebr., U.S., 413 . . . . .308/H3
Malcom, Iowa, U.S., 352 . . . . .274/J4
Malden, Kiri., *island* 175/D2
Malden, Ill., U.S., 343 . . . . .266/D2
Malden, Ind., U.S., 225 . . . . .270/B2
Malden, Mass., U.S., 56,340 . . . . .292/C7, K3
Malden, Mo., U.S., 4,782 . . . . .302/G5
Malden, Wash., U.S., 215 . . . . .358/H2
Malden, W. Va., U.S., 750 . . . . .360/C4
Maldives, *nation* 123
Maldon, Eng., U.K., 15,841 . . . . .70/F3
Maldonado, Uru., *department* 187/C3
Male, Mald., *capital*, 74,069 . . . . .127/A2
Maleb, Alta., Can. 212/E6
Malegaon, India 128/B4
Male Karpaty, Slvk., *mountains* 92/D2
Malham, Eng., U.K. 66/D4
Malheur, Oreg., U.S., *county*, 31,615 . . . . . .334/H4
Malheur, Oreg., U.S., *lake* 334/H4
Malheur, Oreg., U.S., *river* 334/H4
Malheur Natl. For., Oreg., U.S. 334/H3
Malheur N.W.R., Oreg., U.S. 334/H4
Mali, *nation* 144
Mali, India 149/B1
Maliana, E. Timor 122/B1
Malibu, Calif., U.S., 12,575 . . . . .246/G8
Malin, Oreg., U.S., 638 . . . . .334/E5
Malindi, Kenya 157/F5
Malin Head, Ire., *cape* 78/C1
Malinta, Ohio, U.S., 285 . . . . .328/B3
Mali Rajinac, Cro., *mountain* 98/B3
Maljamar, N. Mex., U.S. 317/G5
Mallaig, Alta., Can., 162 . . . . .212/E4
Mallaig, Scot., U.K. 60/B1
Mallard, Iowa, U.S., 298 . . . . .274/E2
Mallawi, Egy. 144/B2
Mallory, W. Va., U.S., 1,143 . . . . .360/C5
Mallow, Ire. 78/B2
Mallwyd, Wales, U.K. 64/D2
Malmberget, Swe. 80/D1
Malmédy, Belg. 85/C2
Malmesbury, Eng., U.K., 4,439 . . . . .73/H1
Malmö, Swe., 262,397, (527,633 metro.) 80/B3
Malmo, Minn., U.S., 60 . . . . .298/D4

Malmo, Nebr., U.S., 109 . . . . .308/H2
Malo, Wash., U.S. 358/G1
Maloelap, Marsh. Is., *island* 173/C2
Malombe, Mal., *lake* 159/C2
Malone, Ala., U.S. 238/D1
Malone, Fla., U.S., 2,00 . . . . .256/C1
Malone, N.Y., U.S., 6,075 . . . . .320/N1
Malone, Tex., U.S., 278 . . . . .346/M4
Maloopolskie, Pol., *province* 83/D4
Malott, Wash., U.S., 250 . . . . .358/F1
Maloy, Iowa, U.S. 274/F6
Malpas, Eng., U.K. 68/B3
Malta, *nation* 95
Malta, Malta, *island* 97/B3
Malta, Ida., U.S., 177 . . . . .264/D7
Malta, Ill., U.S., 969 .266/E2
Malta, Mont., U.S., 2,120 . . . . .306/J1
Malta, Ohio, U.S., 696 . . . . .328/G6
Malta Bend, Mo., U.S., 249 . . . . .302/C2
Maltahöhe, Nam. 160/B3
Maltais, N.B., Can. 217/C1
Maltby, Eng., U.K., 18,158 . . . . .66/F6
Maltby, Eng., U.K., 18,158 . . . . .68/E3
Maltby, Wash., U.S., 8,267 . . . . .358/H4
Maltby le Marsh, Eng., U.K. 66/J6
Maltman's Hill, Eng., U.K. 70/F4
Malton, Ont., Can. 223/J5
Malton, Eng., U.K., 4,294 . . . . .66/G4
Malton, Eng., U.K., 4,294 . . . . .68/F1
Maluku, Indon., *province* 122/E2
Maluti, Leso., *mountains* 161/B2
Malvern, Ark., U.S., 1,215 . . . . .238/D4
Malvern, Ark., U.S., 9,021 . . . . .244/C3
Malvern, Iowa, U.S., 1,256 . . . . .274/C5
Malvern, Ohio, U.S., 1,218 . . . . .328/H4
Malvern, Penn., U.S., 3,059 . . . . .336/K5, K7
Malverne, N.Y., U.S., 8,934 . . . . .320/C2
Malvern Link, Eng., U.K. 68/C5
Mamala, Hawaii, U.S., *bay* 262/E2, J3
Mamãri, Sen. 148/C2
Mamaroneck, N.Y., U.S., 18,752 . . . . .320/C2
Mamawi, Alta., Can., *lake* 212/D2
Mambéré, C.A.R., *river* 154/A2
Mamburao, Phil. 120/B3
Mameyes, P.R. 206/D2
Mamfé, Came. 147/A2
Mamiña, Chile 190/C2
Mammoth, Ariz., U.S., 1,762 . . . . .242/E5
Mammoth Cave, Ky., U.S. 280/D3
Mammoth Cave Natl. Park, Ky., U.S. 280/D3
Mammoth Hot Sprs., Wyo., U.S., 275 . . . . . . .366/A1
Mammoth Lakes, Calif., U.S., 7,093 . . . . .246/G5
Mammoth Spr., Ark., U.S., 1,147 . . . . .244/D1
Mamoré, Bol., *river* 186/A2
Mamou, Guin. 149/A2
Mamou, La., U.S., 3,566 . . . . .282/E5
Mamoudzou, Com., *territorial capital* 163/C2
Mamry, Pol., *lake* 83/C1
Mamuno, Bots. 160/A2
Man, C. d'Iv. 150/C3
Man, Eng., U.K., *island* 66/A5
Man, W. Va., U.S., 770 . . . . .360/C5
Mana, Fr. Gui. 183/B1
Mana, Fr. Gui., *river* 183/B1
Mana, Hawaii, U.S. 262/B1
Manabí, Ecua., *province* 185/A3
Manado, Indon. 122/D1
Managua, Nicar., *capital*, 903,100 . . . . .202/A3
Managua, Nicar., *department* 202/A3
Managua, Nicar., *lake* 202/A2
Manahawkin, N.J., U.S., 2,004 . . . . .314/E4
Manaiki, Hawaii, U.S., *stream* 262/F1
Manakara, Madag. 163/B3
Manakin-Sabot, Va., U.S., 90 . . . . .354/H5
Manalapan, Fla., U.S., 321 . . . . .256/B5
Manalapan, N.J., U.S., 33,423 . . . . .314/E3
Manama, Bahr., *capital*, 140,401 . . . . .137/B1
Manana, Hawaii, U.S., *point* 262/K2
Manannah, Minn., U.S., 100 . . . . .298/C5
Manasquan, N.J., U.S., 6,310 . . . . .314/E3
Manassa, Colo., U.S., 1,042 . . . . .250/E4
Manassas, Ga., U.S., 100 . . . . .260/G7
Manassas, Va., U.S., 35,135 . . . . .354/J3
Manassas Natl. Bfld. Park, Va., U.S. 354/H3
Manassas Park, Va., U.S., 10,290 . . . . .354/J3
Manatee, Fla., U.S., *county*, 264,002 . . .256/D7, F4
Manati, P.R. 206/B2
Manatuto, E. Timor 122/C1
Manatuto, E. Timor, *province* 122/C1
Manaus, Braz., 1,405,835 . . . . .188/C2
Manawa, Wisc., U.S., 1,330 . . . . .364/F4
Manawan, Sask., Can., *lake* 227/G5
Manawatu-Wanganui, N.Z., *region* 171/B3
Manbij, Syria 134/A1
Mancelona, Mich., U.S., 1,408 . . . . .294/D5
Manchac, La., U.S., 70 . . . . .282/J6
Manchaca, Tex., U.S., 1,200 . . . . .346/D2
Manchaug, Mass., U.S., 850 . . . . .292/H4
Manche, Fr., *department* 88/B2
Manchester, Eng., U.K. 60/C3
Manchester, Eng., U.K., 392,819,
   (2,482,352 metro.) 66/D6
Manchester, Eng., U.K., 392,819,
   (2,482,352 metro.) 68/C3
Manchester, Eng., U.K., *unitary authority*,
   392,819 . . . . .66/D6
Manchester, Eng., U.K., *unitary authority*,
   392,819 . . . . .68/C3
Manchester, Calif., U.S., 125 . . . . .246/B4
Manchester, Conn., U.S., 54,740 . . . . .253/E2
Manchester, Ga., U.S., 3,988 . . . . .260/B6
Manchester, Ill., U.S., 354 . . . . .266/C4
Manchester, Iowa, U.S., 5,257 . . . . .274/M3
Manchester, Kans., U.S., 102 . . . . .276/E2
Manchester, Ky., U.S., 1,738 . . . . .280/F3
Manchester, Maine, U.S., 2,465 . . . . .286/C4
Manchester, Md., U.S., 3,329 . . . . .288/G1
Manchester, Mass., U.S., 5,228 . . . . .292/L2
Manchester, Mich., U.S., 2,160 . . . . .294/F7
Manchester, Minn., U.S., 81 . . . . .298/D7
Manchester, Mo., U.S., 19,161 . . . . .302/H3
Manchester, N.H., U.S., 107,006 . . . . .312/D6
Manchester, N.Y., U.S., 1,475 . . . . .320/G5
Manchester, Ohio, U.S., 2,043 . . . . .328/C8
Manchester, Okla., U.S., 100 . . . . .330/D1
Manchester, Penn., U.S., 2,350 . . . . .336/H5
Manchester, S. Dak., U.S. 342/H3
Manchester, Tenn., U.S., 8,294 . . . . .344/H5
Manchester, Vt., U.S., 4,180 . . . . .352/A4
Manchester, Wash., U.S., 4,958 . . . . .358/A4
Manchester-by-the-Sea, Mass., U.S., 3,600 . . .292/L2
Manchester Ctr., Vt., U.S., 2,065 . . . . .352/A4
Manchester Depot, Vt., U.S. 352/A4
Manchester St. For., S.C., U.S. 340/D3
Manchurian, China, *plain* 119/F1
Mancos, Colo., U.S., 1,119 . . . . .250/B4
Mancos, Colo., U.S., *river* 250/B4
Mand, Iran, *river* 130/C4
Mandab, Bab al, Yemen, *strait* 137/A2
Mandalay, Mya., 532,949 . . . . .125/B2
Mandalay, Mya., *division* 125/B2
Mandalgovi, Mong. 118/C2

Mandan, N. Dak., U.S., 16,718 . . . . .326/C3
Mandara, Came., *mountains* 153/B1
Mandaree, N. Dak., U.S., 558 . . . . .326/C2
Mandaue, Phil., 259,728 . . . . .120/B4
Manderfield, Utah, U.S., 90 . . . . .350/B5
Manderson, S. Dak., U.S., 626 . . . . .342/C4
Manderson, Wyo., U.S., 104 . . . . .366/C3
Mandeville, Jam., 39,900 . . . . .206/B2
Mandeville, Ark., U.S., 700 . . . . .244/B4
Mandeville, La., U.S., 10,489 . . . . .282/J6
Mandiana, Guin. 149/D2
Mandra, Gr. 100/Inset
Mandurah, W.A., Austl. 170/A3
Manea, Eng., U.K., 1,186 . . . . .68/H5
Manea, Eng., U.K., 1,186 . . . . .70/E2
Manes, Mo., U.S., 100 . . . . .302/D4
Manfred, N. Dak., U.S. 326/F2
Manfredonia, It. 95/C2
Manga, Niger, *region* 152/C2
Mangalore, India 128/B6
Mangas Sprs., N. Mex., U.S. 317/B5
Mangghystaü, Kaz., *oblast* 131/B2
Mangham, La., U.S., 595 . . . . .282/F2
Mango, Togo 151/B1
Mango, Fla., U.S., 8,842 . . . . .256/D6
Mangoky, Madag., *river* 163/A3
Mangonia Park, Fla., U.S., 1,283 . . . . .256/B6
Mangotsfield, Eng., U.K., 27,860 . . . . .73/H2
Mangum, Okla., U.S., 2,924 . . . . .330/C3
Manhasset, N.Y., U.S., 8,362 . . . . .320/C2
Manhattan, Ill., U.S., 3,330 . . . . .266/F2
Manhattan, Kans., U.S., 44,831 . . . . .276/F2
Manhattan, Mont., U.S., 1,396 . . . . .306/D4
Manhattan, Nev., U.S., 60 . . . . .310/B2
Manhattan Beach, Calif., U.S., 33,852 . . . . . .246/B4
Manhattan Beach, Minn., U.S., 50 . . . . .298/C4
Manheim, Penn., U.S., 4,784 . . . . .336/H5
Maní, P.R. 206/A2
Manicouagan, Que., Can., *reservoir* 225/C3
Manicouagan Deux, Que., Can., *reservoir* . . .226/F2
Maniema, Congo, D.R., *region* 155/C2
Manigotagan, Man., Can., 192 . . . . .215/C3
Manila, Phil., *bay* 120/B3
Manila, Phil., *capital*, 1,581,082,
   (9,932,560 metro.) 120/B3
Manila, Ark., U.S., 3,055 . . . . .244/E2
Manila, Utah, U.S., 308 . . . . .350/E3
Manilla, Iowa, U.S., 839 . . . . .274/D4
Manipur, India, *state* 128/F4
Manisa, Tur., 201,300 . . . . .133/A2
Manisa, Tur., *province* 133/A2
Manish, Scot., U.K. 62/C3
Manistee, Mich., U.S., 6,586 . . . . .294/C5
Manistee, Mich., U.S., *county*, 24,527 . . . . .294/C5
Manistee, Mich., U.S., *river* 294/D5
Manistee Natl. For., Mich., U.S. 294/C5
Manistique, Mich., U.S., 3,583 . . . . .294/C4
Manito, Sask., Can., *lake* 212/C5
Manito, Sask., Can., *lake* 227/A8
Manito, Ill., U.S., 1,733 . . . . .266/D3
Manitoba, Can., *province* 203
Manitoba, Man., Can., *lake* 215/B3, B4, D2
Manitou, Man., Can., 775 . . . . .215/B4
Manitou, Mich., U.S., *island* 294/B2
Manitou, Okla., U.S., 278 . . . . .330/D3
Manitou Beach, (Manitou Beach-Devils Lake),
   Mich., U.S., 2,080 . . . . .294/E8
Manitoulin, Ont., Can. 223/C2
Manitoulin, Ont., Can., *county* 223/C2
Manitoulin, Ont., Can., *island* 223/C2
Manitoulin, Ont., Can., *island* 294/G4
Manitou Sprs., Colo., U.S., 4,980 . . . . .250/F3
Manitouwadge, Ont., Can., 2,949 . . . . .222/C3
Manitowaning, Ont., Can. 223/D2
Manitowish, Wisc., U.S. 364/C2
Manitowoc, Wisc., U.S., 34,053 . . . . .364/F5
Manitowoc, Wisc., U.S., *county*, 82,887 . . . .364/F5
Maniwaki, Que., Can., 3,571 . . . . .225/A4
Maniwaki, Que., Can., 3,571 . . . . .226/A5
Manizales, Col., 362,000 . . . . .184/B3
Mankato, Kans., U.S., 976 . . . . .276/D2
Mankato, Minn., U.S., 32,427 . . . . .298/D6
Mankayane, Swaz. 161/B2
Mankota, Sask., Can., 248 . . . . .227/C11
Mankulam, Sri Lan. .126/B2
Manley, Nebr., U.S., 191 . . . . .308/H3
Manley Hot Sprs., Alaska, U.S., 72 . . . . .240/E1
Manlius, Ill., U.S., 355 . . . . .266/D2
Manlius, N.Y., U.S., 4,819 . . . . .320/K4
Manly, N.S.W., Austl. . . . . .170/Inset IV
Manly, Qnsld., Austl. . . . . .170/Inset III
Manly, Iowa, U.S., 1,342 . . . . .274/H1
Mannar, Sri Lan., *gulf* 128/C7
Mannar, Sri Lan. 126/A3
Mannar, Sri Lan., *gulf* 126/A3
Mannar, Sri Lan., *island* 126/A2
Mannford, Okla., U.S., 2,095 . . . . .330/F1
Mannheim, Ger., 307,730 . . . . .86/B4
Manning, Alta., Can., 1,293 . . . . .212/B3
Manning, Ark., U.S. 244/C4
Manning, Iowa, U.S., 1,490 . . . . .274/D4
Manning, Kans., U.S. 276/B3
Manning, N. Dak., U.S. 326/C2
Manning, S.C., U.S., 4,025 . . . . .340/D3
Manning Prov. Park, Br. Col., Can. 214/M6
Manning Prov. Park, Br. Col., Can. 358/E1
Mannington, Ky., U.S., 80 . . . . .280/C3
Mannington, W. Va., U.S., 2,124 . . . . .360/F1
Manningtree, Eng., U.K., 5,043 . . . . .70/G3
Manns Choice, Penn., U.S., 291 . . . . .336/D6
Manns Harbor, N.C., U.S., 325 . . . . .322/P3
Mannsville, N.Y., U.S., 400 . . . . .320/J3
Mannsville, Okla., U.S., 587 . . . . .330/F3
Mannville, Alta., Can., 722 . . . . .212/E4
Mano, Liber., *river* .149/A2
Mano, N.J., U.S., *river* 149/B2
Manokin, Md., U.S., 100 . . . . .288/G4
Manokwari, Indon. 122/E2
Manomet, Mass., U.S., 2,900 . . . . .292/M5
Manono, Congo, D.R. 155/C2
Manono, Sam., *island* 175/B2
Manor, Ga., U.S., 200 . . . . .260/F9
Manor, Penn., U.S., 2,796 . . . . .336/B5
Manor, Tex., U.S., 1,204 . . . . .346/E2, L5
Manorbier, Wales, U.K. 64/B4
Manorhaven, N.Y., U.S., 6,138 . . . . .128/Inset I
Manori, India, *point* . . . . .128/Inset I
Manor Park, Ont., Can. 223/H5
Manorville, N.Y., U.S., 11,131 . . . . .320/F2
Manorville, Penn., U.S., 401 . . . . .336/B4
Manouane, Que., Can. 226/B4
Manowaialee Forest Reserve, Hawaii, U.S. . . .262/H4
Manp'o, N. Kor. 116/B2
Manra, Kiri., *island* .175/B2
Mansa, Zam. 159/B2
Mansa Konko, Gam. .148/C2
Mansel, Nun., Can., *island* 220/M4
Mansfield, Eng., U.K., 71,858, (154,966 metro.) .68/E3
Mansfield, Ark., U.S., 1,097 . . . . .244/A2

Mansfield, Ga., U.S., 392 . . . . .260/D4
Mansfield, Ill., U.S., 949 . . . . .266/E3
Mansfield, La., U.S., 5,582 . . . . .282/B2
Mansfield, Mass., U.S., 22,414 . . . . .292/K4
Mansfield, Mo., U.S., 1,349 . . . . .302/D4
Mansfield, Ohio, U.S., 49,346, (175,818 metro.) .328/E4
Mansfield, Penn., U.S., 3,411 . . . . .336/G2
Mansfield, S. Dak., U.S., 90 . . . . .342/G2
Mansfield, Tenn., U.S., 150 . . . . .344/E2
Mansfield, Tex., U.S., 28,031 . . . . .346/B10
Mansfield, Vt., U.S., mountain 352/B1
Mansfield, Wash., U.S., 319 . . . . .358/F2
Mansfield Ctr., Conn., U.S., 973 . . . . .253/G2
Mansfield Four Corners, Conn., U.S., 700 . . . . . .68/E3
Mansfield Woodhouse, Eng., U.K., 18,204 . . . . .270/C4
Manson, Ill., U.S., 125 . . . . .274/D1
Manson, Iowa, U.S., 1,893 . . . . .274/E2
Manson, Wash., U.S., 900 . . . . .358/E2
Manson Creek, Br. Col., Can. 214/K3
Manston, Eng., U.K. .70/G4
Mansura, La., U.S., 1,573 . . . . .282/E4
Manta, Ecua. 185/A3
Manta, Ecua., bay 185/A3
Mantachie, Miss., U.S., 1,107 . . . . .300/D1
Mantador, N. Dak., U.S., 71 . . . . .326/J3
Mantaro, Peru, river .185/B3
Manteca, Calif., U.S., 49,258 . . . . .246/C2
Mantee, Miss., U.S., 169 . . . . .300/C2
Manteno, Ill., U.S., 6,414 . . . . .266/F2
Manteo, N.C., U.S., 1,052 . . . . .322/P3
Manter, Kans., U.S., 178 . . . . .276/A4
Manti, Utah, U.S., 3,040 . . . . .350/D4
Manti-La Sal Natl. For., Utah, U.S. . . .350/E5, C4, E6
Mantiqueira, Braz., range 188/D3
Mantoloking, N.J., U.S., 423 . . . . .314/E3
Manton, Eng., U.K. 70/C1
Manton, Calif., U.S., 372 . . . . .246/D2
Manton, Mich., U.S., 1,221 . . . . .294/D5
Mantorville, Minn., U.S., 1,054 . . . . .298/E6
Mantova, It. 95/B1
Mantua (Mantova), It. 95/B1
Mantua, Ohio, U.S., 1,046 . . . . .328/J10
Mantua, Utah, U.S., 791 . . . . .350/D1
Mantua, Va., U.S., 7,485 . . . . .354/M2
Manuelito, N. Mex., U.S., 125 . . . . .317/A2
Manufahi, E. Timor, province 122/B1
Manukau, N.Z., 283,200 . . . . .171/B2
Manumuskin, N.J., U.S. 314/D5
Manus, P.N.G., island 172/A2
Manvel, N. Dak., U.S., 370 . . . . .326/H1
Manvel, Tex., U.S., 3,046 . . . . .346/B7
Manville, N.J., U.S., 10,343 . . . . .314/D2
Manville, R.I., U.S., 3,800 . . . . .339/D2
Manville, Wyo., U.S., 101 . . . . .366/D2
Many, La., U.S., 2,889 . . . . .282/C3
Manyara, Tan., lake .158/C1
Manyberries, Alta., Can. 212/E6
Many Farms, Ariz., U.S., 1,548 . . . . .242/F1
Many Farms, Ariz., U.S., lake 242/F1
Manzanar Natl. Hist. Site, Calif., U.S. 246/G6
Manzanillo, Cuba 204/D3
Manzanillo, Mex., 94,893, (125,143 metro.) . . .200/D4
Manzanillo, Pan., point 203/C2
Manzanita, Oreg., U.S., 564 . . . . .334/C2
Manzano, N. Mex., U.S., 54 . . . . .317/D3
Manzanola, Colo., U.S., 525 . . . . .250/G3
Manzini, Swaz. 161/B2
Mao, Chad 153/A4
Mao, Dom. Rep. 205/A1
Maoke, Indon., mountains 122/E2
Maple, Ont., Can. 223/J5
Maple, Ariz., U.S., peak 242/F4
Maple, Iowa, U.S., river 274/D2
Maple, N. Dak., U.S., river 326/G3, H2
Maple, Tex., U.S., 50 . . . . .346/F2
Maple, Wisc., U.S., 200 . . . . .364/B2
Maple Bay, Minn., U.S., 80 . . . . .298/A3
Maple Bluff, Wisc., U.S., 1,358 . . . . .364/D5
Maple City, Kans., U.S. 276/F4
Maple City, Mich., U.S., 225 . . . . .294/D5
Maple Corner, Vt., U.S., 125 . . . . .352/C2
Maple Creek, Sask., Can., 2,270 . . . . .227M11
Maple Falls, Wash., U.S., 277 . . . . .358/C1
Maple Glen, Penn., U.S., 7,042 . . . . .336/M6
Maple Grove, Maine, U.S., 80 . . . . .286/E2
Maple Grove, Minn., U.S., 50,365 . . . . . . .298/D5, E5
Maple Hts., Ohio, U.S., 26,156 . . . . .328/G3, H9
Maple Hill, Kans., U.S., 469 . . . . .276/G2
Maple Hill, N.C., U.S., 40 . . . . .322/K5
Maple Lake, Minn., U.S., 1,633 . . . . .298/C5
Maple Park, Ill., U.S., 765 . . . . .266/E2
Maple Plain, Minn., U.S., 2,088 . . . . .298/D5
Maple Rapids, Mich., U.S., 643 . . . . .294/E6
Maple Ridge, Ohio, U.S., 910 . . . . .328/H4
Maple Shade, N.J., U.S., 19,079 . . . . . . .314/B3, D4
Maplesville, Ala., U.S., 672 . . . . .238/C3
Mapleton, Ill., U.S., 227 . . . . .266/D3
Mapleton, Iowa, U.S., 1,416 . . . . .274/C3
Mapleton, Kans., U.S., 98 . . . . .276/H3
Mapleton, Maine, U.S., 1,889 . . . . .286/D2
Mapleton, Minn., U.S., 1,678 . . . . .298/D7
Mapleton, N. Dak., U.S., 606 . . . . .326/H3
Mapleton, Oreg., U.S., 300 . . . . .334/C3
Mapleton, Penn., U.S., 473 . . . . .336/F5
Mapleton, Utah, U.S., 5,809 . . . . .350/C4
Maple Valley, Wash., U.S., 14,209 . . . . .358/B4
Maplewood, Maine, U.S., 90 . . . . .286/B5
Maplewood, Minn., U.S., 34,947 . . . . .298/F5
Maplewood, Mo., U.S., 9,228 . . . . .302/H3
Maplewood, N.J., U.S., 23,868 . . . . .314/A2
Maplewood, Wisc., U.S., 175 . . . . .364/F4
Maputo, Moz., capital 966,837,
(2,867,000 metro.) 161/B5
Maquam, Vt., U.S., 175 . . . . .352/A1
Maquela do Zombo, Ang. 159/C2
Maquoketa, Iowa, U.S., 6,112 . . . . .274/N3
Maquon, Ill., U.S., 318 . . . . .266/C3
Mar, Braz., range 188/D4
Mara, Kenya, river 157/C4
Mara, Tan., region 158/B1
Mara, Tan., river 158/B1
Mara, Tur. 133/D3
Marabá, Braz., 41,564, (121,814 metro.) 188/D2
Maracaibo, Ven., 1,219,927, (1,363,863 metro.) .182/B1
Maracaibo, Ven., lake 182/B2
Maracay, Ven., 396,125, (799,884 metro.) 182/C1
Maradi, Niger, 110,739 . . . . .152/B3
Maragarazi, Bur., river 188/D2
Marajó, Braz., island 188/D2
Marakei, Kiri., island .175/A1
Maralik, Arm. 103/C2
Maramasike, Sol. Is., island 173/B1
Maramec, Okla., U.S., 104 . . . . .330/C1
Maramures, Rom., county 101/B2
Marana, Ariz., U.S., 13,556 . . . . .242/D5
Maranhão, Braz., state 188/D2
Marano, It., river 97/C1
Marañón, Peru, river 185/B1, B2
Marathon, Ont., Can., 4,416 . . . . .222/C4
Marathon, Fla., U.S., 10,255 . . . . .256/G7
Marathon, Iowa, U.S., 302 . . . . .274/D2
Marathon, N.Y., U.S., 1,063 . . . . .320/J6

Marathon, Tex., U.S., 455 . . . . .346/E5
Marathon, Wisc., U.S., county, 125,834 . . . . . .364/D4
Marathon City, Wisc., U.S., 1,640 . . . . .364/D4
Marazion, Eng., U.K., 1,381 . . . . .73/B4
Marbella, Sp., 100,036 . . . . .94/D4
Marble, Ark., U.S., 40 . . . . .244/B1
Marble, Colo., U.S., 105 . . . . .250/C2
Marble, Minn., U.S., 695 . . . . .298/D3
Marble, N.C., U.S., 350 . . . . .322/B8
Marble, Wash., U.S. .358/H1
Marble Canyon, Ariz., U.S., 100 . . . . .242/D1
Marble City, Okla., U.S., 242 . . . . .330/E2
Marble Cliff, Ohio, U.S., 646 . . . . .328/D9
Marble Dale, Conn., U.S., 475 . . . . .253/B3
Marble Falls, Tex., U.S., 4,959 . . . . .346/C2
Marblehead, Mass., U.S., 20,377 . . . . .292/L3
Marblehead, Ohio, U.S., 762 . . . . .328/E2
Marble Hill, Mo., U.S., 1,502 . . . . .302/G4
Marble Rock, Iowa, U.S., 326 . . . . .274/J2
Marbleton, Wyo., U.S., 720 . . . . .366/A2
Marburg, Ger. 86/B3
Marbury, Md., U.S., 1,200 . . . . .288/F5
Marcala, Sask., Can., 167 . . . . .227/D8
Marceline, Mo., U.S., 2,558 . . . . .302/D2
Marcell, Minn., U.S., 60 . . . . .298/D3
Marcella, Mich., U.S., 475 . . . . .314/E2
Marcellus, Mich., U.S., 1,162 . . . . .294/D7
Marcellus, N.Y., U.S., 1,826 . . . . .320/J5
Marcellus, Wash., U.S. 358/G2
March, Eng., U.K., 16,221 . . . . .68/H4
March, Eng., U.K., 16,221 . . . . .70/E1
Marche, It., region 95/C2
Marchena, Ecua., island 185/Inset
Marchwood, Eng., U.K., 4,908 . . . . .70/B5
Marco, Fla., U.S., 14,879 . . . . .256/G6
Marcola, Oreg., U.S., 400 . . . . .334/D3
Marcoux, Minn., U.S. 298/A3
Marcross, Wales, U.K. 64/C5
Marcus, Iowa, U.S., 1,139 . . . . .274/C2
Marcus, S. Dak., U.S. 342/C3
Marcus, Wash., U.S., 117 . . . . .358/G1
Marcus Hook, Penn., U.S., 2,314 . . . . .336/L6
Marcy, N.Y., U.S., mountain 320/P2
Mardan, Pak., 245,926 . . . . .129/D2
Mardela Sprs., Md., U.S., 364 . . . . .288/L6
Mar del Plata, Arg., 512,880 . . . . .191/D4
Marden, Eng., U.K., 1,635 . . . . .70/F4
Mardin, Tur. 133/E3
Mardin, Tur., province 133/E3
Marecchia, It., river 97/A1
Maree, Scot., U.K., lake 68/G3
Mareham le Fen, Eng., U.K. 68/G4
Maremma, It., region 95/B2
Marengo, Ala., U.S., county, 22,539 . . . . .238/B3
Marengo, Ill., U.S., 6,355 . . . . .266/E1
Marengo, Ind., U.S., 829 . . . . .270/D8
Marengo, Iowa, U.S., 2,535 . . . . .274/K4
Marengo, Ohio, U.S., 297 . . . . .328/E5
Marengo, Wash., U.S. 358/G2
Marengo, Wisc., U.S., 225 . . . . .364/C2
Marenisco, Mich., U.S., 300 . . . . .294/D2
Maresfield, Eng., U.K. 70/E5
Marfa, Tex., U.S., 2,121 . . . . .346/D5
Margaree Forks, N.S., Can. 221/F1
Margaret, Alta., Can., lake 212/C2
Margaret, Ala., U.S., 1,169 . . . . .238/C2
Margaret, Tex., U.S., 60 . . . . .346/J1
Margaretville, N.Y., U.S., 643 . . . . .320/M6
Margarita, Ven., island 182/D1
Margate, Eng., U.K. .60/D3
Margate, Eng., U.K., 56,734 . . . . .70/G4
Margate, Fla., U.S., 53,909 . . . . .256/B5, H5
Margate City, N.J., U.S., 8,193 . . . . .314/E5
Margherita, Congo, D.R., peak 155/C1
Margherita, Ug., peak 157/A3
Margie, Minn., U.S. 298/D2
Margow, Dasht-e, Afg., desert 129/A2
Marham, Eng., U.K. 70/F1
Marholm, Eng., U.K. .70/D1
Maria, Que., Can., 2,458 . . . . .226/L3
Maria, St. Luc., islands 208/B3
Mariana, Braz. 188/D3
Marianao, Cuba 204/B1
Mariana-glas, Wales, U.K. 64/C1
Marianna, Ark., U.S., 5,181 . . . . .244/E3
Marianna, Fla., U.S., 6,230 . . . . .256/C1
Marianna, Penn., U.S., 626 . . . . .336/A5
Mariano Lake, N. Mex., U.S., 250 . . . . .317/B2
Marías, Mex., islands 200/C3
Marias, Mont., U.S., river 306/E1
María Trinidad Sánchez, Dom. Rep., province . .205/B1
Mariaville, Maine, U.S., 414 . . . . .286/D4
Marib, Yemen 137/B1
Mariba, Ky., U.S., 50 . . . . .280/G3
Maribel, Wisc., U.S., 264 . . . . .364/F4
Maribor, Slove., 108,944 . . . . .98/C2
Maricao, P.R. 206/C2
Maricao Forest Reserve, P.R. 206/B2
Maricopa, Ariz., U.S., 1,040 . . . . .242/C4
Maricopa, Ariz., U.S., county, 3,072,149 . . . . .242/B4
Maricopa, Calif., U.S., 1,111 . . . . .246/F7
Maricopa Ind. Res. (Ak-Chin), Ariz., U.S. 242/C5
Marie, Ark., U.S., 108 . . . . .244/E2
Marie Byrd Land, Antar., region 192/B8
Mariehamn, (Maarianhamina), Fin. 81/A2
Mari El, Russ., region 104/D4
Mariemont, Ohio, U.S., 3,408 . . . . .328/B9
Mariental, Nam. 160/C3
Marienthal, Kans., U.S., 90 . . . . .276/A3
Marienville, Penn., U.S., 350 . . . . .336/C3
Marie-Reine, Alta., Can. 212/B3
Maries, Mo., U.S., county, 8,903 . . . . .302/D3
Marietta, Ga., U.S., 58,748 . . . . .260/B4, H2
Marietta, Ill., U.S., 150 . . . . .266/C3
Marietta, Kans., U.S. 276/F2
Marietta, Minn., U.S., 174 . . . . .298/A5
Marietta, Miss., U.S., 248 . . . . .300/D1
Marietta, N.C., U.S., 164 . . . . .322/C6
Marietta, Ohio, U.S., 14,515 . . . . .328/H7
Marietta, Okla., U.S., 2,445 . . . . .330/E4
Marietta, Penn., U.S., 2,689 . . . . .336/H5
Marietta, S.C., U.S., 2,228 . . . . .340/B1, E1
Marietta, Tex., U.S., 112 . . . . .346/P2
Marietta, (Marietta-Alderwood), Wash.,
U.S., 3,594 . . . . .358/C1
Marigot, Dom. 208/B2
Marijampole, Lith. 82/B2
Marin, Calif., U.S., county, 247,289 . . . . . .246/C4, H1
Marin, Calif., U.S., 25,101 . . . . .246/D6
Marin del Rey, Calif., U.S., 8,176 . . . . .246/C2
Marinduque, Phil., island 120/B3
Marine, Ill., U.S., 910 . . . . .266/B3, D5
Marine City, Mich., U.S., 4,652 . . . . .294/G7
Marineland, Fla., U.S. 256/G2
Marine on St. Croix, Minn., U.S., 602 . . . . .298/E5
Marinette, Wisc., U.S., 11,749 . . . . .364/F3
Marinette, Wisc., U.S., county, 43,384 . . . . . . .364/E3
Maringouin, La., U.S., 1,262 . . . . .282/F6
Marino, Van. 173/C2
Marinwood, Calif., U.S., 6,357 . . . . .246/H1

Marion, S.A., Austl. . . . . .170/Inset II
Marion, Ala., U.S., 3,511 . . . . .238/B3
Marion, Ala., U.S., county, 31,214 . . . . .238/B1
Marion, Ark., U.S., 8,901 . . . . .244/E2
Marion, Ark., U.S., county, 16,140 . . . . .244/C1
Marion, Conn., U.S., 1,900 . . . . .253/D3
Marion, Fla., U.S., county, 258,916 . . . . .256/G2
Marion, Fla., U.S., county, 7,144 . . . . .260/B7
Marion, Ida., U.S., 50 . . . . .264/D7
Marion, Ill., U.S., 16,035 . . . . .266/E6
Marion, Ill., U.S., county, 41,691 . . . . .266/E5
Marion, Ind., U.S., 31,320 . . . . .270/E3
Marion, Ind., U.S., county, 860,454 . . . . .270/D5
Marion, Iowa, U.S., 26,294 . . . . .274/L3
Marion, Iowa, U.S., county, 32,052 . . . . .274/H5
Marion, Kans., U.S., 2,110 . . . . .276/E3
Marion, Kans., U.S., county, 13,361 . . . . .276/E3
Marion, Kans., U.S., lake 276/E3
Marion, Ky., U.S., 3,196 . . . . .280/B3
Marion, Ky., U.S., county, 18,212 . . . . .280/E3
Marion, La., U.S., 806 . . . . .282/E1
Marion, Maine, U.S. .286/E4
Marion, Md., U.S., 600 . . . . .288/L7
Marion, Mass., U.S., 5,123 . . . . .292/L6
Marion, Mich., U.S., 836 . . . . .294/D5
Marion, Mich., U.S., 1,305 . . . . .300/D3
Marion, Miss., U.S., county, 25,595 . . . . .300/C4
Marion, Mo., U.S., 60 . . . . .302/D3
Marion, Mo., U.S., county, 28,289 . . . . .302/E2
Marion, Mont., U.S., 100 . . . . .306/B1
Marion, Nebr., U.S., 50 . . . . .308/D3
Marion, N.Y., U.S., 1,400 . . . . .320/G4
Marion, N.C., U.S., 4,943 . . . . .322/A3
Marion, N. Dak., U.S., 146 . . . . .326/G3
Marion, Ohio, U.S., 35,318 . . . . .328/D4
Marion, Ohio, U.S., county, 66,217 . . . . .328/D4
Marion, Oreg., U.S., county, 284,834 . . . . .334/D3
Marion, Penn., U.S., 1,100 . . . . .340/F6
Marion, S.C., U.S., 7,042 . . . . .340/E2
Marion, S.C., U.S., county, 35,466 . . . . .340/E2
Marion, S.C., U.S., lake 340/D3
Marion, S. Dak., U.S., 892 . . . . .342/H4
Marion, Tenn., U.S., county, 27,776 . . . . .344/K4
Marion, Tex., U.S., 1,099 . . . . .346/B2
Marion, Tex., U.S., county, 10,941 . . . . .346/P3
Marion, Va., U.S., 6,349 . . . . .354/E2
Marion, W. Va., U.S., county, 56,598 . . . . .360/F1
Marion, Wisc., U.S., 1,297 . . . . .364/E4
Marion Bridge, N.S., Can. 221/G2
Marion Ctr., Penn., U.S., 451 . . . . .336/C4
Marion Hts., Penn., U.S., 735 . . . . .336/H4
Marion Forks, Oreg., U.S. 334/E3
Marion Jct., Ala., U.S., 50 . . . . .238/B3
Marion Oaks, Fla., U.S., 100 . . . . .256/F2
Marion Sprs., Mich., U.S., 200 . . . . .294/E6
Marionville, Mo., U.S., 2,113 . . . . .302/C4
Maripasoula, Fr. Gui. 183/A2
Mariposa, Calif., U.S., 1,373 . . . . .246/F5
Mariposa, Calif., U.S., county, 17,130 . . . . . . .246/F5
Mariscal Estigarribia, Para. 187/B3
Marissa, Ill., U.S., 2,141 . . . . .266/D5
Maritime Alps, Fr., range 88/D4
Maritsa, Bul., river 101/D3
Mariupol', Ukr., 491,282 . . . . .102/D3
Mari 'Uyun, Leb. 34/A2
Marj, Lib. 73/G2
Mark, Ill., U.S., 491 .266/D2
Mark, Iowa, U.S., 60 . . . . .274/K6
Marka, Som. 157/A3
Markazi, Iran, province 130/C3
Marked Tree, Ark., U.S., 2,800 . . . . .244/E2
Markesan, Wisc., U.S., 1,396 . . . . .364/E5
Market Deeping, Eng., U.K., 12,068 . . . . .68/G4
Market Deeping, Eng., U.K., 12,068 . . . . .70/D1
Market Drayton, Eng., U.K., 9,482 . . . . .68/E4
Market Harborough, Eng., U.K., 16,563 . . . . . . .68/F5
Market Harborough, Eng., U.K., 16,563 . . . . . . .70/C2
Markethill, N. Ire., U.K., 1,337 . . . . .65/C3
Market Rasen, Eng., U.K., 2,948 . . . . .66/H6
Market Rasen, Eng., U.K., 2,948 . . . . .68/G3
Market Weighton, Eng., U.K., 4,371 . . . . .66/G5
Market Weighton, Eng., U.K., 4,371 . . . . .68/F2
Markham, Que., Can., 208,615 . . . . . . .223/F4, K5
Markham, P.N.G., river 172/A2
Markham, Ill., U.S., 12,620 . . . . .266/C6
Markham, Minn., U.S., 60 . . . . .298/E3
Markham, Wash., U.S., 95 . . . . .358/B3
Markle, Ind., U.S., 1,102 . . . . .270/F3
Markleeville, Calif., U.S., 197 . . . . .246/F4
Marklesburg, Penn., U.S., 216 . . . . .336/E5
Markleville, Ind., U.S., 383 . . . . .270/E5
Markle, Tex., U.S. 346/K2
Markleysburg, Penn., U.S., 282 . . . . .336/C6
Marks, Miss., U.S., 1,551 . . . . .300/B1
Marksbury, Eng., U.K. 73/H2
Marksboro, N.J., U.S., 325 . . . . .314/D2
Markstay, Ont., Can. 223/E1
Mark's Tey, Eng., U.K. 70/F3
Marksville, La., U.S., 5,537 . . . . .282/E4
Mark Twain, Mo., U.S., lake 302/E2
Mark Twain Natl. For.,
Mo., U.S. 302/C5, D3, D4, D5, E4, E5, F4
Mark Twain N.W.R.,
Ill., U.S. 266/B2, B3, B4, C2, C4, C5
Mark Twain N.W.R., Iowa, U.S. 274/M5
Markville, Minn., U.S. 298/E4
Markyate, Eng., U.K., 2,866 . . . . .70/D3
Marl, Ger. 86/A3
Marland, Okla., U.S., 280 . . . . .330/E1
Marlboro, Alta., Can., 160 . . . . .212/B4
Marlboro, Maine, U.S., 70 . . . . .286/D4
Marlboro, N.J., U.S., 36,398 . . . . .314/C5, E3
Marlboro, N.Y., U.S., 2,339 . . . . .320/P7
Marlboro, S.C., U.S., county, 28,818 . . . . .340/E2
Marlboro, Vt., U.S., 978 . . . . .352/B5
Marlborough, N.Z., region 171/B3
Marlborough, Eng., U.K., 6,429 . . . . .73/J2
Marlborough, Conn., U.S., 5,709 . . . . .253/F3
Marlborough, Mass., U.S., 36,255 . . . . .292/H3
Marlborough, Mo., U.S., 2,235 . . . . .302/H3
Marlborough, N.H., U.S., 2,009 . . . . .312/B6
Marlette, Mich., U.S., 2,104 . . . . .294/F6
Marley, Md., U.S., 11,200 . . . . .288/H3
Marlin, Tex., U.S., 6,628 . . . . .346/M4
Marlinton, W. Va., U.S., 1,204 . . . . .360/F4
Marlow, Eng., U.K., 17,771 . . . . .70/C3
Marlow, N.H., U.S., 747 . . . . .312/B5
Marlow, Okla., U.S., 4,592 . . . . .330/E3
Marlow Hts., Md., U.S., 6,059 . . . . .288/C7, G4
Marlton, Md., U.S., 7,792 . . . . .288/H4
Marlton, N.J., U.S., 10,260 . . . . .314/D4
Marmaduke, Ark., U.S., 1,158 . . . . .244/E1
Marmara, Tur., sea 133/B2
Marmarth, N. Dak., U.S., 140 . . . . .326/B3
Marmet, W. Va., U.S., 1,693 . . . . .360/C4
Marmora, Ont., Can., 1,589 . . . . .223/H3
Marmora, N.J., U.S., 1,600 . . . . .314/D5
Marne, Fr., department 88/D2
Marne, Fr., river .88/C2, Inset II
Marne, Iowa, U.S., 149 . . . . .274/D5
Marneuli, Geo. 103/C3

Maroa, Ill., U.S., 1,654 . . . . .266/E3
Maromokotro, Madag., mountain 163/B1
Marondera, Zimb. 160/B2
Maroni, Fr. Gui., river 183/A1
Maros, Hun., river 91/C2
Maroua, Came., 124,000 . . . . .153/B1
Marovoay, Madag. 163/B2
Marowijne, Sur., river 183/B2
Marple, Eng., U.K., 19,829 . . . . .66/D6
Marple, Eng., U.K., 19,829 . . . . .302/F4
Marquesas, Fla., U.S., keys 256/F7
Marquette, Iowa, U.S., 421 . . . . .274/M1
Marquette, Kans., U.S., 542 . . . . .276/E3
Marquette, Mich., U.S., 19,661 . . . . .294/B3
Marquette, Mich., U.S., county, 64,634 . . . . . .294/B3
Marquette, Nebr., U.S., 282 . . . . .308/E3
Marquette, Wisc., U.S., 169 . . . . .364/D5
Marquette, Wisc., U.S., county, 15,832 . . . . . .364/D5
Marquette Hts., Ill., U.S., 2,794 . . . . .266/D3
Marquez, N. Mex., U.S., 250 . . . . .317/C2
Marquez, Tex., U.S., 220 . . . . .346/M4
Marquis, Gren. 209/B2
Marra, Jabal, Sudan, mountains 145/B2
Marrakech, Mor., 602,000 . . . . .147/B2
Marrero, La., U.S., 36,165 . . . . .282/J7, K3
Marrowbone, Ky., U.S., 100 . . . . .280/E4
Mars, Penn., U.S., 1,746 . . . . .336/A4
Marsa al Burayqah, Lib. 145/C1
Marsabit, Kenya 157/E2
Marsala, It. 95/C3
Marsa Matruh, Egy. .144/A1
Marsaxlokk, Malta, bay 97/C3
Marsden, Sask., Can., 276 . . . . .227/A8
Marsden, Eng., U.K., 3,873 . . . . .66/E5
Marsden, Eng., U.K., 3,873 . . . . .68/D5
Marseille, Fr., 807,071, (1,349,772 metro.) 88/D5
Marseilles, Ill., U.S., 4,655 . . . . .266/D2
Marseilles, Ohio, U.S., 124 . . . . .328/D4
Marsh, Eng., U.K. 70/A3
Marsh, La., U.S., island 282/F7
Marsh, Mont., U.S. 306/M3
Marsh, Utah, U.S., peak 350/E3
Marshall, Ala., U.S., county, 82,231 . . . . .238/C1
Marshall, Alaska, U.S., 349 . . . . .240/C2
Marshall, Ark., U.S., 1,313 . . . . .244/C2
Marshall, Colo., U.S. 250/A3
Marshall, Ill., U.S., 3,771 . . . . .266/F4
Marshall, Ill., U.S., county, 13,180 . . . . .266/D2
Marshall, Ind., U.S., 360 . . . . .270/D2
Marshall, Ind., U.S., county, 45,128 . . . . .270/D2
Marshall, Iowa, U.S., county, 39,311 . . . . .274/J3
Marshall, Kans., U.S., county, 10,965 . . . . . . .276/F2
Marshall, Ky., U.S., county, 30,125 . . . . .280/B4
Marshall, Mich., U.S., 7,459 . . . . .294/E7
Marshall, Minn., U.S., 12,735 . . . . .298/B6
Marshall, Minn., U.S., county, 10,155 . . . . .298/A2
Marshall, Miss., U.S., county, 34,993 . . . . .300/C1
Marshall, Mo., U.S., 12,433 . . . . .302/C2
Marshall, N.C., U.S., 840 . . . . .322/E7
Marshall, N. Dak., U.S. 326/C2
Marshall, Ohio, U.S., 150 . . . . .328/D7
Marshall, Okla., U.S., 258 . . . . .330/E1
Marshall, Okla., U.S., county, 13,184 . . . . .330/F3
Marshall, S. Dak., U.S., county, 4,576 . . . . . . .342/H2
Marshall, Tenn., U.S., county, 26,767 . . . . . . .344/H4
Marshall, Tex., U.S., 23,935 . . . . .346/P3
Marshall, Va., U.S., 1,200 . . . . .354/H3
Marshall, Wash., U.S., 175 . . . . .358/H2
Marshall, W. Va., U.S., county, 35,519 . . . .360/E1, K6
Marshall, Wisc., U.S., 3,432 . . . . .364/D5
Marshall, Wyo., U.S. .366/D2
Marshall Islands, nation 165
Marshalls Corner, N.J., U.S., 400 . . . . .314/D3
Marshallton, Del., U.S., 1,700 . . . . .255/B2
Marshalltown, Iowa, U.S., 26,009 . . . . .274/J3
Marshalltown, N.J., U.S., 80 . . . . .314/C4
Marshallville, Ga., U.S., 1,335 . . . . .260/D7
Marshallville, Ohio, U.S., 826 . . . . .328/G4
Marsham, Eng., U.K. .70/G1
Marshaw, Eng., U.K. .68/E6
Marsh-Billings-Rockefeller N.H.P., Vt., U.S. . . .352/B3
Marshchapel, Eng., U.K. 66/J6
Marshfield, P.E.I., Can. 224/B2
Marshfield, Eng., U.K., 1,464 . . . . .73/H2
Marshfield, Wales, U.K., 1,464 . . . . .64/E4
Marshfield, Ind., U.S., 100 . . . . .286/E4
Marshfield, Maine, U.S., 350 . . . . .286/E4
Marshfield, Mass., U.S., 24,324 . . . . .292/M4
Marshfield, Mo., U.S., 5,720 . . . . .302/D4
Marshfield, Vt., U.S., 1,496 . . . . .352/C2
Marshfield, Wisc., U.S., 18,800 . . . . .364/C4
Marshfield Hills, Mass., U.S., 2,369 . . . . .292/M4
Marsh Gibbon, Eng., U.K. 68/E6
Marsh Harbour, Bah. 207/B2
Mars Hill, N.C., U.S., 1,764 . . . . .322/E7
Marshville, N.C., U.S., 2,360 . . . . .322/E5
Marshyhope, Del., U.S., creek 255/A6
Marsing, Ida., U.S., 890 . . . . .264/A6
Marske-by-the-Sea, Eng., U.K., 8,936 . . . . .66/F3
Marsland, Nebr., U.S. 308/A1
Marsoui, Que., Can., 373 . . . . .226/L2
Marston, Eng., U.K. 70/B3
Marston, Mo., U.S., 610 . . . . .302/G5
Marston Magna, Eng., U.K. 73/G3
Marstons Mills, Mass., U.S., 8,000 . . . . .292/N6
Mart, Tex., U.S., 2,273 . . . . .346/M4
Martaban, Mya., gulf 125/C3
Martel, Fla., U.S., 375 . . . . .256/F2
Martel, Ohio, U.S., 200 . . . . .328/E4
Martell, Wisc., U.S., 150 . . . . .364/A4
Martelle, Iowa, U.S., 280 . . . . .274/M3
Marten River, Ont., Can. 223/F1
Martensdale, Iowa, U.S., 467 . . . . .274/G5
Martensville, Sask., Can., 4,365 . . . . .227/D8
Martha, Okla., U.S., 205 . . . . .330/C3
Martha Lake, Wash., U.S., 12,633 . . . . .358/C2
Marthasville, Mo., U.S., 837 . . . . .302/E3
Martha's Vineyard, Mass., U.S. 292/M7
Marthaville, La., U.S., 200 . . . . .282/C3
Martin, Slvk. 92/B2
Martin, Ala., U.S., lake 238/D3
Martin, Fla., U.S., county, 126,731 . . . . . .256/A4, H4
Martin, Ga., U.S., 311 . . . . .260/C4
Martin, Ind., U.S., county, 10,369 . . . . .270/C7
Martin, Ky., U.S., 633 . . . . .280/H3
Martin, Ky., U.S., county, 12,578 . . . . .280/F2
Martin, La., U.S., 625 . . . . .282/C2
Martin, Mich., U.S. 294/D7
Martin, Minn., U.S., county, 21,802 . . . . .298/C7
Martin, N.C., U.S., county, 25,593 . . . . .322/L3
Martin, N. Dak., U.S., 96 . . . . .326/E2
Martin, S.C., U.S. 340/C3
Martin, Tenn., U.S., 10,515 . . . . .344/D2
Martin, Tex., U.S., county, 4,746 . . . . .346/F3
Martin Bluff, Miss., U.S. 300/D5
Martinez, Calif., U.S., 35,866 . . . . .246/C4, K1
Martinez, Ga., U.S., 27,749 . . . . .260/D4

Martinez Lake, Ariz., U.S., 50 ... 242/A5
Martinique, Fr., *overseas department* ... 204/F4
Martin N.W.R., Md., U.S. ... 288/K7
Martins Additions, Md., U.S., 875 ... 288/B6
Martinsburg, Iowa, U.S., 126 ... 274/K5
Martinsburg, Mo., U.S., 326 ... 302/E2
Martinsburg, Nebr., U.S., 103 ... 308/G1
Martinsburg, Ohio, U.S., 185 ... 328/F5
Martinsburg, Penn., U.S., 2,236 ... 336/E4
Martinsburg, W. Va., U.S., 14,972 ... 360/L2
Martins Creek, Penn., U.S., 950 ... 336/L4
Martinsdale, Mont., U.S. ... 306/F3
Martins Ferry, Ohio, U.S., 7,226 ... 328/J5
Martins River, N.S., Can. ... 221/C3
Martinsville, Ill., U.S., 1,225 ... 266/F4
Martinsville, Ind., U.S., 11,698 ... 270/C6
Martinsville, Miss., U.S., 200 ... 300/B4
Martinsville, Mo., U.S. ... 302/B1
Martinsville, N.J., U.S., 1,800 ... 314/D2
Martinsville, Ohio, U.S., 440 ... 328/C7
Martinsville, Va., U.S., 15,416 ... 354/D7
Martinton, Ill., U.S., 375 ... 266/F3
Martin Van Buren N.H.S., N.Y., U.S. ... 320/P6
Martinville, Ark., U.S., 40 ... 244/C2
Martlesham, Eng., U.K. ... 70/G2
Martock, Eng., U.K., 4,051 ... 73/G3
Marton, (Lincolnshire), Eng., U.K. ... 66/G6
Marton, (Lincolnshire), Eng., U.K. ... 68/F3
Marton, (N. Yorkshire), Eng., U.K. ... 66/F4
Marton, (N. Yorkshire), Eng., U.K. ... 68/E1
Martorell, P.R. ... 206/D2
Martuni, Arm. ... 103/C2
Marty, S. Dak., U.S., 421 ... 342/G5
Marvel, Colo., U.S., 80 ... 250/B4
Marvell, Ark., U.S., 1,395 ... 244/E3
Marvin, N.C., U.S., 1,039 ... 322/D5
Marvin, S. Dak., U.S., 66 ... 342/J2
Marvine, Utah, U.S., *mountain* ... 350/C5
Marwayne, Alta., Can., 495 ... 212/E4
Marwick, Scot., U.K. ... 62/L1
Mary, Turkm. ... 132/C3
Mary, Turkm., *province* ... 132/C2
Maryborough, Qnsld., Austl. ... 170/E2
Marydel, Del., U.S. ... 255/B4
Marydel, Md., U.S., 147 ... 288/L3
Mary Esther, Fla., U.S., 4,055 ... 256/B1
Maryfield, Man., Can. ... 215/A4
Maryfield, Sask., Can., 359 ... 227/J11
Maryhill, Wash., U.S., 98 ... 358/E4
Maryhill Estates, Ky., U.S., 175 ... 280/B2
Marykirk, Scot., U.K. ... 62/M5
Maryland, U.S., *state* ... 276
Maryland City, Md., U.S., 6,814 ... 288/D5, G3
Maryland Hts., Mo., U.S., 25,756 ... 302/H3, F3
Maryneal, Tex., U.S., 50 ... 346/H3
Maryport, Eng., U.K., 9,797 ... 66/A3
Marys, Nev., U.S., *river* ... 310/C1
Marys Corner, Wash., U.S., 325 ... 358/C4
Marys Harbour, Nfld., Can., 450 ... 218/D3
Marys Home, Mo., U.S., 80 ... 302/D3
Marystown, Nfld., Can., 5,908 ... 218/D5
Marysvale, Utah, U.S., 381 ... 350/B5
Marysville, Calif., U.S., 12,268 ... 246/D3
Marysville, Iowa, U.S., 54 ... 274/J5
Marysville, Kans., U.S., 3,271 ... 276/F2
Marysville, Mich., U.S., 9,684 ... 294/G7
Marysville, Mont., U.S. ... 306/D3
Marysville, Ohio, U.S., 15,942 ... 328/D5
Marysville, Penn., U.S., 2,306 ... 336/H5
Marysville, Tex., U.S. ... 346/L2
Marysville, Wash., U.S., 25,315 ... 358/C1
Maryville, Ill., U.S., 4,651 ... 266/A3
Maryville, Mo., U.S., 10,581 ... 302/B1
Maryville, Tenn., U.S., 23,120 ... 344/P3
Marywood, (Bel Air North), Md., U.S., 6,000 ... 288/J1
Marzuq, Lib. ... 145/B2
Marzuq Sand Sea, Lib. ... 145/B3
Masada, Isr., *ruins* ... 135/B2
Masai, Tan., *steppe* ... 158/C1
Masaka, Ug., 61,300 ... 157/B4
Masan, S. Kor., 441,242 ... 116/C5
Masardis, Maine, U.S., 255 ... 286/D2
Masaryktown, Fla., U.S., 920 ... 256/F3
Masaya, Nicar., 88,971 ... 202/A3
Masaya, Nicar., *department* ... 202/A2
Masbate, Phil. ... 120/B3
Masbate, Phil., *island* ... 120/B3
Mascot, Tenn., U.S., 2,119 ... 344/P2
Mascotte, Fla., U.S., 2,687 ... 256/G3
Mascouche, Que., Can., 29,556 ... 226/C6
Mascoutah, Ill., U.S., 5,659 ... 266/B3, D5
Maseru, Leso., *capital*, 137,837,
  (373,000 *metro.*) ... 161/A2
Masfut, U.A.E. ... 136/D2
Masham, Eng., U.K. ... 66/E4
Mashhad, Iran, 1,887,405 ... 130/D2
Mashpee, Mass., U.S., 12,946 ... 292/N6
Mashulaville, Miss., U.S., 50 ... 300/D2
Masilah, Wadi al, Yemen, *river* ... 137/B1
Masindi, Ug. ... 157/B3
Masirah, Oman, *gulf* ... 137/C2
Masirah, Oman, *island* ... 137/C2
Mask, Ire., *lake* ... 78/B2
Maskall, Bel. ... 201/B2
Maskell, Nebr., U.S., 67 ... 308/H1
Mason, Ill., U.S., 396 ... 266/E5
Mason, Ill., U.S., *county*, 16,038 ... 266/D3
Mason, Ky., U.S., 125 ... 280/F2
Mason, Ky., U.S., *county*, 16,800 ... 280/G2
Mason, Mich., U.S., 6,714 ... 294/E7
Mason, Mich., U.S., *county*, 28,274 ... 294/C6
Mason, Nev., U.S., 500 ... 310/A2
Mason, N.H., U.S., 1,147 ... 292/M6
Mason, Ohio, U.S., 22,016 ... 328/B7, C9
Mason, Okla., U.S. ... 330/F2
Mason, Tenn., U.S., 1,089 ... 344/B4
Mason, Tex., U.S., 2,134 ... 346/J5
Mason, Tex., U.S., *county*, 3,738 ... 346/J5
Mason, Wash., U.S., *county*, 49,405 ... 358/B2
Mason, W. Va., U.S., 1,064 ... 360/B2
Mason, W. Va., U.S., *county*, 25,957 ... 360/B3
Mason, Wisc., U.S., 72 ... 364/B2
Masonboro, N.C., U.S., 11,812 ... 322/K6
Mason City, Ill., U.S., 2,558 ... 266/D3
Mason City, Iowa, U.S., 29,172 ... 274/H1
Mason City, Nebr., U.S., 178 ... 308/E2
Masontown, Penn., U.S., 3,611 ... 336/B6
Masontown, W. Va., U.S., 647 ... 360/G1
Masonville, Colo., U.S., 500 ... 250/E1
Masonville, Iowa, U.S., 104 ... 274/L3
Masonville, Ky., U.S., 1,075 ... 280/C3
Masonville, N.J., U.S., 7,300 ... 314/D4
Massac, Ill., U.S., *county*, 15,161 ... 266/E6
Massac, Ky., U.S., 3,888 ... 280/B3
Massachusetts, U.S., *state* ... 280
Massachusetts, Mass., U.S., *bay* ... 292/M3
Mass. Tpk., Mass., U.S. ... 292/C4
Massacre, Dom. ... 208/B3
Massacre, Nev., U.S., *lake* ... 310/A1
Massadona, Colo., U.S. ... 250/B1
Mass City, Mich., U.S., 300 ... 294/A3

Massena, Iowa, U.S., 414 ... 274/E5
Massena, N.Y., U.S., 11,209 ... 320/M1
Massenya, Chad ... 153/B5
Masset, Br. Col., Can., 926 ... 214/F4
Massey, Ont., Can. ... 223/C1
Massey, Md., U.S., 200 ... 288/L2
Massies Mill, Va., U.S., 175 ... 354/E5
Massieville, Ohio, U.S., 750 ... 328/E7
Massif Central, Fr., *plateau* ... 88/C4
Massillon, Iowa, U.S., 100 ... 274/N4
Massillon, Ohio, U.S., 31,325 ... 328/C4
Massy, Fr. ... 88/Inset II
Mastens Corner, Del., U.S., 175 ... 255/B5
Masters, Colo., U.S. ... 250/F1
Masterson, Tex., U.S. ... 346/F9
Masterton, N.Z. ... 171/C3
Mastic, N.Y., U.S., 15,436 ... 320/E2
Mastic Beach, N.Y., U.S., 11,543 ... 320/E2
Mastigouche Prov. Reserve, Que., Can. ... 226/C5
Masuda, Jap. ... 114/A3
Masuria, Pol., *region* ... 83/E2
Masvingo, Zimb. ... 160/B2
Mat, Alb., *river* ... 99/B2
Matadi, Congo, D.R., 172,730 ... 155/A2
Matador, Tex., U.S., 740 ... 346/H1
Matagalpa, Nicar. ... 202/B2
Matagalpa, Nicar., *department* ... 202/B2
Matagami, Que., Can., 1,939 ... 225/A4
Matagorda, Tex., U.S., 400 ... 346/N7
Matagorda, Tex., U.S., *county*, 37,957 ... 346/M7
Matale, Sri Lan. ... 126/B4
Matam, Sen. ... 148/C2
Matamoras, Ohio, U.S., 957 ... 328/H6
Matamoras, Penn., U.S., 2,312 ... 336/M3
Matamoros, Mex., 376,279, (418,141 *metro.*) ... 200/F2
Matane, Que., Can., 11,635 ... 225/C4
Matane, Que., Can., 11,635 ... 226/J3
Matane Prov. Reserve, Que., Can. ... 226/J3
Matanzas, Cuba, 124,000 ... 204/B1
Matanzas, Cuba, *province* ... 204/B2
Matapédia, N.B., Can. ... 217/C1
Matapédia, Que., Can., 707 ... 226/K4
Matara, Sri Lan. ... 126/B6
Mataram, Indon. ... 122/C2
Mataró, Sp., 106,358 ... 94/H2
Matautu, Sam. ... 175/C2
Matera, It. ... 95/D2
Matewan, W. Va., U.S., 498 ... 360/B5
Matfield, Mass., U.S. ... 292/L4
Matfield Green, Kans., U.S., 60 ... 276/F3
Mather, Calif., U.S. ... 246/F5
Mather, Penn., U.S., 1,200 ... 336/A6
Mather, Wisc., U.S., 40 ... 364/C4
Matherville, Ill., U.S., 772 ... 266/C2
Matherville, Miss., U.S., 50 ... 300/D4
Matheson, Colo., U.S., 50 ... 250/G2
Mathews, Calif., U.S., *lake* ... 246/F10
Mathews, La., U.S., 2,003 ... 282/H7
Mathews, Va., U.S., 850 ... 354/L6
Mathews, Va., U.S., *county*, 9,207 ... 354/L6
Mathias, W. Va., U.S., 80 ... 360/J3
Mathis, Tex., U.S., 5,034 ... 346/L7
Mathiston, Miss., U.S., 720 ... 300/C2
Mathry, Wales, U.K. ... 64/A4
Mathura, India ... 128/C3
Matinicus, Maine, U.S., *island* ... 286/D5
Matinicus Isle, Maine, U.S., 51 ... 286/D5
Matlacha, Fla., U.S., 735 ... 256/F5
Matlacha Pass N.W.R., Fla., U.S. ... 256/F5
Matlock, Eng., U.K. ... 60/C3
Matlock, Eng., U.K., 14,680 ... 67/F5
Matlock, Iowa, U.S., 83 ... 274/C1
Matlock, Wash., U.S. ... 358/B2
Matoaka, W. Va., U.S., 317 ... 360/D6
Mato Grosso, Braz., *plateau* ... 188/C3
Mato Grosso, Braz., *state* ... 188/C3
Mato Grosso do Sul, Braz., *state* ... 188/C4
Mátra, Hun., *mountains* ... 91/B2
Matrah, Oman ... 137/C1
Matsoku, Leso., *river* ... 161/B2
Matsudo, Jap., 465,000 ... 114/C3
Matsue, Jap. ... 114/B3
Matsumae, Jap. ... 114/D1, Inset I
Matsumoto, Jap. ... 114/C2
Matsuyama, Jap., 473,000 ... 114/B3
Mattamuskeet, N.C., U.S., *lake* ... 322/N3
Mattamuskeet N.W.R., N.C., U.S. ... 322/N4
Mattapoisett, Mass., U.S., 6,268 ... 292/L6
Mattatuck St. For., Conn., U.S. ... 253/C3
Mattawa, Ont., Can., 2,270 ... 223/G1
Mattawa, Wash., U.S., 2,609 ... 358/F3
Mattawamkeag, Maine, U.S., 825 ... 286/D3
Mattawamkeag, Maine, U.S., *river* ... 286/D2
Mattawan, Mich., U.S., 2,536 ... 294/D7
Mattawa River Prov. Park, Ont., Can. ... 223/F1
Mattawin, Que., Can., *river* ... 226/C5
Mattawoman, Md., U.S., 3,100 ... 288/G5
Matterhorn, Switz., *mountain* ... 90/B3
Matterhorn, Nev., U.S., *peak* ... 310/C1
Matteson, Ill., U.S., 12,928 ... 266/B6
Matthew Brake N.W.R., Miss., U.S. ... 300/B2
Matthews, Ind., U.S., 595 ... 270/F4
Matthews, Mo., U.S., 100 ... 288/L4
Matthews, Mo., U.S., 605 ... 302/G5
Matthews, N.C., U.S., 22,127 ... 322/D4
Matthews Ridge, Guy. ... 183/A2
Matthew Town, Bah. ... 207/C4
Matti, Sabkhat, Sa. Arab., *salt flat* ... 136/C2
Matti, U.A.E., *salt flat* ... 136/B3
Mattituck, N.Y., U.S., 4,198 ... 320/F1
Mattoon, Ill., U.S., 18,291 ... 266/E4
Mattoon, Ill., U.S., 100 ... 266/E4
Mattoon, Wisc., U.S., 466 ... 364/D3
Mattson, Miss., U.S., 125 ... 300/B1
Mattydale, N.Y., U.S., 6,367 ... 320/J4
Matunuck, R.I., U.S., 750 ... 339/C5
Maturín, Ven., 218,011, (267,876 *metro.*) ... 182/D2
Mauá, Braz. ... 188/Inset II
Mauchline, Scot., U.K., 4,105 ... 62/H7
Mauckport, Ind., U.S., 83 ... 270/D8
Maud, Scot., U.K., 630 ... 62/M3
Maud, Ohio, U.S., 4,800 ... 328/B9
Maud, Okla., U.S., 1,136 ... 330/F2
Maud, Tex., U.S., 1,028 ... 346/P2
Maudlow, Mont., U.S. ... 306/E3
Maugansville, Md., U.S., 2,295 ... 288/C1
Maui, Hawaii, U.S., 128,094 ... 262/C3, Inset II
Maui, Hawaii, U.S., *island* ... 262/C3, D6
Mauk, Ga., U.S., 60 ... 260/C6
Mauldin, S.C., U.S., 15,224 ... 340/B2, E2
Maule, Chile, *region* ... 190/B5
Maumee, Ind., U.S., *river* ... 270/G2
Maumee, Ohio, U.S., 15,237 ... 328/C2
Maumelle, Ark., U.S., 10,557 ... 244/C3
Maumelle, Ark., U.S., *lake* ... 244/C3
Maumturk, Ire., *mountains* ... 78/B2
Maun, Bots., 26,769 ... 160/A1

Maunabo, P.R. ... 206/D2
Mauna Iki, Hawaii, U.S., *mountain* ... 262/H6
Mauna Kea, Hawaii, U.S., *mountain* ... 262/E6, H5
Mauna Kea Forest Reserve, Hawaii, U.S. ... 262/H4
Maunalani Hts., Hawaii, U.S. ... 262/G2
Maunaloa, Hawaii, U.S., 230 ... 262/A3
Mauna Loa, Hawaii, U.S., *mountain* ... 262/D7, H6
Mauna Loa Forest and Game Reserve,
  Hawaii, U.S. ... 262/H5
Mauna Loa Observatory, Hawaii, U.S. ... 262/H5
Maunalua, Hawaii, U.S., *bay* ... 262/K3
Maunawili, Hawaii, U.S., 4,869 ... 262/K3
Maund Bryan, Eng., U.K. ... 68/B5
Maunie, Ill., U.S., 177 ... 266/E5
Maupin, Oreg., U.S., 411 ... 334/E2
Mauren, Liech. ... 90/B1
Maurepas, Fr. ... 88/Inset II
Maurice, Iowa, U.S., 254 ... 274/B2
Maurice, La., U.S., 642 ... 282/E6
Mauricetown, N.J., U.S., 250 ... 314/D5
Maurine, S. Dak., U.S. ... 342/C2
Mauritania, *nation* ... 141
Mauritius, *nation* ... 157
Maury, N.C., U.S., 400 ... 322/K4
Maury, Tenn., U.S., *county*, 69,498 ... 344/C3
Maury City, Tenn., U.S., 704 ... 344/C3
Mausdale, Penn., U.S., 500 ... 336/H4
Mauston, Wisc., U.S., 3,740 ... 364/C5
Maverick, Tex., U.S., *county*, 47,297 ... 346/H7
Mavinga, Ang. ... 159/C5
Mavisdale, Va., U.S., 550 ... 354/D2
Mawbray, Eng., U.K. ... 66/B3
Max, Minn., U.S., 40 ... 298/C3
Max, Nebr., U.S., 60 ... 308/C3
Max, N. Dak., U.S., 278 ... 326/D2
Maxbass, N. Dak., U.S., 91 ... 326/D1
Maxeys, Ga., U.S., 210 ... 260/E4
Maxfield, Maine, U.S., 87 ... 286/D3
Maxie, La., U.S., 125 ... 282/E6
Maxie, Miss., U.S. ... 300/C5
Max Meadows, Va., U.S., 512 ... 354/B7
Maxton, N.C., U.S., 2,551 ... 322/G5
Maxville, Mont., U.S., 40 ... 306/D3
Maxwell, Ind., U.S., 550 ... 270/E5
Maxwell, Iowa, U.S., 807 ... 274/H4
Maxwell, Nebr., U.S., 315 ... 308/D2
Maxwell, N. Mex., U.S., 274 ... 317/F1
Maxwell Colony, S. Dak., U.S., 100 ... 342/H4
Maxwell N.W.R., N. Mex., U.S. ... 317/F1
May, Scot., U.K., *island* ... 62/M6
May, Ida., U.S. ... 264/D5
May, Okla., U.S. ... 330/C1
Maya, Bel., *mountains* ... 201/A3
Mayaguana, Bah., *island* ... 207/C4
Mayaguana, Bah., *passage* ... 207/C4
Mayagüez, P.R., (253,347 *metro.*) ... 206/A2
Maybee, Mich., U.S., 505 ... 294/F7
Maybell, Colo., U.S., 60 ... 250/B1
Maybeury, W. Va., U.S., 550 ... 360/D6
Maybole, Scot., U.K., 4,552 ... 62/G8
Maybrook, N.Y., U.S., 3,084 ... 320/N8
May City, Iowa, U.S., 100 ... 274/D1
Mayday, Colo., U.S., 40 ... 250/B4
Mayday, Ga., U.S. ... 260/F1
Maydi, Yemen ... 137/A1
Mayenne, Fr., *department* ... 88/B2
Mayer, Ariz., U.S., 1,408 ... 242/C3
Mayersville, Miss., U.S., 795 ... 300/A3
Mayerthorpe, Alta., Can., 1,570 ... 212/C4
Mayes, Okla., U.S., *county*, 38,369 ... 330/G1
Mayesville, S.C., U.S., 1,001 ... 340/D3
Mayetta, Kans., U.S., 312 ... 276/G2
Mayfair, Sask., Can., 48 ... 227/C7
Mayfield, Eng., U.K., 1,954 ... 68/D4
Mayfield, Eng., U.K., 1,954 ... 70/E4
Mayfield, Ga., U.S., 150 ... 260/F5
Mayfield, Ida., U.S. ... 264/B6
Mayfield, Kans., U.S., 113 ... 276/E4
Mayfield, Ky., U.S., 10,349 ... 280/B3
Mayfield, Mich., U.S., 225 ... 294/D5
Mayfield, N.Y., U.S., 800 ... 320/N4
Mayfield, N.C., U.S., 100 ... 322/F2
Mayfield, Ohio, U.S., 3,435 ... 328/H8
Mayfield, Okla., U.S. ... 330/C2
Mayfield, Penn., U.S., 1,756 ... 336/K2
Mayfield, S. Dak., U.S. ... 342/H4
Mayfield, Utah, U.S., 420 ... 350/C4
Mayfield Hts., Ohio, U.S., 19,386 ... 328/H9
Mayflower, Ark., U.S., 1,631 ... 244/C3
Mayhew, Miss., U.S., 40 ... 300/D2
Mayhill, N. Mex., U.S. ... 317/E5
Mayland, Tenn., U.S., 150 ... 344/L2
Maymont, Sask., Can., 164 ... 227/C8
Maymyo (Pyin U Lwin), Mya. ... 125/C2
Mayna, La., U.S., 70 ... 282/F4
Maynard, Ark., U.S., 381 ... 244/E1
Maynard, Iowa, U.S., 500 ... 274/L2
Maynard, Mass., U.S., 10,433 ... 292/J3
Maynard, Minn., U.S., 388 ... 298/B6
Maynardville, Tenn., U.S., 1,782 ... 344/P2
Maynooth, Ont., Can. ... 223/H2
Maynooth, Ire. ... 78/C2
Mayo, Yukon, Can., 366 ... 228/B4
Mayo, Yukon, Can., *lake* ... 228/C4
Mayo, Ire., *county* ... 78/B2
Mayo, Fla., U.S., 988 ... 256/E1
Mayo, Ky., U.S., 200 ... 280/F3
Mayo, Md., U.S., 3,153 ... 288/J4
Mayo, S.C., U.S., 1,842 ... 340/C1
Maybridge, N. Ire., U.K., 933 ... 65/E3
Mayodan, N.C., U.S., 2,417 ... 322/F2
Mayombé, Congo, *massif* ... 155/B5
Mayon, Phil., *volcano* ... 120/B3
Mayotte, Fr., *island* ... 163/C2
Mayoworth, Wyo., U.S. ... 366/C2
May Pen, Jam., 45,900 ... 206/B3
Mayreau, St. Vin.-Gren., *island* ... 208/A4
Mays, Ind., U.S., 225 ... 270/F5
Mays Landing, N.J., U.S., 2,321 ... 314/D5
Mays Lick, Ky., U.S., 100 ... 280/G2
Maysville, Ark., U.S., 50 ... 244/A1
Maysville, Colo., U.S., 40 ... 250/D3
Maysville, Ga., U.S., 1,247 ... 260/D3
Maysville, Iowa, U.S., 163 ... 274/N4
Maysville, Ky., U.S., 8,993 ... 280/G2
Maysville, Mo., U.S., 1,212 ... 302/B2
Maysville, N.C., U.S., 1,002 ... 322/L5
Maysville, Okla., U.S., 1,313 ... 330/E3
Maysville, W. Va., U.S., 125 ... 360/H2
Maytown, Ariz., U.S., 435 ... 238/D1
Mayumba, Gabon ... 155/A4
May Valley, Colo., U.S., 60 ... 250/G2
Mayview, Mo., U.S., 294 ... 302/C2
Mayville, Mich., U.S., 1,055 ... 294/F6
Mayville, N.Y., U.S., 1,756 ... 320/B6
Mayville, N. Dak., U.S., 1,953 ... 326/H2
Mayville, Oreg., U.S. ... 334/F2
Mayville, Wisc., U.S., 4,902 ... 364/E5
Maywood, Calif., U.S., 28,083 ... 246/C9
Maywood, Ill., U.S., 26,987 ... 266/B6
Maywood, Mo., U.S., 225 ... 302/E2
Maywood, Nebr., U.S., 331 ... 308/D3

Maywood, N.J., U.S., 9,523 ... 314/B2
Maywood Park, Oreg., U.S., 777 ... 334/B4
Maza, N. Dak., U.S. ... 326/F1
Mazabuka, Zam. ... 159/B3
Mazama, Wash., U.S. ... 358/E1
Mazandaran, Iran, *province* ... 130/C2
Mazar-e Sharif, Afg., 130,600 ... 129/B1
Mazaruni, Guy., *river* ... 183/A2
Mazatenango, Guat., 43,000 ... 201/B5
Mazatlán, Mex., 327,989, (380,509 *metro.*) ... 200/C3
Mazatzal, Ariz., U.S., *peak* ... 242/D3
Mazeikiai, Lith. ... 82/B1
Mazeppa, Minn., U.S., 778 ... 298/E6
Mazie, Ky., U.S., 300 ... 280/H2
Mazie, Okla., U.S., 88 ... 330/G1
Mazomanie, Wisc., U.S., 1,485 ... 364/D5
Mazon, Ill., U.S., 904 ... 266/E2
Mazowe, Zimb., *river* ... 160/B1
Mazowieckie, Pol., *province* ... 83/E2
Mazyr, Bela. ... 82/D3
Mbabane, Swaz., *capital*, 38,290 ... 161/B2
Mbahiakro, C. d'Iv. ... 150/D3
Mbaiki, C.A.R. ... 154/A3
Mbakaou, Came., *reservoir* ... 153/B1
Mbaké, Sen. ... 148/A2
Mbala, Zam. ... 159/C1
Mbale, Ug., 70,437 ... 157/D3
Mbalmayo, Came. ... 153/B3
Mbandaka, Congo, D.R., 169,841 ... 155/B2
M'banza Congo, Ang. ... 159/B2
Mbanza-Ngungu, Congo, D.R. ... 155/A2
Mbarara, Ug., 69,208 ... 157/B4
Mbé, Congo ... 158/C3
Mbemkuru, Tan., *river* ... 158/C3
Mbeni, Com. ... 163/A1
Mbéré, Came., *river* ... 153/B2
Mbeya, Tan., 152,844 ... 158/B2
Mbeya, Tan., *region* ... 158/B2
Mbini, Eq. Gui. ... 154/B3
Mbini, Eq. Gui., *river* ... 154/C3
Mboro, Came., *river* ... 154/D4
Mboune, Sen., *river* ... 148/B2
Mbour, Sen. ... 148/A2
Mbuji-Mayi, Congo, D.R., 486,235 ... 155/B2
Mbuluzane, Swaz., *river* ... 161/B2
Mbuluzi, Swaz., *river* ... 161/B2
McAdam, N.B., Can., 1,513 ... 217/B3
McAdams, Miss., U.S., 200 ... 300/C2
McAdenville, N.C., U.S., 619 ... 322/C4
McAdoo, Penn., U.S., 2,274 ... 336/J4
McAfee, N.J., U.S., 2,600 ... 314/D1
McAlester, Okla., U.S., 17,783 ... 330/G3
McAlester Army Ammunition Plant, Okla., U.S. ... 330/G3
McAlister, N. Mex., U.S. ... 317/G3
McAlisterville, Penn., U.S., 765 ... 336/H4
McAllen, Tex., U.S., 106,414, (569,463 *metro.*) ... 346/K9
McAllister, Mont., U.S., 150 ... 306/E4
McAllister, Wisc., U.S. ... 364/F3
McAlpin, Fla., U.S., 80 ... 256/E1
McArthur, Calif., U.S., 365 ... 246/D1
McArthur, Ohio, U.S., 1,888 ... 328/F7
McBain, Mich., U.S., 584 ... 294/D5
McBaine, Mo., U.S. ... 302/D3
McBean, Ga., U.S., 125 ... 260/H5
McBee, S.C., U.S., 714 ... 340/D2
McBride, Br. Col., Can., 711 ... 214/M4
McBride, Okla., U.S., 80 ... 330/F4
McBrides, Mich., U.S., 232 ... 294/D6
McCabe, Mont., U.S. ... 306/M1
McCain, N.C., U.S., 400 ... 322/G4
McCall, Ida., U.S., 2,084 ... 264/A5
McCall Creek, Miss., U.S., 125 ... 300/B4
McCallsburg, Iowa, U.S., 318 ... 274/H3
McCallum, Nfld., Can., 134 ... 218/C5
McCallum, Miss., U.S., 40 ... 300/C4
McCamey, Tex., U.S., 1,805 ... 346/F4
McCammon, Ida., U.S., 805 ... 264/E7
McCandless, Penn., U.S., 29,022 ... 336/A4
McCanna, N. Dak., U.S. ... 326/H2
McCarthy, Alaska, U.S., 42 ... 240/G2
McCartys, N. Mex., U.S., 325 ... 317/C2
McCaskill, Ark., U.S., 84 ... 244/B4
McCauley, Tex., U.S., 150 ... 346/H3
McCausland, Iowa, U.S., 299 ... 274/P4
McCaysville, Ga., U.S., 1,071 ... 260/B2
McClain, Okla., U.S., *county*, 27,740 ... 330/E3
McClave, Colo., U.S. ... 250/H3
McCleary, Wash., U.S., 1,454 ... 358/B2
McClellan Creek Natl. Grassland, Tex., U.S. ... 346/G9
McClelland, Iowa, U.S., 129 ... 274/C5
McClellandville, Del., U.S., 2,400 ... 255/A4
McClellanville, S.C., U.S., 459 ... 340/E3
McCloud, Calif., U.S., 1,343 ... 246/C1
McClure, Ohio, U.S., 761 ... 328/C3
McClure, Penn., U.S., 975 ... 336/G4
McClure, Va., U.S., 350 ... 354/D2
McClusky, N. Dak., U.S., 415 ... 326/E2
McColl, S.C., U.S., 2,498 ... 340/E2
McComb, Miss., U.S., 13,337 ... 300/B4
McComb, Ohio, U.S., 1,676 ... 328/C3
McCone, Mont., U.S., *county*, 1,977 ... 306/L2
McConnells, S.C., U.S., 287 ... 340/C2
McConnellsburg, Penn., U.S., 1,073 ... 336/E6
McConnelsville, Ohio, U.S., 1,676 ... 328/G6
McCook, Ill., U.S., 254 ... 266/B6
McCook, Nebr., U.S., 7,994 ... 308/D3
McCook, S. Dak., U.S., *county*, 5,832 ... 342/H4
McCook, Miss., U.S., 182 ... 300/C2
McCool Jct., Nebr., U.S., 385 ... 308/G3
McCord, Okla., U.S., 1,711 ... 330/E1
McCordsville, Ind., U.S., 1,134 ... 270/E5
McCormick, Ill., U.S., 40 ... 266/E6
McCormick, S.C., U.S., 1,489 ... 340/B3
McCormick, S.C., U.S., *county*, 9,958 ... 340/B3
McCoy, Calif., U.S., *mountains* ... 246/K9
McCoy, Colo., U.S. ... 250/D2
McCoy, Tex., U.S. ... 346/G2
McCoy, Va., U.S., 90 ... 354/B6
McCracken, Kans., U.S., 211 ... 276/C3
McCracken, Ky., U.S., *county*, 65,514 ... 280/B3
McCreary, Man., Can., 522 ... 215/B4
McCreary, Ky., U.S., *county*, 17,080 ... 280/F4
McCredie Sprs., Oreg., U.S., 90 ... 334/D4
McCrory, Ark., U.S., 1,850 ... 244/D2
McCulloch, Tex., U.S., *county*, 8,205 ... 346/J4
McCullough, Ala., U.S., 200 ... 238/B4
McCune, Kans., U.S., 426 ... 276/G4
McCuneville, Ohio, U.S., 100 ... 328/F6
McCurtain, Okla., U.S., 466 ... 330/H2
McCurtain, Okla., U.S., *county*, 34,402 ... 330/H3
McDade, Tex., U.S., 325 ... 346/L5
McDame, Br. Col., Can. ... 214/H1
McDaniel, Md., U.S., 425 ... 288/J4
McDaniels, Ky., U.S., 90 ... 280/D3
McDavid, Fla., U.S., 175 ... 256/A1
McDermitt, Nev., U.S., 269 ... 310/B1
McDermitt, Nev., U.S. ... 334/J6
McDermott, Ohio, U.S., 650 ... 328/D8
McDonald, Kans., U.S., 159 ... 276/A2
McDonald, Miss., U.S., 70 ... 300/C3
McDonald, Mo., U.S., *county*, 21,681 ... 302/B5
McDonald, N. Mex., U.S. ... 317/G4

McDonald, N.C., U.S., 119 . . . . .322/G5
McDonald, Ohio, U.S., 3,481 . . . . .328/J3
McDonald, Penn., U.S., 2,281 . . . . .336/A5
McDonough, Ga., U.S., 8,493 . . . . .260/C5, J4
McDonough, Ill., U.S., county, 32,913 . . . . . . .266/C3
McDougal, Ark., U.S., 195 . . . . .244/E1
McDowell, N.C., U.S., county, 42,151 . . . . .322/A3
McDowell, Va., U.S. .354/E4
McDowell, W. Va., U.S., county, 27,329 . . . . . . .360/C6
McDuffie, Ga., U.S., county, 21,231 . . . . .260/F5
McEwen, Tenn., U.S., 1,702 . . . . .344/F2
McEwensville, Penn., U.S., 314 . . . . .336/H3
McFadden, Wyo., U.S. 366/C3
McFaddin, Tex., U.S. .346/L7
McFaddin N.W.R., Tex., U.S. 346/P6
McFall, Mo., U.S., 135 . . . . .302/B1
McFarlan, N.C., U.S., 89 . . . . .322/F5
McFarland, Calif., U.S., 9,618 . . . . .246/F4
McFarland, Kans., U.S., 271 . . . . .276/F2
McFarland, Mich., U.S. 294/B3
McFarland, Wisc., U.S., 6,416 . . . . .364/D5
McGaffey, N. Mex., U.S. 317/B2
McGee, Sask., Can. .227/B9
7cGee, Mo., U.S. 302/F4
McGehee, Ark., U.S., 4,570 . . . . .244/D4
McGill, Nev., U.S., 1,054 . . . . .310/C2
McGrady, N.C., U.S., 250 . . . . .322/C2
McGrath, Alaska, U.S., 401 . . . . .240/D2
McGrath, Minn., U.S., 65 . . . . .298/D4
McGraw, N.Y., U.S., 1,000 . . . . .320/J5
McGraw Brook, N.B., Can. 217/C2
McGregor, Iowa, U.S., 871 . . . . .274/M1
McGregor, Minn., U.S., 404 . . . . .298/D4
McGregor, N. Dak., U.S., 60 . . . . .326/C1
McGregor, Tex., U.S., 4,727 . . . . .346/L4
McGrew, Nebr., U.S., 103 . . . . .308/A2
8cGuffey, Ohio, U.S., 522 . . . . .328/C4
McGuireville, Ariz., U.S. 242/D3
McHenry, Ill., U.S., 21,501 . . . . .266/A4, E1
McHenry, Ill., U.S., county, 260,077 . . . . .266/A5, E1
McHenry, Ky., U.S., 417 . . . . .280/D3
McHenry, Md., U.S. 250 . . . . .288/A3
McHenry, Miss., U.S., 225 . . . . .300/C5
McHenry, N. Dak., U.S., 71 . . . . .326/G2
McHenry, N. Dak., U.S., county, 5,987 . . . . . . .326/E1
Mchinji, Mal. 159/A2
McIndoe Falls, Vt., U.S., 200 . . . . .352/C2
McIntire, Iowa, U.S., 173 . . . . .274/I1
McIntosh, Ala., U.S., 244 . . . . .238/A4
McIntosh, Fla., U.S., 453 . . . . .256/F2
McIntosh, Ga., U.S., county, 10,847 . . . . .260/H9
McIntosh, Minn., U.S., 638 . . . . .298/B3
McIntosh, N. Mex., U.S., 100 . . . . .317/D3
McIntosh, N. Dak., U.S., county, 3,390 . . . . . . .326/F3
McIntosh, Okla., U.S., county, 19,456 . . . . .330/G2
McIntosh, S. Dak., U.S., 217 . . . . .342/D2
McIntyre, Ga., U.S., 718 . . . . .260/E6
McKamie, Ark., U.S. .244/B4
McKay Beach, Wash., U.S., 600 . . . . .288/H7
McKay Creek N.W.R., Oreg., U.S. 334/H2
McKean, Penn., U.S., 389 . . . . .336/E1
McKean, Penn., U.S., county, 45,936 . . . . .336/D2
McKee, Ky., U.S., 878 . . . . .280/G3
McKee City, N.J., U.S., 2,800 . . . . .314/D5
McKeesport, Penn., U.S., 24,040 . . . . .336/E7
McKees Rocks, Penn., U.S., 6,622 . . . . .336/D7
McKenna, Wash., U.S., 800 . . . . .358/C3
McKenney, Va., U.S. 441 . . . . .354/H7
McKenzie, Ala., U.S., 644 . . . . .238/C4
McKenzie, N. Dak., U.S. 326/E3
McKenzie, N. Dak., U.S., county, 5,737 . . . . . . .326/B2
McKenzie, Tenn., U.S., 5,295 . . . . .344/D4
McKenzie Bridge, Oreg., U.S., 150 . . . . .334/D3
McKerrow, Ont., Can. 223/D1
McKibben, Tex., U.S. 346/G8
McKinley, U.S., mountain 193/C11
McKinley, Alaska, U.S., mountain 240/E2
McKinley, N. Mex., U.S., county, 74,798 . . . . . .317/B2
McKinley, Wisc., U.S., 100 . . . . .364/A3
McKinley, Wisc., U.S. 366/D2
McKinley Park, Alaska, U.S. 240/F2
McKinleyville, Calif., U.S., 13,599 . . . . .246/A2
McKinney, Tex., U.S., 54,369 . . . . .346/C8, M2
McKinnon, Ga., U.S., 70 . . . . .260/H9
McKinnon, Tenn., U.S., 40 . . . . .344/F2
McKinnon, Wyo., U.S., 49 . . . . .366/B3
McKittrick, Calif., U.S., 160 . . . . .246/F7
McKittrick, Mo., U.S., 72 . . . . .302/E3
McKnight, Okla., U.S. 330/C3
McLain, Miss., U.S., 603 . . . . .300/D4
McLaughlin, S. Dak., U.S., 775 . . . . .342/E2
McLaurin, Miss., U.S., 250 . . . . .300/C4
McLean, Ill., U.S., 808 . . . . .266/D3
McLean, Ill., U.S., county, 150,433 . . . . .266/E3
McLean, Ky., U.S., county, 9,938 . . . . .280/C3
McLean, Nebr., U.S. .308/G1
McLean, N. Dak., U.S., county, 9,311 . . . . .326/D2
McLean, Tex., U.S., 830 . . . . .346/G9
McLean, Va., U.S., 38,929 . . . . .354/I3, M2
McLean N.W.R., N. Dak., U.S. 326/D2
McLeansboro, Ill., U.S., 2,945 . . . . .266/E5
McLean Settlement, N.B., Can. 217/E2
McLeansville, N.C., U.S., 1,080 . . . . .322/F2
McLeese Lake, Br. Col., Can., 261 . . . . .214/L5
McLemoresville, Tenn., U.S., 259 . . . . .344/D9
McLendon-Chisholm, Tex., U.S., 914 . . . . .346/N2
McLennan, Alta., Can., 804 . . . . .212/B3
McLennan, Tex., U.S., county, 213,517 . . . . . . .346/L4
McLeod, Minn., U.S., county, 34,898 . . . . .298/C6
McLeod, Mont., U.S. 306/F4
McLeod, N. Dak., U.S. 326/H3
McLeod, Tex., U.S., 175 . . . . .346/P3
McLeod Lake, Br. Col., Can. 214/L4
McLeods Corner, Mich., U.S. 294/D3
McLeod Valley, Alta., Can. 212/C4
M'Clintock, Nun., Can., channel 220/H2
McLoud, Okla., U.S., 3,548 . . . . .330/E2
McLoughlin House N.H.S., Oreg., U.S. 334/A3
McLouth, Kans., U.S., 868 . . . . .276/F2
M'Clure, N.W. Terr., Can., strait 220/D2
McManus, La., U.S., 350 . . . . .282/G5
McMillan, Mich., U.S., 100 . . . . .294/D3
McMinn, Tenn., U.S., county, 49,015 . . . . .344/M4
McMinnville, Oreg., U.S., 26,499 . . . . .334/C4
McMinnville, Tenn., U.S., 12,749 . . . . .344/K3
McMullen, Ala., U.S., 66 . . . . .238/A4
McMullen, Tex., U.S., county, 851 . . . . .346/K7
McMurdo, Antar., sound 192/B5
McMurray, Wash., U.S., 150 . . . . .358/C1
McNab, Ark., U.S. 244/B4
McNabb, Ill., U.S., 310 . . . . .266/D3
McNair, Miss., U.S., 50 . . . . .300/A4
McNairy, Tenn., U.S., county, 24,653 . . . . .344/D4
McNally, Maine, U.S. .286/D2
McNary, Ariz., U.S., 349 . . . . .242/F3
McNary, La., U.S., 211 . . . . .282/D5
McNary, Tex., U.S., 40 . . . . .346/C4
McNaughton, Wisc., U.S. 364/D3
McNeal, Ariz., U.S., 100 . . . . .242/F6
McNeil, Ark., U.S., 662 . . . . .244/B4
McNeill, Miss., U.S., 425 . . . . .300/C5

McPherson, Kans., U.S., 13,770 . . . . .276/E3
McPherson, Kans., U.S., county, 29,554 . . . . . .276/E3
McPherson, Nebr., U.S., county, 533 . . . . .308/C2
McPherson, S. Dak., U.S., county, 2,904 . . . . . .342/F2
McQuady, Ky., U.S., 100 . . . . .280/D3
McQueen, Okla., U.S. 330/C3
McQueeney, Tex., U.S., 2,527 . . . . .346/B2
McRae, Alta., Can. 212/E4
McRae, Ark., U.S., 661 . . . . .244/D2
McRae, Ga., U.S., 2,682 . . . . .260/F7
McRoberts, Ky., U.S., 921 . . . . .280/H3
McSherrystown, Penn., U.S., 2,691 . . . . .336/G6
McVeigh, Ky., U.S., 550 . . . . .280/H3
McVeytown, Penn., U.S., 405 . . . . .336/F4
McVille, Miss., U.S. 50 . . . . .300/C3
McVille, N. Dak., U.S., 470 . . . . .326/G2
McWhorter, W. Va., U.S., 175 . . . . .360/F2
McWilliams, Ala., U.S., 125 . . . . .238/B4
McWillie, Okla., U.S. .330/D1
Meacham, Sask., Can., 90 . . . . .227/E8
Meacham, Oreg., U.S. 334/H2
Mead, Ariz., U.S., lake 242/A1
Mead, Colo., U.S., 2,017 . . . . .250/F1
Mead, Nebr., U.S., 564 . . . . .308/H3
Mead, Nev., U.S., lake 310/C3
Mead, Okla., U.S., 123 . . . . .330/F3
Mead, Wash., U.S., 2,100 . . . . .358/H2
Meade, Kans., U.S., 1,672 . . . . .276/B4
Meade, Kans., U.S., county, 4,631 . . . . .276/B4
Meade, Ky., U.S., county, 26,349 . . . . .280/D3
Meade, S. Dak., U.S., county, 24,253 . . . . .342/C3
Meadie, Scot., U.K., lake 62/H2
Meadow, S. Dak., U.S. 342/C2
Meadow, Tex., U.S., 658 . . . . .346/F2
Meadow, Utah, U.S., 254 . . . . .350/B5
Meadow Bridge, W. Va., U.S., 321 . . . . .360/E5
Meadow Brook, N.B., Can. 217/E2
Meadowbrook, Ala., U.S., 4,697 . . . . .238/E1
Meadowbrook Acres, (Woodside East), Del., U.S. . .255/B4
Meadow Creek, W. Va., U.S., 100 . . . . .360/E5
Meadowdale, Wyo., U.S. 366/D2
Meadow Glade, Wash., U.S., 2,225 . . . . .358/C4
Meadow Grove, Nebr., U.S., 311 . . . . .308/G1
Meadow Lake, Sask., Can., 4,582 . . . . .227/B6
Meadow Lake, N. Mex., U.S., 4,491 . . . . .317/D3
Meadow Lake Prov. Park, Sask., Can. 227/A6
Meadowlakes, Tex., U.S., 1,293 . . . . .346/C2
Meadowlands, Minn., U.S., 111 . . . . .298/E3
Meadow Portage, Man., Can., 80 . . . . .215/B3
Meadows, Ida., U.S. .264/A5
Meadows, N.H., U.S., 100 . . . . .312/D3
Meadowview, (Emory-Meadowview), ...354/D3
Va., U.S., 2,266
Meadowview Estates, Ky., U.S., 422 . . . . .280/B2
Meadow Vista, Calif., U.S., 3,096 . . . . .246/D3
Meadview, Ariz., U.S. 242/A2
Meadville, Miss., U.S., 519 . . . . .300/B4
Meadville, Mo., U.S., 457 . . . . .302/C2
Meadville, Penn., U.S., 13,685 . . . . .336/A2
Meaford, Ont., Can., 4,559 . . . . .223/E3
Meagher, Mont., U.S., county, 1,932 . . . . .306/F3
Mealsgate, Eng., U.K. 68/D4
Mealy, Nfld., Can., mountains 218/A3
Meander River, Alta., Can. 212/B1
Meansville, Ga., U.S., 192 . . . . .260/C5
Mears, Mich., U.S., 425 . . . . .294/C6
Measham, Eng., U.K., 3,656 . . . . .68/D4
Measham, Eng., U.K., 3,656 . . . . .70/A1
Meath, Ire., county 78/C2
Mebane, N.C., U.S., 7,284 . . . . .322/G2
Mecca, Sa. Arab., 965,697 . . . . .136/A2
Mecca, Sa. Arab., emirate 136/B2
Mecca, Ind., U.S., 355 . . . . .270/B5
Mecca, Ohio, U.S., 300 . . . . .328/J3
Mechanic Falls, Maine, U.S., 3,138 . . . . .286/B4
Mechanicsburg, Ill., U.S., 456 . . . . .266/D4
Mechanicsburg, Ohio, U.S., 1,744 . . . . .328/C5
Mechanicsburg, Penn., U.S., 9,042 . . . . .336/C5
Mechanicsburg, Va., U.S., 80 . . . . .354/B6
Mechanic Settlement, N.B., Can. 217/D3
Mechanicsville, Iowa, U.S., 1,173 . . . . .274/M4
Mechanicsville, Md., U.S., 750 . . . . .288/G6
Mechanicsville, (Montour County),
Penn., U.S., 3,099 . . . . .336/H4
Mechanicsville, (Schuylkill County),
Penn., U.S., 515 . . . . .336/J4
Mechanicsville, Vt., U.S., 500 . . . . .352/A2
Mechanicville, N.Y., U.S., 5,019 . . . . .320/P5
Mechelen, Belg., 75,946, (307,433 metro.) 85/C1
Mecklenburg, Ger., bay 86/B1
Mecklenburg, N.C., U.S., county, 695,454 . . . . .322/D4
Mecklenburg, Va., U.S., county, 32,380 . . . . . .354/G7
Meckling, S. Dak., U.S., 100 . . . . .342/H5
Mecosta, Mich., U.S., 440 . . . . .294/D6
Mecosta, Mich., U.S., county, 40,553 . . . . .294/D6
Mecsek, Hun., mountains 91/B2
Medan, Indon. 122/A1
Medanales, N. Mex., U.S., 450 . . . . .317/D1
Medart, Fla., U.S., 175 . . . . .256/D1
Medaryville, Ind., U.S., 565 . . . . .270/C2
Medbourne, Eng., U.K. 68/F4
Medborne, Eng., U.K. 73/D3
Meddybemps, Maine, U.S., 150 . . . . .286/E3
Medellín, Col., 1,885,001 . . . . .184/B3
Medfield, Mass., U.S., 12,273 . . . . .292/J4
Medford, Mass., U.S., 55,765 . . . . .292/C7, K3
Medford, Minn., U.S., 984 . . . . .298/D6
Medford, N.J., U.S., 22,253 . . . . .314/D4
Medford, N.Y., U.S., 21,985 . . . . .320/E2
Medford, Okla., U.S., 1,172 . . . . .330/E1
Medford, Oreg., U.S., 63,154, (181,269 metro.) . .334/D6
Medford, Wisc., U.S., 4,350 . . . . .364/C3
Medford Ctr., Maine, U.S. 286/D3
Medford Lakes, N.J., U.S., 4,173 . . . . .314/D4
Medgidia, Rom. 101/E3
Media, Ill., U.S. 130 .266/C3
Media, Penn., U.S., 5,533 . . . . .336/L6, L7
Mediapolis, Iowa, U.S., 1,644 . . . . .274/M5
Medias, Rom. 101/C2
Medical Lake, Wash., U.S., 3,758 . . . . .358/H2
Medical Sprs., Oreg., U.S. 334/J3
Medicine Bow, Colo., U.S., mountains 250/D1
Medicine Bow, Wyo., U.S., 274 . . . . .366/C3
Medicine Bow, Wyo., U.S., river 366/C2
Medicine Bow Natl. For., Wyo., U.S. 366/C3, D2, D3
Medicine Hat, Alta., Can., 51,249 . . . . .212/E6
Medicine Lake, Mont., U.S., 269 . . . . .306/M1
Medicine Lake N.W.R., Mont., U.S. 306/M1
Medicine Lodge, Kans., U.S., 2,193 . . . . .276/D4
Medicine Lodge, Kans., U.S., river 276/C4
Medicine Park, Okla., U.S., 373 . . . . .330/D3
Medika, Man., Can. 215/D4
Medina, Sa. Arab., 608,295 . . . . .136/A1
Medina, Sa. Arab., emirate 136/B1
Medina, Minn., U.S., 4,005 . . . . .298/D5
Medina, N.Y., U.S., 6,415 . . . . .320/E4
Medina, N. Dak., U.S., 335 . . . . .326/F3
Medina, Ohio, U.S., 25,139 . . . . .328/F5
Medina, Ohio, U.S., county, 151,095 . . . . .328/G1, G3

Medina, Tenn., U.S., 969 . . . . .344/D3
Medina, Tex., U.S., county, 39,304 . . . . .346/J6
Medina, Wash., U.S., 3,011 . . . . .358/A4
Medina del Campo, Sp. 94/D2
Medinah, Ill., U.S., 2,500 . . . . .266/B5
Medio, Tex., U.S., creek 346/A3
Medit, Bru. 121/B2
Mediterranean, It., sea 95/C3
Mediterranean, Mor., sea 147/D1
Mediterranean, Sp., sea 94/E4
Mediterranean, Sp., Fr., sea 88/C6, B5
Mediterranean, Syria, sea 134/A2
Mediterranean, Tun., sea 146/A1
Mediterranean, Tur., sea 133/B4
Medjerda, Tun., river .146/B1
Medley, Alta., Can. 212/E4
Medley, Fla., U.S., 1,098 . . . . .256/A6
Medon, Tenn., U.S., 191 . . . . .344/D4
Medora, Man., Can. .215/A4
Medora, Ill., U.S., 501 . . . . .266/A2, C4
Medora, Ind., U.S., 565 . . . . .270/D7
Medora, Kans., U.S., 350 . . . . .276/E3
Medora, N. Dak., U.S., 100 . . . . .326/B3
Meductic, N.B., Can., 189 . . . . .217/B3
Medway, Eng., U.K., river 70/E4
Medway, Eng., U.K., 1,489 . . . . .286/D3
Medway, Mass., U.S., 12,448 . . . . .292/J4
Meeker, Colo., U.S., 2,242 . . . . .250/C1
Meeker, La., U.S., 40 .282/E4
Meeker, Minn., U.S., county, 22,644 . . . . .298/C5
Meeker, Ohio, U.S., 250 . . . . .328/D4
Meeker, Okla., U.S., 978 . . . . .330/F2
Meeks Bay, Calif., U.S., 50 . . . . .246/E3
Meelpaeg, Nfld., Can., reservoir 218/C5
Meeman Shelby Forest St. Park, Tenn., U.S. 344/A4
Meers, Okla., U.S., 40 . . . . .330/D3
Meerut, India, 1,074,229, (1,167,399 metro.) . . .128/C3
Meeteetse, Wyo., U.S., 351 . . . . .366/B1
Meeth, Eng., U.K. 73/D3
Mégantic, Que., Can., lake 286/B3
Mégantic, Maine, U.S., lake 286/B3
Megargel, Ala., U.S., 90 . . . . .238/B4
Megargel, Tex., U.S., 248 . . . . .346/K2
Meggett, S.C., U.S., 1,230 . . . . .340/D4
Meghalaya, India, state 128/F3
Meghna, Bangl., river 127/D5
Meghri, Arm. 103/D4
Mehedinţi, Rom., county 101/B3
Meherrin, Va., U.S., 175 . . . . .354/G6
Mehlville, Mo., U.S., 28,822 . . . . .302/F3, H3
Meidrim, Wales, U.K. .64/C4
Meifod, Wales, U.K. 64/C2
Meiganga, Came. 153/B2
Meighen, Nun., Can., island 220/J1
Meigs, Ga., U.S., 1,090 . . . . .260/C9
Meigs, Ohio, U.S., county, 23,072 . . . . .328/F7
Meigs, Tenn., U.S., county, 11,086 . . . . .344/M4
Meiktila, Mya. 125/B2
Meire Grove, Minn., U.S., 149 . . . . .298/C5
Meissen, Ger. 86/C3
Mejicanos, El. Salv. 203/A2
Mek'ele, Eth., 119,779 . . . . .156/C1
Mékambo, Gabon 155/B1
Mekinock, N. Dak., U.S., 125 . . . . .326/H1
Meknès, Mor., 401,000 . . . . .147/C1
Mekong, Camb., river 124/D3
Mekong, China, river .119/C2
Mekong, Laos, river 124/A1, C4
Mekong, Mya., river .125/C2
Mekong, Thai., river .125/C2
Mekong, Viet., river .123/A4
Mekoryuk, Alaska, U.S., 210 . . . . .240/B2
Mékrou, Ben., river 151/B2
Melaka, Malay. 121/B2
Melba, Ida., U.S., 439 . . . . .264/A6
Melbeta, Nebr., U.S., 105 . . . . .308/A2
Melbourn, Eng., U.K., 4,006 . . . . .68/H5
Melbourn, Eng., U.K., 4,006 . . . . .70/E2
Melbourne, Vic., Austl., state capital,
(3,338,704 metro.) . . . . .170/D3, Inset V
Melbourne, Ark., U.S., 1,673 . . . . .244/D1
Melbourne, Fla., U.S., 71,382, (476,230 metro.) . .256/H3
Melbourne, Iowa, U.S., 794 . . . . .274/H4
Melbourne, Ky., U.S., 457 . . . . .280/G1
Melbourne Beach, Fla., U.S., 3,335 . . . . .256/H3
Melby, Minn., U.S., 80 . . . . .298/B4
Melcher-Dallas, Iowa, U.S., 1,298 . . . . .274/H5
Melcombe Bingham, Eng., U.K. 73/H3
Melder, La., U.S., 90 .282/D4
Meldrum, Ky., U.S., 225 . . . . .280/G4
Meldrum Bay, Ont., Can. 223/B2
Meleb, Man., Can. 215/C4
Melekeok, Palau 172/C3
Mélèzes, Que., Can., river 225/D2
Melfa, Va., U.S., 450 .354/M5
Melfi, Chad 153/B5
Melfort, Sask., Can., 5,559 . . . . .227/F8
Melilla, Sp., 66,411 .94/E5
Melipilla, Chile 190/Inset
Melita, Man., Can., 1,111 . . . . .215/A4
Melitopol', Ukr., 170,017 . . . . .102/D3
Melitota, Md., U.S., 225 . . . . .288/K2
Melksham, Eng., U.K., 13,074 . . . . .73/H2
Mellen, Wisc., U.S., 845 . . . . .364/C2
Mellette, S. Dak., U.S., 248 . . . . .342/G2
Mellette, S. Dak., U.S., county, 2,083 . . . . .342/E4
Mellieha, Malta 97/B2
Mellieha, Malta, bay .97/B2
Melling, Eng., U.K. 66/C4
Mellott, Ind., U.S., 207 . . . . .270/B4
Mellwood, Ark., U.S. .244/E3
Melmerby, Eng., U.K. 66/C3
Melmore, Ohio, U.S., 275 . . . . .328/D3
Melo, Uru., 46,883 . . . . .187/C2
Melody Hill, Ind., U.S., 3,066 . . . . .270/A8
Melplash, Eng., U.K. .73/G3
Melrose, N.B., Can. 221/E2
Melrose, Scot., U.K., 1,656 . . . . .62/L7
Melrose, Iowa, U.S., 130 . . . . .274/H6
Melrose, Kans., U.S., 60 . . . . .276/H4
Melrose, La., U.S., 90 . . . . .282/D3
Melrose, Md., U.S., 750 . . . . .288/G1
Melrose, Mass., U.S., 27,134 . . . . .292/C7, K3
Melrose, Minn., U.S., 3,091 . . . . .298/C5
Melrose, Mont., U.S. .306/D4
Melrose, N. Mex., U.S., 736 . . . . .317/G3
Melrose, Ohio, U.S., 322 . . . . .328/B3
Melrose, Oreg., U.S., 550 . . . . .334/C4
Melrose, Wisc., U.S., 529 . . . . .364/B4
Melrose Park, Ill., U.S., 23,171 . . . . .266/B6
Melrose Park, N.Y., U.S., 2,359 . . . . .320/H5
Melrude, Minn., U.S. .298/E3
Melson, Md., U.S., 225 . . . . .288/N6
Melstone, Mont., U.S., 136 . . . . .306/J3
Melstrand, Mich., U.S. 294/C3
Meltham, Eng., U.K., 7,514 . . . . .66/E5
Meltham, Eng., U.K., 7,514 . . . . .68/D2
Melton Mowbray, Eng., U.K., 24,348 . . . . .68/F4
Melton Mowbray, Eng., U.K., 24,348 . . . . .73/D1
Melun, Fr. . . . . .88/Inset II

Melvaig, Scot., U.K. .62/E3
Melvern, Kans., U.S., 429 . . . . .276/G3
Melvern, Kans., U.S., lake 276/G3
Melvich, Scot., U.K. 62/J1
Melville, Austl., island 170/C1
Melville, W.A., Austl. . . . . .170/Inset I
Melville, Nfld., Can., lake 218/B2
Melville, N.W. Terr., Can., island 220/F1
Melville, Nun., Can., peninsula 220/M3
Melville, Sask., Can., 4,453 . . . . .227/H10
Melville, La., U.S., 1,376 . . . . .282/E5
Melville, Mont., U.S. .306/G3
Melville, N. Dak., U.S. 326/F2
Melvin, Ala., U.S., 60 . . . . .238/A4
Melvin, Ill., U.S., 465 .266/E3
Melvin, Iowa, U.S., 243 . . . . .274/C1
Melvin, Mich., U.S., 160 . . . . .294/G6
Melvin, Tex., U.S., 155 . . . . .346/J4
Melvina, Wisc., U.S., 93 . . . . .364/C5
Melvindale, Mich., U.S., 10,735 . . . . .294/B7
Melvin Mills, N.H., U.S., 125 . . . . .312/C5
Melvin Vil., N.H., U.S., 275 . . . . .312/D4
Memmingen, Ger. 86/B5
Memphis, Tenn., Miss., U.S., 2,555 . . . . .300/C4
Mendes, Ga., U.S., 125 . . . . .260/H8
Mendham, N.J., U.S., borough, 5,097 . . . . .314/D2
Mendi, P.N.G. 172/A2
Mendocino, Calif., U.S., 824 . . . . .246/B3
Mendocino, Calif., U.S., county, 86,265 . . . . . .246/B3
Mendocino Natl. For., Calif., U.S. 246/B3
Mendon, Ill., U.S., 883 . . . . .266/B3
Mendon, Mass., U.S., 5,286 . . . . .292/H4
Mendon, Mich., U.S., 917 . . . . .294/D7
Mendon, Mo., U.S., 208 . . . . .302/C2
Mendon, Ohio, U.S., 697 . . . . .328/A4
Mendon, Utah, U.S., 898 . . . . .350/E2
Mendon, Vt., U.S., 1,028 . . . . .352/B3
Mendota, Calif., U.S., 7,890 . . . . .246/E6
Mendota, Ill., U.S., 7,272 . . . . .266/D2
Mendota, Minn., U.S., 197 . . . . .298/F6
Mendota, Wisc., U.S., lake 354/D3
Mendota Hts., Minn., U.S., 11,434 . . . . .298/F6
Mendoza, Arg., 121,620, (773,113 metro.) 191/B3
Mendoza, Arg., province 191/B3
Mendoza, Tex., U.S., 80 . . . . .346/C3
Menemsha, Mass., U.S., 100 . . . . .292/M7
Meneng, Nauru 174/B3
Meneng, Nauru, point 174/C2
Menfro, Mo., U.S., 60 . . . . .302/G4
Menifee, Ark., U.S., 311 . . . . .244/C2
Menifee, Ky., U.S., county, 6,556 . . . . .280/G3
Menihek, Nfld., Can. .218/D3
Menlo, Ga., U.S., 485 . . . . .260/A3
Menlo, Iowa, U.S., 365 . . . . .274/F4
Menlo, Kans., U.S., 57 . . . . .276/B2
Menlo, Wash., U.S., 225 . . . . .358/B3
Menlo Park, Calif., U.S., 30,785 . . . . .246/J2
Menlo Park, N.J., U.S. 314/E2
Mennecy, Fr. . . . . .88/Inset II
Menneval, N.B., Can., 83 . . . . .217/B1
Menno, S. Dak., U.S., 729 . . . . .342/H4
Meno, Okla., U.S., 195 . . . . .330/D1
Menoken, N. Dak., U.S., 40 . . . . .326/E3
Menominee, Ill., U.S., 237 . . . . .266/C1
Menominee, Mich., U.S., 9,131 . . . . .294/B4
Menominee, Mich., U.S., county, 25,326 . . . . . .294/B4
Menominee, Wisc., U.S., county, 4,562 . . . . . . .364/E4
Menominee Ind. Res., Wisc., U.S. 364/E3
Menominee Falls, Wisc., U.S., 32,647 . . . .364/E5, F1
Menomonie, Wisc., U.S., 14,937 . . . . .364/B4
Menongue, Ang. 159/C4
Mentasta Lake, Alaska, U.S., 142 . . . . .240/G2
Mentawai, Indon., islands 122/A2
Mentmore, N. Mex., U.S., 150 . . . . .317/B2
Mentone, Ala., U.S., 451 . . . . .238/D1
Mentone, Ind., U.S., 898 . . . . .270/D2
Mentone, Tex., U.S. .346/E4
Mentone, Kans., U.S., 100 . . . . .276/E3
Mentor, Ky., U.S., 181 . . . . .280/F2
Mentor, Minn., U.S., 150 . . . . .298/B3
Mentor, Ohio, U.S., 50,278 . . . . .328/H2, J8
Mentor-on-the-Lake, Ohio, U.S., 8,127 . . . . . . .328/J8
Menzel Bourguiba, Tun. 146/B1
Meopham, Eng., U.K., 4,956 . . . . .70/E4
Meppel, Neth. 84/D2
Meppen, Ill., U.S., 60 . . . . .266/C5
Meppershall, Eng., U.K. 70/D2
Mequinenza, Sp., reservoir 95/B1
Mequon, Wisc., U.S., 21,823 . . . . .364/F1, F5
Meramec, Mo., U.S., river 302/E4, G3
Meramo, It. 95/B1
Meraux, La., U.S., 10,192 . . . . .282/K7, L3
Merced, Calif., U.S., 63,893, (210,554 metro.) . .246/E5
Merced, Calif., U.S., county, 210,554 . . . . .246/E5
Merced, Calif., U.S., river 246/E5
Mercedario, Arg., mountain 191/B3
Mercedes, Tex., U.S., 13,649 . . . . .346/L8
Mercedes, Uru. 187/A2
Mercer, Ill., U.S., county, 16,957 . . . . .266/C2
Mercer, Ky., U.S., county, 20,817 . . . . .280/F3
Mercer, Maine, U.S., 647 . . . . .286/C4
Mercer, Mo., U.S., 342 . . . . .302/C1
Mercer, Mo., U.S., county, 3,757 . . . . .302/C1
Mercer, N.J., U.S., county, 350,761 . . . . .314/D3
Mercer, N.Y., U.S., 86 . . . . .302/C2
Mercer, N. Dak., U.S., county, 8,644 . . . . .326/C2
Mercer, Ohio, U.S., county, 40,924 . . . . .328/A4
Mercer, Penn., U.S., 2,391 . . . . .336/A3
Mercer, Penn., U.S., county, 120,293 . . . . .336/A3
Mercer, Tenn., U.S., 225 . . . . .344/C4
Mercer, W. Va., U.S., county, 62,980 . . . . .360/D6
Mercer, Wisc., U.S., 450 . . . . .364/C2
Mercer Island, Wash., U.S., 22,036 . . . . .358/A4
Mercersburg, Penn., U.S., 1,540 . . . . .336/F6

Mercerville, N.J., U.S., 26,419 . . . . .314/D3
Merchantville, N.J., U.S., 3,801 . . . . .314/B3
Mercury, Nev., U.S. 310/C3
Mercury, Tex., U.S. 346/J4
Mere, Eng., U.K., 2,257 . . . . .73/H2
Meredith, Colo., U.S. 250/D2
Meredith, Mich., U.S., 125 . . . . .294/E5
Meredith, N.H., U.S., 5,943 . . . . .312/D4
Meredith, Tex., U.S., lake 346/F9
Meredith Ctr., N.H., U.S., 425 . . . . .312/C4
Meredosia, Ill., U.S., 1,041 . . . . .266/C4
Meredosia N.W.R., Ill., U.S. 266/C4
Mereta, Tex., U.S., 175 . . . . .346/H4
Mergui, (Myeik), Mya. 125/C3
Mergui, Mya., archipelago 125/C4
Mérida, Mex., state capital 662,530,
  (705,055 metro.) 200/G3
Mérida, Sp., 50,271 . . . . .94/C3
Mérida, Ven., 176,200, (178,580 metro.) . .182/B2
Mérida, Ven., mountains 182/B2
Mérida, Ven., state 182/B2
Meridean, Wisc., U.S. 364/B4
Meriden, Conn., U.S., 58,244 . . . . .253/D3
Meriden, Iowa, U.S., 184 . . . . .274/C2
Meriden, Kans., U.S., 706 . . . . .276/G2
Meriden, N.H., U.S., 250 . . . . .312/B4
Meriden, Wyo., U.S. 366/D3
Meridian, Ga., U.S., 300 . . . . .260/J9
Meridian, Ida., U.S., 34,919 . . . . .264/A6
Meridian, Miss., U.S., 39,968 . . . . .300/D4
Meridian, N.Y., U.S., 350 . . . . .320/H4
Meridian, (Logan County), Okla., U.S., 54 . .330/E2
Meridian, (Stephens County), Okla., U.S., 1,485 . .330/E3
Meridian, Tex., U.S., 1,491 . . . . .346/L4
Meridian Hts. (part of East Hill-Meridian),
  Wash., U.S. 358/B4
Meridian Hills, Ind., U.S., 1,713 . . . . .270/D5
Meridian N.A.S., Miss., U.S. 300/D3
Meridianville, Ala., U.S., 4,117 . . . . .238/C1
Merigold, Miss., U.S., 664 . . . . .300/B2
Merigomish, N.S., Can. 221/E2
Merín, Uru., lagoon 187/D2
Merino, Colo., U.S., 246 . . . . .250/G1
Merir, Palau, island 172/A3
Merit, Tex., U.S., 175 . . . . .346/D8
Meriwether, Ga., U.S., county, 22,534 . . . .260/B5
Merkel, Tex., U.S., 2,637 . . . . .346/H3
Merkland, Scot., U.K., lake 62/C2
Merkys, Lith., river 82/C2
Mermentau, La., U.S., 721 . . . . .282/D6
Merna, Ill., U.S. .266/E3
Merna, Nebr., U.S., 391 . . . . .308/E2
Merna, Wyo., U.S. 366/A2
Merom, Ind., U.S., 294 . . . . .270/A6
Meron, Isr., mountain 135/M1
Merredin, W.A., Austl. 170/A3
Merriam, Ind., U.S., 225 . . . . .270/F2
Merriam, Kans., U.S., 11,008 . . . . .276/H1
Merriam Woods, Mo., U.S., 1,142 . . . . . . .302/C5
Merrick, Scot., U.K., mountain 60/E2
Merrick, N.Y., U.S., county, 8,204 . . . . . . .308/G2
Merricourt, N. Dak., U.S. 326/G3
Merridale, Man., Can. 215/A3
Merrifield, Minn., U.S., 275 . . . . .298/C4
Merrifield, Va., U.S., 11,170 . . . . .354/M2
Merrill, Iowa, U.S., 754 . . . . .274/B2
Merrill, Mich., U.S., 782 . . . . .294/E6
Merrill, Miss., U.S. 300/D5
Merrill, N.Y., U.S., 125 . . . . .320/P1
Merrill, Oreg., U.S., 897 . . . . .334/E5
Merrill, Wisc., U.S., 10,146 . . . . .364/C4
Merrillan, Wisc., U.S., 585 . . . . .364/C4
Merrillville, Ga., U.S., 175 . . . . .260/D1
Merrillville, Ind., U.S., 30,560 . . . . .270/B2
Merrimac, Ky., U.S., 40 . . . . .280/E3
Merrimac, Mass., U.S., 6,138 . . . . .292/K1
Merrimac, Va., U.S., 1,751 . . . . .354/C6
Merrimac, Wisc., U.S., 416 . . . . .364/D5
Merrimack, Mass., U.S., river 292/L1
Merrimack, N.H., U.S., 25,119 . . . . .312/D6
Merrimack, N.H., U.S., county, 136,225 . . .312/C5
Merrimack, N.H., U.S., river 312/D6
Merriman, Mich., U.S., 125 . . . . .294/A4
Merriman, Nebr., U.S., 118 . . . . .308/C1
Merrimon, N.C., U.S., 175 . . . . .322/M5
Merrionette Park, Ill., U.S., 1,999 . . . . . . .266/B6
Merriott, Eng., U.K., 1,956 . . . . .73/G2
Merritt, Br. Col., Can., 7,088 . . . . .214/M6
Merritt, Mich., U.S., 90 . . . . .294/E5
Merritt, Wash., U.S. 358/E2
Merritt Island, Fla., U.S., 36,090 . . . . .256/H5
Merritt Parkway, Conn., U.S. 253/A5
Merriweather, Mich., U.S., 125 . . . . .294/D2
Mer Rouge, La., U.S., 721 . . . . .282/F1
Merrow, Conn., U.S., 1,000 . . . . .253/F2
Merrydale, La., U.S., 10,427 . . . . .282/G5
Merry Hill, N.C., U.S. 322/M2
Merryville, La., U.S., 1,126 . . . . .282/B5
Mersch, Lux. 85/B2
Mersey, Eng., U.K., river 60/C3
Mersey, Eng., U.K., river 68/B3
Merseyside, Eng., U.K., unitary authority,
  1,362,034 . . . . .68/B3
Mershon, Ga., U.S., 90 . . . . .260/G9
Merthyr Tydfil, Wales, U.K. 60/B3
Merthyr Tydfil, Wales, U.K., 39,482,
  (44,767 metro) 64/E4
Merthyr Tydfil, Wales, U.K., unitary authority,
  55,983 . . . . .64/E4
Merton, Eng., U.K., 168,470 . . . . .70/D4
Merton, Eng., U.K., 168,470 . . . . .73/D3
Merton, Eng., U.K., unitary authority, 187,908 . .70/D4
Merton, Wisc., U.S., 1,926 . . . . .364/F2
Mertzon, Tex., U.S., 839 . . . . .346/H4
Meru, Kenya 157/D3
Merume, Guy., mountains 183/A2
Merwin, Mo., U.S., 83 . . . . .302/B3
Mesa, Ariz., U.S., 396,375 . . . . .242/D4
Mesa, Colo., U.S., 100 . . . . .250/B3
Mesa, Colo., U.S., county, 116,255 . . . . . .250/B3
Mesa, Ida., U.S. .264/A5
Mesa, Miss., U.S., 90 . . . . .300/B4
Mesa, Wash., U.S., 425 . . . . .358/G3
Mesabi Range, Minn., U.S. 298/D3
Mesaoria, Cyp., plain 133/B1
Mesa Verde Natl. Park, Colo., U.S. 250/B4
Mescalero, N. Mex., U.S., 1,233 . . . . .317/E4
Mescalero Apache Indian Res., N. Mex., U.S. . .317/E4
Meservey, Iowa, U.S., 252 . . . . .274/H2
Meseta, Sp., plateau 94/D3
Meshaw, Eng., U.K. 73/E3
Meshomasic St. For., Conn., U.S. 253/E3
Meshoppen, Penn., U.S., 459 . . . . .336/J2
Mesic, N.C., U.S. 322/M4
Mesick, Mich., U.S., 447 . . . . .294/D5
Mesilla, N. Mex., U.S., 2,180 . . . . .317/D5
Mesita, Colo., U.S. 250/E4
Mesita, N. Mex., U.S., 776 . . . . .317/C2
Mesolongion, Gr. 100/B2
Mesopotamia, Iraq, region 130/B2
Mesquite, Nev., U.S., 9,389 . . . . .310/C3

Mesquite, N. Mex., U.S., 948 . . . . .317/D5
Mesquite, (Borden County), Tex., U.S. 346/G3
Mesquite, (Dallas County), Tex., U.S.,
  124,523 . . . . .346/C9, M3
Messina, It. 95/C3
Messina, It., strait 95/C3
Messina, S. Afr. .162/D1
Messing, Eng., U.K. 70/F3
Messingham, Eng., U.K., 2,952 . . . . .66/G5
Messingham, Eng., U.K., 2,952 . . . . .68/F2
Mesta, Bul. 101/B4
Mesurado, Liber., cape 149/A2
Meta, Col., department 184/B4
Meta, Col., river .184/C3
Meta, Mo., U.S., 249 . . . . .302/D3
Meta, Ven., river 182/C2
Meta, Ven., river 182/C2
Métabetchouan, Que., Can., 4,198 . . . . . .226/E3
Meta Incognita, Nun., Can., peninsula 220/P4
Metairie, La., U.S., 146,136 . . . . . . .282/J7, K3
Metaline, Wash., U.S., 162 . . . . .358/H1
Metaline Falls, Wash., U.S., 223 . . . . .358/H1
Metalton, Ark., U.S. 244/B1
Metamora, Ill., U.S., 2,700 . . . . .266/D3
Metamora, Mich., U.S., 507 . . . . .294/F7
Metamora, Ohio, U.S., 563 . . . . .328/B2
Metcalf, Ga., U.S., 150 . . . . .260/D1
Metcalf, Ill., U.S., 213 . . . . .266/F4
Metcalfe, Ont., Can., 1,610 . . . . .223/K2
Metcalfe, Ky., U.S., county, 10,037 . . . . . .280/E4
Metcalfe, Miss., U.S., 1,109 . . . . .300/B2
Metea, Ind., U.S., 100 . . . . .270/D3
Meteghan, N.S., Can. 221/A3
Metfield, Eng., U.K. 70/G2
Methlick, Scot., U.K. 62/M4
Methow, Wash., U.S., 100 . . . . .358/E1
Methuen, Mass., U.S., 43,789 . . . . .292/K2
Methwold, Eng., U.K. 70/F1
Methwold Hythe, Eng., U.K. 70/F1
Metiskow, Alta., Can. 212/E5
Métis-sur-Mer, Que., Can. 226/J3
Metlakatla, Alaska, U.S., 1,375 . . . . .240/J3
Metolius, Oreg., U.S., 635 . . . . .334/E3
Metropolis, Ill., U.S., 6,482 . . . . .266/E6
Mettawa, Ill., U.S., 367 . . . . .266/B5
Mettawee, N.Y., U.S., river 320/Q3
Mettawee, Vt., U.S., river 352/A4
Metter, Ga., U.S., 3,879 . . . . .260/G7
Mettler, Calif., U.S., 157 . . . . .246/G7
Metuchen, N.J., U.S., 12,840 . . . . .314/E2
Metz, Fr., 127,498, (322,526 metro.) 88/D2
Metz, Ind., U.S., 250 . . . . .270/C1
Metz, Mo., U.S., 67 . . . . .302/B3
Metzger, Oreg., U.S., 3,354 . . . . .334/A2
Meulan, Fr. .88/Inset II
Meurthe-et-Moselle, Fr., department 88/D2
Meuse, Belg., river 88/D2
Meuse, Fr., department 88/D2
Meuse, Fr., river .85/D2
Mevagissey, Eng., U.K., 2,272 . . . . .73/C4
Mexborough, Eng., U.K., 15,282 . . . . .66/F6
Mexborough, Eng., U.K., 15,282 . . . . .68/E3
Mexia, Tex., U.S., 6,563 . . . . .346/M4
Mexiana, Braz., island 188/D1
Mexicali, Mex., state capital, 549,873,
  (764,602 metro.) 200/A1
Mexican Hat, Utah, U.S., 88 . . . . .350/E6
Mexican Sprs., N. Mex., U.S., 250 . . . . . . .317/B2
Mexican Water, Ariz., U.S., 60 . . . . .242/F1
Mexico, gulf 346/N8
Mexico, nation 188
México, Cuba, gulf 204/A1
México, Mex., state . . . . .200/E4, Inset
Mexico, Ala., U.S., gulf 238/B5
Mexico, Fla., U.S., gulf 256/C6, E5
Mexico, Ind., U.S., 984 . . . . .270/D3
Mexico, La., U.S., gulf 282/M7
Mexico, Maine, U.S., 2,959 . . . . .286/B4
Mexico, Miss., U.S., gulf 300/D5
Mexico, Mo., U.S., 11,320 . . . . .302/E2
Mexico, N.Y., U.S., 1,572 . . . . .320/J4
Mexico, N.Y., U.S., bay 66/D1
Mexico Beach, Fla., U.S., 1,017 . . . . .256/C2
Mexico City, Mex., national capital, 8,605,239,
  (16,202,773 metro.) . . . . .200/E4, Inset
Meyersdale, Penn., U.S., 2,473 . . . . .336/C6
Meyers Lake, Ohio, U.S., 565 . . . . .328/H4
Meymaneh, Afg., 38,251 . . . . .129/A1
Meyungs, Palau .172/B3
Mgwavuma, Swaz., river 161/B3
Mhlume, Swaz. 161/B2
Mhor, Scot., U.K., lake 62/H4
Miami, Man., Can. 215/B4
Miami, Ariz., U.S., 1,936 . . . . .242/E4
Miami, Fla., U.S., 362,470,
  (3,876,380 metro.) 256/B6, H6
Miami, Ind., U.S., county, 36,082 . . . . . . .270/D3
Miami, Kans., U.S., county, 28,351 . . . . . .276/H3
Miami, Mo., U.S., 160 . . . . .302/C2
Miami, N. Mex., U.S. 317/F1
Miami, Ohio, U.S., county, 98,868 . . .328/B5, G1
Miami, Okla., U.S., 13,704 . . . . .330/H1
Miami, Tex., U.S., 588 . . . . .346/G9
Miami Beach, Fla., U.S., 87,933 . . . . .256/B6, H6
Miami-Dade, Fla., U.S., county, 2,253,362 .257/A6, H6
Miamisburg, Ohio, U.S., 19,489 . . . . .328/F2
Miami Shores, Fla., U.S., 10,380 . . . . .256/B6
Miami Sprs., Fla., U.S., 13,712 . . . . .256/A6
Mianwali, Pak. 129/D3
Miaoli, Tai. 117/B1
Mica, Wash., U.S., 225 . . . . .358/H2
Mica Creek, Br. Col., Can. 214/N5
Micanopy, Fla., U.S., 653 . . . . .256/F2
Micaville, N.C., U.S., 750 . . . . .322/A3, F7
Micco, Fla., U.S., 9,498 . . . . .256/H4
Miccosukee, Fla., U.S., 150 . . . . .256/D1
Miccosukee Indian Res., Fla., U.S. 256/H5
Michaud, Maine, U.S., 150 . . . . .286/D1
Michaux St. For., Penn., U.S. 336/G6
Micheldever, Eng., U.K. 70/B4
Michelson, Alaska, U.S., mountain 240/U1
Miches, Dom. Rep. 205/C3
Michiana, Mich., U.S., 200 . . . . .294/C8
Michiana Shores, Ind., U.S., 330 . . . . .270/C1
Michie, Tenn., U.S., 647 . . . . .344/E4
Michigamme, Mich., U.S., 287 . . . . .294/A3
Michigamme, Mich., U.S., reservoir 294/A3
Michigan, U.S., state 93
Michigan, Ill., U.S., lake 266/C5, F1
Michigan, Ind., U.S., lake 270/B1
Michigan, Mich., U.S., lake 294/C5
Michigan, N. Dak., U.S., 345 . . . . .326/G1
Michigan, Wisc., U.S., lake 364/F5
Michigan Ctr., Mich., U.S., 4,641 . . . . . . .294/E7
Michigan City, Ind., U.S., 32,900 . . . . . . .270/C1
Michigan City, Miss., U.S., 40 . . . . .300/C1
Michigan Islands N.W.R., Mich., U.S. . .294/D4, F5
Michigantown, Ind., U.S., 406 . . . . .270/D4
Michigan Valley, Kans., U.S., 90 . . . . .276/G3
Michoacán, Mex., state 200/D4
Mickfield, Eng., U.K. 70/G2

Mickleover, Eng., U.K. 70/A1
Mickleton, Eng., U.K., 1,551 . . . . .66/D3
Mickleton, Eng., U.K., 1,551 . . . . .68/D5
Mico, Nicar., river 202/B2
Micoud, St. Luc. .208/B3
Micro, N.C., U.S., 454 . . . . .322/J3
Micronesia, Federated States of, nation 164
Midale, Sask., Can., 496 . . . . .227/G11
Midas, Nev., U.S. 310/B1
Middelburg, Neth. 84/A3
Middelburg, S. Afr. 162/C3
Middle Alkali, Calif., U.S., lake 246/F1
Middle Andaman, India, island 128/F6
Middle Arm, Nfld., Can., 546 . . . . .218/C4
Middle Atlas, Mor., ranges 147/C1
Middleberg, Okla., U.S., 90 . . . . .330/E2
Middlebourne, W. Va., U.S., 870 . . . . .360/F2
Middlebro, Man., Can. 215/D4
Middlebrook, Va., U.S. 354/E4
Middleburg, Fla., U.S., 10,338 . . . . .256/G1
Middleburg, Md., U.S., 350 . . . . .288/F1
Middleburg, N.C., U.S., 162 . . . . .322/J2
Middleburg, Penn., U.S., 1,382 . . . . .336/G4
Middleburgh, N.Y., U.S., 1,398 . . . . .320/N5
Middlebury, Conn., U.S., 6,451 . . . . .253/C3
Middlebury, Ind., U.S., 2,956 . . . . .270/E1
Middlebury, Vt., U.S., 8,183 . . . . .352/A2
Middlebush, N.J., U.S., 500 . . . . .314/D3
Middlefield, Conn., U.S., 4,203 . . . . .253/E3
Middlefield, Mass., U.S., 542 . . . . .292/B3
Middlefield, Ohio, U.S., 2,233 . . . . .328/H3
Middlefork, Ind., U.S., 150 . . . . .270/D4
Middle Fork, Mont., U.S., river 306/C1
Middlegate, Nev., U.S. 310/B2
Middle Haddam, Conn., U.S., 900 . . . . . . .253/E3
Middleham, Eng., U.K. 66/F4
Middle Inlet, Wisc., U.S., 90 . . . . .364/F3
Middle Lake, Sask., Can., 300 . . . . .227/E8
Middle Loch, Hawaii, U.S., harbor 262/E1
Middle Loup, Nebr., U.S., river 308/E2
Middle Musquodoboit, N.S., Can. 221/D2
Middle Pt., Ohio, U.S., 593 . . . . .328/B4
Middleport, N.Y., U.S., 1,917 . . . . .320/E4
Middleport, Ohio, U.S., 2,525 . . . . .328/F7
Middleport, Penn., U.S., 458 . . . . .336/J4
Middle River, Md., U.S., 23,958 . . . . .288/J2
Middle River, Minn., U.S., 319 . . . . .298/A2
Middlesboro, Ky., U.S., 10,384 . . . . .280/G4
Middlesbrough, Eng., U.K., 147,430,
  (456,919 metro.) 66/F3
Middlesbrough, Eng., U.K., unitary authority,
  134,847 . . . . .66/F3
Middlesex, Ont., Can., county 223/D4
Middlesex, Conn., U.S., county, 155,071 . . .253/D3
Middlesex, Mass., U.S., county, 1,465,396 . .292/B7, H2
Middlesex, N.J., U.S., 13,717 . . . . .314/E2
Middlesex, N.J., U.S., county, 750,162 . . . .314/E3
Middlesex, N.Y., U.S., 275 . . . . .320/G5
Middlesex, N.C., U.S., 838 . . . . .322/J3
Middlesex, Vt., U.S., 1,729 . . . . .352/B2
Middlesex, Va., U.S., county, 9,932 . . . . . .354/K5
Middlesmoor, Eng., U.K. 66/F4
Middleton, N.S., Can., 1,744 . . . . .221/B3
Middleton, P.E.I., Can. 224/B2
Middleton, (Derbyshire), Eng., U.K. 68/D3
Middleton, (Manchester), Eng., U.K., 45,621 .68/C2
Middleton, Eng., U.K., 45,621 . . . . .66/D5
Middleton, Eng., U.K. 66/D5
Middleton, Ida., U.S., 2,978 . . . . .264/A6
Middleton, Ky., U.S., 50 . . . . .280/D4
Middleton, Mass., U.S., 7,744 . . . . .292/D5, K2
Middleton, Mich., U.S., 475 . . . . .294/E6
Middleton, Tenn., U.S., 602 . . . . .344/D4
Middleton, Wisc., U.S., 15,770 . . . . .364/D5
Middleton Cheney, Eng., U.K., 3,306 . . . . .70/B2
Middleton Hall, Eng., U.K. 66/D1
Middleton-on-Sea, Eng., U.K. 70/C5
Middletown, N. Ire., 274 . . . . .65/D3
Middletown, Calif., U.S., 1,020 . . . . .246/C4
Middletown, Conn., U.S., 43,167 . . . . .253/E3
Middletown, Del., U.S., 6,161 . . . . .255/B3
Middletown, Ill., U.S., 434 . . . . .266/D3
Middletown, Ind., U.S., 2,488 . . . . .270/E4
Middletown, Iowa, U.S., 535 . . . . .274/M6
Middletown, Ky., U.S., 5,744 . . . . . .280/B2, E2
Middletown, Md., U.S., 2,668 . . . . .288/D2
Middletown, Mich., U.S., 966 . . . . .294/E7
Middletown, Mo., U.S., 199 . . . . .302/E2
Middletown, N.J., U.S., 66,327 . . . . .314/E3
Middletown, N.Y., U.S., 25,388 . . . . .320/N8
Middletown, Ohio, U.S., 51,605 . . . . .328/B6
Middletown, (Dauphin County),
  Penn., U.S., 9,242 . . . . .336/H5
Middletown, (Northampton County),
  Penn., U.S., 7,378 . . . . .336/L4
Middletown, R.I., U.S., 17,334 . . . . .339/F4
Middletown, Va., U.S., 1,015 . . . . .354/G2
Middletown Sprs., Vt., U.S., 823 . . . . .352/A4
Middle Tysoe, Eng., U.K. 70/A2
Middle Valley, Tenn., U.S., 11,854 . . . . . . .344/L4
Middleville, Mich., U.S., 2,721 . . . . .294/D7
Middleville, N.J., U.S., 375 . . . . .314/D1
Middleville, N.Y., U.S., 550 . . . . .320/M4
Middle Wallop, Eng., U.K. 70/A4
Middle Water, Tex., U.S. 346/E8
Middlewich, Eng., U.K., 10,100 . . . . .68/C3
Middleyard, Scot., U.K. 62/H7
Midewin Natl. Tallgrass Prairie, Ill., U.S. . . .266/C4
Midfield, Ala., U.S., 5,626 . . . . .238/C2, D1
Midhurst, Eng., U.K., 6,451 . . . . .70/C5
Midi-Pyrénées, Fr., region 88/C5
Midkiff, Tex., U.S., 100 . . . . .346/G4
Midland, W.A., Austl. . . . . .170/Inset I
Midland, Ont., Can., 16,214 . . . . .223/F3
Midland, Ark., U.S., 253 . . . . .244/A2
Midland, Calif., U.S. 246/L9
Midland, Ind., U.S., 350 . . . . .270/B6
Midland, Md., U.S., 473 . . . . .288/C3
Midland, Mich., U.S., 41,685 . . . . .294/E6
Midland, Mich., U.S., county, 82,874 . . . . .294/E6
Midland, Ohio, U.S., 265 . . . . .328/C7
Midland, Oreg., U.S., 200 . . . . .334/E5
Midland, Penn., U.S., 3,137 . . . . .336/A4
Midland, S. Dak., U.S., 179 . . . . .342/D3
Midland, Tex., U.S., 94,996 . . . . .346/F4
Midland, Tex., U.S., county, 116,009 . . . . .346/F4
Midland, Wash., U.S., 7,414 . . . . .358/C2
Midland City, Ala., U.S., 1,703 . . . . .238/D4
Midland City, Ill., U.S., 100 . . . . .266/D3
Midland Park, Mich., U.S., 475 . . . . .294/D7
Midland Park, N.J., U.S., 6,947 . . . . .314/M, L2
Midlothian, Scot., U.K., unitary authority,
  80,941 . . . . .62/K7
Midlothian, Ill., U.S., 14,315 . . . . .266/B6
Midlothian, Tex., U.S., 7,480 . . . . .346/M3
Midlothian, Va., U.S., 3,300 . . . . .354/H5

Midnight, Miss., U.S., 225 . . . . .300/B2
Midsomer Norton, Eng., U.K. 73/H2
Midvale, Ida., U.S., 176 . . . . .264/A5
Midvale, Ohio, U.S., 547 . . . . .328/H5
Midvale, Utah, U.S., 27,029 . . . . .350/C3, E2
Midvale, Wyo., U.S. 366/B3
Midville, Ga., U.S., 457 . . . . .260/G6
Midway, (Bullock County), Ala., U.S., 457 . .238/D3
Midway, (Monroe County), Ala., U.S. 238/B4
Midway, Del., U.S., 1,500 . . . . .255/D6
Midway, Fla., U.S., 1,446 . . . . .256/D1
Midway, Ga., U.S., 1,100 . . . . .260/J8
Midway, Ky., U.S., 1,620 . . . . .280/F2
Midway, (Bossier Parish), La., U.S. 282/B1
Midway, (La Salle Parish), La., U.S., 1,505 .282/E3
Midway, Minn., U.S. 298/B4
Midway, Miss., U.S., 80 . . . . .300/B3
Midway, N. Mex., U.S., 700 . . . . .317/F4
Midway, Ohio, U.S., 274 . . . . .328/D6
Midway, (Adams County), Penn., U.S., 2,323 .336/G6
Midway, (Washington County), Penn., U.S., 982 .336/A5
Midway, S. Dak., U.S. 342/H4
Midway, (Dawson County), Tex., U.S. 346/E4
Midway, (Madison County), Tex., U.S., 288 .346/N4
Midway, Utah, U.S., 2,121 . . . . .350/C3, E2
Midwest, Wyo., U.S., 408 . . . . .366/C2
Midwest City, Okla., U.S., 54,088 . . . .330/B4, E2
Mid Yell, Scot., U.K. 62/Q1
Mie, Jap., prefecture 114/C3
Miera, N. Mex., U.S., 100 . . . . .317/D3
Miercurea Ciuc, Rom. 101/C2
Mieres, Sp. 94/D1
Miesville, Minn., U.S., 135 . . . . .298/E6
Mifflin, Ohio, U.S., 144 . . . . .328/F4
Mifflin, Penn., U.S., 627 . . . . .336/G4
Mifflin, Penn., U.S., county, 46,486 . . . . . .336/F4
Mifflinburg, Penn., U.S., 3,594 . . . . .336/G4
Mifflintown, Penn., U.S., 861 . . . . .336/G4
Mifflinville, Penn., U.S., 1,213 . . . . .336/J3
Mignon, Ala., U.S., 1,348 . . . . .238/C2
Mikado, Mich., U.S., 175 . . . . .294/F5
Mikana, Wisc., U.S., 100 . . . . .364/B3
Mikkalo, Oreg., U.S. 334/F2
Mikkeli, Fin., 46,727 . . . . .81/C2
Mikkwa, Alta., Can., river 212/C2
Mikomeseng, Eq. Gui. 154/C2
Mykonos, Gr., island 100/C3
Mikura, Jap., island 114/C3
Milaca, Minn., U.S., 2,580 . . . . .298/D5
Miladhunmadulu, Mald., atoll 127/A1
Milagro, Ecua. 185/B4
Milam, Tex., U.S., county, 24,238 . . . . .346/L5
Milam, W. Va., U.S. 360/H3
Milan, It., 1,182,693 . . . . .95/B1
Milan, Ga., U.S., 1,012 . . . . .260/E8
Milan, Ill., U.S., 5,348 . . . . .266/C2
Milan, Ind., U.S., 1,816 . . . . .270/F6
Milan, Kans., U.S., 137 . . . . .276/E4
Milan, Mich., U.S., 4,775 . . . . .294/F7
Milan, Minn., U.S., 326 . . . . .298/B5
Milan, Mo., U.S., 1,958 . . . . .302/C1
Milan, N.H., U.S., 1,331 . . . . .312/D2
Milan, N. Mex., U.S., 1,891 . . . . .317/C2
Milan, Ohio, U.S., 1,445 . . . . .328/E3
Milan, Tenn., U.S., 7,664 . . . . .344/D3
Milan, Wash., U.S., 225 . . . . .358/H2
Milan, Wisc., U.S., 900 . . . . .364/C4
Milan Army Ammunition Plant, Tenn., U.S. .344/D3
Milano, Tex., U.S., 400 . . . . .346/M5
Milbank, S. Dak., U.S., 3,640 . . . . .342/J2
Milborne St. Andrew, Eng., U.K. 73/H3
Milbridge, Maine, U.S., 1,279 . . . . .286/E4
Milburn, Nebr., U.S. 308/E2
Milburn, Okla., U.S., 312 . . . . .330/F3
Milburn, Utah, U.S. 350/C4
Milden, Sask., Can., 196 . . . . .227/D9
Mildenhall, Eng., U.K., 10,468 . . . . .70/F2
Mildred, Kans., U.S. 276/H3
Mildred, Mont., U.S. 306/M3
Mildred, Penn., U.S., 425 . . . . .336/J3
Mildura, Vic., Austl. 170/D3
Mile End, Eng., U.K. 70/F3
Miles, Iowa, U.S., 462 . . . . .274/P3
Miles, Tex., U.S., 850 . . . . .346/H4
Miles, Wash., U.S. 358/G2
Milesburg, Penn., U.S., 1,187 . . . . .336/F4
Miles City, Mont., U.S., 8,487 . . . . .306/L3
Miles Pond, Vt., U.S. 352/D2
Milestone, Sask., Can., 542 . . . . .227/F10
Milesville, S. Dak., U.S. 342/D3
Miley, S.C., U.S. .340/G4
Milford, (Milford/Witley), Eng., U.K., 6,476 .70/C4
Milford, N. Ire., U.K., 458 . . . . .65/D3
Milford, Calif., U.S., 90 . . . . .246/E2
Milford, Conn., U.S., 52,305 . . . . .253/C5
Milford, Del., U.S., 6,732 . . . . .255/C5
Milford, Ga., U.S., 50 . . . . .260/B9
Milford, Ill., U.S., 1,369 . . . . .266/F3
Milford, (Decatur County), Ind., U.S., 121 . .270/E6
Milford, (Kosciusko County), Ind., U.S., 1,550 .270/E2
Milford, Iowa, U.S., 2,474 . . . . .274/D1
Milford, Kans., U.S., 502 . . . . .276/F2
Milford, Kans., U.S., lake 276/F2
Milford, Ky., U.S., 80 . . . . .280/D4
Milford, Maine, U.S., 2,950 . . . . .286/D4
Milford, Md., U.S., 26,527 . . . . .288/G2
Milford, Mass., U.S., 26,799 . . . . .292/H4
Milford, Mich., U.S., 6,272 . . . . .294/F7
Milford, Mo., U.S., 52 . . . . .302/B4
Milford, Nebr., U.S., 2,070 . . . . .308/G3
Milford, N.H., U.S., 13,535 . . . . .312/C6
Milford, N.J., U.S., 1,195 . . . . .314/C2
Milford, N.Y., U.S., 511 . . . . .320/M5
Milford, Ohio, U.S., 6,284 . . . . .328/B7, C6
Milford, Penn., U.S., 1,104 . . . . .336/M3
Milford, Tex., U.S., 685 . . . . .346/M3
Milford, Utah, U.S., 1,451 . . . . .350/A5
Milford, Va., U.S., 375 . . . . .354/J4
Milford, Wyo., U.S. 366/B2
Milford Ctr., Ohio, U.S., 626 . . . . .328/D5
Milford Haven, Wales, U.K. 60/B3
Milford Haven, Wales, U.K., 13,194 . . . . . .64/A4
Milford on Sea, Eng., U.K., 4,434 . . . . .70/A5
Milford Sound, N.Z. 171/A3
Milh, Bahr al, Iraq, lake 130/B2
Mili, Marsh. Is., island 173/C2
Mililani Town, Hawaii, U.S., 28,608 . . . . . .262/J2
Milk, Alta., Can., river 212/E6
Milk, Alta., Can., river 246/F1
Milk, Mont., U.S., river 306/D1, G1, K1
Milk River, Alta., Can., 879 . . . . .212/D6
Milladore, Wisc., U.S., 268 . . . . .364/D4
Millard, Mo., U.S., 75 . . . . .302/D1
Millard, Utah, U.S., county, 12,405 . . . . . .350/A4
Mill Bay, Br. Col., Can., 1,974 . . . . .214/C3
Millboro, Va., U.S. 354/F4
Millboro, Va., U.S., 150 . . . . .354/C5
Millbourne, Penn., U.S., 943 . . . . .336/L2
Millbrae, Calif., U.S., 20,718 . . . . .246/J2

Millbrook, Ala., U.S., 10,386 . . . . .238/C3
Millbrook, N.Y., U.S., 1,429 . . . . .320/P7
Millburn, N.J., U.S., 19,765 . . . . .314/A2, E2
Millbury, Mass., U.S., 12,784 . . . . .292/G4
Millbury, Ohio, U.S., 1,161 . . . . .310/A1
Mill City, Nev., U.S., 300 . . . . .310/A1
Mill City, Oreg., U.S., 1,537 . . . . .334/D3
Mill Corner, Eng., U.K. 70/F5
Mill Creek, Ill., U.S., 76 . . . . .266/D6
Mill Creek, Okla., U.S., 340 . . . . .330/F3
Mill Creek, Penn., U.S., 351 . . . . .336/F5
Millcreek, Utah, U.S., 30,377 . . . . .350/E2
Mill Creek, Wash., U.S., 11,525 . . . . .358/A4
Mill Creek, W. Va., U.S., 662 . . . . .360/G3
Milledgeville, Ill., U.S., 18,757 . . . . .260/E5
Milledgeville, Ill., U.S., 1,016 . . . . .266/D2
Milledgeville, Ohio, U.S., 122 . . . . .328/C6
Milledgeville, Tenn., U.S., 287 . . . . .344/E4
Mille Lacs, Minn., U.S., county, 22,330 . . . . .298/D5
Mille Lacs, Minn., U.S., lake 298/D4
Mille Lacs Ind. Res., Minn., U.S. 298/D4
Millen, Ga., U.S., 3,492 . . . . .260/H6
Mill End, Eng., U.K. 70/C3
Millennium, Kiri., island 175/D2
Miller, Ala., U.S., 40 . . . . .238/B3
Miller, Ark., U.S., county, 40,443 . . . . .244/B4
Miller, Ga., U.S., county, 6,383 . . . . .260/B9
Miller, Iowa, U.S., 80 . . . . .274/C1
Miller, Kans., U.S., 50 . . . . .276/G3
Miller, Miss., U.S., 125 . . . . .300/C1
Miller, Mo., U.S., 754 . . . . .302/C4
Miller, Mo., U.S., county, 23,564 . . . . .302/D3
Miller, Nebr., U.S., 156 . . . . .308/E3
Miller, S. Dak., U.S., 1,530 . . . . .342/G3
Miller City, Ill., U.S. 266/D6
Miller City, Ohio, U.S., 136 . . . . .328/B3
Miller Lake, Ont., Can. 223/D2
Miller Place, N.Y., U.S., 10,580 . . . . .320/E1
Millersburg, Ind., U.S., 868 . . . . .270/E1
Millersburg, Iowa, U.S., 184 . . . . .274/K4
Millersburg, Ky., U.S., 842 . . . . .280/F2
Millersburg, Mich., U.S., 263 . . . . .294/E4
Millersburg, Mo., U.S., 175 . . . . .302/D3
Millersburg, Ohio, U.S., 3,326 . . . . .328/G4
Millersburg, Oreg., U.S., 651 . . . . .334/C3
Millersburg, Penn., U.S., 2,562 . . . . .336/H4
Millers Creek, Ky., U.S., 80 . . . . .280/G3
Millers Creek, N.C., U.S., 2,071 . . . . .322/C2
Millers Falls, Mass., U.S., 1,072 . . . . .292/E2
Millers Ferry, Ala., U.S. 238/B3
Millersport, Ohio, U.S., 963 . . . . .328/E6
Millers Tavern, Va., U.S., 60 . . . . .354/K5
Millerstown, Penn., U.S., 679 . . . . .336/G4
Millersville, Mo., U.S., 250 . . . . .302/G4
Millersville, Penn., U.S., 7,774 . . . . .336/J6
Millersville, Tenn., U.S., 5,308 . . . . .344/H2
Millerton, N.B., Can. 217/D2
Millerton, Iowa, U.S., 48 . . . . .274/H6
Millerton, N.Y., U.S., 925 . . . . .320/P7
Millerton, Okla., U.S., 359 . . . . .330/G4
Millerville, Ala., U.S., 260 . . . . .238/D2
Millerville, Minn., U.S., 115 . . . . .298/B4
Millet, Alta., Can., 2,037 . . . . .212/D4
Millett, S.C., U.S., 80 . . . . .340/C3
Millett, Tex., U.S. 346/J7
Millgrove, Ind., U.S., 200 . . . . .270/F4
Mill Grove, Mo., U.S., 50 . . . . .302/C1
Mill Hall, Penn., U.S., 1,568 . . . . .336/G3
Millhaven, Ga., U.S., 40 . . . . .260/H6
Millheim, Penn., U.S., 749 . . . . .336/G4
Millhousen, Ind., U.S., 136 . . . . .270/F6
Millhurst, N.J., U.S., 300 . . . . .314/E3
Millican, Oreg., U.S. 334/H4
Millican, Tex., U.S., 108 . . . . .346/M5
Milligan, Fla., U.S., 425 . . . . .256/B1
Milligan, Nebr., U.S., 315 . . . . .308/G3
Milligan College, Tenn., U.S. 344/S2
Milliken, Ont., Can. 223/K5
Milliken, Colo., U.S., 2,888 . . . . .250/F1
Millington, Eng., U.K. 68/F2
Millington, Ill., U.S., 458 . . . . .266/E2
Millington, Md., U.S., 416 . . . . .288/L2
Millington, Mich., U.S., 1,137 . . . . .294/F6
Millington, N.J., U.S., 3,500 . . . . .314/D2
Millington, Tenn., U.S., 10,433 . . . . .344/B4
Millinocket, Maine, U.S., 5,203 . . . . .286/D3
Millinocket, Maine, U.S., lake 286/D3
Mill Iron, Mont., U.S. 306/M4
Millis, Mass., U.S., 7,902 . . . . .292/J4
Millisle, N. Ire., U.K., 1,531 . . . . .65/F2
Millom, Eng., U.K., 6,455 . . . . .66/B4
Mill Plain, Conn., U.S. 253/A4
Millport, Scot., U.K., 1,253 . . . . .62/G7
Millport, Ala., U.S., 1,160 . . . . .238/B4
Millport, N.Y., U.S., 297 . . . . .320/H6
Mill River, Mass., U.S., 225 . . . . .292/A4
Millry, Ala., U.S., 615 . . . . .238/A4
Mills, Iowa, U.S., county, 14,547 . . . . .274/C2
Mills, Nebr., U.S. 308/E1
Mills, N. Mex., U.S. 317/F1
Mills, Tex., U.S., county, 5,151 . . . . .346/K4
Mills, Utah, U.S. .350/B4
Mills, Wyo., U.S., 2,591 . . . . .366/C2
Millsap, Tex., U.S., 353 . . . . .346/K3
Millsboro, Del., U.S., 2,360 . . . . .255/C6
Millsboro, (Fredericktown-Millsboro),
  Penn., U.S., 1,094 . . . . .336/A6
Mill Shoals, Ill., U.S., 235 . . . . .266/E5
Mill Spr., Mo., U.S., 219 . . . . .302/F4
Mill Spr., N.C., U.S., 325 . . . . .322/A4
Millstadt, Ill., U.S., 2,794 . . . . .266/A4
Millston, Wisc., U.S., 100 . . . . .364/C4
Millstone, Ky., U.S., 650 . . . . .280/H3
Millstone, N.J., U.S., borough 8,970 . . . . . .314/D3
Millstone, N.J., U.S., 275 . . . . .360/D3
Milltown, Nfld., Can., 884 . . . . .218/D5
Milltown, N. Ire., U.K. 65/D1
Milltown, N. Ire., U.K. 65/F2
Milltown, Ind., U.S., 932 . . . . .270/D8
Milltown, Ky., U.S., 90 . . . . .280/E3
Milltown, Mont., U.S. 306/C3
Milltown, N.J., U.S., 7,000 . . . . .314/E3
Milltown, S. Dak., U.S. 342/H4
Milltown, Tenn., U.S. 344/K2
Milltown, Wisc., U.S., 888 . . . . .364/A3
Millvale, Maine, U.S., 125 . . . . .286/D4
Millvale, Penn., U.S., 4,028 . . . . .336/D7
Mill Valley, Calif., U.S., 13,600 . . . . .246/H1
Mill Vil., N.S., Can. 221/C3
Mill Vil., Penn., U.S., 412 . . . . .336/B2
Mill Vil., Vt., U.S., 125 . . . . .352/C1
Millville, N.B., Can., 319 . . . . .217/B2
Millville, Del., U.S., 259 . . . . .255/D6
Millville, Ill., U.S. 274/M2
Millville, Ky., U.S., 325 . . . . .280/E2
Millville, Mass., U.S., 2,724 . . . . .292/H4
Millville, Minn., U.S., 186 . . . . .298/E6
Millville, N.J., U.S., 26,847 . . . . .314/C5
Millville, Ohio, U.S., 817 . . . . .328/A7
Millville, Penn., U.S., 991 . . . . .336/H3
Millville, Utah, U.S., 1,507 . . . . .350/C2

Millwood, Ark., U.S., lake 244/A4
Millwood, Ga., U.S., 90 . . . . .260/F9
Millwood, Ky., U.S., 125 . . . . .280/D3
Milmay, N.J., U.S., 275 . . . . .314/D5
Milne, P.N.G., bay 172/B3
Milner, Colo., U.S., 150 . . . . .250/C1
Milner, Ga., U.S., 522 . . . . .260/C5
Milnesand, N. Mex., U.S. 317/G4
Milnor, N. Dak., U.S., 711 . . . . .326/H3
Milnthorpe, Eng., U.K., 1,934 . . . . .66/C4
Milo, Alta., Can., 115 . . . . .212/D6
Milo, Guin., river .149/D3
Milo, Iowa, U.S., 839 . . . . .274/H4
Milo, Maine, U.S., 2,383 . . . . .286/D3
Milo, Mo., U.S., 84 . . . . .302/B4
Milo, Okla., U.S. .330/E3
Milo, Oreg., U.S., 40 . . . . .334/C5
Milolii, Hawaii, U.S. 262/C7
Milos, Gr., island .100/C3
Milovaig, Scot., U.K. 62/C4
Milpitas, Calif., U.S., 62,698 . . . . .246/K3
Milroy, Ind., U.S., 800 . . . . .270/F6
Milroy, Minn., U.S., 271 . . . . .298/B6
Milroy, Penn., U.S., 1,386 . . . . .336/F4
Milstead, Ala., U.S. 238/D3
Milton, Ont., Can., 31,471 . . . . .223/F4
Milton, P.E.I., Can. 224/B2
Milton, (Highland), Scot., U.K. 62/G3
Milton, (Tayside), Scot., U.K. 62/J5
Milton, Conn., U.S., 275 . . . . .253/B2
Milton, Del., U.S., 1,657 . . . . .255/C5
Milton, Fla., U.S., 7,045 . . . . .256/A1
Milton, Ill., U.S., 274 . . . . .266/C4
Milton, Ind., U.S., 611 . . . . .270/F5
Milton, Iowa, U.S., 550 . . . . .274/K6
Milton, Kans., U.S., 100 . . . . .276/E4
Milton, Ky., U.S., 525 . . . . .280/E2
Milton, Maine, U.S., 123 . . . . .286/B4
Milton, Mass., U.S., 26,062 . . . . .292/K3
Milton, N.H., U.S., 3,910 . . . . .312/E5
Milton, (Saratoga County), N.Y., U.S., 2,692 .320/P4
Milton, (Ulster County), N.Y., U.S., 1,251 . . .320/P7
Milton, N.C., U.S., 132 . . . . .322/G1
Milton, N. Dak., U.S., 85 . . . . .326/G1
Milton, Penn., U.S., 6,650 . . . . .336/H3
Milton, Vt., U.S., 9,479 . . . . .352/A1
Milton, Wash., U.S., 5,795 . . . . .358/C2
Milton, W. Va., U.S., 2,206 . . . . .360/B4
Milton, Wisc., U.S., 5,132 . . . . .364/E6
Milton, Minn., U.S., 279 . . . . .298/B4
Milton Abbot, Eng., U.K. 73/D3
Milton Ctr., Ohio, U.S., 195 . . . . .328/C3
Milton-Freewater, Oreg., U.S., 6,470 . . . . . .334/H2
Milton Keynes, Eng., U.K., 43,964,
  (156,148 metro.) 68/F5
Milton Keynes, Eng., U.K., 43,964,
  (156,148 metro.) 70/C2
Milton Keynes, Eng., U.K., unitary authority,
  207,063 . . . . .68/F5
Milton Keynes, Eng., U.K., unitary authority,
  207,063 . . . . .70/C2
Milton Mills, N.H., U.S., 300 . . . . .312/E5
Miltonsburg, Ohio, U.S. 328/H6
Miltonvale, Kans., U.S., 523 . . . . .276/E2
Milverton, Ont., Can., 1,707 . . . . .223/E4
Milverton, Eng., U.K. 73/F2
Milwaukee, Wisc., U.S., 596,974,
  (1,689,572 metro.) 364/F2, F5
Milwaukee, Wisc., U.S., county, 940,164 . .364/F2, F5
Milwaukie, Oreg., U.S., 20,490 . . . . .334/A2
Milwich, Eng., U.K. 68/C4
Mimbres, N. Mex., U.S., 50 . . . . .317/C5
Mimico, Ont., Can. 223/J6
Miminegash, P.E.I., Can., 188 . . . . .224/A2
Mimosa Park, La., U.S., 4,500 . . . . .282/J3
Mims, Fla., U.S., 9,147 . . . . .256/H3
Mina, Nev., U.S., 275 . . . . .310/A2
Mina, S. Dak., U.S. 342/G2
Mina Baranis, Egy. 144/C3
Mina, Oreg., U.S. 334/J2
Minami, Jap., island . . . . .114/Inset III
Minard, Scot., U.K. 62/F6
Minas, N.B., Can., channel 217/E3
Minas, N.S., Can., channel 221/C2
Minas, Uru. 187/C3
Mina Salman, Bahr. 137/B1
Minas Gerais, Braz., state 188/D3
Minatare, Nebr., U.S., 810 . . . . .308/A2
Minatitlán, Mex., 109,193, (153,001 metro.) . .200/F4
Minburn, Iowa, U.S., 391 . . . . .274/F4
Minch, Scot., U.K., strait 60/B1
Minchinhampton, Eng., U.K., 3,201 . . . . . . .68/C6
Minco, Okla., U.S., 1,672 . . . . .330/E2
Mindanao, Phil., island 120/C5
Mindelo, C.V., 67,844 . . . . .148/B2
Mindemoya, Ont., Can. 223/C2
Minden, Ont., Can. 223/G3
Minden, Iowa, U.S., 564 . . . . .274/C5
Minden, La., U.S., 13,027 . . . . .282/C1
Minden, Nebr., U.S., 2,964 . . . . .308/E3
Minden, Nev., U.S., 2,836 . . . . .310/A2
Minden City, Mich., U.S., 242 . . . . .294/G6
Mindenmines, Mo., U.S., 409 . . . . .302/B4
Mindoro, Phil., island 120/B3
Mindoro, Phil., strait 120/B3
Mindrum, Eng., U.K. 66/D1
Minehead, Eng., U.K., 9,158 . . . . .73/F2
Mine La Motte, Mo., U.S., 100 . . . . .302/F4
Mineola, Iowa, U.S., 150 . . . . .274/C5
Mineola, N.Y., U.S., 19,234 . . . . .320/C2
Mineola, Tex., U.S., 4,550 . . . . .346/N3
Miner, Yukon, Can., river 228/B3
Miner, Mo., U.S., 1,056 . . . . .302/G5
Miner, Mont., U.S. 306/F4
Miner, S. Dak., U.S., county, 2,884 . . . . . . .342/H3
Mineral, Calif., U.S., 143 . . . . .246/D2
Mineral, Colo., U.S., county, 831 . . . . .250/D4
Mineral, Ill., U.S., 272 . . . . .266/D2
Mineral, Mont., U.S., county, 3,884 . . . . . . .306/B3
Mineral, Nev., U.S., county, 5,071 . . . . .310/A2
Mineral, Tex., U.S., 40 . . . . .346/L7
Mineral, Va., U.S., 424 . . . . .354/H4
Mineral, Wash., U.S., 250 . . . . .358/C3
Mineral, W. Va., U.S., county, 27,078 . . . . . .360/H2
Mineral Bluff, Ga., U.S., 150 . . . . .260/C2
Mineral City, Ohio, U.S., 841 . . . . .328/H4
Mineral Hill, N. Mex., U.S. 317/E2
Mineral Hills, Mich., U.S., 214 . . . . .294/A3
Mineral Hot Sprs., Colo., U.S. 250/E3
Mineral King, Calif., U.S. 246/G6
Mineral Pt., Mo., U.S., 363 . . . . .302/F4
Mineral Pt., Wisc., U.S., 2,617 . . . . .364/C6
Mineral Ridge, Ohio, U.S., 3,900 . . . . .328/J3
Mineral Sprs., Ark., U.S., 1,264 . . . . .244/B4
Mineral Wells, Tex., U.S., 16,946 . . . . .346/K3
Mineralwells, W. Va., U.S., 1,860 . . . . .360/C4
Miners Bay, Ont., Can. 223/G3
Minersville, Penn., U.S., 4,552 . . . . .336/J4
Minersville, Utah, U.S., 817 . . . . .350/B5
Minerva, Ky., U.S., 150 . . . . .280/G2

Minerva, Nev., U.S. 310/C2
Minerva, N.Y., U.S., 125 . . . . .320/P3
Minerva, Ohio, U.S., 3,934 . . . . .328/H4
Minerva Park, Ohio, U.S., 1,288 . . . . .328/E9
Minetto, N.Y., U.S., 1,086 . . . . .320/J4
Mineville, (Mineville-Witherbee),
  N.Y., U.S., 1,747 . . . . .320/P2
Minford, Ohio, U.S., 700 . . . . .328/E8
Mingäçevir, Azer. 103/B2
Mingäçevir, Azer., reservoir 103/B2
Mingan Archipelago Natl. Park Reserve,
  Que., Can. 225/D3
Mingo, Iowa, U.S., 269 . . . . .274/H4
Mingo, Kans., U.S. 276/B2
Mingo, W. Va., U.S., county, 28,253 . . . . . . .360/B5
Mingo Jct., Ohio, U.S., 3,631 . . . . .328/J5
Mingo N.W.R., Mo., U.S. 302/F4
Mingulay, Scot., U.K., island 62/A5
Mingus, Tex., U.S., 246 . . . . .346/K3
Minho, Port., river 93/A1
Minicoy, India, island 128/C3
Minidoka, Ida., U.S., 129 . . . . .264/D7
Minidoka, Ida., U.S., county, 20,174 . . . . . . .264/D7
Minidoka Internment Natl. Mon., Ida., U.S. . . .264/C7
Minidoka N.W.R., Ida., U.S. 264/D7
Minier, Ill., U.S., 1,244 . . . . .266/D3
Minija, Lith., river .82/A2
Miniota, Man., Can. 215/A4
Minitonas, Man., Can., 538 . . . . .215/A3
Mink Creek, Man., Can. 215/A3
Mink Creek, Ida., U.S., 40 . . . . .264/F7
Minna, Nig. 152/D3
Minneapolis, Kans., U.S., 2,046 . . . . .276/E2
Minneapolis, Minn., U.S., 382,618,
  (2,968,806 metro.) 298/D5, E6
Minnedosa, Man., Can., 2,426 . . . . .215/B4
Minnehaha, S. Dak., U.S., county, 148,281 . .342/J4
Minnehaha, Wash., U.S., 7,689 . . . . .358/C4
Minnehaha Sprs., W. Va., U.S. 360/G4
Minneiska, Minn., U.S., 116 . . . . .298/F6
Minneola, Fla., U.S., 5,435 . . . . .256/C4
Minneola, Kans., U.S., 717 . . . . .276/B4
Minneota, Minn., U.S., 1,449 . . . . .298/B6
Minnesota, U.S., state 286
Minnesota, U.S., river 298/B6
Minnesota City, Minn., U.S., 235 . . . . .298/F6
Minnesota Lake, Minn., U.S., 681 . . . . .298/D7
Minnesott Beach, N.C., U.S., 311 . . . . .322/M5
Minnetonka, Minn., U.S., 51,301 . . . . .298/E6
Minnetrista, Minn., U.S., 4,358 . . . . .298/D6
Minnewaukan, N. Dak., U.S., 318 . . . . .326/F1
Miño, Sp., river 94/B1
Minoa, N.Y., U.S., 3,348 . . . . .320/J4
Minocqua, Wisc., U.S., 750 . . . . .364/D3
Minonk, Ill., U.S., 2,168 . . . . .266/D3
Minooka, Ill., U.S., 3,971 . . . . .266/E2
Minorca (Menorca), Sp., island 94/H2
Minor Hill, Tenn., U.S., 437 . . . . .344/C4
Minor Lane Hts., Ky., U.S., 1,435 . . . . .280/A2
Minot, Maine, U.S., 2,248 . . . . .286/B4
Minot, Mass., U.S., 1,100 . . . . .292/L4
Minot, N. Dak., U.S., 36,567 . . . . .326/D1
Minsk, Bela., capital, 1,677,137,
  (1,729,000 metro.) 82/C3
Minsk, Bela., oblast 82/C3
Minster, (Minster/Manston), Eng., U.K., 4,591 .70/G4
Minster, Eng., U.K., 15,448 . . . . .70/F4
Minster, Ohio, U.S., 2,794 . . . . .328/B5
Minsterley, Eng., U.K. 68/A4
Minster Lovell, Eng., U.K. 70/A3
Minter, Ga., U.S., 80 . . . . .238/C3
Minter City, Miss., U.S., 90 . . . . .300/B2
Mint Hill, N.C., U.S., 14,922 . . . . .322/D4
Mintlaw, Scot., U.K., 2,647 . . . . .62/N3
Minto, Man., Can. 215/B4
Minto, N.B., Can., 2,776 . . . . .217/C2
Minto, Que., Can., lake 225/B2
Minto, Yukon, Can. 228/B4
Minto, Alaska, U.S., 258 . . . . .240/F2
Minto, N. Dak., U.S., 657 . . . . .326/H1
Minton, Sask., Can., 95 . . . . .227/F11
Minturn, Ark., U.S., 114 . . . . .244/D2
Minturn, Colo., U.S., 1,068 . . . . .250/D2
Minturn, Maine, U.S., 175 . . . . .286/D4
Minuteman Missile N.H.S., S. Dak., U.S. 342/C4
Minute Man N.H.P., Mass., U.S. 292/J3
Mio, Mo., U.S., 2,016 . . . . .294/E5
Mira, N.S., Can. .221/H1
Mira, La., U.S., 40 . . . . .282/B1
Mirabel, Que., Can., 27,330 . . . . .226/B6
Mirador Nacional, Uru., mountain 187/C3
Miraflores, Col. .184/B4
Miragoâne, Haiti .205/B2
Miramar, Fla., U.S., 72,739 . . . . .256/B6, H6
Miramichi, N.B., Can., 18,508 205
Miramichi, N.B., Can., bay 217/E1
Mira Monte, Calif., U.S. 246/F8
Miranda, Calif., U.S., 225 . . . . .246/B2
Miranda, S. Dak., U.S. 342/G3
Miranda, Ven., state 182/C1
Miranda de Ebro, Sp., 35,925 . . . . .94/E1
Mirando City, Tex., U.S., 493 . . . . .346/K8
Mirbat, Oman 137/B3
Mirebalais, Haiti .205/C2
Mirfield, Eng., U.K., 18,459 . . . . .66/E5
Mirfield, Eng., U.K., 18,459 . . . . .68/D2
Miri, Malay., 87,167 . . . . .121/D2
Mirnyy, Russ. 104/G3
Mirpur Khas, Pak., 189,671 . . . . .119/C5
Mirror, Alta., Can., 492 . . . . .212/D5
Mirror Lake, N.H., U.S., 350 . . . . .312/D4
Mirrormont, Wash., U.S., 3,804 . . . . .358/B4, D2
Miscou, N.B., Can., island 217/E1
Miscouche, P.E.I., Can., 766 . . . . .224/B2
Misenheimer, N.C., U.S., 750 . . . . .322/E4
Misere, Sey. 163/Inset
Misery, St. K.-Nevis, mountain 207/B1
Mishawaka, Ind., U.S., 46,557 . . . . .270/D1
Mishicot, Wisc., U.S., 1,422 . . . . .364/F4
Misiones, Arg., province 191/E2
Misiones, Para., department 187/D5
Miskitos, Nicar., cays 202/C1
Miskolc, Hung., 172,993 . . . . .91/C1
Miskolc, Hung. 91/C1
Misool, Indon., island 122/E2
Misratah, Lib., 360,000 . . . . .145/D1
Missaukee, Mich., U.S., county, 14,478 . . . . .294/D5
Missinipe, Sask., Can. 227/F5
Mission, Kans., U.S., 9,727 . . . . .276/H1
Mission, Oreg., U.S., 1,019 . . . . .334/H2
Mission, S. Dak., U.S., 904 . . . . .342/E4
Mission, Tex., U.S., 45,408 . . . . .346/K9
Mission Bend, Tex., U.S., 30,831 . . . . .346/A6
Mission Hill, S. Dak., U.S., 183 . . . . .342/H5
Mission Hills, Calif., U.S., 3,142 . . . . .246/E8
Mission Hills, Kans., U.S., 3,593 . . . . .276/H1
Mission Ridge, S. Dak., U.S., 70 . . . . .342/E3
Mission Viejo, Calif., U.S., 93,102 . . . . .246/F11

Mission Woods, Kans., U.S., 165 . . . . .276/H1
Missisquoi, Vt., U.S., river 352/B1
Missisquoi N.W.R., Vt., U.S. 352/A1
Mississauga, Ont., Can., 612,925 . . . . . .223/F4, J6
Mississinewa, Ind., U.S., lake 270/E3
Mississippi, Ont., Can., lake 223/J2
Mississippi, Ont., Can., lake 320/J1
Mississippi, U.S., state 288
Mississippi, Ark., U.S., county, 51,979 . . . . .244/E2
Mississippi, Ark., U.S., county 244/E3
Mississippi, Ill., U.S., river 266/B3, D6
Mississippi, La., U.S., river 282/G3, K3
Mississippi, Minn., U.S., river 298/C3, C4, F7
Mississippi, Miss., U.S., river 300/A4, B1
Mississippi, Miss., U.S., sound 300/D5
Mississippi, Mo., U.S., county, 13,427 . . . . .302/G5
Mississippi, Mo., U.S., river 302/G4, J3
Mississippi, Tenn., U.S., river 344/B3
Mississippi, Wisc., U.S., river 274/M2
Miss. Choctaw Ind. Res., Miss., U.S. 300/C3
Miss. Sandhill Crane N.W.R., Miss., U.S. 300/D5
Mississippi State, Miss., U.S., 3,500 . . . . . . .300/D2
Misson, Eng., U.K. 66/G6
Missoula, Mont., U.S., 57,053, (95,802 metro.) .306/C3
Missoula, Mont., U.S., county, 95,802 . . . . . .306/C2
Missouri, U.S., state 290
Missouri, Kans., U.S., river 276/G2, H1
Missouri, Mo., U.S., river 302/C2, G3, J5
Missouri, Mont., U.S., river 306/F2, G2, M1
Missouri, Nebr., U.S., river 308/J3
Missouri, N. Dak., U.S., river 326/H1, D2
Missouri, S. Dak., U.S., river 342/E2, F4, J5
Missouri City, Mo., U.S., 295 . . . . .302/J4
Missouri City, Tex., U.S., 52,913 . . . . .346/A7
Missouri Valley, Iowa, U.S., 2,992 . . . . .274/C4
Mist, Ark., U.S., 50 . . . . .244/D4
Mist, Oreg., U.S. 334/C2
Mistassibi, Que., Can., river 226/D1
Mistassini, Que., Can., 1,814 . . . . .225/B3
Mistassini, Que., Can., 1,814 . . . . .226/D3
Mistassini, Que., Can., lake 225/B3
Mistassini, Que., Can., river 226/D2
Mistatim, Sask., Can., 104 . . . . .227/G8
Mistelbach, Aus. .91/E2
Misterton, Eng., U.K., 1,953 . . . . .68/E3
Mitcham, S.A., Austl. . . . . .170/Inset II
Mitcham, Eng., U.K. 70/D4
Mitcheldean, Eng., U.K., 2,243 . . . . .68/C6
Mitchell, Austl., river 170/D1
Mitchell, Ont., Can., 4,181 . . . . .223/D4
Mitchell, Ala., U.S. 238/D3
Mitchell, Ala., U.S., lake 238/C3
Mitchell, Ga., U.S., 173 . . . . .260/F5
Mitchell, Ga., U.S., county, 23,932 . . . . .260/C9
Mitchell, Ind., U.S., 4,567 . . . . .270/D7
Mitchell, Iowa, U.S., 155 . . . . .274/J1
Mitchell, Iowa, U.S., county, 10,874 . . . . . . .274/J1
Mitchell, Kans., U.S. 276/D3
Mitchell, Kans., U.S., county, 6,932 . . . . . . .276/D2
Mitchell, La., U.S., 100 . . . . .282/B3
Mitchell, Nebr., U.S., 1,831 . . . . .308/A2
Mitchell, N.C., U.S., county, 15,687 . . . . .322/A2, F6
Mitchell, N.C., U.S., mountain 322/A3, F7
Mitchell, Oreg., U.S., 170 . . . . .334/F3
Mitchell, S. Dak., U.S., 14,558 . . . . .342/G4
Mitchell Hts., W. Va., U.S., 301 . . . . .360/B5
Mitchellsburg, Ky., U.S., 175 . . . . .280/F3
Mitchellville, Ill., U.S., 90 . . . . .266/E6
Mitchellville, Iowa, U.S., 497 . . . . .354/D4
Mitchellville, Iowa, U.S., 1,715 . . . . .274/H4
Mitchellville, Md., U.S., 9,611 . . . . .288/C4
Mitchellville, Tenn., U.S., 207 . . . . .344/H1
Mitchinamécus, Que., Can., lake 226/A4
Mito, Jap. 114/D2
Mitsamiouli, Com. 163/A1
Mits'iwa, Erit., 40,000 . . . . .156/B2
Mittelfranken, Ger., department 86/B4
Mittelland, Ger., canal 86/B2
Mittie, La., U.S., 40 . . . . .282/D5
Mitú, Col., 14,000 . . . . .184/C4
Mitumba, Congo, D.R., mountains 155/C2
Mitzic, Gabon 155/A1
Miyagi, Jap., prefecture 114/D2
Miyake, Jap., island 114/C3
Miyako, Jap. 114/D2
Miyako, Jap., island . . . . .114/Inset II
Miyakonojo, Jap. 114/A4
Miyazaki, Jap., 306,000 . . . . .114/A4
Miyazaki, Jap., prefecture 114/A3
Mize, Miss., U.S., 285 . . . . .300/C4
Mizen Head, Ire., cape 78/B3
Mizo, India, hills 128/F4
Mizoram, India, state 128/F4
Mizpah, Minn., U.S., 78 . . . . .298/C3
Mizpah, Mont., U.S., river 306/L3
Mizpah, N.J., U.S., 500 . . . . .314/D5
Mizpe Ramon, Isr. 135/B2
Mjøsa, Nor., lake 80/C3
Mkondvo, Swaz., river 161/B2
Mliba, Swaz. 161/B2
Mmabatho, S. Afr. 162/C2
Mo, Nor. 80/C2
Moa, Indon., island 122/D2
Moa, S.L., river .149/B2
Moab, Utah, U.S., 4,779 . . . . .350/E5
Moala, Fiji, island group 174/B3
Moanda, Gabon, 21,921 . . . . .155/B2
Moapa, Nev., U.S., 928 . . . . .310/C3
Moapa River Ind. Res., Nev., U.S. 310/C3
Moark, Ark., U.S., 125 . . . . .244/E1
Moba, Congo, D.R. 155/C2
Mobaye, C.A.R. .154/B3
Mobeetie, Tex., U.S., 107 . . . . .346/G9
Moberly, Mo., U.S., 11,945 . . . . .302/D2
Mobile, Ala., U.S., 198,915, (540,258 metro.) .238/A5
Mobile, Ala., U.S., bay 238/B5
Mobile, Ala., U.S., county, 399,843 . . . . . . .238/A5
Mobile, Ala., U.S., point 238/A5
Mobile, Ariz., U.S., 40 . . . . .242/C4
Mobile City, Tex., U.S., 196 . . . . .346/D9
Mobjack, Va., U.S., 300 . . . . .354/L6
Mobridge, S. Dak., U.S., 3,574 . . . . .342/F2
Moca, Dom. Rep. 205/B1
Moca, P.R. 206/A2
Moçambique, Moz. 161/D2
Mocaccio, Okla., U.S. 330/B1, D4
Moccasin, Ariz., U.S., 80 . . . . .242/C1
Moccasin, Mont., U.S., 40 . . . . .306/G2
Mochrum, Scot., U.K. 62/G9
Mocímboa da Praia, Moz. 161/D1
Mocksville, N.C., U.S., 4,178 . . . . .322/D3
Moclips, Wash., U.S., 615 . . . . .358/A2
Môco, Morro de, Ang., mountain 159/C4
Mocoa, Col., 30,000 . . . . .184/A4
Modale, Iowa, U.S., 303 . . . . .274/B4
Modbury, Eng., U.K. 73/E4
Moddersville, Mich., U.S., 40 . . . . .294/E5
Model, Colo., U.S. 250/F4
Model, Tenn., U.S. 344/F1

Modena, It. 95/B1
Modena, Penn., U.S., 610 ....336/K6
Modena, Utah, U.S. 350/A6
Modena, Wisc., U.S., 40 ....364/B4
Modeste, La., U.S., 125 ....282/G6
Modesto, Calif., U.S., 188,856, (446,997 metro.) ..246/E5
Modesto, Ill., U.S., 252 ....266/D4
Modoc, Calif., U.S., county, 9,449 ....246/D1
Modoc, Ga., U.S. 260/G6
Modoc, Ind., U.S., 225 ....270/F4
Modoc, Kans., U.S. 276/A3
Modoc, S.C., U.S., 256 ....340/B3
Modoc Natl. For., Calif., U.S. 246/E1
Modoc N.W.R., Calif., U.S. 246/E1
Moengo, Sur. 183/B2
Moenkopi, Ariz., U.S., 901 ....242/D1
Moers, Ger., 106,837 ....86/A3
Moffat, Scot., U.K., 2,135 ....62/K8
Moffat, Colo., U.S., 114 ....250/E4
Moffat, Colo., U.S., county, 13,184 ......250/B1
Moffett, Okla., U.S., 179 ....330/H2
Moffit, N. Dak., U.S., 70 ....326/E3
Mogadishu, Som., capital, 230,000 ....157/B3
Mogadore, Ohio, U.S., 3,893 ....328/H3
Mogami, Jap., river 114/D2
Mogi das Cruzes, Braz. ....188/Inset II
Mogocha, Russ. 104/C4
Mogollon, N. Mex., U.S. 317/B4
Mogollon Rim, Ariz., U.S., cliffs 242/D3
Mogote, Colo., U.S., 50 ....250/D4
Mogotón, Nicar., peak 202/A2
Mohács, Hun. 91/B2
Mohale's Hoek, Leso. 161/A3
Mohall, N. Dak., U.S., 812 ....326/D1
Mohammedia, Mor., 156,000 ....147/C1
Mohave, Ariz., U.S., county, 155,032 .....242/A2
Mohave, Ariz., U.S., lake 242/A2
Mohave, Nev., U.S., lake 310/C4
Mohave Valley, Ariz., U.S., 13,694 ....242/A3
Mohawk, Ariz., U.S. 242/B5
Mohawk, Mich., U.S., 750 ....294/A2
Mohawk, N.Y., U.S., 2,660 ....320/M5
Mohawk, N.Y., U.S., river 320/M5
Mohawk St. For., Conn., U.S. 253/B2
Mohegan, Conn., U.S., 3,500 ....253/G4
Moher, Ire., cliffs 78/B2
Mohican, Alaska, U.S., cape 240/B2
Mohican, Ohio, U.S., river 328/F4
Mohler, Wash., U.S. 358/G2
Mohnton, Penn., U.S., 2,963 ....336/J5
Mohyliv Podil's'kyi, Ukr. 102/C2
Moiese, Mont., U.S. 306/B2
Moiliili, Hawaii, U.S. 262/K2
Moingona, Iowa, U.S., 175 ....274/G3
Moira, N. Ire., U.K., 2,772 ....65/E3
Mojave, Calif., U.S., 3,836 ....246/G4
Mojave, Calif., U.S., river 246/J8
Mojave Desert, Calif., U.S. 246/J7
Mojave Natl. Pres., Calif., U.S. 246/K7
Mojos, Bol. 186/A2
Mokane, Mo., U.S., 188 ....302/E3
Mokapu, Hawaii, U.S., point 262/K2
Mokelumne Hill, Calif., U.S., 774 ....246/L6
Mokena, Ill., U.S., 14,583 ....266/B6
Mokhotlong, Leso. 161/C2
Moko, Ark., U.S., 60 ....244/D1
Mokolii, Hawaii, U.S., island 262/J2
Mokolo, Came. 153/B1
Mokpo, S. Kor., 247,452 ....116/B5
Mokuauia, Hawaii, U.S., island 262/J1
Mokuleia, Hawaii, U.S., 1,839 ....262/H1
Mokulua, Hawaii, U.S., island 262/K2
Moku Manu, Hawaii, U.S., island 262/K2
Molalla, Oreg., U.S., 5,647 ....334/D2
Mold, Wales, U.K. 60/B3
Mold, Wales, U.K., 8,745 ....64/E1
Moldavia, Rom., region 101/D2
Molde, Nor. 80/B3
Moldova, nation 100
Moldoveanu, Rom., mountain 101/C3
Mole Lake, Wisc., U.S., 275 ....364/D1
Molega, Ga., U.S., 475 ....260/C6
Molepolole, Bots., 44,564 ....160/D2
Molesworth, Eng., U.K. 70/D2
Molina, Colo., U.S. 250/B2
Moline, Ill., U.S., 43,768 ....266/C2
Moline, Kans., U.S., 457 ....276/F4
Moline Acres, Mo., U.S., 2,662 ....302/J2
Molino, Fla., U.S., 1,312 ....256/A1
Molise, It., region 95/C2
Mollendo, Peru 185/C4
Mollusk, Va., U.S., 300 ....354/K5
Moloaa Forest Reserve, Hawaii, U.S. 262/C1
Molokai, Hawaii, U.S., island 262/A3, C5
Molokai Forest Reserve, Hawaii, U.S. 262/B3
Molokini, Hawaii, U.S., island 262/C4
Molopo, Bots., river 160/A3
Molopo, S. Afr., river 162/B2
Moloundou, Came. 153/C3
Molson, Man., Can., lake 215/C2
Molson, Wash., U.S. 358/F1
Molt, Mont., U.S. 306/H4
Molucca, Indon., sea 122/D2
Moluccas, Indon., islands 122/D2
Molunkus, Maine, U.S. 286/D3
Molybdenite, Wash., U.S., mountain 358/H1
Mombasa, Kenya, 465,000 ....157/E5
Mombetsu, Jap. ....114/Inset I
Momence, Ill., U.S., 3,171 ....266/F2
Momeyer, N.C., U.S., 291 ....322/J3
Mømlingen, Ger., island 79/D4
Mon, Mya., state 125/C3
Mona, Dom. Rep., passage 205/D2
Mona, P.R., passage 206/A2
Mona, Utah, U.S., 850 ....350/C4
Monaca, Penn., U.S., 6,286 ....336/A4
Monachylemore, Scot., U.K. 62/H6
Monaco, nation 95
Monaco, Mon., district 97/B1
Monaco, Mon., port, 27,063 ....97/B1
Monagas, Ven., state 182/D2
Monaghan, Ire. 78/C1
Monaghan, Ire., county 78/C1
Monahans, Tex., U.S., 6,821 ....346/H4
Monango, N. Dak., U.S. 326/G3
Monar, Scot., U.K., lake 62/F4
Monaragala, Sri Lan. 126/C5
Monarch, Alta., Can., 195 ....212/D6
Monarch, Mont., U.S. 306/F2
Monarch Mills, S.C., U.S., 1,930 ....340/C2
Monarda, Maine, U.S. 286/D3
Monashee Prov. Park, Br. Col., Can. 214/N6
Monastery, N.S., Can. 221/F2
Monastir, Tun. 146/C2
Monatélé, Came. 153/B3
Mona Vale, N.S.W., Austl. ....170/Inset IV
Mönchengladbach, Ger., 263,697 ....86/A3
Moncks Corner, S.C., U.S., 5,952 ....340/D3
Monclova, Mex., 192,554, (193,744 metro.) ..200/D2
Moncton, N.B., Can., 61,046 ....217/E2
Mondamin, Iowa, U.S., 423 ....274/B4

Mondego, Port., cape 93/A2
Mondego, Port., river 93/B2
Mondovi, Wash., U.S. 358/G2
Mondovi, Wisc., U.S., 2,634 ....364/B4
Monee, Ill., U.S., 2,924 ....266/F2
Monell, Wyo., U.S. 366/B3
Monero, N. Mex., U.S. 317/D1
Monessen, Penn., U.S., 8,669 ....336/B5
Moneta, Iowa, U.S. 274/D1
Moneta, Va., U.S., 225 ....354/D6
Moneta, Wyo., U.S. 366/C2
Monett, Mo., U.S., 7,396 ....302/C5
Monetta, S.C., U.S., 220 ....340/C3
Monette, Ark., U.S., 1,179 ....244/E2
Money, Miss., U.S., 80 ....300/B2
Money Creek, Minn., U.S., 70 ....298/F7
Moneymore, N. Ire., U.K., 1,231 ....65/D2
Monforte, Sp. 94/C1
Monfort Hts. East, Ohio, U.S., 3,880 .....328/B9
Mongo, Chad 153/B4
Mongolia, nation 114
Mongolian, Mong., plateau 118/C2
Mongomo, Eq. Gui. 154/D3
Mongu, Zam. 159/A3
Monhegan, Maine, U.S., 75 ....286/C5
Monhegan, Maine, U.S., island 286/C5
Moniac, Ga., U.S., 40 ....62/J8
Moniaive, Scot., U.K. 62/J8
Monico, Wisc., U.S., 175 ....364/D3
Monida, Mont., U.S. 306/D5
Monie, Md., U.S., 50 ....288/L7
Monifieth, Scot., U.K. 62/L6
Monitor, Alta., Can. 212/E5
Monitor, Nev., U.S., range 310/D1
Monitor, Wash., U.S., 375 ....358/E2
Monjolo, Braz. ....188/Inset I
Monkey Bay, Mal. 159/B2
Monkleigh, Eng., U.K. 73/D3
Monksilver, Eng., U.K. 73/F2
Monkton, Eng., U.K. 73/F3
Monkton, Vt., U.S., 1,759 ....352/A2
Monkton Deverill, Eng., U.K. 73/H2
Monkton Up, Eng., U.K. 73/J3
Monmouth, Wales, U.K., 7,246 ....64/F4
Monmouth, Ill., U.S., 9,841 ....266/C3
Monmouth, Iowa, U.S., 180 ....274/N3
Monmouth, Maine, U.S., 3,785 ....286/B4
Monmouth, N.J., U.S., county, 615,301 ....314/E3
Monmouth, Oreg., U.S., 7,741 ....334/C3
Monmouth Beach, N.J., U.S., 3,595 ....314/F3
Monmouth Jct., N.J., U.S., 2,721 ....314/D3
Monmouthshire, Wales, U.K., unitary authority, 84,879 ..64/F4
Monnett, Ohio, U.S., 125 ....328/D4
Mono, Ben., river 151/A4
Mono, Togo, river 151/B2
Mono, Calif., U.S., county, 12,853 ....246/F4
Mono, Calif., U.S., lake 246/G4
Mono Hot Sprs., Calif., U.S., 40 ....246/G5
Monomoy, Mass., U.S., island 292/P6
Monomoy, Mass., U.S., point 292/P6
Monomoy N.W.R., Mass., U.S. 292/Q6
Monon, Ind., U.S., 1,733 ....270/C3
Monona, Iowa, U.S., 1,550 ....274/M1
Monona, Iowa, U.S., county, 10,020 ....274/C3
Monona, Wisc., U.S., 8,018 ....364/D4
Monongah, W. Va., U.S., 939 ....360/F2
Monongahela, Penn., U.S., 4,761 ....336/B5
Monongahela, Penn., U.S., river 336/E7
Monongahela Natl. For., W. Va., U.S. 354/D3
Monongalia, W. Va., U.S., county, 81,866 ..360/F1
Monopoli, It. 95/D2
Monowi, Nebr., U.S. 308/E1
Monponsett, Mass., U.S., 1,700 ....292/L4
Mon Repos, St. Luc. 208/B2
Monroe, Ala., U.S., county, 24,324 ....238/B4
Monroe, Ark., U.S., 90 ....244/D3
Monroe, Ark., U.S., county, 10,254 ....244/D3
Monroe, Conn., U.S., 19,247 ....253/B3
Monroe, Fla., U.S., county, 79,589 ....256/C6, G7
Monroe, Ga., U.S., 11,407 ....260/D4
Monroe, Ga., U.S., county, 21,757 ....260/C6
Monroe, Ill., U.S., county, 27,619 ....266/A4, C5
Monroe, Ind., U.S., 734 ....270/C3
Monroe, Ind., U.S., county, 120,563 ......270/C6
Monroe, Ind., U.S., lake 270/D6
Monroe, Iowa, U.S., 1,808 ....274/H4
Monroe, Iowa, U.S., county, 8,016 ....274/J5
Monroe, Ky., U.S., county, 11,756 ....280/E4
Monroe, La., U.S., 53,107, (147,250 metro.) ..282/E1
Monroe, Maine, U.S., 882 ....286/C4
Monroe, Mich., U.S., 22,076 ....294/F8
Monroe, Mich., U.S., county, 145,945 .....294/A8, F8
Monroe, Miss., U.S., county, 38,014 ......300/D2
Monroe, Mo., U.S., county, 9,311 ....302/D3
Monroe, Nebr., U.S., 307 ....308/G2
Monroe, N.H., U.S., 759 ....312/B3
Monroe, N.Y., U.S., 7,780 ....320/A1
Monroe, N.Y., U.S., county, 735,343 ......320/F4
Monroe, N.C., U.S., 26,228 ....322/D5
Monroe, Ohio, U.S., 7,133 ....328/B7
Monroe, Ohio, U.S., county, 15,180 ....328/H6
Monroe, Okla., U.S., 225 ....330/H2
Monroe, Oreg., U.S., 607 ....334/C3
Monroe, Penn., U.S., county, 138,687 .....336/L3
Monroe, S. Dak., U.S., 163 ....342/H4
Monroe, Tenn., U.S., county, 38,961 ......344/N4
Monroe, Utah, U.S., 1,845 ....350/D5
Monroe, Va., U.S., 1,200 ....354/E5
Monroe, Wash., U.S., 13,795 ....358/B4, D2
Monroe, W. Va., U.S., county, 14,583 .....360/E5
Monroe, Wisc., U.S., 10,843 ....364/D6
Monroe, Wisc., U.S., county, 40,899 ......364/C5
Monroe Bridge, Mass., U.S., 60 ....292/C2
Monroe Ctr., Wisc., U.S., 100 ....364/D4
Monroe City, Ind., U.S., 548 ....270/B7
Monroe City, Mo., U.S., 2,588 ....302/E2
Monroeton, Penn., U.S., 514 ....336/J2
Monroeville, Ala., U.S., 6,862 ....238/B4
Monroeville, Ind., U.S., 1,236 ....270/G3
Monroeville, N.J., U.S., 500 ....314/C4
Monroeville, Ohio, U.S., 1,433 ....328/F3
Monroeville, Penn., U.S., 29,349 ....336/B5, F7
Monrovia, Liber., capital, 421,053 ....149/A2
Monrovia, Calif., U.S., 36,929 ....246/D9
Monrovia, Ind., U.S., 628 ....270/D5
Mons, (Bergen), Belg., 90,955, (248,818 metro.) ..85/B2
Monse, Wash., U.S. 358/F1
Monseñor Nouel, Dom. Rep., province 205/B2
Monson, Maine, U.S., 666 ....286/C3
Monson, Mass., U.S. 292/E4
Montague, P.E.I., Can., 1,945 ....224/D2
Montague, Calif., U.S., 1,456 ....246/D1
Montague, Mass., U.S., 8,489 ....292/D2
Montague, Mich., U.S., 2,407 ....294/C6
Montague, Mont., U.S. 306/F2
Montague, N.J., U.S., 3,412 ....314/D1
Montague, Tex., U.S., 225 ....346/L2

Montague, Tex., U.S., county, 19,117 .....346/L2
Montalto, It., mountain 95/C3
Mont Alto, Penn., U.S., 1,357 ....336/F6
Montana, Bul. 101/B2
Montana, Bul., oblast 101/B2
Montana, U.S., state 294
Montana, Kans., U.S., 80 ....276/G4
Montana City, Mont., U.S., 2,094 ....306/E3
Montara, Calif., U.S., 2,950 ....246/H2
Montargis, Fr. 88/C2
Montauban, Fr. 88/C4
Montauk, N.Y., U.S., 3,851 ....320/H1
Mont Belvieu, Tex., U.S., 2,324 ....346/C6
Montcalm, Mich., U.S., county, 61,266 ....294/D6
Montcalm, W. Va., U.S., 885 ....360/D6
Mont-Carmel, Que., Can., 1,244 ....226/C4
Montclair, Calif., U.S., 33,049 ....246/E9
Montclair, N.J., U.S., 38,977 ....314/B2, E2
Monteagle, Tenn., U.S., 1,238 ....344/K4
Montebello, Que., Can., 1,039 ....226/B6
Montebello, Calif., U.S., 62,150 ....246/D9
Montebello, N.Y., U.S., 3,688 ....320/A1
Monte Carlo, Mon., district 97/B1
Monte Cristi, Dom. Rep. 205/A1
Monte Cristi, Dom. Rep., province 205/A1
Montecristo, It., island 95/B2
Montegiardino, S. Mar. 97/B2
Montego, Jam., bay 206/A2
Montego Bay, Jam., 82,002 ....204/B3
Montego Bay, Jam. 206/B2
Montegut, La., U.S., 1,803 ....282/M8
Monteith, Iowa, U.S., 70 ....274/F4
Montélimar, Fr. 88/D4
Montelindo, Para., river 187/C3
Montello, Nev., U.S. 310/C1
Montello, Wisc., U.S., 1,397 ....364/D4
Montenegro, (republic), Serb.-Mont. 99/A3
Monte Plata, Dom. Rep. 205/C2
Monte Plata, Dom. Rep., province 205/C2
Montepulciano, It. 95/B2
Monterey, Calif., U.S., 29,674 ....246/C6
Monterey, Calif., U.S., bay 246/C6
Monterey, Calif., U.S., county, 401,762 ..246/E6
Monterey, Ind., U.S., 231 ....270/D2
Monterey, Ky., U.S., 167 ....280/F2
Monterey, La., U.S., 80 ....282/F4
Monterey, Mass., U.S., 934 ....292/B4
Monterey, Nebr., U.S. 308/N2
Monterey, Tenn., U.S., 2,717 ....344/L2
Monterey, Va., U.S., 158 ....354/D4
Monterey Park, Calif., U.S., 60,051 ......246/D9
Montero, Col., 321,000 ....184/B2
Montero, Bol. 186/B3
Monterrey, Mex., state capital, 1,110,997, (3,130,596 metro.) ..200/D2
Montesano, Wash., U.S., 3,312 ....358/B3
Montes Claros, Braz., 151,881, (247,286 metro.) ..188/D3
Monte Sereno, Calif., U.S., 3,483 ....246/K3
Montevallo, Ala., U.S., 4,825 ....238/C3
Montevallo, Mo., U.S. 302/B4
Montevideo, Minn., U.S., 5,346 ....298/B5
Montevideo, Uru., capital, 1,303,182 .....187/B3
Montevideo, Uru., department 187/B3
Monteview, Ida., U.S., 40 ....264/E6
Monte Vista, Colo., U.S., 4,529 ....250/D4
Monte Vista N.W.R., Colo., U.S. 250/D4
Montezuma, Colo., U.S., 42 ....250/E2
Montezuma, Colo., U.S., county, 23,830 ...250/B4
Montezuma, Colo., U.S., peak 250/E2
Montezuma, Ga., U.S., 3,999 ....260/C7
Montezuma, Ind., U.S., 1,179 ....270/B5
Montezuma, Iowa, U.S., 1,440 ....274/J4
Montezuma, Kans., U.S., 966 ....276/B4
Montezuma, N. Mex., U.S., 325 ....317/E2
Montezuma, Ohio, U.S., 191 ....328/A5
Montezuma Castle N.M., Ariz., U.S. 242/D3
Montezuma Creek, Utah, U.S., 507 ....350/E6
Montezuma N.W.R., N.Y., U.S. 320/H4
Montfort, Wisc., U.S., 663 ....364/C6
Montgomery, Wales, U.K. 64/E3
Montgomery, Ala., U.S., county, 223,510 ..238/C3
Montgomery, Ala., U.S., state capital, 201,568, (333,055 metro.) ..238/C3
Montgomery, Ark., U.S., county, 9,245 ....244/B3
Montgomery, Ga., U.S., 4,134 ....260/J8
Montgomery, Ga., U.S., county, 8,270 .....260/F7
Montgomery, Ill., U.S., 5,471 ....266/F6
Montgomery, Ill., U.S., county, 30,652 ...266/B2, D4
Montgomery, Ind., U.S., 368 ....270/B7
Montgomery, Ind., U.S., county, 37,629 ...270/C4
Montgomery, Iowa, U.S., county, 11,771 ...274/D5
Montgomery, Kans., U.S., county, 36,252 ..276/G4
Montgomery, Ky., U.S., county, 22,554 ....280/G2
Montgomery, La., U.S., 787 ....282/E2
Montgomery, Md., U.S., county, 873,341 ...288/B5, F3
Montgomery, Mass., U.S., 654 ....292/C4
Montgomery, Mich., U.S., 386 ....294/E8
Montgomery, Minn., U.S., 2,794 ....298/D6
Montgomery, Miss., U.S., county, 12,189 ..300/C2
Montgomery, Mo., U.S., county, 12,136 ....302/E3
Montgomery, N.Y., U.S., 3,636 ....320/N7
Montgomery, N.Y., U.S., county, 49,708 ...320/N5
Montgomery, N.C., U.S., county, 26,822 ...322/D4
Montgomery, Ohio, U.S., 10,163 ....328/B7, B9
Montgomery, Ohio, U.S., county, 559,062 ..328/B6, F2
Montgomery, Penn., U.S., 1,695 ....336/H3
Montgomery, Penn., U.S., county, 750,097 ..336/L5, M6
Montgomery, Tenn., U.S., county, 134,768 ..344/G2
Montgomery, Tex., U.S., 489 ....346/N5
Montgomery, Tex., U.S., county, 293,768 ..346/N5
Montgomery, Va., U.S., 992 ....352/B1
Montgomery, Va., U.S., county, 83,629 ....354/B6
Montgomery, W. Va., U.S., 1,942 ....360/D4
Montgomery Ctr., Vt., U.S., 90 ....352/B1
Montgomery City, Mo., U.S., 2,442 ....302/E3
Montgomery Vil., Md., U.S., 38,051 ....288/F3
Montgomeryville, Penn., U.S., 12,031 .....336/L5
Monticello, P.E.I., Can. 224/C2
Monticello, Ark., U.S., 9,146 ....244/D4
Monticello, Fla., U.S., 2,533 ....256/E1
Monticello, Ga., U.S., 2,428 ....260/D5
Monticello, Ill., U.S., 5,138 ....266/E3
Monticello, Ind., U.S., 5,723 ....270/C3
Monticello, Iowa, U.S., 3,607 ....274/M3
Monticello, Ky., U.S., 5,981 ....280/F4
Monticello, Maine, U.S., 4,763 ....286/E2
Monticello, Maine, U.S. 286/E2
Monticello, Minn., U.S., 7,868 ....298/D5
Monticello, Miss., U.S., 1,726 ....300/B4
Monticello, Mo., U.S., 126 ....302/E1
Monticello, N. Mex., U.S., 50 ....317/C4
Monticello, N.Y., U.S., 6,512 ....320/M7
Monticello, N.C., U.S., 500 ....322/F2
Monticello, S.C., U.S., reservoir 340/C2
Monticello, Utah, U.S., 1,958 ....350/E6
Monticello, Wisc., U.S., 1,146 ....364/D6
Mont Ida, Kans., U.S., 60 ....276/G3
Mont-Joli, Que., Can., 5,886 ....226/C4
Mont-Laurier, Que., Can., 7,365 ....225/A4

Mont-Laurier, Que., Can., 7,365 ....226/A5
Montluçon, Fr. 88/C3
Montmagny, Que., Can., 11,654 ....226/C6
Montmartre, Sask., Can., 465 ....227/G10
Montmorenci, S.C., U.S., 300 ....340/C3
Montmorency, Mich., U.S., county, 10,315 ..294/E4
Montour, Ida., U.S. 264/A6
Montour, Iowa, U.S., 285 ....274/J4
Montour, Penn., U.S., county, 18,236 .....336/H3
Montour Falls, N.Y., U.S., 1,797 ....320/H6
Montoursville, Penn., U.S., 4,777 ....336/H3
Montoya, N. Mex., U.S. 317/F2
Montpelier, Calif., U.S., 50 ....246/L6
Montpelier, Ida., U.S., 2,785 ....264/F7
Montpelier, Ind., U.S., 1,929 ....270/F3
Montpelier, La., U.S., 214 ....282/H5
Montpelier, (S. Laurel), Md., U.S., 11,800 ..288/C6
Montpelier, Miss., U.S. 300/C2
Montpelier, N. Dak., U.S., 103 ....326/G3
Montpelier, Ohio, U.S., 4,320 ....328/A2
Montpelier, Va., U.S., 225 ....354/H5
Montpelier, Vt., U.S., state capital, 8,035 ..352/B2
Montpellier, Fr., 229,025, (287,981 metro.) ..88/C5
Montréal, Que., Can., 1,039,534, (3,548,800 metro.) ..225/B4
Montréal, Que., Can., 1,039,534, (3,548,800 metro.) ..226/C6, J5
Montréal, Que., Can., island, 1,039,534 ..226/J5
Montreal, Sask., Can., lake 227/E6
Montreal, Wisc., U.S., 838 ....364/C2
Montreal-Nord, Que., Can., 83,600 ....226/J5
Montreat, N.C., U.S., 630 ....322/A3
Montreuil, Fr. ....88/Inset II
Montreux, Switz. 90/A2
Montrose, Scot., U.K. 60/C2
Montrose, Scot., U.K., 10,845 ....62/M5
Montrose, Ark., U.S., 526 ....244/D4
Montrose, Colo., U.S., 12,344 ....250/C3
Montrose, Colo., U.S., county, 33,432 ....250/B3
Montrose, Ga., U.S., 154 ....260/E6
Montrose, Ill., U.S., 257 ....266/E4
Montrose, Iowa, U.S., 957 ....274/M6
Montrose, Kans., U.S. 276/D2
Montrose, Md., U.S., 4,800 ....288/A6, F3
Montrose, Mich., U.S., 1,619 ....294/F6
Montrose, Minn., U.S., 1,143 ....298/D5
Montrose, Miss., U.S., 127 ....300/C3
Montrose, Mo., U.S., 417 ....302/B3
Montrose, (Montrose-Ghent), Ohio, U.S., 5,261 ..328/G3
Montrose, Penn., U.S., 1,664 ....336/K2
Montrose, S. Dak., U.S., 460 ....342/H4
Montrose, Va., U.S., 7,018 ....354/J5
Montrose, W. Va., U.S., 156 ....360/G2
Montross, Va., U.S., 315 ....354/K4
Mont-Royal, Que., Can., 18,682 ....226/J5
Mont-St-Michel, Fr. 88/B2
Mont-St-Pierre, Que., Can., 239 ....226/L2
Montserrat, U.K., dependency 204/D3
Montsweag, Maine, U.S. 286/C5
Mont-Tremblant Prov. Park, Que., Can. 226/B5
Mont-Tremblant-Village, Que., Can. 226/B5
Montvale, N.J., U.S., 7,034 ....314/B1, E1
Montvale, Va., U.S., 375 ....354/D6
Montverde, Fla., U.S., 882 ....256/C4
Mont Vernon, N.H., U.S., 2,034 ....312/C6
Montville, Conn., U.S., 18,546 ....253/G4
Montville, Mass., U.S., 60 ....292/B4
Montville, N.J., U.S., 20,839 ....314/E2
Montville, Ohio, U.S., 225 ....328/H2
Monument, Ariz., U.S., valley 242/E1
Monument, Colo., U.S., 1,971 ....250/F2
Monument, Kans., U.S., 80 ....276/C5
Monument, N. Mex., U.S., 125 ....317/G5
Monument, Oreg., U.S., 151 ....334/G3
Monument, Utah, U.S., valley 350/D6
Monument Beach, Mass., U.S., 2,438 ....292/M6
Monument Park, Colo., U.S. 250/E4
Monyash, Eng., U.K. 68/D3
Monywa, Mya., 106,843 ....125/B2
Monza, It. 95/B1
Moodus, Conn., U.S., 1,263 ....253/F4
Moody, Ala., U.S., 8,053 ....238/C3
Moody, Mo., U.S., 1,000 ....286/B5
Moody, Mo., U.S., 125 ....302/E5
Moody, S. Dak., U.S., county, 6,595 ......342/J3
Moody, Tex., U.S., 1,400 ....346/L4
Moody Corner, Mass., U.S. 292/D3
Moodys, Okla., U.S., 125 ....330/H1
Mooers, N.Y., U.S., 440 ....320/P1
Mooleyville, Ky., U.S., 40 ....280/D2
Moon, Ky., U.S., 150 ....280/D3
Moonachie, N.J., U.S., 2,754 ....314/B2
Moonstone, Calif., U.S., 1,044 ....246/A1
Moorabbin, Vic., Austl. ....170/Inset IV
Moorcroft, Wyo., U.S., 807 ....366/D1
Moore, Ida., U.S., 196 ....264/D6
Moore, Mont., U.S., 186 ....306/G3
Moore, N.C., U.S., county, 74,769 ....322/F4
Moore, Okla., U.S., 41,138 ....330/G2
Moore, S.C., U.S., 350 ....340/C2, F2
Moore, Tenn., U.S., county, 5,740 ....344/J4
Moore, Tex., U.S., 644 ....346/J6
Moore, Tex., U.S., county, 20,121 ....346/F8
Moore, Utah, U.S. 350/C5
Moorefield, Ark., U.S., 160 ....244/D2
Moorefield, Ind., U.S., 125 ....270/F7
Moorefield, Nebr., U.S., 52 ....308/D3
Moorefield, W. Va., U.S., 2,375 ....360/J2
Moore Haven, Fla., U.S., 1,635 ....256/C5
Mooreland, Ind., U.S., 1,226 ....270/E5
Moore Park, Man., Can. 215/B4
Mooreland, Okla., U.S., 1,190 ....330/C1
Mooresboro, N.C., U.S., 314 ....322/B4
Moores Bridge, Ala., U.S. 238/B2
Moores Creek Natl. Bfld., N.C., U.S. 322/J6
Moores Hill, Ind., U.S., 635 ....270/F6
Moores Mill, Ala., U.S., 5,178 ....238/C1
Moores Mill, N.B., Can. 217/B3
Moorestown, Mich., U.S., 90 ....294/D5
Moorestown, N.J., U.S., 19,017 ....314/D4
Mooresville, Ala., U.S., 59 ....238/C1
Mooresville, Ind., U.S., 9,273 ....270/D5
Mooresville, Mo., U.S., 89 ....302/C2
Mooresville, N.C., U.S., 18,823 ....322/D3
Mooreton, N. Dak., U.S., 204 ....326/J3
Moorewood, Okla., U.S. 330/C2
Moorfields, N.C., U.S. 286/B5
Morfoot, Eng., U.K., hills 66/B1
Moorhead, Iowa, U.S., 232 ....274/C4
Moorhead, Minn., U.S., 32,177 ....298/A4
Moorhead, Miss., U.S., 2,573 ....300/B2
Moorhead, Mont., U.S. 306/L4
Mooringsport, La., U.S., 833 ....282/B1
Moorland, Iowa, U.S., 197 ....274/F3
Moorman, Ky., U.S., 225 ....280/C3
Moorpark, Calif., U.S., 31,415 ....246/G8
Moose, Ont., Can., river 222/D2
Moose, Wyo., U.S., 80 ....366/A2
Moose Factory, Ont., Can., 1,950 ....222/D2
Moosehead, Maine, U.S. 286/C3

Mt. Oliver 597

Moosehead, Maine, U.S., *lake* 286/C3
Moosehorn, Man., Can. 215/B3
Moosehorn N.W.R., Maine, U.S. 286/E3, E4
Moose Jaw, Sask., Can., 32,131 227/E10
Moose Jct., Wisc., U.S. 364/A2
Moose Lake, Man., Can., 740 215/A2
Moose Lake, Minn., U.S., 2,239 298/E4
Mooselookmeguntic, Maine, U.S., *lake* 286/B4
Moose Mtn. Prov. Park, Sask., Can. 227/H11
Moose River, Maine, U.S., 219 286/B3
Moosic, Penn., U.S., 5,575 336/H7, K3
Moosomin, Sask., Can., 2,361 227/J10
Moosonee, Ont., Can., 936 222/D2
Moosup, Conn., U.S., 3,237 253/H3
Moosup Valley, R.I., U.S., 150 339/B3
Mopti, Mali, 82,202 150/C3
Moqua, Nauru, *well* 174/B2
Moquah, Wisc., U.S., 40 364/B2
Moquegua, Peru 185/C4
Moquegua, Peru, *department* 185/C4
Mora, Minn., U.S., 3,193 298/D5
Mora, N. Mex., U.S., 450 317/E2
Mora, N. Mex., U.S., *county*, 5,180 317/F1
Morada, Calif., U.S., 3,726 246/L1
Moradabad, India, 416,836, (432,434 *metro.*) 128/C3
Moraga, Calif., U.S., 16,290 246/J2
Moraine, Ohio, U.S., 6,897 328/B6, F2
Morales, Tex., U.S. 346/M6
Moran, Kans., U.S., 562 276/G4
Moran, Mich., U.S., 175 294/E4
Moran, Tex., U.S., 233 346/J3
Moran, Wyo., U.S. 366/A2
Morant Bay, Jam. 206/C3
Morar, Scot., U.K., *lake* 62/E5
Morar Moidart and Ardnamurchan N.P., Scot., U.K. 62/D5
Moratuwa, Sri Lan., 177,190 126/A5
Morava, Czh. Rep., *river* 92/C3
Morava, Serb.-Mont., *river* 99/B3
Morava, Slvk., *river* 92/A2
Moravia, Czh. Rep., *region* 92/C3
Moravia, Iowa, U.S., 713 274/J6
Moravia, N.Y., U.S., 1,363 320/J5
Moravian Falls, N.C., U.S., 1,440 322/C2
Moravskoslezský, Czh. Rep., *region* 92/C3
Moray, Scot., U.K., *estuary* 60/B1
Moray, Scot., U.K., *unitary authority*, 86,940 62/K4
Morbihan, Fr., *department* 88/B3
Morcott, Eng., U.K. 70/C1
Morden, Man., Can., 6,142 215/B4
Morden, Eng., U.K. 73/H3
Mordialloc, Vic., Austl. 170/Inset V
Mordiford, Eng., U.K. 68/B5
Mordon, Eng., U.K. 66/E3
Mordovia, Russ., *region* 104/D4
More, Scot., U.K., *lake* 62/J2
Moreau, S. Dak., U.S., *river* 342/C2
Moreauville, La., U.S., 922 282/F4
Morebath, Eng., U.K. 73/F2
Morebattle, Scot., U.K. 62/M8
Morecambe, Eng., U.K., 46,657 66/C4
Morecambe, Eng., U.K., 46,657 68/B1
Morecambe, Eng., U.K., *bay* 66/B5
Morecambe, Eng., U.K., *bay* 68/A2
Moree, N.S.W., Austl. 170/D2
Morehead, P.N.G. 172/A2
Morehead, Kans., U.S. 276/G4
Morehead, Ky., U.S., 5,914 280/G2
Morehead City, N.C., U.S., 7,691 322/M5
Morehouse, La., U.S., *parish*, 31,021 282/F1
Morehouse, Mo., U.S., 1,015 302/G5
Moreland, Ark., U.S., 225 244/C2
Moreland, Ga., U.S., 393 260/B5
Moreland, Ky., U.S., 550 280/F3
Moreland Hills, Ohio, U.S., 3,298 328/H9
Moreleigh, Eng., U.K. 73/E4
Morelia, Mex., *state capital*, 549,996, (620,532 *metro.*) 200/D4
Morell, P.E.I., Can., 332 224/C2
Morelos, Mex., *state* 200/E4
Morena, Sp., *mountains* 94/D3
Morenci, Ariz., U.S., 1,879 242/F4
Morenci, Mich., U.S., 2,398 294/E8
Morenish, Scot., U.K. 62/H6
Moreno Valley, Calif., U.S., 142,381 246/H9
Møre og Romsdal, Nor., *province* 80/B3
Moresby, Br. Col., Can., *island* 214/F5
Moresby, Eng., U.K. 66/A3
Moreton, Austl., *bay* 170/Inset III
Moreton, Eng., U.K. 70/E3
Moreton-in-Marsh, Eng., U.K., 1,895 68/D6
Moretown, Vt., U.S., 1,653 352/B2
Morfa Nefyn, Wales, U.K. 64/B2
Morgan, Ala., U.S., *county*, 111,064 238/C1
Morgan, Calif., U.S., *mountain* 246/G5
Morgan, Colo., U.S., *county*, 27,171 250/A2, G1
Morgan, Ga., U.S., 1,464 260/B8
Morgan, Ga., U.S., *county*, 15,457 260/D4
Morgan, Ill., U.S., *county*, 36,616 266/C4
Morgan, Ind., U.S., *county*, 66,689 270/C5
Morgan, Ky., U.S., 70 280/F2
Morgan, Ky., U.S., *county*, 13,948 280/G3
Morgan, Minn., U.S., 903 298/C6
Morgan, Mo., U.S., 90 302/D4
Morgan, Mo., U.S., *county*, 19,309 302/C3
Morgan, Mont., U.S. 306/J1
Morgan, Ohio, U.S., *county*, 14,897 328/G6
Morgan, Tenn., U.S., *county*, 19,757 344/M2
Morgan, Tex., U.S., 485 346/L4
Morgan, Utah, U.S., 2,635 350/C2, E1
Morgan, Utah, U.S., *county*, 7,129 350/C2, E1
Morgan, Vt., U.S., 669 352/C1
Morgan, W. Va., U.S., *county*, 14,943 360/K1
Morgan Brake N.W.R., Miss., U.S. 300/B2
Morgan Ctr., Vt., U.S., 60 352/D1
Morgan City, Ala., U.S., 550 238/C1
Morgan City, La., U.S., 12,703 282/G7
Morgan City, Miss., U.S., 305 300/B2
Morganfield, Ky., U.S., 3,494 280/C3
Morgan Hill, Calif., U.S., 33,556 246/D5, L3
Morgan's Pt., Tex., U.S., 336 346/C6
Morgan's Pt. Resort, Tex., U.S., 2,989 346/L4
Morganton, Ark., U.S., 80 244/C2
Morganton, Ga., U.S., 299 260/C2
Morganton, N.C., U.S., 17,310 322/B3
Morgantown, Ind., U.S., 964 270/D6
Morgantown, Ky., U.S., 2,544 280/D3
Morgantown, Md., U.S., 275 288/G6
Morgantown, Miss., U.S., 225 300/C4
Morgantown, Ohio, U.S., 60 328/D7
Morgantown, W. Va., U.S., 26,809 360/G1
Morganville, Kans., U.S., 198 276/E2
Morganville, N.J., U.S., 11,255 314/E3
Morganza, La., U.S., 659 282/F5
Morganza, Md., U.S., 500 288/H6
Morges, Switz. 90/A2
Morghab, Afg., *river* 129/A1
Morghob, Taj. 132/B1
Morghob, Taj., *river* 132/B1
Moriah, Nev., U.S., *mountain* 310/C2
Moriarty, N. Mex., U.S., 1,765 317/D3
Morice, Br. Col., Can., *lake* 214/J4
Moricetown, Br. Col., Can. 214/J3
Morie, Scot., U.K., *lake* 62/H3
Morija, Leso. 161/A2
Morinville, Alta., Can., 6,540 212/D4
Morioka, Jap., 289,000 114/D2
Morlaix, Fr. 88/B2
Morland, Kans., U.S., 164 276/B2
Morley, Alta., Can. 212/C5
Morley, Eng., U.K., 47,579 66/E5
Morley, Eng., U.K., 47,579 68/D2
Morley, Iowa, U.S., 88 274/M3
Morley, Mich., U.S., 495 294/D6
Morley, Mo., U.S., 792 302/G4
Mormon, Ariz., U.S., *lake* 242/D3
Mormon Lake, Ariz., U.S., 50 242/D3
Morne Diablotin, Dom., *mountain* 208/B2
Morningdale, Mass., U.S., 2,500 292/G3
Morningside, Qnsld., Austl. 170/Inset III
Morningside, Md., U.S., 1,295 288/C7
Morningside, S. Dak., U.S., 125 342/G3
Morning Sun, Iowa, U.S., 872 274/M5
Moro, Liber., *river* 149/A2
Moro, Phil., *gulf* 120/B5
Moro, Ark., U.S., 241 244/E3
Moro, Maine, U.S., 63 286/D2
Moro, Oreg., U.S., 337 334/F2
Moro Bay, Ark., U.S. 244/C4
Morobe, P.N.G. 172/A2
Morocco, *nation* 141
Morocco, Ind., U.S., 1,127 270/B3
Morogoro, Tan., 117,760 158/C2
Morogoro, Tan., *region* 158/C2
Morombe, Madag. 163/A3
Mörön, Mong. 118/C2
Morón, Cuba 204/D2
Morona-Santiago, Ecua., *province* 185/C4
Morondava, Madag. 163/A3
Morón de la Frontera, Sp. 94/D4
Morongo Valley, Calif., U.S., 1,929 246/J8
Moroni, Com., *capital*, 29,916 163/A1
Moroni, Utah, U.S., 1,280 350/C4
Morotai, Indon., *island* 122/D1
Moroto, Ug. 157/D2
Morovis, P.R. 206/C2
Morpeth, Ont., Can. 223/D5
Morpeth, Eng., U.K., 14,393 66/E2
Morphou, Cyp., *bay* 133/A1
Morral, Ohio, U.S., 388 328/D4
Morrice, Mich., U.S., 882 294/E7
Morrill, Kans., U.S., 277 276/G2
Morrill, Ky., U.S. 280/F3
Morrill, Maine, U.S., 774 286/C4
Morrill, Minn., U.S., 175 298/D5
Morrill, Nebr., U.S., 957 308/A2
Morrill, Nebr., U.S., *county*, 5,440 308/B2
Morrilton, Ark., U.S., 6,550 244/C2
Morrin, Alta., Can., 252 212/D5
Morris, Man., Can., 1,673 215/C4
Morris, Ala., U.S., 1,827 238/C2
Morris, Ga., U.S. 260/B8
Morris, Ill., U.S., 11,928 266/E2
Morris, Kans., U.S., *county*, 6,104 276/F3
Morris, Minn., U.S., 5,068 298/B5
Morris, N.J., U.S., *county*, 470,212 314/D2
Morris, N.Y., U.S., 591 320/L5
Morris, Okla., U.S., 1,294 330/G2
Morris, Penn., U.S., 100 336/G2
Morris, Tex., U.S., *county*, 13,048 346/P2
Morrisburg, Ont., Can., 2,583 223/K3
Morrisey, Wyo., U.S. 366/D2
Morris Jessup, Grld., *cape* 193/A17
Morris Jesup, Grld., *cape* 193/D1
Morrison, Colo., U.S., 430 250/A3
Morrison, Ill., U.S., 4,447 266/D2
Morrison, Iowa, U.S., 97 274/J3
Morrison, Minn., U.S., *county*, 31,712 298/C4
Morrison, Mo., U.S., 123 302/E3
Morrison, Okla., U.S., 636 330/E1
Morrison, Tenn., U.S., 684 344/K3
Morrison Bluff, Ark., U.S., 74 244/B2
Morrisonville, Ill., U.S., 1,068 266/D4
Morrisonville, N.Y., U.S., 1,702 320/P1
Morris Plains, N.J., U.S., 5,236 314/E2
Morriston, Ark., U.S., 40 244/D1
Morriston, Fla., U.S., 125 256/F2
Morristown, Ariz., U.S., 80 242/C4
Morristown, Ind., U.S., 1,133 270/E5
Morristown, Minn., U.S., 981 298/D6
Morristown, N.J., U.S., 18,544 314/E2
Morristown, N.Y., U.S., 456 320/K1
Morristown, Ohio, U.S., 299 328/H5
Morristown, S. Dak., U.S., 82 342/D2
Morristown, Tenn., U.S., 24,965 344/Q2
Morristown, Vt., U.S., 5,139 352/B1
Morristown N.H.P., N.J., U.S. 314/D2
Morrisville, Mo., U.S., 344 302/C4
Morrisville, N.Y., U.S., 2,148 320/K5
Morrisville, N.C., U.S., 5,208 322/H3
Morrisville, (Bucks County), Penn., U.S., 10,023 336/M5
Morrisville, (Greene County), Penn., U.S., 1,443 336/A6
Morrisville, Vt., U.S., 2,009 352/B1
Morrisville, Va., U.S., 550 354/H3
Morro Bay, Calif., U.S., 10,350 246/E7
Morrow, Ga., U.S., 4,882 260/C4, J3
Morrow, La., U.S., 200 282/E5
Morrow, Ohio, U.S., 1,286 328/B7
Morrow, Ohio, U.S., *county*, 31,628 328/E4
Morrow, Oreg., U.S., *county*, 10,995 334/G2
Morrowville, Kans., U.S., 168 276/E2
Mors, Den., *island* 79/B2
Morse, Sask., Can., 248 227/C10
Morse, Iowa, U.S., 125 274/M4
Morse, La., U.S., 759 282/E6
Morse, Tex., U.S., 172 346/F8
Morse, Wisc., U.S. 364/C2
Morse Bluff, Nebr., U.S., 134 308/H2
Morston, Eng., U.K. 70/F1
Mortehoe, Eng., U.K. 73/D2
Mortimer's Cross, Eng., U.K. 68/B5
Mortlach, Sask., Can., 241 227/D10
Mortlock, Micr., *islands* 172/C2
Morton, Eng., U.K. 68/E3
Morton, Eng., U.K. 68/G4
Morton, Eng., U.K. 70/D1
Morton, Ill., U.S., 15,198 266/D3
Morton, Kans., U.S., *county*, 3,496 276/A4
Morton, Minn., U.S., 442 298/C6
Morton, Miss., U.S., 3,482 300/C3
Morton, N. Dak., U.S., *county*, 25,303 326/D3
Morton, Tex., U.S., 2,249 346/F2
Morton, Wash., U.S., 1,045 358/C3
Morton, Wyo., U.S. 366/B2
Morton Grove, Ill., U.S., 22,451 266/B5
Morton Mills, Iowa, U.S., 40 274/E5
Mortons Gap, Ky., U.S., 952 280/C3
Mortonsville, Ky., U.S., 150 280/F3
Moruga, Trin.-To. 209/A2
Morven, Scot., U.K., *hill* 62/J2
Morven, Ga., U.S., 634 260/D1
Morven, N.C., U.S., 579 322/E5
Morven, Va., U.S., 125 354/G6
Morville, Eng., U.K. 68/C4
Mosby, Mo., U.S., 242 302/J4
Mosby, Mont., U.S. 306/J3
Mosca, Colo., U.S., 150 250/E4
Moscow, Russ., *capital*, 8,297,056, (8,537,700 *metro.*) 104/C4
Moscow, Russ., *capital*, 8,297,056, (8,537,700 *metro.*) 193/D2
Moscow, Ark., U.S., 50 244/D3
Moscow, Ida., U.S., 21,291 264/A3
Moscow, Kans., U.S., 247 276/A4
Moscow, Ky., U.S., 60 280/A4
Moscow, Maine, U.S., 577 286/C3
Moscow, Mich., U.S., 250 294/E7
Moscow, Ohio, U.S., 244 328/B8
Moscow, Penn., U.S., 1,883 336/J7, K3
Moscow, Tenn., U.S., 422 344/C4
Moscow, Vt., U.S., 250 352/B2
Moscow Mills, Mo., U.S., 1,742 302/F3
Mosedale, Eng., U.K. 66/C3
Mosel, Ger., *river* 85/B2
Mosel, Ger., *river* 86/A4
Moseley, Va., U.S., 275 354/H6
Moselle, Fr., *department* 88/D2
Moselle, Fr., *river* 88/D2
Moselle, Miss., U.S., 325 300/C4
Moses Lake, Wash., U.S., 14,953 358/F2
Moses Lake North, Wash., U.S., 4,232 358/F2
Moshannon, Penn., U.S., 450 336/E3
Moshannon St. For., Penn., U.S. 336/D3, E4
Mosheim, Tenn., U.S., 1,749 344/R2
Mosher, S. Dak., U.S. 342/E4
Moshi, Tan. 158/C1
Mosier, Oreg., U.S., 410 334/E2
Mosinee, Wisc., U.S., 4,063 364/D4
Mosjøen, Nor. 80/C2
Moskee, Wyo., U.S. 366/D1
Mosman Park, W.A., Austl. 170/Inset I
Mosquero, N. Mex., U.S., 120 317/G2
Mosquito, Hond., *coast* 202/D2
Mosquitos, Nicar., *coast* 202/C3
Mosquitos, Pan., *gulf* 203/B2
Moss, Nor. 80/C4
Moss, Tenn., U.S., 100 344/K1
Mossat, Scot., U.K. 62/L4
Mossbank, Sask., Can., 379 227/E11
Mossbank, Scot., U.K. 62/Q2
Moss Beach, Calif., U.S., 1,953 246/H2
Moss Bluff, La., U.S., 10,535 282/C6
Mossel Bay, S. Afr. 162/B3
Mossendjo, Congo, 16,405 155/B5
Mosses, Ala., U.S., 1,101 238/C3
Moss Landing, Calif., U.S., 300 246/D6
Mossleigh, Alta., Can. 212/D6
Mossley, Eng., U.K., 10,569 66/D5
Mossley, Eng., U.K., 10,569 68/C2
Mossley, N. Ire., U.K., 1,420 65/F2
Mossoró, Braz., 118,007, (191,959 *metro.*) 188/E2
Moss Pt., Miss., U.S., 15,851 300/D5
Mossville, Ill., U.S., 1,000 266/D3
Mossy, Sask., Can., *river* 227/F6
Mossy Head, Fla., U.S., 150 256/B1
Mossyrock, Wash., U.S., 486 358/C3
Most, Czh. Rep., 71,000 92/A2
Mostaganem, Alg., 115,212 146/B1
Mostar, Bos.-Her., 127,034 98/B2
Móstoles, Sp., 196,524 94/Inset II
Mostyn, Wales, U.K., 1,601 64/E1
Mosul, Iraq, 664,221, (879,000 *metro.*) 130/B1
Motagua, Guat., *river* 201/D4
Motcombe, Eng., U.K. 73/H2
Motherwell, Scot., U.K. 60/B2
Motherwell, Scot., U.K., 30,311 62/J7
Motherwell Homestead N.H.S., Sask., Can. 227/G10
Motley, Minn., U.S., 585 298/C4
Motley, Tex., U.S., *county*, 1,426 346/H1
Mott, N. Dak., U.S., 808 326/C3
Mottville, Mich., U.S., 400 294/D8
Mouila, Gabon 155/A2
Mould Bay, N.W. Terr., Can. 220/E1
Moule à Chique, St. Luc., *cape* 208/B3
Moulmein, (Mawlamyine), Mya., 219,961 125/C3
Moulouya, Mor., *river* 147/D1
Moulton, (Cheshire), Eng., U.K., 5,060 68/B3
Moulton, (Lincolnshire), Eng., U.K. 68/G4
Moulton, Eng., U.K., 5,060 70/D1
Moulton, Ala., U.S., 3,260 238/B1
Moulton, Iowa, U.S., 658 274/J6
Moultonborough, N.H., U.S., 4,484 312/D4
Moultonville, N.H., U.S. 312/D4
Moultrie, Ga., U.S., 14,387 260/D9
Moultrie, Ill., U.S., *county*, 14,287 266/E4
Moultrie, S.C., U.S., *lake* 340/D3
Mound, La., U.S. 282/G2
Mound, Minn., U.S., 9,435 298/D6
Mound Bayou, Miss., U.S., 2,102 300/B2
Mound City, Ill., U.S., 692 266/D6
Mound City, Mo., U.S., 1,193 302/A1
Mound City, S. Dak., U.S., 84 342/E2
Moundou, Chad, 103,295, (282,103 *metro.*) 153/B5
Moundridge, Kans., U.S., 1,593 276/E3
Mounds, Ill., U.S., 1,117 266/D6
Mounds, Okla., U.S., 1,153 330/F2
Mounds, Utah, U.S. 350/D4
Mound Sta., (Timewell), Ill., U.S., 127 266/C3
Mounds View, Minn., U.S., 12,738 298/F5
Moundsville, W. Va., U.S., 9,998 360/K5
Mound Valley, Kans., U.S., 418 276/G4
Moundville, Ala., U.S., 1,809 238/B3
Moundville, Mo., U.S., 103 302/B4
Mt. Aetna, Md., U.S., 838 288/D1
Mountain, N. Dak., U.S., 133 326/H1
Mountain, Wisc., U.S., 200 364/E3
Mountainair, N. Mex., U.S., 1,116 317/D3
Mountainaire, Ariz., U.S., 1,014 242/D2
Mtn. Ash, (Mtn. Ash/Abercynon), Wales, U.K., 21,301 64/E4
Mountainboro, Ala., U.S., 338 238/C1
Mtn. Brook, Ala., U.S., 20,604 238/C2, E1
Mountainburg, Ark., U.S., 682 244/A2
Mtn. City, Ga., U.S., 829 260/E2
Mtn. City, Nev., U.S. 310/C1
Mtn. City, Tenn., U.S., 2,383 344/T2
Mtn. City, Tex., U.S., 671 346/D3
Mtn. Creek, Ala., U.S., 300 238/C3
Mountaindale, Md., U.S., 325 288/E1
Mtn. Grove, Mo., U.S., 4,574 302/D4
Mtn. Home, Ark., U.S., 11,012 244/C1
Mtn. Home, Ida., U.S., 11,143 264/B6
Mtn. Home, N.C., U.S., 2,169 322/E8
Mountainhome, Penn., U.S., 1,169 336/L3
Mtn. Home, Tex., U.S. 346/J5
Mtn. Home, Utah, U.S., 100 350/D3
Mtn. Home, Wyo., U.S. 366/C3
Mtn. Iron, Minn., U.S., 2,999 298/E3
Mtn. Lake, Minn., U.S., 2,082 298/C7
Mtn. Lake Park, Md., U.S., 2,248 288/A4
Mtn. Lakes, N.J., U.S., 4,256 314/E2
Mtn. Mesa, Calif., U.S., 716 246/G7
Mtn. Nile, Sudan, *river* 145/C3
Mtn. Nile, Ug., *river* 157/B2
Mtn. Park, Alta., Can. 212/B5
Mtn. Park, (Fulton County), Ga., U.S., 506 260/C3, H1
Mtn. Park, (Gwinnett County), Ga., U.S., 11,753 260/J2
Mtn. Park, Okla., U.S., 390 330/D3
Mtn. Pine, Ark., U.S., 772 244/B3
Mountainside, N.J., U.S., 6,602 314/A3
Mtn. Valley, Ark., U.S., 50 244/B3
Mtn. Valley, Ky., U.S., 40 280/G3
Mtn. View, Ark., U.S., 2,876 244/C2
Mtn. View, Calif., U.S., 70,708 246/K3
Mtn. View, Colo., U.S., 569 250/A3
Mtn. View, (part of Chattanooga Valley), Ga., U.S. 260/A2
Mtn. View, Hawaii, U.S., 2,799 262/J5
Mtn. View, Mo., U.S., 2,430 302/E4
Mtn. View, N.C., U.S., 3,768 322/C3
Mtn. View, Okla., U.S., 880 330/D2
Mtn. View, (Natrona County), Wyo., U.S., 103 366/C2
Mtn. View, (Uinta County), Wyo., U.S., 1,153 366/A3
Mtn. View Acres, Calif., U.S., 2,521 246/H8
Mountain Vil., Alaska, U.S., 755 240/C2
Mountainville, Maine, U.S., 150 286/D4
Mountainville, N.J., U.S., 475 314/D2
Mt. Airy, Ga., U.S., 604 260/E2
Mt. Airy, Md., U.S., 6,425 288/F2
Mt. Airy, N.J., U.S., 250 314/D3
Mt. Airy, N.C., U.S., 8,484 322/D1
Mt. Airy, Va., U.S., 90 354/E7
Mt. Andrew, Ala., U.S., 40 238/D4
Mt. Angel, Oreg., U.S., 3,121 334/D2
Mt. Arlington, N.J., U.S., 4,663 314/D2
Mt. Assiniboine Prov. Park, Br. Col., Can. 214/P6
Mt. Athos, Gr., *autonomous region* 100/C2
Mt. Auburn, Ill., U.S., 515 266/D4
Mt. Auburn, (Shelby County), Ind., U.S., 125 270/E6
Mt. Auburn, (Wayne County), Ind., U.S., 75 270/F5
Mt. Auburn, Iowa, U.S., 160 274/K3
Mt. Ayr, Ind., U.S., 147 270/B3
Mt. Ayr, Iowa, U.S., 1,822 274/F6
Mt. Baker Natl. Rec. Area, Wash., U.S. 358/D1
Mt. Baker-Snoqualmie Natl. For., Wash., U.S. 358/C3, D1
Mt. Barker, S.A., Austl. 170/Inset II
Mountbenger, Scot., U.K. 62/K7
Mt. Berry, Ga., U.S., 225 260/A3
Mt. Bethel, N.J., U.S., 1,000 314/D2
Mt. Blanchard, Ohio, U.S., 484 328/C4
Mt. Blanco, Tex., U.S. 346/G2
Mt. Calm, Tex., U.S., 310 346/M4
Mt. Calvary, Wisc., U.S., 956 364/E5
Mt. Carbon, Penn., U.S., 87 336/J4
Mt. Carleton Prov. Park, N.B., Can. 217/C1
Mt. Carmel, P.E.I., Can. 224/A2
Mt. Carmel, Fla., U.S., 100 256/A1
Mt. Carmel, Ill., U.S., 7,982 266/F5
Mt. Carmel, Ind., U.S., 106 270/G6
Mt. Carmel, Ky., U.S., 125 280/G2
Mt. Carmel, Miss., U.S., 125 300/C4
Mt. Carmel, Ohio, U.S., 4,308 328/C10
Mt. Carmel, Penn., U.S., 6,390 336/J4
Mt. Carmel, S.C., U.S., 237 340/B2
Mt. Carmel, Tenn., U.S., 4,795 344/R1
Mt. Carmel, Utah, U.S., 50 350/B6
Mt. Carmel Jct., Utah, U.S., 40 350/B6
Mt. Carroll, Ill., U.S., 1,832 266/D1
Mt. Clare, Ill., U.S., 433 266/B3
Mt. Clemens, Mich., U.S., 17,312 294/B6, G7
Mt. Cory, Ohio, U.S., 203 328/C4
Mt. Crawford, Va., U.S., 254 354/F4
Mt. Crested Butte, Colo., U.S., 707 250/D3
Mt. Croghan, S.C., U.S., 155 340/D2
Mt. Davis, Penn., U.S., *mountain* 336/C6
Mt. Desert, Maine, U.S., *island* 286/D4
Mt. Dora, Fla., U.S., 9,418 256/C3, G3
Mt. Dora, N. Mex., U.S. 317/G1
Mt. Eaton, Ohio, U.S., 246 328/G4
Mt. Eden, Ky., U.S., 50 280/E2
Mt. Edziza Prov. Park, Br. Col., Can. 214/G2
Mt. Enterprise, Tex., U.S., 525 346/P4
Mt. Ephraim, N.J., U.S., 4,495 314/B3
Mt. Erie, Ill., U.S., 105 266/E5
Mt. Etna, Ind., U.S., 110 270/E3
Mt. Etna, Iowa, U.S., 40 274/E5
Mountfield, N. Ire., U.K. 65/C2
Mt. Forest, Ont., Can., 4,584 223/E4
Mt. Freedom, N.J., U.S., 2,000 314/D2
Mt. Frissell, Conn., U.S., *hill* 253/B1
Mt. Gambier, S.A., Austl. 170/D3
Mt. Gay, W. Va., U.S., 2,623 360/B5
Mt. Gilead, N.C., U.S., 1,389 322/F4
Mt. Gilead, Ohio, U.S., 3,290 328/E4
Mt. Gravatt, Qnsld., Austl. 170/Inset III
Mt. Gretna, Penn., U.S., 242 336/J5
Mt. Hagen, P.N.G. 172/A2
Mt. Hamill, Iowa, U.S., 50 274/L6
Mt. Healthy, Ohio, U.S., 7,149 328/A7, B9
Mt. Hebron, Calif., U.S., 92 246/C1
Mt. Hermon, Ky., U.S., 125 280/E4
Mt. Holly, Ark., U.S., 150 244/C4
Mt. Holly, N.J., U.S., 10,728 314/D4
Mt. Holly, N.C., U.S., 9,618 322/C4
Mt. Holly, Vt., U.S., 1,241 352/B4
Mt. Holly Sprs., Penn., U.S., 1,925 336/G5
Mt. Hood Natl. For., Oreg., U.S. 334/E2
Mt. Hope, Conn., U.S., 275 253/G2
Mt. Hope, Conn., U.S., *river* 253/G2
Mt. Hope, Kans., U.S., 830 276/E4
Mt. Hope, R.I., U.S., *bay* 339/E4
Mt. Hope, W. Va., U.S., 1,487 360/D5
Mt. Hope, Wisc., U.S., 186 364/C6
Mt. Horeb, Wisc., U.S., 5,860 364/D5
Mt. Houston, Tex., U.S., 4,400 346/B6
Mt. Ida, Ark., U.S., 981 244/B3
Mt. Isa, Qnsld., Austl. 170/C2
Mt. Jackson, Va., U.S., 1,664 354/F3
Mt. Jewett, Penn., U.S., 1,070 336/D2
Mountjoy, N. Ire., U.K. 65/C2
Mt. Joy, Penn., U.S., 6,765 336/H5
Mt. Judea, Ark., U.S., 70 244/B2
Mt. Juliet, Tenn., U.S., 12,366 344/H2
Mt. Kisco, N.Y., U.S., 9,983 320/B1
Mt. Laguna, Calif., U.S. 246/J10
Mountlake Terrace, Wash., U.S., 20,362 358/A4
Mt. Laurel, N.J., U.S., 40,221 314/D4
Mt. Laurel, Va., U.S., 125 354/F7
Mt. Lebanon, La., U.S., 73 282/C1
Mt. Lebanon, Penn., U.S., 33,017 336/A5, C7
Mt. Leonard, Mo., U.S., 123 302/C2
Mt. Liberty, Ohio, U.S., 300 328/E5
Mt. Misery, Conn., U.S., *point* 253/C5
Mt. Montgomery, Nev., U.S. 310/A3
Mt. Moriah, Mo., U.S., 143 302/C1
Mt. Morris, Ill., U.S., 3,013 266/D1
Mt. Morris, Mich., U.S., 3,194 294/F6
Mt. Morris, N.Y., U.S., 3,266 320/F5
Mt. Nebo, Qnsld., Austl. 170/Inset III
Mt. Nebo, W. Va., U.S., 300 360/E4
Mt. Olive, Ark., U.S. 244/C2
Mt. Olive, Ill., U.S., 2,150 266/B3, D4
Mt. Olive, Miss., U.S., 893 300/C4
Mt. Olive, N.C., U.S., 4,567 322/J4
Mt. Oliver, Penn., U.S., 3,970 336/D7

Mt. Olivet, Ky., U.S., 289 . . . .280/F2
Mt. Olympus, Utah, U.S., 7,103 . . .350/E2
Mt. Orab, Ohio, U.S., 2,307 . . . .328/C7
Mt. Penn, Penn., U.S., 3,016 . . . .336/K5
Mt. Pleasant, Ark., U.S., 401 . . .244/D2
Mt. Pleasant, Fla., U.S., 150 . . .256/D1
Mt. Pleasant, Iowa, U.S., 8,751 . .274/L6
Mt. Pleasant, Md., U.S., 550 . . .288/F1
Mt. Pleasant, Mich., U.S., 25,946 . .294/E6
Mt. Pleasant, Miss., U.S., 300 . . .300/C1
Mt. Pleasant, N.C., U.S., 1,259 . .322/E4
Mt. Pleasant, Ohio, U.S., 535 . . .328/J5
Mt. Pleasant, Penn., U.S., 4,728 . .336/B5
Mt. Pleasant, S.C., U.S., 47,609 . .340/E4
Mt. Pleasant, Tenn., U.S., 4,491 . .344/G3
Mt. Pleasant, Tex., U.S., 13,935 . .346/P2
Mt. Pleasant, Utah, U.S., 2,707 . .350/C4
Mt. Pleasant, (part of Port Angeles East), Wash., U.S. . . .358/B1
Mt. Plymouth, Fla., U.S., 2,814 . .256/C3
Mt. Pocono, Penn., U.S., 2,742 . .336/L3
Mt. Prospect, Ill., U.S., 56,265 . .266/B5
Mountrail, N. Dak., U.S., county, 6,631 . .326/C1
Mt. Rainier, Md., U.S., 8,498 . . .288/C7
Mt. Rainier Natl. Park, Wash., U.S. . .358/D3
Mt. Repose, Ohio, U.S., 4,102 . . .328/C9
Mt. Revelstoke Natl. Park, Br. Col., Can. . .212/A5
Mt. Revelstoke Natl. Park, Br. Col., Can. . .214/N5
Mt. Robson Prov. Pk., Br. Col., Can. . .212/A5
Mt. Robson Prov. Park, Br. Col., Can. . .214/N5
Mt. Rogers Natl. Rec. Area, Va., U.S. . .354/A7, E3
Mt. Rose, N.J., U.S., 550 . . . .314/D3
Mt. Royal, N.J., U.S., 1,800 . . .314/C4
Mt. Rushmore Natl. Mem., S. Dak., U.S. . .342/B4
Mount's, Eng., U.K., bay 73/B4
Mt. St. Helens Natl. Vol. Mon., Wash., U.S. . .358/C3
Mt. Savage, Md., U.S., 1,200 . . .288/C3
Mt. Shasta, Calif., U.S., 3,621 . .246/C1
Mt. Sidney, Va., U.S., 750 . . . .354/F4
Mt. Sinai, N.Y., U.S., 8,734 . . .320/E1
Mt. Solon, Va., U.S., 200 . . . .354/E4
Mt. Sterling, Ill., U.S., 2,070 . .266/C4
Mt. Sterling, Iowa, U.S., 45 . . .274/L6
Mt. Sterling, Ky., U.S., 5,876 . .280/C2
Mt. Sterling, Ohio, U.S., 1,865 . .328/D6
Mt. Sterling, Wisc., U.S., 215 . .364/C5
Mt. Stewart, P.E.I., Can., 312 . .224/C2
Mt. Storm, W. Va., U.S., 150 . . .360/H2
Mt. Summit, Ind., U.S., 313 . . .270/F4
Mt. Sunapee, N.H., U.S., 150 . . .312/B5
Mt. Sunflower, Kans., U.S. . . .276/A2
Mt. Tabor, Vt., U.S., 203 . . . .352/B4
Mt. Tabor, Wisc., U.S., 80 . . . .364/C5
Mt. Trumbull, Ariz., U.S. 242/B1
Mt. Union, Iowa, U.S., 132 . . .274/M5
Mt. Union, Penn., U.S., 2,504 . .336/F5
Mt. Upton, N.Y., U.S., 175 . . . .320/L6
Mt. Vernon, Ala., U.S., 844 . . .238/A4
Mt. Vernon, Ark., U.S., 144 . . .244/C2
Mt. Vernon, Ga., U.S., 2,082 . . .260/F7
Mt. Vernon, Ill., U.S., 16,269 . .266/E6
Mt. Vernon, Ind., U.S., 7,478 . . .270/A9
Mt. Vernon, Iowa, U.S., 3,390 . .274/M4
Mt. Vernon, Ky., U.S., 2,592 . . .280/F3
Mt. Vernon, Maine, U.S., 1,524 . .286/C4
Mt. Vernon, Md., U.S., 761 . . .288/F1
Mt. Vernon, Mo., U.S., 4,017 . . .302/C4
Mt. Vernon, (Erie County), N.Y., U.S., 4,400 . .320/D5
Mt. Vernon, (Westchester County), N.Y., U.S., 68,381 . . .320/E2
Mt. Vernon, Ohio, U.S., 14,375 . .328/F5
Mt. Vernon, Oreg., U.S., 595 . . .334/G3
Mt. Vernon, S. Dak., U.S., 477 . .342/G4
Mt. Vernon, Tenn., U.S., 225 . . .344/N4
Mt. Vernon, Tex., U.S., 2,286 . .346/N2
Mt. Vernon, Va., U.S., 28,582 . .354/M3
Mt. Vernon, Wash., U.S., 26,232 . .358/C1
Mt. Victory, Ohio, U.S., 600 . . .328/C4
Mt. View, R.I., U.S., 750 . . . .339/D4
Mountville, Ga., U.S. 260/B5
Mountville, Penn., U.S., 2,444 . .336/J5
Mt. Washington, Ky., U.S., 8,485 . .280/E2
Mt. Washington, Mass., U.S., 130 . .292/A4
Mt. Washington St. For., Conn., U.S. . .323/B1
Mt. Westley, Md., U.S., 80 . . .288/N7
Mt. Wolf, Penn., U.S., 1,373 . . .336/H5
Mt. Wynn, St. Vin.-Gren., bay . .208/B2
Mt. Zion, Ga., U.S., 1,275 . . .260/A4
Mt. Zion, Ill., U.S., 4,845 . . .266/E4
Mt. Zion, Iowa, U.S., 40 . . . .274/L6
Mt. Zion, Wisc., U.S., 50 . . . .364/C5
Moura, Port. 93/B3
Mourne, N. Ire., U.K., mountains . .60/A2
Mourne, N. Ire., U.K., mountains . .65/E3
Mourne, N. Ire., U.K., mountains . .78/C1
Mourne, N. Ire., U.K., river . . .65/C2
Mousa, Scot., U.K., island . . .62/G3
Mouscron, Belg. 85/B2
Mouser, Okla., U.S. 330/C4
Mousie, Ky., U.S., 200 . . . .280/H3
Moussa'alli, Dji., mountain . . .156/B1
Mouths of the Danube, Rom., delta . .101/E3
Mouths of the Ganges, Bangl., delta . .127/C7
Mouths of the Ganges, India, delta . .128/E4
Mouths of the Indus, Pak., delta . .129/C5
Mouths of the Irrawaddy, Mya., delta . .125/B2
Moutsamoudou, Com., 16,540 . .163/B2
Moville, Iowa, U.S., 1,583 . . .274/B3
Moweaqua, Ill., U.S., 1,923 . . .266/D4
Mower, Minn., U.S., county, 38,603 . .298/E7
Mowrystown, Ohio, U.S., 373 . .328/C6
Moxahala, Ohio, U.S., 300 . . .328/F6
Moxee, Wash., U.S. 358/E3
Moxee City, Wash., U.S., 821 . .358/E3
Moxico, Ang., province 159/D4
Moy, N. Ire., U.K., 875 . . . .65/D3
Moyale, Kenya 157/E2
Moyamba, S.L. 149/A1
Moyers, Okla., U.S., 90 . . . .330/G3
Moyie, Br. Col., Can. 214/P6
Moyie Sprs., Ida., U.S., 656 . .264/A1
Moyle, N. Ire., U.K., unitary authority, 15,933 . .65/E1
Moyobamba, Peru 185/B2
Moyock, N.C., U.S., 400 . . . .322/N1
Moyowosi, Tan., river 158/B1
Mozambique, nation 155
Mozambique, Com., channel . . .163/B2
Mozambique, Madag., channel . .163/A2
Mozambique, Moz., channel . . .161/C3
Mozelle, Ky., U.S., 125 . . . .280/G4
Mpanda, Tan. 158/B2
Mpika, Zam. 159/C2
Mpoko, C.A.R., river 154/A2
Mporokoso, Zam. 159/C1
Mqinvartsveri, Geo., mountain . .103/C3
Mtkvari, Geo., river 103/C4
Mts'khet'a, Geo. 103/C4
Mtwara, Tan. 158/D3
Mtwara, Tan., region 158/D3

Muş, Tur. 133/E2
Muş, Tur., province 133/E2
Muang Khong, Laos 124/C4
Muang Khôngxédôn, Laos . . .124/C4
Muang Paklay, Laos 124/A2
Muang Vangviang, Laos . . .124/B2
Muang Xai, Laos 124/A1
Muang Xépon, Laos 124/D3
Muang Xon, Laos 124/B1
Muar, Malay. 121/B2
Muara, Bru. 121/C1
Mubende, Ug. 157/B3
Mubi, Nig. 152/G2
Muchinga, Zam., mountains . .159/C2
Much Marcle, Eng., U.K. . . .68/A6
Much Wenlock, Eng., U.K., 1,921 . .68/B4
Muck, Scot., U.K., island . . .62/D5
Muckleramer, N. Ire., U.K. . . .65/C5
Muckle Roe, Scot., U.K., island . .62/P2
Mud, Minn., U.S., lake . . .298/B2
Mud Butte, S. Dak., U.S. . . .342/C3
Muddy, Ill., U.S., 78 . . . .266/E6
Muddy, Mont., U.S., 627 . . .306/K4
Muddy Gap, Wyo., U.S. . . .366/H3
Mud Lake, Ida., U.S., 270 . . .264/E6
Muenster, Tex., U.S., 1,556 . .346/L2
Mufulira, Zam., 204,104 . . .159/B2
Muğla, Tur. 133/B3
Muğla, Tur., province 133/B3
Muhazi, Rwa., lake 158/C1
Muhlenberg, Ky., U.S., county, 31,839 . .280/C3
Mühlhausen, Ger. 86/B3
Mühlviertel, Aus., region . . .91/D2
Mui Bai Bung, Viet., point . .123/A5
Muick, Scot., U.K., lake . . .62/K5
Muir, Scot., U.K. 62/J5
Muir, Alaska, U.S., glacier . .240/F2
Muir, Mich., U.S., 634 . . .294/E6
Muirdrum, Scot., U.K. . . .62/L5
Muirkirk, Scot., U.K., 1,630 . .62/H7
Muir of Ord, Scot., U.K., 1,812 . .62/H3
Mui Wo, H.K., China 117/A2
Mukilteo, Wash., U.S., 18,019 . .358/C2
Muko, Jap., island . . . .114/Inset III
Mukwonago, Wisc., U.S., 6,162 . .364/F2
Mulaku, Mald., atoll 127/A3
Mulberry, Ark., U.S., 1,627 . .244/A2
Mulberry, Fla., U.S., 3,230 . .256/G4
Mulberry, Ind., U.S., 1,387 . .270/C4
Mulberry, Kans., U.S., 577 . .276/H4
Mulberry, N.C., U.S., 2,269 . .322/C2
Mulberry, Ohio, U.S., 3,139 . .328/C9
Mulberry, S.C., U.S., 841 . . .340/D3
Mulberry, Tenn., U.S., 125 . .344/J4
Mulberry Grove, Ill., U.S., 671 . .266/D5
Mulde, Ger., river 86/C2
Muldraugh, Ky., U.S., 1,298 . .280/D3
Muldrow, Okla., U.S., 3,104 . .330/H2
Mule Creek, N. Mex., U.S., 40 . .317/B4
Mule Creek, Wyo., U.S. . . .366/D2
Muleshoe, Tex., U.S., 4,530 . .346/F1
Mulga, Ala., U.S., 973 . . . .238/D1
Mulhall, Okla., U.S., 239 . . .330/E1
Mülheim an der Ruhr, Ger., 173,895 . .86/A3
Mulhouse, Fr., 112,002, (234,445 metro.) . .88/D3
Mull, Scot., U.K., island . . .60/A2
Mull, Scot., U.K., island . . .62/D6
Mullaghcarn, N. Ire., U.K., hill . .65/C3
Mullaittivu, Sri Lan. 126/B2
Mullan, W.A., Austl. . . . .170/Inset I
Mullan, Ida., U.S., 840 . . .264/B2
Mullardoch, Scot., U.K., lake . .62/F4
Mullen, Nebr., U.S., 491 . . .308/C1
Mullens, W. Va., U.S., 1,769 . .360/D5
Mullett Lake, Mich., U.S., 325 . .294/E4
Mullica Hill, N.J., U.S., 1,658 . .314/C4
Mulliken, Mich., U.S., 557 . .294/E7
Mullin, Tex., U.S., 175 . . .346/K4
Mullingar, Ire. 78/C2
Mullins, S.C., U.S., 5,029 . . .340/E2
Mullinville, Kans., U.S., 279 . .276/C4
Mullion, Eng., U.K., 2,040 . . .73/B4
Multan, Pak., 1,197,384 . . .129/D3
Multnomah, Oreg., U.S., county, 660,486 . .334/A2
Multnomah, Oreg., U.S., falls . .334/D2
Mulund, India . . . . .128/Inset I
Mulvane, Kans., U.S., 5,155 . .276/E4
Mulvihill, Man., Can. 215/B4
Mumbai, (Bombay), India, 11,914,398,
(16,368,084 metro.) . .128/B4 Inset I
Mumbai, (Bombay), India, 11,914,398,
(16,368,084 metro.) . .128/B5, Inset I
Mumbra, India . . . . .128/Inset I
Mumbwa, Zam. 159/B3
Mumford, N.Y., U.S., 600 . . .320/F5
Mun, Thai., river 125/C2
Muna, Indon., island 122/D2
Munamägi, Est., mountain . . .81/D3
Muncho Lake, Br. Col., Can. . .214/K2
Muncho Lake Prov. Park, Br. Col., Can. . .214/K1
Muncie, Ill., U.S., 155 . . . .266/F3
Muncie, Ind., U.S., 67,430, (118,769 metro.) . .270/F4
Muncy, Penn., U.S., 2,663 . . .336/H3
Mundare, Alta., Can., 653 . . .212/D4
Munday, Tex., U.S., 1,527 . . .346/J2
Mundelein, Ill., U.S., 30,935 . .266/B5
Munden, Kans., U.S., 122 . . .276/E2
Mundford, Eng., U.K. 70/F1
Munds Park, Ariz., U.S., 1,250 . .242/D3
Munford, Tenn., U.S., 4,708 . .344/B4
Munfordville, Ky., U.S., 1,563 . .280/E3
Munger, Mich., U.S., 350 . . .294/F6
Munhall, Penn., U.S., 12,264 . .336/F2
Munich, (München), Ger., 1,210,200 . .86/B4
Munich, N. Dak., U.S., 268 . . .326/G1
Munising, Mich., U.S., 2,539 . .294/C3
Munjor, Kans., U.S., 325 . . .276/C3
Munnerlyn, Ga., U.S. 260/H6
Munnsville, N.Y., U.S., 437 . . .320/K5
Munroe Falls, Ohio, U.S., 5,314 . .328/H3
Munsan, S. Kor. 116/B4
Munslow, Eng., U.K. 68/B5
Munson, Fla., U.S. 256/B1
Munsons Corners, N.Y., U.S., 2,426 . .320/J5
Munsonville, N.H., U.S., 175 . .312/B5
Munster, Ire., province . . .78/B2
Munster, Ind., U.S., 21,511 . .270/A1
Münster, Ger., 264,670 . . .86/A3
Münster, Ger., department . . .86/A2
Munsungan, Maine, U.S., lake . .286/D2
Munolea, Hawaii, U.S. . . .262/D4
Muonio, Fin. 81/B1
Muonioälven, Swe., river . . .80/D1
Muoniojoki, Fin., river 81/B1
Muoniojoki, Swe., river . . .80/E2
Mur, Aus., river 91/D3
Mura, Slove., river 98/C2
Muramvya, Bur. 158/B2
Murat, Tur., river 133/E2

Murchison, Austl., river 170/A2
Murcia, Sp., 370,745 . . . .94/F4
Murcia, Sp., autonomous community . .94/F4
Murcia, Sp., province 94/F4
Murderkill, Del., U.S., river . .255/B5
Murdo, S. Dak., U.S., 612 . . .342/E4
Murdochville, Que., Can., 1,171 . .226/L3
Murdock, Kans., U.S., 100 . . .276/E4
Murdock, Minn., U.S., 303 . . .298/B5
Murdock, Nebr., U.S., 269 . . .308/H3
Mureş, Rom., county 101/C2
Mureş, Rom., river 101/B2
Murfreesboro, Ark., U.S., 1,764 . .244/B3
Murfreesboro, N.C., U.S., 2,045 . .322/L2
Murfreesboro, Tenn., U.S., 68,816 . .344/J3
Murgab, Turkm., river 132/D3
Muriel, Alta., U.S., lake . . .212/E4
Murilo, Micr., atoll 172/C2
Murmansk, Russ., 378,552 . . .104/C3
Murmansk, Russ. 193/C2
Muroran, Jap. . . . .114/D1, Inset I
Muroto, Jap., cape 114/B3
Murphy, Ga., U.S., 70 . . . .260/D9
Murphy, Ida., U.S., 40 . . .264/A6
Murphy, Mo., U.S., 9,048 . . .302/H4
Murphy, N.C., U.S., 1,568 . . .322/B8
Murphy, Oreg., U.S., 325 . . .334/C5
Murphy, Tex., U.S., 3,099 . . .346/C9
Murphy City, Minn., U.S. . . .298/F3
Murphys, Calif., U.S., 2,061 . .246/E4
Murphysboro, Ill., U.S., 13,295 . .266/D6
Murphytown, W. Va., U.S., 200 . .360/D3
Murray, Austl., river 170/D3
Murray, P.E.I., Can., harbour . .224/C2
Murray, P.N.G., lake 172/A2
Murray, Ga., U.S., county, 36,506 . .260/B2
Murray, Ida., U.S., 60 . . .264/B2
Murray, Iowa, U.S., 766 . . .274/G5
Murray, Ky., U.S., 14,950 . . .280/B4
Murray, Minn., U.S., county, 9,165 . .298/B6
Murray, Nebr., U.S., 481 . . .308/J3
Murray, Okla., U.S., county, 12,623 . .330/E3
Murray, S.C., U.S., lake . . .340/A3, C2
Murray, Tex., U.S. 346/K2
Murray, Utah, U.S., 34,024 . . .350/C3
Murray City, Ohio, U.S., 452 . .328/F6
Murray Harbour, P.E.I., Can., 357 . .224/C3
Murray Hbr. North, P.E.I., Can. . .224/C2
Murray Hill, Ky., U.S., 616 . . .280/B2
Murray River, P.E.I., Can., 435 . .224/C2
Murrayville, Ill., U.S., 644 . . .266/C4
Murrells Inlet, S.C., U.S., 5,519 . .340/E3
Murrieta, Calif., U.S., 44,282 . .246/H9
Murrieta Hot Sprs., Calif., U.S., 2,948 . .246/H9
Murrumbidgee, Austl., river . . .170/D3
Murrysville, Penn., U.S., 18,872 . .336/B5
Murska Sobota, Slove., 19,987 . .98/C2
Mursley, Eng., U.K. 70/C3
Murtaugh, Ida., U.S., 139 . . .264/C7
Mürz, Aus., river 91/D3
Mûša, Lith., river 82/B1
Musala, Bul., mountain . . .101/B3
Musan, N. Kor. 116/C1
Musandam Ra.'s, Oman, cape . .137/C1
Muscat, Oman, capital, 40,856,
(477,211 metro.) . . .137/C1
Muscatatuck N.W.R., Ind., U.S. . .270/E7
Muscatine, Iowa, U.S., 22,697 . .274/M5
Muscatine, Iowa, U.S., county, 41,722 . .274/M5
Muscle Shoals, Ala., U.S., 11,924 . .238/B1
Muscoda, Wisc., U.S., 1,453 . .364/C5
Muscogee, Ga., U.S., county, 186,291 . .260/B6
Muscotah, Kans., U.S., 200 . . .276/G2
Muse, Okla., U.S., 175 . . .330/H3
Musella, Ga., U.S., 125 . . .260/C6
Musgrave, Austl., ranges . . .170/C2
Musgrave Harbour, Nfld., Can., 1,294 . .218/E4
Musgravetown, Nfld., Can., 640 . .218/E5
Mushin, Nig. 152/B4
Muskeget, Mass., U.S., channel . .292/N7
Muskego, Wisc., U.S., 21,397 . .364/E6, F2
Muskegon, Mich., U.S., 40,105 . .294/C6
Muskegon, Mich., U.S., county, 170,200 . .294/C6
Muskegon Hts., Mich., U.S., 12,049 . .294/C6
Muskeg River, Alta., Can. . . .212/A4
Muskingum, Ohio, U.S., county, 84,585 . .328/G6
Muskingum, Ohio, U.S., river . .328/G6
Muskogee, Okla., U.S., 38,310 . .330/G2
Muskogee, Okla., U.S., county, 69,451 . .330/G2
Muskoka, Ont., Can. 223/F2
Muskoka, Ont., Can., county . .223/F2
Muskoka, Ont., Can., lake . . .223/F2
Muskwa, Br. Col., Can., ranges . .214/J2
Muslim Mindanao, Phil., autonomous region . .120/B5
Musoma, Tan. 158/B1
Musquodoboit Harbour, N.S., Can. . .221/D3
Mussau, P.N.G., island 172/A2
Musselshell, Mont., U.S., 60 . .306/H3
Musselshell, Mont., U.S., county, 4,497 . .306/H3
Mustang, Nepal 126/B2
Mustang, Okla., U.S., 13,156 . .330/A4, E2
Mustang Ridge, Tex., U.S., 785 . .346/D3, I5
Mustique, St. Vin.-Gren., island . .208/B3
Mustoe, Va., U.S. 354/D4
Mustvee, Est. 81/D2
Musu dan, N. Kor., point . . .116/C2
Mut, Egy. 144/A2
Mutare, Zimb., 131,367 . . .160/C2
Mutford, Eng., U.K. 70/H2
Muthill, Scot., U.K., 675 . . .62/J6
Mutsu, Jap. 114/D1
Muttontown, N.Y., U.S., 3,412 . .320/C2
Mutual, Ohio, U.S., 132 . . .328/C5
Mutual, Okla., U.S., 76 . . .330/C1
Mutual, Utah, U.S. 350/D5
Muyinga, Bur. 158/C1
Müynoq, Uzb. 132/A2
Muyun Kum, Kaz., desert . . .131/D2
Muzaffarabad, Pak. 129/D2
Muzaffarpur, India 128/E3
Mvurwi, Zimb., range 160/B1
Mwali, (Mohéli), Com., island . .163/A2
Mwanza, Tan., 223,013 . . .158/B1
Mwanza, Tan., region 158/B1
Mwene-Ditu, Congo, D.R. . . .155/B2
Mweneze, Zimb., river 160/B2
Mweru, Congo, D.R., lake . . .155/C3
Mweru, Zam., lake 159/B1
Mwinilunga, Zam. 159/B2
Myakka City, Fla., U.S., 200 . .256/F4
Myakka River St. Park, Fla., U.S. . .256/F4
Myanmar, nation 121
Myddle, Eng., U.K. 68/B4
Myers, Ky., U.S., 50 . . . .280/G2
Myers, Mont., U.S. 306/J3
Myerstown, Penn., U.S., 3,171 . .336/J5
Myersville, Md., U.S., 1,382 . .288/D1
Myingyan, Mya. 125/B2
Myitkyina, Mya. 125/C1
Mykolaiv, Ukr., 510,146 . . .102/C3

Mykolaiv, Ukr., oblast 102/C3
Mylo, N. Dak., U.S. 326/F1
Mymensingh, Bangl., 185,517 . .127/D4
Mynard, Nebr., U.S., 100 . . .308/J3
Mynydd Preseli, Wales, U.K., hill . .64/B4
Myra, Maine, U.S. 286/D4
Myrick, Miss., U.S., 325 . . .300/C4
Myricks, Mass., U.S., 600 . . .292/K5
Myrnam, Alta., Can., 322 . . .212/E4
Myron, Ark., U.S., 40 . . . .244/D1
Myrtle, Ida., U.S., 200 . . .264/A3
Myrtle, Minn., U.S., 63 . . .298/D7
Myrtle, Miss., U.S., 407 . . .300/C1
Myrtle, Mo., U.S., 90 . . . .302/E5
Myrtle, W. Va., U.S. 360/F3
Myrtle Beach, S.C., U.S., 22,759,
(196,629 metro.) . . .340/F3
Myrtle Creek, Oreg., U.S., 3,419 . .334/C4
Myrtle Grove, N.C., U.S., 7,125 . .322/K6
Myrtle Pt., Oreg., U.S., 2,451 . .334/B4
Myrtlewood, Ala., U.S., 139 . .238/B3
Mysore, India, 480,000, (652,246 metro.) . .128/C6
Mystic, Conn., U.S., 4,001 . .253/H4
Mystic, Iowa, U.S., 588 . . .274/J6
Mystic Islands, N.J., U.S., 8,694 . .314/E4
My Tho, Viet., 108,404 . . .123/B4
Mytilini, Gr. 100/C3
Myton, Utah, U.S., 539 . . .350/D3
Mzimba, Mal. 159/B2
Mzuzu, Mal., 86,980 . . . .159/B2
Naalehu, Hawaii, U.S., 919 . .262/H7
Naas, Ire., 18,312 . . . .78/C2
Nabb, Ind., U.S., 200 . . . .270/E6
Naberezhnyye Chelny, Russ., 521,282,
(524,400 metro.) . . .104/D3
Nabeul, Tun. 146/C1
Nabi Shuayb, Jabal an, Yemen, mountain . .137/A1
Naborton, Ky., U.S., 125 . . .282/B2
Nabouwalu, Fiji 174/B2
Naburn, Eng., U.K. 66/F5
Nacala, Moz., 125,208 . . .161/D2
Nacaome, Hond. 202/B3
Naches, Wash., U.S., 643 . . .358/E3
Nacimiento, Calif., U.S., reservoir . .246/D4
Nackawic, N.B., Can., 1,042 . .217/B3
Naco, Ariz., U.S., 833 . . . .242/F5
Nacogdoches, Tex., U.S., 29,914 . .346/P4
Nacogdoches, Tex., U.S., county, 59,203 . .346/P4
Nacton, Eng., U.K. 70/G2
Nada, Tex., U.S., 175 . . . .346/M4
Nadeau, Mich., U.S., 175 . . .294/B4
Nadi, Fiji, 30,791 . . . .174/A2
Nadi, Fiji, bay 174/A2
Nadine, N. Mex., U.S., 175 . . .317/G5
Nadur, Malta 97/B1
Naduri, Fiji 174/B2
Næstved, Den. 79/C3
Nafferton, Eng., U.K., 1,979 . .66/H4
Nafferton, Eng., U.K., 1,979 . .68/G1
Naga, India, hills 128/F3
Nagaland, India, state 128/F3
Nagano, Jap., 360,000 . . . .114/C2
Nagano, Jap., prefecture . . .114/C2
Nagaoka, Jap. 114/C2
Nagarote, Nicar. 202/A2
Nagasaki, Jap., 423,163 . . .114/A3
Nagasaki, Jap., prefecture . .114/A3
Nageezi, N. Mex., U.S., 296 . .317/C1
Nag Hammadi, Egy. 144/C3
Nagoya, Jap., 2,171,378 . . .114/C3
Nagpur, India, 2,051,320, (2,122,965 metro.) . .128/C4
Nags Head, St. K.-Nevis, cape . .207/C2
Nags Head, N.C., U.S., 2,700 . .322/P3
Nagua, Dom. Rep. 205/C1
Naguabo, P.R. 206/D2
Nagykanizsa, Hun. 91/A2
Naha, Jap., 301,000 . . .114/Inset II
Nahanni, N.W. Terr., Can., river . .220/C4
Nahanni Natl. Park, N.W. Terr., Can. . .214/K1
Nahanni Natl. Park, N.W. Terr., Can. . .220/D3
Nahant, Mass., U.S., 3,632 . .292/L3
Nahariyya, Isr. 135/C3
Nahma, Mich., U.S. 294/C4
Nahunta, Ga., U.S., 930 . . .260/H9
Naicam, Sask., Can., 761 . . .227/F8
Naihati, India . . . .128/Inset I
Nail Pond, P.E.I., Can. . . .224/A2
Nailsea, Eng., U.K., 17,919 . .73/G2
Nailsworth, Eng., U.K., 5,242 . .68/C6
Nailsworth, Eng., U.K., 5,242 . .73/H1
Nain, Nfld., Can., 1,159 . . .218/E3
Nairn, Scot., U.K., 8,418 . . .62/J3
Nairn, La., U.S., 350 . . . .282/K8
Nairobi, Kenya, capital, 2,143,254 . .157/D4
Nairobi Area, Kenya, province . .157/D4
Najd, Sa. Arab., region . . .136/B1
Najin, N. Kor. 116/D1
Najran, Sa. Arab. 136/B2
Najran, Sa. Arab., emirate . . .136/B2
Nakadori, Jap., island 114/A3
Nakalele, Hawaii, U.S., point . .262/B3
Nakano, Jap., island 114/A4
Nakdong, S. Kor., river . . .116/B1
Nak'fa, Erit. 156/B1
Nakhodka, Russ., 158,559, (188,150 metro.) . .104/H5
Nakhon Phanom, Thai. . . .125/C2
Nakhon Ratchasima, Thai., (254,900 metro.) . .125/C3
Nakhon Sawan, Thai., (142,500 metro.) . .125/B3
Nakhon Si Thammarat, Thai., (167,400 metro.) . .125/B4
Nakina, Ont., Can. 222/C2
Nakina, N.C., U.S., 90 . . .322/H6
Naknek, Alaska, U.S., 678 . . .240/D3
Nakodu, Fiji 174/B2
Nakskov, Den. 79/C4
Nakuru, Kenya, 162,800 . . .157/D4
Nakusp, Br. Col., Can., 1,698 . .214/O6
Nal, Pak., river 129/B4
Naliikakani, Hawaii, U.S., point . .262/H6
Nalikul, India . . . .128/Inset II
Nallen, W. Va., U.S., 125 . . .360/E4
Namak, Kavir-e, Iran, desert . .130/D3
Namakan, Ont., Can., lake . .298/E2
Namakan, Ont., Can., river . .298/E2
Namangan, Uzb., 376,600 . . .132/D2
Namangan, Uzb., province . .132/D2
Nambe, N. Mex., U.S., 1,200 . .317/E2
Namekagon, Wisc., U.S. . . .364/B2
Namekagon, Wisc., U.S., river . .364/B2
Namew, Sask., Can., lake . . .227/H5
Namib, Nam., desert . . .160/A1, B3
Namib, S. Afr., desert . . .162/A2
Namibe, Ang. 159/B5
Namibe, Ang., province . . .159/B5
Namibia, nation 154
Nam Ngum, Laos, reservoir . .124/B2
Namoluk, Micr., atoll 172/C2
Namonuito, Micr., atoll . . .172/C2
Nampa, Alta., Can., 372 . . .212/B3
Nampa, Ida., U.S., 51,867 . .264/A6

Namp'o, N. Kor. ...116/A3
Namp'o, N. Kor., province ...116/A3
Nampula, Moz., 303,346 ...161/C2
Namsos, Nor. ...80/C3
Nam Tok, Thai. ...125/C3
Namu, Marsh Is., island ...175/B2
Namuli, Moz., highlands ...161/C2
Namur, Belg., 105,393, (285,181 metro.) ...85/C4
Namur, Belg., province ...85/C2
Namur, Alta., Can., lake ...212/D2
Namwala, Zam. ...159/B3
Nan, Thai. ...125/C2
Nan, Thai., river ...125/B2
Nanaimo, Br. Col., Can., 73,000 ...214/L6
Nanakuli, Hawaii, U.S., 10,814 ...262/B5, H2
Nance, Nebr., U.S., county, 4,038 ...308/F2
Nanchang, China, 1,075,710, (2,471,070 metro.) ...119/E3
Nanchong, China ...119/D2
Nan Clar, Scot., U.K., lake ...62/H2
Nancy, Fr., 105,830, (331,363 metro.) ...88/D2
Nancy, Ky., U.S., 200 ...280/F3
Nanda Devi, India, mountain ...128/C2
Nanded, India ...128/C5
Nanga Eboko, Came. ...153/B3
Nanga Parbat, Pak., mountain ...129/E2
Nangi, India ...128/Inset II
Nangnim Sanmaek, N. Kor., mountains ...116/B3
Nanisivik, Nun., Can. ...220/M2
Nanjemoy, Md., U.S., 300 ...288/F6
Nanjing, China, 2,678,363 ...119/E2
Nankin, Ohio, U.S., 550 ...328/E4
Nan Ling, China, mountains ...119/E3
Nanning, China ...119/D3
Nanole, India ...128/Inset I
Nanson, N. Dak., U.S. ...326/F1
Nantahala, U.S., lake ...322/C8
Nantahala Natl. For., N.C., U.S. ...322/C8
Nant-Ddu, Wales, U.K. ...64/E4
Nanterre, Fr. ...88/Inset II
Nantes, Fr., 277,728, (544,932 metro.) ...88/B3
Nanticoke, Ont., Can. ...223/E5
Nanticoke, Del., U.S., river ...255/B6
Nanticoke, Md., U.S., 275 ...288/L6
Nanticoke, Md., U.S., river ...288/L6
Nanticoke, Penn., U.S., 10,955 ...336/J3
Nanticoke Acres, Del., U.S. ...255/B6
Nantlle, Wales, U.K. ...64/C1
Nanton, Alta., Can., 1,841 ...212/D6
Nant'ou, Tai. ...117/B2
Nantucket, Mass., U.S., 9,520 ...292/P7
Nantucket, Mass., U.S., county, 9,520 ...292/P7
Nantucket, Mass., U.S., island ...292/P7
Nantucket, Mass., U.S., sound ...292/N6
Nantucket N.W.R., Mass., U.S. ...292/P7
Nantwich, Eng., U.K., 11,695 ...68/B3
Nantyglo, Wales, U.K. ...64/E4
Nanty Glo, Penn., U.S., 3,054 ...336/D5
Nant-y-moch, Wales, U.K., reservoir ...64/D3
Nanumaga, Tuv., island ...174/B3
Nanumea, Tuv., island ...174/B1
Nanyang, China ...119/E2
Nao, Sp., cape ...94/G3
Napa, Calif., U.S., 72,585 ...246/C4, J1
Napa, Calif., U.S., county, 124,279 ...246/C4, J1
Napadogan, N.B., Can. ...217/C2
Napaktulik, Nun., Can., lake ...220/F3
Na Pali, Hawaii, U.S., coast ...262/B1
Na Pali Kona Forest Reserve, Hawaii, U.S. ...262/C1
Napanee, Ont., Can., 7,760 ...223/J3
Napanoch, N.Y., U.S., 1,168 ...320/N7
Napaskiak, Alaska, U.S., 390 ...240/C2
Napavine, Wash., U.S., 1,361 ...358/C3
Naper, Nebr., U.S., 105 ...308/E1
Naperville, Ill., U.S., 128,358 ...266/A6
Napier, N.Z., 53,661, (113,673 metro.) ...171/C2
Napier Field, Ala., U.S., 404 ...238/D4
Naplate, Ill., U.S., 523 ...266/E2
Naples, It., 993,386 ...95/C2
Naples, It., bay ...95/C2
Naples, Fla., U.S., 20,976, (251,377 metro.) ...256/G5
Naples, Ida., U.S., 175 ...264/A1
Naples, Ill., U.S., 134 ...266/C4
Naples, Maine, U.S., 3,274 ...286/B5
Naples, N.Y., U.S., 1,072 ...320/G5
Naples, S. Dak., U.S. ...342/H3
Naples, Tex., U.S., 1,410 ...346/P2
Naples, Utah, U.S., 1,300 ...350/E4
Naples Manor, Fla., U.S., 5,186 ...256/G5
Naples Park, Fla., U.S., 6,741 ...256/G5
Napo, Ecua., province ...185/C3
Napo, Ecua., river ...185/C3
Napoleon, Ind., U.S., 238 ...270/F6
Napoleon, Mich., U.S., 1,254 ...294/E7
Napoleon, Mo., U.S., 208 ...302/B2
Napoleon, N. Dak., U.S., 857 ...326/F3
Napoleon, Ohio, U.S., 9,318 ...328/B3
Napoleonville, La., U.S., 686 ...282/G7
Naponee, Nebr., U.S., 132 ...308/E3
Nappanee, Ind., U.S., 6,710 ...270/D2
Napton on the Hill, Eng., U.K. ...70/B2
Nara, Jap., 366,196 ...114/B3
Nara, Jap., prefecture ...114/B3
Nara, Pak., canal ...129/C4
Naranja, Fla., U.S., 4,034 ...256/A7, H6
Naranjito, P.R. ...206/C2
Narathiwat, Thai. ...125/C3
Nara Visa, N. Mex., U.S., 70 ...317/Q2
Narayanganj, Bangl., 268,952 ...127/D5
Narayani, Nepal, river ...126/A2
Narberth, Wales, U.K., 1,801 ...64/B4
Narberth, Penn., U.S., 4,233 ...336/L7
Narbonne, Fr. ...88/C5
Narborough, (Leicestershire), Eng., U.K., 6,360 ...70/B1
Narborough, (Norfolk), Eng., U.K. ...70/F1
Narborough, Eng., U.K., 6,360 ...68/E4
Narcisse, Man., Can. ...215/C4
Narcoossee, Fla., U.S., 475 ...256/D4
Nardin, Okla., U.S., 80 ...330/E1
Nares, Nun., Can., strait ...220/O1
Narew, Pol., river ...83/E2
Nariño, Col., department ...184/A4
Narka, Kans., U.S., 93 ...276/E2
Narmada, India, river ...128/C4
Narragansett, R.I., U.S., bay ...339/D4
Narragansett Pier, R.I., U.S., 3,671 ...339/D5
Narrogin, W.A., Austl. ...170/A3
Narrow Hills Prov. Park, Sask., Can. ...227/F6
Narrows, St. K.-Nevis, strait ...207/C2
Narrows, Ky., U.S., 40 ...280/D3
Narrows, Oreg., U.S. ...334/H4
Narrows, Va., U.S., 2,111 ...354/B6
Narrowsburg, N.Y., U.S., 414 ...320/L7
Narsaq, Grld. ...193/C2
Naruna, Va., U.S., 275 ...354/E6
Narva, Est., 68,680 ...81/E1
Narva, Est., river ...81/D1
Narvik, Nor. ...80/D2
Nar'yan-Mar, Russ. ...104/D3
Nar'yan-Mar, Russ. ...193/C3
Naryn, Kyrg. ...131/E2

Naryn, Kyrg., province ...131/D2
Naryn, Kyrg., river ...131/E2
NASA Stennis Space Ctr., Miss., U.S. ...300/C5
Naschitti, N. Mex., U.S., 360 ...317/B1
Naseby, Eng., U.K. ...70/C2
Naselle, Wash., U.S., 377 ...358/B3
Nash, N.C., U.S., county, 87,420 ...322/K2
Nash, N. Dak., U.S., 40 ...326/H1
Nash, Okla., U.S., 224 ...330/D1
Nash, Tex., U.S., 2,169 ...346/P2
Nashaquitsa, Mass., U.S. ...292/L7
Nash Creek, N.B., Can., 279 ...217/C1
Na Shealling, Scot., U.K., lake ...62/F3
Nashik, India, 1,076,967, (1,152,048 metro.) ...128/B4
Nash Lee, Eng., U.K. ...70/C3
Nashoba, Okla., U.S., 50 ...330/G3
Nashotah, Wisc., U.S., 1,266 ...364/E2
Nash Stream St. For., N.H., U.S. ...312/D2
Nashua, Iowa, U.S., 1,618 ...274/F2
Nashua, Minn., U.S., 69 ...298/A4
Nashua, Mont., U.S., 325 ...306/K1
Nashua, N.H., U.S., 86,605 ...312/D6
Nashville, Ark., U.S., 4,878 ...244/B4
Nashville, Ga., U.S., 4,697 ...260/E9
Nashville, Ill., U.S., 3,147 ...266/D5
Nashville, Ind., U.S., 825 ...270/D6
Nashville, Kans., U.S., 111 ...276/D4
Nashville, Maine, U.S., 55 ...286/D2
Nashville, Mich., U.S., 1,684 ...294/D7
Nashville, Mo., U.S., 60 ...302/B4
Nashville, N.C., U.S., 4,309 ...322/K3
Nashville, Ohio, U.S., 172 ...328/F4
Nashville, Tenn., U.S., state capital, 569,891, (1,231,311 metro.) ...344/H2
Nashwaak Bridge, N.B., Can. ...217/C2
Nashwaak Vil., N.B., Can., 255 ...217/C2
Nashwauk, Minn., U.S., 935 ...298/D3
Näsi, Fin., lake ...81/B2
Näsijärvi, Fin., lake ...81/B2
Naskeag, Maine, U.S., 80 ...286/D4
Nason, Ill., U.S., 234 ...266/E5
Nass, Br. Col., Can., river ...214/H3
Nassau, Bah., capital ...204/B1
Nassau, Bah., capital, (210,832 metro.) ...207/B2
Nassau, Del., U.S., 1,600 ...255/D5
Nassau, Fla., U.S., county, 57,663 ...256/C1
Nassau, Minn., U.S., 83 ...298/A5
Nassau, N.Y., U.S., 1,161 ...320/P5
Nassau, N.Y., U.S., county, 1,334,544 ...320/C2
Nassau Bay, Tex., U.S., 4,170 ...346/C7
Nassawadox, Va., U.S., 572 ...354/M6
Nasser, Egy., lake ...144/B3
Nasser, Sudan, lake ...145/C1
Nata, Bots. ...160/B2
Natal, Braz., 712,317 ...188/E2
Natalbany, La., U.S., 1,739 ...282/J5
Natalia, Tex., U.S., 1,663 ...346/K6
Natalkuz, Br. Col., Can., lake ...214/K4
Natashquan, Que., Can. ...225/D3
Natchaug, Conn., U.S., river ...253/G2
Natchaug St. For., Conn., U.S. ...253/G2
Natchez, La., U.S., 583 ...282/C3, G3
Natchez, Miss., U.S., 18,464 ...300/A4
Natchez N.H.P., Miss., U.S. ...300/A4
Natchez Trace St. Park and Forest, Tenn., U.S. ...344/E3
Natchitoches, La., U.S., 17,865 ...282/C3
Natchitoches, La., U.S., parish, 39,080 ...282/C3
Nathalie, Va., U.S., 150 ...354/F7
Nathan, Ark., U.S., 60 ...244/B4
Nathan, Mich., U.S. ...294/B4
Nathrop, Colo., U.S., 100 ...250/D3
Natick, Mass., U.S., 32,170 ...292/J3
Natl. Bison Range, Mont., U.S. ...306/B2
National Capital, Phil., region ...120/B3
National City, Calif., U.S., 54,260 ...246/H10
National City, Ill., U.S. ...266/A6
Natl. Elk Refuge, Wyo., U.S. ...366/A2
National Key Deer Refuge, Fla., U.S. ...256/G7
National Mine, Mich., U.S., 400 ...294/B3
National Park, N.J., U.S., 3,205 ...314/A3
Natitingou, Ben., 57,535 ...151/A2
Natland, Eng., U.K. ...66/C4
Natoma, Kans., U.S., 367 ...276/D3
Natron, Tan., lake ...158/C1
Natrona, Wyo., U.S. ...366/C2
Natrona, Wyo., U.S., county, 66,533 ...366/C2
Natuna Besar, Indon., islands ...122/B1
Natural Bridge, Ala., U.S. ...238/B1
Natural Bridge, N.Y., U.S., 392 ...320/K2
Natural Bridge, Va., U.S., 100 ...354/D5
Natural Bridges Natl. Mon., Utah, U.S. ...350/E6
Natural Bridge Sta., Va., U.S., 250 ...354/D5
Natural Dam, Ark., U.S., 60 ...244/A2
Naturita, Colo., U.S., 635 ...250/B3
Natwick, Wyo., U.S. ...366/D3
Naubinway, Mich., U.S., 175 ...294/D3
Naucalpan de Juárez, Mex., 835,053 ...200/Inset
Naufrage, P.E.I., Can. ...224/C2
Naugatuck, Conn., U.S., 30,989 ...253/C4
Naugatuck, Conn., U.S., river ...253/C4
Naugatuck St. For., Conn., U.S. ...253/C4
Naujoji Akmenė, Lith. ...82/B1
Naumburg, Ger. ...86/B3
Naunton, Eng., U.K. ...68/D6
Naunton Beauchamp, Eng., U.K. ...68/C5
Nauru, nation ...166
Nauvoo, Ala., U.S., 284 ...238/B2
Nauvoo, Ill., U.S., 1,063 ...266/B3
Nauwigewauk, N.B., Can., 1,508 ...217/D3
Navabad, Taj. ...132/A1
Navajo, Ariz., U.S. ...242/F2
Navajo, Ariz., U.S., county, 97,470 ...242/F2
Navajo, Colo., U.S., reservoir ...250/C4
Navajo, N. Mex., U.S., 2,097 ...317/A2
Navajo, N. Mex., U.S., reservoir ...317/C1
Navajo, Utah, U.S., mountain ...350/D6
Navajo, N.M., Ariz., U.S. ...242/E1
Navajo Army Depot, Ariz., U.S. ...242/D2
Navajo Ind. Res., Ariz., U.S. ...242/E1, F2
Navajo Ind. Res., Ariz., Utah, U.S. ...350/E6
Navajo N.M., Ariz., U.S., 80 ...242/F2
Naval Surface Warfare Ctr. Crane Division, Ind., U.S. ...271/C7
Navarino, Wisc., U.S., 100 ...364/E4
Navarra, Sp., autonomous community ...94/F1
Navarra, Sp., province ...94/F1
Navarre, Fla., U.S., 450 ...256/B1
Navarre, Ohio, U.S., 1,440 ...328/G4
Navarro, Kans., U.S., 60 ...276/E3
Navarro, Calif., U.S., 40 ...246/B3
Navarro, Calif., U.S., head ...246/B3
Navarro, Tex., U.S., county, 45,124 ...346/M4
Navasota, Tex., U.S., 6,789 ...346/M5
Navassa, N.C., U.S., 479 ...322/J6
Naver, Scot., U.K., lake ...62/H2
Navojoa, Mex., 98,187, (140,650 metro.) ...200/C2
Navua, Fiji ...174/A3
Navua, Fiji, river ...174/A3
Navy Yard City, Wash., U.S., 2,638 ...358/A4
Nawabshah, Pak., 189,244 ...129/C4
Nawoiy, Uzb., 117,600 ...132/C2
Nawoiy, Uzb., province ...132/B2

Naxçıvan, Azer., autonomous republic ...103/A3
Naxos, Gr., island ...100/C3
Nayarit, Mex., state ...200/C3
Naylor, Ga., U.S., 125 ...260/E1
Naylor, Mo., U.S., 610 ...302/F5
Naytahwaush, Minn., U.S., 583 ...298/B3
Nazareth, Isr. ...135/B1
Nazareth, Ky., U.S., 1,000 ...280/E3
Nazareth, Penn., U.S., 6,023 ...336/L4
Nazareth, Tex., U.S., 356 ...346/F1, F10
Nazca, Peru ...185/C3
Naze, Jap. ...114/Inset II
Nazko, Br. Col., Can. ...214/L5
Nazlini, Ariz., U.S., 397 ...242/F2
Nazret, Eth., 163,533 ...156/C2
Nchelenge, Zam. ...159/B1
Ndalatando, Ang. ...159/B3
Ndélé, C.A.R. ...154/B2
Ndendé, Gabon ...155/A2
N'Djamena, Chad, capital, 546,572, (998,000 metro.) ...153/A4
Ndjolé, Gabon ...155/A2
Ndogo, Gabon, lagoon ...155/A2
Ndola, Zam., 441,624 ...159/B2
Neagh, N. Ire., U.K., lake ...60/A2
Neagh, N. Ire., U.K., lake ...65/E2
Neagh, N. Ire., U.K., lake ...78/C1
Neah Bay, Wash., U.S., 794 ...358/A1
Neal, Kans., U.S., 70 ...276/F4
Nea Liosia, Gr. ...100/Inset
Neal Smith N.W.R., Iowa, U.S. ...274/H4
Neamt, Rom., county ...101/D2
Neapolis, Gr. ...100/B3
Neapolis, Ohio, U.S., 1,000 ...328/C3
Near, Alaska, U.S., islands ...240/Inset
Neath, Wales, U.K., 45,965 ...64/D4
Neath Port Talbot, Wales, U.K., unitary authority, 134,471 ...64/D4
Neavitt, Md., U.S., 250 ...288/J5
Nebish, Minn., U.S., 90 ...298/C3
Nebitdag, Turkm. ...132/B2
Neblina, Braz., mountain ...188/B1
Neblina, Ven., mountain ...182/C3
Nebo, Ill., U.S., 408 ...266/C4
Nebo, Ky., U.S., 220 ...280/C3
Nebo, La., U.S., 125 ...282/E3
Nebo, Utah, U.S., mountain ...350/C4
Nebo Ctr., Calif., U.S., 1,174 ...246/J8
Nebraska, U.S., state ...296
Nebraska City, Nebr., U.S., 7,228 ...308/J3
Nebraska Natl. For., Nebr., U.S. ...308/A1, D2
Nebraska Natl. For., S. Dak., U.S. ...342/B5
Necaise, Miss., U.S., 80 ...300/C5
Necedah, Wisc., U.S., 888 ...364/C4
Necedah N.W.R., Wisc., U.S. ...364/C4
Nechako, Br. Col., Can., river ...214/K4
Neche, N. Dak., U.S., 437 ...326/H1
Neckar, Ger., river ...86/B4
Necochea, Arg. ...191/D4
Nectar, Ala., U.S., 372 ...238/C2
Nederland, Colo., U.S., 1,394 ...250/E2
Nederland, Tex., U.S., 17,422 ...346/P6
Neder Rijn, Neth., river ...85/C3
Nedlands, W.A., Austl. ...170/Inset I
Needham, Ala., U.S. ...238/A4
Needham, Ala., U.S., 97 ...238/A4
Needham, Mass., U.S., 28,911 ...292/K3
Needham Market, Eng., U.K., 4,312 ...70/G2
Needingworth, Eng., U.K., 1,808 ...68/G5
Needingworth, Eng., U.K., 1,808 ...70/D2
Needles, Br. Col., Can. ...214/N6
Needles, Calif., U.S., 4,830 ...246/J9
Needmore, Ga., U.S. ...260/F1
Needmore, Penn., U.S., 225 ...336/E6
Needville, Tex., U.S., 2,609 ...346/N6
Neely, Miss., U.S. ...300/D4
Neely Henry, Ala., U.S., lake ...238/C2
Neelyville, Mo., U.S., 487 ...302/F5
Neembucú, Para., department ...187/C5
Neenah, Wisc., U.S., 24,507 ...364/E4
Neepawa, Man., Can., 3,325 ...215/B4
Neeses, S.C., U.S., 413 ...340/C3
Nee Soon, Sing. ...123/B1
Neffs, Ohio, U.S., 1,138 ...328/J5
Nefta, Tun. ...148/A3
Neganee, Mich., U.S., 4,576 ...294/B3
Negele, Eth. ...156/C3
Negev, Isr., desert ...135/M2
Negley, Tex., U.S., 80 ...346/N2
Negombo, Sri Lan. ...126/A4
Negra, Peru, point ...185/A2
Negra, Uru., lagoon ...187/D2
Negreet, La., U.S., 90 ...282/B4
Negril, Jam. ...206/A2
Negro, Arg., river ...191/B4
Negro, Braz., river ...188/B2
Negro, Uru., river ...187/C2
Negro, Ven., river ...182/B3
Negros, Phil., island ...120/B4
Neguac, N.B., Can., 1,697 ...217/D1
Nehalem, Oreg., U.S., 203 ...334/C2
Nehantic St. For., Conn., U.S. ...253/F4
Nehawka, Nebr., U.S., 232 ...308/J3
Neiafu, Tonga ...175/C2
Neiba, Dom. Rep. ...205/A2
Neiba, Dom. Rep., mountains ...205/A2
Neihart, Mont., U.S., 91 ...306/F3
Neijiang, China ...119/D3
Neilburg, Sask., Can., 366 ...227/A8
Neillsville, Wisc., U.S., 2,731 ...364/C4
Neilton, Wash., U.S., 345 ...358/B2
Neisse, Ger., river ...86/C3
Neisse, Pol., river ...83/B3
Neiva, Col., 322,000 ...184/B4
Nek'emte, Eth. ...156/C2
Nekoma, Kans., U.S. ...276/C3
Nekoma, N. Dak., U.S., 51 ...326/G1
Nekoosa, Wisc., U.S., 2,590 ...364/D4
Nelagoney, Okla., U.S., 40 ...330/F1
Neligh, Nebr., U.S., 1,651 ...308/E1
Nellie, Ohio, U.S., 134 ...328/F5
Nellieburg, Miss., U.S., 1,354 ...300/D3
Nellis A.F.B., Nev., U.S. ...310/C3
Nellis Air Force Range Complex, Nev., U.S. ...310/B3
Nelliston, N.Y., U.S., 622 ...320/M5
Nellore, India ...128/C6
Nelma, Wisc., U.S., 70 ...364/E2
Nelson, Br. Col., Can., 9,298 ...214/O6
Nelson, Man., Can., river ...215/C1, D1
Nelson, N.Z., 41,568, (53,685 metro.) ...171/B4
Nelson, N.Z., region ...171/B3
Nelson, Eng., U.K., 29,120 ...66/D5
Nelson, Eng., U.K., 29,120 ...68/C5
Nelson, Ariz., U.S. ...242/B4
Nelson, Ga., U.S., 626 ...260/C3
Nelson, Ill., U.S., 163 ...266/D2
Nelson, Ky., U.S., county, 37,477 ...280/E3
Nelson, Minn., U.S., 172 ...298/B5
Nelson, Mo., U.S., 212 ...302/C3
Nelson, Mont., U.S. ...306/C4

Nelson, Nebr., U.S., 587 ...308/E3
Nelson, Nev., U.S., 50 ...310/C4
Nelson, N.H., U.S., 634 ...312/B6
Nelson, N. Dak., U.S., county, 3,715 ...326/G2
Nelson, Va., U.S., county, 14,445 ...354/F5
Nelson, Wisc., U.S., 395 ...364/A4
Nelson Forks, Br. Col., Can. ...214/L1
Nelson House, Man., Can., 54 ...215/B1
Nelson-Miramichi, N.B., Can. ...217/D2
Nelsonville, N.Y., U.S., 565 ...320/P8
Nelsonville, Ohio, U.S., 5,230 ...328/F7
Nelsonville, Wisc., U.S., 191 ...364/D4
Nelspruit, S. Afr. ...162/D2
Néma, Maur. ...147/D3
Nemacolin, Penn., U.S., 1,034 ...336/B6
Nemah, Wash., U.S. ...358/B3
Nemaha, Iowa, U.S., 102 ...274/D2
Nemaha, Kans., U.S., county, 10,717 ...276/G2
Nemaha, Nebr., U.S., 178 ...308/J3
Nemaha, Nebr., U.S., county, 7,576 ...308/J3
Nemeiben, Sask., Can., lake ...227/E5
Nemo, S. Dak., U.S. ...342/B3
Nemunas, Lith., river ...82/A2, C2
Nemuro, Jap. ...114/Inset I
Nemuro, Jap., strait ...114/Inset I
Nenagh, Ire. ...78/B2
Nenana, Alaska, U.S., 402 ...240/F2
Nendo, Sol. Is., island ...173/C2
Nene, Eng., U.K., river ...70/E1
Nenetskiy, Russ., autonomous okrug ...104/D3
Nenthead, Eng., U.K. ...66/D3
Nenzel, Nebr., U.S. ...308/C1
Neodesha, Kans., U.S., 2,848 ...276/G4
Neoga, Ill., U.S., 1,854 ...266/E4
Neola, Iowa, U.S., 845 ...274/C5
Neola, Utah, U.S., 533 ...350/D3
Neopit, Wisc., U.S., 839 ...364/E4
Neosho, Kans., U.S., county, 16,997 ...276/G4
Neosho, Mo., U.S., 10,505 ...302/B5
Neosho, Wisc., U.S., 593 ...364/E1, E5
Neosho Falls, Kans., U.S., 179 ...276/G3
Neosho Rapids, Kans., U.S., 274 ...276/G3
Neotsu, Oreg., U.S., 650 ...334/C3
Nepal, nation ...122
Nepalganj, Nepal ...126/B2
Nepaug, Conn., U.S., reservoir ...253/D2
Nepean, Ont., Can. ...223/G6, K2
Nephi, Utah, U.S., 4,733 ...350/C4
Nepisiguit, N.B., Can., river ...217/C1
Neponset, Ill., U.S., 519 ...266/D2
Neptune, N.J., U.S., 27,690 ...314/E3
Neptune, Ohio, U.S., 250 ...328/B4
Neptune City, N.J., U.S., 5,218 ...314/E3
Neretva, Bos.-Her., river ...98/B2
Neris, Lith., river ...82/C2
Nerstrand, Minn., U.S., 233 ...298/D6
Nesbit, Miss., U.S. ...300/C1
Nesbitt, Tex., U.S., 302 ...346/P3
Nesco, N.J., U.S., 375 ...314/D4
Nescopeck, Penn., U.S., 1,528 ...336/J3
Neshanic Sta., N.J., U.S. ...314/D2
Neshkoro, Wisc., U.S., 453 ...364/D5
Neshoba, Miss., U.S., 60 ...300/C3
Neshoba, Miss., U.S., county, 28,684 ...300/C3
Nesika Beach, Oreg., U.S., 200 ...334/B5
Neskowin, Oreg., U.S., 169 ...334/C2
Nesmith, S.C., U.S., 100 ...340/E3
Nespelem, Wash., U.S., 212 ...358/G1
Nespelem Community, Wash., U.S., 290 ...358/F1
Nesquehoning, Penn., U.S., 3,288 ...336/K4
Ness, Scot., U.K., lake ...62/G4
Ness, Scot., U.K., lake ...62/G4
Ness, Kans., U.S., county, 3,454 ...276/C3
Ness City, Kans., U.S., 1,534 ...276/C3
Nesscliffe, Eng., U.K. ...68/B4
Nesselrode, Br. Col., Can., mountain ...214/E1
Nestaocano, Que., Can., river ...226/C2
Neston, Eng., U.K., 15,585 ...66/B6
Neston, Eng., U.K., 15,585 ...68/A3
Nestoria, Mich., U.S. ...294/A3
Nestorville, W. Va., U.S., 150 ...360/G2
Netanya, Isr., 152,200 ...135/B1
Netarts, Oreg., U.S., 744 ...334/C2
Netawaka, Kans., U.S., 170 ...276/G2
Netcong, N.J., U.S., 2,580 ...314/D2
Nether Broughton, Eng., U.K. ...70/C1
Netherfield, Eng., U.K. ...70/C1
Netherlands, nation ...82
Netherlands Antilles, Neth. ...204/D4, F3
Nethers, Va., U.S. ...354/G4
Netherwitton, Eng., U.K. ...66/E2
Nethy Bridge, Scot., U.K. ...62/J4
Netley, Eng., U.K., 6,327 ...70/B5
Nettilling, Nun., Can., lake ...220/O3
Nett Lake, Minn., U.S. ...298/D2
Nett Lake Ind. Res., Minn., U.S. ...298/D2
Nettleham, Eng., U.K., 3,152 ...66/H6
Nettleham, Eng., U.K., 3,152 ...68/D3
Nettleton, Miss., U.S., 1,932 ...300/D1
Netzahualcóyotl, Mex., 1,225,083 ...200/Inset
Neubrandenburg, Ger. ...86/C2
Neuchâtel, Switz. ...90/A2
Neuchâtel, Switz., canton ...90/A2
Neuchâtel, Switz., lake ...90/A2
Neudorf, Sask., Can., 304 ...227/G10
Neufchâteau, Belg. ...85/D3
Neumünster, Ger. ...86/B1
Neunkirchen, Ger. ...86/A4
Neuquén, Arg., 167,296, (183,579 metro.) ...191/B4
Neuquén, Arg., province ...191/B4
Neuse, N.C., U.S., 250 ...322/H3
Neuse, N.C., U.S., river ...322/M5
Neuse Harbor, N.C., U.S., 150 ...322/M5
Neusiedler, Aus., lake ...91/E3
Neusiedler, (Fertő), Hun., lake ...91/A2
Neuss, Ger., 149,702 ...86/A3
Neustadt, Bel. ...201/A2
Neustrelitz, Ger. ...86/C2
Neutral, Kans., U.S. ...276/H4
Nevşehir, Tur. ...133/C2
Nevşehir, Tur., province ...133/C2
Nevada, Sp., mountains ...94/E4
Nevada, U.S., state ...298
Nevada, Iowa, U.S., 6,658 ...274/E3
Nevada, Mo., U.S., 8,607 ...302/B4
Nevada, Ohio, U.S., 814 ...328/D4
Nevada, Tex., U.S., 563 ...346/D8
Nevada City, Calif., U.S., 3,001 ...246/D3
Nevada Test Site, Nev., U.S. ...310/B3
Nevendon, Eng., U.K. ...70/E3
Nevern, Wales, U.K. ...64/B3
Nevers, Fr. ...88/C3
Neves, Braz. ...188/Inset I
Neves, São T.-Prínc. ...154/A4
Nevėžis, Lith., river ...82/B2
Neville, Ohio, U.S., 127 ...328/B8

Nevinville, Iowa, U.S. 274/E5
Nevis, St. K.-Nevis, island 207/C3
Nevis, St. K.-Nevis, peak 62/E5
Nevis, Minn., U.S., 364 . . . . .298/C4
New, Bel., river 201/B1
New, Guy., river 183/C4
New, Jam., bank 206/A3
New Albany, Ind., U.S., 37,603 . . . . . .270/E8
New Albany, Kans., U.S., 73 . . . . .276/G4
New Albany, Miss., U.S., 7,607 . . . . . .300/D1
New Albany, Penn., U.S., 306 . . . . . . .336/J2
New Albin, Iowa, U.S., 527 . . . . .274/M1
Newald, Wisc., U.S., 125 . . . . .364/E3
New Alexandria, Ohio, U.S., 222 . . . . .328/J5
New Alexandria, Penn., U.S., 595 . . . .336/C5
New Alluwe, Okla., U.S., 95 . . . . .330/G1
New Almelo, Kans., U.S., 40 . . . . .276/B2
New Amsterdam, Guy. 183/C2
New Amsterdam, Ind., U.S. 270/D8
Newark, Ark., U.S., 1,219 . . . . .244/D2
Newark, Calif., U.S., 42,471 . . . . .246/K2
Newark, Del., U.S., 28,547 . . . . .255/A2
Newark, Ill., U.S., 887 . . . . .266/E2
Newark, Md., U.S., 339 . . . . .288/N7
Newark, Mo., U.S., 100 . . . . .302/E1
Newark, Nev., U.S., lake 310/C2
Newark, N.J., U.S., 273,546 . . . . .314/B2, E2
Newark, N.Y., U.S., 9,682 . . . . .320/G4
Newark, Ohio, U.S., 46,279 . . . . .328/F5
Newark, Tex., U.S., 887 . . . . .346/A9
Newark, Vt., U.S., 470 . . . . .352/D1
Newark-on-Trent, Eng., U.K., 35,129 . .68/F3
Newark Valley, N.Y., U.S., 1,071 . . . . .320/J6
New Ashford, Mass., U.S., 247 . . . . . .292/B2
New Ash Green, Eng., U.K. 70/E4
New Athens, Ill., U.S., 1,981 . . . . .266/C4
New Athens, Ohio, U.S., 342 . . . . . . .328/H5
New Auburn, Minn., U.S., 488 . . . . . .298/C6
New Auburn, Wisc., U.S., 562 . . . . . . .364/B3
New Augusta, Miss., U.S., 715 . . . . . .300/C4
Newaygo, Mich., U.S., 1,670 . . . . .294/D6
Newaygo, Mich., U.S., county, 47,874 . .294/D6
New Baden, Ill., U.S., 3,001 . . . . .266/B3, D5
New Baltimore, Mich., U.S., 7,405 . .294/C6, G7
New Baltimore, Penn., U.S., 168 . . . . .336/D6
New Bandon, N.B., Can., 968 . . . . . . .217/D1
New Bavaria, Ohio, U.S., 78 . . . . .328/B3
New Beaver, Penn., U.S., 1,677 . . . . . .336/A4
New Bedford, Ill., U.S., 95 . . . . .266/D2
New Bedford, Mass., U.S., 93,768 . . . .292/L6
New Bedford Whaling N.H.P., Mass., U.S. .293/L6
Newberg, Oreg., U.S., 18,064 . . . . . . .334/D2
New Berlin, Ill., U.S., 1,030 . . . . .266/D4
New Berlin, N.Y., U.S., 1,129 . . . . . . .320/L5
New Berlin, Penn., U.S., 838 . . . . .336/H4
New Berlin, Tex., U.S., 467 . . . . .346/B2
New Berlin, Wisc., U.S., 38,220 . . .364/E6, J2
Newbern, Ala., U.S., 231 . . . . .238/B3
New Bern, N.C., U.S., 23,128 . . . . . . .322/L4
Newbern, Tenn., U.S., 2,988 . . . . .344/C2
Newberry, Fla., U.S., 3,316 . . . . .256/F2
Newberry, Ind., U.S., 206 . . . . .270/B7
Newberry, Mich., U.S., 2,686 . . . . . . .294/D3
Newberry, S.C., U.S., 10,580 . . . . . . .340/C2
Newberry, S.C., U.S., county, 36,108 . .340/C2
Newberry Natl. Vol. Mon., Oreg., U.S. .334/E4
Newberry Sprs., Calif., U.S., 40 . . . . . .246/J8
New Bethlehem, Penn., U.S., 1,057 . . .336/C3
Newbiggin, Eng., U.K. 66/D3
Newbiggin-by-the-Sea, Eng., U.K., 7,100 .66/E2
New Bloomfield, Mo., U.S., 599 . . . . . .302/D3
New Bloomfield, Penn., U.S., 1,077 . . .336/G5
New Bloomington, Ohio, U.S., 548 . . . .328/D4
Newborn, Ga., U.S., 520 . . . . .260/D4
Newboro, Ont., Can., 309 . . . . .223/J3
Newboro, Ont., Can., lake, 309 . . . . . .320/J1
Newborough, Eng., U.K. 68/D4
Newborough, Wales, U.K. 64/C1
New Boston, Ill., U.S., 632 . . . . .266/C2
New Boston, Mass., U.S., 200 . . . . . . .292/B4
New Boston, Mo., U.S., 40 . . . . .302/D2
New Boston, N.H., U.S., 4,138 . . . . . . .312/C6
New Boston, Ohio, U.S., 2,340 . . . . . .328/E8
New Boston, Tex., U.S., 4,808 . . . . . . .346/P2
New Braintree, Mass., U.S., 927 . . . . .292/H4
New Branch, Ga., U.S., 50 . . . . .260/G7
New Braunfels, Tex., U.S., 36,494 . .346/B2, K6
New Bremen, Ohio, U.S., 2,909 . . . . . .328/B5
Newbridge on Wye, Wales, U.K. 64/E3
New Brigden, Alta., Can. 212/E5
New Brighton, Minn., U.S., 22,206 . . . .298/F5
New Brighton, Penn., U.S., 6,641 . . . . .336/A4
New Britain, P.N.G., island 172/B2
New Britain, Conn., U.S., 71,538 . . . . .253/D3
New Britain, Penn., U.S., 3,125 . . . . . .336/L5
New Brockton, Ala., U.S., 1,250 . . . . . .238/D4
Newbrook, Alta., Can., 85 . . . . .212/D4
Newbrough, Eng., U.K. 66/D2
New Brunswick, Can., province 205
New Brunswick, N.J., U.S., 48,573 . . . .314/E3
New Buckenham, Eng., U.K. 70/G2
New Buffalo, Mich., U.S., 2,200 . . . . . .294/C8
New Buffalo, Penn., U.S., 123 . . . . . . .336/H5
Newburg, Ark., U.S., 125 . . . . .244/D1
Newburg, Iowa, U.S., 100 . . . . .274/J4
Newburg, Ky., U.S., 20,636 . . . . .280/C4
Newburg, Md., U.S., 300 . . . . .288/G6
Newburg, Mo., U.S., 484 . . . . .302/E4
Newburg, N. Dak., U.S., 88 . . . . .326/E1
Newburg, Penn., U.S., 81 . . . . .336/D4
Newburg, Penn., U.S., 81 . . . . .336/F5
Newburg, W. Va., U.S., 360 . . . . .360/G2
Newburg, Wisc., U.S., 1,119 . . . . .364/E5
Newburgh, Scot., U.K. 62/K6
Newburgh, Ind., U.S., 3,088 . . . . .270/B9
Newburgh, N.Y., U.S., 28,259 . . . . . . .320/N7
Newburgh Hts., Ohio, U.S., 2,389 . . . .328/G9
Newburgh Vil., Maine, U.S., 250 . . . . .286/C4
Newburn, Fla., U.S., 60 . . . . .256/E1
New Burnside, Ill., U.S., 242 . . . . .266/E6
Newbury, Eng., U.K., 33,273 . . . . .70/B4
Newbury, Eng., U.K., unitary authority,
144,445 . . . . .70/B4
Newbury, N.H., U.S., 1,702 . . . . .312/B5
Newbury, Vt., U.S., 1,955 . . . . .352/C2
Newbury Old Town, Mass., U.S., 475 . .292/L1
Newburyport, Mass., U.S., 17,189 . . . .292/L1
Newby Bridge, Eng., U.K. 66/C4
New Caledonia, Fr., dependency 161
New Cambria, Kans., U.S., 150 . . . . . .276/E3
New Cambria, Mo., U.S., 222 . . . . .302/D2
New Canaan, N.B., Can. 217/D2
New Canaan, Conn., U.S., 19,395 . . . .253/A5
New Caney, Tex., U.S. 346/B5
New Canton, Que., U.S., 1,431 . . . . . . .226/L4
New Canton, Va., U.S., 125 . . . . .354/G5
New Carlisle, Que., Can. 226/L4
New Carlisle, Ind., U.S., 1,505 . . . . . . .270/C1
New Carlisle, Ohio, U.S., 5,735 . . . . . .328/B6
New Carrollton, Md., U.S., 12,589 . . . .288/C6

Newcastle, N.S.W., Austl., 255,787,
(416,120 metro.) 170/E3
Newcastle, N.B., Can. 217/D2
Newcastle, St. K.-Nevis 207/C2
Newcastle, S. Afr. 162/C2
Newcastle, N. Ire., U.K., 7,214 . . . . . . .65/F3
Newcastle, Calif., U.S. 246/L5
New Castle, Colo., U.S., 1,984 . . . . . . .250/C2
New Castle, Del., U.S., 4,862 . . . . .255/B2
New Castle, Del., U.S., county, 500,265 .255/B2
New Castle, Ind., U.S., 17,780 . . . . . . .270/F5
New Castle, Ky., U.S., 919 . . . . .280/E2
Newcastle, Maine, U.S., 1,748 . . . . . . .286/C4
Newcastle, Nebr., U.S., 299 . . . . .308/H1
New Castle, Okla., U.S., 5,434 . . . . . . .330/C6
New Castle, Penn., U.S., 26,309 . . . . . .336/A4
Newcastle, Tex., U.S., 575 . . . . .346/K2
Newcastle, Utah, U.S., 90 . . . . .350/A6
New Castle, Va., U.S., 179 . . . . .354/C5
Newcastle, Wash., U.S., 7,737 . . .358/A4, C2
Newcastle, Wyo., U.S., 3,065 . . . . .366/D2
Newcastle Emlyn, Wales, U.K., 1,506 . .64/C3
Newcastleton, Scot., U.K., 772 . . . . . . .62/L8
Newcastle-under-Lyme, Eng., U.K. 60/C3
Newcastle-under-Lyme, Eng., U.K., 73,731 .68/C3
Newcastle upon Tyne, Eng., U.K. 60/C2
Newcastle upon Tyne, Eng., U.K., 189,150,
(1,075,262 metro.) 66/E3
Newcastle upon Tyne, Eng., U.K.,
unitary authority, 259,573 . . . . .66/E2
New Crtville, Penn., U.S., 193 . . . . .336/C6
New Chicago, Ind., U.S., 2,063 . . . . . . .270/B1
New City, N.Y., U.S., 34,038 . . . . .320/B1
New Columbus, Penn., U.S., 215 . . . . .336/J3
Newcomb, Md., U.S., 600 . . . . .288/K4
Newcomb, N. Mex., U.S., 387 . . . . . . .317/B1
Newcomb, N.Y., U.S., 40 . . . . .320/N3
Newcomerstown, Ohio, U.S., 4,008 . . .328/G5
New Concord, Ky., U.S., 150 . . . . .280/B4
New Concord, Ohio, U.S., 2,651 . . . . . .328/G5
New Creek, W. Va., U.S., 275 . . . . .360/H2
New Cumberland, Penn., U.S., 7,349 . .336/H5
New Cumberland, W. Va., U.S., 1,099 . .360/K4
New Cumnock, Scot., U.K., 3,165 . . . . .62/H8
Newdale, Man., Can. 215/A4
Newdale, Ida., U.S., 358 . . . . .264/F6
New Deal, Tex., U.S., 708 . . . . .346/G2
New Deer, Scot., U.K., 519 . . . . .62/M3
New Delhi, India, capital, 294,783 . . . .128/C2
New Denmark, N.B., Can. 217/B2
New Denver, Br. Col., Can., 538 . . . . . .214/O6
New Diggings, Wisc., U.S., 125 . . . . . .364/C6
New Douglas, Ill., U.S., 369 . . . . .266/B3
New Durham, N.H., U.S., 2,220 . . . . . .312/D5
New Duston, Eng., U.K. 70/C2
New Eagle, Penn., U.S., 2,262 . . . . . . .336/B5
New Edinburg, Ark., U.S., 50 . . . . .244/C4
New Effington, S. Dak., U.S., 233 . . . . .342/J2
New Egypt, N.J., U.S., 2,519 . . . . .314/D3
Newell, Alta., Can., lake 212/E6
Newell, Ark., U.S., 250 . . . . .244/C4
Newell, Calif., U.S., 400 . . . . .246/D1
Newell, Iowa, U.S., 887 . . . . .274/D2
Newell, Penn., U.S., 551 . . . . .336/B5
Newell, S. Dak., U.S., 646 . . . . .342/B3
New Ellenton, S.C., U.S., 2,250 . . . . . .340/C3
Newellton, La., U.S., 1,482 . . . . .282/G2
Newenden, Eng., U.K. 70/F4
New England, Austl., range 170/E3
New England, N. Dak., U.S., 555 . . . . .326/C3
Newenham, Alaska, U.S., cape 240/C3
Newent, Eng., U.K., 4,111 . . . . .68/C6
New Era, La., U.S. 282/F4
New Era, Mich., U.S., 461 . . . . .294/C6
New Fairfield, Conn., U.S., 13,953 . . . .253/B4
Newfane, N.Y., U.S., 3,129 . . . . .320/D4
Newfane, Vt., U.S., 1,680 . . . . .352/B5
New Ferolle, Nfld., Can., 345 . . . . .218/C4
Newfield (Fairfield County), Conn., U.S. .253/A5
Newfield (Litchfield County), Conn., U.S. .253/C2
Newfield, Maine, U.S., 1,328 . . . . .286/B5
Newfield, N.J., U.S., 1,616 . . . . .314/C4
Newfield, N.Y., U.S., 647 . . . . .320/H6
Newfields, N.H., U.S., 1,551 . . . . .312/E5
New Fish Creek, Alta., Can. 212/B3
New Florence, Mo., U.S., 764 . . . . . . .302/E3
New Florence, Penn., U.S., 784 . . . . . .336/C5
New Flys Villiage, Tenn., U.S. 344/C3
Newfolden, Minn., U.S., 362 . . . . .298/A2
Newfound, N.H., U.S., lake 312/C4
Newfoundland, Can., province 206
Newfoundland, Ky., U.S., 80 . . . . .280/G2
Newfoundland, N.J., U.S., 250 . . . . . . .314/E1
Newfoundland, Penn., U.S., 400 . . . . . .336/L3
New Franken, Wisc., U.S., 285 . . . . . . .364/F4
New Franklin, Mo., U.S., 1,145 . . . . . . .302/D2
New Freedom, Penn., U.S., 3,512 . . . . .336/H6
New Freeport, Penn., U.S., 50 . . . . . . .336/A6
Newgale, Wales, U.K. 64/A4
New Galilee, Penn., U.S., 424 . . . . .336/A4
Newgate, Scot., U.K. 62/H8
Newgardens, Vat. 96/A2
New Georgia Group, Sol. Is., islands . .173/A1
New Germany, Minn., U.S., 346 . . . . . .298/D6
New Glarus, Wisc., U.S., 2,111 . . . . . . .364/D6
New Glasgow, N.S., Can., 9,432 . . . . . .221/E2
New Gloucester, Maine, U.S., 4,803 . . .286/B5
New Grand Chain, Ill., U.S., 233 . . . . . .266/D6
New Greenleaf, Mich., U.S., 125 . . . . .294/F6
New Gretna, N.J., U.S., 500 . . . . .314/E4
New Guinea, Indon., island 122/E2
New Guinea, P.N.G., island 172/A2
Newhalem, Wash., U.S., 60 . . . . .358/D1
Newhalen, Alaska, U.S., 160 . . . . .240/D3
Newhall, Iowa, U.S., 886 . . . . .274/L4
Newham, Eng., U.K., unitary authority, 243,737 .70/E3
New Hamburg, Ont., Can., 7,003 . . . . .223/E4
New Hampshire, U.S., state 300
New Hampton, Iowa, U.S., 3,692 . . . . .274/K1
New Hampton, Mo., U.S., 349 . . . . . . .302/B1
New Hampton, N.H., U.S., 1,950 . . . . .312/C4
New Hanover, P.N.G., island 172/B2
New Hanover, N.C., U.S., county, 160,307 .322/K6
New Harbor, Maine, U.S., 225 . . . . . . .286/C5
New Harmony, Ind., U.S., 916 . . . . . . .270/A8
New Harmony, Utah, U.S., 190 . . . . . .350/A6
New Hartford, Conn., U.S., 6,088 . . . . .253/D2
New Hartford, Ill., U.S., 60 . . . . .266/C4
New Hartford, Iowa, U.S., 659 . . . . . . .274/J2
New Hartford, N.Y., U.S., 1,886 . . . . . .320/L4
Newhaven, Eng., U.K., 11,208 . . . . . . .70/E5
New Haven, Conn., U.S., 123,626 . . . . .253/D4
New Haven, Conn., U.S., county, 824,008 .253/D4
New Haven, Ill., U.S., 477 . . . . .266/E6
New Haven, Ind., U.S., 12,406 . . . . . . .270/D2
New Haven, Ky., U.S., 100 . . . . .274/I1
New Haven, Ky., U.S., 849 . . . . .280/E3
New Haven, Mich., U.S., 3,071 . . . .294/B6, G7
New Haven, Mo., U.S., 1,867 . . . . .302/E3
New Haven, N.Y., U.S., 375 . . . . .320/J4
New Haven, Vt., U.S., 1,666 . . . . .352/A2

New Haven, W. Va., U.S., 1,559 . . . . . .360/C3
New Haven, Wyo., U.S. 366/D1
New Hebron, Miss., U.S., 447 . . . . .300/C4
New Hempstead, N.Y., U.S., 4,767 . . . .320/B1
New Holland, Ill., U.S., 318 . . . . .266/D3
New Holland, Ohio, U.S., 785 . . . . .328/D6
New Holland, Penn., U.S., 5,092 . . . . . .336/J5
New Holland, S. Dak., U.S., 78 . . . . . . .342/G4
New Holstein, Wisc., U.S., 3,301 . . . . . .364/E5
New Home, Tex., U.S., 320 . . . . .346/G2
New Hope, Ala., U.S., 2,539 . . . . .238/C1
Newhope, Ark., U.S., 90 . . . . .244/A3
New Hope, Ga., U.S., 750 . . . . .260/B4
New Hope, Minn., U.S., 20,873 . . . . . .298/E5
New Hope, Miss., U.S., 1,964 . . . . .300/D2
New Hope, (Wake County), N.C., U.S. . .322/H3
New Hope, (Wayne County), N.C., U.S., 4,500 .322/M5
New Hope, Penn., U.S., 2,252 . . . . .336/M5
New Hope, Tenn., U.S., 1,043 . . . . .344/K4
New Hope, Tex., U.S., 662 . . . . . . .346/C8, M2
New Houlka, Miss., U.S., 710 . . . . .300/C1
New Hradec, N. Dak., U.S., 90 . . . . . . .326/C2
New Hyde Park, N.Y., U.S., 9,523 . . . . .320/C2
New Iberia, La., U.S., 32,623 . . . . .282/F6
Newick, Eng., U.K., 2,445 . . . . .70/E5
Newington, Eng., U.K., 2,454 . . . . .70/F4
Newington, Conn., U.S., 29,306 . . . . . .253/E3
Newington, Ga., U.S., 322 . . . . .260/H6
Newington, N.H., U.S., 1,542 . . . . .312/E5
Newington, Va., U.S., 19,784 . . . . .354/M2
New Ipswich, N.H., U.S., 4,289 . . . . . . .312/C6
New Ireland, P.N.G., island 172/B2
New Jersey, U.S., state 302
N.J. Turnpike, N.J., U.S. 314/C4, D4, E3
New Johnsonville, Tenn., U.S., 1,905 . .344/F2
New Kensington, Penn., U.S., 14,701 . .336/B4
New Kent, Va., U.S., 175 . . . . .354/K5
New Kent, Va., U.S., county, 13,462 . . .354/J6
Newkirk, N. Mex., U.S. 317/F2
Newkirk, Okla., U.S., 2,243 . . . . .330/E1
New Knoxville, Ohio, U.S., 891 . . . . . . .328/B4
New Kowloon, H.K., China 117/B2
New Lancaster, Kans., U.S. 276/H3
Newland, N.C., U.S., 704 . . . . .322/B2
New Lebanon, Ohio, U.S., 4,231 . . . . . .328/A6
New Lebanon, Penn., U.S., 205 . . . . . .336/A3
New Leipzig, N. Dak., U.S., 274 . . . . . .326/D3
New Lenox, Ill., U.S., 17,771 . . . . .266/B6
New Lexington, Ohio, U.S., 4,689 . . . . .328/F6
New Liberty, Iowa, U.S., 121 . . . . .274/N4
New Liberty, Okla., U.S. 330/C2
New Limerick, Maine, U.S., 523 . . . . . .286/E2
Newlin, Tex., U.S. 346/G10, H1
New Lisbon, Ind., U.S., 325 . . . . .270/F5
New Lisbon, N.J., U.S., 450 . . . . .314/D4
New Lisbon, Wisc., U.S., 1,436 . . . . . . .364/C5
New Liskeard, Ont., Can., 4,906 . . . . . .222/E3
New Llano, Tex., U.S., 2,415 . . . . .282/C4
New London, P.E.I., Can. 224/B2
New London, Ark., U.S. 244/C4
New London, Conn., U.S., 25,671,
(293,566 metro.) 253/G4
New London, Conn., U.S., county, 259,088 .253/G3
New London, Minn., U.S., 1,937 . . . . . .274/M6
New London, Minn., U.S., 1,066 . . . . . .298/C5
New London, Mo., U.S., 1,001 . . . . . . .302/E2
New London, N.H., U.S., 4,116 . . . . . . .312/C5
New London, N.C., U.S., 326 . . . . .322/E4
New London, Ohio, U.S., 2,696 . . . . . .328/F3
New London, Wash., U.S. 358/B2
New London, Wisc., U.S., 7,085 . . . . . .364/E4
New Lothrop, Mich., U.S., 603 . . . . . . .294/F6
Newlyn, Eng., U.K. 73/A4
New Lynn, Tex., U.S. 346/G2
New Madison, Ohio, U.S., 817 . . . . . . .328/A6
New Madrid, Mo., U.S., 3,334 . . . . .302/G5
New Madrid, Mo., U.S., county, 19,760 .302/G5
Newman, W.A., Austl. 170/A2
Newman, Calif., U.S., 7,093 . . . . .246/D5
Newman Grove, Nebr., U.S., 797 . . . . .308/G2
Newmarket, Qnsld., Austl. . . . . . .170/Inset III
Newmarket, Ont., Can., 65,788 . . . . . .223/F4
Newmarket, Eng., U.K., 16,498 . . . . . . .70/D2
New Market, Ala., U.S., 1,864 . . . . .238/C1
New Market, Ind., U.S., 659 . . . . .270/C5
New Market, Iowa, U.S., 456 . . . . .274/E6
New Market, Ky., U.S. 280/E3
New Market, Md., U.S., 427 . . . . .288/E2
New Market, Minn., U.S., 332 . . . . .298/D6
New Market, N.H., U.S., 8,027 . . . . . . .312/E5
New Market, Tenn., U.S., 1,234 . . . . . . .344/P2
New Market, Va., U.S., 1,637 . . . . .354/F3
New Marlborough, Mass., U.S., 1,494 . .292/B4
New Martinsville, W. Va., U.S., 5,984 . . .360/E1
New Maryland, N.B., Can., 4,284 . . . . .217/C3
New Matamoras, Ohio, U.S., 957 . . . . .328/H6
Meadows, Ida., U.S., 533 . . . . .264/A4
New Melle, Mo., U.S., 124 . . . . .302/F3
New Memphis, Ill., U.S., 225 . . . . .266/C4
New Mercer, Ill., U.S. 266/C2
New Mexico, U.S., state 305
New Miami, Ohio, U.S., 2,469 . . . . .328/A7
New Middletown, Ind., U.S., 77 . . . . . .270/D8
New Middletown, Ohio, U.S., 1,682 . . . .328/J4
New Milford, Conn., U.S., 27,121 . . . . .253/B3
New Milford, N.J., U.S., 16,400 . . . . . . .314/B2
New Milford, Penn., U.S., 878 . . . . .336/K2
New Milford, Ohio, U.S., 541 . . . . .266/D1
New Mills, N.B., Can. 217/C1
New Mills, Eng., U.K., 9,092 . . . . .66/D6
New Mills, Eng., U.K., 9,092 . . . . .68/E3
New Mills, Wales, U.K., 9,092 . . . . .64/E2
New Milton, (New Milton/Barton-on-Sea),
Eng., U.K., 24,324 . . . . .70/A5
New Milton, W. Va., U.S., 40 . . . . .360/E2
New Minas, N.S., Can. 221/C2
New Minden, Ill., U.S., 204 . . . . .266/D5
New Morgan, Penn., U.S. 336/K5
New Munich, Minn., U.S., 352 . . . . .298/C5
Newnan, Ga., U.S., 16,242 . . . . .260/B5
Newnham, Eng., U.K. 68/C6
New Norway, Alta., Can., 292 . . . . . . .212/D5
New Orleans, La., U.S., 484,674,
(1,337,726 metro.) 282/J7, K3
New Oxford, Penn., U.S., 1,696 . . . . . .336/G6
New Palestine, Ind., U.S., 1,264 . . . . . .270/E5
New Paltz, N.Y., U.S., 6,034 . . . . .320/N7
New Paris, Ind., U.S., 1,006 . . . . .270/E2
New Paris, Ohio, U.S., 1,623 . . . . .328/A6
New Paris, Penn., U.S., 214 . . . . .336/D5
New Pekin, Ind., U.S., 1,334 . . . . .270/D7
New Petersburg, Ohio, U.S. 328/D7
New Philadelphia, Ohio, U.S., 17,056 . .328/H5
New Philadelphia, Penn., U.S., 1,149 . .336/J4
New Pine Creek, Oreg., U.S., 80 . . . . .334/F6
New Plymouth, N.Z. 171/B2
New Plymouth, Ida., U.S., 1,400 . . . . . .264/A6

Newpoint, Ind., U.S., 290 . . . . .270/F6
New Pt., Ind., U.S., 325 . . . . .354/L6
Newport, (Essex), Eng., U.K., 2,178 . . .68/H6
Newport, (Essex), Eng., U.K., 2,178 . . .70/E3
Newport, (Isle of Wight), Eng., U.K., 20,574 .70/B5
Newport, (Shropshire), Eng., U.K. 68/C4
Newport, Wales, U.K. 60/C3
Newport, Wales, U.K. 64/B3
Newport, Wales, U.K., 115,522 . . . . . . .64/F4
Newport, Wales, U.K., unitary authority,
137,017 . . . . .64/F4
Newport, Ark., U.S., 7,811 . . . . .244/D2
Newport, Del., U.S., 1,122 . . . . .255/B2
Newport, Ind., U.S., 578 . . . . .270/B5
Newport, Ky., U.S., 17,048 . . . . .280/C1
Newport, Maine, U.S., 3,017 . . . . .286/C4
Newport, Md., U.S., 175 . . . . .288/G6
Newport, Minn., U.S., 3,715 . . . . .298/G6
Newport, Miss., U.S., 40 . . . . .300/B1
Newport, Nebr., U.S., 98 . . . . .308/E1
Newport, N.H., U.S., 6,269 . . . . .312/B5
Newport, N.J., U.S., 325 . . . . .314/C5
Newport, N.Y., U.S., 640 . . . . .320/L4
Newport, N.C., U.S., 3,349 . . . . .322/M5
Newport, (Shelby County), Ohio, U.S. . .328/B5
Newport, (Washington County), Ohio, U.S. .328/H7
Newport, Oreg., U.S., 9,532 . . . . .334/B3
Newport, Penn., U.S., 1,506 . . . . .336/G5
Newport, R.I., U.S., 26,475 . . . . .339/E5
Newport, R.I., U.S., county, 85,433 . . . .339/E4
Newport, Tenn., U.S., 7,242 . . . . .344/Q3
Newport, Vt., U.S., city, 5,005 . . . . . . .352/C1
Newport, Vt., U.S., town, 1,511 . . . . . . .352/C1
Newport, Wash., U.S., 1,921 . . . . .358/H1
Newport Beach, Calif., U.S., 70,032 . . .246/D11
Newport Ctr., Vt., U.S., 300 . . . . .352/C1
New Portland, Maine, U.S., 785 . . . . . .286/B4
Newport News, Va., U.S., 180,150 . . . .354/L7
Newport-on-Tay, Scot., U.K., 4,214 . . . .62/L6
Newport Pagnell, Eng., U.K., 12,285 . . .68/F5
Newport Pagnell, Eng., U.K., 12,285 . . .70/C2
New Port Richey, Fla., U.S., 16,117 . . . .256/F3
New Post, Wisc., U.S., 367 . . . . .364/B3
New Prague, Minn., U.S., 4,559 . . . . . .298/D6
New Preston, Conn., U.S., 1,110 . . . . . .253/B3
New Providence, Bah., island 204/B1
New Providence, Ind., U.S., 818 . . . . . .270/E8
New Providence, Iowa, U.S., 227 . . . . .274/H3
New Providence, N.J., U.S., 11,907 . . . .314/E2
New Prue, Okla., U.S., 40 . . . . .330/F1
Newquay, Eng., U.K. 60/B4
Newquay, Eng., U.K., 17,390 . . . . .73/B4
New Quay, Wales, U.K. 64/C3
New Radnor, Wales, U.K. 64/E3
New Richland, Minn., U.S., 1,197 . . . . .298/D7
New Richmond, Que., Can., 3,760 . . . .226/L3
New Richmond, Ind., U.S., 349 . . . . . . .270/C4
New Richmond, Ohio, U.S., 2,219 . . . . .328/B8
New Richmond, Wisc., U.S., 6,310 . . . .364/A3
New Riegel, Ohio, U.S., 226 . . . . .328/D3
New Ringgold, Penn., U.S., 291 . . . . . . .336/J4
New Ringgold, Okla., U.S., 50 . . . . .330/G3
New River, Ariz., U.S., 10,740 . . . . .242/C4
New River, Tenn., U.S., 175 . . . . .344/M2
New River Gorge Natl. River, W. Va., U.S. .354/A4
New River Gorge Natl. River, W. Va., U.S. .360/D4
New River Sta., N.C., U.S. 322/L5
New Roads, La., U.S., 4,966 . . . . .282/G5
New Rochelle, N.Y., U.S., 72,182 . . . . . .320/B2
New Rockford, N. Dak., U.S., 1,463 . . . .326/F2
New Rome, Ohio, U.S., 60 . . . . .328/D9
New Romney, Eng., U.K. 70/F4
New Ross, N.S., Can. 221/C3
New Ross, Ind., U.S., 334 . . . . .270/C5
Newry, N. Ire., U.K. 60/A2
Newry, N. Ire., U.K., 22,975 . . . . .65/E3
Newry, Maine, U.S., 344 . . . . .286/B4
Newry, Penn., U.S., 245 . . . . .336/E5
Newry, Wisc., U.S., 60 . . . . .364/C5
Newry and Mourne, N. Ire., U.K.,
unitary authority, 87,058 . . . . .65/E3
New Salem, Ill., U.S., 136 . . . . .266/C4
New Salem, Ind., U.S., 200 . . . . .270/F5
New Salem, Mass., U.S., 929 . . . . .292/E4
New Salem, N.C., U.S., 70 . . . . .322/D3
New Salem, N. Dak., U.S., 938 . . . . . . .326/D3
New Salem, (Fayette County, New Salem-Buffingtion),
Penn., U.S. 336/B6
New Salem, (York County), Penn., U.S., 648 .336/H6
New Sandy Bay, St. Vin.-Gren. 208/B1
New Sarepta, Alta., Can., 382 . . . . . . .212/D4
New Sarpy, La., U.S., 1,568 . . . . . .282/J3, J7
New Schwabenland, Antar., region 192/B16
New Sharon, Iowa, U.S., 1,301 . . . . . . .274/J5
New Sharon, Maine, U.S., 1,297 . . . . . .286/C4
New Sharon, Mo., U.S., 300 . . . . .314/D3
New Siberian, Russ., islands 104/I2
New Siberian, Russ., islands 193/B8
New Site, Ala., U.S., 848 . . . . .238/D2
New Smyrna Beach, Fla., U.S., 20,048 . .256/H2
Newsoms, Va., U.S., 282 . . . . .354/J7
New S. Wales, Austl., state 170/D3
New Square, N.Y., U.S., 4,624 . . . . . . .320/B1
New Stanton, Penn., U.S., 1,906 . . . . . .336/B5
New Straitsville, Ohio, U.S., 774 . . . . . .328/F6
New Strawn, Kans., U.S., 425 . . . . .276/G3
New Stuyahok, Alaska, U.S., 471 . . . . .240/D3
New Sweden, Maine, U.S., 621 . . . . . . .286/D2
New Sweden, Tex., U.S., 100 . . . . .346/G2
New Tazewell, Tenn., U.S., 2,871 . . . . .344/P2
New Territories, H.K., China, island 117/B1
Newtok, Alaska, U.S., 321 . . . . .240/C2
Newton, (Hereford & Worcester), Eng., U.K. .68/B6
Newton, (Lancashire), Eng., U.K. 68/C4
Newton, (Lincolnshire), Eng., U.K. 68/G4
Newton, (Lincolnshire), Eng., U.K. 70/D1
Newton, (Norfolk), Eng., U.K. 70/F1
Newton, Eng., U.K. 66/D5
Newton, Scot., U.K. 62/K8
Newton, Ala., U.S., 1,708 . . . . .238/D4
Newton, Ark., U.S., county, 8,608 . . . . .244/B2
Newton, Ga., U.S., 851 . . . . .260/C6
Newton, Ga., U.S., county, 62,001 . .260/D5, K4
Newton, Ill., U.S., 3,069 . . . . .266/E5
Newton, Ind., U.S., county, 14,566 . . . .270/B3
Newton, Iowa, U.S., 15,579 . . . . .274/H4
Newton, Kans., U.S., 17,190 . . . . .276/E3
Newton, Md., U.S., 250 . . . . .288/L4
Newton, Mass., U.S., 83,829 . . . . . .292/B7, K3
Newton, Miss., U.S., 3,699 . . . . .300/C3
Newton, Miss., U.S., county, 21,838 . . .300/C3
Newton, Mo., U.S., county, 52,636 . . . .302/B5
Newton, N.H., U.S., 4,289 . . . . .312/D6
Newton, N.J., U.S., 8,244 . . . . .314/D1
Newton, N.C., U.S., 12,560 . . . . .322/D4
Newton, Tex., U.S., 2,459 . . . . .346/R5
Newton, Tex., U.S., county, 15,072 . . . .346/R5
Newton, Utah, U.S., 699 . . . . .350/C2
Newton, W. Va., U.S., 80 . . . . .360/D3
Newton, Wisc., U.S., 300 . . . . .364/F5

Newton Abbot, Eng., U.K., 23,801 . . . . .73/E3
Newton Aycliffe, Eng., U.K., 25,085 . . . . .66/E3
Newton Falls, N.Y., U.S., 225 . . . . .320/M2
Newton Falls, Ohio, U.S., 5,002 . . . . .328/J3
Newton Ferrers, Eng., U.K., 1,479 . . . . .73/D4
Newtonferry, Scot., U.K. 62/B1
Newton Grove, N.C., U.S., 606 . . . . .322/J4
Newton Hamilton, Penn., U.S., 272 . . . . .336/F5
Newtonhill, Scot., U.K., 2,940 . . . . .62/M4
Newtonia, Mo., U.S., 231 . . . . .302/B5
Newton-le-Willows, Eng., U.K., 19,416 . . . . . .66/C6
Newton-le-Willows, Eng., U.K., 19,416 . . . . . .68/B5
Newton Longville, Eng., U.K., 1,979 . . . . .70/C3
Newtonmore, Scot., U.K., 982 . . . . .62/H4
Newton-on-the-Moor, Eng., U.K. 66/E2
Newton on Trent, Eng., U.K. 68/F3
Newton Purcell, Eng., U.K. 70/B3
Newton Stewart, Scot., U.K., 3,573 . . . . .62/H9
Newtonsville, Ohio, U.S., 492 . . . . .328/B7
Newtonville, Ala., U.S., 40 . . . . .238/B2
Newtonville, N.J., U.S., 800 . . . . .314/D4
Newtown, N.B., Can. 217/D3
Newtown, Eng., U.K., 10,548 . . . . .68/B5
Newtown, Eng., U.K., 10,548 . . . . .70/B4
Newtown, Wales, U.K., 10,548 . . . . .64/E2
Newtown, Conn., U.S., 25,031 . . . . .253/B4
Newtown, Ind., U.S., 162 . . . . .270/B4
Newtown, Ky., U.S., 90 . . . . .280/E2
Newtown, Md., U.S., 80 . . . . .288/K2
Newtown, Mo., U.S., 209 . . . . .302/C1
New Town, N. Dak., U.S., 1,367 . . . . .326/C2
Newtown, Ohio, U.S., 2,420 . . . . .328/B10
Newtown, Penn., U.S., 2,312 . . . . .336/M5
Newtown, (King and Queen County), Va., U.S. .354/J5
Newtown, (Rockingham County), Va., U.S. 354/F4
Newtownabbey, N. Ire., U.K., 57,103 . . . . . . .65/F2
Newtownabbey, N. Ire., U.K., unitary authority,
    79,995 . . . . .65/F2
Newtownards, N. Ire., U.K., 11,644 . . . . .65/F2
Newtownbreda, N. Ire., U.K. 65/F2
Newtownbutler, N. Ire., U.K., 953 . . . . .65/C3
Newtown Crommelin, N. Ire., U.K. 65/E3
Newtownhamilton, N. Ire., U.K., 761 . . . . .65/D3
Newtown St. Boswells, Scot., U.K., 1,199 . . . . .60/C2
Newtown St. Boswells, Scot., U.K., 1,199 . . . . .62/M7
Newtownstewart, N. Ire., U.K., 1,520 . . . . . . .65/C2
New Trier, Minn., U.S., 116 . . . . .298/E6
New Tulsa, Okla., U.S., 568 . . . . .330/G1
New Ulm, Minn., U.S., 13,594 . . . . .298/C6
New Underwood, S. Dak., U.S., 616 . . . . .342/C3
New Unionville, Ind., U.S., 500 . . . . .270/D6
New Vernon, N.J., U.S., 1,200 . . . . .314/D2
New Vienna, Iowa, U.S., 400 . . . . .274/M2
New Vienna, Ohio, U.S., 1,294 . . . . .328/C7
New Vil., N.J., U.S., 350 . . . . .314/C2
Newville, Ala., U.S., 553 . . . . .238/D4
Newville, Calif., U.S. .246/C3
Newville, Ind., U.S., 200 . . . . .270/G2
Newville, Penn., U.S., 1,367 . . . . .336/G5
New Vineyard, Maine, U.S., 725 . . . . .286/B4
New Virginia, Iowa, U.S., 469 . . . . .274/G5
New Waltham, Eng., U.K., 4,263 . . . . .66/H5
New Waltham, Eng., U.K., 4,263 . . . . .68/G2
New Washington, Ohio, U.S., 987 . . . . .328/E4
New Washington, Penn., U.S., 89 . . . . .336/D4
New Washoe City, Nev., U.S., 2,900 . . . . .310/A2
New Waterford, N.S., Can., 10,185 . . . . .221/G1
New Waterford, Ohio, U.S., 1,391 . . . . .328/J4
New Waterway, Neth., channel 84/B3
New Waverly, Tex., U.S., 950 . . . . .346/N5
New Weston, Ohio, U.S., 133 . . . . .328/A5
New Whiteland, Ind., U.S., 4,579 . . . . .270/D5
New Wilmington, Penn., U.S., 2,452 . . . . .336/A4
New Windsor, Md., U.S., 1,303 . . . . .288/F1
New Windsor, N.Y., U.S., 9,077 . . . . .320/N8
New York, U.S., state 308
New York, N.Y., U.S., 8,008,278,
    (21,199,865 metro.) 320/B2
New York, N.Y., U.S., county, 1,537,195 . . . . .320/B2
New York Mills, Minn., U.S., 1,158 . . . . .298/B4
New York Mills, N.Y., U.S., 3,191 . . . . .320/L4
New Zealand, nation 163
New Zion, S.C., U.S., 200 . . . . .340/D3
Ney, Ohio, U.S., 364 .328/A3
Neyagawa, Jap., 251,000 . . . . .114/B3
Neyland, Wales, U.K., 3,006 . . . . .64/B4
Neyshabur, Iran 130/D2
Nezperce, Ida., U.S., 523 . . . . .264/A3
Nez Perce, Ida., U.S., county, 37,410 . . . . . . .264/A3
Nez Perce Ind. Res., Ida., U.S. 264/B4
Nez Perce Natl. For., Ida., U.S. 264/B4
Nez Perce N.H.P., (East Kamiah Site), Ida., U.S. 264/B4
Nez Perce N.H.P., (East Kamiah Site), Ida., U.S. 306/A3
Nez Perce N.H.P., (Spalding Area), Ida., U.S. . .264/A3
Ngami, Bots., lake 160/A2
Nganyatjara, Austl., aboriginal land 170/B2
Ngaoundéré, Came., 47,508 . . . . .153/B2
Ngara, Tan. 158/B1
Ngaramasch, Palau 172/A4
Ngauruhoe, N.Z., mountain 171/C2
Ngemelis, Palau, islands 172/B3
Ngerkeel, Palau 172/C2
Ngermechau, Palau 172/C2
Ngetbong, Palau 172/C2
Ngiro, Kenya, river 157/D3
Ngoc Linh, Viet., mountain 123/B3
Ngorongoro, Tan., crater 158/C1
Ngonini, Swaz. 161/B1
Ngou nié, Gabon, river 155/A2
Ngozi, Bur. 158/B1
Nguigmi, Niger 152/C3
Ngulu, Micr., atoll 172/A2
Nguru, Nig. 152/F1
Ngwempisi, Swaz., river 161/A2
Nha Trang, Viet., 221,331 . . . . .123/B4
Nhlangano, Swaz. 161/B3
Niagara, Ont., Can. 223/F4
Niagara, Ont., Can., county 223/F4
Niagara, Ky., U.S. 280/C3
Niagara, N.Y., U.S., county, 219,846 . . . . . . .320/D4
Niagara, N. Dak., U.S., 57 . . . . .326/H2
Niagara, Wisc., U.S., 1,880 . . . . .364/E3
Niagara Falls, Ont., Can., 78,815 . . . . .223/F4
Niagara Falls, N.Y., U.S., 55,593 . . . . .320/C4
Niagara-on-the-Lake, Ont., Can., 13,839 . . . .223/F4
Niagassola, Guin. 149/D1
Niamey, Niger, capital, 397,437 . . . . .152/A3
Niamtougou, Togo 151/B2
Niandan, Guin., river .149/C3
Niangua, Mo., U.S., 445 . . . . .302/A4
Niantic, Conn., U.S., 3,085 . . . . .253/G4
Niantic, Ill., U.S., 738 . . . . .266/D4
Niarada, Mont., U.S., 50 . . . . .306/B2
Niari, Congo, river 155/B5
Nias, Indon., island 122/A1
Nibley, Utah, U.S., 2,045 . . . . .350/C2
Nibok, Nauru 174/B2
Nicaragua, nation 190
Nicaragua, Nicar., lake 202/B3
Nicatous, Maine, U.S., lake 286/D3
Nice, Fr., 345,892, (888,784 metro.) 88/D5

Nice, Calif., U.S., 2,509 . . . . .246/C3
Niceville, Fla., U.S., 11,684 . . . . .256/B1
Nicholas, Ky., U.S., county, 6,813 . . . . .280/F2
Nicholas, W. Va., U.S., county, 26,562 . . . . . .360/E4
Nicholasville, Ky., U.S., 19,680 . . . . .280/F3
Nicholls, Ga., U.S., 1,008 . . . . .260/F8
Nicholls Town, Bah. 207/A2
Nichols, Iowa, U.S., 374 . . . . .274/M5
Nichols, N.Y., U.S., 574 . . . . .320/J6
Nichols, S.C., U.S., 408 . . . . .340/E2
Nichols, Wisc., U.S., 307 . . . . .364/E4
Nichols Hills, Okla., U.S., 4,056 . . . . .330/B3, E2
Nicholson, Ga., U.S., 1,247 . . . . .260/E3
Nicholson, Miss., U.S., 1,400 . . . . .300/C5
Nicholson, Penn., U.S., 713 . . . . .336/K2
Nicholville, N.Y., U.S., 150 . . . . .320/M1
Nickel Creek, Tex., U.S. 346/D4
Nickelsville, Va., U.S., 448 . . . . .354/C3
Nickerie, Sur., river 183/A2
Nickerson, Kans., U.S., 1,194 . . . . .276/D3
Nickerson, Minn., U.S., 40 . . . . .298/E4
Nickerson, Nebr., U.S., 431 . . . . .308/H2
Nicklesville, Ga., U.S. 260/E6
Nicksville, Ariz., U.S., 425 . . . . .242/E6
Nicobar, India, islands 128/F7
Nicodemus, Kans., U.S. 276/C2
Nicodemus N.H.S., Kans., U.S. 276/C2
Nicola, Br. Col., Can. .214/M6
Nicolaus, Calif., U.S., 100 . . . . .246/D4
Nicolet, Que., Can., 7,928 . . . . .226/D5
Nicolet Natl. For., Wisc., U.S. 364/E3
Nicollet, Minn., U.S., 889 . . . . .298/C6
Nicollet, Minn., U.S., county, 29,771 . . . . . . .298/C6
Nicoma Park, Okla., U.S., 2,415 . . . . .330/B4
Nicosia, Cyp., capital, 273,129 . . . . .133/B1
Nicoya, C.R., gulf 203/B3
Nicoya, C.R., peninsula 203/A3
Nictau, N.B., Can. 217/B1
Nidže, Mac., mountains 100/B3
Nidwalden, Switz., canton 90/C2
Niederbayern, Ger., department 86/C4
Niederwald, Tex., U.S., 584 . . . . .346/D3
Niefang, Eq. Gui. 154/C3
Nielsville, Minn., U.S., 91 . . . . .298/A3
Nienburg, Ger. 86/B2
Niéri Ko, Sen., river 148/C2
Nieuw Amsterdam, Sur. 183/B2
Nieuw Nickerie, Sur. .183/A2
Nièvre, Fr., department 88/C3
Nigadoo, N.B., Can., 983 . . . . .217/D1
Niğde, Tur. 133/C3
Niğde, Tur., province .133/C3
Niger, nation 146
Niger, Ben., river 151/B1
Niger, Guin., river 149/C2
Niger, Mali, river 150/B3
Niger, Niger, river 152/A3
Niger, Nig., delta 152/C5
Niger, Nig., river .152/C2, D5
Niger, Nig., state 152/C2
Nigeria, nation 146
Nigg, Scot., U.K. 62/J3
Nighthawk, Wash., U.S. 358/F1
Nii, Jap., island 114/C3
Niigata, Jap., 501,000 . . . . .114/C2
Niigata, Jap., prefecture 114/C2
Niihama, Jap. 114/B3
Niihau, Hawaii, U.S., island 262/A2, A5
Nijmegen, Neth., 152,032 . . . . .84/C3
Nikaia, Gr. 100/Inset
Nikep, Md., U.S., 650 . . . . .288/B3
Nikiski, Alaska, U.S., 4,327 . . . . .240/E2
Nikki, Ben. 151/B3
Nikko, Jap. 114/C2
Nikolai, Alaska, U.S., 100 . . . . .240/E2
Nikolayevsk-na-Amure, Russ. 104/I4
Nikolski, Alaska, U.S. 240/B4
Nikopol', Ukr., 149,785 . . . . .102/C2
Nikšić, Serb.-Mont. 99/A3
Nikumaroro, Kiri., island 175/B2
Nikunau, Kiri., island .175/A2
Niland, Calif., U.S., 1,143 . . . . .246/K9
Nile, Egy., river 144/B2
Nile, Sudan, river 145/C1, C2
Nilgiri, India, hills 128/C6
Nilópolis, Braz., 103,033, (157,819 metro.) . .188/Inset I
Nilwood, Ill., U.S., 284 . . . . .266/D4
Nimba, C. d'Iv., mountain 150/B3
Nimba, Guin., mountain 149/D4
Nimba, Guin., mountains 149/D4
Nimba, Liber., mountains 149/B2
Nîmes, Fr., 137,740, (148,889 metro.) 88/C4
Nimmons, Ark., U.S., 100 . . . . .244/E1
Nimrod, Ark., U.S., lake 244/C3
Nimrod, Minn., U.S., 75 . . . . .298/C4
Nina, Ky., U.S., 90 . . . . .280/F3
Ninaview, Colo., U.S. 250/G4
Ninebanks, Eng., U.K. 66/D3
Nine Mile Falls, Wash., U.S., 250 . . . . .358/H2
Nine Mile River, N.S., Can. 221/D2
Ninette, Man., Can. 215/B4
Ninety Six, S.C., U.S., 1,936 . . . . .340/B2
Ninety Six Natl. Hist. Site, S.C., U.S. 340/B2
Nineveh, Eng., U.K. 68/B5
Ninfield, Eng., U.K. 70/E5
Ninga, Man., Can. 215/B4
Ningbo, China, 478,940, (943,460 metro.) . . .119/F3
Ningxia, China, autonomous region 119/D2
Ninigo, P.N.G., group 172/A2
Niniigret N.W.R., R.I., U.S. 339/C5
Ninnekah, Okla., U.S., 994 . . . . .330/E3
Ninole, Hawaii, U.S. .262/J4
Niobe, N. Dak., U.S. .326/C1
Niobrara, Nebr., U.S., 379 . . . . .308/E1
Niobrara, Nebr., U.S., river 308/B1, E1
Niobrara, Wyo., U.S., county, 2,407 . . . . .366/D2
Niono, Mali 150/B3
Nioro du Rip, Sen. 148/B3
Nioro du Sahel, Mali .150/B2
Niort, Fr. 88/B3
Niota, Tenn., U.S., 781 . . . . .344/M3
Niotaze, Kans., U.S., 122 . . . . .276/F4
Nipawin, Sask., Can., 4,275 . . . . .227/F7
Nipigon, Ont., Can., 1,964 . . . . .222/C3
Nipigon, Ont., Can., lake 222/C3
Nipissing, Ont., Can. 223/F1
Nipissing, Ont., Can., county 223/F1
Nipissing, Ont., Can., lake 223/F1
Nipmuck St. For., Conn., U.S. 253/G2
Nipomo, Calif., U.S., 12,626 . . . . .246/K7
Niš, Serb.-Mont., 249,845 . . . . .99/B3
Nišava, Serb.-Mont., river 99/C3
Nishino, Jap., island . . . . .114/Inset III
Nishinomiya, Jap., 438,000 . . . . .114/B3
Niskayuna, N.Y., U.S., 4,892 . . . . .320/P5

Nisland, S. Dak., U.S., 204 . . . . .342/B3
Nisling, Yukon, Can., river 228/B4
Nisqually, Wash., U.S., river 358/C2
Nissequogue, N.Y., U.S., 1,543 . . . . .320/D2
Nisswa, Minn., U.S., 1,953 . . . . .298/C4
Nisula, Mich., U.S., 40 . . . . .294/A3
Niter, Ida., U.S. 264/F7
Niterói, Braz., 459,451 . . . . .188/D4, Inset I
Nitra, Slvk., 163,540 . . . . .92/B2
Nitra, Slvk., river 92/B2
Nitriansky, Slvk., region 92/B2
Nitro, W. Va., U.S., 6,824 . . . . .360/C4
Nitta Yuma, Miss., U.S., 70 . . . . .300/B2
Niuafo'ou, Tonga, island 175/B1
Niuatoputapu, Tonga, island group 175/C1
Niuatoputapu, Tonga, island 175/C1
Niue, N.Z., dependency 161
Niulakita, Tuv., island 174/C4
Niutao, Tuv., island 174/B2
Niverton, Penn., U.S. 336/C6
Niverville, Man., Can., 1,921 . . . . .215/C4
Niverville, N.Y., U.S., 1,737 . . . . .320/P6
Nixa, Mo., U.S., 12,124 . . . . .302/C4
Nixon, Nev., U.S., 418 . . . . .310/A2
Nixon, Tenn., U.S., 400 . . . . .344/A4
Nixon, Tex., U.S., 2,186 . . . . .346/L6
Nizamabad, India 128/C5
Nizhnevartosk, Russ., 238,071 . . . . .104/E3
Nizhniy Novgorod, Russ., 1,357,555,
    (1,366,100 metro.) 104/D4
Nizhniy Tagil, Russ., 392,942 . . . . .104/D4
Nízke Tatry, Slvk., mountains 92/B2
Njazidja, (Grande Comore), Com., island 163/A1
Njombe, Tan., river 158/B2
Nkawkaw, Gha. 150/B3
Nkhata Bay, Mal. 159/B2
Nkhotakota, Mal. 159/B2
Nkongsamba, Came. 153/A2
Noaank, Conn., U.S., 1,830 . . . . .253/H4
Noarlunga, S.A., Austl. . . . . .170/Inset II
Noatak, Alaska, U.S., 428 . . . . .240/C1
Noatak, Alaska, U.S., river 240/D1
Noatak Natl. Pres., Alaska, U.S. 240/C1
Nobeoka, Jap. 114/A3
Noble, Ill., U.S., 746 .266/E5
Noble, Ind., U.S., county, 46,275 . . . . .270/F2
Noble, La., U.S., 259 . . . . .282/B3
Noble, Ohio, U.S., county, 14,058 . . . . .328/H6
Noble, Okla., U.S., 5,260 . . . . .330/E2
Noble, Okla., U.S., county, 11,411 . . . . .330/E1
Nobleboro, Maine, U.S., 1,626 . . . . .286/C4
Nobles, Minn., U.S., county, 20,832 . . . . .298/B7
Noblestown, (Sturgeon-Noblestown),
    Penn., U.S., 1,764 . . . . .336/A5
Noblesville, Ind., U.S., 28,590 . . . . .270/D4
Nobottle, Eng., U.K. 70/B2
Nocatee, Fla., U.S., 700 . . . . .256/G4
Nocona, Tex., U.S., 3,198 . . . . .346/L2
Nodaway, Iowa, U.S., 132 . . . . .274/E6
Nodaway, Mo., U.S., county, 21,912 . . . . . . .302/B1
Node, Wyo., U.S. 366/D2
Noel, Mo., U.S., 1,480 . . . . .302/B5
Noel, N.S., Can. 221/D2
Noelke, Tex., U.S. 346/H4
Nogal, N. Mex., U.S. 317/E4
Nogales, Mex., 156,854, (159,787 metro.) . .200/B1
Nogales, Ariz., U.S., 20,878 . . . . .242/E6
Nógrád, Hung., county 91/B2
Nohili, Hawaii, U.S., point 262/B1
Nohly, Mont., U.S. 306/M2
Nojack, Alta., U.S. 212/B4
Nojima, Jap., cape 114/D3
Nokaneng, Bots. 160/A1
Nok Kundi, Pak. 129/B4
Nokomis, Sask., Can., 436 . . . . .227/E9
Nokomis, Ill., U.S., 2,389 . . . . .266/D4
Nola, C.A.R. 154/A3
Nolan, Tex., U.S. 346/H3
Nolan, Tex., U.S., county, 15,802 . . . . .346/H3
Nolensville, Tenn., U.S., 3,099 . . . . .344/H3
Nolin River, Ky., U.S., lake 280/C3
Noma, Fla., U.S., 213 . . . . .256/C1
Nomansland, Eng., U.K. 70/A5
Nomansland, Eng., U.K. 73/J3
Nome, U.S. 193/C10
Nome, Alaska, U.S., 3,505 . . . . .240/C2
Nome, N. Dak., U.S., 70 . . . . .326/H3
Nonacho, N.W. Terr., Can., lake 220/G4
Nondalton, Alaska, U.S., 221 . . . . .240/E2
Nong Khai, Thai. 125/C2
Nonou Forest Reserve, Hawaii, U.S. 262/D1
Nonquitt, Mass., U.S., 350 . . . . .292/L6
Nonsan, S. Kor. 116/B4
Nonthaburi, Thai., (481,900 metro.) 125/B3
Nonville, Eng., U.K. 66/C2
Noocksack, Wash., U.S., 851 . . . . .358/C1
Noonan, N. Dak., U.S., 154 . . . . .326/B1
Noorvik, Alaska, U.S., 634 . . . . .240/C1
Nootka, Br. Col., Can., island 214/I6
Nopal, Tex., U.S. 346/L6
Nopiming Prov. Park, Man., Can. 215/D4
Nora, Ill., U.S., 118 . . . . .266/D1
Nora, Nebr., U.S. 308/G3
Norak, Taj. 132/A2
Nora Sprs., Iowa, U.S., 1,532 . . . . .274/J1
Norborne, Mo., U.S., 805 . . . . .302/C2
Norbourne Estates, Ky., U.S., 461 . . . . .280/B2
Norcatur, Kans., U.S., 169 . . . . .276/B2
Norco, Calif., U.S., 24,157 . . . . .246/F10
Norco, La., U.S., 3,579 . . . . .282/J3, J6
Norcross, Ga., U.S., 8,410 . . . . .260/C4, J2
Norcross, Maine, U.S. 286/D3
Norcross, Minn., U.S., 59 . . . . .298/A5
Nord, Fr., department 88/C1
Nord, Haiti, department 205/C1
Nordegg, Alta., Can. .212/B5
Nordelph, Eng., U.K. .70/D1
Norden, Neth., U.S. 308/D1
Nordenham, Ger. 86/B2
Nord-Est, Haiti, department 205/C1
Nordhausen, Ger. 86/B3
Nordheim, Tex., U.S., 323 . . . . .346/L7
Nordhorn, Ger. 86/A2
Nordjylland, Den., county 79/B2
Nord-Kivu, Congo, D.R., region 155/C2
Nordland, Nor., province 80/C2
Nord-Ostsee, Ger., canal 86/B1
Nord-Ouest, Haiti, department 205/B1
Nord-Pas-de-Calais, Fr., region 88/C1
Nord-Trøndelag, Nor., province 80/C2
Nordvik, Russ. 104/G2
Norfolk, Austl., island 193/B6
Norfolk, Alta., U.S. 212/D5
Norfolk, Eng., U.K., county 70/D1
Norfolk, Eng., U.K., unitary authority, 796,733 . .68/H4
Norfolk, Eng., U.K., unitary authority, 796,733 . .70/F1
Norfolk, Conn., U.S., 1,660 . . . . .253/C2

Norfolk, Mass., U.S., 10,460 . . . . .292/J4
Norfolk, Mass., U.S., county, 650,308 . .292/B8, J4, L3
Norfolk, Nebr., U.S., 23,516 . . . . .308/G1
Norfolk, N.Y., U.S., 1,334 . . . . .320/M1
Norfolk, Va., U.S., 234,403, (1,569,541 metro.) . .354/L7
Norfork, Ark., U.S., 484 . . . . .244/C1
Norfork, Ark., U.S., lake 244/C1
Norge, Okla., U.S., 82 . . . . .330/D3
Norias, Tex., U.S., 40 . . . . .346/L9
Noril'sk, Russ., 148,797, (244,450 metro.) . . .104/F3
Noril'sk, Russ. 193/C5
Norland, Ont., Can. .223/G3
Norlina, N.C., U.S., 1,107 . . . . .322/J2
Norma, N.J., U.S., 500 . . . . .314/C5
Norma, Tenn., U.S., 80 . . . . .344/N2
Normal, Ill., U.S., 45,386 . . . . .266/E3
Norman, Ark., U.S., 423 . . . . .244/B3
Norman, Minn., U.S., county, 7,442 . . . . .298/A3
Norman, Nebr., U.S., 49 . . . . .308/E3
Norman, N.C., U.S., 72 . . . . .322/F4
Norman, N.C., U.S., lake 322/D3
Norman, Okla., U.S., 95,694 . . . . .330/E2
Normanby, Eng., U.K. 66/G4
Normandin, Que., Can., 3,524 . . . . .226/D3
Normandy, Mo., U.S., 5,153 . . . . .302/H3
Normandy, Tenn., U.S., 141 . . . . .344/J4
Normandy, Tex., U.S., 70 . . . . .346/H7
Normandy Beach, N.J., U.S. 314/E3
Normandy Park, Wash., U.S., 6,392 . . . . .358/C3
Normangee, Tex., U.S., 719 . . . . .346/M4
Norman Park, Ga., U.S., 849 . . . . .260/D9
Normans, Md., U.S., 650 . . . . .288/J4
Normanton, (Derbyshire), Eng., U.K. 68/E4
Normanton, (W. Yorkshire), Eng., U.K., 18,775 . .68/E2
Normanton, Eng., U.K. 66/F5
Normanton, Eng., U.K. 70/B1
Normantown, Qu., U.S., 225 . . . . .260/G2
Norman Wells, N.W. Terr., Can., 666 . . . . .220/C3
Norphlet, Ark., U.S., 822 . . . . .244/C4
Norquay, Sask., Can., 485 . . . . .227/H9
Norra Storfjället, Swe., mountain 80/C1
Norrotten, Swe., county 80/C1
Norridge, Ill., U.S., 14,582 . . . . .266/B5
Norridgewock, Maine, U.S., 3,294 . . . . .286/C4
Norris, Ill., U.S., 194 .266/C3
Norris, Mont., U.S. 306/E4
Norris, S.C., U.S., 847 . . . . .340/B2
Norris, S. Dak., U.S., 150 . . . . .342/D4
Norris, Tenn., U.S., 1,446 . . . . .344/N2
Norris, Tenn., U.S., lake 344/P2
Norris, Wyo., U.S. 366/A1
Norris Arm, Nfld., Can., 843 . . . . .218/D4
Norris City, Ill., U.S., 1,057 . . . . .266/E6
Norris Pt., Nfld., Can., 786 . . . . .218/C4
Norristown, Penn., U.S., 31,282 . . . . .336/L5
Norrisville, Md., U.S., 300 . . . . .288/H1
Norrköping, Swe., 122,896 . . . . .80/C5
Norseland, Minn., U.S., 70 . . . . .298/C6
Norte, P.R., key 206/E2
Norte de Santander, Col., department 184/B2
North, sea 80/C1
North, sea 193/D1
North, Barb., point 209/A1
North, Came., province 153/B2
North, Nfld., Can., river 218/B2
North, N.S., Can., cape 221/G1
North, Ont., Can., channel 223/B1
North, Ont., Can., channel 294/F3
North, P.E.I., Can., cape 224/B1
North, Den., sea 79/A3
North, Ger., sea 86/A1
North, N.Z., cape 171/B1
North, N.Z., island 171/B2
North, Nor., cape 80/F1
North, Nor., cape 81/C1
North, Nor., cape 193/B2
North, Nor., sea 80/A3
North, Eng., U.K., sea 66/H2
North, Eng., U.K., sea 68/H2
North, N. Ire., U.K., channel 65/F1
North, N. Ire., U.K., channel 78/C1, D1
North, Scot., U.K., channel 60/D2
North, Scot., U.K., sea 62/P5, R2
North, La., U.S., pass 282/M8
North, Mich., U.S., point 294/F4
North, S.C., U.S., 813 . . . . .340/C3
North, S.C., U.S., island 340/E3
N. Acomita Vil., N. Mex., U.S., 288 . . . . .317/C2
N. Acton, Mass., U.S., 3,000 . . . . .292/J2
N. Adams, Mass., U.S., 14,681 . . . . .292/B2
N. Adams, Mich., U.S., 514 . . . . .294/E8
N. Adelaide, S.A., Austl. . . . . .170/Inset II
N. Albanian Alps, Alb., range 99/A1
N. Albanian Alps, Serb.-Mont., mountains 99/B3
Northallerton, Eng., U.K. 66/F4
Northallerton, Eng., U.K., 13,774 . . . . .66/F4
Northam, Eng., U.K., 6,167 . . . . .73/D2
N. America, continent 186
N. Amherst, Mass., U.S., 6,019 . . . . .292/D3
N. Amity, Maine, U.S. 286/E3
Northampton, Eng., U.K. 60/C3
Northampton, Eng., U.K., 179,596,
    (183,082 metro.) 68/F5
Northampton, Eng., U.K., 179,596,
    (183,082 metro.) 70/C2
Northampton, Mass., U.S., 28,978 . . . . .292/D3
Northampton, N.C., U.S., county, 22,086 . . . .322/L2
Northampton, Penn., U.S., 9,405 . . . . .336/K4
Northampton, Penn., U.S., county, 267,066 . .336/K4
Northampton, Va., U.S., county, 13,093 . . . . .354/M6
Northamptonshire, Eng., U.K., unitary authority,
    629,676 . . . . .68/E5
Northamptonshire, Eng., U.K., unitary authority,
    629,676 . . . . .70/B2
N. Andaman, India, island 128/F6
N. Andover, Mass., U.S., 27,202 . . . . .292/K2
N. Anson, Maine, U.S., 400 . . . . .286/B3
N. Arlington, N.J., U.S., 15,181 . . . . .314/B2, E2
N. Arran N.P., Scot., U.K. 62/F7
N. Atlanta, Ga., U.S., 38,579 . . . . .260/J2
N. Attleboro, Mass., U.S., 27,143 . . . . .292/J5
N. Augusta, S.C., U.S., 17,574 . . . . .340/C3
N. Aurora, Ill., U.S., 10,585 . . . . .266/A6
N. Ayrshire, Scot., U.K., unitary authority,
    135,817 . . . . .62/F7
N. Baltimore, Ohio, U.S., 3,361 . . . . .328/C3
N. Bancroft, Maine, U.S. 286/E3
N. Barrington, Ill., U.S., 2,918 . . . . .266/L6
N. Battleford, Sask., Can., 13,692 . . . . .227/B8
N. Battle Mountain, Nev., U.S. 310/B1
N. Bay, Ont., Can., 52,771 . . . . .222/E3
N. Bay, Ont., Can., 52,771 . . . . .223/F1
N. Bay, Wisc., U.S., 260 . . . . .364/F6, G2
N. Bay Shore, N.Y., Fla., U.S., 6,733 . . . . . . .288/H5
N. Beach, Md., U.S., 1,880 . . . . .288/H5
N. Beach, Wash., U.S., peninsula 358/A3
N. Beach Haven, N.J., U.S., 2,427 . . . . .314/E4
N. Bedeque, P.E.I., Can. 224/B2
N. Bend, Nebr., U.S., 1,213 . . . . .308/H2

N. Bend, Ohio, U.S., 603 . . . . .328/A9
N. Bend, Oreg., U.S., 9,544 . . . . .334/B4
N. Bend, Penn., U.S., 425 . . . . .336/F3
N. Bend, Wash., U.S., 4,746 . . . . . .358/B4, D2
N. Bend, Wisc., U.S., 100 . . . . .364/A4
N. Bennington, Vt., U.S., 1,428 . . . . .352/A5
N. Bergen, N.J., U.S., 58,092 . . . . .314/B2
N. Berwick, Scot., U.K., 6,223 . . . . .62/L6
N. Berwick, Maine, U.S., 4,293 . . . . .286/B5
N. Bethel, Maine, U.S., 60 . . . . .286/B4
N. Billerica, Mass., U.S., 5,200 . . . . .292/B6, J2
N. Bloomfield, Ohio, U.S., 325 . . . . .328/J3
N. Bonneville, Wash., U.S., 593 . . . . .358/D4
Northboro, Iowa, U.S., 60 . . . . .274/D6
Northborough, Mass., U.S., 14,013 . . . . . .292/H3
N. Boston, N.Y., U.S., 2,680 . . . . .320/D5
N. Brabant, Neth., province 84/C3
N. Braddock, Penn., U.S., 6,410 . . . . .336/E7
N. Bradford, Maine, U.S., 125 . . . . .286/D3
Northbranch, Kans., U.S. 276/D2
N. Branch, Mich., U.S., 1,027 . . . . .294/F6
N. Branch, Minn., U.S., 8,023 . . . . .298/E5
N. Branch, N.H., U.S., 225 . . . . .312/C5
N. Branch, N.J., U.S., 1,500 . . . . .314/D2
N. Branford, Conn., U.S., 13,906 . . . . . . .253/D4
N. Brentwood, Md., U.S., 469 . . . . .288/C7
Northbridge, Mass., U.S., 13,182 . . . . . . .292/H4
N. Bridgton, Maine, U.S., 225 . . . . .286/B4
Northbrook, Ill., U.S., 33,435 . . . . .266/B5
Northbrook, Ohio, U.S., 11,076 . . . . .328/B9
N. Brookfield, Mass., U.S., 4,683 . . . . . . .292/F3
N. Browning, Mont., U.S., 2,200 . . . . .306/D1
N. Brunswick, N.J., U.S., 36,287 . . . . .314/E3
N. Buena Vista, Iowa, U.S., 124 . . . . .274/N2
N. Caldwell, N.J., U.S., 7,375 . . . . . .314/B2, E2
N. Canadian, Okla., U.S., river 330/C1
N. Canton, Conn., U.S., 325 . . . . .253/D2
N. Canton, Ohio, U.S., 16,369 . . . . .328/H4
N. Cape, P.E.I., Can. 224/B1
N. Cape, Wisc., U.S. 364/F2
N. Cape May, N.J., U.S., 3,618 . . . . .314/D6
N. Carolina, U.S., state 310
N. Carrollton, Miss., U.S., 499 . . . . .300/C2
N. Carver, Mass., U.S., 700 . . . . .292/L5
N. Cascades Natl. Park, Br. Col., Can. 214/M7
N. Cascades Natl. Park, Wash., U.S. 358/D1
N. Catasauqua, Penn., U.S., 2,814 . . . . . .336/L4
N. Cave, Eng., U.K. 68/F2
N. Central, Sri Lan., province 126/B3
N. Charleroi, Penn., U.S., 1,409 . . . . .336/B5
N. Charleston, S.C., U.S., 79,641 . . . . . . .340/E4
N. Charlestown, N.H., U.S., 425 . . . . .312/B5
N. Chatham, Mass., U.S., 750 . . . . .292/Q6
N. Chatham, N.H., U.S. 312/D3
N. Chelmsford, Mass., U.S., 4,900 . . . . . . .292/J2
N. Chicago, Ill., U.S., 35,918 . . . . . .266/B4, F1
N. Chichester, N.H., U.S., 700 . . . . .312/D5
N. Chili, N.Y., U.S., 4,300 . . . . .320/F4
N. China, China, plain 119/E2
N. Chungcheong, S. Kor., province 116/B4
North City, Ill., U.S., 630 . . . . .266/D6
N. Clarendon, Vt., U.S., 700 . . . . .352/B3
N. Cleveland, Tex., U.S., 263 . . . . .346/N5
N. Cohasset, Mass., U.S., 1,600 . . . . .292/L3
N. College Hill, Ohio, U.S., 10,082 . . . . . .328/B9
N. Collins, N.Y., U.S., 1,079 . . . . .320/D5
N. Comino, Malta, channel 97/B1
N. Concord, Vt., U.S., 175 . . . . .352/D2
N. Conway, N.H., U.S., 2,069 . . . . .352/B2
N. Corbin, Ky., U.S., 1,662 . . . . .280/F4
Northcote, Vic., Austl. . . . . .170/Inset V
Northcote, Minn., U.S. 298/A2
N. Courtland, Ala., U.S., 799 . . . . .238/B1
N. Cowden, Tex., U.S. 346/F4
N. Creek, N.Y., U.S., 425 . . . . .320/P3
Northcrest, Tex., U.S., 1,700 . . . . .346/L4
N. Crossett, Ark., U.S., 3,581 . . . . .244/D4
N. Crows Nest, Ind., U.S., 42 . . . . .270/D5
N. Curry, Eng., U.K. 73/G2
N. Cutler, Maine, U.S. 286/E4
N. Dakota, U.S., state 314
Northdale, (Greater Northdale), Fla., U.S.,
  20,461 . . . . .256/D6
N. Dalton, Eng., U.K. 66/G5
N. Danville, Vt., U.S., 225 . . . . .352/C2
N. Dartmouth, Mass., U.S., 2,200 . . . . . . .292/L6
N. Decatur, Ga., U.S., 15,270 . . . . .260/J2
N. Derby, Vt., U.S. 352/C1
N. Dighton, Mass., U.S., 1,400 . . . . .292/K5
N. Dorset, Vt., U.S. 352/A4
N. Down, N. Ire., U.K., unitary authority,
  76,323 . . . . .65/F2
N. Downs, Eng., U.K., hills 60/C3
N. Druid Hills, Ga., U.S., 18,852 . . . .260/C4, J2
N. Duxbury, Vt., U.S. 352/B2
N. Eagle Butte, S. Dak., U.S., 2,163 . . . . .342/D3
Northeast, Neth., polder 84/C2
North East, Md., U.S., 2,733 . . . . .288/L1
North East, Penn., U.S., 4,601 . . . . .336/B1
North East Carry, Maine, U.S. 286/C3
North-Eastern, Kenya, province 157/F3
N. Eastham, Mass., U.S., 1,915 . . . . .292/Q5
Northeast Harbor, Maine, U.S., 500 . . . . .286/D4
N. East Lincolnshire, Eng., U.K., unitary authority,
  157,983 . . . . .66/H5
N. East Lincolnshire, Eng., U.K., unitary authority,
  157,983 . . . . .68/G2
N. Easton, Mass., U.S., 3,700 . . . . .292/K4
Northeast Providence, Bah., channel 207/B2
N. Edwards, Calif., U.S., 1,227 . . . . .246/H7
N. Egremont, Mass., U.S., 200 . . . . .292/A4
Northeim, Ger. .86/B3
N. Elmham, Eng., U.K. 70/F1
N. English, Iowa, U.S., 991 . . . . .274/K4
N. Enid, Okla., U.S., 796 . . . . .330/E1
N. Epworth, Mich., U.S., 275 . . . . .294/C6
Northern, Isr., district 135/B1
Northern, Sri Lan., province 126/B2
Northern, Zam., province 159/C2
Northern Areas, Pak. 129/D2
Northern Cheyenne Ind. Res., Mont., U.S. .306/K4
Northern Divina, Russ., river 104/D3
Northern Dvina, Russ., river 193/C3
Northern European, Ger., plain 86/B2
Northern European, Russ., plain 104/C4
Northern Frontier, Sa. Arab., emirate 136/B1
Northern Highland American Legion St. For.,
  Wisc., U.S. 364/D2
Northern Ireland, U.K., country 63
Northern Mariana, U.S., islands 172/B1
Northern Mindanao, Phil., region 120/C4
Northern Ostrobothnia, Fin., region 81/C2
Northern Sporades, Gr., islands 100/C3
Northern Territory, Austl. 170/C2
N. Esk Boom, N.B., Can. 217/D2
N. Fairfield, Ohio, U.S., 573 . . . . .328/G3
N. Falmouth, Mass., U.S., 3,355 . . . . .292/M6
N. Ferrisburg, Vt., U.S., 500 . . . . .352/A2
Northfield, Conn., U.S., 825 . . . . .253/D2
Northfield, Ill., U.S., 5,389 . . . . .266/B5
Northfield, Ky., U.S., 970 . . . . .280/B2

Northfield, Maine, U.S., 131 . . . . .286/E4
Northfield, Mass., U.S., 2,951 . . . . .292/E2
Northfield, Minn., U.S., 17,147 . . . . .298/D6
Northfield, N.H., U.S., 4,548 . . . . .312/C5
Northfield, N.J., U.S., 7,725 . . . . .314/D5
Northfield, Ohio, U.S., 3,827 . . . . .328/H9
Northfield, Tex., U.S. 346/H1
Northfield, Vt., U.S., 5,791 . . . . .352/B2
Northfield, Wisc., U.S., 90 . . . . .364/B4
Northfield Ctr., Vt., U.S. 352/B2
Northfield Falls, Vt., U.S., 650 . . . . .352/B2
Northfields, Va., U.S., 3,700 . . . . .354/G4
Northfleet, Eng., U.K., 21,397 . . . . .70/E4
N. Fond du Lac, Wisc., U.S., 4,557 . . . . . .364/E5
Northford, Conn., U.S., 1,600 . . . . .253/D4
N. Foreland, Eng., U.K., promontory 60/D3
N. Fork, Calif., U.S., 500 . . . . .246/F5
N. Fork, Ida., U.S. 264/C4
N. Fork, Nev., U.S. 310/C1
N. Fork, S. Dak., U.S. 342/C2
Northfork, W. Va., U.S., 519 . . . . .360/D6
N. Fork Cimarron, Colo., U.S., river 250/H4
N. Fork Smoky Hill, Colo., U.S., river 250/H2
N. Ft. Myers, Fla., U.S., 40,214 . . . . .256/G5
N. Foster, R.I., U.S., 275 . . . . .339/B2
N. Franklin, Conn., U.S., 150 . . . . .253/G3
N. Freedom, Wisc., U.S., 649 . . . . .364/D5
N. Frisian, Den., islands 79/B4
N. Frisian, Ger., islands 86/B1
N. Fryeburg, Maine, U.S., 125 . . . . .286/B4
Northgate, Sask., Can. 227/H11
Northgate, N. Dak., U.S. 326/C1
Northglenn, Colo., U.S., 31,575 . . . . .250/A3, F2
N. Grafton, Mass., U.S., 3,600 . . . . .292/H4
N. Granby, Conn., U.S., 1,720 . . . . .253/D2
N. Grosvenor Dale, Conn., U.S., 1,424 . . .253/H2
N. Guilford, Conn., U.S. 253/E4
N. Guilford, Maine, U.S. 286/C3
N. Gyeongsang, S. Kor., province 116/C4
N. Haledon, N.J., U.S., 7,920 . . . . .314/B1
N. Hamgyŏng, N. Kor., province 116/C1
N. Hampton, N.H., U.S., 4,259 . . . . .312/E6
N. Hampton, Ohio, U.S., 370 . . . . .328/C5
N. Hartland, Vt., U.S., 425 . . . . .352/C3
N. Hartsville, S.C., U.S., 3,136 . . . . .340/D2
N. Harwich, Mass., U.S. 292/P6
N. Hatfield, Mass., U.S., 550 . . . . .292/D3
N. Haven, Conn., U.S., 23,035 . . . . .253/D4
N. Haven, Maine, U.S., 381 . . . . .286/D4
N. Haven, N.Y., U.S., 743 . . . . .320/G1
N. Haverhill, N.H., U.S., 450 . . . . .312/B3
N. Henderson, Ill., U.S., 187 . . . . .266/C2
N. Hero, Vt., U.S., 810 . . . . .352/A1
N. Hickory, N.C., U.S., 4,300 . . . . .322/C3
N. Highlands, Calif., U.S., 44,187 . . . . . . .246/K5
N. High Shoals, Ga., U.S., 439 . . . . .260/E4
N. Hill, Wash., U.S. 358/A4
N. Hills, W. Va., U.S., 880 . . . . .360/D2
N. Hodge, La., U.S., 440 . . . . .282/D2
N. Holland, Neth., canal 84/B2
N. Holland, Neth., province 84/B2
N. Holmwood, Eng., U.K. 70/D4
N. Hornell, N.Y., U.S., 851 . . . . .320/F6
N. Houston, Tex., U.S., 4,900 . . . . .346/A6
N. Hudson, N.Y., U.S. 320/P3
N. Hudson, Wisc., U.S., 3,463 . . . . .364/A3
N. Hwanghae, N. Kor., province 116/B3
N. Hyde Park, Vt., U.S., 200 . . . . .352/B1
N. Industry, Ohio, U.S., 1,800 . . . . .328/H4
Northington, Eng., U.K. 70/B4
N. Jay, Maine, U.S., 350 . . . . .286/B4
N. Jeolla, S. Kor., province 116/B5
N. Johns, Ala., U.S., 142 . . . . .238/B1
N. Judson, Ind., U.S., 1,675 . . . . .270/C2
N. Kansas City, Mo., U.S., 4,714 . . . . .302/H5
N. Karelia, Fin., region 81/D2
N. Kazakhstan, Kaz., oblast 131/C1
N. Kelsey, Eng., U.K. 66/H5
N. Kilworth, Eng., U.K. 70/B2
N. Kingstown, R.I., U.S., 26,326 . . . . .339/D4
N. Kingsville, Ohio, U.S., 2,658 . . . . .328/J2
N. Komelik, Ariz., U.S., 100 . . . . .242/D5
N. Kyme, Eng., U.K. 70/D1
N. Lake, P.E.I., Can. 224/C2
Northlake, Ill., U.S., 11,878 . . . . .266/B5
Northlake, Tex., U.S., 921 . . . . .346/B8
Northlakes, R.I., U.S., 1,390 . . . . .322/C3
N. Lanarkshire, Scot., U.K., unitary authority,
  321,067 . . . . .62/J7
N. Lancing, Eng., U.K. 70/D5
Northland, N.Z., region 171/B2
Northland, Mich., U.S., 50 . . . . .294/B3
N. Las Vegas, Nev., U.S., 115,488 . . . . . .310/C3
N. Lauderdale, Fla., U.S., 32,264 . . . . . . .256/B5
N. Lebanon, Maine, U.S., 200 . . . . .286/B5
N. Leigh, Eng., U.K. 70/B2
Northleigh, Eng., U.K. 73/F3
N. Leverett, Mass., U.S., 250 . . . . .292/E2
N. Lewisburg, Ohio, U.S., 1,588 . . . . .328/C5
N. Liberty, Ind., U.S., 1,402 . . . . .270/D1
N. Liberty, Iowa, U.S., 5,367 . . . . .274/L4
N. Lilbourn, Mo., U.S., 95 . . . . .302/G5
N. Lincoln, Maine, U.S., 350 . . . . .286/D3
N. Lincolnshire, Eng., U.K., unitary authority,
  152,839 . . . . .66/G5
N. Lincolnshire, Eng., U.K., unitary authority,
  152,839 . . . . .68/F2
N. Little Rock, Ark., U.S., 60,433 . . . . .244/C3
N. Logan, Utah, U.S., 6,163 . . . . .350/C2
N. Lopham, Eng., U.K. 70/G2
N. Loup, Nebr., U.S., 339 . . . . .308/E2
N. Loup, Nebr., U.S., river 308/C1, E2
N. Lovell, Maine, U.S., 40 . . . . .286/B4
N. Lubec, Maine, U.S. 286/E4
N. Lyndon, Maine, U.S. 286/D3
N. Lynnwood, (Lake Serene-N. Lynnwood),
  Wash., U.S. .358/A4
N. Maalhosmadulu, Mald., atoll 127/A3
North Magnetic Pole 193/B13
N. Male, Mald., atoll 127/A2
N. Manchester, Ind., U.S., 6,260 . . . . .270/E2
N. Manitou, Mich., U.S. 294/C4
N. Manitou, Mich., U.S., island 294/C4
N. Mankato, Minn., U.S., 11,798 . . . . .298/C6
N. Marysville, Wash., U.S., 21,161 . . . . . .358/C1
N. Mayreau, St. Vin.-Gren., channel 208/A3
N. Miami, Fla., U.S., 59,880 . . . . . . .256/B6, H6
N. Miami, Okla., U.S., 433 . . . . .330/H1
N. Miami Beach, Fla., U.S., 40,786 . . . . . .256/B6
N. Middleboro, Mass., U.S., 850 . . . . .292/L5
N. Middletown, Ky., U.S., 562 . . . . .280/F2
N. Minch, Scot., U.K., strait 62/D3
N. Molton, Eng., U.K. 73/E2
N. Montpelier, Vt., U.S., 275 . . . . .352/C2
Northmoor, Mo., U.S., 399 . . . . .302/H5
N. Moose, Man., Can., lake 215/B2
N. Muskegon, Mich., U.S., 4,031 . . . . .294/C6
N. Myrtle Beach, S.C., U.S., 10,974 . . . . . .340/F3
N. Naples, Fla., U.S., 13,400 . . . . .256/G5
N. Newport, Maine, U.S., 60 . . . . .286/C4
N. Newport, N.H., U.S., 300 . . . . .312/B5

N. New Portland, Maine, U.S., 200 . . . . . .286/B4
N. Newry, Maine, U.S. 286/B4
N. New Salem, Mass., U.S., 275 . . . . .292/E2
N. Newton, Kans., U.S., 1,522 . . . . .276/E3
N. Nilandhe, Mald., atoll 127/A3
N. Oakley, Eng., U.K. 70/B4
N. Oaks, Minn., U.S., 3,883 . . . . .298/F5
N. Ogden, Utah, U.S., 15,026 . . . . . . .350/C2, E1
N. Olmsted, Ohio, U.S., 34,113 . . . . .328/F9, G3
N. Omak, Wash., U.S., 688 . . . . .358/F1
Northome, Minn., U.S., 230 . . . . .298/C3
Northop, Wales, U.K. 64/E1
N. Orange, Mass., U.S., 200 . . . . .292/E2
N. Ossetia-Alania, Russ., region 104/D5
N. Otis, Mass., U.S., 40 . . . . .292/B4
N. Oxford, Mass., U.S., 1,200 . . . . .292/G4
N. Palm Beach, Fla., U.S., 12,064 . . . . . . .256/B4
N. Paris, Maine, U.S., 150 . . . . .286/B4
N. Patchogue, N.Y., U.S., 7,825 . . . . .320/E2
N. Pekin, Ill., U.S., 1,574 . . . . .266/D3
N. Pelham, N.H., U.S., 750 . . . . .312/D6
N. Pembroke, Mass., U.S., 2,913 . . . . .292/L4
N. Perry, Maine, U.S., 200 . . . . .286/E4
N. Perry, Ohio, U.S., 838 . . . . .328/H2
N. Pittston, Maine, U.S. 286/C4
N. Plainfield, N.J., U.S., 21,103 . . . . .314/E2
N. Plains, Oreg., U.S., 1,605 . . . . .334/D2
N. Platte, Nebr., U.S., 23,878 . . . . .308/D2
N. Platte, Nebr., U.S., river 308/B2
N. Platte, Wyo., U.S., river 366/C3, D2
N. Platte N.W.R., Nebr., U.S. 308/A1
N. Platte N.W.R., Wyo., U.S. 366/F2
N. Plymouth, Mass., U.S., 3,593 . . . . .292/M5
N. Plympton, Mass., U.S., 475 . . . . .292/L5
North Pole 183
N. Pole, Alaska, U.S., 1,570 . . . . .240/F2
N. Pomfret, Vt., U.S., 175 . . . . .352/C3
Northport, Ala., U.S., 19,435 . . . . .238/B2
N. Port, Fla., U.S., 22,797 . . . . .256/F4
Northport, Mich., U.S., 648 . . . . .294/D4
Northport, Nebr., U.S., 50 . . . . .308/A2
Northport, N.Y., U.S., 7,606 . . . . .320/D2
Northport, Wash., U.S., 336 . . . . .358/H1
N. Portal, Sask., Can., 136 . . . . .227/H11
N. Port Norris, N.J., U.S., 80 . . . . .314/C5
N. Powder, Oreg., U.S., 489 . . . . .334/J2
N. Pownal, Vt., U.S., 300 . . . . .352/A5
N. Prairie, Wisc., U.S., 1,571 . . . . .364/E2
N. Providence, R.I., U.S., 32,411 . . . . .339/D2
N. P'yŏngan, N. Kor., province 116/A2
N. Randall, Ohio, U.S., 906 . . . . .328/H9
N. Randolph, Vt., U.S., 100 . . . . .352/B3
N. Reading, Mass., U.S., 13,837 . . . . .292/C6, K2
N. Redington Beach, Fla., U.S., 1,474 . . . .256/A3
N. Redwood, Minn., U.S. 298/B6
N. Rhine-Westphalia, Ger., state 86/A3
N. Richland Hills, Tex., U.S., 55,635 . . . . .346/A9
N. Richmond, Calif., U.S., 100 . . . . .312/B6
Northridge, (Clark County), Ohio, U.S., 6,853 . .328/C6
Northridge, (Montgomery County), Ohio, U.S.,
  8,487 . . . . .328/F1
N. Ridgeville, Ohio, U.S., 22,338 . . . . .328/F9
N. Rim, Ariz., U.S. 242/C1
N. River, N. Dak., U.S., 65 . . . . .326/J3
N. River Shores, Fla., U.S., 3,101 . . . . . . .256/A3
N. Riverside, Ill., U.S., 6,688 . . . . .266/B6
N. Robinson, Ohio, U.S., 211 . . . . .328/E4
N. Rock Sprs., Wyo., U.S., 1,974 . . . . .366/B3
N. Roe, Scot., U.K. 62/Q1
N. Ronaldsay, Scot., U.K., island 62/N1
Northrop, Minn., U.S., 262 . . . . .298/C7
N. Rose, N.Y., U.S., 700 . . . . .320/H4
N. Royalton, Ohio, U.S., 28,648 . . . . .328/G9
N. Runcton, Eng., U.K. 70/E1
N. Rustico, P.E.I., Can., 637 . . . . .224/B2
N. St. Paul, Minn., U.S., 11,929 . . . . .298/F5
N. Salem, Ind., U.S., 591 . . . . .270/C5
N. Salem, N.H., U.S., 1,600 . . . . .312/D6
Salt Lake, Utah, U.S., 8,749 . . . . . . .350/C3, E2
N. Sanbornton, N.H., U.S., 125 . . . . .312/C4
N. Sandwich, N.H., U.S., 60 . . . . .312/D4
N. Santee, S.C., U.S., 225 . . . . .340/E3
N. San Ysidro, N. Mex., U.S. 317/E2
N. Saskatchewan, Alta., Can., river . . .212/B5, D4
N. Scituate, Mass., U.S., 5,065 . . . . .292/L4
N. Scituate, R.I., U.S., 950 . . . . .339/C3
N. Sea, Neth., canal 84/B2
N. Sea, N.Y., U.S., 4,493 . . . . .320/G1
N. Seekonk, Mass., U.S., 2,598 . . . . .292/J5
N. Shapleigh, Maine, U.S., 100 . . . . .286/B5
N. Shields, Eng., U.K. 60/C2
N. Shields, Eng., U.K., 38,119 . . . . .66/F2
N. Shore, La., U.S., 1,800 . . . . .282/K6
N. Shrewsbury, Vt., U.S., 40 . . . . .352/B3
N. Siberian, Russ., lowland 104/G2
N. Sioux City, S. Dak., U.S., 2,288 . . . . . . .342/J5
N. Slope, Alaska, U.S., plain 240/D1
N. Somercotes, Eng., U.K. 66/J6
N. Spearfish, S. Dak., U.S., 2,306 . . . . . . .342/B3
N. Springfield, Oreg., U.S. 334/C3
N. Springfield, Penn., U.S., 300 . . . . .336/A2
N. Springfield, Vt., U.S., 1,100 . . . . .352/B4
N. Springfield, Va., U.S., 9,173 . . . . .354/M2
N. Stainmore, Eng., U.K. 66/D3
N. Star, Alta., Can. 212/B2
N. Star, Ohio, U.S., 209 . . . . .328/A5
N. Stonington, Conn., U.S., 4,991 . . . . . . .253/H4
N. Stratford, N.H., U.S., 100 . . . . .312/C2
N. Sulawesi, Indon., province 122/D1
N. Sumatra, Indon., province 122/A1
N. Sutton, N.H., U.S., 225 . . . . .312/C5
N. Swansea, Mass., U.S., 1,100 . . . . .292/J5
N. Sydney, N.S.W., Austl. . . . . .170/Inset IV
N. Syracuse, N.Y., U.S., 6,862 . . . . .320/J4
N. Taranaki, N.Z., bight 171/B2
N. Tawton, Eng., U.K. 73/E3
N. Terre Haute, Ind., U.S., 4,606 . . . . .270/B5
N. Thetford, Vt., U.S., 250 . . . . .352/C3
N. Thompson, Br. Col., Can., river 214/N5
N. Thoresby, Eng., U.K. 66/H6
N. Tidworth, Eng., U.K. 73/J2
N. Tidworth, Eng., U.K. 70/A4
N. Tisbury, Mass., U.S., 200 . . . . .292/M7
N. Toiyabe, Nev., U.S., peak 310/B2
N. Tolsta, Scot., U.K. 62/D2
Northton, Scot., U.K. 62/B3
N. Tonawanda, N.Y., U.S., 33,262 . . . . . . .320/D4
N. Topsail Beach, N.C., U.S., 843 . . . . . . .322/L6
N. Troy, Vt., U.S., 593 . . . . .352/C1
N. Truro, Mass., U.S., 500 . . . . .292/P4
N. Tunbridge, Vt., U.S., 125 . . . . .352/C3
N. Tunica, Miss., U.S., 1,450 . . . . .300/B1
N. Turner, Maine, U.S., 400 . . . . .286/B4
N. Tyneside, Eng., U.K., unitary authority,
  191,663 . . . . .66/E2
N. Uist, Scot., U.K., island 60/A1
N. Uist, Scot., U.K., island 62/B3
Northumberland, N.B., Can., county 217/C1
Northumberland, N.B., Can., strait 217/E2

Northumberland, N.S., Can., strait 221/D2
Northumberland, Ont., Can. 223/G3
Northumberland, Ont., Can., county 223/G3
Northumberland, P.E.I., Can., strait 224/C3
Northumberland, Eng., U.K., unitary authority,
  307,186 . . . . .66/D2
Northumberland, N.H., U.S., 2,438 . . . . . .312/C4
Northumberland, Penn., U.S., 3,714 . . . . .336/H4
Northumberland, Penn., U.S., county 94,556 . .336/H4
Northumberland, Va., U.S., county, 12,259 . .354/K5
Northumberland Natl. Park, Eng., U.K. 66/D2
N. Utica, Ill., U.S., 977 . . . . .266/D2
N. Uxbridge, Mass., U.S., 4,200 . . . . .292/H4
N. Vacherie, La., U.S., 2,411 . . . . .282/H7
Northvale, N.J., U.S., 4,460 . . . . .314/C1
N. Valley, N. Mex., U.S., 11,923 . . . . .317/D2
N. Vassalboro, Maine, U.S., 750 . . . . .286/C4
N. Vernon, Ind., U.S., 6,515 . . . . .270/E6
Northview, Mich., U.S., 14,730 . . . . .294/D6
N. Village, N.H., U.S., 125 . . . . .312/C6
Northville, Conn., U.S., 175 . . . . .253/E3
Northville, Mass., U.S., 2,400 . . . . .292/L4
Northville, Mich., U.S., 6,459 . . . . . . .294/A7, F7
Northville, N.Y., U.S., 1,139 . . . . .320/N4
Northville, S. Dak., U.S., 124 . . . . .342/G2
N. Wabasca, Alta., Can., lake 212/D3
N. Wade, Maine, U.S. 286/D2
N. Wakefield, N.H., U.S., 150 . . . . .312/D4
N. Wales, Penn., U.S., 3,342 . . . . .336/L5
Northwall, Scot., U.K. 62/N1
N. Walpole, N.H., U.S., 750 . . . . .312/B5
N. Walsham, Eng., U.K., 9,534 . . . . .70/G1
N. Waltham, Eng., U.K. 70/B4
N. Wardell, Mo., U.S., 170 . . . . .302/G5
N. Washington, Iowa, U.S., 118 . . . . .274/K1
N. Waterford, Maine, U.S., 70 . . . . .286/B4
Northway, Eng., U.K. 68/C6
Northway Jct., (Northway), Alaska, U.S., 95 . .240/G2
N. Weare, N.H., U.S., 350 . . . . .312/C5
N. Webster, Ind., U.S., 1,067 . . . . .270/E2
N. Weissport, (part of Weissport East),
  Penn., U.S. 336/K4
N. West, Austl., cape 170/A3
North-West, Came., province 153/A2
Northwest, Calif., U.S., cape 246/B4
Northwest, Mont., U.S., peak 306/A1
Northwest, N.C., U.S., 671 . . . . .322/J6
N. Westchester, Conn., U.S., 800 . . . . . . .253/F3
Northwest Angle, Minn., U.S., province . . .159/B2
Northwest Gander, Nfld., Can., river 218/D5
Northwest Harbor, N.Y., U.S., 3,059 . . . . . .320/G1
N. Westminster, Vt., U.S., 271 . . . . .352/C4
North West River, Nfld., Can., 551 . . . . . .218/A2
Northwest Sutherland N.P., Scot., U.K. 62/G2
Northwest Territories, Can., territory 208
N. Wheatley, Eng., U.K. 66/G6
Northwich, Eng., U.K., 34,520 . . . . .66/C6
Northwich, Eng., U.K., 34,520 . . . . .68/B3
N. Wildwood, N.J., U.S., 4,935 . . . . .314/D5
N. Wilkesboro, N.C., U.S., 4,116 . . . . .322/C2
N. Williston, N.D., U.S. 352/A2
N. Windham, Conn., U.S., 550 . . . . .253/G3
N. Windham, Maine, U.S., 4,568 . . . . .286/B5
N. Wolcott, Vt., U.S., 200 . . . . .352/C1
Northwood, Eng., U.K., 1,961 . . . . .68/B4
Northwood, Iowa, U.S., 2,050 . . . . .274/H1
Northwood, N.H., U.S., 3,640 . . . . .312/D5
Northwood, N. Dak., U.S., 959 . . . . .326/H2
Northwood, Ohio, U.S., 5,471 . . . . .328/C2
Northwood Ctr., N.H., U.S. 312/C3
Northwoods, Mo., U.S., 4,643 . . . . .302/H4
N. Woodstock, N.H., U.S., 750 . . . . .312/C3
Northwye, Mo., U.S., 550 . . . . .302/H4
N. Yelm, Wash., U.S., 2,793 . . . . .358/C4
N. York, Ont., Can. 223/E4
N. York, Penn., U.S., 1,689 . . . . .336/H6
N. York Moors Natl. Park, Eng., U.K. 66/F4
N. Yorkshire, Eng., U.K., unitary authority,
  569,660 . . . . .66/E4
N. Yorkshire, Eng., U.K., unitary authority,
  569,660 . . . . .68/D1
N. Zanesville, Ohio, U.S., 3,013 . . . . .328/E6
Norton, N.B., Can., 1,370 . . . . .217/D3
Norton, (East Shropshire), Eng., U.K. 68/C4
Norton, (N. Yorkshire), Eng., U.K. 68/F1
Norton, (N. Shropshire), Eng., U.K., 6,342 .68/F1
Norton, (Shropshire), Eng., U.K., 6,342 . . . .66/G4
Norton, Eng., U.K. 70/F2
Norton, Alaska, U.S., sound 240/C2
Norton, Kans., U.S., 3,012 . . . . .276/C2
Norton, Kans., U.S., county, 5,953 . . . . . . .276/C2
Norton, Mass., U.S., 18,056 . . . . .292/K5
Norton, Ohio, U.S., 11,523 . . . . .328/G3
Norton, Vt., U.S., 214 . . . . .352/D1
Norton, Va., U.S., 3,904 . . . . .354/C2
Norton, W. Va., U.S., 275 . . . . .360/G3
Norton, Wisc., U.S. 364/C5
Norton, Zimb. 160/B1
Norton Fitzwarren, Eng., U.K. 73/F2
Norton Heath, Eng., U.K. 70/E4
Norton Shores, Mich., U.S., 22,527 . . . . . .294/C6
Nortonville, Ky., U.S., 620 . . . . .276/G2
Nortonville, Ky., U.S., 1,264 . . . . .280/C3
Nortonville, Kans., U.S., 60 . . . . .326/G3
Norvegia, Antar., cape 192/B14
Norvin Green St. For., N.J., U.S. 314/A1
Norwalk, Calif., U.S., 103,298 . . . . .246/D10
Norwalk, Conn., U.S., 82,951 . . . . .253/B5
Norwalk, Conn., U.S., island 253/B5
Norwalk, Conn., U.S., river 253/B5
Norwalk, Iowa, U.S., 6,884 . . . . .274/G5
Norwalk, Ohio, U.S., 16,238 . . . . .328/E3
Norwalk, Wisc., U.S., 653 . . . . .364/C5
Norway, nation 78
Norway, nation .193/C1
Norway, Iowa, U.S., 601 . . . . .274/L4
Norway, Kans., U.S., 40 . . . . .276/E2
Norway, Maine, U.S., 4,611 . . . . .286/B4
Norway, Mich., U.S., 2,959 . . . . .294/B4
Norway, Oreg., U.S., 40 . . . . .334/B4
Norway, S.C., U.S., 389 . . . . .340/C4
Norway House, Man., Can., 456 . . . . .215/C2
Norwegian, sea .193/C1
Norwegian, Nun., Can., bay 193/C1
Norwegian, Nor., sea 79/Inset
Norwegian, Nor., sea 80/A1
Norwegian, Nor., sea 80/A2
Norwegian, Nor., sea 81/A1
Norwell, Mass., U.S., 9,765 . . . . .292/L4
Norwich, Ont., Can., 2,520 . . . . .223/E4
Norwich, Eng., U.K., 171,304, (185,420 metro.) . .70/G1
Norwich, Conn., U.S., 36,117 . . . . .253/G3
Norwich, Kans., U.S., 551 . . . . .276/E4
Norwich, Mass., U.S., 350 . . . . .292/C3

Oelemari 603

Norwich, N.Y., U.S., 7,355 . . . 320/K5
Norwich, N. Dak., U.S., 80 . . . 326/E1
Norwich, Ohio, U.S., 113 . . . 328/G6
Norwich, Vt., U.S., 3,544 . . . 352/C3
Norwick, Scot., U.K. . . . 62/Q1
Norwood, Colo., U.S., 438 . . . 250/B3
Norwood, Ga., U.S., 299 . . . 260/F5
Norwood, Ill., U.S., 473 . . . 266/D3
Norwood, Iowa, U.S. . . . 274/H5
Norwood, Ky., U.S., 395 . . . 280/B2
Norwood, La., U.S., 337 . . . 282/G5
Norwood, Mass., U.S., 28,587 . . . 292/K4
Norwood, Minn., U.S., 3,108 . . . 298/C6
Norwood, Mo., U.S., 552 . . . 302/D4
Norwood, N.J., U.S., 5,751 . . . 314/C1, F2
Norwood, N.Y., U.S., 1,685 . . . 320/M1
Norwood, N.C., U.S., 2,216 . . . 322/E4
Norwood, Ohio, U.S., 21,675 . . . 328/B7, B9
Norwood, Penn., U.S., 5,985 . . . 336/L7
Nossob, Bots., *river* . . . 160/A3
Nossob, Nam., *river* . . . 160/C3
Nossob, S. Afr., *river* . . . 162/B2
Nosy Be, Madag., *island* . . . 163/B1
Nosy Ste. Marie, Madag., *island* . . . 163/B2
Notasulga, Ala., U.S., 916 . . . 238/D3
Noteć, Pol., *river* . . . 83/C2, D2
Notikewan Prov. Park, Alta., Can. . . . 212/B2
Noto, Jap., *peninsula* . . . 114/C2
Notre-Dame, N.B., Can. . . . 217/E2
Notre Dame, Nfld., Can., *bay* . . . 218/D4
Notre Dame, Maine, U.S. . . . 286/D1
Notre-Dame-de-la-Merci, Que., Can., 811 . . . 226/B5
Notre-Dame-de-la-Salette, Que., Can., 706 . . . 226/A6
Notre-Dame-de-Lorette, Que., Can. . . . 226/D2
Notre Dame de Lourdes, Man., Can., 619 . . . 215/B4
Notre-Dame-du-Bon-Conseil, Que., Can. . . . 226/D5
Notre-Dame-du-Lac, Que., Can., 2,152 . . . 226/H4
Notre-Dame-du-Laus, Que., Can., 1,382 . . . 226/A5
Notre Dame Jct., Nfld., Can. . . . 218/D4
Nottingham, Nun., Can., *island* . . . 220/N4
Nottingham, Eng., U.K. . . . 60/C3
Nottingham, Eng., U.K., 270,222, (613,726 *metro.*) . . . 68/E4
Nottingham, Eng., U.K., 270,222, (613,726 *metro.*) . . . 70/B1
Nottingham, Eng., U.K., *unitary authority*, 266,995 . . . 68/E4
Nottingham, Eng., U.K., *unitary authority*, 266,995 . . . 70/B1
Nottingham, N.H., U.S., 3,701 . . . 312/D5
Nottinghamshire, Eng., U.K., *unitary authority*, 748,503 . . . 66/F6
Nottinghamshire, Eng., U.K., *unitary authority*, 748,503 . . . 68/E3
Nottinghamshire, Eng., U.K., *unitary authority*, 748,503 . . . 70/C1
Nottoway, Va., U.S., *county*, 15,725 . . . 354/G6
Nottoway C.H., (Nottoway), Va., U.S., 100 . . . 354/G6
Notus, Ida., U.S., 458 . . . 264/A6
Nouâdhibou, Maur., (75,976 *metro.*) . . . 147/A2
Nouakchott, Maur., *capital*, (611,883 *metro.*) . . . 147/A3
Nounan, Ida., U.S. . . . 264/F7
Nouvelle, Que., Can., 1,960 . . . 226/K3
Nova, Ohio, U.S., 425 . . . 328/F3
Nova Gorica, Slove., 35,151 . . . 98/A3
Nova Iguaçu, Braz., 915,364 . . . 188/Inset I
Novara, It. . . . 95/B1
Nova Scotia, Can., *province* . . . 209
Novato, Calif., U.S., 47,630 . . . 246/H1
Novaya Zemlya, Russ., *island* . . . 193/B3
Novaya Zemlya, Russ., *islands* . . . 104/D2
Novelty, Mo., U.S., 119 . . . 302/D1
Nové Zámky, Slvk., 149,594 . . . 92/B3
Novi, Mich., U.S., 47,386 . . . 294/A6, F7
Novice, (Coleman County), Tex., U.S., 142 . . . 346/J4
Novice, (Lamar County), Tex., U.S. . . . 346/N2
Novinger, Mo., U.S., 534 . . . 302/D1
Novi Pazar, Serb.-Mont. . . . 99/B3
Novi Sad, Serb.-Mont., 290,589 . . . 99/A2
Novokuznetsk, Russ., 564,353, (579,250 *metro.*) . 104/F4
Novo Mesto, Slove., 40,735 . . . 98/C3
Novosibirsk, Russ., 1,400,328 . . . 104/F4
Novra, Man., Can. . . . 215/A3
Nowata, Okla., U.S., 3,971 . . . 330/G1
Nowata, Okla., U.S., *county*, 10,569 . . . 330/G1
Nowitna N.W.R., Alaska, U.S. . . . 240/E2
Nowlin, S. Dak., U.S., 80 . . . 342/D3
Nowood, Wyo., U.S., *river* . . . 366/C1
Nowshak, Afg., *mountain* . . . 129/C1
Nowshak, Pak., *mountain* . . . 129/D2
Nowy Sącz, Pol. . . . 83/E4
Noxapater, Miss., U.S., 419 . . . 300/C3
Noxen, Penn., U.S., 500 . . . 336/J3
Noxon, Mont., U.S., 230 . . . 306/A2
Noxubee, Miss., U.S., *county*, 12,548 . . . 300/D2
Noxubee, Miss., U.S., *river* . . . 300/D2
Noxubee N.W.R., Miss., U.S. . . . 300/D2
Noxville, Tex., U.S. . . . 346/J5
Noyack, N.Y., U.S., 2,696 . . . 320/G1
Noyes, Minn., U.S. . . . 298/A2
Noyes Terrace, N.H., U.S. . . . 312/D6
Nsanje, Mal. . . . 159/C3
Nsawam, Gha. . . . 150/B4
Nsok, Eq. Gui. . . . 154/D3
Nsoko, Swaz. . . . 161/B3
Nsukka, Nig. . . . 152/D4
Ntem, Came., *river* . . . 153/B3
Nuangola, Penn., U.S., 671 . . . 336/K3
Nuba, Sudan, *mountains* . . . 145/C3
Nubian, Sudan, *desert* . . . 145/C1
Nubieber, Calif., U.S., 50 . . . 246/D1
Nuckolls, Nebr., U.S., *county*, 5,057 . . . 308/F3
Nucla, Colo., U.S., 734 . . . 250/B3
Nueces, Tex., U.S., *county*, 313,645 . . . 346/L8
Nueces, Tex., U.S., *river* . . . 346/K7
Nueltin, Man., Can., *lake* . . . 215/D1
Nueltin, Nun., Can., *lake* . . . 220/J4
Nueva Asunción, Para., *department* . . . 187/B2
Nueva Gerona, Cuba . . . 204/A2
Nueva Gerona, Cuba . . . 204/B2
Nueva Loja, Ecua. . . . 185/C2
Nueva Ocotepeque, Hond. . . . 202/A2
Nueva Palmira, Uru. . . . 187/A2
Nueva Rosita, Mex. . . . 200/D2
Nueva San Salvador, El. Salv., 116,575 . . . 203/A2
Nueva Segovia, Nicar., *department* . . . 202/A2
Nueve Esparta, Ven., *state* . . . 182/D1
Nuevitas, Cuba . . . 204/D2
Nuevo Casas Grandes, Mex., 50,378, (54,390 *metro.*) . . . 200/C1
Nuevo Laredo, Mex., 308,828, (310,915 *metro.*) . . . 200/E2
Nuevo León, Mex., *state* . . . 200/D2
Nuevo Rocafuerte, Ecua. . . . 185/D3
Nugaal, Som., *valley* . . . 157/B2
Nugent, Tex., U.S., 50 . . . 346/J3
Nuguria, P.N.G., *islands* . . . 172/B2
Nui, Tuv., *island* . . . 174/B2
Nuiqsut, Alaska, U.S., 433 . . . 240/E1
Nuku'alofa, Tonga, *capital*, 21,538, (30,336 *metro.*) . . . 175/B4
Nukufetau, Tuv., *island* . . . 174/C2
Nukulaelae, Tuv., *island* . . . 174/C3
Nukuoro, Micr., *atoll* . . . 172/C2
Nukus, Uzb., 199,000 . . . 132/A2
Nulato, Alaska, U.S., 336 . . . 240/D2
Nullarbor, Austl., *plain* . . . 170/B3
Numa, Iowa, U.S., 109 . . . 274/J6
Numazu, Jap. . . . 114/C3
Numila, Hawaii, U.S. . . . 262/C2
Numin, Sask., Can., *lake* . . . 227/H1
Nunavut, Can., *territory* . . . 208
Nunawading, Vic., Austl. . . . 170/Inset V
Nunda, N.Y., U.S., 1,330 . . . 320/F5
Nunda, S. Dak., U.S., 47 . . . 342/H3
Nuneaton, Eng., U.K., 66,715 . . . 68/E4
Nuneaton, Eng., U.K., 66,715 . . . 70/B1
Nunez, Ga., U.S., 131 . . . 260/G7
Nunivak, U.S., *island* . . . 193/D10
Nunivak, Alaska, U.S., *island* . . . 240/B3
Nunn, Colo., U.S., 471 . . . 250/F1
Nunnelly, Tenn., U.S., 150 . . . 344/G3
Nunnington, Eng., U.K. . . . 66/G4
Ñuñoa, Chile . . . 190/Inset
Nunwick, Eng., U.K. . . . 66/D2
Nuoro, It. . . . 95/B2
Nuremberg, Ger., 486,628 . . . 86/B4
Nuremberg, Penn., U.S., 700 . . . 336/J4
Nusayriyah, Jabal an, Syria, *mountains* . . . 134/A2
Nutak, Nfld., Can. . . . 218/E3
Nutbush, Tenn., U.S., 125 . . . 344/C3
Nutley, Eng., U.K. . . . 70/E4
Nutley, N.J., U.S., 27,362 . . . 314/B2, E2
Nutria, Colo., U.S., 100 . . . 250/C4
Nutria, Wyo., U.S. . . . 366/A3
Nutrioso, Ariz., U.S., 40 . . . 242/F4
Nutt, N. Mex., U.S. . . . 317/C5
Nutter Fort, W. Va., U.S., 1,686 . . . 360/F2
Nutting Lake, Mass., U.S., 5,700 . . . 292/B6, J2
Nutt's Corner, N. Ire., U.K. . . . 65/E2
Nuuk, (Godthåb), Grld., *capital*, 13,445 . . . 193/B2
Nuuk, (Godthåb), Grld., *capital*, 13,445 . . . 193/C16
Nu'ulua, Sam., *island* . . . 175/D3
Nu'utele, Sam., *island* . . . 175/D3
Nuwara Eliya, Sri Lan. . . . 126/B5
Nuyaka, Okla., U.S., 60 . . . 330/F2
Nyaba, Rwa., *river* . . . 158/B2
Nyabarongo, Rwa., *river* . . . 158/C2
Nyack, N.Y., U.S., 6,737 . . . 320/B1
Nyala, Sudan, 227,183 . . . 145/B2
Nyala, Nev., U.S. . . . 310/C2
Nyanga, Gabon, *river* . . . 155/A2
Nyanza, Kenya, *province* . . . 157/C4
Nyanza, Rwa. . . . 158/B2
Nyasa, (Malawi), Moz., *lake* . . . 161/B2
Nyasa, (Malawi), Tan., *lake* . . . 158/B3
Nyborg, Den. . . . 79/C3
Nye, Mont., U.S. . . . 306/E4
Nye, Nev., U.S., *county*, 32,485 . . . 310/B3
Nyeri, Kenya, 91,258 . . . 157/D4
Nyetane, Swaz., *river* . . . 161/B2
Nyewood, Eng., U.K. . . . 70/C5
Nyika, Mal., *plateau* . . . 159/B2
Nyíregyháza, Hun., 113,000 . . . 91/C2
Nyíregyháza, Hun. . . . 91/C2
Nykøbing, Den. . . . 79/C4
Nyoman, Bela., *river* . . . 82/B3
Nyong, Came., *river* . . . 153/B3
Nysa, Pol. . . . 83/C3
Nyssa, Oreg., U.S., 3,163 . . . 334/J4
Nzérékoré, Guin., 55,356 . . . 149/D4
Nzeto, Ang. . . . 159/B2
Nzi, C. d'Iv., *river* . . . 150/D3
Nzo, C. d'Iv., *river* . . . 150/C3
Nzoia, Kenya, *river* . . . 157/C3
Nzwani, (Anjouan), Com., *island* . . . 163/B2
Oacoma, S. Dak., U.S., 390 . . . 342/F4
Oadby, Eng., U.K., 18,538 . . . 68/E4
Oadby, Eng., U.K., 18,538 . . . 70/B1
Oahe, N. Dak., U.S., *lake* . . . 326/E3, E4
Oahe, N. Dak., U.S., *lake* . . . 342/E1, E3
Oahe Dam, S. Dak., U.S. . . . 342/E3
Oahu, Hawaii, U.S., *island* . . . 262/B5, D2, K1
Oak, Nebr., U.S., 60 . . . 308/G3
Oak Bluffs, Mass., U.S., 3,713 . . . 292/M7
Oakboro, N.C., U.S., 1,198 . . . 322/E4
Oak Brook, Ill., U.S., 8,702 . . . 266/B6
Oakbrook, Ky., U.S., 7,726 . . . 280/F2
Oakbrook Terrace, Ill., U.S., 2,300 . . . 266/B6
Oak City, N.C., U.S., 339 . . . 322/L3
Oak City, Utah, U.S., 650 . . . 350/B4
Oak Creek, Colo., U.S., 849 . . . 250/D1
Oak Creek, Wisc., U.S., 28,456 . . . 364/F2, F6
Oakdale, Calif., U.S., 15,503 . . . 246/E5
Oakdale, Conn., U.S., 1,100 . . . 253/G4
Oakdale, Fla., U.S., 125 . . . 256/C1
Oakdale, Ill., U.S., 213 . . . 266/D5
Oakdale, Ky., U.S., 4,937 . . . 280/B3
Oakdale, La., U.S., 8,137 . . . 282/D5
Oakdale, Mass., U.S., 1,100 . . . 292/G3
Oakdale, Minn., U.S., 26,653 . . . 298/F5
Oakdale, Nebr., U.S., 345 . . . 308/G1
Oakdale, Penn., U.S., 1,551 . . . 336/A5
Oakdale, Tenn., U.S., 244 . . . 344/M3
Oakdale, Wisc., U.S., 297 . . . 364/C5
Oakes, N. Dak., U.S., 1,979 . . . 326/G3
Oakesdale, Wash., U.S., 420 . . . 358/H2
Oakfield, Ga., U.S., 125 . . . 260/D8
Oakfield, Maine, U.S., 732 . . . 286/D2
Oakfield, N.Y., U.S., 1,805 . . . 320/E4
Oakfield, Tenn., U.S., 100 . . . 344/D3
Oakfield, Wisc., U.S., 1,012 . . . 364/E5
Oakford, Eng., U.K. . . . 73/E3
Oakford, Ill., U.S., 309 . . . 266/D3
Oak Forest, Ill., U.S., 28,051 . . . 266/B6
Oak Grove, Ala., U.S., 457 . . . 238/C2
Oak Grove, Ark., U.S., 376 . . . 244/B1
Oak Grove, Del., U.S. . . . 255/C4
Oak Grove, Ill., U.S., 1,318 . . . 266/C2
Oak Grove, Ky., U.S., 7,064 . . . 280/C4
Oak Grove, (Lincoln Parish), La., U.S. . . . 282/D2
Oak Grove, (W. Carroll Parish), La., U.S., 2,174 . . . 282/G1
Oak Grove, Mich., U.S., 700 . . . 294/E5
Oak Grove, Minn., U.S., 6,903 . . . 298/D5
Oak Grove, Miss., U.S., 1,400 . . . 300/C4
Oak Grove, (Franklin County), Mo., U.S., 382 . . . 302/E3
Oak Grove, (Jackson County), Mo., U.S., 5,535 . . . 302/B3, J5
Oak Grove, Okla., U.S. . . . 330/F1
Oak Grove, Oreg., U.S., 12,808 . . . 334/A3
Oak Grove, S.C., U.S., 8,183 . . . 340/A3, E2
Oak Grove, Tenn., U.S., 4,072 . . . 344/S2
Oak Grove, Va., U.S., 350 . . . 354/J4
Oak Grove Hts., Ark., U.S., 727 . . . 244/E1
Oakham, Eng., U.K., 8,691 . . . 68/F4
Oakham, Eng., U.K., 8,691 . . . 70/C1
Oakham, Mass., U.S., 1,673 . . . 292/F3
Oak Harbor, Ohio, U.S., 2,841 . . . 328/D2
Oak Harbor, Wash., U.S., 19,795 . . . 358/C1
Oakhaven, Ark., U.S., 54 . . . 244/B4
Oak Hill, Ala., U.S. . . . 238/B4
Oak Hill, Fla., U.S., 1,378 . . . 256/H3
Oak Hill, Kans., U.S. . . . 276/E2
Oak Hill, Mo., U.S., 60 . . . 302/E3
Oak Hill, N.C., U.S., 90 . . . 322/H2
Oak Hill, Ohio, U.S., 1,685 . . . 328/E8
Oak Hill, Tenn., U.S., 4,493 . . . 344/H2
Oak Hill, Tex., U.S., 400 . . . 346/D2
Oak Hill, W. Va., U.S., 7,589 . . . 360/D5
Oak Hills, Oreg., U.S., 9,050 . . . 334/A2
Oak Hills Place, La., U.S., 7,996 . . . 282/G6
Oakhurst, Calif., U.S., 2,868 . . . 246/F5
Oakhurst, N.J., U.S., 4,152 . . . 314/E3
Oakhurst, Okla., U.S., 2,731 . . . 330/F1
Oak Lake, Man., Can., 359 . . . 215/A4
Oakland, Ark., U.S., 100 . . . 244/C1
Oakland, Calif., U.S., 399,484 . . . 246/C5, J2
Oakland, Fla., U.S., 936 . . . 256/C4
Oakland, Ill., U.S., 996 . . . 266/E4
Oakland, Iowa, U.S., 1,487 . . . 274/D5
Oakland, Ky., U.S., 260 . . . 280/D3
Oakland, La., U.S. . . . 282/E1
Oakland, Maine, U.S., 5,959 . . . 286/C4
Oakland, (Carroll County), Md., U.S., 2,100 . . . 288/G2
Oakland, (Garrett County), Md., U.S., 1,930 . . . 288/A4
Oakland, Mich., U.S., *county*, 1,194,156 . . . 294/A6, F7
Oakland, Minn., U.S., 60 . . . 298/D7
Oakland, Miss., U.S., 586 . . . 300/C1
Oakland, Mo., U.S., 1,540 . . . 302/H3
Oakland, Nebr., U.S., 1,367 . . . 308/H2
Oakland, N.J., U.S., 12,466 . . . 314/B1, E1
Oakland, Okla., U.S., 674 . . . 330/F3
Oakland, Oreg., U.S., 954 . . . 334/C4
Oakland, (Lawrence County), Penn., U.S., 1,516 . . . 336/A4
Oakland, (Susquehanna County), Penn., U.S., 622 . . . 336/K2
Oakland, Tenn., U.S., 1,279 . . . 344/B4
Oakland, Tex., U.S., 50 . . . 346/M6
Oakland Acres, Iowa, U.S., 166 . . . 274/J4
Oakland City, Ind., U.S., 2,588 . . . 270/B8
Oakland Park, Fla., U.S., 30,966 . . . 256/B5, H5
Oakland Park, Mo., U.S. . . . 302/B4
Oak Lawn, Ill., U.S., 55,245 . . . 266/B6, F2
Oaklawn, (Oaklawn-Sunview), Kans., U.S., 3,135 . . . 276/E4
Oakleigh, Vic., Austl. . . . 170/Inset V
Oak Level, Ky., U.S. . . . 280/B4
Oakley, Eng., U.K. . . . 70/B3
Oakley, Scot., U.K., 4,123 . . . 62/J6
Oakley, Calif., U.S., 25,619 . . . 246/L1
Oakley, Ida., U.S., 668 . . . 264/D7
Oakley, Ill., U.S., 125 . . . 266/E4
Oakley, Kans., U.S., 2,173 . . . 276/B2
Oakley, Mich., U.S., 339 . . . 294/E6
Oakley, Miss., U.S., 250 . . . 300/B3
Oakley, Utah, U.S., 948 . . . 350/C3
Oaklyn, N.J., U.S., 4,188 . . . 314/B3
Oakman, Ala., U.S., 944 . . . 238/B2
Oakman, Ga., U.S. . . . 260/B2
Oakmont, Penn., U.S., 6,911 . . . 336/B4
Oakner, Man., Can. . . . 215/A4
Oak Orchard, Del., U.S., 750 . . . 255/D6
Oak Park, Ga., U.S., 366 . . . 260/G7
Oak Park, Ill., U.S., 52,524 . . . 266/B6, F2
Oak Park, Ind., U.S., 5,379 . . . 270/E8
Oak Park, Mich., U.S., 29,793 . . . 294/A6, F7
Oak Park, Minn., U.S., 125 . . . 298/D5
Oakpark, Va., U.S. . . . 354/G4
Oak Park Hts., Minn., U.S., 3,957 . . . 298/E5
Oak Pt., Man., Can. . . . 215/C4
Oak Pt., N.B., Can. . . . 217/C3
Oak Pt., Tex., U.S., 1,747 . . . 346/B8
Oakport, Minn., U.S., 1,334 . . . 298/A4
Oak Ridge, La., U.S., 142 . . . 282/F1
Oak Ridge, Mo., U.S., 202 . . . 302/G4
Oak Ridge, N.J., U.S., 750 . . . 314/E1
Oakridge, Oreg., U.S., 3,148 . . . 334/D4
Oak Ridge, Tenn., U.S., 27,387 . . . 344/N2
Oak Ridge, Tex., U.S., 400 . . . 346/M3
Oak Ridge North, Tex., U.S., 2,991 . . . 346/A5
Oak River, Man., Can. . . . 215/A4
Oaks, Mo., U.S., 136 . . . 302/H5
Oaks, Okla., U.S., 412 . . . 330/H1
Oak Shade, N.J., U.S., 1,500 . . . 314/D4
Oakshade, Ohio, U.S., 275 . . . 328/B2
Oakton, Ky., U.S., 150 . . . 280/A4
Oakton, Va., U.S., 29,348 . . . 354/L2
Oaktown, Ind., U.S., 633 . . . 270/B7
Oak Vale, Miss., U.S., 150 . . . 300/C4
Oakvale, W. Va., U.S., 142 . . . 360/E6
Oak Valley, Kans., U.S. . . . 276/F4
Oak Valley, N.J., U.S., 3,747 . . . 314/A4
Oakview, Man., Can. . . . 215/B3
Oakview, Mo., U.S., 386 . . . 302/H4
Oakville, Man., Can. . . . 215/C4
Oakville, Ont., Can., 144,738 . . . 223/F4
Oakville, Conn., U.S., 8,618 . . . 253/C3
Oakville, Iowa, U.S., 439 . . . 274/M5
Oakville, La., U.S., 125 . . . 282/J7, K4
Oakville, Md., U.S., 50 . . . 288/M7
Oakville, Mo., U.S., 35,309 . . . 302/F3, H4
Oakville, Tex., U.S. . . . 346/K7
Oakville, Wash., U.S., 675 . . . 358/B3
Oakwood, Ga., U.S., 2,689 . . . 260/D3
Oakwood, Ill., U.S., 1,502 . . . 266/F3
Oakwood, Md., U.S., 425 . . . 288/K1
Oakwood, Mo., U.S., 197 . . . 302/H5
Oakwood, (Cuyahoga County), Ohio, U.S., 3,667 . . . 328/H9
Oakwood, (Montgomery County), Ohio, U.S., 9,215 . . . 328/F2
Oakwood, (Paulding County), Ohio, U.S., 607 . . . 328/B3
Oakwood, Okla., U.S., 72 . . . 330/D2
Oakwood, Penn., U.S., 2,249 . . . 336/A3
Oakwood, Tenn., U.S., 350 . . . 344/F1
Oakwood, Tex., U.S., 471 . . . 346/N4
Oakwood Beach, N.J., U.S., 700 . . . 314/B4
Oakwood Hills, Ill., U.S., 2,194 . . . 266/A5
Oakwood Park, Mo., U.S., 183 . . . 302/H4
Oakworth, Eng., U.K. . . . 66/E5
Oamaru, N.Z. . . . 171/B4
Oark, Ark., U.S., 70 . . . 244/B2
Oasis, Calif., U.S. . . . 246/H5
Oasis, Nev., U.S., 200 . . . 310/C1
Oasis, Utah, U.S., 125 . . . 350/B4
Oatfield, Oreg., U.S., 15,750 . . . 334/A2
Oatland, S.C., U.S., 400 . . . 340/E3
Oatman, Ariz., U.S., 150 . . . 242/A2
Oaxaca, Mex., *state capital*, 251,846, (256,130 *metro.*) . . . 200/E4
Oaxaca, Mex., *state* . . . 200/E4
Ob', Russ., *river* . . . 104/E3
Ob', Russ., *river* . . . 193/C4
Oban, Nig., *hills* . . . 152/E5
Oban, Scot., U.K. . . . 60/B2
Oban, Scot., U.K., 8,120 . . . 62/F6
Obed, Alta., Can. . . . 212/B4
Oberammergau, Ger. . . . 86/B5
Oberbayern, Ger., *department* . . . 86/B4
Oberhausen, Ger., 222,349 . . . 86/A3
Oberlin, Kans., U.S., 1,994 . . . 276/B2
Oberlin, La., U.S., 1,853 . . . 282/D5
Oberlin, Ohio, U.S., 8,195 . . . 328/F3
Oberon, N. Dak., U.S., 81 . . . 326/F2
Oberpfalz, Ger., *department* . . . 86/B4
Oberpfälzer Wald, Ger., *mountains* . . . 86/C4
Obert, Nebr., U.S., 49 . . . 308/G1
Obetz, Ohio, U.S., 3,977 . . . 328/E10
Obi, Indon., *island* . . . 122/D2
Obihiro, Jap. . . . 114/Inset I
Obion, Tenn., U.S., 1,134 . . . 344/C2
Obion, Tenn., U.S., *county*, 32,450 . . . 344/C2
Oblong, Ill., U.S., 1,580 . . . 266/F4
Obo, C.A.R. . . . 154/C2
Obock, Dji. . . . 156/C2
O'Brien, Fla., U.S., 80 . . . 256/F1
O'Brien, Iowa, U.S., *county*, 15,102 . . . 274/C1
O'Brien, Oreg., U.S., 225 . . . 334/C5
O'Brien, Tex., U.S., 132 . . . 346/J2
Obuasi, Gha. . . . 150/B3
Obwalden, Switz., *canton* . . . 90/C2
Ocala, Fla., U.S., 45,943, (258,916 *metro.*) . . . 256/F2
Ocala Natl. For., Fla., U.S. . . . 256/G2
Ocate, N. Mex., U.S., 100 . . . 317/E1
Occidental, Peru, *mountains* . . . 185/B2, C4
Occoquan, Va., U.S., 759 . . . 354/J3, M3
Occoquan, Va., U.S., *reservoir* . . . 354/L2
Ocean, N.J., U.S., *county*, 510,916 . . . 314/E4
Oceana, Mich., U.S., *county*, 26,873 . . . 294/C6
Oceana, W. Va., U.S., 1,550 . . . 360/C5
Ocean Beach, N.Y., U.S., 138 . . . 320/D2
Ocean Bluff, Mass., U.S., 5,100 . . . 292/M4
Ocean Breeze Park, Fla., U.S., 463 . . . 256/A3, H4
Ocean City, Md., U.S., 7,173 . . . 288/P6
Ocean City, N.J., U.S., 15,378 . . . 314/D5
Ocean City, Wash., U.S., 217 . . . 358/A2
Ocean Falls, Br. Col., Can. . . . 214/J5
Ocean Gate, N.J., U.S., 2,076 . . . 314/E4
Ocean Grove, Mass., U.S., 3,012 . . . 292/K6
Ocean Grove, N.J., U.S., 4,256 . . . 314/E3
Oceania, *region* . . . 161
Ocean Isle Beach, N.C., U.S., 426 . . . 322/J7
Oceano, Calif., U.S., 7,260 . . . 246/E7
Ocean Park, Wash., U.S., 1,459 . . . 358/A3
Ocean Pines, Md., U.S., 10,496 . . . 288/P6
Oceanport, N.J., U.S., 5,807 . . . 314/E3
Ocean Ridge, Fla., U.S., 1,636 . . . 256/B5
Ocean Shores, Wash., U.S., 3,836 . . . 358/A3
Oceanside, Calif., U.S., 161,029 . . . 246/H9
Oceanside, N.Y., U.S., 32,733 . . . 320/C2
Oceanside, Oreg., U.S., 326 . . . 334/C2
Ocean Sprs., Miss., U.S., 17,225 . . . 300/D5
Ocean View, Del., U.S., 1,006 . . . 255/D6
Ocean View, N.J., U.S., 450 . . . 314/D5
Oceanville, Maine, U.S., 100 . . . 286/D4
Oceanville, N.J., U.S., 475 . . . 314/E5
Och'amch'ire, Geo. . . . 103/A3
Ochelata, Okla., U.S., 494 . . . 330/G1
Ocheyedan, Iowa, U.S., 536 . . . 274/C1
Ocheyedan Mound, Iowa, U.S. . . . 274/C1
Ochil, Scot., U.K., *hills* . . . 60/B2
Ochiltree, Tex., U.S., *county*, 9,006 . . . 346/G8
Ochlocknee, Ga., U.S., 605 . . . 260/C1
Ochlockonee, Fla., U.S., *river* . . . 256/D1
Ochlockonee, Ga., U.S., *river* . . . 260/C10
Ochoa, Tex., U.S. . . . 346/D6
Ochoco, Oreg., U.S., *mountains* . . . 334/F3
Ochoco Natl. For., Oreg., U.S. . . . 334/F3, G4
Ochopee, Fla., U.S. . . . 256/G6
Ocho Rios, Jam. . . . 206/B2
Ochre River, Man., Can. . . . 215/B3
Ocilla, Ga., U.S., 3,270 . . . 260/E8
Ocmulge, Ga., U.S., *river* . . . 260/E7
Ocmulgee N.M., Ga., U.S. . . . 260/D6
Ocoa, Dom. Rep., *bay* . . . 205/B2
Ocoee, Fla., U.S., 24,391 . . . 256/C4, G3
Ocoee, Tenn., U.S., 400 . . . 344/M4
Oconee, Ga., U.S., 280 . . . 260/F6
Oconee, Ga., U.S., *county*, 26,225 . . . 260/D4
Oconee, Ga., U.S., *lake* . . . 260/E5
Oconee, Ga., U.S., *river* . . . 260/D3, F6
Oconee, Ill., U.S., 202 . . . 266/D4
Oconee, S.C., U.S., *county*, 66,215 . . . 340/A2
Oconee Natl. For., Ga., U.S. . . . 260/D5, E4
Oconomowoc, Wisc., U.S., 12,382 . . . 364/E2, E5
Oconomowoc Lake, Wisc., U.S., 564 . . . 364/E2
Oconto, Nebr., U.S., 141 . . . 308/E2
Oconto, Wisc., U.S., 4,708 . . . 364/F4
Oconto, Wisc., U.S., *county*, 35,634 . . . 364/E3
Oconto Falls, Wisc., U.S., 2,843 . . . 364/E4
Ocotal, Nicar. . . . 202/A2
Ocotepeque, Hond., *department* . . . 202/A2
Ocotillo, Calif., U.S., 296 . . . 246/K10
Ocotillo Wells, Calif., U.S., 100 . . . 246/J9
Ocotlán, Mex., 75,942, (84,200 *metro.*) . . . 200/D3
Ocqueoc, Mich., U.S. . . . 294/E4
Ocracoke, N.C., U.S., 769 . . . 322/N4
Ocracoke, N.C., U.S., *inlet* . . . 322/N4
Octa, Ohio, U.S., 83 . . . 328/C6
Octave, Ariz., U.S., 50 . . . 242/C3
Octavia, Nebr., U.S., 145 . . . 308/G2
Octavia, Okla., U.S., 60 . . . 330/H3
Oda, Gha. . . . 150/B4
Odanah, Wisc., U.S., 254 . . . 364/C2
Odebolt, Iowa, U.S., 1,153 . . . 274/D3
Odei, Man., Can., *river* . . . 215/C1
Odell, Ill., U.S., 1,014 . . . 266/E2
Odell, Ind., U.S., 80 . . . 270/B4
Odell, Nebr., U.S., 345 . . . 308/H3
Odell, Oreg., U.S., 1,849 . . . 334/E2
Odell, Tex., U.S., 80 . . . 346/J1
Odem, Tex., U.S., 2,499 . . . 346/L8
Odemira, Port. . . . 93/A4
Oden, Ark., U.S., 220 . . . 244/B3
Odense, Den., 144,849, (179,487 *metro.*) . . . 79/C3
Odense, Den., *fjord* . . . 79/C3
Odenton, Md., U.S., 20,534 . . . 288/H3
Odenville, Ala., U.S., 1,131 . . . 238/C2
Odenwald, Ger., *forest* . . . 86/B4
Oder, Ger., *river* . . . 86/C2
Oder, Pol., *river* . . . 83/B2, C3
Oderhaff, Ger., *lake* . . . 86/C2
Odesa, Ukr., 1,002,246 . . . 102/C3
Odesa, Ukr., *oblast* . . . 102/B3
Odessa, Del., U.S., 286 . . . 255/B3
Odessa, Fla., U.S., 3,173 . . . 256/D6, F3
Odessa, Minn., U.S., 113 . . . 298/A5
Odessa, Mo., U.S., 4,818 . . . 302/C3
Odessa, Nebr., U.S., 175 . . . 308/E3
Odessa, N.Y., U.S., 617 . . . 320/H6
Odessa, Tex., U.S., 90,943, (237,132 *metro.*) . . . 346/F4
Odessa, Wash., U.S., 957 . . . 358/G2
Odienné, C. d'Iv. . . . 150/C2
Odiham, Eng., U.K., 3,531 . . . 70/C4
Odin, Ill., U.S., 1,122 . . . 266/D5
Odin, Kans., U.S., 100 . . . 276/D3
Odin, Minn., U.S., 125 . . . 298/C7
Odon, Ind., U.S., 1,376 . . . 270/C7
O'Donnell, Tex., U.S., 1,011 . . . 346/G3
Odra, (Oder), Czh. Rep., *river* . . . 92/C3
Odra, Pol., *river* . . . 86/C2
Odum, Ga., U.S., 414 . . . 260/G8
Oeiras, Port. . . . 93/A3
Oelemari, Sur., *river* . . . 183/B3

Oelrichs, S. Dak., U.S., 145 . . . . .342/B4
Oelwein, Iowa, U.S., 6,692 . . . . .274/L2
Ofahoma, Miss., U.S. 300/C3
O'Fallon, Ill., U.S., 21,910 . . . . .266/B3, D5
O'Fallon, Mo., U.S., 46,169 . . . . .302/F3
Offa, Nig. 152/C3
Offaly, Ire., county .78/C2
Offenbach, Ger., 116,627 . . . . .86/B3
Offerle, Kans., U.S., 220 . . . . .276/C4
Offerman, Ga., U.S., 403 . . . . .260/G9
Offord Cluny, Eng., U.K. 68/G3
Ogaden, Eth., region 156/D3
Ogallah, Kans., U.S., 40 . . . . .276/C3
Ogallala, Nebr., U.S., 4,930 . . . . .308/C2
Ogbomoso, Nig., 433,030 . . . . .152/C3
Ogden, Ark., U.S., 214 . . . . .244/A4
Ogden, Ill., U.S., 743 . . . . .266/F3
Ogden, Iowa, U.S., 2,023 . . . . .274/F3
Ogden, Kans., U.S., 1,762 . . . . .276/F2
Ogden, N.C., U.S., 5,481 . . . . .322/K6
Ogden, Utah, U.S., 77,226 . . . . .350/C2, E1
Ogden Dunes, Ind., U.S., 1,313 . . . . .270/B1
Ogdensburg, N.J., U.S., 2,638 . . . . .314/D1
Ogdensburg, N.Y., U.S., 12,364 . . . . .320/L1
Ogdensburg, Wisc., U.S., 224 . . . . .364/D4
Ogeechee, Ga., U.S., river 260/F5
Ogema, Sask., Can., 292 . . . . .227/F11
Ogema, Minn., U.S., 143 . . . . .298/B3
Ogema, Wisc., U.S., 250 . . . . .364/C3
Ogemaw, Ark., U.S., 80 . . . . .244/B4
Ogemaw, Mich., U.S., county, 21,645 . . . . . .294/E5
Ogilby, Calif., U.S., 70 . . . . .246/L10
Ogilvie, Yukon, Can., mountains 228/B3
Ogilvie, Minn., U.S., 474 . . . . .298/D5
Oglala, S. Dak., U.S., 1,229 . . . . .342/C4
Oglala Natl. Grassland, Nebr., U.S. 308/A1
Ogle, Ill., U.S., county, 51,032 . . . . .266/D1
Oglesby, Ill., U.S., 3,647 . . . . .266/D2
Oglesby, Ga., U.S., 175 . . . . .330/G1
Oglethorpe, Ga., U.S., 1,200 . . . . .260/C7
Oglethorpe, Ga., U.S., county, 12,635 . . . . .260/E4
Oglio, It., river 95/B1
Ogmore-by-Sea, Wales, U.K. 64/D5
Ogoki, Ont., Can., river 222/C2
Ogooué, Gabon, river 155/A2
Ogosta, Bul., river 101/B2
Ograżden, Mac., mountains 100/C2
Ogre, Lat. 82/C2
Ogun, Nig., river .152/B3
Ogun, Nig., state .152/B4
Ogunquit, Maine, U.S., 1,226 . . . . .286/B5
Ogwen, Wales, U.K., lake 64/D1
Ohatchee, Ala., U.S., 1,215 . . . . .238/C2
Ohio, U.S., state 316
Ohio, Colo., U.S., 40 . . . . .250/D3
Ohio, Ill., U.S., 540 . . . . .266/D2
Ohio, Ill., U.S., county 266/D6
Ohio, Ind., U.S., county, 5,623 . . . . .270/G7
Ohio, Ky., U.S., river 270/A9, F7
Ohio, Ky., U.S., county, 22,916 . . . . .280/D3
Ohio, Ky., U.S., river 280/A2, B3, G1, G2
Ohio, Ohio, U.S., river 328/A10, D8, J6
Ohio, Penn., U.S., river 336/B5, D7
Ohio, W. Va., U.S., county, 47,427 . . . . .360/K5
Ohio, W. Va., U.S., river 360/E1, K5
Ohio City, Ohio, U.S., 784 . . . . .328/A4
Ohiopyle, Penn., U.S., 77 . . . . .336/B6
Ohiopyle St. Park, Penn., U.S. 336/C6
Ohioville, Penn., U.S., 3,759 . . . . .336/A4
Ohiowa, Nebr., U.S., 142 . . . . .308/G3
O.H. Ivie, Tex., U.S., lake 346/J4
Ohlman, Ill., U.S. .266/D4
Ohman, Ill., U.S. .266/D4
Ohonua, Tonga 175/C4
Ohoopee, Ga., U.S., river 260/G7
Ohrid, Alb., lake 99/B2
Ohrid, Alb., Mac., lake 100/A3
Ohrid, Mac. 100/A2
Oil Ctr., N. Mex., U.S. 317/G5
Oil City, Mich., U.S., 200 . . . . .282/K4
Oil City, Mich., U.S., 200 . . . . .294/E6
Oil City, Okla., U.S., 125 . . . . .330/D3
Oil City, Penn., U.S., 11,504 . . . . .336/B3
Oildale, Calif., U.S., 27,885 . . . . .246/F7
Oilmont, Mont., U.S. 306/E1
Oil Sprs. Ind. Res., N.Y., U.S. 320/E6
Oilton, Okla., U.S., 1,099 . . . . .330/F1
Oilton, Tex., U.S., 310 . . . . .346/K8
Oil Trough, Ark., U.S., 218 . . . . .244/D2
Oise, Fr., department 88/C2
Oise, Fr., river . . . . .88/C2, Inset II
Oistins, Barb. 209/B5
Oita, Jap., 436,000 . . . . .114/A3
Oita, Jap., prefecture 114/A3
Ojai, Calif., U.S., 7,862 . . . . .246/F8
Ojibwa, Wisc., U.S. 364/B3
Ojinaga, Mex., 20,371, (24,307 metro.) 200/D3
Ojito, N. Mex., U.S. 317/C1
Ojo Amarillo, N. Mex., U.S., 829 . . . . .317/B1
Ojo Caliente, (Cibola County), N. Mex., U.S. .317/B3
Ojo Caliente, (Taos County), N. Mex., U.S. . .317/D1
Ojo Feliz, N. Mex., U.S., 90 . . . . .317/E1
Ojos del Salado, Arg., mountain 191/B2
Ojos del Salado, Chile, mountain 190/C3
Oka, Russ., river .104/D4
Okabena, Minn., U.S., 185 . . . . .298/B7
Okahandja, Nam. 160/B2
Okakarara, Nam. 160/B2
Okaloosa, Fla., U.S., county, 170,498 . . . . . .256/B1
Okanagan, Br. Col., Can., lake 214/N6
Okanagan Falls, Br. Col., Can., 1,971 . . . . . .214/N6
Okanogan, Wash., U.S., 2,484 . . . . .358/F1
Okanogan, Wash., U.S., county, 39,564 . . . .358/F1
Okanogan, Wash., U.S., river 358/F1
Okanogan Natl. For., Wash., U.S. 358/E1, F1
Okara, Pak., 201,815 . . . . .129/D3
Okarche, Okla., U.S., 1,110 . . . . .330/E2
Okatibbee, Miss., U.S., lake 300/D3
Okaton, S. Dak., U.S. 342/E4
Okauchee Lake, Wisc., U.S., 3,916 . . . . .364/E2
Okavango, Bots., basin 160/A1
Okavango, Bots., river 160/A1
Okavango, Nam., river 160/C1
Okawville, Ill., U.S., 1,355 . . . . .266/D5
Okay, Okla., U.S., 597 . . . . .330/G2
Okayama, Jap., 627,000 . . . . .114/B3
Okayama, Jap., prefecture 114/B3
Okazaki, Jap., 337,000 . . . . .114/C3
O'Kean, Ark., U.S., 201 . . . . .244/E1
Okeechobee, Fla., U.S., 5,376 . . . . .256/H4
Okeechobee, Fla., U.S., county, 35,910 . . . . .256/H4
Okeechobee, Fla., U.S., lake 256/H5
Okeelanta, Fla., U.S. 256/H5
Okeene, Okla., U.S., 1,240 . . . . .330/D1
Okefenokee, Ga., U.S., swamp 260/G10
Okefenokee, Ga., U.S., swamp 260/G10
Okefenokee N.W.R., Ga., U.S. 260/G10
Okehampton, Eng., U.K., 4,841 . . . . .73/D3
Okemah, Okla., U.S., 3,038 . . . . .330/F2
Okemos, Mich., U.S., 22,805 . . . . .294/E7
Okene, Nig. 152/D4
Oketo, Kans., U.S., 87 . . . . .276/F2

Okfuskee, Okla., U.S. 330/F2
Okfuskee, Okla., U.S., county, 11,814 . . . . . .330/F2
Okha, Russ. 104/I4
Okhotsk, sea 193/D8
Okhotsk, Jap., sea . . . . .114/Inset I
Okhotsk, Russ. 104/I4
Okhotsk, Russ., sea 104/I4
Oki, Jap., islands 114/B2
Okinawa, Jap., island . . . . .114/Inset II
Okinawa, Jap., islands . . . . .114/Inset II
Okinawa, Jap., prefecture . . . . .114/Inset II
Okino Erabu, Jap., island . . . . .114/Inset II
Oklahoma, U.S., state 318
Oklahoma, Okla., U.S., county 660,448 . .330/B3, E2
Oklahoma City, Okla., U.S., state capital,
  506,132, (1,083,346 metro.) 330/B4
Oklahoma City Natl. Mem., Okla., U.S. 330/B4
Oklahoma Lane, Tex., U.S. 346/F1
Oklee, Minn., U.S., 396 . . . . .298/B3
Okmulgee, Okla., U.S., 13,022 . . . . .330/G2
Okmulgee, Okla., U.S., county, 39,685 . . . . .330/G2
Okoboji, Iowa, U.S., 820 . . . . .274/D1
Okolona, Ark., U.S., 160 . . . . .244/B4
Okolona, Ky., U.S., 17,807 . . . . .280/A2, E2
Okolona, Miss., U.S., 3,056 . . . . .300/D1
Okolona, Ohio, U.S., 250 . . . . .328/B3
Okondja, Gabon .155/B2
Okotoks, Alta., Can., 11,664 . . . . .212/C6
Okreek, S. Dak., U.S., 400 . . . . .342/E4
Oktaha, Okla., U.S., 327 . . . . .330/G2
Oktibbeha, Miss., U.S., county, 42,902 . . . . .300/D2
Okushiri, Jap., island . . . . .114/C1, Inset I
Okwa, Bots., river 160/A2
Ola, Ark., U.S., 1,204 . . . . .244/B2
Ola, Ida., U.S. 264/A5
Olafsvík, Ice. 79/A2
Olamon, Maine, U.S., 175 . . . . .286/D3
Olancha, Calif., U.S., 134 . . . . .246/H6
Olanchito, Hond., 17,900 . . . . .202/B2
Olancho, Hond., department 202/B3
Oland, Swe., island 80/D3
Olanta, S.C., U.S., 613 . . . . .340/C3
Olar, S.C., U.S., 237 . . . . .340/C3
Olathe, Colo., U.S., 1,573 . . . . .250/C3
Olathe, Kans., U.S., 92,962 . . . . .276/H1, H3
Olaton, Ky., U.S., 90 . . . . .280/D3
Olavarría, Arg. 191/C4
Olberg, Ariz., U.S., 40 . . . . .242/D4
Olbia, It. 95/B2
Olcott, N.Y., U.S., 1,156 . . . . .320/D4
Old Alresford, Eng., U.K. 70/B4
Old Appleton, Mo., U.S., 82 . . . . .302/G4
Old Basing, Eng., U.K. 70/C4
Old Bennington, Vt., U.S., 232 . . . . .352/A5
Old Brahmaputra, Bangl., river 127/C4
Old Bridge, N.J., U.S., 60,456 . . . . .314/E3
Old Church, Va., U.S., 150 . . . . .354/J5
Oldcotes, Eng., U.K. 66/F6
Old Crow, Yukon, Can., 299 . . . . .228/B2
Old Dock, N.C., U.S., 150 . . . . .322/H6
Oldenburg, Ger., 154,125 . . . . .86/B2
Oldenburg, Ind., U.S., 647 . . . . .270/F6
Old Faithful, Wyo., U.S. 366/A1
Old Field, N.Y., U.S., 947 . . . . .320/D1
Old Fields, W. Va., U.S., 90 . . . . .360/J2
Old Ford, N.C., U.S., 500 . . . . .322/L3
Old Forge, N.Y., U.S., 800 . . . . .320/M3
Old Forge, Penn., U.S., 8,798 . . . . . . .336/H7, K3
Old Fort, N.C., U.S., 963 . . . . .322/A3, F7
Old Gardens, Vat. .96/A1
Oldham, Eng., U.K. 60/C3
Oldham, Eng., U.K., 103,931 . . . . .60/D5
Oldham, Eng., U.K., 103,931 . . . . .68/C2
Oldham, Eng., U.K., unitary authority, 217,393 .60/D5
Oldham, Eng., U.K., unitary authority, 217,393 .68/C2
Oldham, Ky., U.S., county, 46,178 . . . . .280/B1, E2
Oldham, S. Dak., U.S., 206 . . . . .342/H3
Oldham, Tex., U.S., county, 2,185 . . . . .346/E9
Old Harbor, Alaska, U.S., 237 . . . . .240/E3
Old Horse Sprs., N. Mex., U.S. 317/B4
Old House, S.C., U.S., 225 . . . . .340/D4
Oldhurst, Eng., U.K. 70/D2
Old Hutton, Eng., U.K. 66/C4
Old Jefferson, La., U.S., 5,631 . . . . .282/H6
Old Leake, Eng., U.K. 70/E1
Old Lexington, Ark., U.S. 244/C2
Old Lyme, Conn., U.S., 7,406 . . . . .253/F4
Oldman, Alta., Can., river 212/D6
Oldmeldrum, Scot., U.K., 2,003 . . . . .62/M4
Old Mill Creek, Ill., U.S., 251 . . . . .266/B4
Old Mines, Mo., U.S., 350 . . . . .302/F3
Old Monroe, Mo., U.S., 250 . . . . .302/F3
Old Myakka, Fla., U.S., 225 . . . . .256/F4
Old Mystic, Conn., U.S., 3,205 . . . . .253/H4
Old Newton, Eng., U.K. 70/F2
Old Orchard Beach, Maine, U.S., 8,856 . . . . .286/B5
Old Perlican, Nfld., Can., 714 . . . . .218/E5
Old Ripley, Ill., U.S., 127 . . . . .266/D5
Old River-Winfree, Tex., U.S., 1,364 . . . . . . .346/C6
Old Road, Ant.-Bar. 207/D5
Old Road Town, St. K.-Nevis 207/D5
Olds, Alta., Can., 6,607 . . . . .212/C5
Olds, Iowa, U.S., 249 . . . . .274/L5
Old Saybrook, Conn., U.S., 10,367 . . . . .253/F4
Old Shawneetown, Ill., U.S., 278 . . . . .266/E6
Oldsmar, Fla., U.S., 11,910 . . . . .256/C6, F3
Old Somerby, Eng., U.K. 70/C1
Old Tappan, N.J., U.S., 5,482 . . . . .314/C1, F1
Old Town, Fla., U.S. 256/C4
Old Town, Fla., U.S., 100 . . . . .256/F2
Oldtown, Ida., U.S., 190 . . . . .264/A1
Oldtown, Ky., U.S., 60 . . . . .280/H2
Old Town, Maine, U.S., 8,130 . . . . .286/D4
Oldtown, Md., U.S. 288/D3
Old Washington, Ohio, U.S., 265 . . . . .328/H5
Oldwick, N.J., U.S., 250 . . . . .314/D2
Old Windsor, Eng., U.K., 7,497 . . . . .70/E2
Old Wives, Sask., Can., lake 227/D10
Old Wives Lees, Eng., U.K. 70/F4
Old Woman, Calif., U.S., mountains 246/K8
Olean, Mo., U.S., 157 . . . . .302/D3
Olean, N.Y., U.S., 15,347 . . . . .320/E6
O'Leary, P.E.I., Can., 860 . . . . .224/A2
Olena, Ohio, U.S., 250 . . . . .328/E3
Olene, Oreg., U.S., 100 . . . . .334/E5
Olenek, Russ., river 104/G3
Olentangy, Ohio, U.S., river 328/D9
Oléron, Fr., island .88/B4
Oleta, Okla., U.S., 40 . . . . .330/G3
Olex, Oreg., U.S. .334/F2
Olga, N. Dak., U.S. 326/G1
Olga, Wash., U.S., 150 . . . . .358/C1
Olgilvie, Yukon, Can., river 228/B3
Olgiy, Mong. 118/A2
Olifants, S. Afr., river 161/C1
Olifants, S. Afr., river 162/C1
Olin, Iowa, U.S., 716 . . . . .274/M4
Olin, Iowa, U.S. 346/K4
Olinda, Braz. 188/E2
Olive, Mont., U.S. 306/L4
Olive Branch, Ill., U.S., 500 . . . . .266/D6

Olive Branch, Miss., U.S., 21,054 . . . . .300/C1
Olive Hill, Ky., U.S., 1,813 . . . . .280/G2
Olivehurst, Calif., U.S., 11,061 . . . . .246/D3
Oliver, Br. Col., Can., 4,224 . . . . .214/N6
Oliver, Ga., U.S., 253 . . . . .260/H6
Oliver, Ill., U.S., 125 . . . . .266/F4
Oliver, N. Dak., U.S., county, 2,065 . . . . . . .326/D2
Oliver, Penn., U.S., 2,925 . . . . .336/B6
Oliver, Wisc., U.S., 358 . . . . .364/A2
Oliver Sprs., Tenn., U.S., 3,303 . . . . .344/N2
Olivet, Ill., U.S., 400 . . . . .266/F4
Olivet, Kans., U.S., 64 . . . . .276/G3
Olivet, Mich., U.S., 1,758 . . . . .294/E7
Olivet, N.J., U.S., 1,420 . . . . .314/C4
Olivet, S. Dak., U.S., 70 . . . . .342/H4
Olivet Hill, Md., U.S., 250 . . . . .288/L2
Olivette, Mo., U.S., 7,438 . . . . .302/H3
Olivia, Minn., U.S., 2,570 . . . . .298/C6
Olivia, N.C., U.S., 475 . . . . .322/H4
Olla, La., U.S., 1,417 . . . . .282/E3
Ollagüe, Bol., volcano 186/A4
Ollagüe, Chile, volcano 190/C2
Ollei, Palau 172/C2
Ollerton, Eng., U.K. 66/D6
Ollerton, Eng., U.K. 68/F5
Ollie, Iowa, U.S., 224 . . . . .274/K5
Ollie, Mont., U.S. 306/M3
Olmaliq, Uzb. 132/C2
Olmitz, Kans., U.S., 138 . . . . .276/D3
Olmos, Tex., U.S. .346/K7
Olmos Park, Tex., U.S., 2,343 . . . . .346/A2
Olmstead, Ky., U.S., 70 . . . . .280/C4
Olmsted, Ill., U.S., 299 . . . . .266/D6
Olmsted, Minn., U.S., county, 124,277 . . . . .298/E7
Olmsted Falls, Ohio, U.S., 7,962 . . . . .328/G9
Olney, Eng., U.K., 4,484 . . . . .68/F5
Olney, Eng., U.K., 4,484 . . . . .70/C2
Olney, Ill., U.S., 8,631 . . . . .266/E5
Olney, Mo., U.S., 31,438 . . . . .288/F3
Olney, Mo., U.S., 60 . . . . .302/E2
Olney, Mont., U.S., 60 . . . . .306/B1
Olney, Tex., U.S., 3,396 . . . . .346/K2
Olney Sprs., Colo., U.S., 389 . . . . .250/G3
Olomana, Hawaii, U.S. 262/K2
Olomouc, Czh. Rep., 104,000 . . . . .92/C3
Olomoucký, Czh. Rep., region 92/C3
Olongapo, Phil., 194,260 . . . . .120/B3
Olowalu, Hawaii, U.S. 262/B4
Olpe, Kans., U.S., 504 . . . . .276/F3
Olsburg, Kans., U.S., 192 . . . . .276/F2
Olsonville, S. Dak., U.S. 342/E4
Olsztyn, Pol., 171,400 . . . . .83/E2
Olt, Rom., county 101/C3
Olt, Rom., river 101/C3
Oltenita, Rom. 101/D3
Olton, Tex., U.S., 2,288 . . . . .346/F1
Olustee, Okla., U.S., 680 . . . . .330/C3
Olvey, Ark., U.S., 200 . . . . .244/C1
Olympia, N.Y., U.S., 225 . . . . .280/G2
Olympia, Wash., U.S., state capital, 42,514 . .358/C2
Olympia Fields, Ill., U.S., 4,732 . . . . .266/C6
Olympia Hts., Fla., U.S., 13,452 . . . . .256/N6
Olympian Vil., Mo., U.S., 669 . . . . .302/F3
Olympic, Wash., U.S., mountains 358/B1
Olympic Natl. For., Wash., U.S. 358/A1, B2
Olympic Natl. Park, Wash., U.S. 358/A2, B2
Olympus, Cyp., mountain 133/A2
Olympus, Gr., mountain 100/B1
Olympus, Wash., U.S., mountain 358/B1
Olyphant, Ark., U.S. 244/D2
Olyphant, Penn., U.S., 4,978 . . . . .336/H7, K3
Oma, Ark., U.S., 175 . . . . .244/B3
Oma, Miss., U.S., 40 . . . . .300/B4
Omagh, N. Ire., U.K. 60/A2
Omagh, N. Ire., U.K., 17,280 . . . . .65/C2
Omagh, N. Ire., U.K., unitary authority, 47,952 .65/C2
Omaha, Fr., beach .88/B2
Omaha, Ark., U.S., 165 . . . . .244/B1
Omaha, Ga., U.S., 125 . . . . .260/A7
Omaha, Ill., U.S., 263 . . . . .266/E6
Omaha, Nebr., U.S., 390,007, (716,998 metro.) .308/J2
Omaha Ind. Res., Nebr., U.S. 308/H1
Omak, Wash., U.S., 4,721 . . . . .358/F1
Omak, Wash., U.S., mountain 358/F1
Oman, nation 133
Oman, Iran, gulf .130/D2
Oman, Oman, gulf 137/C1
Oman, U.A.E., gulf 136/D2
Omao, Hawaii, U.S., 1,221 . . . . .262/C2
Omaruru, Nam. .160/B2
Omatako, Nam., river 160/C1
Ombersley, Eng., U.K. 68/C5
Omboué, Gabon .155/A2
Omdurman, Sudan, 1,271,403 . . . . .145/C2
Omega, Ga., U.S., 1,340 . . . . .260/D9
Omega, N. Mex., U.S., 60 . . . . .317/B3
Omega, Ohio, U.S., 225 . . . . .328/E7
Omega, Okla., U.S., 40 . . . . .330/D2
Omemee, Ont., Can., 1,319 . . . . .223/G3
Omemee, N. Dak., U.S. 326/E1
Omena, Mich., U.S., 150 . . . . .294/D4
Omer, Mich., U.S., 337 . . . . .294/F5
Ometepe, Nicar., island 202/B3
Omineca, Br. Col., Can., mountains 214/K3
Omineca, Br. Col., Can., river 214/K3
Omiya, Jap., 456,000 . . . . .114/C3
Omo, Eth., river 156/B3
Omoa, Hond. 202/B1
Omok, Russ., 3,177 . . . . .364/E4
Omsk, Russ., 1,153,314, (1,177,000 metro.) .104/E4
Omuta, Jap. 114/A3
Ona, Fla., U.S., 100 . . . . .256/G4
Onaga, Kans., U.S., 704 . . . . .276/F2
Onaka, S. Dak., U.S. 342/F2
Onalaska, Tex., U.S., 1,174 . . . . .346/N5
Onalaska, Wash., U.S., 325 . . . . .358/C3
Onalaska, Wisc., U.S., 14,839 . . . . .364/B5
Onamia, Minn., U.S., 847 . . . . .298/D4
Onancock, Va., U.S., 1,525 . . . . .354/M5
Onanole, Man., Can. 215/B4
Onapa, Okla., U.S., 150 . . . . .330/G2
Onarga, Ill., U.S., 1,438 . . . . .266/F3
Onawa, Iowa, U.S., 3,091 . . . . .274/B3
Onawa, Maine, U.S. 286/C3
Onaway, Ida., U.S., 230 . . . . .264/A3
Onaway, Mich., U.S., 993 . . . . .294/E4
Ondame, Gui.-B. .149/B2
Ondangwa, Nam. 160/B1
Ondava, Slvk., river 93/F2
Ondjiva, Nam. 159/C5
Ondo, Nig. 152/C4
Ondo, Nig., state .152/C4
Ondörhaan, Mong. 118/B2
One and Half Degree, Mald., channel 127/A4
Oneco, Conn., U.S., 475 . . . . .253/H3
Oneco, Fla., U.S., 7,500 . . . . .256/F4
Onecote, Eng., U.K. 68/D3
Onefour, Alta., Can. 212/E6
Onega, Russ., river 104/C3
Onega, Russ., lake 193/C2
Onego, W. Va., U.S., 80 . . . . .360/H3
150 Mile House, Br. Col., Can., 1,142 . . . . . .214/M5

100 Mile House, Br. Col., Can., 1,739 . . . . . .214/M5
Oneida, Ark., U.S., 70 . . . . .244/E3
Oneida, Ida., U.S., county, 4,125 . . . . .264/E7
Oneida, Ill., U.S., 752 . . . . .266/C2
Oneida, Iowa, U.S., 50 . . . . .274/M4
Oneida, Kans., U.S., 70 . . . . .276/G2
Oneida, Ky., U.S., 325 . . . . .280/G3
Oneida, N.Y., U.S., 10,987 . . . . .320/K4
Oneida, N.Y., U.S., county, 235,469 . . . . . . .320/K4
Oneida, N.Y., U.S., lake 320/K4
Oneida, Tenn., U.S., 3,615 . . . . .344/M2
Oneida, Wisc., U.S., county, 36,776 . . . . . . .364/D3
Oneida Castle, N.Y., U.S., 627 . . . . .320/K4
Oneida Ind. Res., Wisc., U.S. 364/E4
Oneill, Mont., U.S. 306/L3
O'Neill, Nebr., U.S., 3,733 . . . . .308/E1
Onekama, Mich., U.S., 647 . . . . .294/C5
Oneonta, Ala., U.S., 5,576 . . . . .238/C2
Oneonta, N.Y., U.S., 13,292 . . . . .320/L6
Ong, Nebr., U.S., 67 . . . . .308/G3
Ongar Hill, Eng., U.K. 70/E1
Ongjin, N. Kor. 116/A4
Ongole, India 128/C5
Onida, S. Dak., U.S., 740 . . . . .342/E3
Onilahy, Madag., river 163/A3
Onion Creek, Tex., U.S., 2,116 . . . . . . .346/D2, L5
Onion Lake, Sask., Can. 227/A7
Onitsha, Nig. 152/D4
Ono, Va., U.S., 496 . . . . .354/M5
Ono, Fiji, island 174/B3
Onon, Mong., river 118/B2
Onondaga, Mich., U.S., 425 . . . . .294/E7
Onondaga, N.Y., U.S., county, 458,336 . . . . .320/J5
Onondaga Ind. Res., N.Y., U.S. 320/J5
Onota, Kiri., island 175/A2
Onoway, Alta., Can., 847 . . . . .212/C4
Onset, Mass., U.S., 1,292 . . . . .292/M6
Onslow, Iowa, U.S., 223 . . . . .274/M4
Onslow, N.C., U.S., bay 322/L5
Onslow, N.C., U.S., county, 150,355 . . . . . . .322/L5
Onsong, N. Kor. 116/C1
Onsted, Mich., U.S., 813 . . . . .294/E7
Ontario, Can., province 222/211
Ontario, Ont., Can., lake 222/E4
Ontario, Ont., Can., lake 223/H4, K4
Ontario, Calif., U.S., 158,007 . . . . .246/H8
Ontario, N.Y., U.S., county, 100,224 . . . . . . .320/G5
Ontario, N.Y., U.S., lake 320/F3
Ontario, Ohio, U.S., 5,303 . . . . .328/C4
Ontario, Oreg., U.S., 10,985 . . . . .334/K3
Ontario, Wisc., U.S., 476 . . . . .364/C5
Ontonagon, Mich., U.S., 1,769 . . . . .294/D1
Ontonagon, Mich., U.S., county, 7,818 . . . . .294/D2
Ontong Java, Atoll, Sol. Is. 173/A1
Onward, Ind., U.S., 81 . . . . .270/D3
Onward, Miss., U.S. 300/B3
Onycha, Ala., U.S., 208 . . . . .238/C4
Onyx, Ark., U.S. 244/B3
Ookala, Hawaii, U.S. 262/H4
Oolitic, Ind., U.S., 1,152 . . . . .270/D6
Oologah, Okla., U.S., 883 . . . . .330/G1
Oologah, Okla., U.S., lake 330/G1
Ooltewah, Tenn., U.S., 5,681 . . . . .344/L4
Oostburg, Wisc., U.S., 2,660 . . . . .364/F5
Oostende, Belg. 85/A1
Oostende-Brugge, Belg., canal 85/B1
Oosterschelde, Neth., channel 84/A3
Ootsa, Br. Col., Can., lake 214/J4
Opal, S. Dak., U.S., 70 . . . . .342/C3
Opal, Wyo., U.S., 102 . . . . .366/A3
Opal Cliffs, Calif., U.S., 6,458 . . . . .246/K4
Opa-Locka, Fla., U.S., 14,951 . . . . .256/B6
Opava, Czh. Rep. 92/C3
Opdyke, Ill., U.S., 300 . . . . .266/E5
Opdyke West, Tex., U.S., 188 . . . . .346/F2
Opelika, Ala., U.S., 23,498 . . . . .238/D3
Opelousas, La., U.S., 22,860 . . . . .282/E5
Opeongo, Ont., Can., lake 223/G2
Opheim, Mont., U.S., 111 . . . . .306/K1
Ophir, Alaska, U.S. 240/D2
Ophir, Colo., U.S., 113 . . . . .250/C4
Ophir, Oreg., U.S., 50 . . . . .334/B5
Ophir, Utah, U.S. .350/B3
Ophikao, Hawaii, U.S. 262/K6
Opihn, Tex., U.S. .346/J3
Opole, Pol., 129,370 . . . . .83/D3
Opolskie, Pol., province 83/C3
Oporto, (Porto), Port., 263,131,
  (1,260,680 metro.) 93/A2
Opp, Ala., U.S., 6,607 . . . . .238/C4
Oppelo, Ark., U.S., 725 . . . . .244/C2
Oppland, Nor., province 80/B3
Opportunity, Wash., U.S., 25,065 . . . . .358/H2
Optima, Okla., U.S., 266 . . . . .330/A1
Optima NW.R., Okla., U.S. 330/A1, C4
Opuwo, Nam. 160/A1
Oqsu, Taj., river 132/C2
Oquawka, Ill., U.S., 1,539 . . . . .266/C3
Oquirrh, Utah, U.S., 10,390 . . . . .350/B3
Oquossoc, Maine, U.S., 50 . . . . .286/B4
Oracle, Ariz., U.S., 3,563 . . . . .242/E5
Oracle Jct., Ariz., U.S., 550 . . . . .242/E5
Oradea, Rom., 220,626 . . . . .101/A2
Oradell, N.J., U.S., 8,047 . . . . .314/B1, E2
Oral, Kaz. 131/B1
Oral, S. Dak., U.S. 342/B4
Oran, Alg., 744,917 . . . . .146/A1
Oran, Mo., U.S., 1,264 . . . . .302/G4
Orange, N.S.W., Austl. 170/D3
Orange, Leso., river 161/A3, B4
Orange, Nam., river 160/C4
Orange, S. Afr., river 162/B2
Orange, Calif., U.S., 128,821 . . . . .246/E10
Orange, Calif., U.S., county, 2,846,289 . . .246/E1, D9
Orange, Conn., U.S., 13,233 . . . . .253/C4
Orange, Fla., U.S. .256/C1
Orange, Fla., U.S., county, 896,344 . . . .256/D4, G3
Orange, Ind., U.S., county, 19,306 . . . . .270/C6
Orange, Mass., U.S., 7,518 . . . . .292/E2
Orange, N.H., U.S., 299 . . . . .312/C4
Orange, (City of Orange), N.J., U.S., 32,868 . .314/B2
Orange, N.J., U.S., county, 341,361 . . . . . . .320/A1
Orange, N.Y., U.S., county, 341,367 . . . . . . .320/N8
Orange, N.C., U.S., county, 118,227 . . . . . . .322/G2
Orange, Ohio, U.S., 3,236 . . . . .328/H9
Orange, Tex., U.S., 18,643 . . . . .346/K5
Orange, Tex., U.S., county, 84,966 . . . . .346/P5
Orange, Vt., U.S., 965 . . . . .352/C2
Orange, Vt., U.S., county, 28,226 . . . . .352/C2
Orange, Va., U.S., 4,123 . . . . .354/G4
Orange, Va., U.S., county, 25,881 . . . . .354/G4
Orange Beach, Ala., U.S., 3,784 . . . . .238/C5
Orangeburg, S.C., U.S., 12,765 . . . . .340/D3
Orangeburg, S.C., U.S., county, 91,582 . . . .340/D3
Orange City, Fla., U.S., 6,604 . . . . .256/G3
Orange City, Iowa, U.S., 5,582 . . . . .274/B1
Orange Cove, Calif., U.S., 7,722 . . . . .246/F6
Orange Grove, Tex., U.S., 1,288 . . . . .346/L8
Orange Hts., Fla., U.S., 150 . . . . .256/F2
Orange Park, Fla., U.S., 9,081 . . . . .256/F1
Orangevale, Calif., U.S., 26,705 . . . . .246/L5

Orangeville, Ont., Can., 25,248 . . . . .223/E4
Orangeville, Ill., U.S., 751 . . . . .266/D1
Orangeville, Ohio, U.S., 189 . . . . .328/J3
Orangeville, Penn., U.S., 500 . . . . .336/J3
Orangeville, Utah, U.S., 1,398 . . . . .350/C4
Orange Walk, Bel., 13,483 . . . . .201/B1
Oranje, Sur., mountains 183/B3
Oranjemund, Nam. 160/B4
Oranjestad, Aruba, capital 204/D4
Orapa, Bots. 160/B2
Orbisonia, Penn., U.S., 425 . . . . .336/F5
Orcas, Wash., U.S., 90 . . . . .358/C1
Orcas, Wash., U.S., island 358/C1
Orchard, Colo., U.S., 100 . . . . .250/F1
Orchard, Ida., U.S. 264/A6
Orchard, Iowa, U.S., 88 . . . . .274/J1
Orchard, Nebr., U.S., 391 . . . . .308/E1
Orchard, Tex., U.S., 408 . . . . .346/N6
Orchard Beach, Md., U.S., 4,400 . . . . . . .288/H3
Orchard Ctr., N.J., U.S., 550 . . . . .314/C5
Orchard City, Colo., U.S., 2,880 . . . . . . .250/C3
Orchard Farm, Mo., U.S., 275 . . . . .302/H2
Orchard Grass Hills, Ky., U.S., 1,031 . . . .280/B1
Orchard Hill, Ga., U.S., 230 . . . . .260/C5
Orchard Homes, Mont., U.S., 5,199 . . . . .306/B3
Orchard Lake, Mich., U.S., 2,215 . . . . . . .294/A6
Orchard Mesa, Colo., U.S., 6,456 . . . . . . .250/B2
Orchard Park, N.Y., U.S., 3,294 . . . . .320/D5
Orchards, (Orchards South), Wash.,
U.S., 17,852 .358/C4
Orchard Valley, Wyo., U.S., 550 . . . . .366/D3
Orchid, Fla., U.S., 140 . . . . .256/H4
Orchila, Ven., island 204/E5
Orcutt, Calif., U.S., 28,830 . . . . .246/E8
Ord, Nebr., U.S., 2,269 . . . . .308/E2
Orderville, Utah, U.S., 596 . . . . .350/B6
Ordino, And. 93/B2
Ordu, Tur. 133/D2
Ordu, Tur., province 133/D2
Ordway, Colo., U.S., 1,248 . . . . .250/H2
Ore, Eng., U.K. .70/F5
Oreana, Ida., U.S., 60 . . . . .264/A6
Oreana, Ill., U.S., 892 . . . . .266/E4
Oreana, Nev., U.S. 310/A1
Örebro, Swe., 124,873 . . . . .80/C3
Örebro, Swe., county 80/B3
Ore City, Tex., U.S., 1,106 . . . . .346/P3
Oregon, U.S., state 322
Oregon, Ill., U.S., 4,060 . . . . .266/D1
Oregon, Mo., U.S., 935 . . . . .302/A2
Oregon, Mo., U.S., county, 10,344 . . . . . .302/E5
Oregon, N.C., U.S., inlet 322/Q3
Oregon, Ohio, U.S., 19,355 . . . . .328/D2
Oregon, Wash., U.S., butte 358/H3
Oregon, Wisc., U.S., 7,514 . . . . .364/D6
Oregon Caves Natl. Mon., Oreg., U.S. 334/C5
Oregon City, Oreg., U.S., 25,754 . . . . . . .334/A3
Oregon Dunes Natl. Rec. Area, Oreg., U.S. .334/B4
Oregonia, Ohio, U.S., 175 . . . . .328/B7
Oreland, Penn., U.S., 5,509 . . . . .336/L6
Orellana, Sp., reservoir 94/D3
Orem, Utah, U.S., 84,324 . . . . .350/C3
Orenburg, Russ., 522,643, (541,500 metro.) .104/D4
Orestes, Ind., U.S., 334 . . . . .270/E4
Øresund, Den., sound 79/D3
Øresund, Den., Swe., sound 80/B3
Oretta, La., U.S., 250 . . . . .282/C5
Orford, Eng., U.K. 70/H2
Orford, N.H., U.S., 1,091 . . . . .312/B4
Orford Ness, Eng., U.K., cape 70/H2
Orfordville, N.H., U.S., 200 . . . . .312/B4
Orfordville, Wisc., U.S., 1,272 . . . . .364/D6
Organ, N. Mex., U.S., 300 . . . . .317/D5
Órganos, Cuba, mountains 204/A2
Organ Pipe Cactus Natl. Mon., Ariz., U.S. .242/C5
Órgãos, Braz., range . . . . .188/Inset I
Orhei, Mol. 102/B2
Orhon, Mong., river 118/C2
Orick, Calif., U.S., 350 . . . . .246/A1
Orient, Conn., U.S., point 253/C5
Orient, Ill., U.S., 296 . . . . .266/E6
Orient, Iowa, U.S., 402 . . . . .274/F5
Orient, Maine, U.S., 145 . . . . .286/E3
Orient, Ohio, U.S., 269 . . . . .328/D6
Orient, S. Dak., U.S., 57 . . . . .342/F3
Orient, Tex., U.S., 80 . . . . .346/H4
Orient, Wash., U.S., 80 . . . . .358/G1
Orienta, Okla., U.S., 50 . . . . .330/D1
Oriental, Dom. Rep., range 205/C2
Oriental, Peru, mountains 185/B2, C3
Oriental, N.C., U.S., 875 . . . . .322/M4
Orientale, Congo, D.R., region 155/C1
Orient Park, (East Lake-Orient Park), Fla.,
U.S., 5,703 . . . . .256/D6
Orilla, Wyo., U.S. 366/D2
Orillia, Ont., Can., 29,121 . . . . .223/F3
Orin, Wyo., U.S. 366/D2
Orinda, Calif., U.S., 17,599 . . . . .246/J1
Orinoco, Col., river 182/C3
Orinoco, Ven., river 182/C3, D2
Oriole, Md., U.S., 200 . . . . .288/L7
Orion, Alta., Can. 212/E6
Orion, Ala., U.S. 238/D4
Orion, Ill., U.S., 1,713 . . . . .266/C2
Orion, Okla., U.S. 330/D1
Oriska, N. Dak., U.S., 128 . . . . .326/H3
Oriskany, N.Y., U.S., 1,459 . . . . .354/D5
Oriskany, Va., U.S., 60 . . . . .354/D5
Oriskany Falls, N.Y., U.S., 698 . . . . .320/L5
Orissa, India, state 128/D4
Oristano, It. 95/B3
Orizaba, Mex., 118,552 . . . . .200/E4
Orizaba, Mex., peak 200/E4
Orkney, Scot., U.K., islands . . . . .60/Inset I
Orkney, Scot., U.K., islands 62/E2
Orkney Islands, Scot., U.K., unitary authority,
19,245 . . . . .62/J1, L2
Orla, Tex., U.S. .346/E4
Orland, Calif., U.S., 6,281 . . . . .246/C3
Orland, Ind., U.S., 341 . . . . .270/F1
Orland, Maine, U.S., 2,134 . . . . .286/D4
Orland, S. Dak., U.S. 342/H4
Orland Hills, Ill., U.S., 6,779 . . . . .266/B6
Orlando, Fla., U.S., 185,951,
(1,644,561 metro.) 256/C4, G3
Orlando, Okla., U.S., 201 . . . . .330/E1
Orlando, W. Va., U.S., 125 . . . . .360/E3
Orland Park, Ill., U.S., 51,077 . . . . .266/B6
Orléans, Que., Can. 226/F5, L5
Orléans, Fr., 116,559, (263,292 metro.) . . .88/C3
Orleans, Calif., U.S., 80 . . . . .246/B1
Orleans, Ind., U.S., 2,273 . . . . .270/D7
Orleans, Iowa, U.S., 583 . . . . .274/D1
Orleans, La., U.S., parish, 484,674 . . .282/K6, L2
Orleans, Mass., U.S., 6,341 . . . . .292/Q5
Orleans, Mich., U.S., 275 . . . . .294/A6
Orleans, Minn., U.S. 298/A2
Orleans, Nebr., U.S., 425 . . . . .308/E3
Orleans, N.Y., U.S., county, 44,171 . . . . . .320/E4
Orleans, Vt., U.S., 826 . . . . .352/C1
Orleans, Vt., U.S., county, 26,277 . . . . . . .352/C1
Orlinda, Tenn., U.S., 594 . . . . .344/H1

Orma, W. Va., U.S., 40 . . . . .360/D3
Orme, Tenn., U.S., 124 . . . . .344/K4
Ormoc, Phil., 154,297 . . . . .120/C4
Ormond Beach, Fla., U.S., 36,301 . . . . . . .256/G2
Ormond-by-the-Sea, Fla., U.S., 8,430 . . . .256/G2
Ormsby, Minn., U.S., 154 . . . . .298/C7
Ormskirk, Eng., U.K., 23,425 . . . . .66/C5
Ormskirk, Eng., U.K., 23,425 . . . . .68/B2
Orne, Fr., department 88/C2
Orne, Fr., river 88/C2
Örnsköldsvik, Swe., 55,364 . . . . .80/C2
Orocovis, P.R. 206/C2
Orocué, Col. 184/C3
Orofino, Ida., U.S., 3,247 . . . . .264/A3
Oro Grande, Calif., U.S., 475 . . . . .246/H8
Orogrande, Ida., U.S. 264/B4
Orogrande, N. Mex., U.S., 70 . . . . .317/D5
Orofuk, Micr., atoll 172/C2
Oromiya, Eth., state 156/C2
Oromocto, N.B., Can., 8,843 . . . . .217/C3
Oron, Nig. 152/E5
Orondo, Wash., U.S., 175 . . . . .358/E2
Orono, Maine, U.S., 9,112 . . . . .286/D4
Orono, Minn., U.S., 7,538 . . . . .298/D6
Oronoco, Minn., U.S., 883 . . . . .298/E6
Oronsay, Scot., U.K., island 62/D7
Orontes, Leb., river 134/B1
Orontes, Syria, river 134/A2
Oroszháza, Hun. 91/C2
Orosi, Calif., U.S., 7,318 . . . . .246/F6
Orovada, Nev., U.S. 310/B1
Oro Valley, Ariz., U.S., 29,700 . . . . .242/E5
Oroville, Calif., U.S., 13,004 . . . . .246/D3
Oroville, Calif., U.S., reservoir 246/D3
Oroville, Wash., U.S., 1,653 . . . . .358/F1
Orpha, Wyo., U.S. 366/D3
Orphir, Scot., U.K. 62/M2
Orpington, Eng., U.K. 70/E4
Orr, Minn., U.S., 249 . . . . .298/E2
Orr, Okla., U.S. .330/E3
Orrefors, Swe. 80/C3
Orrick, Mo., U.S., 889 . . . . .302/B2, J5
Orrin, Scot., U.K., reservoir 62/G3
Orrin, N. Dak., U.S. 326/E1
Orrington, Maine, U.S., 3,526 . . . . .286/D4
Orrs Island, Maine, U.S., 550 . . . . .286/C5
Orrstown, Penn., U.S., 231 . . . . .336/F5
Orrum, N.C., U.S., 79 . . . . .322/G6
Orrville, Ala., U.S., 230 . . . . .238/B3
Orrville, Ohio, U.S., 8,551 . . . . .328/G4
Orsett, Eng., U.K. 70/E3
Orsk, Russ., 274,849, (280,000 metro.) . . .104/D4
Orson, Penn., U.S., 60 . . . . .336/L2
Orston, Eng., U.K. 70/C1
Ortegal, Sp., cape 94/C1
Orting, Wash., U.S., 3,760 . . . . .358/C2
Ortley, S. Dak., U.S., 54 . . . . .342/H2
Orton, Eng., U.K. 66/C4
Ortonville, Mich., U.S., 1,535 . . . . .294/F7
Ortonville, Minn., U.S., 2,158 . . . . .298/A5
Orton Waterville, Eng., U.K. 70/D1
Orumiyeh, (Urmia), Iran, 435,200 . . . . . . .130/A2
Oruro, Bol., 248,000 . . . . .186/A3
Oruro, Bol., department 186/A3
Orwell, P.E.I., Can. 224/C2
Orwell, Eng., U.K. 70/D2
Orwell, Ohio, U.S., 1,519 . . . . .328/J2
Orwell, Vt., U.S., 1,185 . . . . .352/A3
Orwigsburg, Penn., U.S., 3,106 . . . . .336/J4
Oryakhovo, Bul. .101/B2
Os, And., river 93/A3
Osa, C.R., peninsula 203/C4
Osage, Ark., U.S. 244/B1
Osage, Iowa, U.S., 3,451 . . . . .274/J1
Osage, Kans., U.S., county, 16,712 . . . . . .276/G3
Osage, Minn., U.S., 150 . . . . .298/B4
Osage, Mo., U.S., county, 13,062 . . . . . . .302/E3
Osage, Mo., U.S., river 302/B4, D3
Osage, Okla., U.S., 188 . . . . .330/F1
Osage, Okla., U.S., county, 44,437 . . . . . .330/F1
Osage, W. Va., U.S., 175 . . . . .360/F1
Osage, Wyo., U.S., 215 . . . . .366/D2
Osage Beach, Mo., U.S., 3,662 . . . . .302/D3
Osage City, Kans., U.S., 3,034 . . . . .276/G3
Osage Ind. Res., Okla., U.S. 330/F1
Osaka, Jap., 2,598,589 . . . . .114/B3
Osaka, Jap., prefecture 114/B3
Osakis, Minn., U.S., 1,567 . . . . .298/B5
Osasco, Braz., 652,593 . . . . .188/Inset II
Osawatomie, Kans., U.S., 4,645 . . . . .276/H3
Osborn, Maine, U.S., 69 . . . . .286/D4
Osborn, Mo., U.S., 455 . . . . .302/B2
Osborne, Kans., U.S., 1,607 . . . . .276/D2
Osborne, Kans., U.S., county, 4,452 . . . . .276/D2
Osburn, Ida., U.S., 1,545 . . . . .264/A2
Oscar, Okla., U.S. 330/E4
Osceola, Ark., U.S., 8,875 . . . . .244/F2
Osceola, Fla., U.S., county, 172,493 . . .256/D4, G3
Osceola, Ind., U.S., 1,859 . . . . .270/D1
Osceola, Iowa, U.S., 4,659 . . . . .274/G5
Osceola, Iowa, U.S., county, 7,003 . . . . . .274/C1
Osceola, Mich., U.S., county, 23,197 . . . . .294/D6
Osceola, Mo., U.S., 835 . . . . .302/C3
Osceola, Nebr., U.S., 921 . . . . .308/G2
Osceola, N.Y., U.S., 50 . . . . .320/K3
Osceola, S. Dak., U.S. 342/H1
Osceola, Wisc., U.S., 2,421 . . . . .364/A3
Osceola Mills, Penn., U.S., 1,249 . . . . . . .336/E4
Osceola Natl. For., Fla., U.S. 256/F1
Oscoda, Mich., U.S., 992 . . . . .294/F5
Oscoda, Mich., U.S., county, 9,418 . . . . . .294/E5
Oscuro, N. Mex., U.S., 40 . . . . .317/D4
Osgood, Ind., U.S., 1,669 . . . . .270/F6
Osgood, Mo., U.S., 51 . . . . .302/C1
Osgood, Ohio, U.S., 255 . . . . .328/A5
Osh, Kyrg., 212,000 . . . . .131/C2
Osh, Kyrg., province 131/C2
Oshakati, Nam. .160/B1
Oshawa, Ont., Can., 139,051,
(310,000 metro.) 223/G4
Oshima, Jap., peninsula . . . . .114/D1, Inset I
Oshkosh, Nebr., U.S., 887 . . . . .308/B2
Oshkosh, Wisc., U.S., 62,916 . . . . .364/E4
Oshoto, Wyo., U.S. 366/D1
Osierfield, Ga., U.S. 260/E8
Osijek, Cro., 90,411 . . . . .98/D2
Osilinka, Br. Col., Can., river 214/K3
Oskaloosa, Iowa, U.S., 10,938 . . . . .274/J5
Oskaloosa, Kans., U.S., 1,165 . . . . .276/G2
Oskaloosa, Mo., U.S., 40 . . . . .302/B4
Oskamull, Scot., U.K. 62/D6
Öskemen, Kaz. .131/E1
Oslo, Nor., capital, 512,589 . . . . .80/C3
Oslo, Nor., capital 193/D1
Oslo, Nor., province 80/C3
Oslo, Fla., U.S., 1,900 . . . . .256/H4
Oslo, Minn., U.S., 347 . . . . .298/A2
Oslofjord, Nor., fjord 80/C4
Osman, Nebr., U.S. 266/E3
Osmond, Nebr., U.S., 796 . . . . .308/G1

Osnabrock, N. Dak., U.S., 174 . . . . .326/G1
Osnabrück, Ger., 164,539 . . . . .86/B2
Oso, Wash., U.S., 246 . . . . .358/D1
Osogbo, Nig. 152/C4
Osorno, Chile, 124,839 . . . . .190/B6
Osoyoos, Br. Col., Can., 4,295 . . . . .214/N6
Osprey, Fla., U.S., 4,143 . . . . .256/C4
Oss, Neth. 84/C3
Ossabaw, Ga., U.S., island 260/J8
Ossabaw, Ga., U.S., sound 260/J8
Osse, Nig., river .152/C4
Osseo, Mich., U.S., 550 . . . . .294/E8
Osseo, Minn., U.S., 2,434 . . . . .298/E5
Osseo, Wisc., U.S., 1,669 . . . . .364/B4
Ossett, Eng., U.K., 20,405 . . . . .66/E5
Ossett, Eng., U.K., 20,405 . . . . .68/D2
Ossian, Ind., U.S., 2,943 . . . . .270/F3
Ossian, Iowa, U.S., 853 . . . . .274/L1
Ossineke, Mich., U.S., 1,059 . . . . .294/F5
Ossining, N.Y., U.S., 24,010 . . . . .320/B1
Ossipee, N.H., U.S., 4,211 . . . . .312/D4
Ossipee, N.H., U.S., lake 312/D4
Osteen, Fla., U.S., 450 . . . . .256/G3
Österdalälven, Swe. 80/B2
Osterdock, Iowa, U.S., 50 . . . . .274/M2
Östergötland, Swe., county 80/C3
Östersund, Swe., 58,361 . . . . .80/B2
Osterville, Mass., U.S., 2,900 . . . . .292/N6
Østfold, Nor., province 80/C4
Ostrander, Minn., U.S., 212 . . . . .298/E7
Ostrander, Ohio, U.S., 405 . . . . .328/D5
Ostrander, Wash., U.S. 358/C3
Ostrava, Czh. Rep., 319,293 . . . . .92/D3
Ostrobothnia, Fin., region 81/B2
Ostrołęka, Pol. 83/E2
Osum, Alb., river 99/B3
Osum, Bul., river 101/C3
Osumi, Jap., islands 114/A4
Osumi, Jap., peninsula 114/A4
Osumi, Jap., strait 114/A4
Osun, Nig., state 152/C4
Oswayo, Penn., U.S., 159 . . . . .336/E2
Oswego, Ill., U.S., 13,326 . . . . .266/E6
Oswego, Kans., U.S., 2,046 . . . . .276/G4
Oswego, Mont., U.S., 60 . . . . .306/L1
Oswego, N.Y., U.S., 17,954 . . . . .320/J4
Oswego, N.Y., U.S., county, 122,377 . .320/J4, M5
Oswestry, Eng., U.K., 15,612 . . . . .68/A4
Osyka, Miss., U.S., 481 . . . . .300/D3
Otaru, Jap. 114/D1
Otago, N.Z., region 169/B4
Otavalo, Ecua. 185/B2
Otavi, Nam. 160/C1
Otego, N.Y., U.S., 1,052 . . . . .320/L6
Otero, Colo., U.S., county, 20,311 . . . . . . .250/G4
Otero, N. Mex., U.S., county, 62,298 . . . . .317/E5
Otford, (Otford/Kemsing), Eng., U.K., 6,840 .70/E4
Othello, Calif., U.S. 314/C5
Othello, Wash., U.S., 5,847 . . . . .358/F3
Othery, Eng., U.K. 73/G2
Otho, Iowa, U.S., 571 . . . . .274/F3
Oti, Gha., river 150/C2
Oti, Togo, river 151/B1
Otis, Colo., U.S., 534 . . . . .250/H1
Otis, Kans., U.S., 325 . . . . .276/C3
Otis, La., U.S., 90 . . . . .282/D4
Otis, Maine, U.S. 543 . . . . .286/D4
Otis, Mass., U.S., 1,365 . . . . .292/B4
Otis, Mass., U.S., reservoir 292/B4
Otis, N. Mex., U.S., 175 . . . . .317/F5
Otis, Oreg., U.S., 80 . . . . .334/C3
Otisco, Ind., U.S., 325 . . . . .270/E7
Otisco, Minn., U.S., 60 . . . . .298/D7
Otisfield, Maine, U.S., 1,560 . . . . .286/B4
Otis Orchards, (Otis Orchards-East Farms),
Wash., U.S., 6,318 . . . . .358/H2
Otisville, Mich., U.S., 882 . . . . .294/F6
Otisville, N.Y., U.S., 989 . . . . .320/M8
Otjiwarongo, Nam. 160/B2
Otley, Eng., U.K., 13,596 . . . . .66/E5
Otley, Eng., U.K., 13,596 . . . . .68/D2
Otley, Eng., U.K., 13,596 . . . . .70/G2
Otley, Iowa, U.S., 150 . . . . .274/H5
Oto, Iowa, U.S., 145 . . . . .274/D4
Otoe, Nebr., U.S., 217 . . . . .308/H3
Otoe, Nebr., U.S., county, 15,396 . . . . . . .308/H3
Otranto, Alb., strait 99/A3
Otranto, It. 95/D2
Otranto, Iowa, U.S. 274/J1
Otsego, Mich., U.S., 3,933 . . . . .294/D7
Otsego, N.Y., U.S., county, 23,301 . . . . . .294/E5
Otsego, Minn., U.S., 6,389 . . . . .298/D5
Otsego, Ohio, U.S. 328/G5
Otsego Lake, Mich., U.S., 325 . . . . .294/E5
Otselic, N.Y., U.S., 90 . . . . .320/K5
Otsu, Jap., 288,000 . . . . .114/B3
Ottawa, Ont., Can., 774,072,
(1,128,900 metro.) 223/H5, K2
Ottawa, Ont., Can., 774,072,
(1,128,900 metro.) 223/G4
Ottawa, Ont., Can., river 223/G1, G5, H5, K2
Ottawa, Que., Can., river 226/A6
Ottawa, Ill., U.S., 18,307 . . . . .266/E2
Ottawa, Kans., U.S., 11,921 . . . . .276/G3
Ottawa, Kans., U.S., county, 6,163 . . . . . .276/E2
Ottawa, Mich., U.S., county, 238,314 . . . . .294/C7
Ottawa, Minn., U.S., 125 . . . . .298/D6
Ottawa, Ohio, U.S., 4,367 . . . . .328/B3
Ottawa, Ohio, U.S., county, 40,985 . . . . . .328/D2
Ottawa, Okla., U.S., county, 33,194 . . . . . .330/H1
Ottawa-Carleton, Ont., Can. 223/G5, K2
Ottawa-Carleton, Ont., Can., county . . .223/G5, K2
Ottawa Hills, Ohio, U.S., 4,564 . . . . .328/D2
Ottawa Natl. For., Mich., U.S. 294/A3, B3, D2
Ottawa N.W.R., Ohio, U.S. 328/D2
Otter, Mont., U.S. 306/K4
Otter, Mont., U.S., creek 352/A3
Otterbein, Ind., U.S., 1,312 . . . . .270/B4
Otterbourne, Eng., U.K. 70/B4
Otterburn, Eng., U.K. 66/D2
Otter Creek, Fla., U.S., 121 . . . . .256/F2
Otter Creek, Iowa, U.S., 50 . . . . .274/N3
Otter Creek, Maine, U.S., 250 . . . . .286/D4
Otter Ferry, Scot., U.K. 62/F7
Otter Lake, Mich., U.S., 437 . . . . .294/F6
Otterlo, Neth. 84/C2
Otter River, Mass., U.S., 850 . . . . .292/F2
Otter Rock, Oreg., U.S., 175 . . . . .334/B3
Otter Tail, Minn., U.S., 451 . . . . .298/B4
Otter Tail, Minn., U.S., county, 57,159 . . . .298/B4
Otterville, Ill., U.S., 120 . . . . .266/C4
Otterville, Mo., U.S., 476 . . . . .302/C3
Ottery St. Mary, Eng., U.K., 3,253 . . . . . . .73/G2
Otto, Ark., U.S., 50 . . . . .244/C2
Otto, Wyo., U.S., 40 . . . . .366/B1
Ottosen, Iowa, U.S., 61 . . . . .274/F2
Ottoville, Ohio, U.S., 873 . . . . .328/B4
Ottringham, Eng., U.K. 66/H5
Ottumwa, Iowa, U.S., 24,998 . . . . .274/K5
Ottumwa, Kans., U.S. 276/G3
Ottumwa, S. Dak., U.S. 342/D3

Ottusville, Ky., U.S. 280/F2
Otway, N.C., U.S., 700 . . . . .322/M5
Otway, Ohio, U.S., 86 . . . . .328/D8
Otwell, Ark., U.S., 60 . . . . .244/E2
Ötztal Alps, Aus., range 91/B4
Ou, Laos, river 124/B1
Ou, Jap., mountains 114/D2
Ouachita, Ark., U.S., 90 . . . . .244/C4
Ouachita, Ark., U.S., county, 28,790 . . . . .244/B4
Ouachita, Ark., U.S., lake 244/B3
Ouachita, Ark., U.S., mountains 244/A3, C3
Ouachita, La., U.S., parish, 147,250 . . . . .282/E2
Ouachita, La., U.S., river 282/E2
Ouachita, Okla., U.S., mountains 330/G3
Ouachita Natl. For., Ark., Okla., U.S. . .330/H3, H4
Ouachita Natl. For., Tex., U.S. 346/P2
Ouâdâne, Maur. .147/C2
Ouadda, C.A.R. .154/B2
Ouad Naba, Chad, river 153/C4
Ouagadougou, Burkina, capital, 634,479,
(1,026,000 metro.) 151/D2
Ouahigouya, Burkina, 38,604 . . . . .151/C2
Ouaka, C.A.R., river 154/B2
Ouanary, Fr. Gui. 183/C1
Ouango, C.A.R., river 154/C2
Ouargla, Alg. 146/B1
Ouarzazate, Mor. 147/C2
Oudtshoorn, S. Afr. 162/B3
Ouémé, Ben., river 151/B3
Ouesso, Congo, 16,171 . . . . .155/C3
Ouest, Haiti, department 205/C2
Ouezzane, Mor. .147/C1
Ouham, C.A.R., river 154/A2
Ouidah, Ben., 64,408 . . . . .151/B4
Oujda, Mor., 331,000 . . . . .147/D1
Oulton, Eng., U.K. 70/G1
Oulu, Fin., 120,753 . . . . .81/C1
Oulu, Fin., lake .81/C2
Oulu, Fin., province 81/C1
Oulujoki, Fin., river 81/C1
Oum er Rbia, Mor., river 147/C1
Ounasjoki, Fin., river 81/B1
Oundle, Eng., U.K., 3,996 . . . . .68/G5
Oundle, Eng., U.K., 3,996 . . . . .70/D2
Oungre, Sask., Can. 227/G11
Our, Ger., river 85/B3
Ouray, Colo., U.S., 813 . . . . .250/C3
Ouray, Colo., U.S., county, 3,742 . . . . . . .250/C3
Ouray, Utah, U.S. 350/E3
Ouray N.W.R., Utah, U.S. 350/E3
Ourense, Sp., 107,510 . . . . .94/C1
Ourense, Sp., province 94/C1
Ourthe, Belg., river 85/D2
Ousden, Eng., U.K. 70/F2
Ouse, Eng., U.K., river 60/C2
Outagamie, Wisc., U.S., county, 160,971 . .364/E4
Outarde, Que., Can., river 226/H2
Outer, Wisc., U.S., island 364/C1
Outer Hebrides, Scot., U.K., islands 60/A1
Outing, Minn., U.S., 100 . . . . .298/D4
Outjo, Nam. 160/B2
Outland, S.C., U.S., 100 . . . . .340/E3
Outlook, Sask., Can., 2,129 . . . . .227/C9
Outlook, Mont., U.S., 82 . . . . .306/M1
Out Skerries, Scot., U.K., island 62/Q2
Outwell, Eng., U.K., 1,683 . . . . .68/H4
Outwell, Eng., U.K., 1,683 . . . . .70/E1
Ouzinkie, Alaska, U.S., 225 . . . . .240/E3
Ovalau, Fiji, island 174/B2
Ovalle, Chile 190/B4
Ovalo, Tex., U.S., 150 . . . . .346/J3
Ovando, Mont., U.S., 71 . . . . .306/C2
Overall, Tenn., U.S., 800 . . . . .344/J3
Overbrook, Ala., U.S., 400 . . . . .238/C2
Overbrook, Kans., U.S., 947 . . . . .276/G3
Overbrook, Okla., U.S., 80 . . . . .330/E3
Overflakkee, Neth., island 84/B3
Overflowing River, Man., Can. 227/D5
Overflow N.W.R., Ark., U.S. 244/D4
Overgaard, Ariz., U.S., 2,722 . . . . .242/E3
Overijssel, Neth., province 84/D2
Over Kellet, Eng., U.K. 68/B1
Overland, Mo., U.S., 16,838 . . . . .302/H3
Overland Park, Kans., U.S., 149,080 . . . . .276/H1
Overlea, Md., U.S., 12,148 . . . . .288/H2
Overly, N. Dak., U.S. 326/E1
Overseal, Eng., U.K. 70/A1
Overstrand, Eng., U.K. 70/G1
Overton, Eng., U.K., 3,660 . . . . .66/C4
Overton, Eng., U.K., 3,660 . . . . .68/B1
Overton, Eng., U.K., 3,660 . . . . .70/B4
Overton, Wales, U.K., 3,660 . . . . .64/F2
Overton, Nebr., U.S., 646 . . . . .308/E3
Overton, Nev., U.S., 1,700 . . . . .310/C3
Overton, Tenn., U.S., county, 20,118 . . . . .344/L2
Overton, Tex., U.S., 2,350 . . . . .346/P3
Ovett, Miss., U.S., 150 . . . . .300/C4
Ovid, Colo., U.S., 330 . . . . .250/H1
Ovid, Ida., U.S., 50 . . . . .264/F7
Ovid, Mich., U.S., 1,514 . . . . .294/E6
Ovid, N.Y., U.S., 612 . . . . .320/H5
Oviedo, Dom. Rep. 205/A3
Oviedo, Sp., 201,154 . . . . .94/D1
Oviedo, Sp., province 94/C1
Oviedo, Fla., U.S., 26,316 . . . . .256/D4, G3
Ovington, Eng., U.K. 66/D3
Owando, Congo .155/C4
Owaneco, Ill., U.S., 256 . . . . .266/D4
Owanka, S. Dak., U.S. 342/C3
Owasa, Iowa, U.S. 274/H3
Owasso, Okla., U.S., 18,502 . . . . .330/G1
Owatonna, Minn., U.S., 22,434 . . . . .298/D6
Owego, N.Y., U.S., 3,911 . . . . .320/J6
Owen, Ky., U.S., county, 10,547 . . . . .280/F2
Owen, Wisc., U.S., 936 . . . . .364/C4
Owendale, Mich., U.S., 296 . . . . .294/F6
Owendo, Gabon 155/A1
Owens, Del., U.S., 125 . . . . .255/B5
Owens, Tex., U.S., 150 . . . . .346/K4
Owensboro, Ky., U.S., 54,067, (91,545 metro.) .280/C3
Owensburg, Ind., U.S., 225 . . . . .270/C7
Owens Crossroads, Ala., U.S., 1,124 . . . . .238/C1
Owen Sound, Ont., Can., 21,431 . . . . .223/E3
Owen Stanley, P.N.G., range 172/A2
Owensville, Ark., U.S., 70 . . . . .244/C3
Owensville, Ind., U.S., 1,322 . . . . .270/A8
Owensville, Mo., U.S., 2,500 . . . . .302/E3
Owensville, Ohio, U.S., 816 . . . . .328/B7
Owenton, Ky., U.S., 1,387 . . . . .280/E2
Owenton, Va., U.S., 175 . . . . .354/F5
Owerri, Nig. 152/D5
Owings Mills, Md., U.S., 20,193 . . . . .288/G2
Owingsville, Ky., U.S., 1,488 . . . . .280/G2
Owl Creek Mountains, Wyo., U.S. 366/B2
Owls Head, Maine, U.S., 1,601 . . . . .286/C4
Owosso, Mich., U.S., 15,713 . . . . .294/E6
Owslebury, Eng., U.K. 70/B4
Owsley, Ky., U.S., county, 4,858 . . . . .280/G3

Owston Ferry, Eng., U.K. 66/G6
Owyhee, Ida., U.S., *county*, 10,644 . . . . . .264/A7
Owyhee, Ida., U.S., *mountains* 264/A6
Owyhee, Nev., U.S., 1,017 . . . . .310/B1
Owyhee, Nev., U.S., *desert* 310/B1
Owyhee, Nev., U.S., *river* 310/B1
Owyhee, Oreg., U.S. 334/J4
Owyhee, Oreg., U.S., *river* 334/J4, K5
Oxbo, Wisc., U.S. 364/C3
Oxbow, Sask., Can., 1,132 . . . . .227/H11
Oxbow, Maine, U.S., 56 . . . . .286/D2
Oxbow, N. Dak., U.S., 248 . . . . .326/J3
Oxenhope, Eng., U.K. 66/E5
Oxenwood, Eng., U.K. 70/A4
Oxford, Man., Can., *lake* 215/D2
Oxford, N.S., Can., 1,332 . . . . .221/D2
Oxford, Ont., Can. 223/E4
Oxford, Ont., Can., *county* 223/E4
Oxford, Eng., U.K. 60/C3
Oxford, Eng., U.K., 134,248 . . . . .68/E6
Oxford, Eng., U.K., 134,248 . . . . .70/B3
Oxford, Ala., U.S., 14,592 . . . . .238/D2
Oxford, Ark., U.S., 642 . . . . .244/C1
Oxford, Colo., U.S., 70 . . . . .250/C4
Oxford, Conn., U.S., 9,821 . . . . .253/C4
Oxford, Fla., U.S., 350 . . . . .256/F3
Oxford, Ga., U.S., 1,892 . . . . .260/D4
Oxford, Ida., U.S., 53 . . . . .264/E7
Oxford, Ind., U.S., 1,271 . . . . .270/B3
Oxford, Iowa, U.S., 705 . . . . .274/L4
Oxford, Kans., U.S., 1,173 . . . . .276/E4
Oxford, Ky., U.S., 300 . . . . .280/F2
Oxford, La., U.S., 90 . . . . .282/B3
Oxford, Maine, U.S., 3,960 . . . . .286/B4
Oxford, Maine, U.S., *county*, 54,755 . . . . .286/B4
Oxford, Md., U.S., 771 . . . . .288/K5
Oxford, Mass., U.S., 13,352 . . . . .292/G4
Oxford, Mich., U.S., 3,540 . . . . .294/A6, F7
Oxford, Miss., U.S., 11,756 . . . . .300/C1
Oxford, Nebr., U.S., 876 . . . . .308/E3
Oxford, N.J., U.S., 2,307 . . . . .314/D2
Oxford, N.Y., U.S., 1,584 . . . . .320/K6
Oxford, N.C., U.S., 8,338 . . . . .322/H2
Oxford, Ohio, U.S., 21,943 . . . . .328/A6
Oxford, Penn., U.S., 4,315 . . . . .336/K6
Oxford, Tex., U.S. 346/K5
Oxford, Wisc., U.S., 536 . . . . .364/D5
Oxford House, Man., Can. 215/D1, D2
Oxford Jct., Iowa, U.S., 573 . . . . .274/N3
Oxfordshire, Eng., U.K., *unitary authority*,
605,492 . . . . .68/E6
Oxfordshire, Eng., U.K., *unitary authority*,
605,492 . . . . .70/B3
Oxley's Green, Eng., U.K. 70/F5
Oxly, Mo., U.S., 175 . . . . .302/F5
Oxnard, Calif., U.S., 170,358 . . . . .246/F8
Oxon Hill, (Oxon Hill-Glassmanor), Md., U.S.,
35,355 . . . . .288/B7
Oxted, Eng., U.K., 11,117 . . . . .70/E4
Oxton, Eng., U.K. 68/E3
Oyapok, Fr. Gui., *river* 183/B2
Oyem, Gabon, 22,404 . . . . .155/A1
Oyen, Alta., Can., 1,020 . . . . .212/E5
Oyens, Iowa, U.S., 132 . . . . .274/B2
Oylen, Minn., U.S., 50 . . . . .298/C4
Oyo, Nig. 152/B4
Oyo, Nig., *state* 152/B3
Oyster Creek, Tex., U.S., 1,192 . . . . .346/N7
Oysterville, Wash., U.S., 40 . . . . .358/A4
Ozama, Dom. Rep., *river* 205/B2
Ozan, Ark., U.S., 81 . . . . .244/B4
Ozark, Ala., U.S., 15,119 . . . . .238/D4
Ozark, Ark., U.S., 3,525 . . . . .244/B1
Ozark, Ark., U.S., *plateau* 244/A1
Ozark, Mich., U.S. 294/E3
Ozark, Mo., U.S., 9,665 . . . . .302/C4
Ozark, Mo., U.S., *county*, 9,542 . . . . .302/D5
Ozark Natl. For., Ark., U.S. 244/A1, A2, B2, C1
Ozark Natl. Scenic Riverways, Mo., U.S. . . .302/E4
Ozaukee, Wisc., U.S., *county*, 82,317 . . .364/F1, F5
Ozawkie, Kans., U.S., 552 . . . . .276/G2
Ozd, Hun. 91/C1
Ozette, Wash., U.S., *lake* 358/A1
Ozgön, Kyrg. 131/C2
Ozoir-la-Ferrière, Fr. . . . . .88/Inset II
Ozona, Miss., U.S., 425 . . . . .300/C5
Ozona, Tex., U.S., 3,436 . . . . .346/G5
Ozone, Ark., U.S., 225 . . . . .244/B4
Ozone, Tenn., U.S., 125 . . . . .344/M3
Ozurget'i, Geo. 103/A4
Paamiut, (Frederikshåb), Grld. 193/C2
Pa-an, (Hpa-an), Mya. 125/C3
Paauhau, Hawaii, U.S. 262/H4
Paauilo, Hawaii, U.S. 262/H4
Pabbay, Scot., U.K., *island* 62/B3
Pablo, Mont., U.S., 1,814 . . . . .306/B2
Pablo N.W.R., Mont., U.S. 306/B2
Pabna, Bangl., 104,479 . . . . .127/C4
Pacaraima, Ven., *mountains* 182/D3
Pacasmayo, Peru 185/B2
Pachena, Br. Col., Can., *point* 358/A1
Pachuca, Mex., *state capital*, 231,602,
(245,208 *metro*.) 200/E3
Pachuta, Miss., U.S., 245 . . . . .300/D4
Pacific, Calif., U.S., *ocean* 246/B6, C11, H3
Pacific, Mo., U.S., 5,482 . . . . .302/F3
Pacific, Oreg., U.S., *ocean* 334/C2
Pacific, Wash., U.S., 5,527 . . . . .358/C4
Pacific, Wash., U.S., *county*, 20,984 . . . . .358/B3
Pacific, Wash., U.S., *ocean* 358/A3
Pacifica, Calif., U.S., 38,390 . . . . .246/H2
Pacific Beach, Wash., U.S., 375 . . . . .358/A4
Pacific City, Oreg., U.S., 1,027 . . . . .334/C2
Pacific Grove, Calif., U.S., 15,522 . . . . .246/D6
Pacific Hts., Hawaii, U.S. 262/G2
Pacific Jct., Iowa, U.S., 507 . . . . .274/C5
Pacific Palisades, Hawaii, U.S. 262/E1, J2
Pacific Rim Natl. Park Reserve, Br. Col., Can. .214/K7
Pacific Rim Natl. Park Reserve, Br. Col., Can. .358/A1
Packard, Iowa, U.S. 274/J2
Packton, La., U.S. 282/D3
Packwood, Iowa, U.S., 223 . . . . .274/K5
Packwood, Wash., U.S., 550 . . . . .358/D3
Pacolet, S.C., U.S., 2,690 . . . . .340/C2, F2
Pacolet Mills, S.C., U.S. 340/C2, F2
Padang, Indon. 122/B2
Padbury, Eng., U.K. 70/C3
Paddle Prairie, Alta., Can., 581 . . . . .212/D2
Paddock Lake, Wisc., U.S., 3,012 . . . . .364/E4
Paden, Miss., U.S., 106 . . . . .300/D1
Paden, Okla., U.S., 446 . . . . .330/D2
Paden City, W. Va., U.S., 2,860 . . . . .360/E1
Paderborn, Ger., 137,647 . . . . .86/B3
Padiham, Eng., U.K., 12,570 . . . . .66/D5
Padiham, Eng., U.K., 12,570 . . . . .68/D3
Padma, Bangl., *river* 127/D5
Padonia, Kans., U.S. 276/G2

Padova, It. 95/B1
Padre Island Natl. Seashore, Tex., U.S. 346/L8
Padroni, Colo., U.S., 97 . . . . .250/G1
Padstow, Eng., U.K., 2,460 . . . . .73/C3
Padua, (Padova), It. 95/B1
Paducah, Tex., U.S., 1,498 . . . . .346/H1
Paektu san, N. Kor., *mountain* 116/C2
Pagadian, Phil., 142,515 . . . . .120/B5
Page, Ariz., U.S., 6,809 . . . . .242/D1
Page, Iowa, U.S., *county*, 16,976 . . . . . . .274/D6
Page, Nebr., U.S., 157 . . . . .308/E1
Page, N. Dak., U.S., 225 . . . . .326/H2
Page, Okla., U.S. 330/H3
Page, Va., U.S., *county*, 23,177 . . . . .354/F3
Page City, Kans., U.S., 60 . . . . .276/A2
Pagedale, Mo., U.S., 3,616 . . . . .302/H3
Pageland, S.C., U.S., 2,521 . . . . .340/D2
Page Manor, (Overlook-Page Manor), Ohio, U.S. .328/G2
Paglesham Eastend, Eng., U.K. 70/F3
Pagoda, Colo., U.S. 250/C1
Pagosa Jct., Colo., U.S. 250/C4
Pagosa Sprs., Colo., U.S., 1,591 . . . . .250/C4
Paguate, N. Mex., U.S., 474 . . . . .317/C2
Pahala, Hawaii, U.S., 1,378 . . . . .262/H6
Pahang, Malay., *river* 121/B2
Pahaska, Wyo., U.S. 366/B1
Pahoa, Hawaii, U.S., 962 . . . . .262/J6
Pahokee, Fla., U.S., 5,985 . . . . .256/H5
Pahranagat N.W.R., Nev., U.S. 310/C3
Pahrump, Nev., U.S., 24,631 . . . . .310/C3
Paiania, Gr. 100/Inset
Paignton, Eng., U.K., 42,989 . . . . .73/E4
Paijanne, Fin., *lake* 81/C2
Päijät-Häme, Fin., *region* 81/C2
Pailolo, Hawaii, U.S., *channel* 262/B3
Paincourtville, La., U.S., 884 . . . . .282/C6
Painesdale, Mich., U.S., 550 . . . . .294/A2
Painesville, Ohio, U.S., 17,503 . . . . .328/H2, J8
Painshawfield, Eng., U.K., 3,033 . . . . .66/E3
Paint, Man., Can., *lake* 215/B1
Paint, Mich., U.S., *river* 294/A3
Paint, Penn., U.S., 1,103 . . . . .336/D5
Paint Bank, Va., U.S. 354/C5
Painted, Ariz., U.S., *desert* 242/D1
Painted Post, N.Y., U.S., 1,842 . . . . .320/G6
Painter, Va., U.S., 246 . . . . .354/M5
Paintersville, Penn., U.S., 550 . . . . .336/G4
Paint Lake Prov. Rec. Park, Man., Can. 215/C1
Paint Lick, Ky., U.S., 200 . . . . .280/F2
Paint Rock, Ala., U.S., 185 . . . . .238/C1
Paint Rock, Tex., U.S., 320 . . . . .346/H4
Paintsville, Ky., U.S., 4,132 . . . . .280/H3
Paisano, Tex., U.S. 346/E5
Paisley, Scot., U.K. 60/B2
Paisley, Scot., U.K., 74,170 . . . . .62/H7
Paisley, Oreg., U.S., 247 . . . . .334/F5
Paita, Peru 185/A2
Paiute Ind. Res., Ariz., U.S. 242/B1
Paiute Ind. Res., Utah, U.S. 310/C3
Paiute Ind. Res., Utah, U.S. 350/A6
Pajarito, N. Mex., U.S., 2,700 . . . . .317/D2
Pajaro, Calif., U.S., 3,384 . . . . .246/D6
Pakala Vil., Hawaii, U.S., 478 . . . . .262/C2
Pakaraima, Guy., *mountains* 183/A3
Pakenham, Eng., U.K. 70/F2
Pakistan, *nation* 125
Pakowki, Alta., Can., *lake* 212/E6
Paks, Hun. 91/B2
Pakxan, Laos .124/B2
Pakxé, Laos, 47,323 . . . . .124/C4
Pala, Chad 153/A5
Palace, Mon. .97/B2
Palace Holy Office, Vat. 96/B2
Palacios, Tex., U.S., 5,153 . . . . .346/M7
Palaiseau, Fr. . . . . .88/Inset II
Palama, Hawaii, U.S. 262/F2
Palana, Russ. .104/J4
Palanga, Lith. .83/A2
Palangkaraya, Indon. 122/C2
Palaoa, Hawaii, U.S., *point* 262/B4
Palatine, Ill., U.S., 65,479 . . . . .266/B5
Palatine Bridge, N.Y., U.S., 706 . . . . .320/M5
Palatka, Fla., U.S., 10,033 . . . . .256/G2
Palau, *nation* 164
Palawan, Phil., *island* 120/A4
Palco, Kans., U.S., 248 . . . . .276/C2
Paldiski, Est. 81/C1
Pale, Bos.-Her. .98/B2
Pale, Wales, U.K. 64/D2
Palembang, Indon., 1,415,500 . . . . .122/B2
Palena, Chile, *lake* 190/B6
Palencia, Sp., 79,797 . . . . .94/D1
Palencia, Sp., *province* 94/D1
Palenville, N.Y., U.S., 1,120 . . . . .320/N6
Palermo, It., 652,640 . . . . .95/C3
Palermo, Calif., U.S., 5,720 . . . . .246/D3
Palermo, Maine, U.S., 1,220 . . . . .286/C4
Palermo, N.J., U.S., 2,300 . . . . .314/D5
Palermo, N. Dak., U.S., 77 . . . . .326/C1
Palestine, Eng., U.K. 70/A4
Palestine, Ark., U.S., 741 . . . . .244/E3
Palestine, Ill., U.S., 1,366 . . . . .266/F4
Palestine, Ohio, U.S., 170 . . . . .328/A5
Palestine, Tex., U.S., 17,598 . . . . .346/N4
Paley Street, Eng., U.K. 70/C4
Palikir, Micr., *capital*, 6,660 . . . . .172/C2
Palisade, Colo., U.S., 2,579 . . . . .250/B2
Palisade, Minn., U.S., 118 . . . . .298/D4
Palisade, Nebr., U.S., 386 . . . . .308/C3
Palisade, Nev., U.S. 310/B1
Palisades, Ida., U.S. 264/F6
Palisades, Ida., U.S., *reservoir* 264/F6
Palisades, Wash., U.S. 358/F2
Palisades Park, N.J., U.S., 17,073 . . . . .314/C2
Palito Blanco, Tex., U.S., 70 . . . . .346/K8
Palk, India, *strait* 128/C7
Palk, Sri Lan., *strait* 126/A2
Palliser, N.Z., *cape* 171/C3
Pall Mall, Tenn., U.S., 175 . . . . .344/M1
Palm, St. Vin.-Gren., *island* 205/A2
Palma de Mallorca, Sp., 333,801 . . . . .94/H3
Palmarejo, P.R. 206/A2
Palmas, Braz. .188/D3
Palmas, Liber., *cape* 149/C3
Palm Bay, Fla., U.S., 79,413 . . . . .256/H3
Palm Beach, Fla., U.S., 10,468 . . . . . . .256/B4, H5
Palm Beach, Fla., U.S., *county*, 1,131,184 .256/A4, H5
Palm Beach Gardens, Fla., U.S., 35,058 . . . .256/B4
Palm Beach Shores, Fla., U.S., 1,269 . . . . . .256/B4
Palm City, Fla., U.S., 20,097 . . . . .256/A4
Palm Coast, Fla., U.S., 32,732 . . . . .256/G2
Palmdale, Calif., U.S., 116,670 . . . . .246/G8
Palmdale, Fla., U.S., 175 . . . . .256/G5
Palm Desert, Calif., U.S., 41,155 . . . . .246/J9
Palmer, Alaska, U.S., 4,533 . . . . .240/F3
Palmer, Ill., U.S., 248 . . . . .266/D4
Palmer, Iowa, U.S., 214 . . . . .274/E2
Palmer, Kans., U.S., 108 . . . . .276/E2
Palmer, Mass., U.S., 12,497 . . . . .292/E4
Palmer, Mich., U.S., 449 . . . . .294/B3
Palmer, Nebr., U.S., 472 . . . . .308/E2

Palmer, Tenn., U.S., 726 . . . . .344/K4
Palmer, Tex., U.S., 1,774 . . . . .346/M3
Palmer Lake, Colo., U.S., 2,179 . . . . .250/F2
Palmer Land, Antar., *region* 192/B11
Palmer Park, Md., U.S., 7,000 . . . . .288/C7
Palmers, Minn., U.S., 80 . . . . .298/F4
Palmers Crossing, Miss., U.S. 300/C4
Palmerston, Ont., Can., 2,518 . . . . .223/E4
Palmerston North, N.Z., 72,036,
(72,681 *metro*.) 171/C3
Palmersville, Tenn., U.S., 90 . . . . .344/D2
Palmerton, Penn., U.S., 5,248 . . . . .336/K4
Palmetto, Ant.-Bar., *point* 207/C2
Palmetto, Fla., U.S., 12,571 . . . . .256/C6
Palmetto, Ga., U.S., 3,400 . . . . .260/B4, G4
Palmetto, La., U.S., 188 . . . . .282/F5
Palm Harbor, Fla., U.S., 59,248 . . . . . .256/C6, F3
Palmira, Col. .184/A4
Palm River, (Palm River-Clair Mel), Fla.,
U.S., 17,589 . . . . .256/D6
Palm Shores, Fla., U.S., 794 . . . . .256/H3
Palm Sprs., Calif., U.S., 42,807 . . . . .246/J9
Palm Sprs., Fla., U.S., 11,699 . . . . .256/B5
Palmyra, Syria, *ruins* 134/B2
Palmyra, U.S., *atoll* 161
Palmyra, Ark., U.S., 125 . . . . .244/D4
Palmyra, Ill., U.S., 733 . . . . .266/D4
Palmyra, Ind., U.S., 633 . . . . .270/D8
Palmyra, Maine, U.S., 1,953 . . . . .286/C4
Palmyra, Mo., U.S., 3,467 . . . . .302/E2
Palmyra, Nebr., U.S., 546 . . . . .308/H3
Palmyra, N.J., U.S., 7,091 . . . . .314/C3
Palmyra, N.Y., U.S., 3,490 . . . . .320/G4
Palmyra, Penn., U.S., 7,096 . . . . .336/H5
Palmyra, Va., U.S., 100 . . . . .354/G5
Palmyra, Wisc., U.S., 1,766 . . . . .364/E6
Palo, Iowa, U.S., 614 . . . . .274/L3
Palo Alto, Calif., U.S., 58,598 . . . . .246/C5, J3
Palo Alto, Iowa, U.S., *county*, 10,147 . . . .274/E1
Palo Alto, Penn., U.S., 1,052 . . . . .336/J4
Palo Alto Battlefield N.H.S., Tex., U.S. 347/L10
Paloduro, Tex., U.S. 346/G9
Palomas, P.R. .206/B2
Palomas, P.R. .206/C2
Palominas, (part of Sierra Vista Southeast),
Ariz., U.S. 242/E6
Palo Pinto, Tex., U.S., 150 . . . . .346/K3
Palo Pinto, Tex., U.S., *county*, 27,026 . . . .346/K3
Palopo, Indon. 122/D2
Palos, Sp., *cape* 94/F4
Palos Hts., Ill., U.S., 11,260 . . . . .266/B6
Palos Hills, Ill., U.S., 17,665 . . . . .266/B6
Palos Park, Ill., U.S., 4,689 . . . . .266/B6
Palos Verdes Estates, Calif., U.S., 13,340 . . .246/B10
Palouse, Wash., U.S., 1,011 . . . . .358/H3
Palo Verde, Ariz., U.S., 100 . . . . .242/C4
Palo Verde, Calif., U.S., 236 . . . . .246/L9
Palu, Indon. 122/C2
Pamirs, China, *region* 119/A2
Pamirs, Taj., *mountains* 132/B2
Pamlico, N.C., U.S., *county*, 12,934 . . . . .322/M4
Pamlico, N.C., U.S., *river* 322/M4
Pamlico, N.C., U.S., *sound* 322/P4
Pamlico Beach, N.C., U.S., 125 . . . . .322/M4
Pampa, Tex., U.S., 17,887 . . . . .346/G9
Pampas, Arg., *plain* 191/C4
Pamplemousses, Mauritius 163/C2
Pamplico, S.C., U.S., 1,139 . . . . .340/E3
Pamplin City, Va., U.S., 199 . . . . .354/F6
Pamplona, Sp., 183,964 . . . . .94/F1
Pana, Ill., U.S., 5,614 . . . . .266/D4
Panaca, Nev., U.S., 550 . . . . .310/C3
Panacea, Fla., U.S., 550 . . . . .256/D1
Panagyurishte, Bul. 101/C3
Panaji, India 128/B5
Panama, *nation* 191
Panamá, Pan., *bay* 203/C2
Panamá, Pan., *canal* 203/C2
Panamá, Pan., *gulf* 203/C3
Panamá, Pan., *province* 203/C2
Panama, Ill., U.S., 323 . . . . .266/D4
Panama, Iowa, U.S., 212 . . . . .274/D4
Panama, Nebr., U.S., 253 . . . . .308/H3
Panama, N.Y., U.S., 491 . . . . .320/C6
Panama, Okla., U.S., 1,362 . . . . .330/H2
Panama City, Pan., *capital*, 415,964,
(1,002,183 *metro*.) 203/C2
Panama City, Fla., U.S., 36,417,
(148,217 *metro*.) 256/C1
Panama City Beach, Fla., U.S., 7,671 . . . . . .256/C1
Panamint, Calif., U.S., *range* 246/H6
Panamint, Calif., U.S., *valley* 246/H6
Panay, Phil., *gulf* 120/B4
Panay, Phil., *island* 120/B4
Pančevo, Serb.-Mont., 123,884 . . . . .99/B2
Panch'iao, Tai. 117/B1
Panco, Ky., U.S., 80 . . . . .280/G3
Pandale, Tex., U.S. 346/G5
Pandan, Sing., *strait* 123/A2
Pandaruan, Bru., *river* 121/C2
Pando, Bol., *department* 186/A2
Pando, Uru. 187/D3
Pandora, Colo., U.S., 125 . . . . .250/C4
Pandora, Ohio, U.S., 1,188 . . . . .328/C4
Pandora, Tex., U.S., 70 . . . . .346/L6
Panevėžys, Lith., 133,695 . . . . .82/C2
Pangani, Tan., *river* 158/C1
Pangbourne, (Pangbourne/Whitchurch),
Eng., U.K., 3,362 . . . . .70/B4
Pangburn, Ark., U.S., 654 . . . . .244/D2
Pangkalanbuun, Indon. 122/C2
Pangkalpinang, Indon. 122/B2
Pangnirtung, Nun., Can., 1,276 . . . . .220/P3
Panhandle, Tex., U.S., 2,589 . . . . .346/G9
Paniau, Hawaii, U.S., *mountain* 262/A2
Panihati, India . . . . .128/Inset II
Panj, Afg., *river* 129/C1
Panj, Taj., *river* 132/B2
Panjakent, Taj. 132/A1
Panjgur, Pak. .129/A4
Panji Poyon, Taj. 132/A2
P'anmunjŏm, N. Kor. 116/A4
Pan Tak, Ariz., U.S., 40 . . . . .242/C4
Pantanal, Braz., *lowland* 188/C4
Pantano, Ariz., U.S., 350 . . . . .242/D4
Pantego, N.C., U.S., 170 . . . . .322/M3
Pantego, Tex., U.S., 2,318 . . . . .346/B10
Pantelleria, It., *island* 95/C3
Pante Makasar, E. Timor 122/A2
Panther, Ky., U.S., 175 . . . . .280/C3
Panthersville, Ga., U.S., 11,791 . . . . .260/J3

Panther Swamp N.W.R., Miss., U.S. 300/C3
Pant Mawr, Wales, U.K. 64/D3
Panton, Vt., U.S., 682 . . . . .352/A2
Pantperthog, Wales, U.K. 64/D2
Pant-y-dwr, Wales, U.K. 64/E3
Pánuco, Mex., *river* 200/D3
Panxworth, Eng., U.K. 70/G1
Panzhihua, China, 497,330, (795,910 *metro*.) .119/D3
Paoli, Colo., U.S., 5,011 . . . . .276/H3
Paoli, Colo., U.S., 42 . . . . .250/H1
Paoli, Ind., U.S., 3,844 . . . . .270/D7
Paoli, Okla., U.S., 664 . . . . .330/E3
Paoli, Penn., U.S., 5,425 . . . . .336/K7
Paonia, Colo., U.S., 1,497 . . . . .250/C3
Pápa, Hun. 91/A2
Papa, Hawaii, U.S. 262/G6
Papaaloa, Hawaii, U.S. 262/J5
Papagayo, C.R., *gulf* 203/A2
Papaikou, Hawaii, U.S., 1,414 . . . . .262/J5
Papa Stour, Scot., U.K., *island* 62/N2
Papawai, Hawaii, U.S., *point* 262/B4
Papa Westray, Scot., U.K., *island* 62/N1
Paphos, Cyp. .133/A2
Papillion, Nebr., U.S., 16,363 . . . . .308/H2
Papineau, Ill., U.S., 196 . . . . .266/F3
Papineau-Labelle Prov. Reserve, Que., Can. .226/A5
Papua, P.N.G., *gulf* 172/A2
Papua New Guinea, *nation* 164
Papworth Everard, Eng., U.K. 70/D2
Paquetville, N.B., Can., 667 . . . . .217/D1
Pará, Braz., *river* 188/C2
Pará, Braz., *state* 188/C2
Parachute, Colo., U.S., 1,006 . . . . .250/B2
Parade, S. Dak., U.S., 40 . . . . .342/D2
Paradise, Nfld., Can., *river* 218/C3
Paradise, Ariz., U.S. 242/F6
Paradise, Calif., U.S., 26,408 . . . . .246/D3
Paradise, Kans., U.S., 64 . . . . .276/D2
Paradise, Mich., U.S., 125 . . . . .294/D3
Paradise, Mont., U.S., 184 . . . . .306/B2
Paradise, Nev., U.S., 186,070 . . . . .310/C3
Paradise, Penn., U.S., 1,028 . . . . .336/J5
Paradise, Utah, U.S., 759 . . . . .350/C2
Paradise Hill, Sask., Can., 486 . . . . .227/A7
Paradise Hill, Okla., U.S., 100 . . . . .330/G2
Paradise Hills, N. Mex., U.S., 5,500 . . . . . . .317/D2
Paradise Lakes, N.J., U.S., 425 . . . . .314/C4
Paradise River, Nfld., Can. 218/C2
Paradise Valley, Ariz., U.S., 13,664 . . . . . . .242/D4
Paradise Valley, Nev., U.S., 60 . . . . .310/B1
Paradise Valley, Wyo., U.S. 366/G2
Paradox, Colo., U.S., 60 . . . . .250/B3
Paragon, Ind., U.S., 663 . . . . .270/C6
Paragonah, Utah, U.S., 470 . . . . .350/B6
Paragould, Ark., U.S., 22,017 . . . . .244/E1
Paraguá, Bol., *river* 188/C3
Paraguai, Braz., *river* 188/C3
Paraguarí, Para. 187/D4
Paraguarí, Para., *department* 187/D5
Paraguay, *nation* 177
Paraguay, Arg., *river* 191/C2
Paraguay, Bol., *river* 186/C4
Paraguay, Para., *river* 187/C2, C5
Paraíba, Braz., *state* 188/E2
Paraje, N. Mex., U.S. 317/C2
Parakou, Ben., 144,627 . . . . .151/B3
Paraloma, Ark., U.S., 60 . . . . .244/A4
Paramaribo, Sur., *capital*, 219,326,
(290,629 *metro*.) 183/B2
Paramount, Calif., U.S., 55,266 . . . . .246/C10
Paramus, N.J., U.S., 25,737 . . . . .314/B2, B3
Paraná, Arg., 207,041, (211,936 *metro*.) . .191/C3
Paraná, Arg., *river* 191/C3
Paraná, Braz., *river* 188/C4
Paraná, Braz., *state* 188/C4
Paranaguá, Braz., 68,366, (107,583 *metro*.) .188/D4
Paranam, Sur. .183/B2
Parchment, Mich., U.S., 1,936 . . . . .294/D7
Pardee, Va., U.S., 50 . . . . .354/C2
Pardeeville, Wisc., U.S., 1,982 . . . . .364/D5
Pardubice, Czh. Rep., 93,000 . . . . .92/B2
Pardubický, Czh. Rep., *region* 92/B3
Parece Vela, Jap., *island* 172/A1
Parent, Que., Can., 326 . . . . .226/B4
Parent, Maine, U.S. 286/C1
Parepare, Indon. 122/C2
Paria, Trin.-To., *gulf* 209/A2
Paria, Utah, U.S., *river* 350/C6
Paria, Ven., *gulf* 182/D1
Paricutín, Mex., *volcano* 200/D4
Parima, Braz., *range* 188/B1
Parima, Ven., *mountains* 182/D3
Paris, Ont., Can., 9,881 . . . . .223/E4
Paris, Fr., 2,147,857, (9,644,507 *metro*.) .88/C2, Inset II
Paris, Fr., *department* 88/C2
Paris, Ark., U.S., 3,707 . . . . .244/B2
Paris, Ida., U.S., 576 . . . . .264/F7
Paris, Ill., U.S., 9,077 . . . . .266/F4
Paris, Iowa, U.S., 80 . . . . .274/L3
Paris, Ky., U.S., 9,183 . . . . .280/F2
Paris, Maine, U.S., 4,793 . . . . .286/B4
Paris, Mich., U.S., 450 . . . . .294/D6
Paris, Miss., U.S., 175 . . . . .300/C1
Paris, Mo., U.S., 1,520 . . . . .302/D2
Paris, Tenn., U.S., 9,763 . . . . .344/E2
Paris, Tex., U.S., 25,898 . . . . .346/N2
Paris Crossing, Ind., U.S., 200 . . . . .270/E7
Parish, N.Y., U.S., 512 . . . . .320/J4
Parishville, N.Y., U.S., 600 . . . . .320/M1
Parita, Pan., *bay* 203/B2
Park, N. Ire., U.K., 435 . . . . .65/C2
Park, Scot., U.K. 62/F4
Park, Colo., U.S., *county*, 14,523 . . . . . . .250/E2
Park, Colo., U.S., *range* 250/D1
Park, Kans., U.S., 151 . . . . .276/B2
Park, Mont., U.S., *county*, 15,694 . . . . . .306/F4
Park, Wyo., U.S., *county*, 25,786 . . . . . . .366/B1
Park City, Ill., U.S., 6,637 . . . . .266/E4
Park City, Kans., U.S., 5,814 . . . . .276/E4
Park City, Ky., U.S., 517 . . . . .280/D3
Park City, Mont., U.S., 870 . . . . .306/H4
Park City, Utah, U.S., 7,371 . . . . .350/C3, D2
Park Corner, P.E.I., Can. 224/B2
Parkdale, Ark., U.S., 377 . . . . .244/D4
Parkdale, Colo., U.S. 250/E3
Parkdale, Mo., U.S., 205 . . . . .302/G4
Parkdale, Oreg., U.S., 266 . . . . .334/E2
Parke, Ind., U.S., *county*, 17,241 . . . . . . .270/B4
Parkend, Eng., U.K. 68/B6
Parke Prov. Reserve, Que., Can. 226/B3
Parker, Ariz., U.S., 3,140 . . . . .242/A3
Parker, Ariz., U.S., *dam* 242/A3
Parker, Colo., U.S., 23,558 . . . . .250/F2
Parker, Ida., U.S., 319 . . . . .264/F6
Parker, Kans., U.S., 281 . . . . .276/H3
Parker, Penn., U.S., 799 . . . . .336/B3
Parker, S.C., U.S., 10,760 . . . . .340/B2, G2
Parker, S. Dak., U.S., 1,031 . . . . .342/H4
Parker, Tex., U.S., 175 . . . . .346/C8

Parker, Tex., U.S., *county*, 88,495 . . . . .346/L3
Parker, Wash., U.S., 400 . . . . .358/E3
Parker City, Ind., U.S., 1,416 . . . . .270/F4
Parker Dam, Calif., U.S., 100 . . . . .246/L8
Parker Hill, N.H., U.S., 80 . . . . .312/C3
Parker Ridge, N.B., Can. 217/C2
Parker River N.W.R., Mass., U.S. 292/L1
Parkers, Ark., U.S., 3,499 . . . . .244/C3
Parkersburg, Ill., U.S., 234 . . . . .266/E5
Parkersburg, Iowa, U.S., 1,889 . . . . .274/I2
Parkersburg, W. Va., U.S., 33,099,
   (151,237 *metro.*) 360/C2
Parker's Cross Roads, Tenn., U.S., 241 . . . . .344/E3
Parkers Lake, Ky., U.S. 280/F4
Parkers Prairie, Minn., U.S., 991 . . . . .298/B4
Parkerton, Wyo., U.S. 366/D2
Parkertown, Ohio, U.S., 225 . . . . .328/E3
Parkerville, Kans., U.S., 73 . . . . .276/F3
Parkesburg, Penn., U.S., 3,373 . . . . .336/K6
Park Falls, Wisc., U.S., 2,793 . . . . .364/C3
Parkfield, Calif., U.S. 246/E7
Park Forest, Ill., U.S., 23,462 . . . . .266/B6, F2
Park Forest Vil., Penn., U.S., 8,830 . . . . .336/F4
Park Grove, Mont., U.S. 306/K1
Park Hall, Md., U.S., 800 . . . . .288/J7
Parkhill, Ont., Can., 1,752 . . . . .223/D4
Park Hill, N.H., U.S. 312/B6
Park Hill, Okla., U.S., 3,936 . . . . .330/H2
Park Hills, Ky., U.S., 2,977 . . . . .280/G1
Park Hills, Mo., U.S., 7,861 . . . . .302/F4
Parkhurst, Eng., U.K. 70/B5
Parkin, Ark., U.S., 1,602 . . . . .244/E2
Parkindale, N.B., Can. 217/E3
Park Lake, Ky., U.S., 537 . . . . .280/E2
Parkland, Alta., Can. 212/D6
Parkland, Fla., U.S., 13,835 . . . . .256/A5
Parkland, Wash., U.S., 24,053 . . . . .358/C2
Park Lane, Conn., U.S., 650 . . . . .253/B3
Parkman, Maine, U.S., 811 . . . . .286/C3
Parkman, Ohio, U.S., 600 . . . . .328/H3
Parkman, Wyo., U.S., 137 . . . . .366/C1
Park Rapids, Minn., U.S., 3,276 . . . . .298/B4
Park Rapids, Wash., U.S., 70 . . . . .358/H1
Park Ridge, Ill., U.S., 37,775 . . . . .266/B5
Park Ridge, N.J., U.S., 8,708 . . . . .314/B1, J1
Park Ridge, Wisc., U.S., 488 . . . . .364/D4
Park River, N. Dak., U.S., 1,535 . . . . .326/H1
Parks, Ariz., U.S., 1,137 . . . . .242/D2
Parks, Ark., U.S. 244/B3
Parks, La., U.S., 533 . . . . .282/F6
Parks, Nebr., U.S. 308/C3
Parkside, Penn., U.S., 2,267 . . . . .336/L7
Parksley, Va., U.S., 837 . . . . .354/M5
Park Sprs., Tex., U.S. 346/L2
Parkston, S. Dak., U.S., 1,674 . . . . .342/G4
Parksville, Br. Col., Can., 10,323 . . . . .214/K6
Parksville, N.Y., U.S., 150 . . . . .320/M7
Parksville, S.C., U.S., 120 . . . . .340/B3
Parkton, N.C., U.S., 428 . . . . .322/G5
Park Valley, Utah, U.S., 80 . . . . .350/A2
Park View, Iowa, U.S., 2,169 . . . . .274/N4
Parkville, Md., U.S., 31,118 . . . . .288/H2
Parkville, Mo., U.S., 4,059 . . . . .302/H5
Parkville, Penn., U.S., 6,593 . . . . .336/H6
Parkway, (Parkway-S. Sacramento), Calif.,
   U.S., 36,468 . . . . .246/K5
Parkway, Mo., U.S., 280 . . . . .302/F3
Parkway Vil., Ky., U.S., 715 . . . . .280/A2
Parkwood, N.C., U.S. 322/H3
Parkwood, Wash., U.S., 7,213 . . . . .358/A4
Parlier, Calif., U.S., 11,145 . . . . .246/F6
Parlin, Colo., U.S. 250/D3
Parma, It. 95/B1
Parma, Ida., U.S., 1,771 . . . . .264/A6
Parma, Mich., U.S., 907 . . . . .294/E7
Parma, Mo., U.S., 852 . . . . .302/G5
Parma, Ohio, U.S., 85,655 . . . . .328/G3, G9
Parma Hts., Ohio, U.S., 21,659 . . . . .328/G9
Parmele, N.C., U.S., 290 . . . . .322/L3
Parmelee, S. Dak., U.S., 650 . . . . .342/D3
Parmer, Tex., U.S., *county*, 10,016 . . . . .346/E1, F1
Parnaíba, Braz., 78,718, (127,986 *metro.*) 188/D2
Parnaíba, Braz., *river* 188/D2
Parnell, Ill., U.S., 40 . . . . .266/E3
Parnell, Iowa, U.S., 220 . . . . .274/L4
Parnell, Mo., U.S., 197 . . . . .302/B1
Parnell, Tex., U.S. 346/G10, H1
Pärnu, Est., 45,500 . . . . .81/C2
Pärnu, Est., *river* 81/C2
Paro, Bhu. 126/A2
Parole, Md., U.S., 14,031 . . . . .288/H4
Paron, Ark., U.S. 244/C3
Paropamisus, Afg., *range* 129/A2
Paros, Gr., *island* 100/C3
Parowan, Utah, U.S., 2,565 . . . . .350/B6
Parque Nacional Los Novillos, Mex. 346/G6
Parr, Ind., U.S., 150 . . . . .270/B2
Parracombe, Eng., U.K. 73/E2
Parral, Chile 190/B5
Parral, Ohio, U.S., 241 . . . . .328/G4
Parramatta, N.S.W., Austl. . . . . .170/Inset IV
Parran, Nev., U.S. 310/A2
Parrish, Ala., U.S., 1,268 . . . . .238/B2
Parrish, Fla., U.S., 550 . . . . .256/D7, F4
Parrish, Wisc., U.S. 364/D3
Parris Island, S.C., U.S., 4,841 . . . . .340/D4
Parris Island Marine Corps Recruit Depot,
   S.C., U.S. 340/D4
Parrott, Ga., U.S., 156 . . . . .260/B8
Parrott, Va., U.S., 225 . . . . .354/B6
Parrottsville, Tenn., U.S., 207 . . . . .344/Q2
Parrsboro, N.S., Can., 1,529 . . . . .221/C2
Parry, N.W. Terr., Can. 220/D2
Parry, Nun., Can., *channel* 220/J2
Parry Sound, Ont., Can., 6,124 . . . . .223/E2
Parry Sound, Ont., Can., *county* 223/E2
Parryville, Penn., U.S., 478 . . . . .336/K4
Parshall, Colo., U.S., 50 . . . . .250/D1
Parshall, N. Dak., U.S., 981 . . . . .326/C2
Parsippany, (Parsippany-Troy Hills),
   N.J., U.S., 50,649 . . . . .314/E2
Parsnip, Br. Col., Can., *river* 214/L4
Parson Drove, Eng., U.K. 70/E1
Parsons, Kans., U.S., 11,514 . . . . .276/G4
Parsons, Tenn., U.S., 2,452 . . . . .344/E3
Parsons, W. Va., U.S., 1,463 . . . . .360/G2
Parsonsburg, Md., U.S., 600 . . . . .288/N6
Parsonsfield, Maine, U.S., 1,584 . . . . .286/B5
Parsons Pond, Nfld., Can., 427 . . . . .218/C4
Parsonville, Md., U.S. 288/L7
Parthenon, Ark., U.S., 80 . . . . .244/B2
Partlow, N.J., U.S., 200 . . . . .354/H4
Partney, Oreg., U.S. 62/H3
Parton, Scot., U.K. 62/H9
Partridge, Kans., U.S., 259 . . . . .276/D4
Partridge Green, Eng., U.K. 70/D5
Parwich, Eng., U.K. 68/D3
Pasadena, Calif., U.S., 133,936 . . . . .246/D9
Pasadena, Md., U.S., 12,093 . . . . .288/H3

Pasadena, Tex., U.S., 141,674 . . . . .346/B6, N6
Pa Sak, Thai., *river* 125/B3
Pasayten, Wash., U.S., *river* 358/E1
Pascagoula, Miss., U.S., 26,200 . . . . .300/D5
Pascagoula, Miss., U.S., *river* 300/D5
Pasco, Peru, *department* 185/B3
Pasco, Fla., U.S., 100 . . . . .256/F3
Pasco, Fla., U.S., *county*, 344,765 . . . . .256/F3
Pasco, Wash., U.S., 32,066 . . . . .358/F3
Pascoag, R.I., U.S., 4,742 . . . . .339/B2
Pascola, Mo., U.S., 138 . . . . .302/G5
Pas-de-Calais, Fr., *department* 88/C1
Pas de la Casa, And. 93/C2
Pasfield, Sask., Can., *lake* 227/B2
Pasión, Guat., *river* 201/C3
Paskenta, Calif., U.S. 246/C3
Paso de los Toros, Uru. 187/B2
Paso de Palmar, Uru., *lake* 187/B2
Paso Robles, Calif., U.S., 24,297 . . . . .246/E7
Paso Seco, P.R. 206/C2
Pasquotank, N.C., U.S., *county*, 34,897 . . . . .322/N2
Passadumkeag, Maine, U.S., 441 . . . . .286/D3
Passaic, Mo., U.S., 40 . . . . .302/B3
Passaic, N.J., U.S., 67,861 . . . . .314/B2, E2
Passaic, N.J., U.S., *county*, 489,049 . . . . .314/A1, E1
Passamaquoddy Indian Township I.R., Maine, U.S. 286/E3
Passau, Ger. 86/C4
Pass Christian, Miss., U.S., 6,579 . . . . .300/C5
Passero, It., *cape* 95/C3
Passo Fundo, Braz., 103,121, (147,215 *metro.*) 188/C4
Passumpsic, Vt., U.S., 150 . . . . .352/C2
Pastavy, Bela. 82/C2
Pastaza, Ecua., *province* 185/C3
Pastaza, Ecua., *river* 185/C4
Pastaza, Peru, *river* 185/B1
Pastillo, P.R. 206/C2
Pasto, Col., 379,000 . . . . .184/A4
Pastura, N. Mex., U.S. 317/F3
Patagonia, Arg., *region* 191/A6
Patagonia, Ariz., U.S., 881 . . . . .242/E6
Pataha, Wash., U.S., 60 . . . . .358/H3
Patapsco, Md., U.S., *river* 288/H3
Pataskala, Ohio, U.S., 10,249 . . . . .328/E5
Patavilca, Peru 185/B3
Patch Grove, Wisc., U.S., 166 . . . . .364/C6
Patchogue, N.Y., U.S., 11,919 . . . . .320/E2
Patchole, Eng., U.K. 73/E2
Pateley Bridge, Eng., U.K. 66/E4
Pateros, Wash., U.S., 643 . . . . .358/F1
Paterson, N.J., U.S., 149,222 . . . . .314/B2, E2
Paterson, Wash., U.S. 358/F4
Patesville, Ky., U.S., 50 . . . . .280/D3
Patetown, N.C., U.S., 50 . . . . .322/K4
Pathfinder, Wyo., U.S., *reservoir* 366/D2
Pathfinder N.W.R., Wyo., U.S. 366/D2
Pathfork, Ky., U.S., 350 . . . . .280/G4
Patía, Col., *river* 184/A4
Patiala, India 128/C2
Patience, Alta., Can. 212/D4
Patillas, P.R. 206/C2
Patmos, Ark., U.S., 61 . . . . .244/B4
Patna, India, 1,376,950, (1,707,429 *metro.*) 128/E3
Patna, Scot., U.K., 2,179 . . . . .62/H8
Patoka, Ill., U.S., 633 . . . . .266/D5
Patoka, Ind., U.S., 749 . . . . .270/A8
Patoka, Ind., U.S., *river* 270/B8
Paton, Iowa, U.S., 265 . . . . .274/F3
Patos, Braz., *lagoon* 188/C5
Patrai, Gr., 163,446, (170,452 *metro.*) 100/B2
Patricia, Alta., Can., 116 . . . . .212/E6
Patricia, S. Dak., U.S. 342/D4
Patricia, Tex., U.S. 346/G3
Patrick, Nev., U.S. 310/A2
Patrick, S.C., U.S., 354 . . . . .340/C7
Patrick, Va., U.S., *county*, 19,407 . . . . .354/C7
Patricksburg, Ind., U.S., 250 . . . . .270/C6
Patrick Sprs., Va., U.S., 2,068 . . . . .354/C7
Patriot, Ind., U.S., 202 . . . . .270/G7
Patroon, Tex., U.S. 346/R4
Patsville, Nev., U.S. 310/C1
Pattani, Thai. 125/B5
Patten, Maine, U.S., 1,111 . . . . .286/D3
Pattenburg, N.J., U.S., 800 . . . . .314/C2
Patterdale, Eng., U.K. 66/C3
Patterson, Ark., U.S., 467 . . . . .244/D2
Patterson, Calif., U.S., 11,606 . . . . .246/D5
Patterson, Ga., U.S., 627 . . . . .260/G9
Patterson, Ida., U.S. 264/D5
Patterson, Ill., U.S., 120 . . . . .266/C4
Patterson, Iowa, U.S., 126 . . . . .274/G4
Patterson, Kans., U.S. 276/E4
Patterson, La., U.S., 5,130 . . . . .282/G7
Patterson, Mo., U.S., 250 . . . . .302/F4
Patterson, N.Y., U.S., 950 . . . . .320/P7
Patterson, Ohio, U.S., 138 . . . . .328/C4
Patterson Gardens, Mich., U.S., 3,900 . . . . .294/F8
Patterson Hts., Penn., U.S., 670 . . . . .336/A4
Patterson Sprs., N.C., U.S., 620 . . . . .322/B4
Pattishall, Eng., U.K. 68/E5
Pattison, Miss., U.S., 175 . . . . .300/B4
Pattison, Tex., U.S., 447 . . . . .346/N6
Patton, Ill., U.S., 125 . . . . .266/F5
Patton, Mo., U.S., 125 . . . . .302/F4
Patton, Penn., U.S., 2,023 . . . . .336/M4
Pattonsburg, Mo., U.S., 261 . . . . .302/B1
Patton Vil., Tex., U.S., 1,391 . . . . .346/N5
Patuakhali, Bangl. 127/D6
Patuanak, Sask., Can., 72 . . . . .227/C5
Patuca, Hond., *mountains* 202/C2
Patuca, Hond., *river* 202/C2
Patuxent, Md., U.S., *river* 288/D6, H4
Patzau, Wisc., U.S., 80 . . . . .364/A2
Pau, Fr., 80,610, (181,413 *metro.*) 88/B5
Pauchaug St. For., Conn., U.S. 253/H3
Paugnut St. For., Conn., U.S. 253/C4
Paugussett St. For., Conn., U.S. 253/C4
Pauingassi, Man., Can. 215/D3
Paukaa, Hawaii, U.S., 495 . . . . .262/J5
Paul, Ida., U.S., 998 . . . . .264/D7
Paul, Nebr., U.S. 308/J3
Paulatuk, N.W. Terr., Can., 286 . . . . .220/D3
Paulaya, Hond., *river* 202/C2
Paulden, Ariz., U.S., 3,420 . . . . .242/C3
Paulding, Ga., U.S., *county*, 81,678 . . . . .260/B4
Paulding, Mich., U.S., 70 . . . . .294/A3
Paulding, Miss., U.S., 200 . . . . .300/C3
Paulding, Ohio, U.S., 3,595 . . . . .328/A3
Paulding, Ohio, U.S., *county*, 20,293 . . . . .328/A3
Paulerspury, Eng., U.K. 70/C2
Paulette, Miss., U.S. 300/D3
Paulina, Oreg., U.S., 40 . . . . .334/G3
Pauline, Ida., U.S. 264/E3
Pauline, Nebr., U.S., 90 . . . . .308/H4
Pauline, S.C., U.S., 350 . . . . .340/C2, F2
Paulins Kill, N.J., U.S., 1,400 . . . . .314/D1
Paullina, Iowa, U.S., 1,124 . . . . .274/C2
Paulo Afonso, Braz. 188/E2
Paulo Afonso, Braz., *falls* 188/E2

Paulsboro, N.J., U.S., 6,160 . . . . .314/C4
Paul Smiths, N.Y., U.S., 50 . . . . .320/N2
Paul Spur, Ariz., U.S. 242/F6
Pauls Valley, Okla., U.S., 6,256 . . . . .330/E3
Pauma Valley, Calif., U.S., 325 . . . . .246/J9
Pauwela, Hawaii, U.S., 6,578 . . . . .262/C3
Pauwela, Hawaii, U.S., *point* 262/C3
Pavant, Utah, U.S., *range* 350/B5
Pavia, It. 95/B1
Pavilion, N.Y., U.S., 550 . . . . .320/E5
Pavillion, Wyo., U.S., 165 . . . . .366/B2
Pavilosta, Lat. 82/A2
Pavlodar, Kaz., 300,503 . . . . .131/D1
Pavlodar, Kaz., *oblast* 131/D1
Pavo, Ga., U.S., 711 . . . . .260/D1
Pawanee, Kans., U.S., *creek* 276/B3
Pawcatuck, Conn., U.S., 5,474 . . . . .253/H4
Pawhuska, Okla., U.S., 3,629 . . . . .330/F1
Pawlet, Vt., U.S., 1,394 . . . . .352/A4
Pawleys Island, S.C., U.S., 138 . . . . .340/E3
Pawling, N.Y., U.S., 2,233 . . . . .320/P7
Pawnee, Colo., U.S., *creek* 250/G1
Pawnee, Ill., U.S., 2,647 . . . . .266/D4
Pawnee, Kans., U.S., *county*, 7,233 . . . . .276/C3
Pawnee, Nebr., U.S., *county*, 3,087 . . . . .308/H3
Pawnee, Okla., U.S., 2,230 . . . . .330/F1
Pawnee, Okla., U.S., *county*, 16,612 . . . . .330/F1
Pawnee, Tex., U.S., 201 . . . . .346/K7
Pawnee City, Nebr., U.S., 1,033 . . . . .308/H3
Pawnee Natl. Grassland, Colo., U.S. 250/F1, G1
Pawnee Rock, Kans., U.S., 356 . . . . .276/C3
Paw Paw, Ill., U.S., 852 . . . . .266/E2
Paw Paw, Ky., U.S., 175 . . . . .280/H3
Paw Paw, Mich., U.S., 3,363 . . . . .294/D7
Paw Paw, W. Va., U.S., 524 . . . . .360/K1
Paw Paw Lake, Mich., U.S., 3,944 . . . . .294/C7
Pawson, Eng., U.K. 66/D1
Pawtucket, R.I., U.S., 72,958 . . . . .339/D2
Pawtuxet, R.I., U.S. 339/D3
Pax, W. Va., U.S., 174 . . . . .360/D5
Paxbān, Guat. 201/C2
Paxico, Kans., U.S., 211 . . . . .276/F2
Paxson, Alaska, U.S., 43 . . . . .240/F2
Paxton, Scot., U.K. 62/M7
Paxton, Fla., U.S., 656 . . . . .256/B1
Paxton, Ill., U.S., 4,525 . . . . .266/E3
Paxton, Mass., U.S., 4,386 . . . . .292/G3
Paxton, Nebr., U.S., 614 . . . . .308/C2
Paxtonia, Penn., U.S., 5,254 . . . . .336/H5
Paxville, S.C., U.S., 248 . . . . .340/D3
Payar, Sen. 148/B2
Paye, India . . . . .128/Inset I
Payette, Ida., U.S., 7,054 . . . . .264/A5
Payette, Ida., U.S., *county*, 20,578 . . . . .264/A5
Payette, Ida., U.S., *lake* 264/A5
Payette, Ida., U.S., *river* 264/A5
Payette Natl. For., Ida., U.S. 264/A5, B4
Payne, Que., U.S., *lake* 225/B2
Payne, Ga., U.S., 178 . . . . .260/D6
Payne, Minn., U.S. 298/E3
Payne, Ohio, U.S., 1,166 . . . . .328/A3
Payne, Okla., U.S., *county*, 68,190 . . . . .330/E1
Paynes, Miss., U.S., 150 . . . . .300/B2
Paynesville, Mich., U.S., 125 . . . . .294/A3
Paynesville, Minn., U.S., 2,267 . . . . .298/C5
Paynesville, Mo., U.S., 91 . . . . .302/F2
Payneway, Ark., U.S., 225 . . . . .244/E2
Paynton, Sask., Can., 172 . . . . .227/B7
Paysandú, Uru., 74,568 . . . . .187/A1
Paysandú, Uru., *department* 187/B1
Pays de la Loire, Fr., *region* 88/B3
Payson, Ariz., U.S., 13,620 . . . . .242/D3
Payson, Ill., U.S., 1,066 . . . . .266/B4
Payson, Utah, U.S., 12,716 . . . . .350/C3
Paytes, Va., U.S., 250 . . . . .354/H4
Paz, Guat., *river* 201/C6
Pazardzhik, Bul., 128,900 . . . . .101/C3
Pazardzhik, Bul., *oblast* 101/B3
Peč, Serb.-Mont. 99/B3
Peabody, Kans., U.S., 1,384 . . . . .276/E3
Peabody, Mass., U.S., 48,129 . . . . .292/E6, L2
Peace, Alta., Can., *river* 212/A3, C2
Peace, Br. Col., Can., *river* 214/L3
Peace, Fla., U.S., *river* 256/G4
Peacehaven, Eng., U.K., 16,517 . . . . .70/E5
Peace Pt., Alta., Can. 212/D1
Peace River, Alta., Can., 6,240 . . . . .212/B3
Peach, Ga., U.S., *county*, 23,668 . . . . .260/D6
Peacham, Vt., U.S., 665 . . . . .352/C2
Peach Creek, W. Va., U.S., 175 . . . . .360/C5
Peach Lake, N.Y., U.S., 1,671 . . . . .320/C1, P8
Peachland, Br. Col., Can., 4,654 . . . . .214/N6
Peachland, N.C., U.S., 554 . . . . .322/E5
Peach Orchard, Ark., U.S., 195 . . . . .244/E1
Peach Orchard (part of S. Augusta), Ga., U.S. 260/G5
Peach Sprs., Ariz., U.S., 600 . . . . .242/B2
Peachtree City, Ga., U.S., 31,580 . . . . .260/C5
Peacock, Tex., U.S., 40 . . . . .346/H2
Peahala Park, N.J., U.S., 850 . . . . .314/E4
Pea Island N.W.R., N.C., U.S. 322/Q3
Peak, S.C., U.S., 61 . . . . .340/C2
Peak District Natl. Park, Eng., U.K. 66/E6
Peak District Natl. Park, Eng., U.K. 68/D3
Peakes, P.E.I., Can. 224/C2
Peak Forest, Eng., U.K. 66/E6
Peaks Mill, Ky., U.S., 300 . . . . .280/F2
Peale, Colo., U.S., *mountain* 250/A3
Peale, Utah, U.S., *mountain* 350/E3
Peanut, Calif., U.S. 246/B2
Pearcy, Ark., U.S., 175 . . . . .244/B3
Pea Ridge, Ala., U.S., 175 . . . . .238/C2
Pea Ridge, Ark., U.S., 2,346 . . . . .244/A1
Pea Ridge Natl. Mil. Park, Ark., U.S. 244/A1
Pearisburg, Va., U.S., 2,729 . . . . .354/B6
Pearl, Hawaii, U.S., *harbor* 262/E2
Pearl, Ida., U.S. 264/A6
Pearl, Ill., U.S., 187 . . . . .266/C4
Pearl, Miss., U.S., 21,961 . . . . .300/B3
Pearl, Miss., U.S., *river* 300/B4, C3
Pearl, Tex., U.S., 50 . . . . .346/K4
Pearland, Tex., U.S., 37,640 . . . . .346/B7
Pearl Beach, Mich., U.S., 3,224 . . . . .294/G7
Pearl City, Hawaii, U.S., 30,976 . . . . .262/C5, E1, J2
Pearl City, Ill., U.S., 780 . . . . .266/D1
Pearl Harbor N.W.R., Hawaii, U.S. 262/D2, J2
Pearlington, Miss., U.S., 1,684 . . . . .300/C5
Pearl River, La., U.S., 1,839 . . . . .282/K6
Pearl River, Miss., U.S., 3,156 . . . . .300/C5
Pearl River, Miss., U.S., *county*, 48,621 . . . . .300/C5
Pearl River, N.Y., U.S., 15,553 . . . . .320/B1
Pearsall, Tex., U.S., 7,157 . . . . .346/J7
Pearson, Ark., U.S., 70 . . . . .244/C2
Pearson, Ga., U.S., 1,805 . . . . .260/F9
Pearson, Okla., U.S., 50 . . . . .330/F2
Pearson, Wisc., U.S., 80 . . . . .364/D3
Peasedown SaintJohn, Eng., U.K., 3,398 . . . . .73/H2
Peasenhall, Eng., U.K. 71/G1
Pebane, Moz. 161/C3
Pebble Beach, Calif., U.S., 100 . . . . .246/D6

Pecan Acres, Tex., U.S. 346/A9
Pecan Gap, Tex., U.S., 214 . . . . .346/N2
Pecan Grove, Tex., U.S., 13,551 . . . . .346/A7
Pecan Island, La., U.S., 125 . . . . .282/E7
Pecatonica, Ill., U.S., 1,997 . . . . .266/D1
Pecatonica, Wisc., U.S., *river* 274/F2
Pechora, Russ. 104/D3
Pechora, Russ., *river* 104/D3
Pechora, Russ., *river* 193/C3
Peck, Ida., U.S., 186 . . . . .264/A3
Peck, Kans., U.S., 175 . . . . .276/E4
Peck, Mich., U.S., 599 . . . . .294/G6
Peckham, Okla., U.S., 60 . . . . .330/E1
Peconic, N.Y., U.S., 1,081 . . . . .320/F1
Pecos, N. Mex., U.S., 1,441 . . . . .317/E2
Pecos, N. Mex., U.S., *plains* 317/F4
Pecos, N. Mex., U.S., *river* 317/F2, F5
Pecos, Tex., U.S., 9,501 . . . . .346/E4
Pecos, Tex., U.S., *county*, 16,809 . . . . .346/F5
Pecos, Tex., U.S., *river* 346/F4
Pecos N.H.P., N. Mex., U.S. 317/E2
Pecs, Hun., 157,970 . . . . .91/B2
Pécs, Hun. 91/B2
Peculiar, Mo., U.S., 2,604 . . . . .302/B3
Pedernales, Dom. Rep. 205/A2
Pedernales, Dom. Rep., *province* 205/A3
Pedernales, Tex., U.S., *river* 346/C2
Pedja, Est., *river* 81/D2
Pedra Açú, Braz., *mountain* . . . . .188/Inset I
Pedra Lume, C.V. 148/C2
Pedricktown, N.J., U.S., 550 . . . . .314/C4
Pedro, Ohio, U.S., 325 . . . . .328/E8
Pedro, S. Dak., U.S. 342/C3
Pedro Juan Caballero, Para., 64,153 . . . . .187/E3
Pedro Santana, Dom. Rep. 205/A1
Peebles, Sask., Can. 227/H10
Peebles, Scot., U.K., 8,065 . . . . .62/K7
Peebles, Ohio, U.S., 1,739 . . . . .328/D8
Pee Dee, S.C., U.S., *river* 340/E2
Peekskill, N.Y., U.S., 22,441 . . . . .320/B1
Peel, Ont., Can., 223/F4, J5
Peel, Ont., Can., *county* 223/F4, J5
Peel, Yukon, Can., *river* 228/B3, C2
Peel, Eng., U.K. 66/A5
Pe Ell, Wash., U.S., 657 . . . . .358/B3
Peeples Valley, Ariz., U.S., 374 . . . . .242/C3
Peerless, Alta., Can., *lake* 212/C3
Peerless, Mont., U.S., 60 . . . . .306/L1
Peerless Lake, Alta., Can., 402 . . . . .212/C3
Peerless Park, Mo., U.S., 80 . . . . .302/G3
Petz, Colo., U.S., 227 . . . . .250/G1
Peever, S. Dak., U.S., 209 . . . . .342/J2
Pegasus, N.Z., *bay* 171/B3
Peggs, Okla., U.S., 175 . . . . .330/G1
Peggy, Tex., U.S. 346/K7
Pegram, Tenn., U.S., 2,146 . . . . .344/G2
Pegu, (Bago), Mya. 125/C3
Peipus, Est., *lake* 81/D2
Pekalongan, Indon. 122/B2
Pekanbaru, Indon. 122/B1
Pekin, Ill., U.S., 33,857 . . . . .266/D3
Pekin, N. Dak., U.S., 80 . . . . .326/G2
Pelahatchie, Miss., U.S., 1,461 . . . . .300/C3
Peldon, Eng., U.K. 71/G2
Pelee, Ont., Can., *island* 223/C6
Pelee, Ont., Can., *island* 294/G8
Pelee, Ohio, U.S., *island* 328/E2
Pelee, Ohio, U.S., *point* 328/F2
Peleliu, Palau, *island* 172/B4
Peleng, Indon., *island* 122/C2
Pelham, Ala., U.S., 14,369 . . . . .238/C2
Pelham, Ga., U.S., 4,126 . . . . .260/C9
Pelham, Mass., U.S., 1,403 . . . . .292/E3
Pelham, N.H., U.S., 10,914 . . . . .312/D6
Pelham, N.Y., U.S., 6,400 . . . . .320/B2
Pelham, N.C., U.S., 150 . . . . .322/G1
Pelham Manor, N.Y., U.S., 5,466 . . . . .320/B2
Pelican, Sask., Can., *lake* 227/G5
Pelican, Alaska, U.S., 163 . . . . .240/H3
Pelican, La., U.S. 282/B3
Pelican Bay, Tex., U.S., 1,505 . . . . .346/A9
Pelican Lake, Wisc., U.S., 505 . . . . .364/D3
Pelican Narrows, Sask., Can., 690 . . . . .227/H5
Pelican Portage, Alta., Can. 212/D3
Pelican Rapids, Man., Can., 123 . . . . .215/A3
Pelican Rapids, Minn., U.S., 2,374 . . . . .298/A4
Pelion, S.C., U.S., 553 . . . . .340/C3
Pelkan, Man., Can., *lake* 215/A3
Pelkie, Mich., U.S., 40 . . . . .294/A3
Pella, Iowa, U.S., 9,832 . . . . .274/J5
Pella, Tex., U.S., 50 . . . . .364/E4
Pelland, Minn., U.S., 90 . . . . .298/D2
Pell City, Ala., U.S., 9,565 . . . . .238/C2
Pell Lake, Wisc., U.S., 2,988 . . . . .364/E6
Pellston, Mich., U.S., 771 . . . . .294/E4
Pellville, Ky., U.S., 175 . . . . .280/D3
Pelly, Sask., Can., 303 . . . . .227/J9
Pelly, Yukon, Can., *mountains* 228/B4
Pelly, Yukon, Can., *river* 228/C4, C5
Pelly Bay, Nun., Can. 220/L3
Pelly Crossing, Yukon, Can., 328 . . . . .228/B4
Peloponnesus, Gr., *region* 100/B3
Pelotas, Braz., 197,092, (289,494 *metro.*) 188/C5
Pelzer, Ark., U.S. 244/B2
Pelzer, S.C., U.S., 97 . . . . .340/B2
Pemaduncook, Maine, U.S., *lake* 286/C3
Pematangsiantar, Indon. 122/A1
Pemba, Moz. 161/D2
Pemba, Tan., *island* 158/C2
Pemba North, Tan., *region* 158/C2
Pemba South, Tan., *region* 158/C2
Pemberton, Br. Col., Can., 1,637 . . . . .214/L6
Pemberton, Minn., U.S., 246 . . . . .298/D6
Pemberton, N.J., U.S., *borough*, 1,210 . . . . .314/D4
Pemberton Hts., N.J., U.S., 2,512 . . . . .314/D4
Pemberville, Ohio, U.S., 1,365 . . . . .328/D3
Pembina, Alta., Can., *river* 212/B4
Pembina, Man., Can., *river* 215/B4
Pembina, N. Dak., U.S., 642 . . . . .326/H1
Pembina, N. Dak., U.S., *county*, 8,585 . . . . .326/H1
Pembina, N. Dak., U.S., *river* 326/G1
Pembine, Wisc., U.S., 175 . . . . .364/F3
Pembrey, Wales, U.K. 64/C4
Pembridge, Eng., U.K. 68/B5
Pembroke, Ont., Can., 13,490 . . . . .223/H2
Pembroke, Wales, U.K. 60/B4
Pembroke, Wales, U.K., 6,773 . . . . .64/B4
Pembroke, Ga., U.S., 2,379 . . . . .260/H7
Pembroke, Ky., U.S., 797 . . . . .280/C4
Pembroke, Maine, U.S., 897 . . . . .286/E4
Pembroke, Mass., U.S., 16,927 . . . . .292/L4
Pembroke, N.C., U.S., 2,399 . . . . .322/G5
Pembroke, Va., U.S., 1,134 . . . . .354/B6
Pembroke Dock, Wales, U.K., 8,651 . . . . .64/B4
Pembroke Park, Fla., U.S., 6,299 . . . . .256/B6
Pembroke Pines, Fla., U.S., 137,427 . . . . .256/B6
Pembrokeshire, Wales, U.K., *unitary authority*,
   112,901 . . . . .64/B4
Pembrokeshire Coast N.P., Wales, U.K. 64/A4

Pleasantville, N.J., U.S., 19,012 . . . . .314/D5
Pleasantville, N.Y., U.S., 7,172 . . . . .320/B1
Pleasantville, Ohio, U.S., 877 . . . . .328/E6
Pleasantville, (Bedford County),
  Penn., U.S., 211 . . . . .336/D5
Pleasantville, (Venango County),
  Penn., U.S., 850 . . . . .336/B2
Pleasley, Eng., U.K. 68/E3
Pleasure Beach, Conn., U.S., 1,600 . . . . .253/G4
Pleasure Ridge Park, Ky., U.S., 25,776 . . . . . . .280/E2
Pleasureville, Ky., U.S., 869 . . . . .280/E2
Plenty, N.Z., bay .171/C2
Plentywood, Mont., U.S., 2,061 . . . . .306/M1
Plessisville, Que., Can., 6,756 . . . . .226/E5
Pletcher, Ala., U.S., 90 . . . . .238/C3
Pleven, Bul., 150,400 . . . . .101/C2
Pleven, Bul., oblast 101/C2
Plevna, Ont., Can. 223/J3
Plevna, Ala., U.S., 50 . . . . .238/C1
Plevna, Kans., U.S., 99 . . . . .276/D4
Plevna, Mo., U.S., 40 . . . . .302/D2
Plevna, Mont., U.S., 138 . . . . .306/M3
Plibo, Liber. 149/C3
Pljevlja, Serb.-Mont. 99/A3
Ploče, Cro. 98/C3
Plock, Pol., 131,006 . . . . .83/D2
Ploiesti, Rom., 249,054 . . . . .101/D3
Plovdiv, Bul., 339,744 . . . . .101/C3
Plovdiv, Bul., oblast 101/C3
Plover, Iowa, U.S., 95 . . . . .274/E2
Plover, Wisc., U.S., 10,520 . . . . .364/D4
Pluckemin, N.J., U.S., 6,000 . . . . .314/D2
Plum, Ky., U.S. 280/F2
Plum, N.Y., U.S., island 320/G1
Plum, Pa., U.S., 26,940 . . . . .336/B5, F7
Plumas, Man., Can. 215/B4
Plumas, Calif., U.S., county, 20,824 . . . . .246/E3
Plumas Natl. For., Calif., U.S. 246/E2
Plum Branch, S.C., U.S., 98 . . . . .340/B3
Plumbridge, N. Ire., U.K., 257 . . . . .65/C2
Plumb Tree Island NWR., Va., U.S. 354/L6
Plum City, Wisc., U.S., 574 . . . . .364/A4
Plum Coulee, Man., Can., 725 . . . . .215/C4
Plumerville, Ark., U.S., 854 . . . . .244/C2
Plum Grove, Tex., U.S., 930 . . . . .346/N5
Plummer, Ida., U.S., 990 . . . . .264/A2
Plummer, Minn., U.S., 270 . . . . .298/A3
Plum Pt., R.I., U.S., 850 . . . . .339/D4
Plumpton, Eng., U.K. 66/C3
Plum Sprs., Ky., U.S., 447 . . . . .280/D5
Plumville, Penn., U.S., 342 . . . . .336/C4
Plumwood, Ohio, U.S., 300 . . . . .328/D5
Plush, Oreg., U.S. .99/B2
Plymell, Kans., U.S. 276/B4
Plymouth, Montserrat, capital 204/F3
Plymouth, Trin.-To. 209/B1
Plymouth, Eng., U.K. 60/B4
Plymouth, Eng., U.K., 245,295 . . . . .73/D4
Plymouth, Eng., U.K., unitary authority, 240,718 .73/D4
Plymouth, Calif., U.S., 980 . . . . .246/L5
Plymouth, Conn., U.S., 11,634 . . . . .253/C3
Plymouth, Del., U.S., 350 . . . . .255/B4
Plymouth, Ill., U.S., 562 . . . . .266/C3
Plymouth, Ind., U.S., 9,840 . . . . .270/D2
Plymouth, Iowa, U.S., 429 . . . . .274/H1
Plymouth, Iowa, U.S., county, 24,849 . . . . . . .274/B2
Plymouth, Kans., U.S., 90 . . . . .276/F3
Plymouth, Maine, U.S., 1,257 . . . . .286/C4
Plymouth, Mass., U.S., 51,701 . . . . .292/M5
Plymouth, Mass., U.S., county, 472,822 . . . . . .292/L4
Plymouth, Mich., U.S., 9,022 . . . . .294/A7
Plymouth, Minn., U.S., 65,894 . . . . .298/E5
Plymouth, Nebr., U.S., 477 . . . . .308/G3
Plymouth, N.H., U.S., 5,892 . . . . .312/C4
Plymouth, N.C., U.S., 4,107 . . . . .322/M3
Plymouth, Ohio, U.S., 1,852 . . . . .328/E4
Plymouth, Penn., U.S., 6,507 . . . . .336/G7, K3
Plymouth, Utah, U.S., 328 . . . . .350/B2
Plymouth, Vt., U.S., 555 . . . . .352/B3
Plymouth, Wash., U.S., 175 . . . . .358/F4
Plymouth, W. Va., U.S. 360/C3
Plymouth, Wisc., U.S., 7,781 . . . . .364/F5
Plymouth Meeting, Penn., U.S., 5,593 . . . . . . .336/L6
Plymouth Township, Mich., U.S., 27,798 . . . . . .294/A7
Plymouth Union, Vt., U.S. 352/B3
Plympton, Eng., U.K. 73/D4
Plympton, Mass., U.S., 2,637 . . . . .292/L5
Plymptonville, Penn., U.S., 1,040 . . . . .336/E3
Plymstock, Eng., U.K. 73/D4
Plzeň, Czh. Rep., 166,000 . . . . .92/A3
Plzeňský, Czh. Rep., region 92/A3
Po, It., river 88/D4
Po, It., river 95/A1, B1
Požarevac, Serb.-Mont. . . . . .188/Inset II
Poá, Braz. . . . . .188/Inset II
Poamoho, Hawaii, U.S. 262/J2
Pobé, Ben. 151/B4
Poca, W. Va., U.S., 1,013 . . . . .360/C4
Pocahontas, Ark., U.S., 6,518 . . . . .244/E1
Pocahontas, Ill., U.S., 727 . . . . .266/D5
Pocahontas, Iowa, U.S., 1,970 . . . . .274/E2
Pocahontas, Iowa, U.S., county, 8,662 . . . . . . .274/E2
Pocahontas, Miss., U.S., 40 . . . . .300/B3
Pocahontas, Mo., U.S., 127 . . . . .302/G4
Pocahontas, Va., U.S., 441 . . . . .354/E2
Pocahontas, W. Va., U.S., county, 9,131 . . . . . .360/F4
Pocasse N.W.R., S. Dak., U.S. 342/E1
Pocasset, Mass., U.S., 2,671 . . . . .292/M6
Pocasset, Okla., U.S., 192 . . . . .330/E2
Pocatalico, W. Va., U.S., 425 . . . . .360/C4
Pocatello, Ida., U.S., 51,466, (75,565 metro.) . . .264/E7
Pocklington, Eng., U.K., 5,908 . . . . .66/G5
Pocklington, Eng., U.K., 5,908 . . . . .68/F2
Pocola, Okla., U.S., 3,994 . . . . .330/H2
Pocomoke, Va., U.S., sound 354/M5
Pocomoke City, Md., U.S., 4,098 . . . . .288/M7
Pocono Pines, Penn., U.S., 1,013 . . . . .336/L3
Pocosin Lakes N.W.R., N.C., U.S. 322/N3
Podgorica, Serb.-Mont., 173,205 . . . . .99/A3
Podil'ska, Ukr., highlands 102/B2
Podkarpackie, Pol., province 83/F3
Podlaskie, Pol., province 83/F2
Pogradec, Alb. 99/B3
Pohakuloa Training Area, Hawaii, U.S. 262/H5
Pohakupu, Hawaii, U.S. 262/K2
Pohang, S. Kor., 508,899 . . . . .116/C4
Pohnpei, Micr., island 172/D2
Pohnpei, Micr., state 172/C2
Pohoiki, Hawaii, U.S. 262/K6
Poindexter, Ky., U.S., 60 . . . . .280/F2
Poinsett, Antar., cape 192/C2
Poinsett, Ark., U.S., county, 25,614 . . . . .244/E2
Point, N.W. Terr., Can., lake 220/F3
Point, St. Luc., cape 208/E1
Point, Tex., U.S., 175 . . . . .282/F1
Point, Tex., U.S., 792 . . . . .346/N3
Pt. Arena, Calif., U.S., 474 . . . . .246/B4
Pt. au Fer, La., U.S., point 282/G8
Pt. Blank, La., U.S., 559 . . . . .346/N5
Pt. Blue, La., U.S., 175 . . . . .282/C5
Pt. Cedar, Ark., U.S., 80 . . . . .244/B3

Pt. Chevreuil, La., U.S., point 282/F7
Pt. Clear, Ala., U.S., 1,876 . . . . .238/B5
Pt. Comfort, Tex., U.S., 781 . . . . .346/M7
Pointe-a-la-Croix, Que., Can., 1,513 . . . . .226/K3
Pointe a la Hache, La., U.S., 475 . . . . .282/K7
Pointe au Baril, Ont., Can. 223/E2
Pointe Aux Pins, Mich., U.S. 294/E4
Pointe-Claire, Que., Can. 226/H6
Pointe Coupee, La., U.S., parish, 22,763 . . . . . .282/F5
Pointe-des-Monts, Que., Can. 226/J2
Pointe du Bois, Man., Can. 215/D4
Pointe-Lebel, Que., Can., 1,931 . . . . .226/J2
Pointe Michel, Dom. 208/B3
Pointe-Noire, Congo, 298,014, (576,206 metro.) .155/A6
Pointers, N.J., U.S., 550 . . . . .314/C4
Pointe Sapin, N.B., Can., 627 . . . . .217/E2
Pointe-Taillon Prov. Park, Que., Can. 226/D3
Pointe-Verte, N.B., Can., 1,041 . . . . .217/D1
Pt. Fortin, Trin.-To. .209/A2
Pt. Harbor, N.C., U.S., 200 . . . . .322/P2
Pt. Hope, Alaska, U.S., 757 . . . . .240/B1
Pt. Imperial, Ariz., U.S., peak 242/D1
Pt. Isabel, Ind., U.S., 125 . . . . .270/E4
Pt. Judith, R.I., U.S., 900 . . . . .339/D5
Pt. Lay, Alaska, U.S., 247 . . . . .240/D4
Pt. Leamington, Nfld., Can., 685 . . . . .218/D4
Pt. Marion, Penn., U.S., 1,333 . . . . .336/B6
Pt. of Rocks, Md., U.S., 850 . . . . .288/D2
Pt. of Rocks, Wyo., U.S. 366/B3
Pt. Pedro, Sri Lan. .126/B2
Pt. Pelee Natl. Park, Ont., Can. 223/C6
Pt. Pelee N.P., Ont., Can. 294/G8
Pt. Pleasant, N.J., U.S., 19,306 . . . . .314/E3
Pt. Pleasant, W. Va., U.S., 4,637 . . . . .360/B3
Pt. Pleasant Beach, N.J., U.S., 5,314 . . . . .314/E3
Pt. Reyes Natl. Seashore, Calif., U.S. 246/C4
Pt. Reyes Sta., Calif., U.S., 818 . . . . .246/H1
Pt. Roberts, Wash., U.S., 375 . . . . .358/B1
Poipu, Hawaii, U.S., 1,075 . . . . .262/C2
Poisson Blanc, Que., Can., reservoir 226/A6
Poissy, Fr. . . . . .88/Inset II
Poitiers, Fr., 87,012, (119,371 metro.) 88/C3
Poitou-Charentes, Fr., region 88/C3
Pojoaque, N. Mex., U.S., 1,261 . . . . .317/D2
Pokegama, Minn., U.S., lake 298/D3
Pokemouche, N.B., Can., 558 . . . . .217/E1
Pokeshaw, N.B., Can. 217/D1
Pokhara, Nepal 126/B2
Pokiok, N.B., Can. .217/B3
Polacca, Ariz., U.S., 1,100 . . . . .242/E2
Poland, nation 81
Poland, nation 193/D3
Poland, Maine, U.S., 4,866 . . . . .286/B4
Poland, N.Y., U.S., 451 . . . . .320/L4
Poland, Ohio, U.S., 2,866 . . . . .328/J3
Polar, Antar., plateau 192/A14
Polar, Tex., U.S. 346/H2
Polaris, Mont., U.S., 60 . . . . .306/C4
Polatsk, Bela. 82/D2
Polba, India . . . . .128/Inset II
Polebridge, Mont., U.S. 306/B1
Polegate, Eng., U.K. 70/E5
Pole Ojea, P.R. 206/A3
Polesworth, Eng., U.K. 70/A1
Poli, Came. 153/B2
Polis, Cyp. 133/A1
Polk, Ark., U.S., county, 20,229 . . . . .244/A3
Polk, Fla., U.S., county, 483,924 . . . . .256/C4, G3
Polk, Ga., U.S., county, 38,127 . . . . .260/A3
Polk, Iowa, U.S., county, 374,601 . . . . .274/H4
Polk, Minn., U.S., county, 31,369 . . . . .298/A3
Polk, Mo., U.S., county, 26,992 . . . . .302/C4
Polk, Nebr., U.S., 322 . . . . .308/G2
Polk, Nebr., U.S., county, 5,639 . . . . .308/G2
Polk, N.C., U.S., county, 18,324 . . . . .322/A4, F8
Polk, Ohio, U.S., 357 . . . . .328/F4
Polk, Oreg., U.S., county, 62,380 . . . . .334/C3
Polk, Penn., U.S., 1,031 . . . . .336/B3
Polk, Tenn., U.S., county, 16,050 . . . . .344/M4
Polk, Tex., U.S., county, 41,133 . . . . .346/P5
Polk, Wisc., U.S., county, 41,319 . . . . .364/A3
Polk City, Fla., U.S., 1,516 . . . . .256/C3
Polk City, Iowa, U.S., 2,344 . . . . .274/G4
Polkton, N.C., U.S., 1,195 . . . . .322/E4
Polkville, Miss., U.S., 132 . . . . .300/C3
Polkville, N.C., U.S., 535 . . . . .322/B4
Pollard, Ala., U.S., 120 . . . . .238/B4
Pollard, Ark., U.S., 240 . . . . .244/E1
Pollock, Ida., U.S. .264/A4
Pollock, La., U.S., 376 . . . . .282/E3
Pollock, Mo., U.S., 131 . . . . .302/C1
Pollock, S. Dak., U.S., 339 . . . . .342/E1
Pollock Pines, Calif., U.S., 4,728 . . . . .246/E4
Pollocksville, N.C., U.S., 269 . . . . .322/L4
Polo, Ill., U.S., 2,477 . . . . .266/D2
Polo, Mo., U.S., 582 . . . . .302/B2
Polo, S. Dak., U.S. .342/F3
Polonia, Wisc., U.S., 275 . . . . .364/D4
Polonnaruwa, Sri Lan. 126/C4
Polperro, Eng., U.K. .73/C4
Polpis, Mass., U.S., 90 . . . . .292/P7
Polson, Mont., U.S., 4,041 . . . . .306/B2
Poltava, Ukr., 313,199 . . . . .102/C2
Poltava, Ukr., oblast 102/C2
Poltimore, Que., Can. 226/A6
Polvadera, N. Mex., U.S., 250 . . . . .317/D3
Polyphant, Eng., U.K. 73/D3
Pomaria, S.C., U.S., 177 . . . . .340/C2
Pomerania, Ger., state 86/C2
Pomerania, Pol., region 83/C2
Pomeranian, Ger., bay 86/C1
Pomeranian, Pol., bay 83/B1
Pomerene, Ariz., U.S., 40 . . . . .242/E5
Pomeroy, N.B., Can. 217/C3
Pomeroy, N. Ire., U.K., 730 . . . . .65/D2
Pomeroy, Iowa, U.S., 710 . . . . .274/E2
Pomeroy, Ohio, U.S., 1,966 . . . . .328/F7
Pomeroy, Wash., U.S., 1,517 . . . . .358/H3
Pomfret, Conn., U.S., 3,798 . . . . .253/H2
Pomfret, Vt., U.S., 997 . . . . .352/B3
Pomona, Calif., U.S., 149,473 . . . . .246/E9
Pomona, Ill., U.S., 125 . . . . .266/D6
Pomona, Kans., U.S., 923 . . . . .276/K3
Pomona, Md., U.S., 150 . . . . .288/K3
Pomona, Mo., U.S., 300 . . . . .302/E5
Pomona, N.J., U.S., 4,019 . . . . .314/D5
Pomona, N.Y., U.S., 2,726 . . . . .320/B1
Pomona Park, Fla., U.S., 789 . . . . .256/G2
Pomonkey, Md., U.S., 750 . . . . .288/F5
Pomorskie, Pol., province 83/D1
Pompano Beach, Fla., U.S., 78,191 . . . . . . .256/B5, H5
Pompanoosuc, Vt., U.S., 125 . . . . .352/C3
Pompeys Pillar, Mont., U.S. 306/J4
Pompeys Pillar Natl. Mon., Mont., U.S. 306/H3
Pompton Lakes, N.J., U.S., 10,640 . . . . .314/A1
Pompton Plains, N.J., U.S., 6,500 . . . . .314/A1
Ponca, Ark., U.S. 244/B1
Ponca, Nebr., U.S., 1,062 . . . . .308/H1
Ponca City, Okla., U.S., 25,919 . . . . .330/E1
Ponce, P.R. 204/E3
Ponce, P.R., 189,317, (361,094 metro.) 206/B2

Ponce de Leon, Fla., U.S., 457 . . . . .256/C1
Ponce de Leon, Fla., U.S., bay 256/G6
Ponce Inlet, Fla., U.S., 2,513 . . . . .256/H2
Poncha Sprs., Colo., U.S., 466 . . . . .250/D3
Ponchatoula, La., U.S., 5,180 . . . . .282/J6
Pond Cove, Nfld., Can. 218/C3
Pond Creek, Okla., U.S., 896 . . . . .330/E1
Ponder, Tex., U.S., 507 . . . . .346/M8
Pondera, Mont., U.S., county, 6,424 . . . . .306/D1
Ponderay, Ida., U.S., 638 . . . . .264/A1
Ponderosa Park, Colo., U.S., 3,112 . . . . .250/F2
Pondersbridge, Eng., U.K. 70/D1
Pond Gap, W. Va., U.S., 525 . . . . .360/D4
Pond Inlet, Nun., Can., 1,220 . . . . .220/N2
Pondosa, Calif., U.S. 246/D1
Pondville, Ala., U.S., 60 . . . . .238/B3
Ponemah, Minn., U.S., 874 . . . . .298/C2
Ponemah, N.H., U.S., 1,000 . . . . .312/C6
Poneto, Ind., U.S., 240 . . . . .270/F3
Ponferrada, Sp., 62,175 . . . . .94/C1
Ponta Delgada, Port. . . . . .93/Inset II
Pontardawe, Wales, U.K., 18,479 . . . . .64/D4
Pontardulais, Wales, U.K., 7,770 . . . . .64/C4
Pontarsais, Wales, U.K. 64/C4
Pont Cassé, Dom. .208/B3
Pontchartrain, Fr. . . . . .88/Inset II
Pontchartrain, La., U.S., lake 282/J2, J6
Pontefract, Eng., U.K., 28,358 . . . . .66/F5
Pontefract, Eng., U.K., 28,358 . . . . .68/E2
Ponteix, Sask., Can., 550 . . . . .227/C11
Ponteland, Eng., U.K., 9,933 . . . . .66/F2
Ponterwyd, Wales, U.K. 64/D3
Pontesbury, Eng., U.K., 1,956 . . . . .68/B4
Pontevedra, Sp., 74,942 . . . . .94/B1
Pontevedra, Sp., province 94/B1
Pontiac, Ill., U.S., 11,864 . . . . .266/E3
Pontiac, Mich., U.S., 66,337 . . . . .294/A6, F7
Pontianak, Indon. .122/B2
Pontic, Tur., mountains 133/C2
Pontine, It., islands .95/C2
Pont-Lafrance, N.B., Can., 754 . . . . .217/E1
Pontoise, Fr. . . . . .88/Inset II
Ponton, Man., Can. 215/B2
Pontoon Beach, Ill., U.S., 5,620 . . . . .266/A3
Pontoosuc, Ill., U.S., 171 . . . . .266/B3
Pontotoc, Miss., U.S., 5,253 . . . . .300/D1
Pontotoc, Miss., U.S., county, 26,726 . . . . .300/C1
Pontotoc, Miss., U.S., ridge 300/D1
Pontotoc, Okla., U.S., county, 35,143 . . . . . . .330/F3
Pontrhyd-fendigaid, Wales, U.K. 64/D3
Pont-rhyd-y-groes, Wales, U.K. 64/D3
Pontrilas, Eng., U.K. .68/B5
Pont-Rouge, Que., Can., 7,146 . . . . .226/E5
Pontsticill, Wales, U.K., reservoir 64/E4
Pontyclun, Wales, U.K., lake 64/E4
Pontycymer, Wales, U.K., 4,439 . . . . .64/D4
Pontypool, Wales, U.K., 35,564 . . . . .64/E4
Pontypridd, Wales, U.K., 28,487 . . . . .64/E4
Pony, Mont., U.S., 40 . . . . .306/E4
Pool, Eng., U.K. 66/E5
Poole, Eng., U.K. 60/C4
Poole, Eng., U.K., 138,479 . . . . .73/J3
Poole, Eng., U.K., unitary authority, 138,299 . . .73/J3
Poole, Ky., U.S., 275 . . . . .280/C3
Poole, Nebr., U.S. .308/E3
Pooler, Ga., U.S., 6,239 . . . . .260/J7
Poolesville, Md., U.S., 5,151 . . . . .288/E3
Poolewe, Scot., U.K. 62/E1
Pooley Bridge, Eng., U.K. 66/E3
Poopó, Bol., lake 186/A3
Poorman, Alaska, U.S. 240/D2
Popayán, Col., 218,000 . . . . .184/A4
Pope, Ark., U.S., county, 54,469 . . . . .244/B2
Pope, Ill., U.S., county, 4,413 . . . . .266/E6
Pope, Minn., U.S., county, 11,236 . . . . .298/B5
Pope, Miss., U.S., 241 . . . . .300/C1
Popejoy, Iowa, U.S., 78 . . . . .274/H2
Poperinge, Belg. 85/A2
Popes Creek, Md., U.S., 125 . . . . .288/G6
Poplar, Man., Can., river 215/C3
Poplar, Calif., U.S., 1,496 . . . . .246/F6
Poplar, Mont., U.S., 911 . . . . .306/L1
Poplar, N.C., U.S. .322/A2
Poplar, Wisc., U.S., 552 . . . . .364/B2
Poplar Bluff, Mo., U.S., 16,651 . . . . .302/F5
Poplar Branch, N.C., U.S., 225 . . . . .322/P2
Poplar Creek, Miss., U.S., 60 . . . . .300/C2
Poplar Grove, P.E.I., Can. 224/B2
Poplar Grove, Ark., U.S., 325 . . . . .244/E3
Poplar Grove, Ill., U.S., 1,368 . . . . .266/E1
Poplar Hill, Va., U.S. 354/B6
Poplar Hills, Ky., U.S., 396 . . . . .280/A2
Poplar Plains, Ky., U.S., 100 . . . . .280/F2
Poplar River, Man., Can. 215/C3
Poplar Tent, N.C., U.S. 322/D4
Poplarville, Miss., U.S., 2,601 . . . . .300/C5
Popomanaseu, Sol. Is., mountain 173/B1
Popondetta, P.N.G. 172/A2
Popponesset Beach, Mass., U.S., 310 . . . . . . .292/N6
Poprad, Slvk., 104,348 . . . . .92/C2
Poquetanuck, Conn., U.S., 1,100 . . . . .253/G4
Poquonock, Conn., U.S., 2,200 . . . . .253/E2
Poquonock Bridge, Conn., U.S., 1,592 . . . . . . .253/G4
Poquoson, Va., U.S., 11,566 . . . . .354/L5
Poquott, N.Y., U.S., 975 . . . . .320/E1
Porcupine, Yukon, Can., river 228/B2
Porcupine, Alaska, U.S., river 240/G1
Porcupine, Mich., U.S., mountains 294/D2
Porcupine, S. Dak., U.S., 407 . . . . .342/C4
Porcupine Mountains Wilderness St. Park,
  Mich., U.S. 294/D2
Porcupine Plain, Sask., Can., 820 . . . . .227/G8
Pori, Fin., 75,994 . . . . .81/B2
Poringland, Eng., U.K., 4,684 . . . . .70/G1
Porlock Weir, Eng., U.K. 73/E2
Port Adelaide, S.A., Austl. . . . . .170/Inset II
Portadown, N. Ire., U.K. 60/A2
Portadown, N. Ire., U.K., 21,299 . . . . .65/E3
Portaferry, N. Ire., U.K., 2,324 . . . . .65/F3
Portage, P.E.I., Can. 224/A2
Portage, Ind., U.S., 33,496 . . . . .270/D1
Portage, Maine, U.S., 225 . . . . .286/D2
Portage, Mich., U.S., 44,897 . . . . .294/D7
Portage, Mont., U.S. 306/E2
Portage, Ohio, U.S., 428 . . . . .328/E3
Portage, Ohio, U.S., county, 152,061 . . . . . .328/H3, J1
Portage, Penn., U.S., 2,837 . . . . .336/D5
Portage, Utah, U.S., 257 . . . . .350/B2
Portage, Wisc., U.S., county, 67,182 . . . . .364/D4
Portage Lakes, Ohio, U.S., 9,870 . . . . .328/H2
Portage la Prairie, Man., Can., 12,976 . . . . .215/B4, D2
Portageville, Mo., U.S., 3,295 . . . . .302/G5
Portal, Ariz., U.S. 242/F6
Portal, Ga., U.S., 597 . . . . .260/H6

Portal, N. Dak., U.S., 131 . . . . .326/C1
Port Alberni, Br. Col., Can., 17,743 . . . . .214/K3
Portalegre, Port. 93/B3
Portalegre, Port., district 93/B3
Port Alexander, N. Mex., U.S., 11,131 . . . . . . .317/G3
Port Allegany, Penn., U.S., 2,355 . . . . .336/E2
Port Allen, La., U.S., 5,278 . . . . .282/G6
Port Alto, Tex., U.S. 346/M7
Port Angeles, Wash., U.S., 18,397 . . . . .358/B1
Port Antonio, Jam. .206/C2
Port Aransas, Tex., U.S., 3,370 . . . . .346/L8
Port Arthur, Tex., U.S., 57,755 . . . . .346/R6
Port au Choix, Nfld., Can., 1,010 . . . . .218/C4
Port Augusta, S.A., Austl. 170/C3
Port au Port, Nfld., Can. 218/B5
Port-au-Prince, Haiti, bay 205/C2
Port-au-Prince, Haiti, capital 204/C3
Port-au-Prince, Haiti, capital, 990,558,
  (1,699,000 metro.) 205/C2
Port Austin, Mich., U.S., 737 . . . . .294/F5
Portavadie, Scot., U.K. 62/F7
Port Barre, La., U.S., 2,287 . . . . .282/F5
Port Bickerton, N.S., Can. 221/F2
Port Blair, India 128/F6
Port Blandford, Nfld., Can., 580 . . . . .218/D5
Port Bruce, Ont., Can. 223/E5
Port Burwell, Nfld., Can. 218/D4
Port Burwell, Ont., Can. 223/E5
Port Byron, Ill., U.S., 1,535 . . . . .266/C2
Port Byron, N.Y., U.S., 1,297 . . . . .320/H4
Port Carbon, Penn., U.S., 2,019 . . . . .336/H4
Port-Cartier, Que., Can., 6,412 . . . . .225/C3
Port Charlotte, Fla., U.S., 46,451 . . . . .256/F5
Port Chester, N.Y., U.S., 27,867 . . . . .320/C1
Port Clements, Br. Col., Can., 516 . . . . .214/F4
Port Clinton, Ohio, U.S., 6,391 . . . . .328/E2
Port Clinton, Penn., U.S., 288 . . . . .336/J4
Port Clyde, Maine, U.S., 300 . . . . .286/C5
Port Colborne, Ont., Can., 18,450 . . . . .223/F5
Port Coquitlam, Br. Col., Can., 51,257 . . . . . . .214/L6
Port-Daniel Prov. Reserve, Que., Can. 226/M3
Port-de-Paix, Haiti .205/C1
Port Deposit, Md., U.S., 676 . . . . .288/K1
Port Dickinson, N.Y., U.S., 1,697 . . . . .320/K6
Port Dinorwic, Wales, U.K., 1,664 . . . . .64/C1
Port Dufferin, N.S., Can. 221/E3
Port Edward, S. Afr. 162/D3
Port Edwards, Wisc., U.S., 1,944 . . . . .364/D4
Port Elgin, N.B., Can., 436 . . . . .217/E3
Port Elgin, Ont., Can., 6,766 . . . . .223/D3
Port Elizabeth, St. Vin.-Gren. 208/B2
Port Elizabeth, S. Afr., 775,255,
  (1,311,505 metro.) 162/C4
Port Elizabeth, N.J., U.S., 425 . . . . .314/D6
Port Ellen, Scot., U.K., 819 . . . . .62/D7
Porter, Sask., Can., lake 227/C4
Porter, Ind., U.S., 4,972 . . . . .270/D1
Porter, Ind., U.S., county, 146,798 . . . . .270/B2
Porter, Minn., U.S., 190 . . . . .298/A5
Porter, Okla., U.S., 574 . . . . .330/G2
Porter, Wash., U.S., 473 . . . . .358/B3
Porterdale, Ga., U.S., 1,281 . . . . .260/D4
Porter Hts., Tex., U.S., 1,490 . . . . .346/B5
Port Erin, Eng., U.K. 66/C3
Porters Corner, Mont., U.S. 306/C3
Porters Lake, N.S., Can. 221/D3
Portersville, Ala., U.S. 238/C1
Portersville, Penn., U.S., 268 . . . . .336/A4
Porterville, Calif., U.S., 39,615 . . . . .246/G6
Porterville, Miss., U.S., 40 . . . . .300/D3
Porterville, Utah, U.S. 350/D7
Port Ewen, N.Y., U.S., 3,650 . . . . .320/P7
Port-Eynon, Wales, U.K. 64/C4
Port Franks, Ont., Can. 223/D4
Port Gamble, Wash., U.S., 325 . . . . .358/A4, C2
Port-Gentil, Gabon, 79,225 . . . . .155/A2
Port George, N.S., Can. 221/B2
Port Gibson, Miss., U.S., 1,840 . . . . .300/B4
Port Glasgow, Scot., U.K., 16,617 . . . . .62/G7
Port Glaud, Sey. 163/Inset
Portglenone, N. Ire., U.K., 1,243 . . . . .65/E2
Porth, Wales, U.K. 64/E4
Port Hadlock, Wash., U.S., 3,476 . . . . .358/C1
Port Hardy, Br. Col., Can., 4,574 . . . . .214/J6
Port Harcourt, Nig. .152/C5
Port Hawkesbury, N.S., Can., 3,701 . . . . .221/F2
Porthcawl, Wales, U.K., 15,922 . . . . .64/D5
Port Hedland, W.A., Austl. 170/A2
Port Heiden, Alaska, U.S., 119 . . . . .240/D4
Port Henry, N.Y., U.S., 1,152 . . . . .320/Q2
Porthgain, Wales, U.K. 64/A4
Porthill, Ida., U.S. 264/A1
Porthleven, Eng., U.K., 3,123 . . . . .73/B4
Porthmadog, Wales, U.K., 3,048 . . . . .64/C2
Porthmeor, Eng., U.K. 73/A4
Port Hood, N.S., Can. 221/F1
Port Hope, Ont., Can., 11,718 . . . . .223/G4
Port Hope, Mich., U.S., 310 . . . . .294/G6
Port Hope Simpson, Nfld., Can., 509 . . . . .218/C3
Port Hudson, La., U.S., 275 . . . . .282/G5
Port Hueneme, Calif., U.S., 21,845 . . . . .246/F8
Port Huron, Mich., U.S., 32,338 . . . . .294/G7
Portia, Ark., U.S., 483 . . . . .244/D1
Portimão, Port. 93/A4
Portis, Kans., U.S., 123 . . . . .276/D2
Port Isaac, Eng., U.K. 73/C3
Portishead, Eng., U.K., 14,721 . . . . .73/G2
Port Jefferson, N.Y., U.S., 7,837 . . . . .320/E1
Port Jefferson, Ohio, U.S., 321 . . . . .328/B5
Port Jefferson Sta., N.Y., U.S., 7,527 . . . . .320/E1
Port Kent, N.Y., U.S., 250 . . . . .320/Q1
Portknockie, Scot., U.K., 1,217 . . . . .62/J3
Port Lavaca, Tex., U.S., 12,035 . . . . .346/M7
Port Leyden, N.Y., U.S., 665 . . . . .320/L3

Pemiscot, Mo., U.S., *county*, 20,047 . . . . .302/G5
Pena Blanca, N. Mex., U.S., 661 . . . . .317/D2
Penalosa, Kans., U.S. 276/D4
Pen Argyl, Penn., U.S., 3,615 . . . . .336/L4
Penarth, Wales, U.K., 23,434 . . . . .64/E5
Penas, Chile, *gulf* .190/B7
Penasco, N. Mex., U.S., 572 . . . . .317/E1
Pencader, Wales, U.K. 64/C3
Pencer, Minn., U.S. .298/B2
Pendé, C.A.R., *river* 154/A2
Pendennis, Kans., U.S. 276/B3
Pender, Nebr., U.S., 1,148 . . . . .308/H1
Pender, N.C., U.S., *county* 41,082 . . . . .322/K5
Pendergrass, Ga., U.S., 431 . . . . .260/D3
Penderlea, N.C., U.S., 225 . . . . .322/J5
Pendine, Wales, U.K. .64/B4
Pendleton, Ind., U.S., 3,873 . . . . .270/E4
Pendleton, Ky., U.S., 225 . . . . .280/E2
Pendleton, Ky., U.S., *county*, 14,390 . . . . .280/F2
Pendleton, Oreg., U.S., 16,354 . . . . .334/H2
Pendleton, S.C., U.S., 2,966 . . . . .340/B2
Pendleton, W. Va., U.S., *county*, 8,196 . . . . .360/H3
Pend Oreille, Ida., U.S., *lake* 264/A1
Pend Oreille, Ida., U.S., *river* 264/A1
Pend Oreille, Wash., U.S., *county*, 11,732 . . . . . .358/H1
Pend Oreille, Wash., U.S., *river* 358/H1
Pendroy, Mont., U.S. 306/D1
Penermon, Mo., U.S., 75 . . . . .302/G5
Penetanguishene, Ont., Can., 8,316 . . . . .223/F3
Penfield, Penn., U.S., 350 . . . . .336/D3
P'enghu, (Pescadores), Tai., *islands* 117/A2
Pengilly, Minn., U.S., 350 . . . . .298/D3
Penhold, Alta., Can., 1,729 . . . . .212/D5
Penhook, Va., U.S., 726 . . . . .354/D7
Peniche, Port. 93/A3
Penicuik, Scot., U.K., 14,759 . . . . .62/K7
Peninsula, Ohio, U.S., 602 . . . . .328/G3, H10
Penistone, Eng., U.K., 8,627 . . . . .66/E5
Penistone, Eng., U.K., 8,627 . . . . .68/D2
Penkridge, Eng., U.K., 7,212 . . . . .66/D4
Penley, Wales, U.K. 64/F2
Penmachno, Wales, U.K. 64/D1
Penmaenmawr, Wales, U.K., 2,681 . . . . .64/D1
Penmark, Wales, U.K. .64/E5
Penn, N. Dak., U.S., 90 . . . . .326/F1
Pennal, Wales, U.K. 64/D2
Pennan, Scot., U.K. 62/M3
Pennant, Sask., Can., 150 . . . . .227/B10
Penndel, Penn., U.S., 2,420 . . . . .336/M5
Pennell, Utah, U.S., *mountain* 350/D6
Penney Farms, Fla., U.S., 580 . . . . .256/G2
Penn Hills, Penn., U.S., 46,809 . . . . .336/E5
Pennine Alps, Switz., *mountains* 90/B2
Pennines, Eng., U.K., *hills* 66/D3
Pennines, Eng., U.K., *mountains* 60/C2
Pennines, Eng., U.K., *range* 68/D2
Pennington, Ala., U.S., 353 . . . . .238/A3
Pennington, Minn., U.S., *county*, 13,584 . . . . . . .298/A2
Pennington, N.J., U.S., 2,696 . . . . .314/D3
Pennington, S. Dak., U.S., *county*, 88,565 . . . . . .342/C4
Pennington Gap, Va., U.S., 1,781 . . . . .354/B3
Penn Lake Park, Penn., U.S., 269 . . . . .336/K3
Pennock, Minn., U.S., 504 . . . . .298/B5
Pennsauken, N.J., U.S., 35,737 . . . . .314/B3, C4
Pennsboro, W. Va., U.S., 1,199 . . . . .360/E2
Pennsburg, Penn., U.S., 2,732 . . . . .336/K5
Pennsbury Vil., Penn., U.S., 738 . . . . .336/D7
Penns Grove, N.J., U.S., 4,886 . . . . .314/C4
Pennsville, N.J., U.S., 13,194 . . . . .314/B4
Pennsylvania, U.S., *state* 324
Pa. Tpk., Penn., U.S. 336/D6, G5, J5
Pennville, Ind., U.S., 706 . . . . .270/F4
Penn Wynne, Penn., U.S., 5,382 . . . . .336/L6
Penn Wynne, Penn., U.S., 5,382 . . . . .336/L7
Penn Yan, N.Y., U.S., 5,219 . . . . .320/G5
Penny Pot, N.J., U.S., 90 . . . . .314/D4
Pennyrile Forest St. Resort Park, Ky., U.S. 280/C3
Penobscot, Maine, U.S., 1,344 . . . . .286/D4
Penobscot, Maine, U.S., *bay* 286/D4
Penobscot, Maine, U.S., *county*, 144,919 . . . . . . .286/D3
Penobscot, Maine, U.S., *river* 286/D3
Penobsquis, N.B., Can. 217/D3
Penokee, Kans., U.S., 60 . . . . .276/C2
Penonomé, Pan. 203/B2
Penrhyndeu-draeth, Wales, U.K., 1,948 . . . . .64/C2
Penrith, Eng., U.K. 60/C2
Penrith, Eng., U.K., 12,049 . . . . .66/C3
Penrose, Ark., U.S. .244/D2
Penrose, Colo., U.S., 4,070 . . . . .250/E3
Penryn, Eng., U.K., 7,027 . . . . .73/B4
Pensacola, Antar., *mountains* 192/A11
Pensacola, Fla., U.S., 56,255, (412,153 *metro.*) . . .256/A1
Pensacola, Fla., U.S., *bay* 256/A1
Pensacola, Okla., U.S., 141 . . . . .330/G1
Pensacola Beach, Fla., U.S., 750 . . . . .256/A1
Pensaukee, Wisc., U.S., 125 . . . . .364/F4
Pensford, Eng., U.K. .73/C2
Pensilva, Eng., U.K., 1,528 . . . . .73/D4
Pentecost, Man., Can. 173/C2
Penticton, Br. Col., Can., 30,985 . . . . .214/N6
Pentland, Eng., U.K., *hills* 66/A1
Pentland, Scot., U.K., *hills* 62/K7
Penton, Ala., U.S. 238/D2
Penton, Miss., U.S., 40 . . . . .300/B1
Pentre-bach, Wales, U.K. 64/D4
Pentre Berw, Wales, U.K. 64/C1
Pentrefoelas, Wales, U.K. 64/D1
Pentwater, Mich., U.S., 958 . . . . .294/C6
Pen-twyn, Wales, U.K. .64/E4
Peñuelas, P.R. 206/B2
Penwell, Tex., U.S. .346/F4
Pen-y-cae, Wales, U.K. 64/E4
Pen-y-fan, Wales, U.K., *hill* 64/D4
Penygroes, Wales, U.K., 1,796 . . . . .64/C1
Penysarn, Wales, U.K. .64/C1
Penza, Russ., 528,140, (528,500 *metro.*) 104/D4
Penzance, Eng., U.K. .60/B4
Penzance, Eng., U.K., 19,709 . . . . .73/A4
Peoa, Utah, U.S., 125 . . . . .350/C3, E2
Peoples St. For., Conn., U.S. 253/C2
Peoria, Ariz., U.S., 108,364 . . . . .242/C4
Peoria, Ill., U.S., 112,936, (347,387 *metro.*) 266/D3
Peoria, Ill., U.S., *county*, 183,433 . . . . .266/D3
Peoria, Kans., U.S. .276/G3
Peoria, Ohio, U.S., 250 . . . . .328/D5
Peoria, Okla., U.S., 141 . . . . .330/H1
Peoria Hts., Ill., U.S., 6,635 . . . . .266/D3
Peosta, Iowa, U.S., 651 . . . . .274/N3
Peotone, Ill., U.S., 3,385 . . . . .266/F2
Pep, N. Mex., U.S. .317/G4
Pep, Tex., U.S., 40 .346/F2
Pepacton, N.Y., U.S., *reservoir* 320/M6
Pepeekeo, Hawaii, U.S., 1,697 . . . . .262/J5
Pepeekeo, Hawaii, U.S., *point* 262/J5
Pepin, Wisc., U.S., 878 . . . . .364/A4
Pepin, Wisc., U.S., *county* 7,213 . . . . .364/A4
Pepperell, Mass., U.S., 11,142 . . . . .292/H2
Pepper Pike, Ohio, U.S., 6,040 . . . . .328/H9
Pequaming, Mich., U.S. 294/A3
Pequannock, N.J., U.S., 13,888 . . . . .314/A1, E2

Pequop, Nev., U.S. .310/C1
Pequot Lakes, Minn., U.S., 947 . . . . .298/C4
Perak, Malay., *river* .121/A2
Peralta, N. Mex., U.S., 3,750 . . . . .317/D3
Peravia, Dom. Rep., *province* 205/B2
Percé, Que., Can., 3,614 . . . . .225/D4
Percé, Que., Can., 3,614 . . . . .226/M3
Percilla, Tex., U.S., 90 . . . . .346/N4
Percival, Iowa, U.S., 125 . . . . .274/C6
Percy, Ill., U.S., 942 . . . . .266/D5
Percy, Iowa, U.S. 274/H5
Percy, Miss., U.S., 50 . . . . .300/D2
Percy, N.H., U.S., 40 . . . . .312/D2
Perdido, Ala., U.S., 375 . . . . .238/B4
Perdiz, Tex., U.S. 346/E6
Perdue, Sask., Can., 372 . . . . .227/C8
Pereira, Col., 457,000 . . . . .184/B3
Perez, Calif., U.S. 246/D1
Perham, Maine, U.S., 434 . . . . .286/D2
Perham, Minn., U.S., 2,559 . . . . .298/B4
Péribonca, Que., Can., *river* 225/B3
Péribonca, Que., Can., *river* 226/E2
Péribonka, Que., Can., 538 . . . . .226/D3
Perico, Tex., U.S. 346/E8
Peridot, Ariz., U.S., 1,266 . . . . .242/E4
Perigueux, Fr. 88/C4
Perim, Yemen, *island* 137/A2
Peristeri, Gr., 137,288 . . . . .100/Inset
Perkasie, Penn., U.S., 8,828 . . . . .336/L5
Perkins, Ga., U.S., 80 . . . . .260/H6
Perkins, La., U.S., 40 . . . . .282/C6
Perkins, Maine, U.S. 286/C4
Perkins, Mich., U.S., 150 . . . . .294/B4
Perkins, Okla., U.S., 2,272 . . . . .330/E2
Perkins, S. Dak., U.S., *county*, 3,363 . . . . .342/C2
Perkins Corner, Conn., U.S., 1,000 . . . . .253/F3
Perkinston, Miss., U.S., 700 . . . . .242/C3
Perkinsville, Ariz., U.S. 242/C3
Perkinsville, Vt., U.S., 142 . . . . .352/B4
Perla, Ark., U.S., 115 . . . . .244/C3
Perlas, Nicar., *lagoon* 202/C2
Perlas, Nicar., *point* 202/C2
Perlas, Pan., *archipelago* 203/C2
Perley, Minn., U.S., 121 . . . . .298/A3
Perm', Russ., 1,014,360, (1,024,250 *metro.*) 104/D4
Perma, Mont., U.S. .306/B2
Përmet, Alb. 99/B3
Pernambuco, Braz., *state* 188/E2
Pernell, Okla., U.S., 60 . . . . .330/E3
Pernik, Bul., 105,900 . . . . .101/A3
Pernik, Bul., *oblast* 101/A3, B5, E7
Pernitas Pt., Tex., U.S., 269 . . . . .346/L7
Perote, Ala., U.S. 238/D4
Perpignan, Fr. 107,241, (162,678 *metro.*) 88/C5
Perquimans, N.C., U.S., *county*, 11,368 . . . . .322/N2
Perranporth, Eng., U.K., 2,611 . . . . .73/B4
Perrin, Tex., U.S., 100 . . . . .346/K2
Perrine, Fla., U.S., 15,600 . . . . .256/A7, H6
Perrineville, N.J., U.S., 550 . . . . .314/E3
Perrinton, Mich., U.S., 439 . . . . .294/E6
Perris, Calif., U.S., 36,189 . . . . .246/H9
Perronville, Mich., U.S., 100 . . . . .294/M4
Perrot, Que., Can., *island* 226/G6
Perry, Ala., U.S., *county*, 11,861 . . . . .238/B3
Perry, Ark., U.S., 314 . . . . .244/C2
Perry, Ark., U.S., *county*, 10,209 . . . . .244/C3
Perry, Fla., U.S., 6,847 . . . . .256/E1
Perry, Ga., U.S., 9,602 . . . . .260/D7
Perry, Ill., U.S., 437 .266/C4
Perry, Ill., U.S., *county*, 23,094 . . . . .266/D5
Perry, Ill., U.S., *county*, 18,899 . . . . .270/C8
Perry, Iowa, U.S., 7,633 . . . . .274/F4
Perry, Kans., U.S., 901 . . . . .276/G2
Perry, Ky., U.S., *county*, 29,390 . . . . .280/G3
Perry, La., U.S., 1,300 . . . . .282/E4
Perry, Maine, U.S., 847 . . . . .286/E4
Perry, Mich., U.S., 2,065 . . . . .294/E7
Perry, Miss., U.S., *county*, 12,138 . . . . .300/D4
Perry, Mo., U.S., 666 . . . . .302/E2
Perry, Mo., U.S., *county*, 18,132 . . . . .302/F4
Perry, N.Y., U.S., 3,945 . . . . .320/F5
Perry, Ohio, U.S., 1,195 . . . . .328/H2
Perry, Ohio, U.S., *county*, 34,078 . . . . .328/F6
Perry, Okla., U.S., 5,230 . . . . .330/E1
Perry, Penn., U.S., *county*, 43,602 . . . . .336/G5
Perry, S.C., U.S., 237 . . . . .340/C3
Perry, Tenn., U.S., *county*, 7,631 . . . . .344/F3
Perry, Utah, U.S., 2,383 . . . . .350/B2
Perry Hall, Md., U.S., 28,705 . . . . .288/J2
Perry Hts., Ohio, U.S., 8,900 . . . . .328/H4
Perryman, Md., U.S., 2,461 . . . . .288/K2
Perryopolis, Penn., U.S., 1,764 . . . . .336/B5
Perrysburg, Ohio, U.S., 16,945 . . . . .328/C6
Perry's Victory and International Peace Mem.,
Ohio, U.S. 328/E2
Perrysville, Ind., U.S., 502 . . . . .270/B4
Perrysville, Ohio, U.S., 816 . . . . .328/F4
Perryton, Tex., U.S., 7,774 . . . . .346/G8
Perrytown, Ark., U.S., 255 . . . . .244/C4
Perryville, Ark., U.S., 1,458 . . . . .244/C3
Perryville, Ky., U.S., 763 . . . . .280/F3
Perryville, La., U.S., 50 . . . . .282/F1
Perryville, Md., U.S., 3,672 . . . . .288/K1
Perryville, Mo., U.S., 7,667 . . . . .302/G4
Perryville, R.I., U.S., 300 . . . . .339/C5
Perryville, Tenn., U.S., 275 . . . . .344/E3
Pershing, Nev., U.S., *county*, 6,693 . . . . .310/A1
Pershore, Eng., U.K., 7,087 . . . . .68/C5
Persia, Iowa, U.S., 363 . . . . .274/C4
Persian, Iran, *gulf* .130/C4
Persian, Iraq, *gulf* .130/C3
Persian, Kuw., *gulf* .136/C2
Persian, Oman, *gulf* 137/B1
Persian, Sa. Arab., *gulf* 136/C1
Persian, U.A.E., *gulf* 136/B1
Person, N.C., U.S., *county*, 35,623 . . . . .322/G2
Perth, W.A., Austl., *state capital*,
(1,307,196 *metro.*) . . . . .170/A3, Inset I
Perth, Ont., Can., 6,003 . . . . .223/D4
Perth, Ont., Can., 6,003 . . . . .223/J4
Perth, Ont., Can., *county* 223/D3
Perth, Scot., U.K. 60/B2
Perth, Scot., U.K., 43,450 . . . . .62/K6
Perth, N. Dak., U.S. .326/F1
Perth Amboy, N.J., U.S., 47,303 . . . . .314/E2
Perth and Kinross, Scot., U.K., *unitary authority*,
134,949 . . . . .62/H5
Perth-Andover, N.B., Can., 1,908 . . . . .217/B2
Peru, *nation* 175
Peru, Ill., U.S., 9,835 . . . . .266/D2
Peru, Ind., U.S., 12,994 . . . . .270/D3
Peru, Kans., U.S., 183 . . . . .276/F4
Peru, Mass., U.S., 821 . . . . .292/B3
Peru, Nebr., U.S., 569 . . . . .308/J4
Peru, N.Y., U.S., 1,514 . . . . .320/P1
Peru, Vt., U.S., 416 .352/B4
Peru, Wisc., U.S., 90 . . . . .364/D4
Peru, Wyo., U.S. 366/B3

Perugia, It. 95/C2
Pervomais'k, Ukr. 102/C2
Pesaro, It. 95/C2
Pescadero, Calif., U.S., 475 . . . . .246/J3
Pescadores, Tai., *channel* 117/A2
Pescara, It. 95/C2
Peshastin, Wash., U.S., 650 . . . . .358/E2
Peshawar, Pak., 982,816 . . . . .129/D3
Peshawbestown, Mich., U.S., 200 . . . . .294/D4
Peshkopi, Alb. 99/B2
Peshtigo, Wisc., U.S., 3,357 . . . . .364/F3
Peshtigo, Wisc., U.S., *river* 364/E3
Pesotum, Ill., U.S., 521 . . . . .266/E4
Pest, Hun., *county* 91/B2
Petah Tiqwa, Isr., 155,200 . . . . .135/B1
Petal, Miss., U.S., 7,579 . . . . .300/C4
Petaluma, Calif., U.S., 54,548 . . . . .246/C4, H1
Petare, Ven., 338,880, (500,868 *metro.*) 182/C1
Petauke, Zam. 159/C2
Petawawa, Ont., Can., 14,398 . . . . .223/H2
Petén-Itzá, Guat., *lake* 201/D3
Petenwell, Wisc., U.S., *lake* 364/D4
Peterborough, Ont., Can., 71,446 . . . . .222/E4
Peterborough, Ont., Can., 71,446 . . . . .223/G3
Peterborough, Ont., Can., 71,446 . . . . .223/G3
Peterborough, Ont., Can., *county* 223/G3
Peterborough, Eng., U.K. 60/C3
Peterborough, Eng., U.K., 134,788 . . . . .68/G4
Peterborough, Eng., U.K., 134,788 . . . . .70/D1
Peterborough, Eng., U.K., *unitary authority*,
156,060 . . . . .68/G4
Peterborough, Eng., U.K., *unitary authority*,
156,060 . . . . .70/D1
Peterborough, N.H., U.S., 5,883 . . . . .312/C6
Peterculter, Scot., U.K. 62/M4
Peterhead, Scot., U.K. 60/C1
Peterhead, Scot., U.K., 17,947 . . . . .62/N3
Peterlee, Eng., U.K., 31,139 . . . . .66/F3
Peter Lougheed Prov. Park, Alta., Can. 212/C6
Petermann, Austl., *aboriginal land* 170/B2
Peter Pond, Sask., Can., *lake* 212/E3
Petersburg, Alaska, U.S., 3,224 . . . . .240/J3
Petersburg, Del., U.S., 225 . . . . .255/B4
Petersburg, Ill., U.S., 2,299 . . . . .266/D4
Petersburg, Ind., U.S., 2,570 . . . . .270/B8
Petersburg, Ky., U.S., 450 . . . . .280/F1
Petersburg, Md., U.S., 175 . . . . .288/L5
Petersburg, Mich., U.S., 1,157 . . . . .294/F8
Petersburg, Minn., U.S. 298/C7
Petersburg, Nebr., U.S., 374 . . . . .308/E2
Petersburg, N.J., U.S., 650 . . . . .314/D1
Petersburg, N.J., U.S., 650 . . . . .314/D5
Petersburg, N.Y., U.S. 320/Q5
Petersburg, N. Dak., U.S., 195 . . . . .326/H2
Petersburg, Penn., U.S., 455 . . . . .336/E4
Petersburg, Tenn., U.S., 580 . . . . .344/H4
Petersburg, Tex., U.S., 1,262 . . . . .346/G2
Petersburg, Va., U.S., 33,740 . . . . .354/J6
Petersburg, W. Va., U.S., 2,423 . . . . .360/H2
Petersburg N.B., Va., U.S. 343/J6
Petersfield, Man., Can. 215/C4
Petersfield, Eng., U.K., 12,177 . . . . .70/C5
Petersham, Mass., U.S., 1,180 . . . . .292/F3
Peterson, Ala., U.S., 475 . . . . .238/B2
Peterson, Iowa, U.S., 372 . . . . .274/D2
Peterson, Minn., U.S., 269 . . . . .298/F7
Peterstone Wentlooge, Wales, U.K. 64/E4
Peterstown, W. Va., U.S., 499 . . . . .360/E6
Petersville, Ala., U.S., 3,137 . . . . .238/B1
Petersville, Ky., U.S., 80 . . . . .280/G2
Petit Bois, Miss., U.S., *island* 300/D5
Petit Canouan, St. Vin.-Gren., *island* 208/B3
Petitcodiac, N.B., Can., 1,444 . . . . .217/D3
Petite-Cap, N.B., Can. 217/E2
Petite Riviere, N.S., Can. 221/C6
Petit Martinique, Gren., *island* 208/C1
Petit Mustique, St. Vin.-Gren., *island* 208/B3
Petitot, Br. Col., Can., *river* 212/A1
Petit-Rocher, N.B., Can., 1,966 . . . . .217/D1
Petit St. Vincent, St. Vin.-Gren., *island* 208/A4
Petit-Shippegan, N.B., Can. 217/E1
Petlura, Man., Can. .215/A3
Petoskey, Mich., U.S., 6,080 . . . . .294/E4
Petra, Jor., *ruins* 134/A2
Petrey, Ala., U.S., 63 . . . . .238/C4
Petrich, Bul. 101/B4
Petrie, Qnsld., Austl. . . . . .170/Inset III
Petrified Forest Natl. Park, Ariz., U.S. 242/F3
Petrila, Rom. 101/B3
Petroglyph Natl. Mon., N. Mex., U.S. 317/D2
Petroleum, Mont., U.S., *county*, 493 . . . . .306/H2
Petroleum, W. Va., U.S. 360/D2
Petrolia, Ont., Can., 4,849 . . . . .223/C5
Petrolia, Calif., U.S. .246/A2
Petrolia, Kans., U.S., 70 . . . . .276/G4
Petrolia, Tex., U.S., 218 . . . . .336/B3
Petrólina, Braz., 73,436, (174,972 *metro.*) 188/D2
Petronila, Tex., U.S., 83 . . . . .346/L8
Petropavlovsk, Kaz., 203,523 . . . . .131/C1
Petropavlovsk-Kamchatskiy, Russ., 198,424,
(209,650 *metro.*) 104/I4
Petropavlovsk-Kamchatskiy, Russ. 193/D8
Petrópolis, Braz., 149,427,
(255,211 *metro.*) . . . . .188/D4, Inset I
Petros, Tenn., U.S., 650 . . . . .344/N1
Petroşani, Rom. 101/B3
Petrozavodsk, Russ., 282,401, (282,650 *metro.*) . . .104/C3
Pettibone, N. Dak., U.S., 88 . . . . .326/F2
Pettigrew, Ark., U.S. .244/B2
Pettis, Mo., U.S., *county*, 39,403 . . . . .302/C3
Pettit, Tex., U.S., 40 . . . . .346/F2
Pettus, Tex., U.S., 608 . . . . .346/L7
Petty, Tex., U.S. 346/N2
Petworth, Eng., U.K., 2,156 . . . . .70/E5
Pevek, Russ. 104/J3
Pevely, Mo., U.S., 3,768 . . . . .302/F3
Pevensey, Eng., U.K. .70/E5
Pewamo, Mich., U.S., 560 . . . . .294/E6
Pewaukee, Wisc., U.S., 8,170 . . . . .364/B1
Pewee Valley, Ky., U.S., 1,436 . . . . .280/B1
Pewsey, Eng., U.K., 2,452 . . . . .73/J2
Peyia, Cyp. 133/A2
Peyton, Colo., U.S., 150 . . . . .250/F2
Pfeifer, Kans., U.S., 40 . . . . .276/C3
Pflugerville, Tex., U.S., 16,335 . . . . .346/L4
Pforzheim, Ger., 117,227 . . . . .86/B4
Phair, Maine, U.S. 286/E2
Phan Rang, Viet. 123/B4
Phan Thiet, Viet. 123/B4
Pharr, Tex., U.S., 46,660 . . . . .346/K9
Phatthalung, Thai. 125/B5
Phayao, Thai. 125/B2
Pheba, Miss., U.S., 175 . . . . .300/D2
Phelps, Ky., U.S., 1,053 . . . . .280/H3
Phelps, Minn., U.S., 40 . . . . .298/B4
Phelps, Mo., U.S., *county*, 39,825 . . . . .302/E4
Phelps, Nebr., U.S., *county*, 9,747 . . . . .308/E3
Phelps, N.Y., U.S., 1,969 . . . . .320/G5
Phelps, N.C., U.S., *lake* 322/N3

Phelps, Wisc., U.S., 350 . . . . .364/C
Phelps City, Mo., U.S., 40 . . . . .302/A
Phenix, Va., U.S., 200 . . . . .354/H
Phenix City, Ala., U.S., 28,265 . . . . .238/C
Phetchabun, Thai., *range* 125/E
Phetchabun, Thai. 125/B
Phichit, Thai. . . . . .125/B.
Philadelphia, Miss., U.S., 7,303 . . . . .300/C
Philadelphia, Mo., U.S., 250 . . . . .302/E2
Philadelphia, N.Y., U.S., 1,519 . . . . .320/K2
Philadelphia, Penn., U.S., 1,517,550,
(6,188,463 *metro.*) 336/L6, M7
Philadelphia, Penn., U.S., *county*,
1,517,550 .336/L5, M7
Philadelphia, Tenn., U.S., 533 . . . . .344/N
Philbrook, Minn., U.S. 298/C
Phil Campbell, Ala., U.S., 1,091 . . . . .238/
Philip, S. Dak., U.S., 885 . . . . .342/
Philip, W. Va., U.S., 2,870 . . . . .360/
Philippine, Phil., *sea* 120/C
Philippine, Tai., *sea* 117/B
Philippines, *nation* 11
Philipsburg, Mont., U.S., 914 . . . . .306/C
Philipsburg, Penn., U.S., 3,056 . . . . .336/E4
Phillips, Ark., U.S., *county*, 26,445 . . . . .244/E3
Phillips, Colo., U.S., *county*, 4,480 . . . . .250/H1
Phillips, Kans., U.S., *county*, 6,001 . . . . .276/C2
Phillips, Maine, U.S., 990 . . . . .286/B4
Phillips, Mont., U.S., *county*, 4,601 . . . . .306/J1
Phillips, Nebr., U.S., 336 . . . . .308/E3
Phillips, Okla., U.S., 150 . . . . .330/F3
Phillips, Wisc., U.S., 1,675 . . . . .364/C3
Phillipsburg, Ga., U.S., 887 . . . . .260/D9
Phillipsburg, Kans., U.S., 2,668 . . . . .276/C2
Phillipsburg, Ky., U.S. 280/E3
Phillipsburg, Mo., U.S., 201 . . . . .302/D4
Phillipsburg, N.J., U.S., 15,166 . . . . .314/C2
Phillipsburg, Ohio, U.S., 628 . . . . .328/B6
Phillipston, Mass., U.S., 1,621 . . . . .292/F2
Phillipstown, Ill., U.S. 266/E5
Philmont, N.Y., U.S., 1,480 . . . . .320/P6
Philo, Calif., U.S., 325 . . . . .246/B3
Philo, Ill., U.S., 1,314 . . . . .266/E4
Philo, Ohio, U.S., 769 . . . . .328/G6
Philomath, Ga., U.S., 50 . . . . .260/E4
Philomath, Oreg., U.S., 3,838 . . . . .334/C3
Philpot, Ky., U.S., 850 . . . . .280/D3
Phippsburg, Colo., U.S., 150 . . . . .250/D1
Phitsanulok, Thai. 125/B2
Phlox, Wisc., U.S., 150 . . . . .364/D3
Phnom Penh, Camb., *capital*, 999,804 . . . . .124/C4
Phnum Aôral, Camb., *mountain* 124/C3
Phnum Tbêng Méanchey, Camb. 124/C2
Phoenicia, N.Y., U.S., 381 . . . . .320/N6
Phoenix, Kiri., *islands* 175/D2
Phoenix, Ariz., U.S., *state capital*, 1,321,045,
(3,251,876 *metro.*) 242/C4
Phoenix, Ill., U.S., 2,157 . . . . .266/C6
Phoenix, La., U.S., 475 . . . . .282/K7
Phoenix, Md., U.S., 500 . . . . .288/H1
Phoenix, Miss., U.S., 60 . . . . .300/B3
Phoenix, N.Y., U.S., 2,251 . . . . .320/J4
Phoenix, Oreg., U.S., 4,060 . . . . .334/C5
Phoenixville, Conn., U.S., 150 . . . . .253/C2
Phoenixville, Penn., U.S., 14,788 . . . . .336/K5
Phôngsali, Laos 124/B1
Phou Bia, Laos, *mountain* 124/B2
Phrae, Thai. 125/B2
Phra Nakhon Si Ayutthaya, Thai. 125/B3
Phuket, Thai. 125/B5
Phum Sâmraông, Camb. 124/B1
Phuntsholing, Bhu. 126/A3
Piacenza, It. 95/B1
Pianosa, It., *island* 95/B2
Pia Oik, Ariz., U.S., 450 . . . . .242/C6
Piapot, Sask., Can., 55 . . . . .227/A10
Piatra Neamţ, Rom., 124,189 . . . . .101/D2
Piatt, Ill., U.S., *county*, 16,365 . . . . .266/E3
Piauí, Braz., *state* .188/D2
Piave, It., *river* 95/C1
Pibor Post, Sudan 145/C3
Pica, Ariz., U.S. 242/B2
Picabo, Ida., U.S., 60 . . . . .264/C6
Picacho, Ariz., U.S., 475 . . . . .242/D5
Picacho, N. Mex., U.S. 317/E2
Picardie, Fr., *region* 88/C2
Picayune, Miss., U.S., 10,535 . . . . .300/C5
Pic de la Selle, Haiti, *mountain* 205/D2
Picher, Okla., U.S., 1,640 . . . . .330/H1
Pichincha, Ecua., *province* 184/B4
Pickaway, Ohio, U.S., *county*, 52,727 . . . . .328/D6
Pick City, N. Dak., U.S., 166 . . . . .326/D2
Pickens, Ala., U.S., *county*, 20,949 . . . . .238/A2
Pickens, Ark., U.S., 100 . . . . .244/D4
Pickens, Ga., U.S., *county*, 22,983 . . . . .260/B3
Pickens, Miss., U.S., 1,325 . . . . .300/C3
Pickens, Okla., U.S., 50 . . . . .330/G3
Pickens, S.C., U.S., 3,012 . . . . .340/B2
Pickens, S.C., U.S., *county*, 110,757 . . . . .340/B2
Pickens, W. Va., U.S. 360/F3
Pickensville, Ala., U.S., 662 . . . . .238/A2
Pickerel, Wisc., U.S., 100 . . . . .364/E3
Pickering, Eng., U.K., 5,914 . . . . .66/G4
Pickering, Eng., U.K., *valley* 66/G4
Pickering, La., U.S., 400 . . . . .282/C4
Pickering, Mo., U.S., 154 . . . . .302/B1
Pickering Brook, W.A., Austl. . . . . .170/Inset I
Pickerington, Ohio, U.S., 9,792 . . . . .328/E6, E10
Pickett, Tenn., U.S., *county*, 4,945 . . . . .344/J1
Pickett, Wisc., U.S., 200 . . . . .364/E5
Pickford, Mich., U.S., 500 . . . . .294/E4
Pickle Lake, Ont., Can. 222/B2
Pickrell, Nebr., U.S., 182 . . . . .308/H3
Pickstown, S. Dak., U.S., 168 . . . . .342/G4
Pickton, Tex., U.S. 346/N2
Pickwick, Miss., U.S., *lake* 300/D1
Pico, C.V., *volcano* .148/A4
Pico, Port., *island* . . . . .93/Inset II
Pico de la Selle, Haiti, 63,428 . . . . .246/D9
Picton, Ont., Can., 4,563 . . . . .223/H3
Picton, N.Z. 171/B3
Pictou, N.S., Can., 3,875 . . . . .221/E2
Pictou, N.S., Can., *county* 221/E2
Pictured Rocks Natl. Lakeshore, Mich., U.S. 294/C3
Picture Rocks, Penn., U.S., 693 . . . . .336/H3
Pidurutalagala, Sri Lan., *mountain* 126/B4
Pie, Ont., Can., *island* 294/A1
Piedmont, It., *region* .95/A1
Piedmont, Ala., U.S., 5,120 . . . . .238/D2
Piedmont, Calif., U.S., 10,952 . . . . .246/C6
Piedmont, Ga., U.S. .260/C5
Piedmont, Kans., U.S. 276/F4
Piedmont, Mo., U.S., 1,992 . . . . .302/F4
Piedmont, Ohio, U.S., 225 . . . . .328/H5
Piedmont, Okla., U.S., 3,650 . . . . .340/B2, B4
Piedmont, S.C., U.S., 4,684 . . . . .340/B2
Piedmont, S. Dak., U.S., 700 . . . . .342/B3
Piedmont, W. Va., U.S., 1,014 . . . . .360/H2
Piedmont, Wyo., U.S. 366/A3

edmont N.W.R., Ga., U.S. 260/D5
edra, Ariz., U.S. .242/C5
edra, Calif., U.S. 246/F6
edras Blancas, Calif., U.S., point 246/D7
edras Negras, Mex., 126,386,
  (128,130 metro.) 200/D2
edra Sola, Uru. .187/B2
elinen, Fin., lake 81/C2
ierce, Colo., U.S., 884 . . . . .250/F1
ierce, Ida., U.S., 617 . . . . .264/B3
Pierce, Ky., U.S., 200 . . . . .280/E3
Pierce, Nebr., U.S., 1,774 . . . . .308/G1
Pierce, Nebr., U.S., county, 7,857 . . . . .308/G1
Pierce, N. Dak., U.S., county, 4,675 . . . . . . .326/E1
ierce, Okla., U.S. 330/G2
ierce, Wash., U.S., county, 700,820 . . . . . .358/C2
erce, Wisc., U.S., county, 36,804 . . . . .364/A4
orcebridge, Eng., U.K. 66/E3
rce Bridge, N.H., U.S., 80 . . . . .312/C3
rce City, Mo., U.S., 1,385 . . . . .302/B5
ercefield, N.Y., U.S., 150 . . . . .320/M2
erceland, Sask., Can., 449 . . . . .227/A6
ierces Pt., U.S., 125 . . . . .314/D5
ierceton, Ind., U.S., 695 . . . . .270/C2
ierceville, Kans., U.S., 90 . . . . .276/B4
iercy, Calif., U.S., 50 . . . . .246/B3
iermont, N.H., U.S., 709 . . . . .312/B4
Piermont, N.Y., U.S., 2,607 . . . . .320/B1
Pierowall, Scot., U.K. 62/M1
Pierpont, Ohio, U.S., 300 . . . . .328/J2
Pierpont, S. Dak., U.S., 122 . . . . .342/H2
Pierport, Mich., U.S., 70 . . . . .294/C5
Pierre, S. Dak., U.S., state capital, 13,876 . .342/E3
Pierrefonds, Que., Can., 54,963 . . . . .226/G5
Pierre Part, La., U.S., 3,239 . . . . .282/G7
Pierreville, Trin.-To. 209/A2
Pierron, Ill., U.S., 653 . . . . .266/D5
Pierson, Man., Can. 215/A4
Pierson, Fla., U.S., 2,596 . . . . .256/C2
Pierson, Iowa, U.S., 371 . . . . .274/C2
Pierson, Mich., U.S., 185 . . . . .294/D6
Pierz, Minn., U.S., 1,277 . . . . .298/C5
Piešt'any, Slvk. 92/A2
Pietermaritzburg, S. Afr. 162/D2
Pietersburg, S. Afr. 162/C1
Pie Town, N. Mex., U.S. 317/B3
Pigeon, Alta., U.S., lake 212/C4
Pigeon, Ont., Can., lake 223/G3
Pigeon, Tex., U.S., 600 . . . . .282/G6
Pigeon, Mich., U.S., 1,207 . . . . .294/F6
Pigeon Cove, Mass., U.S., 1,700 . . . . .292/M2
Pigeon Falls, Wisc., U.S., 388 . . . . .364/B4
Pigeon Forge, Tenn., U.S., 5,083 . . . . .344/P3
Pigeon Hill, N.B., Can., 537 . . . . .217/E1
Pigeon River, Minn., U.S. 298/F2
Piggott, Ark., U.S., 3,894 . . . . .244/E1
Piggs Peak, Swaz. 161/B1
Pigs Eye, Minn., U.S., lake 298/F6
Pikangikum, Ont., Can. 222/B2
Pike, Ala., U.S., county, 29,605 . . . . .238/D4
Pike, Ark., U.S., county, 11,303 . . . . .244/B3
Pike, Colo., U.S., county, 13,688 . . . . .260/C5
Pike, Ill., U.S., county, 17,384 . . . . .266/C4
Pike, Ind., U.S., 150 . . . . .270/D4
Pike, Ind., U.S., county, 12,837 . . . . .270/B8
Pike, Ky., U.S., county, 68,736 . . . . .280/H3
Pike, Miss., U.S., county, 38,940 . . . . .300/B4
Pike, Mo., U.S., county, 18,351 . . . . .302/E2
Pike, N.Y., U.S., 382 . . . . .320/E5
Pike, Ohio, U.S., county, 27,695 . . . . .328/D7
Pike, Penn., U.S., county, 46,302 . . . . .336/L3
Pike, W. Va., U.S., 125 . . . . .360/D2
Pike City, Ark., U.S., 40 . . . . .244/B3
Pikehall, Eng., U.K. 68/D3
Pike Natl. For., Colo., U.S. 250/E2, F3
Pike Road, Ala., U.S., 310 . . . . .238/C3
Pike Road, N.C., U.S., 275 . . . . .322/M3
Pikes, Colo., U.S., peak 250/E3
Pikesville, Md., U.S., 29,123 . . . . .288/H2
Piketon, Ohio, U.S., 1,907 . . . . .328/D7
Pike View, Ky., U.S., 125 . . . . .280/E3
Pikeville, Ky., U.S., 6,295 . . . . .280/H3
Pikeville, N.C., U.S., 719 . . . . .322/K4
Pikeville, Tenn., U.S., 1,781 . . . . .344/L3
Pikwitonei, Man., Can., 117 . . . . .215/C1
Piła, Pol. 83/C2
Pilar, Para. 187/C5
Pilar, N. Mex., U.S., 90 . . . . .317/E1
Pilaya, Bol., river 186/B4
Pilcomayo, Arg., river 191/C1
Pilcomayo, Bol., river 186/B4
Pilcomayo, Para., river 187/B3, C4
Pilger, Nebr., U.S., 378 . . . . .308/G2
Pilica, Pol., river .83/E3
Pillager, Minn., U.S., 420 . . . . .298/C4
Pillaton, Eng., U.K. 73/D4
Pilling, Eng., U.K. .66/C5
Pillow, Penn., U.S., 304 . . . . .336/H4
Pillsbury, N. Dak., U.S. 326/H2
Pilot, Nev., U.S., peak 310/C1
Pilot Butte, Sask., Can., 1,850 . . . . .227/F10
Pilot Grove, Mo., U.S., 723 . . . . .302/D3
Pilot Hill, Calif., U.S., 200 . . . . .246/L5
Pilot Knob, Mo., U.S., 697 . . . . .302/F4
Pilot Mound, Man., Can., 676 . . . . .215/B4
Pilot Mound, Iowa, U.S., 214 . . . . .274/E3
Pilot Mt., N.C., U.S., 1,281 . . . . .322/E2
Pilot Pt., Alaska, U.S., 100 . . . . .240/D3
Pilot Pt., Tex., U.S., 3,538 . . . . .346/M2
Pilot Rock, Oreg., U.S., 1,532 . . . . .334/H2
Pilot Sta., Alaska, U.S., 550 . . . . .240/C2
Pilottown, La., U.S., 100 . . . . .282/L8
Pilsen, Wisc., U.S., 125 . . . . .364/F4
Pilton, Eng., U.K. .70/C2
Pilton, Eng., U.K. .73/G2
Pima, Ariz., U.S., 1,989 . . . . .242/F5
Pima, Ariz., U.S., county, 843,746 . . . . .242/D5
Pimento, Ind., U.S., 275 . . . . .270/B6
Pimmit Hills, Va., U.S., 6,152 . . . . .354/M2
Pinal, Ariz., U.S., county, 179,727 . . . . .242/D5
Pinang, Malay., island 121/A2
Pinar del Río, Cuba, 133,000 . . . . .204/A2
Pinar del Río, Cuba, province 204/A2
Pinardville, N.H., U.S., 5,779 . . . . .312/C6
Pinawa, Man., Can., 1,500 . . . . .215/D4
Pinch, W. Va., U.S., 2,811 . . . . .360/D4
Pinchbeck, Eng., U.K., 3,655 . . . . .68/G4
Pinchbeck, Eng., U.K., 3,655 . . . . .70/D1
Pinchbeck West, Eng., U.K. 70/D1
Pincher Creek, Alta., Can., 3,666 . . . . .212/D6
Pinckard, Ala., U.S., 667 . . . . .238/C4
Pinckney, Mich., U.S., 2,141 . . . . .294/F7
Pinckneyville, Ill., U.S., 5,464 . . . . .266/D5
Pinckneyville, Miss., U.S., 40 . . . . .300/A4
Pinconning, Mich., U.S., 1,386 . . . . .294/F6
Pindall, Ark., U.S., 95 . . . . .244/C1
Pindus, Gr., mountains 100/B2
Pine, Ariz., U.S., 1,931 . . . . .242/D3
Pine, Colo., U.S., 100 . . . . .250/E2
Pine, Ida., U.S. 264/B6

Pine, Minn., U.S., county, 26,530 . . . . .298/E4
Pine, Miss., U.S., hills 300/B4
Pine, Nebr., U.S., ridge 308/B1
Pine, Oreg., U.S. .334/J3
Pine, S. Dak., U.S., ridge 342/C5
Pine Apple, Ala., U.S., 145 . . . . .238/C4
Pine Barren, Fla., U.S., 150 . . . . .256/A1
Pine Beach, N.J., U.S., 1,950 . . . . .314/E4
Pine Bluff, Ark., U.S., 55,085, (84,278 metro.) . .244/D3
Pinebluff, N.C., U.S., 1,109 . . . . .322/G4
Pine Bluff Arsenal, Ark., U.S. 244/C3
Pine Bluffs, Wyo., U.S., 1,153 . . . . .366/D3
Pine Brook, Minn., U.S., 175 . . . . .298/D5
Pine Bush, N.Y., U.S., 1,539 . . . . .320/N7
Pine Castle, Fla., U.S., 8,803 . . . . .256/C4, B3
Pine Ctr., Minn., U.S., 80 . . . . .298/D4
Pine City, Minn., U.S., 3,043 . . . . .298/E5
Pine City, Wash., U.S. 358/H2
Pinecliffe, Colo., U.S., 50 . . . . .250/D2
Pinecreek, Minn., U.S. 298/B2
Pinecrest, Fla., U.S., 600 . . . . .256/F4
Pine Crest, Tenn., U.S., 2,872 . . . . .344/S2
Pineda, Fla., U.S., 1,100 . . . . .256/H3
Pinedale, Ariz., U.S., 100 . . . . .242/E3
Pinedale, N. Mex., U.S., 70 . . . . .317/B2
Pinedale, Wyo., U.S., 1,412 . . . . .366/B2
Pine Dock, Man., Can., 108 . . . . .215/C3
Pine Falls, Man., Can. 215/C4
Pine Grove, Ky., U.S. 280/F2
Pine Grove, La., U.S., 250 . . . . .282/H5
Pine Grove, Oreg., U.S., 162 . . . . .334/E2
Pine Grove, Penn., U.S., 2,154 . . . . .336/J4
Pine Grove, W. Va., U.S., 571 . . . . .360/E1
Pine Grove Mills, Penn., U.S., 1,141 . . . . . .336/F4
Pine Hall, N.C., U.S., 275 . . . . .322/E2
Pine Haven, Wyo., U.S., 222 . . . . .366/D1
Pine Hill, Ala., U.S., 966 . . . . .238/B4
Pine Hill, N.J., U.S., 10,880 . . . . .314/B4, D4
Pine Hill, N. Mex., U.S., 116 . . . . .317/B2
Pinehouse, Sask., Can., lake 227/D5
Pinehouse Lake, Sask., Can. 227/D5
Pinehurst, Ga., U.S., 307 . . . . .260/D7
Pinehurst, Ida., U.S., 1,661 . . . . .264/A2
Pinehurst, Mass., U.S., 6,941 . . . . .292/B6, K2
Pinehurst, N.C., U.S., 9,706 . . . . .322/G4
Pinehurst, Oreg., U.S. 334/D5
Pinehurst, (Montgomery County),
  Tex., U.S., 4,266 . . . . .346/A5
Pine Island, Minn., U.S., 2,337 . . . . .298/E6
Pine Island, Tex., U.S., 849 . . . . .346/M5
Pine Island Ridge, Fla., U.S., 5,199 . . . . . .256/A6
Pine Knoll Shores, N.C., U.S., 1,524 . . . . . .322/N5
Pine Knot, Ky., U.S., 1,680 . . . . .280/F4
Pine Lake, Alta., Can. 212/D5
Pine Lake, Ga., U.S., 621 . . . . .260/J3
Pine Lake, Wash., U.S. 358/B4
Pine Lake Park, N.J., U.S. 314/E4
Pineland, S.C., U.S., 200 . . . . .340/C4
Pineland, Tex., U.S., 980 . . . . .346/R4
Pine Lawn, Mo., U.S., 4,204 . . . . .302/P2
Pine Level, Ala., U.S., 100 . . . . .238/C3
Pine Level, N.C., U.S., 1,313 . . . . .322/J4
Pinellas, Fla., U.S., county, 921,482 . . .256/C6, F4
Pinellas Park, Fla., U.S., 45,658 . . . . .256/C6
Pine Log, Ga., U.S., 250 . . . . .260/B3
Pine Mountain, Ga., U.S., 1,141 . . . . .260/B6
Pine Mtn. Valley, Ga., U.S., 475 . . . . .260/B6
Pine Plains, N.Y., U.S., 1,412 . . . . .320/P7
Pine Pt., N.W. Terr., Can. 220/F4
Pine Pt., Maine, U.S., 600 . . . . .286/B5
Pine Prairie, La., U.S., 1,087 . . . . .282/E5
Pine Ridge, N.B., Can. 217/D2
Pine Ridge, Ala., U.S., 243 . . . . .238/D1
Pine Ridge, Ark., U.S. 244/B3
Pineridge, S.C., U.S., 1,593 . . . . .340/A3, C3
Pine Ridge, S. Dak., U.S., 3,171 . . . . .342/C4
Pine Ridge Ind. Res., S. Dak., U.S. 342/C4
Pine Ridge Natl. Rec. Area, Nebr., U.S. 308/A1
Pine River, Man., Can. 215/A3
Pine River, Minn., U.S., 928 . . . . .298/C4
Pinesdale, Mont., U.S., 742 . . . . .306/B3
Pine Sprs., Ariz., U.S. 242/C2
Pine Sprs., Minn., U.S., 421 . . . . .298/F5
Pine Sprs., Tex., U.S. 346/A6
Pinetop-Lakeside, Ariz., U.S., 3,582 . . . . . .242/F3
Pinetops, N.C., U.S., 1,419 . . . . .322/K3
Pinetown, Del., U.S., 1,100 . . . . .255/D5
Pinetown, N.C., U.S., 225 . . . . .322/M3
Pinetta, Fla., U.S., 275 . . . . .256/E1
Piney Valley, N.J., U.S. 314/B4
Pine Valley, (Chemung County), N.Y., U.S., 950 . .320/F2
Pine Valley, (Suffolk County), N.Y., U.S. . . .320/F2
Pine Valley, Utah, U.S. 350/A6
Pineview, Ga., U.S., 532 . . . . .260/E7
Pine Vil., Ind., U.S., 255 . . . . .270/B4
Pineville, Ark., U.S., 246 . . . . .244/C1
Pineville, Ky., U.S., 2,093 . . . . .280/G4
Pineville, La., U.S., 13,829 . . . . .282/E4
Pineville, Mo., U.S., 768 . . . . .302/B5
Pineville, N.C., U.S., 3,449 . . . . .322/D4
Pineville, S.C., U.S., 300 . . . . .340/D3
Pineville, W. Va., U.S., 715 . . . . .360/C5
Pinewald, N.J., U.S., 2,500 . . . . .314/E4
Pinewood, Minn., U.S., 50 . . . . .298/B3
Pinewood, S.C., U.S., 459 . . . . .340/D3
Piney, (Garland County), Ark., U.S., 3,988 . .244/B3
Piney, (Johnson County), Ark., U.S., 90 . . . .244/B2
Piney, Fla., U.S., point 256/C2
Piney Green, N.C., U.S., 11,658 . . . . .322/L5
Piney Pt., Fla., U.S. 256/D7
Piney Pt., Md., U.S., 700 . . . . .288/H7
Piney Pt. Vil., Tex., U.S., 3,380 . . . . .346/A6
Piney River, Va., U.S., 200 . . . . .354/E7
Piney View, W. Va., U.S., 1,046 . . . . .360/D5
Piney Woods, Miss., U.S., 80 . . . . .300/C4
Ping, Thai., river .125/B2
Pingree, Ida., U.S., 90 . . . . .264/E6
Pingree, N. Dak., U.S., 66 . . . . .326/G2
Pingree Grove, Ill., U.S., 124 . . . . .266/E1
Pingtung, Tai. 119/B2
Pingxiang, China .119/E3
Pinhook, Mo., U.S., 48 . . . . .302/G5
Pinios, Gr., river .100/B2
Pink, Sask., Can., river 227/F4
Pink, Okla., U.S., 1,165 . . . . .330/E2
Pink Hill, N.C., U.S., 521 . . . . .322/K4
Pink Mountain, Br. Col., Can. 214/L2
Pinkstaff, Ill., U.S., 225 . . . . .266/F5
Pinland, Fla., U.S., 80 . . . . .256/H6
Pinnacle, Ark., U.S., 325 . . . . .244/C3
Pinnacle, Mont., U.S. 306/C1
Pinnacle, N.C., U.S., 550 . . . . .322/E2
Pinnacles, Calif., U.S. 246/E6
Pinnacles N.M., Calif., U.S. 246/E6
Pinnebog, Mich., U.S., 60 . . . . .294/F6
Pinola, Miss., U.S., 150 . . . . .300/C4
Pinole, Calif., U.S., 19,039 . . . . .246/J1
Pinon, Ariz., U.S., 1,190 . . . . .242/E1
Pinon, N. Mex., U.S. 317/E4
Pinos Altos, N. Mex., U.S. 317/B5
Pinsk, Bela. 82/C3

Pinson, Ala., U.S., 5,033 . . . . .238/C2, E1
Pinson, Tenn., U.S., 475 . . . . .344/D4
Pinta, Ecua., island 185/Inset
Pinta, Ariz., U.S. .242/E3
Pintada, N. Mex., U.S., 40 . . . . .317/E3
Pintura, Utah, U.S. 350/A6
Pinwherry, Scot., U.K. 62/G8
Pioche, Nev., U.S., 475 . . . . .310/C3
Pioneer, Iowa, U.S. 274/F2
Pioneer, La., U.S., 171 . . . . .282/G1
Pioneer, Ohio, U.S., 1,460 . . . . .328/A2
Pioneer, Tenn., U.S., 40 . . . . .344/N2
Pioneer Vil., Ky., U.S., 2,555 . . . . .280/E2
Piotrków Trybunalski, Pol. 83/D3
Pipe, Wisc., U.S., 175 . . . . .364/E5
Piper City, Ill., U.S., 781 . . . . .266/E3
Piperton, Tenn., U.S., 589 . . . . .344/B4
Pipe Spr. Natl. Mon., Ariz., U.S. 242/C1
Pipestone, Man., Can. 215/A4
Pipestone, Minn., U.S., 4,280 . . . . .298/A7
Pipestone, Minn., U.S., county, 9,895 . . . . .298/A6
Pipestone N.M., Minn., U.S. 298/A6
Pipmuacan, Que., Can., reservoir 226/F2
Pippa Passes, Ky., U.S., 297 . . . . .280/H3
Piqua, Kans., U.S., 125 . . . . .276/G4
Piqua, Ohio, U.S., 20,738 . . . . .328/B5
Piracicaba, Braz., 179,395, (283,540 metro.) . .188/D4
Pirada, Gui.-B. 149/C1
Piraeus, Gr., 175,697 . . . . .100/B3, Inset
Pirate Harbor, Fla., U.S., 200 . . . . .256/F5
Pireway, N.C., U.S., 100 . . . . .322/H6
Pirkanmaa, Fin., region 81/B2
Pirmasens, Ger. 86/A4
Pirnmill, Scot., U.K. 62/F7
Pirot, Serb.-Mont. .99/C3
Pirris, C.R., river .203/B3
Pirtleville, Ariz., U.S., 1,550 . . . . .242/F6
Pisa, It., 85,379 . . . . .95/B2
Pisagua, Chile 190/B1
Piscataquis, Maine, U.S., county, 17,235 . . .286/C3
Piscataquis, Maine, U.S., river 286/C3
Piscataway, Md., U.S., 150 . . . . .288/F5
Piscataway, N.J., U.S., 50,482 . . . . .314/E2
Pisco, Peru 185/B3
Piseco, N.Y., U.S., lake 320/M4
Pisek, N. Dak., U.S., 96 . . . . .326/H1
Pisgah, Ala., U.S., 706 . . . . .238/D1
Pisgah, Iowa, U.S., 316 . . . . .274/C4
Pisgah, Md., U.S., 175 . . . . .288/F5
Pisgah Forest, N.C., U.S., 1,100 . . . . .322/E8
Pisgah Natl. For., N.C., U.S. 322/B3, D8
Pishill, Eng., U.K. .70/C5
Pisinimo, Ariz., U.S., 237 . . . . .242/C5
Pismo Beach, Calif., U.S., 8,551 . . . . .246/E7
Pistakee Highlands, Ill., U.S., 3,812 . . . . . .266/A4
Pistoia, It. 95/B2
Pistol River, Oreg., U.S., 70 . . . . .334/B5
Pitagowan, Scot., U.K. 62/J5
Pitcairn, U.K., island 161
Pitcairn, Penn., U.S., 3,689 . . . . .336/F7
Pitch, Trin.-To., lake 209/A2
Pitchcombe, Eng., U.K. 68/C6
Pitchfork, Wyo., U.S., 40 . . . . .366/B1
Piteşti, Rom., 186,163 . . . . .101/C3
Pitjantjatjara, Austl., aboriginal land 170/C2
Pitkin, Colo., U.S., 124 . . . . .250/D3
Pitkin, Colo., U.S., county, 14,872 . . . . .250/C2
Pitkin, La., U.S., 400 . . . . .282/D5
Pitlochry, Scot., U.K. 60/B2
Pitlochry, Scot., U.K., 2,564 . . . . .62/J5
Pitman, N.J., U.S., 9,331 . . . . .314/C4
Pitmedden, Scot., U.K., 1,137 . . . . .62/M4
Pitsburg, Ohio, U.S., 392 . . . . .328/B6
Pitsea, Eng., U.K. .70/F3
Pitseng, Leso. 161/B2
Pitsford, Eng., U.K., reservoir 70/C2
Pitstone, Eng., U.K. 70/C3
Pitt, Br. Col., Can., island 214/H4
Pitt, Minn., U.S. 298/C2
Pitt, N.C., U.S., county, 133,798 . . . . .322/L3
Pittman Ctr., Tenn., U.S., 477 . . . . .344/Q3
Pitts, Ga., U.S., 308 . . . . .260/D8
Pittsboro, Ind., U.S., 1,588 . . . . .270/D5
Pittsboro, Miss., U.S., 212 . . . . .300/C2
Pittsboro, N.C., U.S., 2,226 . . . . .322/G3
Pittsburg, Calif., U.S., 56,769 . . . . .246/K1
Pittsburg, Ill., U.S., 575 . . . . .266/E6
Pittsburg, Kans., U.S., 19,243 . . . . .276/H4
Pittsburg, N.H., U.S., 867 . . . . .312/D1
Pittsburg, Okla., U.S., 280 . . . . .330/G3
Pittsburg, Okla., U.S., county, 43,953 . . . . .330/G3
Pittsburg, Tex., U.S., 4,347 . . . . .346/P2
Pittsburgh, Penn., U.S., 334,563,
  (2,358,695 metro.) 336/A5, D7
Pittsfield, Ill., U.S., 4,211 . . . . .266/C4
Pittsfield, Maine, U.S., 4,214 . . . . .286/C4
Pittsfield, Mass., U.S., 45,793, (84,699 metro.) . .292/B3
Pittsfield, N.H., U.S., 3,931 . . . . .312/D5
Pittsfield, Vt., U.S., 427 . . . . .352/B3
Pittsford, N.Y., U.S., 1,418 . . . . .320/F4
Pittsford, Vt., U.S., 3,140 . . . . .352/A3
Pittsford Mills, Vt., U.S. 352/A3
Pittston, Penn., U.S., 8,104 . . . . .336/H7, K3
Pittston Farm, Maine, U.S. 286/C3
Pittstown, N.J., U.S., 550 . . . . .314/D2
Pittsview, Ala., U.S., 70 . . . . .238/D3
Pittsville, Md., U.S., 1,182 . . . . .288/N6
Pittsville, Mo., U.S., 50 . . . . .302/C3
Pittsville, Wisc., U.S., 866 . . . . .364/C4
Pittsylvania, Va., U.S., county, 61,745 . . . . .354/E7
Pittwood, Ill., U.S., 50 . . . . .266/F3
Piura, Peru, 241,427 . . . . .185/A2
Piura, Peru, department 185/A2
Piute, Utah, U.S., county, 1,435 . . . . .350/B5
Pixley, Calif., U.S., 2,586 . . . . .246/F7
Pixley N.W.R., Nev., U.S. 310/A4
Placentia, Bel. 201/B3
Placentia, Nfld., Can., 4,426 . . . . .218/D5
Placentia, Nfld., Can., bay 218/D5
Placentia, Calif., U.S., 46,488 . . . . .246/E10
Placer, Calif., U.S., county, 248,399 . . . .246/E3, K5
Placerville, Calif., U.S., 9,610 . . . . .246/D4, L5
Placerville, Colo., U.S., 40 . . . . .250/B3
Placerville, Ida., U.S., 60 . . . . .264/B6
Placetas, Cuba 204/C2
Placid, Tex., U.S. .346/J4
Placida, Fla., U.S., 325 . . . . .256/F5
Placitas, N. Mex., U.S., 3,452 . . . . .317/D2
Plain, Wash., U.S., 50 . . . . .358/E2
Plain, Wisc., U.S., 792 . . . . .364/C5
Plain City, Ohio, U.S., 2,832 . . . . .328/D5
Plain City, Utah, U.S., 3,489 . . . . .350/B2, B1
Plain Dealing, La., U.S., 1,071 . . . . .282/B1
Plainfield, Conn., U.S., 14,619 . . . . .253/H3
Plainfield, Ill., U.S., 13,038 . . . . .266/A6, E2
Plainfield, Ind., U.S., 18,396 . . . . .270/D5
Plainfield, Iowa, U.S., 438 . . . . .274/J2
Plainfield, Mass., U.S., 589 . . . . .292/C2
Plainfield, Mich., U.S. 294/E7
Plainfield, N.H., U.S., 2,241 . . . . .312/B4
Plainfield, N.J., U.S., 47,829 . . . . .314/E2

Plainfield, Ohio, U.S., 158 . . . . .328/G5
Plainfield, Vt., U.S., 1,286 . . . . .352/C2
Plainfield, Wisc., U.S., 899 . . . . .364/D4
Plains, Ga., U.S., 637 . . . . .260/C7
Plains, Kans., U.S., 1,163 . . . . .276/B4
Plains, Mont., U.S., 1,126 . . . . .306/B2
Plains, Tex., U.S., 1,450 . . . . .346/F2
Plainsboro, N.J., U.S., 20,215 . . . . .314/D3
Plainview, Ark., U.S., 755 . . . . .244/B3
Plainview, Minn., U.S., 3,190 . . . . .298/E6
Plainview, Nebr., U.S., 1,353 . . . . .308/G1
Plainview, N.Y., U.S., 25,637 . . . . .320/C2
Plainview, S. Dak., U.S. 342/C3
Plainview, Tenn., U.S., 1,866 . . . . .344/P2
Plainville, Conn., U.S., 17,328 . . . . .253/D3
Plainville, Ga., U.S., 257 . . . . .260/A3
Plainville, Ill., U.S., 248 . . . . .266/B4
Plainville, Kans., U.S., 2,029 . . . . .276/C2
Plainville, Mass., U.S., 7,683 . . . . .292/J4
Plainville, Wisc., U.S., 150 . . . . .364/D5
Plainwell, Mich., U.S., 3,933 . . . . .294/D7
Plaisted, Maine, U.S., 50 . . . . .286/D1
Plaistow, Eng., U.K. 70/C4
Plaistow, N.H., U.S., 7,747 . . . . .312/D6
Planada, Calif., U.S., 4,369 . . . . .246/E5
Planken, Liech. 90/B1
Plankinton, S. Dak., U.S., 601 . . . . .342/G4
Plano, Ill., U.S., 5,633 . . . . .266/E2
Plano, Iowa, U.S., 58 . . . . .274/H6
Plano, Tex., U.S., 222,030 . . . . .346/C8, M2
Plantagenet, Ont., Can., 1,103 . . . . .223/K2
Plantation, Fla., U.S., 82,934 . . . . .256/A6, H5
Plantation, Ky., U.S., 902 . . . . .280/B2
Plant City, Fla., U.S., 29,915 . . . . .256/F3
Plantersville, Ala., U.S., 325 . . . . .238/C3
Plantersville, Miss., U.S., 1,144 . . . . .300/D1
Plantsville, S.C., U.S., 250 . . . . .340/E3
Plantsville, Conn., U.S., 6,400 . . . . .253/D3
Plaquemine, La., U.S., 7,064 . . . . .282/G6
Plaquemines, La., U.S., parish, 26,757 . .282/K7, L4
Plasencia, Sp. 94/C2
Plaska, Tex., U.S. .346/H1
Plaster Rock, N.B., Can., 1,219 . . . . .217/B2
Plata, Río de la, Arg., estuary 191/D3
Plata, Ecua., island 185/A3
Plata, Tex., U.S. 346/D6
Plata, Uru., river .187/B3
Platea, Penn., U.S., 474 . . . . .336/A2
Plateau, Nig., state 152/E3
Platina, Calif., U.S. 246/C3
Platner, Colo., U.S., 40 . . . . .250/G1
Plato, Minn., U.S., 336 . . . . .298/C6
Plato Ctr., Ill., U.S., 225 . . . . .266/E1
Platoro, Colo., U.S. 250/D4
Platte, Colo., U.S., river 250/D2
Platte, Mo., U.S., county, 73,781 . . . . . .302/B2, H4
Platte, Mo., U.S., river 302/B2
Platte, Nebr., U.S., county, 31,662 . . . . .308/G2
Platte, Nebr., U.S., river 308/D3, G2
Platte, S. Dak., U.S., 1,367 . . . . .342/G4
Platte, Wyo., U.S., county, 8,807 . . . . .366/D3
Platte Ctr., Nebr., U.S., 359 . . . . .308/G2
Platte City, Mo., U.S., 3,866 . . . . .302/B2, H4
Platteville, Colo., U.S., 2,370 . . . . .250/F1
Platteville, Wisc., U.S., 9,989 . . . . .364/C6
Platte Woods, Mo., U.S., 474 . . . . .302/H4
Plattsburg, Mo., U.S., 2,354 . . . . .302/B2
Plattsburgh, N.Y., U.S., 18,816 . . . . .320/Q1
Plattsburgh West, N.Y., U.S., 1,289 . . . . . . .320/P1
Plattsmouth, Nebr., U.S., 6,887 . . . . .308/J2
Plaucheville, La., U.S., 281 . . . . .282/F5
Plauen, Ger. 86/C3
Playas, N. Mex., U.S., lake 317/B6
Play Cu, (Pleiku), Viet. 123/B4
Plaza, N. Dak., U.S., 167 . . . . .326/D1
Plaza, Wash., U.S. 358/H2
Pleak, Tex., U.S., 947 . . . . .346/A7
Pleasant, Ariz., U.S., lake 242/C4
Pleasant Bay, N.S., Can. 221/G1
Pleasant City, Ohio, U.S., 439 . . . . .328/G6
Pleasant Dale, Nebr., U.S., 245 . . . . .308/H3
Pleasant Gap, Penn., U.S., 1,611 . . . . .336/F4
Pleasant Garden, N.C., U.S., 4,714 . . . . . . .322/F3
Pleasant Grove, Ala., U.S., 9,983 . . . . .238/D1
Pleasant Grove, Iowa, U.S., 70 . . . . .274/M6
Pleasant Grove, Kans., U.S., 300 . . . . .276/G3
Pleasant Grove, N.J., U.S., 150 . . . . .314/D2
Pleasant Grove, Utah, U.S., 23,468 . . . . . . .350/C3
Pleasant Groves, Ala., U.S., 447 . . . . .238/D1
Pleasant Hill, Calif., U.S., 32,837 . . . . .246/K1
Pleasant Hill, Ill., U.S., 1,047 . . . . .266/C4
Pleasant Hill, Iowa, U.S., 5,070 . . . . .274/G4
Pleasant Hill, La., U.S., 786 . . . . .282/B3
Pleasant Hill, N. Mex., U.S., 40 . . . . .317/G3
Pleasant Hill, N.C., U.S., 1,109 . . . . .322/D2
Pleasant Hill, Ohio, U.S., 1,134 . . . . .328/B5
Pleasant Hill, Tenn., U.S., 544 . . . . .344/L3
Pleasant Hill, Md., U.S., 2,851 . . . . .288/J2
Pleasant Hills, Penn., U.S., 8,397 . . . . .336/E7
Pleasant Hope, Mo., U.S., 548 . . . . .302/C4
Pleasant Lake, Ind., U.S., 750 . . . . .270/F1
Pleasant Lake, Mass., U.S., 850 . . . . .292/P6
Pleasant Lake, Mich., U.S., 850 . . . . .294/E7
Pleasant Lake, Minn., U.S., 504 . . . . .298/C5
Pleasant Mound, Ill., U.S., 150 . . . . .266/D5
Pleasanton, Calif., U.S., 63,654 . . . . .246/K2
Pleasanton, Iowa, U.S. 274/G6
Pleasanton, Kans., U.S., 1,387 . . . . .276/H3
Pleasanton, Nebr., U.S., 360 . . . . .308/E3
Pleasanton, N. Mex., U.S., 80 . . . . .317/B4
Pleasanton, Tex., U.S., 8,266 . . . . .346/K7
Pleasant Plain, Iowa, U.S., 131 . . . . .274/L5
Pleasant Plain, Ohio, U.S., 156 . . . . .328/B7
Pleasant Plains, Ark., U.S., 267 . . . . .244/D2
Pleasant Plains, Ill., U.S., 777 . . . . .266/D3
Pleasant Plains, N.J., U.S., 2,600 . . . . .314/E4
Pleasant Pt., Maine, U.S., 600 . . . . .286/E4
Pleasant Prairie, Wisc., U.S. 286/C3
Pleasant Prairie, Wisc., U.S., 16,136 . . . . . .364/F6
Pleasant Ridge, Maine, U.S., 83 . . . . .286/C3
Pleasant Ridge, Mich., U.S., 2,594 . . . . . . .294/B6
Pleasant Run, Ohio, U.S., 5,320 . . . . .328/A7
Pleasants, W. Va., U.S., county, 7,514 . . . . .360/D2
Pleasant Site, Ala., U.S., 50 . . . . .238/A1
Pleasant Valley, Conn., U.S., 550 . . . . .253/D2
Pleasant Valley, Mich., U.S. 294/E6
Pleasant Valley, Mo., U.S., 3,321 . . . . .302/H4
Pleasant Valley, N.Y., U.S., 1,839 . . . . .320/J2
Pleasant Valley, Oreg., U.S. 334/J3
Pleasant Valley, Tex., U.S., 408 . . . . .346/K2
Pleasant Valley, W. Va., U.S., 620 . . . . .250/A8
Pleasantview, Ida., U.S., 60 . . . . .264/E7
Pleasant View, Ind., U.S., 500 . . . . .270/E5
Pleasant View, Mich., U.S., 40 . . . . .294/E4
Pleasant View, Utah, U.S., 5,632 . . . . . .350/C2, B1
Pleasant View, Wash., U.S. 358/G3
Pleasantville, Iowa, U.S., 1,539 . . . . .274/H5

Port Lincoln, S.A., Austl. 170/C3
Port Lions, Alaska, U.S., 256 . . . . .240/E3
Port Logan, Scot., U.K. 62/G9
Port Loko, S.L. 149/A1
Portloe, Eng., U.K. .73/D4
Port Loring, Ont., Can. 223/E2
Port Louis, Mauritius, capital, 127,855 . . . . .163/B4
Port Ludlow, Wash., U.S., 1,968 . . . . .358/C2
Port Madison, Wash., U.S. 358/A4
Port Macquarie, N.S.W., Austl. 170/E3
Portmahomack, Scot., U.K. 62/J3
Port Mansfield, Tex., U.S., 415 . . . . .346/L9
Port Maria, Jam. .206/C2
Port Matilda, Penn., U.S., 638 . . . . .336/E4
Port Mayaca, Fla., U.S. 256/H5
Port McNeill, Br. Col., Can., 2,821 . . . . .214/J6
Port Monmouth, N.J., U.S., 3,742 . . . . .314/E3
Port Moody, Br. Col., Can., 23,816 . . . . .214/L6
Port Morant, Jam. 206/C3
Port Moresby, P.N.G., capital, 173,500 . . . . .172/A2
Port Mouton, N.S., Can. 221/C4
Portmuck, N. Ire., U.K. 65/F2
Port Murray, N.J., U.S., 425 . . . . .314/D2
Portnaguran, Scot., U.K. 62/D2
Portnahaven, Scot., U.K. 62/D4
Portnalong, Scot., U.K. 62/C4
Port Neches, Tex., U.S., 13,601 . . . . .346/R6
Portneuf, Que., Can., river 226/G3
Portneuf Prov. Reserve, Que., Can. 226/D4
Port Nolloth, S. Afr. 162/A2
Port Norris, N.J., U.S., 1,507 . . . . .314/C5
Pôrto Alegre, Braz., 1,359,932,
  (3,655,072 metro.) 188/C5
Porto Alegre, São T.-Prínc. 154/B4
Portobelo, Pan. 203/C2
Port O'Connor, Tex., U.S. 346/M7
Port of Ness, Scot., U.K. 62/D1
Port of Spain, Trin.-To., capital 204/F5
Port of Spain, Trin.-To., capital, 48,042 . . . .209/A2
Pôrto Inglês, C.V. 148/C3
Portola, Calif., U.S., 2,227 . . . . .246/E3
Portola Hills, Calif., U.S., 6,391 . . . . .246/F11
Portola Valley, Calif., U.S., 4,462 . . . . .246/J3
Porto-Novo, Ben., capital, 232,756 . . . . .151/B4
Port Orange, Fla., U.S., 45,823 . . . . .256/H2
Port Orchard, Wash., U.S., 7,693 . . . . .358/A4, C2
Port Orford, Oreg., U.S., 1,153 . . . . .334/B5
Porto Santo, Port. . . . . .93/Inset I
Porto Santo, Port., island . . . . .93/Inset I
Porto-Vecchio, It. . . . . .88/Inset I
Pôrto Velho, Braz., 101,644, (286,400 metro.) . .188/B2
Portoviejo, Ecua., 132,937 . . . . .185/A3
Portpatrick, Scot., U.K., 585 . . . . .62/F9
Port Perry, Ont., Can., 7,244 . . . . .223/C3
Port Phillip, Austl., bay . . . . .170/Inset V
Port Pirie, S.A., Austl. 170/C3
Port Reading, N.J., U.S., 3,829 . . . . .314/E2
Portreath, Eng., U.K. 73/B4
Portree, Scot., U.K. 60/A1
Portree, Scot., U.K., 1,917 . . . . .62/D4
Port Renfrew, Br. Col., Can. 214/K7
Port Republic, N.J., U.S., 1,037 . . . . .314/E4
Port Richey, Fla., U.S., 3,021 . . . . .256/F3
Port Rowan, Ont., Can. 223/E5
Port Royal, Ky., U.S., 175 . . . . .280/E2
Port Royal, Penn., U.S., 977 . . . . .336/G4
Port Royal, S.C., U.S., 3,950 . . . . .340/G4
Port Royal, S.C., U.S., sound 340/D4
Port Royal, Va., U.S., 170 . . . . .354/J4
Port Royal Natl. Hist. Park, N.S., Can. 221/B3
Portrush, N. Ire., U.K., 5,703 . . . . .65/D1
Port Said, Egy., 472,335 . . . . .144/A3
Port St. Joe, Fla., U.S., 3,644 . . . . .256/C2
Port St. Lucie, Fla., U.S., 88,769 . . . . .256/A3, H4
Port Salerno, Fla., U.S., 10,141 . . . . . .256/A4, H4
Port-Salut, Haiti .205/B2
Port Sanilac, Mich., U.S., 658 . . . . .294/G6
Port Saunders, Nfld., Can., 812 . . . . .218/E4
Portslade-by-Sea, (Portslade), Eng., U.K., 17,762 . .70/D5
Portsmouth, Dom. 208/A2
Portsmouth, Eng., U.K. 60/C4
Portsmouth, Eng., U.K., 174,690,
  (430,265 metro.) 70/B5
Portsmouth, Eng., U.K., unitary authority,
  186,704 . . . . .70/B5
Portsmouth, Iowa, U.S., 225 . . . . .274/C4
Portsmouth, N.H., U.S., 20,784 . . . . .312/E5
Portsmouth, Ohio, U.S., 20,909 . . . . .328/E8
Portsmouth, R.I., U.S., 17,149 . . . . .339/E4
Portsmouth, Va., U.S., 100,565 . . . . .354/L7
Portsoy, Scot., U.K., 1,734 . . . . .62/L3
Port Stanley, Ont., Can., 2,521 . . . . .223/E5
Portstewart, N. Ire., U.K., 6,459 . . . . .65/D1
Port Sudan, Sudan, 308,195 . . . . .145/H5
Port Sulphur, La., U.S., 3,115 . . . . .282/K8
Port Talbot, Wales, U.K. 60/B3
Port Talbot, Wales, U.K., 37,647 . . . . .64/C3
Port Tobacco, Md., U.S. 288/F5
Port Townsend, Wash., U.S., 8,334 . . . . .358/C1
Portuairk, Scot., U.K. 62/D5
Portugal, nation 91
Portuguesa, Ven., state 182/C2
Port-Vila, Van., capital, 30,139 . . . . .173/C3
Portville, N.Y., U.S., 1,024 . . . . .320/E6
Port Vincent, La., U.S., 463 . . . . .282/H6
Port Vue, Penn., U.S., 4,228 . . . . .336/E7
Port Washington, Ohio, U.S., 552 . . . . .328/G5
Port Washington, Wisc., U.S., 10,467 . . . . . .364/F15
Port Wentworth, Ga., U.S., 3,276 . . . . .260/J7
Port William, Scot., U.K. 62/G9
Port William, Ohio, U.S., 258 . . . . .328/C6
Port Wing, Wisc., U.S., 175 . . . . .364/B2
Porum, Okla., U.S., 725 . . . . .330/G2
Porvenir, Chile 190/B8
Posadas, Arg., 201,273, (210,755 metro.) 191/D2
Posen, Ill., U.S., 4,730 . . . . .266/C6
Posen, Mich., U.S., 292 . . . . .294/F4
Posey, Calif., U.S. 246/G7
Posey, Ind., U.S., county, 27,061 . . . . .270/A8
Poseyville, Ind., U.S., 1,187 . . . . .270/A8
Poseyville, Mich., U.S., 225 . . . . .294/E6
Poskin, Wisc., U.S., 125 . . . . .364/B3
Possum Grape, Ark., U.S., 150 . . . . .244/D2
Post, Oreg., U.S. .334/F3
Post, Tex., U.S., 3,708 . . . . .346/G4
Post Creek, Mont., U.S., 70 . . . . .306/B2
Poste, Mauritius, river 163/C3
Post Falls, Ida., U.S., 17,247 . . . . .264/A2
Post Mills, Vt., U.S., 300 . . . . .352/C3
Post Oak, Mo., U.S., 60 . . . . .302/C3
Postoak, Tex., U.S. 346/K2
Postojna, Slove., 14,559 . . . . .98/B3
Poston, Ariz., U.S., 389 . . . . .242/A4
Poston, Calif., U.S., 175 . . . . .340/E3
Posts, Calif., U.S., 250 . . . . .246/D6
Postville, Nfld., Can. 218/B4
Postville, Iowa, U.S., 2,273 . . . . .274/L1
Postville, Wisc., U.S. 364/D6
Potaro, Guy., river 183/B3
Potatoe Creek, S. Dak., U.S., 40 . . . . .342/D4
Potawatomi Ind. Res., Kans., U.S. 276/G2

Potawatomi Ind. Res., Wisc., U.S. 364/E3
Poteau, Okla., U.S., 7,939 . . . . .330/H2
Poteet, Tex., U.S., 3,305 . . . . .346/K6
Potenza, It. 95/C2
Poth, Tex., U.S., 1,850 . . . . .346/K6
Potholes, Wash., U.S., reservoir 358/F3
P'ot'i, Geo., 54,000 . . . . .103/A3
Potiskum, Nig. 152/D2
Potlatch, Ida., U.S., 791 . . . . .264/A3
Potnarvin, Van. 173/C4
Potomac, Ill., U.S., 681 . . . . .266/F3
Potomac, Md., U.S., 44,822 . . . . .288/A6, F3
Potomac, Md., U.S., river 288/B1, B7, G7
Potomac, N. Branch, Md., U.S., river 288/A2
Potomac, W. Va., U.S., river 354/F2, G1, K4, M2
Potomac, Md., U.S., 125 . . . . .306/C3
Potomac, W. Va., U.S., river 360/J2
Potomac Hts., Md., U.S., 1,154 . . . . .288/F5
Potomac Park, Md., U.S., 1,900 . . . . .288/G6
Potomac View, Md., U.S., 200 . . . . .288/G6
Potosi, Bol., 162,000 . . . . .186/A3
Potosi, Bol., department 186/A4
Potosi, Mo., U.S., 2,662 . . . . .302/F4
Potosi, Wisc., U.S., 711 . . . . .364/C6
Potrerillos, Chile .190/C3
Potsdam, Ger., 128,983 . . . . .86/C2
Potsdam, N.Y., U.S., 9,425 . . . . .320/M1
Potsdam, Ohio, U.S., 203 . . . . .328/B6
Pottawatomie, Kans., U.S., county, 18,209 . . .276/F2
Pottawatomie, Okla., U.S., county, 65,521 . . .330/F2
Pottawattamie, Iowa, U.S., county, 87,704 . . .274/D5
Pottawattamie Park, Ind., U.S., 300 . . . . . . .270/C1
Potter, Ark., U.S., 90 . . . . .244/A3
Potter, Kans., U.S., 90 . . . . .276/G2
Potter, Nebr., U.S., 390 . . . . .308/A2
Potter, Penn., U.S., county, 18,080 . . . . .336/F2
Potter, S. Dak., U.S., county, 2,693 . . . . . . .342/F2
Potter, Tex., U.S., county, 113,546 . . . . .346/F9
Potter, Wisc., U.S., 223 . . . . .364/E4
Potterhawoth, Eng., U.K. 68/G3
Potter Place, N.H., U.S., 150 . . . . .312/C5
Potters Bar, Eng., U.K., 22,414 . . . . .70/D3
Pottersville, Mo., U.S., 50 . . . . .302/D5
Pottersville, N.J., U.S. 314/D2
Potter Valley, Calif., U.S., 650 . . . . .246/B3
Potterville, Ga., U.S., 175 . . . . .260/C6
Potterville, Mich., U.S., 2,168 . . . . .294/E7
Potton, Eng., U.K., 4,230 . . . . .68/G5
Potton, Eng., U.K., 4,230 . . . . .70/D2
Pottsboro, Tex., U.S., 1,579 . . . . .346/M2
Potts Camp, Miss., U.S., 494 . . . . .300/C5
Pottstown, Penn., U.S., 21,859 . . . . .336/K5
Pottsville, Ark., U.S., 1,271 . . . . .244/B2
Pottsville, Penn., U.S., 15,549 . . . . .336/J4
Pottuvil, Sri Lan. .126/C5
Potwin, Kans., U.S., 457 . . . . .276/E4
Pouch Cove, Nfld., Can., 1,669 . . . . .218/E5
Poudre Park, Colo., U.S., 70 . . . . .250/E1
Poughkeepsie, N.Y., U.S., 29,871 . . . . .320/P7
Poulan, Ga., U.S., 946 . . . . .260/D8
Poulsbo, Wash., U.S., 6,813 . . . . .358/A4, C2
Poultney, Vt., U.S., 3,633 . . . . .352/B3
Poulton-le-Fylde, Eng., U.K., 18,939 . . . . . . .66/B5
Poulton-le-Fylde, Eng., U.K., 18,939 . . . . . . .68/A2
Pound, Va., U.S., 1,089 . . . . .354/C2
Pound, Wisc., U.S., 355 . . . . .364/E3
Pound Bank, Eng., U.K. 68/C5
Poutasi, Sam. 175/C3
Poûthisât, Camb. 124/B3
Povazská Bystrica, Slvk. 92/B2
Povungnituk, Que., Can. 225/A1
Powassan, Ont., Can., 3,252 . . . . .223/F1
Poway, Calif., U.S., 48,044 . . . . .246/H10
Powburn, Eng., U.K. 66/E2
Powder, Mont., Wyo., U.S., river 306/K5, L3, L4
Powder, Oreg., U.S., river 334/J3
Powderhorn, Colo., U.S. 250/C3
Powderly, Ky., U.S., 846 . . . . .280/C3
Powderly, Tex., U.S., 175 . . . . .346/N2
Powder River, Mont., U.S., county, 1,858 . . . .306/L4
Powder River, Wyo., U.S., 51 . . . . .366/C2
Powder Sprs., Ga., U.S., 12,481 . . . . .260/B4, G2
Powderville, Mont., U.S. 306/L4
Powder Wash, Colo., U.S., 50 . . . . .250/B1
Powe, Mo., U.S., 100 . . . . .302/F5
Powell, Ala., U.S., 926 . . . . .238/D1
Powell, Ala., U.S., lake 242/D1
Powell, Ky., U.S., county, 13,237 . . . . .280/G3
Powell, Mont., U.S., county, 7,180 . . . . .306/C2
Powell, Nebr., U.S. 308/G3
Powell, Ohio, U.S., 6,247 . . . . .328/D5
Powell, Penn., U.S., 300 . . . . .336/H2
Powell, Tenn., U.S., 7,500 . . . . .344/N2
Powell, Utah, U.S., lake 350/D6
Powell, Wyo., U.S., 5,373 . . . . .366/B1
Powell Butte, Oreg., U.S., 80 . . . . .334/E3
Powell River, Br. Col., Can., 12,983 . . . . . . .214/K6
Powells Crossroads, Tenn., U.S., 1,286 . . . . .344/L4
Powellsville, N.C., U.S., 259 . . . . .322/M2
Powellton, W. Va., U.S., 1,796 . . . . .360/D4
Powellville, Md., U.S., 225 . . . . .288/N6
Powelton, Ga., U.S. 260/F5
Power, Ida., U.S., county, 7,538 . . . . .264/E7
Power, Mont., U.S., 171 . . . . .306/E2
Powers, Mich., U.S., 430 . . . . .294/B4
Powers, Oreg., U.S., 734 . . . . .334/B5
Powers Lake, N. Dak., U.S., 309 . . . . .326/C1
Powersville, Mo., U.S., 86 . . . . .302/C1
Powerview, Man., Can., 750 . . . . .215/C4
Poweshiek, Iowa, U.S., county, 18,815 . . . . . .274/J4
Powhatan, Ark., U.S., 50 . . . . .244/D1
Powhatan, La., U.S., 141 . . . . .282/C2
Powhatan, Va., U.S., 550 . . . . .354/H5
Powhatan, Va., U.S., county, 22,377 . . . . . . .354/H5
Powhatan Pt., Ohio, U.S., 1,744 . . . . .328/J6
Powhattan, Kans., U.S., 91 . . . . .276/G2
Powick, Eng., U.K. 68/C5
Pownal, Vt., U.S., 3,560 . . . . .352/A5
Pownal Ctr., Vt., U.S. 352/A5
Powys, Wales, U.K., unitary authority, 126,344 . .64/E3
Poyang, China, lake 119/E3
Poydras, La., U.S., 3,886 . . . . .282/K7, L3
Poyen, Ark., U.S., 272 . . . . .244/C3
Poygan, Wisc., U.S., lake 364/E4
Poynette, Wisc., U.S., 2,266 . . . . .364/D5
Poynings, Eng., U.K. 70/D5
Poynor, Mo., U.S., 90 . . . . .302/F5
Poynor, Tex., U.S., 314 . . . . .346/N3
Poyntz Pass, N. Ire., U.K., 380 . . . . .65/E3
Poy Sippi, Wisc., U.S., 375 . . . . .364/E4
Poza Rica, Mex., 151,441, (152,838 metro.) . .200/E3
Pozna, Pol., 577,523 . . . . .83/C2
Pozo Colorado, Para. 187/C3
Pra, Gha., river 150/B4
Prachuap Khiri Khan, Thai. 125/B4
Prague, Czh. Rep., capital, 1,178,576 . . . . . . .92/B1
Prague, Czh. Rep., region 92/B1
Prague, Nebr., U.S., 346 . . . . .308/H2
Prague, Okla., U.S., 2,138 . . . . .330/G2
Prahova, Rom., county 101/C3
Prahran, Vic., Austl. . . . . .170/Inset V

Praia, C.V., capital, 103,052 . . . . .148/C4
Prairie, Ark., U.S., county, 9,539 . . . . .244/D3
Prairie, Ida., U.S. .264/B6
Prairie, Maine, U.S. 286/C1
Prairie, Miss., U.S. 300/D2
Prairie, Mont., U.S., county, 1,199 . . . . .306/L3
Prairieburg, Iowa, U.S., 175 . . . . .274/M3
Prairie City, Ill., U.S., 461 . . . . .266/C4
Prairie City, Iowa, U.S., 1,365 . . . . .274/H4
Prairie City, Oreg., U.S., 1,080 . . . . .334/H3
Prairie City, S. Dak., U.S. 342/C2
Prairie Creek, Ark., U.S., 1,849 . . . . .244/A1
Prairie Dog, Kans., U.S., creek 276/B2
Prairie du Chien, Wisc., U.S., 6,018 . . . . . . .364/B5
Prairie du Rocher, Ill., U.S., 613 . . . . .266/C5
Prairie du Sac, Wisc., U.S., 3,231 . . . . .364/D5
Prairie Farm, Wisc., U.S., 508 . . . . .364/B3
Prairie Grove, Ark., U.S., 2,540 . . . . .244/A2
Prairie Grove, Ill., U.S., 960 . . . . .266/A5
Prairie Hill, Mo., U.S., 100 . . . . .302/D2
Prairie Home, Mo., U.S., 220 . . . . .302/D3
Prairie Island Ind. Res., Minn., U.S. 298/E6
Prairie Pt., Miss., U.S. 300/D2
Prairie Rose, N. Dak., U.S., 68 . . . . .326/J3
Prairie View, Kans., U.S., 141 . . . . .276/C2
Prairie View, Tex., U.S., 4,410 . . . . .346/N5
Prairie Vil., Kans., U.S., 22,072 . . . . .276/H1
Prairieville, La., U.S., 950 . . . . .282/H6
Praslin, St. Luc. 208/B2
Praslin, Sey., island 163/C1
Prather, Calif., U.S., 150 . . . . .246/F5
Prathersville, Mo., U.S., 111 . . . . .302/J4
Prato, It. 95/B2
Pratt, Kans., U.S., 6,570 . . . . .276/D4
Pratt, Kans., U.S., county, 9,647 . . . . .276/D4
Pratt, W. Va., U.S., 551 . . . . .360/D4
Pratts, Va., U.S., 225 . . . . .354/C4
Prattsburgh, N.Y., U.S., 650 . . . . .320/G5
Prattsville, Ark., U.S., 282 . . . . .244/C3
Prattsville, N.Y., U.S., 400 . . . . .320/N6
Prattville, Ala., U.S., 24,303 . . . . .238/C3
Prawda, Man., Can. 215/D4
Prawle, Eng., U.K., point 73/E4
Pray, Mont., U.S., 50 . . . . .306/F4
Preble, N.Y., U.S., 325 . . . . .320/J5
Preble, Ohio, U.S., county, 42,337 . . . . .328/A6
Precept, Nebr., U.S. 308/E3
Preeceville, Sask., Can., 1,074 . . . . .227/H9
Preesall, Eng., U.K., 5,168 . . . . .66/C5
Preesall, Eng., U.K., 5,168 . . . . .68/B2
Prees Higher Heath, Eng., U.K. 68/B4
Prelate, Sask., Can., 164 . . . . .227/A10
Premont, Tex., U.S., 2,772 . . . . .346/K8
Prenteg, Wales, U.K. 64/C2
Prentice, Wisc., U.S., 626 . . . . .364/C3
Prentice Cooper St. For., Tenn., U.S. 344/L4
Prentiss, Maine, U.S., 214 . . . . .286/D3
Prentiss, Miss., U.S., 1,158 . . . . .300/C4
Prentiss, Miss., U.S., county, 25,556 . . . . . . .300/D1
Preparis, Mya., island 125/B3
Přerov, Czh. Rep. .92/C3
Prescot, Eng., U.K., 37,486 . . . . .66/C6
Prescot, Eng., U.K., 37,486 . . . . .68/B3
Prescott, Ont., Can., 4,228 . . . . .223/K3
Prescott, Ariz., U.S., 33,938 . . . . .242/C3
Prescott, Ark., U.S., 3,686 . . . . .244/B4
Prescott, Iowa, U.S., 266 . . . . .274/E5
Prescott, Kans., U.S., 280 . . . . .276/H3
Prescott, Mich., U.S., 286 . . . . .294/F5
Prescott, Oreg., U.S., 72 . . . . .334/D1
Prescott, Wash., U.S., 314 . . . . .358/G3
Prescott, Wisc., U.S., 3,764 . . . . .364/A4
Prescott and Russel, Ont., Can., county 223/K2
Prescott and Russel, Ont., Can., county 223/J2
Prescott Natl. For., Ariz., U.S. 242/C3
Prescott Valley, Ariz., U.S., 23,535 . . . . .242/C3
Presidencia Roque Sáenz Peña, Arg. 191/C2
Presidente Hayes, Para., department 187/C4
Presidential, N.H., U.S., range 312/D3
Presidential Lakes, N.J., U.S. 314/D4
Presidential Lakes Estates, N.J., U.S., 2,332 . .314/D4
Presidio, Tex., U.S., 4,167 . . . . .346/D5
Presidio, Tex., U.S., county, 7,304 . . . . .346/D5
Prešov, Slvk., 161,782 . . . . .92/C2
Prešovský, Slvk., region 92/C2
Prespa, Alb., lake .99/C3
Prespa, Gr., lake 100/B1
Prespa, Mac., lake 100/B3
Presque Isle, Maine, U.S., 9,511 . . . . .286/E2
Presque Isle, Mich., U.S., 125 . . . . .294/F4
Presque Isle, Mich., U.S., county, 14,411 . . . .294/E4
Presque Isle, Penn., U.S., peninsula 336/A1
Presque Isle, Wisc., U.S., 70 . . . . .364/D2
Presquile N.W.R., Va., U.S. 354/J6
Prestatyn, Wales, U.K., 15,020 . . . . .64/E1
Prestbury, Eng., U.K., 3,346 . . . . .68/B2
Prestea, Gha. 150/A4
Presteigne, Wales, U.K., 1,815 . . . . .64/E3
Preston, Vic., Austl. . . . . .170/Inset V
Preston, (Dorset), Eng., U.K. 73/H3
Preston, (Hertfordshire), Eng., U.K. 70/D3
Preston, (Humberside), Eng., U.K., 2,040 . . . .66/H5
Preston, (Humberside), Eng., U.K., 2,040 . . . .68/G2
Preston, (Lanc.), Eng., U.K., 177,660,
  (256,411 metro.) 66/C5
Preston, (Lanc.), Eng., U.K., 177,660,
  (256,411 metro.) 68/B2
Preston, Eng., U.K. 68/B2
Preston, Scot., U.K. 62/M7
Preston, Ga., U.S., 453 . . . . .260/B7
Preston, Ida., U.S., 4,682 . . . . .264/F7
Preston, Iowa, U.S., 949 . . . . .274/P3
Preston, Kans., U.S., 164 . . . . .276/D4
Preston, Md., U.S., 566 . . . . .288/L5
Preston, Minn., U.S., 1,426 . . . . .298/E7
Preston, Miss., U.S., 250 . . . . .300/D3
Preston, Mo., U.S., 113 . . . . .302/C4
Preston, Nebr., U.S., 50 . . . . .308/J3
Preston, Nev., U.S. 310/C2
Preston, Okla., U.S., 125 . . . . .330/F2
Preston, Wash., U.S., 200 . . . . .358/B4
Preston, W. Va., U.S., county, 29,334 . . . . . .360/G2
Preston Brockhurst, Eng., U.K. 68/B4
Preston City, Conn., U.S., 425 . . . . .253/H3
Preston Hts., Ill., U.S., 2,527 . . . . .266/B6
Prestonpans, Scot., U.K., 7,153 . . . . .62/L7
Prestonsburg, Ky., U.S., 3,612 . . . . .280/H3
Prestonville, Ky., U.S. 280/E2
Prestwick, Scot., U.K., 13,705 . . . . .62/G8
Prestwood, Eng., U.K. 70/C3
Pretoria, S. Afr., administrative capital,
  692,348, (2,086,279 metro.) 162/C2
Pretoria, Ga., U.S. 260/B7
Prettyboy, Md., U.S., reservoir 288/G1
Pretty Prairie, Kans., U.S., 615 . . . . .276/D4
Preveza, Gr. 100/B2
Prewitt, N. Mex., U.S. 317/B2
Prey Vêng, Camb. 124/C4
Pribilof, Alaska, U.S., islands 240/B3

Priboj, Serb.-Mont. 99/A3
Price, Md., U.S., 100 . . . . .288/L3
Price, N.C., U.S. .322/F1
Price, N. Dak., U.S., 40 . . . . .326/F2
Price, Utah, U.S., 8,402 . . . . .350/D4
Price, Utah, U.S., river 350/D4
Price, Wisc., U.S. .364/B4
Price, Wisc., U.S., county, 15,822 . . . . .364/C3
Pricedale, Miss., U.S., 125 . . . . .300/B4
Price Settlement, N.B., Can. 217/D1
Priceville, Ala., U.S., 1,631 . . . . .238/C1
Prichard, Ala., U.S., 28,633 . . . . .238/A5
Prichard, Miss., U.S. 300/B1
Prichard, W. Va., U.S., 325 . . . . .360/A4
Prickwillow, Eng., U.K. 70/E2
Priddis, Alta., Can. 212/C6
Pride, Ky., U.S., 150 . . . . .280/C3
Pridgen, Ga., U.S., 125 . . . . .260/F8
Priest, Ida., U.S., lake 264/A1
Priest Pt., Wash., U.S., 779 . . . . .358/C1
Priest River, Ida., U.S., 1,754 . . . . .264/A1
Prievidza, Slvk., 140,444 . . . . .92/B2
Prijedor, Bos.-Her. 98/A1
Prilep, Mac., 68,148 . . . . .100/B2
Prim, P.E.I., Can., point 224/B2
Prim, Ark., U.S., 40 . . . . .244/C2
Primehook Beach, Del., U.S. 255/C5
Prime Hook N.W.R., Del., U.S. 255/C5
Primghar, Iowa, U.S., 891 . . . . .274/C1
Primm, Nev., U.S. 310/C4
Primorsko, Bul. 101/F3
Primrose, Sask., Can., lake 212/E4
Primrose, Sask., Can., lake 227/A6
Primrose, Ga., U.S., 175 . . . . .260/B5
Primrose, Ky., U.S. 280/G3
Primrose, Nev., U.S., 69 . . . . .308/E2
Primrose, P.E.I., Can., county 224/A2
Prince, Nev., U.S. 310/C3
Prince Albert, N.W. Terr., Can., peninsula 220/E2
Prince Albert, Sask., Can., 34,291 . . . . .227/E7
Prince Albert, N.W. Terr., Can., hills 220/L3
Prince Charles, Nun., Can., island 220/N3
Prince Edward, Ont., Can. 223/H3
Prince Edward, Ont., Can., county 223/H3
Prince Edward, Va., U.S., county, 19,720 . . . .354/F6
Prince Edward Island, Can., province 212
Prince Edward Island Natl. Park, P.E.I., Can. . .224/B2
Prince Frederick, Md., U.S., 1,432 . . . . .288/H5
Prince George, Br. Col., Can., 72,406 . . . . . .214/L4
Prince George, Va., U.S., 750 . . . . .354/J6
Prince George, Va., U.S., county, 33,047 . . . .354/J6
Prince George's, Md., U.S., county,
  801,515 . . . . .288/D7, G5
Prince of Wales, Nun., Can., island 217/C3
Prince of Wales, Nun., Can., island 220/J2
Prince of Wales, Alaska, U.S., island 240/J3
Prince Patrick, N.W. Terr., Can., island 220/L1
Prince Regent, Aus., Can., inlet 220/K2
Prince Rupert, Br. Col., Can., 14,643 . . . . . .214/G4
Princes Lakes, Ind., U.S., 1,506 . . . . .270/D6
Princess Anne, Md., U.S., 2,313 . . . . .288/M7
Princess Harbour, Man., Can. 215/C3
Princess Margriet, Neth., canal 84/C1
Princess Royal, Br. Col., Can., island 214/H4
Princes Town, Trin.-To. 209/A2
Princethorpe, Eng., U.K. 70/B2
Princeton, Br. Col., Can., 2,610 . . . . .214/M6
Princeton, Ark., U.S. 244/C4
Princeton, Fla., U.S., 10,090 . . . . .256/A7
Princeton, Ill., U.S., 7,501 . . . . .266/D2
Princeton, Ind., U.S., 8,175 . . . . .270/A8
Princeton, Iowa, U.S., 946 . . . . .274/P4
Princeton, Kans., U.S., 317 . . . . .276/G3
Princeton, Ky., U.S., 6,536 . . . . .280/C3
Princeton, La., U.S., 225 . . . . .282/C1
Princeton, Maine, U.S., 892 . . . . .286/E3
Princeton, Mass., U.S., 3,353 . . . . .292/G3
Princeton, Mich., U.S., 200 . . . . .294/B3
Princeton, Minn., U.S., 3,933 . . . . .298/D5
Princeton, Mo., U.S., 1,047 . . . . .302/C1
Princeton, Nebr., U.S. 308/H3
Princeton, N.J., U.S., borough, 14,203 . . . . . .314/D3
Princeton, N.C., U.S., 1,066 . . . . .322/J4
Princeton, Oreg., U.S. 334/H4
Princeton, S.C., U.S., 65 . . . . .340/B2
Princeton, Tenn., U.S., 3,477 . . . . .346/D8
Princeton, W. Va., U.S., 6,347 . . . . .360/D5
Princeton, Wisc., U.S., 1,504 . . . . .364/D5
Princeton Jct., N.J., U.S., 2,382 . . . . .314/D3
Princeton Sta., Mass., U.S., 225 . . . . .292/G3
Princetown, Eng., U.K. 73/E3
Princeville, Que., Can., 5,703 . . . . .226/E5
Princeville, Hawaii, U.S., 1,698 . . . . .262/C1
Princeville, Ill., U.S., 1,621 . . . . .266/D3
Princeville, N.C., U.S., 940 . . . . .322/K3
Prince William, Va., U.S., county, 280,813 . .354/H3, L3
Príncipe, São T.-Prínc., island 154/C1
Prineville, Oreg., U.S., 7,356 . . . . .334/F3
Pringle, Penn., U.S., 991 . . . . .336/G7
Pringle, S. Dak., U.S., 125 . . . . .342/B4
Pringle, Tex., U.S., 50 . . . . .346/F8
Prinsburg, Minn., U.S., 458 . . . . .298/C6
Prinzapolka, Nicar. 202/D2
Prinzapolka, Nicar., river 202/B2
Prior Lake, Minn., U.S., 15,917 . . . . .298/D6
Pripyat, Ukr., river 102/A1
Pripyats, Bela., marshes 82/C3
Pripyats, Bela., river 82/C3
Prismatic, Miss., U.S., 60 . . . . .300/D3
Priština, Serb.-Mont., 46,857 . . . . .99/B3
Pritchett, Colo., U.S., 137 . . . . .250/H4
Privas, Fr. 88/D4
Privett, Eng., U.K. .70/B4
Prizren, Serb.-Mont. 99/B3
Proctor, Colo., U.S. 250/H1
Proctor, Minn., U.S., 2,852 . . . . .298/E4
Proctor, Mont., U.S. 306/B2
Proctor, Vt., U.S., 1,877 . . . . .352/B3
Proctor, W. Va., U.S., 100 . . . . .360/E2, K6
Proctorville, N.C., U.S., 133 . . . . .322/G6
Progress, Penn., U.S., 9,647 . . . . .336/H5
Progress, Tex., U.S., 125 . . . . .346/F1
Progresso, Bel. 201/B1
Progromni, Alaska, U.S., volcano 240/C4
Prokop'evsk, Russ., 236,174, (236,350 metro.) . .104/F4
Prokuplje, Serb.-Mont. 99/B3
Prome, (Pyay), Mya. 125/B2
Promise City, Iowa, U.S., 105 . . . . .274/H6
Promontory, Utah, U.S. 350/B2
Promontory Pt., Utah, U.S., 100 . . . . .350/B2
Prompton, Penn., U.S., 243 . . . . .336/J2
Pronto, Ky., U.S. .310/A1
Prophet River, Br. Col., Can. 214/L2
Prophetstown, Ill., U.S., 2,023 . . . . .266/D2
Prosit, Minn., U.S., 40 . . . . .298/E4
Prospect, Conn., U.S., 8,707 . . . . .253/D4
Prospect, Ky., U.S., 4,657 . . . . .280/E2
Prospect, Maine, U.S., 642 . . . . .286/D4
Prospect, N.Y., U.S., 330 . . . . .320/L4
Prospect, Ohio, U.S., 1,191 . . . . .328/D5

Prospect, Oreg., U.S., 250 . . . . .334/D5
Prospect, Penn., U.S., 1,234 . . . . .336/A4
Prospect, Va., U.S., 250 . . . . .354/F6
Prospect Harbor, Maine, U.S., 200 . . . . .286/D4
Prospect Hts., Colo., U.S. 250/E3
Prospect Hts., Ill., U.S., 17,081 . . . . .266/B5
Prospect Hill, N.C., U.S., 125 . . . . .322/G2
Prospect Park, N.J., U.S., 5,779 . . . . .314/B2
Prospect Park, Penn., U.S., 6,594 . . . . .336/L7
Prospect Plains, N.J., U.S., 550 . . . . .314/B4
Prospect Valley, Colo., U.S., 125 . . . . .250/E3
Prosper, Tex., U.S., 2,097 . . . . .346/C8, L2
Prosperity, Fla., U.S., 70 . . . . .256/C1
Prosperity, Penn., U.S., 200 . . . . .336/A5
Prosperity, S.C., U.S., 1,047 . . . . .340/D4
Prosperity, W. Va., U.S., 1,310 . . . . .360/D5
Prosser, Nebr., U.S., 94 . . . . .308/E3
Prosser, Wash., U.S., 4,838 . . . . .358/F3
Prostějov, Czh. Rep. 92/C3
Protection, Kans., U.S., 558 . . . . .276/C4
Protem, Mo., U.S. 302/D5
Protivin, Iowa, U.S., 317 . . . . .274/K1
Protvino, Russ. 104/K3
Provence-Alpes-Côte-d'Azur, Fr., region 88/D4
Provencal, La., U.S., 708 . . . . .282/C4
Providence, Ala., U.S., 311 . . . . .238/B5
Providence, Fla., U.S., 1,100 . . . . .256/F3
Providence, Ky., U.S., 3,611 . . . . .280/C3
Providence, N.C., U.S., 325 . . . . .322/G2
Providence, R.I., U.S., county, 621,602 . . . . .339/C2
Providence, R.I., U.S., state capital, 173,618,
 (1,188,613 metro.) 339/D3
Providence, Utah, U.S., 4,377 . . . . .350/C3
Providence Bay, Ont., Can. 223/C2
Providence Forge, Va., U.S., 175 . . . . .354/J6
Providencia, Col. 184/Inset
Providenciales, T.-C. Is., island 207/C5
Provideniya, Russ. 104/K3
Provincetown, Mass., U.S., 3,431 . . . . .292/F4
Provo, Ark., U.S., 100 . . . . .244/A3
Provo, S. Dak., U.S. 342/B4
Provo, Utah, U.S., 105,166 (368,536 metro.) . .350/C3
Provost, Alta., Can., 1,980 . . . . .212/E5
Prowers, Colo., U.S. .250/H3
Prowers, Colo., U.S., county, 14,483 . . . . . . .250/H4
Pru, Gha., river 150/B3
Pruden, Tenn., U.S., 60 . . . . .344/P1
Prudence, R.I., U.S., 40 . . . . .339/E4
Prudenville, Mich., U.S., 1,737 . . . . .294/E5
Prudhoe, Eng., U.K., 11,204 . . . . .66/E3
Prudhoe Bay, Alaska, U.S. 240/F1
Pruitt City, Okla., U.S., 200 . . . . .330/F1
Prunedale, Calif., U.S., 16,432 . . . . .246/D6
Pruntytown, W. Va., U.S., 600 . . . . .360/F2
Prut, Mol., river 102/A1, B3
Prut, Rom., river 101/C2
Prut, Ukr., river 102/B2
Pryluky, Ukr. 102/C1
Pryor, Colo., U.S. 250/F4
Pryor, Mont., U.S., 628 . . . . .306/H4
Pryor, Okla., U.S., 8,659 . . . . .330/G1
Pryorsburg, Ky., U.S., 275 . . . . .280/B4
Przemyśl, Pol. 83/F4
Pskov, Est., lake 81/D3
Pskov, Russ., 201,846 . . . . .104/C4
Ps'ol, Ukr., river 102/C1
Ptsich, Bela., river 82/D3
Ptuj, Slove., 23,017 .98/C2
Puako, Hawaii, U.S., 429 . . . . .262/G4
Pu'apu'a, Sam. 175/B2
Public Landing, Md., U.S., 90 . . . . .288/N7
Pubnico, N.S., Can. .221/B4
Pucallpa, Peru, 225,224 . . . . .185/C2
Puck, Pol. 83/D1
Puckett, Miss., U.S., 354 . . . . .300/C3
Puckington, Eng., U.K. 73/G3
Puddledock, Eng., U.K. 70/G2
Puddletown, Eng., U.K. 73/H3
Pudsey, Eng., U.K., 31,636 . . . . .66/E5
Pudsey, Eng., U.K., 31,636 . . . . .68/D2
Puebla, Mex., state capital, 1,271,673,
 (1,346,916 metro.) 200/E4
Puebla, Mex., state 200/E4
Pueblo, Colo., U.S., 102,121, (141,472 metro.) . .250/F3
Pueblo, Colo., U.S., county, 141,472 . . . . . .250/F3
Pueblo, Ky., U.S., 60 . . . . .280/F4
Pueblo, Oreg., U.S., mountains 334/H5
Pueblo Ordnance Depot, Colo., U.S. 250/F3
Pueblo Pintado, N. Mex., U.S., 247 . . . . . . .317/C2
Pueblo West, Colo., U.S., 16,899 . . . . .250/F3
Puente Alto, Chile, 340,639 . . . . .190/Inset
Pueo, Hawaii, U.S., point 262/B2
Puerca, P.R., river .206/D2
Puerto Aisén, Chile 190/B7
Puerto Armuelles, Pan. 203/A2
Puerto Ayacucho, Ven. 182/C2
Puerto Bahía Negra, Para. 187/C2
Puerto Baquerizo Moreno, Ecua. 185/Inset
Puerto Barrios, Guat., 66,848 . . . . .201/E4
Puerto Bolívar, Ecua. 185/B4
Puerto Cabello, Ven., 137,067, (144,666 metro.) . .182/C1
Puerto Cabezas, Nicar. 202/C1
Puerto Carreño, Col., 12,000 . . . . .184/D3
Puerto Cisnes, Chile 190/B6
Puerto Cortés, Hond., 33,500 . . . . .202/B2
Puerto de Luna, N. Mex., U.S., 50 . . . . .317/F3
Puerto Deseado, Arg. 191/B7
Puerto Escondido, Mex. 200/E4
Puerto Inírida, Col., 20,000 . . . . .184/D4
Puerto Jiménez, C.R. 203/C4
Puerto La Cruz, Ven. 182/D1
Puerto Leguízamo, Col. 184/A4
Puerto Lempira, Hond. 202/D2
Puerto Limón, C.R. .203/C3
Puertollano, Sp. 94/C3
Puerto Maldonado, Peru 185/D3
Puerto Montt, Chile, 174,952 . . . . .190/B6
Puerto Natales, Chile 190/B8
Puerto Peñasco, Mex., 30,466, (31,157 metro.) . .200/B1
Puerto Pinasco, Para. 187/D3
Puerto Plata, Dom. Rep. 205/B1
Puerto Plata, Dom. Rep., province 205/B1
Puerto Princesa, Phil., 161,912 . . . . .120/A4
Puerto Quepos, C.R. 203/B3
Puerto Real, P.R. 206/A2
Puerto Rico, U.S., dependency 204/E3
Puerto Rico, U.S., dependency 194
Puerto Sandino, Nicar. 202/A2
Puerto Santa Cruz, Arg. 191/B7
Puerto Suárez, Bol. .186/C3
Puerto Vallarta, Mex., 151,432,
 (184,728 metro.) 200/C3
Puerto Varas, Chile 190/B6
Puerto Williams, Chile 190/C8
Puget, Wash., U.S., sound 358/A4, C1
Pugwash, N.S., Can., 810 . . . . .221/D2
Puhi, Hawaii, U.S., 1,186 . . . . .262/D2
Pujehun, S.L. 149/B2
Pukalani, Hawaii, U.S., 7,380 . . . . . . .262/C3, D6
Pukaskwa Natl. Park, Ont., Can. 222/C3
Pukatawagan, Man., Can. 215/A1

Pukch'ŏng, N. Kor. .116/C2
Pukë, Alb. 99/A1
Pukoo, Hawaii, U.S. 262/B3
Pukwana, S. Dak., U.S., 287 . . . . .342/F4
Pula, Cro. 98/A3
Pulangi, Phil., river 120/C5
Pulaski, Ark., U.S., county, 361,474 . . . . . .244/C3
Pulaski, Ga., U.S., 261 . . . . .260/H7
Pulaski, Ga., U.S., county, 9,588 . . . . .260/D7
Pulaski, Ill., U.S., 274 . . . . .266/D6
Pulaski, Ill., U.S., county, 7,348 . . . . .266/D6
Pulaski, Ind., U.S., 175 . . . . .270/C3
Pulaski, Ind., U.S., county, 13,755 . . . . .270/C3
Pulaski, Iowa, U.S., 249 . . . . .274/K6
Pulaski, Ky., U.S., 425 . . . . .280/F3
Pulaski, Ky., U.S., county, 56,217 . . . . .280/F3
Pulaski, Miss., U.S., 90 . . . . .300/C3
Pulaski, Mo., U.S., county, 41,165 . . . . .302/D4
Pulaski, N.Y., U.S., 2,398 . . . . .320/J3
Pulaski, Tenn., U.S., 7,871 . . . . .344/G4
Pulaski, Va., U.S., 9,473 . . . . .354/B6
Pulaski, Va., U.S., county, 35,127 . . . . .354/B6
Pulaski, Wisc., U.S., 3,060 . . . . .364/E4
Puławy, Pol. 83/E3
Pulehu, Hawaii, U.S. 262/C4
Pulham Market, Eng., U.K. 70/G2
Pullman, Mich., U.S., 700 . . . . .294/C7
Pullman, Wash., U.S., 24,675 . . . . .358/H4
Pullman, W. Va., U.S., 169 . . . . .360/E2
Pulo Anna, Palau, island 172/A3
Pulusuk, Micr., island 172/B2
Pumphrey, Md., U.S., 5,317 . . . . .288/H3
Pumphrey, Tex., U.S. 346/H3
Pumpkin Ctr., N.C., U.S., 2,228 . . . . .322/L5
Pumpkin Ctr., Okla., U.S., 70 . . . . .330/D3
Pumpville, Tex., U.S. 346/G6
Puná, Ecua., island 185/A4
Puna Forest Reserve, Hawaii, U.S. 262/J6
Punakha, Bhu. 126/A2
Punalau, Hawaii, U.S. 262/H7, J1
Punchbowl, Hawaii, U.S., crater 262/G2
Punckbowle, Eng., U.K. 73/C3
Pune, India, 2,540,069, (3,755,525 metro.) . .128/B5
Punggol, Sing. 123/B1
Pulo Anna . . . .
P'ungsan, N. Kor. 116/C2
Punjab, India, state 128/C2
Punjab, Pak., province 129/D3
Punkin Ctr., Ariz., U.S. 242/D4
Punkin Ctr., Colo., U.S. 250/G3
Puno, Peru, 116,710 . . . . .185/C4
Puno, Peru, department 185/C3
Punta, N. Mex., U.S., 40 . . . . .317/D3
Punta Arenas, Chile, 120,891 . . . . .190/B8
Punta Brava, P.R. .206/B2
Punta de Agua, Tex., U.S. 346/E8
Punta del Este, Uru. 187/C3
Punta Delgada, Chile 190/B8
Punta Gorda, Bel., 4,329 . . . . .201/B3
Punta Gorda, Nicar., bay 202/C3
Punta Gorda, Fla., U.S., 14,344, (141,627 metro.) . .256/F5
Puntarenas, C.R., 109,326 . . . . .203/B3
Puntarenas, C.R., province 203/C4
Punta Santiago, P.R. 206/D2
Punto Fijo, Ven., 106,649, (154,015 metro.) . .182/B1
Punxsutawney, Penn., U.S., 6,271 . . . . .336/D4
Puolo, Hawaii, U.S., point 262/C2
Puposky, Minn., U.S., 70 . . . . .298/C3
Pupukea, Hawaii, U.S., 4,250 . . . . .262/J1
Purari, P.N.G., river 172/A2
Purbecks Cove, Nfld., Can. 218/C4
Purcell, Colo., U.S. 250/F1
Purcell, Mo., U.S., 357 . . . . .302/B4
Purcell, Okla., U.S., 5,571 . . . . .330/E2
Purcellville, Va., U.S., 3,584 . . . . .354/H2
Purdin, Mo., U.S., 223 . . . . .302/C2
Purdum, Nebr., U.S. 308/D1
Purdy, Mo., U.S., 1,103 . . . . .302/C5
Purdy, Okla., U.S., 50 . . . . .330/E3
Purdy, Va., U.S., 70 . . . . .354/H7
Purfleet, Eng., U.K. 70/E4
Purgatoire, Colo., U.S., river 250/G4
Purgitsville, W. Va., U.S., 80 . . . . .360/G2
Puriton, Eng., U.K., 1,986 . . . . .73/G2
Purley, Eng., U.K. 70/D4
Purmela, Tex., U.S. 346/L4
Purton, Eng., U.K., 3,879 . . . . .73/J1
Purus, Braz., river .188/B2
Purús, Peru, river .185/C3
Purvis, Miss., U.S., 2,164 . . . . .300/C4
Puryear, Tenn., U.S., 667 . . . . .344/E2
Pushmataha, Okla., U.S., county, 11,667 . . .330/G3
Putao, Mya. 125/C1
Put-in-Bay, Ohio, U.S., 128 . . . . .328/E2
Putnam, Ala., U.S. 238/A3
Putnam, Conn., U.S., 9,002 . . . . .253/H2
Putnam, Fla., U.S., county, 70,423 . . . . . . .256/B2
Putnam, Ga., U.S., county, 18,812 . . . . . . .260/E5
Putnam, Ill., U.S., county, 6,086 . . . . .266/D4
Putnam, Ind., U.S., county, 36,019 . . . . . . .270/C5
Putnam, Mo., U.S., county, 5,223 . . . . .302/C1
Putnam, N.Y., U.S., county, 95,745 . . . . . . .320/P8
Putnam, Ohio, U.S., county, 34,726 . . . . . .328/B3
Putnam, Okla., U.S., 46 . . . . .330/D2
Putnam, Tenn., U.S., county, 62,315 . . . . . .344/L2
Putnam, Tex., U.S., 88 . . . . .346/J3
Putnam, W. Va., U.S., county, 51,589 . . . . .360/C3
Putnam Lake, N.Y., U.S., 3,855 . . . . .320/P8
Putnamville, Ind., U.S. 270/C5
Putnamville, Vt., U.S., 90 . . . . .352/B5
Putney, Ga., U.S., 2,998 . . . . .260/C9
Putney, Ky., U.S., 600 . . . . .280/G4
Putney, S. Dak., U.S. 342/G2
Putney, Vt., U.S., 2,634 . . . . .352/B5
Putre, Chile 190/C1
Puttalam, Sri Lan. .126/A3
Puttenham, Eng., U.K. 70/C4
Puttgarden, Ger. 86/B1
Putu, Liber., range 149/B3
Putumayo, Col., department 184/A4
Putumayo, Col., river 184/B5
Putumayo, Ecua., river 185/D2
Putumayo, Peru, river 185/C1
Puuanahulu, Hawaii, U.S. 262/G5
Puuhonua O Honaunau Natl. Hist. Park,
 Hawaii, U.S. 262/G6
Puuiki, Hawaii, U.S. 262/J1
Puu Kainapuaa, Hawaii, U.S., mountain . . .262/J1
Puu Ka Pele Forest Reserve, Hawaii, U.S. . .262/C1
Puu Kaua, Hawaii, U.S., mountain 262/H2
Puukohola Heiau Natl. Hist. Site, Hawaii, U.S. . .262/G4
Puukolii, Hawaii, U.S. 262/B3
Puu Kukui, Hawaii, U.S., mountain 262/C3
Puu Loa, Hawaii, U.S., mountain 262/H5
Puu Nana, Hawaii, U.S., mountain 262/A3
Puunene, Hawaii, U.S. 262/C4
Puuni, Hawaii, U.S. 262/G4
Puu O Keokeo, Hawaii, U.S., mountain 262/G6
Puupehe, Hawaii, U.S., point 262/B4
Puu Ulaula, Hawaii, U.S., mountain 262/C4

Puu Waawaa, Hawaii, U.S. 262/G5
Puuwai, Hawaii, U.S. 262/A2
Puxico, Mo., U.S., 1,145 . . . . .302/F5
Puyallup, Wash., U.S., 33,011 . . . . .358/D4
Puy-de-Dôme, Fr., department 88/C4
Puyo, Ecua. 185/C3
Puysegur, N.Z., point 171/A4
Pwani, Tan., region 158/C2
Pwllheli, Wales, U.K., 3,974 . . . . .64/C2
Pyatt, Ark., U.S., 253 . . . . .244/C1
Pyatts, Ill., U.S. 266/D5
Pyle, Wales, U.K., 12,331 . . . . .64/D4
Pylesville, Md., U.S., 350 . . . . .288/J1
Pylos, Gr. 100/B3
Pymatuning St. Park, Penn., U.S. 336/A2
P'yŏnggang, N. Kor. 116/B3
P'yŏngsan, N. Kor. 116/A3
P'yŏngsŏng, N. Kor. 116/A3
P'yŏngyang, N. Kor., capital, 2,741,260 . . .116/A3
P'yŏngyang, N. Kor., province 116/A3
Pyote, Tex., U.S., 131 . . . . .346/E4
Pyramid, Nev., U.S., lake 310/A1
Pyramid Lake Ind. Res., Nev., U.S. 310/A1
Pyramid Lake Indian Res., Nev., U.S. 246/F2
Pyrenees, And., range 93/A1
Pyrenees, Fr., range 88/C5
Pyrenees, Sp., range 94/F1
Pyrénées-Atlantiques, Fr., department 88/B5
Pyrénées-Orientales, Fr., department 88/C5
Pyriton, Ala., U.S., 70 . . . . .238/D2
Qaanaaq, (Thule), Grld. 193/B15
Qaanaaq, (Thule), Grld. 193/B3
Qacha's Nek, Leso., 10,000 . . . . .161/B3
Qaidam, China, basin 119/C2
Qal'ai Khum, Taj. .132/B1
Qalansiyah, Yemen 137/C2
Qalat, Afg. 129/B2
Qal'eh Now, Afg. .129/A2
Qal'eh-ye Panjeh, Afg. 129/C1
Qamea, Fiji, island 174/C2
Qandahar, Afg., 225,500 . . . . .129/B2
Qaqortoq, (Julianehåb), Grld. 193/C2
Qaraghandy, Kaz., 436,864 . . . . .131/D2
Qaraghandy, Kaz., oblast 131/C2
Qardho, Som. 157/B2
Qareh, Iran, river .130/B3
Qarokūl, Taj., lake 132/B1
Qarshi, Uzb., 197,600 . . . . .132/C3
Qashqadaryo, Uzb., province 132/C3
Qasigiannguit, (Christianshåb), Grld. 193/B2
Qasim, Sa. Arab., emirate 136/B1
Qasr as Sabiyah, Kuw. 135/B1
Qatar, nation 133
Qattarah, Egy., depression 144/A2
Qazvin, Iran, 291,117 . . . . .130/B2
Qelelevu, Fiji, island 174/C2
Qeshm, Iran, island 130/C3
Qikiqtarjuaq, Nun., Can. 220/Q3
Qilian Shan, China, range 119/C2
Qina, Egy., 171,000 . . . . .144/B2
Qingdao, China, 1,172,370, (4,204,840 metro.) . .119/F2
Qinghai, China, lake 119/C2
Qinghai, China, province 119/C2
Qinhuangdao, China 119/E2
Qin Ling, China, mountains 119/D2
Qiqihar, China 119/F1
Qiryat Gat, Isr. 135/B2
Qiryat Shemona, Isr. 135/B1
Qishm, Yemen 137/C1
Qom, Iran, 777,677 . . . . .130/C3
Qormi, Malta 97/B2
Qostanay, Kaz., 221,429 . . . . .131/C1
Qostanay, Kaz., oblast 131/C1
Quabbin, Mass., U.S., reservoir 292/F3
Quaddick, Conn., U.S., 425 . . . . .253/H2
Quail, Tex., U.S. 346/G9
Quaker City, N.H., U.S. 312/B5
Quaker City, Ohio, U.S., 563 . . . . .328/H6
Quaker Hill, Conn., U.S., 4,200 . . . . .253/G4
Quakertown, N.J., U.S., 400 . . . . .314/D2
Quakertown, Penn., U.S., 8,931 . . . . .336/L5
Quamba, Minn., U.S., 98 . . . . .298/D5
Quanah, Tex., U.S., 3,022 . . . . .346/I1
Quang Ngai, Viet. 123/B3
Quang Tri, Viet. 123/B3
Quantaq, Que., Can. 225/C1
Quantico, Md., U.S., 325 . . . . .288/M6
Quantico, Va., U.S., 561 . . . . .354/J3
Quantico U.S.M.C. Res., Va., U.S. 354/J3
Quanzhou, China .119/E3
Quapaw, Okla., U.S., 984 . . . . .330/H1
Qu'Appelle, Sask., Can., 648 . . . . .227/G10
Qu'Appelle, Sask., Can., river 227/D10
Quarff, Scot., U.K. 62/Q2
Quarndon, Eng., U.K. 70/A1
Quarrville, N.B., Can. 217/D2
Quarryville, Conn., U.S., 2,500 . . . . .253/F2
Quarryville, Penn., U.S., 1,994 . . . . .336/J6
Quartz Hill, Calif., U.S., 9,890 . . . . .246/G8
Quartz Mountain, Oreg., U.S. 334/F5
Quartzsite, Ariz., U.S., 3,354 . . . . .242/A4
Quasqueton, Iowa, U.S., 574 . . . . .274/L3
Quatre Bornes, Mauritius, 72,147 . . . . . . .163/B3
Quay, N. Mex., U.S. 317/G2
Quay, N. Mex., U.S., county, 10,155 . . . . . .317/G2
Quay, Okla., U.S., 47 . . . . .330/F1
Quba, Azer. 103/C2
Quealy, Wyo., U.S., 80 . . . . .366/B3
Québec, Can., province 225/214
Québec, Que., Can., 169,076, (697,800 metro.) . .225/B4
Québec, Que., Can., 169,076,
 (697,800 metro.) 226/E5, L6
Quebeck, Tenn., U.S., 225 . . . . .344/K3
Quebo, Gui.-B. 149/C2
Quebrada, P.R. 206/B2
Quebradillas, P.R. 206/B2
Quechan Ind. Res., Ariz., U.S. 242/A5
Quechan Ind. Res., Calif., U.S. 246/L10
Quechee, Vt., U.S., 550 . . . . .352/C3
Queen, Penn., U.S., 350 . . . . .336/D5
Queen Anne, Md., U.S., 176 . . . . .288/L4
Queen Anne's, Md., U.S., county, 40,563 . . .288/K3
Queenborough, Eng., U.K., 3,689 . . . . .70/F4
Queen Charlotte, Br. Col., Can. 214/G4
Queen Charlotte, Br. Col., Can., islands . . .214/G4
Queen Charlotte, Br. Col., Can., sound 214/H5
Queen Charlotte, Br. Col., Can., strait 214/H5
Queen City, Mo., U.S., 638 . . . . .302/D1
Queen City, Tex., U.S., 1,613 . . . . .346/P2
Queen Creek, Ariz., U.S., 4,316 . . . . .242/D4
Queen Elizabeth, Can., islands 193/B14
Queen Elizabeth, N.W. Terr., Can., islands . .220/H1
Queen Maud, Antar., mountains 192/A5
Queen Maud, Antar., gulf 220/H3
Queen Maud Land, Antar., region 192/B16
Queens, N.B., Can., county 217/D2
Queens, N.S., Can., county 221/B3
Queens, N.Y., U.S., county, 2,229,379 . . . .320/B2
Queensbury, Eng., U.K., 7,424 . . . . .66/E5
Queensbury, Eng., U.K., 7,424 . . . . .68/D2

Queensferry, Wales, U.K. 64/F1
Queensland, Austl., state 170/D3
Queensport, Ga., U.S., 200 . . . . .260/E8
Queenstown, Tas., Austl. 170/D4
Queenstown, N.Z. 171/A3
Queenstown, Sing. 123/B1
Queenstown, S. Afr. 162/C3
Queenstown, Md., U.S., 617 . . . . .288/K4
Queets, Wash., U.S., 175 . . . . .358/A2
Queguay Grande, Uru., river 187/B2
Queimados, Braz. . . . . .188/Inset I
Quelimane, Moz. .161/C2
Quellón, Chile 190/B6
Queluz, Port. 93/A3
Quemado, N. Mex., U.S., 125 . . . . .317/B3
Quemado, Tex., U.S., 243 . . . . .346/H7
Quemeno, Kans., U.S., 648 . . . . .276/G3
Querétaro, Mex., state capital, 536,463,
 (641,386 metro.) 200/D3
Querétaro, Mex., state . . . .
Quesnel, Br. Col., Can., 10,044 . . . . .214/L5
Quesnel, Br. Col., Can., lake 214/M5
Questa, N. Mex., U.S., 1,864 . . . . .317/E1
Quetta, Pak., 565,137 . . . . .129/C3
Quetzaltenango, Guat., 108,605 . . . . .201/B5
Quevedo, Ecua. 185/B3
Quezon City, Phil., 2,173,831 . . . . .120/B3
Quibala, Ang. 159/C3
Quibdó, Col., 123,000 . . . . .184/A3
Quick City, Mo., U.S. 302/B3
Quidnessett, R.I., U.S., 3,600 . . . . .339/D4
Quidnet, Mass., U.S. 292/G2
Quidnick, R.I., U.S., 6,300 . . . . .339/C3
Quietus, Mont., U.S. 306/K4
Quihi, Tex., U.S., 40 . . . . .346/J6
Quijotoa, Ariz., U.S., 150 . . . . .242/C5
Quilcene, Wash., U.S., 591 . . . . .358/C2
Quilchena, Br. Col., Can. 214/M6
Quill, Sask., Can., lakes 227/F8
Quill Lake, Sask., Can., 439 . . . . .227/F8
Quimbele, Ang. 159/C2
Quimby, Iowa, U.S., 368 . . . . .274/C2
Quimby, Maine, U.S., 70 . . . . .286/D2
Quimper, Fr. 88/A2
Quinag, Scot., U.K., hill 62/F2
Quinault, Wash., U.S., 40 . . . . .358/B2
Quinault, Wash., U.S., lake 358/B2
Quinault Ind. Res., Wash., U.S. 358/A2
Quinby, S.C., U.S., 842 . . . . .340/E2
Quince Orchard, (N. Potomac), Md., U.S., 23,044 . .288/F3
Quincy, (Quincy-East Quincy), Calif., U.S., 1,879 . .246/E3
Quincy, Fla., U.S., 6,982 . . . . .256/D1
Quincy, Ill., U.S., 40,366 . . . . .266/B4
Quincy, Ind., U.S., 250 . . . . .270/C6
Quincy, Kans., U.S. 276/F4
Quincy, Mass., U.S., 88,025 . . . . .292/K3
Quincy, Mich., U.S., 1,701 . . . . .294/E8
Quincy, Miss., U.S., 40 . . . . .300/D2
Quincy, Mo., U.S. 302/D3
Quincy, N.H., U.S., 250 . . . . .312/C4
Quincy, Ohio, U.S., 734 . . . . .328/C5
Quincy, Oreg., U.S., 275 . . . . .334/C1
Quincy, Wash., U.S., 5,044 . . . . .358/F2
Quincy, Wash., U.S., department 184/B3
Quinebaug, Conn., U.S., 1,122 . . . . .253/H2
Quinebaug, Conn., U.S., river 253/H3
Quinhagak, Alaska, U.S., 555 . . . . .240/C3
Quinhámel, Gui.-B. 149/B2
Quinlan, Okla., U.S. 330/D1
Quinlan, Tex., U.S., 1,370 . . . . .346/M3
Quinn, Nev., U.S., river 310/B1
Quinn, S. Dak., U.S., 44 . . . . .342/C4
Quinnesec, Mich., U.S., 1,187 . . . . .294/B4
Quinnimont, W. Va., U.S., 40 . . . . .360/D5
Quintana Roo, Mex., state 200/G4
Quinter, Kans., U.S., 961 . . . . .276/B2
Quinton, N.J., U.S., 2,786 . . . . .314/C4
Quinton, Okla., U.S., 1,071 . . . . .330/G2
Quinwood, W. Va., U.S., 435 . . . . .360/E4
Quirke, Ont., Can., lake 294/B3
Quispamsis, N.B., Can., 13,757 . . . . .217/D3
Quitaque, Tex., U.S., 432 . . . . .346/G1
Quitman, Ark., U.S., 714 . . . . .244/C2
Quitman, Ga., U.S., 4,638 . . . . .260/D1
Quitman, Ga., U.S., county, 2,598 . . . . . . .260/A8
Quitman, La., U.S., 168 . . . . .282/D2
Quitman, Miss., U.S., 2,463 . . . . .300/D4
Quitman, Miss., U.S., county, 10,117 . . . . .300/A1
Quitman, Mo., U.S., 46 . . . . .302/A1
Quitman, Tex., U.S., 2,030 . . . . .346/N3
Quito, Ecua., capital, 1,615,809 . . . . .185/B3
Quito, Miss., U.S., 100 . . . . .300/B3
Quitsna, N.C., U.S., 100 . . . . .322/L3
Quivero, Ariz., U.S. 242/C2
Quivira N.W.R., Kans., U.S. 276/D3
Quliin, Mo., U.S., 467 . . . . .302/F5
Qŭnghirot, Uzb. 132/A2
Quoddy, Maine, U.S. 286/E4
Quogue, N.Y., U.S., 1,018 . . . . .320/F2
Quoich, Scot., U.K., lake 62/F4
Quonochontaug, R.I., U.S., 350 . . . . .339/B6
Quorndon, Eng., U.K., 4,614 . . . . .68/E4
Quorndon, Eng., U.K., 4,614 . . . . .70/B1
Qŭqon, Uzb. 132/D2
Qŭrghonteppa, Taj. 132/A2
Qurnat as Sawda, Leb., mountain 134/B1
Qus, Egy. 144/B2
Quthing, Leso. 161/A3
Quy Nhon, Viet., 163,385 . . . . .123/B4
Raahe, Fin. 81/B2
Raanes, Nun., Can., peninsula 220/I1
Raasay, Scot., U.K., island 62/D4
Raas Xaafun, Som., cape 157/C1
Rába, Hun., river 91/A2
Raba, Indon. 122/C2
Rabat, Malta 97/B2
Rabat, Mor., capital, 1,220,000 . . . . .147/C1
Rabaul, P.N.G. 172/B2
Rabbit Lake, Sask., Can., 87 . . . . .227/C5
Rabbit Lake Mine, Sask., Can. 227/G2
Rabi, Fiji, island 174/C2
Rabigh, Sa. Arab. .136/A2
Rabun, Ala., U.S., 100 . . . . .238/B4
Rabun, Ga., U.S., county, 15,050 . . . . .260/D2
Raccoon, Ohio, U.S., creek 328/F7
Raceland, Ky., U.S., 2,355 . . . . .280/H2
Raceland, La., U.S., 10,224 . . . . .282/G7
Race Pond, Ga., U.S. 260/G1
Rachal, Tex., U.S., 80 . . . . .346/K9
Rachel, Nev., U.S., 90 . . . . .310/C3
Rach Gia, Viet., 141,132 . . . . .123/B4
Racine, Minn., U.S., 355 . . . . .298/E7
Racine, Mo., U.S., 200 . . . . .302/B5
Racine, Ohio, U.S., 746 . . . . .328/G8
Racine, W. Va., U.S., 475 . . . . .360/C4
Racine, Wisc., U.S., 81,855 . . . . .364/F6
Racine, Wisc., U.S., county, 188,831 . . . . .364/E6, F2
Rackenford, Eng., U.K. 73/G3
Rackwick, Scot., U.K. 62/L2
Raco, Mich., U.S. .294/E3

Red Rock, Iowa 613

Rădăuţi, Rom. 101/C2
Radcliff, Ky., U.S., 21,961 280/E3
Radcliffe, Iowa, U.S., 607 274/H3
Radcliffe on Trent, Eng., U.K., 7,387 68/E4
Radcliffe on Trent, Eng., U.K., 7,387 70/B1
Radcot, Eng., U.K. 70/A3
Radersburg, Mont., U.S., 70 306/E3
Radford, Va., U.S., 15,859 354/B6
Radisson, Wisc., U.S., 222 364/B3
Radium, Colo., U.S. 250/D2
Radium, Kans., U.S., 40 276/D3
Radium, Minn., U.S. 298/A2
Radium, Tex., U.S. 346/J3
Radium Hot Sprs., Br. Col., Can., 583 214/O6
Radium Sprs., N. Mex., U.S., 1,518 317/D5
Radnor, Ohio, U.S., 225 328/D5
Radnor, Penn., U.S., 30,878 336/L5, L7
Radom, Pol., 232,079 83/E3
Radom, Ill., U.S., 395 266/D5
Radstock, Eng., U.K. 73/H2
Radviliškis, Lith. 82/B2
Radville, Sask., Can., 735 227/F11
Radyr, Wales, U.K., 4,335 64/E4
Rae-Edzo, N.W. Terr., Can., 1,552 220/E4
Raeford, N.C., U.S., 3,386 322/G5
Raemon, N.C., U.S., 212 322/G5
Raeville, Nebr., U.S., 50 308/E2
Rafael Capó, P.R. 206/B2
Rafaï, C.A.R. 154/B2
Rafha, Sa. Arab. 136/B1
Rafter, Man., Can. 215/A1
Rafter J Ranch, Wyo., U.S., 1,138 366/A2
Ragan, Nebr., U.S., 46 308/E3
Ragged, Bah., *island* 204/C2
Ragged, Barb., *point* 209/C3
Raglan, Wales, U.K. 64/F4
Ragland, Ala., U.S., 1,918 238/C2
Ragland, N. Mex., U.S. 317/G3
Ragley, La., U.S., 125 282/C5
Rago, Kans., U.S. 276/D4
Ragueneau, Que., Can. 226/H2
Ragusa, It. 95/C3
Rahimyar Khan, Pak., 233,537 129/D4
Rahway, N.J., U.S., 26,500 314/A3
Raiford, Fla., U.S., 187 256/F1
Raiford, Okla., U.S., 40 330/G2
Rainbow Bridge Natl. Mon., Utah, U.S. 350/D6
Rainbow City, Ala., U.S., 8,428 238/C2
Rainbow Lake, Alta., Can., 976 212/A2
Rainbow Valley, Ariz., U.S. 242/C4
Rainelle, W. Va., U.S., 1,545 360/E5
Raines, Ga., U.S., 50 260/D8
Rainford, Eng., U.K., 6,362 66/C5
Rainford, Eng., U.K., 6,362 68/B2
Rainham, Eng., U.K. 70/E3
Rainier, Oreg., U.S., 1,687 334/D1
Rainier, Wash., U.S., 1,492 358/C3
Rainier, Wash., U.S., *mountain* 358/D3
Rains, S.C., U.S., 650 340/E2
Rains, Tex., U.S., *county*, 9,139 346/N3
Rainsburg, Penn., U.S., 146 336/D6
Rainsville, Ala., U.S., 4,499 238/D1
Rainsville, N. Mex., U.S., 100 317/E2
Rainy, Ont., Can., *river* 298/C2
Raipur, India, 437,887, (461,851 *metro.*) 128/D4
Rajang, Malay., *river* 121/C2
Rajasthan, India, *state* 128/B3
Rajbiraj, Nepal 126/C3
Rajkot, India, 556,137, (1,002,160 *metro.*) 128/B4
Rajpur, India 128/Inset II
Rajshahi, Bangl., 299,671, (756,000 *metro.*) 127/B4
Rajshahi, Bangl., *division* 127/C3
Rakan, Ra's, Qatar, *cape* 137/C1
Rakaposhi, Pak., *mountain* 129/E2
Rake, Eng., U.K. 70/C4
Rake, Iowa, U.S., 227 274/G1
Rakhine, Mya., *state* 125/B2
Raleigh, Fla., U.S., 300 256/F2
Raleigh, Ga., U.S., 125 260/B6
Raleigh, Ill., U.S., 330 266/E6
Raleigh, Miss., U.S., 1,255 300/C3
Raleigh, N.C., U.S., *state capital*, 276,093,
(1,187,941 *metro.*) 322/H3
Raleigh, N. Dak., U.S. 326/D3
Raleigh, W. Va., U.S., *county*, 79,220 360/D5
Raleigh Hills, Oreg., U.S., 5,865 334/A2
Ralik, Marsh. Is., *island chain* 173/A1
Ralls, Mo., U.S., *county*, 9,626 302/E2
Ralls, Tex., U.S., 2,252 346/G2
Ralph, Ala., U.S., 40 238/B2
Ralph, Mich., U.S., 40 294/B3
Ralph, S. Dak., U.S. 342/B2
Ralston, Iowa, U.S., 98 274/E3
Ralston, Nebr., U.S., 6,314 308/H2
Ralston, Okla., U.S., 355 330/F1
Ralston, Penn., U.S., 200 336/H2
Ralston, Wash., U.S. 358/G3
Ralston, Wyo., U.S., 233 366/B1
Rama, Nicar. 202/B2
Ramah, Colo., U.S., 117 250/F2
Ramah, N. Mex., U.S., 407 317/B2
Ramah Navajo Ind. Res., N. Mex., U.S. 317/B3
Ramanbati, India 128/Inset II
Ramapo Mtn. S.F., N.J., U.S. 314/B1
Ramat Gan, Isr., 127,400 135/B1
Ramblewood, N.J., U.S., 6,003 314/B3, D4
Ramea, Nfld., Can., 754 218/C5
Ramer, Ala., U.S., 100 238/C3
Ramer, Tenn., U.S., 354 344/D4
Ramey, Penn., U.S., 525 336/E4
Ramhurst, Ga., U.S., 400 260/B2
Ramirez, Tex., U.S. 346/K8
Ramla, Isr. 135/B2
Ram Lane, Eng., U.K. 70/F4
Ramm, Jabal, Jor., *mountain* 134/A3
Ramon, Isr., *mountain* 135/B2
Ramon, N. Mex., U.S. 317/F3
Ramona, Calif., U.S., 15,691 246/J9
Ramona, Kans., U.S., 94 276/E3
Ramona, Okla., U.S., 564 330/G1
Ramona, S. Dak., U.S., 190 342/H3
Rampart, Alaska, U.S., 45 240/E1
Rampside, Eng., U.K. 66/B4
Ramree, Mya., *island* 125/B2
Ramsay, Mich., U.S., 750 294/C2
Ramsbury, Eng., U.K. 70/A4
Ramsbury, Eng., U.K. 73/J2
Ramseur, N.C., U.S., 1,588 322/F3
Ramsey, Eng., U.K., 7,577 66/B5
Ramsey, Eng., U.K., 7,577 68/G5
Ramsey, Eng., U.K., 7,577 70/D2
Ramsey, Wales, U.K., *island* 64/A4
Ramsey, Ark., U.S., 40 244/C4
Ramsey, Ill., U.S., 1,056 266/D4
Ramsey, Minn., U.S., 18,510 298/D5
Ramsey, Minn., U.S., *county*, 511,035 298/D5, F6
Ramsey, N.J., U.S., 14,351 314/B1, E1
Ramsey, N. Dak., U.S., *county*, 12,066 326/G1
Ramsey St. Mary's, Eng., U.K. 68/G5
Ramsgate, Eng., U.K., 37,895 70/G4
Ramsgill, Eng., U.K. 66/E4
Ramu, Kenya 157/F2
Ramu, P.N.G., *river* 172/A2
Ranburne, Ala., U.S., 459 238/D2
Ranby, Eng., U.K. 66/F6
Rancagua, Chile, 197,879 190/B4
Rance, Fr., *river* 88/B2
Ranchester, Wyo., U.S., 701 366/C1
Ranchettes, Wyo., U.S., 4,869 366/D3
Ranchi, India, 598,498, (614,454 *metro.*) 128/E4
Ranchito, N. Mex., U.S. 317/E1
Rancho Cordova, Calif., U.S., 55,060 246/K5
Rancho Cucamonga, Calif., U.S., 127,743 246/H8
Rancho Mirage, Calif., U.S., 13,249 246/J9
Rancho Murieta, Calif., U.S., 4,193 246/L5
Rancho Palos Verdes, Calif., U.S., 41,145 246/C10
Rancho Rinconada, Calif., U.S., 4,200 246/K3
Rancho Santa Margarita, Calif., U.S., 47,214 246/F11
Ranchos de Taos, N. Mex., U.S., 2,390 317/E1
Ranchvale, N. Mex., U.S. 317/G3
Rancocas, N.J., U.S., 8,400 314/D3
Rand, Colo., U.S. 250/D1
Rand, W. Va., U.S., 2,300 360/C4
Randa, Dji. 156/B2
Randado, Tex., U.S. 346/K8
Randalia, Iowa, U.S., 84 274/L2
Randall, Iowa, U.S., 148 274/G3
Randall, Kans., U.S., 90 276/D2
Randall, Minn., U.S., 535 298/C4
Randall, Tex., U.S., *county*, 104,312 346/F9
Randallstown, Md., U.S., 30,870 288/G2
Randalstown, N. Ire., U.K., 4,290 65/E2
Randers, Den., 56,008 79/C2
Randle, Wash., U.S., 70 358/D3
Randle Cliff Beach, Md., U.S., 800 288/H5
Randleman, N.C., U.S., 3,557 322/F3
Randlett, Okla., U.S., 511 330/D3
Randlett, Utah, U.S., 224 350/E3
Randolph, Ala., U.S. 238/C3
Randolph, Ala., U.S., *county*, 22,380 238/D2
Randolph, Ariz., U.S., 275 242/D5
Randolph, Ark., U.S., *county*, 18,195 244/D1
Randolph, Ga., U.S., *county*, 7,791 260/B8
Randolph, Ill., U.S., *county*, 33,893 266/D5
Randolph, Ind., U.S., *county*, 27,401 270/F4
Randolph, Iowa, U.S., 209 274/C6
Randolph, Kans., U.S., 175 276/F2
Randolph, Maine, U.S., 1,911 286/C4
Randolph, Mass., U.S., 30,963 292/K4
Randolph, Minn., U.S., 318 298/D6
Randolph, Miss., U.S., 150 300/C1
Randolph, Mo., U.S., 47 302/H5
Randolph, Mo., U.S., *county*, 24,663 302/D2
Randolph, Nebr., U.S., 955 308/G1
Randolph, N.H., U.S., 339 312/D3
Randolph, N.Y., U.S., 1,316 320/D6
Randolph, N.C., U.S., *county*, 130,454 322/F3
Randolph, Utah, U.S., 483 350/C2
Randolph, Vt., U.S., 4,853 352/B3
Randolph, W. Va., U.S., *county*, 28,262 360/G3
Randolph, Wisc., U.S., 1,869 364/E5
Randolph Ctr., Vt., U.S., 850 352/B3
Randolph Hills, (N. Bethesda), Md., U.S., 14,300 288/A6
Random Lake, Wisc., U.S., 1,551 364/F5
Rands, Iowa, U.S. 274/E3
Randville, Mich., U.S., 40 294/A3
Randwick, N.S.W., Austl. 170/Inset IV
Ranfurly, Alta., Can., 60 212/E4
Rangamati, Bangl. 127/F6
Range, Ala., U.S., 80 238/B4
Range, Wisc., U.S., 150 364/A3
Rangeley, (plantation), Maine, U.S., 123 286/B4
Rangeley, (town), Maine, U.S., 123 286/B4
Rangely, Colo., U.S., 2,096 250/B1
Ranger, Ont., Can., *lake* 223/B1
Ranger, Ont., Can., *lake* 294/F3
Ranger, Ga., U.S., 85 260/B3
Ranger, Tex., U.S., 2,584 346/K3
Ranger Lake, Ont., Can. 223/B1
Rangitikei, N.Z., *river* 171/C2
Rangoon, (Yangon), Mya., *capital*, 2,513,023 125/C3
Rangoon, (Yangon), Mya., *division* 125/C3
Rangpur, Bangl., 203,931 127/C3
Ranier, Minn., U.S., 188 298/D2
Ranish, Scot., U.K. 62/D2
Rankin, Ill., U.S., 617 266/F3
Rankin, Miss., U.S., *county*, 115,327 300/C3
Rankin, Penn., U.S., 2,315 336/E7
Rankin, Tex., U.S., 800 346/G4
Rankin Inlet, Nun., Can., 2,177 220/K4
Ranlo, N.C., U.S., 2,198 322/C4
Rann of Kutch, India, *mud flat* 128/B4
Ranong, Thai. 125/B4
Ranskill, Eng., U.K. 66/F6
Ransom, Ill., U.S., 409 266/E2
Ransom, Kans., U.S., 338 276/C3
Ransom, N. Dak., U.S., *county*, 5,890 326/H3
Ransom Canyon, Tex., U.S., 1,011 346/G2
Ransomville, N.Y., U.S., 1,488 320/D4
Ranson, W. Va., U.S., 2,951 360/L2
Rantoul, Ill., U.S., 12,857 266/E3
Rantoul, Kans., U.S., 241 276/G3
Raoul, Ga., U.S., 1,816 260/D3
Rapalje, Mont., U.S., 70 306/G4
Rapid City, Man., Can., 424 215/A4
Rapid City, Mich., U.S., 550 294/D5
Rapid City, S. Dak., U.S., 59,607,
(88,565 *metro.*) 342/B3
Rapides, La., U.S., *parish*, 126,337 282/D5
Rapid River, Mich., U.S., 500 294/C4
Rapids, N.Y., U.S., 1,356 320/D4
Rapids City, Ill., U.S., 953 266/C2
Rapid Valley, S. Dak., U.S., 7,043 342/B3
Rapla, Est. 81/C1
Rapness, Scot., U.K. 62/M1
Rappahannock, Va., U.S., *county*, 6,983 354/G3
Rappahannock, Va., U.S., *river* 354/J4
Rapti, Nepal, *river* 126/B2
Raquette Lake, N.Y., U.S., 80 320/M3
Rarden, Ohio, U.S., 176 328/D8
Rardin, Ill., U.S., 100 266/E4
Raritan, Ill., U.S., 140 266/C3
Raritan, (Somerset County), N.J., U.S., 6,338 314/D2
Raritan, N.J., U.S., *bay* 314/E3
Rasa, Arg., *point* 191/C5
Ra's al Khafji, Sa. Arab. 136/C1
Ra's al Khaymah, U.A.E. 136/C2
Ra's an Naqb, Jor. 134/A2
Ras Dashen, Eth., *mountain* 156/C1
Rasharkin, N. Ire., U.K., 923 65/E2
Rashayya, Leb. 134/A2
Rasht, Iran, 417,748 130/B2
Ra's Tannurah, Sa. Arab. 136/C1
Rat, Alaska, U.S., *islands* 240/Inset
Ratak, Marsh. Is., *island chain* 173/B1
Ratchaburi, Thai. 125/B3
Ratcliff, Ark., U.S., 191 244/B2
Rathbun, Iowa, U.S., 88 274/J6
Rathbun, Iowa, U.S., *lake* 274/H6
Rathdrum, Ida., U.S., 4,816 264/A2
Rathen, Scot., U.K. 62/N3
Rathfriland, N. Ire., U.K., 2,126 65/E3
Rathlin, N. Ire., U.K., *island* 60/A2
Rathlin, N. Ire., U.K., *island* 65/E1
Rathlin, N. Ire., U.K., *island* 78/C1
Rathlin, N. Ire., U.K., *sound* 65/E1
Ratingen, Ger. 86/A3
Ratliff City, Okla., U.S., 131 330/E3
Ratnapura, Sri Lan. 126/B5
Raton, N. Mex., U.S., 7,282 317/F1
Rattan, Okla., U.S., 241 330/G3
Rattlesden, Eng., U.K. 70/F2
Rattlesnake N.R.A., Mont., U.S. 306/C2
Rattray, Scot., U.K. 62/K5
Raub, N. Dak., U.S. 326/C2
Raukumara, N.Z., *range* 171/C2
Rauma, Fin., 37,190 81/B2
Raunds, Eng., U.K., 7,493 68/F5
Raunds, Eng., U.K., 7,493 70/C2
Raurkela, India 128/D4
Răut, Mol., *river* 102/B2
Ravalli, Mont., U.S., 119 306/B2
Ravalli, Mont., U.S., *county*, 36,070 306/C3
Raven, Va., U.S., 2,593 354/E2
Ravena, N.Y., U.S., 3,369 320/P6
Ravendale, Calif., U.S. 246/E2
Ravenden, Ark., U.S., 511 244/D1
Ravenden Sprs., Ark., U.S., 137 244/D1
Ravenel, S.C., U.S., 2,214 340/D4
Ravenglass, Eng., U.K. 66/B4
Ravenna, It. 95/C1
Ravenna, Ky., U.S., 693 280/G3
Ravenna, Mich., U.S., 1,206 294/D6
Ravenna, Mont., U.S. 306/C3
Ravenna, Nebr., U.S., 1,341 308/E2
Ravenna, Ohio, U.S., 11,771 328/H3
Ravenna, Tex., U.S., 215 346/M2
Raven Rock, N.J., U.S., 150 314/C3
Ravensburg, Ger. 86/B5
Ravenscar, Eng., U.K. 66/H4
Ravensdale, Wash., U.S., 816 358/B4
Ravenstone, Eng., U.K. 70/C2
Ravenstonedale, Eng., U.K. 66/D4
Ravenswood, W. Va., U.S., 4,031 360/C3
Ravenwood, Mo., U.S., 448 302/B1
Ravi, Pak., *river* 129/D3
Ravia, Okla., U.S., 459 330/F3
Ravinia, S. Dak., U.S., 79 342/G4
Rawaki, Kiri., *island* 175/B2
Rawalpindi, Pak., 1,409,768 129/D3
Rawcliffe, Eng., U.K. 66/G5
Rawdon, N.S., Can. 221/D2
Rawlings, Md., U.S., 750 288/C3
Rawlins, Kans., U.S., *county*, 2,966 276/A2
Rawlins, Wyo., U.S., 8,538 366/C3
Rawmarsh, Eng., U.K., 18,085 66/F6
Rawmarsh, Eng., U.K., 18,085 68/E3
Rawridge, Eng., U.K. 73/F3
Rawson, Arg. 191/B5
Rawson, N. Dak., U.S. 326/B2
Rawson, Ohio, U.S., 465 328/C4
Rawsonville, Vt., U.S., 60 352/B4
Rawtenstall, Eng., U.K., 21,933 66/D5
Rawtenstall, Eng., U.K., 21,933 68/C2
Ray, Minn., U.S. 298/D2
Ray, Mo., U.S., *county*, 23,354 302/C2
Ray, N. Dak., U.S., 534 326/B1
Ray City, Ga., U.S., 746 260/E9
Ray Hubbard, Tex., U.S., *lake* 346/D9
Rayland, Ohio, U.S., 434 328/J5
Rayland, Tex., U.S. 346/J1
Rayle, Ga., U.S., 139 260/F4
Raylees, Eng., U.K. 66/D2
Raymer, Colo., U.S., 91 250/G1
Raymond, Alta., Can., 3,200 212/D6
Raymond, Ga., U.S., 300 260/B5
Raymond, Ida., U.S. 264/F7
Raymond, Ill., U.S., 927 266/B2, D4
Raymond, Ind., U.S., 50 270/G6
Raymond, Iowa, U.S., 537 274/K3
Raymond, Kans., U.S., 95 276/D3
Raymond, Maine, U.S., 4,299 286/B5
Raymond, Minn., U.S., 803 298/B5
Raymond, Miss., U.S., 1,664 300/B3
Raymond, Mont., U.S. 306/M1
Raymond, Nebr., U.S., 186 308/H3
Raymond, N.H., U.S., 9,674 312/D5
Raymond, S. Dak., U.S., 86 342/H3
Raymond, Wash., U.S., 2,975 358/B3
Raymond, Wyo., U.S. 366/A2
Raymondville, Mo., U.S., 442 302/E4
Raymondville, N.Y., U.S., 475 320/M1
Raymondville, Tex., U.S., 9,733 346/L9
Raymore, Sask., Can., 625 227/F9
Raymore, Mo., U.S., 11,146 302/B3
Rayne, La., U.S., 8,552 282/E6
Raynesford, Mont., U.S. 306/F2
Raynham, Mass., U.S., 11,739 292/K5
Raynham, N.C., U.S., 67 322/G5
Raynham Ctr., Mass., U.S., 3,633 292/K5
Rayong, Thai., (104,800 *metro.*) 125/B3
Rayside-Balfour, Ont., Can. 223/D1
Raystown, Penn., U.S., *lake* 336/E5
Raytown, Mo., U.S., 30,388 302/B2, H5
Rayville, La., U.S., 4,234 282/F2
Rayville, Mo., U.S., 204 302/B2
Raywick, Ky., U.S., 144 280/G3
Raz, Fr., *point* 88/A3
Razelm, Rom., *lake* 101/E3
Razgrad, Bul. 101/E2
Razgrad, Bul., *oblast* 101/E2
Rdnyy, Kaz., 109,515 131/C1
Ré, Fr., *island* 88/B3
Rea, Mo., U.S., 56 302/B1
Reader, Ark., U.S., 82 244/B4
Readfield, Maine, U.S., 2,360 286/C4
Reading, Eng., U.K. 60/C3
Reading, Eng., U.K., 213,474, (335,757 *metro.*) 70/C4
Reading, Eng., U.K., *unitary authority*, 143,124 70/B4
Reading, Kans., U.S., 247 276/G3
Reading, Mass., U.S., 23,708 292/C6, K2
Reading, Mich., U.S., 1,134 294/E8
Reading, Minn., U.S., 125 298/B7
Reading, Ohio, U.S., 11,292 328/B7, B9
Reading, Penn., U.S., 81,207, (373,638 *metro.*) 336/K5
Readington, N.J., U.S., 15,803 314/D2
Readland, Ark., U.S., 125 244/D4
Readlyn, Iowa, U.S., 786 274/K2
Readsboro, Vt., U.S., 809 352/B5
Readstown, Wisc., U.S., 395 364/C5
Readsville, Mo., U.S. 302/E3
Ready, Ky., U.S., 70 280/D3
Reagan, Okla., U.S., 90 330/F3
Reagan, Tenn., U.S., 50 344/E3
Reagan, Tex., U.S., *county*, 3,326 346/G4
Reager, Kans., U.S. 276/B2
Real, Tex., U.S., *county*, 3,047 346/J6
Realitos, Tex., U.S., 209 346/K8
Reardan, Wash., U.S., 608 358/H2
Rearsby, Eng., U.K. 70/B1
Reasnor, Iowa, U.S., 194 274/H4
Reaville, N.J., U.S., 1,200 314/D3
Reawick, Scot., U.K. 62/P2
Rebecca, Ga., U.S., 246 260/E8
Rebersburg, Penn., U.S., 492 336/G4
Rebun, Jap., *island* 114/Inset I
Rechytsa, Bela. 82/E3
Recife, Braz., 1,421,947, (3,331,552 *metro.*) 188/E2
Recklinghausen, Ger., 125,022 86/A3
Recluse, Wyo., U.S. 366/D1
Reconquista, Arg. 191/D2
Rector, Ark., U.S., 2,017 244/E1
Rectorville, Ky., U.S., 375 280/G2
Red, Man., Can., *river* 215/C4
Red, Dji., *sea* 156/C1
Red, Egy., *sea* 144/C2
Red, Erit., *sea* 156/C1
Red, Sa. Arab., *sea* 136/A1
Red, Sudan, *sea* 145/D1
Red, N. Ire., U.K., *bay* 65/E1
Red, Ariz., U.S., *lake* 242/B2
Red, Ark., U.S., *river* 244/B4
Red, La., U.S., *river* 282/C3, F4
Red, (Hong), Viet., *river* 123/A2
Red, Yemen, *sea* 137/A2
Redan, Ga., U.S., 33,841 260/J3
Redange, Lux. 85/A2
Red Ash, Va., U.S., 100 354/D2
Red Bank, N.B., Can. 217/D2
Red Bank, Calif., U.S., 40 246/C2
Red Bank, N.J., U.S., 11,844 314/E3
Red Bank, S.C., U.S., 8,811 340/A3
Red Bank, Tenn., U.S., 12,418 344/L4
Red Banks, Miss., U.S., 125 300/C1
Red Bay, Nfld., Can., 264 218/C3
Red Bay, Ala., U.S., 3,374 238/A1
Red Beach, Maine, U.S. 286/E3
Redbird, Okla., U.S., 153 330/G2
Redbird, Wyo., U.S. 366/D2
Red Bluff, Calif., U.S., 13,147 246/C2
Red Bluff, Tex., U.S., *lake* 346/D4
Red Boiling Sprs., Tenn., U.S., 1,023 344/K1
Redbridge, Ont., Can. 223/F1
Redbridge, Eng., U.K., *unitary authority*, 238,628 70/E3
Redbrook, Wales, U.K. 64/F2
Red Bud, Ill., U.S., 3,422 266/D5
Red Buttes, Wyo., U.S. 366/D3
Redby, Minn., U.S., 957 298/C3
Redcar, Eng., U.K., 35,877 66/F3
Redcar and Cleveland, Eng., U.K.,
unitary authority, 139,141 66/G3
Red Chute, La., U.S., 5,984 282/B1
Redcliff, Alta., Can., 4,372 212/E6
Red Cliff, Colo., U.S., 289 250/D2
Red Cliff, Wisc., U.S., 600 364/C2
Redcliffe, Qnsld., Austl. 170/Inset III
Red Cliff Ind. Res., Wisc., U.S. 364/B2
Red Cloud, Nebr., U.S., 1,131 308/E3
Red Creek, N.Y., U.S., 521 320/H4
Red Deer, Alta., Can., 67,707 212/D5
Red Deer, Alta., Can., *river* 212/D5, E6
Red Deer, Man., Can., *lake* 215/A2
Red Deer, Sask., Can., *river* 227/G8
Reddell, La., U.S., 500 282/E5
Redden, Okla., U.S. 330/G3
Redden St. For., Del., U.S. 255/C6
Red Desert, Wyo., U.S. 366/B3
Red Dial, Eng., U.K. 66/B3
Reddick, Fla., U.S., 571 256/F2
Reddick, Ill., U.S., 219 266/E2
Redding, Calif., U.S., 80,865, (163,256 *metro.*) 246/C2
Redding, Conn., U.S., 8,270 253/B4
Redding, Iowa, U.S., 78 274/F6
Redding Ridge, Conn., U.S., 900 253/B4
Redditch, Eng., U.K., 73,372 68/D5
Red Elm, S. Dak., U.S. 342/D2
Red Feather Lakes, Colo., U.S., 525 250/E1
Redfield, Ark., U.S., 1,157 244/C3
Redfield, Iowa, U.S., 833 274/F4
Redfield, Kans., U.S., 140 276/H4
Redfield, N.Y., U.S., 60 320/K3
Redfield, S. Dak., U.S., 2,897 342/G3
Redford, Mich., U.S., 51,622 294/A7
Redford, Tex., U.S., 132 346/D6
Redgranite, Wisc., U.S., 1,040 364/D4
Red Head, Fla., U.S., 60 256/C1
Redhill, Eng., U.K. 70/D4
Redhill, Eng., U.K. 73/G2
Red Hill, Ala., U.S., 350 238/D3
Red Hill, N. Mex., U.S., 90 317/B3
Red Hill, Penn., U.S., 2,196 336/L5
Red Hill, S.C., U.S., 10,509 340/E3
Red Hill-Patrick Henry Natl. Mem., Va., U.S. 354/F6
Red Hook, N.Y., U.S., 1,805 320/P7
Redhouse, Md., U.S. 288/A4
Red House, Nev., U.S. 310/B1
Redig, S. Dak., U.S. 342/B2
Red Indian, Nfld., Can., *lake* 218/C5
Redington, Ariz., U.S. 242/E5
Redington, Nebr., U.S. 308/A2
Redington Beach, Fla., U.S., 1,539 256/C6, F4
Redington Shores, Fla., U.S., 2,338 256/C6
Redisham, Eng., U.K. 70/H2
Red Jacket, W. Va., U.S., 728 360/B5
Redkey, Ind., U.S., 1,427 270/F4
Red Lake, Ariz., U.S., 225 242/C2
Red Lake, Minn., U.S., 1,430 298/B3
Red Lake, Minn., U.S., *county*, 4,299 298/A3
Red Lake Falls, Minn., U.S., 1,590 298/A3
Red Lake Ind. Res., Minn., U.S. 298/B1, B2
Redland, Md., U.S., 16,998 288/F3
Redland Bay, Qnsld., Austl. 170/Inset III
Redlands, Calif., U.S., 63,591 246/H8
Redlands, Colo., U.S., 8,043 250/B2
Red Level, Ala., U.S., 556 238/C4
Red Lick, Miss., U.S., 100 300/B4
Red Lion, Penn., U.S., 6,149 336/H6
Red Lodge, Mont., U.S., 2,177 306/G4
Red Mesa, Ariz., U.S., 237 242/F1
Redmesa, Colo., U.S., 40 250/B4
Red Mills, (Claverack-Red Mills), N.Y., U.S., 1,061 320/P6
Redmon, Ill., U.S., 199 266/F4
Redmond, Oreg., U.S., 13,481 334/E3
Redmond, Utah, U.S., 788 350/C5
Redmond, Wash., U.S., 45,256 358/B4, C2
Red Mountain, Calif., U.S., 150 246/H7
Red Oak, Iowa, U.S., 6,197 274/D5
Red Oak, La., U.S. 282/G6
Red Oak, Mich., U.S., 40 294/E5
Red Oak, N.C., U.S., 2,723 322/K2
Red Oak, Okla., U.S., 581 330/G3
Redonda, Ant.-Bar., *island* 207/A6
Redondo Beach, Calif., U.S., 63,261 246/B10
Redowl, S. Dak., U.S. 342/C3
Red Pt., P.E.I., Can. 224/C2
Redpoint, Scot., U.K. 62/E3
Red River, La., U.S., *parish*, 9,622 282/C2
Red River, N. Mex., U.S., 484 317/E1
Red River, Tex., U.S., *county*, 14,314 346/N2
Red River Hot Sprs., Ida., U.S. 264/B4
Red River of the North, N. Dak., U.S., *river* 298/A3
Red Rock, (Apache County), Ariz., U.S. 242/F1
Red Rock, (Pinal County), Ariz., U.S., 70 242/D5
Red Rock, Iowa, U.S., *lake* 274/J5

Redrock, N. Mex., U.S. 317/B5
Red Rock, Okla., U.S., 293 . . . . .330/E1
Red Rock, Tex., U.S., 100 . . . . .346/E3, L6
Red Rock Canyon N.C.A., Nev., U.S. 310/C4
Red Rock Lakes N.W.R., Mont., U.S. 306/E5
Red Rose, Man., Can. 215/C3
Redruth, Eng., U.K. .73/B4
Red Scaffold, S. Dak., U.S., 80 . . . . .342/D3
Red Sea, Sudan, hills 145/D1
Red Shirt, S. Dak., U.S. 342/C4
Red Sprs., N.C., U.S., 3,493 . . . . .322/G5
Red Star, Ark., U.S. 244/B2
Redstone, Br. Col., Can. 214/L5
Redstone, Colo., U.S. 250/C2
Redstone, Mont., U.S., 40 . . . . .306/M1
Redstone, N.H., U.S. 312/D3
Redstone Arsenal, Ala., U.S. 238/C1
Red Sucker, Man., Can., lake 215/E2
Red Top, Calif., U.S., 40 . . . . .246/E5
Redvale, Colo., U.S., 60 . . . . .250/B3
Redvers, Man., Can. 215/A4
Redvers, Sask., Can., 917 . . . . .227/I11
Red Volta, Burkina, river 151/D3
Red Volta, Gha., river 150/B1
Redwater, Alta., Can., 2,172 . . . . .212/D4
Redwater, Miss., U.S., 409 . . . . .300/C3
Redwater, Tex., U.S., 872 . . . . .346/P2
Redway, Calif., U.S., 1,188 . . . . .246/B2
Redwick, Wales, U.K. 64/F4
Red Willow, Alta., Can., 40 . . . . .212/D5
Red Willow, Nebr., U.S., county, 11,448 . . . .308/D3
Red Willow Cr., Nebr., U.S. 308/C3
Red Wing, Colo., U.S. 250/E4
Red Wing, Minn., U.S., 16,116 . . . . .298/E6
Redwood, Minn., U.S., county, 16,815 . . . .298/B6
Redwood, Miss., U.S., 125 . . . . .300/B3
Redwood, N.Y., U.S., 584 . . . . .320/K2
Redwood, Oreg., U.S., 5,844 . . . . .334/C5
Redwood City, Calif., U.S., 75,402 . . .246/C5, J2
Redwood Estates, Calif., U.S., 1,600 . . . . .246/K3
Redwood Falls, Minn., U.S., 5,459 . . . . . . .298/B6
Redwood N.P., Calif., U.S. 246/A1
Redwood Valley, Calif., U.S., 1,200 . . . . . .246/B3
Ree, Ire., lake 78/B2
Reece, Kans., U.S. 276/F4
Reece City, Ala., U.S., 634 . . . . .238/C1
Reed, Man., Can., lake 215/A2
Reed, Eng., U.K. 70/D2
Reed, Ark., U.S., 275 . . . . .244/D4
Reed, Ky., U.S., 175 . . . . .280/C3
Reed, Maine, U.S., 207 . . . . .286/D3
Reed, Okla., U.S. .330/C3
Reed City, Mich., U.S., 2,430 . . . . .294/D6
Reed Creek, Ga., U.S., 2,148 . . . . .260/F3
Reeder, N. Dak., U.S., 181 . . . . .326/C3
Reedham, Eng., U.K. 70/H1
Reedley, Calif., U.S., 20,756 . . . . .246/F6
Redpoint, Mont., U.S., 185 . . . . .306/G4
Reeds, Mo., U.S., 103 . . . . .302/B4
Reeds, N. Mex., U.S., peak 317/C4
Reeds Beach, N.J., U.S., 100 . . . . .314/D5
Reedsburg, Wisc., U.S., 7,827 . . . . .364/D5
Reeds Ferry, N.H., U.S., 1,400 . . . . .312/D6
Reedsport, Oreg., U.S., 4,378 . . . . .334/B4
Reeds Spr., Mo., U.S., 465 . . . . .302/C5
Reedsville, Ohio, U.S., 175 . . . . .328/G7
Reedsville, Penn., U.S., 858 . . . . .336/F4
Reedsville, W. Va., U.S., 517 . . . . .360/G1
Reedsville, Wisc., U.S., 1,187 . . . . .364/F4
Reedville, Va., U.S., 600 . . . . .354/L5
Reedy, W. Va., U.S., 198 . . . . .360/D3
Reefton, N.Z. 171/B3
Ree Hts., S. Dak., U.S., 85 . . . . .342/F3
Reelsboro, N.C., U.S., 800 . . . . .322/M4
Reese, Mich., U.S., 1,375 . . . . .294/F6
Reeseville, Wisc., U.S., 703 . . . . .364/E5
Reeves, La., U.S., 209 . . . . .282/C5
Reeves, Tex., U.S., county, 13,137 . . . . . . .346/E4
Reeves Crossing, Del., U.S., 450 . . . . .255/B5
Reevesville, Ill., U.S., 70 . . . . .266/E6
Reevesville, S.C., U.S., 207 . . . . .340/D3
Reform, Ala., U.S., 1,978 . . . . .238/A2
Reform, Miss., U.S., 125 . . . . .300/C2
Refugio, Tex., U.S., 2,941 . . . . .346/L7
Refugio, Tex., U.S., county, 7,828 . . . . . . .346/L7
Regal, Minn., U.S., 40 . . . . .298/C5
Regal, Mo., U.S., 50 . . . . .302/C2
Regan, N. Dak., U.S., 43 . . . . .326/E2
Regensburg, Ger., 125,236 . . . . .86/C4
Regent, N. Dak., U.S., 211 . . . . .326/C3
Reggio di Calabria, It. 95/C3
Reggio nell'Emilia, It. 95/B1
Reghin, Rom. 101/C2
Regina, Sask., Can., 178,225, (197,000 metro.) .227/F10
Régina, Fr. Gui. 183/B1
Regina, N. Mex., U.S., 99 . . . . .317/D1
Regional Municipality of Sudbury,
  Ont., Can., county 223/D1
Región Metropolitana, Chile, region . . . .190/B4, Inset
Register, Ga., U.S., 164 . . . . .260/H7
Rehoboth, Nam. .160/C3
Rehoboth, Del., U.S., bay 255/D6
Rehoboth, Mass., U.S., 10,172 . . . . .292/K5
Rehoboth, N. Mex., U.S., 375 . . . . .317/B2
Rehoboth, Va., U.S. 354/G7
Rehoboth Beach, Del., U.S., 1,495 . . . . . .255/D6
Rehovot, Isr. 135/B2
Reidland, Ky., U.S., 4,353 . . . . .280/B3
Reids Grove, Md., U.S., 80 . . . . .288/L5
Reidsville, Ga., U.S., 2,235 . . . . .260/G7
Reidsville, N.C., U.S., 14,485 . . . . .322/F2
Reiff, Scot., U.K. 62/F2
Reigate, (Reigate/Redhill), Eng., U.K., 47,602 . . .70/D4
Reigate, Eng., U.K. . . . . .60/Inset III
Reighton, Eng., U.K. 66/H4
Reile's Acres, N. Dak., U.S., 254 . . . . .326/J3
Reims, Fr., 191,325, (215,581 metro.) 88/D2
Reina Adelaida, Chile, archipelago 190/B8
Reinbeck, Iowa, U.S., 1,751 . . . . .274/J3
Reindeer, Man., Can., island 215/C1
Reindeer, Man., Can., lake 215/C1
Reindeer, Sask., Can., lake 227/H3
Reindeer, Sask., Can., river 227/G4
Reinersville, Ohio, U.S., 70 . . . . .328/G6
Reinerton, (Reinerton-Orwin-Muir),
  Penn., U.S., 1,037 . . . . .336/H4
Reinosa, Sp. 94/D1
Reiss, Scot., U.K. .62/F2
Reisterstown, Md., U.S., 22,438 . . . . .288/G2
Reklaw, Tex., U.S., 327 . . . . .346/P4
Reliance, N.W. Terr., Can. 220/G4
Reliance, Del., U.S. 255/B6
Reliance, Md., U.S. 288/M5
Reliance, S. Dak., U.S., 206 . . . . .342/F4
Reliance, Wyo., U.S., 665 . . . . .366/B3
Remagen, Ger. 86/A3
Rembert, S.C., U.S., 406 . . . . .340/D2
Rembrandt, Iowa, U.S., 228 . . . . .274/D2
Remer, Minn., U.S., 372 . . . . .298/D3
Remerton, Ga., U.S., 847 . . . . .260/E1

Remich, Lux. 85/B2
Reminderville, Ohio, U.S., 2,347 . . . . .328/H9
Remington, Ind., U.S., 1,323 . . . . .270/B3
Remington, Va., U.S., 624 . . . . .354/H3
Rémire, Fr. Gui. 183/B1
Remote, Oreg., U.S., 90 . . . . .334/C4
Remscheid, Ger., 120,125 . . . . .86/A3
Remsen, Iowa, U.S., 1,762 . . . . .274/C2
Remsen, N.Y., U.S., 531 . . . . .320/L4
Remus, Mich., U.S., 250 . . . . .294/D6
Rencona, N. Mex., U.S. 31/F2
Rencontre East, Nfld., Can., 202 . . . . .218/D5
Rend, Ill., U.S., lake 266/D5
Rendville, Ohio, U.S., 46 . . . . .328/F6
Renfrew, Ont., Can., 7,942 . . . . .223/J2
Renfrew, Ont., Can., county 223/H2
Renfrewshire, Scot., U.K., unitary authority,
  172,867 . . . . .62/G7
Renfroe, Ga., U.S. 260/B7
Renfroe, Miss., U.S., 90 . . . . .300/C3
Renfrow, Okla., U.S. 330/E1
Renhold, Eng., U.K. 70/D2
Renick, Mo., U.S., 221 . . . . .302/D2
Renick, W. Va., U.S., 200 . . . . .360/F4
Rennell, Sol. Is., island 173/B2
Rennes, Fr., 212,494, (272,263 metro.) 88/B2
Rennie, Man., Can. 215/D4
Reno, Ill., U.S., 60 . . . . .266/D5
Reno, Kans., U.S., 50 . . . . .276/G2
Reno, Kans., U.S., county, 64,790 . . . . . . .276/D4
Reno, Minn., U.S. .298/F7
Reno, Nev., U.S., 180,480, (339,486 metro.) . .310/A2
Reno, (Lamar County), Tex., U.S., 2,767 . . .346/N2
Reno, (Parker County), Tex., U.S., 2,441 . .346/A9, L3
Renous, N.B., Can., 1,183 . . . . .217/D2
Renova, Miss., U.S., 623 . . . . .300/B2
Renovo, Penn., U.S., 1,318 . . . . .336/F3
Rensselaer, Ind., U.S., 5,294 . . . . .270/B3
Rensselaer, Mo., U.S., 145 . . . . .302/D2
Rensselaer, N.Y., U.S., 7,761 . . . . .320/P5
Rensselaer, N.Y., U.S., county, 152,538 . . .320/Q5
Rensselaer Falls, N.Y., U.S., 337 . . . . .320/L1
Rentiesville, Okla., U.S., 102 . . . . .330/G2
Renton, Wash., U.S., 50,052 . . . . .358/A4, C2
Rentz, Ga., U.S., 304 . . . . .260/F7
Renville, Minn., U.S., 1,323 . . . . .298/B6
Renville, Minn., U.S., county, 17,154 . . . . .298/C6
Renville, N. Dak., U.S., county, 2,610 . . . . .326/D1
Renwick, Eng., U.K. 66/C3
Renwick, Iowa, U.S., 306 . . . . .274/G2
Repaupo, N.J., U.S., 275 . . . . .314/C4
Repentigny, Que., Can., 54,550 . . . . .217/E1
Repton, Ala., U.S., 280 . . . . .238/B4
Repton, Ky., U.S., 80 . . . . .280/B3
Republic, Kans., U.S., 161 . . . . .276/E2
Republic, Kans., U.S., county, 5,835 . . . . . .276/E2
Republic, Mich., U.S., 614 . . . . .294/B3
Republic, Mo., U.S., 8,438 . . . . .302/C4
Republic, Ohio, U.S., 614 . . . . .328/D3
Republic, Penn., U.S., 1,396 . . . . .336/B6
Republic, Wash., U.S., 954 . . . . .358/G1
Republican, S. Fork, Kans., U.S., river 276/A2
Republican, Nebr., U.S., river 308/D3, F3
Republican, Nebr., U.S., 209 . . . . .308/E3
Repulse Bay, Nun., Can., 612 . . . . .220/L3
Requa, Calif., U.S., 100 . . . . .246/A1
Resaca, Ga., U.S., 815 . . . . .260/B2
Reserve, Sask., Can. 227/H8
Reserve, Kans., U.S., 100 . . . . .276/G2
Reserve, La., U.S., 9,111 . . . . .282/H6
Reserve, Mont., U.S. 306/M1
Reserve, N. Mex., U.S., 387 . . . . .317/B4
Resistencia, Arg., 229,212, (292,287 metro.) . .191/D2
Reşiţa, Rom., 92,776 . . . . .101/A3
Resolute, Can. .193/B14
Resolute, Nun., Can., 215 . . . . .220/J2
Resolution, Nun., Can., island 220/P4
Resolven, Wales, U.K., 2,274 . . . . .64/D4
Rest Haven, Ga., U.S., 151 . . . . .260/D3
Restigouche, N.B., Can., county 217/C1
Restigouche, N.B., Can., river 217/B1
Restigouche, Que., Can., river 226/J4
Reston, Man., Can. 215/A4
Reston, Va., U.S., 56,407 . . . . .354/J3, L2
Restoule, Ont., Can., 415 . . . . .223/F1
Retford, Eng., U.K. 66/G6
Retreat, Tex., U.S., 339 . . . . .346/M3
Retrop, Okla., U.S. 330/C2
Rettendon, Eng., U.K. 70/F3
Reubens, Ida., U.S., 72 . . . . .264/A3
Reus, Sp., 89,006 .94/G2
Reuss, Switz., river 90/C2
Reutlingen, Ger., 110,343 . . . . .86/B4
Reva, S. Dak., U.S. 342/B2
Revelstoke, Br. Col., Can., 7,500 . . . . .214/M6
Reventazón, C.R., river 203/C3
Revere, Mass., U.S., 47,283 . . . . .292/D7, K3
Revere, Minn., U.S., 100 . . . . .298/B6
Revere, Mo., U.S., 121 . . . . .302/E1
Revere, Wash., U.S. 358/H2
Revillagigedo, Mex., islands 200/B4
Revillo, S. Dak., U.S., 147 . . . . .342/J2
Rewa, Guy., river .183/B4
Rewe, Eng., U.K. 73/F3
Rewey, Wisc., U.S., 311 . . . . .364/C6
Rexburg, Ida., U.S., 17,257 . . . . .264/F6
Rexdale, Ont., Can. 223/J5
Rexford, Kans., U.S., 157 . . . . .276/B2
Rexford, Mont., U.S., 151 . . . . .306/A1
Rexton, N.B., Can., 810 . . . . .217/E2
Rexton, Mich., U.S., 70 . . . . .294/D3
Rexville, Ind., U.S., 175 . . . . .270/F7
Rey, Pan., island .203/C2
Reydon, Okla., U.S., 177 . . . . .330/C2
Reyes, Calif., U.S., point 246/B5
Reykjavík, Ice., capital, 111,345,
  (174,991 metro.) 79/A2
Reykjavík, Ice., capital, 111,345,
  (174,991 metro.) 193/C17
Reynella, S.A., Austl. . . . . .170/Inset II
Reyno, Ark., U.S., 484 . . . . .244/E1
Reynolds, Ga., U.S., 1,036 . . . . .260/C6
Reynolds, Ida., U.S., 100 . . . . .264/A6
Reynolds, Ill., U.S., 508 . . . . .266/C2
Reynolds, Ind., U.S., 547 . . . . .270/C3
Reynolds, Mo., U.S., 125 . . . . .302/E4
Reynolds, Mo., U.S., county, 6,689 . . . . . .302/E4
Reynolds, Nebr., U.S., 88 . . . . .308/G3
Reynolds, N. Dak., U.S., 350 . . . . .326/H2
Reynoldsburg, Ohio, U.S., 32,069 . . . .328/E6, E9
Reynoldsville, Ga., U.S., 175 . . . . .260/B1
Reynoldsville, Ky., U.S. 280/G2
Reynoldsville, Penn., U.S., 2,710 . . . . .336/D3
Reynosa, Mex., 403,718, (420,463 metro.) . .200/E2
Rēzekne, Lat. 82/D2
Reznas, Lat., lake .82/D2
Rhaetian Alps, Switz., mountains 90/D2
Rhame, N. Dak., U.S., 189 . . . . .326/B3
Rhandirmwyn, Wales, U.K. 64/D3

Rharsa, Tun., salt marsh 146/A2
Rhayader, Wales, U.K., 1,793 . . . . .64/E3
Rhea, Ark., U.S., 100 . . . . .244/A1
Rhea, Okla., U.S. .330/C2
Rhea, Tenn., U.S., county, 28,400 . . . . . . .344/M3
Rhea, Tex., U.S. 346/E10
Rheems, Penn., U.S., 1,557 . . . . .336/H5
Rheinhesen-Pfalz, Ger., department 86/A4
Rhems, S.C., U.S. .340/E3
Rhigos, Wales, U.K. 64/D4
Rhine, Ger., river 84/D3, E4
Rhine, Ger., river 86/A3, A4
Rhine, Ger., river 88/D2
Rhine, Liech., canal 90/B1, B2
Rhine, Liech., river 90/A1, A2
Rhine, Switz., river 90/C1, D2
Rhine, Ger., 422 .260/E8
Rhinebeck, N.Y., U.S., 3,077 . . . . .320/P7
Rhineland, Mo., U.S., 176 . . . . .302/D2
Rhineland, Tex., U.S., 190 . . . . .346/J2
Rhinelander, Wisc., U.S., 7,735 . . . . .364/D3
Rhineland-Palatinate, Ger., state 86/A4
Rhiw, Wales, U.K. 64/B2
Rhode Island, U.S., state 327
Rhode Island, R.I., U.S., sound 339/E5
Rhodell, W. Va., U.S., 234 . . . . .360/D5
Rhodes, Gr. 100/D3
Rhodes, Gr., island 100/D3
Rhodes, Iowa, U.S., 294 . . . . .274/H4
Rhodes, Mich., U.S., 125 . . . . .294/E6
Rhodesdale, Md., U.S., 70 . . . . .288/L5
Rhodhiss, N.C., U.S., 366 . . . . .322/C3
Rhododendron, (part of Mt. Hood Vil.),
  Oreg., U.S. 334/E2
Rhodope, Bul., mountains 101/C4
Rhome, Tex., U.S., 551 . . . . .346/A9
Rhondda, Wales, U.K. 60/B4
Rhondda, Wales, U.K., 59,947 . . . . .64/E4
Rhondda, Cynon, Taff, Wales, U.K.,
  unitary authority, 231,952 . . . . .64/E4
Rhône, Fr., department 88/D4
Rhône, Fr., river 88/D3, D4
Rhône, Switz., river 90/B2
Rhône-Alpes, Fr., region 88/D4
Rhoose, Wales, U.K. 64/E5
Rhos, Wales, U.K. .64/C1
Rhosgoch, Wales, U.K. 64/C1
Rhosllanerch-rugog, Wales, U.K., 12,879 . . .64/E1
Rhosneigr, Wales, U.K. 64/B1
Rhossili, Wales, U.K. 64/C4
Rhuddlan, Wales, U.K., 3,182 . . . . .64/E1
Rhum, Scot., U.K., island 60/A1
Rhum, Scot., U.K., island 62/D5
Rhydcymerau, Wales, U.K. 64/C3
Rhyd-Ddu, Wales, U.K. 64/C1
Rhydowen, Wales, U.K. 64/C3
Rhydymain, Wales, U.K. 64/D2
Rhyl, Wales, U.K., 24,909 . . . . .64/E1
Rhymney, Wales, U.K., 7,991 . . . . .64/E4
Rhynie, Scot., U.K. 62/L4
Riaba, Eq. Gui. 154/A1
Rialto, Calif., U.S., 91,873 . . . . .246/H8
Riau, Indon., province 122/B1
Ribe, Den. 79/B3
Ribe, Den., county .79/B3
Ribeira Brava, C.V. 148/B2
Ribeira Grande, C.V. 148/A1
Ribeirão Pires, Braz. . . . . .188/Inset II
Ribeirão Prêto, Braz., 504,923 . . . . .188/D4
Ribera, N. Mex., U.S., 125 . . . . .317/E2
Riberalta, Bol. 186/A2
Rib Falls, Wisc., U.S. 364/D4
Rib Lake, Wisc., U.S., 878 . . . . .364/C3
Ribnita, Mol. 102/B2
Ricardo, Tex., U.S., 450 . . . . .346/L8
Riccall, Eng., U.K., 1,949 . . . . .66/F5
Riccall, Eng., U.K., 1,949 . . . . .68/E2
Rice, Ont., Can., lake 223/G3
Rice, Calif., U.S. 246/L8
Rice, Kans., U.S. .276/E2
Rice, Kans., U.S., county, 10,761 . . . . .276/D3
Rice, Minn., U.S., 711 . . . . .298/C5
Rice, Minn., U.S., county, 56,665 . . . . .298/D6
Rice, Tex., U.S., 798 . . . . .346/M3
Rice, Va., U.S., 250 . . . . .354/G6
Rice, Wash., U.S., 70 . . . . .358/G1
Riceboro, Ga., U.S., 736 . . . . .260/J8
Rice City, R.I., U.S., 425 . . . . .339/B3
Rice Hill, Oreg., U.S., 150 . . . . .334/C4
Rice Lake, Wisc., U.S., 8,320 . . . . .364/B3
Rice Lake N.W.R., Minn., U.S. 298/D4
Rices Landing, Penn., U.S., 443 . . . . .336/A6
Riceville, Iowa, U.S., 840 . . . . .274/J1
Riceville, Ky., U.S. 280/H3
Riceville, Penn., U.S., 82 . . . . .336/B2
Riceville, Tenn., U.S., 650 . . . . .344/M4
Rich, Miss., U.S., 60 . . . . .300/B1
Rich, Utah, U.S., county, 1,961 . . . . .350/C2
Richard, Sask., Can., lake 227/C1
Richards, Mo., U.S., 95 . . . . .302/B4
Richards, Tex., U.S., 275 . . . . .346/N5
Richards Bay, S. Afr. 162/D2
Richards Landing, Ont., Can. 223/A1
Richardson, Alta., Can., river 212/E2
Richardson, Yukon, Can., mountains 228/B1
Richardson, Maine, U.S., lakes 286/B4
Richardson, Nebr., U.S., county, 9,531 . . .308/J3
Richardson, Tex., U.S., 91,802 . . . . .346/C9
Richardson, Wash., U.S. 358/C1
Richards Spur, Okla., U.S., 200 . . . . .330/D3
Richardsville, Ky., U.S., 425 . . . . .280/D3
Richard Toll, Sen. 148/B1
Richardton, N. Dak., U.S., 619 . . . . .326/C3
Richboro, Penn., U.S., 6,678 . . . . .336/M6
Richburg, N.Y., U.S., 448 . . . . .320/E6
Richburg, S.C., U.S., 332 . . . . .340/C2
Rich Creek, Va., U.S., 665 . . . . .354/B6
Richelieu, Que., Can., river 226/C6
Richer, Man., Can. 215/C4
Richey, Mont., U.S., 189 . . . . .306/L2
Richfield, Ida., U.S., 412 . . . . .264/C6
Richfield, Kans., U.S., 48 . . . . .276/A4
Richfield, Minn., U.S., 34,439 . . . . .298/E6
Richfield, N.C., U.S., 515 . . . . .322/E4
Richfield, Ohio, U.S., 3,286 . . . . .328/H10
Richfield, Penn., U.S., 459 . . . . .336/G4
Richfield, Utah, U.S., 6,847 . . . . .350/D4
Richfield, Wisc., U.S., 500 . . . . .364/F1
Richfield Sprs., N.Y., U.S., 1,255 . . . . .320/M5
Richford, N.Y., U.S., 225 . . . . .320/J6
Richford, Vt., U.S., 2,321 . . . . .352/B1
Richford, Wisc., U.S., 40 . . . . .364/D4
Rich Fountain, Mo., U.S., 90 . . . . .302/E3
Rich Hill, Mo., U.S., 1,461 . . . . .302/B3
Richibucto, N.B., Can., 1,341 . . . . .217/E2
Richill, Eng., U.K. .73/H1
Rich Hill, N. Ire., U.K. 65/D3
Richland, Ga., U.S., 1,794 . . . . .260/B7
Richland, Ill., U.S., county, 16,149 . . . . . . .266/E5
Richland, Iowa, U.S., 587 . . . . .274/K5

Richland, Kans., U.S. 276/G3
Richland, La., U.S., parish, 20,981 . . . . . . .282/F2
Richland, Mich., U.S., 593 . . . . .294/D7
Richland, Miss., U.S., 6,027 . . . . .300/C4
Richland, Mo., U.S., 1,805 . . . . .302/D4
Richland, Mont., U.S. 306/K1
Richland, Mont., U.S., county, 9,667 . . . . .306/M2
Richland, Nebr., U.S., 89 . . . . .308/G2
Richland, N.J., U.S., 750 . . . . .314/D5
Richland, N. Dak., U.S., county, 17,998 . . .326/J3
Richland, Ohio, U.S., county, 128,852 . . . .328/E4
Richland, Oreg., U.S., 147 . . . . .334/J3
Richland, Penn., U.S., 1,508 . . . . .336/J5
Richland, S.C., U.S., county, 320,677 . .340/A3, D3
Richland, S. Dak., U.S., 80 . . . . .342/J5
Richland, Tex., U.S., 291 . . . . .346/M4
Richland, Wash., U.S., 38,708, (191,822 metro.) . .358/F3
Richland, Wisc., U.S., county, 17,924 . . . . .364/C5
Richland Ctr., Wisc., U.S., 5,114 . . . . .364/C5
Richland Hills, Tex., U.S., 8,132 . . . . .346/B9
Richlands, N.C., U.S., 928 . . . . .322/K5
Richlands, Va., U.S., 4,144 . . . . .354/E2
Richland Sprs., Tex., U.S., 350 . . . . .346/K4
Richlandtown, Penn., U.S., 1,283 . . . . .336/L5
Richmond, Br. Col., Can., 164,345 . . . . . . .214/L6
Richmond, Ont., Can., county 221/G2
Richmond, P.E.I., Can. 224/B2
Richmond, Que., Can., 3,424 . . . . .226/D6
Richmond, (Richmond upon Thames),
  Eng., U.K., 160,732 . . . . .70/D4
Richmond, Eng., U.K., 7,862 . . . . .66/E4
Richmond, Ark., U.S., 60 . . . . .244/A4
Richmond, Calif., U.S., 99,216 . . . . .246/J1
Richmond, Ga., U.S., county, 199,775 . . . .260/G5
Richmond, Ill., U.S., 1,091 . . . . .266/A4
Richmond, Ind., U.S., 39,124 . . . . .270/F5
Richmond, Kans., U.S., 510 . . . . .276/G3
Richmond, Ky., U.S., 27,152 . . . . .280/F3
Richmond, La., U.S., 499 . . . . .282/G2
Richmond, Maine, U.S., 3,298 . . . . .286/C4
Richmond, Mass., U.S., 1,604 . . . . .292/A3
Richmond, Mich., U.S., 4,897 . . . . .294/C6, G7
Richmond, Minn., U.S., 1,213 . . . . .298/C5
Richmond, Mo., U.S., 5,616 . . . . .302/C2
Richmond, N.H., U.S., 1,077 . . . . .312/B6
Richmond, N.Y., U.S., county, 443,728 . . . .320/A3
Richmond, N.C., U.S., county, 46,564 . . . .322/F4
Richmond, Ohio, U.S., 471 . . . . .328/J5
Richmond, Tex., U.S., 11,081 . . . . . . .346/A7, N6
Richmond, Utah, U.S., 2,051 . . . . .350/C2
Richmond, Vt., U.S., 4,090 . . . . .352/B2
Richmond, Va., U.S., state capital, 197,790,
  (996,512 metro.) 354/J5
Richmond Dale, Ohio, U.S., 500 . . . . .328/E7
Richmond Hts., Fla., U.S., 8,479 . . . . .256/A7
Richmond Hts., Mo., U.S., 9,602 . . . . .302/H3
Richmond Hts., Ohio, U.S., 10,944 . . . . . .328/H8
Richmond Hill, Ont., Can., 132,030 . . .223/F4, K5
Richmond Hill, Ga., U.S., 6,959 . . . . .260/J8
Richmond N.B.P., Va., U.S. 343/J6
Richmond Park, Alta., Can. 212/D4
Richmond Upon Thames, Eng., U.K.,
  unitary authority, 172,327 . . . . .70/D4
Richmondville, N.Y., U.S., 786 . . . . .320/M5
Rich Pond, Ky., U.S., 425 . . . . .280/D4
Rich Square, N.C., U.S., 931 . . . . .322/L2
Richton, Miss., U.S., 1,038 . . . . .300/D4
Richton Park, Ill., U.S., 12,533 . . . . .266/B6
Rich Valley, Alta., Can. 212/C4
Richview, Ill., U.S., 308 . . . . .266/D5
Richville, Minn., U.S., 124 . . . . .298/B4
Richville, N.Y., U.S., 274 . . . . .320/L2
Richwood, La., U.S., 2,115 . . . . .282/E2
Richwood, Minn., U.S., 100 . . . . .298/B4
Richwood, Ohio, U.S., 2,156 . . . . .328/D5
Richwood, W. Va., U.S., 2,477 . . . . .360/E4
Richwoods, Mo., U.S., 225 . . . . .302/F3
Rickardsville, Iowa, U.S., 191 . . . . .274/N4
Ricketts, Iowa, U.S., 144 . . . . .274/C3
Ricketts Glen St. Park, Penn., U.S. 336/J3
Rickman, Tenn., U.S., 475 . . . . .344/L2
Rickmansworth, Eng., U.K., 10,767 . . . . . . .70/D3
Rico, Colo., U.S., 205 . . . . .250/B4
Ricobayo, Sp., reservoir 94/D2
Rida, Yemen 137/A2
Riddle, Ida., U.S. .264/A7
Riddle, Oreg., U.S., 1,014 . . . . .334/C4
Riddlesburg, Penn., U.S., 100 . . . . .336/E5
Riddleville, Ga., U.S., 124 . . . . .260/F6
Rideau, Ont., Can., lake 223/J3
Rideau, Ont., Can., river 223/H3
Rideau, Ont., Can., river 320/K1
Riderwood, Ala., U.S., 40 . . . . .238/A3
Ridge, Md., U.S., 400 . . . . .288/J7
Ridge, Mont., U.S. 306/L4
Ridgebury, Conn., U.S., 1,200 . . . . .253/A4
Ridgecrest, Calif., U.S., 24,927 . . . . .246/H7
Ridge Farm, Ill., U.S., 912 . . . . .266/F4
Ridgefield, Conn., U.S., 23,643 . . . . .253/B4
Ridgefield, Ill., U.S., 325 . . . . .266/A4
Ridgefield, N.J., U.S., 10,830 . . . . .314/C2
Ridgefield, Wash., U.S., 2,147 . . . . .358/B4
Ridgefield Park, N.J., U.S., 12,873 . . . .314/B2, J2
Ridgeland, Miss., U.S., 20,173 . . . . .300/B3
Ridgeland, S.C., U.S., 2,518 . . . . .340/C4
Ridgeley, W. Va., U.S., 265 . . . . .364/J9
Ridgely, W. Va., U.S., 762 . . . . .360/J1
Ridgely, Md., U.S., 1,352 . . . . .288/L4
Ridgely, Mo., U.S., 64 . . . . .302/B2
Ridgely, Tenn., U.S., 1,667 . . . . .344/C2
Ridge Manor, Fla., U.S., 4,108 . . . . .256/F3
Ridge Spr., S.C., U.S., 823 . . . . .340/C3
Ridgetop, Tenn., U.S., 1,083 . . . . .344/H2
Ridgeview, S. Dak., U.S. 342/E2
Ridgeview, W. Va., U.S., 375 . . . . .360/C4
Ridgeville, Ala., U.S., 158 . . . . .238/C1
Ridgeville, Ind., U.S., 843 . . . . .270/F4
Ridgeville, S.C., U.S., 1,690 . . . . .340/D3
Ridgeway, Iowa, U.S., 293 . . . . .274/L1
Ridgeway, Mo., U.S., 530 . . . . .302/C1
Ridgeway, Ohio, U.S., 354 . . . . .328/C4
Ridgeway, S.C., U.S., 328 . . . . .340/D2
Ridgeway, Va., U.S., 775 . . . . .354/E7
Ridgeway, Wisc., U.S., 689 . . . . .364/D5
Ridgewood, N.J., U.S. 70/E5
Ridgewood, N.J., U.S., 24,936 . . . . . . .314/B1, J1
Ridgway, Colo., U.S., 713 . . . . .250/C3
Ridgway, Ill., U.S., 928 . . . . .266/E6
Ridgway, Penn., U.S., 4,591 . . . . .336/D3
Riding Mill, Eng., U.K. 66/E3
Riding Mtn. Natl. Park, Man., Can. 215/A4, C2
Ridley Park, Penn., U.S., 7,196 . . . . .336/L7
Ridott, Ill., U.S., 159 . . . . .266/C1
Ridsdale, Eng., U.K. 66/D2
Riegelsville, N.J., U.S. 314/C2
Riegelsville, Penn., U.S., 863 . . . . .336/L4
Rienzi, Miss., U.S., 330 . . . . .300/D1
Riesa, Ger. 86/C3

Rieth, Oreg., U.S., 90 . . . . .334/H2
Rieti, It. 95/C2
Riffe, Wash., U.S., lake 358/C3
Rifle, Colo., U.S., 6,784 . . . . .250/C2
Rift Valley, Kenya, province 157/D3
Riga, Est., gulf 81/B3
Riga, Fin., gulf 80/D3
Riga, Lat., capital, 792,508 . . . . . . .82/C2
Riga, Lat., gulf 82/B2
Rigby, Ida., U.S., 2,998 . . . . .264/F6
Rigestan, Afg., region 129/A2
Rigg, Scot., U.K. 62/K9
Riggins, Ida., U.S., 410 . . . . .264/A4
Rigolet, Nfld., Can., 317 . . . . .218/B2
Rigside, Scot., U.K., 741 . . . . .62/J7
Riiser-Larsen, Antar., peninsula 192/C16
Riiser-Larsen Ice Shelf, Antar., glacier . . .292/B14
Rijeka, Cro., 143,800 . . . . .98/B2
Rila, Bul., mountains 101/B3
Riley, Ind., U.S., 160 . . . . .270/B6
Riley, Kans., U.S., 886 . . . . .276/F2
Riley, Kans., U.S., county, 62,843 . . .276/F2
Riley, Ky., U.S., 175 . . . . .280/E3
Riley, Maine, U.S., 375 . . . . .286/B4
Riley, Oreg., U.S., 50 . . . . .334/G4
Riley Brook, N.B., Can., 78 . . . . .217/B1
Rileyville, Va., U.S., 275 . . . . .354/G3
Rillington, Eng., U.K. 68/F1
Rillito, Ariz., U.S., 275 . . . . .242/D5
Rimbey, Alta., Can., 2,118 . . . . .212/C5
Rimersburg, Penn., U.S., 1,051 . . . . .336/B3
Rimington, Eng., U.K. 68/C2
Rimini, It. .95/C1
Rimini, S.C., U.S., 200 . . . . .340/D3
Rîmnicu Vîlcea, Rom., 119,249 . . . . .101/C3
Rimouski, Que., Can., 31,305 . . . . . .225/C4
Rimouski, Que., Can., 31,305 . . . . . .226/H3
Rimouski Prov. Reserve, Que., Can. . .226/H3
Rimrock, Wash., U.S. 358/D3
Rimrock, Wash., U.S., lake 358/D3
Rinard, Ill., U.S., 100 . . . . .266/E5
Rinard, Iowa, U.S., 72 . . . . .274/F3
Rincón, P.R. 206/A2
Rincón, P.R., bay 206/C3
Rincon, Ga., U.S., 4,376 . . . . .260/J7
Rincon, N. Mex., U.S., 220 . . . . .317/C5
Rincón del Bonete, Uru., lake 187/B2
Rinda, Tenn., U.S. 344/F3
Rindal, Minn., U.S., 40 . . . . .298/A3
Rindge, N.H., U.S., 5,451 . . . . .312/B6
Riner, Va., U.S., 300 . . . . .354/C6
Riner, Wyo., U.S. 366/C3
Rineyville, Ky., U.S., 550 . . . . .280/E3
Ringgold, Ga., U.S., 2,422 . . . . .260/A2
Ringgold, Iowa, U.S., county, 5,469 . .274/F6
Ringgold, La., U.S., 1,660 . . . . .282/C2
Ringgold, Nebr., U.S. 308/D2
Ringgold, Tex., U.S., 225 . . . . .346/K2
Ringkøbing, Den. 79/B2
Ringkøbing, Den., county 79/B2
Ringling, Mont., U.S. 306/F3
Ringling, Okla., U.S., 1,135 . . . . .330/E3
Ringmer, Eng., U.K., 3,119 . . . . .70/E5
Ringoes, N.J., U.S., 1,100 . . . . .314/D3
Ringold, Okla., U.S. 330/G3
Ring's End, Eng., U.K. 70/E1
Ringsend, N. Ire., U.K. 65/D1
Ringsted, Iowa, U.S., 436 . . . . .274/E1
Ringtown, Penn., U.S., 826 . . . . .336/J4
Ringville, Mass., U.S., 100 . . . . .292/C3
Ringwood, Vic., Austl. . . . . .170/Inset V
Ringwood, Eng., U.K., 11,959 . . . . . .73/J3
Ringwood, Ill., U.S., 471 . . . . .266/A4
Ringwood, N.J., U.S., 12,396 . . . . . . .314/E1
Ringwood, Okla., U.S., 424 . . . . .330/D1
Ringwood St. Park, N.J., U.S. 314/B1, E1
Rio, Fla., U.S., 1,028 . . . . .256/A3
Rio, Ill., U.S., 240 . . . . .266/C2
Rio, W. Va., U.S., 90 . . . . .360/J2
Rio, Wisc., U.S., 938 . . . . .364/D5
Río Abajo Forest Reserve, P.R. 206/B2
Rio Arriba, N. Mex., U.S., county, 41,190 . .317/C1
Riobamba, Ecua., 94,505 . . . . .185/B3
Rio Blanco, Nicar. 202/E2
Rio Blanco, Colo., U.S. 250/C2
Rio Blanco, Colo., U.S., county, 5,986 . .250/B2
Rio Branco, Braz., 87,462, (196,923 metro.) . .188/B2
Rio Bravo, Tex., U.S., 5,553 . . . . .346/J8
Río Camuy Cave Park, P.R. 206/B2
Rio Casas Grandes, Mex., river 346/A4
Río Claro, Trin.-To. 209/A2
Rio Communities, N. Mex., U.S., 4,213 . .317/D3
Rio Conchos, Mex., river 346/D6
Rio Creek, Wisc., U.S., 150 . . . . .364/F4
Rio Cuarto, Arg., 134,355, (138,853 metro.) . .191/C3
Rio de Janeiro, Braz., 5,850,544,
 (10,611,610 metro.) . . . . .188/D4, Inset I
Rio de Janeiro, Braz., state . . . . . .188/D4, Inset I
Río Dell, Calif., U.S., 3,174 . . . . .246/A2
Rio del Mar, Calif., U.S., 9,198 . . . . .246/K4
Rio Frio, Tex., U.S., 100 . . . . .346/J6
Río Gallegos, Arg. 191/B7
Rio Grande, Braz., 124,706, (172,435 metro.) . .188/C5
Rio Grande, (Río Bravo), Mex., river . .200/D2
Río Grande, Nicar. 202/A2
Río Grande, P.R. 206/D2
Rio Grande, Colo., U.S., county, 12,413 . .250/D4
Rio Grande, Colo., U.S., river 250/E4
Rio Grande, N.J., U.S., 2,444 . . . . . . .314/D5
Rio Grande, Ohio, U.S., 915 . . . . . . .328/F8
Rio Grande, Tex., U.S., river 346/D5, G6
Rio Grande City, Tex., U.S., 11,923 . . .346/K9
Rio Grande do Norte, Braz., state . . .188/E2
Rio Grande do Sul, Braz., state 188/C5
Rio Grande Natl. For., Colo., U.S. . . .250/D4, E4
Rio Grande Vil., Tex., U.S., 250 . . . . .346/F6
Ríohacha, Col., 115,000 . . . . .184/B2
Rio Hondo, N. Mex., U.S., river 317/F4
Rio Linda, Calif., U.S., 10,466 . . . . . .246/K5
Riomedina, Tex., U.S. 346/K6
Río Negro, Arg., province 191/B5
Río Negro, Uru., department 187/B2
Rioni, Geo., river 103/B3
Rio Puerco, N. Mex., U.S., river 317/C2
Rio Rancho, N. Mex., U.S., 51,765 . . .317/D2
Rio Rico, Ariz., U.S., 3,164 . . . . .242/E6
Ríos, Tex., U.S., 40 . . . . .346/K8
Rio Salado, Mex., river 346/H8
Río San Juan, Nicar., department . . .202/B3
Riou, Sask., Can., lake 188/C3
Rio Verde, Braz. 188/C3
Rio Vista, Calif., U.S., 4,571 . . . . . . .246/L1
Rio Vista, Tex., U.S., 656 . . . . .346/L3
Ripley, (Derbyshire), Eng., U.K., 18,310 . .70/B1
Ripley, (Surrey), Eng., U.K. 70/D4
Ripley, Eng., U.K., 18,310 . . . . .68/E3
Ripley, Calif., U.S., 650 . . . . .246/L9
Ripley, Ill., U.S., 103 . . . . .266/C3
Ripley, Ind., U.S., county, 26,523 . . . .270/F6
Ripley, Maine, U.S., 452 . . . . .286/C3

Ripley, Miss., U.S., 5,478 . . . . .300/D1
Ripley, Mo., U.S., county, 13,509 . . . .302/F5
Ripley, N.Y., U.S., 1,030 . . . . .320/B6
Ripley, Ohio, U.S., 1,745 . . . . .328/C8
Ripley, Okla., U.S., 444 . . . . .330/F1
Ripley, Tenn., U.S., 7,844 . . . . .344/B3
Ripley, W. Va., U.S., 3,263 . . . . .360/C3
Riplinger, Wisc., U.S., 125 . . . . .364/C4
Ripon, Eng., U.K., 13,806 . . . . .66/E4
Ripon, Eng., U.K., 13,806 . . . . .68/D1
Ripon, Calif., U.S., 10,146 . . . . .246/D5
Ripon, Wisc., U.S., 6,828 . . . . .364/E5
Rippey, Iowa, U.S., 319 . . . . .274/F4
Rippingale, Eng., U.K. 70/D1
Rippon, W. Va., U.S., 200 . . . . .360/L2
Rippon, Eng., U.K., 2,855 . . . . .66/E5
Ripponden, Eng., U.K., 2,855 . . . . . .68/D2
Ripton, Vt., U.S., 556 . . . . .352/A3
Ririe, Ida., U.S., 545 . . . . .264/F6
Risaralda, Col., department 184/B3
Risby, Eng., U.K. 70/F2
Risca, Wales, U.K., 15,124 . . . . .64/E4
Rişcani, Mol. 102/A2
Risco, Mo., U.S., 392 . . . . .302/G5
Riseley, Eng., U.K. 70/C4
Rishangles, Eng., U.K. 70/F4
Rishiri, Jap., island . . . . .114/Inset I
Rishra, India . . . . .128/Inset II
Rising City, Nebr., U.S., 386 . . . . . . .308/G2
Risingdale, Mass., U.S., 225 . . . . . . .292/A4
Rising Fawn, Ga., U.S., 200 . . . . . . .260/A2
Rising Star, Tex., U.S., 835 . . . . .346/K3
Rising Sun, (Rising Sun-Lebanon),
 Del., U.S., 2,458 . . . . .255/B4
Rising Sun, Ind., U.S., 2,470 . . . . . . .270/G7
Rising Sun, Md., U.S., 1,702 . . . . . . .288/K1
Risingsun, Ohio, U.S., 620 . . . . .328/D3
Riske Creek, Br. Col., Can. 214/L5
Rison, Ark., U.S., 1,271 . . . . .244/C4
Rita Blanca, Tex., U.S., creek 346/E8
Ritchey, Mo., U.S., 76 . . . . .302/B5
Ritchie, Ky., U.S. 280/C3
Ritchie, W. Va., U.S., county, 10,343 . .360/D2
Ritchies, India, archipelago 128/F6
Ritter, Calif., U.S., mountain 246/F5
Ritter, Nev., U.S., mountain 310/A3
Ritter, Oreg., U.S. 334/G3
Ritter, S.C., U.S., 500 . . . . .340/D4
Rittman, Ohio, U.S., 6,314 . . . . .328/G4
Ritzville, Wash., U.S., 1,736 . . . . . . .358/G2
Riva, Md., U.S., 3,966 . . . . .288/H4
Rivas, Nicar. 202/B3
Rivenhall End, Eng., U.K. 70/F3
Rivera, Uru., 62,859 . . . . .187/C1
Rivera, Uru., department 187/C1
Riverbank, Calif., U.S., 15,826 . . . . . .246/E5
River Bend, Mo., U.S. 302/J5
River Bend, N.C., U.S., 2,923 . . . . . .322/L4
River Bluff, Ky., U.S., 402 . . . . .280/E2
River Cess, Liber. 149/B3
Rivercrest, Man., Can. 215/C4
Riverdale, Calif., U.S., 2,416 . . . . . . .246/F6
Riverdale, Ga., U.S., 12,478 . . . . .260/C4, H3
Riverdale, Ill., U.S., 15,055 . . . . .266/C6
Riverdale, Iowa, U.S., 656 . . . . .274/P4
Riverdale, Kans., U.S., 60 . . . . .276/E4
Riverdale, Md., U.S., 6,690 . . . . .288/C6
Riverdale, Nebr., U.S., 213 . . . . .308/E3
Riverdale, N.J., U.S., 2,498 . . . . .314/A1, E2
Riverdale, N. Dak., U.S., 273 . . . . . . .326/D2
Riverdale, Utah, U.S., 7,656 . . . . .350/C2, E1
Riverdale Hts., (East Riverdale), Md., U.S. . .288/C6
River de Chute, N.B., Can. 217/B2
River Edge, N.J., U.S., 10,946 . . . . . .314/B2
River Falls, Ala., U.S., 616 . . . . .238/C4
River Falls, Wisc., U.S., 12,560 . . . . .364/A4
River Forest, Ill., U.S., 11,635 . . . . . .266/B6
River Forest, Ind., U.S. 270/E4
River Grove, Ill., U.S., 10,668 . . . . . .266/B5
Rivergrove, Oreg., U.S., 324 . . . . . . .334/A3
Riverhead, N.Y., U.S., 10,513 . . . . . .320/F1
River Hts., Utah, U.S., 1,496 . . . . . . .350/C2
River Hills, Man., Can. 215/C4
River Hills, Wisc., U.S., 1,631 . . . . . .364/F1
Riverhurst, Sask., Can., 143 . . . . . .227/O10
River John, N.S., Can. 221/D2
Riverlea, Ohio, U.S., 499 . . . . .328/D9
River Oaks, Tex., U.S., 6,985 . . . . . . .346/A9
River Pines, Calif., U.S., 400 . . . . . . .246/D4
River Ridge, La., U.S., 14,588 . . . . .282/J3, J6
River Road, Oreg., U.S. 334/C3
River Rouge, Mich., U.S., 9,917 . . . . .294/B7
Rivers, Man., Can., 1,119 . . . . .215/A4
Rivers, Nig., state 152/D5
Riverside, Ala., U.S., 1,564 . . . . .238/C2
Riverside, Ark., U.S., 40 . . . . .244/D2
Riverside, Calif., U.S., 255,166 . . . . .246/H9
Riverside, Calif., U.S., county, 1,545,387 . .246/F1, H9
Riverside, Ga., U.S., 57 . . . . .260/D9
Riverside, Ill., U.S., 8,895 . . . . .266/B6
Riverside, Iowa, U.S., 928 . . . . .274/L5
Riverside, Maine, U.S., 250 . . . . .286/C4
Riverside, Mo., U.S., 2,979 . . . . .302/H5
Riverside, N.J., U.S., 7,911 . . . . .314/D3
Riverside, (Eddy County), N. Mex., U.S., 40 . .317/F5
Riverside, (Lincoln County), N. Mex., U.S. . .317/E4
Riverside, (Steuben County), N.Y., U.S., 594 . .320/G6
Riverside, (Suffolk County), N.Y., U.S., 2,875 . .320/F2
Riverside, Ohio, U.S., 23,545 . . . . . . .328/G2
Riverside, Oreg., U.S. 334/H4
Riverside, Penn., U.S., 1,861 . . . . . . .336/H5
Riverside, R.I., U.S. 339/D3
Riverside, Tex., U.S., 425 . . . . .346/N5
Riverside, Wash., U.S., 348 . . . . . . .358/F1
Riverside, Wyo., U.S., 59 . . . . .366/C3
Riverside-Albert, N.B., Can., 393 . . . .217/E3
Rivers Inlet, Br. Col., Can. 214/J5
River Sioux, Iowa, U.S., 90 . . . . .274/B4
Riverton, Man., Can., 594 . . . . .215/C3
Riverton, Conn., U.S., 225 . . . . .253/C2
Riverton, Ill., U.S., 3,048 . . . . .266/D4
Riverton, Iowa, U.S., 304 . . . . .274/C6
Riverton, Kans., U.S., 850 . . . . .276/H4
Riverton, La., U.S., 40 . . . . .282/C2
Riverton, Minn., U.S., 115 . . . . .298/C4
Riverton, Mo., U.S. 302/E5
Riverton, Nebr., U.S., 145 . . . . .308/E3
Riverton, N.J., U.S., 2,759 . . . . .314/C3
Riverton, Oreg., U.S., 50 . . . . .334/B4
Riverton, Utah, U.S., 25,011 . . . .350/C3, E2
Riverton, W. Va., U.S., 80 . . . . .360/H3
Riverton, Wyo., U.S., 9,310 . . . . .366/C3
Riverton Hts., Wash., U.S. 358/A4
Rivervale, Ark., U.S., 80 . . . . .244/E2
River Vale, N.J., U.S., 9,449 . . . . . . .314/B1
Riverview, N.B., Can., 17,010 . . . . . .217/E2
Riverview, Ala., U.S., 99 . . . . .238/B4
Riverview, Fla., U.S., 12,035 . . . .256/D6, F4
Riverview, Mich., U.S., 13,272 . . . .294/B7, F7
Riverview, Mo., U.S., 3,146 . . . . .302/J2
Riverview, Wyo., U.S. 366/D2

Riverwood, Ky., U.S., 469 . . . . .280/A2
Riverwoods, Ill., U.S., 3,843 . . . . . . .266/B5
Rives, Mo., U.S., 88 . . . . .302/F5
Rives, Tenn., U.S., 331 . . . . .344/C2
Rives Jct., Mich., U.S., 650 . . . . .294/E7
Rivesville, W. Va., U.S., 913 . . . . . . .360/F1
Riviera, Tex., U.S., 550 . . . . .346/L6
Riviera Beach, Fla., U.S., 29,884 . .256/B4, H5
Riviera Beach, Md., U.S., 12,695 . . . .288/H3
Riviera Beach, Tex., U.S. 346/L8
Rivière-à-Pierre, Que., Can. 226/D4
Rivière-au-Renard, Que., Can. 226/M3
Rivière-aux-Rats, Que., Can. 226/D4
Rivière-Bleue, Que., Can. 226/G4
Rivière-du-Loup, Que., Can., 17,772 . .225/C4
Rivière-du-Loup, Que., Can., 17,772 . .226/G4
Rivière-du-Portage, N.B., Can. 217/E1
Rivière du Rempart, Mauritius 163/C2
Rivière-Matawin, Que., Can. 226/D5
Rivière Noire, Mauritius, mountain . . .163/B3
Rivière-Ste-Marguerite, Que., Can. . . .226/G3
Rivière-Verte, N.B., Can., 856 . . . . . .217/A1
Rivne, Ukr., 244,357 . . . . .102/B1
Rivne, Ukr., oblast 102/B1
Rixeyville, Va., U.S., 50 . . . . .354/H3
Rixford, Penn., U.S., 250 . . . . .336/D2
Riyadh, Sa. Arab., capital, 2,776,096 . .136/B2
Riyadh, Sa. Arab., emirate 136/B2
Riyaq, Leb. 134/B2
Rize, Tur. .133/E2
Rize, Tur., province 133/E2
R.L. Harris, Ala., U.S., reservoir 238/C2
Roachdale, Ind., U.S., 975 . . . . .270/C5
Roachill, Eng., U.K. 73/E3
Roade, Eng., U.K., 2,239 . . . . .68/F5
Roade, Eng., U.K., 2,239 . . . . .70/C2
Roadford, Eng., U.K., reservoir 73/D3
Roads, Ohio, U.S., 225 . . . . .328/E7
Roadstown, N.J., U.S., 175 . . . . .314/C5
Road Town, British Vir. Is., capital . . .204/F4
Roaming Shores, Ohio, U.S., 1,239 . . .328/J2
Roan, Colo., U.S., plateau 250/B2
Roane, N.C., U.S., mountain 322/K2
Roane, Tenn., U.S., county, 51,910 . . .344/M3
Roane, W. Va., U.S., county, 15,446 . .360/D3
Roan Fell, Eng., U.K., hill 66/C2
Roan Mountain, Tenn., U.S., 1,160 . . .344/S2
Roann, Ind., U.S., 400 . . . . .270/E3
Roanne, Fr. 88/D3
Roanoke, Ala., U.S., 6,563 . . . . .238/D2
Roanoke, Ill., U.S., 1,994 . . . . .266/D3
Roanoke, Ind., U.S., 1,495 . . . . .270/F3
Roanoke, N.C., U.S., river 322/K2
Roanoke, Va., U.S., 94,911, (235,932 metro.) . .354/D6
Roanoke, Va., U.S., county, 85,778 . . .354/C6
Roanoke Rapids, N.C., U.S., 16,957 . .322/K2
Roanoke River NWR., N.C., U.S. . . .322/L3, M3
Roaring Gap, N.C., U.S. 322/D2
Roaring Spr., Penn., U.S., 2,418 . . . . .336/E5
Roaring Spr., Tex., U.S., 265 . . . . . . .346/H2
Roatán, Hond. 202/B1
Roatán, Hond., island 202/B1
Robards, Ky., U.S., 564 . . . . .280/C3
Robb, Alta., Can., 183 . . . . .212/B4
Robbin, Minn., U.S., 40 . . . . .298/A2
Robbins, Calif., U.S., 325 . . . . .246/K5
Robbins, Ill., U.S., 6,635 . . . . .266/B6
Robbins, N.C., U.S., 1,195 . . . . .322/F4
Robbins, Tenn., U.S., 500 . . . . .344/M2
Robbins, Tex., U.S., 60 . . . . .346/M4
Robbinsdale, Minn., U.S., 14,123 . . . .298/E5
Robbinston, Maine, U.S., 525 . . . . . . .286/E3
Robbinsville, N.J., U.S., 1,900 . . . . . .314/D3
Robbinsville, N.C., U.S., 747 . . . . . . .322/C8
Robbs, Ill., U.S., 60 . . . . .266/E6
Robe, Wash., U.S., 125 . . . . .358/D1
Robeline, La., U.S., 183 . . . . .282/C3
Robersonville, N.C., U.S., 1,731 . . . . .322/L3
Robert, La., U.S., 375 . . . . .282/J5
Roberta, Ga., U.S., 808 . . . . .260/C6
Robert Lee, Tex., U.S., 1,171 . . . . . .346/H4
Roberts, Ida., U.S., 647 . . . . .264/E6
Roberts, Ill., U.S., 387 . . . . .266/E3
Roberts, Md., U.S., 100 . . . . .288/L3
Roberts, Miss., U.S. 300/G4
Roberts, S. Dak., U.S., county, 10,016 . .342/H2
Roberts, Tex., U.S., county, 887 . . . . .346/G8
Roberts, Wisc., U.S., 1,043 . . . . .364/A4
Robertsbridge, Eng., U.K., 1,923 . . . .70/E5
Robertsburg, W. Va., U.S., 225 . . . . .360/C3
Robertsdale, Ala., U.S., 3,782 . . . . . .238/B5
Robertson, Ky., U.S., county, 2,266 . . .280/F2
Robertson, Tenn., U.S., county, 54,433 . .344/H2
Robertson, Wyo., U.S., county, 16,000 . .366/M5
Robertson, Wyo., U.S., 59 . . . . .366/A3
Robertsport, Liber. 149/A2
Robertsville, Conn., U.S., 225 . . . . . .253/C2
Robertsville, N.J., U.S., 9,800 . . . . . .314/E3
Robertville, N.B., Can., 954 . . . . .217/D1
Roberval, Que., Can., 10,906 . . . . . . .226/D3
Robeson, N.C., U.S., county, 123,339 . .322/G5
Robesonia, Penn., U.S., 2,036 . . . . . .336/J5
Robin, Ida., U.S., 60 . . . . .264/E7
Robins, Iowa, U.S., 1,806 . . . . .274/L3
Robinson, Ill., U.S., 6,822 . . . . .266/F4
Robinson, Iowa, U.S. 274/L3
Robinson, Kans., U.S., 216 . . . . .276/G2
Robinson, Ky., U.S., 125 . . . . .280/E3
Robinson, Minn., U.S. 298/E3
Robinson, N. Dak., U.S., 71 . . . . .326/F2
Robinson, Tex., U.S., 7,845 . . . . .346/L4
Robinsonville, Miss., U.S., 100 . . . . . .300/B1
Robinsonville, N.B., Can. 217/C1
Robinsonville, Miss., U.S., 100 . . . . . .300/B1
Roblin, Man., Can., 1,818 . . . . .215/A3
Roboré, Bol. 186/C3
Robson, Br. Col., Can., mountain, 1,599 . .214/N4
Robstown, Tex., U.S., 12,727 . . . . . . .346/L8
Roby, Mo., U.S., 60 . . . . .302/D4
Roby, Tex., U.S., 673 . . . . .346/H3
Roca, Nebr., U.S., 220 . . . . .308/H3
Rocanville, Sask., Can., 887 . . . . . .227/I10
Rocester, Eng., U.K., 1,432 . . . . .68/D4
Rocha, Uru. 187/C3
Rocha, Uru., department 187/C3
Rochdale, Eng., U.K. 60/C2
Rochdale, Eng., U.K., 94,313 . . . . . . .66/D5
Rochdale, Eng., U.K., 94,313 . . . . . . .68/C2
Rochdale, Eng., U.K., unitary authority, 205,233 . .66/D5
Rochdale, Eng., U.K., unitary authority, 205,233 . .68/C2
Rochdale, Mass., U.S., 1,400 . . . . . . .292/G4
Rochefort, Fr. 88/B4
Rochelle, Ga., U.S., 1,415 . . . . .260/E8
Rochelle, Ill., U.S., 9,424 . . . . .266/B2
Rochelle, La., U.S., 40 . . . . .282/C3
Rochelle, Va., U.S., 400 . . . . .354/G4
Rochelle Park, N.J., U.S., 5,528 . . . . .314/B2
Rocheport, Mo., U.S., 208 . . . . .302/D3

Rochert, Minn., U.S., 350 . . . . .298/B4
Rochester, Alta., Can., 116 . . . . .212/D4
Rochester, Eng., U.K., 23,971 . . . . . .70/E4
Rochester, Ill., U.S., 2,893 . . . . .266/D4
Rochester, Ind., U.S., 6,414 . . . . . . .270/D2
Rochester, Ky., U.S., 186 . . . . .280/D3
Rochester, Mass., U.S., 4,581 . . . . . .292/L6
Rochester, Mich., U.S., 10,467 . . .294/B6, F7
Rochester, Minn., U.S., 85,806, (124,277 metro.) . .298/E6
Rochester, N.H., U.S., 28,461 . . . . . .312/E5
Rochester, N.Y., U.S., 219,773,
 (1,098,201 metro.) 320/F4
Rochester, Ohio, U.S., 190 . . . . .328/F4
Rochester, Penn., U.S., 4,014 . . . . . .336/A4
Rochester, Tex., U.S., 378 . . . . .346/J2
Rochester, Vt., U.S., 1,171 . . . . .352/B3
Rochester, Wash., U.S., 1,829 . . . . . .358/B3
Rochester, Wisc., U.S., 1,149 . . . . . .364/E6
Rochester Hills, Mich., U.S., 68,825 . .294/A6
Rochford, Eng., U.K., 15,081 . . . . . . .70/F3
Rochford, S. Dak., U.S. 342/B3
Rock, Ill., U.S., river 266/D2
Rock, Kans., U.S. 276/E4
Rock, Mass., U.S., 850 . . . . .292/L5
Rock, Mich., U.S., 150 . . . . .294/B3
Rock, Minn., U.S., county, 9,721 . . . . .298/A7
Rock, Nebr., U.S., county, 1,756 . . . . .308/E1
Rock, Wisc., U.S., county, 152,307 . . .364/D6
Rockaway, N.J., U.S., borough, 6,473 . .314/D2
Rockaway Beach, Oreg., U.S., 1,267 . .334/C2
Rockbridge, Ill., U.S., 189 . . . . . .266/A2, C4
Rockbridge, Ohio, U.S., 150 . . . . . . .328/E6
Rockbridge, Va., U.S., county, 20,808 . .354/E5
Rockcastle, Ky., U.S., county, 16,582 . .280/F3
Rock Cave, W. Va., U.S., 300 . . . . . .360/F3
Rock City, Ill., U.S., 313 . . . . .266/D1
Rock Creek, Calif., U.S. 264/E6
Rock Creek, Kans., U.S., 150 . . . . . . .276/G2
Rock Creek, Minn., U.S., 1,119 . . . . . .298/E5
Rock Creek, Ohio, U.S., 584 . . . . . . .328/J2
Rockcreek, Oreg., U.S. 334/A2
Rock Creek, Oreg., U.S. 334/G2
Rockdale, N.S.W., Austl. . . . . . .170/Inset IV
Rockdale, Ga., U.S., county, 70,111 . .260/C4, K3
Rockdale, Ill., U.S., 1,888 . . . . .266/B6
Rockdale, (northern Baltimore County), Md., U.S. . .288/G1
Rockdale, (southern Baltimore County,
 Milford Mill), Md., U.S., 26,527 . . .288/G2
Rockdale, Tex., U.S., 5,439 . . . . .346/M5
Rockdale, Wisc., U.S., 214 . . . . .364/D6
Rockdell, Va., U.S. 354/D2
Rockerville, S. Dak., U.S., 50 . . . . . . .342/B4
Rockfall, Conn., U.S., 1,500 . . . . . . .253/E3
Rock Falls, Ill., U.S., 9,580 . . . . .266/D2
Rock Falls, Iowa, U.S., 170 . . . . .274/H1
Rockfield, Wales, U.K. 64/F4
Rockfield, Ind., U.S., 225 . . . . .270/C3
Rockfield, Wisc., U.S. 364/E6
Rockford, Ala., U.S., 428 . . . . .238/C3
Rockford, Ida., U.S., 350 . . . . .264/E6
Rockford, Ill., U.S., 150,115, (371,236 metro.) . .266/D1
Rockford, Iowa, U.S., 907 . . . . .274/J1
Rockford, Mich., U.S., 4,626 . . . . . . .294/D6
Rockford, Minn., U.S., 3,484 . . . . . . .298/D5
Rockford, Nebr., U.S. 308/H3
Rockford, N.C., U.S., 125 . . . . .322/D2
Rockford, Ohio, U.S., 1,126 . . . . .328/A4
Rockford, Tenn., U.S., 798 . . . . .344/P3
Rockford, Wash., U.S., 413 . . . . .358/H2
Rockglen, Sask., Can., 450 . . . . . . .227/E11
Rock Hall, Md., U.S., 1,396 . . . . .288/K3
Rock Hall, S. Dak., U.S., 53 . . . . .342/G3
Rockhampton, Qnsld., Austl., 56,146,
 (64,000 metro.) 170/E2
Rock Hill, Mo., U.S. 256/B1
Rock Hill, Mo., U.S., 4,765 . . . . .302/H3
Rock Hill, S.C., U.S., 49,765 . . . . . . .340/C2
Rockhill Furnace, Penn., U.S., 414 . . .336/F5
Rockholds, Ky., U.S., 325 . . . . .280/F4
Rockhope, Eng., U.K. 66/D3
Rockingham, Eng., U.K. 70/C1
Rockingham, N.H., U.S., county, 277,359 . .312/D6
Rockingham, N.C., U.S., 9,672 . . . . . .322/F5
Rockingham, N.C., U.S., county, 91,928 . .322/F2
Rockingham, Vt., U.S., 5,309 . . . . . . .352/C4
Rockingham, Va., U.S., county, 67,725 . .354/F3
Rock Island, Que., Can., 1,025 . . . . . .226/D6
Rock Island, Ill., U.S., 39,684 . . . . . .266/C2
Rock Island, Ill., U.S., county, 149,374 . .266/C2
Rock Island, Okla., U.S., 709 . . . . . . .330/H2
Rock Island, Wash., U.S., 863 . . . . . .358/E2
Rocklake, N. Dak., U.S., 194 . . . . . . .326/F1
Rockland, Ont., Can., 8,542 . . . . . . .223/K2
Rockland, Ida., U.S., 316 . . . . .264/E7
Rockland, Maine, U.S., 7,609 . . . . . . .286/C4
Rockland, Mass., U.S., 17,670 . . . . . .292/L4
Rockland, Mich., U.S., 250 . . . . .294/A3
Rockland, N.Y., U.S., county, 286,753 . .320/A1
Rockland, Wisc., U.S., 628 . . . . .364/C5
Rockland All Saints, Eng., U.K. 70/F1
Rockledge, Ala., U.S., 600 . . . . .238/C1
Rockledge, Fla., U.S., 20,170 . . . . . . .256/H3
Rockledge, Penn., U.S., 2,577 . . . . . .336/M6
Rockleigh, N.J., U.S., 391 . . . . . .314/C1, F1
Rocklin, Calif., U.S., 36,330 . . . . .246/L5
Rockmart, Ga., U.S., 3,870 . . . . .260/A3
Rockne, Tex., U.S., 150 . . . . .346/E3
Rock Pt., Ariz., U.S., 724 . . . . .242/F2
Rock Pt., Md., U.S., 750 . . . . .288/G6
Rockport, Ark., U.S., 792 . . . . .244/C3
Rockport, Calif., U.S. 246/B3
Rockport, Ill., U.S., 80 . . . . .266/B4
Rockport, Ind., U.S., 2,160 . . . . .270/B9
Rockport, Ky., U.S., 334 . . . . .280/D3
Rockport, Maine, U.S., 3,209 . . . . . . .286/C4
Rockport, Mass., U.S., 7,767 . . . . . . .292/M2
Rockport, Miss., U.S., 40 . . . . .300/B4
Rock Port, Mo., U.S., 1,395 . . . . . . .302/A1
Rockport, Tex., U.S., 7,385 . . . . .346/L6
Rockport, Wash., U.S., 102 . . . . .358/D1
Rock, W. Va., U.S. 360/C2
Rock Rapids, Iowa, U.S., 2,573 . . . . .274/B1
Rock River, Wyo., U.S., 235 . . . . . . .366/D3
Rock Spr., La., U.S., 550 . . . . .260/A2
Rock Sprs., Ariz., U.S. 242/C3
Rock Sprs., Ark., U.S. 244/C2
Rock Sprs., Mont., U.S. 306/K3
Rocksprings, Tex., U.S., 1,285 . . . . . .346/H5
Rock Sprs., Wisc., U.S., 425 . . . . . . .364/D5
Rock Sprs., Wyo., U.S., 18,708 . . . . .366/B3
Rockton, Ill., U.S., 5,296 . . . . .266/D1
Rocktown, N.J., U.S. 314/D3
Rockvale, Colo., U.S., 426 . . . . .250/E3
Rock Valley, Iowa, U.S., 2,702 . . . . . .274/B1
Rockville, Conn., U.S., 7,708 . . . . . . .253/F2
Rockville, Ind., U.S., 2,650 . . . . .270/B5
Rockville, Md., U.S., 47,388 . . . . .288/A6, F3
Rockville, Minn., U.S., 749 . . . . .298/C5
Rockville, Mo., U.S., 162 . . . . .302/B3

Rockville, Nebr., U.S., 111 . . . . .308/E2
Rockville, R.I., U.S., 425 . . . . .339/B4
Rockville, S.C., U.S., 137 . . . . .340/D4
Rockville, Utah, U.S., 247 . . . . .350/A6
Rockville, Va., U.S., 450 . . . . .354/H5
Rockwall, Tex., U.S., 17,976 . . . . . . .346/D9, M3
Rockwall, Tex., U.S., county, 43,080 . . . . .346/D9, M3
Rockwell, Ark., U.S., 3,024 . . . . .244/B3
Rockwell, Iowa, U.S., 989 . . . . .274/H2
Rockwell, N.C., U.S., 1,971 . . . . .322/E3
Rockwell City, Iowa, U.S., 2,264 . . . . . . .274/E3
Rockwood, Colo., U.S. 250/C4
Rockwood, Ill., U.S., 41 . . . . .266/D6
Rockwood, Maine, U.S. 286/C3
Rockwood, Mich., U.S., 3,442 . . . . .294/F7
Rockwood, Penn., U.S., 954 . . . . .336/C6
Rockwood, Tenn., U.S., 5,774 . . . . .344/M3
Rocky, Alta., Can., mountains 212/A4
Rocky, Br. Col., Can., mountains 214/K2
Rocky, Colo., U.S., mountains 250/D1
Rocky, Conn., U.S., point 253/F5
Rocky, Mont., U.S., mountains 306/C2
Rocky, N.C., U.S., river 322/E4
Rocky, Okla., U.S., 174 . . . . .330/C2
Rocky, Wyo., U.S., mountains 366/B2
Rocky Bar, Ida., U.S. 264/B6
Rocky Boy, Mont., U.S., 175 . . . . .306/G1
Rocky Boy's Ind. Res., Mont., U.S. 306/G1
Rocky Comfort, Mo., U.S., 175 . . . . .302/B5
Rockyford, Alta., Can., 375 . . . . .212/D5
Rocky Ford, Colo., U.S., 4,286 . . . . .250/G3
Rocky Ford, Ga., U.S., 186 . . . . .260/H6
Rocky Fork, Tenn., U.S., 100 . . . . .344/M2
Rocky Gap, Va., U.S., 175 . . . . .354/A6
Rocky Harbour, Nfld., Can., 1,002 . . . . . . .218/C4
Rocky Hill, Conn., U.S., 17,966 . . . . .253/E3
Rocky Hill, N.J., U.S., 662 . . . . .314/D3
Rocky Hill, Ohio, U.S., 70 . . . . .328/E7
Rocky Island, Ont., Can., island 223/B1
Rocky Island, Ont., Can., lake 294/G3
Rocky Mount, N.C., U.S., 55,893,
  (143,026 metro.) 322/K3
Rocky Mount, Va., U.S., 4,066 . . . . .354/D7
Rocky Mtn. House, Alta., Can., 6,208 . . . . .212/C5
Rocky Mtn. Natl. Park, Colo., U.S. 250/E1
Rocky Pt., N.Y., U.S., 10,185 . . . . .320/L1
Rocky Pt., N.C., U.S., 275 . . . . .322/K6
Rockypoint, Wyo., U.S. 366/D1
Rocky Ridge, Md., U.S., 425 . . . . .288/E1
Rocky Ridge, Mo., U.S., 350 . . . . .302/F4
Rocky Ridge, Ohio, U.S., 389 . . . . .328/D2
Rocky Ripple, Ind., U.S., 712 . . . . .270/D5
Rocky River, Ohio, U.S., 20,735 . . . . .328/G9
Rodanthe, N.C., U.S. 322/Q3
Rodarte, N. Mex., U.S., 350 . . . . .317/E1
Roddickton, Nfld., Can., 1,003 . . . . .218/C4
Rode Heath, Eng., U.K., 2,078 . . . . .66/C3
Rodel, Scot., U.K. 62/C3
Roden, Eng., U.K., river 68/B4
Rodeo, Calif., U.S., 8,717 . . . . .246/J1
Rodeo, N. Mex., U.S., 100 . . . . .317/A6
Rodessa, La., U.S., 307 . . . . .282/A1
Rodez, Fr. 88/C4
Rodley, Eng., U.K. 68/C6
Rodman, Iowa, U.S., 56 . . . . .274/E1
Rodman, S.C., U.S., 70 . . . . .340/C2
Rodney, Ont., Can., 1,102 . . . . .223/D5
Rodney, Iowa, U.S., 74 . . . . .274/C3
Rodney, Mich., U.S., 175 . . . . .294/D6
Rodney, Miss., U.S. 300/A4
Rodney Vil., Del., U.S., 1,602 . . . . .255/B4
Rodono, Scot., U.K. 62/K8
Roe, Ark., U.S., 124 . . . . .244/D3
Roebling, N.J., U.S., 8,200 . . . . .314/D3
Roebuck, S.C., U.S., 1,725 . . . . .340/C2, F2
Roeland Park, Kans., U.S., 6,817 . . . . . . .276/H1
Roellen, Tenn., U.S., 350 . . . . .344/C2
Roermond, Neth. 84/D3
Roeselare, Belg. 85/B2
Roesslerville, N.Y., U.S., 10,800 . . . . .320/P5
Roff, Okla., U.S., 734 . . . . .330/F3
Rogaland, Nor., province 80/B4
Rogart, Scot., U.K. 62/H3
Roger Mills, Okla., U.S., county, 3,436 . . . .330/C2
Rogers, Ark., U.S., 38,829 . . . . .244/A1
Rogers, La., U.S. 282/E3
Rogers, Minn., U.S., 3,588 . . . . .298/C5
Rogers, Nebr., U.S., 95 . . . . .308/H2
Rogers, N. Mex., U.S. 317/G4
Rogers, N. Dak., U.S., 61 . . . . .326/G2
Rogers, Ohio, U.S., 266 . . . . .328/J4
Rogers, Okla., U.S., county, 70,641 . . . . . .330/G1
Rogers, Tex., U.S., 1,117 . . . . .346/L5
Rogers, Va., U.S., mountain 354/E3
Rogers City, Mich., U.S., 3,322 . . . . .294/F4
Rogerson, Ida., U.S., 60 . . . . .264/C7
Rogersville, N.B., Can., 1,248 . . . . .217/D2
Rogersville, Ala., U.S., 1,199 . . . . .238/B1
Rogersville, Mo., U.S., 1,508 . . . . .302/C4
Rogersville, Tenn., U.S., 4,240 . . . . .344/Q2
Roger Williams Natl. Mem., R.I., U.S. 339/D3
Roggen, Colo., U.S., 90 . . . . .250/F1
Rogiet, Wales, U.K. 64/F4
Rogue, Oreg., U.S., river 334/C5
Rogue River, Oreg., U.S., 1,847 . . . . .334/C5
Rogue River Natl. For., Oreg., U.S. 334/C4, D5
Rohnert Park, Calif., U.S., 42,236 . . . . . . .246/C4
Rohwer, Ark., U.S., 150 . . . . .244/D4
Roi, Marsh. Is., island 173/B2
Roi Et, Thai. 125/C2
Rojo, P.R., cape 206/A2
Rokel, S.L., river 149/A1
Roland, Man., Can. 215/C4
Roland, Ark., U.S., 200 . . . . .244/C3
Roland, Iowa, U.S., 1,324 . . . . .274/G3
Roland, Okla., U.S., 2,842 . . . . .330/H2
Rolesville, N.C., U.S., 907 . . . . .322/J3
Rolette, N. Dak., U.S., 538 . . . . .326/F1
Rolette, N. Dak., U.S., county, 13,674 . . . .326/F1
Rolfe, Iowa, U.S., 675 . . . . .274/E2
Rolinda, Calif., U.S., 200 . . . . .246/F6
Roll, Ariz., U.S., 70 . . . . .242/B5
Roll, Ind., U.S., 225 . . . . .270/F3
Roll, Okla., U.S., 40 . . . . .330/C2
Rolla, Kans., U.S., 482 . . . . .276/A4
Rolla, Mo., U.S., 16,367 . . . . .302/E4
Rolla, N. Dak., U.S., 1,417 . . . . .326/F1
Rollag, Minn., U.S., 60 . . . . .298/A4
Rolling Fields, Ky., U.S., 648 . . . . .280/C2
Rolling Fork, Miss., U.S., 2,486 . . . . .300/B3
Rolling Hills, Alta., Can., 234 . . . . .212/E6
Rolling Hills, Calif., U.S., 1,871 . . . . .246/C10
Rolling Hills, Ky., U.S., 907 . . . . .280/B2
Rolling Hills, Wyo., U.S., 449 . . . . .366/D2
Rolling Hills Estates, Calif., U.S., 7,676 . . .246/C10
Rolling Meadows, Ill., U.S., 24,604 . . . . . .266/B5
Rolling Prairie, Ind., U.S., 800 . . . . .270/C1
Rollingwood, Tex., U.S., 1,403 . . . . .346/D2
Rollins, Minn., U.S. 298/F3
Rollins, Mont., U.S., 183 . . . . .306/B2
Rollinsford, N.H., U.S., 2,648 . . . . .312/E5

Rollinsville, Colo., U.S., 40 . . . . .250/E2
Rollo, PE.I., Can., bay 224/C2
Rollo Bay, PE.I., Can. 224/C2
Rolphton, Ont., Can. 223/H1
Rolvenden, Eng., U.K. 70/F4
Roma, Qnsld., Austl. 170/D2
Roma, Leso. 161/A2
Roma, Tex., U.S., 9,617 . . . . .346/J9
Roman, Rom. 101/D2
Romancoke, Md., U.S., 800 . . . . .288/J4
Roman Forest, Tex., U.S., 1,279 . . . . .346/B5
Romania, nation 99
Romano, Fla., U.S., cape 256/G6
Rombauer, Mo., U.S., 80 . . . . .302/F5
Rome, It., capital, 2,459,776 . . . . .95/C2
Rome, Ga., U.S., 34,980 . . . . .260/E4
Rome, Ill., U.S., 1,776 . . . . .266/D3
Rome, Iowa, U.S., 113 . . . . .274/L6
Rome, Ky., U.S., 275 . . . . .280/C3
Rome, Maine, U.S., 980 . . . . .286/C4
Rome, Miss., U.S., 90 . . . . .300/B2
Rome, Mo., U.S. 302/D5
Rome, N.Y., U.S., 34,950 . . . . .320/L4
Rome, (Adams County), Ohio, U.S., 117 . . .328/D8
Rome, (Ashtabula County), Ohio, U.S. 328/J2
Rome, Oreg., U.S., 40 . . . . .334/J5
Rome, Penn., U.S., 382 . . . . .336/J2
Rome, Tenn., U.S., 200 . . . . .344/J2
Rome City, Ind., U.S., 1,615 . . . . .270/F1
Romeo, Colo., U.S., 375 . . . . .250/E4
Romeo, Mich., U.S., 3,721 . . . . .294/B6, F7
Romeoville, Ill., U.S., 21,153 . . . . .266/B6
Romero, Tex., U.S. 346/E9
Romeroville, N. Mex., U.S. 317/E2
Romney, W. Va., U.S., 1,940 . . . . .360/J2
Rømø, Den., island 79/B3
Romsey, Eng., U.K., 17,032 . . . . .70/B5
Romulus, Mich., U.S., 22,979 . . . . .294/A7, F7
Rona, Scot., U.K., island 62/D3
Ronan, Mont., U.S., 1,812 . . . . .306/B2
Ronay, Scot., U.K., island 62/B3
Roncador, Braz., range 188/C3
Roncador, Col., cay 184/Inset
Ronceverte, W. Va., U.S., 1,557 . . . . .360/F5
Ronda, N.C., U.S., 460 . . . . .322/D2
Ronda, Sp. 91/C4
Ronde, Gren., island 209/B1
Rondeau Prov. Park, Ont., Can. 223/D5
Rondo, Ark., U.S., 237 . . . . .244/E3
Rondônia, Braz., state 188/B3
Rondonópolis, Braz., 52,185, (125,107 metro.) .188/B3
Rongelap, Marsh. Is., island 173/B1
Rongerik, Marsh. Is., island 173/B1
Rønne, Den. .79/E3
Ronne Ice Shelf, Antar., glacier 192/B11
Ronneby, Swe. 79/D4
Ronne Ice Shelf, Antar., glacier 192/B11
Roodepoort, S. Afr. 162/C2
Roodhouse, Ill., U.S., 2,214 . . . . .266/C4
Rookley, Eng., U.K. 70/B5
Rooks, Kans., U.S., county, 5,685 . . . . . . .276/C2
Roopville, Ga., U.S., 177 . . . . .260/A5
Roosevelt, Antar., island 192/B6
Roosevelt, Ariz., U.S. 242/D4
Roosevelt, Minn., U.S., 166 . . . . .298/B2
Roosevelt, Mont., U.S., county, 10,620 . . . .306/L1
Roosevelt, N.J., U.S., 933 . . . . .314/E3
Roosevelt, N. Mex., U.S., county, 18,018 . . .317/G3
Roosevelt, Okla., U.S., 280 . . . . .330/C3
Roosevelt, Tex., U.S. 346/H5
Roosevelt, Utah, U.S., 4,299 . . . . .350/D3
Roosevelt, Wash., U.S., 79 . . . . .358/E4
Roosevelt Campobello Intl. Hist. Park, N.B., Can. . .217/C4
Roosevelt City, N.J., U.S., 325 . . . . .314/E4
Roosevelt Natl. For., Colo., U.S. 250/E1
Roosevelt Park, Mich., U.S., 3,890 . . . . . .294/C6
Roosevelt Roads Naval Sta., P.R. 206/D2
Root, Minn., U.S., river 298/E7
Roper, Austl., river 170/C1
Roper, Kans., U.S. 276/G4
Roper, N.C., U.S., 613 . . . . .322/M3
Ropesville, Tex., U.S., 517 . . . . .346/F2
Ropley, Eng., U.K. 70/B4
Roque Bluffs, Maine, U.S., 264 . . . . .286/E4
Roraima, Braz., state 188/B1
Roraima, Guy., mountain 183/A3
Roraima, Ven., mountain 182/D2
Rosa, It., mountain 95/A1
Rosa, Ala., U.S. 238/C2
Rosaireville, N.B., Can. 217/D2
Rosalia, Kans., U.S., 100 . . . . .276/F4
Rosalia, Wash., U.S., 648 . . . . .358/H2
Rosalie, Dom. 208/B3
Rosalie, Ala., U.S., 375 . . . . .238/D1
Rosalie, Nebr., U.S., 194 . . . . .308/H1
Rosalind, Alta., Can., 190 . . . . .212/D5
Rosamond, Calif., U.S., 14,349 . . . . .246/G8
Rosario, Arg., 907,718, (1,118,905 metro.) . .191/C3
Rosario, P.R. 206/A2
Rosario, Wash., U.S., 175 . . . . .358/C1
Rosaryville, Md., U.S., 12,322 . . . . .288/G5
Rosati, Mo., U.S., 125 . . . . .302/E3
Rosboro, Ark., U.S. 244/B3
Rosburg, Wash., U.S., 40 . . . . .358/B3
Roscoe, Ill., U.S., 6,244 . . . . .266/D1
Roscoe, Minn., U.S., 116 . . . . .298/C5
Roscoe, Mo., U.S., 112 . . . . .302/C4
Roscoe, Mont., U.S. 306/G4
Roscoe, Nebr., U.S., 70 . . . . .308/C2
Roscoe, N.Y., U.S., 597 . . . . .320/M7
Roscoe, S. Dak., U.S., 324 . . . . .342/F2
Roscoe, Tex., U.S., 1,378 . . . . .346/H3
Roscommon, Ire. 78/B2
Roscommon, Ire. 78/B2
Roscommon, Mich., U.S., 1,133 . . . . .294/E5
Roscommon, Mich., U.S., county, 25,469 . . .294/E5
Roscrea, Ire. 78/C2
Rose, Nebr., U.S. 308/E1
Roseau, Man., Can., river 215/B4
Roseau, Dom., capital 204/F4
Roseau, Dom., capital, 16,243, (24,000 metro.) .208/B3
Roseau, Dom., river 208/B3
Roseau, Minn., U.S., 2,756 . . . . .298/B2
Roseau, Minn., U.S., county, 16,338 . . . . . .298/B2
Rose Belle, Mauritius 163/C3
Rose Blanche, Nfld., Can., 668 . . . . .218/B5
Roseboro, N.C., U.S., 1,267 . . . . .322/H5
Rosebud, Alta., Can., 87 . . . . .212/D5
Rose Bud, Ark., U.S., 429 . . . . .244/C2
Rosebud, Mo., U.S., 364 . . . . .302/E3
Rosebud, Mont., U.S. 306/K3
Rosebud, Mont., U.S., county, 9,383 . . . . .306/K3
Rosebud, N. Mex., U.S. 317/G2
Rosebud, S. Dak., U.S., 1,557 . . . . .342/E4
Rosebud, Tex., U.S., 1,493 . . . . .346/M4
Rosebud Ind. Res., S. Dak., U.S. 342/D4
Roseburg, Oreg., U.S., 20,017 . . . . .334/C4
Rosebush, Mich., U.S., 379 . . . . .294/E6
Rose City, Mich., U.S., 721 . . . . .294/E5
Rose City, Minn., U.S., 90 . . . . .298/B4
Rose Creek, Minn., U.S., 354 . . . . .298/E7
Rosedale, Calif., U.S., 8,445 . . . . .246/F7
Rosedale, Ind., U.S., 750 . . . . .270/B5

Rosedale, La., U.S., 753 . . . . .282/G6
Rosedale, Md., U.S., 19,199 . . . . .288/H2
Rosedale, Mich., U.S., 50 . . . . .294/E3
Rosedale, Miss., U.S., 2,414 . . . . .300/A2
Rosedale, Okla., U.S., 66 . . . . .330/E3
Rosedale, W. Va., U.S., 100 . . . . .360/E3
Rosedale Beach, Del., U.S., 750 . . . . .255/D6
Rosedale Colony, S. Dak., U.S. 342/H4
Rosefield, La., U.S. 282/E3
Roseglen, N. Dak., U.S. 326/D2
Rose Haven, Md., U.S., 1,400 . . . . .288/H5
Rose Hill, Mauritius 163/B2
Rose Hill, Ill., U.S., 79 . . . . .266/E4
Rose Hill, Iowa, U.S., 205 . . . . .274/K5
Rose Hill, Kans., U.S., 3,432 . . . . . . .276/D4, E4
Rose Hill, Miss., U.S., 90 . . . . .300/C3
Rose Hill, N.C., U.S., 1,330 . . . . .322/J5
Rose Hill, (Fairfax County), Va., U.S., 15,058 . .354/M2
Rose Hill, (Lee County), Va., U.S., 714 . . . .354/B3
Rose Lake, Ida., U.S., 40 . . . . .264/A2
Roseland, Calif., U.S., 6,369 . . . . .246/C4
Roseland, Fla., U.S., 1,775 . . . . .256/H4
Roseland, Ind., U.S., 1,809 . . . . .270/D1
Roseland, Kans., U.S., 101 . . . . .276/H4
Roseland, La., U.S., 1,162 . . . . .282/J5
Roseland, Nebr., U.S., 242 . . . . .308/E3
Roseland, N.J., U.S., 5,298 . . . . .314/A2
Roselle, Ill., U.S., 23,115 . . . . .266/B5
Roselle, Mo., U.S. 302/F4
Roselle, N.J., U.S., 21,274 . . . . .314/A3
Roselle Park, N.J., U.S., 13,281 . . . . .314/A3
Rose Lodge, Oreg., U.S., 1,708 . . . . .334/C3
Rosemark, Tenn., U.S., 350 . . . . .344/B4
Rosemary, Alta., Can., 366 . . . . .212/D6
Rosemead, Calif., U.S., 53,505 . . . . .246/D9
Rosemont, Calif., U.S., 22,904 . . . . .246/K5
Rosemont, Ill., U.S., 4,224 . . . . .266/B5
Rosemont, Nebr., U.S., 40 . . . . .308/E3
Rosemont, N.J., U.S., 450 . . . . .314/D3
Rosemount, Minn., U.S., 14,619 . . . . .298/D6
Rosemount, Ohio, U.S., 2,043 . . . . .328/E8
Rosen, Minn., U.S., 60 . . . . .298/A5
Rosenberg, Tex., U.S., 24,043 . . . . . . .346/A7, N6
Rosendale, Minn., U.S., 40 . . . . .298/C5
Rosendale, Mo., U.S., 180 . . . . .302/B1
Rosendale, N.Y., U.S., 1,374 . . . . .320/N7
Rosendale, Wisc., U.S., 923 . . . . .364/E5
Rosenfeld, Man., Can. 215/C4
Rosenhayn, N.J., U.S., 1,099 . . . . .314/C5
Rosenheim, Ger. 86/C5
Rosenort, Man., Can. 215/C4
Rosepine, La., U.S., 1,390 . . . . .282/C5
Roseto, Penn., U.S., 1,653 . . . . .336/L4
Rosetown, Sask., Can., 2,471 . . . . .227/B9
Rosetta, Egy., river 144/B1
Rosetta, Miss., U.S., 70 . . . . .300/A4
Rosette, Utah, U.S., 70 . . . . .350/A2
Rose Valley, Sask., Can., 395 . . . . .227/G8
Rose Valley, Penn., U.S., 944 . . . . .336/L7
Roseville, Calif., U.S., 79,921 . . . . .246/K5
Roseville, Ill., U.S., 1,083 . . . . .266/C3
Roseville, Mich., U.S., 48,129 . . . . . . .294/B6, G7
Roseville, Minn., U.S., 33,690 . . . . .298/F5
Roseville, Ohio, U.S., 1,936 . . . . .328/F6
Roseville, Penn., U.S., 207 . . . . .336/H2
Roseville Park, Del., U.S., 6,200 . . . . .255/B2
Rosewood, Ohio, U.S., 350 . . . . .328/C5
Rosewood Hts., Ill., U.S., 4,262 . . . . .266/A3
Roseworth, Ida., U.S. 264/C7
Rosholt, S. Dak., U.S., 419 . . . . .342/J2
Rosholt, Wisc., U.S., 518 . . . . .364/D4
Rosiclare, Ill., U.S., 1,213 . . . . .266/E6
Rosier, Ga., U.S. 260/G6
Rosine, Ky., U.S., 175 . . . . .280/D3
Rosinish, Scot., U.K., island 62/A5
Rosita, Colo., U.S., 40 . . . . .250/E3
Rosita, (Duval County), Tex., U.S. 346/K8
Rosita, (Starr County), Tex., U.S. 346/K9
Roskilde, Den., 43,210 . . . . .79/D3
Roskilde, Den., county 79/D3
Roslyn, N.Y., U.S., 2,570 . . . . .320/C2
Roslyn, S. Dak., U.S., 225 . . . . .342/H2
Roslyn, Wash., U.S., 1,017 . . . . .358/D2
Rosman, N.C., U.S., 490 . . . . .322/D4
Ross, Antar., island 192/B5
Ross, Antar., sea 192/B6
Ross, Yukon, Can., river 228/C4
Ross, Calif., U.S., 2,329 . . . . .246/H1
Ross, Iowa, U.S., 80 . . . . .274/E4
Ross, Minn., U.S. 298/B2
Ross, N. Dak., U.S., 48 . . . . .326/C1
Ross, Ohio, U.S., 1,971 . . . . .328/A9
Ross, Ohio, U.S., county, 73,345 . . . . .328/D7
Ross, Wash., U.S., lake 358/D1
Ross Barnett, Miss., U.S., reservoir 300/C3
Rossburg, Minn., U.S., 50 . . . . .298/B4
Rossburg, Ohio, U.S., 224 . . . . .328/B5
Rossburn, Man., Can., 568 . . . . .215/A4
Rosseau, Ont., Can., lake 223/F2
Rossel, P.N.G., island 172/B3
Rossendale, Man., Can. 215/B4
Rossett, Wales, U.K., 1,986 . . . . .64/F1
Rossford, Ohio, U.S., 6,406 . . . . .328/C2
Ross Fork, Mont., U.S. 306/G2
Ross Ice Shelf, Antar., glacier 192/A6
Rossie, Iowa, U.S., 58 . . . . .274/D1
Rossignol, N.S., Can., lake 221/B3
Rossiter, Penn., U.S., 790 . . . . .336/D4
Ross Lake Natl. Rec. Area, Wash., U.S. 358/E1
Rossland, Br. Col., Can., 3,646 . . . . .214/O6
Rosslare, Ire. 78/C2
Rosslyn Farms, Penn., U.S., 464 . . . . .336/D7
Rossmoor, Calif., U.S., 10,298 . . . . .246/D10
Rossmoor, N.J., U.S., 3,129 . . . . .314/E3
Rossmor Leisure World, Md., U.S., 7,569 . . .288/F2
Ross N.P., Scot., U.K. 62/F3
Rosso, Maur. 147/B3
Rosson-on-Wye, Eng., U.K., 9,606 . . . . . . .68/B6
Ross River, Yukon, Can., 337 . . . . .228/C4
Rosston, Ark., U.S., 265 . . . . .244/B4
Rosston, Okla., U.S., 66 . . . . .330/C1
Rossville, Ga., U.S., 3,511 . . . . .260/A2
Rossville, Ill., U.S., 1,217 . . . . .266/F3
Rossville, Ind., U.S., 1,513 . . . . .270/C4
Rossville, Iowa, U.S., 125 . . . . .274/M1
Rossville, Kans., U.S., 1,014 . . . . .276/G2
Rossville, Md., U.S., 11,515 . . . . .288/J2
Rossville, Tenn., U.S., 380 . . . . .344/B4
Rosthern, Sask., Can., 1,504 . . . . .227/D8
Rosthwaite, Eng., U.K. 66/B3
Rostock, Ger., 203,279 . . . . .86/C1
Rostov-na-Donu, Russ., 1,003,482 . . . . . . .104/C5
Rostrevor, N. Ire., U.K., 2,269 . . . . .65/C3
Roswell, Ga., U.S., 79,334 . . . . .260/C3, J2

Roswell, N. Mex., U.S., 45,293 . . . . .317/F4
Roswell, Ohio, U.S., 276 . . . . .328/H5
Roswell, S. Dak., U.S. 342/H4
Rotan, Tex., U.S., 1,611 . . . . .346/H3
Rothbury, Eng., U.K., 1,805 . . . . .66/E2
Rothbury, Mich., U.S., 416 . . . . .294/C6
Rotherfield, Eng., U.K. 70/E4
Rotherham, Eng., U.K. 60/C3
Rotherham, Eng., U.K., 121,380 . . . . .66/F6
Rotherham, Eng., U.K., 121,380 . . . . .68/E3
Rotherham, Eng., U.K., unitary authority,
  248,176 . . . . .66/F6
Rotherham, Eng., U.K., unitary authority,
  248,176 . . . . .68/E3
Rothes, Scot., U.K., 1,156 . . . . .62/K4
Rothesay, N.B., Can., 11,505 . . . . .217/D3
Rothesay, Scot., U.K., 5,017 . . . . .62/F7
Rothiemay, Mont., U.S. 306/G3
Rothiesholm, Scot., U.K. 62/N1
Rothrock St. For., Penn., U.S. 336/F4
Rothsay, Minn., U.S., 497 . . . . .298/A4
Rothschild, Wisc., U.S., 4,970 . . . . .364/D4
Rothville, Mo., U.S., 93 . . . . .302/C2
Rothwell, N.B., Can. 217/C2
Rothwell, (Northamptonshire), Eng., U.K., 7,070 . .68/F5
Rothwell, (W. Yorkshire), Eng., U.K., 18,336 . .68/E2
Rothwell, Eng., U.K., 18,336 . . . . .66/F5
Rothwell, Eng., U.K., 7,070 . . . . .70/C2
Rotorua, N.Z., (52,605 metro.) 171/C2
Rotterdam, Neth., 605,950, (987,615 metro.) . .84/B3
Rotterdam, N.Y., U.S., 20,536 . . . . .320/P5
Rottingdean, (Rottingdean/Saltdean),
  Eng., U.K., 21,487 . . . . .70/D5
Roubaix, Fr. .88/C1
Rouen, Fr. 70/B5
Rouen, Fr., 108,758, (389,862 metro.) 88/C2
Rouge-Matawin Prov. Reserve, Que., Can. . .226/B5
Rougemont, N.C., U.S., 600 . . . . .322/H2
Rough, Eng., U.K., river 280/D3
Rough River, Ky., U.S., lake 280/D3
Rough Rock, Ariz., U.S., 469 . . . . .242/F1
Roughsike, Eng., U.K. 66/C2
Rougon, La., U.S., 250 . . . . .282/G5
Rouleau, Sask., Can., 434 . . . . .227/F10
Roulette, Penn., U.S., 650 . . . . .336/E2
Round, Nfld., Can., pond 218/C5
Round, Mauritius, island 163/D1
Roundhead, Ohio, U.S., 125 . . . . .328/C4
Round Hill, Va., U.S., 500 . . . . .354/H2
Round Lake, Fla., U.S., 200 . . . . .256/C1
Round Lake, Ill., U.S., 5,842 . . . . .266/A4
Round Lake, Minn., U.S., 424 . . . . .298/B7
Round Lake, N.Y., U.S., 604 . . . . .320/P5
Round Lake Beach, Ill., U.S., 25,859 . . . . .266/A4
Round Lake Ctr., Ont., Can. 223/H2
Round Lake Hts., Ill., U.S., 1,347 . . . . . . .266/B4
Round Lake Park, Ill., U.S., 6,038 . . . . . . .266/B4
Round Mountain, Maine, U.S. 286/B3
Round Mountain, Nev., U.S., 550 . . . . . . .310/B2
Round Mountain, Tex., U.S., 111 . . . . .346/C2
Round Oak, Ga., U.S. 260/D5
Round Pond, Ark., U.S., 80 . . . . .244/E2
Round Pond, Maine, U.S., 325 . . . . .286/C5
Round Prairie, Minn., U.S., 100 . . . . .298/C5
Round Rock, Ariz., U.S., 601 . . . . .242/F1
Round Rock, Tex., U.S., 61,136 . . . . .346/D2
Round Rock, Tex., U.S., 61,136 . . . . .346/L5
Round Top, Tex., U.S., 77 . . . . .346/M5
Roundup, Mont., U.S., 1,931 . . . . .306/H3
Round Valley Ind. Res., Calif., U.S. 246/B3
Rousay, Scot., U.K., island 62/M1
Rouses Pt., N.Y., U.S., 2,277 . . . . .320/Q1
Rouseville, Penn., U.S., 472 . . . . .336/B3
Rousky, N. Ire., U.K. 65/C2
Rousseau, Mich., U.S. 294/A3
Routhierville, Que., Can. 226/J3
Routt, Colo., U.S., county, 19,690 . . . . . . .250/C1
Routt Natl. For., Colo., U.S. 250/C1, D1
Rouyn-Noranda, Que., Can., 28,270 . . . . . .225/A4
Rouzerville, Penn., U.S., 862 . . . . .336/F6
Rovaniemi, Fin. 81/C1
Rover, Ark., U.S., 175 . . . . .244/B3
Rover, Mo., U.S., 60 . . . . .302/E5
Rover, Tenn., U.S., 125 . . . . .344/H3
Rovigo, It. 95/B1
Rovuma, Moz., river 161/C1
Rowan, Ky., U.S., county, 22,094 . . . . .280/G2
Rowan, N.C., U.S., county, 130,340 . . . . . .322/D3
Rowden, Tex., U.S. 346/J3
Rowdy, Ky., U.S., 150 . . . . .280/G3
Rowe, Mass., U.S., 351 . . . . .292/C2
Rowe, N. Mex., U.S. 317/E2
Rowena, N.B., Can. 217/B2
Rowena, S. Dak., U.S., 100 . . . . .342/J4
Rowena, Tex., U.S., 350 . . . . .346/J4
Rowesville, S.C., U.S., 378 . . . . .340/D3
Rowland, Nev., U.S. 310/C1
Rowland, N.C., U.S., 1,146 . . . . .322/G5
Rowland Hts., Calif., U.S., 48,553 . . . . . . .246/E9
Rowland's Castle, Eng., U.K. 70/C5
Rowlesburg, W. Va., U.S., 613 . . . . .360/G2
Rowlett, Tex., U.S., 44,503 . . . . .346/D9
Rowley, Alta., Can. 212/D5
Rowley, Iowa, U.S., 290 . . . . .274/L3
Rowley, Mass., U.S., 5,500 . . . . .292/C2
Rownham's, Eng., U.K. 70/B5
Rownham, Ohio, U.S., 275 . . . . .328/F4
Rowsley, Eng., U.K. 68/D3
Roxana, Del., U.S., 375 . . . . .255/D7
Roxana, Ill., U.S., 1,547 . . . . .266/A3
Roxas, Phil. .120/B4
Roxboro, N.C., U.S., 8,696 . . . . .322/H2
Roxbury, Conn., U.S., 2,136 . . . . .253/B3
Roxbury, Kans., U.S., 100 . . . . .276/E3
Roxbury, Maine, U.S., 384 . . . . .286/B4
Roxbury, N.Y., U.S., 375 . . . . .320/M6
Roxbury, Penn., U.S., 350 . . . . .336/F5
Roxbury, Vt., U.S., 576 . . . . .352/B2
Roxbury, Wisc., U.S., 200 . . . . .364/D5
Roxie, Miss., U.S., 569 . . . . .300/A4
Roxobel, N.C., U.S., 263 . . . . .322/L2
Roxton, Eng., U.K. 70/D2
Roxton, Tex., U.S., 694 . . . . .346/N2
Roy, La., U.S., 125 . . . . .282/C2
Roy, Mont., U.S., 100 . . . . .306/H2
Roy, N. Mex., U.S., 304 . . . . .317/F2
Roy, Utah, U.S., 32,885 . . . . .350/B2, E1
Roy, Wash., U.S., 260 . . . . .358/C3
Royal, Ire., canal 78/C2
Royal, Colo., U.S., gorge 250/E3
Royal, Ill., U.S., 279 . . . . .266/F3
Royal, Iowa, U.S., 479 . . . . .274/D1
Royal, Nebr., U.S., 75 . . . . .308/E1
Royal Ctr., Ind., U.S., 832 . . . . .270/C3
Royal City, Wash., U.S., 1,823 . . . . .358/F3
Royal Lakes, Ill., U.S., 190 . . . . .266/A3
Royal Leamington Spa, Eng., U.K. 70/A2

Royal Oak, Md., U.S., 750 . . . . .288/K5
Royal Oak, Mich., U.S., 60,062 . . . . .294/B6
Royal Palm Beach, Fla., U.S., 21,523 . . . .256/A4, H5
Royal Pines, N.C., U.S., 5,334 . . . . .322/E7
Royalston, Mass., U.S., 1,254 . . . . .292/F2
Royalton, Ill., U.S., 1,130 . . . . .266/D6
Royalton, Ky., U.S., 325 . . . . .280/G3
Royalton, Minn., U.S., 816 . . . . .298/C5
Royalton, Penn., U.S., 963 . . . . .336/H5
Royalton, Vt., U.S., 2,603 . . . . .352/B3
Royal Tunbridge Wells, Eng., U.K., 60,272 . . . . .70/E4
Royalty, Tex., U.S. 346/F4
Royersford, Penn., U.S., 4,246 . . . . .336/K5
Royse City, Tex., U.S., 2,957 . . . . . . .346/D9, M3
Royston, (Cambridgeshire/Hertfordshire),
 Eng., U.K., 14,087 . . . . .68/G5
Royston, (South/W. Yorkshire), Eng., U.K., 9,638 . .68/E2
Royston, Eng., U.K., 9,638 . . . . .66/F5
Royston, Eng., U.K., 14,087 . . . . .70/D2
Royston, Ga., U.S., 2,493 . . . . .260/E3
Rozel, Kans., U.S., 182 . . . . .276/C3
Rozellville, Wisc., U.S., 275 . . . . .364/C4
Rozet, Wyo., U.S., 90 . . . . .366/D1
Rožňava, Alb. .99/A2
Rrëshen, Alb. .99/A2
Ružomberok, Slvk. 92/B2
Ruabon, Wales, U.K., 2,828 . . . . .64/E2
Ruacana, Nam., falls 160/B1
Ruaha Natl. Park, Tan. 158/B2
Ruahine, N.Z., range 171/C2
Ruapehu, N.Z., mountain 171/C2
Rub al Khali, (Empty Quarter), Sa. Arab., desert . .136/C2
Rubery, Eng., U.K. 68/C5
Rubicon, Wisc., U.S., 350 . . . . .364/E1, E5
Rubio, Iowa, U.S., 50 . . . . .274/L5
Rubonia, Fla., U.S., 1,700 . . . . .256/D7
Rubtsovsk, Russ., 163,252 . . . . .104/F4
Ruby, Alaska, U.S., 188 . . . . .240/D2
Ruby, Nev., U.S., lake 310/C1
Ruby, Nev., U.S., mountains 310/C1
Ruby, S.C., U.S., 348 . . . . .340/D2
Ruby, Wash., U.S., 80 . . . . .358/H1
Ruby Dome, Nev., U.S., peak 310/C1
Ruby Lake N.W.R., Nev., U.S. 310/C1
Rubys Inn, Utah, U.S., 125 . . . . .350/B6
Ruby Valley, Nev., U.S., 50 . . . . .310/C1
Ruch, Oreg., U.S., 700 . . . . .334/C5
Rucker, Tex., U.S. 346/K3
Ruckersville, Va., U.S., 100 . . . . .354/G4
Rudall River Natl. Park, Austl. 170/B2
Ruda Śląska, Pol., 158,498 . . . . .83/D3
Rudd, Iowa, U.S., 431 . . . . .274/J1
Ruddington, Eng., U.K., 6,476 . . . . .68/E4
Rudolph, Ohio, U.S., 600 . . . . .328/C3
Rudolph, Tex., U.S., 40 . . . . .346/L9
Rudolph, Wisc., U.S., 423 . . . . .364/D4
Rudston, Eng., U.K. 66/H4
Rudy, Ark., U.S., 72 . . . . .244/A2
Rudyard, Eng., U.K. 68/C3
Rudyard, Mich., U.S., 500 . . . . .294/E3
Rudyard, Mont., U.S., 275 . . . . .306/F1
Rueter, Mo., U.S. 302/D5
Rufe, Okla., U.S., 80 . . . . .330/G4
Ruff, Wash., U.S. 358/G2
Ruffin, N.C., U.S., 375 . . . . .322/F2
Ruffin, S.C., U.S., 275 . . . . .340/D3
Rufiji, Tan., river 158/C2
Rufisque, Sen. 148/A2
Rufus, Oreg., U.S., 268 . . . . .334/F2
Rugby, Eng., U.K., 61,106 . . . . .68/E5
Rugby, Eng., U.K., 61,106 . . . . .70/B2
Rugby, N. Dak., U.S., 2,939 . . . . .326/F1
Rugby, Tenn., U.S., 60 . . . . .344/M2
Rugeley, Eng., U.K., 22,975 . . . . .68/D4
Rügen, Ger., island 86/C1
Ruggell, Liech. 90/B1
Ruggs, Oreg., U.S. 334/G2
Ruhengeri, Rwa. 158/B1
Ruhr, Ger., river 86/B3
Ruhwa, Rwa., river 158/B2
Ruidosa, Tex., U.S., 40 . . . . .346/D5
Ruidoso, N. Mex., U.S., 7,698 . . . . .317/E4
Ruidoso Downs, N. Mex., U.S., 1,824 . . . . .317/E4
Ruislip, Eng., U.K. 70/D3
Rukwa, Tan., lake 158/B2
Rukwa, Tan., region 158/B2
Rule, Ark., U.S. 244/B1
Rule, Tex., U.S., 698 . . . . .346/J2
Ruleton, Kans., U.S., 40 . . . . .276/A2
Ruleville, Miss., U.S., 3,234 . . . . .300/B2
Rulo, Nebr., U.S., 226 . . . . .308/J3
Rum, Bah., cay 204/C2
Rum, Bah., cay 207/C3
Rum, Minn., U.S., river 298/D3
Ruma, Ill., U.S., 260 . . . . .266/D5
Rumbek, Sudan 145/B3
Rumford, Maine, U.S., 6,472 . . . . .286/B4
Rumford, R.I., U.S. 339/D2
Rumford, S. Dak., U.S. 342/B4
Rumford Ctr., Maine, U.S., 125 . . . . .286/B4
Rumford Pt., Maine, U.S., 50 . . . . .286/B4
Rumney, Wales, U.K. 64/E4
Rumney, N.H., U.S., 1,480 . . . . .312/C4
Rumney Depot, N.H., U.S., 300 . . . . .312/C4
Rumson, N.J., U.S., 7,137 . . . . .314/E3
Runaway Bay, Jam. 206/B2
Runaway Bay, Tex., U.S., 1,104 . . . . .346/L2
Runcorn, Eng., U.K., 64,154 . . . . .66/C6
Runcorn, Eng., U.K., 64,154 . . . . .68/B5
Rundu, Nam., 19,366 . . . . .160/C1
Runge, Tex., U.S., 1,080 . . . . .346/L7
Rungue, Chile 190/Inset
Rungwa, Tan., river 158/B2
Runnells, Iowa, U.S., 352 . . . . .274/H4
Runnels, Tex., U.S., county, 11,495 . . . . .346/J4
Runnelstown, Miss., U.S., 250 . . . . .300/C4
Runnemede, N.J., U.S., 8,533 . . . . .314/B3, C4
Running Water, S. Dak., U.S. 342/G5
Rupel, Belg., river 85/C1
Rupert, Ark., U.S., 100 . . . . .244/C2
Rupert, Ga., U.S. 260/C7
Rupert, Ida., U.S., 5,645 . . . . .264/D7
Rupert, Vt., U.S., 704 . . . . .352/A4
Rupert, W. Va., U.S., 940 . . . . .360/E5
Rur, Ger., river 84/D4
Rural Hall, N.C., U.S., 2,464 . . . . .322/E2
Rural Hill, Tenn., U.S., 2,032 . . . . .344/H2
Rural Valley, Penn., U.S., 922 . . . . .336/C4
Ruse, Bul., 182,565 . . . . .101/D2
Ruse, Bul., oblast 101/E2
Rush, Colo., U.S. 250/F3
Rush, Colo., U.S., creek 250/G3
Rush, Ind., U.S., county, 18,261 . . . . .270/F5
Rush, Kans., U.S., county, 3,551 . . . . .276/C3
Rush, Ky., U.S., 175 . . . . .280/H2
Rush Ctr., Kans., U.S., 175 . . . . .276/C3
Rush City, Minn., U.S., 2,102 . . . . .298/E5
Rushden, Eng., U.K., 23,854 . . . . .68/E5
Rushden, Eng., U.K., 23,854 . . . . .70/C2
Rushford, Minn., U.S., 1,696 . . . . .298/F7
Rushford, N.Y., U.S., 350 . . . . .320/E6

Rushford Vil., Minn., U.S., 714 . . . . .298/F7
Rush Hill, Mo., U.S., 130 . . . . .302/E2
Rush Lake, Wisc., U.S., 175 . . . . .364/E5
Rushmere, Va., U.S., 1,083 . . . . .354/K6
Rushmore, Minn., U.S., 376 . . . . .298/B7
Rush Sprs., Okla., U.S., 1,278 . . . . .330/E3
Rushsylvania, Ohio, U.S., 543 . . . . .328/C5
Rush Valley, Utah, U.S., 453 . . . . .350/B3
Rushville, Ill., U.S., 3,212 . . . . .266/C3
Rushville, Ind., U.S., 5,995 . . . . .270/F5
Rushville, Mo., U.S., 280 . . . . .302/A2
Rushville, Nebr., U.S., 999 . . . . .308/B1
Rushville, N.Y., U.S., 621 . . . . .320/G5
Rushville, Ohio, U.S., 268 . . . . .328/F6
Rushyford, Eng., U.K. 66/C3
Rusizi, Bur., river 158/A1
Rusizi, Rwa., river 158/A2
Rusk, Tex., U.S., 5,085 . . . . .346/N4
Rusk, Tex., U.S., county, 47,372 . . . . .346/P3
Rusk, Wisc., U.S., 90 . . . . .364/B4
Rusk, Wisc., U.S., county, 15,347 . . . . .364/B3
Ruskin, Fla., U.S., 8,321 . . . . .256/D7
Ruskin, Nebr., U.S., 195 . . . . .308/G3
Ruskington, Eng., U.K., 3,530 . . . . .68/G3
Ruskington, Eng., U.K., 3,530 . . . . .70/D1
Ruso, N. Dak., U.S. 326/E2
Russell, Man., Can., 1,587 . . . . .215/A4
Russell, Ala., U.S., county, 49,756 . . . . .238/D3
Russell, Ark., U.S., 228 . . . . .244/D2
Russell, Fla., U.S., 100 . . . . .256/G1
Russell, Ga., U.S. 260/D4
Russell, Ga., U.S., lake 260/F3
Russell, Iowa, U.S., 559 . . . . .274/H6
Russell, Kans., U.S., 4,696 . . . . .276/D3
Russell, Kans., U.S., county, 7,370 . . . . .276/D3
Russell, Ky., U.S., 3,645 . . . . .280/H2
Russell, Ky., U.S., county, 16,315 . . . . .280/F4
Russell, Mass., U.S., 1,657 . . . . .292/C4
Russell, Minn., U.S., 371 . . . . .298/B6
Russell, N.Y., U.S., 125 . . . . .320/L2
Russell, N. Dak., U.S. 326/E1
Russell, Okla., U.S. 330/C3
Russell, Penn., U.S., 1,200 . . . . .336/C2
Russell, S.C., U.S., lake 340/B2
Russell, Va., U.S., county, 30,308 . . . . .354/C3
Russell Cave Natl. Mon., Ala., U.S. 238/D1
Russells Pt., Ohio, U.S., 1,619 . . . . .328/C5
Russell Sprs., Kans., U.S. 276/A3
Russell Sprs., Ky., U.S., 2,399 . . . . .280/E3
Russellville, Ala., U.S., 8,971 . . . . .238/B1
Russellville, Ark., U.S., 23,682 . . . . .244/B2
Russellville, Ill., U.S., 119 . . . . .266/F5
Russellville, Ind., U.S., 340 . . . . .270/C4
Russellville, Ky., U.S., 7,149 . . . . .280/D4
Russellville, Mo., U.S., 758 . . . . .302/D3
Russellville, Ohio, U.S., 453 . . . . .328/C8
Russellville, Tenn., U.S., 1,000 . . . . .344/Q2
Russia, nation .102
Russia, nation 193/A4
Russia, Ohio, U.S., 551 . . . . .328/B5
Russian Mission, Alaska, U.S., 296 . . . . .240/C2
Russiaville, Ind., U.S., 1,092 . . . . .270/D4
Rustad, Minn., U.S., 70 . . . . .298/A4
Rust'avi, Geo., 158,000 . . . . .103/C4
Rustburg, Va., U.S., 1,271 . . . . .354/E6
Rustic, Colo., U.S. 250/E1
Rustington, Eng., U.K. 70/D5
Ruston, La., U.S., 20,546 . . . . .282/D1
Ruston, Wash., U.S., 738 . . . . .358/C2
Rutana, Bur. .158/B2
Ruth, Mich., U.S. 275 . . . . .294/G6
Ruth, Miss., U.S., 500 . . . . .300/B4
Ruth, Nev., U.S., 500 . . . . .310/C2
Ruth, N.C., U.S., 329 . . . . .322/B4
Rutherford, N.J., U.S., 18,110 . . . . .314/B2
Rutherford, N.C., U.S., county, 62,899 . . . . . . .322/B4
Rutherford, Tenn., U.S., 1,272 . . . . .344/D2
Rutherford, Tenn., U.S., county, 182,023 . . . . . .344/J3
Rutherford College, N.C., U.S., 1,293 . . . . . . .322/B3
Rutherfordton, N.C., U.S., 4,131 . . . . .322/B4
Ruther Glen, Va., U.S., 300 . . . . .354/J5
Rutheron, N. Mex., U.S., 90 . . . . .317/D1
Ruthin, Wales, U.K., 5,029 . . . . .64/E1
Ruthsburg, Md., U.S., 125 . . . . .288/L3
Ruthton, Minn., U.S., 284 . . . . .298/A6
Ruthven, Iowa, U.S., 711 . . . . .274/E1
Rutland, Br. Col., Can. 214/N6
Rutland, Eng., U.K., unitary authority, 34,560 . . .68/F4
Rutland, Eng., U.K., unitary authority, 34,560 . . .70/C1
Rutland, Ill., U.S., 354 . . . . .266/D3
Rutland, Iowa, U.S., 145 . . . . .274/F2
Rutland, Mass., U.S., 6,353 . . . . .292/G3
Rutland, N. Dak., U.S., 220 . . . . .326/H3
Rutland, Ohio, U.S., 401 . . . . .328/F7
Rutland, S. Dak., U.S. 342/J3
Rutland, Vt., U.S., city, 17,292 . . . . .352/B3
Rutland, Vt., U.S., county, 63,400 . . . . .352/A3
Rutland Water, Eng., U.K., lake 70/C1
Rutledge, Ala., U.S., 476 . . . . .238/C4
Rutledge, Ga., U.S., 707 . . . . .260/D3
Rutledge, Minn., U.S., 196 . . . . .298/E4
Rutledge, Mo., U.S., 103 . . . . .302/D1
Rutledge, Penn., U.S., 860 . . . . .336/L7
Rutledge, Tenn., U.S., 1,187 . . . . .344/Q2
Ruvubu, Bur., river 158/C2
Ruvuma, Tan., region 158/C2
Ruvuma, Tan., river 158/C3
Ruwenzori, Ug., range 157/B1
Ruyigi, Bur. .158/C2
Ruyton-Xi-Towns, Eng., U.K. 68/B4
Rwanda, nation .152
Rwayakizinga, Rwa., lake 158/C1
Rweru, Rwa., river 158/C2
Ryal, Eng., U.K. 66/B1
Ryall Sprs., (East Brainerd), Tenn., U.S., 4,600 . .344/L4
Ryan, Ida., U.S., peak 264/C6
Ryan, Iowa, U.S., 410 . . . . .274/M3
Ryan, Okla., U.S., 894 . . . . .330/E3
Ryan, Tex., U.S. 346/D5
Ryan Park, Wyo., U.S. 366/C3
Ryazan', Russ., 528,116, (531,200 metro.) 104/C4
Rybnik, Pol., 144,441 . . . . .83/D3
Rycroft, Alta., Can., 609 . . . . .212/A3
Rydal, Eng., U.K. 66/C4
Ryde, N.S.W., Austl. . . . . .170/Inset IV
Ryde, Eng., U.K., 20,502 . . . . .70/B5
Ryder, N. Dak., U.S., 92 . . . . .326/D2
Ryderwood, Wash., U.S., 325 . . . . .358/B3
Rye, Eng., U.K., 3,708 . . . . .70/F5
Rye, Ariz., U.S., 40 . . . . .242/D3
Rye, Ark., U.S., 100 . . . . .244/D4
Rye, Colo., U.S., 202 . . . . .250/F4
Rye, N.H., U.S., 5,182 . . . . .312/E5
Rye, N.Y., U.S., 14,955 . . . . .320/C2
Rye Beach, N.H., U.S., 750 . . . . .312/E6
Rye Brook, N.Y., U.S., 8,602 . . . . .320/C1
Ryegate, Mont., U.S., 268 . . . . .306/G3
Ryegate Corner, Vt., U.S. 352/C2
Rye N. Beach, N.H., U.S., 475 . . . . .312/E5
Rye Patch, Nev., U.S., reservoir 310/A1

Ryhall, Eng., U.K. 70/D1
Ryland Hts., Ky., U.S., 799 . . . . .280/F2
Ryley, Alta., Can., 437 . . . . .212/D4
Rylstone, Eng., U.K. 68/C1
Ryotsu, Jap. .114/C2
Ryton, Eng., U.K., 15,952 . . . . .66/G4
Ryton-on-Dunsmore, (Ryton), Eng., U.K., 15,952 . . .70/A2
Ryton-on-Dunsmore, Eng., U.K. 68/E5
Ryukyu, Jap., islands . . . . .114/A4, Inset II
Rzeszów, Pol., 162,273 . . . . .83/F3
Saale, Ger., river 86/B3
Saar, Ger., river 86/A4
Saar, Ger., river 88/D2
Saarbrücken, Ger., 183,836 . . . . .86/A4
Saaremaa, Est., island 81/B2
Saarland, Ger., state 86/A4
Saba, Neth. Ant., island 204/F3
Sabadell, Sp., 183,788 . . . . .94/H2
Sab Abar, Syria 134/A3
Sabah, Malay., state 121/D2
Sabana de la Mar, Dom. Rep. 205/C1
Sabana Grande, P.R. 206/A2
Sabana Grande, P.R. 206/B2
Sabana Hoyos, P.R. 206/B2
Sabaneta, Dom. Rep. 205/A1
Sabaragamuwa, Sri Lan., province 126/B5
Sabattis, N.Y., U.S. 320/M2
Sabattus, Maine, U.S., 4,486 . . . . .286/B4
Saberi, Hamun-e, Afg., lake 129/A2
Sabetha, Kans., U.S., 2,589 . . . . .276/G2
Sabha, Lib. .145/B2
Sabi, Zimb., river 160/C2
Sabillasville, Md., U.S., 350 . . . . .288/E1
Sabin, Minn., U.S., 421 . . . . .298/A4
Sabina, Ohio, U.S., 2,780 . . . . .328/C7
Sabinal, N. Mex., U.S., 100 . . . . .317/D3
Sabinal, Tex., U.S., 1,586 . . . . .346/J6
Sabine, La., U.S., parish, 23,459 . . . . .282/B3
Sabine, Tex., U.S., county, 10,469 . . . . .346/R4
Sabine, Tex., U.S., pass 346/R6
Sabine, Tex., U.S., river 346/N3, R5
Sabine Natl. For., Tex., U.S. 346/R4
Sabine N.W.R., La., U.S. 282/B7, C7
Sabine Pass, Tex., U.S., 40 . . . . .346/R6
Sabinoso, N. Mex., U.S. 317/F2
Sabinsville, Penn., U.S., 225 . . . . .336/F2
Sable, Fla., U.S., cape 256/G6
Sable River, N.S., Can. 221/B4
Sabula, Iowa, U.S., 670 . . . . .274/P3
Sabula, Mo., U.S. 302/F4
Sabzevar, Iran 130/D2
Sac, Iowa, U.S., county, 11,529 . . . . .274/D3
Sacajawea, Oreg., U.S., peak 334/J2
Sacajawea, Wash., U.S., lake 358/G3
Sac and Fox Ind. Res., Iowa, U.S. 274/J3
Sac and Fox Ind. Res., Nebr., U.S. 308/J3
Sacaton, Ariz., U.S., 1,584 . . . . .242/D4
Sac City, Iowa, U.S., 2,368 . . . . .274/E3
Sachem Head, Conn., U.S., 600 . . . . .253/E5
Sachigo, Ont., Can., river 222/B2
Sachs Harbour, N.W. Terr., Can., 114 . . . . .220/C2
Sachuest Pt. N.W.R., R.I., U.S. 339/E5
Sackets Harbor, N.Y., U.S., 1,386 . . . . .320/J3
Sackville, N.B., Can., 5,361 . . . . .217/E3
Saco, Ala., U.S., 100 . . . . .238/D4
Saco, Maine, U.S., 16,822 . . . . .286/B5
Saco, Maine, U.S., bay 286/B5
Saco, Maine, U.S., river 286/B5
Saco, Mont., U.S., 224 . . . . .306/J1
Sacramento, Calif., U.S., county,
 1,223,499 . . . . .246/D4, K6, L1
Sacramento, Calif., U.S., river 246/C3, K6
Sacramento, Calif., U.S., state capital,
 407,018, (1,796,857 metro.) 246/D4, K5
Sacramento, Ky., U.S., 517 . . . . .280/C3
Sacramento, N. Mex., U.S., 50 . . . . .317/E5
Sacred Heart, Minn., U.S., 549 . . . . .298/B6
Sacriston, Eng., U.K., 4,726 . . . . .66/G4
Sa'dah, Yemen 137/A1
Sadberge, Eng., U.K. 66/F3
Saddleback, Maine, U.S., mountain 286/B4
Saddle Brook, N.J., U.S., 13,155 . . . . .314/B2
Saddle Mtn. N.W.R., Wash., U.S. 358/F3
Saddle River, N.J., U.S., 3,201 . . . . .314/B1
Saddlestring, Wyo., U.S., 40 . . . . .366/C1
Sadie, Tenn., U.S., 325 . . . . .344/S2
Sadieville, Ky., U.S., 263 . . . . .280/E2
Sado, Jap., island 114/C2
Sado, Port., river 93/A3
Sadorus, Ill., U.S., 426 . . . . .266/E4
Saegertown, Penn., U.S., 1,071 . . . . .336/A2
Safata, Sam., bay 175/C3
Safety Harbor, Fla., U.S., 17,203 . . . . .256/C6
Safford, Ala., U.S. 238/B3
Safford, Ariz., U.S., 9,232 . . . . .242/F5
Saffron Walden, Eng., U.K., 13,201 . . . . .68/H5
Saffron Walden, Eng., U.K., 13,201 . . . . .70/E2
Safi, Mor., 278,000 . . . . .147/B1
Safotu, Sam. .175/B1
Saga, Jap. 114/A3
Saga, Jap., prefecture 114/A3
Sagadahoc, Maine, U.S., county, 35,214 . . . . . . .286/C5
Sagaing, Mya. 125/B2
Sagaing, Mya., division 125/B2
Sagamartha, Jap., bay 114/C3
Sagamihara, Jap., 606,000 . . . . .114/C3
Sagamore, Mass., U.S., 3,544 . . . . .292/M5
Sagamore, Penn., U.S., 400 . . . . .336/C4
Sagamore Beach, Mass., U.S., 1,200 . . . . .292/M5
Sagamore Hill N.H.S., N.Y., U.S. 320/C2
Sage, Ark., U.S., 60 . . . . .244/D1
Sage, Wyo., U.S. 366/A3
Sage Creek Jct., Utah, U.S., 50 . . . . .350/C2
Sageville, Iowa, U.S., 203 . . . . .274/N2
Sag Harbor, N.Y., U.S., 2,313 . . . . .320/G1
Saginaw, Ala., U.S., 325 . . . . .238/C2
Saginaw, Mich., U.S., 61,799, (403,070 metro.) . . .294/F6
Saginaw, Mich., U.S., bay 294/F6
Saginaw, Mich., U.S., county, 210,039 . . . . . . .294/E6
Saginaw, Minn., U.S., 150 . . . . .298/E4
Saginaw, Mo., U.S., 276 . . . . .302/B4
Saginaw, Tex., U.S., 12,374 . . . . .346/A9
Sagola, Mich., U.S., 50 . . . . .294/A3
Saguache, Colo., U.S., 578 . . . . .250/D3
Saguache, Colo., U.S., county, 5,917 . . . . .250/D3
Saguache, Colo., U.S., creek 250/D3
Sagua la Grande, Cuba 204/C2
Saguaro N.P., Ariz., U.S. 242/D5, E5
Saguenay, Que., Can., river 226/E3
Saguenay Prov. Park, Que., Can. 226/E3
Saguento, Sp. .94/E3
Sahalee, Wash., U.S. 358/B4, C3
Sahara, Alg., desert 146/B2
Sahara, Chad, desert 153/A2
Sahara, Lib., desert 145/C2

Sahara, Mali, desert 150/C1
Sahara, Maur., desert 147/C1
Sahara, Mor., desert 147/B2
Sahara, Niger, desert 152/A1
Sahara, Sudan, desert 144/A3
Sahara, Tun., desert 146/B4
Sa. W. Sah., desert 147/B1
Saharan Atlas, Alg., mountains 146/A1
Saharanpur Panipat, India 128/C3
Şahbuz, Azer. 103/A3
Sahel, Mali, region 150/C2
Sahel, Niger, region 152/A3
Sahel, Sen., region 148/C2
Sahiwal, Pak., 208,778 . . . . .129/D3
Sahuarita, Ariz., U.S., 3,242 . . . . .242/E6
Sahuayo, Bangl., 102,030 . . . . .127/B3
Sai Kung, H.K., China 117/B1
Sailor Sprs., Ill., U.S., 128 . . . . .266/E5
Saimaa, Fin., lake 81/C2
St. Abb's, Scot., U.K. 62/M7
St. Adolphe, Man., Can., 1,140 . . . . .215/A4
St. Agatha, Maine, U.S., 802 . . . . .286/D1
St. Agnes, Eng., U.K., 2,899 . . . . .73/B4
St. Agnes, Eng., U.K., island 73/A3
St. Alban, Nfld., Can., 1,372 . . . . .218/D5
St. Albans, Eng., U.K. . . . . .60/C3, Inset II
St. Albans, Eng., U.K., 80,376 . . . . .70/D3
St. Albans, Maine, U.S., 1,836 . . . . .286/C4
St. Albans, Vt., U.S., city, 7,650 . . . . .352/A1
St. Albans, Vt., U.S., town, 5,086 . . . . .352/A1
St. Albans, W. Va., U.S., 11,567 . . . . .360/C4
St. Albans Bay, Vt., U.S., 425 . . . . .352/A1
St. Albert, Alta., Can., 53,081 . . . . .212/D4
St. Andrew, Ga., U.S., sound 260/I10
St. Andrews, N.B., Can., 1,869 . . . . .217/B3
St. Andrews, Scot., U.K. 60/C2
St. Andrews, Scot., U.K., 14,209 . . . . .62/L6
St. Andrews, S.C., U.S., 21,814 . . . . .340/A3, C2
St. Ann, Mo., U.S., 13,607 . . . . .302/H3
St. Anne, Sey., island 163/Inset
St. Anne, Eng., U.K. 73/J4
St. Anne, Ill., U.S., 1,212 . . . . .266/F2
St. Ann's Bay, Jam. 206/B2
St. Ansgar, Iowa, U.S., 1,031 . . . . .274/J1
St. Anthony, Nfld., Can., 2,730 . . . . .218/D3
St. Anthony, Ida., U.S., 3,342 . . . . .264/F6
St. Anthony, Iowa, U.S., 109 . . . . .274/H3
St. Anthony, (Hennepin County),
 Minn., U.S., 8,012 . . . . .298/F5
St. Anthony, (Stearns County), Minn., U.S., 90 . . .298/C5
St. Anthony, N. Dak., U.S., 40 . . . . .326/E3
St-Antoine, N.B., Can., 1,472 . . . . .217/E2
St-Antoine, Que., Can. 226/C6
St-Apollinaire, Que., Can., 3,930 . . . . .226/E3
St-Arthur, N.B., Can., 832 . . . . .217/C1
St. Arvans, Wales, U.K. 64/E1
St. Asaph, Wales, U.K. 64/E1
St. Athan, Wales, U.K. 64/E5
St-Augustin, Que., Can., 626 . . . . .209/A2
St. Augustine, Trin.-To. 209/A2
St. Augustine, Ill., U.S., 11,592 . . . . .256/G2
St. Augustine, Ill., U.S., 152 . . . . .266/C3
St. Augustine Beach, Fla., U.S., 4,683 . . . . . . .256/G2
St. Augustine Shores, Fla., U.S., 4,922 . . . . . . .256/G2
St. Austell, Eng., U.K. 60/B4
St. Austell, Eng., U.K., 21,622 . . . . .73/C4
St. Barbe, Nfld., Can., 158 . . . . .218/D3
St-Barthélemy, Fr., island 204/F3
St-Basile, N.B., Can. 217/A1
St. Benedict, Kans., U.S., 80 . . . . .276/F2
St. Bernard, La., U.S., 1,500 . . . . .282/L3
St. Bernard, La., U.S., parish, 67,229 . . . . .282/K7, L3
St. Bernard, Ohio, U.S., 4,924 . . . . .328/B9
St. Bernard's, Nfld., Can., 657 . . . . .218/D5
St. Blazey, (St Blazey/Par), Eng., U.K., 8,837 . . .73/C4
St. Bonaventure, N.Y., U.S., 2,127 . . . . .320/E6
St. Brendan's, Nfld., Can., 251 . . . . .218/E5
St. Bride's, Nfld., Can., 473 . . . . .218/D5
St. Brides, Wales, U.K. 64/A4
St. Bride's, Wales, U.K., bay 64/A4
St-Brieuc, Fr. .88/B2
St. Brieux, Sask., Can., 505 . . . . .227/F8
St-Bruno, Que., Can., 2,384 . . . . .226/E3
St. Catharines, Ont., Can., 129,170,
 (392,300 metro.) 223/F4
St. Catherine, Gren., mountain 209/B2
St. Catherine Creek N.W.R., Miss., U.S. 300/A4
St. Catherine's, Nfld., Can. 218/E5
St. Catherines, Ga., U.S., island 260/J8
St. Charles, N.B., Can., 806 . . . . .217/E2
St-Charles, Que., Can., lake 226/E3
St. Charles, Ark., U.S., 261 . . . . .244/D3
St. Charles, Ida., U.S., 156 . . . . .264/F7
St. Charles, Ill., U.S., 27,896 . . . . .266/A6
St. Charles, Iowa, U.S., 619 . . . . .274/G5
St. Charles, Ky., U.S., 309 . . . . .280/C3
St. Charles, La., U.S., parish, 48,072 . . . . .282/J3, J7
St. Charles, Md., U.S., 33,379 . . . . .288/G6
St. Charles, Mich., U.S., 2,215 . . . . .294/E6
St. Charles, Minn., U.S., 3,295 . . . . .298/E7
St. Charles, Mo., U.S., 60,321 . . . . .302/F3, H2
St. Charles, Mo., U.S., county, 283,883 . . . . . .302/F3, G2
St. Charles, S.C., U.S., 70 . . . . .340/D2
St. Charles, S. Dak., U.S. 342/F4
St. Charles, Va., U.S., 159 . . . . .354/B2
St. Charles Palace, Vat. 96/B2
St-Chrysostome, P.E.I., Can. 224/A2
St. Clair, Ont., Can., lake 223/C5
St. Clair, Ont., Can., river 223/C5
St. Clair, Ala., U.S., county, 64,742 . . . . .238/C2
St. Clair, Ga., U.S. 260/G5
St. Clair, Ill., U.S., county, 256,082 . . . . .266/A3, C5
St. Clair, Mich., U.S., 5,802 . . . . .294/G7
St. Clair, Mich., U.S., county, 164,235 . . . . . .294/F6, G7
St. Clair, Minn., U.S., 827 . . . . .298/D6
St. Clair, Mo., U.S., 4,390 . . . . .302/E3
St. Clair, Mo., U.S., county, 9,652 . . . . .302/C3
St. Clair, Penn., U.S., 3,254 . . . . .336/J4
St. Clair Shores, Mich., U.S., 63,096 . . . . . . .294/B6
St. Clairsville, Ohio, U.S., 5,057 . . . . .328/J5
St. Clairsville, Penn., U.S., 86 . . . . .336/B6
St. Claude, Man., Can., 558 . . . . .215/B4
St. Clears, Wales, U.K. 64/C4
St. Clement Shores, Md., U.S., 800 . . . . .288/H6
St-Cloud, Fr. . . . . .88/Inset II
St. Cloud, Fla., U.S., 20,074 . . . . .256/G3
St. Cloud, Minn., U.S., 59,107, (167,392 metro.) . .298/C5
St. Cloud, Wisc., U.S., 497 . . . . .364/E6
St. Columb Major, Eng., U.K., 2,119 . . . . .73/C4
St-Côme, Que., Can., 1,923 . . . . .226/C5
St-Constant, Que., Can. 226/J6
St. Croix, N.B., Can. 217/B3

St. Croix, Maine, U.S., *river* 286/E3
St. Croix, Wisc., U.S., *county*, 63,155 . . . . .364/A3
St. Croix, Vir. Is., *island* 204/E3
St. Croix Falls, Wisc., U.S., 2,033 . . . . .364/A3
St. Croix Island Intl. Hist. Site, Maine,
N.B., U.S., Can. 286/E3
St. Croix Natl. Scenic River, Minn., U.S. 298/E5
St. Croix Natl. Scenic River, Wisc., U.S. 364/A3
St. Croix St. Park, Minn., U.S. 298/E5
St-Cyprien, Que., Can., 1,231 . . . . .226/H4
St. David, Ariz., U.S., 1,744 . . . . .242/E6
St. David, Ill., U.S., 587 . . . . .266/C3
St. David, Maine, U.S., 125 . . . . .286/D1
St-David-de-Falardeau, Que., Can., 2,347 . . .226/E3
St-David's, Gren. .209/B2
St. David's, Wales, U.K. 60/B3
St. David's, Wales, U.K., 1,627 . . . . .64/A4
St-Denis, Fr. . . . . .88/Inset II
St. Dennis, Eng., U.K., 1,974 . . . . .73/C4
St. Dennis, Ky., U.S., 9,177 . . . . .280/E2
St-Dizier, Fr. 88/D2
St-Donat, Que., Can., 847 . . . . .226/B5
St-Donatus, Iowa, U.S., 140 . . . . .274/N3
Ste. Agathe, Man., Can. 215/C4
Ste-Agathe-des-Monts, Que., Can., 7,116 . . .226/B5
Ste. Amélie, Que., Can. 215/B4
Ste-Angèle-de-Mérici, Que., Can. 226/J3
Ste. Anne, Man., Can., 1,513 . . . . .215/C4
Ste-Anne-de-Kent, N.B., Can., 1,150 . . . . . .217/E2
Ste-Anne-de-Madawaska, N.B., Can., 1,168 . .217/A1
Ste-Anne-des-Monts, Que., Can., 6,835 . . . .226/K2
Ste-Anne-du-Lac, Que., Can., 570 . . . . .226/A5
Ste-Apolline, Que., Can. 226/F5
Ste-Claire, Que., Can., 3,135 . . . . .226/F5
Ste-Croix, Que., Can., 1,533 . . . . .226/E5
St. Edward, P.E.I., Can. 224/A2
St. Edward, Nebr., U.S., 796 . . . . .308/G2
Ste-Eulalie, Que., Can. 226/D5
Ste-Foy, Que., Can., 72,547 . . . . .226/E5, K6
Ste. Genevieve, Mo., U.S., 4,476 . . . . .302/F4
Ste. Genevieve, Mo., U.S., *county*, 17,842 . .302/F4
St. Elias, Br. Col., Can., *mountains* 214/D1
St. Elias, Yukon, Can., *mountains* 228/K5
St. Elias, Alaska, U.S., *cape* 240/G3
St. Elias, Alaska, U.S., *mountain* 240/G2
St-Elie, Fr. Gui. 183/B1
St. Elizabeth, Mo., U.S., 297 . . . . .302/D3
St. Elmo, Colo., U.S. 250/D3
St. Elmo, Ill., U.S., 1,456 . . . . .266/E4
Ste-Luce, Que., Can., 1,478 . . . . .226/H3
Ste-Marie, Que., Can., 11,320 . . . . .226/E5
Ste-Marie, Madag., *cape* 163/B4
Ste. Marie, Ill., U.S., 261 . . . . .266/E4
Ste-Marie-de-Kent, N.B., Can. 217/E2
Ste-Émilie, Que., Can., 10,940 . . . . .226/K5
Ste-Monique, Que., Can., 930 . . . . .226/E3
Ste. Rose du Lac, Man., Can., 1,047 . . . . . . .215/B3
Ste-Rose-du-Nord, Que., Can., 409 . . . . . . .226/F3
Saintes, Fr. 88/B4
Ste-Thérèse, Que., Can. 226/H5
St-Étienne, Fr., 183,522, (291,960 metro.) . . .88/D4
St. Eustache, Man., Can. 215/C4
St-Eustache, Que., Can., 40,378 . . . . .226/H5
St. Eustatius, Neth. Ant., *island* 204/F3
Ste-Véronique, Que., Can., 1,050 . . . . .226/A5
St-Fabien, Que., Can., 1,848 . . . . .226/H3
St-Fabien-de-Panet, Que., Can., 1,021 . . . . .226/F5
St-Félicien, Que., Can., 10,622 . . . . .226/D3
St-Félix-d'Otis, Que. Can., 790 . . . . .226/F3
St. Fergus, Scot., U.K. 62/N3
Saintfield, N. Ire., U.K., 2,168 . . . . .65/F3
St. Florian, Ala., U.S., 335 . . . . .238/B1
St. Francis, Ark., U.S., 250 . . . . .244/E1
St. Francis, Ark., U.S., *county*, 29,329 . . . . .244/D2
St. Francis, Ark., U.S., *river* 244/E1
St. Francis, Kans., U.S., 1,497 . . . . .276/A2
St. Francis, Ky., U.S., 125 . . . . .280/E3
St. Francis, Maine, U.S., 577 . . . . .286/D1
St. Francis, Minn., U.S., 4,910 . . . . .298/D5
St. Francis, Mo., U.S., *river* 302/F4
St. Francis, S. Dak., U.S., 675 . . . . .342/E4
St. Francis, Tex., U.S. 346/F9
St. Francis, Wisc., U.S., 8,662 . . . . .364/F2
St. Francis Natl. For., Ark., U.S. 244/E3
St. Francisville, Ill., U.S., 759 . . . . .266/F5
St. Francisville, La., U.S., 1,712 . . . . .282/G5
St-François, Que., Can., *lake* 226/E6
St-François, Que., Can., *river* 226/D5
St. Francois, Mo., U.S., *county*, 55,641 . . . .302/F4
St-François-de-Madawaska, N.B., Can., 572 . .217/A1
St. Gabriel, La., U.S., 5,514 . . . . .282/G6
St-Gaudens N.H.S., N.H., U.S. 312/B4
St-Gédéon, Que., Can., 1,923 . . . . .226/F6
St. George, N.B., Can., 1,509 . . . . .217/C3
St. George, Alaska, U.S., 152 . . . . .240/B3
St. George, Alaska, U.S., *island* 240/B3
St. George, Fla., U.S., *island* 256/D2
St. George, Ga., U.S., 275 . . . . .260/G1
St. George, Kans., U.S., 434 . . . . .276/F2
St. George, Maine, U.S., 2,580 . . . . .286/C4
St. George, Minn., U.S., 100 . . . . .298/C6
St. George, Mo., U.S., 1,288 . . . . .302/H3
St. George, (see New York), N.Y., U.S. 320/E2
St. George, S.C., U.S., 2,092 . . . . .340/D3
St. George, Utah, U.S., 49,663 . . . . .350/A6
St. George Island, Md., U.S., 275 . . . . .288/H7
St. George's, Nfld., Can., 1,354 . . . . .218/B5
St. George's, Nfld., Can., *bay* 218/B5
St. George's, N.S., Can., *bay* 221/F2
St-Georges, Que., Can., 20,787 . . . . .226/F5
St-Georges, Fr. Gui. 183/C2
St. George's, Gren., *capital* 204/F4
St. George's, Gren., *capital*, 4,621,
(35,559 metro.) 209/A2
Saint George's, Ire., *channel* 78/C3
St. George's, P.N.G., *channel* 172/B2
St-Germain, (St-Germain-de-Grantham),
Que., Can. 226/G4
St-Germain, Wisc., U.S., 225 . . . . .364/D1
St-Germain-en-Laye, Fr. . . . . .88/Inset II
St. Gotthard, Switz., *pass* 90/C2
St. Gotthard, Switz., *tunnel* 90/C2
St. Hedwig, Tex., U.S., 1,875 . . . . .346/B2
St. Helen, Mich., U.S., 2,993 . . . . .294/E2
St. Helena, U.K., *island* 140/B6
St. Helena, Calif., U.S., 5,950 . . . . .246/C4
St. Helena, La., U.S., *parish*, 10,525 . . . . . .282/H5
St. Helena, Nebr., U.S., 86 . . . . .308/G1
St. Helena, N.C., U.S., 395 . . . . .322/K5
St. Helena, S.C., U.S., *sound* 340/D4
St. Helena Island, S.C., U.S., 400 . . . . .340/D4
St. Helens, Eng., U.K. 60/C3
St. Helens, Eng., U.K., 106,293 . . . . .66/C6
St. Helens, Eng., U.K., *unitary authority*, 176,845 . .66/C6
St. Helens, Eng., U.K., *unitary authority*, 176,845 . .68/B3
St. Helens, Oreg., U.S., 10,019 . . . . .334/C3
St. Helens, Wash., U.S., *mountain* 358/C3
St. Helier, Eng., U.K., *territorial capital* . . .60/Inset II
St. Helier, Eng., U.K., *territorial capital* 73/H4
St-Henri-de-Taillon, Que., Can., 776 . . . . . . .226/E3

St. Henry, Ohio, U.S., 2,271 . . . . .328/A5
St-Hilaire, Minn., U.S., 272 . . . . .298/A3
St-Hubert, Que., Can., 75,912 . . . . .226/G4
St-Hyacinthe, Que., Can., 38,739 . . . . .226/D6
St-Ignace, N.B., Can., 651 . . . . .217/D2
St-Ignace, Mich., U.S., 2,678 . . . . .294/E4
St-Ignace-du-Lac, Que., Can. 226/C5
St. Ignatius, Mont., U.S., 788 . . . . .306/B2
St. Inigoes, Md., U.S., 650 . . . . .288/J7
St-Isidore, N.B., Can., 877 . . . . .217/D1
St. Ives, N.S.W., Austl. . . . . .170/Inset IV
St. Ives, Eng., U.K., 16,510 . . . . .68/G5
St. Ives, Eng., U.K., 16,510 . . . . .70/D2
St. Ives, Eng., U.K., 10,092 . . . . .73/B4
St. Jacob, Ill., U.S., 801 . . . . .266/B3
St-Jacques, N.B., Can. 217/A1
St. Jacques, Mich., U.S., 50 . . . . .294/C4
St-Jacques-de-Leeds, Que., Can., 771 . . . . . .226/E5
St. James, Ark., U.S., 125 . . . . .244/D2
St. James, Ill., U.S., 80 . . . . .266/E5
St. James, La., U.S., 275 . . . . .282/H6
St. James, La., U.S., *parish*, 21,216 . . . . . .282/H7
St. James, Mich., U.S., 200 . . . . .294/D4
St. James, Minn., U.S., 4,695 . . . . .298/C7
St. James, Mo., U.S., 3,704 . . . . .302/E4
St. James, Que., Can., *lake* 226/D3
St-Jean Baptiste, Man., Can. 215/C4
St-Jean-Baptiste-de-Restigouche, N.B., Can., 214 . .217/B1
St-Jean-Chrysostome, Que., Can., 17,089 . . .226/L6
St-Jean-de-Matha, Que., Can., 3,602 . . . . . .226/C5
St-Jean-Port-Joli, Que., Can., 1,898 . . . . . . .226/F4
St-Jean-sur-Richelieu, Que., Can., 37,386 . . .226/C6
St-Jérôme, Que., Can., 24,583 . . . . .226/B6
St. Jo, Tex., U.S., 977 . . . . .346/L2
St. Joe, Ark., U.S., 85 . . . . .244/C1
St. Joe, Ida., U.S. 264/A2
St. Joe, Ida., U.S., *river* 264/A2
St. Joe, Ind., U.S., 478 . . . . .270/G2
St. Joe, Kans., U.S., 70 . . . . .276/E4
St. Joe Natl. For., Ida., U.S. 264/A3, B2
Saint John, N.B., Can., 69,661, (127,000 metro.) . .217/C3
Saint John, N.B., Can., *county* 217/D3
Saint John, N.B., Can., *river* 217/B2
St. John, Eng., U.K. 73/H4
St. John, Ind., U.S., 8,382 . . . . .270/B2
St. John, Kans., U.S., 1,318 . . . . .276/D3
St. John, Ky., U.S. 280/E3
Saint John, Maine, U.S., 282 . . . . .286/C2, E2
St. John, Mo., U.S., 6,871 . . . . .302/H3
St. John, N. Dak., U.S., 358 . . . . .326/F1
St. John, Wash., U.S., 548 . . . . .358/H2
St. John's, Ant.-Bar., *capital* 204/F3
St. John's, Ant.-Bar., *capital*, 22,342 . . . . . .207/D5
St. John's, Nfld., Can., 99,182,
(177,200 metro.) 218/E5
St. Johns, Eng., U.K. 66/A5
St. Johns, N. Ire., U.K., *point* 65/F3
St. Johns, Ariz., U.S., 3,269 . . . . .242/F3
St. Johns, Fla., U.S., *county*, 123,135 . . . . .256/G1
St. Johns, Fla., U.S., *river* 256/G2
St. Johns, Ill., U.S., 218 . . . . .266/D5
St. Johns, Mich., U.S., 7,485 . . . . .294/E6
St. Johnsbury, Vt., U.S., 7,571 . . . . .352/C2
St. Johnsbury Ctr., Vt., U.S., 1,000 . . . . .352/C2
St. John's Chapel, Eng., U.K. 66/D3
St. John's Highway, Eng., U.K. 70/E1
St. Johnsville, N.Y., U.S., 1,685 . . . . .320/M4
St. John Baptist, La., U.S., *parish*,
43,044 . . . . .282/H2, H6
St. Joseph, N.B., Can. 217/E2
St. Joseph, Ont., Can., *island* 223/B1
St. Joseph, Ont., Can., *island* 294/F3
Saint Joseph, Dom. 208/A3
St. Joseph, Fla., U.S., *bay* 256/C2
St. Joseph, Fla., U.S., *point* 256/C2
St. Joseph, Ill., U.S., 2,912 . . . . .266/E3
St. Joseph, Ind., U.S., 375 . . . . .270/E8
St. Joseph, Ind., U.S., *county*, 265,559 . . . .270/D1
St. Joseph, Ind., U.S., *river* 270/G2
St. Joseph, La., U.S., 1,340 . . . . .282/G3
St. Joseph, Mich., U.S., 8,789 . . . . .294/C7
St. Joseph, Mich., U.S., *county*, 62,422 . . . .294/D8
St. Joseph, Minn., U.S., 4,681 . . . . .298/C5
St. Joseph, Mo., U.S., 73,990, (102,490 metro.) . .302/B2
St. Joseph, Tenn., U.S., 829 . . . . .344/F4
St-Joseph-de-Beauce, Que., Can., 4,487 . . . .226/F5
St. Just, Eng., U.K., 2,092 . . . . .73/A4
St. Keverne, Eng., U.K. 73/B4
St. Kilda, S.A., Austl. . . . . .170/Inset II
St. Kilda, Vic., Austl. . . . . .170/Inset V
St. Kitts, (St. Christopher), St. K.-Nevis, *island* . .207/B2
St. Kitts and Nevis, *nation* 204/F3
St. Kitts and Nevis, *nation* 195
St. Labre, Man., Can. 215/C4
St-Lambert, Que., Can., 21,051 . . . . .226/J5
St. Landry, La., U.S., 300 . . . . .282/E5
St. Landry, La., U.S., *parish*, 87,700 . . . . . .282/F5
St. Laurent, Man., Can. 215/C4
St-Laurent, Que., Can., 77,391 . . . . .226/J5
St-Laurent du Maroni, Fr. Gui., 19,210 . . . . .183/A1
St. Lawrence, Nfld., Can., 1,558 . . . . .218/D5
St. Lawrence, Nfld., Can., *gulf* 218/B4
St. Lawrence, N.S., Can., *cape* 221/G1
St. Lawrence, Ont., Can., *river* 223/K3
St. Lawrence, P.E.I., Can., *gulf* 224/C2
St. Lawrence, Que., Can., *gulf* 225/D4
St. Lawrence, Que., Can., *river* 226/B6, G3, J6, L6
St. Lawrence, Eng., U.K. 70/B5
St. Lawrence, U.S., *island* 193/C10
St. Lawrence, Alaska, U.S., *island* 240/A2
St. Lawrence, N.Y., U.S., *county*, 111,931 . .320/L2
St. Lawrence, N.Y., U.S., *river* 320/L1
St. Lawrence, S. Dak., U.S., 210 . . . . .342/G3
St. Lawrence, Tex., U.S., 40 . . . . .346/G4
St. Lawrence Islands N.P., Ont., Can. 223/J3
St-Lazare, Man., Can., 265 . . . . .215/A4
St. Leo, Fla., U.S., 595 . . . . .256/F3
St. Leo, Kans., U.S., 70 . . . . .276/D4
St. Leon, Ind., U.S., 387 . . . . .270/G6
St-Léonard, N.B., Can., 1,385 . . . . .217/B1
St-Léonard, Que., Can., 69,604 . . . . .226/J5
St-Léonard, Md., U.S., 536 . . . . .288/H6
St-Léonard-Parent, N.B., Can. 217/B1
St. Leonards, Eng., U.K., 6,136 . . . . .70/F5
St. Lewis, Nfld., Can., 290 . . . . .218/C3
St. Libory, Ill., U.S., 583 . . . . .266/D5
St. Libory, Nebr., U.S., 275 . . . . .308/F2
St-Lô, Fr. 88/B2
St-Louis, P.E.I., Can., 98 . . . . .224/A2
St-Louis, Que., Can., 474 . . . . .226/H6
St-Louis, Sask., Can. 227/E8
St. Louis, Sen., (147,961 metro.) 148/A1
St. Louis, Mich., U.S., 4,494 . . . . .294/E6
St. Louis, Minn., U.S., *county*, 200,528 . . . .298/E2
St. Louis, Minn., U.S., *river* 298/E3

St. Louis, Mo., U.S., *city*, 348,189,
(2,603,607 metro.) 302/F3, J3
St. Louis, Mo., U.S., *county*, 1,016,315 . . .302/F3, H3
St. Louis, Okla., U.S., 206 . . . . .330/F2
St-Louis-de-Kent, N.B., Can., 991 . . . . .217/E2
St. Louis Hts., Hawaii, U.S. 262/G2
St. Louis Park, Minn., U.S., 44,126 . . . . .298/E6
St. Louisville, Ohio, U.S., 346 . . . . .328/F5
St. Lucas, Iowa, U.S., 178 . . . . .274/L1
St. Lucia, *nation* 204/F4
St. Lucia, *nation* 196
Saint Lucia, St. Luc., *channel* 208/B1
St. Lucia, S. Afr., *lake* 162/D2
St. Lucie, Fla., U.S., 604 . . . . .256/H4
St. Lucie, Fla., U.S., *county*, 192,695 . . .256/A3, H4
St-Ludger, Que., Can., 1,203 . . . . .226/F6
St-Ludger-de-Milot, Que., Can., 764 . . . . . . .226/E3
St. Maarten, Neth., *island* 204/F3
St. Malo, Man., Can. 215/C4
St-Malo, Que., Can., 518 . . . . .226/E6
St-Malo, Fr. 88/B2
St-Malo, Fr., *gulf* . . . . .60/Inset II
St-Malo, Fr., *gulf* .88/B2
St-Marc, Haiti 205/C1
St-Marc-du-Lac-Long, Que., Can., 469 . . . . . .226/H4
St-Marcel, Que., Can., 531 . . . . .226/H3
St-Marcel, Fr. Gui., *mountain* 183/B2
St-Marcellin, Que., Can. 226/H3
St. Margarets, N.B., Can., 386 . . . . .217/D2
St. Margaret's at Cliffe, Eng., U.K., 2,415 . . . .70/G4
St. Margaret's Hope, Scot., U.K. 62/M2
St. Marie, Mont., U.S., 183 . . . . .306/K1
St. Maries, Ida., U.S., 2,652 . . . . .264/A2
St. Mark, Kans., U.S. 276/E4
St. Marks, Fla., U.S., 272 . . . . .256/D1
St. Marks N.W.R., Fla., U.S. 256/D1
St. Martha Palace, Vat. 96/B2
St. Martin, Man., Can. 215/B3
St. Martin, Man., Can., *lake* 215/B3
St. Martin, Fr., *island* 204/F3
St. Martin, La., U.S., *parish*, 48,583 . . . .282/F6, G7
St. Martin, Mich., U.S., *island* 294/C4
St. Martin, Minn., U.S., 278 . . . . .298/C5
St. Martin, Miss., U.S., 6,676 . . . . .300/D5
St. Martin, Ohio, U.S., 91 . . . . .328/C7
St-Martin-de-Restigouche, N.B., Can., 14 . . .217/B1
St-Martins, N.B., Can., 374 . . . . .217/D3
St. Martin's, Eng., U.K., 2,513 . . . . .68/A4
St. Martin's, Eng., U.K., *island* 73/B3
St. Martins, Mo., U.S., 1,023 . . . . .302/D3
St. Martinville, La., U.S., 6,989 . . . . .282/F6
St. Mary, La., U.S., *parish*, 53,500 . . . . . . .282/G7
St. Mary, Mo., U.S., 377 . . . . .302/G4
St. Mary, Mont., U.S. 306/C1
St. Mary, Mont., U.S., *river* 306/C1
St. Mary, Nebr., U.S., 60 . . . . .308/H3
St. Mary Bourne, Eng., U.K. 70/B4
St. Marys, Nfld., Can., 505 . . . . .218/E5
St. Mary's, Ont., Can., 6,293 . . . . .223/D4
St. Mary's, Eng., U.K., *island* 73/B3
St. Mary's, Scot., U.K. 62/M2
St. Marys, Alaska, U.S., 500 . . . . .240/C2
St. Marys, Fla., U.S., *river* 256/G1
St. Marys, Ga., U.S., 13,761 . . . . .260/H1
St. Marys, Ga., U.S., *river* 260/H10
St. Marys, Iowa, U.S., 134 . . . . .274/G5
St. Marys, Kans., U.S., 2,198 . . . . .276/F2
St. Mary's, Md., U.S., *county*, 86,211 . . . . .288/H6
St. Marys, Ohio, U.S., 8,342 . . . . .328/B4
St. Marys, Penn., U.S., 14,502 . . . . .336/D3
St. Marys, W. Va., U.S., 2,017 . . . . .360/D2
St. Mary's Bay, Eng., U.K., 3,163 . . . . .70/F4
St. Mary's City, Md., U.S., 900 . . . . .288/J7
St. Marys Pt., Minn., U.S., 344 . . . . .298/E6
St. Matthew, Alaska, U.S., *island* 240/A2
St. Matthews, Ky., U.S., 15,852 . . . . .280/B2
St. Matthews, S.C., U.S., 2,107 . . . . .340/D3
St-Maurice, Que., Can., *river* 226/C4
St. Maurice, La., U.S., 100 . . . . .282/D3
St-Maurice Prov. Reserve, Que., Can. 226/C4
St. Mawes, Eng., U.K. 73/B4
St. Mawgan, Eng., U.K. 73/C4
St. Meinrad, Ind., U.S., 700 . . . . .270/C8
St. Mellion, Eng., U.K. 73/D4
St. Michael, Alaska, U.S., 368 . . . . .240/C2
St. Michael, Minn., U.S., 9,099 . . . . .298/D5
St. Michaels, Ariz., U.S., 1,295 . . . . .242/F2
St. Michaels, Md., U.S., 1,193 . . . . .288/K4
St-Michel, Que., Can., 1,633 . . . . .226/F5
St-Michel-des-Saints, Que., Can., 1,805 . . . .226/C5
St-Milaire, N.B., Can. 217/A1
St-Nazaire, Fr., 68,616, (136,886 metro.) 88/B3
St. Nazianz, Wisc., U.S., 749 . . . . .364/F1
St. Neots, Eng., U.K., 13,471 . . . . .68/G5
St. Neots, Eng., U.K., 13,471 . . . . .70/D2
St-Nicholas, Que., Can., 16,645 . . . . .226/E5
St. Olaf, Iowa, U.S., 136 . . . . .274/M2
St. Onge, S. Dak., U.S., 150 . . . . .342/B3
St. Osyth, Eng., U.K., 2,073 . . . . .70/G3
St. Owen's Cross, Eng., U.K. 68/B6
St-Pacôme, Que., Can., 1,706 . . . . .226/G5
St-Pamphile, Que., Can., 2,847 . . . . .226/G5
St. Paris, Ohio, U.S., 1,998 . . . . .328/C5
St-Pascal, Que., Can., 3,643 . . . . .226/G5
St-Paul, Alta., Can., 5,061 . . . . .212/E4
St. Paul, Nfld., Can., *river* 218/C3
St. Paul, Liber., *river* 149/A2
St. Paul, Minn., U.S., *state capital*, 287,151 . .298/D6, F6
St. Paul, Mo., U.S., 1,634 . . . . .302/D3
St. Paul, Nebr., U.S., 2,218 . . . . .308/F2
St. Paul, Oreg., U.S., 354 . . . . .334/C2
St. Paul, (Collin County), Tex., U.S., 630 . . . .346/C8
St. Paul Park, Minn., U.S., 5,070 . . . . .298/E6
St. Paul's, Malta, *bay* 97/B2
St. Paul's, St. K.-Nevis 207/B2
St. Pauls, N.C., U.S., 2,137 . . . . .322/H5
St. Paul's Walden, Eng., U.K. 70/D3
St. Pete Beach, Fla., U.S., 9,929 . . . . .256/C7, F4
St. Peter, Ill., U.S., 386 . . . . .266/E5
St. Peter, Ind., U.S., 175 . . . . .270/F6
St. Peter, Kans., U.S. 276/B2
St. Peter, Minn., U.S., 9,747 . . . . .298/C6
St. Peter Port, Guernsey, U.K.,
territorial capital . . . . .60/Inset II
St. Peter Port, Guernsey, U.K.,
territorial capital 73/G4
St. Peters, N.S., Can. 221/G2
St. Peters, P.E.I., Can. 224/C2
St. Peters, P.E.I., Can., *bay* 224/C2
St. Peters, P.E.I., Can., *island* 224/B2
St. Peters, Mo., U.S., 51,381 . . . . .302/G2

St. Peter's Basilica, Vat. 96/B2
St. Petersburg, Russ., 4,678,102 . . . . .104/C4
St. Petersburg, Russ. 193/D2
St. Petersburg, Colo., U.S. 250/H1
St. Petersburg, Fla., U.S., 248,232 . . . . .256/C7, F4
St. Petersburg, Penn., U.S., 405 . . . . .336/B3
St. Peter's Square, Vat. 96/B2
St-Philémon, Que., Can., 855 . . . . .226/F5
St. Phillip, Mont., U.S. 306/M3
St. Pierre and Miquelon, Fr.,
territorial collectivity 198/M4
St. Pierre-Jolys, Man., Can., 893 . . . . .215/C4
St-Quentin, N.B., Can., 2,280 . . . . .217/B1
St. Quintin, Eng., U.K. 73/H1
St-Raphaël, Que., Can., 2,231 . . . . .226/F5
St-Rédempteur, Que., Can., 6,349 . . . . .226/K6
St. Regis, Mont., U.S., 315 . . . . .306/A2
St. Regis, Mont., U.S., *river* 306/A2
St. Regis Falls, N.Y., U.S., 750 . . . . .320/M1
St. Regis Mohawk Ind. Res., N.Y., U.S. 320/M1
St. Regis Park, Ky., U.S., 1,520 . . . . .280/B2
St-Rémi-d'Amherst, Que., Can. 226/B5
St. Robert, Mo., U.S., 2,760 . . . . .302/D4
St-Romuald, Que., Can., 10,825 . . . . .226/L6
St. Rosa, Minn., U.S., 44 . . . . .298/C5
St. Rose, Ill., U.S., 350 . . . . .266/D5
St. Rose, La., U.S., 6,540 . . . . .282/J3
St-Sauveur, N.B., Can., 817 . . . . .217/D1
St. Shotts, Nfld., Can., 144 . . . . .218/E5
St-Siméon, Que., Can., 984 . . . . .226/G4
St. Simons, Ga., U.S., *island* 260/J9
St. Simons Island, Ga., U.S., 13,381 . . . . . . .260/J9
St. Stephen, N.B., Can., 4,667 . . . . .217/B3
St. Stephen, Minn., U.S., 860 . . . . .298/C5
St. Stephen, S.C., U.S., 1,776 . . . . .340/E3
St. Stephens, Ala., U.S., 60 . . . . .238/A4
St. Stephens, Nebr., U.S. 308/E3
St. Stephens, N.C., U.S., 9,439 . . . . .322/C3
St. Stephens, Wyo., U.S. 366/B2
St. Tammany, La., U.S., *parish*, 191,268 . . .282/J5
St. Teath, Eng., U.K. 73/C3
St. Teresa, Fla., U.S. 256/D2
St. Thomas, Ont., Can., 33,236 . . . . .223/D5
St. Thomas, Mo., U.S., 287 . . . . .302/D3
St. Thomas, N. Dak., U.S., 447 . . . . .326/H1
St-Tite-des-Caps, Que., Can., 1,426 . . . . . . .226/F4
St-Tropez, Fr. 88/D5
St-Vallier, Que., Can. 226/F5
St. Vincent, Austl., *gulf* . . . . .170/Inset II
Saint Vincent, St. Luc., *passage* 208/B4
St. Vincent, St. Vin.-Gren., *island* 208/B5
St. Vincent, Fla., U.S., *island* 256/C2
St. Vincent, Minn., U.S., 117 . . . . .298/A2
St. Vincent and the Grenadines, *nation* 204/F4
St. Vincent and the Grenadines, *nation* 196
St. Vrain, N. Mex., U.S. 317/C3
St. Walburg, Sask., Can., 672 . . . . .227/A7
St. Weonards, Eng., U.K. 68/B6
St. Xavier, Mont., U.S., 67 . . . . .306/J4
St-Zacharie, Que., Can., 2,100 . . . . .226/F5
Saitama, Jap., *prefecture* 114/C2
Sajama, Bol., *mountain* 186/A3
Sak, S. Afr., *river* 162/B3
Sakai, Jap., 792,000 . . . . .114/B3
Sakakah, Sa. Arab. 136/B1
Sakakawea, N. Dak., U.S., *lake* 326/B2, C2
Sakarya, (Adapazarı), Tur. 133/B2
Sakarya, Tur., *province* 133/B2
Sakarya, Tur., *river* 133/B2
Sakha, (Yakutia), Russ., *region* 104/H3
Sakhalin, Russ., *island* 193/D8
Şaki, Azer. 103/B2
Sakishima, Jap., *islands* . . . . .114/Inset II
Sakon Nakhon, Thai. 125/C2
Sakonnet, R.I., U.S., 125 . . . . .339/E5
Sakonnet, R.I., U.S., *river* 339/E4
Saks, Ala., U.S., 10,698 . . . . .238/D2
Sal, Calif., U.S., *point* 246/E8
Sal, C.V., *island* .148/D2
Salaberry-de-Valleyfield, Que., Can., 26,170 . .226/B6
Salacgrīva, Lat. 82/C2
Salado, Arg., *river* 191/C2
Salado, Ariz., U.S., 125 . . . . .242/F3
Salado, Ark., U.S., 350 . . . . .244/D2
Salaga, Gha. 150/B2
Sala 'Ilua, Sam. 175/A2
Sälaj, Rom., *county* 101/B2
Salalah, Oman 137/B3
Salamá, Guat. 201/C4
Salamanca, Sp., 156,368 . . . . .94/C3
Salamanca, Sp., *province* 94/C2
Salamanca, N.Y., U.S., 6,097 . . . . .320/D6
Salamis, Gr., *island* 100/Inset
Salamiyah, Syria .134/C2
Salamiyah, U.A.E., *salt flat* 136/C3
Salamoni, Ind., U.S., *lake* 270/C4
Salamonia, Ind., U.S., 158 . . . . .270/C4
Salar de Uyuni, Bol., *salt flat* 186/A4
Salavan, Laos 124/D2
Salcedo, Dom. Rep. 205/B1
Salcedo, Dom. Rep., *province* 205/B1
Salcombe, Eng., U.K., 1,921 . . . . .73/E4
Salcott, Eng., U.K. 70/F3
Saldanha, S. Afr. .162/A3
Saldus, Lat. 82/C2
Salé, Mor., 521,000 . . . . .147/C1
Sale, Eng., U.K. 66/C6
Sale City, Ga., U.S., 319 . . . . .260/C9
Sale Creek, Tenn., U.S., 750 . . . . .344/L4
Salekhard, Russ. .104/E3
Salelologa, Sam. .175/B2
Salem, India, 363,934, (573,685 metro.) . . .128/C6
Salem, Ala., U.S., 125 . . . . .238/D3
Salem, (Fulton County), Ark., U.S., 1,591 . . .244/D1
Salem, (Saline County), Ark., U.S., 2,789 . . .244/C3
Salem, Conn., U.S., 3,858 . . . . .253/F4
Salem, Fla., U.S., 80 . . . . .256/E2
Salem, Ill., U.S., 7,909 . . . . .266/E5
Salem, Ind., U.S., 6,172 . . . . .270/D7
Salem, Iowa, U.S., 464 . . . . .274/L6
Salem, Ky., U.S., 769 . . . . .280/B3
Salem, Maine, U.S. 286/B4
Salem, Mass., U.S., 40,407 . . . . .292/L4
Salem, Mo., U.S., 4,854 . . . . .302/E4
Salem, Nebr., U.S., 138 . . . . .308/J3
Salem, N.H., U.S., 28,112 . . . . .312/D6
Salem, N.J., U.S., 5,857 . . . . .314/C4
Salem, N.J., U.S., *county*, 64,285 . . . . . . .314/C4
Salem, N. Mex., U.S., 795 . . . . .317/C5
Salem, N.Y., U.S., 964 . . . . .320/Q4
Salem, Ohio, U.S., 12,197 . . . . .328/J4
Salem, Oreg., U.S., *state capital*, 136,924 . .334/C3
Salem, S.C., U.S., 1,371 . . . . .342/H4
Salem, S. Dak., U.S. 342/J4
Salem, Utah, U.S., 4,372 . . . . .350/C3
Salem, Va., U.S., 24,747 . . . . .354/C6
Salem, W. Va., U.S., 2,006 . . . . .360/E2
Salemburg, N.C., U.S., 469 . . . . .322/H4
Salem Maritime N.H.S., Mass., U.S. 292/L4

Salen, (Highland), Scot., U.K. 62/E5
Salen, (Strathclyde), Scot., U.K. 62/E6
Salerno, It. 95/C2
Salerno, It., gulf 95/C2
Salesville, Ark., U.S., 437 . . . . .328/C1
Salesville, Ohio, U.S., 154 . . . . .60/C3
Salford, Eng., U.K. 66/D5
Salford, Eng., U.K., 79,755 . . . . .66/D5
Salford, Eng., U.K., 79,755 . . . . .68/C2
Salford, Eng., U.K., unitary authority, 216,119 .66/D5
Salford, Eng., U.K., unitary authority, 216,119 .68/C2
Salgótarján, Hun. .91/B1
Salibia, Dom. 208/B2
Salibury, Vt., U.S. 352/A3
Salida, Calif., U.S., 12,560 . . . . .246/D5
Salida, Colo., U.S., 5,504 . . . . .250/E3
Salihorsk, Bela. 82/C3
Salima, Mal. 159/B2
Salina, Ariz., U.S., 150 . . . . .242/F1
Salina, Iowa, U.S. 274/L5
Salina, Kans., U.S., 45,679 . . . . .276/E3
Salina, Okla., U.S., 1,422 . . . . .330/G1
Salina, Utah, U.S., 2,393 . . . . .350/C5
Salina Cruz, Mex., 72,218, (76,452 metro.) . .200/E4
Salinas, P.R. 206/C3
Salinas, Calif., U.S., 151,060, (401,762 metro.) .246/D6
Salinas Pueblo Missions N.M., N. Mex., U.S. .317/D3
Saline, Ark., U.S., county, 83,529 . . . . . . .244/C3
Saline, Ark., U.S., river 244/C3
Saline, Ill., U.S., county, 26,733 . . . . .266/E6
Saline, Kans., U.S., county, 53,597 . . . . . .276/E2
Saline, Kans., U.S., river 276/C2
Saline, La., U.S., 296 . . . . .282/D2
Saline, Mich., U.S., 8,034 . . . . .294/F7
Saline, Mo., U.S., county, 23,756 . . . . . . .302/C2
Saline, Nebr., U.S., county, 13,843 . . . . . .308/G3
Salineno, Tex., U.S., 304 . . . . .346/J9
Salines, Gren., point 209/A2
Salineville, Ohio, U.S., 1,397 . . . . .328/J4
Salisbury, S.A., Austl. . . . . .170/Inset II
Salisbury, N.B., Can., 1,954 . . . . .217/D2
Salisbury, Nun., Can., island 220/N4
Salisbury, Dom. 208/A2
Salisbury, Eng., U.K. 60/C3
Salisbury, Eng., U.K., 39,268 . . . . .73/J2
Salisbury, Conn., U.S. 253/B2
Salisbury, Md., U.S., 23,743 . . . . .288/M6
Salisbury, Mass., U.S., 7,827 . . . . .292/L1
Salisbury, Mo., U.S., 1,726 . . . . .302/D2
Salisbury, N.H., U.S., 1,137 . . . . .312/C5
Salisbury, N.C., U.S., 26,462 . . . . .322/E3
Salisbury, Penn., U.S., 878 . . . . .336/C6
Salisbury Beach, Mass., U.S., 1,300 . . . . .292/L1
Salisbury Hts., N.H., U.S., 150 . . . . .312/C5
Salitpa, Ala., U.S., 150 . . . . .238/A4
Salix, Iowa, U.S., 370 . . . . .274/B3
Salkum, Wash., U.S., 250 . . . . .358/C4
Salladasburg, Penn., U.S., 260 . . . . .336/G3
Salley, S.C., U.S., 410 . . . . .340/C3
Sallis, Miss., U.S., 114 . . . . .300/C2
Sallisaw, Okla., U.S., 7,989 . . . . .330/H2
Salluit, Que., Can., 1,072 . . . . .225/A1
Sallys Cove, Nfld., Can. 218/C4
Salmon, Br. Col., Can., river 214/L4
Salmon, Ida., U.S., 3,122 . . . . .264/D4
Salmon, Ida., U.S., river 264/B4
Salmon, Middle Fork, Ida., U.S., river 264/B5
Salmon Arm, Br. Col., Can., 15,210 . . . . .214/N6
Salmon-Challis Natl. For., Ida., U.S. . .264/C4, C5, C6, D5
Salmon Creek, Wash., U.S., 16,767 . . . . .358/C4
Salmon River, N.S., Can., 2,259 . . . . .221/A3
Salmon River, Ida., U.S., mountains 264/C5
Salmon River N.Y., U.S., reservoir 320/K3
Salmon River St. For., Conn., U.S. 253/F3
Salo, Fin. 81/B2
Salol, Minn., U.S., 100 . . . . .298/B2
Salome, Ariz., U.S., 1,690 . . . . .242/B4
Salonta, Rom. 101/A2
Saloum, Sen., river 148/B2
Sal-Rei, C.V. 148/D2
Salsbury Cove, Maine, U.S., 300 . . . . . . .286/D4
Salsette, India, island . . . . .128/Inset I
Salt, T.-C. Is., cay 207/D4
Salt, Ariz., U.S., river 242/E4
Salt, Hawaii, U.S., lake 262/C4
Salta, Arg., 367,550, (370,904 metro.) . . .191/B1
Salta, Arg., province 191/B2
Saltaire, N.Y., U.S., 43 . . . . .320/D2
Saltash, Eng., U.K., 14,139 . . . . .73/D4
Saltburn-by-the-Sea, Eng., U.K., 6,145 . . . .66/G3
Saltcoats, Sask., Can., 494 . . . . .227/H9
Saltcoats, Scot., U.K., 11,260 . . . . .62/G7
Saltdale, Calif., U.S. 246/H7
Salter Path, N.C., U.S., 450 . . . . .322/M5
Salters, S.C., U.S., 200 . . . . .340/E3
Saltery Bay, Br. Col., Can. 214/K6
Saltese, Mont., U.S. 306/A2
Salt Flat, Tex., U.S. 346/C4
Saltfleet, Eng., U.K. 66/I6
Salt Fork, Ohio, U.S., lake 328/H5
Salt Fork, Okla., U.S. 330/E1
Salthouse, Eng., U.K. 70/G1
Saltillo, Mex., state capital, 562,587, (578,046 metro.) 200/D2
Saltillo, Ind., U.S., 107 . . . . .270/D7
Saltillo, Miss., U.S., 3,393 . . . . .300/D1
Saltillo, Penn., U.S., 343 . . . . .336/F5
Saltillo, Tenn., U.S., 344 . . . . .344/E4
Salt Lake, Utah, U.S., county, 898,387 . . .350/B3, E2
Salt Lake City, Utah, U.S., state capital, 181,743, (1,333,914 metro.) 350/C3, E2
Salt Lick, Ky., U.S., 342 . . . . .280/G2
Salt Marsh, Utah, U.S., lake 350/A4
Salt Meadow N.W.R., Conn., U.S. 253/F4
Saltney, Eng., U.K., 4,144 . . . . .68/B3
Saltney, Wales, U.K., 4,144 . . . . .64/F1
Salto, Uru., 93,117 . . . . .187/B1
Salto, Uru., department 187/B1
Salto del Guairá, Para. 187/E4
Salto Grande, Uru., reservoir 187/B1
Salton, Calif., U.S., sea 246/K9
Salton City, Calif., U.S., 978 . . . . .246/K9
Salt Plains N.W.R., Okla., U.S. 330/D1
Saltsburg, Penn., U.S., 955 . . . . .336/C5
Saltspring, Br. Col., Can., island 358/B1
Salt Sprs., U.S., 600 . . . . .256/G2
Saltville, Va., U.S., 2,204 . . . . .354/F2
Salt Water, India, lake . . . . .128/Inset II
Salt Wells, Nev., U.S. 310/A2
Saluda, N.C., U.S., 575 . . . . .322/E8
Saluda, S.C., U.S., 3,066 . . . . .340/C3
Saluda, S.C., U.S., county, 19,181 . . . . . .340/C2
Saluda, S.C., U.S., river 340/C2
Saluda, S.C., U.S., 250 . . . . .354/K5
Salunga, (Salunga-Landisville), Penn., U.S., 4,771 .336/J5
Salus, Ark., U.S. 244/B2
Salut, Fr. Gui., islands 183/B1
Salvador, Braz., 2,440,886, (3,018,326 metro.) .188/E3
Salvador, La., U.S., lake 282/J4
Salvage, Nfld., Can., 203 . . . . .218/E5
Salvisa, Ky., U.S., 325 . . . . .280/F3

Salvo, N.C., U.S., 250 . . . . .322/Q3
Salwa, Dawhat as, Qatar, bay 137/B3
Salwa, Sa. Arab. 136/C1
Salwayash, Eng., U.K. 73/G3
Salween, China, river 119/C2
Salween, Mya., river 125/C2
Salween, Thai., river 125/A2
Salyan, Azer. 103/C3
Salyer, Calif., U.S., 100 . . . . .246/B2
Salyersville, Ky., U.S., 1,604 . . . . .280/G3
Salzach, Aus., river 91/C3
Salzach, Ger., river 86/C4
Salzburg, Aus., 144,817 . . . . .91/C3
Salzburg, Aus., state 91/C3
Salzburg Alps, Aus., range 91/C3
Salzgitter, Ger., 112,934 . . . . .86/B2
Salzkammergut, Aus., region 91/C3
Samakhixai, Laos 124/D4
Samalga, Alaska, U.S., pass 240/B4
Samana, Bah., cay 207/C3
Samaná, Dom. Rep. 205/C1
Samaná, Dom. Rep., bay 205/C1
Samaná, Dom. Rep., cape 205/C1
Samaná, Dom. Rep., province 205/C1
Samangan, Afg. 129/B1
Samantha, Ala., U.S., 70 . . . . .238/B2
Samar, Phil., island 120/C4
Samar, Phil., sea 120/C3
Samara, Russ., 1,164,859, (1,183,350 metro.) .104/D4
Samaria, Ida., U.S. 264/F7
Samarian, Isr., hills 135/B1
Samarinda, Indon. 122/C2
Samarqand, Uzb., 362,300 . . . . .132/C3
Samarqand, Uzb., province 132/C2
Samarra, Iraq 130/B2
Sambalpur, India 128/D4
Sambre, Belg., river 85/C2
Sambre, Fr., river 88/C1
Samburg, Tenn., U.S., 260 . . . . .344/C2
Samcheok, S. Kor. 116/C4
Same, E. Timor 122/B2
Samford, Qnsld., Austl. . . . . .170/Inset III
Sam Houston Natl. For., Tex., U.S. 346/N5
Samina, Liech., river 90/B2
Sammamish, Wash., U.S., lake 358/B4
Samnorwood, Tex., U.S. 346/H9
Samokov, Bul. .101/B3
Samos, Gr., island 100/C3
Samothraki, Gr., island 100/C1
Sampit, S.C., U.S., 700 . . . . .340/E3
Sampson, N.C., U.S., county, 60,161 . . . .322/J5
Sam Rayburn, Tex., U.S., reservoir 346/P4
Samsø, Den., island 79/C3
Samsø, Den., strait 79/C3
Samson, Ala., U.S., 2,071 . . . . .238/C4
Samsonvale, Austl., lake . . . . .170/Inset III
Samsun, Tur., 338,400 . . . . .133/D2
Samsun, Tur., province 133/C2
Samtredia, Geo. 103/B3
Samuel R. McKelvie Natl. For., Nebr., U.S. .308/D1
Samuels, Ida., U.S., 80 . . . . .264/A1
Samuels, Ky., U.S., 400 . . . . .280/E3
Samur, Azer., river 103/B2
San, Camb., river 124/E2
San, Mali 150/C3
San, Pol., river .83/F3
Sanaa, Yemen, capital, (926,595 metro.) .137/A1
San Acacia, N. Mex., U.S., 100 . . . . .317/D3
San Acacio, Colo., U.S., 60 . . . . .250/E4
Sanaga, Came., river 153/B2
Sanaigmore, Scot., U.K. 62/D7
Sanak, Alaska, U.S., island 240/C4
San Ambrosio, Chile, island 178/B5
Sanandaj, Iran, 277,808 . . . . .130/B2
San Andreas, Calif., U.S., 2,615 . . . . . . .246/E4, L6
San Andrés, Col., island, 61,000 . . . . .184/Inset
San Andres, N. Mex., U.S., mountains . . .317/D5
San Andres N.W.R., Tex., U.S. 317/D5
San Andrés y Providencia, Col., department . . .184/Inset
San Angelo, Tex., U.S., 88,439, (104,010 metro.) 346/H4
San Anselmo, Calif., U.S., 12,378 . . . . . .246/H1
San Antonio, Arg., cape 191/D4
San Antonio, Bel. 201/A3
San Antonio, Chile . . . . .190/B4, Inset
San Antonio, Cuba, cape 204/A2
San Antonio, P.R. 206/A2
San Antonio, P.R. 206/C2
San Antonio, Calif., U.S., reservoir 246/D7
San Antonio, Colo., U.S., 150 . . . . .250/D4
San Antonio, N. Mex., U.S., 125 . . . . . . .317/D4
San Antonio, Tex., U.S., 1,144,646, (1,592,383 metro.) 346/A2, K6
San Antonio, Tex., U.S., river 346/P2
San Antonio Missions N.H.P., Tex., U.S. . .346/A3
San Antonio Oeste, Arg. 191/B5
San Antonito, N. Mex., U.S. 317/D4
San Ardo, Calif., U.S., 501 . . . . .246/E6
Sanatoga, Penn., U.S., 7,734 . . . . .336/K5
Sanatorium, Miss., U.S., 900 . . . . .300/C4
San Augustine, Tex., U.S., 2,475 . . . . . . .346/P4
San Augustine, Tex., U.S., county, 8,946 .346/P4
Sanaw, Yemen 137/C1
San Baudilio de Llobregat, Sp. 94/G2
San Benito, Calif., U.S., county, 53,234 . .246/D6
San Benito, Tex., U.S., 23,444 . . . . .346/L9
San Bernardino, Calif., U.S., county, 1,709,434 . . . . .246/E1, J7
San Bernardino, Calif., U.S., 185,401 . . .246/H8
San Bernardino, Calif., U.S., mountains . .246/J8
San Bernardino Natl. For., Calif., U.S. . . .246/J9
San Bernard N.W.R., Tex., U.S. 346/N7
San Bernardo, Chile, 214,575 . . . . . .190/Inset
San Blas, Pan., mountains 203/C2
San Blas, Pan., province 203/C2
San Blas, Fla., U.S., cape 256/C2
San Borja, Bol. 186/A2
Sanborn, Fla., U.S. 256/D1
Sanborn, Iowa, U.S., 1,353 . . . . .274/C1
Sanborn, Minn., U.S., 434 . . . . .298/B6
Sanborn, N. Dak., U.S., 194 . . . . .326/G3
Sanborn, S. Dak., U.S., county, 2,675 . . .342/G4
Sanborn, Wisc., U.S., 60 . . . . .364/C2
Sanbornton, N.H., U.S., 2,581 . . . . .312/C5
Sanbornville, N.H., U.S., 950 . . . . .312/D4
San Bruno, Calif., U.S., 40,165 . . . . .246/G2
San Carlos, C.R., river 203/B2
San Carlos, Nicar. 202/B3
San Carlos, Phil., 118,259 . . . . .120/B4
San Carlos, Ariz., U.S., 3,716 . . . . .242/E4
San Carlos, Ariz., U.S., lake 242/E4
San Carlos, Calif., U.S., 27,718 . . . . . . .246/J2
San Carlos, Uru. 187/C3
San Carlos, Ven. 182/C2
San Carlos, Coah., Mex., res., Ariz., U.S. .242/E4
San Carlos de Bariloche, Arg. 191/A5
San Carlos Park, Fla., U.S., 16,317 . . . . .256/G5
Sánchez Ramírez, Dom. Rep., province . .205/B1
San Clara, Man., Can. 215/A3
San Clemente, Calif., U.S., 49,936 . . .246/F11, H9

San Clemente, Calif., U.S., island 246/G10
Sanco, Tex., U.S. 346/H3
San Cristóbal, Sol. Is., island 173/B2
San Cristóbal, Ven., 235,753, (257,399 metro.) .182/B2
San Cristóbal, Bol. 186/B2
San Cristóbal, Dom. Rep. 205/B2
San Cristóbal, Dom. Rep., province 205/B2
San Cristóbal, Ecua. 185/Inset
San Cristóbal de las Casas, Mex., 112,442, (132,421 metro.) 200/F4
Sancti Spíritus, Cuba 204/C2
Sancti Spíritus, Cuba, province 204/C2
Sand, Alta., Can., river 212/E3
Sand, Hawaii, U.S., island 262/F2
Sand, Mich., U.S., point 294/E6
Sand, Nebr., U.S., hills 308/B2
Sand, Wisc., U.S., island 364/B2
Sandakan, Malay., 125,841 . . . . .121/D2
Sanday, Scot., U.K., island . . . . .60/Inset I
Sanday, Scot., U.K., island 62/N1
Sandbach, Eng., U.K., 15,839 . . . . .68/C3
Sandbanks, Eng., U.K. 73/J3
Sandborn, Ind., U.S., 451 . . . . .270/B7
Sand Brook, N.J., U.S., 400 . . . . .314/D3
Sand City, Calif., U.S., 261 . . . . .246/D6
Sand Coulee, Mont., U.S., 200 . . . . .306/E2
Sand Creek, Okla., U.S. 330/D1
Sand Creek Massacre N.H.S., Colo., U.S. .250/H3
Sand Draw, Wyo., U.S. 366/B2
San de Fuca, Wash., U.S., 325 . . . . .358/C1
Sanders, Ariz., U.S., 200 . . . . .242/F2
Sanders, Ky., U.S., 246 . . . . .280/F2
Sanders, Mont., U.S., 40 . . . . .306/J3
Sanders, Mont., U.S., county, 10,227 . . .306/A2
Sanderson, Fla., U.S., 500 . . . . .256/F1
Sanderson, Tex., U.S., 861 . . . . .346/F5
Sandersville, Ga., U.S., 6,144 . . . . .260/F6
Sandersville, Miss., U.S., 789 . . . . .300/C4
Sand Fork, (Layopolis), W. Va., U.S., 176 .360/E3
Sandgap, Ky., U.S., 350 . . . . .280/F3
Sandgarth, Qnsld., Austl. . . . . .170/Inset III
Sandgate, Vt., U.S., 353 . . . . .352/A4
Sandgates, Md., U.S., 550 . . . . .288/H6
Sandhill, Miss., U.S., 125 . . . . .300/C3
Sand Hill, Miss., U.S., 125 . . . . .300/D4
Sand Hills, Mass., U.S., 2,400 . . . . .292/M4
Sandhills Str. For., S.C., U.S. 340/D2
Sandhurst, Eng., U.K., 19,153 . . . . .70/C4
Sand Hutton, Eng., U.K. 68/F1
Sandia, N. Mex., U.S. 317/D2
Sandia Pueblo, N. Mex., U.S. 317/D2
San Diego, Calif., U.S., 1,223,400, (2,813,833 metro.) 246/H10
San Diego, Calif., U.S., county, 2,813,833 .246/I9
San Diego, Tex., U.S., 4,753 . . . . .346/K8
San Diego Country Estates, Calif., U.S., 9,262 . . .246/J9
Sandilands, Man., Can. 215/C4
San Dimas, Calif., U.S., 34,980 . . . . . . .246/E9
Sandisfield, Mass., U.S., 824 . . . . .292/A4
Sandisfield St. For., Conn., U.S. 253/C1
Sand Lake, Mich., U.S., 492 . . . . .294/D6
Sand Lake N.W.R., S. Dak., U.S. 342/G2
Sand Lane, Eng., U.K. 73/H2
Sandness, Scot., U.K. 62/P2
Sandon, Eng., U.K. 68/C4
Sandougou, Sen., river 148/B3
Sandoval, Ill., U.S., 1,434 . . . . .266/D5
Sandoval, N. Mex., U.S., county, 89,908 . .317/C2
Sandown, (Sandown/Shanklin), Eng., U.K., 17,305 .70/B5
Sandown, N.H., U.S., 5,143 . . . . .312/D6
Sandoy, Den., island 79/Inset
Sand Pt., Alaska, U.S., 952 . . . . .240/C3
Sandpoint, Ida., U.S., 6,835 . . . . .264/A1
Sandray, Scot., U.K., island 62/B5
Sand Ridge, N.Y., U.S., 906 . . . . .320/J4
Sand River, Mich., U.S., 80 . . . . .294/B3
Sand Rock, Ala., U.S., 509 . . . . .238/D1
Sands, Fla., U.S., key 256/B7, H6
Sands, Mich., U.S., 100 . . . . .294/B3
Sandspit, Br. Col., Can., 435 . . . . .214/G4
Sand Sprs., Ariz., U.S. 242/E2
Sand Sprs., Iowa, U.S., 70 . . . . .274/M3
Sand Sprs., Mont., U.S., 40 . . . . .306/J2
Sand Sprs., Okla., U.S., 17,451 . . . . .330/F1
Sandston, Va., U.S., 3,400 . . . . .354/J5
Sandstone, Minn., U.S., 1,549 . . . . .298/E4
Sandtown, Del., U.S., 325 . . . . .255/B4
Sandur, Den. 79/Inset
Sandusky, Mich., U.S., 2,745 . . . . .294/G6
Sandusky, Ohio, U.S., 27,844 . . . . .328/E3
Sandusky, Ohio, U.S., county, 61,792 . . .328/D3
Sandusky, Ohio, U.S., river 328/D3
Sandwell, Eng., U.K., unitary authority, 282,901 .68/D2
Sandwich, Mass., U.S., bay 218/C2
Sandwich, Eng., U.K., 4,164 . . . . .70/D4
Sandwich, Ill., U.S., 6,509 . . . . .266/F2
Sandwich, Mass., U.S., 20,136 . . . . .292/N5
Sandwich, N.H., U.S., 1,286 . . . . .312/D4
Sandwick, Scot., U.K. 62/Q3
Sandy, Nfld., Can., lake 218/C4
Sandy, Ont., Can., lake 222/B2
Sandy, Gren., island 209/B2
Sandy, Palau, river 172/B2
Sandy, Eng., U.K., 8,554 . . . . .68/G5
Sandy, Eng., U.K., 8,554 . . . . .70/D2
Sandy, Nev., U.S. 310/C4
Sandy, Oreg., U.S., 5,385 . . . . .334/D2
Sandy, R.I., U.S., point 339/C6
Sandy, Utah, U.S., 88,418 . . . . .350/C3
Sandy Bay, Sask., Can., 1,092 . . . . .227/H5
Sandy Cove, N.S., Can. 221/A3
Sandy Creek, Maine, U.S., 125 . . . . .286/B4
Sandy Creek, N.Y., U.S., 789 . . . . .320/J3
Sandy Creek, N.C., U.S., 246 . . . . .322/J6
Sandyfield, N.C., U.S., 340 . . . . .322/J6
Sandygate, Eng., U.K. 66/B5
Sandy Hook, Ky., U.S., 678 . . . . .280/G2
Sandy Hook, Miss., U.S., 50 . . . . .300/C4
Sandy Hook, N.J., U.S. 314/D2
Sandy Lake, Alta., Can. 212/D3
Sandy Lake, Man., Can. 215/A4
Sandy Lake, Ont., Can. 222/B2
Sandy Lake, Penn., U.S., 743 . . . . .336/A3
Sandy Level, Va., U.S., 50 . . . . .354/D7
Sandy Pt., Bah. 207/B2
Sandy Pt., Maine, U.S., 175 . . . . .286/D4
Sandy Pt. Town, St. K.-Nevis 207/A1
Sandy Ridge, Ala., U.S. 238/C3
Sandy Springs, Miss., U.S., 93 . . . . .286/B4
Sandy Spr., (see Ashton), Md., U.S., 3,437 .288/F3
Sandy Sprs., Ga., U.S., 85,781 . . . . .260/H2
Sandy Sprs., S.C., U.S., 750 . . . . .340/B2
Sandyville, Iowa, U.S., 61 . . . . .274/D3
Sandyville, W. Va., U.S., 1,000 . . . . .360/C3
Sandyville, Md., U.S., 1,000 . . . . .288/G1
San Elizario, Tex., U.S., 11,046 . . . . .346/B4
San Felipe, Col. 184/D4
San Felipe, Mex. 200/B1

San Felipe, Tex., U.S., 868 . . . . .346/M6
San Felipe, Ven. 182/C1
San Felipe Pueblo, N. Mex., U.S., 2,080 .317/D2
San Félix, Chile 190/B3
San Félix, Chile, island 178/A5
San Fernando, Phil. 120/B2
San Fernando, Sp., 88,073 . . . . .94/C4
San Fernando, Trin.-To., 28,957 . . . . . . .209/A2
San Fernando, Calif., U.S., 23,564 . .246/B8, G8
San Fernando de Apure, Ven. 182/C2
San Fidel, N. Mex., U.S., 60 . . . . .317/C2
Sanford, Man., Can. 215/C4
Sanford, Ala., U.S., 269 . . . . .238/C4
Sanford, Colo., U.S., 817 . . . . .250/E4
Sanford, Fla., U.S., 38,291 . . . . .256/D3, G3
Sanford, Ga., U.S. 260/B8
Sanford, Kans., U.S. 276/C3
Sanford, Maine, U.S., 20,806 . . . . .286/B5
Sanford, Mich., U.S., 943 . . . . .294/E6
Sanford, Miss., U.S., 300 . . . . .300/C4
Sanford, N.C., U.S., 23,220 . . . . .322/G4
Sanford, Tex., U.S., 203 . . . . .346/F9
San Franicue, Trin.-To. 209/A2
San Francisco, Arg. 191/C3
San Francisco, El Salv., 20,497 . . . . .203/B2
San Francisco, Calif., U.S., 776,733, (7,039,362 metro.) 246/C5, J2
San Francisco, Calif., U.S., county, 776,733 .246/C5, H2
San Francisco, Colo., U.S. 250/E4
San Francisco de Macorís, Dom. Rep., 266,629 .205/B1
San Gabriel, Calif., U.S., 39,804 . . . . . . .246/D9
San Gabriel, Calif., U.S., mountains . .246/C8, G8
San Gabriel, Tex., U.S., river 346/L6
Sangamon, Ill., U.S., county, 188,951 . . .266/D4
Sangamon, Ill., U.S., river 266/C3
Sangay, Ecua., volcano 185/B6
Sanger, Calif., U.S., 18,931 . . . . .246/F6
Sanger, Tex., U.S., 4,534 . . . . .346/L2
Sangerfield, N.Y., U.S., 200 . . . . .320/L5
San Germán, P.R. 206/A2
Sangerville, Maine, U.S., 1,270 . . . . .286/C3
Sangha, Congo, river 155/D2
San Gimignano, It. 95/C2
Sangmelima, Came. 153/B3
Sangre de Cristo, Colo., U.S., mountains .250/E3
Sangre de Cristo, N. Mex., U.S., mountains .317/E1
Sangre Grande, Trin.-To. 209/A2
Sangro, It., river 95/C2
Sangudo, Alta., Can., 377 . . . . .212/C4
Sanibel, Fla., U.S., 6,064 . . . . .256/F5
Sanibel, Fla., U.S., island 256/F5
San Ignacio, Bel., 13,260 . . . . .201/A2
San Ignacio, Bol. 186/B3
San Ignacio, N. Mex., U.S. 317/C2
Sanilac, Mich., U.S., county, 44,547 . . . .294/G6
San Ildefonso Pueblo, N. Mex., U.S., 458 .317/D2
San Isabel Natl. For., Colo., U.S. 250/D3, E3, E4
San Isidro, P.R. 206/D2
San Jacinto, Calif., U.S., 23,779 . . . . . . .246/J9
San Jacinto, Nev., U.S. 310/C1
San Jacinto, Tex., U.S., county, 22,246 . .346/N5
San Joaquin, Calif., U.S., 3,270 . . . . . . .246/E6
San Joaquin, Calif., U.S., county, 563,598 . . . . .246/D5, L2, L6
San Joaquin, Calif., U.S., river 246/E5
San Jon, N. Mex., U.S., 306 . . . . .317/G2
San Jorge, Arg., gulf 191/B6
San José, C.R., capital, 344,349, (1,305,365 metro.) 203/B3
San José, C.R., province 203/B3
San José, Guat. 201/C6
San José, Calif., U.S., 894,943 . . . . .246/D5, K3
San José, Ill., U.S., 696 . . . . .266/D3
San José, N. Mex., U.S. 317/E2
San José, Uru. .187/B3
San José, Uru., department 187/B3
San José, C.R., river 203/B3
San José de Chiquitos, Bol. 186/B3
San José de las Matas, Dom. Rep. 205/A1
San José del Guaviare, Col., 54,000 . . . .184/B4
San Juan, Arg., 119,423, (352,691 metro.) .191/B3
San Juan, Arg., province 191/B3
San Juan, C.R., river 203/B2
San Juan, Dom. Rep. 205/A2
San Juan, Dom. Rep., province 205/A2
San Juan, Eq. Gui., cape 154/A3
San Juan, Nicar., river 202/B3
San Juan, Peru 185/B4
San Juan, P.R., capital 204/E3
San Juan, P.R., capital, 441,401, (2,450,292 metro.) 206/C2
San Juan, P.R., passage 206/D2
San Juan, Colo., U.S., county, 558 . . . . .250/C4
San Juan, Colo., U.S., mountains 250/C4
San Juan, (Grant County), N. Mex., U.S., 50 .317/C5
San Juan, (Rio Arriba County), N. Mex., U.S., 592 . . . . .317/D1
San Juan, N. Mex., U.S., county, 113,801 .317/B1
San Juan, N. Mex., U.S., river 317/B1
San Juan, Tex., U.S., 26,229 . . . . .346/K9
San Juan, Utah, U.S., county, 14,413 . . .350/D6
San Juan, Utah, U.S., river 350/D6
San Juan, Wash., U.S., county, 14,077 . .358/C1
San Juan, Wash., U.S., island 358/B1
San Juan Bautista, Para. 187/D5
San Juan Bautista, Calif., U.S., 1,549 . . .246/D6
San Juan Capistrano, Calif., U.S., 33,826 .246/F11, H9
San Juan del Norte, Nicar. 202/C3
San Juan de los Morros, Ven. 182/B3
San Juan Natl. For., Colo., U.S. 250/C4
San Juan Pueblo, N. Mex., U.S. 317/D1
Sankertown, Penn., U.S., 680 . . . . .336/D5
Sankosh, Bhu., river 126/B2
Sankrail, India . . . . .128/Inset II
Sankt Gallen, Switz. 90/D1
Sankt Gallen, Switz., canton 90/D1
Sankt Pölten, Aus. 91/D2
Sankuru, Congo, D.R., river 155/B2
San Leandro, Calif., U.S., 79,452 . . . . . .246/J2
San Leanna, Tex., U.S., 384 . . . . .346/C7
San Leon, Tex., U.S., 4,365 . . . . .346/C7
Sanlúcar, Tur., province 133/D3
Sanlurfa, Tur. 133/D3
San Lorenzo, Ecua. 185/B2
San Lorenzo, Ecua., cape 185/A3
San Lorenzo, Hond. 202/B2
San Lorenzo, Para., 202,745 . . . . .187/D4
San Lorenzo, P.R. 206/D2
San Lorenzo, Calif., U.S., 21,898 . . . . . .246/J2
San Lorenzo, N. Mex., U.S., 40 . . . . . . .317/C5
San Lucas, Mex., 37,984 . . . . .200/B3
San Lucas, Calif., U.S., 419 . . . . .246/E6
San Luis, Arg. .191/B3
San Luis, Arg., province 191/B3
San Luis, Bol. .186/B2
San Luis, Bol., lake 186/B2
San Luis, Guat. 201/D3
San Luis, (Pima County), Ariz., U.S., 60 . .242/D5

San Luis, (Yuma County), Ariz., U.S., 15,322 . . . .242/A5
San Luis, Colo., U.S., 739 . . . . .250/E4
San Luis, Colo., U.S., valley 250/D3
San Luis Obispo, Calif., U.S., 44,174,
   (246,681 metro.) 246/E7
San Luis Obispo, Calif., U.S., county, 246,681 . . .246/E7
San Luis Obispo Bay, Calif., U.S. 246/D7
San Luis Potosí, Mex., state capital, 629,208,
   (670,532 metro.) 200/D3
San Luis Potosí, Mex., state 200/D3
San Luis Río Colorado, Mex., 126,645,
   (145,006 metro.) 200/B1
San Manuel, Ariz., U.S., 4,375 . . . . .242/E5
San Marcial, N. Mex., U.S., 175 . . . . .317/D4
San Marcos, Calif., U.S., 54,977 . . . . .246/H9
San Marcos, Tex., U.S., 34,733 . . . . .346/B1, L6
San Marino, nation 95
San Marino, S. Mar., capital, 2,822,
   (4,508 metro.) .97/B1
San Marino, S. Mar., river 97/A1
San Marino, Calif., U.S., 12,945 . . . . .246/D9
San Martín, Arg., lake 191/A6
San Martín, Chile, lake 190/B7
San Martín, Peru, department 185/B2
San Martin, Calif., U.S., 4,230 . . . . .246/L4
San Mateo, Calif., U.S., 92,482 . . . . .246/J2
San Mateo, Calif., U.S., county, 707,161 . .246/C5, J3
San Mateo, Fla., U.S., 1,000 . . . . .256/G2
San Mateo, N. Mex., U.S., 225 . . . . .317/C2
San Matías, Arg., gulf 191/C5
San Matías, Bol. 186/C3
San Miguel, El. Salv., 233,036 . . . . .203/B2
San Miguel, Pan., gulf 203/C2
San Miguel, Ariz., U.S., 90 . . . . .242/D6
San Miguel, Calif., U.S., 1,427 . . . . .246/E7
San Miguel, Calif., U.S., island 246/E8
San Miguel, Colo., U.S., county, 6,594 . . . . . . .250/B4
San Miguel, (Doña Ana County),
   N. Mex., U.S., 1,100 . . . . .317/D5
San Miguel, (Rio Arriba County), N. Mex., U.S. . . .317/D1
San Miguel, N. Mex., U.S., county, 30,126 . . . . .317/F2
San Miguel de Tucumán, Arg., 470,809,
   (622,324 metro.) 191/B2
San Miguelito, Pan., 331,692 . . . . .203/C2
Sannar, Sudan 145/C2
San Nicolás, Arg., 119,302 . . . . .191/C3
San Nicolas, Calif., U.S., island 246/F9
Sanostee, N. Mex., U.S., 429 . . . . .317/B1
San Pablo, Bol., river 186/B3
San Pablo, Phil., 207,927 . . . . .120/B3
San Pablo, Calif., U.S., 30,215 . . . . .246/J1
San Pablo, Colo., U.S., 125 . . . . .250/E4
San Patricio, N. Mex., U.S. 317/E4
San Patricio, Tex., U.S., county, 67,138 . . . . . .346/L7
San Pawl il-Baħar, Malta 97/B2
San Pedro, C. d'Iv. 150/C4
San Pedro, Guat., river 201/D2
San Pedro, Para. 187/D4
San Pedro, Para., department 187/D4
San Pedro, Ariz., U.S. 242/D5
San Pedro, Ariz., U.S., river 242/D5
San Pedro, Calif., U.S. 246/C11
San Pedro, Colo., U.S. 250/E4
San Pedro Bay, Calif., U.S. 246/C11
San Pedro de Atacama, Chile 190/C2
San Pedro de las Colonias, Mex., 41,642,
   (88,343 metro.) 200/D2
San Pedro de Macorís, Dom. Rep., 146,413 . . . .205/C2
San Pedro de Macorís, Dom. Rep., province 205/C2
San Pedro Riparian N.C.A., Ariz., U.S. 242/E6
San Pedro Sula, Hond., 444,570 . . . . .202/A2
San Perlita, Tex., U.S., 680 . . . . .346/L9
Sanpete, Utah, U.S., county, 22,763 . . . . .350/C4
San Pierre, Ind., U.S., 156 . . . . .270/C2
San Pietro, It., island 95/B3
Sanpoil, Wash., U.S., river 358/G1
Sanquhar, Scot., U.K., 2,028 . . . . .62/J8
San Rafael, Arg. 191/B3
San Rafael, Calif., U.S., 56,063 . . . . .246/C5, H1
San Rafael, Calif., U.S., mountains 246/F8
San Rafael, N. Mex., U.S., 175 . . . . .317/C2
San Rafael, Utah, U.S., desert 350/D5
San Rafael, Utah, U.S., river 350/D4
San Ramon, Calif., U.S., 44,722 . . . . .246/K2
San Remo, It. 95/A2
San Saba, Tex., U.S., 2,637 . . . . .346/K4
San Saba, Tex., U.S., county, 6,186 . . . . .346/K4
San Salvador, Bah., island 204/C1
San Salvador, Bah., island 207/C3
San Salvador, Ecua., island 185/Inset
San Salvador, El. Salv., capital, 473,372,
   (1,908,921 metro.) 203/A2
San Salvador, Uru., river 187/A2
San Salvador de Jujuy, Arg., 178,748,
   (180,102 metro.) 191/B1
San Sebastián, P.R. 206/B2
San Severo, It. 95/C2
San Simeon, Calif., U.S. 246/D7
San Simon, Ariz., U.S., 125 . . . . .242/F5
Sanski Most, Bos.-Her. 98/A1
Sansom Park, Tex., U.S., 4,181 . . . . .346/A9
Sans Souci, S.C., U.S., 7,836 . . . . .340/E2
Santa, Ida., U.S., 100 . . . . .264/A2
Santa Ana, Bol. 186/A2
Santa Ana, El. Salv., 245,048 . . . . .203/A2
Santa Ana, El. Salv., volcano 203/A2
Santa Ana, Calif., U.S., 337,977 . . . . . . .246/E10, H9
Santa Ana, Calif., U.S., river 246/E10
Santa Ana, Uru., range 187/C1
Santa Ana Pueblo, N. Mex., U.S., 479 . . . . .317/D2
Santa Anna, Tex., U.S., 1,081 . . . . .346/J4
Santa Bárbara, Hond. 202/A2
Santa Bárbara, Hond., department 202/A2
Santa Barbara, Calif., U.S., 92,325,
   (399,347 metro.) 246/F8
Santa Barbara, Calif., U.S., county, 399,347 . . .246/E8
Santa Barbara, Calif., U.S., island 246/G9
Santa Barbara Channel, Calif., U.S. 246/E8
Santa Catalina, Calif., U.S., island 246/G9
Santa Catarina, Braz., state 188/C4
Santa Catarina, Tex., U.S. 346/K9
Santa Clara, Cuba .204/B2
Santa Clara, Cuba, 209,800 . . . . .204/C2
Santa Clara, Calif., U.S., 102,361 . . . . .246/K3
Santa Clara, Calif., U.S., county, 1,682,585 . .246/D5, J3
Santa Clara, N.Y., U.S., 70 . . . . .320/N1
Santa Clara, Oreg., U.S., 12,800 . . . . .334/C3
Santa Clara, Utah, U.S., 4,630 . . . . .350/A6
Santa Clara Pueblo, N. Mex., U.S., 980 . . . . . . .317/D2
Santa Clarita, Calif., U.S., 151,088 . . . . .246/G8
Santa Claus, Ga., U.S., 237 . . . . .260/G7
Santa Claus, Ind., U.S., 2,041 . . . . .270/C8
Santa Coloma de Gramenet, Sp., 112,992 . . . . .94/H2
Santa Cruz, Arg., province 191/A6
Santa Cruz, Arg., river 191/A7
Santa Cruz, Bol., 1,135,526 . . . . .186/B3
Santa Cruz, Bol., department 186/B3
Santa Cruz, C.R. 203/A2
Santa Cruz, Ecua., island 185/Inset
Santa Cruz, Sol. Is., islands 173/C2
Santa Cruz, Ariz., U.S., county, 38,381 . . . . . . .242/E6

Santa Cruz, Ariz., U.S., river 242/D5
Santa Cruz, Calif., U.S., 54,593 . . . . . . .246/C6, K4
Santa Cruz, Calif., U.S., county, 255,602 . .246/C5, J3
Santa Cruz, Calif., U.S., island 246/F8
Santa Cruz, N. Mex., U.S., 423 . . . . .317/D2
Santa Cruz de Tenerife, Sp. . . . . .94/Inset I
Santa Cruz de Tenerife, Sp., province . . . . . .94/Inset I
Santa Elena, Ecua., point 185/A4
Santa Elena, Tex., U.S., 40 . . . . .346/K9
Santa Elena de Uairén, Ven. 182/C3
Santa Fe, Arg., 353,063, (406,388 metro.) 191/C3
Santa Fe, Arg., province 191/C2
Santa Fe, N. Mex., U.S., 70 . . . . .302/E2
Santa Fe, N. Mex., U.S., county, 129,292 . . . . .317/E2
Santa Fe, N. Mex., U.S., state capital, 62,203,
   (147,635 metro.) 317/E2
Santa Fe, Tenn., U.S., 300 . . . . .344/G3
Santa Fe, Tex., U.S., 9,548 . . . . .346/N6
Santa Fe Natl. For., N. Mex., U.S. 317/D1, E2
Santa Fe Sprs., Calif., U.S., 17,438 . . . . .246/D10
Santa Inés, Chile 190/Inset
Santa Inés, Chile, island 190/B8
Santa Isabel, Eq. Gui., peak 154/A1
Santa Isabel, P.R. .206/C3
Santa Isabel, Sol. Is., island 173/A1
Santa Lucía, Uru., river 187/B3
Santa Lucia Range, Calif., U.S. 246/D6
Santa Luzia, C.V., island 148/A2
Santa Margarita, Calif., U.S., 950 . . . . .246/E7
Santa María, Braz., 151,202, (217,565 metro.) . .188/C4
Santa Maria, C.V. .148/D2
Santa María, Ecua., island 185/Inset
Santa Maria, Port., island . . . . .93/Inset II
Santa Maria, Calif., U.S., 77,423 . . . . .246/E8
Santa Maria, Van., island 173/B2
Santa Maria di Leuca, It., cape 95/D3
Santa Marta, Col., 343,000 . . . . .184/B2
Santa Monica, Calif., U.S., 84,084 . . . . .246/B9
Santa Monica Mountains N.R.A., Calif., U.S. 247/B9
Santana do Livramento, Braz. 188/C5
Santander, Col., department 184/B3
Santander, Sp., 180,717 . . . . .94/E1
Santander, Sp., province 94/D1
Sant'Antioco, It., island 95/B3
Santa Paula, Calif., U.S., 28,598 . . . . .246/F8
Santaquin, Utah, U.S., 4,834 . . . . .350/C4
Santarém, Braz., 101,534, (265,105 metro.) . . .188/C4
Santarém, Port., 63,536 . . . . .93/A3
Santarém, Port., district 93/A3
Santa Rita, Hond. .202/B2
Santa Rita, Mont., U.S., 100 . . . . .306/D1
Santa Rosa, Arg. 191/C4
Santa Rosa, Ecua. .185/B4
Santa Rosa, Ariz., U.S. 242/C5
Santa Rosa, Calif., U.S., 147,595 . . . . .246/C4
Santa Rosa, Calif., U.S., island 246/E9
Santa Rosa, Fla., U.S., county, 117,743 . . . . . . .256/A1
Santa Rosa, Fla., U.S., island 256/B1
Santa Rosa, N. Mex., U.S., 2,744 . . . . .317/F3
Santa Rosa and San Jacinto Mtns. Natl. Mon.,
   Calif., U.S. 246/J9
Santa Rosa Beach, Fla., U.S., 300 . . . . .256/B1
Santa Rosa de Copán, Hond., 23,400 . . . . .202/A2
Santa Rosa del Palmar, Bol. 186/B3
Santa Rosalía, Mex., 10,609 . . . . .200/B2
Santa Venetia, Calif., U.S., 4,298 . . . . .246/H1
Santa Ynez, Calif., U.S., 4,584 . . . . .246/E8
Santee, Calif., U.S., 52,975 . . . . .246/J10
Santee, Nebr., U.S., 302 . . . . .308/G1
Santee, S.C., U.S., 740 . . . . .340/D3
Santee, S.C., U.S., river 340/E3
Santee Ind. Res., Nebr., U.S. 308/G1
Santee NWR., S.C., U.S. 340/D3
Santeetlah, N.C., U.S., 67 . . . . .322/B8
Santiago, Chile, capital, 206,044,
   (4,647,444 metro.) . . . . .190/B4, Inset
Santiago, Dom. Rep. 204/D3
Santiago, Dom. Rep., 836,614,
   (1,289,000 metro.) 205/B1
Santiago, Dom. Rep., province 205/B1
Santiago, Ecua., river 185/B4
Santiago, Pan. 203/B2
Santiago, Peru, river 185/B1
Santiago, Minn., U.S., 100 . . . . .298/D5
Santiago, Tex., U.S., peak 346/E6
Santiago de Compostela, Sp., 90,188 . . . . .94/B1
Santiago de Cuba, Cuba 204/D3
Santiago de Cuba, Cuba, 439,669 . . . . .204/E3
Santiago de Cuba, Cuba, province 204/E3
Santiago del Estero, Arg., 189,947,
   (263,471 metro.) 191/C2
Santiago del Estero, Arg., province 191/C2
Santiago Rodríguez, Dom. Rep., province 205/A1
Sant Julià de Lòria, And. 93/A3
Santo André, Braz., 649,331 . . . . .188/Inset II
Santo Antão, C.V., island 148/A1
Santo Domingo, Dom. Rep., capital 204/D3
Santo Domingo, Dom. Rep., capital, 2,677,056,
   (3,523,000 metro.) 205/C2
Santo Domingo, P.R. 206/B2
Santo Domingo de los Colorados, Ecua. 185/B3
Santo Domingo Pueblo, N. Mex., U.S., 2,550 . . .317/D2
Santon Downham, Eng., U.K. 70/F2
Santos, Braz., 417,983 . . . . .188/D4, Inset II
Santos, Fla., U.S., 550 . . . . .256/F2
Santo Tomás de Castilla, Guat. 201/E4
Santuit, Mass., U.S., 375 . . . . .292/N6
San Vicente, El. Salv., 45,842 . . . . .203/B2
San Vicente Chicoloapan de Juárez, Mex. 200/Inset
San Vito, It., cape 95/C3
San Xavier, Ariz., U.S., 50 . . . . .242/D6
Sanyati, Zimb., river 157/A2
San Ygnacio, Tex., U.S., 350 . . . . .346/J8
San Ysidro, N. Mex., U.S., 238 . . . . .317/D2
São Bernardo do Campo, Braz., 703,177 . . . .188/Inset II
São Caetano do Sul, Braz. . . . . .188/Inset II
São Domingos, Gui.-B. 149/A1
São Filipe, C.V. 148/B4
São Francisco, Braz., river 188/D3
São Gonçalo, Braz., 891,119 . . . . .188/Inset I
São João de Meriti, Braz., 449,476 . . . . .188/Inset I
São Jorge, Port., island . . . . .93/Inset II
São José do Rio Prêto, Braz., 171,982,
   (283,281 metro.) 188/D4
São Luís, Braz., 870,028 . . . . .188/D2
São Miguel, Port., island . . . . .93/Inset II
Saona, Dom. Rep., island 205/D2
Saône, Fr., river 86/A5
Saône, Fr., river 88/C3
Saône-et-Loire, Fr., department 88/C3
São Nicolau, C.V., island 148/B2
São Paulo, Braz., 10,406,166,
   (17,833,511 metro.) . . . . .188/D4, Inset II
São Paulo, Braz., state . . . . .188/C4, Inset II
São Tiago, C.V., island 148/C3
São Tomé, São T.-Prínc., capital, 5,714 . . . . . .154/A4
São Tomé, São T.-Prínc., island 154/B4
São Tomé, São T.-Prínc., mountain 154/B4
São Tomé and Príncipe, nation 148
Saoura, Alg., river .146/A1
São Vicente, C.V., island 148/A2

São Vicente, Port., cape 93/A4
São Vicente, Braz. . . . . .188/Inset II
Sapcote, Eng., U.K., 2,628 . . . . .68/E4
Sapcote, Eng., U.K., 2,628 . . . . .70/B1
Sapele, Nig. 152/C5
Sapello, N. Mex., U.S. 317/E2
Sapelo, Ga., U.S., island 260/J9
Sapelo, Ga., U.S., sound 260/J8
Sapelo Island, Ga., U.S. 260/J9
Sapey Common, Eng., U.K. 68/C5
Sapinero, Colo., U.S. 250/C3
Sapitwa, Mal., mountain 159/C3
Saponac, Maine, U.S. 286/D3
Sappa Creek, Kans., U.S. 276/B2
Sappho, Wash., U.S. 358/A1
Sappington, Mo., U.S., 7,287 . . . . .302/H3
Sappington, Mont., U.S. 306/E4
Sapporo, Jap., 1,822,300 . . . . .114/Inset I
Sapulpa, Okla., U.S., 19,166 . . . . .330/F1
Sar, Palau, island .172/B3
Sara Buri, Thai., (125,300 metro.) 125/B3
Saracen's Head, Eng., U.K. 70/D1
Saragosa, Tex., U.S. 346/E4
Sarah, Miss., U.S., 70 . . . . .300/B1
Sarahsville, Ohio, U.S., 198 . . . . .328/H6
Sarajevo, Bos.-Her., capital, 529,021 . . . . .98/B2
Saraland, Ala., U.S., 12,288 . . . . .238/A5
Saramacca, Sur., river 183/B2
Saranac, Mich., U.S., 1,326 . . . . .294/D7
Saranac, Calif., U.S., 275 . . . . .320/P1
Saranac Lake, N.Y., U.S., 5,041 . . . . .320/N2
Sarandë, Alb. 99/A4
Saransk, Russ., 316,086, (344,700 metro.) 104/D4
Sarapiquí river, C.R. 203/B2
Sarasota, Fla., U.S., 52,715, (589,959 metro.) . .256/F4
Sarasota, Fla., U.S., county, 325,957 . . . . .256/F4
Saratoga, Calif., U.S., 29,843 . . . . .246/K3
Saratoga, Ind., U.S., 288 . . . . .270/G4
Saratoga, Iowa, U.S., 100 . . . . .274/K1
Saratoga, N.Y., U.S., county, 200,635 . . . . . . .320/P4
Saratoga, N.Y., U.S., lake 320/P4
Saratoga, N.C., U.S., 379 . . . . .322/K3
Saratoga, Wyo., U.S., 1,726 . . . . .366/C3
Saratoga Natl. Hist. Park, N.Y., U.S. 320/P5
Saratoga Sprs., N.Y., U.S., 26,186 . . . . .320/P4
Saratov, Russ., 875,256 . . . . .104/D4
Sarawak, Malay., state 121/C2
Saraya, Sen. 148/B3
Sarben, Nebr., U.S. .308/C2
Sarbhang, Bhu. 128/C2
Sarcelles, Fr. . . . . .88/Inset II
Sarcoxie, Mo., U.S., 1,354 . . . . .302/A4
Sarda, Nepal, river .126/A2
Sardinia, It., island .95/B2
Sardinia, It., region .95/B3
Sardinia, Ind., U.S., 150 . . . . .270/E6
Sardinia, Ohio, U.S., 862 . . . . .328/C8
Sardis, Ala., U.S., 80 . . . . .238/C3
Sardis, Ark., U.S., lake 244/F3
Sardis, Ky., U.S., 1,171 . . . . .260/H6
Sardis, Miss., U.S., 2,038 . . . . .300/C1
Sardis, Miss., U.S., lake 300/C1
Sardis, Ohio, U.S., 750 . . . . .328/J6
Sardis, Tenn., U.S., 445 . . . . .344/E4
Sardis, W. Va., U.S. 360/F2
Sardis City, Ala., U.S., 1,438 . . . . .238/C1
Sar-e Pol, Afg. 129/B1
Sarepta, La., U.S., 925 . . . . .282/C1
Sarepta, Miss., U.S., 60 . . . . .300/C1
Sargeant, Minn., U.S., 76 . . . . .298/E7
Sargent, Ga., U.S., 700 . . . . .260/B5
Sargent, Nebr., U.S., 524 . . . . .308/E2
Sargent, N. Dak., U.S., county, 4,366 . . . . .326/H3
Sargents, Colo., U.S. 250/D3
Sargodha, Pak., 458,440 . . . . .129/D3
Sarh, Chad, 79,850, (193,753 metro.) 153/B5
Sari, Iran 130/C2
Sarita, Tex., U.S. 346/L8
Sariwŏn, N. Kor. 116/A3
Sarjektjakko, Swe. .80/C1
Sark, Eng., U.K., island . . . . .60/Inset II
Sark, Eng., U.K., island 73/G4
Sarles, N. Dak., U.S. 326/G1
Sarnia, (Sarnia-Clearwater), Ont., Can., 70,876 .223/C5
Sarnia, Ont., Can., 70,876 . . . . .222/D4
Sarona, Wisc., U.S., 100 . . . . .364/B3
Saronic, Gr., gulf .100/Inset
Saronville, Nebr., U.S., 61 . . . . .308/G3
Sarpy, Nebr., U.S., county, 122,595 . . . . .308/H2
Sarre, Eng., U.K. 70/H4
Sarstoon, Bel., river 201/A4
Sarstún, Guat., river 201/D4
Sartell, Minn., U.S., 9,641 . . . . .298/C5
Sarthe, Fr., department 88/C3
Sarygamysh Koli, Turkm., lake 132/B2
Saryshagan, Kaz. 131/D2
Sary Tash, Kyrg. 131/C3
Sasabe, Ariz., U.S. .242/D6
Sasakwa, Okla., U.S., 150 . . . . .330/F3
Sasamungga, Sol. Is. 173/A1
Sasaram, India 128/C3
Sasebo, Jap. 114/A3
Saskatchewan, Can., province 215
Saskatchewan, Man., Can., river 215/A2
Saskatchewan, Sask., Can., river 227/E7
Saskatchewan Landing Prov. Park, Sask., Can. . .227/C10
Saskatoon, Sask., Can., 196,811,
   (231,000 metro.) 227/D8
Sassafras, Md., U.S., 100 . . . . .288/L2
Sassandra, C. d'Iv. .150/C4
Sassandra, C. d'Iv., river 150/C2, C4
Sassari, It. 95/B2
Sasser, Ga., U.S., 393 . . . . .260/C8
Sassnitz, Ger. 86/C1
Sata, Jap., cape 114/A4
Satakunta, Fin., region 81/B2
Satanta, Kans., U.S., 1,239 . . . . .276/B4
Satartia, Miss., U.S., 68 . . . . .300/B3
Satellite Beach, Fla., U.S., 9,577 . . . . .256/H4
Satley, Eng., U.K. .66/E3
Satpura, India, range 128/C4
Satsuma, Jap., peninsula 114/A4
Satsuma, Ala., U.S., 5,687 . . . . .238/A5
Sattahip, Thai. 125/B3
Sattler, Tex., U.S. .346/B1
Satu Mare, Rom., 129,153 . . . . .101/B2
Satu Mare, Rom., county 101/B2
Satus, Wash., U.S., 746 . . . . .358/E3
Sauble Beach, Ont., Can. 223/D3
Saucier, Miss., U.S., 1,303 . . . . .300/C5
Saudárkrókur, Ice. .79/B2
Saudi Arabia, nation 132
Saugatuck, Conn., U.S., reservoir 253/B4
Saugatuck, Mich., U.S., 1,065 . . . . .294/C7
Saugerties, N.Y., U.S., 4,955 . . . . .320/P6
Sauget, Ill., U.S., 249 . . . . .266/B3
Saugus, Mass., U.S., 26,078 . . . . .292/D6, K3
Saugus Iron Works N.H.S., Mass., U.S. 292/D6
Sauk, Minn., U.S., river 298/C5
Sauk, Wisc., U.S., county, 55,225 . . . . .364/D5

Sauk Centre, Minn., U.S., 3,930 . . . . .298/C5
Sauk City, Wisc., U.S., 3,109 . . . . .364/D5
Sauk Rapids, Minn., U.S., 10,213 . . . . .298/C5
Sauk Vil., Ill., U.S., 10,411 . . . . .266/C6
Saukville, Wisc., U.S., 4,068 . . . . .364/F5
Saul, Eng., U.K. 68/C6
Saül, Fr. Gui. 183/B2
Saulsbury, Tenn., U.S., 99 . . . . .344/C4
Sault-au-Mouton, Que., Can., 1,352 . . . . .226/G3
Sault Ste. Marie, Ont., Can., 74,566 . . . . .222/D3
Sault Ste. Marie, Ont., Can., 74,566 . . . . .223/A1
Sault Ste. Marie, Mich., U.S., 16,542 . . . . .294/E3
Saum, Minn., U.S., 60 . . . . .298/C3
Saunders, Kans., U.S. 276/A4
Saunders, Nebr., U.S., county, 19,830 . . . . . . .308/G2
Saundersfoot, Wales, U.K., 3,221 . . . . .64/B4
Saunderstown, R.I., U.S., 1,600 . . . . .339/D5
Saunemin, Ill., U.S., 456 . . . . .266/E3
Saunton, Eng., U.K. 73/D2
Sauquoit, N.Y., U.S., 1,000 . . . . .320/L5
Saurimo, Ang. 159/D3
Sausalito, Calif., U.S., 7,330 . . . . .246/H2
Sauteurs, Gren. 209/B2
Sava, Bos.-Her., river 98/B3
Sava, Cro., river 98/C2
Sava, Serb.-Mont., river 99/A2
Sava, Slove., river .98/A1
Savage, (Savage-Guilford), Md., U.S., 12,918 . . .288/G3
Savage, Minn., U.S., 21,115 . . . . .298/D6
Savage, Miss., U.S., 100 . . . . .300/A1
Savage, Mont., U.S., 250 . . . . .306/M2
Savage Gulf St. Nat. Area, Tenn., U.S. 344/K4
Savage River St. For., Md., U.S. 288/B3
Savageton, Wyo., U.S. 366/D2
Savai'i, Sam., island 175/A2
Savalou, Ben. 151/A3
Savan, St. Vin.-Gren., island 208/B3
Savanna, Ill., U.S., 3,542 . . . . .266/C1
Savanna, Okla., U.S., 730 . . . . .330/G3
Savannah, Ga., U.S., 131,510, (293,000 metro.) .260/J7
Savannah, Ga., U.S., river 260/H5
Savannah, Mo., U.S., 4,762 . . . . .302/B2
Savannah, Ohio, U.S., 372 . . . . .328/F4
Savannah, Tenn., U.S., 6,917 . . . . .344/E4
Savannah Beach, Ga., U.S. 260/K7
Savanna-la-Mar, Jam. 206/A2
Savé, Ben. 151/B3
Save, Moz., river 161/B4
Savery, Wyo., U.S. .366/C3
Savigny-sur-Orge, Fr. . . . . .88/Inset II
Savinja, Slove., river 98/B2
Savo, Fin., region 81/C2
Savoie, Fr., department 88/D4
Savona, Br. Col., Can. 214/M6
Savona, It. 95/B1
Savona, N.Y., U.S., 822 . . . . .320/G6
Savonburg, Kans., U.S., 91 . . . . .276/G4
Savonlinna, Fin. 81/C2
Savonga, Alaska, U.S., 643 . . . . .240/A2
Savoy, Ill., U.S., 4,476 . . . . .266/E3
Savoy, Mass., U.S., 705 . . . . .292/B2
Savoy, Mont., U.S. .306/H2
Savoy, Tex., U.S., 850 . . . . .346/M2
Savu, Indon., sea 122/C4
Sawatch, Colo., U.S., range 250/D2
Sawbridgeworth, Eng., U.K., 9,432 . . . . .70/G3
Sawda, Jabal, Sa. Arab., mountain 136/B2
Sawel, N. Ire., U.K., mountain 65/C2
Sawel, (N. Yorkshire), Eng., U.K. 78/C1
Sawley, (Lancashire), Eng., U.K. 68/C2
Sawley, (N. Yorkshire), Eng., U.K. 68/D1
Sawley, Derby., Eng., U.K. 68/D5
Sawley, Eng., U.K. .66/E4
Sawmill, Ariz., U.S., 612 . . . . .242/F2
Sawmills, N.C., U.S., 4,921 . . . . .322/C3
Sawpit, Colo., U.S. .250/B4
Sawqirah, Oman 137/C2
Sawqirah, Oman, bay 137/C2
Sawston, Eng., U.K., 7,172 . . . . .68/G5
Sawston, Eng., U.K., 7,172 . . . . .70/E2
Sawtooth, Ida., U.S., range 264/C6
Sawtooth Natl. For., Ida., U.S. 264/C6, D7
Sawtooth Natl. For., Utah, U.S. 350/A1, A4
Sawtooth Natl. Rec. Area, Ida., U.S. 264/C5
Sawtry, Eng., U.K., 4,766 . . . . .68/G5
Sawtry, Eng., U.K., 4,766 . . . . .70/D2
Sawyer, Kans., U.S., 124 . . . . .276/D4
Sawyer, Mich., U.S., 200 . . . . .294/C8
Sawyer, Minn., U.S., 175 . . . . .298/E4
Sawyer, N. Dak., U.S., 377 . . . . .326/E3
Sawyer, Okla., U.S., 254 . . . . .330/G3
Sawyer, Wash., U.S., 200 . . . . .358/K4
Sawyer, Wisc., U.S., county, 16,196 . . . . .364/B3
Sawyerville, Ala., U.S., 50 . . . . .238/B4
Sawyerville, Ill., U.S., 295 . . . . .266/B3
Saxapahaw, N.C., U.S., 1,418 . . . . .322/G3
Saxby, Eng., U.K. .70/C1
Saxe, Va., U.S., 70 .354/F7
Saxeville, Wisc., U.S., 200 . . . . .364/D4
Saxilby, Eng., U.K., 3,086 . . . . .66/G6
Saxilby, Eng., U.K., 3,086 . . . . .68/F3
Saxis, Va., U.S., 337 . . . . .354/M5
Saxman, Kans., U.S. 276/D3
Saxmundham, Eng., U.K., 2,529 . . . . .70/G2
Saxon, S.C., U.S., 3,707 . . . . .340/C2
Saxon, Wisc., U.S., 125 . . . . .364/C2
Saxonburg, Penn., U.S., 1,629 . . . . .336/B4
Saxony, Ger., state .86/C2
Saxony-Anhalt, Ger., state 86/B3
Saxthorpe, Eng., U.K. 70/G1
Saxton, Eng., U.K. .66/F5
Saxton, Penn., U.S., 803 . . . . .336/E5
Saxtons River, Vt., U.S., 519 . . . . .352/B4
Sayabec, Que., Can., 1,999 . . . . .226/J3
Sayan, Russ., mountains 104/F4
Saybrook, Ill., U.S., 764 . . . . .266/E3
Saybrook, Ohio, U.S., 850 . . . . .328/J2
Saybrook Manor, Conn., U.S., 1,133 . . . . .253/F4
Sayhut, Yemen 137/C1
Saylesville, R.I., U.S. 339/D2
Saylorsburg, Penn., U.S., 1,100 . . . . .336/E4
Saylorville, Iowa, U.S., 3,238 . . . . .274/G4
Saylorville Res., Iowa, U.S. 274/G4
Sayner, Wisc., U.S., 175 . . . . .364/D3
Sayre, Okla., U.S., 4,114 . . . . .330/D2
Sayre, Penn., U.S., 5,813 . . . . .336/H2
Sayreville, N.J., U.S., 40,377 . . . . .316/H4
Sayward, Br. Col., Can., 379 . . . . .214/K6
Saywun, Yemen 137/B1
Sázava, Czh. Rep., river 92/B3
Scafell, Eng., U.K., hill 66/B4
Scafell Pike, Eng., U.K., hill 60/B4
Scafell Pike, Eng., U.K., hill 66/B4
Scalasaig, Scot., U.K. 62/F4
Scalby, Eng., U.K., 9,019 . . . . .66/H4
Scales Mound, Ill., U.S., 401 . . . . .266/C1
Scallorn, Tex., U.S., 40 . . . . .346/K4
Scalloway, Scot., U.K., 812 . . . . .62/Q2

Scalpay, Scot., U.K., island 62/C3
Scalpay, Scot., U.K. 62/E4
Scalp Level, Penn., U.S., 851 . . . .336/D5
Scaly Mountain, N.C., U.S., 125 . . . .322/D8
Scamblesby, Eng., U.K. 66/H6
Scammon, Kans., U.S., 496 . . . .276/H4
Scammon Bay, Alaska, U.S., 465 . . . .240/B2
Scandia, Alta., Can., 114 . . . .212/D6
Scandia, Kans., U.S., 436 . . . .276/E2
Scandinavia, Wisc., U.S., 349 . . . .364/D4
Scanlon, Minn., U.S., 838 . . . .298/E4
Scantic, Conn., U.S., 200 . . . .253/E2
Scappoose, Oreg., U.S., 4,976 . . . .334/D2
Scar, Scot., U.K. 62/N1
Scaraben, Scot., U.K., hill 62/I2
Scarba, Scot., U.K., island 62/E6
Scarba Lunga and the Garvellachs N.P., Scot., U.K. 62/E6
Scarboro, Ga., U.S., 50 . . . .260/H6
Scarboro, Ill., U.S., 50 . . . .266/D2
Scarborough, W.A., Austl. . . . .170/Inset I
Scarborough, Ont., Can. 223/F4, L5
Scarborough, Trin.-To. 209/B1
Scarborough, Eng., U.K. 60/C2
Scarborough, Eng., U.K., 38,809, (57,536 metro.) 66/H4
Scarborough, Maine, U.S., 16,970 . . . .286/B5
Scarbro, W. Va., U.S., 1,700 . . . .360/D5
Scardroy, Scot., U.K. 62/G3
Scarface, Mont., U.S., peak 306/C2
Scarp, Scot., U.K., island 62/B2
Scarsdale, N.Y., U.S., 17,823 . . . .274/C1
Scarville, Iowa, U.S., 97 . . . .274/C1
Scayne's Hill, Eng., U.K. 70/D5
Scenic, S. Dak., U.S. 342/C4
Scenic Oaks, Tex., U.S., 3,279 . . . .346/A2
Schaal, Ark., U.S., 40 . . . .244/B4
Schaan, Liech. 90/B2
Schaerbeek, Belg. 85/C2
Schaffer, Mich., U.S., 275 . . . .294/B4
Schaffhausen, Switz. 90/C1
Schaffhausen, Switz., canton 90/C1
Schaghticoke, N.Y., U.S., 676 . . . .320/P5
Schaller, Iowa, U.S., 779 . . . .274/D2
Schaumburg, Ill., U.S., 75,386 . . . .84/B3
Schelde, Belg., river 85/B2
Schelde, Belg., river 85/B2
Schell City, Mo., U.S., 286 . . . .302/B3
Schell Creek, Nev., U.S., range 310/C2
Schellenberg, Liech. 90/B1
Schellsburg, Penn., U.S., 316 . . . .336/D5
Schenectady, N.Y., U.S., 61,821 . . . .320/P5
Schenectady, N.Y., U.S., county, 146,555 . . . .320/N5
Schenevus, N.Y., U.S., 500 . . . .320/M5
Schererville, Ind., U.S., 24,851 . . . .270/B2
Scherr, W. Va., U.S., 40 . . . .360/H2
Schertz, Tex., U.S., 18,694 . . . .346/A2
Scheveningen, Neth. 84/B3
Schiedam, Neth. 84/B3
Schiermonnikoog, Neth., island 84/D1
Schiller Park, Ill., U.S., 11,850 . . . .266/B5
Schlater, Miss., U.S., 388 . . . .300/B2
Schleicher, Tex., U.S., county, 2,935 . . . .346/H5
Schleswig, Ger. 86/B1
Schleswig, Iowa, U.S., 833 . . . .274/D3
Schleswig-Holstein, Ger., state 86/B2
Schley, Ga., U.S., county, 3,766 . . . .260/C7
Schley, Iowa, U.S., 40 . . . .274/K1
Schley, Minn., U.S. 298/C3
Schneider, Ind., U.S., 317 . . . .270/B2
Schofield, Wisc., U.S., 2,117 . . . .364/D4
Schofield Barracks Mil. Res., Hawaii, U.S. 262/J2
Schoharie, N.Y., U.S., 1,030 . . . .320/N5
Schoharie, N.Y., U.S., county, 31,582 . . . .320/N5
Schoharie, N.Y., U.S., reservoir 320/N6
Scholle, N. Mex., U.S. 317/D3
Schoolcraft, Mich., U.S., 1,587 . . . .294/D7
Schoolcraft, Mich., U.S., county, 8,903 . . . .294/C3
Schooleys Mountain, N.J., U.S., 1,100 . . . .314/D2
Schouwen, Neth., island 84/A3
Schrag, Wash., U.S. 358/G2
Schram City, Ill., U.S., 653 . . . .266/D4
Schreiber, Ont., Can. 222/C3
Schriever, La., U.S., 5,880 . . . .282/H7
Schroeder, Minn., U.S., 80 . . . .298/F3
Schroon, N.Y., U.S., lake 320/P3
Schroon Lake, N.Y., U.S., 650 . . . .320/P3
Schuchk, Ariz., U.S., 50 . . . .242/D5
Schuler, Alta., Can., 89 . . . .212/E6
Schuline, Ill., U.S., 70 . . . .266/D5
Schulte, Kans., U.S., 125 . . . .276/E4
Schulter, Okla., U.S., 600 . . . .330/G2
Schultz, W. Va., U.S., 125 . . . .360/D2
Schurz, Nev., U.S., 721 . . . .310/A2
Schuyler, Ill., U.S., county, 7,189 . . . .266/C3
Schuyler, Mo., U.S., county, 4,170 . . . .302/D1
Schuyler, Nebr., U.S., 5,371 . . . .308/G2
Schuyler, N.Y., U.S., county, 19,224 . . . .354/F5
Schuyler, Va., U.S., 250 . . . .320/L5
Schuyler Lake, N.Y., U.S., 275 . . . .320/P4
Schuylerville, N.Y., U.S., 1,197 . . . .320/P4
Schuylkill, Penn., U.S., county, 150,336 . . . .336/H4
Schuylkill, Penn., U.S., river 336/K5, L7
Schuylkill Haven, Penn., U.S., 5,548 . . . .336/J4
Schwaben, Ger., department 86/B4
Schwäbisch Gmünd, Ger. 86/B4
Schwedt, Ger. 86/C2
Schweinfurt, Ger. 86/B3
Schwenksville, Penn., U.S., 1,693 . . . .336/L5
Schwerin, Ger., 102,878 . . . .86/B2
Schweriner, Ger., lake 86/B2
Schwyz, Switz. 90/C1
Schwyz, Switz., canton 90/C1
Science Hill, Ky., U.S., 634 . . . .280/F3
Scientists Cliffs, Md., U.S. 288/H5
Scio, Ohio, U.S., 799 . . . .328/H5
Scio, Oreg., U.S., 695 . . . .334/D3
Sciota, Ill., U.S., 58 . . . .266/C3
Scioto, Ohio, U.S., county, 79,195 . . . .328/D8
Scioto, Ohio, U.S., river 328/D4, D8
Sciotodale, Ohio, U.S., 982 . . . .328/E8
Scipio, Ind., U.S., 225 . . . .270/E6
Scipio, Okla., U.S., 70 . . . .330/G2
Scipio, Utah, U.S., 500 . . . .360/B4
Scitico, Conn., U.S., 550 . . . .253/E2
Scituate, Mass., U.S., 17,863 . . . .292/L4
Scituate, R.I., U.S., reservoir 339/C2
Scobey, Miss., U.S. 300/C2
Scobey, Mont., U.S., 1,082 . . . .306/L1
Scofield, Utah, U.S. 360/C4
Scole, Eng., U.K. 70/G2
Scooba, Miss., U.S., 632 . . . .300/D3
Scopwick, Eng., U.K. 68/G3
Scoraig, Scot., U.K. 62/F3
Scotch Corner, Eng., U.K. 66/E4
Scotch Plains, N.J., U.S., 22,732 . . . .314/E2
Scotch Ridge, N.B., Can. 217/B3
Scotchtown, N.Y., U.S., 8,954 . . . .320/N8
Scotforth, Eng., U.K. 66/C2

Scotia, Nebr., U.S., 308 . . . .308/E2
Scotia, N.Y., U.S., 7,957 . . . .320/P5
Scotia, S.C., U.S., 227 . . . .340/C4
Scotland, U.K., country 60
Scotland, Ark., U.S., 100 . . . .244/C2
Scotland, Conn., U.S., 1,556 . . . .253/G3
Scotland, Ga., U.S., 300 . . . .260/F7
Scotland, Md., U.S., 300 . . . .288/J7
Scotland, Mass., U.S., 1,900 . . . .292/K5
Scotland, Mo., U.S., county, 4,983 . . . .302/D1
Scotland, N.H., U.S., 300 . . . .312/B6
Scotland, N.C., U.S., county, 35,998 . . . .322/F5
Scotland, Penn., U.S., 1,700 . . . .336/F6
Scotland, S. Dak., U.S., 891 . . . .342/H4
Scotland, Tex., U.S., 438 . . . .346/K2
Scotland Beach, Md., U.S., 125 . . . .288/J7
Scotland Neck, N.C., U.S., 2,362 . . . .322/L2
Scotstown, Que., Can., 642 . . . .226/G1
Scotswood, Alta., Can. 212/A3
Scott, Antar., island 192/C5
Scott, Ark., U.S., 94 . . . .244/C3
Scott, Ark., U.S., county, 10,996 . . . .244/A3
Scott, Ida., U.S., peak 264/E5
Scott, Ill., U.S., county, 5,537 . . . .266/C4
Scott, Ind., U.S., county, 22,960 . . . .270/E7
Scott, Iowa, U.S., county, 158,668 . . . .274/N4
Scott, Kans., U.S., county, 5,120 . . . .276/B3
Scott, Ky., U.S., county, 33,061 . . . .280/F2
Scott, La., U.S., 7,870 . . . .282/E6
Scott, Mich., U.S., point 294/D4
Scott, Minn., U.S., county, 89,498 . . . .298/D6
Scott, Miss., U.S., 150 . . . .300/A2
Scott, Miss., U.S., county, 28,423 . . . .300/C3
Scott, Mo., U.S., county, 40,422 . . . .302/G5
Scott, Ohio, U.S., 322 . . . .328/A4
Scott, Tenn., U.S., county, 21,127 . . . .344/M2
Scott, Va., U.S., county, 23,403 . . . .354/C3
Scott City, Kans., U.S., 3,855 . . . .276/B3
Scott City, Mo., U.S., 4,591 . . . .302/G4
Scottdale, Ga., U.S., 9,803 . . . .260/J2
Scottdale, Penn., U.S., 4,772 . . . .336/B5
Scott Depot, W. Va., U.S., 2,600 . . . .360/C4
Scotter, Eng., U.K., 2,415 . . . .66/G6
Scotter, Eng., U.K., 2,415 . . . .66/G6
Scottish Borders, Scot., U.K., unitary authority, 106,764 . . . .62/K8
Scotts Bar, Calif., U.S., 40 . . . .246/H1
Scottsbluff, Nebr., U.S., 14,732 . . . .308/A2
Scotts Bluff, Nebr., U.S., county, 36,951 . . . .308/A2
Scotts Bluff N.M., Nebr., U.S. 308/A2
Scottsboro, Ala., U.S., 14,762 . . . .238/C1
Scottsburg, Ind., U.S., 6,040 . . . .270/E7
Scottsburg, Ky., U.S., 125 . . . .280/C3
Scottsburg, Oreg., U.S., 50 . . . .334/C4
Scottsburg, Va., U.S., 145 . . . .354/F7
Scottsdale, Ariz., U.S., 202,705 . . . .242/D5
Scotts Mills, Oreg., U.S., 312 . . . .334/D2
Scottsmoor, Fla., U.S., 600 . . . .256/H3
Scotts Valley, Calif., U.S., 11,385 . . . .246/K4
Scottsville, Ark., U.S., 60 . . . .244/A4
Scottsville, Kans., U.S. 276/E2
Scottsville, Ky., U.S., 4,327 . . . .280/D4
Scottsville, N.Y., U.S., 2,128 . . . .320/F4
Scottsville, Va., U.S., 555 . . . .354/G5
Scottville, Ill., U.S., 140 . . . .266/C4
Scottville, Mich., U.S., 1,266 . . . .294/C6
Scotty's Jct., Nev., U.S. 310/B3
Scourie, Scot., U.K. 62/F2
Scousburgh, Scot., U.K. 62/J1
Scrabster, Scot., U.K. 62/J2
Scraghy, N. Ire., U.K. 65/B2
Scrane End, Eng., U.K. 70/E1
Scranton, Ark., U.S., 222 . . . .244/B2
Scranton, Iowa, U.S., 604 . . . .274/E3
Scranton, Kans., U.S., 724 . . . .276/G3
Scranton, N.C., U.S., 50 . . . .322/N4
Scranton, N. Dak., U.S., 304 . . . .326/B3
Scranton, Penn., U.S., 76,415, (624,776 metro.) 336/H7, K3
Scranton, S.C., U.S., 942 . . . .340/E3
Scraper, Okla., U.S., 475 . . . .330/H1
Screven, Ga., U.S., 702 . . . .260/G9
Screven, Ga., U.S., county, 15,374 . . . .260/H6
Scribner, Nebr., U.S., 971 . . . .308/H2
Scugog, Ont., Can., lake 223/G3
Scullville, N.J., U.S., 600 . . . .314/D5
Scunthorpe, Eng., U.K. 60/C3
Scunthorpe, Eng., U.K., 75,982 . . . .66/G5
Scunthorpe, Eng., U.K., 75,982 . . . .68/F2
Scurry, Tex., U.S., county, 16,361 . . . .346/H3
Scutari, Alb., lake 99/A1
Scutari, Serb.-Mont., lake 99/A3
Sczcecinek, Pol. 83/C2
Seabeck, Wash., U.S., 325 . . . .358/C2
Seaboard, N.C., U.S., 695 . . . .322/L2
Sea Breeze, N.J., U.S., 40 . . . .314/C5
Sea Bright, N.J., U.S., 1,818 . . . .314/F3
Seabrook, (see Lanham), Md., U.S., 18,190 . . . .288/D6
Seabrook, N.H., U.S., 7,934 . . . .312/E6
Seabrook, N.J., U.S., 1,719 . . . .314/C5
Seabrook, Tex., U.S., 9,443 . . . .346/C7
Seabrook Island, S.C., U.S., 1,250 . . . .340/D4
Seacow Pond, P.E.I., Can. 224/B1
Seadrift, Tex., U.S., 1,352 . . . .346/M7
Seaford, Eng., U.K., 19,622 . . . .70/E5
Seaford, Del., U.S., 6,699 . . . .255/B6
Seaford, Va., U.S., 2,000 . . . .354/L6
Seaforth, Ont., Can., 2,692 . . . .223/D4
Seaforth, Minn., U.S., 77 . . . .298/B6
Seagate, N.C., U.S., 4,590 . . . .322/K6
Sea Girt, N.J., U.S., 2,148 . . . .314/E3
Seagoville, Tex., U.S., 10,823 . . . .346/D10
Seagrave, Eng., U.K. 70/B1
Seagraves, Tex., U.S., 2,334 . . . .346/F2
Seagrove, N.C., U.S., 246 . . . .322/F3
Seagrove Beach, Fla., U.S., 150 . . . .256/B1
Seaham, Eng., U.K., 22,130 . . . .66/F3
Seahouses, Eng., U.K. 66/E1
Sea Island, Ga., U.S., 80 . . . .260/J9
Sea Isle City, N.J., U.S., 2,835 . . . .314/D5
Seal, Man., Can., river 246/D10
Seal Beach, Calif., U.S., 24,157 . . . .248/D2
Seal Cove, Nfld., Can., 417 . . . .218/C4
Seale, Ala., U.S. 225 . . . .238/D3
Sealevel, N.C., U.S., 225 . . . .322/N5
Seal Harbor, Maine, U.S., 300 . . . .286/D4
Seal Island N.W.R., Maine, U.S. 286/D4
Seal Rock, Oreg., U.S., 275 . . . .334/B3
Sealy, Tex., U.S., 5,248 . . . .346/M6
Seama, N. Mex., U.S., 333 . . . .317/C2
Seamer, Eng., U.K., 2,178 . . . .66/G4
Sea Palling, Eng., U.K. 70/H1
Sea Ranch Lakes, Fla., U.S., 1,392 . . . .256/B5
Searchlight, Nev., U.S., 596 . . . .310/C4
Searchmont, Ont., Can., 365 . . . .223/A1
Searcy, Ark., U.S., 18,928 . . . .244/C2
Searcy, Ark., U.S., county, 8,261 . . . .244/C2

Searles, Calif., U.S. 246/H7
Searles, Minn., U.S., 225 . . . .298/C6
Sears, Mich., U.S., 100 . . . .294/D6
Searsboro, Iowa, U.S., 155 . . . .274/J4
Searsburg, Vt., U.S., 96 . . . .352/B5
Searsmont, Maine, U.S., 1,174 . . . .286/C4
Searsport, Maine, U.S., 2,641 . . . .286/C4
Seasalter, Eng., U.K. 70/G4
Seascale, Eng., U.K. 66/B4
Seaside, Calif., U.S., 31,696 . . . .246/D6
Seaside, Oreg., U.S., 5,900 . . . .334/C2
Seaside Hts., N.J., U.S., 3,155 . . . .314/E4
Seaside Park, N.J., U.S., 2,263 . . . .314/E4
SeaTac, Wash., U.S., 25,496 . . . .358/A4
Seaton, Eng., U.K., 4,380 . . . .66/A3
Seaton, Eng., U.K., 7,579 . . . .73/F3
Seaton, Ill., U.S., 242 . . . .266/C2
Seaton Delaval, Eng., U.K., 7,333 . . . .66/F1
Seatonville, Ill., U.S., 303 . . . .266/D2
Seat Pleasant, Md., U.S., 4,885 . . . .288/C7, G4
Seattle, Wash., U.S., 563,374, (3,554,760 metro.) 358/A4, C3
Seave Green, Eng., U.K. 66/F4
Seaview, Eng., U.K., 2,181 . . . .70/B5
Seaville, N.J., U.S., 1,700 . . . .314/D5
Seawall, Maine, U.S., 125 . . . .286/D4
Seawell, Barb. 209/C4
Sebago, Maine, U.S., lake 286/B5
Sebago Lake, Maine, U.S., 550 . . . .286/B5
Sebastian, Ark., U.S., county, 115,071 . . . .244/A2
Sebastian, Fla., U.S., 16,181 . . . .256/H4
Sebastián Vizcaíno, Mex., bay 200/E3
Sebastopol, Calif., U.S., 7,774 . . . .246/C4
Sebastopol, Miss., U.S., 233 . . . .300/C3
Sebec, Maine, U.S., 612 . . . .286/C3
Sebec, Maine, U.S., lake 286/C3
Sebec Lake, Maine, U.S. 286/C3
Sebeka, Minn., U.S., 710 . . . .298/B4
Sebergham, Eng., U.K. 66/C3
Seboeis, Maine, U.S., 41 . . . .286/D3
Seboeis, Maine, U.S., lake 286/D3
Seboomook, Maine, U.S. 286/C3
Seboomook, Maine, U.S., lake 286/C3
Sebou, Mor., river 147/C1
Sebree, Ky., U.S., 1,558 . . . .280/C3
Sebrell, Va., U.S. 354/J7
Sebright, Ont., Can. 223/F3
Sebring, Fla., U.S., 9,667 . . . .256/G4
Sebring, Ohio, U.S., 4,912 . . . .328/H5
Secaucus, N.J., U.S., 15,931 . . . .314/B2, E2
Sechura, Peru, desert 185/A2
Second Connecticut, N.H., U.S., lake 312/D1
Second Mesa, Ariz., U.S., 814 . . . .242/E2
Secor, Ill., U.S., 379 . . . .266/D3
Secretary, Md., U.S., 503 . . . .288/L5
Section, Ala., U.S., 769 . . . .238/D1
Security, (Security-Widefield), Colo., U.S., 29,845 . . . .250/F3
Seda, Port., river 93/B3
Sedalia, Alta., Can. 212/E5
Sedalia, Colo., U.S., 211 . . . .250/E2
Sedalia, Ind., U.S., 175 . . . .270/C4
Sedalia, Mo., U.S., 20,339 . . . .302/C3
Sedan, Fr. 88/D2
Sedan, Kans., U.S., 1,342 . . . .276/F4
Sedan, Minn., U.S., 65 . . . .298/B5
Sedan, N. Mex., U.S. 317/G1
Sedbergh, Eng., U.K., 1,670 . . . .66/C4
Sedberrow, Eng., U.K. 68/D5
Sedgefield, Eng., U.K., 4,424 . . . .66/F3
Sedgefield, N.C., U.S., 1,100 . . . .322/F2
Sedgeford, Eng., U.K. 70/F1
Sedge Garden, N.C., U.S. 322/E2
Sedgewick, Alta., Can., 865 . . . .212/E5
Sedgewickville, Mo., U.S., 197 . . . .302/G4
Sedgley, Eng., U.K. 68/C4
Sedgwick, Ark., U.S., 112 . . . .244/E2
Sedgwick, Colo., U.S., 191 . . . .250/H1
Sedgwick, Colo., U.S., county, 2,747 . . . .250/H1
Sedgwick, Kans., U.S., 1,537 . . . .276/E4
Sedgwick, Kans., U.S., county, 452,869 . . . .276/E4
Sedgwick, Maine, U.S., 1,102 . . . .286/D4
Sédhiou, Sen. 148/B3
Sedley, Sask., Can., 322 . . . .227/F10
Sedley, Va., U.S., 500 . . . .354/K7
Sedona, Ariz., U.S., 10,192 . . . .242/D3
Sedro-Woolley, Wash., U.S., 8,658 . . . .358/C1
Seedskadee N.W.R., Wyo., U.S. 366/B3
Seekonk, Mass., U.S., 13,425 . . . .292/J5
Seeley, Wisc., U.S., 100 . . . .364/B2
Seeley Lake, Mont., U.S., 1,436 . . . .306/C2
Seeleys Bay, Ont., Can. 223/J3
Seelyville, Ind., U.S., 1,182 . . . .270/B6
Sefadu, S.L. 149/B1
Seffner, Fla., U.S., 5,467 . . . .256/D6
Sefton, Eng., U.K., unitary authority, 282,956 . . . .66/B5
Sefton, Eng., U.K., unitary authority, 282,956 . . . .68/A2
Segbana, Ben. 151/B2
Ségou, Mali, 87,560 . . . .150/B3
Segovia, Sp., 54,368 . . . .94/D2
Segovia, Sp., province 94/E2
Segovia, Tex., U.S. 346/J5
Seguam, Alaska, U.S., island 240/Inset
Séguéla, C. d'Iv. 150/C3
Seguin, Kans., U.S. 276/B3
Seguin, Tex., U.S., 22,011 . . . .346/B2, L6
Segundo, Colo., U.S., 40 . . . .250/F4
Segura, Sp., river 94/E3
Seibert, Colo., U.S., 180 . . . .250/H2
Seil, Scot., U.K., island 62/E6
Seilebost, Scot., U.K. 62/B3
Seiling, Okla., U.S., 875 . . . .330/D1
Seinäjoki, Fin. 81/B2
Seine, Fr., river . . . .88/C2, Inset II
Seine-et-Marne, Fr., department 88/C2
Seine-Maritime, Fr., department 88/C2
Seine-St-Denis, Fr., department 88/C2
Sekake, Leso. 161/B2
Sekondi, Gha., 33,713, (160,868 metro.) 150/B4
Selah, Wash., U.S., 6,310 . . . .358/E3
Selattyn, Eng., U.K. 68/A4
Selawik, Alaska, U.S., 772 . . . .240/C1
Selawik N.W.R., Alaska, U.S. 240/D1
Selborne, Eng., U.K. 70/C4
Selby, Eng., U.K., 15,292 . . . .66/F5
Selby, Eng., U.K., 15,292 . . . .68/E2
Selby, S. Dak., U.S., 736 . . . .342/F2
Selby-on-the-Bay, Md., U.S., 3,674 . . . .288/H4
Selbyville, Del., U.S., 1,645 . . . .255/D7
Selden, Kans., U.S., 201 . . . .276/C2
Selden, Maine, U.S. 286/E3
Seldovia, Alaska, U.S., 286 . . . .240/E4
Selebi-Phikwe, Bots., 46,766 . . . .160/C2
Selenge, Mong., river 118/C2
Selenge Mörön, Mong., river 118/C2
Selfridge, N. Dak., U.S., 223 . . . .326/E3
Sélibabi, Maur. 147/B4
Seligman, Ariz., U.S., 456 . . . .242/C2

Seligman, Mo., U.S., 877 . . . .302/C5
Selinia, Gr. 100/Inset
Selinsgrove, Penn., U.S., 5,383 . . . .336/H4
Selkirk, Man., Can., 9,752 . . . .215/C4
Selkirk, Scot., U.K., 5,742 . . . .62/K7
Selkirk, Kans., U.S. 276/A3
Selkirk, Mich., U.S., 90 . . . .294/E5
Selkirk, Wash., U.S., mountains 358/H1
Sellafield, Eng., U.K. 66/A4
Selleck, Wash., U.S. 358/B4
Sellers, S.C., U.S., 277 . . . .340/E2
Sellersville, Penn., U.S., 4,564 . . . .336/L5
Sellindge, Eng., U.K. 70/G4
Sells, Ariz., U.S., 2,799 . . . .242/D6
Selly Oak, Eng., U.K. 68/D5
Selma, Ala., U.S., 20,512 . . . .238/B3
Selma, Ark., U.S., 50 . . . .244/D4
Selma, Calif., U.S., 19,444 . . . .246/F6
Selma, Ind., U.S., 880 . . . .270/F4
Selma, Iowa, U.S., 80 . . . .274/K6
Selma, Kans., U.S. 276/G3
Selma, N.C., U.S., 5,914 . . . .322/J3
Selma, Ohio, U.S., 225 . . . .328/C6
Selma, Oreg., U.S., 300 . . . .334/C5
Selma, Tex., U.S., 788 . . . .346/A2
Selman, Okla., U.S., 40 . . . .330/C1
Selmer, Tenn., U.S., 4,541 . . . .344/D4
Selmont, Ala., U.S., 3,502 . . . .238/B3
Selsey, Eng., U.K., 8,754 . . . .70/C5
Selsey Bill, Eng., U.K., cape 70/C5
Selvas, Braz., region 188/B2
Selvin, Ind., U.S., 200 . . . .270/B8
Selway, Ida., U.S., river 264/E3
Selwyn, Yukon, Can., mountains 228/C4
Selz, N. Dak., U.S., 60 . . . .326/F2
Semakau, Sing., island 123/B2
Seman, Alb., river 99/A3
Semarang, Indon., 2,220,000 . . . .122/C2
Sembawang, Sing. 155/C3
Sembe, Congo 159/C2
Semeru, Indon., volcano 122/C2
Seney, Kaz., 269,574 . . . .131/E1
Seminary, Miss., U.S., 335 . . . .300/C4
Seminoe, Wyo., U.S., reservoir 366/C3
Seminoe Dam, Wyo., U.S. 366/C2
Seminole, Ala., U.S., 225 . . . .238/B5
Seminole, Fla., U.S., 10,890 . . . .256/C6
Seminole, Fla., U.S., county, 365,196 . . . .256/D3, G3
Seminole, Ga., U.S., county, 9,369 . . . .260/B1
Seminole, Ga., U.S., lake 260/B10
Seminole, Okla., U.S., 6,899 . . . .330/F2
Seminole, Okla., U.S., county, 24,894 . . . .330/F2
Seminole, Tex., U.S., 5,910 . . . .346/F3
Semisopochnoi, Alaska, U.S., island 240/Inset
Semmering, Aus., pass 91/D3
Semmes, Ala., U.S., 550 . . . .238/A5
Semnan, Iran 130/C2
Semnan, Iran, province 130/C2
Semois, Belg., river 85/D3
Sempach, Switz. 90/C1
Sên, Camb., river 124/D2
Sena, N. Mex., U.S., 250 . . . .317/E2
Senaki, Geo. 103/B3
Senang, Sing., island 123/A2
Senath, Mo., U.S., 1,650 . . . .302/F5
Senatobia, Miss., U.S., 6,682 . . . .300/C1
Sendai, Jap., 1,008,130 . . . .114/D2
Seneca, Ill., U.S., 2,053 . . . .266/E2
Seneca, Kans., U.S., 2,122 . . . .276/F2
Seneca, Mo., U.S., 2,135 . . . .302/B5
Seneca, Nebr., U.S., 51 . . . .308/D1
Seneca, N. Mex., U.S. 317/G1
Seneca, N.Y., U.S., county, 33,342 . . . .320/H5
Seneca, Ohio, U.S., county, 58,683 . . . .328/D3
Seneca, Oreg., U.S., 223 . . . .334/H3
Seneca, Penn., U.S., 966 . . . .336/B3
Seneca, S.C., U.S., 7,652 . . . .340/B2
Seneca, S. Dak., U.S., 58 . . . .342/F2
Seneca, Wisc., U.S., 125 . . . .364/C5
Seneca Falls, N.Y., U.S., 6,861 . . . .320/H5
Seneca Gardens, Ky., U.S., 699 . . . .280/A2
Senecaville, Ohio, U.S., 453 . . . .328/H6
Senecaville, Ohio, U.S., lake 328/H6
Senegal, nation 142
Sénégal, Mali, river 150/A3
Sénégal, Maur., river 147/B3
Sénégal, Sen., river 148/B1, C2
Seney, Iowa, U.S., 100 . . . .274/B2
Seney, Mich., U.S., 70 . . . .294/D3
Seney N.W.R., Mich., U.S. 294/C3
Senkaku, Jap., islands . . . .114/Inset II
Senmonorom, Camb. 124/F3
Senne, Belg., river 85/C2
Sennar, Sudan 73/A4
Senneterre, Que., Can., 3,275 . . . .225/A4
Senoia, Ga., U.S., 1,738 . . . .260/B5
Senta, Serb.-Mont. 99/B2
Sentinel, Ariz., U.S. 242/B5
Sentinel, Okla., U.S., 859 . . . .330/C2
Sentinel Butte, N. Dak., U.S., 62 . . . .326/B3
Sentosa, Sing., island 123/B2
Seongnam, S. Kor., 869,094 . . . .116/B4
Seoul, S. Kor., capital, 9,853,972 . . . .116/B4
Seoul, S. Kor., province 116/B4
Separ, N. Mex., U.S. 317/B5
Sepik, P.N.G., river 172/A2
Septentrional, Dom. Rep., range 205/A1
Sept-Îles, Que., Can., 23,791 . . . .225/C3
Sequatchie, Tenn., U.S., county, 11,370 . . . .344/L4
Sequim, Wash., U.S., 4,334 . . . .358/B1
Sequoia Natl. For., Calif., U.S. 246/G6, G7
Sequoia Natl. Park, Calif., U.S. 246/G6
Sequoyah, Okla., U.S., county, 38,972 . . . .330/H2
Sequoyah N.W.R., Ark., U.S. 244/A2
Sequoyah N.W.R., Okla., U.S. 330/G2
Serafina, N. Mex., U.S., 50 . . . .317/E2
Serangoon, Sing. 123/B1
Serbia, Serb.-Mont., republic 99/B2
Seremban, Malay., 182,869, (193,237 metro.) 121/A2
Serenada, Tex., U.S., 1,847 . . . .346/D11
Serengeti Natl. Park, Tan. 159/C2
Serenje, Zam. 159/C4
Sergeant Bluff, Iowa, U.S., 3,321 . . . .274/B3
Sergeantsville, N.J., U.S., 650 . . . .314/D3
Sergipe, Braz., state 188/E3
Seria, Bru., 21,082 . . . .121/A2
Serov, Russ. 104/E4
Serowe, Bots., 42,444 . . . .160/B1
Serpent, Mauritius, island 163/D1
Serrai, Gr. 100/B1
Serranilla, Col., bank 184/Inset
Serravalle, S. Mar. 97/B1
Serrekunda, Gam., 151,450 . . . .148/C2
Serule, Bots. 160/B2
Sese, Ug., islands 157/C4
Sesheke, Zam. 159/A3
Seskinore, N. Ire., U.K. 65/C2
Sesser, Ill., U.S., 2,128 . . . .266/D5
Seth, W. Va., U.S., 275 . . . .360/C4

Seth Ward, Tex., U.S., 1,926 . . . . .346/G1
Seti, Nepal, *river* 126/A2
Sétif, Alg., 211,859 . . . . .146/B1
Settat, Mor. .147/C1
Settle, Eng., U.K., 3,082 . . . . .66/D4
Settle, Eng., U.K., 3,082 . . . . .68/C1
Settrington, Eng., U.K. 68/F1
Setúbal, Port., 113,934 . . . . .93/A3
Setúbal, Port., *bay* 93/A3
Setúbal, Port., *district* 93/A3
Seul Choix, Mich., U.S., *point* 294/D4
Sevan, Arm. .103/B2
Sevan, Arm., *lake* 103/C2
Sevastopol', Ukr., 350,798 . . . . .102/C4
Sevastopol', Ukr. 102/C4
Seven Corners, Va., U.S., 8,701 . . . . .354/M2
Seven Devils, N.C., U.S., 129 . . . . .322/B4
Seven Hills, Ohio, U.S., 12,080 . . . . .328/G9
Seven Lakes, N. Mex., U.S. 317/C2
Seven Lakes, N.C., U.S., 3,214 . . . . .322/F4
Seven Mile, Ohio, U.S., 678 . . . . .328/A7
Sevenmile Corner, S. Dak., U.S. 342/D4
Seven Oaks, S.C., U.S., 15,755 . . . . .340/A3
Seven Persons, Alta., Can., 245 . . . . .212/E6
Seven Rivers, N. Mex., U.S., 125 . . . . .317/F5
Seven Sisters, Tex., U.S., 60 . . . . .346/K8
Seven Sisters Falls, Man., Can. 215/C4
Severn, N.C., U.S., 86 . . . . .322/K4
Seven Sprs., Penn., U.S., 127 . . . . .336/C5
70 Mile House, Br. Col., Can. 214/M5
Seven Valleys, Penn., U.S., 492 . . . . .336/H6
Severance, Colo., U.S., 597 . . . . .250/F1
Severance, Kans., U.S., 108 . . . . .276/G2
Severance, N.H., U.S., 500 . . . . .312/D5
Severn, Ont., Can., *river* 222/B2
Severn, Eng., U.K., *river* 60/C3
Severn, Eng., U.K., *river* 68/B4, B6
Severn, Eng., U.K., *river* 73/G1
Severn, Wales, U.K., *river* 64/F4
Severn, Md., U.S., 35,076 . . . . .288/H3
Severn, N.C., U.S., 263 . . . . .322/L1
Severna Park, Md., U.S., 28,507 . . . . .288/H3
Severnaya Zemlya, Russ., *island* 193/B5
Severnaya Zemlya, Russ., *islands* 104/F1
Severn Beach, Eng., U.K., 1,468 . . . . .73/G1
Severy, Kans., U.S., 359 . . . . .276/F4
Sevier, Ark., U.S., *county*, 15,757 . . . . . . .244/A4
Sevier, Tenn., U.S., *county*, 71,170 . . . . . . .344/Q3
Sevier, Utah, U.S., 40 . . . . .350/B5
Sevier, Utah, U.S., *county*, 18,842 . . . . . . .350/C4
Sevier, Utah, U.S., *desert* 350/B4
Sevier, Utah, U.S., *lake* 350/A5
Sevierville, Tenn., U.S., 11,757 . . . . .344/P3
Seville, Sp., 684,633 . . . . .94/D4
Seville, Sp., *province* 94/D4
Seville, Fla., U.S., 475 . . . . .256/G2
Seville, Ga., U.S., 200 . . . . .260/D8
Seville, Ohio, U.S., 2,160 . . . . .328/G3
Sevilleta N.W.R., N. Mex., U.S. 317/C3
Sevogle, N.B., Can. 217/D1
Sevran, Fr. .88/Inset II
Sèvres, Fr. . . . . .88/Inset II
Sewa, S.L., *river* 149/B2
Sewal, Iowa, U.S. 274/H6
Sewalls Pt., Fla., U.S., 1,946 . . . . .256/A3
Sewanee, Tenn., U.S., 2,361 . . . . .344/K4
Seward, Alaska, U.S., 2,830 . . . . .240/F2
Seward, Alaska, U.S., *peninsula* 240/C1
Seward, Ill., U.S., 225 . . . . .266/D1
Seward, Kans., U.S., 63 . . . . .276/D3
Seward, Kans., U.S., *county*, 22,510 . . . . . . .276/B4
Seward, Nebr., U.S., 6,319 . . . . .308/G3
Seward, Nebr., U.S., *county*, 16,496 . . . . . . .308/G3
Seward, Okla., U.S., 70 . . . . .330/G4
Seward, Penn., U.S., 484 . . . . .336/C5
Sewaren, N.J., U.S., 2,780 . . . . .314/C4
Sewell, N.J., U.S., 3,400 . . . . .314/C4
Sewickley, Penn., U.S., 3,902 . . . . .336/A4
Sextonville, Wisc., U.S., 250 . . . . .364/C5
Seychelles, *nation* 157
Seyhan, Tur., *river* 133/C3
Seymour, Conn., U.S., 15,454 . . . . .253/C4
Seymour, Ind., U.S., 18,101 . . . . .270/E7
Seymour, Iowa, U.S., 810 . . . . .274/H6
Seymour, Mo., U.S., 1,834 . . . . .302/D4
Seymour, Tenn., U.S., 8,850 . . . . .344/P3
Seymour, Tex., U.S., 2,908 . . . . .346/J2
Seymour, Vt., U.S., *lake* 352/C1
Seymour, (Eau Claire County),
  Wisc., U.S., 1,879 . . . . .364/B4
Seymour, (Outagamie County),
  Wisc., U.S., 3,335 . . . . .364/E4
Seymourville, La., U.S., 2,200 . . . . .282/G6
Sfax, Tun., 248,800, (334,702 metro.) 146/C2
Sîntu Gheorghe, Rom. 101/C3
Sgurr na Lapaich, Scot., U.K., *hill* 62/F4
Shaanxi, China, *province* 119/D2
Shabbona, Ill., U.S., 929 . . . . .266/E2
Shabwah, Yemen 137/B1
Shache, China 119/A2
Shackelford, Tex., U.S., *county*, 3,302 . . . . .346/J3
Shackleton Ice Shelf, Antar., *glacier* 192/C2
Shade, Ohio, U.S., 100 . . . . .328/F7
Shade Gap, Penn., U.S., 97 . . . . .336/F5
Shadehill, S. Dak., U.S. 342/C2
Shadeland, Ind., U.S., 1,682 . . . . .270/C4
Shad Pt., Md., U.S. 288/M6
Shadwell, Va., U.S. 354/G4
Shady Brook, N. Mex., U.S., 200 . . . . .317/E1
Shady Cove, Oreg., U.S., 2,307 . . . . .334/D5
Shady Dale, Ga., U.S., 242 . . . . .260/D5
Shady Grove, Ala., U.S., 40 . . . . .238/C4
Shady Grove, Fla., U.S., 90 . . . . .256/E1
Shady Grove, Ky., U.S. 280/C3
Shady Grove, Okla., U.S., 44 . . . . .330/F1
Shady Pt., Okla., U.S., 848 . . . . .330/H2
Shady Rest, Conn., U.S., 550 . . . . .253/B4
Shady Shores, Tex., U.S., 1,461 . . . . .346/B8
Shady Side, Md., U.S., 5,559 . . . . .288/H4
Shadyside, Ohio, U.S., 3,675 . . . . .328/J6
Shady Spr., W. Va., U.S., 2,078 . . . . .360/D5
Shafter, Calif., U.S., 12,736 . . . . .246/F7
Shafter, Nev., U.S. 310/C1
Shafter, Tex., U.S. 346/D6
Shaftesbury, Eng., U.K., 6,203 . . . . .73/H3
Shaftsbury, Vt., U.S., 3,767 . . . . .352/A4
Shaftsbury Ctr., Vt., U.S., 250 . . . . .352/A5
Shageluk, Alaska, U.S., 129 . . . . .240/D2
Shahr-e Kord, Iran 130/C3
Shaker Hts., Ohio, U.S., 29,405 . . . . . . .328/G3, H9
Shaki, Nig. .152/B3
Shakopee, Minn., U.S., 20,568 . . . . .298/D6
Shaktoolik, Alaska, U.S., 230 . . . . .240/C2
Shalbourne, Eng., U.K. 70/A4
Shalcombe, Eng., U.K. 70/B5
Shaldon, Eng., U.K., 1,581 . . . . .73/E3
Shalfleet, Eng., U.K. 70/B5
Shalimar, Fla., U.S., 718 . . . . .256/B1
Shallotte, N.C., U.S., 1,381 . . . . .322/J7
Shallowater, Tex., U.S., 2,086 . . . . .346/F2

Shallow Water, Kans., U.S., 125 . . . . .276/B3
Shalqar, Kaz. 131/B2
Shalstone, Eng., U.K. 70/B2
Shamattawa, Man., Can. 215/E2
Shambaugh, Iowa, U.S., 188 . . . . .274/D6
Shamokin, Penn., U.S., 8,009 . . . . .336/H4
Shamokin Dam, Penn., U.S., 1,502 . . . . .336/H4
Shamrock, Fla., U.S., 200 . . . . .256/E2
Shamrock, Okla., U.S., 125 . . . . .330/F2
Shamrock, Tex., U.S., 2,029 . . . . .346/H9
Shamrock Lakes, Ind., U.S., 168 . . . . .270/F4
Shan, Mya., *plateau* 125/C2
Shan, Mya., *state* 125/C2
Shanchung, Tai. 117/B1
Shandon, Scot., U.K. 62/G6
Shandon, Calif., U.S., 986 . . . . .246/E7
Shandon, Ohio, U.S., 425 . . . . .328/A9
Shandong, China, *province* 119/E2
Shanghai, China, 8,214,384 . . . . .119/F2
Shanghai, China, *independent municipality* . . .119/F2
Shanghai, W. Va., U.S., 100 . . . . .360/M2
Shaniko, Oreg., U.S. 334/F3
Shanklin, Eng., U.K. 70/B5
Shanksville, Penn., U.S., 245 . . . . .336/C5
Shannock, R.I., U.S., 900 . . . . .339/C5
Shannon, Ire. 78/B2
Shannon, Ire., *river* 78/B2
Shannon, Ga., U.S., 1,682 . . . . .260/A3
Shannon, Ill., U.S., 854 . . . . .266/D1
Shannon, Miss., U.S., 1,657 . . . . .300/D1
Shannon, Mo., U.S., *county*, 8,324 . . . . .302/E4
Shannon, S. Dak., U.S., *county*, 12,466 . . . . .342/C4
Shannon, Tex., U.S. 346/K2
Shannon City, Iowa, U.S., 70 . . . . .274/F6
Shannon Hills, Ark., U.S., 2,005 . . . . .244/C3
Shannontown, S.C., U.S., 4,100 . . . . .340/D3
Shantou, China 119/E3
Shanxi, China 119/E3
Shanxi, China, *province* 119/E2
Shaoguan, China, 370,550, (696,340 *metro.*) . . .119/E3
Shaoxing, China 119/F3
Shaoyang, China 119/E3
Shap, Eng., U.K. 66/C2
Shapinsay, Scot., U.K., *island* 62/N2
Shapleigh, Maine, U.S., 2,326 . . . . .286/B5
Sharbot Lake, Ont., Can. 223/J3
Sharjah, U.A.E. 136/C2
Sharkey, Miss., U.S., *county*, 6,580 . . . . . . .300/B3
Shark River Hills, N.J., U.S., 3,878 . . . . . . .314/E3
Sharnbrook, Eng., U.K., 1,984 . . . . .68/F5
Sharnbrook, Eng., U.K., 1,984 . . . . .70/C2
Sharon, Isr., *plain* 135/B1
Sharon, Conn., U.S., 2,968 . . . . .253/B2
Sharon, Ga., U.S., 105 . . . . .260/D5
Sharon, Kans., U.S., 210 . . . . .276/D4
Sharon, Mass., U.S., 17,408 . . . . .292/K4
Sharon, Miss., U.S. 300/C3
Sharon, N.H., U.S., 360 . . . . .312/C6
Sharon, N. Dak., U.S., 109 . . . . .326/H2
Sharon, Okla., U.S., 122 . . . . .330/C1
Sharon, Penn., U.S., 16,328, (120,293 *metro.*) .336/A3
Sharon, S.C., U.S., 421 . . . . .340/C2
Sharon, Tenn., U.S., 988 . . . . .344/D2
Sharon, Vt., U.S., 1,411 . . . . .352/C3
Sharon, Wisc., U.S., 1,549 . . . . .364/E6
Sharon Hill, Penn., U.S., 5,468 . . . . .336/L7
Sharon Sprs., N.Y., U.S., 547 . . . . .320/M5
Sharonville, Ohio, U.S., 13,804 . . . . .328/B9
Sharp, Ark., U.S., *county*, 17,119 . . . . .244/D1
Sharp, Tex., U.S., 100 . . . . .346/L5
Sharpe, Kans., U.S. 276/C3
Sharpe, Ky., U.S., 300 . . . . .280/B4
Sharpe, S. Dak., U.S., *lake* 342/F3
Sharples, W. Va., U.S., 70 . . . . .360/C5
Sharpness, Eng., U.K. 68/C6
Sharpsburg, Ga., U.S., 316 . . . . .260/B5
Sharpsburg, Iowa, U.S., 98 . . . . .274/E6
Sharpsburg, Ky., U.S., 295 . . . . .280/G2
Sharpsburg, Md., U.S., 691 . . . . .288/C2
Sharpsburg, N.C., U.S., 2,421 . . . . .322/K3
Sharpsburg, Ohio, U.S., 60 . . . . .328/G7
Sharpsburg, Penn., U.S., 3,594 . . . . .336/E7
Sharpsville, Ind., U.S., 618 . . . . .270/D4
Sharpsville, Penn., U.S., 4,500 . . . . .336/A3
Sharptown, Md., U.S., 649 . . . . .288/M5
Sharptown, N.J., U.S., 350 . . . . .314/C4
Shashe, Bots., *river* 160/C2
Shashi, China 119/E2
Shasta, Calif., U.S., 375 . . . . .246/C2
Shasta, Calif., U.S., *county*, 163,256 . . . . .246/D2
Shasta, Calif., U.S., *lake* 246/C2
Shasta, Calif., U.S., *mountain* 246/C1
Shasta Lake, Calif., U.S., 9,008 . . . . .246/C2
Shasta Natl. For., Calif., U.S. 246/D1
Sha Tin, H.K., China 117/B1
Shatt al-Arab, Iran, *river* 130/D2
Shatt al Arab, Iraq, *river* 130/C2
Shatterford, Eng., U.K. 68/C5
Shattuck, Okla., U.S., 1,274 . . . . .330/C1
Shattuckville, Mass., U.S., 225 . . . . .292/D2
Shauck, Ohio, U.S., 400 . . . . .328/E4
Shaunavon, Sask., Can., 1,775 . . . . .227/B11
Shavano Park, Tex., U.S., 1,754 . . . . .346/A2
Shaver Lake, Calif., U.S., 705 . . . . .246/F5
Shavington, Eng., U.K., 4,780 . . . . .68/C3
Shaw, Kans., U.S. 276/G4
Shaw, Minn., U.S. 298/E3
Shaw, Miss., U.S., 2,312 . . . . .300/B2
Shawanee, Tenn., U.S., 2,865 . . . . .344/P1
Shawano, Wisc., U.S., 8,298 . . . . .364/E4
Shawano, Wisc., U.S., *county*, 40,664 . . . . . .364/E4
Shawboro, N.C., U.S., 90 . . . . .322/N2
Shawell, Eng., U.K. 70/B2
Shawhan, Ky., U.S. 280/F2
Shawinigan, Que., Can., 17,535 . . . . .226/D5
Shaw Island, Wash., U.S., 70 . . . . .358/C1
Shawmut, Mont., U.S., 90 . . . . .306/G3
Shawnee, Colo., U.S., 80 . . . . .250/E2
Shawnee, Ga., U.S., 150 . . . . .260/J7
Shawnee, Kans., U.S., 47,996 . . . . .276/H1, H2
Shawnee, Kans., U.S., *county*, 169,871 . . . . .276/G3
Shawnee, Ohio, U.S., 608 . . . . .328/F6
Shawnee, Okla., U.S., 28,692 . . . . .330/F2
Shawnee, Wyo., U.S. 366/G2
Shawnee Hills, (Delaware County),
  Ohio, U.S., 419 . . . . .328/D5
Shawnee Hills, (Greene County),
  Ohio, U.S., 2,355 . . . . .328/C6
Shawnee Natl. For., Ill., U.S. 266/D6, E6
Shawneetown, Ill., U.S., 1,410 . . . . .266/E6
Shawsville, Md., U.S., 275 . . . . .288/H1
Shawsville, Va., U.S., 1,029 . . . . .354/C6
Shawville, Vt., U.S., 200 . . . . .352/B1
Sheakleyville, Penn., U.S., 164 . . . . .336/A3
Shearsby, Eng., U.K. 70/B2
Shebar, Afg., *pass* 129/B2
Shebberan, Eng., U.K. 73/D3
Sheberghan, Afg. 129/B1
Sheboygan, Wisc., U.S., 50,792,
  (112,646 *metro.*) 364/F5

Sheboygan, Wisc., U.S., *county*, 112,646 . . . .364/F5
Sheboygan Falls, Wisc., U.S., 6,772 . . . . .364/F5
Shediac, Oreg., U.S., 90 . . . . .334/C3
Shediac, Alta., Can., 4,892 . . . . .217/E2
Shediac Ridge, N.B., Can. 217/F2
Sheepscot, Maine, U.S. 286/C4
Sheep Sprs., N. Mex., U.S., 237 . . . . .317/B1
Sheerness, Alta., Can. 212/E5
Sheerness, Eng., U.K., 11,653 . . . . .70/F4
Sheet Harbour, N.S., Can. 221/E3
Sheffield, Eng., U.K. 60/C3
Sheffield, Eng., U.K., 431,607, (670,010 metro.) .66/F6
Sheffield, Eng., U.K., 431,607, (670,010 *metro.*) .68/E3
Sheffield, Eng., U.K., *unitary authority*, 513,234 .66/E6
Sheffield, Eng., U.K., *unitary authority*, 513,234 .68/D3
Sheffield, Ala., U.S., 9,652 . . . . .238/B1
Sheffield, Ill., U.S., 946 . . . . .266/D2
Sheffield, Iowa, U.S., 930 . . . . .274/H2
Sheffield, Mass., U.S., 3,335 . . . . .292/A4
Sheffield, Mont., U.S. 306/K3
Sheffield, Penn., U.S., 1,268 . . . . .336/C2
Sheffield, Tex., U.S., 225 . . . . .346/G5
Sheffield, Vt., U.S., 727 . . . . .352/C1
Sheffield Lake, Ohio, U.S., 9,371 . . . . .328/F3
Shefford, Eng., U.K. 70/D2
Sheguianda, Ont., Can. 223/D2
Sheho, Sask., Can., 148 . . . . .227/G9
Sheigra, Scot., U.K. 62/F1
Shek Pik, H.K., China 117/A2
Shelbiana, Ky., U.S., 600 . . . . .280/H3
Shelbina, Mo., U.S., 1,943 . . . . .302/D2
Shelburn, Ind., U.S., 1,268 . . . . .270/B6
Shelburn, La., U.S., 60 . . . . .282/C1
Shelburne, N.S., Can., 2,013 . . . . .221/B4
Shelburne, N.S., Can., *county*, 2,013 . . . . . .221/B4
Shelburne, Ont., Can., 4,122 . . . . .223/E3
Shelburne, Mass., U.S., 2,058 . . . . .292/D2
Shelburne, N.H., U.S., 379 . . . . .312/D3
Shelburne, Vt., U.S., 6,944 . . . . .352/A2
Shelburne Falls, Mass., U.S., 1,951 . . . . .292/D2
Shelburne Falls, Vt., U.S., 1,700 . . . . .352/A2
Shelby, Ala., U.S., *county*, 143,293 . . . .238/C2, E1
Shelby, Ill., U.S., *county*, 22,893 . . . . . . .266/E4
Shelby, Ind., U.S., 475 . . . . .270/B8
Shelby, Ind., U.S., *county*, 43,445 . . . . . . .270/E5
Shelby, Iowa, U.S., 696 . . . . .274/D4
Shelby, Iowa, U.S., *county*, 13,173 . . . . . . .274/D4
Shelby, Ky., U.S., *county*, 33,337 . . . . .280/E2
Shelby, (Macomb County), Mich., U.S., 65,159 . . .294/B6
Shelby, (Oceana County), Mich., U.S., 1,914 . . .294/C6
Shelby, Miss., U.S., 2,926 . . . . .300/B2
Shelby, Mo., U.S., *county*, 6,799 . . . . .302/D2
Shelby, Mont., U.S., 3,216 . . . . .306/E1
Shelby, Nebr., U.S., 690 . . . . .308/G2
Shelby, N.C., U.S., 19,477 . . . . .322/B4
Shelby, Ohio, U.S., 9,821 . . . . .328/E4
Shelby, Ohio, U.S., *county*, 47,910 . . . . . . .328/B5
Shelby, Tenn., U.S., *county*, 897,472 . . . . . .344/B4
Shelby, Tex., U.S., *county*, 25,224 . . . . . . .346/P4
Shelbyville, Ill., U.S., 4,971 . . . . .266/E4
Shelbyville, Ill., U.S., *lake* 266/E4
Shelbyville, Ind., U.S., 17,951 . . . . .270/E5
Shelbyville, Ky., U.S., 10,085 . . . . .280/E2
Shelbyville, Mo., U.S., 682 . . . . .302/D2
Shelbyville, Tenn., U.S., 16,105 . . . . .344/J4
Sheldahl, Iowa, U.S., 336 . . . . .274/G4
Sheldon, Eng., U.K. 68/D5
Sheldon, Ariz., U.S. 242/F5
Sheldon, Ill., U.S., 1,232 . . . . .266/F3
Sheldon, Iowa, U.S., 4,914 . . . . .274/C1
Sheldon, Mo., U.S., 529 . . . . .302/B4
Sheldon, N. Dak., U.S., 135 . . . . .326/H3
Sheldon, S.C., U.S., 225 . . . . .340/D4
Sheldon, Tex., U.S., 1,831 . . . . .346/B6
Sheldon, Vt., U.S., 1,990 . . . . .352/B1
Sheldon, Wisc., U.S., 256 . . . . .364/C3
Sheldon Jct., Vt., U.S., 125 . . . . .352/B1
Sheldon N.W.R., Nev., U.S. 310/A1
Sheldon Pt., (Sheldon Point Nunam Iqua),
  Alaska, U.S. 240/C2
Sheldon Sprs., Vt., U.S., 200 . . . . .352/B1
Sheldonville, Mass., U.S., 500 . . . . .292/J4
Shelf, Eng., U.K., 4,237 . . . . .66/E5
Shelf, Eng., U.K., 4,237 . . . . .68/D2
Shelfanger, Eng., U.K. 70/G2
Shelikhov, Russ., *gulf* 104/I3
Shell, Wyo., U.S., 70 . . . . .366/F1
Shell Beach, La., U.S., 300 . . . . .282/K7
Shellbrook, Sask., Can., 1,276 . . . . .227/D7
Shelley, Ind., U.S., 3,813 . . . . .264/E6
Shell Lake, Sask., Can., 185 . . . . .227/C7
Shell Lake, Wisc., U.S., 1,309 . . . . .364/B3
Shell Lake N.W.R., N. Dak., U.S. 326/C1
Shellman, Ga., U.S., 1,166 . . . . .260/B8
Shellman Bluff, Ga., U.S., 150 . . . . .260/J8
Shell Pt., S.C., U.S., 2,856 . . . . .340/D4
Shell Rock, Iowa, U.S., 1,298 . . . . .274/J2
Shellsburg, Iowa, U.S., 938 . . . . .274/L3
Shelltown, Md., U.S., 40 . . . . .288/M7
Shell Valley, N. Dak., U.S., 395 . . . . .326/F1
Shelly, Minn., U.S., 266 . . . . .298/A3
Shelocta, Penn., U.S., 127 . . . . .336/C4
Shelter Bay, Br. Col., Can. 214/N6
Shelter Bay, Wash., U.S. 358/C1
Shelter Cove, Calif., U.S., 125 . . . . .246/A2
Shelter Island, N.Y., U.S., 1,234 . . . . .320/G1
Shelter Island Hts., N.Y., U.S., 981 . . . . . . .320/G1
Shelton, Conn., U.S., 38,101 . . . . .253/C4
Shelton, Nebr., U.S., 1,140 . . . . .308/E3
Shelton, S.C., U.S. 340/C2
Shelton, Wash., U.S., 8,442 . . . . .358/B2
Sheltons, La., U.S. 282/F1
Shemgang, Bhu. 126/B2
Shemogue, N.B., Can. 217/E2
Shenandoah, Iowa, U.S., 5,546 . . . . .274/D6
Shenandoah, La., U.S., 17,070 . . . . .282/H6
Shenandoah, Penn., U.S., 5,624 . . . . .336/J4
Shenandoah, Tex., U.S., 1,503 . . . . .346/A5
Shenandoah, Va., U.S., 1,878 . . . . .354/F4
Shenandoah, Va., U.S., *county*, 35,075 . . . . .354/F3
Shenandoah, Va., U.S., *mountains* 354/F4
Shenandoah, Va., U.S., *river* 354/F4
Shenandoah, Va., U.S., *mountains* 360/N4
Shenandoah Natl. Park, Va., U.S. 354/G3
Shengjin, Alb. 99/A2
Shenipsit, Conn., U.S., *lake* 253/F2
Shenipsit St. For., Conn., U.S. 253/F2
Shenval, Scot., U.K. 62/K4
Shenyang, China, 4,669,737 . . . . .119/F1
Shepherd, Mich., U.S., 1,536 . . . . .294/E6
Shepherd, Mont., U.S., 193 . . . . .306/H4
Shepherd, Tex., U.S., 2,029 . . . . .346/P5
Shepherdstown, W. Va., U.S., 803 . . . . .360/L2
Shepherdsville, Ky., U.S., 8,334 . . . . .280/E3
Shepshed, Eng., U.K., 12,961 . . . . .68/E4
Shepshed, Eng., U.K., 12,961 . . . . .70/A1
Shepton Mallet, Eng., U.K., 7,581 . . . . .73/G2
Sherack, Minn., U.S. 298/A2
Sherando, Va., U.S., 665 . . . . .354/F5
Sherard, Miss., U.S., 40 . . . . .300/B1
Sherborn, Mass., U.S., 4,200 . . . . .292/J3

Sherborne, Eng., U.K., 7,606 . . . . .73/G3
Sherborne St. John, Eng., U.K. 70/B4
Sherbro, S.L., *island* 149/A2
Sherbrooke, N.S., Can. 221/F2
Sherbrooke, Que., Can., 75,916,
  (156,500 metro.) 226/F6
Sherburn, Eng., U.K., 2,832 . . . . .66/G4
Sherburn, Minn., U.S., 1,082 . . . . .298/D7
Sherburne, Minn., U.S., *county*, 64,417 . . . . .298/D5
Sherburne, N.Y., U.S., 1,455 . . . . .320/E5
Sherburne Ctr., Vt., U.S., 150 . . . . .352/B3
Sherburne N.W.R., Minn., U.S. 298/D5
Sherburn in Elmet, Eng., U.K., 5,396 . . . . . . .66/F5
Sherburn in Elmet, Eng., U.K., 5,396 . . . . . . .68/E2
Sherfield on Loddon, Eng., U.K., 1,233 . . . . . .70/B4
Sheridan, Ark., U.S., 3,872 . . . . .244/C3
Sheridan, Calif., U.S., 750 . . . . .246/D4
Sheridan, Colo., U.S., 5,600 . . . . .250/A3, E2
Sheridan, Ill., U.S., 2,411 . . . . .266/E2
Sheridan, Ind., U.S., 2,520 . . . . .270/D4
Sheridan, Kans., U.S., *county*, 2,813 . . . . . .276/B2
Sheridan, Ky., U.S., 60 . . . . .280/B3
Sheridan, Maine, U.S., 250 . . . . .286/D2
Sheridan, Mich., U.S., 705 . . . . .294/D6
Sheridan, Mo., U.S., 185 . . . . .302/B1
Sheridan, Mont., U.S., 659 . . . . .306/D4
Sheridan, Nebr., U.S., *county*, 6,198 . . . . . .308/B1
Sheridan, N. Dak., U.S., *county*, 1,710 . . . . .326/E2
Sheridan, Oreg., U.S., 3,570 . . . . .334/C2
Sheridan, Tex., U.S., 60 . . . . .346/M6
Sheridan, Wisc., U.S., 150 . . . . .364/D4
Sheridan, Wyo., U.S., 15,804 . . . . .366/C1
Sheridan, Wyo., U.S., *county*, 26,560 . . . . . .366/C1
Sheridan Lake, Colo., U.S., 66 . . . . .250/H3
Sheriff Hutton, Eng., U.K. 66/F4
Sheringham, Eng., U.K., 7,620 . . . . .70/G1
Sherman, Conn., U.S., 3,827 . . . . .253/B3
Sherman, Ill., U.S., 2,871 . . . . .266/D4
Sherman, Kans., U.S., 40 . . . . .276/A2
Sherman, Kans., U.S., *county*, 6,760 . . . . . .276/A2
Sherman, Ky., U.S., 100 . . . . .280/F2
Sherman, Maine, U.S., 937 . . . . .286/D3
Sherman, Miss., U.S., 548 . . . . .300/D1
Sherman, Nebr., U.S., *county*, 3,318 . . . . . .308/E2
Sherman, N. Mex., U.S., 90 . . . . .317/C5
Sherman, N.Y., U.S., 714 . . . . .320/B6
Sherman, Oreg., U.S., *county*, 1,934 . . . . . .334/F2
Sherman, S. Dak., U.S., 87 . . . . .342/J4
Sherman, Tex., U.S., 35,082, (110,595 *metro.*) .346/M2
Sherman, Tex., U.S., *county*, 3,186 . . . . . . .346/F8
Sherman Mills, Maine, U.S., 300 . . . . .286/D3
Sherman Sta., Maine, U.S., 150 . . . . .286/D3
Sherrard, Ill., U.S., 694 . . . . .266/C2
Sherrelwood, Colo., U.S., 17,657 . . . . .250/A3
Sherridon, Man., Can., 113 . . . . .215/A1
Sherrill, Ark., U.S., 126 . . . . .244/C3
Sherrill, Iowa, U.S., 186 . . . . .274/N2
Sherrill, N.Y., U.S., 3,147 . . . . .320/K4
Sherrills Ford, N.C., U.S., 941 . . . . .322/D3
Sherrodsville, Ohio, U.S., 316 . . . . .328/H4
's Hertogenbosch, Neth., 128,522,
  (153,742 metro.) 84/C3
Sherwin, Kans., U.S., 60 . . . . .276/H4
Sherwood, Ark., U.S., 21,511 . . . . .244/C3
Sherwood, Iowa, U.S. 274/E3
Sherwood, Md., U.S., 100 . . . . .288/J4
Sherwood, Mich., U.S., 324 . . . . .294/D7
Sherwood, N. Dak., U.S., 255 . . . . .326/D1
Sherwood, Ohio, U.S., 801 . . . . .328/A3
Sherwood, Oreg., U.S., 11,791 . . . . .334/A3, D2
Sherwood, Tenn., U.S., 150 . . . . .344/K4
Sherwood, Tex., U.S., 90 . . . . .346/H4
Sherwood, Wisc., U.S., 1,550 . . . . .364/E4
Sherwood Manor, Conn., U.S., 5,689 . . . . .253/E1
Sherwood Park, Alta., Can. 212/D4
Sheshebee, Minn., U.S. 298/D4
Shetland, Scot., U.K., *islands* . . . . .60/Inset I
Shetland, Scot., U.K., *islands* 62/P3,
Shetland Islands, Scot., U.K., *unitary authority*,
  21,988 . . . . .62/P3,
Shetucket, Conn., U.S., *river* 253/F3
Sheva, India . . . . .128/Inset I
Shevlin, Minn., U.S., 160 . . . . .298/B3,
Shewa Gimira, Eth. 156/B3,
Sheyenne, N. Dak., U.S., 318 . . . . .326/F2,
Sheyenne, N. Dak., U.S., *river* . .326/E2, G2, H3
Sheyenne Natl. Grassland, N. Dak., U.S. 326/H3
Shiant, Scot., U.K., *islands* 62/D3
Shiawassee, Mich., U.S., *county*, 71,687 . . . .294/E7
Shibin al Kawm, Egy., 160,000 . . . . .144/B1
Shickley, Nebr., U.S., 376 . . . . .308/G3
Shickshinny, Penn., U.S., 959 . . . . .336/J3
Shidler, Okla., U.S., 520 . . . . .330/F1
Shiel, Scot., U.K., *lake* 62/E5
Shiel, Scot., U.K., *lake* 62/F5
Shiel Bridge, Scot., U.K. 62/F3
Shieldaig, Scot., U.K. 62/E3
Shields, Kans., U.S. 276/B3
Shields, Mich., U.S., 6,590 . . . . .294/E6
Shields, N. Dak., U.S. 326/D3
Shifnal, Eng., U.K., 5,893 . . . . .68/C4
Shiga, Jap., *prefecture* 114/C3
Shijiazhuang, China 119/E2
Shikarpur, Pak. 129/C4
Shikoku, Jap., *island* 114/B3
Shilbottle, Eng., U.K. 66/F2
Shildon, Eng., U.K., 11,136 . . . . .66/F3
Shillington, Penn., U.S., 5,059 . . . . .336/K5
Shillong, India 128/F3
Shiloh, Ala., U.S., 289 . . . . .238/D1
Shiloh, Ga., U.S., 423 . . . . .260/B6
Shiloh, Ill., U.S., 7,643 . . . . .266/A3
Shiloh, Md., U.S., 250 . . . . .288/G6
Shiloh, N.J., U.S., 534 . . . . .314/C5
Shiloh, N.C., U.S., 300 . . . . .322/N2
Shiloh, (Montgomery County),
  Ohio, U.S., 11,272 . . . . .328/F1
Shiloh, (Richland County), Ohio, U.S., 721 . . . .328/E4
Shiloh, Penn., U.S., 10,192 . . . . .336/H6
Shiloh, Tenn., U.S., 175 . . . . .344/F4
Shiloh, Tex., U.S. 346/L5
Shiloh Natl. Mil. Park, Tenn., U.S. 344/F4
Shimane, Jap., *prefecture* 114/B3
Shimizu, Jap. 114/C3
Shimla, India 128/C2
Shimonoseki, Jap., 252,000 . . . . .114/A3
Shimonoseki, Jap., *strait* 114/A3
Shin, Scot., U.K., *lake* 62/G2
Shinano, Jap., *river* 114/C2
Shinas, Oman 137/C1
Shindand, Afg. 129/A2
Shinfield, Eng., U.K. 70/C4
Shinglehouse, Penn., U.S., 1,250 . . . . .336/F2
Shingler, Ga., U.S., 60 . . . . .260/D8
Shingle Sprs., Calif., U.S., 2,643 . . . . .246/L5
Shingleton, Mich., U.S., 475 . . . . .294/C3
Shingletown, Calif., U.S., 2,222 . . . . .246/D2
Shinnecock Hills, N.Y., U.S., 1,749 . . . . .320/G2
Shinness, Scot., U.K. 62/H2
Shinnston, W. Va., U.S., 2,295 . . . . .360/F2

Shin Pond, Maine, U.S., 60 . . . . .286/D2
Shinrock, Ohio, U.S., 200 . . . . .328/E3
Shinyanga, Tan., 100,724 . . . . .158/B1
Shinyanga, Tan., region 158/B1
Shiocton, Wisc., U.S., 954 . . . . .364/E4
Shiono, Jap., cape 114/B3
Ship, Miss., U.S., island 300/D5
Ship Bottom, N.J., U.S., 1,384 . . . . .314/E4
Ship Cove, Nfld., Can., 133 . . . . .218/D3
Shipley, Eng., U.K., 28,165 . . . . .66/E5
Shipley, Eng., U.K., 28,165 . . . . .68/D2
Shipley, Iowa, U.S. 274/G4
Shipley, Ky., U.S., 225 . . . . .280/E4
Shipman, Ill., U.S., 655 . . . . .266/A3, C4
Shipman, Va., U.S. 354/F5
Shippagan, N.B., Can., 2,872 . . . . .217/E1
Shippensburg, Penn., U.S., 5,586 . . . . .336/F5
Shippenville, Penn., U.S., 505 . . . . .336/C3
Shippingport, Penn., U.S., 237 . . . . .336/A4
Shiprock, N. Mex., U.S., 8,156 . . . . .317/B1
Shiprock, N. Mex., U.S., peak 317/B1
Shipshewana, Ind., U.S., 536 . . . . .270/E1
Shipston on Stour, Eng., U.K., 3,882 . . . . .68/D5
Shipston on Stour, Eng., U.K., 3,882 . . . . .70/A2
Shipton, Eng., U.K. 66/F4
Shipton, Eng., U.K. 68/D6
Shipton, Eng., U.K. 68/E1
Shirak, Arm., district 103/A2
Shirane, Jap., mountain 114/C3
Shiraz, Iran, 1,053,025 . . . . .130/C4
Shire, Mal., river 159/B3
Shirebrook, Eng., U.K., 10,413 . . . . .68/E3
Shiremanstown, Penn., U.S., 1,521 . . . . .336/H5
Shiretoko, Jap., cape . . . . .114/Inset I
Shirley, Ant.-Bar., cape 207/E6
Shirley, Ark., U.S., 337 . . . . .244/C2
Shirley, Ind., U.S., 806 . . . . .270/E5
Shirley, Mass., U.S., 6,373 . . . . .292/H2
Shirley, Mo., U.S., 125 . . . . .302/F4
Shirley Basin, Wyo., U.S. 366/C2
Shirley Mills, Maine, U.S., 150 . . . . .286/C3
Shirleysburg, Penn., U.S., 140 . . . . .336/F5
Shiro, Tex., U.S. 346/N5
Shirrel Heath, Eng., U.K. 70/B5
Shishaldin, Alaska, U.S., volcano 240/C4
Shishmaref, Alaska, U.S., 562 . . . . .240/B1
Shively, Calif., U.S. 246/B2
Shively, Ky., U.S., 15,157 . . . . .280/C2
Shivers, Miss., U.S., 70 . . . . .300/C4
Shivwits, Ariz., U.S., plateau 242/B1
Shivwits, Utah, U.S. 350/A6
Shizuoka, Jap., 470,000 . . . . .114/C3
Shizuoka, Jap., prefecture 114/C3
Shkhara, Geo., mountain 103/B3
Shkodër, Alb., 82,445 . . . . .99/A1
Shkumbin, Alb., river 99/A2
Shoal, Man., Can., lake 215/D4
Shoal Creek Drive, Mo., U.S., 346 . . . . .302/B4
Shoal Lake, Man., Can., 801 . . . . .215/A4
Shoals, Ind., U.S., 807 . . . . .270/C7
Shobonier, Ill., U.S., 125 . . . . .266/D5
Shoeburyness, Eng., U.K. 70/F3
Shoemakersville, Penn., U.S., 2,124 . . . . .336/K4
Sholes, Nebr., U.S. 308/G1
Shongaloo, La., U.S., 162 . . . . .282/C1
Shonkin, Mont., U.S. 306/F2
Shonto, Ariz., U.S., 568 . . . . .242/E1
Shooks, Minn., U.S. 298/C3
Shopton, Ala., U.S. 238/D3
Shopville, Ky., U.S., 150 . . . . .280/F3
Shore Acres, N.J., U.S., 4,500 . . . . .314/E4
Shoreacres, Tex., U.S., 1,488 . . . . .346/C6
Shoreham, Mich., U.S., 860 . . . . .294/C7
Shoreham, N.Y., U.S., 417 . . . . .320/E1
Shoreham, Vt., U.S., 1,222 . . . . .352/A3
Shoreham Beach, Md., U.S., 1,300 . . . . .288/H4
Shoreham-by-Sea, (Shoreham),
  Eng., U.K., 17,332 . . . . .70/D5
Shoreham Ctr., Vt., U.S. 352/A3
Shoreline, Wash., U.S., 53,025 . . . . .358/A4, C2
Shoreline Park, Miss., U.S., 4,058 . . . . .300/C5
Shoreview, Minn., U.S., 25,924 . . . . .298/F5
Shorewood, Ill., U.S., 7,686 . . . . .266/A6, E2
Shorewood, Minn., U.S., 7,400 . . . . .364/F2
Shorewood, Wisc., U.S., 13,763 . . . . .364/D5
Shorewood Hills, Wisc., U.S., 1,732 . . . . .364/C4
Short Beach, Conn., U.S., 5,100 . . . . .253/D5
Short Creek, Ky., U.S. 280/D3
Shorter, Ala., U.S., 355 . . . . .238/D3
Shorterville, Ala., U.S., 80 . . . . .238/D4
Short Falls, N.H., U.S., 550 . . . . .312/D5
Shortsville, N.Y., U.S., 1,320 . . . . .320/G5
Shoshone, Calif., U.S., 52 . . . . .246/J7
Shoshone, Ida., U.S., 1,398 . . . . .264/C7
Shoshone, Ida., U.S., county, 13,771 . . . . .264/A2
Shoshone, Nev., U.S. 310/C2
Shoshone, Nev., U.S. 310/B2
Shoshone, Nev., U.S., mountains 310/B3
Shoshone, Nev., U.S., range 310/B1
Shoshone Natl. For., Wyo., U.S. 366/B1, B2
Shoshoni, Wyo., U.S., 635 . . . . .366/B2
Shostka, Ukr. 102/C1
Shotley, Minn., U.S. 298/C2
Shotley Street, Eng., U.K. 70/G3
Shottisham, Eng., U.K. 70/G2
Shoup, Ida., U.S. 264/C5
Shovel Lake, Minn., U.S. 298/D4
Showell, Md., U.S., 225 . . . . .288/P6
Show Low, Ariz., U.S., 7,695 . . . . .242/F3
Shreve, Ohio, U.S., 1,582 . . . . .328/F4
Shreveport, La., U.S., 200,145, (392,302 metro.) .282/B1
Shrewsbury, Eng., U.K. 60/C3
Shrewsbury, Eng., U.K., 64,219 . . . . .66/D4
Shrewsbury, Mass., U.S., 31,640 . . . . .292/H3
Shrewsbury, Mo., U.S., 6,644 . . . . .302/H3
Shrewsbury, N.J., U.S., borough, 3,590 . . . . .314/E3
Shrewsbury, Penn., U.S., 3,378 . . . . .336/H6
Shrewsbury, Vt., U.S., 1,108 . . . . .352/B3
Shrirampur, India . . . . .128/Inset II
Shropshire, Eng., U.K., hills 68/A4
Shropshire, Eng., U.K., unitary authority,
  283,240 . . . . .68/B4
Shubenacadie, N.S., Can., 906 . . . . .221/D2
Shubert, Nebr., U.S., 252 . . . . .308/J3
Shubra al Khaymah, Egy., 870,776 . . . . .144/B1
Shubuta, Miss., U.S., 651 . . . . .300/D4
Shueyville, Iowa, U.S., 250 . . . . .274/L4
Shulishader, Scot., U.K. 62/C6
Shullsburg, Wisc., U.S., 1,246 . . . . .364/C6
Shumagin, Alaska, U.S., islands 240/D4
Shumen, Bul., 109,000 . . . . .101/E2
Shumen, Bul., oblast 101/E2
Shumway, Ariz., U.S., 125 . . . . .242/E3
Shumway, Ill., U.S., 217 . . . . .266/E4
Shungnak, Alaska, U.S., 256 . . . . .240/D1
Shungopavi, Ariz., U.S., 632 . . . . .242/E2
Shuqualak, Miss., U.S., 562 . . . . .300/D3
Shurugwi, Zimb. 160/B2
Shutesbury, Mass., U.S., 1,810 . . . . .292/G3
Shwebo, Mya. 125/B2
Shymkent, Kaz., 360,078 . . . . .131/C2
Shū, Kyrg., river 131/D1

Siahan, Pak., range 129/B4
Sialkot, Pak., 421,502 . . . . .129/E3
Siam, Iowa, U.S., 40 . . . . .274/E6
Siargao, Phil., island 120/C4
Siasconset, Mass., U.S., 275 . . . . .292/Q7
Šiauliai, Lith., 146,563 . . . . .82/B2
Šibbald, Alta., Can. 212/E5
Šibenik, Cro. 98/B3
Siberia, Russ., region 104/G3
Siberia, Russ., region 193/C3
Siberut, Indon., island 122/A2
Sibiti, Congo 155/B5
Sibiu, Rom., 167,737 . . . . .101/C3
Sibiu, Rom., county 101/C3
Sible Hedingham, Eng., U.K., 3,947 . . . . .70/F3
Sibley, Ill., U.S. 266/E3
Sibley, La., U.S., 1,098 . . . . .282/C1
Sibley, Minn., U.S., county, 15,356 . . . . .298/C6
Sibley, Miss., U.S., 300 . . . . .300/A4
Sibley, Mo., U.S. 302/J5
Sibley, N. Dak., U.S., 46 . . . . .326/H2
Sibley Prov. Park, Ont., Can. 294/A1
Sibolga, Indon. 122/A1
Sibu, Malay., 126,381 . . . . .121/C2
Sibut, C.A.R. 154/A2
Sibuyan, Phil., island 120/B3
Sibuyan, Phil., sea 214/N6
Sicamous, Br. Col., Can., 2,720 . . . . .119/D2
Sichuan, China, province 116/B1
Sicily, It., island 93/C3
Sicily, It., region 93/C3
Sicily, It., strait 95/B3
Sicily Island, La., U.S., 453 . . . . .282/F3
Sicklerville, N.J., U.S., 6,000 . . . . .314/D4
Sico, Hond., river 202/C2
Sicuani, Peru 185/C3
Sidell, Ill., U.S., 626 . . . . .266/F4
Sidi bel Abbès, Alg., 180,260 . . . . .146/A1
Sidi Bou Zid, Tun. 146/B2
Sidlaw, Scot., U.K., hills 60/D2
Sidlesham, Eng., U.K. 70/C5
Sidmouth, Eng., U.K., 10,767 . . . . .73/F3
Sidnaw, Mich., U.S., 50 . . . . .294/A3
Sidney, Br. Col., Can., 10,929 . . . . .214/L2
Sidney, Man., Can. 215/B4
Sidney, Ark., U.S., 275 . . . . .244/D2
Sidney, Ill., U.S., 1,062 . . . . .266/E3
Sidney, Ind., U.S., 168 . . . . .270/E2
Sidney, Iowa, U.S., 1,300 . . . . .274/C6
Sidney, Maine, U.S., 3 . . . . .286/C4
Sidney, Mont., U.S., 4,774 . . . . .306/M2
Sidney, Nebr., U.S., 6,282 . . . . .308/B2
Sidney, N.Y., U.S., 4,068 . . . . .320/L6
Sidney, Ohio, U.S., 20,211 . . . . .328/B5
Sidney Ctr., N.Y., U.S., 275 . . . . .320/L6
Sidney Lanier, Ga., U.S., lake 260/D3
Sidon, (Saydā), Leb., 38,000 . . . . .134/A2
Sidon, Ark., U.S., 40 . . . . .244/D2
Sidon, Miss., U.S., 672 . . . . .300/B2
Sidra, Lib., gulf 145/C1
Sidvokodvo, Swaz. 161/B2
Siedlce, Pol. 83/F2
Siegas, N.B., Can., 272 . . . . .217/B1
Siegen, Ger., 109,225 . . . . .86/B3
Simpang, Camb. 124/B2
Siména, It. 95/B2
Sieper, La., U.S., 70 . . . . .83/D3
Sieradz, Pol. 83/D2
Sierra, Calif., U.S., county, 3,555 . . . . .246/E3
Sierra, N. Mex., U.S., county, 13,270 . . . . .317/D5
Sierra Army Depot, Calif., U.S. 246/E2
Sierra Blanca, N. Mex., U.S., mountains 317/E4
Sierra Blanca, Tex., U.S., 533 . . . . .346/C4
Sierra Blanca, Tex., U.S., peak 346/C4
Sierra Boca Grande, Mex., range 346/A4
Sierra de Cayey, P.R., mountains 206/C2
Sierra Del Carmen, Tex., U.S., range 346/E6
Sierra de Luquillo, P.R., mountains 206/D2
Sierra El Fresnal, Mex., range 346/A4
Sierra Grande, Mex., range 346/D6
Sierra Leone, nation 143
Sierra Madre, Guat., mountains 201/C5
Sierra Madre, Phil., mountains 120/B2
Sierra Madre, Calif., U.S., 10,578 . . . . .246/D8
Sierra Madre del Sur, Mex., mountains 200/D4
Sierra Madre Occidental, Mex., mountains 200/C2
Sierra Madre Oriental, Mex., mountains 200/D3
Sierra Natl. For., Calif., U.S. 246/F5
Sierra Nevada, Calif., U.S., range . .246/D3, G5
Sierra Nevada de Santa Marta, Col., mountains .184/B2
Sierraville, Calif., U.S. 246/E3
Sierra Vista, Ariz., U.S., 37,775 . . . . .242/E6
Sifton, Man., Can. 215/A3
Sigel, Ill., U.S., 386 . . . . .266/E4
Sigel, Penn., U.S., 100 . . . . .336/C3
Sigglesthorne, Eng., U.K. 66/H5
Sighetul Marmației, Rom. 101/C2
Sighișoara, Rom. 101/C2
Siglufjör…ur, Ice. 79/B1
Signal Hill, Calif., U.S., 9,333 . . . . .246/C10
Signal Mountain, Tenn., U.S., 7,429 . . . . .344/L4
Sigourney, Iowa, U.S., 2,209 . . . . .274/K5
Sigsbee, Ga., U.S., 300 . . . . .260/D9
Siguatepeque, Hond., 37,500 . . . . .202/B2
Siguiri, Guin. 149/D2
Sigurd, Utah, U.S., 430 . . . . .350/C5
Siirt, Tur. 133/E3
Siirt, Tur., province 133/E3
Sikanni Chief, Br. Col., Can. 214/L2
Sikasso, Mali, 156,736 . . . . .150/B3
Sikes, La., U.S., 120 . . . . .282/E2
Sikeston, Mo., U.S., 16,992 . . . . .302/G5
Sikhote Alin, Russ., range 104/H5
Sikkim, India, state 128/E3
Silale, Lith. 82/B2
Silas, Ala., U.S., 529 . . . . .238/A4
Silay, Phil., 107,722 . . . . .120/B4
Sileby, Eng., U.K., 7,190 . . . . .68/E4
Sileby, Eng., U.K., 7,190 . . . . .70/B1
Silecroft, Eng., U.K. 66/B4
Siler City, N.C., U.S., 6,966 . . . . .322/G3
Silerton, Tenn., U.S., 60 . . . . .344/D4
Silesia, Czh. Rep., region 92/B2
Silesia, Pol., region 83/C3
Silesia, Mont., U.S. 306/H4
Silet, Alg. 146/B2
Siletz, Oreg., U.S., 1,133 . . . . .334/C3
Silex, Mo., U.S., 206 . . . . .302/E2
Silgadhi, Nepal 126/B2
Silhouette, Sey., island 163/C1
Siliana, Tun. 146/B1
Silica, Ohio, U.S., 1,100 . . . . .328/C3
Silifke, Tur. 133/C3
Silisili, Sam., mountain 175/B2
Silistra, Bul. 101/F1
Silistra, Bul., oblast 101/E2
Silkeborg, Den. 79/B2
Silk Hope, N.C., U.S., 125 . . . . .322/G3
Sillery, Que., Can., 11,909 . . . . .226/K6

Silloth, Eng., U.K., 2,942 . . . . .66/B3
Sil Nakya, Ariz., U.S., 125 . . . . .242/D5
Silo, Okla., U.S., 282 . . . . .330/F3
Siloam, Ga., U.S., 331 . . . . .260/E4
Siloam Sprs., Ark., U.S., 10,843 . . . . .244/A1
Siloam Sprs., Mo., U.S., 70 . . . . .302/D5
Silsbee, Tex., U.S., 6,393 . . . . .346/P5
Silsden, Eng., U.K., 6,284 . . . . .68/D2
Silt, Colo., U.S., 1,740 . . . . .250/C2
Siltcoos, Oreg., U.S., 40 . . . . .334/B4
Silutè, Lith. 82/A2
Silva, Mo., U.S., 125 . . . . .302/F4
Silvassa, India 128/B4
Silver, Man., Can. 215/C4
Silver, Tex., U.S. 346/H3
Silver, Wash., U.S., lake 358/C4
Silver Bay, Minn., U.S., 2,068 . . . . .298/F3
Silver Beach, Mass., U.S., 500 . . . . .292/M6
Silver Bow, Mont., U.S., county, 34,606 . . . . .306/D4
Silver City, Ida., U.S. 264/C6
Silver City, Iowa, U.S., 259 . . . . .274/C5
Silver City, Mich., U.S. 294/A2
Silver City, Miss., U.S., 337 . . . . .300/B2
Silver City, N. Mex., U.S., 10,545 . . . . .317/B5
Silver City, N.C., U.S., 1,146 . . . . .322/G5
Silver City, Okla., U.S., 100 . . . . .330/F1
Silver City, S. Dak., U.S., 50 . . . . .342/B3
Silver City, Utah, U.S. 350/B4
Silver Cliff, Colo., U.S., 512 . . . . .250/E3
Silver Creek, Miss., U.S., 209 . . . . .300/B4
Silver Creek, Nebr., U.S., 441 . . . . .308/G2
Silver Creek, N.Y., U.S., 2,896 . . . . .320/C5
Silverdale, Kans., U.S., 80 . . . . .276/F4
Silverdale, Penn., U.S., 1,001 . . . . .298/D3
Silverdale, Wash., U.S., 15,816 . . . . .336/L5
Silver Grove, Ky., U.S., 1,215 . . . . .358/C2
Silverhill, Ala., U.S., 616 . . . . .280/L1
Silverhill, Ky., U.S., 100 . . . . .238/B5
Silver Hill, (see Suitland), Md., U.S., 33,515 . .280/A3
Silver Lake, Ind., U.S., 546 . . . . .288/C7
Silver Lake, Kans., U.S., 1,358 . . . . .270/E2
Silver Lake, (Middlesex County),
  Mass., U.S., 1,000 . . . . .276/F2
Silver Lake, (Plymouth County),
  Mass., U.S., 1,000 . . . . .292/B6
Silver Lake, Minn., U.S., 761 . . . . .292/L4
Silver Lake, Mo., U.S., 60 . . . . .298/C6
Silver Lake, N.C., U.S., 5,788 . . . . .302/G4
Silver Lake, Ohio, U.S., 3,019 . . . . .312/D4
Silver Lake, Oreg., U.S., 60 . . . . .322/K6
Silver Lake, (Cowlitz County), Wash., U.S. 334/F4
Silver Lake, (Snohomish County,
  Silver Lake-Fircrest), Wash., U.S. 358/C2
Silver Lake, (Kenosha County),
  Wisc., U.S., 2,341 . . . . .364/E6
Silver Lake, (Waushara County), Wisc., U.S. 364/D4
Silverpeak, Nev., U.S. 310/B3
Silver Plume, Colo., U.S., 203 . . . . .250/E2
Silver Pt., Tenn., U.S. 344/K2
Silver Ridge, N.J., U.S., 1,211 . . . . .314/E4
Silver Run, Miss., U.S. 300/D4
Silver Spr., Md., U.S., 76,540 . . . . . . .288/B6, F4
Silver Sprs., Fla., U.S., 6,400 . . . . .256/F2
Silver Sprs., Nev., U.S., 4,708 . . . . .310/A2
Silver Sprs., N.Y., U.S., 844 . . . . .320/E5
Silver Star Mont., U.S. 306/D4
Silver Star Prov. Park, Br. Col., Can. 214/N6
Silverstone, Eng., U.K. 70/B2
Silverstreet, S.C., U.S., 216 . . . . .340/C2
Silverthorne, Colo., U.S., 3,196 . . . . .250/D2
Silverton, Eng., U.K., 1,222 . . . . .73/F3
Silverton, Colo., U.S., 531 . . . . .250/C4
Silverton, N.J., U.S., 9,200 . . . . .314/E3
Silverton, Ohio, U.S., 5,178 . . . . .328/B9
Silverton, Oreg., U.S., 7,414 . . . . .334/D3
Silverton, Tex., U.S., 771 . . . . . . .346/G1, G10
Silverton, Wash., U.S. 358/D1
Silvies, Oreg., U.S. 334/H4
Silvies, Oreg., U.S., river 334/G4
Silvis, Ill., U.S., 7,269 . . . . .266/C2
Sima, Com. 163/B2
Simcoe, Ont., Can., 14,175 . . . . .223/E5
Simcoe, Ont., Can., 14,175 . . . . .223/F3
Simcoe, Ont., Can., county 223/F3
Simcoe, Ont., Can., lake 222/E4
Simcoe, Ont., Can., lake 223/F3
Simcoe, N. Dak., U.S., lake 122/A1
Simeulue, Indon., island 122/A2
Simferopol', Ukr., 337,118 . . . . .102/C4
Simikot, Nepal 126/B1
Simik Beach, Wash., U.S., 450 . . . . .358/C1
Simi Valley, Calif., U.S., 111,351 . . . . .246/G8
Simla, Colo., U.S., 663 . . . . .250/F2
Simmesport, La., U.S., 2,239 . . . . .282/F5
Simmler, Calif., U.S. 246/F7
Simmons, Mo., U.S. 302/D4
Simms, Mont., U.S., 373 . . . . .306/F2
Simms, Tex., U.S. 346/E9
Simnasho, Oreg., U.S., 70 . . . . .334/E3
Simon, Que., Can., lake 226/A6
Simonette, Alta., Can., river 212/A4
Simonhouse, Man., Can. 215/A2
Simons, Ohio, U.S., 225 . . . . .328/J2
Simonsbath, Eng., U.K. 73/E2
Simonsville, Vt., U.S., 50 . . . . .352/B4
Simonton, Tex., U.S., 718 . . . . .346/N6
Simonton Lake, Ind., U.S., 4,053 . . . . .270/E1
Simpson, Austl., desert 170/C2
Simpson, Ill., U.S., 54 . . . . .266/E6
Simpson, Kans., U.S., 114 . . . . .276/E2
Simpson, Ky., U.S., county, 16,405 . . . . .280/C3
Simpson, La., U.S., 583 . . . . .282/C4
Simpson, Minn., U.S., 70 . . . . .298/E7
Simpson, Miss., U.S., county, 27,639 . . . . .300/C4
Simpson, Mont., U.S. 306/H1
Simpson, N.C., U.S., 464 . . . . .322/L3
Simpson Desert Natl. Park, Austl. 170/C2
Simpsons, Va., U.S. 354/C6
Simpsonville, Ky., U.S., 1,281 . . . . .280/E2
Simpsonville, Md., U.S., 4,400 . . . . .288/G3
Simpsonville, S.C., U.S., 14,352 . . . . . .340/B2, C2
Sims, Ark., U.S., 100 . . . . .244/B3
Sims, Ill., U.S., 273 . . . . .266/E5
Sims, N.C., U.S., 128 . . . . .322/J3
Simsboro, La., U.S., 684 . . . . .282/D1
Simsbury, Conn., U.S., 23,234 . . . . .253/D2
Sims Chapel, Ala., U.S., 80 . . . . .238/A4
Sinai, Egy., peninsula 144/B2
Sinai, S. Dak., U.S., 133 . . . . .342/H3
Sinaloa, Mex., state 200/C3
Sincelejo, Col., 214,000 . . . . .184/B2
Sinclair, Man., Can. 215/A4
Sinclair, Ga., U.S., lake 260/E5
Sinclair, Maine, U.S., 100 . . . . .286/D1
Sinclair, Wyo., U.S., 423 . . . . .366/C3
Sinclair Mills, Br. Col., Can. 214/M4

Sinclairs, Scot., U.K., bay 62/K1
Sinclairston, Scot., U.K. 62/H8
Sinclairville, N.Y., U.S., 665 . . . . .320/C6
Sind, Pak., province 129/C5
Sinderhope, Eng., U.K. 66/D3
Sindhulimadhi, Nepal 126/C2
Sine, Sen., river 148/B2
Sines, Port. 93/A4
Singapore, nation 119
Singapore, Sing., capital, 4,131,200 . . . . .123/B1
Singapore, Sing., island 123/B1
Singapore, Sing., strait 123/B2
Singen, Ger. 86/B5
Singer, La., U.S., 70 . . . . .282/C5
Singida, Tan. 158/B1
Singida, Tan., region 158/B2
Singkawang, Indon. 122/B1
Singleton, Eng., U.K. 66/C5
Singleton, Colo., U.S. 250/E2
Singur, India . . . . .128/Inset II
Sink Creek, Fla., U.S., 50 . . . . .256/C1
Sinking Spr., Ohio, U.S., 158 . . . . .328/D7
Sinking Spr., Penn., U.S., 2,639 . . . . .336/J5
Sinnemahoning, Penn., U.S., 100 . . . . .336/E3
Sinop, Tur. 133/C2
Sinop, Tur., province 133/C2
Sinp'o, N. Kor. 116/C2
Sint-Niklaas, Belg., 68,473, (225,050 metro.) . .85/C1
Sinton, Tex., U.S., 5,676 . . . . .346/L7
Sint-Truiden, Belg. 85/C2
Sinüiju, N. Kor., 326,011 . . . . .116/A2
Sió, Hun., river 91/B2
Siófok, Hun. 91/B2
Sion, Switz. 90/B2
Sion Mills, N. Ire., U.K., 1,998 . . . . .65/C2
Sioux, Iowa, U.S., county, 31,589 . . . . .274/B1
Sioux, Nebr., U.S., county, 1,475 . . . . .308/A1
Sioux, N. Dak., U.S., county, 4,044 . . . . .326/D3
Sioux City, Iowa, U.S., 85,013, (124,130 metro.) .274/B3
Sioux Ctr., Iowa, U.S., 6,002 . . . . .274/B1
Sioux Falls, S. Dak., U.S., 123,975,
  (172,412 metro.) 342/J4
Sioux Lookout, Ont., Can., 5,336 . . . . .222/B2
Sioux Pass, Mont., U.S. 306/M2
Sioux Rapids, Iowa, U.S., 720 . . . . .274/D2
Sioux Valley, Minn., U.S., 50 . . . . .298/B7
Sipaliwini, Sur. 183/A3
Siparia, Trin.-To. 187/A3
Siping, China 119/F1
Sipiwesk, Man., Can., lake 215/C1
Siple, Antar., island 192/B8
Siple, Antar., mountain 192/B8
Sippewisset, Mass., U.S., 950 . . . . .292/M6
Sipsey, Ala., U.S., 552 . . . . .238/B2
Siquia, Nicar., river 202/B2
Sirajganj, Bangl. 127/C4
Sirba, Burkina, river 151/D2
Sirdaryo, Uzb., province 132/C2
Sirdaryo, Uzb., river 132/D2
Siren, Wisc., U.S., 988 . . . . .364/A3
Siret, Rom. 101/D2
Siret, Rom., river 101/E2
Sirhan, Wadi as, Jor., depression 134/B2
Sirinthorn, Thai., reservoir 125/C3
Sirjan, Iran 130/D4
Sirmans, Fla., U.S. 256/E1
Sirmaur, India, river 128/E3
Sirnak, Tur. 133/E3
Sirnak, Tur., province 133/E3
Sisaket, Thai. 125/C3
Sisian, Arm. 103/D3
Sisimiut, (Holsteinsborg), Grld. 193/B2
Sisipuk, Sask., Can., lake 227/J5
Siskiyou, Calif., U.S., county, 44,301 . . . . .246/C1
Siskiyou, Calif., U.S., mountains 246/B1
Siskiyou, Oreg., U.S. 334/B5
Siskiyou Natl. For., Oreg., U.S. 334/B5
Sisophon, Camb. 124/B2
Sisseton, S. Dak., U.S., 2,572 . . . . .342/H2
Sissonville, W. Va., U.S., 4,399 . . . . .360/C3
Sistan and Baluchistan, Iran, province 130/E4
Sister Bay, Wisc., U.S., 886 . . . . .364/F3
Sister Lakes, Mich., U.S., 1,000 . . . . .294/C7
Sisters, Oreg., U.S., 959 . . . . .334/E3
Sistersville, W. Va., U.S., 1,588 . . . . .360/E1
Sistine Chapel, Vat. 96/B2
Siteki, Swaz. 161/B2
Sitgreaves N.F., Ariz., U.S. 242/E3
Sitka, Alaska, U.S., 8,835 . . . . .240/H3
Sitka, Kans., U.S. 276/C4
Sitka, Ky., U.S. 280/H3
Sitka N.H.P., Alaska, U.S. 240/H3
Sitka, Oreg., U.S., 50 . . . . .334/C4
Sitrah, Bahr., island 137/B1
Sittang, Mya., river 125/C2
Sittard, Neth. 84/C4
Sittingbourne, Eng., U.K., 38,771 . . . . .70/F4
Sittwe, (Sittway), Mya. 125/B2
Siuna, Nicar. 202/B2
Siuslaw, Oreg., U.S., river 334/C4
Siuslaw Natl. For., Oreg. 334/C2, C3
Sivas, Tur., 232,400 . . . . .133/D2
Sivas, Tur., province 133/D2
Sivells Bend, Tex., U.S. 346/L2
Siwah, Egy. 144/A2
Siwah, Egy., oasis 144/A2
Sixaola, C.R., river 203/C3
Sixes, Oreg., U.S., 90 . . . . .334/B5
Six Lakes, Mich., U.S., 425 . . . . .294/D6
Six Mile, Ga., U.S., 175 . . . . .260/A3
Six Mile, S.C., U.S., 553 . . . . .340/B2
Sixmilecross, N. Ire., U.K., 264 . . . . .65/C2
Six Rivers Natl. For., Calif., U.S. 246/B1, B2
Sixteen, Mont., U.S. 306/F3
Sjælland, Den., island 79/C3
Skagen, Den. 79/C1
Skagerrak, Den., strait 79/B3
Skagerrak, Nor., strait 80/A3
Skagerrak, Nor., Den., strait 80/A4
Skagit, Wash., U.S., county, 102,979 . . . . .358/D1
Skagit, Wash., U.S., river 358/D1
Skagway, Alaska, U.S., 862 . . . . .240/H3
Skaill, Scot., U.K. 62/N2
Skamania, Wash., U.S., county, 9,872 . . . . .358/D3
Skamokawa, Wash., U.S., 60 . . . . .358/B3
Skandia, Mich., U.S., 325 . . . . .294/B3
Skåne, Swe., county 80/B3
Skåne, Swe., region 80/B3
Skaneateles, N.Y., U.S., 2,616 . . . . .320/J5
Skanee, Mich., U.S., 40 . . . . .294/A3
Skaw, Den., cape 79/C1
Skead, Ont., Can. 223/F1
Skedee, Okla., U.S., 102 . . . . .330/F1
Skeena, Br. Col., Can., mountains 214/H3
Skeena, Br. Col., Can., river 214/H4
Skeffington, Eng., U.K. 70/C1
Skegness, Eng., U.K., 15,149 . . . . .68/H3
Skeleton, Minn., U.S., coast 298/C1
Skellefteå, Swe., 72,035 . . . . .80/D2
Skelleftealven, Swe., river 80/C1
Skellingthorpe, Eng., U.K., 2,776 . . . . .68/F3
Skellytown, Tex., U.S., 610 . . . . .346/G9

Skelmersdale, Eng., U.K., 42,104 . . . . .66/C5
Skelmersdale, Eng., U.K., 42,104 . . . . .68/B2
Skelmorlie, Scot., U.K., 1,828 . . . . .62/G7
Skelton, Eng., U.K., 5,353 . . . . .66/F3
Skelwick, Scot., U.K. .62/M1
Skene, Miss., U.S., 200 . . . . .300/B2
Skerray, Scot., U.K. 62/H1
Skhira, Tun. 146/C2
Skiatook, Okla., U.S., 5,396 . . . . .330/F1
Skibo, Minn., U.S. 298/E3
Skidaway Island, Ga., U.S., 6,914 . . . . .260/J8
Skidby, Eng., U.K. 66/H5
Skiddaw, Eng., U.K., hill 66/B3
Skiddy, Kans., U.S. 276/F3
Skidmore, Mo., U.S., 342 . . . . .302/A1
Skidmore, Tex., U.S., 1,013 . . . . .346/L7
Skidway Lake, Mich., U.S., 3,147 . . . . .294/E5
Skien, Nor. 80/B4
Skierniewice, Pol. 83/E3
Skiff, Alta., U.S. 212/E6
Skigersta, Scot., U.K. .62/D2
Skikda, Alg., 152,335 . . . . .146/B1
Skime, Minn., U.S. 298/B2
Skinner, Maine, U.S. .286/B3
Skinners Pond, P.E.I., Can. 224/A2
Skipsea, Eng., U.K. 66/H5
Skipton, Eng., U.K., 13,583 . . . . .66/D5
Skipton, Eng., U.K., 13,583 . . . . .68/C2
Skipton, Md., U.S., 200 . . . . .288/K4
Skipton-on-Swale, Eng., U.K. 66/F4
Skirmett, Eng., U.K. 70/C2
Skive, Den. 79/B2
Skjern, Den., river 79/B3
Skokholm, Wales, U.K., island 64/A4
Skokie, Ill., U.S., 63,348 . . . . .266/B5
Skokomish, Wash., U.S., 616 . . . . .358/B2
Skomer, Wales, U.K., island 64/A4
Skookumchuck, Br. Col., Can. 214/P6
Skopje, Mac., capital, 545,228 . . . . .100/B2
Skovorodino, Russ. 104/H4
Skowhegan, Maine, U.S., 8,824 . . . . .286/C4
Skownan, Man., Can. .215/B3
Skull Valley, Ariz., U.S., 60 . . . . .242/C3
Skull Valley Ind. Res., Utah, U.S. 350/B3
Skunk, Iowa, U.S., river 274/K5
Skye, Scot., U.K., island 60/A1
Skye, Scot., U.K., island 62/D4
Skykomish, Wash., U.S., 214 . . . . .358/D2
Skykomish, Wash., U.S., river 358/B4, D2
Skyland, N.C., U.S., 50 . . . . .322/E7
Skyline, Ala., U.S., 843 . . . . .238/C1
Skyline, Minn., U.S., 330 . . . . .298/C6
Skyline, Nebr., U.S. 308/H2
Skyros, Gr., island 100/C2
Sky Valley, Ga., U.S., 221 . . . . .260/E2
Skyway, Colo., U.S. 250/B2
Skyway, (Bryn Mawr-Skyway),
   Wash., U.S., 13,977 . . . . .358/A4
Slade, Ky., U.S. 280/G3
Slade N.W.R., N. Dak., U.S. 326/F3
Slagelse, Den. 79/C3
Slaggyford, Eng., U.K. 66/C3
Slagle, La., U.S., 225 .282/C4
Slaley, Eng., U.K. 66/D3
Slaná, Slvk., river 92/C2
Slana, Alaska, U.S., 124 . . . . .240/G2
Slanesville, W. Va., U.S., 90 . . . . .360/J2
Slapout, Okla., U.S. 330/B1
Slapton, Eng., U.K. 73/E4
Slaskie, Pol., province .83/D3
Slater, Colo., U.S. 250/C1
Slater, Iowa, U.S., 1,306 . . . . .274/G4
Slater, Mo., U.S., 2,083 . . . . .302/C2
Slater, S.C., U.S., 2,228 . . . . .340/B1, E1
Slater, Wyo., U.S., 82 . . . . .366/D3
Slatersville, R.I., U.S., 2,600 . . . . .339/C2
Slaterville Sprs., N.Y., U.S., 275 . . . . .320/J6
Slate Spr., Miss., U.S., 121 . . . . .300/C2
Slatina, Rom. 101/C3
Slatington, Penn., U.S., 4,434 . . . . .336/K4
Slaton, Tex., U.S., 6,109 . . . . .346/G2
Slaty Fork, W. Va., U.S. 360/F4
Slaughter, La., U.S., 1,011 . . . . .282/G5
Slaughter Beach, Del., U.S., 198 . . . . .255/C5
Slaughters, Ky., U.S., 238 . . . . .280/C3
Slaughterville, Okla., U.S., 3,609 . . . . .330/E2
Slave, Alta., U.S., river 212/E1
Slave, N.W. Terr., Can., river 220/F4
Slave Lake, Alta., Can., 6,600 . . . . .212/C3
Slavonia, Cro., region .98/C2
Slavonska Požega, Cro. 98/C2
Slavonski Brod, Cro. 98/C2
Slayden, Miss., U.S., 60 . . . . .300/C1
Slayden, Tenn., U.S., 185 . . . . .344/G2
Slayton, Minn., U.S., 2,072 . . . . .298/B7
Sleaford, Eng., U.K., 10,388 . . . . .68/G4
Sleaford, Eng., U.K., 10,388 . . . . .70/D1
Sledge, Miss., U.S., 529 . . . . .300/B1
Sledmere, Eng., U.K. .68/F1
Sleeper, Mo., U.S., 175 . . . . .302/D4
Sleeping Bear Dunes Natl. Lakeshore,
   Mich., U.S. 294/C5
Sleepy Eye, Minn., U.S., 3,515 . . . . .298/C6
Sleepy Hollow, Ill., U.S., 3,553 . . . . .266/A5
Sleepy Hollow, N.Y., U.S., 9,212 . . . . .320/B1
Sleepy Hollow, Wyo., U.S., 1,177 . . . . .366/D1
Sleetmute, Alaska, U.S., 100 . . . . .240/D2
Sleights, Eng., U.K., 2,061 . . . . .66/G4
Slemp, Ky., U.S., 300 . . . . .280/G3
Slick, Okla., U.S., 148 . . . . .330/F2
Slick Rock, Colo., U.S. 250/B3
Slide, N.Y., U.S., mountain 320/N7
Slide, Tex., U.S. 346/G2
Slidell, La., U.S., 25,695 . . . . .282/K6
Sliema, Malta 97/C2
Slieve Donard, N. Ire., U.K., mountain 60/B2
Slieve Donard, N. Ire., U.K., mountain 65/F3
Slieve Donard, N. Ire., U.K., mountain 78/D1
Slieve Gallion, N. Ire., U.K., mountain 65/D2
Slieve Gullion, N. Ire., U.K., mountain 65/E3
Sligachan, Scot., U.K. .62/D4
Sligo, Ire., 18,429 . . . . .78/B1
Sligo, Ire., county 78/B1
Sligo, Penn., U.S., 728 . . . . .336/C3
Slindon, Eng., U.K. 68/C4
Slinger, Wisc., U.S., 3,901 . . . . .364/E5, F1
Slippery Rock, Penn., U.S., 3,068 . . . . .336/A3
Sliven, Bul., 142,400 .101/E3
Sliven, Bul., oblast 101/E3
Sloan, Iowa, U.S., 1,032 . . . . .274/B3
Sloan, Nev., U.S. 310/C4
Sloan, N.Y., U.S., 3,775 . . . . .320/D5
Sloan, Calif., U.S. 246/E4
Sloatsburg, N.Y., U.S., 3,117 . . . . .320/A1
Slobozia, Rom. 101/D3
Slocomb, Ala., U.S., 2,052 . . . . .238/D4
Slocum, R.I., U.S., 350 . . . . .339/C4
Slocum, Tex., U.S., 150 . . . . .346/N4
Slope, N. Dak., U.S., county, 767 . . . . . . .60/Inset III
Slough, Eng., U.K. . . . . .60/Inset III
Slough, Eng., U.K., 110,708 . . . . .70/C3

Slough, Eng., U.K., unitary authority, 119,070 . .70/C3
Slovakia, nation 90
Slovenia, nation 96
Slovenské Rudohorie, Slvk., mountains 92/B2
Sluch', Ukr., river 102/B1
Słupsk, Pol., 102,354 .83/C1
Smackover, Ark., U.S., 2,005 . . . . .244/C4
Småland, Swe., region 80/B3
Small, Maine, U.S., point 286/C5
Small, Tex., U.S. 346/C4
Smalley, Eng., U.K. 70/B1
Smallwood, Nfld., Can., reservoir 218/D3
Smallwood, Md., U.S., 950 . . . . .288/C1
Smalyavichy, Bela. 82/D2
Smarden, Eng., U.K. 70/F4
Smarr, Ga., U.S. 260/D6
Smarts, N.H., U.S., mountain 312/B4
Smeaton, Sask., Can., 178 . . . . .227/F7
Smederevo, Serb.-Mont., 117,050 . . . . .99/B2
Smelterville, Ida., U.S. 264/A2
Smethport, Penn., U.S., 1,684 . . . . .336/E2
Smethwick, Eng., U.K. .68/D5
Smicksburg, Penn., U.S., 49 . . . . .336/C4
Smiley, Tex., U.S., 453 . . . . .346/L6
Smiltene, Lat. 82/C2
Smith, Alta., Can., 262 . . . . .212/C3
Smith, Kans., U.S., county, 4,536 . . . . .276/D2
Smith, Ky., U.S., 50 . . . . .280/G4
Smith, Md., U.S., island 288/K7
Smith, Miss., U.S., county, 16,182 . . . . .300/C4
Smith, Nev., U.S., 1,425 . . . . .310/A2
Smith, N.C., U.S., island 322/J7
Smith, Tenn., U.S., county, 17,712 . . . . .344/K2
Smith, Tex., U.S., county, 174,706 . . . . .346/N3
Smith, Va., U.S., island 354/L4
Smithboro, Ill., U.S., 200 . . . . .266/D5
Smithboro, S.C., U.S., 350 . . . . .340/E2
Smithburg, N.J., U.S., 350 . . . . .314/E3
Smithburg, W. Va., U.S., 350 . . . . .360/E2
Smith Ctr., Kans., U.S., 1,931 . . . . .276/D2
Smith Creek, N.C., U.S. 322/K6
Smithdale, Miss., U.S., 100 . . . . .300/B4
Smithers, Br. Col., Can., 5,414 . . . . .214/J4
Smithers, W. Va., U.S., 904 . . . . .360/D4
Smithers Landing, Br. Col., Can. 214/J3
Smithfield, Eng., U.K. .66/C3
Smithfield, Ill., U.S., 214 . . . . .266/C3
Smithfield, Ky., U.S., 102 . . . . .280/E2
Smithfield, Maine, U.S., 930 . . . . .286/C4
Smithfield, Nebr., U.S., 68 . . . . .308/E3
Smithfield, N.C., U.S., 11,510 . . . . .322/J4
Smithfield, Ohio, U.S., 867 . . . . .328/J5
Smithfield, Penn., U.S., 854 . . . . .336/B6
Smithfield, Utah, U.S., 7,261 . . . . .350/C2
Smithfield, Va., U.S., 6,324 . . . . .354/K7
Smithfield, W. Va., U.S., 177 . . . . .360/D4
Smithland, Iowa, U.S., 221 . . . . .274/C3
Smithland, Ky., U.S., 401 . . . . .280/B3
Smithland, Tex., U.S., 175 . . . . .346/P3
Smith Mills, Ky., U.S., 325 . . . . .280/C3
Smith Mills, Mass., U.S., 4,432 . . . . .292/L6
Smith Mtn., Va., U.S., lake 354/D6
Smith Pt., Tex., U.S. 346/P6
Smith River, Br. Col., Can. 214/J1
Smith River, Calif., U.S., 750 . . . . .246/A1
Smith River N.R.A., Calif., U.S. 246/B1
Smiths, Ala., U.S., 21,756 . . . . .238/D3
Smithsburg, Md., U.S., 2,146 . . . . .288/D1
Smiths Corner, N.B., Can. 217/D2
Smiths Cove, (Smiths Cove Sta.), N.S., Can. 221/B3
Smiths Falls, Ont., Can., 9,140 . . . . .223/J3
Smiths Creek, Ky., U.S., 40 . . . . .280/G2
Smiths Ferry, Ida., U.S. 264/A5
Smiths Grove, Ky., U.S., 784 . . . . .280/D3
Smithton, Ark., U.S., 100 . . . . .244/B4
Smithton, Ill., U.S., 2,248 . . . . .266/A4
Smithton, Mo., U.S., 510 . . . . .302/C3
Smithtown, Conn., U.S., bay 253/B5
Smithtown, N.H., U.S. 312/B6
Smith Vil., Okla., U.S., 40 . . . . .330/B4, E2
Smithville, Ont., Can., 3,317 . . . . .223/F4
Smithville, Ark., U.S., 73 . . . . .244/D1
Smithville, Ga., U.S., 774 . . . . .260/C8
Smithville, Ind., U.S., 750 . . . . .270/C6
Smithville, (Caroline County), Md., U.S., 150 . . .288/M4
Smithville, (Dorchester County), Md., U.S. 288/J6
Smithville, Miss., U.S., 882 . . . . .300/D1
Smithville, Mo., U.S., 5,514 . . . . .302/B2
Smithville, N.H., U.S. .312/C6
Smithville, N.J., U.S., 3,100 . . . . .314/E5
Smithville, Ohio, U.S., 1,333 . . . . .328/G4
Smithville, Okla., U.S., 123 . . . . .330/H3
Smithville, Tenn., U.S., 3,994 . . . . .344/K3
Smithville, Tex., U.S., 3,901 . . . . .346/L5
Smithville, W. Va., U.S., 90 . . . . .360/D2
Smithwick, S. Dak., U.S. 342/B4
Smithwick, Tex., U.S. 346/C2, K5
Smoaks, S.C., U.S., 140 . . . . .340/D3
Smoke Creek, Nev., U.S. 310/A1
Smoke Signal, Ariz., U.S. 242/E2
Smokey Pt., Wash., U.S., 1,556 . . . . .358/C1
Smoky, Alta., Can., river 212/A3a, A4
Smoky Hill, Kans., U.S., river 276/B3
Smoky Lake, Alta., Can., 1,011 . . . . .212/D4
Smolan, Kans., U.S., 219 . . . . .276/E3
Smolensk, Russ., 351,498 . . . . .104/C4
Smoljan, Bul. 101/C4
Smoljan, Bul., oblast 101/C4
Smoot, Wyo., U.S., 182 . . . . .366/A2
Smoothstone, Sask., Can., lake 227/D6
Smoothstone, Sask., Can., river 227/D6
Smugglers Notch, Vt., U.S., pass 352/B1
Smut Eye, Ala., U.S., 40 . . . . .238/C4
Smyer, Tex., U.S., 480 . . . . .346/F2
Smyrna, Ark., U.S. 244/C2
Smyrna, Del., U.S., 5,679 . . . . .255/B3
Smyrna, Del., U.S., river 255/B3
Smyrna, Ga., U.S., 40,999 . . . . .260/B4, H2
Smyrna, Mich., U.S., 275 . . . . .294/D6
Smyrna, N.Y., U.S., 241 . . . . .320/K5
Smyrna, S.C., U.S., 59 . . . . .340/C1
Smyrna, Tenn., U.S., 25,569 . . . . .344/H3
Smyrna, Wash., U.S. 358/F3
Smyrna Mills, Maine, U.S., 200 . . . . .286/D2
Smyth, Va., U.S., county, 33,081 . . . . .354/E2
Snaefell, Eng., U.K., hill 66/B5
Snainton, Eng., U.K. 66/G4
Snaith, Eng., U.K., 2,748 . . . . .66/F5
Snaith, Eng., U.K., 2,748 . . . . .68/F2
Snake, Yukon, Can., river 228/C3
Snake, Ida., U.S., river 264/A4, A5, A6, F6
Snake, Nev., U.S., range 310/C2
Snake, S. Dak., U.S., creek 326/C4,
Snake, Wash., U.S., river 358/H3,
Snake River, Ida., U.S., plain 264/B6,
Snake River, Wash., U.S. 358/G3,
Snake River Birds of Prey Natl. Cons. Area,
   Ida., U.S. 264/A6,
Snaring, Alta., Can. 212/A4,

Snĕžka, Czh. Rep., mountain 92/B2,
Snead, Ala., U.S., 748 . . . . .238/C1,
Sneads, Fla., U.S., 1,919 . . . . .256/D1,
Sneads Ferry, N.C., U.S., 2,248 . . . . .322/L5,
Sneedville, Tenn., U.S., 1,257 . . . . .344/Q1,
Sneek, Neth. 84/C1,
Snee Oosh, Wash., U.S. 358/C1,
Snelling, S.C., U.S., 246 . . . . .340/C3,
Snellville, Ga., U.S., 15,351 . . . . .260/C4, K2
Sniardwy, Pol., lake 83/E2,
Snina, Slvk. 92/C2,
Snipesville, Ga., U.S., 70 . . . . .260/F8,
Snitterfield, Eng., U.K. .70/A2,
S.N.N.P.R.S., Eth., state 156/B3,
Snodland, Eng., U.K., 8,814 . . . . .70/F4,
Snohomish, Wash., U.S., 8,494 . . . . .358/C2,
Snohomish, Wash., U.S., county, 606,024 . .358/B4, D2
Snook, Tex., U.S., 568 . . . . .346/M5,
Snoqualmie, Wash., U.S., 1,631 . . . . .358/B4, D2
Snoqualmie, Wash., U.S., pass 358/D2,
Snoqualmie Pass, Wash., U.S., 201 . . . . .358/D2,
Snover, Mich., U.S., 275 . . . . .294/G6,
Snow, Maine, U.S., mountain 286/B3,
Snow, Okla., U.S. 330/G3,
Snow, Vt., U.S., mountain 352/B5,
Snowball, Ark., U.S., 40 . . . . .244/C2,
Snow Camp, N.C., U.S., 175 . . . . .322/G3,
Snowdon, Wales, U.K., hill 60/B3,
Snowdon, Wales, U.K., hill 64/C1,
Snowdonia Natl. Park, Wales, U.K. 64/D2,
Snowdoun, Ala., U.S., 425 . . . . .238/C3,
Snowflake, Man., Can. 215/B4,
Snowflake, Ariz., U.S., 4,460 . . . . .242/E3,
Snow Hill, Ala., U.S. 238/B3,
Snow Hill, Md., U.S., 2,409 . . . . .288/N7,
Snow Hill, N.C., U.S., 1,514 . . . . .322/K4,
Snow Lake, Man., Can., 1,207 . . . . .215/A2,
Snow Shoe, Penn., U.S., 771 . . . . .336/F3,
Snowville, N.H., U.S., 60 . . . . .312/D4,
Snowville, Utah, U.S., 177 . . . . .350/B2,
S.N.P.J., Penn., U.S. 336/A4,
Snug Harbour, Nfld., Can. 218/D3,
Snuol, Camb. 124/E3,
Snyder, Ark., U.S., 80 . . . . .244/D4,
Snyder, Colo., U.S., 125 . . . . .250/G1,
Snyder, Nebr., U.S., 318 . . . . .308/H2,
Snyder, Okla., U.S., 1,509 . . . . .330/D3,
Snyder, Penn., U.S., county, 37,546 . . . . .336/G4,
Snyder, Tex., U.S., 10,783 . . . . .346/H3,
Snydertown, Penn., U.S., 357 . . . . .336/H4,
Soan, S. Kor., islands .116/B5,
Soap Lake, Wash., U.S., 1,733 . . . . .358/F2,
Soay, Scot., U.K., island 62/D4,
Sobaek Sanmaek, S. Kor., mountains 116/B5,
Sobat, Sudan, river 145/C3,
Sobieski, Minn., U.S., 196 . . . . .298/C5,
Sobieski, Wisc., U.S., 150 . . . . .364/E4,
Sobradinho, Braz., reservoir 188/D3,
Sobral, Braz., 69,072, (127,449 metro.) 188/D2,
Socastee, S.C., U.S., 14,295 . . . . .340/E3,
Sochi, Russ., 334,009, (395,800 metro.) 104/C5,
Social Circle, Ga., U.S., 3,379 . . . . .260/D4,
Social Hill, Ark., U.S., 80 . . . . .244/C3,
Society Hill, Ala., U.S. 238/D3,
Society Hill, S.C., U.S., 700 . . . . .340/E2,
Soco, Dom. Rep., river 205/C2,
Socompa, Chile 190/C2,
Socorro, N. Mex., U.S., 8,877 . . . . .317/D3,
Socorro, N. Mex., U.S., county, 18,078 . . . . . . .317/D3,
Socorro, Tex., U.S., 27,152 . . . . .346/B4,
Socotra, Yemen, island 109/G8,
Soc Trang, Viet. 123/A5,
Soda Sprs., Calif., U.S., 100 . . . . .246/E3,
Soda Sprs., Ida., U.S., 3,381 . . . . .264/F7,
Sodaville, Oreg., U.S., 290 . . . . .334/C3,
Soddy-Daisy, Tenn., U.S., 11,530 . . . . .344/L4,
Söderhamn, Swe. 80/C2,
Södermanland, Swe., county 80/C3,
Sodus, N.Y., U.S., 1,735 . . . . .320/D4,
Sodus Pt., N.Y., U.S., 1,160 . . . . .320/H4,
Sofia, Bul., capital, 1,190,547 . . . . .101/B3,
Sofia, Bul., oblast 101/B3,
Sofia, Madag., river 163/B2,
Sofia, N. Mex., U.S. 317/G1,
Sofia City, Bul., oblast 101/B3,
Sognefjord, Nor., fjord .80/A3,
Sogn og Fjordane, Nor., province 80/A3,
Soham, Eng., U.K., 6,639 . . . . .68/H5,
Soham, Eng., U.K., 6,639 . . . . .70/E2,
Soissons, Fr. 88/C2,
Sŏjosŏn, N. Kor., bay .116/A3,
Sokagoon Chippewa Ind. Comm., Wisc., U.S. . . .364/F3,
Sokcho, S. Kor. 116/C3,
Sokhumi, Geo., 121,000 . . . . .103/A3,
Sokodé, Togo 151/B2,
Sokoto, Nig. 152/C1,
Sokoto, Nig., plains 152/C1,
Sokoto, Nig., river 152/C1,
Sokoto, Nig., state 152/C1,
Sol, Sp., coast 94/C4,
Sola, Van. 173/B1,
Solana Beach, Calif., U.S., 12,979 . . . . . .246/D4, H10,
Solano, Calif., U.S., county, 394,542 . . .246/B4, K1, K6
Solano, N. Mex., U.S. .317/F2,
Solapur, India, 603,870, (620,499 metro.) 128/C5,
Soldeu, And. 93/B2,
Soldier, Iowa, U.S., 207 . . . . .274/C4,
Soldier, Kans., U.S., 122 . . . . .276/G2,
Soldier Pond, Maine, U.S., 100 . . . . .286/D1,
Soldiers Grove, Wisc., U.S., 653 . . . . .364/C5,
Soldier Summit, Utah, U.S. 350/C4,
Soldotna, Alaska, U.S., 3,759 . . . . .240/E2,
Soledad, Calif., U.S., 11,263 . . . . .246/D6,
Solen, N. Dak., U.S., 86 . . . . .326/E3,
Solentiname, Nicar., archipelago 202/B3,
Solihull, Eng., U.K. 60/C3,
Solihull, Eng., U.K., 94,531 . . . . .68/D5,
Solihull, Eng., U.K., unitary authority, 199,521 . .68/D5,
Solingen, Ger., 165,583 . . . . .86/A3,
Solitude, Ind., U.S., 125 . . . . .270/A8,
Sollas, Scot., U.K. 62/C3,
Solomon, P.N.G., river 172/B2,
Solomon, Sol. Is., sea .173/A2,
Solomon, Ariz., U.S., 475 . . . . .242/F5,
Solomon, Kans., U.S., 1,072 . . . . .276/E3,
Solomon, N. Fork, Kans., U.S., river 276/B2,
Solomon, Kans., U.S., river 276/D2,
Solomon Islands, nation 165,
Solomons, Md., U.S., 1,536 . . . . .288/J6,
Solon, Iowa, U.S., 1,177 . . . . .274/M4,
Solon, Maine, U.S., 940 . . . . .286/C4,
Solon, Ohio, U.S., 21,802 . . . . .328/H9,
Solon Sprs., Wisc., U.S., 576 . . . . .364/B2,
Solothurn, Switz., canton 175/C2,
Solvang, Calif., U.S., 5,332 . . . . .246/F8,
Solvay, N.Y., U.S., 6,845 . . . . .320/J4,
Solway, Eng., U.K., coast 66/B3,
Solway, Eng., U.K., estuary 60/B2,

Solway, Eng., U.K., estuary 66/A3
Solway, Minn., U.S., 69 . . . . .298/A5
Solway, Tenn., U.S., 1,200 . . . . .344/N3
Solway Firth, Scot., U.K. 62/J9
Solwezi, Zam. 159/B2
Somali, Eth., state 156/D3
Somalia, nation 151
Sombe, P.R., beach 206/E2
Sombor, Serb.-Mont. 99/A2
Sombra, Ont., Can. 223/C5
Sombrio, Br. Col., Can., point 358/A1
Somerdale, N.J., U.S., 5,192 . . . . .314/B3, C4
Somerdale, Ohio, U.S., 275 . . . . .328/H4
Somerley, Eng., U.K. 70/C5
Somers, Conn., U.S., 10,417 . . . . .253/F2
Somers, Iowa, U.S., 165 . . . . .274/F3
Somers, Mont., U.S., 556 . . . . .306/B1
Somers, Wisc., U.S., 1,100 . . . . .364/F6
Somerset, Man., Can., 459 . . . . .215/B4
Somerset, Nun., Can., island 220/K2
Somerset, Eng., U.K., unitary authority, 498,093 .73/G2
Somerset, Colo., U.S. .250/C3
Somerset, Ky., U.S., 11,352 . . . . .280/F3
Somerset, Maine, U.S., 60 . . . . .286/B3
Somerset, Maine, U.S., county, 50,888 . . . . . . .286/B3
Somerset, Md., U.S., 1,124 . . . . .288/B6
Somerset, Md., U.S., county, 24,747 . . . . .288/M7
Somerset, Mass., U.S., 18,234 . . . . .292/K5
Somerset, N.J., U.S., 23,040 . . . . .314/D2
Somerset, N.J., U.S., county, 297,490 . . . . .314/D2
Somerset, Ohio, U.S., 1,549 . . . . .328/F6
Somerset, Penn., U.S., 6,762 . . . . .336/C5
Somerset, Penn., U.S., county, 80,023 . . . . .336/C5
Somerset, Tex., U.S., 1,550 . . . . .346/A3, K6
Somerset, Vt., U.S., reservoir 352/B5
Somerset, Wisc., U.S., 1,556 . . . . .364/A3
Somersham, Eng., U.K., 3,257 . . . . .70/E2
Somers Pt., N.J., U.S., 11,614 . . . . .314/D5
Somersworth, N.H., U.S., 11,477 . . . . .312/E5
Somerton, Eng., U.K., 4,489 . . . . .68/E6
Somerton, Eng., U.K. .70/B3
Somerton, Eng., U.K. .70/H1
Somerton, Ariz., U.S., 7,266 . . . . .242/A5
Somervell, Tex., U.S., county, 6,809 . . . . .346/L3
Somerville, N.B., Can., 368 . . . . .217/B2
Somerville, Ala., U.S., 347 . . . . .238/C1
Somerville, Ind., U.S., 312 . . . . .270/B8
Somerville, Maine, U.S., 509 . . . . .286/C4
Somerville, Mass., U.S., 77,478 . . . . .292/C7, K3
Somerville, N.J., U.S., 12,423 . . . . .314/D2
Somerville, Ohio, U.S., 250 . . . . .328/A6
Somerville, Tenn., U.S., 2,519 . . . . .344/C4
Somerville, Tex., U.S., 1,704 . . . . .346/M5
Somes, Rom., river 101/B2
Somes Bar, Calif., U.S. 246/B1
Somesville, Maine, U.S., 250 . . . . .286/D4
Somme, Fr., department 88/C2
Somme, Fr., river 88/C2
Somogy, Hun., county .91/A2
Somonauk, Ill., U.S., 1,295 . . . . .266/E2
Somoto, Nicar. 202/A2
Son, India, river 128/C4
Sonarpur, India .128/Inset II
Sønderborg, Den. 79/B4
Sønderjylland, Den., county 79/B3
Sondheimer, La., U.S., 80 . . . . .282/G1
Sondrio, It. 95/B1
Sonestown, Penn., U.S., 225 . . . . .336/H3
Songea, Tan. 159/C2
Songhua, China, river .119/F1
Songkhla, Thai., (294,200 metro.) 125/B5
Songköl, Kyrg. 131/D2
Songnim, N. Kor. 116/A3
Songo Lock, Maine, U.S., 475 . . . . .286/B5
Songwe, Mal., river 159/B1
Son La, Viet. 123/A2
Sonnette, Mont., U.S. .306/L4
Sonning, Eng., U.K. 70/C4
Sonoita, Ariz., U.S., 826 . . . . .242/E6
Sonoma, Calif., U.S., 9,128 . . . . .246/J1
Sonoma, Calif., U.S., county, 458,614 . . .246/B4, J1
Sonora, Mex., state 200/B1
Sonora, Calif., U.S., 4,423 . . . . .246/E5
Sonora, Ky., U.S., 350 . . . . .280/E3
Sonora, Tex., U.S., 2,924 . . . . .346/H5
Sonoran, Ariz., U.S., desert 242/B5
Sonsonate, El. Salv., 76,200 . . . . .203/A2
Sonsoral, Palau, island 172/A3
Sontag, Miss., U.S., 125 . . . . .300/B4
Sooke, Br. Col., Can., 8,735 . . . . .214/L7
Sooner, Okla., U.S., lake 330/F1
Sooy Place, N.J., U.S., 550 . . . . .314/D4
Sopchoppy, Fla., U.S., 426 . . . . .256/D1
Soper, Okla., U.S., 300 . . . . .330/G3
Soperton, Ga., U.S., 2,824 . . . . .260/F7
Sophia, W. Va., U.S., 1,301 . . . . .360/D5
Sopron, Hun. 91/A2
Soquel, Calif., U.S., 5,081 . . . . .246/K4
Sor, Port., river 93/B3
Sorel, Que., U.S., 34,194 . . . . .226/C5
Sorento, Ill., U.S., 601 . . . . .266/D4
Soria, Sp., 35,151 . . . . .94/E2
Soria, Sp., province 94/E2
Soriano, Uru., department 187/B2
Sorisdale, Scot., U.K. .62/D5
Sorø, Den. 79/C3
Soroca, Mol. 102/B1
Sorocaba, Braz., 493,468 . . . . .188/D4
Sorong, Indon. 127/F4
Soroti, Ug., 41,470 . . . . .157/C3
Sorraia, Port., river 93/A3
Sorrel, La., U.S., 550 .282/F7
Sorrento, It. 95/C2
Sorrento, La., U.S., 1,227 . . . . .282/H6
Sorrento, Maine, U.S., 290 . . . . .286/D4
Sør-Trøndelag, Nor., province 80/C3
Sorum, S. Dak., U.S. .342/C2
Sosnowiec, Pol., 243,332 . . . . .83/D3
Soso, Fiji, bay 174/B3
Soso, Miss., U.S., 379 . . . . .300/C4
Sota, Ben., river 151/B2
Sot'k', Arm. 103/C2
Sotouboua, Togo 151/B2
Soubré, C. d'Iv. 150/C4
Soudan, Minn., U.S., 475 . . . . .298/E3
Souderton, Penn., U.S., 6,730 . . . . .336/L5
Soufrière, Dom. 208/B4
Soufrière, St. Luc. 208/A2
Soufrière, St. Luc., volcano 208/A2
Soufrière, St. Vin.-Gren., mountain 208/B1
Souillac, Mauritius 163/C4
Soulbury, Eng., U.K. 70/C2
Souldern, Eng., U.K. 70/B3
Sound Beach, N.Y., U.S., 9,807 . . . . .320/E1
Sound of Eigg, Scot., U.K. 62/D5
Sound of Mull, Scot., U.K. 62/D5
Sound View, Conn., U.S., 1,200 . . . . .253/F4
Soungrougou, Sen., river 148/B3
Sources, Leso., mountain 161/B1

Spencer, Mich. 625

Souris, Man., Can., 1,683 . . . 215/A4
Souris, Man., Can., *river* . . . 215/A4
Souris, P.E.I., Can., 1,248 . . . 224/C2
Souris, Sask., Can., *river* . . . 227/G11
Souris, N. Dak., U.S., 83 . . . 326/E1
Souris, N. Dak., U.S., *river* . . . 326/C1, D1
Sour Lake, Tex., U.S., 1,667 . . . 346/P5
Sous, Mor., *river* . . . 147/B2
Sousse, Tun., 124,990 . . . 146/C2
Sosúa, Dom. Rep. . . . 205/B1
South, Barb., *point* . . . 209/B5
South, Came., *province* . . . 153/B3
South, N.Z., *island* . . . 171/A3
South, La., U.S., *pass* . . . 282/L8
South, Mich., U.S., *point* . . . 294/F5
South, S.C., U.S., *island* . . . 340/E3
S. Acton, Mass., U.S., 2,700 . . . 292/J3
S. Acworth, N.H., U.S., 150 . . . 312/B5
S. Addison, Maine, U.S., 100 . . . 286/E4
S. Africa, *nation* . . . 156
S. Albany, Vt., U.S., 50 . . . 352/C1
Southam, Eng., U.K., 5,304 . . . 68/E5
Southam, Eng., U.K., 5,304 . . . 70/B2
Southam, N. Dak., U.S. . . . 326/G1
S. Amboy, N.J., U.S., 7,913 . . . 314/E3
S. America, *continent* . . . 170
S. Amherst, Mass., U.S., 5,039 . . . 292/D3
S. Amherst, Ohio, U.S., 1,863 . . . 328/F3
Southampton, Nun., Can., *island* . . . 220/L4
Southampton, Ont., Can., 3,360 . . . 223/D3
Southampton, Eng., U.K. . . . 60/C4
Southampton, Eng., U.K., 210,138, (295,220 *metro.*) . . . 70/B5
Southampton, Eng., U.K., *unitary authority*, 217,478 . . . 70/B5
Southampton, Mass., U.S., 5,387 . . . 292/D4
Southampton, N.Y., U.S., 3,965 . . . 320/G2
Southampton, Va., U.S., *county*, 17,482 . . . 354/J7
S. Andaman, India, *island* . . . 128/F6
Southard, Okla., U.S., 70 . . . 330/D1
S. Arm, Maine, U.S. . . . 286/B4
S. Ashburnham, Mass., U.S., 1,013 . . . 292/G2
S. Aulatsivik, Nfld., Can., *island* . . . 218/E3
S. Australia, Austl., *state* . . . 170/C2
Southaven, Miss., U.S., 28,977 . . . 300/B1
S. Ayrshire, Scot., U.K., *unitary authority*, 112,097 . . . 62/F8
S. Baldy, N. Mex., U.S., *peak* . . . 317/C3
S. Bancroft, Maine, U.S. . . . 286/E3
S. Barnstead, N.H., U.S., 150 . . . 312/D5
S. Barre, Vt., U.S., 1,242 . . . 352/B2
S. Barrington, Ill., U.S., 3,760 . . . 266/A5
S. Bay, Fla., U.S., 3,859 . . . 256/H5
S. Baymouth, Ont., Can. . . . 223/C2
S. Beach, Oreg., U.S., 150 . . . 334/B3
S. Belmar, N.J., U.S., 1,806 . . . 314/E3
S. Beloit, Ill., U.S., 5,397 . . . 266/D1
S. Bend, Ind., U.S., 107,789, (265,559 *metro.*) . . . 270/D1
S. Bend, Nebr., U.S., 86 . . . 308/H2
S. Bend, Tex., U.S., 50 . . . 346/K3
S. Bend, Wash., U.S., 1,807 . . . 358/B3
S. Benfleet, Eng., U.K. . . . 70/F3
S. Berlin, Mass., U.S., 800 . . . 292/H3
S. Berwick, Maine, U.S., 6,671 . . . 286/B5
S. Bethany, Del., U.S., 492 . . . 255/D6
S. Bethlehem, Penn., U.S., 444 . . . 336/C4
S. Bloomfield, Ohio, U.S., 1,179 . . . 328/E6
S. Bloomingville, Ohio, U.S., 90 . . . 328/E7
S. Boardman, Mich., U.S., 500 . . . 294/D5
Southborough, Eng., U.K. . . . 70/E4
Southborough, Mass., U.S., 8,781 . . . 292/H3
S. Boston, Va., U.S., 8,491 . . . 354/F7
S. Bound Brook, N.J., U.S., 4,492 . . . 314/D2
S. Branch, Nfld., Can. . . . 218/B5
S. Branch, Mich., U.S., 125 . . . 294/F5
S. Brent, Eng., U.K., 2,087 . . . 73/E4
Southbridge, Mass., U.S., 17,214 . . . 292/F4
S. Bridgeton, Maine, U.S. . . . 286/B5
S. Bridgewater, Mass., U.S., 2,600 . . . 292/L5
S. Bristol, Maine, U.S., 897 . . . 286/C5
S. Broadway, Wash., U.S. . . . 358/E3
S. Brook, Nfld., Can., 578 . . . 218/C4
S. Browning, Mont., U.S., 1,677 . . . 306/C1
S. Burlington, Vt., U.S., 15,814 . . . 352/A2
Southbury, Conn., U.S., 18,567 . . . 253/C4
S. Canaan, Conn., U.S., 125 . . . 253/B2
S. Carolina, U.S., *state* . . . 328
S. Carrollton, Ky., U.S., 184 . . . 280/C3
S. Carthage, Tenn., U.S., 1,302 . . . 344/K2
S. Carver, Mass., U.S., 375 . . . 292/M5
S. Casco, Maine, U.S., 650 . . . 286/B5
S. Cave, Eng., U.K., 2,669 . . . 66/G5
S. Cave, Eng., U.K., 2,669 . . . 68/F2
S. Cerney, Eng., U.K., 2,145 . . . 68/D6
S. Cerney, Eng., U.K., 2,145 . . . 73/J1
S. Chaplin, Conn., U.S., 550 . . . 253/G2
S. Charleston, Ohio, U.S., 1,850 . . . 328/C6
S. Charleston, W. Va., U.S., 13,390 . . . 360/C4
S. Charlestown, N.H., U.S., 175 . . . 312/B5
S. Chatham, Mass., U.S., 800 . . . 292/P6
S. Chatham, N.H., U.S., 40 . . . 312/D3
S. Chicago Hts., Ill., U.S., 3,970 . . . 266/C6
S. China, Bru., *sea* . . . 121/A2
S. China, China, *sea* . . . 119/E4
S. China, H.K., China, *sea* . . . 117/C2
S. China, Indon., *sea* . . . 122/C1
S. China, Phil., *sea* . . . 120/A3
S. China, Tai., *sea* . . . 117/A2
S. China, Maine, U.S., 325 . . . 286/C4
S. Chungcheong, S. Kor., *province* . . . 116/B4
S. Cle Elum, Wash., U.S., 457 . . . 358/E2
S. Cleveland, Tenn., U.S., 6,216 . . . 344/M4
S. Coatesville, Penn., U.S., 997 . . . 336/K6
S. Coffeyville, Okla., U.S., 790 . . . 330/G1
S. Colton, N.Y., U.S., 200 . . . 320/M1
S. Comino, Malta, *channel* . . . 97/B2
S. Congaree, S.C., U.S., 2,266 . . . 340/A3, C3
S. Connellsville, Penn., U.S., 2,281 . . . 336/B6
S. Corinth, Vt., U.S., 50 . . . 352/C2
S. Corning, N.Y., U.S., 1,147 . . . 320/G6
S. Cornish, N.H., U.S., 275 . . . 312/B5
S. Coventry, Conn., U.S. . . . 253/F2
S. Dakota, U.S., *state* . . . 330
S. Danbury, N.H., U.S., 50 . . . 312/C5
S. Danville, N.H., U.S. . . . 312/D6
S. Dartmouth, Mass., U.S., 1,900 . . . 292/L6
S. Dayton, N.Y., U.S., 662 . . . 320/C6
S. Daytona, Fla., U.S., 13,177 . . . 256/G2
S. Decatur, (part of Candler-McAfee), Ga., U.S. . . . 260/C4, J3
S. Deerfield, Mass., U.S., 1,868 . . . 292/D3
S. Deerfield, N.H., U.S. . . . 312/D5
S. Deer Isle, Maine, U.S. . . . 286/D4
S. Dennis, Mass., U.S., 3,679 . . . 292/P6
S. Dennis, N.J., U.S., 600 . . . 314/D5
S. Dorset, Vt., U.S., 125 . . . 352/A4
S. Dos Palos, Calif., U.S., 1,385 . . . 246/E6
S. Dover, Maine, U.S. . . . 286/C3
S. Downs, Eng., U.K., *hills* . . . 60/C3
S. Dublin, Ire., *county* . . . 78/C2
S. Dum-Dum, India . . . 128/Inset II
S. Duxbury, Mass., U.S., 3,062 . . . 292/M4
Southeast, R.I., U.S., *point* . . . 339/C7
S. Easton, Mass., U.S., 3,600 . . . 292/K4
Southeast Sulawesi, Indon., *province* . . . 122/D2
S. Egremont, Mass., U.S., 450 . . . 292/A4
S. Elgin, Ill., U.S., 16,100 . . . 266/A5, E2
S. Eliot, Maine, U.S., 3,445 . . . 286/B5
S. El Monte, Calif., U.S., 21,144 . . . 246/D9
Southend, Sask., Can., 696 . . . 227/G4
Southend, Scot., U.K. . . . 62/E8
Southend-on-Sea, Eng., U.K. . . . 60/D3
Southend-on-Sea, Eng., U.K., 158,517 . . . 70/F3
Southend-on-Sea, Eng., U.K., *unitary authority*, 160,256 . . . 70/F3
S. English, Iowa, U.S., 213 . . . 274/K5
Southern, Isr., *district* . . . 135/B2
Southern, Sri Lan., *province* . . . 126/B5
Southern, Zam., *province* . . . 159/B3
Southern Aegean, Gr., *region* . . . 100/C3
Southern Alps, N.Z., *mountains* . . . 171/A3
Southern Bug, Ukr., *river* . . . 102/B2
Southern Finland, Fin., *province* . . . 81/C2
Southern Mindanao, Phil., *region* . . . 120/C5
Southern Pines, N.C., U.S., 10,918 . . . 322/G4
Southern Shops, S.C., U.S., 3,707 . . . 340/F1
Southern Shores, N.C., U.S., 2,201 . . . 322/P2
Southern Tagalog, Phil., *region* . . . 120/B3
Southern Uplands, Scot., U.K., *mountains* . . . 60/B2
Southern Ute Ind. Res., Colo., U.S. . . . 250/C4
Southern View, Ill., U.S., 1,695 . . . 266/D4
Southery, Eng., U.K. . . . 70/E1
S. Euclid, Ohio, U.S., 23,537 . . . 328/H9
S. Fallsburg, N.Y., U.S., 2,061 . . . 320/M7
S. Ferriby, Eng., U.K. . . . 66/G5
Southfield, Mass., U.S., 100 . . . 292/B4
Southfield, Mich., U.S., 78,296 . . . 294/A6, F7
S. Fork, Colo., U.S., 604 . . . 250/D4
S. Fork, Ky., U.S. . . . 280/F3
S. Fork, Mo., U.S., 50 . . . 302/E5
S. Fork, Mont., U.S., *river* . . . 306/C2
S. Fork, Penn., U.S., 1,138 . . . 336/D5
S. Fork, S. Dak., U.S. . . . 342/B2
S. Fork Cheyenne, Wyo., U.S., *river* . . . 366/D2
S. Fork Powder, Wyo., U.S., *river* . . . 366/C2
S. Fork Republican, Colo., U.S., *river* . . . 250/G2
S. Foster, R.I., U.S., 225 . . . 339/B3
S. Fox, Mich., U.S., *island* . . . 294/D4
S. Fulton, Tenn., U.S., 2,517 . . . 344/D2
S. Gardiner, Maine, U.S., 50 . . . 286/C4
S. Gastonia, N.C., U.S., 5,433 . . . 322/C4
S. Gate, Calif., U.S., 96,375 . . . 246/C10
Southgate, Ky., U.S., 3,472 . . . 280/G1
S. Gate, Md., U.S., 28,672 . . . 288/H3
Southgate, Mich., U.S., 30,136 . . . 294/A7
S. Gifford, Mo., U.S., 72 . . . 302/D1
S. Glastonbury, Conn., U.S., 1,900 . . . 253/E3
Southglenn, Colo., U.S., 43,520 . . . 250/A3, F2
S. Glens Falls, N.Y., U.S., 3,368 . . . 320/P4
S. Gloucestershire, Eng., U.K., *unitary authority*, 245,644 . . . 73/H1
S. Gorin, Mo., U.S., 143 . . . 302/D1
S. Greeley, Wyo., U.S., 4,201 . . . 366/D3
S. Greenfield, Mo., U.S., 136 . . . 302/C4
S. Greensburg, Penn., U.S., 2,280 . . . 336/B5
S. Gut St-Anns, N.S., Can. . . . 221/G1
S. Gyeongsang, S. Kor., *province* . . . 116/C5
S. Hadley, Mass., U.S., 17,196 . . . 292/D3
S. Hadley Falls, Mass., U.S., 4,300 . . . 292/D4
S. Hamgyŏng, N. Kor., *province* . . . 116/B2
S. Haven, Ind., U.S., 5,619 . . . 270/B1
S. Haven, Kans., U.S., 390 . . . 276/E4
S. Haven, Mich., U.S., 5,021 . . . 294/C7
S. Haven, Minn., U.S., 204 . . . 298/C5
S. Hayling, Eng., U.K. . . . 70/C5
S. Heart, N. Dak., U.S., 307 . . . 326/C3
S. Henderson, N.C., U.S., 1,220 . . . 322/J2
S. Henik, Nun., Can., *lake* . . . 220/J4
S. Hero, Vt., U.S., 1,696 . . . 352/A1
S. Hill, N.Y., U.S., 6,003 . . . 320/H6
S. Hill, Va., U.S., 4,403 . . . 354/G7
S. Hiram, Maine, U.S., 900 . . . 286/B5
S. Holland, Neth., *province* . . . 84/B2
S. Holland, Ill., U.S., 22,147 . . . 266/C6
S. Hooksett, N.H., U.S., 5,282 . . . 312/D5
S. Houston, Tex., U.S., 15,833 . . . 346/B6
S. Hutchinson, Kans., U.S., 2,539 . . . 276/E3
S. Hwanghae, N. Kor., *province* . . . 116/A3
S. Indian Lake, Man., Can., 808 . . . 215/D1
Southington, Conn., U.S., 39,728 . . . 253/D3
S. Jacksonville, Ill., U.S., 3,475 . . . 266/C4
S. Jeolla, S. Kor., *province* . . . 116/B5
S. Jordan, Utah, U.S., 29,437 . . . 350/C3, E2
S. Junction, Oreg., U.S. . . . 334/E3
S. Kalimantan, Indon., *province* . . . 122/C2
S. Karelia, Fin., *region* . . . 81/C2
S. Kazakhstan, Kaz., *oblast* . . . 131/C2
S. Kelsey, Eng., U.K. . . . 66/H6
S. Kent, Conn., U.S., 225 . . . 253/B3
S. Killingly, Conn., U.S., 750 . . . 253/H2
S. Komelik, Ariz., U.S., 90 . . . 242/D6
S. Kona Forest Reserve, Hawaii, U.S. . . . 262/G6
S. Lagrange, Maine, U.S., 100 . . . 286/D3
S. Lake, P.E.I., Can. . . . 224/C2
S. Lake, Calif., U.S. . . . 246/G7
Southlake, Tex., U.S., 21,519 . . . 346/B9
S. Lake Tahoe, Calif., U.S., 23,609 . . . 246/F4
S. Lanarkshire, Scot., U.K., *unitary authority*, 302,216 . . . 62/J7
S. Lancaster, Mass., U.S., 1,742 . . . 292/H3
S. Lancing, Eng., U.K. . . . 70/D5
Southland, N.Z., *region* . . . 171/A4
Southland, Tex., U.S. . . . 346/G2
S. Lead Hill, Ark., U.S., 88 . . . 244/C1
S. Lebanon, Maine, U.S., 350 . . . 286/B5
S. Lebanon, Ohio, U.S., 2,538 . . . 328/C9
S. Levant, Maine, U.S., 125 . . . 286/D4
S. Leverton, Eng., U.K. . . . 66/G6
S. Lewis Harris and N. Uist N.P., Scot., U.K. . . . 62/B3
S. Lincoln, Maine, U.S., 150 . . . 286/D3
S. Lincoln, Vt., U.S., 100 . . . 352/B2
S. Lineville, Mo., U.S. . . . 302/C1
S. Lockport, N.Y., U.S., 8,552 . . . 320/D4
S. Londonderry, Vt., U.S., 100 . . . 352/B4
S. Lopham, Eng., U.K. . . . 70/F2
S. Loup, Nebr., U.S., *river* . . . 308/E2
S. Lubec, Maine, U.S., 100 . . . 286/F4
S. Lunenburg, Vt., U.S. . . . 352/D2
S. Lyndeborough, N.H., U.S., 275 . . . 312/C6
S. Lyon, Mich., U.S., 10,036 . . . 294/F7
S. Maalhosmadulu, Mald., *atoll* . . . 127/A2
S. Magnetic Pole, Antar. . . . 192/C3
S. Male, Mald., *atoll* . . . 127/A3
S. Manitou, Mich., U.S., *island* . . . 294/C4
S. Mansfield, La., U.S., 352 . . . 282/B2
S. Merrimack, N.H., U.S., 1,900 . . . 312/C6
S. Miami, Fla., U.S., 10,741 . . . 256/B6
S. Miami Hts., Fla., U.S., 33,522 . . . 256/A7
S. Middleboro, Mass., U.S., 750 . . . 292/L5
S. Milford, N.S., Can. . . . 221/B3
S. Mills, N.C., U.S., 700 . . . 322/N2
S. Milwaukee, Wisc., U.S., 21,256 . . . 364/F6, G2
Southminster, Eng., U.K., 3,374 . . . 70/F3
S. Molton, Eng., U.K., 4,066 . . . 73/E2
S. Monroe, Mich., U.S., 6,370 . . . 294/F8
Southmont, N.C., U.S., 850 . . . 322/E3
Southmont, Penn., U.S., 2,262 . . . 336/D5
S. Montrose, Penn., U.S., 400 . . . 336/K2
S. Moose, Man., Can., *lake* . . . 215/B2
S. Moresby Natl. Park Reserve, Br. Col., Can. . . . 214/G5
S. Mound, Kans., U.S., 80 . . . 276/G4
S. Nation, Ont., Can., *river* . . . 320/L1
S. New Berlin, N.Y., U.S., 400 . . . 320/L5
S. Newbury, Vt., U.S., 100 . . . 352/C2
S. New Castle, Penn., U.S., 808 . . . 336/A4
S. Newfane, Vt., U.S., 100 . . . 352/B5
S. Newport, Ga., U.S. . . . 260/J8
S. Nilandhe, Mald., *atoll* . . . 127/A3
S. Normanton, (S. Normanton/Pinxton), Eng., U.K., 13,044 . . . 68/E3
S. Northfield, Vt., U.S. . . . 352/B2
S. Nyack, N.Y., U.S., 3,473 . . . 320/B1
S. Ogden, Utah, U.S., 14,377 . . . 350/C2, E1
Southold, N.Y., U.S., 5,465 . . . 320/G1
S. Orange, (S. Orange Vil.), N.J., U.S., 16,964 . . . 314/B2
S. Orkney, Antar., *islands* . . . 192/C12
S. Orleans, Mass., U.S., 1,100 . . . 292/Q5
S. Orrington, Maine, U.S., 475 . . . 286/D4
S. Ossetia, Geo., *region* . . . 103/B3
S. Ostrobothnia, Fin., *region* . . . 81/B2
S. Otselic, N.Y., U.S., 300 . . . 320/K5
S. Otterington, Eng., U.K. . . . 66/F4
S. Padre Island, Tex., U.S., 2,422 . . . 346/L9
S. Palm Beach, Fla., U.S., 699 . . . 256/B5
S. Paris, Maine, U.S., 2,237 . . . 286/B4
S. Park View, Ky., U.S., 196 . . . 280/A2
S. Pasadena, Calif., U.S., 24,292 . . . 246/C9
S. Pasadena, Fla., U.S., 5,778 . . . 256/C7
S. Pass City, Wyo., U.S. . . . 366/B2
S. Peacham, Vt., U.S., 150 . . . 352/C2
S. Pekin, Ill., U.S., 1,162 . . . 266/D3
S. Penobscot, Maine, U.S., 125 . . . 286/D4
S. Perrott, Eng., U.K. . . . 73/G3
S. Perry, Ohio, U.S., 150 . . . 328/E6
S. Pickenham, Eng., U.K. . . . 70/F1
S. Pittsburg, Tenn., U.S., 3,295 . . . 344/K4
S. Plainfield, N.J., U.S., 21,810 . . . 314/E2
S. Platte, Colo., U.S. . . . 250/E2
S. Platte, Colo., U.S., *river* . . . 250/E2, G1
S. Point, Ohio, U.S., 3,742 . . . 328/E9
S. Pole, Antar. . . . 192/A17
S. Pomfret, Vt., U.S., 80 . . . 352/B3
S. Ponte Vedra Beach, Fla., U.S., 150 . . . 256/G1
Southport, P.E.I., Can. . . . 224/B2
Southport, Eng., U.K. . . . 60/C3
Southport, Eng., U.K., 90,959 . . . 66/B5
Southport, Eng., U.K., 90,959 . . . 68/B2
Southport, Fla., U.S., 1,500 . . . 256/C1
Southport, Ind., U.S., 1,852 . . . 270/D5
Southport, Maine, U.S., 684 . . . 286/C5
Southport, N.Y., U.S., 7,396 . . . 320/H6
Southport, N.C., U.S., 2,351 . . . 322/J7
S. Portland, Maine, U.S., 23,324 . . . 286/B5
S. Pottstown, Penn., U.S., 2,135 . . . 336/K5
S. Poultney, Vt., U.S., 80 . . . 352/A4
S. Prairie, Wash., U.S., 382 . . . 358/C2
S. Princeton, Maine, U.S. . . . 286/E3
S. P'yŏngan, N. Kor., *province* . . . 116/B3
S. Range, Mich., U.S., 727 . . . 294/A2
S. Range, Wisc., U.S., 250 . . . 364/B2
S. Rawdon, N.S., Can. . . . 221/D3
S. Reading, Vt., U.S., 60 . . . 352/B4
S. Renovo, Penn., U.S., 557 . . . 336/F3
Southrepps, Eng., U.K. . . . 70/G1
S. River, Ont., Can., 1,040 . . . 223/F2
S. River, N.J., U.S., 15,322 . . . 314/E3
S. Robbinston, Maine, U.S., 125 . . . 286/E3
S. Rockwood, Mich., U.S., 1,284 . . . 294/F7
S. Ronaldsay, Scot., U.K., *island* . . . 60/Inset I
S. Ronaldsay, Scot., U.K., *island* . . . 62/M2
S. Rosemary, N.C., U.S., 2,843 . . . 322/K2
S. Roxana, Ill., U.S., 1,888 . . . 266/A3
S. Royalston, Mass., U.S., 300 . . . 292/F2
S. Royalton, Vt., U.S., 800 . . . 352/B3
S. Russell, Ohio, U.S., 4,022 . . . 328/J9
S. Ryegate, Vt., U.S., 275 . . . 352/C2
S. St. Paul, Minn., U.S., 20,167 . . . 298/F6
S. Salem, Ohio, U.S., 213 . . . 328/D7
S. Salt Lake, Utah, U.S., 22,038 . . . 350/C3, E2
S. Sandisfield, Mass., U.S. . . . 292/B4
S. Sanford, Maine, U.S., 4,173 . . . 286/B5
S. San Francisco, Calif., U.S., 60,552 . . . 246/J2
S. Saskatchewan, Alta., Can., *river* . . . 212/E6
S. Saskatchewan, Sask., Can., *river* . . . 227/D8
S. Seaville, N.J., U.S., 600 . . . 314/D5
S. Shaftsbury, Vt., U.S., 772 . . . 352/A5
S. Shetland, Antar., *islands* . . . 192/C12
S. Shields, Eng., U.K. . . . 60/C2
S. Shields, Eng., U.K., 83,704 . . . 66/F3
S. Shore, Ky., U.S., 1,226 . . . 280/H2
S. Shore, S. Dak., U.S., 270 . . . 342/J2
Southside, Ala., U.S., 7,036 . . . 238/C2
Southside, W. Va., U.S. . . . 360/C3
Southside Place, Tex., U.S., 1,546 . . . 346/B6
S. Sioux City, Nebr., U.S., 11,925 . . . 308/H1
S. Skirlaugh, Eng., U.K. . . . 66/H5
S. Solon, Ohio, U.S., 405 . . . 328/C6
S. Springfield, Maine, U.S. . . . 286/D3
S. Strafford, Vt., U.S., 100 . . . 352/C3
S. Sulawesi, Indon., *province* . . . 122/C2
S. Sumatra, Indon., *province* . . . 122/B2
S. Sutton, N.H., U.S., 175 . . . 312/C5
S. Taft, Calif., U.S., 1,898 . . . 246/F7
S. Tamworth, N.H., U.S., 150 . . . 312/D4
S. Taranaki, N.Z., *bight* . . . 171/B2
S. Tetagouche, N.B., Can. . . . 217/D1
S. Toms River, N.J., U.S., 3,634 . . . 314/E4
S. Torrington, Wyo., U.S., 550 . . . 366/D2
S. Trescott, Maine, U.S., 40 . . . 286/E4
S. Truro, Mass., U.S. . . . 292/P5
S. Tucson, Ariz., U.S., 5,490 . . . 242/E5
S. Tunbridge, Vt., U.S., 90 . . . 352/B3
S. Tyneside, Eng., U.K., *unitary authority*, 152,785 . . . 66/F3
S. Uist, Scot., U.K., *island* . . . 60/A1
S. Uist, Scot., U.K., *island* . . . 62/B4
S. Uist Machair N.P., Scot., U.K. . . . 62/B4
S. Umpqua, Oreg., U.S., *river* . . . 334/C5
S. Vacherie, La., U.S., 3,543 . . . 282/H7
S. Venice, Fla., U.S., 13,539 . . . 256/F4
S. Vienna, Ohio, U.S., 469 . . . 328/C6
S. Wallingford, Vt., U.S., 100 . . . 352/B4
S. Wallins, Ky., U.S., 996 . . . 280/G4
S. Walpole, Mass., U.S., 1,900 . . . 292/J4
S. Wareham, Mass., U.S., 375 . . . 292/L5
Southwark, Eng., U.K., *unitary authority*, 244,867 . . . 70/D4
S. Waterford, Maine, U.S., 50 . . . 286/B4
S. Waverly, Penn., U.S., 987 . . . 336/H2
S. Wayne, Wisc., U.S., 484 . . . 364/D6
S. Weare, N.H., U.S., 375 . . . 312/C5
S. Weber, Utah, U.S., 4,260 . . . 350/E1
S. Webster, Ohio, U.S., 764 . . . 328/E8
S. Weldon, N.C., U.S., 1,414 . . . 322/K2
Southwell, Eng., U.K., 6,498 . . . 68/F3
S. Wellfleet, Mass., U.S., 500 . . . 292/P5
S. Wenatchee, Wash., U.S., 1,991 . . . 358/E2
South-West, Came., *province* . . . 153/A2
South West, N.Z., *cape* . . . 171/A4
Southwest, La., U.S., *pass* . . . 282/L8
South West City, Mo., U.S., 855 . . . 302/B5
South-West Finland, Fin., *region* . . . 81/B2
Southwest Harbor, Maine, U.S., 1,966 . . . 286/D4
Southwest Miramichi, N.B., Can., *river* . . . 217/C2
S. Westport, Mass., U.S., 600 . . . 292/K6
Southwest Rift Zone, Hawaii, U.S. . . . 262/G6
S. Weymouth, Mass., U.S., 11,100 . . . 292/L4
S. Whitley, Ind., U.S., 1,782 . . . 270/E2
S. Whittier, Calif., U.S., 55,193 . . . 246/D10
Southwick, Eng., U.K., 11,067 . . . 68/F4
Southwick, Eng., U.K., 11,067 . . . 70/B5
Southwick, Eng., U.K. . . . 70/D1
Southwick, Eng., U.K. . . . 70/D5
Southwick, Ida., U.S. . . . 264/A3
Southwick, Mass., U.S., 8,835 . . . 292/C4
S. Williamson, Ky., U.S., 600 . . . 280/H3
S. Williamsport, Penn., U.S., 6,412 . . . 336/G3
S. Willington, Conn., U.S., 1,700 . . . 253/F2
S. Wilmington, Ill., U.S., 621 . . . 266/E2
S. Windham, Conn., U.S., 1,278 . . . 253/G3
S. Windham, Maine, U.S., 1,792 . . . 286/B5
S. Windham, Vt., U.S., 70 . . . 352/B4
S. Windsor, Conn., U.S., 24,412 . . . 253/E2
S. Windsor, Maine, U.S. . . . 286/C4
Southwold, Eng., U.K., 3,905 . . . 70/H2
S. Wolfeboro, N.H., U.S., 350 . . . 312/D4
Southwood Acres, Conn., U.S., 8,067 . . . 253/E2
S. Woodbury, Vt., U.S., 200 . . . 352/C2
S. Woodham, Eng., U.K. . . . 70/F3
S. Woodstock, Conn., U.S., 1,211 . . . 253/H2
S. Woodstock, Maine, U.S., 125 . . . 286/B4
S. Woodstock, Vt., U.S., 200 . . . 352/B3
S. Woodville, Maine, U.S. . . . 286/D3
S. Wootton, Eng., U.K. . . . 70/E1
S. Worthington, Mass., U.S., 80 . . . 292/C3
S. Yarmouth, Mass., U.S., 11,603 . . . 292/P6
S. Yorkshire, Eng., U.K., *unitary authority*, 1,266,337 . . . 68/E2
S. Zanesville, Ohio, U.S., 1,936 . . . 328/G6
S. Zeal, Eng., U.K. . . . 73/E3
Soutra Mains, Scot., U.K. . . . 62/L7
Sovetskaya Gavan, Russ. . . . 104/I5
Soweto, S. Afr. . . . 162/C2
Soya, Jap., *cape* . . . 114/Inset I
Soyapango, El. Salv. . . . 203/A2
Soyo, Ang. . . . 159/B2
Sozh, Bela., *river* . . . 82/E3
Spa, Belg. . . . 85/D2
Spade, Tex., U.S. . . . 346/H3
Spain, *nation* . . . 92
Spalding, Eng., U.K., 18,731 . . . 68/G4
Spalding, Eng., U.K., 18,731 . . . 70/D1
Spalding, Ga., U.S., *county*, 58,417 . . . 260/C5
Spalding, Ida., U.S., 50 . . . 264/A3
Spalding, Mich., U.S., 475 . . . 294/B4
Spalding, Nebr., U.S., 537 . . . 308/E2
Spaldwick, Eng., U.K. . . . 70/D2
Spanaway, Wash., U.S., 21,588 . . . 358/C2
Spandau, Ger. . . . 86/C2
Spangle, Wash., U.S., 240 . . . 358/H2
Spangler, Penn., U.S. . . . 336/D4
Spanish, Ant.-Bar., *point* . . . 207/E2
Spanish, Ont., Can. . . . 223/C1
Spanish Fork, Utah, U.S., 20,246 . . . 350/C3
Spanish Fort, Ala., U.S., 5,423 . . . 238/B5
Spanish Fort, Tex., U.S., 60 . . . 346/L2
Spanish Lake, Mo., U.S., 21,337 . . . 302/J2
Spanish Town, Jam., 131,056 . . . 206/C3
Spar City, Colo., U.S. . . . 250/D4
Spargursville, Ohio, U.S., 175 . . . 328/D7
Sparkford, Eng., U.K. . . . 73/G2
Sparkman, Ark., U.S., 586 . . . 244/C4
Sparks, Colo., U.S. . . . 250/B1
Sparks, Ga., U.S., 1,755 . . . 260/E9
Sparks, Md., U.S., 1,800 . . . 288/H1
Sparks, Nebr., U.S. . . . 308/D1
Sparks, Nev., U.S., 66,346 . . . 310/A2
Sparks, Okla., U.S., 137 . . . 330/F2
Sparksville, Ind., U.S., 100 . . . 270/D7
Sparland, Ill., U.S., 504 . . . 266/D2
Sparlingville, Mich., U.S. . . . 294/G7
Sparr, Fla., U.S., 400 . . . 256/F2
Sparta, Gr. . . . 100/B3
Sparta, Ga., U.S., 1,522 . . . 260/F5
Sparta, Ill., U.S., 4,486 . . . 266/D5
Sparta, Ky., U.S., 230 . . . 280/F2
Sparta, Mich., U.S., 4,159 . . . 294/D6
Sparta, Mo., U.S., 1,144 . . . 302/C5
Sparta, N.J., U.S., 18,080 . . . 314/D1
Sparta, N.C., U.S., 1,817 . . . 322/C1
Sparta, Ohio, U.S., 191 . . . 328/E5
Sparta, Tenn., U.S., 4,599 . . . 344/L3
Sparta, Va., U.S., 100 . . . 354/J5
Sparta, Wisc., U.S., 8,648 . . . 364/C5
Spartanburg, S.C., U.S., 39,673 . . . 340/C2, F2
Spartanburg, S.C., U.S., *county*, 253,791 . . . 340/C2, F2
Spartansburg, Penn., U.S., 333 . . . 336/B2
Spartivento, It., *cape* . . . 95/D3
Sparwood, Br. Col., Can., 3,812 . . . 214/P6
Spatsizi Plateau Wilderness Prov. Park, Br. Col., Can. . . . 214/H2
Spaulding, Ill., U.S., 559 . . . 266/D4
Spaulding, Maine, U.S. . . . 286/D2
Spavinaw, Okla., U.S., 563 . . . 330/G1
Speaks, Tex., U.S. . . . 346/M6
Spean, Scot., U.K., *river* . . . 62/G5
Spean Bridge, Scot., U.K. . . . 62/G5
Spearfish, S. Dak., U.S., 8,606 . . . 342/B3
Spearman, Tex., U.S., 3,021 . . . 346/G8
Spearsville, La., U.S., 155 . . . 282/D1
Spearville, Kans., U.S., 813 . . . 276/C4
Spearwood, W.A., Austl. . . . 170/Inset I
Speculator, N.Y., U.S., 348 . . . 320/N3
Spedden, Alta., Can. . . . 212/E4
Speed, Kans., U.S., 44 . . . 276/C2
Speed, N.C., U.S., 70 . . . 322/L3
Speedway, Ind., U.S., 12,881 . . . 270/D5
Speedwell, Tenn., U.S., 125 . . . 344/P2
Speedwell, Va., U.S., 450 . . . 354/A7
Speer, Okla., U.S., 50 . . . 330/G3
Speers, Penn., U.S., 1,241 . . . 336/B5
Speight, Ky., U.S., 100 . . . 280/H3
Speightstown, Barb. . . . 209/A2
Speigner, Ala., U.S., 1,700 . . . 238/C3
Spencer, Austl., *gulf* . . . 170/C3
Spencer, Ida., U.S. . . . 264/E5
Spencer, Ind., U.S., 2,508 . . . 270/C6
Spencer, Ind., U.S., *county*, 20,391 . . . 270/B9
Spencer, Iowa, U.S., 11,317 . . . 274/D1
Spencer, Ky., U.S., *county*, 11,766 . . . 280/E2
Spencer, La., U.S., 90 . . . 282/E1
Spencer, Maine, U.S. . . . 286/B3
Spencer, Mass., U.S., 11,691 . . . 292/G3
Spencer, Mich., U.S., 100 . . . 294/D5

Spencer, Nebr., U.S., 541 . . . . .308/E1
Spencer, N.Y., U.S., 731 . . . . .320/J6
Spencer, Ohio, U.S., 747 . . . . .328/F3
Spencer, Okla., U.S., 3,746 . . . . .330/B3, E2
Spencer, S. Dak., U.S., 157 . . . . .342/H4
Spencer, Tenn., U.S., 1,713 . . . . .344/L3
Spencer, Va., U.S., 175 . . . . .354/C7
Spencer, W. Va., U.S., 2,352 . . . . .360/D3
Spencer, Wisc., U.S., 1,932 . . . . .364/C4
Spencer Mountain, N.C., U.S., 51 . . . . . . .322/C4
Spencerport, N.Y., U.S., 3,559 . . . . .320/F4
Spencerville, Ind., U.S., 350 . . . . .270/G2
Spencerville, (Cloverly), Md., U.S., 2,900 . . . .288/G3
Spencerville, Ohio, U.S., 2,235 . . . . .328/B4
Spencerville, Okla., U.S., 40 . . . . .330/G3
Spences Bridge, Br. Col., Can. 214/M6
Spennymoor, Eng., U.K., 17,381 . . . . .66/E3
Speonk, (Remsenburg-Speonk), N.Y.,
  U.S., 2,675 . . . . .320/F2
Sperrin, N. Ire., U.K., mountains 60/A2
Sperrin, N. Ire., U.K., mountains 65/C2
Sperrin, N. Ire., U.K., mountains 78/C1
Sperry, Okla., U.S., 981 . . . . .330/C1
Sperryville, Va., U.S., 250 . . . . .354/G3
Spessart, Ger., mountains 86/B4
Spetchley, Eng., U.K. 68/C5
Spey, Scot., U.K., river 60/B1
Spey, Scot., U.K., river 62/J4
Spey, Scot., U.K., river 62/K3
Spey Bay, Scot., U.K. 62/K3
Speyer, Ger. 86/B4
Spiceland, Ind., U.S., 807 . . . . .270/F5
Spicer, Minn., U.S., 1,126 . . . . .298/C5
Spickard, Mo., U.S., 315 . . . . .302/C1
Spillertown, Ill., U.S., 220 . . . . .266/E6
Spillville, Iowa, U.S., 386 . . . . .274/L1
Spilsby, Eng., U.K., 2,434 . . . . .68/H3
Spindale, N.C., U.S., 4,022 . . . . .322/B4
Spink, S. Dak., U.S., 60 . . . . .342/J5
Spink, S. Dak., U.S., county, 7,454 . . . . . .342/G3
Spirit, Iowa, U.S., lake 274/D1
Spirit Lake, Ida., U.S., 1,376 . . . . .264/A2
Spirit Lake, Iowa, U.S., 4,261 . . . . .274/D1
Spirit Lake I.R., N. Dak., U.S. 326/F2
Spirit River, Alta., Can., 1,100 . . . . .212/A3
Spiritwood, Sask., Can., 907 . . . . .227/C7
Spiritwood, N. Dak., U.S., 50 . . . . .326/G3
Spiritwood Lake, N. Dak., U.S., 72 . . . . . .326/G2
Spiro, Okla., U.S., 2,227 . . . . .330/M2
Spišská Nová Ves, Slvk. 92/C2
Spithead, Eng., U.K., channel 60/C4
Spittal, Wales, U.K. 64/B4
Spittal an der Drau, Aus. 91/C4
Spittal of Glenshee, Scot., U.K. 62/K5
Spivey, Kans., U.S., 80 . . . . .276/C4
Spiveys Corner, N.C., U.S., 448 . . . . .322/J4
Split, Cro., 175,140 . . . . .98/C3
Split Lake, Man., Can. 215/D1
Splügen, Switz., pass 90/D2
Spofford, N.H., U.S., 500 . . . . .312/B6
Spofford, Tex., U.S., 75 . . . . .346/H6
Spofforth, Eng., U.K. 66/F5
Spokane, Mo., U.S., 133 . . . . .302/C5
Spokane, Wash., U.S., 195,629,
  (417,939 metro.) 358/H2
Spokane, Wash., U.S., county, 417,939 . . .358/H2
Spokane, Wash., U.S., river 358/H2
Spokane Ind. Res., Wash., U.S. 358/G2
Spoleto, It. 95/C2
Spoon, Ill., U.S., river 266/C3
Spooner, Wisc., U.S., 2,653 . . . . .364/B3
Sporting Club, Mon. 97/C1
Sportsmen Acres, Okla., U.S., 204 . . . . . .330/G1
Spotswood, N.J., U.S., 7,880 . . . . .314/E3
Spotsylvania, (Spotsylvania Courthouse),
  Va., U.S., 3,833 . . . . .354/H4
Spotsylvania, Va., U.S., county, 90,395 . . .354/H4
Spotted Horse, Wyo., U.S. 366/D1
Spottsville, Ky., U.S., 600 . . . . .280/C3
Spout Sprs., N.C., U.S., 550 . . . . .322/G4
Spraberry, Tex., U.S., 125 . . . . .346/E4
Sprague, Ont., Can. 223/C1
Sprague, Man., Can. 215/D4
Sprague, Ala., U.S., 50 . . . . .238/C3
Sprague, Nebr., U.S., 146 . . . . .308/H3
Sprague, Wash., U.S., 490 . . . . .358/H2
Sprague River, Oreg., U.S. 334/E5
Spragueville, Iowa, U.S., 89 . . . . .274/P3
Spragueville, Maine, U.S. 286/D2
Spragueville, R.I., U.S., 300 . . . . .339/C2
Spratt, Mich., U.S., 60 . . . . .294/F5
Spratton, Eng., U.K. 68/F5
Spray, Oreg., U.S., 140 . . . . .334/G3
Spread Eagle, Wisc., U.S., 250 . . . . .364/E3
Spree, Ger., river 86/C3
Spreyton, Eng., U.K. 73/E3
Spring, Tex., U.S., 36,385 . . . . .346/B5
Spring Arbor, Mich., U.S., 2,188 . . . . .294/E7
Spring Bay, Ont., Can. 223/C2
Spring Bay, Ill., U.S., 436 . . . . .266/D3
Springbok, S. Afr. 162/A2
Springboro, Ohio, U.S., 12,380 . . . . .328/B6
Springboro, Penn., U.S., 491 . . . . .336/A2
Springbrook, Iowa, U.S., 182 . . . . .274/P3
Springbrook, N. Dak., U.S. 326/B1
Springbrook, Wisc., U.S., 60 . . . . .364/B3
Spring City, Penn., U.S., 3,305 . . . . .336/K5
Spring City, Tenn., U.S., 2,025 . . . . .344/M3
Spring City, Utah, U.S., 956 . . . . .350/C4
Spring Coulee, Alta., Can. 212/D6
Spring Creek, Nev., U.S., 10,548 . . . . .310/C1
Spring Creek, Okla., U.S. 330/D2
Spring Creek, S. Dak., U.S., 136 . . . . .342/D4
Spring Creek, Va., U.S. 354/E4
Springdale, Nfld., Can., 3,045 . . . . .218/C4
Springdale, Ark., U.S., 45,798 . . . . .244/A1
Springdale, Mont., U.S., 40 . . . . .306/F4
Springdale, Ohio, U.S., 10,563 . . . . .328/B9
Springdale, (Lancaster County),
  S.C., U.S., 2,864 . . . . .340/D2
Springdale, (Lexington County),
  S.C., U.S., 2,877 . . . . .340/A3, C3
Springdale, Utah, U.S., 457 . . . . .350/B6
Springdale, Wash., U.S., 283 . . . . .358/H1
Springer, N. Mex., U.S., 1,285 . . . . .317/F1
Springer, Okla., U.S., 577 . . . . .330/E3
Springerton, Ill., U.S., 134 . . . . .266/E5
Springerville, Ariz., U.S., 1,972 . . . . .242/F3
Springfield, N.B., Can. 217/D3
Springfield, N. Ire., U.K. 65/B3
Springfield, Ark., U.S., 90 . . . . .244/C2
Springfield, Colo., U.S., 1,562 . . . . .317/H4
Springfield, Fla., U.S., 8,810 . . . . .256/C1
Springfield, Ga., U.S., 1,821 . . . . .260/J7
Springfield, Ida., U.S. 264/E6
Springfield, Ill., U.S., state capital,
  111,454, (201,437 metro.) 266/D4
Springfield, Ky., U.S., 2,634 . . . . .280/E3
Springfield, La., U.S., 395 . . . . .282/H6
Springfield, Maine, U.S., 379 . . . . .286/D3

Springfield, Mass., U.S., 152,082,
  (591,932 metro.) 292/D4
Springfield, Mich., U.S., 5,189 . . . . .294/D7
Springfield, Minn., U.S., 2,215 . . . . .298/C6
Springfield, Mo., U.S., 151,580,
  (325,721 metro.) 302/C4
Springfield, Nebr., U.S., 1,450 . . . . .308/H2
Springfield, N.H., U.S., 945 . . . . .312/B5
Springfield, (Union County),
  N.J., U.S., 14,429 . . . . .314/A2, E2
Springfield, Ohio, U.S., 65,358 . . . . .328/C6
Springfield, Oreg., U.S., 52,864 . . . . .334/D3
Springfield, Penn., U.S., 23,677 . . . . .336/L7
Springfield, S.C., U.S., 504 . . . . .340/C4
Springfield, S. Dak., U.S., 792 . . . . .342/H5
Springfield, Tenn., U.S., 14,329 . . . . .344/H1
Springfield, Vt., U.S. 352/C4
Springfield, Va., U.S., 30,417 . . . . .354/M2
Springfield, W. Va., U.S., 400 . . . . .360/J2
Springfield Armory N.H.S., Mass., U.S. 292/D4
Spring Garden, Va., U.S., 175 . . . . .354/E7
Spring Garden Estates, (Discovery-Spring Garden),
  Md., U.S., 2,400 . . . . .288/E2
Spring Glen, Utah, U.S., 1,000 . . . . .350/D4
Spring Green, Wisc., U.S., 1,444 . . . . .364/C5
Spring Grove, Ill., U.S., 3,880 . . . . .266/A4
Spring Grove, Ind., U.S., 386 . . . . .270/C5
Spring Grove, Minn., U.S., 1,304 . . . . .298/F7
Spring Grove, Penn., U.S., 2,050 . . . . .336/H6
Spring Grove, Va., U.S. 354/K6
Spring Hall, Barb. 209/A2
Springhill, N.S., Can., 4,091 . . . . .221/C2
Springhill, P.E.I., Can. 224/B2
Spring Hill, Ala., U.S., 150 . . . . .238/D4
Spring Hill, Ark., U.S. 244/B4
Spring Hill, Fla., U.S., 69,078 . . . . .256/F3
Spring Hill, Ind., U.S., 97 . . . . .270/D5
Spring Hill, Iowa, U.S., 92 . . . . .274/G5
Spring Hill, Kans., U.S., 2,727 . . . . .276/H3
Springhill, La., U.S., 5,439 . . . . .282/C1
Spring Hill, Minn., U.S., 55 . . . . .298/C5
Spring Hill, Tenn., U.S., 7,715 . . . . .344/H3
Spring Hope, N.C., U.S., 1,261 . . . . .322/J3
Spring Lake, Ind., U.S., 262 . . . . .270/E5
Spring Lake, Mich., U.S., 2,514 . . . . .294/C6
Spring Lake, Minn., U.S. 298/D3
Spring Lake, N.J., U.S., 3,567 . . . . .314/E3
Spring Lake, N.C., U.S., 8,098 . . . . .322/H4
Springlake, Tex., U.S., 135 . . . . .346/F1
Spring Lake Hts., N.J., U.S., 5,227 . . . . . . .314/E3
Spring Lake Park, Minn., U.S., 6,772 . . . . .298/F5
Springlee, Ky., U.S., 426 . . . . .280/B2
Spring Mill, Ky., U.S., 380 . . . . .280/D2
Spring Mills, Penn., U.S., 289 . . . . .336/H4
Spring Mts. N.R.A., Nev., U.S. 310/C3
Springport, Ind., U.S., 174 . . . . .270/F4
Springport, Mich., U.S., 704 . . . . .294/E7
Springs, S. Afr. 162/C2
Springs, N.Y., U.S., 4,950 . . . . .320/G1
Springside, Sask., Can., 525 . . . . .227/H9
Springstead, Wisc., U.S., 60 . . . . .364/C2
Springstein, Man., Can. 215/C4
Springtown, Ark., U.S., 114 . . . . .244/A1
Springtown, N.J., U.S., 250 . . . . .314/C5
Spring Valley, Vic., Austl. . . . . .170/Inset V
Springvale, Vic., Austl. . . . . .170/Inset V
Springvale, Maine, U.S., 3,488 . . . . .286/B5
Spring Valley, Ark., U.S., 50 . . . . .244/B1
Spring Valley, Calif., U.S., 26,663 . . . . . . .246/J10
Spring Valley, Ill., U.S., 5,398 . . . . .266/C3
Spring Valley, Minn., U.S., 2,518 . . . . .298/E7
Spring Valley, Nev., U.S., 117,390 . . . . . . .310/C3
Spring Valley, N.Y., U.S., 25,464 . . . . .320/B1
Spring Valley, Ohio, U.S., 510 . . . . .328/B6
Spring Valley, Tex., U.S., 3,611 . . . . .346/A6
Spring Valley, Wisc., U.S., 1,189 . . . . .364/A4
Springview, Nebr., U.S., 244 . . . . .308/E1
Springville, Ala., U.S., 2,521 . . . . .238/C2
Springville, Iowa, U.S., 1,091 . . . . .274/M3
Springville, Miss., U.S., 90 . . . . .300/C1
Springville, N.Y., U.S., 4,252 . . . . .320/D5
Springville, Penn., U.S., 325 . . . . .336/K2
Springville, Utah, U.S., 20,424 . . . . .350/C3
Springwater, Sask., Can. 227/B9
Springwater, N.Y., U.S., 700 . . . . .320/F5
Sprott, Ala., U.S. 238/B3
Sproul St. For., Penn., U.S. 336/F3
Sprouston, Scot., U.K. 62/M7
Sprout, Ky., U.S. 280/G2
Sprowston, Eng., U.K. 70/G1
Spruce, Mich., U.S., 125 . . . . .294/F5
Spruce Grove, Alta., Can., 15,983 . . . . . . .212/D4
Spruce Head, Maine, U.S., 300 . . . . .286/C5
Spruce Knob, W. Va., U.S., mountain 354/D3
Spruce Knob, W. Va., U.S., peak 360/G3
Spruce Knob-Seneca Rocks Natl. Rec. Area,
  W. Va., U.S. .354/E3
Spruce Knob-Seneca Rocks Natl. Rec. Area,
  W. Va., U.S. .360/H3
Spruce Pine, N.C., U.S., 2,030 . . . . .322/A3
Spruce Woods Prov. Park, Man., Can. 215/B4
Spry, Utah, U.S. 350/B6
Spur, Tex., U.S., 1,088 . . . . .346/H2
Spurgeon, Ind., U.S., 227 . . . . .270/B8
Spurgeon, Tenn., U.S. 344/S2
Spurlockville, W. Va., U.S., 150 . . . . .360/B4
Spy Hill, Sask., Can., 213 . . . . .227/J10
Squam, N.H., U.S., lake 312/C4
Squamish, Br. Col., Can., 14,247 . . . . .214/L6
Squantum, N.H., U.S., 400 . . . . .312/C6
Squa Pan, Maine, U.S. 286/D2
Squa Pan, Maine, U.S., lake 286/D2
Square Butte, Mont., U.S. 306/F2
Square Islands, Nfld., Can. 218/D3
Squaw Brook, Maine, U.S. 286/C3
Squaw Lake, Minn., U.S., 99 . . . . .298/C3
Squaw Valley, Calif., U.S., 2,691 . . . . .246/F6
Squire, W. Va., U.S., 100 . . . . .360/C6
Squires, Mo., U.S. 302/D5
Srê Âmbĕl, Camb. 124/B4
Srebrenica, Bos.-Her. 98/C1
Sredna Gora, Bul., mountains 101/C3
Sremska Mitrovica, Serb.-Mont. 99/A2
Srĕng, Camb., river 124/B2
Srĕpŏk, Viet., river 123/B4
Sri Jayawardenepura, Sri Lan., capital 126/A5
Sri Lanka, nation 122
Srinagar, India, 594,775, (606,002 metro.) . .128/B2
Srinagarind, Thai., reservoir 125/B3
Staatsburg, N.Y., U.S., 911 . . . . .320/P7
Stackpole, Wales, U.K. 64/B4
Stacy, Minn., U.S., 1,278 . . . . .298/E5
Stacy, Tex., U.S. 346/J4
Stacy, Va., U.S., 275 . . . . .354/D2
Stacyville, Iowa, U.S., 469 . . . . .274/J1
Stacyville, Maine, U.S., 405 . . . . .286/D3
Staden København, Den., county 79/D3
Stadhampton, Eng., U.K. 70/B3
Staffin, Scot., U.K. 62/D3
Stafford, Eng., U.K. 60/C3

Stafford, Eng., U.K., 61,885 . . . . .68/C4
Stafford, Conn., U.S., 11,307 . . . . .253/F2
Stafford, Kans., U.S., 1,161 . . . . .276/D4
Stafford, Kans., U.S., county, 4,789 . . . . . .276/D3
Stafford, Ohio, U.S., 86 . . . . .328/H6
Stafford, Okla., U.S., 40 . . . . .330/C2
Stafford, Tex., U.S., 15,681 . . . . .346/A7
Stafford, Va., U.S., 3,000 . . . . .354/J4
Stafford, Va., U.S., county, 92,446 . . . . . . .354/H4
Staffordshire, Eng., U.K., unitary authority,
  806,737 . . . . .68/C4
Stafford Sprs., Conn., U.S., 4,100 . . . . . . .253/F2
Stafford Sprs., Miss., U.S., 175 . . . . .300/D4
Staffordville, Conn., U.S., 550 . . . . .253/F2
Staffordville, N.J., U.S., 425 . . . . .314/E4
Stagecoach, Tex., U.S., 455 . . . . .346/A5
Staindrop, Eng., U.K. 66/D3
Staines, Eng., U.K., 51,167 . . . . .70/C4
Stainmore, Eng., U.K., forest 66/D4
Stalbridge, Eng., U.K., 2,344 . . . . .73/H3
Staley, N.C., U.S., 347 . . . . .322/F3
Stalisfield Green, Eng., U.K. 70/F4
Stallings, N.C., U.S., 3,189 . . . . .322/D4
Stallo, Miss., U.S., 125 . . . . .300/C3
Stalwart, Mich., U.S., 60 . . . . .294/E3
Stambaugh, Mich., U.S., 1,243 . . . . .294/A3
Stamford, Eng., U.K., 17,492 . . . . .70/D1
Stamford, Conn., U.S., 117,083 . . . . .253/A5
Stamford, Nebr., U.S., 202 . . . . .308/E3
Stamford, N.Y., U.S., 1,265 . . . . .320/M6
Stamford, S. Dak., U.S. 342/D4
Stamford, Tex., U.S., 3,636 . . . . .346/J3
Stamford, Vt., U.S. 352/A5
Stamford Bridge, Eng., U.K., 3,099 . . . . . .66/G5
Stamford Bridge, Eng., U.K., 3,099 . . . . . .68/F2
Stamfordham, Eng., U.K. 66/E2
Stamping Ground, Ky., U.S., 566 . . . . .280/F2
Stamps, Ark., U.S., 2,131 . . . . .244/B4
Stanaford, W. Va., U.S., 1,443 . . . . .360/D5
Stanardsville, Va., U.S., 476 . . . . .354/G4
Stanberry, Mo., U.S., 1,243 . . . . .302/B1
Standard, Alta., Can., 389 . . . . .212/D5
Standard, Ill., U.S., 256 . . . . .266/D2
Standard, La., U.S., 250 . . . . .282/E3
Standard City, Ill., U.S., 138 . . . . .266/D4
Standford, Eng., U.K. 70/C4
Standing Indian, N.C., U.S. 322/C8
Standing Pine, Miss., U.S., 509 . . . . .300/C3
Standing Rock, N. Mex., U.S., 60 . . . . .317/B2
Standing Rock Ind. Res., S. Dak., U.S. 342/D2
Standish, Eng., U.K., 12,196 . . . . .66/C5
Standish, Eng., U.K., 12,196 . . . . .68/B2
Standish, Mass., U.S., 425 . . . . .292/L4
Standish, Mich., U.S., 1,581 . . . . .294/F6
Stand Off, Alta., Can. 212/D6
Standon, Eng., U.K., 2,731 . . . . .68/G4
Standon, Eng., U.K., 2,731 . . . . .70/B4
Standrod, Utah, U.S., 40 . . . . .350/A2
Stanfield, Eng., U.K. 70/F1
Stanfield, Ariz., U.S., 651 . . . . .242/D5
Stanfield, N.C., U.S., 1,113 . . . . .322/E4
Stanford, Oreg., U.S., 1,979 . . . . .334/G2
Stanford, Calif., U.S., 13,315 . . . . .246/J3
Stanford, Ill., U.S., 670 . . . . .266/D3
Stanford, Ky., U.S., 3,430 . . . . .280/F3
Stanford, Mont., U.S., 454 . . . . .306/F2
Stanford in the Vale, Eng., U.K., 1,708 . . . .70/A3
Stanford-le-Hope, (Stanford Le Hope/Corringham),
  Eng., U.K., 30,747 . . . . .70/E3
Stanhoe, Eng., U.K. 70/F1
Stanhope, Eng., U.K., 1,342 . . . . .66/D3
Stanhope, Iowa, U.S., 488 . . . . .274/G3
Stanhope, N.J., U.S., 3,584 . . . . .314/D2
Stanion, Eng., U.K. 68/G5
Stanislaus, Calif., U.S., county, 446,997 . .246/D5, L3
Stanislaus Natl. For., Calif., U.S. 246/E4
Stanley, N.B., Can., 460 . . . . .217/C2
Stanley, Eng., U.K., 18,905 . . . . .66/E3
Stanley, Ida., U.S., 100 . . . . .264/C5
Stanley, Iowa, U.S., 128 . . . . .274/L2
Stanley, Kans., U.S. 276/H1, H3
Stanley, Ky., U.S., 400 . . . . .280/C3
Stanley, La., U.S., 145 . . . . .282/B3
Stanley, Mass., U.S. 292/L4
Stanley, N. Mex., U.S. 317/E2
Stanley, N.C., U.S., 3,053 . . . . .322/C4
Stanley, N. Dak., U.S., 1,279 . . . . .326/C1
Stanley, Okla., U.S. 330/G3
Stanley, S. Dak., U.S., county, 2,772 . . . . .342/E3
Stanley, Va., U.S., 1,326 . . . . .354/F3
Stanley, Wisc., U.S., 1,898 . . . . .364/B4
Stanley Corner, S. Dak., U.S. 342/H4
Stanleytown, Va., U.S., 1,515 . . . . .354/D7
Stanleyville, (see Winston-Salem), N.C., U.S. . .322/E2
Stanly, N.C., U.S., county, 58,100 . . . . . . .322/E4
Stanmore, Alta., Can. 212/E5
Stannard, Vt., U.S. 352/C1
Stannards, N.Y., U.S., 868 . . . . .320/F6
Stanovoy, Russ., range 104/H4
Stansbury Park, Utah, U.S., 2,385 . . . . . . .350/B3
Stansted Mountfitchet, Eng., U.K., 4,943 . .70/E3
Stanton, Eng., U.K., 2,131 . . . . .70/F2
Stanton, Eng., U.K., 2,131 . . . . .73/H1
Stanton, Ala., U.S., 90 . . . . .238/C3
Stanton, Calif., U.S., 37,403 . . . . .246/D10
Stanton, Del., U.S., 5,000 . . . . .253/A3
Stanton, Iowa, U.S., 714 . . . . .274/D6
Stanton, Kans., U.S., county, 2,406 . . . . . .276/A4
Stanton, Ky., U.S., 3,029 . . . . .280/G3
Stanton, Mich., U.S., 1,504 . . . . .294/D6
Stanton, Minn., U.S., 100 . . . . .298/D6
Stanton, Miss., U.S., 275 . . . . .300/A4
Stanton, Mo., U.S., 225 . . . . .302/E3
Stanton, Nebr., U.S., 1,627 . . . . .308/G2
Stanton, Nebr., U.S., county, 6,455 . . . . . .308/G2
Stanton, N.J., U.S., 500 . . . . .314/D2
Stanton, N. Dak., U.S., 345 . . . . .326/D2
Stanton, Tenn., U.S., 615 . . . . .344/C4
Stanton, Tex., U.S., 2,556 . . . . .346/G3
Stanton Harcourt, Eng., U.K. 70/B3
Stanton St. John, Eng., U.K. 68/E6
Stantonsburg, N.C., U.S., 726 . . . . .322/J3
Stantonville, Tenn., U.S., 312 . . . . .344/F4
Stanwood, Iowa, U.S., 680 . . . . .274/M4
Stanwood, Mich., U.S., 204 . . . . .294/D6
Stanwood, Wash., U.S., 3,923 . . . . .358/C1
Stapleford, Eng., U.K. 70/B1
Stapleford, Eng., U.K. 73/J2
Staplehurst, Nebr., U.S., 270 . . . . .308/G3
Staples, Eng., U.K. 70/B5
Staples, Minn., U.S., 3,104 . . . . .298/C4
Stapleton, Ala., U.S., 375 . . . . .238/B5
Stapleton, Ga., U.S., 318 . . . . .260/G5
Stapleton, Nebr., U.S., 301 . . . . .308/D2
Star, Idaho, U.S., 1,795 . . . . .264/A6
Star, Miss., U.S., 600 . . . . .300/B3
Star, N.C., U.S., 807 . . . . .322/F4
Star, Tex., U.S., 60 . . . . .346/K4
Stara Zagora, Bul., 173,200 . . . . .101/D3

Stara Zagora, Bul., oblast 101/D3
Starboard, Maine, U.S., 225 . . . . .286/E4
Starbuck, Man., Can. 215/C4
Starbuck, Kiri., island 175/D2
Starbuck, Minn., U.S., 1,314 . . . . .298/B5
Starbuck, Wash., U.S., 130 . . . . .358/G4
Star City, Sask., Can., 482 . . . . .227/F8
Star City, Ark., U.S., 2,471 . . . . .244/D4
Star City, Ind., U.S., 377 . . . . .270/C3
Star City, W. Va., U.S., 1,366 . . . . .360/G1
Starcross, Eng., U.K. 73/F3
Star Cross, N.J., U.S., 1,400 . . . . .314/C4
Star Hill, Del., U.S., 600 . . . . .255/B4
Stark, Ill., U.S., county, 6,332 . . . . .266/D2
Stark, Kans., U.S., 106 . . . . .276/C4
Stark, N. Dak., U.S., county, 22,636 . . . . . .326/C3
Stark, Ohio, U.S., county, 378,098 . . . . . . .328/H4
Stark City, Mo., U.S., 156 . . . . .302/B5
Starke, Fla., U.S., 5,593 . . . . .256/F2
Starke, Ind., U.S., county, 23,556 . . . . . . .270/C2
Starkey, Oreg., U.S. 334/H2
Starkey, Va., U.S., 600 . . . . .354/E6
Starks, La., U.S., 650 . . . . .282/B6
Starks, Maine, U.S., 578 . . . . .286/C4
Starks, Wisc., U.S., 90 . . . . .364/D3
Starksboro, Vt., U.S. 352/A2
Starkville, Colo., U.S., 128 . . . . .250/F4
Starkville, Miss., U.S., 21,869 . . . . .300/D2
Starkweather, N. Dak., U.S., 157 . . . . .326/G1
Star Lake, N. Mex., U.S., 150 . . . . .317/C2
Star Lake, N.Y., U.S., 860 . . . . .320/L2
Star Lake, Wisc., U.S. 364/D2
Starnberg, Ger., lake 86/B5
Star Prairie, Wisc., U.S., 574 . . . . .364/A3
Starr, S.C., U.S., 173 . . . . .340/B2
Starr, Tex., U.S., county, 53,597 . . . . .346/K9
Starr School, Mont., U.S., 248 . . . . .306/C1
Starrs Mill, Ga., U.S., 275 . . . . .260/C5
Start, Eng., U.K., point 60/B4
Start, La., U.S., 475 . . . . .282/E2
Startex, S.C., U.S., 988 . . . . .340/F2
Startforth, Eng., U.K. 66/E3
Star Valley, Ariz., U.S., 550 . . . . .242/D3
State Bridge, Colo., U.S., 60 . . . . .250/D2
State College, Penn., U.S., 38,420,
  (135,758 metro.) 336/F4
State Ctr., Iowa, U.S., 1,349 . . . . .274/H3
State Line, Ida., U.S. 264/A2
State Line, Ky., U.S., 60 . . . . .280/A2
State Line, Miss., U.S., 555 . . . . .300/D4
Stateline, Nev., U.S., 1,215 . . . . .310/A2
State Line, N.H., U.S., 60 . . . . .312/B6
State Line City, Ind., U.S., 141 . . . . .270/A4
Staten, N.Y., U.S., island 320/A3
Statenville, Ga., U.S., 50 . . . . .260/F1
State Road, Maine, U.S., 100 . . . . .286/D2
State Road, N.C., U.S. 322/D2
Statesboro, Ga., U.S., 22,698 . . . . .260/H4
Statesville, N.C., U.S., 23,320 . . . . .322/D3
Statesville, Tenn., U.S. 344/J2
Statham, Ga., U.S., 2,040 . . . . .260/D4
Statue of Liberty N.M., N.Y., U.S. 314/A2
Statue of Liberty N.M., N.Y., U.S. 320/A2
Staubbach, Switz., falls 90/B2
Staunton, Eng., U.K. 68/C6
Staunton, Ill., U.S., 5,030 . . . . .266/B3, D4
Staunton, Va., U.S., 23,853 . . . . .354/F4
Staunton-on-Wye, Eng., U.K. 68/B5
Stavanger, Nor., 162,983 . . . . .80/B4
Staveley, (Derbyshire), Eng., U.K., 27,665 . .68/E3
Staveley, Eng., U.K., 27,665 . . . . .66/F6
Stavely, Alta., Can., 442 . . . . .212/D6
Staverton, Eng., U.K. 70/B2
Staves, Ark., U.S., 125 . . . . .244/C3
Stavropol', Russ., 342,642, (342,700 metro.) . .104/D5
Staxton, Eng., U.K. 66/H4
Staylittle, Wales, U.K. 64/D2
Stayner, Ont., Can., 3,885 . . . . .223/E3
Stayton, Oreg., U.S., 6,816 . . . . .334/D3
Stead, Man., Can. 215/C4
Stead, N. Mex., U.S. 317/C1
Steamboat, Nev., U.S., 1,100 . . . . .310/A2
Steamboat, Oreg., U.S. 334/D4
Steamboat Canyon, Ariz., U.S., 1,100 . . . .242/F2
Steamboat Rock, Iowa, U.S., 336 . . . . . . .274/H3
Steamboat Sprs., Colo., U.S., 9,815 . . . . . .250/D1
Steamtown N.H.S., Penn., U.S. 337/H7
Stearns, Ky., U.S., 1,586 . . . . .280/F4
Stearns, Minn., U.S., county, 133,166 . . . . .298/C5
Stebbins, Alaska, U.S., 547 . . . . .240/C2
Stecker, Okla., U.S., 100 . . . . .330/D3
Stedman, N.C., U.S., 664 . . . . .322/H4
Steele, Ala., U.S., 1,093 . . . . .238/C2
Steele, Minn., U.S., county, 33,680 . . . . . .298/D6
Steele, Mo., U.S., 2,263 . . . . .302/G5
Steele, N. Dak., U.S. 761 . . . . .326/F3
Steele, N. Dak., U.S., county, 2,258 . . . . . .326/H2
Steele City, Nebr., U.S., 84 . . . . .308/G3
Steeleville, Ill., U.S., 2,077 . . . . .266/D5
Steelton, Penn., U.S., 5,858 . . . . .336/H5
Steelville, Mo., U.S., 1,429 . . . . .302/E4
Steen, Minn., U.S., 182 . . . . .298/A7
Steen River, Alta., Can. 212/B1
Steens, Miss., U.S., 70 . . . . .300/D2
Steens, Oreg., U.S., mountain 334/H5
Steens Mtn. Cooperative Management and
  Protection Area, Oreg., U.S. 334/H5
Steeple, Eng., U.K. 70/C4
Steeple Aston, Eng., U.K. 70/B3
Steeple Bumpstead, Eng., U.K. 70/E2
Steeple Claydon, Eng., U.K., 2,269 . . . . . .70/C3
Steeple Morden, Eng., U.K. 70/D2
Steese Natl. Cons. Area, Alaska, U.S. 240/F1
Stefanson, Nun., Can., island 220/G2
Steger, Ill., U.S., 9,682 . . . . .266/F2
Stehekin, Wash., U.S., 60 . . . . .358/E1
Steilacoom, Wash., U.S., 6,049 . . . . .358/C2
Steinauer, Nebr., U.S., 74 . . . . .308/H3
Steinbach, Man., Can., 9,227 . . . . .215/C4
Steinhatchee, Fla., U.S., 700 . . . . .256/E2
Steinkjer, Nor. .80/C3
Steins, N. Mex., U.S. 317/B5
Stella, Ky., U.S., 300 . . . . .280/B4
Stella, Mo., U.S., 178 . . . . .302/B5
Stella, Nebr., U.S., 220 . . . . .308/J3
Stellarton, N.S., Can., 4,809 . . . . .221/E2
Stellenbosch, S. Afr. 162/A3
Stem, N.C., U.S., 229 . . . . .322/H2
Stendal, Ger. 86/B2
Stenness, Scot., U.K. 62/K1
Stennett, Iowa, U.S., 40 . . . . .274/D5
Stepanakert, (Xankändi), Azer. 103/B3
Step'anavan, Arm. 103/B2
Stephan, S. Dak., U.S. 342/H3
Stephen, Minn., U.S., 708 . . . . .298/A2
Stephens, Ark., U.S., 1,152 . . . . .244/B4
Stephens, Ga., U.S., county, 25,435 . . . . . .260/E3

Sudbourne 627

Stephens, Okla., U.S., *county*, 43,182 . . . 330/E3
Stephens, Tex., U.S., *county*, 9,674 . . . 346/K3
Stephensburg, Ky., U.S., 325 . . . 280/D3
Stephens City, Va., U.S., 1,146 . . . 354/G2
Stephenson, Ill., U.S., *county*, 48,979 . . . 266/D1
Stephenson, Mich., U.S., 875 . . . 294/B4
Stephensport, Ky., U.S., 80 . . . 280/D3
Stephenville, Nfld., Can., 7,109 . . . 218/B5
Stephenville, Tex., U.S., 14,921 . . . 346/K3
Steprock, Ark., U.S., 50 . . . 244/D2
Steptoe, Nev., U.S. . . . 310/C2
Steptoe, Wash., U.S., 60 . . . 358/H3
Sterling, Colo., U.S., 11,360 . . . 250/G1
Sterling, Conn., U.S., 3,099 . . . 253/H3
Sterling, Ga., U.S., 550 . . . 260/H9
Sterling, Ida., U.S. . . . 264/E6
Sterling, Ill., U.S., 15,451 . . . 266/D2
Sterling, Kans., U.S., 2,642 . . . 276/D3
Sterling, Mass., U.S., 7,257 . . . 292/G3
Sterling, Mich., U.S., 533 . . . 294/E5
Sterling, Nebr., U.S., 507 . . . 308/H3
Sterling, N. Dak., U.S., 70 . . . 326/E3
Sterling, Okla., U.S., 762 . . . 330/D3
Sterling, Tex., U.S., *county*, 1,393 . . . 346/G4
Sterling, Utah, U.S., 235 . . . 350/C4
Sterling, Va., U.S., 20,500 . . . 354/J2, L1
Sterling City, Tex., U.S., 1,081 . . . 346/H4
Sterling Hts., Mich., U.S., 124,471 . . . 294/B6, F7
Sterling Run, Penn., U.S., 40 . . . 336/E3
Sterlington, La., U.S., 1,276 . . . 282/E1
Sterrett, Ala., U.S., 325 . . . 238/C2
Stetson, Maine, U.S., 981 . . . 286/C4
Stetsonville, Wisc., U.S., 563 . . . 364/C3
Stettler, Alta., Can., 5,215 . . . 212/D5
Steuben, Ind., U.S., *county*, 33,214 . . . 270/F1
Steuben, Maine, U.S., 1,126 . . . 286/E4
Steuben, Mich., U.S. . . . 294/C3
Steuben, N.Y., U.S., *county*, 98,726 . . . 320/G6
Steuben, Wisc., U.S., 177 . . . 364/C5
Steubenville, Ky., U.S., 550 . . . 280/F4
Steubenville, Ohio, U.S., 19,015, (132,008 *metro.*) . . . 328/J5
Stevenage, Eng., U.K. . . . 60/Inset III
Stevenage, Eng., U.K., 76,064 . . . 70/D3
Stevens, Kans., U.S., *county*, 5,463 . . . 276/A4
Stevens, Minn., U.S., *county*, 10,053 . . . 298/A5
Stevens, Wash., U.S., *county*, 40,066 . . . 358/H1
Stevens Creek, Va., U.S., 550 . . . 354/B7
Stevenson, Man., Can., *lake* . . . 215/C2
Stevenson, Ala., U.S., 1,770 . . . 238/D1
Stevenson, Conn., U.S., 800 . . . 253/C4
Stevenson, Wash., U.S., 1,200 . . . 358/D4
Stevens Pt., Wisc., U.S., 24,551 . . . 364/D4
Stevens Pottery, Ga., U.S., 350 . . . 260/E6
Stevenstown, Wisc., U.S., 80 . . . 364/B4
Stevensville, Md., U.S., 5,880 . . . 288/J4
Stevensville, Mich., U.S., 1,191 . . . 294/C7
Stevensville, Mont., U.S., 1,553 . . . 306/B3
Stevensville, Penn., U.S., 125 . . . 336/J2
Stevensville, Va., U.S., 40 . . . 354/K5
Stevensville South, Md., U.S. . . . 288/J4
Steventon, Eng., U.K. . . . 70/B3
Steward, Ill., U.S., 271 . . . 266/D2
Stewardson, Ill., U.S., 747 . . . 266/E4
Stewart, Br. Col., Can., 661 . . . 214/H3
Stewart, Yukon, Can., *river* . . . 228/B4, C3
Stewart, N.Z., *island* . . . 171/A4
Stewart, Ga., U.S., 300 . . . 260/D5
Stewart, Ga., U.S., *county*, 5,252 . . . 260/B7
Stewart, (Lake County), Minn., U.S., 40 . . . 298/F3
Stewart, (McLeod County), Minn., U.S., 564 . . . 298/C6
Stewart, Miss., U.S., 175 . . . 300/C2
Stewart, Ohio, U.S., 225 . . . 328/G7
Stewart, Tenn., U.S., *county*, 12,370 . . . 344/F2
Stewart B. McKinney N.W.R., Conn., U.S. . . . 253/B5, E5
Stewartby, Eng., U.K. . . . 70/D2
Stewart Lake N.W.R., N. Dak., U.S. . . . 326/B3
Stewarton, Scot., U.K., 6,582 . . . 62/H7
Stewart River, Yukon, Can. . . . 228/B4
Stewarts Pt., Calif., U.S. . . . 246/B4
Stewartstown, N. Ire., U.K., 649 . . . 65/D2
Stewartstown, N.H., U.S., 1,012 . . . 312/D2
Stewartstown, Penn., U.S., 1,752 . . . 336/H6
Stewartstown Hollow, N.H., U.S., 50 . . . 312/D2
Stewartsville, Mo., U.S., 759 . . . 302/B2
Stewartsville, N.J., U.S., 650 . . . 314/C2
Stewartville, Ala., U.S., 425 . . . 238/C2
Stewartville, Minn., U.S., 5,411 . . . 298/E7
Stewiacke, N.S., Can., 1,388 . . . 221/D2
Steyr, Aus. . . . 91/D2
Stibb Cross, Eng., U.K. . . . 73/D3
Stickney, N.B., Can. . . . 217/B2
Stickney, Eng., U.K. . . . 68/H3
Stickney, Ill., U.S., 6,148 . . . 266/B6
Stickney, S. Dak., U.S., 334 . . . 342/G4
Stickney Corner, Maine, U.S., 150 . . . 286/C4
Stidham, Okla., U.S. . . . 330/G2
Stiffkey, Eng., U.K. . . . 70/F1
Stigler, Okla., U.S., 2,731 . . . 330/G2
Stikine, Br. Col., Can. . . . 214/G3
Stikine, Br. Col., Can., *river* . . . 214/G2
Stikine, Alaska, U.S., *river* . . . 240/J3
Stiles, Iowa, U.S. . . . 274/K6
Stiles, Tex., U.S., 40 . . . 346/G4
Stiles, Wisc., U.S., 200 . . . 364/E4
Stilesville, Ind., U.S., 261 . . . 270/C5
Stilligarry, Scot., U.K. . . . 62/B4
Stillington, Eng., U.K. . . . 66/F4
Stillman Valley, Ill., U.S., 1,048 . . . 266/D1
Stillmore, Ga., U.S., 730 . . . 260/G7
Still Pond, Md., U.S., 325 . . . 288/K2
Still River, Mass., U.S., 400 . . . 292/H3
Stillwater, Maine, U.S., 1,600 . . . 286/D4
Stillwater, Minn., U.S., 15,143 . . . 298/E5
Stillwater, Mont., U.S., *county*, 8,195 . . . 306/G4
Stillwater, Nev., U.S., 50 . . . 310/A2
Stillwater, N.J., U.S., 4,267 . . . 314/D1
Stillwater, N.Y., U.S., 1,644 . . . 320/P5
Stillwater, N.Y., U.S., *reservoir* . . . 320/L3
Stillwater, Ohio, U.S., 150 . . . 328/H5
Stillwater, Okla., U.S., 39,065 . . . 330/E1
Stillwater, Penn., U.S., 194 . . . 336/J3
Stillwater N.W.R., Nev., U.S. . . . 310/A2
Stillwell, Ga., U.S., 80 . . . 260/J7
Stillwell, Ind., U.S., 375 . . . 270/C1
Stilson, Ga., U.S., 80 . . . 260/H7
Stilson, Iowa, U.S. . . . 274/G1
Stilton, Eng., U.K., 2,219 . . . 68/G5
Stilton, Eng., U.K., 2,219 . . . 70/D2
Stilwell, Kans., U.S., 1,200 . . . 276/H3
Stilwell, Okla., U.S., 3,276 . . . 330/H2
Stimson Crossing, Wash., U.S., 773 . . . 358/C1
Stinesville, Ind., U.S., 194 . . . 270/C6
Stinnett, Ky., U.S., 250 . . . 280/G3
Stinnett, Tex., U.S., 1,936 . . . 346/F8
Stinson Lake, N.H., U.S. . . . 312/C4
Štip, Mac. . . . 100/C2
Stippville, Kans., U.S., 125 . . . 276/H4
Stirling, S.A., Austl. . . . 170/Inset II
Stirling, W.A., Austl. . . . 170/Inset I
Stirling, Alta., Can., 877 . . . 212/D6
Stirling, Ont., Can., 2,149 . . . 223/H3
Stirling, Scot., U.K. . . . 60/B2
Stirling, Scot., U.K., 32,673 . . . 62/J6
Stirling, Scot., U.K., *unitary authority*, 86,212 . . . 62/H6
Stirrat, W. Va., U.S., 90 . . . 360/B5
Stites, Ida., U.S., 226 . . . 264/B3
Stithian's, Eng., U.K., *reservoir* . . . 73/B4
Stitzer, Wisc., U.S., 175 . . . 364/C6
Stock, Eng., U.K., 2,097 . . . 70/E3
Stockbridge, Eng., U.K. . . . 70/B4
Stockbridge, Ga., U.S., 9,853 . . . 260/C4, J3
Stockbridge, Mass., U.S., 2,276 . . . 292/A3
Stockbridge, Mich., U.S., 1,260 . . . 294/E7
Stockbridge, Vt., U.S. . . . 352/B3
Stockbridge, Wisc., U.S., 649 . . . 364/E4
Stockbridge-Munsee Ind. Comm., Wisc., U.S. . . . 364/E4
Stockcross, Eng., U.K. . . . 70/B4
Stockdale, Ohio, U.S., 150 . . . 328/E8
Stockdale, Penn., U.S., 555 . . . 336/B5
Stockdale, Tex., U.S., 1,398 . . . 346/B3, L6
Stockerau, Aus. . . . 91/E2
Stockerston, Eng., U.K. . . . 70/C1
Stockertown, Penn., U.S., 687 . . . 336/L4
Stockett, Mont., U.S., 200 . . . 306/E2
Stockham, Nebr., U.S., 60 . . . 308/G3
Stockholm, Swe., *capital*, 754,948, (1,664,910 *metro.*) . . . 80/C3
Stockholm, Swe., *capital* . . . 193/D1
Stockholm, Swe., *county* . . . 80/C3
Stockholm, Maine, U.S., 271 . . . 286/D1
Stockholm, N.J., U.S., 200 . . . 314/D1
Stockholm, S. Dak., U.S., 105 . . . 342/J2
Stockholm, Wisc., U.S., 97 . . . 364/A4
Stockland, Ill., U.S., 100 . . . 266/F3
Stockport, Eng., U.K., 132,813 . . . 66/D6
Stockport, Eng., U.K., 132,813 . . . 68/C3
Stockport, Eng., U.K., *unitary authority*, 284,544 . . . 66/D6
Stockport, Eng., U.K., *unitary authority*, 284,544 . . . 68/C3
Stockport, Iowa, U.S., 284 . . . 274/L6
Stockport, Ohio, U.S., 540 . . . 328/G6
Stocks, Eng., U.K., *reservoir* . . . 66/C5
Stocks, Eng., U.K., *reservoir* . . . 68/B2
Stocksbridge, Eng., U.K., 13,182 . . . 66/E6
Stocksbridge, Eng., U.K., 13,182 . . . 68/D3
Stockton, Eng., U.K. . . . 70/B2
Stockton, Ala., U.S., 225 . . . 238/B4
Stockton, Calif., U.S., 243,771, (563,598 *metro.*) . . . 246/D5, L1
Stockton, Ga., U.S., 100 . . . 260/F1
Stockton, Ill., U.S., 1,926 . . . 266/C1
Stockton, Iowa, U.S., 182 . . . 274/N4
Stockton, Kans., U.S., 1,558 . . . 276/C2
Stockton, Md., U.S., 143 . . . 288/N7
Stockton, Minn., U.S., 682 . . . 298/F6
Stockton, Mo., U.S., 1,960 . . . 302/C4
Stockton, Mo., U.S., *lake* . . . 302/C4
Stockton, N.J., U.S., 560 . . . 314/D3
Stockton, Tex., U.S., *plateau* . . . 346/F5
Stockton, Utah, U.S., 443 . . . 350/B3
Stockton, Wisc., U.S., *island* . . . 364/C2
Stockton-on-Tees, Eng., U.K., 83,576 . . . 66/F3
Stockton-on-Tees, Eng., U.K., *unitary authority*, 178,405 . . . 66/F3
Stockton Sprs., Maine, U.S., 1,481 . . . 286/D4
Stockville, Nebr., U.S. . . . 308/D3
Stockwell, Ind., U.S., 425 . . . 270/C4
Stockwith, Eng., U.K. . . . 66/G6
Stoddard, Mo., U.S., *county*, 29,705 . . . 302/F5
Stoddard, N.H., U.S., 928 . . . 312/B5
Stoddard, Wisc., U.S., 815 . . . 364/B5
Stody, Eng., U.K. . . . 70/G1
Stoeng Trêng, Camb. . . . 124/D2
Stoke, Eng., U.K. . . . 70/F4
Stoke, Eng., U.K. . . . 73/J2
Stoke Albany, Eng., U.K. . . . 70/C2
Stoke Ash, Eng., U.K. . . . 70/G2
Stoke-by-Nayland, Eng., U.K. . . . 70/F3
Stoke Goldington, Eng., U.K. . . . 70/C2
Stokenchurch, Eng., U.K., 3,775 . . . 68/F6
Stokenchurch, Eng., U.K., 3,775 . . . 70/C3
Stoke-on-Trent, Eng., U.K. . . . 60/C3
Stoke-on-Trent, Eng., U.K., 266,543, (367,976 *metro.*) . . . 68/C3
Stoke-on-Trent, Eng., U.K., *unitary authority*, 240,643 . . . 68/C3
Stoke Prior, Eng., U.K. . . . 68/C5
Stokes, N.C., U.S., *county*, 44,711 . . . 322/E2
Stokesby, Eng., U.K. . . . 70/H1
Stokesdale, N.C., U.S., 3,267 . . . 322/F2
Stokesley, Eng., U.K., 4,008 . . . 66/F4
Stokes St. For., N.J., U.S. . . . 314/D1
Stone, (Staffordshire), Eng., U.K., 12,305 . . . 68/C4
Stone, Ark., U.S., *county*, 11,499 . . . 244/C2
Stone, Ida., U.S. . . . 264/E7
Stone, Miss., U.S., *county*, 13,622 . . . 300/C5
Stone, Mo., U.S., *county*, 28,658 . . . 302/C5
Stoneboro, Penn., U.S., 1,104 . . . 336/A3
Stone City, Colo., U.S. . . . 250/F3
Stonecliffe, Ont., Can. . . . 223/H1
Stone Creek, Ohio, U.S., 184 . . . 328/G5
Stonefort, Ill., U.S., 292 . . . 266/E6
Stonega, Va., U.S., 475 . . . 354/C2
Stoneham, Que., Can. . . . 226/E4
Stoneham, Colo., U.S. . . . 250/G1
Stoneham, Mass., U.S., 22,219 . . . 292/C6, K3
Stone Harbor, N.J., U.S., 1,128 . . . 314/D5
Stonehaven, Scot., U.K., 9,577 . . . 62/M5
Stone Lake, Wisc., U.S., 225 . . . 364/B3
Stonely, Eng., U.K. . . . 70/D2
Stone Mountain, Ga., U.S., 7,145 . . . 260/C4, J2
Stone Mtn. Prov. Park, Br. Col., Can. . . . 214/K2
Stone Mtn. St. Park, Ga., U.S. . . . 260/K2
Stone Park, Ill., U.S., 5,127 . . . 266/B6
Stoner, Colo., U.S. . . . 250/B4
Stones River Natl. Bfld., Tenn., U.S. . . . 344/J3
Stoneville, N.C., U.S., 1,002 . . . 322/F2
Stoneville, S. Dak., U.S. . . . 342/C3
Stonewall, Man., Can., 4,012 . . . 215/C4
Stonewall, Ark., U.S., 70 . . . 244/E1
Stonewall, Colo., U.S., 40 . . . 250/E4
Stonewall, La., U.S., 1,668 . . . 282/B2
Stonewall, Miss., U.S., 1,149 . . . 300/D3
Stonewall, N.C., U.S., 285 . . . 322/M4
Stonewall, Okla., U.S., 465 . . . 330/F3
Stonewall, Tex., U.S., *county*, 1,693 . . . 346/H2
Stonewood, W. Va., U.S., 1,815 . . . 360/F2
Stoney Pt., Ont., Can., 1,316 . . . 223/C5
Stonington, Colo., U.S. . . . 250/H4
Stonington, Conn., U.S., 17,906 . . . 253/H4
Stonington, Ill., U.S., 960 . . . 266/D4
Stonington, Maine, U.S., 1,152 . . . 286/D4
Stony, N.Y., U.S., *island* . . . 320/J3
Stony, N.Y., U.S., *point* . . . 320/J3
Stony Brook, N.Y., U.S., 13,727 . . . 320/D2
Stony Creek, Conn., U.S., 900 . . . 253/E4
Stony Creek, Va., U.S., 202 . . . 354/J7
Stonyford, Calif., U.S., 40 . . . 246/C3
Stony Mountain, Man., Can., 1,700 . . . 215/C4
Stony Plain, Alta., Can., 9,589 . . . 212/D4
Stony Pt., Mich., U.S., 1,775 . . . 294/F8
Stony Pt., N.Y., U.S., 11,744 . . . 320/B1
Stony Pt., N.C., U.S., 1,380 . . . 322/C3
Stony Rapids, Sask., Can., 189 . . . 227/E1
Stony Stratford, Eng., U.K. . . . 70/C2
Storå, Den., *river* . . . 79/B2
Storavan, Swe. . . . 80/C1
Storden, Minn., U.S., 274 . . . 298/B6
Store, Den., *strait* . . . 79/C3
Storey, Nev., U.S., *county*, 3,399 . . . 310/A2
Storkerson, Nun., Can., *peninsula* . . . 220/G2
Storla, S. Dak., U.S. . . . 342/G4
Storm, Iowa, U.S., *lake* . . . 274/D2
Storm Lake, Iowa, U.S., 10,076 . . . 274/D2
Storm Lake N.W.R., N. Dak., U.S. . . . 326/H3
Stormont, Dundas, and Glengarry, Ont., Can., *county* . . . 223/L2
Stornoway, Que., Can., 606 . . . 226/E6
Stornoway, Scot., U.K. . . . 60/A1
Stornoway, Scot., U.K. . . . 62/D2
Storrie, Calif., U.S. . . . 246/D3
Storrs, Conn., U.S., 10,996 . . . 253/F2
Storsjön, Swe., *lake* . . . 80/B2, C3
Storstrøm, Den., *county* . . . 79/C4
Storthoaks, Man., Can. . . . 215/A4
Story, Ark., U.S., 40 . . . 244/B3
Story, Iowa, U.S., *county*, 79,981 . . . 274/H4
Story, Wyo., U.S., 887 . . . 366/C1
Story City, Iowa, U.S., 3,228 . . . 274/G3
Stotesbury, Mo., U.S., 43 . . . 302/B4
Stotfold, Eng., U.K., 6,524 . . . 68/G5
Stotfold, Eng., U.K., 6,524 . . . 70/D2
Stotts City, Mo., U.S., 250 . . . 302/C4
Stottville, N.Y., U.S., 1,355 . . . 320/P6
Stoughton, Sask., Can., 720 . . . 227/G11
Stoughton, Mass., U.S., 27,149 . . . 292/K4
Stoughton, Wisc., U.S., 12,354 . . . 364/D6
Stoulton, Eng., U.K. . . . 68/C5
Stourbridge, Eng., U.K., 55,624 . . . 68/C5
Stourpaine, Eng., U.K. . . . 73/H3
Stourport-on-Severn, Eng., U.K., 18,283 . . . 68/C5
Stout, Eng., U.K., *river* . . . 70/F2
Stout, Iowa, U.S., 217 . . . 274/J2
Stoutland, Mo., U.S., 177 . . . 302/D4
Stoutsville, Mo., U.S., 44 . . . 302/E2
Stoutsville, Ohio, U.S., 581 . . . 328/E6
Stovall, Miss., U.S. . . . 300/B1
Stovall, N.C., U.S., 376 . . . 322/H2
Stover, Mo., U.S., 968 . . . 302/D3
Stow, Eng., U.K. . . . 68/F3
Stow, Scot., U.K., 548 . . . 62/L7
Stow, Maine, U.S., 288 . . . 286/A4
Stow, Mass., U.S., 5,902 . . . 292/H3
Stow, Ohio, U.S., 32,139 . . . 328/H3
Stowe, Penn., U.S., 3,585 . . . 336/K5
Stowe, Vt., U.S. . . . 352/B2
Stowmarket, Eng., U.K., 13,229 . . . 70/F2
Stow-on-the-Wold, Eng., U.K., 1,999 . . . 68/D6
Stoy, Ill., U.S., 119 . . . 266/F5
Stoystown, Penn., U.S., 428 . . . 336/D5
Straad, Scot., U.K. . . . 62/F7
Strabane, N. Ire., U.K., 11,981 . . . 65/C2
Strabane, N. Ire., U.K., *unitary authority*, 38,248 . . . 65/C2
Strachan, Scot., U.K. . . . 62/L4
Stradbroke, Eng., U.K. . . . 70/G2
Stradsett, Eng., U.K. . . . 70/E1
Strafford, Mo., U.S., 1,845 . . . 302/C4
Strafford, N.H., U.S., 3,626 . . . 312/D5
Strafford, N.H., U.S., *county*, 112,233 . . . 312/D5
Strafford, Vt., U.S. . . . 352/C3
Strahan, Iowa, U.S., 40 . . . 274/D6
Straight, Okla., U.S. . . . 330/C4
Straiton, Scot., U.K. . . . 62/G8
Straitsville, Conn., U.S., 1,000 . . . 253/C4
Strakonice, Czh. Rep. . . . 92/A3
Straloch, Scot., U.K. . . . 62/J5
Stralsund, Ger. . . . 86/C1
Strandburg, S. Dak., U.S., 69 . . . 342/J2
Strandquist, Minn., U.S., 88 . . . 298/A2
Strang, Nebr., U.S. . . . 308/G3
Strang, Okla., U.S., 100 . . . 330/G1
Strange Creek, W. Va., U.S., 80 . . . 360/E3
Strangford, N. Ire., U.K., 548 . . . 65/F3
Strangford, N. Ire., U.K., *bay* . . . 78/D1
Strangford, N. Ire., U.K., *lake* . . . 65/F2
Stranraer, Scot., U.K. . . . 60/B2
Stranraer, Scot., U.K., 10,851 . . . 62/F9
Strasbourg, Sask., Can., 760 . . . 227/F9
Strasbourg, Fr., 267,051, (427,245 *metro.*) . . . 88/D2
Strasburg, Colo., U.S., 1,402 . . . 250/F2
Strasburg, Ill., U.S., 603 . . . 266/E4
Strasburg, Mo., U.S., 136 . . . 302/B3
Strasburg, N. Dak., U.S., 549 . . . 326/E3
Strasburg, Ohio, U.S., 2,310 . . . 328/G4
Strasburg, Penn., U.S., 2,800 . . . 336/J6
Strasburg, Va., U.S., 4,017 . . . 354/G3
Stratford, Ont., Can., 29,676 . . . 223/D4
Stratford, (Stratford-Centre), Que., Can. . . . 226/E6
Stratford, Calif., U.S., 1,264 . . . 246/F6
Stratford, Conn., U.S., 49,976 . . . 253/C5
Stratford, Conn., U.S., *point* . . . 253/C5
Stratford, Iowa, U.S., 746 . . . 274/G3
Stratford, N.H., U.S., 942 . . . 312/C2
Stratford, N.J., U.S., 7,271 . . . 314/B3, C4
Stratford, Okla., U.S., 1,474 . . . 330/F3
Stratford, S. Dak., U.S., 96 . . . 342/G2
Stratford, Tex., U.S., 1,991 . . . 346/F8
Stratford, Va., U.S. . . . 354/K4
Stratford, Wash., U.S. . . . 358/F2
Stratford, Wisc., U.S., 1,523 . . . 364/C4
Stratford St. Mary, Eng., U.K. . . . 70/F3
Stratford-upon-Avon, Eng., U.K. . . . 60/C3
Stratford-upon-Avon, Eng., U.K., 22,231 . . . 68/D5
Stratham, N.H., U.S., 6,355 . . . 312/E5
Strathan, Scot., U.K. . . . 62/H1
Strathcarron, Scot., U.K. . . . 62/F4
Strathclair, Man., Can. . . . 215/A4
Strathcoil, Scot., U.K. . . . 62/E6
Strathcona, Minn., U.S. . . . 298/A2
Strathcona Prov. Park, Br. Col., Can. . . . 214/K6
Strathconon Forest, Scot., U.K. . . . 62/F4
Strathdon, Scot., U.K. . . . 62/K4
Strath Kanaird, Scot., U.K. . . . 62/F3
Strathlorne, N.S., Can. . . . 221/F1
Strathmere, N.J., U.S., 175 . . . 314/D5
Strathmoor Manor, Ky., U.S., 333 . . . 280/A2
Strathmoor Vil., Ky., U.S., 625 . . . 280/A2
Strathmore, Alta., Can., 7,621 . . . 212/D5
Strathmore, Calif., U.S., 2,584 . . . 246/F6
Strathmore, N.J., U.S., 6,740 . . . 314/E3
Strathnaver, Br. Col., Can. . . . 214/L4
Strathroy, Ont., Can., 12,805 . . . 223/D5
Strathy, Scot., U.K. . . . 62/J1
Strathyre, Scot., U.K. . . . 62/H6
Stratmoor Hills, (Stratmoor), Colo., U.S., 6,650 . . . 250/F3
Strattanville, Penn., U.S., 542 . . . 336/C3
Stratton, Eng., U.K., 2,298 . . . 73/C3
Stratton, Colo., U.S., 669 . . . 250/H2
Stratton, Maine, U.S., 425 . . . 286/B3
Stratton, Nebr., U.S., 396 . . . 308/C3
Stratton, Ohio, U.S., 277 . . . 328/J4
Stratton Audley, Eng., U.K. . . . 70/B3
Straubing, Ger. . . . 86/C4
Straughn, Ind., U.S., 263 . . . 270/F5
Strausstown, Penn., U.S., 339 . . . 336/J5
Strawberry, Ariz., U.S., 1,028 . . . 242/D3
Strawberry, Ark., U.S., 283 . . . 244/D2
Strawberry, Calif., U.S., 125 . . . 246/F4
Strawberry, Oreg., U.S., *mountain* . . . 334/H3
Strawberry, Utah, U.S., *river* . . . 350/D3
Strawberry Pt., Iowa, U.S., 1,386 . . . 274/L2
Strawn, Ill., U.S., 104 . . . 266/E3
Strawn, Tex., U.S., 739 . . . 346/K3
Streamwood, Ill., U.S., 36,407 . . . 266/A5
Streatham, Eng., U.K. . . . 70/D4
Streatley, Eng., U.K. . . . 70/D3
Streator, Ill., U.S., 14,190 . . . 266/E2
Středočeský, Czh. Rep., *region* . . . 92/B3
Street, Eng., U.K., 10,539 . . . 73/G2
Streeter, N. Dak., U.S., 172 . . . 326/F3
Streeter, Tex., U.S. . . . 346/J5
Streetsboro, Ohio, U.S., 12,311 . . . 328/J10
Strensall, Eng., U.K., 4,432 . . . 66/F4
Strensall, Eng., U.K., 4,432 . . . 68/E1
Strete, Eng., U.K. . . . 73/E4
Stretford, Eng., U.K., 43,953 . . . 66/D6
Stretford, Eng., U.K., 43,953 . . . 68/C3
Stretham, Eng., U.K., 1,471 . . . 68/H5
Stretham, Eng., U.K., 1,471 . . . 70/E2
Stretton, Eng., U.K. . . . 70/C1
Strevell, Ida., U.S. . . . 264/D7
Streymoy, Den., *island* . . . 79/Inset
Strichen, Scot., U.K., 879 . . . 62/M3
Stringer, Miss., U.S., 125 . . . 300/C4
Stringtown, Okla., U.S., 396 . . . 330/F3
Stroh, Ind., U.S., 700 . . . 270/F1
Stroma, Scot., U.K., *island* . . . 62/K1
Stromboli, It., *island* . . . 95/C3
Stromeferry, Scot., U.K. . . . 62/E4
Stromness, Scot., U.K., 1,609 . . . 62/L2
Stromsburg, Nebr., U.S., 1,232 . . . 308/G2
Stronach, Mich., U.S., 350 . . . 294/C5
Stroner, Wyo., U.S. . . . 366/D1
Strong, Ark., U.S., 651 . . . 244/C4
Strong, Maine, U.S., 1,259 . . . 286/B4
Strong, Miss., U.S. . . . 300/D2
Strong City, Kans., U.S., 584 . . . 276/F3
Strong City, Okla., U.S., 42 . . . 330/C2
Stronghurst, Ill., U.S., 896 . . . 266/C3
Strongs, Mich., U.S. . . . 294/E3
Strongsville, Ohio, U.S., 43,858 . . . 328/G3, G9
Stronsay, Scot., U.K., *island* . . . 60/Inset I
Stronsay, Scot., U.K., *island* . . . 62/N1
Strontian, Scot., U.K. . . . 62/E5
Stroud, Eng., U.K., 38,835 . . . 68/C6
Stroud, Ala., U.S., 60 . . . 238/D2
Stroud, Okla., U.S., 2,758 . . . 330/F2
Stroudsburg, Penn., U.S., 5,756 . . . 336/L4
Struble, Iowa, U.S., 85 . . . 274/B2
Struga, Mac. . . . 100/A2
Strum, Wisc., U.S., 1,001 . . . 364/B4
Struma, Bul., *river* . . . 101/A3
Struma, Gr., *river* . . . 100/B1
Strumica, Mac. . . . 100/C2
Struthers, Ohio, U.S., 11,756 . . . 328/J3
Stryama, Bul., *river* . . . 101/C3
Stryker, Mont., U.S. . . . 306/B1
Stryker, Ohio, U.S., 1,406 . . . 328/B2
Stuart, Br. Col., Can., *lake* . . . 214/K4
Stuart, Fla., U.S., 14,633 . . . 256/A3, H4
Stuart, Iowa, U.S., 1,712 . . . 274/F4
Stuart, Nebr., U.S., 625 . . . 308/E1
Stuart, Okla., U.S., 220 . . . 330/F3
Stuart, Va., U.S., 961 . . . 354/C7
Stuart, Wash., U.S., *mountain* . . . 358/E2
Stuarts Draft, Va., U.S., 8,367 . . . 354/E4
Stubbs, St. Vin.-Gren. . . . 208/B2
Stuckey, S.C., U.S., 263 . . . 340/E3
Studland, Eng., U.K. . . . 73/J3
Studley, Eng., U.K., 5,883 . . . 68/D5
Studley, Kans., U.S. . . . 276/B2
Study Butte, Tex., U.S., 267 . . . 346/E6
Stuie, Br. Col., Can. . . . 214/J5
Stukeley, Eng., U.K. . . . 68/G5
Stull, Kans., U.S., 60 . . . 276/G3
Stump Lake N.W.R., N. Dak., U.S. . . . 326/G2
Stumptown, W. Va., U.S., 50 . . . 360/E3
Stumpy Pt., N.C., U.S., 200 . . . 322/P3
Sturbridge, Mass., U.S., 7,837 . . . 292/F4
Sturgeon, P.E.I., Can. . . . 224/C2
Sturgeon, Mich., U.S., *bay* . . . 294/D4
Sturgeon, Mich., U.S., *point* . . . 294/F5
Sturgeon, Mo., U.S., 944 . . . 302/D2
Sturgeon Bay, Wisc., U.S., 9,437 . . . 364/F4
Sturgeon Falls, Ont., Can., 5,978 . . . 222/D3
Sturgeon Falls, Ont., Can., 5,978 . . . 223/F1
Sturgeon Hts., Alta., Can. . . . 212/B3
Sturgeon Lake, Minn., U.S., 347 . . . 298/E4
Sturgis, Sask., Can., 627 . . . 227/H9
Sturgis, Ky., U.S., 2,030 . . . 280/B3
Sturgis, Mich., U.S., 11,285 . . . 294/D8
Sturgis, Miss., U.S., 206 . . . 300/C2
Sturgis, Okla., U.S. . . . 330/B4
Sturgis, S. Dak., U.S., 6,442 . . . 342/B3
Sturkie, Ark., U.S. . . . 244/D1
Sturry, Eng., U.K., 4,847 . . . 70/G4
Sturtevant, Wisc., U.S., 5,287 . . . 364/F6
Sturton by Stow, Eng., U.K. . . . 66/G6
Sturton le Steeple, Eng., U.K. . . . 68/F3
Stutsman, N. Dak., U.S., *county*, 21,908 . . . 326/F3
Stuttgart, Ger., 582,443 . . . 86/B4
Stuttgart, Ger., *department* . . . 86/B4
Stuttgart, Ark., U.S., 9,745 . . . 244/D3
Stuttgart, Kans., U.S., 80 . . . 276/C2
Styria, Aus., *state* . . . 91/D3
Suai, E. Timor . . . 122/B2
Suamico, Wisc., U.S., 950 . . . 364/E4
Subiaco, Ark., U.S., 439 . . . 244/B2
Sublett, Ida., U.S. . . . 264/D7
Sublett, Ky., U.S., 325 . . . 280/G3
Sublette, Ill., U.S., 456 . . . 266/D2
Sublette, Kans., U.S., 1,592 . . . 276/B4
Sublette, Wyo., U.S., *county*, 5,920 . . . 366/B2
Sublimity, Oreg., U.S., 2,148 . . . 334/D3
Subotica, Serb.-Mont., 145,157 . . . 99/A1
Succasunna, N.J., U.S., 12,569 . . . 314/D2
Success, Ark., U.S., 180 . . . 244/E1
Success, Mo., U.S., 100 . . . 302/D4
Suceava, Rom., 117,615 . . . 101/D2
Suceava, Rom., *county* . . . 101/C2
Suches, Ga., U.S., 50 . . . 260/C2
Suchiate, Guat., *river* . . . 201/A5
Sucre, Bol., *judicial capital*, 215,778 . . . 186/A3
Sucre, Col., *department* . . . 184/B2
Sucre, Ven., *state* . . . 182/D1
Sucumbíos, Ecua., *province* . . . 185/C3
Sud, Haiti, *department* . . . 205/B2
Sudan, *nation* . . . 139
Sudan, Tex., U.S., 1,039 . . . 346/F1
Sudborough, Eng., U.K. . . . 70/C2
Sudbourne, Eng., U.K. . . . 70/H2

Sudbury, Ont., Can., 103,879,
 (155,900 metro.) 222/D3
Sudbury, Ont., Can., 103,879,
 (155,900 metro.) 223/E1
Sudbury, Ont., Can., 103,879,
 (155,900 metro.) 223/D1
Sudbury, Ont., Can., county 223/D1
Sudbury, Eng., U.K., 19,512 . . . . . .68/D4
Sudbury, Eng., U.K., 19,512 . . . . . .70/F2
Sudbury, Mass., U.S., 16,841 . . . .292/J3
Sudbury, Vt., U.S. 352/A3
Sudd, Sudan, region 145/B3
Sudden Valley, Wash., U.S., 4,165 . .358/C1
Suddie, Guy. 183/B2
Sud-Est, Haiti, department 205/C2
Sudeten, Czh. Rep., mountains 92/B2
Sudeten, Pol., mountains 83/B3
Sud-Kivu, Congo, D.R., region 155/C2
Sudlersville, Md., U.S., 391 . . . . . .288/L3
Sue, Sudan, river 145/B3
Suez, Egy., 437,000 . . . . .144/B2
Suez, Egy., canal 144/B1
Suez, Egy., gulf 144/B2
Suffern, N.Y., U.S., 11,006 . . . . . .320/A1
Suffield, Alta., Can., 205 . . . . . . .212/E6
Suffield, Conn., U.S., 13,552 . . . . .253/E2
Suffolk, Eng., U.K., unitary authority, 668,548 . .70/G2
Suffolk, Mass., U.S., county, 689,807 . .292/C8, L3
Suffolk, Mont., U.S. 306/G2
Suffolk, N.Y., U.S., county, 1,419,369 . .320/F2
Suffolk, Va., U.S., 63,677 . . . . . . .354/K7
Sugandha, India . . . . .128/Inset II
Sugar, Mich., U.S., mountain 294/A2
Sugar Bush Knolls, Ohio, U.S., 227 . .328/110
Sugar Camp, Wisc., U.S., 90 . . . . .364/D3
Sugar City, Colo., U.S., 279 . . . . . .250/C3
Sugar City, Ida., U.S., 1,242 . . . . . .264/F6
Sugar Creek, Mo., U.S., 3,839 . . . . .302/J5
Sugarcreek, Ohio, U.S., 2,174 . . . . .328/G4
Sugarcreek, Penn., U.S., 5,331 . . . .336/B3
Sugar Grove, Ill., U.S., 3,909 . . . . .266/E2
Sugar Grove, Ky., U.S., 125 . . . . . .280/D3
Sugar Grove, N.C., U.S., 325 . . . . .322/B2
Sugar Grove, Ohio, U.S., 448 . . . . .328/E6
Sugar Grove, Penn., U.S., 613 . . . .336/C2
Sugar Hill, Ga., U.S., 11,399 . . . . .260/C3, K1
Sugar Hill, N.H., U.S., 563 . . . . . . .312/C3
Sugar Land, Tex., U.S., 63,328 . . . .346/A7
Sugarland, Tex., U.S., 63,328 . . . . .346/N6
Sugarland Run, Va., U.S., 9,400 . . . .354/J2, L1
Sugarloaf, Maine, U.S., mountain . . .286/B3
Sugarloaf Key, Fla., U.S. 256/G7
Sugar Mountain, N.C., U.S., 226 . . .322/B2
Sugar Notch, Penn., U.S., 1,023 . . .336/K3
Sugartown, La., U.S., 60 . . . . .282/D5
Sugar Valley, Ga., U.S., 250 . . . . . .260/A2
Sugarville, Utah, U.S. 350/B4
Sugden, Okla., U.S., 59 . . . . .330/E3
Suhaj, Egy. 144/B2
Suhar, Oman 137/C1
Sühbaatar, Mong. 118/C2
Suhl, Ger. 86/B3
Suir, Ire., river 78/C2
Suisun City, Calif., U.S., 26,118 . . . .246/K1
Suita, Jap., 348,000 . . . . .114/B3
Suitland, (Suitland-Silver Hill), Md., U.S.,
 33,515 . . . . .288/C7, G4
Sukabumi, Indon. 122/B2
Sukang, Bru. 121/B3
Sukhothai, Thai. 125/B2
Sukkur, Pak., 335,551 . . . . .129/C4
Sula, Indon., islands 122/D2
Sula, Mont., U.S. 306/C4
Sulaiman, Pak., range 129/C4
Sulby, Eng., U.K. 66/B5
Sulima, S.L. 149/B2
Sullana, Peru, 143,902 . . . . .185/A1
Sulligent, Ala., U.S., 2,151 . . . . . . .238/A2
Sullivan, Alta., Can., lake 212/E5
Sullivan, Ill., U.S., 4,326 . . . . .266/E4
Sullivan, Ind., U.S., 4,617 . . . . . . .270/B6
Sullivan, Ind., U.S., county, 21,751 . .270/B6
Sullivan, Ky., U.S., 125 . . . . .280/C3
Sullivan, Mo., U.S., 6,351 . . . . . . .302/E3
Sullivan, Mo., U.S., county, 7,219 . . .302/C1
Sullivan, N.H., U.S., 746 . . . . .312/B5
Sullivan, N.H., U.S., county, 40,458 . .312/B5
Sullivan, N.Y., U.S., county, 73,966 . .320/M7
Sullivan, Penn., U.S., county, 6,556 . .336/H2
Sullivan, Tenn., U.S., county, 153,048 . .344/S1
Sullivan, Wisc., U.S., 688 . . . . .364/E2
Sullivans Island, S.C., U.S., 1,911 . . .340/E4
Sully, Wales, U.K. 64/E5
Sully, Iowa, U.S., 904 . . . . .274/J4
Sully, S. Dak., U.S., county, 1,556 . . .342/E3
Sullys Hill Natl. Game Pres., N. Dak., U.S. .326/G2
Sulphur, La., U.S., 20,512 . . . . . . .282/C6
Sulphur, Nev., U.S. 310/A1
Sulphur, Okla., U.S., 4,794 . . . . . .330/F3
Sulphur Cone, Hawaii, U.S., mountain . .262/G6
Sulphurdale, Utah, U.S. 350/B5
Sulphur Rock, Ark., U.S., 421 . . . . .244/D2
Sulphur Sprs., Ark., U.S., 671 . . . . .244/A1
Sulphur Sprs., Ind., U.S., 346 . . . . .270/F4
Sulphur Sprs., Ohio, U.S., 400 . . . .328/E4
Sulphur Sprs., Tex., U.S., 14,551 . . .346/N2
Sultan, Wash., U.S., 3,344 . . . . . . .358/D2
Sulu, Indon., sea 122/D1
Sulu, Phil., archipelago 120/B5
Sulu, Phil., sea 120/A4
Sülüktü, Kyrg. 131/K3
Sumach, (see Fairview), Wash., U.S. . .358/E3
Sumas, Wash., U.S., 960 . . . . .358/C1
Sumatra, Indon., island 122/B2
Sumatra, Fla., U.S., 60 . . . . .256/D1
Sumatra, Mont., U.S. 306/J3
Šumava, Czh. Rep., mountains 92/A3
Sumba, Indon., island 122/D2
Sumbar, Turkm., river 132/B2
Sumbawa, Indon., island 122/C2
Sumbawanga, Tan. 158/B2
Sumbe, Ang. 159/B3
Sumburgh, Scot., U.K. 62/Q3
Sumidero, P.R. 206/C2
Sumiton, Ala., U.S., 2,665 . . . . . . .238/B2
Summer, Scot., U.K., islands 62/E2
Summer, Mich., U.S., island 294/C4
Summer, Oreg., U.S., lake 334/F5
Summerbridge, Eng., U.K. 66/E4
Summerdale, Ala., U.S., 655 . . . . . .238/B5
Summerfield, Fla., U.S., 550 . . . . . .256/F2
Summerfield, Ill., U.S., 472 . . . . . .266/B3
Summerfield, Kans., U.S., 211 . . . . .276/F2
Summerfield, La., U.S. 282/D1
Summerfield, N.C., U.S., 7,018 . . . .322/F2
Summerfield, Ohio, U.S., 296 . . . . .328/H6
Summerford, Nfld., Can., 1,010 . . . .218/D2
Summerhaven, Ariz., U.S. 242/E5
Summerhill, Penn., U.S., 521 . . . . .336/D5
Summer Lake, Oreg., U.S. 334/F5
Summerland, Br. Col., Can., 10,713 . .214/N6

Summerland, Calif., U.S., 1,545 . . . .246/F8
Summerland, Miss., U.S. 300/C4
Summers, Ark., U.S., 225 . . . . .244/A2
Summers, W. Va., U.S., county, 12,999 . .360/E5
Summerside, P.E.I., Can., 14,654 . . .224/B2
Summerside, Ohio, U.S., 5,523 . . . .328/C10
Summersville, Ky., U.S., 325 . . . . . .280/E3
Summersville, Mo., U.S., 544 . . . . .302/E4
Summersville, W. Va., U.S., 3,294 . . .360/E4
Summerton, S.C., U.S., 1,061 . . . . .340/D3
Summertown, Ga., U.S., 140 . . . . .260/G6
Summertown, Tenn., U.S., 800 . . . .344/G4
Summerville, Nfld., Can., 541 . . . . .218/E5
Summerville, Ga., U.S., 4,556 . . . . .260/A3
Summerville, La., U.S., 125 . . . . . . .282/E3
Summerville, Oreg., U.S., 117 . . . . .334/J2
Summerville, Penn., U.S., 525 . . . . .336/C3
Summerville, S.C., U.S., 27,752 . . . .340/D3
Summit, Ala., U.S., 125 . . . . .238/C1
Summit, Ark., U.S., 586 . . . . .244/C1
Summit, Colo., U.S., county, 23,548 . .250/D2
Summit, Ill., U.S., 10,637 . . . . .266/B6
Summit, (Boyd County), Ky., U.S., 3,400 . .280/H2
Summit, (Hardin County), Ky., U.S., 300 . .280/D3
Summit, Miss., U.S., 1,428 . . . . . . .300/B4
Summit, Nev., U.S., mountain 310/B2
Summit, N.J., U.S., 21,131 . . . . . . .314/E2
Summit, N. Mex., U.S., 150 . . . . . .317/B5
Summit, Ohio, U.S., county, 542,899 . .328/G3, H1
Summit, Okla., U.S., 226 . . . . .330/G2
Summit, Oreg., U.S. 334/C3
Summit, S.C., U.S., 219 . . . . .340/C3
Summit, S. Dak., U.S., 281 . . . . . . .342/H2
Summit, Utah, U.S., 175 . . . . .350/B6
Summit, Utah, U.S., county, 29,736 . .350/D3, E2
Summit Hill, Penn., U.S., 2,974 . . . .336/K4
Summit Lake, Br. Col., Can. 214/K2
Summit Lake, Br. Col., Can. 214/L4
Summit Lake, Wisc., U.S., 150 . . . . .364/D3
Summit Lake Ind. Res., Calif., U.S. . .246/F1
Summit Lake Ind. Res., Nev., U.S. . .310/A1
Summit Lake Ind. Res., Oreg., U.S. . .334/A1
Summit Pt., Utah, U.S. 350/E5
Summit Sta., Ohio, U.S. 328/E9
Summitville, Colo., U.S. 250/D4
Summitville, Ind., U.S., 1,090 . . . . .270/E4
Summitville, Iowa, U.S., 125 . . . . . .274/M7
Summitville, Ohio, U.S., 108 . . . . . .328/J4
Summitville, Tenn., U.S., 400 . . . . .344/K3
Summum, Ill., U.S., 175 . . . . .266/C3
Sumner, Ga., U.S., 309 . . . . .260/D8
Sumner, Ill., U.S., 1,022 . . . . .266/F5
Sumner, Iowa, U.S., 2,106 . . . . . . .274/K2
Sumner, Kans., U.S., county, 25,946 . .276/E4
Sumner, Maine, U.S., 854 . . . . . . .286/B4
Sumner, Mich., U.S., 300 . . . . .294/C6
Sumner, Miss., U.S., 407 . . . . .300/B2
Sumner, Mo., U.S., 142 . . . . .302/C2
Sumner, Nebr., U.S., 237 . . . . .308/E3
Sumner, N. Mex., U.S., lake 317/F3
Sumner, Okla., U.S., 70 . . . . .330/E1
Sumner, Oreg., U.S., 40 . . . . .334/B4
Sumner, Tenn., U.S., county, 130,449 . .344/H2
Sumner, Tex., U.S., 60 . . . . .346/N2
Sumner, Wash., U.S., 8,504 . . . . . .358/C2
Sumperk, Czh. Rep. 92/C3
Sumpter, Oreg., U.S., 171 . . . . . . .334/H3
Sumqayit, Azer., 281,600 . . . . . . .103/G4
Sumrall, Miss., U.S., 1,005 . . . . . . .300/C4
Sumter, Ala., U.S., county, 14,798 . . .238/A3
Sumter, Fla., U.S., county, 53,345 . . .256/F3
Sumter, Ga., U.S., 60 . . . . .260/C8
Sumter, Ga., U.S., county, 33,200 . . .260/C7
Sumter, S.C., U.S., 39,643, (104,646 metro.) . .340/D3
Sumter, S.C., U.S., county, 104,646 . .340/D3
Sumter Natl. For., S.C., U.S. 340/A2, B3, L4
Sumterville, Fla., U.S., 250 . . . . . . .256/G3
Sumy, Ukr., 296,643 . . . . .102/C1
Sumy, Ukr., oblast 102/C1
Sun, La., U.S., 471 . . . . .282/K5
Sunapee, N.H., U.S., 3,055 . . . . . .312/B5
Sunapee, N.H., U.S., lake 62/E5
Sunart, Scot., U.K., lake 62/E5
Sunbeam, Colo., U.S., 40 . . . . . . .250/B1
Sunbeam, Ida., U.S. 264/C5
Sunbright, Tenn., U.S., 577 . . . . . .344/M2
Sunburg, Minn., U.S., 110 . . . . . . .298/B5
Sunburst, Mont., U.S., 415 . . . . . . .306/E1
Sunbury, N.B., Can., county 217/C3
Sunbury, Ga., U.S. 260/J8
Sunbury, Iowa, U.S., 100 . . . . .274/N4
Sunbury, N.C., U.S., 125 . . . . .322/M2
Sunbury, Ohio, U.S., 2,630 . . . . . . .328/E5
Sunbury, Penn., U.S., 10,610 . . . . .336/H4
Suncheon, S. Kor., 249,263 . . . . . .116/B5
Sun City, S. Afr. 162/C2
Sun City, Ariz., U.S., 38,309 . . . . . .242/C4
Sun City, Calif., U.S., 17,773 . . . . . .246/H9
Sun City, Fla., U.S., 175 . . . . .256/D7, F4
Sun City, Kans., U.S., 81 . . . . .276/D4
Sun City Ctr., Fla., U.S., 16,321 . . . .256/D7
Sun City West, Ariz., U.S., 26,344 . . .242/C4
Suncook, N.H., U.S., 5,362 . . . . . . .312/D5
Sundance, Wyo., U.S., 1,161 . . . . . .366/D1
Sundarbans, Bangl., region 127/C7
Sunderland, Ont., Can. 223/F3
Sunderland, Eng., U.K. 60/C2
Sunderland, Eng., U.K. 66/F3
Sunderland, Eng., U.K., unitary authority,
 280,807 . . . . .66/F3
Sunderland, Md., U.S., 1,400 . . . . .288/H5
Sunderland, Mass., U.S., 3,777 . . . .292/D3
Sunderland, Vt., U.S. 352/A4
Sundi, São T.-Prínc. 154/C1
Sundown, Man., Can. 215/C4
Sundown, Mo., U.S. 302/D5
Sundown, Tex., U.S., 1,505 . . . . . .346/F2
Sundre, Alta., Can., 2,267 . . . . . . .212/C5
Sundridge, Ont., Can., 983 . . . . . .223/F2
Sundsvall, Swe., 93,125 . . . . .80/C2
Sunfield, Ill., U.S., 425 . . . . .266/D5
Sunfield, Mich., U.S., 591 . . . . . . .294/D7
Sunfish Lake, Minn., U.S., 504 . . . . .298/F6
Sunflower, Ariz., U.S. 242/D4
Sunflower, Miss., U.S., 596 . . . . . .300/B2
Sunflower, Miss., U.S., county, 34,369 . .300/B2
Sunizona, Ariz., U.S., 200 . . . . . . .242/F6
Sun Kosi, Nepal, river 126/C2
Sun Lakes, Ariz., U.S., 11,936 . . . . .242/D4
Sunland Park, N. Mex., U.S., 13,309 . .317/D6
Sunman, Ind., U.S., 805 . . . . .270/F6
Sunninghill, Eng., U.K. 70/C4
Sunnybrook, Ky., U.S., 150 . . . . . . .280/F4
Sunnybrook, Md., U.S., 2,300 . . . . .288/H1
Sunny Corner, N.B., Can., 910 . . . . .217/D2
Sunnydale, Alta., Can., 60 . . . . . . .244/D2
Sunnynook, Alta., Can. 212/E5
Sunnyside, (Sunnyside-Tahoe City),
 Calif., U.S., 1,761 . . . . .246/E3
Sunnyside, Fla., U.S. 256/C3
Sunny Side, Ga., U.S., 142 . . . . . . .260/C5

Sunnyside, Ga., U.S., 142 . . . . . . .260/G9
Sunnyside, Nev., U.S. 310/C2
Sunnyside, Oreg., U.S., 6,791 . . . . .334/A2
Sunnyside, Tex., U.S., 70 . . . . .346/F1
Sunnyside, Utah, U.S., 404 . . . . . . .350/D4
Sunnyside, Wash., U.S., 13,905 . . . .358/E3
Sunnyslope, Wash., U.S., 2,521 . . . .358/E2
Sunnyvale, Calif., U.S., 131,760 . . . .246/C5, K3
Sunnyvale, Tex., U.S., 2,693 . . . . . .346/D9
Sunny Valley, Oreg., U.S., 150 . . . . .334/C5
Sunnyview, S. Dak., U.S., 150 . . . . .342/J3
Sunol, Nebr., U.S., 80 . . . . .308/B2
Sun Prairie, (Cascade County), Mont., U.S. .306/E2
Sun Prairie, (Phillips County), Mont., U.S. .306/J2
Sun Prairie, Wisc., U.S., 20,369 . . . .364/D5
Sunray, Tex., U.S., 1,950 . . . . .346/F8
Sunrise, Fla., U.S., 85,779 . . . . . . .256/B6
Sunrise, Ky., U.S., 100 . . . . .280/F2
Sunrise, Minn., U.S., 175 . . . . .298/E5
Sunrise, Wyo., U.S. 366/D2
Sunrise Beach, Mo., U.S., 368 . . . . .302/D3
Sunrise Beach, Tex., U.S., 704 . . . . .346/C2
Sunrise Manor, Nev., U.S., 156,120 . .310/C3
Sunrise Sprs., Ariz., U.S., 40 . . . . . .242/F2
Sun River, Mont., U.S., 131 . . . . . . .306/E2
Sunriver, Oreg., U.S., 450 . . . . . . .334/E4
Sun River Terrace, Ill., U.S., 383 . . . .266/F2
Sunset, Ariz., U.S., 80 . . . . .242/E5
Sunset, Ark., U.S., 348 . . . . .244/E2
Sunset, La., U.S., 2,352 . . . . .282/E6
Sunset, Tex., U.S., 339 . . . . .346/L2
Sunset, Utah, U.S., 5,204 . . . . .350/C2, E1
Sunset Beach, Hawaii, U.S. 262/J1
Sunset Beach, N.C., U.S., 1,824 . . . .322/H7
Sunset Crater Volcano N.M., Ariz., U.S. .242/D2
Sunset Hills, Mo., U.S., 8,267 . . . . .302/H3
Sunset House, Alta., Can. 212/B3
Sunset Valley, Tex., U.S., 365 . . . . .346/C10
Sunshine, Vic., Austl. . . . . .170/Inset V
Sunshine, N. Mex., U.S., 90 . . . . . .317/C5
Sunshine, Wyo., U.S. 366/B4
Sunspot, N. Mex., U.S., 80 . . . . . . .317/E5
Sun Valley, Ariz., U.S. 242/E3
Sun Valley, Fla., U.S. 256/B5
Sun Valley, Ida., U.S., 1,427 . . . . . .264/C6
Sun Valley, Nev., U.S., 19,461 . . . . .310/A2
Sunyani, Gha. 150/A3
Supai, Ariz., U.S. 242/C1
Superior, Ont., Can., lake 222/C3
Superior, Ariz., U.S., 3,254 . . . . . . .242/D4, E4
Superior, Colo., U.S., 9,011 . . . . . . .250/A3, E2
Superior, Iowa, U.S., 142 . . . . .274/E1
Superior, Mich., U.S., lake 294/A2, D1
Superior, Minn., U.S., lake 298/F2, F3
Superior, Mont., U.S., 893 . . . . . . .306/B2
Superior, Nebr., U.S., 2,055 . . . . . .308/E3
Superior, Wisc., U.S., 27,368 . . . . . .364/A2
Superior, Wisc., U.S., lake 364/C1, F1
Superior, Wyo., U.S., 244 . . . . .366/B3
Superior Natl. For., Minn., U.S. 298/E2, E3, F3
Suplee, Oreg., U.S. 334/G3
Supreme, La., U.S., 1,119 . . . . .282/H7
Supung, N. Kor., reservoir 116/A2
Suqualena, Miss., U.S., 150 . . . . . .300/D3
Suquamish, Wash., U.S., 3,510 . . . .358/A4
Sur, Oman 137/C1
Surab, Pak. 129/C4
Surabaya, Indon., 2,801,300 . . . . . .122/C2
Surakarta, Indon. 122/C2
Surat, India, 2,433,787, (2,811,466 metro.) . .128/B4
Surat Thani, Thai., (153,500 metro.) . .125/B4
Şüre, Lux., river 85/A2, B2
Surf City, N.J., U.S., 1,442 . . . . . . .314/E4
Surf City, N.C., U.S., 1,393 . . . . . . .322/K6
Surfside, Fla., U.S., 4,909 . . . . .256/B6
Surfside, Mass., U.S., 175 . . . . .292/P8
Surfside Beach, S.C., U.S., 4,425 . . .340/F3
Surfside Beach, Tex., U.S., 763 . . . . .346/N7
Surginer, Ala., U.S., 150 . . . . .238/B4
Surgoinsville, Tenn., U.S., 1,484 . . . .344/R2
Surgut, Russ., 277,781 . . . . .104/E3
Surigao, Phil. 120/C4
Surin, Thai. 125/C3
Suriname, nation 173
Suriname, Sur., river 183/B3
Suring, Wisc., U.S., 605 . . . . .364/E4
Surkhob, Taj., river 132/B1
Surkhonadaryo, Uzb., province 132/C3
Surma, Bangl., river 127/E3
Surprise, Br. Col., Can. 214/F1
Surprise, Ariz., U.S., 30,848 . . . . . .242/C4
Surprise, Nebr., U.S., 44 . . . . .308/G2
Surrency, Ga., U.S., 237 . . . . .260/G8
Surrey, Eng., U.K., unitary authority, 1,059,015 . .70/D4
Surrey, N. Dak., U.S., 917 . . . . . . .326/E1
Surry, Maine, U.S., 1,361 . . . . .286/D4
Surry, N.H., U.S., 673 . . . . .312/A5
Surry, N.C., U.S., county, 71,219 . . .322/D2
Surry, Va., U.S., 262 . . . . .354/K6
Surry, Va., U.S., county, 6,829 . . . . .354/K6
Surt, Lib. 145/C1
Surtsey, Ice., island 79/A3
Surud Ad, Som., mountain 157/B1
Survey, Nebr., U.S., valley 308/B1
Susan, Va., U.S., 475 . . . . .354/L6
Susank, Kans., U.S., 57 . . . . .276/D3
Susan Moore, Ala., U.S., 721 . . . . . .238/C1, C2
Susanville, Calif., U.S., 13,541 . . . . .246/E2
Susitna, Alaska, U.S., river 232/C2
Susquehanna, Penn., U.S., 1,690 . . .336/K2
Susquehanna, Penn., U.S., county, 42,238 . .336/K2
Susquehanna, Penn., U.S., river 336/G6, J2, J6
Susquehannock St. For., Penn., U.S. . .336/F2
Sussex, N.B., Can., 4,182 . . . . .217/D3
Sussex, Del., U.S., county, 156,638 . .255/C6
Sussex, N.J., U.S., 2,145 . . . . .314/D1
Sussex, N.J., U.S., county, 144,166 . .314/D1
Sussex, Va., U.S., 125 . . . . .354/J7
Sussex, Va., U.S., county, 12,504 . . .354/J7
Sussex, Wisc., U.S., 8,828 . . . . .364/E5, F2
Sussex, Wyo., U.S., 70 . . . . .366/C2
Sussex Corner, N.B., Can., 1,321 . . .217/D3
Susua Forest Reserve, P.R. 206/B2
Susuman, Russ. 104/I3
Sutcliffe, Nev., U.S., 281 . . . . .310/A2
Sutersville, Penn., U.S., 636 . . . . . .336/B5
Sutherland, N.S.W., Austl. . . . . . . .170/Inset IV
Sutherland, Iowa, U.S., 707 . . . . . .274/D2
Sutherland, Ky., U.S., 100 . . . . .280/C3
Sutherland, Nebr., U.S., 1,129 . . . . .308/C2
Sutherland, Va., U.S., 400 . . . . . . .354/H6
Sutherlin, Oreg., U.S., 6,669 . . . . . .334/C4
Sutlej, India, river 128/C2
Sutlej, Pak., river 129/D4
Sutter, Calif., U.S., 2,885 . . . . .246/D3
Sutter, Calif., U.S., county, 78,930 . . .246/D4, K5
Sutter Creek, Calif., U.S., 2,303 . . . .246/L6
Sutton, Eng., U.K. 70/D1
Sutton, Eng., U.K. 238/B3
Sutton, (Cambridgeshire), Eng., U.K., 3,076 . .68/H5

Sutton, (Cambridgeshire), Eng., U.K., 3,076 . .70/E2
Sutton, (London), Eng., U.K., 166,041 . .70/D4
Sutton, (Surrey), Eng., U.K. 70/D4
Sutton, (W. Sussex), Eng., U.K. 70/D5
Sutton, Eng., U.K., unitary authority, 179,667 . .70/D4
Sutton, Mass., U.S., 8,250 . . . . . . .292/C4
Sutton, Nebr., U.S., 1,447 . . . . .308/G3
Sutton, N.H., U.S., 1,544 . . . . .312/C5
Sutton, N. Dak., U.S., 50 . . . . .326/G2
Sutton, Tex., U.S., county, 4,077 . . . .346/H5
Sutton, Vt., U.S. 352/C1
Sutton, W. Va., U.S., 1,011 . . . . . . .360/E3
Sutton, W. Va., U.S., lake 354/E8
Sutton, W. Va., U.S., lake 360/E3
Sutton Bridge, Eng., U.K., 3,457 . . .68/H4
Sutton Bridge, Eng., U.K., 3,457 . . .70/E1
Sutton Coldfield, Eng., U.K., 106,001 . .68/D4
Sutton in Ashfield, Eng., U.K., 37,890 . .68/E5
Sutton on Sea, Eng., U.K. 66/J6
Sutton-on-the-Forest, Eng., U.K. . . .68/E1
Sutton on the Hill, Eng., U.K. 68/D4
Suttons Bay, Mich., U.S., 589 . . . . .294/D5
Sutton Scotney, Eng., U.K. 70/B4
Suttontown, N.C., U.S., 80 . . . . . . .322/J4
Sutton West, Ont., Can. 223/F3
Suuroy, Den., island 79/Inset
Suva, Fiji, capital, 92,012, (196,000 metro.) . .174/B3
Suwałki, Pol. 83/F1
Suwanee, Ga., U.S., 8,725 . . . . . . .260/C3, K1
Suwannee, Fla., U.S., 425 . . . . . . .256/E2
Suwannee, Fla., U.S., county, 34,844 . .256/E1
Suwannee, Fla., U.S., river 256/F1, D2
Suwannee, Ga., U.S., river 260/F10
Suwannee Sprs., Fla., U.S., 70 . . . . .256/F1
Suwanose, Jap., island 114/A4
Suwon, S. Kor., 755,550 . . . . .116/B4
Suzano, Braz. . . . . .188/Inset II
Suzhou, China, 882,677 . . . . .119/F2
Svalbard, Nor., islands 193/B1
Svartka, Czh. Rep., river 92/C3
Svay Ring, Camb. 124/D4
Svea, Minn., U.S., 150 . . . . .298/C6
Svendborg, Den. 79/C3
Šventoji, Lith., river 82/C2
Svetozarevo, Serb.-Mont. 99/B3
Svilengrad, Bul. 101/D4
Svishtov, Bul. 101/D2
Svitavy, Czh. Rep. 92/C3
Svobodnyy, Russ. 104/H4
Swabian Jura, Ger., mountains 86/B4
Swaby, Eng., U.K. 66/J6
Swadlincote, Eng., U.K., 36,859 . . . .68/D4
Swadlincote, Eng., U.K., 36,859 . . . .70/A1
Swaffham, Eng., U.K., 5,332 . . . . . .70/F1
Swaffham Bulbeck, Eng., U.K. 70/E2
Swain, Ark., U.S., 125 . . . . .244/B2
Swain, N.C., U.S., county, 12,968 . . .322/C8
Swainsboro, Ga., U.S., 6,943 . . . . . .260/G6
Swakopmund, Nam., 17,681 . . . . . .159/A1
Swaledale, Iowa, U.S., 174 . . . . . . .274/H2
Swallowcliffe, Eng., U.K. 73/H2
Swampscott, Mass., U.S., 14,412 . . .292/L3
Swan, Austl., river . . . . .170/Inset I
Swan, Man., Can., lake 215/A3
Swan, Man., Can., river 215/A3
Swan, Sask., Can., river 227/J8
Swan, Iowa, U.S., 121 . . . . .274/H5
Swan, Mont., U.S., river 306/C2
Swanage, Eng., U.K., 9,947 . . . . . .73/J3
Swandale, W. Va., U.S. 360/E4
Swan Hills, Alta., Can., 1,807 . . . . .212/C4
Swanlake, Ida., U.S. 264/F7
Swan Lake, Idaho, U.S. 264/F7
Swan Lake, Man., U.S., 60 . . . . . . .300/B2
Swan Lake, Mont., U.S. 306/C2
Swan Lake N.W.R., Mo., U.S. 302/C2
Swannington, Eng., U.K. 70/B1
Swan Quarter, N.C., U.S., 275 . . . . .322/N4
Swan River, Man., Can., 4,032 . . . . .215/A3
Swan River, Minn., U.S. 298/D3
Swan River N.W.R., Mont., U.S. 306/C2
Swans, Maine, U.S., island 286/D4
Swansboro, N.C., U.S., 1,426 . . . . . .322/L5
Swanscombe, Eng., U.K., 5,973 . . . .70/E4
Swansea, Wales, U.K. 60/B3
Swansea, Wales, U.K., 171,038,
 (273,129 metro.) 64/D4
Swansea, Wales, U.K., bay 64/D4
Swansea, Wales, U.K., unitary authority,
 223,293 . . . . .64/C4
Swansea, Ill., U.S., 10,579 . . . . . . .266/C3
Swansea, Mass., U.S., 15,901 . . . . .292/K5
Swansea, S.C., U.S., 533 . . . . .340/C3
Swans Island, Maine, U.S., 327 . . . .286/D4
Swanson, Mich., U.S. 294/B4
Swanton, Nebr., U.S., 106 . . . . . . .308/G3
Swanton, Ohio, U.S., 3,307 . . . . . . .328/C2
Swanton, Vt., U.S. 352/A1
Swan Valley, Ida., U.S., 213 . . . . . .264/F6
Swanville, Maine, U.S., 1,357 . . . . . .286/C4
Swanville, Minn., U.S., 351 . . . . . . .298/C5
Swanwick, Ill., U.S., 150 . . . . .266/C5
Swanzey, N.H., U.S., 6,800 . . . . . . .312/B6
Swarkestone, Eng., U.K. 70/B1
Swartberg, S. Afr., mountains 162/B3
Swarthmore, Penn., U.S., 6,170 . . . .336/L7
Swartswood, N.J., U.S., 500 . . . . . .314/D1
Swartz, La., U.S., 4,247 . . . . .282/F1
Swartz Creek, Mich., U.S., 5,102 . . .294/F7
Swasey, Utah, U.S., peak 350/A4
Swatara, Minn., U.S., 60 . . . . .298/D4
Swaton, Eng., U.K. 70/D1
Sway, Eng., U.K., 2,072 . . . . .70/A5
Swayzee, Ind., U.S., 1,011 . . . . . . .270/E3
Swaziland, nation 155
Swea City, Iowa, U.S., 642 . . . . . . .274/F1
Swearingen, Tex., U.S. 346/H1
Sweatman, Miss., U.S. 300/C2
Swedeborg, Mo., U.S., 250 . . . . . . .302/D4
Swedeburg, Nebr., U.S., 70 . . . . . . .308/H2
Sweden, nation 78
Sweden, nation 193/C1
Sweden, Maine, U.S., 324 . . . . . . .286/D2
Swedesboro, N.J., U.S., 2,055 . . . . .314/C4
Swedesburg, Iowa, U.S., 150 . . . . . .274/L5
Sweeny, Tex., U.S., 3,624 . . . . .346/N6
Sweet, Ida., U.S., 125 . . . . .264/A6
Sweet Briar, Va., U.S., 750 . . . . . . .354/F5
Sweetgrass, Mont., U.S. 306/E1
Sweet Grass, Mont., U.S., county, 3,609 . .306/G4
Sweet Home, Oreg., U.S., 8,016 . . . .334/D3
Sweet Sprs., Mo., U.S., 1,628 . . . . .302/C3
Sweet Sprs., W. Va., U.S., 150 . . . . .360/F5
Sweet Valley, Penn., U.S., 600 . . . . .336/J3
Sweet Water, Ala., U.S., 234 . . . . . .238/B3
Sweetwater, Ariz., U.S. 242/F1
Sweetwater, Fla., U.S., 14,226 . . . . .256/A6, H6

Sweetwater, Nebr., U.S. 308/E2
Sweetwater, Okla., U.S. 330/C2
Sweetwater, Tenn., U.S., 5,586 ...344/N3
Sweetwater, Tex., U.S., 11,415 ...346/H3
Sweetwater, Wyo., U.S., *county*, 37,613 ...366/B2
Sweetwater Sta., Wyo., U.S. ...366/B2
Swenson, Tex., U.S. ...346/H2
Swepsonville, N.C., U.S., 922 ...322/G2
Swett, S. Dak., U.S. ...342/D4
Swietokrzyskie, Pol., *province* ...83/E3
Swift, Mass., U.S., *river* ...292/E4
Swift, Minn., U.S., 90 ...298/B2
Swift, Minn., U.S., *county*, 11,956 ...298/B5
Swift, N.H., U.S., *river* ...312/D4
Swift Current, Nfld., Can., 255 ...218/D5
Swift Current, Sask., Can., 14,821 ...227/C10
Swift Falls, Minn., U.S., 100 ...298/B5
Swifton, Ark., U.S., 871 ...344/D2
Swiftown, Miss., U.S., 80 ...300/B2
Swifts Beach, Mass., U.S., 2,700 ...292/M6
Swift Trail Jct., Ariz., U.S., 2,195 ...242/F5
Swiftwater, N.H., U.S., 175 ...312/C3
Swiftwater, Penn., U.S., 800 ...336/L3
Swindon, Eng., U.K. ...60/C3
Swindon, Eng., U.K., 145,236 ...73/J1
Swindon, Eng., U.K., *unitary authority*, 180,061 ...73/J1
Swineshead, Eng., U.K., 1,576 ...68/G4
Swineshead, Eng., U.K., 1,576 ...70/D1
Swinford, Eng., U.K. ...70/B2
Swink, Colo., U.S., 696 ...250/G3
Swink, Okla., U.S., 83 ...330/C3
Swinoujście, Pol. ...68/D3
Swinscoe, Eng., U.K. ...70/B2
Swinton, Eng., U.K., 15,936 ...66/F6
Swinton, Eng., U.K., 15,936 ...68/E3
Swisher, Iowa, U.S., 813 ...274/L4
Swisher, Tex., U.S., *county*, 8,378 ...346/F1, G1
Swiss Alp, Tex., U.S. ...346/M6
Swisshome, Oreg., U.S., 40 ...334/C3
Swissvale, Penn., U.S., 9,653 ...336/E7
Swithland, Eng., U.K. ...70/B1
Switz City, Ind., U.S., 311 ...270/B6
Switzer, W. Va., U.S., 1,138 ...360/C5
Switzerland, *nation* ...88
Switzerland, Ind., U.S., *county*, 9,065 ...270/F7
Swords, Ire. ...78/C2
Swoyersville, Penn., U.S., 5,157 ...336/G7, K3
Swynnerton, Eng., U.K. ...68/C4
Sycamore, Ala., U.S., 500 ...238/C2
Sycamore, Ga., U.S., 496 ...260/D8
Sycamore, Ill., U.S., 12,020 ...266/E2
Sycamore, Kans., U.S., 125 ...276/G4
Sycamore, Ohio, U.S., 914 ...328/D4
Sycamore, S.C., U.S., 185 ...340/C3
Sycamore Hills, Mo., U.S., 722 ...302/H3
Syderstone, Eng., U.K. ...70/F1
Sydney, N.S.W., Austl., *state capital*, (3,948,015 *metro.*) ...170/E3, Inset IV
Sydney, N.S., Can., 33,913 ...221/G1
Sydnorsville, Va., U.S., 150 ...354/D7
Syerston, Eng., U.K. ...70/C1
Sykeston, N. Dak., U.S., 153 ...326/F2
Sykesville, Md., U.S., 4,197 ...288/G2
Sykesville, N.J., U.S., 375 ...314/D3
Sykesville, Penn., U.S., 1,246 ...336/D3
Syktyvkar, Russ., 229,879, (246,800 *metro.*) ...104/D3
Sylacauga, Ala., U.S., 12,616 ...238/C2
Sylhet, Bangl. ...127/E4
Sylhet, Bangl., *division* ...127/E4
Sylva, N.C., U.S., 2,435 ...322/D8
Sylvan, Wisc., U.S. ...364/C5
Sylvan Beach, N.Y., U.S., 1,071 ...320/K4
Sylvan Grove, Kans., U.S., 324 ...276/D2
Sylvania, Ala., U.S., 1,186 ...238/D1
Sylvania, Ga., U.S., 2,675 ...260/H6
Sylvania, Ohio, U.S., 18,670 ...328/C2
Sylvania, Penn., U.S., 200 ...336/H2
Sylvan Lake, Alta., Can., 7,493 ...212/C5
Sylvan Lake, Mich., U.S., 1,735 ...294/A6
Sylvan Sprs., Ala., U.S., 1,465 ...238/C1
Sylvarena, Miss., U.S., 120 ...300/C3
Sylvester, Ga., U.S., 5,990 ...260/D8
Sylvester, W. Va., U.S., 195 ...360/C4
Sylvia, Kans., U.S., 297 ...276/D4
Symbister, Scot., U.K. ...62/Q2
Symco, Wisc., U.S., 175 ...364/E4
Symerton, Ill., U.S., 106 ...266/E2
Symonds Yat, Eng., U.K. ...68/B6
Symsonia, Ky., U.S., 450 ...280/B4
Synarep, Wash., U.S. ...358/F1
Synod Inn, Wales, U.K. ...64/C3
Syracuse (Siracusa), It. ...95/C3
Syracuse, Ind., U.S., 3,038 ...270/E2
Syracuse, Kans., U.S., 1,824 ...276/A4
Syracuse, Mo., U.S., 172 ...302/D3
Syracuse, Nebr., U.S., 1,762 ...308/H3
Syracuse, N.Y., U.S., 147,306, (732,117 *metro.*) ...320/J4
Syracuse, Ohio, U.S., 879 ...328/G7
Syracuse, Utah, U.S., 9,398 ...350/E1
Syr Darya, Kaz., *river* ...131/C2
Syrdarya, Kaz., *river* ...132/A1, B1
Syre, Scot., U.K. ...62/H2
Syre, Minn., U.S. ...298/A3
Syria, *nation* ...130
Syria, Va., U.S. ...354/G4
Syrian, Iraq, *desert* ...130/B2
Syrian, Jor., *desert* ...134/B1
Syrian, Sa. Arab., *desert* ...136/A1
Syrian, Syria, *desert* ...134/B3
Syston, Eng., U.K. ...70/B1
Syunik', Arm., *district* ...103/D3
Szabolcs-Szatmár-Bereg, Hun., *county* ...91/C1
Szczecin, Pol., 416,682 ...83/B2
Szeged, Hun., 158,646 ...91/C2
Szeged, Hun. ...91/C2
Székesfehérvár, Hun., 106,000 ...91/B2
Székesfehérvár, Hun. ...91/B2
Szekszárd, Hun. ...91/B2
Szentes, Hun. ...91/C2
Szolnok, Hun. ...91/C2
Szombathely, Hun. ...91/A2

Taabo, C. d'Iv., *lake* ...150/D3
Tabar, P.N.G., *islands* ...172/B2
Tabasco, Mex., *state* ...200/F4
Tabassah, Tun., *mountains* ...146/A2
Tabelbala, Alg. ...146/A2
Taber, Alta., Can., 7,671 ...212/D6
Tabernacle, N.J., U.S., 7,170 ...314/D4
Tabernash, Colo., U.S., 165 ...250/E2
Tabiona, Utah, U.S., 149 ...350/F2
Tablas, Phil., *island* ...120/B3
Table Grove, Ill., U.S., 396 ...266/C3
Table Rock, Mo., U.S. ...330/E2
Table Rock, Mo., U.S., 229 ...302/C5
Table Rock, Nebr., U.S., 264 ...308/H3
Table Rock, Wyo., U.S., 82 ...366/B3
Table Rock L., Ark., U.S. ...244/B1
Tabligbo, Togo ...151/B3
Taboão da Serra, Braz. ...188/Inset II

Tábor, Czh. Rep. ...92/B3
Tabor, Iowa, U.S., 993 ...274/C6
Tabor, Minn., U.S., 50 ...298/A2
Tabor, S. Dak., U.S., 417 ...342/H5
Tabora, Tan. ...158/B2
Tabora, Tan., *region* ...158/B2
Tabor City, N.C., U.S., 2,509 ...322/H6
Tabou, C. d'Iv. ...150/C4
Tabriz, Iran, 1,191,043 ...130/B2
Tabuaeran, Kiri., *island* ...175/D1
Tabuk, Sa. Arab. ...136/A1
Tabuk, Sa. Arab., *emirate* ...136/A1
Tabusintac, N.B., Can., 893 ...217/D1
Tabwémasana, Van., *mountain* ...173/B2
Tacaná, Guat., *volcano* ...201/A4
Táchira, Ven., *state* ...182/B2
Tacloban, Phil., 178,639 ...120/C4
Tacna, Peru, 136,774 ...185/C4
Tacna, Peru, *department* ...185/C4
Tacna, Ariz., U.S., 555 ...242/B5
Tacoma, Wash., U.S., 193,556 ...358/C2
Taconic, Conn., U.S., 200 ...253/B1
Taconic, Mass., U.S., *mountains* ...292/A3
Taconic St. Park, ...253/A1
Taconite, Minn., U.S., 315 ...298/D3
Taconite Harbor, Minn., U.S. ...298/F3
Tacuarembó, Uru. ...187/C1
Tacuarembó, Uru., *department* ...187/C2
Tacuarembó, Uru., *river* ...187/C1
Tacuarí, Uru., *river* ...187/D2
Tadcaster, Eng., U.K., 6,915 ...66/F5
Tadcaster, Eng., U.K., 6,915 ...68/E2
Tademait, Alg., *plateau* ...146/B2
Tadjoura, Dji. ...156/C2
Tadjoura, Dji., *gulf* ...156/B2
Tadley, Eng., U.K., 15,520 ...70/B4
Tadlow, Eng., U.K. ...70/D2
Tadmarton, Eng., U.K. ...70/B2
Tadmur, Syria ...134/B2
Tadoussac, Que., Can., 870 ...226/G3
Taebaek Sanmaek, S. Kor., *mountains* ...116/C3
Taedong, N. Kor., *river* ...116/B3
Tafahi, Tonga, *island* ...175/C1
Taft, Calif., U.S., 6,400 ...246/F7
Taft, Fla., U.S., 1,938 ...256/C4, C3
Taft, Okla., U.S., 349 ...330/G2
Taft, Tenn., U.S., 150 ...344/H4
Taft, Tex., U.S., 3,396 ...346/L8
Taft Hts., Calif., U.S., 1,865 ...246/F7
Tafton, Penn., U.S., 200 ...336/L3
Taga, Sam. ...175/A2
Taganrog, Ukr., *gulf* ...102/D3
Tagant, Maur., *region* ...147/C3
Tagish, Br. Col., Can., *lake* ...214/E1
Tagish, Yukon, Can., 206 ...228/C5
Tagula, P.N.G., *island* ...94/D3
Tagus, Sp., *river* ...93/A3, B3
Tagus, N. Dak., U.S. ...326/D1
Tagus, Sp., Port., *river* ...93/A3, B3
Tahan, G., Malay., *mountain* ...121/B2
Tahat, Alg., *mountain* ...146/B2
Tahawus, N.Y., U.S. ...320/N2
Tahiti, Fr. Poly., *island* ...161
Tahlequah, Okla., U.S., 14,458 ...330/H2
Tahlequah, Wash., U.S., 225 ...358/C2
Tahoe, Calif., U.S., *lake* ...246/F3
Tahoe, Nev., U.S., *lake* ...310/A2
Tahoe City, (see Sunnyside), Calif., U.S., 1,761 ...246/E3
Tahoe Natl. For., Calif., U.S. ...246/E3
Tahoka, Tex., U.S., 2,910 ...346/G2
Taholah, Wash., U.S., 824 ...358/A2
Tahoua, Niger ...147/D3
Tahquamenon Falls St. Park, Mich., U.S. ...294/D3
Tahta, Egy. ...144/B2
Tahuya, Wash., U.S., 225 ...358/B2
Tai, Chi., *lake* ...119/F2
Tai'an, China ...119/E2
Taiban, N. Mex., U.S. ...317/F3
T'aichung, Tai. ...117/B1
Tain, Scot., U.K., 3,511 ...62/H3
T'ainan, Tai., 719,701 ...117/B1
Taipei, Tai., *capital*, 2,719,659 ...117/B1
Taitao, Chile, *peninsula* ...190/A7
T'aitung, Tai., 108,196 ...117/B2
Taiwan, *nation* ...113
Taiwan, China, *strait* ...119/E3
Taiwan, Tai., *strait* ...117/A1
Taiyuan, China, 2,051,558 ...119/D2
Ta'izz, Yemen, (290,107 *metro.*) ...137/A2
Tajikistan, *nation* ...128
Tajique, N. Mex., U.S., 148 ...317/D3
Tajumulco, Guat., *volcano* ...201/B4
Tak, Thai. ...125/B2
Taka, Marsh. Is., *island* ...173/B1
Takamaka, Sey. ...163/Inset
Takamatsu, Jap., 333,000 ...114/B3
Takara, Jap., *island* ...114/A4
Takatsuki, Jap., 357,000 ...114/B3
Takeley, Eng., U.K., 1,703 ...70/E3
Takev, Camb. ...124/C5
Takilma, Oreg., U.S., 125 ...334/C5
Takipy, Man., Can. ...215/A1
Takla, Br. Col., Can., *lake* ...214/K3
Takla Makan, China, *desert* ...119/B2
Takoma Park, Md., U.S., 17,299 ...288/B6
Takoradi, Gha. ...150/B4
Takua Pa, Thai. ...125/B4
Takutu, Guy., *river* ...183/B4
Talagante, Chile ...190/Inset
Talak, Niger, *region* ...152/B2
Talala, Okla., U.S., 270 ...203/C3
Talara, Peru ...185/A1
Talas, Kyrg. ...131/C1
Talas, Kyrg., *province* ...131/B1
Talaton, Eng., U.K. ...73/F3
Talaud, Indon., *islands* ...122/D1
Talavera de la Reina, Sp., 75,369 ...94/D3
Talbert, Ky., U.S., 250 ...280/G3
Talbot, Ga., U.S., *county*, 6,498 ...260/B6
Talbot, Md., U.S., *county*, 33,812 ...288/K4
Talbott, Tenn., U.S., 1,400 ...344/Q2
Talbotton, Ga., U.S., 1,019 ...260/B6
Talca, Chile, 172,132 ...190/B5
Talcahuano, Chile, 249,274 ...190/B5
Talco, Tex., U.S., 570 ...346/N2
Talcottville, Conn., U.S., 4,500 ...253/F2
Taldyqorgan, Kaz. ...131/D2
Talent, Oreg., U.S., 5,589 ...334/D5
Talgarth, Wales, U.K., 1,818 ...64/E4
Talihina, Okla., U.S., 1,211 ...330/G3
T'alin, Arm. ...103/A2
Talish, Azer., *mountains* ...103/C3
Talisheek, La., U.S., 60 ...282/K5
Talkeetna, Alaska, U.S., 772 ...240/E2
Talking Rock, Ga., U.S., 49 ...260/C2
Talladale, Scot., U.K. ...62/E3
Talladega, Ala., U.S., 15,143 ...238/C2
Talladega, Ala., U.S., *county*, 80,321 ...238/C2

Talladega Natl. For., Ala., U.S. ...238/D2, B3
Talladega Sprs., Ala., U.S., 124 ...238/C2
Tall Afar, Iraq ...130/B1
Tallahassee, Fla., U.S., *state capital*, 150,624, (284,539 *metro.*) ...256/D1
Tallahatchie, Miss., U.S., *county*, 14,903 ...300/B2
Tallahatchie, Miss., U.S., *river* ...300/B2
Tallahatchie N.W.R., Miss., U.S. ...300/B1, B2
Tallapoosa, Ala., U.S., *county*, 41,475 ...238/D2
Tallapoosa, Ga., U.S., 2,789 ...260/A4
Tallapoosa, Ga., U.S., *river* ...260/A4
Tallapoosa, Mo., U.S., 204 ...302/G5
Tallassee, Ala., U.S., 4,934 ...238/D3
Tallassee, Tenn., U.S. ...344/N3
Talleyville, Del., U.S., 6,300 ...255/B1
Tallgrass Prairie Natl. Pres., Kans., U.S. ...276/F3
Tallington, Eng., U.K. ...70/F1
Tallinn, Est., *capital*, 398,434 ...81/C1
Tallmadge, Ohio, U.S., 16,390 ...328/H3
Tall Timbers, Md., U.S., 275 ...288/H7
Tallula, Ill., U.S., 638 ...266/D4
Tallulah, La., U.S., 9,189 ...282/G2
Tallulah Falls, Ga., U.S., 164 ...260/E2
Talmadge, Maine, U.S., 70 ...286/E3
Talmage, Kans., U.S., 125 ...276/E2
Talmage, Nebr., U.S., 268 ...308/J3
Talmage, Utah, U.S., 60 ...350/D3
Talmo, Ga., U.S., 477 ...260/D3
Talmoon, Minn., U.S., 50 ...298/D3
Taloga, Okla., U.S., 372 ...330/D1
Talowah, Miss., U.S., 100 ...300/C4
Taloyoak, Nun., Can., 720 ...220/K3
Talquin, Fla., U.S., *lake* ...256/D1
Talsarnau, Wales, U.K. ...64/C2
Talsi, Lat. ...82/B2
Taltal, Chile ...190/B3
Taltson, N.W. Terr., Can., *river* ...220/F4
Tal-y-Bont, Wales, U.K. ...64/D1
Tal-y-bont, Wales, U.K. ...64/D3
Talybont, Wales, U.K. ...64/E4
Tal-y-cafn, Wales, U.K. ...64/D1
Tal-y-llyn, Wales, U.K. ...64/C2
Tama, Iowa, U.S., 2,731 ...274/J4
Tama, Iowa, U.S., *county*, 18,103 ...274/K3
Tamaha, Okla., U.S., 198 ...330/H2
Tamale, Gha., 136,828, (168,091 *metro.*) ...150/B2
Tamalpais Valley, (Tamalpais-Homestead Valley), Calif., U.S., 10,691 ...246/H1
Tamanrasset, Alg. ...146/B2
Tamaqua, Penn., U.S., 7,174 ...336/K4
Tamarac, Fla., U.S., 55,588 ...256/A5, H5
Tamarack, Minn., U.S., 59 ...298/D4
Tamarack N.W.R., Minn., U.S. ...298/B4
Tamarin, Mauritius ...163/B3
Tamaroa, Ill., U.S., 740 ...266/D5
Tamaulipas, Mex., *state* ...148/C3
Tambacounda, Sen. ...147/B3
Tambo, Peru, *river* ...185/C3
Tambo, Peru, *river* ...185/C4
Tâmega, Port., *river* ...93/B2
Tamerton Foliot, Eng., U.K. ...73/D4
Tameside, Eng., U.K., *unitary authority*, 213,045 ...66/D6
Tameside, Eng., U.K., *unitary authority*, 213,045 ...68/D6
Tamil Nadu, India, *state* ...128/C6
Tamina, Tex., U.S. ...346/A5
Tamms, Ill., U.S., 724 ...266/D6
Tamo, Ark., U.S., 50 ...244/D3
Tamora, Nebr., U.S., 50 ...308/G3
Tampa, Fla., U.S., 303,447, (2,395,997 *metro.*) ...256/D6, F4
Tampa, Fla., U.S., *bay* ...256/D7, F4
Tampa, Kans., U.S., 144 ...276/E3
Tampere, Fin., 197,774 ...81/B2
Tampico, Mex., 295,442, (519,480 *metro.*) ...200/D3
Tampico, Ill., U.S., 772 ...266/D2
Tampico, Mont., U.S., 60 ...306/K1
Tampico, Wash., U.S., 150 ...358/E3
Tampines, Sing. ...123/B1
Tampok, Fr. Gui., *river* ...183/B2
Tamsagbulag, Mong. ...118/D2
Tamu, Mya. ...125/B1
Tamworth, N.S.W., Austl. ...170/E3
Tamworth, Eng., U.K., 68,440, (72,988 *metro.*) ...68/D4
Tana, Eth., *lake* ...156/B1
Tana, Kenya, *river* ...157/F4
Tana, Nor., *river* ...80/F1
Tanabe, Jap. ...114/B3
Tanacross, Alaska, U.S., 140 ...240/G2
Tanaga, Alaska, U.S., *island* ...240/C6
Tanana, Alaska, U.S., 308 ...240/E1
Tanana, Alaska, U.S., *river* ...240/E2
Tanch'ŏn, N. Kor. ...116/C2
Tandil, Arg. ...191/D4
Tanega, Jap., *island* ...114/A4
Tanen, Thai., *range* ...125/B2
Taney, Mo., U.S., *county*, 39,703 ...302/C5
Taneytown, Md., U.S., 5,128 ...288/F1
Taneyville, Mo., U.S., 359 ...302/C5
Tanezrouft, Alg., *mountains* ...146/A2
Tanga, P.N.G., *islands* ...172/B2
Tanga, Tan., 187,455 ...158/C2
Tanga, Tan., *region* ...158/C2
Tangail, Bangl., 104,387 ...127/C4
Tanganyika, Bur., *lake* ...158/B2
Tanganyika, Congo, D.R., *lake* ...155/C2
Tanganyika, Tan., *lake* ...158/A2
Tanganyika, Zam., *lake* ...159/C1
Tangelo Park, Fla., U.S., 2,430 ...256/C4
Tanggula Shan, China, *range* ...119/C2
Tangent, Oreg., U.S., 933 ...334/C3
Tangier, N.S., Can. ...221/F3
Tangier, Mor. ...147/C1
Tangier, Mor., 307,000 ...147/C1
Tangier, Md., U.S., *sound* ...288/K7
Tangier, Okla., U.S., 40 ...330/C1
Tangier, Va., U.S., 604 ...354/M5
Tangipahoa, La., U.S., 747 ...282/J5
Tangipahoa, La., U.S., *parish*, 100,588 ...282/J5
Tanglewilde, (Tanglewild-Thompson Place), Wash., U.S., 5,670 ...358/C2
Tanglewood, S.C., U.S. ...340/E2
Tanglewood Forest, Tex., U.S. ...346/D2
Tangshan, China ...119/E2
Tanimbar, Indon., *islands* ...122/E2
Tanintharyi, Mya., *division* ...125/B3
Tanjungpandan, Indon. ...122/B2
Tanjungpinang, Indon. ...122/B2
Tankersley, Tex., U.S., 150 ...346/H4
Tanna, Van., *island* ...173/C4
Tannehill, Ala., U.S., 100 ...282/D2
Tanner, W. Va., U.S., 100 ...360/E3
Tannersville, N.Y., U.S., 448 ...320/N6
Tannersville, Penn., U.S., 1,000 ...336/L3
Tano, C. d'Iv., *river* ...150/E3
Tano, Gha., *river* ...150/A3
Tanque, Ariz., U.S., 40 ...242/F5
Tanque Verde, Ariz., U.S., 16,195 ...242/F5
Tanshui, Tai. ...117/B1
Tanshui, Tai., *river* ...117/B1
Tansley, Eng., U.K. ...68/D3

Tanta, Egy., 371,000 ...144/B1
Tantallon, Md., U.S., 7,900 ...288/F5
Tan-Tan, Mor. ...147/B2
Tan-y-groes, Wales, U.K. ...64/B3
Tanzania, *nation* ...152
Taongi, Marsh. Is., *island* ...173/B1
Taopi, Minn., U.S., 93 ...298/E7
Taos, Mo., U.S., 870 ...302/D3
Taos, N. Mex., U.S., 4,700 ...317/E1
Taos, N. Mex., U.S., *county*, 29,979 ...317/E1
Taos Ind. Res., N. Mex., U.S. ...317/E1
Taos Pueblo, N. Mex., U.S., 1,264 ...317/E1
Taoudenni, Mali ...150/C1
T'aoyüan, Tai. ...117/B1
Tapa, Est. ...81/C1
Tapachula, Mex., 179,839, (271,674 *metro.*) ...200/F5
Tapajós, Braz., *river* ...188/C2
Tapanahoni, Sur., *river* ...183/B3
Tapanuli, Sur. ...183/B3
Tapeta, Liber. ...149/B2
Tapiola, Mich., U.S., 40 ...294/A3
Tappahannock, Va., U.S., 2,068 ...354/K5
Tappen, N. Dak., U.S., 210 ...326/F3
Taquari, Braz., *river* ...188/C3
Tar, N.C., U.S., *river* ...322/J2
Tara, Russ. ...104/E4
Tara, Serb.-Mont., *river* ...99/A3
Tara, Iowa, U.S. ...274/F2
Taraba, Nig., *river* ...152/F3
Taraba, Nig., *state* ...152/F3
Tarakan, Indon. ...122/C1
Taranaki, N.Z., *region* ...171/B2
Tarangire Natl. Park, Tan. ...158/C1
Taransay, Scot., U.K., *island* ...62/B3
Taranto, It. ...95/C3
Taranto, It., *gulf* ...95/C3
Tarapacá, Chile, *region* ...190/C1
Tarapoto, Peru ...185/B2
Tararua, N.Z., *range* ...171/C3
Tarat, Alg. ...146/B2
Tarawa, (Bairiki), Kiri., *capital*, (25,380 *metro.*) ...175/A1
Taraz, Kaz., 330,125 ...131/D2,
Taraz, Kaz., *oblast* ...131/D2,
Tarbellville, Vt., U.S., 100 ...352/B4
Tarbert, (Strathclyde), Scot., U.K. ...62/F7,
Tarbert, (Strathclyde), Scot., U.K. ...62/C3,
Tarbert, (Western Isles), Scot., U.K. ...62/C3,
Tarbes, Fr. ...88/C5,
Tarbet, Scot., U.K. ...62/G6,
Tarboro, Ga., U.S., 125 ...260/H9,
Tarboro, N.C., U.S., 11,138 ...322/K3,
Taree, N.S.W., Austl. ...170/E3,
Tarentum, Penn., U.S., 4,993 ...336/E6
Targhee Natl. For., Ida., U.S. ...264/E5, F5, F6
Targovishte, Bul., *oblast* ...101/E2,
Tar Heel, N.C., U.S., 70 ...322/H5,
Tarif, U.A.E. ...136/B2,
Tariffville, Conn., U.S., 1,371 ...253/D2
Tarija, Bol., 163,000 ...186/B4
Tarija, Bol., *department* ...186/B4
Tarim, China, *river* ...119/B1
Tarim Kowt, Afg. ...129/B2
Tarkiln, R.I., U.S., 950 ...339/C2
Tarkio, Mo., U.S., 1,935 ...302/A1
Tarkio, Mont., U.S. ...306/B3
Tarland, Scot., U.K., 520 ...62/L4
Tarlton, Ohio, U.S., 298 ...328/E6
Tarn, Fr., *department* ...88/C5
Tarn-et-Garonne, Fr., *department* ...88/C4
Tarnobrzeg, Pol. ...83/E3
Tarnov, Nebr., U.S., 63 ...308/G2
Tarnów, Pol., 121,391 ...83/E3
Taroudannt, Mor. ...147/B2
Tarpon Sprs., Fla., U.S., 21,003 ...256/C6, F3
Tarporley, Eng., U.K., 2,308 ...68/B3
Tarrafal, C.V. ...148/C2
Tarragona, Sp., 113,129 ...94/G2
Tarragona, Sp., *province* ...94/G2
Tarrant, Tex., U.S., *county*, 1,446,219 ...346/B1, L3
Tarrant City, Ala., U.S., 7,022 ...238/C2, E1
Tarrants, Mo., U.S. ...302/E2
Tarratine, Maine, U.S. ...286/C3
Tarry, Ark., U.S., 250 ...244/D3
Tarryall, Colo., U.S. ...250/E2
Tarrytown, N.Y., U.S., 11,090 ...320/B1
Tarskavaig, Scot., U.K. ...62/E4
Tarsus, Tur. ...133/C3
Tartu, Est., 101,140 ...81/D2
Tartus, Syria ...134/A2
Tarver, Ga., U.S., 425 ...260/F1
Tarvin, Eng., U.K., 2,843 ...68/B3
Tarvo, Bol. ...186/B3
Tarzan, Tex., U.S. ...346/G3
Tasburgh, Eng., U.K. ...70/G1
Tasco, Kans., U.S. ...276/B2
Tasco, Tex., U.S. ...346/F9
Taseko, Br. Col., Can., *lake* ...214/L5
Tashigang, Bhu. ...126/C2
Tashir, Arm. ...103/B1
Tashkent, Uzb., *capital*, 2,142,700 ...132/C2
Tashkent City, Uzb., *province* ...132/C2
Tash Kömür, Kyrg. ...131/C2
Tasikmalaya, Indon. ...122/B2
Tasman, Austl., *sea* ...170/E3
Tasman, N.Z., *bay* ...171/B3
Tasman, N.Z., *region* ...171/A2
Tasman, N.Z., *sea* ...170/D4
Tasmania, Austl., *state* ...170/E4
Tassili-n-Ajjer, Alg., *mountains* ...146/B2
Tata, Mor. ...147/C2
Tatabánya, Hun. ...91/B2
Tatamagouche, N.S., Can., 738 ...221/D2
Tatamy, Penn., U.S., 930 ...336/L4
Tataouine, Tun. ...146/A2
Tatar, Russ., *strait* ...104/I4
Tatarstan, Russ., *region* ...104/D4
Tate, Ga., U.S., 500 ...260/C3
Tate, Miss., U.S., *county*, 25,370 ...300/C1
Tate, N.W. Terr., Can., *lake* ...220/E4
Tatitlek, Alaska, U.S., 107 ...240/F2
Tatla Lake, Br. Col., Can. ...214/K5
Tatlayoko Lake, Br. Col., Can. ...214/K5
Tatra, Slvk., *range* ...92/B2
Tattenhall, Eng., U.K., 1,854 ...68/B3
Tattersett, Eng., U.K. ...70/F1
Tattnall, Ga., U.S., *county*, 22,305 ...260/G8
Tatum, N. Mex., U.S., 683 ...317/G4
Tatum, S.C., U.S., 69 ...340/E2
Tatum, Tex., U.S., 1,175 ...346/P3
Tatums, Okla., U.S., 172 ...330/E3
Tatumaruni, Tur. ...171/C2
Taum Sauk, Mo., U.S., *mountain* ...302/F4
Taungdwingyi, Mya. ...125/C2
Taungoo, Mya. ...125/C2
Taunton, Eng., U.K. ...60/B3
Taunton, Eng., U.K., 58,855 ...73/F2
Taunton, Mass., U.S., 55,976 ...292/K6
Taunton, Minn., U.S., 207 ...298/A6
Taunus, Ger., *mountains* ...86/B3
Taupo, N.Z. ...171/C2

Taupo, N.Z., lake ...171/C2
Taurage, Lith. ...82/B2
Tauranga, N.Z., (95,694 metro.) ...171/C2
Taureau, Que., Can., reservoir ...226/C5
Taurus, Tur., mountains ...133/B3
Tauu, P.N.G., islands ...172/B3
Tavan Bogd Uul, Mong., mountain ...118/A2
Tavares, Fla., U.S., 9,700 ...256/C3, G3
Tavernier, Fla., U.S., 2,173 ...256/H6
Taverny, Fr. ...88/Inset II
Taveuni, Fiji, island ...174/C2
Tavistock, Eng., U.K., 10,222 ...73/D3
Tavistock, N.J., U.S. ...314/B3
Tavoy, (Dawei), Mya. ...125/C3
Tavoy, Mya., point ...125/C3
Tavush, Arm., district ...103/C2
Tawas City, Mich., U.S., 2,005 ...294/F5
Tawau, Malay. ...121/D2
Tawi Tawi, Phil., island ...120/A5
Taxal, Eng., U.K. ...68/D3
Taxco, Mex., 50,488, (100,245 metro.) ...200/E4
Tay, Yukon, Can., river ...228/C2
Tay, Scot., U.K., estuary ...60/C4
Tay, Scot., U.K., lake ...60/B2
Tay, Scot., U.K., lake ...62/H5
Tay, Scot., U.K., river ...60/B2
Tay Creek, N.B., Can. ...217/C2
Tayinloam, Scot., U.K. ...62/E7
Taylor, Ariz., U.S., 1,898 ...238/D4
Taylor, Ariz., U.S., 3,176 ...242/E3
Taylor, Ark., U.S., 566 ...244/B4
Taylor, Fla., U.S., 150 ...256/F1
Taylor, Fla., U.S., county, 19,256 ...256/E1
Taylor, Ga., U.S., county, 8,815 ...260/C6
Taylor, Iowa, U.S., county, 6,958 ...274/C6
Taylor, Ky., U.S., county, 22,927 ...280/E3
Taylor, Mich., U.S., 65,868 ...294/A7
Taylor, Miss., U.S., 289 ...300/C1
Taylor, Nebr., U.S., 207 ...308/E2
Taylor, N. Mex., U.S., mountain ...317/C2
Taylor, N. Dak., U.S., 150 ...326/C3
Taylor, Penn., U.S., 6,475 ...336/H7, K3
Taylor, Tex., U.S., 13,575 ...346/E1, L5
Taylor, Tex., U.S., county, 126,555 ...346/H3
Taylor, W. Va., U.S., county, 16,089 ...360/E4
Taylor, Wisc., U.S., 513 ...364/B4
Taylor, Wisc., U.S., county, 19,680 ...364/D3
Taylor Lake Vil., Tex., U.S., 3,694 ...346/C7
Taylor Mill, Ky., U.S., 6,913 ...280/G1
Taylors, S.C., U.S., 20,125 ...340/B2, F2
Taylors Bridge, Del., U.S. ...255/B3
Taylors Falls, Minn., U.S., 951 ...298/E5
Taylors Island, Md., U.S., 100 ...288/J6
Taylor Sprs., Ill., U.S., 583 ...266/D4
Taylorsville, Ga., U.S., 229 ...260/B3
Taylorsville, Ind., U.S., 936 ...270/E6
Taylorsville, Ky., U.S., 1,009 ...280/E2
Taylorsville, Md., U.S., 900 ...288/F2
Taylorsville, Miss., U.S., 1,341 ...300/C4
Taylorsville, N.C., U.S., 1,799 ...322/C3
Taylorsville, Utah, U.S., 57,439 ...350/E2
Taylortown, N.J., U.S., 1,200 ...314/E2
Taylortown, N.C., U.S., 845 ...322/G4
Taylorville, Ill., U.S., 11,427 ...266/D4
Taymouth, N.B., Can. ...217/C2
Taymyr, Russ., peninsula ...104/G2
Taymyr, Russ., peninsula ...193/B6
Taymyria, Russ., autonomous okrug ...104/F2
Tay Ninh, Viet. ...123/B4
Taynton, Eng., U.K. ...68/C6
Taynton, Eng., U.K. ...70/A3
Tayport, Scot., U.K., 3,847 ...62/L6
Taza, Mor. ...147/C1
Tazewell, Ill., U.S., county, 128,485 ...266/D3
Tazewell, Tenn., U.S., 2,165 ...344/F2
Tazewell, Va., U.S., 4,206 ...354/E2
Tazewell, Va., U.S., county, 44,598 ...354/E2
Tazin, Sask., Can., lake ...227/A1
Tazin, Sask., Can., river ...227/B1
T'bilisi, Geo., capital, 1,398,968 ...103/C4
Tchamba, Togo ...151/B2
Tchaourou, Ben. ...151/B2
Tchentlo, Br. Col., Can., lake ...214/K3
Tchibanga, Gabon ...155/A2
Tchula, Miss., U.S., 2,332 ...300/B2
Tea, S. Dak., U.S., 1,742 ...342/J4
Teachey, N.C., U.S., 245 ...322/J5
Teague, Tex., U.S., 4,557 ...346/M4
Teafwhit Head, Wash., U.S., cape ...358/A2
Te Anau, N.Z., lake ...171/A4
Teaneck, N.J., U.S., 39,260 ...314/C2, E2
Teasdale, Utah, U.S., 100 ...350/G5
Teaticket, Mass., U.S., 1,907 ...292/M6
Tea Tree Gully, S.A., Austl. ...170/Inset II
Teays, W. Va., U.S., 2,400 ...360/C4
Tebay, Eng., U.K. ...66/C4
Tebicuary, Para., river ...187/D5
Tecolote, N. Mex., U.S., 125 ...317/E2
Tecomán, Mex., 74,106, (99,289 metro.) ...200/D4
Tecopa, Calif., U.S., 99 ...246/J7
Tecuci, Rom. ...101/D3
Tecumseh, Kans., U.S., 600 ...276/G2
Tecumseh, Mich., U.S., 8,574 ...294/F7
Tecumseh, Mo., U.S. 50 ...302/D5
Tecumseh, Nebr., U.S., 1,716 ...308/H3
Tecumseh, Okla., U.S., 6,098 ...330/G2
Tedburn St. Mary, Eng., U.K. ...73/E2
Teddington, Eng., U.K. ...68/C6
Teec Nos Pos, Ariz., U.S., 799 ...242/F1
Teeds Grove, Iowa, U.S., 100 ...274/P3
Teepee Creek, Alta., Can. ...212/A3
Tees, Eng., U.K., river ...60/C2
Teesdale, Eng., U.K., valley ...66/D3
Tees Toh, Ariz., U.S. ...242/E2
Teeswater, Ont., Can., 1,109 ...223/D3
Tefé, Braz. ...188/B2
Teffont Magna, Eng., U.K. ...73/H2
Tega Cay, S.C., U.S., 4,044 ...340/C1
Tegal, Indon. ...122/B2
Tegarden, Okla., U.S. ...330/D1
Tegid, Wales, U.K., lake ...64/D2
Tegryn, Wales, U.K. ...64/B4
Tegucigalpa, Hond., capital, 835,294, (919,000 metro.) ...202/B2
Tehachapi, Calif., U.S., 10,957 ...246/G7
Tehachapi, Calif., U.S., mountains ...246/G8
Tehama, Calif., U.S., 432 ...246/C2
Tehama, Calif., U.S., county, 56,039 ...246/C3
Tehek, Nun., Can., lake ...220/J4
Tehkummah, Ont., Can. ...223/D2
Tehran, Iran, capital, 6,758,845 ...130/C2
Tehran, Iran, province ...130/C2
Tehuacán, Mex., 204,598, (226,258 metro.) ...200/E4
Tehuantepec, Mex., gulf ...200/F4
Tehuantepec, Mex., isthmus ...200/F4
Teifi, Wales, U.K., river ...60/B3
Teigen, Mont., U.S. ...306/H2
Teignmouth, Eng., U.K., 13,528 ...73/E3
Tejen, Turkm. ...132/C3
Tejen, Turkm., river ...132/C3

Tekamah, Nebr., U.S., 1,892 ...308/H2
Tekapo, N.Z., lake ...171/B3
Tekeze, Eth., river ...156/B1
Tekirdağ, Tur. ...133/A2
Tekirdağ, Tur., province ...133/A2
Tekoa, Wash., U.S., 826 ...358/H2
Tekong, Sing., island ...123/C1
Tekonsha, Mich., U.S., 712 ...294/E7
Tela, Hond., 24,800 ...202/B2
Telavi, Geo. ...103/C4
Tel Aviv, Isr., district ...135/B1
Tel Aviv-Jaffa, Isr., 348,300, (2,594,700 metro.) ...135/B1
Telde, Sp., 87,949 ...94/Inset I
Telegraph, Tex., U.S. ...346/J5
Telegraph Creek, Br. Col., Can. ...214/G2
Telemark, Nor., province ...80/B4
Teleorman, Rom., county ...101/C3
Telescope, Calif., U.S., peak ...246/H6
Teles Pires, Braz., river ...188/C2
Telfair, Ga., U.S., county, 11,794 ...260/E8
Telferner, Tex., U.S., 550 ...346/M7
Telford, Eng., U.K. ...60/C3
Telford, Eng., U.K., 35,790 ...68/C4
Telford, Penn., U.S., 4,680 ...336/L5
Télimélé, Guin. ...149/B2
Telkwa, Br. Col., Can., 1,371 ...214/J4
Tell, Tex., U.S., 40 ...346/H1
Tell City, Ind., U.S., 7,845 ...270/C9
Teller, Alaska, U.S., 268 ...240/B1
Teller, Colo., U.S., county, 20,555 ...250/E3
Tellico Plains, Tenn., U.S., 859 ...344/H4
Tell Region, Alg. ...146/A1
Telluride, Colo., U.S., 2,221 ...250/C4
Telma, Wash., U.S., 80 ...358/E2
Telocaset, Oreg., U.S., 70 ...334/J2
Telogia, Fla., U.S., 200 ...256/D1
Telok Anson, Malay. ...121/A2
Telos, Maine, U.S., lake ...286/C2
Telšiai, Lith. ...82/B2
Tema, Gha., 109,975 ...150/C4
Temagami, Ont., Can., lake ...223/E1
Tembilahan, Indon. ...122/B2
Tembrong, Bru., river ...121/C2
Temecula, Calif., U.S., 57,716 ...246/H9
Temirtaū, Kaz., 170,481 ...131/D1
Te-Moak Ind. Res., Nev., U.S. ...310/C1
Tempe, Ariz., U.S., 158,625 ...242/D4
Temperance, Mich., U.S., 7,757 ...294/F8
Temperanceville, Va., U.S., 275 ...354/M5
Tempisque, C.R., river ...203/A2
Tempiute, Nev., U.S. ...310/C3
Temple, Ga., U.S., 2,383 ...260/A4
Temple, La., U.S. ...282/D4
Temple, Maine, U.S., 572 ...286/B4
Temple, Mich., U.S., 200 ...294/D5
Temple, N.H., U.S., 1,297 ...312/C6
Temple, Okla., U.S., 1,146 ...330/F3
Temple, Penn., U.S., 1,400 ...336/K5
Temple, Tex., U.S., 54,514 ...346/L4
Temple Bar, Wales, U.K. ...64/C3
Temple Bar, Ariz., U.S. ...242/A1
Temple City, Calif., U.S., 33,377 ...246/D9
Temple Ewell, Eng., U.K. ...70/G4
Temple Hill, Ky., U.S., 175 ...280/E4
Temple Hills, Md., U.S., 7,792 ...288/C7
Templepatrick, N. Ire., U.K., 1,414 ...65/E2
Temple Sowerby, Eng., U.K. ...66/C2
Temple Terrace, Fla., U.S., 20,918 ...256/D6, F3
Templeton, Wales, U.K. ...64/B4
Templeton, Calif., U.S., 4,687 ...246/E7
Templeton, Iowa, U.S., 334 ...274/E4
Templeton, Mass., U.S., 6,799 ...292/F2
Templeville, Md., U.S., 80 ...288/L3
Tempo, N. Ire., U.K., 292 ...65/C3
Temuco, Chile, 246,304 ...190/B5
Temvik, N. Dak., U.S. ...326/E3
Tena, Ecua. ...185/C3
Tenafly, N.J., U.S., 13,806 ...314/C2, F2
Tenaha, Tex., U.S., 1,046 ...346/P4
Tenakee Sprs., Alaska, U.S., 104 ...240/H3
Téna Kourou, Burkina, mountain ...151/B3
Tenants Harbor, Maine, U.S., 500 ...286/C5
Tenbury Wells, Eng., U.K., 2,219 ...68/B5
Tenby, Wales, U.K., 5,619 ...64/B4
Ten Degree, India, channel ...125/C3
Tendoy, Ida., U.S. ...264/D5
Ténéré, Erg du, Niger, desert ...152/B2
Ténéré, Niger, region ...152/C1
Tenerife, Sp., island ...94/Inset I
Tengiz, Kaz., lake ...131/C1
Tenille, Fla., U.S. ...256/E2
Tenino, Wash., U.S., 1,447 ...358/C3
Tenkodogo, Burkina ...151/D3
Tenmile, Oreg., U.S., 225 ...334/C4
Ten Mile, Tenn., U.S., 40 ...344/M3
Tennant, Ala., U.S., 70 ...238/D2
Tennant, Calif., U.S., 63 ...246/D1
Tennant, Iowa, U.S., 73 ...274/D4
Tennant Creek, N.T., Austl. ...170/C1
Tennent, N.J., U.S., 1,100 ...314/E3
Tennessee, U.S., state ...332
Tennessee, Ala., U.S., river ...238/A1
Tennessee, Ill., U.S., 144 ...266/C3
Tennessee, Miss., U.S. ...300/E1
Tennessee City, Tenn., U.S., 175 ...344/F2
Tennessee, Tenn., U.S., river ...344/E5, K5
Tennessee N.W.R., Tenn., U.S. ...344/E2, F3
Tennessee Ridge, Tenn., U.S., 1,334 ...344/F2
Tenney, Minn., U.S. ...298/A4
Tennille, Ga., U.S., 1,505 ...260/F6
Tennyson, Ind., U.S., 290 ...270/B8
Tennyson, Tex., U.S. ...346/H4
Tennyson, Wisc., U.S., 370 ...364/H4
Tenojoki, Fin., river ...81/C1
Tenryu, Jap., river ...114/C3
Tensas, La., U.S., parish, 6,618 ...282/G3
Tensas River N.W.R., La., U.S. ...282/G2
Tensaw, Ala., U.S. ...238/B4
Tensed, Ida., U.S., 126 ...264/A2
Ten Sleep, Wyo., U.S., 304 ...366/C1
Tenstrike, Minn., U.S., 195 ...298/C3
Tenterden, Eng., U.K., 6,803 ...70/F4
Teotihuacán, Mex. ...200/Inset
Tepelenë, Alb. ...99/A3
Tepexpan, Mex. ...200/Inset
Tepic, Mex., state capital, 265,817, (305,176 metro.) ...200/D3
Tequesta, Fla., U.S., 5,273 ...256/M4
Téra, Niger ...152/A3
Teraina, Kiri., island ...175/D1
Teramo, It. ...95/C2
Terceira, Port. ...93/Inset II
Tererro, N. Mex., U.S. ...317/E2
Teresina, Braz., 715,360 ...188/D2
Terlingua, Tex., U.S., 267 ...346/E6
Terlton, Okla., U.S., 85 ...330/F1
Terminous, Calif., U.S. ...246/L1
Termiz, Uzb., 111,500 ...132/C3
Termini, Calif., U.S. ...246/E2
Termoli, It. ...95/C2

Ternhill, Eng., U.K. ...68/B4
Terni, It. ...95/C2
Ternopil', Ukr., 233,152 ...102/B2
Ternopil', Ukr., oblast ...102/B2
Terra Alta, W. Va., U.S., 1,456 ...360/G2
Terra Bella, Calif., U.S., 3,466 ...246/F7
Terrace, Br. Col., Can., 12,109 ...214/H4
Terrace, Minn., U.S., 40 ...298/B5
Terrace Hts., Wash., U.S., 6,447 ...358/E3
Terrace Park, Ohio, U.S., 2,273 ...328/C9
Terral, Okla., U.S., 386 ...330/E4
Terra Nova Natl. Park, Nfld., Can. ...218/D5
Terrassa, Sp., 173,775 ...94/H2
Terrebonne, Que., Can., 43,149 ...226/J5
Terrebonne, La., U.S., bay ...282/H8
Terrebonne, La., U.S., parish, 104,503 ...282/G7
Terrebonne, Minn., U.S., 40 ...298/A3
Terrebonne, Oreg., U.S., 1,469 ...334/E3
Terre Haute, Ind., U.S., 59,614, (149,192 metro.) ...270/B6
Terre Hill, Penn., U.S., 1,237 ...336/J5
Terreiro Velho, São T.-Prínc. ...154/C1
Terrell, Ga., U.S., county, 10,970 ...260/C8
Terrell, Tex., U.S., 13,606 ...346/M3
Terrell, Tex., U.S., county, 1,081 ...346/E5
Terrell Hills, Tex., U.S., 5,019 ...346/A2
Terrenceville, Nfld., Can., 630 ...218/D5
Terreton, Ida., U.S., 125 ...264/E6
Terril, Iowa, U.S., 404 ...274/E1
Terrington, Eng., U.K. ...68/F1
Terry, La., U.S., 225 ...282/C1
Terry, Miss., U.S., 664 ...300/B3
Terry, Mont., U.S., 611 ...306/L3
Terry, Tex., U.S., county, 12,761 ...346/F2
Terrytown, La., U.S., 25,430 ...282/K3
Terrytown, Nebr., U.S., 646 ...308/A2
Terryville, Conn., U.S., 5,360 ...253/C3
Terryville, Tex., U.S. ...346/L6
Terschelling, Neth., island ...84/C1
Teruel, Sp., 31,158 ...94/F2
Teruel, Sp., province ...94/F2
Tescott, Kans., U.S., 339 ...276/E2
Teseney, Erit. ...156/A2
Teshio, Jap., river ...114/Inset
Tesiyn, Mong., river ...118/B2
Teslić, Bos.-Her. ...98/B1
Teslin, Br. Col., Can., lake ...214/F1
Teslin, Br. Col., Can., river ...214/G1
Teslin, Yukon, Can., 123 ...228/C5
Teslin, Yukon, Can., lake ...228/C5
Teslin, Yukon, Can., river ...228/C5
Tes Nez Iah, Ariz., U.S. ...242/F1
Tessalit, Mali ...150/D1
Tessaoua, Niger ...152/B3
Test, Eng., U.K., river ...70/A4
Testa del Gargano, It., point ...95/C2
Teston, Eng., U.K. ...70/E4
Tesuque, N. Mex., U.S., 909 ...317/E2
Tesuque Pueblo, N. Mex., U.S., 225 ...317/E2
Tetbury, Eng., U.K., 4,618 ...68/C6
Tete, Moz. ...161/B3
Tête Jaune Cache, Br. Col., Can. ...214/N5
Teterboro, N.J., U.S. ...314/B2
Teterville, Kans., U.S. ...276/F3
Tetford, Eng., U.K. ...66/H6
Tetlin Jct., (Tetlin), Alaska, U.S., 117 ...240/G2
Tetlin N.W.R., Alaska, U.S. ...240/Inset
Teton, Ida., U.S., 569 ...264/F6
Teton, Ida., U.S., county, 5,999 ...264/F6
Teton, Ida., U.S., river ...264/F6
Teton, Mont., U.S., county, 6,445 ...306/D2
Teton, Mont., U.S., river ...306/F2
Teton, Wyo., U.S., county, 18,251 ...366/A2
Teton, Wyo., U.S., river ...366/A2
Tetonia, Ida., U.S., 247 ...264/F6
Teton Vil., Wyo., U.S., 175 ...366/A2
Tétouan, Mor., 272,000 ...147/C1
Tetovo, Mac., 50,344 ...100/A1
Tetsworth, Eng., U.K. ...68/F6
Teulada, It., cape ...95/B3
Teulon, Man., Can., 1,058 ...215/C4
Teutopolis, Ill., U.S., 1,559 ...266/E4
Teviotdale, Scot., U.K. ...62/K8
Tewaukon N.W.R., N. Dak., U.S. ...326/H3
Tewkesbury, Eng., U.K. ...60/C3
Tewkesbury, Eng., U.K., 9,488 ...68/C5
Tewksbury, Mass., U.S., 28,851 ...292/B5, K2
Texarkana, Ark., U.S., 26,448 ...244/A4
Texarkana, Tex., U.S., 34,782, (129,749 metro.) ...346/P2
Texas, U.S., state ...334
Texas, Mass., U.S., 1,300 ...292/C4
Texas, Mo., U.S., county, 23,003 ...302/D4
Texas, Okla., U.S., county, 20,107 ...330/C4
Texas City, Tex., U.S., 41,521 ...346/C7
Texas Creek, Colo., U.S. ...250/E3
Texas Pt. N.W.R., Tex., U.S. ...346/R6
Texasville, Ala., U.S. ...238/D4
Texcoco, Mex. ...200/Inset
Texel, Neth., island ...84/B1
Texhoma, Okla., U.S., 935 ...330/C4
Texhoma, Tex., U.S., 371 ...346/F8
Texico, N. Mex., U.S., 1,065 ...317/G3
Texline, Tex., U.S., 511 ...346/E8
Texola, Okla., U.S., 47 ...330/C2
Texon, Tex., U.S., 40 ...346/G4
Teyateyaneng, Leso., 14,251 ...161/A2
Teynham, Eng., U.K., 3,038 ...70/F4
Tezoyuca, Mex. ...200/Inset
Tezzeron, Br. Col., Can., lake ...214/K4
Thabana-Ntlenyana, Leso., mountain ...161/A2
Thaba-Tseka, Leso. ...161/B2
Thach, Ala., U.S. ...238/C1
Thacher Island N.W.R., Mass., U.S. ...292/M2
Thackerville, Okla., U.S., 404 ...330/E4
Thailand, nation ...121
Thailand, Camb., gulf ...124/A4
Thailand, Thai., gulf ...125/B4
Thai Nguyen, Viet., 127,643 ...123/A2
Thakhèk, Laos ...124/C3
Thakurgaon, Bngl. ...128/A1
Thale Luang, Thai., lagoon ...125/B5
Thalia, Tex., U.S., 40 ...346/J2
Thalmann, Ga., U.S., 125 ...260/H9
Thame, Eng., U.K., 10,806 ...68/F6
Thame, Eng., U.K., 10,806 ...70/C3
Thames, Ont., Can., river ...223/D5
Thames, Eng., U.K., river ...60/C3, Inset III
Thames, Eng., U.K., river ...68/B3
Thames, Eng., U.K., river ...88/B1, C1
Thames, Conn., U.S., river ...253/C4
Thamesville, Ont., Can., 928 ...223/D5
Thane, India, 1,261,517 ...128/Inset I
Thanh Hoa, Viet. ...123/A2
Thanjavur, India ...128/C6
Thar, Pak., desert ...129/C4
Thasos, Gr. ...100/C1
Thasos, Gr., island ...100/C1
Thatcham, Eng., U.K., 20,726 ...70/B4
Thatcher, Ariz., U.S., 4,022 ...242/F5
Thatcher, Colo., U.S., 40 ...250/F4
Thatcher, Ida., U.S. ...264/F7

Thawville, Ill., U.S., 258 ...266/E3
Thaxted, Eng., U.K., 1,899 ...70/E3
Thaxton, Miss., U.S., 513 ...300/C1
Thayer, Ill., U.S., 750 ...266/D4
Thayer, Iowa, U.S., 66 ...274/F4
Thayer, Kans., U.S., 500 ...276/G4
Thayer, Mo., U.S., 2,201 ...302/E5
Thayer, Nebr., U.S., 71 ...308/G3
Thayer, Nebr., U.S., county, 6,055 ...308/G3
Thayer Jct., Wyo., U.S. ...366/B3
Thayne, Wyo., U.S., 341 ...366/A2
Theale, Eng., U.K., 2,640 ...70/B4
Theba, Ariz., U.S. ...242/C5
The Bage, Eng., U.K. ...68/A5
Theberton, Eng., U.K. ...70/H2
Thebes, Ill., U.S., 478 ...266/D6
The Braes, Scot., U.K. ...62/D4
The Channel Tunnel, Eng., U.K. ...70/G4
The Cheviot, Eng., U.K., hill ...66/D2
The Colony, Tex., U.S., 26,531 ...346/C8
The Crane, Barb. ...209/C4
The Dalles, Oreg., U.S., 12,156 ...334/E2
Thedford, Ont., Can., 755 ...223/D4
Thedford, Nebr., U.S., 211 ...308/D2
The Flatt, Eng., U.K. ...66/C2
The Forks, Maine, U.S. ...286/C3
The Gap, Ariz., U.S., 175 ...242/D1
The Glen, N.Y., U.S. ...320/P3
The Grand Strand, S.C., U.S., beach ...340/F3
The Hague, Neth., 441,094, (608,862 metro.) ...84/B2
The Hamptons, (Hamptons at Boca Raton), Fla., U.S., 11,306 ...256/B5
The Hill, Eng., U.K. ...66/B4
Thekulthili, N.W. Terr., Can., lake ...220/G4
The Landing, Mo., U.S. ...302/E2
The Lhen, Eng., U.K. ...66/B5
Thelma, Tex., U.S. ...346/A3, K6
Thelon, N.W. Terr., Can., river ...220/H4
Thelon, Nun., Can., river ...220/J4
The Medway Towns, Eng., U.K., unitary authority, 249,502 ...70/F4
The Merse, Eng., U.K., river ...66/C1
The Mumbles, Wales, U.K. ...64/D4
The Naze, Eng., U.K., cape ...70/G3
Thendara, N.Y., U.S., 300 ...320/L3
Theodore, Sask., Can., 381 ...227/H3
Theodore, Ala., U.S., 6,811 ...238/A5
Theodore Roosevelt, Ariz., U.S., lake ...242/D4
Theodore Roosevelt Natl. Park, (Elkhorn Ranch Unit), N. Dak., U.S. ...326/B2
Theodore Roosevelt Natl. Park, (N. Unit), N. Dak., U.S. ...326/B2
Theodore Roosevelt Natl. Park, (S. Unit), N. Dak., U.S. ...326/B2
Theodosia, Mo., U.S., 240 ...302/D5
The Ovens, N.S., Can. ...221/C3
The Pas, Man., Can., 5,795 ...215/A2, C2
The Pinery, Colo., U.S., 7,253 ...250/F2
The Plains, Ohio, U.S., 2,931 ...328/F4
The Plains, Va., U.S., 266 ...354/H3
Theresa, N.Y., U.S., 812 ...320/K2
Theresa, Wisc., U.S., 1,252 ...364/E5
Theressa, Fla., U.S., 175 ...256/F2
Therfield, Eng., U.K. ...70/D2
Theriot, La., U.S., 225 ...282/H8
Thermalito, Calif., U.S., 6,045 ...246/D3
Thermopolis, Wyo., U.S., 3,172 ...366/C2
The Rock, Ga., U.S., 80 ...260/C6
The Sheddings, N. Ire., U.K. ...65/E2
The Small Isles, Scot., U.K., islands ...62/C5
Thessalon, Ont., Can., 1,386 ...223/D1
Thessaloniki, Gr., 363,987, (768,000 metro.) ...100/B1
Thessaly, Gr., region ...100/B2
The Temple, N. Ire., U.K. ...65/F3
Thetford, Eng., U.K. ...60/D3
Thetford, Eng., U.K., 20,058 ...70/F2
Thetford, Vt., U.S. ...352/E3
Thetford Ctr., Vt., U.S. ...352/C3
Thetford Mines, Que., Can., 16,628 ...226/E5
The Village, Okla., U.S., 10,157 ...330/B3, E2
The Wash, Eng., U.K., bay ...70/E1
The Wolds, Eng., U.K., hills ...66/G4
The Woodlands, Tex., U.S., 55,649 ...346/A5, N5
The Wrekin, Eng., U.K., unitary authority, 158,285 ...68/B4
Thibodaux, La., U.S., 14,431 ...282/H7
Thicket Ice, Antar. ...192/C3
Thicket, Barb. ...209/C4
Thicket Portage, Man., Can., 137 ...215/C1
Thief River Falls, Minn., U.S., 8,410 ...298/A2
Thielsen, Oreg., U.S., mountain ...334/D4
Thiensville, Wisc., U.S., 3,254 ...364/F1
Thiès, Sen., (256,113 metro.) ...148/A2
Thika, Kenya, 57,603 ...157/D4
Thiladhunmathi, Mald., atoll ...127/A1
Thimbu, Bhu., capital, 28,000 ...126/A2
Thingvellir, Ice. ...79/A2
Thira, (Santorini), Gr., island ...100/C3
Third Lake, Ill., U.S., 1,355 ...266/B4
Thirlmere, Eng., U.K., lake ...66/B3
Thirsk, Eng., U.K., 6,860 ...66/F4
Thiruvananthapuram, India 523,733, (825,682 metro.) ...128/C7
Thisted, Den. ...79/B2
Thistle, Utah, U.S. ...350/G4
Thixendale, Eng., U.K. ...66/G4
Thlewiaza, Nun., Can., river ...215/D1
Tholen, Neth., island ...84/B3
Thomas, Ga., U.S., county, 42,737 ...260/C1
Thomas, Kans., U.S., county, 8,180 ...276/A2
Thomas, Nebr., U.S., county, 729 ...308/D2
Thomas, Okla., U.S., 1,238 ...330/D2
Thomas, S. Dak., U.S., 40 ...342/H3
Thomas, W. Va., U.S., 452 ...360/H2
Thomasboro, Ill., U.S., 1,233 ...266/E3
Thomas Cole N.H.S., N.Y., U.S. ...320/P6
Thomas Hill, Mo., U.S., reservoir ...302/D2
Thomas Stone N.H.S., Md., U.S. ...288/F3
Thomaston, Conn., U.S., 7,503 ...253/C3
Thomaston, Ga., U.S., 9,411 ...260/C6
Thomaston, Maine, U.S., 3,748 ...286/C4
Thomaston, Mich., U.S., 90 ...294/C2
Thomaston, Tex., U.S. ...346/L6
Thomaston Corner, N.B., Can. ...217/B3
Thomastown, Miss., U.S., 100 ...300/C3
Thomasville, Ala., U.S., 4,649 ...238/B4
Thomasville, Ga., U.S., 18,162 ...260/D1
Thomasville, Mo., U.S., 40 ...302/E5
Thomasville, N.C., U.S., 19,788 ...322/E3
Thompson, Br. Col., Can., river ...214/M6
Thompson, Man., Can., 13,256 ...215/C1, D2
Thompson, Conn., U.S. ...253/H2
Thompson, Conn., U.S., 8,878 ...253/H2
Thompson, Iowa, U.S., 596 ...274/G1
Thompson, Mich., U.S. ...294/C4
Thompson, Miss., U.S. ...300/B4
Thompson, N. Dak., U.S., 1,006 ...326/H2
Thompson, Penn., U.S., 299 ...336/K2
Thompson Corners, Maine, U.S. ...286/D3

Thompson Falls, Mont., U.S., 1,321 ......306/A2
Thompson Place, (see Tanglewild),
  Wash., U.S., 5,670 ......358/C2
Thompsons, Tex., U.S., 236 ......346/A7
Thompson Sprs., Utah, U.S., 50 ......350/E5
Thompsons Sta., Tenn., U.S., 1,283 ......344/H3
Thompsontown, Md., U.S., 90 ......288/L5
Thompsontown, Penn., U.S., 711 ......336/G4
Thompsonville, Conn., U.S., 1,600 ......253/E2
Thompsonville, Ill., U.S., 571 ......266/E6
Thompsonville, Mich., U.S., 457 ......294/D5
Thomson, Ga., U.S., 6,828 ......260/G5
Thomson, Ill., U.S., 559 ......266/C2
Thomson, Minn., U.S., 153 ......298/E4
Thong Hoe, Sing. 123/A1
Thor, Iowa, U.S., 174 ......274/F2
Thoreau, N. Mex., U.S., 1,863 ......317/B2
Thorhild, Alta., Can., 462 ......212/D4
Thorn, Miss., U.S., 200 ......300/C2
Thornaby-on-Tees, Eng., U.K., 24,189 ......66/F3
Thornburg, Ark., U.S., 100 ......244/C3
Thornburg, Iowa, U.S., 84 ......274/K5
Thornburg, Penn., U.S., 468 ......336/D7
Thornburg, Va., U.S., 450 ......354/H4
Thornbury, Eng., U.K., 12,108 ......73/G1
Thorndale, Penn., U.S., 3,561 ......336/K5
Thorndale, Tex., U.S., 1,278 ......346/L5
Thorndike, Maine, U.S., 712 ......286/C4
Thorndon, Eng., U.K. 70/G2
Thorne, (Thorne/Moorends), Eng., U.K., 16,751 ......66/G5
Thorne, (Thorne/Moorends), Eng., U.K., 16,751 ......68/E2
Thorne, Nev., U.S. 310/A2
Thorne Bay, Alaska, U.S., 557 ......240/J3
Thorney, Eng., U.K. 70/D1
Thornfield, Mo., U.S., 60 ......302/D5
Thornhill, Ont., Can. 223/K5
Thornhill, Scot., U.K. 62/J8
Thornley, Eng., U.K., 2,970 ......66/F3
Thornthwaite, Eng., U.K. 66/B3
Thornton, (Buckinghamshire), Eng., U.K. 68/F5
Thornton, (Lancashire-Thornton/Cleveleys),
  Eng., U.K., 28,061 ......68/D4
Thornton, Eng., U.K. 66/B5
Thornton, Eng., U.K. 66/E3
Thornton, Eng., U.K. 70/C2
Thornton, Ark., U.S., 517 ......244/C4
Thornton, Calif., U.S., 850 ......246/K6, L1
Thornton, Colo., U.S., 82,384 ......250/A3
Thornton, Ida., U.S., 300 ......264/F6
Thornton, Ill., U.S., 2,582 ......266/C6
Thornton, Iowa, U.S., 422 ......274/H2
Thornton, Miss., U.S. 300/B2
Thornton, (see Farragut), Tenn., U.S. 344/N3
Thornton, Tex., U.S., 525 ......346/M4
Thornton, Wash., U.S., 70 ......358/H2
Thornton, W. Va., U.S., 175 ......360/G2
Thornton, Wisc., U.S., 100 ......312/C6
Thorntons Ferry, N.H., U.S. 292/E2
Thorntonville, Tex., U.S., 442 ......346/F4
Thorntown, Ind., U.S., 1,562 ......270/C4
Thornville, Ohio, U.S., 731 ......328/F6
Thornwood, W. Va., U.S., 50 ......360/F4
Thorofare, N.J., U.S., 1,500 ......314/C4
Thorold, Ont., Can., 18,048 ......223/F4
Thorp, Wash., U.S., 273 ......358/E2
Thorp, Wisc., U.S., 1,536 ......364/C4
Thorpe, Eng., U.K. 68/D3
Thorpe-le-Soken, Eng., U.K., 1,509 ......70/G3
Thorpe Mandeville, Eng., U.K. 70/B2
Thorpeness, Eng., U.K. 70/H2
Thorpe on the Hill, Eng., U.K. 66/F5
Thorpe Salvin, Eng., U.K. 66/F6
Thorrington, Eng., U.K. 70/G3
Thorsby, Alta., Can., 799 ......212/C4
Thorsby, Ala., U.S., 1,820 ......238/C3
Thousand, Ont., Can., islands 320/J2
Thousand Oaks, Calif., U.S., 117,005 ......246/G8
Thousandsticks, Ky., U.S., 70 ......280/G3
Thrace, Bul., region 101/D4
Thrace, Tur., region 133/A2
Thrall, Tex., U.S., 710 ......346/L5
Thrapston, Eng., U.K., 3,912 ......68/F5
Thrapston, Eng., U.K., 3,912 ......70/C2
Thrashers Corner, (part of N. Creek-Canyon Park),
  Wash., U.S. 358/A4
Threapwood, Eng., U.K. 68/B3
Three Bridges, N.J., U.S., 850 ......314/D2
Three Brooks, N.B., Can. 217/B2
Three Creek, Ida., U.S., 50 ......264/F6
Three Creeks, Ark., U.S. 244/C4
Three Forks, Mont., U.S., 1,728 ......306/E4
Three Hills, Alta., Can., 2,902 ......212/D5
Three Kings, N.Z., islands 171/K1
Three Lakes, Mich., U.S. 294/A3
Three Lakes, Wisc., U.S., 600 ......364/D3
Threelinks, Ky., U.S. 280/F3
Three Oaks, Mich., U.S., 1,829 ......294/C8
Three Pts., Ariz., U.S., 5,273 ......242/D5
Three Pts., (see Mascot), Tenn., U.S. 344/P2
Three Rivers, Calif., U.S., 2,248 ......246/G6
Three Rivers, Mass., U.S., 2,939 ......292/E4
Three Rivers, Mich., U.S., 7,328 ......294/D8
Three Rivers, N. Mex., U.S. 317/C4
Three Rivers, Oreg., U.S., 2,445 ......334/E4
Three Rivers, Tex., U.S., 1,878 ......346/K7
Three Rocks, Calif., U.S. 246/E6
Three Sprs., Penn., U.S., 445 ......336/F5
Threlkeld, Eng., U.K. 66/B3
Thringarth, Eng., U.K. 66/D3
Throckmorton, Tex., U.S., 905 ......346/J2
Throckmorton, Tex., U.S., county, 1,850 ......346/J2
Throop, Penn., U.S., 4,010 ......336/H7
Thrumster, Scot., U.K. 62/K1
Thule, Grld., air base 193/B2
Thun, Switz. 90/B2
Thunder, Ont., Can., bay 294/A1, F5
Thunder, Ont., Can., cape 294/A1
Thunder Basin Natl. Grassland, Wyo., U.S. 366/D1, D2
Thunder Bay, Ont., Can., 109,016,
  (125,100 metro.) 222/C3
Thunderbolt, Ga., U.S., 2,340 ......260/J7
Thunder Butte, S. Dak., U.S., 60 ......342/D2
Thunder Hawk, S. Dak., U.S. 342/D2
Thunersee, Switz., lake 90/B2
Thurcroft, Eng., U.K., 905 ......66/F6
Thurcroft, Eng., U.K., 5,115 ......68/E3
Thurgau, Switz., canton 90/C1
Thuringia, Ger., state 86/B3
Thuringian, Ger., forest 86/B3
Thurlestone, Eng., U.K. 73/E4
Thurman, Colo., U.S. 250/G2
Thurman, Iowa, U.S., 236 ......274/C6
Thurmond, W. Va., U.S. 360/D5
Thurmont, Md., U.S., 5,588 ......288/E1,
Thurnby, Eng., U.K. 70/B1,
Thurrock, Eng., U.K., unitary authority,
  143,042 ......70/E3,
Thursby, Eng., U.K. 66/B3,
Thursley, Eng., U.K. 70/C4,
Thurso, Que., Can. 60/B1,
Thurso, Scot., U.K., 7,737 ......62/K1,

Thurston, Antar., island 192/B9,
Thurston, Nebr., U.S., 125 ......308/H1,
Thurston, Nebr., U.S., county, 7,171 ......308/H1,
Thurston, Ohio, U.S., 555 ......328/E6,
Thurston, Wash., U.S., county, 207,355 ......358/C3,
Thurton, Eng., U.K. 70/G1,
Tiadaghton St. For., Penn., U.S. 336/F3, G3, H3
Tiáhuac, Mex. 200/Inset,
Tianjin, China, 5,855,044 ......119/E2,
Tianjin, China, independent municipality 119/E2
Ti'avea, Sam. 175/D2
Tibati, Came. 153/B2
Tibbie, Ala., U.S., 50 ......238/A4
Tiber, It., river 95/C2
Tiberias, Isr. 135/B1
Tiberias, (Galilee), Isr., lake 135/B1
Tiberias, Jor., lake 134/A1
Tibesti, Chad, massif 153/B2
Tibet, (Xizang), China, autonomous region 119/B3
Tibet, China, plateau 119/B2
Tiburon, Calif., U.S., 8,666 ......246/J1
Tiburón, Mex., island 200/B2
Ticaboo, Utah, U.S., 40 ......350/D6
Ticehurst, Eng., U.K. 70/E4
Tichît, Maur. 147/C3
Tichla, W. Sah. 147/A2
Tichnor, Ark., U.S. 244/D3
Ticino, Switz., canton 90/C2
Ticino, Switz., river 90/C2
Tickfaw, La., U.S., 617 ......282/J5
Tickhill, Eng., U.K., 5,572 ......66/F6
Tickhill, Eng., U.K., 5,572 ......68/E3
Ticonderoga, N.Y., U.S., 2,800 ......320/Q3
Tideford, Eng., U.K. 73/D4
Tide Head, N.B., Can., 1,149 ......217/C1
Tideswell, Eng., U.K., 1,717 ......66/E6
Tideswell, Eng., U.K., 1,717 ......68/D3
Tidewater, Oreg., U.S., 100 ......334/C3
Tidioute, Penn., U.S., 792 ......336/C2
Tidjikja, Maur. 147/C3
Tidnish, N.B., Can. 217/E3
Tien Shan, China, range 119/A1
Tien Shan, Kyrg., mountains 131/E2
Tie Plant, Miss., U.S., 450 ......300/C2
Tiernan, Oreg., U.S., 40 ......334/C3
Tierra Amarilla, N. Mex., U.S., 90 ......317/D1
Tierra del Fuego, Arg., province 191/B7
Tierra del Fuego, Chile, island 190/C8
Tie Siding, Wyo., U.S. 366/D3
Tietê, Braz., river ......188/Inset II
Tieton, Wash., U.S., 1,154 ......358/E3
Tiffany, Colo., U.S. 250/C4
Tiff City, Mo., U.S., 125 ......302/B5
Tiffin, Iowa, U.S., 975 ......274/L4
Tiffin, Mo., U.S., 40 ......302/C4
Tiffin, Ohio, U.S., 18,135 ......328/D3
Tift, Ga., U.S., county, 38,407 ......260/D8
Tifton, Ga., U.S., 15,060 ......260/E9
Tigard, Oreg., U.S., 41,223 ......334/A3, D2
Tiger, Ga., U.S., 316 ......260/E2
Tiger, Wash., U.S. 358/H1
Tigerton, Wisc., U.S., 764 ......364/D4
Tigharry, Scot., U.K. 62/A3
Tightwad, Mo., U.S., 63 ......302/C2
Tignall, Ga., U.S., 653 ......260/F4
Tignère, Came. 153/B2
Tignish, P.E.I., Can., 831 ......224/A2
Tigray, Eth., state 156/C1
Tigre, Ecua., river 185/C3
Tigre, Peru, river 185/B1
Tigris, Iraq, river 130/B1
Tigris, Syria, river 134/C1
Tigris, Tur., river 133/C3
Tijeras, N. Mex., U.S., 474 ......317/D2
Tijuana, Mex., 1,148,681, (1,210,820 metro.) 200/A1
Tikal, Guat. 201/D2
Tikchik, Alaska, U.S., lakes 240/D2
Tiki Island, Tex., U.S., 1,016 ......346/P6
Tikrit, Iraq 130/B1
Tiksi, Russ. 104/H2
Tiksi, Russ. 193/B7
Tilburg, Neth., 191,838, (214,143 metro.) 84/C3
Tilbury, Ont., Can., 4,599 ......223/D4
Tilden, Ill., U.S., 922 ......266/D5
Tilden, Ky., U.S. 280/C3
Tilden, Mo., U.S., 100 ......300/D1
Tilden, Nebr., U.S., 1,078 ......308/G1
Tilden, Tex., U.S., 500 ......346/K7
Tilden, Wisc., U.S., 250 ......364/B4
Tilford, S. Dak., U.S. 342/B3
Tilghman, Md., U.S., 854 ......288/J5
Tilghmanton, Md., U.S., 475 ......288/D1
Tiline, Ky., U.S., 40 ......280/B3
Tillabéri, Niger 152/A3
Tillamook, Oreg., U.S., 4,352 ......334/C2
Tillamook, Oreg., U.S., bay 334/C2
Tillamook, Oreg., U.S., county, 24,262 ......334/C2
Tillamook, Oreg., U.S., head 334/B2
Tillar, Ark., U.S., 240 ......244/D4
Tillatoba, Miss., U.S., 121 ......300/C2
Tilleda, Wisc., U.S., 100 ......364/E4
Tiller, Oreg., U.S., 150 ......334/D5
Tillery, N.C., U.S., 40 ......322/L2
Tilley, Alta., Can., 422 ......212/E6
Tillingham, Eng., U.K. 70/F3
Tillman, Okla., U.S., county, 9,287 ......330/C3
Tillman, S.C., U.S., 150 ......340/C4
Tillmans Corner, Ala., U.S., 15,685 ......238/A5
Tillson, N.Y., U.S., 1,709 ......320/N1
Tillsonburg, Ont., Can., 14,052 ......223/E4
Tillomonte, Chile 190/C2
Tilshead, Eng., U.K. 73/J2
Tilston, Man., Can. 68/B3
Tilton, Ark., U.S., 90 ......244/E2
Tilton, Ill., U.S., 2,976 ......266/F3
Tilton, N.H., U.S., 3,477 ......312/C5
Tilton on the Hill, Eng., U.K. 70/C1
Tiltonsville, Ohio, U.S., 1,329 ......328/J5
Timah, Sing., hill 123/B1
Timahat ash Sham, Sa. Arab., plain 136/B2
Timaru, N.Z. 171/B3
Timbalier, La., U.S., bay 282/J8
Timber, Oreg., U.S., 100 ......334/C2
Timbercreek Canyon, Tex., U.S., 406 ......346/F9
Timberlake, N.C., U.S., 225 ......322/H2
Timberlake, Ohio, U.S., 775 ......328/H8
Timber Lake, S. Dak., U.S., 443 ......342/D2
Timberlake, Va., U.S., 10,683 ......354/E6
Timberlane, La., U.S., 11,405 ......282/K5
Timberon, N. Mex., U.S., 309 ......317/E5
Timberville, Va., U.S., 1,739 ......354/F3
Timberwood Park, Tex., U.S., 5,889 ......346/A2
Timblin, Penn., U.S., 151 ......336/C4
Timbo, Ark., U.S., 60 ......244/C2
Timbuktu, Mali 150/C2
Time, Ill., U.S. 266/C4
Timgad, Alg., ruins 146/B1
Timiş, Rom., county 101/A3

Timişoara, Rom., 329,554 ......101/A3
Timken, Kans., U.S., 83 ......276/C3
Timmins, Ont., Can., 43,686 ......222/D3
Timmonsville, S.C., U.S., 2,315 ......340/E2
Timms, Wisc., U.S., hill 364/C3
Timnath, Colo., U.S., 223 ......250/F1
Timonium, (see Lutherville), Md., U.S. 288/H2
Timor, Austl., sea 170/B1
Timor, Indon., island 122/D2
Timor, Indon., sea 122/D3
Timpanogos Cave N.M., Utah, U.S. 350/C3
Timpas, Colo., U.S. 250/G4
Timpie, Utah, U.S. 350/B3
Timpson, Tex., U.S., 1,094 ......346/P4
Timsquarry, Scot., U.K. 62/B2
Timucuan Ecological and Hist. Pres., Fla., U.S. 256/G1
Tina, Mo., U.S., 193 ......302/C2
Tincup, Colo., U.S. 250/D3
Tindall, Mo., U.S., 65 ......302/C1
Tindouf, Alg. 146/A2
Tinghert, Alg., plateau 146/B2
Tinghert, Lib., plateau 145/A2
Tingo María, Peru 185/B2
Tingley, Iowa, U.S., 171 ......274/F6
Tinkerville, N.H., U.S. 312/C3
Tinkisso, Guin., river 149/C2
Tinley Park, Ill., U.S., 48,401 ......266/B6, L2
Tinmouth, Vt., U.S. 352/A4
Tinnie, N. Mex., U.S. 317/E4
Tinsley, Miss., U.S., 50 ......300/B3
Tinsman, Ark., U.S., 75 ......244/C4
Tintagel, Eng., U.K. 73/C3
Tintah, Minn., U.S., 79 ......298/A4
Tintern Parva, Wales, U.K. 64/F4
Tinto, Eng., U.K., hill 66/A1
Tinton Falls, N.J., U.S., 15,053 ......314/E3
Ti-n-Zaouâtène, Alg. 146/B2
T'lo, Erit. 156/C2
Tioga, La., U.S., 1,500 ......282/E4
Tioga, N. Dak., U.S., 1,125 ......326/C1
Tioga, N.Y., U.S., county, 51,784 ......320/J6
Tioga, Penn., U.S., 622 ......336/G2
Tioga, Penn., U.S., county, 41,373 ......336/G2
Tioga, Penn., U.S., river 336/G2
Tioga, W. Va., U.S., 175 ......360/E4
Tioga St. For., Penn., U.S. 336/F2, G2
Tionesta, Calif., U.S. 246/F1
Tionesta, Penn., U.S., 615 ......336/C3
Tipitapa, Nicar., river 202/A2
Tipler, Wisc., U.S., 40 ......364/E3
Tippah, Miss., U.S., county, 20,826 ......300/D1
Tipp City, Ohio, U.S., 9,221 ......328/B6
Tippecanoe, Ind., U.S., 150 ......270/D2
Tippecanoe, Ind., U.S., county, 148,955 ......270/C4
Tippecanoe, Ind., U.S., river 270/C2
Tipperary, Ire. 78/B2
Tipperary N. Riding, Ire., county 78/C2
Tipperary S. Riding, Ire., county 78/B2
Tippett, Nev., U.S. 310/C2
Tipton, Ariz., U.S., mountain 242/A2
Tipton, Calif., U.S., 1,790 ......246/F6
Tipton, Ind., U.S., 5,251 ......270/D4
Tipton, Ind., U.S., county, 16,577 ......270/D4
Tipton, Iowa, U.S., 3,155 ......274/M4
Tipton, Kans., U.S., 243 ......276/D2
Tipton, Mich., U.S., 325 ......294/E7
Tipton, Mo., U.S., 3,261 ......302/D3
Tipton, Okla., U.S., 916 ......330/C3
Tipton, Penn., U.S., 1,225 ......336/E4
Tipton, Tenn., U.S., county, 51,271 ......344/B3
Tiptonville, Tenn., U.S., 2,439 ......344/C2
Tiptop, Va., U.S. 354/E2
Tiptree, Eng., U.K., 7,679 ......70/F3
Tira, S. Dak., U.S., 248 ......346/N2
Tirana, Alb., capital, 244,153 ......99/A2
Tiraspol, Mol., 185,000 ......102/B2
Tiree, Scot., U.K., island 60/A2
Tiree, Scot., U.K., island 62/C5
Tirgovişte, Rom. 101/C3
Tirgu Jiu, Rom. 101/B3
Tirgu Mureş, Rom., 163,184 ......101/C2
Tirgu Neamţ, Rom. 101/D2
Tirgu Ocna, Rom. 101/D2
Tirich Mir, Pak., mountain 129/D2
Tiro, Ohio, U.S., 281 ......328/E4
Tirol, Aus., state 91/B3, C4
Tirso, It., river 95/B3
Tiruchchirappalli, India, 386,628,
  (711,120 metro.) 128/C6
Tisa, Serb.-Mont., river 99/B2
Tisch Mills, Wisc., U.S., 275 ......364/F4
Tisdale, Sask., Can., 3,063 ......227/F8
Tishomingo, Miss., U.S., 316 ......300/D1
Tishomingo, Miss., U.S., county, 19,163 ......300/D1
Tishomingo, Okla., U.S., 3,162 ......330/F3
Tishomingo NWR., Okla., U.S. 330/F3
Tiskilwa, Ill., U.S., 787 ......266/D2
Tissington, Eng., U.K. 68/D3
Tista, Bangl., river 127/C2
Tisza, Hun., river 91/C2
Tisza, Ukr., river 91/C3
Titagarh, India ......128/Inset II
Titano, S. Mar., mountain 97/B1
Titicaca, Bol., lake 186/A3
Titicaca, Peru, lake 185/D4
Titley, Eng., U.K. 64/E1
Titonka, Iowa, U.S., 584 ......274/F1
Titus, Tex., U.S., county, 28,118 ......346/N2
Titusville, Fla., U.S., 40,670 ......256/H3
Titusville, N.J., U.S., 800 ......314/D3
Titusville, Penn., U.S., 6,146 ......336/B2
Tivaouane, Sen. 148/A2
Tiverton, Ont., Can., 743 ......223/D3
Tiverton, Eng., U.K. 60/B4
Tiverton, Eng., U.K., 14,805 ......73/F3
Tiverton, R.I., U.S., 15,260 ......339/D2
Tivoli, Gren. 209/S2
Tivoli, N.Y., U.S., 1,163 ......320/P6
Tivoli, Tex., U.S., 450 ......346/M7
Tizimín, Mex., 39,525, (64,104 metro.) 200/H3
Tiznit, Mor. 147/B2
Tlaipan, Mex. 200/Inset
Tlalnepantla, Mex., 714,735 ......200/Inset
Tlaxcala, Mex., state capital, 73,213 ......200/E4
Tlaxcala, Mex., state 200/E4
Tlemcen, Alg. 146/A1
Toadlena, N. Mex., U.S., 125 ......317/B1
Toad River, Br. Col., Can. 214/K2
Toamasina, Madag., 137,782 ......163/B2
Toano, Va., U.S., 1,400 ......354/K6
Toa Payoh, Sing. 123/B1
Toast, N.C., U.S., 1,922 ......322/D6
Tobacco, Ky., U.S., 275 ......280/D3
Tobaccoville, N.C., U.S., 2,209 ......280/A4
Tobago, St. Vin.-Gren., cays 208/A4
Tobago, Trin.-To., 54,084 ......204/F5
Tobago, Trin.-To., island 209/B1
Toba Kakar, Pak., range 129/C3

Tobermore, N. Ire., U.K., 621 ......65/D2
Tobermory, Ont., Can. 223/D2
Tobermory, Scot., U.K., 980 ......62/D5
Tobi, Palau, island 172/A4
Tobias, Nebr., U.S., 158 ......308/G3
Tobin, Sask., Can., lake 227/G7
Tobin, Nev., U.S., mountain 310/B1
Tobique, Minn., U.S. 298/C3
Tobol, Kaz., river 131/C1
Toboso, Russ. 104/E4
Toboso, Ohio, U.S., 325 ......328/F5
Tobruk, Lib. 145/D1
Tobyhanna, Penn., U.S., 325 ......336/L3
Tocantins, Braz., river 188/D2
Tocantins, Braz., state 188/D3
Toccoa, Ga., U.S., 9,323 ......260/E2
Toccopola, Miss., U.S., 189 ......300/C1
Tochigi, Jap., prefecture 114/C2
Tocito, N. Mex., U.S., 60 ......317/B1
Toco, Trin.-To. 209/B2
Toco, Tex., U.S., 89 ......346/N2
Tocopilla, Chile 190/B2
Tocsin, Ind., U.S., 275 ......270/F3
Todd, Ky., U.S., county, 11,971 ......280/C4
Todd, Minn., U.S., county, 24,426 ......298/C4
Todd, S. Dak., U.S., county, 9,050 ......342/E4
Toddington, Eng., U.K., 3,999 ......68/D6
Toddington, Eng., U.K. 70/C3
Todd Mission, Tex., U.S., 146 ......346/N5
Toddville, Iowa, U.S., 450 ......274/L3
Toddville, Md., U.S., 150 ......288/K6
Toddville, S.C., U.S., 200 ......340/E4
Todhills, Eng., U.K. 66/C3
Todmorden, Eng., U.K., 11,969 ......66/D5
Todmorden, Eng., U.K., 11,969 ......68/C2
Tofield, Alta., Can., 1,818 ......212/D4
Tofino, Br. Col., Can., 1,466 ......214/K6
Toft, Scot., U.K. 62/Q2
Tofua, Tonga, island 175/B3
Toga, Va., U.S., 125 ......354/F6
Togiak, Alaska, U.S., 809 ......240/C3
Togiak NWR., Alaska, U.S. 240/C3
Togo, nation 145
Togo, Minn., U.S. 298/D3
Tohatchi, N. Mex., U.S., 1,037 ......317/B2
Tohono O'Odham (Gila Bend) Ind. Res.,
  Ariz., U.S. 242/C4
Tohono O'Odham (Gila Bend) Ind. Res.,
  Ariz., U.S. 242/C4
Tohono O'Odham Ind. Res., Ariz., U.S. 242/C5
Tohono O'Odham (San Xavier) Ind. Res.,
  Ariz., U.S. 242/D5
Toimi, Minn., U.S. 298/F3
Toivola, Mich., U.S. 294/A2
Toivola, Minn., U.S., 50 ......298/E3
Toiyabe, Nev., U.S., range 310/B2
Tok, Alaska, U.S., 1,393 ......240/H2
Tokachi, Jap., river ......114/Inset I
Tokaj, Hun. 91/C1
Tokara, Jap., islands 114/A4
Tokat, Tur. 133/D2
Tokat, Tur., province 133/D2
Tokeland, Wash., U.S., 194 ......358/B3
Tokio, Ark., U.S. 244/B4
Tokio, N. Dak., U.S., 100 ......326/G2
Tokio, Tex., U.S., 40 ......346/F2
Tokmok, Kyrg., 71,200 ......131/D1
Tokorozawa, Jap., 330,000 ......114/C3
Toksook Bay, Alaska, U.S., 532 ......240/C2
Toktogul, Kyrg. 131/C2
Toku, Tonga, island 175/B2
Tokuno, Jap., island ......114/Inset II
Tokushima, Jap., 268,000 ......114/B3
Tokushima, Jap., prefecture 114/B3
Tokuyama, Jap. 114/A3
Tokyo, Jap., capital, 8,130,408,
  (12,059,237 metro.) 114/C3
Tokyo, Jap., prefecture 114/C3
Tôlanaro, Madag. 163/B3
Tolar, N. Mex., U.S. 317/G3
Tolar, Tex., U.S., 504 ......346/L3
Tolchester Beach, Md., U.S., 175 ......288/K3
Toledo, Sp., 68,382 ......94/D3
Toledo, Sp., mountains 94/D3
Toledo, Sp., province 94/D3
Toledo, Ill., U.S., 1,166 ......266/E4
Toledo, Iowa, U.S., 2,539 ......274/J4
Toledo, Ohio, U.S., 313,619, (618,203 metro.) 328/C2
Toledo, Oreg., U.S., 3,472 ......334/C3
Toledo, Wash., U.S., 653 ......358/C3
Toledo Bend, Tex., U.S., reservoir 346/R4
Toledo Vil., Tex., U.S. 346/R4
Toliara, Madag., 61,460 ......163/A3
Tolima, Col., department 184/B4
Tolima, Col., mountain 184/B3
Tolland, Alta., Can. 212/E4
Tolland, Conn., U.S., 13,146 ......253/F2
Tolland, Conn., U.S., county, 136,364 ......253/F2
Tolland, Mass., U.S., 426 ......292/B4
Tolles, Conn., U.S. 253/C3
Tolleson, Ariz., U.S., 4,974 ......242/C4
Tollette, Ariz., U.S. 244/B4
Tolley, N. Dak., U.S., 63 ......326/D1
Tollhouse, Calif., U.S., 275 ......246/F5
Toll of Birness, Scot., U.K. 62/N4
Tollville, Ark., U.S. 244/D3
Tolna, Hun., county 91/B2
Tolna, N. Dak., U.S., 202 ......326/G2
Tolono, Ill., U.S., 2,700 ......266/E4
Tolstoy, S. Dak., U.S., 64 ......342/F2
Toltec, Ariz., U.S. 242/D5
Tolú, Ky., U.S., 100 ......280/B3
Toluca, Mex., state capital, 435,125,
  (666,569 metro.) 200/E4
Toluca, Ill., U.S., 1,339 ......266/D3
Tol'yatti, Russ., 720,430, (734,300 metro.) 104/D4
Tom, Okla., U.S., 225 ......330/H4
Tomah, Maine, U.S. 286/E3
Tomah, Wisc., U.S., 8,419 ......364/C5
Tomahawk, Ala., U.S., 61 ......238/D3
Tomahawk, Wisc., U.S., 3,770 ......364/D3
Tomakomai, Jap. ......114/Inset I
Tomales, Calif., U.S., 210 ......246/C4
Tomanivi, Fiji, mountain 174/B2
Tomatin, Scot., U.K. 62/J4
Tomato, Ark., U.S. 244/F2
Tomball, Tex., U.S., 9,089 ......346/A5
Tombigbee, Ala., U.S., river 238/A2, A4
Tombigbee Natl. For., Miss., U.S. 300/C2, D1
Tombstone, Ariz., U.S., 1,504 ......242/E6
Tombua, Ang. 159/B5
Tomé, Chile 190/B5
Tome, N. Mex., U.S., 2,211 ......317/D3
Tom Green, Tex., U.S., county, 104,010 ......346/H4
Tomiko, Ont., Can., lake 223/F1
Tomintoul, Scot., U.K. 62/K4
Tomnolen, Miss., U.S., 90 ......300/C2

Tompkins, Sask., Can., 191 . . . . .227/B10
Tompkins, N.Y., U.S., *county*, 96,501 . . . . . . .320/J5
Tompkinsville, Ky., U.S., 2,660 . . . . .280/E4
Tom Price, W.A., Austl. 170/A2
Toms Brook, Va., U.S., 255 . . . . .354/G3
Toms Place, Calif., U.S., 125 . . . . .246/G5
Toms River, N.J., U.S., 86,327 . . . . .314/E4
Tonalá, Mex., 31,212, (78,438 *metro.*) 200/F4
Tonasket, Wash., U.S., 994 . . . . .358/F1
Tonawanda, N.Y., U.S., 16,136 . . . . .320/D4
Tonawanda Ind. Res., N.Y., U.S. 320/E4
Tonbridge, Eng., U.K. . . . . .60/Inset III
Tonbridge, Eng., U.K., 34,260 . . . . .70/E4
Tone, Jap., *river* 114/C2
Tonga, *nation* 167
Tonganoxie, Kans., U.S., 2,728 . . . . .276/G2
Tongariro, N.Z., *mountain* 171/C2
Tongass Natl. For., Alaska, U.S. 240/H3
Tongatapu, Tonga, *island group* 175/B4
Tongatapu, Tonga, *island* 175/B4
Tonge, Eng., U.K. 70/B1
Tongham, Eng., U.K. 70/C4
Tonghua, China 119/F1
Tongjosŏn, N. Kor., *bay* 116/B3
Tongland, Scot., U.K. 62/H9
Tongliao, China 119/F1
Tongsa, Bhu. 126/B2
Tongsa, Bhu., *river* 126/B2
Tongue, Scot., U.K. .62/H2
Tongue, Mont., U.S., *river* 306/K4
Tonica, Ill., U.S., 685 . . . . .266/D4
Tonkawa, Okla., U.S., 3,299 . . . . .330/E1
Tonkin, China, *gulf* 119/D4
Tonkin, Viet., *gulf* .123/B2
Tonle Sap, Camb., *lake* 124/B2, C3
Tonle Sap, Camb., *river* 124/B2
Tonolea, Ariz., U.S., 562 . . . . .242/E1
Tonopah, Ariz., U.S. 242/C4
Tonopah, Nev., U.S., 2,627 . . . . .310/D2
Tonopah Test Range, Nev., U.S. 310/B3, C3
Tontitown, Ark., U.S., 942 . . . . .244/A1
Tontogany, Ohio, U.S., 364 . . . . .328/C3
Tonto Natl. For., Ariz., U.S. 242/D3
Tonto N.M., Ariz., U.S. 242/D4
Tony, Wisc., U.S., 105 . . . . .364/B3
Tonyrefail, Wales, U.K., 8,815 . . . . .64/E4
Tonytank, Md., U.S., 3,500 . . . . .288/M6
Tooele, Utah, U.S., 22,502 . . . . .350/B3
Tooele, Utah, U.S., *county*, 40,735 . . . . .350/A3
Tool, Tex., U.S., 2,275 . . . . .346/M3
Toole, Mont., U.S., *county*, 5,267 . . . . .306/E1
Toombs, Ga., U.S., *county*, 26,067 . . . . .260/G7
Toome, N. Ire., U.K. .65/E2
Toomsboro, Ga., U.S., 622 . . . . .260/E6
Toomsuba, Miss., U.S., 175 . . . . .300/D3
Toone, Tenn., U.S., 330 . . . . .344/D4
Toonerville, Colo., U.S. 250/G4
Toot Hill, Eng., U.K. .70/E3
Toowoomba, Qnsld., Austl. 170/E2
Topawa, Ariz., U.S., 150 . . . . .242/D6
Topaz Lake, Nev., U.S., 60 . . . . .310/A2
Topeka, Ind., U.S., 1,159 . . . . .270/E1
Topeka, Kans., U.S., *state capital*, 122,377,
  (169,871 *metro.*) 276/G2
Topinabee, Mich., U.S., 250 . . . . .294/E4
Topley Landing, Br. Col., Can. 214/J4
Topmost, Ky., U.S., 250 . . . . .280/H3
Topock, Ariz., U.S. .242/A3
Toponas, Colo., U.S. 250/D1
Toppenish, Wash., U.S., 8,946 . . . . .358/E3
Toppenish NWR, Wash., U.S. 358/E3
Topsail Beach, N.C., U.S., 471 . . . . .322/K6
Topsfield, Maine, U.S., 225 . . . . .286/E3
Topsfield, Mass., U.S., 6,141 . . . . .292/L2
Topsham, Maine, U.S., 9,100 . . . . .286/C5
Topton, N.C., U.S. 322/C8
Topton, Penn., U.S., 1,948 . . . . .336/K4
Toquerville, Utah, U.S., 910 . . . . .350/A6
Toquima, Nev., U.S., *range* 310/B2
Torbay, Nfld., U.S., 5,474 . . . . .218/E5
Torbay, Eng., U.K., 59,587 . . . . .60/B4
Torbay, Eng., U.K., 59,587 . . . . .73/E4
Torbay, Eng., U.K., *unitary authority*, 129,702 . .73/E4
Torch Lake, Mich., U.S., 175 . . . . .294/D4
Torcross, Eng., U.K. .73/E4
Tore, Scot., U.K. 62/H3
Torfaen, Wales, U.K., *unitary authority*, 90,967 . .64/E4
Torghay, Kaz., *plateau* 131/C1
Tormarton, Eng., U.K. 73/H1
Tornado, W. Va., U.S., 1,111 . . . . .360/C4
Torneälven, Swe., *river* 80/D1
Torngat, Nfld., Can., *mountains* 218/D3
Tornillo, Tex., U.S., 1,609 . . . . .346/B4
Tornio, Fin. 81/B1
Torniojoki, Fin., *river* 81/B1
Torniojoki, Swe., *river* 80/E2
Toro, La., U.S. 282/B4
Toro Negro Forest Reserve, P.R. 206/C2
Toronto, Ont., Can., 2,481,494,
  (5,029,900 *metro.*) 222/E4
Toronto, Ont., Can., 2,481,494,
  (5,029,900 *metro.*) 223/F4, K5
Toronto, Iowa, U.S., 134 . . . . .274/N4
Toronto, Kans., U.S., 312 . . . . .276/G4
Toronto, Ohio, U.S., 5,676 . . . . .328/J5
Toronto, S. Dak., U.S., 202 . . . . .342/J3
Toronto Islands Park, Ont., Can. 223/K6
Tororo, Ug., 42,473 . . . . .157/D3
Torphins, Scot., U.K., 1,094 . . . . .62/L4
Torpoint, Eng., U.K., 8,238 . . . . .73/D4
Torquay, Sask., Can., 231 . . . . .227/G11
Torquay, Eng., U.K. .60/B4
Torquay, Eng., U.K., 59,587, (102,576 *metro.*) . .73/E4
Torrance, Calif., U.S., 137,946 . . . . . . .246/C10, G9
Torrance, N. Mex., U.S., *county*, 16,911 . . . .317/E3
Torre del Greco, It. 95/C2
Torrejón de Ardoz, Sp., 97,887 . . . . .94/Inset II
Torrelavega, Sp. 94/D1
Torrens, Austl., *lake* 170/C2
Torrens, Austl., *river* 170/C2
Torreón, Sp., 65,417 . . . . .94/F3
Torreón, (Sandoval County), N. Mex., U.S., 297 . .317/C2
Torreón, (Torrance County), N. Mex., U.S., 244 . .317/D3
Torreón, Mex., 502,964, (529,512 *metro.*) . . .200/D3
Torres, Austl., *strait* 170/D1
Torres, P.N.G., *strait* 172/A2
Torres, Van., *islands* 173/B1
Torrey, Utah, U.S., 171 . . . . .350/C5
Torr Head, N. Ire., U.K., *cape* 65/E1
Torrin, Scot., U.K. 62/D4
Torrington, Alta., Can. 212/D5
Torrington, Conn., U.S., 35,202 . . . . .253/C2
Torrington, Wyo., U.S., 5,776 . . . . .366/D2
Tórshavn, Den., *territorial capital* 79/Inset
Tortilla Flat, Ariz., U.S., 40 . . . . .242/D4
Tortosa, Sp. 94/G2
Tortosa, Sp., *cape* .94/G2
Tortuga, Haiti, *island* 205/C1

Tortuga, Ven., *island* 204/E5
Toru, Pol., 206,283 .83/D1
Tõrva, Est. 81/C2
Torver, Eng., U.K. 66/B4
Tory Hill, Ont., Can. 223/G3
Tosa, Jap., *bay* 114/B3
Toscaig, Scot., U.K. .62/E4
Toston, Mont., U.S., 105 . . . . .306/E3
Totavi, N. Mex., U.S. 317/D2
Totland, Eng., U.K. 70/A5
Totley, Eng., U.K. 68/D3
Totness, Sur. 183/A2
Totowa, N.J., U.S., 9,892 . . . . .314/B2
Tottori, Jap. 114/B3
Tottori, Jap., *prefecture* 114/B3
Totz, Ky., U.S., 325 .280/G4
Touchet, Wash., U.S., 396 . . . . .358/G3
Touggourt, Alg. 146/B1
Toughkenamon, Penn., U.S., 1,375 . . . . .336/K6
Touhy, Nebr., U.S., 50 . . . . .308/H2
Toulaman, Dom., *river* 208/B2
Touliu, Tai. 117/B2
Toulon, Fr., 166,442, (519,640 *metro.*) 88/D5
Toulon, Ill., U.S., 1,400 . . . . .266/C4
Toulouse, Fr., 398,423, (761,090 *metro.*) 88/C5
Toura, C. d'Iv., *mountains* 150/C2
Tourcoing, Fr. 88/C1
Tournai, Belg., 67,232, (140,830 *metro.*) 85/B2
Touro Synagogue N.H.S., R.I., U.S. 339/E5
Tours, Fr., 137,046, (297,631 *metro.*) 88/C3
Toussaint, C.A.R., *mountain* 154/B2
Toutes Aides, Man., Can. 215/B3
Toutle, Wash., U.S., 125 . . . . .358/C3
Tovey, Ill., U.S., 516 . . . . .266/D4
Tovuz, Azer. 103/A2
Towaco, N.J., U.S., 2,700 . . . . .314/A2, E2
Towada, Jap., *lake* 114/D1
Towanda, Ill., U.S., 493 . . . . .266/E3
Towanda, Kans., U.S., 1,338 . . . . .276/E4
Towanda, Penn., U.S., 3,024 . . . . .336/J2
Towaoc, Colo., U.S., 1,097 . . . . .250/B4
Toward, Scot., U.K. .62/F7
Tower, Mich., U.S., 375 . . . . .294/E4
Tower, Minn., U.S., 479 . . . . .298/E3
Tower City, N. Dak., U.S., 252 . . . . .326/H3
Tower City, Penn., U.S., 1,396 . . . . .336/H4
Tower Hamlets, Eng., U.K., *unitary authority*,
  196,121 . . . . .70/D3
Tower Hill, Ill., U.S., 609 . . . . .266/E5
Tower Jct., Wyo., U.S. 366/A1
Tower Lakes, Ill., U.S., 1,310 . . . . .266/A5
Tow Law, Eng., U.K., 2,204 . . . . .66/E3
Town and Country, Mo., U.S., 10,894 . . . . . . .302/H3
Town and Country, Wash., U.S., 4,452 . . . . . . .358/H3
Town Bank, N.J., U.S., 552 . . . . .314/D6
Town Creek, Ala., U.S., 1,216 . . . . .238/B1
Towner, Colo., U.S., 40 . . . . .250/H3
Towner, N. Dak., U.S., 574 . . . . .326/E1
Towner, N. Dak., U.S., *county*, 2,876 . . . . . .326/F1
Town of Pines, Ind., U.S., 798 . . . . .270/C1
Town Pt., Md., U.S., 550 . . . . .288/L2
Towns, Ga., U.S., 70 . . . . .260/F8
Towns, Ga., U.S., *county*, 9,319 . . . . .260/D2
Townsbury, N.J., U.S., 550 . . . . .314/D2
Townsend, Del., U.S., 346 . . . . .255/B3
Townsend, Ga., U.S., 90 . . . . .260/H8
Townsend, Mass., U.S., 9,198 . . . . .292/H2
Townsend, Mont., U.S., 1,867 . . . . .306/E3
Townsend, Tenn., U.S., 244 . . . . .344/P3
Townsend, Wisc., U.S., 225 . . . . .364/E3
Townsend Harbor, Mass., U.S., 1,700 . . . . . . .292/H2
Townsends Inlet, N.J., U.S. 314/D6
Townshend, Vt., U.S. 352/B4
Townsville, Qnsld., Austl., 114,094,
  (118,000 *metro.*) 170/D1
Townsville, N.C., U.S., 175 . . . . .322/J1
Townville, Penn., U.S., 306 . . . . .336/B2
Townville, S.C., U.S., 300 . . . . .340/B2
Town West, Tex., U.S. 346/A7
Town Yetholm, Scot., U.K. 62/M7
Towson, Md., U.S., 51,793 . . . . .288/H2
Toxey, Ala., U.S., 152 . . . . .238/A4
Toxkan, Kyrg., *river* 131/E2
Toyah, Tex., U.S., 100 . . . . .346/E4
Toyahvale, Tex., U.S. 346/E5
Toyama, Jap., 326,000 . . . . .114/C2
Toyama, Jap., *bay* 114/C2
Toyama, Jap., *prefecture* 114/C2
Toyei, Ariz., U.S., 70 . . . . .242/F2
Toyohashi, Jap., 365,000 . . . . .114/C3
Toyonaka, Jap., 392,000 . . . . .114/B3
Toyota, Jap., 351,000 . . . . .114/C3
Tozeur, Tun. 146/B3
Tqvarcheli, Geo. 103/A3
Trabuco Highlands, Calif., U.S. 246/F11
Trabzon, Tur. 133/D2
Trabzon, Tur., *province* 133/D2
Tracadie, P.E.I., Can. 224/C2
Tracadie-Sheila, N.B., Can., 4,724 . . . . .217/E1
Tracy, N.B., Can., 601 . . . . .217/C3
Tracy, Que., Can. 226/C5
Tracy, Calif., U.S., 56,929 . . . . .246/L2
Tracy, Iowa, U.S., 275 . . . . .274/J5
Tracy, Ky., U.S., 80 .280/E4
Tracy, Minn., U.S., 2,268 . . . . .298/B6
Tracy, Mo., U.S., 213 . . . . .302/B2
Tracy, Mont., U.S., 150 . . . . .306/E2
Tracy City, Tenn., U.S., 1,679 . . . . .344/K4
Tracyton, Wash., U.S., 3,267 . . . . .358/A4
Trade Lake, Wisc., U.S., 100 . . . . .364/A3
Trade River, Wisc., U.S., 80 . . . . .364/A3
Tradesville, S.C., U.S., 200 . . . . .340/D2
Trading Post, Kans., U.S., 60 . . . . .276/H3
Traer, Iowa, U.S., 1,594 . . . . .274/K3
Traer, Kans., U.S. 276/B2
Trafalgar, Tas., Can. 221/E2
Trafalgar, Ind., U.S., 798 . . . . .270/D6
Trafford, Eng., U.K., *unitary authority*, 210,135 . .66/D6
Trafford, Eng., U.K., *unitary authority*, 210,135 . .68/C5
Trafford, Ala., U.S., 523 . . . . .238/C2
Trafford, Penn., U.S., 3,236 . . . . .336/F7
Trail, Br. Col., Can., 7,575 . . . . .214/O6
Trail, Minn., U.S., 62 . . . . .298/B3
Trail, Okla., U.S. 330/C2
Trail, Oreg., U.S., 100 . . . . .334/D5
Trail City, S. Dak., U.S., 40 . . . . .342/E2
Trail Creek, Ind., U.S., 2,296 . . . . .270/C1
Traill, N. Dak., U.S., *county*, 8,477 . . . . .326/H2
Trainer, Penn., U.S., 1,901 . . . . .336/K7, L6
Tralee, Ire., 20,362 .78/A2
Trammel, Va., U.S. 354/D2
Tramway, N.C., U.S., 750 . . . . .322/G4
Tranent, Scot., U.K., 8,892 . . . . .62/L7
Trang, Thai. 125/B5
Tranquility, N.J., U.S., 425 . . . . .314/D2
Transantarctic, Antar., *mountains* 192/B4
Transylvania, Rom., *region* 101/B2
Transylvania, La., U.S., 90 . . . . .282/G1
Transylvania, N.C., U.S., *county*, 29,334 . . . .322/D8
Transylvanian Alps, Rom., *mountains* 101/B3

Trapani, It. 95/C3
Trappe, Md., U.S., 1,146 . . . . .288/K5
Trasimeno, It., *lake* 95/C2
Traskwood, Ark., U.S., 548 . . . . .244/C3
Trat, Thai. 125/C3
Traun, Aus., *river* 91/D2
Traunik, Mich., U.S. 294/C6
Travelers Rest, S.C., U.S., 4,099 . . . . . . .340/B2, E2
Traverse, Mich., U.S., *point* 294/A2
Traverse, Minn., U.S., 60 . . . . .298/C6
Traverse, Minn., U.S., *county*, 4,134 . . . . . .298/A5
Traverse, Wisc., U.S., *point* 364/E1
Traverse City, Mich., U.S., 14,532 . . . . .294/D5
Travis, Tex., U.S., *county*, 812,280 . . . .346/E2, K5
Travis, Tex., U.S., *lake* 346/D2
Trawden, Eng., U.K. .66/D5
Trawsfynydd, Wales, U.K. 64/B1
Trearddur Bay, Wales, U.K. 64/B1
Treasure, Mont., U.S., *county*, 861 . . . . . . .306/I3
Treasure Island, Fla., U.S., 7,450 . . . . .256/C7, F4
Trebinje, Bos.-Her. 98/A2
Trebloc, Miss., U.S., 40 . . . . .300/D2
Treece, Kans., U.S., 149 . . . . .276/H4
Treen, Eng., U.K. 73/A4
Trees, La., U.S. 282/A1
Trefecca, Wales, U.K. 64/E4
Trefegiwys, Wales, U.K. 64/D3
Trefnant, Wales, U.K. 64/E1
Trefriw, Wales, U.K. .64/D1
Trego, Kans., U.S., *county*, 3,319 . . . . .276/C3
Trego, Mont., U.S. 306/B1
Trego, Nev., U.S. 310/A1
Trego, Wisc., U.S., 200 . . . . .364/B3
Tregony, Eng., U.K. .73/C4
Treherne, Man., Can., 644 . . . . .215/B4
Treig, Scot., U.K., *lake* 62/G5
Treinta y Tres, Uru. .187/C2
Treinta y Tres, Uru., *department* 187/C2
Trellech, Wales, U.K. .64/F4
Tremadoc, Wales, U.K., *bay* 64/C2
Tremblear, Br. Col., Can., *lake* 214/K4
Trementina, N. Mex., U.S. 317/F2
Tremont, Ill., U.S., 2,029 . . . . .266/D4
Tremont, Miss., U.S., 390 . . . . .300/D1
Tremont, Penn., U.S., 1,784 . . . . .336/J4
Tremont City, Ohio, U.S., 349 . . . . .328/C5
Tremonton, Utah, U.S., 5,592 . . . . .350/B2
Trempealeau, Wisc., U.S., 1,319 . . . . .364/B4
Trempealeau, Wisc., U.S., *county*, 27,010 . . .364/B4
Trenary, Mich., U.S., 125 . . . . .294/C3
Trenche, Que., Can., *river* 226/C3
Trenčiansky, Slvk., *region* 92/A2
Trenčín, Slvk., 112,767 . . . . .92/B2
Trent, Eng., U.K., *river* 60/C3
Trent, Ky., U.S., 150 . . . . .280/G3
Trent, S. Dak., U.S., 254 . . . . .342/J4
Trent, Tex., U.S., 318 . . . . .346/H3
Trentham, Eng., U.K. 68/C4
Trentino-Alto Adige, It., *region* 95/B1
Trento, It. 95/B1
Trenton, N.S., Can., 2,798 . . . . .221/E2
Trenton, Ont., Can. .223/H3
Trenton, Fla., U.S., 1,617 . . . . .256/F2
Trenton, Ga., U.S., 1,942 . . . . .260/A2
Trenton, Ill., U.S., 2,610 . . . . .266/D5
Trenton, Iowa, U.S., 125 . . . . .274/L5
Trenton, Ky., U.S., 419 . . . . .280/C4
Trenton, Maine, U.S., 1,370 . . . . .286/D4
Trenton, Mich., U.S., 19,584 . . . . .294/B7, F7
Trenton, Mo., U.S., 6,216 . . . . .302/C1
Trenton, Nebr., U.S., 507 . . . . .308/C3
Trenton, N.J., U.S., *state capital*, 85,403 . . . .314/D3
Trenton, N.C., U.S., 206 . . . . .322/L4
Trenton, N. Dak., U.S., 350 . . . . .326/B1
Trenton, Ohio, U.S., 8,746 . . . . .328/B7
Trenton, S.C., U.S., 226 . . . . .340/C3
Trenton, Tenn., U.S., 4,683 . . . . .344/D3
Trenton, Utah, U.S., 449 . . . . .350/C2
Trentwood, Wash., U.S., 4,388 . . . . .358/H2
Trent Woods, N.C., U.S., 4,192 . . . . .322/L4
Trepassey, Nfld., Can., 889 . . . . .218/E5
Tresckow, Penn., U.S., 964 . . . . .336/K4
Tresco, Eng., U.K., *island* 73/A3
Tres Hermanos, P.R. 206/A2
Treska, Mac., *river* 100/B2
Tres Piedras, N. Mex., U.S. 317/E1
Tres Puntas, Arg., *cape* 191/B6
Tres Ritos, N. Mex., U.S. 317/E1
Tre-Taliesin, Wales, U.K. 64/D2
Treuddyn, Wales, U.K. 64/E1
Treutlen, Ga., U.S., *county*, 6,854 . . . . .260/F7
Trevilians, Va., U.S., 100 . . . . .354/G4
Treviso, It. 95/C1
Trevlac, Ind., U.S., 350 . . . . .270/D6
Trevor, Wales, U.K. 64/E2
Trevose, Eng., U.K., *point* 73/B3
Trevose, (see Feasterville), Penn., U.S., 6,525 . .336/M6
Treynor, Iowa, U.S., 950 . . . . .274/C5
Trezevant, Tenn., U.S., 901 . . . . .344/D2
Triana, Ala., U.S., 458 . . . . .238/C1
Triangle, Va., U.S., 5,500 . . . . .354/J3
Tribbey, Okla., U.S., 273 . . . . .330/E2
Trident, Mont., U.S. .306/E4
Trier, Ger. 86/A4
Trier, Ger., *department* 86/A3
Triesen, Liech. 90/B2
Triesenberg, Liech. 90/B2
Trieste, It., 209,520 .95/C1
Trieste, Slove., *gulf* .98/A3
Trigg, Ky., U.S., *county*, 12,597 . . . . .280/C4
Triglav, Slove., *mountain* 98/A2
Trikala, Gr. 100/B2
Tri-Lakes, Ind., U.S., 3,925 . . . . .270/F2
Trillick, N. Ire., U.K., 434 . . . . .65/C2
Trim, Ire. 78/C2
Trimbelle, Wisc., U.S., 175 . . . . .364/A4
Trimble, Colo., U.S., 650 . . . . .250/C4
Trimble, Ill., U.S., 125 . . . . .266/F4
Trimble, Ky., U.S., *county*, 8,125 . . . . .280/E2
Trimble, Mo., U.S., 451 . . . . .302/B2
Trimble, Ohio, U.S., 466 . . . . .328/F7
Trimble, Tenn., U.S., 728 . . . . .344/C2
Trimdon, Eng., U.K., 3,049 . . . . .66/F3
Trimingham, Eng., U.K. 70/G1
Trimont, Minn., U.S., 754 . . . . .298/C7
Trinchera, Colo., U.S. 250/F4
Trincomalee, Sri Lan. 126/C3
Trincomalee, Sri Lan., *harbor* 126/C3
Trinidad, Bol. 186/B2
Trinidad, Cuba 204/C2
Trinidad, Cuba, *mountains* 204/C2
Trinidad, Trin.-To., *island* 204/F5
Trinidad, Trin.-To., *island* 209/A2
Trinidad, Calif., U.S., 311 . . . . .246/A1
Trinidad, Colo., U.S., 9,078 . . . . .250/F4
Trinidad, Uru. 187/B2
Trinidad and Tobago, *nation* 204/F5
Trinidad and Tobago, *nation* 197
Trinity, Nfld., Can., *bay* 218/E5

Trinity, Ala., U.S., 1,841 . . . . .238/B1
Trinity, Alaska, U.S., *islands* 240/E3
Trinity, Calif., U.S., *county*, 13,022 . . . . .246/B2
Trinity, Calif., U.S., *river* 246/B2
Trinity, N.C., U.S., 6,690 . . . . .322/F3
Trinity, Tex., U.S., 2,721 . . . . .346/N5
Trinity, Tex., U.S., *bay* 346/C6
Trinity, Tex., U.S., *county*, 13,779 . . . . .346/N5
Trinity, Tex., U.S., *river* 346/C5, C9, C10
Trinity Ctr., Calif., U.S., 50 . . . . .246/B2
Trinity East, Nfld., Can. 218/E5
Trinity Natl. For., Calif., U.S. 246/B2
Trinway, Ohio, U.S., 450 . . . . .328/F5
Trio, S.C., U.S., 50 .340/E3
Triolet, Mauritius 163/C2
Trion, Ga., U.S., 1,993 . . . . .260/A2
Tripoli, (Tarabulus), Leb., 127,611 . . . . .134/A1
Tripoli, Lib., *capital*, 1,500,000 . . . . .145/B1
Tripoli, Iowa, U.S., 1,310 . . . . .274/K2
Tripoli, Wisc., U.S., 40 . . . . .364/D3
Tripolitania, Lib., *region* 145/B1
Tripp, S. Dak., U.S., 711 . . . . .342/H4
Tripp, S. Dak., U.S., *county*, 6,430 . . . . .342/F4
Tripura, India, *state* 128/C2
Triton, Nfld., Can., 1,102 . . . . .218/D4
Triumph, Ill., U.S., 225 . . . . .266/D4
Triumph, (see Buras), La., U.S., 3,358 . . . . . .282/L8
Trnava, Slvk. 92/A2
Trnavský, Slvk., *region* 92/A2
Trobriand, P.N.G., *islands* 172/B2
Trochu, Alta., Can., 1,033 . . . . .212/D5
Trois-Pistoles, Que., Can., 3,635 . . . . .226/G3
Trois-Rivières, Que., Can., 46,264,
  (141,400 *metro.*) 225/B4
Trois-Rivières, Que., Can., 46,264,
  (141,400 *metro.*) 226/D5
Troisvierges, Lux. 85/B3
Trollhättan, Swe. 80/B3
Trombay, India .128/Inset I
Trommald, Minn., U.S., 125 . . . . .298/C4
Tromsø, Nor. 80/D2
Tromsø, Nor., *province* 193/C1
Trona, Calif., U.S., 650 . . . . .246/H7
Trondheim, Nor., 151,408 . . . . .80/C3
Trondheimsfjord, Nor., *fjord* 80/B3
Trongisvágur, Den. 79/Inset
Troödos, Cyp., *mountains* 133/A2
Troon, Scot., U.K., 14,766 . . . . .62/G7
Trooper, Penn., U.S., 6,061 . . . . .336/L5
Trophy Club, Tex., U.S., 6,350 . . . . .346/B9
Tropic, Utah, U.S., 508 . . . . .350/B6
Trosky, Minn., U.S., 116 . . . . .298/A7
Trossachs, Sask., Can. 227/F11
Trostan, N. Ire., U.K., *hill* 65/E1
Trotternish N.P., Scot., U.K. 62/D3
Trotters, N. Dak., U.S. 326/B2
Trotwood, Ohio, U.S., 27,420 . . . . .328/F2
Troup, Ga., U.S., *county*, 58,779 . . . . .260/A6
Troup, Tex., U.S., 1,949 . . . . .346/N3
Trousdale, Kans., U.S. 276/C4
Trousdale, Tenn., U.S., *county*, 7,259 . . . . . .344/J2
Trout, N.W. Terr., Can., *lake* 214/M1
Trout, N.W. Terr., Can., *lake* 220/D4
Trout, Ont., Can., *lake* 222/B2
Trout, La., U.S., 350 . . . . .282/E3
Trout, W. Va., U.S., 50 . . . . .360/F4
Trout, Wyo., U.S., *peak* 366/B1
Troutbeck, Eng., U.K. 66/C4
Trout Creek, Ont., Can., 591 . . . . .223/F1
Trout Creek, Mich., U.S., 225 . . . . .294/A3
Trout Creek, Mont., U.S., 261 . . . . .306/A2
Trout Creek, Oreg., U.S., *mountains* 334/H5
Trout Creek, Utah, U.S. 350/A4
Troutdale, Maine, U.S. 286/C3
Troutdale, Oreg., U.S., 13,777 . . . . .334/B2, D2
Troutdale, Va., U.S., 1,230 . . . . .354/E3
Trout Lake, Alta., Can., 315 . . . . .212/C3
Trout Lake, Mich., U.S., 175 . . . . .294/D3
Trout Lake, Wash., U.S., 494 . . . . .358/D4
Troutman, N.C., U.S., 1,592 . . . . .322/D3
Trout River, Nfld., Can., 616 . . . . .218/B4
Trout Run, Penn., U.S., 300 . . . . .336/G3
Troutville, Penn., U.S., 224 . . . . .336/D3
Troutville, Va., U.S., 432 . . . . .354/F4
Trouville, Fr. 88/C2
Trowbridge, Eng., U.K. 60/C3
Trowbridge, Eng., U.K., 29,334 . . . . .73/H2
Trowbridge, Ill., U.S., 100 . . . . .266/E4
Trowbridge Park, Mich., U.S., 2,012 . . . . .294/B3
Troy, Ala., U.S., 13,935 . . . . .238/D4
Troy, Ida., U.S., 779 . . . . .264/A3
Troy, Ill., U.S., 8,524 . . . . .266/A3
Troy, Ind., U.S., 392 . . . . .270/C8
Troy, Iowa, U.S., 60 . . . . .274/K6
Troy, Kans., U.S., 1,054 . . . . .276/G2
Troy, Maine, U.S., 963 . . . . .286/C4
Troy, Mich., U.S., 80,959 . . . . .294/B6, F7
Troy, Minn., U.S., 40 . . . . .298/E7
Troy, Miss., U.S., 60 . . . . .300/D1
Troy, Mo., U.S., 6,737 . . . . .302/F3
Troy, Mont., U.S., 957 . . . . .306/A1
Troy, N.H., U.S., 1,962 . . . . .312/B6
Troy, N.Y., U.S., 49,170 . . . . .320/P5
Troy, N.C., U.S., 3,430 . . . . .322/F4
Troy, Ohio, U.S., 21,999 . . . . .328/B5
Troy, Oreg., U.S. 334/J2
Troy, Penn., U.S., 1,508 . . . . .336/H2
Troy, S.C., U.S., 105 . . . . .340/B3
Troy, S. Dak., U.S. .342/J2
Troy, Tenn., U.S., 1,273 . . . . .344/C2
Troy, Tex., U.S., 1,378 . . . . .346/L4
Troy, Vt., U.S. 352/C1
Troyes, Fr., 62,612, (128,945 *metro.*) 88/D2
Troy Grove, Ill., U.S., 305 . . . . .266/D2
Truby, Tex., U.S. 346/J3
Truchas, N. Mex., U.S., 125 . . . . .317/E1
Truckee, Calif., U.S., 13,864 . . . . .246/F3
Truesdale, Iowa, U.S., 91 . . . . .274/D2
Truesdale, Mo., U.S., 397 . . . . .302/E3
Trufant, Mich., U.S., 600 . . . . .294/D6
Trujillo, Hond. 202/B2
Trujillo, Peru, 273,239, (733,722 *metro.*) 185/B2
Trujillo, N. Mex., U.S. 317/F2
Trujillo, Ven., 44,425 . . . . .182/B2
Trujillo, Ven., *state* 182/B2
Trujillo Alto, P.R. 206/B2
Truman, Minn., U.S., 1,259 . . . . .298/C7
Trumann, Ark., U.S., 6,889 . . . . .244/E2
Trumansburg, N.Y., U.S., 1,581 . . . . .320/H5
Trumbauersville, Penn., U.S., 1,059 . . . . .336/L5
Trumbull, Ariz., U.S., *mountain* 242/B1
Trumbull, Conn., U.S., 34,243 . . . . .253/C3
Trumbull, Nebr., U.S., 212 . . . . .308/E3
Trumbull, Ohio, U.S., *county*, 225,116 . . . . .328/J3
Trumpan, Scot., U.K. 62/C3
Trumpet, Eng., U.K. .68/C5
Trumpington, Eng., U.K. 70/E2
Truro, N.S., Can., 11,457 . . . . .221/D2
Truro, Eng., U.K. 60/B4

Truro, Eng., U.K., 18,966 . . . . .73/B4
Truro, Iowa, U.S., 427 . . . . .274/G5
Truro, Mass., U.S., 2,087 . . . . .292/P5
Truscott, Tex., U.S., 90 . . . . .346/J2
Trussville, Ala., U.S., 12,924 . . . . .238/C2, E1
Trust, N.C., U.S. 322/D7
Trustom Pond N.W.R., R.I., U.S. 339/C5
Trutch, Br. Col., Can. 214/L2
Truth or Consequences, N. Mex., U.S., 7,289 . .317/C4
Trutnov, Czh. Rep. 92/B2
Truxton, Ariz., U.S. 242/B2
Truxton, Mo., U.S., 96 . . . . .302/E2
Tryon, P.E.I., Can. .224/B2
Tryon, Nebr., U.S., 100 . . . . .308/D2
Tryon, N.C., U.S., 1,760 . . . . .322/A4, F8
Tryon, Okla., U.S., 448 . . . . .330/F2
Tsaile, Ariz., U.S., 1,078 . . . . .242/F1
Tsaratanana, Madag., mountains 163/B1
Tsavo, Kenya 157/E5
Tschetter Colony, S. Dak., U.S. 342/H4
Tsedike, Leso., river 161/B3
Tsengwen, Tai., river 117/B2
Tsetserleg, Mong. .118/C2
Tsévié, Togo 151/B3
Tshabong, Bots. 160/A3
Tshane, Bots. 160/A3
Tshaneni, Swaz. 161/B1
Tshikapa, Congo, D.R., 180,860 . . . . .155/B2
Tshuapa, Congo, D.R., river 155/B2
Tsingoni, Col. 163/C2
Tsiribihina, Madag., river 163/B2
Tsiroanomandidy, Madag. 163/B2
Tsitéli-Tsqaro, Geo. 103/D4
Ts'khinvali, Geo. 103/B3
Tsnori, Geo. 103/C4
Tsu, Jap., island 114/A3
Tsuen Wan, H.K., China 117/B1
Tsugaru, Jap., strait . . . . .114/D1, Inset I
Tsumeb, Nam. 160/C1
Tsumkwe, Nam. 160/D1
Tsuruga, Jap. 114/C3
Tsuruoka, Jap. 114/C2
Tualatin, Oreg., U.S., 22,791 . . . . .334/A3, D2
Tuam, Ire. 78/B2
Tuas, Sing. 123/A1
Tuasivi, Sam. 175/B2
Tubac, Ariz., U.S., 949 . . . . .242/D6
Tuba City, Ariz., U.S., 8,225 . . . . .242/D1
Tubarão, Braz. 188/D4
Tübingen, Ger. 86/B4
Tübingen, Ger., department 86/B4
Tubmanburg, Liber. 149/A2
Tuckahoe, N.J., U.S., 600 . . . . .314/D5
Tuckahoe (Suffolk County), N.Y., U.S., 1,741 .320/G1
Tuckahoe, (Westchester County),
   N.Y., U.S., 6,211 . . . . .320/B2
Tuckasegee, N.C., U.S., 50 . . . . .322/D8
Tucker, Ga., U.S., 26,532 . . . . .260/C4, J2
Tucker, Miss., U.S., 934 . . . . .300/C4
Tucker, Okla., U.S. 330/H2
Tucker, W. Va., U.S., county, 7,321 . . . . .360/H2
Tuckerman, Ark., U.S., 1,757 . . . . .244/G2
Tuckers Crossing, Miss., U.S., 350 . . . . .300/C4
Tuckerton, N.J., U.S., 3,517 . . . . .314/E4
Tucson, Ariz., U.S., 486,699, (843,746 metro.) .242/E5
Tucumán, Arg., province 191/B2
Tucumcari, N. Mex., U.S., 5,989 . . . . .317/G2
Tucupita, Ven., 81,749 . . . . .182/D2
Tucuruí, Braz., reservoir 188/D2
Tuen Mun, H.K., China 117/A1
Tuftonboro, N.H., U.S., 2,148 . . . . .312/D4
Tugela, S. Afr., river 162/D2
Tuguegarao, Phil. .120/B2
Tuira, Pan., river 203/D2
Tuktoyaktuk, N.W. Terr., Can., 930 . . . . .220/B3
Tukums, Lat. 82/B2
Tukwila, Wash., U.S., 17,181 . . . . .358/A4
Tula, Mex., ruins 200/C4
Tula, Russ., 506,147, (554,650 metro.) 104/C4
Tula, Miss., U.S., 200 . . . . .300/C4
Tulalip (Tulalip Bay), Wash., U.S., 1,561 . . . . .358/C1
Tulare, Calif., U.S., 43,994 . . . . .246/F6
Tulare, Calif., U.S., county, 368,021 . . . . . . .246/G6
Tulare, S. Dak., U.S., 221 . . . . .342/G3
Tularosa, N. Mex., U.S., 2,864 . . . . .317/D4
Tulcán, Ecua. 185/C2
Tulcea, Rom. 101/E3
Tulcea, Rom., county 101/E3
Tule, Calif., U.S., river 246/F6
Tulelake, Calif., U.S., 1,020 . . . . .246/D1
Tule River Ind. Res., Calif., U.S. 246/G6
Tulia, Tex., U.S., 5,117 . . . . .346/F10, G1
Tulip, Tex., U.S. 346/M2
Tulita, N.W. Terr., Can., 473 . . . . .220/C4
Tull, Ark., U.S., 358 . . . . .244/C3
Tulla, Scot., U.K., lake 62/G5
Tullahassee, Okla., U.S., 106 . . . . .330/G2
Tullahoma, Tenn., U.S., 17,994 . . . . .348/J4
Tullamore, Ire., 10,260 . . . . .78/C2
Tullos, La., U.S., 419 . . . . .282/E3
Tully, Mass., U.S., 275 . . . . .292/E2
Tully, N.Y., U.S., 924 . . . . .320/J5
Tullytown, Penn., U.S., 2,031 . . . . .336/M5
Tulsa, Okla., U.S., 393,049, (803,235 metro.) .330/G1
Tulsa, Okla., U.S., county, 563,299 . . . . .330/G1
Tulsequah, Br. Col., Can. 214/F2
Tulsipur, Nepal 126/B2
Tultitlán, Mex. .200/Inset
Tulun, Russ. 104/G4
Tuma, Nicar., river .202/D2
Tumacacori, Ariz., U.S., 569 . . . . .242/D6
Tumacacori N.H.P., Ariz., U.S. 242/D6
Tumaco, Col. 184/A4
Tumalo, Oreg., U.S., 375 . . . . .334/E3
Tumba, Congo, D.R., lake 155/B2
Tumbes, Peru 185/A1
Tumbes, Peru, department 185/A1
Tumble, Wales, U.K. 64/C4
Tumbler Ridge, Br. Col., Can., 1,851 . . . . . . .214/M3
Tumen, N. Kor., river 116/C1
Tummel, Scot., U.K., lake 62/J5
Tumtum, Wash., U.S., 40 . . . . .358/H2
Tumuc-Humac, Braz., mountains 188/C1
Tumuc-Humac, Fr. Gui., mountains 183/B3
Tumuc-Humac, Braz., mountains 183/B3
Tumwater, Wash., U.S., 12,698 . . . . .358/C3
Tunas, Mo., U.S., 50 . . . . .302/C4
Tunbridge, Vt., U.S. 352/C3
Tunbridge Wells, Eng., U.K. 60/D3
Tunceli, Tur., province 133/D2
Tundzha, Bul., river 101/E3
Tungurahua, Ecua., province 185/B3
Tunica, La., U.S., 90 . . . . .282/F5
Tunica, Miss., U.S., 1,132 . . . . .300/B1
Tunica, Miss., U.S., county, 9,227 . . . . .300/B1
Tunis, Tun., capital, 702,330,
   (1,394,749 metro.) 146/C1
Tunis, Tun., gulf 146/C1
Tunisia, nation 140
Tunis Mills, Md., U.S., 225 . . . . .288/K4

Tunja, Col., 118,000 . . . . .184/B3
Tunkhannock, Penn., U.S., 1,911 . . . . .336/K2
Tunk Lake, Maine, U.S., 40 . . . . .286/D4
Tunnel City, Wisc., U.S., 225 . . . . .364/C4
Tunnel Hill, Ga., U.S., 1,209 . . . . .260/C4
Tunnel Hill, Ill., U.S., 80 . . . . .266/E6
Tunnel Sprs., Ala., U.S., 80 . . . . .238/B4
Tunnelton, W. Va., U.S., 336 . . . . .360/G2
Tunstall, Eng., U.K. .66/C4
Tunstall, Eng., U.K. .70/G2
Tununak, Alaska, U.S., 325 . . . . .240/B2
Tunxis St. For., Conn., U.S. 253/D1
Tuolumne, Calif., U.S., 1,865 . . . . .246/E5
Tuolumne, Calif., U.S., county, 54,501 . . . . . .246/F4
Tupelo, Ark., U.S., 177 . . . . .244/D2
Tupelo, Miss., U.S., 34,211 . . . . .300/D1
Tupelo, Okla., U.S., 377 . . . . .330/F3
Tupelo N.B., Miss., U.S. 300/D1
Tupiza, Bol. 186/A4
Tupman, Calif., U.S., 227 . . . . .246/F7
Tupper, N.Y., U.S., lake 320/M2
Tupper Lake, N.Y., U.S., 3,935 . . . . .320/N2
Tupungato, Arg., mountain 191/B3
Tura, Russ. 104/G3
Turan, Turkm., lowland 132/C2
Turan, Uzb., lowland 132/A2
Turayf, Sa. Arab. 136/A1
Turbeville, S.C., U.S., 602 . . . . .340/D3
Turbeville, Va., U.S., 70 . . . . .354/E7
Turbo, Col. 184/A2
Turbotville, Penn., U.S., 691 . . . . .336/K4
Turda, Rom. 101/B2
Turgovishte, Bul. 101/E2
Turgovishte, Bul., oblast 101/E2
Türi, Est. 81/C2
Turin, Alta., Can., 123 . . . . .212/D6
Turin, It. 95/A1
Turin, Ga., U.S., 165 . . . . .260/B5
Turin, Iowa, U.S., 75 . . . . .274/C3
Turin, N.Y., U.S., 263 . . . . .320/L3
Turkana, Eth., lake .156/B3
Turkana, (Rudolf), Kenya, lake 157/D2
Turkestan, Taj., mountains 132/A1
Turkey, nation 129
Turkey, Iowa, U.S., river 274/L2
Turkey, Ky., U.S., 125 . . . . .280/G3
Turkey, N.C., U.S., 262 . . . . .322/J5
Turkey, Tex., U.S., 494 . . . . .346/H1
Turkey Creek, La., U.S., 356 . . . . .282/E5
Turkey Flat, Ariz., U.S. 242/F5
Turkey Ridge, S. Dak., U.S. 342/H4
Türkmenabat, Turkm., 164,000 . . . . .132/B2
Türkmenbashy, Turkm. 132/A2
Turkmenistan, nation 128
Turks, T.-C. Is., islands 204/C2
Turks, T.-C. Is., islands 207/D4
Turks and Caicos Islands, U.K., dependency . . .204/D2
Turku, Fin., 173,686 . . . . .81/B2
Turkville, Kans., U.S. 276/C2
Turkwel, Kenya, river 157/C2
Turley, N. Mex., U.S., 425 . . . . .317/C1
Turley, Okla., U.S., 3,231 . . . . .330/G1
Turlock, Calif., U.S., 55,810 . . . . .246/E5
Turn, N. Mex., U.S., 125 . . . . .317/D3
Turnberry, Man., Can. 215/A2
Turnberry, Scot., U.K. 62/G8
Turnbull, Man., Can. 215/B2
Turnbull N.W.R., Wash., U.S. 358/H2
Turnditch, Eng., U.K. 68/D3
Turneffe, Bel., islands 201/C2
Turner, Kans., U.S., county, 9,504 . . . . .260/D8
Turner, Maine, U.S., 4,972 . . . . .286/B4
Turner, Mich., U.S., 139 . . . . .294/F5
Turner, Mont., U.S., 80 . . . . .306/H1
Turner, Oreg., U.S., 1,199 . . . . .334/D3
Turner, S. Dak., U.S., county, 8,849 . . . . .342/H4
Turner, Wash., U.S. 358/H3
Turners Falls, Mass., U.S., 4,441 . . . . .292/D2
Turnersville, N.J., U.S., 3,867 . . . . .314/C4
Turner Valley, Alta., Can., 1,608 . . . . .212/C6
Turnerville, Ga., U.S., 150 . . . . .260/E2
Turnerville, Miss., U.S. 300/C3
Turnerville, Wyo., U.S., 155 . . . . .366/A2
Turney, Mo., U.S., 155 . . . . .302/B2
Turnhout, Belg. 85/C1
Turnor Lake, Sask., Can., 155 . . . . .227/B4
Turnu Măgurele, Rom. 101/C4
Turon, Kans., U.S., 436 . . . . .276/C4
Turpan, China, depression 119/C1
Turpin, Okla., U.S., 475 . . . . .330/B1, A4
Turpin Hills, Ohio, U.S., 4,960 . . . . .328/B10
Turquino, Cuba, mountain 204/B3
Turrell, Ark., U.S., 957 . . . . .244/E2
Turriff, Scot., U.K., 4,454 . . . . .62/M3
Tursunzoda, Taj. 132/A1
Turtle, Sask., Can., lake 227/B7
Turtle, S.C., U.S., islands 149/A2
Turtle, S.C., U.S., mountains 246/L8
Turtle Creek, N.B. Can. 21/E3
Turtle Creek, Penn., U.S., 6,076 . . . . .336/E7
Turtleford, Sask., Can., 465 . . . . .227/B7
Turtle Lake, N. Dak., U.S., 580 . . . . .326/E2
Turtle Lake, Wisc., U.S., 1,065 . . . . .364/A3
Turtle Mtn. Ind. Res., N. Dak., U.S. 326/F1
Turtle Mtn. Prov. Park, Man., Can. 215/A4
Turtle Mtn. Prov. Park, Man., Can. 326/E1
Turtle River, Minn., U.S., 75 . . . . .298/C3
Turton, S. Dak., U.S., 61 . . . . .342/G2
Turvey, Eng., U.K. 70/C2
Tusayan, Ariz., U.S., 562 . . . . .242/D2
Tuscaloosa, Ala., U.S., 77,906, (164,875 metro.) .238/B2
Tuscaloosa, Ala., U.S., county, 164,875 . . . . .238/B2
Tuscaloosa, Ala., U.S., lake 238/B2
Tuscany, It., region .95/B2
Tuscarawas, Ohio, U.S., 934 . . . . .328/H5
Tuscarawas, Ohio, U.S., county, 90,914 . . . . .328/G5
Tuscarora, Nev., U.S. 310/B1
Tuscarora, Nev., U.S., mountains 310/B1
Tuscarora Ind. Res., N.Y., U.S. 320/D4
Tuscarora St. For., Penn., U.S. 336/F5
Tuscola, Ill., U.S., 4,448 . . . . .266/E4
Tuscola, Mich., U.S., county, 58,266 . . . . . . .294/F6
Tuscola, Miss., U.S. 300/C3
Tuscola, Tex., U.S., 714 . . . . .346/J3
Tusculum, Tenn., U.S., 2,004 . . . . .244/R2
Tuscumbia, Ala., U.S., 7,856 . . . . .238/B1
Tuscumbia, Mo., U.S., 218 . . . . .302/D3
Tushka, Okla., U.S., 345 . . . . .330/F3
Tuskahoma, Okla., U.S., 125 . . . . .330/G3
Tuskegee, Ala., U.S., 11,846 . . . . .238/D3
Tuskegee Institute N.H.S., Ala., U.S. 238/D3
Tuskegee Natl. For., Ala., U.S. 238/D3
Tuskegee Natl. For., Ga., U.S. 260/A7
Tusket, N.S., Can. .221/B4
Tustin, Calif., U.S., 67,504 . . . . .246/E10
Tustin, Mich., U.S., 237 . . . . .294/D5
Tutbury, (Tutbury/Hatton), Eng., U.K., 5,646 . . .68/D4
Tuthill, S. Dak., U.S., 40 . . . . .342/D4
Tuticorin, India 128/C7
Tutong, Bru. 121/B2

Tutong, Bru., river .121/B2
Tutshill, (Tutshill/Sedbury), Eng., U.K., 3,361 . . .68/B6
Tuttle, Ida., U.S. 264/C7
Tuttle, N. Dak., U.S. 106 . . . . .326/E2
Tuttle, Okla., U.S., 4,294 . . . . .330/E2
Tuttle Creek, Kans., U.S., lake 276/F2
Tutwiler, Miss., U.S., 1,364 . . . . .300/B1
Tuul, Mong., river .118/C2
Tuvalu, nation 166
Tuwayq, Jabal, Sa. Arab., mountains 136/B2
Tuxedo, N.C., U.S., 475 . . . . .322/E8
Tuxedo, Tex., U.S. .346/J3
Tuxedo Park, N.Y., U.S., 731 . . . . .320/A1
Tuxford, Eng., U.K., 2,577 . . . . .66/G6
Tuxpan, Mex., 74,527, (126,616 metro.) 200/E3
Tuxtepec, Mex. 200/E4
Tuxtla Gutiérrez, Mex., state capital,
   424,579, (434,143 metro.) 200/F4
Tuy, Br. Col., Can., lake 214/G1
Tuy Hoa, Viet. 123/B4
Tuz Gölü, Tur., lake .133/C2
Tuzigoot N.M., Ariz., U.S. 242/C3
Tuzla, Bos.-Her. 98/B1
Twain Harte, Calif., U.S., 2,586 . . . . .246/E4
Twatt, Scot., U.K. 62/M1
Tweed, Ont., Can., 1,539 . . . . .223/H3
Tweed, Eng., U.K., river 66/B1
Tweed, Scot., U.K., river 60/C2
Tweedmouth, Eng., U.K., river 62/K7
Tweedmouth, Eng., U.K. 60/C2
Tweedside, N.B., Can. 21/B3
Tweedsmuir, Eng., U.K., hills 66/B1
Tweedsmuir, Scot., U.K. 62/K8
Tweedsmuir Prov. Park, Br. Col., Can. 214/J4
Twelve Pins, Ire., mountain 78/B2
Twentynine Palms, Calif., U.S., 14,764 . . . . . .246/J8
Twentynine Palms Marine Corps Air Ground
   Combat Ctr., Calif., U.S. 246/J8
Twichell, Tex., U.S. .346/G8
Twickenham, Eng., U.K. 70/D4
Twig, Minn., U.S., 350 . . . . .298/E4
Twiggs, Ga., U.S., county, 10,590 . . . . .260/D6
Twigworth, Eng., U.K. 68/C6
Twillingate, Nfld., Can., 2,611 . . . . .218/D4
Twin Bridges, Mo., U.S., 42 . . . . .302/D4
Twin Bridges, Mont., U.S., 400 . . . . .306/D4
Twin Brooks, S. Dak., U.S., 55 . . . . .342/J2
Twin Butte, Alta., Can. 212/D6
Twin Buttes, N. Dak., U.S., 80 . . . . .326/C2
Twin City, Ga., U.S., 1,752 . . . . .260/D6
Twin Falls, Ida., U.S., 34,469 . . . . .264/C7
Twin Falls, Ida., U.S., county, 64,284 . . . . . . .264/C7
Twin Groves, Ark., U.S., 276 . . . . .244/C2
Twining, Mich., U.S., 192 . . . . .294/F5
Twin Lake, Mich., U.S., 1,613 . . . . .294/C6
Twin Lakes, Calif., U.S., 5,533 . . . . .246/K4
Twin Lakes, Colo., U.S. 250/D2
Twin Lakes, Ga., U.S., 750 . . . . .260/E1
Twin Lakes, Mich., U.S. 294/A3
Twin Lakes, Minn., U.S., 168 . . . . .298/D4
Twin Lakes, N. Mex., U.S., 1,069 . . . . .317/B2
Twin Lakes, Wisc., U.S., 5,124 . . . . .364/E6
Twin Mountain, N.H., U.S., 100 . . . . .312/C3
Twin Oaks, Mo., U.S., 362 . . . . .302/H3
Twin Rivers, N.J., U.S., 7,422 . . . . .314/E3
Twinsburg, Ohio, U.S., 17,006 . . . . .328/H3, H9
Twin Sisters, Tex., U.S. 346/C3
Twin Valley, Minn., U.S., 865 . . . . .298/A3
Twisp, Wash., U.S., 938 . . . . .358/H1
Two Bridges, Eng., U.K. 73/E3
Two Buttes, Colo., U.S., 67 . . . . .250/H4
Two Buttes, Colo., U.S., creek 250/H4
Two Creeks, Man., Can. 215/A4
Two Creeks, Wisc., U.S., 125 . . . . .364/F4
Two Dales, Eng., U.K. 68/D3
Two Guns, Ariz., U.S. 242/D2
Two Harbors, Minn., U.S., 3,613 . . . . .298/F3
Two Hills, Alta., Can., 1,091 . . . . .212/E4
Two Inlets, Minn., U.S., 40 . . . . .298/B3
Twomile, Colo., U.S., creek 250/G1
Two Rivers, Wisc., U.S., 12,639 . . . . .364/F4
Two Strike, S. Dak., U.S. 342/E4
Tyaskin, Md., U.S., 250 . . . . .288/L6
Tybee, Ga., U.S., island 260/K8
Tybee Island, Ga., U.S., 3,392 . . . . .260/K8
Tyberton, Eng., U.K. .68/B5
Tychy, Pol., 133,134 . . . . .83/D3
Tye, Tex., U.S., 1,158 . . . . .346/J3
Tyger, S.C., U.S., river 340/E1
Tygh Valley, Oreg., U.S., 224 . . . . .334/E2
Tyler, Minn., U.S., 1,218 . . . . .298/A6
Tyler, Tex., U.S., 83,650, (174,706 metro.) . . .346/N3
Tyler, Tex., U.S., county, 20,871 . . . . .346/P5
Tyler, Wash., U.S. 358/H2
Tyler, W. Va., U.S., county, 9,592 . . . . .360/F2
Tylersville, Ohio, U.S., 2,900 . . . . .328/B9
Tylersville, Penn., U.S., 100 . . . . .336/G4
Tylertown, Miss., U.S., 1,910 . . . . .300/B4
Tynan, Tex., U.S., 301 . . . . .346/L7
Ty-nant, Wales, U.K. 64/D2
Tynda, Russ. 104/H4
Tyndall, Man., Can. .215/C4
Tyndall, S. Dak., U.S., 1,239 . . . . .342/H5
Tyndall A.F.B., Fla., U.S. 256/C2
Tyne, Eng., U.K., river 60/C2
Tynemouth, Eng., U.K., 17,422 . . . . .66/F2
Tyner, Ind., U.S., 300 . . . . .270/D2
Tyner, N.C., U.S., 100 . . . . .322/M2
Tyne Valley, P.E.I., Can., 223 . . . . .222/J2
Tyngsborough, Mass., U.S., 11,081 . . . . .292/J2
Tyre, (Sur), Leb. 134/A2
Tyre, Mich., U.S., 60 . . . . .294/G6
Tyringham, Mass., U.S., 350 . . . . .292/B4
Tyro, Ark., U.S., 40 . . . . .244/D4
Tyro, Kans., U.S., 226 . . . . .276/G4
Tyro, Miss., U.S. 300/C1
Tyrone, Colo., U.S. .250/F6
Tyrone, Ga., U.S., 3,916 . . . . .260/B5, H4
Tyrone, N. Mex., U.S., 500 . . . . .317/A4
Tyrone, Okla., U.S., 880 . . . . .330/A1, C4
Tyrone, Penn., U.S., 5,528 . . . . .336/E4
Tyronza, Ark., U.S., 918 . . . . .244/F2
Tyrrell, N.C., U.S., county, 4,149 . . . . .322/N3
Tyrrhenian, It., sea 95/B2
Tyson, W. Va., U.S., 100 . . . . .352/B4
Tysons Corner, Va., U.S., 18,540 . . . . .354/M2
Tytherleigh, Eng., U.K. 73/G4
Ty Ty, Ga., U.S., 714 . . . . .260/D9
Tyumen', Russ., 502,214, (556,200 metro.) . . .104/F4
Tyva, Russ., region .104/F4
Tywi, Wales, U.K., river 60/B3
Tywyn, Wales, U.K., 2,864 . . . . .64/C2
Užice, Serb.-Mont. 99/A3
Uşak, Tur., province 133/B2
Uaboe, Nauru 174/B1
Ualapue, Hawaii, U.S. 262/B3
Uaoa, Hawaii, U.S., bay 262/C3
Ubangi, C.A.R., river 154/A3
Ubangi, Congo, D.R., river 155/B1

Ubangi, Congo, river 155/E2
Ube, Jap. 114/A3
Ubeda, Sp. 94/E3
Uberaba, Braz., 180,296, (210,803 metro.) . . .188/D3
Uberlândia, Braz., 501,214 . . . . .188/D3
Ubin, Sing., island .123/B1
Ubly, Mich., U.S., 873 . . . . .294/G6
Ubon Ratchathani, Thai., (149,700 metro.) 125/C3
Ucayali, Peru, department 185/C2
Ucayali, Peru, river .185/C2
Uccle, Belg. 85/C2
Uchiura, Jap., bay . . . . .114/Inset I
Uchquduq, Uzb. 132/B2
Uckfield, Eng., U.K., 13,531 . . . . .70/E5
Uckington, Eng., U.K. 68/C6
Ucluelet, Br. Col., Can., 1,559 . . . . .214/K7
Ucolo, Utah, U.S. 350/E6
Ucon, Ida., U.S., 943 . . . . .264/F6
Ucross, Wyo., U.S. .366/C1
Udaipur, India 128/B4
Udall, Kans., U.S., 794 . . . . .276/E4
Uddevalla, Swe., 49,255 . . . . .80/B3
Uddjaur, Swe. 80/C1
Udell, Iowa, U.S., 58 . . . . .274/J6
Udine, It. 95/C1
Udmurtia, Russ., region 104/D4
Udon Thani, Thai., (153,200 metro.) 125/C2
Udu, Fiji, point 174/C2
Uehling, Nebr., U.S., 275 . . . . .308/H2
Uele, Congo, D.R., river 155/C1
Uelzen, Ger. 86/B2
Ufa, Russ., 1,087,788, (1,093,700 metro.) . . .104/D4
Uffington, Eng., U.K. .70/A3
Ugab, Nam., river 160/B2
Ugalla, Tan., river 158/B2
Uganda, nation 151
Uhland, Tex., U.S., 386 . . . . .346/D3, L6
Uhrichsville, Ohio, U.S., 5,662 . . . . .328/H5
Uíge, Ang. 159/C2
Uíge, Ang., province 159/C2
Uinta, Utah, U.S., mountains 350/D3,
Uinta, Wyo., U.S., county, 19,742 . . . . .366/A3,
Uintah, Utah, U.S., county, 25,224 . . . . .350/E5
Uintah and Ouray Ind. Res., Utah, U.S. .350/D3, D4
Uinta Natl. For., Utah, U.S. 350/C3, C4
Uitenhage, S. Afr. 162/C3,
Ujae, Marsh. Is., island 173/B2,
Ujelang, Marsh. Is., island 173/A2,
Ujjain, India, 366,787, (367,154 metro.) 128/C4,
Ukhta, Russ., 101,192, (109,200 metro.) 104/D3,
Ukiah, Calif., U.S., 15,497 . . . . .246/B3,
Ukiah, Oreg., U.S., 255 . . . . .334/H2,
Ukmergė, Lith. 82/C2,
Ukraine, nation 100/,
Ukraine, nation 193/A2
Ulaanbaatar, Mong., capital, 760,077 . . . . . . .118/C2
Ulaangom, Mong. 118/B2
Ulaan-Uul, Mong. 118/D2
Ulan, N.C., U.S., 800 . . . . .322/F3
Ulansuhai, China, lake 119/D1
Ulan-Ude, Russ., 370,175, (394,400 metro.) . .104/G4
Ulceby, Eng., U.K. 66/H5
Ulen, Ind., U.S., 123 . . . . .270/D4
Ulen, Minn., U.S., 532 . . . . .298/A3
Ulgham, Eng., U.K. 66/E2
Ulhas, India, river . . . . .128/Inset I
Uliastay, Mong. 118/B2
Ulithi, Micr., atoll 172/B2
Uljin, S. Kor. 116/C4
Ullapool, Scot., U.K. .60/B1
Ullapool, Scot., U.K., 1,308 . . . . .62/F3
Ulleung-do, S. Kor., island 116/D4
Ullin, Ill., U.S., 779 .266/D6
Ullswater, Eng., U.K., lake 66/C3
Ulm, Ger., 116,103 . . . . .86/B4
Ulm, Ark., U.S., 205 . . . . .244/D3
Ulm, Mont., U.S., 750 . . . . .306/E2
Ulm, Wyo., U.S. 366/C1
Ulmer, S.C., U.S., 102 . . . . .340/C3
Ulpha, Eng., U.K. 66/B4
Ulsan, S. Kor., 967,429 . . . . .116/C5
Ulsan, S. Kor., province 116/C5
Ulsta, Scot., U.K. 62/Q2
Ulster, Ire., province .78/C1
Ulster, N.Y., U.S., county, 177,749 . . . . .320/N12
Ulster, Penn., U.S., 325 . . . . .336/H2
Ulúa, Hond., river 202/B2
Ulubaria, India .128/Inset II
Ulu Dağ, (Mt. Olympus), Tur., mountain 133/B2
Ulupalakua, Hawaii, U.S. 262/C4
Uluru, (Ayers Rock), Austl. 170/C2
Ulva, Scot., U.K., island 62/D6
Ulverston, Eng., U.K., 11,866 . . . . .66/B4
Ulysses, Kans., U.S., 5,960 . . . . .276/A4
Ulysses, Ky., U.S., 175 . . . . .280/H3
Ulysses, Nebr., U.S., 276 . . . . .308/G2
Ulysses, Penn., U.S., 684 . . . . .336/F2
Uman', Ukr. 102/C2
Umapine, Oreg., U.S., 250 . . . . .334/H2
Umatilla, Fla., U.S., 2,214 . . . . .256/G3
Umatilla, Oreg., U.S., 4,978 . . . . .334/G2
Umatilla, Oreg., U.S., county, 70,548 . . . . . . .334/G2
Umatilla, Oreg., U.S., river 334/G2
Umatilla Ind. Res., Oreg., U.S. 334/G2, H2
Umatilla Natl. For., Oreg., U.S. 334/H2
Umatilla N.W.R., Wash., U.S. 358/F4
Umbagog, Maine, U.S., lake 286/C3
Umbagog, N.H., U.S., lake 312/D2
Umbeluzi, Swaz., river 161/B2
Umber View Hts., Mo., U.S., 52 . . . . .302/C4
Umbria, It., region 172/A2
Umbria, It., region 95/C2
Umeå, Swe., 105,006 . . . . .80/C2
Umealven, Swe., river 80/C2
Umm al Qaywayn, U.A.E. 136/C2
Umm an Na'san, Bahr., island 137/A1
Umm as Samim, Sa. Arab., salt flat 136/C2
Umm Bab, Qatar 137/B3
Umm Lajj, Sa. Arab. 136/A1
Umm Qasr, Iraq 130/C2
Umm Sa'id, Qatar 137/D4
Umnak, Alaska, U.S. 240/Inset
Umniati, Zimb., river 160/D2
Umpire, Ark., U.S., 100 . . . . .244/A3
Umpqua, Oreg., U.S. 334/C4
Umpqua Natl. For., Oreg., U.S. 334/D4
Umtata, S. Afr. 162/C3
Umuahia, Nig. 152/D5
Umzingwani, Zimb., river 160/B2
Una, Bos.-Her., river .98/A1
Unadilla, Ga., U.S., 2,772 . . . . .260/D7
Unadilla, Nebr., U.S., 342 . . . . .308/H3
Unadilla, N.Y., U.S., 1,127 . . . . .320/L6
Unadilla, N.Y., U.S., river 320/L5
Unalakleet, Alaska, U.S. 240/B2
Unalaska, Alaska, U.S., 4,283 . . . . .240/B4
Unalaska, Alaska, U.S., island 240/B4
Unayzah, Sa. Arab. .136/B1
Uncasville, Conn., U.S., 1,500 . . . . .253/G4
Uncertain, Tex., U.S., 150 . . . . .346/P3

Uncompahgre, Colo., U.S., peak 250/C3
Uncompahgre, Colo., U.S., plateau 250/B3
Uncompahgre Natl. For., Colo., U.S. 250/C3
Underbarrow, Eng., U.K. 66/C4
Underhill, Vt., U.S. 352/B1
Underhill Ctr., Vt., U.S., 500 . . . . .352/B1
Underwood, Eng., U.K., 2,177 . . . . .68/D4
Underwood, Eng., U.K. 68/E3
Underwood, Eng., U.K., 2,177 . . . . .70/B1
Underwood, Ind., U.S., 425 . . . . .270/E7
Underwood, Iowa, U.S., 688 . . . . .274/C5
Underwood, Minn., U.S., 319 . . . . .298/B4
Underwood, N. Dak., U.S., 812 . . . . .326/D2
Unga, Alaska, U.S., island 240/C3
Ungava, Nfld., Can., bay 218/D3
Ungava, Nun., Can., bay 220/P5
Ungava, Que., Can., bay 225/C2
Ungheni, Mol. 102/A2
Unicoi, Tenn., U.S., 3,519 . . . . .344/S2
Unicoi, Tenn., U.S., county, 17,667 . . . . .344/R2
Unimak, Alaska, U.S., island 240/C4
Union, St. Vin.-Gren., island 208/A4
Union, Ala., U.S., 227 . . . . .238/B3
Union, Ark., U.S., county, 45,629 . . . . .244/C4
Union, Conn., U.S., 693 . . . . .253/G2
Union, Fla., U.S., county, 13,442 . . . . .256/F1
Union, Ga., U.S., county, 17,289 . . . . .260/C2
Union, Ill., U.S., 576 .266/E1
Union, Ill., U.S., county, 18,293 . . . . .266/D6
Union, Ind., U.S., county, 7,349 . . . . .270/G5
Union, Iowa, U.S., 427 . . . . .274/H3
Union, Iowa, U.S., county, 12,309 . . . . .274/F6
Union, Ky., U.S., 2,893 . . . . .280/F2
Union, Ky., U.S., county, 15,637 . . . . .280/C3
Union, La., U.S., 500 . . . . .282/H6
Union, La., U.S., parish, 22,803 . . . . .282/E1
Union, Maine, U.S., 2,209 . . . . .286/C4
Union, Mich., U.S., 475 . . . . .294/D8
Union, Miss., U.S., 2,021 . . . . .300/C3
Union, Miss., U.S., county, 25,362 . . . . .300/C1
Union, Mo., U.S., 7,757 . . . . .302/F3
Union, Nebr., U.S., 260 . . . . .308/J3
Union, N.H., U.S., 425 . . . . .312/D5
Union, (Union County), N.J., U.S., 54,405 . . .314/B2, J2
Union, N.J., U.S., county, 522,541 . . . . .314/E2
Union, N. Mex., U.S., county, 4,174 . . . . .317/C1
Union, N.C., U.S., county, 123,677 . . . . .322/D5
Union, Ohio, U.S., 5,574 . . . . .328/B6
Union, Ohio, U.S., county, 40,909 . . . . .328/D5
Union, Oreg., U.S., 1,926 . . . . .334/J2
Union, Oreg., U.S., county, 24,530 . . . . .334/H2
Union, Penn., U.S., county, 41,624 . . . . .336/G4
Union, S.C., U.S., 8,793 . . . . .340/C2
Union, S.C., U.S., county, 29,881 . . . . .340/C2
Union, S. Dak., U.S., county, 12,584 . . . . . . .342/J5
Union, Tenn., U.S., county, 17,808 . . . . .344/P2
Union, (Scurry County), Tex., U.S. 346/G3
Union, (Terry County), Tex., U.S. 346/E3
Union, (Wilson County), Tex., U.S. 346/L6
Union, Utah, U.S. 350/E2
Union, Wash., U.S., 375 . . . . .358/B2
Union, W. Va., U.S., 548 . . . . .360/E5
Unión, Chile 190/C2
Union Beach, N.J., U.S., 6,649 . . . . .314/E3
Union Bridge, Md., U.S., 989 . . . . .288/F1
Union Ctr., S. Dak., U.S., 50 . . . . .342/C3
Union Ctr., Wisc., U.S., 214 . . . . .364/C5
Union Church, Miss., U.S., 50 . . . . .300/B4
Union City, Calif., U.S., 66,869 . . . . .246/K2
Union City, Ind., U.S., 3,622 . . . . .270/G4
Union City, Ky., U.S., 175 . . . . .280/F3
Union City, Mich., U.S., 1,804 . . . . .294/D7
Union City, N.J., U.S., 67,088 . . . . .314/B2, E2
Union City, Ohio, U.S., 1,767 . . . . .328/A5
Union City, Okla., U.S., 1,375 . . . . .330/E2
Union City, Penn., U.S., 3,463 . . . . .336/B2
Union City, Tenn., U.S., 10,876 . . . . .344/C2
Union Creek, Oreg., U.S. 334/D5
Uniondale, Ind., U.S., 277 . . . . .270/F4
Union Dale, Penn., U.S., 368 . . . . .336/L2
Union Gap, Wash., U.S., 5,621 . . . . .358/E4
Union Grove, Ala., U.S., 94 . . . . .238/C1
Union Grove, N.C., U.S., 350 . . . . .322/D2
Union Grove, Wisc., U.S., 4,322 . . . . .364/E6
Union Hill, Ill., U.S., 66 . . . . .266/E2
Union Hill, La., U.S., 60 . . . . .282/D4
Union Lake, Mich., U.S., 2,500 . . . . .294/A6
Union Level, Va., U.S., 125 . . . . .354/G7
Union Mills, Md., U.S., 300 . . . . .288/F1
Union Pt., Ga., U.S., 1,669 . . . . .260/E4
Union Slough N.W.R., Iowa, U.S. 274/F1
Union Sprs., Ala., U.S., 3,670 . . . . .238/D3
Union Sprs., N.Y., U.S., 1,074 . . . . .320/H5
Union Star, Mo., U.S., 433 . . . . .302/B2
Uniontown, Ala., U.S., 1,636 . . . . .238/B3
Uniontown, Ark., U.S., 150 . . . . .244/A2
Uniontown, Kans., U.S., 288 . . . . .276/H4
Uniontown, Ky., U.S., 1,064 . . . . .280/C3
Uniontown, Md., U.S., 275 . . . . .288/F1
Uniontown, Penn., U.S., 12,422 . . . . .336/B6
Uniontown, Wash., U.S., 345 . . . . .358/H4
Unionvale, Ohio, U.S., 80 . . . . .328/J5
Union Vil., Vt., U.S., 125 . . . . .352/E3
Unionville, Conn., U.S., 5,100 . . . . .253/D3
Unionville, Ga., U.S., 2,074 . . . . .260/D9
Unionville, Iowa, U.S., 127 . . . . .274/J6
Unionville, Maine, U.S., 60 . . . . .286/E4
Unionville, Md., U.S., 175 . . . . .288/K4
Unionville, Mich., U.S., 605 . . . . .294/F6
Unionville, Mo., U.S., 2,041 . . . . .302/C1
Unionville, Mont., U.S., 175 . . . . .306/D3
Unionville, Nev., U.S., 250 . . . . .310/A1
Unionville, Penn., U.S., 313 . . . . .336/F4
Unionville, Va., U.S., 175 . . . . .354/H4
Unionville Ctr., Ohio, U.S., 299 . . . . .328/B5
Uniopolis, Ohio, U.S., 256 . . . . .328/B4
United Arab Emirates, nation 132
United Kingdom, nation 58
United Kingdom, nation 193/D18
UK Sovereign Base Area, Cyp. 133/A2, B2
U.S. Air Force Academy, Colo., U.S. 250/F2
U.S. Dept. of Energy Hanford Site, Wash., U.S. .358/F3
U.S. Dept. of Energy Savannah River Site,
  S.C., U.S. 340/C3
U.S. Mil. Res. Yakima Training Ctr., Wash., U.S. .358/F4
U.S. Naval Base Guantánamo Bay, Cuba 204/C3
U.S. Naval Base Guantánamo Bay, Cuba 204/C3
U.S. Naval Res. Hawaii, U.S. 262/E1, E2
U.S. Naval Res., Calif., U.S. 246/G10, K10
U.S. Naval Res., S.C., U.S. 340/E4
United States of America, nation 220
U.S.S. Arizona Mem., Hawaii, U.S. 262/E1
Unity, Sask., Can., 2,243 . . . . .227/A8
Unity, (Kennebec Co.) Maine, U.S. 286/C4
Unity, (Waldo Co.) Maine, U.S., 1,889 . . . . . .286/C4
Unity, N.H., U.S., 1,530 . . . . .312/B5
Unity, Oreg., U.S., 131 . . . . .334/H3
Unity, Wisc., U.S., 368 . . . . .364/C4
Unity Vil., Mo., U.S., 140 . . . . .302/J5
Unityville, S. Dak., U.S., 40 . . . . .342/H4

Universal, Ind., U.S., 419 . . . . .270/B5
Universal City, Tex., U.S., 14,849 . . . . .346/A2, K6
Universal City, Mo., U.S., 37,428 . . . . .302/H3
University Hts., Iowa, U.S., 987 . . . . .274/L4
University Hts., Ohio, U.S., 14,146 . . . . .328/H9
University Park, Ill., U.S., 6,662 . . . . .266/F2
University Park, Iowa, U.S., 536 . . . . .274/J5
University Park, Md., U.S., 2,318 . . . . .288/C6
University Park, N. Mex., U.S., 2,732 . . . . . . .317/D5
University Park, Tex., U.S., 23,324 . . . . .346/C9
University Place, Wash., U.S., 29,933 . . . . . . .358/C2
University West, Fla., U.S. 256/D6
Unley, S.A., Austl. . . . . .170/Inset II
Unnamed, Austl., aboriginal land 170/B2
Unnamed, Austl., aboriginal land 170/C1
Unnamed, Austl., aboriginal land 170/D1
Unst, Scot., U.K., island . . . . .60/Inset I
Unst, Scot., U.K., island 62/B1
Unterfranken, Ger., department 86/B3
Unthank, Eng., U.K. .66/C3
Upalco, Utah, U.S. 350/D3
Upatoi, Ga., U.S. 260/B6
Upemba, Congo, D.R., lake 155/C3
Upernavik, Grld. 193/B2
Upham, N. Dak., U.S., 155 . . . . .326/E1
Upington, S. Afr. 162/B2
Upland, Calif., U.S., 68,393 . . . . .246/H8
Upland, Ind., U.S., 3,803 . . . . .270/F4
Upland, Kans., U.S. .276/E2
Upland, Nebr., U.S., 179 . . . . .308/E3
Upland, Penn., U.S., 2,977 . . . . .336/L7
Uplands Park, Mo., U.S., 460 . . . . .302/H3
Uplowman, Eng., U.K. 73/F3
Upolu, Sam., island .175/C2
Upolu, Sam., point 262/D6, G3
Upper, Calif., U.S., lake 246/E1
Upper Arlington, Ohio, U.S., 33,686 . . . . .328/D5, D9
Upper Arrow, Br. Col., Can., lake 214/O6
Upper Austria, Aus., state 91/C2
Upper Blackville, N.B., Can. 217/D2
Upper Brockway, N.B., Can. 217/B3
Upper Broughton, Eng., U.K. 70/B1
Upper Cokeham, Eng., U.K. 70/D5
Upper Darby, Penn., U.S., 1,900 . . . . .336/L7
Upper Dicker, Eng., U.K. 70/E5
Upper Drew, Maine, U.S. 286/D3
Upper Elkstone, Eng., U.K. 68/D3
Upper Erne, N. Ire., U.K., lake 60/A2
Upper Erne, N. Ire., U.K., lake 78/C1
Upper Frenchville, Maine, U.S., 125 . . . . .286/D1
Upper Gagetown, N.B., Can., 314 . . . . .217/C3
Upper Gloucester, Maine, U.S., 475 . . . . .286/B4
Upper Hainesville, N.B., Can. 217/B2
Upper Hill, Md., U.S., 175 . . . . .288/L7
Upper Kent, N.B., Can., 167 . . . . .217/B2
Upper Klamath, Oreg., U.S., lake 334/E5
Upper Klamath N.W.R., Oreg., U.S. 334/E5
Upper Liard, Yukon, Can., 159 . . . . .228/D5
Upper Lough Erne, N. Ire., U.K., lake 65/B3
Upper Marlboro, Md., U.S., 648 . . . . .288/D7, G4
Upper Mississippi River Natl. Wildlife &
  Fish Refuge, Wisc., U.S. 274/M1, P3
Upper Missouri River Breaks Natl. Mon.,
  Mont., U.S. 306/G2
Upper Musquodoboit, N.S., Can. 221/E2
Upper Nutria, N. Mex., U.S. 317/B2
Upper Nyack, N.Y., U.S., 1,863 . . . . .320/B1
Upper Ohio, N.S., Can. 221/B4
Upper Ouachita N.W.R., La., U.S. 282/E1
Upper Poppleton, Eng., U.K. 66/F5
Upper Red, Minn., U.S., lake 298/C2
Upper Saddle River, N.J., U.S., 7,741 . . . . . . .314/B1, E1
Upper Sandusky, Ohio, U.S., 6,533 . . . . .328/D4
Upper Saranac, N.Y., U.S., lake 320/N2
Upper Soda, Oreg., U.S. 334/D3
Upper Souris N.W.R., N. Dak., U.S. 326/D1
Upper Street, Eng., U.K. 70/H1
Upper Tract, W. Va., U.S., 175 . . . . .360/H3
Upper Tweeddale N.P. Eng., U.K. 66/B1
Upper Tweeddale N.P. Scot., U.K. 62/K7
Upperville, Va., U.S., 150 . . . . .354/H4
Upper Waiakea Forest Reserve, Hawaii, U.S. .262/J5
Upper Woodstock, N.B., Can. 217/B2
Uppingham, Eng., U.K., 3,140 . . . . .68/F4
Uppingham, Eng., U.K., 3,140 . . . . .70/C1
Uppsala, Swe., 191,110 . . . . .81/D3
Uppsala, Swe., county 80/C2
Upsala, Minn., U.S., 424 . . . . .298/C5
Upshur, Tex., U.S., county, 35,291 . . . . .346/N3
Upshur, W. Va., U.S., county, 23,404 . . . . . . .360/F3
Upson, Ga., U.S., county, 27,597 . . . . .260/C6
Upson, Wisc., U.S., 50 . . . . .364/C2
Upton, Eng., U.K., 5,422 . . . . .68/F6
Upton, Eng., U.K., 5,422 . . . . .70/C3
Upton, Eng., U.K. 73/F2
Upton, Eng., U.K., 5,422 . . . . .70/H3
Upton, Ky., U.S., 654 . . . . .280/E3
Upton, Maine, U.S., 62 . . . . .286/A4
Upton, Mass., U.S., 5,642 . . . . .292/H4
Upton, N.J., U.S. 314/D4
Upton, Tex., U.S., county, 3,404 . . . . .346/F4
Upton, Wyo., U.S., 872 . . . . .366/D1
Upton Cross, Eng., U.K. 73/D3
Upton Grey, Eng., U.K. 70/C4
Upton upon Severn, Eng., U.K., 1,756 . . . . . .68/C5
Upwell, Eng., U.K. 70/E1
Upwood, Eng., U.K. .70/D3
Ural, Russ., mountains 104/D4
Ural, Russ., mountains 193/C4
Ural, Russ., river 104/D5
Uran, India . . . . .128/Inset I
Urania, La., U.S., 700 . . . . .282/E3
Uranium City, Sask., Can. 227/B1
Uravan, Colo., U.S. .250/B3
Urawa, Jap., 485,000 . . . . .114/C3
Urbana, Ark., U.S., 90 . . . . .244/C4
Urbana, Ill., U.S., 36,395 . . . . .266/E3
Urbana, Ind., U.S., 325 . . . . .270/E3
Urbana, Iowa, U.S., 1,019 . . . . .274/L3
Urbana, Kans., U.S. .276/K4
Urbana, Md., U.S., 400 . . . . .288/E2
Urbana, Mo., U.S., 407 . . . . .302/C4
Urbana, Ohio, U.S., 11,613 . . . . .328/C5
Urbancrest, Ohio, U.S., 868 . . . . .328/D9
Urbandale, Iowa, U.S., 29,072 . . . . .274/G4
Urbanette, Ark., U.S., 175 . . . . .244/B2
Urbank, Minn., U.S., 59 . . . . .298/B4
Urbanna, Va., U.S., 543 . . . . .354/K5
Urganch, Uzb., 139,100 . . . . .132/B2
Uri, Switz., canton 90/C2
Uriah, Ala., U.S., 200 . . . . .238/B4
Urich, Mo., U.S., 499 . . . . .302/B3
Urmia, Iran, lake 130/D2
Uroševac, Serb.-Mont. 99/B3
Uroteppa, Taj. 132/A1
Ursa, Ill., U.S., 595 .266/B3
Ursina, Penn., U.S., 254 . . . . .336/C6
Ursine, Nev., U.S., 90 . . . . .310/C3
Uruapan, Mex., 225,816, (265,699 metro.) . .200/D4
Urubamba, Peru, river 185/C3
Uruguai, Braz., river .188/C4

Uruguay, nation 177
Uruguay, Arg., river .191/D3
Uruguay, Uru., river .187/A1
Urukthapel, Palau, island 172/B3
Ürümqi, China, 961,240, (1,084,060 metro.) . .119/B3
Usak, Tur. 133/B2
Ushuaia, Arg. 191/B7
Usk, Wales, U.K., 2,187 . . . . .64/F4
Usk, Wales, U.K., reservoir 64/D4
Usk, Wales, U.K., river 60/C3
Usk, Wash., U.S., 100 . . . . .358/H1
Üsküdar, Tur. 133/B2
Usmas, Lat., lake 82/B2
Usquepaug, R.I., U.S., 350 . . . . .339/C5
Ussuri, Russ., river 104/H5
Ussuriysk, Russ. 104/H5
Ustecký, Czh. Rep., region 92/C2
Uster, Switz. 90/C1
Ustica, It., island 95/C3
Ust'-Ilimsk, Russ. 104/G4
Ústí nad Labem, Czh. Rep., 97,000 . . . . .92/B2
Ustka, Pol. 83/C1
Ust'-Kamchatsk, Russ. 104/J4
Ust'-Kut, Russ. 104/G4
Ust'-Ordynskiy, Russ. 104/G4
Ust'-Ordynskiy Buryat, Russ.,
  autonomous okrug 104/G4
Ustyurt, Kaz., plateau 131/B2
Ustyurt, Uzb., plateau 132/A2
Usulután, El Salv., 62,967 . . . . .203/B2
Usumacinta, Guat., river 201/C3
Usumacinta, Mex., river 200/F4
Utah, Fr., beach 88/B2
Utah, U.S., state 338
Utah, Utah, U.S., county, 368,536 . . . . .350/B3
Utah, Utah, U.S., lake 350/C3
Utah Test and Training Range, Utah, U.S. . . .350/A2, A3
Utan, India . . . . .128/Inset I
Ute, Iowa, U.S., 378 . . . . .274/C3
Ute Mtn. Ind. Res., Colo., U.S. 250/B4
Utena, Lith. 82/C2
Ute Park, N. Mex., U.S. 317/E1
Utica, Ind., U.S., 591 . . . . .270/E8
Utica, Kans., U.S., 223 . . . . .276/B3
Utica, Mich., U.S., 4,577 . . . . .294/B6, F7
Utica, Minn., U.S., 230 . . . . .298/F7
Utica, Miss., U.S., 966 . . . . .300/B3
Utica, Mo., U.S., 274 . . . . .302/C2
Utica, Mont., U.S. 306/F3
Utica, Nebr., U.S., 844 . . . . .308/G3
Utica, N.Y., U.S., 60,651, (299,896 metro.) . .320/L14
Utica, Ohio, U.S., 2,130 . . . . .328/F5
Utica, Penn., U.S., 211 . . . . .336/B3
Utica, S.C., U.S., 1,322 . . . . .340/B2
Utica, S. Dak., U.S., 86 . . . . .342/H5
Utikuma, Alta., Can., lake 212/C3
Utila, Hond., island .202/B1
Utley, Tex., U.S. 346/E2
Utleyville, Colo., U.S. 250/G4
Utopia, Tex., U.S., 241 . . . . .346/J6
Utrecht, Neth., 258,370, (364,762 metro.) . . .84/C4, J6
Utrecht, Neth., province 84/C2
Utsunomiya, Jap., 444,000 . . . . .114/C2
Uttaradit, Thai. 125/B2
Uttar Pradesh, India, state 128/C3
Uttoxeter, Eng., U.K., 10,329 . . . . .68/D4
Utuado, P.R. 206/D2
Utukok, Alaska, U.S., river 240/C1
Utupua, Sol. Is., island 173/C2
Uummannaq, Grld. 193/B2
Uusimaa, Fin., region 81/D2
Uva, Sri Lan., province 126/C5
Uvada, Utah, U.S., 60 . . . . .350/A6
Uvalda, Ga., U.S., 530 . . . . .260/F7
Uvalde, Tex., U.S., 14,929 . . . . .346/J6
Uvalde, Tex., U.S., county, 25,926 . . . . .346/J6
Uvira, Congo, D.R. 155/C2
Uvs, Mong., lake 118/B1
Uwajima, Jap. 114/B3
Uwaynat, Jabal al, Lib., mountain 145/D3
Uwharrie Natl. For., N.C., U.S. 322/F4
Uxbridge, Eng., U.K. .70/D3
Uxbridge, Mass., U.S., 11,156 . . . . .292/H4
Uyo, Nig. 152/D5
Uyuni, Bol. 186/A4
Uzbekistan, nation 128
Uzhhorod, Ukr., 125,585 . . . . .102/A2

Vaal, S. Afr., reservoir 162/C2
Vaal, S. Afr., river 162/B2
Vaalserberg, Neth., mountain 84/D4
Vaasa, Fin., 56,737 .81/D2
Vác, Hun. 92/E2
Vacaville, Calif., U.S., 88,625 . . . . .246/D4, K1
Vache, Haiti, island .205/B2
Vacherie, La., U.S., 250 . . . . .282/H6
Vada, Ga., U.S., 50 .260/C9
Vader, Wash., U.S., 590 . . . . .358/C3
Vadito, N. Mex., U.S., 242 . . . . .317/E1
Vadnais Hts., Minn., U.S., 13,069 . . . . .298/E6
Vado, N. Mex., U.S., 3,003 . . . . .317/D5
Vadodara, India, 1,306,035, (1,492,398 metro.) .128/B4
Vadsø, Nor. 80/F1
Vaduz, Liech., capital, 5,097 . . . . .90/B2
Vágar, Den., island 79/Inset
Váh, Slvk., river 92/A2
Vahsh, Taj., river 132/A1
Vaich, Scot., U.K., lake 62/G3
Vaiden, Miss., U.S., 840 . . . . .300/C2
Vail, Ariz., U.S., 2,484 . . . . .242/E5
Vail, Colo., U.S., 4,531 . . . . .250/D2
Vail, Iowa, U.S., 452 . . . . .274/D3
Vail, Wash., U.S., 225 . . . . .358/C3
Vaitupu, Tuv., island 174/C2
Vakhan, Afg., region 129/C1
Valais, Switz., canton 90/B2
Valatie, N.Y., U.S., 1,712 . . . . .320/P6
Val Comeau, N.B., Can., 823 . . . . .217/E1
Valcourt, Que., Can., 2,411 . . . . .226/D6
Valdecañas, Sp., reservoir 94/D3
Val-de-Marne, Fr., department 88/C2
Valdepeñas, Sp. 94/E3
Valders, Wisc., U.S., 948 . . . . .364/F4
Valdés, Arg., peninsula 191/C5
Val-des-Bois, Que., Can., 732 . . . . .226/A6
Valdese, N.C., U.S., 4,485 . . . . .322/B3
Valdez, Alaska, U.S., 4,036 . . . . .240/F2
Valdez, N. Mex., U.S. 317/E1
Valdivia, Chile, 120,786 . . . . .190/B5
Val-d'Oise, Fr., department 88/C2
Val-d'Or, Que., Can., 22,748 . . . . .225/A4
Valdosta, Ga., U.S., 43,724 . . . . .260/E1
Vale, Oreg., U.S., 1,976 . . . . .334/J4
Vale, S. Dak., U.S., 50 . . . . .342/B3
Valeene, Ind., U.S., 200 . . . . .270/D8
Valemount, Br. Col., Can., 1,195 . . . . .214/N5
Valença, Port. 93/A1
Valence, Fr., 66,568, (117,448 metro.) 88/D4
Valencia, Sp., 738,441 . . . . .94/F3
Valencia, Sp., autonomous community 94/F2, F3
Valencia, Sp., gulf 94/G3

Valencia, Sp., province 94/F3
Valencia, N. Mex., U.S., 4,500 . . . . .317/C3
Valencia, N. Mex., U.S., county, 66,152 . . . . .317/C3
Valencia, Penn., U.S., 384 . . . . .336/B4
Valencia, Ven., 742,145 . . . . .182/C1
Valencia Hts., U.S. 340/E2
Valenciennes, Fr., 42,343, (357,395 metro.) . .88/C1
Valentine, Ariz., U.S. 242/B2
Valentine, Mont., U.S. 306/H2
Valentine, Nebr., U.S., 2,820 . . . . .308/D1
Valentine, Tex., U.S., 187 . . . . .346/D5
Valentine N.W.R., Nebr., U.S. 308/D1
Valentines, Va., U.S. .354/H7
Vale of Glamorgan, Wales, U.K.,
  unitary authority, 119,293 . . . . .64/E5
Valera, Tex., U.S. 346/H4
Valera, Ven., 97,931, (110,395 metro.) 182/B2
Valeria, Iowa, U.S., 62 . . . . .274/H4
Valeria, Ky., U.S. 280/G3
Valga, Est. 81/D3
Valhalla, N.C., U.S., 90 . . . . .322/M2
Valier, Ill., U.S., 662 .266/D5
Valier, Mont., U.S., 498 . . . . .306/D1
Valira, And., river 93/B2
Valira d'Orient, And., river 93/B2
Valjevo, Serb.-Mont. .99/A2
Valka, Lat. 82/C1
Valkaria, Fla., U.S., 200 . . . . .256/H4
Valladolid, Mex., 37,332, (56,776 metro.) . . .200/G3
Valladolid, Sp., 316,580 . . . . .94/D2
Valladolid, Sp., province 94/D2
Valle, Hond., department 202/B3
Vallecito, Colo., U.S. .250/C4
Vallecitos, N. Mex., U.S., 200 . . . . .317/D1
Valle d'Aosta, It., region 95/A1
Valle del Cauca, Col., department 184/A3
Valledupar, Col., 297,000 . . . . .184/B2
Vallejo, Calif., U.S., 116,760 . . . . .246/C4, J1
Vallenar, Chile 190/B3
Vallersville, Mass., U.S., 2,000 . . . . .292/M5
Valles Mines, Mo., U.S., 275 . . . . .302/F3
Valletta, Malta, capital, 7,625 . . . . .97/C3
Valley, Man., Can., river 215/A3
Valley, Wales, U.K. 64/B1
Valley, Ala., U.S., 9,198 . . . . .238/D3
Valley, Ida., U.S., county, 7,651 . . . . .264/B5
Valley, Mont., U.S., county, 7,675 . . . . .306/K1
Valley, Nebr., U.S., 1,788 . . . . .308/H2
Valley, Oreg., U.S. 334/G2
Valley, Wash., U.S., 125 . . . . .358/H1
Valley, Wyo., U.S. 366/G5
Valley Brook, Okla., U.S., 817 . . . . .330/B4, E2
Valley Ctr., Kans., U.S., 4,883 . . . . .276/C4
Valley City, Ill., U.S. .266/C4
Valley City, N. Dak., U.S., 6,826 . . . . .326/H3
Valley City, Ohio, U.S., 650 . . . . .328/F10
Valley Falls, Kans., U.S., 1,254 . . . . .276/H2
Valley Falls, N.Y., U.S., 491 . . . . .320/P5
Valley Falls, Oreg., U.S. 334/F5
Valley Falls, R.I., U.S., 11,599 . . . . .339/D2
Valley Falls, S.C., U.S., 3,990 . . . . .340/C1, F1
Valley Farm, Tex., U.S. 346/E4
Valley Farms, Ariz., U.S., 300 . . . . .242/D4
Valley Forge N.H.P., Penn., U.S. 336/K6, L5
Valley Head, Ala., U.S., 611 . . . . .238/D1
Valley Head, W. Va., U.S., 200 . . . . .360/F3
Valley Hi, Ohio, U.S., 244 . . . . .328/C5
Valley-Hi, Penn., U.S. 336/E5
Valley Hill, N.C., U.S., 2,137 . . . . .322/E8
Valley Mills, Tex., U.S., 1,123 . . . . .346/L4
Valley of Fire St. Park, Nev., U.S. 310/C3
Valley Park, Miss., U.S., 60 . . . . .300/B3
Valley Park, Mo., U.S., 6,518 . . . . .302/H3
Valley Park, Okla., U.S. 330/G1
Valley Spr., Tex., U.S., 50 . . . . .346/K5
Valley Sprs., Ark., U.S., 167 . . . . .244/B1
Valley Sprs., Calif., U.S., 2,560 . . . . .246/L6
Valley Sprs., S. Dak., U.S., 792 . . . . .342/J4
Valley Stream, N.Y., U.S., 36,368 . . . . .320/C2
Valleyview, Alta., Can., 1,856 . . . . .212/B3
Valley View, Ky., U.S., 70 . . . . .280/F3
Valleyview, Ohio, U.S., 601 . . . . .328/D9
Valley View, Ohio, U.S., 601 . . . . .328/H9
Valley View, Penn., U.S., 1,677 . . . . .336/H4
Valley View, Tex., U.S., 737 . . . . .346/L2
Valley View, Tex., U.S. 346/J7
Valliant, Okla., U.S., 771 . . . . .330/G5
Val Marie, Sask., Can., 134 . . . . .227/C11
Valmeyer, Ill., U.S., 608 . . . . .266/C5
Valmiera, Lat. 82/C2
Valmont, N. Mex., U.S., 100 . . . . .317/E5
Valmora, N. Mex., U.S., 125 . . . . .317/F2
Valmy, Nev., U.S., 100 . . . . .310/B1
Valparaíso, Chile, 270,242 . . . . .190/B4, Inset
Valparaíso, Chile, region . . . . .190/B4, Inset
Valparaiso, Fla., U.S., 6,408 . . . . .256/B1
Valparaiso, Ind., U.S., 27,428 . . . . .270/B2
Valparaiso, Nebr., U.S., 563 . . . . .308/H2
Valsetz, Oreg., U.S. .334/C3
Valton, Wisc., U.S., 100 . . . . .364/C5
Val Verde, Utah, U.S. 350/C3, E2
Val Verde, Tex., U.S., county, 44,856 . . . . . . .346/G5
Vamori, Ariz., U.S., 60 . . . . .242/D6
Van, Tur., 227,000 . . . . .133/E2
Van, Tur., lake 133/E2
Van, Tur., province 133/E2
Van, Tex., U.S., 2,362 . . . . .346/N3
Van, W. Va., U.S., 250 . . . . .360/D4
Vanadzor, Arm., 172,800 . . . . .103/B2
Van Alstyne, Tex., U.S., 2,502 . . . . .346/M2
Vananda, Mont., U.S. 306/K3
Van Bibber, Md., U.S. 288/J2
Van Buren, Ark., U.S., 18,986 . . . . .244/A2
Van Buren, Ark., U.S., county, 16,192 . . . . . .244/C2
Van Buren, Ind., U.S., 935 . . . . .270/E3
Van Buren, Iowa, U.S., county, 7,809 . . . . . . .274/K6
Van Buren, Ky., U.S. .280/E3
Van Buren, Maine, U.S., 2,631 . . . . .286/E1
Van Buren, Mich., U.S., county, 76,263 . . . . .294/C7
Van Buren, Mo., U.S., 845 . . . . .302/E4
Van Buren, Ohio, U.S., 313 . . . . .328/C3
Van Buren, Tenn., U.S., county, 5,508 . . . . . .344/L3
Vance, Ala., U.S., 500 . . . . .238/B2
Vance, Miss., U.S., 80 . . . . .300/B1
Vance, N.C., U.S., county, 42,954 . . . . .322/J2
Vance, S.C., U.S., 208 . . . . .340/D3
Vanceboro, Maine, U.S., 147 . . . . .286/E3
Vanceboro, N.C., U.S., 898 . . . . .322/L4
Vanceburg, Ky., U.S., 1,731 . . . . .280/G2
Vancleave, Miss., U.S., 4,910 . . . . .300/D5
Vancleve, Ky., U.S. 280/G3
Vancorum, Colo., U.S., 40 . . . . .250/B3
Vancouver, Br. Col., Can., 545,671,
  (2,122,700 metro.) 214/L6
Vancouver, Br. Col., Can., island, 545,671 . . .214/I6
Vancouver, Br. Col., Can., island, 545,671 . . .358/B1
Vancouver, Wash., U.S., 143,560 . . . . .358/C4

Vandalia, Ill., U.S., 6,975 . . . . .266/D5
Vandalia, Mich., U.S., 429 . . . . .294/D8
Vandalia, Mo., U.S., 2,529 . . . . .302/E2
Vandalia, Mont., U.S. 306/K1
Vandalia, Ohio, U.S., 14,603 . . . . .328/B6
Vandemere, N.C., U.S., 289 . . . . .322/M4
Vandenberg Vil., Calif., U.S., 5,802 . . . . .246/E8
Vandenburg A.F.B., Calif., U.S. 246/E8
Vander, N.C., U.S., 1,204 . . . . .322/H4
Vanderbilt, Mich., U.S., 587 . . . . .294/E4
Vanderbilt, Penn., U.S., 553 . . . . .336/B5
Vanderbilt, Tex., U.S., 411 . . . . .346/M7
Vanderbilt Mansion N.H.S., N.Y., U.S. 321/P7
Vanderburgh, Ind., U.S., county, 171,922 . . . . .270/A8
Vandercook Lake, Mich., U.S., 4,809 . . . . .294/E7
Vandergrift, Penn., U.S., 5,455 . . . . .336/B4
Vanderhoof, Br. Col., Can., 4,390 . . . . .214/K4
Vanderpool, Tex., U.S. 346/J6
Vandiver, Mo., U.S., 83 . . . . .302/E2
Vandling, Penn., U.S., 738 . . . . .336/L2
Vanduser, Mo., U.S., 217 . . . . .302/G5
Van Dyne, Wisc., U.S., 250 . . . . .364/E5
Vänern, Swe., lake 80/B3
Van Etten, N.Y., U.S., 581 . . . . .320/H6
Vanguard, Sask., Can., 187 . . . . .227/C11
Vanhiseville, N.J., U.S., 700 . . . . .314/E3
Van Horn, Tex., U.S., 2,435 . . . . .346/D4
Van Horne, Iowa, U.S., 716 . . . . .274/K3
Vanier, Ont., Can. 223/H5
Vanier, Que., Can., 11,054 . . . . .226/L5
Vanikolo, Sol. Is., islands 173/C2
Vanimo, P.N.G. 172/A2
Van Lear, Ky., U.S., 1,100 . . . . .280/H3
Vanleer, Tenn., U.S., 310 . . . . .344/G2
Vanlue, Ohio, U.S., 371 . . . . .328/D4
Van Meter, Iowa, U.S., 866 . . . . .274/G4
Van Metre, S. Dak., U.S. 342/E3
Vanndale, Ark., U.S., 325 . . . . .244/E2
Vannes, Fr. 88/B3
Van Norman, Mont., U.S. 306/K2
Vanoss, Okla., U.S., 100 . . . . .330/F3
Vanrhynsdorp, S. Afr. 162/A3
Vansant, Va., U.S., 989 . . . . .354/D2
Vanscoy, Sask., Can., 345 . . . . .227/D8
Vansittart, Nun., Can., island 220/M3
Vantaa, Fin., 178,471 . . . . .81/B2
Vantage, Wash., U.S., 70 . . . . .358/F3
Van Tassell, Wyo., U.S. 366/D2
Vanua Balavu, Fiji, island 174/C2
Vanua Lava, Van., island 173/B1
Vanua Levu, Fiji, island 174/B2
Vanuatu, nation 165
Van Wert, Iowa, U.S., 231 . . . . .274/G6
Van Wert, Ohio, U.S., 10,690 . . . . .328/A4
Van Wert, Ohio, U.S., county, 29,659 . . . . . . .328/A4
Van Zandt, Tex., U.S., county, 48,140 . . . . . . .346/N3
Van Zandt, Wash., U.S., 200 . . . . .358/C1
Vanzant, Mo., U.S. .302/D5
Var, Fr., department .88/D5
Varaždin, Cro. 98/C2
Varanasi, India, 1,100,748, (1,211,749 metro.) .128/D3
Vardaman, Miss., U.S., 1,065 . . . . .300/C2
Vardar, Mac., river 100/C2
Varde, Den., river 79/B3
Vardenis, Arm. 103/C2
Varese, It. 95/B1
Variadero, N. Mex., U.S. 317/F2
Varina, Iowa, U.S., 90 . . . . .274/E2
Varkaus, Fin. 81/C2
Värmland, Swe., county 80/B3
Varna, Bul., 304,559 . . . . .101/F2
Varna, Bul., oblast 101/F2
Varna, Ill., U.S., 436 . . . . .266/D2
Varnado, La., U.S., 342 . . . . .282/K5
Varnamtown, N.C., U.S., 481 . . . . .322/J7
Varnell, Ga., U.S., 1,491 . . . . .260/B2
Varner, Kans., U.S. .276/D4
Varnville, S.C., U.S., 2,074 . . . . .340/C4
Varysburg, N.Y., U.S., 375 . . . . .320/D5
Vas, Hun., county 91/A2
Vasai, India . . . . .128/Inset I
Vasai, India, creek . . . . .128/Inset I
Vashon Hts., Wash., U.S., 1,100 . . . . .358/A4
Vaslui, Rom. 101/D2
Vaslui, Rom., county 101/D2
Vass, N.C., U.S., 750 . . . . .322/G4
Vassar, Man., Can. .215/D4
Vassar, Kans., U.S., 175 . . . . .276/G3
Vassar, Mich., U.S., 2,823 . . . . .294/F6
Västerås, Swe., 127,799 . . . . .80/C3
Västerbotten, Swe., county 80/C2
Västernorrland, Swe., county 80/C2
Västmanland, Swe., county 80/C3
Västra Götaland, Swe., county 80/B3
Vatersay, Scot., U.K., island 62/A5
Vatican City, nation 94
Vatican Museums, Vat. 96/B1
Vatnajökull, Ice., ice cap 79/B2
Vättern, Swe., lake 80/B3
Vatulele, Fiji, island .174/A3
Vaucluse, Fr., department 88/D4
Vaucluse, S.C., U.S., 125 . . . . .340/C3
Vaud, Switz., canton 90/A2
Vaudreuil, Que., Can., 19,920 . . . . .226/C6
Vaughan, Miss., U.S., 60 . . . . .300/B3
Vaughan, N.C., U.S., 90 . . . . .322/J2
Vaughn, Mont., U.S., 70 . . . . .306/F2
Vaughn, N. Mex., U.S., 539 . . . . .317/E3
Vaughn, Wash., U.S., 400 . . . . .358/A4
Vaughns Mill, Ky., U.S., 275 . . . . .280/G3
Vaupés, Col., department 184/C4
Vaupés, Col., river 184/B4
Vauxhall, Alta., Can., 1,112 . . . . .212/D6
Vava'u, Tonga, island group 175/C2
Vava'u, Tonga, island 175/C2
Vavenby, Br. Col., Can. 214/N5
Vavuniya, Sri Lan. 126/D3
Vawkavysk, Bela. 82/B3
Växjö, Swe. 80/B3
Vaya Chin, Ariz., U.S., 70 . . . . .242/C5
Vayk', Arm. 103/C3
Vayots' Dzor, Arm., district 103/C3
Vázquez, P.R. 206/C2
Vealmoor, Tex., U.S. 346/G3
Veazie, Maine, U.S., 1,744 . . . . .286/D4
Veblen, S. Dak., U.S., 281 . . . . .342/H2
Veedersburg, Ind., U.S., 2,299 . . . . .270/B4
Vega, Alta., Can. 212/C4
Vega, Tex., U.S., 936 . . . . .346/F9
Vega Alta, P.R. 206/C2
Vega Baja, P.R. 206/C2
Vegreville, Alta., Can., 5,376 . . . . .212/D4
Veguita, N. Mex., U.S., 100 . . . . .317/D3
Veimandu, Mald., channel 127/A3
Vejle, Den., 48,402 .79/B3
Vejle, Den., county 79/B3
Velarde, N. Mex., U.S., 325 . . . . .317/E1
Velas, Port. . . . . .93/Inset II
Velda City, Mo., U.S., 1,616 . . . . .302/H3
Veles, Mac. 100/B2

Velika Morava, Serb.-Mont., river 99/B2
Veliki, Serb.-Mont., canal 99/A2
Velikiy Novgorod, Russ. 104/C4
Veliko Tarnovo, Bul. .101/D2
Veliko Tarnovo, Bul., oblast 99
Velindre, Wales, U.K. 64/E3
Vélingara, Sen. 148/B2
Vélingara, Sen. 148/B3
Vella Lavella, Sol. Is., island 173/A1
Vellore, India 128/C6
Velma, Miss., U.S. .300/C1
Velma, Okla., U.S., 664 . . . . .330/E1
Velva, N. Dak., U.S., 1,049 . . . . .326/E1
Venango, Nebr., U.S., 175 . . . . .308/B3
Venango, Penn., U.S., 288 . . . . .336/A2
Venango, Penn., U.S., county, 57,565 . . . . . . .336/B3
Vendée, Fr., department 88/B3
Venedocia, Ohio, U.S., 160 . . . . .328/B4
Venedy, Ill., U.S., 137 . . . . .266/D5
Veness, Scot., U.K. .62/N1
Veneta, Oreg., U.S., 2,755 . . . . .334/C3
Venetian Vil., Ill., U.S., 3,082 . . . . .266/B4
Venetie, Alaska, U.S., 202 . . . . .240/F1
Veneto, It., region 95/B1
Venezuela, nation 172
Venice, It., 266,181 .95/C1
Venice, It., gulf 95/C1
Venice, Fla., U.S., 17,764 . . . . .256/F4
Venice, Ill., U.S., 2,528 . . . . .266/A3
Venice, (see Boothville), La., U.S., 2,220 . . . . .282/L8
Venlo, Neth. 84/D3
Venta, Lith., river 82/B1
Ventana, Ariz., U.S., 70 . . . . .242/C5
Ventana, Ariz., U.S., cave 242/C5
Ventimiglia, It. 95/A2
Ventnor, Eng., U.K., 5,710 . . . . .70/B5
Ventnor City, N.J., U.S., 12,910 . . . . .314/E5
Ventspils, Lat., 46,600 . . . . .82/A1
Ventucopa, Calif., U.S. 246/F8
Ventura, Calif., U.S., 100,916 . . . . .246/F8
Ventura, Calif., U.S., county, 753,197 . . . . . . .246/F8
Ventura, Iowa, U.S., 670 . . . . .274/H1
Venturia, N. Dak., U.S. 326/F3
Venus, Fla., U.S. 256/G4
Vera, Ill., U.S., 125 .266/D4
Vera, Okla., U.S., 188 . . . . .330/G1
Vera, Tex., U.S., 100 . . . . .346/J2
Veracruz, Mex., 411,582, (457,377 metro.) . . .200/E4
Veracruz, Mex., state 200/E4
Vera Cruz, Ind., U.S., 55 . . . . .270/F3
Veradale, Wash., U.S., 9,387 . . . . .358/H2
Veraguas, Pan., province 203/B3
Verbena, Ala., U.S., 250 . . . . .260/C2
Verbena, Tex., U.S., 60 . . . . .346/G2
Vercelli, It. 95/B1
Verda, La., U.S., 275 . . . . .282/D3
Verde, Para., river 187/C3
Verde, Ariz., U.S., river 242/D3
Verdel, Nebr., U.S., 58 . . . . .308/E1
Verden, Okla., U.S., 659 . . . . .330/D2
Verdery, S.C., U.S., 175 . . . . .340/B2
Verdi, Kans., U.S. 276/E2
Verdi, Minn., U.S., 60 . . . . .298/A6
Verdi, Nev., U.S., 2,949 . . . . .310/A2
Verdigre, Nebr., U.S., 519 . . . . .308/E1
Verdigris, Kans., U.S., river 276/F3
Verdon, Nebr., U.S., 223 . . . . .308/J3
Verdon, S. Dak., U.S. 342/G2
Verdun, Que., Can., 60,564 . . . . .226/J6
Verdun, Fr. 88/D2
Vereeniging, S. Afr. .162/C2
Vergas, Minn., U.S., 311 . . . . .298/B4
Vergennes, Ill., U.S., 491 . . . . .266/D6
Vergennes, Vt., U.S. 352/A2
Verhalen, Tex., U.S. 346/E4
Verkhoyansk, Russ. .104/H3
Verkhoyansk, Russ., range 104/H3
Verkhoyansk, Russ., range 193/C2
Vermilion, Alta., Can., 3,948 . . . . .212/E4
Vermilion, Ill., U.S., 239 . . . . .266/F4
Vermilion, Ill., U.S., county, 83,919 . . . . .266/F4
Vermilion, La., U.S., bay 282/E7
Vermilion, La., U.S., parish, 53,807 . . . . .282/E7
Vermilion, Minn., U.S., range 298/E3
Vermilion, Ohio, U.S., 10,927 . . . . .328/F3
Vermilion Cliffs Natl. Mon., Ariz., U.S. 242/D1
Vermilion Lake Ind. Res., Minn., U.S. 298/E3
Vermillion, Que., Can., river 226/C4
Vermillion, Ind., U.S., county, 16,788 . . . . . . .270/A5
Vermillion, Kans., U.S., 107 . . . . .276/F2
Vermillion, Minn., U.S., 437 . . . . .298/E6
Vermillion, S. Dak., U.S., 9,765 . . . . .342/J5
Vermillion, S. Dak., U.S., river 342/H4
Vermont, U.S., state 340
Vermont, Ill., U.S., 792 . . . . .266/C3
Vermontville, Mich., U.S., 789 . . . . .294/D7
Verna, Fla., U.S. 256/F4
Vernal, Utah, U.S., 7,714 . . . . .350/E3
Vernalis, Calif., U.S., 70 . . . . .246/L2
Verndale, Minn., U.S., 575 . . . . .298/C4
Verne, Wyo., U.S. 366/A3
Verner, Ont., Can. 223/E1
Vernham Dean, Eng., U.K. 70/A4
Vernon, Br. Col., Can., 33,494 . . . . .214/N6
Vernon, Ala., U.S., 2,143 . . . . .238/A2
Vernon, Ariz., U.S. .242/F3
Vernon, Calif., U.S., 91 . . . . .246/C9
Vernon, Colo., U.S., 40 . . . . .250/H2
Vernon, Conn., U.S., 28,063 . . . . .253/F2
Vernon, Fla., U.S., 743 . . . . .256/C1
Vernon, Ill., U.S., 178 . . . . .266/D5
Vernon, Ind., U.S., 330 . . . . .270/E7
Vernon, Kans., U.S. 276/G4
Vernon, Ky., U.S. 280/E2
Vernon, La., U.S. 282/D2
Vernon, La., U.S., parish, 52,531 . . . . .282/C4
Vernon, Mich., U.S., 847 . . . . .294/E7
Vernon, Mo., U.S., county, 20,454 . . . . .302/B4
Vernon, N.J., U.S., 24,686 . . . . .314/E1
Vernon, N.Y., U.S., 1,155 . . . . .320/K4
Vernon, Tex., U.S., 11,660 . . . . .346/J1
Vernon, Utah, U.S., 236 . . . . .350/D4
Vernon, Vt., U.S. 352/B5
Vernon, Wisc., U.S., county, 28,056 . . . . .364/C5
Vernon Bridge, P.E.I., Can. 224/C2
Vernonburg, Ga., U.S., 138 . . . . .260/J8
Vernon Ctr., Minn., U.S., 359 . . . . .298/C7
Vernon Hills, Ill., U.S., 20,120 . . . . .266/B5
Vernonia, Oreg., U.S., 2,228 . . . . .334/C2
Vernon River, P.E.I., Can. 224/C2
Vernon Valley, N.J., U.S., 1,737 . . . . .314/E1
Vero Beach, Fla., U.S., 17,705 . . . . .256/H4
Veroia, Gr. 100/B1
Verona, Ont., Can. .223/J3
Verona, It. 95/B1
Verona, Ill., U.S., 257 . . . . .266/E2
Verona, Ky., U.S., 175 . . . . .280/F2
Verona, Maine, U.S., 533 . . . . .286/D4
Verona, Mich., U.S., 90 . . . . .294/G6
Verona, Miss., U.S., 3,334 . . . . .300/D1
Verona, Mo., U.S., 714 . . . . .302/C5

Verona, N.J., U.S., 13,533 . . . . .314/B2
Verona, N.C., U.S., 700 . . . . .322/L5
Verona, N. Dak., U.S., 108 . . . . .326/G3
Verona, Ohio, U.S., 430 . . . . .328/B6
Verona, Penn., U.S., 3,124 . . . . .336/E7
Verona, Va., U.S., 3,638 . . . . .354/E4
Verona, Wisc., U.S., 7,052 . . . . .364/E6
Versailles, Fr. . . . . .88/C2, Inset II
Versailles, Conn., U.S., 750 . . . . .253/G3
Versailles, Ill., U.S., 567 . . . . .266/C4
Versailles, Ind., U.S., 1,784 . . . . .270/F6
Versailles, Ky., U.S., 7,511 . . . . .280/F2
Versailles, Mo., U.S., 2,565 . . . . .302/D3
Versailles, Ohio, U.S., 2,589 . . . . .328/B6
Versailles, Penn., U.S., 1,724 . . . . .336/E7
Verse, Wyo., U.S. 366/D2
Vershire, Vt., U.S. 352/C3
Vert, Sen., cape 148/A2
Verviers, Belg. 85/D2
Verwood, Eng., U.K., 8,926 . . . . .73/J3
Veryan, Eng., U.K. 73/C4
Vesoul, Fr. 88/D3
Vesper, Kans., U.S. .276/D2
Vesper, Wisc., U.S., 541 . . . . .364/D4
Vesta, Ga., U.S. 260/F4
Vesta, Minn., U.S., 339 . . . . .298/B6
Vesta, Nebr., U.S., 40 . . . . .308/H3
Vesta, Va., U.S., 125 . . . . .354/C7
Vestaburg, Mich., U.S., 550 . . . . .294/E6
Vest-Agder, Nor., province 80/B4
Vestal, N.Y., U.S., 3,900 . . . . .320/J6
Vestal Ctr., N.Y., U.S., 850 . . . . .320/J6
Vestavia Hills, Ala., U.S., 24,476 . . . . . . .238/C2, E1
Vesterålen, Nor., islands 80/C2
Vestfjorden, Nor. 81/A1
Vestfold, Nor., province 80/C4
Vestmanna, Den. 79/Inset
Vestmannaeyjar, Ice., 4,522 . . . . .79/A3
Vestsjælland, Den., county 79/C3
Vesuvius, It., volcano 95/C2
Vesuvius, Va., U.S., 200 . . . . .354/E5
Veszprém, Hun. 91/A2
Veszprém, Hun., county 91/A2
Vetal, S. Dak., U.S. .342/D4
Vetauua, Fiji, island .174/C1
Veteran, Alta., Can., 292 . . . . .212/E5
Veteran, Wyo., U.S. 366/D3
Vevay, Ind., U.S., 1,735 . . . . .270/F7
Veyo, Utah, U.S., 200 . . . . .350/A6
Vian, Okla., U.S., 1,362 . . . . .330/H2
Viana do Castelo, Port. 93/A2
Viana Do Castelo, Port., district 93/A2
Vianden, Lux. 85/B2
Vibank, Sask., Can., 381 . . . . .227/G10
Viboras, Tex., U.S., 60 . . . . .346/K9
Viborg, Den. 79/B2
Viborg, Den., county 79/B2
Viborg, S. Dak., U.S., 832 . . . . .342/H4
Viburnum, Mo., U.S., 825 . . . . .302/E4
Vic, Sp. 94/H2
Vicco, Ky., U.S., 318 . . . . .280/G3
Vicenza, It. 95/B1
Vichada, Col., department 184/C3
Vichada, Col., river .184/C3
Vichy, Fr. 88/C3
Vichy, Mo., U.S., 668 . . . . .302/E3
Vick, Ark., U.S. 244/C4
Vick, La., U.S., 50 .282/E4
Vick, Tex., U.S. 346/H4
Vickerstown, Eng., U.K. 66/B4
Vickery, Ohio, U.S., 300 . . . . .328/E3
Vicksburg, Ariz., U.S. 242/B4
Vicksburg, Mich., U.S., 2,320 . . . . .294/D7
Vicksburg, Miss., U.S., 26,407 . . . . .300/B3
Vicksburg N.M.P., Miss., U.S. 300/B3
Victor, Colo., U.S., 445 . . . . .250/E3
Victor, Ida., U.S., 840 . . . . .264/F6
Victor, Iowa, U.S., 952 . . . . .274/K4
Victor, Mont., U.S., 859 . . . . .306/B3
Victor, N.Y., U.S., 2,433 . . . . .320/G5
Victor, S. Dak., U.S. 342/J2
Victoria, Austl., river 170/C1
Victoria, Austl., state 170/G3
Victoria, Bel., peak .201/B3
Victoria, Can., island 193/B13
Victoria, Br. Col., Can., 74,125, ...
  (318,900 metro.) .214/L7
Victoria, N.B., Can., county 217/B1
Victoria, N.W. Terr., Can., island 220/F2
Victoria, N.S., Can., county 221/G1
Victoria, Ont., Can. .223/G3
Victoria, Ont., Can., county 223/G3
Victoria, P.E.I., Can., 119 . . . . .224/C2
Victoria, Chile 190/B5
Victoria, Kenya, lake 157/B4
Victoria, (Rabat), Malta 97/A1
Victoria, Sey., capital, 24,701 . . . . .163/Inset
Victoria, Tan., lake .158/B3
Victoria, Ug., lake 157/C4
Victoria, Ark., U.S., 59 . . . . .244/E2
Victoria, Ill., U.S., 323 . . . . .266/C2
Victoria, Kans., U.S., 1,208 . . . . .276/C3
Victoria, Mich., U.S. 294/A3
Victoria, Minn., U.S., 4,025 . . . . .298/D6
Victoria, Tenn., U.S., 175 . . . . .344/K4
Victoria, Tex., U.S., 60,603, (84,088 metro.) . .346/M7
Victoria, Tex., U.S., county, 84,088 . . . . .346/L7
Victoria, Va., U.S., 1,821 . . . . .354/G7
Victoria, Zam., falls .159/B3
Victoria, Zimb., falls 160/A1
Victoria Beach, Man., Can. 215/C4
Victoria Beach, N.S., Can. 221/B3
Victoria Land, Antar., region 192/B5
Victoria Nile, Ug., river 157/B2, C3
Victoria Park, W.A., Austl. . . . . .170/Inset I
Victoria Pt., Qnsld., Austl. . . . . .170/Inset III
Victoriaville, Que., Can., 38,841 . . . . .226/E5
Victorville, Calif., U.S., 64,029 . . . . .246/H8
Victory, N.Y., U.S., 250 . . . . .320/H4
Victory, Okla., U.S. .330/C3
Victory, Wisc., U.S., 90 . . . . .364/B5
Victory Gardens, N.J., U.S., 1,546 . . . . .314/D2
Victory Lakes, N.J., U.S., 2,118 . . . . .314/D4
Victory Mills, N.Y., U.S., 544 . . . . .320/P4
Vida, Mont., U.S. 306/L2
Vida, Oreg., U.S., 200 . . . . .334/D3
Vidal, Calif., U.S. 246/L8
Vidalia, Ga., U.S., 10,491 . . . . .260/G7
Vidalia, La., U.S., 4,543 . . . . .282/G3
Vidal Jct., Calif., U.S. 246/L8
Vidaurri, Tex., U.S. .346/L7
Vidette, Ga., U.S., 112 . . . . .260/G5
Vidin, Bul. 101/A2
Vidin, Bul., oblast 101/A2
Vidor, Tex., U.S., 11,440 . . . . .346/P5
Vidrine, La., U.S., 225 . . . . .282/E5
Viedma, Arg. 191/C5
Viedma, Arg., lake 191/A6
Vieille Case, Dom. 208/A1

Vienna, Aus., capital, 1,562,482 . . . . .91/E2
Vienna, Aus., state .91/E2
Vienna, Ga., U.S., 2,973 . . . . .260/D7
Vienna, Ill., U.S., 1,234 . . . . .266/E6
Vienna, La., U.S., 424 . . . . .282/D1
Vienna, Maine, U.S., 527 . . . . .286/C4
Vienna, Md., U.S., 280 . . . . .288/L6
Vienna, Mo., U.S., 628 . . . . .302/E3
Vienna, N.J., U.S., 1,264 . . . . .314/D2
Vienna, (Vienna Ctr), Ohio, U.S., 650 . . . . . . .328/J3
Vienna, S. Dak., U.S., 78 . . . . .342/H3
Vienna, Tex., U.S. 346/M6
Vienna, Va., U.S., 14,453 . . . . .354/M2
Vienna, W. Va., U.S., 10,861 . . . . .360/C2
Vienne, Fr., department 88/C3
Vienne, Fr., river 88/C3
Vientiane, Laos, capital, 330,798, ...
  (640,000 metro.) .124/B3
Vieques, P.R. 206/D2
Vieques, P.R., island 206/E2
Vieques, P.R., passage 206/D2
Vieques, P.R., sound 206/E2
Vierzon, Fr. 88/C3
Vietnam, nation 119
Viet Tri, Viet. 123/A2
Vieux Fort, St. Luc., 1,802 . . . . .208/B3
View, Tex., U.S., 50 . . . . .346/J3
Viewfield, S. Dak., U.S. 342/C3
Vigan, Phil. 120/B2
Vigil, Colo., U.S. 250/F4
Vignemale, Fr., mountain 88/B5
Vigo, Sp., 280,186 .94/B1
Vigo, Ind., U.S., county, 105,848 . . . . .270/B6
Vigo Park, Tex., U.S. 346/F10, G1
Vijayawada, India, 701,351, ...
  (1,011,152 metro.) 128/D5
Vijosë, Alb., river 99/A3
Vikeke, E. Timor 122/C1
Vikeke, E. Timor, province 122/C1
Viking, Alta., Can., 1,052 . . . . .212/E4
Viking, Minn., U.S., 92 . . . . .298/A2
Vila do Conde, Port. 93/A2
Vilaine, Fr., river 88/B3
Vilanculos, Moz. 161/B4
Vilano Beach, Fla., U.S., 2,533 . . . . .256/G2
Vila Nova de Gaia, Port. 93/A2
Vila Real, Port. 93/B2
Vila Real, Port., district 93/B2
Vila Real de Santo Antonio, Port. 93/B4
Vilas, Colo., U.S., 110 . . . . .250/H4
Vilas, Fla., U.S. 256/D1
Vilas, Kans., U.S. 276/G4
Vilas, S. Dak., U.S. .342/H4
Vilas, Wisc., U.S., county, 21,033 . . . . .364/D2
Vilcabamba, Peru, mountains 185/C3
Vilcea, Rom., county 101/C3
Viljandi, Est. 81/C2
Vilkaviškis, Lith. 82/B2
Villa Ahumada, Mex. 200/C1
Villach, Aus. 91/C2
Villa Clara, Cuba, province 204/C2
Village, Ark., U.S., 125 . . . . .244/B4
Village Green, N.Y., U.S., 3,945 . . . . .320/J4
Village Green, (Village Green-Green Ridge), . .
  Penn., U.S., 8,279 . . . . .336/K7
Village of Clarkston, Mich., U.S., 962 . . .294/A6, F7
Village of Superior, Wisc., U.S., 500 . . . . . . .364/A2
Village of the Branch, N.Y., U.S., 1,895 . . . . .320/D2
Village St. George, La., U.S., 6,993 . . . . .282/G6
Village Shires, Penn., U.S., 4,137 . . . . .336/M6
Villages of Oriole, Fla., U.S., 4,758 . . . . .256/B5
Villa Grove, Colo., U.S. 250/E3
Villa Grove, Ill., U.S., 2,553 . . . . .266/E4
Villa Hayes, Para. 187/D4
Villahermosa, Mex., state capital, ...
  330,846, (520,308 metro.) 200/F4
Villa Hills, Ky., U.S., 7,948 . . . . .280/G1
Villalba, P.R. 206/C2
Villa María, Arg. 191/C3
Villanueva, N. Mex., U.S., 70 . . . . .317/E2
Villa Park, Calif., U.S., 5,999 . . . . .246/E10
Villa Park, Ill., U.S., 22,075 . . . . .266/B6
Villard, Minn., U.S., 244 . . . . .298/B5
Villa Rica, Ga., U.S., 4,134 . . . . .260/B4
Villa Ridge, Mo., U.S., 2,417 . . . . .302/F3
Villarreal de los Infantes, Sp. 94/F3
Villarrica, Para., 38,151 . . . . .187/D4
Villas, N.J., U.S., 9,064 . . . . .314/D5
Villavicencio, Col., 314,000 . . . . .184/B3
Villazón, Bol. 186/A4
Villegreen, Colo., U.S. 250/G4
Ville-Marie, Que., Can., 2,770 . . . . .225/A4
Villeneuve-St-Georges, Fr. . . . . .88/Inset II
Ville Platte, La., U.S., 8,145 . . . . .282/E5
Villeroy, Que., Can., 519 . . . . .226/E5
Villisca, Iowa, U.S., 1,344 . . . . .274/E6
Vilnius, Lith., capital, 578,334 . . . . .82/C2
Vilonia, Ark., U.S., 2,106 . . . . .244/C2
Vilyuy, Russ., river .104/G3
Vilyuysk, Russ. 104/H3
Vimy Ridge, Ark., U.S., 600 . . . . .244/C3
Vina, Ala., U.S., 400 . . . . .238/A1
Vina, Calif., U.S., 175 . . . . .246/C4
Viña del Mar, Chile, 298,828 . . . . .190/B4, Inset
Vinalhaven, Maine, U.S., 1,235 . . . . .286/D4
Vinalhaven, Maine, U.S., island 286/D4
Vincennes, Fr. . . . . .88/Inset II
Vincennes, Ind., U.S., 18,701 . . . . .270/A7
Vincent, Ala., U.S., 1,853 . . . . .238/C2
Vincent, Iowa, U.S., 158 . . . . .274/F2
Vincent, Tex., U.S. .346/G3
Vincente de Carvalho, Braz. . . . . .188/Inset II
Vincentown, N.J., U.S., 750 . . . . .314/D4
Vinces, Ecua. 185/B3
Vindelälven, Swe. 80/C1
Vindhya, India, range 128/C4
Vinegar Bend, Ala., U.S. 238/A4
Vine Grove, Ky., U.S., 4,169 . . . . .280/E3
Vineland, Minn., U.S. 298/D4
Vineland, N.J., U.S., 56,271 . . . . .314/C5
Vinemont, Ala., U.S., 425 . . . . .238/C1
Vineyard, Mass., U.S., sound 292/L7
Vineyard, Utah, U.S., 150 . . . . .350/C3
Vineyard Haven, Mass., U.S., 2,048 . . . . .292/M7
Vinh, Viet., 112,455 . . . . .123/A2
Vining, Iowa, U.S., 70 . . . . .274/K4
Vining, Kans., U.S., 58 . . . . .276/E2
Vining, Minn., U.S., 68 . . . . .298/B4
Vinings, Ga., U.S., 9,677 . . . . .260/H2
Vinita, Okla., U.S., 6,472 . . . . .330/G1
Vinita Park, Mo., U.S., 1,924 . . . . .302/H3
Vinita Terrace, Mo., U.S., 292 . . . . .302/H3
Vinland, Kans., U.S. 276/G3
Vinnytsia, Ukr., 383,250 . . . . .102/B2
Vinnytsia, Ukr., oblast 102/B2
Vinson, Okla., U.S. .330/C3
Vinson Massif, Antar., mountain 192/B10
Vinton, Ohio, U.S., 387 . . . . .246/E3
Vinton, Iowa, U.S., 5,102 . . . . .274/K3
Vinton, La., U.S., 3,338 . . . . .282/B6
Vinton, Ohio, U.S., 324 . . . . .328/F8

Vinton, Ohio, U.S., *county*, 12,806 . . . . .328/E7
Vinton, Tex., U.S., 1,892 . . . . .346/B4
Vinton, Va., U.S., 7,782 . . . . .354/D6
Vintondale, Penn., U.S., 528 . . . . .336/D5
Viola, Ark., U.S., 381 .244/D1
Viola, Del., U.S., 156 .255/B4
Viola, Ida., U.S., 80 . . . . .264/A3
Viola, Ill., U.S., 956 . . . . .266/C2
Viola, Iowa, U.S., 70 .274/M3
Viola, Kans., U.S., 211 . . . . .276/E4
Viola, Minn., U.S., 70 . . . . .298/E6
Viola, Tenn., U.S., 129 . . . . .344/K3
Viola, Wisc., U.S., 667 . . . . .364/C5
Violet, La., U.S., 8,555 . . . . .282/K7, L3
Violet Hill, Ark., U.S. 244/D1
Viper, Ky., U.S., 250 .280/Q3
Virden, Man., Can., 3,109 . . . . .215/A4
Virden, Ill., U.S., 3,488 . . . . .266/D4
Virden, N. Mex., U.S., 143 . . . . .317/B5
Virgelle, Mont., U.S. .306/F1
Vírgenes, Arg., *cape* 191/B7
Vírgenes, Chile, *cape* 190/C8
Virgil, Ill., U.S., 266 .266/E2
Virgil, Kans., U.S., 113 . . . . .276/F4
Virgil, S. Dak., U.S. .342/G3
Virgilina, Va., U.S., 159 . . . . .354/F7
Virgin, Sask., Can., *river* 227/C3
Virgin, Ariz., U.S., *river* 242/A1
Virgin, Nev., U.S., *river* 310/C3
Virgin, Utah, U.S., 394 . . . . .350/A6
Virginia, U.S., *state* 342
Virginia, Ida., U.S., 80 . . . . .264/E7
Virginia, Ill., U.S., 1,728 . . . . .266/C4
Virginia, Minn., U.S., 9,157 . . . . .298/E3
Virginia, Nebr., U.S. .308/H3
Virginia Beach, Va., U.S., 425,257 . . . . .354/M7
Virginia City, Mont., U.S., 130 . . . . .306/L4
Virginia City, Nev., U.S., 800 . . . . .310/A2
Virginia Dale, Colo., U.S. 250/E1
Virginia Gardens, Fla., U.S., 2,348 . . . . .256/A6
Virgin Islands, U.S. 172
Viroqua, Wisc., U.S., 4,335 . . . . .364/C5
Virtsu, Est. 81/B2
Virunga, Rwa., *mountains* 158/B1
Visakhapatnam, India, 750,024,
  (1,329,472 *metro*.) 128/D5
Visalia, Calif., U.S., 91,565, (368,021 *metro*.) 246/F6
Visalia, Ky., U.S., 111 . . . . .280/F2
Visayan, Phil., *islands* 120/B4
Visayan, Phil., *sea* .120/B4
Visby, Swe. 80/C3
Viscount Melville, N.W. Terr., Can., *sound* . . .220/F2
Viseu, Port. 93/B2
Viseu, Port., *district* 93/B2
Vista, Man., Can. 215/A4
Vista, Calif., U.S., 89,857 . . . . .246/H9
Vista, Mo., U.S., 55 .302/C4
Vista Hermosa, Col. .184/B4
Vistula, Pol., *lagoon* 83/D1
Vistula, Pol., *river* 83/D2, E3
Vita, Man., Can. 215/C4
Viterbo, It. 95/C2
Viti Levu, Fiji, *island* 174/A2
Vitória, Braz. 188/D4
Vitória da Conquista, Braz., 125,717,
  (262,494 *metro*.) 188/D3
Vitoria-Gasteiz, Sp., 216,852 . . . . .94/E1
Vitsyebsk, Bela., 358,800 . . . . .82/C2
Vitsyebsk, Bela., *oblast* 82/C2
Vivian, Man., Can. 215/C4
Vivian, La., U.S., 4,031 . . . . .282/B1
Vivian, S. Dak., U.S., 131 . . . . .342/E4
Vixen, La., U.S. 282/E2
Vizcaíno, Mex., *desert* 200/B2
Vizcaíno, Calif., U.S., *cape* 246/B3
Vizcaya, Sp., *province* 94/E1
Vlaardingen, Neth. 84/B3
Vladivostok, Russ., 606,895, (636,600 *metro*.) . .104/H5
Vlieland, Neth., *island* 84/A3
Vlissingen, Neth. 84/A3
Vlorë, Alb., 77,691 . . . . .99/A3
Vltava, Czh. Rep., *river* 92/B3
Voca, Tex., U.S., 40 .346/J5
Vöcklabruck, Aus. 91/C2
Voda, Kans., U.S. 276/B2
Voe, Scot., U.K. 62/Q2
Vogel Ctr., Mich., U.S., 175 . . . . .294/D5
Voinjama, Liber. 149/B1
Vojvodina, Serb.-Mont., *autonomous province* . .99/A2
Volant, Penn., U.S., 113 . . . . .336/A3
Volborg, Mont., U.S. 306/L1
Volcano, Jap., *islands* . . . . .114/Inset III
Volcano, Hawaii, U.S., 2,231 . . . . .262/J6
Volens, Va., U.S., 80 .354/F7
Volga, Russ., *river* .104/D5
Volga, Russ., *river* .193/D3
Volga, Iowa, U.S., 247 . . . . .274/L2
Volga, S. Dak., U.S., 1,435 . . . . .342/J3
Volgograd, Russ., 992,341, (1,024,900 *metro*.) . .104/D5
Volin, S. Dak., U.S., 207 . . . . .342/H5
Volland, Kans., U.S. .276/F3
Volo, Ill., U.S., 180 . . . . .266/A4
Vologda, Russ., 300,449, (309,750 *metro*.) 104/C4
Volos, Gr., 71,378, (106,142 *metro*.) 100/B2
Volt, Mont., U.S. 306/L1
Volta, Gha., *lake* 150/C3
Volta, Gha., *river* 150/C3
Volta, Calif., U.S., 125 . . . . .246/E5
Voltaire, N. Dak., U.S., 51 . . . . .326/E1
Volta Redonda, Braz., 177,772,
  (220,086 *metro*.) 188/D4
Voluntown, Conn., U.S., 2,528 . . . . .253/H3
Volusia, Fla., U.S., *county*, 443,343 . . . . .256/G2
Volyn, Ukr., *oblast* .102/A1
Vona, Colo., U.S., 95 . . . . .250/H2
Vonda, Sask., Can., 322 . . . . .227/D8
Vonore, Tenn., U.S., 1,162 . . . . .344/N3
Voorheesville, N.Y., U.S., 2,705 . . . . .320/P3
Voorhies, Iowa, U.S., 90 . . . . .274/K3
Vorarlberg, Aus., *state* 91/A3
Vorkuta, Russ. 104/E3
Voronezh, Russ., 903,224, (978,100 *metro*.) . . .104/C4
Vorotan, Arm., *river* 103/C3
Vorskla, Ukr., *river* .102/C1
Vortex, Ky., U.S. 280/Q3
Võrts Järv, Est., *lake* 81/D2
Võru, Est. 81/D3
Vosges, Fr., *department* 88/D2
Vosges, Fr., *mountains* 88/D2
Voss, N. Dak., U.S., 70 . . . . .326/H1
Vossburg, Miss., U.S., 80 . . . . .300/D4
Vostok, Kiri., *island* 175/D3
Votaw, Tex., U.S., 90 . . . . .346/P5
Voyageurs Natl. Park, Minn., U.S. 298/E2
Vraca, Bul. 101/B2
Vraca, Bul., *oblast* .101/B2
Vranje, Serb.-Mont. 99/B3
Vrbas, Bos.-Her., *river* 98/B1
Vrbas, Serb.-Mont. 99/A2
Vredenburgh, Ala., U.S., 327 . . . . .238/B4

Vršac, Serb.-Mont. 99/B2
Vryburg, S. Afr. 162/B2
Vukovar, Cro. 98/D2
Vulcan, Alta., Can., 1,762 . . . . .212/D6
Vunaniu, Fiji, *bay* 174/A3
Vung Tau, Viet., 145,145 . . . . .123/B4
Vunisea, Fiji 174/B3
Vuntut Natl. Park, Yukon, Can. 228/A1
Vya, Nev., U.S. 310/A1
Vysočina, Czh. Rep., *region* 92/B3
Wa, Gha. 150/A1
Waal, Neth., *river* 84/C3
Waani/Garawa, Austl., *aboriginal land* 170/C1
Wabag, P.N.G. 172/A2
Wabamun, Alta., Can., 601 . . . . .212/C4
Wabamun, Alta., Can., *lake* 212/C4
Wabana, Nfld., Can., 2,679 . . . . .218/E5
Wabasca, Alta., Can. 212/C2
Wabasca-Desmarais, Alta., Can. 212/D3
Wabash, Ark., U.S. 244/E3
Wabash, Ill., U.S., *county*, 12,937 . . . . .266/F5
Wabash, Ill., U.S., *river* 266/E6
Wabash, Ind., U.S., 11,743 . . . . .270/E3
Wabash, Ind., U.S., *county*, 34,960 . . . . .270/E3
Wabash, Ind., U.S., *river* 270/A8, B4, F3
Wabash, Ohio, U.S., 175 . . . . .328/A4
Wabasha, Minn., U.S., 2,599 . . . . .298/E6
Wabasha, Minn., U.S., *county*, 21,610 . . . . . .298/E6
Wabasso, Fla., U.S., 918 . . . . .256/H4
Wabasso, Minn., U.S., 643 . . . . .298/B6
Wabaunsee, Kans., U.S., 60 . . . . .276/F2
Wabaunsee, Kans., U.S., *county*, 6,885 . . . . .276/F3
Wabbaseka, Ark., U.S., 323 . . . . .244/D3
Wabe Gestro, Eth., *river* 156/C3
Wabeno, Wisc., U.S., 475 . . . . .364/E3
Wabe Shebele, Eth., *river* 156/D3
Wabowden, Man., Can., 497 . . . . .215/B2
Wabush, Nfld., Can., 1,894 . . . . .218/D4
Wabuska, Nev., U.S. .310/A2
Waccamaw, N.C., U.S., *lake* 322/J6
Waccasassa, Fla., U.S., *bay* 256/F2
Wachapreague, Va., U.S., 236 . . . . .354/M5
Wachusett, Mass., U.S., *mountain* 292/H3
Wachusett, Mass., U.S., *reservoir* 292/H3
Wacissa, Fla., U.S., 350 . . . . .256/E1
Waco, Ga., U.S., 469 . . . . .260/A4
Waco, Mo., U.S., 86 . . . . .302/B4
Waco, Nebr., U.S., 256 . . . . .308/G3
Waco, N.C., U.S., 328 . . . . .322/C4
Waco, Tex., U.S., 113,726, (213,517 *metro*.) . .346/L4
Waconda, Kans., U.S., *lake* 276/D2
Waconia, Minn., U.S., 6,814 . . . . .298/D6
Wacouta, Minn., U.S., 200 . . . . .298/E6
Waddan, Lib. 145/C2
Waddenzee, Neth., *sound* 84/C1
Waddesdon, Eng., U.K. 70/C3
Waddington, Br. Col., Can., *mountain* 214/K5
Waddington, Eng., U.K., 4,781 . . . . .66/D5
Waddington, Eng., U.K., 4,781 . . . . .68/C2
Waddington, Eng., U.K. 68/F3
Waddington, N.Y., U.S., 923 . . . . .320/L1
Waddy, Ky., U.S., 275 . . . . .280/E2
Wade, Miss., U.S., 491 . . . . .300/D5
Wade, N.C., U.S., 480 . . . . .322/H4
Wade, Okla., U.S. 330/F4
Wadebridge, Eng., U.K., 5,291 . . . . .73/C3
Wadena, Sask., Can., 1,412 . . . . .227/G9
Wadena, Iowa, U.S., 243 . . . . .274/L2
Wadena, Minn., U.S., 4,294 . . . . .298/B4
Wadena, Minn., U.S., *county*, 13,713 . . . . . .298/B4
Wadesboro, N.C., U.S., 3,552 . . . . .322/E5
Wades Corner, Mass., U.S., 150 . . . . .292/K5
Wadesville, Ind., U.S., 500 . . . . .270/A8
Wadi al Malik, Sudan, *river* 145/B2
Wadi Halfa, Sudan 145/C1
Wadi Howar, Sudan, *river* 145/B2
Wad Madani, Sudan .145/C2
Wading River, N.J., U.S. 314/E4
Wadley, Ala., U.S., 640 . . . . .238/D2
Wadley, Ga., U.S., 2,088 . . . . .260/G6
Wadshelf, Eng., U.K. .68/D3
Wadsworth, Ill., U.S., 3,083 . . . . .266/B4
Wadsworth, Nev., U.S., 881 . . . . .310/A2
Wadsworth, Ohio, U.S., 18,437 . . . . .328/C3
Wadworth, Eng., U.K. 66/F6
Waelder, Tex., U.S., 947 . . . . .346/L6
Wagarville, Ala., U.S., 100 . . . . .238/A4
Wagener, S.C., U.S., 863 . . . . .340/C3
Waggaman, La., U.S., 9,435 . . . . .282/J3, J7
Wagga Wagga, N.S.W., Austl. 170/D3
Waggoner, Ill., U.S., 245 . . . . .266/D4
Wagner, Mont., U.S. 306/H1
Wagner, S. Dak., U.S., 1,675 . . . . .342/G4
Wagoner, Ariz., U.S. .242/C4
Wagoner, Okla., U.S., 7,669 . . . . .330/G2
Wagoner, Okla., U.S., *county*, 57,491 . . . . . .330/G2
Wagon Mound, N. Mex., U.S., 369 . . . . .317/F1
Wagontire, Oreg., U.S. 334/G4
Wagon Wheel Gap, Colo., U.S. 250/D4
Wagram, N.C., U.S., 801 . . . . .322/G5
Wagstaff, Kans., U.S. 276/H3
Waha, Ida., U.S., 100 . . . . .264/D4
Wahiawa, Hawaii, U.S., 16,151 . . . . . . .262/B5, J2
Wahkiakum, Wash., U.S., *county*, 3,824 . . . .358/B3
Wahkon, Minn., U.S., 314 . . . . .298/D4
Wahoo, Nebr., U.S., 3,942 . . . . .308/H2
Wahpeton, Iowa, U.S., 462 . . . . .274/D1
Wahpeton, N. Dak., U.S., 8,586 . . . . .326/J3
Wahsatch, Utah, U.S. 350/C2
Waiahole, Hawaii, U.S. 262/J2
Waiahole Forest Reserve, Hawaii, U.S. 262/J5
Waiakea Forest Reserve, Hawaii, U.S. 262/J5
Waialeale, Hawaii, U.S., *mountain* 262/A5, C1
Waialee, Hawaii, U.S. 262/J1
Waialua, Hawaii, U.S., 3,761 . . . . .262/B3, H1
Waianae, Hawaii, U.S., 10,506 . . . . .262/H1
Waianae Range, Hawaii, U.S., *mountains* 262/H1
Waiawa, Hawaii, U.S., *stream* 262/E1
Waiehu, Hawaii, U.S., 7,310 . . . . .262/C3
Waigeo, Indon., *island* 122/E2
Waihee, (Waihee-Waiehue), Hawaii, U.S., 7,310 . .262/C3
Waikane, Hawaii, U.S., 726 . . . . .262/J2
Waikapu, Hawaii, U.S., 1,115 . . . . .262/C3
Waikato, N.Z., *region* 171/B2
Waikato, N.Z., *river* 171/C2
Waikiki, Hawaii, U.S. 262/G3
Waikoloa Vil., Hawaii, U.S., 4,806 . . . . .262/J5
Wailua, Hawaii, U.S., 2,083 . . . . .262/C3, D1
Wailuku, Hawaii, U.S., 12,296 . . . . .262/C3, D6
Wailuku, Hawaii, U.S., *river* 262/J5
Waimalu, Hawaii, U.S., 29,371 . . . . . . .262/E1, J2
Waimalu, Hawaii, U.S., *stream* 262/F1,
Waimanalo, Hawaii, U.S., 3,664 . . . . .262/K2,
Waimanalo Beach, Hawaii, U.S., 4,271 . . . . . .262/K2,
Waimea, Hawaii, U.S., *canyon* 262/C2,
Waimea, Hawaii, U.S. 262/C2, D6, H1
Waimea, Hawaii, U.S., 1,227 . . . . .262/H4
Wainfleet All Saints, Eng., U.K. 68/H3,
Waingapu, Indon. 122/D2,

Wainwright, Alta., Can., 5,117 . . . . .212/E5
Wainwright, Alaska, U.S., 546 . . . . .240/C1
Wainwright, Okla., U.S., 197 . . . . .330/G2,
Waiohinu, Hawaii, U.S. 262/H7,
Waipahu, Hawaii, U.S., 33,108 . . . . . . .262/E1, J2
Waipio, Hawaii, U.S. .262/H4,
Waipio, Hawaii, U.S. .262/H4,
Waipio Acres, Hawaii, U.S., 5,298 . . . . .262/J2
Wairau, N.Z., *river* .171/B3
Wairoa, N.Z. 171/C2
Waitaki, N.Z., *river* .171/B3
Waite, Maine, U.S., 105 . . . . .286/E3
Waite Hill, Ohio, U.S., 446 . . . . .328/H8
Waite Park, Minn., U.S., 6,568 . . . . .298/C5
Waiteville, W. Va., U.S. 360/F6
Waitsburg, Wash., U.S., 1,212 . . . . .358/G4
Waitsfield, Vt., U.S. 352/B2
Waits River, Vt., U.S., 80 . . . . .352/C2
Wajir, Kenya 157/F3
Waka, Tex., U.S., 125 . . . . .346/G8
Wakarusa, Ind., U.S., 1,618 . . . . .270/D1
Wakarusa, Kans., U.S., 150 . . . . .276/G3
Wakasa, Jap., *bay* .114/B3
Wakaw, Sask., Can., 884 . . . . .227/E8
Wakayama, Jap., 387,000 . . . . .114/B3
Wakayama, Jap., *prefecture* 114/B3
Wake, U.S., *island* .172/C1
Wake, N.C., U.S., *county*, 627,846 . . . . .322/H3
Wakeby, Mass., U.S., 1,600 . . . . .292/N6
Wakeeney, Kans., U.S., 1,924 . . . . .276/C2
Wakefield, Eng., U.K., 73,955 . . . . .60/C3
Wakefield, Eng., U.K., 73,955 . . . . .68/D2
Wakefield, Eng., U.K., *unitary authority*, 315,173 . .66/E5
Wakefield, Eng., U.K., *unitary authority*, 315,173 . .68/E2
Wakefield, Kans., U.S., 838 . . . . .276/E2
Wakefield, La., U.S., 150 . . . . .282/G5
Wakefield, Mass., U.S., 24,804 . . . . .292/C6, K2
Wakefield, Mich., U.S., 2,085 . . . . .294/C2
Wakefield, Nebr., U.S., 1,411 . . . . .308/H1
Wakefield, N.H., U.S., 4,252 . . . . .312/D4
Wakefield, Ohio, U.S. 328/D8
Wakefield, R.I., U.S., 8,468 . . . . .339/C5
Wakefield, Tex., U.S. 346/P4
Wakefield, Va., U.S., 1,038 . . . . .354/K7
Wake Forest, N.C., U.S., 12,588 . . . . .322/H3
Wakeman, Ohio, U.S., 951 . . . . .328/F3
Wakenda, Mo., U.S., 90 . . . . .302/C2
Wakerley, Eng., U.K. .68/F4
Wake Vil., Tex., U.S., 5,129 . . . . .346/P2
Wakita, Okla., U.S., 420 . . . . .330/E1
Wakkanai, Jap. .114/Inset I
Wakomata, Ont., Can., *lake* 223/B1
Wakonda, S. Dak., U.S., 374 . . . . .342/H4
Wakpala, S. Dak., U.S., 225 . . . . .342/E2
Wakulla, Fla., U.S., 175 . . . . .256/D1
Wakulla, Fla., U.S., *county*, 22,863 . . . . .256/D1
Walberswick, Eng., U.K. 70/H2
Walbridge, Ohio, U.S., 2,546 . . . . .328/C2
Wałbrzych, Pol., 136,411 . . . . .83/C3
Walcheren, Neth., *island* 84/A3
Walcott, Iowa, U.S., 1,528 . . . . .274/N4
Walcott, N. Dak., U.S., 189 . . . . .326/J3
Walcott, Wyo., U.S. .366/C3
Walden, Ont., Can. 223/D1
Walden, Colo., U.S., 734 . . . . .250/D1
Walden, N.Y., U.S., 6,164 . . . . .320/N7
Walden, Tenn., U.S., 1,960 . . . . .344/L4
Waldenburg, Ark., U.S., 80 . . . . .244/E2
Walden Hts., Vt., U.S., 1,900 . . . . .352/C2
Waldersee, Man., Can. 215/B4
Waldheim, Sask., Can., 889 . . . . .227/D8
Waldo, Ala., U.S., 281 . . . . .238/C2
Waldo, Ark., U.S., 1,594 . . . . .244/B4
Waldo, Fla., U.S., 821 . . . . .256/F2
Waldo, Kans., U.S., 48 . . . . .276/D2
Waldo, Maine, U.S., *county*, 36,280 . . . . . . .286/C4
Waldo, Ohio, U.S., 332 . . . . .328/D5
Waldo, Oreg., U.S., *lake* 334/D4
Waldo, Wisc., U.S., 450 . . . . .364/F5
Waldoboro, Maine, U.S., 4,916 . . . . .286/C4
Waldorf, Md., U.S., 22,312 . . . . .288/C6
Waldorf, Minn., U.S., 242 . . . . .298/D7
Waldport, Oreg., U.S., 2,050 . . . . .334/B3
Waldron, Ark., U.S., 3,508 . . . . .244/A3
Waldron, Ind., U.S., 1,100 . . . . .270/E6
Waldron, Kans., U.S. .276/D4
Waldron, Mich., U.S., 590 . . . . .294/E8
Waldron, Mo., U.S., 175 . . . . .302/B2
Waldron, Wash., U.S. 358/B1
Waldwick, N.J., U.S., 9,622 . . . . .314/B1, E1
Waldwick, Wisc., U.S. 364/C6
Walensee, Switz., *lake* 90/D1
Wales, U.K., *country* .62
Wales, Alaska, U.S., 152 . . . . .240/B1
Wales, Mass., U.S., 1,737 . . . . .292/F4
Wales, Minn., U.S. 298/F3
Wales, N. Dak., U.S. .326/G1
Wales, Utah, U.S., 219 . . . . .350/C4
Wales, Wisc., U.S., 2,523 . . . . .364/E2
Wales Ctr., Maine, U.S. 286/B4
Waleska, Ga., U.S., 616 . . . . .260/B3
Walford, Eng., U.K. 68/B5
Walford, Iowa, U.S., 1,224 . . . . .274/L4
Walgrave, Eng., U.K. .70/C2
Walhalla, Mich., U.S., 275 . . . . .294/C6
Walhalla, N. Dak., U.S., 1,057 . . . . .326/H1
Walhalla, S.C., U.S., 3,801 . . . . .340/A2
Walhalla, S.C., U.S., *county*, 70,713 . . . . . . .238/B2
Walker, Ga., U.S., *county*, 61,053 . . . . .260/A2
Walker, Iowa, U.S., 750 . . . . .274/L3
Walker, La., U.S., 4,801 . . . . .282/H6
Walker, Maine, U.S. .286/B2
Walker, Mich., U.S., 21,842 . . . . .294/D7
Walker, Minn., U.S., 1,069 . . . . .298/C3
Walker, Mo., U.S., 275 . . . . .302/B4
Walker, Nev., U.S., *lake* 310/A2
Walker, S. Dak., U.S. 342/D2
Walker, Tex., U.S., *county*, 61,758 . . . . .346/N5
Walker, W. Va., U.S., 80 . . . . .360/D2
Walker Mill, Md., U.S., 11,104 . . . . .288/C7
Walkern, Eng., U.K. 70/D3
Walker River Ind. Res., Calif., U.S. 246/G3
Walker River Ind. Res., Nev., U.S. 310/A2
Walker Sprs., Ala., U.S. 238/B4
Walkersville, Md., U.S., 5,192 . . . . .288/F2
Walkersville, W. Va., U.S., 50 . . . . .360/F3
Walkerton, Ont., Can., 4,970 . . . . .223/D3
Walkerton, Ind., U.S., 2,274 . . . . .270/D2
Walkertown, N.C., U.S., 4,009 . . . . .322/E2
Walkerville, Mich., U.S., 254 . . . . .294/C6
Walkerville, Mont., U.S., 714 . . . . .306/H3
Walkington, Eng., U.K., 1,934 . . . . .66/G5
Wall, Penn., U.S., 727 . . . . .336/F7
Wall, S. Dak., U.S., 818 . . . . .342/C3
Wall, Tex., U.S., 250 .346/H4
Wallace, N.S., Can. .221/D4
Wallace, Calif., U.S., 220 . . . . .246/E4, L6

Wallace, Ida., U.S., 960 . . . . .264/B2
Wallace, Ind., U.S., 100 . . . . .270/C4
Wallace, Kans., U.S., 67 . . . . .276/A3
Wallace, Kans., U.S., *county*, 1,749 . . . . .276/A3
Wallace, Mich., U.S., 200 . . . . .294/B4
Wallace, N.C., U.S., 3,344 . . . . .322/K5
Wallace, S.C., U.S., 550 . . . . .340/D4
Wallace, S. Dak., U.S., 86 . . . . .342/H2
Wallace, Va., U.S., 550 . . . . .354/D3
Wallace, W. Va., U.S., 150 . . . . .360/F2
Wallaceburg, Ont., Can., 11,114 . . . . .223/C5
Wallaceton, Penn., U.S., 350 . . . . .336/D4
Wallachia, Rom., *region* 101/B3
Wallagrass, Maine, U.S., 561 . . . . .286/D1
Wallasey, Eng., U.K., 60,895 . . . . .66/B6
Wallasey, Eng., U.K., 60,895 . . . . .68/A3
Walla Walla, Wash., U.S., 29,686 . . . . .358/G3
Walla Walla, Wash., U.S., *county*, 55,180 . . .358/G3
Walla Walla East, Wash., U.S., 2,479 . . . . .358/G3
Walled Lake, Mich., U.S., 6,713 . . . . .294/M6
Wallend, Eng., U.K. 70/F4
Waller, Tex., U.S., 2,092 . . . . .346/M6
Waller, Tex., U.S., *county*, 32,663 . . . . .346/M6
Wallerville, Miss., U.S. 300/D3
Wallingford, Eng., U.K., 9,315 . . . . .70/B3
Wallingford, Conn., U.S., 43,026 . . . . .253/D4
Wallingford, Iowa, U.S., 210 . . . . .274/E1
Wallingford, Vt., U.S. 352/B4
Wallingford, N.J., U.S., 11,583 . . . . .314/B2
Wallins Creek, Ky., U.S., 257 . . . . .280/G4
Wallis, Tex., U.S., 1,172 . . . . .346/M6
Wallis and Futuna, Fr., *dependency* 161
Wallis Sands, N.H., U.S., 850 . . . . .312/C6
Wallkill, N.Y., U.S., 2,143 . . . . .320/N7
Wall Lake, Iowa, U.S., 841 . . . . .274/F3
Wallonia, Belg., *region* 85/C2
Walloon Lake, Mich., U.S., 375 . . . . .294/E4
Wallowa, Oreg., U.S., 869 . . . . .334/J2
Wallowa, Oreg., U.S., *county*, 7,226 . . . . . . .334/J2
Wallowa, Oreg., U.S., *mountains* 334/J2
Wallowa-Whitman Natl. For., Oreg., U.S. . . .334/H2, J2
Wallpack Ctr., N.J., U.S. 314/D1
Walls, Scot., U.K. 62/P2
Walls, Miss., U.S., 200 . . . . .300/B1
Wallsboro, Ala., U.S., 200 . . . . .238/C3
Wallsburg, Utah, U.S., 274 . . . . .350/C3
Wallsend, Eng., U.K., 45,280 . . . . .66/E3
Wallula, Wash., U.S., 197 . . . . .358/G3
Wallula, Wash., U.S., *lake* 358/F3
Walmer, Eng., U.K. 70/G4
Walmley, Eng., U.K. 68/D4
Walney, Eng., U.K., *island* 66/B4
Walnut, Calif., U.S., 30,004 . . . . .246/E9
Walnut, Ill., U.S., 1,461 . . . . .266/D2
Walnut, Iowa, U.S., 778 . . . . .274/D5
Walnut, Kans., U.S., 221 . . . . .276/G4
Walnut, Kans., U.S., *creek* 276/C3
Walnut, Miss., U.S., 754 . . . . .300/D1
Walnut, N.C., U.S., 450 . . . . .322/F6
Walnut Bottom, Penn., U.S., 650 . . . . .336/G6
Walnut Canyon N.M., Ariz., U.S. 242/D2
Walnut Cove, N.C., U.S., 1,465 . . . . .322/E2
Walnut Creek, Calif., U.S., 64,296 . . . . .246/K3
Walnut Creek, N.C., U.S., 859 . . . . .322/K4
Walnut Grove, Ala., U.S., 710 . . . . .238/C1
Walnut Grove, Calif., U.S., 669 . . . . .246/L1, K6
Walnut Grove, Ga., U.S., 1,241 . . . . .260/D4
Walnut Grove, Minn., U.S., 599 . . . . .298/B6
Walnut Grove, Miss., U.S., 488 . . . . .300/C3
Walnut Grove, Mo., U.S., 630 . . . . .302/C4
Walnut Grove, Wash., U.S., 7,164 . . . . .358/C4
Walnut Hill, Fla., U.S., 375 . . . . .256/A4
Walnut Hill, Ill., U.S., 109 . . . . .266/D5
Walnut Hill, Tenn., U.S., 2,756 . . . . .344/S1
Walnutport, Penn., U.S., 2,043 . . . . .336/K4
Walnut Ridge, Ark., U.S., 4,925 . . . . .244/E1
Walnut Sprs., Tex., U.S., 755 . . . . .346/L3
Walpole, Eng., U.K. 70/G2
Walpole, Mass., U.S., 22,824 . . . . .292/J4
Walpole, N.H., U.S., 3,594 . . . . .312/B5
Walsall, Eng., U.K. 60/C3
Walsall, Eng., U.K., 174,739 . . . . .68/C4
Walsall, Eng., U.K., *unitary authority*, 253,502 . .68/C4
Walsenburg, Colo., U.S., 4,182 . . . . .250/F4
Walsh, Alta., Can., 70 . . . . .212/E6
Walsh, Colo., U.S., 723 . . . . .250/H4
Walsh, N. Dak., U.S., *county*, 12,389 . . . . . . .326/H1
Walshville, Ill., U.S., 89 . . . . .266/D4
Walstonburg, N.C., U.S., 224 . . . . .322/K3
Walt Disney World, Fla., U.S., *resort* 256/C4
Walterboro, S.C., U.S., 5,153 . . . . .340/C4
Walter E. Long, Tex., U.S., *lake* 346/E2
Walter F. George, Ala., U.S., *reservoir* 238/C4
Walter F. George, Ga., U.S., *reservoir* 260/A8
Walterhill, Tenn., U.S., 1,523 . . . . .344/J3
Walters, La., U.S. 282/F3
Walters, Minn., U.S., 88 . . . . .298/D7
Walters, Okla., U.S., 2,657 . . . . .330/D3
Walters, Va., U.S., 275 . . . . .354/K7
Waltersville, Miss., U.S. 300/A3
Walterville, Oreg., U.S., 350 . . . . .334/D3
Walthall, Miss., U.S., 170 . . . . .300/C2
Walthall, Miss., U.S., *county*, 15,156 . . . . . . .300/B4
Waltham, Eng., U.K., 6,157 . . . . .66/H5
Waltham, Eng., U.K. .68/G2
Waltham, Maine, U.S., 306 . . . . .286/D4
Waltham, Mass., U.S., 59,226 . . . . .292/B7, J3
Waltham, Minn., U.S., 196 . . . . .298/E7
Waltham Abbey, Eng., U.K., 15,629 . . . . .70/E3
Waltham Forest, Eng., U.K., *unitary authority*,
  218,277 . . . . .70/D3
Waltham on the Wolds, Eng., U.K. 70/C1
Waltham St. Lawrence, Eng., U.K. 70/C3
Walthill, Nebr., U.S., 909 . . . . .308/H1
Walthourville, Ga., U.S., 4,030 . . . . .260/H8
Waltman, Wyo., U.S. 366/C2
Walton, N.S., Can. 221/C2
Walton, Ont., Can. 223/D4
Walton, Eng., U.K., 3,323 . . . . .68/E3
Walton, Fla., U.S., 100 . . . . .256/H4
Walton, Fla., U.S., *county*, 40,601 . . . . .256/B1
Walton, Ga., U.S., *county*, 60,687 . . . . .260/D4
Walton, Ind., U.S., 1,069 . . . . .270/D3
Walton, Kans., U.S., 284 . . . . .276/E3
Walton, Ky., U.S., 2,450 . . . . .280/F2
Walton, N.Y., U.S., 3,070 . . . . .320/L6
Walton, Oreg., U.S. .334/C3
Walton, W. Va., U.S., 250 . . . . .360/D3
Walton Hills, Ohio, U.S., 2,400 . . . . .328/H9
Walton-on-Thames, (Walton and Weybridge),
  Eng., U.K., 52,802 . . . . .70/D4
Walton-on-the-Naze, Eng., U.K. 70/G3
Waltonville, Ill., U.S., 422 . . . . .266/D5
Waltreak, Ark., U.S., 100 . . . . .244/B3
Walum, N. Dak., U.S. 326/G2
Walvis Bay, Nam. 160/A2

Walworth, S. Dak., U.S., county, 5,974 . . . . . . .342/E2
Walworth, Wisc., U.S., 2,304 . . . . .364/E6
Walworth, Wisc., U.S., county, 93,759 . . . . . . .364/E6
Wamac, Ill., U.S., 1,378 . . . . .266/D5
Wamego, Kans., U.S., 4,246 . . . . .276/F2
Wami, Tan., river 158/C2
Wamic, Oreg., U.S. 334/E2
Wampsville, N.Y., U.S., 561 . . . . .320/K4
Wamsutter, Wyo., U.S., 261 . . . . .366/C3
Wanaka, N.Z., lake 171/A3
Wanakah, N.Y., U.S., 3,200 . . . . .320/D5
Wanamassa, N.J., U.S., 4,551 . . . . .314/E3
Wanamingo, Minn., U.S., 1,007 . . . . .298/E6
Waapitei, Ont., Can., lake 223/E1
Wanaque, N.J., U.S., 10,266 . . . . .314/A1, E1
Wanaque, N.J., U.S., reservoir 314/A1
Wanatah, Ind., U.S., 1,013 . . . . .270/C2
Wanblee, S. Dak., U.S., 641 . . . . .342/D4
Wanchese, N.C., U.S., 1,527 . . . . .322/P3
Wanda, Minn., U.S., 103 . . . . .298/B6
Wandering River, Alta., Can. 212/D3
Wanderoos, Wisc., U.S., 200 . . . . .364/A3
Wando, S. Kor. .116/B5
Wando, S.C., U.S., 375 . . . . .340/E4
Wandsworth, Eng., U.K., 252,425 . . . . .70/D4
Wandsworth, Eng., U.K., unitary authority,
260,383 . . . . .70/D4
Wanette, Okla., U.S., 402 . . . . .330/E3
Wanganui, N.Z. .171/C2
Wangford, Eng., U.K. 70/H2
Wanham, Alta., Can. 212/A3
Wanilla, Miss., U.S., 90 . . . . .300/B4
Wann, Nebr., U.S., 80 . . . . .308/H2
Wann, Okla., U.S., 132 . . . . .330/G1
Wannaska, Minn., U.S. 298/B2
Wanneroo, W.A., Austl. . . . . .170/Inset I
Wansford, Eng., U.K. 70/D1
Wanship, Utah, U.S., 175 . . . . .350/C3, E2
Wanstrow, Eng., U.K. 70/B3
Wantage, Eng., U.K., 9,452 . . . . .70/B3
Wapakoneta, Ohio, U.S., 9,474 . . . . .328/B4
Wapanucka, Okla., U.S., 445 . . . . .330/F3
Wapato, Wash., U.S., 4,582 . . . . .358/E3
Wapawekka, Sask., Can., lake 227/F5
Wapawsik, Man., Can. 215/B1
Wapella, Ill., U.S., 651 . . . . .266/E3
Wapello, Iowa, U.S., 2,124 . . . . .274/M5
Wapello, Iowa, U.S., county, 36,051 . . . . .274/K5
Wapiti, Alta., Can., river 212/A4
Wapiti, Alta., Can., river 214/N4
Wapiti, Wyo., U.S. 366/B1
Wappingers Falls, N.Y., U.S., 4,929 . . . . .320/P7
Wapsipinicon, Iowa, U.S., river 274/K2
Wapusk Natl. Park, Man., Can. 215/D1
War, W. Va., U.S., 788 . . . . .360/C6
Waramaug, Conn., U.S., lake 253/B3
Warangal, India, 446,760, (466,877 metro.) . . .128/C5
Warba, Minn., U.S., 183 . . . . .298/D3
Warbah, Kuw., island 136/C1
Warboys, Eng., U.K., 2,945 . . . . .68/G5
Warboys, Eng., U.K., 2,945 . . . . .70/D2
Warburg, Alta., Can., 560 . . . . .212/C4
Warcop, Eng., U.K. 66/D3
Ward, Ala., U.S. .238/A3
Ward, Ark., U.S., 2,580 . . . . .244/D2
Ward, Colo., U.S., 169 . . . . .250/E1
Ward, N. Dak., U.S., county, 58,795 . . . . .326/D1
Ward, S.C., U.S., 110 . . . . .340/C3
Ward, S. Dak., U.S., 41 . . . . .342/J3
Ward, Tex., U.S., county, 10,909 . . . . .346/E4
Ward, W. Va., U.S. 360/D4
Warda, Tex., U.S. 346/M5
Wardell, Mo., U.S., 278 . . . . .302/G5
Warden, La., U.S., 150 . . . . .282/G1
Warden, Wash., U.S., 2,544 . . . . .358/F3
Wardensville, W. Va., U.S., 246 . . . . .360/J2
Wardington, Eng., U.K. 70/B2
Wardlow, Alta., Can. 212/E6
Wardlow, Eng., U.K. 66/E6
Wardner, Alta., Can. 264/A2
Wardner, Ida., U.S., 215 . . . . .264/A2
Ward Ridge, Fla., U.S., 60 . . . . .256/C2
Wardsboro, Vt., U.S. 352/B4
Wardsboro Ctr., Vt., U.S., 125 . . . . .352/B4
Wards Corner, N.C., U.S., 40 . . . . .322/J5
Ward Sprs., Minn., U.S., 125 . . . . .298/C5
Wardsville, Mo., U.S., 976 . . . . .302/D3
Wardville, Okla., U.S., 50 . . . . .330/F3
Ware, Br. Col., Can. 214/K2
Ware, Eng., U.K., 17,000 . . . . .70/D3
Ware, Ga., U.S., county, 35,483 . . . . .260/F9
Ware, Ill., U.S., 125 . . . . .266/D6
Ware, Iowa, U.S. 274/E2
Ware, Mass., U.S., 9,707 . . . . .292/F3
Ware, Tex., U.S. .346/E8
War Eagle, Ark., U.S., 60 . . . . .244/B1
Wareham, Eng., U.K., 2,454 . . . . .73/H3
Wareham, Mass., U.S., 20,335 . . . . .292/L5, M5
Waresboro, Ga., U.S., 125 . . . . .260/G9
Ware Shoals, S.C., U.S., 2,363 . . . . .340/B2
Waretown, N.J., U.S., 1,582 . . . . .314/E4
Warfield, Ky., U.S., 284 . . . . .280/H3
Wargrave, Eng., U.K., 3,221 . . . . .73/H3
War Horse N.W.R., Mont., U.S. 306/H2, H3
Wark, Eng., U.K. 66/D2
Warkworth, Eng., U.K., 1,642 . . . . .66/E2
Warley, Eng., U.K. 68/D5
Warlingham, Eng., U.K. 70/D4
Warman, Sask., Can., 3,481 . . . . .227/D8
Warman, Minn., U.S., 70 . . . . .298/D4
Warm Beach, Wash., U.S., 2,040 . . . . .358/C1
Warmington, Eng., U.K. 70/D1
Warmińsko-Mazurskie, Pol., province 83/E1
Warminster, Eng., U.K., 16,379 . . . . .73/H2
Warminster, Penn., U.S., 650 . . . . .336/M6
Warm Lake, Ida., U.S. 264/B5
Warm River, Ida., U.S. 264/F5
Warm Sprs., Ga., U.S., 485 . . . . .260/B6
Warm Sprs., Nev., U.S. 310/B2
Warm Sprs., Oreg., U.S., 2,431 . . . . .334/E3
Warm Sprs., Oreg., U.S., reservoir 334/H4
Warm Sprs., Va., U.S., 200 . . . . .354/D4
Warm Sprs. Ind. Res., Oreg., U.S. 334/E3
Warmwell, Eng., U.K. 73/H3
Warner, Alta., Can., 379 . . . . .212/D6
Warner, N.H., U.S., 2,760 . . . . .312/C5
Warner, Okla., U.S., 1,430 . . . . .330/G2
Warner, S. Dak., U.S., 419 . . . . .342/G2
Warner Robins, Ga., U.S., 48,804 . . . . .260/D6
Warnerton, La., U.S., 50 . . . . .282/J5
Warnford, Eng., U.K. 70/B5
Warr Acres, Okla., U.S., 9,735 . . . . .330/B3, E2
Warren, Man., Can. 215/C4
Warren, Ont., Can. 223/E1
Warren, Wales, U.K. 64/A4
Warren, Ariz., U.S. 242/F6
Warren, Ark., U.S., 6,442 . . . . .244/C4
Warren, Conn., U.S., 1,254 . . . . .253/B3
Warren, Ga., U.S., county, 6,336 . . . . .260/F5
Warren, Ida., U.S. 264/B4
Warren, Ill., U.S., 1,496 . . . . .266/D1
Warren, Ill., U.S., county, 18,735 . . . . .266/C3

Warren, Ind., U.S., 1,272 . . . . .270/F3
Warren, Ind., U.S., county, 8,419 . . . . .270/B4
Warren, Iowa, U.S., county, 40,671 . . . . .274/G5
Warren, Ky., U.S., county, 92,522 . . . . .280/D4
Warren, Maine, U.S., 3,794 . . . . .286/C4
Warren, Mass., U.S., 4,776 . . . . .292/F4
Warren, Mich., U.S., 138,247 . . . . .294/B6
Warren, Minn., U.S., 1,678 . . . . .298/A2
Warren, Miss., U.S., county, 49,644 . . . . .300/B3
Warren, Mo., U.S., county, 24,525 . . . . .302/E3
Warren, Mont., U.S. 306/H4
Warren, Mont., U.S., peak 306/C4
Warren, N.H., U.S., 873 . . . . .312/C4
Warren, N.J., U.S., county, 102,437 . . . . .314/D2
Warren, N.Y., U.S., county, 63,303 . . . . .320/P3
Warren, N.C., U.S., county, 19,972 . . . . .322/J2
Warren, Ohio, U.S., 46,832 . . . . .328/J3
Warren, Ohio, U.S., county, 158,383 . . . .328/B7, C9
Warren, Okla., U.S., 80 . . . . .330/C3
Warren, Penn., U.S., 10,259 . . . . .336/C2
Warren, Penn., U.S., county, 43,863 . . . . .336/C2
Warren, R.I., U.S., 11,360 . . . . .339/E3
Warren, Tenn., U.S., county, 38,276 . . . . .344/K3
Warren, Vt., U.S. 352/B2
Warren, Va., U.S., county, 31,584 . . . . .354/C3
Warren Glen, N.J., U.S., 650 . . . . .314/C2
Warren Grove, N.J., U.S., 150 . . . . .314/E4
Warren Landing, Man., Can. 215/C2
Warren Park, Ind., U.S., 1,656 . . . . .270/D5
Warrenpoint, N. Ire., U.K., 5,637 . . . . .65/E3
Warrens, Wisc., U.S., 286 . . . . .364/C4
Warrensburg, Ill., U.S., 1,289 . . . . .266/D4
Warrensburg, Mo., U.S., 16,340 . . . . .302/C3
Warrensburg, N.Y., U.S., 3,208 . . . . .320/P4
Warrensville, N.C., U.S., 275 . . . . .322/B2
Warrensville Hts., Ohio, U.S., 15,109 . . . . .328/H9
Warrenton, Ga., U.S., 2,013 . . . . .260/F5
Warrenton, Mo., U.S., 5,281 . . . . .302/E3
Warrenton, N.C., U.S., 811 . . . . .322/J2
Warrenton, Oreg., U.S., 4,096 . . . . .334/C1
Warrenton, Va., U.S., 6,670 . . . . .354/H3
Warrentown, Mass., U.S., 400 . . . . .292/L5
Warrenville, Conn., U.S., 350 . . . . .253/G2
Warrenville, Ill., U.S., 13,363 . . . . .266/A6
Warri, Nig. 152/C5
Warrick, Ind., U.S., county, 52,383 . . . . .270/B8
Warrington, Eng., U.K., 82,812,
(152,458 metro.) 60/C3
Warrington, Eng., U.K., 82,812,
(152,458 metro.) 66/C6
Warrington, Eng., U.K., 82,812,
(152,458 metro.) 68/B3
Warrington, Eng., U.K., unitary authority,
191,084 . . . . .66/C6
Warrington, Eng., U.K., unitary authority,
191,084 . . . . .68/B3
Warrington, Fla., U.S., 15,207 . . . . .256/A1
Warrior, Ala., U.S., 3,169 . . . . .238/C2
Warrior Run, Penn., U.S., 624 . . . . .336/K3
Warriors Mark, Penn., U.S., 375 . . . . .336/E4
Warrnambool, Vic., Austl. 170/D3
Warroad, Minn., U.S., 1,722 . . . . .298/B2
Warsash, Eng., U.K. 70/B5
Warsaw, Pol., capital, 1,609,780 . . . . .83/E2
Warsaw, Ill., U.S., 1,793 . . . . .266/B3
Warsaw, Ind., U.S., 12,415 . . . . .270/E2
Warsaw, Ky., U.S., 1,811 . . . . .280/F2
Warsaw, Minn., U.S., 550 . . . . .298/D6
Warsaw, Mo., U.S., 2,070 . . . . .302/C3
Warsaw, N.Y., U.S., 3,814 . . . . .320/E5
Warsaw, N.C., U.S., 3,051 . . . . .322/J5
Warsaw, Ohio, U.S., 781 . . . . .328/G5
Warsaw, Va., U.S., 1,375 . . . . .354/K5
Warslow, Eng., U.K. 68/D3
Warson Woods, Mo., U.S., 1,983 . . . . .302/H3
Warsop, Eng., U.K., 10,083 . . . . .68/E3
Warta, Pol., river 83/B2, C2
Warta, Pol., river .86/C2
Wartburg, Tenn., U.S., 890 . . . . .344/M2
Warter, Eng., U.K. 66/F4
Warthen, Ga., U.S., 40 . . . . .260/F5
Warton, Eng., U.K. 66/C4
Wartrace, Tenn., U.S., 548 . . . . .344/J3
Warwick, Eng., U.K. 60/C3
Warwick, Eng., U.K., 22,476, (77,872 metro.) . .68/D5
Warwick, Eng., U.K., 22,476, (77,872 metro.) . .70/A2
Warwick, Ga., U.S., 430 . . . . .260/D8
Warwick, Md., U.S., 300 . . . . .288/L2, L
Warwick, Mass., U.S., 750 . . . . .292/E2, E
Warwick, N.Y., U.S., 6,412 . . . . .320/N7
Warwick, N. Dak., U.S., 75 . . . . .326/G2
Warwick, Okla., U.S., 235 . . . . .330/F2
Warwick, R.I., U.S., 85,808 . . . . .339/D3, D
Warwickshire, Eng., U.K., unitary authority,
505,885 . . . . .68/D5, D
Warwickshire, Eng., U.K., unitary authority,
505,885 . . . . .70/A2
Wasa, Br. Col., Can., 259 . . . . .214/P6
Wasaga Beach, Ont., Can., 12,419 . . . . .223/F3
Wasagaming, Man., Can. 215/B4
Wasatch, Utah, U.S., county, 15,215 . . . .350/C3, E2
Wasatch, Utah, U.S., plateau 350/C5
Wasatch-Cache Natl. For., Ida., U.S. 264/F7
Wasatch-Cache Natl. For.,
Utah, U.S. 350/C3, C2, B3, E1
Wasbister, Scot., U.K. 62/M1
Wasco, Calif., U.S., 21,263 . . . . .246/F7
Wasco, Oreg., U.S., 381 . . . . .334/F2
Wasco, Oreg., U.S., county, 23,791 . . . . .334/E2
Wascott, Wisc., U.S. 364/B2
Waseca, Minn., U.S., 8,493 . . . . .298/D6
Waseca, Minn., U.S., county, 19,526 . . . . .298/D6
Wash, The, Eng., U.K., bay 60/D3
Wash, The, Eng., U.K., bay 68/H4
Washago, Ont., Can. 223/F3
Washakie, Wyo., U.S., county, 8,289 . . . . .366/C2
Washburn, Ark., U.S., 80 . . . . .244/A2
Washburn, Ill., U.S., 1,147 . . . . .266/D3
Washburn, Iowa, U.S., 1,000 . . . . .274/K3
Washburn, Maine, U.S., 1,627 . . . . .286/D2
Washburn, Mo., U.S., 448 . . . . .302/C5
Washburn, N. Dak., U.S., 1,389 . . . . .326/D2
Washburn, Tenn., U.S., 125 . . . . .344/P2
Washburn, Tex., U.S., 150 . . . . .346/F9
Washburn, Wisc., U.S., 2,280 . . . . .364/C2
Washburn, Wisc., U.S., county, 16,036 . . . . . . .364/B2
Washingborough, Eng., U.K. 68/G3
Washington, Fiji, cape 174/A3
Washington, Eng., U.K., 56,848 . . . . .66/E3
Washington, Eng., U.K., 56,848 . . . . .70/D5
Washington, U.S., state 346
Washington, Ala., U.S., county, 18,097 . . . . . .238/A4
Washington, Ark., U.S., 148 . . . . .244/B4
Washington, Ark., U.S., county, 157,715 . . . . . .244/A2
Washington, Calif., U.S., 125 . . . . .246/E3
Washington, Colo., U.S., county, 4,926 . . . . . . .250/G2
Washington, Conn., U.S., 3,596 . . . . .253/B3
Washington, D.C., U.S., capital, 572,059,
(7,608,070 metro.) 288/B7, F4
Washington, Fla., U.S., county, 20,973 . . . . . . .256/C1

Washington, Ga., U.S., 4,295 . . . . .260/F4
Washington, Ga., U.S., county, 21,176 . . . . . . .260/F6
Washington, Ida., U.S., county, 9,977 . . . . . . .264/A5
Washington, Ill., U.S., 10,841 . . . . .266/D3
Washington, Ill., U.S., county, 15,148 . . . . . . .266/D5
Washington, Ind., U.S., 11,380 . . . . .270/B7
Washington, Ind., U.S., county, 27,223 . . . . . . .270/D7
Washington, Iowa, U.S., 7,047 . . . . .274/L5
Washington, Iowa, U.S., county, 20,670 . . . . . .274/L5
Washington, Kans., U.S., 1,223 . . . . .276/E2
Washington, Kans., U.S., county, 6,483 . . . . . .276/E2
Washington, Ky., U.S., county, 10,916 . . . . . . .280/E3
Washington, La., U.S., 1,082 . . . . .282/E5
Washington, La., U.S., parish, 43,926 . . . . . . .282/J5
Washington, Maine, U.S., 1,345 . . . . .286/C4
Washington, Maine, U.S., county, 33,941 . . . . .286/E4
Washington, Md., U.S., county, 131,923 . . . . . .288/C1
Washington, Mass., U.S., 544 . . . . .292/B3
Washington, Minn., U.S., county, 201,130 . . .298/E5, F5
Washington, Miss., U.S., 250 . . . . .300/A4
Washington, Miss., U.S., county, 62,977 . . . . . .300/B3
Washington, Mo., U.S., 13,243 . . . . .302/E3
Washington, Mo., U.S., county, 23,344 . . . . . . .302/J4
Washington, Nebr., U.S., 126 . . . . .308/H2
Washington, Nebr., U.S., county, 18,780 . . . . . .308/H2
Washington, N.H., U.S., 895 . . . . .312/B5
Washington, N.H., U.S., mountain 312/D3
Washington, (Bergen County), N.J., U.S., 8,938 . .314/B1
Washington, (township, Warren County),
N.J., U.S., 6,248 . . . . .314/D2
Washington, N.Y., U.S., county, 61,042 . . . . . . .320/Q4
Washington, N.C., U.S., 9,583 . . . . .322/L3
Washington, N.C., U.S., county, 13,723 . . . . . .322/M3
Washington, Ohio, U.S., county, 63,251 . . . . . .328/G7
Washington, Okla., U.S., 520 . . . . .330/E2
Washington, Okla., U.S., county, 48,996 . . . . . .330/G1
Washington, Oreg., U.S., county, 445,342 . .334/A3, C2
Washington, Penn., U.S., 15,268 . . . . .336/A5
Washington, Penn., U.S., county, 202,897 . . . . .336/A5
Washington, R.I., U.S. 339/C3
Washington, R.I., U.S., county, 123,546 . . . . . .339/C4
Washington, Tenn., U.S., county, 107,198 . . . . .344/R2
Washington, Tex., U.S., county, 30,373 . . . . . .346/M5
Washington, Utah, U.S., 8,186 . . . . .350/A6
Washington, Utah, U.S., county, 90,354 . . . . . .350/A6
Washington, Vt., U.S. 352/C2
Washington, Vt., U.S., county, 58,039 . . . . . . .352/B2
Washington, Va., U.S., 183 . . . . .354/D3
Washington, Va., U.S., county, 51,103 . . . . . . .354/D3
Washington, Wash., U.S., lake 358/A4
Washington, W. Va., U.S., 1,170 . . . . .360/C2
Washington, Wisc., U.S., county, 117,493 . .364/E5, F1
Washington, Wisc., U.S., island 364/G3
Washington C.H., Ohio, U.S., 13,524 . . . . . . .328/D6
Washington Crossing, N.J., U.S., 950 . . . . . . .314/D3
Washington Depot, Conn., U.S., 550 . . . . . . .253/B3
Washington Grove, Md., U.S., 515 . . . . .288/F3
Washington Island, Wisc., U.S., 150 . . . . .364/G3
Washington Park, Ill., U.S., 5,345 . . . . .266/A3
Washington Park, N.C., U.S., 440 . . . . .322/L3
Washington Terrace, Utah, U.S., 8,551 . . . . . .350/E1
Washingtonville, N.Y., U.S., 5,851 . . . . .320/N8
Washingtonville, Ohio, U.S., 789 . . . . .328/J4
Washingtonville, Penn., U.S., 201 . . . . .336/H3
Washita, Okla., U.S., county, 11,508 . . . . .330/D2
Washita, Tex., U.S., river 346/G9
Washita Battlefield N.H.S., Okla., U.S. 330/C2
Washita N.W.R., Okla., U.S. 330/C2
Washoe, Mont., U.S. 306/G4
Washoe, Nev., U.S., county, 339,486 . . . . .310/A1
Washoe City, Nev., U.S., 225 . . . . .310/A2
Washoe Ind. Res., Calif., U.S. 246/F4
Washoe Ind. Res., Nev., U.S. 310/A2
Washougal, Wash., U.S., 8,595 . . . . .358/C4
Washta, Iowa, U.S., 282 . . . . .274/C2
Washtenaw, Mich., U.S., county, 322,895 . . . . .294/F7
Washtucna, Wash., U.S., 260 . . . . .358/G3
Wasilla, Alaska, U.S., 5,469 . . . . .240/F2
Wasilla, Man., Can., 208 . . . . .215/A4
Waskaganish, Que., Can., 1,699 . . . . .225/A3
Waskerley, Eng., U.K. 66/E3
Waskish, Minn., U.S., 50 . . . . .298/C2
Waskom, Tex., U.S., 2,068 . . . . .346/P3
Wasola, Mo., U.S., 90 . . . . .302/D5
Waspam, Nicar. .202/C1
Wassaw, Ga., U.S., island 260/K8
Wassaw N.W.R., Ga., U.S. 260/J8
Wasson, Ill., U.S., 300 . . . . .266/E6
Wasta, S. Dak., U.S., 75 . . . . .342/C3
Wast Water, Eng., U.K., lake 66/B4
Watab, Minn., U.S., 425 . . . . .298/C5
Wataga, Ill., U.S., 857 . . . . .266/C3
Watauga, N.C., U.S., county, 42,695 . . . . .322/B2
Watauga, S. Dak., U.S. 342/D2
Watauga, Tenn., U.S., 403 . . . . .344/S2
Watauga, Tex., U.S., 21,908 . . . . .346/A9
Watchet, Eng., U.K., 3,147 . . . . .73/F2
Watchfield, Eng., U.K. 70/A3
Watchfield, Eng., U.K. 73/J1
Watch Hill, R.I., U.S., 325 . . . . .339/A6
Watchung, N.J., U.S., 5,613 . . . . .314/E2
Water, Bah., cays 207/A3
Waterbeach, Eng., U.K., 4,148 . . . . .68/H5
Waterbeach, Eng., U.K., 4,148 . . . . .70/E2
Waterboro, Maine, U.S., 6,214 . . . . .286/B5
Waterborough, N.B., Can. 217/C3
Waterbury, Sask., Can., lake 227/F2
Waterbury, Conn., U.S., 107,271 . . . . .253/C3
Waterbury, Nebr., U.S., 89 . . . . .308/H1
Waterbury, Vt., U.S. 352/B2
Waterbury, Vt., U.S., reservoir 352/B2
Waterbury Ctr., Vt., U.S., 850 . . . . .352/B2
Wateree, S.C., U.S., lake 340/D2
Wateree, S.C., U.S., river 340/D2
Waterflow, N. Mex., U.S., 175 . . . . .317/B1
Waterford, Ire., 44,564 . . . . .78/C2
Waterford, Ire., county 78/C2
Waterford, Calif., U.S., 6,924 . . . . .246/E5
Waterford, Conn., U.S., 19,152 . . . . .253/G4
Waterford, Ind., U.S., 2,200 . . . . .270/C1
Waterford, Maine, U.S., 1,455 . . . . .286/B4
Waterford, Mich., U.S., 73,150 . . . . .294/A6
Waterford, Miss., U.S., 90 . . . . .300/C1
Waterford, N.Y., U.S., 2,204 . . . . .320/P5
Waterford, Penn., U.S., 1,449 . . . . .336/B2
Waterford, Wisc., U.S., 4,048 . . . . .364/E6
Waterford County Borough, Ire., county 78/C2
Waterford Works, N.J., U.S., 1,000 . . . . .314/D4
Watergap, Ky., U.S., 150 . . . . .280/H3
Waterhen, Man., Can., lake, 171 . . . . .215/B3
Waterloo, Ont., Can., 86,543 . . . . .223/E4
Waterloo, Ont., Can., 86,543 . . . . .223/E4
Waterloo, Que., Can., 3,993 . . . . .226/D2
Waterloo, Ala., U.S., 208 . . . . .238/A1
Waterloo, Ark., U.S., 50 . . . . .244/B4
Waterloo, Ill., U.S., 7,614 . . . . .266/C5
Waterloo, Ind., U.S., 2,200 . . . . .270/F1
Waterloo, Iowa, U.S., 68,747, (128,012 metro.) . .274/K3
Waterloo, Kans., U.S. 276/E4

Waterloo, Mont., U.S. 306/D4
Waterloo, Nebr., U.S., 459 . . . . .308/H2
Waterloo, N.H., U.S. 312/C5
Waterloo, N.Y., U.S., 5,111 . . . . .320/H5
Waterloo, Oreg., U.S., 239 . . . . .334/D3
Waterloo, S.C., U.S., 203 . . . . .340/B2
Waterloo, Wisc., U.S., 3,259 . . . . .364/E5
Waterman, Ill., U.S., 1,224 . . . . .266/E2
Water Mill, N.Y., U.S., 1,724 . . . . .320/U1
Waterproof, La., U.S., 834 . . . . .282/G3
Waters, Mich., U.S., 225 . . . . .294/E5
Watersfield, Eng., U.K. 70/C5
Waterside, N.B., Can. 217/E3
Waterside, N. Ire., U.K. 65/C2
Watersmeet, Mich., U.S., 450 . . . . .294/A3
Waterstock, Eng., U.K. 70/B3
Waterton Lakes Natl. Park, Alta., Can. 212/D6
Waterton Park, Alta., Can., 155 . . . . .212/D6
Watertown, Conn., U.S., 21,661 . . . . .253/C3
Watertown, Fla., U.S., 2,837 . . . . .256/F1
Watertown, Mass., U.S., 32,986 . . . . . . .292/C7, K3
Watertown, Mich., U.S., 225 . . . . .294/C6
Watertown, Minn., U.S., 3,029 . . . . .298/D6
Watertown, N.Y., U.S., 26,705 . . . . .320/K3
Watertown, Ohio, U.S., 225 . . . . .328/G7
Watertown, S. Dak., U.S., 20,237 . . . . .342/H3
Watertown, Tenn., U.S., 1,358 . . . . .344/J2
Watertown, Wisc., U.S., 21,598 . . . . .364/E5
Water Valley, Alta., Can. 212/C5
Water Valley, Ky., U.S., 316 . . . . .280/B4
Water Valley, Miss., U.S., 3,677 . . . . .300/C1
Water Valley, Tex., U.S., 125 . . . . .346/H4
Waterview, Md., U.S., 100 . . . . .288/L7
Waterville, Kans., U.S., 681 . . . . .276/F2
Waterville, Maine, U.S., 15,605 . . . . .286/C4
Waterville, Mass., U.S., 950 . . . . .292/F2
Waterville, Minn., U.S., 1,833 . . . . .298/D6
Waterville, N.Y., U.S., 1,721 . . . . .320/L5
Waterville, Ohio, U.S., 4,828 . . . . .328/C2
Waterville, Vt., U.S. 352/B1
Waterville Valley, N.H., U.S., 257 . . . . .312/C4
Watervliet, Mich., U.S., 1,843 . . . . .294/C7
Watervliet, N.Y., U.S., 10,207 . . . . .320/P5
Watford, Ont., Can., 1,625 . . . . .223/D4
Watford, Eng., U.K. . . . . .60/Inset III
Watford, Eng., U.K., 113,080 . . . . .68/G6
Watford, Eng., U.K., 113,080 . . . . .70/D3
Watford City, N. Dak., U.S., 1,435 . . . . .326/B2
Watha, Eng., U.K., 151 . . . . .322/K5
Wathaman, Sask., Can., lake 227/G3
Wathena, Kans., U.S., 1,348 . . . . .276/H2
Wath upon Dearne, Eng., U.K., 16,070 . . . . . . .66/F5
Wath upon Dearne, Eng., U.K., 16,070 . . . . . . .68/E5
Watino, Alta., Can. 212/B3
Watkins, Colo., U.S., 80 . . . . .250/F2
Watkins, Minn., U.S., 880 . . . . .298/C5
Watkins Glen, N.Y., U.S., 2,149 . . . . .320/H6
Watkinsville, Ga., U.S., 2,097 . . . . .260/E4
Watonga, Okla., U.S., 4,658 . . . . .330/D2
Watonwan, Minn., U.S., county, 11,876 . . . . . .298/C6
Watova, Okla., U.S., 100 . . . . .330/G1
Watrous, Sask., Can., 1,808 . . . . .227/E9
Watrous, N. Mex., U.S. 317/F2
Watrousville, Mich., U.S., 200 . . . . .294/F6
Watsa, Congo, D.R. 155/C1
Watseka, Ill., U.S., 5,670 . . . . .266/E4
Watson, Sask., Can., 794 . . . . .227/F8
Watson, Ark., U.S., 288 . . . . .244/D4
Watson, Ill., U.S., 729 . . . . .266/E4
Watson, La., U.S., 1,400 . . . . .282/H5
Watson, Mass., U.S., 80 . . . . .292/C2
Watson, Minn., U.S., 209 . . . . .298/B5
Watson, Mo., U.S., 121 . . . . .302/A1
Watson, Okla., U.S., 70 . . . . .330/H3
Watson Lake, Yukon, Can., 912 . . . . .228/D5
Watsontown, Penn., U.S., 2,255 . . . . .336/H3
Watsonville, Calif., U.S., 44,265 . . . . .246/D6
Watten, Scot., U.K. 62/K2
Watten, Scot., U.K., lake 62/K1
Wattenberg, Colo., U.S. 250/A2, F1
Watterson Park, Ky., U.S., 953 . . . . .280/A2
Wattis, Utah, U.S., 60 . . . . .350/C4
Watton, Mich., U.S. 294/A3
Watts, Okla., U.S., 316 . . . . .330/H1
Watts Bar, Tenn., U.S., lake 344/M3
Wattsburg, Penn., U.S., 378 . . . . .336/B1
Watts Mills, S.C., U.S., 1,479 . . . . .340/B2
Watuppa, Mass., U.S., pond 292/K6
Wau, P.N.G. 172/A2
Waubay, S. Dak., U.S., 662 . . . . .342/H2
Waubay, S. Dak., U.S., lake 342/H2
Waubay N.W.R., S. Dak., U.S. 342/H2
Waubun, Minn., U.S., 403 . . . . .298/B3
Wauceda, Mich., U.S., 175 . . . . .294/B4
Wauchula, Fla., U.S., 4,368 . . . . .256/C4
Waucoma, Iowa, U.S., 299 . . . . .274/K1
Wauconda, Ill., U.S., 9,448 . . . . .266/A5
Wauconda, Wash., U.S. 358/F1
Waukau, Wisc., U.S., 300 . . . . .364/E5
Waukee, Iowa, U.S., 5,126 . . . . .274/G4
Waukegan, Ill., U.S., 87,901 . . . . .266/B4, F1
Waukena, Calif., U.S., 225 . . . . .246/F6
Waukesha, Wisc., U.S., 64,825 . . . . .364/E5, F2
Waukesha, Wisc., U.S., county, 360,767 . .364/E6, F2
Waukomis, Okla., U.S., 1,261 . . . . .330/E1
Waukon, Iowa, U.S., 4,131 . . . . .274/M1
Waukon, Wash., U.S., 70 . . . . .358/H2
Waumandee, Wisc., U.S. 364/C4
Waunakee, Wisc., U.S., 8,995 . . . . .364/D5
Wauneta, Kans., U.S. 276/F4
Wauneta, Nebr., U.S., 625 . . . . .308/C3
Waupaca, Wisc., U.S., 5,676 . . . . .364/D4
Waupaca, Wisc., U.S., county, 51,731 . . . . . . .364/D4
Waupun, Wisc., U.S., 10,718 . . . . .364/D5
Wauregan, Conn., U.S., 1,085 . . . . .253/H3
Waurika, Okla., U.S., 1,988 . . . . .330/D4
Wausa, Nebr., U.S., 636 . . . . .308/G1
Wausau, Fla., U.S., 398 . . . . .256/C1
Wausau, Wisc., U.S., 38,426, (125,834 metro.) . .364/D4
Wausaukee, Wisc., U.S., 572 . . . . .364/F3
Wauseon, Ohio, U.S., 7,091 . . . . .328/B2
Waushara, Wisc., U.S., county, 23,154 . . . . . . .364/D4
Wautoma, Wisc., U.S., 1,998 . . . . .364/D4
Wauwatosa, Wisc., U.S., 47,271 . . . . . . .364/F2, F3
Wauwinet, Mass., U.S. 292/P7
Wauzeka, Wisc., U.S., 768 . . . . .364/C5
Waveland, Ark., U.S. 244/B2
Waveland, Ind., U.S., 416 . . . . .270/B5
Waveland, Miss., U.S., 6,674 . . . . .300/C5
Waverley, Vic., Austl. . . . . .170/Inset V
Waverly, Ala., U.S., 184 . . . . .238/D3
Waverly, Colo., U.S. 250/D4
Waverly, Ga., U.S., 60 . . . . .260/H9
Waverly, Ill., U.S., 1,346 . . . . .266/D4
Waverly, Iowa, U.S., 8,968 . . . . .274/K2
Waverly, Kans., U.S., 589 . . . . .276/G3
Waverly, Ky., U.S., 297 . . . . .280/C3

Waverly, La., U.S., 40 ....282/G2
Waverly, Mich., U.S., 16,194 ....294/E7
Waverly, Minn., U.S., 732 ....298/D5
Waverly, Mo., U.S., 806 ....302/C2
Waverly, Nebr., U.S., 2,448 ....308/H3
Waverly, N.Y., U.S., 4,607 ....320/H6
Waverly, Ohio, U.S., 4,433 ....328/E7
Waverly, Tenn., U.S., 4,028 ....344/F2
Waverly, Va., U.S., 2,309 ....354/J6
Waverly, Wash., U.S., 121 ....358/H2
Waverly Hall, Ga., U.S., 709 ....260/B6
Wavre, Belg. 85/C2
Waw, Sudan 145/B3
Wawa, Ont., Can., 3,279 ....222/D3
Wawa, Nicar., river 202/B1
Wawanesa, Man., Can., 516 ....215/B4
Wawasee, Ind., U.S., lake 270/E2
Wawawai, Wash., U.S. 358/H3
Wawayanda, N.J., U.S. 314/E1
Wawayanda St. Park, N.J., U.S. 314/E1
Wawina, Minn., U.S. 298/D3
Wawona, Calif., U.S. 246/F5
Wax, Ky., U.S., 70 ....280/D3
Waxahachie, Tex., U.S., 21,426 ....346/M3
Waxhaw, N.C., U.S., 2,625 ....322/D5
Way, Miss., U.S. 300/B3
Wayan, Ida., U.S. 264/F7
Waycross, Ga., U.S., 15,333 ....260/G9
Wayland, Iowa, U.S., 945 ....274/L5
Wayland, Ky., U.S., 298 ....280/H3
Wayland, Mass., U.S., 13,100 ....292/J3
Wayland, Mich., U.S., 3,939 ....294/D7
Wayland, Mo., U.S., 425 ....302/E1
Wayland, N.Y., U.S., 1,893 ....320/F5
Waymart, Penn., U.S., 1,429 ....336/L2
Wayne, Ga., U.S., county, 26,565 ......260/G8
Wayne, Ill., U.S., 2,137 ....266/A5
Wayne, Ill., U.S., county, 17,151 .....266/K5
Wayne, Ind., U.S., county, 71,097 .....270/F5
Wayne, Iowa, U.S., county, 6,730 ......274/H6
Wayne, Kans., U.S. 276/E2
Wayne, Ky., U.S., county, 19,923 ......280/F4
Wayne, Maine, U.S., 1,112 ....286/B4
Wayne, Mich., U.S., 19,051 ....294/A7, F7
Wayne, Mich., U.S., county, 2,061,162 .294/A7, F7
Wayne, Mo., U.S., county, 21,216 ......300/D4
Wayne, Mo., U.S., county, 13,259 ......302/F4
Wayne, Nebr., U.S., 5,583 ....308/G1
Wayne, Nebr., U.S., county, 9,851 .....308/G1
Wayne, N.J., U.S., 54,069 ....314/A2, J2
Wayne, N.Y., U.S., county, 93,765 .....320/C4
Wayne, N.C., U.S., county, 113,329 ....322/J4
Wayne, (Ashtabula County), Ohio, U.S. .328/J2
Wayne, (Wood County), Ohio, U.S., 842 .328/D3
Wayne, Ohio, U.S., county, 111,564 ....328/G4,
Wayne, Okla., U.S., 714 ....330/E3,
Wayne, Penn., U.S., 1,000 ....336/L7,
Wayne, Penn., U.S., county, 47,722 ....336/L2,
Wayne, Tenn., U.S., county, 16,842 ....344/F4,
Wayne, Utah, U.S., county, 2,509 ......350/D5,
Wayne, W. Va., U.S., 1,105 ....360/B4,
Wayne, W. Va., U.S., county, 42,903 ...360/B4,
Wayne City, Ill., U.S., 1,089 ....266/E5,
Wayne Lakes, Ohio, U.S., 684 ....328/A5,
Wayne Natl. For., Ohio, U.S. 328/F7, J8, H6
Waynesboro, Ga., U.S., 5,813 ....260/G5,
Waynesboro, Miss., U.S., 5,197 ....300/D4,
Waynesboro, Penn., U.S., 9,614 ....336/F6,
Waynesboro, Tenn., U.S., 2,228 ....344/F4,
Waynesboro, Va., U.S., 19,520 ....354/F4,
Waynesburg, Ky., U.S., 400 ....280/F3,
Waynesburg, Ohio, U.S., 1,003 ....328/H4
Waynesburg, Penn., U.S., 4,184 ....336/A6
Waynesfield, Ohio, U.S., 803 ....328/C4
Waynesville, Ill., U.S., 452 ....266/D3
Waynesville, Mo., U.S., 3,507 ....302/D4
Waynesville, N.C., U.S., 9,232 ....322/D7
Waynesville, Ohio, U.S., 2,558 ....328/B6
Waynetown, Ind., U.S., 909 ....270/B4
Waynewood, Va., U.S., 6,000 ....354/M2
Waynoka, Okla., U.S., 993 ....330/D1
Wayside, Ga., U.S., 125 ....260/D6
Wayside, Kans., U.S. 276/G4
Wayside, Miss., U.S., 70 ....300/A2
Wayside, Tex., U.S. 346/F9
Wayside, Wisc., U.S., 275 ....364/F4
Wayzata, Minn., U.S., 4,113 ....298/D6
Weagamow Lake, Ont., Can. 222/B2
Weakley, Tenn., U.S., county, 34,895 ..344/D2
Weardale, Eng., U.K., valley 66/D3
Weare, N.H., U.S., 7,776 ....312/C5
Weatherby, Mo., U.S., 123 ....302/B2
Weatherby Lake, Mo., U.S., 1,873 ......302/H4
Weatherford, Okla., U.S., 9,859 ....330/D2
Weatherford, Tex., U.S., 19,000 ....346/L3
Weatherly, Penn., U.S., 2,612 ....336/K4
Weathers, Ark., U.S. 244/D4
Weathersby, Miss., U.S. 300/C4
Weatogue, Conn., U.S., 2,805 ....253/D2
Weaubleau, Mo., U.S., 518 ....302/C4
Weaver, Ala., U.S., 2,619 ....238/D2
Weaverham, Eng., U.K., 6,604 ....66/C6
Weaverham, Eng., U.K., 6,604 ....68/B3
Weaverthorpe, Eng., U.K. 66/G4
Weaverville, Calif., U.S., 3,554 ......246/B2
Weaverville, N.C., U.S., 2,416 ....322/F7
Webb, Ala., U.S., 1,398 ....238/D4
Webb, Iowa, U.S., 165 ....274/D4
Webb, Miss., U.S., 587 ....300/B2
Webb, Okla., U.S. 330/C2
Webb, Tex., U.S. 346/J8
Webb, Tex., U.S., county, 193,117 .....346/J8
Webb, W. Va., U.S. 360/B5
Webb City, Ark., U.S., 200 ....244/D4
Webb City, Mo., U.S., 9,812 ....302/B4
Webb City, Okla., U.S., 95 ....330/F1
Webber, Kans., U.S. 276/D2
Webbers Falls, Okla., U.S., 726 ....330/G2
Webberville, Mich., U.S., 1,503 ....294/E7
Webb Lake, Wisc., U.S., 40 ....364/A2
Webbville, Ky., U.S. 280/H2
Webbwood, Ont., Can., 507 ....223/D1
Webequie, Ont., Can., 600 ....222/C2
Weber, Minn., U.S., 90 ....298/D3
Weber, Utah, U.S., county, 196,533 ....350/B2, E1
Weber City, Va., U.S., 1,333 ....354/C3
Webi Shabeelle, Som., river 157/B3
Webster, Fla., U.S., 805 ....256/F3
Webster, Ga., U.S., county, 2,390 .....260/B7
Webster, Ind., U.S., 550 ....270/G5
Webster, Iowa, U.S., 110 ....274/K5
Webster, Iowa, U.S., county, 40,235 ...274/F2
Webster, Kans., U.S. 276/C3
Webster, Ky., U.S., county, 14,120 ....280/C3
Webster, La., U.S., parish, 41,831 ....282/C1
Webster, Maine, U.S., 82 ....286/B4
Webster, Md., U.S., 1,200 ....288/K1
Webster, Mass., U.S., 16,415 ....292/G4
Webster, Miss., U.S., county, 10,294 ..300/C2
Webster, Mo., U.S., county, 31,045 ....302/D4
Webster, Mont., U.S. 306/M3

Webster, Nebr., U.S., county, 4,061 ...308/F3
Webster, N.H., U.S., 1,579 ....312/C5
Webster, N.Y., U.S., 5,216 ....320/G4
Webster, N.C., U.S., 486 ....322/D8
Webster, N. Dak., U.S., 40 ....326/G1
Webster, S. Dak., U.S., 1,952 ....342/H2
Webster, Tex., U.S., 9,083 ....346/B7
Webster, W. Va., U.S., county, 9,719 ..360/F3
Webster, Wisc., U.S., 653 ....364/A3
Webster City, Iowa, U.S., 8,176 ....274/G3
Webster Groves, Mo., U.S., 23,230 .....302/H3
Webster Sprs., W. Va., U.S., 808 ......360/F4
Websterville, Vt., U.S., 1,200 ....352/C2
Weches, Tex., U.S. 346/N4
Wecota, S. Dak., U.S. 342/F2
Weddell, Antar., sea 192/B12
Wedderburn, Oreg., U.S., 300 ....334/B5
Weddington, S.C., U.S., 6,696 ....322/D4
Wedgefield, S.C., U.S., 275 ....340/D3
Wedgeport, N.S., Can., 1,217 ....221/A4
Wedhampton, Eng., U.K. 73/J2
Wedmore, Eng., U.K., 2,222 ....73/G2
Wednesbury, Eng., U.K. 68/C4
Wednesfield, Eng., U.K. 68/C4
Wedowee, Ala., U.S., 818 ....238/D2
Wedron, Ill., U.S., 300 ....266/E2
Weed, Calif., U.S., 2,978 ....246/C1
Weed, N. Mex., U.S., 60 ....317/E5
Weed Hts., Nev., U.S. 310/A2
Weedon Bec, Eng., U.K., 2,363 ....68/E5
Weedon Bec, Eng., U.K., 2,363 ....70/B2
Weedonville, Va., U.S. 354/J4
Weedsport, N.Y., U.S., 2,017 ....320/H4
Weedville, Penn., U.S., 400 ....336/E3
Weehawken, N.J., U.S., 13,501 ....314/B2
Weekapaug, R.I., U.S., 350 ....339/B6
Weeki Wachee, Fla., U.S. 256/F3
Weeks, La., U.S. 282/F7
Week St. Mary, Eng., U.K. 73/C3
Weeks Mills, Maine, U.S., 150 ....286/C4
Weekstown, N.J., U.S., 150 ....314/D4
Weeksville, N.C., U.S., 150 ....322/N2
Weems Creek, Md., U.S. 288/H4
Weeping Water, Nebr., U.S., 1,103 .....308/H3
Weert, Neth. 84/C3
Wegdahl, Minn., U.S., 50 ....298/B6
Wei, China, river 119/D2
Weiden, Ger. 86/C4
Weidman, Mich., U.S., 879 ....294/E6
Weifang, China 119/E2
Weimar, Ger. 86/B3
Weimar, Tex., U.S., 1,981 ....346/M6
Weiner, Ark., U.S., 760 ....244/E2
Weinert, Tex., U.S., 177 ....346/J2
Weipa, Qnsld., Austl. 170/D1
Weippe, Ida., U.S., 416 ....264/B3
Weir, Kans., U.S., 780 ....276/H4
Weir, Ky., U.S., 60 ....280/C3
Weir, Miss., U.S., 553 ....300/C2
Weir, Tex., U.S., 591 ....346/D1, L5
Weir Farm N.H.S., Conn., U.S. 253/B5
Weirsdale, Fla., U.S., 750 ....256/G3
Weirton, W. Va., U.S., 20,411 ....360/K4
Weiser, Ida., U.S., 5,343 ....264/A5
Weiser, Ida., U.S., river 264/A5
Weiss, Ala., U.S., lake 238/D1
Weiss, Ga., U.S., lake 260/A3
Weissert, Nebr., U.S. 308/E2
Weitzel, Sask., Can., lake 227/D3
Wekusko, Man., Can. 215/B2
Wekusko, Man., Can., lake 215/B2
Wekweti, N.W. Terr., Can., 131 ....220/F4
Welaka, Fla., U.S., 586 ....256/G2
Welbourn, Eng., U.K. 68/F3
Welby, Eng., U.K. 70/C1
Welby, Colo., U.S., 12,973 ....250/A3
Welch, Okla., U.S., 597 ....330/G1
Welch, Tex., U.S., 275 ....346/F3
Welch, W. Va., U.S., 2,683 ....360/C3
Welchville, N.J., U.S. 314/C4
Welcome, La., U.S., 950 ....282/H6
Welcome, Md., U.S., 175 ....288/F6
Welcome, Minn., U.S., 721 ....298/C7
Welcome, N.C., U.S., 3,538 ....322/E3
Weld, Colo., U.S., county, 180,926 ....250/F1
Weld, Maine, U.S., 402 ....286/B4
Welda, Kans., U.S., 60 ....276/G3
Weld Corner, Maine, U.S. 286/B4
Weldiya, Eth. 156/C2
Weldon, Eng., U.K. 70/C2
Weldon, Ark., U.S., 100 ....244/D2
Weldon, Ill., U.S., 440 ....266/E3
Weldon, Iowa, U.S., 145 ....274/G6
Weldon, La., U.S. 282/D1
Weldon, Mo., U.S., river 302/C2
Weldon, Mont., U.S. 306/L2
Weldon, N.C., U.S., 1,374 ....322/K2
Weldona, Colo., U.S., 175 ....250/G1
Weldon Spr., Mo., U.S., 5,270 ....302/G3
Weldon Spr. Hts., Mo., U.S., 79 ....302/G3
Weleetka, Okla., U.S., 1,014 ....330/F2
Welkom, S. Afr. 162/C2
Welland, Eng., U.K. 68/C5
Welland, Eng., U.K., river 70/D1
Wellborn, Fla., U.S., 350 ....256/F1
Wellborn, Tex., U.S., 300 ....346/M5
Wellersburg, Penn., U.S., 176 ....336/D6
Wellesley, Mass., U.S., 26,613 ....292/B8, J3
Wellfleet, Mass., U.S., 2,749 ....292/P5
Wellfleet, Nebr., U.S., 76 ....308/D3
Wellford, S.C., U.S., 2,030 ....340/B2, F2
Wellingborough, Eng., U.K., 41,602 ....68/F5
Wellingborough, Eng., U.K., 41,602 ....70/C2
Wellingore, Eng., U.K. 68/F3
Wellington, Ont., Can., 1,943 ....223/E4
Wellington, Ont., Can., county 223/E4
Wellington, P.E.I., Can., 382 ....224/A2
Wellington, Chile, island 190/A7
Wellington, N.Z., capital, 163,824,
(339,747 metro.) 171/B3
Wellington, N.Z., region 171/C3
Wellington, (Shropshire), Eng., U.K., 18,494 ..68/B4
Wellington, Eng., U.K., 9,621 ....73/F3
Wellington, Ala., U.S. 238/D2
Wellington, Colo., U.S., 2,672 ....250/E1
Wellington, Fla., U.S., 38,216 ....256/A5
Wellington, Ill., U.S., 264 ....266/F3
Wellington, Kans., U.S., 8,647 ....276/E4
Wellington, Ky., U.S., 561 ....280/A2
Wellington, Maine, U.S., 258 ....286/C3
Wellington, Mo., U.S., 784 ....302/C2
Wellington, Nev., U.S. 310/A2
Wellington, Ohio, U.S., 4,511 ....328/F5
Wellington, Tex., U.S., 2,275 ....346/H9
Wellington, Utah, U.S., 1,666 ....350/D4
Wellman, Iowa, U.S., 1,393 ....274/L5
Wellman, Tex., U.S., 203 ....346/F2
Wellpinit, Wash., U.S., 60 ....358/H2
Wells, Eng., U.K., 9,763 ....73/G2
Wells, Ind., U.S., county, 27,600 .....270/F3
Wells, Kans., U.S., 40 ....276/E2

Wells, Maine, U.S., 9,400 ....286/B5
Wells, Minn., U.S., 2,494 ....298/D7
Wells, Nev., U.S., 1,346 ....310/C1
Wells, N.Y., U.S., 300 ....320/N4
Wells, N. Dak., U.S., county, 5,102 ...326/F2
Wells, (Cherokee), Tex., U.S., 769 ....346/P4
Wells, (Lynn County), Tex., U.S. 346/G2
Wells, Vt., U.S. 352/A4
Wellsboro, Ind., U.S., 600 ....270/C2
Wellsboro, Penn., U.S., 3,328 ....336/C2
Wellsburg, Iowa, U.S., 716 ....274/J3
Wellsburg, N.Y., U.S., 631 ....320/H6
Wellsburg, N. Dak., U.S. 326/F2
Wellsburg, W. Va., U.S., 2,891 ....360/K5
Wellsford, Kans., U.S. 276/C4
Wells Gray Prov. Park, Br. Col., Can. .214/M5
Wells Gray Prov. Pk, Br. Col., Can. ...212/A5
Wells-next-the-Sea, Eng., U.K., 2,400 .70/F1
Wells River, Vt., U.S., 325 ....352/C2
Wellston, Mich., U.S., 425 ....294/D5
Wellston, Mo., U.S., 2,460 ....302/H3
Wellston, Ohio, U.S., 6,078 ....328/E7
Wellston, Okla., U.S., 825 ....330/E2
Wellsville, Kans., U.S., 1,606 ....276/G3
Wellsville, Mo., U.S., 1,423 ....302/E2
Wellsville, N.Y., U.S., 5,171 ....320/F6
Wellsville, Ohio, U.S., 4,133 ....328/J4
Wellsville, Utah, U.S., 2,728 ....350/C2
Wellton, Ariz., U.S., 1,829 ....242/A5
Welney, Eng., U.K. 70/E1
Wels, Aus. 91/C2
Welsford, N.B., Can. 217/C3
Welsh, La., U.S., 3,380 ....282/D6
Welshampton, Eng., U.K. 68/B4
Welshfield, Ohio, U.S., 350 ....328/H3, J9
Welshpool, Wales, U.K. 60/B3
Welshpool, Wales, U.K., 5,725 ....64/E2
Welton, (Humberside), Eng., U.K. 66/E4
Welton, (Lincolnshire-Welton/Dunholme),
Eng., U.K., 3,695 ....68/G3
Welton, (Welton/Dunholme), Eng., U.K., 3,695 ..66/H6
Welton, Iowa, U.S. 66/G5
Welton, Eng., U.K. 70/B2
Welton, Iowa, U.S., 159 ....274/N4
Welty, Okla., U.S., 80 ....330/F2
Welwyn, Man., Can. 215/A4
Welwyn Garden City, Eng., U.K., 42,087 ..70/D3
Wem, Eng., U.K., 4,882 ....68/B4
Wembere, Tan., river 158/B1
Wembley, Alta., Can., 1,497 ....212/A5
Wembley, Eng., U.K. 70/D3
Weme, Minn., U.S. 298/B3
Wenasoga, Miss., U.S., 175 ....300/D1
Wenatchee, Wash., U.S., 27,856 ....358/E2
Wenatchee, Wash., U.S., lake 358/E2
Wenatchee, Wash., U.S., mountains 358/E2
Wenatchee, Wash., U.S., river 358/E2
Wenatchee Natl. For., Wash., U.S. 358/E2, B4
Wenchi, Gha. 150/A3
Wendell, Ida., U.S., 2,338 ....264/C7
Wendell, Mass., U.S., 986 ....292/F2
Wendell, Minn., U.S., 177 ....298/A4
Wendell, N.C., U.S., 4,247 ....322/J3
Wendover, Ariz., U.S., 556 ....242/B4
Wendover, Eng., U.K., 6,985 ....70/C3
Wendover, Utah, U.S., 1,537 ....350/A3
Wendte, S. Dak., U.S. 342/E3
Wenham, Mass., U.S., 4,440 ....292/L2
Weno, Micr., 15,253 ....172/C2
Weno, Micr., island 172/C2
Wenona, Ga., U.S., 175 ....260/D8
Wenona, Ill., U.S., 1,065 ....266/D2
Wenona, Md., U.S., 475 ....288/L7
Wenonah, N.J., U.S., 2,317 ....314/C4
Wenshan, China 119/D3
Wensleydale, Eng., U.K., valley 66/D4
Wentworth, N.S., Can. 221/D2
Wentworth, Mo., U.S., 141 ....302/B5
Wentworth, (Grafton County), N.H., U.S., 798 ..312/C4
Wentworth, N.C., U.S., 2,779 ....322/F2
Wentworth, S. Dak., U.S., 188 ....342/J3
Wentworth, Wisc., U.S., 70 ....364/B2
Wentzel, Alta., Can., lake 212/C1
Wentzville, Mo., U.S., 6,896 ....302/F3
Wenvoe, Wales, U.K. 64/E3
Wenzhou, China, 515,560, (5,948,130 metro.) ..119/F3
Weobley, Eng., U.K. 68/B5
Weogufka, Ala., U.S., 70 ....238/C2
Weona, Ark., U.S. 244/E2
Weott, Calif., U.S., 125 ....246/B2
Werder, Eth. 156/D3
Werley, Wisc., U.S., 40 ....364/C2
Werra, Ger., river 86/B3
Weser, Ger., river 86/B2
Weser, Tex., U.S., 40 ....346/L7
Weser-Ems, Ger., department 86/A2
Weskan, Kans., U.S. 276/A3
Weslaco, Tex., U.S., 26,935 ....346/L9
Wesley, Dom. 208/B2
Wesley, Ark., U.S., 175 ....244/B1
Wesley, Ga., U.S., 60 ....260/G2
Wesley, Iowa, U.S., 467 ....274/F1
Wesley, Maine, U.S., 114 ....286/E4
Wesley, Md., U.S., 80 ....288/K6
Wesley Hills, N.Y., U.S., 4,848 ....320/B1
Wesleyville, Nfld., Can. 218/E4
Wesleyville, Penn., U.S., 3,617 ....336/A1
Wessington, S. Dak., U.S., 248 ....342/G3
Wessington Sprs., S. Dak., U.S., 1,011 ..342/G3
Wesson, Ark., U.S., 100 ....244/C4
Wesson, Miss., U.S., 1,693 ....300/B4
West, Came., province 153/B2
West, Miss., U.S., 220 ....300/C2
West, Vt., U.S., river 352/B4
W. Alexander, Penn., U.S., 320 ....336/A5
W. Alexandria, Ohio, U.S., 1,395 ......328/A6
W. Allis, Wisc., U.S., 61,254 ....364/F2, F5
W. Alton, Mo., U.S., 573 ....302/F3, J2
W. Andover, N.H., U.S., 100 ....312/C5
W. Antarctica, Antar. 192/A8
W. Athens, Maine, U.S., 60 ....286/C4
W. Augusta, Va., U.S., 80 ....354/E4
W. Azerbaijan, Iran, province 130/A2
W. Babylon, N.Y., U.S., 43,452 ....320/D2
W. Baden Sprs., Ind., U.S., 618 ....270/C7
Westbank, Br. Col., Can., 15,700 ......214/N6
W. Baraboo, Wisc., U.S., 1,248 ....364/D5
W. Barnet, Vt., U.S., 225 ....352/C2
W. Barnstable, Mass., U.S., 1,500 .....292/N6
W. Baton Rouge, La., U.S., parish, 21,601 ..339/D3
W. Bay, Fla., U.S., 225 ....256/C1
W. Becket, Mass., U.S. 292/G3
W. Beckham, Eng., U.K. 70/G1
W. Belmar, N.J., U.S., 2,606 ....314/E3
W. Bend, Iowa, U.S., 834 ....274/F2
Westbend, Ky., U.S., 250 ....280/G3

W. Bend, Wisc., U.S., 28,152 ....364/E5
W. Bengal, India, state 128/A3
W. Berkshire, Eng., U.K., 125 ....352/B1
W. Berlin, N.J., U.S., 4,000 ....314/A4
W. Berlin, Vt., U.S., 150 ....352/C2
W. Bethel, Maine, U.S., 150 ....286/B4
W. Blocton, Ala., U.S., 1,372 ....238/B2
W. Bloomfield, Wisc., U.S., 100 ....364/E4
W. Bloomfield Township, Mich., U.S., 64,862 ..294/A6
W. Bolton, Vt., U.S., 150 ....352/B2
W. Boothbay Harbor, Maine, U.S. 286/C5
Westboro, Mo., U.S., 163 ....302/A1
Westboro, Wisc., U.S., 200 ....364/C3
Westborough, Mass., U.S., 17,997 ......292/H3
W. Bountiful, Utah, U.S., 4,484 ....350/E2
Westbourne, Man., Can. 215/B4
W. Boxford, Mass., U.S., 1,200 ....292/K2
W. Boylston, Mass., U.S., 7,481 ....292/G3
W. Braintree, Vt., U.S., 70 ....352/B3
W. Branch, Iowa, U.S., 2,188 ....274/M4
W. Branch, Mich., U.S., 1,926 ....294/E5
W. Brattleboro, Vt., U.S., 3,222 ......352/B3
W. Bridgewater, Mass., U.S., 6,634 ....292/K4
W. Bridgewater, Vt., U.S. 352/B3
W. Bridgford, Eng., U.K., 33,843 ......68/C4
W. Bridgford, Eng., U.K., 33,843 ......70/B1
W. Brimfield, Mass., U.S. 292/E4
W. Bromwich, Eng., U.K., 146,386 ......68/C4
Westbrook, Conn., U.S., 6,292 ....253/F4
Westbrook, Maine, U.S., 16,142 ....286/B5
Westbrook, Minn., U.S., 755 ....298/B6
Westbrook, Tex., U.S., 203 ....346/G2
W. Brookfield, Mass., U.S., 3,804 .....292/F4
W. Brookfield, Vt., U.S., 60 ....352/B2
W. Brooklyn, Ill., U.S., 174 ....266/D2
W. Brownsville, Penn., U.S., 1,075 ....336/B5
W. Buechel, Ky., U.S., 1,301 ....280/A2
W. Burke, Vt., U.S., 364 ....352/D1
W. Burlington, Iowa, U.S., 3,161 ......274/M6
W. Burton, Eng., U.K. 66/E4
Westbury, Eng., U.K., 11,863 ....68/B4
Westbury, Eng., U.K., 11,863 ....73/H2
Westbury, Minn., U.S. 298/A4
Westbury, N.Y., U.S., 14,263 ....320/C2
Westbury-on-Severn, Eng., U.K. 68/C6
W. Buxton, Maine, U.S., 425 ....286/B5
Westby, Mont., U.S., 172 ....306/M1
Westby, Wisc., U.S., 2,045 ....364/C5
W. Calder, Scot., U.K., 2,818 ....62/I7
W. Caldwell, N.J., U.S., 11,233 ....314/A2
W. Campton, N.H., U.S., 225 ....312/C4
W. Canaan, N.H., U.S., 225 ....312/B4
W. Cape May, N.J., U.S., 1,095 ....314/D6
W. Carroll, La., U.S., parish, 12,314 .282/E1
W. Carrollton City, Ohio, U.S., 13,818 ..328/F2
W. Carthage, N.Y., U.S., 2,102 ....320/K3
W. Castleton, Vt., U.S. 352/A3
W. Charleston, Vt., U.S., 150 ....352/C1
W. Ctr. Harbor, N.H., U.S., 175 ....312/C4
W. Chazy, N.Y., U.S., 600 ....320/Q1
W. Chelmsford, Mass., U.S., 1,400 .....292/J2
Westchester, Fla., U.S., 30,271 ....256/A6
Westchester, Ill., U.S., 16,824 ....266/B6
W. Chester, Iowa, U.S., 159 ....274/L5
Westchester, N.Y., U.S., county, 923,459 ..320/D1
W. Chester, Penn., U.S., 17,861 ....336/K6
W. Chesterfield, Mass., U.S., 100 .....292/C3
W. Chesterfield, N.H., U.S., 500 ......312/A6
W. Chicago, Ill., U.S., 23,469 ....266/A6
West City, Ill., U.S., 716 ....266/E6
W. Clandon, Eng., U.K. 70/C4
W. Clarkston, (W. Clarkston-Highland),
Wash., U.S., 4,707 ....358/H3
W. Clarksville, N.Y., U.S., 125 ....320/E6
Westcliffe, Colo., U.S., 417 ....250/E3
W. Coast, N.Z., region 171/B4
W. College Corner, Ind., U.S., 634 ....270/G5
W. Columbia, S.C., U.S., 13,064 ....340/A3
W. Columbia, Tex., U.S., 4,255 ....346/N6
W. Concord, Mass., U.S., 5,632 ....292/J3
W. Concord, Minn., U.S., 836 ....298/E6
W. Conshohocken, Penn., U.S., 1,446 ...336/L7
W. Cornwall, Conn., U.S., 40 ....253/B2
W. Cornwall, Vt., U.S., 150 ....352/A3
W. Cote Blanche, La., U.S., bay 282/F7
W. Covina, Calif., U.S., 105,080 ......246/E9
Westcreek, Colo., U.S., 105 ....250/E2
W. Creek, N.J., U.S., 1,500 ....314/E4
W. Crossett, Ark., U.S., 1,664 ....244/C4
W. Cumberland, Maine, U.S. 286/B5
W. Cummington, Mass., U.S., 125 ....292/C3
Westdale, La., U.S. 282/C2
W. Danville, Vt., U.S., 125 ....352/C2
W. Decatur, Penn., U.S., 600 ....336/E4
W. Dennis, Mass., U.S., 2,570 ....292/P6
W. Denton, Md., U.S., 325 ....288/J4
W. Des Moines, Iowa, U.S., 46,403 .....274/G4
W. Devon, P.E.I., Can. 224/A2
W. Dover, Vt., U.S., 175 ....352/B5
W. Down, Eng., U.K. 73/D2
W. Dresden, Maine, U.S. 286/C4
W. Dummerston, Vt., U.S., 325 ....352/B5
W. Dunbartonshire, Scot., U.K.,
unitary authority, 93,378 ....62/G7
W. Dundee, Ill., U.S., 5,428 ....266/A5
Westel, Tenn., U.S., 375 ....344/M3
W. Elkton, Ohio, U.S., 194 ....328/A6
W. Elmira, N.Y., U.S., 5,136 ....320/H6
W. End, Ala., U.S., 3,924 ....238/D2
Westend, Calif., U.S., 175 ....246/H7
W. End, N.Y., U.S., 1,813 ....320/F2
W. End, N.C., U.S., 450 ....322/F4
W. Enfield, Maine, U.S., 350 ....286/D3
W. Enosburg, Vt., U.S., 100 ....352/B1
W. Epping, N.H., U.S., 1,200 ....312/D5
Westerdale, Scot., U.K. 62/K2
Westerlo, N.Y., U.S., 275 ....320/N5
Westerly, R.I., U.S., 22,966 ....339/B5
Western, Egy., desert 144/A2
Western, Kenya, province 157/C3
Western, S. Kor., channel 116/C5
Western, Sri Lan., province 126/A4
Western, Nebr., U.S., 287 ....308/G3
Western, Zam., province 159/A3
Western Australia, Austl., state 170/B2
Western Dvina, Bela., river 82/D2
Western Dvina, Lat., river 81/B3
Western Finland, Fin., province 81/B2
Western Ghats, India, mountains 128/B5
Western Greece, Gr., region 100/B3
Western Grove, Ark., U.S., 407 ....244/C1
Western Macedonia, Gr., region 100/B1
Western Mindanao, Phil., region 120/B4
Western Sahara, dependency 141
Western Samoa, nation 167
Western Sprs., Ill., U.S., 12,493 .....266/B6
Western Visayas, Phil., region 120/B4
Westerose, Alta., Can. 212/D5
Westerschelde, Neth., channel 84/A3

Westerville, Nebr., U.S. ...308/E2
Westerville, Ohio, U.S., 35,318 ...328/E5, E9
W. Fairlee, Vt., U.S. ...352/C3
Westfall, Kans., U.S., 40 ...276/D3
Westfall, Oreg., U.S. ...334/J3
W. Falmouth, Mass., U.S., 1,867 ...292/M6
W. Fargo, N. Dak., U.S., 14,940 ...326/J3
W. Farmington, Maine, U.S., 3,500 ...286/B4
W. Farmington, Ohio, U.S., 519 ...328/J3
W. Feliciana, La., U.S., parish, 15,111 ...282/G5
W. Felton, Eng., U.K. ...68/B4
Westfield, N.B., Can. ...217/C3
Westfield, Ill., U.S. ...70/F5
Westfield, Ill., U.S., 678 ...266/F4
Westfield, Ind., U.S., 9,293 ...270/D4
Westfield, Iowa, U.S., 189 ...274/A2
Westfield, Maine, U.S., 559 ...286/E2
Westfield, Mass., U.S., 40,072 ...292/D4
Westfield, N.J., U.S., 29,644 ...314/A3, E2
Westfield, N.Y., U.S., 3,481 ...320/B6
Westfield, N. Dak., U.S., 40 ...326/E3
Westfield, Penn., U.S., 1,190 ...336/F2
Westfield, Tex., U.S., 1,700 ...346/B6
Westfield, Vt., U.S. ...352/C1
Westfield, Wisc., U.S., 1,217 ...364/D5
Westfield Ctr., Ohio, U.S., 1,054 ...328/G3
Westfir, Oreg., U.S., 276 ...334/D4
W. Flanders, Belg., province ...85/B1
Westford, Conn., U.S., 175 ...253/G2
Westford, Mass., U.S., 20,754 ...292/G2
Westford, Vt., U.S. ...352/A1
W. Fork, Ark., U.S., 2,042 ...244/A2
W. Forks, Maine, U.S., 47 ...286/C3
W. Frankfort, Ill., U.S., 8,196 ...266/E6
W. Freehold, N.J., U.S., 12,498 ...314/E3
W. Friendship, Md., U.S., 700 ...288/G2
W. Frisian, Neth., islands ...84/B1
W. Frostproof, Fla., U.S., 125 ...256/G4
W. Gardiner, Maine, U.S., 2,902 ...286/C4
Westgate, Iowa, U.S., 234 ...274/L2
W. Gate of Lomond, Va., U.S., 7,493 ...354/H3
W. Glacier, Mont., U.S., 125 ...306/B1
W. Glens Falls, N.Y., U.S., 6,721 ...320/P4
W. Glocester, R.I., U.S., 175 ...339/B2
W. Glover, Vt., U.S., 90 ...352/C1
W. Granby, Conn., U.S., 450 ...253/D2
W. Grand, Maine, U.S., lake ...286/E3
W. Granville, Mass., U.S. ...292/C4
W. Green, Ga., U.S., 225 ...260/F8
W. Grinstead, Eng., U.K. ...70/D5
W. Groton, Mass., U.S., 750 ...292/H2
W. Grove, Penn., U.S., 2,652 ...336/K6
W. Halifax, Vt., U.S., 175 ...352/B5
W. Hall, Eng., U.K. ...66/C2
Westham, (part of Tuckahoe), Va., U.S. ...354/H5
W. Hamlin, W. Va., U.S., 696 ...360/B4
W. Hampstead, N.H., U.S., 700 ...312/D6
Westhampton, Mass., U.S., 1,468 ...292/C3
Westhampton, N.Y., U.S., 2,869 ...320/F2
Westhampton Beach, N.Y., U.S., 1,902 ...320/F2
W. Hampton Dunes, N.Y., U.S. ...320/F2
W. Harrison, Ind., U.S., 284 ...270/G6
W. Hartford, Conn., U.S., 63,589 ...253/E2
W. Hartford, Vt., U.S., 375 ...352/C3
W. Hartland, Conn., U.S., 175 ...253/D1
W. Harwich, Mass., U.S. ...292/P6
Westhaven, (Humboldt County, Westhaven-Moonstone), Calif., U.S., 1,044 ...246/A1
W. Haven, Conn., U.S., 52,360 ...253/D4
W. Haven, Utah, U.S., 3,976 ...350/E1
W. Haven, Vt., U.S. ...352/A3
W. Haven-Sylvan, Oreg., U.S., 7,147 ...334/A2
W. Haverstraw, N.Y., U.S., 10,295 ...320/B1
W. Hawley, Mass., U.S., 50 ...292/C2
W. Hazleton, Penn., U.S., 3,542 ...336/J4
W. Helena, Ark., U.S., 8,689 ...244/E3
W. Heslerton, Eng., U.K. ...66/G4
W. Hickory, Penn., U.S., 200 ...336/C2
W. Hill, Eng., U.K. ...73/F3
Westhill, Scot., U.K., 9,498 ...62/M4
W. Hills, Penn., U.S., 1,229 ...336/B4
W. Hoathly, Eng., U.K. ...70/D4
Westhoff, Tex., U.S., 175 ...346/L6
W. Hollywood, Calif., U.S., 35,716 ...246/C9
W. Homestead, Penn., U.S., 2,197 ...336/B5
Westhope, N. Dak., U.S., 533 ...326/D1
W. Hopkinton, N.H., U.S., 175 ...312/C5
W. Hurley, N.Y., U.S., 2,105 ...320/N6
West Ice Shelf, Antar., glacier ...192/C1
West Indies ...192
W. Islip, N.Y., U.S., 28,907 ...320/D2
W. Java, Indon., province ...122/B2
W. Jefferson, Ala., U.S., 344 ...238/B2
W. Jefferson, N.C., U.S., 1,081 ...322/B2
W. Jefferson, Ohio, U.S., 4,331 ...328/C6
W. Jersey, Ill., U.S., 50 ...266/C4
W. Jordan, Utah, U.S., 68,336 ...350/E2
W. Kalimantan, Indon., province ...122/C2
W. Kazakhstan, Kaz., oblast ...131/A2
W. Keal, Eng., U.K. ...68/H3
W. Kennebunk, Maine, U.S., 809 ...286/B5
W. Kilbride, Scot., U.K., 4,393 ...62/G7
W. Kingston, R.I., U.S., 500 ...339/C3
W. Kirby, Eng., U.K. ...66/B6
W. Kittanning, Penn., U.S., 1,199 ...336/B4
W. Knoyle, Eng., U.K. ...73/H2
W. Lafayette, Ind., U.S., 28,778 ...270/C4
W. Lafayette, Ohio, U.S., 2,313 ...328/G5
Westlake, La., U.S., 4,668 ...282/C6
Westlake, Ohio, U.S., 31,719 ...328/F9, G3
Westlake, Tex., U.S., 207 ...346/B9
W. Lake Hills, Tex., U.S., 3,116 ...346/D2
W. Lake Sammamish, Wash., U.S., 5,937 ...358/B4
W. Lake Stevens, Wash., U.S., 18,071 ...358/C2
Westlake Vil., Calif., U.S., 8,368 ...246/C9
Westland, Mich., U.S., 86,602 ...294/A7, F7
W. Lebanon, Ind., U.S., 793 ...270/B4
W. Lebanon, Maine, U.S., 350 ...286/B5
W. Leechburg, Penn., U.S., 1,290 ...336/B4
W. Leipsic, Ohio, U.S., 271 ...328/B3
Westleton, Eng., U.K. ...70/H2
Westley, Calif., U.S., 747 ...246/L3
W. Liberty, Iowa, U.S., 3,332 ...274/M4
W. Liberty, Ky., U.S., 3,277 ...280/G3
W. Liberty, Ohio, U.S., 325 ...288/H1
W. Liberty, Ohio, U.S., 1,813 ...328/C5
W. Liberty, Penn., U.S., 325 ...336/A3
W. Line, Mo., U.S., 95 ...302/B3
Westline, Penn., U.S. ...336/D2
W. Linn, Oreg., U.S., 22,261 ...334/A3
W. Linton, Scot., U.K., 1,459 ...62/K7
W. Loch, Hawaii, U.S., harbor ...262/E1
Westlock, Alta., Can., 4,819 ...212/D4
W. Logan, W. Va., U.S., 418 ...360/B5
W. Long Branch, N.J., U.S., 8,258 ...314/E3
Westlothian, Wash., U.S., 2,882 ...358/B3
W. Lothian, Scot., U.K., unitary authority, 158,714 ...62/J7
W. Louisville, Ky., U.S., 150 ...280/C3
W. Lubec, Maine, U.S., 150 ...286/E4
W. Lulworth, Eng., U.K. ...73/H3

W. Malling, Eng., U.K., 2,056 ...70/E4
Westmanland, Maine, U.S., 71 ...286/D2
W. Mansfield, Ohio, U.S., 700 ...328/C5
W. Marion, N.C., U.S., 1,556 ...322/A3
W. Maui, Hawaii, U.S., mountains ...262/B3
W. Maui Forest Reserve, Hawaii, U.S. ...262/B3
W. Mayfield, Penn., U.S., 1,187 ...336/A4
Westmeath, Ire., county ...78/C2
W. Medway, Mass., U.S., 3,500 ...292/J4
W. Melbourne, Fla., U.S., 9,824 ...256/H3
W. Memphis, Ark., U.S., 27,666 ...244/E2
Westmere, N.Y., U.S., 7,188 ...320/P5
W. Mersea, Eng., U.K., 6,602 ...70/F3
Westmeston, Eng., U.K. ...70/D5
W. Miami, Fla., U.S., 5,863 ...256/A6
W. Middlesex, Penn., U.S., 929 ...336/A3
W. Middletown, Penn., U.S., 144 ...336/A5
W. Mifflin, Penn., U.S., 22,464 ...336/E7
Milan, N.H., U.S., 100 ...312/D2
W. Milford, N.J., U.S., 26,410 ...314/E1
W. Milford, W. Va., U.S., 651 ...360/F2
W. Millgrove, Ohio, U.S., 78 ...328/D3
W. Mills, Maine, U.S., 90 ...286/B4
W. Milton, Ohio, U.S., 4,645 ...328/B6
W. Milton, Vt., U.S., 600 ...352/A1
W. Milwaukee, Wisc., U.S., 4,201 ...364/F2
W. Mineral, Kans., U.S., 243 ...276/H4
W. Minot, Maine, U.S., 175 ...286/B4
Westminster, Eng., U.K. ...60/Inset III
Westminster, City of, Eng., U.K., unitary authority, 181,279 ...70/D3
Westminster, Calif., U.S., 88,207 ...246/D10
Westminster, Colo., U.S., 100,940 ...250/A3, E2
Westminster, Md., U.S., 16,731 ...288/G1
Westminster, Mass., U.S., 6,907 ...292/G2
Westminster, S.C., U.S., 2,743 ...340/A2
Westminster, Vt., U.S. ...352/C4
Westminster West, Vt., U.S., 80 ...352/B4
W. Monroe, La., U.S., 13,250 ...282/E1
Westmont, Calif., U.S., 31,623 ...246/C10
Westmont, Ill., U.S., 24,554 ...266/B6
Westmont, Penn., U.S., 5,523 ...336/D5
W. Moors, Eng., U.K. ...73/J3
Westmore, Vt., U.S. ...352/C1
Westmoreland, N.H., U.S., 1,747 ...312/B6
Westmoreland, Penn., U.S., county, 369,993 ...336/B5, F7
Westmoreland, Tenn., U.S., 2,093 ...344/J1
Westmoreland, Va., U.S., county, 16,718 ...354/K4
Westmorland, N.B., Can., county ...217/D2
Westmorland, Calif., U.S., 2,131 ...246/K9
W. Mystic, Conn., U.S., 3,600 ...253/H4
W. Newbury, Mass., U.S., 4,149 ...292/K1
W. Newfield, Maine, U.S., 90 ...286/B5
Westnewton, Eng., U.K. ...66/B3
W. Newton, Penn., U.S., 3,083 ...336/B5
W. New York, N.J., U.S., 45,768 ...314/C2, E2
W. Nishnabotna, Iowa, U.S., river ...274/C5
W. Norfolk, Conn., U.S., 275 ...253/C1
W. Northfield, Mass., U.S. ...292/F2
W. Nottingham, N.H., U.S., 300 ...312/D5
W. Nusa Tenggara, Indon., province ...122/C2
W. Ocean City, Md., U.S., 3,311 ...288/P6
W. Odessa, Tex., U.S., 17,799 ...346/F4
W. Okoboji, Iowa, U.S., 432 ...274/D1
W. Old Town, Maine, U.S. ...286/D4
Weston, Ont., Can. ...223/J5
Weston, Eng., U.K. ...68/C4
Weston, Colo., U.S. ...250/F4
Weston, Conn., U.S., 10,037 ...253/B5
Weston, Ga., U.S., 75 ...260/B8
Weston, Ida., U.S., 425 ...264/E7
Weston, Iowa, U.S., 175 ...274/C5
Weston, La., U.S., 150 ...282/D2
Weston, Maine, U.S., 203 ...286/E3
Weston, Mass., U.S., 11,469 ...292/B7, J3
Weston, Mich., U.S., 300 ...294/E8
Weston, Mo., U.S., 1,631 ...302/B2
Weston, Nebr., U.S., 310 ...308/H2
Weston, Ohio, U.S., 1,659 ...328/C3
Weston, Oreg., U.S., 717 ...334/F2
Weston, Vt., U.S. ...352/B4
Weston, W. Va., U.S., 4,317 ...360/F2
Weston, (Dunn County), Wisc., U.S. ...364/A4
Weston, (Marathon County), Wisc., U.S., 12,079 ...364/D4
Weston, Wyo., U.S. ...366/D1
Weston Heath, Eng., U.K. ...68/C4
Weston Mills, N.Y., U.S., 1,608 ...320/E6
Weston-on-the-Green, Eng., U.K. ...70/B3
Weston-Super-Mare, Eng., U.K., 69,372 ...73/G2
Westonzoyland, Eng., U.K., 1,769 ...73/F2
W. Orange, N.J., U.S., 44,943 ...314/A2, E2
W. Orange, Tex., U.S., 4,111 ...346/R5
W. Ossipee, N.H., U.S., 325 ...312/D4
W. Otis, Mass., U.S., 125 ...292/B4
Westover, Md., U.S., 100 ...288/M7
Westover, Penn., U.S., 458 ...336/D4
Westover, Tenn., U.S., 900 ...344/D3
Westover, Tex., U.S. ...346/J2
Westover, W. Va., U.S., 3,941 ...360/C3, D2
Westover Hills, Tex., U.S., 658 ...346/A10
Westow, Eng., U.K. ...68/F1
W. Palm Beach, Fla., U.S., 82,103, (1,131,184 metro.) ...256/B4, H5
W. Paris, Maine, U.S., 1,722 ...286/B4
W. Pasco, Wash., U.S., 4,629 ...358/F3
W. Paterson, N.J., U.S., 10,987 ...314/B2, E2
W. Pawlet, Vt., U.S., 40 ...352/A3
W. Pelham, Mass., U.S., 1,300 ...292/E3
W. Pelzer, S.C., U.S., 879 ...340/B2
W. Pensacola, Fla., U.S., 21,939 ...256/A1
W. Peoria, Ill., U.S., 4,762 ...266/D3
W. Perry, Eng., U.K. ...68/G5
W. Peru, Maine, U.S., 350 ...286/B4
W. Peterborough, N.H., U.S., 650 ...312/C6
Westphalia, Iowa, U.S., 160 ...274/D4
Westphalia, Kans., U.S., 165 ...276/G3
Westphalia, Mich., U.S., 876 ...294/E7
Westphalia, Mo., U.S., 320 ...302/E3
W. Pike, Penn., U.S., 70 ...336/F2
W. Pittsburg, Calif., U.S. ...246/K1
W. Pittston, Penn., U.S., 5,072 ...336/H7
W. Plains, Mo., U.S., 10,866 ...302/E5
W. Plymouth, N.H., U.S., 100 ...312/C4
W. Point, P.E.I., Can. ...224/A2
W. Point, Ala., U.S., 295 ...238/C1
W. Point, Ala., U.S., lake ...238/D2
W. Point, Ga., U.S., 164 ...244/D2
W. Point, Calif., U.S., 746 ...246/E4
W. Point, Ga., U.S., 3,382 ...260/A6
W. Point, Ga., U.S., lake ...260/A6
W. Point, Ill., U.S., 195 ...266/B3
Westpoint, Ind., U.S., 425 ...270/B4
W. Point, Iowa, U.S., 1,100 ...274/M6
W. Point, Ky., U.S., 900 ...280/E2
W. Point, Miss., U.S., 175 ...286/C5
W. Point, Miss., U.S., 12,145 ...300/D2
W. Point, Nebr., U.S., 3,660 ...308/H2
W. Point, N.Y., U.S. ...320/P8

W. Point, Ohio, U.S., 375 ...328/J4
Westpoint, Tenn., U.S., 250 ...344/F4
W. Point, Tex., U.S. ...346/F2
W. Point, Utah, U.S., 6,033 ...350/E1
W. Point, Va., U.S., 2,866 ...354/K5
W. Point Military Academy, N.Y., U.S. ...320/A1
W. Poland, Maine, U.S., 350 ...286/B4
Westport, Ont., Can., 647 ...223/J3
Westport, Ire. ...78/B2
Westport, N.Z. ...171/B3
Westport, Calif., U.S., 70 ...246/B3
Westport, Conn., U.S., 25,749 ...253/B5
Westport, Ind., U.S., 1,515 ...270/E6
Westport, Ky., U.S., 250 ...280/E2
Westport, Maine, U.S., 745 ...286/C5
Westport, Mass., U.S., 14,183 ...292/K6
Westport, Minn., U.S., 72 ...298/B5
Westport, N.H., U.S. ...312/B6
Westport, N.Y., U.S., 550 ...320/Q2
Westport, N.C., U.S., 2,006 ...322/D4
Westport, Okla., U.S., 264 ...330/F1
Westport, Oreg., U.S., 500 ...334/C1
Westport, Penn., U.S. ...336/F3
Westport, S. Dak., U.S., 125 ...342/G2
Westport, Wash., U.S., 2,137 ...358/A3
W. Portal, N.J., U.S., 225 ...314/C2
Westport Point, Mass., U.S., 350 ...292/K6
W. Portsmouth, Ohio, U.S., 3,458 ...328/D8
W. Pownal, Maine, U.S. ...286/B4
W. Princeton, Maine, U.S. ...286/E3
W. Quaco, N.B., Can. ...217/D3
W. Quoddy Head, Maine, U.S., point ...286/F4
W. Rasen, Eng., U.K. ...66/H6
W. Redding, Conn., U.S., 500 ...253/B4
W. Richland, Wash., U.S., 8,385 ...358/F3
W. Rindge, N.H., U.S., 475 ...312/B6
W. Riverside, (see Bonner), Mont., U.S., 1,693 ...306/C3
W. Road, Br. Col., Can., river ...214/K4
W. Rockport, Maine, U.S., 425 ...286/C4
W. Royalston, Mass., U.S., 40 ...292/F2
W. Rudham, Eng., U.K. ...70/F1
W. Rumney, N.H., U.S., 175 ...312/C4
W. Rupert, Vt., U.S., 125 ...352/A4
W. Rushville, Ohio, U.S., 132 ...328/F6
Westruther, Scot., U.K. ...62/L7
W. Rutland, Vt., U.S. ...352/A3
W. Rye, N.H., U.S., 1,400 ...312/E5
W. Sacramento, Calif., U.S., 31,615 ...246/K5
W. St. Modeste, Nfld., Can., 175 ...218/C3
W. St. Paul, Minn., U.S., 19,405 ...298/F6
W. Salem, Ill., U.S., 1,001 ...266/F5
W. Salem, Ohio, U.S., 1,501 ...328/F4
W. Salem, Wisc., U.S., 4,540 ...364/B5
W. Seboeis, Maine, U.S. ...286/D3
W. Selmont, Ala., U.S., 3,502 ...238/B3
W. Seneca, N.Y., U.S., 45,943 ...320/D5
W. Shiloh, Tenn., U.S., 125 ...344/E4
West Siberian, Russ., plain ...104/E3
Westside, Ga., U.S. ...260/D3
Westside, Iowa, U.S., 327 ...274/D3
W. Siloam Sprs., Okla., U.S., 877 ...330/H1
W. Simsbury, Conn., U.S., 2,395 ...253/D2
W. Slope, Oreg., U.S., 6,442 ...334/A2
W. Smithfield, N.C., U.S., 59 ...322/J3
W. Springfield, Mass., U.S., 27,899 ...292/D4
W. Springfield, Va., U.S., 28,378 ...354/M2
W. Stafford, Conn., U.S., 375 ...253/F2
W. Sterling, Mass., U.S., 450 ...292/G3
W. Stewartstown, N.H., U.S. ...312/D2
W. Stockbridge, Mass., U.S., 1,416 ...292/A3
W. Suffield, Conn., U.S., 600 ...253/E2
W. Sumatra, Indon., province ...122/A2
W. Sunbury, Penn., U.S., 104 ...336/B3
W. Sussex, Eng., U.K., unitary authority, 753,612 ...70/C5
W. Sutton, Mass., U.S., 350 ...292/G4
W. Swanzey, N.H., U.S., 1,118 ...312/B6
W. Tanfield, Eng., U.K. ...66/E4
W. Terre Haute, Ind., U.S., 2,330 ...270/B6
W. Thornton, N.H., U.S., 225 ...312/C4
W. Thumb, Wyo., U.S. ...366/A1
W. Tisbury, Mass., U.S., 2,467 ...292/M7
W. Topsham, Vt., U.S., 175 ...352/C2
W. Townsend, Mass., U.S., 1,300 ...292/H2
W. Townshend, Vt., U.S., 150 ...352/B4
W. Tytherley, Eng., U.K. ...70/A4
W. Union, Ill., U.S., 300 ...266/F4
W. Union, Iowa, U.S., 2,549 ...274/L2
W. Union, Minn., U.S., 87 ...298/B5
W. Union, Ohio, U.S., 2,903 ...328/C8
W. Union, S.C., U.S., 297 ...340/A2
W. Union, W. Va., U.S., 806 ...360/E2
W. Unity, Ohio, U.S., 1,790 ...328/B2
W. University Place, Tex., U.S., 14,211 ...346/B6
W. Upton, Mass., U.S., 2,326 ...292/H4
Westvaco, Wyo., U.S. ...366/B3
Westvale, N.Y., U.S., 5,166 ...320/J4
W. Valley City, Utah, U.S., 108,896 ...350/C3, E2
W. View, Penn., U.S., 7,277 ...336/D6
Westville, Ill., U.S., 3,175 ...266/F3
Westville, Ind., U.S., 2,116 ...270/C1
Westville, N.H., U.S., 2,100 ...312/D6
Westville, N.J., U.S., 4,500 ...314/A3
Westville, Okla., U.S., 1,596 ...330/H1
Westville, S.C., U.S., 275 ...340/D2
W. Virginia, U.S., state ...348
W. Walton, Eng., U.K. ...68/H4
W. Wardsboro, Vt., U.S., 125 ...352/B4
W. Wareham, Mass., U.S., 1,908 ...292/L5
W. Warren, Mass., U.S., 1,100 ...292/F4
W. Warwick, R.I., U.S., 29,581 ...339/C3
Westwater, Utah, U.S. ...350/E4
Westway, Tex., U.S., 3,829 ...346/B4
Westwego, La., U.S., 10,763 ...282/J7, K3
W. Wellow, Eng., U.K., 2,151 ...70/A5
W. Wenatchee, Wash., U.S., 1,681 ...358/E2
W. Wendover, Nev., U.S., 4,721 ...310/C1
W. Wildwood, N.J., U.S., 448 ...314/D5
W. Willington, Conn., U.S., 450 ...253/F2
W. Wilton, N.H., U.S., 175 ...312/C6
W. Winfield, N.Y., U.S., 862 ...320/L5
W. Wittering, Eng., U.K., 1,551 ...70/C5
Westwood, Eng., U.K. ...66/G5
Westwood, Calif., U.S., 1,998 ...246/E2
Westwood, Iowa, U.S., 127 ...274/L6
Westwood, Kans., U.S., 1,533 ...276/H1
Westwood, (Boyd County), Ky., U.S., 4,888 ...280/D2
Westwood, (Jefferson County), Ky., U.S., 612 ...280/B2
Westwood, Mass., U.S., 14,117 ...292/K4
Westwood, Mich., U.S., 9,122 ...294/D7
Westwood, N.J., U.S., 10,999 ...314/B1
Westwood Acres, Fla., U.S., 125 ...256/F2
W. Woodburn, Eng., U.K. ...66/D2
Westwood Hills, Kans., U.S., 378 ...276/H1

Westworth Vil., Tex., U.S., 2,124 ...346/A9
W. Wyoming, Penn., U.S., 2,833 ...336/G7
W. Yarmouth, Mass., U.S., 6,460 ...292/P6
W. Yellowstone, Mont., U.S., 1,177 ...306/C5
W. York, Ill., U.S., 225 ...266/F4
W. York, Penn., U.S., 4,321 ...336/H6
W. Yorkshire, Eng., U.K., unitary authority, 2,079,217 ...68/D2
Wetar, Indon., island ...122/D3
Wetaskiwin, Alta., Can., 11,154 ...212/D5
Wete, Tan. ...158/C1
Wetheral, Eng., U.K. ...66/C3
Wetherby, Eng., U.K., 8,154 ...66/F5
Wetherden, Eng., U.K., 8,154 ...68/E2
Wethersfield, Eng., U.K. ...70/E3
Wethersfield, Conn., U.S., 26,271 ...253/E3
Wetipquin, Md., U.S., 100 ...288/L6
Wetmore, Colo., U.S., 100 ...250/E8
Wetmore, Kans., U.S., 362 ...276/G2
Wetmore, Mich., U.S., 300 ...294/C3
Wetmore, Tex., U.S. ...346/A2
Wetonka, S. Dak., U.S. ...342/G2
Wetumka, Okla., U.S., 1,451 ...330/F2
Wetumpka, Ala., U.S., 5,726 ...238/C3
Wetwang, Eng., U.K. ...66/G4
Wetzel, W. Va., U.S., county, 17,693 ...360/E1, K6
Wetzlar, Ger. ...86/B3
Wever, Iowa, U.S., 250 ...274/M6
Wewahitchka, Fla., U.S., 1,722 ...256/C1
Wewak, P.N.G. ...172/A1
Wewela, S. Dak., U.S. ...342/F4
Wewoka, Okla., U.S., 3,562 ...330/F2
Wexford, Ire., 9,443 ...78/C2
Wexford, Ire., county ...78/C2
Wexford, Mich., U.S., county, 30,484 ...294/D5
Weyakwin, Sask., Can., 183 ...227/E6
Weyauwega, Wisc., U.S., 1,806 ...364/E4
Weybridge, Eng., U.K. ...70/D4
Weybridge, Vt., U.S. ...352/A2
Weyburn, Sask., Can., 9,534 ...227/G11
Weyerhaeuser, Wisc., U.S., 353 ...364/B3
Weymouth, N.S., Can. ...221/A3
Weymouth, Eng., U.K., 46,065 ...73/H3
Weymouth, Mass., U.S., 53,988 ...292/L4
Weymouth, N.J., U.S., 2,257 ...314/D4
Whakatane, N.Z. ...171/C2
Whalan, Minn., U.S., 64 ...298/F7
Whale Cove, Nun., Can., 305 ...220/K4
Whaletown, Br. Col., Can. ...214/K6
Whaley Bridge, Eng., U.K., 4,530 ...66/E6
Whaley Bridge, Eng., U.K., 4,530 ...68/D3
Whaleysville, Md., U.S., 250 ...288/N6
Whalsay, Scot., U.K., island ...62/Q2
Whalton, Eng., U.K. ...66/E2
Wham, Eng., U.K. ...66/D4
Whaness, Scot., U.K. ...62/L2
Whangarei, N.Z., (46,047 metro.) ...171/B2
Wharfedale, Eng., U.K., valley ...66/D4
Wharfedale, Eng., U.K., valley ...68/C1
Wharncliffe, W. Va., U.S., 150 ...360/C5
Wharton, Eng., U.K. ...68/B3
Wharton, N.J., U.S., 6,298 ...314/D2
Wharton, Ohio, U.S., 409 ...328/D4
Wharton, Tex., U.S., 9,237 ...346/M6
Wharton, Tex., U.S., county, 41,188 ...346/M6
Wharton St. For., N.J., U.S. ...314/D4
Whashton, Eng., U.K. ...66/E4
What Cheer, Iowa, U.S., 678 ...274/K5
Whatcom, Wash., U.S., county, 166,814 ...358/D1
Whately, Mass., U.S., 1,573 ...292/D3
Whatfield, Eng., U.K. ...70/F2
Wha Ti, N.W. Terr., Can., 453 ...220/E4
Whatley, Ala., U.S., 125 ...238/B4
Wheatcroft, Ky., U.S., 173 ...280/C3
Wheatfield, Ind., U.S., 772 ...270/B2
Wheatland, Man., Can. ...215/A4
Wheatland, Calif., U.S., 2,275 ...246/D3
Wheatland, Ind., U.S., 504 ...270/B7
Wheatland, Iowa, U.S., 772 ...274/N4
Wheatland, Mo., U.S., 388 ...302/C4
Wheatland, Mont., U.S., county, 2,259 ...317/C3
Wheatland, N. Mex., U.S. ...330/A3
Wheatland, Penn., U.S., 748 ...336/A3
Wheatland, Tex., U.S. ...346/A10
Wheatland, Wyo., U.S., 3,548 ...366/D2
Wheatley, Ont., Can., 1,920 ...223/C5
Wheatley, Eng., U.K., 3,661 ...68/E6
Wheatley, Eng., U.K., 3,661 ...70/B3
Wheatley, Ark., U.S., 372 ...244/D3
Wheatley, Ky., U.S., 80 ...280/F2
Wheaton, Ill., U.S., 55,416 ...266/A6, E2
Wheaton, Kans., U.S., 92 ...276/F2
Wheaton, Md., U.S., 57,694 ...288/B6, F3
Wheaton, Minn., U.S., 1,619 ...298/A5
Wheaton, Mo., U.S., 721 ...302/B5
Wheat Ridge, Colo., U.S., 32,913 ...250/A3, E2
Wheeler, Ala., U.S., lake ...238/B1
Wheeler, Ga., U.S., county, 6,179 ...260/F7
Wheeler, Ill., U.S., 119 ...266/E4
Wheeler, Kans., U.S. ...276/A2
Wheeler, Ky., U.S., 90 ...280/G4
Wheeler, Miss., U.S., 300 ...300/D1
Wheeler, Mont., U.S. ...306/K2
Wheeler, Nebr., U.S., county, 886 ...308/F2
Wheeler, Nev., U.S., peak ...310/C2
Wheeler, N. Mex., U.S., peak ...317/E1
Wheeler, Oreg., U.S., 391 ...334/C3
Wheeler, Oreg., U.S., county, 1,547 ...334/F3
Wheeler, Tex., U.S., 1,378 ...346/H9
Wheeler, Tex., U.S., county, 5,284 ...346/G9
Wheeler, Wash., U.S. ...358/G9
Wheeler, Wisc., U.S., 317 ...364/B3
Wheeler Air Force Base, Hawaii, U.S. ...262/J2
Wheeler N.W.R., Ala., U.S. ...238/C1
Wheeler Ridge, Calif., U.S. ...246/G8
Wheelersburg, Ohio, U.S., 6,471 ...328/E8
Wheeless, Okla., U.S. ...330/A1
Wheeling, Ill., U.S., 34,496 ...266/B5, F1
Wheeling, Mo., U.S., 268 ...302/C2
Wheeling, W. Va., U.S., 31,419, (153,172 metro.) ...360/K5
Wheelock, Maine, U.S. ...286/D1
Wheelock, N. Dak., U.S. ...326/B1
Wheelock, Vt., U.S. ...352/C1
Wheelwright, Ky., U.S., 1,042 ...280/H3
Wheelwright, Mass., U.S., 425 ...292/F3
Wheldrake, Eng., U.K. ...66/G5
Whelen Sprs., Ark., U.S., 84 ...244/B4
Whepstead, Eng., U.K. ...70/F2
Wherwell, Eng., U.K. ...70/B4
Whichard Beach, (River Road), N.C., U.S. ...322/M3
Whickham, Eng., U.K., 17,428 ...66/F3
Whiddon Down, Eng., U.K. ...73/E3
Whigham, Ga., U.S., 631 ...260/D8
Whigville, Ohio, U.S., 850 ...253/D3
Whinburgh, Eng., U.K. ...70/F1
Whipholt, Minn., U.S., 60 ...298/C3
Whippany, N.J., U.S., 3,800 ...314/E2
Whippingham, Eng., U.K. ...70/B5
Whipple, Ohio, U.S., 225 ...328/H6

Whipsnade, Eng., U.K. 70/C3
Whiskey, Wyo., U.S., *peak* 366/C2
Whiskeytown-Shasta-Trinity N.R.A., Calif., U.S. ..246/D1
Whispering Pines, N.C., U.S., 2,090 ....322/G4
Whistler, Br. Col., Can., 8,896 ....214/L6
Whitaker, Penn., U.S., 1,338 ....336/E7
Whitakers, N.C., U.S., 799 ....322/K4
Whitbourne, Nfld., Can., 930 ....218/E5
Whitburn, Scot., U.K., 10,391 ....62/J7
Whitby, Ont., Can., 87,413 ....223/G4
Whitby, Eng., U.K., 13,640 ....66/G4
Whitchurch, (Hereford & Worcester), Eng., U.K. ..68/B6
Whitchurch, (Shropshire), Eng., U.K., 7,868 ..68/B4
Whitchurch, Eng., U.K. 70/C3
White, Nfld., Can., *bay* 218/C4
White, Nun., Can., *island* 220/L3
White, Yukon, Can., *river* 228/A4
White, Russ., *sea* 104/C3
White, Ariz., U.S., *mountains* 242/F4
White, Ark., U.S. 244/D4
White, Ark., U.S., *county*, 67,165 ....244/D2
White, Ark., U.S., *river* 244/C2, D3
White, Calif., U.S., *mountains* 246/G5
White, Colo., U.S., *river* 250/D1
White, Ga., U.S., 693 ....260/B3
White, Ga., U.S., *county*, 19,944 ....260/D2
White, Ill., U.S., *county*, 15,371 ....266/E5
White, Ind., U.S., *county*, 25,267 ....270/C3
White, Ind., U.S., *river* 270/C6
White, La., U.S., *lake* 282/E7
White, Maine, U.S., *mountains* 286/C4
White, Nev., U.S., *river* 310/C3
White, N.H., U.S., *mountains* 312/C3
White, N. Dak., U.S., *butte* 326/B3
White, S. Dak., U.S., 530 ....342/J3
White, S. Dak., U.S., *river* 342/C4, E4
White, Tenn., U.S., *county*, 23,102 ....344/L3
White, Utah, U.S., *river* 350/E4
White, Vt., U.S., *river* 352/B3
White, Wash., U.S., *pass* 358/D3
White Apple, Miss., U.S., 80 ....300/A4
Whiteash, Ill., U.S., 268 ....266/E6
White Bead, Okla., U.S., 150 ....330/E3
White Bear, Minn., U.S., *lake* 298/F5
White Bear Lake, Minn., U.S., 24,325 ....298/E5, F5
White Bird, Ida., U.S., 106 ....264/A4
White Bluff, Tenn., U.S., 2,142 ....344/G2
Whitebridge, Scot., U.K. 62/H4
Whiteburg, Md., U.S. 288/M7
White Butte, S. Dak., U.S. 342/C2
White Canyon, Utah, U.S. 350/D6
White Cap, Maine, U.S., *mountain* 286/C3
White Castle, La., U.S., 1,946 ....282/G6
White Ctr., (White Ctr.-Shorewood),
   Wash., U.S., 20,975 ....358/A4
White Church, Mo., U.S., 50 ....302/E5
White City, Fla., U.S., 275 ....256/C6
White City, Ill., U.S., 221 ....266/B3
White City, Kans., U.S., 518 ....276/F3
White City, Ky., U.S. 280/E3
White City, Oreg., U.S., 5,466 ....334/D5
White City, Utah, U.S., 5,988 ....350/E2
Whiteclay, Nebr., U.S., 40 ....308/B1
White Cloud, Kans., U.S., 239 ....276/G2
White Cloud, Mich., U.S., 1,420 ....294/D6
White Cone, Ariz., U.S. 242/E2
White Coomb, Eng., U.K., *hill* 66/B2
Whitecourt, Alta., Can., 8,334 ....212/C4
White Crystal Beach, Md., U.S. 288/L2
White Deer, Tex., U.S., 1,060 ....346/G9
White Earth, Minn., U.S., 424 ....298/B3
White Earth, N. Dak., U.S., 63 ....326/C1
White Earth Ind. Res., Minn., U.S. 298/B3
Whiteface, Minn., U.S. 298/E3
Whiteface, N.H., U.S. 312/D4
Whiteface, Tex., U.S., 465 ....346/F2
Whitefield, Maine, U.S., 2,273 ....286/C4
Whitefield, N.H., U.S., 2,038 ....312/C3
Whitefield, Okla., U.S., 231 ....330/G2
Whitefish, Ont., Can. 223/A1
Whitefish, Mich., U.S., *bay* 294/E3
Whitefish, Mont., U.S., 5,032 ....306/B1
Whitefish Bay, (Door County), Wisc., U.S., 50 ..364/F4
Whitefish Bay, (Milwaukee County),
   Wisc., U.S., 14,163 ....364/F2, F5
Whitefish Falls, Ont., Can., 273 ....223/D1
Whitefish Pt., Mich., U.S. 294/E3
Whiteflat, Tex., U.S. 346/H1
Whiteford, Md., U.S., 700 ....288/J1
White Fox, Sask., Can., 436 ....227/F7
Whitehall, Scot., U.K. 62/N1
White Hall, Ala., U.S., 1,014 ....238/C3
White Hall, Ark., U.S., 80 ....244/E2
Whitehall, Ark., U.S. 244/E2
Whitehall, (part of Gaines School), Ga., U.S. ..260/E4
White Hall, Ill., U.S., 2,629 ....266/C4
Whitehall, Ind., U.S., 175 ....270/C6
Whitehall, (La Salle Parish), La., U.S., 150 ..282/E3
Whitehall, (Livingston Parish), La., U.S., 275 ..282/H6
White Hall, Md., U.S., 300 ....288/H1
Whitehall, Mich., U.S., 2,884 ....294/C6
Whitehall, Mont., U.S., 1,044 ....306/D4
Whitehall, N.Y., U.S., 2,667 ....320/Q3
Whitehall, Ohio, U.S., 19,201 ....328/E9
Whitehall, (Allegheny County), Penn., U.S.,
   14,444 ....336/D7
Whitehall, (Lehigh County), Penn., U.S., 14,268 ..336/L4
Whitehall, Wisc., U.S., 1,651 ....364/B4
Whitehaven, Eng., U.K. 60/D2
Whitehaven, Eng., U.K., 26,542 ....66/A3
Whitehaven, Md., U.S., 70 ....288/L6
White Haven, Penn., U.S., 1,182 ....336/K3
Whitehead, N. Ire., U.K., 3,761 ....65/F2
White Heath, Ill., U.S., 375 ....266/E3
Whitehorse, Yukon, Can., 19,058 ....228/C5
White Horse, N.J., U.S., 9,373 ....314/D3
White Horse, N. Mex., U.S. 317/C2
Whitehorse, S. Dak., U.S. 342/E2
White Horse, S. Dak., U.S., 141 ....342/E4
White Horse Beach, Mass., U.S., 2,300 ....292/M5
Whitehouse, Scot., U.K. 62/F7
Whitehouse, Scot., U.K. 62/J4
Whitehouse, N.J., U.S. 314/D2
Whitehouse, Ohio, U.S., 2,733 ....328/C2
White House, Tenn., U.S., 7,220 ....344/H2
Whitehouse, Tex., U.S., 5,346 ....346/N3
White House Ruin, Ariz., U.S. 242/F1
White House Sta., N.J., U.S., 1,951 ....314/D2
White Island Shores, Mass., U.S., 2,133 ......292/M5
Whitekirk, Scot., U.K. 62/L6
White Lake, Ont., Can. 223/J2
White Lake, N.C., U.S., 529 ....322/J5
White Lake, S. Dak., U.S., 405 ....342/G4
White Lake, Wisc., U.S., 329 ....364/E4
White Lake N.W.R., N. Dak., U.S. 326/B3
White Lakes, N. Mex., U.S. 317/E2
Whiteland, Ind., U.S., 3,958 ....270/D5
Whitelaw, Alta., Can., 124 ....212/A3
Whitelaw, Wisc., U.S., 730 ....364/F4
Whiteman, P.N.G., *range* 172/A2

White Marsh, Md., U.S., 8,485 ....288/J2
White Marsh, Va., U.S., 600 ....354/K6
White Marsh Island, Ga., U.S., 5,824 ....260/J7
White Meadow Lake, N.J., U.S., 9,052 ....314/D2
White Mountain, Alaska, U.S., 203 ....240/C2
White Mtn. Natl. For., Maine, U.S. 286/A4
White Mtn. Natl. For., N.H., U.S. 312/C3, D2
White Mountains Natl. Rec. Area, Alaska, U.S. ..240/F1
Whitemouth, Man., Can. 215/D4
Whitemouth, Man., Can., *lake* 298/B1
White Nile, Sudan, *river* 145/C3
White Oak, Ga., U.S., 125 ....260/H9
White Oak, Ky., U.S., 125 ....280/C3
White Oak, Md., U.S., 20,973 ....288/B6
White Oak, Ohio, U.S., 13,277 ....328/A9
White Oak, Penn., U.S., 8,437 ....336/E7
White Oak, S.C., U.S., 40 ....340/C2
White Oak, Tex., U.S., 5,624 ....346/P3
White Oaks, N. Mex., U.S. 317/E4
White Owl, S. Dak., U.S. 342/C3
White Pigeon, Mich., U.S., 1,627 ....294/D8
White Pine, Mich., U.S., 700 ....294/D2
White Pine, Mont., U.S., 70 ....306/A2
White Pine, Nev., U.S., *county*, 9,181 ......310/C2
White Pine, Tenn., U.S., 1,997 ....344/Q2
White Plains, Ga., U.S., 283 ....260/E5
White Plains, Ky., U.S., 800 ....280/C3
White Plains, Md., U.S., 3,600 ....288/G5
White Plains, N.Y., U.S., 53,077 ....320/C1
White Plains, N.C., U.S., 1,049 ....322/D4
White Pt. Beach, Md., U.S., 200 ....288/H7
Whiterashes, Scot., U.K. 62/M4
Whiteriver, Ariz., U.S., 5,220 ....242/F4
White River, S. Dak., U.S., 598 ....342/E4
White River Jct., Vt., U.S., 2,569 ....352/C3
White River Natl. For., Colo., U.S. 250/C2, D2
White River N.W.R., Ark., U.S. 244/D3
White Rock, Br. Col., Can., 18,250 ....214/L6
White Rock, Minn., U.S., 90 ....298/E6
White Rock, (Los Alamos County),
   N. Mex., U.S., 6,045 ....317/D2
White Rock, (San Juan County), N. Mex., U.S. .317/B1
White Rock, S. Dak., U.S. 342/J2
Whiterocks, Utah, U.S., 341 ....350/E3
White Rocks N.R.A., Vt., U.S. 352/B4
White Roding, Eng., U.K. 70/E3
White Salmon, Wash., U.S., 2,193 ....358/D4
White Sands, P.E.I., Can. 224/C3
White Sands, N. Mex., U.S. 317/D5
White Sands Missile Range, N. Mex., U.S. 317/D4
White Sands Natl. Mon., N. Mex., U.S. 317/D5
Whitesbog, N.J., U.S., 70 ....314/D4
Whitesboro, N.J., U.S., 1,836 ....314/D5
Whitesboro, N.Y., U.S., 3,943 ....320/H4
Whitesboro, Okla., U.S., 70 ....330/H3
Whitesboro, Tex., U.S., 3,760 ....346/M2
Whites Brook, N.B., Can., 158 ....217/B1
Whitesburg, Ga., U.S., 596 ....260/B5
Whitesburg, Ky., U.S., 1,600 ....280/H3
Whites City, N. Mex., U.S., 40 ....317/F5
White Settlement, Tex., U.S., 14,831 ....346/A10
Whiteshell Prov. Park, Man., Can. 215/D4
White Shield, N. Dak., U.S., 348 ....326/D2
Whiteside, Ill., U.S., *county*, 60,653 ......266/D2
Whiteside, Mo., U.S., 67 ....302/E2
White Signal, N. Mex., U.S. 317/B5
White Sprs., Fla., U.S., 819 ....256/F1
Whitestone, Yukon, Can., *river* 228/B3
White Stone, Va., U.S., 358 ....354/L5
Whitestown, Ind., U.S., 471 ....270/D5
White Sulphur Sprs., Mont., U.S., 984 ....306/F3
White Sulphur Sprs., W. Va., U.S., 2,315 .....360/F5
Whitesville, Del., U.S., 125 ....255/D7
Whitesville, Ky., U.S., 632 ....280/D3
Whitesville, N.Y., U.S., 400 ....320/F6
Whitesville, Vt., U.S. 352/B4
Whitesville, W. Va., U.S., 520 ....360/C5
White Swan, Wash., U.S., 3,033 ....358/E3
Whitetail, Mont., U.S. 306/L1
Whitethorn, Calif., U.S. 246/B2
Whitetop, Va., U.S., 125 ....354/F7
Whiteville, Ind., U.S., 80 ....282/E5
Whiteville, N.C., U.S., 5,148 ....322/H6
Whiteville, Tenn., U.S., 3,148 ....344/C4
White Volta, Burkina, *river* 151/D2
White Volta, Gha., *river* 150/B1
Whitewater, Colo., U.S., 50 ....250/B3
Whitewater, Ind., U.S., 78 ....270/G5
Whitewater, Ind., U.S., *river* 270/F6
Whitewater, Kans., U.S., 653 ....276/E4
Whitewater, Mo., U.S., 113 ....302/G4
Whitewater, Mont., U.S., 40 ....306/J1
Whitewater, (Grant County), N. Mex., U.S. 317/B5
Whitewater, (McKinley County), N. Mex., U.S. ..317/B2
Whitewater, Wisc., U.S., 13,437 ....364/E6
Whitewater Baldy, N. Mex., U.S., *peak* 317/B4
Whitewood, Sask., Can., 947 ....227/H10
Whitewood, S. Dak., U.S., 844 ....342/B3
Whitewood, S. Dak., U.S., *lake* 342/H3
Whitfield, Ala., U.S., 50 ....238/A3
Whitfield, Ga., U.S., *county*, 83,525 ....260/A2
Whitfield, Miss., U.S., 90 ....300/C4
Whithorn, Scot., U.K., 867 ....62/H9
Whiting, Ind., U.S., 5,137 ....270/B1
Whiting, Iowa, U.S., 707 ....274/B3
Whiting, Kans., U.S., 206 ....276/G2
Whiting, Maine, U.S., 430 ....286/H4
Whiting, N.J., U.S., 1,800 ....314/E4
Whiting, Vt., U.S. 352/A3
Whiting, Wisc., U.S., 1,760 ....364/D4
Whiting Bay, Scot., U.K. 62/F8
Whitingham, Vt., U.S. 352/B5
Whitinsville, Mass., U.S., 6,340 ....292/H4
Whitland, Wales, U.K., 1,518 ....64/B4
Whitlash, Mont., U.S. 306/E1
Whitley, Ind., U.S., *county*, 30,707 ....270/F2
Whitley, Ky., U.S., *county*, 35,865 ....280/F4
Whitley Bay, Eng., U.K., 33,335 ....66/F2
Whitley City, Ky., U.S., 1,111 ....280/F4
Whitley Row, Eng., U.K. 70/E4
Whitman, Mass., U.S., 13,882 ....292/L4
Whitman, Nebr., U.S. 308/C1
Whitman, N. Dak., U.S. 326/C1
Whitman, Wash., U.S., *county*, 40,740 ....358/H3
Whitman Mission Natl. Hist. Site, Wash., U.S. ..358/G3
Whitminster, Eng., U.K. 68/C6
Whitmire, S.C., U.S., 1,512 ....340/C2
Whitmore, Calif., U.S. 246/D2
Whitmore, Mich., U.S. 294/F7
Whitmore Lake, Mich., U.S., 6,574 ....294/F7
Whitmore Vil., Hawaii, U.S., 4,057 ....262/J2
Whitney, Ont., Can. 223/G2
Whitney, Calif., U.S., *mountain* 246/G6
Whitney, Eng., U.K. 68/A5
Whitney, Ida., U.S. 350/E4
Whitney, Nebr., U.S., 87 ....308/A1
Whitney, Tex., U.S., 1,833 ....346/L4
Whitney Pt., N.Y., U.S., 965 ....320/K6
Whitneyville, Maine, U.S., 262 ....286/E4
Whiton, Md., U.S. 288/N6
Whitsett, N.C., U.S., 686 ....322/F2

Whitsett, Tex., U.S., 50 ....346/K7
Whitstable, Eng., U.K., 28,907 ....70/G4
Whitstone, Eng., U.K. 73/D3
Whittemore, Iowa, U.S., 530 ....274/F1
Whittemore, Mich., U.S., 476 ....294/F5
Whitten, Iowa, U.S., 160 ....274/J3
Whittier, Alaska, U.S., 182 ....240/F2
Whittier, Calif., U.S., 83,680 ....246/D9
Whittier, N.H., U.S., 275 ....312/D4
Whittingham, Eng., U.K. 66/E2
Whittington, Eng., U.K., 2,350 ....66/C4
Whittington, Eng., U.K., 2,350 ....68/B4
Whittington, Ill., U.S., 250 ....266/E5
Whittlesey, Eng., U.K., 10,275 ....68/E4
Whittlesey, Eng., U.K., 10,275 ....70/D1
Whittlesey, Wisc., U.S., 125 ....364/C3
Whitton, Eng., U.K. 68/E3
Whitton, Wales, U.K. 64/C3
Whitwell, Eng., U.K., 4,016 ....68/E3
Whitwell, Tenn., U.S., 1,660 ....344/K4
Wholdaia, N.W. Terr., Can., *lake* 220/H4
Why, Ariz., U.S., 225 ....242/C5
Whyalla, S.A., Austl. 170/C3
Whycocomagh, N.S., Can. 221/F2
Whyte, Minn., U.S. 298/F3
Wiarton, Ont., Can., 2,349 ....223/D3
Wiay, Scot., U.K., *island* 62/B4
Wibaux, Mont., U.S., 567 ....306/M3
Wibaux, Mont., U.S., *county*, 1,068 ....306/M3
Wibtoft, Eng., U.K. 70/B2
Wichita, Kans., U.S., 344,284, (545,220 *metro*.) ..276/E4
Wichita, Kans., U.S., *county*, 2,531 ....276/A3
Wichita, Kans., U.S., *county*, 131,664 ......346/K2
Wichita Falls, Tex., U.S., 104,197,
   (140,518 *metro*.) 346/K2
Wick, Scot., U.K. 60/B1
Wick, Scot., U.K., 7,333 ....62/K2
Wick, Wales, U.K., 1,940 ....64/C4
Wick, W. Va., U.S., 500 ....360/E2
Wickenburg, Ariz., U.S., 5,082 ....242/C4
Wickersham, Wash., U.S., 125 ....358/C1
Wickes, Ark., U.S., 675 ....244/A3
Wickett, Tex., U.S., 455 ....346/F4
Wickford, Eng., U.K., 26,294 ....70/F3
Wickford, R.I., U.S., 1,900 ....339/D4
Wickham Market, Eng., U.K., 2,243 ....70/G2
Wickliffe, Ky., U.S., 794 ....280/A4
Wickliffe, Ohio, U.S., 13,484 ....328/H8
Wicklow, Ire., 7,007 ....78/C3
Wicklow, Ire., *county* 78/C2
Wicklow, Ire., *mountains* 78/C2
Wicklow Head, Ire., *cape* 78/D2
Wickwar, Eng., U.K. 73/H1
Wicomico, Md., U.S., *county*, 84,644 ....288/M6
Wicomico, Md., U.S., *river* 288/G6
Wicomico Church, Va., U.S., 250 ....354/L5
Widdrington, Eng., U.K. 66/E2
Widecombe in the Moor, Eng., U.K. 73/E3
Wideman, Ark., U.S., 40 ....244/D1
Widener, Ark., U.S., 335 ....244/E2
Widford, Eng., U.K. 70/E3
Widnes, Eng., U.K., 57,162 ....66/C6
Widnes, Eng., U.K., 57,162 ....68/B3
Wiederkehr Vil., Ark., U.S., 46 ....244/B2
Wielkopolskie, Pol., *province* 83/C2
Wien, Mo., U.S., 50 ....302/D2
Wiener Neustadt, Aus. 91/E3
Wien, Neustadt, Aus. 83/F3
Wieprz, Pol., *river* 83/F3
Wiesbaden, Ger., 268,716 ....86/B3
Wigan, Eng., U.K. 60/C3
Wigan, Eng., U.K., 85,819 ....66/C5
Wigan, Eng., U.K., 85,819 ....68/B2
Wigan, Eng., U.K., *unitary authority*, 301,417 ..66/C5
Wigan, Eng., U.K., *unitary authority*, 301,417 ..68/B3
Wiggins, Colo., U.S., 838 ....250/F1
Wiggins, (Leake County), Miss., U.S., 100 ....300/C3
Wiggins, (Stone County), Miss., U.S., 3,849 ..300/C5
Wiggington, Eng., U.K. 66/F
Wigginton, Eng., U.K. 70/B3
Wigglesworth, Eng., U.K. 66/D4
Wight, Eng., U.K., *island* 60/C4
Wigstthorpe, Eng., U.K. 70/D2
Wigston, Eng., U.K., 32,864 ....68/E4
Wigston, Eng., U.K., 32,864 ....70/B1
Wigton, Eng., U.K., 5,306 ....66/B3
Wigtown, Scot., U.K., 987 ....62/H9
Wikieup, Ariz., U.S. 242/B3
Wilbarger, Tex., U.S., *county*, 14,676 ......346/J2
Wilbarston, Eng., U.K. 68/F5
Wilber, Nebr., U.S., 1,761 ....308/H3
Wilberforce, Ont., Can. 223/G2
Wilberforce, Ohio, U.S., 1,579 ....328/C6
Wilberfoss, Eng., U.K. 66/F4
Wilbraham, Mass., U.S., 13,473 ....292/E4
Wilbur, Oreg., U.S., 125 ....334/C4
Wilbur, Wash., U.S., 914 ....358/G2
Wilbur Cross Parkway, Conn., U.S. 253/C4
Wilbur Park, Mo., U.S., 475 ....302/H3
Wilburton, Okla., U.S., 2,972 ....330/G3
Wilcox, Ala., U.S., *county*, 13,183 ....238/B4
Wilcox, Ga., U.S., *county*, 8,577 ....260/D7
Wilcox, Nebr., U.S., 360 ....308/E3
Wilcox, Penn., U.S., 500 ....336/D2
Wilcox, Wyo., U.S. 366/D1
Wildcat, Wyo., U.S. 366/D1
Wild Cherry, Ark., U.S. 244/C1
Wilder, Ida., U.S., 1,462 ....280/C1
Wilder, Ky., U.S., 2,624 ....280/C1
Wilder, Minn., U.S., 69 ....298/B7
Wilder, Tenn., U.S. 344/L2
Wilder, Vt., U.S., 1,636 ....352/C3
Wilderness, Mo., U.S., 40 ....302/E5
Wilderness, Va., U.S., 300 ....354/H4
Wild Horse, Colo., U.S. 250/G3
Wild Horse, Tex., U.S. 346/D4
Wildomar, Calif., U.S., 14,064 ....246/H9
Wildorado, Tex., U.S., 150 ....346/F9
Wild Rice, N. Dak., U.S., *river* 326/H3
Wildrose, N. Dak., U.S., 129 ....326/B1
Wild Rose, Wisc., U.S., 765 ....364/D4
Wildwood, Calif., U.S. 246/B2
Wildwood, Fla., U.S., 3,924 ....256/C4
Wildwood, Ky., U.S., 247 ....280/B2
Wildwood, N.J., U.S., 5,436 ....314/D6
Wildwood, Tex., U.S., 550 ....346/P5
Wildwood Crest, N.J., U.S., 3,980 ....314/D6
Wiley, Colo., U.S., 483 ....250/H3
Wiley, Okla., U.S. 330/J1
Wiley City, Wash., U.S. 358/E3
Wiley Ford, W. Va., U.S., 1,095 ....360/J1
Wilge, S. Afr., *river* 162/C2
Wilhelm, P.N.G., *mountain* 172/A2
Wilhelmina, Neth., *canal* 84/B3
Wilhelmina Rise, Hawaii, U.S. 262/G2
Wilhelmshaven, Ger. 86/B2
Wilhoit, Ariz., U.S., 664 ....242/C3
Wilkes, Ga., U.S., *county*, 10,687 ....260/F4
Wilkes, N.C., U.S., *county*, 65,632 ....322/C2
Wilkes-Barre, Penn., U.S., 43,123 ....336/G7, K3

Wilkesboro, N.C., U.S., 3,159 ....322/C2
Wilkes Land, Antar., *region* 192/C3
Wilkeson, Wash., U.S., 395 ....358/C2
Wilkesville, Ohio, U.S., 151 ....328/F7
Wilkhaven, Scot., U.K. 62/J3
Wilkie, Sask., Can., 1,282 ....227/B3
Wilkin, Minn., U.S., *county*, 7,138 ....298/A4
Wilkins, Nev., U.S. 310/C1
Wilkinsburg, Penn., U.S., 19,196 ....336/E7
Wilkinson, Ga., U.S., *county*, 10,220 ....260/E6
Wilkinson, Ind., U.S., 356 ....270/E5
Wilkinson, Minn., U.S., 50 ....298/C3
Wilkinson, Miss., U.S., 125 ....300/A4
Wilkinson, Miss., U.S., *county*, 10,312 .....300/A4
Wilkinson Hts., S.C., U.S., 3,068 ....340/D3
Will, Ill., U.S., *county*, 502,266 ....266/B6, E2
Willacoochee, Ga., U.S., 1,434 ....260/E9
Willacy, Tex., U.S., *county*, 20,082 ....346/L9
Willaha, Ariz., U.S. 242/C2
Willamar, Tex., U.S. 346/L9
Willamette, Oreg., U.S., *river* 334/A2, C3
Willamette Natl. For., Oreg., U.S. 334/D3
Willamina, Oreg., U.S., 1,844 ....334/D3
Willand, Eng., U.K., 2,232 ....73/F3
Willapa, Wash., U.S., *bay* 358/B3
Willapa N.W.R., Wash., U.S. 358/B3
Willard, Colo., U.S. 250/G1
Willard, Kans., U.S., 86 ....276/G2
Willard, Ky., U.S., 90 ....280/H2
Willard, Mo., U.S., 3,193 ....302/C4
Willard, Mont., U.S., 50 ....306/M3
Willard, N. Mex., U.S., 240 ....317/D3
Willard, N.C., U.S., 300 ....322/K5
Willard, Ohio, U.S., 6,806 ....328/E3
Willard, Utah, U.S., 1,630 ....350/B2
Willard, Wisc., U.S., 100 ....364/C4
Willards, Md., U.S., 938 ....288/N6
Willcox, Ariz., U.S., 3,733 ....242/F5
Willcox Playa Bombing Range, Ariz., U.S. 242/F5
Willemstad, Neth. Ant., *capital*, 123,000 ...204/D4
Willenhall, Eng., U.K. 68/E5
Willernie, Minn., U.S., 549 ....298/F5
Willette, Tenn., U.S., 100 ....344/K2
Willey, Eng., U.K. 70/B2
Willey, Iowa, U.S., 103 ....274/E4
Willey House, N.H., U.S. 312/D3
William, Sask., Can., *river* 227/B2
William B. Bankhead Natl. For., Ala., U.S. ...238/B1
William Bill Dannelly, Ala., U.S., *reservoir* ..238/B3
William H. Taft N.H.S., Ohio, U.S. 329/B10
William L. Finley N.W.R., Oreg., U.S. 334/C3
Williams, Ariz., U.S., 2,842 ....242/C2
Williams, Calif., U.S., 3,670 ....246/C3
Williams, Ind., U.S., 275 ....270/C7
Williams, Iowa, U.S., 427 ....274/G3
Williams, Minn., U.S., 210 ....298/C2
Williams, N. Dak., U.S., *county*, 19,761 ....326/B1
Williams, Ohio, U.S., *county*, 39,188 ....328/B2
Williams, Oreg., U.S., 200 ....334/C5
Williams, S.C., U.S., 116 ....340/D4
Williams, Tex., U.S. 346/K3
Williams Bay, Wisc., U.S., 2,415 ....364/E6
Williamsburg, N.B., Can. 217/C2
Williamsburg, Colo., U.S., 714 ....250/E3
Williamsburg, Iowa, U.S., 2,622 ....274/L4
Williamsburg, Kans., U.S., 351 ....276/F3
Williamsburg, Ky., U.S., 5,143 ....280/F4
Williamsburg, Md., U.S., 60 ....288/L5
Williamsburg, Mass., U.S., 2,427 ....292/D3
Williamsburg, Mich., U.S., 350 ....294/D5
Williamsburg, Miss., U.S., 90 ....300/C4
Williamsburg, N. Mex., U.S., 527 ....317/C4
Williamsburg, Ohio, U.S., 2,358 ....328/B6
Williamsburg, Penn., U.S., 1,345 ....336/E6
Williamsburg, S.C., U.S., *county*, 37,217 ...340/E3
Williamsburg, Va., U.S., 11,998 ....354/K6
Williams Creek, Ind., U.S., 413 ....270/C4
Williamsfield, Ill., U.S., 620 ....266/C3
Williams Harbour, Nfld., Can., 61 ....218/D3
Williams Lake, Br. Col., Can., 11,153 ....214/L5
Williamson, Ga., U.S., 297 ....260/C5
Williamson, Ill., U.S., 251 ....266/B3
Williamson, Ill., U.S., *county*, 61,296 .....266/E6
Williamson, Iowa, U.S., 163 ....274/H5
Williamson, N.Y., U.S., 2,100 ....320/G4
Williamson, Tenn., U.S., *county*, 126,638 ...344/H3
Williamson, Tex., U.S., *county*, 249,967 ....346/D2, L5
Williamson, W. Va., U.S., 3,414 ....360/B5
Williamsport, Nfld., Can. 218/C4
Williamsport, Ind., U.S., 1,935 ....270/B4
Williamsport, Md., U.S., 1,868 ....288/C1
Williamsport, (Morrow County), Ohio, U.S. 328/E3
Williamsport, (Pickaway County), Ohio, U.S.,
   1,002 ....328/D6
Williamsport, Penn., U.S., 30,706,
   (120,044 *metro*.) 336/G3
Williamston, Mich., U.S., 3,441 ....294/E7
Williamston, N.C., U.S., 5,843 ....322/L3
Williamston, S.C., U.S., 3,791 ....340/B2
Williamstown, Kans., U.S. 276/G2
Williamstown, Ky., U.S., 3,227 ....280/F2
Williamstown, Mass., U.S., 8,424 ....292/C2
Williamstown, Mo., U.S., 100 ....302/E1
Williamstown, N.J., U.S., 11,812 ....314/D4
Williamstown, N.Y., U.S., 475 ....320/K4
Williamstown, Vt., U.S. 352/B2
Williamstown, W. Va., U.S., 2,996 ....360/D2
Williamsville, (Kent County), Del., U.S., 300 ..255/B5
Williamsville, (Sussex County), Del., U.S., 300 ..255/D7
Williamsville, Ill., U.S., 1,439 ....266/D4
Williamsville, Mass., U.S., 225 ....292/F4
Williamsville, Mo., U.S., 379 ....302/F5
Williamsville, N.Y., U.S., 5,573 ....320/D5
Williamsville, Vt., U.S., 200 ....352/B5
Williamsville, Va., U.S. 354/D4
Williford, Ark., U.S., 63 ....244/D1
Willimantic, Conn., U.S., 15,823 ....253/G3
Willimantic, Maine, U.S., 135 ....286/C3
Willingboro, N.J., U.S., 33,008 ....314/D3
Willingdon, Alta., Can., 287 ....212/D4
Willingdon, Eng., U.K. 70/E5
Willingham, Eng., U.K., 3,317 ....68/H5
Willingham, Eng., U.K., 3,317 ....70/E2
Willingham by Stow, Eng., U.K. 66/G4
Willington, Eng., U.K., 4,913 ....66/E3
Willington, Eng., U.K., 2,292 ....66/E3
Willington, Eng., U.K., 2,292 ....70/A1
Williows, Md., U.S. 288/N6
Willis, Kans., U.S., 69 ....276/G2
Willis, Tex., U.S., 3,985 ....346/N5
Willis, Va., U.S., 100 ....354/C7
Willisburg, Ky., U.S., 304 ....280/E3
Williston, Br. Col., Can., *lake* 214/K3
Williston, Fla., U.S., 2,297 ....256/F2
Williston, Md., U.S., 425 ....288/L4
Williston, N. Dak., U.S., 12,512 ....326/B1
Williston, Ohio, U.S., 800 ....328/D2
Williston, S.C., U.S., 3,307 ....340/C3

Williston, Tenn., U.S., 341 344/C4
Williston, Vt., U.S. 352/A2
Willisville, Ark., U.S., 188 244/B4
Willisville, Ill., U.S., 694 266/D6
Williton, Eng., U.K., 2,025 73/F2
Willits, Calif., U.S., 5,073 246/B3
Willmar, Minn., U.S., 18,351 298/B5
Willmore Wilderness Park, Alta., Can. 212/A4
Willmore Wilderness Prov. Pk., Alta., Can. 214/N4
Willoughby, Ant.-Bar., *bay* 207/E5
Willoughby, N.S.W., Austl. 170/Inset IV
Willoughby, Ohio, U.S., 22,621 328/H8
Willoughby, Vt., U.S., *lake* 352/C1
Willoughby Hills, Ohio, U.S., 8,595 328/H8
Willow, Ark., U.S., 50 244/C3
Willow, Okla., U.S., 114 330/C2
Willow, Wisc., U.S., *reservoir* 364/D3
Willow Beach, Ariz., U.S. 242/A2
Willowbrook, Calif., U.S., 34,138 246/C10
Willowbrook, Ill., U.S., 8,967 266/B6
Willowbrook, Kans., U.S. 276/E3
Willow Bunch, Sask., Can., 395 227/E11
Willowbunch, Sask., Can., *lake* 227/E11
Willow City, N. Dak., U.S., 221 326/E1
Willow City, Tex., U.S. 346/K5
Willow Creek, Sask., Can. 227/A11
Willow Creek, Calif., U.S., 1,743 246/B2
Willow Creek, Mont., U.S., 209 306/E4
Willow Creek, Oreg., U.S., 125 334/J3
Willowdale, Kans., U.S., 50 276/D4
Willowdale, Oreg., U.S. 334/F3
Willow Glen, La., U.S., 175 282/E4
Willow Grove, Penn., U.S., 16,234 336/M6
Willow Hill, Ill., U.S., 250 266/E5
Willowick, Ohio, U.S., 14,361 328/H8
Willow Island, Nebr., U.S. 308/D3
Willow Lake, S. Dak., U.S., 294 342/H3
Willow Lake N.W.R., N. Dak., U.S. 326/E1
Willow River, Minn., U.S., 309 298/E4
Willows, Calif., U.S., 6,220 246/C3
Willow Sprs., Ill., U.S., 5,027 266/B6
Willow Sprs., Mo., U.S., 2,147 302/E4
Willow Street, Penn., U.S., 7,258 336/J6
Willshire, Ohio, U.S., 463 328/A4
Wills Pt., Tex., U.S., 3,496 346/M3
Willwood, Wyo., U.S., 100 366/B1
Wilma, Fla., U.S. 256/D1
Wilmar, Ark., U.S., 571 244/D4
Wilmer, Ala., U.S., 500 238/A5
Wilmer, La., U.S., 60 282/J5
Wilmer, Tex., U.S., 3,393 346/C10
Wilmerding, Penn., U.S., 2,145 336/E7
Wilmeth, Tex., U.S. 346/H4
Wilmette, Ill., U.S., 27,651 266/B5
Wilmington, Del., U.S., 72,664 255/B1
Wilmington, Ill., U.S., 5,134 266/E2
Wilmington, Mass., U.S., 21,363 292/C6, K2
Wilmington, N.C., U.S., 75,838, (233,450 *metro.*) 322/K6
Wilmington, Ohio, U.S., 11,921 328/C7
Wilmington, Vt., U.S. 352/B5
Wilmington Island, Ga., U.S., 14,213 260/K7
Wilmington Manor, Del., U.S., 8,262 255/B2
Wilmont, Minn., U.S., 332 298/B7
Wilmore, Kans., U.S., 57 276/C4
Wilmore, Ky., U.S., 5,905 280/F3
Wilmore, Penn., U.S., 252 336/D5
Wilmot, N.S., Can. 221/B3
Wilmot, Ark., U.S., 786 244/D4
Wilmot, Kans., U.S., 60 276/F4
Wilmot, N.H., U.S., 1,144 312/C5
Wilmot, Ohio, U.S., 335 328/G4
Wilmot, S. Dak., U.S., 543 342/J2
Wilmot Flat, N.H., U.S. 312/C5
Wilmslow, Eng., U.K., 28,604 66/D6
Wilmslow, Eng., U.K., 28,604 68/C3
Wilno, Minn., U.S. 298/A6
Wilsall, Mont., U.S., 237 306/F4
Wilsey, Kans., U.S., 191 276/F3
Wilshamstead, Eng., U.K., 2,188 68/F5
Wilshamstead, Eng., U.K., 2,188 70/D2
Wilson, Ala., U.S., *lake* 238/B1
Wilson, Ark., U.S., 939 244/E2
Wilson, Colo., U.S., *mountain* 250/B4
Wilson, Kans., U.S., 799 276/D3
Wilson, Kans., U.S., *county*, 10,332 276/G4
Wilson, Kans., U.S., *lake* 276/D3
Wilson, La., U.S., 668 282/G5
Wilson, Minn., U.S., 100 298/F7
Wilson, N.Y., U.S., 1,213 320/D4
Wilson, N.C., U.S., 44,405 322/K3
Wilson, N.C., U.S., *county*, 73,814 322/K3
Wilson, Ohio, U.S., 118 328/H6
Wilson, Okla., U.S., 1,584 330/E3
Wilson, Penn., U.S., 7,682 336/L4
Wilson, Tenn., U.S., *county*, 88,809 344/J2
Wilson, Tex., U.S., 532 346/G2
Wilson, Tex., U.S., *county*, 32,408 346/B3, K6
Wilson, Wisc., U.S., 176 364/A4
Wilson, Wyo., U.S., 1,294 366/A2
Wilson City, Mo., U.S., 165 302/G5
Wilson Creek, Wash., U.S., 227 358/F2
Wilsonia, Calif., U.S., 50 246/G6
Wilsons, Va., U.S., 100 354/H6
Wilsons Beach, N.B., Can. 217/C4
Wilson's Creek Natl. Bfld., Mo., U.S. 302/C4
Wilsons Mills, Maine, U.S. 286/A4
Wilsonville, Ala., U.S., 1,551 238/C2
Wilsonville, Ill., U.S., 604 266/B3
Wilsonville, Nebr., U.S., 118 308/D3
Wilsonville, Oreg., U.S., 13,991 334/D2
Wilton, Eng., U.K., 3,717 73/J2
Wilton, Ala., U.S., 580 238/C2
Wilton, Ark., U.S., 439 244/A4
Wilton, Calif., U.S., 4,551 246/K5, L1
Wilton, Conn., U.S., 17,633 253/B5
Wilton, Iowa, U.S., 2,829 274/M4
Wilton, Maine, U.S., 4,123 286/B4
Wilton, Minn., U.S., 186 298/C3
Wilton, Mo., U.S., 70 302/D3
Wilton, N.H., U.S., 3,743 312/C6
Wilton, N.C., U.S., 125 322/H2
Wilton, N. Dak., U.S., 807 326/E2
Wilton, Wisc., U.S., 519 364/C5
Wilton Ctr., Ill., U.S., 125 266/F2
Wilton Ctr., N.H., U.S. 312/C6
Wiltondale, Nfld., Can. 218/C4
Wilton Manors, Fla., U.S., 12,697 256/B6
Wiltshire, Eng., U.K., *unitary authority*, 432,973 73/J2
Wiltz, Lux. 85/A2
Wimauma, Fla., U.S., 4,246 256/D7
Wimberley, Tex., U.S., 3,797 346/D3
Wimbleball, Eng., U.K., *lake* 73/E2
Wimbledon, Eng., U.K. 70/D4
Wimbledon, N. Dak., U.S., 237 326/G2
Wimblington, Eng., U.K. 70/E1
Wimborne Minster, Eng., U.K., 15,274 73/H3
Winamac, Ind., U.S., 2,418 270/C2
Winborn, Miss., U.S. 300/C1
Wincanton, Eng., U.K., 3,973 73/H2
Winchcombe, Eng., U.K., 4,243 68/D6
Winchell, Tex., U.S., 40 346/J4
Winchelsea, Eng., U.K. 70/F5
Winchendon, Mass., U.S., 9,611 292/F2
Winchester, Ont., Can., 2,427 223/K2
Winchester, Eng., U.K. 60/C3
Winchester, Eng., U.K., 36,121 70/B4
Winchester, Ark., U.S., 191 244/D4
Winchester, Ida., U.S., 308 264/A3
Winchester, Ill., U.S., 1,650 266/C4
Winchester, Ind., U.S., 5,037 270/G4
Winchester, Kans., U.S., 579 276/G2
Winchester, Ky., U.S., 16,724 280/F3
Winchester, Mass., U.S., 20,810 292/C7, K3
Winchester, Miss., U.S., 50 300/D4
Winchester, Mo., U.S., 1,651 302/G3
Winchester, Nev., U.S., 26,958 310/C3
Winchester, N.H., U.S., 4,144 312/B6
Winchester, Ohio, U.S., 1,025 328/C8
Winchester, Okla., U.S., 424 330/G2
Winchester, Oreg., U.S., 275 334/C4
Winchester, Tenn., U.S., 7,329 344/J4
Winchester, Tex., U.S., 80 346/M6
Winchester, Va., U.S., 23,585 354/G2
Winchester, Wash., U.S., 70 358/F2
Winchester, Wisc., U.S., 100 364/D2
Winchester, Wyo., U.S., 60 366/B2
Winchester Bay, Oreg., U.S., 488 334/B4
Winchester Ctr., Conn., U.S., 275 253/C2
Wind, Yukon, Can., *river* 228/B3
Wind, Wyo., U.S., *river* 366/B2
Windber, Penn., U.S., 4,395 336/D5
Wind Cave Natl. Park, S. Dak., U.S. 342/B4
Windcrest, Tex., U.S., 5,105 346/A2
Windemere, N.C., U.S. 322/K6
Windemere, Tex., U.S., 6,868 346/D2
Winder, Ga., U.S., 10,201 260/D4
Windermere, Br. Col., Can., 1,060 214/O6
Windermere, Ont., Can. 223/F2
Windermere, Eng., U.K., 6,847 66/C4
Windermere, Eng., U.K., *lake* 66/C4
Windermere, Fla., U.S., 1,897 256/C4
Windfall, Alta., Can. 212/B4
Windfall, Ind., U.S., 712 270/E4
Wind Gap, Penn., U.S., 2,812 336/L4
Windham, Conn., U.S., 22,857 253/G3
Windham, Conn., U.S., *county*, 109,091 253/G2
Windham, Mont., U.S., 50 306/F2
Windham, N.H., U.S., 10,709 312/D6
Windham, Ohio, U.S., 2,806 328/H3
Windham, Vt., U.S. 352/B4
Windham, Vt., U.S., *county*, 44,216 352/B4
Windham Depot, N.H., U.S. 312/D6
Windham Sprs., Ala., U.S., 100 238/B2
Windhoek, Nam., *capital*, 147,056 160/C2
Windhorst, Kans., U.S. 276/C4
Winding Falls, Ky., U.S. 280/B2
Winding Stair N.R.A., Okla., U.S. 330/H3
Wind Lake, Wisc., U.S., 5,202 364/F2
Windlesham, Eng., U.K., 4,109 70/C4
Windom, Kans., U.S., 137 276/E3
Windom, Minn., U.S., 4,490 298/B7
Window Rock, Ariz., U.S., 3,059 242/F2
Wind Pt., Wisc., U.S., 1,853 364/F6, G2
Wind Ridge, Penn., U.S., 90 336/A6
Wind River, Wyo., U.S., *range* 366/B2
Wind River Ind. Res., Wyo., U.S. 366/B2
Windrush, Eng., U.K. 68/D6
Windsor, N.B., Can. 217/B2
Windsor, N.S., Can., 3,778 221/C3
Windsor, Ont., Can., 208,402, (319,900 *metro.*) 222/D4
Windsor, Ont., Can., 208,402, (319,900 *metro.*) 223/C5
Windsor, Que., Can., 5,321 226/D6
Windsor, (Windsor/Eton), Eng., U.K., 30,136 70/C4
Windsor, Eng., U.K. 60/Inset III
Windsor, Calif., U.S., 22,744 246/C4
Windsor, Colo., U.S., 9,896 250/F1
Windsor, Conn., U.S., 28,237 253/E2
Windsor, Ill., U.S., 1,125 266/E4
Windsor, Mass., U.S., 875 292/B2
Windsor, Mo., U.S., 3,087 302/C3
Windsor, N.Y., U.S., 901 320/K6
Windsor, N.C., U.S., 2,283 322/M3
Windsor, Penn., U.S., 1,331 336/H6
Windsor, S.C., U.S., 127 340/C3
Windsor, Vt., U.S. 352/C4
Windsor, Vt., U.S., *county*, 57,418 352/B3
Windsor, Va., U.S., 916 354/K7
Windsor and Maidenhead, Eng., U.K., *unitary authority*, 133,606 70/C4
Windsor Hts., Iowa, U.S., 4,805 274/G4
Windsor Hts., W. Va., U.S., 431 360/K5
Windsor Locks, Conn., U.S., 12,043 253/E2
Windthorst, Tex., U.S., 440 346/K2
Windward, *islands* 204/F4
Windward, *passage* 204/C3
Windward, Cuba, *passage* 204/F3
Windward, Haiti, *passage* 205/B1
Windward, St. Vin.-Gren., *islands* 208/B4
Windward Group, C.V. 148/B2
Windy Hills, Ky., U.S., 2,480 280/B2
Windyville, Mo., U.S. 302/D4
Winefred, Alta., Can., *lake* 212/E3
Winegars, Mich., U.S., 50 294/E6
Winema Natl. For., Oreg., U.S. 334/E4
Winfall, N.C., U.S., 554 322/N2
Winfield, Br. Col., Can. 214/N6
Winfield, Ala., U.S., 4,540 238/B2
Winfield, Fla., U.S., 225 256/F1
Winfield, Ill., U.S., 8,718 266/A6
Winfield, Ind., U.S., 2,298 270/B2
Winfield, Iowa, U.S., 1,131 274/M5
Winfield, Kans., U.S., 12,206 276/F4
Winfield, Mo., U.S., 723 302/F2
Winfield, Tenn., U.S., 911 344/N1
Winfield, Tex., U.S., 499 346/N2
Winfield, W. Va., U.S., 1,858 360/C3
Winfred, S. Dak., U.S., 50 342/H4
Wing, Eng., U.K., 2,805 70/C3
Wing, Ala., U.S., 50 238/C4
Wing, Ill., U.S., 80 266/E3
Wing, N. Dak., U.S., 124 326/E2
Wingate, Eng., U.K., 4,541 66/F3
Wingate, Ind., U.S., 299 270/B4
Wingate, N.C., U.S., 2,406 322/E5
Winger, Minn., U.S., 205 298/B3
Wingham, Ont., Can., 2,885 223/D4
Wingham, Eng., U.K., 1,553 70/G4
Wingina, Va., U.S. 354/F5
Wingo, Ky., U.S., 581 280/B4
Winifred, Kans., U.S. 276/F2
Winifred, Mont., U.S., 156 306/G2
Winigan, Mo., U.S. 302/D1
Winisk, Ont., Can. 222/C1
Winisk, Ont., Can., *lake* 222/C2
Winisk, Ont., Can., *river* 222/C2
Wink, Tex., U.S., 919 346/E4
Winkelman, Ariz., U.S., 443 242/E5
Winkle, Ohio, U.S. 328/C7
Winkleigh, Eng., U.K. 73/E3
Winkler, Man., Can., 7,943 215/C4
Winkler, Tex., U.S., *county*, 7,173 346/E4
Winlock, Wash., U.S., 1,166 358/C3
Winn, La., U.S., *parish*, 16,894 282/D3
Winn, Maine, U.S., 420 286/D3
Winn, Mich., U.S., 275 294/E6
Winnabow, N.C., U.S., 125 322/J6
Winneba, Gha. 150/B4
Winnebago, Ill., U.S., 2,958 266/D1
Winnebago, Ill., U.S., *county*, 278,418 266/D1
Winnebago, Iowa, U.S., *county*, 11,723 274/G1
Winnebago, Minn., U.S., 1,487 298/C7
Winnebago, Nebr., U.S., 768 308/H1
Winnebago, Wisc., U.S., *county*, 156,763 364/E4
Winnebago, Wisc., U.S., *lake* 364/E4
Winnebago Ind. Res., Nebr., U.S. 308/H1
Winneconne, Wisc., U.S., 2,401 364/E4
Winnecook, Mont., U.S., 40 306/G3
Winnecunnet, Mass., U.S., 750 292/K5
Winnemucca, Nev., U.S., 7,174 310/B1
Winnemucca, Nev., U.S., *lake* 310/A1
Winner, S. Dak., U.S., 3,137 342/F4
Winneshiek, Iowa, U.S., *county*, 21,310 274/L1
Winnetka, Ill., U.S., 12,419 266/B5
Winnetoon, Nebr., U.S., 70 308/G1,
Winnett, Mont., U.S., 185 306/H2,
Winnfield, La., U.S., 5,749 282/D3,
Winnibigoshish, Minn., U.S., *lake* 298/D3,
Winnipeg, Man., Can., 619,544, (685,500 *metro.*) 215/C4, D2
Winnipeg, Man., Can., *lake* 215/B3, C4, D2
Winnipeg, Man., Can., *river* 215/D4,
Winnipeg Beach, Man., Can., 801 215/C4,
Winnipegosis, Man., Can., 621 215/B3,
Winnipegosis, Man., Can., *lake* 215/A3,
Winnipesaukee, N.H., U.S., *lake* 312/D4,
Winnisquam, N.H., U.S., 850 312/C4,
Winnisquam, N.H., U.S., *lake* 312/C4,
Winnsboro, La., U.S., 5,344 282/F2,
Winnsboro, S.C., U.S., 3,599 340/C2,
Winnsboro, Tex., U.S., 3,584 346/N3,
Winnsboro Mills, S.C., U.S., 2,263 340/C2
Winokur, Ga., U.S. 260/G9
Winona, Ariz., U.S. 242/D2
Winona, Kans., U.S., 228 276/A2
Winona, Mich., U.S. 294/A3
Winona, Minn., U.S., 27,069 298/F6
Winona, Minn., U.S., *county*, 49,985 298/F7
Winona, Miss., U.S., 5,482 300/C2
Winona, Mo., U.S., 1,290 302/E4
Winona, N.H., U.S., 150 312/C4
Winona, Ohio, U.S., 475 328/J4
Winona, Tex., U.S., 582 346/N3
Winona, Wash., U.S., 40 358/H3
Winona Lake, Ind., U.S., 3,987 270/E2
Winooski, Vt., U.S. 352/A1
Winsford, Eng., U.K., 26,839 68/B3
Winsford, Eng., U.K., 26,839 73/E2
Winside, Nebr., U.S., 468 308/G1
Winslow, Eng., U.K., 4,005 68/F6
Winslow, Eng., U.K., 4,005 70/C3
Winslow, Ariz., U.S., 9,520 242/E2
Winslow, Ark., U.S., 399 244/A2
Winslow, Ill., U.S., 345 266/D1
Winslow, Ind., U.S., 881 270/B8
Winslow, Maine, U.S., 7,743 286/C4
Winslow, Nebr., U.S., 104 308/H2
Winslow, N.J., U.S., 34,611 314/D4
Winsted, Conn., U.S., 7,321 253/C2
Winsted, Minn., U.S., 2,094 298/C6
Winster, Eng., U.K. 68/D3
Winston, Ala., U.S., *county*, 24,843 238/B1
Winston, Miss., U.S., *county*, 20,160 300/C2
Winston, Mo., U.S., 247 302/B2
Winston, Mont., U.S., 73 306/E3
Winston, N. Mex., U.S. 317/C4
Winston, Oreg., U.S., 4,613 334/C4
Winston-Salem, N.C., U.S., 185,776 322/E2
Winstonville, Miss., U.S., 319 300/B2
Winter, Wisc., U.S., 344 364/B3
Winter Beach, Fla., U.S., 965 256/H4
Winterboro, Ala., U.S., 150 238/C2
Winterbourne, (County Avon), Eng., U.K. 73/G1
Winterbourne, (County Wiltshire), Eng., U.K. 73/H2
Winterbourne, Eng., U.K., 2,241 70/B4
Winter Garden, Fla., U.S., 14,351 256/C4, G3
Winter Harbor, Maine, U.S., 988 286/D4
Winter Harbour, Br. Col., Can. 214/H6
Winter Haven, Fla., U.S., 26,487 256/G3
Winter Haven, Tex., U.S. 346/J7
Winteringham, Eng., U.K. 68/F2
Winter Park, Colo., U.S., 662 250/E2
Winter Park, Fla., U.S., 24,090 256/D4, G3
Winterpock, Va., U.S., 125 354/H6
Winterport, Maine, U.S., 3,602 286/D4
Winters, Calif., U.S., 6,125 246/D4
Winters, Tex., U.S., 2,880 346/J4
Wintersburg, Ariz., U.S., 125 242/C4
Winterset, Iowa, U.S., 4,768 274/F5
Winter Sprs., Fla., U.S., 31,666 256/D4
Winterstown, Penn., U.S., 546 336/H6
Wintersville, Ohio, U.S., 4,067 328/J5
Winterthur, Switz., 89,612, (118,152 *metro.*) 90/C1
Winterton, Eng., U.K., 4,895 66/G5
Winterton, Eng., U.K., 4,895 68/F2
Winterville, Ga., U.S., 1,068 260/E4
Winterville, Maine, U.S., 196 286/D2
Winterville, Miss., U.S., 175 300/A2
Winterville, N.C., U.S., 4,791 322/L3
Winthrop, Ark., U.S., 186 244/A4
Winthrop, Conn., U.S., 400 253/F4
Winthrop, Iowa, U.S., 772 274/L3
Winthrop, Maine, U.S., 6,232 286/C4
Winthrop, Mass., U.S., 18,303 292/D7, L3
Winthrop, Minn., U.S., 1,367 298/C6
Winthrop, Wash., U.S., 349 358/E1
Winthrop Harbor, Ill., U.S., 6,670 266/B4
Winton, Calif., U.S., 8,832 246/E5
Winton, Minn., U.S., 185 298/F3
Winton, N.C., U.S., 956 322/M2
Winton, Wash., U.S. 358/E2
Winton, Wyo., U.S. 366/B3
Wintringham, Eng., U.K. 66/G4
Wiota, Iowa, U.S., 149 274/E5
Wiota, Wisc., U.S., 80 364/D6
Wirksworth, Eng., U.K., 4,235 68/D3
Wirral, Eng., U.K., *unitary authority*, 312,289 66/B6
Wirt, Minn., U.S. 298/D3
Wirt, W. Va., U.S., *county*, 5,873 360/D2
Wisbech, Eng., U.K., 24,981 68/H4
Wisbech, Eng., U.K., 24,981 70/E1
Wisbech St. Mary, Eng., U.K. 70/E1
Wisborough Green, Eng., U.K. 70/C4
Wiscasset, Maine, U.S., 3,603 286/C5
Wisconsin, U.S., *state* 352
Wisconsin, Wisc., U.S., *river* 274/N1
Wisconsin, Wisc., U.S., *river* 364/C5
Wisconsin, Wisc., U.S., *river* 364/D3
Wisconsin Dells, Wisc., U.S., 2,418 364/D5
Wisconsin Rapids, Wisc., U.S., 18,435 364/D4
Wisdom, Mont., U.S., 114 306/C4
Wise, N.C., U.S., 250 322/J2
Wise, Tex., U.S., *county*, 48,793 346/A9, L2
Wise, Va., U.S., 3,255 354/C2
Wise, Va., U.S., *county*, 40,123 354/C2
Wise River, Mont., U.S., 60 306/D4
Wishart Pt., N.B., Can. 217/E1
Wishek, N. Dak., U.S., 1,122 326/F3
Wishram, Wash., U.S., 324 358/E4
Wismar, Ger. 86/B2
Wisner, La., U.S., 1,140 282/F3
Wisner, Mich., U.S., 200 294/F6
Wisner, Nebr., U.S., 1,270 308/H2
Wistaston, Eng., U.K. 68/C3
Wister, Okla., U.S., 1,002 330/H3
Witchampton, Eng., U.K. 73/H3
Witch Lake, Mich., U.S., 60 294/A3
Witco, Tex., U.S. 346/G4
Witham, Eng., U.K., 22,684 70/F3
Withamsville, Ohio, U.S., 3,145 328/C10
Withee, Wisc., U.S., 508 364/C4
Witherbee, N.Y., U.S., 1,747 320/P2
Withern, Eng., U.K. 66/J6
Withernsea, Eng., U.K., 6,433 66/J5
Withernsea, Eng., U.K., 6,433 68/H2
Withington, Eng., U.K. 68/B5
Withington, N. Mex., U.S., *mountain* 317/C4
Withlacoochee, Fla., U.S., *river* 256/E1
Withlacoochee, Ga., U.S., *river* 260/E10
Withrow, Wash., U.S. 358/F2
Witjira Natl. Park, Austl. 170/C2
Witless Bay, Nfld., Can., 1,056 218/E5
Witley, Eng., U.K. 70/C4
Witney, Eng., U.K., 20,377 68/E6
Witney, Eng., U.K., 20,377 70/B3
Witoka, Minn., U.S., 100 298/F7
Witt, Ill., U.S., 991 266/D4
Witt, Tenn., U.S., 500 344/Q2
Witten, Ger., 103,384 86/A3
Witten, S. Dak., U.S., 51 342/E4
Wittenberg, Ger. 86/C3
Wittenberg, Mo., U.S. 302/G4
Wittenberg, Wisc., U.S., 1,177 364/D4
Wittenberge, Ger. 86/B2
Witter, Ark., U.S., 40 244/B2
Wittering, Eng., U.K., 2,379 68/G4
Wittman, Md., U.S., 325 288/J4
Wittmann, Ariz., U.S., 550 242/C4
Witts Sprs., Ark., U.S., 40 244/C2
Witu, P.N.G., *islands* 172/A2
Wiveliscombe, Eng., U.K., 1,753 73/F2
Wivenhoe, Eng., U.K., 7,073 70/F3
Wiwili, Nicar. 202/B2
Wix, Eng., U.K. 70/G3
Wixom, Mich., U.S., 13,263 294/A6, F7
Wixom, Mich., U.S., *lake* 294/E6
Wixon Valley, Tex., U.S., 235 346/M5
W.J. van Blommestein, Sur., *lake* 183/B2
Władysławowo, Pol. 83/D1
Włocławek, Pol., 123,292 83/D2
Woburn, Que., Can. 226/F6
Woburn, Eng., U.K. 70/C3
Woburn, Mass., U.S., 37,258 292/C6, K3
Woburn Sands, Eng., U.K., 4,961 68/F5
Woburn Sands, Eng., U.K., 4,961 70/C2
Woden, Iowa, U.S., 243 274/G1
Wodzisław Śląski, Pol. 83/D3
Wofford, Ky., U.S., 375 280/F4
Wofford Hts., Calif., U.S., 2,276 246/G7
Woking, Alta., Can., 87 212/A3
Woking, (Woking/Byfleet), Eng., U.K., 98,138 70/C4
Wokingham, Eng., U.K., 38,063 70/C4
Wokingham, Eng., U.K., *unitary authority*, 150,257 70/C4
Wolbach, Nebr., U.S., 287 308/E2
Wolcott, Colo., U.S., 50 250/D2
Wolcott, Conn., U.S., 15,215 253/D3
Wolcott, Ind., U.S., 989 270/B3
Wolcott, Kans., U.S. 276/H1, H2
Wolcott, N.Y., U.S., 1,712 320/H4
Wolcott, Vt., U.S. 352/C1
Wolcottville, Ind., U.S., 933 270/F1
Wolds, The, Eng., U.K., *hills* 68/F1
Wolf, Yukon, Can., *lake* 214/G1
Wolf, Yukon, Can., *lake* 228/C5
Wolf, Ecua., *volcano* 185/Inset
Wolf, Kans., U.S. 276/A3
Wolf, Wisc., U.S., *river* 364/E4
Wolf, Wyo., U.S., 40 366/C1
Wolf Bayou, Ark., U.S., 70 244/D2
Wolf Creek, Ky., U.S., 90 280/D2
Wolf Creek, Mont., U.S. 306/D2
Wolf Creek, Oreg., U.S., 175 334/C5
Wolfdale, Penn., U.S., 2,873 336/A5
Wolfe, Ont., Can., *island* 320/J2
Wolfe, Ky., U.S., *county*, 7,065 280/G3
Wolfeboro, N.H., U.S., 6,083 312/D4
Wolfeboro Ctr., N.H., U.S., 80 312/D4
Wolfeboro Falls, N.H., U.S., 1,000 312/D4
Wolfe City, Tex., U.S., 1,566 346/M2
Wolfforth, Tex., U.S., 2,554 346/G2
Wolf Island N.W.R., Ga., U.S. 260/J9
Wolflake, Ind., U.S., 350 270/F2
Wolf Lake, Mich., U.S., 4,455 294/C6
Wolf Lake, Minn., U.S. 298/B4
Wolford, N. Dak., U.S., 50 326/F1
Wolf Pt., Mont., U.S., 2,663 306/L1
Wolfsberg, Aus. 91/D4
Wolfsburg, Ger., 121,954 86/B2
Wolfville, N.S., Can., 3,658 221/C2
Wollaston, N.W. Terr., Can., *peninsula* 220/E3
Wollaston, Sask., Can., *lake* 227/H2
Wollaston, Eng., U.K., 2,982 68/A4
Wollaston, Eng., U.K. 68/F5
Wollaston, Eng., U.K., 2,982 70/C2
Wollaston Lake, Sask., Can. 227/G2
Wollongong, N.S.W., Austl. 170/E3
Wolseley, Sask., Can., 766 227/G10
Wolsey, S. Dak., U.S., 418 342/G3
Wolsingham, Eng., U.K., 1,286 66/E3
Wolverhampton, Eng., U.K. 60/C3
Wolverhampton, Eng., U.K., 257,943 68/C4
Wolverhampton, Eng., U.K., *unitary authority*, 236,573 68/C4
Wolverine, Mich., U.S., 359 294/E4
Wolverine Lake, Mich., U.S., 4,415 294/A6, F7
Wolverton, (Buckinghamshire-Wolverton/ Stony Stratford), Eng., U.K., 55,733 70/C2
Wolverton, (Hampshire), Eng., U.K. 70/B4
Wolverton, Eng., U.K., 55,733 68/F5
Wolverton, Minn., U.S., 122 298/A4
Wolviston, Eng., U.K. 66/F3
Wombwell, Eng., U.K., 15,462 66/E5
Wombwell, Eng., U.K., 15,462 68/E2
Womelsdorf, Penn., U.S., 2,599 336/J5
Women's Rights N.H.P., N.Y., U.S. 320/H5
Wonalancet, N.H., U.S., 40 312/D4
Wonder, Oreg., U.S. 334/C5
Wonder Lake, Ill., U.S., 1,345 266/E1
Wonersh, Eng., U.K. 70/C4
Wonewoc, Wisc., U.S., 834 364/C5
Wong, Bhu., *river* 126/A2

Wonju, S. Kor., 237,460 . . . . .116/B4
Wonnie, Ky., U.S., 250 . . . . .280/G3
Wonowon, Br. Col., Can. 214/M3
Wŏnsan, N. Kor., 300,148 . . . . .116/B3
Wood, Eng., U.K. 70/E4
Wood, Ohio, U.S., county, 121,065 . . . .328/C3
Wood, S. Dak., U.S., 66 . . . . .342/E4
Wood, Tex., U.S., county, 36,752 . . . . .346/N3
Wood, W. Va., U.S., county, 87,986 . . . .360/C2
Wood, Wisc., U.S., county, 75,555 . . . . .364/C4
Woodacre, Calif., U.S., 1,393 . . . . .246/H1
Woodberry, Ark., U.S., 80 . . . . .244/C4
Woodbine, Ga., U.S., 1,218 . . . . .260/H1
Woodbine, Iowa, U.S., 1,564 . . . . .274/C4
Woodbine, Kans., U.S., 207 . . . . .276/F3
Woodbine, Ky., U.S., 550 . . . . .280/F4
Woodbine, Md., U.S., 425 . . . . .288/F2
Woodbine, N.J., U.S., 2,716 . . . . .314/D5
Woodboro, Wisc., U.S., 325 . . . . .364/C3
Woodborough, Eng., U.K., 1,691 . . . . . .68/E3
Woodbourne, N.Y., U.S., 1,600 . . . . . . .320/M7
Woodbourne, (Woodbourne-Hyde Park),
  Ohio, U.S., 7,910 . . . . .328/C2
Woodbranch, Tex., U.S., 1,305 . . . . . . .346/B5
Woodbridge, Ont., Can. 223/J5
Woodbridge, Eng., U.K., 10,950 . . . . . .70/G2
Woodbridge, Calif., U.S. 246/K6, L1
Woodbridge, Conn., U.S., 8,983 . . . . . .253/C4
Woodbridge, N.J., U.S., 97,203 . . . . . . .314/E2
Woodbridge, N.J., U.S., 31,941 . . . .354/J3, M3
Wood Buffalo Natl. Park, Alta., Can. . . .212/D1
Wood Buffalo Natl. Park, Alta., Can. . . .214/H1
Wood Buffalo Natl. Park, N.W. Terr., Can. . .220/F4
Woodburn, Ind., U.S., 1,579 . . . . .270/G2
Woodburn, Iowa, U.S., 244 . . . . .274/G5
Woodburn, Ky., U.S., 323 . . . . .280/D4
Woodburn, Oreg., U.S., 20,100 . . . . . . .334/D2
Woodbury, Eng., U.K. 73/F3
Woodbury, Conn., U.S., 9,198 . . . . .253/C3
Woodbury, Ga., U.S., 1,184 . . . . .260/B6
Woodbury, Iowa, U.S., county, 103,877 . .274/B4
Woodbury, Ky., U.S., 87 . . . . .280/D3
Woodbury, Mich., U.S., 175 . . . . .294/D7
Woodbury, Minn., U.S., 46,463 . . . . . . .298/F6
Woodbury, N.J., U.S., 10,307 . . . . . .314/A3, C4
Woodbury, Penn., U.S., 269 . . . . .336/E5
Woodbury, Tenn., U.S., 2,428 . . . . .344/J3
Woodbury, Vt., U.S. 352/C2
Woodbury Hts., N.J., U.S., 2,988 . . . . . .314/A4
Woodchurch, Eng., U.K., 1,419 . . . . . . .70/F4
Woodcliff Lake, N.J., U.S., 5,745 . . . . . .314/E1
Woodcock, Penn., U.S., 146 . . . . .336/A2
Woodcote, Eng., U.K., 2,608 . . . . .68/C4
Woodcreek, Tex., U.S., 1,274 . . . . .346/D3
Wood Dale, Ill., U.S., 13,535 . . . . .266/B5
Wood End, Eng., U.K. 68/D5
Woodend, Eng., U.K. 70/C5
Woodenhawk, Del., U.S., 200 . . . . .255/B4
Woodfield, Md., U.S., 2,500 . . . . .288/F3
Woodfield, S.C., U.S., 9,238 . . . . .238/F4
Woodfin, N.C., U.S., 3,162 . . . . .322/E7
Woodford, Ill., U.S., county, 35,469 . . . .266/D3
Woodford, Ky., U.S., county, 23,208 . . . .280/F2
Woodford, S.C., U.S., 196 . . . . .340/C3
Woodford, Vt., U.S. 352/A5
Woodford, Wisc., U.S., 150 . . . . .364/D6
Woodfords, Calif., U.S., 50 . . . . .246/F4
Woodhall Spa, Eng., U.K., 3,337 . . . . . .68/G3
Woodham Mortimer, Eng., U.K. 70/F3
Woodhaven, Mich., U.S., 12,530 . . . .294/A7, F7
Woodhull, Ill., U.S., 809 . . . . .266/C2
Woodhull, N.Y., U.S., 400 . . . . .320/G6
Woodingdean, Eng., U.K. 70/D5
Woodinville, Wash., U.S., 9,194 . . . . . . .358/A4
Wood Islands, P.E.I., Can. 224/C3
Woodlake, Calif., U.S., 6,651 . . . . .246/F6
Wood Lake, Minn., U.S., 436 . . . . .298/B6
Wood Lake, Nebr., U.S., 72 . . . . .308/D1
Woodland, Ala., U.S., 192 . . . . .238/D2
Woodland, Calif., U.S., 49,151 . . . . . . .246/D4
Woodland, Ga., U.S., 432 . . . . .260/B6
Woodland, Ill., U.S., 319 . . . . .266/F3
Woodland, La., U.S., 70 . . . . .282/H5
Woodland, Maine, U.S., 1,403 . . . . .286/E3
Woodland, Mich., U.S., 495 . . . . .294/D7
Woodland, (Hennepin County), Minn., U.S., 480 . .298/D6
Woodland, (Kanabec County), Minn., U.S. . . .302/D3
Woodland, Miss., U.S., 159 . . . . .300/C2
Woodland, N.C., U.S., 833 . . . . .322/L2
Woodland, Penn., U.S., 550 . . . . .336/E3
Woodland, Tex., U.S. 346/N2
Woodland, Wash., U.S., 3,780 . . . . .358/C4
Woodland Beach, Del., U.S., 100 . . . . . .255/C3
Woodland Beach, Mich., U.S., 2,179 . . . .294/F8
Woodland Hts., Penn., U.S., 1,402 . . . . .336/E5
Woodland Hills, Calif., U.S. 246/A9
Woodland Hills, Ky., U.S., 657 . . . . .280/B2
Woodland Hills, Utah, U.S., 941 . . . . . . .350/C3
Woodland Mills, Tenn., U.S., 296 . . . . . .344/C2
Woodland Park, Colo., U.S., 6,515 . . . . .250/E3
Woodland Park, Mich., U.S., 150 . . . . . .244/C2
Woodland Pt., Md., U.S., 125 . . . . .288/C6
Woodlands, Man. Can. 215/C4
Woodlands, Sing. 123/B1
Woodlands, W. Va., U.S., 100 . . . . .360/E1
Woodlark, (Muyua), P.N.G., island 172/B2
Woodlawn, Hawaii, U.S. 262/G2
Woodlawn, Ill., U.S., 630 . . . . .266/D5
Woodlawn, (Campbell County), Ky., U.S., 268 . .280/G1
Woodlawn, (McCracken County),
  Ky., U.S., 4,937 . . . . .280/A3
Woodlawn, La., U.S., 100 . . . . .282/D6
Woodlawn, (Baltimore County),
  Md., U.S., 36,079 . . . . .288/G2
Woodlawn, (Cecil County), Md., U.S., 1,600 . .288/K1
Woodlawn, N.C., U.S., 250 . . . . .322/A3
Woodlawn, Ohio, U.S., 2,816 . . . . .328/B9
Woodlawn Hts., Ind., U.S., 73 . . . . .270/E4
Woodlawn Park, Ky., U.S., 1,033 . . . . . .280/B2
Woodlawn Park, Okla., U.S., 161 . . . . . .330/B4
Woodleaf, N.C., U.S., 350 . . . . .322/D3
Woodloch, Tex., U.S., 247 . . . . .346/N5
Woodlyn, Penn., U.S., 10,036 . . . . .336/L7
Woodlynne, N.J., U.S., 2,796 . . . . .314/B3
Woodman, Wisc., U.S., 96 . . . . .364/C5
Woodmere, N.H., U.S. 312/B6
Woodmere, N.J., U.S., 150 . . . . .314/B4
Woodmere, Ohio, U.S., 828 . . . . .328/H9
Woodmont, Conn., U.S., 1,711 . . . . .253/D5
Woodmont Beach, Wash., U.S. 358/A4
Woodmoor, Md., U.S., 6,077 . . . . .288/D7
Woodnewton, Eng., U.K. 70/D1
Woodnorth, Man., Can. 215/A4
Woodport, N.J., U.S., 2,000 . . . . .314/D2
Woodridge, Man., Can. 215/C4
Woodridge, Ill., U.S., 30,934 . . . . .266/B6
Wood-Ridge, N.J., U.S., 7,644 . . . . .314/B2
Woodridge, N.Y., U.S., 902 . . . . .320/M7
Wood River, Ill., U.S., 11,296 . . . . . .266/A3, C5
Wood River, Nebr., U.S., 1,204 . . . . . . .308/E3

Woodrow, Colo., U.S. 250/G2
Woodruff, Ariz., U.S., 150 . . . . .242/E3
Woodruff, Ark., U.S., county, 8,741 . . . .244/D2
Woodruff, Ida., U.S., 50 . . . . .264/E7
Woodruff, Kans., U.S. 276/C2
Woodruff, S.C., U.S., 4,229 . . . . . . .340/B2, F2
Woodruff, Utah, U.S., 194 . . . . .350/C2
Woodruff, Wisc., U.S., 1,300 . . . . .364/D3
Woods, Man., Can., lake 215/D4
Woods, Ont., Can., lake 222/B3
Woods, Kans., U.S. 276/A4
Woods, Okla., U.S., county, 9,089 . . . . .330/C1
Woods, Tenn., U.S., reservoir 344/J4
Woods, Tex., U.S., 150 . . . . .346/P3
Woodsboro, Md., U.S., 846 . . . . .288/E1
Woodsboro, Tex., U.S., 1,685 . . . . .346/L7
Woods Cross, Utah, U.S., 6,419 . . . .350/C3, E2
Woodseaves, Eng., U.K. 68/C4
Woodsfield, Ohio, U.S., 2,598 . . . . .328/H6
Woods Hole, Mass., U.S., 925 . . . . .292/M6
Woodside, S.A., Austl. . . . . .170/Inset II
Woodside, Calif., U.S., 5,352 . . . . .246/J3
Woodside, Del., U.S., 184 . . . . .255/B4
Woodside, La., U.S. 282/F5
Woodside, Mont., U.S., 175 . . . . .306/B3
Woodside, Utah, U.S. 350/D4
Woods Landing, Wyo., U.S., 100 . . . . . .366/C3
Woodson, Ark., U.S., 445 . . . . .244/C3
Woodson, Ill., U.S., 559 . . . . .266/C4
Woodson, Kans., U.S., county, 3,788 . . .276/C4
Woodson, Tex., U.S., 296 . . . . .346/J2
Woodson Terrace, Mo., U.S., 4,189 . . . .302/H3
Woodstock, N.B., Can., 5,198 . . . . .217/B2
Woodstock, Ont., Can., 33,061 . . . . . . .223/E4
Woodstock, P.E.I., Can. 224/A2
Woodstock, Eng., U.K., 2,898 . . . . .68/E6
Woodstock, Eng., U.K., 2,898 . . . . .70/B3
Woodstock, Ala., U.S., 986 . . . . .238/B2
Woodstock, Conn., U.S., 7,221 . . . . .253/H2
Woodstock, Ga., U.S., 10,050 . . . . . .260/B3, H1
Woodstock, Ill., U.S., 20,151 . . . . .266/E1
Woodstock, Minn., U.S., 132 . . . . .298/A6
Woodstock, N.H., U.S., 1,139 . . . . .312/C4
Woodstock, N.Y., U.S., 2,187 . . . . .320/N6
Woodstock, Ohio, U.S., 317 . . . . .328/C5
Woodstock, Vt., U.S. 352/B2
Woodstock, Va., U.S., 3,952 . . . . .354/F3
Woodstock Valley, Conn., U.S., 750 . . . .253/G2
Woodston, Kans., U.S., 116 . . . . .276/C2
Woodstown, N.J., U.S., 3,136 . . . . .314/C4
Woodsville, N.H., U.S., 1,081 . . . . .312/B3
Wood-Tikchik St. Park, Alaska, U.S. 240/D2
Woodton, Eng., U.K. 70/G2
Wood Valley, Hawaii, U.S. 262/H6
Wood Vil., Oreg., U.S., 2,860 . . . . .334/B2
Woodville, S.A., Austl. . . . . .170/Inset II
Woodville, Ala., U.S., 761 . . . . .238/C1
Woodville, Calif., U.S., 1,678 . . . . .246/F6
Woodville, Conn., U.S., 225 . . . . .253/B3
Woodville, Fla., U.S., 3,006 . . . . .256/D1
Woodville, Ga., U.S., 400 . . . . .260/E4
Woodville, Mass., U.S., 500 . . . . .292/H4
Woodville, Miss., U.S., 1,192 . . . . .300/A4
Woodville, Ohio, U.S., 1,977 . . . . .328/D3
Woodville, Okla., U.S., 150 . . . . .330/F4
Woodville, Tex., U.S., 2,415 . . . . .346/P5
Woodville, Va., U.S., 60 . . . . .354/G3
Woodville, Wisc., U.S., 1,104 . . . . .364/A4
Woodward, Iowa, U.S., 1,200 . . . . .274/G4
Woodward, Okla., U.S., 11,853 . . . . . . .330/C1
Woodward, Okla., U.S., county, 18,486 . .330/C1
Woodway, Tex., U.S., 8,733 . . . . .346/L4
Woodway, Wash., U.S., 936 . . . . .358/A4
Woodworth, Ill., U.S. 150 . . . . .266/F3
Woodworth, La., U.S., 1,080 . . . . .282/E4
Woodworth, N. Dak., U.S., 80 . . . . .326/F2
Woody, Calif., U.S. 246/G7
Woodyard, Md., U.S. 288/G4
Woodyates, Eng., U.K. 73/J3
Woody Creek, Colo., U.S., 275 . . . . .250/D2
Woody Pt., Nfld., Can., 366 . . . . .218/C4
Woofferton, Eng., U.K. 68/B5
Wookey, Eng., U.K. 73/G2
Wool, Eng., U.K., 2,097 . . . . .73/H3
Woolacombe, Eng., U.K. 73/D2
Wooldridge, Mo., U.S., 47 . . . . .302/D3
Woolford, Md., U.S., 150 . . . . .288/K5
Wool Market, Miss., U.S. 300/C5
Woolsey, Ga., U.S., 175 . . . . .260/C5
Woolsey, Nev., U.S. 310/A1
Woolstock, Iowa, U.S., 204 . . . . .274/G2
Woolwich, Eng., U.K. 70/E4
Woolwich, Maine, U.S., 2,810 . . . . .286/C5
Woolwine, Va., U.S., 175 . . . . .354/C7
Woomera, S.A., Austl. 170/C3
Woonsocket, R.I., U.S., 43,224 . . . . . . .339/C1
Woonsocket, S. Dak., U.S., 720 . . . . . . .342/G3
Wooperton, Eng., U.K. 66/E2
Woore, Eng., U.K. 68/C4
Wooster, Ark., U.S., 516 . . . . .244/C2
Wooster, Ohio, U.S., 24,811 . . . . .328/C4
Woosung, Ill., U.S. 266/D2
Wootton, (Hampshire), Eng., U.K., 4,353 . .70/A5
Wootton, (N. Oxford), Eng., U.K. 68/E6
Wootton, (Oxfordshire), Eng., U.K. 70/B3
Wootton, (S. Oxford), Eng., U.K. 68/E6
Wootton, Eng., U.K. 73/J3
Worcester, S. Afr. 162/A3
Worcester, Eng., U.K. 60/C3
Worcester, Eng., U.K., 82,661 . . . . .68/C5
Worcester, Md., U.S., county, 46,543 . . .288/N7
Worcester, Mass., U.S., 172,648 . . . . . .292/G3
Worcester, Mass., U.S., county, 750,963 . .292/F3
Worcester, N.Y., U.S., 900 . . . . .320/M5
Worcester, Vt., U.S. 352/B2
Worcestershire, Eng., U.K., unitary authority,
  542,107 . . . . .68/C5
Worden, Ill., U.S., 905 . . . . .266/B3, D5
Worden, Mont., U.S., 506 . . . . .306/H4
Worden, Oreg., U.S. 334/E5
Worden, R.I., U.S., pond 339/C5
Workington, Eng., U.K., 25,579 . . . . . . .66/A3
Workmans Corners, Del., U.S., 400 . . . . .255/C6
Worksop, Eng., U.K., 37,247 . . . . .66/F6
Worksop, Eng., U.K., 37,247 . . . . .68/G2
Worlaby, Eng., U.K. 68/G2
Worley, Ida., U.S., 223 . . . . .264/B3
Wormingford, Eng., U.K. 70/F3
Worminghall, Eng., U.K. 70/B3
Wormleysburg, Penn., U.S., 2,607 . . . . .336/H5
Worms, Ger. 86/B4
Worplesdon, Eng., U.K. 70/C4
Worsley, Alta., Can. 212/A3
Worth, Eng., U.K. 70/G4
Worth, Ga., U.S., county, 21,967 . . . . . .260/D8
Worth, Ill., U.S., 11,047 . . . . .266/B6
Worth, Iowa, U.S., county, 7,909 . . . . . .274/H1
Worth, Mo., U.S., 94 . . . . .302/B1

Worth, Mo., U.S., county, 2,382 . . . . . .302/B1
Worth, Tex., U.S., lake 346/A9
Wortham, Eng., U.K. 70/G2
Wortham, Tex., U.S., 1,082 . . . . .346/M4
Worthing, Eng., U.K., 95,732 . . . . .70/D5
Worthing, S. Dak., U.S., 585 . . . . .342/J4
Worthington, Ind., U.S., 1,481 . . . . .270/D5
Worthington, Iowa, U.S., 381 . . . . .274/M3
Worthington, Ky., U.S., 1,673 . . . . .280/H2
Worthington, Minn., U.S., 11,283 . . . . . .298/B7
Worthington, Mo., U.S., 89 . . . . .302/D1
Worthington, Ohio, U.S., 14,125 . . . .328/D5, D9
Worthington, Penn., U.S., 778 . . . . .336/B4
Worthington, W. Va., U.S., 170 . . . . . . .360/F2
Worthington Ctr., Mass., U.S. 292/C3
Worthington Corners, Mass., U.S., 250 . .292/C3
Worthington Hills, Ky., U.S., 1,594 . . . . .280/B1
Worthington Sprs., Fla., U.S., 193 . . . . .256/F2
Worthville, Ga., U.S., 215 . . . . .280/E2
Worthville, Penn., U.S., 85 . . . . .336/C3
Worton, Md., U.S., 225 . . . . .288/K2
Wotho, Marsh. Is., island 173/B1
Wotje, Marsh. Is., island 173/B2
Wotton-under-Edge, Eng., U.K., 5,316 . . .68/C6
Wotton-under-Edge, Eng., U.K. 73/H1
Wounded Knee, S. Dak., U.S., 328 . . . . .342/C4
Wrangel, Russ., island 104/J2
Wrangel, Russ., island 193/B10
Wrangell, Alaska, U.S., 2,308 . . . . .240/I3
Wrangell, Alaska, U.S., cape 240/Inset
Wrangell, Alaska, U.S., mountains 240/I2
Wrangell-St. Elias Natl. Park and Preserve,
  Alaska, U.S. 240/I2
Wrangle, China, U.S. 70/E1
Wrantage, Eng., U.K. 73/G3
Wrath, Scot., U.K., cape 60/B1
Wraxall, Eng., U.K. 73/G2
Wray, Eng., U.K. 66/B1
Wray, Colo., U.S., 2,187 . . . . .250/H1
Wreay, Eng., U.K. 66/C3
Wreck Cove, Nfld., Can. 218/D5
Wrelton, Eng., U.K. 66/G4
Wren, Ala., U.S., 100 . . . . .238/B1
Wren, Ohio, U.S., 199 . . . . .328/A4
Wrens, Ga., U.S., 2,314 . . . . .260/G5
Wrenshall, Minn., U.S., 308 . . . . .298/E4
Wrentham, Alta., Can. 212/D6
Wrentham, Eng., U.K. 70/H2
Wrentham, Mass., U.S., 10,554 . . . . . . .292/J4
Wressle, Eng., U.K. 66/G5
Wrexham, Wales, U.K., 40,614 . . . . .64/F1
Wrexham, Wales, U.K., unitary authority,
  128,477 . . . . .64/E1
Wright, Iowa, U.S., 80 . . . . .274/J5
Wright, Iowa, U.S., county, 14,334 . . . . .274/G2
Wright, Kans., U.S., 200 . . . . .276/C4
Wright, Minn., U.S., 93 . . . . .298/D4
Wright, Minn., U.S., county, 89,986 . . . .298/D5
Wright, Mo., U.S., county, 17,955 . . . . . .302/D4
Wright, Wyo., U.S., 1,347 . . . . .366/D2
Wright Brothers Natl. Mem., N.C., U.S. . .322/K6
Wright City, Mo., U.S., 1,532 . . . . .302/E3
Wright City, Okla., U.S., 848 . . . . .330/H3
Wrightsboro, N.C., U.S., 4,496 . . . . .322/K6
Wrightstown, Minn., U.S., 50 . . . . .298/B4
Wrightstown, N.J., U.S., 748 . . . . .314/D3
Wrightstown, Wisc., U.S., 1,934 . . . . . . .364/E4
Wrightsville, Ark., U.S., 1,368 . . . . .244/C3
Wrightsville, Ga., U.S., 2,223 . . . . .260/F6
Wrightsville, Penn., U.S., 2,223 . . . . . . .336/H5
Wrightsville Beach, N.C., U.S., 2,593 . . .322/K6
Wrightwood, Calif., U.S., 3,837 . . . . . . .246/H8
Wrigley, N.W. Terr., Can., 165 . . . . .220/D4
Wrigley, Tenn., U.S., 475 . . . . .344/G3
Writtle, Eng., U.K., 5,128 . . . . .70/E3
Wrocław, Pol., 634,047 . . . . .83/C3
Wroot, Eng., U.K. 66/G5
Wroughton, Eng., U.K., 7,111 . . . . .73/J1
Wroxall, Eng., U.K., 1,656 . . . . .68/D5
Wroxall, Eng., U.K., 1,656 . . . . .70/B5
Wroxham, (Wroxham/Hoveton),
  Eng., U.K., 3,247 . . . . .70/G1
Wuhan, China, 4,040,113 . . . . .119/E2
Wuhu, China, 449,070, (944,150 metro.) . .119/E2
Wukari, Nig. 152/E4
Wupatki Natl. Mon., Ariz., U.S. 242/D2
Wuppertal, Ger., 368,993 . . . . .86/A3
Wurtland, Ky., U.S., 1,049 . . . . .280/H2
Wurtsboro, N.Y., U.S., 1,234 . . . . .320/N7
Wurtsmith A.F.B., Mich., U.S. 294/F5
Würzburg, Ger., 127,350 . . . . .86/B4
Wutivi, Liber., mountain 149/B1
Wuwei, China .119/D2
Wuxi, China 119/F2
Wuzhong, China 119/D2
Wuzhou, China 119/E3
Wyaconda, Mo., U.S. 310 . . . . .302/E1
Wyalusing, Penn., U.S., 564 . . . . .336/J2
Wyalusing, Wisc., U.S. 364/B6
Wyandot, Ohio, U.S., county, 22,908 . . . .328/D4
Wyandotte, Ind., U.S., cave 270/D8
Wyandotte, Kans., U.S., county, 157,882 . .276/H1, H2
Wyandotte, Mich., U.S., 28,006 . . . . .294/B7, F7
Wyandotte, Okla., U.S., 363 . . . . .330/H1
Wyanet, Ill., U.S., 1,028 . . . . .266/D2
Wyano, Penn., U.S. 336/B6
Wyantenock St. For., Conn., U.S. 253/B3
Wyarno, Wyo., U.S. 366/C1
Wyaston, Eng., U.K. 68/D4
Wyatt, Ind., U.S., 225 . . . . .270/D1
Wyatt, La., U.S., 70 . . . . .282/D2
Wyatt, Mo., U.S., 364 . . . . .302/G5
Wyatte, Miss., U.S. 300/C1
Wyattville, Minn., U.S., 50 . . . . .298/F7
Wych Cross, Eng., U.K. 70/E4
Wyckoff, N.J., U.S., 16,508 . . . . .314/B1, E1
Wyddial, Eng., U.K. 70/E3
Wye, Eng., U.K., 1,608 . . . . .70/F4
Wye, Eng., U.K., river 60/C3
Wye Mills, Md., U.S., 325 . . . . .288/K4
Wyeville, Wisc., U.S., 146 . . . . .364/C4
Wykoff, Minn., U.S., 460 . . . . .298/E7
Wyldwood, Tex., U.S., 2,310 . . . . .346/D9
Wylie, Minn., U.S. 298/A3
Wylie, Tex., U.S., 15,132 . . . . .346/D9
Wylliesburg, Va., U.S., 125 . . . . .354/F7
Wylye, Eng., U.K. 73/J2
Wyman, Iowa, U.S., 50 . . . . .274/M5
Wyman, Maine, U.S., 70 . . . . .286/E4
Wymark, Sask., Can. 358/E3
Wymondham, (Leicestershire),
  Eng., U.K., 10,159 . . . . .70/C1
Wymondham, (Norfolk), Eng., U.K. 70/G1
Wymondham, Eng., U.K., 10,159 . . . . . .68/F1
Wymore, Nebr., U.S., 1,656 . . . . .308/H3
Wyncote, Penn., U.S., 3,046 . . . . .336/M6
Wyndham, W.A., Austl. 170/B1
Wyndmere, N. Dak., U.S., 533 . . . . .326/H3
Wyndmoor, Penn., U.S., 5,601 . . . . .336/M6
Wynnburg, Tenn., U.S., 175 . . . . .344/C2
Wynne, Ark., U.S., 8,615 . . . . .244/E2

Wynnedale, Ind., U.S., 275 . . . . .270/D5
Wynnewood, Okla., U.S., 2,367 . . . . . . .330/E3
Wynnum, Qnsld., Austl. . . . . .170/Inset III
Wynona, Okla., U.S., 531 . . . . .330/F1
Wynot, Nebr., U.S., 191 . . . . .308/G1
Wynyard, Sask., Can., 1,919 . . . . .227/I9
Wyocena, Wisc., U.S., 668 . . . . .364/D5
Wyodak, Wyo., U.S., 125 . . . . .366/D1
Wyola, Mont., U.S., 186 . . . . .306/I4
Wyoming, U.S., state 354
Wyoming, Del., U.S., 1,141 . . . . .255/B4
Wyoming, Ill., U.S., 1,424 . . . . .266/D2
Wyoming, Iowa, U.S., 626 . . . . .274/M3
Wyoming, Mich., U.S., 69,368 . . . . .294/D7
Wyoming, Minn., U.S., 3,048 . . . . .298/E5
Wyoming, N.Y., U.S., 513 . . . . .320/E5
Wyoming, N.Y., U.S., county, 43,424 . . .320/E5
Wyoming, Ohio, U.S., 8,261 . . . . .328/B9
Wyoming, Penn., U.S., 3,221 . . . . .336/G7
Wyoming, Penn., U.S., county, 28,080 . .336/G7, J3
Wyoming, R.I., U.S., 475 . . . . .339/B4
Wyoming, W. Va., U.S., county, 25,708 . .360/C5
Wyoming, Wyo., U.S. 366/D3
Wyoming St. For., Penn., U.S. 336/J5
Wytheville, Va., U.S., 7,804 . . . . .354/A7
Wythe, Va., U.S., county, 27,599 . . . . . .354/A7
Wytopitlock, Maine, U.S., 40 . . . . .286/E3
Xaçmaz, Azer. 103/C2
Xaignabouli, Laos 124/A2
Xai-Xai, Moz. .161/B5
Xalapa, Mex., state capital, 373,076,
  (390,590 metro.) 200/D4
Xam-Nua, Laos 124/C1
Xampongo, Ang. 159/C5
Xanthi, Gr. 100/C1
Xau, Bots., lake 160/B2
Xenia, Ill., U.S., 407 . . . . .266/E5
Xenia, Kans., U.S. 276/H4
Xenia, Ohio, U.S., 24,164 . . . . .328/C6
Xi, China, river 119/E3
Xiamen, China, 507,390, (961,650 metro.) . .119/E3
Xi'an, China, 2,185,040, (2,911,580 metro.) . .119/D2
Xiangfan, China 119/E2
Xiangkhoang, Laos 124/B2
Xiangkhoang, Laos, plateau 124/B2
Xiangtan, China 119/E3
Xigazê, China .119/B3
Xingu, Braz., river 188/C3
Xining, China .119/D2
Xinjiang, (Sinkiang), China, autonomous region . .119/B1
Xinxiang, China 119/E2
Xinyang, China 119/E2
XI Ranch Ind. Res., Calif., U.S. 246/E1
Xochimilco, Mex. 200/Inset
Xuddur, Som. .157/A3
Xuzhou, China 119/E2
Yaak, Mont., U.S. 306/A1
Ya'an, China 119/D2
Yablonovyy, Russ., range 104/G4
Yabucoa, P.R. .206/D2
Yachats, Oreg., U.S., 617 . . . . .334/B3
Yacolt, Wash., U.S., 1,055 . . . . .358/C4
Yacuiba, Bol. .186/B4
Yadkin, N.C., U.S., county, 36,348 . . . . .322/C2
Yadkin, N.C., U.S., river 322/D2
Yadkinville, N.C., U.S., 2,818 . . . . .322/D2
Yafran, Lib. 145/B1
Yaguaí, Uru., river 187/C1
Yaguarón, Uru., river 187/D2
Yahk, Br. Col., Can., 168 . . . . .214/O6
Yah-Tah-Hey, N. Mex., U.S., 580 . . . . . .317/B2
Yakama Ind. Res., Wash., U.S. 358/E3
Yakima, Wash., U.S., 71,845, (222,581 metro.) . .358/E3
Yakima, Wash., U.S., county, 222,581 . . .358/E3
Yakima, Wash., U.S., river 358/E3
Yaku, Jap., island 114/A4
Yakutat, Alaska, U.S., 680 . . . . .240/H3
Yakutsk, Russ., 196,417, (228,350 metro.) . .104/H3
Yakutsk, Russ. 193/C7
Yala, Thai. 125/B5
Yalaha, Fla., U.S., 1,175 . . . . .256/C3
Yalding, Eng., U.K. 70/E4
Yale, Br. Col., Can., 171 . . . . .214/M6
Yale, Ark., U.S. 244/B2
Yale, Ill., U.S., 97 . . . . .266/E4
Yale, Iowa, U.S., 287 . . . . .274/F4
Yale, Mich., U.S., 2,063 . . . . .294/G6
Yale, Okla., U.S., 1,342 . . . . .330/F1
Yale, S. Dak., U.S., 118 . . . . .342/H3
Yale, Va., U.S., 60 . . . . .354/J7
Yale, Wash., U.S., lake 358/C3
Yalesville, Conn., U.S. 253/D4
Yalinga, C.A.R. 154/B2
Yalobusha, Miss., U.S., county, 13,051 . .300/C1
Yalobusha, Miss., U.S., river 300/C2
Yalta, Ukr. 102/C4
Yalu, China, river 119/F1
Yalu, N. Kor., river 116/B2
Yamagata, Jap. 114/D2
Yamagata, Jap., prefecture 114/C2
Yamaguchi, Jap. 114/A3
Yamaguchi, Jap., prefecture 114/A3
Yamal, Russ., peninsula 104/E3
Yamalo-Nenetsia, Russ., autonomous okrug . .104/E3
Yamanashi, Jap., prefecture 114/C3
Yambio, Sudan 145/B4
Yamhill, Oreg., U.S., 794 . . . . .334/C2
Yamhill, Oreg., U.S., county, 84,992 . . . .334/C2
Yamoussoukro, C. d'Iv., capital, 106,786 . .150/D3
Yampa, Colo., U.S., 443 . . . . .250/D1
Yampa, Colo., U.S., river 250/D1
Yampai, Ariz., U.S. 242/B2
Yampi, Austl., sound 170/B1
Yamuna, India, river 128/C2
Yan, Sri Lan., river 126/B3
Yanbu al Bahr, Sa. Arab. 136/A1
Yancey, N.C., U.S., county, 17,774 . . .322/A3, E7
Yancey, Tex., U.S., 200 . . . . .346/J6
Yanceyville, N.C., U.S., 2,091 . . . . .322/G2
Yancopin, Ark., U.S., 40 . . . . .244/D4
Yandeyarra, Austl., aboriginal land 170/A2
Yangambi, Congo, D.R. 155/C1
Yangdŏk, N. Kor. 116/B3
Yanggang, N. Kor., province 116/B2
Yangquan, China 119/E2
Yangtze, China, river 119/C2, D2
Yangzhou, China 119/E2
Yankee Lake, Ohio, U.S., 99 . . . . .328/J3
Yankeetown, Fla., U.S., 629 . . . . .256/F2
Yankeetown, Ind., U.S., 375 . . . . .270/B9
Yankton, S. Dak., U.S., 13,528 . . . . .342/H4
Yankton, S. Dak., U.S., county, 21,652 . .342/H4
Yankton Ind. Res., S. Dak., U.S. 342/H4
Yantai, China .119/F2
Yantic, Conn., U.S., river 253/F3
Yantley, Ala., U.S., 125 . . . . .238/A3
Yantra, Bul., river 101/D2

Yanush, Okla., U.S., 50 . . . . .330/G3
Yao, Jap., 275,000 . . . . .114/B3
Yaoundé, Came., *capital*, 649,000,
 (1,120,000 metro.) 153/B3
Yap, Micr., *islands* 172/A4
Yap, Micr., *state* 172/A2
Yapen, Indon., *island* 122/E2
Yaque del Norte, Dom. Rep., *river* 205/A1
Yaque del Sur, Dom. Rep., *river* 205/A2
Yaqui, Mex., *river* 200/C2
Yaquina, Oreg., U.S., *bay* 334/B3
Yaracuy, Ven., *state* 182/C1
Yarbo, Ala., U.S., 70 . . . . .238/A4
Yarburgh, Eng., U.K. 66/J6
Yardley, Penn., U.S., 2,498 . . . . .336/M5
Yardley Gobion, Eng., U.K. 70/C2
Yardley Hastings, Eng., U.K. 70/C2
Yardville, N.J., U.S., 9,208 . . . . .314/D3
Yare, Eng., U.K., *river* 60/D3
Yaren, Nauru, *capital* 174/B3
Yariga take, Jap., *mountain* 114/C2
Yarmouth, N.S., Can., 7,561 . . . . .221/A4
Yarmouth, N.S., Can., *county* 221/B3
Yarmouth, Eng., U.K. 70/B5
Yarmouth, Iowa, U.S., 100 . . . . .274/M5
Yarmouth, Maine, U.S., 8,360 . . . . .286/B5
Yarmouth, Mass., U.S., 24,807 . . . . . . .292/P6
Yarmouth Port, Mass., U.S., 5,395 . . . . .292/P6
Yarnell, Ariz., U.S., 645 . . . . .242/C3
Yarnton, Eng., U.K., 2,431 . . . . .68/E6
Yarnton, Eng., U.K., 2,431 . . . . .70/B3
Yaroslavl', Russ., 614,095 . . . . .104/C4
Yarrow Pt., Wash., U.S., 1,008 . . . . .358/A4
Yasawa, Fiji, *island group* 174/A2
Yasuj, Iran .130/C3
Yata, Bol., *river* 186/A2
Yate, Eng., U.K. 73/H1
Yateley, Eng., U.K., 15,663 . . . . .70/C4
Yates, Alta., Can. 212/B4
Yates, N. Mex., U.S. 317/G1
Yates, N.Y., U.S., *county*, 24,621 . . . . .320/G5
Yatesboro, Penn., U.S., 275 . . . . .336/C4
Yates Ctr., Kans., U.S., 1,599 . . . . .276/G4
Yates City, Ill., U.S., 725 . . . . .266/C3
Yatesville, Ga., U.S., 408 . . . . .260/C6
Yatesville, Penn., U.S., 649 . . . . .336/H7
Yathkyed, Nun., Can., *lake* 220/J4
Yatsushiro, Jap. 114/A3
Yatta, Kenya, *plateau* 157/E5
Yattendon, Eng., U.K. 70/B4
Yatton, Eng., U.K., 6,826 . . . . .68/B6
Yatton, Eng., U.K., 6,826 . . . . .73/G2
Yatton Keynell, Eng., U.K. 73/H2
Yauco, P.R. 206/B2
Yauhannah, S.C., U.S., 50 . . . . .340/E3
Yaupon Beach, N.C., U.S. 322/J7
Yaurel, P.R. 206/C2
Yavapai, Ariz., U.S., *county*, 167,517 . . .242/C3
Yavari, Peru, *river* 185/C1
Yaviza, Pan. 203/D2
Yawri, S.L., *bay* 149/A2
Yazd, Iran, 326,776 . . . . .130/C3
Yazd, Iran, *province* 130/C3
Yazoo, Miss., U.S., *county*, 28,149 . . . .300/B3
Yazoo, Miss., U.S., *river* 300/B2
Yazoo City, Miss., U.S., 14,550 . . . . . . .300/B3
Yazoo N.W.R., Miss., U.S. 300/B2
Ybbs, Aus., *river* 91/D2
Y City, Ark., U.S., 60 . . . . .244/A3
Yding Skovhøj, Den., *hill* 79/B2
Ye, Mya. 125/C3
Yeadon, Penn., U.S., 11,762 . . . . .336/L7
Yeager, Okla., U.S., 67 . . . . .330/F2
Yeagertown, Penn., U.S., 1,035 . . . . . . .336/F4
Yecla, Sp. .94/F3
Yeddo, Ind., U.S., 200 . . . . .270/D3
Yedingham, Eng., U.K. 66/C4
Yeehaw Jct., Fla., U.S. 256/H4
Yegheknadzor, Arm. 103/C3
Yeguas, P.R., *point* 206/D2
Yekaterinburg, Russ., 1,267,393,
 (1,313,750 metro.) 104/E4
Yekepa, Liber. 149/B2
Yelden, Eng., U.K. 68/F5
Yell, Scot., U.K., *island* . . . . .60/Inset I
Yell, Scot., U.K., *island* 62/Q2
Yell, Ark., U.S., *county*, 21,139 . . . . . .244/B2
Yellow, China, *sea* 119/F2
Yellow, Fla., U.S., *river* 256/B1
Yellow, Wisc., U.S., *river* 364/C4
Yellow Bluff, Ala., U.S., 181 . . . . .238/B4
Yellow Grass, Sask., Can., 422 . . . . . . .227/F11
Yellow Jacket, Colo., U.S. 250/B4
Yellowknife, N.W. Terr., Can., 16,541 . . . .220/F4
Yellow Lake, Wisc., U.S., 90 . . . . .364/A3
Yellow Medicine, Minn., U.S., *county*, 11,080 . .298/B6
Yellow Pine, Ala., U.S., 70 . . . . .238/A4
Yellow Pine, Ida., U.S., 60 . . . . .264/B5
Yellow Sprs., Md., U.S., 1,100 . . . . .288/E2
Yellow Sprs., Ohio, U.S., 3,761 . . . . . . .328/C6
Yellowstone, Mont., U.S., *county*, 129,352 . .306/H3
Yellowstone, Mont., U.S., *river* . . .306/H3, L3
Yellowstone, Wyo., U.S., *lake* 366/A1
Yellowstone Natl. Park, Wyo., U.S. 366/A1
Yellville, Ark., U.S., 1,312 . . . . .244/C1
Yelm, Wash., U.S., 3,289 . . . . .358/C4
Yelverton, Eng., U.K. 73/D4
Yemassee, S.C., U.S., 807 . . . . .340/D4
Yemen, *nation* 133
Yen Bai, Viet. 123/A2
Yendi, Gha. 150/B2
Yeni Erenköy, (Yialousa), Cyp. 133/C1
Yenisey, Russ., *river* 104/F3
Yenisey, Russ., *river* 193/C5
Yeoman, Ind., U.S., 96 . . . . .270/C3
Yeongju, S. Kor. 116/C4
Yeosu, S. Kor., 183,596 . . . . .116/B5
Yeovil, Eng., U.K. 60/C4
Yeovil, Eng., U.K., 38,805 . . . . .73/G3
Yerevan, Arm., *capital*, 1,247,200 . . . . .103/B2
Yerevan, Arm., *district* 103/B2
Yerington, Nev., U.S., 2,883 . . . . .310/A2
Yerington Ind. Res., Nev., U.S. 310/A2
Yerkes, Ky., U.S., 500 . . . . .280/C3
Yesilırmak, Tur., *river* 133/D2
Yeso, N. Mex., U.S. 317/F3
Yetminster, Eng., U.K. 73/G3
Yetter, Iowa, U.S. 274/E3
Yeu, Fr., *island* 88/B3
Yevlax, Azer. 103/B2
Yevpatoria, Ukr. 102/C3
Yevrey, (Birobidzhan) A.O., Russ.,
 autonomous oblast 104/H5
Yewed, Okla., U.S. 330/D1
Yí, Uru., *river* 187/C2
Yibin, China 119/D3
Yichang, China 119/E2
Yichun, China, 755,830, (1,167,020 metro.) .119/F1
Yinchuan, China 119/D2
Yingkou, China, 422,590, (2,788,690 metro.) .119/F1
Yining, China 119/B1

Yin Shan, China, *mountains* 119/E1
Ylikitka, Fin., *lake* 81/C1
Ylivieska, Fin. 81/B2
Ynyslas, Wales, U.K. 64/C2
Yoakum, Tex., U.S., 5,731 . . . . .346/L6
Yoakum, Tex., U.S., *county*, 7,322 . . . . .346/F2
Yobe, Nig., *state* 152/F2
Yoboki, Dji. 156/B2
Yocemento, Kans., U.S., 70 . . . . .276/C3
Yoder, Colo., U.S. 250/F3
Yoder, Ind., U.S., 300 . . . . .270/F3
Yoder, Kans., U.S., 200 . . . . .276/E4
Yoder, Wyo., U.S., 169 . . . . .366/D3
Yoe, Penn., U.S., 1,022 . . . . .336/H6
Yogyakarta, Indon., 431,300 . . . . .122/C2
Yogyakarta, Indon., *province* 122/C2
Yoho Natl. Park, Br. Col., Can. 212/B5
Yoho Natl. Park, Br. Col., Can. 214/O5
Yojoa, Hond., *lake* 202/B2
Yokadouma, Came. 153/B3
Yokkaichi, Jap., 291,000 . . . . .114/C3
Yokohama, Jap., 3,426,506 . . . . .114/C3
Yokosuka, Jap., 429,000 . . . . .114/C3
Yola, Nig. .152/G3
Yolo, Calif., U.S., 550 . . . . .246/D4
Yolo, Calif., U.S., *county*, 168,660 . . . .246/C4, K5
Yom, Thai., *river* 125/B2
Yomba Ind. Res., Nev., U.S. 310/B2
Yomou, Guin. 149/D4
Yonago, Jap. 114/B3
Yonaguni, Jap., *island* . . . . .114/Inset II
Yoncalla, Oreg., U.S., 1,052 . . . . .334/C4
Yonges Island, S.C., U.S., 80 . . . . .340/D4
Yonkers, N.Y., U.S., 196,086 . . . . .320/B2
Yonne, Fr., *department* 88/C3
Yonne, Fr., *river* 88/C2
Yopal, Col., 69,000 . . . . .184/B3
Yorba Linda, Calif., U.S., 58,918 . . . . . .246/E10
York, Austl., *cape* 170/D1
York, N.B., Can., *county* 217/B3
York, Ont., Can. 223/F4, J5
York, Ont., Can. 223/K5
York, Ont., Can., *county* 223/F4, J5
York, P.E.I., Can. 224/B2
York, Grld., *cape* 193/A2
York, Eng., U.K. 60/C3
York, Eng., U.K., 124,609 . . . . .66/F5
York, Eng., U.K., 124,609 . . . . .68/F2
York, Eng., U.K., *unitary authority*, 181,131 . .66/F5
York, Eng., U.K., *unitary authority*, 181,131 . .68/E1
York, Ala., U.S., 2,854 . . . . .238/A3
York, Ariz., U.S., 50 . . . . .242/F5
York, Ky., U.S. 280/G2
York, Maine, U.S., 12,854 . . . . .286/B5
York, Maine, U.S., *county*, 186,742 . . . .286/B5
York, Nebr., U.S., 8,081 . . . . .308/G3
York, Nebr., U.S., *county*, 14,598 . . . . .308/G3
York, N.Y., U.S., 450 . . . . .320/F5
York, N. Dak., U.S. 326/F1
York, Penn., U.S., 40,862, (381,751 metro.) . .336/H6
York, Penn., U.S., *county*, 381,751 . . . .336/H5
York, S.C., U.S., 6,985 . . . . .340/C2
York, S.C., U.S., *county*, 164,614 . . . . .340/C2
York, Va., U.S., *county*, 56,297 . . . . . . .354/K6
York, Va., U.S., *river* 354/K6
Yorkana, Penn., U.S., 239 . . . . .336/H6
York Beach, Maine, U.S., 1,400 . . . . . . .286/B5
York Ctr., Ill., U.S. 266/B6
York Corner, Maine, U.S. 286/B5
Yorketown, N.J., U.S., 6,712 . . . . .314/E3
York Factory, Man., Can. 215/E1
York Harbor, Maine, U.S., 3,321 . . . . . . .286/B5
York Haven, Penn., U.S., 809 . . . . .336/H5
Yorkley, Eng., U.K. 68/B6
York Mills, N.B., Can. 217/B3
Yorkshire, N.Y., U.S., 1,403 . . . . .320/E5
Yorkshire, Ohio, U.S., 110 . . . . .328/B5
Yorkshire, Va., U.S., 6,732 . . . . .354/J3
Yorkshire Dales Natl. Park, Eng., U.K. . . .66/D4
Yorkshire Dales Natl. Park, Eng., U.K. . . .68/C1
York Sprs., Penn., U.S., 574 . . . . .336/G5
Yorkton, Sask., Can., 15,107 . . . . .227/H9
Yorktown, Ark., U.S., 90 . . . . .244/D3
Yorktown, Ind., U.S., 4,785 . . . . .270/F4
Yorktown, Iowa, U.S., 82 . . . . .274/D6
Yorktown, N.J., U.S., 250 . . . . .314/C4
Yorktown, N.Y., U.S., 14,891 . . . . .320/B1
Yorktown, Tex., U.S., 2,271 . . . . .346/L7
Yorktown, Va., U.S., 203 . . . . .354/K6
Yorktown Hts., N.Y., U.S., 7,972 . . . . . . .320/B1
York Vil., Maine, U.S., 2,000 . . . . .286/B5
Yorkville, Ga., U.S., 150 . . . . .260/B4
Yorkville, Ill., U.S., 6,189 . . . . .266/E2
Yorkville, N.Y., U.S., 2,675 . . . . .320/L4
Yorkville, Ohio, U.S., 1,230 . . . . .328/J5
Yorkville, Tenn., U.S., 293 . . . . .344/C2
Yoro, Hond. 202/B2
Yoro, Hond., *department* 202/B2
Yoron, Jap., *island* . . . . .114/Inset II
Yosemite, Ky., U.S., 175 . . . . .280/F3
Yosemite Natl. Park, Calif., U.S. 246/F5
Yosemite Vil., Calif., U.S., 265 . . . . .246/F5
Yoshino, Jap., *river* 114/B3
Yoshkar-Ola, Russ., 249,550, (278,500 metro.) . .104/D4
Yost, Utah, U.S. 350/A2
Yotvata, Isr. 135/B3
Youghal, Ire. 78/C3
Youghiogheny, Md., U.S., *river* 288/A3
Youlgreave, Eng., U.K. 68/D3
Young, Sask., Can., 299 . . . . .227/E9
Young, Ariz., U.S., 561 . . . . .242/E3
Young, Tex., U.S., *county*, 17,943 . . . . .346/K2
Young America, Ind., U.S., 300 . . . . . . .270/D3
Young America, Minn., U.S., 3,108 . . . . .298/D6
Young Harris, Ga., U.S., 604 . . . . .260/D2
Youngs Cove, N.B., Can. 217/D2
Youngstown, Alta., Can., 184 . . . . .212/E5
Youngstown, Fla., U.S., 40 . . . . .256/C1
Youngstown, N.Y., U.S., 1,957 . . . . .320/C4
Youngstown, Ohio, U.S., 82,026,
 (594,746 metro.) 328/J3
Youngsville, Penn., U.S., 400 . . . . .336/C5
Youngsville, La., U.S., 3,992 . . . . .282/F6
Youngsville, N. Mex., U.S. 317/D1
Youngsville, N.C., U.S., 651 . . . . .322/J2
Youngsville, Penn., U.S., 1,834 . . . . . . .336/C2
Youngtown, Ariz., U.S., 3,010 . . . . .242/C4
Youngwood, Penn., U.S., 4,138 . . . . . . .336/B5
Yountville, Calif., U.S., 2,916 . . . . .246/C4
Yoxall, Eng., U.K., 1,421 . . . . .68/D4
Yozgat, Tur. 133/C2
Yozgat, Tur., *province* 133/C2
Ypané, Para., *river* 187/D4
Ypoá, Para., *lake* 187/D4
Ypres, Belg. 85/A2
Ypsilanti, Mich., U.S., 22,362 . . . . .294/F7
Ypsilanti, N. Dak., U.S., 125 . . . . .326/G3
Yreka, Calif., U.S., 7,290 . . . . .246/C1
Ysbyty Ifan, Wales, U.K. 64/D1
Ysbyty Ystwyth, Wales, U.K. 64/D3
Ystalyfera, Wales, U.K. 64/D4

Ystradfellte, Wales, U.K. 64/D4
Ystradgynlais, (Ystradgynlais/Ystalyfera),
 Wales, U.K., 9,577 . . . . .64/D4
Ystradmeurig, Wales, U.K. 64/D3
Ysyk-Köl, Kyrg., *lake* 131/E1
Ysyk-Köl, Kyrg., *province* 131/E2
Yuan, China, *river* 119/D3
Yuba, Calif., U.S., *county*, 60,219 . . . . .246/D3
Yuba, Wisc., U.S., 92 . . . . .364/C5
Yuba City, Calif., U.S., 36,758,
 (139,149 metro.) 246/D3
Yubari, Jap. . . . . .114/Inset I
Yucaipa, Calif., U.S., 41,207 . . . . .246/H8
Yucatán, Cuba, *channel* 204/A2
Yucatán, Mex., *peninsula* 200/G4
Yucatán, Mex., *state* 200/G3
Yucca, Ariz., U.S., 100 . . . . .242/A3
Yucca House N.M., Colo., U.S. 250/B4
Yucca Valley, Calif., U.S., 16,865 . . . . . .246/J8
Yuen Long, H.K., China 117/B1
Yueyang, China 119/E3
Yugoslavia, *nation* 97
Yukon, Can., *territory* 216
Yukon, Yukon, Can., *river* 228/B4
Yukon, U.S., *river* 193/C11
Yukon, Alaska, U.S., *river* 240/C2
Yukon, Mo., U.S., 60 . . . . .302/E4
Yukon, Okla., U.S., 21,043 . . . . .330/E2
Yukon-Charley Rivers Natl. Pres., Alaska, U.S. . .240/C2
Yukon Delta N.W.R., Alaska, U.S. 240/C2
Yukon Flats N.W.R., Alaska, U.S. 240/F1
Yulee, Fla., U.S., 8,392 . . . . .256/G1
Yuscarán, Hond. 202/B3
Yü Shan, Tai., *mountain* 117/B2
Yuma, Ariz., U.S., 77,515, (160,026 metro.) .242/A5
Yuma, Ariz., U.S., *county*, 160,026 . . . . .242/A5
Yuma, Colo., U.S., *desert* 242/A5
Yuma, Colo., U.S. 250/H1
Yuma, Colo., U.S., *county*, 9,841 . . . . .250/H2
Yuma Proving Ground, Ariz., U.S. . . .242/A4, A5
Yumen, China 119/C2
Yuna, Dom. Rep., *river* 205/B2
Yunaska, Alaska, U.S., *island* 240/Inset
Yundum, Gam. 148/B2
Yungas, Bol., *region* 186/A3
Yungho, Tai. 117/B1
Yunnan, China, *province* 119/C3
Yurimaguas, Peru 185/B2
Yurok Ind. Res., Calif., U.S. 246/B1
Yuxian, Hond. 202/B3
Yutan, Nebr., U.S., 1,216 . . . . .308/H2
Yuzhno-Sakhalinsk, Russ., 176,515,
 (184,500 metro.) 104/I5
Yvelines, Fr., *department* 88/C2
Yverdon, Switz. 90/A2
Zaanstad, Neth., 135,444 . . . . .84/B2
Zabbar, Malta 97/C2
Zabid, Yemen 137/A2
Zabol, Iran .130/E3
Zabrze, Pol., 199,725 . . . . .83/D3
Zacapa, Guat. 201/D5
Zacatecas, Mex., *state capital*, 113,947,
 (123,899 metro.) 200/D3
Zacatecas, Mex., *state* 200/D3
Zacatecoluca, El. Salv., 57,032 . . . . . . .203/B2
Zachary, La., U.S., 11,275 . . . . .282/G5
Zachodnio-Pomorskie, Pol., *province* . . .83/B2
Zadar, Cro. 98/B3
Zafra, Sp. .94/C3
Zag, Ky., U.S. 280/G3
Zagazig, Egy., 267,000 . . . . .144/B1
Zaghouan, Tun. 146/C1
Zagreb, Cro., *capital*, 691,724,
 (1,047,000 metro.) 98/B2
Zagros, Iran, *mountains* 130/B3
Zahedan, Iran, 419,518 . . . . .130/E4
Zahl, N. Dak., U.S. 326/B1
Zahlah, Leb., 45,000 . . . . .134/A2
Zaire, *nation* 149
Zaire, Ang., *province* 159/B2
Zaječar, Serb.-Mont. 99/C3
Zakarpattia, Ukr., *oblast* 102/A2
Zakynthos, Gr., *island* 100/B3
Zakopane, Pol. 83/D4
Zala, Hun., *county* 91/A2
Zala, Hun., *river* 91/A2
Zalaegerszeg, Hun. 91/A2
Zalău, Rom. 101/B2
Zaleski, Ohio, U.S., 375 . . . . .328/F7
Zalma, Mo., U.S., 93 . . . . .302/F4
Zama, Miss., U.S., 40 . . . . .300/C3
Zambales, Phil., *mountains* 120/B4
Zambezi, Ang., *river* 159/E3
Zambezi, Moz., *river* 161/B3
Zambezi, Zam. 159/A2
Zambezi, Zam., *river* 159/A3, B3
Zambezi, Zimb., *river* 160/A1, B1
Zambia, *nation* 153
Zamboanga, Phil., 608,794 . . . . .120/B5
Zamboanga, Phil., *peninsula* 120/B5
Zamora, Ecua. 185/B5
Zamora, Sp. 185/B4
Zamora, Sp., 64,845 . . . . .94/C2
Zamora, Sp., *province* 94/D2
Zamora-Chinchipe, Ecua., *province* 185/B5
Zamość, Pol. 83/F3
Zanderij, Sur. 183/B2
Zane, Utah, U.S. 350/A6
Zanesfield, Ohio, U.S., 220 . . . . .328/C5
Zanesville, Ind., U.S., 602 . . . . .270/F3
Zanesville, Ohio, U.S., 25,586 . . . . .328/F6
Zanjan, Iran, 286,295 . . . . .130/B2
Zanjan, Iran, *province* 130/B2
Zanoni, Mo., U.S., 50 . . . . .302/D5
Zanzibar, Tan., 157,634 . . . . .158/C2
Zanzibar, Tan., *island* 158/C2
Zanzibar Central/South, Tan., *region* . . .158/C1
Zanzibar North, Tan., *region* 158/C1
Zanzibar Urban/West, Tan., *region* 114/D2
Zao san, Jap., *volcano* 114/D2
Zap, N. Dak., U.S., 231 . . . . .326/D2
Zapadna Morava, Serb.-Mont., *river* 99/B3
Zapata, Tex., U.S., 4,856 . . . . .346/J9
Zapata, Tex., U.S., *county*, 12,182 . . . .346/J8
Zapatera, Nicar., *island* 202/B3
Zaporizhzhia, Ukr., 850,118 . . . . .102/D2
Zaporizhzhia, Ukr., *oblast* 102/D2
Zaqatala, Azer. 103/B2
Zarafobod, Taj. 132/A1
Zarafshon, Uzb. 132/B2
Zaragoza, Sp., 614,905 . . . . .94/F2
Zaragoza, Sp., *province* 94/F2
Zaranj, Afg. 129/A2
Zareh Sharan, Afg. 129/B2
Zaria, Nig. .152/B2
Zarzis, Tun. 146/C3
Zavala, Tex., U.S., *county*, 11,600 . . . . .346/J7
Zavalla, Tex., U.S., 647 . . . . .346/N4
Zavidovići, Bos.-Her. 98/B1
Zaysan, Kaz. 131/E2
Zaysan, Kaz., *lake* 131/E2

Zaza, Cuba, *river* 204/C2
Zealand, N.B., Can. 217/C2
Zearing, Iowa, U.S., 617 . . . . .274/H3
Zebbug, Malta 97/A1
Zebulon, Ga., U.S., 1,181 . . . . .260/C5
Zebulon, Ky., U.S., 700 . . . . .280/H1
Zeebrugge, Belg. 85/B1
Zeeland, Neth., *province* 84/A3
Zeeland, Mich., U.S., 5,805 . . . . .294/C7
Zeeland, N. Dak., U.S., 141 . . . . .326/F4
Zefat, Isr. .135/B1
Zeigler, Ill., U.S., 1,669 . . . . .266/D6
Zela, W. Va., U.S., 200 . . . . .360/E4
Zelienople, Penn., U.S., 4,123 . . . . .336/A4
Zell, S. Dak., U.S., 70 . . . . .342/G3
Zell am See, Aus. 91/C3
Zellwood, Fla., U.S., 2,540 . . . . .256/C3
Zémio, C.A.R. 154/C2
Zemple, Minn., U.S., 75 . . . . .298/D3
Zemun, Serb.-Mont. 99/B3
Zena, Okla., U.S., 123 . . . . .330/H1
Zenda, Kans., U.S., 123 . . . . .276/D4
Zenia, Calif., U.S. 246/B2
Zenica, Bos.-Her., 96,238 . . . . .98/B1
Zephyr, Tex., U.S., 125 . . . . .346/K4
Zephyr Cove, Nev., U.S., 1,649 . . . . . . .310/A2
Zephyrhills, Fla., U.S., 10,833 . . . . .256/F3
Zeravshan, Taj., *mountains* 132/A1
Zeravshan, Taj., *river* 132/A1
Zeravshan, Uzb., *river* 132/B2
Zereh, Gowd-e, Afg., *lake* 129/A3
Zerkel, Minn., U.S., 60 . . . . .298/B3
Zermatt, Switz. 90/B2
Zestaponi, Geo. 103/B3
Zetland, Scot., U.K., *island* 62/P2
Zêzere, Port., *river* 93/A3
Zhangjiakou, China 119/E1
Zhangye, China 119/D2
Zhanjiang, China 119/E3
Zhejiang, China, *province* 119/E3
Zhelaniya, Russ., *cape* 104/E2
Zhengzhou, China, 1,796,843 . . . . .119/E2
Zhenjiang, China 119/E2
Zhezqazgan, Kaz. 131/C2
Zhlobin, Bela. 102/B2
Zhob, Pak., *river* 129/C3
Zhoda, Man., Can. 215/C4
Zhu, China, *river* 119/E3
Zhuzhou, China 119/E3
Zhytomyr, Ukr., 297,651 . . . . .102/B1
Zhytomyr, Ukr., *oblast* 102/B1
Zia Ind. Res., N. Mex., U.S. 317/D2
Zia Pueblo, N. Mex., U.S., 646 . . . . .317/D2
Zibo, China 119/E2
Ziebach, S. Dak., U.S., *county*, 2,519 . . .342/D3
Zielona Góra, Pol., 188,244 . . . . .83/B3
Zigong, China, 866,020, (1,673,300 metro.) .119/D3
Ziguinchor, Sen., (199,871 metro.) 148/A3
Žilina, Slvk., 156,361 . . . . .92/B2
Žilinský, Slvk., *region* 92/B2
Zillah, Lib. .145/C2
Zillah, Wash., U.S., 2,198 . . . . .358/E3
Zillertal Alps, Aus., *range* 91/B3
Zilwaukee, Mich., U.S., 1,799 . . . . .294/F6
Zim, Minn., U.S., 90 . . . . .298/E3
Zima, Alta., Can., *lake* 212/A2
Zimbabwe, *nation* 154
Zimmerman, La., U.S., 125 . . . . .282/D4
Zimmerman, Minn., U.S., 2,851 . . . . . . .298/D5
Zinc, Ark., U.S., 76 . . . . .244/C1
Zinder, Niger, 120,160 . . . . .152/B3
Zion, St. K.-Nevis 207/C3
Zion, Ark., U.S., 125 . . . . .244/D2
Zion, Ill., U.S., 22,866 . . . . .266/B4, F1
Zion, Ky., U.S., 550 . . . . .280/C3
Zion, Mo., U.S. 302/F4
Zion, Penn., U.S., 2,054 . . . . .336/F4
Zion Crossroads, Va., U.S., 375 . . . . . . .354/G5
Zion Natl. Park, Utah, U.S. 350/A6
Zionsville, Ind., U.S., 8,775 . . . . .270/D5
Zirkel, Colo., U.S., *mountain* 250/D1
Zittau, Ger. 86/C3
Ziwa Magharibi, Tan., *region* 158/B1
Ziway, Eth., *lake* 156/C3
Zlatibor, Serb.-Mont., *mountains* 99/A3
Zlín, Czh. Rep., 83,000 . . . . .92/C3
Zlínský, Czh. Rep., *region* 92/C3
Znojmo, Czh. Rep. 92/C4
Zoar, Mass., U.S., 175 . . . . .292/C2
Zoar, Ohio, U.S., 193 . . . . .328/H4
Zolfo Sprs., Fla., U.S., 1,641 . . . . .256/G4
Zomba, Mal., 65,915 . . . . .161/B3
Zonguldak, Tur. 133/B2
Zonguldak, Tur., *province* 133/C2
Zook, Kans., U.S., 40 . . . . .276/C3
Zorn, Tex., U.S., 70 . . . . .346/B1
Zortman, Mont., U.S., 175 . . . . .306/H2
Zorzor, Liber. 149/B2
Zouar, Chad 153/B2
Zouérat, Maur. 147/B2
Zrenjanin, Serb.-Mont., 132,712 . . . . . . .99/B2
Zug, Switz. 90/C1
Zug, Switz., *canton* 90/C1
Zugdidi, Geo. 103/A3
Zugspitze, Ger., *mountain* 86/B5
Zuid-Willemsvaart, Neth., *canal* 84/C3
Zújar, Sp., *reservoir* 94/D3
Zulia, Ven., *state* 182/B2
Zululand, S. Afr., *region* 162/D2
Zumbro Falls, Minn., U.S., 177 . . . . .298/E6
Zumbrota, Minn., U.S., 2,789 . . . . .298/E6
Zuni, N. Mex., U.S., *mountains* 317/B2
Zuni, N. Mex., U.S., *river* 354/K7
Zuni Ind. Res., N. Mex., U.S. 317/B2
Zuni Pueblo, N. Mex., U.S., 6,367 . . . . . .346/L7
Zunkerville, Tex., U.S. 346/L7
Zunyi, China 119/D3
Zurich, Kans., U.S., 126 . . . . .276/C2
Zurich, Mont., U.S. 306/G1
Zürich, Switz., 340,873, (932,681 metro.) . .90/C1
Zürich, Switz., *canton* 90/C1
Zürichsee, Switz., *lake* 90/C1
Zurrieq, Malta 97/B2
Zuwarah, Lib. 145/B1
Zvishavane, Zimb. 160/B2
Zvolen, Slvk. 92/C1
Zvornik, Bos.-Her. 99/B2
Zwedru, Liber. 149/B2
Zwickau, Ger., 104,146 . . . . .86/C3
Zwingle, Iowa, U.S., 100 . . . . .274/N3
Zwolle, Neth., 105,116 . . . . .84/C2
Zwolle, La., U.S., 1,783 . . . . .282/B3
Zyryanka, Russ. 104/I3

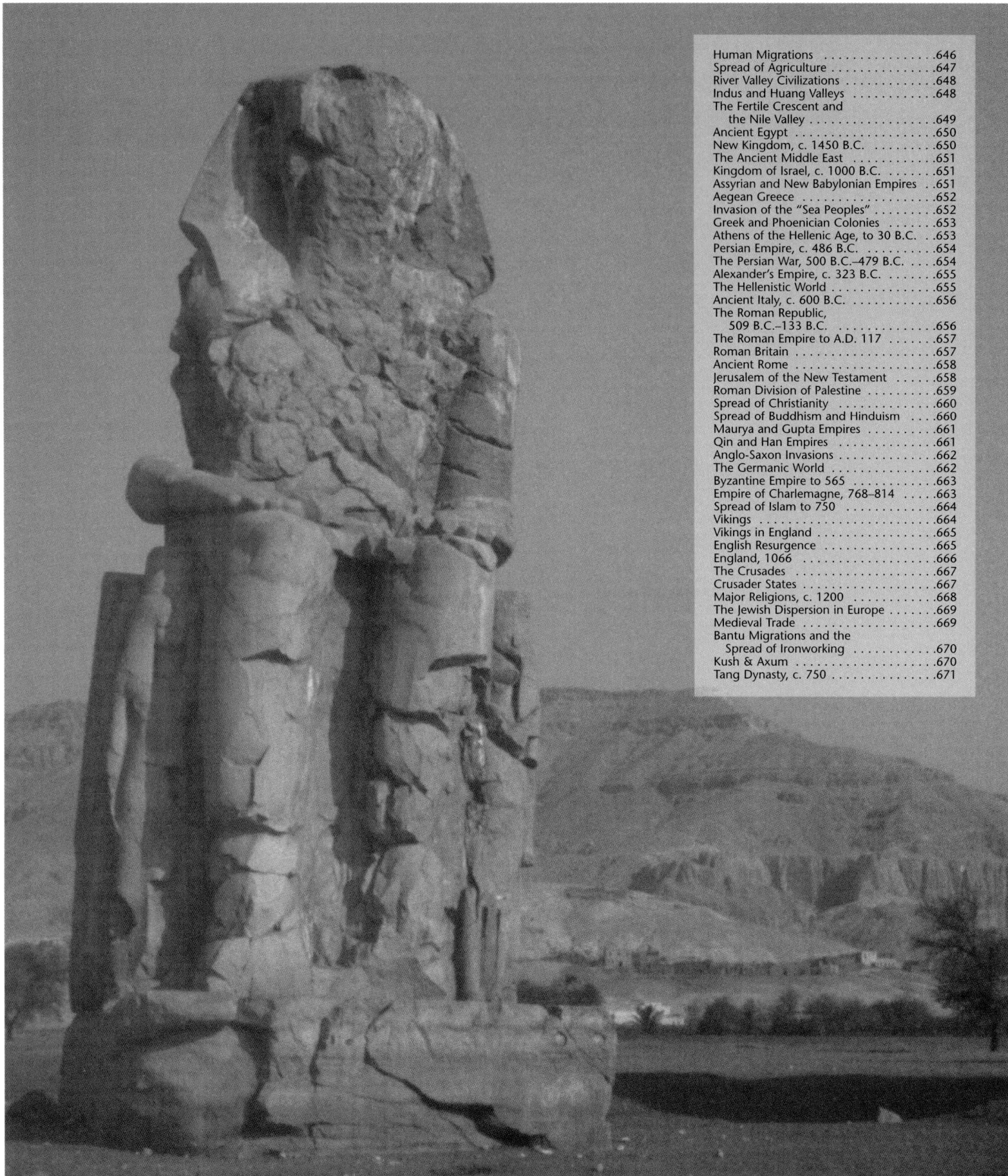

Human Migrations 646
Spread of Agriculture 647
River Valley Civilizations 648
Indus and Huang Valleys 648
The Fertile Crescent and
   the Nile Valley 649
Ancient Egypt 650
New Kingdom, c. 1450 B.C. 650
The Ancient Middle East 651
Kingdom of Israel, c. 1000 B.C. 651
Assyrian and New Babylonian Empires . .651
Aegean Greece 652
Invasion of the "Sea Peoples" 652
Greek and Phoenician Colonies 653
Athens of the Hellenic Age, to 30 B.C. . .653
Persian Empire, c. 486 B.C. 654
The Persian War, 500 B.C.–479 B.C. 654
Alexander's Empire, c. 323 B.C. 655
The Hellenistic World 655
Ancient Italy, c. 600 B.C. 656
The Roman Republic,
   509 B.C.–133 B.C. 656
The Roman Empire to A.D. 117 657
Roman Britain 657
Ancient Rome 658
Jerusalem of the New Testament 658
Roman Division of Palestine 659
Spread of Christianity 660
Spread of Buddhism and Hinduism 660
Maurya and Gupta Empires 661
Qin and Han Empires 661
Anglo-Saxon Invasions 662
The Germanic World 662
Byzantine Empire to 565 663
Empire of Charlemagne, 768–814 663
Spread of Islam to 750 664
Vikings 664
Vikings in England 665
English Resurgence 665
England, 1066 666
The Crusades 667
Crusader States 667
Major Religions, c. 1200 668
The Jewish Dispersion in Europe 669
Medieval Trade 669
Bantu Migrations and the
   Spread of Ironworking 670
Kush & Axum 670
Tang Dynasty, c. 750 671

Colossi of Amonhotep III, Thebes, Egypt

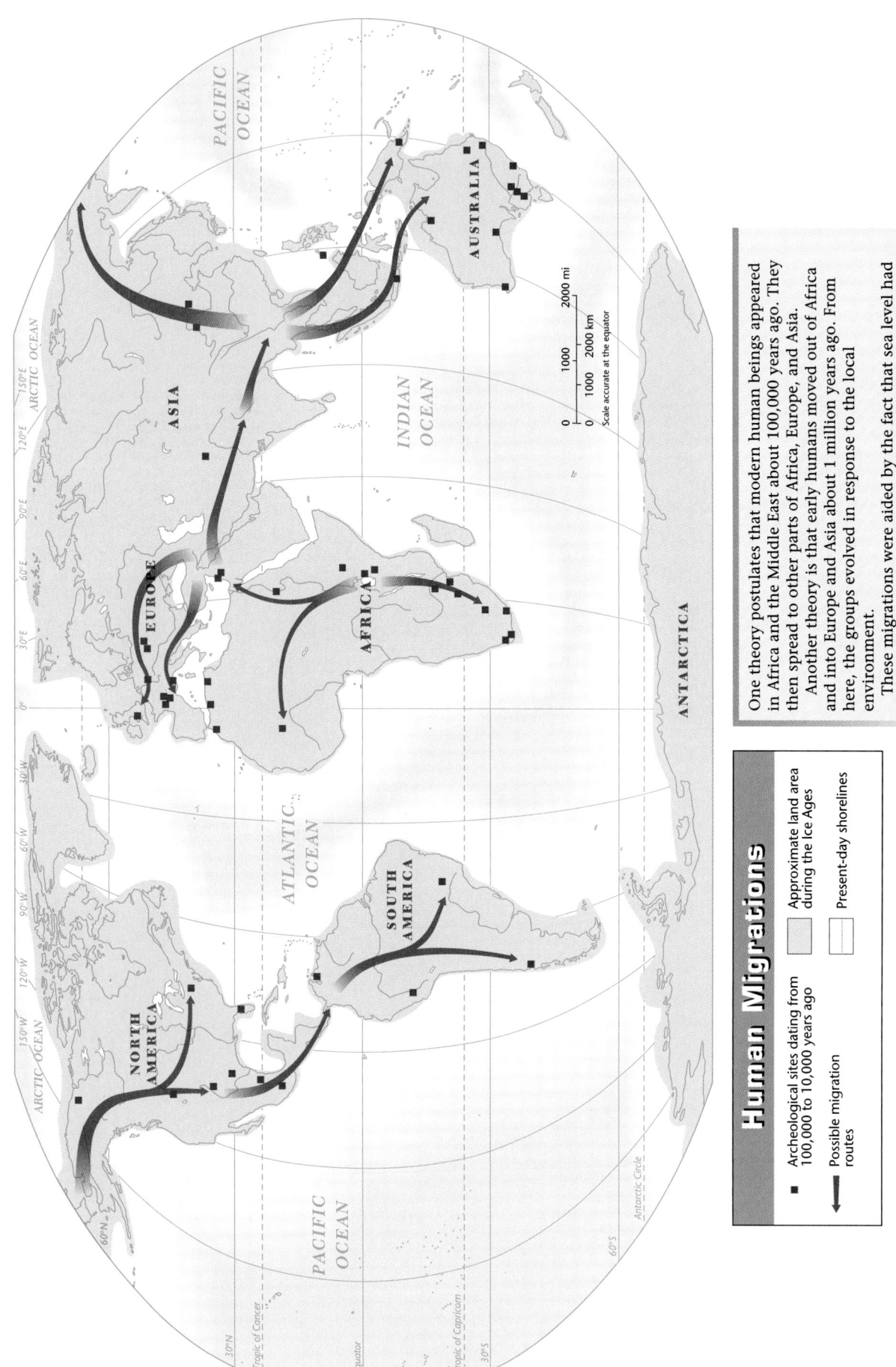

Human Migrations

Archeological sites dating from 100,000 to 10,000 years ago

Possible migration routes

Approximate land area during the Ice Ages

Present-day shorelines

One theory postulates that modern human beings appeared in Africa and the Middle East about 100,000 years ago. They then spread to other parts of Africa, Europe, and Asia. Another theory is that early humans moved out of Africa and into Europe and Asia about 1 million years ago. From here, the groups evolved in response to the local environment.

These migrations were aided by the fact that sea level had dropped during the Ice Ages. This exposed land bridges that enabled people to reach more isolated areas.

© MapQuest.com, Inc.

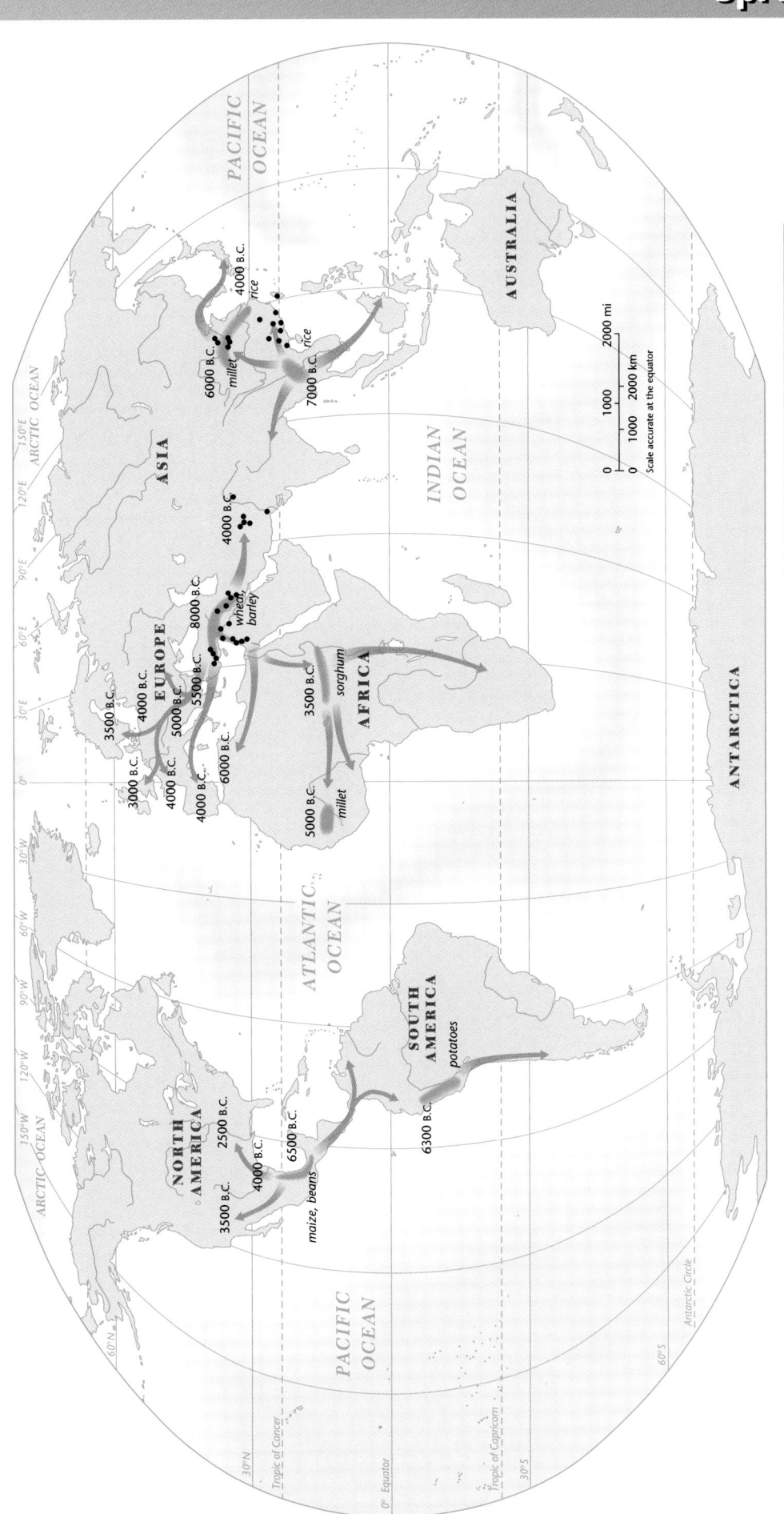

According to most scientists, agriculture developed in the Fertile Crescent of the Middle East about 11,000 to 10,000 years ago (9000 B.C. to 8000 B.C.) and several thousand years later in Southeast Asia and Mesoamerica. Recent research has indicated that agriculture might have developed independently in west and central Africa and Peru.

Before the advent of agriculture, people, as hunters and gatherers, relied on the productivity of the natural environment. Through observation, these people learned the manner of plant reproduction and worked to preserve and increase the yields. With a more reliable source of food, people were able to stay in one place for a longer period of time. Thus, villages were established.

Any surplus of food enabled people to do jobs not directly related to agriculture. People could become craftsmen, miners, teachers, or bureaucrats. It was the efforts of all these people that helped turn villages into cities, and in turn, make groups of cities into states and civilizations.

Spread of Agriculture

▮ Core areas of agriculture

→ General direction of agricultural dispersal

8000 B.C. Approximate date of agricultural development

• Early settlements

wheat Important crop

© MapQuest.com, Inc.

Civilization refers to a life style that consists of economic, governmental, and social systems. During the prehistoric period people probably lived in familial groups. With the development of agriculture people began to settle down, and this often took place along rivers.

Rivers provided food, fresh water, and the promise of irrigated agriculture. But in order to implement any form of irrigation, it was necessary for people to cooperate. It is believed that this might have been one of the main reasons government evolved.

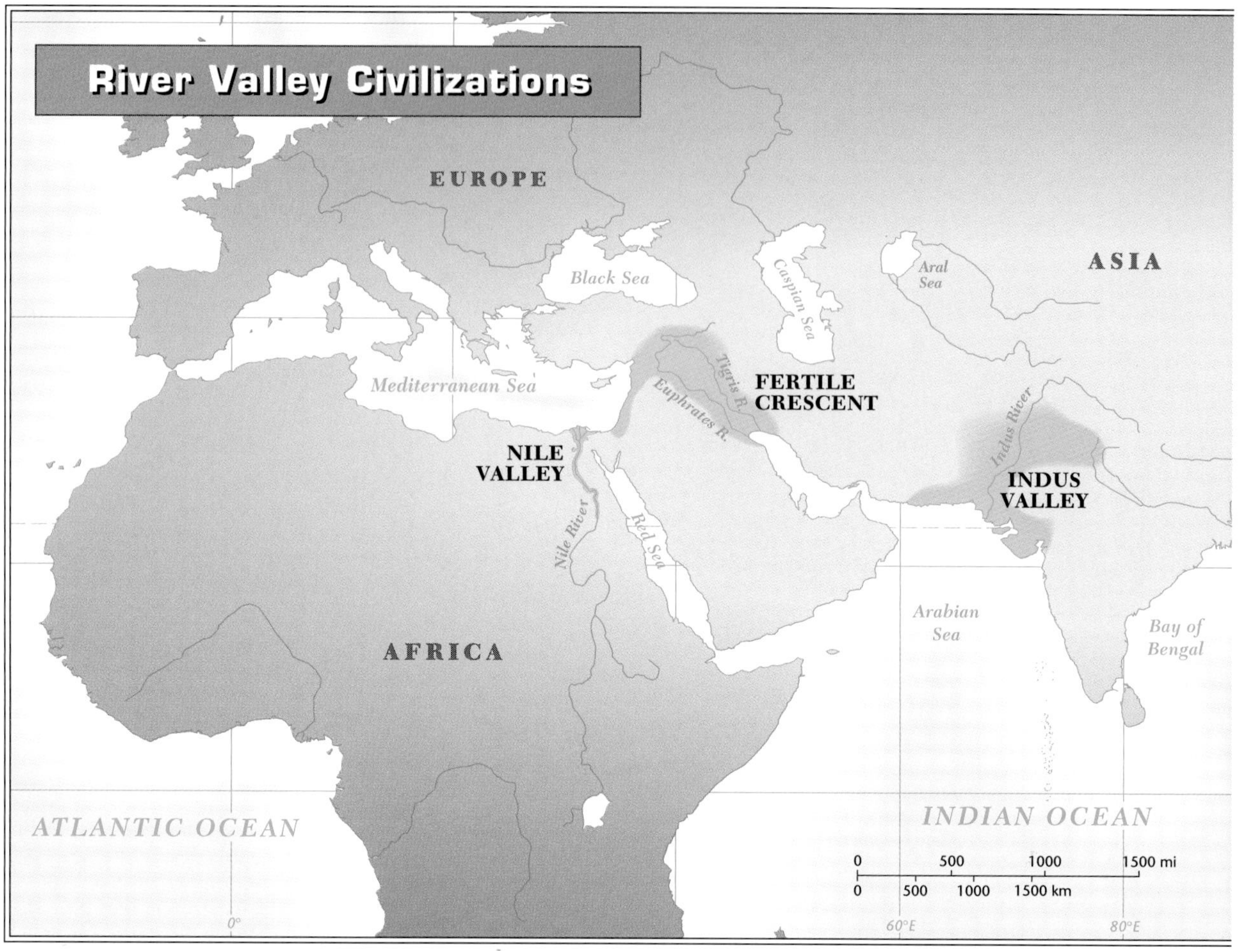

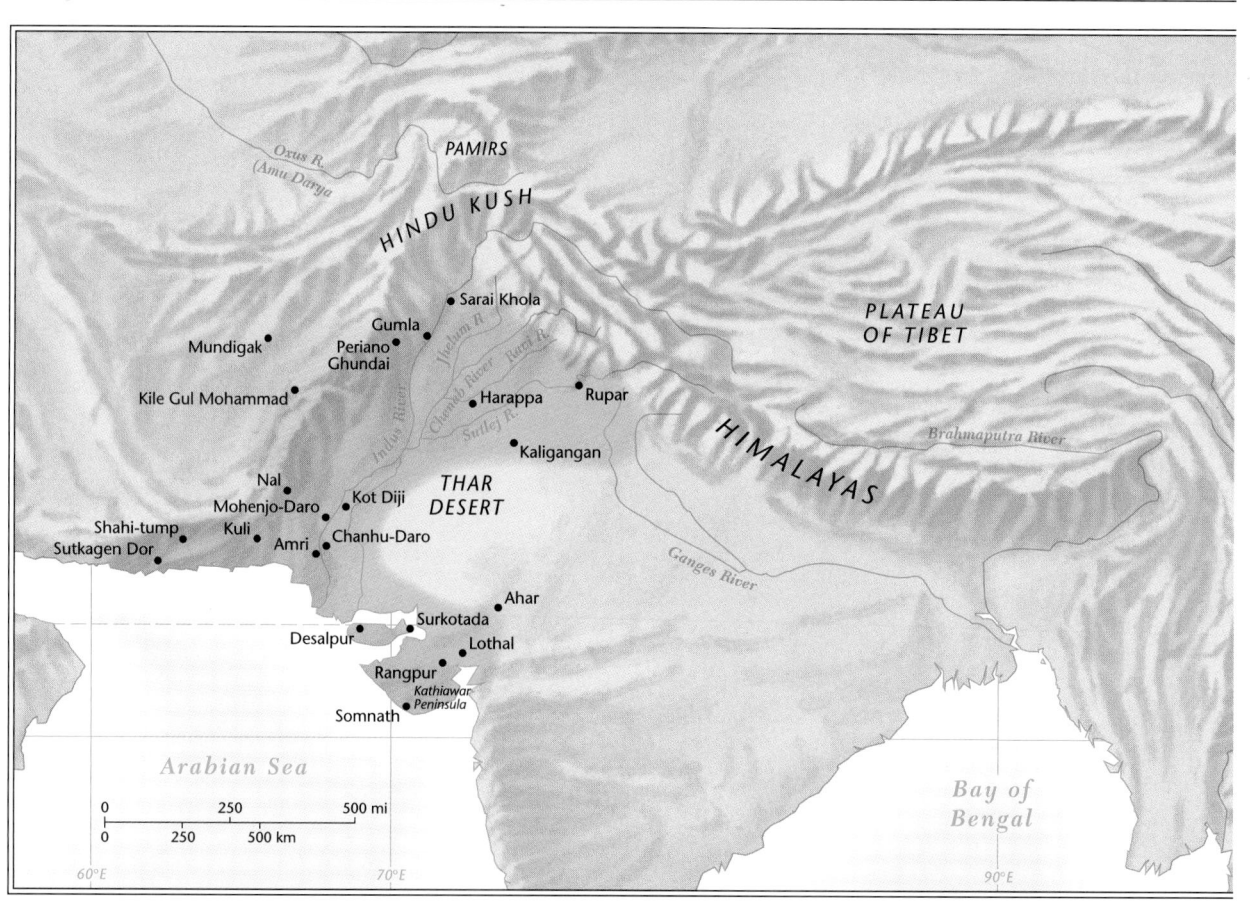

River Valley Civilizations

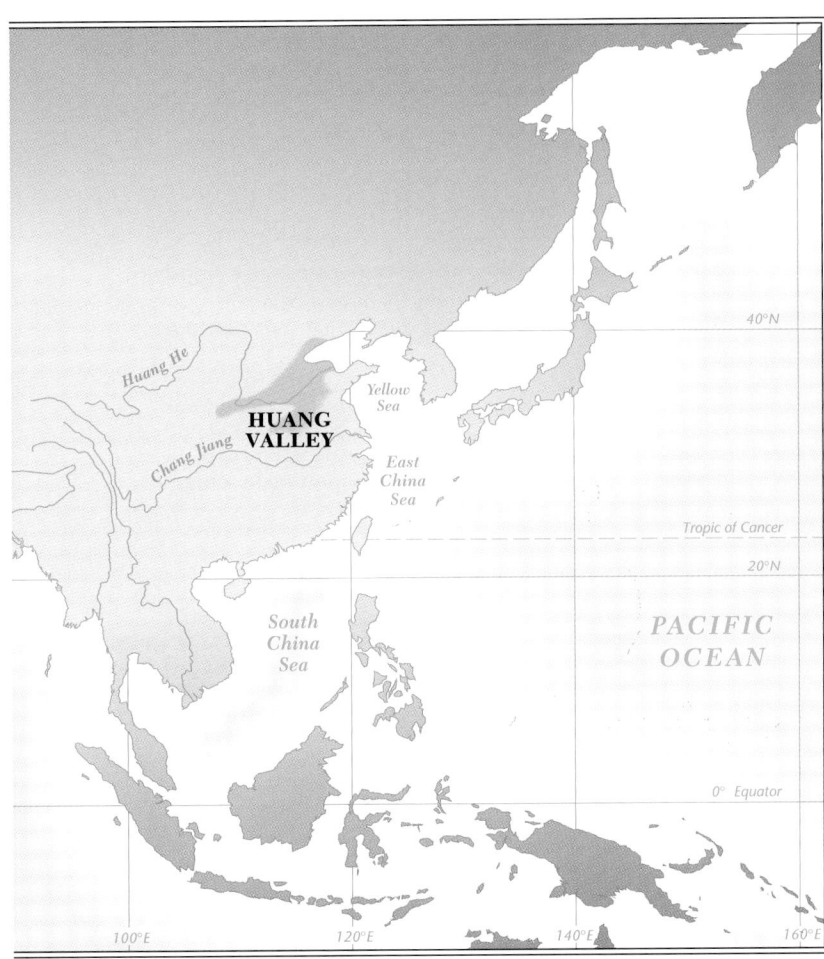

The Fertile Crescent & the Nile Valley

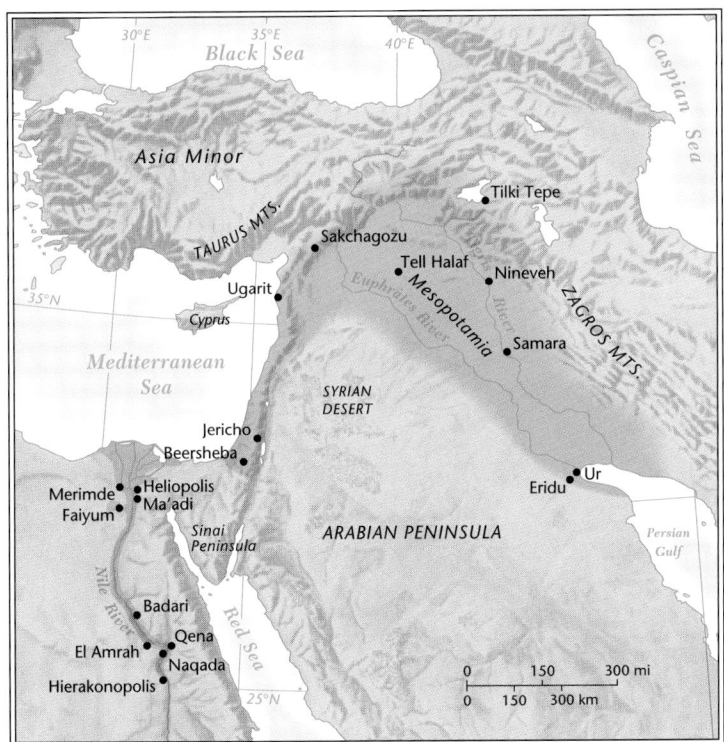

Sometime in the first half of the 4th millennium B.C., civilization began to develop in Mesopotamia. In this region the land was fertile, but the rainfall amounts were low. At first, irrigation was probably intended to reduce the uncertainties of agriculture, but it also helped the people to produce a food surplus. This surplus promoted the growth of population and the number of villages.

The Sumerians migrated from the north and settled in southern Mesopotamia. They developed traditions of religion, politics, and social organizations that would outlast their own civilization.

Farther to the west, another civilization developed along the Nile River around 3000 B.C. The Nile was revered for its yearly flooding that irrigated crops and deposited rich silt. Perhaps because of this focus, Egypt looked inward and developed a tightly knit political organization, one that did not extend too far beyond the valley of the Nile.

Civilization probably developed in the Indus Valley in the middle of the 3rd millennium B.C. Rivers from the Himalayas provided water for irrigation and deposited soils to enrich the land. Harappa and Mohenjo-Daro were the two major cities of the region. Both were major trading centers and were dominated by a powerful priestly class.

Legend has it that the Indus civilization was destroyed by Aryan invaders from central Asia. While this did occur, it is more likely that the civilization gradually declined because of climatic change and natural disasters.

In China civilization developed around the Huang He. The river deposited rich layers of loess—wind-blown glacial soils. While this was beneficial, the river was infamous for raging floods. For those living in the river valley, the construction and maintenance of levees was a major concern.

Unlike the Harappan civilization that disappeared from history, the small kingdoms that developed along the Huang He were consolidated into the Shang Dynasty. These formed the base for the civilization that would last for years to come.

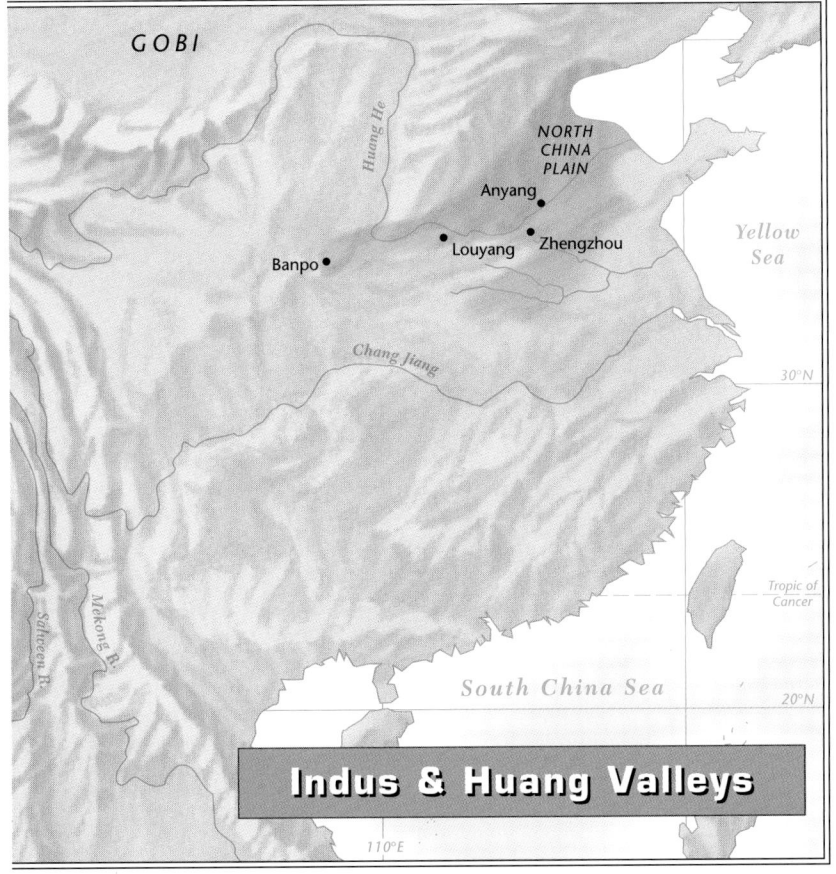

Indus & Huang Valleys

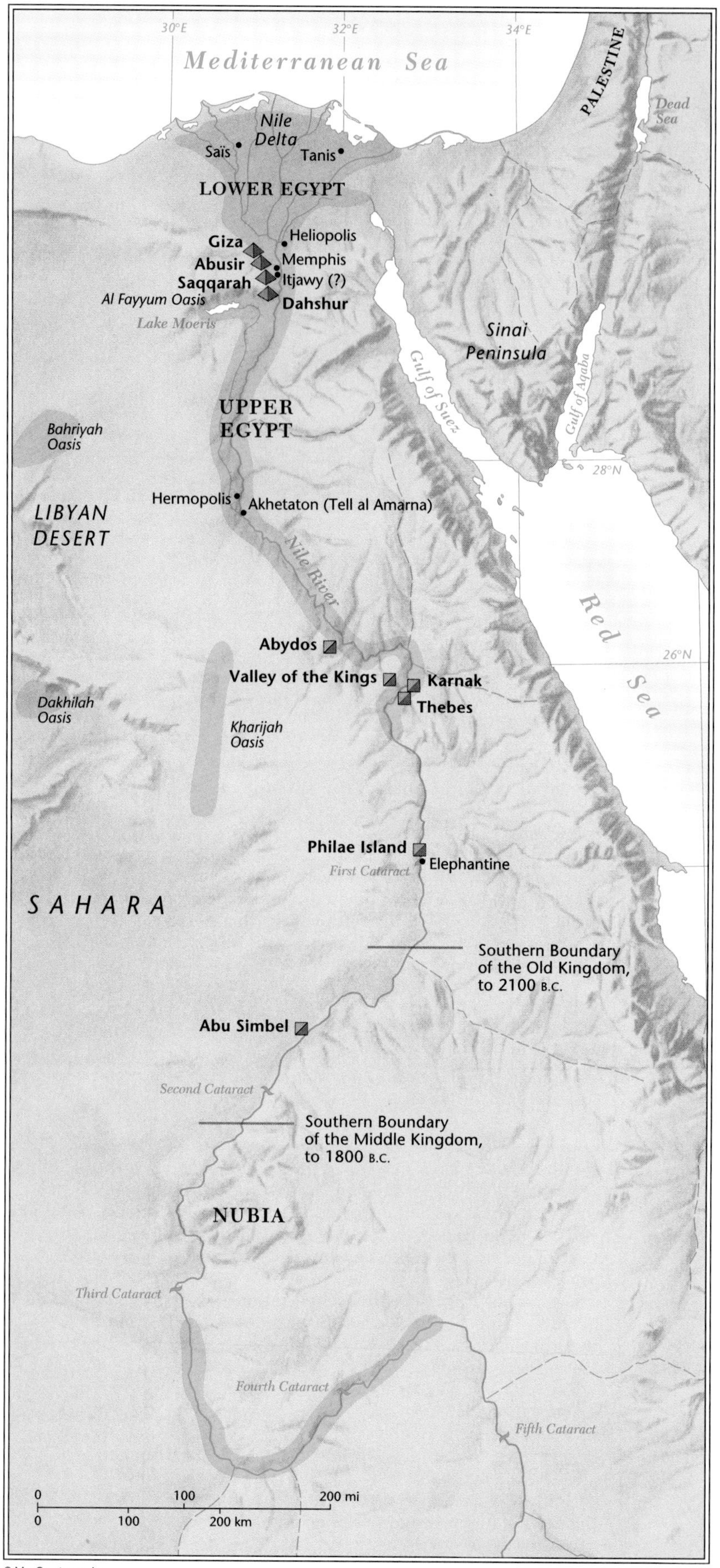

Map of Ancient Egypt showing the Nile River, Lower Egypt (Nile Delta region) and Upper Egypt, with the Mediterranean Sea to the north, the Red Sea and Sinai Peninsula to the east, the Libyan Desert and Sahara to the west, and Nubia to the south.

Locations marked on the main map:

Lower Egypt: Saïs, Tanis, Nile Delta, Giza, Heliopolis, Memphis, Abusir, Itjawy (?), Saqqarah, Dahshur, Al Fayyum Oasis, Lake Moeris

Upper Egypt: Bahriyah Oasis, Hermopolis, Akhetaton (Tell al Amarna), Dakhilah Oasis, Abydos, Valley of the Kings, Karnak, Thebes, Kharijah Oasis, Philae Island, Elephantine (First Cataract), Abu Simbel (Second Cataract)

Southern Boundary of the Old Kingdom, to 2100 B.C.

Southern Boundary of the Middle Kingdom, to 1800 B.C.

NUBIA — Third Cataract, Fourth Cataract, Fifth Cataract

Scale: 0 — 100 — 200 mi / 0 — 100 — 200 km

© MapQuest.com, Inc.

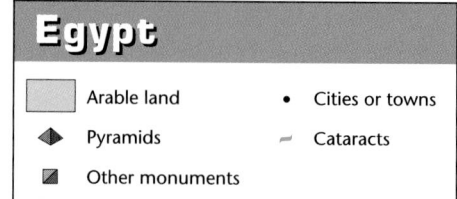

Egypt

▨ Arable land	• Cities or towns
◆ Pyramids	～ Cataracts
▨ Other monuments	

The Nile river was a unifying element in ancient Egypt. Everybody depended on the rich soils that the yearly flooding provided.

Around 3100 B.C. Menes (Narmer), a king in Upper Egypt, conquered the fragmented northern kingdoms of Lower Egypt and created a unified state that would last, in one form or another, for nearly 3000 years. He established the capital at Memphis, on the dividing line between the two regions.

New Kingdom, c. 1450 B.C.

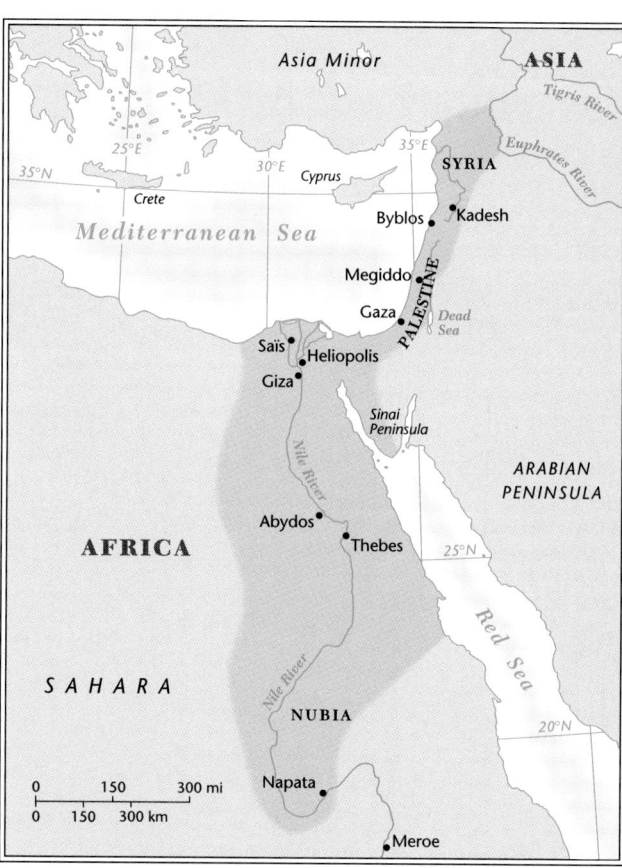

Map of the New Kingdom showing Asia Minor, Asia, Africa, the Mediterranean Sea, Red Sea, and locations including Crete, Cyprus, Byblos, Kadesh, Syria, Megiddo, Gaza, Palestine, Dead Sea, Saïs, Heliopolis, Giza, Sinai Peninsula, Arabian Peninsula, Abydos, Thebes, Nubia, Napata, Meroe. Rivers: Tigris River, Euphrates River, Nile River.

Scale: 0 — 150 — 300 mi / 0 — 150 — 300 km

Following the period of the Middle Kingdom, Egypt was ruled by foreigners called *Hyksos*. Ahmose of Thebes liberated Egypt, founded the New Kingdom, and expanded his empire northward to Syria and southward to Nubia.

It was during this period that a system of slavery was established. Among those that fell into slavery were the Hebrews. Sometime during the 13th century B.C., Moses led his people out of Egypt.

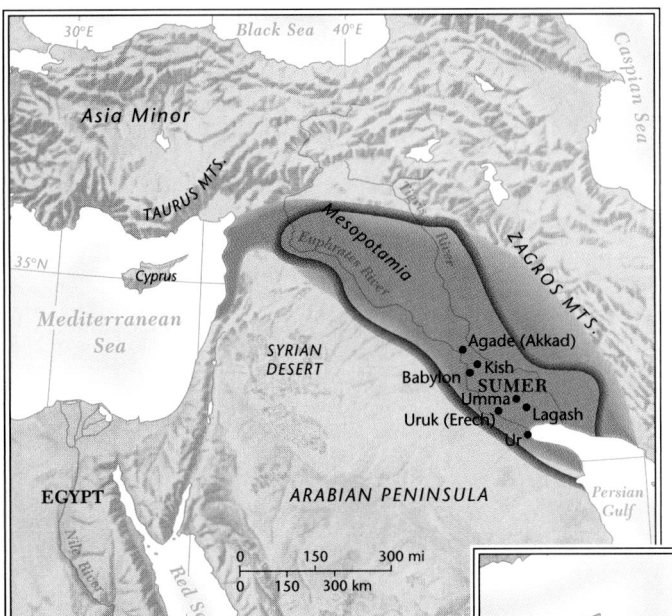

The Ancient Middle East

Akkadian Empire c. 2300 B.C.	Babylonian Empire c. 1750 B.C.

The rulers of Sumerian city-states fought amongst themselves for control of the region, and they were unable to unify themselves against outside pressures. It was Sargan of Agade (Akkad) who was able to conquer the cites of Sumer and become its lord. He then extended the new empire northward and westward, thus creating the first nation-state in the West.

Dynastic disputes and peoples' quest for automony weakened the empire until Hammurabi established the first Babylonian Empire. More famous than the empire itself was the Code of Hammurabi. This was a body of laws, together with a network of officials and judges, that attempted to preserve the existing social and economic order.

Kingdom of Israel c. 1000 B.C.

After arriving from Egypt, the Israelites occupied Palestine as a loose confederation of tribes. This disorganization put them at a disadvantage in fighting their neighbors, so they formed a kingdom under the leadership of David and his son Solomon.

The kingdom split in two after the death of Solomon: Israel in the north and Judah in the South. But the two kingdoms could not stand up to the new power in Mesopotamia—the Assyrians. Israel was defeated in 722 B.C., and Judah became a client state one hundred years later. But even under foreign domination, they were able to maintain their cultural and religious traditions.

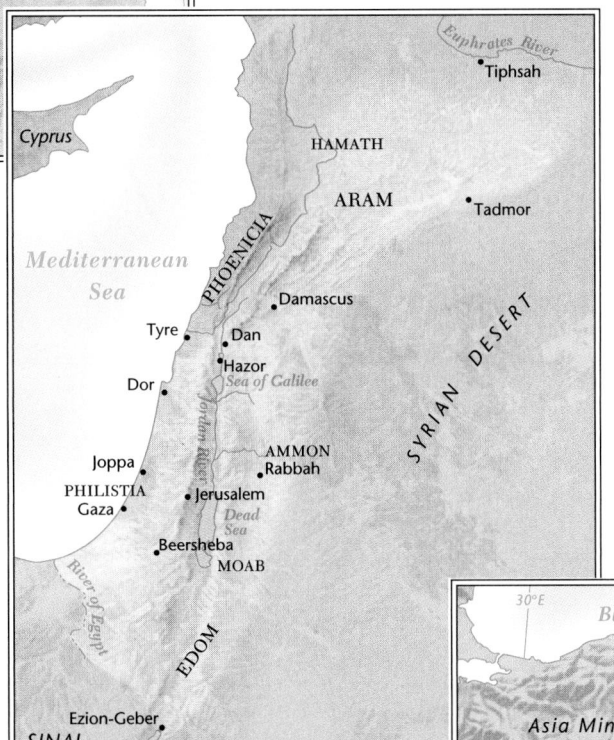

Assyrian & New Babylonian Empires

Assyrian Empire, c. 650 B.C.	New Babylonian Empire, c. 562 B.C.

The Assyrian state was like no other. Previous states and empires tended to be collections of city-states, but the Assyrians reorganized the conquered territories and remade them in the manner of the central government. Through unprecedented cruelty the Assyrians maintained control, but in the end, the hatred this engendered led to the eventual downfall of the empire.

The Babylonians, with the help of the Medes, destroyed the Assyrian capital of Nineveh and established the New Babylonian Empire.

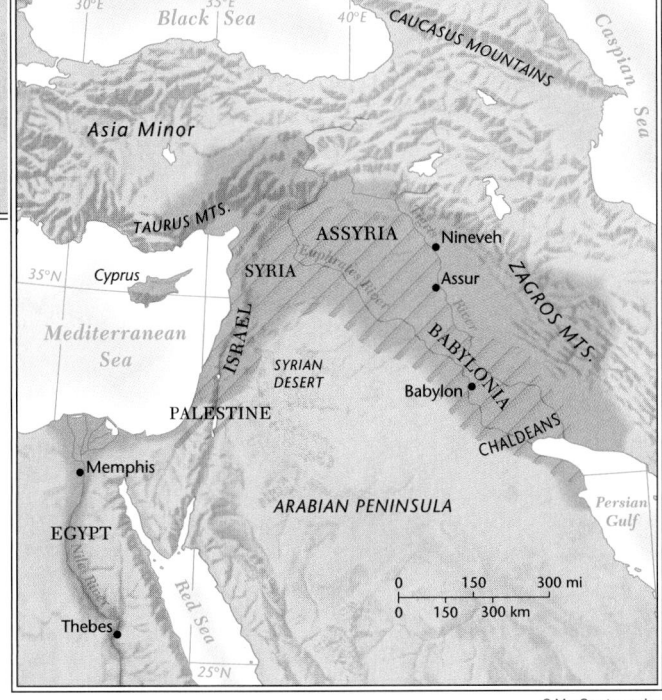

© MapQuest.com, Inc.

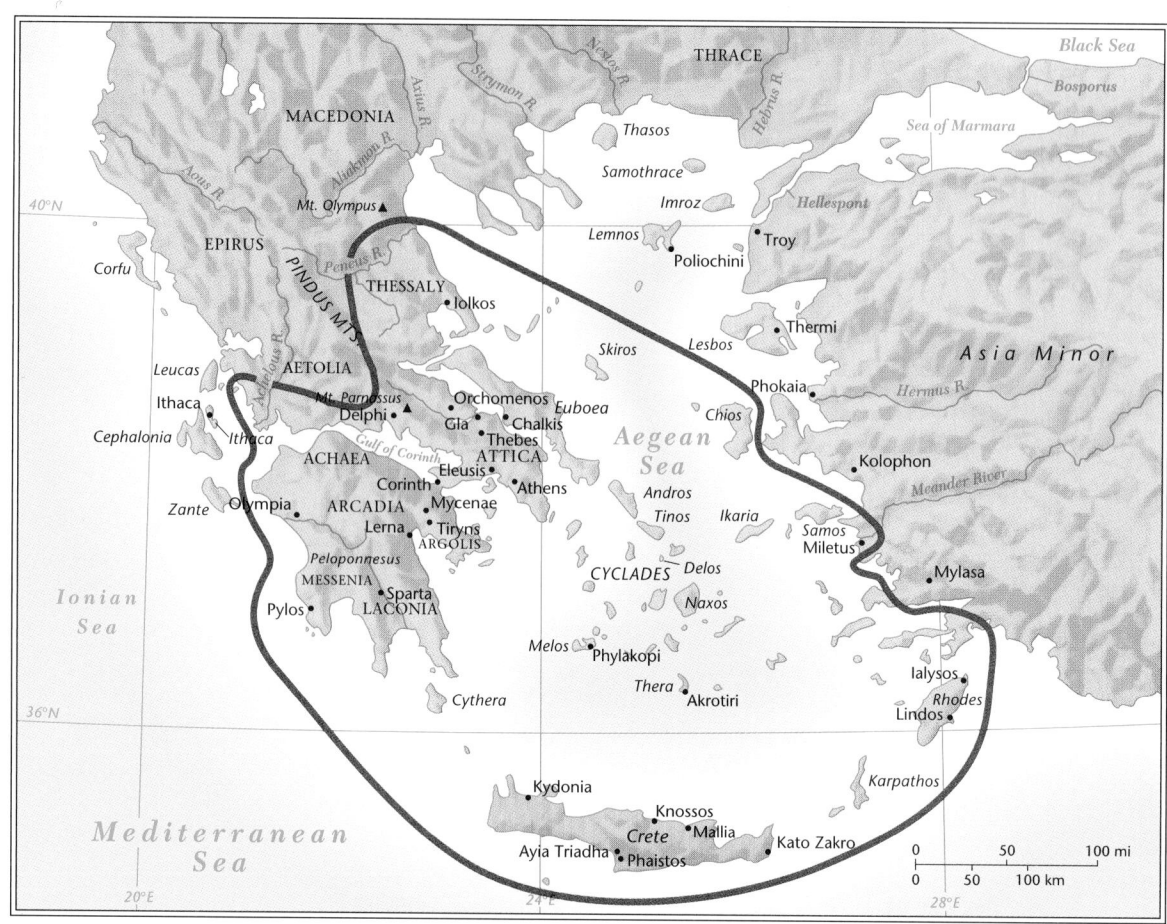

Aegean Greece

Minoan culture
c. 2000 B.C.–c. 1500 B.C.

Mycenaean culture
c. 1250 B.C.

• Major Greek centers

Europe's first major civilization (named for King Minos of Knossos) developed on the island of Crete some-time before 2000 B.C.

Crete's location, between Egyptian and Mesopotamian civilizations and the barbarian world to the north and west, made it a center of trade.

In the vicinity of Mycenae on the mainland there developed a civilization ruled by warrior kings. Taking advantage of the Minoans' lack of a martial tradition, the mainland Greeks conquered the island around 1500 B.C.

But the Mycenaean domination of the Aegean did not last for long. Starting around 1200 B.C., centralized government, urban life, and literacy all but disappeared.

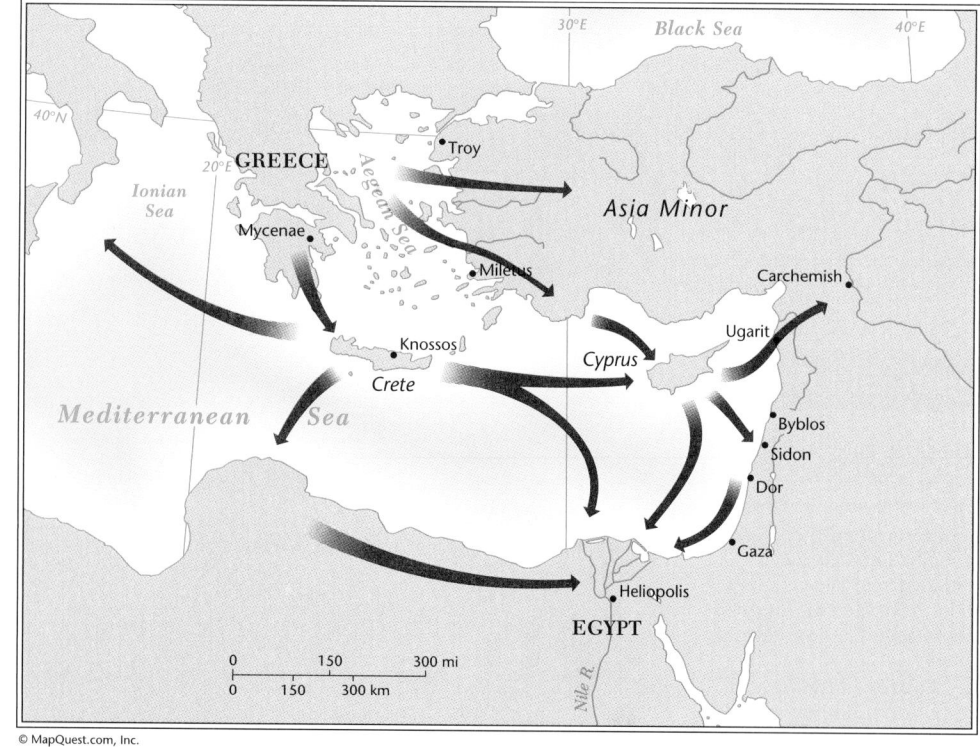

Invasion of the "Sea Peoples"

At one time it was believed that the Mycenaean civilization was destroyed by Dorians from northern Greece. It is true that there were invaders, but it is more likely that they arrived as Mycenae was collapsing.

This was a time of crisis in the Eastern Mediterranean. States throughout the region collapsed or were destroyed. Raiders were called "Sea Peoples," but rather than being one people, they probably were various peoples in flight. And in the general anarchy that followed, other groups took to raiding their neighbors.

© MapQuest.com, Inc.

Greek & Phoenician Colonies

- Major Greek mother city
- □ Greek colony
- Phoenician city
- Phoenician colony

As the Mycenaean culture collapsed, some Greeks migrated to Asia Minor and established cities there. More colonies were founded as trade grew. The population on the Greek mainland increased, putting more pressure on the land.

The Phoenicians were famous sailors and traders. They founded numerous colonies throughout the Mediterranean, the most famous of which was Carthage.

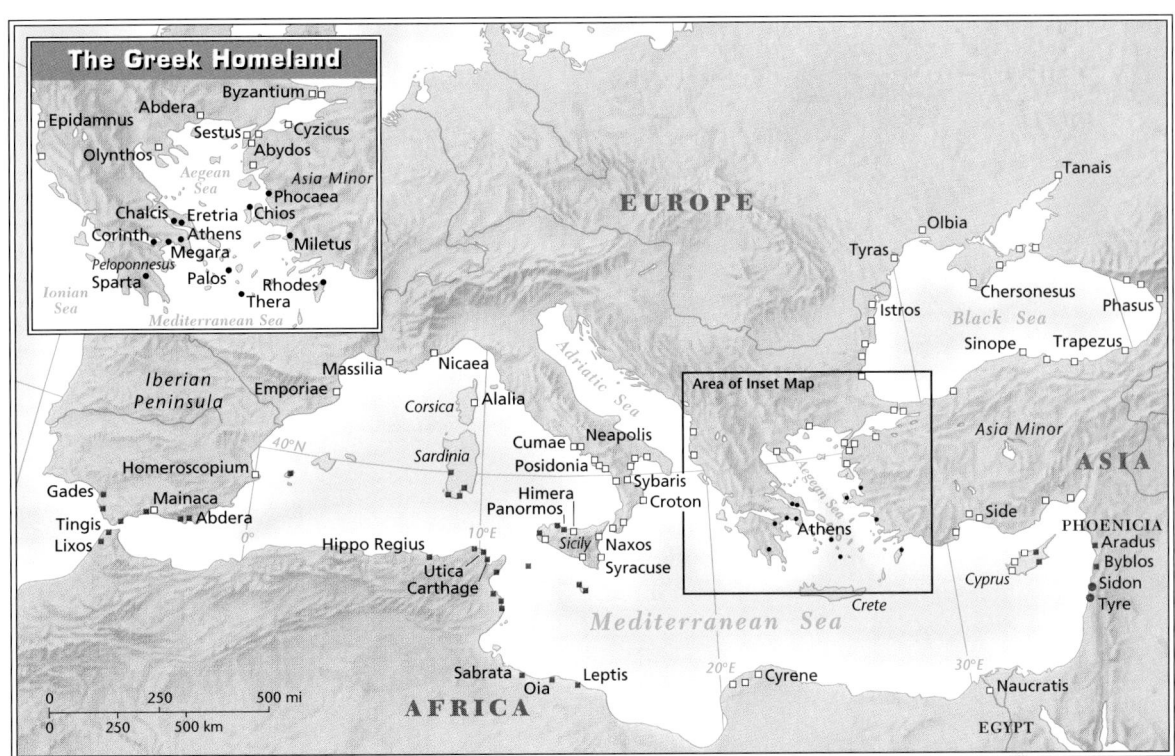

The Greek Homeland

Byzantium, Epidamnus, Abdera, Sestus, Cyzicus, Olynthos, Abydos, Aegean Sea, Asia Minor, Phocaea, Chalcis, Chios, Corinth, Eretria, Athens, Peloponnesus, Megara, Miletus, Sparta, Palos, Rhodes, Thera, Ionian Sea, Mediterranean Sea

EUROPE, Tanais, Olbia, Tyras, Chersonesus, Istros, Black Sea, Phasus, Sinope, Trapezus, Area of Inset Map, Asia Minor, ASIA, Side, PHOENICIA, Aradus, Byblos, Sidon, Cyprus, Tyre

Massilia, Nicaea, Adriatic Sea, Iberian Peninsula, Emporiae, Corsica, Alalia, Cumae, Neapolis, Sardinia, Posidonia, Homeroscopium, Himera, Sybaris, Gades, Panormos, Croton, Mainaca, Abdera, Tingis, Sicily, Naxos, Lixos, Hippo Regius, Syracuse, Utica, Carthage, Athens, Crete, Mediterranean Sea, Sabrata, Oia, Leptis, Cyrene, Naucratis, AFRICA, EGYPT

0 250 500 mi
0 250 500 km

Athens of the Hellenic Age to 30 B.C.

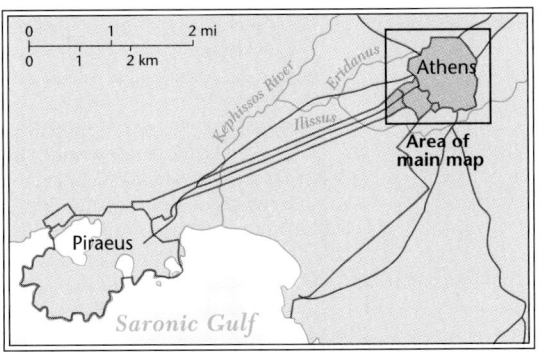

0 1 2 mi
0 1 2 km

Kephissos River, Eridanus, Ilissus, Athens, Area of main map, Piraeus, Saronic Gulf

Athens was named after Athena, the goddess of wisdom, and was one of the earliest city-states in Greece. Under the leadership of Cleisthenese, the city was made into a democracy. Every qualified citizen had the opportunity to help run the government.

Athens played a leading role in the defeat of the Persian Empire, and the half century following that war was called the Golden Age. Although a loss to Sparta in the Peloponnesian War led to a slow decline in its political leadership among the Greeks, Athens remained the intellectual center.

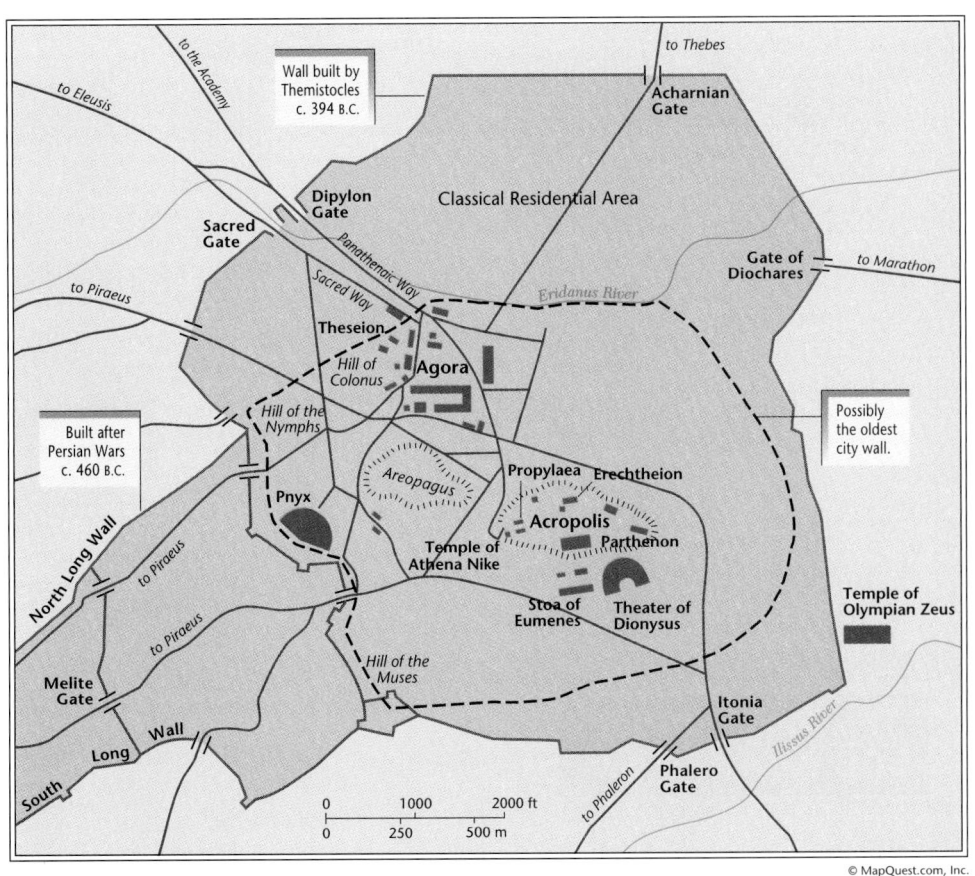

to the Academy, to Thebes, to Eleusis, Wall built by Themistocles c. 394 B.C., Acharnian Gate, Dipylon Gate, Classical Residential Area, Sacred Gate, Panathenaic Way, to Piraeus, Sacred Way, Gate of Diochares, to Marathon, Eridanus River, Theseion, Hill of Colonus, Agora, Hill of the Nymphs, Built after Persian Wars c. 460 B.C., Possibly the oldest city wall, Areopagus, Propylaea, Erechtheion, Pnyx, Acropolis, Parthenon, North Long Wall, to Piraeus, Temple of Athena Nike, Temple of Olympian Zeus, Stoa of Eumenes, Theater of Dionysus, Hill of the Muses, Melite Gate, Itonia Gate, Ilissus River, Long Wall, South, Phalero Gate, to Phaleron

0 1000 2000 ft
0 250 500 m

© MapQuest.com, Inc.

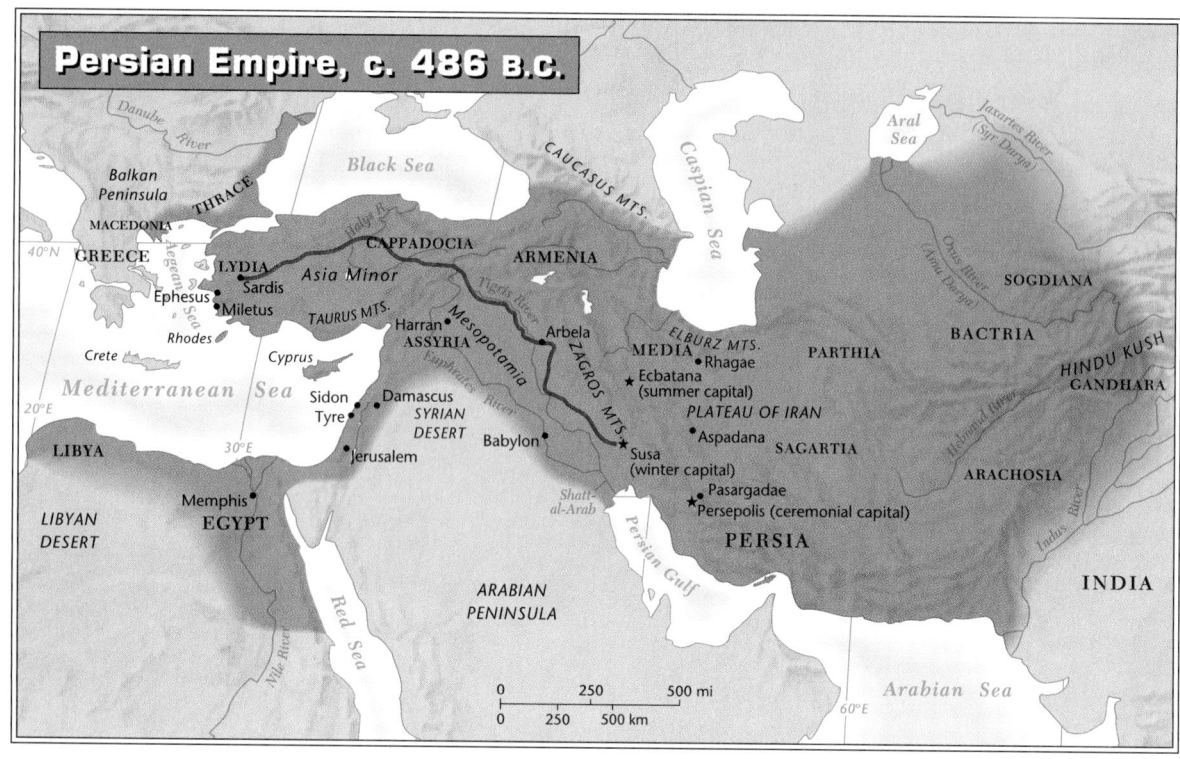

Persian Empire, c. 486 B.C.

Capital city ⋆   Royal Road ▬

Starting from southern Persia, the Persians conquered much of southwest Asia in a twenty year period. Later kings would add northwest India and part of southeast Europe.

For the most part, the Persians were tolerant of the conquered peoples' customs, and often adopted them as their own.

The empire was divided into provinces and ruled by officials, but final authority rested with the king.

Unsuccessful attempts to further extend the empire might have been one of the reasons for the empire's decline.

The Persian War 500 B.C.–479 B.C.

Persian Empire
Rebellious Ionian city-states
Greek city-states allied against the Persians
Neutral and pro-Persian city-states
Greek victory
Persian victory

The Persians had extended their rule to include the Greek colonies of Ionia. For a time, foreign domination was tolerated, but eventually Ionia rebelled and asked Athens for aid.

By 494 B.C. Persia had crushed the revolt and set out to do the same on the Greek mainland. But an outnumbered Athenian army defeated the Persians at the battle of Marathon.

In 480 B.C. the Persians were victorious at Thermopylae and then burned Athens. The Greeks, led by Sparta, defeated the Persians at Salamis and Plataea. The Greeks, for once, had shown they could unite against a common foe.

Alexander's Empire c. 323 B.C.

→ Route of Alexander and his armies

♦ City founded by Alexander

🔱 Major battle site

In 334 B.C. Alexander put into action his father's dream of conquering Persia. Within three years he had captured the capital at Persepolis and assumed the role of king of Persia. As Alexander moved eastward he ventured into lands that lay beyond the realm of Greek geographic knowledge.

Alexander used his military expertise to create a vast empire, but he felt that the Macedonians were spread too thinly to rule effectively. By combining east and west through the creation of a class of mixed-blood nobles he hoped to unify the empire. This fusion of the races might have worked if Alexander had lived long enough to personally oversee it. But he died at 32, and without him, the Macedonians rejected the concept.

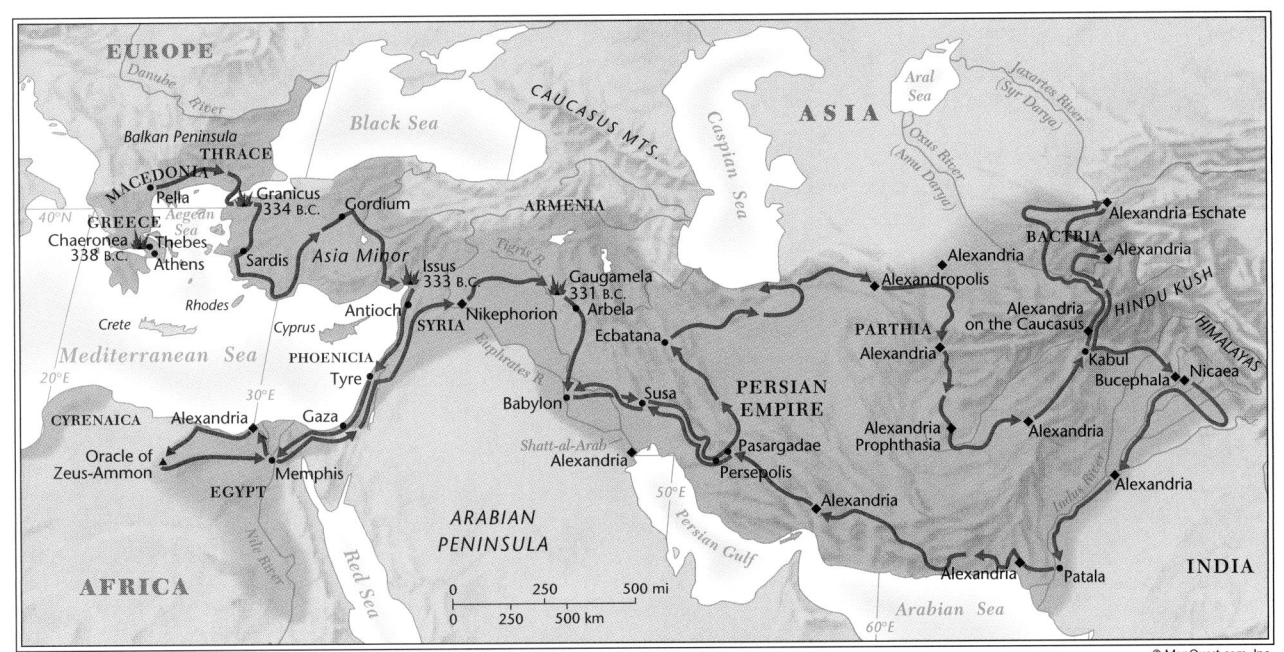

© MapQuest.com, Inc.

The Hellenistic World

Alexander left no heir; his empire would go to the "strongest." The empire quickly broke apart into separate kingdoms, most of which were ruled by Macedonian generals. Despite constant fighting, newly created cities became centers for the diffusion of Greek culture. This influence would outlive the Hellenistic period and continue to influence cultures in southwest Asia and northern Africa for ages to come.

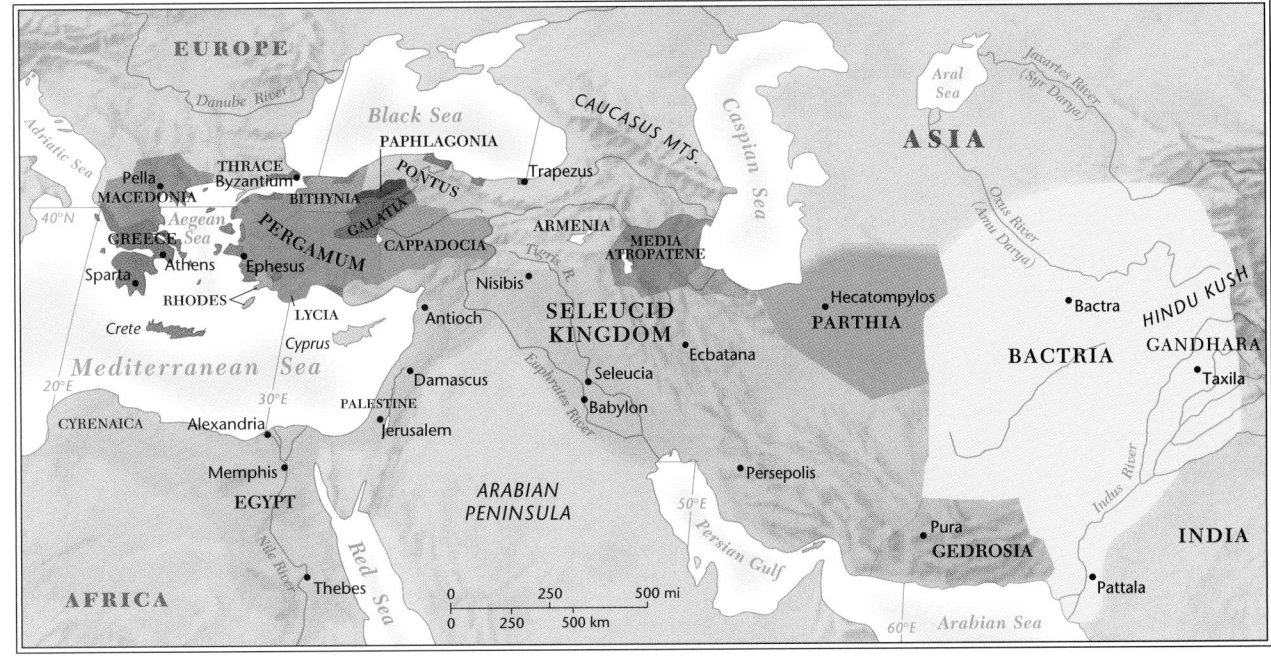

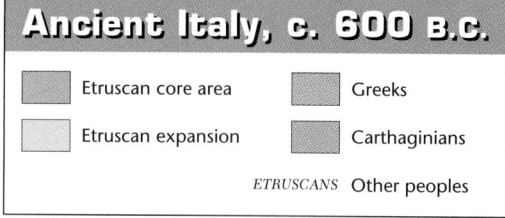

The Etruscan civilization, centered in Etruria, was the first to develop in Italy. Eventually their control of the peninsula extended from the Po Valley southward to Campania.

By the middle of the seventh century B.C., the Etruscans ruled the region around Rome, and they established a strong central government. Around 509 B.C., as tradition says, a local aristocracy rebelled, and a constitution was formulated to create a republic.

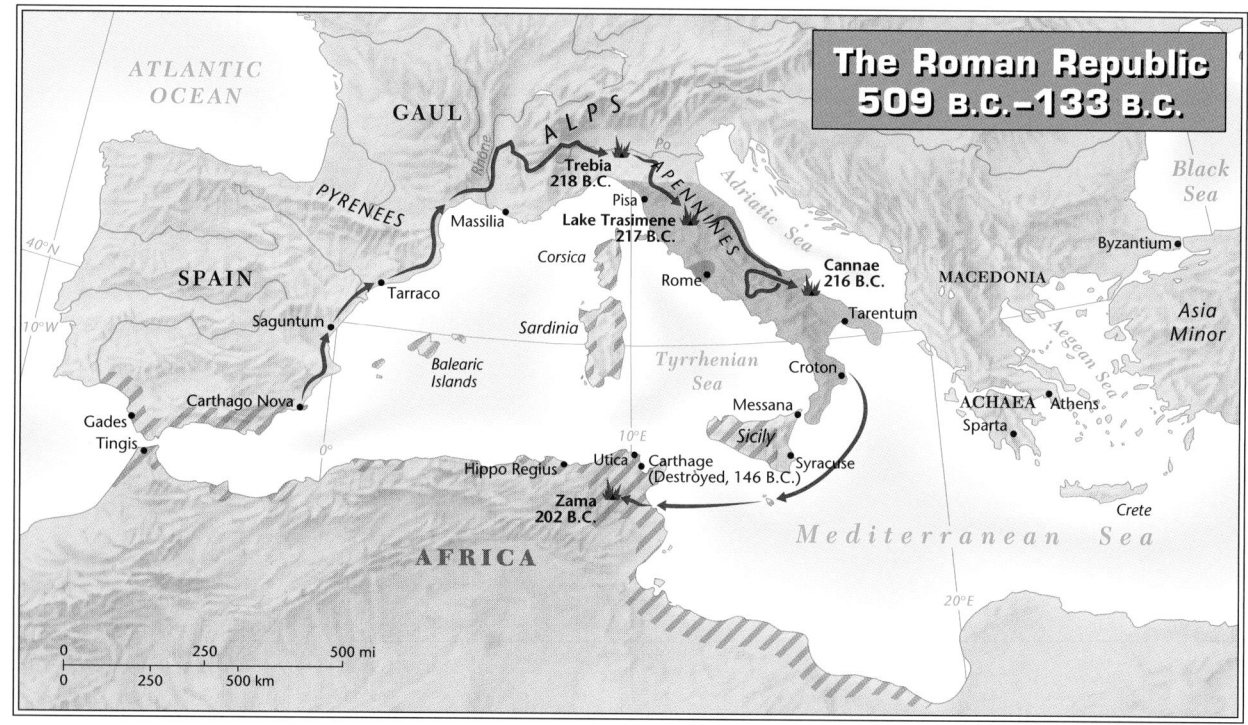

The Roman Republic 509 B.C.–133 B.C.

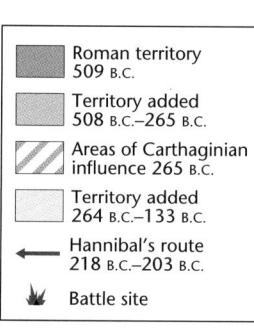

- Roman territory 509 B.C.
- Territory added 508 B.C.–265 B.C.
- Areas of Carthaginian influence 265 B.C.
- Territory added 264 B.C.–133 B.C.
- Hannibal's route 218 B.C.–203 B.C.
- Battle site

Unlike Greece, Rome embraced the idea of expansion. As Rome gained control of the peninsula, it came into conflict with the other power in the western Mediterranean—Carthage.

A series of wars ensued and in the process Rome built a navy to fight the seaborne Carthaginians. Rome was victorious in the first two wars, and Carthage was reduced to being a Roman subject state. But some Roman politicians wanted total destruction, and that was accomplished in the Third Punic War that ended in 146 B.C.

The Roman Empire to A.D. 117

- ☐ Roman Empire, A.D. 14
- ▨ Territory added by A.D. 117

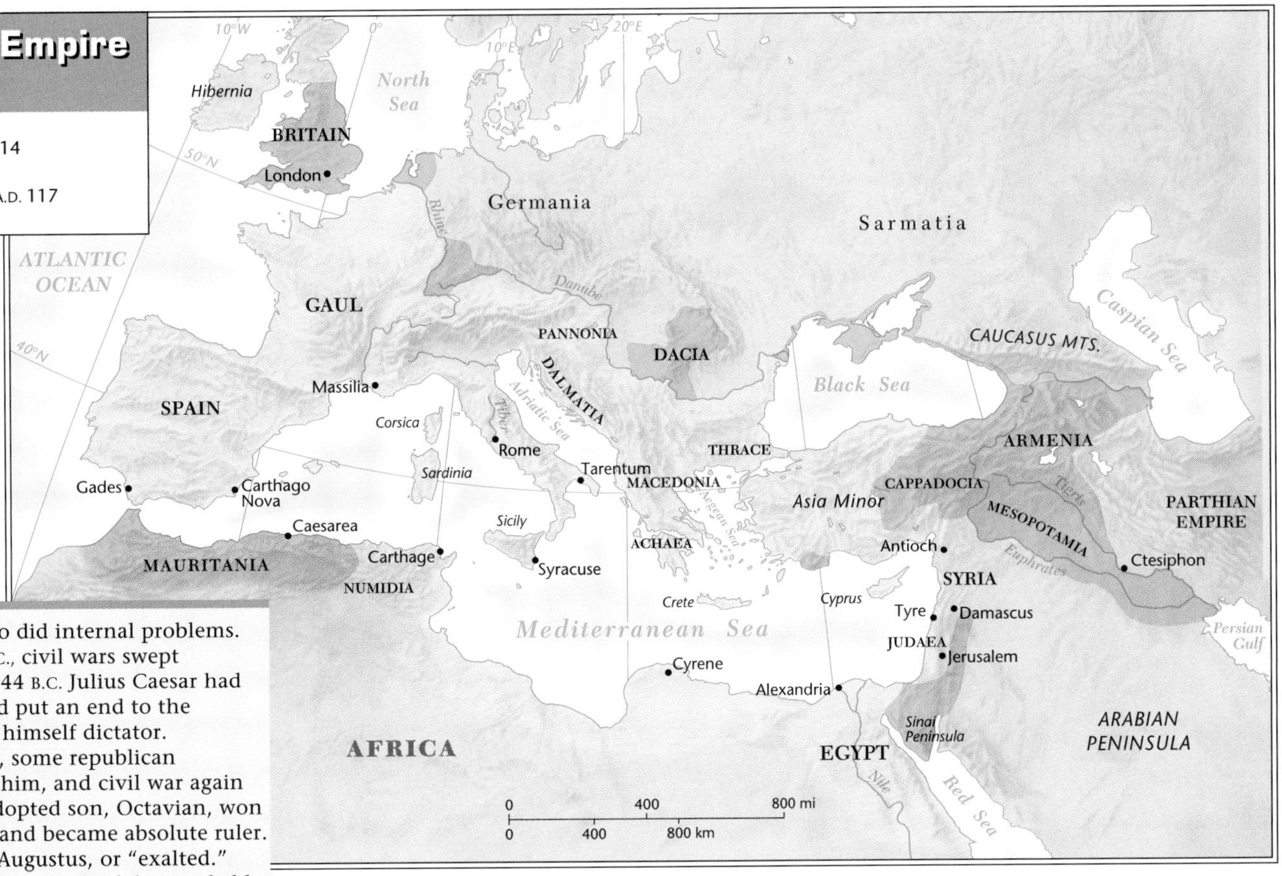

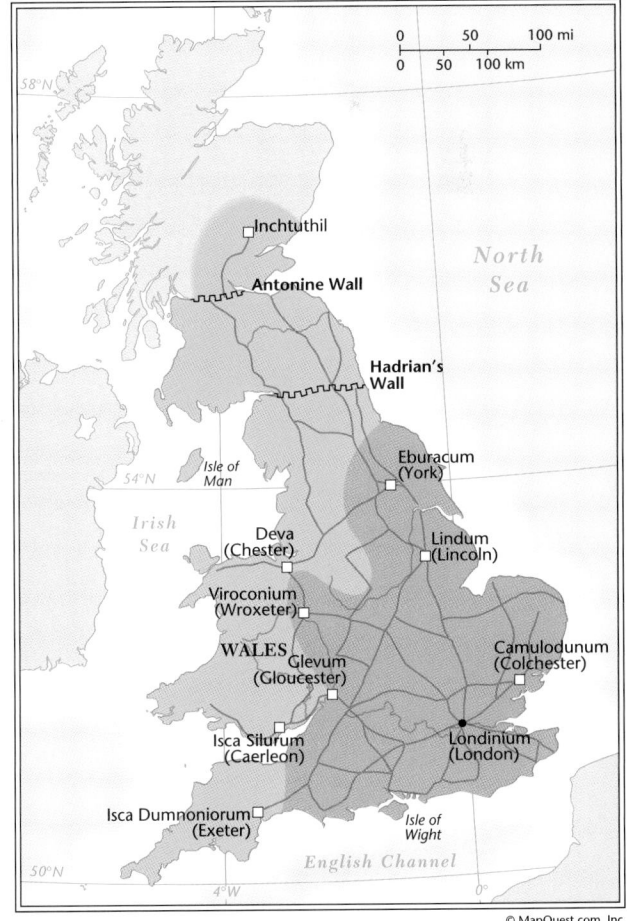

Hibernia

North Sea

BRITAIN
London •

ATLANTIC OCEAN

Germania

Sarmatia

GAUL

PANNONIA

DACIA

CAUCASUS MTS.

Caspian Sea

Massilia •

SPAIN

Corsica

DALMATIA

Adriatic Sea

Rome •

THRACE

Black Sea

ARMENIA

MACEDONIA

Tarentum •

CAPPADOCIA

Asia Minor

MESOPOTAMIA

PARTHIAN EMPIRE

Sardinia

Gades •

Carthago Nova •

MAURITANIA

Caesarea •

Carthage •

NUMIDIA

Sicily

Syracuse •

ACHAEA

Aegean Sea

Crete

Antioch •

Cyprus

SYRIA
Tyre • • Damascus

JUDAEA
• Jerusalem

Ctesiphon •

Euphrates

Tigris

Persian Gulf

• Cyrene

Alexandria •

Mediterranean Sea

AFRICA

EGYPT

Nile

Sinai Peninsula

Red Sea

ARABIAN PENINSULA

0		400		800 mi
0	400		800 km	

As the empire grew, so did internal problems. Starting around 79 B.C., civil wars swept through the land. By 44 B.C. Julius Caesar had defeated his rivals and put an end to the republic by declaring himself dictator.

But soon thereafter, some republican senators assassinated him, and civil war again broke out. Caesar's adopted son, Octavian, won out against his rivals and became absolute ruler. He assumed the title Augustus, or "exalted." Once again the republic was dead, but probably few regretted it.

Although Augustus' power was absolute, he did not greatly abuse it. Under his leadership and that of his successors, Rome enjoyed nearly two centuries of relative peace.

By A.D. 117, the empire had expanded as much as it would. But this would not last for long. The cost of maintaining this vast empire put a strain on the economy. Soon the empire had to assume a defensive stance rather than an expansionist one.

Roman Britain

- ▨ Area of military occupation
- ▨ Area of civilian government
- ☐ Forts
- 〰 Walls
- — Roads

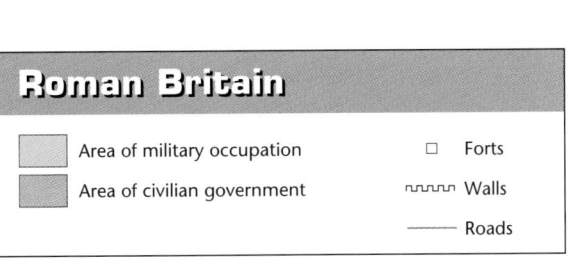

When Rome invaded in A.D. 43 there was no unified defense because the British kingdoms had been battling each other. Southern Britain was overrun and those who resisted were pushed back towards Wales. The Roman governors then set about securing the frontier and "civilizing" the people.

South of Hadrian's Wall, the landscape was dotted with Roman towns and villas. Many of the towns were established by traders who had settled near forts.

Inchtuthil •

Antonine Wall

North Sea

Hadrian's Wall

Eburacum (York) •

Isle of Man

Deva (Chester) ☐

Lindum (Lincoln) ☐

Viroconium (Wroxeter) ☐

WALES
Glevum (Gloucester) ☐

Camulodunum (Colchester) ☐

Irish Sea

Isca Silurum (Caerleon) ☐

Londinium (London) •

Isca Dumnoniorum (Exeter) ☐

Isle of Wight

English Channel

0		50		100 mi
0	50		100 km	

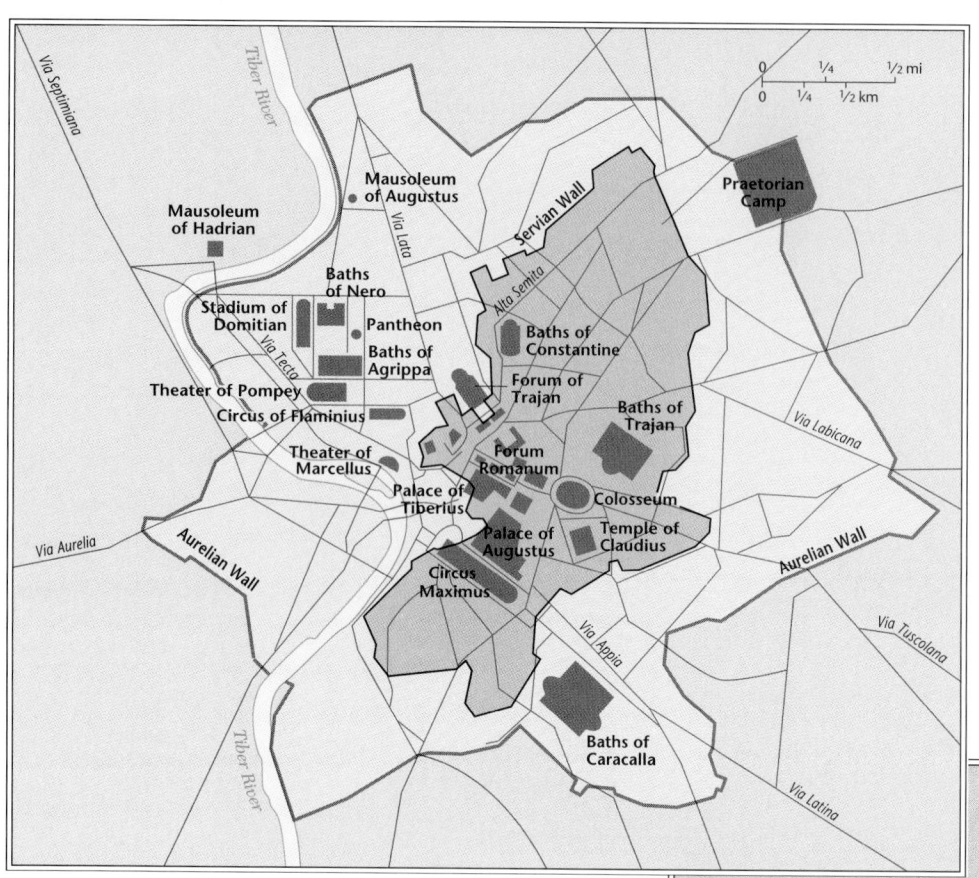

Ancient Rome

Extent of Rome to 550 B.C.
Extent of Rome in A.D. 271

The city of Rome started as an Alban village of shepherds. It was situated on one of the hills that rose above the marshy land that bordered the Tiber River. When the Etruscans took control of the region, Rome was just a collection of small villages. Within two centuries Rome had become an important urban center in Italy.

After expelling the Etruscans, the Romans created a republic. From this point, Rome eventually came to control not only the Italian peninsula, but also the Mediterranean basin and western Europe.

The many monuments and buildings that were constructed in the city reflected the grandeur of the Roman empire.

Jerusalem of the New Testament

— City of David

City at the time of Jesus

Area enclosed by Agrippa I, A.D. 41–44

Jerusalem first came to prominence around 1000 B.C. when David made it the capital of the Israelite tribes. His son Solomon built a magnificent temple that would be the focal point for the city. When Israel split in two, Jerusalem remained as the capital of the Kingdom of Judah.

By the 5th century B.C., control of the city was in the hands of priests, and it became a religious center. Although Judah itself was ruled by foreign empires, the authority of the priests was usually respected by the foreign kings.

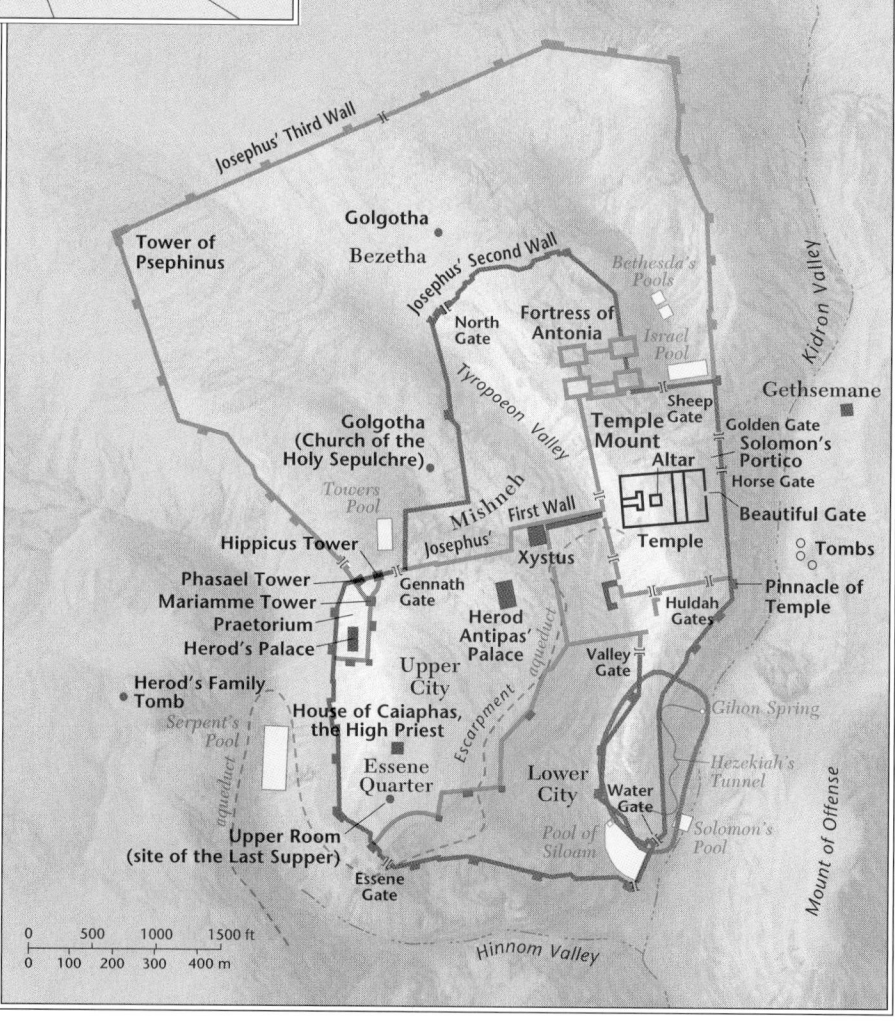

Roman Division of Palestine

- Boundary of Herod's kingdom 37 B.C.–4 B.C.
- ■ Herodian fortress
- Proconsul of Syria

Division of Herod's Kingdom Among His Sons
- Archelaus
- Herod Antipas
- Philip

When the Romans took the city of Jerusalem in 63 B.C., they tried not to interfere with the Jews and their religion. Eventually the Jewish kingdom of Judah was renamed Judaea and Herod, nominally a Jew, was installed as king. But the Jews disliked him for his acceptance of Hellenic culture and his obvious cooperation with the Romans.

By ruthlessly suppressing all opposition, Herod, at great cost, brought stability and prosperity to the kingdom. Upon his death, his kingdom was divided among his sons, and soon thereafter the Jews would revolt.

© MapQuest.com, Inc.

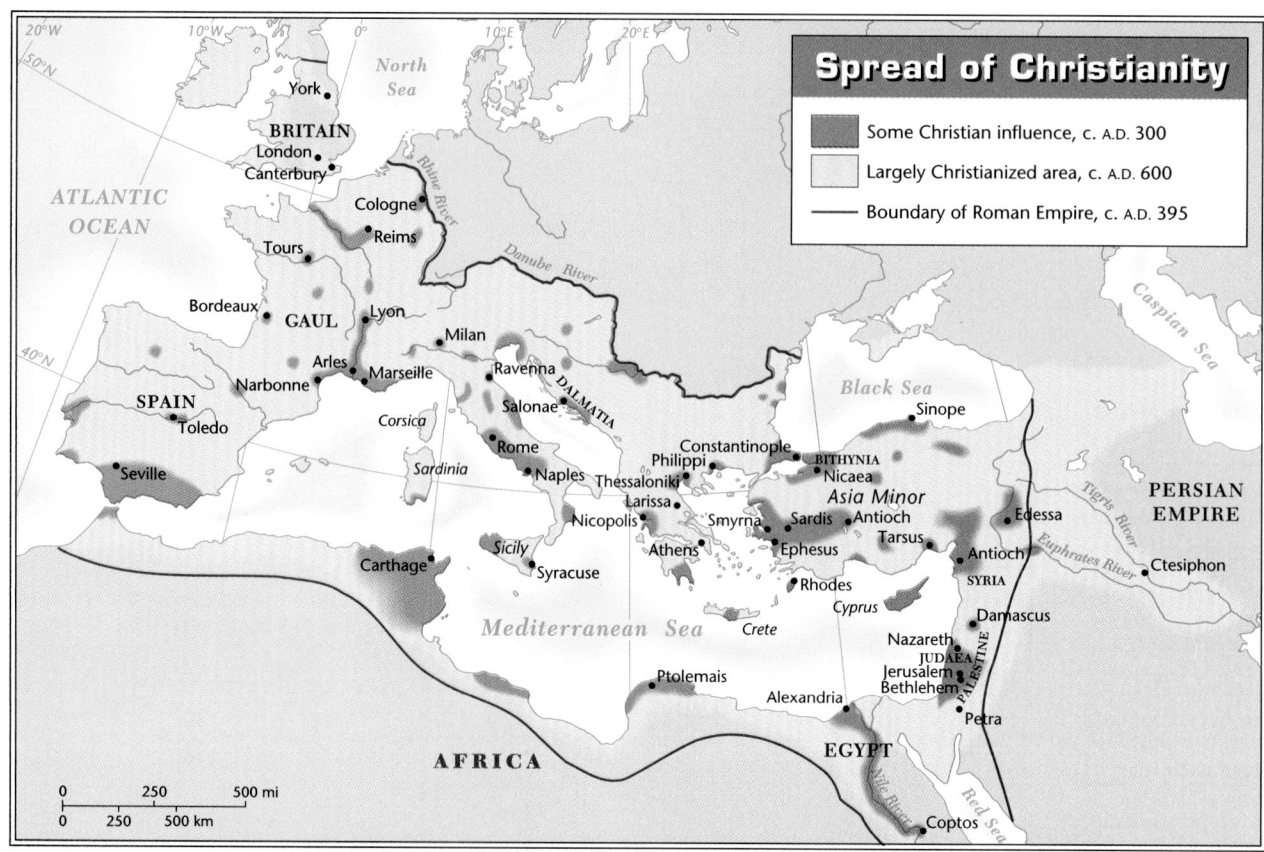

Spread of Christianity

- ■ Some Christian influence, c. A.D. 300
- □ Largely Christianized area, c. A.D. 600
- — Boundary of Roman Empire, c. A.D. 395

Early converts to Christianity were persecuted because they placed duty to God over duty to the emperor. Despite this, the new religion appealed to the spiritual needs of many, and the following grew. Emperor Constantine legalized Christianity in A.D. 313, making it easier to spread the faith.

With the Roman Empire in decay, people joined the church because it was the one institution that could provide leadership. The church benefited from an increasingly educated membership and the implementation of a well organized Roman system of administration.

Spread of Buddhism & Hinduism

- ■ Important Buddhist site
- ← Spread of Buddhism to the 9th century A.D.
- ▨ Area of Hindu influence c. A.D. 500

Siddhartha Gautama, known as Buddha (which means *Enlightened One*), founded a religion that was to be the cornerstone for many in south and east Asia.

Ashoka of the Mauryan Empire embraced the new religion and helped spread it beyond the Indian subcontinent. Buddhism reached China at a time of political and economic uncertainty, and as Christianity did for the Roman Empire, provided society with some cohesion.

Hinduism developed from traditional Indian religions, making it one of the world's oldest. Hinduism, more than Buddhism, tried to appeal to ordinary people. As the Mauryan and later empires collapsed, taking Buddhism along with it, the Hindu faith remained among the people. There was a resurgence in Hinduism in the third century A.D., when the Guptas, supporters of the religion, came to power.

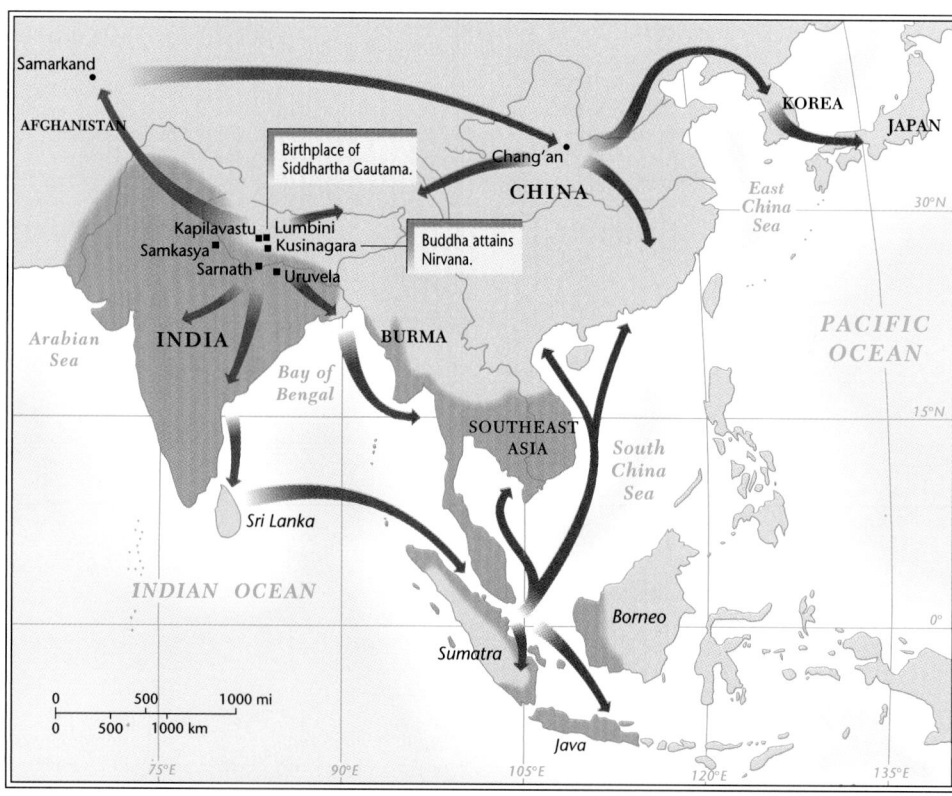

Maurya & Gupta Empires

- **Maurya Empire** c. 232 B.C.
- **Gupta Empire** c. A.D. 400

When Alexander the Great crossed the Indus River in 327 B.C., he threw the region into turmoil. His hasty departure created a vacuum, and the Mauryans stepped in to take control. Under Ashoka, the empire reached its greatest extent. But lesser rulers followed him, and internal strife weakened the empire.

India was invaded by peoples from central Asia, and it wasn't until the fourth century A.D. that an Indian family was able to unite northern India. The Gupta domain was not as extensive as the Mauryan, and they had less control over regional kings. The Guptas were content to be acknowledged as being supreme, and to draw as much tribute as possible.

In the fifth century the Huns began to threaten India from the north. While the Guptas focused on this, they ignored internal strife. Soon the empire broke up into small, warring kingdoms.

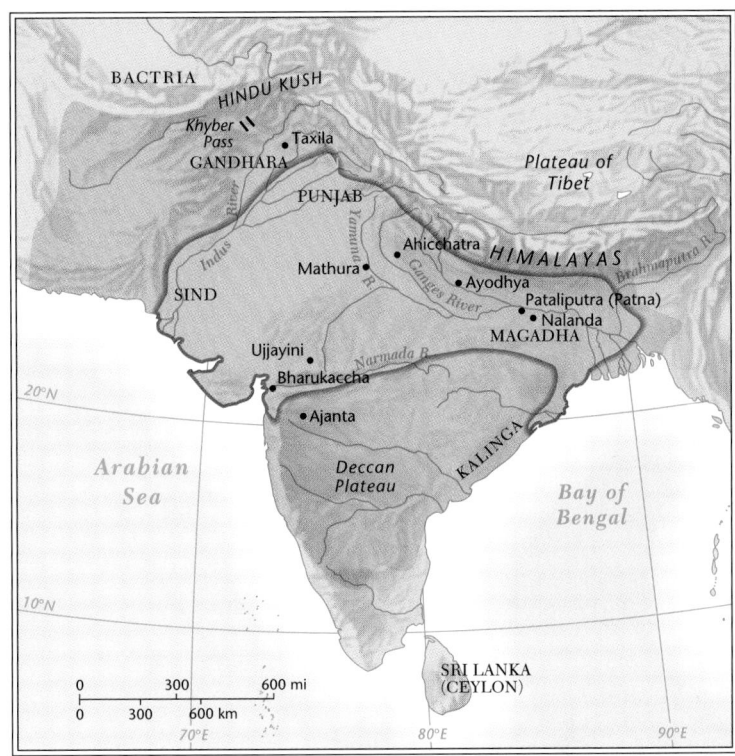

Qin & Han Empires

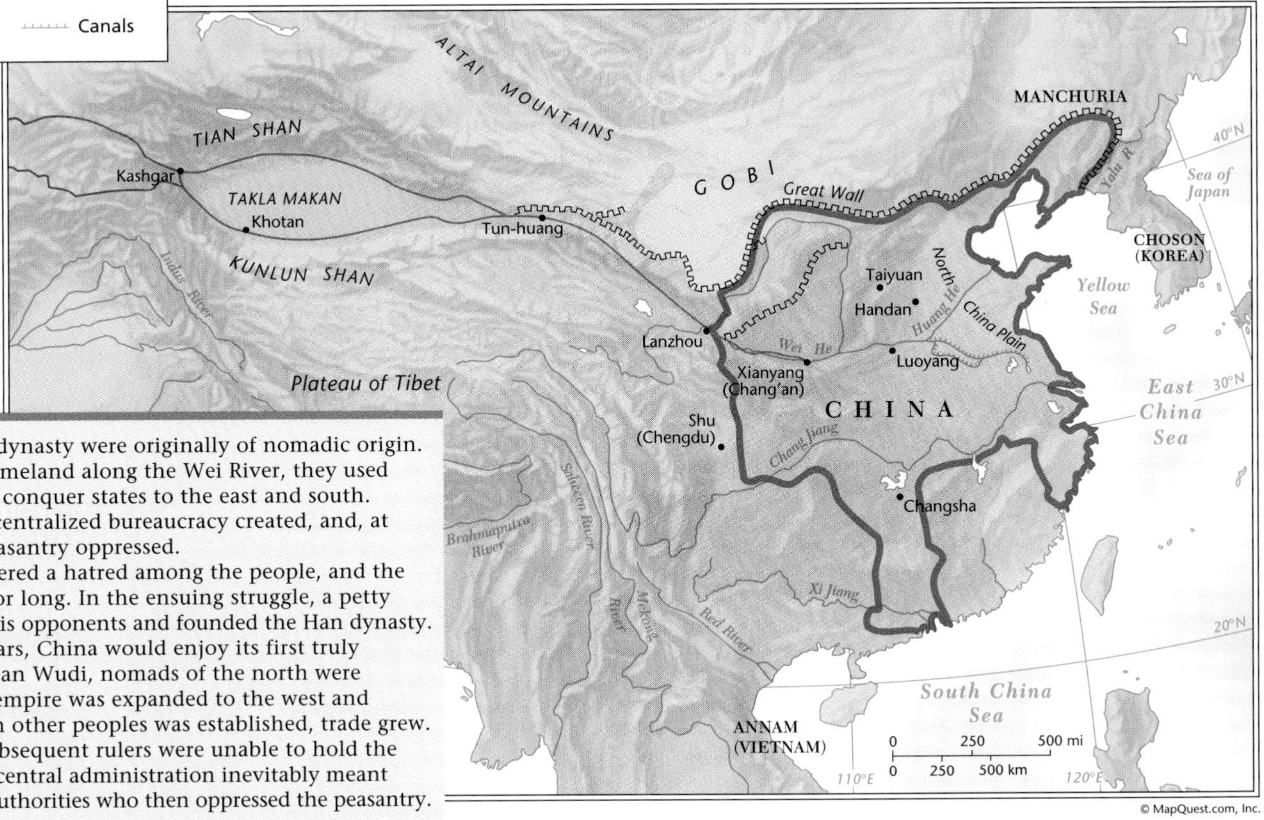

- **Qin dynasty** 221 B.C.–206 B.C.
- **Han dynasty** 202 B.C.–A.D. 220
- —— Roads
- ······ Canals

The rulers of the Qin dynasty were originally of nomadic origin. Starting from their homeland along the Wei River, they used their military skills to conquer states to the east and south. China was unified, a centralized bureaucracy created, and, at the same time, the peasantry oppressed.

The oppression fostered a hatred among the people, and the dynasty did not last for long. In the ensuing struggle, a petty Qin official defeated his opponents and founded the Han dynasty.

For the next 400 years, China would enjoy its first truly imperial age. Under Han Wudi, nomads of the north were driven back, and the empire was expanded to the west and south. As contact with other peoples was established, trade grew.

As was common, subsequent rulers were unable to hold the empire together. Less central administration inevitably meant more power for local authorities who then oppressed the peasantry.

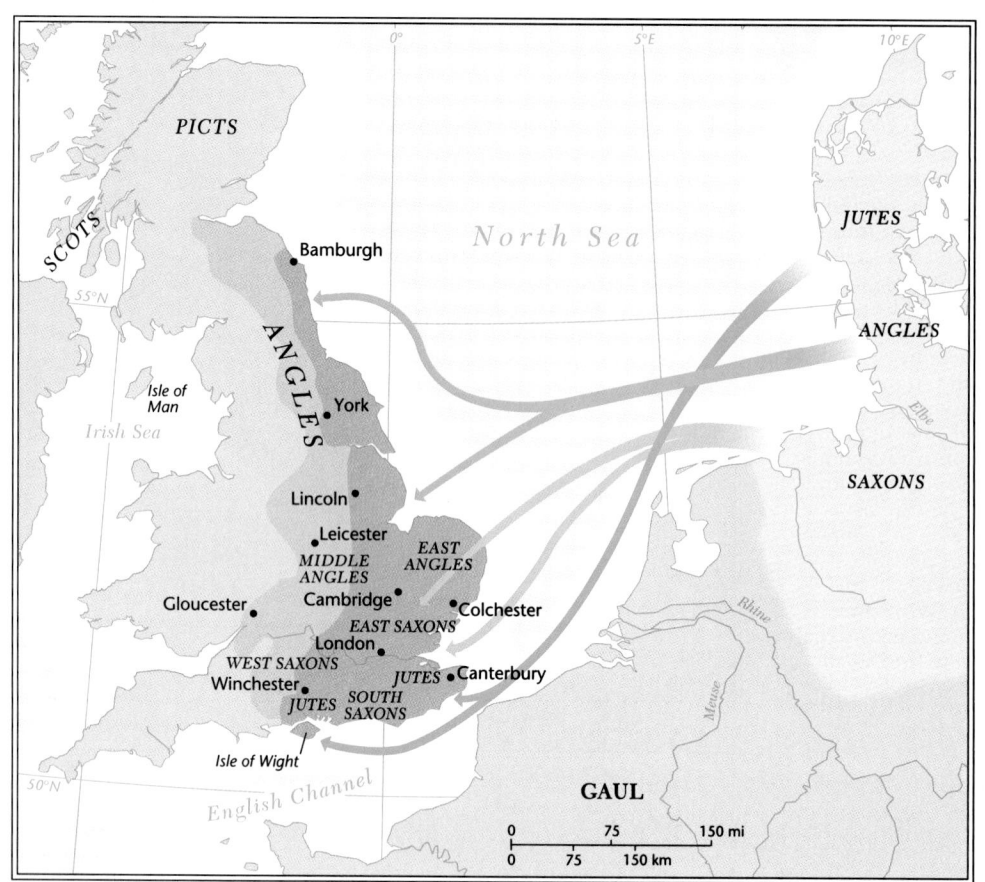

Anglo-Saxon Invasions

Conquered c. 550   Conquered c. 600

In the beginning of the fifth century, many Roman troops were removed from Britain to defend Gaul from Germanic invaders. Those who remained were unable to prevent the Picts and Scots from invading. British pleas for assistance were turned down, and this, in a sense, marked the end of Roman Britain.

Although Britain was still officially Roman, it became independent, and power passed to local rulers. In order to defend against Pictish raiders, one of the rulers allowed Saxon mercenaries to settle and protect areas along the eastern seaboard. Around 442, the Saxons and their allies rebelled, throwing Britain into a period of warfare. The revolt led to additional migrations of Germanic peoples from the continent.

The Britons were driven westward, and the fabled King Arthur was perhaps among the Britons who resisted the invaders.

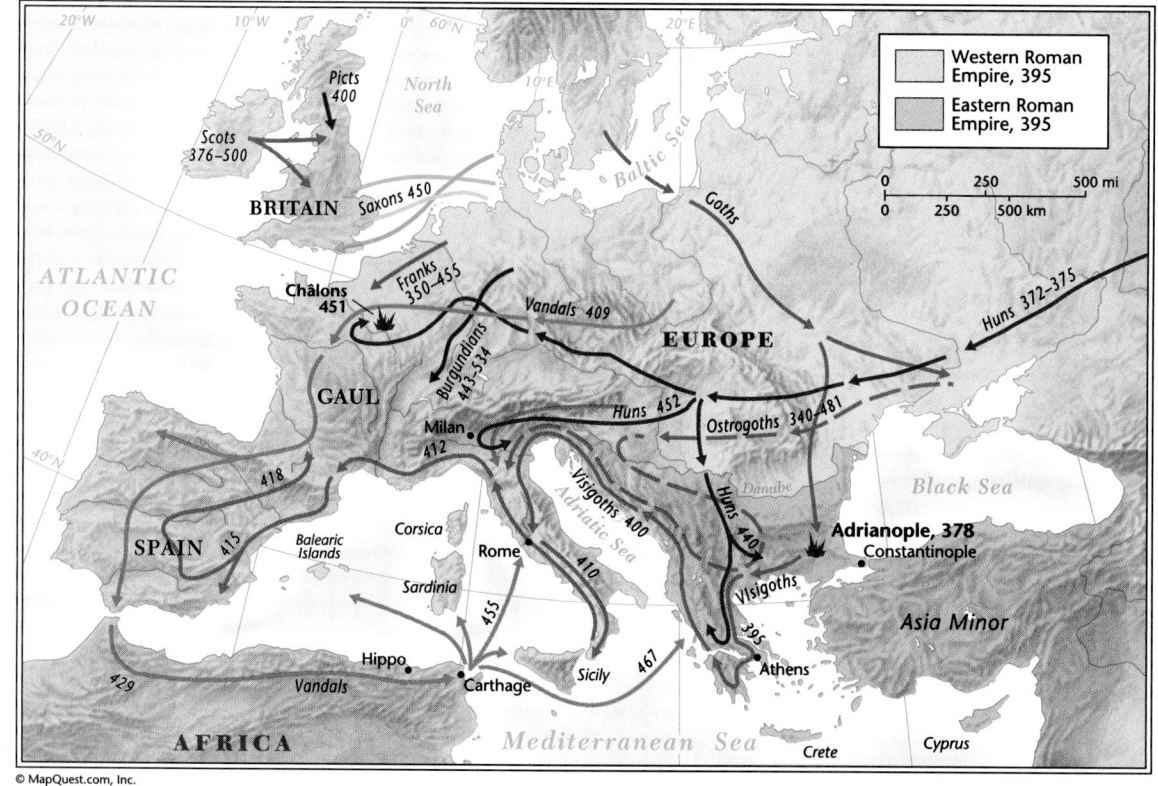

The Germanic World

Little is known about the people who inhabited the Germanic world before they came in contact with the Romans.

Sometime towards the end of the fourth century, the Huns, forced from central Asia, arrived in the Black Sea region. This set off a chain reaction of events. The Goths were threatened, and the Visigoths sought protection from Rome. Eventually they were permitted to settle within the empire's boundaries.

In Gaul, many Germanic peoples were already serving in the Roman army, some as commanders. In 497 Theodoric, an Ostrogoth, was officially recognized by the eastern emperor as ruler of the western empire.

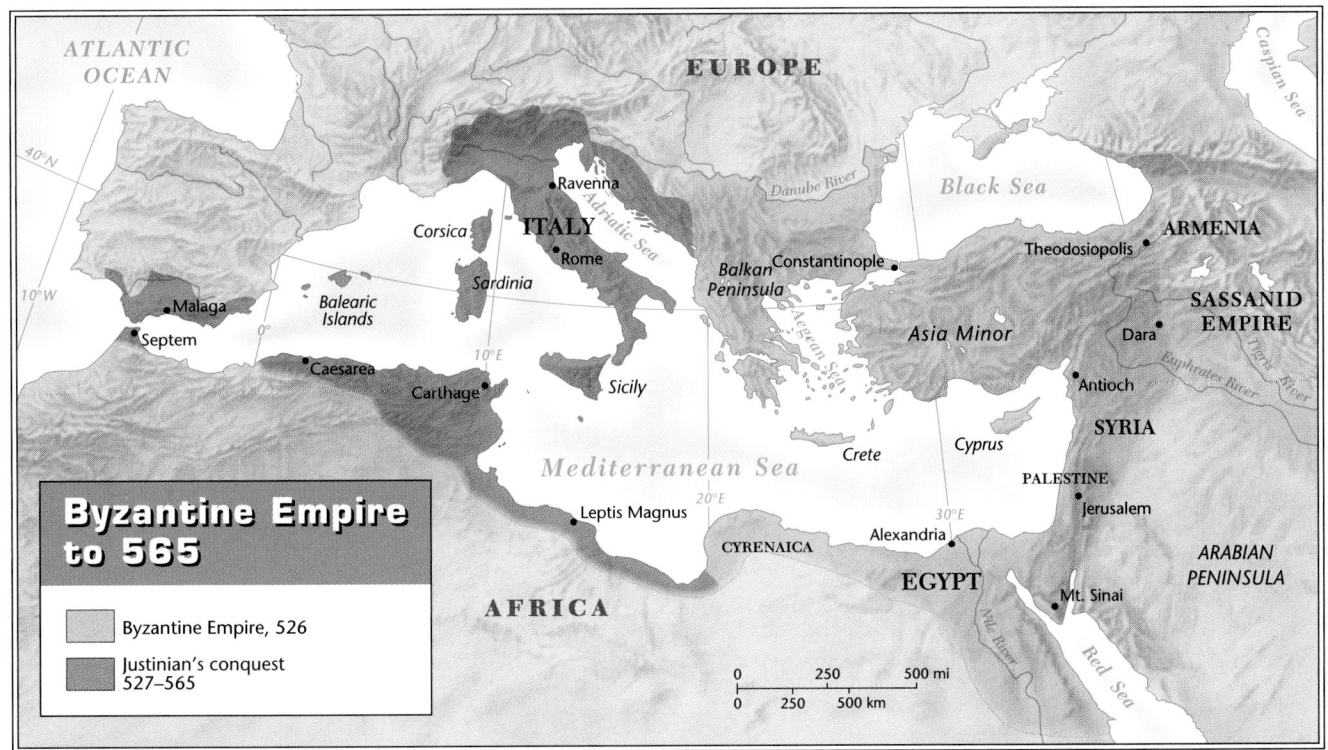

Byzantine Empire to 565

Byzantine Empire, 526

Justinian's conquest 527–565

The roots of the Byzantine Empire go back to the end of the third century when the emperor Diocletian divided the Roman Empire. But in 324, Constantine became emperor of both halves. Because the eastern half was now more important, he made Byzantium the sole capital, and renamed the city Constantinople.

The success of the east may be attributed to several things. The area was wealthier and more urbanized than the west. The empire also benefited from the Hellenic civilization that had been planted earlier. And for whatever reason, the east faced less pressure from the Germanic tribes.

Justinian tried to reclaim portions of the west that had been lost. Although he was successful at first, these gains were soon lost to the Germanic peoples.

Empire of Charlemagne 768–814

Frankish Kingdom 768

Territories added by Charlemagne 768–814

Marches (frontier county or buffer zone)

Division of the empire, 843

Charlemagne inherited a kingdom that was originally founded by Clovis, a Frank who had been a commander in the Roman army. In the process of expanding his empire, Charlemagne's armies proved to be virtually invincible.

During his reign, Charlemagne maintained close relations with the church. In order to further strengthen this alliance, Pope Leo III crowned Charlemagne, emperor of the Romans.

Charlemagne died in 814, and in 843 the empire was divided between his three grandsons. The growing power of local aristocrats and raids led by Vikings, Saracens, and Magyars weakened the empire. By the end of the ninth century, the empire that at one time appeared to be the revival of the Roman Empire in the west was no more.

© MapQuest.com, Inc.

Spread of Islam to 750

Arabs had long been looked upon as barbarians of the desert. But now the Islamic faith that many came to embrace provided a common cause and strength.

Muslims raided the edges of the deserts. They found booty, and their probes also revealed weaknesses in the Byzantine and Sassanid empires.

Muhammad had believed in the need to expand the faith, and these empires happened to be militarily weak and their populations were diverse with deep religious divisions. This made their conquest a little easier.

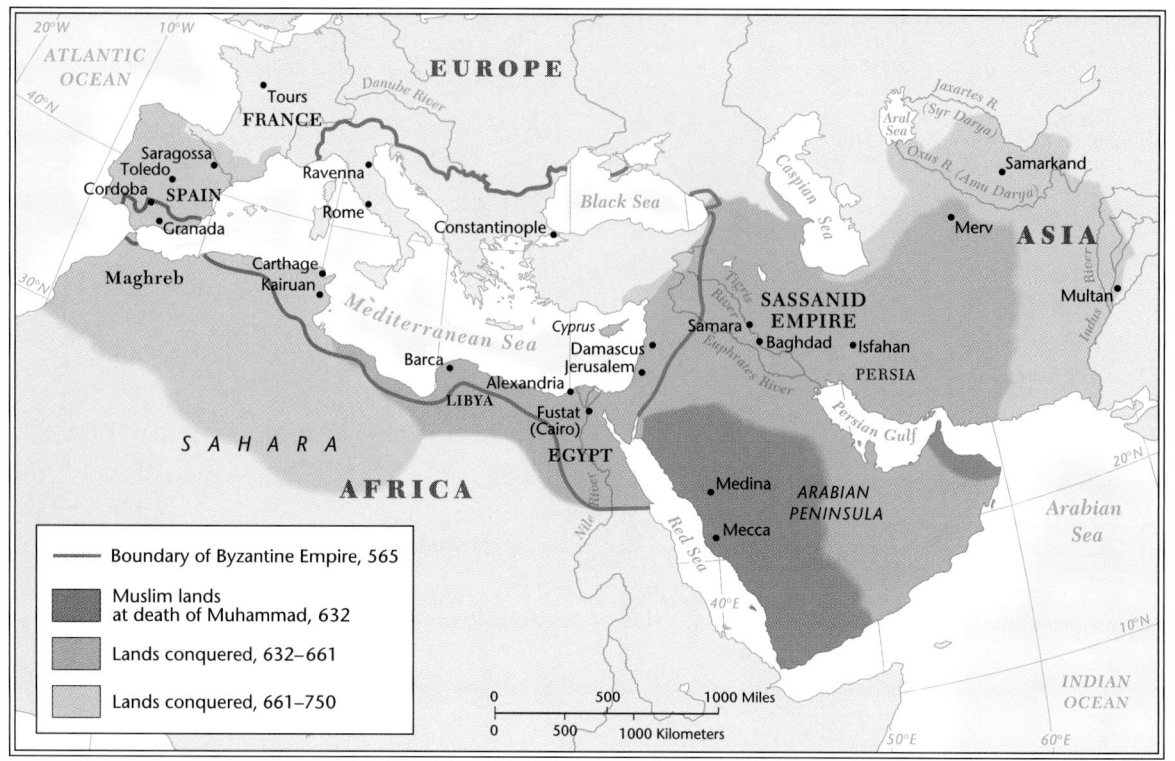

Boundary of Byzantine Empire, 565

Muslim lands at death of Muhammad, 632

Lands conquered, 632–661

Lands conquered, 661–750

Vikings

Viking homeland

Viking invasions

Areas of Viking activity

In the late 8th century, Vikings from Scandinavia began to raid coastal and riverine settlements throughout Europe. They were superb sailors and fierce warriors.

The reasons for these migrations are several. Overpopulation was probably the main reason; local feuds and wars was another. Other Scandinavians might have seen raiding as a way to obtain wealth and prestige.

In many instances, Vikings colonized areas that they had previously plundered. Sometimes they became traders. Once settled down, they often became Christianized, and this helped to integrate them into European society. Others took the religion back to Scandinavia.

The Vikings did not confine themselves to Europe. Around 1000, Leif Ericson landed in Newfoundland, and established a settlement. But the Native Americans were hostile, and it was too far away to be adequately maintained.

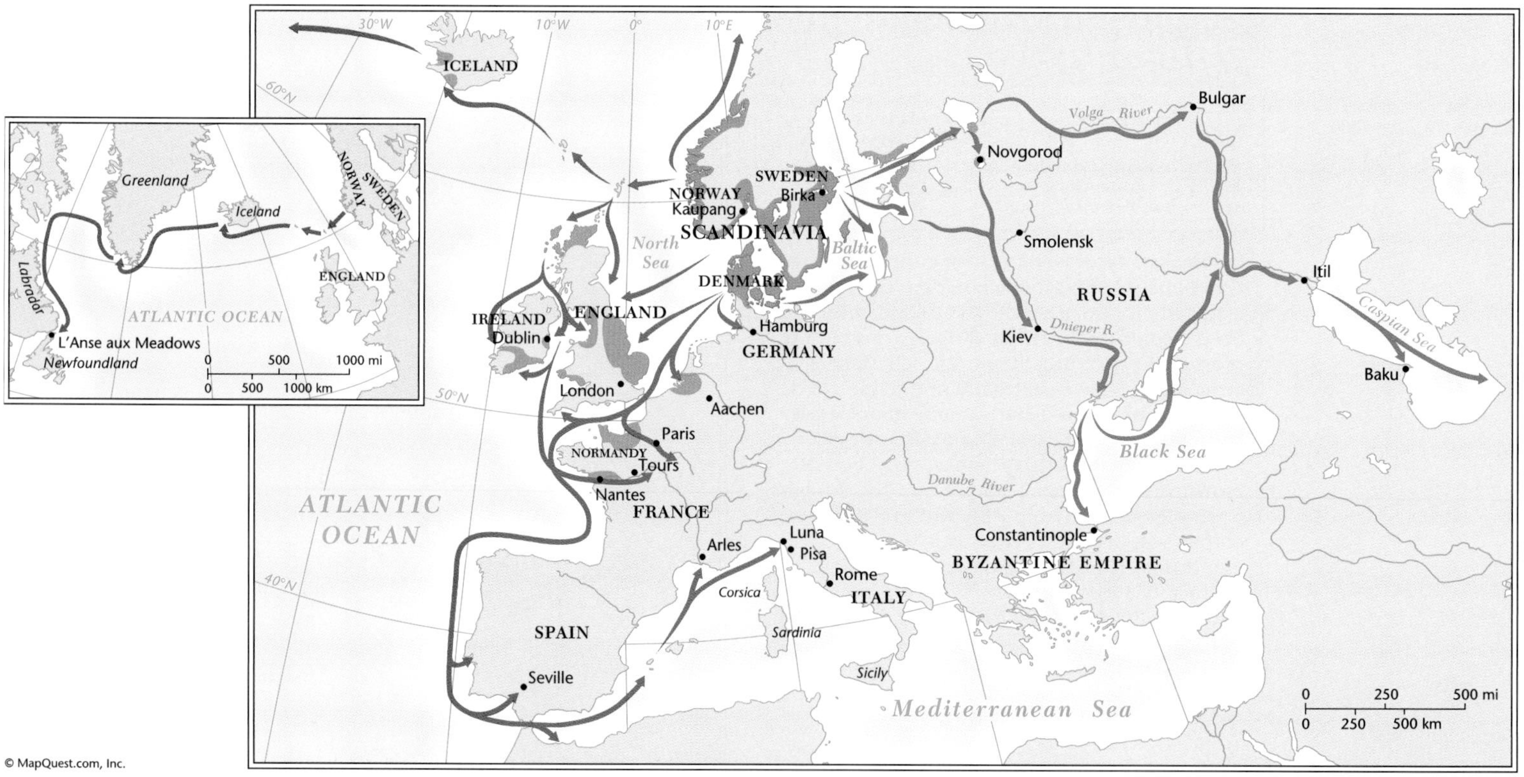

Vikings in England

Viking raiders appeared in England and Ireland at the end of the 8th century. At first plunder was the main objective. But towards the middle of the next century the raids were larger and more systematic. Conquest was now a more likely goal.

York, Mercia, East Anglia, and Northumberland were controlled by the Danes. But they were unable to defeat Alfred the Great of Wessex, although they did exact a tribute.

In the early 870s, Wessex remained the only independent kingdom. With a concerted effort in 878, the Danes under Guthrum forced Alfred to retreat. Many of Alfred's subjects fled to the continent, making this a low point in Alfred's reign.

English Resurgence

After being defeated by Guthrum, Alfred retreated and reorganized what remained of his forces. At Edington in 878 he defeated the Danes, who were forced to withdraw from Wessex.

Around 886 a boundary was established dividing England: the Danes controlled almost all of the north and midlands, but they acknowledged the independence of Wessex.

But the Danes continued their pressure. Despite their attacks in 892 and again in 910, Alfred's descendents continued to work to secure the north.

Athelstan, Alfred's grandson, took York and prepared to invade Scotland. An army led by Olaf, a Norse-Irishman, and composed of Scots, Welsh, and Cumbrians countered. This army was defeated at Brunanburh in 937. Despite being one of the most famous battles, its location is not known.

Scandinavian troubles continued, but the tenacity of Alfred's successors won out, and by 955 England was united.

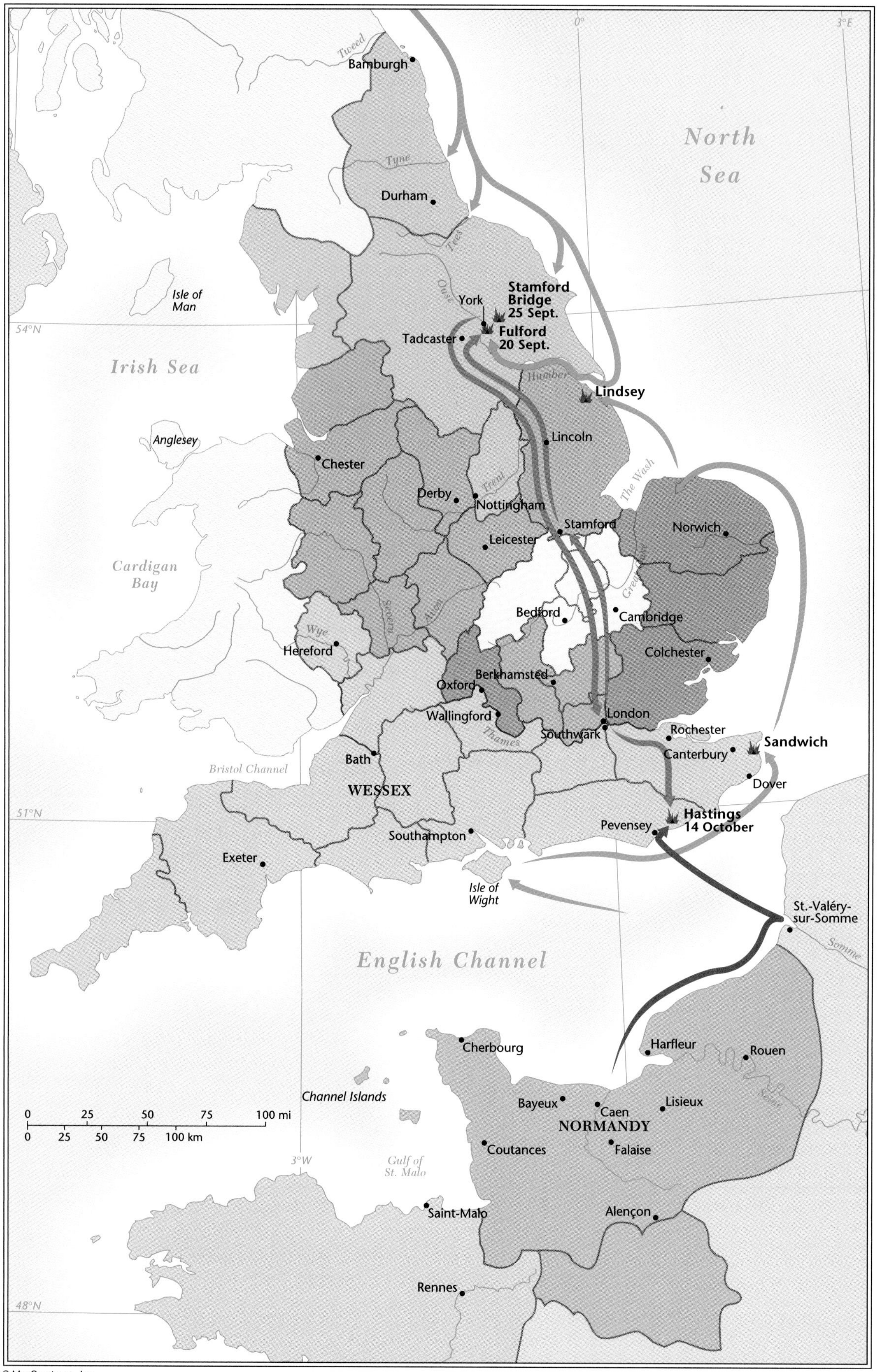

England, 1066

In England

Earldom of Morkere

Earldom of Edwin

Earldom of Waltheof

Earldom of Gyrth

Earldom of Leofwine

Earldom of Harold

In France

Dominions of William I

Land dependent on William I

⟵ Tostig Godwineson and Harald of Norway

⟵ William I

⟵ Harold II Godwineson

✹ Battle

In 1016, England became part of the Danish Empire, but this soon fell apart. The last Danish ruler had no heir so he called upon Edward, heir of the native house, to rule.

But the earls were powerful; especially the Godwines of Wessex. Although they were defeated in battle, their power continued to grow.

Edward, like his predecessor, had no heir. William, Duke of Normandy, claimed to be the personally appointed successor. But Harold II of the Godwine family was able to take the throne. His first challenge came from his brother, Tostig, who had the help of the Norwegians.

Harold II was victorious at Stamford Bridge, but had to immediately march south to meet William, who had just landed. William was victorious, and Harold died. On Christmas Day, William I was crowned king of England.

For the English, it was the year of three kings.

Map labels

North Sea

Tweed

Bamburgh

Tyne

Durham

Tees

Isle of Man

Stamford Bridge 25 Sept.

York

Fulford 20 Sept.

Tadcaster

Irish Sea

Ouse

Humber

Lindsey

Lincoln

Anglesey

Chester

Trent

Derby

Nottingham

Stamford

Norwich

Leicester

Cardigan Bay

The Wash

Wye

Severn

Avon

Bedford

Cambridge

Hereford

Colchester

Great Ouse

Berkhamsted

Oxford

Wallingford

London

Rochester

Thames

Southwark

Canterbury

Sandwich

Bath

Dover

WESSEX

Hastings 14 October

Southampton

Pevensey

Exeter

Isle of Wight

St.-Valéry-sur-Somme

English Channel

Somme

Cherbourg

Harfleur

Rouen

Channel Islands

Bayeux

Lisieux

Caen

Seine

NORMANDY

Coutances

Falaise

Saint-Malo

Alençon

Gulf of St. Malo

Rennes

Bristol Channel

0 25 50 75 100 mi
0 25 50 75 100 km

3°W

54°N

51°N

48°N

0°

3°E

In 1095 Pope Urban II called upon western knights to free the Holy Land from Muslim occupation. The First Crusade was successful largely because the Arabs did not provide a unified defense. The Crusaders took Jerusalem in 1099. Although most Crusaders returned home, some remained to establish Latin states.

During the Fourth Crusade, knights attacked Constantinople and installed a new leader. The Greek and Latin churches had recently split apart, and this made that division permanent.

For the Muslims, the Crusades were a minor event; they never really threatened their Islamic religion.

Although the Crusades enriched European life, it is not true that there was a wholesale introduction of new goods. Trade between Europeans, Byzantines, and Muslims had begun years before the Crusades.

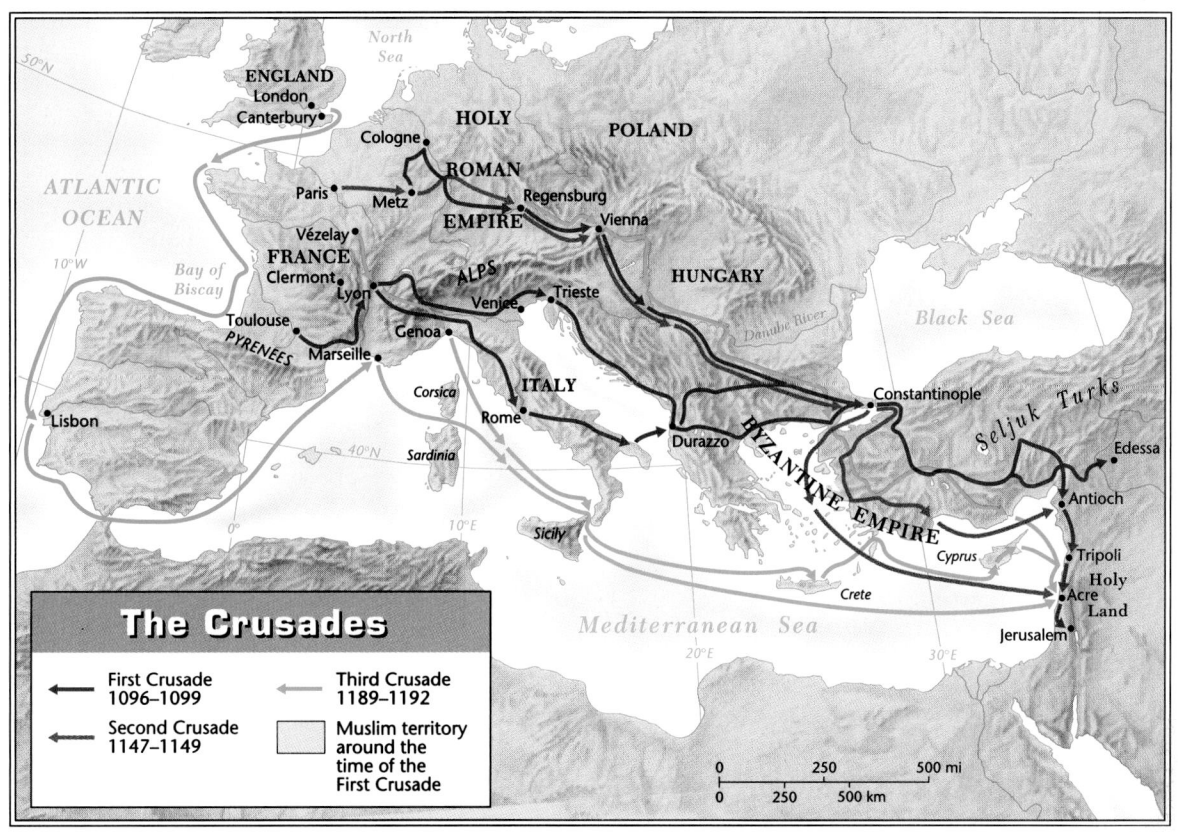

The Crusades

← First Crusade 1096–1099

← Second Crusade 1147–1149

← Third Crusade 1189–1192

▢ Muslim territory around the time of the First Crusade

0   250   500 mi
0   250   500 km

Crusader States

After having taken the Holy Land in 1099, the Crusaders who remained established Latin states at Jerusalem, Tripoli, Antioch, and Edessa. These states were set up much like European feudal manors, where the land was divided into fiefs and ruled by feudal lords.

Godfrey of Bouillon was made ruler of Jerusalem, and he and his men had to face a hostile population of Arabs, Jews, and heretical Christians.

In 1144, Edessa fell to the Muslims, and a second crusade was launched to protect the remaining states.

But in 1187, Jerusalem was lost to the Muslims of Saladin, and the last outpost along the Levant fell to the Mamelukes in 1288.

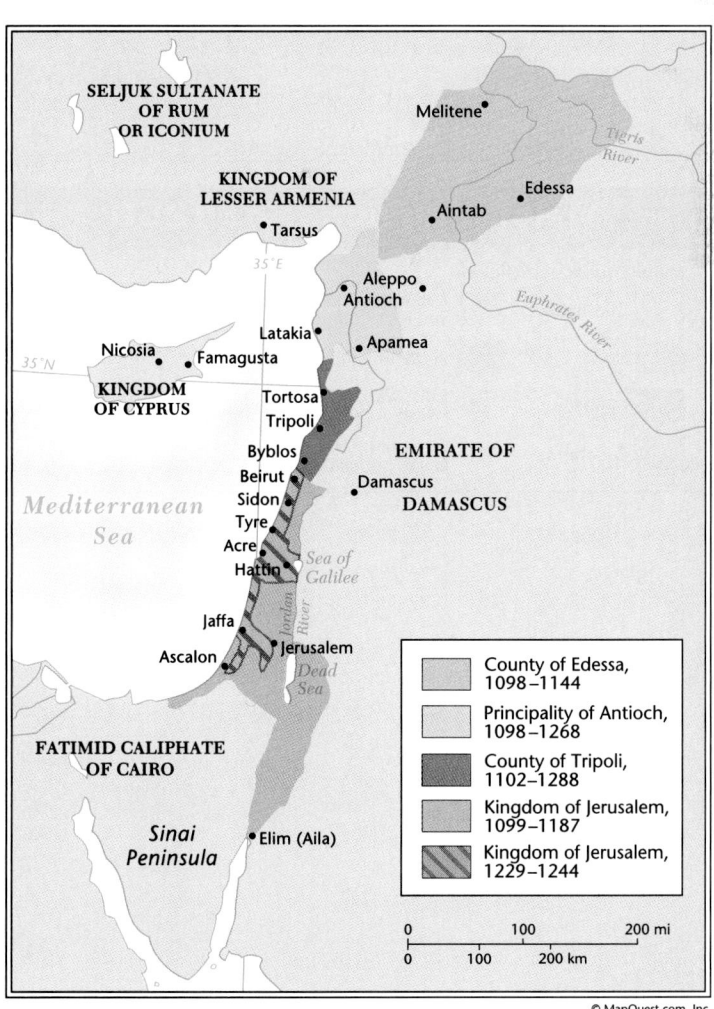

County of Edessa, 1098–1144

Principality of Antioch, 1098–1268

County of Tripoli, 1102–1288

Kingdom of Jerusalem, 1099–1187

Kingdom of Jerusalem, 1229–1244

0   100   200 mi
0   100   200 km

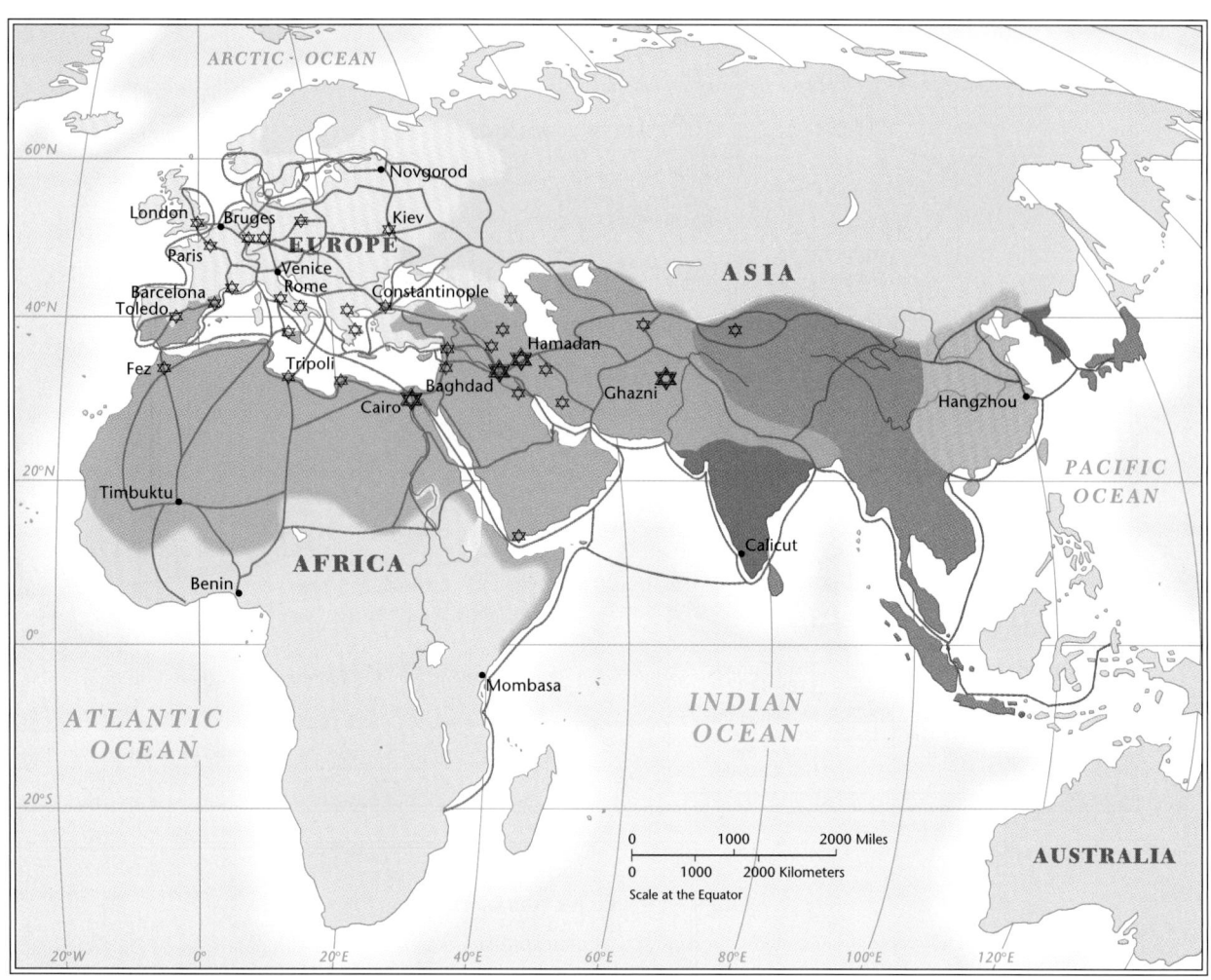

Major Religions, c. 1200

Major Organized Religions

	Christianity		Buddhism, Taoism, and Neo-Confucianism	—— Trade routes
	Islam		Buddhism and Taoism	
	Hinduism	✡	Cities with major Jewish populations	
	Buddhism	✡	Cities with some Jewish population	

This period marked the spread of religions through trade, evangelism, and warfare. The conflict between Christianity and Islam that had started with the Crusades continued. At the same time, the West was becoming more aware of the scholarship of the Muslim and Hindu realms.

Soon after the start of the 13th century, the Mongol onslaught would begin. Their conquests would extend through much of Eurasia and touch all major religions.

© MapQuest.com, Inc.

Jewish Migrations & Expulsions 1000–1500

In the early centuries A.D., the Jews spread throughout Europe, and in most places they constituted only a small minority. Even so, their existence was often dependent on the attitude of the local rulers and their acceptance by the populace in general.

The Crusades stirred a wave of resentment against non-Christians, and the Jews were victims of this. In a number of cities, Jews were forced to live in separate communities known as ghettos.

Beginning in the 1200s, many Jews were forced to leave western Europe.

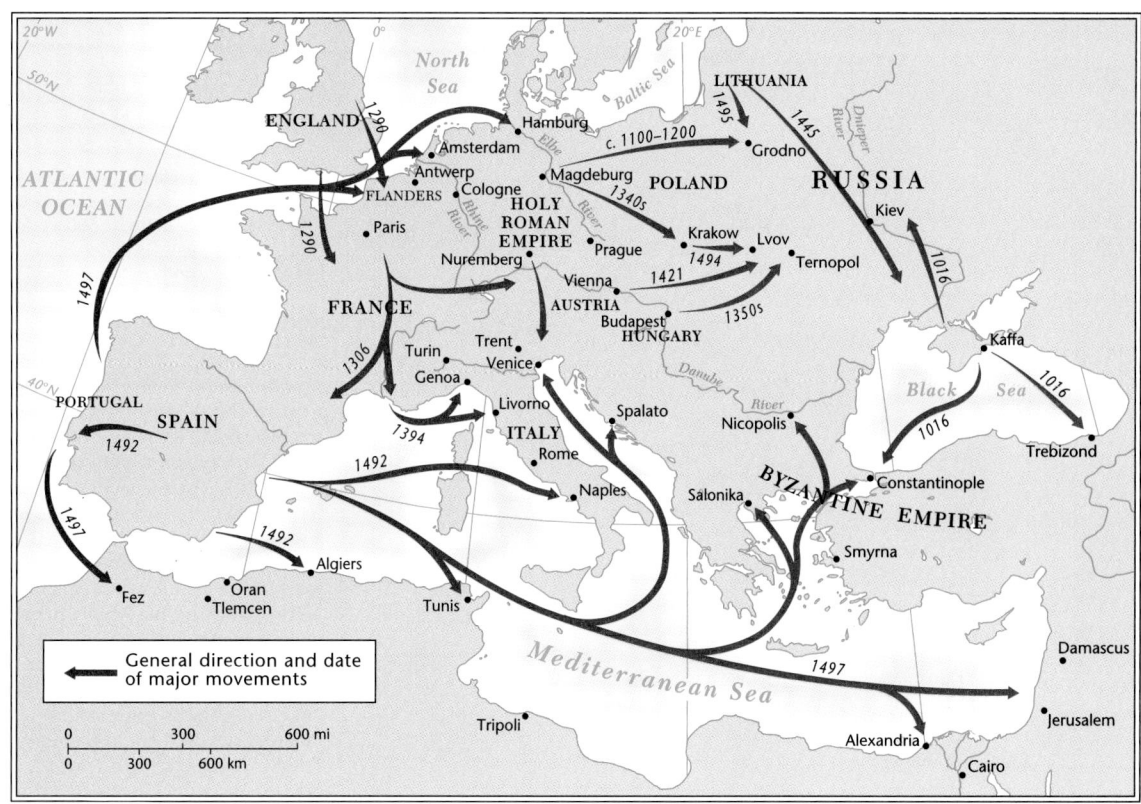

General direction and date of major movements

Medieval Trade

- ● Towns holding fairs
- ○ Major commercial centers
- —— Major trade routes

Cities grew during the Middle Ages. Government, commerce, and industry tended to gather there. The flourishing urban environment encouraged farmers to grow crops that could be sold in the markets.

In the High Middle Ages, commercial fairs were held in France. Here, products of northern Europe such as wool and furs were traded for products from the Mediterranean.

However, carrying goods overland was very expensive. As ships became more dependable, seaborne transport was preferred. Towards the end of the 13th century, ships from the Mediterranean were plying the waters of the North Sea, effectively ending the system of land-based commercial fairs.

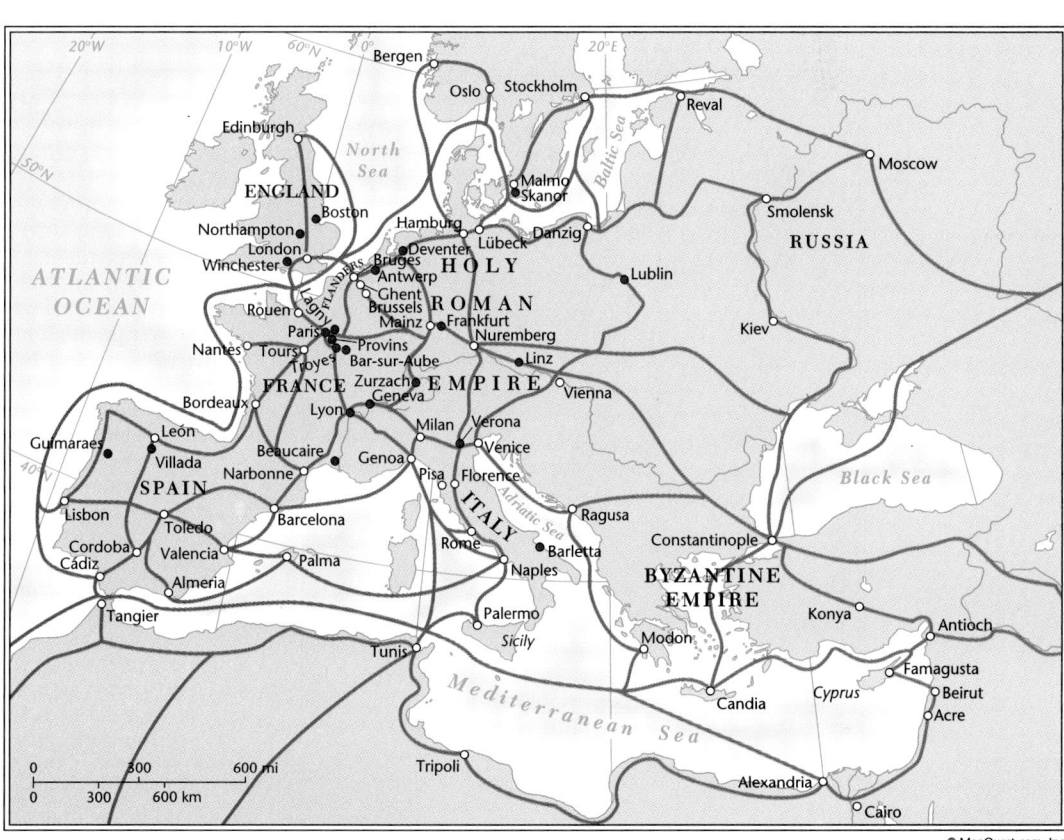

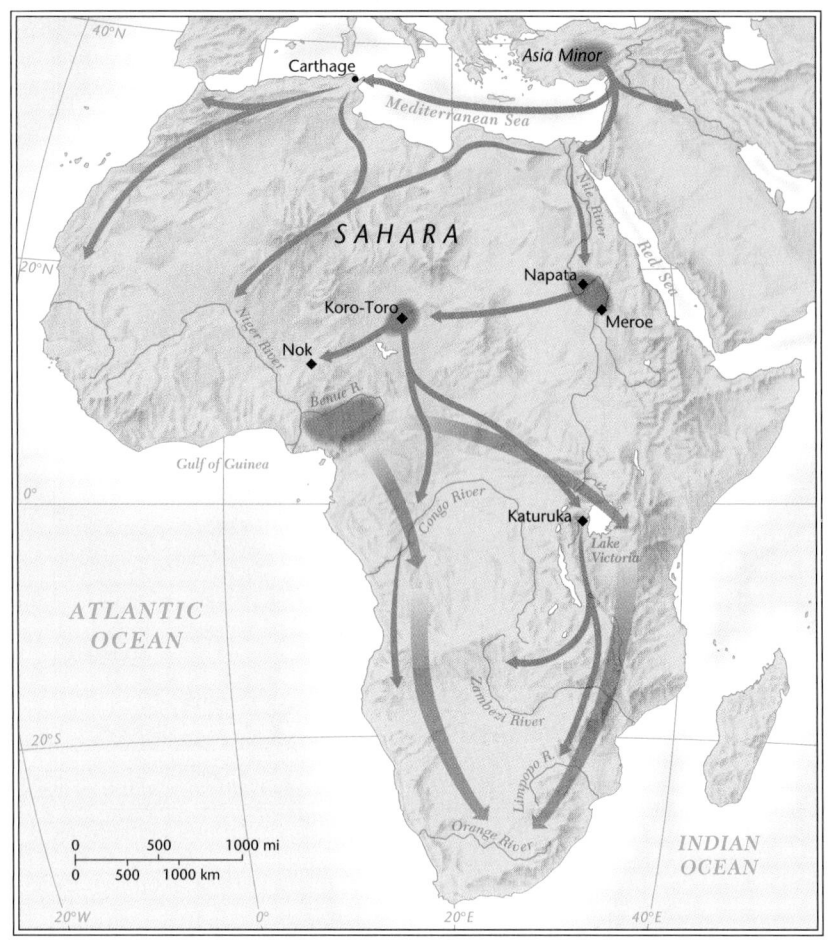

Bantu Migrations and the Spread of Ironworking

- Bantu homeland
- ← Bantu migrations, c. 500 B.C.–A.D. 200
- ◆ Iron-working centers
- ← Spread of ironworking c. 500 B.C.–150 B.C.

Iron-working technology came from western Asia. The Phoenicians took it to Carthage and from there it spread to West Africa along the trade routes. It also spread down the Nile to Meroe, and this might have been another center from which iron-working technology spread.

Iron-working may have been moved south and eastward along with the Bantus. These people moved from what is now eastern Nigeria. Perhaps population pressures caused them to migrate. They moved eastward towards central Sudan and southward to the Congo Basin. It was a gradual process, and eventually they pushed southward past the Zambezi River and into southern Africa.

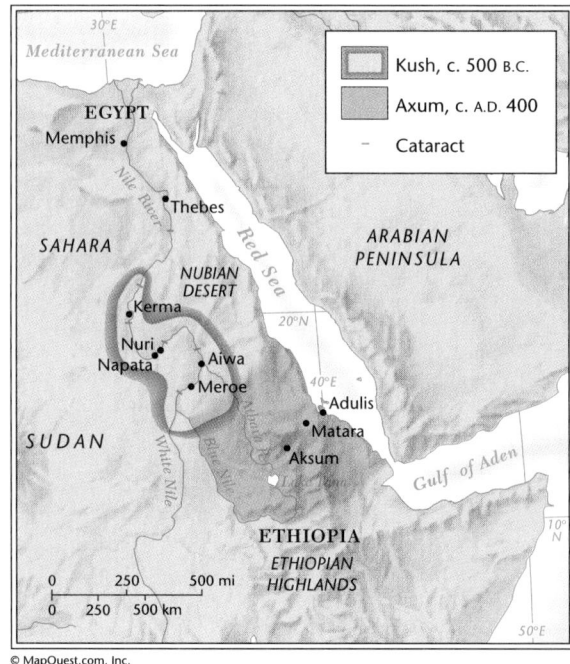

Kush, c. 500 B.C.
Axum, c. A.D. 400
- Cataract

© MapQuest.com, Inc.

Kush & Axum

Kush developed as a province on the frontier of Egypt, but sometime around 1000 B.C. it became independent. Located between Egypt and Sub-Saharan Africa, Kush served as a transfer point along the trade routes. Because of its location, the culture was a mixture of Egyptian and African elements.

Axum based its strength on trade. Adulis was a major trading center located between Egypt and the states along the Indian Ocean.

It is possible that some of the people of Axum may have come from southern Arabia. Sometime in the 4th century A.D., Christianity became the state religion.

As Muslim traders began to dominate the Red Sea, Axum declined and its people retreated inland to the highlands.

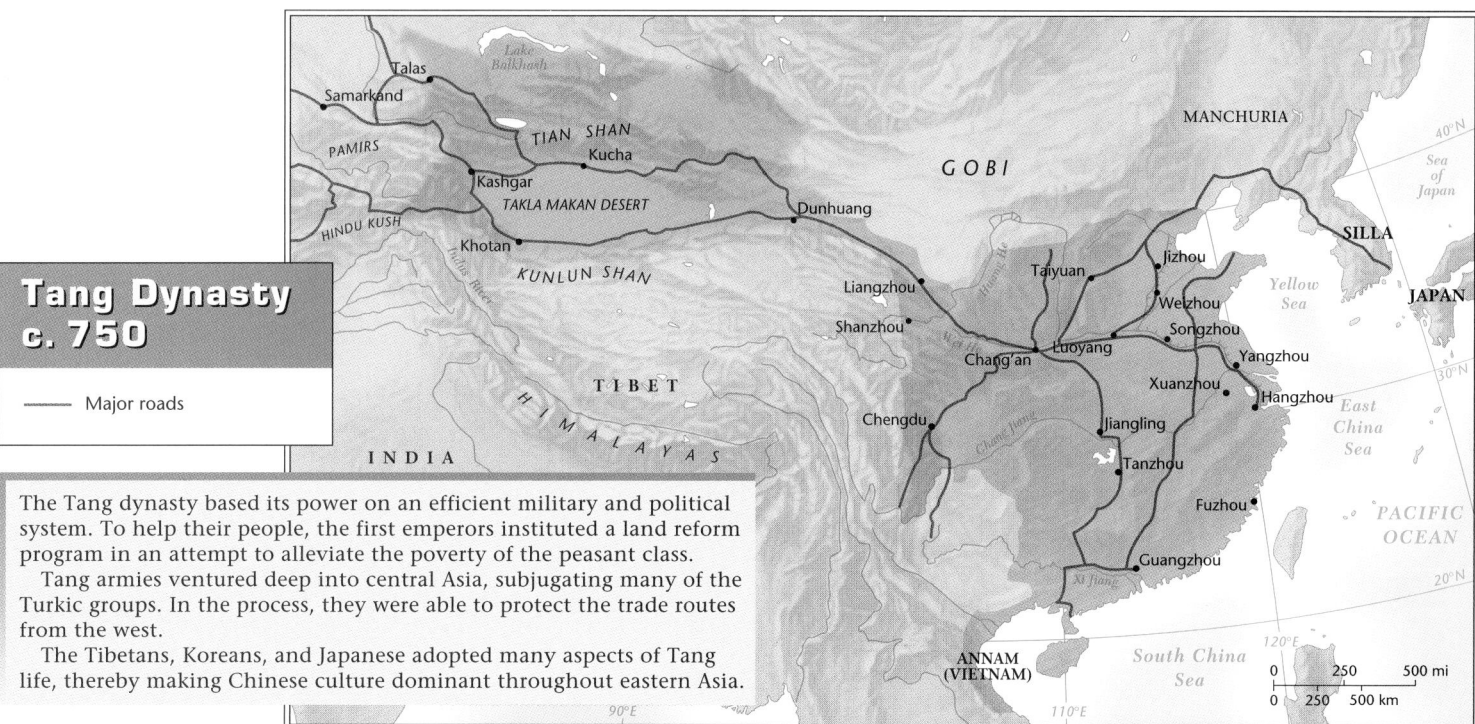

Tang Dynasty c. 750

—— Major roads

The Tang dynasty based its power on an efficient military and political system. To help their people, the first emperors instituted a land reform program in an attempt to alleviate the poverty of the peasant class.

Tang armies ventured deep into central Asia, subjugating many of the Turkic groups. In the process, they were able to protect the trade routes from the west.

The Tibetans, Koreans, and Japanese adopted many aspects of Tang life, thereby making Chinese culture dominant throughout eastern Asia.

The last Tang emperor abdicated in 907, and it wasn't until 960 that a new ruler would emerge to unify China under the banner of the Song dynasty. But he could not defeat the nomadic Khitans. They forced the Song to pay an annual tribute in return for a promise not to raid the Song lands.

In 1115 the Juchens defeated the Khitans and established the Jin dynasty. They then forced the Song dynasty southwards. But they, and the Jin too, could not move far enough away to avoid the Mongols.

Delhi Sultanate

By 1206, the Ghurid dynasty of Afghanistan had conquered part of northern India. A slave-general left in charge became the first sultan of Delhi. Later sultans expanded the area and at the same time fought off Mongol invasions. Now a Muslim dynasty was based in the heart of India.

The sultanate reached its greatest extent under Muhammad bin Tughluq. But there were difficulties in maintaining such a large empire; factional struggles were commonplace. The invasion of Tamerlane, a Mongol, greatly weakened the dynasty. The end came when the Mughals of Babur were victorious over the Delhi forces.

Song & Jin Dynasties

☐ Song dynasty (960–1126)
◻ Southern Song dynasty (1127–1279)
◻ Jin dynasty (1115–1234)

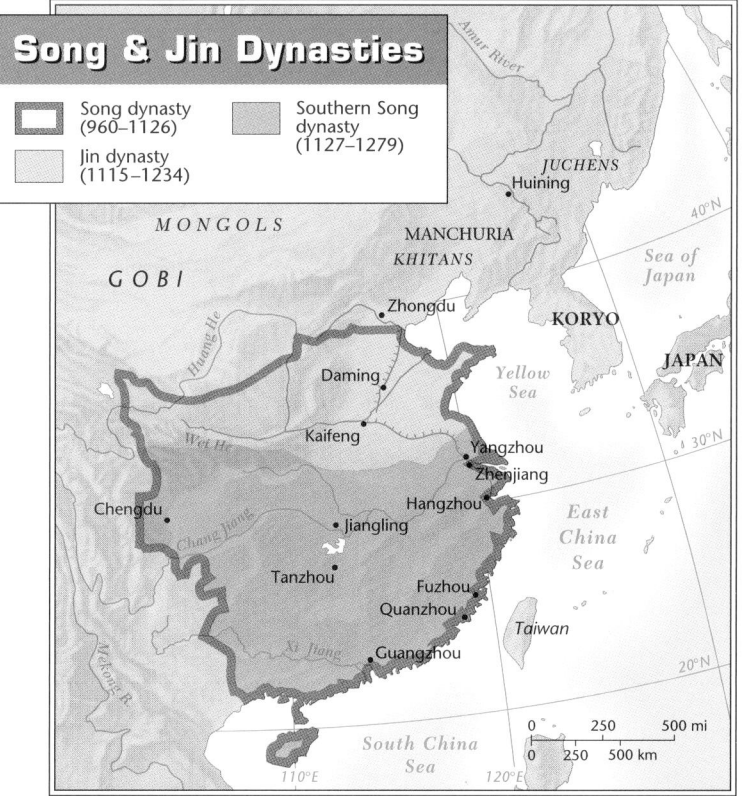

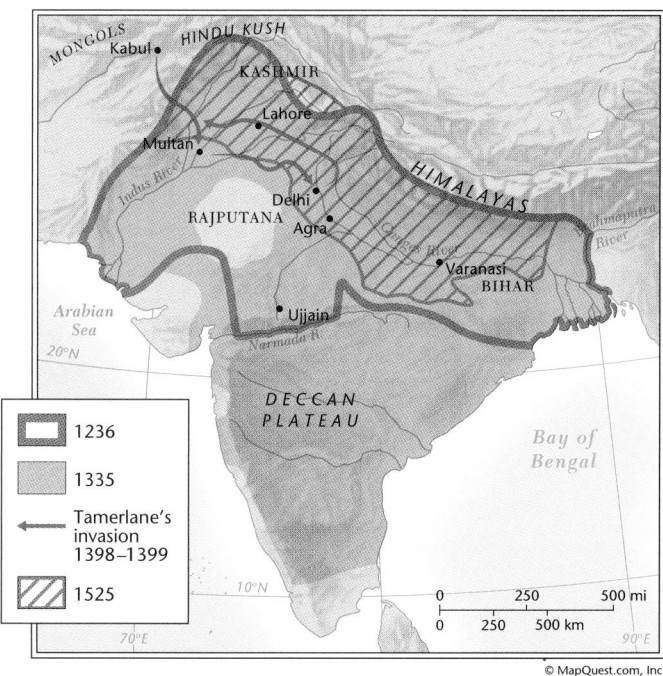

☐ 1236
◻ 1335
← Tamerlane's invasion 1398–1399
▨ 1525

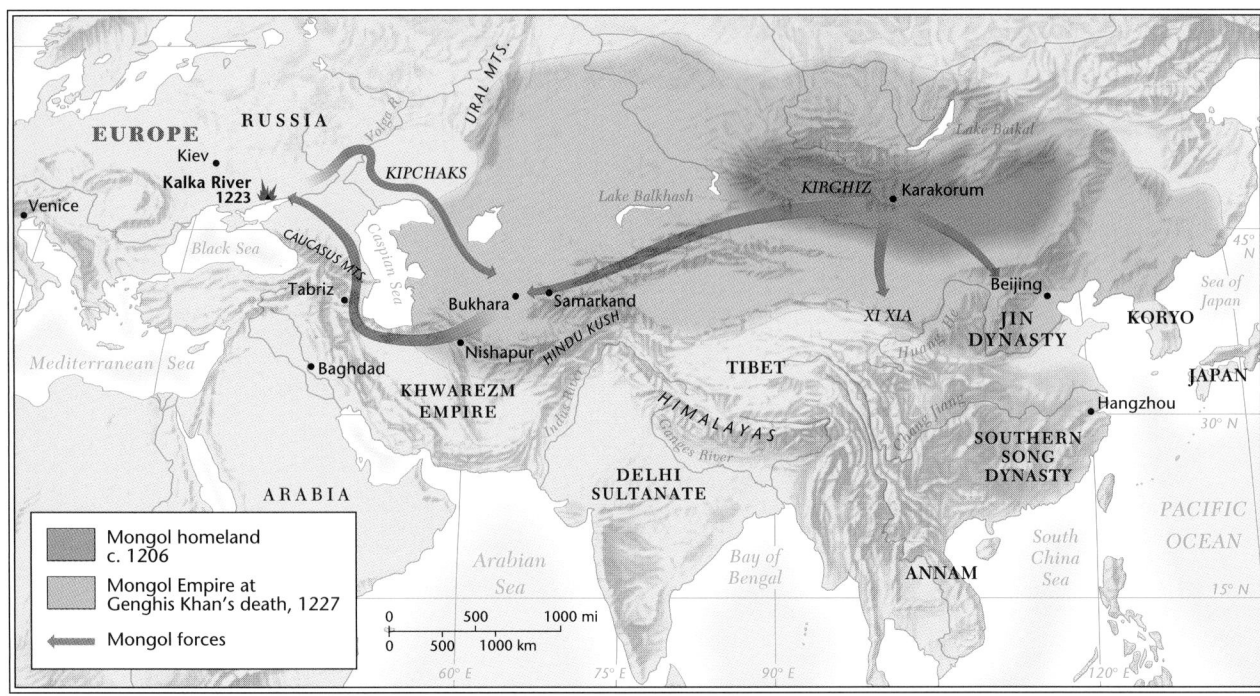

The Empire of Genghis Khan

Mongol Khanates c. 1290

By 1206, Genghis Khan had united the nomadic Mongol tribes. He then defeated the Xi Xia kingdom and took the Jin capital at Beijing in 1215. He then focused his attention westward. Many of the commercial centers of central Asia fell before him. Two of his armies circled the Caspian Sea and defeated the Russians at the Kalka River.

Under his grandsons, Kublai and Hulegu, the empire continued to expand. Hulegu defeated the Abbasids, but the Mamelukes stopped him at Ain Jalut, saving Syria, Egypt, and perhaps even Spain from Mongol rule.

Kublai undertook the conquest of China. Although he was successful, the Song proved to be a determined foe. Around 1259 Kublai took the title of the Great Khan, but his relatives in the other khanates did not recognize his rule.

The Mongols were indeed fierce and disciplined fighters, and they could be unusually cruel to those who opposed them. At the same time, the strength of Mongol rule forced former enemies to live together in relative peace, and the empire served to link the civilizations of Eurasia. Merchants, such as Marco Polo, could travel with little fear.

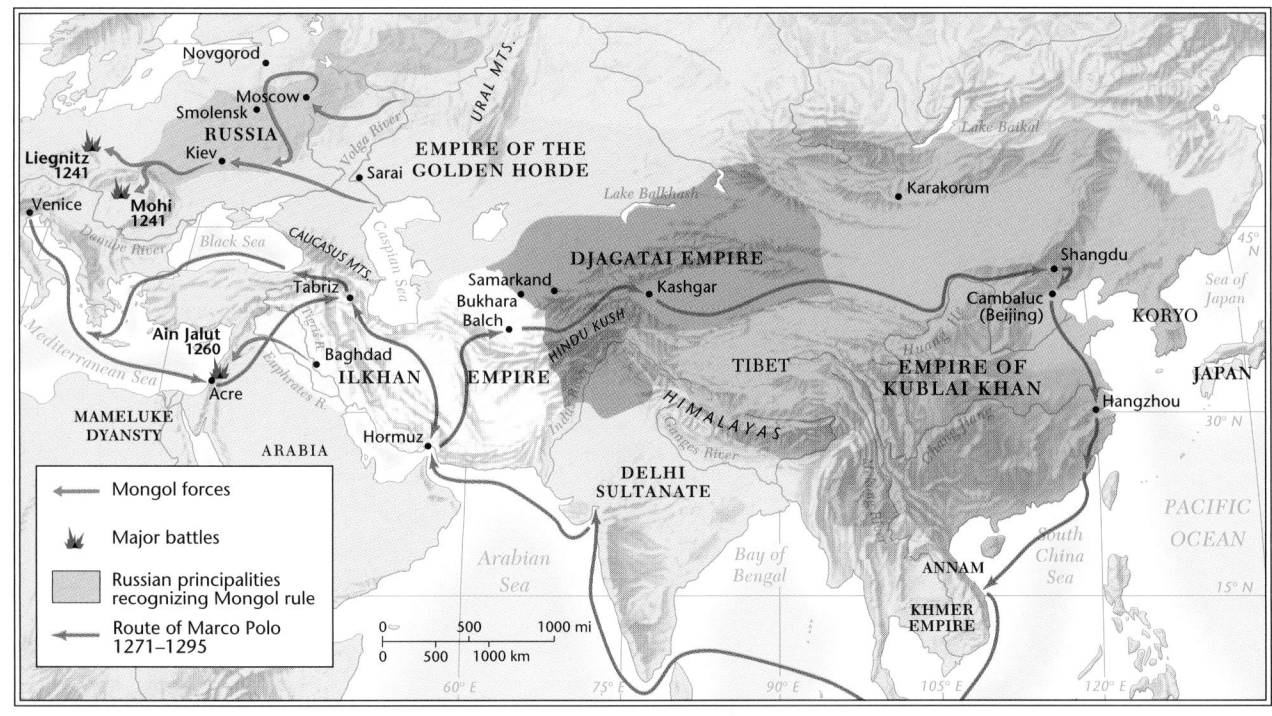

© MapQuest.com, Inc.

The Black Death in Europe

It is certainly possible that the Mongol conquests were partially responsible for transmitting the fleas that carried the plague from central Asia to Europe. Merchants and sailors brought the disease from the Black Sea region to Sicily and Italy. From there it followed trade routes into western Europe.

Mortality statistics are not available, but it is likely that Europe lost one-third to one-half of its population. The plague was all the more frightening because its cause, means of transmission, and cure would not be known for another 500 years.

No aspect of life was untouched. Social, economic, cultural, and even familial bonds were broken by the plague.

But when the plague was over, the survivors often found themselves richer in terms of lands and goods.

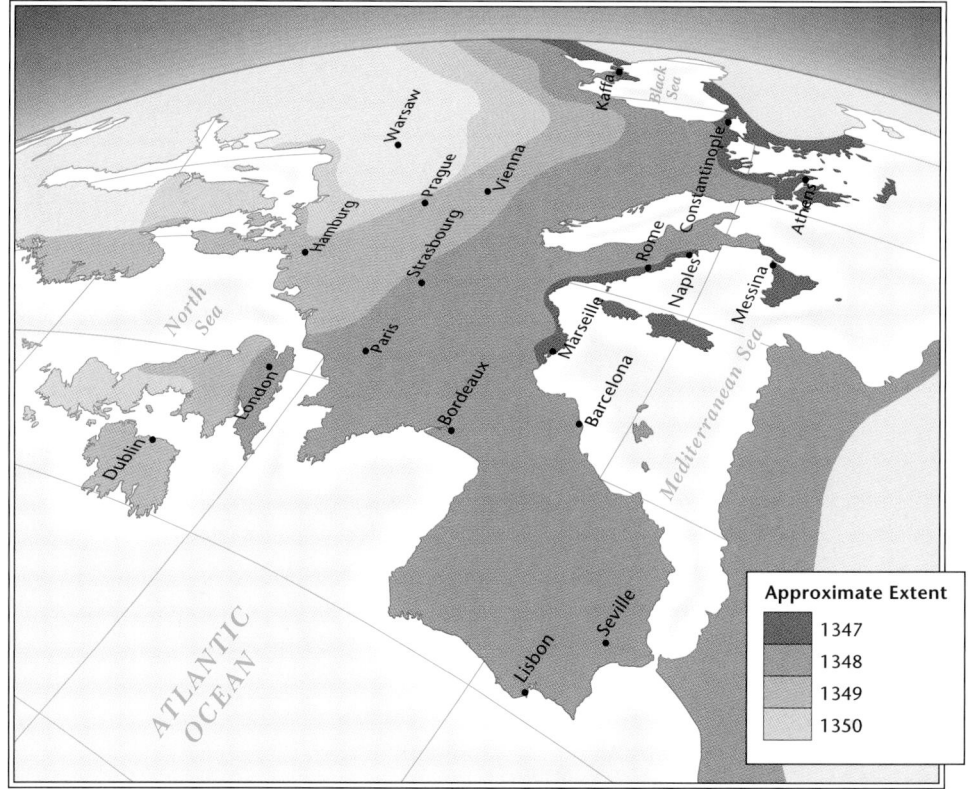

Approximate Extent
- 1347
- 1348
- 1349
- 1350

Renaissance Italy c. 1500

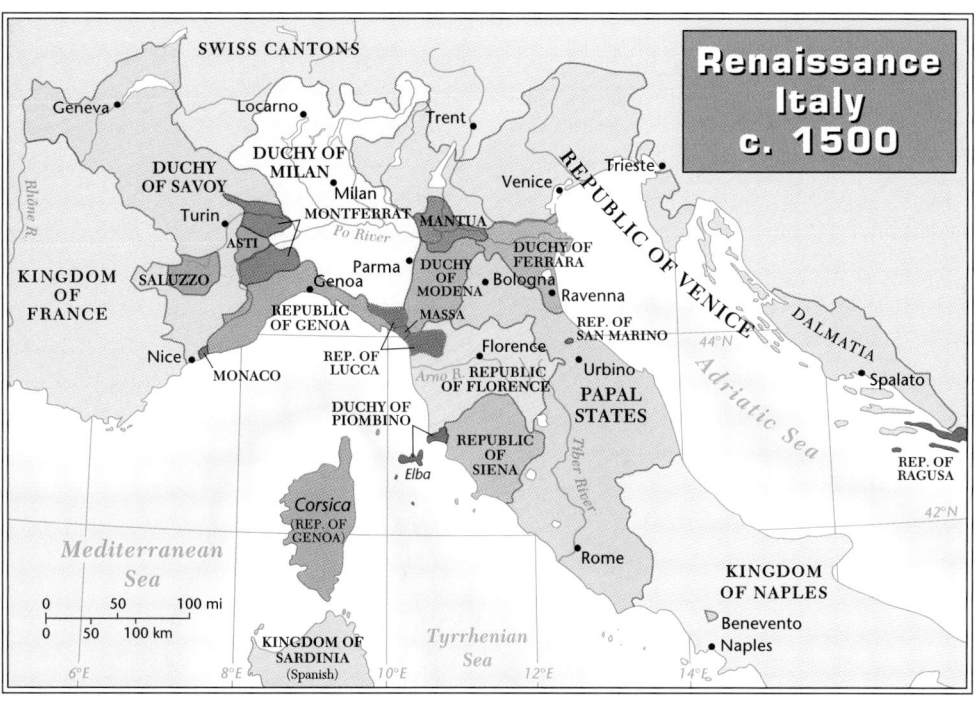

Italy was more urban than the rest of Europe, and through economic growth many of the cities had amassed great wealth. But in the vacuum left by the papal schism, and the weakening of the Holy Roman Empire, there was no central authority in the peninsula. Most Italians were very loyal to their individual city and these in turn governed by their own rules, isolated from others, thus making it difficult to form a unified state.

This disunity made the peninsula an inviting target for the ambitions of other states, and Italy was to be the battleground for a dynastic struggle between France and Spain.

The Spread of Printing in Europe

Printing Centers Established
- 1448–1475
- △ 1476–1500
- • After 1500

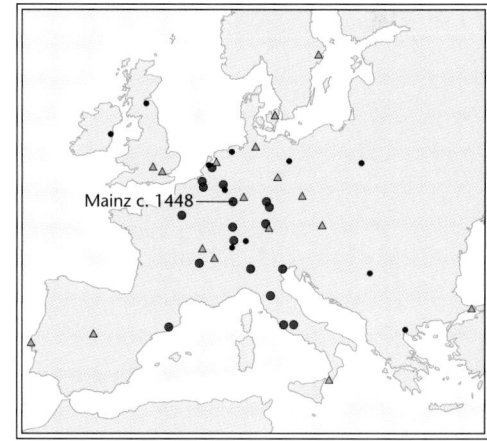

Mainz c. 1448

Until the 1450s, books and other texts had to be laboriously hand-copied, or entire pages had to be carved in wooden blocks. Movable type made printing easier.

Not only did printing make classical literature available to the masses, but because identical copies could be made, it was easier to standardize laws, codes, and theories. Printing also played an important role in the dissemination of ideas, particularly during the Reformation.

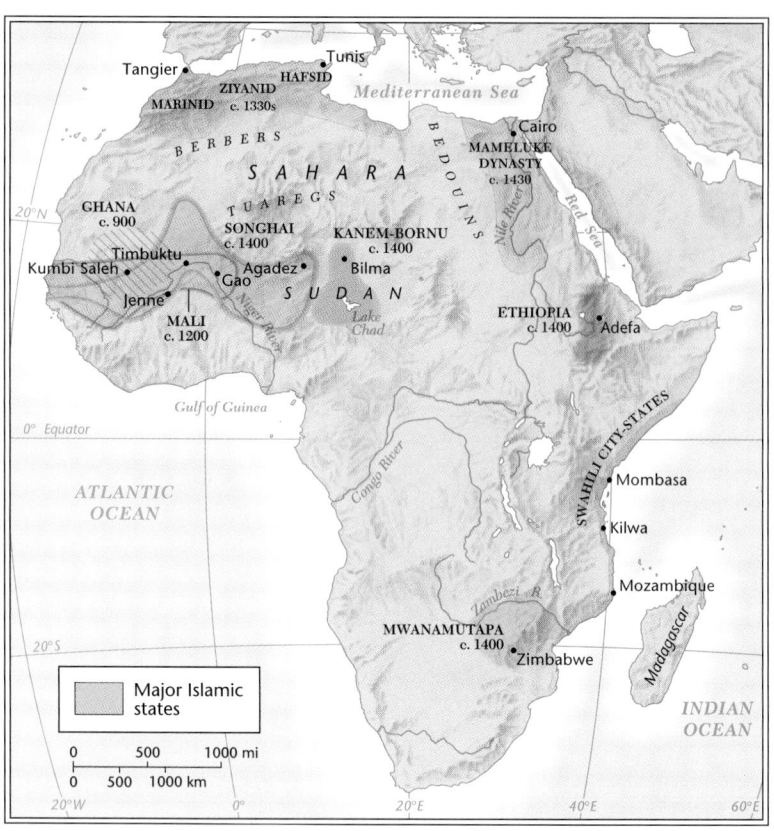

Africa c. 900s–1400s

Islam arrived in northern Africa in the late 600s. By the fourteenth century it had made its way south of the Sahara.

As early as the eighth century, states had developed in western Africa south of the Sahara. Ghana was the most famous of these early states. Mali was the successor to Ghana and the first major state in the region to peacefully convert to Islam.

Along the east coast, Arab Muslim traders settled and developed trade links with states that bordered the Indian Ocean. The intermingling of Arab culture and indigenous Bantu culture gave rise to the Swahili civilization.

Latin America c. 800–1500s

The Maya produced one of the great civilizations of the Americas. Although its peak was probably in the third century, it lasted for many more years.

The Aztecs were nomadic people from northern Mexico. They migrated southward and settled in the Valley of Mexico about 1325. They gained dominance over their neighbors and soon extended their power over most of central Mexico.

In South America, the Inca, from their capital of Cuzco, began to expand. In the mid-1460s they defeated the kingdom of Chimú, their main rival. By the end of the century they held sway over nearly 3,000 miles of coastline, and this included nearly 100 ethnic groups.

As mighty as the Aztecs and Inca were, their empires were both relatively short-lived. By the early 1500s, both had been defeated by the Spaniards.

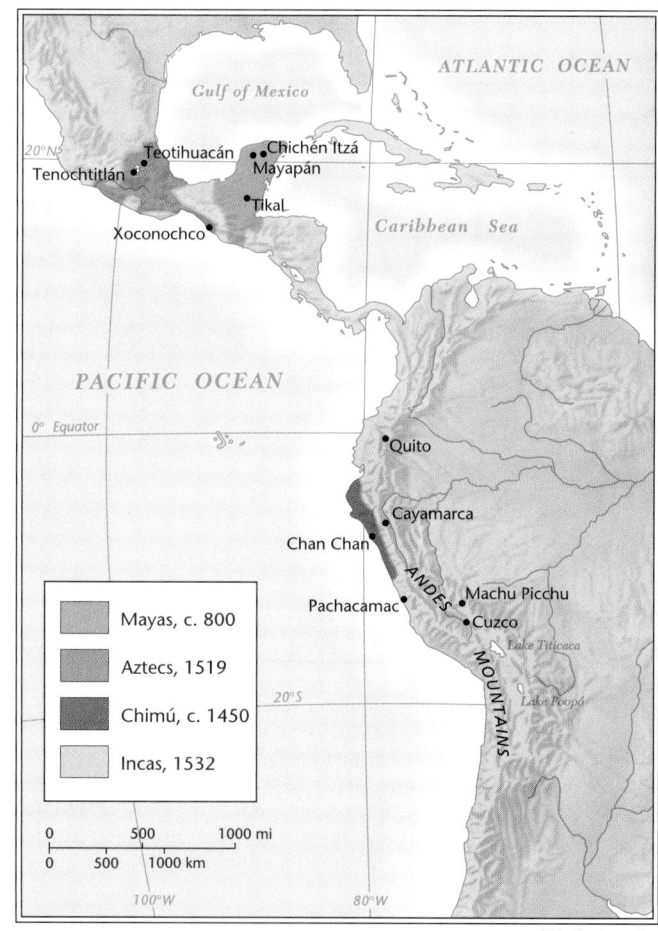

North American Culture Areas During the Pre-Columbian Period

This map covers a long period of time, and the Indian groups that are shown here might not have lived in the same time period.

The peopling of North America probably began during the last glacial period. Because the climate was colder than it is today, much of the world's moisture existed as ice. Sea level dropped and land bridges that would otherwise have been underwater were exposed. This is one method by which people moved from Asia.

When the native peoples first arrived, they were hunters and gatherers. But signs of agriculture appeared in Central America sometime between 8000 and 5000 B.C.

Over the ages isolated groups developed their own cultures and lifestyles to fit their unique environment. For example, fishing was common in the Pacific Northwest, hunting remained the way of life in the Great Plains, and agriculture was relied upon in the arid Southwest.

With the development of agriculture, the food supply became more dependable and the population increased rapidly. At the time of Columbus' arrival, there may have been between two and four million Native Americans (or Indians as the Europeans called them).

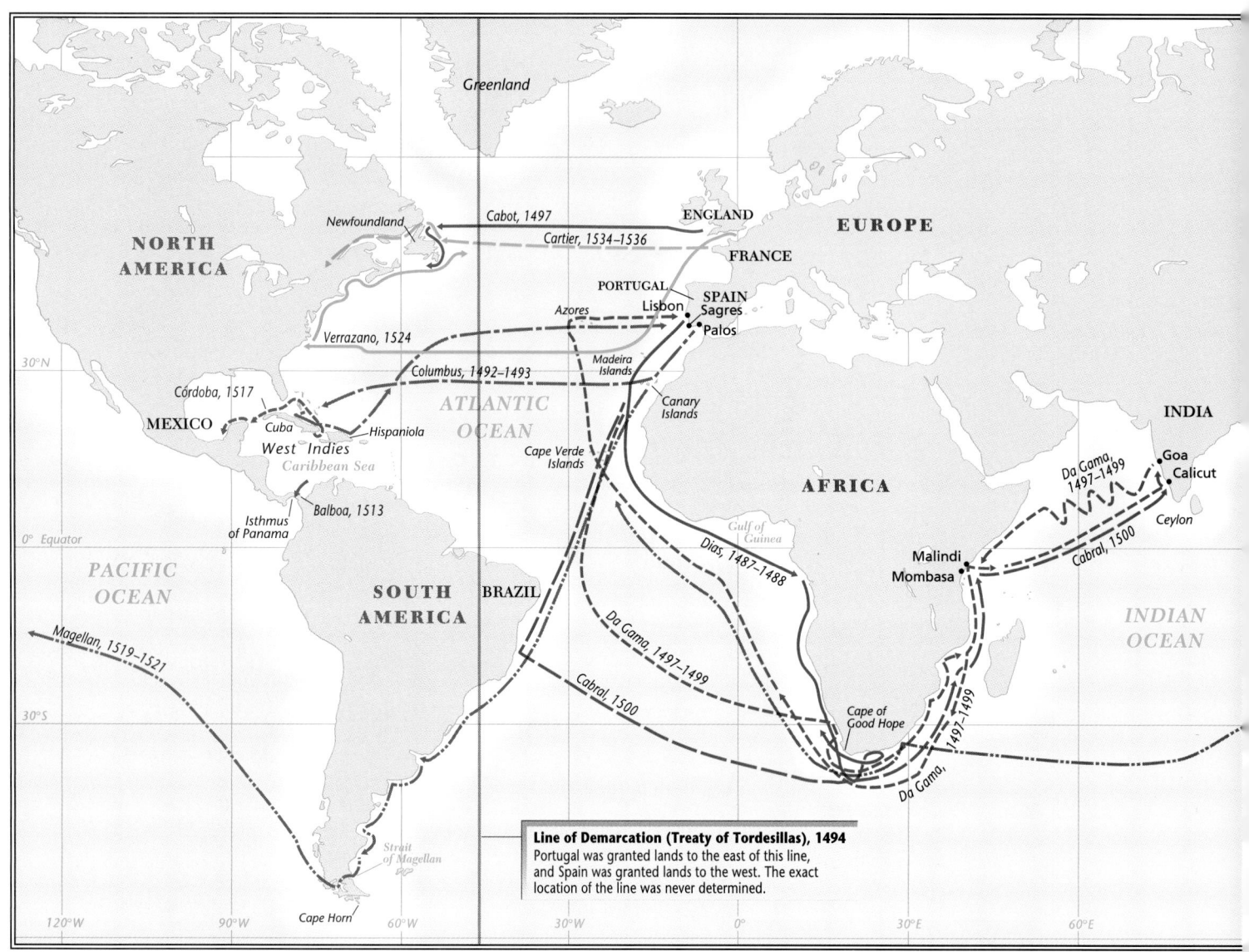

Greenland

NORTH AMERICA

EUROPE

Cabot, 1497 ENGLAND
Cartier, 1534–1536 FRANCE
Newfoundland

PORTUGAL
Azores Lisbon SPAIN Sagres Palos
Verrazano, 1524

30°N

Córdoba, 1517 Columbus, 1492–1493 Madeira Islands
MEXICO ATLANTIC OCEAN
Cuba Canary Islands
West Indies Hispaniola
Caribbean Sea Cape Verde Islands
AFRICA INDIA

Isthmus of Panama Balboa, 1513 Da Gama, 1497–1499 Goa Calicut

0° Equator Gulf of Guinea Ceylon
Dias, 1487–1488 Cabral, 1500

PACIFIC OCEAN SOUTH AMERICA BRAZIL Da Gama, 1497–1499 Malindi Mombasa INDIAN OCEAN

Magellan, 1519–1521 Cabral, 1500 Da Gama, 1497–1499

30°S Cape of Good Hope

Da Gama, 1497–1499

Line of Demarcation (Treaty of Tordesillas), 1494
Portugal was granted lands to the east of this line, and Spain was granted lands to the west. The exact location of the line was never determined.

Strait of Magellan

120°W 90°W Cape Horn 60°W 30°W 0° 30°E 60°E

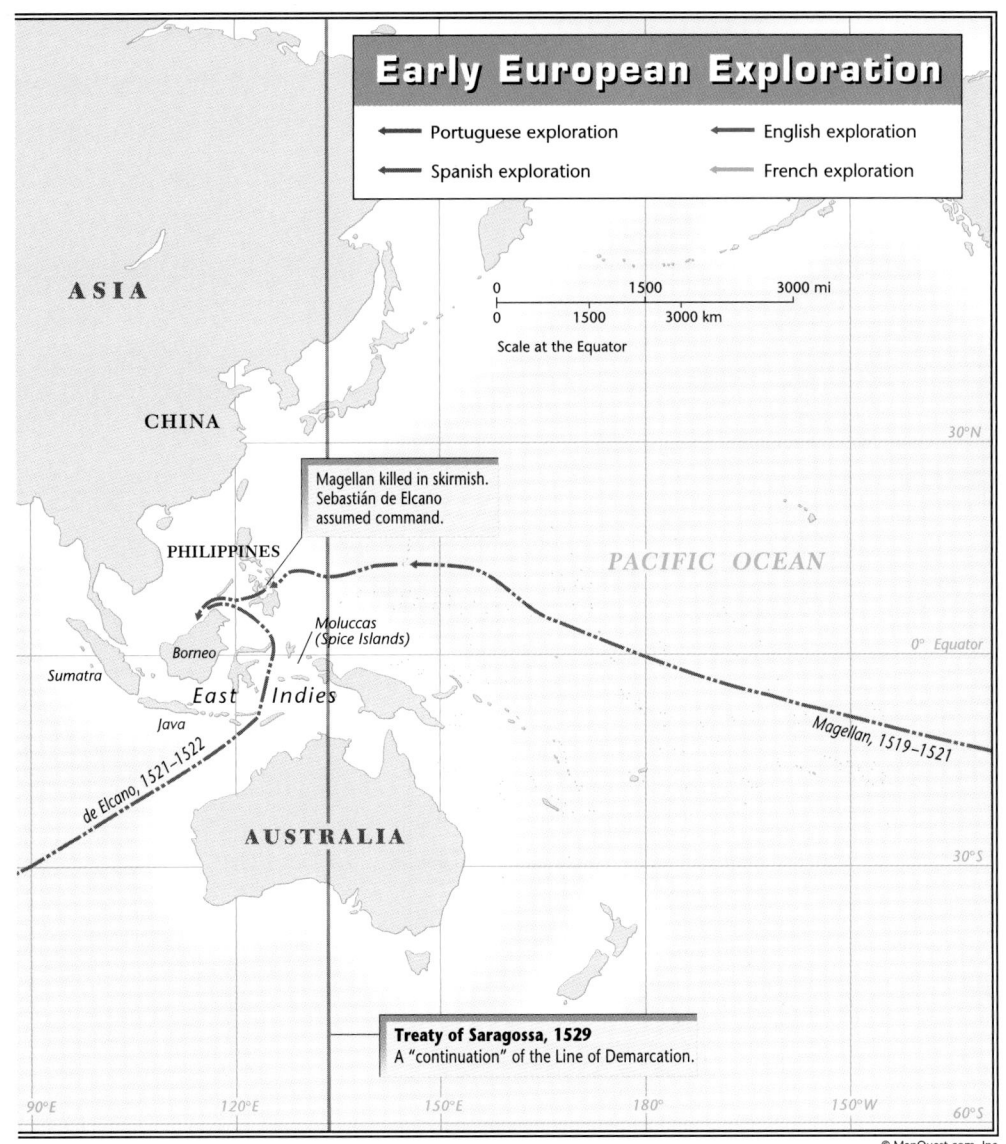

Early European Exploration

→ Portuguese exploration   ← English exploration

← Spanish exploration   ← French exploration

ASIA

CHINA

0   1500   3000 mi
0   1500   3000 km

Scale at the Equator

30°N

Magellan killed in skirmish.
Sebastián de Elcano
assumed command.

PHILIPPINES

PACIFIC OCEAN

Moluccas
(Spice Islands)

0° Equator

Borneo

Sumatra

East Indies

Java

de Elcano, 1521–1522

Magellan, 1519–1521

AUSTRALIA

30°S

Treaty of Saragossa, 1529
A "continuation" of the Line of Demarcation.

90°E   120°E   150°E   180°   150°W   60°S

© MapQuest.com, Inc.

1450 ushered in what is commonly called the "Age of Discovery." The next 200 years would also be called the "Age of Expansion." In terms of discovery, there were major advances in the Europeans' geographical knowledge and navigational technology. As to expansion, there would be European colonization of coastal portions of African, Asia, and the Americas.

The motivations for exploration are varied. The desire to convert Muslim and other pagan peoples to Christianity was certainly one factor, especially in Spain and Portugal.

The desire for spices and other goods such as porcelain and silk was another reason Europeans wanted to travel to the East. The Turks had made land travel difficult, and some European states were determined to find a direct sea route to the East.

But the search for profit was probably the most important reason. The chance to find precious metals was an opportunity some Europeans could not resist.

The reasons for exploration were there, and technology provided the means. The compass (invented in China) had only recently been introduced to Europe. Astrolabes were also important in aiding navigators to find their latitudinal position. Dead reckoning was more accurate than ever in determining distances traveled.

The Portuguese and Spanish caravels were the first non-oared, European ships that could safely and efficiently sail the open ocean.

The Portuguese were the first Europeans to develop a systematic program of exploration. The Portuguese logically looked eastward to find the Indies, and Christopher Columbus convinced the Spanish crown that he could reach them by sailing westward.

European Exploration of North America

→ Spanish exploration
→ French exploration
→ English exploration
→ Dutch exploration

Hudson & Bylot 1610–1611
Bylot 1611
Hudson 1609
Greenland
Hudson Bay
Newfoundland
NORTH AMERICA
Quebec
Champlain 1615
Nova Scotia
Great Lakes
St. Lawrence R.
Mississippi R.
Marquette & Jolliet 1673
La Salle 1679–1682
Coronado 1540–1542
De Soto 1539–1542
Cabrillo 1542
Colorado River
Rio Grande
ATLANTIC OCEAN
PACIFIC OCEAN
Drake 1577
Gulf of Mexico
Ponce de León 1513
Cortés 1519
Cuba
Puerto Rico
Tenochtitlán
Hispaniola
Caribbean Sea
SOUTH AMERICA

0   500   1000 mi
0   500   1000 km

© MapQuest.com, Inc.

By the late 1400s, the Spanish monarchs consolidated several kingdoms to form a united Spain. The monarchy, now stronger than ever, wanted to develop overseas trading. They had decided to leave Africa to the Portuguese, who had already explored much of its western coast.

In service to Spain, Columbus sailed westward in hopes of finding India, but discovered the Americas without knowing it. Magellan and de Elcano circled the globe and brought back enough spices to more than cover the cost of the expedition. But in the long run the Pacific passage was uneconomical. Spain gave up any claim to the East Indies and concentrated on finding gold, silver, and converts in the Americas.

Spanish conquistadors established settlements in the West Indies. Bernal Díaz said that his goal and that of many others was, "To serve God and His Majesty, to give light to those who were in darkness, and to grow rich, as all men desire to do."

Rumors abounded as to the fabulous wealth to be found inland. Cortés' victory over the Aztecs and Pizarro's conquest of the Incas of Peru would bring untold riches to the mother country. But Spanish expeditions to the north found little exploitable wealth.

The French sought a northwest passage to the East. By going in this direction they could avoid conflicts with New Spain. Although they found no gold or silver in Canada, they did establish, in alliance with the Native Americans, a thriving fur trade. But any dream of a French colonial empire was hampered by royal indifference to any plans.

English claims to North America were based on John Cabot's voyage of 1497. But it would be about 80 years before England would challenge Spain's domination of the Americas. The English would begin colonization plans towards the end of the sixteenth century, but without success until the next century.

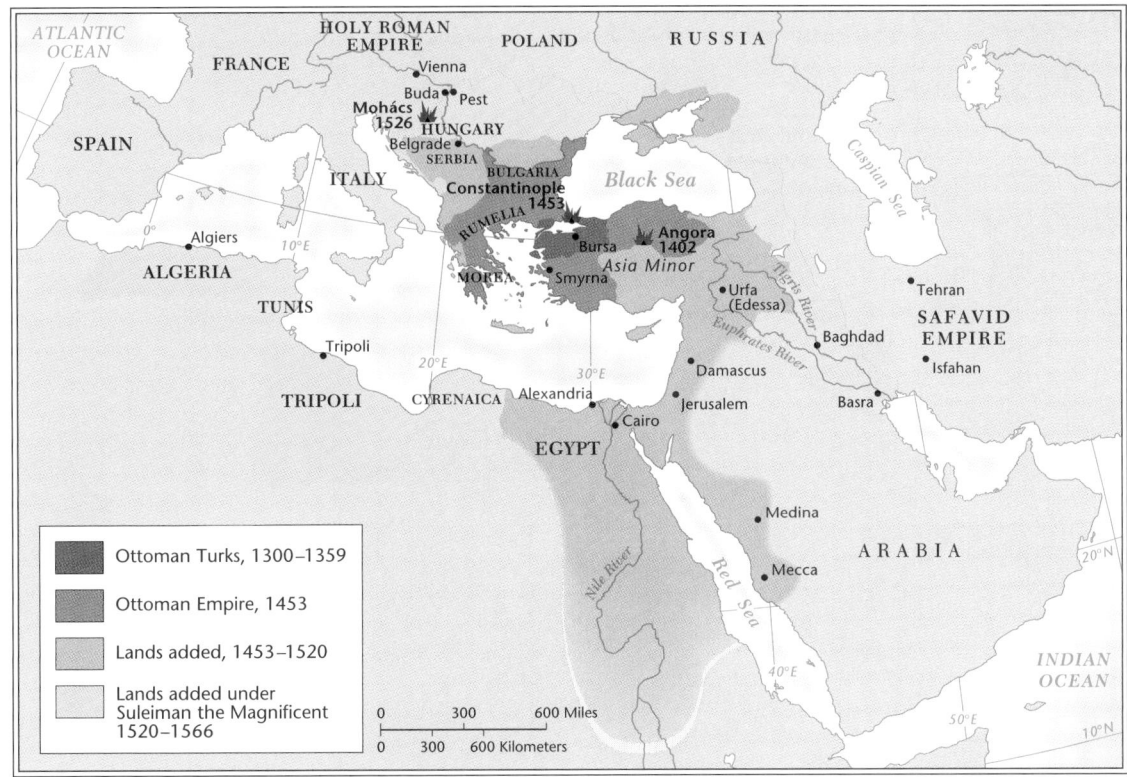

The Ottoman Empire

The Ottomans were nomadic Turkish-speaking peoples who migrated to Asia Minor from central Asia. They rose to power following the break-up of the empire of the Seljuk Turks.

In their expansion, the Ottomans bypassed Constantinople and moved into Europe. But in 1453 the city—and with it the Byzantine Empire—fell to their siege. From there they moved to consolidate their conquests in southeast Europe. There is no doubt that Ottoman success in Europe was in part due to the political disunity that was prevalent there. Nonetheless, at its peak, the Ottoman Empire was more powerful than any European state.

Its inability to keep up with the newly burgeoning European economic growth contributed to the stagnation of the empire.

Legend (Ottoman map):
- Ottoman Turks, 1300–1359
- Ottoman Empire, 1453
- Lands added, 1453–1520
- Lands added under Suleiman the Magnificent 1520–1566

European Religions in the Late 1500s

Prior to the 1500s there was really only one church in Europe, and that was the Catholic Church. Despite its strength, its sheer size required a great deal of money to underwrite it. To raise this money, clerical positions were sold, as were "indulgences"—the pardon or remission of sins. It was specifically the sale of these indulgences that prompted Martin Luther to attack the church.

At first, Luther hoped to reform the church, but his theology soon became a movement, and was to be called Protestantism. Many people, especially peasants, embraced his concept of "freedom" for the Christian man, because they felt this extended to economic and social matters as well.

In Geneva, John Calvin gave the Protestant church discipline and a well-organized governmental framework. It was the Calvinist Church that would be the model for other churches throughout Europe.

The Huguenots, as the Calvinists in France were called, faced persecution from the monarchy, and there would be nearly thirty years of warfare before they were granted some degree of toleration.

Predominant Religions (legend):
- Lutheran
- Calvinist (Reformed)
- Church of England
- Roman Catholic
- C Calvinist minorities
- H Huguenot minorities

© MapQuest.com, Inc.

The English Civil War 1642–1646

Areas controlled by Royalists

Areas controlled by Parliamentarians

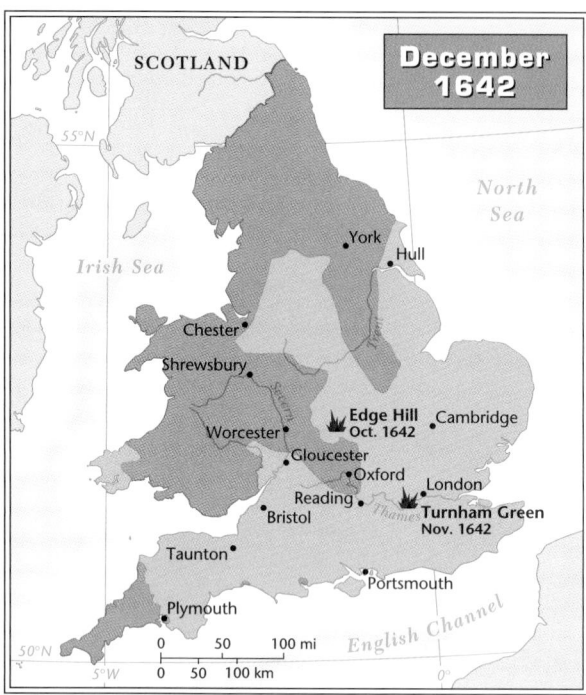

The Stuarts, as rulers of Scotland and England, believed that their right to rule came from God, and not from the people. Parliament refused to grant funds to Charles I unless he was willing to address a number of political grievances. He refused and civil war broke out.

The supporters of the king were called *Cavaliers*, and the supporters of Parliament were called *Roundheads*. Among those who supported Parliament were the Puritans.

Oliver Cromwell led the Parliament forces and won a series of victories. Charles was captured in 1646, condemned to death, and beheaded in 1649. Upon his execution, England became a republic to be known as the Commonwealth of England.

Fighting continued as Cromwell defeated resisting forces in Scotland and Ireland.

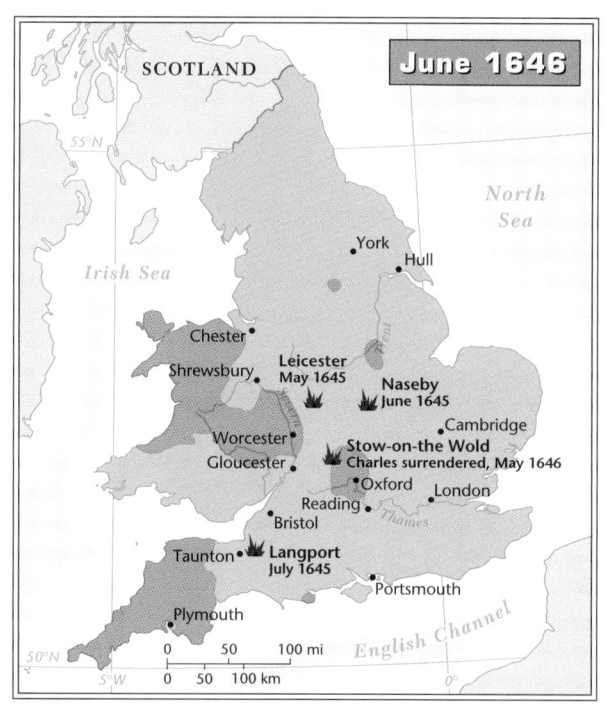

Europeans in the
Eastern Hemisphere
c. 1714

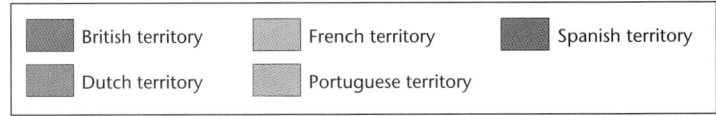

British territory   French territory   Spanish territory

Dutch territory   Portuguese territory

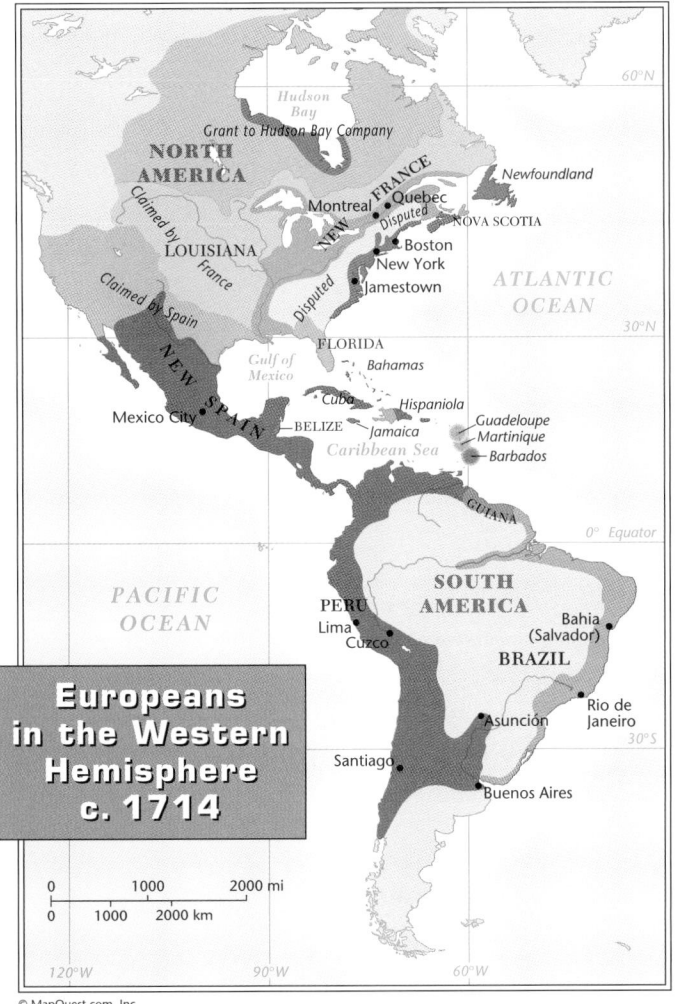

Europeans
in the Western
Hemisphere
c. 1714

European discovery of the Americas and of a passage to the East
Indies laid the foundation for the commercial empires of western
European nations. The hope for each nation was to monopolize
trade in order to maximize profits. Colonies were established for
the purpose of economic gain.

The Portuguese pushed south along the west coast of Africa and
into the Indian Ocean. They established fortified towns that
would serve as naval bases and places where products could be
stored prior to shipment to Europe. The Portuguese overextended
themselves however, and were soon overtaken by the Dutch.
Although they followed the Portuguese example of posts and
naval presence, the Dutch improved upon them.

In the last half of the seventeenth century, the Dutch, English,
and later the French would become involved in a series of
mercantile wars. The growing commercial strength of the English
was in large part due to the success of their North American colonies.

English claim to North America was based on John Cabot's
voyage of 1497. But it was not until 1607 that a permanent
settlement was established. The founding of Plymouth in 1620 by
the Pilgrims was a momentous event, for it opened the way for
large numbers of religious dissenters. Instead of being populated
by men whose sole interest was the acquisition of wealth, the
New England colonies were populated by educated and
responsible families. Thus English law, language, and customs
became established.

Tobacco and sugar were major products of North America, and
their importation enriched the British government's coffers. The
economy of the colonies was booming, and British manufactured
goods were in demand.

British Colonies 1764

Beginning in the 1600s, the English crown began to grant charters for the purpose of founding colonies in North America. In contrast to Spain and France, who desired a monolithic, centralized empire, English grants went to a variety of peoples: merchants, religious dissenters, and aristocrats.

Because these charters were granted with little knowledge of North America's geography there would soon be boundary disputes, and these would continue until the late eighteenth century.

By the mid-1700s, the French had established a chain of forts and settlements from Quebec to the mouth of the Mississippi River. Soon they built forts in the Ohio River valley, lands that the British colonists coveted. But the colonists were divided into separate governments and lacked the leadership to challenge the French. Nonetheless, war came, and working in concert with the British, the French were defeated.

Following the war, the British government, in hopes of avoiding costly Indian wars, established a proclamation line: lands to the west were to be "reserved for Indians."

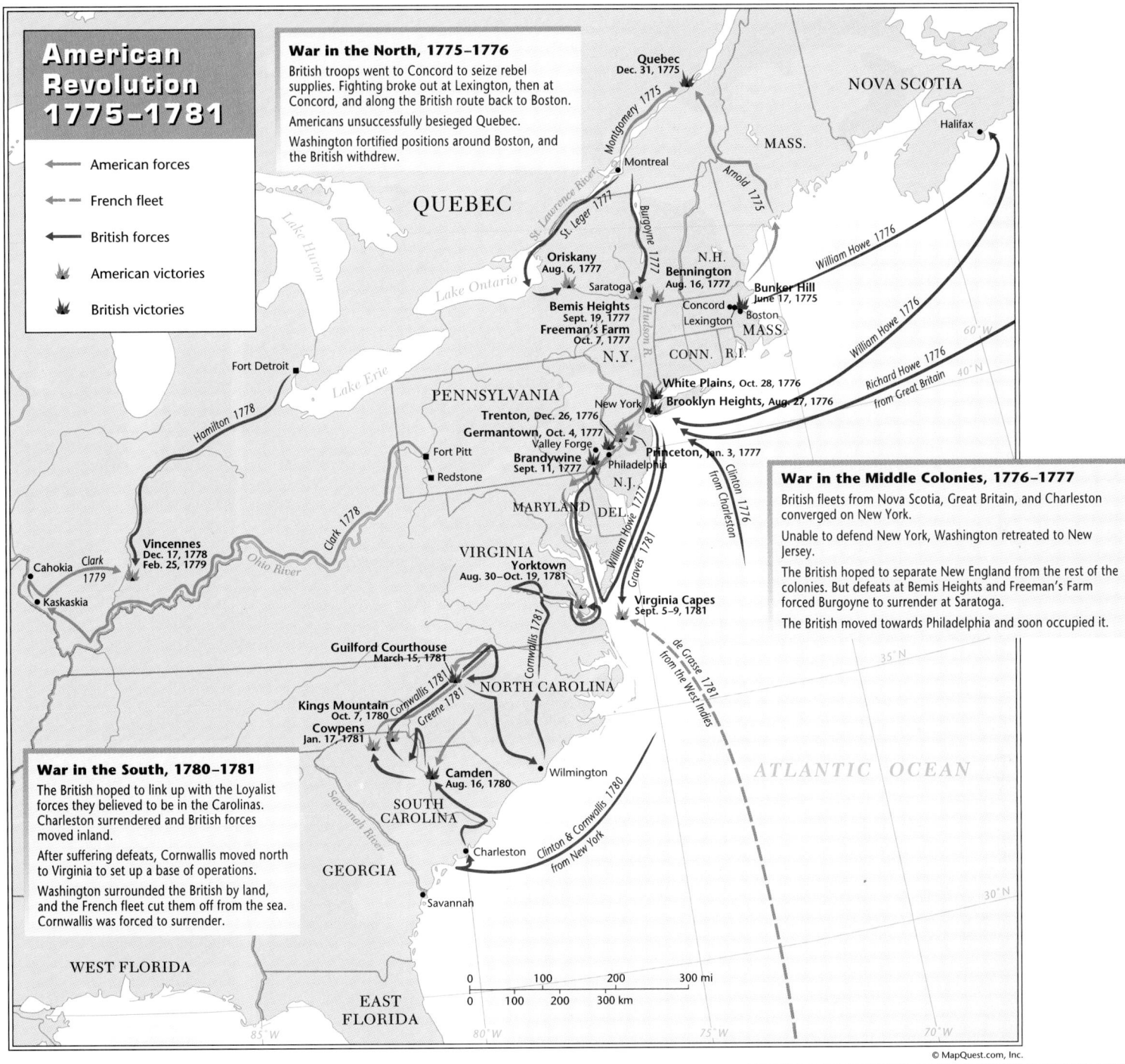

American Revolution 1775–1781

→ American forces
→ French fleet
→ British forces
🔥 American victories
🔥 British victories

War in the North, 1775–1776

British troops went to Concord to seize rebel supplies. Fighting broke out at Lexington, then at Concord, and along the British route back to Boston.

Americans unsuccessfully besieged Quebec.

Washington fortified positions around Boston, and the British withdrew.

War in the Middle Colonies, 1776–1777

British fleets from Nova Scotia, Great Britain, and Charleston converged on New York.

Unable to defend New York, Washington retreated to New Jersey.

The British hoped to separate New England from the rest of the colonies. But defeats at Bemis Heights and Freeman's Farm forced Burgoyne to surrender at Saratoga.

The British moved towards Philadelphia and soon occupied it.

War in the South, 1780–1781

The British hoped to link up with the Loyalist forces they believed to be in the Carolinas. Charleston surrendered and British forces moved inland.

After suffering defeats, Cornwallis moved north to Virginia to set up a base of operations.

Washington surrounded the British by land, and the French fleet cut them off from the sea. Cornwallis was forced to surrender.

© MapQuest.com, Inc.

In the 1760s, probably nobody considered the possibility of independence for the colonies. But the bonds that existed slowly began to unravel. The British continued to garrison troops in the Americas, and frontier posts were expensive to maintain. Believing that the colonists should bear some of this burden, Parliament passed a series of revenue bills to do just that.

It is easy to oversimplify the origins of war, but the anger over increased taxes was certainly an immediate one. As colonists, and Bostonians in particular, became more "rebellious," Parliament enacted the *Coercive Acts* to suppress this movement. Americans believed that some of the provisions denied them constitutional liberties. The first Continental Congress convened in 1774 called for a redress of grievances. But none would be forthcoming from Parliament.

In July 1776, the Continental Congress adopted the Declaration of Independence. Now the Americans would have to win it.

There was no colonial army or navy: only militias made up of citizen-soldiers. George Washington would have to build an army of soldiers. In light of this, the British forces entered the war believing all that was needed to win was a demonstration of military force. But the rigid European-style tactics were not always suitable to the forests of America where the opponent was often more flexible and adaptable. Because each colony had its own government, there was no one "strategic heart" in the colonies that the British needed to conquer. Instead, they would have to occupy and control large expanses of territory, and the British lacked the resources to do this.

Following victories in 1777, the French signed an alliance with the Americans in 1778. Soon the Spanish and Dutch would enter on the American side. Now it was an imperial war, and once the last major British army surrendered at Yorktown, the British were willing to cut their losses and end the war.

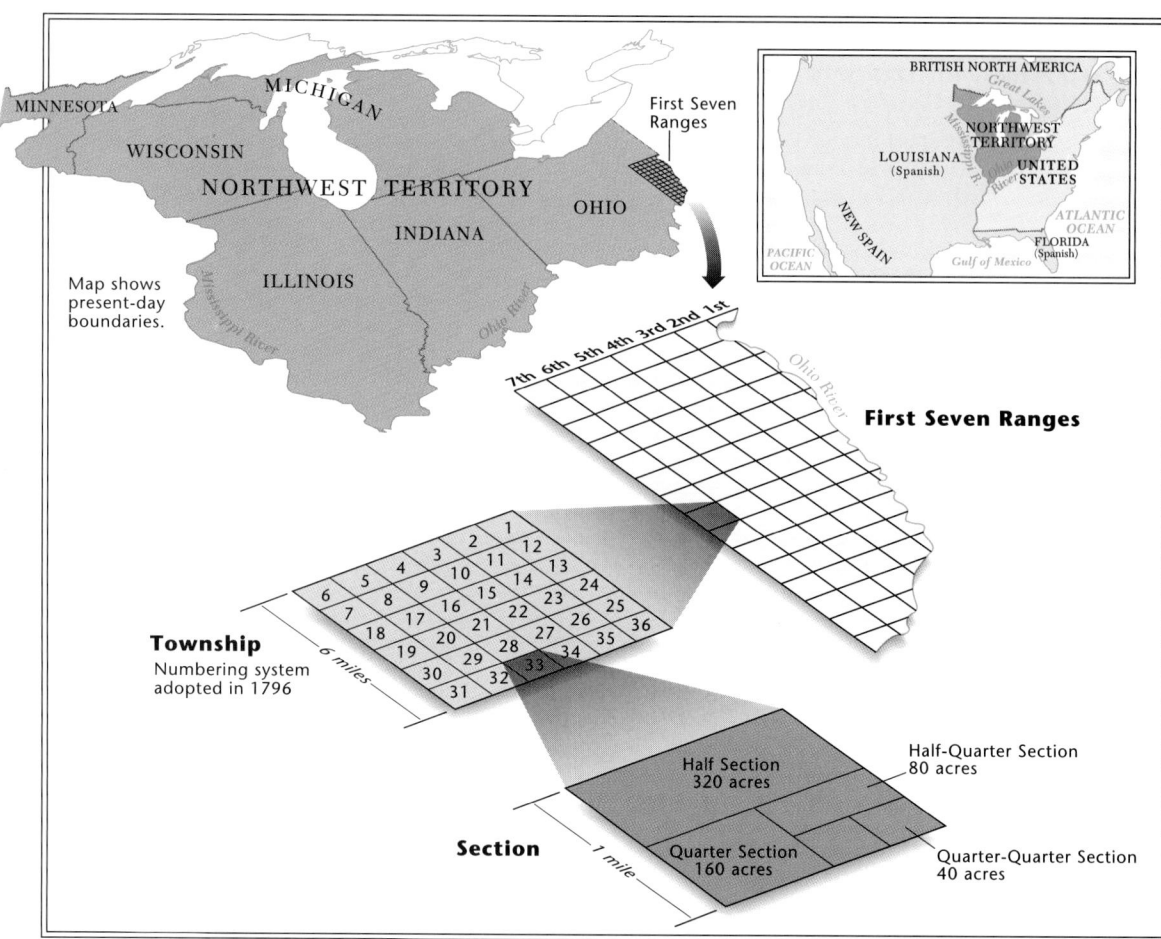

Map shows present-day boundaries.

First Seven Ranges

7th 6th 5th 4th 3rd 2nd 1st

Township
Numbering system adopted in 1796

6 miles

1	12	
2	11	13
3	14	24
4	15	23

Section

1 mile

Half Section
320 acres

Half-Quarter Section
80 acres

Quarter Section
160 acres

Quarter-Quarter Section
40 acres

The Northwest Territory

Congress faced the issue of sorting out conflicting claims to lands west of the Appalachians. Virginia was one of the first states to relinquish its claims, and the "Old Northwest," was ceded to the United States.

The Ordinance of 1784 established the means by which settlers in the Northwest Territory could form governments and apply for statehood.

Congress needed money and the Land Ordinance of 1785 established an orderly system of survey (ranges, townships and sections) so that land could be sold.

The Northwest Ordinance of 1787 further refined the governmental arrangements and banned slavery north of the Ohio River.

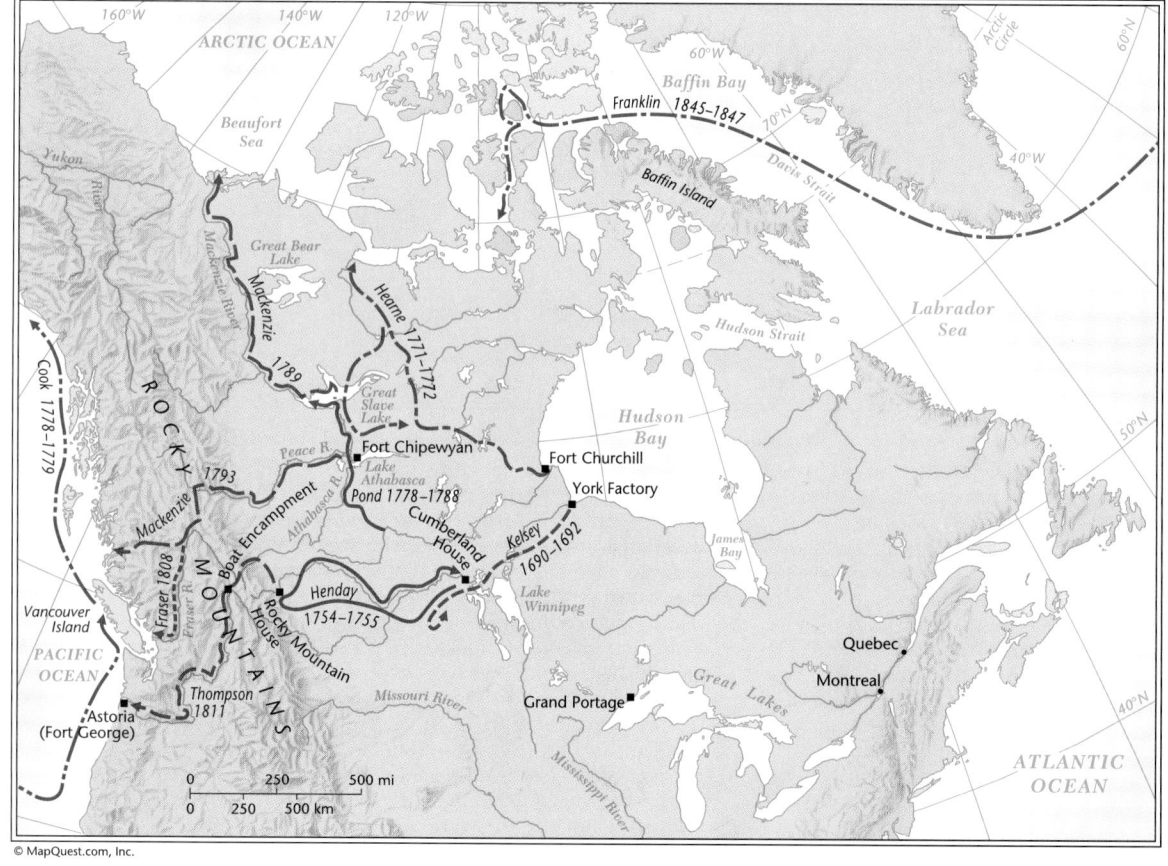

Exploration of Canada

← British exploration

■ Trading post after 1821

Following the American Revolution, many of the rich fur areas were assigned to the United States, and new sources of furs needed to be found.

In 1784 the North West Company was founded, and its intention was to establish trade in those areas to the north and west of the Great Lakes. This brought them into direct—and sometimes violent—competition with the firmly established Hudson Bay Company. It was this competition for better fur-trading areas and trade routes that led to the exploration of the West.

In 1821 the North West Company and Hudson Bay Company merged. After the merger the Hudson Bay Company consolidated many of the competing posts.

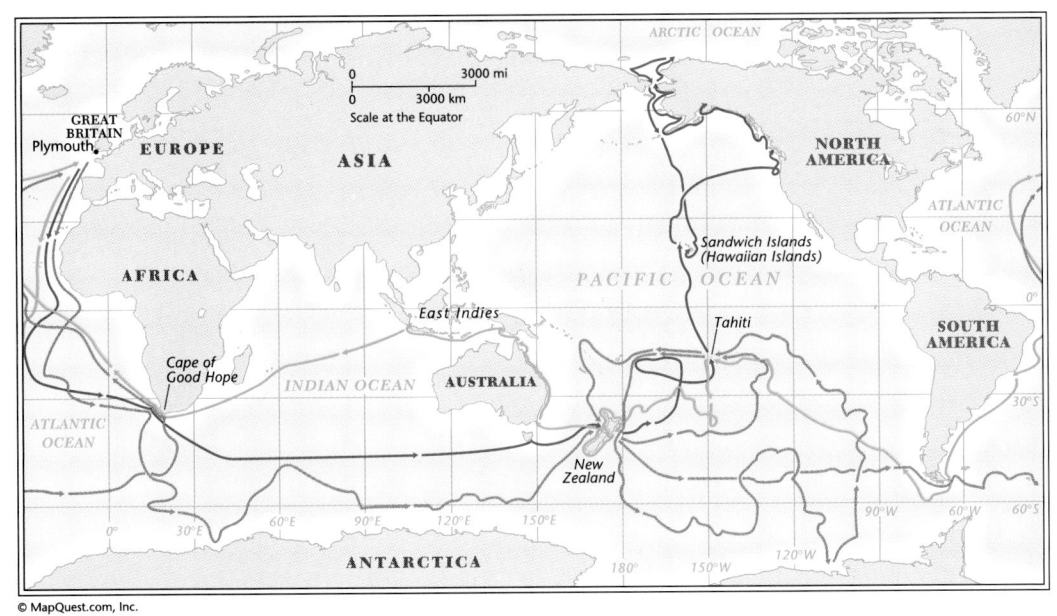

© MapQuest.com, Inc.

Voyages of Captain James Cook

→ First voyage, 1768–1771

→ Second voyage, 1772–1775

→ Third voyage, 1776–1779

Captain James Cook, a British naval officer, commanded three voyages to the Pacific Ocean. On two of them he circumnavigated the globe.

The aim of the first two voyages was to find the southern continent (Antarctica) and to claim any lands in the South Pacific. On the first voyage he explored the eastern coast of Australia and claimed the land for Great Britain. On the second voyage, Cook sailed farther south than any European before him, but he did not actually see Antarctica.

On his third voyage he set out to find the *Northwest Passage*, a sea link that could connect Europe with Asia. But once through the Bering Strait, his way was blocked by ice. On his return he stopped at the Hawaiian Islands. There was an altercation with the islanders, and Cook was fatally stabbed. He was buried at sea.

Voyages in the Pacific

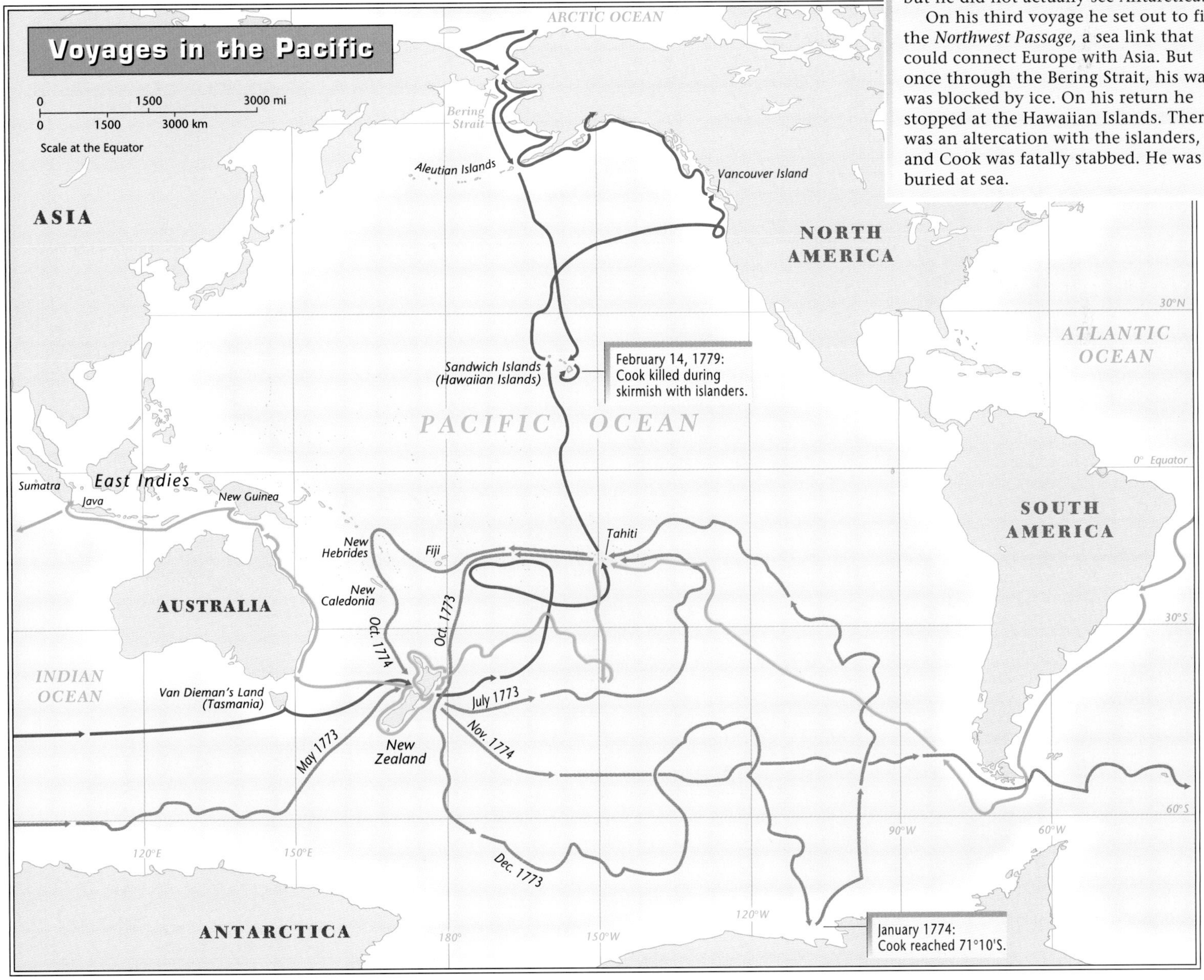

ARCTIC OCEAN

Bering Strait

Aleutian Islands

Vancouver Island

ASIA

NORTH AMERICA

30°N

Sandwich Islands (Hawaiian Islands)

February 14, 1779: Cook killed during skirmish with islanders.

PACIFIC OCEAN

ATLANTIC OCEAN

0° Equator

Sumatra
Java   East Indies   New Guinea

New Hebrides   Fiji   Tahiti

SOUTH AMERICA

New Caledonia

Oct. 1773

AUSTRALIA

Oct. 1774

30°S

INDIAN OCEAN

Van Dieman's Land (Tasmania)

July 1773

May 1773

New Zealand

Nov. 1774

Dec. 1773

60°S

90°W   60°W

ANTARCTICA   180°   150°W   120°W

January 1774: Cook reached 71°10'S.

0   1500   3000 mi
0   1500   3000 km
Scale at the Equator

30°E   60°E   90°E   120°E   150°E   180   150°W   120°W   90°W   60°W   60°S

GREAT BRITAIN
Plymouth

EUROPE   ASIA

NORTH AMERICA

60°N

AFRICA

ATLANTIC OCEAN

Sandwich Islands (Hawaiian Islands)

PACIFIC OCEAN

Tahiti

East Indies

SOUTH AMERICA

0°

Cape of Good Hope

INDIAN OCEAN   AUSTRALIA

30°S

ATLANTIC OCEAN

New Zealand

60°S

ANTARCTICA

0°   30°E   60°E   90°E   120°E   150°E   180   150°W   120°W

0   3000 mi
0   3000 km
Scale at the Equator

Louisiana Purchase 1803

→ Lewis & Clark's route to the Pacific

--→ Lewis & Clark's return to St. Louis

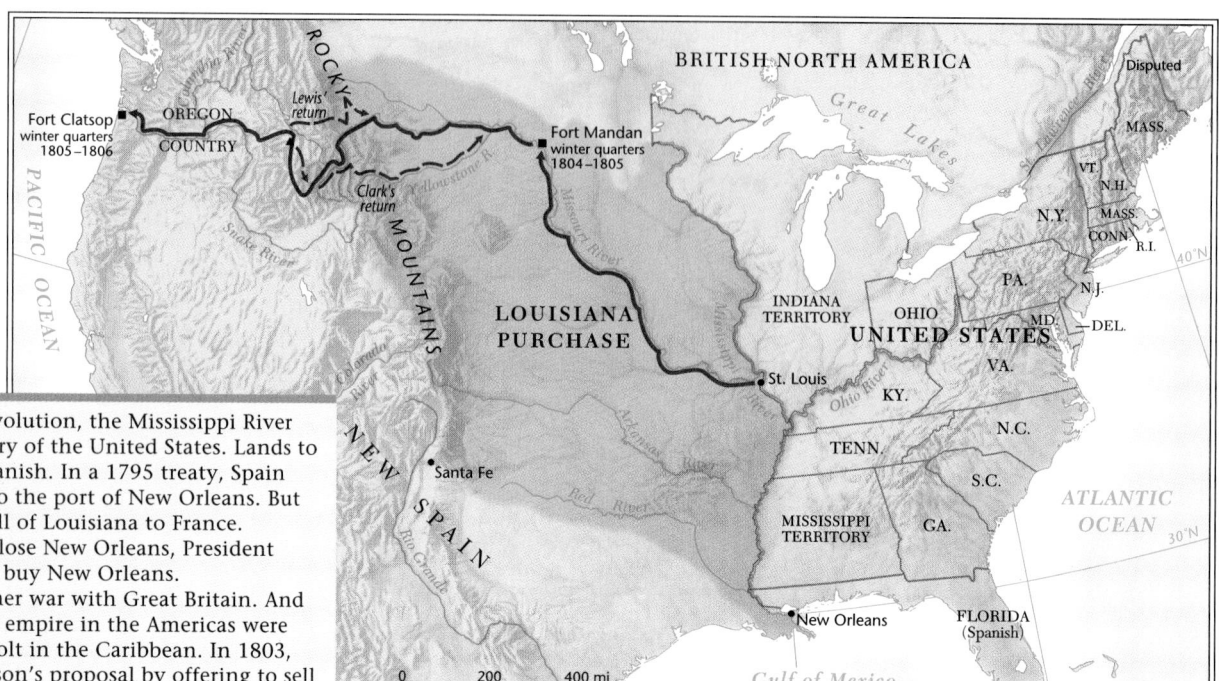

Following the American Revolution, the Mississippi River formed the western boundary of the United States. Lands to the south and west were Spanish. In a 1795 treaty, Spain gave the Americans access to the port of New Orleans. But in 1800, Spain transferred all of Louisiana to France. Fearing that France would close New Orleans, President Thomas Jefferson offered to buy New Orleans.

But Napoleon faced another war with Great Britain. And his hopes of establishing an empire in the Americas were dashed by a costly slave revolt in the Caribbean. In 1803, the French countered Jefferson's proposal by offering to sell all of Louisiana.

Jefferson chose Meriwether Lewis (who in turn chose William Clark) to lead an expedition to determine the boundaries of the newly acquired territory, find a route to the Pacific, and lay claim to the Oregon country.

Napoleonic Empire, 1804–1815

- France, 1804
- Added to France by 1812
- States under Napoleon's control 1812
- States allied with Napoleon, 1812
- States allied against Napoleon 1812
- ⚜ Battles

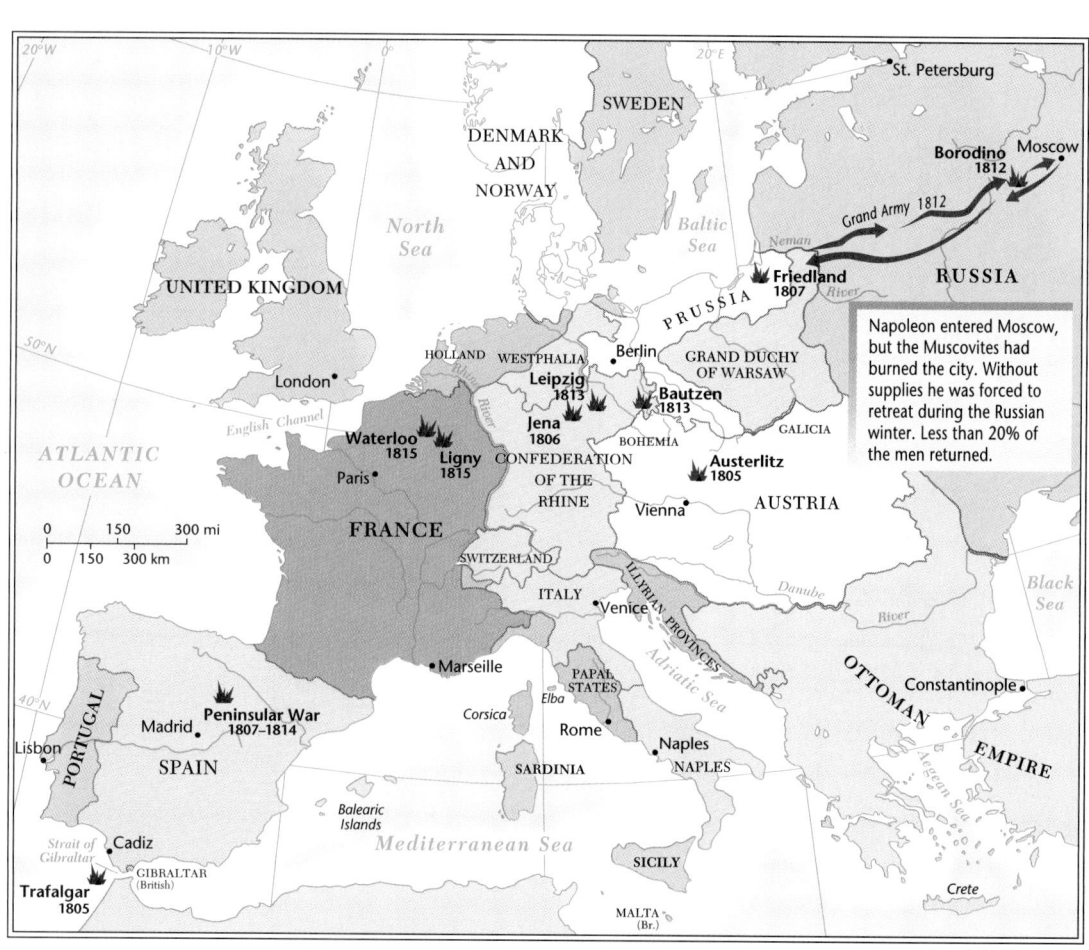

Napoleon entered Moscow, but the Muscovites had burned the city. Without supplies he was forced to retreat during the Russian winter. Less than 20% of the men returned.

Napoleon's rise to power changed the revolutionary French republic into an authoritarian empire. After establishing a power base at home, he turned to expansion abroad. Austria fell in 1805 and Prussia in 1806. In 1807 he invaded Spain in order to drive out British troops who were poised to invade France. By 1812, the French Empire held or controlled most of western Europe. A failed invasion of Russia was a sign of Napoleon's vulnerability. An alliance led by Britain defeated Napoleon in 1813. He was exiled to Elba, but returned to Paris. In 1815, a combined army of British and Prussian troops finally defeated him at Waterloo.

The British-American War of 1812

⬅ American forces
⬅ British forces
╌╌ British blockade
🌿 American victories
🌿 British victories

In 1803, France declared war on Britain. At first the Americans profited; due to being a neutral nation, American ships transported goods to all ports. However, Americans were soon angered by the British seizure of their ships and the impressment of sailors who were thought to be British subjects. Even the French declared that ships carrying British goods were liable to be seized.

Anti-British sentiment ran high in the western states where it was believed that British agents in Canada were fueling Indian hostilities. By 1812, President Madison believed war to be inevitable.

The "War Hawks" were confident of sweeping the British out of Canada, but early defeats showed how unprepared America was for war. American victories at Lake Erie and Thames River buoyed spirits.

By 1814, Napoleon seemed to have been defeated, and Britain now had forces available for an invasion of the United States. Americans stopped the British near Niagara and Lake Champlain, but the British were able to enter Chesapeake Bay and burn the city of Washington.

Britain was weary of wars, and believed the American war was not worth the effort. On December 24, 1814, the Treaty of Ghent ended the war. But news traveled slowly: in January 1815, Andrew Jackson defeated a major British force on the outskirts of New Orleans.

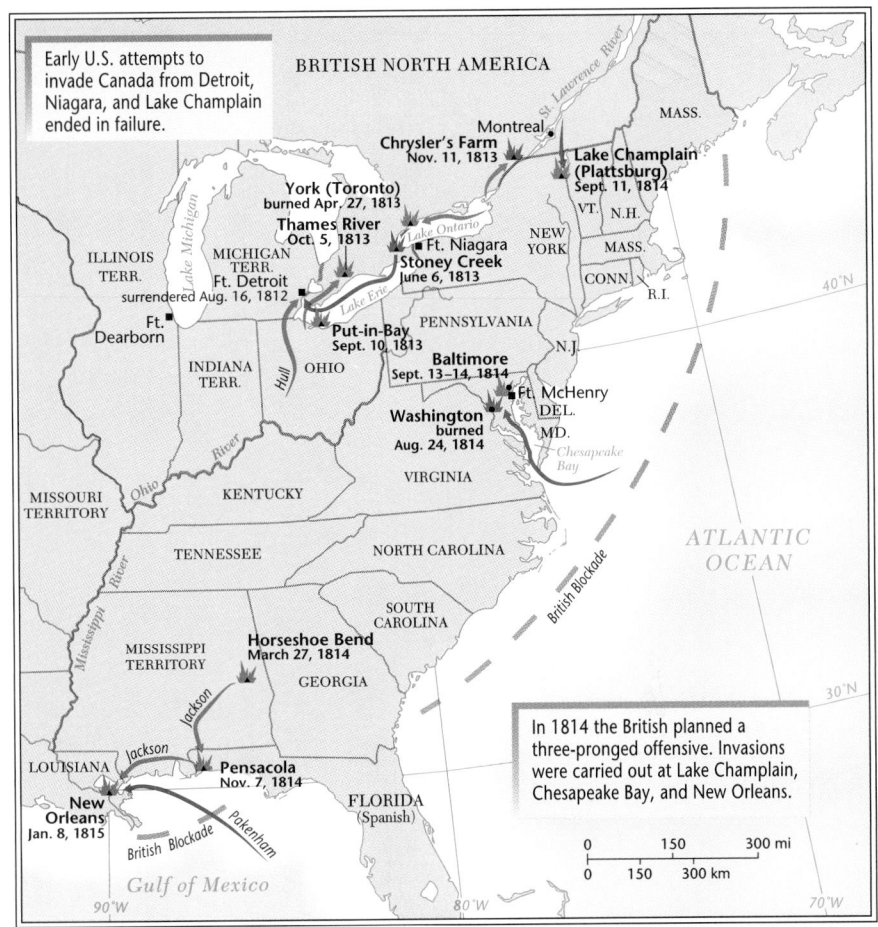

Early U.S. attempts to invade Canada from Detroit, Niagara, and Lake Champlain ended in failure.

BRITISH NORTH AMERICA

Chrysler's Farm Nov. 11, 1813
Montreal
Lake Champlain (Plattsburg) Sept. 11, 1814
York (Toronto) burned Apr. 27, 1813
Thames River Oct. 5, 1813
Ft. Niagara
Stoney Creek June 6, 1813
Ft. Detroit surrendered Aug. 16, 1812
Put-in-Bay Sept. 10, 1813
Baltimore Sept. 13–14, 1814
Ft. McHenry
Washington burned Aug. 24, 1814
Horseshoe Bend March 27, 1814
Pensacola Nov. 7, 1814
New Orleans Jan. 8, 1815

In 1814 the British planned a three-pronged offensive. Invasions were carried out at Lake Champlain, Chesapeake Bay, and New Orleans.

0 150 300 mi
0 150 300 km

United States, 1820

— Convention of 1818
— Adams-Onís Treaty 1819
▨ Ceded by Great Britain
▨ Ceded by Spain

The United States and Great Britain jointly occupied the Oregon Country until 1846.

To Britain, 1818
To U.S., 1818
BRITISH NORTH AMERICA
Lake of the Woods
Disputed
49th Parallel
MAINE
OREGON COUNTRY
ROCKY MOUNTAINS
42nd Parallel
SPANISH TERRITORY MEXICO 1821
MISSOURI TERRITORY
UNITED STATES
MICHIGAN TERRITORY
APPALACHIAN MOUNTAINS
ARKANSAS TERRITORY
SPANISH WEST FLORIDA
SPANISH EAST FLORIDA
FLORIDA TERR. 1822
TEXAS

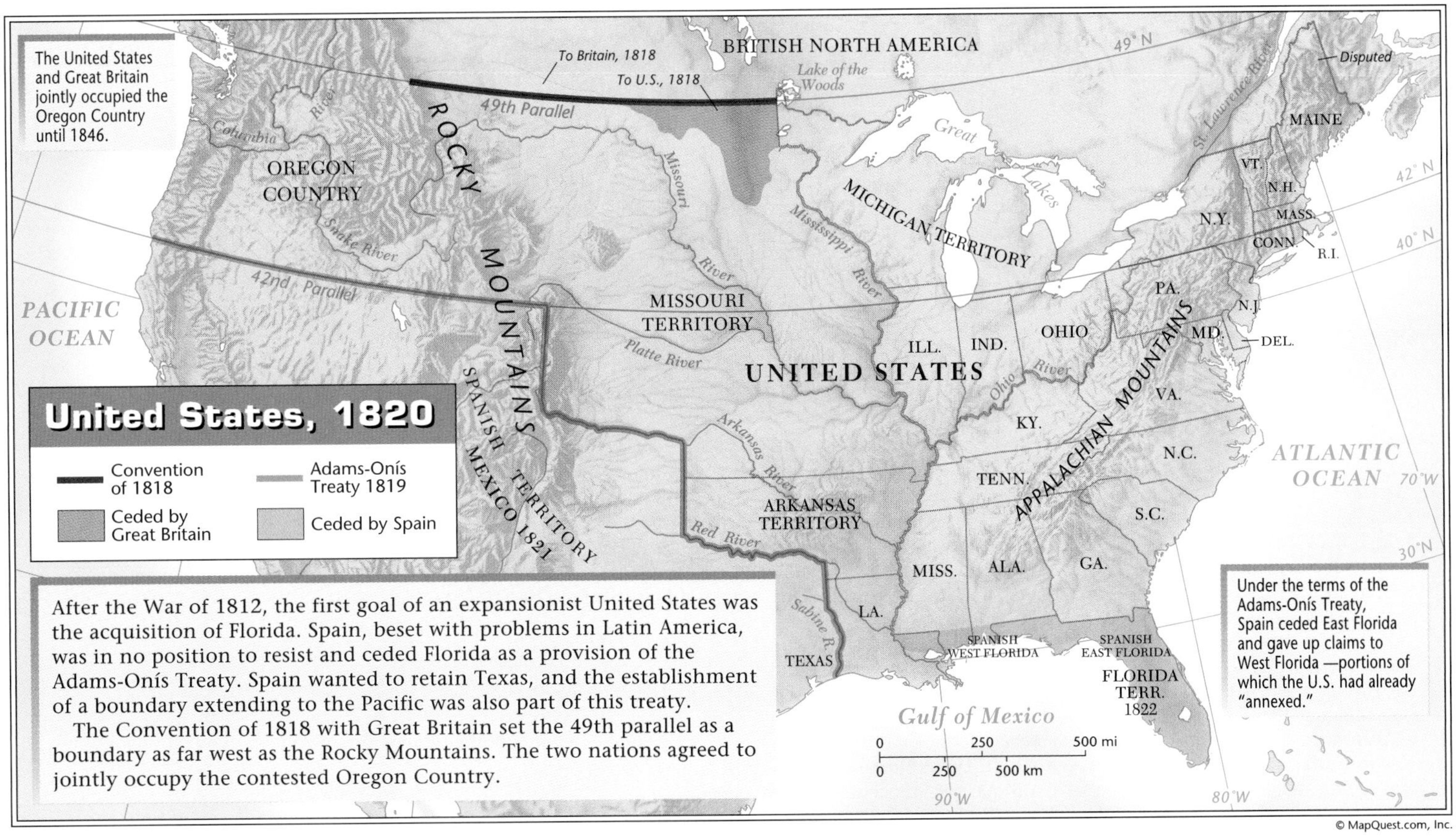

After the War of 1812, the first goal of an expansionist United States was the acquisition of Florida. Spain, beset with problems in Latin America, was in no position to resist and ceded Florida as a provision of the Adams-Onís Treaty. Spain wanted to retain Texas, and the establishment of a boundary extending to the Pacific was also part of this treaty.

The Convention of 1818 with Great Britain set the 49th parallel as a boundary as far west as the Rocky Mountains. The two nations agreed to jointly occupy the contested Oregon Country.

Under the terms of the Adams-Onís Treaty, Spain ceded East Florida and gave up claims to West Florida —portions of which the U.S. had already "annexed."

0 250 500 mi
0 250 500 km

Growth of Canada

1791

ALASKA (Russian)

Hudson Bay

RUPERT'S LAND

LOWER CANADA

NEWFOUNDLAND

ST. JOHN'S I.
CAPE BRETON ISLAND

UPPER CANADA

NOVA SCOTIA

NEW BRUNSWICK

SPANISH LOUISIANA

UNITED STATES

ATLANTIC OCEAN

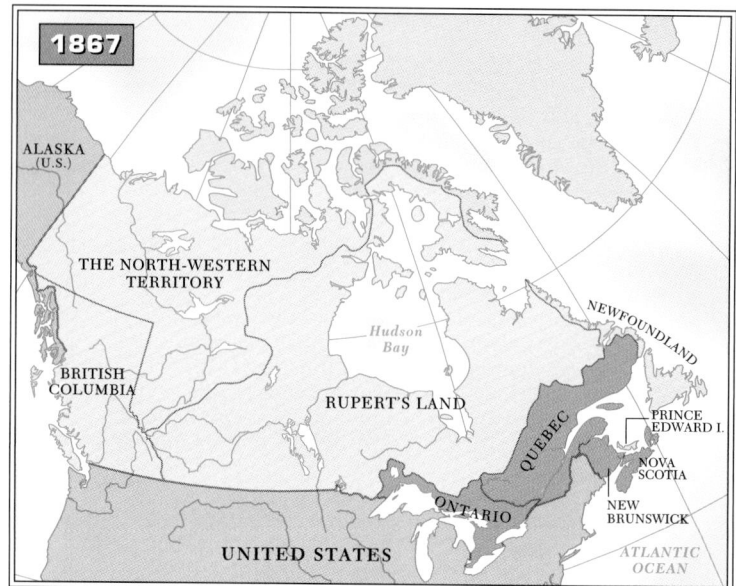

1867

ALASKA (U.S.)

THE NORTH-WESTERN TERRITORY

Hudson Bay

BRITISH COLUMBIA

RUPERT'S LAND

NEWFOUNDLAND

QUEBEC

PRINCE EDWARD I.

NOVA SCOTIA

ONTARIO

NEW BRUNSWICK

UNITED STATES

ATLANTIC OCEAN

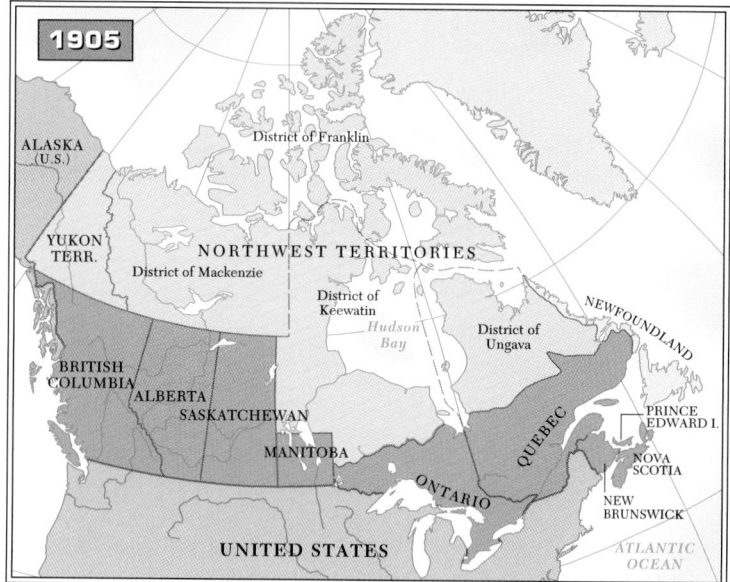

1905

ALASKA (U.S.)

District of Franklin

YUKON TERR.

NORTHWEST TERRITORIES

District of Mackenzie

District of Keewatin

Hudson Bay

District of Ungava

NEWFOUNDLAND

BRITISH COLUMBIA

ALBERTA

SASKATCHEWAN

MANITOBA

QUEBEC

PRINCE EDWARD I.

NOVA SCOTIA

ONTARIO

NEW BRUNSWICK

UNITED STATES

ATLANTIC OCEAN

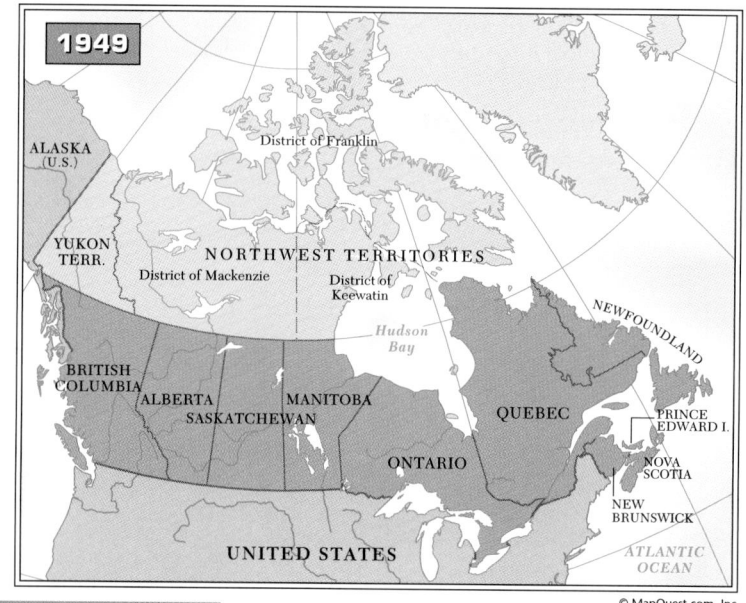

1949

ALASKA (U.S.)

District of Franklin

YUKON TERR.

NORTHWEST TERRITORIES

District of Mackenzie

District of Keewatin

Hudson Bay

NEWFOUNDLAND

BRITISH COLUMBIA

ALBERTA

SASKATCHEWAN

MANITOBA

QUEBEC

PRINCE EDWARD I.

ONTARIO

NOVA SCOTIA

NEW BRUNSWICK

UNITED STATES

ATLANTIC OCEAN

© MapQuest.com, Inc.

When the American Revolution began, many Loyalists (Americans who had remained loyal to the crown), moved to Canada. In response to their call for their own colony, the British, in 1784, created New Brunswick out of western Nova Scotia. To appease Loyalists in Quebec, the British divided Quebec into two colonies in 1791: Upper Canada and Lower Canada.

In 1867, Great Britain created the Dominion of Canada. There would be four provinces: Nova Scotia, New Brunswick, Quebec, and Ontario. The remaining territories would continue to be governed by Britain.

In 1870, Canada assumed control of Rupert's Land and the North-West Territory. Manitoba was created from a portion of Rupert's Land. In 1871 British Columbia, a colony since 1858, became the first Pacific province. Prince Edward Island joined the dominion as the seventh province in 1873.

Although Saskatchewan and Alberta were created in 1905, it wasn't until 1949 that Newfoundland became the tenth province. In 1999, Nunavut became the newest territory, embracing most of Franklin, Keewatin, and part of Mackenzie (see page 208).

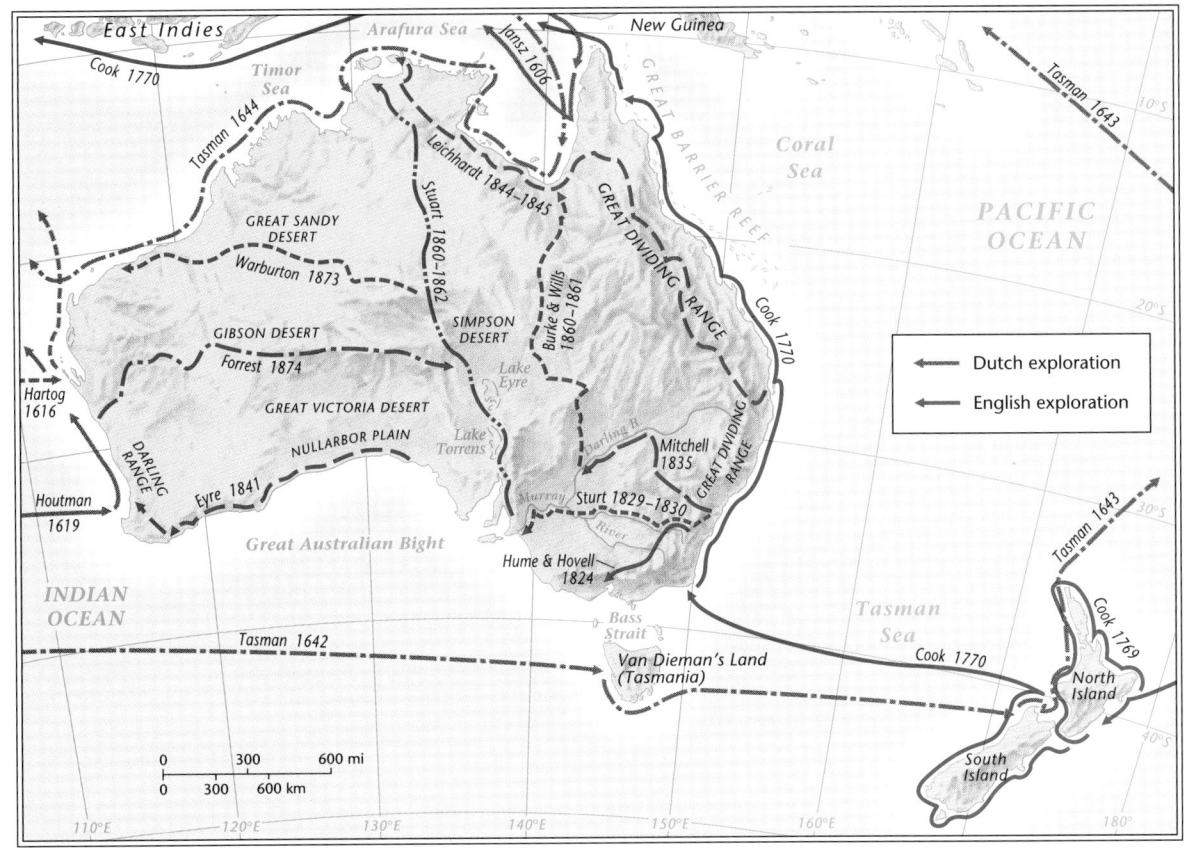

European Exploration of Australia & New Zealand

Europeans had believed in the existence of *Terra Australis Incognita* (Unknown Southern Land), but it was not easily found. Spanish and Portuguese explorers had been through the East Indies during the 1500s. But it was probably the Dutch captain Willem Jansz who was the first European to make landfall on Australia.

The Dutch continued to sail the western coast of the continent, but it was James Cook, sailing under the British flag who explored and claimed the eastern portion for Great Britain.

Growth of Australia

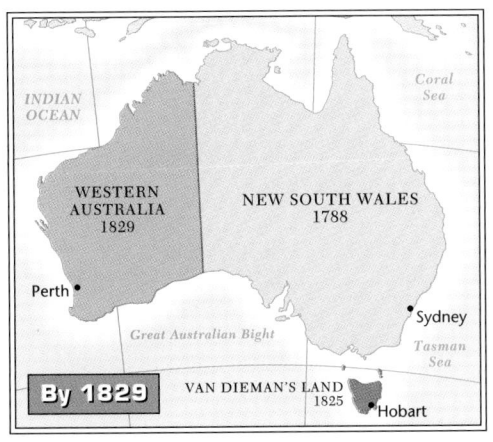

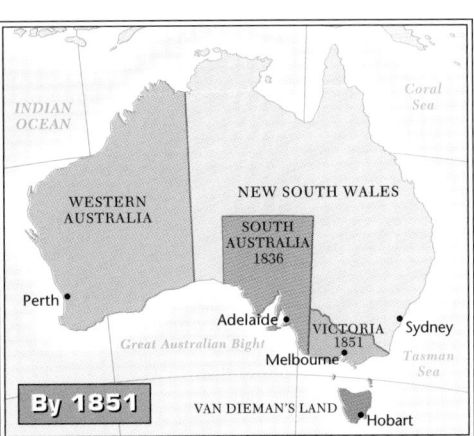

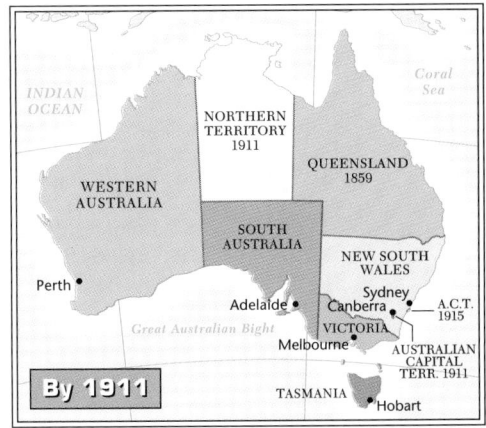

© MapQuest.com, Inc.

Once America had won its independence, Great Britain needed a place to send its convicts. This practice of exiling criminals was called *transportation*. In 1787 a fleet of ships carrying convicts left Great Britain, bound for Australia. On January 26, 1788, the first settlement was established where Sydney now stands.

In 1829 the British claimed the western portion of Australia, and a colony, centered around Perth, was founded. In the 1830s settlers (mostly sheep farmers) converged on the area around present-day Melbourne. They prospered and petitioned Great Britain for colonial status, and this was granted in 1851.

By the end of the 1890s, now that the colonies were self-governing, there was movement towards federation. The people voted for it, and Great Britain agreed. On January 1, 1901, the Commonwealth of Australia was established.

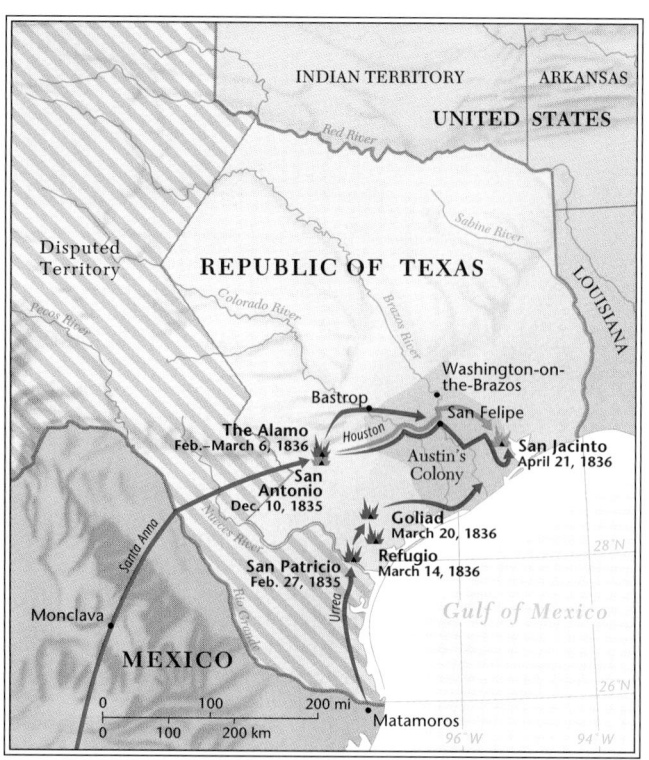

Texas Revolution 1835–1836

← Texan troops	⚔ Texan victory
← Mexican troops	⚔ Mexican victory

Mexico gained its independence from Spain in 1821. At this time Texas was largely underpopulated. By granting large tracts of land to Americans, Mexican officials hoped to make the land productive and control the Native American population. But quarrels soon developed, especially over the issues of conversion to Catholicism (which the Mexican government required of all immigrants) and slavery (which had been abolished in Mexico).

Texans wanted self-government, but the Mexicans would not permit this. Tension increased and by the end of September 1835, the fighting had begun. In March 1836, Texans declared their independence and created the Republic of Texas. In little more than a month's time the Texans won the battle of San Jacinto and their independence.

President Sam Houston of Texas welcomed annexation to the United States, but the admission of such a large, potential slave state was not possible at this time.

Mexican War 1846–1847

In 1844 James Polk, an avowed expansionist, was elected president. One of the first items on his agenda was the annexation of Texas, which was approved just a few days before his inauguration.

The land between the Nueces River and Rio Grande had been disputed between Texas and Mexico for years. When Congress established the Rio Grande as the southern boundary, Mexico broke off diplomatic relations. And when American troops entered the disputed area, Mexico declared war.

By the time the fighting ended in September 1847, California, New Mexico and all of Texas were in American hands. Back in 1845, Polk had offered to buy these lands. Now in the peace treaty, the United States gained these same lands at a cost of $15 million and the assumption of Texan claims against the Mexican government.

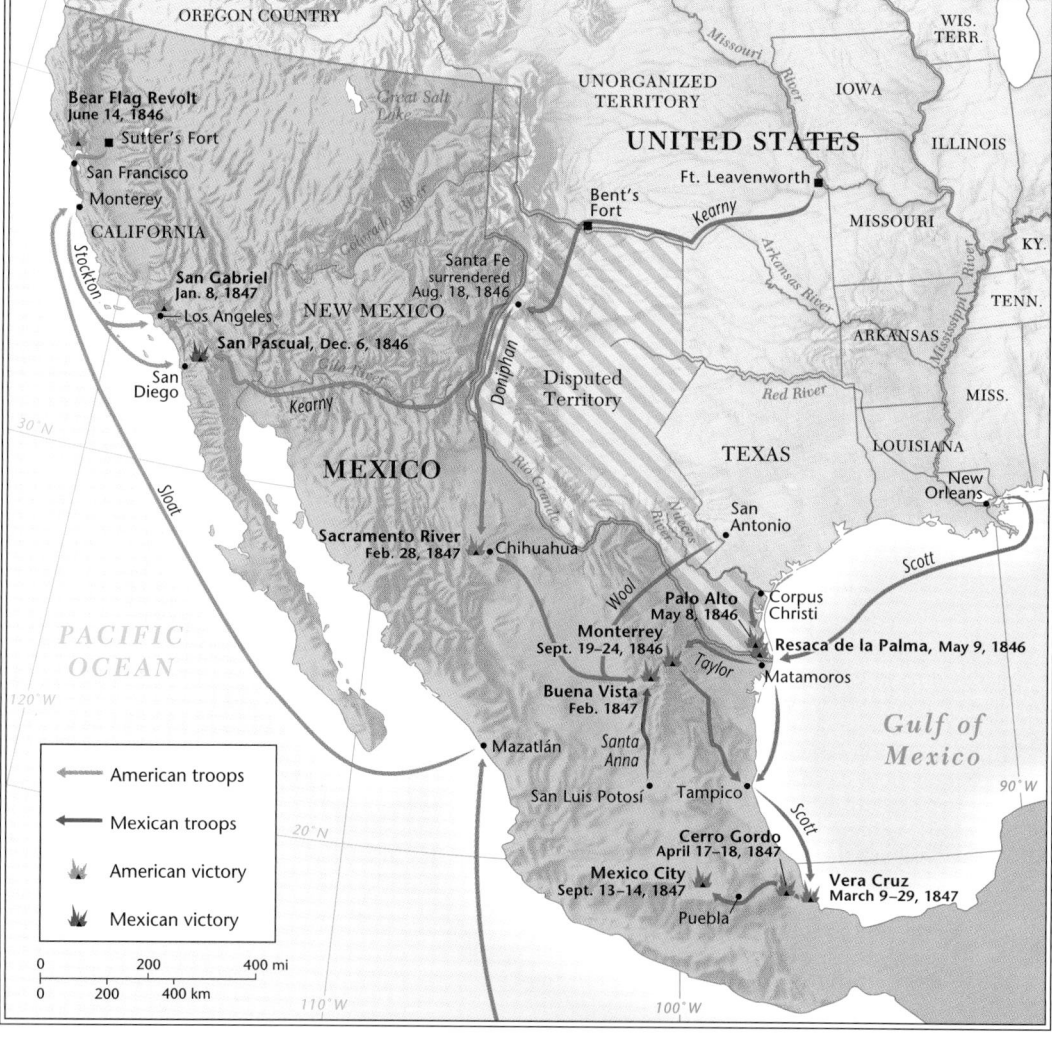

© MapQuest.com, Inc.

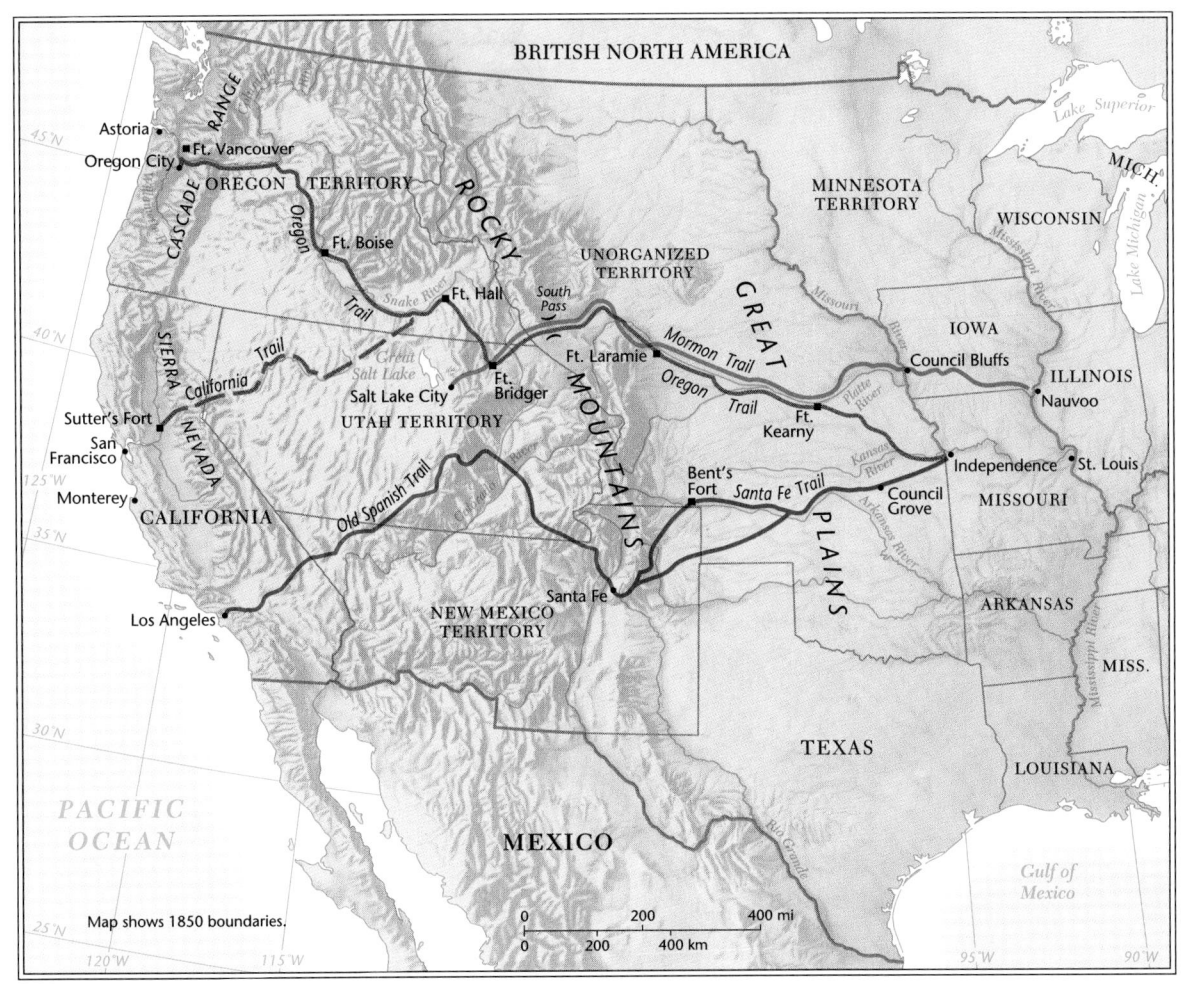

Map shows 1850 boundaries.

© MapQuest.com, Inc.

Western Trails

In 1806 the Lewis and Clark expedition was homeward bound. Along the upper reaches of the Missouri, Capt. Clark met two men who were heading upstream to trap furs in the Rocky Mountains.

The fur traders played an important role in the opening of the West. They blazed the trails and opened the passes. And their tales of the fertile lands caught the attention of many Americans.

The chance for economic advancement prompted many to take to the trails. The first organized party of settlers left Missouri in 1841.

Most pioneers headed directly for the West, bypassing the Great Plains. Here the Native Americans tended to be more hostile, and it was believed that the land was not as fertile as land in the West.

Although increased economic opportunity was the reason most Americans migrated, the Mormons sought freedom from religious persecution out west in the "wilderness."

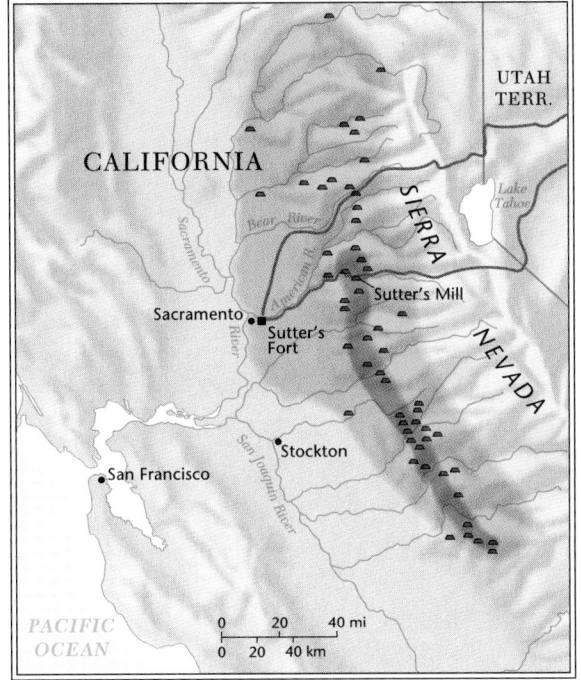

California Gold Mining

▢ Gold mining region	▲	Mining sites
▢ "Mother Lode"	—	California Trail

On January 24, 1848, while overseeing the construction of a sawmill, John Marshall discovered gold. Although there was an attempt to keep it a secret, word soon leaked out, and the rush was on.

Fortune-seekers (often called "Forty-Niners") traveled overland or by sea from the east coast. About half of the men who came were foreigners. The population of California swelled. San Francisco's population grew by a factor of 40 in less than a year.

But the "easy-pickings" soon played out and large mining companies replaced the lone prospector with his pick and shovel.

Latin America c. 1830

Over a period of three centuries, Spain and Portugal had created colonial empires. A multiethnic society of Indians, Europeans, and Africans existed within an Iberian governmental framework.

People of Spanish descent who were born in Latin America were called *Creoles*, and they resented the fact that Spanish officials held most of the top governmental posts. The other ethnic groups had their grievances too, but class divisions prevented people from working together.

The movements toward independence were spurred on by the ideological concepts of the American and French revolutions. In the early 1800s, Napoleon invaded Portugal and Spain. In the power vacuum that ensued, Latin American colonies began the fight for their independence.

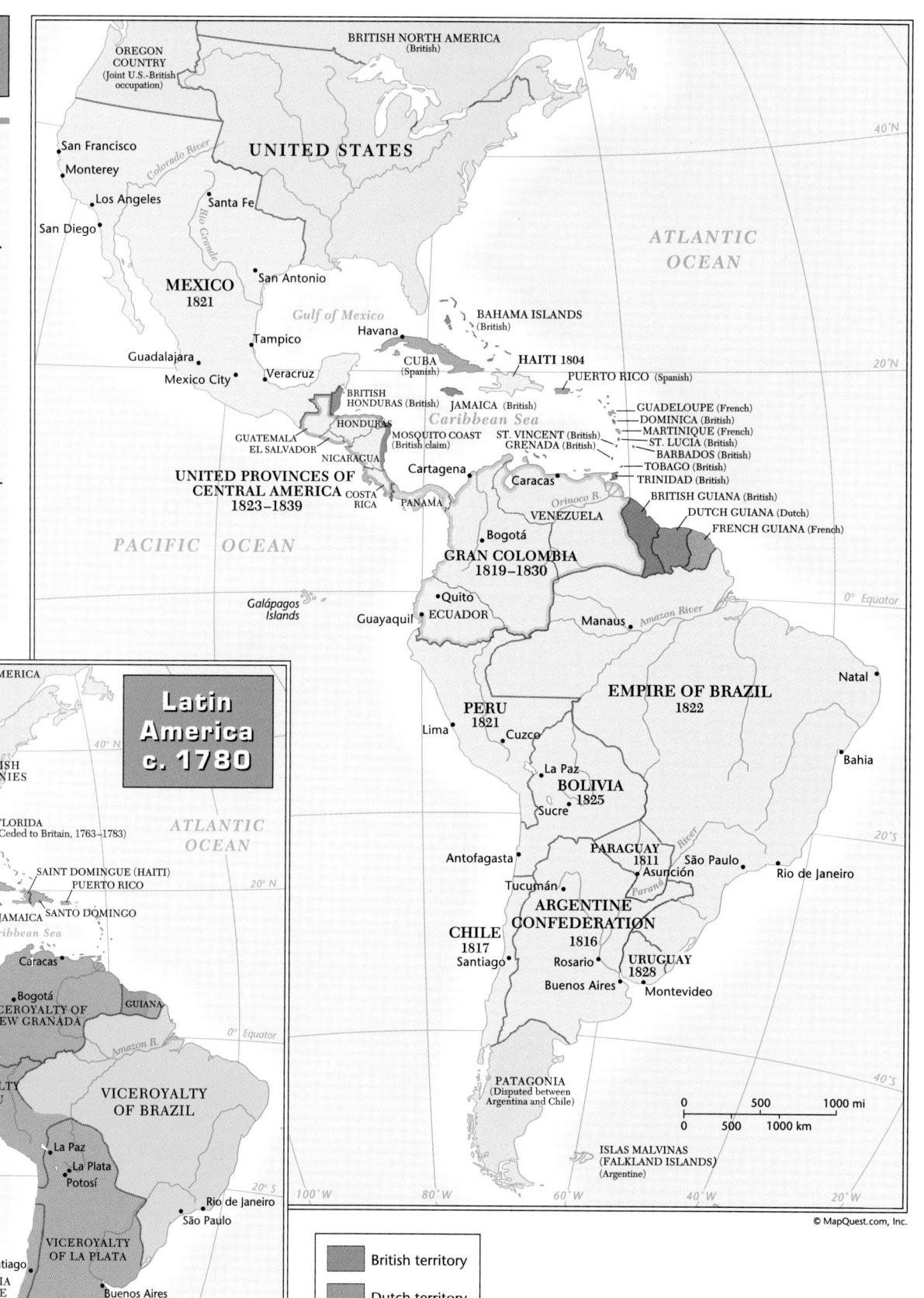

© MapQuest.com, Inc.

Legend:
- British territory
- Dutch territory
- French territory
- Portuguese territory
- Spanish territory

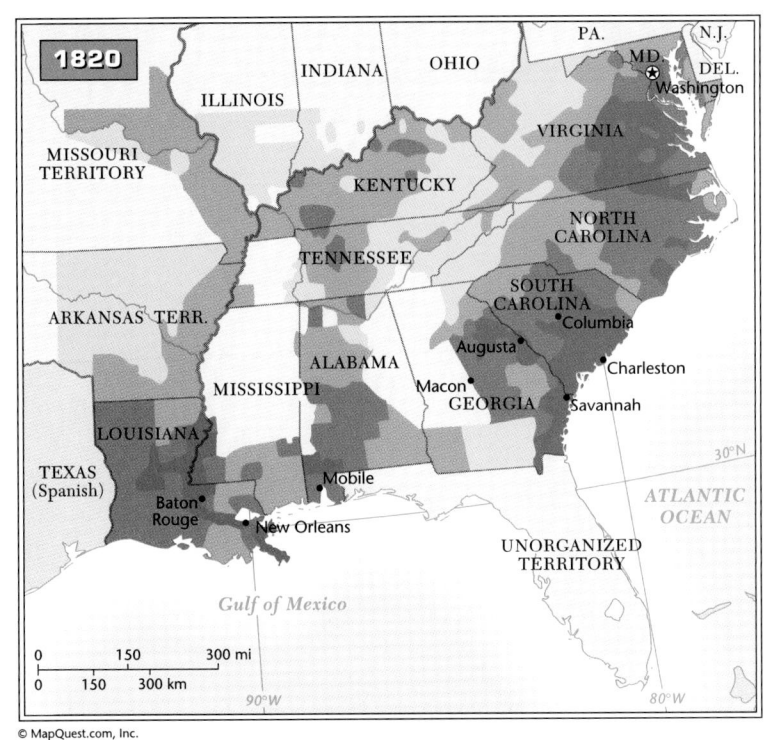

1820

MISSOURI TERRITORY
ILLINOIS
INDIANA
OHIO
PA.
N.J.
MD.
⊛ Washington
DEL.
VIRGINIA
KENTUCKY
NORTH CAROLINA
TENNESSEE
ARKANSAS TERR.
ALABAMA
MISSISSIPPI
SOUTH CAROLINA
•Columbia
Augusta•
Macon•
GEORGIA
•Charleston
Savannah•
LOUISIANA
TEXAS (Spanish)
•Mobile
Baton Rouge•
•New Orleans
UNORGANIZED TERRITORY
ATLANTIC OCEAN
Gulf of Mexico
30°N
90°W
80°W

0　150　300 mi
0　150　300 km

© MapQuest.com, Inc.

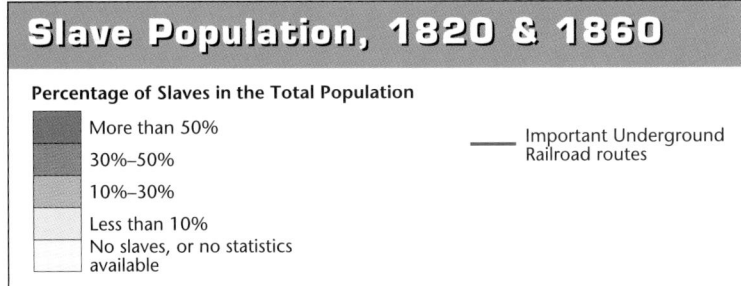

Slave Population, 1820 & 1860

Percentage of Slaves in the Total Population

- More than 50%
- 30%–50%
- 10%–30%
- Less than 10%
- No slaves, or no statistics available

— Important Underground Railroad routes

In the South, cotton was king. Cotton was well-suited to plantation labor: although the work was hard, it was easy to supervise and there was work to be done year-round. This made slave labor practical.

Cotton growing started in Georgia and South Carolina, but in time it moved westward. The slave population probably mirrored the existence of large cotton plantations, where most of the slaves lived.

But not all African Americans were slaves. Perhaps 10% were "free blacks." These people along with whites (in the North and the South) who opposed slavery helped many slaves escape. If slaves could find their way to the border of the free states, there existed an "underground railroad" that would help them make their way to safety farther north. Even without any formal organization, the underground railroad helped thousands of African Americans escape slavery during the period between the 1830s through the 1850s.

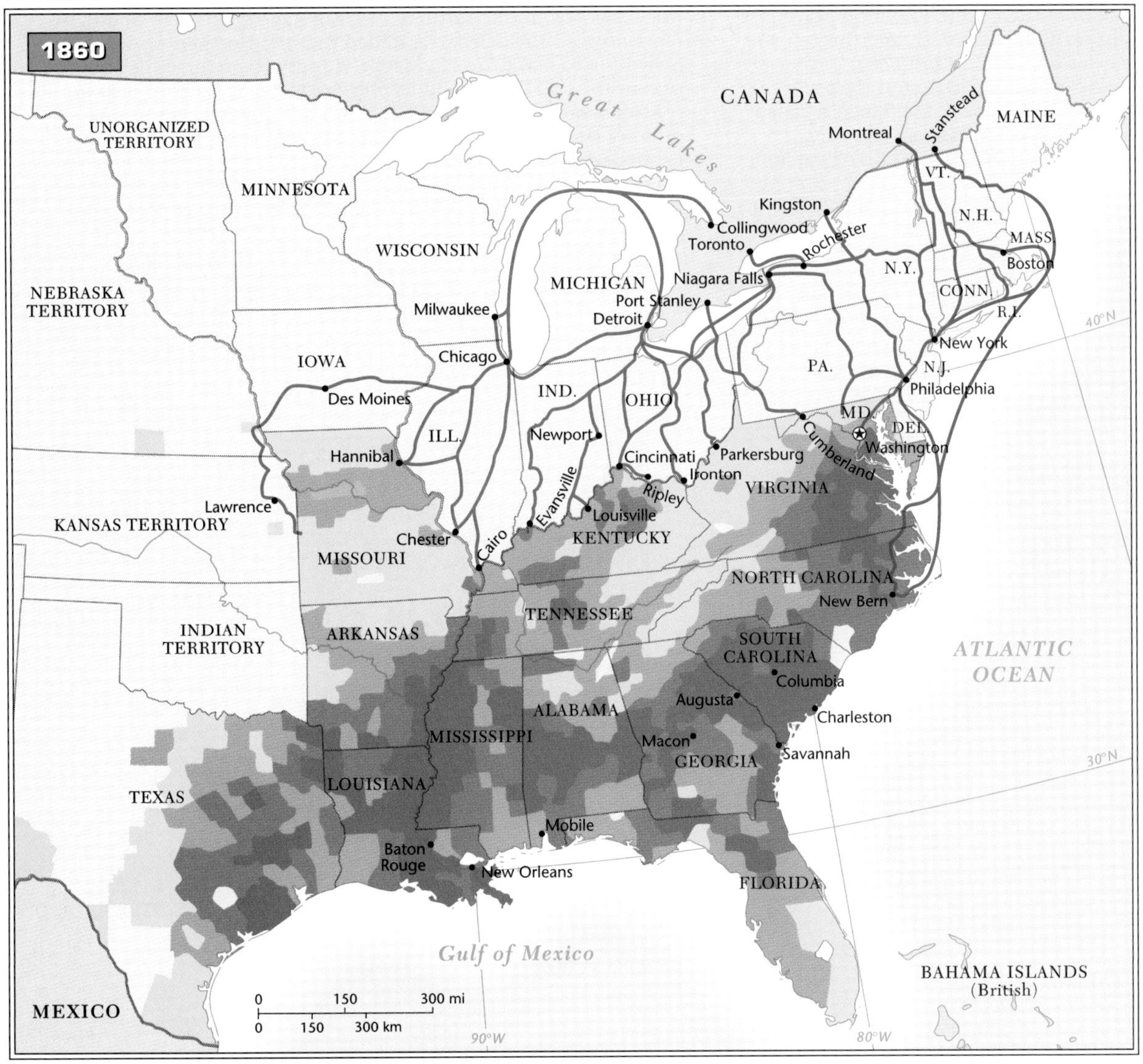

1860

UNORGANIZED TERRITORY
MINNESOTA
WISCONSIN
Great Lakes
CANADA
MAINE
Montreal
Stanstead
VT.
Kingston
Collingwood
Toronto
Rochester
N.H.
MASS
Boston
Niagara Falls
N.Y.
CONN.
R.I.
NEBRASKA TERRITORY
MICHIGAN
Milwaukee
Port Stanley
Detroit
Chicago
IOWA
Des Moines
IND.
OHIO
PA.
New York
N.J.
Philadelphia
MD.
⊛ Washington
DEL.
ILL.
Newport
Cincinnati
Parkersburg
Cumberland
Ironton
Lawrence
Evansville
Ripley
VIRGINIA
KANSAS TERRITORY
Hannibal
Chester
Louisville
Cairo
KENTUCKY
MISSOURI
TENNESSEE
NORTH CAROLINA
New Bern
INDIAN TERRITORY
ARKANSAS
SOUTH CAROLINA
ALABAMA
Augusta•
Columbia•
MISSISSIPPI
Macon•
GEORGIA
Charleston•
Savannah•
ATLANTIC OCEAN
TEXAS
LOUISIANA
•Mobile
Baton Rouge•
•New Orleans
FLORIDA
40°N
30°N
MEXICO
Gulf of Mexico
BAHAMA ISLANDS (British)
90°W
80°W

0　150　300 mi
0　150　300 km

Civil War/War Between the States

Union & Confederacy, 1861

- Union states
- Confederate states before the fall of Fort Sumter
- States joining the Confederacy after the fall of Fort Sumter
- Slave states loyal to the Union
- Territories

⟵ Union forces   ⟵ Confederate forces   ✹ Major battles

When Abraham Lincoln was elected in 1860, many Southerners feared that he would abolish slavery. In December of that year, South Carolina was the first to secede from the Union. Five more states in the "Deep South" followed suit early the next year, and the Confederate States of America was formed. In April 1861, Confederate forces attacked Fort Sumter in Charleston Harbor, causing the small garrison to surrender. In response, Lincoln called upon Union troops to suppress the rebellion. The states of the "Upper South" viewed Lincoln's decision as a declaration of war and joined the Confederacy.

In order to reunite the states, Lincoln had to invade and defeat the Confederacy. To its advantage, the South "only" had to defend its territory, and Southerners could say that they were protecting themselves from the northern "War of Aggression." The South, by remaining on the defensive, hoped that the Northerners would not be willing to make the sacrifices necessary to preserve the Union, and that in the end they would let the Confederacy do as it pleased.

After some consideration, Lincoln's administration formulated a military strategy whose aims were: the capture of Richmond, the Confederate capitol; controlling the length of the Mississippi River, thereby splitting the Confederacy; and a blockade of Southern ports in order to prevent Confederate commerce with European powers.

War in the East, 1861–1862

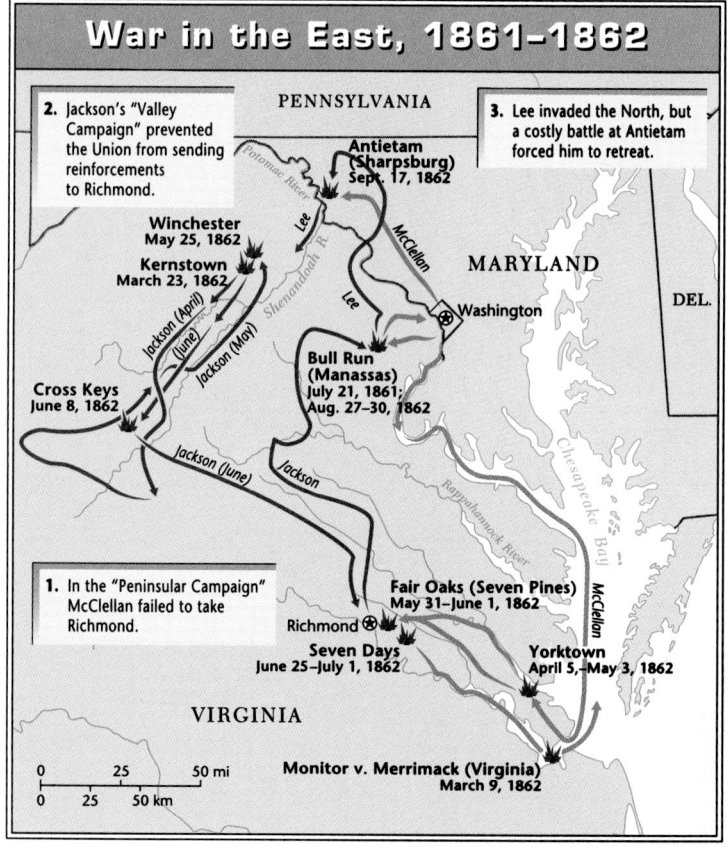

2. Jackson's "Valley Campaign" prevented the Union from sending reinforcements to Richmond.

3. Lee invaded the North, but a costly battle at Antietam forced him to retreat.

1. In the "Peninsular Campaign" McClellan failed to take Richmond.

War in the West, 1861–1863

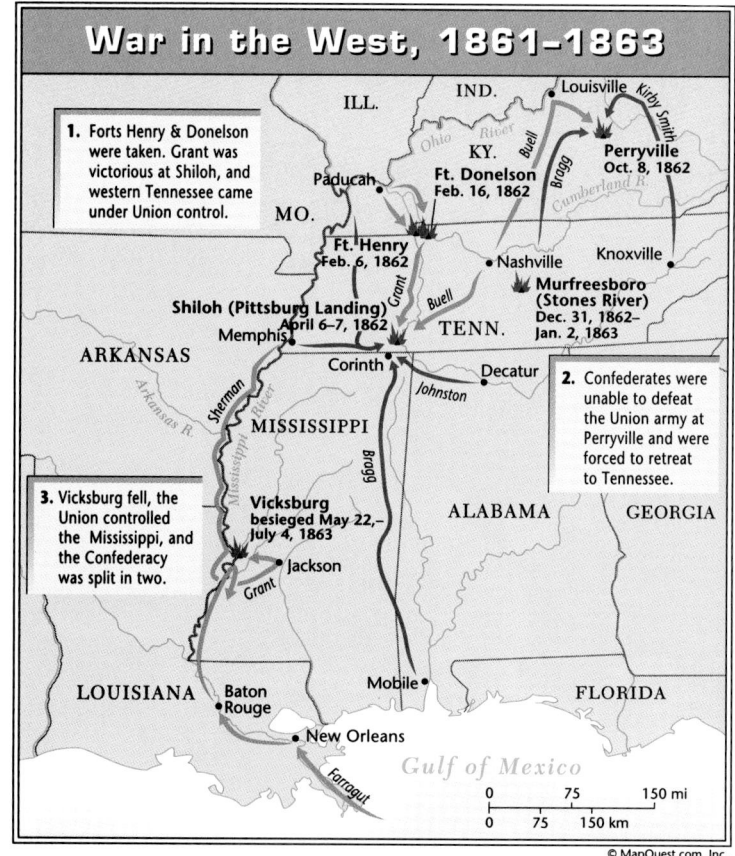

1. Forts Henry & Donelson were taken. Grant was victorious at Shiloh, and western Tennessee came under Union control.

2. Confederates were unable to defeat the Union army at Perryville and were forced to retreat to Tennessee.

3. Vicksburg fell, the Union controlled the Mississippi, and the Confederacy was split in two.

War in the East 1862-1863

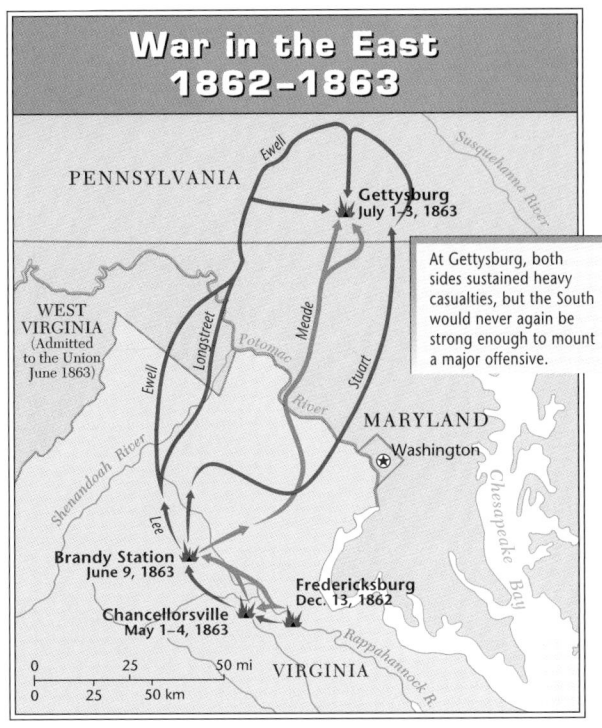

PENNSYLVANIA

Ewell

Gettysburg July 1-3, 1863

Susquehanna River

WEST VIRGINIA (Admitted to the Union June 1863)

At Gettysburg, both sides sustained heavy casualties, but the South would never again be strong enough to mount a major offensive.

Longstreet

Meade

Ewell

Potomac River

Stuart

MARYLAND

Washington ⊛

Lee

Shenandoah River

Chesapeake Bay

Brandy Station June 9, 1863

Fredericksburg Dec. 13, 1862

Chancellorsville May 1-4, 1863

Rappahannock R.

VIRGINIA

| 0 | 25 | 50 mi |
| 0 | 25 | 50 km |

When the fighting started, it seemed that the North had a tremendous advantage. With respect to manpower, the North had nearly four times as many men of fighting age. The North produced almost 20 times as much iron and 32 times as many firearms. Clearly the South did not have the industrial base that the North had.

The South did have an advantage in terms of military leadership. Prior to the war, a large proportion of officers were of southern origin, and many joined the Confederate army.

Through strength of numbers, the North was able to wear down the South. By 1863 the Confederate economy and society were under strain. Union victories in the South would soon fragment the Confederacy. Confederate remedies proposed by the government in Richmond, led by Jefferson Davis, were often opposed by governors who staunchly upheld the tradition of states' rights.

Gettysburg, July 1-3, 1863

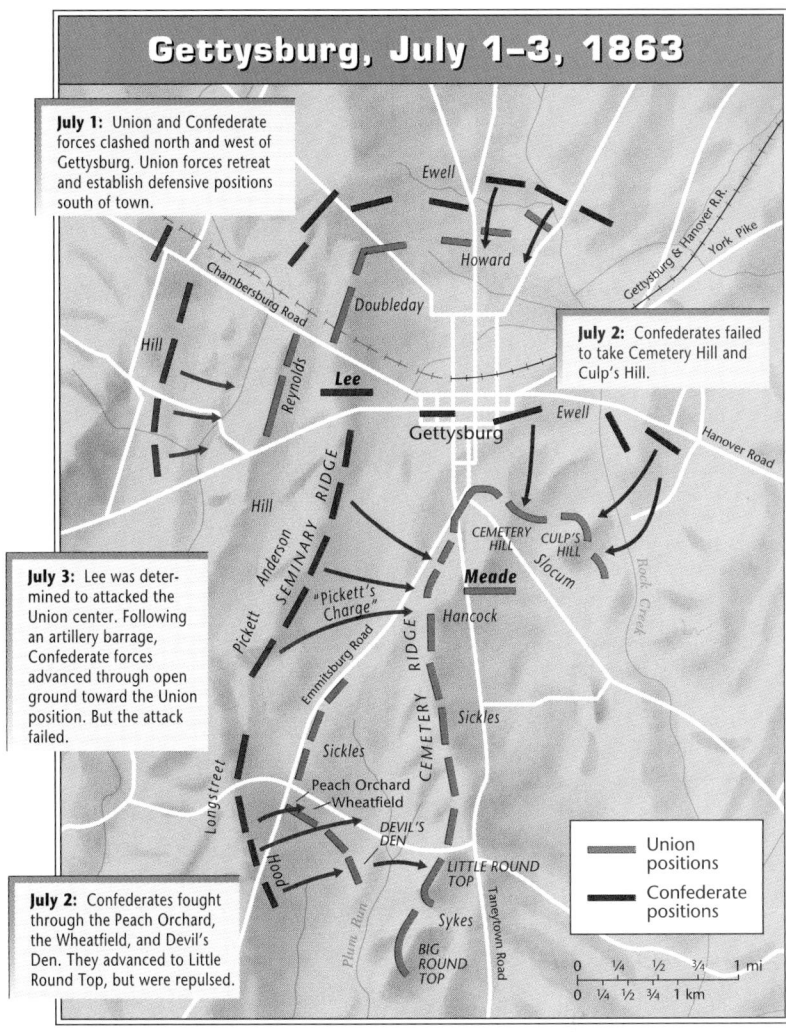

July 1: Union and Confederate forces clashed north and west of Gettysburg. Union forces retreat and establish defensive positions south of town.

Ewell

Howard

Chambersburg Road

Doubleday

Gettysburg & Hanover R.R.

York Pike

Hill

Reynolds

Lee

Gettysburg

Ewell

Hanover Road

July 2: Confederates failed to take Cemetery Hill and Culp's Hill.

Hill

SEMINARY RIDGE

Anderson

CEMETERY HILL

CULP'S HILL

Rock Creek

Pickett

"Pickett's Charge"

Meade

Slocum

July 3: Lee was determined to attacked the Union center. Following an artillery barrage, Confederate forces advanced through open ground toward the Union position. But the attack failed.

Emmitsburg Road

Hancock

CEMETERY RIDGE

Sickles

Longstreet

Sickles

Peach Orchard Wheatfield

DEVIL'S DEN

LITTLE ROUND TOP

Plum Run

Hood

Sykes

Taneytown Road

| | Union positions |
| | Confederate positions |

July 2: Confederates fought through the Peach Orchard, the Wheatfield, and Devil's Den. They advanced to Little Round Top, but were repulsed.

BIG ROUND TOP

| 0 | 1/4 | 1/2 | 3/4 | 1 mi |
| 0 | 1/4 | 1/2 | 3/4 | 1 km |

War in the Southeast, 1863-1865

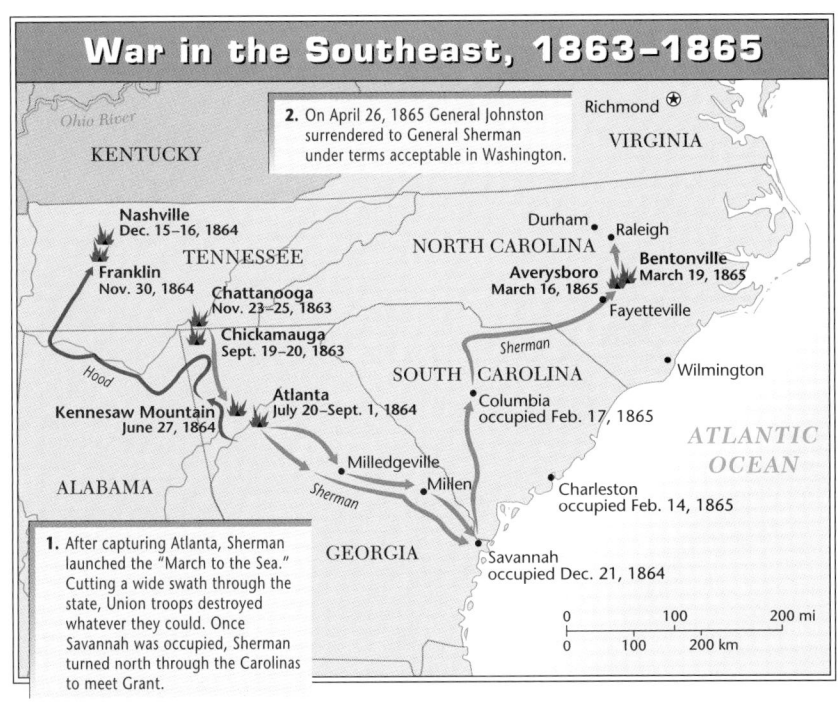

Ohio River

2. On April 26, 1865 General Johnston surrendered to General Sherman under terms acceptable in Washington.

Richmond ⊛

VIRGINIA

KENTUCKY

Nashville Dec. 15-16, 1864

Durham

Raleigh

NORTH CAROLINA

Bentonville March 19, 1865

Franklin Nov. 30, 1864

TENNESSEE

Averysboro March 16, 1865

Chattanooga Nov. 23-25, 1863

Chickamauga Sept. 19-20, 1863

Fayetteville

Sherman

Hood

SOUTH CAROLINA

Wilmington

Atlanta July 20-Sept. 1, 1864

Columbia occupied Feb. 17, 1865

Kennesaw Mountain June 27, 1864

ATLANTIC OCEAN

Milledgeville

ALABAMA

Sherman

Millen

Charleston occupied Feb. 14, 1865

GEORGIA

Savannah occupied Dec. 21, 1864

1. After capturing Atlanta, Sherman launched the "March to the Sea." Cutting a wide swath through the state, Union troops destroyed whatever they could. Once Savannah was occupied, Sherman turned north through the Carolinas to meet Grant.

| 0 | 100 | 200 mi |
| 0 | 100 | 200 km |

The Road to Appomattox 1864-1865

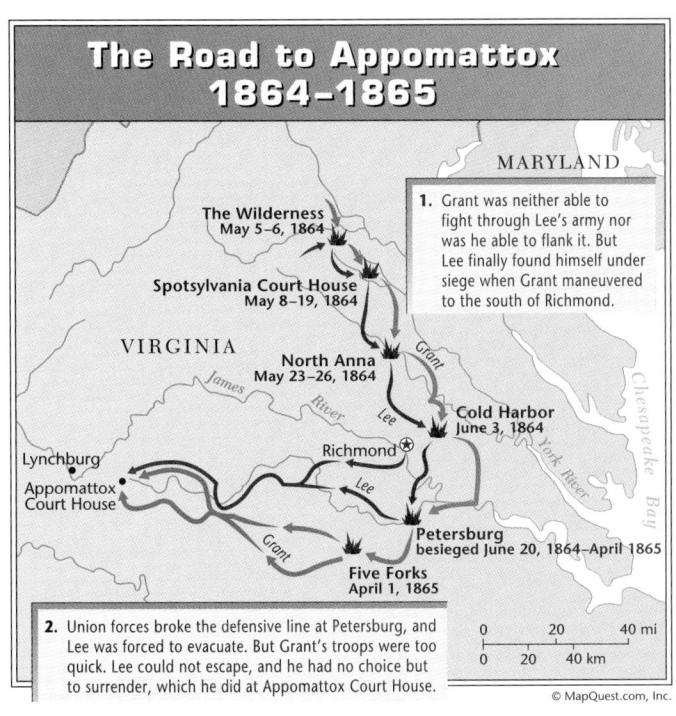

MARYLAND

The Wilderness May 5-6, 1864

1. Grant was neither able to fight through Lee's army nor was he able to flank it. But Lee finally found himself under siege when Grant maneuvered to the south of Richmond.

Spotsylvania Court House May 8-19, 1864

VIRGINIA

James River

North Anna May 23-26, 1864

Grant

Lee

Cold Harbor June 3, 1864

Lynchburg

Richmond ⊛

Lee

York River

Appomattox Court House

Lee

Petersburg besieged June 20, 1864-April 1865

Grant

Chesapeake Bay

Five Forks April 1, 1865

2. Union forces broke the defensive line at Petersburg, and Lee was forced to evacuate. But Grant's troops were too quick. Lee could not escape, and he had no choice but to surrender, which he did at Appomattox Court House.

| 0 | 20 | 40 mi |
| 0 | 20 | 40 km |

© MapQuest.com, Inc.

Federal Land Grants to Railroads

After the Civil War, the West became the focus of the railroad industry. But settlement had leapfrogged across the plains and mountains to the west coast. This meant that railroads would have to be built across areas that offered almost no traffic. The government saw the need for transcontinental routes and offered land grants as incentives to construction.

Within the "primary" limits of the land grants (as much as 40 miles wide), the railroads gained title to alternating sections of land (one-mile square). Some of the land was sold to investors to raise capital, but the preferred customer was the farmer, who would someday have products to ship.

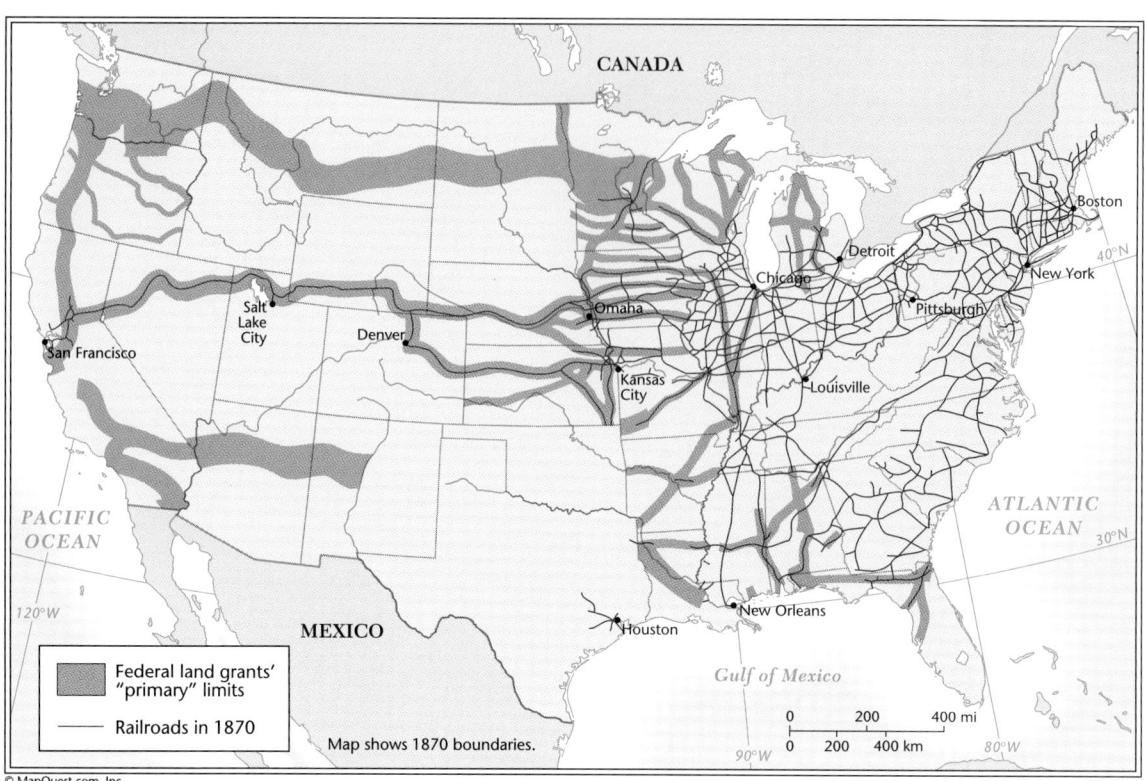

Federal land grants' "primary" limits

Railroads in 1870

Map shows 1870 boundaries.

© MapQuest.com, Inc.

Cattle Trails 1870s

Cattle were introduced to Texas from Mexico (then New Spain). The animals flourished on the unfenced ranges.

Meat was in demand in the East. The best way to get the cattle to market was to "drive" them to the railheads and load them on trains for shipment to slaughterhouses.

The earliest cattle drives were to Sedalia. As the railroads pushed westward, other cattle towns developed in Kansas, Nebraska, and Colorado.

Although most of the cattle driven north from Texas were herded onto trains, some continued northward to Wyoming and Montana.

Towards the end of the 1880s, conditions changed. Farmers arrived and fenced their lands. Disastrous weather during 1885–1887 forced cattlemen to gain title to land, and fence it so they could grow hay to provide for their herds. This marked the end of the "open range."

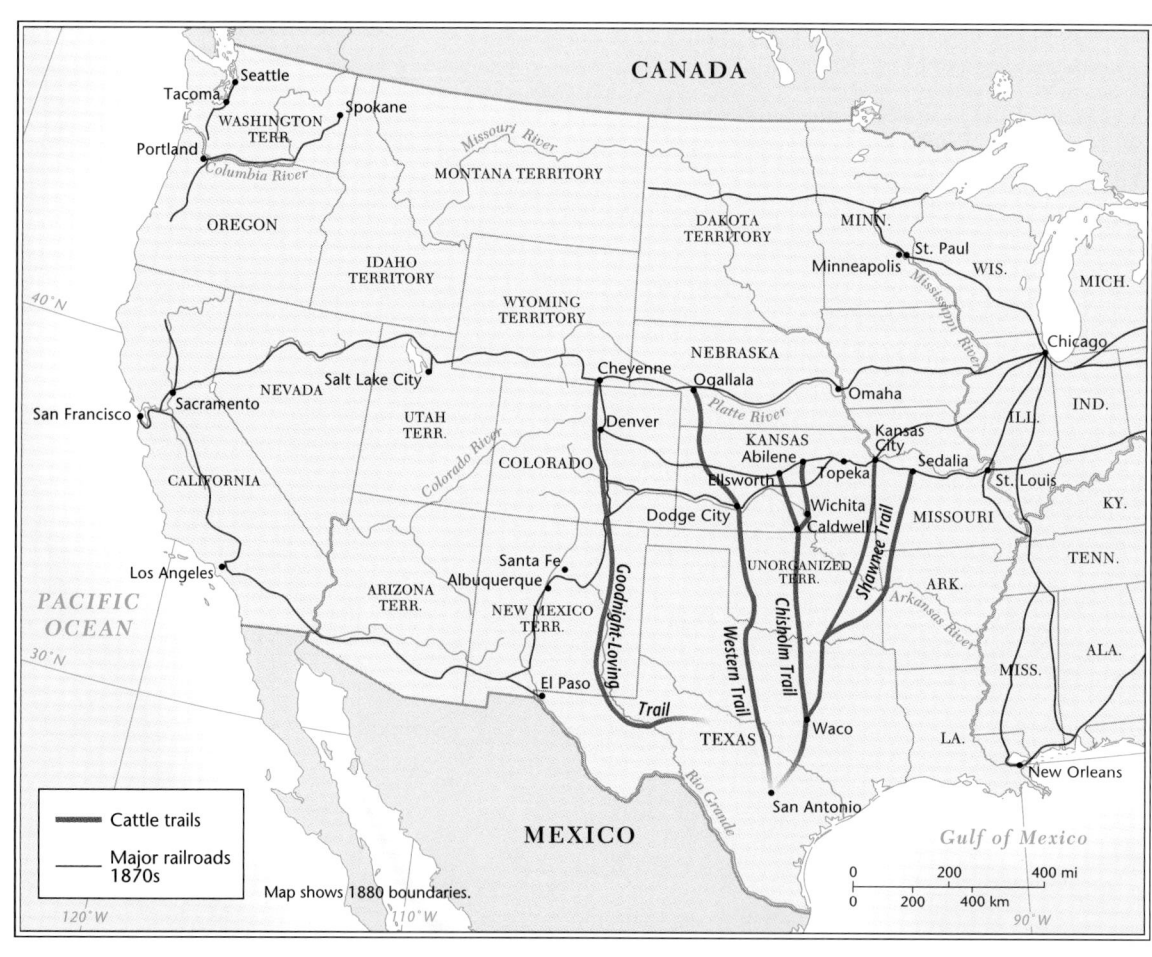

Cattle trails

Major railroads 1870s

Map shows 1880 boundaries.

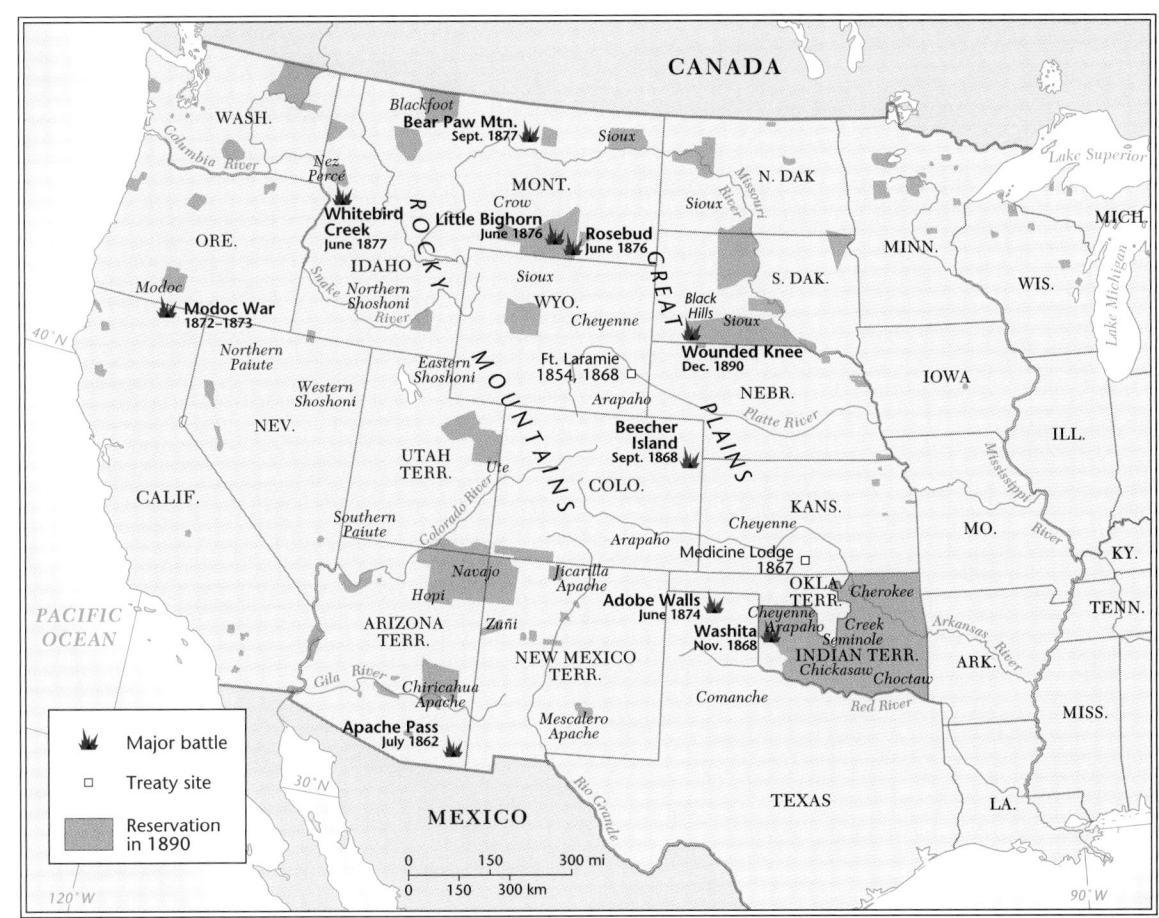

Indian Reservations 1890

During the 1850s, in order to open the West for settlement, the government instituted a policy of concentrating the Plains Indians in specific areas. But most of the Indians were nomadic and moved out of their designated areas in order to hunt. Settlers who had moved into the former Indian lands asked the government for protection.

The discovery of gold in Colorado brought more whites to Indian land, and more confrontations were inevitable.

Under the terms of treaties in 1867 and 1868, Indians had little choice but to accept reservations in Indian Territory and South Dakota. Yet many still refused to accept the terms imposed upon them and drifted back to their plains. Warfare soon broke out, and by the end of the 1870s, most of the Indians had been either killed or subdued.

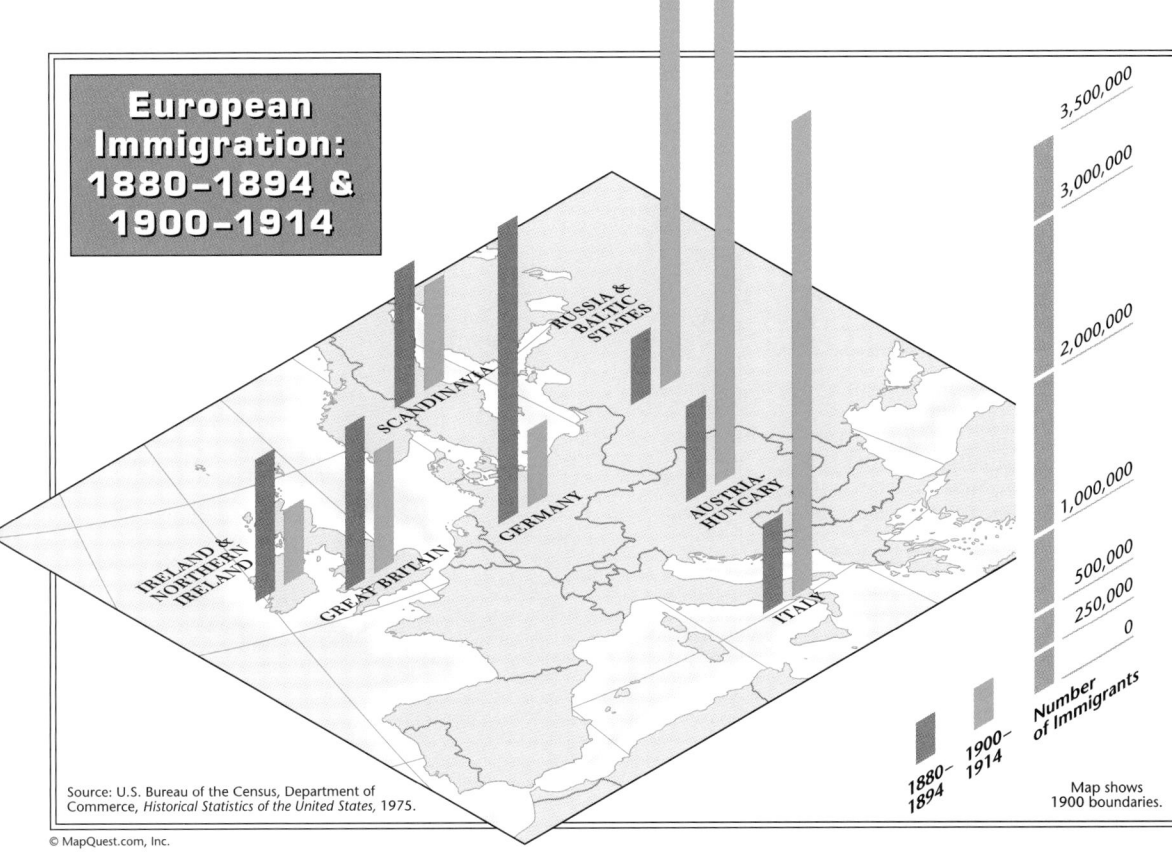

European Immigration: 1880–1894 & 1900–1914

Source: U.S. Bureau of the Census, Department of Commerce, *Historical Statistics of the United States*, 1975.

Map shows 1900 boundaries.

There were two phases of European immigration: the old and the new. The old phase consisted of people from northern and western Europe. Because the foundations of American society were built by people from this part of Europe, these immigrants were assimilated relatively easily.

The new immigrants were from southern and eastern Europe. Democratic forms of government were slower to develop there, and until such time, peasants were probably not free to emigrate. Culturally they differed from native-born Americans and earlier immigrants. Many were poor, uneducated, and unskilled. Their assimilation into America was more difficult.

Many immigrants came without plans to stay. They wanted to make enough money in order to live a better life back home. But others fled unbearable hardship and had little attachment to their native land.

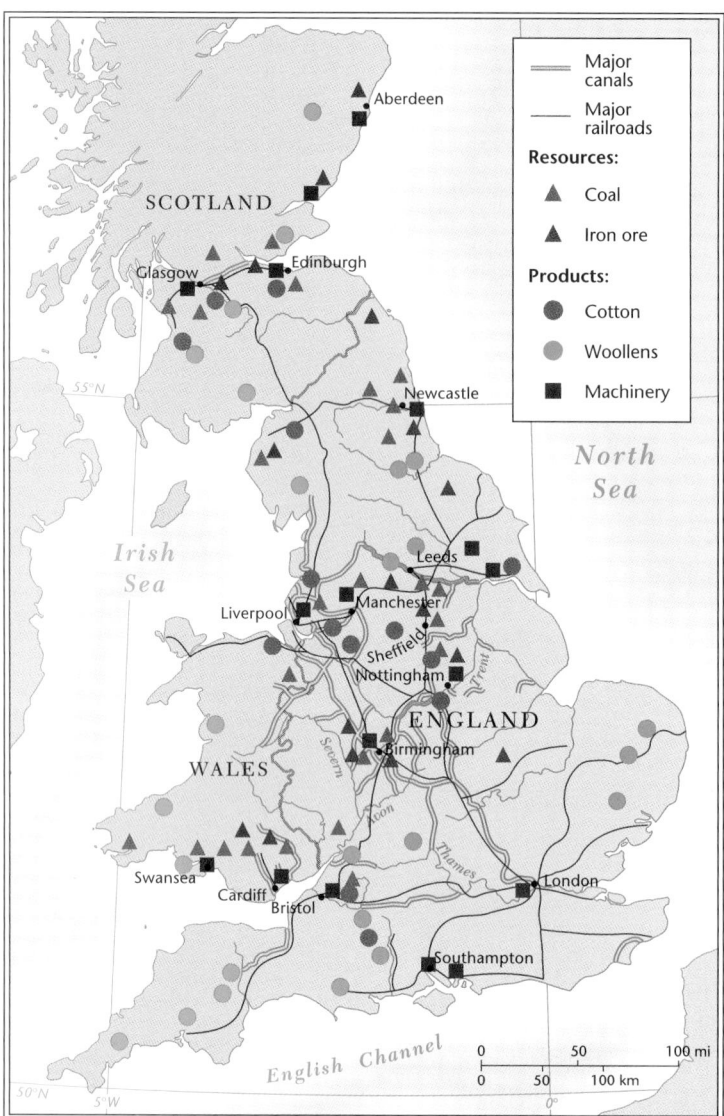

Great Britain: Industrial Revolution to 1851

Industrial development in Great Britain had its beginnings in the textile industries that had started as early as the sixteenth century.

But without the resources of coal and iron, the Industrial Revolution—as we now know it— might never have happened. Britain had ample supplies of both and was fortunate that its iron ore deposits were near the coal fields, thus making transportation less of a problem. Canals and railroads were an integral part of the British transportation network.

Technological advances also "fueled" the Industrial Revolution. Coal-powered engines were applied to the many production processes, replacing people- and animal-power as a source of energy.

Britain also had other advantages that enabled it to lead the revolution. Britain was a leader in international trade, and this trade brought in capital and provided a means of importing raw materials and exporting manufactured products. Britain's well-established banking system made it possible to provide capital for industrial investments.

Great Britain: Population Growth 1861–1891

The Industrial Revolution changed Europe from a largely rural/agricultural society into a largely urban/industrial one. Prior to the revolution, perhaps less than 10 percent of the people lived in cities. By 1851, over 50 percent of the English population lived in cities, and by 1870, that number reached 70 percent.

Great Britain was already experiencing a population explosion. An adequate food supply and improvements in hygiene and health care have been cited as factors in the population increase.

London was the main focus of the population growth and attracted many migrants from other parts of the country. Other growth centers were Glasgow, Liverpool, and Manchester. Although many people migrated to cities in search of jobs, other migrated overseas, particularly to America.

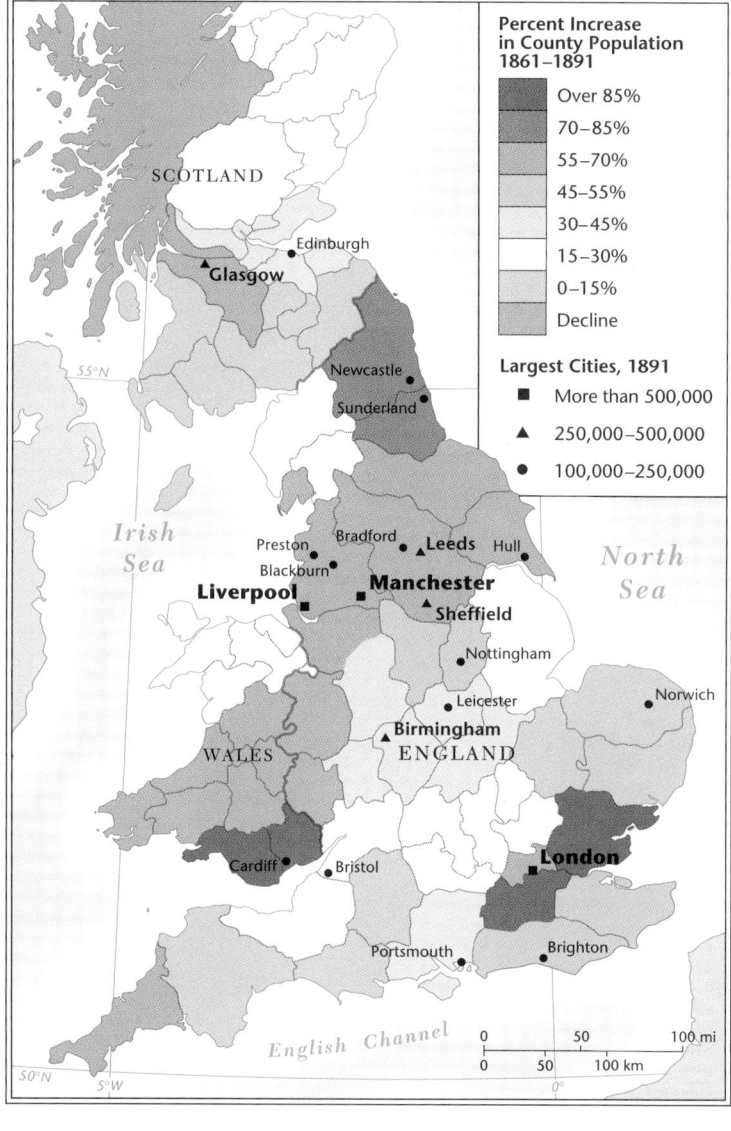

German Unification 1865–1871

Sedan Aug.–Sept. 1870

Metz besieged Aug.–Oct. 1870

Paris besieged Sept. 1870– Jan. 1871

FRANCE

0   75   150 mi
0   75   150 km

Legend:
- Kingdom of Prussia 1865
- States annexed by Prussia, 1866
- States joining the North German Confederation, 1867
- States joining the German Empire 1871
- Annexed, 1871
- Major battles

Otto von Bismarck, as prime minister of Prussia, worked to make Prussia the foremost German state. His first move was to go to war with Denmark over the German-speaking duchies of Schleswig and Holstein.

Prussia then successfully went to war against Austria. Bismarck did not want to destroy Austria, he just wanted to keep it out of German affairs.

Bismarck dethroned rulers of other German states and formed the North German Confederation in 1867.

France saw a united Germany as a threat. And Bismarck saw war with France as a way of uniting more German states. The Franco-Prussian War ended in January 1871, and France ceded Alsace-Lorraine. South German states joined the North German Confederation, and the German Empire was created.

Italian Unification, 1858–1870

Legend:
- Kingdom of Sardinia 1858
- Austrian territory annexed by Sardinia, 1859
- Territory annexed by Sardinia, 1860 (Kingdom of Italy formed, 1861)
- Austrian territory annexed by Italy, 1866
- Territory annexed by Italy, 1870
- Major battles

In the mid-1800s, portions of northern Italy were controlled by Austria. In 1848, revolutions broke out in Italy and throughout central Europe. In time, Austria was able to suppress those in Italy.

Italians realized they would need to expel the Austrians if they had any hopes of creating a united republican Italy. The Kingdom of Sardinia entered into a defensive agreement with France. Fearful of French intervention, Austria declared war on the Kingdom of Sardinia in 1859. Italian and French forces defeated the Austrians. Lombardy was annexed, but Austria held on to Venetia.

The successes against Austria encouraged other revolutionaries in Italy. In 1860, revolutionized areas joined the Kingdom of Sardinia, and in 1861, the Kingdom of Italy was proclaimed. When Austria was defeated by Prussia in 1866, Italy annexed Venetia.

Rome had been protected by French troops, but in 1870, when French troops were withdrawn to fight Prussia, Italian troops moved upon Rome. The pope remained in the Vatican, opposed to this united Italy.

© MapQuest.com, Inc.

British Empire, 1914

British possessions 1914

Major British bases or coaling stations

Major cities

Major British trade routes

The empire-building that began in the sixteenth century and tapered off in the mid-eighteenth century underwent a resurgence during the last quarter of the nineteenth century. Most states in the Americas had attained their independence by this time, so Europeans focused their interest on Africa and Asia. Many historians refer to this era as a time of "new imperialism."

There were a number of possible motives for this new wave of imperialism.

Many European leaders believed that colonies could provide guaranteed markets for manufactured goods. Unfortunately most colonies were too poor to buy these goods. But very few colonies were ever abandoned because of this. Almost any colony was important for political or nationalistic reasons.

Geopolitics was a keyword in this period's international relations. The idea was that certain areas of the world were important for political purposes. Some colonies were established solely to protect older, more important colonies, or to protect vital sea routes.

Nationalism was another factor. Empires, it was believed, would enhance national prestige. If one nation began the process of colonization, other nations, based on feelings of fear, suspicion, and jealousy, would soon follow suit.

Europeans also believed that imperialism had an altruistic theme. Once in contact with Africans and Asians, they saw their own material culture as superior. Europeans thought they could "civilize" non-whites by introducing a better standard of living. But the concept of cultural superiority was just a short step away from that of racial superiority. Social Darwinists applied ideas of human development to nations. The concept of "survival of the fittest" was used to justify conquest of the non-Western world.

For many years Britain had maintained its position as the world's leading economic power. By the 1870s, France, Germany, and the United States were becoming global economic powers. Fearing increased competition, Britain took renewed interest in its existing colonies, specifically Canada, India, and Australia.

India was Britain's "Jewel in the Crown," and Britain maintained Mediterranean and East African outposts in order to protect access to India.

Britain's leading role in the Industrial Revolution helped the country build the world's largest naval fleet. To provide supplies for the fleets, depots and coaling stations were established around the world. And Britain's manufacturing strength gave it capital to invest in overseas development. London soon became the world's banker.

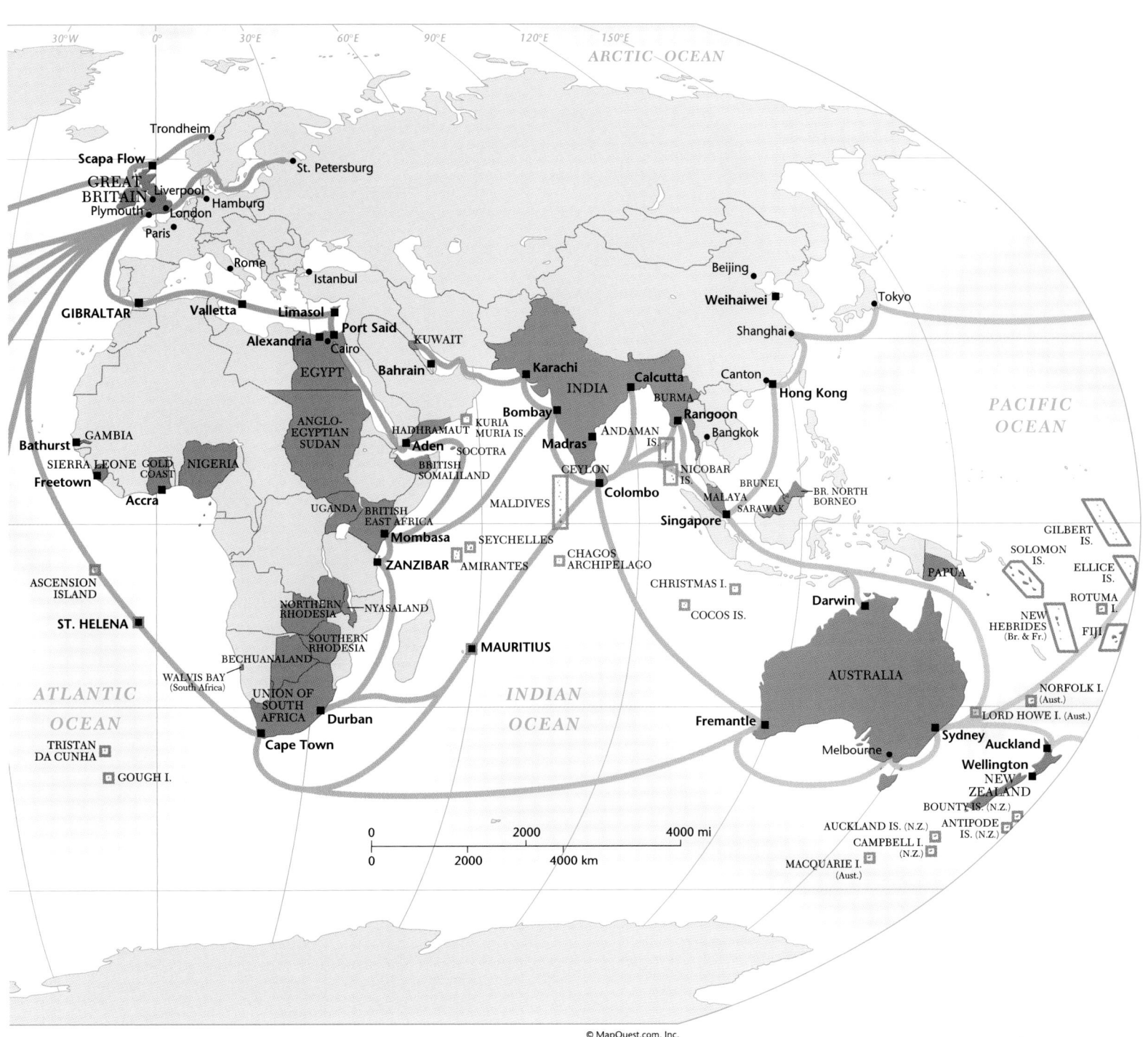

ARCTIC OCEAN

30°W   0°   30°E   60°E   90°E   120°E   150°E

Trondheim

Scapa Flow

GREAT BRITAIN   Liverpool   St. Petersburg

Plymouth   Hamburg

London

Paris

Rome

Istanbul

Beijing

Weihaiwei

Tokyo

GIBRALTAR   Valletta   **Limasol**

Shanghai

PACIFIC OCEAN

Alexandria   **Port Said**

Cairo   **KUWAIT**

EGYPT   **Bahrain**   **Karachi**   **Calcutta**   Canton

INDIA   **Hong Kong**

ANGLO-EGYPTIAN SUDAN   BURMA

GAMBIA   HADHRAMAUT   KURIA MURIA IS.   **Bombay**   **Rangoon**

Bathurst   **Aden**   SOCOTRA   **Madras**   ANDAMAN IS.   Bangkok

SIERRA LEONE   **GOLD COAST**   **NIGERIA**   BRITISH SOMALILAND   CEYLON   NICOBAR IS.

Freetown   **Accra**   UGANDA   MALDIVES   **Colombo**   BRUNEI

BRITISH EAST AFRICA   **Singapore**   MALAYA   BR. NORTH BORNEO

Mombasa   SEYCHELLES   SARAWAK

ASCENSION ISLAND   **ZANZIBAR**   AMIRANTES   CHAGOS ARCHIPELAGO

CHRISTMAS I.

GILBERT IS.

SOLOMON IS.

ELLICE IS.

ROTUMA I.

St. HELENA   NORTHERN RHODESIA   NYASALAND   COCOS IS.   **PAPUA**

Darwin   NEW HEBRIDES (Br. & Fr.)   FIJI

SOUTHERN RHODESIA   **MAURITIUS**

BECHUANALAND   **AUSTRALIA**

WALVIS BAY (South Africa)

INDIAN OCEAN   NORFOLK I. (Aust.)

ATLANTIC OCEAN   **UNION OF SOUTH AFRICA**   **Durban**   **Fremantle**   LORD HOWE I. (Aust.)

TRISTAN DA CUNHA   **Cape Town**   Melbourne   **Sydney**   **Auckland**

GOUGH I.   **Wellington**   **NEW ZEALAND**

BOUNTY IS. (N.Z.)

AUCKLAND IS. (N.Z.)   ANTIPODE IS. (N.Z.)

CAMPBELL I. (N.Z.)

MACQUARIE I. (Aust.)

0   2000   4000 mi

0   2000   4000 km

© MapQuest.com, Inc.

Imperialism in Africa c. 1914

Prior to 1880, western European nations controlled about 10 percent of Africa. After 1880, state-supported seizure of territory began anew.

Conflict over control of the Congo River prompted European nations and the United States to meet in Berlin to establish ground rules for the colonization of Africa. Claims would be recognized on the basis of effective control. Unfortunately most European nations lacked the resources to effectively govern an African colony.

Under European political and economic leadership, African society disintegrated. Boundaries were established where none had existed before. Ethnic groups were often split apart. And sometimes peoples with long-held animosities were grouped together within a colony.

African weapons were no match for those that the Europeans carried. In conventional battle, the Africans faced overwhelming odds. Guerrilla-style resistance was about all the Africans could muster in the face of the European onslaught.

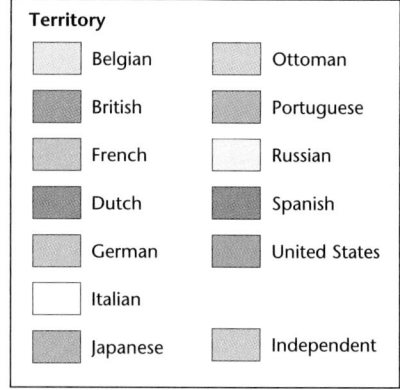

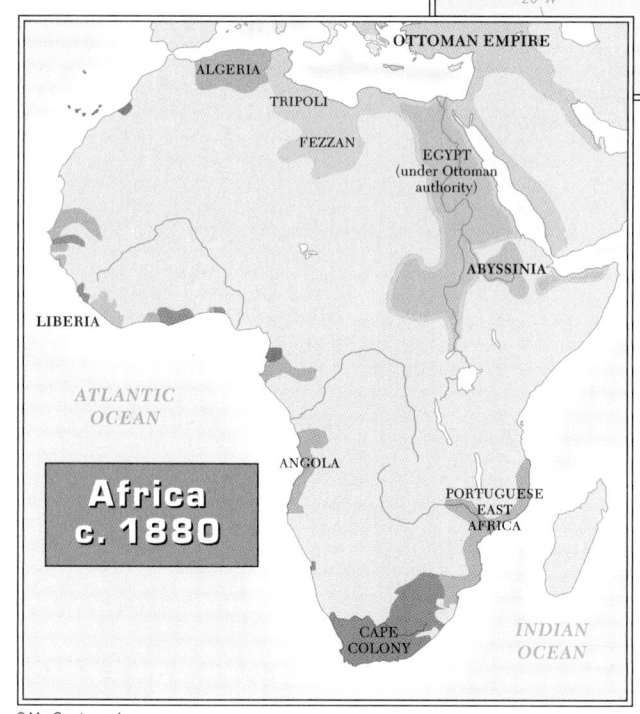

Africa c. 1880

Territory

Belgian	Ottoman
British	Portuguese
French	Russian
Dutch	Spanish
German	United States
Italian	
Japanese	Independent

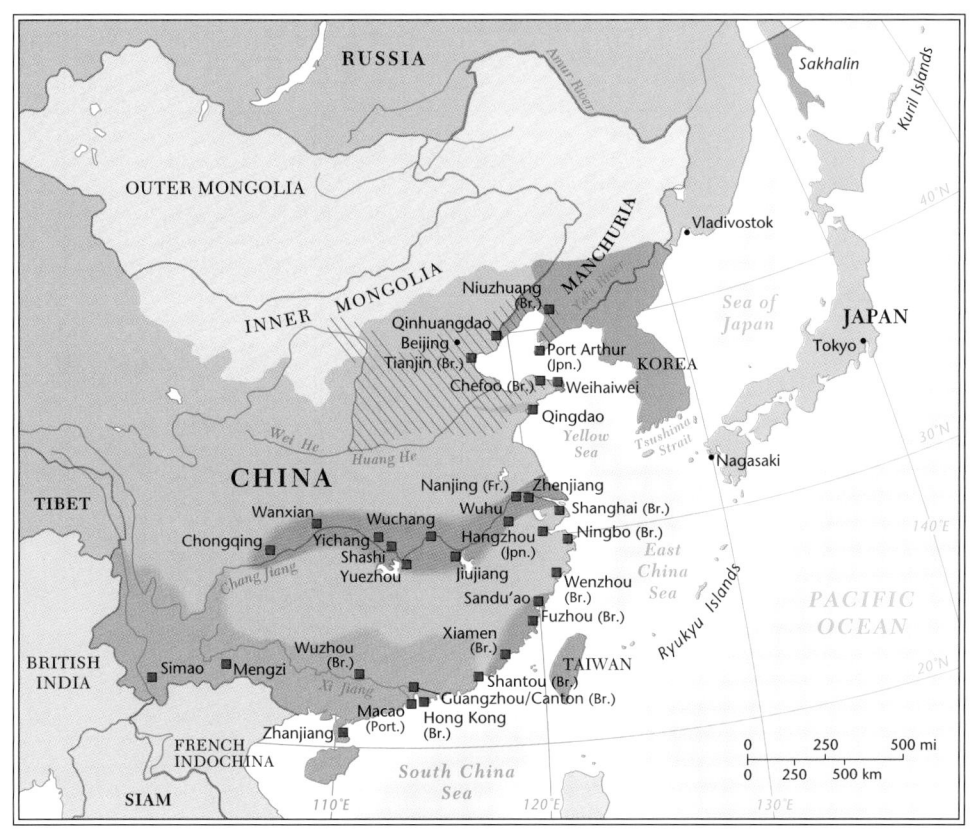

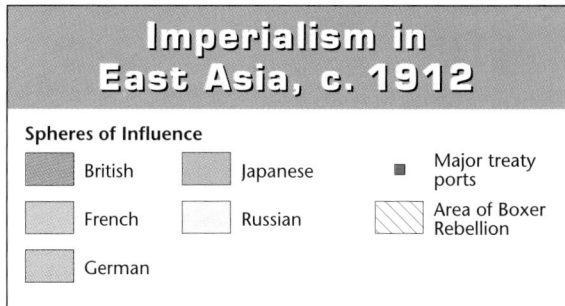

Imperialism in East Asia, c. 1912

Spheres of Influence

- British
- French
- German
- Japanese
- Russian
- ■ Major treaty ports
- ▨ Area of Boxer Rebellion

China found itself on the losing end of a series of wars in the last half of the 1880s. The result was that Britain, France, Germany, Russia, and Japan were able to establish treaty ports and "spheres of influence." In the treaty ports, the rule of extraterritoriality applied—foreigners were exempt from Chinese law.

China survived this period because no single power could control all of China, and each state acted as a check against the other. The United States supported an "Open Door" policy. This would recognize Chinese sovereignty and guarantee equal access to Chinese markets.

Japan was able to escape European domination because it westernized and modernized. And like other European nations, it took up the banner of imperialism against other Asian states.

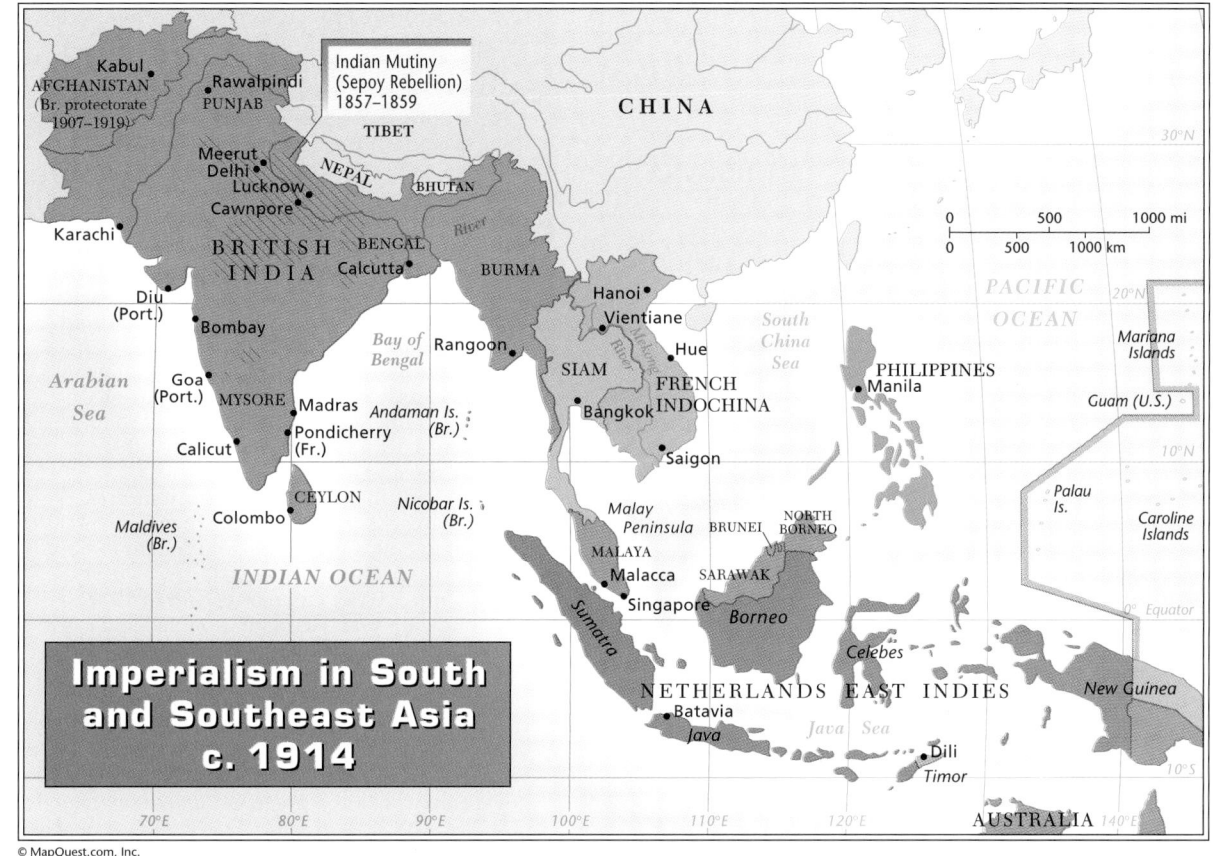

Imperialism in South and Southeast Asia c. 1914

The East Indies had been one of the first prizes in the age of European expansion, but until the last third of the 1800s, only Java was under Dutch control. The drive by other nations to establish world-wide empires spurred the Dutch to establish control over the entire archipelago.

In India, British officials often took control of local states, but retained Indian princes as heads of state. Following the Indian Mutiny, the British government took direct control of India.

The British introduced improvements in education, communication, transportation, and agriculture. Many Hindus rose in the ranks of government service. But not surprisingly, they could never hope to achieve equal status with the whites.

The United States joined the ranks of imperialists when the Philippines were taken following the Spanish-American War in 1898.

World War I
1914–1918

Allied Powers
Central Powers
Neutral countries
Major areas of fighting
Major battle

NORWAY
SWEDEN
FINLAND
Petrograd
ATLANTIC OCEAN
North Sea
DENMARK
Baltic Sea
GREAT BRITAIN
NETHERLANDS
Lusitania sunk May 7, 1915
London
Berlin
Tannenberg Aug. 1914
EASTERN FRONT
RUSSIA
GERMANY
BELGIUM
LUXEMBOURG
Paris
WESTERN FRONT
Danube R.
Vienna
Caspian Sea
FRANCE
SWITZ.
AUSTRIA-HUNGARY
Caporetto Oct. 1917
ITALIAN FRONT
Danube R.
ROMANIA
ROMANIAN CAMPAIGN
Black Sea
CAUCASUS CAMPAIGN
Bay of Biscay
Sarajevo
SERBIA
BULGARIA
PORT.
SPAIN
Corsica (French)
ITALY
Rome
MONTENEGRO
BALKAN CAMPAIGN
ALBANIA
GREECE
Constantinople
DARDANELLES CAMPAIGN
Gallipoli April 1915–Jan. 1916
OTTOMAN EMPIRE
Tigris R.
Euphrates R.
MESOPOTAMIAN CAMPAIGN
Baghdad
Balearic Islands (Spanish)
Sardinia (Italian)
Sicily (Italian)
Crete (Greek)
Cyprus (British)
PALESTINIAN CAMPAIGN
Jerusalem
Mediterranean Sea

0   250   500 mi
0   250   500 km

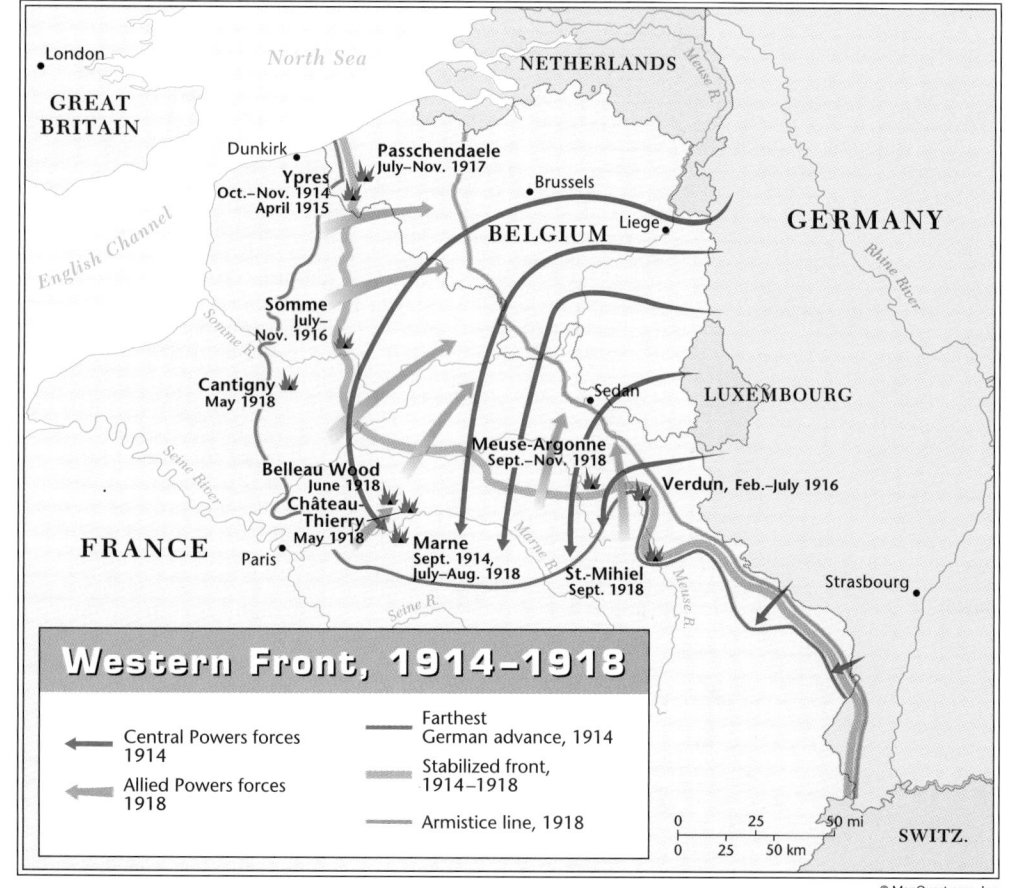

London
GREAT BRITAIN
North Sea
NETHERLANDS
Dunkirk
Ypres Oct.–Nov. 1914 April 1915
Passchendaele July–Nov. 1917
Brussels
BELGIUM
Liege
GERMANY
English Channel
Somme July–Nov. 1916
Rhine River
Cantigny May 1918
Sedan
LUXEMBOURG
Belleau Wood June 1918
Meuse-Argonne Sept.–Nov. 1918
Château-Thierry May 1918
Verdun, Feb.–July 1916
FRANCE
Paris
Marne Sept. 1914, July–Aug. 1918
St.-Mihiel Sept. 1918
Strasbourg
Seine R.

Western Front, 1914–1918

Central Powers forces 1914
Allied Powers forces 1918
Farthest German advance, 1914
Stabilized front, 1914–1918
Armistice line, 1918

0   25   50 mi
0   25   50 km
SWITZ.

Prior to World War I, an increase in international rivalries led to tensions throughout Europe. Nations were competing for overseas colonies, and they were also engaged in a massive arms race.

As nations kept a wary eye on the actions of their neighbors, they often established alliances with countries with whom they had common interests. Although it was hoped that this would provide protection, it also meant that more than one nation could be drawn into a war caused by a dispute in which it was not directly involved. And this is what happened when Austria-Hungary declared war on Serbia.

Most European nations were quickly drawn into this war. In the West, Germany invaded France, hoping for a quick victory, but the war settled into deadly stalemate that would last for over three years.

In the East, the Russians had early success, but they were soon rolled back. The country was undergoing a revolution and sought a separate peace with Germany.

The United States entered the war in 1917. The following year, Germany gambled and launched an offensive along the Western Front. The Allies, with American assistance, pushed the Germans back. With America in the war, Germany could not match the Allied strength. Because the country was weak and wracked with internal dissension, the government sought a peace settlement.

Europe After World War I

- Germany in 1914
- Austria-Hungary in 1914
- Russia in 1914
- —— Boundaries of new and reconstituted nations
- ···· Other post-war boundaries

In the treaty settlements following the war, the defeated empires were forced to surrender territory, and from this, new nations were created. Adhering to the principle of self-determination, an attempt was made to consider national groups in drawing the new boundaries. But inevitably most new nations ended up with a substantial national minority group within its bounds. This would cause friction in the years to come.

Former German colonies and Ottoman territories became mandates to be governed by Western powers with the aim of eventually gaining independence.

Not only did the vanquished lose territory, but they were forced to pay punitive reparations. European nations, especially France, had suffered terribly during the war years, and they wanted to be repaid. The German government's ability to rule was undermined because it had been forced to accept responsibility for the war. Many German leaders vowed revenge on France for the severity of the terms of the Treaty of Versailles.

Mandate System c. 1926

- Belgian
- British
- French
- Australian
- Japanese
- South African

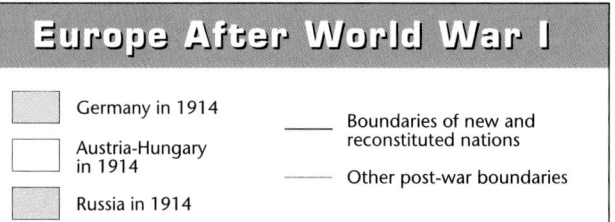

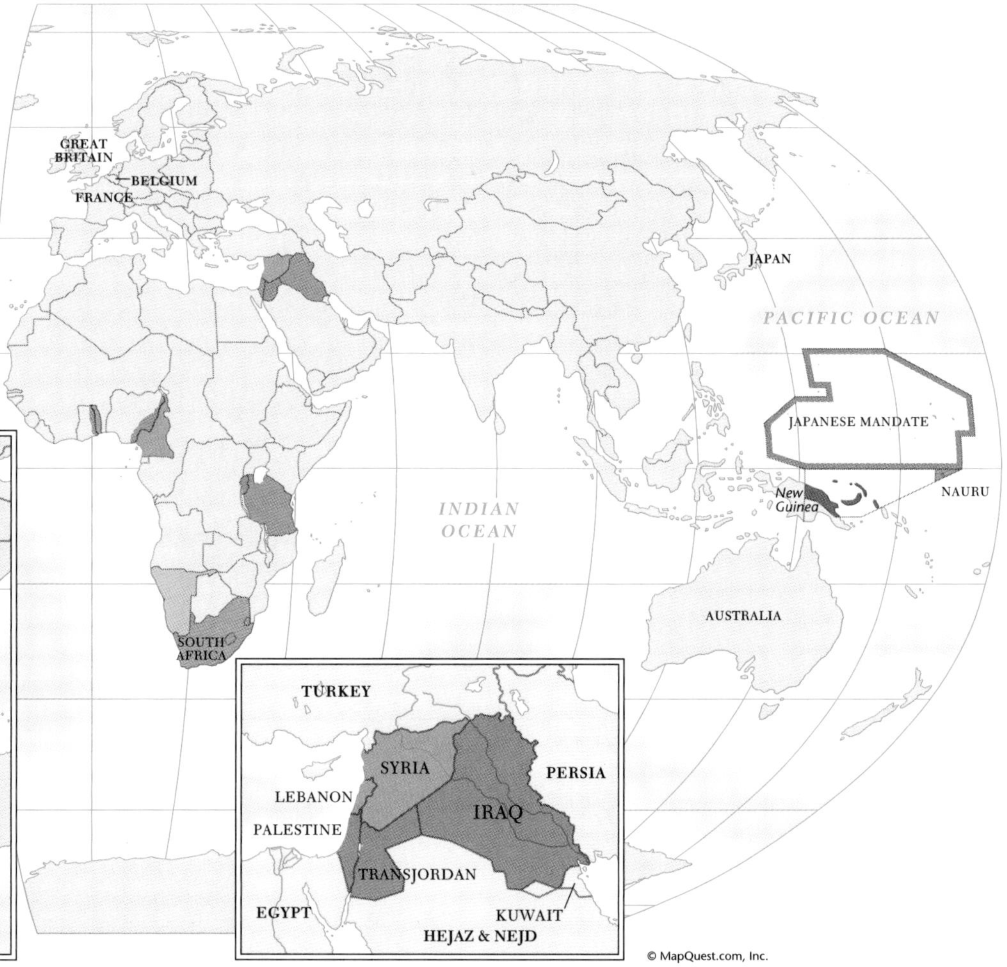

Russian Civil War, 1917–1921

- ⚡ Bolshevik uprising, 1917
- ◀── Foreign forces
- ◀── Bolshevik counterattacks
- ▨ Area controlled by Bolsheviks October 1919
- ◀── Whites Russian forces
- —— Boundaries 1921

Russia was not prepared for World War I. Efforts to provide for its army caused severe hardships for its people, and long-standing animosities between the classes erupted. The monarchy fell in March, 1917. Then in November, the provisional government fell to the *Bolsheviks*. Lenin, as the new leader, made peace with Germany. The treaty that the Germans imposed was unusually harsh, and many Russians considered it to be a betrayal.

Disgruntled soldiers formed the "White Armies" to fight the Bolsheviks. Western nations wanted to keep the Eastern Front in operation and sent supplies to the Whites. Aid continued after the end of World War I. This attempt to undermine the new Soviet state made the citizens forever suspicious of capitalist countries.

In the anarchy caused by civil war, the government became more repressive and dictatorial. By 1920 the determined Red Army had defeated most of the opposition. This done, the government established a system of socialist republics, and Russia became the Union of Soviet Socialist Republics.

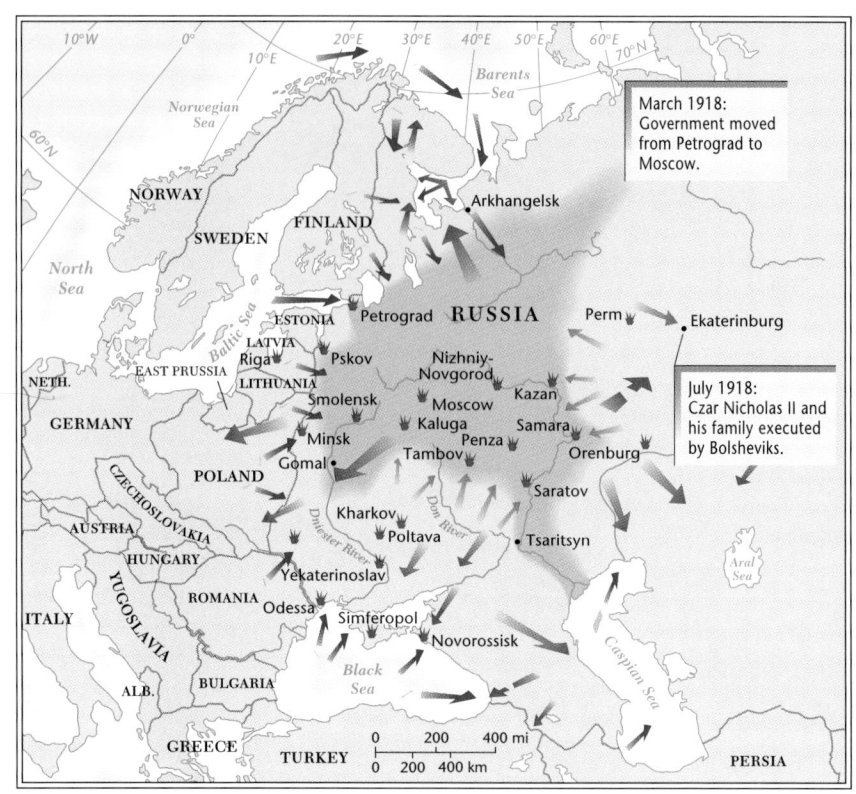

March 1918: Government moved from Petrograd to Moscow.

July 1918: Czar Nicholas II and his family executed by Bolsheviks.

The Great Depression

The Great Depression refers to the worldwide economic crisis of the 1930s. Following World War I, resources were drained from Europe to pay war debts. Nations established tariffs to protect home industries, reducing market opportunities as a whole.

Funds earmarked for European recovery were invested in the booming U.S. stock market. When the market collapsed in 1929, more money was withdrawn from Europe to pay off debts, and this further strained European banks.

Percentage of the Work Force Unemployed
- 1929
- 1932

CANADA — 2.9% / 17.6%
UNITED STATES — 3.2% / 23.6%
GREAT BRITAIN — 11.0% / 22.5%
NORWAY — 15.4% / 30.8%
DENMARK — 15.5% / 31.7%
BELGIUM — 1.9% / 23.5%
GERMANY — 13.1% / 30.1%
POLAND — 4.9% / 15.6%
ITALY (1929 & 1931) — 7.2% / 20.5%

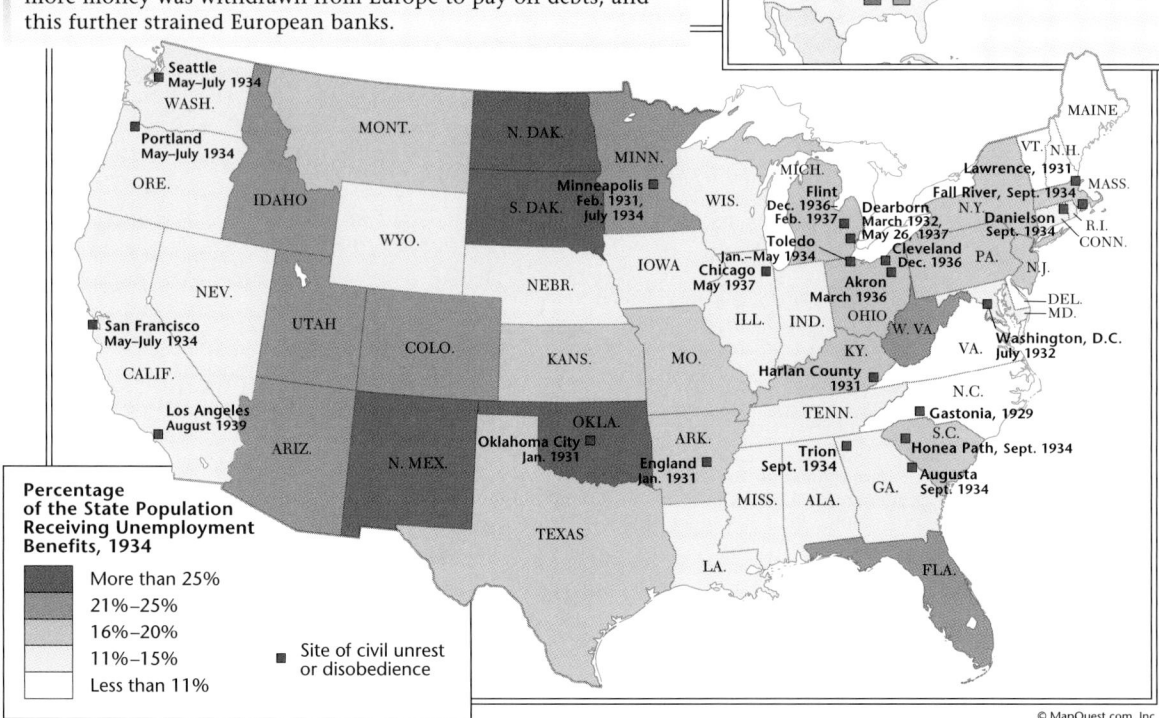

Percentage of the State Population Receiving Unemployment Benefits, 1934
- ▨ More than 25%
- ▨ 21%–25%
- ▨ 16%–20%
- ▨ 11%–15%
- ☐ Less than 11%
- ■ Site of civil unrest or disobedience

During World War I and the early 1920s, U.S. farmers overproduced. Prices fell and farmers lost money. In the industrial sector, production had been increasing, but wages had not. People were unable to afford products.

President Hoover felt that the business sector could correct the economic distress. But states lacked federal assistance and did not have enough money to provide relief for the people. Roosevelt was elected and instituted a policy whereby the federal government took the responsibility of combating the depression. The government used deficit spending to help provide relief for the people.

Europe 1936–1939

- Germany, 1933
- Rhineland remilitarized by Germany, 1936
- Annexed by Germany, 1938
- Acquired by Poland, 1938
- Annexed by Hungary 1938–1939
- Annexed by Germany, 1939
- Occupied by Germany September 1939
- Occupied by Soviet Union September 1939
- Italy, 1933
- Acquired by Italy, 1939

© MapQuest.com, Inc.

It is possible to trace some of the causes of World War II to problems created by the treaties that ended World War I.

The punitive nature of some treaties fostered animosities between victors and losers. Germany was forced to accept the blame for World War I.

Most of the new nations that were created ended up with substantial minority groups, and this would lead to tension within nations and between nations.

When the economic system collapsed in the 1930s, democratic governments were hard pressed to find solutions. Some dictatorships arose in these times of political and economic instability.

Prelude to War

Jan. 1933: Adolf Hitler became Chancellor of Germany. Within two months he gained dictatorial power, and Germany became a police state.

Oct. 1933: Germany withdrew from the League of Nations.

March 1934: Germany instituted conscription in the face of increased French and Soviet militarization.

March 1936: Germany reoccupied and remilitarized the Rhineland.

May 1936: Italian army occupied Ethiopia's capital. The failure of the League of Nations to defend a member nation signaled the end of the institution's effectiveness.

July 1936: The Spanish Civil War began, and Europe was divided into fascist and non-fascist nations.

Oct. 1936: Germany and Italy formed the "Berlin-Italy Axis."

March 1938: Germany annexed Austria. There was virtually no opposition from other European nations.

Sept. 1938: Germany demanded self-determination for Germans living in the Sudetenland. Prime Minister Chamberlain of Great Britain convinced Czechoslovakia and France to yield to Hitler's demands, telling them that this action would redress some of the wrongs done to Germany after World War I. This policy of *appeasement* was based on Britain's unwillingness and inability to go to war over this issue.

March 1939: Germany annexed Czechoslovakia and Memel.

April 1939: Italy invaded Albania.

August 1939: Germany continued its demands for the return of Danzig. Germany and the USSR signed a non-aggression pact. They secretly agreed to divide Poland.

Sept. 1, 1939: Germany invaded Poland. Britain and France reiterated their pledges to Poland that were made earlier in the year. They hoped to negotiate if Germany would withdraw. Germany refused.

Sept. 3, 1939: Great Britain and France declared war on Germany.

Sept. 17, 1939: Russian troops invaded Poland.

Sept. 27, 1939: Poland surrendered.

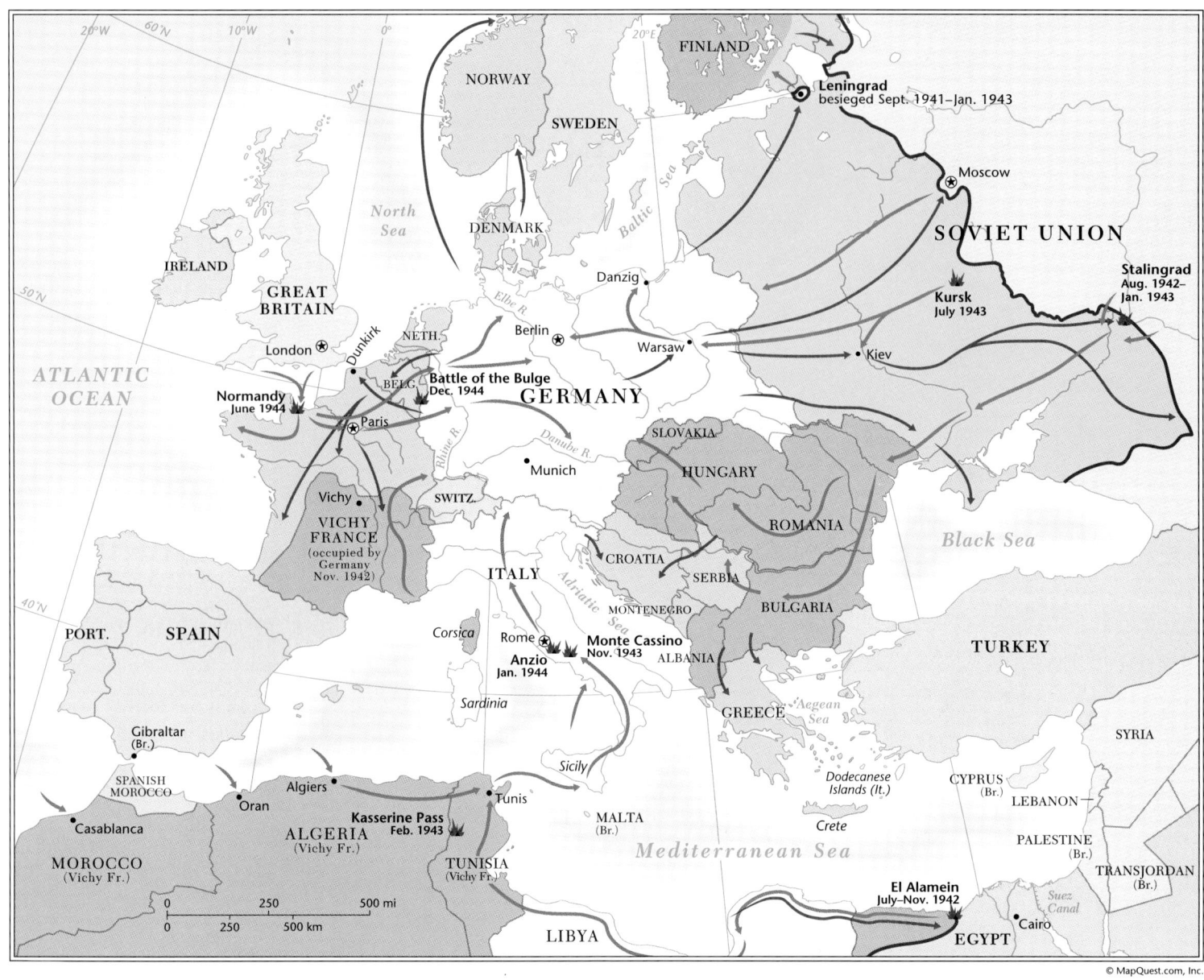

© MapQuest.com, Inc.

World War II in Europe

Axis countries, 1942

Axis satellite states and allies

Axis controlled areas

Allies and allied controlled areas, 1942

Neutral countries

→ Axis offensives, 1940–1942

→ Allied offensives, 1942–1945

— Farthest Axis advance, 1942

⚜ Major battle

Following the fall of Poland, poor weather conditions forced Germany to postpone any military offensives. But when spring arrived Germany invaded Denmark and Norway. In May, 1940, Germany launched its invasion of Belgium, the Netherlands, and France. These countries were quickly overrun. In France, Germany occupied the northern portion and set up a collaborationist government headquartered in Vichy.

Despite a non-aggression pact, neither Germany nor the Soviet Union trusted each other. The June 1941 invasion of the Soviet Union caught the Soviets by surprise. The Germans reached Moscow, but the Russian winter helped save the city. In February, 1943, the Germans were defeated at Stalingrad, marking the end of Germany's eastward advance.

In the meantime the U.S. had entered the war. The Allies agreed that the first offensive against the Axis would be through Italy, Germany's "soft underbelly." The next major thrust would be through northern France. The Germans expected an invasion, but were unsure of the location. Operations began on June 6, 1944, and a small beachhead was quickly established, but beyond that, the advance was slow. On August 25, Paris was liberated.

The drive to the Rhine was on. The Germans caught the Allies by surprise in December, 1944, but lacked the troop strength to halt the advance. In the East, following the victories at Stalingrad and Kursk, the Red Army began the slow process of driving the Germans back. In April, 1945, Allied and Soviet troops met south of Berlin. The Russians took Berlin on April 25, 1945. Germany surrendered on May 7, and the next day was declared Victory in Europe, or V-E, Day.

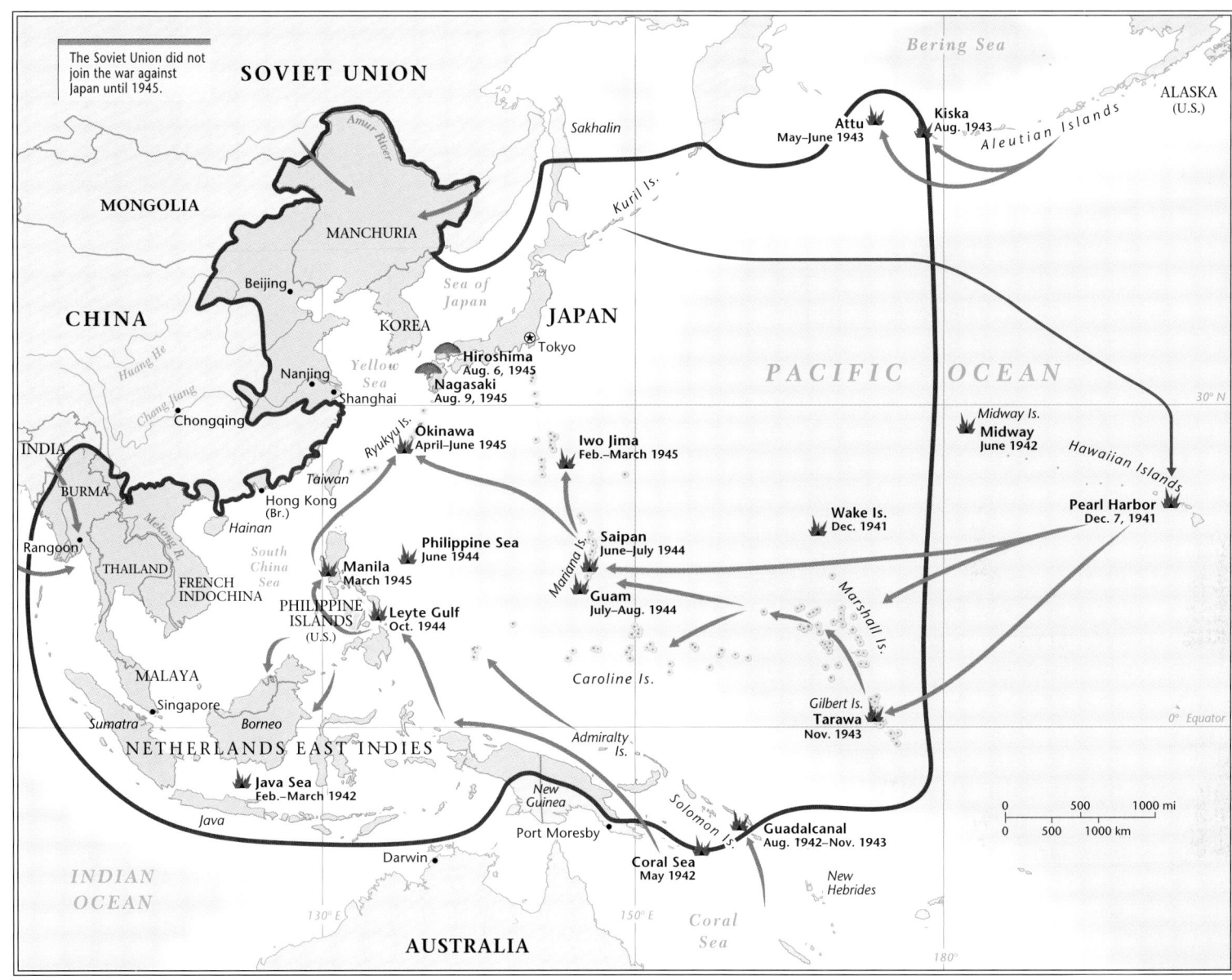

The Soviet Union did not join the war against Japan until 1945.

Although the United States' foremost concerns and interests were in Europe, it was Japan's bombing of Pearl Harbor that brought the U.S. into World War II.

In 1937, Japan invaded China, and the U.S. threatened to impose economic sanctions. In July, 1941, Japanese assets in the U.S. were frozen. Exports of steel and oil were cut off. The two nations tried to negotiate, but the Japanese government fell, and militarists took control. They felt that the U.S. stood in the way of their expansion in Asia, and that one quick strike would cripple the U.S. That strike would come at Pearl Harbor. Although the U.S. navy suffered greatly, the attack fulfilled Roosevelt's wish of enraging and then mobilizing the American people to action.

The Japanese had early victories in Southeast Asia where defenders were not prepared. But the tide quickly turned in the Pacific. In 1942, Japan suffered major defeats at Midway and the Coral Sea.

Japanese expansion had already reached its peak.

Now the Allies faced the task of removing Japanese troops from the many islands that Japan held. The Allies became experts at amphibious assaults as they battled through the South Pacific. Once the U.S. had control of the Marianas, they were within bombing range of Japan. Even so, the Allies continued taking Japanese-held islands. The Philippines, Iwo Jima, and Okinawa all fell at a great price to the U.S., but they set the stage for the impending invasion of Japan.

At home, scientists had developed a possible means of ending the war without losing large numbers of Allied troops. The Allies warned Japan that they had a new device that could destroy the country, but Japan ignored the warning. Two bombs were dropped, one at Hiroshima and another at Nagasaki, before Japan sued for peace. Although Japan experienced the devastation of the atomic bombs, the Allies were able to show the Soviets the power they had at their disposal.

World War II in the Pacific

- Japan and Japanese controlled areas, May 1942
- Allied countries
- Japanese fleet, Dec. 1941
- Allied offensives
- Farthest Japanese advance 1942
- Major battle
- Atomic bombing site

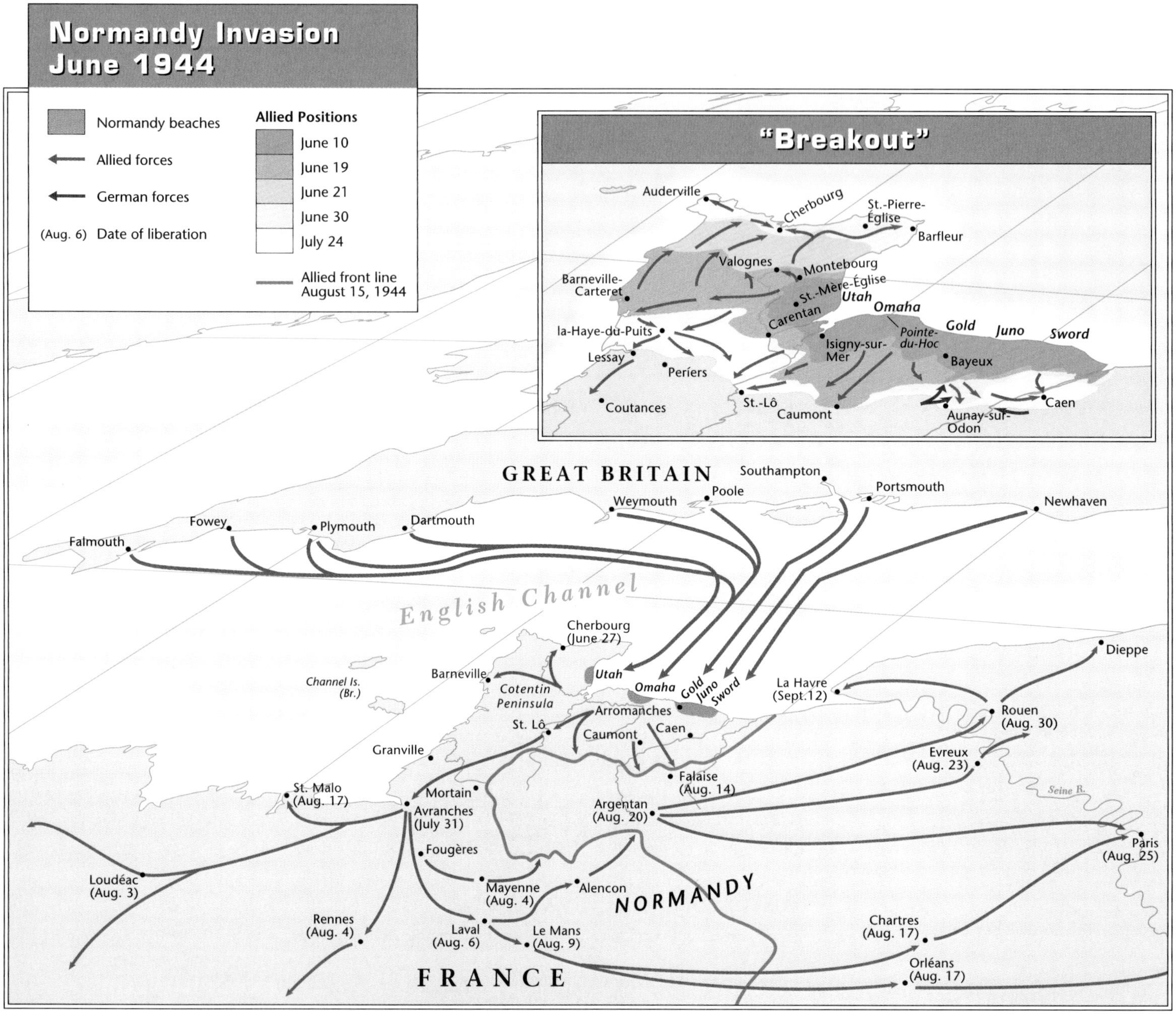

Normandy Invasion
June 1944

Legend:
- Normandy beaches
- ← Allied forces
- ← German forces
- (Aug. 6) Date of liberation

Allied Positions
- June 10
- June 19
- June 21
- June 30
- July 24
- Allied front line August 15, 1944

"Breakout"

Auderville • Cherbourg • St.-Pierre-Église • Barfleur
Valognes • Montebourg
Barneville-Carteret • St.-Mère-Église • *Utah* • *Omaha* • *Gold* • *Juno* • *Sword*
la-Haye-du-Puits • Carentan • Pointe-du-Hoc
Lessay • Isigny-sur-Mer • Bayeux
Périers
Coutances • St.-Lô • Caumont • Aunay-sur-Odon • Caen

GREAT BRITAIN

Falmouth • Fowey • Plymouth • Dartmouth • Weymouth • Poole • Southampton • Portsmouth • Newhaven

English Channel

Cherbourg (June 27)
Channel Is. (Br.)
Barneville
Cotentin Peninsula
Utah • *Omaha* • *Gold* • *Juno* • *Sword*
Dieppe
St. Lô • Arromanches • Caen • La Havre (Sept.12)
Granville • Caumont
Rouen (Aug. 30)
Evreux (Aug. 23)
Seine R.
St. Malo (Aug. 17) • Mortain • Falaise (Aug. 14)
Avranches (July 31) • Argentan (Aug. 20)
Paris (Aug. 25)
Fougères
Loudéac (Aug. 3)
Mayenne (Aug. 4) • Alencon
NORMANDY
Rennes (Aug. 4) • Laval (Aug. 6) • Le Mans (Aug. 9)
Chartres (Aug. 17)
FRANCE
Orléans (Aug. 17)

North Sea
GREAT BRITAIN
London
Calais
Cherbourg • Le Havre
Paris
ATLANTIC OCEAN
FRANCE
GERMANY

Joseph Stalin had pushed the Allies to open a second front to relieve pressure on Soviet troops. The Allied offensive in Italy did little to help the Soviets. In November, 1943, Roosevelt and Churchill committed themselves to a major offensive in France. General Eisenhower was given command of what would be the largest invasion fleet in history, and his task was to establish a beachhead from which to launch the final assault on Germany.

The German command knew an attack was imminent, but they could not determine the location. Eisenhower tried to deceive them into thinking that the attack would come at the narrowest part of the English Channel, near Calais. Eisenhower's actual target was farther west in Normandy, between Le Havre and Cherbourg.

The assault began before dawn on June 6, 1944. Airborne troops arrived first and then the armada of nearly 5,000 ships. Four beaches were quickly taken, but there was strong German resistance at "Bloody Omaha." By nightfall, the beaches were secured, but it took a week to link up all five locations.

Allied progress was slower than expected, but the Germans were unable to mount a counteroffensive before the Allies were firmly established. Allied air forces had destroyed the transportation network in northern France, preventing the Germans from sending reinforcements.

Through June and most of July, the Allied advances were confined to the Cotentin Peninsula. Finally, toward the end of the July, U.S. troops, under General Patton, with Allied bomber support were able to break the German defensive perimeter near St.-Lô. They quickly swept southward through Avranches.

Now moving in a broad front, the Allies advanced toward the Seine. On August 25, American forces and Free French armored forces liberated Paris.

Divided Germany 1945–1949

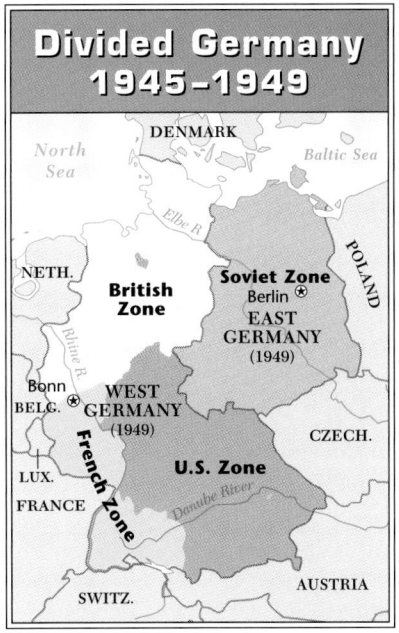

Berlin

European Alliances 1955

NATO nations

Warsaw Pact nations

Other Communist nations

Non-aligned nations

After World War II, the Allies and the Soviet Union disagreed on German policy. Both sides began to organize occupation zones in Germany and Berlin. The western Allies worked to rebuild Germany and, in 1949, West Germany was formed from the former occupation zones.

Facing an increased Soviet threat in Europe, some European nations and the U.S. formed the North Atlantic Treaty Organization (NATO) to provide a common defense. In response, Soviet bloc nations allied themselves in 1955 under the Warsaw Pact.

Israel Since 1947

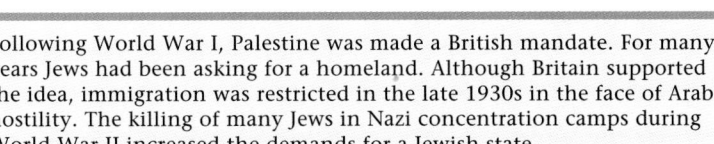

Jewish state under 1947 UN partition plan for Palestine

Acquired by Israel in War of Independence, 1948–1949

Acquired by Israel in Six-Day War, 1967

Self-declared security zones

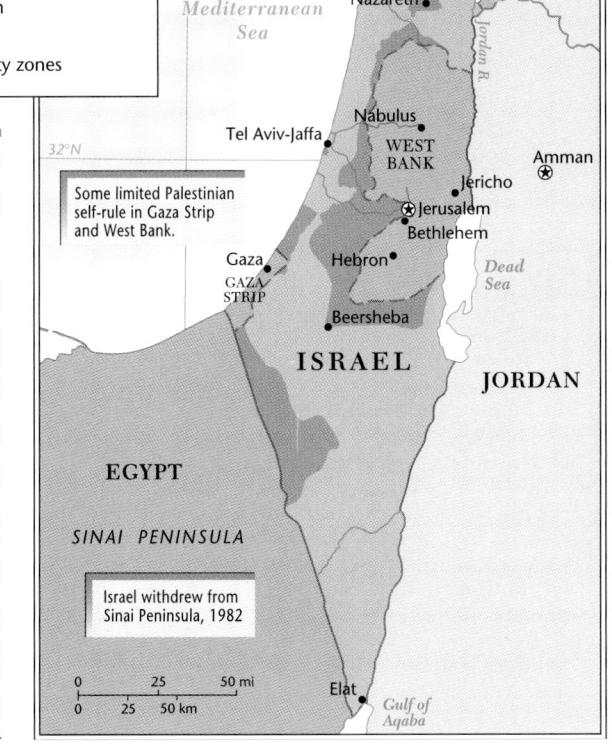

Following World War I, Palestine was made a British mandate. For many years Jews had been asking for a homeland. Although Britain supported the idea, immigration was restricted in the late 1930s in the face of Arab hostility. The killing of many Jews in Nazi concentration camps during World War II increased the demands for a Jewish state.

In 1947, the UN proposed a plan to divide Palestine into two states: one Arab and one Jewish. From the very beginning, the new state of Israel had to fight, not only for survival, but for its right to exist.

In 1948–1949, Israel fended off attacks from Arab neighbors and seized much of the land for the planned Arab state in Palestine. Many Arabs fled or were expelled. There developed a great bitterness towards Israel and its main benefactors—Britain and the United States.

For many years border clashes continued. These escalated into the Six-Day War in 1967, and Israel quickly demonstrated its military superiority. The next war occurred in 1973. Although it was a victory for Israel, the economy suffered and many Israelis questioned the government's role in the war.

In territories that the Israelis had taken, the Palestinian population remained hostile. During the late 1980s, a widespread series of violent demonstrations known as the *Intifada* (uprising) erupted.

In 1993, Israel inaugurated plans for giving self-rule to the Gaza Strip and the West Bank.

Chinese Civil War, 1947–1949

Areas Occupied by Communists

- By April 1947
- By July 1948
- By 1949

← Spread of communism

- ✪ Communist capital, 1949
- ★ Nationalist capitals
- ⊛ Nationalist capital 1949

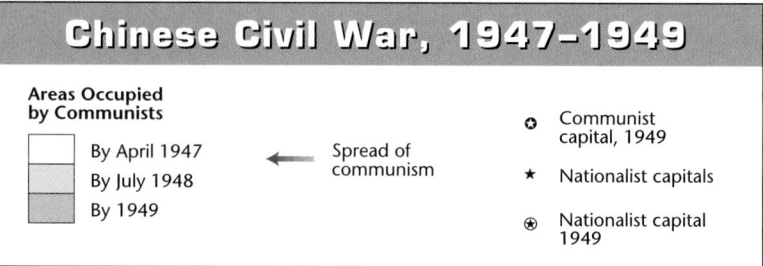

During World War II, Japan had expanded through northern China, but lacked the manpower to actually control such a large area. The Communist Chinese stepped into this vacuum.

When the war ended, the Communist and Nationalist Chinese struggled for control of the country. The U.S. needed an ally in the region to counterbalance the newly resurgent Soviet Union and attempted to get the two sides to reconcile their differences. But neither side saw the other as deserving a role in China's future.

The Communists had preached a social revolution and with their superior forces, they drove the Nationalists southward. Eventually the Nationalists fled to the island of Taiwan. On October 1, 1949, Mao Zedong proclaimed the establishment of the People's Republic of China.

With China now a communist state, the rebuilding of Japan took on added importance because the U.S. needed a strong ally in East Asia.

Korean War, 1950–1953

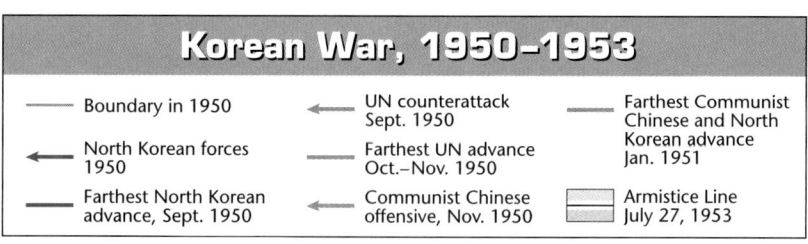

— Boundary in 1950

← North Korean forces 1950

— Farthest North Korean advance, Sept. 1950

← UN counterattack Sept. 1950

— Farthest UN advance Oct.–Nov. 1950

← Communist Chinese offensive, Nov. 1950

— Farthest Communist Chinese and North Korean advance Jan. 1951

▨ Armistice Line July 27, 1953

After World War II, Soviet troops occupied Korea north of the 38th parallel, and American troops occupied the south. The people of the south established the Republic of Korea, and the Soviets installed a communist government in the north. Both sides claimed the entire country, and border clashes were common.

In June, 1950, North Koreans attacked across the 38th parallel. The Soviet role had been debated, and President Truman saw this attack as a case of blatant Soviet aggression. A UN resolution condemned North Korea, and called for a collective-security action.

Early North Korean successes were reversed, and Truman felt the time had come to unify the two nations by force. China warned the U.S. against invading North Korea, but General MacArthur convinced Truman that there was nothing to fear. The UN forces advanced to the Yalu River, but were routed by a massive Communist Chinese winter attack.

UN forces were able to stabilize the front near the 38th parallel. Truman's policy of containment had been successful, but his plans for liberation were not. Peace talks began in July, 1951, and would drag on for two years.

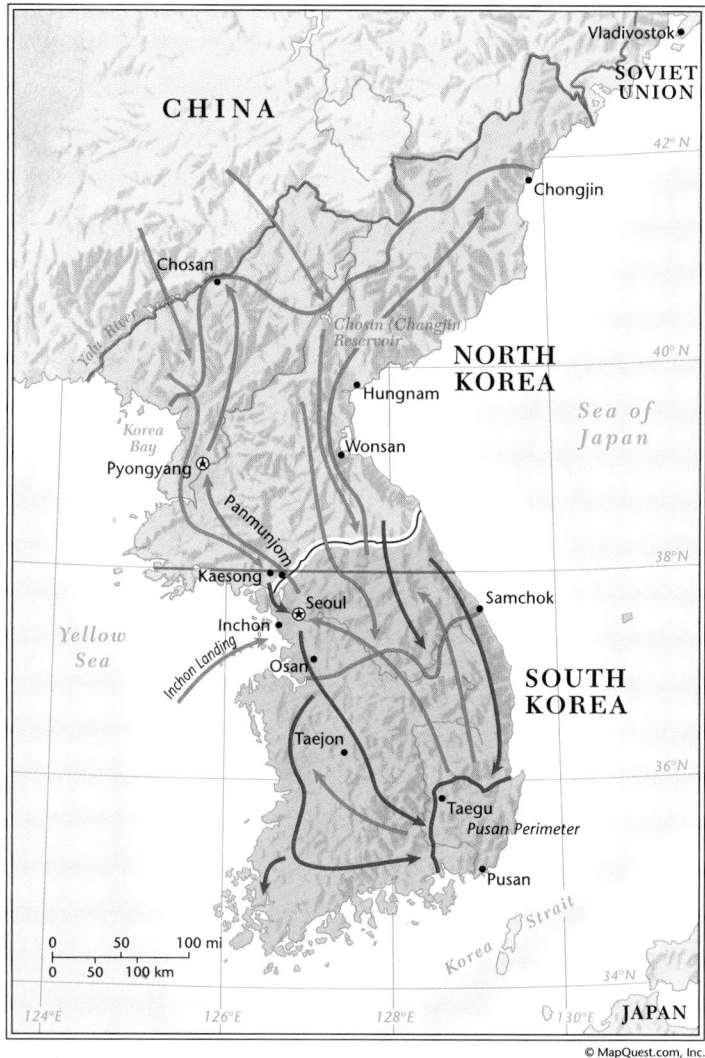

© MapQuest.com, Inc.

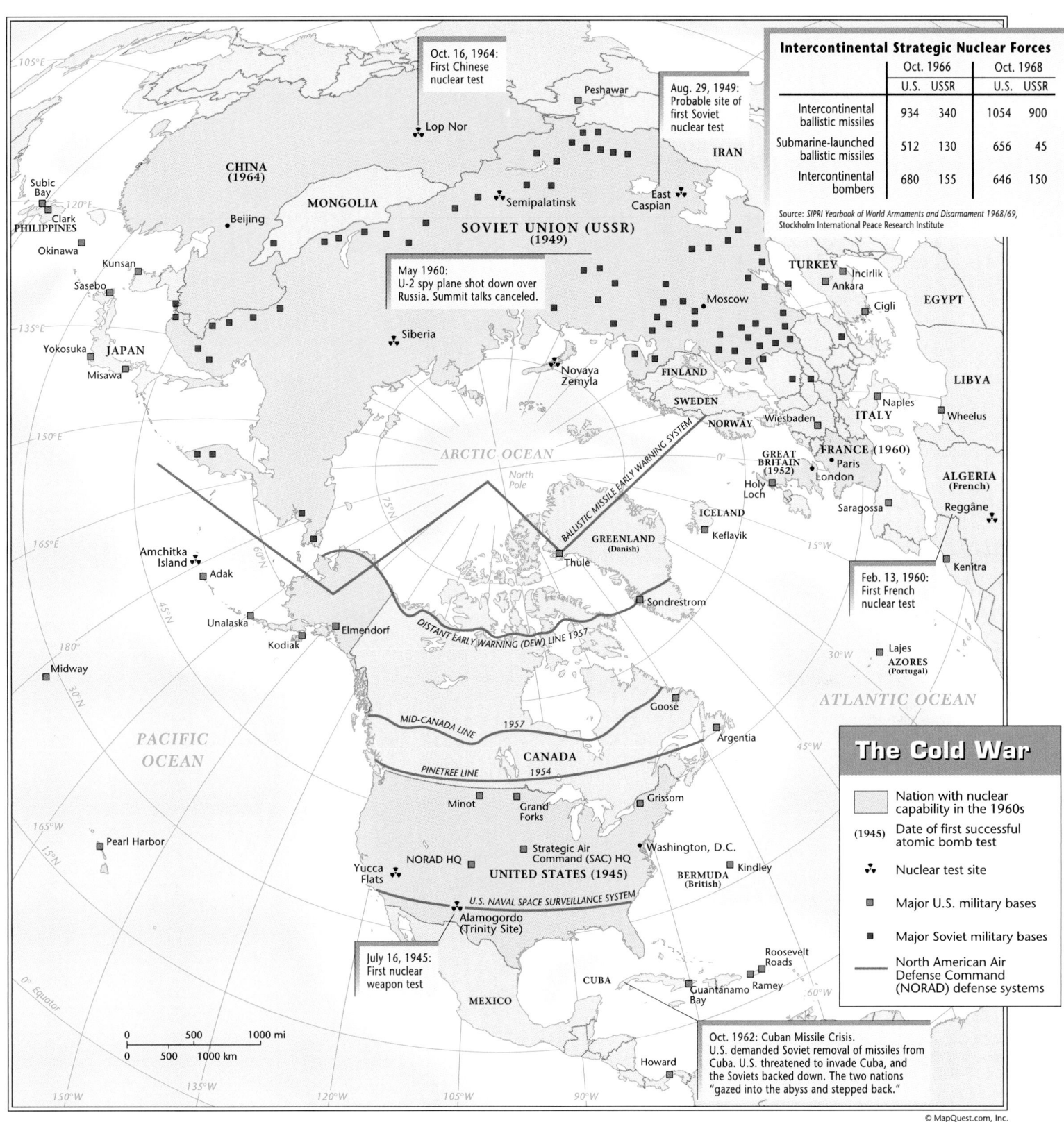

Intercontinental Strategic Nuclear Forces

	Oct. 1966		Oct. 1968	
	U.S.	USSR	U.S.	USSR
Intercontinental ballistic missiles	934	340	1054	900
Submarine-launched ballistic missiles	512	130	656	45
Intercontinental bombers	680	155	646	150

Source: *SIPRI Yearbook of World Armaments and Disarmament 1968/69,* Stockholm International Peace Research Institute

Oct. 16, 1964: First Chinese nuclear test

Aug. 29, 1949: Probable site of first Soviet nuclear test

May 1960: U-2 spy plane shot down over Russia. Summit talks canceled.

Feb. 13, 1960: First French nuclear test

July 16, 1945: First nuclear weapon test

Oct. 1962: Cuban Missile Crisis. U.S. demanded Soviet removal of missiles from Cuba. U.S. threatened to invade Cuba, and the Soviets backed down. The two nations "gazed into the abyss and stepped back."

The Cold War

- Nation with nuclear capability in the 1960s
- (1945) Date of first successful atomic bomb test
- Nuclear test site
- Major U.S. military bases
- Major Soviet military bases
- North American Air Defense Command (NORAD) defense systems

© MapQuest.com, Inc.

After World War II, the Soviet Union continued to expand its power by instituting communist governments in many eastern European nations. In the face of this growing threat, the U.S. continued military aid to its western allies.

In 1949 the Soviets exploded their first nuclear bomb, and the nuclear arms race began. New strategies were being developed to deal with new weapons. "Massive retaliation" was one means by which the U.S. would counter any communist aggression. In the mid-1950s, both sides realized the disastrous effects of nuclear war and relations settled into a pattern of "peaceful coexistence."

The Cold War continued: tensions would ease, but then something would occur that increased the friction. Did the Cold War end in 1992 when Russia and the United States declared that they no longer viewed each others as enemies?

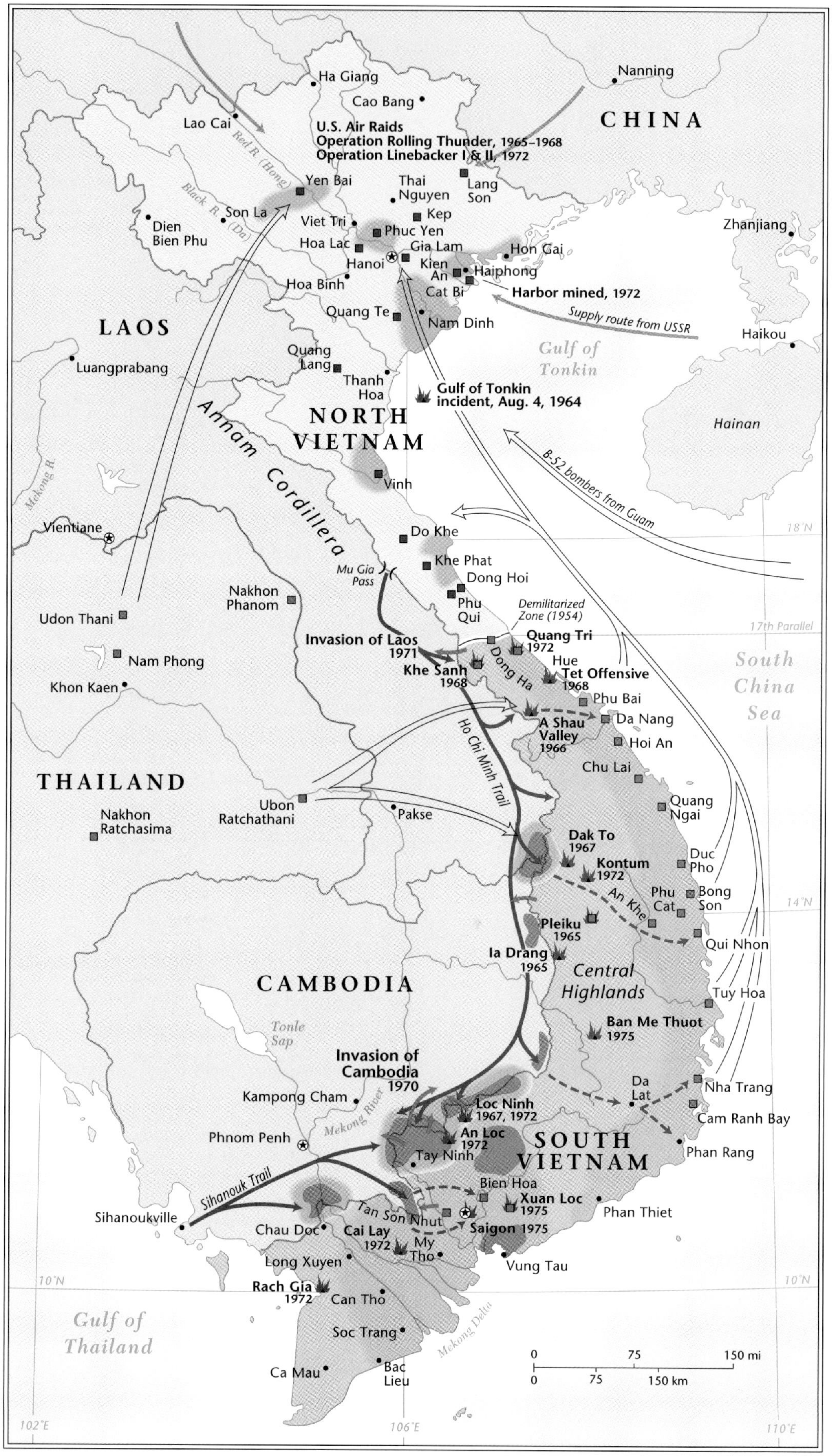

Vietnam War

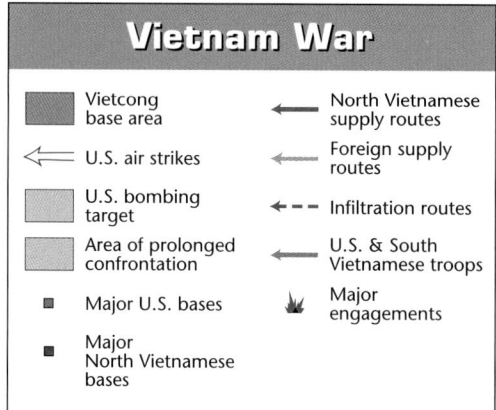

■ Vietcong base area	← North Vietnamese supply routes
← U.S. air strikes	← Foreign supply routes
U.S. bombing target	◄- - Infiltration routes
Area of prolonged confrontation	← U.S. & South Vietnamese troops
■ Major U.S. bases	✷ Major engagements
■ Major North Vietnamese bases	

After Japan's defeat in World War II, Ho Chi Minh and the *Vietminh* organized a revolt to fight the French attempt to reestablish control. War broke out and the French were defeated in 1954. The peace treaty divided the country in two until elections could be held to reunify the country. Ho Chi Minh set up a communist regime in the north. The government in the south was anti-communist and supported by the United States. Free elections were never held.

Vietnamese who were loyal to Ho and remained in the south were called the *Vietcong*, or Vietnamese Communists. Supplied from the north, they began to attack the South Vietnamese army. U.S. support to the South was mostly military; very little went to the people.

American military advisors had been in South Vietnam since the late 1950s. Presidents Kennedy and Johnson continued the commitment to "save" South Vietnam. Johnson wanted a free hand to fight a more aggressive war. After hearing that two destroyers had been attacked, Congress passed the Gulf of Tonkin Resolution in 1964. Although it was not a declaration of war, Johnson used it to increase U.S. involvement.

The U.S. hoped that its superior firepower would convince the North Vietnamese to stop fighting. Knowing they were deficient in firepower, the North Vietnamese avoided direct battles and depended on guerrilla warfare. In contrast to previous American wars, it was a war without fixed front lines.

President Nixon's plan to get the U.S. out of the war was called "Vietnamization." The direct American role would be reduced, while expanded aid would be given to the South Vietnamese forces. In 1972, a North Vietnamese invasion brought South Vietnam close to collapse. The U.S. stepped up its bombing of the north. Both sides suffered greatly and peace negotiations, which had stalled earlier, began again.

On January 27, 1973, a peace treaty was signed. The U.S. withdrew its troops and later decreased its military aid. North Vietnam took advantage of this, and attacked. On April 30, 1975, South Vietnam surrendered.

Soviet Ethnic Groups

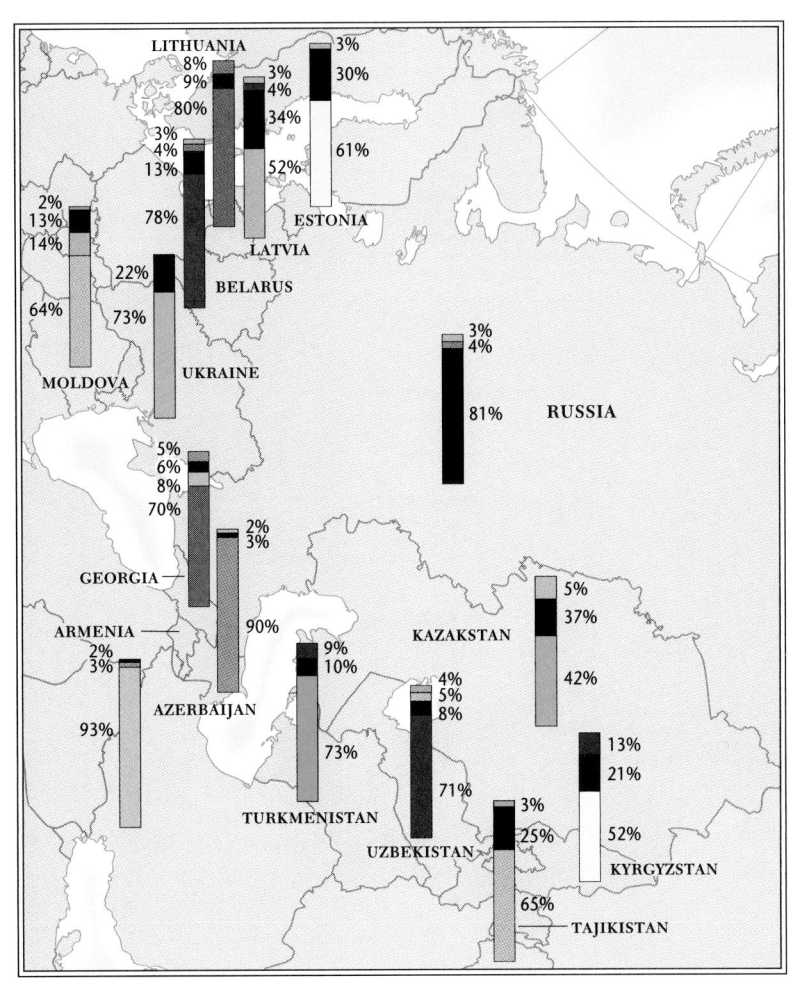

Percentage of Total Population

5%	The height of the bars is consistent throughout and does not represent the total population. Therefore, the numbers do not add up to 100 percent.
37%	
42%	

Major Ethnic Groups

- Armenian
- Azeri
- Bulgarian
- Byelorussian
- Estonian
- Georgian
- Kazak
- Kirghiz
- Latvian
- Lithuanian
- Moldavian
- Polish
- Russian
- Tajik
- Tatar
- Turkmen
- Ukrainian
- Uzbek

Source: *World Factbook 1995*, Central Intelligence Agency,

When the Soviet Union was created, it consisted of a number of multicultural republics. The monolithic nature of the Soviet state made this easy to forget.

In 1985, Mikhail Gorbachev became head of the Communist Party. In 1988, he stated that "Freedom of choice was a universal principle." The next year Poland held free elections. In 1990, Lithuania, Latvia, and Estonia began the process of separation from the Soviet Union. Borders were literally coming down.

If the Soviet government allowed a degree of self-determination for its former satellites in Eastern Europe, how could it deny some measure of the same to its own republics? The people of the Baltic, central Asia, and the Caucasus had voiced grievances since the formation of the country.

A number of republics demanded greater freedom. Even Russia declared that its laws took precedence over those of the Soviet government. In mid-1991, the republics were given a degree of self-government. By the end of the year, it was declared that the Soviet Union no longer existed.

© MapQuest.com, Inc.

Breakup of the Soviet Union

——	Boundary of the former Soviet Union
▨	Former East European satellites of Soviet Union

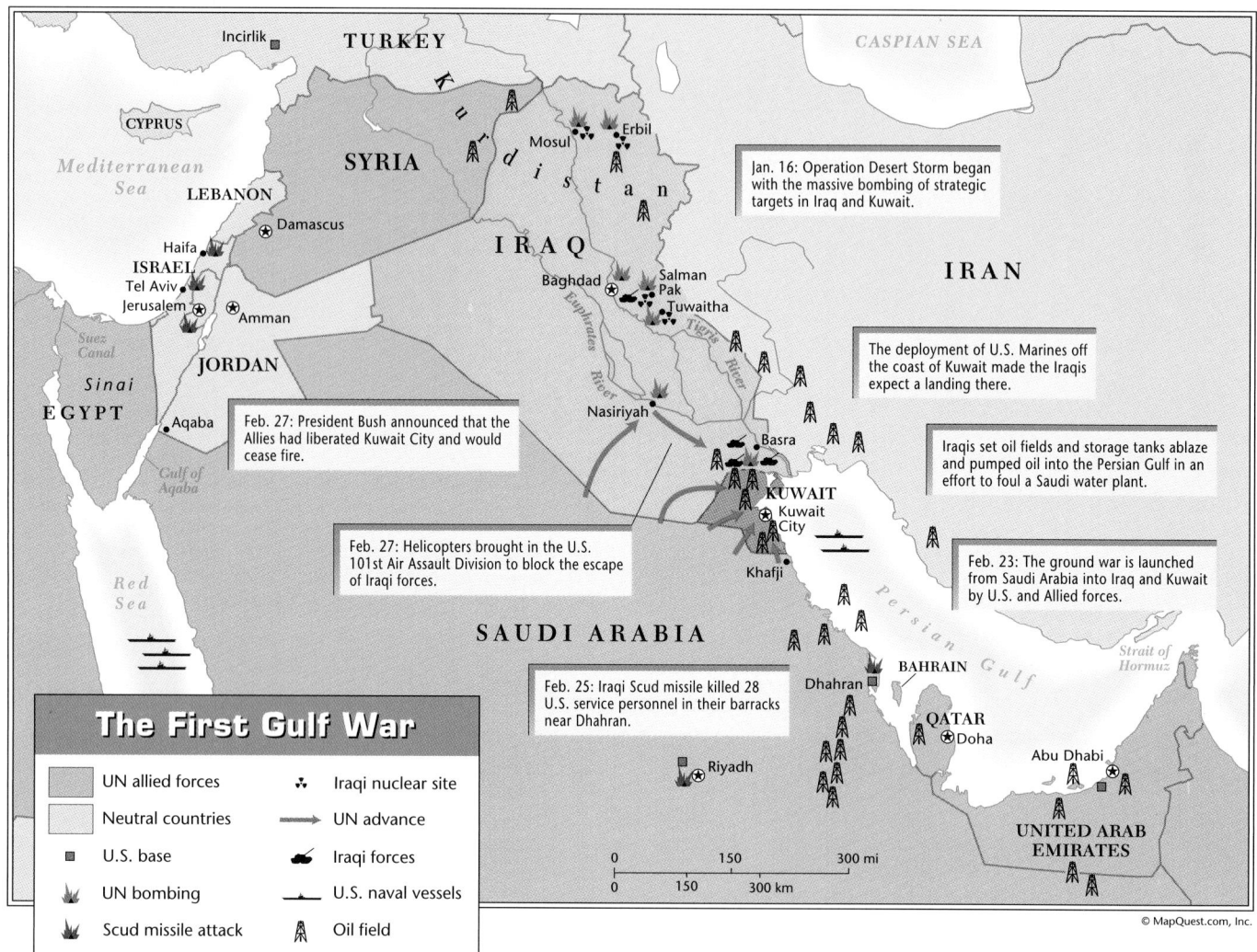

The First Gulf War

Legend:
- UN allied forces
- Neutral countries
- ■ U.S. base
- UN bombing
- Scud missile attack
- ❖ Iraqi nuclear site
- → UN advance
- Iraqi forces
- U.S. naval vessels
- Oil field

Jan. 16: Operation Desert Storm began with the massive bombing of strategic targets in Iraq and Kuwait.

The deployment of U.S. Marines off the coast of Kuwait made the Iraqis expect a landing there.

Iraqis set oil fields and storage tanks ablaze and pumped oil into the Persian Gulf in an effort to foul a Saudi water plant.

Feb. 27: President Bush announced that the Allies had liberated Kuwait City and would cease fire.

Feb. 23: The ground war is launched from Saudi Arabia into Iraq and Kuwait by U.S. and Allied forces.

Feb. 27: Helicopters brought in the U.S. 101st Air Assault Division to block the escape of Iraqi forces.

Feb. 25: Iraqi Scud missile killed 28 U.S. service personnel in their barracks near Dhahran.

© MapQuest.com, Inc.

On August 2, 1990, Iraq invaded and overran neighboring Kuwait. The United Nations immediately demanded Iraq's withdrawl and imposed a trade embargo that shut down virtually all trade with Iraq. On August 7, the United States began sending troops to the Persian Gulf to defend Saudi Arabia from a possible Iraqi attack. Operation *Desert Shield* was the name utilized for the American deployment. On the following day, August 8, Iraq declared Kuwait an annexed Iraqi province. However, the U.N. declared such annexation void and approved an international military response to liberate Kuwait if Iraq did not withdraw by January 15, 1991.

Given Iraq's failure to withdraw from Kuwait by the U.N. deadline, a coalition of 39 NATO and Middle Eastern countries, led by the United States, launched bomb and missile attacks on strategic targets in Iraq; renaming the mission *Desert Shield*. Iraq responded by launching "Scud" missiles into Israel in an effort to draw the Israelis into the conflict, thereby possibly undermining Arab participation in the coalition. The Iraqi strategy failed, as American diplomacy persuaded Israel not to retaliate in exchange for the deployment of anti-missile systems, known as "Patriots". Live news coverage of these attacks and the ensuing war made this the first war in history to be viewed on television, internationally, as it was fought.

In addition to launching "Scuds" at populated targets in Saudi Arabia and Israel, Iraq ignited hundreds of oil wells in Kuwait, creating massive oil slicks in the Persian Gulf. Horrific ecological damage resulted from this Iraqi effort.

After over a month-long air campaign against Iraq, the coalition's ground offensive began on February 23. The Iraqis, expecting coalition assualts from the sea and into Kuwait from Saudi Arabia, were caught by surprise due to American flanking maneuvers. Unknown to Iraqi military leaders, the U.S. had deployed its ground forces westward, opposite Iraq, in order to surround the Iraqi troops in Kuwait and cut off their lines of supply, reinforcement, and retreat.

Kuwait City was first liberated by Arab forces, driving north from Saudi Arabia along the Kuwaiti coast, on February 27. Due to the rout and mass surrender of Iraqi troops, the coalition ended military operations only 100 hours after the ground attack had begun. Coalition forces flew more than 116,000 air sorties during this brief war. The coalition suffered a loss of 370 lives whereas estimates of Iraqi deaths approach as high as 100,000.

Iraq agreed to the provisions of a cease-fire that took effect on April 11. However, Iraq failed to respect many of the terms of the cease-fire agreement, resulting in continued conflict with the United States through the 1990s.

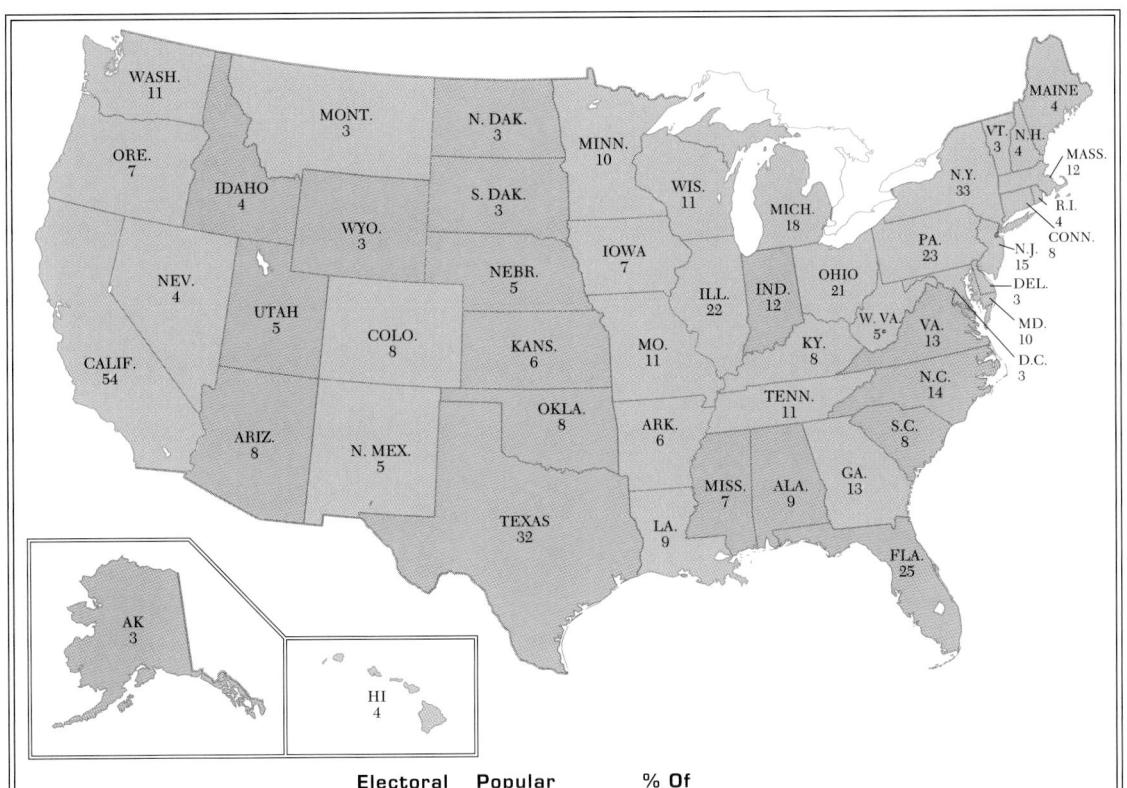

© MapQuest.com, Inc.

Candidate	Party	Electoral Vote	Popular Vote	% Of Popular Vote
Bush	Republican	168	38,117,331	36.46
Clinton	Democratic	370	43,682,624	41.78
Perot	Independant		19,217,213	18.38
Other candidates			3,535,568	3.38

*West Virginia had one electoral vote go to Lloyd Bentsen.

Source: Federal Election Commission

The Electoral College was set up in the Constitution as the body that elects Presidents and Vice Presidents of the United States. Each state appoints as many electors as it has Senators and Congressional Representatives. The electors are chosen by political parties and are elected by voters.

The Constitution requires that an elector may vote for only one candidate who is a resident of his same state. A majority of 270 electoral votes is necessary to elect the President and Vice President. If no candidate receives a majority, the House of Representatives chooses the President (with each state casting one vote) from the three top candidates. Similarly, if no Vice Presidential candidate receives a majority, the Senate chooses from the top two candidates (with each state casting one vote). Due to the nature of this system, a candidate with a majority of the popular vote may still not be elected by the Electoral College, as occured in the 2000 election.

Electoral College Cartogram

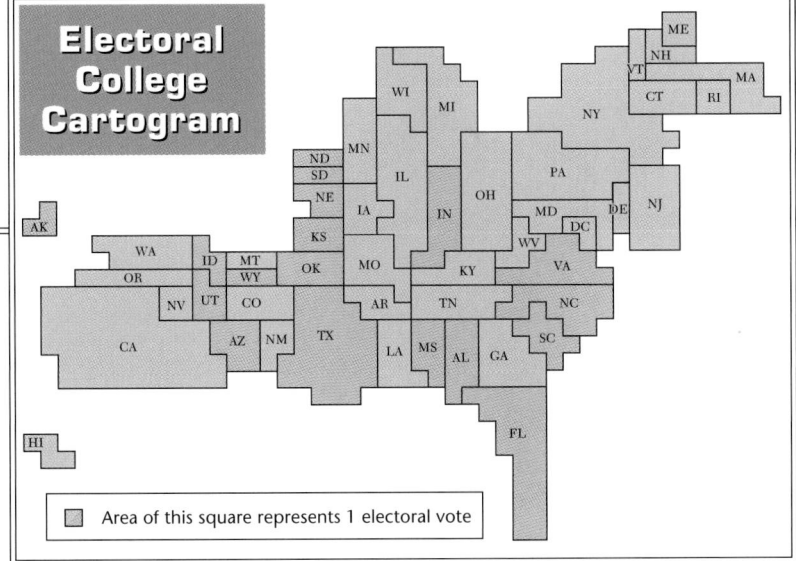

Area of this square represents 1 electoral vote

President Bush's Job Approval Rating

Source: The Gallup Poll Public Opinion 1991, 1992

Although President George Bush had enjoyed sweeping political popularity in 1991 as a result of the American-led expulsion of Iraq from Kuwait in February; persistent economic stagnation, beginning in 1990, began to erode Bush's public support. Criticism mounted as Bush's optimistic assessments of an economic recovery failed to materialize. Democratic challenger Bill Clinton campaigned on the theme of a need for change and a new generation of leadership, chastising Bush for neglecting domestic matters. Independent candidate Ross Perot polled well at the onset of his campaign, attacking Bush on the mounting federal deficit, until he unexpectedly withdrew then reentered the race.

By Election Day in November, Clinton's focus on domestic issues won for him the 1992 election with a plurality of votes and a decisive Electoral College victory, thereby ending 12 years of Republican occupancy of the White House. Perot won the largest percentage of votes for a third-party candidate since 1912.

The Balkans in 1914

The Balkans in 1919

© MapQuest.com, Inc.

The Ottoman Empire controlled most of the Balkan Peninsula by 1400 A.D. In the 1800s the peoples of the Balkans began to seek independence.

The First Balkan War started in 1912, when Bulgaria and Serbia made a secret alliance to wage war on the Ottomans and divide the territory they would win. This first war culminated in a May 1913 peace treaty, overseen by the United Kingdom, France, and Austria-Hungary, that forced the Ottoman Empire to surrender almost all of its territory in Europe (except the European portion of Turkey). The Ottomans loss was to the territorial benefit of Serbia, Bulgaria, and Greece. The Second Balkan War began a

month later due to continued discord among the Balkan peoples over boundaries. Though this second conflict lasted only five weeks, it caused terrible losses. The Treaty of Bucharest, in August 1913, created as many disputes as it solved, paving the way for World War I to break out in 1914.

In the treaty agreements following World War I, an attempt was made to consider national groups in creating new states within the former Austro-Hungarian Empire. However, most of these new nations, especially Yugoslavia, ended up with substantial national minorities within its bounds. This would cause friction between the different religious and ethnic groups in the Balkans in future years.

Balkan Ethnic Groups

- Albanians
- Bulgarians
- Croatians
- Hungarians
- Macedonians
- Montenegrins
- Bosnians or Sandzak Muslims
- Romanians
- Serbs
- Slovenes
- No majority present
- —— Yugoslavia in 1991
- –·–·– Republic boundaries
- – – – Autonomous region boundaries

Following World War II, led by Communist partisan Josip Tito, a new constitution in Yugoslavia organized the nation as a federal state in which the six republics oversaw most internal affairs. Tito and the Communist Party firmly ruled the nation until his death in 1980. No new political entity appeared during the 1980s to unite the country. As a result, once dormant nationalist movements and ethnic tensions grew. By 1990 the Communist party formally voted to end its monopoly on power in the country.

Slovenia and Croatia declared independence in June 1991. The Serbian-led Yugoslav Army attacked Slovenia the next day, but a truce was concluded after two weeks, allowing Slovenia to secede from the federation. The war was not protracted in Slovenia due to its relatively homogenous ethnic population in comparison to other parts of the country.

At the onset of the war in Croatia, Serbs comprised about 10% of the population. By the end of 1991, Serb secessionists, with the support of the Yugoslav army, had gained control of almost 30% of Croatian territory. In January 1992, the warring parties signed a truce providing for the introduction of U.N. peacekeeping forces to maintain order. The last Serb troops left Croatia in 1998 under supervision of the United Nations.

The ethnic composition of Bosnia-Herzegovina was much more mixed as Yugoslavia began to unravel. Muslims accounted for roughly 40% of the population in the republic, Serbs 30% and Croats 20%. A Muslim-Croat supported referendum on independence in February 1992 was rejected by the Serbian minority, who vowed to militarily resist the secession. During the first few weeks of the ensuing conflict, the Yugoslav army played a direct role in the fighting in Bosnia, both on the ground and in aerial attacks on Muslim and Croat towns. Later the Yugoslav army withdrew, but continued to provide air cover to the Bosnian Serb forces. Given this aid, the Serbs drove Muslims and Croats out of their villages in a process known as *ethnic cleansing*. After three years of intense fighting among the parties, the republic remained geographically unified, though politically divided between the parties.

Following separatist ambitions in Kosovo, which is 90% ethnic Albanian, the U.N. interceded on behalf of the Kosovars in 1999. Kosovo's final status has yet to be determined, though the U.N. has transferred an increasing number of responsibilities to the province's provisional institutions.

Breakup and Conflict in Yugoslavia

- —— Boundary of the former Yugoslavia
- 1991 Date of independence
- ⚔ Major engagements

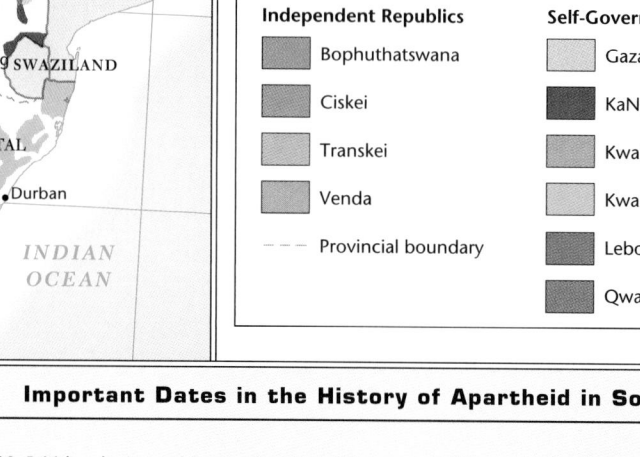

South Africa Provinces and Homelands Before 1993

Independent Republics
- Bophuthatswana
- Ciskei
- Transkei
- Venda
- - - - Provincial boundary

Self-Governing Territories
- Gazankulu
- KaNgwane
- KwaNdebele
- KwaZulu
- Lebowa
- QwaQwa

© MapQuest.com, Inc.

In the Afrikaans language, the word *apartheid* means separateness.

Important Dates in the History of Apartheid in South Africa

1910 British colonies and former Boer Republics create the Union of South Africa; blacks denied vote; areas that are now Lesotho and Swaziland remain British protectorates until the 1960s

1948 Afrikaner National Party wins control of the government and apartheid becomes law

1960 Anti-apartheid uprisings culminate in the Sharpeville massacre of 69 black protestors by government troops; African National Congress (ANC) banned

1961 South Africa becomes a republic and leaves the British Commonwealth

1963 Nelson Mandela and other ANC leaders receive life imprisonment sentences

1976 Violent uprisings erupt in Soweto when students organize protests against the use of the Afrikaans language in black schools

1977 Steve Biko, leader of the Black Consciousness Movement, is tortured to death by police while in custody

1985 Government declares state of emergency

1990 President F.W. de Klerk lifts ban on the ANC and restrictions on other anti-apartheid groups; Nelson Mandela freed from prison

1992 Last all-white election is held, giving government the authority to negotiate a new constitution with the ANC and other groups; political violence escalates during the negotiating phase

1993 Transitional constitution ends apartheid system

1994 First multi-racial, democratic election held in South African history; Mandela becomes president

In 1948, South Africa officially adopted the racist, separatist system of apartheid that had existed unofficially since Dutch and British colonization. The white South African minority used apartheid until the early 1990s to control, oppress, and persecute the vast non-white majority. Under the apartheid system, South Africans were classified by their race as black, white, colored (mixed race), or Asian. Non-whites had limited rights to own and occupy land, were not allowed to vote or run for any political office, were very limited in the occupations they could pursue, were paid less than whites for similar work, and could not travel freely within the country without documentation. Opposition protests, boycotts, strikes, and demonstrations led to horrific government-supported and intraracial violence during the apartheid years.

International opposition to and condemnation of apartheid caused South Africa to become more and more isolated in the world community. In 1962 the United Nations urged its members to break political and economic ties with South Africa until apartheid was abolished.

Slow to respond to domestic and international pressure, the South African government continued to violently suppress the African National Congress (ANC) and other anti-apartheid groups. The first significant step to repeal apartheid laws came in 1984, when a new constitution extended voting rights to the colored and Asian minorities. In the second half of the 1980s, however, violence escalated and a state of emergency was in force. It was not until 1990 that newly elected South African President F.W. de Klerk lifted the ban on the ANC and restrictions on other opposition groups and freed political prisoners, including ANC leader Nelson Mandela.

In 1991 the last of the apartheid laws were repealed and the country entered into a period of transition that saw new violence erupt as various groups sought political power. The black "homelands" that had been created under the 1913 Native Lands Act–where 13% of the territory was reserved for 75% of the population– by the Afrikaners were dissolved and incorporated into a nine region national system.

The country's first multi-racial general election was held in 1994 with the ANC winning 63% of the vote and Nelson Mandela becoming president. The ANC, under the leadership of Thabo Mbeki, retained the presidency in the general elections held in 1999.

The effects of decades of segregation, terror and upheaval continue despite apartheid's repeal. The Mandela and Mbeki governments have made efforts to improve the economic and educational opportunities available to all South Africans as well as address crimes and grievances during the apartheid period in order to combat continued discrimination.

After World War II, key European leaders became convinced that the only way to foster lasting peace between their nations was to unite them economically and politically.

In 1951 the European Coal and Steel Community (ECSC) was formed by six nations (Belgium, France, Italy, Luxembourg, the Netherlands, and West Germany); and in 1957 these same members formed the European Economic Community (EEC), creating a common market economy that represented the West's largest trading entity. A European Parliament was founded in 1967. The Maastricht Treaty created the European Union (EU) in 1992, and the Euro was adopted as the EU's common currency.

The EU will welcome ten new member nations in 2004, and there are three applicant countries pending, as well as 17 other, non-member countries.

© MapQuest.com, Inc.

European Union

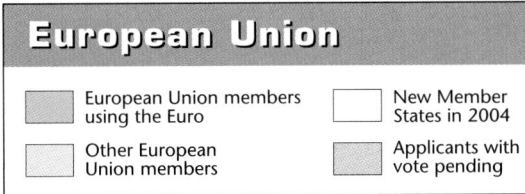

- European Union members using the Euro
- Other European Union members
- New Member States in 2004
- Applicants with vote pending

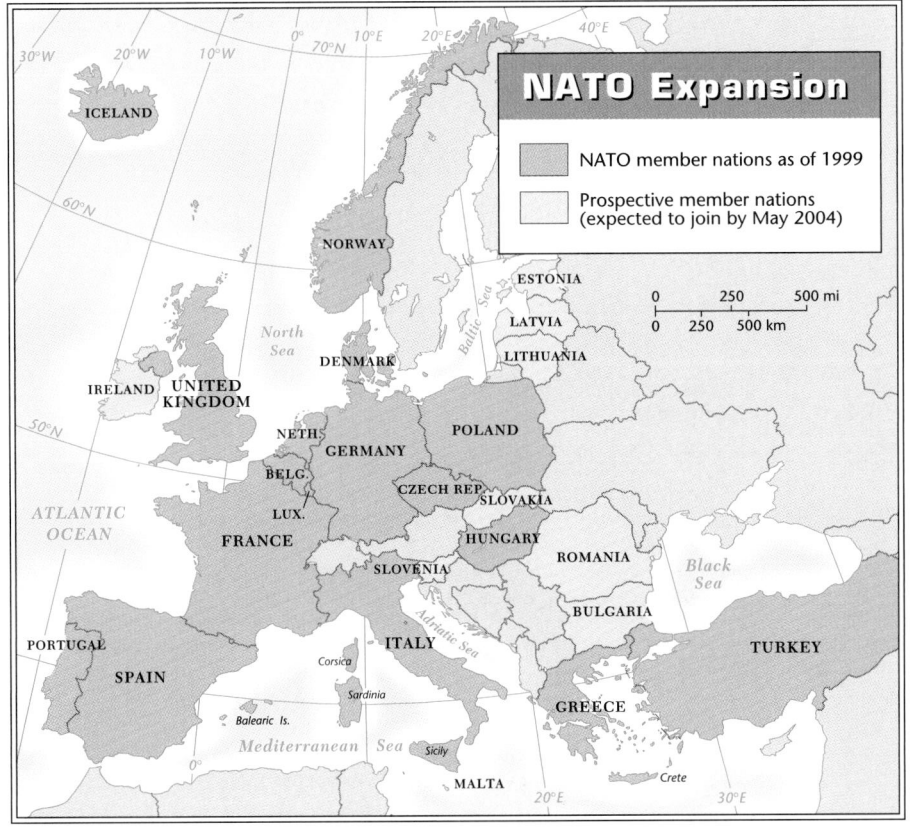

NATO Expansion

- NATO member nations as of 1999
- Prospective member nations (expected to join by May 2004)

NATO Partners
(Euro-Atlantic Partnership Council)

Albania	Ireland	The Former Yugoslav Republic of Macedonia
Armenia	Kazakhstan	
Austria	Kyrghyz Republic	Tadjikistan
Azerbaijan	Moldova	Turkmenistan
Belarus	Russia	Ukraine
Croatia	Sweden	Uzbekistan
Finland	Switzerland	

The North Atlantic Treaty Organization (NATO) is an alliance of 19 countries from North America and Europe committed to fulfilling the goals of the North Atlantic Treaty that was signed on April 4, 1949. In accordance with the treaty, the fundamental role of NATO is to safeguard the freedom and security of its member countries by political and military means.

Since the end of the Cold War, NATO has developed partnerships with neighboring countries to encourage dialogue and cooperation between NATO and non-NATO nations. During the last 15 years, NATO has also played an increasingly important role in crisis management and peacekeeping. NATO is also deepening and broadening its cooperation with partner countries (see box), and is developing a strategic partnership with the European Union.

© MapQuest.com, Inc.

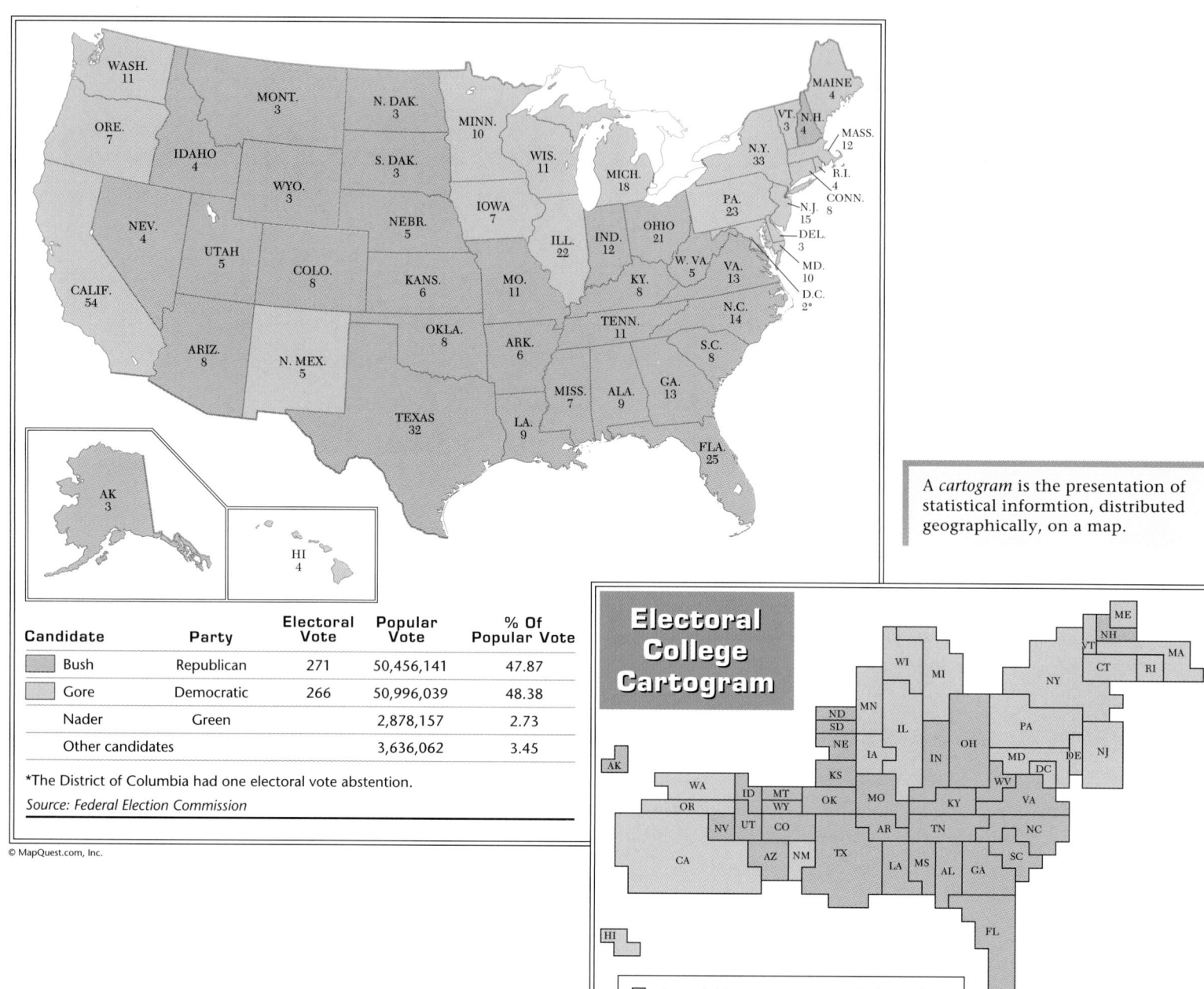

A *cartogram* is the presentation of statistical informtion, distributed geographically, on a map.

Candidate	Party	Electoral Vote	Popular Vote	% Of Popular Vote
Bush	Republican	271	50,456,141	47.87
Gore	Democratic	266	50,996,039	48.38
Nader	Green		2,878,157	2.73
Other candidates			3,636,062	3.45

*The District of Columbia had one electoral vote abstention.

Source: Federal Election Commission

© MapQuest.com, Inc.

Electoral College Cartogram

Area of this square represents 1 electoral vote

The U.S. presidential election of November 7, 2000 was one of the closest and most controversial elections in the history of the United States. Vice President Al Gore, the Democratic candidate, received some 540,000 more popular votes than his Republican opponent, Texas Governor George W. Bush. Yet Gore lost the election.

The key to this unusual outcome was who won Florida's 25 electoral votes. Early in the evening of the election, television newscasters predicted that Gore would win Florida, then recanted that prediction as additional precincts reported, showing Bush taking the lead in votes. Gore phoned Bush, about to concede the election, only to see the vote count rise again in his own favor. The vote was so close that Florida law called for a recount of votes. Because voting machines did not always count votes on ballots that were partially punched and left a small *chad* of paper dangling, Gore requested that ballots be recounted by hand rather than by machine in four counties where the results were in dispute. Bush protested the recounts. On November 26, Florida Secretary of State Katherine Harris declared that Bush had won the Florida vote, despite the fact that only two of the four counties recounting ballots had turned in final results. Gore contested Harris' decision, and the Florida Supreme Court ordered a hand recount of all state ballots that had not registered a vote for president by machine. Bush appealed the Florida Supreme Court's ruling to the U. S. Supreme Court and, on December 12, the U.S. Supreme Court voted 5 to 4 that the Florida recounts should not continue because there was not a consistent statewide standard for recounting votes. Thus, on December 13, Gore conceded the election to Bush.

War in Afghanistan

Areas Controlled by Northern Alliance

- By November 5, 2001
- By November 12, 2001
- By November 17, 2001
- By December, 2001

U.S. bombing
Northern Alliance movement
Taliban movement

© MapQuest.com, Inc.

In December 1979, Soviet troops invaded Afghanistan and installed a pro-Soviet government. Aided by the United States, armed Islamic opposition groups, called *mujahidin*, fought against the Soviet and pro-Soviet Afghan forces; causing the government to collapse in 1992.

The victorious mujahidin forces declared an Islamic state. However, fighting between different factions of the mujahidin and the rise to power of the Taliban–composed of armed, religious students–led to the Taliban capturing Kabul, executing the former president, and creating a severe, fundamentalist Islamic government in 1996. Those opposing the Taliban retreated northwards and formed the Northern Alliance from the four primary mujahidin groups. By the end of the 1990s, the Taliban controlled 90% of the country, leaving the Northern Alliance in possession of a small area northeast of Kabul.

In March 2001, the Taliban, thought to be supported by Pakistan and Saudi Arabia, was severely condemned by the international community for destroying precious ancient monuments that it deemed un-Islamic. Soon afterwards, the Taliban refused to extradite known Saudi terrorist Osama bin Laden to the United States to face charges connected to the 1998 bombings of American embassies in Kenya and Tanzania. Bin Laden's al Qaeda organization was also the prime suspect in conducting the terrorist attacks on the United States on September 11, 2001. Repeated demands for bin Laden's extradition were refused by the Taliban. As a result, American and British forces launched air strikes against Taliban and al Qaeda targets on October 7, 2001.

The Taliban regime quickly collapsed as the number of air strikes mounted and the Northern Alliance advanced upon Kabul and other major cities. In December 2001, representatives of numerous anti-Taliban factions met at United Nations-sponsored talks, and named a multiethnic interim government to be led by Pashtun tribal leader Hamid Karzai. After six months as interim president, Karzai was voted to lead the transitional government in June 2002. Due to ongoing violence and assassination attempts, Karzai is heavily guarded and a U.N.-authorized multinational security force remains in Afghanistan.

Despite intense efforts by the United States to locate and capture Osama bin Laden and Taliban leader Mullah Omar, by early 2004 neither had been found.

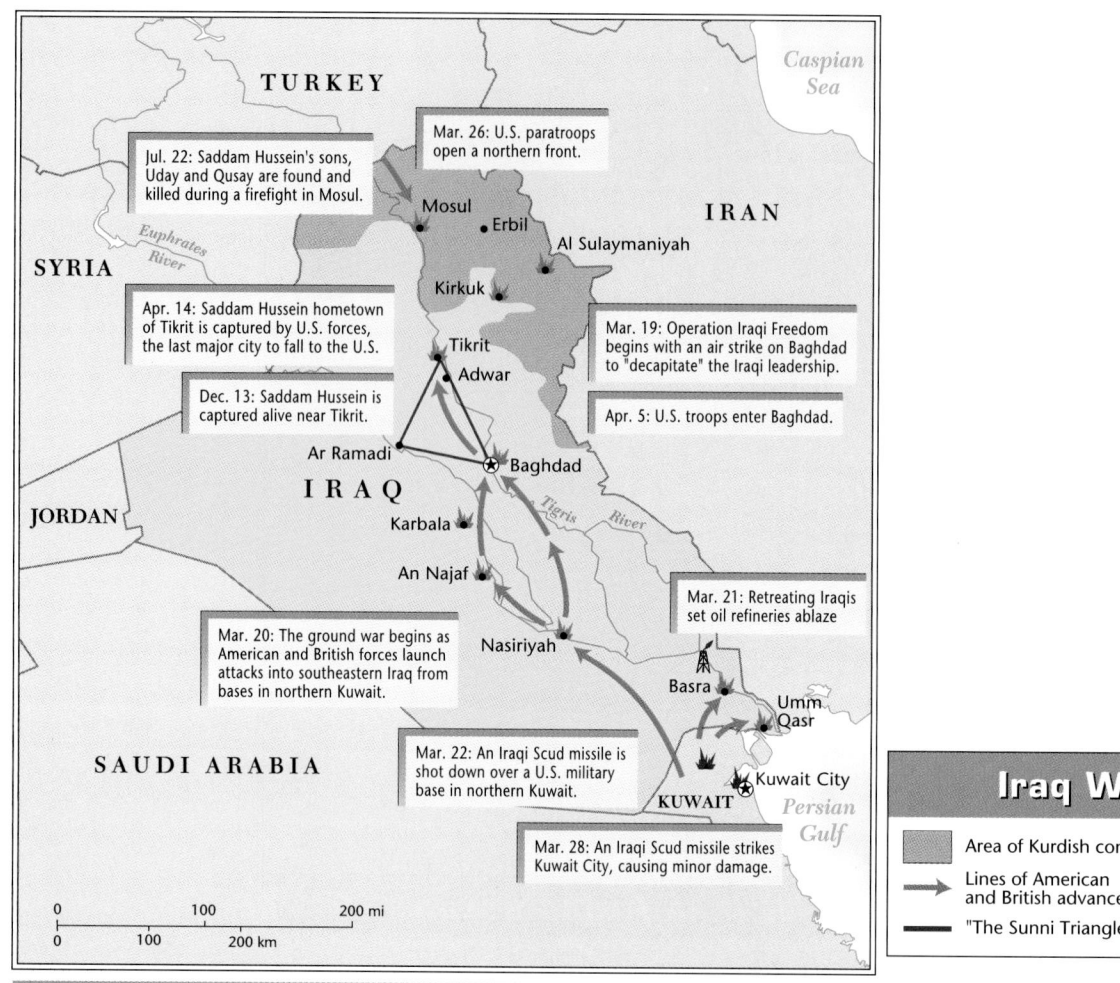

Jul. 22: Saddam Hussein's sons, Uday and Qusay are found and killed during a firefight in Mosul.

Mar. 26: U.S. paratroops open a northern front.

Apr. 14: Saddam Hussein hometown of Tikrit is captured by U.S. forces, the last major city to fall to the U.S.

Mar. 19: Operation Iraqi Freedom begins with an air strike on Baghdad to "decapitate" the Iraqi leadership.

Dec. 13: Saddam Hussein is captured alive near Tikrit.

Apr. 5: U.S. troops enter Baghdad.

Mar. 21: Retreating Iraqis set oil refineries ablaze

Mar. 20: The ground war begins as American and British forces launch attacks into southeastern Iraq from bases in northern Kuwait.

Mar. 22: An Iraqi Scud missile is shot down over a U.S. military base in northern Kuwait.

Mar. 28: An Iraqi Scud missile strikes Kuwait City, causing minor damage.

Iraq War, 2003

- Area of Kurdish control
- Lines of American and British advance
- "The Sunni Triangle"
- Major battles
- Scud missile attack

© MapQuest.com, Inc.

The ongoing and escalating conflict between the United States and Iraq during the 1990s culminated in another war with Iraq beginning in March 2003.

President George W. Bush's justification for war varied in the months preceeding the conflict as he sought to gain U.N. and allied support. Generally, the issues surrounded Iraq's failure to abide by United Nations resolutions and inspections concerning its alleged weapons of mass destruction (WMD) programs and Iraq's support of international terrorist groups–including al Qaeda. International support of American policy was not as forthcoming as it had been during the Gulf War in 1991. American and British troops, numbering over 300,000, made up the bulk of the invading force; with much smaller contingents from Australia and Poland.

The Iraq War began on the evening of March 19, 2003 with an air strike on one of Hussein's Baghdad palaces, where he was believed to be staying. Though unsuccessful in decapitating the Iraqi leadership at the onset of the war, the ground campaign began the following day as forces moved into Iraq from bases in northern Kuwait. Countering sporadic Iraqi resistance, by March 22 American forces were already halfway to Baghdad. Advance elements of American troops, advancing on routes along the Tigris and Euphrates rivers, entered Baghdad on April 5. Hussein's threat to use chemical and biological weapons in a final battle on the outskirts of Baghdad never materialized. The U.S. continued its advance north on Tikrit, capturing it on April 14. Tikrit had served as the center of Ba'ath Party support and was Saddam Hussein's hometown.

On May 1, President Bush declared that the major hostilities in Iraq had ended, although Hussein had not been captured and skirmishes between coalition troops and Saddam-loyalists continued. Instead, the U.S. and its partners would refocus on the task of rebuilding the Iraqi infrastructure damaged during the war, searching for Iraqi political and military leaders and weapons of mass destruction, and beginning the process of establishing a democratic Iraqi regime.

On July 22, Saddam's sons, Uday and Qusay Hussein, were killed in a firefight with U.S. forces in the city of Mosul. Their role in their father's reign of terror was significant and, in an effort to convince a skeptical Iraqi public that the two had really been killed, the Pentagon released graphic photos and video footage of their dead bodies. International and domestic criticism of the war and its aftermath mounted against President Bush and British Prime Minister Tony Blair as the summer and fall stretched on without the capture of Hussein, mounting coalition casualties, and a lack of hard evidence of a WMD weapons program.

In an unexpected discovery, Saddam was captured in a camoflaged tunnel underground near Tikrit on December 13. Taken alive, he is currently awaiting his fate as a prisoner of war. Unfortunately his capture has not marked the end of the conflict or casualties. At the end of January 2004, there had been some 600 coalition deaths, most of which have been Americans though included in that tally are troops from Britain, Bulgaria, Denmark, Italy, Spain, Thailand, and Ukraine. Some 3,000 Americans had been wounded as well.

The effort to rebuild Iraq and return power to the Iraqis has thus far proven to be a massive and complicated effort, especially in an area now commonly known as "the Sunni Triangle". Between Baghdad and Tikrit, it has become the area of heaviest fighting as Iraqis and terrorists from other nations, using a variety of guerrilla tactics, attempt to undermine the coalition occupation.

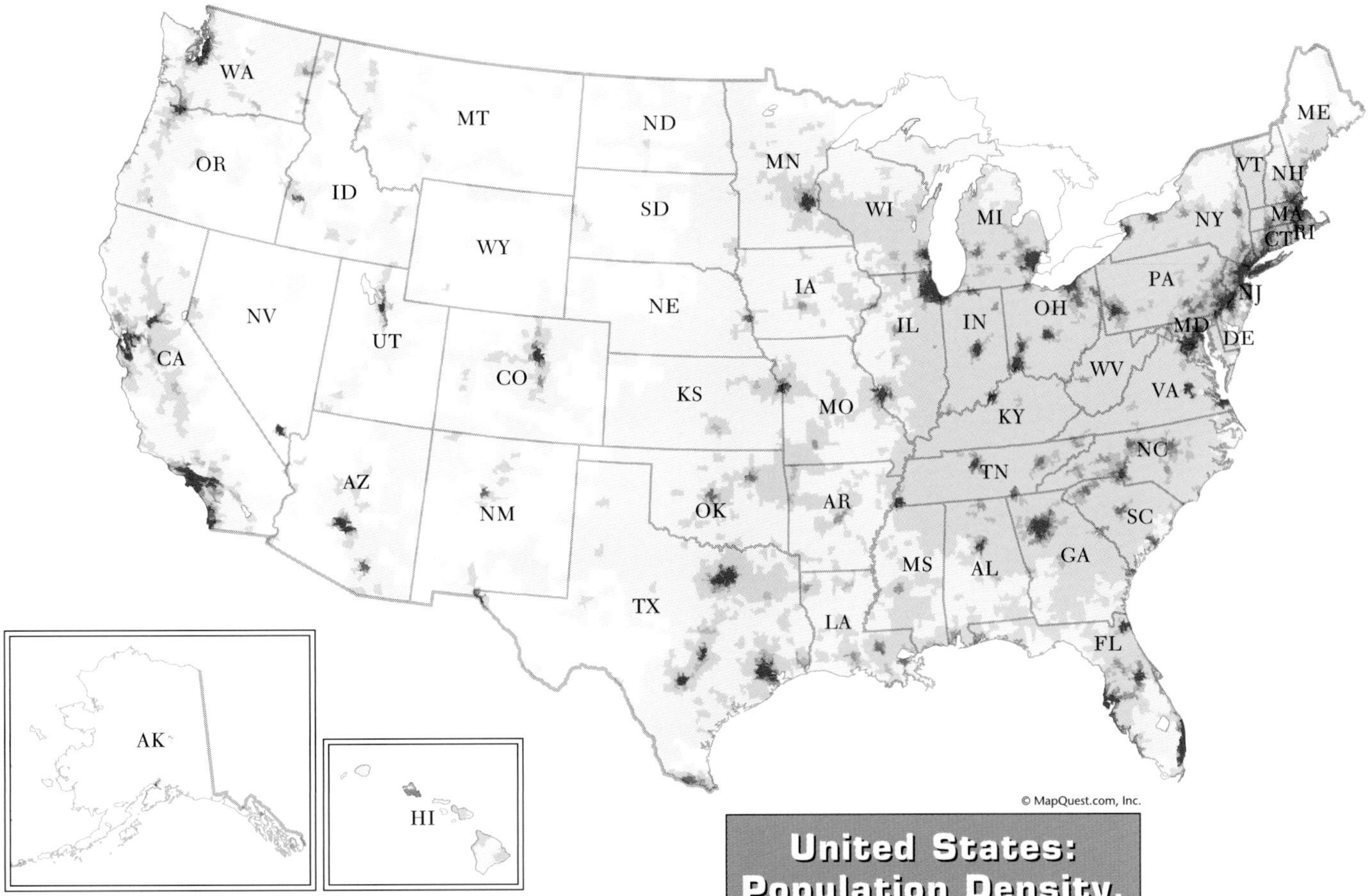

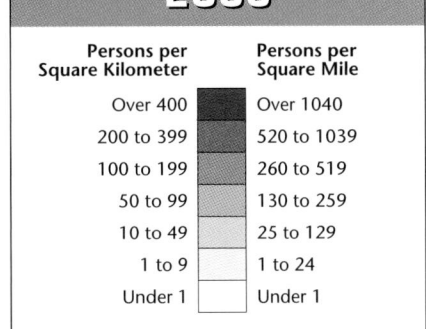

© MapQuest.com, Inc.

United States: Population Density, 2000

Persons per Square Kilometer	Persons per Square Mile
Over 400	Over 1040
200 to 399	520 to 1039
100 to 199	260 to 519
50 to 99	130 to 259
10 to 49	25 to 129
1 to 9	1 to 24
Under 1	Under 1

A new population density map of the United States can be created whenever a census is taken. Although the extent of conurbations continues to grow, it is interesting to note that the basic pattern of settlement has not changed in nearly 100 years.

The Northeast remains the most densely populated region and the West Coast's population pattern is clearly visible. The 20 inch isohyet (rainfall line) runs from North Dakota to Texas and the population pattern still follows this line, which in the past was roughly the division between irrigated and non-irrigated agriculture.

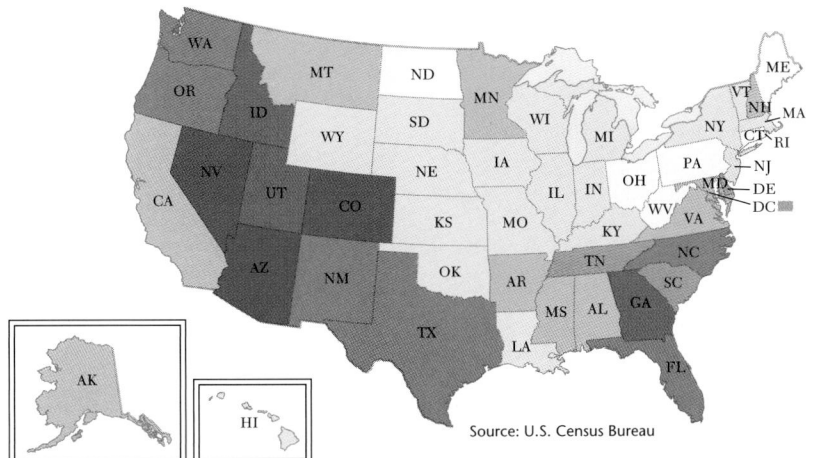

Source: U.S. Census Bureau

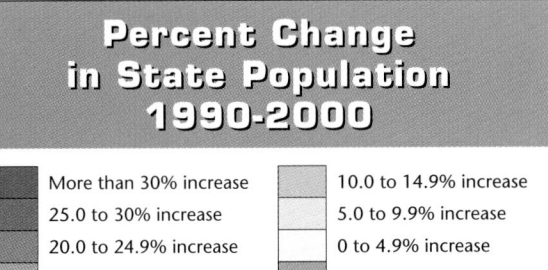

Percent Change in State Population 1990-2000

More than 30% increase	10.0 to 14.9% increase
25.0 to 30% increase	5.0 to 9.9% increase
20.0 to 24.9% increase	0 to 4.9% increase
15.0 to 19.9% increase	Decrease

Current World Issues

Aerial view of Sydney, Australia

World Conflict Today

The United Nations (U.N.) is responsible for maintaining international peace and security; developing friendly relations among nations; cooperating in solving international economic, social, cultural, and humanitarian problems; and in promoting respect for human rights.

Currently the U.N. is involved in several peacekeeping missions (see box) around the world. In the last decade, 90% of conflicts have taken place within, rather than between, states. Many of the disputes in Africa and Asia are border related, a legacy of European colonialism where boundaries disregarded the cultural landscape.

Environmental problems, refugees, organized crime, drug trafficking, and AIDS are all issues that the United Nations views as global problems requiring action. The U.N. is concentrating on emphasizing conflict prevention and strengthening post-conflict peace building between its members.

Though conflict between states has endured for centuries around the world, there has been a rise in unconventional methods of conflict in the late 20th and early 21st centuries. Terrorism and civil disobediance are examples of ways that groups promote their political agendas against national governments.

Current United Nations Peacekeeping Missions

	Date mission began	Strength
AFRICA		
UN Mission for the Referendum in Western Sahara (MINURSO)	April 1991	518
UN Mission in Sierra Leone (UNAMSIL)	Oct. 22, 1999	16,427
UN Organization Mission in the Democratic Republic of the Congo and the subregion (MONUC)	Nov. 30, 1999	12,030
UN Mission in Ethiopia and Eritrea (UNMEE)	July 31, 2000	4,573
UN Mission in Liberia (UNMIL)	September, 2003	5,798
ASIA		
UN Military Observer Group in India and Pakistan (UNMOGIP)	January 1949	117
UN Mission of Support in East Timor (UNMISET)	May 20, 2002	4,290
EUROPE		
UN Peacekeeping Force in Cyprus (UNFICYP)	March 1964	1,407
UN Observer Mission in Georgia (UNOMIG)	August 1993	403
UN Interim Administration Mission in Kosovo (UNMIK)	June 10, 1999	11,249
MIDDLE EAST		
UN Truce Supervision Organization (UNTSO)	May 1948	369
UN Disengagement Observer Force (UNDOF)	May 1974	1,246
UN Lebanon Interim Force in Lebanon (UNIFIL)	March 1978	2,473

Source: United Nations

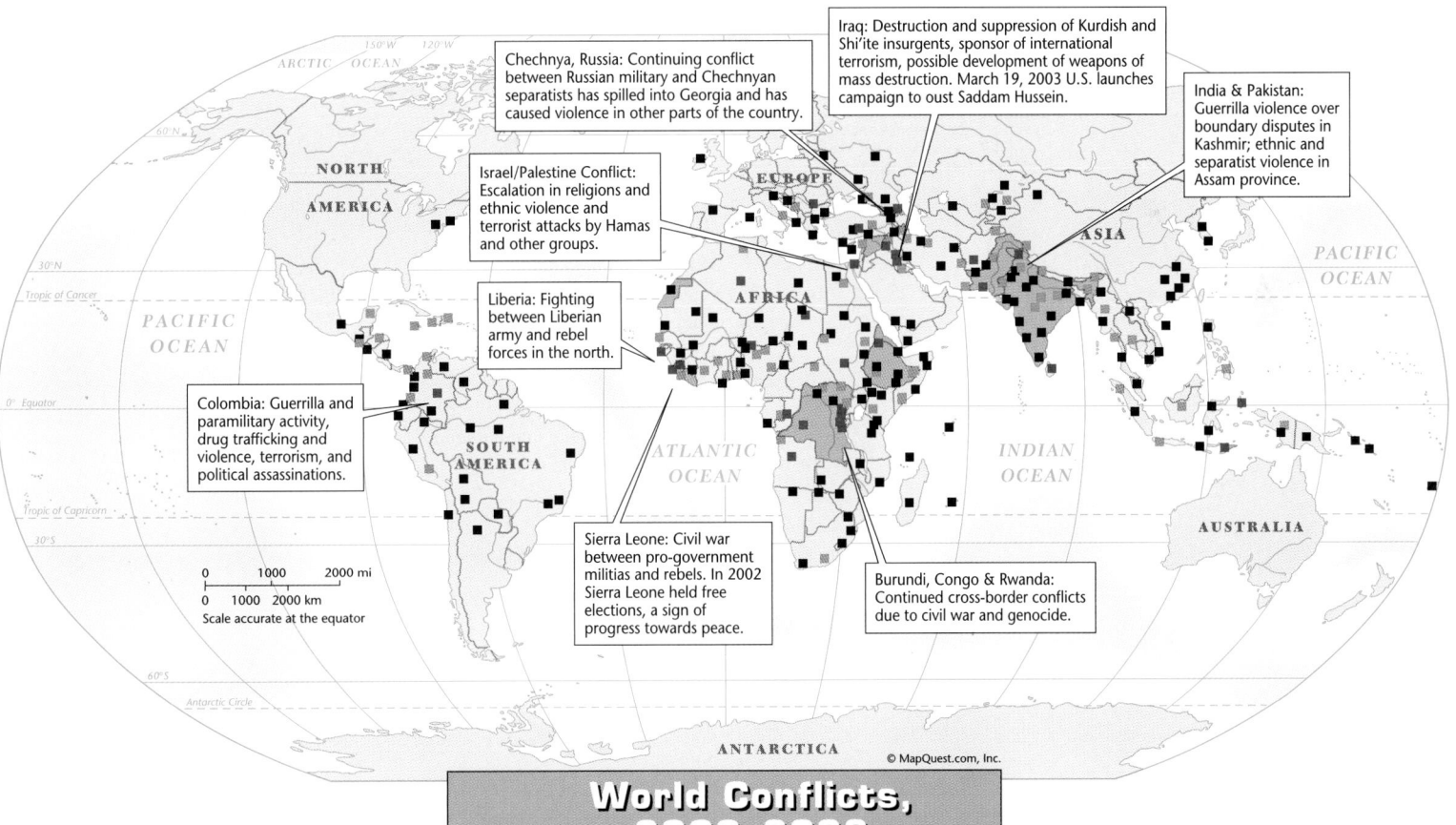

Chechnya, Russia: Continuing conflict between Russian military and Chechnyan separatists has spilled into Georgia and has caused violence in other parts of the country.

Iraq: Destruction and suppression of Kurdish and Shi'ite insurgents, sponsor of international terrorism, possible development of weapons of mass destruction. March 19, 2003 U.S. launches campaign to oust Saddam Hussein.

India & Pakistan: Guerrilla violence over boundary disputes in Kashmir; ethnic and separatist violence in Assam province.

Israel/Palestine Conflict: Escalation in religions and ethnic violence and terrorist attacks by Hamas and other groups.

Liberia: Fighting between Liberian army and rebel forces in the north.

Colombia: Guerrilla and paramilitary activity, drug trafficking and violence, terrorism, and political assassinations.

Sierra Leone: Civil war between pro-government militias and rebels. In 2002 Sierra Leone held free elections, a sign of progress towards peace.

Burundi, Congo & Rwanda: Continued cross-border conflicts due to civil war and genocide.

© MapQuest.com, Inc.

World Conflicts, 2000–2002

- ■ Violent political conflict
- ■ High-intensity conflict
- ■ Low-intensity conflict
- ▨ Countries where the United Nations is involved in Peacekeeping

Source: Interdisciplinary Research Programme on Causes of Human Rights Violations (PIOMM), National Defense Council Foundation

0   1000   2000 mi
0   1000   2000 km
Scale accurate at the equator

Terrorism Today

International terrorism extends to all corners of the world. As globalization brings peoples of all nations together through business and military interests; racial, religious, and political tensions are a source of conflict.

Since 1990, bombings and hijackings have claimed the lives of thousands of people around the world. Since the al Qaeda attack on the United States in 2001, the U.S. has led the effort to form cooperative partnerships with countries around the world to combat terrorism both at home and abroad.

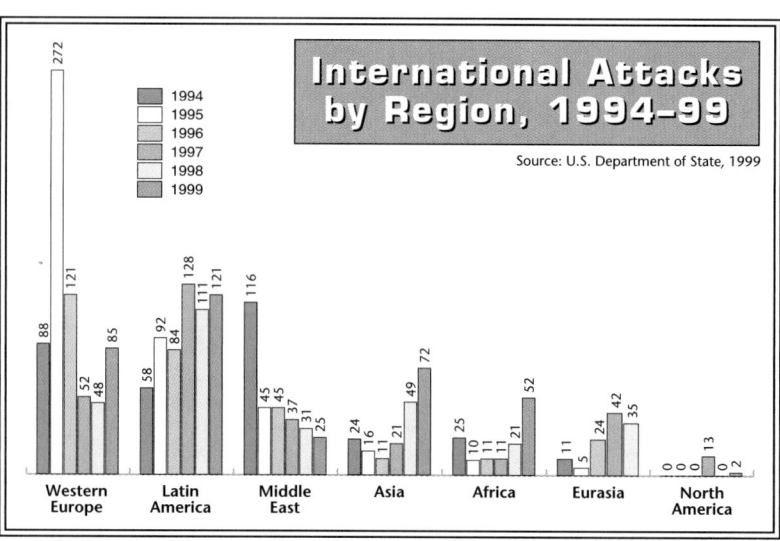

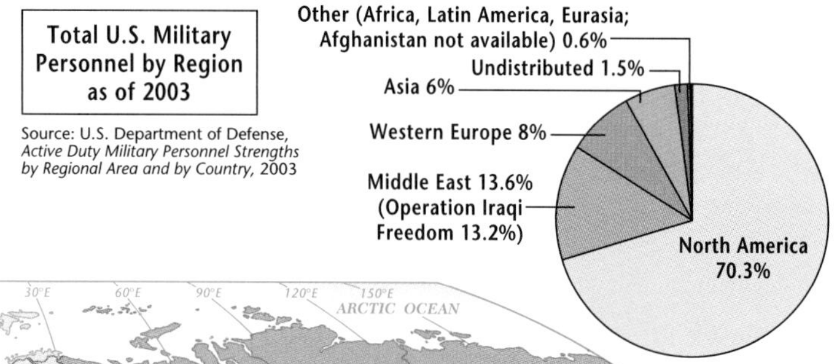

International Attacks by Region, 1994–99

Source: U.S. Department of State, 1999

Legend: 1994, 1995, 1996, 1997, 1998, 1999

Western Europe: 88, 121, 52, 48, 85, 272
Latin America: 58, 92, 84, 128, 111, 121
Middle East: 116, 45, 45, 37, 31, 25
Asia: 24, 16, 11, 21, 49, 72
Africa: 25, 10, 11, 11, 21, 52
Eurasia: 11, 5, 24, 42, 35
North America: 0, 0, 0, 13, 2

Total U.S. Military Personnel by Region as of 2003

Source: U.S. Department of Defense, *Active Duty Military Personnel Strengths by Regional Area and by Country*, 2003

- Other (Africa, Latin America, Eurasia; Afghanistan not available) 0.6%
- Undistributed 1.5%
- Asia 6%
- Western Europe 8%
- Middle East 13.6% (Operation Iraqi Freedom 13.2%)
- North America 70.3%

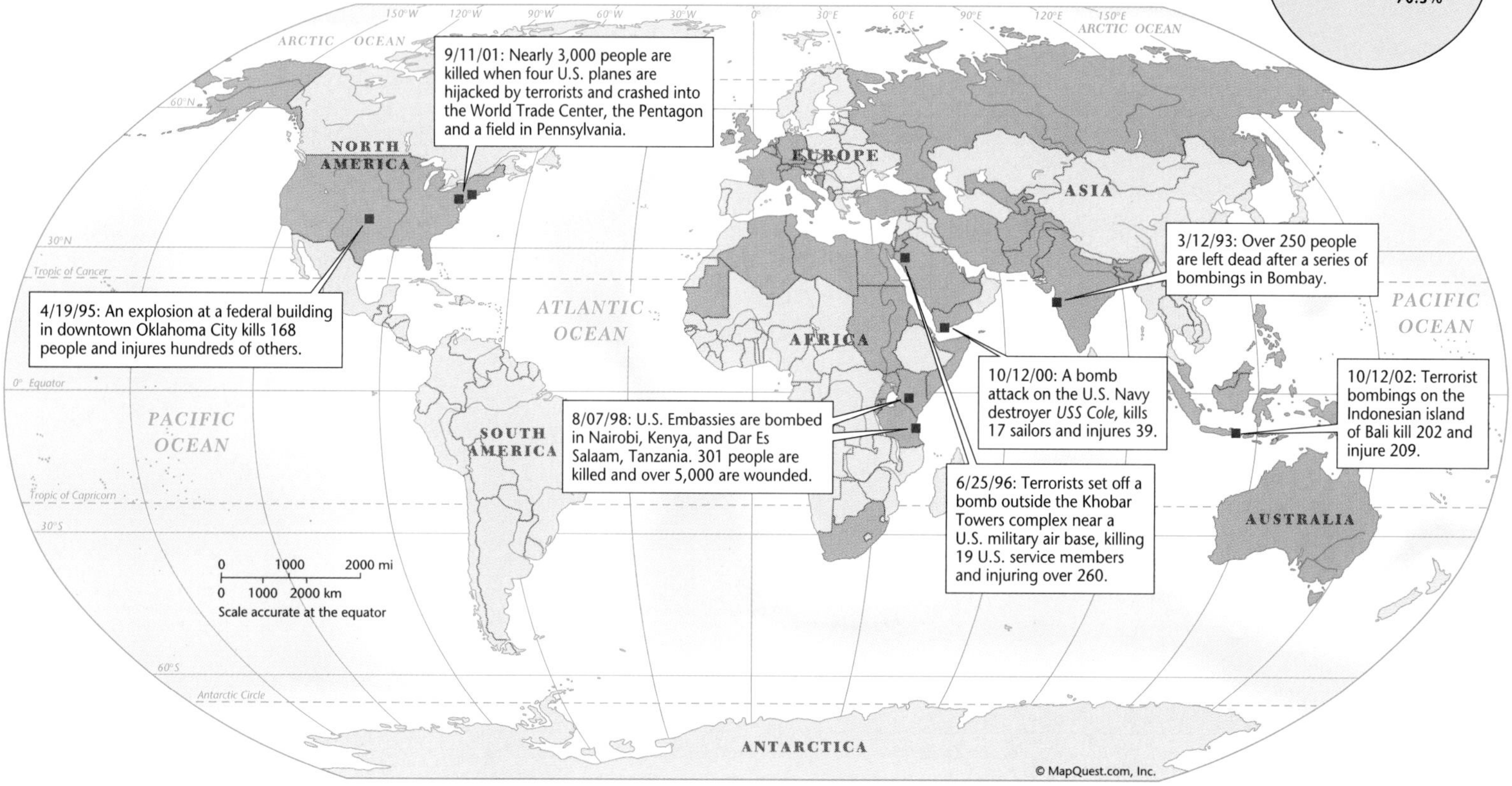

9/11/01: Nearly 3,000 people are killed when four U.S. planes are hijacked by terrorists and crashed into the World Trade Center, the Pentagon and a field in Pennsylvania.

4/19/95: An explosion at a federal building in downtown Oklahoma City kills 168 people and injures hundreds of others.

3/12/93: Over 250 people are left dead after a series of bombings in Bombay.

8/07/98: U.S. Embassies are bombed in Nairobi, Kenya, and Dar Es Salaam, Tanzania. 301 people are killed and over 5,000 are wounded.

10/12/00: A bomb attack on the U.S. Navy destroyer *USS Cole*, kills 17 sailors and injures 39.

6/25/96: Terrorists set off a bomb outside the Khobar Towers complex near a U.S. military air base, killing 19 U.S. service members and injuring over 260.

10/12/02: Terrorist bombings on the Indonesian island of Bali kill 202 and injure 209.

0 1000 2000 mi
0 1000 2000 km
Scale accurate at the equator

© MapQuest.com, Inc.

Terrorist Incidents

- ■ Significant terrorist incident since 1990
- Countries where al Qaeda is known to have operated

Events of the Morning of September 11, 2001

8:45 a.m. (all times are EDT): A hijacked passenger jet, American Airlines Flight 11 out of Boston, Massachusetts, crashes into the north tower of the World Trade Center, tearing a gaping hole in the building and setting it afire.

9:03 a.m.: A second hijacked airliner, United Airlines Flight 175 from Boston, crashes into the south tower of the World Trade Center and explodes. Both buildings are burning.

9:17 a.m.: The Federal Aviation Administration shuts down all New York City area airports.

9:21 a.m.: The Port Authority of New York and New Jersey orders all bridges and tunnels in the New York area closed.

9:30 a.m.: President Bush, speaking in Sarasota, Florida, says the country has suffered an "apparent terrorist attack."

9:40 a.m.: The FAA halts all flight operations at U.S. airports, the first time in U.S. history that air traffic nationwide has been halted.

9:43 a.m.: American Airlines Flight 77 crashes into the Pentagon, sending up a huge plume of smoke. Evacuation begins immediately.

9:45 a.m.: The White House evacuates.

9:57 a.m.: Bush departs from Florida.

10:05 a.m.: The south tower of the World Trade Center collapses, plummeting into the streets below. A massive cloud of dust and debris forms and slowly drifts away from the building.

10:08 a.m.: Secret Service agents armed with automatic rifles are deployed into Lafayette Park across from the White House.

10:10 a.m.: A portion of the Pentagon collapses.

10:10 a.m.: United Airlines Flight 93, also hijacked, crashes in Somerset County, Pennsylvania, southeast of Pittsburgh.

10:13 a.m.: The United Nations building evacuates, including 4,700 people from the headquarters building and 7,000 total from UNICEF and U.N. development programs.

10:22 a.m.: In Washington, the State and Justice Departments are evacuated, along with the World Bank.

10:24 a.m.: The FAA reports that all inbound transatlantic aircraft flying into the United States are being diverted to Canada.

10:28 a.m.: The World Trade Center's north tower collapses from the top down as if it were being peeled apart, releasing a tremendous cloud of debris and smoke.

Casualties of 9/11/01

Airplanes: Total of 265 people killed on four planes

World Trade Center: 2,605 people killed; 6,291 people treated for injuries

Pentagon: 126 staffers killed; 88 people treated for injuries

Source: CNN.com

Terrorist Incidents

The number of foreign-sponsored and domestic terrorist attacks has increased within the United States in recent years. Racial tenions, religious and moral beliefs, and political differences have all been responsible for many *terrorist incidents*, defined by the FBI as any "violent act or an act dangerous to human life, in violation of the criminal laws of the United States, or of any state, to intimidate or coerce a government, the civilian population, or any segment thereof."

Although the terrorist organization al Qaeda is perhaps the most widely publicized in the United States, due to their attacks of September 11, 2001; other domestic groups operate at a much more localized level in terms of their target selection. Much of the increase in domestic terrorism can be attributed to extremist environmental groups in the western United States who attack business, scholarly and governmental institutions.

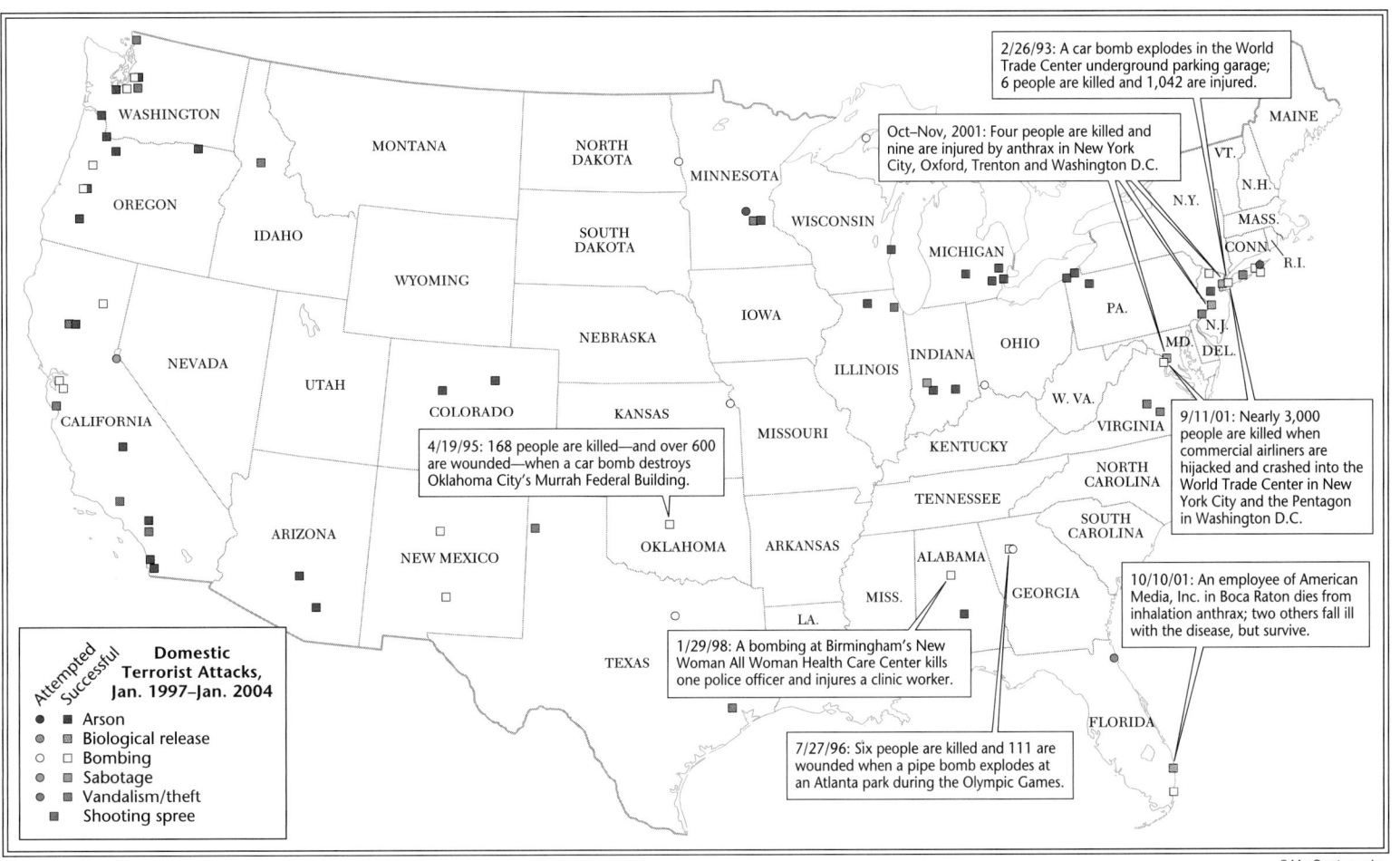

2/26/93: A car bomb explodes in the World Trade Center underground parking garage; 6 people are killed and 1,042 are injured.

Oct–Nov, 2001: Four people are killed and nine are injured by anthrax in New York City, Oxford, Trenton and Washington D.C.

4/19/95: 168 people are killed—and over 600 are wounded—when a car bomb destroys Oklahoma City's Murrah Federal Building.

9/11/01: Nearly 3,000 people are killed when commercial airliners are hijacked and crashed into the World Trade Center in New York City and the Pentagon in Washington D.C.

10/10/01: An employee of American Media, Inc. in Boca Raton dies from inhalation anthrax; two others fall ill with the disease, but survive.

1/29/98: A bombing at Birmingham's New Woman All Woman Health Care Center kills one police officer and injures a clinic worker.

7/27/96: Six people are killed and 111 are wounded when a pipe bomb explodes at an Atlanta park during the Olympic Games.

Domestic Terrorist Attacks, Jan. 1997–Jan. 2004

Attempted / Successful
- Arson
- Biological release
- Bombing
- Sabotage
- Vandalism/theft
- Shooting spree

© MapQuest.com, Inc.

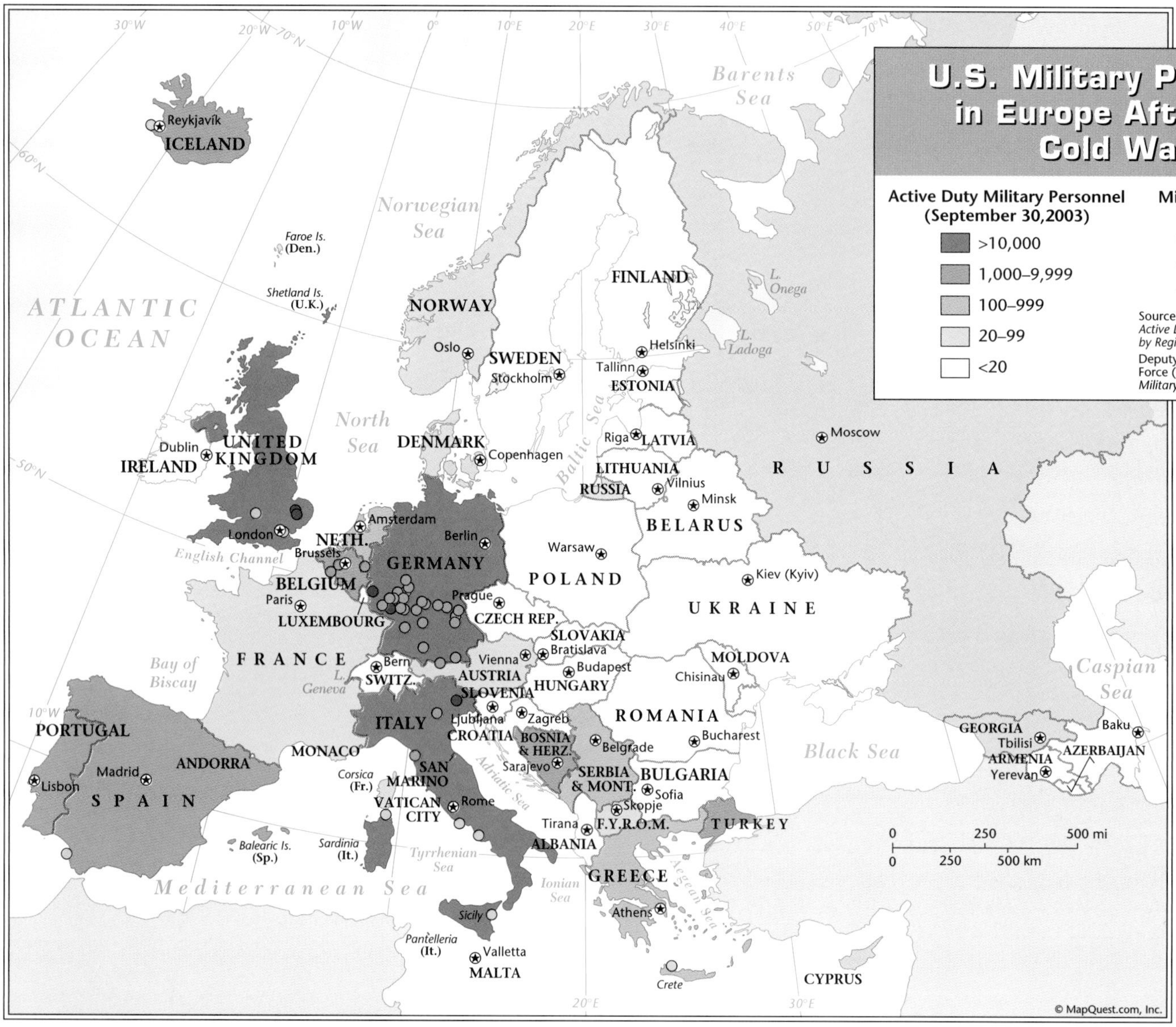

U.S. Military Presence in Europe After the Cold War

Active Duty Military Personnel (September 30, 2003)

- >10,000
- 1,000–9,999
- 100–999
- 20–99
- <20

Military Installations, 2002

- ● Air Force
- ◐ Army
- ○ Navy/Marines

Source: U.S. Department of Defense, *Active Duty Military Personnel Strengths by Regional Area and by Country*, 2003
Deputy Assistant Secretary of the Air Force (Installations), *United States Military Installations in 2002*, 2002

ICELAND — Reykjavík
Faroe Is. (Den.)
Shetland Is. (U.K.)
ATLANTIC OCEAN
Norwegian Sea
NORWAY — Oslo
SWEDEN — Stockholm
FINLAND — Helsinki
North Sea
DENMARK — Copenhagen
ESTONIA — Tallinn
L. Onega
L. Ladoga
Moscow
IRELAND — Dublin
UNITED KINGDOM — London
NETH. — Amsterdam
Brussels — BELGIUM
LUXEMBOURG
Paris
FRANCE
GERMANY — Berlin
Prague — CZECH REP.
POLAND — Warsaw
LATVIA — Riga
LITHUANIA — Vilnius
RUSSIA
BELARUS — Minsk
UKRAINE — Kiev (Kyiv)
SLOVAKIA — Bratislava
Bern — SWITZ.
AUSTRIA — Vienna
Geneva
L.
HUNGARY — Budapest
SLOVENIA — Ljubljana
MOLDOVA — Chisinau
PORTUGAL — Lisbon
SPAIN — Madrid
ANDORRA
MONACO
Corsica (Fr.)
SAN MARINO
ITALY — Rome
VATICAN CITY
CROATIA — Zagreb
BOSNIA & HERZ. — Sarajevo
Belgrade
SERBIA & MONT.
ROMANIA — Bucharest
Black Sea
GEORGIA — Tbilisi
ARMENIA — Yerevan
AZERBAIJAN — Baku
Caspian Sea
Bay of Biscay
Balearic Is. (Sp.)
Sardinia (It.)
Tyrrhenian Sea
Adriatic Sea
Skopje
F.Y.R.O.M.
BULGARIA — Sofia
Tirana — ALBANIA
TURKEY
English Channel
Mediterranean Sea
Sicily
Pantelleria (It.)
Valletta — MALTA
Ionian Sea
GREECE — Athens
Aegean Sea
Crete
CYPRUS
Barents Sea
Baltic Sea

© MapQuest.com, Inc.

0 — 250 — 500 mi
0 — 250 — 500 km

European Energy Dependence

Source: European Commission, *Energy: Let Us Overcome our Dependence*, 2002

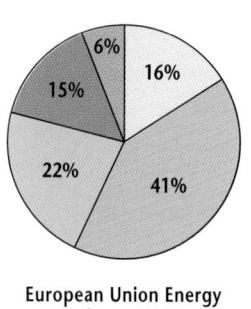

European Union Energy Balance, 1998

- 16%
- 41%
- 22%
- 15%
- 6%

- ☐ Solid fuels
- ☐ Oil & oil products
- ☐ Natural gas
- ☐ Nuclear
- ☐ Renewable energy

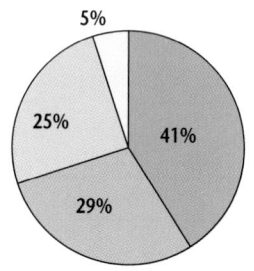

Natural Gas Imports from Non-European Union Countries, 1999

- 5%
- 41%
- 29%
- 25%

- ☐ Russia & Commonwealth of Independent States
- ☐ Algeria
- ☐ Norway
- ☐ Others

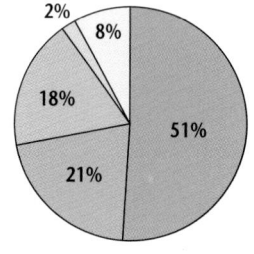

Oil Imports from Non-European Union Countries, 1999

- 2%
- 8%
- 51%
- 21%
- 18%

- ☐ OPEC
- ☐ Norway
- ☐ Russia & Commonwealth of Independent States
- ☐ Mexico
- ☐ Others

Europeans are becoming more concerned with overcoming their dependence on energy from non-European Union countries. Energy consumption is currently rising by one to two percent a year, and dependence on non-EU countries is approaching fifty percent. Europe's dependence on fossil fuels (oil, gas, and coal) has contributed to problems such as high prices, pollution, and social protest.

Many countries in Europe are exploring alternative energy sources, such as wind and solar power, that would reduce their foreign dependence.

In 2000, there were approximately 376 million people living in the European Union. About five percent of those were citizens of a country other than where they resided. Of those non-nationals, 32 percent were citizens of another E.U. country. The population composition differs widely by country. For example, in Luxembourg only 64 percent of the population were nationals; while in Greece, Finland, Portugal, and Spain almost all of the population were citizens of their resident country.

About one-third of all E.U. nationals living in the European Union, but outside of their home country, reside in Germany. Roughly 20 percent live in France, and 15 percent live in the United Kingdom. Many natives of Portugal live in France, and many Italians live in Germany, because of labor recruitment efforts that occured during the 1960s.

Many neighboring countries share residents; for example, about 60 percent of the non-nationals in Finland are Swedish. Turkish natives are the most representative among non-E.U. nationals, living primarily in Germany.

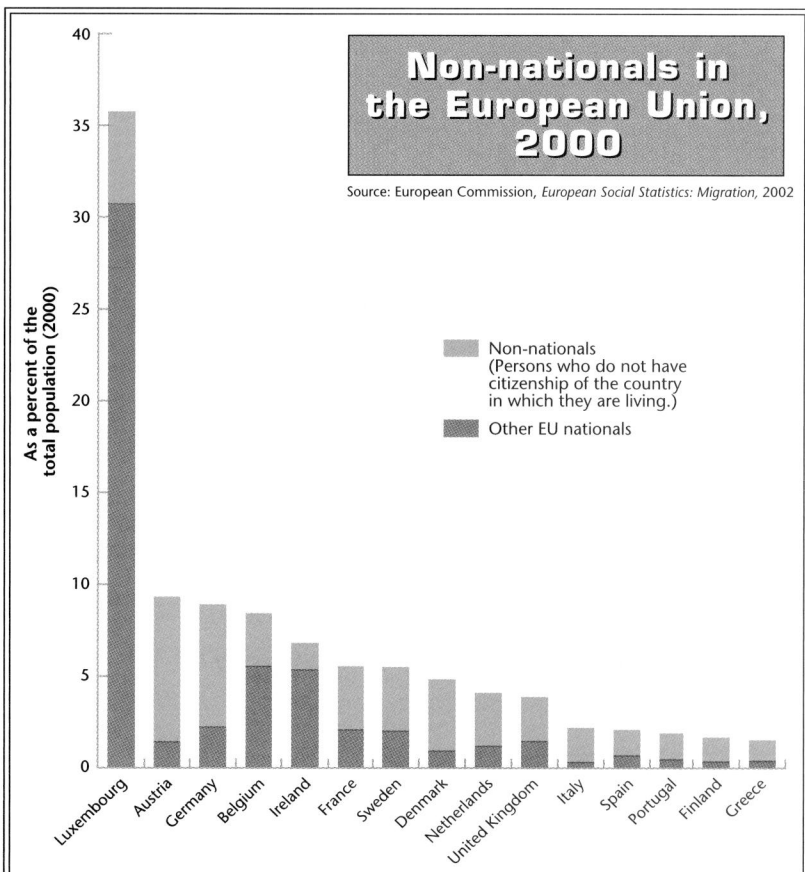

Non-nationals in the European Union, 2000

Source: European Commission, *European Social Statistics: Migration*, 2002

As a percent of the total population (2000)

■ Non-nationals
(Persons who do not have citizenship of the country in which they are living.)
■ Other EU nationals

Luxembourg, Austria, Germany, Belgium, Ireland, France, Sweden, Denmark, Netherlands, United Kingdom, Italy, Spain, Portugal, Finland, Greece

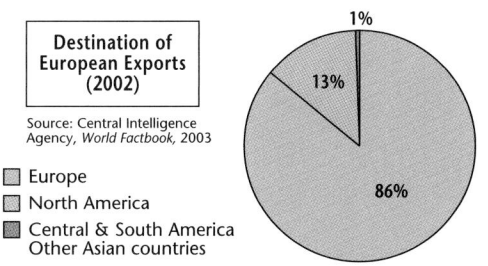

Destination of European Exports (2002)

Source: Central Intelligence Agency, *World Factbook*, 2003

□ Europe
□ North America
□ Central & South America
Other Asian countries

1%
13%
86%

Gross Domestic Product (per capita, US dollars)

■ >$30,000
■ $26,000–$29,999
▨ $19,000–$25,999
▨ $9,000–$18,999
□ $4,000–$8,999
□ <$4,000

ICELAND

ATLANTIC OCEAN

NORWAY
FINLAND
SWEDEN
ESTONIA
IRELAND   UNITED KINGDOM   DENMARK   LATVIA
LITHUANIA
RUSSIA
NETH.   BELARUS
BELGIUM   GERMANY   POLAND
LUXEMBOURG   CZECH REP.   UKRAINE
SLOVAKIA
FRANCE   SWITZ.   AUSTRIA   HUNGARY   MOLDOVA
SLOVENIA   ROMANIA
CROATIA
PORTUGAL   ANDORRA   BOSNIA & HERZ.   SERBIA & MONT.   BULGARIA
SPAIN   ITALY   F.Y.R.O.M.   TURKEY
ALBANIA
GREECE

RUSSIA

GEORGIA   AZERBAIJAN
ARMENIA

0   250   500 mi
0   250   500 km

Source: Central Intelligence Agency, *World Factbook*, 2003

MALTA   CYPRUS

Switzerland is known for its stable economy, low unemployment, and highly skilled labor force. Another wealthy nation, Norway has many natural resources, including petroleum, hydropower, fish, forests, and minerals. Abundant resources and a skilled, highly educated workforce are key factors in maintaining a prosperous economy.

Eastern European nations, having shed communism and their centralized economies only a little over a decade ago, are making strides in catching the West thanks to their new reliance on capitalism and international investment.

Many of the former Yugoslav republics, which gained their independence in the early 1990s, are struggling to keep pace with the rest of Europe, due to problems resulting from interethnic warfare and economic mismanagement. Unemployment and damage to infrastructure and industry caused during the war years remain unresolved there.

© MapQuest.com, Inc.

Israeli Settlements in the Occupied Territories

- Palestinian Autonomous Area (Area A: full civil and security control)
- Palestinian Autonomous Area (Area B: full civil control, joint Israeli-Palestinian security control)
- Israeli civil and security control (Area C)
- Israeli settlement/built-up area

Source: Foundation for Middle East Peace

In 1993, Israel and the Palestine Liberation Organization (PLO) signed an agreement to resolve their conflict and work towards Palestinian self-rule. As a result of this agreement, in 1994 and 1995 Israel withdrew from the Gaza Strip and began to withdraw from the West Bank. By 1996, though, Israel again planned to expand Israeli settlements in the West Bank, resulting in Palestinian protests.

In 1998, Israel and the Palestinians signed another agreement that called for Israel to turn over more territory in the West Bank to Palestinian control. However, by 2000, Palestinian Authority leader Yasir Arafat and Israeli Prime Minister Ehud Barak failed to reach a final peace settlement.

Since 2002, Israeli troops have reoccupied land in the West Bank that it had earlier relinquished because of a wave of suicide bombings performed by Palestinians. Among Israel's demands is that the Palestinian Authority stop these series of attacks against Israelis before negotiations can proceed.

Another obstacle to achieving a lasting peace between Israelis and Palestinians is the Israeli government's decision to construct a wall to protect its citizens from continued violence. However, the wall does not follow a recognized boundary, in places it cuts deep into the West Bank, trapping many Palestinians on the Israeli side. These areas, between the old border and the wall have been declared "closed zones", where Palestinian residents must apply for a permit to live or work.

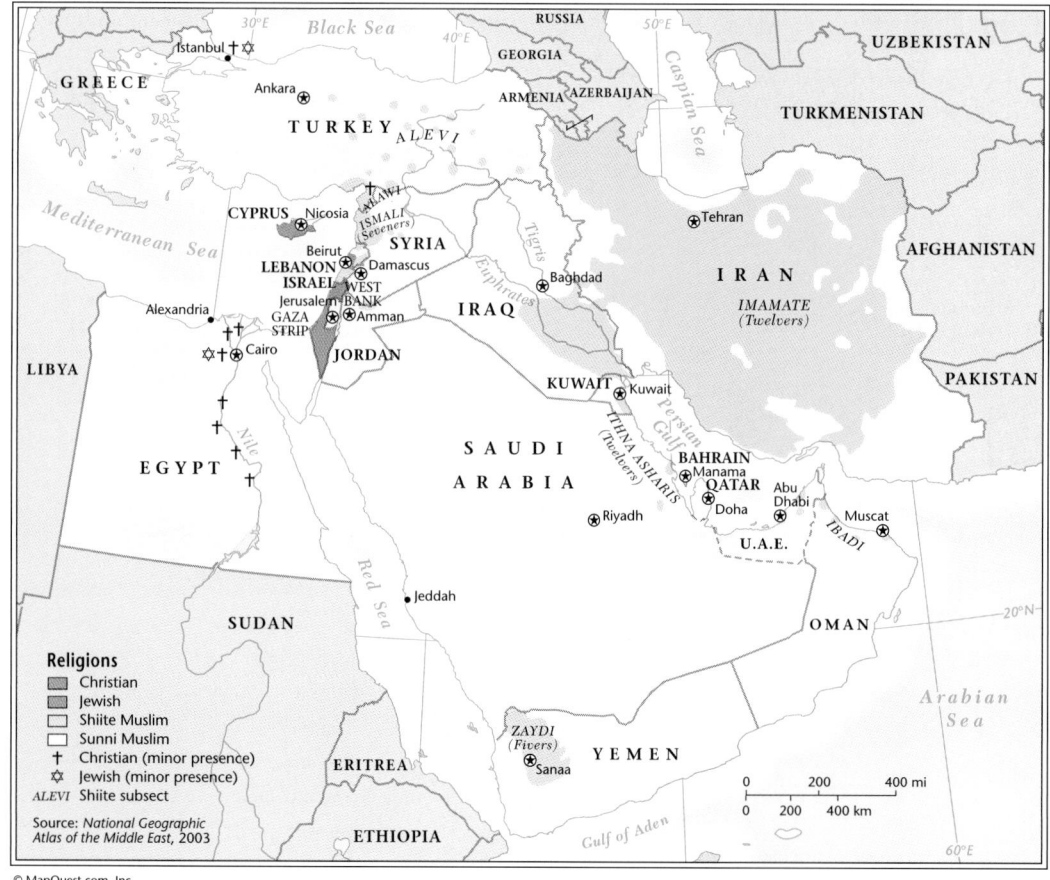

Religions
- Christian
- Jewish
- Shiite Muslim
- Sunni Muslim
- † Christian (minor presence)
- ✡ Jewish (minor presence)
- ALEVI Shiite subset

Source: National Geographic Atlas of the Middle East, 2003

Religious tensions are very common in the Middle East. Israel, a nation composed mostly of Jews, grants fewer privileges to Muslims. Christian emigration has been a result of harassment from Muslims. Many governments, such as Saudi Arabia, center their rule on Islamic law and do not allow its citizens religious freedom.

Religious Adherents in the Middle East

Source: *Britannica Book of the Year*

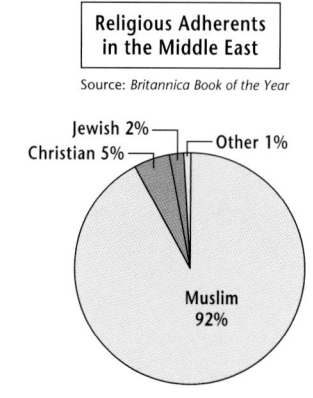

Jewish 2%
Christian 5%
Other 1%
Muslim 92%

Saudi Arabia is home to one quarter of the world's oil reserves, making it by far the largest oil producer, followed by neighboring countries bordering the Persian Gulf.

Conflicts have developed between nations over oil ownership, such as Iraq's invasion of Kuwait in 1990.

With most of the world dependent on oil from this region, resource depletion is a considerable threat.

Major Oil Reserves in the Middle East

Saudi Arabia 261.8 billion barrels

Iraq 112.5 billion barrels

United Arab Emirates 97.8 billion barrels

Kuwait 96.5 billion barrels

Iran 89.7 billion barrels

Qatar 15.2 billion barrels

Oman 5.5 billion barrels

Neutral Zone (Kuwait/Saudi Arabia) 5 billion barrels

Yemen 4 billion barrels

Egypt 2.9 billion barrels

Syria 2.5 billion barrels

Source: Penwell Corporation, *International Petroleum Encyclopedia*, 2002

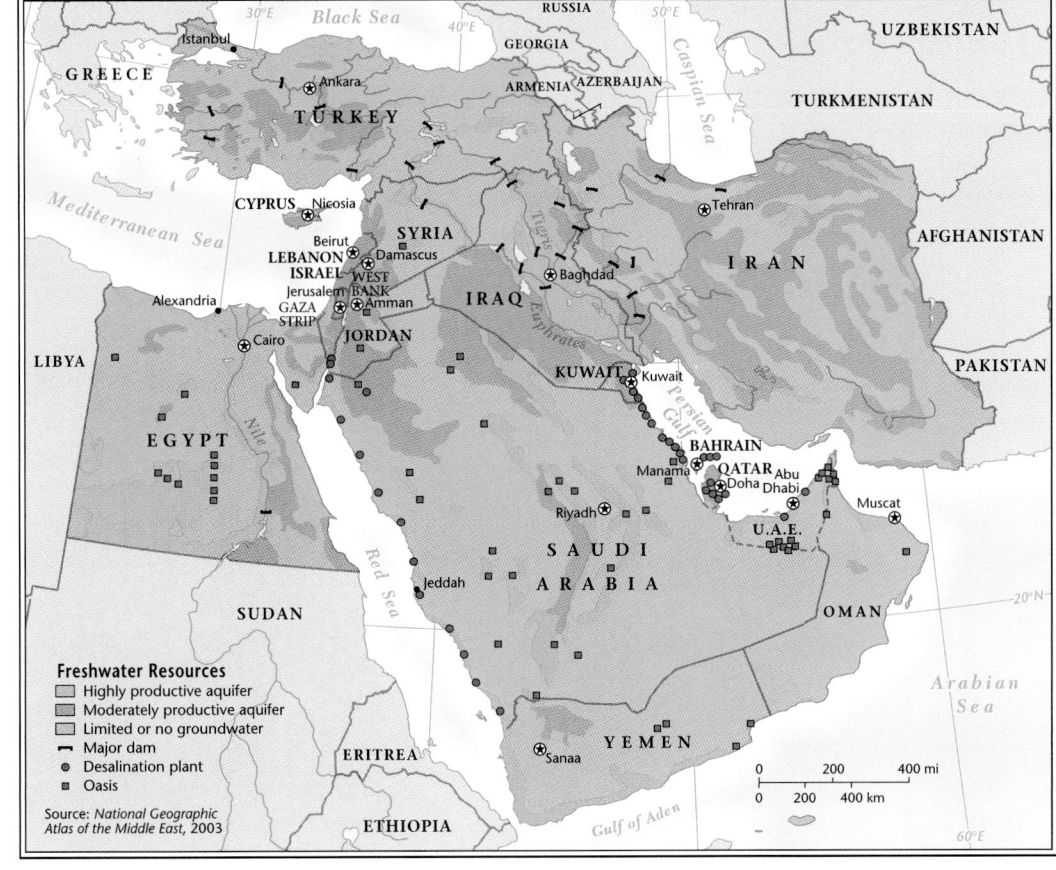

Bosporus/Turkish Straits 2 million barrels/day

Sumed Pipeline 2.5 million barrels/day

Suez Canal 1.3 million barrels/day

Strait of Hormuz 13 million barrels/day

Bab el-Mandab 3.2–3.3 million barrels/day

Energy Resources
- Oil or gas field
- Oil pipeline
- Oil transit chokepoint

Chokepoints are relatively narrow shipping lanes. If any of these routes were closed or disrupted, there could be a significant impact on world oil prices.

Source: *National Geographic Atlas of the Middle East*, 2003

The Middle East is a very arid region that depends highly on groundwater and desalination processes to provide water suitable for drinking and agriculture. There is a future risk of over-exploiting groundwater supplies, which is a nonrenewable resource. Greater energy resources are required to provide power to the desalination plants.

Nations that share water resources are not always in agreement about resource conservation, which can cause conflict.

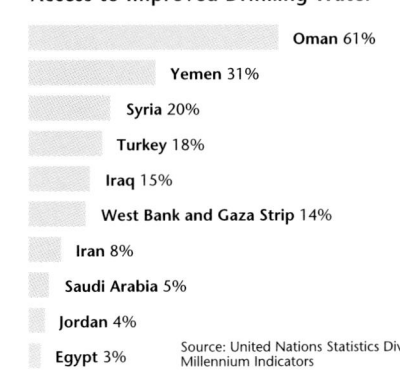

Freshwater Resources
- Highly productive aquifer
- Moderately productive aquifer
- Limited or no groundwater
- Major dam
- Desalination plant
- Oasis

Source: *National Geographic Atlas of the Middle East*, 2003

Percentage of Population without Access to Improved Drinking Water

Oman 61%

Yemen 31%

Syria 20%

Turkey 18%

Iraq 15%

West Bank and Gaza Strip 14%

Iran 8%

Saudi Arabia 5%

Jordan 4%

Egypt 3%

Source: United Nations Statistics Division, Millennium Indicators

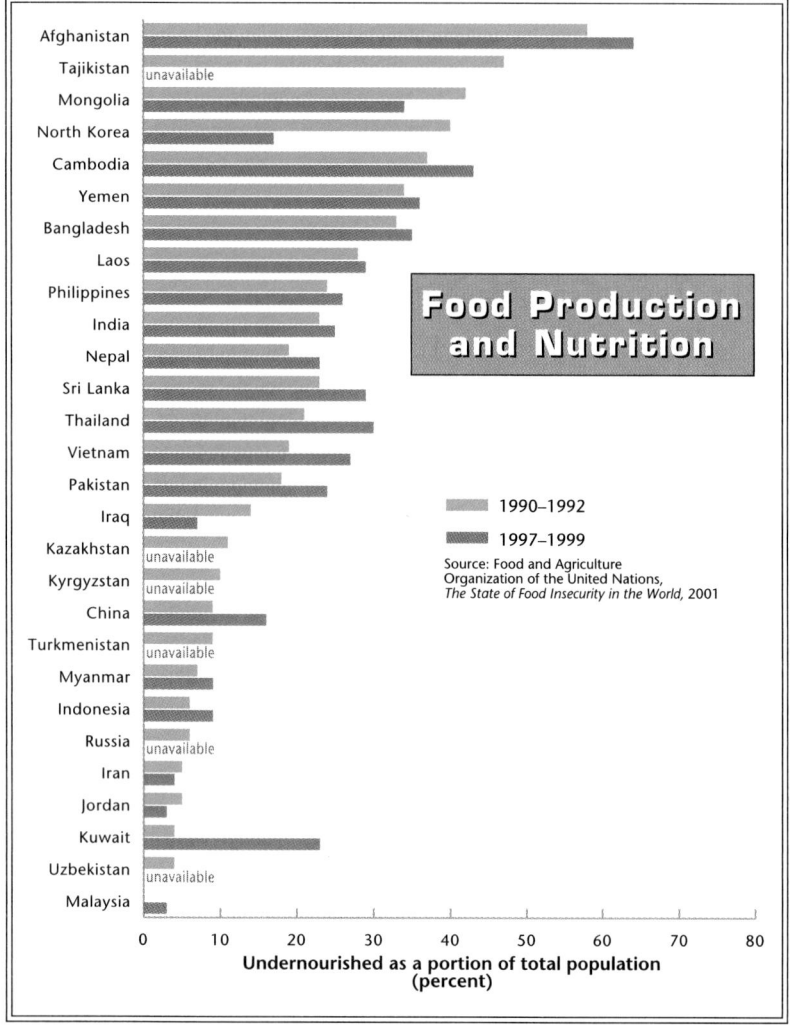

Food Production and Nutrition

Undernourished as a portion of total population (percent)

- 1990–1992
- 1997–1999

Source: Food and Agriculture Organization of the United Nations, *The State of Food Insecurity in the World*, 2001

In general, a greater proportion of the Asian population is now undernourished as compared to ten years ago. Reasons behind this trend include persistent drought in some areas (such as Afghanistan), overpopulation in some countries (Bangladesh), warfare, and increasing domestic military expenditures–thereby limiting a government's ability to respond to a food emergency.

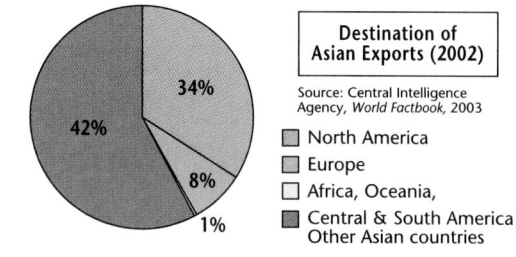

Destination of Asian Exports (2002)

Source: Central Intelligence Agency, *World Factbook*, 2003

- North America
- Europe
- Africa, Oceania,
- Central & South America Other Asian countries

34%
42%
8%
1%

Military Expenditures (as percent of GDP)

- >30%
- 8%–30%
- 4%–7.9%
- 2%–3.9%
- <2%
- data unavailable

Countries with the Highest Military Expenditures as a % of GDP	
North Korea	33.9 %
Saudi Arabia	13.0 %
Oman	12.2 %
Qatar	10.0 %
Israel	8.8 %
Jordan	8.6 %

Countries with the Lowest Military Expenditures as a % of GDP	
Kyrgyzstan	1.4 %
Thailand	1.4 %
Indonesia	1.3 %
Nepal	1.1 %
Japan	1.0 %
Kazakhstan	0.9 %

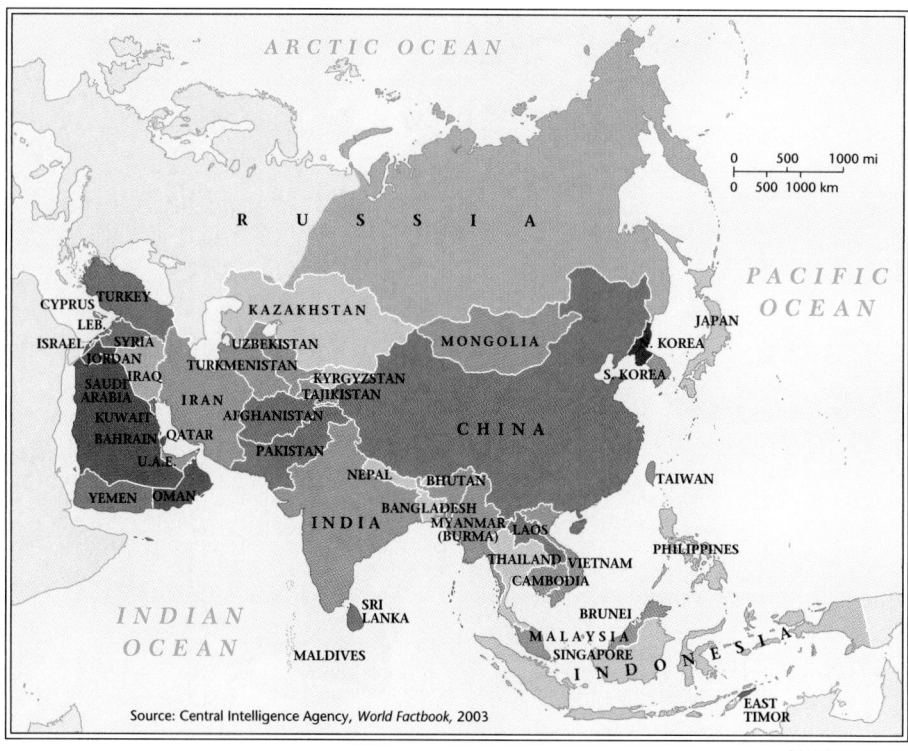

Source: Central Intelligence Agency, *World Factbook*, 2003

ARCTIC OCEAN

R U S S I A

CYPRUS
TURKEY
LEBANON
SYRIA
ISRAEL
JORDAN
IRAQ
SAUDI
ARABIA
KUWAIT
BAHRAIN QATAR
UNITED ARAB
EMIRATES
YEMEN OMAN
IRAN
TURKMENISTAN
UZBEKISTAN
KAZAKHSTAN
KYRGYZSTAN
TAJIKISTAN
AFGHANISTAN
PAKISTAN
MONGOLIA
CHINA
N. KOREA
S. KOREA
JAPAN
NEPAL
BHUTAN
BANGLADESH
INDIA
MYANMAR
(BURMA)
LAOS
THAILAND
CAMBODIA
VIETNAM
TAIWAN
PHILIPPINES
SRI
LANKA
MALDIVES
BRUNEI
M A L A Y S I A
SINGAPORE
I N D O N E S I A
EAST
TIMOR

PACIFIC
OCEAN

INDIAN
OCEAN

0   500   1000 mi
0   500   1000 km

Source: Central Intelligence Agency, *World Factbook*, 2003

The Gross Domestic Product of several Asian countries rival those of European and North American states, most notably Bahrain, Japan, Qatar, Saudi Arabia, and the United Arab Emirates. Oil and natural gas exports have been an enormous source of wealth for those countries bordering the Persian Gulf. Japan is known for its strong work ethic and technological mastery, though industries there are very dependent on imported raw materials and fuels.

Afghanistan is extremely poor and highly reliant on foreign aid. For the past twenty years this nation has suffered a Soviet military occupation, a repressive religious regime, and conflict involving the United States in its pursuit of terrorist groups. As a result, many Afghanis have fled to neighboring Pakistan and Iran to flee these conflicts. Yemen is also one of the poorest countries in Asia, though its future economic fate will certainly improve with the onset of oil production there.

Gross Domestic Product (per capita, US dollars)

<$1,000	$5,000–$9,999
$1,000–$1,999	$10,000–$20,000
$2,000–$4,999	>$20,000

© MapQuest.com, Inc.

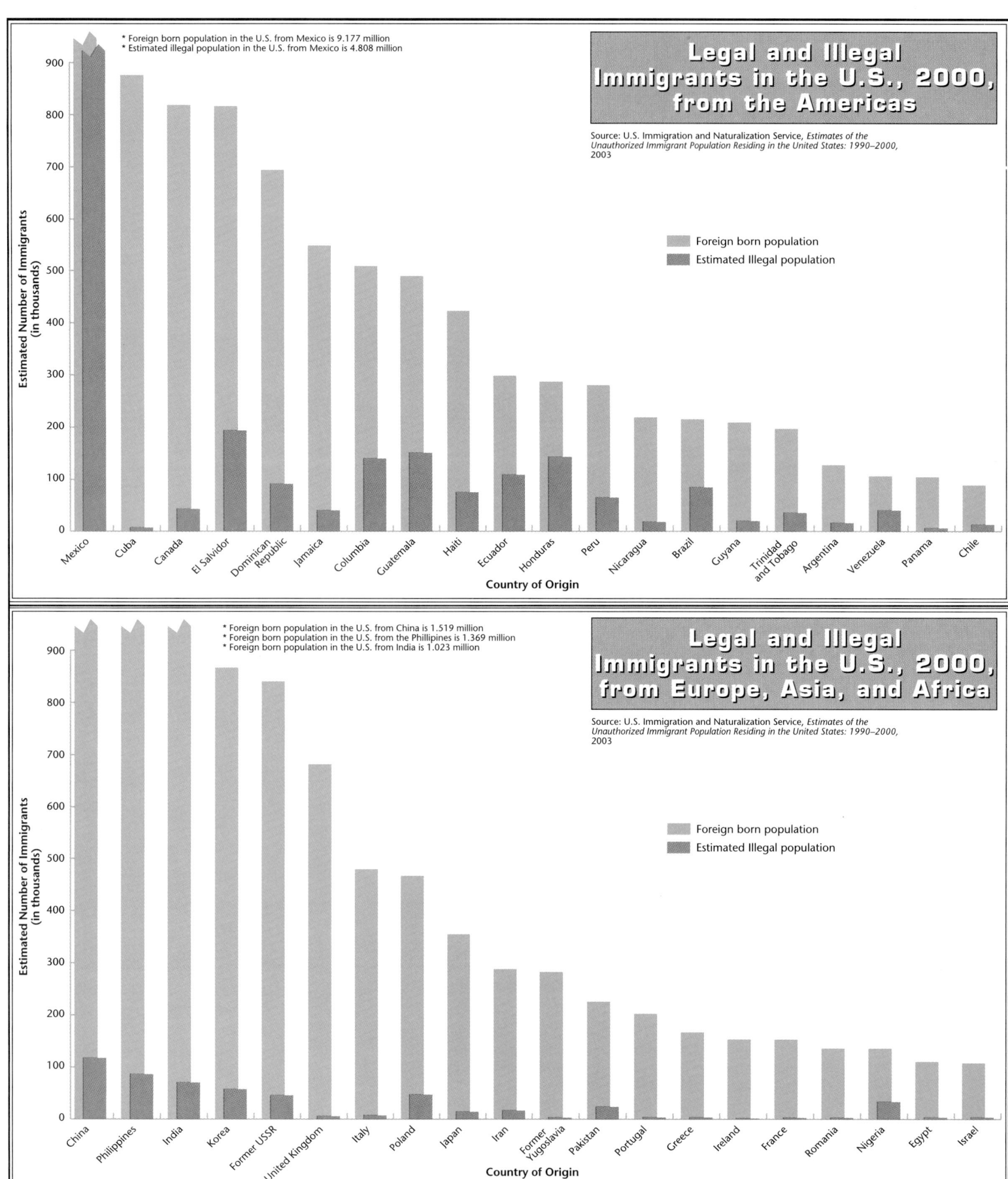

Legal and Illegal Immigrants in the U.S., 2000, from the Americas

Source: U.S. Immigration and Naturalization Service, *Estimates of the Unauthorized Immigrant Population Residing in the United States: 1990–2000,* 2003

* Foreign born population in the U.S. from Mexico is 9.177 million
* Estimated illegal population in the U.S. from Mexico is 4.808 million

Foreign born population
Estimated Illegal population

Estimated Number of Immigrants (in thousands)

Country of Origin

Mexico, Cuba, Canada, El Salvidor, Dominican Republic, Jamaica, Columbia, Guatemala, Haiti, Ecuador, Honduras, Peru, Nicaragua, Brazil, Guyana, Trinidad and Tobago, Argentina, Venezuela, Panama, Chile

Legal and Illegal Immigrants in the U.S., 2000, from Europe, Asia, and Africa

Source: U.S. Immigration and Naturalization Service, *Estimates of the Unauthorized Immigrant Population Residing in the United States: 1990–2000,* 2003

* Foreign born population in the U.S. from China is 1.519 million
* Foreign born population in the U.S. from the Phillipines is 1.369 million
* Foreign born population in the U.S. from India is 1.023 million

Foreign born population
Estimated Illegal population

Estimated Number of Immigrants (in thousands)

Country of Origin

China, Philippines, India, Korea, Former USSR, United Kingdom, Italy, Poland, Japan, Iran, Former Yugoslavia, Pakistan, Portugal, Greece, Ireland, France, Romania, Nigeria, Egypt, Israel

How to Study

CONTENTS

739 Study Skills: Take Charge of Your Future

740 First Things First: Know Yourself

746 Basic Study Skills

750 Study Tips: By Subject Area

755 Taking Tests: A Fact of Life

758 College Entrance Exams

758 Overview

762 SAT I: Reasoning Test

780 ACT Assessment

792 SAT II: Subject Tests

804 Other Exams

804 Advanced Placement Exams

816 GED

818 GCSE

830 A Levels

831 GNVQ

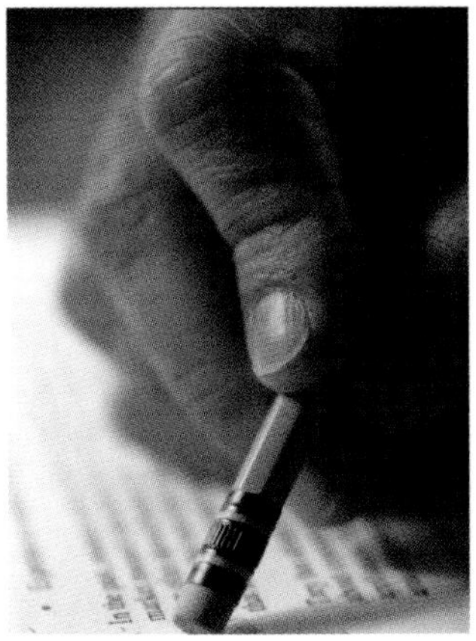

To students:

A popular teacher once was asked for the three most important pieces of advice she could offer today's students. Her reply? "Learn how to study. Learn how to study. Learn how to study." Students who ignore this sound advice will have problems not only in school but in adult life, both on the job and at home.

The following pages can help you take charge of your future through the use of study skills. Some of you may feel that you need help because you are lagging behind your classmates. If so, you'll want to check out a special boxed feature called "In a Bind?" Others may be doing well already and simply want an extra boost. In that case, look for "Fast Track." In either case, you will find that improving your study skills will help not only for school but also for the world into which you are moving.

Learning how to learn really is important in both school and life. We wish you great success in the adventure of learning!

To parents and guardians:

For the past several years, we have conducted a tutorial program matching the skills of academically successful students with those who are struggling in school. As director of that program, I noticed that when we started using study skills in our training, we began to see students at all levels become independent learners. The real problem became apparent: failure in mathematics or English was just a symptom. Behind all the academic struggle was the simple fact that students did not know how to study.

We also discovered that as we related study skills to life, students became more interested. They began to see, for example, that listening is an important skill for success in the classroom, and it is equally important for success in the workplace. Put another way, poor study skills in school could earn students an F, while poor study skills at work could cost them a job.

The following pages will help students not only in school but also in the world where they live. Ultimately, that's the most important measure of educational success.

Emory Register
Director, Governor's Study Partner Program
Tennessee Department of Education

Authors

Study Skills: Take Charge of Your Future

SUSAN W. KNOWLES, *S.W. Knowles & Associates,*
Nashville, Tennessee

EMORY REGISTER, *Tennessee Department of Education,*
Nashville, Tennessee

GCSE, A Levels, GNVQ

GEORGE LOW, *Publisher, Education Journal,*
Middlesex, England

Study Skills: Take Charge of Your Future

This chapter could change your life. No, really. It's not about school, it's about your life after school. Doing well in school can be a matter of simply adjusting your perspective. Once you realize that school is a steppingstone to the rest of your life, you may see your studies in a totally different light.

I'm living my life backwards!
What if someone suggested to you that school actually comes at the wrong time of life—that you can't really know what you need to learn until you've been out on your own for awhile? What if you decided that they were right? Well, there is a way to overcome this dilemma.

Take a few minutes now to imagine what you might be doing in the future. More than likely, you'll be working at a job for a good portion of every day in order to earn enough money to support yourself. Maybe you'll have a family, and a household to manage as well.

School is an important stop on the highway of life.
Now, what if you imagine school to be simply a stop—though an important one—on the highway of life? What if you know that you have just a few years to fuel up for the work that awaits you after you leave school? Your time now becomes more valuable. You don't feel stuck in the endless fast lane of school if you know you are going to turn off just a few exits down the road.

Coming to this realization could change the way you approach school. You might decide to begin taking advantage of school opportunities because (1) they're available, (2) you'll be spending time there anyway, and (3) at the moment you have more time than money. You might begin to demand what you deserve of the school system by asking questions about things that are confusing or unclear.

Treat school as if it were your job.
At this point in your life, school *is* your job! See what happens if you think of your teachers as your employers. Listen carefully to hear what they expect of you, then try to produce it. This may not only gain you better grades now; later, in the workplace, it will likely result in promotions and pay increases.

Try dedicating the hours between 8 a.m. and 5 p.m. to your schoolwork, as if it were a job. "Punch in" to class on time every day, and while you're there, work hard. Use your time away from class efficiently as well. If you can do most of your studying before and after school, during study halls, and between classes, you might be able to avoid working nights and weekends. But be prepared for some overtime during finals and other busy periods.

If you are especially good at managing time and have your homework completely under control, then and only then should you consider taking on extracurricular activities, such as sports, theater, cheerleading, drill team, band, the school newspaper, or the student government.

Employers like the combination of good grades *and* a résumé or CV filled with additional activities and responsibilities, but good grades must always come first.

The school/job analogy isn't so far-fetched; after all, if your grades are good enough, they can literally be worth money—in scholarships, as well as in better-paying jobs down the road. If you really make a point of studying hard, perhaps your future "job" could even be as a self-employed entrepreneur, business owner, or founder of a nonprofit organization.

10 Reasons Why Good Study Habits Pay Off

1. You will feel great about yourself and how much you've accomplished.
2. Your friends will be impressed with how much you know (even if they won't admit it).
3. Your family will brag about how smart you are.
4. Your parents will stop lecturing you on all the reasons you need to study.
5. Your parents will be so pleased with the way you accept responsibility that they may grant you extra privileges—a private phone, a later curfew, more computer or television time.
6. Your teachers will stop teasing you about turning in your homework late.
7. If you're planning to continue your education, you're more likely to be accepted at the college you'd like to attend.
8. You stand a far better chance of getting the job you want once you're out of school.
9. Chances are you will make more money in your lifetime than your friends who don't study. More money means nicer clothes, better and longer vacations, nice stereo and television equipment, and a really neat car.
10. You can use "I'm studying" as an excuse to get out of just about anything.

First Things First: Know Yourself

How you feel affects how you do . . . and you know what? How you do affects how you feel. As you improve your study skills, you also increase your feelings of self-worth. Many students adopt a whole new outlook on life as a result of just practicing how to study.

Memory and How It Works

The immediate source of memory is *sensory* or *surface memory*. Your senses take in a smell or sight or sound, and for a few moments you can remember a related experience; however, events in sensory memory occur all the time, so they are quickly forgotten.

The *short-term memory* is where you store things that you hear in class or that you have read and understood. If your reading has consisted of merely going through the motions without engaging the thought process, the material probably wasn't retained in your short-term memory at all.

Short-term memory is a useful tool that processes all recent learning. Since it is intended only for the short term, new memories are constantly moving in to take up space. While you can usually pass a test using only the short-term part of your memory, it's not likely that you could pass the same test a few months later.

The *long-term memory* works like a filing system. It puts things related to the same topic in the same place. That's why it's important to link any new

knowledge to what you already know on the topic, or even to anything you think might be related. This practice will bring related subjects into the active part of the brain and make you better able to understand and remember what you are learning.

In order to "save" something you have learned so that it can be used in the future, you'll want to take some action to move it from short-term memory into long-term memory. For exam-

ple, instead of just hearing something and moving on, you might want to write it down, enter it into your daily agenda, or talk to a friend about it.

Your attitude is important. One of the most critical factors in long-term memory storage is your attitude toward what you are learning. If you do not believe something, your long-term memory is going to have trouble storing it. Rather than dismissing it outright, try allowing for the possibility that there might be two ways of looking at the subject, so that your memory can place the new view alongside the old one. If you are visually oriented, imagine the material as a chart or table comparing and contrasting your beliefs and those with which you disagree. If images don't help, ask yourself why you think this point of view might be incorrect or unacceptable.

Storage is nothing without retrieval. As you learn new information, think about occasions when you will want to retrieve it in the future. Will it be part of a larger course of study, such as medicine, engineering, or political science? Will it be more likely to come up in managing your own home or pursuing a hobby such as hang-gliding or piloting your own plane? Or is it simply a unique fact that belongs to a group of related facts? If so, try to think of a device to help you recall it.

Train your brain. Thinking is, quite simply, making your mind work. If you are not paying attention and your mind is wandering, you are not applying your brain to the task at hand. Many factors can be responsible for lack of concentration—noise, hunger, lack of sleep, emotional upset—and can interfere with your mental readiness.

Just Memorize It!

Here are ten tried-and-true methods for memorizing:

1. **Repeat, repeat, repeat!** Say the word or words over and over out loud, until they sound as familiar as your own name. (This technique is most often used to learn foreign words but can just as easily be applied to terms in the sciences or in mathematics.)
2. **Write it out.** If you write a new term repeatedly (or type it on a word processor) you are more likely to remember how the term is spelled and to recognize it when you see it again.
3. **Draw a picture.** Make a sketch or diagram that explains the term. For example, you might remember the parts of an atom by drawing an atom and placing protons and neutrons within it.
4. **Break down big words into small words.** Let's say you're trying to remember *hematite*, an iron ore. Think of the hem of an iron-colored coat being pulled tight.
5. **Create strange, funny mental pictures.** If you associate an outlandish image with a fact you're trying to learn, you'll be more likely to recall it. For example, you might remember Richard the Lion-Heart by envisioning a lion leaping out of a man's chest.
6. **Use acronyms.** Acronyms, words in which each letter stands for another word, can be created to help you remember lists of things. For example, the made-up name Roy G. Biv can help you remember the colors of the spectrum in order: red, orange, yellow, green, blue, indigo, vermillion.
7. **Make up sentences.** If you can't think of an acronym, create a sentence in which the first letter of each word stands for an idea. For example, "Please excuse my dear Aunt Sally" tells the order of operations in mathematics—parentheses, exponents, multiplication, division, addition, and subtraction.
8. **Play mental charades.** Act out things you'd like to remember in a mock game of charades; the body motions will help you store information and retrieve it. For example, the name Czestokowski could be broken into syllables and acted out as chest-toe-cow-ski.
9. **Take a walk through your house.** Think of a route you might take through your house. Then, when you're trying to remember a list of items, form a mental picture of each successive item in the appropriate room. For example, you could remember the first three presidents by imagining a washing machine in your entryway (George Washington), an atom in your den (John Adams), and a tom-tom in your kitchen (Thomas Jefferson).
10. **Make up songs—the sillier the better.** Putting new words to a familiar melody can help you remember things. For example, the following ditty is sung to the tune of "Row, Row, Row Your Boat":

I will not forget
Alkalinity,
Bases have high, acids have low (PH),
Seven's neutrality.

How You Learn

The latest research in education (and there's a ton of it out there) tells us that people learn in a number of different ways. Three of the major ways are visual, auditory, and kinesthetic. The particular style that suits you has to do with the way you receive and process information. For example, if you prefer to listen to a book being read aloud rather than to read it yourself, chances are that you are more of an auditory than a visual learner.

Visual learners. People who are visual learners grasp information best when it's presented in a written or graphic form. They are often heard to say things such as "I *see* what you're getting at" or "I *see* what you mean." The majority of students are visual learners. If you are in this group, you should try to remember things by putting them on paper—in pictures, symbols, charts, or visual maps.

Auditory learners. If you find it easiest to remember things that you have heard, chances are that you are primarily an auditory learner. People who learn best in this manner often say things such as "I *hear* you" or "That *sounds* right." If you are in this group, techniques for learning include studying with friends so you can listen to each other's comments, or making up stories, songs, and rhymes that you can remember and recite to yourself.

Kinesthetic learners. If you have trouble sitting still or can pick up a dance step or basketball pattern on the first try, you are likely a kinesthetic (movement-based) learner. People who are kinesthetic learners can be heard to say such things as "That *feels* right," and they best grasp information through motion or hands-on practice. If you are a kinesthetic learner and need to memorize dates, you might try making up a pattern of gestures keyed to the dates or role-play a character in history who is actually there witnessing the activity.

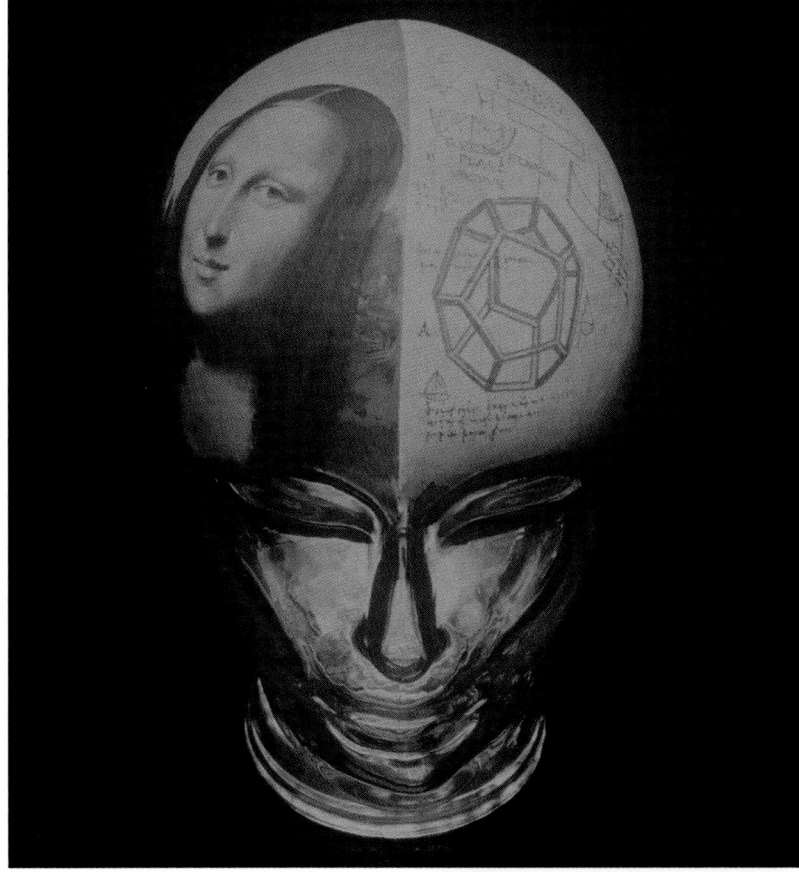

Although each of us has elements of all three types of learners, chances are that one type is dominant. You'll want to discover which type you are so that you can understand why some subjects and styles of teaching work better for you, and to help you determine ways to bridge the gap if a teacher's style or topic doesn't lend itself readily to your way of processing information.

THIS FLUTE player is probably an auditory learner.

≡FAST Track Your Awesome Brain

Did you know that your mind can process information at a rate of anywhere from 400 to 800 words per minute, and that the average person speaks at a speed of approximately 125 words per minute? Since our brains work much faster than anyone can speak, we should be able not just to listen but to listen actively and effectively. Practice active listening on a daily basis—your friends and family will appreciate it!

---

10 Study Tips

1. Find a quiet, well-lit place to work. Ask your parents and other family members to respect your privacy, and don't answer the phone. (Some experts say that ten minutes of study in a quiet place is equal to an hour of study in front of the television.)
2. Try to study when you are at your best. Some people find that they are freshest and least distracted in the morning. Others feel that they can recall things best if they study as soon as they come home from school. Others prefer a two-hour study period after dinner.
3. Give yourself a break. Stand up and stretch every half hour. Drinking water also keeps you alert. If you need a snack, wait until halfway through your study session and use it as a reward.
4. Alternate the subjects you are studying. If you have been reading intensively in social studies, switch to your mathematics homework before proceeding to your English literature assignment. This will help keep your mind refreshed.
5. Make sure you get enough exercise. If you're burned out on studying, take a ten-minute walk around the block. As you walk, summarize what you have learned, or make up a rhyme that will help you remember it.
6. If you are too upset to study, talk with someone (parent, friend, school counselor) or write about it in a journal so that it will no longer be quite so distracting. Then go back to your work and focus on one thing at a time.
7. Study with a friend. Any task is made easier when you're sharing it with someone you like.
8. Present the material to others as though you were the teacher, then switch places and have them teach. Communicating information to others is an excellent way to learn.
9. Get it right the first time. It's a lot easier and faster to learn something right the first time than it is to relearn it.
10. Take the time to work through sample problems, which are designed to walk you step-by-step through the correct solution. Before you apply yourself to the real problems, make sure that your methods and answers to the sample are correct.

Breaking the Barriers to Learning

There are a number of common reasons why students give up trying to earn high grades. An important task in developing good study habits is to determine if any of these reasons apply to you and, if so, to develop a plan to overcome them.

Poor self-image. Many students wrongly think that they simply aren't smart enough. The truth is that the desire to learn is often as important as a high I.Q. Regardless of what you've decided or been told about your intelligence level, you can still achieve realistic goals through perseverance, determination, and effective study habits.

Distractions stemming from personal issues. Many students grapple with problems involving friends or family. If this is the case with you, try jotting down what's bothering you. Just writing it out and deciding to deal with it at some point will help to ease your mind. If you don't have a solution to the problem, talk to your school counselor or a trusted friend. What you are confronting may be more common and therefore more easily solvable than you think—but you'll never know until you tell someone else.

"Boring" topics. No student gets equally excited about all the subjects in school. When you encounter a subject that doesn't appeal to you, remind yourself that it's just a class, not your life's work. In the meantime, look for ways to make the topic more interesting. Try to find other resources—books, videotapes, information from the Internet—in which the information is presented in a more appealing way. If you disagree with what you're reading, try to grasp the author's viewpoint and contrast it with your own. As you read on, you may actually find yourself arguing with the author. That's good, because it means you're beginning to form your own point of view.

Lack of time or space. With household chores, family responsibilities, and extracurricular activities, you may feel that you simply don't have enough time to study. Or maybe you have the time but lack a quiet place, what with your sister's noisy friends or your brother's loud stereo. If either of these is the case, don't hesitate to ask a parent for help. They may set up a study area where you won't be disturbed or begin planning family events at more convenient times. If that doesn't work, search for quiet study areas outside your home—the library, an empty classroom, a friend's house.

 **Don't Panic**

Do you feel as if you're dropping behind the other students in your class? This can happen for lots of reasons—illness, stress at home, extra-curricular activities, even pressure from your other classes. Don't be hard on yourself, and don't give up. Sometimes academic problems have nothing to do with ability. Many well-known individuals had trouble in school—even Albert Einstein. Use the tips in this chapter as a special boost, and if you need help, find a study partner or a tutor. Remember, failure isn't falling down—it's staying down.

your turn ➡ Study Trouble?

The following students are having trouble studying. What advice would you give them?

- Sue simply can't study at home: her parents argue a lot; her sister (with whom she shares a bedroom) plays her radio too loud; and her brother practices the drums.
- Rashad wants to study for the algebra test tomorrow, but there's a great movie on television tonight that he's been dying to see.
- Hanna wants to be a television reporter but is convinced that she's just not a good enough writer.
- Michael knows that he needs to do well in school in order to have a chance at getting into his first-choice college. Unfortunately, he has managed to put off all the necessary classes that he hates: foreign language, civics, and physics.

Ready! Set! Go!

Success produces success, and failure produces failure. When successful students are asked how many of them are making much better grades today than in primary school, more than 95 percent indicate that their grades are basically the same. This is also true with those who are not achieving.

One good way to break the cycle of failure is to use goal setting. If one reaches a goal, then success has been achieved. Let the reaching of one goal help you reach another goal. Remember these points about goals: they must be realistic, and they should include at least some short-term components.

Setting goals. (Ready!) Someone once said that you can't build a bridge to a cloud. You need to have tangible goals or objectives if you're to have any chance reaching them. When one goal leads to another in this way, life is like a series of stepping stones. The ability to state and achieve short-term goals (*Get an* A *on my English project*) results in the ability to achieve mid-term goals (*Get accepted to my first-choice university*), which in turn leads to the achievement of long-term goals (*Become a sportswriter for a major newspaper*).

Adjusting your attitude and honing your skills. (Set!) Think about life after school. Ask yourself what activities during the school day might be most useful later on, then make an extra effort to learn those things.

Would you like to be smarter at making change when you are handling money? Could you get excited about starting your own home-building business? Are you interested in the breakthrough field of genetic engineering? Do you think you might want to work in another country? Do you want to become involved in ecological issues? Would you like to make a career for yourself through selling products on the Internet?

The answers to these and other career-related questions may spark your interest in subjects which up to now have seemed boring.

Know your strengths. You can succeed in learning by (1) identifying your strengths, (2) using your time efficiently and strategically, and (3) prioritizing your work. Everyone has unique qualities that affect learning. Finding out what yours are and working with them will prove far more useful than striking out in the first direction that comes along.

Recognize your weaknesses. If you have a learning difficulty, such as poor reading skills or a hearing problem, get help right away. Problems such as these are far more common than you might think. (A surprising number of actors and visual artists are dyslexic!)

Just think how much further you will get if your energies are directed in a forward direction rather than trying to make up a deficit.

Look at the big picture. Before you begin studying, step back and take in the whole picture. Do you understand the assignment? What is your teacher expecting you to learn, and by when? Do you have all the books and other sources that are called for? If you need more information and don't have it, call someone for help! (Many schools have a homework hotline.)

Plan your study session. Some successful students like to tackle the hardest subject first, figuring that it will take less time than at the end of the session when they are tired. Other students prefer to knock off the fast and easy subjects first, then ride that momentum like a wave into the more difficult subjects. Only you know which approach works best for you. By taking a few minutes to plan, you can take the measure of what you must do and figure out how to get it done most successfully.

Have the tools you need. When you sit down to study, you'll want to make sure you have all the tools you need to be successful. Of course, there are the usual things—paper, pencils, pens, textbooks. In addition to these, however, you'll want access to other reference books and equipment that can make your life easier. These include a good dictionary, a thesaurus, an encyclopedia, and a style manual for grammar and writing.

Don't be alarmed if you don't have all these items at home. Simply become acquainted with your school library or public library, where you can use these items for free. Another handy tool is a diary with enough space to write down assignment due dates and test dates. You can also use the calendar to keep track of social engagements and other important events in your life.

Strengths
① Organized
② Prompt and efficient
③ Good writing skills
④ Team player
⑤ Enjoy a challenge

Weaknesses
① Shy
② Verbal skills weak
③ Sometimes passive
④ Get bogged down in details

Don't Give Up

Researchers tell us that neither I.Q. nor aptitude test scores can predict later success in life. These methods measure certain kinds of abilities, but they do not account for self-discipline and the ability to work steadily at something until it is finished. As Winston Churchill once said, "Never, never give up." You know what? He went on to win a war!

Try teamwork. Studying with others can be either a boon or a bust. As the old saying goes, the more the merrier. So watch out for distracting social situations that can result in too much fun and too little studying.

As a rule, it's more effective to partner with classmates you don't know very well—you probably will be more formal in manner and a little more respectful of each other. In addition, since you won't have as much in common as you would with close friends, it will also be easier to stick to the subject at hand.

When you study with others, it's important to plan what you wish to accomplish. Make up a structure that suits your plan. For example, everyone might come prepared to share their favorite study method, and five minutes will be spent discussing each and deciding which to use. Or you might divide the group in half, pair up with someone in the opposite group, and act as though you are that person's tutor. Teach what you have learned about the subject you are studying, then switch roles and let the other person teach you.

Don't be afraid to ask for help. If you're struggling, you can always ask someone for help. Being willing to admit that you don't know something is a sign of maturity. Besides, watching someone else solve a problem is a great way to learn. Keep in mind, though, that you are still in charge. If the first person you go to cannot help you to solve the problem, you can always approach someone else or do additional research yourself and try again.

≡FAST Track Explore on Your Own

Try using your essay-writing skills to explore an interesting topic. For example, do some market research to find out how people feel about television reception through satellite dishes—what they like about them, what they don't like, and what questions they have.

Talk to potential customers, then write an essay about whether or not you think there is a market for satellite dishes in your hometown.

Exploring on your own will help to bring any subject to life.

Just do it. (Go!) Once you have taken charge of your own learning, you will find that you'll waste less time "lost in space." You'll be surprised how much easier it is to remember things and retain what you've read if you know ahead of time what it is that you're learning and why.

Taking control of your own schooling is an empowering act. Try it now. Formulate your own example: I want to learn *this* so I can do *that*. Start with something simple: for example, I want to learn multiplication and division by heart, without a calculator, so that I can calculate my remaining air supply at various water depths when I'm scuba diving.

When the going gets tough, hang in there. Education is a life-long process of asking questions and then stubbornly hanging in there until you find the answers. Once you realize that, you can do almost anything.

Simple persistence has propelled many ordinary people to the top of their professions. Give yourself an incentive to get to the next step. Reward yourself for small accomplishments. Make yourself study an extra half hour and then call your best friend, or dial up the Internet, or watch television, or read a chapter in your favorite novel.

Do what you can. If simply going to class and listening is all you can manage right now because of circumstances beyond your control, then at least give it your best. Don't miss a day. Try to recall as much as you can of what you hear in class. You'll be surprised how much you can remember if you stay alert in class and ask questions when you need to.

*Do*s and *Don't*s for Success in School

Do
Attend every class
Listen, pay attention, and control your mind
Take notes and review them daily
Ask questions
Isolate yourself from distractions and trouble

Don't
Miss school
Get distracted or daydream in class
Put off reviewing or get behind
Compare yourself with others
Isolate yourself from those who can help

Computers: To Use or Not to Use?

A computer is a tool, not a substitute brain. Can it help in studying? Definitely yes, with some limitations:

Use a computer to edit. Enter the first draft of a paper or essay into the computer so that you can make changes and edits to your written work on-screen. Use the spell-check feature to save you from embarrassing spelling errors. Keep in mind, though, that spell-check has its limitations. For example, it can't distinguish between finding insects in the *desert* and finding insects in the *dessert!*

Use a computer to help produce term papers. A computer can help you create a title page and table of contents for your term papers. Using a database program to create a list of sources or bibliography will save you time, since it can sort the entries into alphabetical order. Some software will provide an automatic footnoting feature as well.

Use a computer to summarize and review notes. By typing in your class notes, you will force yourself to re-see them in a different format. (You will, literally, re-view them.) If you are a computer whiz, you can use a computer spreadsheet to break down your topic into easily viewed parts, such as a numerical sequence top to bottom and a word sequence left to right. But don't focus too much energy on the construction of the spreadsheet instead of the contents.

Use a computer to research. If your topic is well defined, or if you know a specific website that can provide the information you need, you actually can do research on the Internet via the World Wide Web. Be sure to cite your source address and author clearly.

There are a number of websites and CD-ROM programs that promote active learning by using lesson plans designed by teachers. You may already have seen examples of these in school. Some are designed by teams of scientists, historians, or professionals in other fields. Many of these lesson plans promote the kinds of thinking that you will be asked to do as part of a career in that profession. Use these resources as a supplement to your assigned textbook, to reinforce and extend what you have learned.

Although a computer can be valuable in studying, watch out for these possible pitfalls:

First-draft writing. Many writers do their first draft on the computer. However, this requires some discipline, because computer operations may prove distracting. Focus on what you're trying to say, not on the mechanics of word processing.

Loosely searching the Internet. Before you start searching the Internet, have a good ideal of what you need and where must go to get it before you log onto the computer. If you start a search of the World Wide Web with only a vague idea that it might help you with your homework, you are likely to waste a lot of valuable time.

Basic Study Skills

Contrary to what you might have been led to believe, there is nothing especially mysterious about learning. Gathering clues about the world in which we live is a basic human instinct. Babies naturally explore everything they can reach—first, whatever they can focus on, then their own fingers and toes, and then whatever they can crawl to. All humans keep a curious eye out for anything that might seem interesting, fun, or worthy of exploration.

In order to increase the pleasure and success of the exploration and learning process, there are four basic skills that one needs to master: listening, taking notes, reading, and writing.

Active Listening

 Listening has three parts: hearing information, seeing nonverbal cues, and making connections with what you already know. Active listening is what happens when you are doing all three parts at the same time.

FAST Track Read Ahead

Get a leg up on the lecture. If you know that the teacher is going to cover the next chapter in tomorrow's class, read ahead or skim the material so that you'll know what's to be covered. You'll be amazed how much it helps to be familiar with the basic content and vocabulary of a lecture before it begins.

Understanding what people are saying, even in a casual conversation, results not only from hearing the words but also from watching face and body language for additional clues. You might ask a question to make sure you are on the same wavelength, or, if you are really interested in what they are saying, you might try chiming in with something similar from your own experience.

Since listening and paying attention are things you already know how to do, becoming an active listener in the classroom is mostly a matter of practice. At times, you may find yourself drifting because you have already absorbed what the teacher is saying. There are several ways to counteract this tendency to daydream:

Direct your gaze. Direct your attention to the speaker to let the person know you are paying attention and that you care about what he or she is saying. If you look closely, you may even get some ideas as to what the speaker thinks is most important about the subject.

Find out what it means. Sometimes we lose track simply because we hear too many technical terms at once. When the teacher mentions a word or phrase that is unfamiliar to you, jot it down. Then, as soon as you can, look it up in the back of your textbook or in a dictionary. Better yet, raise your hand and ask for clarification while you're in class—the other students probably will appreciate your asking!

Efficient Note Taking

If you think that taking notes and looking directly at your teacher cannot be done at the same time, you are 100 percent correct! Try this. Just jot down key concepts, then wait until the end of class to copy whatever the teacher has put on the board. Your notes will contain the major concepts, or "bare bones." When you go back and look at them later, you can test yourself by filling in details and "fleshing out the skeleton."

Graphic notes. Have you ever noticed how, when you are reading a textbook, your eyes will jump to charts and graphs before reading the text alongside them? Well, why not make a graphic representation while you are listening in class?

Using graphics rather than words can help simplify something that seems overwhelmingly complicated. While this is especially true in mathematics and science, it works equally well for English and social studies.

One effective type of note taking is a visual map. A visual map is a graphic organizer that simplifies concepts to the bare essentials and gives you a picture to use as a memory device. In addition, a visual map forces you to establish relationships among the different parts of your topic.

Some examples of visual maps are: a *spider map*, which has a center with legs protruding in different directions; a *chain of events,* featuring links that connect other chains that might intersect; a *timeline* that plots out a sequence of events in the chronological order in which they took place; and a *pie chart* that shows how a whole item breaks down into separate components.

You can also invent your own visual maps by using geometric shapes; forms from nature, such as simple tree and flower diagrams; and mechanical or architectural models.

Summarizing information. As a way to review what you've heard in class, write out your notes in a very compressed form. Take a few minutes to do this soon after learning the information—if possible, the same day. Then, when you read your homework assignment or do more reading on the same topic, you can put in additional information that you learn.

As a review before an exam, condense what you know about the topic down to a bare-bones skeleton. By putting your mind to work, forcing yourself to decide what are the most important points, you'll find that you are gaining control over the material.

Obviously, the fewer points you have to remember, the easier it will be to recall them. You'll be amazed at how much will come back to you when you need to flesh out the skeleton on an essay test. This technique is used effectively by many professional public speakers, who step up to the podium with only a few key words written on an index card.

Here are four basic steps to summarizing:

1. Substitute general concepts for specific details. Narrow down the material to what is most important. Be brutal; pick out only the top ideas.
2. Write a short sentence that describes the topic in terms of a simple overall idea.
3. Write a second sentence that covers the next most important aspect.
4. Write a third sentence dealing with one or more additional points that should be mentioned (if necessary), and your summary is complete.

Example:

Mesopotamia, which in Greek means "the land between two rivers," is sometimes called the "Cradle of Civilization," because the region was home to the earliest known civilization. The Tigris and Euphrates rivers run for more than 1,000 miles southward through the Fertile Crescent, in modern-day Iraq, into the Persian Gulf, carrying fertile silt with them. Each year, they overflow their banks, flooding the land of Mesopotamia and renewing its soil with their silt.

By 5000 B.C., numerous farming villages dotted Mesopotamia, and by 4500 B.C., artisans there had discovered how to extract metal from copper ore by heating it with charcoal. With this discovery, the Neolithic Age ended in Mesopotamia as metal tools and weapons replaced primitive stone ones. About 3000 B.C., Mesopotamian metalworkers made another technological breakthrough. They found that copper could be made harder and could hold a sharper edge by the addition of tin, thus producing bronze. With this discovery, the Bronze Age began in Mesopotamia.

(from Volume 13: "History of the World," in *Volume Library 1)*

Summary:

1. *General concepts:* Mesopotamia made up of land between Tigris and Euphrates rivers; farming land created by silt from river overflow; farmers used first stone tools, then copper, then bronze.
2. *Main idea:* Mesopotamia, the "Cradle of Civilization," moved out of the Neolithic Age around 4500 B.C. and into the Bronze Age around 3000 B.C.
3. *Secondary idea:* It was a farming region because of silt created from the yearly overflow of the Tigris and Euphrates rivers.
4. *Other points:*
   a. Region consists of part of modern-day Iraq and the area around the Persian Gulf
   b. Metal first extracted from copper ore by heating it with charcoal
   c. Bronze was created from copper by the addition of tin

More note-taking tips. Here are some other tips that you might find useful.

Review notes daily. It's helpful to look over your notes each day after school. This cuts down the amount of time that's required to study for tests, since you'll find that you're already well prepared.

Ask for overheads. If the teacher has used overheads, ask if you may borrow them to have copies made. Often these overheads do an excellent job of summarizing the information that the teacher has presented.

Develop your own shorthand. It is helpful to have your own personal shorthand, using symbols that will help you plow through your notes and quickly find the information you need. Examples of these symbols might include: a star for noting a key point; a large question mark for identifying information that you don't understand and need to look up; a capital letter *L* indicating reference books from the library that can offer additional information on the topic.

AN EXAMPLE of graphic notes

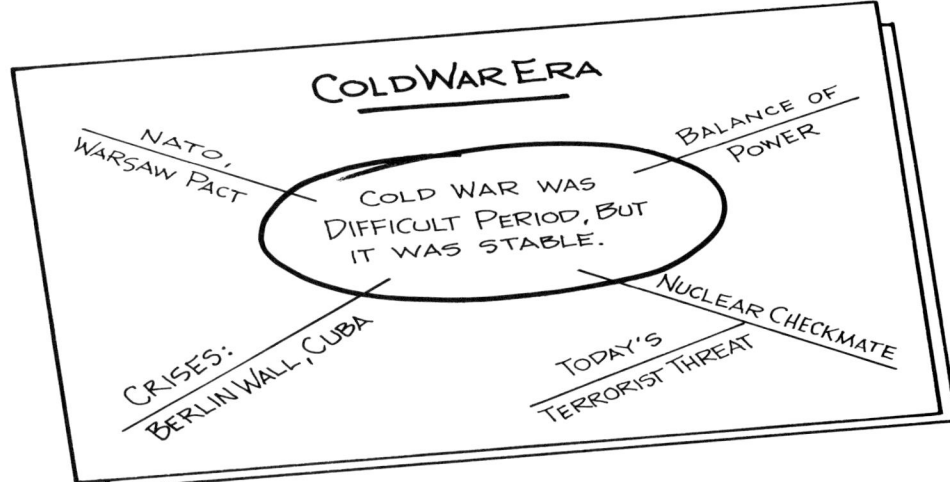

Reading for Comprehension

 Reading affects learning more than any other factor. Think of reading as independence; that is, being able to read and retain information keeps you from having to rely on someone else to tell you. When you read, you are in control of your time and what you are putting into your mind. In fact, reading is the most valuable tool you have outside the classroom.

Skim first, then read for real. The brain works in an amazing way, taking in far more information than we realize. Its ability to process material subliminally, or below the surface, has been proven by the use of television advertising. A subliminal message is an image that flashes on the screen so fast that the conscious mind does not acknowledge it, but it registers on the brain. This type of below-the-surface mental processing is why pre-reading—the practice of skimming the material before you read it in detail—works so well. Your brain will intuitively start to organize the material once it realizes the scope of what will be covered.

Pre-reading consists of:

1. *Skimming the table of contents.* Get a feel for the overall approach to the subject, and note how your chapter relates to the whole.
2. *Looking at every page quickly.* Flip through the chapter you are about to read, looking at titles, subheadings, tables, and charts. This will take just a few minutes, but it will tell you where the chapter is going and how much material is to be covered.
3. *Reading the review questions at the end of the chapter.* This will tell you what the important points are.

Read to understand, then to remember. When you do get around to reading the material in depth, keep in mind that the key to remembering what you've read is first to understand the material. To do this, keep your mind focused on the topic and make sure you follow what the author is trying to say before you move on.

Make sure you are reading at a pace that allows you to digest the information. Whenever possible, try to make a connection to something you already know. Once you comprehend the information, it will be a lot easier to remember it.

More Reading Tips. Here are some more reading tips you might find useful.

Jot down what you already know about the topic. Before starting, write down what you think is probably going to be covered in the chapter and try to connect it with things that may be related. Do this quickly, with just a few words. Don't judge your responses, as they may be more on target than you think. Even if they're not, at least you'll be thinking about the topic and ready to learn.

Read with pencil or highlighter in hand. When you are reading, underline or highlight the points that you think are the most important. Later, when you are studying for a test, this will make it easier to spot likely test items. However, save this technique for the key points; an entire chapter of underlined or highlighted material will do you little good.

Put yourself in the author's shoes. What is the author's point of view? How does the author approach the material? Why would the author want to tell this particular story in this particular way? Questions such as these can help make you a more active reader.

Look up things as you go. If you don't know or can't remember the meaning of a word, look it up in a good dictionary. Don't get stumped on the first word and wonder about it all the way through your reading. That single word that you don't understand may be the key to understanding the whole assignment.

Write your own review questions. When you finish the reading assignment, make up a few questions of your own to address what you feel is most important about the topic. Try out the questions on your classmates or parents.

Consult another source if you need to. If you are still unclear about what you have read, find a different textbook, an encyclopedia, or a library book on the subject. Ask your teacher or librarian if you need assistance.

When possible, pick something that interests you. When given the choice, try reading something you would enjoy, such as a book about rock climbing, a short story about someone your age, or a novel from which a favorite movie was made.

Don't be shy about problems. If you have trouble reading, you may need glasses or a new prescription, or you may have a visual disorder such as dyslexia. In either case, once diagnosed, the problem is treatable.

Practice, practice, practice. You weren't born able to walk, and the same thing goes for reading. Like any skill, it takes practice, and the more you practice, the better you'll be. If you have difficulty reading, practice improving your skills by reading magazines or books on topics that appeal to you.

Effective Writing

Good writing skills are essential for letting other people know how you think and how well you understand a particular topic. Only through good writing and effective presentation skills can you show teachers and future employers or customers your mastery of a given subject. While term papers and essay tests on "boring" topics may have seemed like a waste of time up to now, think of them as practice for the future and a tangible way to demonstrate your skills.

Start with a problem or question.
If you treat any piece of writing as a question to answer or a problem to solve, things will tend to fall into place. The statement of the problem becomes your topic sentence. The final answer becomes your conclusion. Your exploration of possible solutions—or, in mathematics, your presentation of the proof—becomes the body or text.

Do not attempt to start writing until you know specifically the question or problem you are trying to address. If you skip this first, important step, you're in for a bumpy and frustrating ride.

Organize your thoughts before you write.
Most writers claim that preliminary organization is the most important part of the writing process. Many writers produce an outline showing key topics to be covered and the main points to be addressed under each topic. This outline serves as a map to guide them from point *A* to point *B* as they work on their paper.

Other writers put their thoughts onto note cards. Then, when they have listed all the points they want to make, they organize the cards into the order they would like to use in the final paper. Make sure to format your paper by using headlines and subheads, paragraph breaks, or more formal outlining techniques, such as roman numerals and letters, so that readers can see clearly how your paper is organized.

Edit later.
You may find that, in order to develop your thoughts, you'll write more than you will actually use and then cut it down to size. This is standard procedure for most writers. In fact, editing, or selecting the best of what you have written, is a valuable skill that will be useful throughout your schooling and career.

State your conclusion.
No matter what you are writing, don't forget to state a conclusion or summarize your thoughts. You can place this at the beginning and use the rest of the paper to substantiate your findings, or you can place it at the end, using the beginning of the paper to build your case. Either way, stating a conclusion will make readers feel satisfied that you have told them something. In fact, many of the best speakers in the world follow this sage advice in organizing presentations: Tell the audience what you're going to say; say it; then tell them what you just said.

Keep track of the reference material.
Be sure to keep a list of the books you consulted in your research, along with the page numbers where you found the information. You will need title, author, publisher, place of publication, and year published in order to prepare your footnotes and bibliography. It's a lot easier to keep track of these as you go along than to re-create them at the end.

Make a good impression.
Whether you're writing a short essay or a long term paper, go that extra mile to make the presentation as impressive as possible. Use good penmanship, type on clean and uncrumpled paper, or print out from a computer using a neat, readable typeface. Check spelling carefully. Use a cover sheet showing the title of the paper, the name of the class, the teacher, your own name, and the date.

A professional-looking presentation may impress teachers enough that they will overlook shaky logic or minor inconsistencies. Have a classmate critique your work before you turn it in, on the basis of both content and presentation quality.

Make it interesting.
Don't think of writing as drudgery. When you are allowed to choose a topic, pick something that is relevant and interesting to you. If you think your topic is too wacky, check with your teacher—you may be surprised to find that it's approved! If it's not approved, at least the teacher may help you come up with an interesting alternative.

Realize that writing is a process of revision.
In the workplace, projects are done in stages and are usually revised several times along the way. Once you have written a first draft by hand, show it to friends and ask for constructive criticism.

A computer can also be helpful in the editing process, especially if you're planning to revise your work more than once. Sometimes just seeing it on the computer screen or printed out will enable you to spot mistakes. Reading your own writing on a computer can also help you see how to rearrange and improve it.

In a Bind?

Try the Morning

One secret to good concentration is having few distractions. Lots of writers work best in the early morning. Try waking up an hour early and dedicating this time to your writing. Who knows? You might discover that you're a morning person.

---

your turn

Want to Improve?

Below, under *My Strengths*, list three aspects of studying that you do exceptionally well. Under *Things to Improve*, list three things that you would like to do better or need to work on. For each of the three things to be improved, list at least two methods under *Ways to Improve*.

	My Strengths	Things to Improve	Ways to Improve
1.			
2.			
3.			

Study Tips: By Subject Area

No matter what subject you're studying, the assignments can be broken down into several types: those that concentrate on problem solving, those that require interpretation, and those that are primarily informational. Different subject areas require different types of study skills.

Problem solving is the process of finding a solution to a specific question. Coming to the correct answer in a timely, efficient way requires understanding basic principles and being able to prove them, often by working them out on paper. It's easy to see that the study of mathematics and science will probably require lots of problem solving.

Interpretation means speculating about, analyzing, and explaining a given topic. Writing and reading are the most important skills that come into play. Interpretation is a major component of the study of literature, art, religion, philosophy, or any other subject involving a symbolic vocabulary.

Informational subject areas are those in which you concentrate on learning facts: events, names, dates, definitions. These subjects often require a certain amount of memorizing, thus lending themselves to the use of visual organizers such as visual maps, which will help imprint information on the memory.

Before you continue reading, try to guess which of the three skills you will be using in each of the following subject areas: mathematics, English, science, and social studies. This will help focus your attention and put you in a receptive frame of mind as you read about each of these four subjects.

Mathematics: The Way We Get Things Done

Why mathematics? Mathematics was invented by the Egyptians in order to measure the world around them and build structures they could use. Mathematics is a language all its own that is made up of logic and computation. It's a universal language and can be understood by people in all parts of the world. In fact, many people who have only a rudimentary grasp of the English language work in highly paid mathematics and engineering positions in the United States.

Mathematics is a continuum that begins with simple addition and subtraction and builds to higher mathematics such as algebra, geometry, trigonometry, and calculus. These and other forms of mathematics involve solving problems through the use of formulas and algorithms. (An algorithm is a series of steps to follow, usually involving mathematical operations, in order to find the solution to a particular type of problem.)

Computation and measurement. Making change, keeping up with your checkbook, organizing your earnings into a budget so that you don't run out of money before your next paycheck—all these require you to add, subtract, multiply, and divide. You will use these basic computational skills your whole life, so make

10 Jobs Requiring Strong Mathematical Skills

1. Biochemist
2. Architect
3. Musician
4. Doctor
5. Aerospace engineer
6. Chef
7. Electrician
8. Fashion designer
9. Accountant
10. Mapmaker

Biochemist

sure you learn them now. Farmers, carpenters, clerks, and many other workers use computation many times each day.

It's also important to become familiar with weights and measures of all kinds. Since people in different parts of the world use different systems, we must learn to convert measurements from one to another. In many countries the metric system is used (meters, grams, liters), while other countries use the English system (feet, pounds, gallons).

Converting from one system to another is done by means of a formula in which the number you know is inserted, and a calculation converts the number into its equivalent in the other system. Using a formula with calculations in mathematics is only one of the many facets of mathematics called algebra.

Units of measure enable us to compare things to each other, such as distances between pairs of cities. Formulas for describing distance are contained in geometry, which literally means *world measuring*.

Mathematics for the future. The language of computer programming is based on mathematics, and that fact alone makes it essential for the twenty-first-century workplace. You may not need to know how to program your own computer in order to use it, but the more you understand the basic principles of mathematics, the more comfortable you will feel with computers.

Space exploration, which was made possible through mathematics, has vividly demonstrated many new and exciting ways in which mathematics can be used and applied. If mathematics comes easily to you, challenge yourself to stick with it. Perhaps you will become an inventor of technology for the twenty-second century!

How to study mathematics. Here are some tips that may prove useful as you study mathematics.

Even in mathematics, reading is key. Reading comprehension is a fundamental skill that must be mastered for mathematics—for example, to pick out the operative (key) words when detecting what mathematical principle the text explains. To understand your reading in mathematics, try to form a mental picture of the idea so that it will stick in your mind. A slope in geometry can be pictured as the incline of a ski slope, a wheelchair ramp, or a mountain road.

Hone your memorizing skills. Mathematics is, in many ways, like a foreign language. Just as in learning a new language, *memorizing* is imperative. Even terms that seem familiar may have an entirely different meaning in a mathematical context, and you must sometimes practice operations you don't fully understand over and over until they finally become second nature.

To assist you in memorizing a new word or formula, write it down on the left side of a clean sheet of notebook paper. On the right side, show the definition or sample calculations that demonstrate how the formula works. In time, you will develop a personalized glossary of terms and formulas that you need to know.

Accuracy is a basic mathematical skill. Learn to check your work as you go, since this will, in the long term, save you time and frustration. Mathematical problems often involve a series of steps that build on one another. By the time you notice an error, you may be way off the track, performing some operation that is not even required by the problem.

Think of word problems as situations in life. Word problems in mathematics are often based on things we can relate to, such as how long it will take to get from one place to another if we drive at a certain speed, or

how many cookies we can make from a recipe if the cookie size is changed. We construct similar scenarios in our day-to-day life, whether we realize it or not. The first time you see yourself "living" a word problem you'll probably laugh—but you'll be glad that you paid attention in mathematics class!

Use a calculator as a tool, not a crutch. In most schools, the ability to use (or not to use) a calculator is dictated by school policy. If you are allowed to use a calculator you should definitely take advantage of it to solve problems, but make sure you understand the basic principles behind each problem and could work it out on paper if you had to. There's always the chance that the calculator batteries might die at the worst possible moment—during a test or in a real-life situation, where you need to make a calculation that could save money, time, or even your life.

English: The Language We Can't Live Without

Spoken language is what we use to communicate with other people. English is the international language of business and, as such, is used all over the world.

Writing and speaking in understandable English is a requirement in almost all "service industry" business situations today. After all, service means helping others, and businesses must communicate with their customers. Being able to compose a business letter, knowing how to address someone formally, using correct grammar, punctuation, and spelling—these are no longer optional; they are required!

Not only must you be prepared to speak and write in standard English; you must also be able to understand the different ways in which English is spoken. In the United States there are many regional dialects that may be difficult to follow. Learn how to listen carefully to what is being said, particularly if the person speaks English haltingly or with a heavy accent.

Courtesy is also a part of good listening. Paying attention to the customs and manners of other people may save you from embarrassing yourself. This is also true in classroom situations. How many times have you heard someone ask a question that had already been asked?

English has both Latin and Germanic roots. Consider taking a course in one or both of those languages; you'll find that they actually help your English skills!

How to study English. Studying English really involves three different subjects: learning a language, reading literature, and writing.

Update the basics. Learning about language—how we speak and what we say—may seem like a "slam dunk," since talking is an everyday activity that we tend to take for granted. After all, most of us learned to speak just by listening to the members of our family when we were tiny babies. Using the language correctly, however, may be another matter. Be aware that you may be faced with correcting what you've been doing all these years!

You'll also learn rules that explain the way English works—for example, *i* before *e* except after *c*. As we pointed out before, this is informational learning. Repeat these rules over and over again, using flashcards or other memory techniques, until they become second nature. Keep in mind, though, that even experienced writers and editors keep a good style manual close at hand so that they can look up the rules.

Use interpretive skills. Studying literature calls for interpretive skills as well. You'll be called upon to analyze what you have read, using additional sources, then give your own opinions about the material. Keep in mind that the way an idea is expressed (style) might turn out to be nearly as important as the idea itself (content).

Don't be afraid to ask questions about your reading assignments. If you've read the assigned passages and are still confused, chances are the rest of the class is, too. You may be surprised at how relieved everyone else will be when you ask a simple question.

At home, keep a log in your notebook as you read, jotting down things that strike you as odd or interesting. Write down questions. Map out character relationships. Show the sequence of events (*plot*) along a timeline.

Practice reading a computer manual. At some point, you'll need to learn how to use a computer or a new piece of computer software. Chances are, your introduction to it will include reading an instruction book or manual. This may be some of the most difficult and detailed reading that you ever do. As you plow through it, practice your reading comprehension. Reading for understanding as you learn something new will increase your reading comprehension skills overall.

Practice writing letters and reports. Composing your own business letters and reports can be a good way to practice English skills. First, locate a model or "template" that shows the correct form—for example, in a style manual. If you're working on a computer, use desktop publishing features to enhance your work, including choice of type, style, and color.

When you get ready to write, remember the adage: Tell them what you're going to say; say it; then tell them what you just said.

See a movie; read the book. Notice how many current movies are being made from works that were originally published as books. If you like a movie that was adapted in this way, go back and read the book. You may be surprised to see how much different it is from the movie.

Foreign Languages: They May Be Easier Than You Ever Imagined!

Studying a foreign language involves more memorizing than any other subject. Just as you learned English, however, you can pick up a lot merely by listening and repeating.

- Learn through repetitive exercises: listen, repeat; listen, repeat. If you're having trouble remembering pronunciations, make some notes to yourself using phonetic spelling.

- If a language lab is available, use it! You are probably going to encounter recorded tapes that your teacher will play in a language lab. Repetition and imitation of the spoken words you hear are best done by regular practice, and the language lab is a great place to do it.

- Drill for vocabulary. Read the word to yourself, then write it in a sentence. Then repeat the word without looking at it, and write it out while saying it aloud.

- Practice listening and speaking. Rent a film in the language you are studying, or try to find someone to talk to, perhaps at a restaurant where the staff speaks the language. Use recorded children's books and music to help you "hear" the language and distinquish words and phrases.

- Find something written in the language that interests you, such as the French *Climbing* magazine or the Italian *Vogue*, and see how much easier reading becomes.

10 Jobs Requiring Strong English Skills

1. Television news anchor
2. Public relations executive
3. Minister or rabbi
4. Office manager
5. Union official
6. Museum curator
7. Sales representative
8. Teacher
9. Athletic coach
10. Telemarketer

Telemarketer

Escape through reading. One of the pleasures of mastering English is being able to read the great works of literature. Reading fiction is a good way to learn about people and places. It can also provide a feeling of independence, since you can explore worlds very different from your own. Try recreational reading as a break from your studies; you'll be building vocabulary and improving your reading skills all the while.

Develop a writing style of your own. If you are lucky enough to have a creative writing unit in your English course, make the most of it. When skillfully practiced, writing can be as much an art form as music, dance, or the visual arts. You do have to learn techniques, just as painters and sculptors do, but once those techniques are mastered you will have a wonderful way of expressing yourself artfully.

When you're writing creatively, don't be discouraged by criticism. Listen to the comments of friends, family, and teachers, but remember that you are the ultimate judge of your work. It may help you to know that every famous author has a drawer full of rejection letters.

Social Studies: People, Places, and Governments

Why social studies? Social studies is the study of people and the way they organize and relate. Unless you're planning to spend your life as a hermit, this study will be extremely valuable, no matter what career you choose.

Social studies includes not only past history but also current events in such subjects as government and civics. You can make this up-to-the-minute interesting by applying it to the city or town in which you live.

The use of the word *social* to describe these areas of study is no coincidence. Because all the professions listed above require that you work with other people, often in a public capacity, your communications skills will be critical.

How to study social studies. Social studies includes history, geography, and civics, and so it has the widest range of informational learning of any group of subjects. Proper names will often need to be memorized; therefore, memory devices such as acronyms and association will sometimes help.

"Map" your textbooks. Textbooks can be mapped according to headings and subheadings in order to keep track of the basic divisions of any long portion of a book. Making up questions that you can use for review later is another good way to keep your mind working while you read. It will also make studying for tests a lot easier.

Use graphs, charts, and tables. Because of the diversity of subjects included under the umbrella of social studies, it also encompasses almost every other type of learning skill. In economics, sociology, and psychology, for example, it is important to look at graphs, charts, and tables in order to determine trends over a period of time. The design of these visual structures calls for problem-solving skills; their interpretation involves interpretive skills; and the statistics on which they are based require computational mathematics skills.

Bring subjects alive. Many textbooks include maps and tables that will help you visualize a subject. Maps and demographic charts of a population can make a country come alive, as you begin to compare and relate it to where you live. For example, you might learn from a chart that the population density in an Asian city is one thousand people per square block. When you think that in your own town a block might contain four houses with an average of four people per house, you begin to see just how crowded that Asian city really is.

Study your own community. If you are studying the various levels of government in a civics class, get out the phone book and look up the office where you would go to get a passport, a driver's license, and a building permit for a swimming pool. In which section of the phone book did you find each one? What does that tell you? Whom would you contact if a rabid animal was prowling your neighborhood? Where would you go to get an automobile registration?

Basing your study on real examples will leave a more lasting impression and may actually be helpful later on in your life.

10 Jobs Requiring Strong Social Studies Skills

1. Marriage and family counselor
2. Librarian
3. Newspaper reporter
4. Diplomat
5. Historian
6. Paralegal
7. Social worker
8. Politician
9. Anthropologist
10. Focus group moderator

Librarian

Science: The World Around Us

Why science? Science is in many ways the most useful of all subjects. It is, simply, the methods which humans have devised over the years for understanding and explaining the world around us.

Because our planet and the universe are so complex, separate disciplines of science have been developed: life sciences (biology, botany) dealing with living matter and physical sciences (geology, chemistry, physics) for non-living matter. Environmental science, which explores the way the two interact, is a newly developing field of its own.

As we begin the twenty-first century, a working knowledge of science will be more important than ever before. Among the scientific terms we will be hearing more about are cloning (the artificial creation of living things through genetic duplication), genetic alteration (changing the features of plants or animals by means of DNA manipulation) and global warming (the effect of atmospheric pollution on the world climate).

How to study science. The study of science combines all three learning styles: it's informational and interpretive and requires problem solving.

Analyze words. Become familiar with Greek and Latin roots, as these are often used in scientific terminology—for example, bio/logy (life/study, from Greek). Once you've learned a term in this way, you're more likely to recognize it when you see it again, and you'll have an easier time spelling it. You'll also have a headstart in defining other words that use those same roots.

Define all terms. Definitions in science are very specific and sometimes differ from everyday definitions. For example, when a scientific theory is described as elegant, the word is being used quite differently from its use in, say, the fashion industry.

Think like a scientist. Many people think science is a permanent set of facts that never change. Wrong! Scientists are posing new questions every day, based on what they observe and what they do or don't understand. Among their activities are the following:

- Observation: What do you see?
- Classification: How can it be arranged or sorted?
- Questioning: What questions can be posed based on what you have seen?
- Predicting: What do you think might happen based on what you have seen?
- Measuring: How can you calculate what has happened?
- Reporting: How will you communicate the results?
- Interpreting: What patterns do you observe, and what, if anything, can you hypothesize?
- Hypothesizing: What can you pose as a question that an experiment might answer?
- Experimenting: What methods will you use in trying to prove the hypothesis?
- Formulating a model: What conclusion can you make based on this process of inquiry?

Learn the "art" of science. As you can see, in this quest for truth that we call science, the ability to interpret is critical. Does this sound vaguely familiar? Perhaps that's because, at the cutting edge, the work of scientists is closer to the artistic process than any other discipline.

Keep notes on experiments. In the sciences, problem solving often

 **Watch TV!**

This is one time when watching television can actually be good for you. Some channels often broadcast specials on hot scientific topics. The field of science is expanding rapidly, and true discoveries can be fascinating entertainment.

involves experiments, done either in the lab by the student or in class by the teacher. In either case, here are a couple of pointers:

- Draw a diagram of the lab setup and label all the parts. Make the diagram large enough to label with additional information that you'll be gathering later.

- As the experiment is conducted, write out and number the steps. If you can, connect those steps to the scientific principles being demonstrated. Then, after the experiment, review your notes and form conclusions.

Calculate carefully. Science is done in steps, like mathematics, and reasoning is done in sequence in order to reach conclusions. If you make a mistake early on, it can throw the whole process off. Always check your figures and equations carefully!

10 Jobs Requiring Strong Science Skills

1. Veterinarian
2. Computer software designer
3. Geologist
4. Park ranger
5. Pharmacist
6. Printer
7. Geneticist
8. Recording engineer
9. Astronaut
10. Lab technician

Astronaut

Taking Tests: A Fact of Life

Taking tests is a necessity not just in school but in life after school as well. Most employers conduct on-the-job testing of some kind, whether it's in the form of a typing test or a supervisor's accompanying you on sales rounds. Since tests take many different forms, try to determine in advance what skills they will require.

One example is the driver's test. You must be able to read through the driver's manual and answer questions related to it. This requires *reading comprehension skills*. Some of the questions may require you to analyze cause and effect; others, to apply a rule that you are supposed to know. These demand *analytical thinking skills*. There's usually a section on traffic laws that requires *memory skills*. Finally, there is the driving test itself, in which you actually demonstrate *physical skills*. In this exam, as in daily driving, you are applying your knowledge.

Keep in mind that test taking is a natural part of any learning process, whether at school or on the job.

Before the test

Find out what kind of test you'll be taking. For example, if you know the test involves only multiple-choice questions, you won't want to waste a lot of time memorizing information. Then determine its scope: How much material will be covered, and at what level of detail?

Start early. Begin far enough in advance with a preliminary review, even if you can't devote much time to it. This process will remind your brain to be working on the material in the meantime. Allowing a subject to percolate in your mind can yield surprising results.

Get help if you need it. Ask a classmate to help you review a section or memorize the most important points.

Be good to yourself along the way. Don't panic. Make sure you take a break when you need one. Get enough sleep before a test. If you are calm and well rested, you are more likely to be able to think logically. You're also more likely to remember what you learned in the classroom, even if you haven't had time to review it.

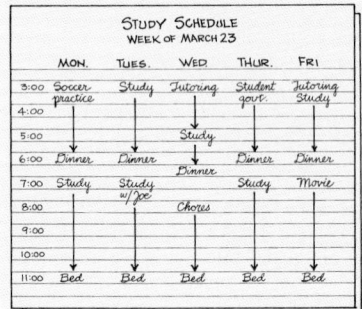

AN IMPORTANT part of planning for a test is making a study schedule.

At the test

Give yourself a pep talk. Remind yourself that tests are merely an extension of the study process. When you make up your own questions for review, you are self testing. When you summarize your reading into a skeleton, you are getting ready to flesh it out on a test.

Be confident of your ability to remember what you've learned. Picture your visual maps. Think about the ways in which your brain has formed relationships between new and old knowledge. A test isn't a life-or-death situation, so relax and try your best, knowing you did what you could to prepare.

Make a strategic plan. Take a moment to preview the test mentally. Determine what types of skills you will need and put them into action.

Plan Your Strategy

Planning your study strategy is still worthwhile even if you have very little time to devote to it. Devise a plan that makes sense for you. You might decide to spend your limited study time concentrating on what you don't know, and leave what you know best for just a final review the night before the test.

Remind yourself that a test is a way to demonstrate what you have learned. If you aren't sure what answer the teacher is looking for, try at least to show that you have some knowledge of the material.

10 Test-Taking Tips

1. Stop studying at least a half hour before the test.
2. Try not to talk to others about the material while waiting for the test to begin.
3. As soon as you are allowed to begin, before you even read the test, jot down anything you have on the tip of your tongue so you don't lose it—facts, formulas, dates.
4. Read the test directions thoroughly. Ask about anything you do not understand.
5. Look through the entire test, note how many parts there are, and budget your time on each section accordingly.
6. If there are essay questions, read them and briefly outline the points you want to cover. That way you won't forget anything important when you start writing.
7. Go through the test once quickly, answering everything you know for sure. Then go back and spend time on items you're unsure of.
8. When you're not sure of an answer, make your best guess and put a mark in the margin so you can come back for a final look at it if you have time.
9. Estimate the answer to computations before you solve them, to insure that you don't make decimal-place errors.
10. Check your work. Make sure crossed-out answers are fully hidden and all your other answers are legible. Don't change answers unless you are absolutely sure; first impulses are generally correct.

Test strategies, by type of test

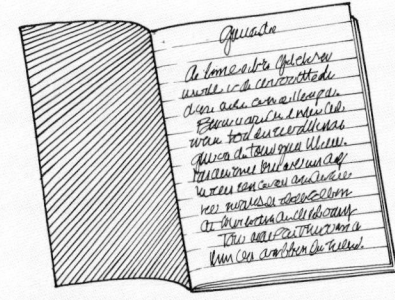

MULTIPLE CHOICE

- Read all the choices, even though the first one may be correct. It is possible that all the answers are correct and that the correct choice is "all of the above."
- Make a note in the margin, such as a star or dash, for the questions you haven't answered, so you don't miss them later.
- Reread the questions you're struggling with to make sure you understand them. Can you eliminate one or more of the answer choices?
- Try to think of or visualize the context in which you learned the information. Perhaps that will provide some clues.
- If there is no penalty for guessing, then do so if you are sure you do not know the answer.

TRUE-FALSE

- Keep in mind that if any part of a statement is false, then the entire statement is considered false.
- Watch out for absolutes, such as all, always, never, and only; they often are used in false statements.
- Two-part true/false questions often involve logical thinking or pretend to be logical when they are not. Reword them to make certain that you are not fooled by the way they are written. (For example: A train is faster than a car, and a bike is faster than a train.)

ESSAY (LONGER ANSWERS)

- Read all questions thoroughly, noting key concepts and any terms you do not understand. Ask for clarification if you are allowed to do so.
- Before you start to write, briefly outline the points you want to make, so you don't forget any of them.
- Think about what you can add to your answers to make them distinctive and unusual, such as a quotation or unusual example.
- Begin each answer with a statement that either answers the question or tells what you are proposing to accomplish in your essay.
- Avoid writing just to fill space.
- Give your best answer first. Doing a good job on one question will give you momentum and confidence for the others.
- Check the time periodically to make sure you are progressing at a good pace. If you have extra time at the end, go back over the questions and do some editing, stressing key points.

WORD PROBLEMS IN MATHEMATICS AND SCIENCE

- Read all the problems thoroughly, underlining the key concepts.
- Jot down any formulas, equations, or principles that will jog your memory later.
- Note whether any problems are worth more points than others, and allow yourself more time to do those.
- If you find yourself spending too much time on one problem, leave it and move on to the others. You can come back to it once you have finished.
- Try to predict the range of possible answers before you solve a problem. This will help to prevent careless errors.
- Double-check computation, units of measure, and other simple things you might have overlooked.
- Use a drawing or diagram to help you think out a problem.
- Check your work, making sure that errors are completely crossed out.
- Even if you can't solve a problem, show that you have some understanding of the principles involved by inserting the correct formula or drawing a diagram.

WORD PROBLEMS IN OTHER SUBJECTS

- Decide how much time you have for each problem.
- Notice the way the problems are worded. Do they in fact mean what they appear to say, or or they "trick" questions?
- Watch for flaws in logic that tell you something could not possibly be true.
- If you can't remember the meaning of a term, try to infer its meaning from the related ideas and terms surrounding it.

SHORT ANSWERS

- Read questions carefully. Make sure you know what is being asked.
- If you are given explicit instructions (such as list, define, or identify), make sure you follow them exactly.
- If you don't know the answer but know something related to it, write it down; perhaps you will receive partial credit.
- If you have some notion of what is being asked and there is no penalty for wrong answers, make an educated guess. Never leave it blank!

College Entrance Exams

College entrance exams are one way in which most colleges evaluate students who apply for admission. In addition, students and counselors frequently use scores to help them determine colleges and universities to which students can apply realistically.

Test scores are not the be-all and end-all for getting into college, and how they are used varies from one school to the next. They are, however, an important part of the college admissions process, and students should be familiar with them.

This section will give an overview of the entrance exams used by most colleges and universities in the United States, including registration procedures, scoring information, and advice on preparing for and taking the exams. The three major exams then will be described. For each exam, pages of sample test items will be provided, along with tips for answering them correctly.

Overview

Most colleges in the United States will specify that students take either the SAT I: Reasoning Test (Scholastic Aptitude Test) or the ACT (American College Test). Some schools also require the SAT II: Subject Tests, previously known as the Achievement Tests, which cover specific subject areas. (The PSAT, a preliminary version of the SAT I, enables students to prepare for the SAT I and helps students select colleges where they will apply.)

Entrance exams are offered several times during each academic year. The SAT I generally is offered in October, November, December, January, March, May, and June; the SAT II tests are on many of the same dates as the SAT I; and the ACT, in September, October, December, February, April, and June.

Many locations are used to administer entrance exams. High schools and colleges are the most frequently used test sites. You may need to travel a substantial distance from home to get to the test site; if this is the case, you will need to make travel arrangements in advance.

How to Register

During your sophomore or junior year, talk with your counselor about which tests to take, when to take them, and how to register. Your counselor should have the forms and information that you will need. Also, you can write to the appropriate testing company to request registration information.

In the case of the SAT I and II, you need the *SAT Program Registration Bulletin*, which provides registration information and forms for both SAT I and SAT II.

For the SAT I, you also will need *Taking the SAT I Reasoning Test*, which provides background, tips for taking the test, sample questions, and an explanation of the scoring system. A similar booklet about the SAT II is available, called *Taking the SAT II: Subject Tests*.

Corresponding information is available for the ACT, in the form of the booklets *Registering for the ACT Assessment* and *Preparing for the ACT Assessment*.

Select your test date and center. Be sure to file the forms by the deadline and pay the appropriate fees. Students can register either by mail or Online (http://www.collegeboard.org) and pay using Visa, MasterCard, or American Express. If you are retaking the SAT, you can reregister either Online or by phone (800-728-7267).

Most tests have a date for late registration, for which the fee is higher. You may be able to register on a standby basis on the day of the test, though the fee will be still higher, with no assurance of space. Going standby is strongly discouraged.

After registering, you will receive from the testing company confirmation as well as an admission ticket, which you will need to get into the test. If you do not receive this packet, or if you lose the ticket, call the testing company.

Registration forms. Follow directions carefully when you complete exam registration forms. The forms are processed by machine; you will need to use a No. 2 pencil to complete them.

The forms ask for routine information such as your name, address, phone number, Social Security number, date of birth, and grade level. You enter codes that represent the high school you attend and the center where you want to take the test. Obtain your school code from your counselor. The test center code, as well as codes for scholarships and colleges where you would like to have scores sent, are in the registration bulletin. The fee covers the cost of sending scores to several schools; you can send them to more locations at additional cost. You may be able to list a first and second choice for the test center. Register early.

The registration form for the SAT I and SAT II includes the Student Descriptive Questionnaire (SDQ), which you complete once, not each time you register. The SDQ is a voluntary form; it asks questions about your courses, grades, activities, goals, and interests. By completing this questionnaire, you can share information with colleges and your counselor; colleges often use this information to recruit students. You may update the information on the SDQ whenever you want, for example, when you finish courses taken since first completing the form.

Registration fees. A set fee is charged each time you take an entrance exam; the fee can be paid by check or money order (credit card for phone or electronic registration). Late fees are charged if you do not register on time. Other fees may be required for additional services. Some of these charges are for sending scores to additional colleges or sending them after you have taken the test.

You may have an option to receive a scoring sheet for your test or to have your test scored by hand rather than machine. Other services, such as informational books or guides, carry additional costs. If you cannot afford the test fee, speak with your counselor; you may be eligible for a fee-waiver card.

Special circumstances. Sometimes students have circumstances that require special accommodations. For example, students whose religious practices prevent their taking the test on Saturday may request a Sunday test date. Students who are hearing impaired can make arrangements to have a signer available at the test site. Students with visual impairments can arrange to take the test in large type, Braille, or on cassette; they also may be allowed to have a reader with them or take the test at their own school rather than one of the regularly scheduled test centers. Students with learning disabilities may need additional test time to accommodate their circumstances. Weather conditions, ill-

Scores Are Personal

Entrance exams are only one part of how colleges evaluate you. Your scores are your business. Only the people and schools you choose to notify need to find out how you performed. Don't feel pressured to tell others your scores and don't pressure others to tell you theirs.

ness or injury, or a death in the family may require a student to reschedule a test.

These accommodations are not available for all tests, nor at all times. Read the test bulletin to learn more about them. If you find that you need a special accomodation, first speak with your counselor to determine what arrangements can be made.

Scoring

Entrance exams are scored and reported in a variety of ways. For the SAT I and II, the first step in scoring determines a raw score based on the number of correct answers within a section minus a fraction of the incorrect answers. This fraction varies from one-fourth to one-third. The total raw scores are rounded to whole numbers, then converted to scores ranging from 200 to 800. Scores are reported in multiples of ten (500, 510, 520, and so on).

NOTE: On the SAT I and II, students are penalized for incorrect answers; therefore, random guessing may result in lower scores than skipping questions.

On the SAT I, your combined score is the sum of your verbal and math scores. For example, a verbal score of 600 and a math score of 540 produce a combined score of 1140. Colleges may seek students with certain combined scores. They also may set minimal cutoffs for verbal and math scores.

The ACT converts raw scores to overall scores, on a scale of 1 to 36. Students receive scores for each of the four major sections and a composite score for the whole test. They also receive subscores, on a range of 1 to 18, for different parts of tests. There are seven subscores, including two within the English test (one subscore for usage and mechanics and another for rhetorical skills). Within the mathematics test, students receive three subscores (one for pre-algebra and elementary algebra, one for intermediate algebra and coordinate geometry, and one for plane geometry and trigonometry). The reading test has two subscores (one for arts and literature and the other for social studies and sciences). Unlike the SAT I and II, the ACT does not penalize for incorrect answers.

The information packets from the testing companies explain the scoring process in more detail.

Who receives scores? Students receive their scores approximately three weeks after taking their entrance exams. The information they receive includes not only their scores but information about how their scores compare nationally to other students. Scores are also sent to the high school, provided the high school code is listed on the registration forms. Students can receive and send scores by phone. Call toll-free at 800-728-7267.

Students can designate colleges and scholarship programs where scores should be sent. Unless they cancel such requests, the scores are sent at about the same time they are sent to students. In addition, subsequent to taking the test, students can request that scores be sent to additional locations.

Sending scores. Test scores should be sent to all colleges where you plan to apply and which require or recommend that you take a particular test. You may want to send scores to colleges where you are thinking of applying.

For example, when you take the SAT I, your fees include sending your scores to four colleges or scholarship programs. If you are sure of only two but are strongly considering other colleges, then go ahead and send your scores to two more, because you've already paid to have scores sent to four locations.

If possible, choose these locations at the time that you register. If you don't designate where to send scores at the time of registration, they can be sent later by phone instructions or with Online service. This takes approximately three weeks once tests are scored. For a $20 fee plus $6.50 per college or university, scores can be rushed within two working days of the phone call, once tests have been scored.

Test scores are cumulative. Suppose you take the SAT I three times. If you report scores to a particular college the third time you take the SAT I, your scores from the first two times will be reported as well.

Canceling scores. Frequently students complete a test sensing they did poorly on it. They have an option when leaving the test center to cancel scores altogether. If you choose this option on the day of the test, ask the test supervisor for a form to complete. You generally will have a few days more after the test to cancel scores; check the information packet for more details.

When you cancel scores, you are canceling the entire test, not just one section. Your scores will not be reported anywhere; it will be as if you never took the test.

Because you will not receive your scores, you will not know how you did. Therefore, unless you are absolutely sure that you did poorly on the test and are confident that you would do significantly better on another date, you should not cancel your scores.

Preparing for and Taking the Test

There are several ways to prepare for exams. At minimum, go to your high school counselor to obtain sample materials from the testing companies. Assess your test-taking skills. Are you self-motivated? Are you confident when approaching tests? How well do you manage your time when taking tests? Know the format of the test that you are taking; be familiar with the types of questions to be asked and the types of directions.

Preparation beyond this minimal level involves more practice. Take the practice tests that are available from the testing companies. Diagnose your weaker areas and focus on them. For the first time you get ready to take an exam, purchase a preparation book or software program.

When you practice a test for the first time, focus on accuracy and understanding test content and directions, rather than watching the clock. The second time, focus on timing and strategies that help you improve speed. The third time, combine accuracy with speed. Try to recreate test conditions as closely as possible. Take the test, calculate your results, and determine whether more structured measures are necessary, such as a course or tutoring.

Books, software, and courses.
Numerous study books can be found at most bookstores, some including software to help break up the monotony of test preparation. Keep in mind, however, that using paper and pencil is the best way to practice, since it most closely replicates exam conditions.

Many students enroll in special preparation or coaching courses. These can be helpful, especially in developing test-taking strategies, but do not expect them to substitute for schoolwork in terms of developing content knowledge and basic skills.

Evaluate courses before investing time and money. Ask students who have attended previously about their experience and success. Compare course offerings and fees with what is available free from the testing companies and your high school. The advantage of courses is that they provide structure. For this reason, if you have performed poorly on an entrance exam, courses are often a good way to reverse poor performance on the next test.

Exam day. A key testing strategy is preparing for the test day itself. Prior to the test, make a list of required materials. Gather these materials in advance.

Arrange transportation in advance. If you are not familiar with the location of the test center, try to visit it prior to test day to ensure you have proper directions and have allotted adequate travel time. If you are taking public transportation, remember that weekend and weekday schedules may differ.

Do not cram the night before the test. Try to relax and get to bed early. If you do review the night before, you probably will do best to focus on test directions and strategies.

Arriving at the test site. Plan to arrive early, though not so early that you become anxious. Find a seat that has good lighting and few distractions. Find a comfortable seat, because you will be sitting for several hours with few breaks.

Follow the supervisor's directions carefully. Avoid talking with others or letting your eyes wander. Any suspicion of cheating, whether or not warranted,

What to Pack

- Test admission ticket
- Driver's license or other photo I.D.
- School identification
- Other identification, as needed
- Test bulletin
- Test registration information
- Directions to test site
- Map
- Two or three sharpened No. 2 pencils
- Good eraser
- Pencil sharpener
- Watch
- Calculator, if test permits
- Comfortable layered clothing
- Change for phone calls and vending machines
- Gum or hard candy, if desired
- Medicine, if needed (such as inhaler for asthma)
- Reading glasses, if needed

could cause you to be dismissed from the test or result in cancellation of your scores.

Test-taking strategies. Be careful how you mark answer sheets. Each marking should be dark and match the question you intend to answer. Mismarking answer sheets is a common and serious test error. Working in blocks of questions helps you ensure that your answer matches the question. If you skip a question, be sure you also skip the corresponding space on the answer sheet. Do not make stray marks on the page. Periodically stop to double-check that the question you are answering corresponds to your place on the answer sheet. When you erase incorrect marks, be sure to erase them completely.

MANY TEST preparation programs now include computer software.

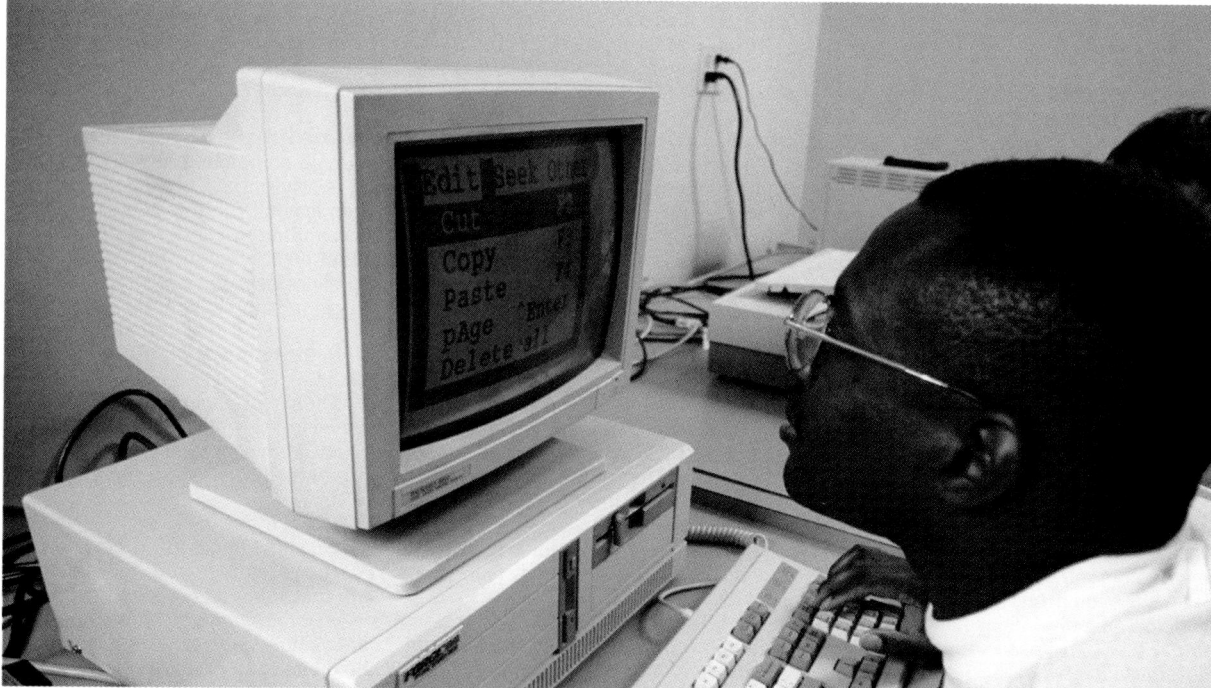

Except for reading comprehension sections, questions are ordered easiest to most difficult. Complete the easy questions first. If a question is taking too much time, skip it and come back to it later. Do not get bogged down.

You may write in your exam book. Use that space effectively, especially for mathematical questions. If you have started a question and then decide to move on and return if time permits, what you write in the book might save you time when you return to the question.

Practice time management. At the start of each section, have a sense of the number of questions versus the amount of time. The ratio will change from section to section. Consulting your watch is a must.

Never waste valuable test time learning directions that you could know in advance. Use sample materials to study directions ahead of time. Read each question carefully; be sure you are clear about what is being asked. Identify key words that point you in the right direction.

If you know an answer immediately, and you are sure of it, mark it and move on. When you are not sure of an answer, see if you can eliminate wrong answers. Doing so improves the likelihood of guessing correctly. Cross out wrong answers in the test book (not on the answer sheet). Then if you skip a question and return to it later, you can pick up from where you left off. If you plan to change an answer which you have already marked, be sure that your reasoning is logical; often, your initial hunches are correct.

You are not allowed to go back to sections you completed earlier. Nor are you allowed to look at upcoming sections. If you are caught doing either, you could find yourself being dismissed from the test. If you have extra time at the end of a section, review your work or take advantage of the time to relax in your seat.

If you possibly can, try to leave time at the end to recheck your work. This may be even more valuable than trying to answer one more hard question. You do not have to answer all the questions to do well.

After the test. At the end of the test you will turn in your answer sheet and test booklet. You are not allowed to take the booklet out of the room with you.

You will know ahead of time when the test period will end. Schedule difference are affected only by the time it takes the supervisor to distribute and collect materials and to give directions.

You should receive your test scores about six weeks following the exam. You may feel pressure to talk about your performance, both immediately after the test or when scores are mailed. Do so only if you feel comfortable. Do not be pressured into talking about it if you do not want to. At the same time, do not pressure others into talking about their

Should You Guess?

SAT I and II
In both tests, one point is added to your raw score for a correct answer and one-fourth of a point is subtracted for an incorrect answer if the question has five choices. One-third of a point is subtracted for an incorrect answer if the question has four choices. (Your raw score is then converted to the test score.)

ACT
The ACT has no penalty for guessing.

GENERAL STRATEGY
There is disagreement about the issue of whether you should guess on the SAT I or II if you cannot eliminate any of the choices. However, most experts will tell you that you should guess if you can eliminate at least one of the choices. Since the ACT has no penalty, you should provide an answer for every question. Do not guess randomly, even on the ACT. Always try to eliminate as many choices as you can before guessing; this will dramatically improve your chances of answering correctly. Focus on questions you know. Save guessing for the end.

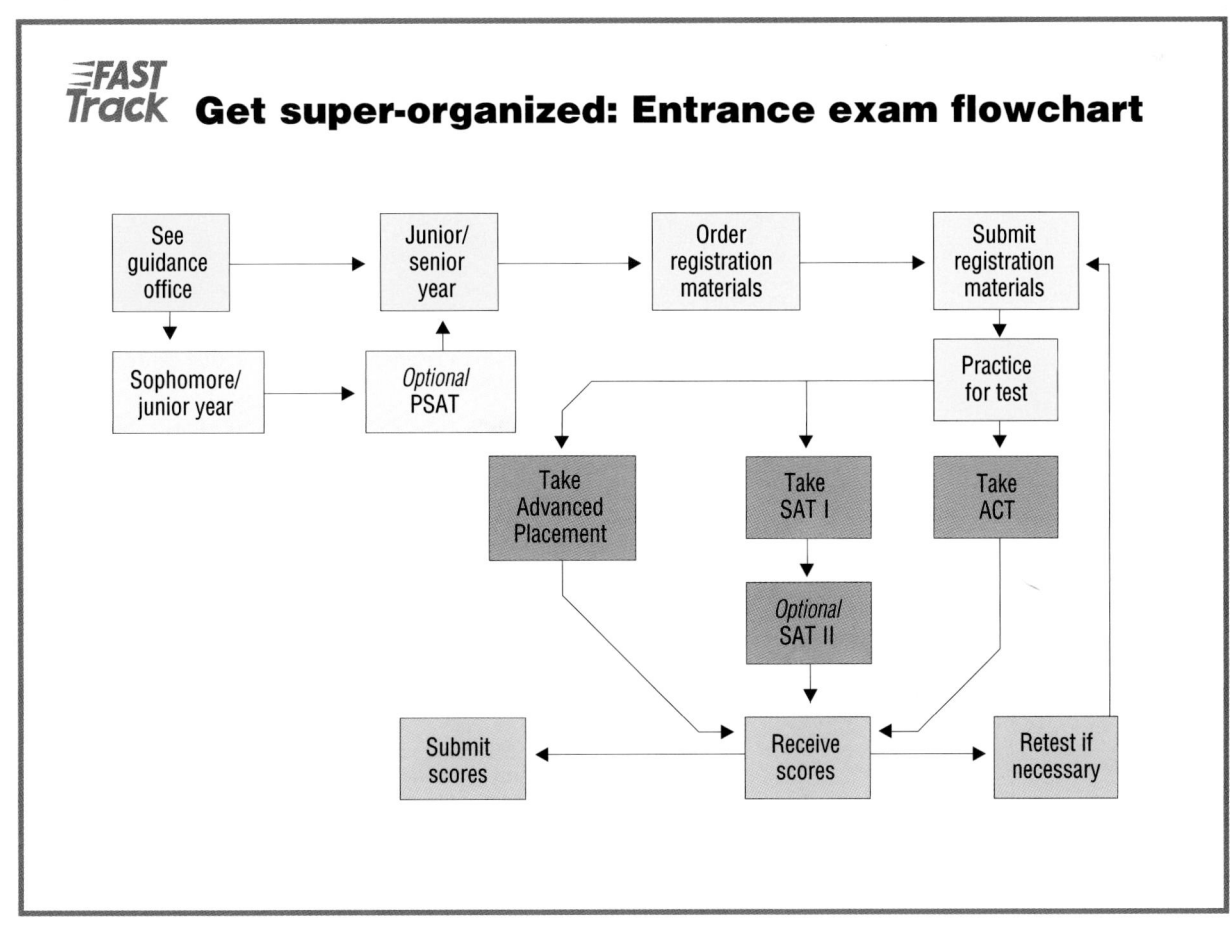

≡FAST Track Get super-organized: Entrance exam flowchart

SAT I: Reasoning Test

VISUALIZING
the problem can be helpful in answering analogy questions. The analogy here is bat : crow. For this problem it is important to remember that a bat is a mammal and a crow is a brid. Therefore the answer is D, seal : penguin.

The following information is based on the latest information available at time of publication.

The SAT I has seven parts: three verbal, three mathematical, and one additional part. The three verbal parts cover analogies (thirty minutes), sentence completion (thirty minutes), and critical reading (fifteen minutes). All questions in these parts are multiple choice.

The mathematical component covers standard computational skills and quantitative comparisons; it consists of two thirty-minute parts and one fifteen-minute part. Most questions in the math component are multiple choice; however, some are open-ended, requiring you to develop your own answers and use the answer sheet grids to fill them in. Calculator use is permitted.

The seventh part of the test might be either verbal or mathematical. Its scores do not count toward your total score. Instead, its purpose is either to validate prior exam questions or to experiment with questions to be used for future exams. Because the order of these seven parts varies from test to test, you will not know which section is the experimental part.

Omitting a question does not affect the SAT score. However, incorrect answers do lower the score. Questions are sequenced from easy to difficult, except for critical reading.

Verbal Examples

The combined verbal section consists of seventy-eight questions presented in one fifteen-minute and two thirty-minute parts. These include nineteen analogies, nineteen sentence completions, and forty questions evaluating critical reading skills. No specific knowledge of other fields is needed, even for reading passages, but well-read students will have a vocabulary and comprehension advantage.

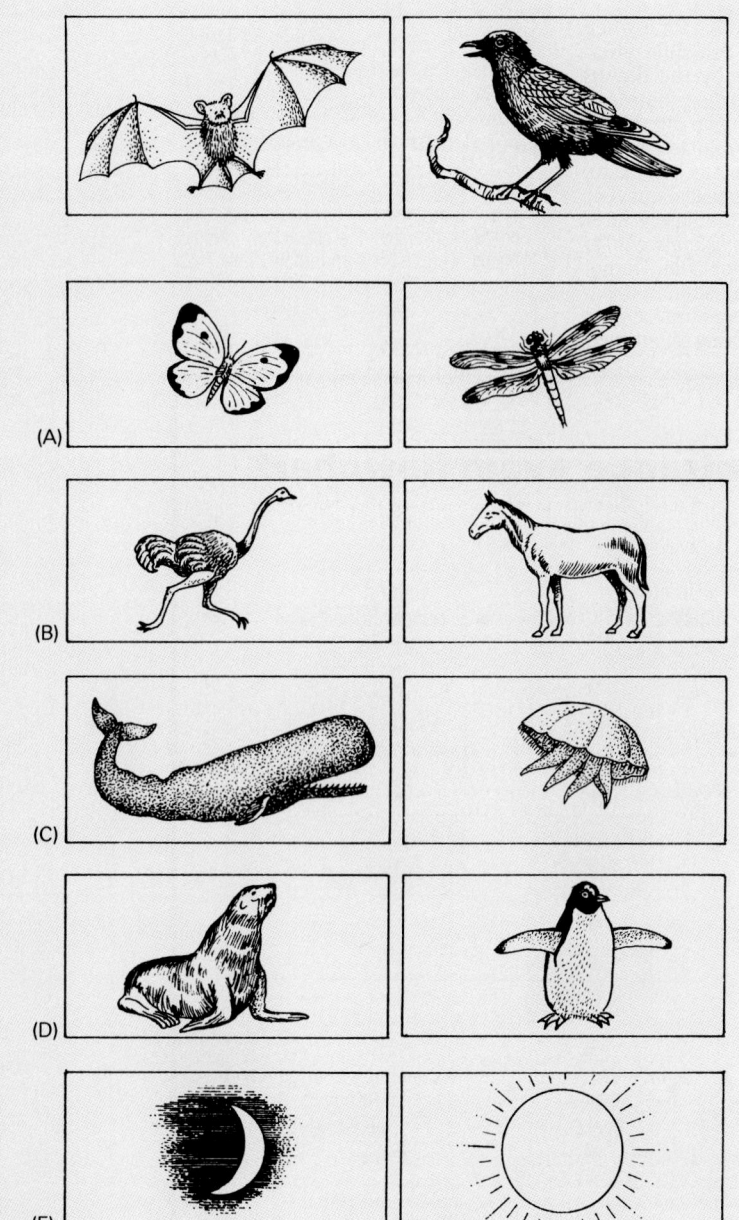

Analogies. These are words or phrases that have a relationship similar to other words or phrases. In the context of the SAT I, a pair of words that bear a certain relationship to each other will be presented. This pair will be followed by five more pairs of words. The student must select from these five the pair that has a relationship similar to (analogous to) the original pair.

When working with analogies, it is often helpful to develop a sentence that states the relationship between the original pair of words. Then see if another pair can be substituted into the sentence. The sentence should be as specific as possible, using as precise a meaning as possible for each word. Keep in mind that the relationship is between the first word and the second word within the pair, not between a word from one pair and a word from the second pair.

Words often have more than one meaning, and all must be considered. For example, the word *fast* can suggest many things, including a description of speed or the act of going without food. If you were to see the word pair *fast : food*, you would need to determine which meaning was intended.

Fast has many meanings and can be any of several parts of speech. Other words are clearly nouns or verbs or other parts of speech. With analogies, parts of speech are as important as meanings and relationships. The correct answer likely will be a pair of words that not only have a similar relationship but also represent the same parts of speech.

<u>Directions:</u> Each question below consists of a related pair of words or phrases, followed by five pairs of words or phrases labeled A through E. Select the lettered pair that <u>best</u> expresses a relationship similar to that expressed in the original pair.

DOG : PUPPY :: (A) poodle : terrier (B) horse : lamb (C) rooster : hen (D) cat : kitten (E) fawn : deer

The relationship is that the second word is the name given to a young version of the first. The words can be used in the sentence "A young <u>dog</u> is called a <u>puppy</u>." <u>Poodle</u> and <u>terrier</u> are types of dogs, but they do not bear an age relationship to each other. A <u>horse</u> is a mature animal and a <u>lamb</u> is a young animal; that choice may be tempting. But a lamb is a young sheep, not a horse. The relationship between <u>rooster</u> and <u>hen</u> is gender, not age. The relationship between <u>fawn</u> and <u>deer</u> is age, but the younger animal is listed first. The relationship between <u>cat</u> and <u>kitten</u> is also age. The statement "A young cat is called a kitten" is true; the relationship between this pair of words most parallels the original pair. (D) is correct.

NOTES : MELODY :: (A) bricks : fireplace (B) stadium : baseball (C) chef : pastry (D) oven : bread (E) hose : fire fighter

When <u>notes</u> are assembled in a particular order, they form a <u>melody</u>. Answer (C) may be tempting because a <u>chef</u> makes <u>pastry</u>. But the chef assembles ingredients such as flour and sugar to form the pastry; the chef is not part of the final product. (A) is correct.

TENSION : ARGUMENT :: (A) war : peace
(B) symphony : coda (C) story : conclusion
(D) thunder : lightning (E) recklessness : accident

Choices (B) and (C) might be considered similar in that a coda comes at the end of a symphony and a conclusion comes at the end of a story, much like an argument can come toward the end of tension. However, more precisely, if tension is not brought under control, it results in an argument. Similarly, if recklessness is not brought under control, it results in an accident. This comparison is more precise; (E) is correct.

NYLON : FABRIC :: (A) sweater : wool
(B) notebook : paper (C) statue : marble
(D) oxygen : air (E) carrot : vegetable

A good way to find the correct choice in analogy items is to put the relationship of a word pair into a sentence. For example, the relationship "kind of fiber:fabric" can be expressed as "Nylon is a kind of fabric." Then find another pair of words related in the same way by testing them in the same sentence. For example, "A sweater is a kind of wool"; "a notebook is a kind of paper"; "a statue is a kind of marble"; "oxygen is a kind of air"; and "a carrot is a kind of vegetable." The only one that works is choice (E), carrot:vegetable. If you started with "Some fabrics are made from nylon," the test sentences for the other suggested choices would then become "some wool is made of sweaters"; "some paper is made of notebooks"; "some marble is made of statues"; "some air is made of oxygen"; and "some vegetables are made of carrots." The only candidate in that groups is "Some air is made from oxygen," but that has to be rejected because air is a mixture or gases. The only acceptable choice, then, still is (E).

CLUB : GOLF :: (A) racket : tennis (B) pitcher : baseball
(C) strike : bowling (D) track : racing
(E) touchdown : football

Although a person may belong to a golf club, none of the choices concerns an association or membership. Thus, club in this analogy refers to the device used to hit the ball in the game of golf. Your sentence has to be as specific as possible to work here. A sentence such as "A club is used in golf" does not discriminate among the choices. A sentence such as "A club is used to hit the ball in the game of golf precisely indicates that choice (A), racket:tennis, is correct.

VETERINARIAN : ANIMALS :: (A) doctor : medicine
(B) pediatrician : children (C) surgeon : hospital
(D) psychiatrist : schizophrenia (E) dermatologist : skin

The only meaning that makes sense here is "A veterinarian is a doctor who treats animals," which easily eliminates choices (A) and (C), but leaves the other three as possibilities. You need to make the original relationship more specific, such as "A veterinarian is a doctor who treats diseases of animals." The more specific sentence rules out choices (D) and (E) and leaves (B) as the correct choice.

CHAPTER : NOVEL :: (A) student : auditorium
(B) story : word (C) song : medley (D) crowd : outcry
(E) artist : painting

State the relationship as, "A chapter is part of a novel." Similarly, a song is part of a medley. Although a word is part of a story, choice (B) reverses that order, and a story is not a part of a word. Only choice (C) exactly expresses the perceived relationship.

ASTRONOMER : TELESCOPE :: (A) teacher : blackboard
(B) dentist : tooth (C) soldier : canteen
(D) doctor : stethoscope (E) singer : voice

It is always important to get a specific relationship. If you say "An astronomer uses a telescope," you haven't eliminated any choices. If you say "An astronomer uses a telescope to gather information," you have limited your choices. Looking over the available choices, you can spot (D), and think "A doctor uses a stethoscope to gather information." None of the other choices works that way, so choice (D) is correct.

BOXER : RING :: (A) dancer : music (B) actor : stage
(C) golfer : tee (D) skater : skates (E) comedian : jokes

The given relationship is "A boxer performs in a ring." The only choice with the same relationship is (B), "An actor performs on a stage." Although one statement uses in and the other uses on, this small discrepancy would be important only if it were needed to help decide among choices that are close. Since the relationship is between a performer and the place where the performance occurs, choice (B) is correct.

BEAVER : LODGE :: (A) snake : grass (B) cow : farm
(C) fish : ocean (D) insect : garden (E) hornet : nest

You need to choose between "A beaver lives in a lodge" and "A beaver builds a lodge." The first sentence does not make any discrimination among choices available. The second sentence has the same relationship as choice (E), hornet:nest, but the other choices do not. Snakes do not build grass, cows do not build farms, and so forth. Choice (E) is correct.

COIN : PAYMENT :: (A) stamp : letter
(B) umbrella : protection (C) shoe : leather
(D) camera : picture (E) purse : money

A coin can be used as a form of payment. Although it is easy to see that each pair describes a close relationship, only "An umbrella is a form of protection" makes sense and has the same relation, that of performing a function, as coin does to payment. Choice (B) is correct.

BEE : SWARM :: (A) salmon : fish (B) dog : puppy
(C) bear : carnivore (D) bison : herd (E) cat : feline

One possibility for the relationship between bee and swarm would be that between an animal and a form of motion. The choices do not support that relationship. Another relationship between bee and swarm is that a group of bees is called a swarm. Since a bison is part of a herd, choice (D) is correct.

GULLIBLE : FOOLED :: (A) inquisitive : questioned
(B) mysterious : understood (C) argumentative : ignored
(D) dependable : admired (E) sensitive : offended

A gullible person is easily fooled. While someone who is inquisitive can be questioned, someone who is mysterious can sometimes be understood, someone who is argumentative can be ignored, and someone who is dependable is admired, these relationships are not always true. The only pair that surely has this relationship is sensitive:offended, for one definition of sensitive is "easily offended." The correct choice is (E).

ZEPHYR : WIND :: (A) flakes : snow (B) ice : hail
(C) drizzle : rain (D) warmth : sun (E) shade : cloud

A zephyr is a "gentle breeze." Thus, its relationship to wind is that it is a kind of wind that is not very strong. A shade is not a kind of cloud (choice E). The pairs flakes:snow, drizzle:rain, and warmth:sun are plausible candidates; but flakes make up a heavy snow as well as the few flakes that constitute a weak snow; and, while warmth might be a mild form of the sun's heart, it is not a form of the sun itself. A drizzle is a small amount of light rain, just as a zephyr is a small amount of light wind. Thus, the only correct choice is (C).

STORY : RESOLUTION :: (A) treaty : peace
(B) train : caboose (C) piano : key
(D) confession : sentence (E) cabin : log

The connection between story and resolution is that the end of a story is its resolution. (While there might be a story about someone's resolution, this sort of connection is not inevitable. In looking for the correct choice in an analogy item, it is important to look for connections that always happen, not those that might happen. Then to discriminate among the possible choices, pay attention to details.) It is tempting to think that peace follows a treaty, choice (A), or a sentence usually follows a confession, choice (D), but unlike the resolution of a story, which is part of the story, the peace and the sentence are not part of the things they follow. Similarly, although a key can be part of a piano, choice (C), or a log may be part of a cabin, choice (E), neither one is the final part. Only train:caboose shows a relationship in which the caboose is the final part of the train, so the correct choice is (B).

MALNUTRITION : FOOD :: (A) pneumonia : bacteria
(B) atrophy : exercise (C) headache : pain
(D) virus : stomach (E) depression : grief

The relationship "Malnutrition is caused by inadequate food" is very precise, and there are no alternatives in meaning involved. None of the other relationships is exactly the same, but one cause of atrophy (of muscles) is inadequate exercise. Because the other pairs can easily be ruled out, the correct choice is (B), *atrophy:exercise*.

DEER : DOE :: (A) sheep : ewe (B) cat : kitten
(C) buck : stag (D) bull : cow (E) horse : stallion

A doe is a female deer. If you also know that a ewe is a female sheep, then you will recognize it immediately as the correct choice. In that case you can move on to the next item to save time, although if you feel you are not going to have a problem with time, you might want to examine the other choices to see if there could be some sort of trick. Also, if you are unsure of what a ewe is, you may have to go carefully through the other choices to eliminate them: A kitten is a baby cat; a stag is a buck; a cow is female, but it is a bovine animal, not a bull; and a stallion is a male horse. Since a doe is a female deer, the only possibility is choice (A), *sheep:ewe*.

ANGUISH : SORROW :: (A) friendliness : friendship
(B) ecstasy : happiness (C) carelessness : clumsiness
(D) revenge : revolution (E) adviser : consultant

Although anguish and sorrow are close synonyms, anguish is an intense form of psychic pain, while sorrow is a generalized sadness. In this case, pure synonyms such as choices (A), (C), (D), and (E) would therefore be incorrect. Choice (B), in contrast, has the same relationship as *anguish:sorrow*. Ecstasy is an intense form of joy, and happiness is a generalized feeling. Further, one would expect both anguish and ecstasy to be short-lived, while both sorrow and happiness can pervade a person's life for long periods of time. Choice (B) is correct.

QUARRY : LION :: (A) range : buffalo (B) mine : gold
(C) kitten : cat (D) gravel : chicken (E) prey : falcon

The word quarry has several meanings, both as a noun and a verb. In relation to lion, however, it makes sense only when it refers to the animals that the lion hunts and eats. While a buffalo eats the grass on the range, choice (A), it does not hunt or consume the range itself. One meaning of quarry suggests the word mine, but that is not the meaning in this analogy. Thus, choice (B) is wrong. Similarly, a lion is a kind of cat, but a cat's relation to its kitten is far different from that of lion to its quarry, making choice (C) wrong. Gravel also suggests another meaning of quarry, but even though a chicken does consume some *gravel*, it cannot be said to hunt it, making choice (D) wrong. Choice (E), *prey:falcon*, is an exact match. Just as a lion hunts its quarry, a falcon hunts its prey.

CLOAK : DAGGER :: (A) spy : counterspy
(B) paper : gift (C) pin : dress (D) cover : book
(E) stamp : letter

While the expression "cloak and dagger" refers to spying, the relationship between a cloak and a dagger is not the same as the antagonistic relationship between a spy and a counterspy, choice (A). Similarly, although you could put a dagger through a cloak and a pin through a dress, the order is reversed in choice (C). A cover is part of a book, choice (D), but a cloak is not a part of a dagger. A stamp can be attached to a letter, choice (E), but a dagger could only be wrapped in or concealed by a cloak. The correct choice is (B), since a gift can be wrapped in paper, just as a dagger can be wrapped in a cloak.

BLACK : GRAY :: (A) white : bright (B) noise : sound
(C) sun : planet (D) mountain : hill (E) pink : red

In essence, gray is a diminution or a less intense form of black, but bright is more intense than white, so choice (A) is not correct. Noise is not necessarily more or less intense (loud) than other sounds—just more annoying—so choice (B) is wrong. The sun is different from a planet in a basic way, since it is undergoing thermonuclear reactions that produce vast amounts of energy, so choice (C) is wrong. While pink can be watered-down red, the relationship is in the other direction from that of *black:gray*, making choice (E) wrong. The correct choice is (D), since a hill is the same thing as a mountain, only less so, just as gray is the same thing as black, only less so.

Sentence completion. These questions provide a statement with one or two blank spaces. The answers are words or sets of words that fit into the blanks. The questions check not only a student's understanding of the words but also the ability to place the words correctly into a sentence, given the content and structure of the sentence.

If a sentence has two blanks, then the words must be substituted in the order they appear, the first word in the first blank, the second word in the second blank. Even if one of the words makes sense, do not assume it is the correct answer; *both* words must fit.

Sometimes one choice fits, but another fits even better. Try all answers before choosing one. Be sure the entire sentence makes sense. Watch for transitional words and phrases like *despite*, *even though*, and *however*. They signal that one part of the sentence is in contrast to another.

Directions: Each sentence below has one or two blanks, each blank indicating that something has been omitted. Beneath the sentence are five words or sets of words labeled A through E. Choose the word or set of words that, when inserted in the sentence, best fits the meaning of the sentence as a whole.

Even though she is not a football fan, Rita said she would go to the _____ with the others.

(A) museum (B) restaurant (C) game (D) movies
(E) store

The phrase even though suggests that Rita will do something she would not normally do. From the sentence, Rita does not like football. Unless (A), (D), and (E) were referring to a special exhibit on football, a movie with a football theme, or a store that sells football memorabilia, these choices do not make sense. (B) might make sense in that Rita might join others at a restaurant before or after football. However, football is most associated with game; Rita would go to the game with the others, even though she is not a fan of football. (C) is correct.

Mr. Rodriguez recommended that all his American history students read the _____ book about the Battle of Antietam that describes the conflict in _____ detail.

(A) brief . . painstaking (B) dull . . exciting
(C) tedious . . snappy (D) comprehensive . . considerable
(E) tragic . . humorous

The adjective that describes detail must support the adjective that describes book. For example, in answer (A), if the book is brief, then it would not have painstaking detail, which would add length. Painstaking does not support brief. The correct answer is (D).

Because of his need for _____, he agrees to make public appearances only when he is assured of a supportive audience.

(A) attention (B) competition (C) approval
(D) involvement (E) diversity

Think of the needs of a person who would make public appearance only when assured of a supportive audience. This should suggest that you can eliminate choices (B), (D), and (E). In addition, a need for attention, choice (A), would not cause him to limit his public appearances. Since he will appear only before a supportive audience, he needs approval, choice (C).

With his team trailing by a point in the final seconds of the game, Kevin lunged for the ball, scooped it up, and flung it _____ toward the hoop.

(A) willingly (B) desperately (C) crazily
(D) peculiarly (E) mercilessly

Every clue in this sentence points to a desperate situation, so choice (B) is the correct choice. A check of the other choices shows that none makes sense in the sentence no matter what Kevin was feeling at the time.

Although the food was _____ prepared, the meal was a _____ culinary experience.

(A) hastily . . crude
(B) painstakingly . . memorable
(C) eagerly . . fascinating
(D) exquisitely . . disappointing
(E) lavishly . . delightful

Once again the word *although* suggests that there should be a contrast between the two clauses in the sentence. The way the meal turned out was not consistent with the way the food was prepared. Therefore, you should look for words that are opposites or near opposites. The words in choice (D) come closest to being opposites and, when inserted into the sentence, make a logical statement.

After restlessly listening to what Eddie called his parents' old-fashioned music, he was _____ finally to have a chance to play some of the more _____ tunes.

(A) relieved . . current
(B) resigned . . childish
(C) delighted . . unfamiliar
(D) reluctant . . sprightly
(E) willing . . popular

If Eddie has been "restlessly listening" to something, one would assume he would be glad to hear something completely different. Choices (B) and (D) begin with words that suggest something that Eddie also does not want to do, so neither is correct. Choice (E) begins with a word that, while not as negative as those that start choices (B) and (D), suggests that Eddie is going along somewhat reluctantly with listening to the more popular tunes. While choice (C) starts with a positive note in delighted, the unfamiliar does not seem to fit the rest of the sentence. Only choice (A), in which Eddie is relieved to play current tunes, correctly reflects the expectation of how Eddie might feel after listening to his parents' music.

The candidate's inability to gain the support of any major newspaper resulted in a feeling of _____ among her opponents.

(A) rejection   (B) disappointment   (C) optimism
(D) hostility   (E) urgency

Even before looking at the choices on an item like this, you should think about how the candidate's opponents would feel, based on the first part of the sentence. Would they be encouraged if the newspapers did not support their rivals? Would they be depressed? Since lack of newspaper support is said to give the opponents a better chance to win the election, look for a word among the choices that expresses a feeling representative of this. Choice (C), optimism, fits such a feeling, while the others do not.

Although aluminum is a competitive material in the market-place, its presence is _____ in the recycling of steel.

(A) destructive   (B) unnoticed   (C) overshadowed
(D) stabilized   (E) beneficial

The word *although* suggests that the effect of aluminum on the recycling of steel somehow stands in contrast to the competition between the two met-als. Since the first part of the sentence sets up this contrast, the second part of the sentence must show the other side of the relationship. As a compet-itive material, aluminum is in some way harmful to steel, so the contrasting word, and correct choice, is beneficial, choice (E).

During a blackout, most people are forced to substitute _____ plans for their usual life-styles.

(A) common   (B) interesting   (C) drastic
(D) alternative   (E) whimsical

The word *substitute* suggests that the plans during a blackout will be dif-ferent from those when there is no blackout. The choices common, inter-esting, drastic, and whimsical fail to suggest this difference. The correct choice is alternative, choice (D).

Her dream of becoming the first female basketball player on the team was _____ by an insensitive coaching staff.

(A) fulfilled   (B) acknowledged   (C) encouraged
(D) revolutionized   (E) thwarted

An insensitive coaching staff would not be interested in fulfilling, choice (A); encouraging, choice (C); revolutionizing, choice (D); or even acknowl-edging, choice (B) her dream. An insensitive staff would most likely thwart the dream. The choice that completes the logic of the sentence is (E).

The 1980 United States Olympic hockey team _____ the world by defeating the highly favored and _____ unbeatable Soviet team.

(A) amused . . probably
(B) stunned . . seemingly
(C   angered . . absolutely
(D) explored . . evidently
(E) represented . . hardly

By looking at the second word in each pair, you can use the fact that the Soviet team was soundly beaten to eliminate choices (A), (C), and (D). Choice (E) does not make sense, since the United States team would be unlikely to represent the world, and hardly is a peculiar modifier for *unbeat-able*. Choice (B) makes sense because, although the Soviet team was seem-ingly unbeatable, it was in fact beaten, and this is the kind of event that could have stunned the world.

Criticism does not _____ but _____ his determination, driving him to elevate his efforts to new heights.

(A) encourage . . augments
(B) produce . . involves
(C) impede . . enhances
(D) lessen . . ridicules
(E) invoke . . overlooks

The signal word *but* suggests that you are looking for two words with opposite meanings. Therefore, you can eliminate choices (A), (B), and (D). The second word of the missing pair should show a positive effect on his determination. Based on this, you can now eliminate choice (E). Test the words for choice (C) in the sentence. They work, so choice (C) is correct.

An outstanding baseball player in his day, Slugger was
_____ as he helplessly watched his talent _____ over the
years.

(A) outraged . . evolve
(B) enthusiastic . . surge
(C) undecided . . ridiculed
(D) devastated . . diminish
(E) flattered . . imitated

This sentence suggests that the first blank must be filled by a word with
strong negative feelings, which eliminates all choices but (A) and (D).
While it makes no sense that Slugger would be <u>outraged</u> to see his skills
<u>evolve</u>—a positive conclusion should not make a person angry—he would
be <u>devastated</u> to watch the skills <u>diminish</u>. Choice (D) is correct.

Most people growing up in the 1960's failed to realize that
the baseball cards they should have _____ would some day
be valuable collector's items.

(A) hoarded   (B) discarded   (C) shared   (D) abused
(E) inspected

From the sentence it is apparent that baseball cards worth little in the
1960's can be sold to collectors today for large sums. If people knew that
this situation would arrive more than a quarter of a century later, they
would have wanted to save the cards. Choice (A), <u>hoarded</u>, is the correct
answer.

Our guide made no effort to be _____ as he rushed us
through the museum, rattling off information while
_____ our questions.

(A) diplomatic . . honoring
(B) courteous . . ignoring
(C) informative . . inviting
(D) flippant . . dismissing
(E) impatient . . distorting

As this sentence is phrased, the first word of the pair must describe what
the museum guide "made no effort to be." You can easily reject choices (D)
and (E). Choice (C) is debatable since he did give information, though it
was rattled off. Based on the guide's actions, you can assume that he did
not invite questions. You can now eliminate choices (A) and (C). Only
choice (B) completes a logical sentence.

Most people thought of the young lawyer as arrogant, since
she _____ to _____ to even the slightest error in judgment.

(A) decided . . conform
(B) refused . . admit
(C) confessed . . adjust
(D) returned . . adhere
(E) feared . . react

Here, the correct word pair will complete a statement to illustrate the definition of *arrogant*. Since arrogance involves a pretension of superiority, first-
word choices <u>confessed</u> (C) and <u>feared</u> (E) can be eliminated. Of the
remaining word pairs, only choice (B) is consistent with the definition of
arrogant.

In an attempt to increase public _____, some advertisers
suggest that their products are _____ by doctors.

(A) confidence . . recommended
(B) indignation . . treated
(C) apathy . . endorsed
(D) awareness . . misused
(E) skepticism . . rejected

Since it is illogical to assume that advertisers would want to increase public <u>indignation</u>, <u>apathy</u>, or <u>skepticism</u> directed a their products, you can
eliminate choices (B), (C), and (E). The word pair for choice (D), when
inserted in the sentence, also produces an illogical statement. Choice (A)
makes the only logical statement within the context of the sentence.

He considers himself an original thinker, never allowing
the findings of others to _____ his judgment.

(A) support   (B) contradict   (C) influence
(D) reinforce   (E) reflect

Anyone who considers himself an original thinker probably would not care
whether the findings of others <u>support</u>, <u>contradict</u>, <u>reinforce</u>, or <u>reflect</u> his
judgment. His status as an original thinker would be threatened, however,
if he allowed the findings of others to <u>influence</u> his judgment. Therefore,
the best choice is (C).

When the first mailboxes were erected in Paris, in 1653,
messengers _____ for their _____ put mice in the boxes
to destroy the mail.

(A) thrilled . . future
(B) thankful . . pets
(C) searching . . homes
(D) fearful . . livelihoods
(E) collecting . . hobbies

Consider the effect the first mailboxes must have had on the lives of people
who delivered messages for a living. This new development would not
have caused them to be <u>thrilled</u> or <u>thankful</u>. The best choice is (D), <u>fearful
. . . livelihoods</u>.

Even though the enemy troops _____ at his border, the
young ruler _____ to change his policies.

(A) frolicked . . began
(B) fought . . continued
(C) gathered . . refused
(D) debated . . elected
(E) retreated . . declined

Even though, like *although*, suggests that there will be a contrast between
the two clauses in the sentence. Furthermore, while troops might be
expected to fight, gather, or retreat, one does not expect them to frolic or
debate. Also, choices (A) and (D) do not supply the desired contrast.
Choice (E) is unsuitable, since if the enemy troops are retreating, it seems
reasonable that the ruler would continue the policies that caused the
retreat. A similar situation prevails with choice (B). The correct choice is
(C): Even though the enemy troops <u>gathered</u> at his border, the young
ruler <u>refused</u> to change his policies.

The most _____ outcome of Alfred's action was that his
company would soon _____ as its financial situation
deteriorated.

(A) unexpected . . falter
(B) damaging . . prosper
(C) important . . complain
(D) incredible . . repeat
(E) likely . . fold

In this sentence the key word is the last one: *deteriorated*. Once you accept
the premise that the company is now in increasing financial trouble, you
can reject choice (B), especially since prospering would not be damaging.
Looking at choice (A), one would expect that a company in financial trouble
would <u>falter</u>, so that would not be <u>unexpected</u>. For choice (C), it is difficult
to see how a company's complaining would be important. Choice (D) does
not make any sense. The correct choice is (E). It is <u>likely</u> that a company
with a deteriorating financial condition will <u>fold</u>.

Critical reading. These items provide you with passages to read and then several questions to answer based on the passage. Sometimes two passages will be given and the questions will draw on both. The passages range from 400 to about 850 words in length.

All the information you need to answer questions is contained within the passage. You will not need additional, outside information. Passages generally are drawn from existing materials. They may be narratives or arguments or essays in fields such as physical science, biological science, social studies, or humanities.

Read the entire passage. Make sure the question you answer is the one that is asked. Sometimes wrong answers are true statements, but they do not answer the question. Similarly, a correct answer may include a false statement; the question could be about what the author says, and the author may have said something wrong. Key words will help you find correct answers.

Try to answer an entire block of questions at one time so that you do not have to reread the passage later. Read all answers. Some may be partly true, but one will be best. If a passage is especially difficult, skip it and return to it later.

Directions: The passages below are followed by questions based on their content; questions following a pair of related passages may also be based on the relationship between the paired passages. Answer the questions on the basis of what is <u>stated</u> or <u>implied</u> in the passages and in any introductory materials that may be provided.

Dandelion is what we named the woodchuck that makes its home under our garage. (It's easy to guess his major food passion!) He's a fine specimen, too. His thick, glossy fur shades from light brown on his belly to deep red-brown along his spine. Both back feet and front feet are black, with strong claws for digging burrows and defending himself. His ears are small, round, and close to his head. His eyes are large, and his nose is black. We assume Dandelion is a male, since we've seen no offspring.

It's characteristic of a marmot to sit upright on its rear legs, and Dandelion does that after every few bites during his frequent meals. Marmots are described as lazy and slow-moving. He is both. In the morning sunlight he is a rug flung across the stones, feet spread wide, and eyes closed. As summer wears on, he grows fatter and fatter, preparing for his winter's sleep. We don't know if we'll see this groundhog on February 2, but probably we won't, since the snow will still be deep then.

Dandelion is quite a charming animal. He will continue to be charming—and welcome—as long as he doesn't raid the garden. So far, he hasn't. As other squirrels do, Dandelion likes seeds, grass, and nuts. He is especially fond of popcorn, when he can get it.

Based on this passage, names for this kind of animal include

(A) dandelion, marmot, lazybones, squirrel
(B) woodchuck, dandelion, groundhog, animal
(C) woodchuck, marmot, groundhog, squirrel
(D) specimen, rug, groundhog, squirrel
(E) dandelion, specimen, lazybones, popcorn

The first sentence clearly states that "we named" this particular animal Dandelion, so that's a proper name and can be eliminated, making choices (A), (B), and (E) incorrect. Choice (D) includes <u>specimen</u>, which may refer to any representative of a kind of thing or animal. Choice (C) includes only names for this type of animal.

It can be inferred that a woodchuck's favorite food is

(A) dandelions
(B) popcorn
(C) seeds
(D) nuts
(E) grass

The clues to the correct answer appear in the first two sentences. Choice (A) is correct. While all the foods mentioned are foods that a woodchuck eats, only dandelions are specifically referred to as "his major food passion." The woodchuck loves popcorn, too, but that's apparently not a regular item in his diet, since he eats it "when he can get it."

The sentence "He has a short, rather broad tail" would best be placed

(A) in paragraph one because paragraph one contains mostly short sentences
(B) in paragraph one because paragraph one gives Dandelion's physical description
(C) in paragraph two because paragraph two contains many longer, more complex sentences
(D) in paragraph two because paragraph two is about Dandelion's behavior
(E) in paragraph three because paragraph three is about human reactions to Dandelion

Each answer includes a reason for making the choice. The determining factor is not likely to be sentence length, so choices (A) and (C) can be eliminated. Also, paragraph one has long sentences as well as short ones. If you evaluate the content of the sentence, it's clearly part of a physical description of the animal. Most of the physical description is in paragraph one, so choice (B) is the best answer.

The actual meaning of "he is a rug flung across the stones" in the second paragraph is that the animal

(A) lacks normal strength
(B) has fur that would make a nice rug
(C) finds the hard stones uncomfortable
(D) is relaxed and limp as he sleeps in the sun
(E) is furry and very warm, like many rugs

The actual meaning of the description is not the same as the literal meaning of the words. To determine what the author is saying, look at the context of the description. The woodchuck is lazy and slow-moving, he is in the morning sunlight, his feet are spread wide, and his eyes are closed. You can conclude that he is probably warm and that he is asleep. Therefore, choice (D) is the best one.

The best title for this passage would be

(A) "A Woodchuck's Favorite Foods"
(B) "Animals That Hibernate"
(C) "One Fine Woodchuck"
(D) "Ground Squirrels of All Kinds"
(E) "Marmots Around the World"

To determine the correct answer, review each paragraph to see if each title covers it well. Choice (A) does not cover paragraphs one and two. Choices (B) and (D) can be eliminated because no other hibernating animals or ground squirrels are mentioned in the passage. Choice (E) also refers to more than the passage contains (no other marmots are mentioned in the passage). Only choice (C) includes all the information in the passage but no more than that.

Nearly 2000 years ago, the Roman Empire included much of the island now known as Great Britain. Julius Caesar invaded Britain in 55 B.C. and defeated its ruler. His heir, the emperor Augustus, negotiated a settlement with the British leaders under which they would pay taxes but keep their independence. This treaty, settled in 27 B.C., lasted only until 43 A.D., when the emperor Claudius invaded and conquered the southern part of the island we call England. By 83 A.D., the entire island group was ruled by the Romans. It was known as the province of Britannia.

But Britannia was a long way from Rome, and it was not easy for the Romans to maintain their rule without a great deal of fighting. In 122 A.D., the emperor Hadrian visited his province with the intention of settling matters. He ordered the army to build a wall across the island between what today are England and Scotland. The wall separated the "civilized" Romans and the northern "barbarians."

Hadrian's Wall, as we call it, is 80 miles long. It varies in thickness from 8 to 10 feet and averages 15 feet in height. At each Roman mile a milecastle was built, an enclosed structure with gates, barracks, and a cooking area. Each milecastle was about 60 feet square. Evenly spaced between each pair of milecastles, two turrets were built into the wall. A turret was 20 feet square and had stairs leading up from the ground level. In addition, two ditches ran along Hadrian's Wall, one to the north and the other to the south.

(1) Contrary to long-held belief, Hadrian's Wall was probably not intended primarily as part of a defense system in time of war. (2) Many Roman soldiers married local women and had families in Britannia. (3) Instead, the wall most likely marked a political and economic boundary. (4) Smugglers trying to avoid paying taxes, travelers who wanted to avoid being seen, and others who had reason to keep their movements quiet were the probable targets for the wall's guardians.

HADRIAN'S WALL

According to the passage, for a long time people believed that Hadrian's Wall was intended to be primarily

(A) a political boundary
(B) a military defense
(C) an economic defense
(D) all of these
(E) both (A) and (C)

The sentence numbered (1) in the last paragraph of the passage begins "Contrary to long-held belief." This implies that a clause following that phrase and including the word *not* will include an idea that people believed for a long time. "Hadrian's Wall was probably *not* intended primarily as part of a defense system. . . ." In other words, for a long time people believed that Hadrian's Wall was primarily a military defense. Although the passage implies that the belief was incorrect, the item does not ask what the primary purpose of the wall was. It asks what people believed it was for a long period of time. Choices (A) and (C) or both—choice (E)—reflect present-day thinking. Choice (B) is correct.

It can be inferred from the passage that soldiers lived

(A) on top of the wall
(B) in the milecastles
(C) in the turrets
(D) behind the wall
(E) in the nearby towns

The word *inferred* tells you that the needed information is not directly given in the passage. However, everything you need is given. In paragraph three, each milecastle is described as having "gates, barracks, and a cooking area." Barracks were living quarters for soldiers, so the inclusion of a cooking area makes it likely that soldiers lived in the milecastles, which is choice (B). The other choices may be possible but are less likely.

It was not easy for the Romans to maintain their rule over Great Britain because

(A) Hadrian's Wall was 80 miles long
(B) many smugglers traveled between north and south
(C) Rome is a long way from Great Britain
(D) the Romans thought Britain was populated by uncivilized people and was not worth fighting for
(E) the Roman soldiers were unwilling to fight

To find the answer, look for the phrase "maintain their rule" or something similar. (In this case, it's the exact wording, but it may not be exact in other items.) You can eliminate choice (E) right away, since nothing is ever said about the fighting quality of Roman soldiers. Choices (A), (B), and (D) are all mentioned in the passage, but are not given as reasons for difficulty in maintaining Rome's rule. The correct choice is (C).

The sentence that does not belong in the last paragraph of the passage is

(A) sentence (1)
(B) sentence (2)
(C) sentence (3)
(D) sentence (4)
(E) all the sentences belong in the last paragraph

This question requires that you understand the main idea of the paragraph. Then you must decide if all the sentences are about the main idea, which is choice (E), or if one sentence does not belong. In this case, the correct answer is choice (B); the soldiers' families have little or nothing to do with why Hadrian's Wall was built.

According to the passage, the Roman ruler who conquered Great Britain was

(A) Julius Caesar
(B) Augustus
(C) Claudius
(D) Hadrian
(E) the passage does not specify

The correct answer is choice (E). Julius Caesar, choice (A), invaded Britain, while Augustus, choice (B), negotiated a treaty with the British rulers. Claudius, who is choice (C), conquered only the southern part. The remaining choice, (D), is Hadrian, who did not conquer any of England; he built the wall.

No one knows why sleep is necessary, though it clearly is. Studies show that people who have been deprived of sleep for several days develop various symptoms such as irritability, confusion, lack of eye focus, and hand tremors. These relatively mild symptoms virtually disappear after only one good night's sleep, however. In more serious cases, several days' lack of sleep may lead to hallucinations in a small group of individuals.

Whatever the purpose of sleep may be, it is not to rest the brain, for the brain is as active during sleep as in waking hours—perhaps even more so. We know this from readings taken by the electroencephalograph (EEG), a device that measures the brain's electrical activity. It shows that during the course of a normal night's sleep, the brain produces several different kinds of brain waves and that they correspond to different stages of sleep.

The first sleep stage, immediately after falling asleep, is called Stage One. At this level, the body is somewhat relaxed and the sleeper can be easily reawakened. The sleeper then passes through Stage Two and Stage Three, becoming ever more relaxed and more difficult to awaken, to Stage Four, the deepest stage of sleep, characterized by total relaxation and extreme difficulty in awakening. At each of these stages the EEG registers a noticeably different kind of brain wave.

Throughout the sleep period, the sleeper moves from one sleep stage to another. After the first period of Stage Four sleep, the sleeper moves briefly to Stage One or Two, then, typically, back to Stage Four. After two or three such cycles, which take place in the first hours of sleep, the remainder of the sleeping period is spent mainly at Stage One and Stage Two.

At Stage One there are two distinct kinds of sleep: REM (rapid eye movement) and NREM (non-rapid eye movement). During REM sleep, the eyes move about rapidly beneath the closed lids. Brain wave measurements suggest a high level of activity in the brain, but the sleeper is as difficult to awaken as in Stage Four. As the sleep period progresses, the periods of REM sleep become longer. Sleepers awakened from the various stages of sleep during experiments indicate that REM sleep is typically a time of emotional and pictorially vivid dreams. (It has been suggested that the moving eyes may be following the action of a dream.)

During NREM sleep, many people who have been awakened also report dreamlike activity, sometimes as vivid as that of REM sleep but much more often of a less emotional character. It appears that many people are mentally active through most or all of the night, and that almost all people are active during REM sleep. It seems almost certain, then, that all normal people dream; their ability to recall dreams on awakening, however, varies considerably.

Information on the content of dreams is gathered in two ways: by asking people to write about their dreams after they wake up or, in a laboratory setting, by waking them up and taking an immediate report. The second method produces better data but is much more expensive and time-consuming.

(1) The content of a person's dreams seems to be considerably influenced by that person's waking concerns. It can also, at least in some cases, be influenced by stimuli in the sleeper's environment, such as the music or talk of a radio left on overnight. Interestingly, the content of about two-thirds of reported dreams is emotionally negative, characterized by anger, fear, and hostility.

The purpose of dreaming is not clear. Sigmund Freud theorized that what he called the manifest content of a dream—essentially its action and story line—is the surface manifestation, disguised and dramatized, of the latent content. The latent content is the hidden desires and motives that, according to Freud's theory, the conscious mind has repressed. If the latent content is not sufficiently disguised, the result is frightening to the dreamer—a nightmare. Freud's hypothesis has been partially supported by subsequent research, but much of it has also been questioned.

Another theory about dreams suggests that approximately every 90 minutes—the frequency with which REM sleep recurs—the brain goes through a period of consolidating recent experiences with the information already stored there. It is a process, not unlike that of a computer, of inserting new data in the memory. In the course of the process, so the theory goes, the mind searches the memory for the most appropriate place to store the new information. Dreams, then, may be simply a by-product of the memory search.

Whatever its purpose, REM sleep is not limited to humans; all mammals seem to experience it, and in roughly the same proportions to humans. Newborn babies (and the newborn young of other mammals) experience more REM sleep than do older people and older animals. From this it has been inferred that REM sleep may play some role in the development of the central nervous system in infants.

The purpose of sleep, according to this passage is

(A) to rest the brain
(B) to help infants' nervous systems develop
(C) to dream
(D) not yet known
(E) to prevent hand tremors

Though the passage advances theories about why people sleep and dream, it clearly states in the very first sentence that "No one knows why sleep is necessary," making choice (D) the best response.

You might reasonably infer from the paragraph marked (1) that

(A) all people who dream have had a bad day
(B) dreaming is often a way of releasing negative emotions about what happened during the day
(C) two-thirds of the people listened to a radio talk show in their sleep
(D) people with bad dreams had a lot of REM sleep that night
(E) people remember bad dreams only after they wake up

Choices (A) and (E) can be eliminated immediately because the paragraph says that about two-thirds of reported dreams are emotionally negative. That means about a third of reported dreams are good, making both (A) and (E) false. Choice (D) can be eliminated because while elsewhere in the passage REM sleep is linked with dream activity, it is not always connected with negative dreams. Paragraph (1) also states that only "in some cases" is there a link with sleep environment stimuli, such as a radio left on, eliminating (C). The only reasonable inference is choice (B).

How many stages of sleep are there?

(A) one
(B) two
(C) three
(D) four
(E) none of the above

The passage talks about four different sleep stages, making choice (D) the only correct answer.

We know that people's brains remain active during sleep because

(A) researchers can see sleepers' eyes moving under closed eyelids during REM sleep
(B) people report having dreams, indicating mental activity
(C) stimulus in the sleep environment, such as music, can affect dreams
(D) dreaming can also take place in NREM sleep, showing brain activity at that time
(E) EEG readings taken during sleep cycles show it

Choices (A) through (D) all offer signs of brain activity at some time or other during sleep, but it is only through EEG readings of brain waves, as mentioned early in the passage, that we know just how active the brain is during sleep. Choice (E) is correct.

Stories attest to the ancient belief that music had magical powers: It could work natural miracles, cure the sick, and purify the souls of worshipers. The ancient Greeks traced music to their mythical gods. In fact, the modern word *music* probably come form the *Muses*, the nine goddesses the Greeks believed watched over the arts and sciences.

In ancient Greece, the *lyre* (a simple harp) and the *kithara* (grandfather of the guitar) figured in the worship of Apollo, who was devoted to the rational, harmonious spirit of man and nature. Cult members played alone or strummed their instruments in accompaniment with singing or reciting of epic poems.

But the pleasure-seeking followers of Dionysus, god of wine and fertility, preferred the shrill sounds of the *aulos*, a double-pipe reed instrument. Its music accompanied a form of poetry that may have given birth to Greek drama. In fact, writings and vase paintings of the time tell us that performances of Sophocles' and Euripides' plays were traditionally laced with the harsh sound of the aulos.

In this period of antiquity, 500 years before Christ, music gradually began to break loose from its strict ceremonial ties. The lyre and the aulos were played as solo instruments and in music festivals and competitions. Music education stressed skillful techniques, and more and more virtuosos appeared before the public. Music became increasingly complex.

The shift away from the "noble" use of music worried the older generation. For example, Aristotle warned in a very modern-sounding lecture:

(1) . . . students of music [should] stop short of the arts which are practiced in professional contests . . . those fantastic marvels of execution. . . . Let the young practice . . . such music as we have prescribed, only until they are able to feel delight in noble melodies and rhythms.

Soon the pendulum of style and attitude swung the other way. Music practice became simplified and, most important of all, writers on the subject of music formulated clear, fundamental theories about the nature of music, its composition, its use in society, and its place in the universe.

Pythagoras thought music to be inseparable from mathematical laws, and that to understand numbers was to understand not only music but the cosmos and everything in it. Aristotle spoke of the unbreakable bond between melody and poetry, and of the overwhelming influence of music on our attitudes and passions. Plato believed that to change the foundations of music was to invite chaos in art and education and anarchy in society and politics. "Let me make the songs of a nation," he said, "and I care not who makes the laws."

This Greek doctrine of *ethos*—that is, the moral qualities and effects of music, of its emotional power, and of its relationship to the universal mathematical laws—was no passing chapter in the history of musical theory. It was to influence the development of music for more than 20 centuries.

(2) Mathematical laws underlie our study of acoustics, musical intervals, and harmonics. They determine the way instruments are constructed, the tuning of pianos, and the design of electronic synthesizers, and they are the foundation of modern theories of orchestration—the way instruments of different timbre can be most effectively combined.

Ancient theory also suggested that music was related to the path of the sun, moon, and stars. This idea flowed down through the centuries, influencing poets of the Middle Ages, Shakespeare, Milton, and even some of the more mystical composers of our time.

The bond between melody and poetry has found sublime expression in the great romantic art songs of the 19th century, especially in the works of Franz Schubert and Hugo Wolf, and in Wagner's romantic music drama: a union of language, philosophy, drama, and music.

The power of music to influence human emotion (the very basis of contemporary music therapy) has remained unchanged throughout the ages. We still pray in church against the background of solemn music, make merry to rollicking songs, fall in love to sentimental strings, and march to a vigorous beat. In fact, on a very basic level, our music has continued to express the two faces of human nature symbolized by the opposing cults of ancient Greece. In the music we call "classic," we follow the Apollonian ideal of logic, orderliness, and spiritual uplift. In the music we call "romantic," we celebrate the Dionysian ideal of sensuality, fantasy, and stimulation. These opposite ideals have interacted throughout the history of music.

The expression "the kithara (grandfather of the guitar)" as used in the passage means

(A) the kithara is a living thing that gave birth to the guitar's father
(B) the kithara is older than the lyre
(C) the kithara was an early form of guitar
(D) the kithara played "noble" music better than new music
(E) the guitar was the product of the kithara and some other instrument

From the passage, the kithara is an instrument and not a living thing, so choice (A) can be eliminated. Choices (B) and (E) might possibly be true, but the passage does not provide the necessary information to say one way or the other. Choice (D) certainly could be true, but the statement is not relevant to the expression. Only choice (C) gives a reasonable approximation of the expression.

In the quotation which is marked (1), Aristotle said
that the young

(A) should spend more time increasing their technical
    skills
(B) get too much allowance
(C) should practice playing "noble" music
(D) spend too much time playing music in professional
    contests
(E) should learn the joys that come from playing the
    new music

Aristotle said that students had become too concerned with technical mastery and the new music, so that choices (A) and (E) are wrong. Choice (B)
is not relevant and can also be eliminated. Choice (D) is a possibility, but
(C) comes closer to Aristotle's overall intent.

Based on the passage, when Plato said "Let me make the
songs of a nation, and I care not who makes the laws," he
probably meant

(A) the emotional power of music is greater than even the
    laws of a nation
(B) he would be so happy writing music that nothing else
    would matter
(C) there is more to life than law
(D) that he is a better songwriter than lawmaker
(E) that he has no interest in law

If you read only the quote, choices (B) through (E) might in some way
seem possible answers. But in the passage itself, the sentence immediately before the quote sets up Plato's intent. He is concerned about the fundamental power of music, and thus choice (A) is the best answer.

According to the passage, what two forms of modern
music express the division between "noble" and "new"
music of ancient Greece?

(A) church music and love songs
(B) Schubert's words and those of Wagner
(C) works played on the lyre and on the aulos
(D) classical and romantic music
(E) folk and rock music

Choice (A) is incorrect because the two types of music do not relate to the
division between rational and harmonious music (classical), as opposed to
stimulating and sensual music (romantic). Choice (B) is incorrect because
both composers wrote romantic works, while (C) refers to ancient music
only. Choice (E) is wrong because neither of these types of music is mentioned in the passage, while classical and romantic music are. Choice (D),
then, is correct.

Although they lived far from other people, the rest of the
world still intruded from time to time. Sometimes they
heard a horse clattering past on the distant road; another
time a gunshot brought their heads up sharply. Once they
stumbled on an abandoned building deep in the woods. Its
roof was open to the sky and the window holes gaped darkly.
The door hung at a slight slant on its hinges. They left without saying a word. Long association made speech unnecessary most of the time. In this instance, both knew there was
nothing here for them and did not even look to see if they
were of the same mind. The old house made them uncomfortable, as if it might somehow be theirs. Their lives did not
include the concept of neglect or abandonment: It wasn't
they who had been neglected or abandoned, but instead
they had neglected and abandoned the world. So they rejected this visible sign of humans once present but now gone,
choosing to continue instead in the solitary, speechless
patterns developed over long years.

This passage is about

(A) one character
(B) two characters
(C) three characters
(D) many characters
(E) no characters

This is a straightforward question about a detail. In order to choose the
answer, you must look for clues to number. The words "they" and "them"
indicate more than one character, so you can eliminate choices (A) and (E).
The word "both" indicates that choice (B) is correct.

It appears that the setting for this passage is

(A) a wooded area
(B) a ghost town
(C) a desert
(D) a small town
(E) a beach near an ocean

This is a question about a detail, but it requires an inference to answer it.
The clues are "the distant road" and "deep in the woods." These clues
make choice (A) the best answer, although we are not certain the others
are wrong.

To the characters, it seemed that the house they found symbolized their

(A) frustration, anger and guilt toward each other
(B) happiness and fulfillment in their lives
(C) loneliness and longing for the company of other
    people
(D) need to find a place to live and be happy
(E) rejection of others and acceptance of solitude

To answer this question, look for key words such as "symbol," "represent,"
"sign," or "signal" with respect to the house. You can eliminate choice (B),
because the house made them uncomfortable. There is no indication of the
emotions mentioned in choices (A) or (C) anywhere in the passage. Choice
(D) might be possible, but the word "rejected" in the last sentence indicates
that choice (E) is the better of the two.

It can be inferred that the characters in the passage

(A) cannot speak to each other
(B) do not want company or any change in their lives
(C) abandoned and neglected the house in the woods
(D) are frightened by horses and guns
(E) are superstitious about old, abandoned buildings

This inference question asks for an evaluation of the overall effect of the
passage rather than a conclusion about a specific part of the passage. The
mood of the passage is set by the descriptive words and the actions of the
characters. It is clear that the characters could speak if they wished
("speech unnecessary"), so choice (A) can be eliminated. The house was
abandoned and neglected before they "stumbled" on it. Since that word
suggests that they had not known it was there, we can eliminate choice (C).
They may be frightened of guns, but they don't seem to be alarmed by
horses, and their motives for leaving the house seem to have nothing to do
with superstition. With choices (D) and (E) eliminated, choice (B) is left.

According to the passage, the characters are living where
they are

(A) by their own choice
(B) because they have been exiled
(C) because they have nowhere else to go
(D) as a punishment
(E) temporarily, until they find a better place

The information to answer the question is given in the passage, although it
may not be given in exactly the words used in the question. The best
choice is (A) because the passage directly states that "they had neglected
and abandoned the world. . .choosing to continue instead. . . ." All the
other choices might be possible, but they are not supported by the choice
of words in the passage.

Mathematical Examples

The combined mathematical section consists of sixty questions presented in one fifteen-minute and two thirty-minute parts. Of these sixty questions, thirty-five are standard multiple-choice questions that cover topics from arithmetic, algebra, and geometry, as well as logic, symbols and operations, and probability and counting. Another fifteen questions involve quantitative comparison. The remaining questions require students to produce their own answers rather than choose one from a selection provided in the test.

Use the test booklet itself for scratch paper, rather than performing calculations in your head. Seeing the calculation on paper helps reinforce that an answer is correct. Having the calculations on paper also helps in the latter part of the test, when questions that were tried and skipped are retried. Remember, too, that you now may use a calculator; check in advance to determine which kinds you may bring.

Most concepts needed for the mathematical portion are reviewed in the SAT I information packet. They include odd and even numbers, integers, and prime numbers; percents, including those over 100 and less than 1; averages, including weighted averages; distance/rate/time problems; squares of integers and properties of signed numbers; and factoring. Key geometric concepts include parallel lines; relationships of angles; the Pythagorean theorem and the relationship of sides of a triangle; formulas for area and perimeter of rectangles, triangles, and circles; and volume of rectangular solids. Questions also cover topics such as slope, median, and mode.

Directions for the mathematical section include a guide to symbols and key concepts, including area of a circle; the degree measure of circles, straight angles, and triangles; the area of a right triangle; and the Pythagorean theorem. The figures that are included in questions are not always drawn to scale.

Standard multiple choice. Most of the time, numerical answers will list values either from smallest to greatest or from greatest to smallest. In either case, answer (C) will generally be the middle value. Sometimes plugging a number into a problem is a faster way to approach a question than setting up an equation, solving it, and then finding an answer that matches. When using this approach, start with answer (C) if the numbers are arranged in order. Then if (C) is too high, work next with the two smaller values; if (C) is too low, work with the two greater values.

When preparing for the mathematical section, practice estimation skills. They can often help save time on the test, especially when answers are not close together. For example, suppose a question is to find 48 percent of 794. Note that 48 percent rounds to 50 percent, while 794 rounds to 800. It is much faster to calculate 50 percent of 800, which equals 400. The answer should be fairly close to 400, and lower than 400, since the original numbers are lower than 50 percent and 800. Thus, answers over 400 can be eliminated quickly, as can answers that are much smaller than 400. If the choice of answers is 165.42, 360.64, 381.12, 404, and 536.84, then all but 360.64 and 381.12 can be eliminated fairly quickly.

Directions: In this section solve each problem using any available space on the page for scratchwork. Then decide which is the best of the choices given and fill in the corresponding oval on the answer sheet.

If $3a = 4b = 6c$, what is $8a + 8c$ in terms of b?

(A) $10b$ (B) $12b$ (C) $14b$ (D) $16b$ (E) $18b$

Estimating can help you eliminate some answers. If $3a = 4b$, then $6a = 8b$. Thus, $6a + 6c = 8b + 4b = 12b$. This is too little, so both (A) and (B) can be cut from the choices. Note that $3a = 6c = 2\ (3c)$; in turn, $8a = 2\ (8c) = 16c$. Thus, $8a + 8c = 16c + 8c = 24c$. Now the problem has become to state $24c$ in terms of b. Note that $24c = 4\ (6c)$; since $4b = 6c$, we have $24c = 4\ (6c) = 4\ (4b) = 16b$. Thus, (D) is correct. There are several other ways to solve this problem.

Denise sold pottery at the outdoor market on two Saturdays. On the first Saturday, she earned \$120. On the second Saturday, she earned \$160. What percent increase were her second Saturday's earnings over her first Saturday's earnings?

(A) 20% (B) 25% (C) $33\frac{1}{3}$% (D) 40% (E) 75%

To find the percent increase, find the amount of the increase. Then write a fraction for the amount of increase over the original earnings. Finally, change the fraction to a percent.

$$\$160 - \$120 = \$40$$

$$\frac{\$40}{\$120} = \frac{1}{3} = 33\frac{1}{3}\%$$

The correct choice is (C).

George scored 80, 78, 85, and 86 on his social studies quizzes. He would like to have an average of 85 after his next quiz. What score must he get?

(A) 85 (B) 90 (C) 91 (D) 96 (E) 100

The average is found by adding all the scores and dividing by the number of scores. If George wants to get an average of 85, he must have all five scores add up to 5×85, or 425. The total of his first four scores is 329. Subtracting 329 from $425 = 96$. The correct choice is (D).

If $12 \cdot 12 \cdot 12 = 6 \cdot 6 \cdot Q$, then $Q =$

(A) 6 (B) 12 (C) 36 (D) 48 (E) 72

There are several ways to approach this problem. You might multiply 12 by 12 by 12 and divide by 6 times 6. You would save a lot of time by simply comparing both sides of the equation and determining the missing factors.
$$12 \cdot 12 \cdot 12 = 6 \cdot 6 \cdot Q$$
$$6(2) \cdot 6(2) \cdot 6(2) = 6 \cdot 6 \cdot Q$$
The factors on the left that are missing from the right are 2, 2, and 6(2). So Q must equal the product of 2, 2, and 12. The correct choice is (D).

Louise borrowed \$2000 for 6 months at 8% simple annual interest. She must repay the loan in full with interest at the end of 6 months. How much will she have to pay then?

(A) \$2008 (B) \$2080 (C) \$2160 (D) \$2320
(E) \$4000

To find out how much she must repay, first find the interest. Use the formula $i = p \times r \times t$, where p is the principal, r is the rate, and t is the time in years.
$$i = \$2000 \times 0.08 \times \frac{6}{12} = 160 \times \frac{1}{2} = 80$$

The total to be repaid is the principal plus interest: $\$2000 + \$80$. The correct choice is (B).

A number is divisible by 4 if its last two digits are divisible by 4. Only one of the following is divisible by 12. Which number is divisible by 12?

(A) 32,013   (B) 31,248   (C) 30,020   (D) 36,028
(E) 36,114

If a number is divisible by 12, it must be divisible by 4 and by 3. If it is divisible by 3, the sum of its digits is divisible by 3. These two divisibility tests, for 4 and for 3, can be used to determine which of the numbers is divisible by 12. This is much faster than dividing each of the numbers by 12. Using the divisibility test for 4, we can eliminate (A) and (E). The sums of the digits for (B), (C), and (D) are 18, 5, and 19 respectively. Therefore, the correct choice is (B).

If $\frac{12}{x} = 3$ and $\frac{y}{4} = 2$, then $\frac{5+x}{y+4} =$

(A) $\frac{5}{8}$ (B) $\frac{5}{4}$ (C) $\frac{1}{2}$ (D) $\frac{9}{4}$ (E) $\frac{3}{4}$

First, solve for each variable. Then substitute their values in the expression on the right and simplify it.

$$\frac{12}{x} = 3 \qquad \frac{y}{4} = 2$$
$$x = 4 \qquad\qquad y = 8$$
$$\frac{5+x}{y+4} = \frac{5+4}{8+4}$$
$$= \frac{9}{12} = \frac{3}{4}$$

The correct choice is (E).

The sum of two consecutive even integers is 30. Which of the following is the larger number in the pair?

(A) 14   (B) 15   (C) 16   (D) 18   (E) 20

Solve this problem by letting $n =$ the smaller even number and $n + 2$ the larger even number.

$$n + n + 2 = 30$$
$$2n + 2 = 30$$
$$2n = 28$$
$$n = 14$$
$$n + 2 = 16$$

The correct choice is (C).

Find the average of $2x + 5$ and $6x - 1$.

(A) $3x + 2$ (B) $4x + 4$ (C) $4x + 3$ (D) $8x + 4$
(E) $4x + 2$

To find the average of two algebraic expressions, add the expressions and divide by 2. Then simplify the expression.

$$\frac{2x + 5 + 6x - 1}{2} = \frac{2x + 6x + 5 - 1}{2} = \frac{8x + 4}{2}$$
$$= \frac{4(2x + 1)}{2}$$
$$= 2(2x + 1) = 4x + 2$$

The correct choice is (E).

If x and y are positive integers such that $x^2 + y^2 = 20$ and $x > y$, then $x - y =$

(A) 1   (B) 2   (C) 3   (D) 4   (E) 6

This problem requires some reasoning. Since x and y are positive integers, x^2 and y^2 are both perfect squares. Perfect squares less than 20 are 1, 4, 9, and 16. The two perfect squares that add to 20 are 4 and 16. Since $x > y$, $x^2 = 16$, $x = 4$; $y^2 = 4$, $y = 2$ and $x - y = 4 - 2 = 2$. The correct choice is (B).

If the operation # is defined for all positive x and y by

$$x \,\#\, y = \frac{2xy}{x + y},$$

which of the following is true for positive x, y, and z?
I. $x \,\#\, x = x$
II. $x \,\#\, y = y \,\#\, x$
III. $x \,\#\, (y \,\#\, z) = (x \,\#\, y) \,\#\, z$

(A) I only   (B) I and II only   (C) I and III only
(D) II and III only   (E) I, II, and III

This is a newly defined operation. Apply the operation correctly.

I $x \,\#\, x = \dfrac{2x(x)}{x + x} = \dfrac{2x(x)}{2x} = x$

I is true.

II $x \,\#\, y = \dfrac{2xy}{x + y}$; $y \,\#\, x = \dfrac{2yx}{y + x}$

II is true because of the commutative properties for multiplication and addition.

III This expression is more complicated. Instead of working it out algebraically, substitute any three values of x, y, and z. Let $x = 2$, $y = 3$ and $z = 4$:

$$x \,\#\, (y \,\#\, z) = 2 \,\#\, (3 \,\#\, 4)$$
$$= 2 \,\#\, \frac{(2 \cdot 3 \cdot 4)}{3 + 4}$$
$$= 2 \,\#\, \frac{24}{7} = \frac{\left(2 \cdot 2 \cdot \frac{24}{7}\right)}{2 + \frac{24}{7}} = \frac{\frac{96}{7}}{\frac{38}{7}} = \frac{96}{38}$$

$$(x \,\#\, y) \,\#\, z = (2 \,\#\, 3) \,\#\, 4$$
$$= \frac{2 \cdot 2 \cdot 3}{2 + 3} \,\#\, 4$$
$$= \frac{12}{5} \,\#\, 4$$
$$= \frac{2 \cdot \frac{12}{5} \cdot 4}{\frac{12}{5} + 4} = \frac{\frac{96}{5}}{\frac{32}{5}} = \frac{96}{32}$$

Since the results are different, III is not true. The correct choice is (B).

If 50% of x is 25% of y, then y is what percent of x?

(A) $12\frac{1}{2}\%$ (B) 25%   (C) 50%   (D) 75%   (E) 200%

The best way to have a clear picture of the problem is to write an algebraic expression for it.

$$0.5x = 0.25y$$

To find what percent y is of x, solve the equation for $\frac{y}{x}$.

$$\frac{0.5x}{0.25} = y \qquad \frac{0.5}{0.25} = \frac{y}{x} \qquad 2 = \frac{y}{x}$$

Change 2 to a percent. The correct choice is (E).

Find the value of x if $2x^2 - 7x = 4$.

(A) $-\frac{1}{2}$ or 4   (B) $\frac{1}{2}$ or 4   (C) $-\frac{1}{2}$ or -4 (D) -1 or 4
(E) -1 or -4

Many quadratic equations can be solved by factoring. First, rewrite the equation so that one side equals 0. Factor the expression on the other side. Let both factors equal 0 and solve for x.

$$2x^2 - 7x - 4 = 0$$
$$(2x + 1)(x - 4) = 0$$
$$2x + 1 = 0 \qquad x - 4 = 0$$
$$2x = -1 \qquad\qquad x = 4$$
$$x = -\frac{1}{2}$$

The correct choice is (A).

Simplify the expression $\dfrac{12x^4yz^5}{3x^6z^4}$

(A) $15x^{10}z^9$ (B) $9x^2yz$ (C) $4x^2yz$ (D) $\dfrac{4yz}{x^2}$ (E) $\dfrac{4x^2y}{z}$

Use the laws of exponents to simplify this expression. Consider each part of the expression separately.

$$\frac{12x^4yz^5}{3x^6z^4} = \frac{12 \cdot x^4 \cdot y \cdot z^5}{3x^6z^4} = \frac{4yz}{x^2}$$

The correct choice is (D).

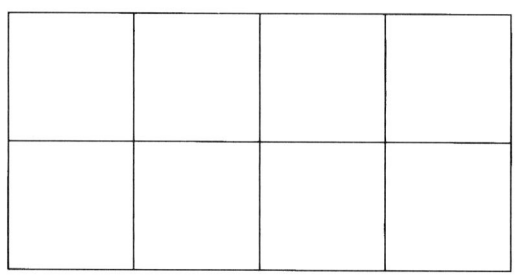

The figure above is a rectangle divided into eight equal squares. If the perimeter of the rectangle is 3, what is the perimeter of one of the squares?

(A) $\frac{3}{11}$ (B) $\frac{1}{4}$ (C) $\frac{3}{8}$ (D) 1   (E) 4

The perimeter of the rectangle is the sum of all the line segments around the rectangle. There are twelve segments in all in the perimeter. Since the figure is composed of squares, all the line segments are congruent. Therefore, the measure of each line segment in the figure is 3 divided by 12, or $\frac{1}{4}$. The perimeter of one square is $4(\frac{1}{4})$. The correct choice is (D).

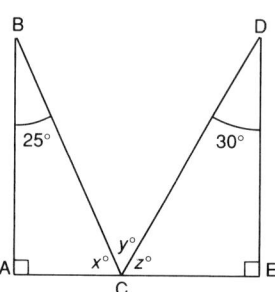

In the figure above, AE is a line segment. What is the measure of y?

(A) 55°   (B) 60°   (C) 65°   (D) 125°   (E) 180°

There are two right triangles. In each, you are given the measure of one acute angle. In order to find x and z, use the fact that the acute angles in a right triangle are complements. Then $y = 180 - (x + z)$, since the three angles form a straight angle.

$$x = 90 - 25 = 65; z = 90 - 30 = 60$$
$$y = 180 - (65 + 60)$$
$$y = 180 - 125$$
$$y = 55$$

The correct choice is (A).

If $6x + 8y = 12$, then $3x + 4y =$

(A) 3/4 (B) 4/3 (C) 6 (D) 14 (E) 24

First, note the relationship between $6x + 8y$ and $3x + 4y$. Factoring $6x + 8y$ leads to $2(3x + 4y)$. Also $12 = 2(6)$. Thus $2(3x + 4y) = 2(6)$. Divide both sides by 2 to find that $3x + 4y = 6$. (C) is correct.

Circle O has a diameter of 4. Circle P has a radius of 3. What is the ratio of the area of circle O to the area of circle P?

(A) 4 to 3   (B) 2 to 3   (C) 3 to 4   (D) 16 to 9   (E) 4 to 9

The formula for the area of a circle is $A = \pi r^2$. The area of circle O is $2^2\pi$. The area of circle P is $3^2\pi$. The ratio of their areas is 4π to 9π or 4 to 9. The answer is (E).

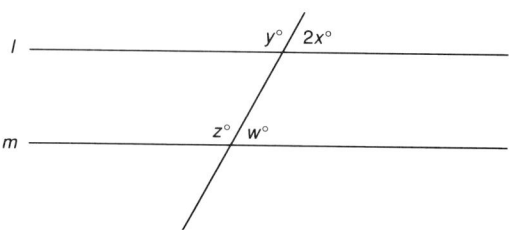

In the figure above, lines l and m are parallel. Which of the following must equal $180 - x$?

(A) $x + y$ (B) $x + w$ (C) $y + z$ (D) $y + w$ (E) $w + z$

Since the lines are parallel, $2x$ and w are equal, y and z are equal, and $2x$ is supplementary to y and z. This gives us a few equations that involve 180 and x:

$$180 - 2x = y \quad \text{and} \quad 180 - 2x = z$$
$$180 - x - x = y \qquad\qquad 180 - x - x = z$$
$$180 - x = y + x \qquad\qquad 180 - x = z + x$$

Therefore, the correct choice is (A), since $180 - x = y + x = x + y$.

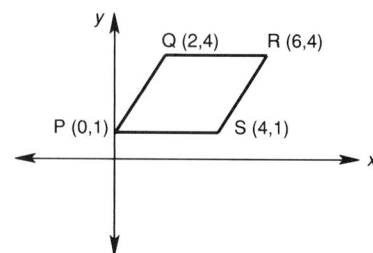

In the figure above, what is the area of parallelogram $PQRS$?

(A) 4   (B) 8   (C) 12   (D) 16
(E) It cannot be determined from the information given.

The formula for the area of a parallelogram is $A = bh$, where b is the base and h is the height. The height is the measure of a perpendicular from one vertex to the base. If PS is the base, the height can be measured by the distance parallel to the y-axis.

$$A = bh$$
$$A = 4(3) = 12$$

The correct choice is (C).

The graph of the equation $y = 2x - 3$ can be described as

(A) a circle with its center at $(2, 3)$
(B) a line that goes through the points $(0, -3)$ and $(\frac{3}{2}, 0)$
(C) a circle that has a radius of 3 and a center at $(0, 2)$
(D) a line parallel to the x-axis
(E) an angle with its vertex at $(2, -3)$

Since this is an equation that has only the first power of both x and y, it must be a line, which eliminates choices (A), (C), and (D). The slope-intercept form of a line is $y = mx + b$, where m is the slope and b is the y intercept. For the given equation, the slope would be 2 and the y intercept would be -3, which eliminates choice (D)—where the slope is 0—and strongly implies choice (B). Checking both points in the equation confirms this choice.

Suppose a \$10 bill measures 6 by 3 inches and a bundle of 50 of them is $\frac{1}{4}$-inch thick. How much room would \$1 million in tens take up (in cubic inches)?

(A) 9,000   (B) 144,000   (C) 3,400   (D) 19,600   (E) 36,000

To find the volume (in cubic inches), change all measurements into quarters and multiply:
$$\frac{24}{4} \times \frac{12}{4} \times \frac{1}{4} = \frac{288}{64}$$
$$\frac{288}{64} = 4.5 \text{ cubic inches per bundle.}$$
Since one bundle contains \$500, there are 2,000 bundles in \$1 million, which would take up 9,000 cubic inches. Choice (A) is correct.

A jar filled with jelly beans contains 35 red ones, 15 green ones, 27 yellow ones, and 13 purple ones. What are the chances of randomly selecting any color but the green ones?

(A) 7 in 10   (B) 80 in 100   (C) 75 in 90   (D) 65 in 70
(E) 15 in 90

To find the answer, add up the number of possible outcomes (picking any color jelly bean) and divide it into the number of ways a particular outcome can occur (picking any color except green).
So, $35 + 27 + 13 = 75$
and $35 + 15 + 27 + 13 = 90$ for $\frac{75}{90}$.
Choice (C) is correct.

A teacher named Ms. Jackson grades q papers an hour for $5m$ hours. She stops for lunch and then grades h papers an hour for m additional hours. What was the total number of papers Ms. Jackson graded expressed in terms of q, m, and h?

(A) $5m(q + h)$ (B) $m(q + 5h)$ (C) $5m(5q + h)$
(D) $m(5q + h)$ (E) $m(q + h)/5$

Ms. Jackson grades q papers per hour for $5m$ hours in the first session and then grades h papers per hour for m more hours—a total of $(q \times 5m) + (h \times m)$. The answer does not appear in this form among the choices, so divide the product within the parentheses by m and multiply the resulting sum by m, producing choice (D).

A farmer mixes 12 gallons of an insecticide with 36 gallons of water before discovering he should have made a 45 percent solution of insecticide. Which of the following equations would tell him how many gallons of insecticide to add, where x represents the number of gallons?

(A) $12 + \frac{x}{36} = \frac{45}{100}$ (B) $12 + \frac{x}{48} + x = \frac{45}{100}$
(C) $\frac{12}{36} + x = \frac{45}{100}$ (D) $12 + \frac{x}{36} + x = \frac{45}{100}$
(E) $12 + \frac{x}{48} = \frac{45}{100}$

Set up this equation with $\frac{45}{100}$ on one side. On the other side put the current amount of insecticide and the total gallons, $\frac{12}{48}$, and add x gallons to it. The important thing to remember here is that x must be added to both 12 *and* 48. The resulting equation is given in choice (B).

A wire supporting a telephone pole forms a 60-degree angle with the ground. If the wire is anchored to the ground 10 feet from the telephone pole, what is the length in feet of the wire from the ground to its attachment on the pole?

(A) 15   (B) 3.16   (C) 100   (D) 20   (E) 36

The important clue here is the 60-degree angle, because the wire forms a 30-60-90-degree triangle with the telephone pole. The 10-foot distance from the pole to the anchor point on the ground is the triangle's short side, and in 30-60-90-degree triangles, the hypotenuse is two times the short side. Choice (D) is correct.

Get Real

Sometimes it's hard to see the relevance of what you are doing. When this happens, ask your teacher how the topic is important in real life. For example, trigonometry can be used for figuring distances in outer space and for determining whether or not a tree will hit the house when it is cut down! Learning something as simple as that can make all the difference in your study attitude.

Quantitative comparison. These items list two quantities, one in column A and one in column B. You must determine if either of the two quantities has a greater value, if the two are of equal value, or if there is insufficient information to compare the quantities.

Unlike other questions on the SAT I, quantitative comparisons have only four possible answers. While (E) is not considered wrong, it is treated as an omission. If you choose to use a guessing strategy toward the end of a test, realize that marking in (E) will have no impact on your score.

For many comparisons, you will have to calculate both quantities in order to answer the question. On other comparisons, though, other skills can help you out. Suppose the question compares $\sqrt{5} + 1$ with $\sqrt{6} + 1$. By subtracting 1 from both sides, you realize that you are comparing $\sqrt{5}$ and $\sqrt{6}$. Even at this point, you may forget how to compare them. However, you can compare $\sqrt{4}$ and $\sqrt{9}$, which equal 2 and 3 respectively. In making this comparison, you remind yourself that the square root of the larger number is greater than the square root of the smaller number, and with assurance choose the answer that $\sqrt{6} + 1$ is the greater quantity.

Your preparation should include practicing shortcuts that will help you narrow your choices. When you take the test, see if one answer jumps out at you as being correct; then see if you can quickly demonstrate to yourself that the choice is correct. If so, mark it and move on. As in the verbal section, if a question is difficult, but you are able to eliminate some answers, cross them out in the test booklet and move on. When you return to the question later, you will not have to start at the beginning.

<u>Directions:</u> Each of the following questions consists of two quantities in boxes, one in Column A and one in Column B. You are to compare the two quantities and on the answer sheet fill in oval

A   if the quantity in column A is greater;
B   if the quantity in column B is greater;
C   if the two quantities are equal;
D   if the relationship cannot be determined from the information given.

Notes: 1. In certain questions, information concerning one or both of the quantities to be compared is centered above the two columns.
2. In a given question, a symbol that appears in both columns represents the same thing in Column A as it does in Column B.
3. Letters such as x, n, and k stand for real numbers.

Column A	Column B
$(374 + 62)^2$	$(374 - 62)^2$

You could take the time to add within the parenthesis and square the sum, but that would take considerable time. Instead note that $(374 + 62)$ and $(374 - 62)$ are both positive and that $(374 + 62)$ is greater than $(374 - 62)$. If two positive numbers are squared, the square of the larger number will be greater than the square of the smaller number. Thus, the quantity in column A is greater and (A) is correct.

Column A	Column B

$$a = -\frac{1}{3}$$

$$b = \frac{1}{5}$$

$\dfrac{b}{a}$	$\dfrac{a}{b}$

Substitute the given values for a and b in each expression. Simplify the expressions and compare.

$$\frac{b}{a} = \frac{1/5}{-1/3} \qquad\qquad \frac{a}{b} = \frac{-1/3}{1/5}$$

$$= \frac{1}{5} \div \frac{1}{3} \qquad\qquad = -\frac{1}{3} \div \frac{1}{5}$$

$$= \frac{1}{5} \cdot -3 = -\frac{3}{5} \qquad = -\frac{1}{3} \cdot 5 = -\frac{5}{3} = -1\frac{2}{3}$$

The correct choice is (A) since $-\dfrac{3}{5} > -1\dfrac{2}{3}$.

$\dfrac{2}{3} - \dfrac{1}{6}$	$\dfrac{7}{18}$

Evaluate the expression in Column A and compare it with the expression in Column B.

$$\frac{2}{3} - \frac{1}{6} = \frac{4}{6} - \frac{1}{6}$$

$$= \frac{3}{6} \text{ or } \frac{1}{2} \qquad \frac{1}{2} > \frac{7}{18}$$

The answer is (A).

---

x is an integer less than 0.

$3x$	$\dfrac{x}{x} + x$

One approach is to make a table of values for x and look for a pattern in the values of the two given expressions.

x	-1	-2	-3	-4
$3x$	-3	-6	-9	-12
$\dfrac{x}{x} + x$	0	-1	-2	-3

From the table, you can see that the expression in Column B is always greater than the expression in Column A, and that relationship will continue to be true for all values of x that are less than 0. The correct choice is (B).

$$S = \{0, 2, 4, 6, 8\}$$
$$T = \{2, 4, 6, 8\}$$

A number that is a member of S but not of T.	A number that is a member of both S and T.

The only number that is a member of S but not of T is 0. The numbers that are members of both sets are 2, 4, 6, and 8. Any of the numbers described in Column B are greater than the number described in Column A. The choice is (B).

Column A	Column B

A die with the numbers 1 through 6 on each of its faces is to be rolled.

The probability of obtaining an odd number.	The probability of obtaining a number that is 3 or less.

There are six possible outcomes of this experiment that are all equally likely. Three of the possibilities are odd. Three of the possibilities are 3 or less. Therefore, the probabilities of the two events described in Columns A and B are equal. The correct choice is (C).

---

x	$-x^3$

For this type of problem, it is important to consider the range of values of x. Think of the two graphs:

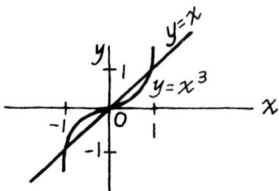

If x is a positive number greater than 1, Column B's expression will be greater than Column A's. If x is less than -1, Column A's expression will be greater than Column B's. Between -1 and 1, the situation changes from $x^3 > x$ to $x < x^3$ at 0. For $x = 0$, 1, or -1, the two expressions are equal. Therefore, the correct choice is (D).

$$x = 500$$
$$y = 499$$

$(x + y)(x - y)$	1000

Although the given values of x and y are large, the problem can be solved mentally. The sum of x and y is 999; the difference between x and y is 1. Therefore, $(x + y)(x - y) = 999 \times 1 = 999$. The correct choice is (B).

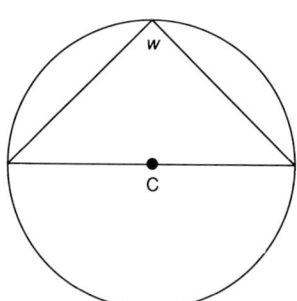

C is the center of the circle; $w > 0$.

$90°$	w

w is the measure of an angle inscribed in a semicircle. Its measure is half the measure of its arc of 180°, which is 90°. Therefore, the correct choice is (C).

3.14	π

While 3.14 is a useful, often used approximation for π, it does not equal π. π is an irrational number with an infinite number of decimal places that begins 3.14159.... The correct choice is (B).

Column A	Column B

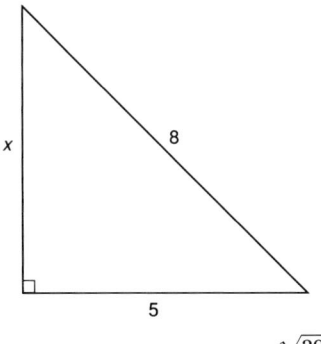

x $\sqrt{39}$

In a right triangle, the Pythagorean relationship states that
$a^2 + b^2 = c^2$ Substitute the values given in the drawing.

$x^2 + 5^2 = 8^2$
$x^2 + 25 = 64$
$x^2 = 39$
$x = \sqrt{39}$ The correct choice is (C).

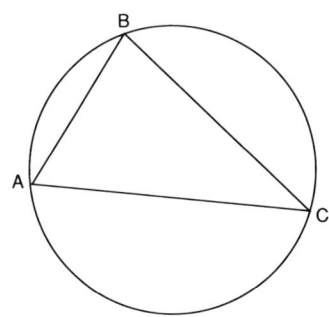

The diameter of the circle is 1.
A, B, and C are on the circumference.

The perimeter of triangle ABC.	3

If the diameter is 1, then the largest possible value of AC is 1. The measures of AB and BC must each be less than 1, since if $AC = 1$, $\angle B = 90°$, and AC is the hypotenuse of a right triangle. Therefore, the perimeter of ABC must be less than 3. The correct choice is (B).

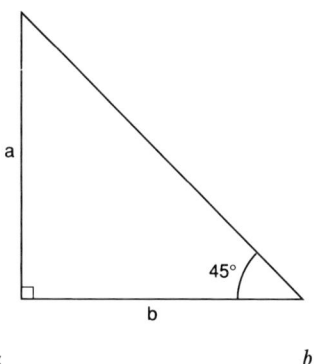

a b

Since the figure is a right triangle, the angle opposite b measures $90° - 45° = 45°$. Since the two acute angles are equal, the triangle is isosceles. The correct choice is (C).

Student-produced responses. This part contains ten questions that are similar to other items in the mathematics section. The difference here is that instead of choosing the correct answer, you solve the problem and then write your answer in special grids provided on the answer sheet as shown below.

For the most part, the grids allow you to write your answer in the form you obtain it—as a fraction, decimal, or whole number—and usually it is a good idea to write the answer in that form. (The grid holds numbers from 0 to 9999 as well as fractions and decimals.) But in practice you sometimes must adjust your answers; these types of cases are covered later.

Spend some time now becoming familiar with the directions for filling in answers. The more you learn about the system now, the less time it will cost you during the actual examination.

1. It is a good idea to write in your answer first at the top of the grid, then fill in the bubbles. *Fill in only one bubble per column,* and remember that your answer counts only if you have filled in the bubbles correctly.

2. Usually it is best to start your answer in the left column, but you may begin in any column so long as you have enough spaces to finish it. Do not fill in bubbles that are in leftover columns.

3. For student-produced response items, answer questions even if you are unsure; no points are deducted for incorrect responses.

4. For fractions you must mark a bubble with a slash mark. For answers with decimals, fill in a bubble with a decimal point. Do not fill in any other bubbles in the column you have used to indicate either of these symbols.

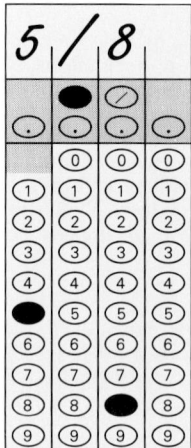

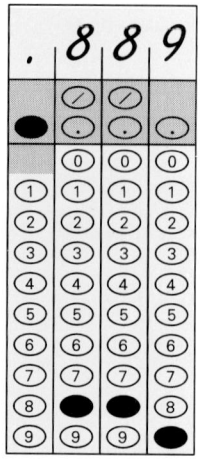
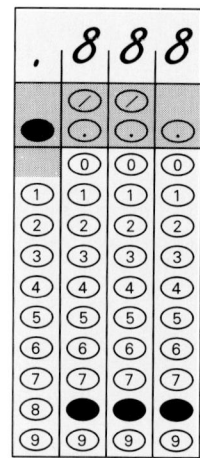

5. Where problems have more than one solution, mark only one answer in the answer grid.

6. Note that you can enter 0 in any column but the leftmost one. That is to discourage you from filling up a column with a meaningless 0, as in 0.59. Also notice that there is no provision for a negative sign. No correct answer in this section will have a negative number.

7. Mixed answers, those with whole numbers and fractions, must be adjusted before entering them on the grid. Convert them into a single fraction or a decimal. For example, change $5\frac{1}{2}$ into $\frac{11}{2}$. This is important. If you write in $5\frac{1}{2}$ on the answer grid, the machine will read it as $\frac{51}{2}$ and record your answer as incorrect. You could also write $5\frac{1}{2}$ as 5.5.

WRONG

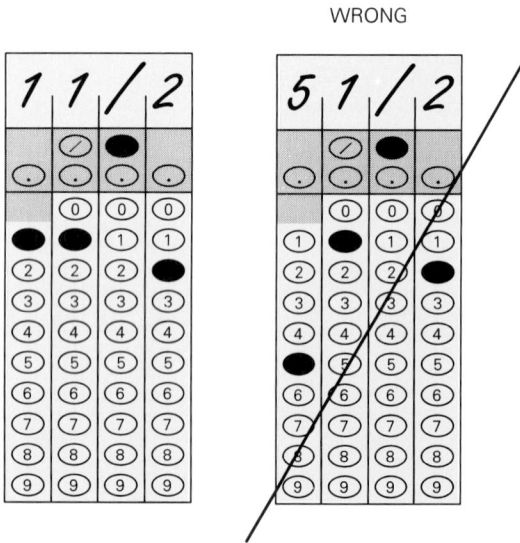

8. Be sure your answer is correct before you start writing it into the grid. If you must change an answer, completely erase the marks so that they will not be read by the scoring machine.

9. Always write in the most accurate decimal you can fit in the answer grid. For example, .88888… can be entered on the grid as .889 or .888. Writing .88 or .89 will be incorrect.

Sally made 40% of the number of cookies baked by Mary, who finished baking 120 that day. The next day, Sally doubled her output. How many did Sally bake the second day?

Multiply .40 × 120 to find out what Sally made the first day: 48. The next day Sally made 2 × 48, or 96 cookies. The answer is entered on the grid:

In $6(p - 2) - 3p = 16$, what is the value of p?

First multiply out $6(p - 2)$, which produces $6p - 3p - 12 = 16$. Add 12 to both sides of the equation and get $3p = 28$. Thus, $p = 9.3333…$, which you should grid as 9.33 or 9.34.

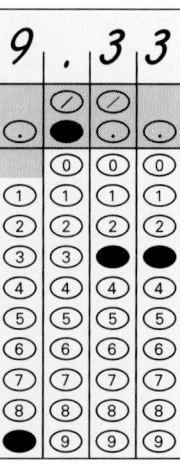

 **Clarify Mathematical Examples**

Identify two questions or things you don't understand about the SAT I mathematical examples. For each, state what you will do within the next week to find out the information you need.

Find a fraction that is larger than $\frac{1}{4}$ and less than $\frac{1}{3}$.

Convert both fractions to twelfths first, making them $\frac{3}{12}$ and $\frac{4}{12}$. To find a fraction between them, go to twenty-fourths, or $\frac{6}{24}$ and $\frac{8}{24}$. So $\frac{7}{24}$ is one fraction between $\frac{1}{4}$ and $\frac{1}{3}$, but there are others. If, for example, you converted the fractions to forty-eighths, you would have $\frac{12}{48}$ and $\frac{16}{48}$, with three correct answers. Grid only one correct answer, here $\frac{7}{24}$.

Gridded answer: 7 / 2 4

A line is marked with four points, W, X, Y, and Z in that order. The line segment WX = 11, XY = 5, and XZ = 8. Determine the value of WY/YZ.

Sketch the line with points WXYZ and the known values. The value of YZ is unknown, but can be found easily because XY = 5 and XZ = 8. Find the length of YZ by subtracting XY from XZ. The result is a length of 3. WY = WX + XY = 11 + 5. The value of WY/YZ then is $\frac{16}{3}$ or, if you use a decimal approximation, 5.33. The answer $\frac{16}{3}$ is gridded:

Gridded answer: 1 6 / 3

Suppose one interior angle of a triangle is 66° and a second is twice the third. How many degrees does the second angle measure?

Remember: (1) the sum of the interior angles of a triangle is 180 degrees and (2) the second angle is twice the third. Set up the equation:
$$x + 2x + 66 = 180$$
$$3x = 180 - 66$$
$$x = \frac{114}{3} \qquad x = 38.$$
To find the second angle, multiply 38 by 2 to get 76 degrees.

Gridded answer: 7 6

Suppose a large drum contains 48 gallons of oil and that a spigot allows $\frac{1}{2}$ gallon of oil to flow out each minute it is left open. What percent of the oil will have flowed out after the spigot has been left open 24 minutes? (Ignore the percent sign when gridding the answer.)

First, calculate how much oil flows out in 24 minutes, or $\frac{1}{2} \times 24 = 12$ gallons. Then set up the equation $\frac{12}{48} = \frac{x}{100}$ to find the percent of the original 48 gallons. Multiply both sides by 100 to get $x = 12 \times \frac{100}{48}$, and the resulting answer, 25 percent.

Gridded answer: 2 5

ACT Assessment

The ACT differs in format from the SAT I and is somewhat more content oriented. The test has four sections: English, mathematics, reading, and science reasoning.

The English section tests grammar, writing, and rhetorical skills. Students have forty-five minutes to answer seventy-five questions. (The SAT I includes reading comprehension as part of the verbal section.) The mathematics section has sixty questions and a sixty-minute time frame. The reading section includes passages from arts and litera-ture as well as from social studies and science, and students have thirty-five minutes to answer forty questions. The science reasoning section consists of forty questions in a thirty-five-minute time frame.

The ACT tests somewhat different skills than the SAT I. Unlike the SAT I, the ACT English section includes material covering usage and mechanics. The mathematics section relies more on geometry and trigonometry skills. Reading is a section unto itself, rather than being included as part of the verbal section. The section on science reasoning does not have a counterpart in the SAT I.

Another key difference is that there is no penalty for a wrong answer on the ACT, while there is a fractional deduction on the SAT I. Thus, while you might hesitate to answer an SAT I question if you cannot eliminate any choices, you should always answer an ACT question, since doing so can never hurt your score.

English. In the English section of the ACT, seventy-five questions are presented to test skills in punctuation, grammar, and sentence structure (which make up the subsection on usage and mechanics) and on strategy, organization, and style (which make up the subsection on rhetorical skills).

You will read a passage consisting of several paragraphs. Several words and phrases in each passage will be underlined. The usage and mechanics section asks about the specific underlined portions. Four choices are given. Three of the choices suggest changes to be made; the other choice is to accept the passage as is with no change.

The rhetorical skills section asks about broader issues. These issues might include whether quotation marks have been used effectively throughout the passage, how the paragraphs could be better ordered to provide a more logical structure, who the intended audience is, and how the author could make an individual point stronger.

Directions: In the passage that follows, certain words and phrases are underlined and numbered. In the right-hand column you will find alternatives for each underlined part. You are to choose the one that best expresses the idea, makes the statement appropriate for standard written English, or is worded most consistently with the style and tone of the passage as a whole. If you think the original version is best, choose "NO CHANGE."

You will also find questions about a section of the passage or about the passage as a whole. These questions do not refer to an underlined portion of the passage, but rather are identified by a number or numbers in a box.

Read the passage through once before you begin to answer the questions that accompany it. You cannot determine most answers without reading several sentences beyond the question. Be sure that you have read far enough ahead each time you choose an alternative.

Once upon a time, many people thought no one should read science fiction stories. Parents didn't want children to read "escapist" magazines. Such far-fetched adventure stories were <u>not literature they</u>
                             1
were not fit for young minds to read.

Of course, much science fiction *is* poorly written. Many stories have shallow plots, stereotyped characters, and <u>not interestingly written</u>. But are all westerns well
  2
written and interesting? Consider mystery stories, spy <u>novels, just</u> plain mainstream
               3
novels. How many of them could be called <u>"great literature?"</u>
         4
    The truth is that most books are not great literature. They are amusing or interesting or frightening <u>but not thought provoking</u>. This is
         5
neither <u>more but not less</u> true of
        6
science fiction than of other types of stories and novels.

Certainly, in the past, some science fiction magazines featured <u>stories and</u>
                 7
<u>tales</u> about "bug-eyed monsters" and "invasions from Mars." These events are unlikely. But "being swept off your feet by a handsome millionaire" is hardly more likely. Few people have "<u>single-handedly stopping</u> an illegal arms sale."
  8
    Open a modern science fiction <u>novel. You're</u> likely to find a story about
  9

---

1. A. NO CHANGE
    B. not. Literature they
    C. not literature but they
    D. not literature; they

D. is correct. Choice A. is wrong because two related thoughts are expressed and they must be separated. Choice B. puts a period at the wrong place. In Choice C. the conjunction *but* results in nonsense.

---

2. F. NO CHANGE
    G. uninteresting writing
    H. not interesting written
    J. are written uninterestingly

G. is correct because it sets up a parallel construction (modifier and noun) with the other descriptions. Choice H. is ungrammatical. Choice J. is wrong because it results in a construction that is not parallel.

---

3. A. NO CHANGE
    B. novels. Just
    C. novels just
    D. novels, and just

D. is correct. Choices A. and C. are wrong because each word is part of a different item in a list, and items must be separated. Choice B. creates a sentence fragment.

---

4. F. NO CHANGE
    G. "great literature"?
    H. "great literature?
    J. "great literature."?

G. is correct. When quotation marks fall at the end of a sentence, the punctuation mark that ends the sentence usually goes inside the quotation marks. The exceptions are question marks and exclamation points that punctuate the sentences they are in, rather than the quotations.

---

5. A. NO CHANGE
    B. and not thought provoking
    C. but thought provoking
    D. or not thought provoking

A. is correct. All the other choices make nonsense out of the sentence.

---

6. F. NO CHANGE
    G. more and less
    H. more nor less
    J. more or less

H. is correct. Choices F. and G. do not make sense with *neither*. Although choice J. makes sense, *or* is the wrong word to use with *neither* (either/or, neither/nor).

---

7. A. NO CHANGE
    B. stories, and tales
    C. stories
    D. stories and, tales

C. is correct because *stories* and *tales* have the same meaning, so only one of them is needed. Adding a comma just adds another problem.

---

8. F. NO CHANGE
    G. single-handedly stop
    H. single-handed stopped
    J. single-handedly stopped

J. is correct. Choices F. and G. result in wrong verb tenses (*have stopping* and *have stop*). In both choices H. and J., *stopped* is correct, but choice H. uses the wrong modifier (an adjective instead of an adverb).

---

9. A. NO CHANGE
    B. novel. Your
    C. novel, you're
    D. novel you're

A. is correct. Choice B. uses *your*, a possessive adjective, instead of *you're*, a contraction of *you are*. Choices C. and D. incorrectly combine the two sentences.

how people act and react in new situations. These new situations just happen to be on another planet or on a space ship or in the future, instead of taking place on Earth right now. Often the plot of a science fiction story would work equally well in another kind of novel.

[1] Furthermore, science fiction helps stretches the imagination. [2]
                                    10
Both writers and readers get a chance to try out some far-fetched ideas. [3] Most of these will never become reality. [4]
                        11
But television, submarines, and computers are among the things that first made they're public appearances in
                                              12
science fiction stories. [13]

Is science fiction "escapist" reading? Perhaps it is. Yet everyone needs to escape, at times, isn't that what travel advertisements
                                    14
offer? "Get away to a magic island!" or "Escape to paradise!" are familiar themes.

Well I don't need to travel to magic islands or
    15
paradise. I can escape to my favorite distant planet or an entirely new place. Depending
                                              16
on whether I want something familiar or something new. Its the best vacation I can
                              17
find, then I can go out into space myself to
    18
see what wonderful things actually exist there.

---

10. F. NO CHANGE
    G. stretches
    H. help stretch
    J. helps, stretches

G. is correct. Only one verb is needed, so choice F. is wrong. In choice H., both verbs are plural instead of singular. Adding a comma in choice J. only adds another mistake.

---

11. The antecedent of the pronoun *these* is:
    A. science fiction writers
    B. science fiction readers
    C. televisions
    D. far-fetched ideas

D. is correct. Put each of the suggested antecedents into the sentence after these to see how it fits. (*Most of these ideas* is the only one that makes sense when it's added.)

---

12. F. NO CHANGE
    G. there public appearances
    H. their public appearances
    J. public appearance

H. is correct. Choice F. uses *they're* instead of *their*, a possessive adjective. Choice G. uses an adverb (*there*) in place of *their*. Choice J. would have been correct if the subject of the subordinate clause (*that*) did not have a plural antecedent (*things*), making *that* plural. For this reason, *appearances* is correct.

---

13. In order to maintain the flow of ideas, sentence [3] should be:
    A. put after sentence [1]
    B. kept where it is now
    C. put after sentence [4]
    D. removed entirely

B. is correct. Sentence [3] provides a good transition from the idea in sentence [2] to the idea in sentence [4]. If sentence [3] came after sentence [1] or after sentence [4], the ideas would be confusing. If it were removed, the ideas in sentences [2] and [4] would not be connected very well.

---

14. F. NO CHANGE
    G. escape at times, isn't
    H. escape, at times isn't
    J. escape at times. Isn't

J. is correct. The two ideas need to be in separate sentences. All the other choices simply move unneeded commas into different places without making the thought clear.

---

15. A. NO CHANGE
    B. Well, I
    C. Well. I
    D. Well; I

B. is correct. In this sentence, *well* is an interjection that must be set off by a comma. It is not, however, emphatic enough to be set off in a clause or sentence of its own.

---

16. F. NO CHANGE
    G. new place depending
    H. new place, depending
    J. new, place depending

H. is correct. If it is not changed, then *Depending* is the first word of a sentence fragment. Choice G. is wrong because the dependent clause should be set off from the main clause. In choice J., the comma is in the wrong place.

---

17. A. NO CHANGE
    B. It's
    C. its
    D. it's

B. is correct. Choice A. leaves a possessive adjective (*Its*) where a contraction of *it is* should be. Notice that both choices C. and D. start the sentence with small letters.

---

18. F. NO CHANGE
    G. find. Then
    H. find, when
    J. find until

J. is correct. The word *then* doesn't make sense in the sentence, nor does the word *when*. The word *until* continues the idea already expressed in the sentence.

Mathematics. The sixty math questions cover topics from pre-algebra, elementary and intermediate algebra, coordinate and plane geometry, and trigonometry. Use the ACT information packets and any guidebooks to identify individual topics that will be covered, such as fractions, inequalities, literal expressions, percent, conics, and problem solving. Then take practice tests to build skills and identify areas of weakness. When you see which questions are difficult for you, talk with your counselor or math teacher about them. Identify specific topics that you need to review. You may even borrow texts from earlier courses in order to review specific topics and solve related exercises.

Wrong answers are provided for a reason. They reflect common errors made when solving a problem. For example, if the question asks the value of $4 + 6 \div 2$, the correct answer is 7 (divide before you add, so $(4 + [6 \div 2] = 4 + 3 = 7$); however, 5 is likely to be given, in case students add $4 + 6$ before dividing by 2. An answer cannot just appear correct; solve the problem to ensure you have selected the correct answer.

Directions: Solve each problem and choose the correct answer. Do not linger over problems that take too much time. Solve as many as you can; then return to the others in the time you have left for this test.

Note: Unless otherwise stated, all of the following should be assumed.
1. Illustrative figures are NOT necessarily drawn to scale.
2. Geometric figures lie in a plane.
3. The word *line* indicates a straight line.
4. The word *average* indicates an arithmetic mean.

During his last four basketball games, Peter scored 28, 24, 31, and 36 points. Peter wants to have an average of 30 points after his next game. How many points must he score in the fifth game?

F. 28
G. 29
H. 30
J. 31
K. 32

The correct choice is J. To obtain an average of 30 over five games, Peter must score a total of 5×30, or 150 points in all. He has already scored 119 points $(28 + 24 + 31 + 36)$. $150 - 119 = 31$.

The area of a square with a side x is 3. What is the area of a square with side $2x$?

F. $2\sqrt{3}$
G. 6
H. 12
J. 18
K. 36

If the area of a square with side x is 3, you know that $x^2 = 3$. The area of a square with side $2x$ is $(2x)^2 = 4x^2$. If $x^2 = 3$, $4x^2 = 4 \times 3 = 12$. The correct choice is H.

If $2^{n+2} = 16$, then n equals

F. 0
G. 1
H. 2
J. 4
K. 6

The correct choice is H. To solve equations with exponents, it is important to remember that each side of the equation must have the same base.

$$2^{n+2} = 16 \qquad 2^{n+2} = 2^4$$
$$n + 2 = 4$$
$$n = 2$$

If the area of a circle is 16π, what is the diameter?

A. ± 4
B. 4
C. 8
D. 16

$A = \pi r^2$ is the area of a circle where r is the radius. Thus, $16\pi = \pi r^2$, leading to $16 = r^2$. While both 4^2 and $(-4)^2$ equal 16, a radius is a physical length and must be positive. Thus, $r = 4$. Now go back to the question; it asks for the diameter, not the radius. The diameter is twice the radius, or 8. (C) is the correct answer.

Cal scored 84, 96, and 88 on his first three tests. If he wants to end the term with an average of 91, what score must he receive on the remaining test?

A. 86
B. 91
C. 93
D. 96

Set up an equation for averages. The average score is the sum of his scores divided by the number of scores. Let s represent the fourth test score. The sum of the scores is $84 + 96 + 88 + s$. The number of scores is 4, the number of tests. Thus, $91 = (84 + 96 + 88 + s) \div 4$. Multiply both sides by 4; $4 \times 91 = 84 + 96 + 88 + s$ or $364 = 268 + s$. Subtract 268 from both sides to find that $96 = s$. Thus, (D) is the answer.

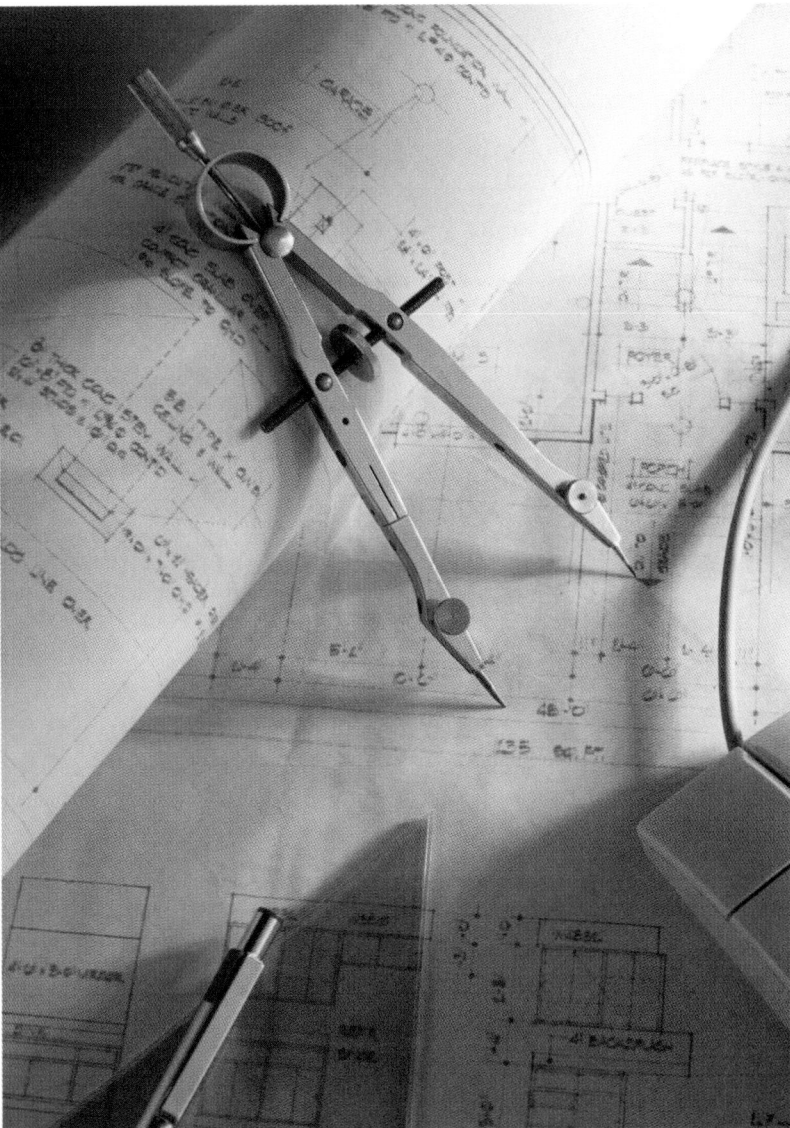

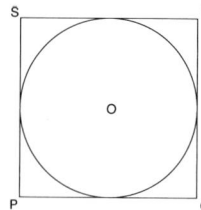

The area of square *PQRS* is 64 square inches. Find the area of circle *O*.

F. 16π
G. 32π
H. 64π
J. $32\pi^2$
K. $64\pi^2$

The circle is inscribed in the square. The diameter of the circle has the same length as the side of the square. Find the diameter first. The diameter is the same length as one side of the square, which we will designate as *s*. Since $s^2 = 64$, $s = 8$. Therefore, the diameter of *O* is 8. The area of a circle is found using the formula $A = \pi r^2$, where *r* is the radius. The radius of a circle is half the diameter, or 4.

$$A = \pi r^2$$
$$A = \pi \cdot 4^2$$
$$= 16\pi$$

The correct choice is F.

Two trains leave Bay City at noon. One travels due east at 60 mph. The other travels due north at 80 mph. How many miles apart are the trains at 2 P.M.?

A. 100 mi.
B. 140 mi.
C. 200 mi.
D. 240 mi.
E. 340 mi.

Draw a diagram. In two hours, one train covers 120 miles and the other 160 miles. Their paths and a line connecting their new positions form a right triangle.

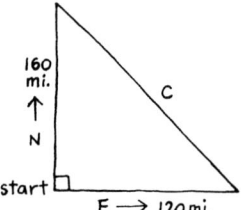

You could compute the hypotenuse, but there is an easier way. Since all the choices are whole numbers, the sides of the right triangle must be proportional to one of the common right triangles with all integral sides, such as a 3-4-5 right triangle or a 5-12-13 right triangle. Note that $120 = 3(40)$; $160 = 4(40)$. The distance between them, *c*, must therefore be $5(40) = 200$. The correct choice is C.

What number added to 70% of itself is equal to 136?

A. 76
B. 80
C. 96
D. 106
E. 206

It is useful to write and solve an equation for this problem.
$$\text{Let } x = \text{the number}$$
$$x + 0.70x = 136$$
$$1.7x = 136$$
$$x = \frac{136}{1.7}$$
$$x = 80$$

The correct choice is B.

The Clark family spent \$92,000 to build a house. Of this cost, 12% was for plumbing and heating, 4% for electrical wiring, and 8% for kitchen appliances. How much money was spent on other items?

F. \$76,000
G. \$22,080
H. \$69,920
J. \$24,000
K. \$84,200

The other items amount to $100\% - 12\% - 4\% - 8\%$, *or* 76%, of the total. 76% of \$92,000 = \$69,920. The correct choice is H.

Since 76% is very close to 75%, you might estimate $\frac{3}{4}$ of 92,000 to find the correct choice:

$$\tfrac{3}{4} \times 92{,}000 = 3 \times 23{,}000 = 69{,}000.$$

The only choice close to this number is H.

If $(x - y)^2 = 60$ and $xy = 20$, find $x^2 + y^2$.

F. -40
G. 40
H. 80
J. 100
K. 140

Begin by squaring $x - y$:
$$(x - y)^2 = (x - y)(x - y)$$
$$= x^2 - 2xy + y^2$$
$$= x^2 + y^2 - 2xy$$
We know the value of $(x - y)^2$ and of xy.
$$60 = x^2 + y^2 - 2(20)$$
$$60 + 2(20) = x^2 + y^2$$
$$60 + 40 = x^2 + y^2$$
$$100 = x^2 + y^2$$

The correct choice is J.

If $2(x + 4) = 12$, find $x - 3$.

A. -2
B. -1
C. 1
D. 2
E. none of these

It is important to read the whole question. You not only must solve for *x*, but you are asked to find the value of $x - 3$.
$$2(x + 4) = 12$$
$$2x + 8 = 12$$
$$2x + 8 - 8 = 12 - 8$$
$$2x = 4$$
$$\tfrac{2x}{2} = \tfrac{4}{2}$$
$$x = 2$$
If $x = 2$, $x - 3 = 2 - 3 = -1$.

The correct choice is B.

If the angles of a triangle are in the ratio 1:2:3, the triangle is

F. acute
G. isosceles
H. right
J. equilateral
K. obtuse

Write an equation using the fact that the sum of the angles of a triangle is 180°. The angles of the triangles can be represented by *x*, 2*x*, and 3*x*.
$$x + 2x + 3x = 180$$
$$6x = 180$$
$$x = 30$$
If $x = 30$, $2x = 60$ and $3x = 90$. So the angles of the triangle measure 30°, 60°, and 90°. The correct choice is H.

How much more is $\frac{1}{2}$ of $\frac{5}{6}$ than $\frac{5}{6}$ of $\frac{1}{2}$?

A. $\frac{5}{6}$

B. $\frac{1}{2}$

C. $\frac{1}{3}$

D. $\frac{1}{12}$

E. 0

While you can get the correct choice by computing
$$\frac{1}{2} \times \frac{5}{6} - \frac{5}{6} \times \frac{1}{2},$$
a little reasoning will save you some time. Since the order of the factors does not affect the product, $\frac{1}{2}$ times $\frac{5}{6}$ and $\frac{5}{6}$ times $\frac{1}{2}$ will have the same product. Therefore, their difference is 0. The correct choice is E.

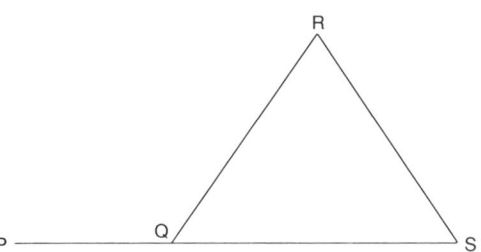

In triangle RQS, $QR = RS$. QS is a segment of PS. Angle RQP measures $125°$. Find the number of degrees in angle R.

A. 45

B. 55

C. 70

D. 110

E. 125

Since $QR = RS$, angle RQS = angle RSQ. Angle RQP and angle RQS form a straight angle, so the sum of their measures is 180.

$180 - 125 = 55$

angle RQS + angle RSQ + angle R = 180

    55   +   55   + angle R = 180

            110   + angle R = 180

                    angle R = $180 - 110 = 70$.

The correct choice is C.

A town council wants to form a subcommittee of three members to investigate a way of improving the recreation facilities of the town. There are six members of the council. In how many different ways can the subcommittee be formed?

A. 2

B. 3

C. 6

D. 20

E. 120

The order in which council members are named to the subcommittee does not matter. Here, you need to find out how many combinations of three can be made from a total of six. Remember that the number of combinations of n items taken r at a time is $n!/(r!(n-r)!)$, where the sign ! means to take the factorial.

$$\frac{6!}{3! \times 3!} = \frac{6 \times 5 \times 4 \times 3 \times 2 \times 1}{(3 \times 2 \times 1)(3 \times 2 \times 1)} = 5 \times 4 = 20.$$

The correct choice is D.

The value of $[9 - (6 - 11)] + [(14 - 3) - (3 - 6)]$ is:

A. -10

B. -6

C. 12

D. 18

E. 28

With this type of exercise, it is important to work carefully. There are parentheses inside brackets. Work in the innermost parentheses first. Be careful to record the correct signs.

$$[9 - (6 - 11)] + [(14 - 3) - (3 - 6)] = [9 - (-5)] + [11 - (-3)]$$
$$= [9 + 5] + [11 + 3]$$
$$= 14 + 14$$
$$= 28$$

The correct choice is E.

What is the value of b if $5a^2b = -135$ and a $= -3$?

A. -9

B. -3

C. 3

D. 9

First substitute -3 for a. Thus $5(-3)^2b = -135$. This leads to $5 \bullet 9 \bullet b = -135$ and $45b = -135$. Divide -135 by 45 to find that (B) is the correct answer. Follow the order of operations (parentheses, exponents, multiplication and division, addition and subtraction) and take care with negative signs.

Reading. The reading section of the ACT includes four passages, each followed by ten questions. The passages cover different types of reading that college students are likely to encounter and are drawn from four broad areas: fiction, humanities, social sciences, and natural sciences. Questions might ask about the broad themes of a passage, specific factual content, implied arguments and perspectives that are not directly stated, meanings of words and phrases, and style. There are forty questions to complete in thirty-five minutes. This is less than one minute per question; therefore, balance a close, careful reading with the need to keep pace.

For each passage, first read the questions that will be asked; this helps focus your reading. Do not take the time at this point to read the answers. Next, read the passage. Underline key phrases and ideas that pertain to the questions. Then go back to the questions and answer each. Often it is helpful to eliminate wrong answers as a way to close in on the correct one; be sure that you read all possible answers.

<u>Directions</u>: There are four passages in this test. Each passage is followed by several questions. After reading a passage, choose the best answer to each question. You may refer to the passages as often as necessary.

Passage I

Only a few hundred years ago, most of the people in the world could neither read nor write. Furthermore, they had no need for these skills. Each family raised much of its own food and hunted animals for meat. Money earned
5 by family members was used to buy items for which the family's homemade or homegrown goods could not be traded. Only people who did not have to earn a living had the time or the need to learn to read and write.

There were always exceptions to this. Sometimes
10 parents saw that reading and writing were keys to better jobs or social advancement, so they insisted that their children learn. Some individuals have such a thirst for knowledge that they will learn in spite of all obstacles.

Within the past few hundred years, there has been a
15 change in educational opportunities. The modern world demands basic reading and writing skills, especially in the industrialized nations. As developing nations progress beyond mere subsistence for most of their populations, these nations also create a situation in which all citizens
20 must have basic skills in order to function productively.

Think about it. If you walk into a supermarket and cannot read the labels, what can you buy? Cereal boxes have cartoon characters or other fanciful pictures on them; it you cannot read the names, would you know the
25 boxes contain cereals? Your child is ill and the doctor tells you what medicine to get for her. If you can't read, can you find and use the medicine you are told to buy? Think about all the things you do easily and quickly that require reading.
30 In spite of this emphasis on reading, in spite of our culture's assumption that everyone can read, there are millions of people in the United States who cannot read well enough to function effectively. Without including the rest of the world, if 250 million people live in the United
35 States, then at least 3 million people are adult nonreaders. This is a conservative estimate; the actual number is probably much higher.

The nonreaders are not children in school—they are parents and grandparents. It is an appalling statistic for a
40 nation as wealthy as the United States. Perhaps the most appalling thing, though, is that the adult nonreader is a person who is ashamed to admit his or her illiteracy. Fear of ridicule and loss of a job often keep the people who
45 need help most from asking for it.

According to the passage, the assumption that everyone can read and write is

A. based on conditions from long ago.
B. true only in industrialized nations.
C. not true even in the United States.
D. true everywhere in the modern world.

The correct answer is C. In the paragraph beginning on line 30, the author says that "there are millions of people in the United States who cannot read well enough to function effectively." A. is incorrect because most people long ago could neither read nor write. B. is incorrect because in the United States, one of the industrialized nations, millions of people cannot read well. D. is absurd.

In the past, people who could not read or write were uneducated because they

F. didn't have time or money for learning.
G. were unable to learn.
H. didn't want to learn to read and write.
J. were ashamed and afraid of asking for help.

F. is correct. This question requires you to infer the answer from clues given in the first paragraph. Answers G. and H. are not supported by any statement in the passage. J. refers to the last line of the passage, which is about people in today's world.

One example in the passage of a place where reading skills are essential is in

A. a developing nation.
B. a family.
C. a church.
D. a supermarket.

The answer is D. The question asks for a *place mentioned in the passage*, so A. and B. are wrong. Choice C. is wrong because churches are not mentioned in the passage.

The most likely change in educational opportunities today, compared with the past, is that

F. more adults need education than in the past.
G. education takes less time today.
H. education is more widely available.
J. fewer people need to be educated.

The question deals with "change in educational opportunities." H. is the only choice that addresses opportunity. Since the other choices do not, they are incorrect.

The figure of 3 million nonreaders includes

A. nonreading children only.
B. nonreading adults only.
C. both nonreading children and nonreading adults.
D. only people living in developing nations.

The answer is B. It can be found in the sentence beginning on line 33. A. and C. are incorrect because children are specifically excluded in line 35. D. is incorrect because the information given refers to the U.S. population.

The second paragraph of this passage implies that

F. people who cannot read are not interested in knowledge.
G. a few people learn to read despite societal obstacles.
H. people who cannot read should blame their parents.
J. no parents make their children learn to read for altruistic reasons.

Although the stem of this item asks what the passage implies, you should not read more into something than it suggests. The context is still a few hundred years ago. At that time there were obstacles to learning to read, but some people learned anyway for reasons stated in the passage, so the correct choice is G. Because of the obstacles, no judgment was made on the people who failed to learn to read, so neither choice F. or choice H. is correct. Although the passage specified other reasons than altruism for parents making their children learn, it did not rule out that possibility, so choice J. is also wrong.

Passage II

A permit? Just to put in a new water heater? Yes, you may need a permit for that, and for many other things as well. Many communities now require plumbing permits for nearly all plumbing work, whether new or replace-
5 ment. If a pipe is moved or replaced, if a fixture is added or moved, or if a building is attached to an existing city sewer system, a permit is probably needed.

Some people grumble, saying that government is getting too involved in people's lives. Well, maybe it is. But
10 think about some of the horror stories you've heard about badly done work that causes damage to someone's home and possessions. Permits can't prevent broken pipes or fixtures. But if issuing permits and inspecting the work
15 can help minimize damage, isn't the inconvenience worth it!

Think about that water heater again. A water heater seems like a simple enough device. Why should someone need a permit to replace a failed water heater? Water heaters keep water at a high temperature, in many cases
20 above 140 degrees. As long as you control the use of the water, it's fine to have it that hot. But suppose something breaks. Water at that temperature can badly hurt some-

one nearby unless it can be channeled away from living areas.
25   Furthermore, water heaters must be installed care- fully. If they're installed improperly, they can explode and hurt or even kill home owners and their families. Issuing permits won't prevent all problems, but they may prevent some.
30   Other plumbing fixtures aren't as dangerous, of course, but badly installed pipes or fixtures can cause a lot of annoying and expensive damage. External work, such as providing septic tanks and leach fields, needs to be done properly, or tanks and fields will fail quickly and cost
35 a great deal more than necessary. Even a hookup to an existing sewer system can be a problem if it's not done correctly.

The author of this passage feels that government

F. is too involved in people's lives.
G. is not involved enough in people's lives.
H. is protecting people by requiring some permits.
J. should not allow individuals to have plumbing businesses.

H. is the correct answer. This question requires you to make an inference to find the answer. The last sentence in the second paragraph gives the clue to choosing the correct answer. F. is what the author says many people think, while G. and J. have no basis in the passage at all.

According to the passage, plumbing permits may prevent

A. water heaters from exploding.
B. fixtures from breaking down.
C. government from getting too involved in our lives.
D. some problems caused by badly done work.

The correct answer is D. The sentence beginning on line 12 contradicts answers A. and B. C. is incorrect because it states that plumbing permits may encourage, not prevent, excessive government interference.

One reason for issuing plumbing permits that is NOT given in the passage is

F. to protect the consumer.
G. to ensure that work is done properly.
H. to help prevent damage or injury.
J. to generate income for a community.

The answer is J. All the other answers can be found in the passage, although the passage may not use exactly the same words as the answers do.

The first paragraph leads one to believe that a permit is needed if

A. a new sink is installed.
B. a broken pipe is replaced with a same kind of pipe.
C. a new water heater is correctly installed.
D. any of A., B., or C. is undertaken.

The answer is D. since the first paragraph specifies both B. and C.: pipe replacement requires a permit, as does a new water heater. While A. is not specified, it is strongly implied.

Plumbing permits for external work help protect people against

F. problems with bathroom plumbing.
G. premature failure of septic tanks and leach fields.
H. problems with town-owned treatment plants.
J. injury from failure of water heaters.

G. is the correct answer, which can be found in the sentence starting on line 32. Answers F. and J. are both internal plumbing problems, and H. is not discussed.

Passage III

They hop, they gnaw, they have long ears and large eyes, and they love carrots and apples and seeds. But they are not rodents at all, although most people think they are. Rabbits are lagomorphs. They do have some
5 similarities to rodents, such as the need to gnaw in order to keep their teeth from growing too long.

What's the attraction of rabbits? Well, they are cute. Their big eyes and round shape appeal to humans' protective instincts. Rabbit fur is soft and warm, ideal for
10 winter wear for humans as well as for rabbits. Many people also think rabbit is delicious to eat. Rabbit meat is certainly nutritious, although it is not a complete protein and humans cannot live on rabbit alone. Still, eaten with beans or rice, rabbit provides all the nutrients you need
15 with less fat and cholesterol than present in other meats.

It goes without saying that many people are uncomfortable with the idea of eating rabbits because, they say, rabbits are so cute and helpless and furry. They may also like rabbit fur better when it's on a person. How
20 about angora wool, then? It's soft and fine and warm, and the rabbit is not hurt at all by the collection process. It does take a great deal of wool to make any garment, so angora rabbit wool is expensive, but somehow that
25 seems to make it more attractive rather than less.

As pets, rabbits are great. They can be housebroken as cats are, and rabbits are quiet. Their major drawback as house pets is their need to gnaw. Rabbit food is made to be hard to satisfy the animal's need to use its teeth,
30 but the instinct is always there. House rabbits have been known to bite through electric wires and take mouthfuls of wooden furniture.

Don't keep your rabbit too warm. Remember that the animal's fur is effective as an insulator. Temperatures
35 that humans find comfortable for bare skin are too much too hot for that furry little body. Rabbits also need to be dry and protected against drafts. An all-metal wire cage

is a good home: It makes the rabbit feel safe, the rabbit cannot eat its home, the cage is easy to keep clean, and
40 the owner can check on the rabbit easily and quickly.

According to the article, rabbits are

A. pests that humans want to get rid of.
B. an excellent food source for humans.
C. cute but not useful in any way.
D. useful as food, as pets, and for fur and wool.

The answer is D. Clues to this answer appear throughout the passage. A. is incorrect because nothing in the passage supports this statement. B. is incorrect because rabbit meat is not a complete protein. C. is incorrect because rabbits are useful.

The difference between lagomorphs and rodents is

A. lagomorphs gnaw but rodents do not.
B. both lagomorphs and rodents gnaw.
C. rabbits are lagomorphs.
D. not given in the passage.

D. is correct. The passage says only that lagomorphs are not rodents, not how they are different. A. is directly contradicted by information in the passage. B. is not a difference but a similarity. C. is true but does not state a difference.

It can be inferred from the passage that rabbits may die if they are

F. kept warm and bathed once a week.
G. kept cool, dry, and out of drafts.
H. housed in all-metal wire cages.
J. raised for their wool.

The answer is F. This is a somewhat tricky question because it asks you for the opposite of what the passage states. G. and H. state what the passage says rabbits need. J. is directly contradicted in the information given in the sentence beginning on line 20.

From the tone of the passage, it can be inferred that the author

F. likes rabbits very much.
G. thinks rabbits do not make good pets.
H. neither likes nor dislikes rabbits.
J. dislikes rabbits.

F. is the correct answer. Again, the answer is supported by clues throughout the passage. G. is directly contradicted by the first sentence on line 26. H. and J. are both inferences that are not supported by clues in the passage.

According to the passage, some people do not like to eat rabbit because

A. rabbit meat tastes awful.
B. rabbit meat isn't nutritious.
C. they think rabbits are cute.
D. rabbits aren't rodents at all.

The answer is C. A. is an opinion not stated in the passage. B. is incorrect, according to the passage. D. is true but has nothing to do with why people do or don't eat rabbit.

Passage IV

In South America, on a grassy plain between the Amazon and Tocantins rivers, lie the remains of an ancient civilization. Great mounds rising above the floor of the floodplain are covered by ruined dwellings. The
5 mounds themselves, usually oval, rise about 20 feet above the forest floor, above the level of seasonal flooding. The tallest one rises about 65 feet. These mounds are not simply piles of earth; most of them are at least 10 acres in area, and the largest mound known covers more than 50 acres.
10 With 30 or 40 ancient people living in each of 8 to 12 houses, there would have been 200 to 400 people living on an average mound. Larger mounds could have housed 1,000 residents. Many mounds were built separate from nearby mounds, but there were also clusters of mounds.
15 Such a cluster might have housed 10,000 or more people. Thus, the total population of the area may have been more than 100,000 people.
These indigenous South Americans maintained a highly developed civilization for more than a thousand
20 years. The people raised and stored food. They produced beautiful, carefully modeled pottery decorated with many colors and formed into a variety of shapes for many uses. They used precious and semiprecious stones as ornaments and made stone tools of all kinds. The people traded
25 with each other and with people of other cultures from distant parts of South America.
We have not been able thus far to discover why this ancient civilization vanished. It had disappeared by 1300 A.D., long before European explorers arrived in South
30 America. As one would expect, by the time the Europeans arrived, other civilizations had spread across the territory once held by the Mound Builders. These later civilizations owed much in their art, tools, and other cultural artifacts to their predecessors.

According to the passage, most mounds were built

F. after the Europeans arrived.
G. to house one or two families.
H. large enough for hundreds of people.
J. for people to farm, not as living quarters.

H. is correct. The passage clearly states that an average mound would have had 200 to 400 people living on it. Since this civilization disappeared before the Europeans arrived, F. can be ruled out. G. is a possible answer, but it is contradicted by information in the passage. J. is not discussed anywhere in the passage.

The civilization discussed in the passage was mostly located

A. in the Andes Mountains.
B. in the Amazon River floodplain.
C. in the jungles near the Amazon River.
D. along the South American coastline.

The correct answer is B. Again, the passage clearly states that the mounds were built on the floodplain between the Amazon and Tocantins rivers. The Andes Mountains and the South American coastline, mentioned in A. and D., are never discussed in the passage. C. is plausible, but the passage supports B. more closely.

It can be inferred that the mounds were built in order to

F. protect the inhabitants from floods.
G. provide a defense against animals and invaders.
H. create better farmland for people.
J. keep people busy, since most people had no jobs.

F. is the answer, and the clue to choosing F. is found at the end of the sentence beginning on line 4. G. may also be true, but nowhere in the passage is there any clue to support this. H. is incorrect since people lived in houses on the mounds and nothing is said about where they farmed. J. is not supported in any way by the information in the passage.

Based on information in the passage, it is fair to say that an ancient civilization can be described as highly developed if it

A. supported more than 10,000 people.
B. lasted more than a thousand years.
C. built mounds at least 20 feet high and 10 acres in size.
D. created artifacts that are beautiful and as well as useful.

The correct answer is D. All the statements here are true with respect to the Mound Builders, but only D. is relevant to cultural development. The clue to this is found in paragraph 3. By inference, the correct answer must also be applicable to other highly developed cultures. Again, only D. is generally applicable to other cultures.

According to the passage, the Mound Builders' civilization disappeared because

F. the Europeans arrived.
G. other civilizations invaded their territories.
H. of diseases and crime.
J. of factors not yet discovered by us.

J. is the correct answer. The last paragraph of the passage states specifically that there is no indication of why the civilization disappeared. F. cannot be true, since the Europeans arrived after the Mound Builders disappeared. G. and H. may be true, but there is no way to know at this time.

Science reasoning. The science reasoning section of the ACT is perhaps what distinguishes it most from the SAT I. While you are not asked to show specific knowledge of biology, chemistry, earth science, and physics, you do need to demonstrate knowledge and understanding of the scientific process.

This section presents several passages, followed by questions about the passages, which fall into three broad categories: data representation, research summaries, and conflicting viewpoints. In the first category, information is presented in tables and graphs. Questions center around understanding and interpreting the data and then drawing conclusions.

In the second area, descriptions of related experiments are presented. Questions involve comparing and contrasting the experiments and summarizing the information presented. These questions complement the data representation section, since not all experiments and data can be presented easily in tables and graphs.

In the third area, general questions are asked, such as, Is there life on other planets? Two different scientific perspectives about the question follow. Students are asked about various assumptions in each perspective, as well as conclusions that can be drawn. Some questions are about the argument itself, evaluating the evidence needed to justify the different conclusions that the authors reach, and whether the assumptions that have been made are valid.

As with the reading section, it is often helpful to read the questions first. Next, read the passages or evaluate the data, keeping the questions in mind. Then answer the questions. By reading the questions first, you can focus on the most important infomation.

<u>Directions:</u> There are two passages in this test. Each passage is followed by several questions. After reading a passage, choose the best answer to each question. You may refer to the passage as often as necessary. You are NOT permitted to use a calculator on this test.

Passage I

Some scientists are experimenting with marine organisms harvested from the ocean and think that these sea-dwelling creatures may someday provide a source for new drugs. In the blue-green waters of the Caribbean Sea,
5 marine biologists dive along the coral reefs for samples of algae and marine invertebrates such as sponges and mollusks. Back aboard the research ship, cells taken from each organism are ground up and mixed with alcohol. The cell extracts then are placed in separate culture dish-
10 es containing viruses and bacteria, the microorganisms that cause many diseases. Surprisingly, some of the algae and sponge extracts show that they can inhibit the growth of these microorganisms. Other marine invertebrates

show the ability to stop the growth of cancer cells in a lab-
15 oratory dish. When a marine organism shows potential for use as a drug, it is taken to other laboratories, where further testing is done. There, some algae have shown the ability to stimulate the immune systems of test animals to fight disease more effectively. However, it will take more
20 time and research to isolate the active agent from each extract and to convert it into a drug that people can take. Once that is done, the new drug will have to undergo extensive testing. Despite the time involved in the development process, there is great potential for obtaining
25 drugs from the sea.

According to the passage, which organisms show potential as a source of useful drugs?

A. algae and viruses
B. sponges and bacteria
C. coral and marine vertebrates
D. algae and marine invertebrates

D. is correct. In the second sentence of the passage, the author states that samples of algae and marine invertebrates such as sponges and mollusks were taken as samples. Although algae are mentioned in choice A. and sponges are mentioned in choice B., each is paired with an incorrect answer; microorganisms are mentioned later in the passage as disease-causing organisms. Choice C. is incorrect because no mention is made of marine vertebrates.

Which statement best describes the scientific research reported in the passage?

F. Scientists have been testing drugs that are derived from the extracts of marine organisms.
G. Marine scientists dive throughout the Caribbean to get samples of algae, sponges, and mollusks that are in danger of extinction.
H. Using extracts, scientists test the ability of marine organisms to inhibit the growth of disease-causing organisms.
J. Marine invertebrates are grown in laboratories and tested for their ability to inhibit the growth of disease-causing organisms.

H. is correct. The author says that extracts, and not drugs, are used in tests, so F. is incorrect. No mention is made that the marine organisms being tested are endangered, nor are they grown in laboratories, making choices G. and J. incorrect.

Which organisms do scientists classify in the same kingdom?

A. sponges and mollusks
B. bacteria and viruses
C. algae and sponges
D. algae and bacteria

A. is correct. Sponges and mollusks are both in the animal kingdom. The passage describes sponges and mollusks as examples of invertebrates, animals without backbones. Bacteria are classified as monerans; algae are plantlike protists; and viruses are not classified in any kingdom. Thus B., C., and D. are incorrect.

The immune system of an animal

F. fights disease.
G. inhibits the animal's growth.
H. kills all bacterial cells.
J. is usually stimulated by algae.

F. is correct. The immune system may inhibit bacterial growth, but not the growth of the animal itself, so G. is incorrect. The immune system may kill some harmful bacteria, but not all bacteria, especially helpful bacteria in the intestinal tract. For this reason, H. is incorrect. Only the immune systems of animals being tested under laboratory conditions were found to be stimulated by some algae, so J. is incorrect.

A group of cells ground up and mixed with alcohol is referred to in this passage as

A. an invertebrate.
B. an extract.
C. a microorganism.
D. a drug.

B. is correct. In the third sentence of the passage, the author describes how an extract is made. All other choices are wrong.

From this passage, what can you infer about the process of producing a safe, useful drug?

F. It is a simple procedure that can be done easily.
G. With scientific cooperation, a drug can be produced immediately after its source is discovered.
H. Producing a drug involves quite a lot of time and research.
J. No inference from the passage can be made.

H. is correct. Although no precise time is established in the passage, it can be inferred that collecting the organisms, isolating the active agent, and producing and testing a drug takes a good deal of time. Certainly, the procedure is not simple (choice F.), a drug cannot be produced immediately after finding its source (choice G.), and H. supplies a valid inference (choice J.).

Passage II
Lasers have become part of our everyday life and have many uses. These concentrated beams of light are used in scanners at supermarket checkouts. Carbon dioxide lasers produce the intense heat needed to weld air-
5 plane and automobile parts. Argon gas lasers are used to perform the delicate task of repairing a retina during eye surgery. Still another kind of laser is bounced off satellites in order to measure tiny changes in Earth's crust, enabling geologists to determine the probability of an earthquake.
10 A laser has three basic parts. Each laser has a lasing medium, a substance that will emit light when it is properly stimulated. The lasing medium can be a solid, liquid, or gas. Secondly, a laser has a pump, something that can provide the laser with energy. The third component is a mir-
15 ror or other device used to control the direction of the laser beam.
The laser gets its name from the first letters of the five main words that describe how it works: light amplification by stimulated emission of radiation. Before the
20 laser is turned on, the electrons of the lasing medium are in a low-energy, unexcited state. When the pump is turned on, it emits radiation—light energy—which stimulates some of the unexcited electrons, causing them to jump to a higher energy state. The excited state is not a stable
25 one, so the electrons soon drop back to the low-energy state. As they do, they release energy in the form of light. Because the electrons are stimulated by light of a particular color or wavelength, they emit light of the same wavelength as the light that stimulated them. The light emis-
30 sions from many electrons join together to amplify the light and form a laser beam.

According to the passage, the three parts of a laser are

A. a lasing medium, a pump, and a mirror.
B. a solid, a liquid, and a gas.
C. stimulation, emission, and radiation.
D. light, amplification, and stimulation.

A. is correct, as shown in the second paragraph. B. is incorrect; the lasing medium may consist of any of these states of matter, but these are not parts of a laser. C. and D. offer several of the terms that describe how a laser works, but they are not parts of a laser.

Electrons emit radiation

A. when they jump to a higher energy state.
B. when they return to a low-energy state from a high-energy state.
C. only when they are stimulated by a different wavelength.
D. when the pump is turned off.

B. is correct. In the third paragraph, the author states that an excited electron emits light or radiation when it leaves the unstable high-energy state and returns to the low-energy state. Electrons do not emit radiation when they jump to a high energy state, so A. is incorrect. C. is incorrect because electrons emit radiation of the same wavelength as the stimulating radiation. The laser beam is formed while the electrons are stimulated by the pump, so D. is incorrect.

Eye surgery can be performed, and airplane parts can be welded. These functions

F. use the same laser technology.
G. are the most important applications of lasers.
H. require lasers that produce the same wavelength.
J. use different types of gas lasers.

J. is correct. In the first paragraph, the author states that argon gas lasers are used in eye surgery and carbon dioxide lasers are used in welding. Carbon dioxide and argon are gases. The two applications do not use the same laser technology, nor do they operate at the same wavelength, because the lasing media differ. These facts make choices F. and H. incorrect. No indication of the relative importance of laser technologies is given in the passage, so choice G. is incorrect.

Visible radiation made of all the same wavelength would appear to your eye as

A. an intense beam of red light.
B. a flash of white light.
C. light of one color.
D. all the colors of the visible spectrum.

C. is correct. The wavelength of radiation determines its color as suggested in the third paragraph. The wavelength is not specified, so the answer cannot be red light, making choice A. incorrect. Both white light (B.) and all the colors of the visible spectrum (D.) consist of light of may different wavelengths.

When laser light is amplified, it is

F. strengthened.
G. pointed in one direction.
H. reduced to a lower energy state.
J. made unstable.

F. is correct. Many emissions at the same wavelength strengthen the beam. The direction of the light is controlled by the mirror, so G. is incorrect. Electrons jump from an unstable high-energy state to a lower energy state and emit radiation. This fact makes H. and J. incorrect.

SAT II: Subject Tests

Introduction

As of publication, these Subject Tests are offered: two in English (writing and literature), twelve in foreign languages (Chinese with listening, French with and without listening, German with and without listening, Modern Hebrew, Italian, Japanese with listening, Korean with listening, Latin, and Spanish with and without listening), two in history and social studies (American history and social studies, and world history), two in mathematics (levels IC and IIC), and four in sciences (biology, biology e/m, chemistry, and physics).

Scheduling

You can take the Subject Tests on the same day as the SAT I, or you can take them separately. College admission requirements or personal choice determine which ones you take. The tests assess content knowledge in specific disciplines. They provide a means of comparing students in subject areas, thus getting past texts, grades, and teaching styles.

Not all tests are offered every time. For example, the Modern Hebrew test is offered only in June. Check to find out when individual tests are offered. Also, be aware of the requirements for admission; some colleges require the tests be taken at certain times.

Description of Tests

The number of questions varies from subject to subject. For example, the literature test has about sixty questions;

the physics test, seventy-five questions; and the Spanish test, eighty-five questions. The writing test combines forty minutes of multiple-choice questions with a twenty-minute essay.

The information packet provides details regarding content coverage for each of the tests. For example, the American history and social studies test asks varying numbers of questions on political history, economic history, social history, intellectual and cultural history, and foreign policy. Furthermore, the questions are categorized by historic period: one-fifth of the questions covers pre-Columbian history to 1789, another two-fifths cover from the period 1790 to 1898, while the remainder covers 1899 to the present.

Other than the essay component of the writing test, all questions are multiple choice. However, in addition to figures, students may encounter maps, posters, drawings, tables, and other visual information during the test.

In addition, not all of the questions are straightforward multiple choice. Some are multiple-multiple choice: the question is followed by a set of answers in which none, some, or all may be correct. A second set of answers follows that lists various combinations of the first group as being correct.

The math tests allow the use of calculators. Not all calculators are allowed, however; so it is important to confirm which calculators may be used for a given test. The registration materials provide information about the types of calculators that may be used as well as those that are not permitted.

Other tests have distinctive features. Know these features and directions in advance. For example, one type of question in the chemistry test provides an

assertion and a reason: something happens because of something else. The first part of the question asks you whether the assertion (statement I) is true or false. The second part asks you whether the reason (statement II) is true or false. The third part then asks whether statement II correctly explains statement I. (For example, $2 + 2 = 4$ because Paris is the capital of France; both the assertion $2 + 2 = 4$ and the reason Paris is the capital of France are true, but the reason is not a correct explanation of the assertion.)

Another type of question that appears in both chemistry and physics is similar to a matching question; it lists a group of five choices—for example, properties in physical science. The group is followed by questions asking which of the choices has a particular characteristic. The group of choices may be a group of graphs or other figures.

The foreign language listening tests offer a unique challenge. Students listen to something being said and then answer a question related to what they have heard. They may hear the passage only once or twice, and from that must answer the question. The spoken words will not appear in print anywhere; students will not be able to return to the question in the usual way, as they can in other tests.

Because of the number and variety of Subject Tests offered, we cannot give examples from every test. Instead, we present tips on four of the most popular tests, along with sample items and explanations of how to approach the items. The four tests are writing; mathematics, level IC; American history and social studies; and world history. Many of the tips for test taking apply to the other tests as well.

Writing Subject Test

Directions: The following sentences contain problems in grammar, usage, word choice, and idiom.

> Some sentences are correct.
>
> No sentence contains more than one error.
>
> You will find that the error, if there is one, is underlined and lettered. Assume that all other elements of the sentence are correct and cannot be changed. In choosing answers, follow the requirements of standard written English.
>
> If there is an error, select the <u>one underlined part</u> that must be changed in order to make the sentence correct.
>
> If there is no error, choice E is correct.

A minor disagreement <u>between</u> good friends may
　　　　　　　　　　　　A

<u>eventually develop</u> into a <u>real</u> serious and <u>irreconcilable</u>
　　　　B　　　　　　　　C　　　　　　　　　　D

difference of opinion. <u>No error</u>.
　　　　　　　　　　　　　　E

The adjective *serious* must be modified by an adverb—*really*, not the adjective *real*. (Remember that adverbs modify adjectives, verbs, and other adverbs.) Choice (C) should read "a <u>really</u> serious…"

Jenny <u>forgot</u> to pick up her package <u>although</u> the post office
　　　　A　　　　　　　　　　　　　　　B

<u>sent</u> her three notices <u>during</u> the past week. <u>No error</u>.
　C　　　　　　　　　　D　　　　　　　　　　E

When two actions have taken place in the past, the past perfect tense is used to indicate the earlier of the two actions. Choice (C) should read "… the post office <u>had sent</u> her…"

When <u>discussing</u> the accomplishments of Babe Ruth and
　　　　A

Henry Aaron, baseball fans <u>seldom agree</u> on who <u>was</u> the
　　　　　　　　　　　　　　　　B　　　　　　　　　C

<u>best</u> of the two. <u>No error</u>.
　D　　　　　　　　E

When a sentence compares two persons or things, you must use the comparative degree (better) rather than the superlative degree (best). Since two people are being compared, Choice (D) should read "… the <u>better</u> of the two."

Mrs. Jennings was startled <u>to learn</u> <u>that</u> her dinner
　　　　　　　　　　　　　　　A　　　B

<u>was ruined</u> <u>while talking</u> on the phone. <u>No error</u>.
　C　　　　　　D　　　　　　　　　　　E

This sentence contains a dangling elliptical clause. More simply stated, something was left out, making the sentence appear to suggest one thing while meaning another. As it is written, the sentence seems to say that the dinner was talking on the phone. You must make clear that Mrs. Jennings was doing the talking. Choice (D) should read "… while <u>she was talking</u> on the phone."

The liver, one of the <u>body's</u> <u>most complex</u> organs, <u>function</u>
　　　　　　　　　　　　A　　　　B　　　　　　　　　　C

as the <u>main</u> food-processing center. <u>No error</u>.
　　　　D　　　　　　　　　　　　　　E

A verb must agree with its subject, regardless of any intervening phrase. The subject of this sentence, *liver*, is singular, and therefore takes a singular verb, *functions*. Choice (C) should read, "The liver, one of the body's most complex organs, <u>functions</u> …"

The judge told the jury that the trial <u>could have come</u> to a
　　　　　　　　　　　　　　　　　　　　A

<u>speedier</u> conclusion if they <u>would have studied</u> the tran-
　B　　　　　　　　　　　　　　　　C

scripts <u>more thoroughly</u>. <u>No error</u>.
　　　　　D　　　　　　　　E

This sentence contains an "if" clause ("… if they would have studied…" as part of a contrary-to-fact past tense sentence. Therefore, the verb *had studied*, not *would have studied*, is required. Choice (C) should read "… if they <u>had studied</u> …"

<u>Each</u> teacher <u>and</u> guidance counselor <u>were</u> expected to
　A　　　　　　B　　　　　　　　　　　　C

report to school early to make final preparations for

<u>the arrival</u> of the students. <u>No error</u>.
　D　　　　　　　　　　　　　E

When singular subjects are joined by <u>and</u>, they generally take a plural verb. However, when preceded by <u>each</u>, the subjects are treated as a singular and require a singular verb. Choice (C) should read, "Each teacher and guidance counselor <u>was</u> …"

Directions: In each of the following sentences, some part of the sentence or the entire sentence is underlined. Beneath each sentence you will find five ways of phrasing the underlined part. The first of these repeats the original; the other four are different. If you think the original is the best of the alternatives, choose answer A; otherwise choose one of the others. Select the best version.

<u>By working after school and on weekends, his income increased dramatically.</u>

(A) By working after school and on weekends, his income increased dramatically.
(B) His income increased dramatically by working after school and on weekends.
(C) His income, by working after school and on weekends, increased dramatically.
(D) His income after school and on weekends increased dramatically.
(E) By working after school and on weekends, he increased his income dramatically.

Choice (A) is incorrect because the position of the gerund phrase seems to suggest that his income was doing the working. The same is true for choices (B) and (C). Choice (D) changes the intended meaning of the original sentence. Choice (E) is correct because inserting the word *he* makes clear who worked "after school and on weekends."

<u>Although it looks very much like a garden cucumber, the sea cucumber is actually an aquatic animal.</u>

(A) Although it looks very much like a garden cucumber, the sea cucumber is actually an aquatic animal.
(B) Because it looks very much like a garden cucumber, the sea cucumber is actually an aquatic animal.
(C) The sea cucumber looks very much like an aquatic animal but is actually a garden cucumber.
(D) The sea cucumber looks very much like a garden cucumber, which is actually an aquatic animal.
(E) The sea cucumber looks very much like a garden cucumber, so it is really an aquatic animal.

Choice (A) is correct. The word *although* suggests that the sentence will present contrasting ideas. Choice (B) changes the meaning of the original sentence by suggesting a ludicrous causal relationship. Choices (C), (D), and (E) drastically change the meaning of the original sentence.

William Roentgen called his invention x-rays <u>because at first he did not understand</u> what they were, and "x" is a scientific symbol for the unknown.

(A) because at first he did not understand
(B) without understanding
(C) although at first he did not understand
(D) and at first he did not understand
(E) which he did not understand at first

Choice (A) is correct. The word *because* shows the causal relationship between the two parts of the sentence. None of the other choices indicates a causal relationship. Choices (D) and (E) create awkward constructions.

After reviewing the evidence, the jury <u>had no choice but to imply that the defendant was guilty</u>.

(A) had no choice but to imply that the defendant was guilty
(B) had chosen to imply that the defendant was guilty
(C) had no choice but to infer that the defendant was guilty
(D) chose to infer that the defendant was guilty
(E) was guilty of implying that the defendant had no choice

Choice (A) is incorrect because it uses *imply* instead of *infer*. These words are often confused. *Imply* means "suggest"; *infer* means "come to a conclusion." Choice (B) is wrong for the same reason. Choices (D) and (E) change the intended meaning of the sentence. Choice (C) is the correct answer.

Our neighbor's dog kept us awake as it either <u>barked or was whining all night</u>.

(A) barked or was whining all night
(B) was barking or whined all night
(C) barked or whined all night
(D) was barking all night or whining
(E) barks or whines all night

Choices (A) and (B) are incorrect because of faulty parallelism. The two related parts of the sentence must use the same verb form. Choice (D) is an awkward attempt at parallelism. Choice (E) is an example of parallel structure, but has incorrectly introduced verbs in the present tense. Only choice (C) uses parallelism correctly to express the meaning of the original sentence.

<u>Directions:</u> The following passage contains errors or parts that could be improved. After reading the passage, select the best answer to the questions that follow.

(1) For most students, freshman year at college is there first time living away from home. (2) It is a time when they must adjust to many new things, especially the freedoms. (3) They have complete control of their lives and lots of fun new things they can do on the campus.

(4) Young college student have many freedoms. (5) They also have responsibilities. (6) Or so my brother tells me. (7) He goes to the University of Virginia. (8) The classes are much harder there and there is far more homework too. (9) My brother said it costs so much money, you have to try doing the best you can.

What change should be made to sentence (1), reproduced below?

For most students, freshman year at college is there first time living away from home.

(A) For some students, . . .
(B) . . . freshman year at college is there first time living in some place other then home.
(C) . . . freshman year at college is a new experience.
(D) . . . freshman year at college is their first time living away from home.
(E) . . . freshman year at college is there first time away from home.

Choice (A) takes issue with how many students live away from home, but there is no way here to judge that based on the passage. Choice (C) eliminates an important element (first time away from home) and therefore is also not a good answer. Choices (B) and (E) change the wording slightly, but preserve the error in which "there" is used for "their." Only choice (D) includes that change, making it the correct answer.

What is the best way to revise and combine the three sentences reproduced below?

(4) Young college students have many freedoms. (5) They also have responsibilities. (6) Or so my brother tells me.

(A) Young college students have many freedoms; they also have many responsibilities, or so my brother tells me.
(B) In addition to freedoms, young college students also have many responsibilities, or so my older brother tells me.
(C) Young college students have many freedoms, but they also have responsibilities, or so my older brother tells me.
(D) Young college students have many freedoms, however they also have responsibilities, or so my older brother tells me.
(E) No changes needed.

With the exception of (E), the choices above all represent an improvement over the original. However, choice (B) is more tightly written and serves as a better topic sentence for the paragraph.

In context, choose the best way to revise the sentences reproduced below.

(7) He goes to the University of Virginia. (8) The classes are much harder there and there is far more homework too.

(A) He goes to the University of Virginia. His classes are harder and he has far more homework.
(B) A University of Virginia student, he said his classes are much harder and he has far more homework than in high school.
(C) The classwork is much harder at the University of Virginia where he goes and there is far more homework too.
(D) The University of Virginia has harder classes and more homework than high school.
(E) At the University of Virginia, the classes are much harder and there is far more homework too.

All five choices eliminate the repeated "there" problem in sentence (8). But the purpose of this sentence is to say something more about a college student's responsibilities while also (secondarily) explaining more about the writer's brother. Choices (C), (D), and (E) all talk primarily about the University of Virginia and the responsibilities, not the brother and the responsibilities. Choice (A) brings the brother into the picture, but does so in a way that is disconnected. Choice (B) makes the connection between the brother, the college, and the responsibilities and is the best choice.

Given the context of the passage, what is the most likely meaning of "it" in sentence (9) reproduced below?

My brother said it costs so much money, you have to try doing the best you can.

(A) skipping class
(B) not doing your homework
(C) getting behind
(D) a high school education
(E) going to college

Choices (A), (B), and (C) might be candidates based on the previous sentence, but they do not make sense in this sentence. Choice (D) does not fit either because we usually think of high school as free (though public education is paid for through taxes). Choice (E) is correct.

Mathematics Subject Test

<u>Directions:</u> For each of the following problems, decide which is the best of the choices given.

<u>Notes:</u>
(1) Figures that accompany problems in this test are intended to provide information useful in solving the problems. They are drawn as accurately as possible EXCEPT when it is stated in a specific problem that the figure is not drawn to scale. All figures lie in a plane unless otherwise indicated.
(2) Unless otherwise specified, the domain of a function f is assumed to be the set of all real numbers x for which $f(x)$ is a real number.

If $ab + a = 12$ and $b + 1 = 3$, then $a =$

(A) 36   (B) 15   (C) 9   (D) 4   (E) 2

Notice that the first expression can be factored: $ab + a = 12$
$$a(b + 1) = 12$$
Substitute 3 for $b + 1$: $a(3) = 12$
$$a = 4$$
The correct answer is (D).

The solution of the pair of equations
$$jx + ky = 1$$
$$kx + jy = 4$$
is $x = -1, y = 2$. What are the values of j and k?

(A) $j = 3,$ (B) $j = 2,$ (C) $j = 1,$ (D) $j = 2,$
$\quad k = 2$ $\quad k = 3$ $\quad k = 1$ $\quad k = -2$

(E) $j = -1,$
$\quad k = 1$

Substituting the given solutions results in a new system of equations in variables j and k.
$$j(-1) + k(2) = 1 \qquad -j + 2k = 1$$
$$k(-1) + j(2) = 4 \qquad -k + 2j = 4$$
Solve for j and k by adding 2 times the first equation to the second, which eliminates j.
$$-2j + 4k = 2$$
$$\underline{2j - k = 4}$$
$$3k = 6,$$
$$k = 2$$
$$-(2) + 2j = 4$$
$$2j = 6$$
$$j = 3$$
The correct choice is (A).

How many integers are in the solution set of $|3x + 1| > 2$?

(A) None (B) One (D) Two (D) Three
(E) Infinitely many

To solve an absolute value inequality, remember that absolute value is a measure of distance along the number line. This sentence states that the distance from some point is greater than 2 units, a description that would fit infinitely many points. You can also tackle this problem algebraically. If the absolute value of $3x + 1$ is greater than 2, then the expression itself must be either greater than 2 or less than -2. This enables you to rewrite the sentence as two separate inequalities.
$$3x + 1 < -2 \qquad 3x + 1 > 2$$
$$3x < -3 \qquad 3x > 1$$
$$x < -1 \qquad x > \tfrac{1}{3}$$
Again, there are infinitely many integers that fit these conditions. The correct choice is (E).

If the points $A(-1, 1)$, $B(2, 4)$, and $C(5, 1)$ are connected to form triangle ABC with sides AB, BC, and CA, the area of the triangle will be:

(A) 2   (B) 6   (C) 9   (D) 12   (E) 40

Sketch the points on a grid. To find the area of a triangle, use the formula $A = \frac{1}{2}bh$. AC is convenient to use as the base; its length is 6. The height from B to the base is 3.
$$A = \frac{1(6)(3)}{2} = 9$$
The correct answer is (C).

If a and b are even integers, which of the following must be an odd integer?

$$\text{I } \frac{ab}{2} \qquad \text{II } ab + 1 \qquad \text{III } \frac{ab + 1}{2}$$

(A) I only   (B) II only   (C) I and II only
(D) II and III only   (E) I, II, and III

This problem requires some careful reasoning. The product of any two even integers is an even integer. The expression in I will always be even, since both a and b have a factor of 2. Dividing out one factor of 2 will leave at least one other, which makes the quotient even. The expression in II will always be odd. The product, ab, is even. Adding 1 to any even number will produce an odd number. The expression in III will certainly never be even, since an odd number is being divided by 2. However, it will not always be an odd number since it may very well not be an integer at all. Therefore, the correct answer is (B).

Which of the following is the equation of a line that is perpendicular to the line with equation $3x + y = 7$?

(A) $3x - y = 7$ (B) $3y - x = 4$ (C) $3y + x = 7$
(D) $3x - 3y = 5$ (E) $3x + y =$
-2

Two lines are perpendicular if their slopes are negative reciprocals. The slope of the given line is found by using the form $y = mx + b$. $3x + y = 7$ can be rewritten as $y = -3x + 7$, so the slope is -3. The negative reciprocal of -3 is $\frac{1}{3}$. Any equation that can be rewritten as $y = \frac{1}{3}x + b$ will yield a line that is perpendicular to the given line.
$$y = \frac{1}{3}x + b$$
$$3y = x + 3b$$
$$3y - x = 3b$$
The only equation that matches this form is (B).

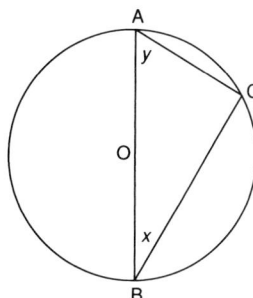

AB is a diameter of circle O. What is the measure of angle y if $x = 30°$?

(A) 30°   (B) 45°   (C) 50°   (D) 60°   (E) 90°

Since angle C is inscribed in a semicircle, it measures 90°. Therefore, ABC is a right triangle and angles x and y are complementary. $y = 90° - 30° = 60°$. The correct answer is (D).

What is the area of a triangle whose sides measure 5, 5, and 8?

(A) 10   (B) 12   (C) 20   (D) 24   (E) 40

Begin by making a drawing.

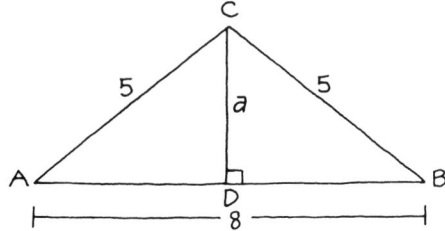

To find the area of a triangle, you need to know the base and the altitude. The altitude is perpendicular to the base. This triangle is isosceles, so the altitude bisects the base, making $AD = DB = 4$. Use the Pythagorean theorem to find the altitude.

$$a^2 + 4^2 = 5^2$$
$$a^2 + 16 = 25$$
$$a^2 = 9$$
$$a = 3$$

To find the area of the triangle, use the equation $A = \frac{1}{2}ba$, where A is the area, b is the base, and a is the altitude. The area is $\frac{1(3)(8)}{2} = 12$. The correct choice is (B).

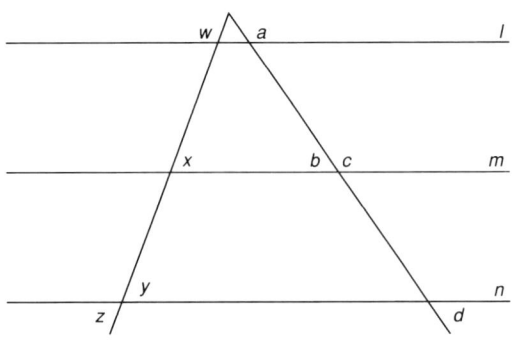

Lines l, m, and n are parallel. Which labeled angles are equal?

(A) x, y, and z
(B) w, x, and y
(C) w, a, and c
(D) a, b, and c
(E) b, d, and z

Three parallel lines are cut by two different transversals. It may help to mark the figure, indicating which angles are necessarily equal. Two kinds of angles formed when a transversal crosses parallel lines are equal: alternating angles (such as w and x) and corresponding angles (such as a and c). There are four different angle measures here, marked as 1, 2, 3, and 4.

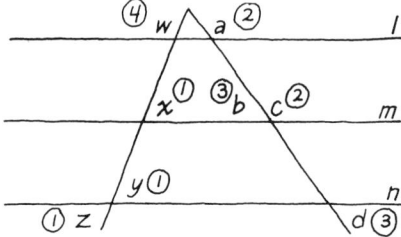

The correct answer is (A).

One side of a cube measures $x + 2$. What is the surface area of the cube?

(A) $6x + 12$ (B) $x^2 + 4x + 4$ (C) $6x^2 + 4$
(D) $4x^2 + 16x + 16$ (E) $6x^2 + 24x + 24$

A cube is a solid figure with 6 congruent faces. Each face is a square. The surface area is 6 times the area of one of these squares.

$$\text{area of one square: } (x + 2)^2 = x^2 + 4x + 4$$
$$\text{area of 6 squares: } 6(x^2 + 4x + 4) = 6x^2 + 24x + 24$$

The correct answer is (E).

If a line contains the points $(-2, 1)$ and $(3, 6)$, then its x-intercept is

(A) -3 (B) 0   (C) 1   (D) 3   (E) 4

To find the x-intercept, find the equation of the line. This x-intercept is the value of x when $y = 0$ in that equation. Use the slope-intercept equation. First find the slope, m.

$$\text{Slope } m = \frac{y_2 - y_1}{x_2 - x_1}$$
$$= \frac{6 - 1}{3 - (-2)}$$
$$= \frac{5}{5} = 1$$

Substitute the slope into the slope-intercept equation $y = mx + b$, where $m = 1$ and b is the y-intercept.

$$y = x + b$$

Choose one point, say $(3, 6)$, for (x, y). So, $x = 3$ and $y = 6$, and the equation becomes

$$6 = 3 + b$$
$$3 = b$$

The equation of the line is $y = x + 3$.
Substituting 0 for y, $0 = x + 3$, or $-3 = x$.
The correct choice is (A).

In the right triangle below,

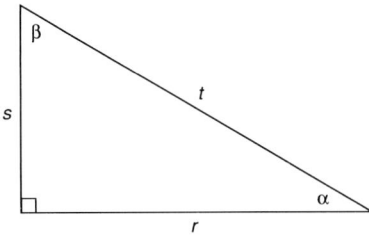

cosine α is equal to which of the following?

$$\text{I } \sin \beta \qquad \text{II } \frac{r}{t} \qquad \text{III } \frac{s}{t}$$

(A) I only   (B) II only   (C) III only   (D) I and II
(E) I and III

The cosine of an angle is the ratio of its adjacent side to its hypotenuse. In this drawing, the side adjacent to α is r and the hypotenuse is t. It is also true that the cosine of an angle is equal to the sine of its complement. So $\cos \alpha = \sin \beta$. Therefore, the correct answer is (D).

If θ is an acute angle and $\sin \theta = \dfrac{3}{5}$, then $\tan \theta =$

(A) $\dfrac{2}{5}$ (B) $\dfrac{4}{5}$ (C) $\dfrac{5}{3}$ (D) $\dfrac{3}{4}$ (E) $\dfrac{4}{3}$

The sine of an angle is the ratio of its opposite side to its hypotenuse.

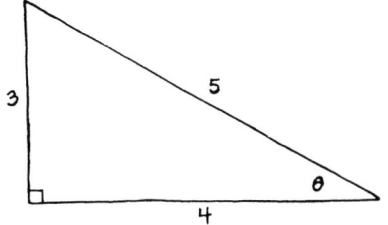

The sketch labels the corresponding parts of the right triangle for θ. The adjacent side is 4, since this is a 3-4-5 right triangle. The tangent is the ratio of the opposite side to the adjacent side. The correct choice is (D).

If $f(x) = \dfrac{x+2}{x}$ and $g(x) = \dfrac{x^2}{2}$, then $f(g(4)) =$

(A) $1\dfrac{1}{8}$ (B) $1\dfrac{1}{4}$ (C) $2\dfrac{1}{2}$ (D) 8   (E) 12

To find the value of function f of function g, first find the value of $g(4)$. Then use that value for x in $f(x)$.

$$g(4) = \frac{4^2}{2} \qquad g(4) = 8$$
$$f(8) = \frac{8+2}{8} = \frac{10}{8} = 1\frac{1}{4}$$

The correct answer is (B).

If $f(x) = 2x - 3$ and $g(x) = 3x - 5$, for what value of a will $f(a) = g(a)$?

(A) -8 (B) 0   (C) 2   (D) 3   (E) 8

To find out which value of a gives the same result for function f and function g, solve this equation:

$$2a - 3 = 3a - 5$$
$$-3 + 5 = 3a - 2a$$
$$2 = a$$

The correct choice is (C).

If an operation * is defined for all real numbers x and y by the equation $x * y = 2x - xy$, then $3 * (-1) =$

(A) 9   (B) 7   (C) 2   (D) 3   (E) 0

Substitute 3 for x and -1 for y.

$$2(3) - (3)(-1) = 6 - (-3) = 6 + 3 = 9$$

The correct choice is (A).

"If p, then q" is a true statement under which of the following conditions?

$$\begin{array}{l}
\text{I } p \text{ is true and } q \text{ is true} \\
\text{II } p \text{ is true and } q \text{ is false} \\
\text{III } p \text{ is false and } q \text{ is true} \\
\text{IV } p \text{ is false and } q \text{ is false}
\end{array}$$

(A) I only   (B) I and II   (C) I and III   (D) I and IV

(E) I, III, and IV

Think of the truth table for "if p, then q." It may help to use some common-language example such as, "If it is raining, then I will go to the movies."

$$p = \text{It is raining}$$
$$q = \text{I will go to the movies}$$

In the table, T means "true" and F means "false." So the first line of the table means that each part and the combined statement are true.

If p, then q	p	q
T	T	T
F	T	F
T	F	T
T	F	F

The logical statement "If p, then q" is true except in the case where p is true and q is false. So, the correct choice is (E).

In the figure below, a cone is inscribed in a cylinder. If the volume of the cylinder is 90π, what is the volume of the cone?

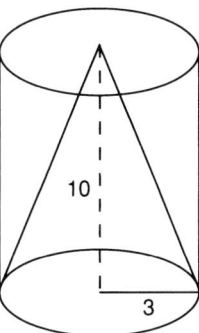

(A) 90π (B) 45π (C) 30π (D) $30\pi^2$ (E) 45

The volume of a cylinder is 3 times the volume of a cone with the same base and height, so the easy way to solve this is to think $\frac{1}{3}$ of 90π is 30π; the correct choice is (C). You could also—but using up more time—calculate the volume of the cone from the formula $V = \frac{1}{3} Bh$, where B is the base of the cone and h is the height.

American History and Social Studies Subject Test

Directions: Each of the questions or incomplete statements below is followed by five suggested answers or completions. Select the one that is best in each case.

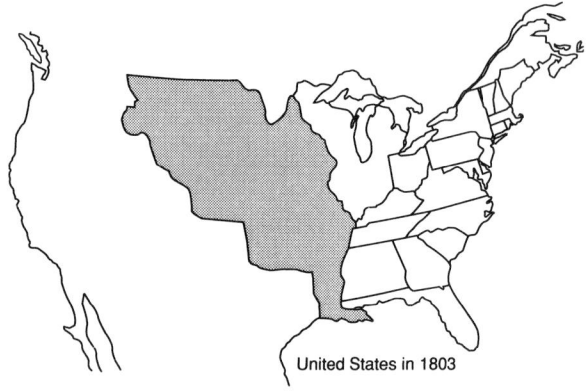

United States in 1803

In 1803 the United States bought the territory shown on the map for $15 million. This land acquisition came to be known as

(A) The Gadsden Purchase
(B) 54-40 or Fight
(C) Seward's Folly
(D) The Louisiana Purchase
(E) The Northwest Passage

There are two clues in the stem of this item: the map itself and the date of the land acquisition. In 1803 Thomas Jefferson was president. Jefferson sent Lewis and Clark off to explore the newly acquired territory of Louisiana. The Gadsden Purchase came much later, shortly before the Civil War (it was intimately involved in the issues that led to the war). "54-40 or Fight" was a slogan for Americans who wanted to expand into western Canada. Seward's Folly was another major land purchase, but it was Alaska and it came much later than 1803. The Northwest Passage, which is a sea route to the Pacific from the Atlantic north of North America, might be confused with the Northwest Territories, a large part of the land bought in the Louisiana Purchase, but it is certainly not the same. The correct choice is (D).

The land forces shown above included a future president as second in command. They played an important part in a war that was, however, won largely at sea, a war that resulted in control of several large islands by the winner of the war. This war is best known as

(A) the Hawaiian War
(B) the Spanish-American War
(C) the Pacific Theater
(D) the Bay of Pigs
(E) the Russo-Japanese War

There are a number of clues in the stem. The picture shows soldiers dressed as a casual expeditionary force around the turn of the century. Therefore, the future U.S. president could not be Lincoln (who served in the Blackhawk War) or any other 19th-century president. The lack of standard uniforms suggests that neither world war, in each of which future presidents served (e.g., Truman, Eisenhower, Kennedy), could be involved. Large islands that have been controlled by another nation include the Hawaiian Islands, which were annexed at about the right time, but no war was involved. The Pacific Theater refers to the part of World War II fought against the Japanese in the Pacific Ocean; this resulted in short-term control of the large islands of Japan, but it does not match the time frame of the photograph. The Russo-Japanese War occurred at about the right time, but these troops are gathered around an American flag. In any case, the Japanese won that war and did not acquire additional whole islands (although they were awarded half the large island of Sakhalin). The Bay of Pigs was a battle in Cuba that troops supported by the United States lost, so no

islands were acquired. The correct choice, therefore must be (B), the Spanish-American War. The troops pictured are the Rough Riders, whose second in command was Teddy Roosevelt. They fought in Cuba, but is was the U.S. Navy that won control of Cuba, Puerto Rico, and the Philippines. The words *control of* in the stem are an additional clue, since the islands were not incorporated into the United States. Cuba became independent after the war, but the United States ran Cuba's foreign policy and stationed troops there (troops remain there to this day). The Philippines were controlled by the United States until after World War II, and Puerto Rico remains a commonwealth of the United States.

During the Civil War, Northern Democrats opposed to the war effort were known as

(A) Butternuts
(B) Carpetbaggers
(C) Copperheads
(D) Know Nothings
(E) Sons of Liberty

All the terms refer to people who believed in or did something. To find the correct choice, we need only look at terms from the Civil War years. The Sons of Liberty date from the American Revolution, long before the Civil War, thus eliminating choice (E). Carpetbaggers were Northerners who went South after the Civil War to take jobs under Reconstruction governments, so choice (B) is not correct. Choices (A) and (C) are both from the Civil War. Butternuts were soldiers or supporters of the Confederacy. Copperheads were Northern Democrats who opposed the war, making choice (C) the correct one.

The importance of ships like the one shown above in American history is that they brought

(A) the pilgrims to New England
(B) European immigrants to Ellis Island
(C) Columbus and other early explorers to the New World
(D) Leif Ericson and the Vikings to the coast of North America
(E) the United States to a position as the second largest international trader

It is easy to reject choice (B), since the great waves of European immigrants came by steamship, not by sailing ship. Also, the ship pictured does not resemble the simple "dragon ships" of the Vikings (choice D). While both the Spanish galleons (choice C) and ships like the *Mayflower* (choice A) were full-rigged sailing ships, these early ships were short and stubby, not long and sleek like the U.S. clipper ship pictured. These speedy sailboats traded all over the world and put the United States just behind Great Britain in international trade during the 1840's and 1850's. After the Civil War, however, various advances by other nations resulted in the loss of the dominant position of the clippers. The correct choice is (E).

Aaron Burr was

(A) vice president during Jefferson's two terms
(B) tried and convicted of treason
(C) tied with Jefferson in the election of 1800
(D) Alexander Hamilton's brother-in-law
(E) elected governor of New York in 1804

Aaron Burr is one of the most colorful figures of the postcolonial period. He was a New Yorker, a vice president, tried for treason, and involved with Alexander Hamilton, giving each of the choices a veneer of truth. Although Burr was vice president, he served only during Jefferson's first term, making choice (A) incorrect. His involvement with Hamilton was not through family but through a feud that ended with Burr killing Hamilton in a duel. Thus, choice (D) is out. Burr ran for governor but lost—just in case choice (E) looks attractive. The correct answer is choice (C). Burr tied with Jefferson in the electoral college in 1800, whereupon the House of Representatives chose Jefferson as president and Burr as vice president.

The word "Okay" (or OK) probably derives from

(A) all correct
(B) a musical by George Gershwin
(C) a World War II military code
(D) a Martin Van Buren campaign organization
(E) a boxing term

This calls for a bit of knowledge of the presidential campaign of 1840. This said, we can eliminate the incorrect choices. Gershwin wrote a musical entitled *Oh, Kay!* in 1926, which eliminates choice (B). World War II came long after 1936, so eliminate (C). Choice (E) is a test writer's bit of fun since the boxing term is "KO." This leaves us with two possibilities. Choice (A) is the meaning OK has come to have and seems to have come from a misinterpretation of the word's correct origin. The correct answer is (D). Martin Van Buren (who lost his bid for reelection) lived near Albany, New York, in a house called Old Kinderhook. The initials O.K. became a secret name for the Democratic clubs in New York. The opposition Whigs somehow never figured this out and invented the meaning "oll korrect," attributing the misspelling to former President Jackson.

The American Colonization Society was concerned with

(A) *Mayflower* descendants' genealogies
(B) encouraging Americans to settle Mexican Texas
(C) transporting freed American slaves to Africa
(D) teaching English to Filipinos after the Spanish-American War
(E) encouraging revolutions against Spain and Portugal in South America

All of the choices seem plausible. The society was supported mainly by Southern slaveholders who sought to resettle freed slaves in Africa. Although very few slaves were sent back, the result was the founding of the West African republic of Liberia. The correct choice is (C).

Luther Burbank was a

(A) horticulturalist
(B) cosmetologist
(C) mortician
(D) evangelist
(E) cinematographer

The correct choice is (A). Luther Burbank developed over 800 new plant varieties, including the commercially valuable Idaho potato.

The Society of the Cincinnati comprises

(A) Ohio businessmen
(B) American Indian tribal chieftains
(C) descendants of Revolutionary War officers
(D) retired Roman legionnaires
(E) Midwestern farmers

Choice (C) is correct. The society was founded by officers who fought in the American Revolution, and it was named for the Roman general Cincinnatus. George Washington was its first president general. Membership is restricted to the oldest male descendants in direct or collateral lines. The city of Cincinnati, Ohio, was named after the society.

This strange shape is made of raised earth and is 1348 feet long if measured along the curves. It was most likely made by

(A) Native Americans in the Midwest or Southern United States
(B) early settlers as a defense against Native Americans
(C) Native Americans of the Four Corners regions or the American desert
(D) unknown visitors to the desert near Nazca, Peru
(E) Native Americans of the northwest coast of the United States

The easiest choice to reject is (D), for this is a test of American history, so Peru could not be involved. In any case, the large, fanciful figures in the Nazca region are made by scraping away the top layer of the desert soil, not by building large mounds. Also, choice (B) makes no sense, since most of the mound could easily be walked around—it is only about a tenth of a mile long. Therefore, it must be one of the three choices that involve Native Americans. The early inhabitants of the Four Corners regions and American desert built large communal pueblos and round kivas, but no mounds. The Northwest is noted for totem poles. The Mound Builders were pre-Columbian Native Americans of the Midwest and South, so the correct choice is (A). In fact, the illustration shows Serpent Mound, in Ohio.

The Articles of Confederation refer to

(A) the first Constitution of the United States
(B) the secession of the Southern states
(C) the merging of Southern and Northern Baptist conventions
(D) the unification of the AFL-CIO
(E) fund-raising rules for umbrella organizations such as United Fund and Community Chest

If you recall that the Southern states formed the Confederate States of America, choice (B) is tempting although it is wrong. And just as wrong are choices (C), (D), and (E). The correct one is (A). The Articles defined the United States government from 1781 to 1789, when the present Constitution was adopted.

The *CSS Alabama*

(A) was sunk at Pearl Harbor
(B) is a major tourist attraction in Mobile Bay
(C) was sunk off the coast of France
(D) was an ironclad ship in the Confederate Navy
(E) played a major role in the Barbary Coast wars

Knowing that the *CSS Alabama* was a Confederate Navy raider during the Civil War, choice (E) is quickly eliminated since the Barbary Coast troubles took place decades before the Civil War. Likewise, choice (A) is out since the Pearl Harbor attack took place in 1941. Choice (D) is a possibility except that the *Alabama* was not an ironclad. Choice (B) might be believable except for the fact that the *Alabama* was sunk by the U.S. Navy off the French coast. Choice (C) is correct.

The Trail of Tears refers to

(A) the Lewis and Clark expedition
(B) the Wilkes expedition to Antarctica
(C) Commodore Perry's entry into Tokyo Bay
(D) pre-Union-Pacific route to California
(E) forced removal of American Indians to the Oklahoma Territory

Although the name might, with some stretching at times, apply to all the choices, (E) is the correct one. Thousands of displaced people died during the winter of 1838 when the Indians were forced to move to Oklahoma.

The Hartford Convention of 1815 resulted in

(A) attempted secession by New England states
(B) successful conclusion of the War of 1812
(C) industrial expansion in the Northeast
(D) the end of the Federalist Party
(E) adoption of a states' rights platform by the Federalist Party

Although some leaders of the convention had the secession of New England in mind, it did not happen, so choice (A) is not right. The War of 1812 ended after the convention, eliminating (B). Despite their protestations, the war did not harm manufacturing in New England, and the convention certainly had no effect on it. Thus, (C) is incorrect too. Although the convention had much to do with states' rights, the Federalist Party did not adopt a platform as the convention was not, in theory, a party meeting. Choice (E) is, therefore, ruled out. The unintended result of the Hartford Convention was the attachment of a stigma of unpatriotism to the Federalist Party in the aftermath of the War of 1812. From this the party, which by then was a regional party, never recovered. (D) is the correct choice.

Andrew Jackson's wife, Rachel, shown above,

(A) gave the first Easter egg roll on the White House lawn
(B) served ice cream for the first time at the White House
(C) was an important champion of the American Indian
(D) gave boisterous receptions in the Blue Room
(E) died before Jackson's first inauguration

The correct choice is (E). Rachel Jackson died in December, 1828, before her husband's inauguration. This eliminates choices (A), (B), and (D), since she never lived in the White House. Remembering Andrew Jackson's campaigns against Native Americans, it is not only highly unlikely that Mrs. Jackson would have been one of their champions, it is untrue.

World History Subject Test

<u>Directions</u>. Each of the questions or incomplete statements below is followed by five suggested answers or completions. Select the one that is best in each case.

How did the Norman Conquest most affect the development of the English language?

(A) Words lost inflectional endings.
(B) Syntax changed.
(C) Many Latin words were borrowed.
(D) Many French words were borrowed.
(E) Many Norse words were borrowed.

While this question is interpretive, it helps to understand the reference to the Norman Conquest. It is the invasion of England by William of Normandy, leading to the Battle of Hastings in 1066, which established the British monarchy that has continued to this day. While the Normans' roots were originally Scandinavian (Northmen or Norsemen), they had settled in France; the invasion was from French Normandy. The Latin impact would have been a thousand years earlier when the Romans invaded Britain. (D) is correct.

"The princes act therefore as ministers of God and as His lieutenants on earth. It is by His ministers that He exercises His sway. . . . For such a reason the royal throne is not the throne of man, but of God Himself. . ."

The author of this passage is justifying which of the following political doctrines?

(A) Caesaropapism
(B) Popular sovereignty
(C) Christian democracy
(D) Divine right of kings
(E) Theocracy

Even if you are not sure of the distinctions between these doctrines, there are clues that can help you answer this question. In the passage, God is central, the people are not mentioned. Therefore, both (B) and (C) can seemingly be eliminated; the passage seems to run counter to popular sovereignty and democracy. The royal throne suggests a king and the passage refers to the relation between God and royalty. (D) emerges as the answer.

Athens won a decisive victory over Persia during the Persian War at

(A) Philippi
(B) Tours
(C) Marathon
(D) Issus
(E) Zama

The correct choice is (C), Marathon. Choice (A), Philippi, was the city in Macedonia where Marc Antony and Octavian defeated the murderers of Caesar. At Tours, (B), Charles Martel defeated the Muslims. At Issus, (D), Alexander the Great defeated the Persians, and at Zama, (E), the Romans defeated Hannibal.

Western Europe during the ninth to twelfth centuries was characterized by

(A) breakdown of feudalism
(B) the rise of capitalism
(C) the ravages of the Black Plague
(D) the flourishing of Romanesque architecture
(E) the development of strong nation-states

The correct choice is (D). This period was the high point of feudalism, so (A) is incorrect. Choice (B), the rise of capitalism, did not begin until later, and (C), the Black Plague, did not ravage Europe until the 14th century. Choice (E), the development of strong nation-states, came with the decline of feudalism.

"His Majesty's Government view with favor the establishment in Palestine of a national home for the Jewish people, and will use their best endeavors to facilitate the achievement of this object. . . ." These words come from

(A) Wilson's Fourteen Points
(B) the Balfour Declaration
(C) the Constitution of Israel
(D) the Entente Cordiale
(E) the Camp David accords

The correct answer is (B), the Balfour Declaration, which stated Britain's support for a Jewish state. Wilson's Fourteen Points, (A), did not deal specifically with a Jewish state although they did include the idea of national self-determination. Although Britain did administer Palestine, it is unlikely that the Israeli Constitution would mention the British government, so (C) is incorrect. (D) was an agreement between Britain and France in 1904, and (E) refers to agreements between Israel, Egypt, and the United States in 1978.

One of the few democracies in Africa is the government of

(A) Qatar
(B) Suriname
(C) Libya
(D) Tonga
(E) Botswana

The correct choice is Botswana, (E), which is a parliamentary democracy. Qatar, (A), is a kingdom on the Arabian peninsula. Suriname, (B), currently has a democratic government, but it is in South America. Libya, (C), is in Africa, but has long been controlled by the dictator Muammar al-Qaddafi. Tonga, (D), although a democracy, is in the South Pacific.

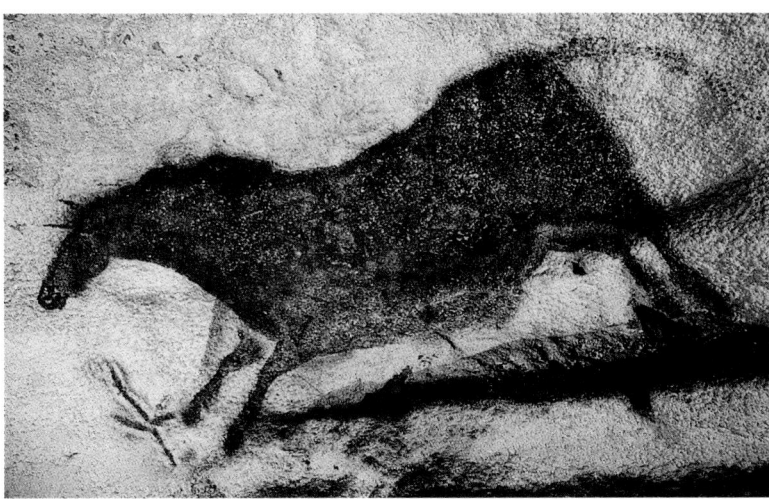

The people who made this painting on a rock wall were

(A) of a type called the Neanderthals
(B) people much like ourselves who lived near the end of the last Ice Age
(C) Australian Aborigines
(D) modern artists living in Paris in the early 20th century
(E) people who lived in a large cave near Peking (now Beijing), China

Choices (A) and (E) refer to human ancestors or relatives that are not known to have any art at all. Although this is a part of a cave painting, so-called Peking man, who lived in caves, was of a species called *Homo erectus* that made only very primitive tools such as hand axes. Australian aborigines made and continue to make many paintings on rocks, but their paintings are not as representational as those shown here. Modern artists may have been influenced somewhat by these paintings, but they are not known to paint on rock walls of caves. The correct choice is (B). The Cro-Magnons were physically the same as modern humans. Toward the end of the last Ice Age, some 11,000 years ago, they created many paintings and some sculptures in the caves of northern Spain and southern France.

Peter the Great brought each of the following changes to Russia EXCEPT

(A)   mercantilist policies
(B)   freedom for the serfs
(C)   a new capital city
(D)   an army modeled on western military traditions
(E)   an expanding central government

(B) is the correct answer. Choices (A), (C), (D), and (E) describe changes wrought by Peter during his reign (1682-1725). The serfs, however, did not obtain their freedom until 1861.

This cartoon shows

(A)   riots created by publication of Adam Smith's *Wealth of Nations*
(B)   agitation over the planting of corn from the New World in fields that had been planted with wheat
(C)   abolitionists in the United States during the 1840's and 1850's
(D)   an organized effort in England to repeal laws forbidding the import of cheap grain
(E)   the Glorious Revolution

The main clues are the posters that say "Anti-cornlaw League." The Corn Laws were laws designed to protect British agricultural and landowning interests by setting a floor on the price at which grains such as wheat (all such grains are called *corn* in England) could be imported. They were abolished in 1846 as a result of a concerted, well-organized campaign against them. They had nothing to do with the grain the Americans call *corn*, choice (B). The time period is right for the American abolitionists, but the posters are wrong. The Glorious Revolution occurred about 150 years earlier and saw the replacement of King James II with William and Mary (see item next page). Adam Smith's 18th-century book advocating, among other things, free trade caused no riots upon publication. The correct choice is (D).

The region marked on this map was all under the dominion of one ruler at this point in history. What does this region represent?

(A)   the Roman Empire
(B)   the Ottoman Empire
(C)   the empire of Charlemagne
(D)   the Spanish Empire
(E)   the empire of Peter the Great

Both the Roman Empire and the Ottoman Empire included regions to the east of the boundary of the area marked on this map, so it could not be choices (A) or (B). The Spanish Empire was largely in the New World, not in Europe. Peter the Great's empire was Russia. Therefore, the correct choice is (C), the empire of Charlemagne. In a sense this is a trick question, because the Holy Roman Empire of about a hundred years later had similar boundaries, but the Holy Roman Empire was not among the choices.

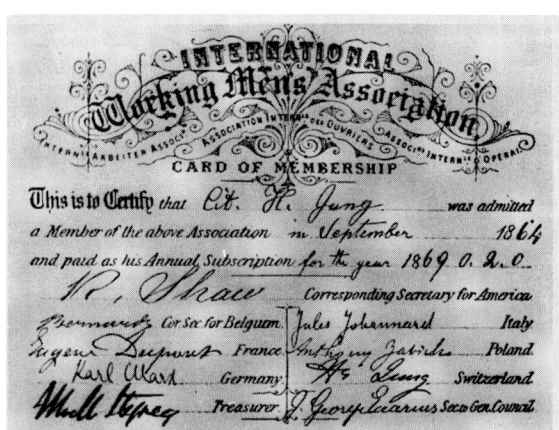

This card represents membership in an organization that is remembered as

(A)   the Wobblies
(B)   the First International
(C)   the Paris Commune
(D)   the Comintern
(E)   the A.F.L.-C.I.O.

A major clue is the signature of Karl Marx as the corresponding secretary for Germany. Marx was one of the founders of the First International, so choice (B) is correct. The Wobblies (choice A) were the International Workers of the World, a rival organization to the A.F.L. (American Federation of Labor) early in the 20th century. The Paris Commune (choice C) of 1871 was also too late for this card, and in any case was not an international organization, although it had members of the International Working Men's Association active in the commune. The Third International, or Comintern (choice D), was created shortly after the Communist revolution in Russia as a partly disguised arm of the new Soviet Union. The A.F.L.-C.I.O. (choice E) is the parent organization of labor unions in the United States today and was founded much later than the 19th century.

The superiority of the longbow over mounted knights protected by armor was demonstrated at

(A) Crécy
(B) Blenheim
(C) Trafalgar
(D) Actium
(E) the Marne

The correct choice is (A), Crécy, where an important battle was fought in 1346, when knighthood was in flower. Blenheim, (B), and Trafalgar, (C), were both fought after the development of gunpowder, which had made the longbow obsolete. Actium, (D), occurred in 31 B.C. before the longbow was invented, and the Marne, (E), was one of the opening battles of World War I.

The most important result of England's Glorious Revolution in 1688 was

(A) a victory for Protestantism
(B) the expulsion of James II
(C) the supremacy of parliamentary government
(D) universal manhood suffrage
(E) the establishment of cabinet government

The Glorious Revolution did mark a victory for Protestantism (A) by the expulsion of Catholic King James II (B). However, the most important result was that the supremacy of parliamentary government (C) was secure in England. Choices (D), universal manhood suffrage, and (E), cabinet government, would come later.

One man who rose to rule a nation as a consequence of the revolutions of 1848 was

(A) Metternich
(B) Napoleon III
(C) Garibaldi
(D) Castlereagh
(E) Louis Philippe

It was Napoleon III, (B), who became the ruler of France. Choice (A), Metternich, the Austrian leader, was overthrown in the revolution and a similar fate befell the French king Louis Philippe, (E). Choice (C), Garibaldi, fought in the Revolution of 1848 in Italy but did not rise to rule a nation, nor did Castlereagh, (D).

As emperor, Augustus did each of the following, EXCEPT

(A) preserve the old republican forms
(B) extend Roman roads in the empire
(C) build magnificent buildings in Rome
(D) reduce piracy at sea
(E) plot the death of Julius Caesar

Augustus smoothed the transition from republic to empire by preserving the old republican forms (A). He also improved the Roman world (B), brought peace to it (D), and beautified the capital (C). Not only did Julius Caesar die before Augustus became emperor, but Augustus—then known as Octavian—was neither in Rome at the time nor one of the plotters. Thus, choice (E) is correct.

After British India was partitioned into India and Pakistan, their two governments were initially led by

(A) Mountbatten and Gandhi
(B) Nehru and Jinnah
(C) Zia and Singh
(D) Sukarno and Magsaysay
(E) Nkrumah and Marcos

The correct choice is (B). Nehru and Jinnah were directly involved in the establishment of India and Pakistan and became the first to head the new governments. Lord Mountbatten, (A), was the last British viceroy of India, while Gandhi was a spiritual leader but never head of the Indian government. Sukarno and Magsaysay, (D), and Nkrumah and Marcos, (E), were leaders of other nations. Zia and Singh, (C), are recent leaders of Pakistan and India.

After World War II, which of the following did NOT occur in France's overseas empire?

(A) war in Algeria
(B) fall of Dien Bien Phu
(C) independence for the Ivory Coast
(D) the Fashoda affair
(E) independence of Guinea

War in Algeria, (A), occurred during the 1950's, while France lost Dien Bien Phu, (B), in Vietnam in 1954. After World War II, France granted independence to all the nations in its African empire, which included the Ivory Coast, (C), in 1960 and Guinea, (E), in 1958. However, the Fashoda affair, (D), occurred in 1898, when France and Britain confronted each other in an area of the Sudan claimed by both countries.

The immediate cause of the Franco-Prussian War in 1870 was

(A) the Ems dispatch
(B) the fall of Bismarck
(C) French defeat in Mexico
(D) the Dreyfus affair
(E) the Zimmerman telegram

The correct choice is (A). Since the dispatch was published by Bismarck to precipitate war, (B) is clearly incorrect. The French defeat in Mexico, (C), may have induced France to regain its lost prestige by going to war with Prussia, but is was not the immediate cause of the conflict. The Dreyfus affair, (D), did not occur in France until the 1890's, more than 20 years after the war; and the Zimmerman telegram, (E), was sent during World War I.

Of the following hypotheses about the stone bas-relief shown above, which is most likely to be valid?

(A) It was taken from an ancient Egyptian tomb
(B) It is from a New England tombstone
(C) It is a fine example of stone carvings found in Central America
(D) It is the work of a cubist artist—Pablo Picasso, for example
(E) It is a representation of one of the kings of Babylon

Although (B), (C), (D), and (E) deal with stone carvings, typical Egyptian art, as in (A), is usually painted or rounded sculpture, so (A) is unlikely. New England tombstones, if they featured drawings cut in stone at all, generally had recognizable Christian religious symbols, such as angels. This makes (B) unlikely. The ornate style of this engraving is incompatible with the very plain style of bas-reliefs from Mesopotamia, which rules out (E). The general style of this carving is basically that of the Central American Maya. Thus, choice (C) is correct. Although (D) might be possible—a modern artist could, for example, copy the art of a non-Western civilization—no work of modern art has used the Mayan style as its basis.

Other Exams

There are many important exams offered besides the SAT I, SAT II, and ACT. In this section we will focus on five of these: The Advanced Placement Exams, GED, GCSE, A levels, and GNVQ.

The Advanced Placement Exams are tests which can be taken by high school students to qualify them for college credits. The Tests of General Educational Development (GED) enable those passing it to be awarded the equivalent of a high school diploma.

The GCSE, A levels, and GNVQ are exams that are offered in the United Kingdom. The final exams of the General Certificate of Secondary Education (GCSE) are taken by most U.K. students soon after they reach their sixteenth birthday and mark the end point to eleven years of compulsory school attendance. The General Certificate of Education Advanced level exams (known as the A levels) are taken by students seeking admittance to Britain's universities. The General National Vocational Qualification (GNVQ) is a broad work-related qualification linked to particular industries or sectors of the economy; it is intended for those students who are not interested in or well suited to the academic curriculum provided by the GCSE and A levels.

Advanced Placement Exams

The Advanced Placement Exams are part of a program in which colleges and universities across the United States cooperate with high schools to offer the equivalent of college-level courses to high school students, and then to test students on that material for possible college credit.

There are thirty-one different AP Exams in eighteen subject areas. These exams cover most of the freshman courses commonly offered in college. Typically, an AP Exam consists of two parts: a multiple-choice part and a free-response part. In the multiple-choice section, wrong answers are penalized by small deductions, so unless you can eliminate some of the choices you should not guess. Free-response items can take the form of essays, solutions to problems or programs, audiotaped responses, or, in the case of Studio Art, portfolios.

The AP Exams are difficult, so most students have little hope of passing them without having taken AP courses in high school for those same subject areas. The more technical a course is, the less likely it is that a student can pass the AP Exam without having taken the AP course. Thus, it is possible to pass the AP Exam in literature or American history with only the ordinary secondary school courses, while it is nearly impossible to pass AP Exams in calculus or chemistry without taking a course designed for this purpose.

Different schools require different scores for college credit. Scores are granted on a five-point scale:

5 extremely well qualified
4 well qualified
3 qualified
2 possibly qualified
1 no recommendations

Almost all schools accept a score of 4 or 5 for college credit; however, many schools also accept a score of 3, or in some cases 2 if combined with other requirements. Check with the college you plan to attend to find out what its policy is.

AP Exams generally are given in May, and grades are reported in July. You should discuss your plans in January with the college counselor or AP Coordinator at your school, who can supply you with registration materials. To prepare, besides taking the AP course itself, you can review a copy of the appropriate Course Description, available from your college counselor or AP Coordinator. There is a fee for each exam taken. Note that exams may be taken in the junior year if you are taking AP courses in that year.

Generally, grades are reported in July to you, to your school, and to a college that you have authorized. You may have a transcript of grades sent to an additional college after the exam, for a fee.

More detailed information about the AP Program and AP Exams may be found in the AP Program Bulletin for Students and Parents.

On the following pages you will find sample test items similar to those you would find on some of the most commonly taken AP Exams: English Language and Composition, English Literature and Composition, Calculus AB and BC, United States History, Biology, and Chemistry.

Advanced Placement Exam Subjects

Art	English	International English Language
History of Art	Language and Composition	Latin
Studio Art	Literature and Composition	Vergil
Biology	Environmental Science	Latin Literature
Calculus	French	Music Theory
Calculus AB	Language	Physics
Calculus BC	Literature	Physics B
Chemistry	German Language	Physics C (Mechanics)
Computer Science	Government and Politics	Physics C (Electricity and Magnetism)
Computer Science A	Comparative Government and Politics	Psychology
Computer Science AB	United States Government and Politics	Spanish
Economics	History	Language
Macroeconomics	European	Literature
Microeconomics	United States	Statistics

English Language and Composition

Ordinarily, this 3-hour exam consists of two parts: 60 minutes for multiple-choice questions that test the student's skills in analyzing the rhetoric of prose passages and 120 minutes for essay questions calling for student compositions in a variety of rhetorical modes. The essay questions count for 55 percent of your score, the multiple-choice questions for 45 percent.

Here are some multiple-choice test items similar to those you might find in an actual AP Exam:

Directions: Read prose passage carefully and answer the accompanying questions.

The first group of questions is based on the following passage.

From *The Interpretation of Dreams*
Sigmund Freud (1856-1939)

It is a proverbial fact that dreams melt away in the morning. They can, of course, be remembered; for we only know dreams from our memory of them after we are awake. But we very often have a feeling that we
5 have only remembered a dream in part and that there was more of it during the night; we can observe, too, how recollection of a dream, which was still lively in the morning, will melt away, except for a few small frag-ments, in the course of the day; we often know we have
10 dreamt, without knowing *what* we have dreamt; and we are so familiar with the fact of dreams being liable to be forgotten, that we see no absurdity in the possibility of someone having had a dream in the night and of his not being aware in the morning either of what he has
15 dreamt or even of the fact that he has dreamt at all. On the other hand, it sometimes happens that dreams show an extraordinary persistence in the memory. I have analyzed dreams in my patients which occurred twenty-five or more years earlier; and I can remember a
20 dream of my own separated by at least thirty-seven years from today and yet as fresh as ever in my memo-ry. All of this is very remarkable and not immediately intelligible.

This passage can best be defined as

(A) narration
(B) exposition
(C) description
(D) argumentation
(E) didacticism

Choice (B), exposition, is correct. Exposition is a form of writing in which the author attempts to explain a subject. Other forms of writing may enter into exposition. For example, a writer may describe a person, a setting, or an event to illustrate a point of view. In this passage, description, as well as narration and argumentation are subdued—the overall approach being to communicate information. A didactic writer projects his or her opinion in a preachy or moralizing tone, often to the extent that style overshadows sub-ject matter. This is clearly not evident here.

The word "melt" in line 8 is used

(A) ironically
(B) literally
(C) metaphorically
(D) symbolically
(E) pedantically

Choice (C), metaphorically, is correct. A metaphor is an implied compari-son between two dissimilar objects. Here, the author implies a comparison between the dwindling recollection (or melting) of dreams and a solid, but transient, object (like a chunk of ice) that diminishes "except for a few small fragments, in the course of the day."

The subject of the verb "will melt" in lines 7-8 is

(A) we
(B) recollection
(C) dream
(D) lively
(E) morning

The correct choice is (B), recollection. Choice (A), we, is the subject of the entire independent clause between the two semicolons and has "can observe" as its verb. Choice (C), dream, may appear at first to be a good candidate, but dream is the object of a preposition, which makes it ineligi-ble to be a subject. Choice (D), lively, is an adjective (despite the -ly suffix that makes it seem to be an adverb) and so cannot be a subject. Choice (E), morning, like dream, is the object of a preposition.

The last sentence of the passage implies that the writer

(A) is more impressed with his own dreams than with the dreams of others
(B) finds the concept of dreams extremely confusing
(C) would like to encourage the readers to suggest their opinions on the subject of dreams
(D) is going to present a more detailed explanation in the pages that follow
(E) is extremely proud of the fact that he is able to recall a thirty-seven-year-old dream

The correct choice is (D), is going to present a more detailed explanation in the pages that follow. By referring to the remarkable nature of dream recall and saying that this phenomenon is not immediately intelligible, he suggests that it will become intelligible as one reads on. The writer is obvi-ously knowledgeable in his subject, eliminating choice (B). He refers to his own and his patients' recollections of dreams to illustrate the longevity of certain dreams, thus eliminating choices (A) and (E). There is no sugges-tion that the author seeks to elicit the dreams of his readers (C).

A person is most likely to remember a dream

(A) during the night
(B) after many years
(C) during the course of a day
(D) immediately on awakening
(E) after it is analyzed

The correct choice is (D), immediately on awakening. The author says in lines 7-9, "the recollection of a dream, which was still lively in the morning, will melt away . . . in the course of the day." Although he speaks of dreams that show "an extraordinary persistence in the memory" (lines 16-17), these are suggested as being exceptional.

The author refers to his own dream to illustrate a kind of

(A) partiality
(B) selfishness
(C) arrogance
(D) irony
(E) sophistication

The correct answer is (D), irony. After establishing the ephemeral nature of dreams, he introduces the seemingly contradictory nature of a personal dream that has not faded in nearly four decades. His purpose is not to sep-arate his experience from those of others, but to use his experience to sug-gest the remarkable potential for the occasional longevity of dreams.

According to this passage, most people, on hearing that someone is unable to recall a dream, would probably

(A) tend to think the person was hiding the truth
(B) try to help the person remember his/her dream
(C) be unable to understand the problem
(D) empathize through personal experience
(E) consider the person to be ignorant

The correct answer is (D), empathize through personal experience. The author suggests in lines 10-15 that we would empathize with this common experience: ". . . and we are so familiar with the fact of dreams being liable to be forgotten, that we see no absurdity in the possibility of someone hav-ing had a dream in the night and of his not being aware in the morning either of what he has dreamt or even of the fact that he has dreamt at all."

English Literature and Composition

Ordinarily, this 3-hour exam consists of two parts: 60 minutes for multiple-choice questions that test the student's critical reading of selected passages and 120 minutes for essay questions that test the student's ability to read and interpret literature and to use other forms of discourse effectively. The essay questions count for 55 percent of your score, the multiple-choice questions for 45 percent.

Here are some multiple-choice test items similar to those you might find in an actual AP Exam:

Directions: Read each poem or prose passage carefully and answer the accompanying questions.

The next group of questions refers to the following poem.

"The River of Life"
Thomas Campbell (1774-1844)

The more we live, more brief appear
    Our life's succeeding stages:
A day to childhood seems a year,
    And years like passing ages.

The gladsome current of our youth,
    Ere passion yet disorders,
Steals lingering like a river smooth
    Along its grassy borders.

But as the care-worn cheeks grow wan,
    And sorrow's shafts fly thicker,
Ye stars, that measure life to man,
    Why seem your courses quicker?

When joys have lost their bloom and breath
    And life itself is vapid,
Why, as we reach the Falls of Death,
    Feel we its tide more rapid?

It may be strange—yet who would change
    Time's course to slower speeding,
When one by one our friends have gone
    And left our bosoms bleeding?

Heaven gives our years of fading strength
    Indemnifying fleetness;
And those of youth, a seeming length,
    Proportion'd to their sweetness.

"The River of Life" should be classified as a(n)

(A) sonnet
(B) elegy
(C) lyric
(D) ballad
(E) epic

The correct choice is (C) lyric. A lyric poem is a reflective work with a regular rhyme scheme and meter. It reveals poet's feeling about a subject. A sonnet is a 14-line poem, an elegy is a poem of lamentation, a ballad tells a story in verse, and an epic is along narrative poem that gives an account of a hero or heroine.

"Sorrow's shafts" (stanza three, line 2) is a metaphor for

(A) old age
(B) death
(C) river
(D) pain
(E) life

Choice (D) pain is correct. The line "And sorrow's shafts fly thicker" refers to the pain of sorrow. this pain is metaphorically compared to the pain inflicted by a "shaft," or spear.

The last two lines in the third stanza exemplify the technique of

(A) hyperbole
(B) irony
(C) synecdoche
(D) metonymy
(E) apostrophe

The correct choice is (E) apostrophe. An apostrophe is a direct address (usually as a digression) to someone not present, or to a personified object or idea. In this poem, Campbell digresses briefly to speak directly to "Ye stars." The remaining choices name other literary techniques: hyperbole uses exaggeration for emphasis, irony offers a contrast between actual and suggested meaning, synecdoche uses a part to represent an entire object or idea, and metonymy substitutes a related work for an entire object or idea.

The poem shifts its focus to the seemingly more rapid passages of time in stanza

(A) two
(B) three
(C) four
(D) five
(E) six

The correct choice is (B) three. After a brief mention of the overall theme, the first two stanzas dwell on the apparent slowness of time in our youth. Stanza three shifts the focus with the signal word "But" and focuses entirely on elderly people's perception of time. It is they whose "courses [seem] quicker."

This poem is about each of the following EXCEPT

(A) bereavement
(B) reflection
(C) acceptance
(D) repression
(E) changes

The correct choice is (D) repression. The poet neither represses his feelings nor alludes to repression. Bereavement is suggested in stanza five, lines 3 and 4; reflection is exhibited as the poet thinks back to the days of his youth. (In a larger sense, this is a poem of reflection.) The poet shows total acceptance of the apparent changes in the flow of time as one grows older.

The theme of this poem is that the passage of time

(A) is fair only to the young
(B) is unfair to everyone
(C) is more fair as we grow older
(D) is unfair to the old
(E) is fair to people of all ages

The correct choice is (E) is fair to people of all ages. The poet speaks of time moving slowly—"lingering like a river smooth" etc. when we are young, and moving quickly as we grow older—"its tide more rapid" etc. The poem suggests throughout that this is as it should be. The theme of fairness in time's varying rate of movement is summarized in the final stanza.

"The River of Life" can be classified as a poem in the style of

(A) the Romantic movement
(B) the modernist movement
(C) the transcendentalists
(D) the Elizabethans
(E) the Cavaliers

While all of the five groups of poets frequently wrote lyric poetry, it is fairly easy to eliminate the modernists (B), the Elizabethans (D), and the Cavaliers (E), since the language and diction is not modern and does not reflect the 16th or 17th centuries. The dates for Thomas Campbell—a poet vastly popular in his time whose reputation has declined considerably since—suggest either the early Romantic movement or the very early transcendentalist movements. If you recall that Campbell was a Scot, you will know the correct choice is (A), since all the transcendentalists were Americans. Another way to eliminate choice (C) is to recall that most transcendental poetry was heavily influenced by Buddhism and Hinduism, whose central ideas are contrary to the central idea of "The River of Life."

Let's Get Together

When a book, story, or play has been assigned in English class, get together with a study partner or two and discuss it. If the discussion goes well, pick another work by the same author and make another book club date. If the work was made into a film, rent it and view the film together, discussing it afterward.

The next group of questions refers to the following passage.

From "The Coketown Population," *Hard Times*
Charles Dickens (1812-1870)

It was a town of red brick, or of brick that would have
been red if the smoke and ashes had allowed it; but as
matters stood it was a town of unnatural red and black
like the painted face of a savage. It was a town of
5 machinery and tall chimneys, out of which interminable
serpents of smoke trailed themselves forever and ever,
and never got uncoiled. It had a black canal in it, and a
river that ran purple with ill-smelling dye, and vast piles
of buildings full of windows where there was a rattling
10 and a trembling all day long, and where the piston of
the steam-engine worked monotonously up and down
like the head of an elephant in a state of melancholy
madness. It contained several large streets all very like
one another, and many small streets still more like one
15 another, inhabited by people equally like one another,
who all went in and out at the same hours, with the
same sound upon the same pavements, to do the same
work, and to whom every day was the same as yester-
day and tomorrow, and every year the counterpart of
the last and the next. . .
20   You saw nothing in Coketown but what was severely
workful. If the members of a religious persuasion built
a chapel there—as the members of eighteen religious
persuasions had done—they made it a pious warehouse
of red brick, with sometimes (but this is only in highly
25 ornamental examples) a bell in a birdcage on the top of
it. The solitary exception was the New Church; a stuc-
coed edifice with a square steeple over the door, termi-
nating in four short pinnacles like florid wooden legs.
All the public inscriptions in the town were painted
30 alike, in severe characters of black and white. The jail
might have been the infirmary, the infirmary might
have been the jail, the townhall might have been either,
or both, or anything else, for anything that appeared to
the contrary in the graces of their construction.

The style of writing employed in this selection is an example of

(A) humanism
(B) naturalism
(C) impressionism
(D) romanticism
(E) transcendentalism

Choice (B) naturalism is correct. Naturalism is often used synonymously with realism, depicting life as the author sees it. However, naturalism tends to focus on the negative, even repulsive, aspects of reality. Humanism takes an optimistic view of human potential; impressionism emphasizes immediate aspects of life without careful examination; romanticism depicts idealized characters and events; and transcendentalism is a more philosophical form of romanticism.

"It was a town of machinery and tall chimneys, out of which interminable serpents of smoke trailed themselves forever and ever, and never got uncoiled." This sentence (lines 4-7) means each of the following EXCEPT

(A) the town was being strangled by the effects of industrialization
(B) the town was taking on a monstrous appearance
(C) the town was reverting to primitive customs
(D) the town's plight appeared endless
(E) smoke from the chimneys reminded one of coiled serpents

The correct choice is (C), the town was reverting to primitive customs. The Industrial Revolution, with all its negative manifestations, still represented the most advanced technology of the time.

The description of "the piston of the steam-engine" (lines 10–12) is an example of

(A) paradox
(B) metaphor
(C) irony
(D) simile
(E) personification

The correct answer is (D), simile. Simile is a comparison between two unlike objects, using the word "like" or "as" as part of the comparison. A metaphor makes a similar comparison without using the word "like" or "as"; both irony and paradox suggest contradictions. Personification, choice (E), appears attractive, but this figurative device gives human qualities to object, animals, ideas, or natural occurrences. Furthermore, it attributes these qualities directly, without employing "like" or "as."

CHARLES DICKENS

Calculus AB and BC

There are two different AP Exams in calculus. Each exam lasts 3 hours and 15 minutes and consists of 105 minutes of multiple-choice questions and 90 minutes of free-response questions.

Calculus AB covers differential and integral calculus topics that one typically might find in an introductory Calculus I college course. Calculus BC covers the Calculus AB topics, in addition to topics in differential and integral calculus and series; combined, these topics are ones that typically might be included in a two-semester sequence of college courses (Calculus I and II). Both the Calculus AB and Calculus BC exams require the use of a graphing calculator.

Following are some test items similar to those you might find in an actual AP Exam. Items that would be included only in the Calculus BC examination are marked **[BC]**.

Multiple-choice examples
Choose the correct answer.

$$\int_1^3 x^{-2}\, dx =$$

(A) $-\dfrac{4}{3}$ (B) $\dfrac{4}{3}$ (C) $-\dfrac{2}{3}$ (D) $\dfrac{2}{3}$ (E) $\dfrac{1}{6}$

This item asks for the value of a <u>definite integral</u>. For a function $f(x)$—in this case $f(x) = x^{-2}$—the definite integral can be found by first finding the <u>antiderivative</u> of $f(x)$, usually indicated by $F(x)$—in this case, $F(x) = -x^{-1} + C = \frac{-1}{x} + C$. The constant C for the antiderivative drops out when evaluating a definite integral. The formula for a definite integral is

$$\int_a^b f(x)\, dx = F(x)\Big|_a^b = F(b) - F(a)$$

Then, for $F(x)\qquad = \dfrac{-1}{x}$

$$\dfrac{-1}{x}\Big|_a^b = \dfrac{-1}{3} - \left(\dfrac{-1}{1}\right) = -\dfrac{1}{3} + 1 = \dfrac{2}{3}$$

The correct choice is (D).

$$\int_1^7 \dfrac{1}{x+1}\, dx =$$

(A) $\ln 8$ (B) $\ln 2$ (C) $2\ln 2$ (D) $3\ln 2$ (E) $\ln 6$

Again the problem is to evaluate a definite integral. You need to remember the correct antiderivative for $\frac{1}{x+1}$

$$\int_1^7 \dfrac{1}{x+1}\, dx = \ln [x+1]\,\Big|_1^7$$

There are a number of formulas for derivatives and antiderivatives in calculus. You need to memorize the basic ones for this test. You will not be given formulas on the test.

$$\ln [7+1] - \ln [1+1] = \ln 8 - \ln 2$$

While this answer is correct, it is not one of the choices given. Note that $\ln 8$ is the same as $\ln 2^3 = 3 \ln 2$.

$$3\ln 2 - \ln 2 = 2\ln 2$$

The correct choice is (C).

 **Try an Encyclopedia**

If you are having trouble reading the textbook or simply want to know more about a topic, look it up in an encyclopedia. Chances are good that you will find a short and complete explanation of your subject, along with references to related encyclopedia articles that will give you additional insights.

If $y = \dfrac{2}{x^3 - 3}$, then $\dfrac{dy}{dx} =$

(A) $\dfrac{2}{(x^3-3)^2}$ (B) $\dfrac{-6x^2}{(x^3-3)^2}$ (C) $\dfrac{6x^2}{(x^3-3)^2}$

(D) $-6x^2$ (E) 0

You need to remember the rule for the derivative of a quotient. If the quotient is $\frac{u}{v}$, the numerator of the derivative is the difference of the expression in the denominator times the derivative of the numerator minus the expression in the numerator times the derivative of the denominator, or $v \cdot \frac{du}{dx} - u \cdot \frac{dv}{dx}$, while the denominator is the square of the denominator, or v^2. Thus, when $u = 2$ and $v = x^3 - 3$, then $\dfrac{dy}{dx} = \dfrac{(x^3-3)(0) - 2(3x^2)}{(x^3-3)^2}$, or $\dfrac{-6x^2}{(x^3-3)^2}$. The correct choice is (B).

If $f(x) = (3x+2)^3$, then the third derivative of $f(x)$ at $x = 1$ is

(A) 18 (B) 0 (C) 270 (D) 162 (E) 54

To find the third derivative, you need to find the derivative of the function, which will be another function, generally designated as $f'(x)$. Then find the derivative of that function, $f''(x)$, which is called the second derivative. The third derivative, $f'''(x)$, is the derivative of the second derivative.
$$f'(x) = 3(3x+2)^2(3) = 9(3x+2)^2$$
$$f''(x) = 18(3x+2)^1(3) = 54(3x+2)$$
$$f'''(x) = 54(3x+2)^0(3) = 162$$
Notice that the third derivative is a constant. The qualification "at $x = 1$" was not needed for the correct choice, (D), but was inserted so that various incorrect choices could be evaluated.

Note that you should expect the nth derivative of a polynomial function of degree n to be a constant. In this item, you would still have to take the three derivatives to determine which constant, but knowing that the answer should be a constant might help to avoid some of the possible incorrect choices.

If $\dfrac{dy}{dx} = \sin 3x$, then $y =$

(A) $3\cos 3x + C$ (B) $\cos 3x + C$ (C) $\dfrac{1}{3}\sin 3x$
(D) $\dfrac{1}{3}\cos 3x$ (E) $-\dfrac{1}{3}\cos 3x + C$

For this item you are given the derivative and asked to find the antiderivative, which is essentially the same as the indefinite integral. It is easy to eliminate choices (C) and (D), since they do not have a constant of integration. All indefinite integrals have such a constant. Now take the derivatives of the other three choices to see which one works. To select among the three remaining choices, begin by noticing that $u = 3x$ is a function of x and $\cos 3x$ is a function of u. In other words, the chain rule applies:

$$\dfrac{dy}{dx} = \dfrac{dy}{du}\dfrac{du}{dx}$$

so $\frac{d}{dx}\cos 3x = -3\sin 3x$. The factor for $\cos 3x$ varies in the three choices from 3 to $\frac{1}{3}$ to $-\frac{1}{3}$. If you look at the three as multiplied by $-3\sin x$, the only one that gives you $\sin 3x$ by itself is $-\frac{1}{3}$. Therefore, the correct choice is (E), since $-\frac{1}{3}(-3\sin 3x) = \sin 3x$. In other words, $\frac{d}{dx}(-\frac{1}{3}\cos 3x + C) = \sin 3x$.

$$\lim_{x\to\infty} \dfrac{2x^3}{100\,x - x^3} =$$

(A) 0 (B) -2 (C) $-\infty$ (D) 2 (E) ∞

One usually finds limits of complicated expressions by using various tricks that have been developed over the years. For the limit of a rational expression, the trick is to divide both the numerator and the denominator by the highest power of the variable—in this case, by x^3. The result is that you can find the limit for an equivalent expression that is much easier to find than the limit for the original expression:

$$\lim_{x\to\infty} \dfrac{2}{100/x^2 - 1} = \dfrac{2}{-1} = -2$$

The correct choice is (B).

If $x^3 + xy + y^2 = 0$, then in terms of x and y, $\dfrac{dy}{dx} =$

(A) $\dfrac{-3x^2 + y}{x + 2y}$ (B) $\dfrac{-3x^2 - y}{3}$ (C) $\dfrac{3x^2 + y}{3}$

(D) $\dfrac{x + 2y}{3x^2 + y}$ (E) $\dfrac{-3x^2 - y}{x + 2y}$

Since you are given an equation that is in terms of both x and y instead of a function of x, implicit differentiation is involved. Instead of solving for y, which is difficult because of the presence of both the xy and the y^2 terms, differentiate the given equation with regard to x. In this case, keep in mind that xy is a product and follows that rule, while y^2 has the basic form u^n. The first form of the derivative is

$$3x^2 + x \cdot \tfrac{dy}{dx} + y(1) + 2y \cdot \tfrac{dy}{dx} = 0, \text{ or}$$
$$x \cdot \tfrac{dy}{dx} + 2y \cdot \tfrac{dy}{dx} = -3x^2 - y$$
$$(x + 2y)\tfrac{dy}{dx} = -3x^2 - y$$
$$\tfrac{dy}{dx} = \tfrac{-3x^2 + y}{x + 2y}$$

The correct choice is (A).

$\displaystyle\int_0^1 (e^x + e^{-x})\,dx =$

(A) 0 (B) $\dfrac{e^2 + 1}{e}$ (C) $\dfrac{e^2 - 1}{e}$ (D) $\dfrac{1}{e^2}$ (E) 1

To begin with, you need to know that the derivative of e^x is the same function, e^x, but if u is some function of x, then the derivative with respect to x of e^u is

$$y' = \tfrac{du}{dx}$$

Applying this rule to the definite integral gives

$$\int_0^1 (e^x + e^{-x})\,dx = [e^x - e^{-x}]\Big|_0^1, \text{ so } F(b) - F(a) \text{ is}$$
$$\left(e^1 - \tfrac{1}{e^1}\right) - \left(e^0 - \tfrac{1}{e^0}\right) = \tfrac{e^2 - 1}{e} - (1 - 1) = \tfrac{e^2 - 1}{e}$$

The correct choice is (C).

[BC] Describe the curve given by the parametric equations

$$x = 2 \cos t, y = 3 \sin t$$

(A) a circle centered at the origin with the radius 6
(B) an ellipse centered at the origin with a major axis of 6 and a minor axis of 4
(C) a hyperbola centered at the origin with vertices at $(-3, 0)$ and $(0, 3)$
(D) a parabola with a vertex at the origin
(E) a sinusoidal curve with a period of 2π and an amplitude of 3

You can eliminate some possibilities by plotting the easiest points, the points for which $t = 0$ and $t = \tfrac{\pi}{2}$. For $t = 0$, $(x, y) = (2, 0)$; while for $t = \tfrac{\pi}{2}$, $(x, y) = (0, 3)$. This eliminates choice (A) because a circle centered at the origin could not go through both $(2, 0)$ and $(0, 3)$. Choice (D) is also eliminated on the same grounds. The other choices, however, could conceivably include the two points. By finding other points, you could continue to narrow the choices down until you had just one. There is a better strategy, however.

In general, to find the graph of parametric equations without plotting a lot of points, find the Cartesian or rectangular equation that has the same graph. Often this will be an easily recognized equation in Cartesian coordinates.

When parametric equations include both the sine and cosine, it generally helps to start with the trigonometric identity.

$$\sin^2 t + \cos^2 t = 1$$

The given parametric equation can be rewritten as

$$\cos t = \tfrac{x}{2}, \sin t = \tfrac{y}{3}$$

When you substitute these values into the trigonometric identity, you get

$$\tfrac{x^2}{2^2} + \tfrac{y^2}{3^2} = 1$$

This should be immediately recognizable as the equation of an ellipse centered at the origin with vertices at $(2,0)$, $(-2,0)$, $(0,3)$, and $(0,-3)$. Note that two of these points are the ones found earlier by looking at easily calculated values of the parametric equations. Since this ellipse also has a major axis of 6 and a minor axis of 4, the correct choice is (B).

If $y = 2 \sin x \cos x$, then $dy/dx =$

(A) $2 \sec^2 x$ (B) $2 \cos x$ (C) $2 \cos 2x$ (D) $\cos 2x$ (E) 1

There are two ways to approach this problem. The easier way depends on recognizing that $2 \sin x \cos x$ is one side of the trigonometric identity for the sine of a double angle: $\sin 2x = 2 \sin x \cos x$. Thus, instead of differentiating the product $2 \sin x \cos x$, you can differentiate the easier composite function $\sin 2x$.

$$y = \sin 2x$$
$$dy/dx = \cos 2x(2) = 2 \cos 2x,$$

so the correct choice is (C).

If you fail to recognize the double-angle formula, you can use the rule for differentiating a product.

$$y = 2(\sin x \cos x)$$
$$dy/dx = 2[\sin x \,(-\sin x) + \cos x \cos x]$$
$$= 2(\cos^2 x - \sin^2 x)$$

This is correct, but the answer in this form is not shown among the choices. You *still* have to remember a double-angle formula from trigonometry:

$$\cos 2x = \cos^2 x - \sin^2 x$$

Therefore, $dy/dx = 2 \cos 2x$, choice (C).

If $f(x) = x^2 - 2x^3$ is defined for all real numbers x, then if there is a relative maximum of the function, it is at $x =$

(A) 0 (B) $-\dfrac{1}{3}$ (C) $\dfrac{1}{6}$ (D) $\dfrac{1}{3}$
(E) there is no relative maximum

A relative maximum occurs in a region where a graph that has been increasing reaches its local high point and begins to descend. At the top of its path, so long as the path is continuous and smooth, the slope (or first derivative) will be 0. A slope can also be 0, however, at a point of inflection, where the graph levels off and then continues rising or falling, whichever way it is moving before the point of inflection. Thus, there are two things to look for in solving this problem: (1) places where the derivative is 0 and (2) the change in sign of the derivative at those places. Finally, examine that second derivative to make sure that the apparent relative maximum is not a point of inflection.

First-derivative (f') test: $f'(x) = 2x - 6x^2$
Set f' equal to 0 and solve: $0 = 2x - 6x^2$
$$0 = 2x(1 - 3x)$$
$$0 = 2x \text{ or } 0 = 1 - 3x$$
$$x = 0 \text{ or } x = \tfrac{1}{3}$$

Number-line test:
The function f' changes sign when $f' = 0$, so it separates the real number line into three intervals: the interval of the line to the left of 0, the interval between 0 and $\tfrac{1}{3}$, and the interval to the right of $\tfrac{1}{3}$. By examining the behavior of f' for sample values in those intervals, you can tell how the function behaves for the whole interval. You only need to know the sign of f' at the sample value, not the value itself. Easy values to compute would be for $f'(-1), f'(0.1)$, and $f'(1)$.

Second derivative (f'') test:
A point of inflection occurs when the second derivative changes sign, which for a smooth curve can happen only when the second derivative is 0. Find the second derivative. Set it equal to 0, and solve.
$$f''(x) = 2 - 12x$$
$$0 = 2 - 12x$$
$$12x = 2$$
$$x = \tfrac{1}{6}$$

The only point of inflection is where $x = \tfrac{1}{6}$.

Therefore, the correct choice is (D), $x = \tfrac{1}{3}$.

The area bounded by $y = x^3$ and $y = x$ on the domain $[0, 1]$ is

(A) $\dfrac{1}{2}$ (B) $\dfrac{1}{8}$ (C) $\dfrac{1}{16}$ (D) $\dfrac{1}{4}$ (E) $\dfrac{3}{4}$

The area under a single curve is the definite integral for the given domain, but this problem involves the area between two curves. If you designate the function for the upper curve as f_u and the function for the lower curve as f_l, then the area above the interval $[a, b]$ is

$$\int_a^b (f_u - f_l)\, dx$$

You may want to sketch the two graphs on the same grid to see which is the upper curve and which is the lower. Since the upper curve in this region is the graph of $y = x$, it its f_u in the definite integral.

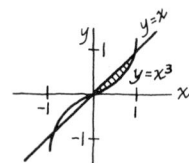

$$\int_0^1 (x - x^3)\, dx = \dfrac{x^2}{2} - \dfrac{x^4}{4}\,\Big|_0^1$$

$$= \left[\dfrac{1}{2} - \dfrac{1}{4}\right] = \dfrac{1}{4}$$

The correct choice is (D), $\frac{1}{4}$.

If $y = 2x^3 - x^2$, then the slope of the tangent line at the inflection point is

(A) $\dfrac{1}{3}$ (B) $-\dfrac{1}{6}$ (C) $\dfrac{1}{6}$ (D) $-\dfrac{1}{3}$ (E) 0

The second derivative is 0 at points of inflection, while the first derivative gives the slope of the curve at any point. Therefore, first find the second derivative and then find the value that makes it equal to 0. Use that value and the first derivative to find the slope.

$$y = 2x^3 - x^2$$
$$y' = 6x^2 - 2x$$
$$y'' = 12x - 2$$

Set y'' equal to 0.

$$12x - 2 = 0$$
$$12x = 2$$
$$x = \tfrac{1}{6}$$

Now evaluate y' for $x = \tfrac{1}{6}$.

$$y' = 6x^2 - 2x$$
$$y' = 6(\tfrac{1}{6})^2 - 2(\tfrac{1}{6})$$
$$= \tfrac{1}{6} - \tfrac{2}{6}$$
$$= -\tfrac{1}{6}$$

The correct choice is (B).

[BC] Find the interval of convergence of the series

$$\sum_{n=1}^{\infty} \dfrac{x^n}{n}$$

(A) $-1 \le x < 1$ (B) $x \le -1 \text{ or } x \ge 1$
(C) $-1 \le x \le 1$ (D) $-1 < x < 1$ (E) $-1 < x \le 1$

First of all you should recognize that x^n/n is a power series. A power series either converges at 0 and diverges everywhere else (not one of the choices), converges absolutely everywhere (not one of the choices), or converges in an interval of the form $|x| < c$, where c is some real number, and possibly at c and $-c$ as well. This theorem about power series means that you can reject choice (B) immediately, since it is of the form $|x| \ge c$. (A), (C), (D), and (E) are all still possible. To choose among them, you need to check the series for $x = -1$ and $x = 1$. For $x = -1$, the series becomes

$$-1 + \tfrac{1}{2} - \tfrac{1}{3} + \tfrac{1}{4} - \ldots$$

or

$$-(1 - \tfrac{1}{2} + \tfrac{1}{3} - \tfrac{1}{4} + \ldots)$$

This is a well-known series that you should recognize as converging; or use Leibnitz's theorem to show that it converges. For $x = 1$, the series becomes

$$1 + \tfrac{1}{2} + \tfrac{1}{3} + \tfrac{1}{4} + \ldots$$

a series well-known as divergent. Therefore, the correct choice is (A), $-1 \le x < 1$.

[BC] A particle moves in two dimensions according to a path defined by the equations

$$x = 2 \cosh 3t \times y = 2 \sinh 3t$$

where t represents time. What is the acceleration of the particle at time t?

First note that the position of any particle at all times can be expressed by the vector

$$R = ix + jy$$

where i and j are the unit vectors for two dimensions. By substituting for x and y, one gets

$$R = i(2 \cosh 3t) + j(2 \sinh 3t).$$

Differentiating the position vector once with respect to time gives the velocity vector v.

$$v = i(6 \sinh 3t) + j(6 \cosh 3t)$$

Differentiating with respect to time again gives the acceleration.

$$a = i(18 \cosh 3t) + j(18 \sinh 3t)$$
$$= 9[i(2 \cosh 3t) + j(2 \sinh 3t)]$$
$$= 9R$$

Therefore the acceleration vector is nine times the position vector.

Free-response examples

Find the area bounded by the curve $y = x^3 - 5x^2 + 2x + 8$ and the lines $x = 1$, $x = 3$, and the x-axis.

This is a case in which a graph or a sketch of a graph is almost essential. To make the sketch, first evaluate $y = x^3 - 5x^2 + 2x + 8$ for $x = 1$ and $x = 3$.

$$1^3 - 5(1^2) + 2(1) + 8 = 1 - 5 + 2 + 8 = 6$$
$$3^3 - 5(3^2) + 2(3) + 8 = 27 - 45 + 6 + 8 = -4$$

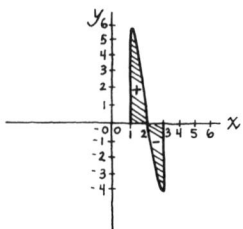

To find the intervals on which you should evaluate the definite integral, you need to know where the graph of $y = x^3 - 5x^2 + 2x + 8$ crosses the x-axis. Use your test-taking skills here. It is unlikely that the test maker would ask for a value here that is not an integer, and the only integer between 1 and 3 is 2. See whether 2 is a zero of $y = x^3 - 5x^2 + 2x + 8$.

$$2^3 - 5(2^2) + 2(2) + 8 = 8 - 20 + 4 + 8 = 0$$

It is, so the interval for the upper region is $[1, 2]$, and the interval for the lower region is $[2, 3]$. Note that the definite interval for a region below the x-axis will be negative. To get the total area of the figure described, you need to use the absolute value of the region below the axis. In other words, if you define

$$\int_1^2 (x^3 - 5x^2 + 2x + 8)\, dx = A_1$$

and

$$\int_2^3 (x^3 - 5x^2 + 2x + 8)\, dx = A_2$$

then

$$A_{total} = A_1 + |A_2|$$

With this in mind, you can proceed to compute the definite integrals, taking great care with the arithmetic, which involves fractions.

$$A_{total} = \tfrac{37}{12} + \left|-\tfrac{29}{12}\right| = \tfrac{66}{12} = \tfrac{11}{2}$$

Find the volume generated when the area bounded by $y = x^3$, $y = 8$, and $x = 0$ is rotated about the x-axis.

As in the last item, a sketch is helpful. First make a sketch of the indicated area.

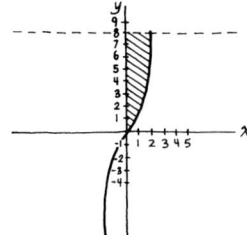

Now picture that figure rotated about the x-axis. Except for the origin, there will be a hole in the solid of revolution. This indicates that you will need to use the method of evaluating the volume that is variously called the "washer," "ring," or "shell" method. If R is the radius of the outside of the "washer" formed when a typical slice of the region is graphed and r is the radius of the hole, then

$$\pi \int (R^2 - r^2)\, dx$$

is the required volume, since the area of each entire washer is πR^2 and the area of each hole is πr^2. In this case $R = 8$ and $r = y = x^3$.

$$\pi \int_0^2 (8^2 - [x^3]^2)\, dx$$

$$\pi \int_0^2 (64 - x^6)\, dx = \left[64x - \frac{x^7}{7} \right]\Big|_0^2 \cdot \pi$$

$$= ([128 - \tfrac{128}{7}] - [0])(\pi)$$

$$= \left(\tfrac{896}{7} - \tfrac{128}{7} \right)\pi = \tfrac{768\pi}{7}$$

For the function $f(x) = 5 - 6x^2 - 2x^3$ defined on the interval $-3 \le x \le 1$, find (a) the maximum points; (b) the minimum points; (c) any points of inflection; (d) any intervals of upward concavity; then (e) graph the function over the given interval.

First, in both the first and second derivatives.

$$f(x) = 5 - 6x^2 - 2x^3$$
$$f'(x) = -12x - 6x^2$$
$$f''(x) = -12 - 12x$$

Then set each derivative equal to 0 to find the x coordinates of the maxima, minima, and points of inflection.

$$f'(x) = -12x - 6x^2 = 0$$
$$-6x(2 + x) = 0$$
$$-6x = 0 \ or \ 2 + x = 0$$
$$x = 0 \ or \ x = -2$$

This means that the tangent is horizontal at $x = 0$ and -2, but it does not tell you whether the points on the curve are maxima, minima, or points of inflection.

$$f''(x) = -12 - 12x = 0$$
$$-12x = 12$$
$$x = -1$$

This implies that the curve has a point of inflection at $x = -1$, and furthermore that the two points located by setting the first derivative equal to 0 must be either maxima or minima. Check the second derivative at each of the values for x. At $x = 0$, $-12 - 12x$ is negative, which implies that the point on the curve is a relative maximum. Similarly, at $x = -2$, $-12 - 12x$ is positive, so the point on the curve is a relative minimum.

These are not all the relative maxima and minima that must be identified, since relative maxima and minima also occur at the ends of the domain, that is at $x = -3$ and $x = 1$. You now have almost all the information needed to answer the five parts of the item. You still need to locate the actual points, not just the x values for the points. The easiest way to do this is to use synthetic division.

	-2	-6	0	5
-3	-2	0	0	5
-2	-2	-2	4	-3
-1	-2	-4	4	1
0	-2	-6	0	5
1	-2	-8	-8	-3

Finally, remember that the interval of upward concavity will be the region for which the second derivative is negative. Since the second derivative is

0 at $x = -1$ and negative at $x = 0$, it must be negative for all values of x to the right of -1.

Putting all this information together, you can answer:
(a) the maximum points are $(-3, 5)$ and $(0, 5)$
(b) the minimum points are $(-2, -3)$ and $(1, -3)$
(c) the point of inflection is $(-1, 1)$
(d) the graph is concave upward for $-3 < x < -1$
(e)

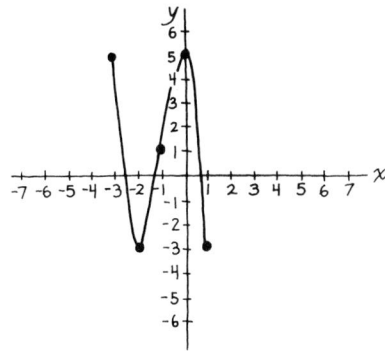

Given $f(x) = \dfrac{x^2}{x^2 - 1}$

(a) give the equation(s) of vertical asymptote(s)
(b) give the equation of the horizontal asymptote
(c) locate the relative maximum point or points
(d) sketch the graph

Note that this is a rational function (the ratio of two polynomials). Vertical asymptotes will occur when the function is undefined. For rational functions, this will occur when the denominator is 0. Solve $x^2 - 1 = 0$ to find when this will occur: $x = \pm 1$ is the solution to that equation, so the function will be undefined if $x = 1$ or -1.
(a) The equations of the vertical asymptotes are $x = 1$ and $x = -1$. For rational functions, horizontal asymptotes can be found by comparing the degrees of the polynomials and the ratio of the coefficients of the highest degree terms, but a more general rule is that the limit of a function as x goes to infinity, if such a limit exists, is a horizontal asymptote.

$$\lim_{x \to \infty} \frac{x^2}{x^2 - 1}$$

Often, a good way to find the limit of a rational function is to divide both numerator and denominator by the highest power of the denominator, which does not change the limit's value.

$$\lim_{x \to \infty} \frac{1}{1 - \dfrac{1}{x^2}} = 1$$

(b) The horizontal asymptote is $y = 1$. To find the relative maximum point(s), you usually find the value(s) for which the first derivative is 0. Then examine the second derivative. For rational functions in which you know the asymptotes, there is an easier way. The two vertical asymptotes separate the graph into three strips. Within each of these strips, the function will have the same sign. You can examine the values at suitable points in each of the three strips to find the sign of the function.

For $x < -1$, use -2: $f(-2) = \frac{(-2)^2}{(-2)^2 - 1} = \frac{4}{3}$, so the function is positive in this strip.

For $-1 < x < 1$, use 0: $f(0) = \frac{0^2}{0^2 - 1} = 0$, which does not tell what we need to know. Try some other number, such as $\frac{1}{2}$: $f(\frac{1}{2}) = \frac{(1/2)^2}{(1/2)^2 - 1} = -\frac{1}{3}$. Thus, the function is negative in the interval except for the point $(0, 0)$, which is a relative maximum.

For $x > 1$, use 2: $f(2) = \frac{2^2}{2^2 - 1} = \frac{4}{3}$, so the function is positive in this interval.
(c) The three tests above imply that the only relative maximum is at the origin. This is made clearer when you sketch the graph.

To sketch the graph, return to the behavior of the function in the three strips defined by the vertical asymptotes. In the left-most strip, there are two asymptotes—one vertical and one horizontal—that the graph must approach, and the graph is all above the x-axis (which implies in this case that it is above the horizontal asymptote at $y = 1$). The same is true of the right-most strip. The only places that the graph can go is to approach each asymptote "at infinity."

Meanwhile, between the vertical asymptotes, the graph is entirely negative except for its relative maximum at $(0, 0)$. This part of the graph must also approach both asymptotes, approaching each asymptote at "negative infinity."

United States History

This exam consists of two parts: 55 minutes of multiple-choice questions testing students' factual knowledge, breadth of preparation, and knowledge-based analytical skills; and 130 minutes of free-response questions allowing students to demonstrate their mastery of historical interpretation and their ability to express their views and knowledge in writing, by responding to a document-based essay question (DBQ) and two standard essay questions. The multiple-choice and free-response sections of the exam each account for half of the student's score.

Here are some multiple-choice test items similar to those you might find in an actual AP Exam:

Directions: Each of the questions or incomplete statements below is followed by five suggested answers or completions. Select the one that is best in each case.

The Harding administration is, unfortunately, known best for the Teapot Dome scandal. The Teapot Dome was

- (A) the cover of a teapot into which bribe money was placed
- (B) a derogatory reference to the well-bred Eastern Republicans who uncovered the scandal
- (C) a reference to the Capitol's dome, under which lobbyists were able to influence the Congress
- (D) an oil reserve in Wyoming leased to an oil company in return for payments to the secretary of the Interior
- (E) the old symbol of the Republican Party

Even if you don't know the answer, you can come close to it by eliminating incorrect choices. Choice (B) is unlikely since Harding was a Republican and members of a party, wherever they are from, are usually not eager to publicize their own wrongdoing. Choice (C) can be ruled out, since lobbyists have influenced legislators since long before and long after Harding's time. Also, congressional scandals do not attach themselves to the executive branch. Choice (E) is a bit of nonsense thrown in for the fun of it; the elephant has long been the party's symbol. Choices (A) and (D) are harder to deal with. In all likelihood, if bribe money had been left in a teapot, it would be called the Teapot scandal, not the Teapot Dome scandal. The correct choice is (D). It was the lease of this Wyoming oil reserve that blew the lid off everything.

President Tyler is best remembered for

- (A) the admission of Texas as a state
- (B) the beginning of the Civil War
- (C) changing from one political party to another
- (D) saying "I would rather be right than be President"
- (E) the end of slavery

Remembering that President Tyler was in office before the Civil War eliminates choices (B) and (E). Choice (C) is tricky. Tyler did change parties while in office but it is not what he is best remembered for. As for choice (D), it was Henry Clay who said this and he never did become President. During the years before the Civil War, a number of states joined the Union, and Tyler pushed strongly for the admission of Texas. Thus, the correct choice is (A).

As a result of World War II, the United States remained as an occupying power in which European country until 1990?

- (A) Poland
- (B) England
- (C) Albania
- (D) Italy
- (E) Germany

Choices (A), (B), and (C) were not enemy states, and one does not occupy the "good guys." Italy, choice (D), actually fought on the Allied side in the end and thus escaped any occupation. The correct choice is (E). Until the reunification of Germany in 1990 with the approval of the four World War II Allies (U.S., France, England, and the Soviet Union), the United States, along with England, France, and the Soviet Union, occupied the wartime German capital of Berlin.

The triangular building shown in the photograph is

- (A) an example of typical work by Frank Lloyd Wright
- (B) an early example of a skyscraper
- (C) a Tudor-revival building from the early 20th century
- (D) an innovative building by I.M. Pei
- (E) an 18th-century building preserved in a city setting

The Flatiron Building, shown in the photograph, is a well-known early skyscraper in New York, so the correct choice is (B). Although Frank Lloyd Wright, choice (A), designed a skyscraper that was never built, his typical work includes many private homes and several public buildings using patterned concrete or cantilevered sections. Tudor-revival, choice (C), is marked by a combination of wood and stucco or rock that is called half-timbered and is generally used for private residences. I.M. Pei, choice (D), is noted for his use of glass-wall construction; a typical skyscraper of his design would be the John Hancock Tower in Boston, which is covered with reflective glass. Since it is apparent that this building has more than ten stories, it could not be an 18th-century building, choice (E). Buildings with ten or more floors were not put up until after the invention of safe elevators in 1852, half a century after the end of the 18th century.

All of the following states gained at least part of their territory as a result of the Louisiana Purchase EXCEPT

- (A) Montana
- (B) Iowa
- (C) Mississippi
- (D) Missouri
- (E) Arkansas

The key to answering this question is to remember that the Mississippi River formed the western border of the United States prior to the Louisiana Purchase. The correct answer is, therefore, (C). The state of Mississippi is east of the river.

The Great Plains is also knows as America's

- (A) Vacationland
- (B) Milkbucket
- (C) Breadbasket
- (D) Sunbelt
- (E) Hunter's Paradise

The key to answering this question is knowing that the main industry in this area of North America is agriculture. The main crops of the Great Plains are wheat, corn, and soybeans. From the first of these comes the nickname shown in choice (C), the correct choice. As for the other choices, (A) is found on Maine's automobile license plates; (B) seemed to be a good foil to breadbasket; (D) refers to the economically growing Southern tier of states; and (E) may have been true once, but the vast bison herds are long gone.

Biology

This 3-hour exam consists of two parts: 90 minutes of multiple-choice questions covering topics found in a typical full-year introductory college biology course with laboratory; and 90 minutes for four required essay questions on broader topics, including molecules and cells; heredity and evolution; and organisms and populations.

Here are some multiple-choice test items similar to those you might find in an actual AP Exam:

Directions: Each of the questions or incomplete statements in this section is followed by five suggested answers or completions. Select the ONE that is BEST in each case.

A polypeptide chain is likely to form which of the following organic molecules?

(A) monosaccharide
(B) disaccharide
(C) polysaccharide
(D) protein
(E) nucleic acid

Choice (D) is correct. Polypeptides are chains of amino acids joined together. A chain of approximately 75 amino acids or more constitutes a protein. Monosaccharides, disaccharides, and polysaccharides are carbohydrates. Nucleic acids are polymers of nucleotide chains.

Which blood vessel is likely to carry blood with the highest proportion of deoxygenated hemoglobin?

(A) right pulmonary vein
(B) left pulmonary vein
(C) aorta
(D) inferior vena cava
(E) internal carotid artery

Choice (D) is correct. The inferior vena cava leads to the heart, transporting blood that has already delivered oxygen to cells in the lower portion of the body, so the blood is substantially deoxygenated. The pulmonary veins are rich in oxygenated blood because they enter the heart directly from the lungs. Both the aorta and the internal carotid, the artery that leads to the brain, contain a high proportion of oxygenated blood.

All chordates are characterized by

(A) a ventral nerve cord and embryological gill slits
(B) a bony vertebral column and closed circulatory system
(C) an endoskeleton made of bone and cartilage
(D) internal fertilization and development within the placenta
(E) a dorsal nerve cord and embryological gill slits

Choice (E) is correct. Chordates have a dorsal rather than ventral nerve cord, making choice (A) incorrect. Although all vertebrates are chordates, there are some invertebrate chordates that lack a vertebral column and bony skeleton, so choices (B) and (C) are incorrect. Only vertebrate mammals have the characteristics described in choice (D).

Which process is most likely to be important during an immune response to disease?

(A) phagocytosis
(B) erythroblastosis
(C) transduction
(D) oogenesis
(E) photophosphorylation

Choice (A) correctly identifies the process of white blood cells engulfing bacteria. Choice (B) is the attack of Rh negative cells on Rh positive cells. Choice (C) is the transfer of DNA. Choice (D) is the formation of egg cells, and choice (E) is ATP production that uses energy.

The two organelles most associated with the energy needs of a cell are

(A) chloroplasts and mitochondria
(B) Golgi apparatus and vacuoles
(C) endoplasmic reticulum and ribosomes
(D) cell nucleus and nucleolus
(E) chromosomes and chromatin

Choice (A) is correct. Chloroplasts are the sites of photosynthesis, and mitochondria are the sites of cellular respiration. These two processes are associated with converting energy into a form useful to the cell. Organelles in choice (B) are for storage and transport; choice (C), for protein synthesis; choice (D), for control of cell activities and reproduction; and choice (E), for reproduction.

Which process is described by the following equation?

$$38\ ADP + 38P \longrightarrow 38\ ATP$$

$$C_6H_{12}O_6 + 6O_2 + 6O_2 \rightarrow 6CO_2 + 6H_2O$$

(A) photosynthesis
(B) deamination
(C) anaerobic respiration
(D) aerobic respiration
(E) hydrolysis

Choice (D) is correct. During aerobic respiration, glucose combines with oxygen to yield stored energy in the form of ATP molecules; carbon dioxide and water are produced as waste products. Anaerobic respiration does not require oxygen; photosynthesis is basically this equation in reverse. Deamination is the removal of nitrogen, and hydrolysis is the splitting of water molecules.

The chrysanthemum is a plant that generally flowers in the autumn. Which statement best describes why?

(A) The flowering of a chrysanthemum depends on the loss of chlorophyll and the appearance of other pigments in the fall.
(B) The flowering of a chrysanthemum depends on the decrease in the amount of carbohydrates transported through the phloem from the leaves.
(C) The chrysanthemum flowers when the photoperiod is shorter than a critical length.
(D) The chrysanthemum flowers when the photoperiod is longer than a critical length.
(E) The flowering of a chrysanthemum does not depend on the photoperiod.

Choice (C) is correct. The decrease in the amount of daylight during the autumn shortens the photoperiod and stimulates the chrysanthemum to flower. The changes in photosynthesis or transport brought on by the change of season are not factors that stimulate flowering.

CHRYSANTHEMUM

Chemistry

This 3-hour exam consists of two parts: 90 minutes of seventy-five multiple-choice questions covering topics found in a typical full-year introductory college chemistry course with laboratory; and 90 minutes of comprehensive problems, essay topics, and questions requiring the determination of products of chemical reactions. Calculators are not permitted in the multiple-choice section; however, for the first two free-response questions, students are allowed to bring most types of scientific, programmable, and graphing calculators.

Here are some test items similar to those you might find in an actual AP Exam:

Multiple-choice examples
Directions: Select and answer from the five choices given.

Which of the following samples contains the largest number of atoms?

(A) 10.0 g of Cl_2
(B) 10.0 g of H_2O
(C) 10.0 g of C_6H_6
(D) 10.0 g of CCl_4
(E) Each sample contains the same number of atoms.

The correct answer is (B). Reasoning alone will not give the answer to this question. It is necessary to compare the number of moles of atoms in each sample. Therefore, the correct answer requires finding the molar mass of each compound by using atomic weights from the periodic table, calculating the number of moles in each sample, and finding the number of moles of atoms. The calculation for choice (B) is shown below.

$$\text{Molar mass of } H_2O = [2 \times (1 \tfrac{g}{H} \text{ atom})] + 16 \tfrac{g}{O} \text{ atom}$$
$$= 18 \tfrac{g}{1} \text{ mol } H_2O$$
$$\left(\frac{1 \text{ mol } H_2O}{18 \text{ g } H_2O}\right)(10 \text{ g } H_2O)\left(\frac{3 \text{ mol atoms}}{1 \text{ mol } H_2O}\right) = 1.6 \text{ mol atoms}$$

The other answers, found in the same manner, are (A) 0.28 mol atoms, (C) 1.5 mol atoms, and (D) 0.32 mol atoms

---

Atoms of A have a high electronegativity and high electron affinity. Atoms of B have a low electronegativity and low electron affinity. What kind of bond forms between A and B?

(A) coordinate covalent bond
(B) covalent bond
(C) hydrogen bond
(D) ionic bond
(E) metallic bond

The correct answer is choice (D). Ionic bonds form between metals of low electronegativity and low electron affinity, such as Na^+ or Ca^{2+}, and nonmetals of high electronegativity and high electron affinity, such as F^- or O^{2-}.

Because of hydrolysis, solutions of most salts are acidic or basic. Which of the following salts will give a basic solution?

(A) KBr
(B) NH_4Cl
(C) $NaC_2H_3O_2$
(D) $CuSO_4$
(E) $KHCO_3$

The correct answers are (C) and (E). To answer this question requires remembering that the acidity or basicity of a solution is not affected by the cations of alkali metals or alkaline earth metals, or by the anions of strong acids. Also, you must know that hydrolysis of other cations gives acidic solutions, and hydrolysis of other anions gives basic solutions. Compounds (A), (B), and (D) can be eliminated because KBr, HCl, and H_2SO_4 are strong acids, and their anions do not hydrolyze. Compounds (C) and (E) will both give basic solutions because they contain the anions of weak acids combined with cations that do not affect acidity or basicity.

Which one of the following mixtures will be a buffer solution?

(A) 50.0 mL of 0.10 M NaOH
    + 50.0 mL of 0.20 M $HC_2H_3O_2$

(B) 50.0 mL of 0.10 M KOH + 50.0 mL of 0.20 M HCl

(C) 50.0 mL of 0.10 M NH_4OH + 50.0 mL of 0.20 M HCl

(D) 50.0 mL of 0.10 M NaCl
    + 50.0 mL of 0.20 M $HC_2H_3O_2$

(E) 50.0 mL of 0.10 M HNO_3
    + 50.0 mL of 0.01 M $NaNO_3$

The correct answer is choice (A). This question requires knowing what a buffer is, knowing which are strong and weak acids, and also some careful analysis because the answer is not as obvious as it seems. A buffer solution, one that resists changes in pH when small amounts of acid or base are added, contains equal molar amounts of a weak acid and a salt of that acid. You might immediately settle on choice (E) as the right answer because it is the only mixture that contains equal molar amounts of an acid and a salt, but this would be wrong because HNO_3 is a strong acid. Choices (B) and (C) can also be eliminated because the solutions contain strong, not weak, acids. This leaves (A) and (D). Choice (D) cannot be a buffer because it contains a weak acid, but no salt of that acid. To verify that choice (A) is correct, you must see that half the acetic acid ($HC_2H_3O_2$) will react with the NaOH to give a solution of equal molar amounts of acetic acid and its salt, sodium acetate.

The reaction below is first order in A_2 and second order in B.

$$A_2 + 2B \rightarrow 2AB$$

Which equation represents the rate of this equation?

(A) $-\dfrac{\Delta[B]}{\Delta t} = -\dfrac{1}{2}\dfrac{\Delta[A_2]}{\Delta t} = k\,[AB]^2$

(B) $-\dfrac{1}{2}\dfrac{\Delta[B]}{\Delta t} = -\dfrac{\Delta[A_2]}{\Delta t} = k[B]^2[A_2]$

(C) $-\dfrac{1}{2}\dfrac{\Delta[AB]}{\Delta t} = +\dfrac{\Delta[A_2]}{\Delta t} = k[B]^2[A_2]$

(D) $+\dfrac{1}{2}\dfrac{\Delta[AB]}{\Delta t} = -\dfrac{\Delta[B]}{\Delta t} = k[A_2]^2\,[B]$

The correct answer is choice (B). Answering this question requires remembering the meaning of first and second order, and remembering how to write the concentration changes of reactants and products with time. First, checking the rate law part of the expression, which must be $k[B]^2[A_2]$ because the reaction is second order in B and first order in A_2, shows that choices (A) and (D) can be eliminated. Next, choice (C) can be eliminated because it has a + sign for $\Delta[A_2]/\Delta t$—since A_2 is a reactant, its concentration must decrease with time (− sign) not increase (+ sign). This leaves choice (B) as the correct answer. To check, note that it has minus signs for both reactant concentrations and a half factor to account for the two molecules of B.

Free-response examples

What is the volume at standard temperature and pressure of a gas that occupies 16.5 L at 350°C and 0.275 atm?

In this gas law problem, the quantity of gas is constant, the initial volume is known, and the initial and final temperature and pressure are known, since at standard temperature and pressure, $T = 273$ K and $P = 1.00$ atm.

$$P_1 = 0.275 \text{ atm} \qquad V_1 = 16.5 \text{ L} \qquad T_1 = 350 + 273 = 623 \text{ K}$$
$$P_2 = 1.00 \text{ atm} \qquad V_2 = ? \qquad T_2 = 273 \text{ K}$$

Since volume decreases with increasing pressure and also decreases with decreasing temperature, V_2 is

$$V_2 = V_1 \left(\frac{P_1}{P_2}\right)\left(\frac{T_2}{T_1}\right) = (16.5 \text{ L})\left(\frac{0.275 \text{ atm}}{1.00 \text{ atm}}\right)\left(\frac{273 \text{ K}}{623 \text{ K}}\right)$$
$$= 1.99 \text{ L}$$

Given the following equations

$$\frac{1}{2} N_2 + \frac{1}{2} O_2 \rightarrow NO \qquad \Delta H° = 91 \text{ kJ}$$
$$2 NO_2 \rightarrow 2NO + O_2 \qquad \Delta H° = 114 \text{ kJ}$$

find $\Delta H°$ for the reaction

$$\frac{1}{2} N2 + O_2 \rightarrow NO_2$$

The equations given must be manipulated so that their sum gives the desired equation and its $\Delta H°$ value. You must know the relationships between how equations are written and their $\Delta H°$ values. Since $\frac{1}{2}N_2$ is a reactant and NO is a product, the first equation need not be reversed. Since NO_2 is a product, the second equation must be reversed.

$$\frac{1}{2}N_2 + \frac{1}{2}O_2 \rightarrow NO \qquad \Delta H° = 91 \text{ kJ}$$
$$2NO + O_2 \rightarrow 2NO2 \qquad \Delta H° = -114 \text{ kJ}$$

To eliminate the unwanted intermediate NO and to give the desired equation, the second equation must be divided by 2.

$$\frac{1}{2}(2NO + O_2 \rightarrow 2NO_2) \qquad \Delta H° = \frac{1}{2}(-114 \text{ kJ})$$

which gives

$$NO + \frac{1}{2}O_2 \rightarrow NO_2 \qquad \Delta H° = -57 \text{ kJ}$$

The desired equation, therefore, is found as follows:

$$\frac{1}{2}N_2 + \frac{1}{2}O_2 \rightarrow NO \qquad \Delta H° = 91 \text{ kJ}$$
$$NO + \frac{1}{2}O_2 \rightarrow NO_2 \qquad \Delta H° = -57 \text{ kJ}$$
$$\frac{1}{2}N_2 + \frac{1}{2}O_2 \rightarrow NO_2 \qquad \Delta H° = 34 \text{ kJ}$$

When ethane, C_2H_6, is burned completely, it combines with oxygen to give carbon dioxide and water. How many grams of water can be formed from 5.00 g of ethane and 5.00 g of oxygen?

Any question involving quantities of reactants or products is a stoichiometry problem, and the balanced equation is needed:

$$2C_2H_6 + 7O_2 \rightarrow 4CO_2 + 6 H_2O$$

Since the quantities of both reactants are given, this is a limiting reactant problem. Before grams of water as a product can be found, it is necessary to determine which is the limiting reactant by calculating the grams of one reactant required by the other.

$$5.00 \text{ g } O_2 \left(\frac{1 \text{ mol } O_2}{32.0 \text{ g } O_2}\right)\left(\frac{2 \text{ mol } C_2H_6}{7 \text{ mol } O_2}\right)\left(\frac{30 \text{ g } C_2H_6}{1 \text{ mol } C_2H_6}\right)$$
$$= 1.34 \text{ g } C_2H_6$$

Since 5.00 g of oxygen only require 1.34 g of ethane, the oxygen is in excess and ethane is the limiting reactant. Therefore, the 5.00 g of ethane is used to calculate the grams of water formed:

$$5.00 \text{ g } C_2H_6 \left(\frac{1 \text{ mol } C_2H_6}{30.0 \text{ g } C_2H_6}\right)\left(\frac{6 \text{ mol } H_2O}{2 \text{ mol} C_2H_6}\right)\left(\frac{18.0 \text{ g } H_2O}{1 \text{ mol } H_2O}\right)$$
$$= 9.00 \text{ g } H_2O$$

Write a net ionic equation for the reaction of an excess of hydrochloric acid with calcium carbonate.

To answer this question, you must know that solid $CaCO_3$ reacts with HCl to form $CaCl_2$ and carbonic acid, H_2CO_3, which immediately decomposes to H_2O and CO_2. Then you must know which reactants and products are solids, gases, or liquids and remember that the formulas of these compounds are written in full. You must also know which are soluble ionic compounds. Write them as ions in solution, and drop any spectator ions. Here, $CaCO_3$ is a solid, $CaCl_2$ is a soluble ionic compound, CO_2 is a gas, H_2O is a liquid, and the Cl^- ions are spectator ions.

$$2H^+ + 2Cl^- + CaCO_3 \rightarrow Ca^2 + 2Cl^- + CO_2 + H_2O$$
$$2H^+ + CaCO_3 \rightarrow Ca^{2+} + CO_2 + H_2O$$

The K_{sp} of silver sulfate is 1.5×10^{-15} at 25°C. Calculate the molarity of a saturated silver sulfate solution at this temperature.

The answer to this question must be calculated from the K_{sp} expression for silver sulfate. To write this expression you must know the formula for silver sulfate and write the equation for its equilibrium with water so you can choose the exponents for the concentrations.

$$Ag_2SO_4 \longleftrightarrow 2Ag^+ + SO_4^{2-} \quad K_{sp} = [Ag^+]^2[SO_4^{2-}] = 1.5 \times 10^{-15}$$

To calculate the answer, let x equal the desired molarity. Taking into account both the number of ions formed and the exponents in the K_{sp} expression gives

$$K_{sp} = [Ag^+]^2[SO_4^{2-}] = 1.5 \times 10^{-15}$$
$$(2x)^2(x) = 1.5 \times 10^{-15}$$
$$4x^3 = 1.5 \times 10^{-15}$$
$$x = 1.1 \times 10^{-5}$$

The net ionic equation below is balanced. Which reactant is the oxidizing agent?

$$5BiO_3^- + 2Mn^+ + 14H^+ \rightarrow 5Bi^{3+} + 2MnO_4^- + 7H_2O$$

In a redox reaction, the oxidizing agent undergoes reduction, which is a decrease in oxidation state. Two quick ways to answer this question are to know that BiO_3^- is an oxidizing agent or to recognize that Mn^+ must increase in oxidation state in forming MnO_4^-, meaning BiO_3^- is the oxidizing agent. Otherwise, the answer can be figured out from changes in oxidation state. Both Bi and Mn change oxidation states. In BiO_3^-, based on an oxidation number of -2 for oxygen, and knowing that the sum of the oxidation numbers must equal the charge on the ion, the oxidation number of bismuth is $+5$:

For O in BiO_3^-: oxidation number $-2 \times 3 = -6$
For Bi in BiO_3^-: oxidation number $= +5$
-1

The oxidation number of Bi in Bi^{3+} is $+3$ (equal to the charge). Bismuth, therefore, undergoes an oxidation number change of $+5 \rightarrow +3$. Since this is reduction, BiO_3^- is the oxidizing agent.

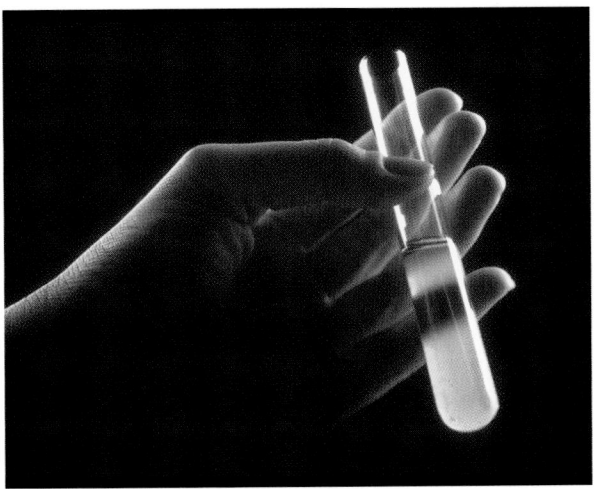

GED

The Tests of General Educational Development, known as the GED, are also called the high school equivalency test. The five GED tests are Writing Skills, Social Studies, Science, Interpreting Literature and the Arts, and Mathematics.

Anyone who is not a high school student or graduate may take the GED if he or she meets certain simple requirements of states, territories, or provinces for age, time out of school,

and resident status. All U.S. states, the District of Columbia, Puerto Rico, eight U.S. territories or possessions, and provinces and territories of Canada, except Quebec and Ontario, accept the GED. There are slight differences from place to place on what is considered a passing score.

A person who passes the test receives an official document that is equivalent to a high school diploma. In any given year, roughly three-quarters

of a million people take the test and over half a million people earn their equivalency certificates.

Each test is scored separately, on a scale of 20 to 80. Passing scores are set by the state, province, or territory where you live. For more information, please contact your local GED Testing Center or adult education program.

Following are sample test items similar to those you would find on an actual GED Test:

Test Examples

Writing Skills. This 2-hour exam consists of two parts: 75 minutes for fifty-five multiple-choice questions requiring you to correct or revise sentences that appear in a writing selection; and 45 minutes for an essay question about a subject or issue that is familiar to you. Here is a sample multiple-choice test item similar to those you might find in an actual GED Test:

<u>Directions:</u> Choose the <u>one best answer</u> to each item.

(1) When writing a letter of complaint, remember that a direct and courteous letter will most likely receive prompt attention. (2) State your specific problem. (3) And suggest how you would like to see it rectified.
(4) Your letter shouldn't imply that a company has deliberately tried to cheat you. (5) A fine company will often honor reasonable letters of complaint.

Sentences 2 and 3: State your specific <u>problem. And suggest</u> how you would like to see it rectified.

Which of the following is the best way to write the underlined portion of these two sentences?

(1) problem. And suggest
(2) problem or suggest
(3) problem and suggest
(4) problem; and suggest
(5) problem suggest

Choice (3) is correct. It uses <u>and</u> to connect independent clauses having the same subject, <u>you</u> (understood). Most teachers will not accept a sentence beginning with <u>And</u> (choice 1). Choice (2) changes the meaning. Choice (4) uses a semicolon followed by <u>and</u>, which is avoided in punctuating short independent clauses. Choice (5) leads to a run-on sentence.

Sentence 4: Your letter shouldn't imply that a company has deliberately tried to cheat you.

What correction should be made in this sentence?

(1) change <u>has</u> to <u>have</u>
(2) change <u>Your</u> to <u>One's</u>
(3) change <u>should'nt</u> to <u>shouldn't</u>
(4) change <u>you.</u> to <u>you!</u>
(5) no correction is necessary

Choice (3) is correct. In a contraction, an apostrophe is used in place of a missing letter. In <u>shouldn't</u> the apostrophe replaces the mission <u>o</u> in <u>not</u>. Choice (1) uses a plural verb, <u>have</u>, with a singular noun, <u>company</u>. Choice (2) mistakenly mixes the pronoun <u>one</u> with the pronoun <u>you</u> at the end of the sentence. Choice (4) adds an unnecessary exclamation point and does not correct the misspelling of <u>shouldn't</u>.

<u>Sentence 5</u>: A fine company will often honor reasonable letters of complaint.

If you rewrote sentence 5 to make it begin with <u>Reasonable letters of complaint</u>, the next words should be

(1) are often honored
(2) is often honored
(3) were often honored
(4) often become honored
(5) gets honored often

Choice (1) is correct. The plural verb <u>are</u> agrees with the plural subject <u>letters</u>. In choices (2) and (5), the verbs are singular. Choice (3) uses a past verb in a paragraph that is in the present tense. Choice (4) is incorrect because <u>become honored</u> is an awkward expression in this sentence.

Social Studies. This 85-minute exam consists of sixty-four multiple-choice questions in history, economics, political science, geography, anthropology, psychology, and sociology. Here is a sample multiple-choice test item similar to those you might find in an actual GED Test:

<u>Directions</u>: Read the following passage and answer the questions that appears after it.

In most of tropical South America, rain forests are being cleared for the creation of new crop and grazing land that yield food for a growing population. Many people criticize policies that let this happen. Rain forests absorb carbon dioxide that could contribute to global warming, and they produce oxygen that almost all animals require. Rain forests contain a host of species found nowhere else on earth, as well as some of the last people living as they did in the Stone Age. Finally, conversion of rain forests to agriculture fosters the loss of soil, either to the forces of erosion or to a form of hardening that endangers tropical soils.

Each of the answers below is an unhappy result of the destruction of South America's rain forests EXCEPT:

(1) loss of oxygen producing plants
(2) loss of potentially valuable animal and plant species
(3) creation of new crop and grazing land
(4) soil erosion
(5) displacement of people living there

This question demands careful reading. The key word is EXCEPT, which asks you to find the answer that is not unhappy, that is, not always the same as happy. Choices (1), (2), (4) and (5) are unhappy results of deforestation. The correct answer, choice (3), may or may not be a happy result. While it has dangerous effects on soil, it feeds populations—at least for a while.

Science.
This 95-minute exam consists of sixty-six multiple-choice questions in biology, earth science, physics, and chemistry. Here are sample multiple-choice test items similar to those you might find in an actual GED Test:

Directions: Choose the one best answer to each item. The items below refer to the following article.

If you were to travel to Colorado, you might visit Cliff Palace, a natural shelf carved into a high sandstone cliff. This rocky ledge was the home of Native American Pueblos hundreds of years ago. Sandstone, a sedimentary rock made mostly of the mineral quartz, varies in color from golden yellow to red to brown. Impurities or other minerals give the sandstone its color. Unlike igneous rock, such as granite, sedimentary rock forms in layers. When sedimentary rock wears away, or erodes, it splits along these layers. Because of the way sandstone erodes, the Pueblos were able to use loose pieces of sandstone as block to make walls within the rocky ledge, forming many rooms that can still be seen today.

The golden yellow color of Cliff Palace shows that it is made of what type of rock?

(1) granite
(2) quartz
(3) sandstone
(4) sedimentary
(5) igneous

Choice (3) is correct. The first sentence states that Cliff Palace is made of sandstone. Choice (2) is incorrect because, although sandstone is mostly quartz, quartz is a mineral not a rock. Although sandstone is a sedimentary rock, choice (4) is incorrect because the question specifies the golden yellow color of the rock. Choice (5) is incorrect, since the only mention of igneous rock in the passage comes in classifying granite as igneous.

The property of sandstone that enable the Pueblos to make use of it for shelter is that sandstone

(1) forms and erodes in layers.
(2) is made of quartz, which has many other uses.
(3) has many impurities
(4) can be yellow, red, or brown.
(5) is less likely to erode than granite.

Choice (1) is correct. The eroding sandstone formed the blocks used to build Cliff Palace. Although quartz might have had other uses, choice (2) does not explain that it helped the Pueblos build the dwelling. Choices (3) and (4) are true, but they have nothing to do with the question. Choice (5) is incorrect. Sandstone is more likely to erode than granite.

What is the principal difference between sandstone and granite?

(1) Both contain quartz.
(2) Sandstone is a sedimentary rock, and granite is an igneous rock.
(3) Both rocks are found in Cliff Palace.
(4) Sandstone and granite both form in layers.
(5) Sandstone and granite have a variety of colors.

Choice (2) is correct. The passage clearly makes this distinction between the two types of rock. Although both contain quartz (choice 1), and may vary in color (choice 5), these are similarities, not differences. Choice (3) is incorrect. It is not mentioned that granite is found in Cliff Palace. Even if it were found there, this answer would not answer the question. Choice (4) also is not correct as a statement and does not establish a difference between the rocks.

Interpreting Literature and the Arts.
This 65-minute exam consists of forty-five multiple-choice questions in popular literature, classical literature, and commentary. Here is a sample multiple-choice test item similar to those you might find in an actual GED Test:

Directions: Choose the one best answer to each item.

> Fog creeps,
> Slow, soundless.
> It oozes, it seeps
> Along river beds.
> Like a dream,
> Fog drifts into sleep.

In this poem, fog is compared to

(1) a river bed
(2) a road bed
(3) a dream
(4) sleep
(5) all of these

In comparison, two things ae said to be alike. In this poem, the word like is actually used in the sixth line, so choice (3) is correct. If like is not used, look for other clues. For example, the poem might have said "As quiet as a dream / Fog drifts into sleep," or "Fog is a dream / That drifts into sleep." In both cases, fog is still being compared to a dream.

Mathematics.
This 90-minute exam consists of fifty-six multiple-choice questions in arithmetic (measurement, numeration, and data analysis), algebra, and geometry. Here is a sample multiple-choice test item similar to those you might find in an actual GED Test:

Directions: Choose the one best answer to each item.

A room is 15 feet wide, 24 feet long, and 9 feet high. How many square yards of carpeting are needed to cover the floor?

(1) 40
(2) 45
(3) 120
(4) 360
(5) 1080

This problem has more information than you need. You do not need to know how high the room is in order to find the area of the floor. The area of the floor is found by multiplying length x width.

$$A = 15 \times 24$$
$$= 360 \text{ square feet}$$

The unit is important. The problem asks for the area in square yards. There are 3 feet in one yard, so there are 9 square feet in one square yard.

$$360 \div 9 = 40$$

The correct choice is (1).

For GED Information

By mail:
GED Testing Service
American Council on Education
One Dupont Circle, Suite 250
Washington, DC 20036

By telephone:
202-939-9490
800-626-9433 toll free

GCSE

Overview

The General Certificate of Secondary Education (GCSE) is the most important qualification in England, Wales and Northern Ireland. The GCSE examinations are taken by nearly one million students each year. In addition, they are taken in many other countries in Africa, Asia and the British Commonwealth.

For most of the students in the United Kingdom, the final examinations are taken soon after the age of 16 and mark the end point to 11 years of compulsory school attendance. These examinations also test the final two years of the programmes of study in the national curriculum, which was introduced in 1988. Because of their importance to the country, all courses of study leading to the GCSE must be approved by the minister for education in London (who is called the Secretary of State) through an agency known as the Qualifications and Curriculum Authority.

For individual students the GCSE opens up the first gate to further study at school or college leading to university. A good set of GCSE grades is also vital for most white-collar jobs, and recent studies have shown that achievement at GCSE is closely related to future employment, as well as to financial, family and social life up to the age of 35 and beyond.

Although the exam is usually taken at the age of 16, older students often take individual subjects later on in life to update and improve their qualifications, and it is quite common for 17- and 18-

year-olds in further education colleges to take one or two GCSE subjects as well as Advanced level subjects, known as A levels.

Description. The GCSE is a two-year course consisting of 90 hours of teaching a year in the core subjects of the national curriculum, and either 63 or 45 hours in other subjects. Some of the GCSE courses are split up into modules of one or two terms, and there is a test or assessment at the end of each module. There are also end-of-year assess-

ments and 'mock' exams in nearly all schools. These and termly reports from teachers will give students and parents feedback on how they are doing. But the the bulk of a student's GCSE score is based upon the final examinations, which take place in May and June (or December in some cases) of the final year of compulsory schooling.

The GCSE examinations consist of a range of exams in single subjects, including the 10 subjects of the national curriculum and 50 or 60 additional subjects. There are no limits to the number of subjects that can be taken at any one time, and the decision to enter for the examinations rests with the parents and students at about the age of 15, although this will usually depend on a previous decision to enter for a two-year course of study at the age of 14.

Because of the importance of gaining good grades at GCSE for most kinds of jobs, students are encouraged to take at least the three 'core subjects' (English, maths and science) at GCSE and two or three of the other compulsory subjects at this stage of the national curriculum (such as design technology, information technology, a modern foreign language and physical education). Religious education is also a compulsory subject up to the age of 16, but students do not have to take it as an exam qualification. In recent years some students have also been encouraged to take vocational courses as well as their GCSE exams.

For the individual student there is still a fairly wide choice of what exami-

nation to take and what examination board to use. These decisions can have a small but important effect on what grades a student gets, and it is worth seeking advice from experienced teachers and career advisers on what subjects to take. The choice of exam board is usually left to the teacher or head of department in school. But it is well worth parents and students' finding out more about the examination syllabuses and the way the marks are distributed among different areas of the subject.

For example, in the English GCSE examination, there are three elements which are separately graded: speaking and listening, reading, and writing. At least 60 per cent of the marks must be awarded for the final examination (50 per cent in exceptional cases), 20 per cent of them for speaking and listening and 40 per cent for each of the other two areas of study. The reading list must include a work by Shakespeare and at least one work of literature published before 1900 and one after that date.

Understanding these requirements, which all the exam boards must follow in setting their examination papers, should help both teachers and students to organise their study time efficiently. In the English examination described above, for example, students would be well advised to spend more study time on reading and writing than on speaking and listening, since the former count for more.

Similarly, some subjects are split up into two or three different levels, and these determine a lower or higher grade. It may not be worth students' spending time on a lower level paper when they can achieve a higher grade taking a more advanced paper.

Grading. A separate certificate is awarded in each subject, listing the grade which a student has achieved. The results take the form of an alphabetical grade: A*, A, B, C, D, E, F and G. Those who do not reach the minimum standard for grade G are recorded as U for 'unclassified' and do not receive a certificate.

The C-D boundary is all-important, since it is widely perceived as a pass-fail boundary. A grade of C or above is usually referred to as a good grade, those below C as low grade passes. All schools report their pass rates at two levels—students gaining passes at grade C and above and those gaining passes at grade G and above. Most students who decide to take a GCSE subject will hope to gain a grade C at least, because many employers and further education colleges demand Cs as a minimum. Nevertheless, a lower grade GCSE is by no means worthless.

The starred A (A*) was introduced four years ago as an additional incentive to excellence, because it was found that many students were getting a whole string of A grades (sometimes as many as 10), and there were complaints that the GCSE had become too easy. The

starred A is now awarded to the top 5 per cent of the candidates in any subject according to the final examination marks.

Choosing an exam board. The selection of an exam board is usually done by the school or college, but different subject teachers may choose a different board so that a school may have up to five GCSE boards on its books. This sometimes presents difficulties in the administration of the exams at school or college level. There is now pressure on the boards to merge and combine forces to achieve economies of scale and standardisation of grades.

Up until the present there have been five GCSE groups, which were originally set up on an area basis (South and London, Midlands and North of England, plus Wales and Northern Ireland). But over the past 10 years of the GCSE this area map has changed considerably, although there are still some local loyalties to a particular board, often because schools like the syllabus it offers.

It is worth remembering too that some boards offer more than one syllabus in any subject, with different set books or with differing amounts of coursework. Exam boards often prepare special syllabuses to fit particular curriculum innovations—for example, in chemistry or technology. Some GCSE subjects (for example, science) are sometimes called 'double award' because of the extra content in the syllabus, and several are now half-courses (for example, in modern foreign languages) and take half the time of a full GCSE; the grades in these courses are worth half those of a full GCSE.

There are many books on the market claiming to tell the public which exam board is the easiest or 'the best buy'. Be aware that such claims no longer have any validity. The grades awarded by each exam board are rigorously monitored by independent assessors, and there has to be uniformity of grades at all grade levels as well as a complete description of the standard of work expected at grades F, C and A.

Many of the set books for reading are now standardised across the examination although there is some flexibility

for individual boards and schools. Schools do not choose their boards on the basis of difficulty or easiness but on the basis of price (subject entries cost about £15 per student) and on the kind of administrative services and support the board offers to hard-pressed teachers. Most boards now offer teacher's guides to their syllabuses and provide training courses at weekends or in the evenings.

Nevertheless, for students wishing to take an individual course at a college or those studying part-time or in evening classes, it is certainly worth studying the GCSE prospectus put out by the college or the exam board to see which type of syllabus meets their needs. For example, some GCSE courses are designed to be taken in one year instead of the usual two and by distance learning and continuous assessment rather than by regular tuition. Most colleges offer flexibility in teaching and learning arrangements. For distance-learning methods it is worth applying to the National Extension College in Cambridge for their prospectus.

Choosing a subject and syllabus.

Up to a few years ago the GCSE was the first major public examination most students took, and often they were unprepared for it. Now, however, students are tested on the national curriculum at the age of 14, and these tests, which are administered by the exam boards, are in many ways a good indicator of what subjects and syllabuses to take up to 16.

Students can take as many GCSE subjects as they like, but in practice eight subjects is usually enough. The core subjects (English, maths and science) are essential, and they take up 90 hours of teaching time a year for two years and the same amount of private study, reading, preparation and coursework. Getting a good grade (C or above) in these subjects is extremely important.

Outside the core subjects, information technology has now been made a mandatory subject up to the age of 16 and is becoming vitally important for most jobs in industry and commerce. In Wales the study of Welsh is mandatory up to the age of 16 in all schools from 1999.

The other subjects students take will depend on their career choices and interests. A modern foreign language (French, Spanish or German) is becoming more and more important inside the European Union, and most employers like to see a GCSE in one well-known modern language. A budding scientist may take an extra science subject or a mathematical qualification. Those with an interest in the arts should consider drama, English literature, art or history of art. The standard of art entries has risen dramatically over the years, and many teachers encourage students to take it as a relaxation and an opportunity for exploration and self-expression amongst young people.

For those who are looking for a career in engineering or industrial design, design technology is an essential subject (it can now be taken as half a GCSE course), and students can specialise in technical drawing, computer aided design or food technology. Design technology is one of the few subjects where coursework accounts for more than 50 per cent of the marks—usually in the form of a design project which builds up into a portfolio of work and a finished product or display. The final written exam is of lesser importance.

Spelling, punctuation and grammar (SPAG).

In the old days spelling, punctuation and grammar were left to the English teacher, and even he or she often left it as an afterthought in the syllabus. But for the past six years SPAG has been given much greater emphasis in the national curriculum and in all subjects. Today it is a major ingredient in all English GCSE syllabuses, and this requirement is spelled out as follows:

A syllabus must include objectives for writing which require candidates to demonstrate their ability to:
- communicate clearly, adapting their writing for a wide range of purposes and audiences;
- use and adapt forms and genres for specific purposes and effects;
- organise ideas into sentences, paragraphs and whole texts;
- use accurate spelling and punctuation and present work neatly and clearly;
- use the grammatical structures of standard English and a wide vocabulary to express meanings with clarity and precision.

This requirement means that students must pay regular attention to their spelling, punctuation and grammar and that colloquial and non-standard English will be marked down. The crackdown on English standards does not only affect English and English literature, it has been extended to all subjects of the national curriculum, and 5 per cent of the marking schemes in all examinations is now devoted to SPAG. Although there is some variation in how this marking is applied—for example, in how much poor spelling is tolerated, provided the meaning is clear—this added element in the marking scheme can mean the loss of a grade across several subjects if a candidate is not proficient in SPAG. It applies both to final examinations and to coursework.

Some students, of course, have specific learning difficulties in reading and writing, such as dyslexia. They can get a medical certificate and present it to the exam board some time before the examination. Then they will be allowed to use a typewriter keyboard with a spelling checker, and they will be given extra time in their exams (usually 30 minutes).

For other students who have a particular problem with spelling it is worth making a note of the key words in a subject—in history, for example, words such as *monastery*, *renaissance* or *dictator*—and check and memorise them before taking exams. The Basic Skills Agency has produced a spelling pack which contains a list of commonly misspelt words and grammatical and other errors, such as *to* for *two* or *too*; *right* for *write*; and *no* for *know*.

Ask your teacher for a wordlist and make a note of words you spell incorrectly in your class assignments. It is a good idea always to have a dictionary nearby when you are working on coursework. Remember, though, that you cannot use a dictionary in your examination. Likewise, spelling checkers may be useful in coursework, but they will not be allowed in final examinations. So your list of key words and their spellings should be learned alongside the other facts and dates during your revision.

Common Spelling Errors

Type of Error	Example	Tip
Right sound but wrong letters	menshun - **mention**	Keep lists of similarly spelt words and look at them regularly.
Didn't apply a spelling rule	comeing - **coming** (drop the *e*)	Get to know which rules you need to learn or which you often forget.
Missing letters Extra letters	becase - **because** everery - **every**	Highlight or mark the parts which you tend to confuse.
Wrong word	two much work **(too)**	Use memory hooks (*mnemonics*) to help and learn each word separately.
Reversed letters	Firday - **Friday**	Look at the difficult parts of the word and sound them out or underline them.
Spelt the way you speak; accent or dialect	somefing - **something** flim - **film**	Keep lists of your typical errors and know your weak spots.

Improving Your Exam Technique

In all the subjects of the GCSE, students are tested primarily on their understanding, knowledge and skills. There is no shortcut to exam success; it will come only through patient and careful study. Lord Puttnam, the famous film director, said recently that exams were like producing plays—a lot of learning and hard work, followed by rehearsals leading up to the first night. Like actors, students have to hope that their performance on the first night will be their best ever—because on that they will be judged.

The following chapter, based on the guidance of George Turnbull, a veteran examiner with the Associated Examining Board (now part of the AQA), is intended to help GCSE candidates improve their techniques and make the best of themselves as the weeks of learning pass and the final examination looms into sight. Unfortunately, however, these tips and pieces of advice on examsmanship will not make up for a lack of work or effort in the past.

Planning. Do not pretend that everything can be done in a rush the night before each exam. Work out how long you have got for revision before the exams and plan how to use your time. (Your mock exam scores can prove valuable in this regard because they will give you an idea of weaknesses that should be addressed.) You may want to try the following technique:

1. Make a calendar for your wall.
2. Put the dates and times of all your exams, using a distinctive colour, such as red.
3. Black out times when you know already that revision will not be possible, such as holidays, field trips or other school activities.
4. Put in your revision programme, working back from the exam. Be precise about the subject and topic for each day's revision.

Once you have planned your time, set target tasks and dates, then place these on your wall next to the calendar. You may also find it helpful to assemble fact sheets for each of your GCSE subjects and post these as well.

Whatever method you use to set out your plans, be sure that you
• set realistic targets for yourself and then work to achieve them;
• remember that making plans and sticking to them enables you to do more;
• tick off what you have achieved and feel good about it.

Remember the old saying attributed to the Duke of Wellington: "Napoleon made his plans out of gold; when they broke, he was done for. I made my plans out of rope; when they broke, I tied a knot in them and went on." In other words, leave some flexibility in your study and revision plans, review them

regularly and then you can make any necessary adjustments to cope with emergencies or events outside your control, such as illness.

If all goes well, you will have about four months for revision after you have finished the syllabus of your course, but sometimes this may be less. If the teaching has gone on too long, never mind! It's still a good idea to plan the use of what time does remain. A last-minute rush will leave you panicky and tired. You need to fit in time for relaxation as well as revision.

As the exams approach, you may get the feeling that time is running out. If you do, try making a chart of what you must accomplish each day from 9am to 10pm, being sure to include both work and relaxation. Most people have difficulty saying where the time went. But there is more time than you think, provided you have a plan. A half-hour here and a half-hour there can add up to several hours of revision. It might even leave you time to go out for an evening!

Start by planning for tomorrow and then for the day and week after. Don't try to do too much too soon or you may disappoint yourself. Start slowly with achievable targets, and then you will feel good as you tick them off. Above all, don't delay your revision until the last minute.

Fact Sheet (Sample)

ENGLISH

What percentage of total marks for written papers?	80%	
How many written papers?	3	
How long for each paper?	Paper 1: Paper 2: Paper 3:	2 hours; 20% 3 hours; 40% 2 hours; 20%
Sections/topics on each paper?	Paper 1: Paper 2: Paper 3:	Comprehension Literature Creative writing
How many questions to be answered?	Paper 1: Paper 2: Paper 3:	Comprehension passage, 15 short questions (compulsory). Any other 3 from 6 longer questions 4, one from each section (essays) 2, from 10 questions (essays)
Coursework	Drama project, 20 % of total marks Check hand-in day with Miss Tomlinson	
Dates of exams	Paper 1: Paper 2: Paper 3:	9am 1 June 2pm 2 June 9am 3 June
Place of exams	Old Library (all papers)	

Target Task Sheet (Sample)

By the end of April I will complete revision cards on:

Biology

Geography

French

I will have tried to understand circulation of the blood percentages.

I will complete the compulsory section of a past maths paper, working against the clock.

Revision. You probably have been accumulating notes from various subjects you are studying, although some of these notes will be better organised than others. Even if they are poorly organised, it is important that you should use them to make your own revision notes.

Although you can buy revision notes that are commercially produced by publishers such as Letts and Penguin, you will find it more effective to make your own notes as an aid to memorising key facts. You can make your own abbreviations and use colours and symbols that are meaningful to you personally.

However your revision notes are organised and coded, make sure to relate them to the syllabus and topics of past exam papers so that your memory is focused on the right topics.

Make a collection of revision notes on separate cards for each of your exam subjects. This will take time and is not something that should be done at the very last minute. You can then use the cards to test yourself, or you can get a friend or member of the family to test you. These notes should include definitions and key ideas, not just facts. They can even take the form of a diagram, especially in economics, maths, geography and chemistry.

≡FAST Track   Memory Aids

Rhymes
Mary, Bessy, James the Vain, Charlie, Charlie, James again (Tudor and Stuart kings and queens)

Word association
Boynty, Boynty, sixteen-noynty (Battle of the Boyne, 1690)

Acroynyms
ANGELA (Oil-producing countries of Africa: Algeria, Nigeria, Gabon, Egypt, Libya, Angola)

First letters of words in a sentence
Richard of York gave battles in vain. (Colours of the rainbow: red, orange, yellow, green, blue, indigo and violet)

It is easy to revise in a mechanical way by simply reading and rereading texts or old notes. It's a little more difficult, but probably far more effective, to organise your notes by theme, so you can use them to plan answers in an exam paper and even time yourself writing an answer.

Remember that if you run out of time answering questions, you can always write out an answer in note form and at least get partial marks.

Easter revision classes. Many local education authorities and schools run Easter revision classes of one or two weeks. These can be especially helpful to students who need to brush up on particular aspects of their GCSE courses which they cannot revise from books—for example, spoken French or information technology. Ring up the education department of your local council; even if they do not offer classes they may know where the classes are being held. Easter revision classes are usually free, and sometimes bus transport is provided. Many schools have found that these revision classes can add one or even two grades to the school average.

In addition, the British Broadcasting Corporation (BBC) runs a series of Easter revision programmes accompanied by revision booklets in all the main GCSE subjects. These run from April through to the beginning of May and can be recorded from the 'Learning Zone' late at night either in school or in the home. Most schools have a timeswitch for recording them. All schools are sent details of these programmes, so you should be able to get the information from your teacher or from the newspapers. If not, then the BBC Education Department at White City, London W12 will send you the information.

Essay writing. Many of the questions in the GCSE exam require an essay form of answer. Here your notes will come in handy. Following is a suggested method for writing essays of 600 to 800 words, which is about the average in a 2-3 hour paper.

1. Read the question carefully, then draft out notes covering the main points you want to discuss in your answer, numbering each point.
2. Write an initial paragraph which answers the question as simply as possible.
3. Write additional paragraphs, each picking up a numbered topic or theme from your notes. The paragraphs should be about three sentences long, or longer if you can remember direct quotations from a book text.
4. When you have exhausted your themes, bring together the ideas in a final paragraph, referring to the ideas presented in your first paragraph, if possible.
5. Look over the result for spelling and punctuation. Organising your material in this way will help to improve your SPAG marks.

Revision Notes (Sample)

Topic:	Location of industry
Questions:	Why are industries located in one place rather than another? Why are certain industries seen more in some towns and parts of the country than in others?
What affects location of industry?	Transport costs: Raw materials/markets Power: Type/amount Available labour Available space

Examination Tips

Before the examination

- Make sure you know what will be examined in each subject and the way in which the questions are likely to be asked. Have a look at the syllabus for this year and look back on past exam papers.
- Find out what you will need for each exam: both what is provided for you, such as maps, and what you must provide yourself, such as drawing pens.
- Verify where and when your exams are to be held.
- Familiarise yourself with the rules for each exam. Never be tempted to break them! Remember that the exam board can take you to court if you cheat or infringe the regulations.
- Dress comfortably before going into an exam. Take a bottle of still water if the weather is hot and sultry. Don't take in a bleeping clock or portable phone. Calculators will probably be banned for some mathematics papers. Give yourself time to lay out your equipment (pens, watch, rulers) and get settled.

In the exam room

- Pay close attention to the instructions. Do the right number of questions from the right sections and answer compulsory questions.
- Plan your time in the exam. If you only attempt half the questions needed, your best possible mark is only 50 per cent, however good the answers.
- Make sure you know how many marks each question carries. Don't spend too long on any one question. Use the number of marks as a guide.
- Read questions carefully *before* you start writing, not halfway through your answer. The examiners allow time for you to read the paper when they plan the exam, so don't think that you are wasting time.
- Answer the questions set, not the ones you hoped for. However good your work, you will get no marks if you don't answer the examiner's questions. Do not try to make jokes in your answer, especially about the questions or what you think of the examiner!
- Do not panic! Remember, exams such as the GCSE are not designed to catch you out. Being calm and thoughtful will help you to get the most out of your preparation.

After the examination

- Don't worry about the exam you have just taken. For now there's nothing more you can do.
- Do not stand around talking with friends and other candidates. There are always people who claim to have known all the answers and tackled all the questions. Listening to them talking can be a depressing and unnerving experience. Concentrate instead on your next exam paper.
- Tell your school straight away about illness or other circumstances which might have affected your performance.
- If you were ill and could not take the exam, you should apply for a certificate, called an aegrotat (I-grow-tat). This will enable you to take a special paper a few weeks later, which is not the same one as the main exam paper.

Examination Results

The GCSE exam papers take two months to mark. So you can go away for a summer holiday or break, knowing that the results will not come out until the third week in August. It is best to make contact with the school or college a day or two beforehand, and they will tell you when to come in for the results. Or you can give them a stamped envelope with your address, in which case the results will take a day or two longer to arrive.

Certificates and records.
When you have gained your GCSEs you will receive a summary of the subjects and grades from the examining board or boards. Keep this safely and make some copies for sending to the school, college or university you are hoping to attend, or to potential employers if you are looking for a job. In a few months' time the exam board will send you an official certificate for each subject which also includes the grade. Keep these safely and also make copies of them. Do *not* send the originals to universities or employers, or you may never get them back. Send a photocopy instead, which is nearly always accepted as evidence of a pass.

The school or college is required by law to keep records on all their students and to provide copies on request to that student (or to the parent if the student is under 16). Students have rights to prevent the school or college from divulging pass-fail information to a third party. Exam boards also keep records, and they will send copies to students on request (in some cases for a small payment). Exam boards will also send information to the school, student or parent. But they will not reveal this information to anyone else, except possibly to the police in special circumstances.

If you should fail.
When you get the results, you may find that you have failed in one or two subjects or done less well than you had hoped—for example, you got a D instead of a C. All is not lost! If you ask your teacher, you may find that several other students have suffered the same fate. Although much time and effort is taken to moderate the marking so as to make the grades consistent, there may be a 'rogue' marker who is out of line with the rest. (See 'Appeals' for information about the appeals process.)

If after exhausting the appeals process you have still failed (or failed to get the grade you want or need), then it may be worth resitting the examination. Fortunately, you do not have to complete all the coursework and study time all over again. You may be able to resit the examination four or five months later, using the time to revise your weaker areas and get a pass or improve your grades. Or you can go to a college and

take a one-year course. Students often do this to improve their grades in English or maths. (A grade of C is now almost essential for clerical and commercial jobs.) Or they may improve their grades in other subjects in order to start an A level course; many schools and colleges demand a C grade, and sometimes even a B grade, before students can start A level.

Failure is not a disaster, even if it sometimes can damage a student's self-esteem or standing amongst family, friends and schoolmates. When this happens, it is sometimes best for the student to go and take another quite different course in a different school or college and make a fresh start.

Improving your grades.
Grades can be improved by student counselling and by systematic self-improvement routines in and out of school. The low-achievement culture in some schools can often be changed by outdoor activity and mentoring from role-model adults such as famous athletes or sports men and women. Students who are encouraged to achieve excellence in sport or athetics can often transfer this sense of achievement into the classroom. The 'no pain, no gain' philosophy of athletics training can be applied to academic study and, especially, to revision.

Of course, some students do not respond well to this type of self-improvement regime. Others simply do not relate to academic subjects. These students should consider a different sort of course from the age of 14—perhaps a

short or half-course GCSE or one with a modular structure, so that the students can feel they are achieving results as they go along, building up their knowledge and skills in short stages.

Alternatively, these students could consider a more vocational course such as the General National Vocational Qualifications (GNVQs), which are now being offered from age 14 onwards. These courses build up success from the bottom and do not have a pass-fail testing regime. They will lead on to other vocational qualifications from 18 onwards (NVQs).

The GNVQ vocational courses may be combined with GCSEs and A levels. They include a special element on key skills, which enables students to improve their writing, reading, maths and information technology while applying these skills to business or commerce. Many students find these courses more motivating, because the work is more closely related to the 'real world' and life after school, especially employment.

Young people who fail their GCSEs often feel rejected by society and believe they will never get a worthwhile job or make a career. But help is at hand. All they need to do is speak to the admissions officer at their local college of further education, where there are trained guidance and careers counsellors who can put them back on the road to success. Staff in these colleges of further education usually subscribe to Sir Winston Churchill's philosophy that "there is no such thing as failure—only another chance for success".

 **Appeals**

There are well-established procedures for checking results and making appeals. Here are some of the steps that can be taken:

- You can get a breakdown of your marks.
- You can get your coursework remarked.
- You can get a clerical check of the addition and subtraction of your marks. These marks are normally checked at the board, but occasionally a simple sum is miscalculated!
- You can get a remark of the script. This can cost about £30, but it could be worth it. You can also get an examiner's report on the script.
- The school or college can get a remark and report that covers a whole group of candidates.
- The school or college can then appeal on your behalf, if you are still not satisfied. This can cost up to £50.
- If you are still not satisfied, the appeal can go to the Independent Appeals Authority for School Examinations (IAASE), which will give an independent view. This will not only cost more money (another £50), it will also take a year or more. So if you are in a hurry to get on with further study or make decisions about your career, it is seldom worth it. However, a school or college can sometimes improve their exam results by one grade across a whole subject area and occasionally a whole area of the country can be regraded, affecting thousands of candidates. Of course, the appeal authority may sometimes find that the marks awarded were too generous. But fortunately they do not insist that the original grades are revised downwards. So you can't lose anything by appealing—except quite a lot of time and money!

GCSE Subjects

The GCSE is essentially a subject-based examination. Since 1990 it has been linked to the final two years (key stage 4) of the national curriculum. This means that the subject content of the syllabuses is laid down by Parliament and is the law of the land. But outside the 10 subjects of the national curriculum the subject matter is less clear. Even within the national curriculum history and geography are now optional from age 14 onwards and students can now drop design technology, art, music and a foreign language if they wish.

Only the following subjects are now compulsory for all students up to the age of 16: English, maths, science, information technology and physical education. Welsh is also now mandatory in Wales. Religious education is also mandatory, but students do not have to take an exam in this subject.

Aside from compulsory subjects, there is now considerable choice in what subjects can be taken. Some able students take as many as 10 GCSE subjects at a time (some of them a year early), but teachers usually discourage this because of the workload and examination strain. Between six and eight subjects is usually considered the optimum number, enabling students to get the best grades in as many subjects as possible.

Obviously, there is a limit to the number of subjects that you can take: not only is the school and college timetable limited in hours per week and teaching staff, but the final examinations at the end of the course become too onerous, and there are likely to be clashes between exam times. (In theory all exams are sat together on the same day during May and June, but there are still likely to be clashes between papers where colleges are using several different boards and syllabuses.)

Here are the syllabus and exam specifications for the main subjects, in summarised form, and some comments on the career and study considerations students should bear in mind.

Art. This is a popular subject in the national curriculum, and teachers encourage all students to consider taking it to develop their creative and practical potential. Art is interpreted as including crafts and design as well—for example, pottery and modelling. Besides developing ideas through creative work, students are expected to identify works of art and to write about art and design, making judgements about what is beautiful and pleasing and what is not.

Students are expected to express ideas and feelings in visual form, in a range of processes and in two and three dimensions. Up to 60 per cent of the work can be coursework, usually involving a finished piece of artwork from the conception to the finished product. The final exam is a timed piece of work on a

given theme or a design brief. Art is a highly valued GCSE for many jobs in the creative field, and standards of work have risen in recent years.

Business studies and economics.
This is a common subject in further education colleges. Economics is more theoretical and business studies are based on real-life situations, but the knowledge, skills and understanding are the same for both and the subjects are sometimes combined. Between 75 and 80 per cent of the work is tested by final examination.

Classical subjects.
This category covers Greek, Latin and classical civilisation—subjects which are making a comeback, especially in the colleges and in the independent schools. A few years ago classical subjects were nearly squeezed out by other subjects of the national curriculum. The category is still considered useful for entry to the ancient universities, Oxford and Cambridge, but is no longer compulsory. It is favoured as an entry qualification for the law and English literature degrees. It is also a useful background subject for history degrees or the study of modern French, Italian and Spanish.

Design and technology.
This is the most practically based subject in the national curriculum and also one of the most controversial. The subject is divided into designing (40 per cent) and making (60 per cent) a product to a specification. Students have to display knowledge of processes and techniques and skill in the use of materials, tools and other equipment (especially computers).

There is now a short course in this subject. The final exam accounts for 40 per cent of the marks. Sadly, this subject has sometimes been squeezed out and scaled down in the national curriculum through budget cuts and resource constraints because it is time- and equipment-intensive and requires specialist workshops and skilled staff who are in short supply.

English.
This is probably the most important, but also the most politically sensitive, subject of the national curriculum. It is divided into three parts: speaking and listening, reading, and writing. These account for 20 per cent, 40 per cent and 40 per cent of the marks, respectively. Coursework must not account for more than 40 per cent of the marks, although some of the most successful English teaching is done through coursework.

Students must read a range of English prose, poetry and dramatic works, a play by Shakespeare, and the work of one great author published before 1900 (from a list of about 20 authors, including such novelists as Jane Austen and Charles Dickens). The range of reading must include non-fiction, media, and texts from other cultures and traditions (American, African or Indian, for example).

Students are encouraged to use a range of styles and forms and to be creative. English teaching can reach a very high quality, but there has been persistent criticism that standards of spelling, punctuation and grammar (SPAG) have been allowed to fall. The Government has now told schools to concentrate more teaching time on this aspect of the subject, especially in coursework, and examiners are expected to penalise poor spelling, punctuation and grammar.

English literature. This subject is distinct from but complementary to the English GCSE, requiring a wider range of reading and writing. There is no requirement for speaking and listening and most of the coursework must be in writing. Further, there is more opportunity for creative and imaginative work and students are expected to show a range of styles and forms in their writing. Reading should include a range of prose, poetry and dramatic works before and after 1900, but some works in translation can also be included, Homer's *Iliad* and *Odyssey*, for example.

Geography. This subject is sliping out of the national curriculum at key stage 4 (ages 14 to 16), which is a pity, as it is the principal subject for learning about environmental and 'green' issues. Students are expected to study a range of geographical patterns and environments from local to global; ways in which people and environments interact; and the effects on industry and commerce. They must acquire and apply a number of skills and techniques, including mapwork, fieldwork and information technology. Coursework (20 to 25 per cent) must include a geographical investigation supported by fieldwork. Students must be able to draw simple maps and also know the main city and country names. They must also be able to interpret diagrams, charts and photographs.

History. This is another subject fighting for its life in the national curriculum. Originally a mandatory subject from ages 5 to 16, it is now a requirement only from ages 11 to 14. The subject is still a battleground for the politicians, some of whom want a British perspective, while others want a European and international dimension. It is a subject that requires a lot of reading and this puts some students off. In recent times there has been an increased emphasis on British history, including kings and dates, but the Labour Government is trying to introduce a more European and international element. The final examination takes up 75 per cent of the marks, but since many history syllabuses are now modular (to match specific periods and themes) coursework can account for 50 per cent of modular schemes. The exam papers require extended essay writing as well as commentaries on historical passages. The subject contains a wide variety of options—for example, the history of art, technology or religion—in many countries. It is a difficult subject, but a rewarding one that is highly valued by universities.

Home economics. This was once seen as a girl's subject, then as a part of technology and then it nearly got squeezed out of the national curriculum. It is still a useful and under-rated subject in which it is possible for both girls and boys to do well and acquire practical skills for a wide range of careers. The subject is now back in vogue because of public interest in food and nutrition and some new curricula have been developed to stimulate a better understanding of the relationship between health and nutrition. Home economics is divided into four separate and optional syllabuses: child development; consumer studies; food and nutrition; and textiles. It is also often taught alongside science. Because of its practical nature the terminal examination only accounts for 50 per cent of the work.

Information technology (IT). This subject is now mandatory up to the age of 16, even though some students need only take a half-course. It is a hands-on subject, reflected in the coursework element which can represent between 40 and 60 per cent of the work. Students are expected to develop an understanding of computers and how to use them to solve problems. They are also required to be aware of the potential and applications of IT in the present and future. With every school and college shortly to be linked on the Internet, it is likely that this topic will become part of the subject criteria. Students are also expected to consider the social, legal, ethical and moral issues surrounding recent advances in IT. Some religious groups, such as the Plymouth Brethren, are allowed to withdraw their children from this subject as being contrary to their beliefs in the same way that parents can withdraw their children from religious education on grounds of conscience.

Mathematics. This is a mandatory subject that is part of the core curriculum right the way through from ages 5 to 16. It has now been given even more time in primary schools and in the final two years of secondary school at key stage 4. More emphasis has now been put on mental and written calculations, and calculators are expected to be banned from at least one final paper so that candidates have to rely solely on their mental calcuations. Recent international research studies have shown that British students perform poorly on mental and written mathematics but quite well on understanding and applying mathematics to solve problems.

All mathematics syllabuses and exams must cover the following: using and applying mathematics; number and algebra, functions, equations and formulae; shape space and measures; and handling data, estimating, interpreting and calculating probabilities. Most of the syllabuses are at least 80 per cent terminally assessed by exam papers at three levels: a foundation tier which goes from grades G to D (that is, students cannot get more than a D); an intermediate tier for grades E to B; and a higher tier for grades C to A*. Students take the advice of their teacher about six months before the exam in deciding which tier of exam paper to attempt, although they can change their mind. At the top level students must know Pythagoras's theorem, sine, cosine and tangent, algebraic formulae and equations, sampling and probability.

Modern foreign languages. Up until recently all students were expected to take a modern foreign language, especially a European one, up until the age of 16. But now this rule has been relaxed for the less able students altogether, and there is a minimum requirement only to study a half-course GCSE (one hour a week). Nevertheless, able students may study two foreign languages for at least four hours a week. There is in theory a wide range of possible languages to study, but in practice French is much the most common, followed by German and Spanish. The final examination tests understanding and speech in the language (an oral paper) and understanding and writing in the language (a written paper). The oral part of the assessment covers one of five areas of experience (such as travelling, buying food, holiday). In most exams candidates can bring in a dictionary to help them read and write the language. For higher marks students will be expected to read newspapers and understand radio programmes in the foreign language, narrate events and give factual information, such as train times, using a range of vocabulary and good pronunciation and intonation. Some errors of spelling and grammar are permissible and students are not marked down for them.

Music. This is a subject that has recently been downgraded in the national curriculum, even though it is a popular subject and one in which high standards have commonly been reached. Students taking instrumental qualifications do not take the GCSE but a specialist exam from, for example, the Royal College of Music. But GCSE music candidates are still expected to perform a solo part or piece and play in a group. They must recognise and appreciate a wide range of music. For the top grades they must be able to read music and compose some pieces of their own. Music is an important subject for emotional development and is especially valuable for many special needs children.

Physical education (PE). This is a mandatory subject right the way through the national curriculum and has been upgraded as a result of several recent reports on the nation's health. Team games, such as football and rounders, have also been made compulsory for part of the primary and secondary curriculum. Nevertheless, not all students are expected to take PE as an exam subject, which requires a study of health, training, coaching and dangers as well as a minimum level of performance of a game or sport. The final examination only accounts for 30 to 40 per cent and practical coursework activity can be up to 60 per cent. This can include a coursework investigation (in a topic such as heartbeat or breathing) accounting for 20 per cent of the marks. This subject is gaining in importance as sports studies degrees increase in prominence and the sporting and leisure industry expands. Once a subject despised by employers as being for the less able, it is now a requirement for some post-16 and university courses.

Religious studies (RS). Religious education is a mandatory subject right through the national curriculum from ages 5 to 16 and it must be mainly Christian in character and also follow an agreed syllabus laid down by a committee in different regional areas. But the GCSE exam is optional and only a minority of students take the course, preferring to concentrate their efforts on other subjects. The RS syllabus is broad and involves the study of one living religion, not necessarily Christianity. It involves developing an understanding of and enthusiasm for the study of religion and skills relevant to religion, which could be singing hymns or memorising texts and prayers. It also includes the ability to discuss moral issues. The largest portion of the marking (40 per cent) is given to the study of the one living religion. It is easy for an able student to pass this exam but less easy to get a high grade.

Science. Most students now take double award science, which enables them to study a broad and balanced mix of physics, chemistry and biology, including the applications of science and its environmental impact. But some independent and grammar schools still teach three separate subjects for the most able students, especially those wanting to study medicine or go on to take science at A level and university. The single award science is usually for the less able or for the arts students who want to do the minimum and concentrate instead on English literature or modern languages. There is a high level of experimental and investigative work in the laboratory and outside, and this accounts for 25 per cent of the marks. The recall of knowledge and the application of scientific theories, formulae and ideas account for 60 per cent of the assessment, though much of this is in coursework and modular schemes. Communicating scientific observations, ideas and arguments using scientific and technical vocabulary and conventions and evaluating scientific information and making judgements on it accounts for 30 per cent, but this is distributed through the other activities. There are variations on the science syllabus covering environmental, rural and geological science.

The coursework for double award science covers life processes and living things, materials and their properties and physical processes to ensure the scientific coverage is broad and balanced. Shortcomings in one area can be made up by better performance in the others for grading purposes. The double award science is a popular course motivating both girls and boys, but sometimes students going on to A level in one or more of the specialised science subjects struggle to survive or find the content boring. Sometimes the mathematical skills and knowledge required in science, for example, mechanics, are neglected, or students have forgotten them by the time of the final examination.

Social sciences. These syllabuses are often offered under the titles of law, politics, psychology or sociology. Social sciences is a broad and low-level course concerned with the nature of individual and family life, work, groups, institutions and societies. Apart from the understanding of simple psychology and sociology, the course aims to enable students to acquire and handle information and develop skills associated with social research and political attitudes, the law and the economy. The final exam accounts for at least 80 per cent of the marks. In the coursework students are expected to design and administer questionnaires, carry out interviews and write up case studies. This subject has had a bad press because it has been seen as a soft option. There are two tiers of assessment—one for the less and one for more able students.

Welsh. This is now a compulsory subject in Wales in all schools up to 16. The subject includes speaking and listening, reading and writing Welsh. Students whose mother tongue is not Welsh are not expected to show a high level of vocabulary, spelling and grammar, but they are expected to carry out an informed conversation and to be able to read Welsh papers and public notices. There is a slightly easier syllabus called Welsh as a Second Language and a harder one entitled Welsh Literature for budding journalists, bards and singers.

Useful Addresses and Telephone Numbers

Qualifications and Curriculum Authority
Newcombe House
45 Notting Hill Gate
London W11 3JB
Tel. 0207 229 1234

Assessment and Qualifications Alliance (AQA)
Stag Hill House, Guildford
Surrey GU2 5XJ
Tel. 0148 350 6506

Edexcel Foundation
Stewart House
32 Russell Square
London WC1B 5DN
Tel. 0207 393 4500

OCR
Syndicate Buildings
1 Hills Road
Cambridge CB1 2EU
Tel. 0845 604 2000

Questions and Model Answers

CHEMISTRY. Chemistry questions may be short or long, but answers often need equations and formulae as well. It is important to read the question carefully to see if a long or short answer is required.

Question:
A deep blue crystalline solid *A* decomposed on heating to give a mixture of three vapours: a brown gas *B*; a colourless gas *C*, which rekindled a glowing splint; and a third substance *D*. The solid residue *E* was black and dissolved in dilute sulphuric acid to give a blue solution *F*. When aqueous ammonia was added to the solution *F*, a light blue precipitate *G* first appeared, but this dissolved in excess aqueous ammonia to give a deep blue solution of a substance *H*.

Name substances *A*, *B*, *C*, *D*, *E*, *F*, *G* and *H*.

Answer:
A. Copper (II) nitrate
B. Nitrogen dioxide
C. Oxygen

D. Water vapour
E. Copper (II) oxide
F. Copper (II) sulphate solution
G. Copper hydroxide
H. Tetraamine copper ion

If you need to show your reasons, then:

1. Blue compounds suggest a copper compound.
2. A brown gas is nitrogen dioxide.
3. Oxygen rekindles a glowing splint.
4. Third substance is probably water vapour.
5. Nitrates give off nitrogen dioxide on heating.
6. Black compounds are unusual and are often carbon or copper oxide.
7. Copper oxide would react with sulphuric acid to form a salt.
8. Ammonia solution is used to identify copper ions.

Note also that you may be asked to write equations for the reactions that have taken place.

Which Study Style Works Best for You?

Some people find it easiest to work in the same place all the time, while others find it useful to shift around, working for an hour in one place, then having a break and working somewhere else and on a different topic.

Remember that your concentration is limited (everyone's is), so have a timed break. But make sure you start again promptly, and don't get hooked on a TV programme during the break!

ENGLISH LITERATURE. Questions in this subject often call for the student to analyse and discuss a character from literature.

Question:
Assess the influence of Banquo on the course of the tragedy in Shakespeare's *Macbeth*.

Answer:
Banquo is a great soldier, second only to Macbeth. At the start of the play we are told by Duncan that he and Macbeth are "captains" of the forces fighting the rebels. When we first see Banquo it is as Macbeth's companion. It is he who seems to glimpse the witches first and he informs us of Macbeth's response. Banquo questions them about his own future but the witches' reply is particularly ambiguous: he will be "lesser than Macbeth, and greater", and "not so happy, yet much happier". He is also told: "Thou shalt get kings, though thou be none".

These predictions come true. Banquo will not become king, but by preserving his integrity he will be the greater man. He will not murder, he will be murdered but will be spared Macbeth's guilty suffering. The third prophecy explains why Macbeth fears Banquo and has him murdered: Banquo is destined to be the father of a line of kings.

Banquo is far more suspicious of the witches than Macbeth is and gives him a warning: "Oftentimes, to win us to our harm, The instruments of darkness tell us truths, Win us with honest trifles, to betray us In deepest consequence". Banquo is brave and shrewd, loyal and suspicious at the same time. He guesses that Macbeth has murdered his way to the throne. He realises Macbeth's wickedness and also that the prophecies have been fulfilled.

Macbeth comes to hate and fear his old friend. He realises that he has sold his soul and seized the throne for nothing, because Banquo's children will succeed him. He deceives Banquo and murders him on his way to Macbeth's own castle for a feast. But Banquo's son Fleance escapes, thereby confirming the last prophecy.

Banquo's last and most dramatic role is to return at Macbeth's feast to haunt his murderer. The closest friend has become Macbeth's cruellest tormentor—his conscience.

HISTORY. Examiners in history expect names and dates and a broad view over time as well as specific incidents. For the best marks students must take more than one point of view.

Question:
Why did France and Britain suddenly become friends at the beginning of the twentieth century when they had been enemies during the eighteenth and nineteenth centuries?

Answer:
At the end of the nineteenth century Great Britain did not want any foreign alliances, and had not wanted any for many years. The Government believed in 'splendid isolation'. This was because its eyes were focussed on the Empire. With the largest of the world's navies it felt in need of no friends.

But, as Germany grew in power, Britain became worried. The German royalty had been allied to Britain's through Queen Victoria's marriage to Prince Albert. There was even talk of an alliance with the Germans. But German naval building after 1900 upset the British Government, who after Victoria's death three years later turned to France as a counterbalance.

In 1907 the British Government went a step further when the Foreign Secretary Sir Edward Grey announced an alliance with Russia, with whom the royal family also had family ties. In 1911 the British Foreign Secretary Sir Edward Grey described the new foreign policy as follows: "After discussions lasting a long time, the result was an Anglo-French agreement of 1904. This agreement at once removed all risk of a quarrel with France and brought the two nations to realise that there was no reason why they should not be the best of friends".

The agreement was known as the *entente cordiale,* and together with Russia the three nations made up a triple entente. Germany found it hard to believe that Britain and France, so long rivals, could be allies, so the Germans twice tested out the strength of the friendship by causing small incidents against French power in North Africa in 1905 and 1911. Each time Germany contested the right to French sovereignty in an area, and both times the British stood by their new ally, following up with more military and naval talks about how the two countries could help each other.

Germany in turn allied with Austria-Hungary and Italy in its own triple alliance. All of these countries were suspicious that Russia wanted to take over control of the Balkans. This left a balance of power in Europe which needed only a small spark to ignite into war in 1914.

As for the French, they forgot their traditional rivalry with the British in the Crimean War during the 1850s. They were potential rivals again in Africa. But many Frenchmen wanted revenge for the defeat the Germans had inflicted on them in 1871, when the French lost Alsace and Lorraine. As a result, France made an alliance first with Russia and then with Britain.

A Levels

General Certificate of Education Advanced level examinations (known as A levels) are the gold standard for entry to Britain's universities. They are a currency that has not been devalued for 40 years and they seem likely to remain so until the next millennium. Like GCSEs they are single-subject examinations and they have a similar grading scale—A to E. Failures are graded U and there is a grade N for 'narrowly failed'.

Most students aiming for university take three A level subjects, usually basing their choice of subjects on their best grades at GCSE or on specific requirements of a university course. The A level syllabuses are designed to lock into the first year of university undergraduate degrees, and this correspondence has meant that British undergraduates can take their degrees in three years instead of four or more, as is usual in other countries. For more than 20 years this exam system has remained largely untouched, and various attempts to broaden the curriculum and increase the number of subjects taken from three to five have failed.

The Gap

In spite of the A levels' success, several problems have arisen in the last 10 years. So long as the exams were taken only by the top 20 per cent of the school students, they passed through easily into the first year of the university. But in the last 10 years the percentage of the age group going on to university has doubled and these students include many older people and 18-year-olds without the neat set of three high-grade A levels needed to qualify.

The changes to the examinations at age 16 occurred 10 years ago with the creation of the GCSE, but changes for those at age 18 did not. The GCSE became broader and more designed for coursework, which meant that there was no longer a close match between the end of GCSE and the first year of A

levels. Many students found there was a substantial gap between the curriculum and examinations before and after 16. Many struggled with the subject matter and found they did not have the depth of knowledge to survive, others found the discipline and teaching at A level dry and dusty and too academic. Students started to drop out of the A levels at an alarming rate—sometimes 20 per cent at the end of the first term of the two-year course and 30 per cent at the end of the first year. The rate of decline in completion of A levels was just too steep. Something had to be done.

A recent Government consultation paper on the future of the country's exams said: "The very strengths of A levels have meant that many 16- to 18-year-olds have been tempted to follow an over-narrow curriculum, which does not help them to develop the full range of skills and competencies needed for adult and working life. Increasing numbers of learners are following mixed programmes of three or four A levels drawn from different curriculum areas. But others fail to complete their programmes and may achieve less than two A levels or drop out without adding to their qualifications. This is a waste of their talents and the nation's resources."

In 1989 the Government introduced the Advanced Supplementary (AS) level to give more choice of subjects and create a broader curriculum. These AS levels held to the same standard as A level but with half the content, taking half the study time. For example, a student studying two A levels in maths and economics could take two AS levels in French and history. But this has been only partially successful. The Government's latest proposal is to create a new form of AS level with half the standard, so that it could be taken in one year. If this proposal went into effect, it would mean that students could change courses completely after the first year and take three new AS levels in the first year and then two A levels and another AS level in the second year.

Study Tips

For today's student there is a bewildering choice of courses—A and AS levels and the GNVQ (see next section). But certain principles still hold good whatever mix of subjects you choose to study from ages 16 to 18.
- If you find the A level too difficult, seek help or advice early. It is better to change before Christmas than at the end of the first year. If you need some extra help with mathematics or English, there are extra short courses and modules that you can take to bring you up to speed. Some of them are available from the National Extension College and some from the Open

University, and you can study them in your spare time.
- A levels are designed for five hours of teaching a week and about three or four hours of reading and private study. Don't rely on the teacher to do all the work. You will need to get into a regular reading and study habit at home and in the library. The same is true of science and technology courses, where only half the work is done in the laboratory or workshop. You will need to get used to carting books back and forth from home. If you can, get a small portable computer and take a disk home at night to continue working.
- Get a reading list early on with both the set books and the recommended reading. Then look out for second-hand books to buy from other students. There is often so much demand for books and seats in the college or school library that they are unavailable when students need them for an assignment.
- Make rough notes for your assignments that you can use later for revision in 12 months' time. Keep your essays and assignments and the teacher's notes and marks.
- Don't leave all the work until the second year of the course. The mock A levels come in December of the second year, and the grades you get then will determine your offers of a place from university, which will be conditional on your getting good grades in your A levels. If you leave your study to the last five months from January until the final exams in June, you will almost certainly lose out on revision.
- It has been said that getting a university place is a lottery. There is an element of chance certainly; but there is plenty you can do to improve the odds in your favour. Remember that university admissions tutors do not just look at A or AS level results, they also look at other skills and qualifications. You should have about three hours each week (possibly an afternoon) to pursue some other course—a foreign language, perhaps, or a computer course.

At the end of your first year of A level, take time to review the situation. Your teacher will give you an assessment and award some grades. These may not mean very much to you, but that is the time to remedy weaknesses, catch up and plan ahead. Most students take the opportunity to earn some money in the long summer vacation and to travel or lie on a beach. But build in some study time—a week or fortnight, if you can—between work and vacation or in September before the term begins. Try to keep reading over the summer, even if it means taking a book on the Costa Brava or in your knapsack up a mountain.

GNVQ

There are many young people who are not suited to the academic curriculum tested by the GCSE and A levels. These students are often very able but simply not motivated by the idea of earning grades through listening to lessons in a classroom and poring over books late at night. Many employers, too, look for young people who have skills and competences rather than knowledge learned from books.

To cater for the educational and training needs of this group, the Government introduced the General National Vocational Qualification (GNVQ) in 1993 as a broad work-related qualification linked to a particular industry or sector of the economy.

Description

The GNVQ has 15 subject areas in all, and students choose one of them to study at the age of 16 for a one- or two-year course of about 16 hours a week. These courses involve work experience and a project in the chosen area of employment. The 15 areas of study are shown below; only a handful of them are taken in most schools and the rest in colleges of further education.

The GNVQ has three levels of difficulty: Foundation and Intermediate, which usually take one year, and Advanced, which takes two years. The Foundation level is set as equivalent in standard to four GCSEs of grades D to G, the Intermediate as equivalent to four GCSEs of grades A* to C, and the Advanced level as equivalent to two A level passes. As an integral part of the course, all students must demonstrate competence in the key skills of communication (written and spoken English), application of number and information technology.

The GNVQ has already established itself firmly in the areas of business, health and social care, and leisure and tourism, but less well in science and engineering. Altogether some 200,000 young people are engaged on GNVQ courses at any one time. In addition, a pilot programme called GNVQ Part 1, involving 5,000 students in 600 schools, has just started for 14- to 16-year-olds.

The system of assessment used in the GNVQ is completely different from that of the GCSE and A levels. Instead of a final examination marked by exam boards, the GNVQs are marked according to demonstrated skills and knowledge in each unit. The final assessment is done on the basis of a portfolio of work completed and assessed as up to the required standard. The study skills and techniques are also quite different: they are more like those required for GCSE coursework and involve organising and presenting a portfolio of work rather than taking an examination paper.

Changes

Despite the differences between the GNVQ on one side and the GCSE and A levels on the other, the Government is now talking about harmonising the two examination systems in a common framework, using certain units—for example, key skills—in both qualifications. As a first step, the academic exam boards who run the GCSE and A levels and the vocational bodies who run the GNVQs have been brought together into three joint boards. The universities are also working out a common scoring and grading structure which will put GNVQ and A level students on an equal footing in the lottery for university places.

With so many changes taking place, students would be well advised to get the latest information on the GNVQ, as well as on the GCSE and A levels, when making their plans for education and career.

GNVQ Subject Areas

1. Art and design
2. Business
3. Construction and built environment
4. Distribution
5. Engineering
6. Health and social care
7. Hospitality and catering
8. Information technology
9. Land-based and environmental industries
10. Leisure and tourism
11. Management studies
12. Manufacturing
13. Media, communication and production
14. Science
15. Performing arts

Here are some examples of how GeoHelp™ can help you:

Let's suppose you have a project on the European country Moldova and you need to know where it fits into Europe, its capital, and one or two of its other major cities. Just click TO THE WORLD, and you'll get a world map. Move the cursor to the word "Europe" and double-click. You'll get a map of Europe; click on the button that says MAP INFO and then click COUNTRY NAMES. You'll get all the countries in Europe.

Then, click on Moldova. Click MAP INFO, and choose what you need: capital city, rivers, names of surrounding countries, landforms, or major cities. And you can print anything you see at any time! If you only need the country outline and name, you can print it. If you need the capital city shown, you can print it. If you need the countries around it, you can print them, too. Print whatever you see.

So, what if you were absent from school the day the assignment was given and don't have a clue where to find Moldova? Go to WHERE IN THE WORLD and start typing M-O-L-... and before you know it, Moldova will appear in the box and you can just click OK. Want to know where a major city is located? Go to WHERE IN THE WORLD again and select CITIES.

If you want to know everything available about a country, a region in Britain, a Canadian province, or any American state, just click MAX INFO and everything appears at once. You can take information off, too. If you want the rivers to disappear, just click RIVERS and voilà, they dry up.

Have fun creating your own maps with STAMPS. Left click and drag your stamps onto your map. Double-click on the stamps to add text. The "T" in the corner is for adding plain text to your map. Don't like what you just added? Click on the stamp and hit the DELETE key on your keyboard. If you scroll your cursor over the stamps, you'll see their names appear. But don't let that limit you. Use your imagination. For example, the airplane could represent an airport or airplane manufacturing. The possibilities are endless.

Need a map for your report? With GeoHelp™, its not a problem. Just click COPY to put your customized map on the Microsoft Windows clipboard. You can now paste your map directly into another Windows application like Word, WordPerfect, or Paint. So, let's suppose your report was done in Word. You would open Word, click EDIT and PASTE, and watch your map appear! Need to take a break? You can save your maps in GeoHelp™ by clicking SAVE. When you want to use your map again, just click on the OPEN button.

You can click your way around the whole world. You can go state to state, province to province, country to country; as long as the cursor turns to a finger when you point to the name of a place, you can just click, and you're there.

Have fun. Get better grades. That's what GeoHelp™ is for!

PRINTING

You can print a map by clicking the PRINT button. The default printer and its options are used to print the map. One option you can change is orientation. If the orientation is portrait, the map is printed from left to right across the page with the top of the map along the top of the page. If the orientation is landscape, the map is rotated so that the top of the map is along the right margin of the page.

To change the printing orientation in Windows, follow these steps.

- Click the Windows START button.
- Click Settings.
- Click Printers.
- Click on the printer with your right mouse button. This displays the Context Menu.
- From the Context Menu, click on the "Properties" menu item.
- At the top of the dialog box, click the "Paper" tab.
- Now, click the word "Landscape" to change the orientation to landscape or "Portrait" to change the orientation to portrait.
- Click OK to confirm your changes.

How to Study (Revised edition) was developed by Kidd & Company, Inc., Nashville, Tennessee.

Executive editor	Ronald Kidd
Design, layout, typesetting	Schatz + Schatz
Additional typesetting	Dale Sprenkle, Laurie Beers
Illustrations	Joel Snyder, Lloyd Birmingham (p. 762 only)
Copyediting, proofreading	Jeannie Crawford-Lee, Christine Benagh, Nina Young

The original edition, portions of which are included in this volume, was developed by the Hudson Group, Inc., Pleasantville, New York.